To my wonderful
BROTHER
AND my GOOD FRIEND.
I love you Always –
Pam

The NIV MESSAGE

PARALLEL BIBLE

ZONDERVAN®

CONTENTS

CONTENTS

PREFACE

THE NEW INTERNATIONAL VERSION is a completely new translation of the Holy Bible made by over a hundred scholars working directly from the best available Hebrew, Aramaic and Greek texts. It had its beginning in 1965 when, after several years of exploratory study by committees from the Christian Reformed Church and the National Association of Evangelicals, a group of scholars met at Palos Heights, Illinois, and concurred in the need for a new translation of the Bible in contemporary English. This group, though not made up of official church representatives, was transdenominational. Its conclusion was endorsed by a large number of leaders from many denominations who met in Chicago in 1966.

Responsibility for the new version was delegated by the Palos Heights group to a self-governing body of fifteen, the Committee on Bible Translation, composed for the most part of biblical scholars from colleges, universities and seminaries. In 1967 the New York Bible Society (now the International Bible Society) generously undertook the financial sponsorship of the project—a sponsorship that made it possible to enlist the help of many distinguished scholars. The fact that participants from the United States, Great Britain, Canada, Australia and New Zealand worked together gave the project its international scope. That they were from many denominations—including Anglican, Assemblies of God, Baptist, Brethren, Christian Reformed, Church of Christ, Evangelical Free, Lutheran, Mennonite, Methodist, Nazarene, Presbyterian, Wesleyan and other churches—helped to safeguard the translation from sectarian bias.

How it was made helps to give the New International Version its distinctiveness. The translation of each book was assigned to a team of scholars. Next, one of the Intermediate Editorial Committees revised the initial translation, with constant reference to the Hebrew, Aramaic or Greek. Their work then went to one of the General Editorial Committees, which checked it in detail and made another thorough revision. This revision in turn was carefully reviewed by the Committee on Bible Translation, which made further changes and then released the final version for publication. In this way the entire Bible underwent three revisions, during each of which the translation was examined for its faithfulness to the original languages and for its English style.

All this involved many thousands of hours of research and discussion regarding the meaning of the texts and the precise way of putting them into English. It may well be that no other translation has been made by a more thorough process of review and revision from committee to committee than this one.

From the beginning of the project, the Committee on Bible Translation held to certain goals for the New International Version: that it would be an accurate translation and one that would have clarity and literary quality and so prove suitable for public and private reading, teaching, preaching, memorizing and liturgical use. The Committee also sought to preserve some measure of continuity with the long tradition of translating the Scriptures into English.

In working toward these goals, the translators were united in their commitment to the authority and infallibility of the Bible as God's Word in written form. They believe that it contains the divine answer to the deepest needs of humanity, that it sheds unique light on our path in a dark world, and that it sets forth the way to our eternal well-being.

The first concern of the translators has been the accuracy of the translation and its fidelity to the thought of the biblical writers. They have weighed the significance of the lexical and grammatical details of the Hebrew, Aramaic and Greek texts. At the same time, they have striven for more than a word-for-word translation. Because thought patterns and syntax differ from language to language, faithful communication of the meaning of the writers of the Bible demands frequent modifications in sentence structure and constant regard for the contextual meanings of words.

A sensitive feeling for style does not always accompany scholarship. Accordingly the Committee on Bible Translation submitted the developing version to a number of stylistic consultants. Two of them read every book of both Old and New Testaments twice—once before and once after the last major revision—and made invaluable suggestions. Samples of the translation were tested for clarity and ease of reading by various kinds of people—young and old, highly educated and less well educated, ministers and laymen.

Concern for clear and natural English—that the New International Version should be idiomatic but not idiosyncratic, contemporary but not dated—motivated the translators and consultants. At the same time, they tried to reflect the differing styles of the biblical writers. In view of the international use of English, the translators sought to avoid obvious Americanisms on the one hand and obvious Anglicisms on the other. A British edition reflects the comparatively few differences of significant idiom and of spelling.

As for the traditional pronouns "thou," "thee" and "thine" in reference to the Deity, the translators judged that to use these archaisms (along with the old verb forms such as "doest," "wouldest" and "hadst") would violate accuracy in translation. Neither Hebrew, Aramaic nor Greek uses special pronouns for the persons of the Godhead. A present-day translation is not enhanced by forms that in the time of the King James Version were used in everyday speech, whether referring to God or man.

For the Old Testament the standard Hebrew text, the Masoretic Text as published in the latest editions of *Biblia Hebraica,* was used throughout. The Dead Sea Scrolls contain material bearing on an earlier stage of the Hebrew text. They were consulted, as were the Samaritan Pentateuch and the ancient scribal traditions relating to textual changes. Sometimes a variant Hebrew reading in the margin of the Masoretic Text was followed instead of the text itself. Such instances, being variants within the Masoretic tradition, are not specified by footnotes. In rare cases, words in the consonantal text were divided differently from the way they appear in the Masoretic Text. Footnotes indicate this. The translators also consulted the more important early versions—the Septuagint; Aquila, Symmachus and Theodotion; the Vulgate; the Syriac Peshitta; the Targums; and for the Psalms the *Juxta Hebraica* of Jerome. Readings from these versions were occasionally followed where the Masoretic Text seemed doubtful and where accepted principles of textual criticism showed that one or more of these textual witnesses appeared to provide the correct reading. Such instances are footnoted. Sometimes vowel letters and vowel signs did not, in the judgment of the translators, represent the correct vowels for the original consonantal text. Accordingly some words were read with a different set of vowels. These instances are usually not indicated by footnotes.

The Greek text used in translating the New Testament was an eclectic one. No other piece of ancient literature has such an abundance of manuscript witnesses as does the New Testament. Where existing manuscripts differ, the translators made their choice of readings according to accepted principles of New Testament textual criticism. Footnotes call attention to places where there was uncertainty about what the original text was. The best current printed texts of the Greek New Testament were used.

There is a sense in which the work of translation is never wholly finished. This applies to all great literature and uniquely so to the Bible. In 1973 the New Testament in the New International Version was published. Since then, suggestions for corrections and revisions have been received from various sources. The Committee on Bible Translation carefully considered the suggestions and adopted a number of them. These were incorporated in the first printing of the entire Bible in 1978. Additional revisions were made by the Committee on Bible Translation in 1983 and appear in printings after that date.

As in other ancient documents, the precise meaning of the biblical texts is sometimes uncertain. This is more often the case with the Hebrew and Aramaic texts than with the Greek text. Although archaeological and linguistic discoveries in this century aid in understanding difficult passages, some uncertainties remain. The more significant of these have been called to the reader's attention in the footnotes.

In regard to the divine name YHWH, commonly referred to as the *Tetragrammaton,* the translators adopted the device used in most English versions of rendering that name as "Lord" in capital letters to distinguish it from *Adonai,* another Hebrew word rendered "Lord," for which small letters are used. Wherever the two names stand together in the Old Testament as a compound name of God, they are rendered "Sovereign Lord."

Because for most readers today the phrases "the Lord of hosts" and "God of hosts" have little meaning, this version renders them "the Lord Almighty" and "God Almighty." These renderings convey the sense of the Hebrew, namely, "he who is sovereign over all the 'hosts' (powers) in heaven and on earth, especially over the 'hosts' (armies) of Israel." For readers unacquainted with Hebrew this does not make clear the distinction between *Sabaoth* ("hosts" or "Almighty") and *Shaddai* (which can also be translated "Almighty"), but the latter occurs infrequently and is always footnoted. When *Adonai* and *YHWH Sabaoth* occur together, they are rendered "the Lord, the LORD Almighty."

As for other proper nouns, the familiar spellings of the King James Version are generally retained. Names traditionally spelled with "ch," except where it is final, are usually spelled in this translation with "k" or "c," since the biblical languages do not have the sound that "ch" frequently indicates in English—for example, in *chant*. For well-known names such as Zechariah, however, the traditional spelling has been retained. Variation in the spelling of names in the original languages has usually not been indicated. Where a person or place has two or more different names in the Hebrew, Aramaic or Greek texts, the more familiar one has generally been used, with footnotes where needed.

To achieve clarity the translators sometimes supplied words not in the original texts but required by the context. If there was uncertainty about such material, it is enclosed in brackets. Also for the sake of clarity or style, nouns, including some proper nouns, are sometimes substituted for pronouns, and vice versa. And though the Hebrew writers often shifted back and forth between first, second and third personal pronouns without change of antecedent, this translation often makes them uniform, in accordance with English style and without the use of footnotes.

Poetical passages are printed as poetry, that is, with indentation of lines and with separate stanzas. These are generally designed to reflect the structure of Hebrew poetry. This poetry is normally characterized by parallelism in balanced lines. Most of the poetry in the Bible is in the Old Testament, and scholars differ regarding the scansion of Hebrew lines. The translators determined the stanza divisions for the most part by analysis of the subject matter. The stanzas therefore serve as poetic paragraphs.

As an aid to the reader, italicized sectional headings are inserted in most of the books. They are not to be regarded as part of the NIV text, are not for oral reading, and are not intended to dictate the interpretation of the sections they head.

The footnotes in this version are of several kinds, most of which need no explanation. Those giving alternative translations begin with "Or" and generally introduce the alternative with the last word preceding it in the text, except when it is a single-word alternative; in poetry quoted in a footnote a slant mark indicates a line division. Footnotes introduced by "Or" do not have uniform significance. In some cases two possible translations were considered to have about equal validity. In other cases, though the translators were convinced that the translation in the text was correct, they judged that another interpretation was possible and of sufficient importance to be represented in a footnote.

In the New Testament, footnotes that refer to uncertainty regarding the original text are introduced by "Some manuscripts" or similar expressions. In the Old Testament, evidence for the reading chosen is given first and evidence for the alternative is added after a semicolon (for example: Septuagint; Hebrew *father*). In such notes the term "Hebrew" refers to the Masoretic Text.

It should be noted that minerals, flora and fauna, architectural details, articles of clothing and jewelry, musical instruments and other articles cannot always be identified with precision. Also measures of capacity in the biblical period are particularly uncertain (see the table of weights and measures following the text).

Like all translations of the Bible, made as they are by imperfect man, this one undoubtedly falls short of its goals. Yet we are grateful to God for the extent to which he has enabled us to realize these goals and for the strength he has given us and our colleagues to complete our task. We offer this version of the Bible to him in whose name and for whose glory it has been made. We pray that it will lead many into a better understanding of the Holy Scriptures and a fuller knowledge of Jesus Christ the incarnate Word, of whom the Scriptures so faithfully testify.

The Committee on Bible Translation

June 1978
(Revised August 1983)

Names of the translators and editors may be secured
from the International Bible Society,
translation sponsors of the New International Version,
1820 Jet Stream Drive, Colorado Springs, Colorado
80921-3696 U.S.A.

PREFACE TO THE READER

If there is anything distinctive about *The Message*, perhaps it is because the text is shaped by the hand of a working pastor. For most of my adult life I have been given a primary responsibility for getting the message of the Bible into the lives of the men and women with whom I worked. I did it from pulpit and lectern, in home Bible studies and at mountain retreats, through conversations in hospitals and nursing homes, over coffee in kitchens and while strolling on an ocean beach. *The Message* grew from the soil of forty years of pastoral work.

As I worked at this task, this Word of God, which forms and transforms human lives, did form and transform human lives. Planted in the soil of my congregation and community the seed words of the Bible germinated and grew and matured. When it came time to do the work that is now *The Message*, I often felt that I was walking through an orchard at harvest time, plucking fully formed apples and peaches and plums from laden branches. There's hardly a page in the Bible I did not see lived in some way or other by the men and women, saints and sinners, to whom I was pastor—and then verified in my nation and culture.

I didn't start out as a pastor. I began my vocational life as a teacher and for several years taught the biblical languages of Hebrew and Greek in a theological seminary. I expected to live the rest of my life as a professor and scholar, teaching and writing and studying. But then my life took a sudden vocational turn to pastoring in a congregation.

I was now plunged into quite a different world. The first noticeable difference was that nobody seemed to care much about the Bible, which so recently people had been paying me to teach them. Many of the people I worked with now knew virtually nothing about it, had never read it, and weren't interested in learning. Many others had spent years reading it but for them it had gone flat through familiarity, reduced to clichés. Bored, they dropped it. And there weren't many people in between. Very few were interested in what I considered my primary work, getting the words of the Bible into their heads and hearts, getting the message lived. They found newspapers and magazines, videos and pulp fiction more to their taste.

Meanwhile I had taken on as my life work the responsibility of getting these very people to listen, really listen, to the message in this book. I knew I had my work cut out for me.

I lived in two language worlds, the world of the Bible and the world of Today. I had always assumed they were the same world. But these people didn't see it that way. So out of necessity I became a "translator" (although I wouldn't have called it that then), daily standing on the border between two worlds, getting the language of the Bible that God uses to create and save us, heal and bless us, judge and rule over us, into the language of Today that we use to gossip and tell stories, give directions and do business, sing songs and talk to our children.

And all the time those old biblical languages, those powerful and vivid Hebrew and Greek originals, kept working their way underground in my speech, giving energy and sharpness to words and phrases, expanding the imagination of the people with whom I was working to hear the language of the Bible in the language of Today and the language of Today in the language of the Bible.

I did that for thirty years in one congregation. And then one day (it was April 30, 1990) I got a letter from an editor asking me to work on a new version of the Bible along the lines of what I had been doing as a pastor. I agreed. The next ten years was harvest time. *The Message* is the result.

The Message is a reading Bible. It is not intended to replace the excellent study Bibles that are available. My intent here (as it was earlier in my congregation and community) is simply to get people reading it who don't know that the Bible is readable at all, at least by them, and to get people who long ago lost interest in the Bible to read it again. I leave out verse numbers to encourage unimpeded reading (no Bibles had verse numbers for the first 1,500 years). But I haven't tried to make it easy—there is much in the Bible that is hard to understand. So at some point along the way, soon or late, it will be important to get a standard study Bible to facilitate further study. Meanwhile, read in order to live, praying as you read, "God, let it be with me just as you say."

THE MESSAGE

INTRODUCTION

Reading is the first thing, just reading the Bible. As we read we enter a new world of words and find ourselves in on a conversation in which God has the first and last words. We soon realize that we are included in the conversation. We didn't expect this. But this is precisely what generation after generation of Bible readers do find: The Bible is not only written about us but to us. In these pages we become insiders to a conversation in which God uses words to form and bless us, to teach and guide us, to forgive and save us.

We aren't used to this. We are used to reading books that explain things, or tell us what to do, or inspire or entertain us. But this is different. This is a world of revelation: God revealing to people just like us—men and women created in God's image—how God works and what is going on in this world in which we find ourselves. At the same time that God reveals all this, God draws us in by invitation and command to participate in God's working life. We gradually (or suddenly) realize that we are insiders in the most significant action of our time as God establishes his grand rule of love and justice on this earth (as it is in heaven). "Revelation" means that we are reading something we couldn't have guessed or figured out on our own. Revelation is what makes the Bible unique.

And so just reading this Bible, *The Message*, and listening to what we read, is the first thing. There will be time enough for study later on. But first, it is important simply to read, leisurely and thoughtfully. We need to get a feel for the way these stories and songs, these prayers and conversations, these sermons and visions, invite us into this large, large world in which the invisible God is behind and involved in everything visible, and illuminates what it means to live here—really live, not just get across the street. As we read, and the longer we read, we begin to "get it"—we are in conversation with God. We find ourselves listening and answering in matters that most concern us: who we are, where we came from, where we are going, what makes us tick, the texture of the world and the communities we live in, and—most of all—the incredible love of God among us, doing for us what we cannot do for ourselves.

Through reading the Bible, we see that there is far more to the world, more to us, more to what we see and more to what we don't see—more to everything!—than we had ever dreamed, and that this "more" has to do with God.

This is new for many of us, a different sort of book—a book that reads us even as we read it. We are used to picking up and reading books for what we can get out of them: information we can use, inspiration to energize us, instructions on how to do something or other, entertainment to while away a rainy day, wisdom that will guide us into living better. These things can and do take place when reading the Bible, but the Bible is given to us in the first place simply to invite us to make ourselves at home in the world of God, God's word and world, and become familiar with the way God speaks and the ways in which we answer him with our lives.

Our reading turns up some surprises. The biggest surprise for many is how accessible this book is to those who simply open it up and read it. Virtually anyone can read this Bible with understanding. The reason that new translations are made every couple of generations or so is to keep the language of the Bible current with the common speech we use, the very language in which it was first written. We don't have to be smart or well educated to understand it, for it is written in the words and sentences we hear in the marketplace, on school playgrounds, and around the dinner table. Because the Bible is so famous and revered, many assume that we need experts to explain and interpret it for us—and, of course, there are some things that need to be explained. But the first men and women who listened to these words now written in our Bibles were ordinary, everyday, working-class people. One of the greatest of the early translators of the Bible into English, William Tyndale, said that he was translating so that "the boy that driveth the plough" would be able to read the Scriptures.

One well-educated African man, who later became one of the most influential Bible teachers in our history (Augustine), was greatly offended when he first read the Bible. Instead of a book cultivated and polished in the literary style he admired so much, he found it full of homespun, earthy stories of plain, unimportant people. He read it in a Latin translation full of slang and jargon. He took one look at what he considered the "unspiritual" quality of so many of its characters and the everydayness of Jesus, and contemptuously abandoned it. It was years before he realized that God had not taken the form of a sophisticated intellectual to teach us about highbrow heavenly culture so we could appreciate the finer things of God. When he saw that God entered our lives as a Jewish servant in order to save us from our sins, he started reading the Book gratefully and believingly.

Some are also surprised that Bible reading does not introduce us to a "nicer" world. This biblical world is decidedly not an ideal world, the kind we see advertised in travel posters. Suffering and injustice and ugliness are not purged from the world in which God works and loves and saves. Nothing is glossed over. God works patiently and deeply, but often in hidden ways, in the mess of our humanity and history. Ours is not a neat and tidy world in which we are assured that we can get everything under our control. This takes considerable getting used to—there is mystery everywhere. The Bible does not give us a predictable cause-effect world in which we can plan our careers and secure our futures. It is not a dream world in which everything works out according to our adolescent expectations—there is pain and poverty and abuse at which we cry out in indignation, "You can't let this happen!" For most of us it takes years and years and years to exchange our dream world for this real world of grace and mercy, sacrifice and love, freedom and joy—the God-saved world.

Yet another surprise is that the Bible does not flatter us. It is not trying to sell us anything that promises to make life easier. It doesn't offer secrets to what we often think of as prosperity or pleasure or high adventure. The reality that comes into focus as we read the Bible has to do with what God is doing in a saving love that includes us and everything we do. This is quite different from what our sin-stunted and culture-cluttered minds imagined. But our Bible reading does not give us access to a mail order catalog of idols from which we can pick and choose to satisfy our fantasies. The Bible begins with God speaking creation and us into being. It continues with God entering into personalized and complex relationships with us, helping and blessing us, teaching and training us, correcting and disciplining us, loving and saving us. This is not an escape from reality but a plunge into more reality—a sacrificial but altogether better life all the way.

God doesn't force any of this on us: God's word is personal address, inviting, commanding, challenging, rebuking, judging, comforting, directing—but not forcing. Not coercing. We are given space and freedom to answer, to enter the conversation. For more than anything else the Bible invites our participation in the work and language of God.

As we read, we find that there is a connection between the Word Read and the Word Lived. Everything in this book is livable. Many of us find that the most important question we ask as we read is not "What does it mean?" but "How can I live it?" So we read personally, not impersonally. We read in order to live our true selves, not just get information that we can use to raise our standard of living. Bible reading is a means of listening to and obeying God, not gathering religious data by which we can be our own gods.

You are going to hear stories in this Book that will take you out of your preoccupation with yourself and into the spacious freedom in which God is working the world's salvation. You are going to come across words and sentences that stab you awake to a beauty and hope that will connect you with your real life.

Be sure to answer.

OLD TESTAMENT

GENESIS   # GENESIS

THE BEGINNING

1 In the beginning God created the heavens and the earth. ²Now the earth was[a] formless and empty, darkness was over the surface of the deep, and the Spirit of God was hovering over the waters.

³And God said, "Let there be light," and there was light. ⁴God saw that the light was good, and he separated the light from the darkness. ⁵God called the light "day," and the darkness he called "night." And there was evening, and there was morning—the first day.

⁶And God said, "Let there be an expanse between the waters to separate water from water." ⁷So God made the expanse and separated the water under the expanse from the water above it. And it was so. ⁸God called the expanse "sky." And there was evening, and there was morning—the second day.

⁹And God said, "Let the water under the sky be gathered to one place, and let dry ground appear." And it was so. ¹⁰God called the dry ground "land," and the gathered waters he called "seas." And God saw that it was good.

¹¹Then God said, "Let the land produce vegetation: seed-bearing plants and trees on the land that bear fruit with seed in it, according to their various kinds." And it was so. ¹²The land produced vegetation: plants bearing seed according to their kinds and trees bearing fruit with seed in it according to their kinds. And God saw that it was good. ¹³And there was evening, and there was morning—the third day.

HEAVEN AND EARTH

1.1-2 **1** First this: God created the Heavens and Earth—all you see, all you don't see. Earth was a soup of nothingness, a bottomless emptiness, an inky blackness. God's Spirit brooded like a bird above the watery abyss.

1.3-5 God spoke: "Light!"
    And light appeared.
God saw that light was good
    and separated light from dark.
God named the light Day,
    he named the dark Night.
It was evening, it was morning—
Day One.

1.6-8 God spoke: "Sky! In the middle of the
       waters;
    separate water from water!"
God made sky.
He separated the water under sky
    from the water above sky.
And there it was:
    he named sky the Heavens;
It was evening, it was morning—
Day Two.

1.9-10 God spoke: "Separate!
    Water-beneath-Heaven, gather into one
       place;
Land, appear!"
    And there it was.
God named the land Earth.
    He named the pooled water Ocean.
God saw that it was good.

1.11-13 God spoke: "Earth, green up! Grow all
       varieties
    of seed-bearing plants,
Every sort of fruit-bearing tree."
And there it was.
Earth produced green seed-bearing plants,
    all varieties,
And fruit-bearing trees of all sorts.
    God saw that it was good.
It was evening, it was morning—
Day Three.

---

a 2 Or possibly *became*

NEW INTERNATIONAL VERSION

14 And God said, "Let there be lights in the expanse of the sky to separate the day from the night, and let them serve as signs to mark seasons and days and years, 15and let them be lights in the expanse of the sky to give light on the earth." And it was so. 16God made two great lights—the greater light to govern the day and the lesser light to govern the night. He also made the stars. 17God set them in the expanse of the sky to give light on the earth, 18to govern the day and the night, and to separate light from darkness. And God saw that it was good. 19And there was evening, and there was morning—the fourth day.

20 And God said, "Let the water teem with living creatures, and let birds fly above the earth across the expanse of the sky." 21So God created the great creatures of the sea and every living and moving thing with which the water teems, according to their kinds, and every winged bird according to its kind. And God saw that it was good. 22God blessed them and said, "Be fruitful and increase in number and fill the water in the seas, and let the birds increase on the earth." 23And there was evening, and there was morning—the fifth day.

24 And God said, "Let the land produce living creatures according to their kinds: livestock, creatures that move along the ground, and wild animals, each according to its kind." And it was so. 25God made the wild animals according to their kinds, the livestock according to their kinds, and all the creatures that move along the ground according to their kinds. And God saw that it was good.

26Then God said, "Let us make man in our image, in our likeness, and let them rule over the fish of the sea and the birds of the air, over the livestock, over all the earth,ᵃ and over all the creatures that move along the ground."

27 So God created man in his own image, in the image of God he created him; male and female he created them.

28God blessed them and said to them, "Be fruitful and increase in number; fill the earth and subdue it. Rule over the fish of

THE MESSAGE

1.14-15 God spoke: "Lights! Come out!
Shine in Heaven's sky!
Separate Day from Night.
Mark seasons and days and years,
Lights in Heaven's sky to give light to
Earth."
And there it was.

1.16-19 God made two big lights, the larger
to take charge of Day,
The smaller to be in charge of Night;
and he made the stars.
God placed them in the heavenly sky
to light up Earth
And oversee Day and Night,
to separate light and dark.
God saw that it was good.
It was evening, it was morning—
Day Four.

1.20-23 God spoke: "Swarm, Ocean, with fish and
all sea life!
Birds, fly through the sky over Earth!"
God created the huge whales,
all the swarm of life in the waters,
And every kind and species of flying birds.
God saw that it was good.
God blessed them: "Prosper! Reproduce!
Fill Ocean!
Birds, reproduce on Earth!"
It was evening, it was morning—
Day Five.

1.24-25 God spoke: "Earth, generate life! Every sort
and kind: cattle and reptiles and
wild animals—all kinds."
And there it was:
wild animals of every kind,
Cattle of all kinds, every sort of reptile and
bug.
God saw that it was good.

1.26-28 God spoke: "Let us make human beings in
our image, make them
reflecting our nature
So they can be responsible for the fish in
the sea,
the birds in the air, the cattle,
And, yes, Earth itself,
and every animal that moves on the face
of Earth."
God created human beings;
he created them godlike,
Reflecting God's nature.
He created them male and female.
God blessed them:
"Prosper! Reproduce! Fill Earth! Take
charge!

ᵃ 26 Hebrew; Syriac *all the wild animals*

NEW INTERNATIONAL VERSION

the sea and the birds of the air and over every living creature that moves on the ground."

²⁹Then God said, "I give you every seed-bearing plant on the face of the whole earth and every tree that has fruit with seed in it. They will be yours for food. ³⁰And to all the beasts of the earth and all the birds of the air and all the creatures that move on the ground—everything that has the breath of life in it—I give every green plant for food." And it was so.

³¹God saw all that he had made, and it was very good. And there was evening, and there was morning—the sixth day.

2 Thus the heavens and the earth were completed in all their vast array.

²By the seventh day God had finished the work he had been doing; so on the seventh day he rested^a from all his work. ³And God blessed the seventh day and made it holy, because on it he rested from all the work of creating that he had done.

ADAM AND EVE

⁴This is the account of the heavens and the earth when they were created.

When the LORD God made the earth and the heavens— ⁵and no shrub of the field had yet appeared on the earth^b and no plant of the field had yet sprung up, for the LORD God had not sent rain on the earth^b and there was no man to work the ground, ⁶but streams^c came up from the earth and watered the whole surface of the ground— ⁷the LORD God formed the man^d from the dust of the ground and breathed into his nostrils the breath of life, and the man became a living being.

⁸Now the LORD God had planted a garden in the east, in Eden; and there he put the man he had formed. ⁹And the LORD God made all kinds of trees grow out of the ground—trees that were pleasing to the eye and good for food. In the middle of the garden were the tree of life and the tree of the knowledge of good and evil.

¹⁰A river watering the garden flowed from Eden; from there it was separated into four head-

^a 2 Or *ceased*; also in verse 3   ^b 5 Or *land*; also in verse 6
^c 6 Or *mist*   ^d 7 The Hebrew for *man (adam)* sounds like and may be related to the Hebrew for *ground (adamah)*; it is also the name *Adam* (see Gen. 2:20).

THE MESSAGE

Be responsible for fish in the sea and birds
  in the air,
  for every living thing that moves on the
    face of Earth."

1.29-30 Then God said, "I've given you
  every sort of seed-bearing plant on Earth
And every kind of fruit-bearing tree,
  given them to you for food.
To all animals and all birds,
  everything that moves and breathes,
I give whatever grows out of the ground for
    food."
  And there it was.

1.31 God looked over everything he had made;
  it was so good, so very good!
It was evening, it was morning—
  Day Six.

2 Heaven and Earth were finished,
  down to the last detail.

2.2-4 By the seventh day
  God had finished his work.
On the seventh day
  he rested from all his work.
God blessed the seventh day.
  He made it a Holy Day
Because on that day he rested from his
    work,
  all the creating God had done.

This is the story of how it all started,
  of Heaven and Earth when they were
    created.

ADAM AND EVE

2.5-7 At the time GOD made Earth and Heaven, before any grasses or shrubs had sprouted from the ground—GOD hadn't yet sent rain on Earth, nor was there anyone around to work the ground (the whole Earth was watered by underground springs)—GOD formed Man out of dirt from the ground and blew into his nostrils the breath of life. The Man came alive—a living soul!

2.8-9 Then GOD planted a garden in Eden, in the east. He put the Man he had just made in it. GOD made all kinds of trees grow from the ground, trees beautiful to look at and good to eat. The Tree-of-Life was in the middle of the garden, also the Tree-of-Knowledge-of-Good-and-Evil.

2.10-14 A river flows out of Eden to water the garden and from there divides into four rivers. The

NEW INTERNATIONAL VERSION

waters. [11]The name of the first is the Pishon; it winds through the entire land of Havilah, where there is gold. [12](The gold of that land is good; aromatic resin[a] and onyx are also there.) [13]The name of the second river is the Gihon; it winds through the entire land of Cush.[b] [14]The name of the third river is the Tigris; it runs along the east side of Asshur. And the fourth river is the Euphrates.

[15]The LORD God took the man and put him in the Garden of Eden to work it and take care of it. [16]And the LORD God commanded the man, "You are free to eat from any tree in the garden; [17]but you must not eat from the tree of the knowledge of good and evil, for when you eat of it you will surely die."

[18]The LORD God said, "It is not good for the man to be alone. I will make a helper suitable for him."

[19]Now the LORD God had formed out of the ground all the beasts of the field and all the birds of the air. He brought them to the man to see what he would name them; and whatever the man called each living creature, that was its name. [20]So the man gave names to all the livestock, the birds of the air and all the beasts of the field.

But for Adam[c] no suitable helper was found. [21]So the LORD God caused the man to fall into a deep sleep; and while he was sleeping, he took one of the man's ribs[d] and closed up the place with flesh. [22]Then the LORD God made a woman from the rib[e] he had taken out of the man, and he brought her to the man.

[23]The man said,

"This is now bone of my bones
    and flesh of my flesh;
she shall be called 'woman,'[f]
    for she was taken out of man."

[24]For this reason a man will leave his father and mother and be united to his wife, and they will become one flesh. [25]The man and his wife were both naked, and they felt no shame.

THE FALL OF MAN

3 Now the serpent was more crafty than any of the wild animals the LORD God had made. He said to the woman, "Did God really say, 'You must not eat from any tree in the garden'?"

[2]The woman said to the serpent, "We may eat fruit from the trees in the garden, [3]but God did

THE MESSAGE

first is named Pishon; it flows through Havilah where there is gold. The gold of this land is good. The land is also known for a sweet-scented resin and the onyx stone. The second river is named Gihon; it flows through the land of Cush. The third river is named Hiddekel and flows east of Assyria. The fourth river is the Euphrates.

2.15   GOD took the Man and set him down in the Garden of Eden to work the ground and keep it in order.

2.16-17   GOD commanded the Man, "You can eat from any tree in the garden, except from the Tree-of-Knowledge-of-Good-and-Evil. Don't eat from it. The moment you eat from that tree, you're dead."

2.18-20   GOD said, "It's not good for the Man to be alone; I'll make him a helper, a companion." So GOD formed from the dirt of the ground all the animals of the field and all the birds of the air. He brought them to the Man to see what he would name them. Whatever the Man called each living creature, that was its name. The Man named the cattle, named the birds of the air, named the wild animals; but he didn't find a suitable companion.

2.21-22   GOD put the Man into a deep sleep. As he slept he removed one of his ribs and replaced it with flesh. GOD then used the rib that he had taken from the Man to make Woman and presented her to the Man.

2.23-25   The Man said,
"Finally! Bone of my bone,
    flesh of my flesh!
Name her Woman
    for she was made from Man."
Therefore a man leaves his father and
    mother and embraces his wife. They
    become one flesh.
The two of them, the Man and his Wife,
    were naked, but they felt no shame.

3.1   3 The serpent was clever, more clever than any wild animal GOD had made. He spoke to the Woman: "Do I understand that God told you not to eat from any tree in the garden?"

3.2-3   The Woman said to the serpent, "Not at all. We can eat from the trees in the garden. It's

---

[a] 12 Or *good; pearls*   [b] 13 Possibly southeast Mesopotamia   [c] 20 Or *the man*   [d] 21 Or *took part of the man's side*   [e] 22 Or *part*   [f] 23 The Hebrew for *woman* sounds like the Hebrew for *man.*

NEW INTERNATIONAL VERSION

say, 'You must not eat fruit from the tree that is in the middle of the garden, and you must not touch it, or you will die.' "

⁴"You will not surely die," the serpent said to the woman. ⁵"For God knows that when you eat of it your eyes will be opened, and you will be like God, knowing good and evil."

⁶When the woman saw that the fruit of the tree was good for food and pleasing to the eye, and also desirable for gaining wisdom, she took some and ate it. She also gave some to her husband, who was with her, and he ate it. ⁷Then the eyes of both of them were opened, and they realized they were naked; so they sewed fig leaves together and made coverings for themselves.

⁸Then the man and his wife heard the sound of the Lord God as he was walking in the garden in the cool of the day, and they hid from the Lord God among the trees of the garden. ⁹But the Lord God called to the man, "Where are you?"

¹⁰He answered, "I heard you in the garden, and I was afraid because I was naked; so I hid."

¹¹And he said, "Who told you that you were naked? Have you eaten from the tree that I commanded you not to eat from?"

¹²The man said, "The woman you put here with me—she gave me some fruit from the tree, and I ate it."

¹³Then the Lord God said to the woman, "What is this you have done?"

The woman said, "The serpent deceived me, and I ate."

¹⁴So the Lord God said to the serpent, "Because you have done this,

"Cursed are you above all the livestock
  and all the wild animals!
You will crawl on your belly
  and you will eat dust
  all the days of your life.
¹⁵And I will put enmity
  between you and the woman,
  and between your offspring ᵃ and hers;
he will crush ᵇ your head,
  and you will strike his heel."

¹⁶To the woman he said,

"I will greatly increase your pains in
  childbearing;
with pain you will give birth to children.
Your desire will be for your husband,
  and he will rule over you."

¹⁷To Adam he said, "Because you listened to your wife and ate from the tree about which I commanded you, 'You must not eat of it,'

THE MESSAGE

only about the tree in the middle of the garden that God said, 'Don't eat from it; don't even touch it or you'll die.'"

3.4-5 The serpent told the Woman, "You won't die. God knows that the moment you eat from that tree, you'll see what's really going on. You'll be just like God, knowing everything, ranging all the way from good to evil."

3.6 When the Woman saw that the tree looked like good eating and realized what she would get out of it—she'd know everything!—she took and ate the fruit and then gave some to her husband, and he ate.

3.7 Immediately the two of them did "see what's really going on"—saw themselves naked! They sewed fig leaves together as makeshift clothes for themselves.

3.8 When they heard the sound of God strolling in the garden in the evening breeze, the Man and his Wife hid in the trees of the garden, hid from God.

3.9 God called to the Man: "Where are you?"

3.10 He said, "I heard you in the garden and I was afraid because I was naked. And I hid."

3.11 God said, "Who told you you were naked? Did you eat from that tree I told you not to eat from?"

3.12 The Man said, "The Woman you gave me as a companion, she gave me fruit from the tree, and, yes, I ate it."

God said to the Woman, "What is this that you've done?"

3.13 "The serpent seduced me," she said, "and I ate."

3.14-15 God told the serpent:
"Because you've done this, you're cursed,
  cursed beyond all cattle and wild
    animals,
Cursed to slink on your belly
  and eat dirt all your life.
I'm declaring war between you and the
    Woman,
  between your offspring and hers.
He'll wound your head,
  you'll wound his heel."

3.16 He told the Woman:
"I'll multiply your pains in childbirth;
  you'll give birth to your babies in pain.
You'll want to please your husband,
  but he'll lord it over you."

3.17-19 He told the Man:
"Because you listened to your wife
  and ate from the tree
That I commanded you not to eat from,
  'Don't eat from this tree,'

ᵃ 15 Or *seed*   ᵇ 15 Or *strike*

NEW INTERNATIONAL VERSION

"Cursed is the ground because of you;
  through painful toil you will eat of it
  all the days of your life.
18 It will produce thorns and thistles for you,
  and you will eat the plants of the field.
19 By the sweat of your brow
  you will eat your food
until you return to the ground,
  since from it you were taken;
for dust you are
  and to dust you will return."

20 Adam[a] named his wife Eve,[b] because she would become the mother of all the living.

21 The LORD God made garments of skin for Adam and his wife and clothed them. 22 And the LORD God said, "The man has now become like one of us, knowing good and evil. He must not be allowed to reach out his hand and take also from the tree of life and eat, and live forever." 23 So the LORD God banished him from the Garden of Eden to work the ground from which he had been taken. 24 After he drove the man out, he placed on the east side[c] of the Garden of Eden cherubim and a flaming sword flashing back and forth to guard the way to the tree of life.

CAIN AND ABEL

4 Adam[a] lay with his wife Eve, and she became pregnant and gave birth to Cain.[d] She said, "With the help of the LORD I have brought forth[e] a man." 2 Later she gave birth to his brother Abel.

Now Abel kept flocks, and Cain worked the soil. 3 In the course of time Cain brought some of the fruits of the soil as an offering to the LORD. 4 But Abel brought fat portions from some of the firstborn of his flock. The LORD looked with favor on Abel and his offering, 5 but on Cain and his offering he did not look with favor. So Cain was very angry, and his face was downcast.

6 Then the LORD said to Cain, "Why are you angry? Why is your face downcast? 7 If you do what is right, will you not be accepted? But if you do not do what is right, sin is crouching at your door; it desires to have you, but you must master it."

8 Now Cain said to his brother Abel, "Let's go out to the field."[f] And while they were in the field, Cain attacked his brother Abel and killed him.

---

a 20,4 Or *The man*   b 20 *Eve* probably means *living*.
c 24 Or *placed in front*   d 1 *Cain* sounds like the Hebrew for *brought forth* or *acquired*.   e 1 Or *have acquired*
f 8 Samaritan Pentateuch, Septuagint, Vulgate and Syriac; Masoretic Text does not have "*Let's go out to the field.*"

THE MESSAGE

The very ground is cursed because of you;
  getting food from the ground
Will be as painful as having babies is for
  your wife;
  you'll be working in pain all your life
  long.
The ground will sprout thorns and weeds,
  you'll get your food the hard way,
Planting and tilling and harvesting,
  sweating in the fields from dawn to dusk,
Until you return to that ground yourself,
  dead and buried;
  you started out as dirt, you'll end up dirt."

3.20 The Man, known as Adam, named his wife Eve because she was the mother of all the living.

3.21 GOD made leather clothing for Adam and his wife and dressed them.

3.22 GOD said, "The Man has become like one of us, capable of knowing everything, ranging from good to evil. What if he now should reach out and take fruit from the Tree-of-Life and eat, and live forever? Never—this cannot happen!"

3.23-24 So GOD expelled them from the Garden of Eden and sent them to work the ground, the same dirt out of which they'd been made. He threw them out of the garden and stationed angel-cherubim and a revolving sword of fire east of it, guarding the path to the Tree-of-Life.

4.1 4 Adam slept with Eve his wife. She conceived and had Cain. She said, "I've gotten a man, with GOD's help!"

4.2 Then she had another baby, Abel. Abel was a herdsman and Cain a farmer.

4.3-5 Time passed. Cain brought an offering to GOD from the produce of his farm. Abel also brought an offering, but from the firstborn animals of his herd, choice cuts of meat. GOD liked Abel and his offering, but Cain and his offering didn't get his approval. Cain lost his temper and went into a sulk.

4.6-7 GOD spoke to Cain: "Why this tantrum? Why the sulking? If you do well, won't you be accepted? And if you don't do well, sin is lying in wait for you, ready to pounce; it's out to get you, you've got to master it."

4.8 Cain had words with his brother. They were out in the field; Cain came at Abel his brother and killed him.

NEW INTERNATIONAL VERSION

⁹Then the LORD said to Cain, "Where is your brother Abel?"

"I don't know," he replied. "Am I my brother's keeper?"

¹⁰The LORD said, "What have you done? Listen! Your brother's blood cries out to me from the ground. ¹¹Now you are under a curse and driven from the ground, which opened its mouth to receive your brother's blood from your hand. ¹²When you work the ground, it will no longer yield its crops for you. You will be a restless wanderer on the earth."

¹³Cain said to the LORD, "My punishment is more than I can bear. ¹⁴Today you are driving me from the land, and I will be hidden from your presence; I will be a restless wanderer on the earth, and whoever finds me will kill me."

¹⁵But the LORD said to him, "Not so*ᵃ*; if anyone kills Cain, he will suffer vengeance seven times over." Then the LORD put a mark on Cain so that no one who found him would kill him. ¹⁶So Cain went out from the LORD's presence and lived in the land of Nod,*ᵇ* east of Eden.

¹⁷Cain lay with his wife, and she became pregnant and gave birth to Enoch. Cain was then building a city, and he named it after his son Enoch. ¹⁸To Enoch was born Irad, and Irad was the father of Mehujael, and Mehujael was the father of Methushael, and Methushael was the father of Lamech.

¹⁹Lamech married two women, one named Adah and the other Zillah. ²⁰Adah gave birth to Jabal; he was the father of those who live in tents and raise livestock. ²¹His brother's name was Jubal; he was the father of all who play the harp and flute. ²²Zillah also had a son, Tubal-Cain, who forged all kinds of tools out of*ᶜ* bronze and iron. Tubal-Cain's sister was Naamah.

²³Lamech said to his wives,

"Adah and Zillah, listen to me;
    wives of Lamech, hear my words.
I have killed*ᵈ* a man for wounding me,
    a young man for injuring me.
²⁴If Cain is avenged seven times,
    then Lamech seventy-seven times."

²⁵Adam lay with his wife again, and she gave birth to a son and named him Seth,*ᵉ* saying, "God has granted me another child in place of Abel, since Cain killed him." ²⁶Seth also had a son, and he named him Enosh.

At that time men began to call on*ᶠ* the name of the LORD.

THE MESSAGE

⁴·⁹ GOD said to Cain, "Where is Abel your brother?"

He said, "How should I know? Am I his babysitter?"

⁴·¹⁰⁻¹² GOD said, "What have you done! The voice of your brother's blood is calling to me from the ground. From now on you'll get nothing but curses from this ground; you'll be driven from this ground that has opened its arms to receive the blood of your murdered brother. You'll farm this ground, but it will no longer give you its best. You'll be a homeless wanderer on Earth."

⁴·¹³⁻¹⁴ Cain said to GOD, "My punishment is too much. I can't take it! You've thrown me off the land and I can never again face you. I'm a homeless wanderer on Earth and whoever finds me will kill me."

⁴·¹⁵ GOD told him, "No. Anyone who kills Cain will pay for it seven times over." GOD put a mark on Cain to protect him so that no one who met him would kill him.

⁴·¹⁶ Cain left the presence of GOD and lived in No-Man's-Land, east of Eden.

⁴·¹⁷⁻¹⁸ Cain slept with his wife. She conceived and had Enoch. He then built a city and named it after his son, Enoch.

Enoch had Irad,
Irad had Mehujael,
Mehujael had Methushael,
Methushael had Lamech.

⁴·¹⁹⁻²² Lamech married two wives, Adah and Zillah. Adah gave birth to Jabal, the ancestor of all who live in tents and herd cattle. His brother's name was Jubal, the ancestor of all who play the lyre and flute. Zillah gave birth to Tubal-Cain, who worked at the forge making bronze and iron tools. Tubal-Cain's sister was Naamah.

⁴·²³⁻²⁴ Lamech said to his wives,
Adah and Zillah, listen to me;
    you wives of Lamech, hear me out:
I killed a man for wounding me,
    a young man who attacked me.
If Cain is avenged seven times,
    for Lamech it's seventy-seven!

⁴·²⁵⁻²⁶ Adam slept with his wife again. She had a son whom she named Seth. She said, "God has given me another child in place of Abel whom Cain killed." And then Seth had a son whom he named Enosh.

That's when men and women began praying and worshiping in the name of GOD.

ᵃ 15 Septuagint, Vulgate and Syriac; Hebrew *Very well*
ᵇ 16 *Nod* means *wandering* (see verses 12 and 14).
ᶜ 22 Or *who instructed all who work in*   *ᵈ* 23 Or *I will kill*
ᵉ 25 *Seth* probably means *granted*.   *ᶠ* 26 Or *to proclaim*

NEW INTERNATIONAL VERSION

FROM ADAM TO NOAH

5 This is the written account of Adam's line.

When God created man, he made him in the likeness of God. ²He created them male and female and blessed them. And when they were created, he called them "man.ᵃ"

³When Adam had lived 130 years, he had a son in his own likeness, in his own image; and he named him Seth. ⁴After Seth was born, Adam lived 800 years and had other sons and daughters. ⁵Altogether, Adam lived 930 years, and then he died.

⁶When Seth had lived 105 years, he became the fatherᵇ of Enosh. ⁷And after he became the father of Enosh, Seth lived 807 years and had other sons and daughters. ⁸Altogether, Seth lived 912 years, and then he died.

⁹When Enosh had lived 90 years, he became the father of Kenan. ¹⁰And after he became the father of Kenan, Enosh lived 815 years and had other sons and daughters. ¹¹Altogether, Enosh lived 905 years, and then he died.

¹²When Kenan had lived 70 years, he became the father of Mahalalel. ¹³And after he became the father of Mahalalel, Kenan lived 840 years and had other sons and daughters. ¹⁴Altogether, Kenan lived 910 years, and then he died.

¹⁵When Mahalalel had lived 65 years, he became the father of Jared. ¹⁶And after he became the father of Jared, Mahalalel lived 830 years and had other sons and daughters. ¹⁷Altogether, Mahalalel lived 895 years, and then he died.

¹⁸When Jared had lived 162 years, he became the father of Enoch. ¹⁹And after he became the father of Enoch, Jared lived 800 years and had other sons and daughters. ²⁰Altogether, Jared lived 962 years, and then he died.

²¹When Enoch had lived 65 years, he became the father of Methuselah. ²²And after he became the father of Methuselah, Enoch walked with God 300 years and had other sons and daughters. ²³Altogether, Enoch lived 365 years. ²⁴Enoch walked with God; then he was no more, because God took him away.

²⁵When Methuselah had lived 187 years, he became the father of Lamech. ²⁶And after he became the father of Lamech, Methuselah lived 782 years and had other sons and daughters. ²⁷Altogether, Methuselah lived 969 years, and then he died.

²⁸When Lamech had lived 182 years, he had a son. ²⁹He named him Noahᶜ and said, "He will comfort us in the labor and painful toil of our

THE MESSAGE

THE FAMILY TREE OF THE HUMAN RACE

5.1-2 **5** This is the family tree of the human race: When God created the human race, he made it godlike, with a nature akin to God. He created both male and female and blessed them, the whole human race.

5.3-5 When Adam was 130 years old, he had a son who was just like him, his very spirit and image, and named him Seth. After the birth of Seth, Adam lived another 800 years, having more sons and daughters. Adam lived a total of 930 years. And he died.

5.6-8 When Seth was 105 years old, he had Enosh. After Seth had Enosh, he lived another 807 years, having more sons and daughters. Seth lived a total of 912 years. And he died.

5.9-11 When Enosh was ninety years old, he had Kenan. After he had Kenan, he lived another 815 years, having more sons and daughters. Enosh lived a total of 905 years. And he died.

5.12-14 When Kenan was seventy years old, he had Mahalalel. After he had Mahalalel, he lived another 840 years, having more sons and daughters. Kenan lived a total of 910 years. And he died.

5.15-17 When Mahalalel was sixty-five years old, he had Jared. After he had Jared, he lived another 830 years, having more sons and daughters. Mahalalel lived a total of 895 years. And he died.

5.18-20 When Jared was 162 years old, he had Enoch. After he had Enoch, he lived another 800 years, having more sons and daughters. Jared lived a total of 962 years. And he died.

5.21-23 When Enoch was sixty-five years old, he had Methuselah. Enoch walked steadily with God. After he had Methuselah, he lived another 300 years, having more sons and daughters. Enoch lived a total of 365 years.

5.24 Enoch walked steadily with God. And then one day he was simply gone: God took him.

5.25-27 When Methuselah was 187 years old, he had Lamech. After he had Lamech, he lived another 782 years. Methuselah lived a total of 969 years. And he died.

5.28-31 When Lamech was 182 years old, he had a son. He named him Noah, saying, "This one will give us a break from the hard work of

---

ᵃ *2* Hebrew *adam*   ᵇ *6 Father* may mean *ancestor*; also in verses 7-26.   ᶜ *29 Noah* sounds like the Hebrew for *comfort.*

NEW INTERNATIONAL VERSION

hands caused by the ground the LORD has cursed." ³⁰After Noah was born, Lamech lived 595 years and had other sons and daughters. ³¹Altogether, Lamech lived 777 years, and then he died.

³²After Noah was 500 years old, he became the father of Shem, Ham and Japheth.

THE FLOOD

6 When men began to increase in number on the earth and daughters were born to them, ²the sons of God saw that the daughters of men were beautiful, and they married any of them they chose. ³Then the LORD said, "My Spirit will not contend with*ᵃ* man forever, for he is mortal*ᵇ*; his days will be a hundred and twenty years."

⁴The Nephilim were on the earth in those days—and also afterward—when the sons of God went to the daughters of men and had children by them. They were the heroes of old, men of renown.

⁵The LORD saw how great man's wickedness on the earth had become, and that every inclination of the thoughts of his heart was only evil all the time. ⁶The LORD was grieved that he had made man on the earth, and his heart was filled with pain. ⁷So the LORD said, "I will wipe mankind, whom I have created, from the face of the earth—men and animals, and creatures that move along the ground, and birds of the air—for I am grieved that I have made them." ⁸But Noah found favor in the eyes of the LORD.

⁹This is the account of Noah.

Noah was a righteous man, blameless among the people of his time, and he walked with God. ¹⁰Noah had three sons: Shem, Ham and Japheth.

¹¹Now the earth was corrupt in God's sight and was full of violence. ¹²God saw how corrupt the earth had become, for all the people on earth had corrupted their ways. ¹³So God said to Noah, "I am going to put an end to all people, for the earth is filled with violence because of them. I am surely going to destroy both them and the earth. ¹⁴So make yourself an ark of cypress*ᶜ* wood; make rooms in it and coat it with pitch inside and out. ¹⁵This is how you are to build it: The ark is to be 450 feet long, 75 feet wide and 45 feet high.*ᵈ* ¹⁶Make a roof for it and finish*ᵉ* the ark to within 18 inches*ᶠ* of the top. Put a door in the side of the ark and make lower, middle and upper decks. ¹⁷I am going to bring floodwaters on the earth to destroy all life under the heavens,

---

ᵃ 3 Or *My spirit will not remain in*   *ᵇ 3* Or *corrupt*
ᶜ 14 The meaning of the Hebrew for this word is uncertain.
ᵈ 15 Hebrew *300 cubits long, 50 cubits wide and 30 cubits high* (about 140 meters long, 23 meters wide and 13.5 meters high)   *ᵉ 16* Or *Make an opening for light by finishing*   *ᶠ 16* Hebrew *a cubit* (about 0.5 meter)

THE MESSAGE

farming the ground that GOD cursed." After Lamech had Noah, he lived another 595 years, having more sons and daughters. Lamech lived a total of 777 years. And he died.

5.32 When Noah was 500 years old, he had Shem, Ham, and Japheth.

GIANTS IN THE LAND

6.1-2 **6** When the human race began to increase, with more and more daughters being born, the sons of God noticed that the daughters of men were beautiful. They looked them over and picked out wives for themselves.

6.3 Then GOD said, "I'm not going to breathe life into men and women endlessly. Eventually they're going to die; from now on they can expect a life span of 120 years."

6.4 This was back in the days (and also later) when there were giants in the land. The giants came from the union of the sons of God and the daughters of men. These were the mighty men of ancient lore, the famous ones.

NOAH AND HIS SONS

6.5-7 GOD saw that human evil was out of control. People thought evil, imagined evil—evil, evil, evil from morning to night. GOD was sorry that he had made the human race in the first place; it broke his heart. GOD said, "I'll get rid of my ruined creation, make a clean sweep: people, animals, snakes and bugs, birds—the works. I'm sorry I made them."

6.8 But Noah was different. GOD liked what he saw in Noah.

6.9-10 This is the story of Noah: Noah was a good man, a man of integrity in his community. Noah walked with God. Noah had three sons: Shem, Ham, and Japheth.

6.11-12 As far as God was concerned, the Earth had become a sewer; there was violence everywhere. God took one look and saw how bad it was, everyone corrupt and corrupting—life itself corrupt to the core.

6.13 God said to Noah, "It's all over. It's the end of the human race. The violence is everywhere; I'm making a clean sweep.

6.14-16 "Build yourself a ship from teakwood. Make rooms in it. Coat it with pitch inside and out. Make it 450 feet long, seventy-five feet wide, and forty-five feet high. Build a roof for it and put in a window eighteen inches from the top; put in a door on the side of the ship; and make three decks, lower, middle, and upper.

6.17 "I'm going to bring a flood on the Earth that

NEW INTERNATIONAL VERSION

every creature that has the breath of life in it. Everything on earth will perish. [18]But I will establish my covenant with you, and you will enter the ark—you and your sons and your wife and your sons' wives with you. [19]You are to bring into the ark two of all living creatures, male and female, to keep them alive with you. [20]Two of every kind of bird, of every kind of animal and of every kind of creature that moves along the ground will come to you to be kept alive. [21]You are to take every kind of food that is to be eaten and store it away as food for you and for them."

[22]Noah did everything just as God commanded him.

7 The LORD then said to Noah, "Go into the ark, you and your whole family, because I have found you righteous in this generation. [2]Take with you seven[a] of every kind of clean animal, a male and its mate, and two of every kind of unclean animal, a male and its mate, [3]and also seven of every kind of bird, male and female, to keep their various kinds alive throughout the earth. [4]Seven days from now I will send rain on the earth for forty days and forty nights, and I will wipe from the face of the earth every living creature I have made."

[5]And Noah did all that the LORD commanded him.

[6]Noah was six hundred years old when the floodwaters came on the earth. [7]And Noah and his sons and his wife and his sons' wives entered the ark to escape the waters of the flood. [8]Pairs of clean and unclean animals, of birds and of all creatures that move along the ground, [9]male and female, came to Noah and entered the ark, as God had commanded Noah. [10]And after the seven days the floodwaters came on the earth.

[11]In the six hundredth year of Noah's life, on the seventeenth day of the second month—on that day all the springs of the great deep burst forth, and the floodgates of the heavens were opened. [12]And rain fell on the earth forty days and forty nights.

[13]On that very day Noah and his sons, Shem, Ham and Japheth, together with his wife and the wives of his three sons, entered the ark. [14]They had with them every wild animal according to its kind, all livestock according to their kinds, every creature that moves along the ground according to its kind and every bird according to its kind, everything with wings. [15]Pairs of all creatures that have the breath of life in them came to Noah and entered the ark. [16]The animals going in were male and female of every living thing, as God had commanded Noah. Then the LORD shut him in.

[a] 2 Or seven pairs; also in verse 3

THE MESSAGE

will destroy everything alive under Heaven. Total destruction.

6.18-21 "But I'm going to establish a covenant with you: You'll board the ship, and your sons, your wife and your sons' wives will come on board with you. You are also to take two of each living creature, a male and a female, on board the ship, to preserve their lives with you: two of every species of bird, mammal, and reptile—two of everything so as to preserve their lives along with yours. Also get all the food you'll need and store it up for you and them."

6.22 Noah did everything God commanded him to do.

7.1 7 Next GOD said to Noah, "Now board the ship, you and all your family—out of everyone in this generation, you're the righteous one.

7.2-4 "Take on board with you seven pairs of every clean animal, a male and a female; one pair of every unclean animal, a male and a female; and seven pairs of every kind of bird, a male and a female, to insure their survival on Earth. In just seven days I will dump rain on Earth for forty days and forty nights. I'll make a clean sweep of everything that I've made."

7.5 Noah did everything GOD commanded him.

7.6-10 Noah was 600 years old when the floodwaters covered the Earth. Noah and his wife and sons and their wives boarded the ship to escape the flood. Clean and unclean animals, birds, and all the crawling creatures came in pairs to Noah and to the ship, male and female, just as God had commanded Noah. In seven days the floodwaters came.

7.11-12 It was the six-hundredth year of Noah's life, in the second month, on the seventeenth day of the month that it happened: all the underground springs erupted and all the windows of Heaven were thrown open. Rain poured for forty days and forty nights.

7.13-16 That's the day Noah and his sons Shem, Ham, and Japheth, accompanied by his wife and his sons' wives, boarded the ship. And with them every kind of wild and domestic animal, right down to all the kinds of creatures that crawl and all kinds of birds and anything that flies. They came to Noah and to the ship in pairs—everything and anything that had the breath of life in it, male and female of every creature came just as God had commanded Noah. Then GOD shut the door behind him.

NEW INTERNATIONAL VERSION

¹⁷For forty days the flood kept coming on the earth, and as the waters increased they lifted the ark high above the earth. ¹⁸The waters rose and increased greatly on the earth, and the ark floated on the surface of the water. ¹⁹They rose greatly on the earth, and all the high mountains under the entire heavens were covered. ²⁰The waters rose and covered the mountains to a depth of more than twenty feet.*ᵃ,ᵇ* ²¹Every living thing that moved on the earth perished—birds, livestock, wild animals, all the creatures that swarm over the earth, and all mankind. ²²Everything on dry land that had the breath of life in its nostrils died. ²³Every living thing on the face of the earth was wiped out; men and animals and the creatures that move along the ground and the birds of the air were wiped from the earth. Only Noah was left, and those with him in the ark.

²⁴The waters flooded the earth for a hundred and fifty days.

8 But God remembered Noah and all the wild animals and the livestock that were with him in the ark, and he sent a wind over the earth, and the waters receded. ²Now the springs of the deep and the floodgates of the heavens had been closed, and the rain had stopped falling from the sky. ³The water receded steadily from the earth. At the end of the hundred and fifty days the water had gone down, ⁴and on the seventeenth day of the seventh month the ark came to rest on the mountains of Ararat. ⁵The waters continued to recede until the tenth month, and on the first day of the tenth month the tops of the mountains became visible.

⁶After forty days Noah opened the window he had made in the ark ⁷and sent out a raven, and it kept flying back and forth until the water had dried up from the earth. ⁸Then he sent out a dove to see if the water had receded from the surface of the ground. ⁹But the dove could find no place to set its feet because there was water over all the surface of the earth; so it returned to Noah in the ark. He reached out his hand and took the dove and brought it back to himself in the ark. ¹⁰He waited seven more days and again sent out the dove from the ark. ¹¹When the dove returned to him in the evening, there in its beak was a freshly plucked olive leaf! Then Noah knew that the water had receded from the earth. ¹²He waited seven more days and sent the dove out again, but this time it did not return to him.

¹³By the first day of the first month of Noah's six hundred and first year, the water had dried up

THE MESSAGE

7.17-23 The flood continued forty days and the waters rose and lifted the ship high over the Earth. The waters kept rising, the flood deepened on the Earth, the ship floated on the surface. The flood got worse until all the highest mountains were covered—the high water mark reached twenty feet above the crest of the mountains. Everything died. Anything that moved—dead. Birds, farm animals, wild animals, the entire teeming exuberance of life—dead. And all people—dead. Every living, breathing creature that lived on dry land died; he wiped out the whole works—people and animals, crawling creatures and flying birds, every last one of them, gone. Only Noah and his company on the ship lived.

7.24 The floodwaters took over for 150 days.

8.1-3 **8** Then God turned his attention to Noah and all the wild animals and farm animals with him on the ship. God caused the wind to blow and the floodwaters began to go down. The underground springs were shut off, the windows of Heaven closed and the rain quit. Inch by inch the water lowered. After 150 days the worst was over.

8.4-6 On the seventeenth day of the seventh month, the ship landed on the Ararat mountain range. The water kept going down until the tenth month. On the first day of the tenth month the tops of the mountains came into view. After forty days Noah opened the window that he had built into the ship.

8.7-9 He sent out a raven; it flew back and forth waiting for the floodwaters to dry up. Then he sent a dove to check on the flood conditions, but it couldn't even find a place to perch—water still covered the Earth. Noah reached out and caught it, brought it back into the ship.

8.10-11 He waited seven more days and sent out the dove again. It came back in the evening with a freshly picked olive leaf in its beak. Noah knew that the flood was about finished.

8.12 He waited another seven days and sent the dove out a third time. This time it didn't come back.

8.13-14 In the six-hundred-first year of Noah's life, on the first day of the first month, the flood

---

ᵃ 20 Hebrew *fifteen cubits* (about 6.9 meters)   *ᵇ 20* Or *rose more than twenty feet, and the mountains were covered*

NEW INTERNATIONAL VERSION

from the earth. Noah then removed the covering from the ark and saw that the surface of the ground was dry. ¹⁴By the twenty-seventh day of the second month the earth was completely dry.

¹⁵Then God said to Noah, ¹⁶"Come out of the ark, you and your wife and your sons and their wives. ¹⁷Bring out every kind of living creature that is with you—the birds, the animals, and all the creatures that move along the ground—so they can multiply on the earth and be fruitful and increase in number upon it."

¹⁸So Noah came out, together with his sons and his wife and his sons' wives. ¹⁹All the animals and all the creatures that move along the ground and all the birds—everything that moves on the earth—came out of the ark, one kind after another.

²⁰Then Noah built an altar to the LORD and, taking some of all the clean animals and clean birds, he sacrificed burnt offerings on it. ²¹The LORD smelled the pleasing aroma and said in his heart: "Never again will I curse the ground because of man, even though*ᵃ* every inclination of his heart is evil from childhood. And never again will I destroy all living creatures, as I have done.

²² "As long as the earth endures,
   seedtime and harvest,
   cold and heat,
   summer and winter,
   day and night
   will never cease."

GOD'S COVENANT WITH NOAH

9 Then God blessed Noah and his sons, saying to them, "Be fruitful and increase in number and fill the earth. ²The fear and dread of you will fall upon all the beasts of the earth and all the birds of the air, upon every creature that moves along the ground, and upon all the fish of the sea; they are given into your hands. ³Everything that lives and moves will be food for you. Just as I gave you the green plants, I now give you everything.

⁴"But you must not eat meat that has its lifeblood still in it. ⁵And for your lifeblood I will surely demand an accounting. I will demand an accounting from every animal. And from each man, too, I will demand an accounting for the life of his fellow man.

⁶ "Whoever sheds the blood of man,
   by man shall his blood be shed;
   for in the image of God
   has God made man.

⁷As for you, be fruitful and increase in number; multiply on the earth and increase upon it."

ᵃ *21 Or man, for*

THE MESSAGE

had dried up. Noah opened the hatch of the ship and saw dry ground. By the twenty-seventh day of the second month, the Earth was completely dry.

8.15-17 God spoke to Noah: "Leave the ship, you and your wife and your sons and your sons' wives. And take all the animals with you, the whole menagerie of birds and mammals and crawling creatures, all that brimming prodigality of life, so they can reproduce and flourish on the Earth."

8.18-19 Noah disembarked with his sons and wife and his sons' wives. Then all the animals, crawling creatures, birds—every creature on the face of the Earth—left the ship family by family.

8.20-21 Noah built an altar to GOD. He selected clean animals and birds from every species and offered them as burnt-offerings on the altar. GOD smelled the sweet fragrance and thought to himself, "I'll never again curse the ground because of people. I know they have this bent toward evil from an early age, but I'll never again kill off everything living as I've just done.

8.22   For as long as Earth lasts,
         planting and harvest, cold and heat,
         Summer and winter, day and night
         will never stop."

9.1-4   **9** God blessed Noah and his sons: He said, "Prosper! Reproduce! Fill the Earth! Every living creature—birds, animals, fish—will fall under your spell and be afraid of you. You're responsible for them. All living creatures are yours for food; just as I gave you the plants, now I give you everything else. Except for meat with its lifeblood still in it—don't eat that.

9.5   "But your own lifeblood I will avenge; I will avenge it against both animals and other humans.

9.6-7   Whoever sheds human blood,
         by humans let his blood be shed,
         Because God made humans in his image
         reflecting God's very nature.
         You're here to bear fruit, reproduce,
         lavish life on the Earth, live
         bountifully!"

NEW INTERNATIONAL VERSION

⁸Then God said to Noah and to his sons with him: ⁹"I now establish my covenant with you and with your descendants after you ¹⁰and with every living creature that was with you—the birds, the livestock and all the wild animals, all those that came out of the ark with you—every living creature on earth. ¹¹I establish my covenant with you: Never again will all life be cut off by the waters of a flood; never again will there be a flood to destroy the earth."

¹²And God said, "This is the sign of the covenant I am making between me and you and every living creature with you, a covenant for all generations to come: ¹³I have set my rainbow in the clouds, and it will be the sign of the covenant between me and the earth. ¹⁴Whenever I bring clouds over the earth and the rainbow appears in the clouds, ¹⁵I will remember my covenant between me and you and all living creatures of every kind. Never again will the waters become a flood to destroy all life. ¹⁶Whenever the rainbow appears in the clouds, I will see it and remember the everlasting covenant between God and all living creatures of every kind on the earth."

¹⁷So God said to Noah, "This is the sign of the covenant I have established between me and all life on the earth."

THE SONS OF NOAH

¹⁸The sons of Noah who came out of the ark were Shem, Ham and Japheth. (Ham was the father of Canaan.) ¹⁹These were the three sons of Noah, and from them came the people who were scattered over the earth.

²⁰Noah, a man of the soil, proceeded*ᵃ* to plant a vineyard. ²¹When he drank some of its wine, he became drunk and lay uncovered inside his tent. ²²Ham, the father of Canaan, saw his father's nakedness and told his two brothers outside. ²³But Shem and Japheth took a garment and laid it across their shoulders; then they walked in backward and covered their father's nakedness. Their faces were turned the other way so that they would not see their father's nakedness.

²⁴When Noah awoke from his wine and found out what his youngest son had done to him, ²⁵he said,

"Cursed be Canaan!
The lowest of slaves
will he be to his brothers."

²⁶He also said,

"Blessed be the LORD, the God of Shem!
May Canaan be the slave of Shem.*ᵇ*

THE MESSAGE

9.8-11 Then God spoke to Noah and his sons: "I'm setting up my covenant with you including your children who will come after you, along with everything alive around you—birds, farm animals, wild animals—that came out of the ship with you. I'm setting up my covenant with you that never again will everything living be destroyed by floodwaters; no, never again will a flood destroy the Earth."

9.12-16 God continued, "This is the sign of the covenant I am making between me and you and everything living around you and everyone living after you. I'm putting my rainbow in the clouds, a sign of the covenant between me and the Earth. From now on, when I form a cloud over the Earth and the rainbow appears in the cloud, I'll remember my covenant between me and you and everything living, that never again will floodwaters destroy all life. When the rainbow appears in the cloud, I'll see it and remember the eternal covenant between God and everything living, every last living creature on Earth."

9.17 And God said, "This is the sign of the covenant that I've set up between me and everything living on the Earth."

9.18-19 The sons of Noah who came out of the ship were Shem, Ham, and Japheth. Ham was the father of Canaan. These are the three sons of Noah; from these three the whole Earth was populated.

9.20-23 Noah, a farmer, was the first to plant a vineyard. He drank from its wine, got drunk and passed out, naked in his tent. Ham, the father of Canaan, saw that his father was naked and told his two brothers who were outside the tent. Shem and Japheth took a cloak, held it between them from their shoulders, walked backwards and covered their father's nakedness, keeping their faces turned away so they did not see their father's exposed body.

9.24-27 When Noah woke up with his hangover, he learned what his youngest son had done. He said,

Cursed be Canaan! A slave of slaves,
a slave to his brothers!
Blessed be GOD, the God of Shem,
but Canaan shall be his slave.

ᵃ 20 Or *soil, was the first*   *ᵇ 26* Or *be his slave*

NEW INTERNATIONAL VERSION	THE MESSAGE

NEW INTERNATIONAL VERSION

[27] May God extend the territory of Japheth[a];
   may Japheth live in the tents of Shem,
   and may Canaan be his[b] slave."

[28] After the flood Noah lived 350 years. [29] Altogether, Noah lived 950 years, and then he died.

THE TABLE OF NATIONS

10 This is the account of Shem, Ham and Japheth, Noah's sons, who themselves had sons after the flood.

THE JAPHETHITES

[2] The sons[c] of Japheth:
   Gomer, Magog, Madai, Javan, Tubal, Meshech and Tiras.
[3] The sons of Gomer:
   Ashkenaz, Riphath and Togarmah.
[4] The sons of Javan:
   Elishah, Tarshish, the Kittim and the Rodanim.[d] [5](From these the maritime peoples spread out into their territories by their clans within their nations, each with its own language.)

THE HAMITES

[6] The sons of Ham:
   Cush, Mizraim,[e] Put and Canaan.
[7] The sons of Cush:
   Seba, Havilah, Sabtah, Raamah and Sabteca.
   The sons of Raamah:
   Sheba and Dedan.

[8] Cush was the father[f] of Nimrod, who grew to be a mighty warrior on the earth. [9] He was a mighty hunter before the LORD; that is why it is said, "Like Nimrod, a mighty hunter before the LORD." [10] The first centers of his kingdom were Babylon, Erech, Akkad and Calneh, in[g] Shinar.[h] [11] From that land he went to Assyria, where he built Nineveh, Rehoboth Ir,[i] Calah [12] and Resen, which is between Nineveh and Calah; that is the great city.

[13] Mizraim was the father of
   the Ludites, Anamites, Lehabites, Naph-

THE MESSAGE

God prosper Japheth,
   living spaciously in the tents of Shem.
But Canaan shall be his slave.

9.28-29   Noah lived another 350 years following the flood. He lived a total of 950 years. And he died.

THE FAMILY TREE OF NOAH'S SONS

10.1 **10** This is the family tree of the sons of Noah: Shem, Ham, and Japheth. After the flood, they themselves had sons.

10.2   The sons of Japheth: Gomer, Magog, Madai, Javan, Tubal, Meshech, Tiras.
10.3   The sons of Gomer: Ashkenaz, Riphath, Togarmah.
10.4-5   The sons of Javan: Elishah, Tarshish, Kittim, Rodanim. The seafaring peoples developed from these, each in its own place by family, each with its own language.

10.6   The sons of Ham: Cush, Egypt, Put, Canaan.
10.7   The sons of Cush: Seba, Havilah, Sabtah, Raamah, Sabteca.
   The sons of Raamah: Sheba, Dedan.
10.8-12   Cush also had Nimrod. He was the first great warrior on Earth. He was a great hunter before GOD. There was a saying, "Like Nimrod, a great hunter before GOD." His kingdom got its start with Babel; then Erech, Akkad, and Calneh in the country of Shinar. From there he went up to Asshur and built Nineveh, Rehoboth Ir, Calah, and Resen between Nineveh and the great city Calah.
10.13-14   Egypt was ancestor to the Ludim, the Anamim, the Lehabim, the Naphtuhim, the

---

a 27 Japheth sounds like the Hebrew for *extend.*
b 27 Or *their*   *c 2 Sons* may mean *descendants* or *successors* or *nations;* also in verses 3, 4, 6, 7, 20-23, 29 and 31.   *d 4* Some manuscripts of the Masoretic Text and Samaritan Pentateuch (see also Septuagint and 1 Chron. 1:7); most manuscripts of the Masoretic Text *Dodanim*
e 6 That is, Egypt; also in verse 13   *f 8 Father* may mean *ancestor* or *predecessor* or *founder;* also in verses 13, 15, 24 and 26.   *g 10* Or *Erech and Akkad—all of them in*
h 10 That is, Babylonia   *i 11* Or *Nineveh with its city squares*

NEW INTERNATIONAL VERSION

tuhites, [14]Pathrusites, Casluhites (from whom the Philistines came) and Caphtorites.

[15]Canaan was the father of
Sidon his firstborn,[a] and of the Hittites, [16]Jebusites, Amorites, Girgashites, [17]Hivites, Arkites, Sinites, [18]Arvadites, Zemarites and Hamathites.

Later the Canaanite clans scattered [19]and the borders of Canaan reached from Sidon toward Gerar as far as Gaza, and then toward Sodom, Gomorrah, Admah and Zeboiim, as far as Lasha.

[20]These are the sons of Ham by their clans and languages, in their territories and nations.

THE SEMITES

[21]Sons were also born to Shem, whose older brother was[b] Japheth; Shem was the ancestor of all the sons of Eber.

[22]The sons of Shem:
Elam, Asshur, Arphaxad, Lud and Aram.
[23]The sons of Aram:
Uz, Hul, Gether and Meshech.[c]
[24]Arphaxad was the father of[d] Shelah, and Shelah the father of Eber.
[25]Two sons were born to Eber:
One was named Peleg,[e] because in his time the earth was divided; his brother was named Joktan.
[26]Joktan was the father of
Almodad, Sheleph, Hazarmaveth, Jerah, [27]Hadoram, Uzal, Diklah, [28]Obal, Abimael, Sheba, [29]Ophir, Havilah and Jobab. All these were sons of Joktan.

[30]The region where they lived stretched from Mesha toward Sephar, in the eastern hill country.

[31]These are the sons of Shem by their clans and languages, in their territories and nations.

[32]These are the clans of Noah's sons, according to their lines of descent, within their nations. From these the nations spread out over the earth after the flood.

THE TOWER OF BABEL

11 Now the whole world had one language and a common speech. [2]As men moved eastward,[f] they found a plain in Shinar[g] and settled there.

[3]They said to each other, "Come, let's make bricks and bake them thoroughly." They used brick instead of stone, and tar for mortar. [4]Then

THE MESSAGE

Pathrusim, the Casluhim (the origin of the Philistines), and the Kaphtorim.

10.15-19 Canaan had Sidon his firstborn, Heth, the Jebusites, the Amorites, the Girgashites, the Hivites, the Arkites, the Sinites, the Arvadites, the Zemarites, and the Hamathites. Later the Canaanites spread out, going from Sidon toward Gerar, as far south as Gaza, and then east all the way over to Sodom, Gomorrah, Admah, Zeboiim, and on to Lasha.

10.20 These are the descendants of Ham by family, language, country, and nation.

10.21 Shem, the older brother of Japheth, also had sons. Shem was ancestor to all the children of Eber.

10.22 The sons of Shem: Elam, Asshur, Arphaxad, Lud, and Aram.

10.23 The sons of Aram: Uz, Hul, Gether, Meshech.

10.24-25 Arphaxad had Shelah and Shelah had Eber. Eber had two sons, Peleg (so named because in his days the human race divided) and Joktan.

10.26-30 Joktan had Almodad, Sheleph, Hazarmaveth, Jerah, Hadoram, Uzal, Diklah, Obal, Abimael, Sheba, Ophir, Havilah, and Jobab—all sons of Joktan. Their land goes from Mesha toward Sephar as far as the mountain ranges in the east.

10.31 These are the descendants of Shem by family, language, country, and nation.

10.32 This is the family tree of the sons of Noah as they developed into nations. From them nations developed all across the Earth after the flood.

"GOD TURNED THEIR LANGUAGE INTO 'BABBLE'"

11.1-2 11 At one time, the whole Earth spoke the same language. It so happened that as they moved out of the east, they came upon a plain in the land of Shinar and settled down.

11.3 They said to one another, "Come, let's make bricks and fire them well." They used brick for stone and tar for mortar.

---

a 15 Or *of the Sidonians, the foremost*   b 21 Or *Shem, the older brother of*   c 23 See Septuagint and 1 Chron. 1:17; Hebrew *Mash*   d 24 Hebrew; Septuagint *father of Cainan, and Cainan was the father of*   e 25 *Peleg* means division.
f 2 Or *from the east;* or *in the east*   g 2 That is, Babylonia

NEW INTERNATIONAL VERSION

they said, "Come, let us build ourselves a city, with a tower that reaches to the heavens, so that we may make a name for ourselves and not be scattered over the face of the whole earth."

⁵But the LORD came down to see the city and the tower that the men were building. ⁶The LORD said, "If as one people speaking the same language they have begun to do this, then nothing they plan to do will be impossible for them. ⁷Come, let us go down and confuse their language so they will not understand each other."

⁸So the LORD scattered them from there over all the earth, and they stopped building the city. ⁹That is why it was called Babelᵃ—because there the LORD confused the language of the whole world. From there the LORD scattered them over the face of the whole earth.

FROM SHEM TO ABRAM

¹⁰This is the account of Shem.

Two years after the flood, when Shem was 100 years old, he became the fatherᵇ of Arphaxad. ¹¹And after he became the father of Arphaxad, Shem lived 500 years and had other sons and daughters.

¹²When Arphaxad had lived 35 years, he became the father of Shelah. ¹³And after he became the father of Shelah, Arphaxad lived 403 years and had other sons and daughters.ᶜ

¹⁴When Shelah had lived 30 years, he became the father of Eber. ¹⁵And after he became the father of Eber, Shelah lived 403 years and had other sons and daughters.

¹⁶When Eber had lived 34 years, he became the father of Peleg. ¹⁷And after he became the father of Peleg, Eber lived 430 years and had other sons and daughters.

¹⁸When Peleg had lived 30 years, he became the father of Reu. ¹⁹And after he became the father of Reu, Peleg lived 209 years and had other sons and daughters.

²⁰When Reu had lived 32 years, he became the father of Serug. ²¹And after he became the father of Serug, Reu lived 207 years and had other sons and daughters.

²²When Serug had lived 30 years, he became the father of Nahor. ²³And after he became the father of Nahor, Serug lived 200 years and had other sons and daughters.

ᵃ 9 That is, Babylon; *Babel* sounds like the Hebrew for *confused.* ᵇ 10 *Father* may mean *ancestor;* also in verses 11-25. ᶜ 12,13 Hebrew; Septuagint (see also Luke 3:35, 36 and note at Gen. 10:24) *35 years, he became the father of Cainan.* ¹³And after he became the father of Cainan, Arphaxad lived 430 years and had other sons and daughters, and then he died. When Cainan had lived 130 years, he became the father of Shelah. And after he became the father of Shelah, Cainan lived 330 years and had other sons and daughters

THE MESSAGE

11.4 Then they said, "Come, let's build ourselves a city and a tower that reaches Heaven. Let's make ourselves famous so we won't be scattered here and there across the Earth."

11.5 GOD came down to look over the city and the tower those people had built.

11.6-9 GOD took one look and said, "One people, one language; why, this is only a first step. No telling what they'll come up with next—they'll stop at nothing! Come, we'll go down and garble their speech so they won't understand each other." Then GOD scattered them from there all over the world. And they had to quit building the city. That's how it came to be called Babel, because there GOD turned their language into "babble." From there GOD scattered them all over the world.

✝

11.10-11 This is the story of Shem. When Shem was 100 years old, he had Arphaxad. It was two years after the flood. After he had Arphaxad, he lived 500 more years and had other sons and daughters.

11.12-13 When Arphaxad was thirty-five years old, he had Shelah. After Arphaxad had Shelah, he lived 403 more years and had other sons and daughters.

11.14-15 When Shelah was thirty years old, he had Eber. After Shelah had Eber, he lived 403 more years and had other sons and daughters.

11.16-17 When Eber was thirty-four years old, he had Peleg. After Eber had Peleg, he lived 430 more years and had other sons and daughters.

11.18-19 When Peleg was thirty years old, he had Reu. After he had Reu, he lived 209 more years and had other sons and daughters.

11.20-21 When Reu was thirty-two years old, he had Serug. After Reu had Serug, he lived 207 more years and had other sons and daughters.

11.22-23 When Serug was thirty years old, he had Nahor. After Serug had Nahor, he lived 200 more years and had other sons and daughters.

NEW INTERNATIONAL VERSION

24When Nahor had lived 29 years, he became the father of Terah. 25And after he became the father of Terah, Nahor lived 119 years and had other sons and daughters.

26After Terah had lived 70 years, he became the father of Abram, Nahor and Haran.

27This is the account of Terah.

Terah became the father of Abram, Nahor and Haran. And Haran became the father of Lot. 28While his father Terah was still alive, Haran died in Ur of the Chaldeans, in the land of his birth. 29Abram and Nahor both married. The name of Abram's wife was Sarai, and the name of Nahor's wife was Milcah; she was the daughter of Haran, the father of both Milcah and Iscah. 30Now Sarai was barren; she had no children.

31Terah took his son Abram, his grandson Lot son of Haran, and his daughter-in-law Sarai, the wife of his son Abram, and together they set out from Ur of the Chaldeans to go to Canaan. But when they came to Haran, they settled there.

32Terah lived 205 years, and he died in Haran.

THE CALL OF ABRAM

12 The LORD had said to Abram, "Leave your country, your people and your father's household and go to the land I will show you.

2 "I will make you into a great nation
   and I will bless you;
I will make your name great,
   and you will be a blessing.
3 I will bless those who bless you,
   and whoever curses you I will curse;
and all peoples on earth
   will be blessed through you."

4So Abram left, as the LORD had told him; and Lot went with him. Abram was seventy-five years old when he set out from Haran. 5He took his wife Sarai, his nephew Lot, all the possessions they had accumulated and the people they had acquired in Haran, and they set out for the land of Canaan, and they arrived there.

6Abram traveled through the land as far as the site of the great tree of Moreh at Shechem. At that time the Canaanites were in the land. 7The LORD appeared to Abram and said, "To your offspring[a] I will give this land." So he built an altar there to the LORD, who had appeared to him.

8From there he went on toward the hills east of Bethel and pitched his tent, with Bethel on the west and Ai on the east. There he built an altar to the LORD and called on the name of the

THE MESSAGE

11.24-25 When Nahor was twenty-nine years old, he had Terah. After Nahor had Terah, he lived 119 more years and had other sons and daughters.

11.26 When Terah was seventy years old, he had Abram, Nahor, and Haran.

THE FAMILY TREE OF TERAH

11.27-28 This is the story of Terah. Terah had Abram, Nahor, and Haran.

Haran had Lot. Haran died before his father, Terah, in the country of his family, Ur of the Chaldees.

11.29 Abram and Nahor each got married. Abram's wife was Sarai; Nahor's wife was Milcah, the daughter of his brother Haran. Haran had two daughters, Milcah and Iscah.

11.30 Sarai was barren; she had no children.

11.31 Terah took his son Abram, his grandson Lot (Haran's son), and Sarai his daughter-in-law (his son Abram's wife) and set out with them from Ur of the Chaldees for the land of Canaan. But when they got as far as Haran, they settled down there.

11.32 Terah lived 205 years. He died in Haran.

ABRAM AND SARAI

12.1 **12** GOD told Abram: "Leave your country, your family, and your father's home for a land that I will show you.

12.2-3 I'll make you a great nation
   and bless you.
I'll make you famous;
   you'll be a blessing.
I'll bless those who bless you;
   those who curse you I'll curse.
All the families of the Earth
   will be blessed through you."

12.4-6 So Abram left just as GOD said, and Lot left with him. Abram was seventy-five years old when he left Haran. Abram took his wife Sarai and his nephew Lot with him, along with all the possessions and people they had gotten in Haran, and set out for the land of Canaan and arrived safe and sound.

Abram passed through the country as far as Shechem and the Oak of Moreh. At that time the Canaanites occupied the land.

12.7 GOD appeared to Abram and said, "I will give this land to your children." Abram built an altar at the place GOD had appeared to him.

12.8 He moved on from there to the hill country east of Bethel and pitched his tent between Bethel to the west and Ai to the east. He built an altar there and prayed to GOD.

---

a 7 Or *seed*

NEW INTERNATIONAL VERSION

LORD. ⁹Then Abram set out and continued toward the Negev.

ABRAM IN EGYPT

¹⁰Now there was a famine in the land, and Abram went down to Egypt to live there for a while because the famine was severe. ¹¹As he was about to enter Egypt, he said to his wife Sarai, "I know what a beautiful woman you are. ¹²When the Egyptians see you, they will say, 'This is his wife.' Then they will kill me but will let you live. ¹³Say you are my sister, so that I will be treated well for your sake and my life will be spared because of you."

¹⁴When Abram came to Egypt, the Egyptians saw that she was a very beautiful woman. ¹⁵And when Pharaoh's officials saw her, they praised her to Pharaoh, and she was taken into his palace. ¹⁶He treated Abram well for her sake, and Abram acquired sheep and cattle, male and female donkeys, menservants and maidservants, and camels.

¹⁷But the LORD inflicted serious diseases on Pharaoh and his household because of Abram's wife Sarai. ¹⁸So Pharaoh summoned Abram. "What have you done to me?" he said. "Why didn't you tell me she was your wife? ¹⁹Why did you say, 'She is my sister,' so that I took her to be my wife? Now then, here is your wife. Take her and go!" ²⁰Then Pharaoh gave orders about Abram to his men, and they sent him on his way, with his wife and everything he had.

ABRAM AND LOT SEPARATE

13 So Abram went up from Egypt to the Negev, with his wife and everything he had, and Lot went with him. ²Abram had become very wealthy in livestock and in silver and gold.

³From the Negev he went from place to place until he came to Bethel, to the place between Bethel and Ai where his tent had been earlier ⁴and where he had first built an altar. There Abram called on the name of the LORD.

⁵Now Lot, who was moving about with Abram, also had flocks and herds and tents. ⁶But the land could not support them while they stayed together, for their possessions were so great that they were not able to stay together. ⁷And quarreling arose between Abram's herdsmen and the herdsmen of Lot. The Canaanites and Perizzites were also living in the land at that time.

⁸So Abram said to Lot, "Let's not have any quarreling between you and me, or between your herdsmen and mine, for we are brothers. ⁹Is not the whole land before you? Let's part company. If you go to the left, I'll go to the right; if you go to the right, I'll go to the left."

THE MESSAGE

12.9 Abram kept moving, steadily making his way south, to the Negev.

12.10-13 Then a famine came to the land. Abram went down to Egypt to live; it was a hard famine. As he drew near to Egypt, he said to his wife, Sarai, "Look. We both know that you're a beautiful woman. When the Egyptians see you they're going to say, 'Aha! That's his wife!' and kill me. But they'll let you live. Do me a favor: tell them you're my sister. Because of you, they'll welcome me and let me live."

12.14-15 When Abram arrived in Egypt, the Egyptians took one look and saw that his wife was stunningly beautiful. Pharaoh's princes raved over her to Pharaoh. She was taken to live with Pharaoh.

12.16-17 Because of her, Abram got along very well: he accumulated sheep and cattle, male and female donkeys, men and women servants, and camels. But GOD hit Pharaoh hard because of Abram's wife Sarai; everybody in the palace got seriously sick.

12.18-19 Pharaoh called for Abram, "What's this that you've done to me? Why didn't you tell me that she's your wife? Why did you say, 'She's my sister' so that I'd take her as my wife? Here's your wife back—take her and get out!"

12.20 Pharaoh ordered his men to get Abram out of the country. They sent him and his wife and everything he owned on their way.

13 So Abram left Egypt and went back to the Negev, he and his wife and everything he owned, and Lot still with him. By now Abram was very rich, loaded with cattle and silver and gold.

13.3-4 He moved on from the Negev, camping along the way, to Bethel, the place he had first set up his tent between Bethel and Ai and built his first altar. Abram prayed there to GOD.

13.5-7 Lot, who was traveling with Abram, was also rich in sheep and cattle and tents. But the land couldn't support both of them; they had too many possessions. They couldn't both live there—quarrels broke out between Abram's shepherds and Lot's shepherds. The Canaanites and Perizzites were also living on the land at the time.

13.8-9 Abram said to Lot, "Let's not have fighting between us, between your shepherds and my shepherds. After all, we're family. Look around. Isn't there plenty of land out there? Let's separate. If you go left, I'll go right; if you go right, I'll go left."

NEW INTERNATIONAL VERSION

¹⁰Lot looked up and saw that the whole plain of the Jordan was well watered, like the garden of the LORD, like the land of Egypt, toward Zoar. (This was before the LORD destroyed Sodom and Gomorrah.) ¹¹So Lot chose for himself the whole plain of the Jordan and set out toward the east. The two men parted company: ¹²Abram lived in the land of Canaan, while Lot lived among the cities of the plain and pitched his tents near Sodom. ¹³Now the men of Sodom were wicked and were sinning greatly against the LORD.

¹⁴The LORD said to Abram after Lot had parted from him, "Lift up your eyes from where you are and look north and south, east and west. ¹⁵All the land that you see I will give to you and your offspring[a] forever. ¹⁶I will make your offspring like the dust of the earth, so that if anyone could count the dust, then your offspring could be counted. ¹⁷Go, walk through the length and breadth of the land, for I am giving it to you."

¹⁸So Abram moved his tents and went to live near the great trees of Mamre at Hebron, where he built an altar to the LORD.

ABRAM RESCUES LOT

14 At this time Amraphel king of Shinar,[b] Arioch king of Ellasar, Kedorlaomer king of Elam and Tidal king of Goiim ²went to war against Bera king of Sodom, Birsha king of Gomorrah, Shinab king of Admah, Shemeber king of Zeboiim, and the king of Bela (that is, Zoar). ³All these latter kings joined forces in the Valley of Siddim (the Salt Sea[c]). ⁴For twelve years they had been subject to Kedorlaomer, but in the thirteenth year they rebelled.

⁵In the fourteenth year, Kedorlaomer and the kings allied with him went out and defeated the Rephaites in Ashteroth Karnaim, the Zuzites in Ham, the Emites in Shaveh Kiriathaim ⁶and the Horites in the hill country of Seir, as far as El Paran near the desert. ⁷Then they turned back and went to En Mishpat (that is, Kadesh), and they conquered the whole territory of the Amalekites, as well as the Amorites who were living in Hazazon Tamar.

⁸Then the king of Sodom, the king of Gomorrah, the king of Admah, the king of Zeboiim and the king of Bela (that is, Zoar) marched out and drew up their battle lines in the Valley of Siddim ⁹against Kedorlaomer king of Elam, Tidal king of Goiim, Amraphel king of Shinar and Arioch king of Ellasar—four kings against five. ¹⁰Now the

[a] 15 Or *seed*; also in verse 16   [b] 1 That is, Babylonia; also in verse 9   [c] 3 That is, the Dead Sea

THE MESSAGE

13.10-11 Lot looked. He saw the whole plain of the Jordan spread out, well watered (this was before GOD destroyed Sodom and Gomorrah), like GOD's garden, like Egypt, and stretching all the way to Zoar. Lot took the whole plain of the Jordan. Lot set out to the east.

13.11-12 That's how they came to part company, uncle and nephew. Abram settled in Canaan; Lot settled in the cities of the plain and pitched his tent near Sodom.

13.13 The people of Sodom were evil—flagrant sinners against GOD.

13.14-17 After Lot separated from Abram, GOD said to Abram, "Open your eyes, look around. Look north, south, east, and west. Everything you see, the whole land spread out before you, I will give to you and your children forever. I'll make your descendants like dust—counting your descendants will be as impossible as counting the dust of the Earth. So—on your feet, get moving! Walk through the country, its length and breadth; I'm giving it all to you."

13.18 Abram moved his tent. He went and settled by the Oaks of Mamre in Hebron. There he built an altar to GOD.

✝

14.1-2 **14** Then this: Amraphel king of Shinar, Arioch king of Ellasar, Kedorlaomer king of Elam, and Tidal king of Goiim went off to war to fight Bera king of Sodom, Birsha king of Gomorrah, Shinab king of Admah, Shemeber king of Zeboiim, and the king of Bela, that is, Zoar.

14.3-4 This second group of kings, the attacked, came together at the Valley of Siddim, that is, the Salt Sea. They had been under the thumb of Kedorlaomer for twelve years. In the thirteenth year, they revolted.

14.5-7 In the fourteenth year, Kedorlaomer and the kings allied with him set out and defeated the Rephaim in Ashteroth Karnaim, the Zuzim in Ham, the Emim in Shaveh Kiriathaim, and the Horites in their hill country of Seir as far as El Paran on the far edge of the desert. On their way back they stopped at En Mishpat, that is, Kadesh, and conquered the whole region of the Amalekites as well as that of the Amorites who lived in Hazazon Tamar.

14.8-9 That's when the king of Sodom marched out with the king of Gomorrah, the king of Admah, the king of Zeboiim, and the king of Bela, that is, Zoar. They drew up in battle formation against their enemies in the Valley of Siddim—against Kedorlaomer king of Elam, Tidal king of Goiim, Amraphel king of Shinar, and Arioch king of Ellasar, four kings against five.

NEW INTERNATIONAL VERSION

Valley of Siddim was full of tar pits, and when the kings of Sodom and Gomorrah fled, some of the men fell into them and the rest fled to the hills. ¹¹The four kings seized all the goods of Sodom and Gomorrah and all their food; then they went away. ¹²They also carried off Abram's nephew Lot and his possessions, since he was living in Sodom.

¹³One who had escaped came and reported this to Abram the Hebrew. Now Abram was living near the great trees of Mamre the Amorite, a brother*ᵃ* of Eshcol and Aner, all of whom were allied with Abram. ¹⁴When Abram heard that his relative had been taken captive, he called out the 318 trained men born in his household and went in pursuit as far as Dan. ¹⁵During the night Abram divided his men to attack them and he routed them, pursuing them as far as Hobah, north of Damascus. ¹⁶He recovered all the goods and brought back his relative Lot and his possessions, together with the women and the other people.

¹⁷After Abram returned from defeating Kedorlaomer and the kings allied with him, the king of Sodom came out to meet him in the Valley of Shaveh (that is, the King's Valley).

¹⁸Then Melchizedek king of Salem*ᵇ* brought out bread and wine. He was priest of God Most High, ¹⁹and he blessed Abram, saying,

"Blessed be Abram by God Most High,
    Creator*ᶜ* of heaven and earth.
²⁰And blessed be*ᵈ* God Most High,
    who delivered your enemies into your
        hand."

Then Abram gave him a tenth of everything.

²¹The king of Sodom said to Abram, "Give me the people and keep the goods for yourself."

²²But Abram said to the king of Sodom, "I have raised my hand to the LORD, God Most High, Creator of heaven and earth, and have taken an oath ²³that I will accept nothing belonging to you, not even a thread or the thong of a sandal, so that you will never be able to say, 'I made Abram rich.' ²⁴I will accept nothing but what my men have eaten and the share that belongs to the men who went with me—to Aner, Eshcol and Mamre. Let them have their share."

GOD'S COVENANT WITH ABRAM

15 After this, the word of the LORD came to Abram in a vision:

"Do not be afraid, Abram.
    I am your shield,*ᵉ*
    your very great reward.*ᶠ*"

THE MESSAGE

14.10-12   The Valley of Siddim was full of tar pits. When the kings of Sodom and Gomorrah fled, they fell into the tar pits, but the rest escaped into the mountains. The four kings captured all the possessions of Sodom and Gomorrah, all their food and equipment, and went on their way. They captured Lot, Abram's nephew who was living in Sodom at the time, taking everything he owned with them.

14.13-16   A fugitive came and reported to Abram the Hebrew. Abram was living at the Oaks of Mamre the Amorite, brother of Eshcol and Aner. They were allies of Abram. When Abram heard that his nephew had been taken prisoner, he lined up his servants, all of them born in his household—there were 318 of them—and chased after the captors all the way to Dan. Abram and his men split into small groups and attacked by night. They chased them as far as Hobah, just north of Damascus. They recovered all the plunder along with nephew Lot and his possessions, including the women and the people.

14.17-20   After Abram returned from defeating Kedorlaomer and his allied kings, the king of Sodom came out to greet him in the Valley of Shaveh, the King's Valley. Melchizedek, king of Salem, brought out bread and wine—he was priest of The High God—and blessed him:

Blessed be Abram by The High God,
    Creator of Heaven and Earth.
And blessed be The High God,
    who handed your enemies over to you.

Abram gave him a tenth of all the recovered plunder.

14.21   The king of Sodom said to Abram, "Give me back the people but keep all the plunder for yourself."

14.22-24   But Abram told the king of Sodom, "I swear to GOD, The High God, Creator of Heaven and Earth, this solemn oath, that I'll take nothing from you, not so much as a thread or a shoestring. I'm not going to have you go around saying, 'I made Abram rich.' Nothing for me other than what the young men ate and the share of the men who went with me, Aner, Eshcol, and Mamre; they're to get their share of the plunder."

✠

15.1   **15** After all these things, this word of GOD came to Abram in a vision: "Don't be afraid, Abram. I'm your shield. Your reward will be grand!"

ᵃ 13 Or *a relative; or an ally*   *ᵇ 18* That is, Jerusalem
ᶜ 19 Or *Possessor;* also in verse 22   *ᵈ 20* Or *And praise be to*
ᵉ 1 Or *sovereign*   *ᶠ 1* Or *shield;* / *your reward will be very great*

NEW INTERNATIONAL VERSION

²But Abram said, "O Sovereign LORD, what can you give me since I remain childless and the one who will inherit *a* my estate is Eliezer of Damascus?" ³And Abram said, "You have given me no children; so a servant in my household will be my heir."

⁴Then the word of the LORD came to him: "This man will not be your heir, but a son coming from your own body will be your heir." ⁵He took him outside and said, "Look up at the heavens and count the stars—if indeed you can count them." Then he said to him, "So shall your offspring be."

⁶Abram believed the LORD, and he credited it to him as righteousness.

⁷He also said to him, "I am the LORD, who brought you out of Ur of the Chaldeans to give you this land to take possession of it."

⁸But Abram said, "O Sovereign LORD, how can I know that I will gain possession of it?"

⁹So the LORD said to him, "Bring me a heifer, a goat and a ram, each three years old, along with a dove and a young pigeon."

¹⁰Abram brought all these to him, cut them in two and arranged the halves opposite each other; the birds, however, he did not cut in half. ¹¹Then birds of prey came down on the carcasses, but Abram drove them away.

¹²As the sun was setting, Abram fell into a deep sleep, and a thick and dreadful darkness came over him. ¹³Then the LORD said to him, "Know for certain that your descendants will be strangers in a country not their own, and they will be enslaved and mistreated four hundred years. ¹⁴But I will punish the nation they serve as slaves, and afterward they will come out with great possessions. ¹⁵You, however, will go to your fathers in peace and be buried at a good old age. ¹⁶In the fourth generation your descendants will come back here, for the sin of the Amorites has not yet reached its full measure."

¹⁷When the sun had set and darkness had fallen, a smoking firepot with a blazing torch appeared and passed between the pieces. ¹⁸On that day the LORD made a covenant with Abram and said, "To your descendants I give this land, from the river *b* of Egypt to the great river, the Euphrates— ¹⁹the land of the Kenites, Kenizzites, Kadmonites, ²⁰Hittites, Perizzites, Rephaites, ²¹Amorites, Canaanites, Girgashites and Jebusites."

HAGAR AND ISHMAEL

16 Now Sarai, Abram's wife, had borne him no children. But she had an Egyptian maidservant named Hagar; ²so she said to Abram, "The LORD has kept me from having children. Go,

a 2 The meaning of the Hebrew for this phrase is uncertain.
b 18 Or *Wadi*

THE MESSAGE

15.2-3   Abram said, "GOD, Master, what use are your gifts as long as I'm childless and Eliezer of Damascus is going to inherit everything?" Abram continued, "See, you've given me no children, and now a mere house servant is going to get it all."

15.4   Then GOD's Message came: "Don't worry, he won't be your heir; a son from your body will be your heir."

15.5   Then he took him outside and said, "Look at the sky. Count the stars. Can you do it? Count your descendants! You're going to have a big family, Abram!"

15.6   And he believed! Believed GOD! God declared him "Set-Right-with-God."

15.7   GOD continued, "I'm the same GOD who brought you from Ur of the Chaldees and gave you this land to own."

15.8   Abram said, "Master GOD, how am I to know this, that it will all be mine?"

15.9   GOD said, "Bring me a heifer, a goat, and a ram, each three years old, and a dove and a young pigeon."

15.10-12   He brought all these animals to him, split them down the middle, and laid the halves opposite each other. But he didn't split the birds. Vultures swooped down on the carcasses, but Abram scared them off. As the sun went down a deep sleep overcame Abram and then a sense of dread, dark and heavy.

15.13-16   GOD said to Abram, "Know this: your descendants will live as outsiders in a land not theirs; they'll be enslaved and beaten down for 400 years. Then I'll punish their slave masters; your offspring will march out of there loaded with plunder. But not you; you'll have a long and full life and die a good and peaceful death. Not until the fourth generation will your descendants return here; sin is still a thriving business among the Amorites."

15.17-21   When the sun was down and it was dark, a smoking firepot and a flaming torch moved between the split carcasses. That's when GOD made a covenant with Abram: "I'm giving this land to your children, from the Nile River in Egypt to the River Euphrates in Assyria—the country of the Kenites, Kenizzites, Kadmonites, Hittites, Perizzites, Rephaim, Amorites, Canaanites, Girgashites, and Jebusites."

✝

16.1   **16** Sarai, Abram's wife, hadn't yet produced a child.

16.1-2   She had an Egyptian maid named Hagar. Sarai said to Abram, "GOD has not seen fit to let

NEW INTERNATIONAL VERSION

sleep with my maidservant; perhaps I can build a family through her."

Abram agreed to what Sarai said. ³So after Abram had been living in Canaan ten years, Sarai his wife took her Egyptian maidservant Hagar and gave her to her husband to be his wife. ⁴He slept with Hagar, and she conceived.

When she knew she was pregnant, she began to despise her mistress. ⁵Then Sarai said to Abram, "You are responsible for the wrong I am suffering. I put my servant in your arms, and now that she knows she is pregnant, she despises me. May the LORD judge between you and me."

⁶"Your servant is in your hands," Abram said. "Do with her whatever you think best." Then Sarai mistreated Hagar; so she fled from her.

⁷The angel of the LORD found Hagar near a spring in the desert; it was the spring that is beside the road to Shur. ⁸And he said, "Hagar, servant of Sarai, where have you come from, and where are you going?"

"I'm running away from my mistress Sarai," she answered.

⁹Then the angel of the LORD told her, "Go back to your mistress and submit to her." ¹⁰The angel added, "I will so increase your descendants that they will be too numerous to count."

¹¹The angel of the LORD also said to her:

"You are now with child
    and you will have a son.
You shall name him Ishmael,ᵃ
    for the LORD has heard of your misery.
¹²He will be a wild donkey of a man;
    his hand will be against everyone
    and everyone's hand against him,
and he will live in hostility
    towardᵇ all his brothers."

¹³She gave this name to the LORD who spoke to her: "You are the God who sees me," for she said, "I have now seenᶜ the One who sees me." ¹⁴That is why the well was called Beer Lahai Roiᵈ; it is still there, between Kadesh and Bered.

¹⁵So Hagar bore Abram a son, and Abram gave the name Ishmael to the son she had borne. ¹⁶Abram was eighty-six years old when Hagar bore him Ishmael.

THE COVENANT OF CIRCUMCISION

17 When Abram was ninety-nine years old, the LORD appeared to him and said, "I am God Almightyᵉ; walk before me and be blameless. ²I will confirm my covenant between me and you and will greatly increase your numbers."

THE MESSAGE

me have a child. Sleep with my maid. Maybe I can get a family from her." Abram agreed to do what Sarai said.

16.3-4 So Sarai, Abram's wife, took her Egyptian maid Hagar and gave her to her husband Abram as a wife. Abram had been living ten years in Canaan when this took place. He slept with Hagar and she got pregnant. When Hagar learned she was pregnant, she looked down on her mistress.

16.5 Sarai told Abram, "It's all your fault that I'm suffering this abuse. I put my maid in bed with you and the minute she knows she's pregnant, she treats me like I'm nothing. May GOD decide which of us is right."

16.6 "You decide," said Abram. "Your maid is your business."

Sarai was abusive to Hagar and Hagar ran away.

16.7-8 An angel of GOD found her beside a spring in the desert; it was the spring on the road to Shur. He said, "Hagar, maid of Sarai, what are you doing here?"

She said, "I'm running away from Sarai my mistress."

16.9-12 The angel of GOD said, "Go back to your mistress. Put up with her abuse." He continued, "I'm going to give you a big family, children past counting.

From this pregnancy, you'll get a son: Name
    him Ishmael;
    for GOD heard you, GOD answered you.
He'll be a bucking bronco of a man,
    a real fighter, fighting and being fought,
Always stirring up trouble,
    always at odds with his family."

16.13 She answered GOD by name, praying to the
    God who spoke to her,
"You're the God who sees me!
    "Yes! He saw me; and then I saw him!"

16.14 That's how that desert spring got named
    "God-Alive-Sees-Me Spring." That
    spring is still there, between
    Kadesh and Bered.

16.15-16 Hagar gave Abram a son. Abram named him Ishmael. Abram was eighty-six years old when Hagar gave him his son, Ishmael.

☩

17.1-2 **17** When Abram was ninety-nine years old, GOD showed up and said to him, "I am The Strong God, live entirely before me, live to the hilt! I'll make a covenant between us and I'll give you a huge family."

ᵃ 11 Ishmael means God hears.   ᵇ 12 Or live to the east / of
ᶜ 13 Or seen the back of   ᵈ 14 Beer Lahai Roi means well of
the Living One who sees me.   ᵉ 1 Hebrew El-Shaddai

NEW INTERNATIONAL VERSION

³Abram fell facedown, and God said to him, ⁴"As for me, this is my covenant with you: You will be the father of many nations. ⁵No longer will you be called Abram*ᵃ*; your name will be Abraham,*ᵇ* for I have made you a father of many nations. ⁶I will make you very fruitful; I will make nations of you, and kings will come from you. ⁷I will establish my covenant as an everlasting covenant between me and you and your descendants after you for the generations to come, to be your God and the God of your descendants after you. ⁸The whole land of Canaan, where you are now an alien, I will give as an everlasting possession to you and your descendants after you; and I will be their God."

⁹Then God said to Abraham, "As for you, you must keep my covenant, you and your descendants after you for the generations to come. ¹⁰This is my covenant with you and your descendants after you, the covenant you are to keep: Every male among you shall be circumcised. ¹¹You are to undergo circumcision, and it will be the sign of the covenant between me and you. ¹²For the generations to come every male among you who is eight days old must be circumcised, including those born in your household or bought with money from a foreigner—those who are not your offspring. ¹³Whether born in your household or bought with your money, they must be circumcised. My covenant in your flesh is to be an everlasting covenant. ¹⁴Any uncircumcised male, who has not been circumcised in the flesh, will be cut off from his people; he has broken my covenant."

¹⁵God also said to Abraham, "As for Sarai your wife, you are no longer to call her Sarai; her name will be Sarah. ¹⁶I will bless her and will surely give you a son by her. I will bless her so that she will be the mother of nations; kings of peoples will come from her."

¹⁷Abraham fell facedown; he laughed and said to himself, "Will a son be born to a man a hundred years old? Will Sarah bear a child at the age of ninety?" ¹⁸And Abraham said to God, "If only Ishmael might live under your blessing!"

¹⁹Then God said, "Yes, but your wife Sarah will bear you a son, and you will call him Isaac.*ᶜ* I will establish my covenant with him as an everlasting covenant for his descendants after him. ²⁰And as for Ishmael, I have heard you: I will surely bless him; I will make him fruitful and will greatly increase his numbers. He will be the father of twelve rulers, and I will make him into

ᵃ 5 Abram means exalted father.   ᵇ 5 Abraham means father of many.   ᶜ 19 Isaac means he laughs.

THE MESSAGE

17.3-8   Overwhelmed, Abram fell flat on his face.

Then God said to him, "This is my covenant with you: You'll be the father of many nations. Your name will no longer be Abram, but Abraham, meaning that 'I'm making you the father of many nations.' I'll make you a father of fathers—I'll make nations from you, kings will issue from you. I'm establishing my covenant between me and you, a covenant that includes your descendants, a covenant that goes on and on and on, a covenant that commits me to be your God and the God of your descendants. And I'm giving you and your descendants this land where you're now just camping, this whole country of Canaan, to own forever. And I'll be their God."

17.9-14   God continued to Abraham, "And you: You will honor my covenant, you and your descendants, generation after generation. This is the covenant that you are to honor, the covenant that pulls in all your descendants: Circumcise every male. Circumcise by cutting off the foreskin of the penis; it will be the sign of the covenant between us. Every male baby will be circumcised when he is eight days old, generation after generation—this includes house-born slaves and slaves bought from outsiders who are not blood kin. Make sure you circumcise both your own children and anyone brought in from the outside. That way my covenant will be cut into your body, a permanent mark of my permanent covenant. An uncircumcised male, one who has not had the foreskin of his penis cut off, will be cut off from his people—he has broken my covenant."

17.15-16   God continued speaking to Abraham, "And Sarai your wife: Don't call her Sarai any longer; call her Sarah. I'll bless her—yes! I'll give you a son by her! Oh, how I'll bless her! Nations will come from her; kings of nations will come from her."

17.17   Abraham fell flat on his face. And then he laughed, thinking, "Can a hundred-year-old man father a son? And can Sarah, at ninety years, have a baby?"

17.18   Recovering, Abraham said to God, "Oh, keep Ishmael alive and well before you!"

17.19   But God said, "That's not what I mean. Your wife, Sarah, will have a baby, a son. Name him Isaac (Laughter). I'll establish my covenant with him and his descendants, a covenant that lasts forever.

17.20-21   "And Ishmael? Yes, I heard your prayer for him. I'll also bless him; I'll make sure he has plenty of children—a huge family. He'll father twelve princes; I'll make him a great nation.

NEW INTERNATIONAL VERSION

a great nation. ²¹But my covenant I will establish with Isaac, whom Sarah will bear to you by this time next year." ²²When he had finished speaking with Abraham, God went up from him.

²³On that very day Abraham took his son Ishmael and all those born in his household or bought with his money, every male in his household, and circumcised them, as God told him. ²⁴Abraham was ninety-nine years old when he was circumcised, ²⁵and his son Ishmael was thirteen; ²⁶Abraham and his son Ishmael were both circumcised on that same day. ²⁷And every male in Abraham's household, including those born in his household or bought from a foreigner, was circumcised with him.

THE THREE VISITORS

18 The LORD appeared to Abraham near the great trees of Mamre while he was sitting at the entrance to his tent in the heat of the day. ²Abraham looked up and saw three men standing nearby. When he saw them, he hurried from the entrance of his tent to meet them and bowed low to the ground.

³He said, "If I have found favor in your eyes, my lord,ᵃ do not pass your servant by. ⁴Let a little water be brought, and then you may all wash your feet and rest under this tree. ⁵Let me get you something to eat, so you can be refreshed and then go on your way—now that you have come to your servant."

"Very well," they answered, "do as you say."

⁶So Abraham hurried into the tent to Sarah. "Quick," he said, "get three seahsᵇ of fine flour and knead it and bake some bread."

⁷Then he ran to the herd and selected a choice, tender calf and gave it to a servant, who hurried to prepare it. ⁸He then brought some curds and milk and the calf that had been prepared, and set these before them. While they ate, he stood near them under a tree.

⁹"Where is your wife Sarah?" they asked him.

"There, in the tent," he said.

¹⁰Then the LORDᶜ said, "I will surely return to you about this time next year, and Sarah your wife will have a son."

Now Sarah was listening at the entrance to the tent, which was behind him. ¹¹Abraham and Sarah were already old and well advanced in years, and Sarah was past the age of childbearing. ¹²So Sarah laughed to herself as she thought, "After I am worn out and my masterᵈ is old, will I now have this pleasure?"

THE MESSAGE

But I'll establish my covenant with Isaac whom Sarah will give you about this time next year."

17.22 God finished speaking with Abraham and left.

17.23 Then Abraham took his son Ishmael and all his servants, whether houseborn or purchased—every male in his household—and circumcised them, cutting off their foreskins that very day, just as God had told him.

17.24-27 Abraham was ninety-nine years old when he was circumcised. His son Ishmael was thirteen years old when he was circumcised. Abraham and Ishmael were circumcised the same day together with all the servants of his household, those born there and those purchased from outsiders—all were circumcised with him.

✟

18.1-2 **18** GOD appeared to Abraham at the Oaks of Mamre while he was sitting at the entrance of his tent. It was the hottest part of the day. He looked up and saw three men standing. He ran from his tent to greet them and bowed before them.

18.3-5 He said, "Master, if it please you, stop for a while with your servant. I'll get some water so you can wash your feet. Rest under this tree. I'll get some food to refresh you on your way, since your travels have brought you across my path."

They said, "Certainly. Go ahead."

18.6 Abraham hurried into the tent to Sarah. He said, "Hurry. Get three cups of our best flour; knead it and make bread."

18.7-8 Then Abraham ran to the cattle pen and picked out a nice plump calf and gave it to the servant who lost no time getting it ready. Then he got curds and milk, brought them with the calf that had been roasted, set the meal before the men, and stood there under the tree while they ate.

18.9 The men said to him, "Where is Sarah your wife?"

He said, "In the tent."

18.10 One of them said, "I'm coming back about this time next year. When I arrive, your wife Sarah will have a son." Sarah was listening at the tent opening, just behind the man.

18.11-12 Abraham and Sarah were old by this time, very old. Sarah was far past the age for having babies. Sarah laughed within herself, "An old woman like me? Get pregnant? With this old man of a husband?"

ᵃ 3 Or *O Lord*   ᵇ 6 That is, probably about 20 quarts (about 22 liters)   ᶜ 10 Hebrew *Then he*
ᵈ 12 Or *husband*

NEW INTERNATIONAL VERSION

¹³Then the Lord said to Abraham, "Why did Sarah laugh and say, 'Will I really have a child, now that I am old?' ¹⁴Is anything too hard for the Lord? I will return to you at the appointed time next year and Sarah will have a son."

¹⁵Sarah was afraid, so she lied and said, "I did not laugh."

But he said, "Yes, you did laugh."

ABRAHAM PLEADS FOR SODOM

¹⁶When the men got up to leave, they looked down toward Sodom, and Abraham walked along with them to see them on their way. ¹⁷Then the Lord said, "Shall I hide from Abraham what I am about to do? ¹⁸Abraham will surely become a great and powerful nation, and all nations on earth will be blessed through him. ¹⁹For I have chosen him, so that he will direct his children and his household after him to keep the way of the Lord by doing what is right and just, so that the Lord will bring about for Abraham what he has promised him."

²⁰Then the Lord said, "The outcry against Sodom and Gomorrah is so great and their sin so grievous ²¹that I will go down and see if what they have done is as bad as the outcry that has reached me. If not, I will know."

²²The men turned away and went toward Sodom, but Abraham remained standing before the Lord.^a ²³Then Abraham approached him and said: "Will you sweep away the righteous with the wicked? ²⁴What if there are fifty righteous people in the city? Will you really sweep it away and not spare^b the place for the sake of the fifty righteous people in it? ²⁵Far be it from you to do such a thing—to kill the righteous with the wicked, treating the righteous and the wicked alike. Far be it from you! Will not the Judge^c of all the earth do right?"

²⁶The Lord said, "If I find fifty righteous people in the city of Sodom, I will spare the whole place for their sake."

²⁷Then Abraham spoke up again: "Now that I have been so bold as to speak to the Lord, though I am nothing but dust and ashes, ²⁸what if the number of the righteous is five less than fifty? Will you destroy the whole city because of five people?"

"If I find forty-five there," he said, "I will not destroy it."

²⁹Once again he spoke to him, "What if only forty are found there?"

He said, "For the sake of forty, I will not do it."

---

a 22 Masoretic Text; an ancient Hebrew scribal tradition but the Lord remained standing before Abraham
b 24 Or forgive; also in verse 26   c 25 Or Ruler

THE MESSAGE

18.13-14   God said to Abraham, "Why did Sarah laugh saying, 'Me? Have a baby? An old woman like me?' Is anything too hard for God? I'll be back about this time next year and Sarah will have a baby."

18.15   Sarah lied. She said, "I didn't laugh," because she was afraid.

But he said, "Yes you did; you laughed."

✝

18.16   When the men got up to leave, they set off for Sodom. Abraham walked with them to say goodbye.

18.17-19   Then God said, "Shall I keep back from Abraham what I'm about to do? Abraham is going to become a large and strong nation; all the nations of the world are going to find themselves blessed through him. Yes, I've settled on him as the one to train his children and future family to observe God's way of life, live kindly and generously and fairly, so that God can complete in Abraham what he promised him."

18.20-21   God continued, "The cries of the victims in Sodom and Gomorrah are deafening; the sin of those cities is immense. I'm going down to see for myself, see if what they're doing is as bad as it sounds. Then I'll know."

18.22   The men set out for Sodom, but Abraham stood in God's path, blocking his way.

18.23-25   Abraham confronted him, "Are you serious? Are you planning on getting rid of the good people right along with the bad? What if there are fifty decent people left in the city; will you lump the good with the bad and get rid of the lot? Wouldn't you spare the city for the sake of those fifty innocents? I can't believe you'd do that, kill off the good and the bad alike as if there were no difference between them. Doesn't the Judge of all the Earth judge with justice?"

18.26   God said, "If I find fifty decent people in the city of Sodom, I'll spare the place just for them."

18.27-28   Abraham came back, "Do I, a mere mortal made from a handful of dirt, dare open my mouth again to my Master? What if the fifty fall short by five—would you destroy the city because of those missing five?"

He said, "I won't destroy it if there are forty-five."

18.29   Abraham spoke up again, "What if you only find forty?"

"Neither will I destroy it if for forty."

NEW INTERNATIONAL VERSION

³⁰Then he said, "May the Lord not be angry, but let me speak. What if only thirty can be found there?"

He answered, "I will not do it if I find thirty there."

³¹Abraham said, "Now that I have been so bold as to speak to the Lord, what if only twenty can be found there?"

He said, "For the sake of twenty, I will not destroy it."

³²Then he said, "May the Lord not be angry, but let me speak just once more. What if only ten can be found there?"

He answered, "For the sake of ten, I will not destroy it."

³³When the LORD had finished speaking with Abraham, he left, and Abraham returned home.

SODOM AND GOMORRAH DESTROYED

19 The two angels arrived at Sodom in the evening, and Lot was sitting in the gateway of the city. When he saw them, he got up to meet them and bowed down with his face to the ground. ²"My lords," he said, "please turn aside to your servant's house. You can wash your feet and spend the night and then go on your way early in the morning."

"No," they answered, "we will spend the night in the square."

³But he insisted so strongly that they did go with him and entered his house. He prepared a meal for them, baking bread without yeast, and they ate. ⁴Before they had gone to bed, all the men from every part of the city of Sodom—both young and old—surrounded the house. ⁵They called to Lot, "Where are the men who came to you tonight? Bring them out to us so that we can have sex with them."

⁶Lot went outside to meet them and shut the door behind him ⁷and said, "No, my friends. Don't do this wicked thing. ⁸Look, I have two daughters who have never slept with a man. Let me bring them out to you, and you can do what you like with them. But don't do anything to these men, for they have come under the protection of my roof."

⁹"Get out of our way," they replied. And they said, "This fellow came here as an alien, and now he wants to play the judge! We'll treat you worse than them." They kept bringing pressure on Lot and moved forward to break down the door.

¹⁰But the men inside reached out and pulled Lot back into the house and shut the door. ¹¹Then they struck the men who were at the door of the house, young and old, with blindness so that they could not find the door.

THE MESSAGE

18.30 He said, "Master, don't be irritated with me, but what if only thirty are found?"

"No, I won't do it if I find thirty."

18.31 He pushed on, "I know I'm trying your patience, Master, but how about for twenty?"

"I won't destroy it for twenty."

18.32 He wouldn't quit, "Don't get angry, Master—this is the last time. What if you only come up with ten?"

"For the sake of only ten, I won't destroy the city."

18.33 When GOD finished talking with Abraham, he left. And Abraham went home.

19 The two angels arrived at Sodom in the evening. Lot was sitting at the city gate. He saw them and got up to welcome them, bowing before them and said, "Please, my friends, come to my house and stay the night. Wash up. You can rise early and be on your way refreshed."

19.3 They said, "No, we'll sleep in the street."

But he insisted, wouldn't take no for an answer; and they relented and went home with him. Lot fixed a hot meal for them and they ate.

19.4-5 Before they went to bed men from all over the city of Sodom, young and old, descended on the house from all sides and boxed them in. They yelled to Lot, "Where are the men who are staying with you for the night? Bring them out so we can have our sport with them!"

19.6-8 Lot went out, barring the door behind him, and said, "Brothers, please, don't be vile! Look, I have two daughters, virgins; let me bring them out; you can take your pleasure with them, but don't touch these men—they're my guests."

19.9 They said, "Get lost! You drop in from nowhere and now you're going to tell us how to run our lives. We'll treat you worse than them!" And they charged past Lot to break down the door.

19.10-11 But the two men reached out and pulled Lot inside the house, locking the door. Then they struck blind the men who were trying to break down the door, both leaders and followers, leaving them groping in the dark.

NEW INTERNATIONAL VERSION

¹²The two men said to Lot, "Do you have any-one else here—sons-in-law, sons or daughters, or anyone else in the city who belongs to you? Get them out of here, ¹³because we are going to destroy this place. The outcry to the LORD against its people is so great that he has sent us to destroy it."

¹⁴So Lot went out and spoke to his sons-in-law, who were pledged to marry ᵃ his daughters. He said, "Hurry and get out of this place, be-cause the LORD is about to destroy the city!" But his sons-in-law thought he was joking.

¹⁵With the coming of dawn, the angels urged Lot, saying, "Hurry! Take your wife and your two daughters who are here, or you will be swept away when the city is punished."

¹⁶When he hesitated, the men grasped his hand and the hands of his wife and of his two daughters and led them safely out of the city, for the LORD was merciful to them. ¹⁷As soon as they had brought them out, one of them said, "Flee for your lives! Don't look back, and don't stop anywhere in the plain! Flee to the mountains or you will be swept away!"

¹⁸But Lot said to them, "No, my lords,ᵇ please! ¹⁹Yourᶜ servant has found favor in yourᶜ eyes, and youᶜ have shown great kindness to me in sparing my life. But I can't flee to the mountains; this disaster will overtake me, and I'll die. ²⁰Look, here is a town near enough to run to, and it is small. Let me flee to it—it is very small, isn't it? Then my life will be spared."

²¹He said to him, "Very well, I will grant this request too; I will not overthrow the town you speak of. ²²But flee there quickly, because I can-not do anything until you reach it." (That is why the town was called Zoar.ᵈ)

²³By the time Lot reached Zoar, the sun had risen over the land. ²⁴Then the LORD rained down burning sulfur on Sodom and Gomor-rah—from the LORD out of the heavens. ²⁵Thus he overthrew those cities and the entire plain, including all those living in the cities—and also the vegetation in the land. ²⁶But Lot's wife looked back, and she became a pillar of salt.

²⁷Early the next morning Abraham got up and returned to the place where he had stood before the LORD. ²⁸He looked down toward Sodom and Gomorrah, toward all the land of the plain, and he saw dense smoke rising from the land, like smoke from a furnace.

²⁹So when God destroyed the cities of the plain, he remembered Abraham, and he brought Lot out of the catastrophe that overthrew the cit-ies where Lot had lived.

ᵃ 14 Or were married to   ᵇ 18 Or No, Lord; or No, my lord
ᶜ 19 The Hebrew is singular.   ᵈ 22 Zoar means small.

THE MESSAGE

19.12-13   The two men said to Lot, "Do you have any other family here? Sons, daughters—anybody in the city? Get them out of here, and now! We're going to destroy this place. The outcries of victims here to GOD are deafening; we've been sent to blast this place into oblivion."

19.14   Lot went out and warned the fiancés of his daughters, "Evacuate this place; GOD is about to destroy this city!" But his daughters' would-be husbands treated it as a joke.

19.15   At break of day, the angels pushed Lot to get going, "Hurry. Get your wife and two daughters out of here before it's too late and you're caught in the punishment of the city."

19.16-17   Lot was dragging his feet. The men grabbed Lot's arm, and the arms of his wife and daugh-ters—GOD was so merciful to them!—and dragged them to safety outside the city. When they had them outside, Lot was told, "Now run for your life! Don't look back! Don't stop any-where on the plain—run for the hills or you'll be swept away."

19.18-20   But Lot protested, "No, masters, you can't mean it! I know that you've taken a liking to me and have done me an immense favor in sav-ing my life, but I can't run for the mountains—who knows what terrible thing might happen to me in the mountains and leave me for dead. Look over there—that town is close enough to get to. It's a small town, hardly anything to it. Let me escape there and save my life—it's a mere wide place in the road."

19.21-22   "All right, Lot. If you insist. I'll let you have your way. And I won't stamp out the town you've spotted. But hurry up. Run for it! I can't do anything until you get there." That's why the town was called Zoar, that is, Smalltown.

19.23   The sun was high in the sky when Lot ar-rived at Zoar.

19.24-25   Then GOD rained brimstone and fire down on Sodom and Gomorrah—a river of lava from GOD out of the sky!—and destroyed these cities and the entire plain and everyone who lived in the cities and everything that grew from the ground.

19.26   But Lot's wife looked back and turned into a pillar of salt.

19.27-28   Abraham got up early the next morning and went to the place he had so recently stood with GOD. He looked out over Sodom and Gomor-rah, surveying the whole plain. All he could see was smoke belching from the Earth, like smoke from a furnace.

19.29   And that's the story: When God destroyed the Cities of the Plain, he was mindful of Abra-ham and first got Lot out of there before he blasted those cities off the face of the Earth.

NEW INTERNATIONAL VERSION

LOT AND HIS DAUGHTERS

³⁰Lot and his two daughters left Zoar and settled in the mountains, for he was afraid to stay in Zoar. He and his two daughters lived in a cave. ³¹One day the older daughter said to the younger, "Our father is old, and there is no man around here to lie with us, as is the custom all over the earth. ³²Let's get our father to drink wine and then lie with him and preserve our family line through our father."

³³That night they got their father to drink wine, and the older daughter went in and lay with him. He was not aware of it when she lay down or when she got up.

³⁴The next day the older daughter said to the younger, "Last night I lay with my father. Let's get him to drink wine again tonight, and you go in and lie with him so we can preserve our family line through our father." ³⁵So they got their father to drink wine that night also, and the younger daughter went and lay with him. Again he was not aware of it when she lay down or when she got up.

³⁶So both of Lot's daughters became pregnant by their father. ³⁷The older daughter had a son, and she named him Moab*ᵃ*; he is the father of the Moabites of today. ³⁸The younger daughter also had a son, and she named him Ben-Ammi*ᵇ*; he is the father of the Ammonites of today.

ABRAHAM AND ABIMELECH

20 Now Abraham moved on from there into the region of the Negev and lived between Kadesh and Shur. For a while he stayed in Gerar, ²and there Abraham said of his wife Sarah, "She is my sister." Then Abimelech king of Gerar sent for Sarah and took her.

³But God came to Abimelech in a dream one night and said to him, "You are as good as dead because of the woman you have taken; she is a married woman."

⁴Now Abimelech had not gone near her, so he said, "Lord, will you destroy an innocent nation? ⁵Did he not say to me, 'She is my sister,' and didn't she also say, 'He is my brother'? I have done this with a clear conscience and clean hands."

⁶Then God said to him in the dream, "Yes, I know you did this with a clear conscience, and so I have kept you from sinning against me. That is why I did not let you touch her. ⁷Now return the man's wife, for he is a prophet, and he will pray for you and you will live. But if you do not return her, you may be sure that you and all yours will die."

ᵃ 37 Moab sounds like the Hebrew for *from father.*
ᵇ 38 Ben-Ammi means *son of my people.*

THE MESSAGE

19.30   Lot left Zoar and went into the mountains to live with his two daughters; he was afraid to stay in Zoar. He lived in a cave with his daughters.

19.31-32   One day the older daughter said to the younger, "Our father is getting old and there's not a man left in the country by whom we can get pregnant. Let's get our father drunk with wine and lie with him. We'll get children through our father—it's our only chance to keep our family alive."

19.33-35   They got their father drunk with wine that very night. The older daughter went and lay with him. He was oblivious, knowing nothing of what she did. The next morning the older said to the younger, "Last night I slept with my father. Tonight, it's your turn. We'll get him drunk again and then you sleep with him. We'll both get a child through our father and keep our family alive." So that night they got their father drunk again and the younger went in and slept with him. Again he was oblivious, knowing nothing of what she did.

19.36-38   Both daughters became pregnant by their father, Lot. The older daughter had a son and named him Moab, the ancestor of the present-day Moabites. The younger daughter had a son and named him Ben-Ammi, the ancestor of the present-day Ammonites.

⁜

20.1-2   **20** Abraham traveled from there south to the Negev and settled down between Kadesh and Shur. While he was camping in Gerar, Abraham said of his wife Sarah, "She's my sister."

20.2-3   So Abimelech, king of Gerar, sent for Sarah and took her. But God came to Abimelech in a dream that night and told him, "You're as good as dead—that woman you took, she's a married woman."

20.4-5   Now Abimelech had not yet slept with her, hadn't so much as touched her. He said, "Master, would you kill an innocent man? Didn't he tell me, 'She's my sister'? And didn't she herself say, 'He's my brother'? I had no idea I was doing anything wrong when I did this."

20.6-7   God said to him in the dream, "Yes, I know your intentions were pure, that's why I kept you from sinning against me; I was the one who kept you from going to bed with her. So now give the man's wife back to him. He's a prophet and will pray for you—pray for your life. If you don't give her back, know that it's certain death both for you and everyone in your family."

NEW INTERNATIONAL VERSION

⁸Early the next morning Abimelech summoned all his officials, and when he told them all that had happened, they were very much afraid. ⁹Then Abimelech called Abraham in and said, "What have you done to us? How have I wronged you that you have brought such great guilt upon me and my kingdom? You have done things to me that should not be done." ¹⁰And Abimelech asked Abraham, "What was your reason for doing this?"

¹¹Abraham replied, "I said to myself, 'There is surely no fear of God in this place, and they will kill me because of my wife.' ¹²Besides, she really is my sister, the daughter of my father though not of my mother; and she became my wife. ¹³And when God had me wander from my father's household, I said to her, 'This is how you can show your love to me: Everywhere we go, say of me, "He is my brother." ' "

¹⁴Then Abimelech brought sheep and cattle and male and female slaves and gave them to Abraham, and he returned Sarah his wife to him. ¹⁵And Abimelech said, "My land is before you; live wherever you like."

¹⁶To Sarah he said, "I am giving your brother a thousand shekels*ᵃ* of silver. This is to cover the offense against you before all who are with you; you are completely vindicated."

¹⁷Then Abraham prayed to God, and God healed Abimelech, his wife and his slave girls so they could have children again, ¹⁸for the Lᴏʀᴅ had closed up every womb in Abimelech's household because of Abraham's wife Sarah.

THE BIRTH OF ISAAC

21 Now the Lᴏʀᴅ was gracious to Sarah as he had said, and the Lᴏʀᴅ did for Sarah what he had promised. ²Sarah became pregnant and bore a son to Abraham in his old age, at the very time God had promised him. ³Abraham gave the name Isaac*ᵇ* to the son Sarah bore him. ⁴When his son Isaac was eight days old, Abraham circumcised him, as God commanded him. ⁵Abraham was a hundred years old when his son Isaac was born to him.

⁶Sarah said, "God has brought me laughter, and everyone who hears about this will laugh with me." ⁷And she added, "Who would have said to Abraham that Sarah would nurse children? Yet I have borne him a son in his old age."

THE MESSAGE

20.8-9 Abimelech was up first thing in the morning. He called all his house servants together and told them the whole story. They were shocked. Then Abimelech called in Abraham and said, "What have you done to us? What have I ever done to you that you would bring on me and my kingdom this huge offense? What you've done to me ought never to have been done."

20.10 Abimelech went on to Abraham, "Whatever were you thinking of when you did this thing?"

20.11-13 Abraham said, "I just assumed that there was no fear of God in this place and that they'd kill me to get my wife. Besides, the truth is that she is my half sister; she's my father's daughter but not my mother's. When God sent me out as a wanderer from my father's home, I told her, 'Do me a favor; wherever we go, tell people that I'm your brother.'"

20.14-15 Then Abimelech gave Sarah back to Abraham, and along with her sent sheep and cattle and servants, both male and female. He said, "My land is open to you; live wherever you wish."

20.16 And to Sarah he said, "I've given your brother a thousand pieces of silver—that clears you of even a shadow of suspicion before the eyes of the world. You're vindicated."

20.17-18 Then Abraham prayed to God and God healed Abimelech, his wife and his maidservants, and they started having babies again. For Gᴏᴅ had shut down every womb in Abimelech's household on account of Sarah, Abraham's wife.

⊹

21.1-4 **21** Gᴏᴅ visited Sarah exactly as he said he would; Gᴏᴅ did to Sarah what he promised: Sarah became pregnant and gave Abraham a son in his old age, and at the very time God had set. Abraham named him Isaac. When his son was eight days old, Abraham circumcised him just as God had commanded.

21.5-6 Abraham was a hundred years old when his son Isaac was born.

Sarah said,

God has blessed me with laughter
and all who get the news will laugh with me!

21.7 She also said,

Whoever would have suggested to Abraham
that Sarah would one day nurse a baby!
Yet here I am! I've given the old man a son!

ᵃ 16 That is, about 25 pounds (about 11.5 kilograms)
ᵇ 3 *Isaac* means *he laughs.*

| NEW INTERNATIONAL VERSION | THE MESSAGE |

HAGAR AND ISHMAEL SENT AWAY

⁸The child grew and was weaned, and on the day Isaac was weaned Abraham held a great feast. ⁹But Sarah saw that the son whom Hagar the Egyptian had borne to Abraham was mocking, ¹⁰and she said to Abraham, "Get rid of that slave woman and her son, for that slave woman's son will never share in the inheritance with my son Isaac."

¹¹The matter distressed Abraham greatly because it concerned his son. ¹²But God said to him, "Do not be so distressed about the boy and your maidservant. Listen to whatever Sarah tells you, because it is through Isaac that your offspring*a* will be reckoned. ¹³I will make the son of the maidservant into a nation also, because he is your offspring."

¹⁴Early the next morning Abraham took some food and a skin of water and gave them to Hagar. He set them on her shoulders and then sent her off with the boy. She went on her way and wandered in the desert of Beersheba.

¹⁵When the water in the skin was gone, she put the boy under one of the bushes. ¹⁶Then she went off and sat down nearby, about a bowshot away, for she thought, "I cannot watch the boy die." And as she sat there nearby, she*b* began to sob.

¹⁷God heard the boy crying, and the angel of God called to Hagar from heaven and said to her, "What is the matter, Hagar? Do not be afraid; God has heard the boy crying as he lies there. ¹⁸Lift the boy up and take him by the hand, for I will make him into a great nation."

¹⁹Then God opened her eyes and she saw a well of water. So she went and filled the skin with water and gave the boy a drink.

²⁰God was with the boy as he grew up. He lived in the desert and became an archer. ²¹While he was living in the Desert of Paran, his mother got a wife for him from Egypt.

THE TREATY AT BEERSHEBA

²²At that time Abimelech and Phicol the commander of his forces said to Abraham, "God is with you in everything you do. ²³Now swear to me here before God that you will not deal falsely with me or my children or my descendants. Show to me and the country where you are living as an alien the same kindness I have shown to you."

²⁴Abraham said, "I swear it."

²⁵Then Abraham complained to Abimelech about a well of water that Abimelech's servants had seized. ²⁶But Abimelech said, "I don't know who has done this. You did not tell me, and I heard about it only today."

21.8 The baby grew and was weaned. Abraham threw a big party on the day Isaac was weaned.

21.9-10 One day Sarah saw the son that Hagar the Egyptian had borne to Abraham, poking fun at her son Isaac. She told Abraham, "Get rid of this slave woman and her son. No child of this slave is going to share inheritance with my son Isaac!"

21.11-13 The matter gave great pain to Abraham—after all, Ishmael was his son. But God spoke to Abraham, "Don't feel badly about the boy and your maid. Do whatever Sarah tells you. Your descendants will come through Isaac. Regarding your maid's son, be assured that I'll also develop a great nation from him—he's your son too."

21.14-16 Abraham got up early the next morning, got some food together and a canteen of water for Hagar, put them on her back and sent her away with the child. She wandered off into the desert of Beersheba. When the water was gone, she left the child under a shrub and went off, fifty yards or so. She said, "I can't watch my son die." As she sat, she broke into sobs.

21.17-18 Meanwhile, God heard the boy crying. The angel of God called from Heaven to Hagar, "What's wrong, Hagar? Don't be afraid. God has heard the boy and knows the fix he's in. Up now; go get the boy. Hold him tight. I'm going to make of him a great nation."

21.19 Just then God opened her eyes. She looked. She saw a well of water. She went to it and filled her canteen and gave the boy a long, cool drink.

21.20-21 God was on the boy's side as he grew up. He lived out in the desert and became a skilled archer. He lived in the Paran wilderness. And his mother got him a wife from Egypt.

21.22-23 At about that same time, Abimelech and the captain of his troops, Phicol, spoke to Abraham: "No matter what you do, God is on your side. So swear to me that you won't do anything underhanded to me or any of my family. For as long as you live here, swear that you'll treat me and my land as well as I've treated you."

21.24 Abraham said, "I swear it."

21.25-26 At the same time, Abraham confronted Abimelech over the matter of a well of water that Abimelech's servants had taken. Abimelech said, "I have no idea who did this; you never told me about it; this is the first I've heard of it."

---

a 12 Or *seed*   *b 16* Hebrew; Septuagint *the child*

NEW INTERNATIONAL VERSION

²⁷So Abraham brought sheep and cattle and gave them to Abimelech, and the two men made a treaty. ²⁸Abraham set apart seven ewe lambs from the flock, ²⁹and Abimelech asked Abraham, "What is the meaning of these seven ewe lambs you have set apart by themselves?"

³⁰He replied, "Accept these seven lambs from my hand as a witness that I dug this well."

³¹So that place was called Beersheba,*ᵃ* because the two men swore an oath there.

³²After the treaty had been made at Beersheba, Abimelech and Phicol the commander of his forces returned to the land of the Philistines. ³³Abraham planted a tamarisk tree in Beersheba, and there he called upon the name of the LORD, the Eternal God. ³⁴And Abraham stayed in the land of the Philistines for a long time.

ABRAHAM TESTED

22 Some time later God tested Abraham. He said to him, "Abraham!"

"Here I am," he replied.

²Then God said, "Take your son, your only son, Isaac, whom you love, and go to the region of Moriah. Sacrifice him there as a burnt offering on one of the mountains I will tell you about."

³Early the next morning Abraham got up and saddled his donkey. He took with him two of his servants and his son Isaac. When he had cut enough wood for the burnt offering, he set out for the place God had told him about. ⁴On the third day Abraham looked up and saw the place in the distance. ⁵He said to his servants, "Stay here with the donkey while I and the boy go over there. We will worship and then we will come back to you."

⁶Abraham took the wood for the burnt offering and placed it on his son Isaac, and he himself carried the fire and the knife. As the two of them went on together, ⁷Isaac spoke up and said to his father Abraham, "Father?"

"Yes, my son?" Abraham replied.

"The fire and wood are here," Isaac said, "but where is the lamb for the burnt offering?"

⁸Abraham answered, "God himself will provide the lamb for the burnt offering, my son." And the two of them went on together.

⁹When they reached the place God had told him about, Abraham built an altar there and arranged the wood on it. He bound his son Isaac and laid him on the altar, on top of the wood. ¹⁰Then he reached out his hand and took the knife to slay his son. ¹¹But the angel of the LORD called out to him from heaven, "Abraham! Abraham!"

ᵃ *31* Beersheba *can mean* well of seven *or* well of the oath.

THE MESSAGE

21.27-28 So the two of them made a covenant. Abraham took sheep and cattle and gave them to Abimelech. Abraham set aside seven sheep from his flock.

21.29 Abimelech said, "What does this mean? These seven sheep you've set aside."

21.30 Abraham said, "It means that when you accept these seven sheep, you take it as proof that I dug this well, that it's my well."

21.31-32 That's how the place got named Beersheba (the Oath-Well), because the two of them swore a covenant oath there. After they had made the covenant at Beersheba, Abimelech and his commander, Phicol, left and went back to Philistine territory.

21.33-34 Abraham planted a tamarisk tree in Beersheba and worshiped GOD there, praying to the Eternal God. Abraham lived in Philistine country for a long time.

✝

22.1 **22** After all this, God tested Abraham. God said, "Abraham!"

"Yes?" answered Abraham. "I'm listening."

22.2 He said, "Take your dear son Isaac whom you love and go to the land of Moriah. Sacrifice him there as a burnt offering on one of the mountains that I'll point out to you."

22.3-5 Abraham got up early in the morning and saddled his donkey. He took two of his young servants and his son Isaac. He had split wood for the burnt offering. He set out for the place God had directed him. On the third day he looked up and saw the place in the distance. Abraham told his two young servants, "Stay here with the donkey. The boy and I are going over there to worship; then we'll come back to you."

22.6 Abraham took the wood for the burnt offering and gave it to Isaac his son to carry. He carried the flint and the knife. The two of them went off together.

22.7 Isaac said to Abraham his father, "Father?"

"Yes, my son."

"We have flint and wood, but where's the sheep for the burnt offering?"

22.8 Abraham said, "Son, God will see to it that there's a sheep for the burnt offering." And they kept on walking together.

22.9-10 They arrived at the place to which God had directed him. Abraham built an altar. He laid out the wood. Then he tied up Isaac and laid him on the wood. Abraham reached out and took the knife to kill his son.

22.11 Just then an angel of GOD called to him out of Heaven, "Abraham! Abraham!"

NEW INTERNATIONAL VERSION	THE MESSAGE

NEW INTERNATIONAL VERSION

"Here I am," he replied.

¹²"Do not lay a hand on the boy," he said. "Do not do anything to him. Now I know that you fear God, because you have not withheld from me your son, your only son."

¹³Abraham looked up and there in a thicket he saw a ram*a* caught by its horns. He went over and took the ram and sacrificed it as a burnt offering instead of his son. ¹⁴So Abraham called that place The LORD Will Provide. And to this day it is said, "On the mountain of the LORD it will be provided."

¹⁵The angel of the LORD called to Abraham from heaven a second time ¹⁶and said, "I swear by myself, declares the LORD, that because you have done this and have not withheld your son, your only son, ¹⁷I will surely bless you and make your descendants as numerous as the stars in the sky and as the sand on the seashore. Your descendants will take possession of the cities of their enemies, ¹⁸and through your offspring*b* all nations on earth will be blessed, because you have obeyed me."

¹⁹Then Abraham returned to his servants, and they set off together for Beersheba. And Abraham stayed in Beersheba.

NAHOR'S SONS

²⁰Some time later Abraham was told, "Milcah is also a mother; she has borne sons to your brother Nahor: ²¹Uz the firstborn, Buz his brother, Kemuel (the father of Aram), ²²Kesed, Hazo, Pildash, Jidlaph and Bethuel." ²³Bethuel became the father of Rebekah. Milcah bore these eight sons to Abraham's brother Nahor. ²⁴His concubine, whose name was Reumah, also had sons: Tebah, Gaham, Tahash and Maacah.

THE DEATH OF SARAH

23 Sarah lived to be a hundred and twenty-seven years old. ²She died at Kiriath Arba (that is, Hebron) in the land of Canaan, and Abraham went to mourn for Sarah and to weep over her.

³Then Abraham rose from beside his dead wife and spoke to the Hittites.*c* He said, ⁴"I am an alien and a stranger among you. Sell me some property for a burial site here so I can bury my dead."

⁵The Hittites replied to Abraham, ⁶"Sir, listen to us. You are a mighty prince among us. Bury your dead in the choicest of our tombs. None of us will refuse you his tomb for burying your dead."

THE MESSAGE

22.12 "Yes, I'm listening."

"Don't lay a hand on that boy! Don't touch him! Now I know how fearlessly you fear God; you didn't hesitate to place your son, your dear son, on the altar for me."

22.13 Abraham looked up. He saw a ram caught by its horns in the thicket. Abraham took the ram and sacrificed it as a burnt offering instead of his son.

22.14 Abraham named that place GOD-Yireh (GOD-Sees-to-It). That's where we get the saying, "On the mountain of GOD, he sees to it."

22.15-18 The angel of GOD spoke from Heaven a second time to Abraham: "I swear—GOD's sure word!—because you have gone through with this, and have not refused to give me your son, your dear, dear son, I'll bless you—oh, how I'll bless you! And I'll make sure that your children flourish—like stars in the sky! like sand on the beaches! And your descendants will defeat their enemies. All nations on Earth will find themselves blessed through your descendants because you obeyed me."

22.19 Then Abraham went back to his young servants. They got things together and returned to Beersheba. Abraham settled down in Beersheba.

✝

22.20-23 After all this, Abraham got the news: "Your brother Nahor is a father! Milcah has given him children: Uz, his firstborn, his brother Buz, Kemuel (he was the father of Aram), Kesed, Hazo, Pildash, Jidlaph, and Bethuel." (Bethuel was the father of Rebekah.) Milcah gave these eight sons to Nahor, Abraham's brother.

22.24 His concubine, Reumah, gave him four more children: Tebah, Gaham, Tahash, and Maacah.

✝

23.1-2 **23** Sarah lived 127 years. Sarah died in Kiriath Arba, present-day Hebron, in the land of Canaan. Abraham mourned for Sarah and wept.

23.3-4 Then Abraham got up from mourning his dead wife and spoke to the Hittites: "I know I'm only an outsider here among you, but sell me a burial plot so that I can bury my dead decently."

23.5-6 The Hittites responded, "Why, you're no mere outsider here with us, you're a prince of God! Bury your dead wife in the best of our burial sites. None of us will refuse you a place for burial."

---

a 13 Many manuscripts of the Masoretic Text, Samaritan Pentateuch, Septuagint and Syriac; most manuscripts of the Masoretic Text *a ram behind ⌊him⌋*   *b 18* Or *seed*
c 3 Or *the sons of Heth*; also in verses 5, 7, 10, 16, 18 and 20

NEW INTERNATIONAL VERSION

⁷Then Abraham rose and bowed down before the people of the land, the Hittites. ⁸He said to them, "If you are willing to let me bury my dead, then listen to me and intercede with Ephron son of Zohar on my behalf ⁹so he will sell me the cave of Machpelah, which belongs to him and is at the end of his field. Ask him to sell it to me for the full price as a burial site among you."

¹⁰Ephron the Hittite was sitting among his people and he replied to Abraham in the hearing of all the Hittites who had come to the gate of his city. ¹¹"No, my lord," he said. "Listen to me; I give*a* you the field, and I give*a* you the cave that is in it. I give*a* it to you in the presence of my people. Bury your dead."

¹²Again Abraham bowed down before the people of the land ¹³and he said to Ephron in their hearing, "Listen to me, if you will. I will pay the price of the field. Accept it from me so I can bury my dead there."

¹⁴Ephron answered Abraham, ¹⁵"Listen to me, my lord; the land is worth four hundred shekels*b* of silver, but what is that between me and you? Bury your dead."

¹⁶Abraham agreed to Ephron's terms and weighed out for him the price he had named in the hearing of the Hittites: four hundred shekels of silver, according to the weight current among the merchants.

¹⁷So Ephron's field in Machpelah near Mamre—both the field and the cave in it, and all the trees within the borders of the field—was deeded ¹⁸to Abraham as his property in the presence of all the Hittites who had come to the gate of the city. ¹⁹Afterward Abraham buried his wife Sarah in the cave in the field of Machpelah near Mamre (which is at Hebron) in the land of Canaan. ²⁰So the field and the cave in it were deeded to Abraham by the Hittites as a burial site.

ISAAC AND REBEKAH

24 Abraham was now old and well advanced in years, and the LORD had blessed him in every way. ²He said to the chief*c* servant in his household, the one in charge of all that he had, "Put your hand under my thigh. ³I want you to swear by the LORD, the God of heaven and the God of earth, that you will not get a wife for my son from the daughters of the Canaanites, among whom I am living, ⁴but will go to my country and my own relatives and get a wife for my son Isaac."

⁵The servant asked him, "What if the woman is unwilling to come back with me to this land?

THE MESSAGE

23.7-9   Then Abraham got up, bowed respectfully to the people of the land, the Hittites, and said, "If you're serious about helping me give my wife a proper burial, intercede for me with Ephron son of Zohar. Ask him to sell me the cave of Machpelah that he owns, the one at the end of his land. Ask him to sell it to me at its full price for a burial plot, with you as witnesses."

23.10-11   Ephron was part of the local Hittite community. Then Ephron the Hittite spoke up, answering Abraham with all the Hittites who were part of the town council listening: "Oh no, my master! I couldn't do that. The field is yours—a gift. I'll give it and the cave to you. With my people as witnesses, I give it to you. Bury your deceased wife."

23.12-13   Abraham bowed respectfully before the assembled council and answered Ephron: "Please allow me—I want to pay the price of the land; take my money so that I can go ahead and bury my wife."

23.14-15   Then Ephron answered Abraham, "If you insist, master. What's four hundred silver shekels between us? Now go ahead and bury your wife."

23.16   Abraham accepted Ephron's offer and paid out the sum that Ephron had named before the town council of Hittites—four hundred silver shekels at the current exchange rate.

23.17-20   That's how Ephron's field next to Mamre—the field, its cave, and all the trees within its borders—became Abraham's property. The town council of Hittites witnessed the transaction. Abraham then proceeded to bury his wife Sarah in the cave in the field of Machpelah that is next to Mamre, present-day Hebron, in the land of Canaan. The field and its cave went from the Hittites into Abraham's possession as a burial plot.

ISAAC AND REBEKAH

24.1   **24** Abraham was now an old man. GOD had blessed Abraham in every way.

24.2-4   Abraham spoke to the senior servant in his household, the one in charge of everything he had, "Put your hand under my thigh and swear by GOD—God of Heaven, God of Earth—that you will not get a wife for my son from among the young women of the Canaanites here, but will go to the land of my birth and get a wife for my son Isaac."

24.5   The servant answered, "But what if the woman refuses to leave home and come with

a 11 Or sell   b 15 That is, about 10 pounds (about 4.5 kilograms)   c 2 Or oldest

NEW INTERNATIONAL VERSION

Shall I then take your son back to the country you came from?"

⁶"Make sure that you do not take my son back there," Abraham said. ⁷"The LORD, the God of heaven, who brought me out of my father's household and my native land and who spoke to me and promised me on oath, saying, 'To your offspring*a* I will give this land'—he will send his angel before you so that you can get a wife for my son from there. ⁸If the woman is unwilling to come back with you, then you will be released from this oath of mine. Only do not take my son back there." ⁹So the servant put his hand under the thigh of his master Abraham and swore an oath to him concerning this matter.

¹⁰Then the servant took ten of his master's camels and left, taking with him all kinds of good things from his master. He set out for Aram Naharaim*b* and made his way to the town of Nahor. ¹¹He had the camels kneel down near the well outside the town; it was toward evening, the time the women go out to draw water.

¹²Then he prayed, "O LORD, God of my master Abraham, give me success today, and show kindness to my master Abraham. ¹³See, I am standing beside this spring, and the daughters of the townspeople are coming out to draw water. ¹⁴May it be that when I say to a girl, 'Please let down your jar that I may have a drink,' and she says, 'Drink, and I'll water your camels too'—let her be the one you have chosen for your servant Isaac. By this I will know that you have shown kindness to my master."

¹⁵Before he had finished praying, Rebekah came out with her jar on her shoulder. She was the daughter of Bethuel son of Milcah, who was the wife of Abraham's brother Nahor. ¹⁶The girl was very beautiful, a virgin; no man had ever lain with her. She went down to the spring, filled her jar and came up again.

¹⁷The servant hurried to meet her and said, "Please give me a little water from your jar."

¹⁸"Drink, my lord," she said, and quickly lowered the jar to her hands and gave him a drink.

¹⁹After she had given him a drink, she said, "I'll draw water for your camels too, until they have finished drinking." ²⁰So she quickly emptied her jar into the trough, ran back to the well to draw more water, and drew enough for all his camels. ²¹Without saying a word, the man watched her closely to learn whether or not the LORD had made his journey successful.

²²When the camels had finished drinking, the man took out a gold nose ring weighing a beka*c*

THE MESSAGE

me? Do I then take your son back to your home country?"

24.6-8 Abraham said, "Oh no. Never. By no means are you to take my son back there. GOD, the God of Heaven, took me from the home of my father and from the country of my birth and spoke to me in solemn promise, 'I'm giving *this* land to your descendants.' This God will send his angel ahead of you to get a wife for my son. And if the woman won't come, you are free from this oath you've sworn to me. But under no circumstances are you to take my son back there."

24.9 So the servant put his hand under the thigh of his master Abraham and gave his solemn oath.

24.10-14 The servant took ten of his master's camels and, loaded with gifts from his master, traveled to Aram Naharaim and the city of Nahor. Outside the city, he made the camels kneel at a well. It was evening, the time when the women came to draw water. He prayed, "O GOD, God of my master Abraham, make things go smoothly this day; treat my master Abraham well! As I stand here by the spring while the young women of the town come out to get water, let the girl to whom I say, 'Lower your jug and give me a drink,' and who answers, 'Drink, and let me also water your camels'—let her be the woman you have picked out for your servant Isaac. Then I'll know that you're working graciously behind the scenes for my master."

24.15-17 It so happened that the words were barely out of his mouth when Rebekah, the daughter of Bethuel whose mother was Milcah the wife of Nahor, Abraham's brother, came out with a water jug on her shoulder. The girl was stunningly beautiful, a pure virgin. She went down to the spring, filled her jug, and came back up. The servant ran to meet her and said, "Please, can I have a sip of water from your jug?"

24.18-21 She said, "Certainly, drink!" And she held the jug so that he could drink. When he had satisfied his thirst she said, "I'll get water for your camels, too, until they've drunk their fill." She promptly emptied her jug into the trough and ran back to the well to fill it, and she kept at it until she had watered all the camels.

The man watched, silent. Was this GOD's answer? Had GOD made his trip a success or not?

24.22-23 When the camels had finished drinking, the man brought out gifts, a gold nose ring weighing a little over a quarter of an ounce and two

a 7 Or seed   *b 10 That is, Northwest Mesopotamia*
c 22 That is, about 1/5 ounce (about 5.5 grams)

NEW INTERNATIONAL VERSION

and two gold bracelets weighing ten shekels. *a*
²³Then he asked, "Whose daughter are you?
Please tell me, is there room in your father's
house for us to spend the night?"

²⁴She answered him, "I am the daughter of
Bethuel, the son that Milcah bore to Nahor."
²⁵And she added, "We have plenty of straw and
fodder, as well as room for you to spend the
night."

²⁶Then the man bowed down and worshiped
the LORD, ²⁷saying, "Praise be to the LORD, the
God of my master Abraham, who has not abandoned his kindness and faithfulness to my master.
As for me, the LORD has led me on the journey to
the house of my master's relatives."

²⁸The girl ran and told her mother's household about these things. ²⁹Now Rebekah had a
brother named Laban, and he hurried out to the
man at the spring. ³⁰As soon as he had seen the
nose ring, and the bracelets on his sister's arms,
and had heard Rebekah tell what the man said
to her, he went out to the man and found him
standing by the camels near the spring. ³¹"Come,
you who are blessed by the LORD," he said. "Why
are you standing out here? I have prepared the
house and a place for the camels."

³²So the man went to the house, and the camels were unloaded. Straw and fodder were
brought for the camels, and water for him and
his men to wash their feet. ³³Then food was set
before him, but he said, "I will not eat until I
have told you what I have to say."

"Then tell us," ⌐Laban⌐ said.

³⁴So he said, "I am Abraham's servant. ³⁵The
LORD has blessed my master abundantly, and he
has become wealthy. He has given him sheep and
cattle, silver and gold, menservants and maidservants, and camels and donkeys. ³⁶My master's
wife Sarah has borne him a son in her *b* old age,
and he has given him everything he owns. ³⁷And
my master made me swear an oath, and said,
'You must not get a wife for my son from the
daughters of the Canaanites, in whose land I
live, ³⁸but go to my father's family and to my
own clan, and get a wife for my son.'

³⁹"Then I asked my master, 'What if the woman will not come back with me?'

⁴⁰"He replied, 'The LORD, before whom I have
walked, will send his angel with you and make
your journey a success, so that you can get a
wife for my son from my own clan and from my
father's family. ⁴¹Then, when you go to my clan,
you will be released from my oath even if they
refuse to give her to you—you will be released
from my oath.'

THE MESSAGE

arm bracelets weighing about four ounces, and
gave them to her. He asked her, "Tell me about
your family? Whose daughter are you? Is there
room in your father's house for us to stay the
night?"

24.24-25 She said, "I'm the daughter of Bethuel the
son of Milcah and Nahor. And there's plenty of
room in our house for you to stay—and lots of
straw and feed besides."

24.26-27 At this the man bowed in worship before
GOD and prayed, "Blessed be GOD, God of my
master Abraham: How generous and true
you've been to my master; you've held nothing
back. You led me right to the door of my master's brother!"

24.28 And the girl was off and running, telling
everyone in her mother's house what had happened.

24.29-31 Rebekah had a brother named Laban. Laban
ran outside to the man at the spring. He had
seen the nose ring and the bracelets on his sister and had heard her say, "The man said this
and this and this to me." So he went to the man
and there he was, still standing with his camels
at the spring. Laban welcomed him: "Come on
in, blessed of GOD! Why are you standing out
here? I've got the house ready for you; and
there's also a place for your camels."

24.32-33 So the man went into the house. The camels
were unloaded and given straw and feed. Water
was brought to bathe the feet of the man and
the men with him. Then Laban brought out
food. But the man said, "I won't eat until I tell
my story."

Laban said, "Go ahead; tell us."

24.34-41 The servant said, "I'm the servant of Abraham. GOD has blessed my master—he's a great
man; GOD has given him sheep and cattle, silver and gold, servants and maidservants,
camels and donkeys. And then to top it off, Sarah, my master's wife, gave him a son in her old
age and he has passed everything on to his son.
My master made me promise, 'Don't get a wife
for my son from the daughters of the Canaanites in whose land I live. No, go to my father's
home, back to my family, and get a wife for my
son there.' I said to my master, 'But what if the
woman won't come with me?' He said, 'GOD
before whom I've walked faithfully will send
his angel with you and he'll make things work
out so that you'll bring back a wife for my son
from my family, from the house of my father.
Then you'll be free from the oath. If you go to
my family and they won't give her to you, you
will also be free from the oath.'

---

a 22 That is, about 4 ounces (about 110 grams)
b 36 Or *his*

NEW INTERNATIONAL VERSION

⁴²"When I came to the spring today, I said, 'O LORD, God of my master Abraham, if you will, please grant success to the journey on which I have come. ⁴³See, I am standing beside this spring; if a maiden comes out to draw water and I say to her, "Please let me drink a little water from your jar," ⁴⁴and if she says to me, "Drink, and I'll draw water for your camels too," let her be the one the LORD has chosen for my master's son.'

⁴⁵"Before I finished praying in my heart, Rebekah came out, with her jar on her shoulder. She went down to the spring and drew water, and I said to her, 'Please give me a drink.'

⁴⁶"She quickly lowered her jar from her shoulder and said, 'Drink, and I'll water your camels too.' So I drank, and she watered the camels also.

⁴⁷"I asked her, 'Whose daughter are you?'

"She said, 'The daughter of Bethuel son of Nahor, whom Milcah bore to him.'

"Then I put the ring in her nose and the bracelets on her arms, ⁴⁸and I bowed down and worshiped the LORD. I praised the LORD, the God of my master Abraham, who had led me on the right road to get the granddaughter of my master's brother for his son. ⁴⁹Now if you will show kindness and faithfulness to my master, tell me; and if not, tell me, so I may know which way to turn."

⁵⁰Laban and Bethuel answered, "This is from the LORD; we can say nothing to you one way or the other. ⁵¹Here is Rebekah; take her and go, and let her become the wife of your master's son, as the LORD has directed."

⁵²When Abraham's servant heard what they said, he bowed down to the ground before the LORD. ⁵³Then the servant brought out gold and silver jewelry and articles of clothing and gave them to Rebekah; he also gave costly gifts to her brother and to her mother. ⁵⁴Then he and the men who were with him ate and drank and spent the night there.

When they got up the next morning, he said, "Send me on my way to my master."

⁵⁵But her brother and her mother replied, "Let the girl remain with us ten days or so; then you*a* may go."

⁵⁶But he said to them, "Do not detain me, now that the LORD has granted success to my journey. Send me on my way so I may go to my master."

⁵⁷Then they said, "Let's call the girl and ask her about it." ⁵⁸So they called Rebekah and asked her, "Will you go with this man?"

"I will go," she said.

a 55 Or she

THE MESSAGE

24.42-44 "Well, when I came this very day to the spring, I prayed, 'GOD, God of my master Abraham, make things turn out well in this task I've been given. I'm standing at this well. When a young woman comes here to draw water and I say to her, Please, give me a sip of water from your jug, and she says, Not only will I give you a drink, I'll also water your camels—let that woman be the wife GOD has picked out for my master's son.'

24.45-48 "I had barely finished offering this prayer, when Rebekah arrived, her jug on her shoulder. She went to the spring and drew water and I said, 'Please, can I have a drink?' She didn't hesitate. She held out her jug and said, 'Drink; and when you're finished I'll also water your camels.' I drank, and she watered the camels. I asked her, 'Whose daughter are you?' She said, 'The daughter of Bethuel whose parents were Nahor and Milcah.' I gave her a ring for her nose, bracelets for her arms, and bowed in worship to GOD. I praised GOD, the God of my master Abraham who had led me straight to the door of my master's family to get a wife for his son.

24.49 "Now, tell me what you are going to do. If you plan to respond with a generous yes, tell me. But if not, tell me plainly so I can figure out what to do next."

24.50-51 Laban and Bethuel answered, "This is totally from GOD. We have no say in the matter, either yes or no. Rebekah is yours: Take her and go; let her be the wife of your master's son, as GOD has made plain."

24.52-54 When Abraham's servant heard their decision, he bowed in worship before GOD. Then he brought out gifts of silver and gold and clothing and gave them to Rebekah. He also gave expensive gifts to her brother and mother. He and his men had supper and spent the night. But first thing in the morning they were up. He said, "Send me back to my master."

24.55 Her brother and mother said, "Let the girl stay a while, say another ten days, and then go."

24.56 He said, "Oh, don't make me wait! GOD has worked everything out so well—send me off to my master."

24.57 They said, "We'll call the girl; we'll ask her."

24.58 They called Rebekah and asked her, "Do you want to go with this man?"

She said, "I'm ready to go."

NEW INTERNATIONAL VERSION

⁵⁹So they sent their sister Rebekah on her way, along with her nurse and Abraham's servant and his men. ⁶⁰And they blessed Rebekah and said to her,

"Our sister, may you increase
   to thousands upon thousands;
may your offspring possess
   the gates of their enemies."

⁶¹Then Rebekah and her maids got ready and mounted their camels and went back with the man. So the servant took Rebekah and left. ⁶²Now Isaac had come from Beer Lahai Roi, for he was living in the Negev. ⁶³He went out to the field one evening to meditate,ᵃ and as he looked up, he saw camels approaching. ⁶⁴Rebekah also looked up and saw Isaac. She got down from her camel ⁶⁵and asked the servant, "Who is that man in the field coming to meet us?"

"He is my master," the servant answered. So she took her veil and covered herself.

⁶⁶Then the servant told Isaac all he had done. ⁶⁷Isaac brought her into the tent of his mother Sarah, and he married Rebekah. So she became his wife, and he loved her; and Isaac was comforted after his mother's death.

THE DEATH OF ABRAHAM

25 Abraham tookᵇ another wife, whose name was Keturah. ²She bore him Zimran, Jokshan, Medan, Midian, Ishbak and Shuah. ³Jokshan was the father of Sheba and Dedan; the descendants of Dedan were the Asshurites, the Letushites and the Leummites. ⁴The sons of Midian were Ephah, Epher, Hanoch, Abida and Eldaah. All these were descendants of Keturah.

⁵Abraham left everything he owned to Isaac. ⁶But while he was still living, he gave gifts to the sons of his concubines and sent them away from his son Isaac to the land of the east.

⁷Altogether, Abraham lived a hundred and seventy-five years. ⁸Then Abraham breathed his last and died at a good old age, an old man and full of years; and he was gathered to his people. ⁹His sons Isaac and Ishmael buried him in the cave of Machpelah near Mamre, in the field of Ephron son of Zohar the Hittite, ¹⁰the field Abraham had bought from the Hittites.ᶜ There Abraham was buried with his wife Sarah. ¹¹After Abraham's death, God blessed his son Isaac, who then lived near Beer Lahai Roi.

ISHMAEL'S SONS

¹²This is the account of Abraham's son Ish-

ᵃ 63 The meaning of the Hebrew for this word is uncertain.
ᵇ 1 Or had taken   ᶜ 10 Or the sons of Heth

THE MESSAGE

24.59-60   So they sent them off, their sister Rebekah with her nurse, and Abraham's servant with his men. And they blessed Rebekah saying,

You're our sister—live bountifully!
And your children, triumphantly!

24.61   Rebekah and her young maids mounted the camels and followed the man. The servant took Rebekah and set off for home.

24.62-65   Isaac was living in the Negev. He had just come back from a visit to Beer Lahai Roi. In the evening he went out into the field; while meditating he looked up and saw camels coming. When Rebekah looked up and saw Isaac, she got down from her camel and asked the servant, "Who is that man out in the field coming toward us?"

"That is my master."

She took her veil and covered herself.

24.66-67   After the servant told Isaac the whole story of the trip, Isaac took Rebekah into the tent of his mother Sarah. He married Rebekah and she became his wife and he loved her. So Isaac found comfort after his mother's death.

✠

25.1-2   **25** Abraham married a second time; his new wife was named Keturah. She gave birth to Zimran, Jokshan, Medan, Midian, Ishbak, and Shuah.

25.3   Jokshan had Sheba and Dedan.

25.3   Dedan's descendants were the Asshurim, the Letushim, and the Leummim.

25.4   Midian had Ephah, Epher, Hanoch, Abida, and Eldaah—all from the line of Keturah.

25.5-6   But Abraham gave everything he possessed to Isaac. While he was still living, he gave gifts to the sons he had by his concubines, but then sent them away to the country of the east, putting a good distance between them and his son Isaac.

25.7-11   Abraham lived 175 years. Then he took his final breath. He died happy at a ripe old age, full of years, and was buried with his family. His sons Isaac and Ishmael buried him in the cave of Machpelah in the field of Ephron son of Zohar the Hittite, next to Mamre. It was the field that Abraham had bought from the Hittites. Abraham was buried next to his wife Sarah. After Abraham's death, God blessed his son Isaac. Isaac lived at Beer Lahai Roi.

THE FAMILY TREE OF ISHMAEL

25.12   This is the family tree of Ishmael son of Abra-

NEW INTERNATIONAL VERSION

mael, whom Sarah's maidservant, Hagar the Egyptian, bore to Abraham.

¹³These are the names of the sons of Ishmael, listed in the order of their birth: Nebaioth the firstborn of Ishmael, Kedar, Adbeel, Mibsam, ¹⁴Mishma, Dumah, Massa, ¹⁵Hadad, Tema, Jetur, Naphish and Kedemah. ¹⁶These were the sons of Ishmael, and these are the names of the twelve tribal rulers according to their settlements and camps. ¹⁷Altogether, Ishmael lived a hundred and thirty-seven years. He breathed his last and died, and he was gathered to his people. ¹⁸His descendants settled in the area from Havilah to Shur, near the border of Egypt, as you go toward Asshur. And they lived in hostility toward*a* all their brothers.

JACOB AND ESAU

¹⁹This is the account of Abraham's son Isaac.

Abraham became the father of Isaac, ²⁰and Isaac was forty years old when he married Rebekah daughter of Bethuel the Aramean from Paddan Aram*b* and sister of Laban the Aramean. ²¹Isaac prayed to the LORD on behalf of his wife, because she was barren. The LORD answered his prayer, and his wife Rebekah became pregnant. ²²The babies jostled each other within her, and she said, "Why is this happening to me?" So she went to inquire of the LORD. ²³The LORD said to her,

"Two nations are in your womb,
    and two peoples from within you will be
        separated;
one people will be stronger than the other,
    and the older will serve the younger."

²⁴When the time came for her to give birth, there were twin boys in her womb. ²⁵The first to come out was red, and his whole body was like a hairy garment; so they named him Esau.*c* ²⁶After this, his brother came out, with his hand grasping Esau's heel; so he was named Jacob.*d* Isaac was sixty years old when Rebekah gave birth to them.

²⁷The boys grew up, and Esau became a skillful hunter, a man of the open country, while Jacob was a quiet man, staying among the tents. ²⁸Isaac, who had a taste for wild game, loved Esau, but Rebekah loved Jacob.

²⁹Once when Jacob was cooking some stew, Esau came in from the open country, famished. ³⁰He said to Jacob, "Quick, let me have some of that red stew! I'm famished!" (That is why he was also called Edom.*e*)

---

a 18 Or *lived to the east of*   *b 20* That is, Northwest Mesopotamia   *c 25* *Esau* may mean *hairy;* he was also called Edom, which means *red.*   *d 26* *Jacob* means *he grasps the heel* (figuratively, *he deceives*).   *e 30* *Edom* means *red.*

THE MESSAGE

ham, the son that Hagar the Egyptian, Sarah's maid, bore to Abraham.

25.13-16 These are the names of Ishmael's sons in the order of their births: Nebaioth, Ishmael's firstborn, Kedar, Adbeel, Mibsam, Mishma, Dumah, Massa, Hadad, Tema, Jetur, Naphish, and Kedemah—all the sons of Ishmael. Their settlements and encampments were named after them. Twelve princes with their twelve tribes.

25.17-18 Ishmael lived 137 years. When he breathed his last and died he was buried with his family. His children settled down all the way from Havilah near Egypt eastward to Shur in the direction of Assyria. The Ishmaelites didn't get along with any of their kin.

JACOB AND ESAU

25.19-20 This is the family tree of Isaac son of Abraham: Abraham had Isaac. Isaac was forty years old when he married Rebekah daughter of Bethuel the Aramean of Paddan Aram. She was the sister of Laban the Aramean.

25.21-23 Isaac prayed hard to GOD for his wife because she was barren. GOD answered his prayer and Rebekah became pregnant. But the children tumbled and kicked inside her so much that she said, "If this is the way it's going to be, why go on living?" She went to GOD to find out what was going on. GOD told her,

Two nations are in your womb,
    two peoples butting heads while still in
        your body.
One people will overpower the other,
    and the older will serve the younger.

25.24-26 When her time to give birth came, sure enough, there were twins in her womb. The first came out reddish, as if snugly wrapped in a hairy blanket; they named him Esau (Hairy). His brother followed, his fist clutched tight to Esau's heel; they named him Jacob (Heel). Isaac was sixty years old when they were born.

25.27-28 The boys grew up. Esau became an expert hunter, an outdoorsman. Jacob was a quiet man preferring life indoors among the tents. Isaac loved Esau because he loved his game, but Rebekah loved Jacob.

25.29-30 One day Jacob was cooking a stew. Esau came in from the field, starved. Esau said to Jacob, "Give me some of that red stew—I'm starved!" That's how he came to be called Edom (Red).

NEW INTERNATIONAL VERSION

³¹Jacob replied, "First sell me your birthright."

³²"Look, I am about to die," Esau said. "What good is the birthright to me?"

³³But Jacob said, "Swear to me first." So he swore an oath to him, selling his birthright to Jacob.

³⁴Then Jacob gave Esau some bread and some lentil stew. He ate and drank, and then got up and left.

So Esau despised his birthright.

ISAAC AND ABIMELECH

26 Now there was a famine in the land—besides the earlier famine of Abraham's time—and Isaac went to Abimelech king of the Philistines in Gerar. ²The LORD appeared to Isaac and said, "Do not go down to Egypt; live in the land where I tell you to live. ³Stay in this land for a while, and I will be with you and will bless you. For to you and your descendants I will give all these lands and will confirm the oath I swore to your father Abraham. ⁴I will make your descendants as numerous as the stars in the sky and will give them all these lands, and through your offspring*a* all nations on earth will be blessed, ⁵because Abraham obeyed me and kept my requirements, my commands, my decrees and my laws." ⁶So Isaac stayed in Gerar.

⁷When the men of that place asked him about his wife, he said, "She is my sister," because he was afraid to say, "She is my wife." He thought, "The men of this place might kill me on account of Rebekah, because she is beautiful."

⁸When Isaac had been there a long time, Abimelech king of the Philistines looked down from a window and saw Isaac caressing his wife Rebekah. ⁹So Abimelech summoned Isaac and said, "She is really your wife! Why did you say, 'She is my sister'?"

Isaac answered him, "Because I thought I might lose my life on account of her."

¹⁰Then Abimelech said, "What is this you have done to us? One of the men might well have slept with your wife, and you would have brought guilt upon us."

¹¹So Abimelech gave orders to all the people: "Anyone who molests this man or his wife shall surely be put to death."

¹²Isaac planted crops in that land and the same year reaped a hundredfold, because the LORD blessed him. ¹³The man became rich, and his wealth continued to grow until he became very wealthy. ¹⁴He had so many flocks and herds and servants that the Philistines envied him. ¹⁵So

a 4 Or seed

THE MESSAGE

25.31 Jacob said, "Make me a trade: my stew for your rights as the firstborn."

25.32 Esau said, "I'm starving! What good is a birthright if I'm dead?"

25.33-34 Jacob said, "First, swear to me." And he did it. On oath Esau traded away his rights as the firstborn. Jacob gave him bread and the stew of lentils. He ate and drank, got up and left. That's how Esau shrugged off his rights as the firstborn.

✠

26.1 **26** There was a famine in the land, as bad as the famine during the time of Abraham. And Isaac went down to Abimelech, king of the Philistines, in Gerar.

26.2-5 GOD appeared to him and said, "Don't go down to Egypt; stay where I tell you. Stay here in this land and I'll be with you and bless you. I'm giving you and your children all these lands, fulfilling the oath that I swore to your father Abraham. I'll make your descendants as many as the stars in the sky and give them all these lands. All the nations of the Earth will get a blessing for themselves through your descendants. And why? Because Abraham obeyed my summons and kept my charge—my commands, my guidelines, my teachings."

26.6 So Isaac stayed put in Gerar.

26.7 The men of the place questioned him about his wife. He said, "She's my sister." He was afraid to say "She's my wife." He was thinking, "These men might kill me to get Rebekah, she's so beautiful."

26.8-9 One day, after they had been there quite a long time, Abimelech, king of the Philistines, looked out his window and saw Isaac fondling his wife Rebekah. Abimelech sent for Isaac and said, "So, she's your wife. Why did you tell us 'She's my sister'?"

Isaac said, "Because I thought I might get killed by someone who wanted her."

26.10 Abimelech said, "But think of what you might have done to *us*! Given a little more time, one of the men might have slept with your wife; you would have been responsible for bringing guilt down on us."

26.11 Then Abimelech gave orders to his people: "Anyone who so much as lays a hand on this man or his wife dies."

26.12-15 Isaac planted crops in that land and took in a huge harvest. GOD blessed him. The man got richer and richer by the day until he was very wealthy. He accumulated flocks and herds and many, many servants, so much so that the Philistines began to envy him. They got back at

NEW INTERNATIONAL VERSION

all the wells that his father's servants had dug in the time of his father Abraham, the Philistines stopped up, filling them with earth.

¹⁶Then Abimelech said to Isaac, "Move away from us; you have become too powerful for us."

¹⁷So Isaac moved away from there and encamped in the Valley of Gerar and settled there. ¹⁸Isaac reopened the wells that had been dug in the time of his father Abraham, which the Philistines had stopped up after Abraham died, and he gave them the same names his father had given them.

¹⁹Isaac's servants dug in the valley and discovered a well of fresh water there. ²⁰But the herdsmen of Gerar quarreled with Isaac's herdsmen and said, "The water is ours!" So he named the well Esek,ᵃ because they disputed with him. ²¹Then they dug another well, but they quarreled over that one also; so he named it Sitnah.ᵇ ²²He moved on from there and dug another well, and no one quarreled over it. He named it Rehoboth,ᶜ saying, "Now the Lᴏʀᴅ has given us room and we will flourish in the land."

²³From there he went up to Beersheba. ²⁴That night the Lᴏʀᴅ appeared to him and said, "I am the God of your father Abraham. Do not be afraid, for I am with you; I will bless you and will increase the number of your descendants for the sake of my servant Abraham."

²⁵Isaac built an altar there and called on the name of the Lᴏʀᴅ. There he pitched his tent, and there his servants dug a well.

²⁶Meanwhile, Abimelech had come to him from Gerar, with Ahuzzath his personal adviser and Phicol the commander of his forces. ²⁷Isaac asked them, "Why have you come to me, since you were hostile to me and sent me away?"

²⁸They answered, "We saw clearly that the Lᴏʀᴅ was with you; so we said, 'There ought to be a sworn agreement between us'—between us and you. Let us make a treaty with you ²⁹that you will do us no harm, just as we did not molest you but always treated you well and sent you away in peace. And now you are blessed by the Lᴏʀᴅ."

³⁰Isaac then made a feast for them, and they ate and drank. ³¹Early the next morning the men swore an oath to each other. Then Isaac sent them on their way, and they left him in peace.

³²That day Isaac's servants came and told him about the well they had dug. They said, "We've found water!" ³³He called it Shibah,ᵈ and to this day the name of the town has been Beersheba.ᵉ

ᵃ 20 *Esek* means *dispute.*   ᵇ 21 *Sitnah* means *opposition.*
ᶜ 22 *Rehoboth* means *room.*   ᵈ 33 *Shibah* can mean *oath* or *seven.*   ᵉ 33 *Beersheba* can mean *well of the oath* or *well of seven.*

THE MESSAGE

him by throwing dirt and debris into all the wells that his father's servants had dug back in the days of his father Abraham, clogging up all the wells.

26.16   Finally, Abimelech told Isaac: "Leave. You've become far too big for us."

26.17-18   So Isaac left. He camped in the valley of Gerar and settled down there. Isaac dug again the wells which were dug in the days of his father Abraham but had been clogged up by the Philistines after Abraham's death. And he renamed them, using the original names his father had given them.

26.19-24   One day, as Isaac's servants were digging in the valley, they came on a well of spring water. The shepherds of Gerar quarreled with Isaac's shepherds, claiming, "This water is ours." So Isaac named the well Esek (Quarrel) because they quarreled over it. They dug another well and there was a difference over that one also, so he named it Sitnah (Accusation). He went on from there and dug yet another well. But there was no fighting over this one so he named it Rehoboth (Wide-Open Spaces), saying, "Now Gᴏᴅ has given us plenty of space to spread out in the land." From there he went up to Beersheba. That very night Gᴏᴅ appeared to him and said,

I am the God of Abraham your father;
   don't fear a thing because I'm with you.
I'll bless you and make your children flourish
   because of Abraham my servant.

26.25 Isaac built an altar there and prayed, calling on Gᴏᴅ by name. He pitched his tent and his servants started digging another well.

26.26-27   Then Abimelech came to him from Gerar with Ahuzzath his advisor and Phicol the head of his troops. Isaac asked them, "Why did you come to me? You hate me; you threw me out of your country."

26.28-29   They said, "We've realized that Gᴏᴅ is on your side. We'd like to make a deal between us—a covenant that we maintain friendly relations. We haven't bothered you in the past; we treated you kindly and let you leave us in peace. So—Gᴏᴅ's blessing be with you!"

26.30-31   Isaac laid out a feast and they ate and drank together. Early in the morning they exchanged oaths. Then Isaac said goodbye and they parted as friends.

26.32-33   Later that same day, Isaac's servants came to him with news about the well they had been digging, "We've struck water!" Isaac named the well Sheba (Oath), and that's the name of the city, Beersheba (Oath-Well), to this day.

☩

NEW INTERNATIONAL VERSION

³⁴When Esau was forty years old, he married Judith daughter of Beeri the Hittite, and also Basemath daughter of Elon the Hittite. ³⁵They were a source of grief to Isaac and Rebekah.

JACOB GETS ISAAC'S BLESSING

27 When Isaac was old and his eyes were so weak that he could no longer see, he called for Esau his older son and said to him, "My son."

"Here I am," he answered.

²Isaac said, "I am now an old man and don't know the day of my death. ³Now then, get your weapons—your quiver and bow—and go out to the open country to hunt some wild game for me. ⁴Prepare me the kind of tasty food I like and bring it to me to eat, so that I may give you my blessing before I die."

⁵Now Rebekah was listening as Isaac spoke to his son Esau. When Esau left for the open country to hunt game and bring it back, ⁶Rebekah said to her son Jacob, "Look, I overheard your father say to your brother Esau, ⁷'Bring me some game and prepare me some tasty food to eat, so that I may give you my blessing in the presence of the LORD before I die.' ⁸Now, my son, listen carefully and do what I tell you: ⁹Go out to the flock and bring me two choice young goats, so I can prepare some tasty food for your father, just the way he likes it. ¹⁰Then take it to your father to eat, so that he may give you his blessing before he dies."

¹¹Jacob said to Rebekah his mother, "But my brother Esau is a hairy man, and I'm a man with smooth skin. ¹²What if my father touches me? I would appear to be tricking him and would bring down a curse on myself rather than a blessing."

¹³His mother said to him, "My son, let the curse fall on me. Just do what I say; go and get them for me."

¹⁴So he went and got them and brought them to his mother, and she prepared some tasty food, just the way his father liked it. ¹⁵Then Rebekah took the best clothes of Esau her older son, which she had in the house, and put them on her younger son Jacob. ¹⁶She also covered his hands and the smooth part of his neck with the goatskins. ¹⁷Then she handed to her son Jacob the tasty food and the bread she had made.

¹⁸He went to his father and said, "My father."

"Yes, my son," he answered. "Who is it?"

¹⁹Jacob said to his father, "I am Esau your firstborn. I have done as you told me. Please sit up and eat some of my game so that you may give me your blessing."

THE MESSAGE

26.34-35 When Esau was forty years old he married Judith, daughter of Beeri the Hittite, and Basemath, daughter of Elon the Hittite. They turned out to be thorns in the sides of Isaac and Rebekah.

27.1 **27** When Isaac had become an old man and was nearly blind, he called his eldest son, Esau, and said, "My son."

"Yes, Father?"

27.2-4 "I'm an old man," he said; "I might die any day now. Do me a favor: Get your quiver of arrows and your bow and go out in the country and hunt me some game. Then fix me a hearty meal, the kind that you know I like, and bring it to me to eat so that I can give you my personal blessing before I die."

27.5-7 Rebekah was eavesdropping as Isaac spoke to his son Esau. As soon as Esau had gone off to the country to hunt game for his father, Rebekah spoke to her son Jacob. "I just overheard your father talking with your brother, Esau. He said, 'Bring me some game and fix me a hearty meal so that I can eat and bless you with GOD's blessing before I die.'

27.8-10 "Now, my son, listen to me. Do what I tell you. Go to the flock and get me two young goats. Pick the best; I'll prepare them into a hearty meal, the kind that your father loves. Then you'll take it to your father, he'll eat and bless you before he dies."

27.11-12 "But Mother," Jacob said, "my brother Esau is a hairy man and I have smooth skin. What happens if my father touches me? He'll think I'm playing games with him. I'll bring down a curse on myself instead of a blessing."

27.13 "If it comes to that," said his mother, "I'll take the curse on myself. Now, just do what I say. Go and get the goats."

27.14 So he went and got them and brought them to his mother and she cooked a hearty meal, the kind his father loved so much.

27.15-17 Rebekah took the dress-up clothes of her older son Esau and put them on her younger son Jacob. She took the goatskins and covered his hands and the smooth nape of his neck. Then she placed the hearty meal she had fixed and fresh bread she'd baked into the hands of her son Jacob.

27.18 He went to his father and said, "My father!"

"Yes?" he said. "Which son are you?"

27.19 Jacob answered his father, "I'm your firstborn son Esau. I did what you told me. Come now; sit up and eat of my game so you can give me your personal blessing."

NEW INTERNATIONAL VERSION

²⁰Isaac asked his son, "How did you find it so quickly, my son?"

"The LORD your God gave me success," he replied.

²¹Then Isaac said to Jacob, "Come near so I can touch you, my son, to know whether you really are my son Esau or not."

²²Jacob went close to his father Isaac, who touched him and said, "The voice is the voice of Jacob, but the hands are the hands of Esau." ²³He did not recognize him, for his hands were hairy like those of his brother Esau; so he blessed him. ²⁴"Are you really my son Esau?" he asked.

"I am," he replied.

²⁵Then he said, "My son, bring me some of your game to eat, so that I may give you my blessing."

Jacob brought it to him and he ate; and he brought some wine and he drank. ²⁶Then his father Isaac said to him, "Come here, my son, and kiss me."

²⁷So he went to him and kissed him. When Isaac caught the smell of his clothes, he blessed him and said,

"Ah, the smell of my son
    is like the smell of a field
    that the LORD has blessed.
²⁸May God give you of heaven's dew
    and of earth's richness—
    an abundance of grain and new wine.
²⁹May nations serve you
    and peoples bow down to you.
Be lord over your brothers,
    and may the sons of your mother bow
        down to you.
May those who curse you be cursed
    and those who bless you be blessed."

³⁰After Isaac finished blessing him and Jacob had scarcely left his father's presence, his brother Esau came in from hunting. ³¹He too prepared some tasty food and brought it to his father. Then he said to him, "My father, sit up and eat some of my game, so that you may give me your blessing."

³²His father Isaac asked him, "Who are you?"

"I am your son," he answered, "your firstborn, Esau."

³³Isaac trembled violently and said, "Who was it, then, that hunted game and brought it to me? I ate it just before you came and I blessed him— and indeed he will be blessed!"

³⁴When Esau heard his father's words, he burst out with a loud and bitter cry and said to his father, "Bless me—me too, my father!"

³⁵But he said, "Your brother came deceitfully and took your blessing."

THE MESSAGE

27.20   Isaac said, "So soon? How did you get it so quickly?"

"Because your GOD cleared the way for me."

27.21   Isaac said, "Come close, son; let me touch you—are you really my son Esau?"

27.22-23   So Jacob moved close to his father Isaac. Isaac felt him and said, "The voice is Jacob's voice but the hands are the hands of Esau." He didn't recognize him because his hands were hairy, like his brother Esau's.

27.23-24   But as he was about to bless him he pressed him, "You're sure? You are my son Esau?"

27.24   "Yes. I am."

27.25   Isaac said, "Bring the food so I can eat of my son's game and give you my personal blessing." Jacob brought it to him and he ate. He also brought him wine and he drank.

27.26   Then Isaac said, "Come close, son, and kiss me."

27.27-29   He came close and kissed him and Isaac smelled the smell of his clothes. Finally, he blessed him,

Ahhh. The smell of my son
    is like the smell of the open country
    blessed by GOD.
May God give you
    of Heaven's dew
    and Earth's bounty of grain and wine.
May peoples serve you
    and nations honor you.
You will master your brothers,
    and your mother's sons will honor you.
Those who curse you will be cursed,
    those who bless you will be blessed.

27.30-31   And then right after Isaac had blessed Jacob and Jacob had left, Esau showed up from the hunt. He also had prepared a hearty meal. He came to his father and said, "Let my father get up and eat of his son's game, that he may give me his personal blessing."

27.32   His father Isaac said, "And who are you?"

"I am your son, your firstborn, Esau."

27.33   Isaac started to tremble, shaking violently. He said, "Then who hunted game and brought it to me? I finished the meal just now, before you walked in. And I blessed him—he's blessed for good!"

27.34   Esau, hearing his father's words, sobbed violently and most bitterly, and cried to his father, "My father! Can't you also bless me?"

27.35   "Your brother," he said, "came here falsely and took your blessing."

NEW INTERNATIONAL VERSION

³⁶Esau said, "Isn't he rightly named Jacob*a*? He has deceived me these two times: He took my birthright, and now he's taken my blessing!" Then he asked, "Haven't you reserved any blessing for me?"

³⁷Isaac answered Esau, "I have made him lord over you and have made all his relatives his servants, and I have sustained him with grain and new wine. So what can I possibly do for you, my son?"

³⁸Esau said to his father, "Do you have only one blessing, my father? Bless me too, my father!" Then Esau wept aloud.

³⁹His father Isaac answered him,

"Your dwelling will be
    away from the earth's richness,
    away from the dew of heaven above.
⁴⁰You will live by the sword
    and you will serve your brother.
But when you grow restless,
    you will throw his yoke
    from off your neck."

JACOB FLEES TO LABAN

⁴¹Esau held a grudge against Jacob because of the blessing his father had given him. He said to himself, "The days of mourning for my father are near; then I will kill my brother Jacob."

⁴²When Rebekah was told what her older son Esau had said, she sent for her younger son Jacob and said to him, "Your brother Esau is consoling himself with the thought of killing you. ⁴³Now then, my son, do what I say: Flee at once to my brother Laban in Haran. ⁴⁴Stay with him for a while until your brother's fury subsides. ⁴⁵When your brother is no longer angry with you and forgets what you did to him, I'll send word for you to come back from there. Why should I lose both of you in one day?"

⁴⁶Then Rebekah said to Isaac, "I'm disgusted with living because of these Hittite women. If Jacob takes a wife from among the women of this land, from Hittite women like these, my life will not be worth living."

28 So Isaac called for Jacob and blessed*b* him and commanded him: "Do not marry a Canaanite woman. ²Go at once to Paddan Aram,*c* to the house of your mother's father Bethuel. Take a wife for yourself there, from among the daughters of Laban, your mother's brother. ³May God Almighty*d* bless you and make you fruitful and increase your numbers until you be-

THE MESSAGE

27.36 Esau said, "Not for nothing was he named Jacob, the Heel. Twice now he's tricked me: first he took my birthright and now he's taken my blessing."

He begged, "Haven't you kept back any blessing for me?"

27.37 Isaac answered Esau, "I've made him your master, and all his brothers his servants, and lavished grain and wine on him. I've given it all away. What's left for you, my son?"

27.38 "But don't you have just one blessing for me, Father? Oh, bless me my father! Bless me!" Esau sobbed inconsolably.

27.39-40 Isaac said to him,

You'll live far from Earth's bounty,
    remote from Heaven's dew.
You'll live by your sword, hand-to-mouth,
    and you'll serve your brother.
But when you can't take it any more
    you'll break loose and run free.

27.41 Esau seethed in anger against Jacob because of the blessing his father had given him; he brooded, "The time for mourning my father's death is close. And then I'll kill my brother Jacob."

27.42-45 When these words of her older son Esau were reported to Rebekah, she called her younger son Jacob and said, "Your brother Esau is plotting vengeance against you. He's going to kill you. Son, listen to me. Get out of here. Run for your life to Haran, to my brother Laban. Live with him for a while until your brother cools down, until his anger subsides and he forgets what you did to him. I'll then send for you and bring you back. Why should I lose both of you the same day?"

27.46 Rebekah spoke to Isaac, "I'm sick to death of these Hittite women. If Jacob also marries a native Hittite woman, why live?"

28 So Isaac called in Jacob and blessed him. Then he ordered him, "Don't take a Caananite wife. Leave at once. Go to Paddan Aram to the family of your mother's father, Bethuel. Get a wife for yourself from the daughters of your uncle Laban.

28.3-4 "And may The Strong God bless you and give you many, many children, a congregation

---

a 36 Jacob means *he grasps the heel* (figuratively, *he deceives*).   *b 1* Or *greeted*   *c 2* That is, Northwest Mesopotamia; also in verses 5, 6 and 7   *d 3* Hebrew *El-Shaddai*

NEW INTERNATIONAL VERSION

come a community of peoples. ⁴May he give you and your descendants the blessing given to Abraham, so that you may take possession of the land where you now live as an alien, the land God gave to Abraham." ⁵Then Isaac sent Jacob on his way, and he went to Paddan Aram, to Laban son of Bethuel the Aramean, the brother of Rebekah, who was the mother of Jacob and Esau.

⁶Now Esau learned that Isaac had blessed Jacob and had sent him to Paddan Aram to take a wife from there, and that when he blessed him he commanded him, "Do not marry a Canaanite woman," ⁷and that Jacob had obeyed his father and mother and had gone to Paddan Aram. ⁸Esau then realized how displeasing the Canaanite women were to his father Isaac; ⁹so he went to Ishmael and married Mahalath, the sister of Nebaioth and daughter of Ishmael son of Abraham, in addition to the wives he already had.

JACOB'S DREAM AT BETHEL

¹⁰Jacob left Beersheba and set out for Haran. ¹¹When he reached a certain place, he stopped for the night because the sun had set. Taking one of the stones there, he put it under his head and lay down to sleep. ¹²He had a dream in which he saw a stairway*a* resting on the earth, with its top reaching to heaven, and the angels of God were ascending and descending on it. ¹³There above it*b* stood the LORD, and he said: "I am the LORD, the God of your father Abraham and the God of Isaac. I will give you and your descendants the land on which you are lying. ¹⁴Your descendants will be like the dust of the earth, and you will spread out to the west and to the east, to the north and to the south. All peoples on earth will be blessed through you and your offspring. ¹⁵I am with you and will watch over you wherever you go, and I will bring you back to this land. I will not leave you until I have done what I have promised you."

¹⁶When Jacob awoke from his sleep, he thought, "Surely the LORD is in this place, and I was not aware of it." ¹⁷He was afraid and said, "How awesome is this place! This is none other than the house of God; this is the gate of heaven." ¹⁸Early the next morning Jacob took the stone he had placed under his head and set it up as a pillar and poured oil on top of it. ¹⁹He called that place Bethel,*c* though the city used to be called Luz.

²⁰Then Jacob made a vow, saying, "If God will be with me and will watch over me on this journey I am taking and will give me food to eat and clothes to wear ²¹so that I return safely to my fa-

a 12 Or ladder   b 13 Or There beside him   c 19 Bethel means house of God.

THE MESSAGE

of peoples; and pass on the blessing of Abraham to you and your descendants so that you will get this land in which you live, this land God gave Abraham."

28.5   So Isaac sent Jacob off. He went to Paddan Aram, to Laban son of Bethuel the Aramean, the brother of Rebekah who was the mother of Jacob and Esau.

28.6-9   Esau learned that Isaac had blessed Jacob and sent him to Paddan Aram to get a wife there, and while blessing him commanded, "Don't marry a Canaanite woman," and that Jacob had obeyed his parents and gone to Paddan Aram. When Esau realized how deeply his father Isaac disliked the Canaanite women, he went to Ishmael and married Mahalath the sister of Nebaioth and daughter of Ishmael, Abraham's son. This was in addition to the wives he already had.

✢

28.10-12 Jacob left Beersheba and went to Haran. He came to a certain place and camped for the night since the sun had set. He took one of the stones there, set it under his head and lay down to sleep. And he dreamed: A stairway was set on the ground and it reached all the way to the sky; angels of God were going up and going down on it.

28.13-15   Then GOD was right before him, saying, "I am GOD, the God of Abraham your father and the God of Isaac. I'm giving the ground on which you are sleeping to you and to your descendants. Your descendants will be as the dust of the Earth; they'll stretch from west to east and from north to south. All the families of the Earth will bless themselves in you and your descendants. Yes. I'll stay with you, I'll protect you wherever you go, and I'll bring you back to this very ground. I'll stick with you until I've done everything I promised you."

28.16-17   Jacob woke up from his sleep. He said, "GOD is in this place—truly. And I didn't even know it!" He was terrified. He whispered in awe, "Incredible. Wonderful. Holy. This is God's House. This is the Gate of Heaven."

28.18-19   Jacob was up first thing in the morning. He took the stone he had used for his pillow and stood it up as a memorial pillar and poured oil over it. He christened the place Bethel (God's House). The name of the town had been Luz until then.

28.20-22   Jacob vowed a vow: "If God stands by me and protects me on this journey on which I'm setting out, keeps me in food and clothing, and brings me back in one piece to my father's

NEW INTERNATIONAL VERSION

ther's house, then the LORD[a] will be my God [22]and[b] this stone that I have set up as a pillar will be God's house, and of all that you give me I will give you a tenth."

JACOB ARRIVES IN PADDAN ARAM

29 Then Jacob continued on his journey and came to the land of the eastern peoples. [2]There he saw a well in the field, with three flocks of sheep lying near it because the flocks were watered from that well. The stone over the mouth of the well was large. [3]When all the flocks were gathered there, the shepherds would roll the stone away from the well's mouth and water the sheep. Then they would return the stone to its place over the mouth of the well.

[4]Jacob asked the shepherds, "My brothers, where are you from?"

"We're from Haran," they replied.

[5]He said to them, "Do you know Laban, Nahor's grandson?"

"Yes, we know him," they answered.

[6]Then Jacob asked them, "Is he well?"

"Yes, he is," they said, "and here comes his daughter Rachel with the sheep."

[7]"Look," he said, "the sun is still high; it is not time for the flocks to be gathered. Water the sheep and take them back to pasture."

[8]"We can't," they replied, "until all the flocks are gathered and the stone has been rolled away from the mouth of the well. Then we will water the sheep."

[9]While he was still talking with them, Rachel came with her father's sheep, for she was a shepherdess. [10]When Jacob saw Rachel daughter of Laban, his mother's brother, and Laban's sheep, he went over and rolled the stone away from the mouth of the well and watered his uncle's sheep. [11]Then Jacob kissed Rachel and began to weep aloud. [12]He had told Rachel that he was a relative of her father and a son of Rebekah. So she ran and told her father.

[13]As soon as Laban heard the news about Jacob, his sister's son, he hurried to meet him. He embraced him and kissed him and brought him to his home, and there Jacob told him all these things. [14]Then Laban said to him, "You are my own flesh and blood."

JACOB MARRIES LEAH AND RACHEL

After Jacob had stayed with him for a whole month, [15]Laban said to him, "Just because you are a relative of mine, should you work for me for nothing? Tell me what your wages should be."

THE MESSAGE

house, *this* GOD will be my God. This stone that I have set up as a memorial pillar will mark this as a place where God lives. And everything you give me, I'll return a tenth to you."

29 [29.1-3] Jacob set out again on his way to the people of the east. He noticed a well out in an open field with three flocks of sheep bedded down around it. This was the common well from which the flocks were watered. The stone over the mouth of the well was huge. When all the flocks were gathered, the shepherds would roll the stone from the well and water the sheep; then they would return the stone, covering the well.

[29.4] Jacob said, "Hello friends. Where are you from?"

They said, "We're from Haran."

[29.5] Jacob asked, "Do you know Laban son of Nahor?"

"We do."

[29.6] "Are things well with him?" Jacob continued.

"Very well," they said. "And here is his daughter Rachel coming with the flock."

[29.7] Jacob said, "There's a lot of daylight still left; it isn't time to round up the sheep yet, is it? So why not water the flocks and go back to grazing?"

[29.8] "We can't," they said. "Not until all the shepherds get here. It takes all of us to roll the stone from the well. Not until then can we water the flocks."

[29.9-13] While Jacob was in conversation with them, Rachel came up with her father's sheep. She was the shepherd. The moment Jacob spotted Rachel, daughter of Laban his mother's brother, saw her arriving with his uncle Laban's sheep, he went and single-handedly rolled the stone from the mouth of the well and watered the sheep of his uncle Laban. Then he kissed Rachel and broke into tears. He told Rachel that he was related to her father, that he was Rebekah's son. She ran and told her father. When Laban heard the news—Jacob, his sister's son!—he ran out to meet him, embraced and kissed him and brought him home. Jacob told Laban the story of everything that had happened.

[29.14] Laban said, "You're family! My flesh and blood!"

[29.14-15] When Jacob had been with him for a month, Laban said, "Just because you're my nephew, you shouldn't work for me for nothing. Tell me what you want to be paid. What's a fair wage?"

[a] 20,21 Or *Since God . . . father's house, the* LORD
[b] 21,22 Or *house, and the* LORD *will be my God,* [22]*then*

NEW INTERNATIONAL VERSION

¹⁶Now Laban had two daughters; the name of the older was Leah, and the name of the younger was Rachel. ¹⁷Leah had weak*ᵃ* eyes, but Rachel was lovely in form, and beautiful. ¹⁸Jacob was in love with Rachel and said, "I'll work for you seven years in return for your younger daughter Rachel."

¹⁹Laban said, "It's better that I give her to you than to some other man. Stay here with me." ²⁰So Jacob served seven years to get Rachel, but they seemed like only a few days to him because of his love for her.

²¹Then Jacob said to Laban, "Give me my wife. My time is completed, and I want to lie with her."

²²So Laban brought together all the people of the place and gave a feast. ²³But when evening came, he took his daughter Leah and gave her to Jacob, and Jacob lay with her. ²⁴And Laban gave his servant girl Zilpah to his daughter as her maidservant.

²⁵When morning came, there was Leah! So Jacob said to Laban, "What is this you have done to me? I served you for Rachel, didn't I? Why have you deceived me?"

²⁶Laban replied, "It is not our custom here to give the younger daughter in marriage before the older one. ²⁷Finish this daughter's bridal week; then we will give you the younger one also, in return for another seven years of work."

²⁸And Jacob did so. He finished the week with Leah, and then Laban gave him his daughter Rachel to be his wife. ²⁹Laban gave his servant girl Bilhah to his daughter Rachel as her maidservant. ³⁰Jacob lay with Rachel also, and he loved Rachel more than Leah. And he worked for Laban another seven years.

JACOB'S CHILDREN

³¹When the LORD saw that Leah was not loved, he opened her womb, but Rachel was barren. ³²Leah became pregnant and gave birth to a son. She named him Reuben,*ᵇ* for she said, "It is because the LORD has seen my misery. Surely my husband will love me now."

³³She conceived again, and when she gave birth to a son she said, "Because the LORD heard that I am not loved, he gave me this one too." So she named him Simeon.*ᶜ*

³⁴Again she conceived, and when she gave birth to a son she said, "Now at last my husband will become attached to me, because I have borne him three sons." So he was named Levi.*ᵈ*

ᵃ 17 Or delicate   ᵇ 32 Reuben sounds like the Hebrew for he has seen my misery; the name means see, a son.
ᶜ 33 Simeon probably means one who hears.   ᵈ 34 Levi sounds like and may be derived from the Hebrew for attached.

THE MESSAGE

29.16-18   Now Laban had two daughters; Leah was the older and Rachel the younger. Leah had nice eyes, but Rachel was stunningly beautiful. And it was Rachel that Jacob loved.

So Jacob answered, "I will work for you seven years for your younger daughter Rachel."

29.19   "It is far better," said Laban, "that I give her to you than marry her to some outsider. Yes. Stay here with me."

29.20   So Jacob worked seven years for Rachel. But it only seemed like a few days, he loved her so much.

29.21-24   Then Jacob said to Laban, "Give me my wife; I've completed what we agreed I'd do. I'm ready to consummate my marriage." Laban invited everyone around and threw a big feast. At evening, though, he got his daughter Leah and brought her to the marriage bed, and Jacob slept with her. (Laban gave his maid Zilpah to his daughter Leah as her maid.)

29.25   Morning came: There was Leah in the marriage bed!

Jacob confronted Laban, "What have you done to me? Didn't I work all this time for the hand of Rachel? Why did you cheat me?"

29.26-27   "We don't do it that way in our country," said Laban. "We don't marry off the younger daughter before the older. Enjoy your week of honeymoon, and then we'll give you the other one also. But it will cost you another seven years of work."

29.28-30   Jacob agreed. When he'd completed the honeymoon week, Laban gave him his daughter Rachel to be his wife. (Laban gave his maid Bilhah to his daughter Rachel as her maid.) Jacob slept with her. And he loved Rachel more than Leah. He worked for Laban another seven years.

29.31-32   When GOD realized that Leah was unloved, he opened her womb. But Rachel was barren. Leah became pregnant and had a son. She named him Reuben (Look-It's-a-Boy!). "This is a sign," she said, "that GOD has seen my misery; and a sign that now my husband will love me."

29.33-35   She became pregnant again and had another son. "GOD heard," she said, "that I was unloved and so he gave me this son also." She named this one Simeon (GOD-Heard). She became pregnant yet again—another son. She said, "Now maybe my husband will connect with me—I've given him three sons!" That's why she named him Levi (Connect). She became preg-

NEW INTERNATIONAL VERSION

³⁵She conceived again, and when she gave birth to a son she said, "This time I will praise the LORD." So she named him Judah.*ᵃ* Then she stopped having children.

30 When Rachel saw that she was not bearing Jacob any children, she became jealous of her sister. So she said to Jacob, "Give me children, or I'll die!"

²Jacob became angry with her and said, "Am I in the place of God, who has kept you from having children?"

³Then she said, "Here is Bilhah, my maidservant. Sleep with her so that she can bear children for me and that through her I too can build a family."

⁴So she gave him her servant Bilhah as a wife. Jacob slept with her, ⁵and she became pregnant and bore him a son. ⁶Then Rachel said, "God has vindicated me; he has listened to my plea and given me a son." Because of this she named him Dan.*ᵇ*

⁷Rachel's servant Bilhah conceived again and bore Jacob a second son. ⁸Then Rachel said, "I have had a great struggle with my sister, and I have won." So she named him Naphtali.*ᶜ*

⁹When Leah saw that she had stopped having children, she took her maidservant Zilpah and gave her to Jacob as a wife. ¹⁰Leah's servant Zilpah bore Jacob a son. ¹¹Then Leah said, "What good fortune!"*ᵈ* So she named him Gad.*ᵉ*

¹²Leah's servant Zilpah bore Jacob a second son. ¹³Then Leah said, "How happy I am! The women will call me happy." So she named him Asher.*ᶠ*

¹⁴During wheat harvest, Reuben went out into the fields and found some mandrake plants, which he brought to his mother Leah. Rachel said to Leah, "Please give me some of your son's mandrakes."

¹⁵But she said to her, "Wasn't it enough that you took away my husband? Will you take my son's mandrakes too?"

"Very well," Rachel said, "he can sleep with you tonight in return for your son's mandrakes."

¹⁶So when Jacob came in from the fields that evening, Leah went out to meet him. "You must sleep with me," she said. "I have hired you with my son's mandrakes." So he slept with her that night.

¹⁷God listened to Leah, and she became pregnant and bore Jacob a fifth son. ¹⁸Then Leah

---

ᵃ 35 Judah sounds like and may be derived from the Hebrew for praise. *ᵇ 6 Dan here means he has vindicated.*
ᶜ 8 Naphtali means my struggle. *ᵈ 11 Or "A troop is coming!"* *ᵉ 11 Gad can mean good fortune or a troop.*
ᶠ 13 Asher means happy.

THE MESSAGE

nant a final time and had a fourth son. She said, "This time I'll praise GOD." So she named him Judah (Praise-GOD). Then she stopped having children.

✝

30.1 **30** When Rachel realized that she wasn't having any children for Jacob, she became jealous of her sister. She told Jacob, "Give me sons or I'll die!"

30.2 Jacob got angry with Rachel and said, "Am I God? Am I the one who refused you babies?"

30.3-5 Rachel said, "Here's my maid Bilhah. Sleep with her. Let her substitute for me so I can have a child through her and build a family." So she gave him her maid Bilhah for a wife and Jacob slept with her. Bilhah became pregnant and gave Jacob a son.

30.6-8 Rachel said, "God took my side and vindicated me. He listened to me and gave me a son." She named him Dan (Vindication). Rachel's maid Bilhah became pregnant again and gave Jacob a second son. Rachel said, "I've been in an all-out fight with my sister—and I've won." So she named him Naphtali (Fight).

30.9-13 When Leah saw that she wasn't having any more children, she gave her maid Zilpah to Jacob for a wife. Zilpah had a son for Jacob. Leah said, "How fortunate!" and she named him Gad (Lucky). When Leah's maid Zilpah had a second son for Jacob, Leah said, "A happy day! The women will congratulate me in my happiness." So she named him Asher (Happy).

30.14 One day during the wheat harvest Reuben found some mandrakes in the field and brought them home to his mother Leah. Rachel asked Leah, "Could I please have some of your son's mandrakes?"

30.15 Leah said, "Wasn't it enough that you got my husband away from me? And now you also want my son's mandrakes?"

Rachel said, "All right. I'll let him sleep with you tonight in exchange for your son's love-apples."

30.16-21 When Jacob came home that evening from the fields, Leah was there to meet him: "Sleep with me tonight; I've bartered my son's mandrakes for a night with you." So he slept with her that night. God listened to Leah; she became pregnant and gave Jacob a fifth son. She

NEW INTERNATIONAL VERSION

said, "God has rewarded me for giving my maid-servant to my husband." So she named him Issachar.[a]

¹⁹Leah conceived again and bore Jacob a sixth son. ²⁰Then Leah said, "God has presented me with a precious gift. This time my husband will treat me with honor, because I have borne him six sons." So she named him Zebulun.[b]

²¹Some time later she gave birth to a daughter and named her Dinah.

²²Then God remembered Rachel; he listened to her and opened her womb. ²³She became pregnant and gave birth to a son and said, "God has taken away my disgrace." ²⁴She named him Joseph,[c] and said, "May the LORD add to me another son."

JACOB'S FLOCKS INCREASE

²⁵After Rachel gave birth to Joseph, Jacob said to Laban, "Send me on my way so I can go back to my own homeland. ²⁶Give me my wives and children, for whom I have served you, and I will be on my way. You know how much work I've done for you."

²⁷But Laban said to him, "If I have found favor in your eyes, please stay. I have learned by divination that[d] the LORD has blessed me because of you." ²⁸He added, "Name your wages, and I will pay them."

²⁹Jacob said to him, "You know how I have worked for you and how your livestock has fared under my care. ³⁰The little you had before I came has increased greatly, and the LORD has blessed you wherever I have been. But now, when may I do something for my own household?"

³¹"What shall I give you?" he asked.

"Don't give me anything," Jacob replied. "But if you will do this one thing for me, I will go on tending your flocks and watching over them: ³²Let me go through all your flocks today and remove from them every speckled or spotted sheep, every dark-colored lamb and every spotted or speckled goat. They will be my wages. ³³And my honesty will testify for me in the future, whenever you check on the wages you have paid me. Any goat in my possession that is not speckled or spotted, or any lamb that is not dark-colored, will be considered stolen."

³⁴"Agreed," said Laban. "Let it be as you have said." ³⁵That same day he removed all the male goats that were streaked or spotted, and all the speckled or spotted female goats (all that had white on them) and all the dark-colored lambs,

THE MESSAGE

said, "God rewarded me for giving my maid to my husband." She named him Issachar (Bartered). Leah became pregnant yet again and gave Jacob a sixth son, saying, "God has given me a great gift. This time my husband will honor me with gifts—I've given him six sons!" She named him Zebulun (Honor). Last of all she had a daughter and named her Dinah.

30.22-24 And then God remembered Rachel. God listened to her and opened her womb. She became pregnant and had a son. She said, "God has taken away my humiliation." She named him Joseph (Add), praying, "May GOD add yet another son to me."

30.25-26 After Rachel had had Joseph, Jacob spoke to Laban, "Let me go back home. Give me my wives and children for whom I've served you. You know how hard I've worked for you."

30.27-28 Laban said, "If you please, I have learned through divine inquiry that GOD has blessed me because of you." He went on, "So name your wages. I'll pay you."

30.29-30 Jacob replied, "You know well what my work has meant to you and how your livestock has flourished under my care. The little you had when I arrived has increased greatly; everything I did resulted in blessings for you. Isn't it about time that I do something for my own family?"

30.31-33 "So, what should I pay you?"

Jacob said, "You don't have to pay me a thing. But how about this? I will go back to pasture and care for your flocks. Go through your entire flock today and take out every speckled or spotted sheep, every dark-colored lamb, every spotted or speckled goat. They will be my wages. That way you can check on my honesty when you assess my wages. If you find any goat that's not speckled or spotted or a sheep that's not black, you will know that I stole it."

30.34 "Fair enough," said Laban. "It's a deal."

30.35-36 But that very day Laban removed all the mottled and spotted billy goats and all the speckled and spotted nanny-goats, every animal that had even a touch of white on it plus

---

^a 18 Issachar sounds like the Hebrew for reward.
^b 20 Zebulun probably means honor.   ^c 24 Joseph means may he add.   ^d 27 Or possibly have become rich and

NEW INTERNATIONAL VERSION

and he placed them in the care of his sons. ³⁶Then he put a three-day journey between himself and Jacob, while Jacob continued to tend the rest of Laban's flocks.

³⁷Jacob, however, took fresh-cut branches from poplar, almond and plane trees and made white stripes on them by peeling the bark and exposing the white inner wood of the branches. ³⁸Then he placed the peeled branches in all the watering troughs, so that they would be directly in front of the flocks when they came to drink. When the flocks were in heat and came to drink, ³⁹they mated in front of the branches. And they bore young that were streaked or speckled or spotted. ⁴⁰Jacob set apart the young of the flock by themselves, but made the rest face the streaked and dark-colored animals that belonged to Laban. Thus he made separate flocks for himself and did not put them with Laban's animals. ⁴¹Whenever the stronger females were in heat, Jacob would place the branches in the troughs in front of the animals so they would mate near the branches, ⁴²but if the animals were weak, he would not place them there. So the weak animals went to Laban and the strong ones to Jacob. ⁴³In this way the man grew exceedingly prosperous and came to own large flocks, and maidservants and menservants, and camels and donkeys.

JACOB FLEES FROM LABAN

31 Jacob heard that Laban's sons were saying, "Jacob has taken everything our father owned and has gained all this wealth from what belonged to our father." ²And Jacob noticed that Laban's attitude toward him was not what it had been.

³Then the LORD said to Jacob, "Go back to the land of your fathers and to your relatives, and I will be with you."

⁴So Jacob sent word to Rachel and Leah to come out to the fields where his flocks were. ⁵He said to them, "I see that your father's attitude toward me is not what it was before, but the God of my father has been with me. ⁶You know that I've worked for your father with all my strength, ⁷yet your father has cheated me by changing my wages ten times. However, God has not allowed him to harm me. ⁸If he said, 'The speckled ones will be your wages,' then all the flocks gave birth to speckled young; and if he said, 'The streaked ones will be your wages,' then all the flocks bore streaked young. ⁹So God has taken away your father's livestock and has given them to me.

¹⁰"In breeding season I once had a dream in which I looked up and saw that the male goats mating with the flock were streaked, speckled

THE MESSAGE

all the black sheep and placed them under the care of his sons. Then he put a three-day journey between himself and Jacob. Meanwhile Jacob went on tending what was left of Laban's flock.

30.37-42 But Jacob got fresh branches from poplar, almond, and plane trees and peeled the bark, leaving white stripes on them. He stuck the peeled branches in front of the watering troughs where the flocks came to drink. When the flocks were in heat, they came to drink and mated in front of the streaked branches. Then they gave birth to young that were streaked or spotted or speckled. Jacob placed the ewes before the dark-colored animals of Laban. That way he got distinctive flocks for himself which he didn't mix with Laban's flocks. And when the sturdier animals were mating, Jacob placed branches at the troughs in view of the animals so that they mated in front of the branches. But he wouldn't set up the branches before the feebler animals. That way the feeble animals went to Laban and the sturdy ones to Jacob.

30.43 The man got richer and richer, acquiring huge flocks, lots and lots of servants, not to mention camels and donkeys.

31.1-2 **31** Jacob learned that Laban's sons were talking behind his back: "Jacob has used our father's wealth to make himself rich at our father's expense." At the same time, Jacob noticed that Laban had changed toward him. He wasn't treating him the same.

31.3 That's when GOD said to Jacob, "Go back home where you were born. I'll go with you."

31.4-9 So Jacob sent word for Rachel and Leah to meet him out in the field where his flocks were. He said, "I notice that your father has changed toward me; he doesn't treat me the same as before. But the God of my father hasn't changed; he's still with me. You know how hard I've worked for your father. Still, your father has cheated me over and over, changing my wages time and again. But God never let him really hurt me. If he said, 'Your wages will consist of speckled animals' the whole flock would start having speckled lambs and kids. And if he said, 'From now on your wages will be streaked animals' the whole flock would have streaked ones. Over and over God used your father's livestock to reward me.

31.10-11 "Once, while the flocks were mating, I had a dream and saw the billy goats, all of them streaked, speckled, and mottled, mounting

NEW INTERNATIONAL VERSION

or spotted. ¹¹The angel of God said to me in the dream, 'Jacob.' I answered, 'Here I am.' ¹²And he said, 'Look up and see that all the male goats mating with the flock are streaked, speckled or spotted, for I have seen all that Laban has been doing to you. ¹³I am the God of Bethel, where you anointed a pillar and where you made a vow to me. Now leave this land at once and go back to your native land.' "

¹⁴Then Rachel and Leah replied, "Do we still have any share in the inheritance of our father's estate? ¹⁵Does he not regard us as foreigners? Not only has he sold us, but he has used up what was paid for us. ¹⁶Surely all the wealth that God took away from our father belongs to us and our children. So do whatever God has told you."

¹⁷Then Jacob put his children and his wives on camels, ¹⁸and he drove all his livestock ahead of him, along with all the goods he had accumulated in Paddan Aram,ᵃ to go to his father Isaac in the land of Canaan.

¹⁹When Laban had gone to shear his sheep, Rachel stole her father's household gods. ²⁰Moreover, Jacob deceived Laban the Aramean by not telling him he was running away. ²¹So he fled with all he had, and crossing the River,ᵇ he headed for the hill country of Gilead.

LABAN PURSUES JACOB

²²On the third day Laban was told that Jacob had fled. ²³Taking his relatives with him, he pursued Jacob for seven days and caught up with him in the hill country of Gilead. ²⁴Then God came to Laban the Aramean in a dream at night and said to him, "Be careful not to say anything to Jacob, either good or bad."

²⁵Jacob had pitched his tent in the hill country of Gilead when Laban overtook him, and Laban and his relatives camped there too. ²⁶Then Laban said to Jacob, "What have you done? You've deceived me, and you've carried off my daughters like captives in war. ²⁷Why did you run off secretly and deceive me? Why didn't you tell me, so I could send you away with joy and singing to the music of tambourines and harps? ²⁸You didn't even let me kiss my grandchildren and my daughters good-by. You have done a foolish thing. ²⁹I have the power to harm you; but last night the God of your father said to me, 'Be careful not to say anything to Jacob, either good or bad.' ³⁰Now you have gone off because you longed to return to your father's house. But why did you steal my gods?"

³¹Jacob answered Laban, "I was afraid, be-

THE MESSAGE

their mates. In the dream an angel of God called out to me, 'Jacob!'

"I said, 'Yes?'

31.12-13 "He said, 'Watch closely. Notice that all the goats in the flock that are mating are streaked, speckled, and mottled. I know what Laban's been doing to you. I'm the God of Bethel where you consecrated a pillar and made a vow to me. Now be on your way, get out of this place, go home to your birthplace.'"

31.14-16 Rachel and Leah said, "Has he treated us any better? Aren't we treated worse than outsiders? All he wanted was the money he got from selling us, and he's spent all that. Any wealth that God has seen fit to return to us from our father is justly ours and our children's. Go ahead. Do what God told you."

31.17-18 Jacob did it. He put his children and his wives on camels and gathered all his livestock and everything he had gotten, everything acquired in Paddan Aram, to go back home to his father Isaac in the land of Canaan.

31.19-21 Laban was off shearing sheep. Rachel stole her father's household gods. And Jacob had concealed his plans so well that Laban the Aramean had no idea what was going on—he was totally in the dark. Jacob got away with everything he had and was soon across the Euphrates headed for the hill country of Gilead.

31.22-24 Three days later, Laban got the news: "Jacob's run off." Laban rounded up his relatives and chased after him. Seven days later they caught up with him in the hill country of Gilead. That night God came to Laban the Aramean in a dream and said, "Be careful what you do to Jacob, whether good or bad."

31.25 When Laban reached him, Jacob's tents were pitched in the Gilead mountains; Laban pitched his tents there too.

31.26-30 "What do you mean," said Laban, "by keeping me in the dark and sneaking off, hauling my daughters off like prisoners of war? Why did you run off like a thief in the night? Why didn't you tell me? Why, I would have sent you off with a great celebration—music, timbrels, flutes! But you wouldn't permit me so much as a kiss for my daughters and grandchildren. It was a stupid thing for you to do. If I had a mind to, I could destroy you right now, but the God of your father spoke to me last night, 'Be careful what you do to Jacob, whether good or bad.' I understand. You left because you were homesick. But why did you steal my household gods?"

31.31-32 Jacob answered Laban, "I was afraid. I

ᵃ 18 That is, Northwest Mesopotamia   ᵇ 21 That is, the Euphrates

NEW INTERNATIONAL VERSION

cause I thought you would take your daughters away from me by force. ³²But if you find anyone who has your gods, he shall not live. In the presence of our relatives, see for yourself whether there is anything of yours here with me; and if so, take it." Now Jacob did not know that Rachel had stolen the gods.

³³So Laban went into Jacob's tent and into Leah's tent and into the tent of the two maidservants, but he found nothing. After he came out of Leah's tent, he entered Rachel's tent. ³⁴Now Rachel had taken the household gods and put them inside her camel's saddle and was sitting on them. Laban searched through everything in the tent but found nothing.

³⁵Rachel said to her father, "Don't be angry, my lord, that I cannot stand up in your presence; I'm having my period." So he searched but could not find the household gods.

³⁶Jacob was angry and took Laban to task. "What is my crime?" he asked Laban. "What sin have I committed that you hunt me down? ³⁷Now that you have searched through all my goods, what have you found that belongs to your household? Put it here in front of your relatives and mine, and let them judge between the two of us.

³⁸"I have been with you for twenty years now. Your sheep and goats have not miscarried, nor have I eaten rams from your flocks. ³⁹I did not bring you animals torn by wild beasts; I bore the loss myself. And you demanded payment from me for whatever was stolen by day or night. ⁴⁰This was my situation: The heat consumed me in the daytime and the cold at night, and sleep fled from my eyes. ⁴¹It was like this for the twenty years I was in your household. I worked for you fourteen years for your two daughters and six years for your flocks, and you changed my wages ten times. ⁴²If the God of my father, the God of Abraham and the Fear of Isaac, had not been with me, you would surely have sent me away empty-handed. But God has seen my hardship and the toil of my hands, and last night he rebuked you."

⁴³Laban answered Jacob, "The women are my daughters, the children are my children, and the flocks are my flocks. All you see is mine. Yet what can I do today about these daughters of mine, or about the children they have borne? ⁴⁴Come now, let's make a covenant, you and I, and let it serve as a witness between us."

⁴⁵So Jacob took a stone and set it up as a pillar. ⁴⁶He said to his relatives, "Gather some stones." So they took stones and piled them in a heap, and they ate there by the heap. ⁴⁷Laban called it Jegar Sahadutha,ᵃ and Jacob called it Galeed.ᵇ

ᵃ 47 The Aramaic *Jegar Sahadutha* means *witness heap.*
ᵇ 47 The Hebrew *Galeed* means *witness heap.*

THE MESSAGE

thought you would take your daughters away from me by brute force. But as far as your gods are concerned, if you find that anybody here has them, that person dies. With all of us watching, look around. If you find anything here that belongs to you, take it." Jacob didn't know that Rachel had stolen the gods.

31.33-35   Laban went through Jacob's tent, Leah's tent, and the tents of the two maids but didn't find them. He went from Leah's tent to Rachel's. But Rachel had taken the household gods, put them inside a camel cushion, and was sitting on them. When Laban had gone through the tent, searching high and low without finding a thing, Rachel said to her father, "Don't think I'm being disrespectful, my master, that I can't stand before you, but I'm having my period." So even though he turned the place upside down in his search, he didn't find the household gods.

31.36-37   Now it was Jacob's turn to get angry. He lit into Laban: "So what's my crime, what wrong have I done you that you badger me like this? You've ransacked the place. Have you turned up a single thing that's yours? Let's see it—display the evidence. Our two families can be the jury and decide between us.

31.38-42   "In the twenty years I've worked for you, ewes and she-goats never miscarried. I never feasted on the rams from your flock. I never brought you a torn carcass killed by wild animals but that I paid for it out of my own pocket—actually, you made me pay whether it was my fault or not. I was out in all kinds of weather, from torrid heat to freezing cold, putting in many a sleepless night. For twenty years I've done this: I slaved away fourteen years for your two daughters and another six years for your flock and you changed my wages ten times. If the God of my father, the God of Abraham and the Fear of Isaac, had not stuck with me, you would have sent me off penniless. But God saw the fix I was in and how hard I had worked and last night rendered his verdict."

31.43-44   Laban defended himself: "The daughters are my daughters, the children are my children, the flock is my flock—everything you see is mine. But what can I do about my daughters or for the children they've had? So let's settle things between us, make a covenant—God will be the witness between us."

31.45   Jacob took a stone and set it upright as a pillar.
31.46-47   Jacob called his family around, "Get stones!" They gathered stones and heaped them up and then ate there beside the pile of stones. Laban named it in Aramaic, Yegar-sahadutha (Witness Monument); Jacob echoed the naming in Hebrew, Galeed (Witness Monument).

NEW INTERNATIONAL VERSION

⁴⁸Laban said, "This heap is a witness between you and me today." That is why it was called Galeed. ⁴⁹It was also called Mizpah,ᵃ because he said, "May the LORD keep watch between you and me when we are away from each other. ⁵⁰If you mistreat my daughters or if you take any wives besides my daughters, even though no one is with us, remember that God is a witness between you and me."

⁵¹Laban also said to Jacob, "Here is this heap, and here is this pillar I have set up between you and me. ⁵²This heap is a witness, and this pillar is a witness, that I will not go past this heap to your side to harm you and that you will not go past this heap and pillar to my side to harm me. ⁵³May the God of Abraham and the God of Nahor, the God of their father, judge between us."

So Jacob took an oath in the name of the Fear of his father Isaac. ⁵⁴He offered a sacrifice there in the hill country and invited his relatives to a meal. After they had eaten, they spent the night there.

⁵⁵Early the next morning Laban kissed his grandchildren and his daughters and blessed them. Then he left and returned home.

JACOB PREPARES TO MEET ESAU

32 Jacob also went on his way, and the angels of God met him. ²When Jacob saw them, he said, "This is the camp of God!" So he named that place Mahanaim.ᵇ

³Jacob sent messengers ahead of him to his brother Esau in the land of Seir, the country of Edom. ⁴He instructed them: "This is what you are to say to my master Esau: 'Your servant Jacob says, I have been staying with Laban and have remained there till now. ⁵I have cattle and donkeys, sheep and goats, menservants and maidservants. Now I am sending this message to my lord, that I may find favor in your eyes.'"

⁶When the messengers returned to Jacob, they said, "We went to your brother Esau, and now he is coming to meet you, and four hundred men are with him."

⁷In great fear and distress Jacob divided the people who were with him into two groups,ᶜ and the flocks and herds and camels as well. ⁸He thought, "If Esau comes and attacks one group,ᵈ the groupᵈ that is left may escape."

⁹Then Jacob prayed, "O God of my father Abraham, God of my father Isaac, O LORD, who said to me, 'Go back to your country and your relatives, and I will make you prosper,' ¹⁰I am unworthy of all the kindness and faithfulness you have shown your servant. I had only my

THE MESSAGE

31.48-50   Laban said, "This monument of stones will be a witness, beginning now, between you and me." (That's why it is called Galeed—Witness Monument.) It is also called Mizpah (Watchtower) because Laban said, "GOD keep watch between you and me when we are out of each other's sight. If you mistreat my daughters or take other wives when there's no one around to see you, God will see you and stand witness between us."

31.51-53   Laban continued to Jacob, "This monument of stones and this stone pillar that I have set up is a witness, a witness that I won't cross this line to hurt you and you won't cross this line to hurt me. The God of Abraham and the God of Nahor (the God of their ancestor) will keep things straight between us."

31.53-55   Jacob promised, swearing by the Fear, the God of his father Isaac. Then Jacob offered a sacrifice on the mountain and worshiped, calling in all his family members to the meal. They ate and slept that night on the mountain. Laban got up early the next morning, kissed his grandchildren and his daughters, blessed them, and then set off for home.

32.1-2   **32** And Jacob went his way. Angels of God met him. When Jacob saw them he said, "Oh! God's Camp!" And he named the place Mahanaim (Campground).

32.3-5   Then Jacob sent messengers on ahead to his brother Esau in the land of Seir in Edom. He instructed them: "Tell my master Esau this, 'A message from your servant Jacob: I've been staying with Laban and couldn't get away until now. I've acquired cattle and donkeys and sheep; also men and women servants. I'm telling you all this, my master, hoping for your approval.'"

32.6   The messengers came back to Jacob and said, "We talked to your brother Esau and he's on his way to meet you. But he has four hundred men with him."

32.7-8   Jacob was scared. Very scared. Panicked, he divided his people, sheep, cattle, and camels into two camps. He thought, "If Esau comes on the first camp and attacks it, the other camp has a chance to get away."

32.9-12   And then Jacob prayed, "God of my father Abraham, God of my father Isaac, GOD who told me, 'Go back to your parents' homeland and I'll treat you well.' I don't deserve all the love and loyalty you've shown me. When I left

---

ᵃ 49 *Mizpah* means *watchtower.*   ᵇ 2 *Mahanaim* means *two camps.*   ᶜ 7 Or *camps*; also in verse 10   ᵈ 8 Or *camp*

NEW INTERNATIONAL VERSION

staff when I crossed this Jordan, but now I have become two groups. [11]Save me, I pray, from the hand of my brother Esau, for I am afraid he will come and attack me, and also the mothers with their children. [12]But you have said, 'I will surely make you prosper and will make your descendants like the sand of the sea, which cannot be counted.' "

[13]He spent the night there, and from what he had with him he selected a gift for his brother Esau: [14]two hundred female goats and twenty male goats, two hundred ewes and twenty rams, [15]thirty female camels with their young, forty cows and ten bulls, and twenty female donkeys and ten male donkeys. [16]He put them in the care of his servants, each herd by itself, and said to his servants, "Go ahead of me, and keep some space between the herds."

[17]He instructed the one in the lead: "When my brother Esau meets you and asks, 'To whom do you belong, and where are you going, and who owns all these animals in front of you?' [18]then you are to say, 'They belong to your servant Jacob. They are a gift sent to my lord Esau, and he is coming behind us.' "

[19]He also instructed the second, the third and all the others who followed the herds: "You are to say the same thing to Esau when you meet him. [20]And be sure to say, 'Your servant Jacob is coming behind us.' " For he thought, "I will pacify him with these gifts I am sending on ahead; later, when I see him, perhaps he will receive me." [21]So Jacob's gifts went on ahead of him, but he himself spent the night in the camp.

JACOB WRESTLES WITH GOD

[22]That night Jacob got up and took his two wives, his two maidservants and his eleven sons and crossed the ford of the Jabbok. [23]After he had sent them across the stream, he sent over all his possessions. [24]So Jacob was left alone, and a man wrestled with him till daybreak. [25]When the man saw that he could not overpower him, he touched the socket of Jacob's hip so that his hip was wrenched as he wrestled with the man. [26]Then the man said, "Let me go, for it is daybreak."

But Jacob replied, "I will not let you go unless you bless me."

[27]The man asked him, "What is your name?"

"Jacob," he answered.

[28]Then the man said, "Your name will no longer be Jacob, but Israel,[a] because you have struggled with God and with men and have overcome."

[29]Jacob said, "Please tell me your name."

[a] 28 Israel means he struggles with God.

THE MESSAGE

here and crossed the Jordan I only had the clothes on my back, and now look at me—two camps! Save me, please, from the violence of my brother, my angry brother! I'm afraid he'll come and attack us all, me, the mothers and the children. You yourself said, 'I will treat you well; I'll make your descendants like the sands of the sea, far too many to count.'"

32.13-16   He slept the night there. Then he prepared a present for his brother Esau from his possessions: two hundred female goats, twenty male goats, two hundred ewes and twenty rams, thirty camels with their nursing young, forty cows and ten bulls, twenty female donkeys and ten male donkeys. He put a servant in charge of each herd and said, "Go ahead of me and keep a healthy space between each herd."

32.17-18   Then he instructed the first one out: "When my brother Esau comes close and asks, 'Who is your master? Where are you going? Who owns these?'—answer him like this, 'Your servant Jacob. They are a gift to my master Esau. He's on his way.'"

32.19-20   He gave the same instructions to the second servant and to the third—to each in turn as they set out with their herds: "Say 'Your servant Jacob is on his way behind us.'" He thought, "I will soften him up with the succession of gifts. Then when he sees me face-to-face, maybe he'll be glad to welcome me."

32.21   So his gifts went before him while he settled down for the night in the camp.

32.22-23   But during the night he got up and took his two wives, his two maidservants, and his eleven children and crossed the ford of the Jabbok. He got them safely across the brook along with all his possessions.

32.24-25   But Jacob stayed behind by himself, and a man wrestled with him until daybreak. When the man saw that he couldn't get the best of Jacob as they wrestled, he deliberately threw Jacob's hip out of joint.

32.26   The man said, "Let me go; it's daybreak."

Jacob said, "I'm not letting you go 'til you bless me."

32.27   The man said, "What's your name?"

He answered, "Jacob."

32.28   The man said, "But no longer. Your name is no longer Jacob. From now on it's Israel (God-Wrestler); you've wrestled with God and you've come through."

32.29   Jacob asked, "And what's your name?"

NEW INTERNATIONAL VERSION

But he replied, "Why do you ask my name?" Then he blessed him there.

³⁰So Jacob called the place Peniel,ᵃ saying, "It is because I saw God face to face, and yet my life was spared."

³¹The sun rose above him as he passed Peniel,ᵇ and he was limping because of his hip. ³²Therefore to this day the Israelites do not eat the tendon attached to the socket of the hip, because the socket of Jacob's hip was touched near the tendon.

JACOB MEETS ESAU

33 Jacob looked up and there was Esau, coming with his four hundred men; so he divided the children among Leah, Rachel and the two maidservants. ²He put the maidservants and their children in front, Leah and her children next, and Rachel and Joseph in the rear. ³He himself went on ahead and bowed down to the ground seven times as he approached his brother.

⁴But Esau ran to meet Jacob and embraced him; he threw his arms around his neck and kissed him. And they wept. ⁵Then Esau looked up and saw the women and children. "Who are these with you?" he asked.

Jacob answered, "They are the children God has graciously given your servant."

⁶Then the maidservants and their children approached and bowed down. ⁷Next, Leah and her children came and bowed down. Last of all came Joseph and Rachel, and they too bowed down.

⁸Esau asked, "What do you mean by all these droves I met?"

"To find favor in your eyes, my lord," he said.

⁹But Esau said, "I already have plenty, my brother. Keep what you have for yourself."

¹⁰"No, please!" said Jacob. "If I have found favor in your eyes, accept this gift from me. For to see your face is like seeing the face of God, now that you have received me favorably. ¹¹Please accept the present that was brought to you, for God has been gracious to me and I have all I need." And because Jacob insisted, Esau accepted it.

¹²Then Esau said, "Let us be on our way; I'll accompany you."

¹³But Jacob said to him, "My lord knows that the children are tender and that I must care for the ewes and cows that are nursing their young. If they are driven hard just one day, all the animals will die. ¹⁴So let my lord go on ahead of his servant, while I move along slowly at the pace of the droves before me and that of the children, until I come to my lord in Seir."

ᵃ 30 Peniel means face of God.   ᵇ 31 Hebrew Penuel, a variant of Peniel

THE MESSAGE

32.30   The man said, "Why do you want to know my name?" And then, right then and there, he blessed him.

32.31-32   Jacob named the place Peniel (God's Face) because, he said, "I saw God face-to-face and lived to tell the story!"

The sun came up as he left Peniel, limping because of his hip. (This is why Israelites to this day don't eat the hip muscle; because Jacob's hip was thrown out of joint.)

33.1-4   **33** Jacob looked up and saw Esau coming with his four hundred men. He divided the children between Leah and Rachel and the two maidservants. He put the maidservants out in front, Leah and her children next, and Rachel and Joseph last. He led the way and, as he approached his brother, bowed seven times, honoring his brother. But Esau ran up and embraced him, held him tight and kissed him. And they both wept.

33.5   Then Esau looked around and saw the women and children: "And who are these with you?"

Jacob said, "The children that God saw fit to bless me with."

33.6-7   Then the maidservants came up with their children and bowed; then Leah and her children, also bowing; and finally, Joseph and Rachel came up and bowed to Esau.

33.8   Esau then asked, "And what was the meaning of all those herds that I met?"

"I was hoping that they would pave the way for my master to welcome me."

33.9   Esau said, "Oh, brother. I have plenty of everything—keep what is yours for yourself."

33.10-11   Jacob said, "Please. If you can find it in your heart to welcome me, accept these gifts. When I saw your face, it was as the face of God smiling on me. Accept the gifts I have brought for you. God has been good to me and I have more than enough." Jacob urged the gifts on him and Esau accepted.

33.12   Then Esau said, "Let's start out on our way; I'll take the lead."

33.13-14   But Jacob said, "My master can see that the children are frail. And the flocks and herds are nursing, making for slow going. If I push them too hard, even for a day, I'd lose them all. So, master, you go on ahead of your servant, while I take it easy at the pace of my flocks and children. I'll catch up with you in Seir."

NEW INTERNATIONAL VERSION

¹⁵Esau said, "Then let me leave some of my men with you."

"But why do that?" Jacob asked. "Just let me find favor in the eyes of my lord."

¹⁶So that day Esau started on his way back to Seir. ¹⁷Jacob, however, went to Succoth, where he built a place for himself and made shelters for his livestock. That is why the place is called Succoth. *a*

¹⁸After Jacob came from Paddan Aram, *b* he arrived safely at the *c* city of Shechem in Canaan and camped within sight of the city. ¹⁹For a hundred pieces of silver, *d* he bought from the sons of Hamor, the father of Shechem, the plot of ground where he pitched his tent. ²⁰There he set up an altar and called it El Elohe Israel. *e*

DINAH AND THE SHECHEMITES

34 Now Dinah, the daughter Leah had borne to Jacob, went out to visit the women of the land. ²When Shechem son of Hamor the Hivite, the ruler of that area, saw her, he took her and violated her. ³His heart was drawn to Dinah daughter of Jacob, and he loved the girl and spoke tenderly to her. ⁴And Shechem said to his father Hamor, "Get me this girl as my wife."

⁵When Jacob heard that his daughter Dinah had been defiled, his sons were in the fields with his livestock; so he kept quiet about it until they came home.

⁶Then Shechem's father Hamor went out to talk with Jacob. ⁷Now Jacob's sons had come in from the fields as soon as they heard what had happened. They were filled with grief and fury, because Shechem had done a disgraceful thing in *f* Israel by lying with Jacob's daughter—a thing that should not be done.

⁸But Hamor said to them, "My son Shechem has his heart set on your daughter. Please give her to him as his wife. ⁹Intermarry with us; give us your daughters and take our daughters for yourselves. ¹⁰You can settle among us; the land is open to you. Live in it, trade *g* in it, and acquire property in it."

¹¹Then Shechem said to Dinah's father and brothers, "Let me find favor in your eyes, and I will give you whatever you ask. ¹²Make the price for the bride and the gift I am to bring as great as you like, and I'll pay whatever you ask me. Only give me the girl as my wife."

THE MESSAGE

33.15 Esau said, "Let me at least lend you some of my men."

"There's no need," said Jacob. "Your generous welcome is all I need or want."

33.16 So Esau set out that day and made his way back to Seir.

33.17 And Jacob left for Succoth. He built a shelter for himself and sheds for his livestock. That's how the place came to be called Succoth (Sheds).

33.18-20 And that's how it happened that Jacob arrived all in one piece in Shechem in the land of Canaan—all the way from Paddan Aram. He camped near the city. He bought the land where he pitched his tent from the sons of Hamor, the father of Shechem. He paid a hundred silver coins for it. Then he built an altar there and named it El-Elohe-Israel (Mighty Is the God of Israel).

✝

34 One day Dinah, the daughter Leah had given Jacob, went to visit some of the women in that country. Shechem, the son of Hamor the Hivite who was chieftain there, saw her and raped her. Then he felt a strong attraction to Dinah, Jacob's daughter, fell in love with her and wooed her. Shechem went to his father Hamor, "Get me this girl for my wife."

34.5-7 Jacob heard that Shechem had raped his daughter Dinah, but his sons were out in the fields with the livestock so he didn't say anything until they got home. Hamor, Shechem's father, went to Jacob to work out marriage arrangements. Meanwhile Jacob's sons on their way back from the fields heard what had happened. They were outraged, explosive with anger. Shechem's rape of Jacob's daughter was intolerable in Israel and not to be put up with.

34.8-10 Hamor spoke with Jacob and his sons, "My son Shechem is head over heels in love with your daughter—give her to him as his wife. Intermarry with us. Give your daughters to us and we'll give our daughters to you. Live together with us as one family. Settle down among us and make yourselves at home. Prosper among us."

34.11-12 Shechem then spoke for himself, addressing Dinah's father and brothers: "Please, say yes. I'll pay anything. Set the bridal price as high as you will—the sky's the limit! Only give me this girl for my wife."

---

a 17 Succoth means *shelters.* *b 18* That is, Northwest Mesopotamia   *c 18* Or *arrived at Shalem, a*
d 19 Hebrew *hundred kesitahs*; a kesitah was a unit of money of unknown weight and value.   *e 20 El Elohe Israel* can mean *God, the God of Israel* or *mighty is the God of Israel.*
f 7 Or *against*   *g 10* Or *move about freely*; also in verse 21

NEW INTERNATIONAL VERSION

¹³Because their sister Dinah had been defiled, Jacob's sons replied deceitfully as they spoke to Shechem and his father Hamor. ¹⁴They said to them, "We can't do such a thing; we can't give our sister to a man who is not circumcised. That would be a disgrace to us. ¹⁵We will give our consent to you on one condition only: that you become like us by circumcising all your males. ¹⁶Then we will give you our daughters and take your daughters for ourselves. We'll settle among you and become one people with you. ¹⁷But if you will not agree to be circumcised, we'll take our sister^a and go."

¹⁸Their proposal seemed good to Hamor and his son Shechem. ¹⁹The young man, who was the most honored of all his father's household, lost no time in doing what they said, because he was delighted with Jacob's daughter. ²⁰So Hamor and his son Shechem went to the gate of their city to speak to their fellow townsmen. ²¹"These men are friendly toward us," they said. "Let them live in our land and trade in it; the land has plenty of room for them. We can marry their daughters and they can marry ours. ²²But the men will consent to live with us as one people only on the condition that our males be circumcised, as they themselves are. ²³Won't their livestock, their property and all their other animals become ours? So let us give our consent to them, and they will settle among us."

²⁴All the men who went out of the city gate agreed with Hamor and his son Shechem, and every male in the city was circumcised.

²⁵Three days later, while all of them were still in pain, two of Jacob's sons, Simeon and Levi, Dinah's brothers, took their swords and attacked the unsuspecting city, killing every male. ²⁶They put Hamor and his son Shechem to the sword and took Dinah from Shechem's house and left. ²⁷The sons of Jacob came upon the dead bodies and looted the city where^b their sister had been defiled. ²⁸They seized their flocks and herds and donkeys and everything else of theirs in the city and out in the fields. ²⁹They carried off all their wealth and all their women and children, taking as plunder everything in the houses.

³⁰Then Jacob said to Simeon and Levi, "You have brought trouble on me by making me a stench to the Canaanites and Perizzites, the people living in this land. We are few in number, and if they join forces against me and attack me, I and my household will be destroyed."

THE MESSAGE

34.13-17 Jacob's sons answered Shechem and his father with cunning. Their sister, after all, had been raped. They said, "This is impossible. We could never give our sister to a man who was uncircumcised. Why, we'd be disgraced. The only condition on which we can talk business is if all your men become circumcised like us. Then we will freely exchange daughters in marriage and make ourselves at home among you and become one big, happy family. But if this is not an acceptable condition, we will take our sister and leave."

34.18 That seemed fair enough to Hamor and his son Shechem.

34.19 The young man was so smitten with Jacob's daughter that he proceeded to do what had been asked. He was also the most admired son in his father's family.

34.20-23 So Hamor and his son Shechem went to the public square and spoke to the town council: "These men like us; they are our friends. Let them settle down here and make themselves at home; there's plenty of room in the country for them. And, just think, we can even exchange our daughters in marriage. But these men will only accept our invitation to live with us and become one big family on one condition, that all our males become circumcised just as they themselves are. This is a very good deal for us—these people are very wealthy with great herds of livestock and we're going to get our hands on it. So let's do what they ask and have them settle down with us."

34.24 Everyone who was anyone in the city agreed with Hamor and his son, Shechem; every male was circumcised.

34.25-29 Three days after the circumcision, while all the men were still very sore, two of Jacob's sons, Simeon and Levi, Dinah's brothers, each with his sword in hand, walked into the city as if they owned the place and murdered every man there. They also killed Hamor and his son Shechem, rescued Dinah from Shechem's house, and left. When the rest of Jacob's sons came on the scene of slaughter, they looted the entire city in retaliation for Dinah's rape. Flocks, herds, donkeys, belongings—everything, whether in the city or the fields—they took. And then they took all the wives and children captive and ransacked their homes for anything valuable.

34.30 Jacob said to Simeon and Levi, "You've made my name stink to high heaven among the people here, these Canaanites and Perizzites. If they decided to gang up on us and attack, as few as we are we wouldn't stand a chance; they'd wipe me and my people right off the map."

^a 17 Hebrew *daughter*   ^b 27 Or *because*

NEW INTERNATIONAL VERSION

³¹But they replied, "Should he have treated our sister like a prostitute?"

JACOB RETURNS TO BETHEL

35 Then God said to Jacob, "Go up to Bethel and settle there, and build an altar there to God, who appeared to you when you were fleeing from your brother Esau."

²So Jacob said to his household and to all who were with him, "Get rid of the foreign gods you have with you, and purify yourselves and change your clothes. ³Then come, let us go up to Bethel, where I will build an altar to God, who answered me in the day of my distress and who has been with me wherever I have gone." ⁴So they gave Jacob all the foreign gods they had and the rings in their ears, and Jacob buried them under the oak at Shechem. ⁵Then they set out, and the terror of God fell upon the towns all around them so that no one pursued them.

⁶Jacob and all the people with him came to Luz (that is, Bethel) in the land of Canaan. ⁷There he built an altar, and he called the place El Bethel,ᵃ because it was there that God revealed himself to him when he was fleeing from his brother.

⁸Now Deborah, Rebekah's nurse, died and was buried under the oak below Bethel. So it was named Allon Bacuth.ᵇ

⁹After Jacob returned from Paddan Aram,ᶜ God appeared to him again and blessed him. ¹⁰God said to him, "Your name is Jacob,ᵈ but you will no longer be called Jacob; your name will be Israel.ᵉ" So he named him Israel.

¹¹And God said to him, "I am God Almightyᶠ; be fruitful and increase in number. A nation and a community of nations will come from you, and kings will come from your body. ¹²The land I gave to Abraham and Isaac I also give to you, and I will give this land to your descendants after you." ¹³Then God went up from him at the place where he had talked with him.

¹⁴Jacob set up a stone pillar at the place where God had talked with him, and he poured out a drink offering on it; he also poured oil on it. ¹⁵Jacob called the place where God had talked with him Bethel.ᵍ

THE DEATHS OF RACHEL AND ISAAC

¹⁶Then they moved on from Bethel. While they were still some distance from Ephrath, Rachel began to give birth and had great difficulty.

ᵃ 7 *El Bethel* means *God of Bethel.*   ᵇ 8 *Allon Bacuth* means *oak of weeping.*   ᶜ 9 That is, Northwest Mesopotamia; also in verse 26   ᵈ 10 *Jacob* means *he grasps the heel* (figuratively, *he deceives*).   ᵉ 10 *Israel* means *he struggles with God.*   ᶠ 11 Hebrew *El-Shaddai*   ᵍ 15 *Bethel* means *house of God.*

THE MESSAGE

34.31 They said, "Nobody is going to treat our sister like a whore and get by with it."

✝

35.1 **35** God spoke to Jacob: "Go back to Bethel. Stay there and build an altar to the God who revealed himself to you when you were running for your life from your brother Esau."

35.2-3 Jacob told his family and all those who lived with him, "Throw out all the alien gods which you have, take a good bath and put on clean clothes, we're going to Bethel. I'm going to build an altar there to the God who answered me when I was in trouble and has stuck with me everywhere I've gone since."

35.4-5 They turned over to Jacob all the alien gods they'd been holding on to, along with their lucky-charm earrings. Jacob buried them under the oak tree in Shechem. Then they set out. A paralyzing fear descended on all the surrounding villages so that they were unable to pursue the sons of Jacob.

35.6-7 Jacob and his company arrived at Luz, that is, Bethel, in the land of Canaan. He built an altar there and named it El-Bethel (God-of-Bethel) because that's where God revealed himself to him when he was running from his brother.

35.8 And that's when Rebekah's nurse, Deborah, died. She was buried just below Bethel under the oak tree. It was named Allon-Bacuth (Weeping-Oak).

35.9-10 God revealed himself once again to Jacob, after he had come back from Paddan Aram and blessed him: "Your name is Jacob (Heel); but that's your name no longer. From now on your name is Israel (God-Wrestler)."

35.11-12 God continued,

I am The Strong God.
    Have children! Flourish!
A nation—a whole company of nations!—
    will come from you.
Kings will come from your loins;
    the land I gave Abraham and Isaac
I now give to you,
    and pass it on to your descendants.

35.13 And then God was gone, ascended from the place where he had spoken with him.

35.14-15 Jacob set up a stone pillar on the spot where God had spoken with him. He poured a drink offering on it and anointed it with oil. Jacob dedicated the place where God had spoken with him, Bethel (God's-House).

✝

35.16-17 They left Bethel. They were still quite a ways from Ephrath when Rachel went into labor—

NEW INTERNATIONAL VERSION

¹⁷And as she was having great difficulty in child-birth, the midwife said to her, "Don't be afraid, for you have another son." ¹⁸As she breathed her last—for she was dying—she named her son Ben-Oni.^a But his father named him Benjamin.^b

¹⁹So Rachel died and was buried on the way to Ephrath (that is, Bethlehem). ²⁰Over her tomb Jacob set up a pillar, and to this day that pillar marks Rachel's tomb.

²¹Israel moved on again and pitched his tent beyond Migdal Eder. ²²While Israel was living in that region, Reuben went in and slept with his father's concubine Bilhah, and Israel heard of it.

Jacob had twelve sons:

²³The sons of Leah:
> Reuben the firstborn of Jacob,
> Simeon, Levi, Judah, Issachar and Zebu-lun.

²⁴The sons of Rachel:
> Joseph and Benjamin.

²⁵The sons of Rachel's maidservant Bilhah:
> Dan and Naphtali.

²⁶The sons of Leah's maidservant Zilpah:
> Gad and Asher.

These were the sons of Jacob, who were born to him in Paddan Aram.

²⁷Jacob came home to his father Isaac in Mamre, near Kiriath Arba (that is, Hebron), where Abraham and Isaac had stayed. ²⁸Isaac lived a hundred and eighty years. ²⁹Then he breathed his last and died and was gathered to his people, old and full of years. And his sons Esau and Jacob buried him.

ESAU'S DESCENDANTS

36
This is the account of Esau (that is, Edom).

²Esau took his wives from the women of Canaan: Adah daughter of Elon the Hit-tite, and Oholibamah daughter of Anah and granddaughter of Zibeon the Hivite—

THE MESSAGE

hard, hard labor. When her labor pains were at their worst, the midwife said to her, "Don't be afraid—you have another boy."

35.18 With her last breath, for she was now dy-ing, she named him Ben-oni (Son-of-My-Pain), but his father named him Ben-jamin (Son-of-Good-Fortune).

35.19-20 Rachel died and was buried on the road to Ephrath, that is, Bethlehem. Jacob set up a pil-lar to mark her grave. It is still there today, "Ra-chel's Grave Stone."

✝

35.21-22 Israel kept on his way and set up camp at Mig-dal Eder. While Israel was living in that region, Reuben went and slept with his father's concu-bine, Bilhah. And Israel heard of what he did.

✝

35.22-26 There were twelve sons of Jacob.
The sons by Leah:
> Reuben, Jacob's firstborn
> Simeon
> Levi
> Judah
> Issachar
> Zebulun.

The sons by Rachel:
> Joseph
> Benjamin.

The sons by Bilhah, Rachel's maid:
> Dan
> Naphtali.

The sons by Zilpah, Leah's maid:
> Gad
> Asher.

These were Jacob's sons, born to him in Paddan Aram.

✝

35.27-29 Finally, Jacob made it back home to his father Isaac at Mamre in Kiriath Arba, present-day He-bron, where Abraham and Isaac had lived. Isaac was now 180 years old. Isaac breathed his last and died—an old man full of years. He was buried with his family by his sons Esau and Jacob.

✝

36.1 # 36
This is the family tree of Esau, who is also called Edom.

36.2-3 Esau married women of Canaan: Adah, daughter of Elon the Hittite; Oholibamah, daughter of Anah and the granddaughter of

---

^a 18 Ben-Oni means *son of my trouble*.   ^b 18 Benjamin means *son of my right hand*.

NEW INTERNATIONAL VERSION

³also Basemath daughter of Ishmael and sister of Nebaioth.

⁴Adah bore Eliphaz to Esau, Basemath bore Reuel, ⁵and Oholibamah bore Jeush, Jalam and Korah. These were the sons of Esau, who were born to him in Canaan.

⁶Esau took his wives and sons and daughters and all the members of his household, as well as his livestock and all his other animals and all the goods he had acquired in Canaan, and moved to a land some distance from his brother Jacob. ⁷Their possessions were too great for them to remain together; the land where they were staying could not support them both because of their livestock. ⁸So Esau (that is, Edom) settled in the hill country of Seir.

⁹This is the account of Esau the father of the Edomites in the hill country of Seir.

¹⁰These are the names of Esau's sons:
Eliphaz, the son of Esau's wife Adah, and Reuel, the son of Esau's wife Basemath.
¹¹The sons of Eliphaz:
Teman, Omar, Zepho, Gatam and Kenaz.
¹²Esau's son Eliphaz also had a concubine named Timna, who bore him Amalek. These were grandsons of Esau's wife Adah.
¹³The sons of Reuel:
Nahath, Zerah, Shammah and Mizzah. These were grandsons of Esau's wife Basemath.
¹⁴The sons of Esau's wife Oholibamah daughter of Anah and granddaughter of Zibeon, whom she bore to Esau:
Jeush, Jalam and Korah.

¹⁵These were the chiefs among Esau's descendants:
The sons of Eliphaz the firstborn of Esau:
Chiefs Teman, Omar, Zepho, Kenaz, ¹⁶Korah,ᵃ Gatam and Amalek. These were the chiefs descended from Eliphaz in Edom; they were grandsons of Adah.
¹⁷The sons of Esau's son Reuel:
Chiefs Nahath, Zerah, Shammah and Mizzah. These were the chiefs descended from Reuel in Edom; they were grandsons of Esau's wife Basemath.
¹⁸The sons of Esau's wife Oholibamah:
Chiefs Jeush, Jalam and Korah. These were the chiefs descended from Esau's wife Oholibamah daughter of Anah.

ᵃ 16 Masoretic Text; Samaritan Pentateuch (see also Gen. 36:11 and 1 Chron. 1:36) does not have *Korah*.

THE MESSAGE

Zibeon the Hivite; and Basemath, daughter of Ishmael and sister of Nebaioth.

36.4 Adah gave Esau Eliphaz;
Basemath had Reuel;
36.5 Oholibamah had Jeush, Jalam, and Korah.
These are the sons of Esau who were born to him in the land of Canaan.

36.6-8 Esau gathered up his wives, sons and daughters, and everybody in his household, along with all his livestock—all the animals and possessions he had gotten in Canaan—and moved a considerable distance away from his brother Jacob. The brothers had too many possessions to live together in the same place; the land couldn't support their combined herds of livestock. So Esau ended up settling in the hill country of Seir (Esau and Edom are the same).

36.9-10 So this is the family tree of Esau, ancestor of the people of Edom, in the hill country of Seir. The names of Esau's sons:
Eliphaz, son of Esau's wife Adah;
Reuel, son of Esau's wife Basemath.
36.11-12 The sons of Eliphaz: Teman, Omar, Zepho, Gatam, and Kenaz. (Eliphaz also had a concubine Timna, who had Amalek.) These are the grandsons of Esau's wife Adah.
36.13 And these are the sons of Reuel: Nahath, Zerah, Shammah, and Mizzah—grandsons of Esau's wife Basemath.
36.14 These are the sons of Esau's wife Oholibamah, daughter of Anah the son of Zibeon. She gave Esau his sons Jeush, Jalam, and Korah.

36.15-16 These are the chieftains in Esau's family tree. From the sons of Eliphaz, Esau's firstborn, came the chieftains Teman, Omar, Zepho, Kenaz, Korah, Gatam, and Amalek—the chieftains of Eliphaz in the land of Edom; all of them sons of Adah.
36.17 From the sons of Esau's son Reuel, came the chieftains Nahath, Zerah, Shammah, and Mizzah. These are the chieftains of Reuel in the land of Edom; all these were sons of Esau's wife Basemath.
36.18 These are the sons of Esau's wife Oholibamah: the chieftains Jeush, Jalam, and Korah—chieftains born of Esau's wife Oholibamah, daughter of Anah.

NEW INTERNATIONAL VERSION

¹⁹These were the sons of Esau (that is, Edom), and these were their chiefs.

²⁰These were the sons of Seir the Horite, who were living in the region:
Lotan, Shobal, Zibeon, Anah, ²¹Dishon, Ezer and Dishan. These sons of Seir in Edom were Horite chiefs.
²²The sons of Lotan:
Hori and Homam.ᵃ Timna was Lotan's sister.
²³The sons of Shobal:
Alvan, Manahath, Ebal, Shepho and Onam.
²⁴The sons of Zibeon:
Aiah and Anah. This is the Anah who discovered the hot springsᵇ in the desert while he was grazing the donkeys of his father Zibeon.
²⁵The children of Anah:
Dishon and Oholibamah daughter of Anah.
²⁶The sons of Dishonᶜ:
Hemdan, Eshban, Ithran and Keran.
²⁷The sons of Ezer:
Bilhan, Zaavan and Akan.
²⁸The sons of Dishan:
Uz and Aran.
²⁹These were the Horite chiefs:
Lotan, Shobal, Zibeon, Anah, ³⁰Dishon, Ezer and Dishan. These were the Horite chiefs, according to their divisions, in the land of Seir.

THE RULERS OF EDOM

³¹These were the kings who reigned in Edom before any Israelite king reignedᵈ:
³²Bela son of Beor became king of Edom. His city was named Dinhabah.
³³When Bela died, Jobab son of Zerah from Bozrah succeeded him as king.
³⁴When Jobab died, Husham from the land of the Temanites succeeded him as king.
³⁵When Husham died, Hadad son of Bedad, who defeated Midian in the country of Moab, succeeded him as king. His city was named Avith.
³⁶When Hadad died, Samlah from Masrekah succeeded him as king.
³⁷When Samlah died, Shaul from Rehoboth on the riverᵉ succeeded him as king.
³⁸When Shaul died, Baal-Hanan son of Acbor succeeded him as king.

ᵃ 22 Hebrew *Hemam,* a variant of *Homam* (see 1 Chron. 1:39)   ᵇ 24 Vulgate; Syriac *discovered water;* the meaning of the Hebrew for this word is uncertain.   ᶜ 26 Hebrew *Dishan,* a variant of *Dishon*   ᵈ 31 Or *before an Israelite king reigned over them*   ᵉ 37 Possibly the Euphrates

THE MESSAGE

36.19   These are the sons of Esau, that is, Edom, and these are their chieftains.

36.20-21   This is the family tree of Seir the Horite, who were native to that land: Lotan, Shobal, Zibeon, Anah, Dishon, Ezer, and Dishan. These are the chieftains of the Horites, the sons of Seir in the land of Edom.

36.22   The sons of Lotan were Hori and Homam; Lotan's sister was Timna.

36.23   The sons of Shobal were Alvan, Manahath, Ebal, Shepho, and Onam.

36.24   The sons of Zibeon were Aiah and Anah—this is the same Anah who found the hot springs in the wilderness while herding his father Zibeon's donkeys.

36.25   The children of Anah were Dishon and his daughter Oholibamah.

36.26   The sons of Dishon were Hemdan, Eshban, Ithran, and Keran.

36.27   The sons of Ezer: Bilhan, Zaavan, and Akan.

36.28   The sons of Dishan: Uz and Aran.

36.29-30   And these were the Horite chieftains: Lotan, Shobal, Zibeon, Anah, Dishon, Ezer, and Dishan—the Horite chieftains clan by clan in the land of Seir.

36.31-39   And these are the kings who ruled in Edom before there was a king in Israel: Bela son of Beor was the king of Edom; the name of his city was Dinhabah. When Bela died, Jobab son of Zerah from Bozrah became the next king. When Jobab died, he was followed by Hushan from the land of the Temanites. When Hushan died, he was followed by Hadad son of Bedad; he was the king who defeated the Midianites in Moab; the name of his city was Avith. When Hadad died, Samlah of Masrekah became the next king. When Samlah died, Shaul from Rehoboth-on-the-River became king. When Shaul died, he was followed by Baal-Hanan son of Ac-

NEW INTERNATIONAL VERSION

³⁹When Baal-Hanan son of Acbor died, Hadad*ᵃ* succeeded him as king. His city was named Pau, and his wife's name was Mehetabel daughter of Matred, the daughter of Me-Zahab.

⁴⁰These were the chiefs descended from Esau, by name, according to their clans and regions:
Timna, Alvah, Jetheth, ⁴¹Oholibamah, Elah, Pinon, ⁴²Kenaz, Teman, Mibzar, ⁴³Magdiel and Iram. These were the chiefs of Edom, according to their settlements in the land they occupied.

This was Esau the father of the Edomites.

JOSEPH'S DREAMS

37 Jacob lived in the land where his father had stayed, the land of Canaan.

²This is the account of Jacob.

Joseph, a young man of seventeen, was tending the flocks with his brothers, the sons of Bilhah and the sons of Zilpah, his father's wives, and he brought their father a bad report about them.
³Now Israel loved Joseph more than any of his other sons, because he had been born to him in his old age; and he made a richly ornamented*ᵇ* robe for him. ⁴When his brothers saw that their father loved him more than any of them, they hated him and could not speak a kind word to him.
⁵Joseph had a dream, and when he told it to his brothers, they hated him all the more. ⁶He said to them, "Listen to this dream I had: ⁷We were binding sheaves of grain out in the field when suddenly my sheaf rose and stood upright, while your sheaves gathered around mine and bowed down to it."
⁸His brothers said to him, "Do you intend to reign over us? Will you actually rule us?" And they hated him all the more because of his dream and what he had said.
⁹Then he had another dream, and he told it to his brothers. "Listen," he said, "I had another dream, and this time the sun and moon and eleven stars were bowing down to me."
¹⁰When he told his father as well as his brothers, his father rebuked him and said, "What is this dream you had? Will your mother and I and your brothers actually come and bow down to the ground before you?" ¹¹His brothers were jealous of him, but his father kept the matter in mind.

ᵃ 39 Many manuscripts of the Masoretic Text, Samaritan Pentateuch and Syriac (see also 1 Chron. 1:50); most manuscripts of the Masoretic Text *Hadar*
ᵇ 3 The meaning of the Hebrew for *richly ornamented* is uncertain; also in verses 23 and 32.

THE MESSAGE

bor. When Baal-Hanan son of Acbor died, Hadad became king; the name of his city was Pau; his wife's name was Mehetabel daughter of Matred, daughter of Me-Zahab.

36.40-43   And these are the chieftains from the line of Esau, clan by clan, region by region: Timna, Alvah, Jetheth, Oholibamah, Elah, Pinon, Kenaz, Teman, Mibzar, Magdiel, and Iram—the chieftains of Edom as they occupied their various regions.

This accounts for the family tree of Esau, ancestor of all Edomites.

37.1   **37** Meanwhile Jacob had settled down where his father had lived, the land of Canaan.

JOSEPH AND HIS BROTHERS

37.2   This is the story of Jacob. The story continues with Joseph, seventeen years old at the time, helping out his brothers in herding the flocks. These were his half brothers actually, the sons of his father's wives Bilhah and Zilpah. And Joseph brought his father bad reports on them.

37.3-4   Israel loved Joseph more than any of his other sons because he was the child of his old age. And he made him an elaborately embroidered coat. When his brothers realized that their father loved him more than them, they grew to hate him—they wouldn't even speak to him.

37.5-7   Joseph had a dream. When he told it to his brothers, they hated him even more. He said, "Listen to this dream I had. We were all out in the field gathering bundles of wheat. All of a sudden my bundle stood straight up and your bundles circled around it and bowed down to mine."

37.8   His brothers said, "So! You're going to rule us? You're going to boss us around?" And they hated him more than ever because of his dreams and the way he talked.

37.9   He had another dream and told this one also to his brothers: "I dreamed another dream—the sun and moon and eleven stars bowed down to me!"

37.10-11   When he told it to his father and brothers, his father reprimanded him: "What's with all this dreaming? Am I and your mother and your brothers all supposed to bow down to you?" Now his brothers were really jealous; but his father brooded over the whole business.

NEW INTERNATIONAL VERSION

JOSEPH SOLD BY HIS BROTHERS

¹²Now his brothers had gone to graze their father's flocks near Shechem, ¹³and Israel said to Joseph, "As you know, your brothers are grazing the flocks near Shechem. Come, I am going to send you to them."

"Very well," he replied.

¹⁴So he said to him, "Go and see if all is well with your brothers and with the flocks, and bring word back to me." Then he sent him off from the Valley of Hebron.

When Joseph arrived at Shechem, ¹⁵a man found him wandering around in the fields and asked him, "What are you looking for?"

¹⁶He replied, "I'm looking for my brothers. Can you tell me where they are grazing their flocks?"

¹⁷"They have moved on from here," the man answered. "I heard them say, 'Let's go to Dothan.' "

So Joseph went after his brothers and found them near Dothan. ¹⁸But they saw him in the distance, and before he reached them, they plotted to kill him.

¹⁹"Here comes that dreamer!" they said to each other. ²⁰"Come now, let's kill him and throw him into one of these cisterns and say that a ferocious animal devoured him. Then we'll see what comes of his dreams."

²¹When Reuben heard this, he tried to rescue him from their hands. "Let's not take his life," he said. ²²"Don't shed any blood. Throw him into this cistern here in the desert, but don't lay a hand on him." Reuben said this to rescue him from them and take him back to his father.

²³So when Joseph came to his brothers, they stripped him of his robe—the richly ornamented robe he was wearing— ²⁴and they took him and threw him into the cistern. Now the cistern was empty; there was no water in it.

²⁵As they sat down to eat their meal, they looked up and saw a caravan of Ishmaelites coming from Gilead. Their camels were loaded with spices, balm and myrrh, and they were on their way to take them down to Egypt.

²⁶Judah said to his brothers, "What will we gain if we kill our brother and cover up his blood? ²⁷Come, let's sell him to the Ishmaelites and not lay our hands on him; after all, he is our brother, our own flesh and blood." His brothers agreed.

²⁸So when the Midianite merchants came by, his brothers pulled Joseph up out of the cistern and sold him for twenty shekels[a] of silver to the Ishmaelites, who took him to Egypt.

THE MESSAGE

37.12-13 His brothers had gone off to Shechem where they were pasturing their father's flocks. Israel said to Joseph, "Your brothers are with flocks in Shechem. Come, I want to send you to them."

Joseph said, "I'm ready."

37.14 He said, "Go and see how your brothers and the flocks are doing and bring me back a report." He sent him off from the valley of Hebron to Shechem.

37.15 A man met him as he was wandering through the fields and asked him, "What are you looking for?"

37.16 "I'm trying to find my brothers. Do you have any idea where they are grazing their flocks?"

37.17 The man said, "They've left here, but I overheard them say, 'Let's go to Dothan.'" So Joseph took off, tracked his brothers down, and found them in Dothan.

37.18-20 They spotted him off in the distance. By the time he got to them they had cooked up a plot to kill him. The brothers were saying, "Here comes that dreamer. Let's kill him and throw him into one of these old cisterns; we can say that a vicious animal ate him up. We'll see what his dreams amount to."

37.21-22 Reuben heard the brothers talking and intervened to save him, "We're not going to kill him. No murder. Go ahead and throw him in this cistern out here in the wild, but don't hurt him." Reuben planned to go back later and get him out and take him back to his father.

37.23-24 When Joseph reached his brothers, they ripped off the fancy coat he was wearing, grabbed him, and threw him into a cistern. The cistern was dry; there wasn't any water in it.

37.25-27 Then they sat down to eat their supper. Looking up, they saw a caravan of Ishmaelites on their way from Gilead, their camels loaded with spices, ointments, and perfumes to sell in Egypt. Judah said, "Brothers, what are we going to get out of killing our brother and concealing the evidence? Let's sell him to the Ishmaelites, but let's not kill him—he is, after all, our brother, our own flesh and blood." His brothers agreed.

37.28 By that time the Midianite traders were passing by. His brothers pulled Joseph out of the cistern and sold him for twenty pieces of silver to the Ishmaelites who took Joseph with them down to Egypt.

---

a 28 That is, about 8 ounces (about 0.2 kilogram)

NEW INTERNATIONAL VERSION

²⁹When Reuben returned to the cistern and saw that Joseph was not there, he tore his clothes. ³⁰He went back to his brothers and said, "The boy isn't there! Where can I turn now?"

³¹Then they got Joseph's robe, slaughtered a goat and dipped the robe in the blood. ³²They took the ornamented robe back to their father and said, "We found this. Examine it to see whether it is your son's robe."

³³He recognized it and said, "It is my son's robe! Some ferocious animal has devoured him. Joseph has surely been torn to pieces."

³⁴Then Jacob tore his clothes, put on sackcloth and mourned for his son many days. ³⁵All his sons and daughters came to comfort him, but he refused to be comforted. "No," he said, "in mourning will I go down to the grave[a] to my son." So his father wept for him.

³⁶Meanwhile, the Midianites[b] sold Joseph in Egypt to Potiphar, one of Pharaoh's officials, the captain of the guard.

JUDAH AND TAMAR

38 At that time, Judah left his brothers and went down to stay with a man of Adullam named Hirah. ²There Judah met the daughter of a Canaanite man named Shua. He married her and lay with her; ³she became pregnant and gave birth to a son, who was named Er. ⁴She conceived again and gave birth to a son and named him Onan. ⁵She gave birth to still another son and named him Shelah. It was at Kezib that she gave birth to him.

⁶Judah got a wife for Er, his firstborn, and her name was Tamar. ⁷But Er, Judah's firstborn, was wicked in the LORD's sight; so the LORD put him to death.

⁸Then Judah said to Onan, "Lie with your brother's wife and fulfill your duty to her as a brother-in-law to produce offspring for your brother." ⁹But Onan knew that the offspring would not be his; so whenever he lay with his brother's wife, he spilled his semen on the ground to keep from producing offspring for his brother. ¹⁰What he did was wicked in the LORD's sight; so he put him to death also.

¹¹Judah then said to his daughter-in-law Tamar, "Live as a widow in your father's house until my son Shelah grows up." For he thought, "He may die too, just like his brothers." So Tamar went to live in her father's house.

¹²After a long time Judah's wife, the daughter of Shua, died. When Judah had recovered from his grief, he went up to Timnah, to the men who

THE MESSAGE

37.29-30 Later Reuben came back and went to the cistern—no Joseph! He ripped his clothes in despair. Beside himself, he went to his brothers. "The boy's gone! What am I going to do!"

37.31-32 They took Joseph's coat, butchered a goat, and dipped the coat in the blood. They took the fancy coat back to their father and said, "We found this. Look it over—do you think this is your son's coat?"

37.33 He recognized it at once. "My son's coat—a wild animal has eaten him. Joseph torn limb from limb!"

37.34-35 Jacob tore his clothes in grief, dressed in rough burlap, and mourned his son a long, long time. His sons and daughters tried to comfort him but he refused their comfort. "I'll go to the grave mourning my son." Oh, how his father wept for him.

37.36 In Egypt the Midianites sold Joseph to Potiphar, one of Pharaoh's officials, manager of his household affairs.

✠

38.1-5 **38** About that time, Judah separated from his brothers and hooked up with a man in Adullam named Hirah. While there, Judah met the daughter of a Canaanite named Shua. He married her, they went to bed, she became pregnant and had a son named Er. She got pregnant again and had a son named Onan. She had still another son; she named this one Shelah. They were living at Kezib when she had him.

38.6-7 Judah got a wife for Er, his firstborn. Her name was Tamar. But Judah's firstborn, Er, grievously offended GOD and GOD took his life.

38.8-10 So Judah told Onan, "Go and sleep with your brother's widow; it's the duty of a brother-in-law to keep your brother's line alive." But Onan knew that the child wouldn't be his, so whenever he slept with his brother's widow he spilled his semen on the ground so he wouldn't produce a child for his brother. GOD was much offended by what he did and also took his life.

38.11 So Judah stepped in and told his daughter-in-law Tamar, "Live as a widow at home with your father until my son Shelah grows up." He was worried that Shelah would also end up dead, just like his brothers. So Tamar went to live with her father.

38.12 Time passed. Judah's wife, Shua's daughter, died. When the time of mourning was over, Ju-

---

a 35 Hebrew *Sheol*   *b 36* Samaritan Pentateuch, Septuagint, Vulgate and Syriac (see also verse 28); Masoretic Text *Medanites*

NEW INTERNATIONAL VERSION

were shearing his sheep, and his friend Hirah the Adullamite went with him.

¹³When Tamar was told, "Your father-in-law is on his way to Timnah to shear his sheep," ¹⁴she took off her widow's clothes, covered herself with a veil to disguise herself, and then sat down at the entrance to Enaim, which is on the road to Timnah. For she saw that, though Shelah had now grown up, she had not been given to him as his wife.

¹⁵When Judah saw her, he thought she was a prostitute, for she had covered her face. ¹⁶Not realizing that she was his daughter-in-law, he went over to her by the roadside and said, "Come now, let me sleep with you."

"And what will you give me to sleep with you?" she asked.

¹⁷"I'll send you a young goat from my flock," he said.

"Will you give me something as a pledge until you send it?" she asked.

¹⁸He said, "What pledge should I give you?"

"Your seal and its cord, and the staff in your hand," she answered. So he gave them to her and slept with her, and she became pregnant by him. ¹⁹After she left, she took off her veil and put on her widow's clothes again.

²⁰Meanwhile Judah sent the young goat by his friend the Adullamite in order to get his pledge back from the woman, but he did not find her. ²¹He asked the men who lived there, "Where is the shrine prostitute who was beside the road at Enaim?"

"There hasn't been any shrine prostitute here," they said.

²²So he went back to Judah and said, "I didn't find her. Besides, the men who lived there said, 'There hasn't been any shrine prostitute here.'"

²³Then Judah said, "Let her keep what she has, or we will become a laughingstock. After all, I did send her this young goat, but you didn't find her."

²⁴About three months later Judah was told, "Your daughter-in-law Tamar is guilty of prostitution, and as a result she is now pregnant."

Judah said, "Bring her out and have her burned to death!"

²⁵As she was being brought out, she sent a message to her father-in-law. "I am pregnant by the man who owns these," she said. And she added, "See if you recognize whose seal and cord and staff these are."

²⁶Judah recognized them and said, "She is more righteous than I, since I wouldn't give her to my son Shelah." And he did not sleep with her again.

²⁷When the time came for her to give birth,

THE MESSAGE

dah with his friend Hirah of Adullam went to Timnah for the sheep shearing.

38.13-14 Tamar was told, "Your father-in-law has gone to Timnah to shear his sheep." She took off her widow's clothes, put on a veil to disguise herself, and sat at the entrance to Enaim which is on the road to Timnah. She realized by now that even though Shelah was grown up, she wasn't going to be married to him.

38.15 Judah saw her and assumed she was a prostitute since she had veiled her face. He left the road and went over to her. He said, "Let me sleep with you." He had no idea that she was his daughter-in-law.

38.16 She said, "What will you pay me?"

38.17 "I'll send you," he said, "a kid goat from the flock."

She said, "Not unless you give me a pledge until you send it."

38.18 "So what would you want in the way of a pledge?"

She said, "Your personal seal-and-cord and the staff you carry."

He handed them over to her and slept with her. And she got pregnant.

38.19 She then left and went home. She removed her veil and put her widow's clothes back on.

38.20-21 Judah sent the kid goat by his friend from Adullam to recover the pledge from the woman. But he couldn't find her. He asked the men of that place, "Where's the prostitute that used to sit by the road here near Enaim?"

They said, "There's never been a prostitute here."

38.22 He went back to Judah and said, "I couldn't find her. The men there said there never has been a prostitute there."

38.23 Judah said, "Let her have it then. If we keep looking, everyone will be poking fun at us. I kept my part of the bargain—I sent the kid goat but you couldn't find her."

38.24 Three months or so later, Judah was told, "Your daughter-in-law has been playing the whore—and now she's a pregnant whore."

Judah yelled, "Get her out here. Burn her up!"

38.25 As they brought her out, she sent a message to her father-in-law, "I'm pregnant by the man who owns these things. Identify them, please. Who's the owner of the seal-and-cord and the staff?"

38.26 Judah saw they were his. He said, "She's in the right; I'm in the wrong—I wouldn't let her marry my son Shelah." He never slept with her again.

38.27-30 When her time came to give birth, it turned

NEW INTERNATIONAL VERSION	THE MESSAGE

there were twin boys in her womb. ²⁸As she was giving birth, one of them put out his hand; so the midwife took a scarlet thread and tied it on his wrist and said, "This one came out first." ²⁹But when he drew back his hand, his brother came out, and she said, "So this is how you have broken out!" And he was named Perez.*a* ³⁰Then his brother, who had the scarlet thread on his wrist, came out and he was given the name Zerah.*b*

JOSEPH AND POTIPHAR'S WIFE

39 Now Joseph had been taken down to Egypt. Potiphar, an Egyptian who was one of Pharaoh's officials, the captain of the guard, bought him from the Ishmaelites who had taken him there.

²The LORD was with Joseph and he prospered, and he lived in the house of his Egyptian master. ³When his master saw that the LORD was with him and that the LORD gave him success in everything he did, ⁴Joseph found favor in his eyes and became his attendant. Potiphar put him in charge of his household, and he entrusted to his care everything he owned. ⁵From the time he put him in charge of his household and of all that he owned, the LORD blessed the household of the Egyptian because of Joseph. The blessing of the LORD was on everything Potiphar had, both in the house and in the field. ⁶So he left in Joseph's care everything he had; with Joseph in charge, he did not concern himself with anything except the food he ate.

Now Joseph was well-built and handsome, ⁷and after a while his master's wife took notice of Joseph and said, "Come to bed with me!"

⁸But he refused. "With me in charge," he told her, "my master does not concern himself with anything in the house; everything he owns he has entrusted to my care. ⁹No one is greater in this house than I am. My master has withheld nothing from me except you, because you are his wife. How then could I do such a wicked thing and sin against God?" ¹⁰And though she spoke to Joseph day after day, he refused to go to bed with her or even be with her.

¹¹One day he went into the house to attend to his duties, and none of the household servants was inside. ¹²She caught him by his cloak and said, "Come to bed with me!" But he left his cloak in her hand and ran out of the house.

¹³When she saw that he had left his cloak in her hand and had run out of the house, ¹⁴she called her household servants. "Look," she said to them, "this Hebrew has been brought to us to make sport of us! He came in here to sleep with

out that there were twins in her womb. As she was giving birth, one put his hand out; the midwife tied a red thread on his hand, saying, "This one came first." But then he pulled it back and his brother came out. She said, "Oh! A breakout!" So she named him Perez (Breakout). Then his brother came out with the red thread on his hand. They named him Zerah (Bright).

✝

^{39.1} **39** After Joseph had been taken to Egypt by the Ishmaelites, Potiphar an Egyptian, one of Pharaoh's officials and the manager of his household, bought him from them.

^{39.2-6} As it turned out, GOD was with Joseph and things went very well with him. He ended up living in the home of his Egyptian master. His master recognized that GOD was with him, saw that GOD was working for good in everything he did. He became very fond of Joseph and made him his personal aide. He put him in charge of all his personal affairs, turning everything over to him. From that moment on, GOD blessed the home of the Egyptian—all because of Joseph. The blessing of GOD spread over everything he owned, at home and in the fields, and all Potiphar had to concern himself with was eating three meals a day.

^{39.6-7} Joseph was a strikingly handsome man. As time went on, his master's wife became infatuated with Joseph and one day said, "Sleep with me."

^{39.8-9} He wouldn't do it. He said to his master's wife, "Look, with me here, my master doesn't give a second thought to anything that goes on here—he's put me in charge of everything he owns. He treats me as an equal. The only thing he hasn't turned over to me is you. You're his wife, after all! How could I violate his trust and sin against God?"

^{39.10} She pestered him day after day after day, but he stood his ground. He refused to go to bed with her.

^{39.11-15} On one of these days he came to the house to do his work and none of the household servants happened to be there. She grabbed him by his cloak, saying, "Sleep with me!" He left his coat in her hand and ran out of the house. When she realized that he had left his coat in her hand and run outside, she called to her house servants: "Look—this Hebrew shows up and before you know it he's trying to seduce us. He tried to make love to me but I yelled as

---

a 29 Perez means *breaking out.*   *b 30 Zerah* can mean *scarlet* or *brightness.*

NEW INTERNATIONAL VERSION

me, but I screamed. ¹⁵When he heard me scream for help, he left his cloak beside me and ran out of the house."

¹⁶She kept his cloak beside her until his master came home. ¹⁷Then she told him this story: "That Hebrew slave you brought us came to me to make sport of me. ¹⁸But as soon as I screamed for help, he left his cloak beside me and ran out of the house."

¹⁹When his master heard the story his wife told him, saying, "This is how your slave treated me," he burned with anger. ²⁰Joseph's master took him and put him in prison, the place where the king's prisoners were confined.

But while Joseph was there in the prison, ²¹the LORD was with him; he showed him kindness and granted him favor in the eyes of the prison warden. ²²So the warden put Joseph in charge of all those held in the prison, and he was made responsible for all that was done there. ²³The warden paid no attention to anything under Joseph's care, because the LORD was with Joseph and gave him success in whatever he did.

THE CUPBEARER AND THE BAKER

40 Some time later, the cupbearer and the baker of the king of Egypt offended their master, the king of Egypt. ²Pharaoh was angry with his two officials, the chief cupbearer and the chief baker, ³and put them in custody in the house of the captain of the guard, in the same prison where Joseph was confined. ⁴The captain of the guard assigned them to Joseph, and he attended them.

After they had been in custody for some time, ⁵each of the two men—the cupbearer and the baker of the king of Egypt, who were being held in prison—had a dream the same night, and each dream had a meaning of its own.

⁶When Joseph came to them the next morning, he saw that they were dejected. ⁷So he asked Pharaoh's officials who were in custody with him in his master's house, "Why are your faces so sad today?"

⁸"We both had dreams," they answered, "but there is no one to interpret them."

Then Joseph said to them, "Do not interpretations belong to God? Tell me your dreams."

⁹So the chief cupbearer told Joseph his dream. He said to him, "In my dream I saw a vine in front of me, ¹⁰and on the vine were three branches. As soon as it budded, it blossomed, and its clusters ripened into grapes. ¹¹Pharaoh's cup was in my hand, and I took the grapes, squeezed them into Pharaoh's cup and put the cup in his hand."

¹²"This is what it means," Joseph said to him.

THE MESSAGE

loud as I could. With all my yelling and screaming, he left his coat beside me here and ran outside."

39.16-18 She kept his coat right there until his master came home. She told him the same story. She said, "The Hebrew slave, the one you brought to us, came after me and tried to use me for his plaything. When I yelled and screamed, he left his coat with me and ran outside."

39.19-23 When his master heard his wife's story, telling him, "These are the things your slave did to me," he was furious. Joseph's master took him and threw him into the jail where the king's prisoners were locked up. But there in jail GOD was still with Joseph: He reached out in kindness to him; he put him on good terms with the head jailer. The head jailer put Joseph in charge of all the prisoners—he ended up managing the whole operation. The head jailer gave Joseph free rein, never even checked on him, because GOD was with him; whatever he did GOD made sure it worked out for the best.

✝

40.1-4 **40** As time went on, it happened that the cupbearer and the baker of the king of Egypt crossed their master, the king of Egypt. Pharaoh was furious with his two officials, the head cupbearer and the head baker, and put them in custody under the captain of the guard; it was the same jail where Joseph was held. The captain of the guard assigned Joseph to see to their needs.

40.4-7 After they had been in custody for a while, the king's cupbearer and baker, while being held in the jail, both had a dream on the same night, each dream having its own meaning. When Joseph arrived in the morning, he noticed that they were feeling low. So he asked them, the two officials of Pharaoh who had been thrown into jail with him, "What's wrong? Why the long faces?"

40.8 They said, "We dreamed dreams and there's no one to interpret them."

Joseph said, "Don't interpretations come from God? Tell me the dreams."

40.9-11 First the head cupbearer told his dream to Joseph: "In my dream there was a vine in front of me with three branches on it: It budded, blossomed, and the clusters ripened into grapes. I was holding Pharaoh's cup; I took the grapes, squeezed them into Pharaoh's cup, and gave the cup to Pharaoh."

40.12-15 Joseph said, "Here's the meaning. The three

NEW INTERNATIONAL VERSION

"The three branches are three days. ¹³Within three days Pharaoh will lift up your head and restore you to your position, and you will put Pharaoh's cup in his hand, just as you used to do when you were his cupbearer. ¹⁴But when all goes well with you, remember me and show me kindness; mention me to Pharaoh and get me out of this prison. ¹⁵For I was forcibly carried off from the land of the Hebrews, and even here I have done nothing to deserve being put in a dungeon."

¹⁶When the chief baker saw that Joseph had given a favorable interpretation, he said to Joseph, "I too had a dream: On my head were three baskets of bread.ᵃ ¹⁷In the top basket were all kinds of baked goods for Pharaoh, but the birds were eating them out of the basket on my head."

¹⁸"This is what it means," Joseph said. "The three baskets are three days. ¹⁹Within three days Pharaoh will lift off your head and hang you on a tree.ᵇ And the birds will eat away your flesh."

²⁰Now the third day was Pharaoh's birthday, and he gave a feast for all his officials. He lifted up the heads of the chief cupbearer and the chief baker in the presence of his officials: ²¹He restored the chief cupbearer to his position, so that he once again put the cup into Pharaoh's hand, ²²but he hangedᶜ the chief baker, just as Joseph had said to them in his interpretation.

²³The chief cupbearer, however, did not remember Joseph; he forgot him.

PHARAOH'S DREAMS

41 When two full years had passed, Pharaoh had a dream: He was standing by the Nile, ²when out of the river there came up seven cows, sleek and fat, and they grazed among the reeds. ³After them, seven other cows, ugly and gaunt, came up out of the Nile and stood beside those on the riverbank. ⁴And the cows that were ugly and gaunt ate up the seven sleek, fat cows. Then Pharaoh woke up.

⁵He fell asleep again and had a second dream: Seven heads of grain, healthy and good, were growing on a single stalk. ⁶After them, seven other heads of grain sprouted—thin and scorched by the east wind. ⁷The thin heads of grain swallowed up the seven healthy, full heads. Then Pharaoh woke up; it had been a dream.

⁸In the morning his mind was troubled, so he sent for all the magicians and wise men of Egypt. Pharaoh told them his dreams, but no one could interpret them for him.

⁹Then the chief cupbearer said to Pharaoh, "Today I am reminded of my shortcomings.

THE MESSAGE

branches are three days. Within three days, Pharaoh will get you out of here and put you back to your old work—you'll be giving Pharaoh his cup just as you used to do when you were his cupbearer. Only remember me when things are going well with you again—tell Pharaoh about me and get me out of this place. I was kidnapped from the land of the Hebrews. And since I've been here, I've done nothing to deserve being put in this hole."

⁴⁰·¹⁶⁻¹⁷ When the head baker saw how well Joseph's interpretation turned out, he spoke up: "My dream went like this: I saw three wicker baskets on my head; the top basket had assorted pastries from the bakery and birds were picking at them from the basket on my head."

⁴⁰·¹⁸⁻¹⁹ Joseph said, "This is the interpretation: The three baskets are three days; within three days Pharaoh will take off your head, impale you on a post, and the birds will pick your bones clean."

⁴⁰·²⁰⁻²² And sure enough, on the third day it was Pharaoh's birthday and he threw a feast for all his servants. He set the head cupbearer and the head baker in places of honor in the presence of all the guests. Then he restored the head cupbearer to his cupbearing post; he handed Pharaoh his cup just as before. And then he impaled the head baker on a post, following Joseph's interpretations exactly.

⁴⁰·²³ But the head cupbearer never gave Joseph another thought; he forgot all about him.

41 ⁴¹·¹⁻⁴ Two years passed and Pharaoh had a dream: He was standing by the Nile River. Seven cows came up out of the Nile, all shimmering with health, and grazed on the marsh grass. Then seven other cows, all skin and bones, came up out of the river after them and stood by them on the bank of the Nile. The skinny cows ate the seven healthy cows. Then Pharaoh woke up.

⁴¹·⁵⁻⁷ He went back to sleep and dreamed a second time: Seven ears of grain, full-bodied and lush, grew out of a single stalk. Then seven more ears grew up, but these were thin and dried out by the east wind. The thin ears swallowed up the full, healthy ears. Then Pharaoh woke up—another dream.

⁴¹·⁸ When morning came, he was upset. He sent for all the magicians and sages of Egypt. Pharaoh told them his dreams, but they couldn't interpret them to him.

⁴¹·⁹⁻¹³ The head cupbearer then spoke up and said to Pharaoh, "I just now remembered some-

---

ᵃ 16 Or *three wicker baskets*   ᵇ 19 Or *and impale you on a pole*   ᶜ 22 Or *impaled*

NEW INTERNATIONAL VERSION

¹⁰Pharaoh was once angry with his servants, and he imprisoned me and the chief baker in the house of the captain of the guard. ¹¹Each of us had a dream the same night, and each dream had a meaning of its own. ¹²Now a young Hebrew was there with us, a servant of the captain of the guard. We told him our dreams, and he interpreted them for us, giving each man the interpretation of his dream. ¹³And things turned out exactly as he interpreted them to us: I was restored to my position, and the other man was hanged.ᵃ"

¹⁴So Pharaoh sent for Joseph, and he was quickly brought from the dungeon. When he had shaved and changed his clothes, he came before Pharaoh.

¹⁵Pharaoh said to Joseph, "I had a dream, and no one can interpret it. But I have heard it said of you that when you hear a dream you can interpret it."

¹⁶"I cannot do it," Joseph replied to Pharaoh, "but God will give Pharaoh the answer he desires."

¹⁷Then Pharaoh said to Joseph, "In my dream I was standing on the bank of the Nile, ¹⁸when out of the river there came up seven cows, fat and sleek, and they grazed among the reeds. ¹⁹After them, seven other cows came up—scrawny and very ugly and lean. I had never seen such ugly cows in all the land of Egypt. ²⁰The lean, ugly cows ate up the seven fat cows that came up first. ²¹But even after they ate them, no one could tell that they had done so; they looked just as ugly as before. Then I woke up.

²²"In my dreams I also saw seven heads of grain, full and good, growing on a single stalk. ²³After them, seven other heads sprouted—withered and thin and scorched by the east wind. ²⁴The thin heads of grain swallowed up the seven good heads. I told this to the magicians, but none could explain it to me."

²⁵Then Joseph said to Pharaoh, "The dreams of Pharaoh are one and the same. God has revealed to Pharaoh what he is about to do. ²⁶The seven good cows are seven years, and the seven good heads of grain are seven years; it is one and the same dream. ²⁷The seven lean, ugly cows that came up afterward are seven years, and so are the seven worthless heads of grain scorched by the east wind: They are seven years of famine.

²⁸"It is just as I said to Pharaoh: God has shown Pharaoh what he is about to do. ²⁹Seven years of great abundance are coming throughout the land of Egypt, ³⁰but seven years of famine will follow them. Then all the abundance in Egypt will be forgotten, and the famine will rav-

ᵃ 13 Or impaled

THE MESSAGE

thing—I'm sorry, I should have told you this long ago. Once when Pharaoh got angry with his servants, he locked me and the head baker in the house of the captain of the guard. We both had dreams on the same night, each dream with its own meaning. It so happened that there was a young Hebrew slave there with us; he belonged to the captain of the guard. We told him our dreams and he interpreted them for us, each dream separately. Things turned out just as he interpreted. I was returned to my position and the head baker was impaled."

41.14 Pharaoh at once sent for Joseph. They brought him on the run from the jail cell. He cut his hair, put on clean clothes, and came to Pharaoh.

41.15 "I dreamed a dream," Pharaoh told Joseph. "Nobody can interpret it. But I've heard that just by hearing a dream you can interpret it."

41.16 Joseph answered, "Not I, but God. God will set Pharaoh's mind at ease."

41.17-21 Then Pharaoh said to Joseph, "In my dream I was standing on the bank of the Nile. Seven cows, shimmering with health, came up out of the river and grazed on the marsh grass. On their heels seven more cows, all skin and bones, came up. I've never seen uglier cows anywhere in Egypt. Then the seven skinny, ugly cows ate up the first seven healthy cows. But you couldn't tell by looking—after eating them up they were just as skinny and ugly as before. Then I woke up.

41.22-24 "In my second dream I saw seven ears of grain, full-bodied and lush, growing out of a single stalk, and right behind them, seven other ears, shriveled, thin, and dried out by the east wind. And the thin ears swallowed up the full ears. I've told all this to the magicians but they can't figure it out."

41.25-27 Joseph said to Pharaoh, "Pharaoh's two dreams both mean the same thing. God is telling Pharaoh what he is going to do. The seven healthy cows are seven years and the seven healthy ears of grain are seven years—they're the same dream. The seven sick and ugly cows that followed them up are seven years and the seven scrawny ears of grain dried out by the east wind are the same—seven years of famine.

41.28-32 "The meaning is what I said earlier: God is letting Pharaoh in on what he is going to do. Seven years of plenty are on their way throughout Egypt. But on their heels will come seven years of famine, leaving no trace of the Egyp-

NEW INTERNATIONAL VERSION

age the land. ³¹The abundance in the land will not be remembered, because the famine that follows it will be so severe. ³²The reason the dream was given to Pharaoh in two forms is that the matter has been firmly decided by God, and God will do it soon.

³³"And now let Pharaoh look for a discerning and wise man and put him in charge of the land of Egypt. ³⁴Let Pharaoh appoint commissioners over the land to take a fifth of the harvest of Egypt during the seven years of abundance. ³⁵They should collect all the food of these good years that are coming and store up the grain under the authority of Pharaoh, to be kept in the cities for food. ³⁶This food should be held in reserve for the country, to be used during the seven years of famine that will come upon Egypt, so that the country may not be ruined by the famine."

³⁷The plan seemed good to Pharaoh and to all his officials. ³⁸So Pharaoh asked them, "Can we find anyone like this man, one in whom is the spirit of God*ᵃ*?"

³⁹Then Pharaoh said to Joseph, "Since God has made all this known to you, there is no one so discerning and wise as you. ⁴⁰You shall be in charge of my palace, and all my people are to submit to your orders. Only with respect to the throne will I be greater than you."

JOSEPH IN CHARGE OF EGYPT

⁴¹So Pharaoh said to Joseph, "I hereby put you in charge of the whole land of Egypt." ⁴²Then Pharaoh took his signet ring from his finger and put it on Joseph's finger. He dressed him in robes of fine linen and put a gold chain around his neck. ⁴³He had him ride in a chariot as his second-in-command,*ᵇ* and men shouted before him, "Make way*ᶜ*!" Thus he put him in charge of the whole land of Egypt.

⁴⁴Then Pharaoh said to Joseph, "I am Pharaoh, but without your word no one will lift hand or foot in all Egypt." ⁴⁵Pharaoh gave Joseph the name Zaphenath-Paneah and gave him Asenath daughter of Potiphera, priest of On,*ᵈ* to be his wife. And Joseph went throughout the land of Egypt.

⁴⁶Joseph was thirty years old when he entered the service of Pharaoh king of Egypt. And Joseph went out from Pharaoh's presence and traveled throughout Egypt. ⁴⁷During the seven years of abundance the land produced plentifully. ⁴⁸Joseph collected all the food produced in those

THE MESSAGE

tian plenty. As the country is emptied by famine, there won't be even a scrap left of the previous plenty—the famine will be total. The fact that Pharaoh dreamed the same dream twice emphasizes God's determination to do this and do it soon.

41.33-36 "So: Pharaoh needs to look for a wise and experienced man and put him in charge of the country. Then Pharaoh needs to appoint managers throughout the country of Egypt to organize it during the years of plenty. Their job will be to collect all the food produced in the good years ahead and stockpile the grain under Pharaoh's authority, storing it in the towns for food. This grain will be held back to be used later during the seven years of famine that are coming on Egypt. This way the country won't be devastated by the famine."

41.37 This seemed like a good idea to Pharaoh and his officials.

41.38 Then Pharaoh said to his officials, "Isn't this the man we need? Are we going to find anyone else who has God's spirit in him like this?"

41.39-40 So Pharaoh said to Joseph, "You're the man for us. God has given you the inside story—no one is as qualified as you in experience and wisdom. From now on, you're in charge of my affairs; all my people will report to you. Only as king will I be over you."

41.41-43 So Pharaoh commissioned Joseph: "I'm putting you in charge of the entire country of Egypt." Then Pharaoh removed his signet ring from his finger and slipped it on Joseph's hand. He outfitted him in robes of the best linen and put a gold chain around his neck. He put the second-in-command chariot at his disposal, and as he rode people shouted "Bravo!"

Joseph was in charge of the entire country of Egypt.

41.44 Pharaoh told Joseph, "I am Pharaoh, but no one in Egypt will make a single move without your stamp of approval."

41.45 Then Pharaoh gave Joseph an Egyptian name, Zaphenath-Paneah (God Speaks and He Lives). He also gave him an Egyptian wife, Asenath, the daughter of Potiphera, the priest of On (Heliopolis).

And Joseph took up his duties over the land of Egypt.

41.46 Joseph was thirty years old when he went to work for Pharaoh the king of Egypt. As soon as Joseph left Pharaoh's presence, he began his work in Egypt.

✠

41.47-49 During the next seven years of plenty the land produced bumper crops. Joseph gathered up the

---

ᵃ 38 Or of the gods   ᵇ 43 Or in the chariot of his second-in-command; or in his second chariot   ᶜ 43 Or Bow down
ᵈ 45 That is, Heliopolis; also in verse 50

NEW INTERNATIONAL VERSION

seven years of abundance in Egypt and stored it in the cities. In each city he put the food grown in the fields surrounding it. [49]Joseph stored up huge quantities of grain, like the sand of the sea; it was so much that he stopped keeping records because it was beyond measure.

[50]Before the years of famine came, two sons were born to Joseph by Asenath daughter of Potiphera, priest of On. [51]Joseph named his firstborn Manasseh[a] and said, "It is because God has made me forget all my trouble and all my father's household." [52]The second son he named Ephraim[b] and said, "It is because God has made me fruitful in the land of my suffering."

[53]The seven years of abundance in Egypt came to an end, [54]and the seven years of famine began, just as Joseph had said. There was famine in all the other lands, but in the whole land of Egypt there was food. [55]When all Egypt began to feel the famine, the people cried to Pharaoh for food. Then Pharaoh told all the Egyptians, "Go to Joseph and do what he tells you."

[56]When the famine had spread over the whole country, Joseph opened the storehouses and sold grain to the Egyptians, for the famine was severe throughout Egypt. [57]And all the countries came to Egypt to buy grain from Joseph, because the famine was severe in all the world.

JOSEPH'S BROTHERS GO TO EGYPT

42 When Jacob learned that there was grain in Egypt, he said to his sons, "Why do you just keep looking at each other?" [2]He continued, "I have heard that there is grain in Egypt. Go down there and buy some for us, so that we may live and not die."

[3]Then ten of Joseph's brothers went down to buy grain from Egypt. [4]But Jacob did not send Benjamin, Joseph's brother, with the others, because he was afraid that harm might come to him. [5]So Israel's sons were among those who went to buy grain, for the famine was in the land of Canaan also.

[6]Now Joseph was the governor of the land, the one who sold grain to all its people. So when Joseph's brothers arrived, they bowed down to him with their faces to the ground. [7]As soon as Joseph saw his brothers, he recognized them, but he pretended to be a stranger and spoke harshly to them. "Where do you come from?" he asked.

"From the land of Canaan," they replied, "to buy food."

[8]Although Joseph recognized his brothers, they did not recognize him. [9]Then he remem-

THE MESSAGE

food of the seven good years in Egypt and stored the food in cities. In each city he stockpiled surplus from the surrounding fields. Joseph collected so much grain—it was like the sand of the ocean!—that he finally quit keeping track.

41.50-52 Joseph had two sons born to him before the years of famine came. Asenath, daughter of Potiphera the priest of On, was their mother. Joseph named the firstborn Manasseh (Forget), saying, "God made me forget all my hardships and my parental home." He named his second son Ephraim (Double Prosperity), saying, "God has prospered me in the land of my sorrow."

41.53-54 Then Egypt's seven good years came to an end and the seven years of famine arrived, just as Joseph had said. All countries experienced famine; Egypt was the only country that had bread.

41.55 When the famine spread throughout Egypt, the people called out in distress to Pharaoh, calling for bread. He told the Egyptians, "Go to Joseph. Do what he tells you."

41.56-57 As the famine got worse all over the country, Joseph opened the storehouses and sold emergency supplies to the Egyptians. The famine was very bad. Soon the whole world was coming to buy supplies from Joseph. The famine was bad all over.

⊹

42.1-2 **42** When Jacob learned that there was food in Egypt, he said to his sons, "Why do you sit around here and look at one another? I've heard that there is food in Egypt. Go down there and buy some so that we can survive and not starve to death."

42.3-5 Ten of Joseph's brothers went down to Egypt to get food. Jacob didn't send Joseph's brother Benjamin with them; he was afraid that something bad might happen to him. So Israel's sons joined everyone else that was going to Egypt to buy food, for Canaan, too, was hit hard by the famine.

42.6-7 Joseph was running the country; he was the one who gave out rations to all the people. When Joseph's brothers arrived, they treated him with honor, bowing to him. Joseph recognized them immediately, but treated them as strangers and spoke roughly to them.

He said, "Where do you come from?"

"From Canaan," they said. "We've come to buy food."

42.8 Joseph knew who they were, but they didn't know who he was.

---

[a] 51 Manasseh sounds like and may be derived from the Hebrew for forget.   [b] 52 Ephraim sounds like the Hebrew for twice fruitful.

NEW INTERNATIONAL VERSION

bered his dreams about them and said to them, "You are spies! You have come to see where our land is unprotected."

¹⁰"No, my lord," they answered. "Your servants have come to buy food. ¹¹We are all the sons of one man. Your servants are honest men, not spies."

¹²"No!" he said to them. "You have come to see where our land is unprotected."

¹³But they replied, "Your servants were twelve brothers, the sons of one man, who lives in the land of Canaan. The youngest is now with our father, and one is no more."

¹⁴Joseph said to them, "It is just as I told you: You are spies! ¹⁵And this is how you will be tested: As surely as Pharaoh lives, you will not leave this place unless your youngest brother comes here. ¹⁶Send one of your number to get your brother; the rest of you will be kept in prison, so that your words may be tested to see if you are telling the truth. If you are not, then as surely as Pharaoh lives, you are spies!" ¹⁷And he put them all in custody for three days.

¹⁸On the third day, Joseph said to them, "Do this and you will live, for I fear God: ¹⁹If you are honest men, let one of your brothers stay here in prison, while the rest of you go and take grain back for your starving households. ²⁰But you must bring your youngest brother to me, so that your words may be verified and that you may not die." This they proceeded to do.

²¹They said to one another, "Surely we are being punished because of our brother. We saw how distressed he was when he pleaded with us for his life, but we would not listen; that's why this distress has come upon us."

²²Reuben replied, "Didn't I tell you not to sin against the boy? But you wouldn't listen! Now we must give an accounting for his blood." ²³They did not realize that Joseph could understand them, since he was using an interpreter.

²⁴He turned away from them and began to weep, but then turned back and spoke to them again. He had Simeon taken from them and bound before their eyes.

²⁵Joseph gave orders to fill their bags with grain, to put each man's silver back in his sack, and to give them provisions for their journey. After this was done for them, ²⁶they loaded their grain on their donkeys and left.

²⁷At the place where they stopped for the night one of them opened his sack to get feed for his donkey, and he saw his silver in the mouth of his sack. ²⁸"My silver has been returned," he said to his brothers. "Here it is in my sack."

Their hearts sank and they turned to each other trembling and said, "What is this that God has done to us?"

THE MESSAGE

⁴²·⁹ Joseph, remembering the dreams he had dreamed of them, said, "You're spies. You've come to look for our weak spots."

⁴²·¹⁰⁻¹¹ "No, master," they said. "We've only come to buy food. We're all the sons of the same man; we're honest men; we'd never think of spying."

⁴²·¹² He said, "No. You're spies. You've come to look for our weak spots."

⁴²·¹³ They said, "There were twelve of us brothers—sons of the same father in the country of Canaan. The youngest is with our father, and one is no more."

⁴²·¹⁴⁻¹⁶ But Joseph said, "It's just as I said, you're spies. This is how I'll test you. As Pharaoh lives, you're not going to leave this place until your younger brother comes here. Send one of you to get your brother while the rest of you stay here in jail. We'll see if you're telling the truth or not. As Pharaoh lives, I say you're spies."

⁴²·¹⁷ Then he threw them into jail for three days.

⁴²·¹⁸⁻²⁰ On the third day, Joseph spoke to them. "Do this and you'll live. I'm a God-fearing man. If you're as honest as you say you are, one of your brothers will stay here in jail while the rest of you take the food back to your hungry families. But you have to bring your youngest brother back to me, confirming the truth of your speech—and not one of you will die." They agreed.

⁴²·²¹ Then they started talking among themselves. "Now we're paying for what we did to our brother—we saw how terrified he was when he was begging us for mercy. We wouldn't listen to him and now we're the ones in trouble."

⁴²·²² Reuben broke in. "Didn't I tell you, 'Don't hurt the boy'? But no, you wouldn't listen. And now we're paying for his murder."

⁴²·²³⁻²⁴ Joseph had been using an interpreter, so they didn't know that Joseph was understanding every word. Joseph turned away from them and cried. When he was able to speak again, he took Simeon and had him tied up, making a prisoner of him while they all watched.

⁴²·²⁵ Then Joseph ordered that their sacks be filled with grain, that their money be put back in each sack, and that they be given rations for the road. That was all done for them.

⁴²·²⁶ They loaded their food supplies on their donkeys and set off.

⁴²·²⁷⁻²⁸ When they stopped for the night, one of them opened his sack to get food for his donkey; there at the mouth of his bag was his money. He called out to his brothers, "My money has been returned; it's right here in my bag!" They were puzzled—and frightened. "What's God doing to us?"

NEW INTERNATIONAL VERSION

²⁹When they came to their father Jacob in the land of Canaan, they told him all that had happened to them. They said, ³⁰"The man who is lord over the land spoke harshly to us and treated us as though we were spying on the land. ³¹But we said to him, 'We are honest men; we are not spies. ³²We were twelve brothers, sons of one father. One is no more, and the youngest is now with our father in Canaan.'

³³"Then the man who is lord over the land said to us, 'This is how I will know whether you are honest men: Leave one of your brothers here with me, and take food for your starving households and go. ³⁴But bring your youngest brother to me so I will know that you are not spies but honest men. Then I will give your brother back to you, and you can trade*ᵃ* in the land.' "

³⁵As they were emptying their sacks, there in each man's sack was his pouch of silver! When they and their father saw the money pouches, they were frightened. ³⁶Their father Jacob said to them, "You have deprived me of my children. Joseph is no more and Simeon is no more, and now you want to take Benjamin. Everything is against me!"

³⁷Then Reuben said to his father, "You may put both of my sons to death if I do not bring him back to you. Entrust him to my care, and I will bring him back."

³⁸But Jacob said, "My son will not go down there with you; his brother is dead and he is the only one left. If harm comes to him on the journey you are taking, you will bring my gray head down to the grave*ᵇ* in sorrow."

THE SECOND JOURNEY TO EGYPT

43 Now the famine was still severe in the land. ²So when they had eaten all the grain they had brought from Egypt, their father said to them, "Go back and buy us a little more food."

³But Judah said to him, "The man warned us solemnly, 'You will not see my face again unless your brother is with you.' ⁴If you will send our brother along with us, we will go down and buy food for you. ⁵But if you will not send him, we will not go down, because the man said to us, 'You will not see my face again unless your brother is with you.' "

⁶Israel asked, "Why did you bring this trouble on me by telling the man you had another brother?"

⁷They replied, "The man questioned us closely about ourselves and our family. 'Is your father still living?' he asked us. 'Do you have another brother?' We simply answered his questions. How were we to know he would say, 'Bring your brother down here'?"

THE MESSAGE

⁴²·²⁹⁻³² When they got back to their father Jacob, back in the land of Canaan, they told him everything that had happened, saying, "The man who runs the country spoke to us roughly and accused us of being spies. We told him, 'We are honest men and in no way spies. There were twelve of us brothers, sons of one father; one is gone and the youngest is with our father in Canaan.'

⁴²·³³⁻³⁴ "But the master of the country said, 'Leave one of your brothers with me, take food for your starving families, and go. Bring your youngest brother back to me, proving that you're honest men and not spies. And then I'll give your brother back to you and you'll be free to come and go in this country.'"

⁴²·³⁵ As they were emptying their food sacks, each man came on his purse of money. On seeing their money, they and their father were upset.

⁴²·³⁶ Their father said to them, "You're taking everything I've got! Joseph's gone, Simeon's gone, and now you want to take Benjamin. If you have your way, I'll be left with nothing."

⁴²·³⁷ Reuben spoke up: "I'll put my two sons in your hands as hostages. If I don't bring Benjamin back, you can kill them. Trust me with Benjamin; I'll bring him back."

⁴²·³⁸ But Jacob refused. "My son will not go down with you. His brother is dead and he is all I have left. If something bad happens to him on the road, you'll put my gray, sorrowing head in the grave."

43 ⁴³·¹⁻² The famine got worse. When they had eaten all the food they had brought back from Egypt, their father said, "Go back and get some more food."

⁴³·³⁻⁵ But Judah said, "The man warned us most emphatically, 'You won't so much as see my face if you don't have your brother with you.' If you're ready to release our brother to go with us, we'll go down and get you food. But if you're not ready, we aren't going. What would be the use? The man told us, 'You won't so much as see my face if you don't have your brother with you.'"

⁴³·⁶ Israel said, "Why are you making my life so difficult! Why did you ever tell the man you had another brother?"

⁴³·⁷ They said, "The man pressed us hard, asking pointed questions about our family: 'Is your father alive? Do you have another brother?' So we answered his questions. How did we know that he'd say, 'Bring your brother here'?"

ᵃ 34 Or *move about freely*   *ᵇ 38* Hebrew *Sheol*

NEW INTERNATIONAL VERSION

⁸Then Judah said to Israel his father, "Send the boy along with me and we will go at once, so that we and you and our children may live and not die. ⁹I myself will guarantee his safety; you can hold me personally responsible for him. If I do not bring him back to you and set him here before you, I will bear the blame before you all my life. ¹⁰As it is, if we had not delayed, we could have gone and returned twice."

¹¹Then their father Israel said to them, "If it must be, then do this: Put some of the best products of the land in your bags and take them down to the man as a gift—a little balm and a little honey, some spices and myrrh, some pistachio nuts and almonds. ¹²Take double the amount of silver with you, for you must return the silver that was put back into the mouths of your sacks. Perhaps it was a mistake. ¹³Take your brother also and go back to the man at once. ¹⁴And may God Almighty*ᵃ* grant you mercy before the man so that he will let your other brother and Benjamin come back with you. As for me, if I am bereaved, I am bereaved."

¹⁵So the men took the gifts and double the amount of silver, and Benjamin also. They hurried down to Egypt and presented themselves to Joseph. ¹⁶When Joseph saw Benjamin with them, he said to the steward of his house, "Take these men to my house, slaughter an animal and prepare dinner; they are to eat with me at noon."

¹⁷The man did as Joseph told him and took the men to Joseph's house. ¹⁸Now the men were frightened when they were taken to his house. They thought, "We were brought here because of the silver that was put back into our sacks the first time. He wants to attack us and overpower us and seize us as slaves and take our donkeys."

¹⁹So the men went up to Joseph's steward and spoke to him at the entrance to the house. ²⁰"Please, sir," they said, "we came down here the first time to buy food. ²¹But at the place where we stopped for the night we opened our sacks and each of us found his silver—the exact weight—in the mouth of his sack. So we have brought it back with us. ²²We have also brought additional silver with us to buy food. We don't know who put our silver in our sacks."

²³"It's all right," he said. "Don't be afraid. Your God, the God of your father, has given you treasure in your sacks; I received your silver." Then he brought Simeon out to them.

²⁴The steward took the men into Joseph's house, gave them water to wash their feet and provided fodder for their donkeys. ²⁵They pre-

ᵃ 14 Hebrew *El-Shaddai*

THE MESSAGE

43:8-10 Judah pushed his father Israel. "Let the boy go; I'll take charge of him. Let us go and be on our way—if we don't get going, we're all going to starve to death—we and you and our children too! I'll take full responsibility for his safety; it's my life on the line for his. If I don't bring him back safe and sound, I'm the guilty one; I'll take all the blame. If we had gone ahead in the first place instead of procrastinating like this, we could have been there and back twice over."

43:11-14 Their father Israel gave in. "If it has to be, it has to be. But do this: stuff your packs with the finest products from the land you can find and take them to the man as gifts—some balm and honey, some spices and perfumes, some pistachios and almonds. And take plenty of money—pay back double what was returned to your sacks; that might have been a mistake. Take your brother and get going. Go back to the man. And may The Strong God give you grace in that man's eyes so that he'll send back your other brother along with Benjamin. For me, nothing's left; I've lost everything."

43:15-16 The men took the gifts, double the money, and Benjamin. They lost no time in getting to Egypt and meeting Joseph. When Joseph saw that they had Benjamin with them, he told his house steward, "Take these men into the house and make them at home. Butcher an animal and prepare a meal; these men are going to eat with me at noon."

43:17-18 The steward did what Joseph had said and took them inside. But they became anxious when they were brought into Joseph's home, thinking, "It's the money; he thinks we ran off with the money on our first trip down here. And now he's got us where he wants us—he's going to turn us into slaves and confiscate our donkeys."

43:19-22 So they went up to Joseph's house steward and talked to him in the doorway. They said, "Listen, master. We came down here one other time to buy food. On our way home, the first night out we opened our bags and found our money at the mouth of the bag—the exact amount we'd paid. We've brought it all back and have plenty more to buy more food with. We have no idea who put the money in our bags."

43:23 The steward said, "Everything's in order. Don't worry. Your God and the God of your father must have given you a bonus. I was paid in full." And with that, he presented Simeon to them.

43:24-25 He then took them inside Joseph's house and made them comfortable—gave them water to wash their feet and saw to the feeding of their

NEW INTERNATIONAL VERSION

pared their gifts for Joseph's arrival at noon, because they had heard that they were to eat there.

²⁶When Joseph came home, they presented to him the gifts they had brought into the house, and they bowed down before him to the ground. ²⁷He asked them how they were, and then he said, "How is your aged father you told me about? Is he still living?"

²⁸They replied, "Your servant our father is still alive and well." And they bowed low to pay him honor.

²⁹As he looked about and saw his brother Benjamin, his own mother's son, he asked, "Is this your youngest brother, the one you told me about?" And he said, "God be gracious to you, my son." ³⁰Deeply moved at the sight of his brother, Joseph hurried out and looked for a place to weep. He went into his private room and wept there.

³¹After he had washed his face, he came out and, controlling himself, said, "Serve the food."

³²They served him by himself, the brothers by themselves, and the Egyptians who ate with him by themselves, because Egyptians could not eat with Hebrews, for that is detestable to Egyptians. ³³The men had been seated before him in the order of their ages, from the firstborn to the youngest; and they looked at each other in astonishment. ³⁴When portions were served to them from Joseph's table, Benjamin's portion was five times as much as anyone else's. So they feasted and drank freely with him.

A SILVER CUP IN A SACK

44 Now Joseph gave these instructions to the steward of his house: "Fill the men's sacks with as much food as they can carry, and put each man's silver in the mouth of his sack. ²Then put my cup, the silver one, in the mouth of the youngest one's sack, along with the silver for his grain." And he did as Joseph said.

³As morning dawned, the men were sent on their way with their donkeys. ⁴They had not gone far from the city when Joseph said to his steward, "Go after those men at once, and when you catch up with them, say to them, 'Why have you repaid good with evil? ⁵Isn't this the cup my master drinks from and also uses for divination? This is a wicked thing you have done.'"

⁶When he caught up with them, he repeated these words to them. ⁷But they said to him, "Why does my lord say such things? Far be it from your servants to do anything like that! ⁸We even brought back to you from the land of Ca-

THE MESSAGE

donkeys. The brothers spread out their gifts as they waited for Joseph to show up at noon—they had been told that they were to have dinner with him.

43.26 When Joseph got home, they presented him with the gifts they had brought and bowed respectfully before him.

43.27 Joseph welcomed them and said, "And your old father whom you mentioned to me, how is he? Is he still alive?"

43.28 They said, "Yes—your servant our father is quite well, very much alive." And they again bowed respectfully before him.

43.29 Then Joseph picked out his brother Benjamin, his own mother's son. He asked, "And is this your youngest brother that you told me about?" Then he said, "God be gracious to you, my son."

43.30-31 Deeply moved on seeing his brother and about to burst into tears, Joseph hurried out into another room and had a good cry. Then he washed his face, got a grip on himself, and said, "Let's eat."

43.32-34 Joseph was served at his private table, the brothers off by themselves and the Egyptians off by themselves (Egyptians won't eat at the same table with Hebrews; it's repulsive to them). The brothers were seated facing Joseph, arranged in order of their age, from the oldest to the youngest. They looked at one another wide-eyed, wondering what would happen next. When the brothers' plates were served from Joseph's table, Benjamin's plate came piled high, far more so than his brothers. And so the brothers feasted with Joseph, drinking freely.

44.1-2 **44** Joseph ordered his house steward: "Fill the men's bags with food—all they can carry—and replace each one's money at the top of the bag. Then put my chalice, my silver chalice, in the top of the bag of the youngest, along with the money for his food." He did as Joseph ordered.

44.3-5 At break of day the men were sent off with their donkeys. They were barely out of the city when Joseph said to his house steward, "Run after them. When you catch up with them, say, 'Why did you pay me back evil for good? This is the chalice my master drinks from; he also uses it for divination. This is outrageous!'"

44.6 He caught up with them and repeated all this word for word.

44.7-9 They said, "What is my master talking about? We would never do anything like that! Why, the money we found in our bags earlier, we brought back all the way from Canaan—do

NEW INTERNATIONAL VERSION

naan the silver we found inside the mouths of our sacks. So why would we steal silver or gold from your master's house? ⁹If any of your servants is found to have it, he will die; and the rest of us will become my lord's slaves."

¹⁰"Very well, then," he said, "let it be as you say. Whoever is found to have it will become my slave; the rest of you will be free from blame."

¹¹Each of them quickly lowered his sack to the ground and opened it. ¹²Then the steward proceeded to search, beginning with the oldest and ending with the youngest. And the cup was found in Benjamin's sack. ¹³At this, they tore their clothes. Then they all loaded their donkeys and returned to the city.

¹⁴Joseph was still in the house when Judah and his brothers came in, and they threw themselves to the ground before him. ¹⁵Joseph said to them, "What is this you have done? Don't you know that a man like me can find things out by divination?"

¹⁶"What can we say to my lord?" Judah replied. "What can we say? How can we prove our innocence? God has uncovered your servants' guilt. We are now my lord's slaves—we ourselves and the one who was found to have the cup."

¹⁷But Joseph said, "Far be it from me to do such a thing! Only the man who was found to have the cup will become my slave. The rest of you, go back to your father in peace."

¹⁸Then Judah went up to him and said: "Please, my lord, let your servant speak a word to my lord. Do not be angry with your servant, though you are equal to Pharaoh himself. ¹⁹My lord asked his servants, 'Do you have a father or a brother?' ²⁰And we answered, 'We have an aged father, and there is a young son born to him in his old age. His brother is dead, and he is the only one of his mother's sons left, and his father loves him.'

²¹"Then you said to your servants, 'Bring him down to me so I can see him for myself.' ²²And we said to my lord, 'The boy cannot leave his father; if he leaves him, his father will die.' ²³But you told your servants, 'Unless your youngest brother comes down with you, you will not see my face again.' ²⁴When we went back to your servant my father, we told him what my lord had said.

²⁵"Then our father said, 'Go back and buy a little more food.' ²⁶But we said, 'We cannot go down. Only if our youngest brother is with us will we go. We cannot see the man's face unless our youngest brother is with us.'

THE MESSAGE

you think we'd turn right around and steal it back from your master? If that chalice is found on any of us, he'll die; and the rest of us will be your master's slaves."

⁴⁴.¹⁰ The steward said, "Very well then, but we won't go that far. Whoever is found with the chalice will be my slave; the rest of you can go free."

⁴⁴.¹¹⁻¹² They outdid each other in putting their bags on the ground and opening them up for inspection. The steward searched their bags, going from oldest to youngest. The chalice showed up in Benjamin's bag.

⁴⁴.¹³ They ripped their clothes in despair, loaded up their donkeys, and went back to the city.

⁴⁴.¹⁴ Joseph was still at home when Judah and his brothers got back. They threw themselves down on the ground in front of him.

⁴⁴.¹⁵ Joseph accused them: "How can you have done this? You have to know that a man in my position would have discovered this."

⁴⁴.¹⁶ Judah as spokesman for the brothers said, "What can we say, master? What is there to say? How can we prove our innocence? God is behind this, exposing how bad we are. We stand guilty before you and ready to be your slaves—we're all in this together, the rest of us as guilty as the one with the chalice."

⁴⁴.¹⁷ "I'd never do that to you," said Joseph. "Only the one involved with the chalice will be my slave. The rest of you are free to go back to your father."

⁴⁴.¹⁸⁻²⁰ Judah came forward. He said, "Please, master; can I say just one thing to you? Don't get angry. Don't think I'm presumptuous—you're the same as Pharaoh as far as I'm concerned. You, master, asked us, 'Do you have a father and a brother?' And we answered honestly, 'We have a father who is old and a younger brother who was born to him in his old age. His brother is dead and he is the only son left from that mother. And his father loves him more than anything.'

⁴⁴.²¹⁻²² "Then you told us, 'Bring him down here so I can see him.' We told you, master, that it was impossible: 'The boy can't leave his father; if he leaves, his father will die.'

⁴⁴.²³ "And then you said, 'If your youngest brother doesn't come with you, you won't be allowed to see me.'

⁴⁴.²⁴⁻²⁶ "When we returned to our father, we told him everything you said to us. So when our father said, 'Go back and buy some more food,' we told him flatly, 'We can't. The only way we can go back is if our youngest brother is with us. We aren't allowed to even see the man if our youngest brother doesn't come with us.'

NEW INTERNATIONAL VERSION

27"Your servant my father said to us, 'You know that my wife bore me two sons. 28One of them went away from me, and I said, "He has surely been torn to pieces." And I have not seen him since. 29If you take this one from me too and harm comes to him, you will bring my gray head down to the grave[a] in misery.'

30"So now, if the boy is not with us when I go back to your servant my father and if my father, whose life is closely bound up with the boy's life, 31sees that the boy isn't there, he will die. Your servants will bring the gray head of our father down to the grave in sorrow. 32Your servant guaranteed the boy's safety to my father. I said, 'If I do not bring him back to you, I will bear the blame before you, my father, all my life!'

33"Now then, please let your servant remain here as my lord's slave in place of the boy, and let the boy return with his brothers. 34How can I go back to my father if the boy is not with me? No! Do not let me see the misery that would come upon my father."

JOSEPH MAKES HIMSELF KNOWN

45 Then Joseph could no longer control himself before all his attendants, and he cried out, "Have everyone leave my presence!" So there was no one with Joseph when he made himself known to his brothers. 2And he wept so loudly that the Egyptians heard him, and Pharaoh's household heard about it.

3Joseph said to his brothers, "I am Joseph! Is my father still living?" But his brothers were not able to answer him, because they were terrified at his presence.

4Then Joseph said to his brothers, "Come close to me." When they had done so, he said, "I am your brother Joseph, the one you sold into Egypt! 5And now, do not be distressed and do not be angry with yourselves for selling me here, because it was to save lives that God sent me ahead of you. 6For two years now there has been famine in the land, and for the next five years there will not be plowing and reaping. 7But God sent me ahead of you to preserve for you a remnant on earth and to save your lives by a great deliverance.[b]

8"So then, it was not you who sent me here, but God. He made me father to Pharaoh, lord of his entire household and ruler of all Egypt. 9Now hurry back to my father and say to him, 'This is what your son Joseph says: God has made me lord of all Egypt. Come down to me; don't delay. 10You shall live in the region of Goshen and be near me—you, your children and

THE MESSAGE

44.27-29 "Your servant, my father, told us, 'You know very well that my wife gave me two sons. One turned up missing. I concluded that he'd been ripped to pieces. I've never seen him since. If you now go and take this one and something bad happens to him, you'll put my old gray, grieving head in the grave for sure.'

44.30-32 "And now, can't you see that if I show up before your servant, my father, without the boy, this son with whom his life is so bound up, the moment he realizes the boy is gone, he'll die on the spot. He'll die of grief and we, your servants who are standing here before you, will have killed him. And that's not all. I got my father to release the boy to show him to you by promising, 'If I don't bring him back, I'll stand condemned before you, Father, all my life.'

44.33-34 "So let me stay here as your slave, not this boy. Let the boy go back with his brothers. How can I go back to my father if the boy is not with me? Oh, don't make me go back and watch my father die in grief!"

45.1-2 **45** Joseph couldn't hold himself in any longer, keeping up a front before all his attendants. He cried out, "Leave! Clear out—everyone leave!" So there was no one with Joseph when he identified himself to his brothers. But his sobbing was so violent that the Egyptians couldn't help but hear him. The news was soon reported to Pharaoh's palace.

45.3 Joseph spoke to his brothers: "I am Joseph. Is my father really still alive?" But his brothers couldn't say a word. They were speechless—they couldn't believe what they were hearing and seeing.

45.4-8 "Come closer to me," Joseph said to his brothers. They came closer. "I am Joseph your brother whom you sold into Egypt. But don't feel badly, don't blame yourselves for selling me. God was behind it. God sent me here ahead of you to save lives. There has been a famine in the land now for two years; the famine will continue for five more years—neither plowing nor harvesting. God sent me on ahead to pave the way and make sure there was a remnant in the land, to save your lives in an amazing act of deliverance. So you see, it wasn't you who sent me here but God. He set me in place as a father to Pharaoh, put me in charge of his personal affairs, and made me ruler of all Egypt.

45.9-11 "Hurry back to my father. Tell him, 'Your son Joseph says: I'm master of all of Egypt. Come as fast as you can and join me here. I'll give you a place to live in Goshen where you'll be close to me—you, your children, your

---

[a] 29 Hebrew *Sheol*; also in verse 31   [b] 7 Or *save you as a great band of survivors*

NEW INTERNATIONAL VERSION

grandchildren, your flocks and herds, and all you have. 11I will provide for you there, because five years of famine are still to come. Otherwise you and your household and all who belong to you will become destitute.'

12"You can see for yourselves, and so can my brother Benjamin, that it is really I who am speaking to you. 13Tell my father about all the honor accorded me in Egypt and about everything you have seen. And bring my father down here quickly."

14Then he threw his arms around his brother Benjamin and wept, and Benjamin embraced him, weeping. 15And he kissed all his brothers and wept over them. Afterward his brothers talked with him.

16When the news reached Pharaoh's palace that Joseph's brothers had come, Pharaoh and all his officials were pleased. 17Pharaoh said to Joseph, "Tell your brothers, 'Do this: Load your animals and return to the land of Canaan, 18and bring your father and your families back to me. I will give you the best of the land of Egypt and you can enjoy the fat of the land.'

19"You are also directed to tell them, 'Do this: Take some carts from Egypt for your children and your wives, and get your father and come. 20Never mind about your belongings, because the best of all Egypt will be yours.' "

21So the sons of Israel did this. Joseph gave them carts, as Pharaoh had commanded, and he also gave them provisions for their journey. 22To each of them he gave new clothing, but to Benjamin he gave three hundred shekels*a* of silver and five sets of clothes. 23And this is what he sent to his father: ten donkeys loaded with the best things of Egypt, and ten female donkeys loaded with grain and bread and other provisions for his journey. 24Then he sent his brothers away, and as they were leaving he said to them, "Don't quarrel on the way!"

25So they went up out of Egypt and came to their father Jacob in the land of Canaan. 26They told him, "Joseph is still alive! In fact, he is ruler of all Egypt." Jacob was stunned; he did not believe them. 27But when they told him everything Joseph had said to them, and when he saw the carts Joseph had sent to carry him back, the spirit of their father Jacob revived. 28And Israel said, "I'm convinced! My son Joseph is still alive. I will go and see him before I die."

THE MESSAGE

grandchildren, your flocks, your herds, and anything else you can think of. I'll take care of you there completely. There are still five more years of famine ahead; I'll make sure all your needs are taken care of, you and everyone connected with you—you won't want for a thing.'

45.12-13 "Look at me. You can see for yourselves, and my brother Benjamin can see for himself, that it's me, my own mouth, telling you all this. Tell my father all about the high position I hold in Egypt, tell him everything you've seen here, but don't take all day—hurry up and get my father down here."

45.14-15 Then Joseph threw himself on his brother Benjamin's neck and wept, and Benjamin wept on his neck. He then kissed all his brothers and wept over them. Only then were his brothers able to talk with him.

45.16 The story was reported in Pharaoh's palace: "Joseph's brothers have come." It was good news to Pharaoh and all who worked with him.

45.17-18 Pharaoh said to Joseph, "Tell your brothers, 'This is the plan: Load up your pack animals; go to Canaan, get your father and your families and bring them back here. I'll settle you on the best land in Egypt—you'll live off the fat of the land.'

45.19-20 "Also tell them this: 'Here's what I want you to do: Take wagons from Egypt to carry your little ones and your wives and load up your father and come back. Don't worry about having to leave things behind; the best in all of Egypt will be yours.'"

45.21-23 And they did just that, the sons of Israel. Joseph gave them the wagons that Pharaoh had promised and food for the trip. He outfitted all the brothers in brand-new clothes, but he gave Benjamin three hundred pieces of silver and several suits of clothes. He sent his father these gifts: ten donkeys loaded with Egypt's best products and another ten donkeys loaded with grain and bread, provisions for his father's journey back.

45.24 Then he sent his brothers off. As they left he told them, "Take it easy on the journey; try to get along with each other."

45.25-28 They left Egypt and went back to their father Jacob in Canaan. When they told him, "Joseph is still alive—and he's the ruler over the whole land of Egypt!" he went numb; he couldn't believe his ears. But the more they talked, telling him everything that Joseph had told them and when he saw the wagons that Joseph had sent to carry him back, the blood started to flow again—their father Jacob's spirit revived. Israel said, "I've heard enough—my son Joseph is still alive. I've got to go and see him before I die."

✠

---

a 22 That is, about 7 1/2 pounds (about 3.5 kilograms)

NEW INTERNATIONAL VERSION

Jacob Goes to Egypt

46 So Israel set out with all that was his, and when he reached Beersheba, he offered sacrifices to the God of his father Isaac.

²And God spoke to Israel in a vision at night and said, "Jacob! Jacob!"

"Here I am," he replied.

³"I am God, the God of your father," he said. "Do not be afraid to go down to Egypt, for I will make you into a great nation there. ⁴I will go down to Egypt with you, and I will surely bring you back again. And Joseph's own hand will close your eyes."

⁵Then Jacob left Beersheba, and Israel's sons took their father Jacob and their children and their wives in the carts that Pharaoh had sent to transport him. ⁶They also took with them their livestock and the possessions they had acquired in Canaan, and Jacob and all his offspring went to Egypt. ⁷He took with him to Egypt his sons and grandsons and his daughters and grand-daughters—all his offspring.

⁸These are the names of the sons of Israel (Jacob and his descendants) who went to Egypt:

Reuben the firstborn of Jacob.
⁹ The sons of Reuben:
Hanoch, Pallu, Hezron and Carmi.
¹⁰ The sons of Simeon:
Jemuel, Jamin, Ohad, Jakin, Zohar and Shaul the son of a Canaanite woman.
¹¹ The sons of Levi:
Gershon, Kohath and Merari.
¹² The sons of Judah:
Er, Onan, Shelah, Perez and Zerah (but Er and Onan had died in the land of Canaan).
The sons of Perez:
Hezron and Hamul.
¹³ The sons of Issachar:
Tola, Puah,ᵃ Jashubᵇ and Shimron.
¹⁴ The sons of Zebulun:
Sered, Elon and Jahleel.

¹⁵These were the sons Leah bore to Jacob in Paddan Aram,ᶜ besides his daughter Dinah. These sons and daughters of his were thirty-three in all.

¹⁶ The sons of Gad:
Zephon,ᵈ Haggi, Shuni, Ezbon, Eri, Arodi and Areli.

THE MESSAGE

46.1 **46** So Israel set out on the journey with everything he owned. He arrived at Beersheba and worshiped, offering sacrifices to the God of his father Isaac.

46.2   God spoke to Israel in a vision that night: "Jacob! Jacob!"

"Yes?" he said. "I'm listening."

46.3-4   God said, "I am the God of your father. Don't be afraid of going down to Egypt. I'm going to make you a great nation there. I'll go with you down to Egypt; I'll also bring you back here. And when you die, Joseph will be with you; with his own hand he'll close your eyes."

46.5-7   Then Jacob left Beersheba. Israel's sons loaded their father and their little ones and their wives on the wagons Pharaoh had sent to carry him. They arrived in Egypt with the livestock and the wealth they had accumulated in Canaan. Jacob brought everyone in his family with him—sons and grandsons, daughters and granddaughters. Everyone.

46.8   These are the names of the Israelites, Jacob and his descendants, who went to Egypt:
Reuben, Jacob's firstborn.

46.9   Reuben's sons: Hanoch, Pallu, Hezron, and Carmi.

46.10   Simeon's sons: Jemuel, Jamin, Ohad, Jakin, Zohar, and Shaul the son of a Canaanite woman.

46.11   Levi's sons: Gershon, Kohath, and Merari.

46.12   Judah's sons: Er, Onan, Shelah, Perez, and Zerah (Er and Onan had already died in the land of Canaan). The sons of Perez were Hezron and Hamul.

46.13   Issachar's sons: Tola, Puah, Jashub, and Shimron.

46.14   Zebulun's sons: Sered, Elon, and Jahleel.

46.15   These are the sons that Leah bore to Jacob in Paddan Aram. There was also his daughter Dinah. Altogether, sons and daughters, they numbered thirty-three.

46.16   Gad's sons: Zephon, Haggi, Shuni, Ezbon, Eri, Arodi, and Areli.

ᵃ 13 Samaritan Pentateuch and Syriac (see also 1 Chron. 7:1); Masoretic Text *Puvah*   *ᵇ 13* Samaritan Pentateuch and some Septuagint manuscripts (see also Num. 26:24 and 1 Chron. 7:1); Masoretic Text *Iob*   *ᶜ 15* That is, Northwest Mesopotamia   *ᵈ 16* Samaritan Pentateuch and Septuagint (see also Num. 26:15); Masoretic Text *Ziphion*

NEW INTERNATIONAL VERSION

¹⁷The sons of Asher:

Imnah, Ishvah, Ishvi and Beriah.
Their sister was Serah.
The sons of Beriah:
Heber and Malkiel.

¹⁸These were the children born to Jacob by Zilpah, whom Laban had given to his daughter Leah—sixteen in all.

¹⁹The sons of Jacob's wife Rachel:

Joseph and Benjamin. ²⁰In Egypt, Manasseh and Ephraim were born to Joseph by Asenath daughter of Potiphera, priest of On.^a

²¹The sons of Benjamin:

Bela, Beker, Ashbel, Gera, Naaman, Ehi, Rosh, Muppim, Huppim and Ard.

²²These were the sons of Rachel who were born to Jacob—fourteen in all.

²³The son of Dan:

Hushim.

²⁴The sons of Naphtali:

Jahziel, Guni, Jezer and Shillem.

²⁵These were the sons born to Jacob by Bilhah, whom Laban had given to his daughter Rachel—seven in all.

²⁶All those who went to Egypt with Jacob—those who were his direct descendants, not counting his sons' wives—numbered sixty-six persons. ²⁷With the two sons^b who had been born to Joseph in Egypt, the members of Jacob's family, which went to Egypt, were seventy^c in all.

²⁸Now Jacob sent Judah ahead of him to Joseph to get directions to Goshen. When they arrived in the region of Goshen, ²⁹Joseph had his chariot made ready and went to Goshen to meet his father Israel. As soon as Joseph appeared before him, he threw his arms around his father^d and wept for a long time.

³⁰Israel said to Joseph, "Now I am ready to die, since I have seen for myself that you are still alive."

³¹Then Joseph said to his brothers and to his father's household, "I will go up and speak to Pharaoh and will say to him, 'My brothers and my father's household, who were living in the land of Canaan, have come to me. ³²The men are shepherds; they tend livestock, and they have brought along their flocks and herds and everything they own.' ³³When Pharaoh calls you in and asks, 'What is your occupation?' ³⁴you

---

^a 20 That is, Heliopolis   ^b 27 Hebrew; Septuagint *the nine children*   ^c 27 Hebrew (see also Exodus 1:5 and footnote); Septuagint (see also Acts 7:14) *seventy-five*   ^d 29 Hebrew *around him*

THE MESSAGE

46.17   Asher's sons: Imnah, Ishvah, Ishvi, and Beriah. Also their sister Serah, and Beriah's sons, Heber and Malkiel.

46.18   These are the children that Zilpah, the maid that Laban gave to his daughter Leah, bore to Jacob—sixteen of them.

46.19-21   The sons of Jacob's wife Rachel were Joseph and Benjamin. Joseph was the father of two sons, Manasseh and Ephraim, from his marriage to Asenath daughter of Potiphera, priest of On. They were born to him in Egypt. Benjamin's sons were Bela, Beker, Ashbel, Gera, Naaman, Ehi, Rosh, Muppim, Huppim, and Ard.

46.22   These are the children born to Jacob through Rachel—fourteen.

46.23   Dan's son: Hushim.

46.24   Naphtali's sons: Jahziel, Guni, Jezer, and Shillem.

46.25   These are the children born to Jacob through Bilhah, the maid Laban had given to his daughter Rachel—seven.

46.26-27   Summing up, all those who went down to Egypt with Jacob—his own children, not counting his sons' wives—numbered sixty-six. Counting in the two sons born to Joseph in Egypt, the members of Jacob's family who ended up in Egypt numbered seventy.

✝

46.28-29 Jacob sent Judah on ahead to get directions to Goshen from Joseph. When they got to Goshen, Joseph gave orders for his chariot and went to Goshen to meet his father Israel. The moment Joseph saw him, he threw himself on his neck and wept. He wept a long time.

46.30   Israel said to Joseph, "I'm ready to die. I've looked into your face—you are indeed alive."

46.31-34 Joseph then spoke to his brothers and his father's family. "I'll go and tell Pharaoh, 'My brothers and my father's family, all of whom lived in Canaan, have come to me. The men are shepherds; they've always made their living by raising livestock. And they've brought their flocks and herds with them, along with everything else they own.' When Pharaoh calls you in and asks what kind of work you do, tell

NEW INTERNATIONAL VERSION

should answer, 'Your servants have tended live-stock from our boyhood on, just as our fathers did.' Then you will be allowed to settle in the re-gion of Goshen, for all shepherds are detestable to the Egyptians."

47 Joseph went and told Pharaoh, "My fa-ther and brothers, with their flocks and herds and everything they own, have come from the land of Canaan and are now in Goshen." ²He chose five of his brothers and presented them before Pharaoh.

³Pharaoh asked the brothers, "What is your occupation?"

"Your servants are shepherds," they replied to Pharaoh, "just as our fathers were." ⁴They also said to him, "We have come to live here awhile, because the famine is severe in Canaan and your servants' flocks have no pasture. So now, please let your servants settle in Goshen."

⁵Pharaoh said to Joseph, "Your father and your brothers have come to you, ⁶and the land of Egypt is before you; settle your father and your brothers in the best part of the land. Let them live in Goshen. And if you know of any among them with special ability, put them in charge of my own livestock."

⁷Then Joseph brought his father Jacob in and presented him before Pharaoh. After Jacob blessed*ᵃ* Pharaoh, ⁸Pharaoh asked him, "How old are you?"

⁹And Jacob said to Pharaoh, "The years of my pilgrimage are a hundred and thirty. My years have been few and difficult, and they do not equal the years of the pilgrimage of my fathers." ¹⁰Then Jacob blessed*ᵇ* Pharaoh and went out from his presence.

¹¹So Joseph settled his father and his brothers in Egypt and gave them property in the best part of the land, the district of Rameses, as Pharaoh directed. ¹²Joseph also provided his father and his brothers and all his father's household with food, according to the number of their children.

JOSEPH AND THE FAMINE

¹³There was no food, however, in the whole region because the famine was severe; both Egypt and Canaan wasted away because of the famine. ¹⁴Joseph collected all the money that was to be found in Egypt and Canaan in payment for the grain they were buying, and he brought it to Phar-aoh's palace. ¹⁵When the money of the people of Egypt and Canaan was gone, all Egypt came to Jo-seph and said, "Give us food. Why should we die before your eyes? Our money is used up."

ᵃ 7 Or greeted   ᵇ 10 Or said farewell to

THE MESSAGE

him, 'Your servants have always kept livestock for as long as we can remember—we and our parents also.' That way he'll let you stay apart in the area of Goshen—for Egyptians look down on anyone who is a shepherd."

47 Joseph went to Pharaoh and told him, ⁴⁷·¹ "My father and brothers with their flocks and herds and everything they own have come from Canaan. Right now they are in Go-shen."

He had taken five of his brothers with him ⁴⁷·²⁻³ and introduced them to Pharaoh. Pharaoh asked them, "What kind of work do you do?"

"Your servants are shepherds, the same as ⁴⁷·³⁻⁴ our fathers were. We have come to this country to find a new place to live. There is no pasture for our flocks in Canaan. The famine has been very bad there. Please, would you let your ser-vants settle in the region of Goshen?"

Pharaoh looked at Joseph. "So, your father ⁴⁷·⁵⁻⁶ and brothers have arrived—a reunion! Egypt welcomes them. Settle your father and brothers on the choicest land—yes, give them Goshen. And if you know any among them that are es-pecially good at their work, put them in charge of my own livestock."

Next Joseph brought his father Jacob in and ⁴⁷·⁷⁻⁸ introduced him to Pharaoh. Jacob blessed Pharaoh. Pharaoh asked Jacob, "How old are you?"

Jacob answered Pharaoh, "The years of my ⁴⁷·⁹⁻¹⁰ sojourning are 130—a short and hard life and not nearly as long as my ancestors were giv-en." Then Jacob blessed Pharaoh and left.

Joseph settled his father and brothers in ⁴⁷·¹¹⁻¹² Egypt, made them proud owners of choice land—it was the region of Rameses (that is, Goshen)—just as Pharaoh had ordered. Joseph took good care of them—his father and broth-ers and all his father's family, right down to the smallest baby. He made sure they had plenty of everything.

✠

The time eventually came when there was no ⁴⁷·¹³⁻¹⁵ food anywhere. The famine was very bad. Egypt and Canaan alike were devastated by the famine. Joseph collected all the money that was to be found in Egypt and Canaan to pay for the distribution of food. He banked the money in Pharaoh's palace. When the money from Egypt and Canaan had run out, the Egyptians came to Joseph. "Food! Give us food! Are you going to watch us die right in front of you? The money is all gone."

NEW INTERNATIONAL VERSION

16"Then bring your livestock," said Joseph. "I will sell you food in exchange for your livestock, since your money is gone." 17So they brought their livestock to Joseph, and he gave them food in exchange for their horses, their sheep and goats, their cattle and donkeys. And he brought them through that year with food in exchange for all their livestock.

18When that year was over, they came to him the following year and said, "We cannot hide from our lord the fact that since our money is gone and our livestock belongs to you, there is nothing left for our lord except our bodies and our land. 19Why should we perish before your eyes—we and our land as well? Buy us and our land in exchange for food, and we with our land will be in bondage to Pharaoh. Give us seed so that we may live and not die, and that the land may not become desolate."

20So Joseph bought all the land in Egypt for Pharaoh. The Egyptians, one and all, sold their fields, because the famine was too severe for them. The land became Pharaoh's, 21and Joseph reduced the people to servitude,[a] from one end of Egypt to the other. 22However, he did not buy the land of the priests, because they received a regular allotment from Pharaoh and had food enough from the allotment Pharaoh gave them. That is why they did not sell their land.

23Joseph said to the people, "Now that I have bought you and your land today for Pharaoh, here is seed for you so you can plant the ground. 24But when the crop comes in, give a fifth of it to Pharaoh. The other four-fifths you may keep as seed for the fields and as food for yourselves and your households and your children."

25"You have saved our lives," they said. "May we find favor in the eyes of our lord; we will be in bondage to Pharaoh."

26So Joseph established it as a law concerning land in Egypt—still in force today—that a fifth of the produce belongs to Pharaoh. It was only the land of the priests that did not become Pharaoh's.

27Now the Israelites settled in Egypt in the region of Goshen. They acquired property there and were fruitful and increased greatly in number.

28Jacob lived in Egypt seventeen years, and the years of his life were a hundred and forty-seven. 29When the time drew near for Israel to die, he called for his son Joseph and said to him, "If I have found favor in your eyes, put your hand under my thigh and promise that you will

---

a 21 Samaritan Pentateuch and Septuagint (see also Vulgate); Masoretic Text *and he moved the people into the cities*

THE MESSAGE

47.16-17   Joseph said, "Bring your livestock. I'll trade you food for livestock since your money's run out." So they brought Joseph their livestock. He traded them food for their horses, sheep, cattle, and donkeys. He got them through that year in exchange for all their livestock.

47.18-19   When that year was over, the next year rolled around and they were back, saying, "Master, it's no secret to you that we're broke: our money's gone and we've traded you all our livestock. We've nothing left to barter with but our bodies and our farms. What use are our bodies and our land if we stand here and starve to death right in front of you? Trade us food for our bodies and our land. We'll be slaves to Pharaoh and give up our land—all we ask is seed for survival, just enough to live on and keep the farms alive."

47.20-21   So Joseph bought up all the farms in Egypt for Pharaoh. Every Egyptian sold his land—the famine was that bad. That's how Pharaoh ended up owning all the land and the people ended up slaves; Joseph reduced the people to slavery from one end of Egypt to the other.

47.22   Joseph made an exception for the priests. He didn't buy their land because they received a fixed salary from Pharaoh and were able to live off of that salary. So they didn't need to sell their land.

47.23-24   Joseph then announced to the people: "Here's how things stand: I've bought you and your land for Pharaoh. In exchange I'm giving you seed so you can plant the ground. When the crops are harvested, you must give a fifth to Pharaoh and keep four-fifths for yourselves, for seed for yourselves and your families—you're going to be able to feed your children!"

47.25   They said, "You've saved our lives! Master, we're grateful and glad to be slaves to Pharaoh."

47.26   Joseph decreed a land law in Egypt that is still in effect, *A Fifth Goes to Pharaoh*. Only the priests' lands were not owned by Pharaoh.

✛

47.27-28   And so Israel settled down in Egypt in the region of Goshen. They acquired property and flourished. They became a large company of people. Jacob lived in Egypt for seventeen years. In all, he lived 147 years.

47.29   When the time came for Israel to die, he called his son Joseph and said, "Do me this favor. Put your hand under my thigh, a sign that

NEW INTERNATIONAL VERSION

show me kindness and faithfulness. Do not bury me in Egypt, [30]but when I rest with my fathers, carry me out of Egypt and bury me where they are buried."

"I will do as you say," he said.

[31]"Swear to me," he said. Then Joseph swore to him, and Israel worshiped as he leaned on the top of his staff.[a]

MANASSEH AND EPHRAIM

48 Some time later Joseph was told, "Your father is ill." So he took his two sons Manasseh and Ephraim along with him. [2]When Jacob was told, "Your son Joseph has come to you," Israel rallied his strength and sat up on the bed.

[3]Jacob said to Joseph, "God Almighty[b] appeared to me at Luz in the land of Canaan, and there he blessed me [4]and said to me, 'I am going to make you fruitful and will increase your numbers. I will make you a community of peoples, and I will give this land as an everlasting possession to your descendants after you.'

[5]"Now then, your two sons born to you in Egypt before I came to you here will be reckoned as mine; Ephraim and Manasseh will be mine, just as Reuben and Simeon are mine. [6]Any children born to you after them will be yours; in the territory they inherit they will be reckoned under the names of their brothers. [7]As I was returning from Paddan,[c] to my sorrow Rachel died in the land of Canaan while we were still on the way, a little distance from Ephrath. So I buried her there beside the road to Ephrath" (that is, Bethlehem).

[8]When Israel saw the sons of Joseph, he asked, "Who are these?"

[9]"They are the sons God has given me here," Joseph said to his father.

Then Israel said, "Bring them to me so I may bless them."

[10]Now Israel's eyes were failing because of old age, and he could hardly see. So Joseph brought his sons close to him, and his father kissed them and embraced them.

[11]Israel said to Joseph, "I never expected to see your face again, and now God has allowed me to see your children too."

[12]Then Joseph removed them from Israel's knees and bowed down with his face to the ground. [13]And Joseph took both of them, Ephraim on his right toward Israel's left hand and Manasseh on his left toward Israel's right hand, and brought them close to him. [14]But Israel reached

THE MESSAGE

you're loyal and true to me to the end. Don't bury me in Egypt. When I lie down with my fathers, carry me out of Egypt and bury me alongside them."

"I will," he said. "I'll do what you've asked."

47.31   Israel said, "Promise me." Joseph promised. Israel bowed his head in submission and gratitude from his bed.

48.1-2 **48** Some time after this conversation, Joseph was told, "Your father is ill." He took his two sons, Manasseh and Ephraim, and went to Jacob. When Jacob was told, "Your son Joseph has come," he roused himself and sat up in bed.

48.3-7   Jacob said to Joseph, "The Strong God appeared to me at Luz in the land of Canaan and blessed me. He said, 'I'm going to make you prosperous and numerous, turn you into a congregation of tribes; and I'll turn this land over to your children coming after you as a permanent inheritance.' I'm adopting your two sons who were born to you here in Egypt before I joined you; they have equal status with Reuben and Simeon. But any children born after them are yours; they will come after their brothers in matters of inheritance. I want it this way because, as I was returning from Paddan, your mother Rachel, to my deep sorrow, died as we were on our way through Canaan when we were only a short distance from Ephrath, now called Bethlehem."

48.8   Just then Jacob noticed Joseph's sons and said, "Who are these?"

48.9-11   Joseph told his father, "They are my sons whom God gave to me in this place."

"Bring them to me," he said, "so I can bless them." Israel's eyesight was poor from old age; he was nearly blind. So Joseph brought them up close. Old Israel kissed and embraced them and then said to Joseph, "I never expected to see your face again, and now God has let me see your children as well!"

48.12-16   Joseph took them from Israel's knees and bowed respectfully, his face to the ground. Then Joseph took the two boys, Ephraim with his right hand setting him to Israel's left, and Manasseh with his left hand setting him to Israel's right, and stood them before him. But Is-

---

[a] 31 Or *Israel bowed down at the head of his bed*
[b] 3 Hebrew *El-Shaddai*   [c] 7 That is, Northwest Mesopotamia

NEW INTERNATIONAL VERSION

out his right hand and put it on Ephraim's head, though he was the younger, and crossing his arms, he put his left hand on Manasseh's head, even though Manasseh was the firstborn. ¹⁵Then he blessed Joseph and said,

"May the God before whom my fathers
Abraham and Isaac walked,
the God who has been my shepherd
all my life to this day,
¹⁶ the Angel who has delivered me from all
harm
—may he bless these boys.
May they be called by my name
and the names of my fathers Abraham and
Isaac,
and may they increase greatly
upon the earth."

¹⁷When Joseph saw his father placing his right hand on Ephraim's head he was displeased; so he took hold of his father's hand to move it from Ephraim's head to Manasseh's head. ¹⁸Joseph said to him, "No, my father, this one is the firstborn; put your right hand on his head."

¹⁹But his father refused and said, "I know, my son, I know. He too will become a people, and he too will become great. Nevertheless, his younger brother will be greater than he, and his descendants will become a group of nations." ²⁰He blessed them that day and said,

"In your*ᵃ* name will Israel pronounce this
blessing:
'May God make you like Ephraim and
Manasseh.' "

So he put Ephraim ahead of Manasseh.

²¹Then Israel said to Joseph, "I am about to die, but God will be with you*ᵇ* and take you*ᵇ* back to the land of your*ᵇ* fathers. ²²And to you, as one who is over your brothers, I give the ridge of land*ᶜ* I took from the Amorites with my sword and my bow."

JACOB BLESSES HIS SONS

49 Then Jacob called for his sons and said: "Gather around so I can tell you what will happen to you in days to come.

² "Assemble and listen, sons of Jacob;
listen to your father Israel.

³ "Reuben, you are my firstborn,
my might, the first sign of my strength,
excelling in honor, excelling in power.

ᵃ 20 The Hebrew is singular.   *ᵇ 21* The Hebrew is plural.
ᶜ 22 Or *And to you I give one portion more than to your
brothers—the portion*

THE MESSAGE

rael crossed his arms and put his right hand on the head of Ephraim who was the younger and his left hand on the head of Manasseh, the firstborn. Then he blessed them:

The God before whom walked
my fathers Abraham and Isaac,
The God who has been my shepherd
all my lifelong to this very day,
48.17-18 The Angel who delivered me from every
evil,
Bless the boys.
May my name be echoed in their lives,
and the names of Abraham and Isaac,
my fathers,
And may they grow
covering the Earth with their children.

When Joseph saw that his father had placed his right hand on Ephraim's head, he thought he had made a mistake, so he took hold of his father's hand to move it from Ephraim's head to Manasseh's, saying, "That's the wrong head, Father; the other one is the firstborn; place your right hand on his head."

48.19-20 But his father wouldn't do it. He said, "I know, my son; but I know what I'm doing. He also will develop into a people, and he also will be great. But his younger brother will be even greater and his descendants will enrich nations." Then he blessed them both:

Israel will use your names to give
blessings:
May God make you like Ephraim and
Manasseh.

In that he made it explicit: he put Ephraim
ahead of Manasseh.

48.21-22 Israel then said to Joseph, "I'm about to die. God be with you and give you safe passage back to the land of your fathers. As for me, I'm presenting you, as the first among your brothers, the ridge of land I took from Amorites with my sword and bow."

✠

49.1 **49** Jacob called his sons and said, "Gather around. I want to tell you what you can expect in the days to come."

49.2 Come together, listen sons of Jacob,
listen to Israel your father.

49.3-4 Reuben, you're my firstborn,
my strength, first proof of my manhood,
at the top in honor and at the top in
power,

NEW INTERNATIONAL VERSION

⁴Turbulent as the waters, you will no longer excel,
  for you went up onto your father's bed,
  onto my couch and defiled it.

⁵"Simeon and Levi are brothers—
  their swordsᵃ are weapons of violence.
⁶Let me not enter their council,
  let me not join their assembly,
for they have killed men in their anger
  and hamstrung oxen as they pleased.
⁷Cursed be their anger, so fierce,
  and their fury, so cruel!
I will scatter them in Jacob
  and disperse them in Israel.

⁸"Judah,ᵇ your brothers will praise you;
  your hand will be on the neck of your
    enemies;
  your father's sons will bow down to you.
⁹You are a lion's cub, O Judah;
  you return from the prey, my son.
Like a lion he crouches and lies down,
  like a lioness—who dares to rouse him?
¹⁰The scepter will not depart from Judah,
  nor the ruler's staff from between his feet,
until he comes to whom it belongsᶜ
  and the obedience of the nations is his.
¹¹He will tether his donkey to a vine,
  his colt to the choicest branch;
he will wash his garments in wine,
  his robes in the blood of grapes.
¹²His eyes will be darker than wine,
  his teeth whiter than milk.ᵈ

¹³"Zebulun will live by the seashore
  and become a haven for ships;
  his border will extend toward Sidon.

¹⁴"Issachar is a rawbonedᵉ donkey
  lying down between two saddlebags.ᶠ
¹⁵When he sees how good is his resting place
  and how pleasant is his land,
he will bend his shoulder to the burden
  and submit to forced labor.

¹⁶"Danᵍ will provide justice for his people
  as one of the tribes of Israel.
¹⁷Dan will be a serpent by the roadside,
  a viper along the path,
that bites the horse's heels
  so that its rider tumbles backward.

¹⁸"I look for your deliverance, O LORD.

ᵃ 5 The meaning of the Hebrew for this word is uncertain.
ᵇ 8 Judah sounds like and may be derived from the Hebrew
for praise.   ᶜ 10 Or until Shiloh comes; or until he comes to
whom tribute belongs   ᵈ 12 Or will be dull from wine, / his
teeth white from milk   ᵉ 14 Or strong   ᶠ 14 Or campfires
ᵍ 16 Dan here means he provides justice.

THE MESSAGE

But like a bucket of water spilled,
  you'll be at the top no more,
Because you climbed into your father's
    marriage bed,
  mounting that couch, and you defiled it.

49.5-6   Simeon and Levi are two of a kind,
  ready to fight at the drop of a hat.
I don't want anything to do with their
    vendettas,
  want no part in their bitter feuds;
They kill men in fits of temper,
  slash oxen on a whim.

49.7   A curse on their uncontrolled anger,
  on their indiscriminate wrath.
I'll throw them out with the trash;
  I'll shred and scatter them like confetti
    throughout Israel.

49.8-12   You, Judah, your brothers will praise you:
  Your fingers on your enemies' throat,
  while your brothers honor you.
You're a lion's cub, Judah,
  home fresh from the kill, my son.
Look at him, crouched like a lion, king of
    beasts;
  who dares mess with him?
The scepter shall not leave Judah;
  he'll keep a firm grip on the command staff
Until the ultimate ruler comes
  and the nations obey him.
He'll tie up his donkey to the grapevine,
  his purebred prize to a sturdy branch.
He will wash his shirt in wine
  and his cloak in the blood of grapes,
His eyes will be darker than wine,
  his teeth whiter than milk.

49.13   Zebulun settles down on the seashore;
  he's a safe harbor for ships,
  right alongside Sidon.

49.14-15   Issachar is one tough donkey
  crouching between the corrals;
When he saw how good the place was,
  how pleasant the country,
He gave up his freedom
  and went to work as a slave.

49.16-17   Dan will handle matters of justice for his
    people;
  he will hold his own just fine among the
    tribes of Israel.
Dan is only a small snake in the grass,
  a lethal serpent in ambush by the road
When he strikes a horse in the heel,
  and brings its huge rider crashing down.

49.18   I wait in hope
  for your salvation, GOD.

NEW INTERNATIONAL VERSION

¹⁹ "Gad^a will be attacked by a band of raiders,
but he will attack them at their heels.

²⁰ "Asher's food will be rich;
he will provide delicacies fit for a king.

²¹ "Naphtali is a doe set free
that bears beautiful fawns.^b

²² "Joseph is a fruitful vine,
a fruitful vine near a spring,
whose branches climb over a wall.^c
²³ With bitterness archers attacked him;
they shot at him with hostility.
²⁴ But his bow remained steady,
his strong arms stayed^d limber,
because of the hand of the Mighty One of
Jacob,
because of the Shepherd, the Rock of Israel,
²⁵ because of your father's God, who helps you,
because of the Almighty,^e who blesses you
with blessings of the heavens above,
blessings of the deep that lies below,
blessings of the breast and womb.
²⁶ Your father's blessings are greater
than the blessings of the ancient
mountains,
than^f the bounty of the age-old hills.
Let all these rest on the head of Joseph,
on the brow of the prince among^g his
brothers.

²⁷ "Benjamin is a ravenous wolf;
in the morning he devours the prey,
in the evening he divides the plunder."

²⁸ All these are the twelve tribes of Israel, and this is what their father said to them when he blessed them, giving each the blessing appropriate to him.

THE DEATH OF JACOB

²⁹ Then he gave them these instructions: "I am about to be gathered to my people. Bury me with my fathers in the cave in the field of Ephron the Hittite, ³⁰ the cave in the field of Machpelah, near Mamre in Canaan, which Abraham bought as a burial place from Ephron the Hittite, along with the field. ³¹ There Abraham and his wife Sarah were buried, there Isaac and his wife Rebekah were buried, and there I buried Leah. ³² The field and the cave in it were bought from the Hittites.^h"

THE MESSAGE

49.19 Gad will be attacked by bandits,
but he will trip them up.

49.20 Asher will become famous for rich foods,
candies and sweets fit for kings.

49.21-26 Naphtali is a deer running free
that gives birth to lovely fawns.

Joseph is a wild donkey,
a wild donkey by a spring,
spirited donkeys on a hill.
The archers with malice attacked,
shooting their hate-tipped arrows;
But he held steady under fire,
his bow firm, his arms limber,
With the backing of the Champion of
Jacob,
the Shepherd, the Rock of Israel.
The God of your father—may he help you!
And may The Strong God—may he give
you his blessings,
Blessings tumbling out of the skies,
blessings bursting up from the Earth—
blessings of breasts and womb.
May the blessings of your father
exceed the blessings of the ancient
mountains,
surpass the delights of the eternal hills;
May they rest on the head of Joseph,
on the brow of the one consecrated
among his brothers.

49.27 Benjamin is a ravenous wolf;
all morning he gorges on his kill,
at evening divides up what's left over.

49.28 All these are the tribes of Israel, the twelve tribes. And this is what their father said to them as he blessed them, blessing each one with his own special farewell blessing.

⁜

49.29-32 Then he instructed them: "I am about to be gathered to my people. Bury me with my fathers in the cave which is in the field of Ephron the Hittite, the cave in the field of Machpelah facing Mamre in the land of Canaan, the field Abraham bought from Ephron the Hittite for a burial plot. Abraham and his wife Sarah were buried there; Isaac and his wife Rebekah were buried there; I also buried Leah there. The field and the cave were bought from the Hittites."

---

^a 19 *Gad* can mean *attack* and *band of raiders*.
^b 21 Or *free; / he utters beautiful words* ^c 22 Or *Joseph is a wild colt, / a wild colt near a spring, / a wild donkey on a terraced hill* ^d 23,24 Or *archers will attack . . . will shoot . . . will remain . . . will stay* ^e 25 Hebrew *Shaddai* ^f 26 Or *of my progenitors, / as great as* ^g 26 Or *the one separated from* ^h 32 Or *the sons of Heth*

NEW INTERNATIONAL VERSION

33When Jacob had finished giving instructions to his sons, he drew his feet up into the bed, breathed his last and was gathered to his people.

50 Joseph threw himself upon his father and wept over him and kissed him. 2Then Joseph directed the physicians in his service to embalm his father Israel. So the physicians embalmed him, 3taking a full forty days, for that was the time required for embalming. And the Egyptians mourned for him seventy days.

4When the days of mourning had passed, Joseph said to Pharaoh's court, "If I have found favor in your eyes, speak to Pharaoh for me. Tell him, 5'My father made me swear an oath and said, "I am about to die; bury me in the tomb I dug for myself in the land of Canaan." Now let me go up and bury my father; then I will return.' "

6Pharaoh said, "Go up and bury your father, as he made you swear to do."

7So Joseph went up to bury his father. All Pharaoh's officials accompanied him—the dignitaries of his court and all the dignitaries of Egypt— 8besides all the members of Joseph's household and his brothers and those belonging to his father's household. Only their children and their flocks and herds were left in Goshen. 9Chariots and horsemen*d* also went up with him. It was a very large company.

10When they reached the threshing floor of Atad, near the Jordan, they lamented loudly and bitterly; and there Joseph observed a seven-day period of mourning for his father. 11When the Canaanites who lived there saw the mourning at the threshing floor of Atad, they said, "The Egyptians are holding a solemn ceremony of mourning." That is why that place near the Jordan is called Abel Mizraim.*b*

12So Jacob's sons did as he had commanded them: 13They carried him to the land of Canaan and buried him in the cave in the field of Machpelah, near Mamre, which Abraham had bought as a burial place from Ephron the Hittite, along with the field. 14After burying his father, Joseph returned to Egypt, together with his brothers and all the others who had gone with him to bury his father.

JOSEPH REASSURES HIS BROTHERS

15When Joseph's brothers saw that their father was dead, they said, "What if Joseph holds a grudge against us and pays us back for all the

a 9 Or charioteers   b 11 Abel Mizraim means mourning of the Egyptians.

THE MESSAGE

49.33   Jacob finished instructing his sons, pulled his feet into bed, breathed his last, and was gathered to his people.

✝

50.1 50 Joseph threw himself on his father, wept over him, and kissed him.

✝

50.2-3 Joseph then instructed the physicians in his employ to embalm his father. The physicians embalmed Israel. The embalming took forty days, the period required for embalming. There was public mourning by the Egyptians for seventy days.

50.4-5   When the period of mourning was completed, Joseph petitioned Pharaoh's court: "If you have reason to think kindly of me, present Pharaoh with my request: My father made me swear, saying, 'I am ready to die. Bury me in the grave plot that I prepared for myself in the land of Canaan.' Please give me leave to go up and bury my father. Then I'll come back."

50.6   Pharaoh said, "Certainly. Go and bury your father as he made you promise under oath."

50.7-9   So Joseph left to bury his father. And all the high-ranking officials from Pharaoh's court went with him, all the dignitaries of Egypt, joining Joseph's family—his brothers and his father's family. Their children and flocks and herds were left in Goshen. Chariots and horsemen accompanied them. It was a huge funeral procession.

50.10   Arriving at the Atad Threshing Floor just across the Jordan River, they stopped for a period of mourning, letting their grief out in loud and lengthy lament. For seven days, Joseph engaged in these funeral rites for his father.

50.11   When the Canaanites who lived in that area saw the grief being poured out at the Atad Threshing Floor, they said, "Look how deeply the Egyptians are mourning." That is how the site at the Jordan got the name Abel Mizraim (Egyptian Lament).

50.12-13   Jacob's sons continued to carry out his instructions to the letter. They took him on into Canaan and buried him in the cave in the field of Machpelah facing Mamre, the field that Abraham had bought as a burial plot from Ephron the Hittite.

✝

50.14-15 After burying his father, Joseph went back to Egypt. All his brothers who had come with him to bury his father returned with him. After the funeral, Joseph's brothers talked among themselves: "What if Joseph is carrying a grudge and

NEW INTERNATIONAL VERSION

wrongs we did to him?" [16]So they sent word to Joseph, saying, "Your father left these instructions before he died: [17]'This is what you are to say to Joseph: I ask you to forgive your brothers the sins and the wrongs they committed in treating you so badly.' Now please forgive the sins of the servants of the God of your father." When their message came to him, Joseph wept.

[18]His brothers then came and threw themselves down before him. "We are your slaves," they said.

[19]But Joseph said to them, "Don't be afraid. Am I in the place of God? [20]You intended to harm me, but God intended it for good to accomplish what is now being done, the saving of many lives. [21]So then, don't be afraid. I will provide for you and your children." And he reassured them and spoke kindly to them.

THE DEATH OF JOSEPH

[22]Joseph stayed in Egypt, along with all his father's family. He lived a hundred and ten years [23]and saw the third generation of Ephraim's children. Also the children of Makir son of Manasseh were placed at birth on Joseph's knees.[a]

[24]Then Joseph said to his brothers, "I am about to die. But God will surely come to your aid and take you up out of this land to the land he promised on oath to Abraham, Isaac and Jacob." [25]And Joseph made the sons of Israel swear an oath and said, "God will surely come to your aid, and then you must carry my bones up from this place."

[26]So Joseph died at the age of a hundred and ten. And after they embalmed him, he was placed in a coffin in Egypt.

---

[a] 23 That is, were counted as his

THE MESSAGE

decides to pay us back for all the wrong we did him?"

50.16-17   So they sent Joseph a message, "Before his death, your father gave this command: Tell Joseph, 'Forgive your brothers' sin—all that wrongdoing. They did treat you very badly.' Will you do it? Will you forgive the sins of the servants of your father's God?"

When Joseph received their message, he wept.

50.18   Then the brothers went in person to him, threw themselves on the ground before him and said, "We'll be your slaves."

50.19-21   Joseph replied, "Don't be afraid. Do I act for God? Don't you see, you planned evil against me but God used those same plans for my good, as you see all around you right now—life for many people. Easy now, you have nothing to fear; I'll take care of you and your children." He reassured them, speaking with them heart-to-heart.

50.22-23   Joseph continued to live in Egypt with his father's family. Joseph lived 110 years. He lived to see Ephraim's sons into the third generation. The sons of Makir, Manasseh's son, were also recognized as Joseph's.

50.24   At the end, Joseph said to his brothers, "I am ready to die. God will most certainly pay you a visit and take you out of this land and back to the land he so solemnly promised to Abraham, Isaac, and Jacob."

50.25   Then Joseph made the sons of Israel promise under oath, "When God makes his visitation, make sure you take my bones with you as you leave here."

50.26   Joseph died at the age of 110 years. They embalmed him and placed him in a coffin in Egypt.

EXODUS

EXODUS

THE ISRAELITES OPPRESSED

1 These are the names of the sons of Israel who went to Egypt with Jacob, each with his family: ²Reuben, Simeon, Levi and Judah; ³Issachar, Zebulun and Benjamin; ⁴Dan and Naphtali; Gad and Asher. ⁵The descendants of Jacob numbered seventy*ᵃ* in all; Joseph was already in Egypt.

⁶Now Joseph and all his brothers and all that generation died, ⁷but the Israelites were fruitful and multiplied greatly and became exceedingly numerous, so that the land was filled with them.

⁸Then a new king, who did not know about Joseph, came to power in Egypt. ⁹"Look," he said to his people, "the Israelites have become much too numerous for us. ¹⁰Come, we must deal shrewdly with them or they will become even more numerous and, if war breaks out, will join our enemies, fight against us and leave the country."

¹¹So they put slave masters over them to oppress them with forced labor, and they built Pithom and Rameses as store cities for Pharaoh. ¹²But the more they were oppressed, the more they multiplied and spread; so the Egyptians came to dread the Israelites ¹³and worked them ruthlessly. ¹⁴They made their lives bitter with hard labor in brick and mortar and with all kinds of work in the fields; in all their hard labor the Egyptians used them ruthlessly.

¹⁵The king of Egypt said to the Hebrew midwives, whose names were Shiphrah and Puah, ¹⁶"When you help the Hebrew women in childbirth and observe them on the delivery stool, if it is a boy, kill him; but if it is a girl, let her live." ¹⁷The midwives, however, feared God and did not do what the king of Egypt had told them to do; they let the boys live. ¹⁸Then the king of Egypt summoned the midwives and asked them,

---

ᵃ 5 Masoretic Text (see also Gen. 46:27); Dead Sea Scrolls and Septuagint (see also Acts 7:14 and note at Gen. 46:27) *seventy-five*

1.1-5   1 These are the names of the Israelites who went to Egypt with Jacob, each bringing his family members:

    Reuben, Simeon, Levi, and Judah,
    Issachar, Zebulun, and Benjamin,
    Dan and Naphtali, Gad and Asher.

Seventy persons in all generated by Jacob's seed. Joseph was already in Egypt.

1.6-7   Then Joseph died, and all his brothers—that whole generation. But the children of Israel kept on reproducing. They were very prolific—a population explosion in their own right—and the land was filled with them.

"A NEW KING . . . WHO DIDN'T KNOW JOSEPH"

1.8-10 A new king came to power in Egypt who didn't know Joseph. He spoke to his people in alarm, "There are way too many of these Israelites for us to handle. We've got to do something: Let's devise a plan to contain them, lest if there's a war they should join our enemies, or just walk off and leave us."

1.11-14   So they organized them into work-gangs and put them to hard labor under gang-foremen. They built the storage cities Pithom and Rameses for Pharaoh. But the harder the Egyptians worked them the more children the Israelites had—children everywhere! The Egyptians got so they couldn't stand the Israelites and treated them worse than ever, crushing them with slave labor. They made them miserable with hard labor—making bricks and mortar and back-breaking work in the fields. They piled on the work, crushing them under the cruel workload.

1.15-16   The king of Egypt had a talk with the two Hebrew midwives; one was named Shiphrah and the other Puah. He said, "When you deliver the Hebrew women, look at the sex of the baby. If it's a boy, kill him; if it's a girl, let her live."

1.17-18   But the midwives had far too much respect for God and didn't do what the king of Egypt ordered; they let the boy babies live. The king of Egypt called in the midwives. "Why didn't

NEW INTERNATIONAL VERSION

"Why have you done this? Why have you let the boys live?"

¹⁹The midwives answered Pharaoh, "Hebrew women are not like Egyptian women; they are vigorous and give birth before the midwives arrive."

²⁰So God was kind to the midwives and the people increased and became even more numerous. ²¹And because the midwives feared God, he gave them families of their own.

²²Then Pharaoh gave this order to all his people: "Every boy that is born^a you must throw into the Nile, but let every girl live."

THE BIRTH OF MOSES

2 Now a man of the house of Levi married a Levite woman, ²and she became pregnant and gave birth to a son. When she saw that he was a fine child, she hid him for three months. ³But when she could hide him no longer, she got a papyrus basket for him and coated it with tar and pitch. Then she placed the child in it and put it among the reeds along the bank of the Nile. ⁴His sister stood at a distance to see what would happen to him.

⁵Then Pharaoh's daughter went down to the Nile to bathe, and her attendants were walking along the river bank. She saw the basket among the reeds and sent her slave girl to get it. ⁶She opened it and saw the baby. He was crying, and she felt sorry for him. "This is one of the Hebrew babies," she said.

⁷Then his sister asked Pharaoh's daughter, "Shall I go and get one of the Hebrew women to nurse the baby for you?"

⁸"Yes, go," she answered. And the girl went and got the baby's mother. ⁹Pharaoh's daughter said to her, "Take this baby and nurse him for me, and I will pay you." So the woman took the baby and nursed him. ¹⁰When the child grew older, she took him to Pharaoh's daughter and he became her son. She named him Moses,^b saying, "I drew him out of the water."

MOSES FLEES TO MIDIAN

¹¹One day, after Moses had grown up, he went out to where his own people were and watched them at their hard labor. He saw an Egyptian beating a Hebrew, one of his own people. ¹²Glancing this way and that and seeing no one, he killed the Egyptian and hid him in the sand. ¹³The next day he went out and saw two He-

THE MESSAGE

you obey my orders? You've let those babies live!"

1.19   The midwives answered Pharaoh, "The Hebrew women aren't like the Egyptian women; they're vigorous. Before the midwife can get there, they've already had the baby."

1.20-21   God was pleased with the midwives. The people continued to increase in number—a very strong people. And because the midwives honored God, God gave them families of their own.

1.22   So Pharaoh issued a general order to all his people: "Every boy that is born, drown him in the Nile. But let the girls live."

MOSES

2.1-3   **2** A man from the family of Levi married a Levite woman. The woman became pregnant and had a son. She saw there was something special about him and hid him. She hid him for three months. When she couldn't hide him any longer she got a little basket-boat made of papyrus, waterproofed it with tar and pitch, and placed the child in it. Then she set it afloat in the reeds at the edge of the Nile.

2.4-6   The baby's older sister found herself a vantage point a little way off and watched to see what would happen to him. Pharaoh's daughter came down to the Nile to bathe; her maidens strolled on the bank. She saw the basket-boat floating in the reeds and sent her maid to get it. She opened it and saw the child—a baby crying! Her heart went out to him. She said, "This must be one of the Hebrew babies."

2.7   Then his sister was before her: "Do you want me to go and get a nursing mother from the Hebrews so she can nurse the baby for you?"

2.8   Pharaoh's daughter said, "Yes. Go." The girl went and called the child's mother.

2.9   Pharaoh's daughter told her, "Take this baby and nurse him for me. I'll pay you." The woman took the child and nursed him.

2.10   After the child was weaned, she presented him to Pharaoh's daughter who adopted him as her son. She named him Moses (Pulled-Out), saying, "I pulled him out of the water."

2.11-12   Time passed. Moses grew up. One day he went and saw his brothers, saw all that hard labor. Then he saw an Egyptian hit a Hebrew—one of his relatives! He looked this way and then that; when he realized there was no one in sight, he killed the Egyptian and buried him in the sand.

2.13   The next day he went out there again. Two

---

^a 22 Masoretic Text; Samaritan Pentateuch, Septuagint and Targums *born to the Hebrews*   ^b 10 *Moses* sounds like the Hebrew for *draw out*.

NEW INTERNATIONAL VERSION

brews fighting. He asked the one in the wrong, "Why are you hitting your fellow Hebrew?"

¹⁴The man said, "Who made you ruler and judge over us? Are you thinking of killing me as you killed the Egyptian?" Then Moses was afraid and thought, "What I did must have become known."

¹⁵When Pharaoh heard of this, he tried to kill Moses, but Moses fled from Pharaoh and went to live in Midian, where he sat down by a well. ¹⁶Now a priest of Midian had seven daughters, and they came to draw water and fill the troughs to water their father's flock. ¹⁷Some shepherds came along and drove them away, but Moses got up and came to their rescue and watered their flock.

¹⁸When the girls returned to Reuel their father, he asked them, "Why have you returned so early today?"

¹⁹They answered, "An Egyptian rescued us from the shepherds. He even drew water for us and watered the flock."

²⁰"And where is he?" he asked his daughters. "Why did you leave him? Invite him to have something to eat."

²¹Moses agreed to stay with the man, who gave his daughter Zipporah to Moses in marriage. ²²Zipporah gave birth to a son, and Moses named him Gershom,[a] saying, "I have become an alien in a foreign land."

²³During that long period, the king of Egypt died. The Israelites groaned in their slavery and cried out, and their cry for help because of their slavery went up to God. ²⁴God heard their groaning and he remembered his covenant with Abraham, with Isaac and with Jacob. ²⁵So God looked on the Israelites and was concerned about them.

MOSES AND THE BURNING BUSH

3 Now Moses was tending the flock of Jethro his father-in-law, the priest of Midian, and he led the flock to the far side of the desert and came to Horeb, the mountain of God. ²There the angel of the LORD appeared to him in flames of fire from within a bush. Moses saw that though the bush was on fire it did not burn up. ³So Moses thought, "I will go over and see this strange sight—why the bush does not burn up."

---

a 22 *Gershom* sounds like the Hebrew for *an alien there.*

THE MESSAGE

Hebrew men were fighting. He spoke to the man who started it: "Why are you hitting your neighbor?"

2.14 The man shot back: "Who do you think you are, telling us what to do? Are you going to kill me the way you killed that Egyptian?"

Then Moses panicked: "Word's gotten out—people know about this."

✠

2.15 Pharaoh heard about it and tried to kill Moses, but Moses got away to the land of Midian. He sat down by a well.

2.16-17 The priest of Midian had seven daughters. They came and drew water, filling the troughs and watering their father's sheep. When some shepherds came and chased the girls off, Moses came to their rescue and helped them water their sheep.

2.18 When they got home to their father, Reuel, he said, "That didn't take long. Why are you back so soon?"

2.19 "An Egyptian," they said, "rescued us from a bunch of shepherds. Why, he even drew water for us and watered the sheep."

2.20 He said, "So where is he? Why did you leave him behind? Invite him so he can have something to eat with us."

2.21-22 Moses agreed to settle down there with the man, who then gave his daughter Zipporah (Bird) to him for his wife. She had a son, and Moses named him Gershom (Sojourner), saying, "I'm a sojourner in a foreign country."

✠

2.23 Many years later the king of Egypt died. The Israelites groaned under their slavery and cried out. Their cries for relief from their hard labor ascended to God:

2.24 God listened to their groanings.

God remembered his covenant with Abraham, with Isaac, and with Jacob.

2.25 God saw what was going on with Israel.

God understood.

✠

3.1-2 **3** Moses was shepherding the flock of Jethro, his father-in-law, the priest of Midian. He led the flock to the west end of the wilderness and came to the mountain of God, Horeb. The angel of GOD appeared to him in flames of fire blazing out of the middle of a bush. He looked. The bush was blazing away but it didn't burn up.

3.3 Moses said, "What's going on here? I can't believe this! Amazing! Why doesn't the bush burn up?"

NEW INTERNATIONAL VERSION

⁴When the LORD saw that he had gone over to look, God called to him from within the bush, "Moses! Moses!"

And Moses said, "Here I am."

⁵"Do not come any closer," God said. "Take off your sandals, for the place where you are standing is holy ground." ⁶Then he said, "I am the God of your father, the God of Abraham, the God of Isaac and the God of Jacob." At this, Moses hid his face, because he was afraid to look at God.

⁷The LORD said, "I have indeed seen the misery of my people in Egypt. I have heard them crying out because of their slave drivers, and I am concerned about their suffering. ⁸So I have come down to rescue them from the hand of the Egyptians and to bring them up out of that land into a good and spacious land, a land flowing with milk and honey—the home of the Canaanites, Hittites, Amorites, Perizzites, Hivites and Jebusites. ⁹And now the cry of the Israelites has reached me, and I have seen the way the Egyptians are oppressing them. ¹⁰So now, go. I am sending you to Pharaoh to bring my people the Israelites out of Egypt."

¹¹But Moses said to God, "Who am I, that I should go to Pharaoh and bring the Israelites out of Egypt?"

¹²And God said, "I will be with you. And this will be the sign to you that it is I who have sent you: When you have brought the people out of Egypt, you*a* will worship God on this mountain."

¹³Moses said to God, "Suppose I go to the Israelites and say to them, 'The God of your fathers has sent me to you,' and they ask me, 'What is his name?' Then what shall I tell them?"

¹⁴God said to Moses, "I AM WHO I AM.*b* This is what you are to say to the Israelites: 'I AM has sent me to you.' "

¹⁵God also said to Moses, "Say to the Israelites, 'The LORD,*c* the God of your fathers—the God of Abraham, the God of Isaac and the God of Jacob—has sent me to you.' This is my name forever, the name by which I am to be remembered from generation to generation.

¹⁶"Go, assemble the elders of Israel and say to them, 'The LORD, the God of your fathers—the God of Abraham, Isaac and Jacob—appeared to me and said: I have watched over you and have seen what has been done to you in Egypt. ¹⁷And I have promised to bring you up out of your misery in Egypt into the land of the Canaanites, Hit-

THE MESSAGE

3.4 GOD saw that he had stopped to look. God called to him from out of the bush, "Moses! Moses!"

3.4 He said, "Yes? I'm right here!"

3.5 God said, "Don't come any closer. Remove your sandals from your feet. You're standing on holy ground."

3.6 Then he said, "I am the God of your father: The God of Abraham, the God of Isaac, the God of Jacob."

Moses hid his face, afraid to look at God.

3.7-8 GOD said, "I've taken a good, long look at the affliction of my people in Egypt. I've heard their cries for deliverance from their slave masters; I know all about their pain. And now I have come down to help them, pry them loose from the grip of Egypt, get them out of that country and bring them to a good land with wide-open spaces, a land lush with milk and honey, the land of the Canaanite, the Hittite, the Amorite, the Perizzite, the Hivite, and the Jebusite.

3.9-10 "The Israelite cry for help has come to me, and I've seen for myself how cruelly they're being treated by the Egyptians. It's time for you to go back: I'm sending you to Pharaoh to bring my people, the People of Israel, out of Egypt."

3.11 Moses answered God, "But why me? What makes you think that I could ever go to Pharaoh and lead the children of Israel out of Egypt?"

3.12 "I'll be with you," God said. "And this will be the proof that I am the one who sent you: When you have brought my people out of Egypt, you will worship God right here at this very mountain."

3.13 Then Moses said to God, "Suppose I go to the People of Israel and I tell them, 'The God of your fathers sent me to you'; and they ask me, 'What is his name?' What do I tell them?"

3.14 God said to Moses, "I-AM-WHO-I-AM. Tell the People of Israel, 'I-AM sent me to you.' "

3.15 God continued with Moses: "This is what you're to say to the Israelites: 'GOD, the God of your fathers, the God of Abraham, the God of Isaac, and the God of Jacob sent me to you.' This has always been my name, and this is how I always will be known.

3.16-17 "Now be on your way. Gather the leaders of Israel. Tell them, 'GOD, the God of your fathers, the God of Abraham, Isaac, and Jacob, appeared to me, saying, "I've looked into what's being done to you in Egypt, and I've determined to get you out of the affliction of Egypt and take you to the land of the Canaanite, the

---

a 12 The Hebrew is plural.   *b* 14 Or *I WILL BE WHAT I WILL BE*   *c* 15 The Hebrew for LORD sounds like and may be derived from the Hebrew for *I AM* in verse 14.

NEW INTERNATIONAL VERSION

tites, Amorites, Perizzites, Hivites and Jebusites—a land flowing with milk and honey.'

¹⁸"The elders of Israel will listen to you. Then you and the elders are to go to the king of Egypt and say to him, 'The LORD, the God of the Hebrews, has met with us. Let us take a three-day journey into the desert to offer sacrifices to the LORD our God.' ¹⁹But I know that the king of Egypt will not let you go unless a mighty hand compels him. ²⁰So I will stretch out my hand and strike the Egyptians with all the wonders that I will perform among them. After that, he will let you go.

²¹"And I will make the Egyptians favorably disposed toward this people, so that when you leave you will not go empty-handed. ²²Every woman is to ask her neighbor and any woman living in her house for articles of silver and gold and for clothing, which you will put on your sons and daughters. And so you will plunder the Egyptians."

SIGNS FOR MOSES

4 Moses answered, "What if they do not believe me or listen to me and say, 'The LORD did not appear to you'?"

²Then the LORD said to him, "What is that in your hand?"

"A staff," he replied.

³The LORD said, "Throw it on the ground."

Moses threw it on the ground and it became a snake, and he ran from it. ⁴Then the LORD said to him, "Reach out your hand and take it by the tail." So Moses reached out and took hold of the snake and it turned back into a staff in his hand. ⁵"This," said the LORD, "is so that they may believe that the LORD, the God of their fathers—the God of Abraham, the God of Isaac and the God of Jacob—has appeared to you."

⁶Then the LORD said, "Put your hand inside your cloak." So Moses put his hand into his cloak, and when he took it out, it was leprous,ᵃ like snow.

⁷"Now put it back into your cloak," he said. So Moses put his hand back into his cloak, and when he took it out, it was restored, like the rest of his flesh.

⁸Then the LORD said, "If they do not believe you or pay attention to the first miraculous sign, they may believe the second. ⁹But if they do not believe these two signs or listen to you, take some water from the Nile and pour it on the dry ground. The water you take from the river will become blood on the ground."

THE MESSAGE

Hittite, the Amorite, the Perizzite, the Hivite, and the Jebusite, a land brimming over with milk and honey." '

3.18   "Believe me, they will listen to you. Then you and the leaders of Israel will go to the king of Egypt and say to him: 'GOD, the God of the Hebrews, has met with us. Let us take a three-day journey into the wilderness where we will worship GOD—*our* God.'

3.19-22   "I know that the king of Egypt won't let you go unless forced to, so I'll intervene and hit Egypt where it hurts—oh, my miracles will send them reeling!—after which they'll be glad to send you off. I'll see to it that this people get a hearty send-off by the Egyptians—when you leave, you won't leave empty-handed! Each woman will ask her neighbor and any guests in her house for objects of silver and gold, for jewelry and extra clothes; you'll put them on your sons and daughters. Oh, you'll clean the Egyptians out!"

4.1   4 Moses objected, "They won't trust me. They won't listen to a word I say. They're going to say, 'GOD? Appear to him? Hardly!' "

4.2   So GOD said, "What's that in your hand?"

"A staff."

4.3   "Throw it on the ground." He threw it. It became a snake; Moses jumped back—fast!

4.4-5   GOD said to Moses, "Reach out and grab it by the tail." He reached out and grabbed it—and he was holding his staff again. "That's so they will trust that GOD appeared to you, the God of their fathers, the God of Abraham, the God of Isaac, and the God of Jacob."

4.6   GOD then said, "Put your hand inside your shirt." He slipped his hand under his shirt, then took it out. His hand had turned leprous, like snow.

4.7   He said, "Put your hand back under your shirt." He did it, then took it back out—as healthy as before.

4.8-9   "So if they don't trust you and aren't convinced by the first sign, the second sign should do it. But if it doesn't, if even after these two signs they don't trust you and listen to your message, take some water out of the Nile and pour it out on the dry land; the Nile water that you pour out will turn to blood when it hits the ground."

ᵃ 6 The Hebrew word was used for various diseases affecting the skin—not necessarily leprosy.

NEW INTERNATIONAL VERSION

¹⁰Moses said to the LORD, "O Lord, I have never been eloquent, neither in the past nor since you have spoken to your servant. I am slow of speech and tongue."

¹¹The LORD said to him, "Who gave man his mouth? Who makes him deaf or mute? Who gives him sight or makes him blind? Is it not I, the LORD? ¹²Now go; I will help you speak and will teach you what to say."

¹³But Moses said, "O Lord, please send someone else to do it."

¹⁴Then the LORD's anger burned against Moses and he said, "What about your brother, Aaron the Levite? I know he can speak well. He is already on his way to meet you, and his heart will be glad when he sees you. ¹⁵You shall speak to him and put words in his mouth; I will help both of you speak and will teach you what to do. ¹⁶He will speak to the people for you, and it will be as if he were your mouth and as if you were God to him. ¹⁷But take this staff in your hand so you can perform miraculous signs with it."

MOSES RETURNS TO EGYPT

¹⁸Then Moses went back to Jethro his father-in-law and said to him, "Let me go back to my own people in Egypt to see if any of them are still alive."

Jethro said, "Go, and I wish you well."

¹⁹Now the LORD had said to Moses in Midian, "Go back to Egypt, for all the men who wanted to kill you are dead." ²⁰So Moses took his wife and sons, put them on a donkey and started back to Egypt. And he took the staff of God in his hand.

²¹The LORD said to Moses, "When you return to Egypt, see that you perform before Pharaoh all the wonders I have given you the power to do. But I will harden his heart so that he will not let the people go. ²²Then say to Pharaoh, 'This is what the LORD says: Israel is my firstborn son, ²³and I told you, "Let my son go, so he may worship me." But you refused to let him go; so I will kill your firstborn son.' "

²⁴At a lodging place on the way, the LORD met ⌊Moses⌋ᵃ and was about to kill him. ²⁵But Zipporah took a flint knife, cut off her son's foreskin and touched ⌊Moses'⌋ feet with it.ᵇ "Surely you are a bridegroom of blood to me," she said. ²⁶So the LORD let him alone. (At that time she said "bridegroom of blood," referring to circumcision.)

ᵃ 24 Or ⌊Moses' son⌋; Hebrew him   ᵇ 25 Or and drew near ⌊Moses'⌋ feet

THE MESSAGE

4.10   Moses raised another objection to GOD: "Master, please, I don't talk well. I've never been good with words, neither before nor after you spoke to me. I stutter and stammer."

4.11-12   GOD said, "And who do you think made the human mouth? And who makes some mute, some deaf, some sighted, some blind? Isn't it I, GOD? So, get going. I'll be right there with you—with your mouth! I'll be right there to teach you what to say."

4.13   He said, "Oh, Master, please! Send somebody else!"

4.14-17   GOD got angry with Moses: "Don't you have a brother, Aaron the Levite? He's good with words, I know he is. He speaks very well. In fact, at this very moment he's on his way to meet you. When he sees you he's going to be glad. You'll speak to him and tell him what to say. I'll be right there with you as you speak and with him as he speaks, teaching you step by step. He will speak to the people for you. He'll act as your mouth, but you'll decide what comes out of it. Now take this staff in your hand; you'll use it to do the signs."

4.18   Moses went back to Jethro his father-in-law and said, "I need to return to my relatives who are in Egypt. I want to see if they're still alive." Jethro said, "Go. And peace be with you."

4.19   GOD said to Moses in Midian: "Go. Return to Egypt. All the men who wanted to kill you are dead."

4.20   So Moses took his wife and sons and put them on a donkey for the return trip to Egypt. He had a firm grip on the staff of God.

4.21-23   GOD said to Moses, "When you get back to Egypt, be prepared: All the wonders that I will do through you, you'll do before Pharaoh. But I will make him stubborn so that he will refuse to let the people go. Then you are to tell Pharaoh, 'GOD's Message: Israel is my son, my firstborn! I told you, "Free my son so that he can serve me." But you refused to free him. So now I'm going to kill your son, your firstborn.' "

✛

4.24-26   On the journey back, as they camped for the night, GOD met Moses and would have killed him but Zipporah took a flint knife and cut off her son's foreskin, and touched Moses' member with it. She said, "Oh! You're a bridegroom of blood to me!" Then GOD let him go. She used the phrase "bridegroom of blood" because of the circumcision.

✛

NEW INTERNATIONAL VERSION

²⁷The Lord said to Aaron, "Go into the desert to meet Moses." So he met Moses at the mountain of God and kissed him. ²⁸Then Moses told Aaron everything the Lord had sent him to say, and also about all the miraculous signs he had commanded him to perform.

²⁹Moses and Aaron brought together all the elders of the Israelites, ³⁰and Aaron told them everything the Lord had said to Moses. He also performed the signs before the people, ³¹and they believed. And when they heard that the Lord was concerned about them and had seen their misery, they bowed down and worshiped.

Bricks Without Straw

5 Afterward Moses and Aaron went to Pharaoh and said, "This is what the Lord, the God of Israel, says: 'Let my people go, so that they may hold a festival to me in the desert.' "

²Pharaoh said, "Who is the Lord, that I should obey him and let Israel go? I do not know the Lord and I will not let Israel go." ³Then they said, "The God of the Hebrews has met with us. Now let us take a three-day journey into the desert to offer sacrifices to the Lord our God, or he may strike us with plagues or with the sword."

⁴But the king of Egypt said, "Moses and Aaron, why are you taking the people away from their labor? Get back to your work!" ⁵Then Pharaoh said, "Look, the people of the land are now numerous, and you are stopping them from working."

⁶That same day Pharaoh gave this order to the slave drivers and foremen in charge of the people: ⁷"You are no longer to supply the people with straw for making bricks; let them go and gather their own straw. ⁸But require them to make the same number of bricks as before; don't reduce the quota. They are lazy; that is why they are crying out, 'Let us go and sacrifice to our God.' ⁹Make the work harder for the men so that they keep working and pay no attention to lies."

¹⁰Then the slave drivers and the foremen went out and said to the people, "This is what Pharaoh says: 'I will not give you any more straw. ¹¹Go and get your own straw wherever you can find it, but your work will not be reduced at all.' " ¹²So the people scattered all over Egypt to gather stubble to use for straw. ¹³The slave drivers kept pressing them, saying, "Complete the work required of you for each day, just as when you had straw." ¹⁴The Israelite foremen appointed by Pharaoh's slave drivers were beaten

THE MESSAGE

4.27-28 God spoke to Aaron, "Go and meet Moses in the wilderness." He went and met him at the mountain of God and kissed him. Moses told Aaron the message that God had sent him to speak and the wonders he had commanded him to do.

4.29-31 So Moses and Aaron proceeded to round up all the leaders of Israel. Aaron told them everything that God had told Moses and demonstrated the wonders before the people. And the people trusted and listened believingly that God was concerned with what was going on with the Israelites and knew all about their affliction. They bowed low and they worshiped.

Moses and Aaron and Pharaoh

5.1 5 After that Moses and Aaron approached Pharaoh. They said, "God, the God of Israel, says, 'Free my people so that they can hold a festival for me in the wilderness.' "

5.2 Pharaoh said, "And who is God that I should listen to him and send Israel off? I know nothing of this so-called 'God' and I'm certainly not going to send Israel off."

5.3 They said, "The God of the Hebrews has met with us. Let us take a three-day journey into the wilderness so we can worship our God lest he strike us with either disease or death."

5.4-5 But the king of Egypt said, "Why on earth, Moses and Aaron, would you suggest the people be given a holiday? Back to work!" Pharaoh went on, "Look, I've got all these people bumming around, and now you want to reward them with time off?"

5.6-9 Pharaoh took immediate action. He sent down orders to the slave-drivers and their underlings: "Don't provide straw for the people for making bricks as you have been doing. Make them get their own straw. And make them produce the same number of bricks—no reduction in their daily quotas! They're getting lazy. They're going around saying, 'Give us time off so we can worship our God.' Crack down on them. That'll cure them of their whining, their god-fantasies."

5.10-12 The slave-drivers and their underlings went out to the people with their new instructions. "Pharaoh's orders: No more straw provided. Get your own straw wherever you can find it. And not one brick less in your daily work quota!" The people scattered all over Egypt scrabbling for straw.

5.13 The slave-drivers were merciless, saying, "Complete your daily quota of bricks—the same number as when you were given straw."

5.14 The Israelite foremen whom the slave-drivers had appointed were beaten and badgered.

NEW INTERNATIONAL VERSION

and were asked, "Why didn't you meet your quota of bricks yesterday or today, as before?"

¹⁵Then the Israelite foremen went and appealed to Pharaoh: "Why have you treated your servants this way? ¹⁶Your servants are given no straw, yet we are told, 'Make bricks!' Your servants are being beaten, but the fault is with your own people."

¹⁷Pharaoh said, "Lazy, that's what you are—lazy! That is why you keep saying, 'Let us go and sacrifice to the LORD.' ¹⁸Now get to work. You will not be given any straw, yet you must produce your full quota of bricks."

¹⁹The Israelite foremen realized they were in trouble when they were told, "You are not to reduce the number of bricks required of you for each day." ²⁰When they left Pharaoh, they found Moses and Aaron waiting to meet them, ²¹and they said, "May the LORD look upon you and judge you! You have made us a stench to Pharaoh and his officials and have put a sword in their hand to kill us."

GOD PROMISES DELIVERANCE

²²Moses returned to the LORD and said, "O Lord, why have you brought trouble upon this people? Is this why you sent me? ²³Ever since I went to Pharaoh to speak in your name, he has brought trouble upon this people, and you have not rescued your people at all."

6 Then the LORD said to Moses, "Now you will see what I will do to Pharaoh: Because of my mighty hand he will let them go; because of my mighty hand he will drive them out of his country."

²God also said to Moses, "I am the LORD. ³I appeared to Abraham, to Isaac and to Jacob as God Almighty,ᵃ but by my name the LORDᵇ I did not make myself known to them.ᶜ ⁴I also established my covenant with them to give them the land of Canaan, where they lived as aliens. ⁵Moreover, I have heard the groaning of the Israelites, whom the Egyptians are enslaving, and I have remembered my covenant.

⁶"Therefore, say to the Israelites: 'I am the LORD, and I will bring you out from under the yoke of the Egyptians. I will free you from being slaves to them, and I will redeem you with an outstretched arm and with mighty acts of judgment. ⁷I will take you as my own people, and I will be your God. Then you will know that I am the LORD your God, who brought you out from

THE MESSAGE

"Why didn't you finish your quota of bricks yesterday or the day before—and now again today!"

⁵·¹⁵⁻¹⁶ The Israelite foremen came to Pharaoh and cried out for relief: "Why are you treating your servants like this? Nobody gives us any straw and they tell us, 'Make bricks!' Look at us—we're being beaten. And it's not our fault."

⁵·¹⁷⁻¹⁸ But Pharaoh said, "Lazy! That's what you are! Lazy! That's why you whine, 'Let us go so we can worship GOD.' Well then, go—go back to work. Nobody's going to give you straw, and at the end of the day you better bring in your full quota of bricks."

⁵·¹⁹ The Israelite foremen saw that they were in a bad way, having to go back and tell their workers, "Not one brick short in your daily quota."

⁵·²⁰⁻²¹ As they left Pharaoh, they found Moses and Aaron waiting to meet them. The foremen said to them, "May GOD see what you've done and judge you—you've made us stink before Pharaoh and his servants! You've put a weapon in his hand that's going to kill us!"

⁵·²²⁻²³ Moses went back to GOD and said, "My Master, why are you treating this people so badly? And why did you ever send me? From the moment I came to Pharaoh to speak in your name, things have only gotten worse for this people. And rescue? Does this look like rescue to you?"

⁶·¹ **6** GOD said to Moses, "Now you'll see what I'll do to Pharaoh: With a strong hand he'll send them out free; with a strong hand he'll drive them out of his land."

⁶·²⁻⁶ God continued speaking to Moses, reassuring him, "I am GOD. I appeared to Abraham, Isaac, and Jacob as The Strong God, but by my name GOD (I-Am-Present) I was not known to them. I also established my covenant with them to give them the land of Canaan, the country in which they lived as sojourners. But now I've heard the groanings of the Israelites whom the Egyptians continue to enslave and I've remembered my covenant. Therefore tell the Israelites:

⁶·⁶⁻⁸ "I am GOD. I will bring you out from under the cruel hard labor of Egypt. I will rescue you from slavery. I will redeem you, intervening with great acts of judgment. I'll take you as my own people and I'll be God to you. You'll know that I am GOD, *your* God who brings you out

---

ᵃ 3 Hebrew *El-Shaddai*   ᵇ 3 See note at Exodus 3:15.
ᶜ 3 Or *Almighty, and by my name the LORD did I not let myself be known to them?*

NEW INTERNATIONAL VERSION

under the yoke of the Egyptians. ⁸And I will bring you to the land I swore with uplifted hand to give to Abraham, to Isaac and to Jacob. I will give it to you as a possession. I am the LORD.' "

⁹Moses reported this to the Israelites, but they did not listen to him because of their discouragement and cruel bondage.

¹⁰Then the LORD said to Moses, ¹¹"Go, tell Pharaoh king of Egypt to let the Israelites go out of his country."

¹²But Moses said to the LORD, "If the Israelites will not listen to me, why would Pharaoh listen to me, since I speak with faltering lips*?"

FAMILY RECORD OF MOSES AND AARON

¹³Now the LORD spoke to Moses and Aaron about the Israelites and Pharaoh king of Egypt, and he commanded them to bring the Israelites out of Egypt.

¹⁴These were the heads of their families*ᵇ*:

The sons of Reuben the firstborn son of Israel were Hanoch and Pallu, Hezron and Carmi. These were the clans of Reuben.

¹⁵The sons of Simeon were Jemuel, Jamin, Ohad, Jakin, Zohar and Shaul the son of a Canaanite woman. These were the clans of Simeon.

¹⁶These were the names of the sons of Levi according to their records: Gershon, Kohath and Merari. Levi lived 137 years.

¹⁷The sons of Gershon, by clans, were Libni and Shimei.

¹⁸The sons of Kohath were Amram, Izhar, Hebron and Uzziel. Kohath lived 133 years.

¹⁹The sons of Merari were Mahli and Mushi.

These were the clans of Levi according to their records.

²⁰Amram married his father's sister Jochebed, who bore him Aaron and Moses. Amram lived 137 years.

²¹The sons of Izhar were Korah, Nepheg and Zicri.

²²The sons of Uzziel were Mishael, Elzaphan and Sithri.

²³Aaron married Elisheba, daughter of Amminadab and sister of Nahshon, and she bore him Nadab and Abihu, Eleazar and Ithamar.

²⁴The sons of Korah were Assir, Elkanah and Abiasaph. These were the Korahite clans.

THE MESSAGE

from under the cruel hard labor of Egypt. I'll bring you into the land that I promised to give Abraham, Isaac, and Jacob and give it to you as your own country. *I AM GOD.*"

6.9   But when Moses delivered this message to the Israelites, they didn't even hear him—they were that beaten down in spirit by the harsh slave conditions.

6.10-11   Then GOD said to Moses, "Go and speak to Pharaoh king of Egypt so that he will release the Israelites from his land."

6.12   Moses answered GOD, "Look—the Israelites won't even listen to me. How do you expect Pharaoh to? And besides, I stutter."

6.13   But GOD again laid out the facts to Moses and Aaron regarding the Israelites and Pharaoh king of Egypt, and he again commanded them to lead the Israelites out of the land of Egypt.

THE FAMILY TREE OF MOSES AND AARON

6.14   These are the heads of the tribes:

The sons of Reuben, Israel's firstborn: Hanoch, Pallu, Hezron, and Carmi—these are the families of Reuben.

6.15   The sons of Simeon: Jemuel, Jamin, Ohad, Jakin, Zohar, and Saul, the son of a Canaanite woman—these are the families of Simeon.

6.16   These are the names of the sons of Levi in the order of their birth: Gershon, Kohath, and Merari. Levi lived 137 years.

6.17   The sons of Gershon by family: Libni and Shimei.

6.18   The sons of Kohath: Amram, Izhar, Hebron, and Uzziel. Kohath lived to be 133.

6.19   The sons of Merari: Mahli and Mushi.

These are the sons of Levi in the order of their birth.

6.20   Amram married his aunt Jochebed and she had Aaron and Moses. Amram lived to be 137.

6.21   The sons of Izhar: Korah, Nepheg, and Zicri.

6.22   The sons of Uzziel: Mishael, Elzaphan, and Sithri.

6.23   Aaron married Elisheba, the daughter of Amminadab and sister of Nahshon, and she had Nadab and Abihu, Eleazar and Ithamar.

6.24   The sons of Korah: Assir, Elkanah, and Abiasaph. These are the families of the Korahites.

ᵃ 12 Hebrew *I am uncircumcised of lips*; also in verse 30
ᵇ 14 The Hebrew for *families* here and in verse 25 refers to units larger than clans.

NEW INTERNATIONAL VERSION

²⁵Eleazar son of Aaron married one of the daughters of Putiel, and she bore him Phinehas.

These were the heads of the Levite families, clan by clan.

²⁶It was this same Aaron and Moses to whom the LORD said, "Bring the Israelites out of Egypt by their divisions." ²⁷They were the ones who spoke to Pharaoh king of Egypt about bringing the Israelites out of Egypt. It was the same Moses and Aaron.

AARON TO SPEAK FOR MOSES

²⁸Now when the LORD spoke to Moses in Egypt, ²⁹he said to him, "I am the LORD. Tell Pharaoh king of Egypt everything I tell you."

³⁰But Moses said to the LORD, "Since I speak with faltering lips, why would Pharaoh listen to me?"

7 Then the LORD said to Moses, "See, I have made you like God to Pharaoh, and your brother Aaron will be your prophet. ²You are to say everything I command you, and your brother Aaron is to tell Pharaoh to let the Israelites go out of his country. ³But I will harden Pharaoh's heart, and though I multiply my miraculous signs and wonders in Egypt, ⁴he will not listen to you. Then I will lay my hand on Egypt and with mighty acts of judgment I will bring out my divisions, my people the Israelites. ⁵And the Egyptians will know that I am the LORD when I stretch out my hand against Egypt and bring the Israelites out of it."

⁶Moses and Aaron did just as the LORD commanded them. ⁷Moses was eighty years old and Aaron eighty-three when they spoke to Pharaoh.

AARON'S STAFF BECOMES A SNAKE

⁸The LORD said to Moses and Aaron, ⁹"When Pharaoh says to you, 'Perform a miracle,' then say to Aaron, 'Take your staff and throw it down before Pharaoh,' and it will become a snake."

¹⁰So Moses and Aaron went to Pharaoh and did just as the LORD commanded. Aaron threw his staff down in front of Pharaoh and his officials, and it became a snake. ¹¹Pharaoh then summoned wise men and sorcerers, and the Egyptian magicians also did the same things by their secret arts: ¹²Each one threw down his staff and it became a snake. But Aaron's staff swallowed up their staffs. ¹³Yet Pharaoh's heart became hard and he would not listen to them, just as the LORD had said.

THE MESSAGE

6.25 Aaron's son Eleazar married one of the daughters of Putiel and she had Phinehas.

These are the heads of the Levite families, family by family.

6.26-27 This is the Aaron and Moses whom GOD ordered: "Bring the Israelites out of the land of Egypt clan by clan." These are the men, Moses and Aaron, who told Pharaoh king of Egypt to release the Israelites from Egypt.

"I'LL MAKE YOU AS A GOD TO PHARAOH"

6.28 And that's how things stood when GOD next spoke to Moses in Egypt.

6.29 God addressed Moses, saying, "I am GOD. Tell Pharaoh king of Egypt everything I say to you."

6.30 And Moses answered, "Look at me. I stutter. Why would Pharaoh listen to me?"

7 GOD told Moses, "Look at me. I'll make you as a god to Pharaoh and your brother Aaron will be your prophet. You are to speak everything I command you, and your brother Aaron will tell it to Pharaoh. Then he will release the Israelites from his land. At the same time I am going to put Pharaoh's back up and follow it up by filling Egypt with signs and wonders. Pharaoh is not going to listen to you, but I will have my way against Egypt and bring out my soldiers, my people the Israelites, from Egypt by mighty acts of judgment. The Egyptians will realize that I am GOD when I step in and take the Israelites out of their country."

7.6-7 Moses and Aaron did exactly what GOD commanded. Moses was eighty and Aaron eighty-three when they spoke to Pharaoh.

✝

7.8-9 Then GOD spoke to Moses and Aaron. He said, "When Pharaoh speaks to you and says, 'Prove yourselves. Perform a miracle,' then tell Aaron, 'Take your staff and throw it down in front of Pharaoh: It will turn into a snake.'"

7.10 Moses and Aaron went to Pharaoh and did what GOD commanded. Aaron threw his staff down in front of Pharaoh and his servants, and it turned into a snake.

7.11-12 Pharaoh called in his wise men and sorcerers. The magicians of Egypt did the same thing by their incantations: each man threw down his staff and they all turned into snakes. But then Aaron's staff swallowed their staffs.

7.13 Yet Pharaoh was as stubborn as ever—he wouldn't listen to them, just as GOD had said.

NEW INTERNATIONAL VERSION

THE PLAGUE OF BLOOD

¹⁴Then the Lord said to Moses, "Pharaoh's heart is unyielding; he refuses to let the people go. ¹⁵Go to Pharaoh in the morning as he goes out to the water. Wait on the bank of the Nile to meet him, and take in your hand the staff that was changed into a snake. ¹⁶Then say to him, 'The Lord, the God of the Hebrews, has sent me to say to you: Let my people go, so that they may worship me in the desert. But until now you have not listened. ¹⁷This is what the Lord says: By this you will know that I am the Lord: With the staff that is in my hand I will strike the water of the Nile, and it will be changed into blood. ¹⁸The fish in the Nile will die, and the river will stink; the Egyptians will not be able to drink its water.' "

¹⁹The Lord said to Moses, "Tell Aaron, 'Take your staff and stretch out your hand over the waters of Egypt—over the streams and canals, over the ponds and all the reservoirs'—and they will turn to blood. Blood will be everywhere in Egypt, even in the wooden buckets and stone jars."

²⁰Moses and Aaron did just as the Lord had commanded. He raised his staff in the presence of Pharaoh and his officials and struck the water of the Nile, and all the water was changed into blood. ²¹The fish in the Nile died, and the river smelled so bad that the Egyptians could not drink its water. Blood was everywhere in Egypt.

²²But the Egyptian magicians did the same things by their secret arts, and Pharaoh's heart became hard; he would not listen to Moses and Aaron, just as the Lord had said. ²³Instead, he turned and went into his palace, and did not take even this to heart. ²⁴And all the Egyptians dug along the Nile to get drinking water, because they could not drink the water of the river.

THE PLAGUE OF FROGS

²⁵Seven days passed after the Lord struck the Nile.

8 ¹Then the Lord said to Moses, "Go to Pharaoh and say to him, 'This is what the Lord says: Let my people go, so that they may worship me. ²If you refuse to let them go, I will plague your whole country with frogs. ³The Nile will teem with frogs. They will come up into your palace and your bedroom and onto your bed, into the houses of your officials and on your people, and into your ovens and kneading troughs. ⁴The frogs will go up on you and your people and all your officials.' "

THE MESSAGE

STRIKE ONE: BLOOD

7.14-18 God said to Moses: "Pharaoh is a stubborn man. He refuses to release the people. First thing in the morning, go and meet Pharaoh as he goes down to the river. At the shore of the Nile take the staff that turned into a snake and say to him, 'God, the God of the Hebrews, sent me to you with this message, "Release my people so that they can worship me in the wilderness." So far you haven't listened. This is how you'll know that I am God. I am going to take this staff that I'm holding and strike this Nile River water: The water will turn to blood; the fish in the Nile will die; the Nile will stink; and the Egyptians won't be able to drink the Nile water.' "

7.19 God said to Moses, "Tell Aaron, 'Take your staff and wave it over the waters of Egypt—over its rivers, its canals, its ponds, all its bodies of water—so that they turn to blood.' There'll be blood everywhere in Egypt—even in the pots and pans."

7.20-21 Moses and Aaron did exactly as God commanded them. Aaron raised his staff and hit the water in the Nile with Pharaoh and his servants watching. All the water in the Nile turned into blood. The fish in the Nile died; the Nile stank; and the Egyptians couldn't drink the Nile water. The blood was everywhere in Egypt.

7.22-25 But the magicians of Egypt did the same thing with their incantations. Still Pharaoh remained stubborn. He wouldn't listen to them as God had said. He turned on his heel and went home, never giving it a second thought. But all the Egyptians had to dig inland from the river for water because they couldn't drink the Nile water.

Seven days went by after God had struck the Nile.

STRIKE TWO: FROGS

8.1-4 **8** God said to Moses, "Go to Pharaoh and tell him, 'God's Message: Release my people so they can worship me. If you refuse to release them, I'm warning you, I'll hit the whole country with frogs. The Nile will swarm with frogs—they'll come up into your houses, into your bedrooms and into your beds, into your servants' quarters, among the people, into your ovens and pots and pans. They'll be all over you, all over everyone—frogs everywhere, on and in everything!' "

NEW INTERNATIONAL VERSION

⁵Then the LORD said to Moses, "Tell Aaron, 'Stretch out your hand with your staff over the streams and canals and ponds, and make frogs come up on the land of Egypt.' "

⁶So Aaron stretched out his hand over the waters of Egypt, and the frogs came up and covered the land. ⁷But the magicians did the same things by their secret arts; they also made frogs come up on the land of Egypt.

⁸Pharaoh summoned Moses and Aaron and said, "Pray to the LORD to take the frogs away from me and my people, and I will let your people go to offer sacrifices to the LORD."

⁹Moses said to Pharaoh, "I leave to you the honor of setting the time for me to pray for you and your officials and your people that you and your houses may be rid of the frogs, except for those that remain in the Nile."

¹⁰"Tomorrow," Pharaoh said.

Moses replied, "It will be as you say, so that you may know there is no one like the LORD our God. ¹¹The frogs will leave you and your houses, your officials and your people; they will remain only in the Nile."

¹²After Moses and Aaron left Pharaoh, Moses cried out to the LORD about the frogs he had brought on Pharaoh. ¹³And the LORD did what Moses asked. The frogs died in the houses, in the courtyards and in the fields. ¹⁴They were piled into heaps, and the land reeked of them. ¹⁵But when Pharaoh saw that there was relief, he hardened his heart and would not listen to Moses and Aaron, just as the LORD had said.

THE PLAGUE OF GNATS

¹⁶Then the LORD said to Moses, "Tell Aaron, 'Stretch out your staff and strike the dust of the ground,' and throughout the land of Egypt the dust will become gnats." ¹⁷They did this, and when Aaron stretched out his hand with the staff and struck the dust of the ground, gnats came upon men and animals. All the dust throughout the land of Egypt became gnats. ¹⁸But when the magicians tried to produce gnats by their secret arts, they could not. And the gnats were on men and animals.

¹⁹The magicians said to Pharaoh, "This is the finger of God." But Pharaoh's heart was hard and he would not listen, just as the LORD had said.

THE PLAGUE OF FLIES

²⁰Then the LORD said to Moses, "Get up early in the morning and confront Pharaoh as he goes to the water and say to him, 'This is what the LORD says: Let my people go, so that they may worship me. ²¹If you do not let my people go, I

THE MESSAGE

8.5 GOD said to Moses, "Tell Aaron, 'Wave your staff over the rivers and canals and ponds. Bring up frogs on the land of Egypt.' "

8.6 Aaron stretched his staff over the waters of Egypt and a mob of frogs came up and covered the country.

8.7 But again the magicians did the same thing using their incantations—they also produced frogs in Egypt.

8.8 Pharaoh called in Moses and Aaron and said, "Pray to GOD to rid us of these frogs. I'll release the people so that they can make their sacrifices and worship GOD."

8.9 Moses said to Pharaoh, "Certainly. Set the time. When do you want the frogs out of here, away from your servants and people and out of your houses? You'll be rid of frogs except for those in the Nile."

8.10-11 "Make it tomorrow."

Moses said, "Tomorrow it is—so you'll realize that there is no God like our GOD. The frogs will be gone. You and your houses and your servants and your people, free of frogs. The only frogs left will be the ones in the Nile."

8.12-14 Moses and Aaron left Pharaoh, and Moses prayed to GOD about the frogs he had brought on Pharaoh. GOD responded to Moses' prayer: The frogs died off—houses, courtyards, fields, all free of frogs. They piled the frogs in heaps. The country reeked of dead frogs.

8.15 But when Pharaoh saw that he had some breathing room, he got stubborn again and wouldn't listen to Moses and Aaron. Just as GOD had said.

STRIKE THREE: GNATS

8.16 GOD said to Moses, "Tell Aaron, 'Take your staff and strike the dust. The dust will turn into gnats all over Egypt.' "

8.17 He did it. Aaron grabbed his staff and struck the dust of the Earth; it turned into gnats, gnats all over people and animals. All the dust of the Earth turned into gnats, gnats everywhere in Egypt.

8.18 The magicians tried to produce gnats with their incantations but this time they couldn't do it. There were gnats everywhere, all over people and animals.

8.19 The magicians said to Pharaoh, "This is God's doing." But Pharaoh was stubborn and wouldn't listen. Just as GOD had said.

STRIKE FOUR: FLIES

8.20-23 GOD said to Moses, "Get up early in the morning and confront Pharaoh as he goes down to the water. Tell him, 'GOD's Message: Release my people so they can worship me. If you don't re-

NEW INTERNATIONAL VERSION

will send swarms of flies on you and your officials, on your people and into your houses. The
houses of the Egyptians will be full of flies, and
even the ground where they are.

22 " 'But on that day I will deal differently with
the land of Goshen, where my people live; no
swarms of flies will be there, so that you will
know that I, the LORD, am in this land. 23I will
make a distinction[a] between my people and your
people. This miraculous sign will occur tomorrow.' "

24And the LORD did this. Dense swarms of
flies poured into Pharaoh's palace and into the
houses of his officials, and throughout Egypt the
land was ruined by the flies.

25Then Pharaoh summoned Moses and Aaron
and said, "Go, sacrifice to your God here in the
land."

26But Moses said, "That would not be right.
The sacrifices we offer the LORD our God would
be detestable to the Egyptians. And if we offer
sacrifices that are detestable in their eyes, will
they not stone us? 27We must take a three-day
journey into the desert to offer sacrifices to the
LORD our God, as he commands us."

28Pharaoh said, "I will let you go to offer sacrifices to the LORD your God in the desert, but
you must not go very far. Now pray for me."

29Moses answered, "As soon as I leave you, I
will pray to the LORD, and tomorrow the flies
will leave Pharaoh and his officials and his people. Only be sure that Pharaoh does not act deceitfully again by not letting the people go to offer sacrifices to the LORD."

30Then Moses left Pharaoh and prayed to the
LORD, 31and the LORD did what Moses asked: The
flies left Pharaoh and his officials and his people;
not a fly remained. 32But this time also Pharaoh
hardened his heart and would not let the people go.

THE PLAGUE ON LIVESTOCK

9 Then the LORD said to Moses, "Go to Pharaoh and say to him, 'This is what the LORD,
the God of the Hebrews, says: "Let my people
go, so that they may worship me." 2If you refuse
to let them go and continue to hold them back,
3the hand of the LORD will bring a terrible plague
on your livestock in the field—on your horses
and donkeys and camels and on your cattle and
sheep and goats. 4But the LORD will make a distinction between the livestock of Israel and that
of Egypt, so that no animal belonging to the Israelites will die.' "

5The LORD set a time and said, "Tomorrow the
LORD will do this in the land." 6And the next day

THE MESSAGE

lease my people, I'll release swarms of flies on
you, your servants, your people, and your
homes. The houses of the Egyptians and even
the ground under their feet will be thick with
flies. But when it happens, I'll set Goshen
where my people live aside as a sanctuary—no
flies in Goshen. That will show you that I am
GOD in this land. I'll make a sharp distinction
between your people and mine. This sign will
occur tomorrow.' "

8.24 And GOD did just that. Thick swarms of flies
in Pharaoh's palace and the houses of his servants. All over Egypt, the country ruined by
flies.

8.25 Pharaoh called in Moses and Aaron and said,
"Go ahead. Sacrifice to your God—but do it
here in this country."

8.26-27 Moses said, "That would not be wise. What
we sacrifice to our GOD would give great offense to Egyptians. If we openly sacrifice what
is so deeply offensive to Egyptians, they'll kill
us. Let us go three days' journey into the
wilderness and sacrifice to our GOD, just as he
instructed us."

8.28 Pharaoh said, "All right. I'll release you to go
and sacrifice to your GOD in the wilderness.
Only don't go too far. Now pray for me."

8.29 Moses said, "As soon as I leave here, I will
pray to GOD that tomorrow the flies will leave
Pharaoh, his servants, and his people. But don't
play games with us and change your mind
about releasing us to sacrifice to GOD."

8.30-32 Moses left Pharaoh and prayed to GOD. GOD
did what Moses asked. He got rid of the flies
from Pharaoh and his servants and his people.
There wasn't a fly left. But Pharaoh became
stubborn once again and wouldn't release the
people.

STRIKE FIVE: ANIMALS

9.1-4 9 GOD said to Moses, "Go to Pharaoh and tell
him, 'GOD, the God of the Hebrews, says:
Release my people so they can worship me. If
you refuse to release them and continue to hold
on to them, I'm giving you fair warning: GOD
will come down hard on your livestock out in
the fields—horses, donkeys, camels, cattle,
sheep—striking them with a severe disease.
GOD will draw a sharp line between the livestock of Israel and the livestock of Egypt. Not
one animal that belongs to the Israelites will
die.' "

9.5 Then GOD set the time: "Tomorrow GOD will
do this thing."

9.6-7 And the next day GOD did it. All the live-

---

a 23 Septuagint and Vulgate; Hebrew will put a deliverance

NEW INTERNATIONAL VERSION	THE MESSAGE

the LORD did it: All the livestock of the Egyptians died, but not one animal belonging to the Israelites died. ⁷Pharaoh sent men to investigate and found that not even one of the animals of the Israelites had died. Yet his heart was unyielding and he would not let the people go.

THE PLAGUE OF BOILS

⁸Then the LORD said to Moses and Aaron, "Take handfuls of soot from a furnace and have Moses toss it into the air in the presence of Pharaoh. ⁹It will become fine dust over the whole land of Egypt, and festering boils will break out on men and animals throughout the land."

¹⁰So they took soot from a furnace and stood before Pharaoh. Moses tossed it into the air, and festering boils broke out on men and animals. ¹¹The magicians could not stand before Moses because of the boils that were on them and on all the Egyptians. ¹²But the LORD hardened Pharaoh's heart and he would not listen to Moses and Aaron, just as the LORD had said to Moses.

THE PLAGUE OF HAIL

¹³Then the LORD said to Moses, "Get up early in the morning, confront Pharaoh and say to him, 'This is what the LORD, the God of the Hebrews, says: Let my people go, so that they may worship me, ¹⁴or this time I will send the full force of my plagues against you and against your officials and your people, so you may know that there is no one like me in all the earth. ¹⁵For by now I could have stretched out my hand and struck you and your people with a plague that would have wiped you off the earth. ¹⁶But I have raised you up*ᵃ* for this very purpose, that I might show you my power and that my name might be proclaimed in all the earth. ¹⁷You still set yourself against my people and will not let them go. ¹⁸Therefore, at this time tomorrow I will send the worst hailstorm that has ever fallen on Egypt, from the day it was founded till now. ¹⁹Give an order now to bring your livestock and everything you have in the field to a place of shelter, because the hail will fall on every man and animal that has not been brought in and is still out in the field, and they will die.' "

²⁰Those officials of Pharaoh who feared the word of the LORD hurried to bring their slaves and their livestock inside. ²¹But those who ignored the word of the LORD left their slaves and livestock in the field.

²²Then the LORD said to Moses, "Stretch out your hand toward the sky so that hail will fall all over Egypt—on men and animals and on everything growing in the fields of Egypt." ²³When

stock of Egypt died, but not one animal of the Israelites had died. Pharaoh sent men to find out what had happened and there it was: none of the livestock of the Israelites had died—not one death. But Pharaoh stayed stubborn. He wouldn't release the people.

STRIKE SIX: BOILS

9.8-11 GOD said to Moses and Aaron, "Take fistfuls of soot from a furnace and have Moses throw it into the air right before Pharaoh's eyes; it will become a film of fine dust all over Egypt and cause sores, an eruption of boils on people and animals throughout Egypt." So they took soot from a furnace, stood in front of Pharaoh, and threw it up into the air. It caused boils to erupt on people and animals. The magicians weren't able to compete with Moses this time because of the boils—they were covered with boils just like everyone else in Egypt.

9.12 GOD hardened Pharaoh in his stubbornness. He wouldn't listen, just as GOD had said to Moses.

STRIKE SEVEN: HAIL

9.13-19 GOD said to Moses, "Get up early in the morning and confront Pharaoh. Tell him, 'GOD, the God of the Hebrews, says: Release my people so they can worship me. This time I am going to strike you and your servants and your people with the full force of my power so you'll get it into your head that there's no one like me anywhere in all the Earth. You know that by now I could have struck you and your people with deadly disease and there would be nothing left of you, not a trace. But for one reason only I've kept you on your feet: To make you recognize my power so that my reputation spreads in all the Earth. You are still building yourself up at my people's expense. You are not letting them go. So here's what's going to happen: At this time tomorrow I'm sending a terrific hailstorm—there's never been a storm like this in Egypt from the day of its founding until now. So get your livestock under roof—everything exposed in the open fields, people and animals, will die when the hail comes down.' "

9.20-21 All of Pharaoh's servants who had respect for GOD's word got their workers and animals under cover as fast as they could, but those who didn't take GOD's word seriously left their workers and animals out in the field.

9.22 GOD said to Moses: "Stretch your hands to the skies. Signal the hail to fall all over Egypt on people and animals and crops exposed in the fields of Egypt."

ᵃ 16 Or have spared you

NEW INTERNATIONAL VERSION

Moses stretched out his staff toward the sky, the LORD sent thunder and hail, and lightning flashed down to the ground. So the LORD rained hail on the land of Egypt; 24hail fell and lightning flashed back and forth. It was the worst storm in all the land of Egypt since it had become a nation. 25Throughout Egypt hail struck everything in the fields—both men and animals; it beat down everything growing in the fields and stripped every tree. 26The only place it did not hail was the land of Goshen, where the Israelites were.

27Then Pharaoh summoned Moses and Aaron. "This time I have sinned," he said to them. "The LORD is in the right, and I and my people are in the wrong. 28Pray to the LORD, for we have had enough thunder and hail. I will let you go; you don't have to stay any longer."

29Moses replied, "When I have gone out of the city, I will spread out my hands in prayer to the LORD. The thunder will stop and there will be no more hail, so you may know that the earth is the LORD's. 30But I know that you and your officials still do not fear the LORD God."

31(The flax and barley were destroyed, since the barley had headed and the flax was in bloom. 32The wheat and spelt, however, were not destroyed, because they ripen later.)

33Then Moses left Pharaoh and went out of the city. He spread out his hands toward the LORD; the thunder and hail stopped, and the rain no longer poured down on the land. 34When Pharaoh saw that the rain and hail and thunder had stopped, he sinned again: He and his officials hardened their hearts. 35So Pharaoh's heart was hard and he would not let the Israelites go, just as the LORD had said through Moses.

THE PLAGUE OF LOCUSTS

10 Then the LORD said to Moses, "Go to Pharaoh, for I have hardened his heart and the hearts of his officials so that I may perform these miraculous signs of mine among them 2that you may tell your children and grandchildren how I dealt harshly with the Egyptians and how I performed my signs among them, and that you may know that I am the LORD."

3So Moses and Aaron went to Pharaoh and said to him, "This is what the LORD, the God of the Hebrews, says: 'How long will you refuse to humble yourself before me? Let my people go, so that they may worship me. 4If you refuse to let them go, I will bring locusts into your country tomorrow. 5They will cover the face of the ground so that it cannot be seen. They will devour what little you have left after the hail, in-

THE MESSAGE

9.23-26 Moses lifted his staff to the skies and GOD sent peals of thunder and hail shot through with lightning strikes. GOD rained hail down on the land of Egypt. The hail came, hail and lightning—a fierce hailstorm. There had been nothing like it in Egypt in its entire history. The hail hit hard all over Egypt. Everything exposed out in the fields, people and animals and crops, was smashed. Even the trees in the fields were shattered. Except for Goshen where the Israelites lived; there was no hail in Goshen.

9.27-28 Pharaoh summoned Moses and Aaron. He said, "I've sinned for sure this time—GOD is in the right and I and my people are in the wrong. Pray to GOD. We've had enough of GOD's thunder and hail. I'll let you go. The sooner you're out of here the better."

9.29-30 Moses said, "As soon as I'm out of the city, I'll stretch out my arms to GOD. The thunder will stop and the hail end so you'll know that the land is GOD's land. Still, I know that you and your servants have no respect for GOD."

9.31-32 (The flax and the barley were ruined, for they were just ripening, but the wheat and spelt weren't hurt—they ripen later.)

9.33 Moses left Pharaoh and the city and stretched out his arms to GOD. The thunder and hail stopped; the storm cleared.

9.34-35 But when Pharaoh saw that the rain and hail and thunder had stopped, he kept right on sinning, stubborn as ever, both he and his servants. Pharaoh's heart turned rock-hard. He refused to release the Israelites, as GOD had ordered through Moses.

STRIKE EIGHT: LOCUSTS

10.1-2 10 GOD said to Moses: "Go to Pharaoh. I've made him stubborn, him and his servants, so that I can force him to look at these signs and so you'll be able to tell your children and grandchildren how I toyed with the Egyptians, like a cat with a mouse; you'll tell them the stories of the signs that I brought down on them, so that you'll all know that I am GOD."

10.3-6 Moses and Aaron went to Pharaoh and said to him, "GOD, the God of the Hebrews, says, 'How long are you going to refuse to knuckle under? Release my people so that they can worship me. If you refuse to release my people, watch out; tomorrow I'm bringing locusts into your country. They'll cover every square inch of ground; no one will be able to see the ground. They'll devour everything left over from the

NEW INTERNATIONAL VERSION

cluding every tree that is growing in your fields. ⁶They will fill your houses and those of all your officials and all the Egyptians—something neither your fathers nor your forefathers have ever seen from the day they settled in this land till now.' " Then Moses turned and left Pharaoh.

⁷Pharaoh's officials said to him, "How long will this man be a snare to us? Let the people go, so that they may worship the LORD their God. Do you not yet realize that Egypt is ruined?"

⁸Then Moses and Aaron were brought back to Pharaoh. "Go, worship the LORD your God," he said. "But just who will be going?"

⁹Moses answered, "We will go with our young and old, with our sons and daughters, and with our flocks and herds, because we are to celebrate a festival to the LORD."

¹⁰Pharaoh said, "The LORD be with you—if I let you go, along with your women and children! Clearly you are bent on evil.ᵃ ¹¹No! Have only the men go; and worship the LORD, since that's what you have been asking for." Then Moses and Aaron were driven out of Pharaoh's presence.

¹²And the LORD said to Moses, "Stretch out your hand over Egypt so that locusts will swarm over the land and devour everything growing in the fields, everything left by the hail."

¹³So Moses stretched out his staff over Egypt, and the LORD made an east wind blow across the land all that day and all that night. By morning the wind had brought the locusts; ¹⁴they invaded all Egypt and settled down in every area of the country in great numbers. Never before had there been such a plague of locusts, nor will there ever be again. ¹⁵They covered all the ground until it was black. They devoured all that was left after the hail—everything growing in the fields and the fruit on the trees. Nothing green remained on tree or plant in all the land of Egypt.

¹⁶Pharaoh quickly summoned Moses and Aaron and said, "I have sinned against the LORD your God and against you. ¹⁷Now forgive my sin once more and pray to the LORD your God to take this deadly plague away from me."

¹⁸Moses then left Pharaoh and prayed to the LORD. ¹⁹And the LORD changed the wind to a very strong west wind, which caught up the locusts and carried them into the Red Sea.ᵇ Not a locust was left anywhere in Egypt. ²⁰But the LORD hardened Pharaoh's heart, and he would not let the Israelites go.

THE MESSAGE

hailstorm, even the saplings out in the fields—they'll clear-cut the trees. And they'll invade your houses, filling the houses of your servants, filling every house in Egypt. Nobody will have ever seen anything like this, from the time your ancestors first set foot on this soil until today.' "

Then he turned on his heel and left Pharaoh.

10.7   Pharaoh's servants said to him, "How long are you going to let this man harass us? Let these people go and worship their GOD. Can't you see that Egypt is on its last legs?"

10.8   So Moses and Aaron were brought back to Pharaoh. He said to them, "Go ahead then. Go worship your GOD. But just who exactly is going with you?"

10.9   Moses said, "We're taking young and old, sons and daughters, flocks and herds—this is our worship-celebration of GOD."

10.10-11   He said, "I'd sooner send you off with GOD's blessings than let you go with your children. Look, you're up to no good—it's written all over your faces. Nothing doing. Just the men are going—go ahead and worship GOD. That's what you want so badly." And they were thrown out of Pharaoh's presence.

10.12   GOD said to Moses: "Stretch your hand over Egypt and signal the locusts to cover the land of Egypt, devouring every blade of grass in the country, everything that the hail didn't get."

10.13   Moses stretched out his staff over the land of Egypt. GOD let loose an east wind. It blew that day and night. By morning the east wind had brought in the locusts.

10.14-15   The locusts covered the country of Egypt, settling over every square inch of Egypt; the place was thick with locusts. There never was an invasion of locusts like it in the past, and never will be again. The ground was completely covered, black with locusts. They ate everything, every blade of grass, every piece of fruit, anything that the hail didn't get. Nothing left but bare trees and bare fields—not a sign of green in the whole land of Egypt.

10.16-17   Pharaoh had Moses and Aaron back in no time. He said, "I've sinned against your GOD and against you. Overlook my sin one more time. Pray to your GOD to get me out of this—get death out of here!"

10.18-19   Moses left Pharaoh and prayed to GOD. GOD reversed the wind—a powerful west wind took the locusts and dumped them into the Red Sea. There wasn't a single locust left in the whole country of Egypt.

10.20   But GOD made Pharaoh stubborn as ever. He still didn't release the Israelites.

ᵃ 10 Or *Be careful, trouble is in store for you!*   ᵇ 19 Hebrew *Yam Suph*; that is, Sea of Reeds

NEW INTERNATIONAL VERSION

The Plague of Darkness

²¹Then the LORD said to Moses, "Stretch out your hand toward the sky so that darkness will spread over Egypt—darkness that can be felt." ²²So Moses stretched out his hand toward the sky, and total darkness covered all Egypt for three days. ²³No one could see anyone else or leave his place for three days. Yet all the Israelites had light in the places where they lived.

²⁴Then Pharaoh summoned Moses and said, "Go, worship the LORD. Even your women and children may go with you; only leave your flocks and herds behind."

²⁵But Moses said, "You must allow us to have sacrifices and burnt offerings to present to the LORD our God. ²⁶Our livestock too must go with us; not a hoof is to be left behind. We have to use some of them in worshiping the LORD our God, and until we get there we will not know what we are to use to worship the LORD."

²⁷But the LORD hardened Pharaoh's heart, and he was not willing to let them go. ²⁸Pharaoh said to Moses, "Get out of my sight! Make sure you do not appear before me again! The day you see my face you will die."

²⁹"Just as you say," Moses replied, "I will never appear before you again."

The Plague on the Firstborn

11 Now the LORD had said to Moses, "I will bring one more plague on Pharaoh and on Egypt. After that, he will let you go from here, and when he does, he will drive you out completely. ²Tell the people that men and women alike are to ask their neighbors for articles of silver and gold." ³(The LORD made the Egyptians favorably disposed toward the people, and Moses himself was highly regarded in Egypt by Pharaoh's officials and by the people.)

⁴So Moses said, "This is what the LORD says: 'About midnight I will go throughout Egypt. ⁵Every firstborn son in Egypt will die, from the firstborn son of Pharaoh, who sits on the throne, to the firstborn son of the slave girl, who is at her hand mill, and all the firstborn of the cattle as well. ⁶There will be loud wailing throughout Egypt—worse than there has ever been or ever will be again. ⁷But among the Israelites not a dog will bark at any man or animal.' Then you will know that the LORD makes a distinction between Egypt and Israel. ⁸All these officials of yours will

THE MESSAGE

Strike Nine: Darkness

10.21 GOD said to Moses: "Stretch your hand to the skies. Let darkness descend on the land of Egypt—a darkness so dark you can touch it."

10.22-23 Moses stretched out his hand to the skies. Thick darkness descended on the land of Egypt for three days. Nobody could see anybody. For three days no one could so much as move. Except for the Israelites: they had light where they were living.

10.24 Pharaoh called in Moses: "Go and worship GOD. Leave your flocks and herds behind. But go ahead and take your children."

10.25-26 But Moses said, "You have to let us take our sacrificial animals and offerings with us so we can sacrifice them in worship to our GOD. Our livestock has to go with us with not a hoof left behind; they are part of the worship of our GOD. And we don't know just what will be needed until we get there."

10.27 But GOD kept Pharaoh stubborn as ever. He wouldn't agree to release them.

10.28 Pharaoh said to Moses: "Get out of my sight! And watch your step. I don't want to ever see you again. If I lay eyes on you again, you're dead."

10.29 Moses said, "Have it your way. You won't see my face again."

Strike Ten: Death

11.1 **11** GOD said to Moses: "I'm going to hit Pharaoh and Egypt one final time, and then he'll let you go. When he releases you, that will be the end of Egypt for you; he won't be able to get rid of you fast enough.

11.2-3 "So here's what you do. Tell the people to ask, each man from his neighbor and each woman from her neighbor, for things made of silver and gold." GOD saw to it that the Egyptians liked the people. Also, Moses was greatly admired by the Egyptians, a respected public figure among both Pharaoh's servants and the people at large.

11.4-7 Then Moses confronted Pharaoh: "GOD's Message: 'At midnight I will go through Egypt and every firstborn child in Egypt will die, from the firstborn of Pharaoh, who sits on his throne, to the firstborn of the slave girl working at her hand mill. Also the firstborn of animals. Widespread wailing will erupt all over the country, lament such as has never been and never will be again. But against the Israelites—man, woman, or animal—there won't be so much as a dog's bark, so that you'll know that GOD makes a clear distinction between Egypt and Israel.'

11.8 "Then all these servants of yours will go to

NEW INTERNATIONAL VERSION

come to me, bowing down before me and saying, 'Go, you and all the people who follow you!' After that I will leave." Then Moses, hot with anger, left Pharaoh.

⁹The Lord had said to Moses, "Pharaoh will refuse to listen to you—so that my wonders may be multiplied in Egypt." ¹⁰Moses and Aaron performed all these wonders before Pharaoh, but the Lord hardened Pharaoh's heart, and he would not let the Israelites go out of his country.

THE PASSOVER

12 The Lord said to Moses and Aaron in Egypt, ²"This month is to be for you the first month, the first month of your year. ³Tell the whole community of Israel that on the tenth day of this month each man is to take a lamb*a* for his family, one for each household. ⁴If any household is too small for a whole lamb, they must share one with their nearest neighbor, having taken into account the number of people there are. You are to determine the amount of lamb needed in accordance with what each person will eat. ⁵The animals you choose must be year-old males without defect, and you may take them from the sheep or the goats. ⁶Take care of them until the fourteenth day of the month, when all the people of the community of Israel must slaughter them at twilight. ⁷Then they are to take some of the blood and put it on the sides and tops of the doorframes of the houses where they eat the lambs. ⁸That same night they are to eat the meat roasted over the fire, along with bitter herbs, and bread made without yeast. ⁹Do not eat the meat raw or cooked in water, but roast it over the fire—head, legs and inner parts. ¹⁰Do not leave any of it till morning; if some is left till morning, you must burn it. ¹¹This is how you are to eat it: with your cloak tucked into your belt, your sandals on your feet and your staff in your hand. Eat it in haste; it is the Lord's Passover.

¹²"On that same night I will pass through Egypt and strike down every firstborn—both men and animals—and I will bring judgment on all the gods of Egypt. I am the Lord. ¹³The blood will be a sign for you on the houses where you are; and when I see the blood, I will pass over you. No destructive plague will touch you when I strike Egypt.

¹⁴"This is a day you are to commemorate; for the generations to come you shall celebrate it as

THE MESSAGE

their knees, begging me to leave, 'Leave! You and all the people who follow you!' And I will most certainly leave."

Moses, seething with anger, left Pharaoh.

11.9 God said to Moses, "Pharaoh's not going to listen to a thing you say so that the signs of my presence and work are going to multiply in the land of Egypt."

11.10 Moses and Aaron had performed all these signs in Pharaoh's presence, but God turned Pharaoh more stubborn than ever—yet again he refused to release the Israelites from his land.

✝

12.1-10 **12** God said to Moses and Aaron while still in Egypt,"This month is to be the first month of the year for you. Address the whole community of Israel; tell them that on the tenth of this month each man is to take a lamb for his family, one lamb to a house. If the family is too small for a lamb, then share it with a close neighbor, depending on the number of persons involved. Be mindful of how much each person will eat. Your lamb must be a healthy male, one year old; you can select it from either the sheep or the goats. Keep it penned until the fourteenth day of this month and then slaughter it—the entire community of Israel will do this—at dusk. Then take some of the blood and smear it on the two doorposts and the lintel of the houses in which you will eat it. You are to eat the meat, roasted in the fire, that night, along with bread, made without yeast, and bitter herbs. Don't eat any of it raw or boiled in water; make sure it's roasted—the whole animal, head, legs, and innards. Don't leave any of it until morning; if there are leftovers, burn them in the fire.

12.11 "And here is how you are to eat it: Be fully dressed with your sandals on and your stick in your hand. Eat in a hurry; it's the Passover to God.

12.12-13 "I will go through the land of Egypt on this night and strike down every firstborn in the land of Egypt, whether human or animal, and bring judgment on all the gods of Egypt. I am God. The blood will serve as a sign on the houses where you live. When I see the blood I will pass over you—no disaster will touch you when I strike the land of Egypt.

12.14-16 "This will be a memorial day for you; you will celebrate it as a festival to God down

---

a 3 The Hebrew word can mean *lamb* or *kid*; also in verse 4.

NEW INTERNATIONAL VERSION

a festival to the LORD—a lasting ordinance. ¹⁵For seven days you are to eat bread made without yeast. On the first day remove the yeast from your houses, for whoever eats anything with yeast in it from the first day through the seventh must be cut off from Israel. ¹⁶On the first day hold a sacred assembly, and another one on the seventh day. Do no work at all on these days, except to prepare food for everyone to eat—that is all you may do.

¹⁷"Celebrate the Feast of Unleavened Bread, because it was on this very day that I brought your divisions out of Egypt. Celebrate this day as a lasting ordinance for the generations to come. ¹⁸In the first month you are to eat bread made without yeast, from the evening of the fourteenth day until the evening of the twenty-first day. ¹⁹For seven days no yeast is to be found in your houses. And whoever eats anything with yeast in it must be cut off from the community of Israel, whether he is an alien or native-born. ²⁰Eat nothing made with yeast. Wherever you live, you must eat unleavened bread."

²¹Then Moses summoned all the elders of Israel and said to them, "Go at once and select the animals for your families and slaughter the Passover lamb. ²²Take a bunch of hyssop, dip it into the blood in the basin and put some of the blood on the top and on both sides of the doorframe. Not one of you shall go out the door of his house until morning. ²³When the LORD goes through the land to strike down the Egyptians, he will see the blood on the top and sides of the doorframe and will pass over that doorway, and he will not permit the destroyer to enter your houses and strike you down.

²⁴"Obey these instructions as a lasting ordinance for you and your descendants. ²⁵When you enter the land that the LORD will give you as he promised, observe this ceremony. ²⁶And when your children ask you, 'What does this ceremony mean to you?' ²⁷then tell them, 'It is the Passover sacrifice to the LORD, who passed over the houses of the Israelites in Egypt and spared our homes when he struck down the Egyptians.'" Then the people bowed down and worshiped. ²⁸The Israelites did just what the LORD commanded Moses and Aaron.

²⁹At midnight the LORD struck down all the firstborn in Egypt, from the firstborn of Pharaoh, who sat on the throne, to the firstborn of the prisoner, who was in the dungeon, and the firstborn of all the livestock as well. ³⁰Pharaoh and all his officials and all the Egyptians got up during the night, and there was loud wailing in Egypt, for there was not a house without someone dead.

THE MESSAGE

through the generations, a fixed festival celebration to be observed always. You will eat unraised bread (matzoth) for seven days: On the first day get rid of all yeast from your houses—anyone who eats anything with yeast from the first day to the seventh day will be cut off from Israel. The first and the seventh days are set aside as holy; do no work on those days. Only what you have to do for meals; each person can do that.

12.17-20 "Keep the Festival of Unraised Bread! This marks the exact day I brought you out in force from the land of Egypt. Honor the day down through your generations, a fixed festival to be observed always. In the first month, beginning on the fourteenth day at evening until the twenty-first day at evening, you are to eat unraised bread. For those seven days not a trace of yeast is to be found in your houses. Anyone, whether a visitor or a native of the land, who eats anything raised shall be cut off from the community of Israel. Don't eat anything raised. Only matzoth."

12.21-23 Moses assembled all the elders of Israel. He said, "Select a lamb for your families and slaughter the Passover lamb. Take a bunch of hyssop and dip it in the bowl of blood and smear it on the lintel and on the two doorposts. No one is to leave the house until morning. GOD will pass through to strike Egypt down. When he sees the blood on the lintel and the two door posts, GOD will pass over the doorway; he won't let the destroyer enter your house to strike you down with ruin.

12.24-27 "Keep this word. It's the law for you and your children, forever. When you enter the land which GOD will give you as he promised, keep doing this. And when your children say to you, 'Why are we doing this?' tell them: 'It's the Passover-sacrifice to GOD who passed over the homes of the Israelites in Egypt when he hit Egypt with death but rescued us.'"

The people bowed and worshiped.

12.28 The Israelites then went and did what GOD had commanded Moses and Aaron. They did it all.

✠

12.29 At midnight GOD struck every firstborn in the land of Egypt, from the firstborn of Pharaoh, who sits on his throne, right down to the firstborn of the prisoner locked up in jail. Also the firstborn of the animals.

12.30 Pharaoh got up that night, he and all his servants and everyone else in Egypt—what wild wailing and lament in Egypt! There wasn't a house in which someone wasn't dead.

NEW INTERNATIONAL VERSION

THE EXODUS

31During the night Pharaoh summoned Moses and Aaron and said, "Up! Leave my people, you and the Israelites! Go, worship the LORD as you have requested. **32**Take your flocks and herds, as you have said, and go. And also bless me."

33The Egyptians urged the people to hurry and leave the country. "For otherwise," they said, "we will all die!" **34**So the people took their dough before the yeast was added, and carried it on their shoulders in kneading troughs wrapped in clothing. **35**The Israelites did as Moses instructed and asked the Egyptians for articles of silver and gold and for clothing. **36**The LORD had made the Egyptians favorably disposed toward the people, and they gave them what they asked for; so they plundered the Egyptians.

37The Israelites journeyed from Rameses to Succoth. There were about six hundred thousand men on foot, besides women and children. **38**Many other people went up with them, as well as large droves of livestock, both flocks and herds. **39**With the dough they had brought from Egypt, they baked cakes of unleavened bread. The dough was without yeast because they had been driven out of Egypt and did not have time to prepare food for themselves.

40Now the length of time the Israelite people lived in Egypt[a] was 430 years. **41**At the end of the 430 years, to the very day, all the LORD's divisions left Egypt. **42**Because the LORD kept vigil that night to bring them out of Egypt, on this night all the Israelites are to keep vigil to honor the LORD for the generations to come.

PASSOVER RESTRICTIONS

43The LORD said to Moses and Aaron, "These are the regulations for the Passover:

"No foreigner is to eat of it. **44**Any slave you have bought may eat of it after you have circumcised him, **45**but a temporary resident and a hired worker may not eat of it.

46"It must be eaten inside one house; take none of the meat outside the house. Do not break any of the bones. **47**The whole community of Israel must celebrate it.

48"An alien living among you who wants to celebrate the LORD's Passover must have all the males in his household circumcised; then he may take part like one born in the land. No uncircumcised male may eat of it. **49**The same law

---

a **40** Masoretic Text; Samaritan Pentateuch and Septuagint *Egypt and Canaan*

THE MESSAGE

12.31-32 Pharaoh called in Moses and Aaron that very night and said, "Get out of here and be done with you—you and your Israelites! Go worship GOD on your own terms. And yes, take your sheep and cattle as you've insisted, but go. And bless me."

12.33 The Egyptians couldn't wait to get rid of them; they pushed them to hurry up, saying, "We're all as good as dead."

12.34-36 The people grabbed their bread dough before it had risen, bundled their bread bowls in their cloaks and threw them over their shoulders. The Israelites had already done what Moses had told them; they had asked the Egyptians for silver and gold things and clothing. GOD saw to it that the Egyptians liked the people and so readily gave them what they asked for. Oh yes! They picked those Egyptians clean.

12.37-39 The Israelites moved on from Rameses to Succoth, about 600,000 on foot, besides their dependents. There was also a crowd of riffraff tagging along, not to mention the large flocks and herds of livestock. They baked unraised cakes with the bread dough they had brought out of Egypt; it hadn't raised—they'd been rushed out of Egypt and hadn't time to fix food for the journey.

THE PASSOVER

12.40-42 The Israelites had lived in Egypt 430 years. At the end of the 430 years, to the very day, GOD's entire army left Egypt. GOD kept watch all night, watching over the Israelites as he brought them out of Egypt. Because GOD kept watch, all Israel for all generations will honor GOD by keeping watch this night—a watchnight.

☩

12.43-47 GOD said to Moses and Aaron, "These are the rules for the Passover:

No foreigners are to eat it.
Any slave, if he's paid for and circumcised,
   can eat it.
No casual visitor or hired hand can eat it.
Eat it in one house—don't take the meat
   outside the house.
Don't break any of the bones.
The whole community of Israel is to be
   included in the meal.

12.48 "If an immigrant is staying with you and wants to keep the Passover to GOD, every male in his family must be circumcised, then he can participate in the Meal—he will then be treated as a native son. But no uncircumcised person can eat it.

NEW INTERNATIONAL VERSION	THE MESSAGE

applies to the native-born and to the alien living among you."

⁵⁰All the Israelites did just what the LORD had commanded Moses and Aaron. ⁵¹And on that very day the LORD brought the Israelites out of Egypt by their divisions.

CONSECRATION OF THE FIRSTBORN

13 The LORD said to Moses, ²"Consecrate to me every firstborn male. The first offspring of every womb among the Israelites belongs to me, whether man or animal."

³Then Moses said to the people, "Commemorate this day, the day you came out of Egypt, out of the land of slavery, because the LORD brought you out of it with a mighty hand. Eat nothing containing yeast. ⁴Today, in the month of Abib, you are leaving. ⁵When the LORD brings you into the land of the Canaanites, Hittites, Amorites, Hivites and Jebusites—the land he swore to your forefathers to give you, a land flowing with milk and honey—you are to observe this ceremony in this month: ⁶For seven days eat bread made without yeast and on the seventh day hold a festival to the LORD. ⁷Eat unleavened bread during those seven days; nothing with yeast in it is to be seen among you, nor shall any yeast be seen anywhere within your borders. ⁸On that day tell your son, 'I do this because of what the LORD did for me when I came out of Egypt.' ⁹This observance will be for you like a sign on your hand and a reminder on your forehead that the law of the LORD is to be on your lips. For the LORD brought you out of Egypt with his mighty hand. ¹⁰You must keep this ordinance at the appointed time year after year.

¹¹"After the LORD brings you into the land of the Canaanites and gives it to you, as he promised on oath to you and your forefathers, ¹²you are to give over to the LORD the first offspring of every womb. All the firstborn males of your livestock belong to the LORD. ¹³Redeem with a lamb every firstborn donkey, but if you do not redeem it, break its neck. Redeem every firstborn among your sons.

¹⁴"In days to come, when your son asks you, 'What does this mean?' say to him, 'With a mighty hand the LORD brought us out of Egypt, out of the land of slavery. ¹⁵When Pharaoh stubbornly refused to let us go, the LORD killed every firstborn in Egypt, both man and animal. This is why I sacrifice to the LORD the first male offspring of every womb and redeem each of my

12.49   "The same law applies both to the native and the immigrant who is staying with you."

12.50-51   All the Israelites did exactly as GOD commanded Moses and Aaron. That very day GOD brought the Israelites out of the land of Egypt, tribe by tribe.

✝

13.1-2 **13** GOD spoke to Moses, saying, "Consecrate every firstborn to me—the first one to come from the womb among the Israelites, whether person or animal, is mine."

13.3   Moses said to the people, "Always remember this day. This is the day when you came out of Egypt from a house of slavery. GOD brought you out of here with a powerful hand. Don't eat any raised bread.

13.4-5   "You are leaving in the spring month of Abib. When GOD brings you into the land of the Canaanite, the Hittite, the Amorite, the Hivite, and the Jebusite, which he promised to your fathers to give you, a land lavish with milk and honey, you are to observe this service during this month:

13.6   "You are to eat unraised bread for seven days; on the seventh day there is a festival celebration to GOD.

13.7   "Only unraised bread is to be eaten for seven days. There is not to be a trace of anything fermented—no yeast anywhere.

13.8   "Tell your child on that day: 'This is because of what GOD did for me when I came out of Egypt.'

13.9-10   "The day of observance will be like a sign on your hand, a memorial between your eyes, and the teaching of GOD in your mouth. It was with a powerful hand that GOD brought you out of Egypt. Follow these instructions at the set time, year after year after year.

13.11-13   "When GOD brings you into the land of the Canaanites, as he promised you and your fathers, and turns it over to you, you are to set aside the first birth out of every womb to GOD. Every first birth from your livestock belongs to GOD. You can redeem every first birth of a donkey if you want to by substituting a lamb; if you decide not to redeem it, you must break its neck.

13.13-16   "Redeem every firstborn child among your sons. When the time comes and your son asks you, 'What does this mean?' you tell him, 'GOD brought us out of Egypt, out of a house of slavery, with a powerful hand. When Pharaoh stubbornly refused to let us go, GOD killed every firstborn in Egypt, the firstborn of both humans and animals. That's why I make a sacrifice for every first male birth from the womb to

NEW INTERNATIONAL VERSION

firstborn sons.' ¹⁶And it will be like a sign on your hand and a symbol on your forehead that the LORD brought us out of Egypt with his mighty hand."

CROSSING THE SEA

¹⁷When Pharaoh let the people go, God did not lead them on the road through the Philistine country, though that was shorter. For God said, "If they face war, they might change their minds and return to Egypt." ¹⁸So God led the people around by the desert road toward the Red Sea.ᵃ The Israelites went up out of Egypt armed for battle.

¹⁹Moses took the bones of Joseph with him because Joseph had made the sons of Israel swear an oath. He had said, "God will surely come to your aid, and then you must carry my bones up with you from this place."ᵇ

²⁰After leaving Succoth they camped at Etham on the edge of the desert. ²¹By day the LORD went ahead of them in a pillar of cloud to guide them on their way and by night in a pillar of fire to give them light, so that they could travel by day or night. ²²Neither the pillar of cloud by day nor the pillar of fire by night left its place in front of the people.

14 Then the LORD said to Moses, ²"Tell the Israelites to turn back and encamp near Pi Hahiroth, between Migdol and the sea. They are to encamp by the sea, directly opposite Baal Zephon. ³Pharaoh will think, 'The Israelites are wandering around the land in confusion, hemmed in by the desert.' ⁴And I will harden Pharaoh's heart, and he will pursue them. But I will gain glory for myself through Pharaoh and all his army, and the Egyptians will know that I am the LORD." So the Israelites did this.

⁵When the king of Egypt was told that the people had fled, Pharaoh and his officials changed their minds about them and said, "What have we done? We have let the Israelites go and have lost their services!" ⁶So he had his chariot made ready and took his army with him. ⁷He took six hundred of the best chariots, along with all the other chariots of Egypt, with officers over all of them. ⁸The LORD hardened the heart of Pharaoh king of Egypt, so that he pursued the Israelites, who were marching out boldly. ⁹The Egyptians—all Pharaoh's horses and chariots, horsemenᶜ and troops—pursued the Is-

THE MESSAGE

GOD and redeem every firstborn son.' The observance functions like a sign on your hands or a symbol on the middle of your forehead: GOD brought us out of Egypt with a powerful hand."

13.17 It so happened that after Pharaoh released the people, God didn't lead them by the road through the land of the Philistines, which was the shortest route, for God thought, "If the people encounter war, they'll change their minds and go back to Egypt."

13.18 So God led the people on the wilderness road, looping around to the Red Sea. The Israelites left Egypt in military formation.

13.19 Moses took the bones of Joseph with him, for Joseph had made the Israelites solemnly swear to do it, saying, "God will surely hold you accountable, so make sure you bring my bones from here with you."

13.20-22 They moved on from Succoth and then camped at Etham at the edge of the wilderness. GOD went ahead of them in a Pillar of Cloud during the day to guide them on the way, and at night in a Pillar of Fire to give them light; thus they could travel both day and night. The Pillar of Cloud by day and the Pillar of Fire by night never left the people.

THE STORY AND SONG OF SALVATION

14.1-2 **14** GOD spoke to Moses: "Tell the Israelites to turn around and make camp at Pi Hahiroth, between Migdol and the sea. Camp on the shore of the sea opposite Baal Zephon.

14.3-4 "Pharaoh will think, 'The Israelites are lost; they're confused. The wilderness has closed in on them.' Then I'll make Pharaoh's heart stubborn again and he'll chase after them. And I'll use Pharaoh and his army to put my Glory on display. Then the Egyptians will realize that I am GOD."

And that's what happened.

14.5-7 When the king of Egypt was told that the people were gone, he and his servants changed their minds. They said, "What have we done, letting Israel, our slave labor, go free?" So he had his chariots harnessed up and got his army together. He took six hundred of his best chariots, with the rest of the Egyptian chariots and their drivers coming along.

14.8-9 GOD made Pharaoh king of Egypt stubborn, determined to chase the Israelites as they walked out on him without even looking back. The Egyptians gave chase and caught up with them where they had made camp by the sea— all Pharaoh's horse-drawn chariots and their

---

ᵃ 18 Hebrew *Yam Suph*; that is, Sea of Reeds
ᵇ 19 See Gen. 50:25.   ᶜ 9 Or *charioteers*; also in verses 17, 18, 23, 26 and 28

NEW INTERNATIONAL VERSION

raelites and overtook them as they camped by the sea near Pi Hahiroth, opposite Baal Zephon.

¹⁰As Pharaoh approached, the Israelites looked up, and there were the Egyptians, marching after them. They were terrified and cried out to the LORD. ¹¹They said to Moses, "Was it because there were no graves in Egypt that you brought us to the desert to die? What have you done to us by bringing us out of Egypt? ¹²Didn't we say to you in Egypt, 'Leave us alone; let us serve the Egyptians'? It would have been better for us to serve the Egyptians than to die in the desert!"

¹³Moses answered the people, "Do not be afraid. Stand firm and you will see the deliverance the LORD will bring you today. The Egyptians you see today you will never see again. ¹⁴The LORD will fight for you; you need only to be still."

¹⁵Then the LORD said to Moses, "Why are you crying out to me? Tell the Israelites to move on. ¹⁶Raise your staff and stretch out your hand over the sea to divide the water so that the Israelites can go through the sea on dry ground. ¹⁷I will harden the hearts of the Egyptians so that they will go in after them. And I will gain glory through Pharaoh and all his army, through his chariots and his horsemen. ¹⁸The Egyptians will know that I am the LORD when I gain glory through Pharaoh, his chariots and his horsemen."

¹⁹Then the angel of God, who had been traveling in front of Israel's army, withdrew and went behind them. The pillar of cloud also moved from in front and stood behind them, ²⁰coming between the armies of Egypt and Israel. Throughout the night the cloud brought darkness to the one side and light to the other side; so neither went near the other all night long.

²¹Then Moses stretched out his hand over the sea, and all that night the LORD drove the sea back with a strong east wind and turned it into dry land. The waters were divided, ²²and the Israelites went through the sea on dry ground, with a wall of water on their right and on their left.

²³The Egyptians pursued them, and all Pharaoh's horses and chariots and horsemen followed them into the sea. ²⁴During the last watch of the night the LORD looked down from the pillar of fire and cloud at the Egyptian army and threw it into confusion. ²⁵He made the wheels of their chariots come off ᵃ so that they had difficulty driving. And the Egyptians said, "Let's get away

---

ᵃ 25 Or He jammed the wheels of their chariots (see Samaritan Pentateuch, Septuagint and Syriac)

THE MESSAGE

riders, all his foot soldiers there at Pi Hahiroth opposite Baal Zephon.

14.10-12 As Pharaoh approached, the Israelites looked up and saw them—Egyptians! Coming at them!

They were totally afraid. They cried out in terror to GOD. They told Moses, "Weren't the cemeteries large enough in Egypt so that you had to take us out here in the wilderness to die? What have you done to us, taking us out of Egypt? Back in Egypt didn't we tell you this would happen? Didn't we tell you, 'Leave us alone here in Egypt—we're better off as slaves in Egypt than as corpses in the wilderness.'"

14.13 Moses spoke to the people: "Don't be afraid. Stand firm and watch GOD do his work of salvation for you today. Take a good look at the Egyptians today for you're never going to see them again.

14.14 GOD will fight the battle for you.
And you? You keep your mouths shut!"

☩

14.15-16 GOD said to Moses: "Why cry out to me? Speak to the Israelites. Order them to get moving. Hold your staff high and stretch out your hand over the sea: Split the sea! The Israelites will walk through the sea on dry ground.

14.17-18 "Meanwhile I'll make sure the Egyptians keep up their stubborn chase—I'll use Pharaoh and his entire army, his chariots and horsemen, to put my Glory on display so that the Egyptians will realize that I am GOD."

14.19-20 The angel of God that had been leading the camp of Israel now shifted and got behind them. And the Pillar of Cloud that had been in front also shifted to the rear. The Cloud was now between the camp of Egypt and the camp of Israel. The Cloud enshrouded one camp in darkness and flooded the other with light. The two camps didn't come near each other all night.

14.21 Then Moses stretched out his hand over the sea and GOD, with a terrific east wind all night long, made the sea go back. He made the sea dry ground. The seawaters split.

14.22-25 The Israelites walked through the sea on dry ground with the waters a wall to the right and to the left. The Egyptians came after them in full pursuit, every horse and chariot and driver of Pharaoh racing into the middle of the sea. It was now the morning watch. GOD looked down from the Pillar of Fire and Cloud on the Egyptian army and threw them into a panic. He clogged the wheels of their chariots; they were stuck in the mud.

NEW INTERNATIONAL VERSION

from the Israelites! The LORD is fighting for them against Egypt."

²⁶Then the LORD said to Moses, "Stretch out your hand over the sea so that the waters may flow back over the Egyptians and their chariots and horsemen." ²⁷Moses stretched out his hand over the sea, and at daybreak the sea went back to its place. The Egyptians were fleeing toward*ᵃ* it, and the LORD swept them into the sea. ²⁸The water flowed back and covered the chariots and horsemen—the entire army of Pharaoh that had followed the Israelites into the sea. Not one of them survived.

²⁹But the Israelites went through the sea on dry ground, with a wall of water on their right and on their left. ³⁰That day the LORD saved Israel from the hands of the Egyptians, and Israel saw the Egyptians lying dead on the shore. ³¹And when the Israelites saw the great power the LORD displayed against the Egyptians, the people feared the LORD and put their trust in him and in Moses his servant.

THE SONG OF MOSES AND MIRIAM

15 Then Moses and the Israelites sang this song to the LORD:

"I will sing to the LORD,
  for he is highly exalted.
The horse and its rider
  he has hurled into the sea.
²The LORD is my strength and my song;
  he has become my salvation.
He is my God, and I will praise him,
  my father's God, and I will exalt him.
³The LORD is a warrior;
  the LORD is his name.
⁴Pharaoh's chariots and his army
  he has hurled into the sea.
The best of Pharaoh's officers
  are drowned in the Red Sea.*ᵇ*
⁵The deep waters have covered them;
  they sank to the depths like a stone.

⁶"Your right hand, O LORD,
  was majestic in power.
Your right hand, O LORD,
  shattered the enemy.
⁷In the greatness of your majesty
  you threw down those who opposed you.
You unleashed your burning anger;
  it consumed them like stubble.
⁸By the blast of your nostrils
  the waters piled up.

^a 27 Or *from*   ^b 4 Hebrew *Yam Suph*; that is, Sea of Reeds;
also in verse 22

THE MESSAGE

The Egyptians said, "Run from Israel! GOD is fighting on their side and against Egypt!"

14.26 GOD said to Moses, "Stretch out your hand over the sea and the waters will come back over the Egyptians, over their chariots, over their horsemen."

14.27-28 Moses stretched his hand out over the sea: As the day broke and the Egyptians were running, the sea returned to its place as before. GOD dumped the Egyptians in the middle of the sea. The waters returned, drowning the chariots and riders of Pharaoh's army that had chased after Israel into the sea. Not one of them survived.

14.29-31 But the Israelites walked right through the middle of the sea on dry ground, the waters forming a wall to the right and to the left. GOD delivered Israel that day from the oppression of the Egyptians. And Israel looked at the Egyptian dead, washed up on the shore of the sea, and realized the tremendous power that GOD brought against the Egyptians. The people were in reverent awe before GOD and trusted in GOD and his servant Moses.

✝

15.1-8 **15** Then Moses and the Israelites sang this song to GOD, giving voice together,

I'm singing my heart out to GOD—what a
    victory!
  He pitched horse and rider into the sea.
GOD is my strength, GOD is my song,
  and, yes! GOD is my salvation.
This is the kind of God I have
  and I'm telling the world!
This is the God of my father—
  I'm spreading the news far and wide!
GOD is a fighter,
  pure GOD, through and through.
Pharaoh's chariots and army
  he dumped in the sea,
The elite of his officers
  he drowned in the Red Sea.
Wild ocean waters poured over them;
  they sank like a rock in the deep blue
    sea.
Your strong right hand, GOD, shimmers
    with power;
  your strong right hand shatters the
    enemy.
In your mighty majesty
  you smash your upstart enemies,
You let loose your hot anger
  and burn them to a crisp.
At a blast from your nostrils
  the waters piled up;

NEW INTERNATIONAL VERSION

The surging waters stood firm like a wall;
　　the deep waters congealed in the heart of
　　　the sea.

9 "The enemy boasted,
　'I will pursue, I will overtake them.
I will divide the spoils;
　I will gorge myself on them.
I will draw my sword
　and my hand will destroy them.'
10 But you blew with your breath,
　and the sea covered them.
They sank like lead
　in the mighty waters.

11 "Who among the gods is like you, O LORD?
　Who is like you—
　　majestic in holiness,
　　awesome in glory,
　　working wonders?
12 You stretched out your right hand
　and the earth swallowed them.

13 "In your unfailing love you will lead
　the people you have redeemed.
In your strength you will guide them
　to your holy dwelling.
14 The nations will hear and tremble;
　anguish will grip the people of Philistia.
15 The chiefs of Edom will be terrified,
　the leaders of Moab will be seized with
　　trembling,
the people a of Canaan will melt away;
16 　terror and dread will fall upon them.
By the power of your arm
　they will be as still as a stone—
until your people pass by, O LORD,
　until the people you bought b pass by.
17 You will bring them in and plant them
　on the mountain of your inheritance—
the place, O LORD, you made for your
　　dwelling,
　the sanctuary, O Lord, your hands
　　established.
18 The LORD will reign
　for ever and ever."

19 When Pharaoh's horses, chariots and horsemen c went into the sea, the LORD brought the
waters of the sea back over them, but the Israelites walked through the sea on dry ground.
20 Then Miriam the prophetess, Aaron's sister,

a 15 Or rulers　　b 16 Or created　　c 19 Or charioteers

THE MESSAGE

Tumbling streams dammed up,
　wild oceans curdled into a swamp.

15.9　The enemy spoke,
　"I'll pursue, I'll hunt them down,
I'll divide up the plunder,
　I'll glut myself on them;
I'll pull out my sword,
　my fist will send them reeling."

15.10-11　You blew with all your might
　and the sea covered them.
They sank like a lead weight
　in the majestic waters.
Who compares with you
　among gods, O GOD?
Who compares with you in power,
　in holy majesty,
In awesome praises,
　wonder-working God?

15.12-13　You stretched out your right hand
　and the Earth swallowed them up.
But the people you redeemed,
　you led in merciful love;
You guided them under your protection
　to your holy pasture.

15.14-18　When people heard, they were scared;
　Philistines writhed and trembled;
Yes, even the head men in Edom were
　　shaken,
　and the big bosses in Moab.
Everybody in Canaan
　panicked and fell faint.
Dread and terror
　sent them reeling.
Before your brandished right arm
　they were struck dumb like a stone,
Until your people crossed over and entered,
　O GOD,
　until the people you made crossed over
　　and entered.
You brought them and planted them
　on the mountain of your heritage,
The place where you live,
　the place you made,
Your sanctuary, Master,
　that you established with your own
　　hands.
Let GOD rule
　forever, for eternity!

15.19　Yes, Pharaoh's horses and chariots and riders
went into the sea and GOD turned the waters
back on them; but the Israelites walked on dry
land right through the middle of the sea.

✛

15.20-21　Miriam the prophetess, Aaron's sister, took a

NEW INTERNATIONAL VERSION

took a tambourine in her hand, and all the women followed her, with tambourines and dancing. 21Miriam sang to them:

"Sing to the LORD,
for he is highly exalted.
The horse and its rider
he has hurled into the sea."

THE WATERS OF MARAH AND ELIM

22Then Moses led Israel from the Red Sea and they went into the Desert of Shur. For three days they traveled in the desert without finding water. 23When they came to Marah, they could not drink its water because it was bitter. (That is why the place is called Marah. a) 24So the people grumbled against Moses, saying, "What are we to drink?"

25Then Moses cried out to the LORD, and the LORD showed him a piece of wood. He threw it into the water, and the water became sweet.

There the LORD made a decree and a law for them, and there he tested them. 26He said, "If you listen carefully to the voice of the LORD your God and do what is right in his eyes, if you pay attention to his commands and keep all his decrees, I will not bring on you any of the diseases I brought on the Egyptians, for I am the LORD, who heals you."

27Then they came to Elim, where there were twelve springs and seventy palm trees, and they camped there near the water.

MANNA AND QUAIL

16 The whole Israelite community set out from Elim and came to the Desert of Sin, which is between Elim and Sinai, on the fifteenth day of the second month after they had come out of Egypt. 2In the desert the whole community grumbled against Moses and Aaron. 3The Israelites said to them, "If only we had died by the LORD's hand in Egypt! There we sat around pots of meat and ate all the food we wanted, but you have brought us out into this desert to starve this entire assembly to death."

4Then the LORD said to Moses, "I will rain down bread from heaven for you. The people are to go out each day and gather enough for that day. In this way I will test them and see whether they will follow my instructions. 5On the sixth day they are to prepare what they bring in, and that is to be twice as much as they gather on the other days."

6So Moses and Aaron said to all the Israelites, "In the evening you will know that it was the LORD who brought you out of Egypt, 7and in the

---

a 23 *Marah* means *bitter.*

THE MESSAGE

tambourine, and all the women followed her with tambourines, dancing. Miriam led them in singing,

Sing to GOD—
what a victory!
He pitched horse and rider
into the sea!

TRAVELING THROUGH THE WILDERNESS

15.22-24 Moses led Israel from the Red Sea on to the Wilderness of Shur. They traveled for three days through the wilderness without finding any water. They got to Marah, but they couldn't drink the water at Marah; it was bitter. That's why they called the place Marah (Bitter). And the people complained to Moses, "So what are we supposed to drink?"

15.25 So Moses cried out in prayer to GOD. GOD pointed him to a stick of wood. Moses threw it into the water and the water turned sweet.

15.26 That's the place where GOD set up rules and procedures; that's where he started testing them.

GOD said, "If you listen, listen obediently to how GOD tells you to live in his presence, obeying his commandments and keeping all his laws, then I won't strike you with all the diseases that I inflicted on the Egyptians; I am GOD your healer."

15.27 They came to Elim where there were twelve springs of water and seventy palm trees. They set up camp there by the water.

16.1-3 **16** On the fifteenth day of the second month after they had left Egypt, the whole company of Israel moved on from Elim to the Wilderness of Sin which is between Elim and Sinai. The whole company of Israel complained against Moses and Aaron there in the wilderness. The Israelites said, "Why didn't GOD let us die in comfort in Egypt where we had lamb stew and all the bread we could eat? You've brought us out into this wilderness to starve us to death, the whole company of Israel!"

16.4-5 GOD said to Moses, "I'm going to rain bread down from the skies for you. The people will go out and gather each day's ration. I'm going to test them to see if they'll live according to my Teaching or not. On the sixth day, when they prepare what they have gathered, it will turn out to be twice as much as their daily ration."

16.6-7 Moses and Aaron told the People of Israel, "This evening you will know that it is GOD who brought you out of Egypt; and in the morning

NEW INTERNATIONAL VERSION

morning you will see the glory of the LORD, because he has heard your grumbling against him. Who are we, that you should grumble against us?" ⁸Moses also said, "You will know that it was the LORD when he gives you meat to eat in the evening and all the bread you want in the morning, because he has heard your grumbling against him. Who are we? You are not grumbling against us, but against the LORD."

⁹Then Moses told Aaron, "Say to the entire Israelite community, 'Come before the LORD, for he has heard your grumbling.' "

¹⁰While Aaron was speaking to the whole Israelite community, they looked toward the desert, and there was the glory of the LORD appearing in the cloud.

¹¹The LORD said to Moses, ¹²"I have heard the grumbling of the Israelites. Tell them, 'At twilight you will eat meat, and in the morning you will be filled with bread.' Then you will know that I am the LORD your God.' "

¹³That evening quail came and covered the camp, and in the morning there was a layer of dew around the camp. ¹⁴When the dew was gone, thin flakes like frost on the ground appeared on the desert floor. ¹⁵When the Israelites saw it, they said to each other, "What is it?" For they did not know what it was.

Moses said to them, "It is the bread the LORD has given you to eat. ¹⁶This is what the LORD has commanded: 'Each one is to gather as much as he needs. Take an omer*ᵃ* for each person you have in your tent.' "

¹⁷The Israelites did as they were told; some gathered much, some little. ¹⁸And when they measured it by the omer, he who gathered much did not have too much, and he who gathered little did not have too little. Each one gathered as much as he needed.

¹⁹Then Moses said to them, "No one is to keep any of it until morning."

²⁰However, some of them paid no attention to Moses; they kept part of it until morning, but it was full of maggots and began to smell. So Moses was angry with them.

²¹Each morning everyone gathered as much as he needed, and when the sun grew hot, it melted away. ²²On the sixth day, they gathered twice as much—two omers*ᵇ* for each person—and the leaders of the community came and reported this to Moses. ²³He said to them, "This is what the LORD commanded: 'Tomorrow is to be a day of rest, a holy Sabbath to the LORD. So bake

THE MESSAGE

you will see the Glory of GOD. Yes, he's listened to your complaints against him. You haven't been complaining against us, you know, but against GOD."

16.8   Moses said, "Since it will be GOD who gives you meat for your meal in the evening and your fill of bread in the morning, it's GOD who will have listened to your complaints against him. Who are we in all this? You haven't been complaining to us—you've been complaining to GOD!"

16.9   Moses instructed Aaron: "Tell the whole company of Israel: 'Come near to GOD. He's heard your complaints.' "

16.10   When Aaron gave out the instructions to the whole company of Israel, they turned to face the wilderness. And there it was: the Glory of GOD visible in the Cloud.

16.11-12   GOD spoke to Moses, "I've listened to the complaints of the Israelites. Now tell them: 'At dusk you will eat meat and at dawn you'll eat your fill of bread; and you'll realize that I am GOD, *your* God.' "

16.13-15   That evening quail flew in and covered the camp and in the morning there was a layer of dew all over the camp. When the layer of dew had lifted, there on the wilderness ground was a fine flaky something, fine as frost on the ground. The Israelites took one look and said to one another, *man-hu* (What is it?). They had no idea what it was.

16.15-16   So Moses told them, "It's the bread GOD has given you to eat. And these are GOD's instructions: 'Gather enough for each person, about two quarts per person; gather enough for everyone in your tent.' "

16.17-18   The People of Israel went to work and started gathering, some more, some less, but when they measured out what they had gathered, those who gathered more had no extra and those who gathered less weren't short—each person had gathered as much as was needed.

16.19   Moses said to them, "Don't leave any of it until morning."

16.20   But they didn't listen to Moses. A few of the men kept back some of it until morning. It got wormy and smelled bad. And Moses lost his temper with them.

16.21-22   They gathered it every morning, each person according to need. Then the sun heated up and it melted. On the sixth day they gathered twice as much bread, about four quarts per person.

Then the leaders of the company came to Moses and reported.

16.23-24   Moses said, "This is what GOD was talking about: Tomorrow is a day of rest, a holy Sabbath to GOD. Whatever you plan to bake, bake

---

ᵃ 16 That is, probably about 2 quarts (about 2 liters); also in verses 18, 32, 33 and 36   *ᵇ 22* That is, probably about 4 quarts (about 4.5 liters)

NEW INTERNATIONAL VERSION

what you want to bake and boil what you want to boil. Save whatever is left and keep it until morning.' "

²⁴So they saved it until morning, as Moses commanded, and it did not stink or get maggots in it. ²⁵"Eat it today," Moses said, "because today is a Sabbath to the LORD. You will not find any of it on the ground today. ²⁶Six days you are to gather it, but on the seventh day, the Sabbath, there will not be any."

²⁷Nevertheless, some of the people went out on the seventh day to gather it, but they found none. ²⁸Then the LORD said to Moses, "How long will you*ᵃ* refuse to keep my commands and my instructions? ²⁹Bear in mind that the LORD has given you the Sabbath; that is why on the sixth day he gives you bread for two days. Everyone is to stay where he is on the seventh day; no one is to go out." ³⁰So the people rested on the seventh day.

³¹The people of Israel called the bread manna.*ᵇ* It was white like coriander seed and tasted like wafers made with honey. ³²Moses said, "This is what the LORD has commanded: 'Take an omer of manna and keep it for the generations to come, so they can see the bread I gave you to eat in the desert when I brought you out of Egypt.' "

³³So Moses said to Aaron, "Take a jar and put an omer of manna in it. Then place it before the LORD to be kept for the generations to come." ³⁴As the LORD commanded Moses, Aaron put the manna in front of the Testimony, that it might be kept. ³⁵The Israelites ate manna forty years, until they came to a land that was settled; they ate manna until they reached the border of Canaan.

³⁶(An omer is one tenth of an ephah.)

WATER FROM THE ROCK

17 The whole Israelite community set out from the Desert of Sin, traveling from place to place as the LORD commanded. They camped at Rephidim, but there was no water for the people to drink. ²So they quarreled with Moses and said, "Give us water to drink."

Moses replied, "Why do you quarrel with me? Why do you put the LORD to the test?"

³But the people were thirsty for water there, and they grumbled against Moses. They said, "Why did you bring us up out of Egypt to make us and our children and livestock die of thirst?"

THE MESSAGE

today; and whatever you plan to boil, boil today. Then set aside the leftovers until morning." They set aside what was left until morning, as Moses had commanded. It didn't smell bad and there were no worms in it.

16.25-26 Moses said, "Now eat it; this is the day, a Sabbath for GOD. You won't find any of it on the ground today. Gather it every day for six days, but the seventh day is Sabbath; there won't be any of it on the ground."

16.27 On the seventh day, some of the people went out to gather anyway but they didn't find anything.

16.28-29 GOD said to Moses, "How long are you going to disobey my commands and not follow my instructions? Don't you see that GOD has given you the Sabbath? So on the sixth day he gives you bread for *two* days. So, each of you, stay home. Don't leave home on the seventh day."

16.30 So the people quit working on the seventh day.

16.31 The Israelites named it manna (What is it?). It looked like coriander seed, whitish. And it tasted like a cracker with honey.

16.32 Moses said, "This is GOD's command: 'Keep a two-quart jar of it, an omer, for future generations so they can see the bread that I fed you in the wilderness after I brought you out of Egypt.' "

16.33 Moses told Aaron, "Take a jar and fill it with two quarts of manna. Place it before GOD, keeping it safe for future generations."

16.34 Aaron did what GOD commanded Moses. He set it aside before The Testimony to preserve it.

16.35 The Israelites ate the manna for forty years until they arrived at the land where they would settle down. They ate manna until they reached the border into Canaan.

16.36 According to ancient measurements, an omer is one-tenth of an ephah.

✛

17.1-2 **17** Directed by GOD, the whole company of Israel moved on by stages from the Wilderness of Sin. They set camp at Rephidim. And there wasn't a drop of water for the people to drink. The people took Moses to task: "Give us water to drink." But Moses said, "Why pester me? Why are you testing GOD?"

17.3 But the people were thirsty for water there. They complained to Moses, "Why did you take us from Egypt and drag us out here with our children and animals to die of thirst?"

ᵃ 28 The Hebrew is plural.   *ᵇ 31 Manna* means *What is it?* (see verse 15).

NEW INTERNATIONAL VERSION

⁴Then Moses cried out to the LORD, "What am I to do with these people? They are almost ready to stone me."

⁵The LORD answered Moses, "Walk on ahead of the people. Take with you some of the elders of Israel and take in your hand the staff with which you struck the Nile, and go. ⁶I will stand there before you by the rock at Horeb. Strike the rock, and water will come out of it for the people to drink." So Moses did this in the sight of the elders of Israel. ⁷And he called the place Massah*a* and Meribah*b* because the Israelites quarreled and because they tested the LORD saying, "Is the LORD among us or not?"

THE AMALEKITES DEFEATED

⁸The Amalekites came and attacked the Israelites at Rephidim. ⁹Moses said to Joshua, "Choose some of our men and go out to fight the Amalekites. Tomorrow I will stand on top of the hill with the staff of God in my hands."

¹⁰So Joshua fought the Amalekites as Moses had ordered, and Moses, Aaron and Hur went to the top of the hill. ¹¹As long as Moses held up his hands, the Israelites were winning, but whenever he lowered his hands, the Amalekites were winning. ¹²When Moses' hands grew tired, they took a stone and put it under him and he sat on it. Aaron and Hur held his hands up— one on one side, one on the other—so that his hands remained steady till sunset. ¹³So Joshua overcame the Amalekite army with the sword.

¹⁴Then the LORD said to Moses, "Write this on a scroll as something to be remembered and make sure that Joshua hears it, because I will completely blot out the memory of Amalek from under heaven."

¹⁵Moses built an altar and called it The LORD is my Banner. ¹⁶He said, "For hands were lifted up to the throne of the LORD. The*c* LORD will be at war against the Amalekites from generation to generation."

JETHRO VISITS MOSES

18 Now Jethro, the priest of Midian and father-in-law of Moses, heard of everything God had done for Moses and for his people Israel, and how the LORD had brought Israel out of Egypt.

²After Moses had sent away his wife Zipporah, his father-in-law Jethro received her ³and her two sons. One son was named Gershom,*d*

THE MESSAGE

17.4 Moses cried out in prayer to GOD, "What can I do with these people? Any minute now they'll kill me!"

17.5-6 GOD said to Moses, "Go on out ahead of the people, taking with you some of the elders of Israel. Take the staff you used to strike the Nile. And go. I'm going to be present before you there on the rock at Horeb. You are to strike the rock. Water will gush out of it and the people will drink."

17.6-7 Moses did what he said, with the elders of Israel right there watching. He named the place Massah (Testing-Place) and Meribah (Quarreling) because of the quarreling of the Israelites and because of their testing of GOD when they said, "Is GOD here with us, or not?"

✛

17.8-9 Amalek came and fought Israel at Rephidim. Moses ordered Joshua: "Select some men for us and go out and fight Amalek. Tomorrow I will take my stand on top of the hill holding God's staff."

17.10-13 Joshua did what Moses ordered in order to fight Amalek. And Moses, Aaron, and Hur went to the top of the hill. It turned out that whenever Moses raised his hands, Israel was winning, but whenever he lowered his hands, Amalek was winning. But Moses' hands got tired. So they got a stone and set it under him. He sat on it and Aaron and Hur held up his hands, one on each side. So his hands remained steady until the sun went down. Joshua defeated Amalek and its army in battle.

17.14 GOD said to Moses, "Write this up as a reminder to Joshua, to keep it before him, because I will most certainly wipe the very memory of Amalek off the face of the Earth."

17.15-16 Moses built an altar and named it "GOD My Banner." He said,

Salute GOD's rule!
GOD at war with Amalek
Always and forever!

✛

18.1-4 **18** Jethro, priest of Midian and father-in-law to Moses, heard the report of all that God had done for Moses and Israel his people, the news that GOD had delivered Israel from Egypt. Jethro, Moses' father-in-law, had taken in Zipporah, Moses' wife who had been sent back home, and her two sons. The name of the one was Gershom (Sojourner) for he had

---

a 7 Massah means *testing.*   *b 7* Meribah means *quarreling.*
c 16 Or *"Because a hand was against the throne of the LORD, the   d 3* Gershom sounds like the Hebrew for *an alien there.*

NEW INTERNATIONAL VERSION

for Moses said, "I have become an alien in a foreign land"; [4]and the other was named Eliezer,[a] for he said, "My father's God was my helper; he saved me from the sword of Pharaoh."

[5]Jethro, Moses' father-in-law, together with Moses' sons and wife, came to him in the desert, where he was camped near the mountain of God. [6]Jethro had sent word to him, "I, your father-in-law Jethro, am coming to you with your wife and her two sons."

[7]So Moses went out to meet his father-in-law and bowed down and kissed him. They greeted each other and then went into the tent. [8]Moses told his father-in-law about everything the LORD had done to Pharaoh and the Egyptians for Israel's sake and about all the hardships they had met along the way and how the LORD had saved them.

[9]Jethro was delighted to hear about all the good things the LORD had done for Israel in rescuing them from the hand of the Egyptians. [10]He said, "Praise be to the LORD, who rescued you from the hand of the Egyptians and of Pharaoh, and who rescued the people from the hand of the Egyptians. [11]Now I know that the LORD is greater than all other gods, for he did this to those who had treated Israel arrogantly." [12]Then Jethro, Moses' father-in-law, brought a burnt offering and other sacrifices to God, and Aaron came with all the elders of Israel to eat bread with Moses' father-in-law in the presence of God.

[13]The next day Moses took his seat to serve as judge for the people, and they stood around him from morning till evening. [14]When his father-in-law saw all that Moses was doing for the people, he said, "What is this you are doing for the people? Why do you alone sit as judge, while all these people stand around you from morning till evening?"

[15]Moses answered him, "Because the people come to me to seek God's will. [16]Whenever they have a dispute, it is brought to me, and I decide between the parties and inform them of God's decrees and laws."

[17]Moses' father-in-law replied, "What you are doing is not good. [18]You and these people who come to you will only wear yourselves out. The work is too heavy for you; you cannot handle it alone. [19]Listen now to me and I will give you some advice, and may God be with you. You must be the people's representative before God and bring their disputes to him. [20]Teach them the decrees and laws, and show them the way to live and the duties they are to perform. [21]But select capable men from all the people—men who fear God, trustworthy men who hate dishonest

a 4 *Eliezer* means *my God is helper.*

THE MESSAGE

said, "I'm a sojourner in a foreign land"; the name of the other was Eliezer (God's-Help) because "The God of my father is my help and saved me from death by Pharaoh."

18.5-6 Jethro, Moses' father-in-law, brought Moses his sons and his wife there in the wilderness where he was camped at the mountain of God. He had sent a message ahead to Moses: "I, your father-in-law, am coming to you with your wife and two sons."

18.7-8 Moses went out to welcome his father-in-law. He bowed to him and kissed him. Each asked the other how things had been with him. Then they went into the tent. Moses told his father-in-law the story of all that GOD had done to Pharaoh and Egypt in helping Israel, all the trouble they had experienced on the journey, and how GOD had delivered them.

18.9-11 Jethro was delighted in all the good that GOD had done for Israel in delivering them from Egyptian oppression. Jethro said, "Blessed be GOD who has delivered you from the power of Egypt and Pharaoh, who has delivered his people from the oppression of Egypt. Now I know that GOD is greater than all gods because he's done this to all those who treated Israel arrogantly."

18.12 Jethro, Moses' father-in-law, brought a Whole-Burnt-Offering and sacrifices to God. And Aaron, along with all the elders of Israel, came and ate the meal with Moses' father-in-law in the presence of God.

18.13-14 The next day Moses took his place to judge the people. People were standing before him all day long, from morning to night. When Moses' father-in-law saw all that he was doing for the people, he said, "What's going on here? Why are you doing all this, and all by yourself, letting everybody line up before you from morning to night?"

18.15-16 Moses said to his father-in-law, "Because the people come to me with questions about God. When something comes up, they come to me. I judge between a man and his neighbor and teach them God's laws and instructions."

18.17-23 Moses' father-in-law said, "This is no way to go about it. You'll burn out, and the people right along with you. This is way too much for you—you can't do this alone. Now listen to me. Let me tell you how to do this so that God will be in this with you. Be there for the people before God, but let the matters of concern be presented to God. Your job is to teach them the rules and instructions, to show them how to live, what to do. And then you need to keep a sharp eye out for competent men—men who fear God, men of integrity, men who are incor-

NEW INTERNATIONAL VERSION

gain—and appoint them as officials over thousands, hundreds, fifties and tens. ²²Have them serve as judges for the people at all times, but have them bring every difficult case to you; the simple cases they can decide themselves. That will make your load lighter, because they will share it with you. ²³If you do this and God so commands, you will be able to stand the strain, and all these people will go home satisfied."

²⁴Moses listened to his father-in-law and did everything he said. ²⁵He chose capable men from all Israel and made them leaders of the people, officials over thousands, hundreds, fifties and tens. ²⁶They served as judges for the people at all times. The difficult cases they brought to Moses, but the simple ones they decided themselves.

²⁷Then Moses sent his father-in-law on his way, and Jethro returned to his own country.

AT MOUNT SINAI

19 In the third month after the Israelites left Egypt—on the very day—they came to the Desert of Sinai. ²After they set out from Rephidim, they entered the Desert of Sinai, and Israel camped there in the desert in front of the mountain.

³Then Moses went up to God, and the LORD called to him from the mountain and said, "This is what you are to say to the house of Jacob and what you are to tell the people of Israel: ⁴'You yourselves have seen what I did to Egypt, and how I carried you on eagles' wings and brought you to myself. ⁵Now if you obey me fully and keep my covenant, then out of all nations you will be my treasured possession. Although the whole earth is mine, ⁶you*ᵃ* will be for me a kingdom of priests and a holy nation.' These are the words you are to speak to the Israelites."

⁷So Moses went back and summoned the elders of the people and set before them all the words the LORD had commanded him to speak. ⁸The people all responded together, "We will do everything the LORD has said." So Moses brought their answer back to the LORD.

⁹The LORD said to Moses, "I am going to come to you in a dense cloud, so that the people will hear me speaking with you and will always put their trust in you." Then Moses told the LORD what the people had said.

¹⁰And the LORD said to Moses, "Go to the people and consecrate them today and tomorrow.

ᵃ 5,6 Or possession, for the whole earth is mine. ⁶You

THE MESSAGE

ruptible—and appoint them as leaders over groups organized by the thousand, by the hundred, by fifty, and by ten. They'll be responsible for the everyday work of judging among the people. They'll bring the hard cases to you, but in the routine cases they'll be the judges. They will share your load and that will make it easier for you. If you handle the work this way, you'll have the strength to carry out whatever God commands you, and the people in their settings will flourish also."

18.24-27   Moses listened to the counsel of his father-in-law and did everything he said. Moses picked competent men from all Israel and set them as leaders over the people who were organized by the thousand, by the hundred, by fifty, and by ten. They took over the everyday work of judging among the people. They brought the hard cases to Moses, but in the routine cases they were the judges. Then Moses said goodbye to his father-in-law who went home to his own country.

MOUNT SINAI

19.1-2 **19** Three months after leaving Egypt the Israelites entered the Wilderness of Sinai. They followed the route from Rephidim, arrived at the Wilderness of Sinai, and set up camp. Israel camped there facing the mountain.

19.3-6   As Moses went up to meet God, GOD called down to him from the mountain: "Speak to the House of Jacob, tell the People of Israel: 'You have seen what I did to Egypt and how I carried you on eagles' wings and brought you to me. If you will listen obediently to what I say and keep my covenant, out of all peoples you'll be my special treasure. The whole Earth is mine to choose from, but you're special: a kingdom of priests, a holy nation.'

"This is what I want you to tell the People of Israel."

19.7   Moses came back and called the elders of Israel together and set before them all these words which GOD had commanded him.

19.8   The people were unanimous in their response: "Everything GOD says, we will do." Moses took the people's answer back to GOD.

✛

19.9   GOD said to Moses, "Get ready. I'm about to come to you in a thick cloud so that the people can listen in and trust you completely when I speak with you." Again Moses reported the people's answer to GOD.

19.10-13   GOD said to Moses, "Go to the people. For the next two days get these people ready to

NEW INTERNATIONAL VERSION

Have them wash their clothes ¹¹and be ready by the third day, because on that day the LORD will come down on Mount Sinai in the sight of all the people. ¹²Put limits for the people around the mountain and tell them, 'Be careful that you do not go up the mountain or touch the foot of it. Whoever touches the mountain shall surely be put to death. ¹³He shall surely be stoned or shot with arrows; not a hand is to be laid on him. Whether man or animal, he shall not be permitted to live.' Only when the ram's horn sounds a long blast may they go up to the mountain."

¹⁴After Moses had gone down the mountain to the people, he consecrated them, and they washed their clothes. ¹⁵Then he said to the people, "Prepare yourselves for the third day. Abstain from sexual relations."

¹⁶On the morning of the third day there was thunder and lightning, with a thick cloud over the mountain, and a very loud trumpet blast. Everyone in the camp trembled. ¹⁷Then Moses led the people out of the camp to meet with God, and they stood at the foot of the mountain. ¹⁸Mount Sinai was covered with smoke, because the LORD descended on it in fire. The smoke billowed up from it like smoke from a furnace, the whole mountain*ᵃ* trembled violently, ¹⁹and the sound of the trumpet grew louder and louder. Then Moses spoke and the voice of God answered him.*ᵇ*

²⁰The LORD descended to the top of Mount Sinai and called Moses to the top of the mountain. So Moses went up ²¹and the LORD said to him, "Go down and warn the people so they do not force their way through to see the LORD and many of them perish. ²²Even the priests, who approach the LORD, must consecrate themselves, or the LORD will break out against them."

²³Moses said to the LORD, "The people cannot come up Mount Sinai, because you yourself warned us, 'Put limits around the mountain and set it apart as holy.' "

²⁴The LORD replied, "Go down and bring Aaron up with you. But the priests and the people must not force their way through to come up to the LORD, or he will break out against them."

²⁵So Moses went down to the people and told them.

THE MESSAGE

meet the Holy GOD. Have them scrub their clothes so that on the third day they'll be fully prepared, because on the third day GOD will come down on Mount Sinai and make his presence known to all the people. Post boundaries for the people all around, telling them, 'Warning! Don't climb the mountain. Don't even touch its edge. Whoever touches the mountain dies—a certain death. And no one is to touch that person, he's to be stoned. That's right— stoned. Or shot with arrows, shot to death. Animal or man, whichever—put to death.'

"A long blast from the horn will signal that it's safe to climb the mountain."

19.14-15 Moses went down the mountain to the people and prepared them for the holy meeting. They gave their clothes a good scrubbing. Then he addressed the people: "Be ready in three days. Don't sleep with a woman."

19.16 On the third day at daybreak, there were loud claps of thunder, flashes of lightning, a thick cloud covering the mountain, and an ear-piercing trumpet blast. Everyone in the camp shuddered in fear.

19.17 Moses led the people out of the camp to meet God. They stood at attention at the base of the mountain.

19.18-20 Mount Sinai was all smoke because GOD had come down on it as fire. Smoke poured from it like smoke from a furnace. The whole mountain shuddered in huge spasms. The trumpet blasts grew louder and louder. Moses spoke and God answered in thunder. GOD descended to the peak of Mount Sinai. GOD called Moses up to the peak and Moses climbed up.

19.21-22 GOD said to Moses, "Go down. Warn the people not to break through the barricades to get a look at GOD lest many of them die. And the priests also, warn them to prepare themselves for the holy meeting, lest GOD break out against them."

19.23 Moses said to GOD, "But the people can't climb Mount Sinai. You've already warned us well telling us: 'Post boundaries around the mountain. Respect the holy mountain.' "

19.24 GOD told him, "Go down and then bring Aaron back up with you. But make sure that the priests and the people don't break through and come up to GOD, lest he break out against them."

19.25 So Moses went down to the people. He said to them:

ᵃ 18 Most Hebrew manuscripts; a few Hebrew manuscripts and Septuagint *all the people*   *ᵇ 19* Or *and God answered him with thunder*

NEW INTERNATIONAL VERSION

THE TEN COMMANDMENTS

20 And God spoke all these words:

² "I am the LORD your God, who brought you out of Egypt, out of the land of slavery.

³ "You shall have no other gods before*ᵃ* me.

⁴ "You shall not make for yourself an idol in the form of anything in heaven above or on the earth beneath or in the waters below. ⁵You shall not bow down to them or worship them; for I, the LORD your God, am a jealous God, punishing the children for the sin of the fathers to the third and fourth generation of those who hate me, ⁶but showing love to a thousand ⌊generations⌋ of those who love me and keep my commandments.

⁷ "You shall not misuse the name of the LORD your God, for the LORD will not hold anyone guiltless who misuses his name.

⁸ "Remember the Sabbath day by keeping it holy. ⁹Six days you shall labor and do all your work, ¹⁰but the seventh day is a Sabbath to the LORD your God. On it you shall not do any work, neither you, nor your son or daughter, nor your manservant or maidservant, nor your animals, nor the alien within your gates. ¹¹For in six days the LORD made the heavens and the earth, the sea, and all that is in them, but he rested on the seventh day. Therefore the LORD blessed the Sabbath day and made it holy.

¹² "Honor your father and your mother, so that you may live long in the land the LORD your God is giving you.

¹³ "You shall not murder.

¹⁴ "You shall not commit adultery.

¹⁵ "You shall not steal.

¹⁶ "You shall not give false testimony against your neighbor.

¹⁷ "You shall not covet your neighbor's house. You shall not covet your neighbor's wife, or his manservant or maidservant, his ox or donkey, or anything that belongs to your neighbor."

¹⁸When the people saw the thunder and lightning and heard the trumpet and saw the mountain in smoke, they trembled with fear. They stayed at a distance ¹⁹and said to Moses, "Speak

THE MESSAGE

20 GOD spoke all these words:
²⁰·¹⁻² I am GOD, your God,
who brought you out of the land of Egypt,
out of a life of slavery.

²⁰·³ No other gods, only me.

²⁰·⁴⁻⁶ No carved gods of any size, shape, or form of anything whatever, whether of things that fly or walk or swim. Don't bow down to them and don't serve them because I am GOD, your God, and I'm a most jealous God, punishing the children for any sins their parents pass on to them to the third, and yes, even to the fourth generation of those who hate me. But I'm unswervingly loyal to the thousands who love me and keep my commandments.

²⁰·⁷ No using the name of GOD, your God, in curses or silly banter; GOD won't put up with the irreverent use of his name.

²⁰·⁸⁻¹¹ Observe the Sabbath day, to keep it holy. Work six days and do everything you need to do. But the seventh day is a Sabbath to GOD, your God. Don't do any work—not you, nor your son, nor your daughter, nor your servant, nor your maid, nor your animals, not even the foreign guest visiting in your town. For in six days GOD made Heaven, Earth, and Sea, and everything in them; he rested on the seventh day. Therefore GOD blessed the Sabbath day; he set it apart as a holy day.

²⁰·¹² Honor your father and mother so that you'll live a long time in the land that GOD, your God, is giving you.

²⁰·¹³ No murder.

²⁰·¹⁴ No adultery.

²⁰·¹⁵ No stealing.

²⁰·¹⁶ No lies about your neighbor.

²⁰·¹⁷ No lusting after your neighbor's house—or wife or servant or maid or ox or donkey. Don't set your heart on anything that is your neighbor's.

✛

²⁰·¹⁸⁻¹⁹ All the people, experiencing the thunder and lightning, the trumpet blast and the smoking mountain, were afraid—they pulled back and stood at a distance. They said to Moses, "You

---

ᵃ 3 Or *besides*

NEW INTERNATIONAL VERSION

to us yourself and we will listen. But do not have God speak to us or we will die."

20Moses said to the people, "Do not be afraid. God has come to test you, so that the fear of God will be with you to keep you from sinning."

21The people remained at a distance, while Moses approached the thick darkness where God was.

IDOLS AND ALTARS

22Then the LORD said to Moses, "Tell the Israelites this: 'You have seen for yourselves that I have spoken to you from heaven: 23Do not make any gods to be alongside me; do not make for yourselves gods of silver or gods of gold.

24 'Make an altar of earth for me and sacrifice on it your burnt offerings and fellowship offerings,*a* your sheep and goats and your cattle. Wherever I cause my name to be honored, I will come to you and bless you. 25If you make an altar of stones for me, do not build it with dressed stones, for you will defile it if you use a tool on it. 26And do not go up to my altar on steps, lest your nakedness be exposed on it.'

21

"These are the laws you are to set before them:

HEBREW SERVANTS

2"If you buy a Hebrew servant, he is to serve you for six years. But in the seventh year, he shall go free, without paying anything. 3If he comes alone, he is to go free alone; but if he has a wife when he comes, she is to go with him. 4If his master gives him a wife and she bears him sons or daughters, the woman and her children shall belong to her master, and only the man shall go free.

5"But if the servant declares, 'I love my master and my wife and children and do not want to go free,' 6then his master must take him before the judges.*b* He shall take him to the door or the doorpost and pierce his ear with an awl. Then he will be his servant for life.

7"If a man sells his daughter as a servant, she is not to go free as menservants do. 8If she does not please the master who has selected her for himself,*c* he must let her be redeemed. He has no right to sell her to foreigners, because he has broken faith with her. 9If he selects her for his son, he must grant her the rights of a daughter. 10If he marries another woman, he must not deprive the first one of her food, clothing and marital rights. 11If he does not provide her with

---

a 24 Traditionally peace offerings   b 6 Or before God
c 8 Or master so that he does not choose her

THE MESSAGE

speak to us and we'll listen, but don't have God speak to us or we'll die."

20.20   Moses spoke to the people: "Don't be afraid. God has come to test you and instill a deep and reverent awe within you so that you won't sin."

20.21   The people kept their distance while Moses approached the thick cloud where God was.

20.22-26   GOD said to Moses, "Give this Message to the People of Israel: 'You've experienced first-hand how I spoke with you from Heaven. Don't make gods of silver and gods of gold and then set them alongside me. Make me an earthen Altar. Sacrifice your Whole-Burnt-Offerings, your Peace-Offerings, your sheep, and your cattle on it. Every place where I cause my name to be honored in your worship, I'll be there myself and bless you. If you use stones to make my Altar, don't use dressed stones. If you use a chisel on the stones you'll profane the Altar. Don't use steps to climb to my Altar because that will expose your nakedness.'

✝

21.1   21 "These are the laws that you are to place before them:

21.2-6   "When you buy a Hebrew slave, he will serve six years. The seventh year he goes free, for nothing. If he came in single he leaves single. If he came in married he leaves with his wife. If the master gives him a wife and she gave him sons and daughters, the wife and children stay with the master and he leaves by himself. But suppose the slave should say, 'I love my master and my wife and children—I don't want my freedom,' then his master is to bring him before God and to a door or doorpost and pierce his ear with an awl, a sign that he is a slave for life.

21.7-11   "When a man sells his daughter to be a handmaid, she doesn't go free after six years like the men. If she doesn't please her master, her family must buy her back; her master doesn't have the right to sell her to foreigners since he broke his word to her. If he turns her over to his son, he has to treat her like a daughter. If he marries another woman, she retains all her full rights to meals, clothing, and marital relations.

NEW INTERNATIONAL VERSION

these three things, she is to go free, without any payment of money.

PERSONAL INJURIES

12 "Anyone who strikes a man and kills him shall surely be put to death. 13 However, if he does not do it intentionally, but God lets it happen, he is to flee to a place I will designate. 14 But if a man schemes and kills another man deliberately, take him away from my altar and put him to death.

15 "Anyone who attacks*a* his father or his mother must be put to death.

16 "Anyone who kidnaps another and either sells him or still has him when he is caught must be put to death.

17 "Anyone who curses his father or mother must be put to death.

18 "If men quarrel and one hits the other with a stone or with his fist*b* and he does not die but is confined to bed, 19 the one who struck the blow will not be held responsible if the other gets up and walks around outside with his staff; however, he must pay the injured man for the loss of his time and see that he is completely healed.

20 "If a man beats his male or female slave with a rod and the slave dies as a direct result, he must be punished, 21 but he is not to be punished if the slave gets up after a day or two, since the slave is his property.

22 "If men who are fighting hit a pregnant woman and she gives birth prematurely*c* but there is no serious injury, the offender must be fined whatever the woman's husband demands and the court allows. 23 But if there is serious injury, you are to take life for life, 24 eye for eye, tooth for tooth, hand for hand, foot for foot, 25 burn for burn, wound for wound, bruise for bruise.

26 "If a man hits a manservant or maidservant in the eye and destroys it, he must let the servant go free to compensate for the eye. 27 And if he knocks out the tooth of a manservant or maidservant, he must let the servant go free to compensate for the tooth.

28 "If a bull gores a man or a woman to death, the bull must be stoned to death, and its meat must not be eaten. But the owner of the bull will not be held responsible. 29 If, however, the bull has had the habit of goring and the owner has been warned but has not kept it penned up and it kills a man or woman, the bull must be stoned and the owner also must be put to death. 30 However, if payment is demanded of him, he may re-

THE MESSAGE

If he won't do any of these three things for her, she goes free, for nothing.

21.12-14 "If someone hits another and death results, the penalty is death. But if there was no intent to kill—if it was an accident, an 'act of God'—I'll set aside a place to which the killer can flee for refuge. But if the murder was premeditated, cunningly plotted, then drag the killer away, even if it's from my Altar, to be put to death.

21.15 "If someone hits father or mother, the penalty is death.

21.16 "If someone kidnaps a person, the penalty is death, regardless of whether the person has been sold or is still held in possession.

21.17 "If someone curses father or mother, the penalty is death.

21.18-19 "If a quarrel breaks out and one hits the other with a rock or a fist and the injured one doesn't die but is confined to bed and then later gets better and can get about on a crutch, the one who hit him is in the clear, except to pay for the loss of time and make sure of complete recovery.

21.20-21 "If a slave owner hits a slave, male or female, with a stick and the slave dies on the spot, the slave must be avenged. But if the slave survives a day or two, he's not to be avenged—the slave is the owner's property.

21.22-25 "When there's a fight and in the fight a pregnant woman is hit so that she miscarries but is not otherwise hurt, the one responsible has to pay whatever the husband demands in compensation. But if there is further damage, then you must give life for life—eye for eye, tooth for tooth, hand for hand, foot for foot, burn for burn, wound for wound, bruise for bruise.

21.26-27 "If a slave owner hits the eye of a slave or handmaid and ruins it, the owner must let the slave go free because of the eye. If the owner knocks out the tooth of the male or female slave, the slave must be released and go free because of the tooth.

21.28-32 "If an ox gores a man or a woman to death, the ox must be stoned. The meat cannot be eaten but the owner of the ox is in the clear. But if the ox has a history of goring and the owner knew it and did nothing to guard against it, then if the ox kills a man or a woman, the ox is to be stoned and the owner given the death penalty. If a ransom is agreed upon instead of death, he must pay it in full as a redemption for

---

a 15 Or kills   *b* 18 Or with a tool   *c* 22 Or she has a miscarriage

NEW INTERNATIONAL VERSION

deem his life by paying whatever is demanded. [31] This law also applies if the bull gores a son or daughter. [32] If the bull gores a male or female slave, the owner must pay thirty shekels[a] of silver to the master of the slave, and the bull must be stoned.

[33] "If a man uncovers a pit or digs one and fails to cover it and an ox or a donkey falls into it, [34] the owner of the pit must pay for the loss; he must pay its owner, and the dead animal will be his.

[35] "If a man's bull injures the bull of another and it dies, they are to sell the live one and divide both the money and the dead animal equally. [36] However, if it was known that the bull had the habit of goring, yet the owner did not keep it penned up, the owner must pay, animal for animal, and the dead animal will be his.

PROTECTION OF PROPERTY

22 "If a man steals an ox or a sheep and slaughters it or sells it, he must pay back five head of cattle for the ox and four sheep for the sheep.

[2] "If a thief is caught breaking in and is struck so that he dies, the defender is not guilty of bloodshed; [3] but if it happens[b] after sunrise, he is guilty of bloodshed.

"A thief must certainly make restitution, but if he has nothing, he must be sold to pay for his theft.

[4] "If the stolen animal is found alive in his possession—whether ox or donkey or sheep— he must pay back double.

[5] "If a man grazes his livestock in a field or vineyard and lets them stray and they graze in another man's field, he must make restitution from the best of his own field or vineyard.

[6] "If a fire breaks out and spreads into thornbushes so that it burns shocks of grain or standing grain or the whole field, the one who started the fire must make restitution.

[7] "If a man gives his neighbor silver or goods for safekeeping and they are stolen from the neighbor's house, the thief, if he is caught, must pay back double. [8] But if the thief is not found, the owner of the house must appear before the judges[c] to determine whether he has laid his hands on the other man's property. [9] In all cases of illegal possession of an ox, a donkey, a sheep, a garment, or any other lost property about which somebody says, 'This is mine,' both parties are to bring their cases before the judges. The one whom the judges declare[d] guilty must pay back double to his neighbor.

---

[a] 32 That is, about 12 ounces (about 0.3 kilogram)
[b] 3 Or *if he strikes him*   [c] 8 Or *before God*; also in verse 9
[d] 9 Or *whom God declares*

THE MESSAGE

his life. If a son or daughter is gored, the same judgment holds. If it is a slave or a handmaid the ox gores, thirty shekels of silver is to be paid to the owner and the ox stoned.

21.33-34 "If someone uncovers a cistern or digs a pit and leaves it open and an ox or donkey falls into it, the owner of the pit must pay whatever the animal is worth to its owner but can keep the dead animal.

22.35-36 "If someone's ox injures a neighbor's ox and the ox dies, they must sell the live ox and split the price; they must also split the dead animal. But if the ox had a history of goring and the owner knew it and did nothing to guard against it, the owner must pay an ox for an ox but can keep the dead animal.

22.1-3 **22** "If someone steals an ox or a lamb and slaughters or sells it, the thief must pay five cattle in place of the ox and four sheep in place of the lamb. If the thief is caught while breaking in and is hit hard and dies, there is no bloodguilt. But if it happens after daybreak, there is bloodguilt.

22.3-4 "A thief must make full restitution for what is stolen. The thief who is unable to pay is to be sold for his thieving. If caught red-handed with the stolen goods, and the ox or donkey or lamb is still alive, the thief pays double.

22.5 "If someone grazes livestock in a field or vineyard but lets them loose so they graze in someone else's field, restitution must be made from the best of the owner's field or vineyard.

22.6 "If fire breaks out and spreads to the brush so that the sheaves of grain or the standing grain or even the whole field is burned up, whoever started the fire must pay for the damages.

22.7-8 "If someone gives a neighbor money or things for safekeeping and they are stolen from the neighbor's house, the thief, if caught, must pay back double. If the thief is not caught, the owner must be brought before God to determine whether the owner was the one who took the neighbor's goods.

22.9 "In all cases of stolen goods, whether oxen, donkeys, sheep, clothing, anything in fact missing of which someone says, 'That's mine,' both parties must come before the judges. The one the judges pronounce guilty must pay double to the other.

NEW INTERNATIONAL VERSION

¹⁰"If a man gives a donkey, an ox, a sheep or any other animal to his neighbor for safekeeping and it dies or is injured or is taken away while no one is looking, ¹¹the issue between them will be settled by the taking of an oath before the LORD that the neighbor did not lay hands on the other person's property. The owner is to accept this, and no restitution is required. ¹²But if the animal was stolen from the neighbor, he must make restitution to the owner. ¹³If it was torn to pieces by a wild animal, he shall bring in the remains as evidence and he will not be required to pay for the torn animal.

¹⁴"If a man borrows an animal from his neighbor and it is injured or dies while the owner is not present, he must make restitution. ¹⁵But if the owner is with the animal, the borrower will not have to pay. If the animal was hired, the money paid for the hire covers the loss.

SOCIAL RESPONSIBILITY

¹⁶"If a man seduces a virgin who is not pledged to be married and sleeps with her, he must pay the bride-price, and she shall be his wife. ¹⁷If her father absolutely refuses to give her to him, he must still pay the bride-price for virgins.

¹⁸"Do not allow a sorceress to live.

¹⁹"Anyone who has sexual relations with an animal must be put to death.

²⁰"Whoever sacrifices to any god other than the LORD must be destroyed.ᵃ

²¹"Do not mistreat an alien or oppress him, for you were aliens in Egypt.

²²"Do not take advantage of a widow or an orphan. ²³If you do and they cry out to me, I will certainly hear their cry. ²⁴My anger will be aroused, and I will kill you with the sword; your wives will become widows and your children fatherless.

²⁵"If you lend money to one of my people among you who is needy, do not be like a moneylender; charge him no interest.ᵇ ²⁶If you take your neighbor's cloak as a pledge, return it to him by sunset, ²⁷because his cloak is the only covering he has for his body. What else will he sleep in? When he cries out to me, I will hear, for I am compassionate.

²⁸"Do not blaspheme Godᶜ or curse the ruler of your people.

²⁹"Do not hold back offerings from your granaries or your vats.ᵈ

ᵃ 20 The Hebrew term refers to the irrevocable giving over of things or persons to the LORD, often by totally destroying them.   ᵇ 25 Or excessive interest   ᶜ 28 Or Do not revile the judges   ᵈ 29 The meaning of the Hebrew for this phrase is uncertain.

THE MESSAGE

22.10-13 "If someone gives a donkey or ox or lamb or any kind of animal to another for safekeeping and it dies or is injured or lost and there is no witness, an oath before GOD must be made between them to decide whether one has laid hands on the property of the other. The owner must accept this and no damages are assessed. But if it turns out it was stolen, the owner must be compensated. If it has been torn by wild beasts, the torn animal must be brought in as evidence; no damages have to be paid.

22.14-15 "If someone borrows an animal from a neighbor and it gets injured or dies while the owner is not present, he must pay for it. But if the owner was with it, he doesn't have to pay. If the animal was hired, the payment covers the loss.

✠

22.16-17 "If a man seduces a virgin who is not engaged to be married and sleeps with her, he must pay the marriage price and marry her. If her father absolutely refuses to give her away, the man must still pay the marriage price for virgins.

22.18 "Don't let a sorceress live.

22.19 "Anyone who has sex with an animal gets the death penalty.

22.20 "Anyone who sacrifices to a god other than GOD alone must be put to death.

22.21 "Don't abuse or take advantage of strangers; you, remember, were once strangers in Egypt.

22.22-24 "Don't mistreat widows or orphans. If you do and they cry out to me, you can be sure I'll take them most seriously; I'll show my anger and come raging among you with the sword, and your wives will end up widows and your children orphans.

22.25 "If you lend money to my people, to any of the down-and-out among you, don't come down hard on them and gouge them with interest.

22.26-27 "If you take your neighbor's coat as security, give it back before nightfall; it may be your neighbor's only covering—what else does the person have to sleep in? And if I hear the neighbor crying out from the cold, I'll step in— I'm compassionate.

22.28 "Don't curse God; and don't damn your leaders.

22.29 "Don't be stingy as your wine vats fill up.

NEW INTERNATIONAL VERSION

"You must give me the firstborn of your sons. [30]Do the same with your cattle and your sheep. Let them stay with their mothers for seven days, but give them to me on the eighth day.

[31]"You are to be my holy people. So do not eat the meat of an animal torn by wild beasts; throw it to the dogs.

LAWS OF JUSTICE AND MERCY

23 "Do not spread false reports. Do not help a wicked man by being a malicious witness.

[2]"Do not follow the crowd in doing wrong. When you give testimony in a lawsuit, do not pervert justice by siding with the crowd, [3]and do not show favoritism to a poor man in his lawsuit.

[4]"If you come across your enemy's ox or donkey wandering off, be sure to take it back to him. [5]If you see the donkey of someone who hates you fallen down under its load, do not leave it there; be sure you help him with it.

[6]"Do not deny justice to your poor people in their lawsuits. [7]Have nothing to do with a false charge and do not put an innocent or honest person to death, for I will not acquit the guilty.

[8]"Do not accept a bribe, for a bribe blinds those who see and twists the words of the righteous.

[9]"Do not oppress an alien; you yourselves know how it feels to be aliens, because you were aliens in Egypt.

SABBATH LAWS

[10]"For six years you are to sow your fields and harvest the crops, [11]but during the seventh year let the land lie unplowed and unused. Then the poor among your people may get food from it, and the wild animals may eat what they leave. Do the same with your vineyard and your olive grove.

[12]"Six days do your work, but on the seventh day do not work, so that your ox and your donkey may rest and the slave born in your household, and the alien as well, may be refreshed.

[13]"Be careful to do everything I have said to you. Do not invoke the names of other gods; do not let them be heard on your lips.

THE THREE ANNUAL FESTIVALS

[14]"Three times a year you are to celebrate a festival to me.

[15]"Celebrate the Feast of Unleavened Bread; for seven days eat bread made without yeast, as I commanded you. Do this at the appointed time in the month of Abib, for in that month you came out of Egypt.

THE MESSAGE

22.29-30 "Dedicate your firstborn sons to me. The same with your cattle and sheep—they are to stay for seven days with their mother, then give them to me.

22.31 "Be holy for my sake.

"Don't eat mutilated flesh you find in the fields; throw it to the dogs.

✝

23.1-3 23 "Don't pass on malicious gossip. "Don't link up with a wicked person and give corrupt testimony. Don't go along with the crowd in doing evil and don't fudge your testimony in a case just to please the crowd. And just because someone is poor, don't show favoritism in a dispute.

23.4-5 "If you find your enemy's ox or donkey loose, take it back to him. If you see the donkey of someone who hates you lying helpless under its load, don't walk off and leave it. Help it up.

23.6 "When there is a dispute concerning your poor, don't tamper with the justice due them.

23.7 "Stay clear of false accusations. Don't contribute to the death of innocent and good people. I don't let the wicked off the hook.

23.8 "Don't take bribes. Bribes blind perfectly good eyes and twist the speech of good people.

23.9 "Don't take advantage of a stranger. You know what it's like to be a stranger; you were strangers in Egypt.

23.10-11 "Sow your land for six years and gather in its crops, but in the seventh year leave it alone and give it a rest so that your poor may eat from it. What they leave, let the wildlife have. Do the same with your vineyards and olive groves.

23.12 "Work for six days and rest the seventh so your ox and donkey may rest and your servant and migrant workers may have time to get their needed rest.

23.13 "Listen carefully to everything I tell you. Don't pay attention to other gods—don't so much as mention their names.

✝

23.14 "Three times a year you are to hold a festival for me.

23.15 "Hold the spring Festival of Unraised Bread when you eat unraised bread for seven days at the time set for the month of Abib, as I commanded you. That was the month you came

NEW INTERNATIONAL VERSION

"No one is to appear before me empty-handed.
¹⁶"Celebrate the Feast of Harvest with the firstfruits of the crops you sow in your field.

"Celebrate the Feast of Ingathering at the end of the year, when you gather in your crops from the field.

¹⁷"Three times a year all the men are to appear before the Sovereign LORD.

¹⁸"Do not offer the blood of a sacrifice to me along with anything containing yeast.

"The fat of my festival offerings must not be kept until morning.

¹⁹"Bring the best of the firstfruits of your soil to the house of the LORD your God.

"Do not cook a young goat in its mother's milk.

GOD'S ANGEL TO PREPARE THE WAY

²⁰"See, I am sending an angel ahead of you to guard you along the way and to bring you to the place I have prepared. ²¹Pay attention to him and listen to what he says. Do not rebel against him; he will not forgive your rebellion, since my Name is in him. ²²If you listen carefully to what he says and do all that I say, I will be an enemy to your enemies and will oppose those who oppose you. ²³My angel will go ahead of you and bring you into the land of the Amorites, Hittites, Perizzites, Canaanites, Hivites and Jebusites, and I will wipe them out. ²⁴Do not bow down before their gods or worship them or follow their practices. You must demolish them and break their sacred stones to pieces. ²⁵Worship the LORD your God, and his blessing will be on your food and water. I will take away sickness from among you, ²⁶and none will miscarry or be barren in your land. I will give you a full life span.

²⁷"I will send my terror ahead of you and throw into confusion every nation you encounter. I will make all your enemies turn their backs and run. ²⁸I will send the hornet ahead of you to drive the Hivites, Canaanites and Hittites out of your way. ²⁹But I will not drive them out in a single year, because the land would become desolate and the wild animals too numerous for you. ³⁰Little by little I will drive them out before you, until you have increased enough to take possession of the land.

³¹"I will establish your borders from the Red Sea*ᵃ* to the Sea of the Philistines,*ᵇ* and from the desert to the River.*ᶜ* I will hand over to you the people who live in the land and you will drive them out before you. ³²Do not make a covenant

ᵃ 31 Hebrew *Yam Suph*; that is, Sea of Reeds   *ᵇ 31* That is, the Mediterranean   *ᶜ 31* That is, the Euphrates

THE MESSAGE

out of Egypt. No one should show up before me empty-handed.

23.16   "Hold the summer Festival of Harvest when you bring in the firstfruits of all your work in the fields.

"Hold the autumn Festival of Ingathering at the end of the season when you bring in the year's crops.

23.17   "Three times a year all your males are to appear before the Master, GOD.

23.18   "Don't offer the blood of a sacrifice to me with anything that has yeast in it.

"Don't leave the fat from my festival offering out overnight.

23.19   "Bring the choice first produce of the year to the house of your GOD.

"Don't boil a kid in its mother's milk.

✛

23.20-24 "Now get yourselves ready. I'm sending my Angel ahead of you to guard you in your travels, to lead you to the place that I've prepared. Pay close attention to him. Obey him. Don't go against him. He won't put up with your rebellions because he's acting on my authority. But if you obey him and do everything I tell you, I'll be an enemy to your enemies, I'll fight those who fight you. When my Angel goes ahead of you and leads you to the land of the Amorites, the Hittites, the Perizzites, the Canaanites, the Hivites, and the Jebusites, I'll clear the country of them. So don't worship or serve their gods; don't do anything they do because I'm going to wipe them right off the face of the Earth and smash their sacred phallic pillars to bits.

23.25-26   "But you—you serve your GOD and he'll bless your food and your water. I'll get rid of the sickness among you; there won't be any miscarriages nor barren women in your land. I'll make sure you live full and complete lives.

23.27   "I'll send my Terror on ahead of you and throw those peoples you're approaching into a panic. All you'll see of your enemies is the backs of their necks.

23.28-31   "And I'll send Despair on ahead of you. It will push the Hivites, the Canaanites, and the Hittites out of your way. I won't get rid of them all at once lest the land grow up in weeds and the wild animals take over. Little by little I'll get them out of there while you have a chance to get your crops going and make the land your own. I will make your borders stretch from the Red Sea to the Mediterranean Sea and from the Wilderness to the Euphrates River. I'm turning everyone living in that land over to you; go ahead and drive them out.

NEW INTERNATIONAL VERSION

with them or with their gods. ³³Do not let them live in your land, or they will cause you to sin against me, because the worship of their gods will certainly be a snare to you."

THE COVENANT CONFIRMED

24 Then he said to Moses, "Come up to the LORD, you and Aaron, Nadab and Abihu, and seventy of the elders of Israel. You are to worship at a distance, ²but Moses alone is to approach the LORD; the others must not come near. And the people may not come up with him."

³When Moses went and told the people all the LORD's words and laws, they responded with one voice, "Everything the LORD has said we will do." ⁴Moses then wrote down everything the LORD had said.

He got up early the next morning and built an altar at the foot of the mountain and set up twelve stone pillars representing the twelve tribes of Israel. ⁵Then he sent young Israelite men, and they offered burnt offerings and sacrificed young bulls as fellowship offerings*a* to the LORD. ⁶Moses took half of the blood and put it in bowls, and the other half he sprinkled on the altar. ⁷Then he took the Book of the Covenant and read it to the people. They responded, "We will do everything the LORD has said; we will obey."

⁸Moses then took the blood, sprinkled it on the people and said, "This is the blood of the covenant that the LORD has made with you in accordance with all these words."

⁹Moses and Aaron, Nadab and Abihu, and the seventy elders of Israel went up ¹⁰and saw the God of Israel. Under his feet was something like a pavement made of sapphire,*b* clear as the sky itself. ¹¹But God did not raise his hand against these leaders of the Israelites; they saw God, and they ate and drank.

¹²The LORD said to Moses, "Come up to me on the mountain and stay here, and I will give you the tablets of stone, with the law and commands I have written for their instruction."

¹³Then Moses set out with Joshua his aide, and Moses went up on the mountain of God. ¹⁴He said to the elders, "Wait here for us until we come back to you. Aaron and Hur are with you, and anyone involved in a dispute can go to them."

¹⁵When Moses went up on the mountain, the cloud covered it, ¹⁶and the glory of the LORD settled on Mount Sinai. For six days the cloud covered the mountain, and on the seventh day the LORD called to Moses from within the cloud. ¹⁷To

THE MESSAGE

^{23.32-33} "Don't make any deals with them or their gods. They are not to stay in the same country with you lest they get you to sin by worshiping their gods. Beware. That's a huge danger."

24 ^{24.1-2} He said to Moses, "Climb the mountain to GOD, you and Aaron, Nadab, Abihu, and seventy of the elders of Israel. They will worship from a distance; only Moses will approach GOD. The rest are not to come close. And the people are not to climb the mountain at all."

^{24.3} So Moses went to the people and told them everything GOD had said—all the rules and regulations. They all answered in unison: "Everything GOD said, we'll do."

^{24.4-6} Then Moses wrote it all down, everything GOD had said. He got up early the next morning and built an Altar at the foot of the mountain using twelve pillar-stones for the twelve tribes of Israel. Then he directed young Israelite men to offer Whole-Burnt-Offerings and sacrifice Peace-Offerings of bulls. Moses took half the blood and put it in bowls; the other half he threw against the Altar.

^{24.7} Then he took the Book of the Covenant and read it as the people listened. They said, "Everything GOD said, we'll do. Yes, we'll obey."

^{24.8} Moses took the rest of the blood and threw it out over the people, saying, "This is the blood of the covenant which GOD has made with you out of all these words I have spoken."

^{24.9-11} Then they climbed the mountain—Moses and Aaron, Nadab and Abihu, and seventy of the elders of Israel—and saw the God of Israel. He was standing on a pavement of something like sapphires—pure, clear sky-blue. He didn't hurt these pillar-leaders of the Israelites: They saw God; and they ate and drank.

^{24.12-13} GOD said to Moses, "Climb higher up the mountain and wait there for me; I'll give you tablets of stone, the teachings and commandments that I've written to instruct them." So Moses got up, accompanied by Joshua his aide. And Moses climbed up the mountain of God.

^{24.14} He told the elders of Israel, "Wait for us here until we return to you. You have Aaron and Hur with you; if there are any problems, go to them."

^{24.15-17} Then Moses climbed the mountain. The Cloud covered the mountain. The Glory of GOD settled over Mount Sinai. The Cloud covered it for six days. On the seventh day he called out of the Cloud to Moses. In the view of

---

a 5 Traditionally *peace offerings*   *b 10* Or *lapis lazuli*

NEW INTERNATIONAL VERSION

the Israelites the glory of the LORD looked like a consuming fire on top of the mountain. ¹⁸Then Moses entered the cloud as he went on up the mountain. And he stayed on the mountain forty days and forty nights.

OFFERINGS FOR THE TABERNACLE

25 The LORD said to Moses, ²"Tell the Israelites to bring me an offering. You are to receive the offering for me from each man whose heart prompts him to give. ³These are the offerings you are to receive from them: gold, silver and bronze; ⁴blue, purple and scarlet yarn and fine linen; goat hair; ⁵ram skins dyed red and hides of sea cows*a*; acacia wood; ⁶olive oil for the light; spices for the anointing oil and for the fragrant incense; ⁷and onyx stones and other gems to be mounted on the ephod and breastpiece.

⁸"Then have them make a sanctuary for me, and I will dwell among them. ⁹Make this tabernacle and all its furnishings exactly like the pattern I will show you.

THE ARK

¹⁰"Have them make a chest of acacia wood— two and a half cubits long, a cubit and a half wide, and a cubit and a half high.*b* ¹¹Overlay it with pure gold, both inside and out, and make a gold molding around it. ¹²Cast four gold rings for it and fasten them to its four feet, with two rings on one side and two rings on the other. ¹³Then make poles of acacia wood and overlay them with gold. ¹⁴Insert the poles into the rings on the sides of the chest to carry it. ¹⁵The poles are to remain in the rings of this ark; they are not to be removed. ¹⁶Then put in the ark the Testimony, which I will give you.

¹⁷"Make an atonement cover*c* of pure gold— two and a half cubits long and a cubit and a half wide.*d* ¹⁸And make two cherubim out of hammered gold at the ends of the cover. ¹⁹Make one cherub on one end and the second cherub on the other; make the cherubim of one piece with the cover, at the two ends. ²⁰The cherubim are to have their wings spread upward, overshadowing the cover with them. The cherubim are to face each other, looking toward the cover. ²¹Place the cover on top of the ark and put in the ark the Testimony, which I will give you. ²²There, above the cover between the two cherubim that are

---

a 5 That is, dugongs   b 10 That is, about 3 3/4 feet (about 1.1 meters) long and 2 1/4 feet (about 0.7 meter) wide and high   c 17 Traditionally a mercy seat   d 17 That is, about 3 3/4 feet (about 1.1 meters) long and 2 1/4 feet (about 0.7 meter) wide

THE MESSAGE

the Israelites below, the Glory of God looked like a raging fire at the top of the mountain.
24.18   Moses entered the middle of the Cloud and climbed the mountain. Moses was on the mountain forty days and forty nights.

INSTRUCTIONS ON THE MOUNTAIN: THE OFFERINGS

25.1-9 **25** GOD spoke to Moses: "Tell the Israelites that they are to set aside offerings for me. Receive the offerings from everyone who is willing to give. These are the offerings I want you to receive from them: gold, silver, bronze; blue, purple, and scarlet material; fine linen; goats' hair; tanned rams' skins; dolphin skins; acacia wood; lamp oil; spices for anointing oils and for fragrant incense; onyx stones and other stones for setting in the Ephod and the Breastpiece. Let them construct a Sanctuary for me so that I can live among them. You are to construct it following the plans I've given you, the design for The Dwelling and the design for all its furnishings.

THE CHEST

25.10-15 "First let them make a Chest using acacia wood: make it three and three-quarters feet long and two and one-quarter feet wide and deep. Cover it with a veneer of pure gold inside and out and make a molding of gold all around it. Cast four gold rings and attach them to its four feet, two rings on one side and two rings on the other. Make poles from acacia wood and cover them with a veneer of gold and insert them into the rings on the sides of the Chest for carrying the Chest. The poles are to stay in the rings; they must not be removed.

25.16   "Place The Testimony that I give you in the Chest.

25.17   "Now make a lid of pure gold for the Chest, an Atonement-Cover, three and three-quarters feet long and two and one-quarter feet wide.

25.18-22   "Sculpt two winged angels out of hammered gold for either end of the Atonement-Cover, one angel at one end, one angel at the other. Make them of one piece with the Atonement-Cover. Make the angels with their wings spread, hovering over the Atonement-Cover, facing one another but looking down on it. Set the Atonement-Cover as a lid over the Chest and place in the Chest The Testimony that I will give you. I will meet you there at set times and speak with you from above the Atonement-Cover and from between the angel-fig-

NEW INTERNATIONAL VERSION	THE MESSAGE

NEW INTERNATIONAL VERSION

over the ark of the Testimony, I will meet with you and give you all my commands for the Israelites.

THE TABLE

23"Make a table of acacia wood—two cubits long, a cubit wide and a cubit and a half high. *a* 24Overlay it with pure gold and make a gold molding around it. 25Also make around it a rim a handbreadth *b* wide and put a gold molding on the rim. 26Make four gold rings for the table and fasten them to the four corners, where the four legs are. 27The rings are to be close to the rim to hold the poles used in carrying the table. 28Make the poles of acacia wood, overlay them with gold and carry the table with them. 29And make its plates and dishes of pure gold, as well as its pitchers and bowls for the pouring out of offerings. 30Put the bread of the Presence on this table to be before me at all times.

THE LAMPSTAND

31"Make a lampstand of pure gold and hammer it out, base and shaft; its flowerlike cups, buds and blossoms shall be of one piece with it. 32Six branches are to extend from the sides of the lampstand—three on one side and three on the other. 33Three cups shaped like almond flowers with buds and blossoms are to be on one branch, three on the next branch, and the same for all six branches extending from the lampstand. 34And on the lampstand there are to be four cups shaped like almond flowers with buds and blossoms. 35One bud shall be under the first pair of branches extending from the lampstand, a second bud under the second pair, and a third bud under the third pair—six branches in all. 36The buds and branches shall all be of one piece with the lampstand, hammered out of pure gold.

37"Then make its seven lamps and set them up on it so that they light the space in front of it. 38Its wick trimmers and trays are to be of pure gold. 39A talent *c* of pure gold is to be used for the lampstand and all these accessories. 40See that you make them according to the pattern shown you on the mountain.

THE TABERNACLE

26 "Make the tabernacle with ten curtains of finely twisted linen and blue, purple and scarlet yarn, with cherubim worked into them by a skilled craftsman. 2All the curtains are to be the same size—twenty-eight cubits long

a 23 That is, about 3 feet (about 0.9 meter) long and 1 1/2 feet (about 0.5 meter) wide and 2 1/4 feet (about 0.7 meter) high   b 25 That is, about 3 inches (about 8 centimeters)   c 39 That is, about 75 pounds (about 34 kilograms)

THE MESSAGE

ures that are on it, speaking the commands that I have for the Israelites.

THE TABLE

25.23-28 "Next make a Table from acacia wood. Make it three feet long, one and one-half feet wide and two and one-quarter feet high. Cover it with a veneer of pure gold. Make a molding all around it of gold. Make the border a handbreadth wide all around it and a rim of gold for the border. Make four rings of gold and attach the rings to the four legs parallel to the table top. They will serve as holders for the poles used to carry the Table. Make the poles of acacia wood and cover them with a veneer of gold. They will be used to carry the Table.

25.29   "Make plates, bowls, jars, and jugs for pouring out offerings. Make them of pure gold.

25.30   "Always keep fresh Bread of the Presence on the Table before me.

THE LAMPSTAND

25.31-36 "Make a Lampstand of pure hammered gold. Make its stem and branches, cups, calyxes, and petals all of one piece. Give it six branches, three from one side and three from the other; put three cups shaped like almond blossoms, each with calyx and petals, on one branch, three on the next, and so on—the same for all six branches. On the main stem of the Lampstand, make four cups shaped like almonds, with calyx and petals, a calyx extending from under each pair of the six branches, the entire Lampstand fashioned from one piece of hammered pure gold.

25.37-38   "Make seven of these lamps for the Table. Arrange the lamps so they throw their light out in front. Make the candle snuffers and trays out of pure gold.

25.39-40   "Use a seventy-five-pound brick of pure gold to make the Lampstand and its accessories. Study the design you were given on the mountain and make everything accordingly.

THE DWELLING

26 "Make The Dwelling itself from ten panels of tapestry woven from fine twisted linen, blue and purple and scarlet material, with an angel-cherubim design. A skilled craftsman should do it. The panels of tapestry are each to be forty-six feet long and six feet

NEW INTERNATIONAL VERSION	THE MESSAGE

and four cubits wide.[a] [3]Join five of the curtains together, and do the same with the other five. [4]Make loops of blue material along the edge of the end curtain in one set, and do the same with the end curtain in the other set. [5]Make fifty loops on one curtain and fifty loops on the end curtain of the other set, with the loops opposite each other. [6]Then make fifty gold clasps and use them to fasten the curtains together so that the tabernacle is a unit.

[7]"Make curtains of goat hair for the tent over the tabernacle—eleven altogether. [8]All eleven curtains are to be the same size—thirty cubits long and four cubits wide.[b] [9]Join five of the curtains together into one set and the other six into another set. Fold the sixth curtain double at the front of the tent. [10]Make fifty loops along the edge of the end curtain in one set and also along the edge of the end curtain in the other set. [11]Then make fifty bronze clasps and put them in the loops to fasten the tent together as a unit. [12]As for the additional length of the tent curtains, the half curtain that is left over is to hang down at the rear of the tabernacle. [13]The tent curtains will be a cubit[c] longer on both sides; what is left will hang over the sides of the tabernacle so as to cover it. [14]Make for the tent a covering of ram skins dyed red, and over that a covering of hides of sea cows.[d]

[15]"Make upright frames of acacia wood for the tabernacle. [16]Each frame is to be ten cubits long and a cubit and a half wide,[e] [17]with two projections set parallel to each other. Make all the frames of the tabernacle in this way. [18]Make twenty frames for the south side of the tabernacle [19]and make forty silver bases to go under them—two bases for each frame, one under each projection. [20]For the other side, the north side of the tabernacle, make twenty frames [21]and forty silver bases—two under each frame. [22]Make six frames for the far end, that is, the west end of the tabernacle, [23]and make two frames for the corners at the far end. [24]At these two corners they must be double from the bottom all the way to the top, and fitted into a single ring; both shall be like that. [25]So there will be eight frames and sixteen silver bases—two under each frame.

[26]"Also make crossbars of acacia wood: five for the frames on one side of the tabernacle, [27]five for those on the other side, and five for the frames on the west, at the far end of the tabernacle. [28]The center crossbar is to extend from

wide. Join five of the panels together, and then the other five together. Make loops of blue along the edge of the outside panel of the first set and the same on the outside panel of the second set. Make fifty loops on each panel. Then make fifty gold clasps and join the tapestries together so that The Dwelling is one whole.

26.7-11 "Next make tapestries of goat hair for a tent that will cover The Dwelling. Make eleven panels of these tapestries. The length of each panel will be forty-five feet long and six feet wide. Join five of the panels together, and then the other six. Fold the sixth panel double at the front of the tent. Now make fifty loops along the edge of the end panel and fifty loops along the edge of the joining panel. Make fifty clasps of bronze and connect the clasps with the loops, bringing the tent together.

26.12-14 "Hang half of the overlap of the tapestry panels over the rear of The Dwelling. The eighteen inches of overlap on either side will cover the sides of the tent. Finally, make a covering for the tapestries of tanned rams' skins dyed red and over that a covering of dolphin skins.

26.15-25 "Frame The Dwelling with planks of acacia wood, each section of frame fifteen feet long and two and one-quarter feet wide, with two pegs for securing them. Make all the frames identical: twenty frames for the south side with forty silver sockets to receive the two pegs from each of the twenty frames; the same construction on the north side of The Dwelling; for the rear of The Dwelling, which faces west, make six frames with two additional frames for the rear corners. Both of the two corner frames need to be double in thickness from top to bottom and fit into a single ring—eight frames altogether with sixteen sockets of silver, two under each frame.

26.26-30 "Now make crossbars of acacia wood, five for the frames on one side of The Dwelling, five for the other side, and five for the back side facing west. The center crossbar runs from end

---

[a] 2 That is, about 42 feet (about 12.5 meters) long and 6 feet (about 1.8 meters) wide   [b] 8 That is, about 45 feet (about 13.5 meters) long and 6 feet (about 1.8 meters) wide   [c] 13 That is, about 1 1/2 feet (about 0.5 meter)   [d] 14 That is, dugongs   [e] 16 That is, about 15 feet (about 4.5 meters) long and 2 1/4 feet (about 0.7 meter) wide

NEW INTERNATIONAL VERSION	THE MESSAGE

end to end at the middle of the frames. ²⁹Overlay the frames with gold and make gold rings to hold the crossbars. Also overlay the crossbars with gold.

³⁰"Set up the tabernacle according to the plan shown you on the mountain.

³¹"Make a curtain of blue, purple and scarlet yarn and finely twisted linen, with cherubim worked into it by a skilled craftsman. ³²Hang it with gold hooks on four posts of acacia wood overlaid with gold and standing on four silver bases. ³³Hang the curtain from the clasps and place the ark of the Testimony behind the curtain. The curtain will separate the Holy Place from the Most Holy Place. ³⁴Put the atonement cover on the ark of the Testimony in the Most Holy Place. ³⁵Place the table outside the curtain on the north side of the tabernacle and put the lampstand opposite it on the south side.

³⁶"For the entrance to the tent make a curtain of blue, purple and scarlet yarn and finely twisted linen—the work of an embroiderer. ³⁷Make gold hooks for this curtain and five posts of acacia wood overlaid with gold. And cast five bronze bases for them.

The Altar of Burnt Offering

27 "Build an altar of acacia wood, three cubits[a] high; it is to be square, five cubits long and five cubits wide.[b] ²Make a horn at each of the four corners, so that the horns and the altar are of one piece, and overlay the altar with bronze. ³Make all its utensils of bronze—its pots to remove the ashes, and its shovels, sprinkling bowls, meat forks and firepans. ⁴Make a grating for it, a bronze network, and make a bronze ring at each of the four corners of the network. ⁵Put it under the ledge of the altar so that it is halfway up the altar. ⁶Make poles of acacia wood for the altar and overlay them with bronze. ⁷The poles are to be inserted into the rings so they will be on two sides of the altar when it is carried. ⁸Make the altar hollow, out of boards. It is to be made just as you were shown on the mountain.

The Courtyard

⁹"Make a courtyard for the tabernacle. The south side shall be a hundred cubits[c] long and is to have curtains of finely twisted linen, ¹⁰with twenty posts and twenty bronze bases and with

26.31-35 to end halfway up the frames. Cover the frames with a veneer of gold and make gold rings to hold the crossbars. And cover the crossbars with a veneer of gold. Then put The Dwelling together, following the design you were shown on the mountain.

"Make a curtain of blue, purple, and scarlet material and fine twisted linen. Have a design of angel-cherubim woven into it by a skilled craftsman. Fasten it with gold hooks to four posts of acacia wood covered with a veneer of gold, set on four silver bases. After hanging the curtain from the clasps, bring the Chest of The Testimony in behind the curtain. The curtain will separate the Holy Place from the Holy-of-Holies. Now place the Atonement-Cover lid on the Chest of The Testimony in the Holy-of-Holies. Place the Table and the Lampstand outside the curtain, the Lampstand on the south side of The Dwelling and the Table opposite it on the north side.

26.36-37 "Make a screen for the door of the tent. Weave it from blue, purple, and scarlet material and fine twisted linen. Frame the weaving with five poles of acacia wood covered with a veneer of gold and make gold hooks to hang the weaving. Cast five bronze bases for the poles.

The Altar

27.1-8 **27** "Make an Altar of acacia wood. Make it seven and a half feet square and four and a half feet high. Make horns at each of the four corners. The horns are to be of one piece with the Altar and covered with a veneer of bronze. Make buckets for removing the ashes, along with shovels, basins, forks, and fire pans. Make all these utensils from bronze. Make a grate of bronze mesh and attach bronze rings at each of the four corners. Put the grate under the ledge of the Altar at the halfway point of the Altar. Make acacia wood poles for the Altar and cover them with a veneer of bronze. Insert the poles through the rings on the two sides of the Altar for carrying. Use boards to make the Altar, keeping the interior hollow.

The Courtyard

27.9-11 "Make a Courtyard for The Dwelling. The south side is to be 150 feet long. The hangings for the Courtyard are to be woven from fine twisted linen, with their twenty posts, twenty

---

a 1 That is, about 4 1/2 feet (about 1.3 meters) *b 1* That is, about 7 1/2 feet (about 2.3 meters) long and wide *c 9* That is, about 150 feet (about 46 meters); also in verse 11

NEW INTERNATIONAL VERSION

silver hooks and bands on the posts. [11]The north side shall also be a hundred cubits long and is to have curtains, with twenty posts and twenty bronze bases and with silver hooks and bands on the posts.

[12]"The west end of the courtyard shall be fifty cubits[a] wide and have curtains, with ten posts and ten bases. [13]On the east end, toward the sunrise, the courtyard shall also be fifty cubits wide. [14]Curtains fifteen cubits[b] long are to be on one side of the entrance, with three posts and three bases, [15]and curtains fifteen cubits long are to be on the other side, with three posts and three bases.

[16]"For the entrance to the courtyard, provide a curtain twenty cubits[c] long, of blue, purple and scarlet yarn and finely twisted linen—the work of an embroiderer—with four posts and four bases. [17]All the posts around the courtyard are to have silver bands and hooks, and bronze bases. [18]The courtyard shall be a hundred cubits long and fifty cubits wide,[d] with curtains of finely twisted linen five cubits[e] high, and with bronze bases. [19]All the other articles used in the service of the tabernacle, whatever their function, including all the tent pegs for it and those for the courtyard, are to be of bronze.

OIL FOR THE LAMPSTAND

[20]"Command the Israelites to bring you clear oil of pressed olives for the light so that the lamps may be kept burning. [21]In the Tent of Meeting, outside the curtain that is in front of the Testimony, Aaron and his sons are to keep the lamps burning before the LORD from evening till morning. This is to be a lasting ordinance among the Israelites for the generations to come.

THE PRIESTLY GARMENTS

28 "Have Aaron your brother brought to you from among the Israelites, along with his sons Nadab and Abihu, Eleazar and Ithamar, so they may serve me as priests. [2]Make sacred garments for your brother Aaron, to give him dignity and honor. [3]Tell all the skilled men to whom I have given wisdom in such matters that they are to make garments for Aaron, for his consecration, so he may serve me as priest. [4]These are the garments they are to make: a breastpiece, an ephod, a robe, a woven tunic, a turban and a sash. They are to make these sacred garments for your brother Aaron and his sons, so

---

a 12 That is, about 75 feet (about 23 meters); also in verse 13   *b 14* That is, about 22 1/2 feet (about 6.9 meters); also in verse 15   *c 16* That is, about 30 feet (about 9 meters)   *d 18* That is, about 150 feet (about 46 meters) long and 75 feet (about 23 meters) wide   *e 18* That is, about 7 1/2 feet (about 2.3 meters)

THE MESSAGE

bronze bases, and fastening hooks and bands of silver. The north side is to be exactly the same.

27.12-19 "For the west end of the Courtyard you will need seventy-five feet of hangings with their ten posts and bases. Across the seventy-five feet at the front, or east end, you will need twenty-two and a half feet of hangings, with their three posts and bases on one side and the same for the other side. At the door of the Courtyard make a screen thirty feet long woven from blue, purple, and scarlet stuff, with fine twisted linen, embroidered by a craftsman, and hung on its four posts and bases. All the posts around the Courtyard are to be banded with silver, with hooks of silver and bases of bronze. The Courtyard is to be 150 feet long and seventy-five feet wide. The hangings of fine twisted linen set on their bronze bases are to be seven and a half feet high. All the tools used for setting up The Holy Dwelling, including all the pegs in it and the Courtyard, are to be made of bronze.

27.20-21 "Now, order the Israelites to bring you pure, clear olive oil for light so that the lamps can be kept burning. In the Tent of Meeting, the area outside the curtain that veils The Testimony, Aaron and his sons will keep this light burning from evening until morning before GOD. This is to be a permanent practice down through the generations for Israelites.

THE VESTMENTS

28.1-5 **28** "Get your brother Aaron and his sons from among the Israelites to serve me as priests: Aaron and his sons Nadab, Abihu, Eleazar, Ithamar. Make sacred vestments for your brother Aaron to symbolize glory and beauty. Consult with the skilled craftsmen, those whom I have gifted in this work, and arrange for them to make Aaron's vestments, to set him apart as holy, to act as priest for me. These are the articles of clothing they are to make: Breastpiece, Ephod, robe, woven tunic, turban, sash. They are making holy vestments for your brother Aaron and his sons as they

NEW INTERNATIONAL VERSION

they may serve me as priests. ⁵Have them use gold, and blue, purple and scarlet yarn, and fine linen.

The Ephod

⁶"Make the ephod of gold, and of blue, purple and scarlet yarn, and of finely twisted linen—the work of a skilled craftsman. ⁷It is to have two shoulder pieces attached to two of its corners, so it can be fastened. ⁸Its skillfully woven waistband is to be like it—of one piece with the ephod and made with gold, and with blue, purple and scarlet yarn, and with finely twisted linen.

⁹"Take two onyx stones and engrave on them the names of the sons of Israel ¹⁰in the order of their birth—six names on one stone and the remaining six on the other. ¹¹Engrave the names of the sons of Israel on the two stones the way a gem cutter engraves a seal. Then mount the stones in gold filigree settings ¹²and fasten them on the shoulder pieces of the ephod as memorial stones for the sons of Israel. Aaron is to bear the names on his shoulders as a memorial before the LORD. ¹³Make gold filigree settings ¹⁴and two braided chains of pure gold, like a rope, and attach the chains to the settings.

The Breastpiece

¹⁵"Fashion a breastpiece for making decisions—the work of a skilled craftsman. Make it like the ephod: of gold, and of blue, purple and scarlet yarn, and of finely twisted linen. ¹⁶It is to be square—a span[a] long and a span wide—and folded double. ¹⁷Then mount four rows of precious stones on it. In the first row there shall be a ruby, a topaz and a beryl; ¹⁸in the second row a turquoise, a sapphire[b] and an emerald; ¹⁹in the third row a jacinth, an agate and an amethyst; ²⁰in the fourth row a chrysolite, an onyx and a jasper.[c] Mount them in gold filigree settings. ²¹There are to be twelve stones, one for each of the names of the sons of Israel, each engraved like a seal with the name of one of the twelve tribes.

²²"For the breastpiece make braided chains of pure gold, like a rope. ²³Make two gold rings for it and fasten them to two corners of the breastpiece. ²⁴Fasten the two gold chains to the rings at the corners of the breastpiece, ²⁵and the other ends of the chains to the two settings, attaching them to the shoulder pieces of the ephod at the front. ²⁶Make two gold rings and attach them to the other two corners of the breastpiece on the

THE MESSAGE

work as priests for me. They will need gold; blue, purple, and scarlet material; and fine linen.

The Ephod

28.6-14 "Have the Ephod made from gold; blue, purple, and scarlet material; and fine twisted linen by a skilled craftsman. Give it two shoulder pieces at two of the corners so it can be fastened. The decorated band on it is to be just like it and of one piece with it: made of gold; blue, purple, and scarlet material; and of fine twisted linen. Next take two onyx stones and engrave the names of the sons of Israel on them in the order of their birth, six names on one stone and the remaining six on the other. Engrave the names of the sons of Israel on the two stones the way a jeweler engraves a seal. Then mount the stones in settings of filigreed gold. Fasten the two stones on the shoulder pieces of the Ephod—they are memorial stones for the Israelites. Aaron will wear these names on his shoulders as a memorial before GOD. Make the settings of gold filigree. Make two chains of pure gold and braid them like cords, then attach the corded chains to the settings.

The Breastpiece

28.15-20 "Now make a Breastpiece of Judgment, using skilled craftsmen, the same as with the Ephod. Use gold; blue, purple, and scarlet material; and fine twisted linen. Make it nine inches square and folded double. Mount four rows of precious gemstones on it.

> First row: carnelian, topaz, emerald.
> Second row: ruby, sapphire, crystal.
> Third row: jacinth, agate, amethyst.
> Fourth row: beryl, onyx, jasper.

28.20-21 "Set them in gold filigree. The twelve stones correspond to the names of the Israelites, with twelve names engraved, one on each, as on a seal for the twelve tribes.

28.22-28 "Then make braided chains of pure gold for the Breastpiece, like cords. Make two rings of gold for the Breastpiece and fasten them to the two ends. Fasten the two golden cords to the rings at the ends of the Breastpiece. Then fasten the other ends of the two cords to the two settings of filigree, attaching them to the shoulder pieces of the Ephod in front. Then make two rings of gold and fasten them to the two ends of the Breastpiece on its inside edge facing the

---

a 16 That is, about 9 inches (about 22 centimeters)
b 18 Or *lapis lazuli*   *c 20* The precise identification of some of these precious stones is uncertain.

NEW INTERNATIONAL VERSION

inside edge next to the ephod. ²⁷Make two more gold rings and attach them to the bottom of the shoulder pieces on the front of the ephod, close to the seam just above the waistband of the ephod. ²⁸The rings of the breastpiece are to be tied to the rings of the ephod with blue cord, connecting it to the waistband, so that the breastpiece will not swing out from the ephod.

²⁹"Whenever Aaron enters the Holy Place, he will bear the names of the sons of Israel over his heart on the breastpiece of decision as a continuing memorial before the LORD. ³⁰Also put the Urim and the Thummim in the breastpiece, so they may be over Aaron's heart whenever he enters the presence of the LORD. Thus Aaron will always bear the means of making decisions for the Israelites over his heart before the LORD.

OTHER PRIESTLY GARMENTS

³¹"Make the robe of the ephod entirely of blue cloth, ³²with an opening for the head in its center. There shall be a woven edge like a collarᵃ around this opening, so that it will not tear. ³³Make pomegranates of blue, purple and scarlet yarn around the hem of the robe, with gold bells between them. ³⁴The gold bells and the pomegranates are to alternate around the hem of the robe. ³⁵Aaron must wear it when he ministers. The sound of the bells will be heard when he enters the Holy Place before the LORD and when he comes out, so that he will not die.

³⁶"Make a plate of pure gold and engrave on it as on a seal: HOLY TO THE LORD. ³⁷Fasten a blue cord to it to attach it to the turban; it is to be on the front of the turban. ³⁸It will be on Aaron's forehead, and he will bear the guilt involved in the sacred gifts the Israelites consecrate, whatever their gifts may be. It will be on Aaron's forehead continually so that they will be acceptable to the LORD.

³⁹"Weave the tunic of fine linen and make the turban of fine linen. The sash is to be the work of an embroiderer. ⁴⁰Make tunics, sashes and headbands for Aaron's sons, to give them dignity and honor. ⁴¹After you put these clothes on your brother Aaron and his sons, anoint and ordain them. Consecrate them so they may serve me as priests.

⁴²"Make linen undergarments as a covering for the body, reaching from the waist to the thigh. ⁴³Aaron and his sons must wear them whenever they enter the Tent of Meeting or approach the altar to minister in the Holy Place, so that they will not incur guilt and die.

"This is to be a lasting ordinance for Aaron and his descendants.

ᵃ 32 The meaning of the Hebrew for this word is uncertain.

THE MESSAGE

Ephod. Then make two more rings of gold and fasten them in the front of the Ephod to the lower part of the two shoulder pieces, near the seam above the decorated band. Fasten the Breastpiece in place by running a cord of blue through its rings to the rings of the Ephod so that it rests secure on the decorated band of the Ephod and won't come loose.

28.29-30 "Aaron will regularly carry the names of the sons of Israel on the Breastpiece of Judgment over his heart as he enters the Sanctuary into the presence of GOD for remembrance. Place the Urim and Thummim in the Breastpiece of Judgment. They will be over Aaron's heart when he enters the presence of GOD. In this way Aaron will regularly carry the Breastpiece of Judgment into the presence of GOD.

THE ROBE

28.31-35 "Make the robe for the Ephod entirely of blue, with an opening for the head at the center and a hem on the edge so that it won't tear. For the edge of the skirts make pomegranates of blue, purple, and scarlet material all around and alternate them with bells of gold—gold bell and pomegranate, gold bell and pomegranate—all around the hem of the robe. Aaron has to wear it when he does his priestly work. The bells will be heard when he enters the Holy Place and comes into the presence of GOD, and again when he comes out so that he won't die.

THE TURBAN, TUNIC, UNDERWEAR

28.36-38 "Make a plate of pure gold. Engrave on it as on a seal: 'Holy to GOD.' Tie it with a blue cord to the front of the turban. It is to rest there on Aaron's forehead. He'll take on any guilt involved in the sacred offerings that the Israelites consecrate, no matter what they bring. It will always be on Aaron's forehead so that the offerings will be acceptable before GOD.

28.39-41 "Weave the tunic of fine linen. Make the turban of fine linen. The sash will be the work of an embroiderer. Make tunics, sashes, and hats for Aaron's sons to express glory and beauty. Dress your brother Aaron and his sons in them. Anoint, ordain, and consecrate them to serve me as priests.

28.42-43 "Make linen underwear to cover their nakedness from waist to thigh. Aaron and his sons must wear it whenever they enter the Tent of Meeting or approach the Altar to minister in the Holy Place so that they won't incur guilt and die. This is a permanent rule for Aaron and all his priest-descendants.

NEW INTERNATIONAL VERSION

CONSECRATION OF THE PRIESTS

29 "This is what you are to do to consecrate them, so they may serve me as priests: Take a young bull and two rams without defect. ²And from fine wheat flour, without yeast, make bread, and cakes mixed with oil, and wafers spread with oil. ³Put them in a basket and present them in it—along with the bull and the two rams. ⁴Then bring Aaron and his sons to the entrance to the Tent of Meeting and wash them with water. ⁵Take the garments and dress Aaron with the tunic, the robe of the ephod, the ephod itself and the breastpiece. Fasten the ephod on him by its skillfully woven waistband. ⁶Put the turban on his head and attach the sacred diadem to the turban. ⁷Take the anointing oil and anoint him by pouring it on his head. ⁸Bring his sons and dress them in tunics ⁹and put headbands on them. Then tie sashes on Aaron and his sons.ᵃ The priesthood is theirs by a lasting ordinance. In this way you shall ordain Aaron and his sons.

¹⁰"Bring the bull to the front of the Tent of Meeting, and Aaron and his sons shall lay their hands on its head. ¹¹Slaughter it in the LORD's presence at the entrance to the Tent of Meeting. ¹²Take some of the bull's blood and put it on the horns of the altar with your finger, and pour out the rest of it at the base of the altar. ¹³Then take all the fat around the inner parts, the covering of the liver, and both kidneys with the fat on them, and burn them on the altar. ¹⁴But burn the bull's flesh and its hide and its offal outside the camp. It is a sin offering.

¹⁵"Take one of the rams, and Aaron and his sons shall lay their hands on its head. ¹⁶Slaughter it and take the blood and sprinkle it against the altar on all sides. ¹⁷Cut the ram into pieces and wash the inner parts and the legs, putting them with the head and the other pieces. ¹⁸Then burn the entire ram on the altar. It is a burnt offering to the LORD, a pleasing aroma, an offering made to the LORD by fire.

¹⁹"Take the other ram, and Aaron and his sons shall lay their hands on its head. ²⁰Slaughter it, take some of its blood and put it on the lobes of the right ears of Aaron and his sons, on the thumbs of their right hands, and on the big toes of their right feet. Then sprinkle blood against the altar on all sides. ²¹And take some of the blood on the altar and some of the anointing oil and sprinkle it on Aaron and his garments and on his sons and their garments. Then he and his sons and their garments will be consecrated.

ᵃ 9 Hebrew; Septuagint *on them*

THE MESSAGE

CONSECRATION OF PRIESTS

29.1-4 **29** "This is the ceremony for consecrating them as priests. Take a young bull and two rams, healthy and without defects. Using fine wheat flour but no yeast make bread and cakes mixed with oil and wafers spread with oil. Place them in a basket and carry them along with the bull and the two rams. Bring Aaron and his sons to the entrance of the Tent of Meeting and wash them with water.

29.5-9 "Then take the vestments and dress Aaron in the tunic, the robe of the Ephod, the Ephod, and the Breastpiece, belting the Ephod on him with the embroidered waistband. Set the turban on his head and place the sacred crown on the turban. Then take the anointing oil and pour it on his head, anointing him. Then bring his sons, put tunics on them and gird them with sashes, both Aaron and his sons, and set hats on them. Their priesthood is upheld by law and is permanent.

29.9-14 "This is how you will ordain Aaron and his sons: Bring the bull to the Tent of Meeting. Aaron and his sons will place their hands on the head of the bull. Then you will slaughter the bull in the presence of GOD at the entrance to the Tent of Meeting. Take some of the bull's blood and smear it on the horns of the Altar with your finger; pour the rest of the blood on the base of the Altar. Next take all the fat that covers the innards, fat from around the liver and the two kidneys, and burn it on the Altar. But the flesh of the bull, including its hide and dung, you will burn up outside the camp. It is an Absolution-Offering.

29.15-18 "Then take one of the rams. Have Aaron and his sons place their hands on the head of the ram. Slaughter the ram and take its blood and throw it against the Altar, all around. Cut the ram into pieces; wash its innards and legs, then gather the pieces and its head and burn the whole ram on the Altar. It is a Whole-Burnt-Offering to GOD, a pleasant fragrance, an offering by fire to GOD.

29.19-21 "Then take the second ram. Have Aaron and his sons place their hands on the ram's head. Slaughter the ram. Take some of its blood and rub it on Aaron's right earlobe and on the right earlobes of his sons, on the thumbs of their right hands and on the big toes of their right feet. Sprinkle the rest of the blood against all sides of the Altar. Then take some of the blood that is on the Altar, mix it with some of the anointing oil, and splash it on Aaron and his clothes and on his sons and their clothes so that Aaron and his clothes and his sons and his sons' clothes will be made holy.

NEW INTERNATIONAL VERSION

22"Take from this ram the fat, the fat tail, the fat around the inner parts, the covering of the liver, both kidneys with the fat on them, and the right thigh. (This is the ram for the ordination.) 23From the basket of bread made without yeast, which is before the LORD, take a loaf, and a cake made with oil, and a wafer. 24Put all these in the hands of Aaron and his sons and wave them before the LORD as a wave offering. 25Then take them from their hands and burn them on the altar along with the burnt offering for a pleasing aroma to the LORD, an offering made to the LORD by fire. 26After you take the breast of the ram for Aaron's ordination, wave it before the LORD as a wave offering, and it will be your share.

27"Consecrate those parts of the ordination ram that belong to Aaron and his sons: the breast that was waved and the thigh that was presented. 28This is always to be the regular share from the Israelites for Aaron and his sons. It is the contribution the Israelites are to make to the LORD from their fellowship offerings.[a]

29"Aaron's sacred garments will belong to his descendants so that they can be anointed and ordained in them. 30The son who succeeds him as priest and comes to the Tent of Meeting to minister in the Holy Place is to wear them seven days.

31"Take the ram for the ordination and cook the meat in a sacred place. 32At the entrance to the Tent of Meeting, Aaron and his sons are to eat the meat of the ram and the bread that is in the basket. 33They are to eat these offerings by which atonement was made for their ordination and consecration. But no one else may eat them, because they are sacred. 34And if any of the meat of the ordination ram or any bread is left over till morning, burn it up. It must not be eaten, because it is sacred.

35"Do for Aaron and his sons everything I have commanded you, taking seven days to ordain them. 36Sacrifice a bull each day as a sin offering to make atonement. Purify the altar by making atonement for it, and anoint it to consecrate it. 37For seven days make atonement for the altar and consecrate it. Then the altar will be most holy, and whatever touches it will be holy.

38"This is what you are to offer on the altar regularly each day: two lambs a year old. 39Offer one in the morning and the other at twilight. 40With the first lamb offer a tenth of an ephah[b] of fine flour mixed with a quarter of a hin[c] of oil from pressed olives, and a quarter of a hin of wine as a drink offering. 41Sacrifice the other

THE MESSAGE

29.22-23 "Take the fat from the ram, the fat tail, the fat that covers the innards, the long lobe of the liver, the two kidneys and the fat on them, and the right thigh: this is the ordination ram. Also take one loaf of bread, an oil cake, and a wafer from the breadbasket that is in the presence of GOD.

29.24-25 "Place all of these in the open hands of Aaron and his sons who will wave them before GOD, a Wave-Offering. Then take them from their hands and burn them on the Altar with the Whole-Burnt-Offering—a pleasing fragrance before GOD, a gift to GOD.

29.26 "Now take the breast from Aaron's ordination ram and wave it before GOD, a Wave-Offering. That will be your portion.

29.27-28 "Consecrate the Wave-Offering breast and the thigh that was held up. These are the parts of the ordination ram that are for Aaron and his sons. Aaron and his sons are always to get this offering from the Israelites; the Israelites are to make this offering regularly from their Peace-Offerings.

29.29-30 "Aaron's sacred garments are to be handed down to his descendants so they can be anointed and ordained in them. The son who succeeds him as priest is to wear them for seven days and enter the Tent of Meeting to minister in the Holy Place.

29.31-34 "Take the ordination ram and boil the meat in the Holy Place. At the entrance to the Tent of Meeting, Aaron and his sons will eat the boiled ram and the bread that is in the basket. Atoned by these offerings, ordained and consecrated by them, they are the only ones who are to eat them. No outsiders are to eat them; they're holy. Anything from the ordination ram or from the bread that is left over until morning you are to burn up. Don't eat it; it's holy.

29.35-37 "Do everything for the ordination of Aaron and his sons exactly as I've commanded you throughout the seven days. Offer a bull as an Absolution-Offering for atonement each day. Offer it on the Altar when you make atonement for it: Anoint and consecrate it. Make atonement for the Altar and consecrate it for seven days; the Altar will become soaked in holiness—anyone who so much as touches the Altar will become holy.

29.38-41 "This is what you are to offer on the Altar: two year-old lambs each and every day, one lamb in the morning and the second lamb at evening. With the sacrifice of the first lamb offer two quarts of fine flour with a quart of virgin olive oil, plus a quart of wine for a Drink-Offering. The sacrifice of the second lamb, the

---

a 28 Traditionally *peace offerings*   *b 40* That is, probably about 2 quarts (about 2 liters)   *c 40* That is, probably about 1 quart (about 1 liter)

NEW INTERNATIONAL VERSION

lamb at twilight with the same grain offering and its drink offering as in the morning—a pleasing aroma, an offering made to the LORD by fire.

⁴²"For the generations to come this burnt offering is to be made regularly at the entrance to the Tent of Meeting before the LORD. There I will meet you and speak to you; ⁴³there also I will meet with the Israelites, and the place will be consecrated by my glory.

⁴⁴"So I will consecrate the Tent of Meeting and the altar and will consecrate Aaron and his sons to serve me as priests. ⁴⁵Then I will dwell among the Israelites and be their God. ⁴⁶They will know that I am the LORD their God, who brought them out of Egypt so that I might dwell among them. I am the LORD their God.

THE ALTAR OF INCENSE

30 "Make an altar of acacia wood for burning incense. ²It is to be square, a cubit long and a cubit wide, and two cubits high *a*—its horns of one piece with it. ³Overlay the top and all the sides and the horns with pure gold, and make a gold molding around it. ⁴Make two gold rings for the altar below the molding—two on opposite sides—to hold the poles used to carry it. ⁵Make the poles of acacia wood and overlay them with gold. ⁶Put the altar in front of the curtain that is before the ark of the Testimony—before the atonement cover that is over the Testimony— where I will meet with you.

⁷"Aaron must burn fragrant incense on the altar every morning when he tends the lamps. ⁸He must burn incense again when he lights the lamps at twilight so incense will burn regularly before the LORD for the generations to come. ⁹Do not offer on this altar any other incense or any burnt offering or grain offering, and do not pour a drink offering on it. ¹⁰Once a year Aaron shall make atonement on its horns. This annual atonement must be made with the blood of the atoning sin offering for the generations to come. It is most holy to the LORD."

ATONEMENT MONEY

¹¹Then the LORD said to Moses, ¹²"When you take a census of the Israelites to count them, each one must pay the LORD a ransom for his life at the time he is counted. Then no plague will come on them when you number them. ¹³Each one who crosses over to those already counted is to give a half shekel, *b* according to the sanctuary shekel, which weighs twenty ge-

THE MESSAGE

one at evening, is also to be accompanied by the same Grain-Offering and Drink-Offering of the morning sacrifice to give a pleasing fragrance, a gift to GOD.

29.42-46 "This is to be your regular, daily Whole-Burnt-Offering before GOD, generation after generation, sacrificed at the entrance of the Tent of Meeting. That's where I'll meet you; that's where I'll speak with you; that's where I'll meet the Israelites, at the place made holy by my Glory. I'll make the Tent of Meeting and the Altar holy. I'll make Aaron and his sons holy in order to serve me as priests. I'll move in and live with the Israelites. I'll be their God. They'll realize that I am their GOD who brought them out of the land of Egypt so that I could live with them. I am GOD, *your* God.

THE ALTAR OF INCENSE

30.1-5 **30** "Make an Altar for burning incense. Construct it from acacia wood, one and one-half feet square and three feet high with its horns of one piece with it. Cover it with a veneer of pure gold, its top, sides, and horns, and make a gold molding around it with two rings of gold beneath the molding. Place the rings on the two opposing sides to serve as holders for poles by which it will be carried. Make the poles of acacia wood and cover them with a veneer of gold.

30.6-10 "Place the Altar in front of the curtain that hides the Chest of The Testimony, in front of the Atonement-Cover that is over The Testimony where I will meet you. Aaron will burn fragrant incense on it every morning when he polishes the lamps, and again in the evening as he prepares the lamps for lighting, so that there will always be incense burning before GOD, generation after generation. But don't burn on this Altar any unholy incense or Whole-Burnt-Offering or Grain-Offering. And don't pour out Drink-Offerings on it. Once a year Aaron is to purify the Altar horns. Using the blood of the Absolution-Offering of atonement, he is to make this atonement every year down through the generations. It is most holy to GOD."

THE ATONEMENT-TAX

30.11-16 GOD spoke to Moses: "When you take a head count of the Israelites to keep track of them, all must pay an atonement-tax to GOD for their life at the time of being registered so that nothing bad will happen because of the registration. Everyone who gets counted is to give a half-shekel (using the standard Sanctuary shekel of

---

a 2 That is, about 1 1/2 feet (about 0.5 meter) long and wide and about 3 feet (about 0.9 meter) high   *b* 13 That is, about 1/5 ounce (about 6 grams); also in verse 15

<table>
<tr><td>

NEW INTERNATIONAL VERSION

rahs. This half shekel is an offering to the LORD. [14]All who cross over, those twenty years old or more, are to give an offering to the LORD. [15]The rich are not to give more than a half shekel and the poor are not to give less when you make the offering to the LORD to atone for your lives. [16]Receive the atonement money from the Israelites and use it for the service of the Tent of Meeting. It will be a memorial for the Israelites before the LORD, making atonement for your lives."

BASIN FOR WASHING

[17]Then the LORD said to Moses, [18]"Make a bronze basin, with its bronze stand, for washing. Place it between the Tent of Meeting and the altar, and put water in it. [19]Aaron and his sons are to wash their hands and feet with water from it. [20]Whenever they enter the Tent of Meeting, they shall wash with water so that they will not die. Also, when they approach the altar to minister by presenting an offering made to the LORD by fire, [21]they shall wash their hands and feet so that they will not die. This is to be a lasting ordinance for Aaron and his descendants for the generations to come."

ANOINTING OIL

[22]Then the LORD said to Moses, [23]"Take the following fine spices: 500 shekels*a* of liquid myrrh, half as much (that is, 250 shekels) of fragrant cinnamon, 250 shekels of fragrant cane, [24]500 shekels of cassia—all according to the sanctuary shekel—and a hin*b* of olive oil. [25]Make these into a sacred anointing oil, a fragrant blend, the work of a perfumer. It will be the sacred anointing oil. [26]Then use it to anoint the Tent of Meeting, the ark of the Testimony, [27]the table and all its articles, the lampstand and its accessories, the altar of incense, [28]the altar of burnt offering and all its utensils, and the basin with its stand. [29]You shall consecrate them so they will be most holy, and whatever touches them will be holy.

[30]"Anoint Aaron and his sons and consecrate them so they may serve me as priests. [31]Say to the Israelites, 'This is to be my sacred anointing oil for the generations to come. [32]Do not pour it on men's bodies and do not make any oil with the same formula. It is sacred, and you are to consider it sacred. [33]Whoever makes perfume like it and whoever puts it on anyone other than a priest must be cut off from his people.' "

INCENSE

[34]Then the LORD said to Moses, "Take fragrant

</td><td>

THE MESSAGE

a fifth of an ounce to the shekel)—a half-shekel offering to GOD. Everyone counted, age twenty and up, is to make the offering to GOD. The rich are not to pay more nor the poor less than the half-shekel offering to GOD, the atonement-tax for your lives. Take the atonement-tax money from the Israelites and put it to the maintenance of the Tent of Meeting. It will be a memorial fund for the Israelites in honor of GOD, making atonement for your lives."

THE WASHBASIN

30.17-21 GOD spoke to Moses: "Make a bronze Washbasin; make it with a bronze base. Place it between the Tent of Meeting and the Altar. Put water in it. Aaron and his sons will wash their hands and feet in it. When they enter the Tent of Meeting or approach the Altar to serve there or offer gift offerings to GOD, they are to wash so they will not die. They are to wash their hands and their feet so they will not die. This is the rule forever, for Aaron and his sons down through the generations."

HOLY ANOINTING OIL

30.22-25 GOD spoke to Moses: "Take the best spices: twelve and a half pounds of liquid myrrh; half that much, six and a quarter pounds, of fragrant cinnamon; six and a quarter pounds of fragrant cane; twelve and a half pounds of cassia—using the standard Sanctuary weight for all of them—and a gallon of olive oil. Make these into a holy anointing oil, a perfumer's skillful blend.

30.26-29   "Use it to anoint the Tent of Meeting, the Chest of The Testimony, the Table and all its utensils, the Lampstand and its utensils, the Altar of Incense, the Altar of Whole-Burnt-Offerings and all its utensils, and the Washbasin and its base. Consecrate them so they'll be soaked in holiness, so that anyone who so much as touches them will become holy.

30.30-33   "Then anoint Aaron and his sons. Consecrate them as priests to me. Tell the Israelites, 'This will be my holy anointing oil throughout your generations.' Don't pour it on ordinary men. Don't copy this mixture to use for yourselves. It's holy; keep it holy. Whoever mixes up anything like it, or puts it on an ordinary person, will be expelled."

HOLY INCENSE

30.34-38 GOD spoke to Moses: "Take fragrant spices—

</td></tr>
</table>

a 23 That is, about 12 1/2 pounds (about 6 kilograms)
b 24 That is, probably about 4 quarts (about 4 liters)

NEW INTERNATIONAL VERSION	THE MESSAGE

spices—gum resin, onycha and galbanum—and pure frankincense, all in equal amounts, ³⁵and make a fragrant blend of incense, the work of a perfumer. It is to be salted and pure and sacred. ³⁶Grind some of it to powder and place it in front of the Testimony in the Tent of Meeting, where I will meet with you. It shall be most holy to you. ³⁷Do not make any incense with this formula for yourselves; consider it holy to the LORD. ³⁸Whoever makes any like it to enjoy its fragrance must be cut off from his people."

BEZALEL AND OHOLIAB

31 Then the LORD said to Moses, ²"See, I have chosen Bezalel son of Uri, the son of Hur, of the tribe of Judah, ³and I have filled him with the Spirit of God, with skill, ability and knowledge in all kinds of crafts— ⁴to make artistic designs for work in gold, silver and bronze, ⁵to cut and set stones, to work in wood, and to engage in all kinds of craftsmanship. ⁶Moreover, I have appointed Oholiab son of Ahisamach, of the tribe of Dan, to help him. Also I have given skill to all the craftsmen to make everything I have commanded you: ⁷the Tent of Meeting, the ark of the Testimony with the atonement cover on it, and all the other furnishings of the tent— ⁸the table and its articles, the pure gold lampstand and all its accessories, the altar of incense, ⁹the altar of burnt offering and all its utensils, the basin with its stand— ¹⁰and also the woven garments, both the sacred garments for Aaron the priest and the garments for his sons when they serve as priests, ¹¹and the anointing oil and fragrant incense for the Holy Place. They are to make them just as I commanded you."

THE SABBATH

¹²Then the LORD said to Moses, ¹³"Say to the Israelites, 'You must observe my Sabbaths. This will be a sign between me and you for the generations to come, so you may know that I am the LORD, who makes you holy.^a

¹⁴" 'Observe the Sabbath, because it is holy to you. Anyone who desecrates it must be put to death; whoever does any work on that day must be cut off from his people. ¹⁵For six days, work is to be done, but the seventh day is a Sabbath of rest, holy to the LORD. Whoever does any work on the Sabbath day must be put to death. ¹⁶The Israelites are to observe the Sabbath, celebrating it for the generations to come as a lasting covenant. ¹⁷It will be a sign between me and the Israelites forever, for in six days the LORD made

---

BEZALEL AND OHOLIAB

31.1-5 **31** GOD spoke to Moses: "See what I've done; I've personally chosen Bezalel son of Uri, son of Hur of the tribe of Judah. I've filled him with the Spirit of God, giving him skill and know-how and expertise in every kind of craft to create designs and work in gold, silver, and bronze; to cut and set gemstones; to carve wood—he's an all-around craftsman.

31.6-11 "Not only that, but I've given him Oholiab, son of Ahisamach of the tribe of Dan, to work with him. And to all who have an aptitude for crafts I've given the skills to make all the things I've commanded you: the Tent of Meeting, the Chest of The Testimony and its Atonement-Cover, all the implements for the Tent, the Table and its implements, the pure Lampstand and all its implements, the Altar of Incense, the Altar of Whole-Burnt-Offering and all its implements, the Washbasin and its base, the official vestments, the holy vestments for Aaron the priest and his sons in their priestly duties, the anointing oil, and the aromatic incense for the Holy Place—they'll make everything just the way I've commanded you."

SABBATH

31.12-17 GOD spoke to Moses: "Tell the Israelites, 'Above all, keep my Sabbaths, the sign between me and you, generation after generation, to keep the knowledge alive that I am the GOD who makes you holy. Keep the Sabbath; it's holy to you. Whoever profanes it will most certainly be put to death. Whoever works on it will be excommunicated from the people. There are six days for work but the seventh day is Sabbath, pure rest, holy to GOD. Anyone who works on the Sabbath will most certainly be put to death. The Israelites will keep the Sabbath, observe Sabbath-keeping down through the generations, as a standing covenant. It's a fixed sign between me and the Israelites. Yes, because in six days GOD made the Heavens and the Earth

---

^a 13 Or *who sanctifies you; or who sets you apart as holy*

NEW INTERNATIONAL VERSION

the heavens and the earth, and on the seventh day he abstained from work and rested.' "

¹⁸When the LORD finished speaking to Moses on Mount Sinai, he gave him the two tablets of the Testimony, the tablets of stone inscribed by the finger of God.

THE GOLDEN CALF

32 When the people saw that Moses was so long in coming down from the mountain, they gathered around Aaron and said, "Come, make us gods*ᵃ* who will go before us. As for this fellow Moses who brought us up out of Egypt, we don't know what has happened to him."

²Aaron answered them, "Take off the gold earrings that your wives, your sons and your daughters are wearing, and bring them to me." ³So all the people took off their earrings and brought them to Aaron. ⁴He took what they handed him and made it into an idol cast in the shape of a calf, fashioning it with a tool. Then they said, "These are your gods,*ᵇ* O Israel, who brought you up out of Egypt."

⁵When Aaron saw this, he built an altar in front of the calf and announced, "Tomorrow there will be a festival to the LORD." ⁶So the next day the people rose early and sacrificed burnt offerings and presented fellowship offerings.*ᶜ* Afterward they sat down to eat and drink and got up to indulge in revelry.

⁷Then the LORD said to Moses, "Go down, because your people, whom you brought up out of Egypt, have become corrupt. ⁸They have been quick to turn away from what I commanded them and have made themselves an idol cast in the shape of a calf. They have bowed down to it and sacrificed to it and have said, 'These are your gods, O Israel, who brought you up out of Egypt.'

⁹"I have seen these people," the LORD said to Moses, "and they are a stiff-necked people. ¹⁰Now leave me alone so that my anger may burn against them and that I may destroy them. Then I will make you into a great nation."

¹¹But Moses sought the favor of the LORD his God. "O LORD," he said, "why should your anger burn against your people, whom you brought out of Egypt with great power and a mighty hand? ¹²Why should the Egyptians say, 'It was with evil intent that he brought them out, to kill them in the mountains and to wipe them off the face of the earth'? Turn from your fierce anger; relent and do not bring disaster on your people. ¹³Remember your servants Abraham, Isaac and

---

ᵃ 1 Or a god; also in verses 23 and 31   ᵇ 4 Or This is your god; also in verse 8   ᶜ 6 Traditionally peace offerings

THE MESSAGE

and on the seventh day he stopped and took a long, deep breath.' "

31.18   When he finished speaking with him on Mount Sinai, he gave Moses two tablets of Testimony, slabs of stone, written with the finger of God.

"MAKE GODS FOR US"

32.1 **32** When the people realized that Moses was taking forever in coming down off the mountain, they rallied around Aaron and said, "Do something. Make gods for us who will lead us. That Moses, the man who got us out of Egypt—who knows what's happened to him?"

32.2-4   So Aaron told them, "Take off the gold rings from the ears of your wives and sons and daughters and bring them to me." They all did it; they removed the gold rings from their ears and brought them to Aaron. He took the gold from their hands and cast it in the form of a calf, shaping it with an engraving tool.

The people responded with enthusiasm: "These are your gods, O Israel, who brought you up from Egypt!"

32.5   Aaron, taking in the situation, built an altar before the calf.

Aaron then announced, "Tomorrow is a feast day to GOD!"

32.6   Early the next morning, the people got up and offered Whole-Burnt-Offerings and brought Peace-Offerings. The people sat down to eat and drink and then began to party. It turned into a wild party!

32.7-8   GOD spoke to Moses, "Go! Get down there! Your people whom you brought up from the land of Egypt have fallen to pieces. In no time at all they've turned away from the way I commanded them: They made a molten calf and worshiped it. They've sacrificed to it and said, 'These are the gods, O Israel, that brought you up from the land of Egypt!' "

32.9-10   GOD said to Moses, "I look at this people—oh! what a stubborn, hard-headed people! Let me alone now, give my anger free reign to burst into flames and incinerate them. But I'll make a great nation out of you."

32.11-13   Moses tried to calm his GOD down. He said, "Why, GOD, would you lose your temper with your people? Why, you brought them out of Egypt in a tremendous demonstration of power and strength. Why let the Egyptians say, 'He had it in for them—he brought them out so he could kill them in the mountains, wipe them right off the face of the Earth.' Stop your anger. Think twice about bringing evil against your people! Think of Abraham, Isaac, and Israel,

NEW INTERNATIONAL VERSION

Israel, to whom you swore by your own self: 'I will make your descendants as numerous as the stars in the sky and I will give your descendants all this land I promised them, and it will be their inheritance forever.' " ¹⁴Then the LORD relented and did not bring on his people the disaster he had threatened.

¹⁵Moses turned and went down the mountain with the two tablets of the Testimony in his hands. They were inscribed on both sides, front and back. ¹⁶The tablets were the work of God; the writing was the writing of God, engraved on the tablets.

¹⁷When Joshua heard the noise of the people shouting, he said to Moses, "There is the sound of war in the camp."

¹⁸Moses replied:

"It is not the sound of victory,
  it is not the sound of defeat;
  it is the sound of singing that I hear."

¹⁹When Moses approached the camp and saw the calf and the dancing, his anger burned and he threw the tablets out of his hands, breaking them to pieces at the foot of the mountain. ²⁰And he took the calf they had made and burned it in the fire; then he ground it to powder, scattered it on the water and made the Israelites drink it.

²¹He said to Aaron, "What did these people do to you, that you led them into such great sin?"

²²"Do not be angry, my lord," Aaron answered. "You know how prone these people are to evil. ²³They said to me, 'Make us gods who will go before us. As for this fellow Moses who brought us up out of Egypt, we don't know what has happened to him.' ²⁴So I told them, 'Whoever has any gold jewelry, take it off.' Then they gave me the gold, and I threw it into the fire, and out came this calf!"

²⁵Moses saw that the people were running wild and that Aaron had let them get out of control and so become a laughingstock to their enemies. ²⁶So he stood at the entrance to the camp and said, "Whoever is for the LORD, come to me." And all the Levites rallied to him.

²⁷Then he said to them, "This is what the LORD, the God of Israel, says: 'Each man strap a sword to his side. Go back and forth through the camp from one end to the other, each killing his brother and friend and neighbor.' " ²⁸The Levites did as Moses commanded, and that day about three thousand of the people died. ²⁹Then Moses said, "You have been set apart to the LORD today, for you were against your own sons and brothers, and he has blessed you this day."

THE MESSAGE

your servants to whom you gave your word, telling them 'I will give you many children, as many as the stars in the sky, and I'll give this land to your children as their land forever.' "

32.14   And GOD did think twice. He decided not to do the evil he had threatened against his people.

32.15-16   Moses turned around and came down from the mountain, carrying the two tablets of The Testimony. The tablets were written on both sides, front and back. God made the tablets and God wrote the tablets—engraved them.

32.17   When Joshua heard the sound of the people shouting noisily, he said to Moses, "That's the sound of war in the camp!"

32.18   But Moses said,

Those aren't songs of victory,
And those aren't songs of defeat,
I hear songs of people throwing a party.

32.19-20   And that's what it was. When Moses came near to the camp and saw the calf and the people dancing, his anger flared. He threw down the tablets and smashed them to pieces at the foot of the mountain. He took the calf that they had made, melted it down with fire, pulverized it to powder, then scattered it on the water and made the Israelites drink it.

32.21   Moses said to Aaron, "What on Earth did these people ever do to you that you involved them in this huge sin?"

32.22-23   Aaron said, "Master, don't be angry. You know this people and how set on evil they are. They said to me, 'Make us gods who will lead us. This Moses, the man who brought us out of Egypt, we don't know what's happened to him.'

32.24   "So I said, 'Who has gold?' And they took off their jewelry and gave it to me. I threw it in the fire and out came this calf."

32.25-26   Moses saw that the people were simply running wild—Aaron had let them run wild, disgracing themselves before their enemies. He took up a position at the entrance to the camp and said, "Whoever is on GOD's side, join me!" All the Levites stepped up.

32.27   He then told them, "GOD's orders, the God of Israel: 'Strap on your swords and go to work. Crisscross the camp from one end to the other: Kill brother, friend, neighbor.' "

32.28   The Levites carried out Moses' orders. Three thousand of the people were killed that day.

32.29   Moses said, "You confirmed your ordination today—and at great cost, even killing your sons and brothers! And God has blessed you."

NEW INTERNATIONAL VERSION

³⁰The next day Moses said to the people, "You have committed a great sin. But now I will go up to the LORD; perhaps I can make atonement for your sin."

³¹So Moses went back to the LORD and said, "Oh, what a great sin these people have committed! They have made themselves gods of gold. ³²But now, please forgive their sin—but if not, then blot me out of the book you have written."

³³The LORD replied to Moses, "Whoever has sinned against me I will blot out of my book. ³⁴Now go, lead the people to the place I spoke of, and my angel will go before you. However, when the time comes for me to punish, I will punish them for their sin."

³⁵And the LORD struck the people with a plague because of what they did with the calf Aaron had made.

33 Then the LORD said to Moses, "Leave this place, you and the people you brought up out of Egypt, and go up to the land I promised on oath to Abraham, Isaac and Jacob, saying, 'I will give it to your descendants.' ²I will send an angel before you and drive out the Canaanites, Amorites, Hittites, Perizzites, Hivites and Jebusites. ³Go up to the land flowing with milk and honey. But I will not go with you, because you are a stiff-necked people and I might destroy you on the way."

⁴When the people heard these distressing words, they began to mourn and no one put on any ornaments. ⁵For the LORD had said to Moses, "Tell the Israelites, 'You are a stiff-necked people. If I were to go with you even for a moment, I might destroy you. Now take off your ornaments and I will decide what to do with you.' " ⁶So the Israelites stripped off their ornaments at Mount Horeb.

THE TENT OF MEETING

⁷Now Moses used to take a tent and pitch it outside the camp some distance away, calling it the "tent of meeting." Anyone inquiring of the LORD would go to the tent of meeting outside the camp. ⁸And whenever Moses went out to the tent, all the people rose and stood at the entrances to their tents, watching Moses until he entered the tent. ⁹As Moses went into the tent, the pillar of cloud would come down and stay at the entrance, while the LORD spoke with Moses. ¹⁰Whenever the people saw the pillar of cloud

THE MESSAGE

32.30   The next day Moses addressed the people: "You have sinned an enormous sin! But I am going to go up to GOD; maybe I'll be able to clear you of your sin."

32.31-32   Moses went back to GOD and said, "This is terrible. This people has sinned—it's an enormous sin! They made gods of gold for themselves. And now, if you will only forgive their sin. . . . But if not, erase me out of the book you've written."

32.33-34   GOD said to Moses, "I'll only erase from my book those who sin against me. For right now, you go and lead the people to where I told you. Look, my Angel is going ahead of you. On the day, though, when I settle accounts, their sins will certainly be part of the settlement."

32.35   GOD sent a plague on the people because of the calf they and Aaron had made.

✛

33 GOD said to Moses: "Now go. Get on your way from here, you and the people you brought up from the land of Egypt. Head for the land which I promised to Abraham, Isaac, and Jacob, saying 'I will give it to your descendants.' I will send an angel ahead of you and I'll drive out the Canaanites, Amorites, Hittites, Perizzites, Hivites, and Jebusites. It's a land flowing with milk and honey. But I won't be with you in person—you're such a stubborn, hard-headed people!—lest I destroy you on the journey."

33.4   When the people heard this harsh verdict, they were plunged into gloom and wore long faces. No one put on jewelry.

33.5-6   GOD said to Moses, "Tell the Israelites, 'You're one hard-headed people. I couldn't stand being with you for even a moment—I'd destroy you. So take off all your jewelry until I figure out what to do with you.' " So the Israelites stripped themselves of their jewelry from Mount Horeb on.

✛

33.7-10   Moses used to take the Tent and set it up outside the camp, some distance away. He called it the Tent of Meeting. Anyone who sought GOD would go to the Tent of Meeting outside the camp. It went like this: When Moses would go to the Tent, all the people would stand at attention; each man would take his position at the entrance to his tent with his eyes on Moses until he entered the Tent; whenever Moses entered the Tent, the Pillar of Cloud descended to the entrance to the Tent and GOD spoke with Moses. All the people would see the Pillar of

NEW INTERNATIONAL VERSION

standing at the entrance to the tent, they all stood and worshiped, each at the entrance to his tent. ¹¹The LORD would speak to Moses face to face, as a man speaks with his friend. Then Moses would return to the camp, but his young aide Joshua son of Nun did not leave the tent.

MOSES AND THE GLORY OF THE LORD

¹²Moses said to the LORD, "You have been telling me, 'Lead these people,' but you have not let me know whom you will send with me. You have said, 'I know you by name and you have found favor with me.' ¹³If you are pleased with me, teach me your ways so I may know you and continue to find favor with you. Remember that this nation is your people."

¹⁴The LORD replied, "My Presence will go with you, and I will give you rest."

¹⁵Then Moses said to him, "If your Presence does not go with us, do not send us up from here. ¹⁶How will anyone know that you are pleased with me and with your people unless you go with us? What else will distinguish me and your people from all the other people on the face of the earth?"

¹⁷And the LORD said to Moses, "I will do the very thing you have asked, because I am pleased with you and I know you by name."

¹⁸Then Moses said, "Now show me your glory."

¹⁹And the LORD said, "I will cause all my goodness to pass in front of you, and I will proclaim my name, the LORD, in your presence. I will have mercy on whom I will have mercy, and I will have compassion on whom I will have compassion. ²⁰But," he said, "you cannot see my face, for no one may see me and live."

²¹Then the LORD said, "There is a place near me where you may stand on a rock. ²²When my glory passes by, I will put you in a cleft in the rock and cover you with my hand until I have passed by. ²³Then I will remove my hand and you will see my back; but my face must not be seen."

THE NEW STONE TABLETS

34 The LORD said to Moses, "Chisel out two stone tablets like the first ones, and I will write on them the words that were on the first tablets, which you broke. ²Be ready in the morning, and then come up on Mount Sinai. Present yourself to me there on top of the mountain. ³No one is to come with you or be seen anywhere on the mountain; not even the flocks and herds may graze in front of the mountain."

⁴So Moses chiseled out two stone tablets like

THE MESSAGE

Cloud at the entrance to the Tent, stand at attention, and then bow down in worship, each man at the entrance to his tent.

33.11 And GOD spoke with Moses face-to-face, as neighbors speak to one another. When he would return to the camp, his attendant, the young man Joshua, stayed—he didn't leave the Tent.

✝

33.12-13 Moses said to GOD, "Look, you tell me, 'Lead this people,' but you don't let me know whom you're going to send with me. You tell me, 'I know you well and you are special to me.' If I am so special to you, let me in on your plans. That way, I will continue being special to you. Don't forget, this is *your* people, your responsibility."

33.14 GOD said, "My presence will go with you. I'll see the journey to the end."

33.15-16 Moses said, "If your presence doesn't take the lead here, call this trip off right now. How else will it be known that you're with me in this, with me and your people? Are you traveling with us or not? How else will we know that we're special, I and your people, among all other people on this planet Earth?"

33.17 GOD said to Moses: "All right. Just as you say; this also I will do, for I know you well and you are special to me. I know you by name."

33.18 Moses said, "Please. Let me see your Glory."

33.19 GOD said, "I will make my Goodness pass right in front of you; I'll call out the name, GOD, right before you. I'll treat well whomever I want to treat well and I'll be kind to whomever I want to be kind."

33.20 GOD continued, "But you may not see my face. No one can see me and live."

33.21-23 GOD said, "Look, here is a place right beside me. Put yourself on this rock. When my Glory passes by, I'll put you in the cleft of the rock and cover you with my hand until I've passed by. Then I'll take my hand away and you'll see my back. But you won't see my face."

✝

34.1-3 **34** GOD spoke to Moses: "Cut out two tablets of stone just like the originals and engrave on them the words that were on the original tablets you smashed. Be ready in the morning to climb Mount Sinai and get set to meet me on top of the mountain. Not a soul is to go with you; the whole mountain must be clear of people, even animals—not even sheep or oxen can be grazing in front of the mountain."

34.4-7 So Moses cut two tablets of stone just like

NEW INTERNATIONAL VERSION

the first ones and went up Mount Sinai early in the morning, as the LORD had commanded him; and he carried the two stone tablets in his hands. ⁵Then the LORD came down in the cloud and stood there with him and proclaimed his name, the LORD. ⁶And he passed in front of Moses, proclaiming, "The LORD, the LORD, the compassionate and gracious God, slow to anger, abounding in love and faithfulness, ⁷maintaining love to thousands, and forgiving wickedness, rebellion and sin. Yet he does not leave the guilty unpunished; he punishes the children and their children for the sin of the fathers to the third and fourth generation."

⁸Moses bowed to the ground at once and worshiped. ⁹"O Lord, if I have found favor in your eyes," he said, "then let the Lord go with us. Although this is a stiff-necked people, forgive our wickedness and our sin, and take us as your inheritance."

¹⁰Then the LORD said: "I am making a covenant with you. Before all your people I will do wonders never before done in any nation in all the world. The people you live among will see how awesome is the work that I, the LORD, will do for you. ¹¹Obey what I command you today. I will drive out before you the Amorites, Canaanites, Hittites, Perizzites, Hivites and Jebusites. ¹²Be careful not to make a treaty with those who live in the land where you are going, or they will be a snare among you. ¹³Break down their altars, smash their sacred stones and cut down their Asherah poles.ᵃ ¹⁴Do not worship any other god, for the LORD, whose name is Jealous, is a jealous God.

¹⁵"Be careful not to make a treaty with those who live in the land; for when they prostitute themselves to their gods and sacrifice to them, they will invite you and you will eat their sacrifices. ¹⁶And when you choose some of their daughters as wives for your sons and those daughters prostitute themselves to their gods, they will lead your sons to do the same.

¹⁷"Do not make cast idols.

¹⁸"Celebrate the Feast of Unleavened Bread. For seven days eat bread made without yeast, as I commanded you. Do this at the appointed time in the month of Abib, for in that month you came out of Egypt.

¹⁹"The first offspring of every womb belongs to me, including all the firstborn males of your livestock, whether from herd or flock. ²⁰Redeem the firstborn donkey with a lamb, but if you do not redeem it, break its neck. Redeem all your firstborn sons.

THE MESSAGE

the originals. He got up early in the morning and climbed Mount Sinai as GOD had commanded him, carrying the two tablets of stone. GOD descended in the cloud and took up his position there beside him and called out the name, GOD. GOD passed in front of him and called out, "GOD, GOD, a God of mercy and grace, endlessly patient—so much love, so deeply true—loyal in love for a thousand generations, forgiving iniquity, rebellion, and sin. Still, he doesn't ignore sin. He holds sons and grandsons responsible for a father's sins to the third and even fourth generation."

34.8-9 At once, Moses fell to the ground and worshiped, saying, "Please, O Master, if you see anything good in me, please Master, travel with us, hard-headed as these people are. Forgive our iniquity and sin. Own us, possess us."

34.10-12 And GOD said, "As of right now, I'm making a covenant with you: In full sight of your people I will work wonders that have never been created in all the Earth, in any nation. Then all the people with whom you're living will see how tremendous GOD's work is, the work I'll do for you. Take careful note of all I command you today. I'm clearing your way by driving out Amorites, Canaanites, Hittites, Perizzites, Hivites, and Jebusites. Stay vigilant. Don't let down your guard lest you make covenant with the people who live in the land that you are entering and they trip you up.

34.13-16 "Tear down their altars, smash their phallic pillars, chop down their fertility poles. Don't worship any other god. GOD—his name is The-Jealous-One—is a jealous God. Be careful that you don't make a covenant with the people who live in the land and take up with their sex-and-religion life, join them in meals at their altars, marry your sons to their women, women who take up with any convenient god or goddess and will get your sons to do the same thing.

34.17 "Don't make molten gods for yourselves.

34.18 "Keep the Feast of Unraised Bread. Eat only unraised bread for seven days in the month of Abib—it was in the month of Abib that you came out of Egypt.

34.19 "Every firstborn from the womb is mine, all the males of your herds, your firstborn oxen and sheep.

34.20 "Redeem your firstborn donkey with a lamb. If you don't redeem it you must break its neck.

"Redeem each of your firstborn sons.

ᵃ 13 That is, symbols of the goddess Asherah

NEW INTERNATIONAL VERSION

"No one is to appear before me empty-handed.
²¹"Six days you shall labor, but on the seventh day you shall rest; even during the plowing season and harvest you must rest.

²²"Celebrate the Feast of Weeks with the firstfruits of the wheat harvest, and the Feast of Ingathering at the turn of the year.[a] ²³Three times a year all your men are to appear before the Sovereign LORD, the God of Israel. ²⁴I will drive out nations before you and enlarge your territory, and no one will covet your land when you go up three times each year to appear before the LORD your God.

²⁵"Do not offer the blood of a sacrifice to me along with anything containing yeast, and do not let any of the sacrifice from the Passover Feast remain until morning.

²⁶"Bring the best of the firstfruits of your soil to the house of the LORD your God.

"Do not cook a young goat in its mother's milk."

²⁷Then the LORD said to Moses, "Write down these words, for in accordance with these words I have made a covenant with you and with Israel." ²⁸Moses was there with the LORD forty days and forty nights without eating bread or drinking water. And he wrote on the tablets the words of the covenant—the Ten Commandments.

THE RADIANT FACE OF MOSES

²⁹When Moses came down from Mount Sinai with the two tablets of the Testimony in his hands, he was not aware that his face was radiant because he had spoken with the LORD. ³⁰When Aaron and all the Israelites saw Moses, his face was radiant, and they were afraid to come near him. ³¹But Moses called to them; so Aaron and all the leaders of the community came back to him, and he spoke to them. ³²Afterward all the Israelites came near him, and he gave them all the commands the LORD had given him on Mount Sinai.

³³When Moses finished speaking to them, he put a veil over his face. ³⁴But whenever he entered the LORD's presence to speak with him, he removed the veil until he came out. And when he came out and told the Israelites what he had been commanded, ³⁵they saw that his face was radiant. Then Moses would put the veil back over his face until he went in to speak with the LORD.

THE MESSAGE

"No one is to show up in my presence empty-handed.

34.21 "Work six days and rest the seventh. Stop working even during plowing and harvesting.

34.22 "Keep the Feast of Weeks with the first cutting of the wheat harvest, and the Feast of Ingathering at the turn of the year.

34.23-24 "All your men are to appear before the Master, the GOD of Israel, three times a year. You won't have to worry about your land when you appear before your GOD three times each year, for I will drive out the nations before you and give you plenty of land. Nobody's going to be hanging around plotting ways to get it from you.

34.25 "Don't mix the blood of my sacrifices with anything fermented.

"Don't leave leftovers from the Passover Feast until morning.

34.26 "Bring the finest of the firstfruits of your produce to the house of your GOD.

"Don't boil a kid in its mother's milk."

34.27 GOD said to Moses: "Now write down these words, for by these words I've made a covenant with you and Israel."

34.28 Moses was there with GOD forty days and forty nights. He didn't eat any food; he didn't drink any water. And he wrote on the tablets the words of the covenant, the Ten Words.

34.29-30 When Moses came down from Mount Sinai carrying the two Tablets of The Testimony, he didn't know that the skin of his face glowed because he had been speaking with GOD. Aaron and all the Israelites saw Moses, saw his radiant face, and held back, afraid to get close to him.

34.31-32 Moses called out to them. Aaron and the leaders in the community came back and Moses talked with them. Later all the Israelites came up to him and he passed on the commands, everything that GOD had told him on Mount Sinai.

34.33-35 When Moses finished speaking with them, he put a veil over his face, but when he went into the presence of GOD to speak with him, he removed the veil until he came out. When he came out and told the Israelites what he had been commanded, they would see Moses' face, its skin glowing, and then he would again put the veil on his face until he went back in to speak with GOD.

[a] 22 That is, in the fall

NEW INTERNATIONAL VERSION

SABBATH REGULATIONS

35 Moses assembled the whole Israelite community and said to them, "These are the things the LORD has commanded you to do: ²For six days, work is to be done, but the seventh day shall be your holy day, a Sabbath of rest to the LORD. Whoever does any work on it must be put to death. ³Do not light a fire in any of your dwellings on the Sabbath day."

MATERIALS FOR THE TABERNACLE

⁴Moses said to the whole Israelite community, "This is what the LORD has commanded: ⁵From what you have, take an offering for the LORD. Everyone who is willing is to bring to the LORD an offering of gold, silver and bronze; ⁶blue, purple and scarlet yarn and fine linen; goat hair; ⁷ram skins dyed red and hides of sea cows ᵃ; acacia wood; ⁸olive oil for the light; spices for the anointing oil and for the fragrant incense; ⁹and onyx stones and other gems to be mounted on the ephod and breastpiece.

¹⁰"All who are skilled among you are to come and make everything the LORD has commanded: ¹¹the tabernacle with its tent and its covering, clasps, frames, crossbars, posts and bases; ¹²the ark with its poles and the atonement cover and the curtain that shields it; ¹³the table with its poles and all its articles and the bread of the Presence; ¹⁴the lampstand that is for light with its accessories, lamps and oil for the light; ¹⁵the altar of incense with its poles, the anointing oil and the fragrant incense; the curtain for the doorway at the entrance to the tabernacle; ¹⁶the altar of burnt offering with its bronze grating, its poles and all its utensils; the bronze basin with its stand; ¹⁷the curtains of the courtyard with its posts and bases, and the curtain for the entrance to the courtyard; ¹⁸the tent pegs for the tabernacle and for the courtyard, and their ropes; ¹⁹the woven garments worn for ministering in the sanctuary—both the sacred garments for Aaron the priest and the garments for his sons when they serve as priests."

²⁰Then the whole Israelite community withdrew from Moses' presence, ²¹and everyone who was willing and whose heart moved him came and brought an offering to the LORD for the work on the Tent of Meeting, for all its service, and for the sacred garments. ²²All who were willing, men and women alike, came and brought gold jewelry of all kinds: brooches, earrings, rings and ornaments. They all presented their gold as a wave offering to the LORD. ²³Everyone who had blue, purple or scarlet yarn or fine linen, or goat hair, ram skins dyed red or hides of sea cows

THE MESSAGE

BUILDING THE PLACE OF WORSHIP

35.1 **35** Moses spoke to the entire congregation of Israel, saying, "These are the things that GOD has commanded you to do:

35.2-3 "Work six days, but the seventh day will be a holy rest day, GOD's holy rest day. Anyone who works on this day must be put to death. Don't light any fires in your homes on the Sabbath day."

THE OFFERINGS

35.4 Moses spoke to the entire congregation of Israel, saying, "This is what GOD has commanded:

35.5-9 "Gather from among you an offering for GOD. Receive on GOD's behalf what everyone is willing to give as an offering: gold, silver, bronze; blue, purple, and scarlet material; fine linen; goats' hair; tanned rams' skins; dolphin skins; acacia wood; lamp oil; spices for anointing oils and for fragrant incense; onyx stones and other stones for setting in the Ephod and the Breastpiece.

35.10-19 "Come—all of you who have skills—come and make everything that GOD has commanded: The Dwelling with its tent and cover, its hooks, frames, crossbars, posts, and bases; the Chest with its poles, the Atonement-Cover and veiling curtain; the Table with its poles and implements and the Bread of the Presence; the Lampstand for giving light with its furnishings and lamps and the oil for lighting; the Altar of Incense with its poles, the anointing oil, the fragrant incense; the screen for the door at the entrance to The Dwelling; the Altar of Whole-Burnt-Offering with its bronze grate and poles and all its implements; the Washbasin with its base; the tapestry hangings for the Courtyard with the posts and bases, the screen for the Courtyard gate; the pegs for The Dwelling, the pegs for the Courtyard with their cords; the official vestments for ministering in the Holy Place, the sacred vestments for Aaron the priest and for his sons serving as priests."

35.20-26 So everyone in the community of Israel left the presence of Moses. Then they came back, every one whose heart was roused, whose spirit was freely responsive, bringing offerings to GOD for building the Tent of Meeting, furnishing it for worship and making the holy vestments. They came, both men and women, all the willing spirits among them, offering brooches, earrings, rings, necklaces—anything made of gold—offering up their gold jewelry to GOD. And anyone who had blue, purple, and scarlet fabrics; fine linen; goats' hair; tanned leather; and dolphin skins brought them.

ᵃ 7 That is, dugongs; also in verse 23

NEW INTERNATIONAL VERSION

brought them. ²⁴Those presenting an offering of silver or bronze brought it as an offering to the LORD, and everyone who had acacia wood for any part of the work brought it. ²⁵Every skilled woman spun with her hands and brought what she had spun—blue, purple or scarlet yarn or fine linen. ²⁶And all the women who were willing and had the skill spun the goat hair. ²⁷The leaders brought onyx stones and other gems to be mounted on the ephod and breastpiece. ²⁸They also brought spices and olive oil for the light and for the anointing oil and for the fragrant incense. ²⁹All the Israelite men and women who were willing brought to the LORD freewill offerings for all the work the LORD through Moses had commanded them to do.

BEZALEL AND OHOLIAB

³⁰Then Moses said to the Israelites, "See, the LORD has chosen Bezalel son of Uri, the son of Hur, of the tribe of Judah, ³¹and he has filled him with the Spirit of God, with skill, ability and knowledge in all kinds of crafts— ³²to make artistic designs for work in gold, silver and bronze, ³³to cut and set stones, to work in wood and to engage in all kinds of artistic craftsmanship. ³⁴And he has given both him and Oholiab son of Ahisamach, of the tribe of Dan, the ability to teach others. ³⁵He has filled them with skill to do all kinds of work as craftsmen, designers, embroiderers in blue, purple and scarlet yarn and fine linen, and weavers—all of them master craftsmen and designers.

36 ¹So Bezalel, Oholiab and every skilled person to whom the LORD has given skill and ability to know how to carry out all the work of constructing the sanctuary are to do the work just as the LORD has commanded."

²Then Moses summoned Bezalel and Oholiab and every skilled person to whom the LORD had given ability and who was willing to come and do the work. ³They received from Moses all the offerings the Israelites had brought to carry out the work of constructing the sanctuary. And the people continued to bring freewill offerings morning after morning. ⁴So all the skilled craftsmen who were doing all the work on the sanctuary left their work ⁵and said to Moses, "The people are bringing more than enough for doing the work the LORD commanded to be done."

⁶Then Moses gave an order and they sent this

THE MESSAGE

Everyone who wanted to offer up silver or bronze as a gift to GOD brought it. Everyone who had acacia wood that could be used in the work, brought it. All the women skilled at weaving brought their weavings of blue and purple and scarlet fabrics and their fine linens. And all the women who were gifted in spinning, spun the goats' hair.

^{35.27-29} The leaders brought onyx and other precious stones for setting in the Ephod and the Breastpiece. They also brought spices and olive oil for lamp oil, anointing oil, and incense. Every man and woman in Israel whose heart moved them freely to bring something for the work that GOD through Moses had commanded them to make, brought it, a voluntary offering for GOD.

BEZALEL AND OHOLIAB

^{35.30-35} Moses told the Israelites, "See, GOD has selected Bezalel son of Uri, son of Hur, of the tribe of Judah. He's filled him with the Spirit of God, with skill, ability, and know-how for making all sorts of things, to design and work in gold, silver, and bronze; to carve stones and set them; to carve wood, working in every kind of skilled craft. And he's also made him a teacher, he and Oholiab son of Ahisamach, of the tribe of Dan. He's gifted them with the know-how needed for carving, designing, weaving, and embroidering in blue, purple, and scarlet fabrics, and in fine linen. They can make anything and design anything.

36 ^{36.1} "Bezalel and Oholiab, along with everyone whom GOD has given the skill and know-how for making everything involved in the worship of the Sanctuary as commanded by GOD, are to start to work."

^{36.2-3} Moses summoned Bezalel and Oholiab along with all whom GOD had gifted with the ability to work skillfully with their hands. The men were eager to get started and engage in the work. They took from Moses all the offerings that the Israelites had brought for the work of constructing the Sanctuary. The people kept on bringing in their freewill offerings, morning after morning.

^{36.4-5} All the artisans who were at work making everything involved in constructing the Sanctuary came, one after another, to Moses, saying, "The people are bringing more than enough for doing this work that GOD has commanded us to do!"

^{36.6-7} So Moses sent out orders through the camp:

NEW INTERNATIONAL VERSION	THE MESSAGE

NEW INTERNATIONAL VERSION

word throughout the camp: "No man or woman is to make anything else as an offering for the sanctuary." And so the people were restrained from bringing more, 7because what they already had was more than enough to do all the work.

THE TABERNACLE

8All the skilled men among the workmen made the tabernacle with ten curtains of finely twisted linen and blue, purple and scarlet yarn, with cherubim worked into them by a skilled craftsman. 9All the curtains were the same size— twenty-eight cubits long and four cubits wide. *a* 10They joined five of the curtains together and did the same with the other five. 11Then they made loops of blue material along the edge of the end curtain in one set, and the same was done with the end curtain in the other set. 12They also made fifty loops on one curtain and fifty loops on the end curtain of the other set, with the loops opposite each other. 13Then they made fifty gold clasps and used them to fasten the two sets of curtains together so that the tabernacle was a unit.

14They made curtains of goat hair for the tent over the tabernacle—eleven altogether. 15All eleven curtains were the same size—thirty cubits long and four cubits wide. *b* 16They joined five of the curtains into one set and the other six into another set. 17Then they made fifty loops along the edge of the end curtain in one set and also along the edge of the end curtain in the other set. 18They made fifty bronze clasps to fasten the tent together as a unit. 19Then they made for the tent a covering of ram skins dyed red, and over that a covering of hides of sea cows. *c*

20They made upright frames of acacia wood for the tabernacle. 21Each frame was ten cubits long and a cubit and a half wide, *d* 22with two projections set parallel to each other. They made all the frames of the tabernacle in this way. 23They made twenty frames for the south side of the tabernacle 24and made forty silver bases to go under them—two bases for each frame, one under each projection. 25For the other side, the north side of the tabernacle, they made twenty frames 26and forty silver bases—two under each frame. 27They made six frames for the far end, that is, the west end of the tabernacle, 28and two frames were made for the corners of the tabernacle at the far end. 29At these two corners the frames were double from the bottom all the way

THE MESSAGE

"Men! Women! No more offerings for the building of the Sanctuary!"

The people were ordered to stop bringing offerings! There was plenty of material for all the work to be done. Enough and more than enough.

THE TAPESTRIES

36.8-13 Then all the skilled artisans on The Dwelling made ten tapestries of fine twisted linen and blue, purple, and scarlet fabric with an angel-cherubim design worked into the material. Each panel of tapestry was forty-six feet long and six feet wide. Five of the panels were joined together, and then the other five. Loops of blue were made along the edge of the outside panel of the first set, and the same on the outside panel of the second set. They made fifty loops on each panel, with the loops opposite each other. Then they made fifty gold clasps and joined the tapestries together so that The Dwelling was one whole.

36.14-19 Next they made tapestries of woven goat hair for a tent that would cover The Dwelling. They made eleven panels of these tapestries. The length of each panel was forty-five feet long and six feet wide. They joined five of the panels together, and then the other six, by making fifty loops along the edge of the end panel and fifty loops along the edge of the joining panel, then making fifty clasps of bronze, connecting the clasps to the loops, bringing the tent together. They finished it off by covering the tapestries with tanned rams' skins dyed red, and covered that with dolphin skins.

THE FRAMING

36.20-30 They framed The Dwelling with vertical planks of acacia wood, each section of frame fifteen feet long and two and a quarter feet wide, with two pegs for securing them. They made all the frames identical: twenty frames for the south side, with forty silver sockets to receive the two tenons from each of the twenty frames; they repeated that construction on the north side of The Dwelling. For the rear of The Dwelling facing west, they made six frames, with two additional frames for the rear corners. Both of the two corner frames were double in thickness

---

a 9 That is, about 42 feet (about 12.5 meters) long and 6 feet (about 1.8 meters) wide   *b 15* That is, about 45 feet (about 13.5 meters) long and 6 feet (about 1.8 meters) wide   *c 19* That is, dugongs   *d 21* That is, about 15 feet (about 4.5 meters) long and 2 1/4 feet (about 0.7 meter) wide

NEW INTERNATIONAL VERSION

to the top and fitted into a single ring; both were made alike. ³⁰So there were eight frames and sixteen silver bases—two under each frame.

³¹They also made crossbars of acacia wood: five for the frames on one side of the tabernacle, ³²five for those on the other side, and five for the frames on the west, at the far end of the tabernacle. ³³They made the center crossbar so that it extended from end to end at the middle of the frames. ³⁴They overlaid the frames with gold and made gold rings to hold the crossbars. They also overlaid the crossbars with gold.

³⁵They made the curtain of blue, purple and scarlet yarn and finely twisted linen, with cherubim worked into it by a skilled craftsman. ³⁶They made four posts of acacia wood for it and overlaid them with gold. They made gold hooks for them and cast their four silver bases. ³⁷For the entrance to the tent they made a curtain of blue, purple and scarlet yarn and finely twisted linen—the work of an embroiderer; ³⁸and they made five posts with hooks for them. They overlaid the tops of the posts and their bands with gold and made their five bases of bronze.

THE ARK

37 Bezalel made the ark of acacia wood— two and a half cubits long, a cubit and a half wide, and a cubit and a half high.ᵃ ²He overlaid it with pure gold, both inside and out, and made a gold molding around it. ³He cast four gold rings for it and fastened them to its four feet, with two rings on one side and two rings on the other. ⁴Then he made poles of acacia wood and overlaid them with gold. ⁵And he inserted the poles into the rings on the sides of the ark to carry it.

⁶He made the atonement cover of pure gold— two and a half cubits long and a cubit and a half wide.ᵇ ⁷Then he made two cherubim out of hammered gold at the ends of the cover. ⁸He made one cherub on one end and the second cherub on the other; at the two ends he made them of one piece with the cover. ⁹The cherubim had their wings spread upward, overshadowing the cover with them. The cherubim faced each other, looking toward the cover.

THE TABLE

¹⁰Theyᶜ made the table of acacia wood—two cubits long, a cubit wide, and a cubit and a half high.ᵈ ¹¹Then they overlaid it with pure gold and

ᵃ 1 That is, about 3 3/4 feet (about 1.1 meters) long and 2 1/4 feet (about 0.7 meter) wide and high   ᵇ 6 That is, about 3 3/4 feet (about 1.1 meters) long and 2 1/4 feet (about 0.7 meter) wide   ᶜ 10 Or He; also in verses 11-29
ᵈ 10 That is, about 3 feet (about 0.9 meter) long, 1 1/2 feet (about 0.5 meter) wide, and 2 1/4 feet (about 0.7 meter) high

THE MESSAGE

from top to bottom and fit into a single ring— eight frames altogether with sixteen sockets of silver, two under each frame.

36.31-34 They made crossbars of acacia wood, five for the frames on one side of The Dwelling, five for the other side, and five for the back side facing west. The center crossbar ran from end to end halfway up the frames. They covered the frames with a veneer of gold, made gold rings to hold the crossbars, and covered the crossbars with a veneer of gold.

36.35-36 They made the curtain of blue, purple, and scarlet material and fine twisted linen. They wove a design of angel-cherubim into it. They made four posts of acacia wood, covered them with a veneer of gold, and cast four silver bases for them.

36.37-38 They made a screen for the door of the tent, woven from blue, purple, and scarlet material and fine twisted linen with embroidery. They framed the weaving with five poles of acacia wood covered with a veneer of gold, and made gold hooks to hang the weaving and five bronze bases for the poles.

THE CHEST

37.1-5 **37** Bezalel made the Chest using acacia wood: He made it three and three-quarters feet long and two and a quarter feet wide and deep. He covered it inside and out with a veneer of pure gold and made a molding of gold all around it. He cast four gold rings and attached them to its four feet, two rings on one side and two rings on the other. He made poles from acacia wood, covered them with a veneer of gold, and inserted the poles for carrying the Chest into the rings on the sides.

37.6 Next he made a lid of pure gold for the Chest, an Atonement-Cover, three and three-quarters feet long and two and a quarter feet wide.

37.7-9 He sculpted two winged angel-cherubim out of hammered gold for the ends of the Atonement-Cover, one angel at one end, one angel at the other. He made them of one piece with the Atonement-Cover. The angels had outstretched wings and appeared to hover over the Atonement-Cover, facing one another but looking down on the Atonement-Cover.

THE TABLE

37.10-15 He made the Table from acacia wood. He made it three feet long, one and a half feet wide and two and a quarter feet high. He covered it with a veneer of pure gold and made a molding of

NEW INTERNATIONAL VERSION

made a gold molding around it. [12]They also made around it a rim a handbreadth[a] wide and put a gold molding on the rim. [13]They cast four gold rings for the table and fastened them to the four corners, where the four legs were. [14]The rings were put close to the rim to hold the poles used in carrying the table. [15]The poles for carrying the table were made of acacia wood and were overlaid with gold. [16]And they made from pure gold the articles for the table—its plates and dishes and bowls and its pitchers for the pouring out of drink offerings.

THE LAMPSTAND

[17]They made the lampstand of pure gold and hammered it out, base and shaft; its flowerlike cups, buds and blossoms were of one piece with it. [18]Six branches extended from the sides of the lampstand—three on one side and three on the other. [19]Three cups shaped like almond flowers with buds and blossoms were on one branch, three on the next branch and the same for all six branches extending from the lampstand. [20]And on the lampstand were four cups shaped like almond flowers with buds and blossoms. [21]One bud was under the first pair of branches extending from the lampstand, a second bud under the second pair, and a third bud under the third pair—six branches in all. [22]The buds and the branches were all of one piece with the lampstand, hammered out of pure gold.

[23]They made its seven lamps, as well as its wick trimmers and trays, of pure gold. [24]They made the lampstand and all its accessories from one talent[b] of pure gold.

THE ALTAR OF INCENSE

[25]They made the altar of incense out of acacia wood. It was square, a cubit long and a cubit wide, and two cubits high[c]—its horns of one piece with it. [26]They overlaid the top and all the sides and the horns with pure gold, and made a gold molding around it. [27]They made two gold rings below the molding—two on opposite sides—to hold the poles used to carry it. [28]They made the poles of acacia wood and overlaid them with gold.

[29]They also made the sacred anointing oil and the pure, fragrant incense—the work of a perfumer.

THE MESSAGE

gold all around it. He made a border a handbreadth wide all around it and a rim of gold for the border. He cast four rings of gold for it and attached the rings to the four legs parallel to the table top. They will serve as holders for the poles used to carry the Table. He made the poles of acacia wood and covered them with a veneer of gold. They will be used to carry the Table.

37.16 Out of pure gold he made the utensils for the Table: its plates, bowls, jars, and jugs used for pouring.

THE LAMPSTAND

37.17-23 He made a Lampstand of pure hammered gold, making its stem and branches, cups, calyxes, and petals all of one piece. It had six branches, three from one side and three from the other; three cups shaped like almond blossoms with calyxes and petals on one branch, three on the next, and so on—the same for all six branches. On the main stem of the Lampstand, there were four cups shaped like almonds, with calyxes and petals, a calyx extending from under each pair of the six branches. The entire Lampstand with its calyxes and stems was fashioned from one piece of hammered pure gold. He made seven of these lamps with their candle snuffers, all out of pure gold.

37.24 He used a seventy-five-pound brick of pure gold to make the Lampstand and its accessories.

THE ALTAR OF INCENSE

37.25-28 He made an Altar for burning incense from acacia wood. He made it a foot and a half square and three feet high, with its horns of one piece with it. He covered it with a veneer of pure gold, its top, sides, and horns, and made a gold molding around it with two rings of gold beneath the molding. He placed the rings on the two opposing sides to serve as holders for poles by which it will be carried. He made the poles of acacia wood and covered them with a veneer of gold.

37.29 He also prepared with the art of a perfumer the holy anointing oil and the pure aromatic incense.

---

[a] 12 That is, about 3 inches (about 8 centimeters)
[b] 24 That is, about 75 pounds (about 34 kilograms)
[c] 25 That is, about 1 1/2 feet (about 0.5 meter) long and wide, and about 3 feet (about 0.9 meter) high

NEW INTERNATIONAL VERSION

The Altar of Burnt Offering

38 They[a] built the altar of burnt offering of acacia wood, three cubits[b] high; it was square, five cubits long and five cubits wide.[c] ²They made a horn at each of the four corners, so that the horns and the altar were of one piece, and they overlaid the altar with bronze. ³They made all its utensils of bronze—its pots, shovels, sprinkling bowls, meat forks and firepans. ⁴They made a grating for the altar, a bronze network, to be under its ledge, halfway up the altar. ⁵They cast bronze rings to hold the poles for the four corners of the bronze grating. ⁶They made the poles of acacia wood and overlaid them with bronze. ⁷They inserted the poles into the rings so they would be on the sides of the altar for carrying it. They made it hollow, out of boards.

Basin for Washing

⁸They made the bronze basin and its bronze stand from the mirrors of the women who served at the entrance to the Tent of Meeting.

The Courtyard

⁹Next they made the courtyard. The south side was a hundred cubits[d] long and had curtains of finely twisted linen, ¹⁰with twenty posts and twenty bronze bases, and with silver hooks and bands on the posts. ¹¹The north side was also a hundred cubits long and had twenty posts and twenty bronze bases, with silver hooks and bands on the posts.

¹²The west end was fifty cubits[e] wide and had curtains, with ten posts and ten bases, with silver hooks and bands on the posts. ¹³The east end, toward the sunrise, was also fifty cubits wide. ¹⁴Curtains fifteen cubits[f] long were on one side of the entrance, with three posts and three bases, ¹⁵and curtains fifteen cubits long were on the other side of the entrance to the courtyard, with three posts and three bases. ¹⁶All the curtains around the courtyard were of finely twisted linen. ¹⁷The bases for the posts were bronze. The hooks and bands on the posts were silver, and their tops were overlaid with silver; so all the posts of the courtyard had silver bands.

¹⁸The curtain for the entrance to the courtyard was of blue, purple and scarlet yarn and finely twisted linen—the work of an embroiderer. It was twenty cubits[g] long and, like the curtains of the courtyard, five cubits[h] high, ¹⁹with

---

a 1 Or *He;* also in verses 2-9   *b 1* That is, about 4 1/2 feet (about 1.3 meters)   *c 1* That is, about 7 1/2 feet (about 2.3 meters) long and wide   *d 9* That is, about 150 feet (about 46 meters)   *e 12* That is, about 75 feet (about 23 meters)   *f 14* That is, about 22 1/2 feet (about 6.9 meters)   *g 18* That is, about 30 feet (about 9 meters)   *h 18* That is, about 7 1/2 feet (about 2.3 meters)

THE MESSAGE

The Altar of Whole-Burnt-Offering

38.1-7 **38** He made the Altar of Whole-Burnt-Offering from acacia wood. He made it seven and a half feet square and four and a half feet high. He made horns at each of the four corners. The horns were made of one piece with the Altar and covered with a veneer of bronze. He made from bronze all the utensils for the Altar: the buckets for removing the ashes, shovels, basins, forks, and fire pans. He made a grate of bronze mesh under the ledge halfway up the Altar. He cast four rings at each of the four corners of the bronze grating to hold the poles. He made the poles of acacia wood and covered them with a veneer of bronze. He inserted the poles through the rings on the two sides of the Altar for carrying it. The Altar was made out of boards; it was hollow.

The Washbasin

38.8 He made the Bronze Washbasin and its bronze stand from the mirrors of the women's work group who were assigned to serve at the entrance to the Tent of Meeting.

The Courtyard

38.9-11 And he made the Courtyard. On the south side the hangings for the Courtyard, woven from fine twisted linen, were 150 feet long, with their twenty posts and twenty bronze bases, and fastening hooks and bands of silver. The north side was exactly the same.

38.12-20 The west end of the Courtyard had seventy-five feet of hangings with ten posts and bases, and fastening hooks and bands of silver. Across the seventy-five feet at the front, or east end, were twenty-two and a half feet of hangings, with their three posts and bases on one side and the same for the other side. All the hangings around the Courtyard were of fine twisted linen. The bases for the posts were bronze and the fastening hooks and bands on the posts were of silver. The posts of the Courtyard were both capped and banded with silver. The screen at the door of the Courtyard was embroidered in blue, purple, and scarlet fabric with fine twisted linen. It was thirty feet long and seven and a half feet high, matching the hangings of

NEW INTERNATIONAL VERSION

four posts and four bronze bases. Their hooks and bands were silver, and their tops were overlaid with silver. 20All the tent pegs of the tabernacle and of the surrounding courtyard were bronze.

THE MATERIALS USED

21These are the amounts of the materials used for the tabernacle, the tabernacle of the Testimony, which were recorded at Moses' command by the Levites under the direction of Ithamar son of Aaron, the priest. 22(Bezalel son of Uri, the son of Hur, of the tribe of Judah, made everything the LORD commanded Moses; 23with him was Oholiab son of Ahisamach, of the tribe of Dan—a craftsman and designer, and an embroiderer in blue, purple and scarlet yarn and fine linen.) 24The total amount of the gold from the wave offering used for all the work on the sanctuary was 29 talents and 730 shekels,*a* according to the sanctuary shekel.

25The silver obtained from those of the community who were counted in the census was 100 talents and 1,775 shekels,*b* according to the sanctuary shekel— 26one beka per person; that is, half a shekel,*c* according to the sanctuary shekel, from everyone who had crossed over to those counted, twenty years old or more, a total of 603,550 men. 27The 100 talents*d* of silver were used to cast the bases for the sanctuary and for the curtain—100 bases from the 100 talents, one talent for each base. 28They used the 1,775 shekels*e* to make the hooks for the posts, to overlay the tops of the posts, and to make their bands.

29The bronze from the wave offering was 70 talents and 2,400 shekels.*f* 30They used it to make the bases for the entrance to the Tent of Meeting, the bronze altar with its bronze grating and all its utensils, 31the bases for the surrounding courtyard and those for its entrance and all the tent pegs for the tabernacle and those for the surrounding courtyard.

THE PRIESTLY GARMENTS

39 From the blue, purple and scarlet yarn they made woven garments for ministering in the sanctuary. They also made sacred garments for Aaron, as the LORD commanded Moses.

THE MESSAGE

the Courtyard. There were four posts with bases of bronze and fastening hooks of silver; they were capped and banded in silver. All the pegs for The Dwelling and the Courtyard were made of bronze.

✝

38.21-23 This is an inventory of The Dwelling that housed The Testimony drawn up by order of Moses for the work of the Levites under Ithamar, son of Aaron the priest. Bezalel, the son of Uri, son of Hur, of the tribe of Judah, made everything that GOD had commanded Moses. Working with Bezalel was Oholiab, the son of Ahisamach, of the tribe of Dan, an artisan, designer, and embroiderer in blue, purple, and scarlet fabrics and fine linen.

38.24 Gold. The total amount of gold used in construction of the Sanctuary, all of it contributed freely, weighed out at 1,900 pounds according to the Sanctuary standard.

38.25-28 Silver. The silver from those in the community who were registered in the census came to 6,437 pounds according to the Sanctuary standard—that amounted to a *beka*, or half-shekel, for every registered person aged twenty and over, a total of 603,550 men. They used the three and one-quarter tons of silver to cast the bases for the Sanctuary and for the hangings, one hundred bases at sixty-four pounds each. They used the remaining thirty-seven pounds to make the connecting hooks on the posts, and the caps and bands for the posts.

38.29-31 Bronze. The bronze that was brought in weighed 4,522 pounds. It was used to make the door of the Tent of Meeting, the Bronze Altar with its bronze grating, all the utensils of the Altar, the bases around the Courtyard, the bases for the gate of the Courtyard, and all the pegs for The Dwelling and the Courtyard.

39.1 **39** Vestments. Using the blue, purple, and scarlet fabrics, they made the woven vestments for ministering in the Sanctuary. Also they made the sacred vestments for Aaron, as GOD had commanded Moses.

---

a 24 The weight of the gold was a little over one ton (about 1 metric ton). *b 25* The weight of the silver was a little over 3 3/4 tons (about 3.4 metric tons). *c 26* That is, about 1/5 ounce (about 5.5 grams) *d 27* That is, about 3 3/4 tons (about 3.4 metric tons) *e 28* That is, about 45 pounds (about 20 kilograms) *f 29* The weight of the bronze was about 2 1/2 tons (about 2.4 metric tons).

NEW INTERNATIONAL VERSION

The Ephod

[2]They[a] made the ephod of gold, and of blue, purple and scarlet yarn, and of finely twisted linen. [3]They hammered out thin sheets of gold and cut strands to be worked into the blue, purple and scarlet yarn and fine linen—the work of a skilled craftsman. [4]They made shoulder pieces for the ephod, which were attached to two of its corners, so it could be fastened. [5]Its skillfully woven waistband was like it—of one piece with the ephod and made with gold, and with blue, purple and scarlet yarn, and with finely twisted linen, as the LORD commanded Moses.

[6]They mounted the onyx stones in gold filigree settings and engraved them like a seal with the names of the sons of Israel. [7]Then they fastened them on the shoulder pieces of the ephod as memorial stones for the sons of Israel, as the LORD commanded Moses.

The Breastpiece

[8]They fashioned the breastpiece—the work of a skilled craftsman. They made it like the ephod: of gold, and of blue, purple and scarlet yarn, and of finely twisted linen. [9]It was square—a span[b] long and a span wide—and folded double. [10]Then they mounted four rows of precious stones on it. In the first row there was a ruby, a topaz and a beryl; [11]in the second row a turquoise, a sapphire[c] and an emerald; [12]in the third row a jacinth, an agate and an amethyst; [13]in the fourth row a chrysolite, an onyx and a jasper.[d] They were mounted in gold filigree settings. [14]There were twelve stones, one for each of the names of the sons of Israel, each engraved like a seal with the name of one of the twelve tribes.

[15]For the breastpiece they made braided chains of pure gold, like a rope. [16]They made two gold filigree settings and two gold rings, and fastened the rings to two of the corners of the breastpiece. [17]They fastened the two gold chains to the rings at the corners of the breastpiece, [18]and the other ends of the chains to the two settings, attaching them to the shoulder pieces of the ephod at the front. [19]They made two gold rings and attached them to the other two corners of the breastpiece on the inside edge next to the ephod. [20]Then they made two more gold rings and attached them to the bottom of the shoulder pieces on the front of the ephod, close to the seam just above the waistband of the ephod. [21]They tied the rings of the breastpiece to the

THE MESSAGE

39.2-5 Ephod. They made the Ephod using gold and blue, purple, and scarlet fabrics and finely twisted linen. They hammered out gold leaf and sliced it into threads that were then worked into designs in the blue, purple, and scarlet fabric and fine linen. They made shoulder pieces fastened at the two ends. The decorated band was made of the same material—gold, blue, purple, and scarlet material, and of fine twisted linen—and of one piece with it, just as GOD had commanded Moses.

39.6-7 They mounted the onyx stones in a setting of filigreed gold and engraved the names of the sons of Israel on them, then fastened them on the shoulder pieces of the Ephod as memorial stones for the Israelites, just as GOD had commanded Moses.

39.8-10 Breastpiece. They made a Breastpiece designed like the Ephod from gold, blue, purple, and scarlet material and fine twisted linen. Doubled, the Breastpiece was nine inches square. They mounted four rows of precious gemstones on it.

First row: carnelian, topaz, emerald.
39.11 Second row: ruby, sapphire, crystal.
39.12 Third row: jacinth, agate, amethyst.
39.13-14 Fourth row: beryl, onyx, jasper.

The stones were mounted in a gold filigree. The twelve stones corresponded to the names of the sons of Israel, twelve names engraved as on a seal, one for each of the twelve tribes.

39.15-21 They made braided chains of pure gold for the Breastpiece, like cords. They made two settings of gold filigree and two rings of gold, put the two rings at the two ends of the Breastpiece, and fastened the two ends of the cords to the two rings at the end of the Breastpiece. Then they fastened the cords to the settings of filigree, attaching them to the shoulder pieces of the Ephod in front. Then they made two rings of gold and fastened them to the two ends of the Breastpiece on its inside edge facing the Ephod. They made two more rings of gold and fastened them in the front of the Ephod to the lower part of the two shoulder pieces, near the seam above the decorated band of the Ephod. The Breastpiece was fastened by running a cord

---

[a] 2 Or *He*; also in verses 7, 8 and 22   [b] 9 That is, about 9 inches (about 22 centimeters)   [c] 11 Or *lapis lazuli*
[d] 13 The precise identification of some of these precious stones is uncertain.

NEW INTERNATIONAL VERSION

rings of the ephod with blue cord, connecting it to the waistband so that the breastpiece would not swing out from the ephod—as the LORD commanded Moses.

OTHER PRIESTLY GARMENTS

22They made the robe of the ephod entirely of blue cloth—the work of a weaver— 23with an opening in the center of the robe like the opening of a collar,[a] and a band around this opening, so that it would not tear. 24They made pomegranates of blue, purple and scarlet yarn and finely twisted linen around the hem of the robe. 25And they made bells of pure gold and attached them around the hem between the pomegranates. 26The bells and pomegranates alternated around the hem of the robe to be worn for ministering, as the LORD commanded Moses.

27For Aaron and his sons, they made tunics of fine linen—the work of a weaver— 28and the turban of fine linen, the linen headbands and the undergarments of finely twisted linen. 29The sash was of finely twisted linen and blue, purple and scarlet yarn—the work of an embroiderer— as the LORD commanded Moses.

30They made the plate, the sacred diadem, out of pure gold and engraved on it, like an inscription on a seal: HOLY TO THE LORD. 31Then they fastened a blue cord to it to attach it to the turban, as the LORD commanded Moses.

MOSES INSPECTS THE TABERNACLE

32So all the work on the tabernacle, the Tent of Meeting, was completed. The Israelites did everything just as the LORD commanded Moses. 33Then they brought the tabernacle to Moses: the tent and all its furnishings, its clasps, frames, crossbars, posts and bases; 34the covering of ram skins dyed red, the covering of hides of sea cows[b] and the shielding curtain; 35the ark of the Testimony with its poles and the atonement cover; 36the table with all its articles and the bread of the Presence; 37the pure gold lampstand with its row of lamps and all its accessories, and the oil for the light; 38the gold altar, the anointing oil, the fragrant incense, and the curtain for the entrance to the tent; 39the bronze altar with its

THE MESSAGE

of blue through its rings to the rings of the Ephod so that it rested secure on the decorated band of the Ephod and wouldn't come loose, just as GOD had commanded Moses.

39.22-26   Robe. They made the robe for the Ephod entirely of blue. The opening of the robe at the center was like a collar, the edge hemmed so that it wouldn't tear. On the hem of the robe they made pomegranates of blue, purple, and scarlet material and fine twisted linen. They also made bells of pure gold and alternated the bells and pomegranates—a bell and a pomegranate, a bell and a pomegranate—all around the hem of the robe that was worn for ministering, just as GOD had commanded Moses.

39.27-29   They also made the tunics of fine linen, the work of a weaver, for Aaron and his sons, the turban of fine linen, the linen hats, the linen underwear made of fine twisted linen, and sashes of fine twisted linen, blue, purple, and scarlet material and embroidered, just as GOD had commanded Moses.

39.30-31   They made the plate, the sacred crown, of pure gold and engraved on it as on a seal: "Holy to GOD." They attached a blue cord to it and fastened it to the turban, just as GOD had commanded Moses.

39.32   That completed the work of The Dwelling, the Tent of Meeting. The People of Israel did what GOD had commanded Moses. They did it all.

39.33-41   They presented The Dwelling to Moses, the Tent and all its furnishings:

fastening hooks
frames
crossbars
posts
bases
tenting of tanned ram skins
tenting of dolphin skins
veil of the screen
Chest of The Testimony
    with its poles
    and Atonement-Cover
Table
    with its utensils
    and the Bread of the Presence
Lampstand of pure gold
    and its lamps all fitted out
    and all its utensils
    and the oil for the light
Gold Altar
anointing oil
fragrant incense
screen for the entrance to the Tent
Bronze Altar
    with its bronze grate

---

a 23 The meaning of the Hebrew for this word is uncertain.
b 34 That is, dugongs

NEW INTERNATIONAL VERSION

bronze grating, its poles and all its utensils; the basin with its stand; ⁴⁰the curtains of the courtyard with its posts and bases, and the curtain for the entrance to the courtyard; the ropes and tent pegs for the courtyard; all the furnishings for the tabernacle, the Tent of Meeting; ⁴¹and the woven garments worn for ministering in the sanctuary, both the sacred garments for Aaron the priest and the garments for his sons when serving as priests.

⁴²The Israelites had done all the work just as the LORD had commanded Moses. ⁴³Moses inspected the work and saw that they had done it just as the LORD had commanded. So Moses blessed them.

SETTING UP THE TABERNACLE

40 Then the LORD said to Moses: ²"Set up the tabernacle, the Tent of Meeting, on the first day of the first month. ³Place the ark of the Testimony in it and shield the ark with the curtain. ⁴Bring in the table and set out what belongs on it. Then bring in the lampstand and set up its lamps. ⁵Place the gold altar of incense in front of the ark of the Testimony and put the curtain at the entrance to the tabernacle.

⁶"Place the altar of burnt offering in front of the entrance to the tabernacle, the Tent of Meeting; ⁷place the basin between the Tent of Meeting and the altar and put water in it. ⁸Set up the courtyard around it and put the curtain at the entrance to the courtyard.

⁹"Take the anointing oil and anoint the tabernacle and everything in it; consecrate it and all its furnishings, and it will be holy. ¹⁰Then anoint the altar of burnt offering and all its utensils; consecrate the altar, and it will be most holy. ¹¹Anoint the basin and its stand and consecrate them.

¹²"Bring Aaron and his sons to the entrance to the Tent of Meeting and wash them with water. ¹³Then dress Aaron in the sacred garments, anoint him and consecrate him so he may serve me as priest. ¹⁴Bring his sons and dress them in tunics. ¹⁵Anoint them just as you anointed their father, so they may serve me as priests. Their anointing will be to a priesthood that will continue for all generations to come." ¹⁶Moses did everything just as the LORD commanded him.

¹⁷So the tabernacle was set up on the first day of the first month in the second year. ¹⁸When Moses set up the tabernacle, he put the bases in place, erected the frames, inserted the crossbars

THE MESSAGE

its poles and all its utensils
Washbasin
and its base
hangings for the Courtyard
its posts and bases
screen for the gate of the Courtyard
its cords and its pegs
utensils for ministry in The Dwelling, the
Tent of Meeting
woven vestments for ministering in the
Sanctuary
sacred vestments for Aaron the priest,
and his sons when serving as priests

^{39.42-43} The Israelites completed all the work, just as GOD had commanded. Moses saw that they had done all the work and done it exactly as GOD had commanded. Moses blessed them.

"MOSES FINISHED THE WORK"

40 GOD spoke to Moses: "On the first day of the first month, set up The Dwelling, the Tent of Meeting. Place the Chest of The Testimony in it and screen the Chest with the curtain.

^{40.4} "Bring in the Table and set it, arranging its Lampstand and lamps.

^{40.5} "Place the Gold Altar of Incense before the Chest of The Testimony and hang the curtain at the door of The Dwelling.

^{40.6} "Place the Altar of Whole-Burnt-Offering at the door of The Dwelling, the Tent of Meeting.

^{40.7} "Place the Washbasin between the Tent of Meeting and the Altar and fill it with water.

^{40.8} "Set up the Courtyard on all sides and hang the curtain at the entrance to the Courtyard.

^{40.9-11} "Then take the anointing oil and anoint The Dwelling and everything in it; consecrate it and all its furnishings so that it becomes holy. Anoint the Altar of Whole-Burnt-Offering and all its utensils, consecrating the Altar so that it is completely holy. Anoint the Washbasin and its base: consecrate it.

^{40.12-15} "Finally, bring Aaron and his sons to the entrance of the Tent of Meeting and wash them with water. Dress Aaron in the sacred vestments. Anoint him. Consecrate him to serve me as priest. Bring his sons and put tunics on them. Anoint them, just as you anointed their father, to serve me as priests. Their anointing will bring them into a perpetual priesthood, down through the generations."

^{40.16} Moses did everything GOD commanded. He did it all.

^{40.17-19} On the first day of the first month of the second year, The Dwelling was set up. Moses set it up: He laid its bases, erected the frames, placed

NEW INTERNATIONAL VERSION

and set up the posts. ¹⁹Then he spread the tent over the tabernacle and put the covering over the tent, as the LORD commanded him.

²⁰He took the Testimony and placed it in the ark, attached the poles to the ark and put the atonement cover over it. ²¹Then he brought the ark into the tabernacle and hung the shielding curtain and shielded the ark of the Testimony, as the LORD commanded him.

²²Moses placed the table in the Tent of Meeting on the north side of the tabernacle outside the curtain ²³and set out the bread on it before the LORD, as the LORD commanded him.

²⁴He placed the lampstand in the Tent of Meeting opposite the table on the south side of the tabernacle ²⁵and set up the lamps before the LORD, as the LORD commanded him.

²⁶Moses placed the gold altar in the Tent of Meeting in front of the curtain ²⁷and burned fragrant incense on it, as the LORD commanded him. ²⁸Then he put up the curtain at the entrance to the tabernacle.

²⁹He set the altar of burnt offering near the entrance to the tabernacle, the Tent of Meeting, and offered on it burnt offerings and grain offerings, as the LORD commanded him.

³⁰He placed the basin between the Tent of Meeting and the altar and put water in it for washing, ³¹and Moses and Aaron and his sons used it to wash their hands and feet. ³²They washed whenever they entered the Tent of Meeting or approached the altar, as the LORD commanded Moses.

³³Then Moses set up the courtyard around the tabernacle and altar and put up the curtain at the entrance to the courtyard. And so Moses finished the work.

THE GLORY OF THE LORD

³⁴Then the cloud covered the Tent of Meeting, and the glory of the LORD filled the tabernacle. ³⁵Moses could not enter the Tent of Meeting because the cloud had settled upon it, and the glory of the LORD filled the tabernacle.

³⁶In all the travels of the Israelites, whenever the cloud lifted from above the tabernacle, they would set out; ³⁷but if the cloud did not lift, they did not set out—until the day it lifted. ³⁸So the cloud of the LORD was over the tabernacle by day, and fire was in the cloud by night, in the sight of all the house of Israel during all their travels.

THE MESSAGE

the crossbars, set the posts, spread the tent over The Dwelling, and put the covering over the tent, just as GOD had commanded Moses.

40.20-21 He placed The Testimony in the Chest, inserted the poles for carrying the Chest, and placed the lid, the Atonement-Cover, on it. He brought the Chest into The Dwelling and set up the curtain, screening off the Chest of The Testimony, just as GOD had commanded Moses.

40.22-23 He placed the Table in the Tent of Meeting on the north side of The Dwelling, outside the curtain, and arranged the Bread there before GOD, just as GOD had commanded him.

40.24-25 He placed the Lampstand in the Tent of Meeting opposite the Table on the south side of The Dwelling and set up the lamps before GOD, just as GOD had commanded him.

40.26-27 Moses placed the Gold Altar in the Tent of Meeting in front of the curtain and burned fragrant incense on it, just as GOD had commanded him.

40.28 He placed the screen at the entrance to The Dwelling.

40.29 He set the Altar of Whole-Burnt-Offering at the door of The Dwelling, the Tent of Meeting, and offered up the Whole-Burnt-Offerings and the Grain-Offerings, just as GOD had commanded Moses.

40.30-32 He placed the Washbasin between the Tent of Meeting and the Altar, and filled it with water for washing. Moses and Aaron and his sons washed their hands and feet there. When they entered the Tent of Meeting and when they served at the Altar, they washed, just as GOD had commanded Moses.

40.33 Finally, he erected the Courtyard all around The Dwelling and the Altar, and put up the screen for the Courtyard entrance.

Moses finished the work.

40.34-35 The Cloud covered the Tent of Meeting, and the Glory of GOD filled The Dwelling. Moses couldn't enter the Tent of Meeting because the Cloud was upon it, and the Glory of GOD filled The Dwelling.

40.36-38 Whenever the Cloud lifted from The Dwelling, the People of Israel set out on their travels, but if the Cloud did not lift, they wouldn't set out until it did lift. The Cloud of GOD was over The Dwelling during the day and the fire was in it at night, visible to all the Israelites in all their travels.

LEVITICUS

LEVITICUS

THE BURNT OFFERING

1 The LORD called to Moses and spoke to him from the Tent of Meeting. He said, ²"Speak to the Israelites and say to them: 'When any of you brings an offering to the LORD, bring as your offering an animal from either the herd or the flock.

³"'If the offering is a burnt offering from the herd, he is to offer a male without defect. He must present it at the entrance to the Tent of Meeting so that it*ᵃ* will be acceptable to the LORD. ⁴He is to lay his hand on the head of the burnt offering, and it will be accepted on his behalf to make atonement for him. ⁵He is to slaughter the young bull before the LORD, and then Aaron's sons the priests shall bring the blood and sprinkle it against the altar on all sides at the entrance to the Tent of Meeting. ⁶He is to skin the burnt offering and cut it into pieces. ⁷The sons of Aaron the priest are to put fire on the altar and arrange wood on the fire. ⁸Then Aaron's sons the priests shall arrange the pieces, including the head and the fat, on the burning wood that is on the altar. ⁹He is to wash the inner parts and the legs with water, and the priest is to burn all of it on the altar. It is a burnt offering, an offering made by fire, an aroma pleasing to the LORD.

¹⁰"'If the offering is a burnt offering from the flock, from either the sheep or the goats, he is to offer a male without defect. ¹¹He is to slaughter it at the north side of the altar before the LORD, and Aaron's sons the priests shall sprinkle its blood against the altar on all sides. ¹²He is to cut it into pieces, and the priest shall arrange them, including the head and the fat, on the burning wood that is on the altar. ¹³He is to wash the inner parts and the legs with water, and the priest is to bring all of it and burn it on the altar. It is a burnt offering, an offering made by fire, an aroma pleasing to the LORD.

¹⁴"'If the offering to the LORD is a burnt offering of birds, he is to offer a dove or a young pigeon. ¹⁵The priest shall bring it to the altar, wring off the head and burn it on the altar; its

WHOLE-BURNT-OFFERING

1 GOD called Moses and spoke to him from the Tent of Meeting: "Speak to the People of Israel. Tell them, When anyone presents an offering to GOD, present an animal from either the herd or the flock.

1.1-2

1.3-9 "If the offering is a Whole-Burnt-Offering from the herd, present a male without a defect at the entrance to the Tent of Meeting that it may be accepted by GOD. Lay your hand on the head of the Whole-Burnt-Offering so that it may be accepted on your behalf to make atonement for you. Slaughter the bull in GOD's presence. Aaron's sons, the priests, will make an offering of the blood by splashing it against all sides of the Altar that stands at the entrance to the Tent of Meeting. Next, skin the Whole-Burnt-Offering and cut it up. Aaron's sons, the priests, will prepare a fire on the Altar, carefully laying out the wood, and then arrange the body parts, including the head and the suet, on the wood prepared for the fire on the Altar. Scrub the entrails and legs clean. The priest will burn it all on the Altar: a Whole-Burnt-Offering, a Fire-Gift, a pleasing fragrance to GOD.

1.10-13 "If the Whole-Burnt-Offering comes from the flock, whether sheep or goat, present a male without defect. Slaughter it on the north side of the Altar in GOD's presence. The sons of Aaron, the priests, will throw the blood against all sides of the Altar. Cut it up and the priest will arrange the pieces, including the head and the suet, on the wood prepared for burning on the Altar. Scrub the entrails and legs clean. The priest will offer it all, burning it on the Altar: a Whole-Burnt-Offering, a Fire-Gift, a pleasing fragrance to GOD.

1.14-17 "If a bird is presented to GOD for the Whole-Burnt-Offering it can be either a dove or a pigeon. The priest will bring it to the Altar, wring off its head, and burn it on the Altar. But he

NEW INTERNATIONAL VERSION

blood shall be drained out on the side of the altar. ¹⁶He is to remove the crop with its contents*ᵃ* and throw it to the east side of the altar, where the ashes are. ¹⁷He shall tear it open by the wings, not severing it completely, and then the priest shall burn it on the wood that is on the fire on the altar. It is a burnt offering, an offering made by fire, an aroma pleasing to the LORD.

THE GRAIN OFFERING

2 " 'When someone brings a grain offering to the LORD, his offering is to be of fine flour. He is to pour oil on it, put incense on it ²and take it to Aaron's sons the priests. The priest shall take a handful of the fine flour and oil, together with all the incense, and burn this as a memorial portion on the altar, an offering made by fire, an aroma pleasing to the LORD. ³The rest of the grain offering belongs to Aaron and his sons; it is a most holy part of the offerings made to the LORD by fire.

⁴" 'If you bring a grain offering baked in an oven, it is to consist of fine flour: cakes made without yeast and mixed with oil, or*ᵇ* wafers made without yeast and spread with oil. ⁵If your grain offering is prepared on a griddle, it is to be made of fine flour mixed with oil, and without yeast. ⁶Crumble it and pour oil on it; it is a grain offering. ⁷If your grain offering is cooked in a pan, it is to be made of fine flour and oil. ⁸Bring the grain offering made of these things to the LORD; present it to the priest, who shall take it to the altar. ⁹He shall take out the memorial portion from the grain offering and burn it on the altar as an offering made by fire, an aroma pleasing to the LORD. ¹⁰The rest of the grain offering belongs to Aaron and his sons; it is a most holy part of the offerings made to the LORD by fire.

¹¹" 'Every grain offering you bring to the LORD must be made without yeast, for you are not to burn any yeast or honey in an offering made to the LORD by fire. ¹²You may bring them to the LORD as an offering of the firstfruits, but they are not to be offered on the altar as a pleasing aroma. ¹³Season all your grain offerings with salt. Do not leave the salt of the covenant of your God out of your grain offerings; add salt to all your offerings.

¹⁴" 'If you bring a grain offering of firstfruits to the LORD, offer crushed heads of new grain roasted in the fire. ¹⁵Put oil and incense on it; it is a grain offering. ¹⁶The priest shall burn the memorial portion of the crushed grain and the oil, together with all the incense, as an offering made to the LORD by fire.

ᵃ 16 Or crop and the feathers; the meaning of the Hebrew for this word is uncertain.   *ᵇ 4 Or and*

THE MESSAGE

will first drain the blood on the side of the Altar, remove the gizzard and its contents, and throw them on the east side of the Altar where the ashes are piled. Then rip it open by its wings but leave it in one piece and burn it on the Altar on the wood prepared for the fire: a Whole-Burnt-Offering, a Fire-Gift, a pleasing fragrance to GOD.

GRAIN-OFFERING

2.1-3 2 "When you present a Grain-Offering to GOD, use fine flour. Pour oil on it, put incense on it, and bring it to Aaron's sons, the priests. One of them will take a handful of the fine flour and oil, with all the incense, and burn it on the Altar for a memorial: a Fire-Gift, a pleasing fragrance to GOD. The rest of the Grain-Offering is for Aaron and his sons—a most holy part of the Fire-Gifts to GOD.

2.4 "When you present a Grain-Offering of oven-baked loaves, use fine flour, mixed with oil but no yeast. Or present wafers made without yeast and spread with oil.

2.5-6 "If you bring a Grain-Offering cooked on a griddle, use fine flour mixed with oil but without yeast. Crumble it and pour oil on it—it's a Grain-Offering.

2.7 "If you bring a Grain-Offering deep-fried in a pan, make it of fine flour with oil.

2.8-10 "Bring the Grain-Offering you make from these ingredients and present it to the priest. He will bring it to the Altar, break off a memorial piece from the Grain-Offering, and burn it on the Altar: a Fire-Gift, a pleasing fragrance to GOD. The rest of the Grain-Offering is for Aaron and his sons—a most holy part of the gifts to GOD.

2.11-13 "All the Grain-Offerings that you present to GOD must be made without yeast; you must never burn any yeast or honey as a Fire-Gift to GOD. You may offer them to GOD as an offering of firstfruits but not on the Altar as a pleasing fragrance. Season every presentation of your Grain-Offering with salt. Don't leave the salt of the covenant with your God out of your Grain-Offerings. Present all your offerings with salt.

2.14-16 "If you present a Grain-Offering of firstfruits to GOD, bring crushed heads of the new grain roasted. Put oil and incense on it—it's a Grain-Offering. The priest will burn some of the mixed grain and oil with all the incense as a memorial—a Fire-Gift to GOD.

NEW INTERNATIONAL VERSION

THE FELLOWSHIP OFFERING

3 " 'If someone's offering is a fellowship offering,[a] and he offers an animal from the herd, whether male or female, he is to present before the LORD an animal without defect. [2]He is to lay his hand on the head of his offering and slaughter it at the entrance to the Tent of Meeting. Then Aaron's sons the priests shall sprinkle the blood against the altar on all sides. [3]From the fellowship offering he is to bring a sacrifice made to the LORD by fire: all the fat that covers the inner parts or is connected to them, [4]both kidneys with the fat on them near the loins, and the covering of the liver, which he will remove with the kidneys. [5]Then Aaron's sons are to burn it on the altar on top of the burnt offering that is on the burning wood, as an offering made by fire, an aroma pleasing to the LORD.

[6]" 'If he offers an animal from the flock as a fellowship offering to the LORD, he is to offer a male or female without defect. [7]If he offers a lamb, he is to present it before the LORD. [8]He is to lay his hand on the head of his offering and slaughter it in front of the Tent of Meeting. Then Aaron's sons shall sprinkle its blood against the altar on all sides. [9]From the fellowship offering he is to bring a sacrifice made to the LORD by fire: its fat, the entire fat tail cut off close to the backbone, all the fat that covers the inner parts or is connected to them, [10]both kidneys with the fat on them near the loins, and the covering of the liver, which he will remove with the kidneys. [11]The priest shall burn them on the altar as food, an offering made to the LORD by fire.

[12]" 'If his offering is a goat, he is to present it before the LORD. [13]He is to lay his hand on its head and slaughter it in front of the Tent of Meeting. Then Aaron's sons shall sprinkle its blood against the altar on all sides. [14]From what he offers he is to make this offering to the LORD by fire: all the fat that covers the inner parts or is connected to them, [15]both kidneys with the fat on them near the loins, and the covering of the liver, which he will remove with the kidneys. [16]The priest shall burn them on the altar as food, an offering made by fire, a pleasing aroma. All the fat is the LORD's.

[17]" 'This is a lasting ordinance for the generations to come, wherever you live: You must not eat any fat or any blood.' "

THE SIN OFFERING

4 The LORD said to Moses, [2]"Say to the Israelites: 'When anyone sins unintentionally and does what is forbidden in any of the LORD's commands—

---

[a] 1 Traditionally *peace offering*; also in verses 3, 6 and 9

THE MESSAGE

THE PEACE-OFFERING

3.1-5 3 "If your offering is a Peace-Offering and you present an animal from the herd, either male or female, it must be an animal without any defect. Lay your hand on the head of your offering and slaughter it at the entrance of the Tent of Meeting. Aaron's sons, the priests, will throw the blood on all sides of the Altar. As a Fire-Gift to GOD from the Peace-Offering, present all the fat that covers or is connected to the entrails, the two kidneys and the fat around them at the loins, and the lobe of the liver that is removed along with the kidneys. Aaron and his sons will burn it on the Altar along with the Whole-Burnt-Offering that is on the wood prepared for the fire: a Fire-Gift, a pleasing fragrance to GOD.

3.6-11 "If your Peace-Offering to GOD comes from the flock, bring a male or female without defect. If you offer a lamb, offer it to GOD. Lay your hand on the head of your offering and slaughter it at the Tent of Meeting. The sons of Aaron will throw its blood on all sides of the Altar. As a Fire-Gift to GOD from the Peace-Offering, present its fat, the entire fat tail cut off close to the backbone, all the fat on and connected to the entrails, the two kidneys and the fat around them on the loins, and the lobe of the liver which is removed along with the kidneys. The priest will burn it on the Altar: a meal, a Fire-Gift to GOD.

3.12-16 "If the offering is a goat, bring it into the presence of GOD, lay your hand on its head, and slaughter it in front of the Tent of Meeting. Aaron's sons will throw the blood on all sides of the Altar. As a Fire-Gift to GOD present the fat that covers and is connected to the entrails, the two kidneys and the fat which is around them on the loins, and the lobe of the liver which is removed along with the kidneys. The priest will burn them on the Altar: a meal, a Fire-Gift, a pleasing fragrance.

3.16-17 "All the fat belongs to GOD. This is the fixed rule down through the generations, wherever you happen to live: Don't eat the fat; don't eat the blood. None of it."

THE ABSOLUTION-OFFERING

4.1-12 4 GOD spoke to Moses, "Tell the Israelites: When a person sins unintentionally by straying from any of GOD's commands, break-

NEW INTERNATIONAL VERSION

³" 'If the anointed priest sins, bringing guilt on the people, he must bring to the LORD a young bull without defect as a sin offering for the sin he has committed. ⁴He is to present the bull at the entrance to the Tent of Meeting before the LORD. He is to lay his hand on its head and slaughter it before the LORD. ⁵Then the anointed priest shall take some of the bull's blood and carry it into the Tent of Meeting. ⁶He is to dip his finger into the blood and sprinkle some of it seven times before the LORD, in front of the curtain of the sanctuary. ⁷The priest shall then put some of the blood on the horns of the altar of fragrant incense that is before the LORD in the Tent of Meeting. The rest of the bull's blood he shall pour out at the base of the altar of burnt offering at the entrance to the Tent of Meeting. ⁸He shall remove all the fat from the bull of the sin offering—the fat that covers the inner parts or is connected to them, ⁹both kidneys with the fat on them near the loins, and the covering of the liver, which he will remove with the kidneys— ¹⁰just as the fat is removed from the ox*ᵃ* sacrificed as a fellowship offering.*ᵇ* Then the priest shall burn them on the altar of burnt offering. ¹¹But the hide of the bull and all its flesh, as well as the head and legs, the inner parts and offal— ¹²that is, all the rest of the bull—he must take outside the camp to a place ceremonially clean, where the ashes are thrown, and burn it in a wood fire on the ash heap.

¹³" 'If the whole Israelite community sins unintentionally and does what is forbidden in any of the LORD's commands, even though the community is unaware of the matter, they are guilty. ¹⁴When they become aware of the sin they committed, the assembly must bring a young bull as a sin offering and present it before the Tent of Meeting. ¹⁵The elders of the community are to lay their hands on the bull's head before the LORD, and the bull shall be slaughtered before the LORD. ¹⁶Then the anointed priest is to take some of the bull's blood into the Tent of Meeting. ¹⁷He shall dip his finger into the blood and sprinkle it before the LORD seven times in front of the curtain. ¹⁸He is to put some of the blood on the horns of the altar that is before the LORD in the Tent of Meeting. The rest of the blood he shall pour out at the base of the altar of burnt offering at the entrance to the Tent of Meeting. ¹⁹He shall remove all the fat from it and burn it on the altar, ²⁰and do with this bull just as he did with the bull for the sin offering. In this way the priest will make atonement for them, and they will be forgiven. ²¹Then he shall take the bull outside

---

ᵃ 10 The Hebrew word can include both male and female.
ᵇ 10 Traditionally *peace offering*; also in verses 26, 31 and 35

THE MESSAGE

ing what must not be broken, if it's the anointed priest who sins and so brings guilt on the people, he is to bring a bull without defect to GOD as an Absolution-Offering for the sin he has committed. Have him bring the bull to the entrance of the Tent of Meeting in the presence of GOD, lay his hand on the bull's head, and slaughter the bull before GOD. He is then to take some of the bull's blood, bring it into the Tent of Meeting, dip his finger in the blood, and sprinkle some of it seven times before GOD, before the curtain of the Sanctuary. He is to smear some of the blood on the horns of the Altar of Fragrant Incense before GOD which is in the Tent of Meeting. He is to pour the rest of the bull's blood out at the base of the Altar of Whole-Burnt-Offering at the entrance of the Tent of Meeting. He is to remove all the fat from the bull of the Absolution-Offering, the fat which covers and is connected to the entrails, the two kidneys and the fat that is around them at the loins, and the lobe of the liver which he takes out along with the kidneys—the same procedure as when the fat is removed from the bull of the Peace-Offering. Finally, he is to burn all this on the Altar of Burnt Offering. Everything else—the bull's hide, meat, head, legs, organs, and guts—he is to take outside the camp to a clean place where the ashes are dumped and is to burn it on a wood fire.

4.13-21 "If the whole congregation sins unintentionally by straying from one of the commandments of GOD that must not be broken, they become guilty even though no one is aware of it. When they do become aware of the sin they've committed, the congregation must bring a bull as an Absolution-Offering and present it at the Tent of Meeting. The elders of the congregation will lay their hands on the bull's head in the presence of GOD and one of them will slaughter it before GOD. The anointed priest will then bring some of the blood into the Tent of Meeting, dip his finger in the blood, and sprinkle some of it seven times before GOD in front of the curtain. He will smear some of the blood on the horns of the Altar which is before GOD in the Tent of Meeting and pour the rest of it at the base of the Altar of Whole-Burnt-Offering at the entrance of the Tent of Meeting. He will remove all the fat and burn it on the Altar. He will follow the same procedure with this bull as with the bull for the Absolution-Offering. The priest makes atonement for them and they are forgiven. They then will take the bull outside the camp and burn it just as

NEW INTERNATIONAL VERSION

the camp and burn it as he burned the first bull. This is the sin offering for the community.

22" 'When a leader sins unintentionally and does what is forbidden in any of the commands of the LORD his God, he is guilty. 23When he is made aware of the sin he committed, he must bring as his offering a male goat without defect. 24He is to lay his hand on the goat's head and slaughter it at the place where the burnt offering is slaughtered before the LORD. It is a sin offering. 25Then the priest shall take some of the blood of the sin offering with his finger and put it on the horns of the altar of burnt offering and pour out the rest of the blood at the base of the altar. 26He shall burn all the fat on the altar as he burned the fat of the fellowship offering. In this way the priest will make atonement for the man's sin, and he will be forgiven.

27" 'If a member of the community sins unintentionally and does what is forbidden in any of the LORD's commands, he is guilty. 28When he is made aware of the sin he committed, he must bring as his offering for the sin he committed a female goat without defect. 29He is to lay his hand on the head of the sin offering and slaughter it at the place of the burnt offering. 30Then the priest is to take some of the blood with his finger and put it on the horns of the altar of burnt offering and pour out the rest of the blood at the base of the altar. 31He shall remove all the fat, just as the fat is removed from the fellowship offering, and the priest shall burn it on the altar as an aroma pleasing to the LORD. In this way the priest will make atonement for him, and he will be forgiven.

32" 'If he brings a lamb as his sin offering, he is to bring a female without defect. 33He is to lay his hand on its head and slaughter it for a sin offering at the place where the burnt offering is slaughtered. 34Then the priest shall take some of the blood of the sin offering with his finger and put it on the horns of the altar of burnt offering and pour out the rest of the blood at the base of the altar. 35He shall remove all the fat, just as the fat is removed from the lamb of the fellowship offering, and the priest shall burn it on the altar on top of the offerings made to the LORD by fire. In this way the priest will make atonement for him for the sin he has committed, and he will be forgiven.

5 " 'If a person sins because he does not speak up when he hears a public charge to testify regarding something he has seen or learned about, he will be held responsible.

THE MESSAGE

they burned the first bull. It's the Absolution-Offering for the congregation.

4.22-26 "When a ruler sins unintentionally by straying from one of the commands of his GOD which must not be broken, he is guilty. When he becomes aware of the sin he has committed, he must bring a goat for his offering, a male without any defect, lay his hand on the head of the goat, and slaughter it in the place where they slaughter the Whole-Burnt-Offering in the presence of GOD—it's an Absolution-Offering. The priest will then take some of the blood of the Absolution-Offering with his finger, smear it on the horns of the Altar of Whole-Burnt-Offering, and pour the rest at the base of the Altar. He will burn all its fat on the Altar, the same as with the fat of the Peace-Offering.

"The priest makes atonement for him on account of his sin and he's forgiven.

4.27-31 "When an ordinary member of the congregation sins unintentionally, straying from one of the commandments of GOD which must not be broken, he is guilty. When he is made aware of his sin, he shall bring a goat, a female without any defect, and offer it for his sin, lay his hand on the head of the Absolution-Offering, and slaughter it at the place of the Whole-Burnt-Offering. The priest will take some of its blood with his finger, smear it on the horns of the Altar of Whole-Burnt-Offering, and pour the rest at the base of the Altar. Finally, he'll take out all the fat, the same as with the Peace-Offerings, and burn it on the Altar for a pleasing fragrance to GOD.

"In this way, the priest makes atonement for him and he's forgiven.

4.32-35 "If he brings a lamb for an Absolution-Offering, he shall present a female without any defect, lay his hand on the head of the Absolution-Offering, and slaughter it at the same place they slaughter the Whole-Burnt-Offering. The priest will take some of the blood of the Absolution-Offering with his finger, smear it on the horns of the Altar of Burnt-Offering, and pour the rest at the base of the Altar. He shall remove all the fat, the same as for the lamb of the Peace-Offering. Finally, the priest will burn it on the Altar on top of the gifts to GOD.

"In this way, the priest makes atonement for him on account of his sin and he's forgiven.

✛

5.1 5 "If you sin by not stepping up and offering yourself as a witness to something you've heard or seen in cases of wrongdoing, you'll be held responsible.

NEW INTERNATIONAL VERSION

2 " 'Or if a person touches anything ceremonially unclean—whether the carcasses of unclean wild animals or of unclean livestock or of unclean creatures that move along the ground—even though he is unaware of it, he has become unclean and is guilty.

3 " 'Or if he touches human uncleanness—anything that would make him unclean—even though he is unaware of it, when he learns of it he will be guilty.

4 " 'Or if a person thoughtlessly takes an oath to do anything, whether good or evil—in any matter one might carelessly swear about—even though he is unaware of it, in any case when he learns of it he will be guilty.

5 " 'When anyone is guilty in any of these ways, he must confess in what way he has sinned 6and, as a penalty for the sin he has committed, he must bring to the LORD a female lamb or goat from the flock as a sin offering; and the priest shall make atonement for him for his sin.

7 " 'If he cannot afford a lamb, he is to bring two doves or two young pigeons to the LORD as a penalty for his sin—one for a sin offering and the other for a burnt offering. 8He is to bring them to the priest, who shall first offer the one for the sin offering. He is to wring its head from its neck, not severing it completely, 9and is to sprinkle some of the blood of the sin offering against the side of the altar; the rest of the blood must be drained out at the base of the altar. It is a sin offering. 10The priest shall then offer the other as a burnt offering in the prescribed way and make atonement for him for the sin he has committed, and he will be forgiven.

11 " 'If, however, he cannot afford two doves or two young pigeons, he is to bring as an offering for his sin a tenth of an ephah *a* of fine flour for a sin offering. He must not put oil or incense on it, because it is a sin offering. 12He is to bring it to the priest, who shall take a handful of it as a memorial portion and burn it on the altar on top of the offerings made to the LORD by fire. It is a sin offering. 13In this way the priest will make atonement for him for any of these sins he has committed, and he will be forgiven. The rest of the offering will belong to the priest, as in the case of the grain offering.' "

THE GUILT OFFERING

14The LORD said to Moses: 15 "When a person commits a violation and sins unintentionally in regard to any of the LORD's holy things, he is to bring to the LORD as a penalty a ram from the flock, one without defect and of the proper value

a 11 That is, probably about 2 quarts (about 2 liters)

THE MESSAGE

5.2   "Or if you touch anything ritually unclean, like the carcass of an unclean animal, wild or domestic, or a dead reptile, and you weren't aware of it at the time, but you're contaminated and you're guilty;

5.3   "Or if you touch human uncleanness, any sort of ritually contaminating uncleanness, and you're not aware of it at the time, but later you realize it and you're guilty;

5.4   "Or if you impulsively swear to do something, whether good or bad—some rash oath that just pops out—and you aren't aware of what you've done at the time, but later you come to realize it and you're guilty in any of these cases;

5.5-6   "When you are guilty, immediately confess the sin that you've committed and bring as your penalty to GOD for the sin you have committed, a female lamb or goat from the flock for an Absolution-Offering.

"In this way, the priest will make atonement for your sin.

5.7-10   "If you can't afford a lamb, bring as your penalty to GOD for the sin you have committed, two doves or two pigeons, one for the Absolution-Offering and the other for the Whole-Burnt-Offering. Bring them to the priest who will first offer the one for the Absolution-Offering: He'll wring its neck but not sever it, splash some of the blood of the Absolution-Offering against the Altar, and squeeze the rest of it out at the base. It's an Absolution-Offering. He'll then take the second bird and offer it as a Whole-Burnt-Offering, following the procedures step-by-step.

"In this way, the priest will make atonement for your sin and you're forgiven.

5.11-12   "If you cannot afford the two doves or pigeons, bring two quarts of fine flour for your Absolution-Offering. Don't put oil or incense on it—it's an Absolution-Offering. Bring it to the priest; he'll take a handful from it as a memorial and burn it on the Altar with the gifts for GOD. It's an Absolution-Offering.

5.13   "The priest will make atonement for you and any of these sins you've committed and you're forgiven. The rest of the offering belongs to the priest, the same as with the Grain-Offering."

COMPENSATION-OFFERING

5.14-16   GOD spoke to Moses, "When a person betrays his trust and unknowingly sins by straying against any of the holy things of GOD, he is to bring as his penalty to GOD a ram without any defect from the flock, the value of the ram as-

NEW INTERNATIONAL VERSION

in silver, according to the sanctuary shekel. *a* It is a guilt offering. ¹⁶He must make restitution for what he has failed to do in regard to the holy things, add a fifth of the value to that and give it all to the priest, who will make atonement for him with the ram as a guilt offering, and he will be forgiven.

¹⁷"If a person sins and does what is forbidden in any of the LORD's commands, even though he does not know it, he is guilty and will be held responsible. ¹⁸He is to bring to the priest as a guilt offering a ram from the flock, one without defect and of the proper value. In this way the priest will make atonement for him for the wrong he has committed unintentionally, and he will be forgiven. ¹⁹It is a guilt offering; he has been guilty of *b* wrongdoing against the LORD."

6 The LORD said to Moses: ²"If anyone sins and is unfaithful to the LORD by deceiving his neighbor about something entrusted to him or left in his care or stolen, or if he cheats him, ³or if he finds lost property and lies about it, or if he swears falsely, or if he commits any such sin that people may do— ⁴when he thus sins and becomes guilty, he must return what he has stolen or taken by extortion, or what was entrusted to him, or the lost property he found, ⁵or whatever it was he swore falsely about. He must make restitution in full, add a fifth of the value to it and give it all to the owner on the day he presents his guilt offering. ⁶And as a penalty he must bring to the priest, that is, to the LORD, his guilt offering, a ram from the flock, one without defect and of the proper value. ⁷In this way the priest will make atonement for him before the LORD, and he will be forgiven for any of these things he did that made him guilty."

THE BURNT OFFERING

⁸The LORD said to Moses: ⁹"Give Aaron and his sons this command: 'These are the regulations for the burnt offering: The burnt offering is to remain on the altar hearth throughout the night, till morning, and the fire must be kept burning on the altar. ¹⁰The priest shall then put on his linen clothes, with linen undergarments next to his body, and shall remove the ashes of the burnt offering that the fire has consumed on the altar and place them beside the altar. ¹¹Then he is to take off these clothes and put on others,

THE MESSAGE

sessed in shekels, according to the Sanctuary shekel for a Compensation-Offering. He is to make additional compensation for the sin he has committed against any holy thing by adding twenty percent to the ram and giving it to the priest.

"Thus the priest will make atonement for him with the ram of the Compensation-Offering and he's forgiven.

5.17-18 "If anyone sins by breaking any of the commandments of GOD which must not be broken, but without being aware of it at the time, the moment he does realize his guilt he is held responsible. He is to bring to the priest a ram without any defect, assessed at the value of the Compensation-Offering.

5.18-19 "Thus the priest will make atonement for him for his error that he was unaware of and he's forgiven. It is a Compensation-Offering; he was surely guilty before God."

6.1-6 **6** GOD spoke to Moses, "When anyone sins by betraying trust with GOD by deceiving his neighbor regarding something entrusted to him, or by robbing or cheating or threatening him; or if he has found something lost and lies about it and swears falsely regarding any of these sins that people commonly commit— when he sins and is found guilty, he must return what he stole or extorted, restore what was entrusted to him, return the lost thing he found, or anything else about which he swore falsely. He must make full compensation, add twenty percent to it, and hand it over to the owner on the same day he brings his Compensation-Offering. He must present to GOD as his Compensation-Offering a ram without any defect from the flock, assessed at the value of a Compensation-Offering.

6.7 "Thus the priest will make atonement for him before GOD and he's forgiven of any of the things that one does that bring guilt."

FURTHER INSTRUCTIONS

6.8-13 GOD spoke to Moses, "Command Aaron and his sons. Tell them, These are the instructions for the Whole-Burnt-Offering. Leave the Whole-Burnt-Offering on the Altar hearth through the night until morning, with the fire kept burning on the Altar. Then dress in your linen clothes with linen underwear next to your body. Remove the ashes remaining from the Whole-Burnt-Offering and place them beside the Altar. Then change clothes and carry the ashes out-

---

a 15 That is, about 2/5 ounce (about 11.5 grams)
b 19 Or *has made full expiation for his*

NEW INTERNATIONAL VERSION	THE MESSAGE

NEW INTERNATIONAL VERSION

and carry the ashes outside the camp to a place that is ceremonially clean. [12]The fire on the altar must be kept burning; it must not go out. Every morning the priest is to add firewood and arrange the burnt offering on the fire and burn the fat of the fellowship offerings[a] on it. [13]The fire must be kept burning on the altar continuously; it must not go out.

THE GRAIN OFFERING

[14]" 'These are the regulations for the grain offering: Aaron's sons are to bring it before the LORD, in front of the altar. [15]The priest is to take a handful of fine flour and oil, together with all the incense on the grain offering, and burn the memorial portion on the altar as an aroma pleasing to the LORD. [16]Aaron and his sons shall eat the rest of it, but it is to be eaten without yeast in a holy place; they are to eat it in the courtyard of the Tent of Meeting. [17]It must not be baked with yeast; I have given it as their share of the offerings made to me by fire. Like the sin offering and the guilt offering, it is most holy. [18]Any male descendant of Aaron may eat it. It is his regular share of the offerings made to the LORD by fire for the generations to come. Whatever touches them will become holy.[b] "

[19]The LORD also said to Moses, [20]"This is the offering Aaron and his sons are to bring to the LORD on the day he[c] is anointed: a tenth of an ephah[d] of fine flour as a regular grain offering, half of it in the morning and half in the evening. [21]Prepare it with oil on a griddle; bring it well-mixed and present the grain offering broken[e] in pieces as an aroma pleasing to the LORD. [22]The son who is to succeed him as anointed priest shall prepare it. It is the LORD's regular share and is to be burned completely. [23]Every grain offering of a priest shall be burned completely; it must not be eaten."

THE SIN OFFERING

[24]The LORD said to Moses, [25]"Say to Aaron and his sons: 'These are the regulations for the sin offering: The sin offering is to be slaughtered before the LORD in the place the burnt offering is slaughtered; it is most holy. [26]The priest who offers it shall eat it; it is to be eaten in a holy place, in the courtyard of the Tent of Meeting. [27]Whatever touches any of the flesh will become holy, and if any of the blood is spattered on a garment, you must wash it in a holy place. [28]The clay pot the meat is cooked in must be broken; but if it is

THE MESSAGE

side the camp to a clean place. Meanwhile keep the fire on the Altar burning; it must not go out. Replenish the wood for the fire every morning, arrange the Whole-Burnt-Offering on it, and burn the fat of the Peace-Offering on top of it all. Keep the fire burning on the Altar continuously. It must not go out.

╬

6.14-18 "These are the instructions for the Grain-Offering. Aaron's sons are to present it to GOD in front of the Altar. The priest takes a handful of the fine flour of the Grain-Offering with its oil and all its incense and burns this as a memorial on the Altar, a pleasing fragrance to GOD. Aaron and his sons eat the rest of it. It is unraised bread and so eaten in a holy place—in the Courtyard of the Tent of Meeting. They must not bake it with yeast. I have designated it as their share of the gifts presented to me. It is very holy, like the Absolution-Offering and the Compensation-Offering. Any male descendant among Aaron's sons may eat it. This is a fixed rule regarding GOD's gifts, stretching down the generations. Anyone who touches these offerings must be holy."

╬

6.19-23 GOD spoke to Moses, "This is the offering which Aaron and his sons each are to present to GOD on the day he is anointed: two quarts of fine flour as a regular Grain-Offering, half in the morning and half in the evening. Prepare it with oil on a griddle. Bring it well-mixed and then present it crumbled in pieces as a pleasing fragrance to GOD. Aaron's son who is anointed to succeed him offers it to GOD—this is a fixed rule. The whole thing is burned. Every Grain-Offering of a priest is burned completely; it must not be eaten."

╬

6.24-30 GOD spoke to Moses, "Tell Aaron and his sons: These are the instructions for the Absolution-Offering. Slaughter the Absolution-Offering in the place where the Whole-Burnt-Offering is slaughtered before GOD—the offering is most holy. The priest in charge eats it in a holy place, the Courtyard of the Tent of Meeting. Anyone who touches any of the meat must be holy. A garment that gets blood spattered on it must be washed in a holy place. Break the clay pot in which the meat was cooked. If it was cooked in

---

^a *12* Traditionally *peace offerings*   ^b *18* Or *Whoever touches them must be holy*; similarly in verse 27
^c *20* Or *each*   ^d *20* That is, probably about 2 quarts (about 2 liters)   ^e *21* The meaning of the Hebrew for this word is uncertain.

NEW INTERNATIONAL VERSION	THE MESSAGE

NEW INTERNATIONAL VERSION

cooked in a bronze pot, the pot is to be scoured and rinsed with water. ²⁹Any male in a priest's family may eat it; it is most holy. ³⁰But any sin offering whose blood is brought into the Tent of Meeting to make atonement in the Holy Place must not be eaten; it must be burned.

THE GUILT OFFERING

7 " 'These are the regulations for the guilt offering, which is most holy: ²The guilt offering is to be slaughtered in the place where the burnt offering is slaughtered, and its blood is to be sprinkled against the altar on all sides. ³All its fat shall be offered: the fat tail and the fat that covers the inner parts, ⁴both kidneys with the fat on them near the loins, and the covering of the liver, which is to be removed with the kidneys. ⁵The priest shall burn them on the altar as an offering made to the LORD by fire. It is a guilt offering. ⁶Any male in a priest's family may eat it, but it must be eaten in a holy place; it is most holy.

⁷" 'The same law applies to both the sin offering and the guilt offering: They belong to the priest who makes atonement with them. ⁸The priest who offers a burnt offering for anyone may keep its hide for himself. ⁹Every grain offering baked in an oven or cooked in a pan or on a griddle belongs to the priest who offers it, ¹⁰and every grain offering, whether mixed with oil or dry, belongs equally to all the sons of Aaron.

THE FELLOWSHIP OFFERING

¹¹" 'These are the regulations for the fellowship offering*ᵃ* a person may present to the LORD:

¹²" 'If he offers it as an expression of thankfulness, then along with this thank offering he is to offer cakes of bread made without yeast and mixed with oil, wafers made without yeast and spread with oil, and cakes of fine flour wellkneaded and mixed with oil. ¹³Along with his fellowship offering of thanksgiving he is to present an offering with cakes of bread made with yeast. ¹⁴He is to bring one of each kind as an offering, a contribution to the LORD; it belongs to the priest who sprinkles the blood of the fellowship offerings. ¹⁵The meat of his fellowship offering of thanksgiving must be eaten on the day it is offered; he must leave none of it till morning.

¹⁶" 'If, however, his offering is the result of a vow or is a freewill offering, the sacrifice shall be eaten on the day he offers it, but anything left over may be eaten on the next day. ¹⁷Any meat of the sacrifice left over till the third day must be burned up. ¹⁸If any meat of the fellowship offering is eaten on the third day, it will not be accepted. It will not be credited to the one who

ᵃ 11 Traditionally peace offering; also in verses 13-37

THE MESSAGE

a bronze pot, scour it and rinse it with water. Any male among the priestly families may eat it; it is most holy. But any Absolution-Offering whose blood is brought into the Tent of Meeting to make atonement in the Sanctuary must not be eaten, it has to be burned.

✠

7.1-6 **7** "These are the instructions for the Compensation-Offering. It is most holy. Slaughter the Compensation-Offering in the same place that the Whole-Burnt-Offering is slaughtered. Splash its blood against all sides of the Altar. Offer up all the fat: the fat tail, the fat covering the entrails, the two kidneys and the fat encasing them at the loins, and the lobe of the liver that is removed with the kidneys. The priest burns them on the Altar as a gift to GOD. It is a Compensation-Offering. Any male from among the priests' families may eat it. But it must be eaten in a holy place; it is most holy.

7.7-10 "The Compensation-Offering is the same as the Absolution-Offering—the same rules apply to both. The offering belongs to the priest who makes atonement with it. The priest who presents a Whole-Burnt-Offering for someone gets the hide for himself. Every Grain-Offering baked in an oven or prepared in a pan or on a griddle belongs to the priest who presents it. It's his. Every Grain-Offering, whether dry or mixed with oil, belongs equally to all the sons of Aaron.

✠

7.11-15 "These are the instructions for the Peace-Offering which is presented to GOD. If you bring it to offer thanksgiving, then along with the Thanksgiving-Offering present unraised loaves of bread mixed with oil, unraised wafers spread with oil, and cakes of fine flour, well-kneaded and mixed with oil. Along with the Peace-Offering of thanksgiving, present loaves of yeast bread as an offering. Bring one of each kind as an offering, a Contribution-Offering to GOD; it goes to the priest who throws the blood of the Peace-Offering. Eat the meat from the Peace-Offering of thanksgiving the same day it is offered. Don't leave any of it overnight.

7.16-21 "If the offering is a Votive-Offering or a Freewill-Offering, it may be eaten the same day it is sacrificed and whatever is left over on the next day may also be eaten. But any meat from the sacrifice that is left to the third day must be burned up. If any of the meat from the Peace-Offering is eaten on the third day, the person who has brought it will not be accepted. It won't benefit him a bit—it has become defiled

NEW INTERNATIONAL VERSION

offered it, for it is impure; the person who eats any of it will be held responsible.

¹⁹" 'Meat that touches anything ceremonially unclean must not be eaten; it must be burned up. As for other meat, anyone ceremonially clean may eat it. ²⁰But if anyone who is unclean eats any meat of the fellowship offering belonging to the LORD, that person must be cut off from his people. ²¹If anyone touches something unclean—whether human uncleanness or an unclean animal or any unclean, detestable thing—and then eats any of the meat of the fellowship offering belonging to the LORD, that person must be cut off from his people.' "

EATING FAT AND BLOOD FORBIDDEN

²²The LORD said to Moses, ²³"Say to the Israelites: 'Do not eat any of the fat of cattle, sheep or goats. ²⁴The fat of an animal found dead or torn by wild animals may be used for any other purpose, but you must not eat it. ²⁵Anyone who eats the fat of an animal from which an offering by fire may be[a] made to the LORD must be cut off from his people. ²⁶And wherever you live, you must not eat the blood of any bird or animal. ²⁷If anyone eats blood, that person must be cut off from his people.' "

THE PRIESTS' SHARE

²⁸The LORD said to Moses, ²⁹"Say to the Israelites: 'Anyone who brings a fellowship offering to the LORD is to bring part of it as his sacrifice to the LORD. ³⁰With his own hands he is to bring the offering made to the LORD by fire; he is to bring the fat, together with the breast, and wave the breast before the LORD as a wave offering. ³¹The priest shall burn the fat on the altar, but the breast belongs to Aaron and his sons. ³²You are to give the right thigh of your fellowship offerings to the priest as a contribution. ³³The son of Aaron who offers the blood and the fat of the fellowship offering shall have the right thigh as his share. ³⁴From the fellowship offerings of the Israelites, I have taken the breast that is waved and the thigh that is presented and have given them to Aaron the priest and his sons as their regular share from the Israelites.' "

³⁵This is the portion of the offerings made to the LORD by fire that were allotted to Aaron and his sons on the day they were presented to serve the LORD as priests. ³⁶On the day they were anointed, the LORD commanded that the Israelites give this to them as their regular share for the generations to come.

³⁷These, then, are the regulations for the

a 25 Or *fire is*

THE MESSAGE

meat. And whoever eats it must take responsibility for his iniquity. Don't eat meat that has touched anything ritually unclean; burn it up. Any other meat can be eaten by those who are ritually clean. But if you're not ritually clean and eat meat from the Peace-Offering for GOD, you will be excluded from the congregation. And if you touch anything ritually unclean, whether human or animal uncleanness or an obscene object, and go ahead and eat from a Peace-Offering for GOD, you'll be excluded from the congregation."

✝

7.22-27 GOD spoke to Moses, "Speak to the People of Israel. Tell them, Don't eat any fat of cattle or sheep or goats. The fat of an animal found dead or torn by wild animals can be put to some other purpose, but you may not eat it. If you eat fat from an animal from which a gift has been presented to GOD, you'll be excluded from the congregation. And don't eat blood, whether of birds or animals, no matter where you end up living. If you eat blood you'll be excluded from the congregation."

✝

7.28-34 GOD spoke to Moses, "Speak to the People of Israel. Tell them: When you present a Peace-Offering to GOD, bring some of your Peace-Offering as a special sacrifice to GOD, a gift to GOD in your own hands. Bring the fat with the breast and then wave the breast before GOD as a Wave-Offering. The priest will burn the fat on the Altar; Aaron and his sons get the breast. Give the right thigh from your Peace-Offerings as a Contribution-Offering to the priest. Give a portion of the right thigh to the son of Aaron who offers the blood and fat of the Peace-Offering as his portion. From the Peace-Offerings of Israel, I'm giving the breast of the Wave-Offering and the thigh of the Contribution-Offering to Aaron the priest and his sons. This is their fixed compensation from the People of Israel."

7.35-36 From the day they are presented to serve as priests to GOD, Aaron and his sons can expect to receive these allotments from the gifts of GOD. This is what GOD commanded the People of Israel to give the priests from the day of their anointing. This is the fixed rule down through the generations.

7.37-38 These are the instructions for the Whole-

NEW INTERNATIONAL VERSION

burnt offering, the grain offering, the sin offering, the guilt offering, the ordination offering and the fellowship offering, ³⁸which the LORD gave Moses on Mount Sinai on the day he commanded the Israelites to bring their offerings to the LORD, in the Desert of Sinai.

THE ORDINATION OF AARON AND HIS SONS

8 The LORD said to Moses, ²"Bring Aaron and his sons, their garments, the anointing oil, the bull for the sin offering, the two rams and the basket containing bread made without yeast, ³and gather the entire assembly at the entrance to the Tent of Meeting." ⁴Moses did as the LORD commanded him, and the assembly gathered at the entrance to the Tent of Meeting.

⁵Moses said to the assembly, "This is what the LORD has commanded to be done." ⁶Then Moses brought Aaron and his sons forward and washed them with water. ⁷He put the tunic on Aaron, tied the sash around him, clothed him with the robe and put the ephod on him. He also tied the ephod to him by its skillfully woven waistband; so it was fastened on him. ⁸He placed the breastpiece on him and put the Urim and Thummim in the breastpiece. ⁹Then he placed the turban on Aaron's head and set the gold plate, the sacred diadem, on the front of it, as the LORD commanded Moses.

¹⁰Then Moses took the anointing oil and anointed the tabernacle and everything in it, and so consecrated them. ¹¹He sprinkled some of the oil on the altar seven times, anointing the altar and all its utensils and the basin with its stand, to consecrate them. ¹²He poured some of the anointing oil on Aaron's head and anointed him to consecrate him. ¹³Then he brought Aaron's sons forward, put tunics on them, tied sashes around them and put headbands on them, as the LORD commanded Moses.

¹⁴He then presented the bull for the sin offering, and Aaron and his sons laid their hands on its head. ¹⁵Moses slaughtered the bull and took some of the blood, and with his finger he put it on all the horns of the altar to purify the altar. He poured out the rest of the blood at the base of the altar. So he consecrated it to make atonement for it. ¹⁶Moses also took all the fat around the inner parts, the covering of the liver, and both kidneys and their fat, and burned it on the altar. ¹⁷But the bull with its hide and its flesh and its offal he burned up outside the camp, as the LORD commanded Moses.

¹⁸He then presented the ram for the burnt offering, and Aaron and his sons laid their hands

THE MESSAGE

Burnt-Offering, the Grain-Offering, the Absolution-Offering, the Compensation-Offering, the Ordination-Offering, and the Peace-Offering which GOD gave Moses at Mount Sinai on the day he commanded the People of Israel to present their offerings to GOD in the wilderness of Sinai.

THE ORDINATION OF PRIESTS

8.1-4 **8** GOD spoke to Moses. He said, "Take Aaron and with him his sons, the garments, the anointing oil, the bull for the Absolution-Offering, the two rams, and the basket of unraised bread. Gather the entire congregation at the entrance of the Tent of Meeting." Moses did just as GOD commanded him and the congregation gathered at the entrance of the Tent of Meeting.

8.5 Moses addressed the congregation: "This is what GOD has commanded to be done."

8.6-9 Moses brought Aaron and his sons forward and washed them with water. He put the tunic on Aaron and tied it around him with a sash. Then he put the robe on him and placed the Ephod on him. He fastened the Ephod with a woven belt, making it snug. He put the Breastpiece on him and put the Urim and Thummim in the pouch of the Breastpiece. He placed the turban on his head with the gold plate fixed to the front of it, the holy crown, just as GOD had commanded Moses.

8.10-12 Then Moses took the anointing oil and anointed The Dwelling and everything that was in it, consecrating them. He sprinkled some of the oil on the Altar seven times, anointing the Altar and all its utensils, the Washbasin and its stand, consecrating them. He poured some of the anointing oil on Aaron's head, anointing him and thus consecrating him.

8.13 Moses brought Aaron's sons forward and put tunics on them, belted them with sashes, and put caps on them, just as GOD had commanded Moses.

8.14-17 Moses brought out the bull for the Absolution-Offering. Aaron and his sons placed their hands on its head. Moses slaughtered the bull and purified the Altar by smearing the blood on each of the horns of the Altar with his finger. He poured out the rest of the blood at the base of the Altar. He consecrated it so atonement could be made on it. Moses took all the fat on the entrails and the lobe of liver and the two kidneys with their fat and burned it all on the Altar. The bull with its hide and meat and guts he burned outside the camp, just as GOD had commanded Moses.

8.18-21 Moses presented the ram for the Whole-Burnt-Offering. Aaron and his sons laid their

NEW INTERNATIONAL VERSION

on its head. ¹⁹Then Moses slaughtered the ram and sprinkled the blood against the altar on all sides. ²⁰He cut the ram into pieces and burned the head, the pieces and the fat. ²¹He washed the inner parts and the legs with water and burned the whole ram on the altar as a burnt offering, a pleasing aroma, an offering made to the LORD by fire, as the LORD commanded Moses.

²²He then presented the other ram, the ram for the ordination, and Aaron and his sons laid their hands on its head. ²³Moses slaughtered the ram and took some of its blood and put it on the lobe of Aaron's right ear, on the thumb of his right hand and on the big toe of his right foot. ²⁴Moses also brought Aaron's sons forward and put some of the blood on the lobes of their right ears, on the thumbs of their right hands and on the big toes of their right feet. Then he sprinkled blood against the altar on all sides. ²⁵He took the fat, the fat tail, all the fat around the inner parts, the covering of the liver, both kidneys and their fat and the right thigh. ²⁶Then from the basket of bread made without yeast, which was before the LORD, he took a cake of bread, and one made with oil, and a wafer; he put these on the fat portions and on the right thigh. ²⁷He put all these in the hands of Aaron and his sons and waved them before the LORD as a wave offering. ²⁸Then Moses took them from their hands and burned them on the altar on top of the burnt offering as an ordination offering, a pleasing aroma, an offering made to the LORD by fire. ²⁹He also took the breast—Moses' share of the ordination ram—and waved it before the LORD as a wave offering, as the LORD commanded Moses.

³⁰Then Moses took some of the anointing oil and some of the blood from the altar and sprinkled them on Aaron and his garments and on his sons and their garments. So he consecrated Aaron and his garments and his sons and their garments.

³¹Moses then said to Aaron and his sons, "Cook the meat at the entrance to the Tent of Meeting and eat it there with the bread from the basket of ordination offerings, as I commanded, saying,ᵃ 'Aaron and his sons are to eat it.' ³²Then burn up the rest of the meat and the bread. ³³Do not leave the entrance to the Tent of Meeting for seven days, until the days of your ordination are completed, for your ordination will last seven days. ³⁴What has been done today was commanded by the LORD to make atonement for you. ³⁵You must stay at the entrance to the Tent of Meeting day and night for seven days and do what the LORD requires, so you will not die; for

ᵃ 31 Or I was commanded:

THE MESSAGE

hands on the head of the ram. Moses slaughtered it and splashed the blood against all sides of the Altar. He cut the ram up into pieces and then burned the head, the pieces, and the fat. He washed the entrails and the legs with water and then burned the whole ram on the Altar. It was a Whole-Burnt-Offering, a pleasing fragrance—a gift to GOD, just as GOD had commanded Moses.

8.22-29   Moses then presented the second ram, the ram for the Ordination-Offering. Aaron and his sons laid their hands on the ram's head. Moses slaughtered it and smeared some of its blood on the lobe of Aaron's right ear, on the thumb of his right hand, and on the big toe of his right foot. Then Aaron's sons were brought forward and Moses smeared some of the blood on the lobes of their right ears, on the thumbs of their right hands, and on the big toes of their right feet. Moses threw the remaining blood against each side of the Altar. He took the fat, the fat tail, all the fat that was on the entrails, the lobe of the liver, the two kidneys with their fat, and the right thigh. From the basket of unraised bread that was in the presence of GOD he took one loaf of the unraised bread made with oil and one wafer. He placed these on the fat portions and the right thigh. He put all this in the hands of Aaron and his sons who waved them before GOD as a Wave-Offering. Then Moses took it all back from their hands and burned them on the Altar on top of the Whole-Burnt-Offering. These were the Ordination-Offerings, a pleasing fragrance to GOD, a gift to GOD. Then Moses took the breast and raised it up as a Wave-Offering before GOD; it was Moses' portion from the Ordination-Offering ram, just as GOD had commanded Moses.

8.30   Moses took some of the anointing oil and some of the blood from the Altar and sprinkled Aaron and his garments, and his sons and their garments, consecrating Aaron and his garments and his sons and their garments.

8.31-35   Moses spoke to Aaron and his sons: "Boil the meat at the entrance of the Tent of Meeting and eat it there with the bread from the basket of ordination, just as I commanded, saying, 'Aaron and his sons are to eat it.' Burn up the leftovers from the meat and bread. Don't leave through the entrance of the Tent of Meeting for the seven days that will complete your ordination. Your ordination will last seven days. GOD commanded what has been done this day in order to make atonement for you. Stay at the entrance of the Tent of Meeting day and night for seven days. Be sure to do what GOD re-

NEW INTERNATIONAL VERSION

that is what I have been commanded." ³⁶So Aaron and his sons did everything the LORD commanded through Moses.

THE PRIESTS BEGIN THEIR MINISTRY

9 On the eighth day Moses summoned Aaron and his sons and the elders of Israel. ²He said to Aaron, "Take a bull calf for your sin offering and a ram for your burnt offering, both without defect, and present them before the LORD. ³Then say to the Israelites: 'Take a male goat for a sin offering, a calf and a lamb—both a year old and without defect—for a burnt offering, ⁴and an ox*ᵃ* and a ram for a fellowship offering*ᵇ* to sacrifice before the LORD, together with a grain offering mixed with oil. For today the LORD will appear to you.' "

⁵They took the things Moses commanded to the front of the Tent of Meeting, and the entire assembly came near and stood before the LORD. ⁶Then Moses said, "This is what the LORD has commanded you to do, so that the glory of the LORD may appear to you."

⁷Moses said to Aaron, "Come to the altar and sacrifice your sin offering and your burnt offering and make atonement for yourself and the people; sacrifice the offering that is for the people and make atonement for them, as the LORD has commanded."

⁸So Aaron came to the altar and slaughtered the calf as a sin offering for himself. ⁹His sons brought the blood to him, and he dipped his finger into the blood and put it on the horns of the altar; the rest of the blood he poured out at the base of the altar. ¹⁰On the altar he burned the fat, the kidneys and the covering of the liver from the sin offering, as the LORD commanded Moses; ¹¹the flesh and the hide he burned up outside the camp.

¹²Then he slaughtered the burnt offering. His sons handed him the blood, and he sprinkled it against the altar on all sides. ¹³They handed him the burnt offering piece by piece, including the head, and he burned them on the altar. ¹⁴He washed the inner parts and the legs and burned them on top of the burnt offering on the altar.

¹⁵Aaron then brought the offering that was for the people. He took the goat for the people's sin offering and slaughtered it and offered it for a sin offering as he did with the first one. ¹⁶He brought the burnt offering and offered it in the prescribed way. ¹⁷He also brought the grain offering, took a handful of it and burned it

---

ᵃ 4 The Hebrew word can include both male and female; also in verses 18 and 19.   *ᵇ 4* Traditionally *peace offering*; also in verses 18 and 22

THE MESSAGE

quires, lest you die. This is what I have been commanded."

8.36 Aaron and his sons did everything that GOD had commanded by Moses.

THE PRIESTS GO TO WORK

9.1-2 **9** On the eighth day, Moses called in Aaron and his sons and the leaders of Israel. He spoke to Aaron: "Take a bull-calf for your Absolution-Offering and a ram for your Whole-Burnt-Offering, both without defect, and offer them to GOD.

9.3-4 "Then tell the People of Israel, Take a male goat for an Absolution-Offering and a calf and a lamb, both yearlings without defect, for a Whole-Burnt-Offering and a bull and a ram for a Peace-Offering, to be sacrificed before GOD with a Grain-Offering mixed with oil, because GOD will appear to you today."

9.5-6 They brought the things that Moses had ordered to the Tent of Meeting. The whole congregation came near and stood before GOD. Moses said, "This is what GOD commanded you to do so that the Shining Glory of GOD will appear to you."

9.7 Moses instructed Aaron, "Approach the Altar and sacrifice your Absolution-Offering and your Whole-Burnt-Offering. Make atonement for yourself and for the people. Sacrifice the offering that is for the people and make atonement for them, just as GOD commanded."

9.8-11 Aaron approached the Altar and slaughtered the calf as an Absolution-Offering for himself. Aaron's sons brought the blood to him. He dipped his finger in the blood and smeared some of it on the horns of the Altar. He poured out the rest of the blood at the base of the Altar. He burned the fat, the kidneys, and the lobe of the liver from the Absolution-Offering on the Altar, just as GOD had commanded Moses. He burned the meat and the skin outside the camp.

9.12-14 Then he slaughtered the Whole-Burnt-Offering. Aaron's sons handed him the blood and he threw it against each side of the Altar. They handed him the pieces and the head and he burned these on the Altar. He washed the entrails and the legs and burned them on top of the Whole-Burnt-Offering on the Altar.

9.15-21 Next Aaron presented the offerings of the people. He took the male goat, the Absolution-Offering for the people, slaughtered it, and offered it as an Absolution-Offering just as he did with the first offering. He presented the Whole-Burnt-Offering following the same procedures. He presented the Grain-Offering by taking a

NEW INTERNATIONAL VERSION

on the altar in addition to the morning's burnt offering.

¹⁸He slaughtered the ox and the ram as the fellowship offering for the people. His sons handed him the blood, and he sprinkled it against the altar on all sides. ¹⁹But the fat portions of the ox and the ram—the fat tail, the layer of fat, the kidneys and the covering of the liver— ²⁰these they laid on the breasts, and then Aaron burned the fat on the altar. ²¹Aaron waved the breasts and the right thigh before the LORD as a wave offering, as Moses commanded.

²²Then Aaron lifted his hands toward the people and blessed them. And having sacrificed the sin offering, the burnt offering and the fellowship offering, he stepped down.

²³Moses and Aaron then went into the Tent of Meeting. When they came out, they blessed the people; and the glory of the LORD appeared to all the people. ²⁴Fire came out from the presence of the LORD and consumed the burnt offering and the fat portions on the altar. And when all the people saw it, they shouted for joy and fell facedown.

THE DEATH OF NADAB AND ABIHU

10 Aaron's sons Nadab and Abihu took their censers, put fire in them and added incense; and they offered unauthorized fire before the LORD, contrary to his command. ²So fire came out from the presence of the LORD and consumed them, and they died before the LORD. ³Moses then said to Aaron, "This is what the LORD spoke of when he said:

" 'Among those who approach me
  I will show myself holy;
in the sight of all the people
  I will be honored.' "

Aaron remained silent.

⁴Moses summoned Mishael and Elzaphan, sons of Aaron's uncle Uzziel, and said to them, "Come here; carry your cousins outside the camp, away from the front of the sanctuary." ⁵So they came and carried them, still in their tunics, outside the camp, as Moses ordered.

⁶Then Moses said to Aaron and his sons Eleazar and Ithamar, "Do not let your hair become unkempt,ᵃ and do not tear your clothes, or you will die and the LORD will be angry with the whole community. But your relatives, all the house of Israel, may mourn for those the LORD has destroyed by fire. ⁷Do not leave the entrance to the Tent of Meeting or you will die, because the LORD's anointing oil is on you." So they did as Moses said.

ᵃ 6 Or Do not uncover your heads

THE MESSAGE

handful of it and burning it on the Altar along with the morning Whole-Burnt-Offering. He slaughtered the bull and the ram, the people's Peace-Offerings. Aaron's sons handed him the blood and he threw it against each side of the Altar. The fat pieces from the bull and the ram—the fat tail and the fat that covers the kidney and the lobe of the liver—they laid on the breasts and Aaron burned it on the Altar. Aaron waved the breasts and the right thigh before GOD as a Wave-Offering, just as GOD commanded.

9.22-24 Aaron lifted his hands over the people and blessed them. Having completed the rituals of the Absolution-Offering, the Whole-Burnt-Offering, and the Peace-Offering, he came down from the Altar. Moses and Aaron entered the Tent of Meeting. When they came out they blessed the people and the Glory of GOD appeared to all the people. Fire blazed out from GOD and consumed the Whole-Burnt-Offering and the fat pieces on the Altar. When all the people saw it happen they cheered loudly and then fell down, bowing in reverence.

NADAB AND ABIHU

10.1-2 **10** That same day Nadab and Abihu, Aaron's sons, took their censers, put hot coals and incense in them, and offered "strange" fire to GOD—something GOD had not commanded. Fire blazed out from GOD and consumed them—they died in GOD's presence.

10.3 Moses said to Aaron, "This is what GOD meant when he said,

To the one who comes near me,
  I will show myself holy;
Before all the people,
  I will show my glory."

Aaron was silent.

10.4-5 Moses called for Mishael and Elzaphan, sons of Uzziel, Aaron's uncle. He said, "Come. Carry your dead cousins outside the camp, away from the Sanctuary." They came and carried them off, outside the camp, just as Moses had directed.

10.6-7 Moses then said to Aaron and his remaining sons, Eleazar and Ithamar, "No mourning rituals for you—unkempt hair, torn clothes—or you'll also die and GOD will be angry with the whole congregation. Your relatives—all the People of Israel, in fact—will do the mourning over those GOD has destroyed by fire. And don't leave the entrance to the Tent of Meeting lest you die, because GOD's anointing oil is on you." They did just as Moses said.

☩

NEW INTERNATIONAL VERSION

[8]Then the LORD said to Aaron, [9]"You and your sons are not to drink wine or other fermented drink whenever you go into the Tent of Meeting, or you will die. This is a lasting ordinance for the generations to come. [10]You must distinguish between the holy and the common, between the unclean and the clean, [11]and you must teach the Israelites all the decrees the LORD has given them through Moses."

[12]Moses said to Aaron and his remaining sons, Eleazar and Ithamar, "Take the grain offering left over from the offerings made to the LORD by fire and eat it prepared without yeast beside the altar, for it is most holy. [13]Eat it in a holy place, because it is your share and your sons' share of the offerings made to the LORD by fire; for so I have been commanded. [14]But you and your sons and your daughters may eat the breast that was waved and the thigh that was presented. Eat them in a ceremonially clean place; they have been given to you and your children as your share of the Israelites' fellowship offerings.[a] [15]The thigh that was presented and the breast that was waved must be brought with the fat portions of the offerings made by fire, to be waved before the LORD as a wave offering. This will be the regular share for you and your children, as the LORD has commanded."

[16]When Moses inquired about the goat of the sin offering and found that it had been burned up, he was angry with Eleazar and Ithamar, Aaron's remaining sons, and asked, [17]"Why didn't you eat the sin offering in the sanctuary area? It is most holy; it was given to you to take away the guilt of the community by making atonement for them before the LORD. [18]Since its blood was not taken into the Holy Place, you should have eaten the goat in the sanctuary area, as I commanded."

[19]Aaron replied to Moses, "Today they sacrificed their sin offering and their burnt offering before the LORD, but such things as this have happened to me. Would the LORD have been pleased if I had eaten the sin offering today?" [20]When Moses heard this, he was satisfied.

CLEAN AND UNCLEAN FOOD

11 The LORD said to Moses and Aaron, [2]"Say to the Israelites: 'Of all the animals that live on land, these are the ones you may eat: [3]You may eat any animal that has a split hoof completely divided and that chews the cud.

[4]"'There are some that only chew the cud or

THE MESSAGE

10.8-11 GOD instructed Aaron, "When you enter the Tent of Meeting, don't drink wine or strong drink, neither you nor your sons, lest you die. This is a fixed rule down through the generations. Distinguish between the holy and the common, between the ritually clean and unclean. Teach the People of Israel all the decrees that GOD has spoken to them through Moses."

10.12-15 Moses spoke to Aaron and his surviving sons, Eleazar and Ithamar, "Take the leftovers of the Grain-Offering from the Fire-Gifts for GOD and eat beside the Altar that which has been prepared without yeast, for it is most holy. Eat it in the Holy Place because it is your portion and the portion of your sons from the Fire-Gifts for GOD. This is what GOD commanded me. Also, you and your sons and daughters are to eat the breast of the Wave-Offering and the thigh of the Contribution-Offering in a clean place. They are provided as your portion and the portion of your children from the Peace-Offerings presented by the People of Israel. Bring the thigh of the Contribution-Offering and the breast of the Wave-Offering and the fat pieces of the Fire-Gifts and lift them up as a Wave-Offering. This will be the regular share for you and your children as ordered by GOD."

10.16-18 When Moses looked into the matter of the goat of the Absolution-Offering, he found that it had been burned up. He became angry with Eleazar and Ithamar, Aaron's remaining sons, and asked, "Why didn't you eat the Absolution-Offering in the Holy Place since it is most holy? The offering was given to you for taking away the guilt of the community by making atonement for them before GOD. Since its blood was not taken into the Holy Place, you should have eaten the goat in the Sanctuary as I commanded."

10.19 Aaron replied to Moses, "Look. They sacrificed their Absolution-Offering and Whole-Burnt-Offering before GOD today, and you see what has happened to me—I've lost two sons. Do you think GOD would have been pleased if I had gone ahead and eaten the Absolution-Offering today?"

10.20 When Moses heard this response, he accepted it.

FOODS

11.1-2 11 GOD spoke to Moses and Aaron: "Speak to the People of Israel. Tell them: Of all the animals on Earth, these are the animals that you may eat:

11.3-8 "You may eat any animal that has a split hoof, divided in two, and that chews the cud,

---

[a] 14 Traditionally *peace offerings*

NEW INTERNATIONAL VERSION

only have a split hoof, but you must not eat them. The camel, though it chews the cud, does not have a split hoof; it is ceremonially unclean for you. [5]The coney,[a] though it chews the cud, does not have a split hoof; it is unclean for you. [6]The rabbit, though it chews the cud, does not have a split hoof; it is unclean for you. [7]And the pig, though it has a split hoof completely divided, does not chew the cud; it is unclean for you. [8]You must not eat their meat or touch their carcasses; they are unclean for you.

[9]" 'Of all the creatures living in the water of the seas and the streams, you may eat any that have fins and scales. [10]But all creatures in the seas or streams that do not have fins and scales—whether among all the swarming things or among all the other living creatures in the water—you are to detest. [11]And since you are to detest them, you must not eat their meat and you must detest their carcasses. [12]Anything living in the water that does not have fins and scales is to be detestable to you.

[13]" 'These are the birds you are to detest and not eat because they are detestable: the eagle, the vulture, the black vulture, [14]the red kite, any kind of black kite, [15]any kind of raven, [16]the horned owl, the screech owl, the gull, any kind of hawk, [17]the little owl, the cormorant, the great owl, [18]the white owl, the desert owl, the osprey, [19]the stork, any kind of heron, the hoopoe and the bat.[b]

[20]" 'All flying insects that walk on all fours are to be detestable to you. [21]There are, however, some winged creatures that walk on all fours that you may eat: those that have jointed legs for hopping on the ground. [22]Of these you may eat any kind of locust, katydid, cricket or grasshopper. [23]But all other winged creatures that have four legs you are to detest.

[24]" 'You will make yourselves unclean by these; whoever touches their carcasses will be unclean till evening. [25]Whoever picks up one of their carcasses must wash his clothes, and he will be unclean till evening.

[26]" 'Every animal that has a split hoof not completely divided or that does not chew the cud is unclean for you; whoever touches ʟthe carcass ofʟ any of them will be unclean. [27]Of all the animals that walk on all fours, those that walk on their paws are unclean for you; whoever touches their carcasses will be unclean till evening. [28]Anyone who picks up their carcasses must wash his clothes, and he will be unclean till evening. They are unclean for you.

THE MESSAGE

but not an animal that only chews the cud or only has a split hoof. For instance, the camel chews the cud but doesn't have a split hoof, so it's unclean. The rock badger chews the cud but doesn't have a split hoof and so it's unclean. The rabbit chews the cud but doesn't have a split hoof so is unclean. The pig has a split hoof, divided in two, but doesn't chew the cud and so is unclean. You may not eat their meat nor touch their carcasses; they are unclean to you.

11.9-12   "Among the creatures that live in the water of the seas and streams, you may eat any that have fins and scales. But anything that doesn't have fins and scales, whether in seas or streams, whether small creatures in the shallows or huge creatures in the deeps, you are to detest. Yes, detest them. Don't eat their meat; detest their carcasses. Anything living in the water that doesn't have fins and scales is detestable to you.

11.13-19   "These are the birds you are to detest. Don't eat them. They are detestable: eagle, vulture, osprey, kite, all falcons, all ravens, ostrich, nighthawk, sea gull, all hawks, owl, cormorant, ibis, water hen, pelican, Egyptian vulture, stork, all herons, hoopoe, bat.

11.20-23   "All flying insects that walk on all fours are detestable to you. But you can eat some of these, namely, those that have jointed legs for hopping on the ground: all locusts, katydids, crickets, and grasshoppers. But all the other flying insects that have four legs you are to detest.

11.24-25   "You will make yourselves ritually unclean until evening if you touch their carcasses. If you pick up one of their carcasses you must wash your clothes and you'll be unclean until evening.

11.26   "Every animal that has a split hoof that's not completely divided, or that doesn't chew the cud is unclean for you; if you touch the carcass of any of them you become unclean.

11.27-28   "Every four-footed animal that goes on its paws is unclean for you; if you touch its carcass you are unclean until evening. If you pick up its carcass you must wash your clothes and are unclean until evening. They are unclean for you.

NEW INTERNATIONAL VERSION

29" 'Of the animals that move about on the ground, these are unclean for you: the weasel, the rat, any kind of great lizard, 30the gecko, the monitor lizard, the wall lizard, the skink and the chameleon. 31Of all those that move along the ground, these are unclean for you. Whoever touches them when they are dead will be unclean till evening. 32When one of them dies and falls on something, that article, whatever its use, will be unclean, whether it is made of wood, cloth, hide or sackcloth. Put it in water; it will be unclean till evening, and then it will be clean. 33If one of them falls into a clay pot, everything in it will be unclean, and you must break the pot. 34Any food that could be eaten but has water on it from such a pot is unclean, and any liquid that could be drunk from it is unclean. 35Anything that one of their carcasses falls on becomes unclean; an oven or cooking pot must be broken up. They are unclean, and you are to regard them as unclean. 36A spring, however, or a cistern for collecting water remains clean, but anyone who touches one of these carcasses is unclean. 37If a carcass falls on any seeds that are to be planted, they remain clean. 38But if water has been put on the seed and a carcass falls on it, it is unclean for you.

39" 'If an animal that you are allowed to eat dies, anyone who touches the carcass will be unclean till evening. 40Anyone who eats some of the carcass must wash his clothes, and he will be unclean till evening. Anyone who picks up the carcass must wash his clothes, and he will be unclean till evening.

41" 'Every creature that moves about on the ground is detestable; it is not to be eaten. 42You are not to eat any creature that moves about on the ground, whether it moves on its belly or walks on all fours or on many feet; it is detestable. 43Do not defile yourselves by any of these creatures. Do not make yourselves unclean by means of them or be made unclean by them. 44I am the LORD your God; consecrate yourselves and be holy, because I am holy. Do not make yourselves unclean by any creature that moves about on the ground. 45I am the LORD who brought you up out of Egypt to be your God; therefore be holy, because I am holy.

46" 'These are the regulations concerning animals, birds, every living thing that moves in the water and every creature that moves about on the ground. 47You must distinguish between the unclean and the clean, between living creatures that may be eaten and those that may not be eaten.' "

THE MESSAGE

11.29-38 "Among the creatures that crawl on the ground, the following are unclean for you: weasel, rat, all lizards, gecko, monitor lizard, wall lizard, skink, chameleon. Among the crawling creatures, these are unclean for you. If you touch them when they are dead, you are ritually unclean until evening. When one of them dies and falls on something, that becomes unclean no matter what it's used for, whether it's made of wood, cloth, hide, or sackcloth. Put it in the water—it's unclean until evening, and then it's clean. If one of these dead creatures falls into a clay pot, everything in the pot is unclean and you must break the pot. Any food that could be eaten but has water on it from such a pot is unclean, and any liquid that could be drunk from it is unclean. Anything that one of these carcasses falls on is unclean—an oven or cooking pot must be broken up; they're unclean and must be treated as unclean. A spring, though, or a cistern for collecting water remains clean, but if you touch one of these carcasses you're ritually unclean. If a carcass falls on any seeds that are to be planted, they remain clean. But if water has been put on the seed and a carcass falls on it, you must treat it as unclean.

11.39-40 "If an animal that you are permitted to eat dies, anyone who touches the carcass is ritually unclean until evening. If you eat some of the carcass you must wash your clothes and you are unclean until evening. If you pick up the carcass you must wash your clothes and are unclean until evening.

11.41-43 "Creatures that crawl on the ground are detestable and not to be eaten. Don't eat creatures that crawl on the ground, whether on their belly or on all fours or on many feet—they are detestable. Don't make yourselves unclean or be defiled by them, because I am your GOD.

11.44-45 "Make yourselves holy for I am holy. Don't make yourselves ritually unclean by any creature that crawls on the ground. I am GOD who brought you up out of the land of Egypt. Be holy because I am holy.

11.46-47 "These are the instructions on animals, birds, fish, and creatures that crawl on the ground. You have to distinguish between the ritually unclean and the clean, between living creatures that can be eaten and those that cannot be eaten."

NEW INTERNATIONAL VERSION

PURIFICATION AFTER CHILDBIRTH

12 The LORD said to Moses, [2]"Say to the Israelites: 'A woman who becomes pregnant and gives birth to a son will be ceremonially unclean for seven days, just as she is unclean during her monthly period. [3]On the eighth day the boy is to be circumcised. [4]Then the woman must wait thirty-three days to be purified from her bleeding. She must not touch anything sacred or go to the sanctuary until the days of her purification are over. [5]If she gives birth to a daughter, for two weeks the woman will be unclean, as during her period. Then she must wait sixty-six days to be purified from her bleeding.

[6]" 'When the days of her purification for a son or daughter are over, she is to bring to the priest at the entrance to the Tent of Meeting a year-old lamb for a burnt offering and a young pigeon or a dove for a sin offering. [7]He shall offer them before the LORD to make atonement for her, and then she will be ceremonially clean from her flow of blood.

" 'These are the regulations for the woman who gives birth to a boy or a girl. [8]If she cannot afford a lamb, she is to bring two doves or two young pigeons, one for a burnt offering and the other for a sin offering. In this way the priest will make atonement for her, and she will be clean.' "

REGULATIONS ABOUT INFECTIOUS SKIN DISEASES

13 The LORD said to Moses and Aaron, [2]"When anyone has a swelling or a rash or a bright spot on his skin that may become an infectious skin disease,[a] he must be brought to Aaron the priest or to one of his sons[b] who is a priest. [3]The priest is to examine the sore on his skin, and if the hair in the sore has turned white and the sore appears to be more than skin deep,[c] it is an infectious skin disease. When the priest examines him, he shall pronounce him ceremonially unclean. [4]If the spot on his skin is white but does not appear to be more than skin deep and the hair in it has not turned white, the priest is to put the infected person in isolation for seven days. [5]On the seventh day the priest is to examine him, and if he sees that the sore is unchanged and has not spread in the skin, he is to keep him in isolation another seven days. [6]On the seventh day the priest is to examine him again, and if the sore has faded and has not spread in the skin, the priest shall pronounce

---

THE MESSAGE

CHILDBIRTH

12.1-5 **12** GOD spoke to Moses: "Tell the People of Israel: A woman who conceives and gives birth to a boy is ritually unclean for seven days, the same as during her menstruation. On the eighth day circumcise the boy. The mother must stay home another thirty-three days for purification from her bleeding. She may not touch anything consecrated or enter the Sanctuary until the days of her purification are complete. If she gives birth to a girl, she is unclean for fourteen days, the same as during her menstruation. She must stay home for sixty-six days for purification from her bleeding.

12.6-7 "When the days for her purification for either a boy or a girl are complete, she will bring a yearling lamb for a Whole-Burnt-Offering and a pigeon or dove for an Absolution-Offering to the priest at the entrance of the Tent of Meeting. He will offer it to GOD and make atonement for her. She is then clean from her flow of blood.

"These are the instructions for a woman who gives birth to either a boy or a girl.

12.8 "If she can't afford a lamb, she can bring two doves or two pigeons, one for the Whole-Burnt-Offering and one for the Absolution-Offering. The priest will make atonement for her and she will be clean."

INFECTIONS

13.1-3 **13** GOD spoke to Moses and Aaron, "When someone has a swelling or a blister or a shiny spot on the skin that might signal a serious skin disease on the body, bring him to Aaron the priest or to one of his priest sons. The priest will examine the sore on the skin. If the hair in the sore has turned white and the sore appears more than skin deep, it is a serious skin disease and infectious. After the priest has examined it, he will pronounce the person unclean.

13.4-8 "If the shiny spot on the skin is white but appears to be only on the surface and the hair has not turned white, the priest will quarantine the person for seven days. On the seventh day the priest will examine it again; if, in his judgment, the sore is the same and has not spread, the priest will keep him in quarantine for another seven days. On the seventh day the priest will examine him a second time; if the sore has faded and hasn't spread, the priest will declare him clean—it is a harmless rash. The

---

[a] 2 Traditionally *leprosy*; the Hebrew word was used for various diseases affecting the skin—not necessarily leprosy; also elsewhere in this chapter.   [b] 2 Or *descendants*
[c] 3 Or *be lower than the rest of the skin*; also elsewhere in this chapter

NEW INTERNATIONAL VERSION

him clean; it is only a rash. The man must wash his clothes, and he will be clean. [7]But if the rash does spread in his skin after he has shown himself to the priest to be pronounced clean, he must appear before the priest again. [8]The priest is to examine him, and if the rash has spread in the skin, he shall pronounce him unclean; it is an infectious disease.

[9]"When anyone has an infectious skin disease, he must be brought to the priest. [10]The priest is to examine him, and if there is a white swelling in the skin that has turned the hair white and if there is raw flesh in the swelling, [11]it is a chronic skin disease and the priest shall pronounce him unclean. He is not to put him in isolation, because he is already unclean.

[12]"If the disease breaks out all over his skin and, so far as the priest can see, it covers all the skin of the infected person from head to foot, [13]the priest is to examine him, and if the disease has covered his whole body, he shall pronounce that person clean. Since it has all turned white, he is clean. [14]But whenever raw flesh appears on him, he will be unclean. [15]When the priest sees the raw flesh, he shall pronounce him unclean. The raw flesh is unclean; he has an infectious disease. [16]Should the raw flesh change and turn white, he must go to the priest. [17]The priest is to examine him, and if the sores have turned white, the priest shall pronounce the infected person clean; then he will be clean.

[18]"When someone has a boil on his skin and it heals, [19]and in the place where the boil was, a white swelling or reddish-white spot appears, he must present himself to the priest. [20]The priest is to examine it, and if it appears to be more than skin deep and the hair in it has turned white, the priest shall pronounce him unclean. It is an infectious skin disease that has broken out where the boil was. [21]But if, when the priest examines it, there is no white hair in it and it is not more than skin deep and has faded, then the priest is to put him in isolation for seven days. [22]If it is spreading in the skin, the priest shall pronounce him unclean; it is infectious. [23]But if the spot is unchanged and has not spread, it is only a scar from the boil, and the priest shall pronounce him clean.

[24]"When someone has a burn on his skin and a reddish-white or white spot appears in the raw flesh of the burn, [25]the priest is to examine the spot, and if the hair in it has turned white, and it appears to be more than skin deep, it is an infectious disease that has broken out in the burn. The priest shall pronounce him unclean; it is an infectious skin disease. [26]But if the priest examines it and there is no white hair in the spot and

THE MESSAGE

person can go home and wash his clothes; he is clean. But if the sore spreads after he has shown himself to the priest and been declared clean, he must come back again to the priest who will conduct another examination. If the sore has spread, the priest will pronounce him unclean—it is a serious skin disease and infectious.

13.9-17   "Whenever someone has a serious and infectious skin disease, you must bring him to the priest. The priest will examine him; if there is a white swelling in the skin, the hair is turning white, and there is an open sore in the swelling, it is a chronic skin disease. The priest will pronounce him unclean. But he doesn't need to quarantine him because he's already given his diagnosis of unclean. If a serious disease breaks out that covers all the skin from head to foot, wherever the priest looks, the priest will make a thorough examination; if the disease covers his entire body, he will pronounce the person with the sore clean—since it has turned all white, he is clean. But if they are open, running sores, he is unclean. The priest will examine the open sores and pronounce him unclean. The open sores are unclean; they are evidence of a serious skin disease. But if the open sores dry up and turn white, he is to come back to the priest who will reexamine him; if the sores have turned white, the priest will pronounce the person with the sores clean. He is clean.

13.18-23   "When a person has a boil and it heals and in place of the boil there is white swelling or a reddish-white shiny spot, the person must present himself to the priest for an examination. If it looks like it has penetrated the skin and the hair in it has turned white, the priest will pronounce him unclean. It is a serious skin disease that has broken out in the boil. But if the examination shows that there is no white hair in it and it is only skin deep and has faded, the priest will put him in quarantine for seven days. If it then spreads over the skin, the priest will diagnose him as unclean. It is infectious. But if the shiny spot has not changed and hasn't spread, it's only a scar from the boil. The priest will pronounce him clean.

13.24-28   "When a person has a burn on his skin and the raw flesh turns into a reddish-white or white shiny spot, the priest is to examine it. If the hair has turned white in the shiny spot and it looks like it's more than skin deep, a serious skin disease has erupted in the area of the burn. The priest will pronounce him unclean; it is a serious skin disease and infectious. But if on examination there is no white hair in the shiny

NEW INTERNATIONAL VERSION

if it is not more than skin deep and has faded, then the priest is to put him in isolation for seven days. ²⁷On the seventh day the priest is to examine him, and if it is spreading in the skin, the priest shall pronounce him unclean; it is an infectious skin disease. ²⁸If, however, the spot is unchanged and has not spread in the skin but has faded, it is a swelling from the burn, and the priest shall pronounce him clean; it is only a scar from the burn.

²⁹"If a man or woman has a sore on the head or on the chin, ³⁰the priest is to examine the sore, and if it appears to be more than skin deep and the hair in it is yellow and thin, the priest shall pronounce that person unclean; it is an itch, an infectious disease of the head or chin. ³¹But if, when the priest examines this kind of sore, it does not seem to be more than skin deep and there is no black hair in it, then the priest is to put the infected person in isolation for seven days. ³²On the seventh day the priest is to examine the sore, and if the itch has not spread and there is no yellow hair in it and it does not appear to be more than skin deep, ³³he must be shaved except for the diseased area, and the priest is to keep him in isolation another seven days. ³⁴On the seventh day the priest is to examine the itch, and if it has not spread in the skin and appears to be no more than skin deep, the priest shall pronounce him clean. He must wash his clothes, and he will be clean. ³⁵But if the itch does spread in the skin after he is pronounced clean, ³⁶the priest is to examine him, and if the itch has spread in the skin, the priest does not need to look for yellow hair; the person is unclean. ³⁷If, however, in his judgment it is unchanged and black hair has grown in it, the itch is healed. He is clean, and the priest shall pronounce him clean.

³⁸"When a man or woman has white spots on the skin, ³⁹the priest is to examine them, and if the spots are dull white, it is a harmless rash that has broken out on the skin; that person is clean.

⁴⁰"When a man has lost his hair and is bald, he is clean. ⁴¹If he has lost his hair from the front of his scalp and has a bald forehead, he is clean. ⁴²But if he has a reddish-white sore on his bald head or forehead, it is an infectious disease breaking out on his head or forehead. ⁴³The priest is to examine him, and if the swollen sore on his head or forehead is reddish-white like an infectious skin disease, ⁴⁴the man is diseased and is unclean. The priest shall pronounce him unclean because of the sore on his head.

⁴⁵"The person with such an infectious disease must wear torn clothes, let his hair be unkempt,^a cover the lower part of his face and cry

^a 45 Or *clothes, uncover his head*

THE MESSAGE

spot and it doesn't look to be more than skin deep but has faded, the priest will put him in quarantine for seven days. On the seventh day the priest will reexamine him. If by then it has spread over the skin, the priest will diagnose him as unclean; it is a serious skin disease and infectious. If by that time the shiny spot has stayed the same and has not spread but has faded, it is only a swelling from the burn. The priest will pronounce him clean; it's only a scar from the burn.

13.29-37   "If a man or woman develops a sore on the head or chin, the priest will offer a diagnosis. If it looks as if it is under the skin and the hair in it is yellow and thin, he will pronounce the person ritually unclean. It is an itch, an infectious skin disease. But if when he examines the itch, he finds it is only skin deep and there is no black hair in it, he will put the person in quarantine for seven days. On the seventh day he will reexamine the sore; if the itch has not spread, there is no yellow hair in it, and it looks as if the itch is only skin deep, the person must shave, except for the itch; the priest will send him back to quarantine for another seven days. If the itch has not spread, and looks to be only skin deep, the priest will pronounce him clean. The person can go home and wash his clothes; he is clean. But if the itch spreads after being pronounced clean, the priest must reexamine it; if the itch has spread in the skin, he doesn't have to look any farther, for yellow hair, for instance; he is unclean. But if he sees that the itch is unchanged and black hair has begun to grow in it, the itch is healed. The person is clean and the priest will pronounce him clean.

13.38-39   "When a man or woman gets shiny or white shiny spots on the skin, the priest is to make an examination; if the shiny spots are dull white, it is only a rash that has broken out: The person is clean.

13.40-44   "When a man loses his hair and goes bald, he is clean. If he loses his hair from his forehead, he is bald and he is clean. But if he has a reddish-white sore on scalp or forehead, it means a serious skin disease is breaking out. The priest is to examine it; if the swollen sore on his scalp or forehead is reddish-white like the appearance of the sore of a serious skin disease, he has a serious skin disease and is unclean. The priest has to pronounce him unclean because of the sore on his head.

13.45-46   "Any person with a serious skin disease must wear torn clothes, leave his hair loose and unbrushed, cover his upper lip, and cry out,

NEW INTERNATIONAL VERSION

out, 'Unclean! Unclean!' ⁴⁶As long as he has the infection he remains unclean. He must live alone; he must live outside the camp.

REGULATIONS ABOUT MILDEW

⁴⁷"If any clothing is contaminated with mildew—any woolen or linen clothing, ⁴⁸any woven or knitted material of linen or wool, any leather or anything made of leather— ⁴⁹and if the contamination in the clothing, or leather, or woven or knitted material, or any leather article, is greenish or reddish, it is a spreading mildew and must be shown to the priest. ⁵⁰The priest is to examine the mildew and isolate the affected article for seven days. ⁵¹On the seventh day he is to examine it, and if the mildew has spread in the clothing, or the woven or knitted material, or the leather, whatever its use, it is a destructive mildew; the article is unclean. ⁵²He must burn up the clothing, or the woven or knitted material of wool or linen, or any leather article that has the contamination in it, because the mildew is destructive; the article must be burned up.

⁵³"But if, when the priest examines it, the mildew has not spread in the clothing, or the woven or knitted material, or the leather article, ⁵⁴he shall order that the contaminated article be washed. Then he is to isolate it for another seven days. ⁵⁵After the affected article has been washed, the priest is to examine it, and if the mildew has not changed its appearance, even though it has not spread, it is unclean. Burn it with fire, whether the mildew has affected one side or the other. ⁵⁶If, when the priest examines it, the mildew has faded after the article has been washed, he is to tear the contaminated part out of the clothing, or the leather, or the woven or knitted material. ⁵⁷But if it reappears in the clothing, or in the woven or knitted material, or in the leather article, it is spreading, and whatever has the mildew must be burned with fire. ⁵⁸The clothing, or the woven or knitted material, or any leather article that has been washed and is rid of the mildew, must be washed again, and it will be clean."

⁵⁹These are the regulations concerning contamination by mildew in woolen or linen clothing, woven or knitted material, or any leather article, for pronouncing them clean or unclean.

CLEANSING FROM INFECTIOUS SKIN DISEASES

14 The LORD said to Moses, ²"These are the regulations for the diseased person at the time of his ceremonial cleansing, when he is brought to the priest: ³The priest is to go outside the camp and examine him. If the person has

THE MESSAGE

'Unclean! Unclean!' As long as anyone has the sores, that one continues to be ritually unclean. That person must live alone; he or she must live outside the camp.

13.47-58 "If clothing—woolen or linen clothing, woven or knitted cloth of linen or wool, leather or leatherwork—is infected with a patch of serious fungus and if the spot in the clothing or the leather or the woven or the knitted material or anything made of leather is greenish or rusty, that is a sign of serious fungus. Show it to the priest. The priest will examine the spot and then confiscate the material for seven days. On the seventh day he will reexamine the spot. If it has spread in the garment—the woven or knitted or leather material—it is the spot of a persistent serious fungus and the material is unclean. He must burn the garment. Because of the persistent and contaminating fungus, the material must be burned. But if when the priest examines it the spot has not spread in the garment, the priest will command the owner to wash the material that has the spot, and he will confiscate it for another seven days. He'll then make another examination after it has been washed; if the spot hasn't changed in appearance, even though it hasn't spread, it is still unclean. Burn it up, whether the fungus has affected the back or the front. If, when the priest makes his examination, the spot has faded after it has been washed, he is to tear the spot from the garment. But if it reappears, it is a fresh outbreak—throw whatever has the spot in the fire. If the garment is washed and the spot has gone away, then wash it a second time; it is clean.

13.59 "These are the instructions regarding a spot of serious fungus in clothing of wool or linen, woven or knitted material, or any article of leather, for pronouncing them clean or unclean."

14.1-9 **14** GOD spoke to Moses, "These are the instructions for the infected person at the time of his cleansing. First, bring him to the priest. The priest will take him outside the camp and make an examination; if the infected

NEW INTERNATIONAL VERSION

been healed of his infectious skin disease,[a] 4the priest shall order that two live clean birds and some cedar wood, scarlet yarn and hyssop be brought for the one to be cleansed. 5Then the priest shall order that one of the birds be killed over fresh water in a clay pot. 6He is then to take the live bird and dip it, together with the cedar wood, the scarlet yarn and the hyssop, into the blood of the bird that was killed over the fresh water. 7Seven times he shall sprinkle the one to be cleansed of the infectious disease and pronounce him clean. Then he is to release the live bird in the open fields.

8"The person to be cleansed must wash his clothes, shave off all his hair and bathe with water; then he will be ceremonially clean. After this he may come into the camp, but he must stay outside his tent for seven days. 9On the seventh day he must shave off all his hair; he must shave his head, his beard, his eyebrows and the rest of his hair. He must wash his clothes and bathe himself with water, and he will be clean.

10"On the eighth day he must bring two male lambs and one ewe lamb a year old, each without defect, along with three-tenths of an ephah[b] of fine flour mixed with oil for a grain offering, and one log[c] of oil. 11The priest who pronounces him clean shall present both the one to be cleansed and his offerings before the LORD at the entrance to the Tent of Meeting.

12"Then the priest is to take one of the male lambs and offer it as a guilt offering, along with the log of oil; he shall wave them before the LORD as a wave offering. 13He is to slaughter the lamb in the holy place where the sin offering and the burnt offering are slaughtered. Like the sin offering, the guilt offering belongs to the priest; it is most holy. 14The priest is to take some of the blood of the guilt offering and put it on the lobe of the right ear of the one to be cleansed, on the thumb of his right hand and on the big toe of his right foot. 15The priest shall then take some of the log of oil, pour it in the palm of his own left hand, 16dip his right forefinger into the oil in his palm, and with his finger sprinkle some of it before the LORD seven times. 17The priest is to put some of the oil remaining in his palm on the lobe of the right ear of the one to be cleansed, on the thumb of his right hand and on the big toe of his right foot, on top of the blood of the guilt offering. 18The rest of the oil in his palm the priest shall put on the head of the one to be cleansed and make atonement for him before the LORD.

---

[a] 3 Traditionally leprosy; the Hebrew word was used for various diseases affecting the skin—not necessarily leprosy; also elsewhere in this chapter.   [b] 10 That is, probably about 6 quarts (about 6.5 liters)   [c] 10 That is, probably about 2/3 pint (about 0.3 liter); also in verses 12, 15, 21 and 24

THE MESSAGE

person has been healed of the serious skin disease, the priest will order two live, clean birds, some cedar wood, scarlet thread, and hyssop to be brought for the one to be cleansed. The priest will order him to kill one of the birds over fresh water in a clay pot. The priest will then take the live bird with the cedar wood, the scarlet thread, and the hyssop and dip them in the blood of the dead bird over fresh water and then sprinkle the person being cleansed from the serious skin disease seven times and pronounce him clean. Finally, he will release the live bird in the open field. The cleansed person, after washing his clothes, shaving off all his hair, and bathing with water, is clean. Afterwards he may again enter the camp, but he has to live outside his tent for seven days. On the seventh day, he must shave off all his hair—from his head, beard, eyebrows, all of it. He then must wash his clothes and bathe all over with water. He will be clean.

14:10-18 "The next day, the eighth day, he will bring two lambs without defect and a yearling ewe without defect, along with roughly six quarts of fine flour mixed with oil. The priest who pronounces him clean will place him and the materials for his offerings in the presence of GOD at the entrance to the Tent of Meeting. The priest will take one of the lambs and present it and the pint of oil as a Compensation-Offering and lift them up as a Wave-Offering before GOD. He will slaughter the lamb in the place where the Absolution-Offering and the Whole-Burnt-Offering are slaughtered, in the Holy Place, because like the Absolution-Offering, the Compensation-Offering belongs to the priest; it is most holy. The priest will now take some of the blood of the Compensation-Offering and put it on the right earlobe of the man being cleansed, on the thumb of his right hand, and on the big toe of his right foot. Following that he will take some oil and pour it into the palm of his left hand and then with the finger of his right hand sprinkle oil seven times before GOD. The priest will put some of the remaining oil on the right earlobe of the one being cleansed, on the thumb of his right hand, and on the big toe of his right foot, placing it on top of the blood of the Compensation-Offering. He will put the rest of the oil on the head of the man being cleansed and make atonement for him before GOD.

NEW INTERNATIONAL VERSION

¹⁹"Then the priest is to sacrifice the sin offering and make atonement for the one to be cleansed from his uncleanness. After that, the priest shall slaughter the burnt offering ²⁰and offer it on the altar, together with the grain offering, and make atonement for him, and he will be clean.

²¹"If, however, he is poor and cannot afford these, he must take one male lamb as a guilt offering to be waved to make atonement for him, together with a tenth of an ephah*a* of fine flour mixed with oil for a grain offering, a log of oil, ²²and two doves or two young pigeons, which he can afford, one for a sin offering and the other for a burnt offering.

²³"On the eighth day he must bring them for his cleansing to the priest at the entrance to the Tent of Meeting, before the LORD. ²⁴The priest is to take the lamb for the guilt offering, together with the log of oil, and wave them before the LORD as a wave offering. ²⁵He shall slaughter the lamb for the guilt offering and take some of its blood and put it on the lobe of the right ear of the one to be cleansed, on the thumb of his right hand and on the big toe of his right foot. ²⁶The priest is to pour some of the oil into the palm of his own left hand, ²⁷and with his right forefinger sprinkle some of the oil from his palm seven times before the LORD. ²⁸Some of the oil in his palm he is to put on the same places he put the blood of the guilt offering—on the lobe of the right ear of the one to be cleansed, on the thumb of his right hand and on the big toe of his right foot. ²⁹The rest of the oil in his palm the priest shall put on the head of the one to be cleansed, to make atonement for him before the LORD. ³⁰Then he shall sacrifice the doves or the young pigeons, which the person can afford, ³¹one*b* as a sin offering and the other as a burnt offering, together with the grain offering. In this way the priest will make atonement before the LORD on behalf of the one to be cleansed."

³²These are the regulations for anyone who has an infectious skin disease and who cannot afford the regular offerings for his cleansing.

CLEANSING FROM MILDEW

³³The LORD said to Moses and Aaron, ³⁴"When you enter the land of Canaan, which I am giving you as your possession, and I put a spreading mildew in a house in that land, ³⁵the owner of the house must go and tell the priest, 'I have seen something that looks like mildew in my house.' ³⁶The priest is to order the house to be emptied

a 21 That is, probably about 2 quarts (about 2 liters)
b 31 Septuagint and Syriac; Hebrew *³¹such as the person can afford, one*

THE MESSAGE

14.19-20   "Finally the priest will sacrifice the Absolution-Offering and make atonement for the one to be cleansed from his uncleanness, slaughter the Whole-Burnt-Offering and offer it with the Grain-Offering on the Altar. He has made atonement for him. He is clean.

14.21-22   "If he is poor and cannot afford these offerings, he will bring one male lamb as a Compensation-Offering to be offered as a Wave-Offering to make atonement for him, and with it a couple of quarts of fine flour mixed with oil for a Grain-Offering, a pint of oil, and two doves or pigeons which he can afford, one for an Absolution-Offering and the other for a Whole-Burnt-Offering.

14.23-29   "On the eighth day he will bring them to the priest at the entrance to the Tent of Meeting before the presence of GOD. The priest will take the lamb for the Compensation-Offering together with the pint of oil and wave them before GOD as a Wave-Offering. He will slaughter the lamb for the Compensation-Offering, take some of its blood and put it on the lobe of the right ear of the one to be cleansed, on the thumb of his right hand, and on the big toe of his right foot. The priest will pour some of the oil into the palm of his left hand, and with his right finger sprinkle some of the oil from his palm seven times before GOD. He will put some of the oil that is in his palm on the same places he put the blood of the Compensation-Offering, on the lobe of the right ear of the one to be cleansed, on the thumb of his right hand, and on the big toe of his right foot. The priest will take what is left of the oil in his palm and put it on the head of the one to be cleansed, making atonement for him before GOD.

14.30-31   "At the last, he will sacrifice the doves or pigeons which are within his means, one as an Absolution-Offering and the other as a Whole-Burnt-Offering along with the Grain-Offering. Following this procedure the priest will make atonement for the one to be cleansed before GOD."

14.32   These are the instructions to be followed for anyone who has a serious skin disease and cannot afford the regular offerings for his cleansing.

✝

14.33-42   GOD spoke to Moses and Aaron, "When you enter the land of Canaan, which I'm giving to you as a possession, and I put a serious fungus in a house in the land of your possession, the householder is to go and tell the priest, 'I have some kind of fungus in my house.' The priest is to order the house vacated until he can come to

NEW INTERNATIONAL VERSION

before he goes in to examine the mildew, so that nothing in the house will be pronounced unclean. After this the priest is to go in and inspect the house. ³⁷He is to examine the mildew on the walls, and if it has greenish or reddish depressions that appear to be deeper than the surface of the wall, ³⁸the priest shall go out the doorway of the house and close it up for seven days. ³⁹On the seventh day the priest shall return to inspect the house. If the mildew has spread on the walls, ⁴⁰he is to order that the contaminated stones be torn out and thrown into an unclean place outside the town. ⁴¹He must have all the inside walls of the house scraped and the material that is scraped off dumped into an unclean place outside the town. ⁴²Then they are to take other stones to replace these and take new clay and plaster the house.

⁴³"If the mildew reappears in the house after the stones have been torn out and the house scraped and plastered, ⁴⁴the priest is to go and examine it and, if the mildew has spread in the house, it is a destructive mildew; the house is unclean. ⁴⁵It must be torn down—its stones, timbers and all the plaster—and taken out of the town to an unclean place.

⁴⁶"Anyone who goes into the house while it is closed up will be unclean till evening. ⁴⁷Anyone who sleeps or eats in the house must wash his clothes.

⁴⁸"But if the priest comes to examine it and the mildew has not spread after the house has been plastered, he shall pronounce the house clean, because the mildew is gone. ⁴⁹To purify the house he is to take two birds and some cedar wood, scarlet yarn and hyssop. ⁵⁰He shall kill one of the birds over fresh water in a clay pot. ⁵¹Then he is to take the cedar wood, the hyssop, the scarlet yarn and the live bird, dip them into the blood of the dead bird and the fresh water, and sprinkle the house seven times. ⁵²He shall purify the house with the bird's blood, the fresh water, the live bird, the cedar wood, the hyssop and the scarlet yarn. ⁵³Then he is to release the live bird in the open fields outside the town. In this way he will make atonement for the house, and it will be clean."

⁵⁴These are the regulations for any infectious skin disease, for an itch, ⁵⁵for mildew in clothing or in a house, ⁵⁶and for a swelling, a rash or a bright spot, ⁵⁷to determine when something is clean or unclean.

These are the regulations for infectious skin diseases and mildew.

THE MESSAGE

examine the fungus, so that nothing in the house is declared unclean. When the priest comes and examines the house, if the fungus on the walls of the house has greenish or rusty swelling that appears to go deeper than the surface of the wall, the priest is to walk out the door and shut the house up for seven days. On the seventh day he is to come back and conduct another examination; if the fungus has spread in the walls of the house, he is to order that the stones affected by the fungus be torn out and thrown in a garbage dump outside the city. He is to make sure the entire inside of the house is scraped and the plaster that is removed be taken away to the garbage dump outside the city. Then he is to replace the stones and replaster the house.

14.43-47   "If the fungus breaks out again in the house after the stones have been torn out and the house has been scraped and plastered, the priest is to come and conduct an examination; if the fungus has spread, it is a malignant fungus. The house is unclean. The house has to be demolished—its stones, wood, and plaster are to be removed to the garbage dump outside the city. Anyone who enters the house while it is closed up is unclean until evening. Anyone who sleeps or eats in the house must wash his clothes.

14.48-53   "But if when the priest comes and conducts his examination, he finds that the fungus has not spread after the house has been replastered, the priest is to declare that the house is clean; the fungus is cured. He then is to purify the house by taking two birds, some cedar wood, scarlet thread, and hyssop. He will slaughter one bird over fresh water in a clay pot. Then he will take the cedar wood, the hyssop, the scarlet thread, and the living bird, dip them in the blood of the killed bird and the fresh water and sprinkle the house seven times, cleansing the house with the blood of the bird, the fresh water, the living bird, the cedar wood, the hyssop, and the scarlet thread. Last of all, he will let the living bird loose outside the city in the open field. He has made atonement for the house; the house is clean.

14.54-57   "These are the procedures to be followed for every kind of serious skin disease or itch, for mildew or fungus on clothing or in a house, and for a swelling or blister or shiny spot in order to determine when it is unclean and when it is clean. These are the procedures regarding infectious skin diseases and mildew and fungus."

NEW INTERNATIONAL VERSION

DISCHARGES CAUSING UNCLEANNESS

15 The LORD said to Moses and Aaron, ²"Speak to the Israelites and say to them: 'When any man has a bodily discharge, the discharge is unclean. ³Whether it continues flowing from his body or is blocked, it will make him unclean. This is how his discharge will bring about uncleanness:

⁴"'Any bed the man with a discharge lies on will be unclean, and anything he sits on will be unclean. ⁵Anyone who touches his bed must wash his clothes and bathe with water, and he will be unclean till evening. ⁶Whoever sits on anything that the man with a discharge sat on must wash his clothes and bathe with water, and he will be unclean till evening.

⁷"'Whoever touches the man who has a discharge must wash his clothes and bathe with water, and he will be unclean till evening.

⁸"'If the man with the discharge spits on someone who is clean, that person must wash his clothes and bathe with water, and he will be unclean till evening.

⁹"'Everything the man sits on when riding will be unclean, ¹⁰and whoever touches any of the things that were under him will be unclean till evening; whoever picks up those things must wash his clothes and bathe with water, and he will be unclean till evening.

¹¹"'Anyone the man with a discharge touches without rinsing his hands with water must wash his clothes and bathe with water, and he will be unclean till evening.

¹²"'A clay pot that the man touches must be broken, and any wooden article is to be rinsed with water.

¹³"'When a man is cleansed from his discharge, he is to count off seven days for his ceremonial cleansing; he must wash his clothes and bathe himself with fresh water, and he will be clean. ¹⁴On the eighth day he must take two doves or two young pigeons and come before the LORD to the entrance to the Tent of Meeting and give them to the priest. ¹⁵The priest is to sacrifice them, the one for a sin offering and the other for a burnt offering. In this way he will make atonement before the LORD for the man because of his discharge.

¹⁶"'When a man has an emission of semen, he must bathe his whole body with water, and he will be unclean till evening. ¹⁷Any clothing or leather that has semen on it must be washed with water, and it will be unclean till evening. ¹⁸When a man lies with a woman and there is an emission of semen, both must bathe with water, and they will be unclean till evening.

¹⁹"'When a woman has her regular flow of

THE MESSAGE

BODILY DISCHARGES

15.1-3 **15** GOD spoke to Moses and Aaron, "Speak to the People of Israel. Tell them: When a man has a discharge from his genitals, the discharge is unclean. Whether it comes from a seepage or an obstruction he is unclean. He is unclean all the days his body has a seepage or an obstruction.

15.4-7 "Every bed on which he lies is ritually unclean, everything on which he sits is unclean. If someone touches his bed or sits on anything he's sat on, or touches the man with the discharge, he has to wash his clothes and bathe in water; he remains unclean until evening.

15.8-11 "If the man with the discharge spits on someone who is clean, that person has to wash his clothes and bathe in water; he remains unclean until evening. Every saddle on which the man with the discharge rides is unclean. Whoever touches anything that has been under him becomes unclean until evening. Anyone who carries such an object must wash his clothes and bathe with water; he remains unclean until evening. If the one with the discharge touches someone without first rinsing his hands with water, the one touched must wash his clothes and bathe with water; he remains unclean until evening.

15.12 "If a pottery container is touched by someone with a discharge, you must break it; a wooden article is to be rinsed in water.

15.13-15 "When a person with a discharge is cleansed from it, he is to count off seven days for his cleansing, wash his clothes, and bathe in running water. Then he is clean. On the eighth day he is to take two doves or two pigeons and come before GOD at the entrance of the Tent of Meeting and give them to the priest. The priest then offers one as an Absolution-Offering and one as a Whole-Burnt-Offering and makes atonement for him in the presence of GOD because of his discharge.

15.16-18 "When a man has an emission of semen, he must bathe his entire body in water; he remains unclean until evening. Every piece of clothing and everything made of leather which gets semen on it must be washed with water; it remains unclean until evening. When a man sleeps with a woman and has an emission of semen, both are to wash in water; they remain unclean until evening.

15.19-23 "When a woman has a discharge of blood,

NEW INTERNATIONAL VERSION

blood, the impurity of her monthly period will last seven days, and anyone who touches her will be unclean till evening.

20 " 'Anything she lies on during her period will be unclean, and anything she sits on will be unclean. 21Whoever touches her bed must wash his clothes and bathe with water, and he will be unclean till evening. 22Whoever touches anything she sits on must wash his clothes and bathe with water, and he will be unclean till evening. 23Whether it is the bed or anything she was sitting on, when anyone touches it, he will be unclean till evening.

24 " 'If a man lies with her and her monthly flow touches him, he will be unclean for seven days; any bed he lies on will be unclean.

25 " 'When a woman has a discharge of blood for many days at a time other than her monthly period or has a discharge that continues beyond her period, she will be unclean as long as she has the discharge, just as in the days of her period. 26Any bed she lies on while her discharge continues will be unclean, as is her bed during her monthly period, and anything she sits on will be unclean, as during her period. 27Whoever touches them will be unclean; he must wash his clothes and bathe with water, and he will be unclean till evening.

28 " 'When she is cleansed from her discharge, she must count off seven days, and after that she will be ceremonially clean. 29On the eighth day she must take two doves or two young pigeons and bring them to the priest at the entrance to the Tent of Meeting. 30The priest is to sacrifice one for a sin offering and the other for a burnt offering. In this way he will make atonement for her before the LORD for the uncleanness of her discharge.

31 " 'You must keep the Israelites separate from things that make them unclean, so they will not die in their uncleanness for defiling my dwelling place,*a* which is among them.' "

32These are the regulations for a man with a discharge, for anyone made unclean by an emission of semen, 33for a woman in her monthly period, for a man or a woman with a discharge, and for a man who lies with a woman who is ceremonially unclean.

THE DAY OF ATONEMENT

16 The LORD spoke to Moses after the death of the two sons of Aaron who died when they approached the LORD. 2The LORD said to Moses: "Tell your brother Aaron not to come whenever he chooses into the Most Holy Place behind the curtain in front of the atonement

a 31 Or my tabernacle

THE MESSAGE

the impurity of her menstrual period lasts seven days. Anyone who touches her is unclean until evening. Everything on which she lies or sits during her period is unclean. Anyone who touches her bed or anything on which she sits must wash his clothes and bathe in water; he remains unclean until evening.

15.24 "If a man sleeps with her and her menstrual blood gets on him, he is unclean for seven days and every bed on which he lies becomes unclean.

15.25-27 "If a woman has a discharge of blood for many days, but not at the time of her monthly period, or has a discharge that continues beyond the time of her period, she is unclean the same as during the time of her period. Every bed on which she lies during the time of the discharge and everything on which she sits becomes unclean the same as in her monthly period. Anyone who touches these things becomes unclean and must wash his clothes and bathe in water; he remains unclean until evening.

15.28-30 "When she is cleansed from her discharge, she is to count off seven days; then she is clean. On the eighth day she is to take two doves or two pigeons and bring them to the priest at the entrance to the Tent of Meeting. The priest will offer one for an Absolution-Offering and the other for a Whole-Burnt-Offering. The priest will make atonement for her in the presence of GOD because of the discharge that made her unclean.

15.31 "You are responsible for keeping the People of Israel separate from that which makes them ritually unclean, lest they die in their unclean condition by defiling my Dwelling which is among them.

15.32-33 "These are the procedures to follow for a man with a discharge or an emission of semen that makes him unclean, and for a woman in her menstrual period—any man or woman with a discharge and also for a man who sleeps with a woman who is unclean."

THE DAY OF ATONEMENT

16.1-2 **16** After the death of Aaron's two sons— they died when they came before GOD with strange fire—GOD spoke to Moses: "Tell your brother Aaron not to enter into the Holy of Holies, barging inside the curtain that's before

NEW INTERNATIONAL VERSION

cover on the ark, or else he will die, because I appear in the cloud over the atonement cover.

³"This is how Aaron is to enter the sanctuary area: with a young bull for a sin offering and a ram for a burnt offering. ⁴He is to put on the sacred linen tunic, with linen undergarments next to his body; he is to tie the linen sash around him and put on the linen turban. These are sacred garments; so he must bathe himself with water before he puts them on. ⁵From the Israelite community he is to take two male goats for a sin offering and a ram for a burnt offering.

⁶"Aaron is to offer the bull for his own sin offering to make atonement for himself and his household. ⁷Then he is to take the two goats and present them before the LORD at the entrance to the Tent of Meeting. ⁸He is to cast lots for the two goats—one lot for the LORD and the other for the scapegoat.ᵃ ⁹Aaron shall bring the goat whose lot falls to the LORD and sacrifice it for a sin offering. ¹⁰But the goat chosen by lot as the scapegoat shall be presented alive before the LORD to be used for making atonement by sending it into the desert as a scapegoat.

¹¹"Aaron shall bring the bull for his own sin offering to make atonement for himself and his household, and he is to slaughter the bull for his own sin offering. ¹²He is to take a censer full of burning coals from the altar before the LORD and two handfuls of finely ground fragrant incense and take them behind the curtain. ¹³He is to put the incense on the fire before the LORD, and the smoke of the incense will conceal the atonement cover above the Testimony, so that he will not die. ¹⁴He is to take some of the bull's blood and with his finger sprinkle it on the front of the atonement cover; then he shall sprinkle some of it with his finger seven times before the atonement cover.

¹⁵"He shall then slaughter the goat for the sin offering for the people and take its blood behind the curtain and do with it as he did with the bull's blood: He shall sprinkle it on the atonement cover and in front of it. ¹⁶In this way he will make atonement for the Most Holy Place because of the uncleanness and rebellion of the Israelites, whatever their sins have been. He is to do the same for the Tent of Meeting, which is among them in the midst of their uncleanness. ¹⁷No one is to be in the Tent of Meeting from the time Aaron goes in to make atonement in the Most Holy Place until he comes out, having made atonement for himself, his household and the whole community of Israel.

¹⁸"Then he shall come out to the altar that is

ᵃ 8 That is, the goat of removal; Hebrew *azazel*; also in verses 10 and 26

THE MESSAGE

the Atonement-Cover on the Chest whenever he feels like it, lest he die, because I am present in the Cloud over the Atonement-Cover.

16.3-5 "This is the procedure for Aaron when he enters the Holy Place: He will bring a young bull for an Absolution-Offering and a ram for a Whole-Burnt-Offering; he will put on the holy linen tunic and the linen underwear, tie the linen sash around him, and put on the linen turban. These are the sacred vestments so he must bathe himself with water before he puts them on. Then from the Israelite community he will bring two male goats for an Absolution-Offering and a Whole-Burnt-Offering.

16.6-10 "Aaron will offer the bull for his own Absolution-Offering in order to make atonement for himself and his household. Then he will set the two goats before GOD at the entrance to the Tent of Meeting and cast lots over the two goats, one lot for GOD and the other lot for Azazel. He will offer the goat on which the lot to GOD falls as an Absolution-Offering. The goat on which the lot for Azazel falls will be sent out into the wilderness to Azazel to make atonement.

16.11-14 "Aaron will present his bull for an Absolution-Offering to make atonement for himself and his household. He will slaughter his bull for the Absolution-Offering. He will take a censer full of burning coals from the Altar before GOD and two handfuls of finely ground aromatic incense and bring them inside the curtain and put the incense on the fire before GOD; the smoke of the incense will cover the Atonement-Cover which is over The Testimony so that he doesn't die. He will take some of the bull's blood and sprinkle it with his finger on the front of the Atonement-Cover, then sprinkle the blood before the Atonement-Cover seven times.

16.15-17 "Next he will slaughter the goat designated as the Absolution-Offering for the people and bring the blood inside the curtain. He will repeat what he does with the bull's blood, sprinkling it on and before the Atonement-Cover. In this way he will make atonement for the Holy of Holies because of the uncleannesses of the Israelites, their acts of rebellion, and all their other sins. He will do the same thing for the Tent of Meeting which dwells among the people in the midst of their uncleanness. There is to be no one in the Tent of Meeting from the time Aaron goes in to make atonement in the Holy of Holies until he comes out, having made atonement for himself, his household, and the whole community of Israel.

16.18-19 "Then he will come out to the Altar that is

NEW INTERNATIONAL VERSION

before the LORD and make atonement for it. He shall take some of the bull's blood and some of the goat's blood and put it on all the horns of the altar. ¹⁹He shall sprinkle some of the blood on it with his finger seven times to cleanse it and to consecrate it from the uncleanness of the Israelites.

²⁰"When Aaron has finished making atonement for the Most Holy Place, the Tent of Meeting and the altar, he shall bring forward the live goat. ²¹He is to lay both hands on the head of the live goat and confess over it all the wickedness and rebellion of the Israelites—all their sins— and put them on the goat's head. He shall send the goat away into the desert in the care of a man appointed for the task. ²²The goat will carry on itself all their sins to a solitary place; and the man shall release it in the desert.

²³"Then Aaron is to go into the Tent of Meeting and take off the linen garments he put on before he entered the Most Holy Place, and he is to leave them there. ²⁴He shall bathe himself with water in a holy place and put on his regular garments. Then he shall come out and sacrifice the burnt offering for himself and the burnt offering for the people, to make atonement for himself and for the people. ²⁵He shall also burn the fat of the sin offering on the altar.

²⁶"The man who releases the goat as a scapegoat must wash his clothes and bathe himself with water; afterward he may come into the camp. ²⁷The bull and the goat for the sin offerings, whose blood was brought into the Most Holy Place to make atonement, must be taken outside the camp; their hides, flesh and offal are to be burned up. ²⁸The man who burns them must wash his clothes and bathe himself with water; afterward he may come into the camp.

²⁹"This is to be a lasting ordinance for you: On the tenth day of the seventh month you must deny yourselves ᵃ and not do any work—whether native-born or an alien living among you— ³⁰because on this day atonement will be made for you, to cleanse you. Then, before the LORD, you will be clean from all your sins. ³¹It is a sabbath of rest, and you must deny yourselves; it is a lasting ordinance. ³²The priest who is anointed and ordained to succeed his father as high priest is to make atonement. He is to put on the sacred linen garments ³³and make atonement for the Most Holy Place, for the Tent of Meeting and the

ᵃ 29 Or must fast; also in verse 31

THE MESSAGE

before GOD and make atonement for it. He will take some of the bull's blood and some of the goat's blood and smear it all around the four horns of the Altar. With his finger he will sprinkle some of the blood on it seven times to purify and consecrate it from the uncleannesses of the Israelites.

16.20-22 "When Aaron finishes making atonement for the Holy of Holies, the Tent of Meeting, and the Altar, he will bring up the live goat, lay both hands on the live goat's head, and confess all the iniquities of the People of Israel, all their acts of rebellion, all their sins. He will put all the sins on the goat's head and send it off into the wilderness, led out by a man standing by and ready. The goat will carry all their iniquities to an empty wasteland; the man will let him loose out there in the wilderness.

16.23-25 "Finally, Aaron will come into the Tent of Meeting and take off the linen clothes in which he dressed to enter the Holy of Holies and leave them there. He will bathe in water in a Holy Place, put on his priestly vestments, offer the Whole-Burnt-Offering for himself and the Whole-Burnt-Offering for the people, making atonement for himself and the people, and burn the fat of the Absolution-Offering on the Altar.

16.26-28 "The man who takes the goat out to Azazel in the wilderness then will wash his clothes and bathe himself with water. After that he will be permitted to come back into the camp. The bull for the Absolution-Offering and the goat for the Absolution-Offering, whose blood has been taken into the Holy of Holies to make atonement, are to be taken outside the camp and burned—their hides, their meat, and their entrails. The man assigned to burn them up will then wash his clothes and bathe himself in water. Then he is free to come back into the camp.

16.29-31 "This is standard practice for you, a perpetual ordinance. On the tenth day of the seventh month, both the citizen and the foreigner living with you are to enter into a solemn fast and refrain from all work, because on this day atonement will be made for you, to cleanse you. In the presence of GOD you will be made clean of all your sins. It is a Sabbath of all Sabbaths. You must fast. It is a perpetual ordinance.

16.32 "The priest who is anointed and ordained to succeed his father is to make the atonement:

He puts on the sacred linen garments;

16.33 He purges the Holy of Holies by making atonement;

He purges the Tent of Meeting and the Altar by making atonement;

NEW INTERNATIONAL VERSION

altar, and for the priests and all the people of the community. ³⁴"This is to be a lasting ordinance for you: Atonement is to be made once a year for all the sins of the Israelites."

And it was done, as the LORD commanded Moses.

EATING BLOOD FORBIDDEN

17 The LORD said to Moses, ²"Speak to Aaron and his sons and to all the Israelites and say to them: 'This is what the LORD has commanded: ³Any Israelite who sacrifices an ox,*ᵃ* a lamb or a goat in the camp or outside of it ⁴instead of bringing it to the entrance to the Tent of Meeting to present it as an offering to the LORD in front of the tabernacle of the LORD—that man shall be considered guilty of bloodshed; he has shed blood and must be cut off from his people. ⁵This is so the Israelites will bring to the LORD the sacrifices they are now making in the open fields. They must bring them to the priest, that is, to the LORD, at the entrance to the Tent of Meeting and sacrifice them as fellowship offerings.*ᵇ* ⁶The priest is to sprinkle the blood against the altar of the LORD at the entrance to the Tent of Meeting and burn the fat as an aroma pleasing to the LORD. ⁷They must no longer offer any of their sacrifices to the goat idols*ᶜ* to whom they prostitute themselves. This is to be a lasting ordinance for them and for the generations to come.'

⁸"Say to them: 'Any Israelite or any alien living among them who offers a burnt offering or sacrifice ⁹and does not bring it to the entrance to the Tent of Meeting to sacrifice it to the LORD—that man must be cut off from his people.

¹⁰" 'Any Israelite or any alien living among them who eats any blood—I will set my face against that person who eats blood and will cut him off from his people. ¹¹For the life of a creature is in the blood, and I have given it to you to make atonement for yourselves on the altar; it is the blood that makes atonement for one's life. ¹²Therefore I say to the Israelites, "None of you may eat blood, nor may an alien living among you eat blood."

¹³" 'Any Israelite or any alien living among you who hunts any animal or bird that may be eaten must drain out the blood and cover it with earth, ¹⁴because the life of every creature is its blood. That is why I have said to the Israelites, "You must not eat the blood of any creature, because the life of every creature is its blood; anyone who eats it must be cut off."

¹⁵" 'Anyone, whether native-born or alien,

THE MESSAGE

He makes atonement for the priests and all the congregation.

16.34 "This is a perpetual ordinance for you: Once a year atonement is to be made for all the sins of the People of Israel."

And Aaron did it, just as GOD commanded Moses.

HOLY LIVING: SACRIFICES AND BLOOD

17.1-7 **17** GOD spoke to Moses, "Speak to Aaron and his sons and all the Israelites. Tell them, This is what GOD commands: Any and every man who slaughters an ox or lamb or goat inside or outside the camp instead of bringing it to the entrance of the Tent of Meeting to offer it to GOD in front of The Dwelling of GOD—that man is considered guilty of bloodshed; he has shed blood and must be cut off from his people. This is so the Israelites will bring to GOD the sacrifices that they're in the habit of sacrificing out in the open fields. They must bring them to GOD and the priest at the entrance to the Tent of Meeting and sacrifice them as Peace-Offerings to GOD. The priest will splash the blood on the Altar of GOD at the entrance to the Tent of Meeting and burn the fat as a pleasing fragrance to GOD. They must no longer offer their sacrifices to goat-demons—a kind of religious orgy. This is a perpetual decree down through the generations.

17.8-9 "Tell them: Any Israelite or foreigner living among them who offers a Whole-Burnt-Offering or Peace-Offering but doesn't bring it to the entrance of the Tent of Meeting to sacrifice it to GOD, that person must be cut off from his people.

17.10-12 "If any Israelite or foreigner living among them eats blood, I will disown that person and cut him off from his people, for the life of an animal is in the blood. I have provided the blood for you to make atonement for your lives on the Altar; it is the blood, the life, that makes atonement. That's why I tell the People of Israel, 'Don't eat blood.' The same goes for the foreigner who lives among you, 'Don't eat blood.'

17.13-14 "Any and every Israelite—this also goes for the foreigners—who hunts down an animal or bird that is edible, must bleed it and cover the blood with dirt, because the life of every animal is its blood—the blood is its life. That's why I tell the Israelites, 'Don't eat the blood of any animal because the life of every animal is its blood. Anyone who eats the blood must be cut off.'

17.15-16 "Anyone, whether native or foreigner, who

ᵃ 3 The Hebrew word can include both male and female.
ᵇ 5 Traditionally *peace offerings*   *ᶜ 7* Or *demons*

NEW INTERNATIONAL VERSION

who eats anything found dead or torn by wild animals must wash his clothes and bathe with water, and he will be ceremonially unclean till evening; then he will be clean. ¹⁶But if he does not wash his clothes and bathe himself, he will be held responsible.' "

UNLAWFUL SEXUAL RELATIONS

18 The LORD said to Moses, ²"Speak to the Israelites and say to them: 'I am the LORD your God. ³You must not do as they do in Egypt, where you used to live, and you must not do as they do in the land of Canaan, where I am bringing you. Do not follow their practices. ⁴You must obey my laws and be careful to follow my decrees. I am the LORD your God. ⁵Keep my decrees and laws, for the man who obeys them will live by them. I am the LORD.

⁶" 'No one is to approach any close relative to have sexual relations. I am the LORD.

⁷" 'Do not dishonor your father by having sexual relations with your mother. She is your mother; do not have relations with her.

⁸" 'Do not have sexual relations with your father's wife; that would dishonor your father.

⁹" 'Do not have sexual relations with your sister, either your father's daughter or your mother's daughter, whether she was born in the same home or elsewhere.

¹⁰" 'Do not have sexual relations with your son's daughter or your daughter's daughter; that would dishonor you.

¹¹" 'Do not have sexual relations with the daughter of your father's wife, born to your father; she is your sister.

¹²" 'Do not have sexual relations with your father's sister; she is your father's close relative.

¹³" 'Do not have sexual relations with your mother's sister, because she is your mother's close relative.

¹⁴" 'Do not dishonor your father's brother by approaching his wife to have sexual relations; she is your aunt.

¹⁵" 'Do not have sexual relations with your daughter-in-law. She is your son's wife; do not have relations with her.

¹⁶" 'Do not have sexual relations with your brother's wife; that would dishonor your brother.

¹⁷" 'Do not have sexual relations with both a woman and her daughter. Do not have sexual relations with either her son's daughter or her daughter's daughter; they are her close relatives. That is wickedness.

¹⁸" 'Do not take your wife's sister as a rival wife and have sexual relations with her while your wife is living.

¹⁹" 'Do not approach a woman to have sexual

THE MESSAGE

eats from an animal that is found dead or mauled must wash his clothes and bathe in water; he remains unclean until evening and is then clean. If he doesn't wash or bathe his body, he'll be held responsible for his actions."

SEX

18 18.1-5 GOD spoke to Moses, "Speak to the People of Israel. Tell them: I am GOD, your God. Don't live like the people of Egypt where you used to live, and don't live like the people of Canaan where I'm bringing you. Don't do what they do. Obey my laws and live by my decrees. I am your GOD. Keep my decrees and laws: The person who obeys them lives by them. I am GOD.

18.6 "Don't have sex with a close relative. I am GOD.

18.7 "Don't violate your father by having sex with your mother. She is your mother. Don't have sex with her.

18.8 "Don't have sex with your father's wife. That violates your father.

18.9 "Don't have sex with your sister, whether she's your father's daughter or your mother's, whether she was born in the same house or elsewhere.

18.10 "Don't have sex with your son's daughter or your daughter's daughter. That would violate your own body.

18.11 "Don't have sex with the daughter of your father's wife born to your father. She is your sister.

18.12 "Don't have sex with your father's sister; she is your aunt, closely related to your father.

18.13 "Don't have sex with your mother's sister; she is your aunt, closely related to your mother.

18.14 "Don't violate your father's brother, your uncle, by having sex with his wife. She is your aunt.

18.15 "Don't have sex with your daughter-in-law. She is your son's wife; don't have sex with her.

18.16 "Don't have sex with your brother's wife; that would violate your brother.

18.17 "Don't have sex with both a woman and her daughter. And don't have sex with her granddaughters either. They are her close relatives. That is wicked.

18.18 "Don't marry your wife's sister as a rival wife and have sex with her while your wife is living.

18.19 "Don't have sex with a woman during the

NEW INTERNATIONAL VERSION

relations during the uncleanness of her monthly period.

20 " 'Do not have sexual relations with your neighbor's wife and defile yourself with her.

21 " 'Do not give any of your children to be sacrificed*a* to Molech, for you must not profane the name of your God. I am the LORD.

22 " 'Do not lie with a man as one lies with a woman; that is detestable.

23 " 'Do not have sexual relations with an animal and defile yourself with it. A woman must not present herself to an animal to have sexual relations with it; that is a perversion.

24 " 'Do not defile yourselves in any of these ways, because this is how the nations that I am going to drive out before you became defiled. 25Even the land was defiled; so I punished it for its sin, and the land vomited out its inhabitants. 26But you must keep my decrees and my laws. The native-born and the aliens living among you must not do any of these detestable things, 27for all these things were done by the people who lived in the land before you, and the land became defiled. 28And if you defile the land, it will vomit you out as it vomited out the nations that were before you.

29 " 'Everyone who does any of these detestable things—such persons must be cut off from their people. 30Keep my requirements and do not follow any of the detestable customs that were practiced before you came and do not defile yourselves with them. I am the LORD your God.' "

VARIOUS LAWS

19 The LORD said to Moses, 2"Speak to the entire assembly of Israel and say to them: 'Be holy because I, the LORD your God, am holy.

3 " 'Each of you must respect his mother and father, and you must observe my Sabbaths. I am the LORD your God.

4 " 'Do not turn to idols or make gods of cast metal for yourselves. I am the LORD your God.

5 " 'When you sacrifice a fellowship offering*b* to the LORD, sacrifice it in such a way that it will be accepted on your behalf. 6It shall be eaten on the day you sacrifice it or on the next day; anything left over until the third day must be burned up. 7If any of it is eaten on the third day, it is impure and will not be accepted. 8Whoever eats it will be held responsible because he has desecrated what is holy to the LORD; that person must be cut off from his people.

9 " 'When you reap the harvest of your land, do not reap to the very edges of your field or

THE MESSAGE

time of her menstrual period when she is unclean.

18.20   "Don't have sex with your neighbor's wife and violate yourself by her.

18.21   "Don't give any of your children to be burned in sacrifice to the god Molech—an act of sheer blasphemy of your God. I am GOD.

18.22   "Don't have sex with a man as one does with a woman. That is abhorrent.

18.23   "Don't have sex with an animal and violate yourself by it.

"A woman must not have sex with an animal. That is perverse.

18.24-28   "Don't pollute yourself in any of these ways. This is how the nations became polluted, the ones that I am going to drive out of the land before you. Even the land itself became polluted and I punished it for its iniquities—the land vomited up its inhabitants. You must keep my decrees and laws—natives and foreigners both. You must not do any of these abhorrent things. The people who lived in this land before you arrived did all these things and polluted the land. And if you pollute it, the land will vomit you up just as it vomited up the nations that preceded you.

18.29-30   "Those who do any of these abhorrent things will be cut off from their people. Keep to what I tell you; don't engage in any of the abhorrent acts that were practiced before you came. Don't pollute yourselves with them. I am GOD, *your* God."

"I AM GOD, YOUR GOD"

19.1-2   **19** GOD spoke to Moses: "Speak to the congregation of Israel. Tell them: Be holy because I, GOD, your God, am holy.

19.3   "Every one of you must respect his mother and father.

"Keep my Sabbaths. I am GOD, your God.

19.4   "Don't take up with no-god idols. Don't make gods of cast metal. I am GOD, your God.

19.5-8   "When you sacrifice a Peace-Offering to GOD, do it as you've been taught so it is acceptable. Eat it on the day you sacrifice it and the day following. Whatever is left until the third day is to be burned up. If it is eaten on the third day it is polluted meat and not acceptable. Whoever eats it will be held responsible because he has violated what is holy to GOD. That person will be cut off from his people.

19.9-10   "When you harvest your land, don't harvest right up to the edges of your field or gather the

---

a 21 Or *to be passed through ⌊the fire⌋*   *b* 5 Traditionally *peace offering*

NEW INTERNATIONAL VERSION

gather the gleanings of your harvest. ¹⁰Do not go over your vineyard a second time or pick up the grapes that have fallen. Leave them for the poor and the alien. I am the LORD your God.

¹¹" 'Do not steal.

" 'Do not lie.

" 'Do not deceive one another.

¹²" 'Do not swear falsely by my name and so profane the name of your God. I am the LORD.

¹³" 'Do not defraud your neighbor or rob him.

" 'Do not hold back the wages of a hired man overnight.

¹⁴" 'Do not curse the deaf or put a stumbling block in front of the blind, but fear your God. I am the LORD.

¹⁵" 'Do not pervert justice; do not show partiality to the poor or favoritism to the great, but judge your neighbor fairly.

¹⁶" 'Do not go about spreading slander among your people.

" 'Do not do anything that endangers your neighbor's life. I am the LORD.

¹⁷" 'Do not hate your brother in your heart. Rebuke your neighbor frankly so you will not share in his guilt.

¹⁸" 'Do not seek revenge or bear a grudge against one of your people, but love your neighbor as yourself. I am the LORD.

¹⁹" 'Keep my decrees.

" 'Do not mate different kinds of animals.

" 'Do not plant your field with two kinds of seed.

" 'Do not wear clothing woven of two kinds of material.

²⁰" 'If a man sleeps with a woman who is a slave girl promised to another man but who has not been ransomed or given her freedom, there must be due punishment. Yet they are not to be put to death, because she had not been freed. ²¹The man, however, must bring a ram to the entrance to the Tent of Meeting for a guilt offering to the LORD. ²²With the ram of the guilt offering the priest is to make atonement for him before the LORD for the sin he has committed, and his sin will be forgiven.

²³" 'When you enter the land and plant any kind of fruit tree, regard its fruit as forbidden.ᵃ For three years you are to consider it forbiddenᵃ; it must not be eaten. ²⁴In the fourth year all its fruit will be holy, an offering of praise to the LORD. ²⁵But in the fifth year you may eat its fruit. In this way your harvest will be increased. I am the LORD your God.

²⁶" 'Do not eat any meat with the blood still in it.

" 'Do not practice divination or sorcery.

THE MESSAGE

gleanings from the harvest. Don't strip your vineyard bare or go back and pick up the fallen grapes. Leave them for the poor and the foreigner. I am GOD, your God.

19.11   "Don't steal.

"Don't lie.

"Don't deceive anyone.

19.12   "Don't swear falsely using my name, violating the name of your God. I am GOD.

19.13   "Don't exploit your friend or rob him.

"Don't hold back the wages of a hired hand overnight.

19.14   "Don't curse the deaf; don't put a stumbling block in front of the blind; fear your God. I am GOD.

19.15   "Don't pervert justice. Don't show favoritism to either the poor or the great. Judge on the basis of what is right.

19.16   "Don't spread gossip and rumors.

"Don't just stand by when your neighbor's life is in danger. I am GOD.

19.17   "Don't secretly hate your neighbor. If you have something against him, get it out into the open; otherwise you are an accomplice in his guilt.

19.18   "Don't seek revenge or carry a grudge against any of your people.

"Love your neighbor as yourself. I am GOD.

19.19   "Keep my decrees.

"Don't mate two different kinds of animals.

"Don't plant your fields with two kinds of seed.

"Don't wear clothes woven of two kinds of material.

19.20-22   "If a man has sex with a slave girl who is engaged to another man but has not yet been ransomed or given her freedom, there must be an investigation. But they aren't to be put to death because she wasn't free. The man must bring a Compensation-Offering to GOD at the entrance to the Tent of Meeting, a ram of compensation. The priest will perform the ritual of atonement for him before GOD with the ram of compensation for the sin he has committed. Then he will stand forgiven of the sin he committed.

19.23-25   "When you enter the land and plant any kind of fruit tree, don't eat the fruit for three years; consider it inedible. By the fourth year its fruit is holy, an offering of praise to GOD. Beginning in the fifth year you can eat its fruit; you'll have richer harvests this way. I am GOD, your God.

19.26   "Don't eat meat with blood in it.

"Don't practice divination or sorcery.

ᵃ 23 Hebrew *uncircumcised*

NEW INTERNATIONAL VERSION

27" 'Do not cut the hair at the sides of your head or clip off the edges of your beard.

28" 'Do not cut your bodies for the dead or put tattoo marks on yourselves. I am the LORD.

29" 'Do not degrade your daughter by making her a prostitute, or the land will turn to prostitution and be filled with wickedness.

30" 'Observe my Sabbaths and have reverence for my sanctuary. I am the LORD.

31" 'Do not turn to mediums or seek out spiritists, for you will be defiled by them. I am the LORD your God.

32" 'Rise in the presence of the aged, show respect for the elderly and revere your God. I am the LORD.

33" 'When an alien lives with you in your land, do not mistreat him. 34The alien living with you must be treated as one of your native-born. Love him as yourself, for you were aliens in Egypt. I am the LORD your God.

35" 'Do not use dishonest standards when measuring length, weight or quantity. 36Use honest scales and honest weights, an honest ephah*a* and an honest hin.*b* I am the LORD your God, who brought you out of Egypt.

37" 'Keep all my decrees and all my laws and follow them. I am the LORD.' "

PUNISHMENTS FOR SIN

20 The LORD said to Moses, 2"Say to the Israelites: 'Any Israelite or any alien living in Israel who gives*c* any of his children to Molech must be put to death. The people of the community are to stone him. 3I will set my face against that man and I will cut him off from his people; for by giving his children to Molech, he has defiled my sanctuary and profaned my holy name. 4If the people of the community close their eyes when that man gives one of his children to Molech and they fail to put him to death, 5I will set my face against that man and his family and will cut off from their people both him and all who follow him in prostituting themselves to Molech.

6" 'I will set my face against the person who turns to mediums and spiritists to prostitute himself by following them, and I will cut him off from his people.

7" 'Consecrate yourselves and be holy, because I am the LORD your God. 8Keep my decrees and follow them. I am the LORD, who makes you holy.*d*

9" 'If anyone curses his father or mother, he must be put to death. He has cursed his father or

THE MESSAGE

19.27 "Don't cut the hair on the sides of your head or trim your beard.

19.28 "Don't gash your bodies on behalf of the dead.

"Don't tattoo yourselves. I am GOD.

19.29 "Don't violate your daughter by making her a whore—the whole country would soon become a brothel, filled with sordid sex.

19.30 "Keep my Sabbaths and revere my Sanctuary: I am GOD.

19.31 "Don't dabble in the occult or traffic with mediums; you'll pollute your souls. I am GOD, your God.

19.32 "Show respect to the aged; honor the presence of an elder; fear your God. I am GOD.

19.33-34 "When a foreigner lives with you in your land, don't take advantage of him. Treat the foreigner the same as a native. Love him like one of your own. Remember that you were once foreigners in Egypt. I am GOD, your God.

19.35-36 "Don't cheat when measuring length, weight, or quantity. Use honest scales and weights and measures. I am GOD, your God. I brought you out of Egypt.

19.37 "Keep all my decrees and all my laws. Yes, *do* them. I am GOD."

✝

20.1-5 **20** GOD spoke to Moses: "Tell the Israelites, Each and every Israelite and foreigner in Israel who gives his child to the god Molech must be put to death. The community must kill him by stoning. I will resolutely reject that man and cut him off from his people. By giving his child to the god Molech he has polluted my Sanctuary and desecrated my holy name. If the people of the land look the other way as if nothing had happened when that man gives his child to the god Molech and fail to kill him, I will resolutely reject that man and his family, and him and all who join him in prostituting themselves in the rituals of the god Molech I will cut off from their people.

20.6 "I will resolutely reject persons who dabble in the occult or traffic with mediums, prostituting themselves in their practices. I will cut them off from their people.

20.7-8 "Set yourselves apart for a holy life. *Live* a holy life, because I am GOD, your God. Do what I tell you; *live* the way I tell you. I am the GOD who makes you holy.

20.9 "Any and every person who curses his father or mother must be put to death. By curs-

---

a 36 An ephah was a dry measure. *b* 36 A hin was a liquid measure. *c* 2 Or *sacrifices*; also in verses 3 and 4 *d* 8 Or *who sanctifies you*; or *who sets you apart as holy*

NEW INTERNATIONAL VERSION

his mother, and his blood will be on his own head.

10 " 'If a man commits adultery with another man's wife—with the wife of his neighbor—both the adulterer and the adulteress must be put to death.

11 " 'If a man sleeps with his father's wife, he has dishonored his father. Both the man and the woman must be put to death; their blood will be on their own heads.

12 " 'If a man sleeps with his daughter-in-law, both of them must be put to death. What they have done is a perversion; their blood will be on their own heads.

13 " 'If a man lies with a man as one lies with a woman, both of them have done what is detestable. They must be put to death; their blood will be on their own heads.

14 " 'If a man marries both a woman and her mother, it is wicked. Both he and they must be burned in the fire, so that no wickedness will be among you.

15 " 'If a man has sexual relations with an animal, he must be put to death, and you must kill the animal.

16 " 'If a woman approaches an animal to have sexual relations with it, kill both the woman and the animal. They must be put to death; their blood will be on their own heads.

17 " 'If a man marries his sister, the daughter of either his father or his mother, and they have sexual relations, it is a disgrace. They must be cut off before the eyes of their people. He has dishonored his sister and will be held responsible.

18 " 'If a man lies with a woman during her monthly period and has sexual relations with her, he has exposed the source of her flow, and she has also uncovered it. Both of them must be cut off from their people.

19 " 'Do not have sexual relations with the sister of either your mother or your father, for that would dishonor a close relative; both of you would be held responsible.

20 " 'If a man sleeps with his aunt, he has dishonored his uncle. They will be held responsible; they will die childless.

21 " 'If a man marries his brother's wife, it is an act of impurity; he has dishonored his brother. They will be childless.

22 " 'Keep all my decrees and laws and follow them, so that the land where I am bringing you to live may not vomit you out. 23You must not live according to the customs of the nations I am going to drive out before you. Because they did all these things, I abhorred them. 24But I said to you, "You will possess their land; I will give it

THE MESSAGE

ing his father or mother he is responsible for his own death.

20.10   "If a man commits adultery with another man's wife—the wife, say, of his neighbor— both the man and the woman, the adulterer and adulteress, must be put to death.

20.11   "If a man has sex with his father's wife, he has violated his father. Both the man and woman must be put to death; they are responsible for their own deaths.

20.12   "If a man has sex with his daughter-in-law, both of them must be put to death. What they have done is perverse. And they are responsible for their own deaths.

20.13   "If a man has sex with a man as one does with a woman, both of them have done what is abhorrent. They must be put to death; they are responsible for their own deaths.

20.14   "If a man marries both a woman and her mother, that's wicked. All three of them must be burned at the stake, purging the wickedness from the community.

20.15   "If a man has sex with an animal, he must be put to death and you must kill the animal.

20.16   "If a woman has sex with an animal, you must kill both the woman and the animal. They must be put to death. And they are responsible for their deaths.

20.17   "If a man marries his sister, the daughter of either his father or mother, and they have sex, that's a disgrace. They must be publicly cut off from their people. He has violated his sister and will be held responsible.

20.18   "If a man sleeps with a woman during her period and has sex with her, he has uncovered her 'fountain' and she has revealed her 'fountain'—both of them must be cut off from their people.

20.19   "Don't have sex with your aunt on either your mother's or father's side. That violates a close relative. Both of you are held responsible.

20.20   "If a man has sex with his aunt, he has dishonored his uncle. They will be held responsible and die childless.

20.21   "If a man marries his brother's wife, it's a defilement. He has shamed his brother. They will be childless.

20.22-23   "Do what I tell you, all my decrees and laws; live by them so that the land where I'm bringing you won't vomit you out. You simply must not live like the nations I'm driving out before you. They did all these things and I hated every minute of it.

20.24-26   "I've told you, remember, that you will possess their land that I'm giving to you as an in-

NEW INTERNATIONAL VERSION

to you as an inheritance, a land flowing with milk and honey." I am the LORD your God, who has set you apart from the nations.

²⁵ "'You must therefore make a distinction between clean and unclean animals and between unclean and clean birds. Do not defile yourselves by any animal or bird or anything that moves along the ground—those which I have set apart as unclean for you. ²⁶You are to be holy to me*a* because I, the LORD, am holy, and I have set you apart from the nations to be my own.

²⁷ "'A man or woman who is a medium or spiritist among you must be put to death. You are to stone them; their blood will be on their own heads.'"

RULES FOR PRIESTS

21 The LORD said to Moses, "Speak to the priests, the sons of Aaron, and say to them: 'A priest must not make himself ceremonially unclean for any of his people who die, ²except for a close relative, such as his mother or father, his son or daughter, his brother, ³or an unmarried sister who is dependent on him since she has no husband—for her he may make himself unclean. ⁴He must not make himself unclean for people related to him by marriage,*b* and so defile himself.

⁵ "'Priests must not shave their heads or shave off the edges of their beards or cut their bodies. ⁶They must be holy to their God and must not profane the name of their God. Because they present the offerings made to the LORD by fire, the food of their God, they are to be holy.

⁷ "'They must not marry women defiled by prostitution or divorced from their husbands, because priests are holy to their God. ⁸Regard them as holy, because they offer up the food of your God. Consider them holy, because I the LORD am holy—I who make you holy.*c*

⁹ "'If a priest's daughter defiles herself by becoming a prostitute, she disgraces her father; she must be burned in the fire.

¹⁰ "'The high priest, the one among his brothers who has had the anointing oil poured on his head and who has been ordained to wear the priestly garments, must not let his hair become unkempt*d* or tear his clothes. ¹¹He must not enter a place where there is a dead body. He must not make himself unclean, even for his father or mother, ¹²nor leave the sanctuary of his God or desecrate it, because he has been dedicated by the anointing oil of his God. I am the LORD.

¹³ "'The woman he marries must be a virgin.

---

a 26 Or be my holy ones   b 4 Or unclean as a leader among his people   c 8 Or who sanctify you; or who set you apart as holy   d 10 Or not uncover his head

THE MESSAGE

heritance, a land flowing with milk and honey. I am GOD, your God, who has distinguished you from the nations. So live like it: Distinguish between ritually clean and unclean animals and birds. Don't pollute yourselves with any animal or bird or crawling thing which I have marked out as unclean for you. Live holy lives before me because I, GOD, am holy. I have distinguished you from the nations to be my very own.

20.27   "A man or woman who is a medium or sorcerer among you must be put to death. You must kill them by stoning. They're responsible for their own deaths."

HOLY PRIESTS

21.1-4 **21** GOD spoke to Moses: "Speak to the priests, the sons of Aaron. Tell them, A priest must not ritually contaminate himself by touching the dead, except for close relatives: mother, father, son, daughter, brother, or an unmarried sister who is dependent on him since she has no husband; for these he may make himself ritually unclean, but he must not contaminate himself with the dead who are only related to him by marriage and thus profane himself.

21.5-6   "Priests must not shave their heads or trim their beards or gash their bodies. They must be holy to their God and must not profane the name of their God. Because their job is to present the gifts of GOD, the food of their God, they are to be holy.

21.7-8   "Because a priest is holy to his God he must not marry a woman who has been a harlot or a cult prostitute or a divorced woman. Make sure he is holy because he serves the food of your God. Treat him as holy because I, GOD, who make you holy, am holy.

21.9   "If a priest's daughter defiles herself in prostitution, she disgraces her father. She must be burned at the stake.

21.10-12 "The high priest, the one among his brothers who has received the anointing oil poured on his head and been ordained to wear the priestly vestments, must not let his hair go wild and tangled nor wear ragged and torn clothes. He must not enter a room where there is a dead body. He must not ritually contaminate himself, even for his father or mother; and he must neither abandon nor desecrate the Sanctuary of his God because of the dedication of the anointing oil which is upon him. I am GOD.

21.13-15 "He is to marry a young virgin, not a widow,

NEW INTERNATIONAL VERSION

¹⁴He must not marry a widow, a divorced woman, or a woman defiled by prostitution, but only a virgin from his own people, ¹⁵so he will not defile his offspring among his people. I am the LORD, who makes him holy.ᵃ' "

¹⁶The LORD said to Moses, ¹⁷"Say to Aaron: 'For the generations to come none of your descendants who has a defect may come near to offer the food of his God. ¹⁸No man who has any defect may come near: no man who is blind or lame, disfigured or deformed; ¹⁹no man with a crippled foot or hand, ²⁰or who is hunchbacked or dwarfed, or who has any eye defect, or who has festering or running sores or damaged testicles. ²¹No descendant of Aaron the priest who has any defect is to come near to present the offerings made to the LORD by fire. He has a defect; he must not come near to offer the food of his God. ²²He may eat the most holy food of his God, as well as the holy food; ²³yet because of his defect, he must not go near the curtain or approach the altar, and so desecrate my sanctuary. I am the LORD, who makes them holy.ᵇ' "

²⁴So Moses told this to Aaron and his sons and to all the Israelites.

22 The LORD said to Moses, ²"Tell Aaron and his sons to treat with respect the sacred offerings the Israelites consecrate to me, so they will not profane my holy name. I am the LORD.

³"Say to them: 'For the generations to come, if any of your descendants is ceremonially unclean and yet comes near the sacred offerings that the Israelites consecrate to the LORD, that person must be cut off from my presence. I am the LORD.

⁴" 'If a descendant of Aaron has an infectious skin diseaseᶜ or a bodily discharge, he may not eat the sacred offerings until he is cleansed. He will also be unclean if he touches something defiled by a corpse or by anyone who has an emission of semen, ⁵or if he touches any crawling thing that makes him unclean, or any person who makes him unclean, whatever the uncleanness may be. ⁶The one who touches any such thing will be unclean till evening. He must not eat any of the sacred offerings unless he has bathed himself with water. ⁷When the sun goes down, he will be clean, and after that he may eat the sacred offerings, for they are his food. ⁸He must not eat anything found dead or torn by wild animals, and so become unclean through it. I am the LORD.

THE MESSAGE

not a divorcee, not a cult prostitute—he is only to marry a virgin from his own people. He must not defile his descendants among his people because I am GOD who makes him holy."

21.16-23 GOD spoke to Moses: "Tell Aaron, None of your descendants, in any generation to come, who has a defect of any kind may present as an offering the food of his God. That means anyone who is blind or lame, disfigured or deformed, crippled in foot or hand, hunchbacked or dwarfed, who has anything wrong with his eyes, who has running sores or damaged testicles. No descendant of Aaron the priest who has any defect is to offer gifts to GOD; he has a defect and so must not offer the food of his God. He may eat the food of his God, both the most holy and the holy, but because of his defect he must not go near the curtain or approach the Altar. It would desecrate my Sanctuary. I am GOD who makes them holy."

21.24 Moses delivered this message to Aaron, his sons, and to all the People of Israel.

✠

22 GOD spoke to Moses, "Tell Aaron and his sons to treat the holy offerings that the Israelites consecrate to me with reverence so they won't desecrate my holy name. I am GOD.

22.3 "Tell them, From now on, if any of your descendants approaches in a state of ritual uncleanness the holy offerings that the Israelites consecrate to GOD, he will be cut off from my presence. I am GOD.

22.4-8 "Each and every one of Aaron's descendants who has an infectious skin disease or a discharge may not eat any of the holy offerings until he is clean. Also, if he touches anything defiled by a corpse, or has an emission of semen, or is contaminated by touching a crawling creature, or touches a person who is contaminated for whatever reason—a person who touches any such thing will be ritually unclean until evening and may not eat any of the holy offerings unless he has washed well with water. After the sun goes down he is clean and may go ahead and eat the holy offerings; they are his food. But he must not contaminate himself by eating anything found dead or torn by wild animals. I am GOD.

ᵃ 15 Or *who sanctifies him; or who sets him apart as holy*
ᵇ 23 Or *who sanctifies them; or who sets them apart as holy*
ᶜ 4 Traditionally *leprosy*; the Hebrew word was used for various diseases affecting the skin—not necessarily leprosy.

NEW INTERNATIONAL VERSION

9" 'The priests are to keep my requirements so that they do not become guilty and die for treating them with contempt. I am the LORD, who makes them holy.*

10" 'No one outside a priest's family may eat the sacred offering, nor may the guest of a priest or his hired worker eat it. 11But if a priest buys a slave with money, or if a slave is born in his household, that slave may eat his food. 12If a priest's daughter marries anyone other than a priest, she may not eat any of the sacred contributions. 13But if a priest's daughter becomes a widow or is divorced, yet has no children, and she returns to live in her father's house as in her youth, she may eat of her father's food. No unauthorized person, however, may eat any of it.

14" 'If anyone eats a sacred offering by mistake, he must make restitution to the priest for the offering and add a fifth of the value to it. 15The priests must not desecrate the sacred offerings the Israelites present to the LORD 16by allowing them to eat the sacred offerings and so bring upon them guilt requiring payment. I am the LORD, who makes them holy.' "

UNACCEPTABLE SACRIFICES

17The LORD said to Moses, 18"Speak to Aaron and his sons and to all the Israelites and say to them: 'If any of you—either an Israelite or an alien living in Israel—presents a gift for a burnt offering to the LORD, either to fulfill a vow or as a freewill offering, 19you must present a male without defect from the cattle, sheep or goats in order that it may be accepted on your behalf. 20Do not bring anything with a defect, because it will not be accepted on your behalf. 21When anyone brings from the herd or flock a fellowship offering*b* to the LORD to fulfill a special vow or as a freewill offering, it must be without defect or blemish to be acceptable. 22Do not offer to the LORD the blind, the injured or the maimed, or anything with warts or festering or running sores. Do not place any of these on the altar as an offering made to the LORD by fire. 23You may, however, present as a freewill offering an ox*c* or a sheep that is deformed or stunted, but it will not be accepted in fulfillment of a vow. 24You must not offer to the LORD an animal whose testicles are bruised, crushed, torn or cut. You must not do this in your own land, 25and you must not accept such animals from the hand of a foreigner and offer them as the food of your God. They will not be accepted on your behalf, because they are deformed and have defects.' "

---

a 9 Or *who sanctifies them*; or *who sets them apart as holy*; also in verse 16   *b 21* Traditionally *peace offering*
c 23 The Hebrew word can include both male and female.

THE MESSAGE

22.9   "The priests must observe my instructions lest they become guilty and die by treating the offerings with irreverence. I am GOD who makes them holy.

22.10-13   "No layperson may eat anything set apart as holy. Nor may a priest's guest or his hired hand eat anything holy. But if a priest buys a slave, the slave may eat of it; also the slaves born in his house may eat his food. If a priest's daughter marries a layperson, she may no longer eat from the holy contributions. But if the priest's daughter is widowed or divorced and without children and returns to her father's household as before, she may eat of her father's food. But no layperson may eat of it.

22.14   "If anyone eats from a holy offering accidentally, he must give back the holy offering to the priest and add twenty percent to it.

22.15-16   "The priests must not treat with irreverence the holy offerings of the Israelites that they contribute to GOD lest they desecrate themselves and make themselves guilty when they eat the holy offerings. I am GOD who makes them holy."

✝

22.17-25   GOD spoke to Moses, "Tell Aaron and his sons and all the People of Israel, Each and every one of you, whether native born or foreigner, who presents a Whole-Burnt-Offering to GOD to fulfill a vow or as a Freewill-Offering, must make sure that it is a male without defect from cattle, sheep, or goats for it to be acceptable. Don't try slipping in some creature that has a defect—it won't be accepted. Whenever anyone brings an offering from cattle or sheep as a Peace-Offering to GOD to fulfill a vow or as a Freewill-Offering, it has to be perfect, without defect, to be acceptable. Don't try giving GOD an animal that is blind, crippled, mutilated, an animal with running sores, a rash, or mange. Don't place any of these on the Altar as a gift to GOD. You may, though, offer an ox or sheep that is deformed or stunted as a Freewill-Offering, but it is not acceptable in fulfilling a vow. Don't offer to GOD an animal with bruised, crushed, torn, or cut-off testicles. Don't do this in your own land but don't accept them from foreigners and present them as food for your GOD either. Because of deformities and defects they will not be acceptable."

NEW INTERNATIONAL VERSION

²⁶The LORD said to Moses, ²⁷"When a calf, a lamb or a goat is born, it is to remain with its mother for seven days. From the eighth day on, it will be acceptable as an offering made to the LORD by fire. ²⁸Do not slaughter a cow or a sheep and its young on the same day.

²⁹"When you sacrifice a thank offering to the LORD, sacrifice it in such a way that it will be accepted on your behalf. ³⁰It must be eaten that same day; leave none of it till morning. I am the LORD.

³¹"Keep my commands and follow them. I am the LORD. ³²Do not profane my holy name. I must be acknowledged as holy by the Israelites. I am the LORD, who makes*ᵃ* you holy*ᵇ* ³³and who brought you out of Egypt to be your God. I am the LORD."

23
The LORD said to Moses, ²"Speak to the Israelites and say to them: 'These are my appointed feasts, the appointed feasts of the LORD, which you are to proclaim as sacred assemblies.

THE SABBATH

³" 'There are six days when you may work, but the seventh day is a Sabbath of rest, a day of sacred assembly. You are not to do any work; wherever you live, it is a Sabbath to the LORD.

THE PASSOVER AND UNLEAVENED BREAD

⁴" 'These are the LORD's appointed feasts, the sacred assemblies you are to proclaim at their appointed times: ⁵The LORD's Passover begins at twilight on the fourteenth day of the first month. ⁶On the fifteenth day of that month the LORD's Feast of Unleavened Bread begins; for seven days you must eat bread made without yeast. ⁷On the first day hold a sacred assembly and do no regular work. ⁸For seven days present an offering made to the LORD by fire. And on the seventh day hold a sacred assembly and do no regular work.' "

FIRSTFRUITS

⁹The LORD said to Moses, ¹⁰"Speak to the Israelites and say to them: 'When you enter the land I am going to give you and you reap its harvest, bring to the priest a sheaf of the first grain you harvest. ¹¹He is to wave the sheaf before the LORD so it will be accepted on your behalf; the priest is to wave it on the day after the Sabbath. ¹²On the day you wave the sheaf, you must sacrifice as a burnt offering to the LORD a lamb a year

THE MESSAGE

²²·²⁶⁻³⁰   GOD spoke to Moses: "When a calf or lamb or goat is born, it is to stay with its mother for seven days. After the eighth day, it is acceptable as an offering, a gift to GOD. Don't slaughter both a cow or ewe and its young on the same day. When you sacrifice a Thanksgiving-Offering to GOD, do it right so it will be acceptable. Eat it on the same day; don't leave any leftovers until morning. I am GOD.

²²·³¹   "Do what I tell you; *live* what I tell you. I am GOD.

²²·³²⁻³³   "Don't desecrate my holy name. I insist on being treated with holy reverence among the People of Israel. I am GOD who makes you holy and brought you out of Egypt to be your God. I am GOD."

THE FEASTS

²³·¹⁻²   ## 23
GOD spoke to Moses: "Tell the People of Israel, These are my appointed feasts, the appointed feasts of GOD which you are to decree as sacred assemblies.

²³·³   "Work six days. The seventh day is a Sabbath, a day of total and complete rest, a sacred assembly. Don't do any work. Wherever you live, it is a Sabbath to GOD.

²³·⁴   "These are the appointed feasts of GOD, the sacred assemblies which you are to announce at the times set for them:

²³·⁵   "GOD's Passover, beginning at sundown on the fourteenth day of the first month.

²³·⁶⁻⁸   "GOD's Feast of Unraised Bread, on the fifteenth day of this same month. You are to eat unraised bread for seven days. Hold a sacred assembly on the first day; don't do any regular work. Offer Fire-Gifts to GOD for seven days. On the seventh day hold a sacred assembly; don't do any regular work."

²³·⁹⁻¹⁴   GOD spoke to Moses: "Tell the People of Israel, When you arrive at the land that I am giving you and you reap its harvest, bring to the priest a sheaf of the first grain that you harvest. He will wave the sheaf before GOD for acceptance on your behalf; on the morning after Sabbath, the priest will wave it. On the same day that you wave the sheaf, offer a year-old male lamb without defect for a Whole-Burnt-Offering to

---

ᵃ 32 Or made   *ᵇ 32 Or who sanctifies you; or who sets you apart as holy*

NEW INTERNATIONAL VERSION

old without defect, ¹³together with its grain offering of two-tenths of an ephah*a* of fine flour mixed with oil—an offering made to the LORD by fire, a pleasing aroma—and its drink offering of a quarter of a hin*b* of wine. ¹⁴You must not eat any bread, or roasted or new grain, until the very day you bring this offering to your God. This is to be a lasting ordinance for the generations to come, wherever you live.

FEAST OF WEEKS

¹⁵" 'From the day after the Sabbath, the day you brought the sheaf of the wave offering, count off seven full weeks. ¹⁶Count off fifty days up to the day after the seventh Sabbath, and then present an offering of new grain to the LORD. ¹⁷From wherever you live, bring two loaves made of two-tenths of an ephah of fine flour, baked with yeast, as a wave offering of firstfruits to the LORD. ¹⁸Present with this bread seven male lambs, each a year old and without defect, one young bull and two rams. They will be a burnt offering to the LORD, together with their grain offerings and drink offerings—an offering made by fire, an aroma pleasing to the LORD. ¹⁹Then sacrifice one male goat for a sin offering and two lambs, each a year old, for a fellowship offering.*c* ²⁰The priest is to wave the two lambs before the LORD as a wave offering, together with the bread of the firstfruits. They are a sacred offering to the LORD for the priest. ²¹On that same day you are to proclaim a sacred assembly and do no regular work. This is to be a lasting ordinance for the generations to come, wherever you live.

²²" 'When you reap the harvest of your land, do not reap to the very edges of your field or gather the gleanings of your harvest. Leave them for the poor and the alien. I am the LORD your God.' "

FEAST OF TRUMPETS

²³The LORD said to Moses, ²⁴"Say to the Israelites: 'On the first day of the seventh month you are to have a day of rest, a sacred assembly commemorated with trumpet blasts. ²⁵Do no regular work, but present an offering made to the LORD by fire.' "

DAY OF ATONEMENT

²⁶The LORD said to Moses, ²⁷"The tenth day of this seventh month is the Day of Atonement. Hold a sacred assembly and deny yourselves,*d* and present an offering made to the LORD by fire.

---

a 13 That is, probably about 4 quarts (about 4.5 liters); also in verse 17   b 13 That is, probably about 1 quart (about 1 liter)   c 19 Traditionally peace offering   d 27 Or and fast; also in verses 29 and 32

THE MESSAGE

GOD and with it the Grain-Offering of four quarts of fine flour mixed with oil—a Fire-Gift to GOD, a pleasing fragrance—and also a Drink-Offering of a quart of wine. Don't eat any bread or roasted or fresh grain until you have presented this offering to your God. This is a perpetual decree for all your generations to come, wherever you live.

23.15-21   "Count seven full weeks from the morning after the Sabbath when you brought the sheaf as a Wave-Offering, fifty days until the morning of the seventh Sabbath. Then present a new Grain-Offering to GOD. Bring from wherever you are living two loaves of bread made from four quarts of fine flour and baked with yeast as a Wave-Offering of the first ripe grain to GOD. In addition to the bread, offer seven yearling male lambs without defect, plus one bull and two rams. They will be a Whole-Burnt-Offering to GOD together with their Grain-Offerings and Drink-Offerings—offered as Fire-Gifts, a pleasing fragrance to GOD. Offer one male goat for an Absolution-Offering and two yearling lambs for a Peace-Offering. The priest will wave the two lambs before GOD as a Wave-Offering, together with the bread of the first ripe grain. They are sacred offerings to GOD for the priest. Proclaim the day as a sacred assembly. Don't do any ordinary work. It is a perpetual decree wherever you live down through your generations.

23.22   "When you reap the harvest of your land, don't reap the corners of your field or gather the gleanings. Leave them for the poor and the foreigners. I am GOD, *your* God."

23.23-25   GOD said to Moses: "Tell the People of Israel, On the first day of the seventh month, set aside a day of rest, a sacred assembly—mark it with loud blasts on the ram's horn. Don't do any ordinary work. Offer a Fire-Gift to GOD."

23.26-32   GOD said to Moses, "The tenth day of the seventh month is the Day of Atonement. Hold a sacred assembly, fast, and offer a Fire-Gift to

NEW INTERNATIONAL VERSION

²⁸Do no work on that day, because it is the Day of Atonement, when atonement is made for you before the LORD your God. ²⁹Anyone who does not deny himself on that day must be cut off from his people. ³⁰I will destroy from among his people anyone who does any work on that day. ³¹You shall do no work at all. This is to be a lasting ordinance for the generations to come, wherever you live. ³²It is a sabbath of rest for you, and you must deny yourselves. From the evening of the ninth day of the month until the following evening you are to observe your sabbath."

FEAST OF TABERNACLES

³³The LORD said to Moses, ³⁴"Say to the Israelites: 'On the fifteenth day of the seventh month the LORD's Feast of Tabernacles begins, and it lasts for seven days. ³⁵The first day is a sacred assembly; do no regular work. ³⁶For seven days present offerings made to the LORD by fire, and on the eighth day hold a sacred assembly and present an offering made to the LORD by fire. It is the closing assembly; do no regular work.

³⁷(" 'These are the LORD's appointed feasts, which you are to proclaim as sacred assemblies for bringing offerings made to the LORD by fire— the burnt offerings and grain offerings, sacrifices and drink offerings required for each day. ³⁸These offerings are in addition to those for the LORD's Sabbaths and *a* in addition to your gifts and whatever you have vowed and all the freewill offerings you give to the LORD.)

³⁹" 'So beginning with the fifteenth day of the seventh month, after you have gathered the crops of the land, celebrate the festival to the LORD for seven days; the first day is a day of rest, and the eighth day also is a day of rest. ⁴⁰On the first day you are to take choice fruit from the trees, and palm fronds, leafy branches and poplars, and rejoice before the LORD your God for seven days. ⁴¹Celebrate this as a festival to the LORD for seven days each year. This is to be a lasting ordinance for the generations to come; celebrate it in the seventh month. ⁴²Live in booths for seven days: All native-born Israelites are to live in booths ⁴³so your descendants will know that I had the Israelites live in booths when I brought them out of Egypt. I am the LORD your God.' "

⁴⁴So Moses announced to the Israelites the appointed feasts of the LORD.

THE MESSAGE

GOD. Don't work on that day because it is a day of atonement to make atonement for you before your GOD. Anyone who doesn't fast on that day must be cut off from his people. I will destroy from among his people anyone who works on that day. Don't do any work that day—none. This is a perpetual decree for all the generations to come, wherever you happen to be living. It is a Sabbath of complete and total rest, a fast day. Observe your Sabbath from the evening of the ninth day of the month until the following evening."

23.33-36   GOD said to Moses, "Tell the People of Israel, GOD's Feast of Booths begins on the fifteenth day of the seventh month. It lasts seven days. The first day is a sacred assembly; don't do any ordinary work. Offer Fire-Gifts to GOD for seven days. On the eighth day hold a sacred assembly and offer a gift to GOD. It is a solemn convocation. Don't do any ordinary work.

23.37-38   "These are the appointed feasts of GOD which you will decree as sacred assemblies for presenting Fire-Gifts to GOD: the Whole-Burnt-Offerings, Grain-Offerings, sacrifices, and Drink-Offerings assigned to each day. These are in addition to offerings for GOD's Sabbaths and also in addition to other gifts connected with whatever you have vowed and all the Freewill-Offerings you give to GOD.

23.39-43   "So, summing up: On the fifteenth day of the seventh month, after you have brought your crops in from your fields, celebrate the Feast of GOD for seven days. The first day is a complete rest and the eighth day is a complete rest. On the first day, pick the best fruit from the best trees; take fronds of palm trees and branches of leafy trees and from willows by the brook and celebrate in the presence of your GOD for seven days—yes, for seven full days celebrate it as a festival to GOD. Every year from now on, celebrate it in the seventh month. Live in booths for seven days—every son and daughter of Israel is to move into booths so that your descendants will know that I made the People of Israel live in booths when I brought them out of the land of Egypt. I am GOD, *your* God."

23.44   Moses posted the calendar for the annual appointed feasts of GOD which Israel was to celebrate.

---

a 38 Or These feasts are in addition to the LORD's Sabbaths, and these offerings are

NEW INTERNATIONAL VERSION

Oil and Bread Set Before the Lord

24 The Lord said to Moses, 2"Command the Israelites to bring you clear oil of pressed olives for the light so that the lamps may be kept burning continually. 3Outside the curtain of the Testimony in the Tent of Meeting, Aaron is to tend the lamps before the Lord from evening till morning, continually. This is to be a lasting ordinance for the generations to come. 4The lamps on the pure gold lampstand before the Lord must be tended continually.

5"Take fine flour and bake twelve loaves of bread, using two-tenths of an ephah*a* for each loaf. 6Set them in two rows, six in each row, on the table of pure gold before the Lord. 7Along each row put some pure incense as a memorial portion to represent the bread and to be an offering made to the Lord by fire. 8This bread is to be set out before the Lord regularly, Sabbath after Sabbath, on behalf of the Israelites, as a lasting covenant. 9It belongs to Aaron and his sons, who are to eat it in a holy place, because it is a most holy part of their regular share of the offerings made to the Lord by fire."

A Blasphemer Stoned

10Now the son of an Israelite mother and an Egyptian father went out among the Israelites, and a fight broke out in the camp between him and an Israelite. 11The son of the Israelite woman blasphemed the Name with a curse; so they brought him to Moses. (His mother's name was Shelomith, the daughter of Dibri the Danite.) 12They put him in custody until the will of the Lord should be made clear to them.

13Then the Lord said to Moses: 14"Take the blasphemer outside the camp. All those who heard him are to lay their hands on his head, and the entire assembly is to stone him. 15Say to the Israelites: 'If anyone curses his God, he will be held responsible; 16anyone who blasphemes the name of the Lord must be put to death. The entire assembly must stone him. Whether an alien or native-born, when he blasphemes the Name, he must be put to death.

17" 'If anyone takes the life of a human being, he must be put to death. 18Anyone who takes the life of someone's animal must make restitution—life for life. 19If anyone injures his neighbor, whatever he has done must be done to him: 20fracture for fracture, eye for eye, tooth for tooth. As he has injured the other, so he is to be injured. 21Whoever kills an animal must make restitution, but whoever kills a man must be put to death. 22You are to have the same law for the

---

a 5 That is, probably about 4 quarts (about 4.5 liters)

THE MESSAGE

Light and Bread

24 God spoke to Moses: "Order the People of Israel to bring you virgin olive oil for light so that the lamps may be kept burning continually. Aaron is in charge of keeping these lamps burning in front of the curtain that screens The Testimony in the Tent of Meeting from evening to morning continually before God. This is a perpetual decree down through the generations. Aaron is responsible for keeping the lamps burning continually on the Lampstand of pure gold before God.

24.5-9 "Take fine flour and bake twelve loaves of bread, using about four quarts of flour to a loaf. Arrange them in two rows of six each on the Table of pure gold before God. Along each row spread pure incense, marking the bread as a memorial; it is a gift to God. Regularly, every Sabbath, this bread is to be set before God, a perpetual covenantal response from Israel. The bread then goes to Aaron and his sons, who are to eat it in a Holy Place. It is their most holy share from the gifts to God. This is a perpetual decree."

✛

24.10-12 One day the son of an Israelite mother and an Egyptian father went out among the Israelites. A fight broke out in the camp between him and an Israelite. The son of the Israelite woman blasphemed the Name of God and cursed. They brought him to Moses. His mother's name was Shelomith, daughter of Dibri of the tribe of Dan. They put him in custody waiting for God's will to be revealed to them.

24.13-16 Then God spoke to Moses: "Take the blasphemer outside the camp. Have all those who heard him place their hands on his head; then have the entire congregation stone him. Then tell the Israelites, Anyone who curses God will be held accountable; anyone who blasphemes the Name of God must be put to death. The entire congregation must stone him. It makes no difference whether he is a foreigner or a native, if he blasphemes the Name, he will be put to death.

24.17-22 "Anyone who hits and kills a fellow human must be put to death. Anyone who kills someone's animal must make it good—a life for a life. Anyone who injures his neighbor will get back the same as he gave: fracture for fracture, eye for eye, tooth for tooth. What he did to hurt that person will be done to him. Anyone who hits and kills an animal must make it good, but whoever hits and kills a fellow human will be put to death. And no double stan-

NEW INTERNATIONAL VERSION

alien and the native-born. I am the LORD your God.'"

²³Then Moses spoke to the Israelites, and they took the blasphemer outside the camp and stoned him. The Israelites did as the LORD commanded Moses.

THE SABBATH YEAR

25 The LORD said to Moses on Mount Sinai, ²"Speak to the Israelites and say to them: 'When you enter the land I am going to give you, the land itself must observe a sabbath to the LORD. ³For six years sow your fields, and for six years prune your vineyards and gather their crops. ⁴But in the seventh year the land is to have a sabbath of rest, a sabbath to the LORD. Do not sow your fields or prune your vineyards. ⁵Do not reap what grows of itself or harvest the grapes of your untended vines. The land is to have a year of rest. ⁶Whatever the land yields during the sabbath year will be food for you— for yourself, your manservant and maidservant, and the hired worker and temporary resident who live among you, ⁷as well as for your livestock and the wild animals in your land. Whatever the land produces may be eaten.

THE YEAR OF JUBILEE

⁸" 'Count off seven sabbaths of years—seven times seven years—so that the seven sabbaths of years amount to a period of forty-nine years. ⁹Then have the trumpet sounded everywhere on the tenth day of the seventh month; on the Day of Atonement sound the trumpet throughout your land. ¹⁰Consecrate the fiftieth year and proclaim liberty throughout the land to all its inhabitants. It shall be a jubilee for you; each one of you is to return to his family property and each to his own clan. ¹¹The fiftieth year shall be a jubilee for you; do not sow and do not reap what grows of itself or harvest the untended vines. ¹²For it is a jubilee and is to be holy for you; eat only what is taken directly from the fields.

¹³" 'In this Year of Jubilee everyone is to return to his own property.

¹⁴" 'If you sell land to one of your countrymen or buy any from him, do not take advantage of each other. ¹⁵You are to buy from your countryman on the basis of the number of years since the Jubilee. And he is to sell to you on the basis of the number of years left for harvesting crops. ¹⁶When the years are many, you are to increase the price, and when the years are few, you are to

THE MESSAGE

dards: the same rule goes for foreigners and natives. I am GOD, *your* God."

24.23 Moses then spoke to the People of Israel. They brought the blasphemer outside the camp and stoned him. The People of Israel followed the orders GOD had given Moses.

"THE LAND WILL OBSERVE A SABBATH TO GOD"

25.1-7 **25** GOD spoke to Moses at Mount Sinai, "Speak to the People of Israel. Tell them: When you enter the land which I am going to give you, the land will observe a Sabbath to GOD. Sow your fields, prune your vineyards, and take in your harvests for six years. But the seventh year the land will take a Sabbath of complete and total rest, a Sabbath to GOD; you will not sow your fields or prune your vineyards. Don't reap what grows of itself; don't harvest the grapes of your untended vines. The land gets a year of complete and total rest. But you can eat from what the land volunteers during the Sabbath year—you and your men and women servants, your hired hands, and the foreigners who live in the country, and, of course, also your livestock and the wild animals in the land can eat from it. Whatever the land volunteers of itself can be eaten.

"THE FIFTIETH YEAR SHALL BE A JUBILEE FOR YOU"

25.8-12 "Count off seven Sabbaths of years—seven times seven years: Seven Sabbaths of years adds up to forty-nine years. Then sound loud blasts on the ram's horn on the tenth day of the seventh month, the Day of Atonement. Sound the ram's horn all over the land. Sanctify the fiftieth year; make it a holy year. Proclaim freedom all over the land to everyone who lives in it—a Jubilee for you: Each person will go back to his family's property and reunite with his extended family. The fiftieth year is your Jubilee year: Don't sow; don't reap what volunteers itself in the fields; don't harvest the untended vines because it's the Jubilee and a holy year for you. You're permitted to eat from whatever volunteers itself in the fields.

25.13 "In this year of Jubilee everyone returns home to his family property.

25.14-17 "If you sell or buy property from one of your countrymen, don't cheat him. Calculate the purchase price on the basis of the number of years since the Jubilee. He is obliged to set the sale price on the basis of the number of harvests remaining until the next Jubilee. The more years left, the more money; you can raise the price. But the fewer years left, the less money; decrease the price. What you are buying

NEW INTERNATIONAL VERSION

decrease the price, because what he is really selling you is the number of crops. [17]Do not take advantage of each other, but fear your God. I am the LORD your God.

[18]" 'Follow my decrees and be careful to obey my laws, and you will live safely in the land. [19]Then the land will yield its fruit, and you will eat your fill and live there in safety. [20]You may ask, "What will we eat in the seventh year if we do not plant or harvest our crops?" [21]I will send you such a blessing in the sixth year that the land will yield enough for three years. [22]While you plant during the eighth year, you will eat from the old crop and will continue to eat from it until the harvest of the ninth year comes in.

[23]" 'The land must not be sold permanently, because the land is mine and you are but aliens and my tenants. [24]Throughout the country that you hold as a possession, you must provide for the redemption of the land.

[25]" 'If one of your countrymen becomes poor and sells some of his property, his nearest relative is to come and redeem what his countryman has sold. [26]If, however, a man has no one to redeem it for him but he himself prospers and acquires sufficient means to redeem it, [27]he is to determine the value for the years since he sold it and refund the balance to the man to whom he sold it; he can then go back to his own property. [28]But if he does not acquire the means to repay him, what he sold will remain in the possession of the buyer until the Year of Jubilee. It will be returned in the Jubilee, and he can then go back to his property.

[29]" 'If a man sells a house in a walled city, he retains the right of redemption a full year after its sale. During that time he may redeem it. [30]If it is not redeemed before a full year has passed, the house in the walled city shall belong permanently to the buyer and his descendants. It is not to be returned in the Jubilee. [31]But houses in villages without walls around them are to be considered as open country. They can be redeemed, and they are to be returned in the Jubilee.

[32]" 'The Levites always have the right to redeem their houses in the Levitical towns, which they possess. [33]So the property of the Levites is redeemable—that is, a house sold in any town they hold—and is to be returned in the Jubilee, because the houses in the towns of the Levites are their property among the Israelites. [34]But the pastureland belonging to their towns must not be sold; it is their permanent possession.

[35]" 'If one of your countrymen becomes poor and is unable to support himself among you, help him as you would an alien or a temporary resident, so he can continue to live among you.

THE MESSAGE

and selling in fact is the number of crops you're going to harvest. Don't cheat each other. Fear your God. I am GOD, your God.

25.18-22 "Keep my decrees and observe my laws and you will live secure in the land. The land will yield its fruit; you will have all you can eat and will live safe and secure. Do I hear you ask, 'What are we going to eat in the seventh year if we don't plant or harvest?' I assure you, I will send such a blessing in the sixth year that the land will yield enough for three years. While you plant in the eighth year, you will eat from the old crop and continue until the harvest of the ninth year comes in.

25.23-24 "The land cannot be sold permanently because the land is mine and you are foreigners—you're my tenants. You must provide for the right of redemption for any of the land that you own.

25.25-28 "If one of your brothers becomes poor and has to sell any of his land, his nearest relative is to come and buy back what his brother sold. If a man has no one to redeem it but he later prospers and earns enough for its redemption, he is to calculate the value since he sold it and refund the balance to the man to whom he sold it; he can then go back to his own land. If he doesn't get together enough money to repay him, what he sold remains in the possession of the buyer until the year of Jubilee. In the Jubilee it will be returned and he can go back and live on his land.

25.29-31 "If a man sells a house in a walled city, he retains the right to buy it back for a full year after the sale. At any time during that year he can redeem it. But if it is not redeemed before the full year has passed, it becomes the permanent possession of the buyer and his descendants. It is not returned in the Jubilee. However, houses in unwalled villages are treated the same as fields. They can be redeemed and have to be returned at the Jubilee.

25.32-34 "As to the Levitical cities, houses in the cities owned by the Levites are always subject to redemption. Levitical property is always redeemable if it is sold in a town that they hold and reverts to them in the Jubilee, because the houses in the towns of the Levites are their property among the People of Israel. The pastures belonging to their cities may not be sold; they are their permanent possession.

25.35-38 "If one of your brothers becomes indigent and cannot support himself, help him, the same as you would a foreigner or a guest so that he can continue to live in your neighbor-

NEW INTERNATIONAL VERSION

³⁶Do not take interest of any kind*ᵃ* from him, but fear your God, so that your countryman may continue to live among you. ³⁷You must not lend him money at interest or sell him food at a profit. ³⁸I am the LORD your God, who brought you out of Egypt to give you the land of Canaan and to be your God.

³⁹ "If one of your countrymen becomes poor among you and sells himself to you, do not make him work as a slave. ⁴⁰He is to be treated as a hired worker or a temporary resident among you; he is to work for you until the Year of Jubilee. ⁴¹Then he and his children are to be released, and he will go back to his own clan and to the property of his forefathers. ⁴²Because the Israelites are my servants, whom I brought out of Egypt, they must not be sold as slaves. ⁴³Do not rule over them ruthlessly, but fear your God.

⁴⁴ "Your male and female slaves are to come from the nations around you; from them you may buy slaves. ⁴⁵You may also buy some of the temporary residents living among you and members of their clans born in your country, and they will become your property. ⁴⁶You can will them to your children as inherited property and can make them slaves for life, but you must not rule over your fellow Israelites ruthlessly.

⁴⁷ "If an alien or a temporary resident among you becomes rich and one of your countrymen becomes poor and sells himself to the alien living among you or to a member of the alien's clan, ⁴⁸he retains the right of redemption after he has sold himself. One of his relatives may redeem him: ⁴⁹An uncle or a cousin or any blood relative in his clan may redeem him. Or if he prospers, he may redeem himself. ⁵⁰He and his buyer are to count the time from the year he sold himself up to the Year of Jubilee. The price for his release is to be based on the rate paid to a hired man for that number of years. ⁵¹If many years remain, he must pay for his redemption a larger share of the price paid for him. ⁵²If only a few years remain until the Year of Jubilee, he is to compute that and pay for his redemption accordingly. ⁵³He is to be treated as a man hired from year to year; you must see to it that his owner does not rule over him ruthlessly.

⁵⁴ "Even if he is not redeemed in any of these ways, he and his children are to be released in the Year of Jubilee, ⁵⁵for the Israelites belong to me as servants. They are my servants, whom I brought out of Egypt. I am the LORD your God.

THE MESSAGE

hood. Don't gouge him with interest charges; out of reverence for your God help your brother to continue to live with you in the neighborhood. Don't take advantage of his plight by running up big interest charges on his loans, and don't give him food for profit. I am your GOD who brought you out of Egypt to give you the land of Canaan and to be your God.

25.39-43   "If one of your brothers becomes indigent and has to sell himself to you, don't make him work as a slave. Treat him as a hired hand or a guest among you. He will work for you until the Jubilee, after which he and his children are set free to go back to his clan and his ancestral land. Because the People of Israel are my servants whom I brought out of Egypt, they must never be sold as slaves. Don't tyrannize them; fear your God.

25.44-46   "The male and female slaves which you have are to come from the surrounding nations; you are permitted to buy slaves from them. You may also buy the children of foreign workers who are living among you temporarily and from their clans which are living among you and have been born in your land. They become your property. You may will them to your children as property and make them slaves for life. But you must not tyrannize your brother Israelites.

25.47-53   "If a foreigner or temporary resident among you becomes rich and one of your brothers becomes poor and sells himself to the foreigner who lives among you or to a member of the foreigner's clan, he still has the right of redemption after he has sold himself. One of his relatives may buy him back. An uncle or cousin or any close relative of his extended family may redeem him. Or, if he gets the money together, he can redeem himself. What happens then is that he and his owner count out the time from the year he sold himself to the year of Jubilee; the buy-back price is set according to the wages of a hired hand for that number of years. If many years remain before the Jubilee, he must pay back a larger share of his purchase price, but if only a few years remain until the Jubilee, he is to calculate his redemption price accordingly. He is to be treated as a man hired from year to year. You must make sure that his owner does not tyrannize him.

25.54-55   "If he is not redeemed in any of these ways, he goes free in the year of Jubilee, he and his children, because the People of Israel are my servants, my servants whom I brought out of Egypt. I am GOD, *your* God.

✝

NEW INTERNATIONAL VERSION

Reward for Obedience

26 " 'Do not make idols or set up an image or a sacred stone for yourselves, and do not place a carved stone in your land to bow down before it. I am the Lord your God.

² " 'Observe my Sabbaths and have reverence for my sanctuary. I am the Lord.

³ " 'If you follow my decrees and are careful to obey my commands, ⁴I will send you rain in its season, and the ground will yield its crops and the trees of the field their fruit. ⁵Your threshing will continue until grape harvest and the grape harvest will continue until planting, and you will eat all the food you want and live in safety in your land.

⁶ " 'I will grant peace in the land, and you will lie down and no one will make you afraid. I will remove savage beasts from the land, and the sword will not pass through your country. ⁷You will pursue your enemies, and they will fall by the sword before you. ⁸Five of you will chase a hundred, and a hundred of you will chase ten thousand, and your enemies will fall by the sword before you.

⁹ " 'I will look on you with favor and make you fruitful and increase your numbers, and I will keep my covenant with you. ¹⁰You will still be eating last year's harvest when you will have to move it out to make room for the new. ¹¹I will put my dwelling place*ᵃ* among you, and I will not abhor you. ¹²I will walk among you and be your God, and you will be my people. ¹³I am the Lord your God, who brought you out of Egypt so that you would no longer be slaves to the Egyptians; I broke the bars of your yoke and enabled you to walk with heads held high.

Punishment for Disobedience

¹⁴ " 'But if you will not listen to me and carry out all these commands, ¹⁵and if you reject my decrees and abhor my laws and fail to carry out all my commands and so violate my covenant, ¹⁶then I will do this to you: I will bring upon you sudden terror, wasting diseases and fever that will destroy your sight and drain away your life. You will plant seed in vain, because your enemies will eat it. ¹⁷I will set my face against you so that you will be defeated by your enemies; those who hate you will rule over you, and you will flee even when no one is pursuing you.

¹⁸ " 'If after all this you will not listen to me, I will punish you for your sins seven times over. ¹⁹I will break down your stubborn pride and make the sky above you like iron and the ground beneath you like bronze. ²⁰Your strength will be

ᵃ 11 Or my tabernacle

THE MESSAGE

26 "Don't make idols for yourselves; don't set up an image or a sacred pillar for yourselves, and don't place a carved stone in your land that you can bow down to in worship. I am God, *your* God.

²⁶.² "Keep my Sabbaths; treat my Sanctuary with reverence. I am God.

"If You Live by My Decrees . . . "

²⁶.³⁻⁵ "If you live by my decrees and obediently keep my commandments, I will send the rains in their seasons, the ground will yield its crops and the trees of the field their fruit. You will thresh until the grape harvest and the grape harvest will continue until planting time; you'll have more than enough to eat and will live safe and secure in your land.

²⁶.⁶⁻¹⁰ "I'll make the country a place of peace—you'll be able to go to sleep at night without fear; I'll get rid of the wild beasts; I'll eliminate war. You'll chase out your enemies and defeat them: Five of you will chase a hundred, and a hundred of you will chase ten thousand and do away with them. I'll give you my full attention: I'll make sure you prosper, make sure you grow in numbers, and keep my covenant with you in good working order. You'll still be eating from last year's harvest when you have to clean out the barns to make room for the new crops.

²⁶.¹¹⁻¹³ "I'll set up my residence in your neighborhood; I won't avoid or shun you; I'll stroll through your streets. I'll be your God; you'll be my people. I am God, your personal God who rescued you from Egypt so that you would no longer be slaves to the Egyptians. I ripped off the harness of your slavery so that you can move about freely.

"But If You Refuse to Obey Me . . . "

²⁶.¹⁴⁻¹⁷ "But if you refuse to obey me and won't observe my commandments, despising my decrees and holding my laws in contempt by your disobedience, making a shambles of my covenant, I'll step in and pour on the trouble: debilitating disease, high fevers, blindness, your life leaking out bit by bit. You'll plant seed but your enemies will eat the crops. I'll turn my back on you and stand by while your enemies defeat you. People who hate you will govern you. You'll run scared even when there's no one chasing you.

²⁶.¹⁸⁻²⁰ "And if none of this works in getting your attention, I'll discipline you seven times over for your sins. I'll break your strong pride: I'll make the skies above you like a sheet of tin and the ground under you like cast iron. No

NEW INTERNATIONAL VERSION

spent in vain, because your soil will not yield its crops, nor will the trees of the land yield their fruit.

21 " 'If you remain hostile toward me and refuse to listen to me, I will multiply your afflictions seven times over, as your sins deserve. 22I will send wild animals against you, and they will rob you of your children, destroy your cattle and make you so few in number that your roads will be deserted.

23 " 'If in spite of these things you do not accept my correction but continue to be hostile toward me, 24I myself will be hostile toward you and will afflict you for your sins seven times over. 25And I will bring the sword upon you to avenge the breaking of the covenant. When you withdraw into your cities, I will send a plague among you, and you will be given into enemy hands. 26When I cut off your supply of bread, ten women will be able to bake your bread in one oven, and they will dole out the bread by weight. You will eat, but you will not be satisfied.

27 " 'If in spite of this you still do not listen to me but continue to be hostile toward me, 28then in my anger I will be hostile toward you, and I myself will punish you for your sins seven times over. 29You will eat the flesh of your sons and the flesh of your daughters. 30I will destroy your high places, cut down your incense altars and pile your dead bodies on the lifeless forms of your idols, and I will abhor you. 31I will turn your cities into ruins and lay waste your sanctuaries, and I will take no delight in the pleasing aroma of your offerings. 32I will lay waste the land, so that your enemies who live there will be appalled. 33I will scatter you among the nations and will draw out my sword and pursue you. Your land will be laid waste, and your cities will lie in ruins. 34Then the land will enjoy its sabbath years all the time that it lies desolate and you are in the country of your enemies; then the land will rest and enjoy its sabbaths. 35All the time that it lies desolate, the land will have the rest it did not have during the sabbaths you lived in it.

36 " 'As for those of you who are left, I will make their hearts so fearful in the lands of their enemies that the sound of a windblown leaf will put them to flight. They will run as though fleeing from the sword, and they will fall, even though no one is pursuing them. 37They will stumble over one another as though fleeing from the sword, even though no one is pursuing them. So you will not be able to stand before your enemies. 38You will perish among the nations; the land of your enemies will devour you.

THE MESSAGE

matter how hard you work, nothing will come of it: No crops out of the ground, no fruit off the trees.

26.21-22   "If you defy me and refuse to listen, your punishment will be seven times more than your sins: I'll set wild animals on you; they'll rob you of your children, kill your cattle, and decimate your numbers until you'll think you are living in a ghost town.

26.23-26   "And if even this doesn't work and you refuse my discipline and continue your defiance, then it will be my turn to defy you. I, yes I, will punish you for your sins seven times over: I'll let war loose on you, avenging your breaking of the covenant; when you huddle in your cities for protection, I'll send a deadly epidemic on you and you'll be helpless before your enemies; when I cut off your bread supply, ten women will bake bread in one oven and ration it out. You'll eat, but barely—no one will get enough.

26.27-35   "And if this—*even this!*—doesn't work and you still won't listen, still defy me, I'll have had enough and in hot anger will defy you, punishing you for your sins seven times over: famine will be so severe that you'll end up cooking and eating your sons in stews and your daughters in barbecues; I'll smash your sex-and-religion shrines and all the paraphernalia that goes with them, and then stack your corpses and the idol-corpses in the same piles—I'll abhor you; I'll turn your cities into rubble; I'll clean out your sanctuaries; I'll hold my nose at the "pleasing aroma" of your sacrifices. I'll turn your land into a lifeless moonscape—your enemies who come in to take over will be shocked at what they see. I'll scatter you all over the world and keep after you with the point of my sword in your backs. There'll be nothing left in your land, nothing going on in your cities. With you gone and dispersed in the countries of your enemies, the land, empty of you, will finally get a break and enjoy its Sabbath years. All the time it's left there empty, the land will get rest, the Sabbaths it never got when you lived there.

26.36-39   "As for those among you still alive, I'll give them over to fearful timidity—even the rustle of a leaf will throw them into a panic. They'll run here and there, back and forth, as if running for their lives even though no one is after them, tripping and falling over one another in total confusion. You won't stand a chance against an enemy. You'll perish among the nations; the land of your enemies will eat you up.

NEW INTERNATIONAL VERSION

³⁹Those of you who are left will waste away in the lands of their enemies because of their sins; also because of their fathers' sins they will waste away.

⁴⁰" 'But if they will confess their sins and the sins of their fathers—their treachery against me and their hostility toward me, ⁴¹which made me hostile toward them so that I sent them into the land of their enemies—then when their uncircumcised hearts are humbled and they pay for their sin, ⁴²I will remember my covenant with Jacob and my covenant with Isaac and my covenant with Abraham, and I will remember the land. ⁴³For the land will be deserted by them and will enjoy its sabbaths while it lies desolate without them. They will pay for their sins because they rejected my laws and abhorred my decrees. ⁴⁴Yet in spite of this, when they are in the land of their enemies, I will not reject them or abhor them so as to destroy them completely, breaking my covenant with them. I am the LORD their God. ⁴⁵But for their sake I will remember the covenant with their ancestors whom I brought out of Egypt in the sight of the nations to be their God. I am the LORD.' "

⁴⁶These are the decrees, the laws and the regulations that the LORD established on Mount Sinai between himself and the Israelites through Moses.

REDEEMING WHAT IS THE LORD'S

27 The LORD said to Moses, ²"Speak to the Israelites and say to them: 'If anyone makes a special vow to dedicate persons to the LORD by giving equivalent values, ³set the value of a male between the ages of twenty and sixty at fifty shekels^a of silver, according to the sanctuary shekel^b; ⁴and if it is a female, set her value at thirty shekels. ^c ⁵If it is a person between the ages of five and twenty, set the value of a male at twenty shekels^d and of a female at ten shekels. ^e ⁶If it is a person between one month and five years, set the value of a male at five shekels^f of silver and that of a female at three shekels^g of silver. ⁷If it is a person sixty years old or more, set the value of a male at fifteen shekels^h and of a female at ten shekels. ⁸If anyone making the vow is too poor to pay the specified amount, he is to

---

^a 3 That is, about 1 1/4 pounds (about 0.6 kilogram); also in verse 16 ^b 3 That is, about 2/5 ounce (about 11.5 grams); also in verse 25 ^c 4 That is, about 12 ounces (about 0.3 kilogram) ^d 5 That is, about 8 ounces (about 0.2 kilogram) ^e 5 That is, about 4 ounces (about 110 grams); also in verse 7 ^f 6 That is, about 2 ounces (about 55 grams) ^g 6 That is, about 1 1/4 ounces (about 35 grams) ^h 7 That is, about 6 ounces (about 170 grams)

THE MESSAGE

Any who are left will slowly rot away in the enemy lands. Rot. And all because of their sins, their sins compounded by their ancestors' sins.

"ON THE OTHER HAND, IF THEY CONFESS . . ."

26.40-42 "On the other hand, if they confess their sins and the sins of their ancestors, their treacherous betrayal, the defiance that set off my defiance that sent them off into enemy lands; if by some chance they soften their hard hearts and make amends for their sin, I'll remember my covenant with Jacob, I'll remember my covenant with Isaac, and, yes, I'll remember my covenant with Abraham. And I'll remember the land.

26.43-45 "The land will be empty of them and enjoy its Sabbaths while they're gone. They'll pay for their sins because they refused my laws and treated my decrees with contempt. But in spite of their behavior, while they are among their enemies I won't reject or abhor or destroy them completely. I won't break my covenant with them: I am GOD, their God. For their sake I will remember the covenant with their ancestors whom I, with all the nations watching, brought out of Egypt in order to be their God. I am GOD."

26.46 These are the decrees, laws, and instructions that GOD established between himself and the People of Israel through Moses at Mount Sinai.

VOWS, DEDICATIONS, AND REDEMPTIONS

27.1-8 **27** GOD spoke to Moses. He said, "Speak to the People of Israel. Tell them: If anyone wants to vow the value of a person to the service of GOD, set the value of a man between the ages of twenty and sixty at fifty shekels of silver, according to the Sanctuary shekel. For a woman the valuation is thirty shekels. If the person is between the ages of five and twenty, set the value at twenty shekels for a male and ten shekels for a female. If the person is between one month and five years, set the value at five shekels of silver for a boy and three shekels of silver for a girl. If the person is over sixty, set the value at fifteen shekels for a man and ten shekels for a woman. If anyone is too poor to pay the stated amount, he is to present

NEW INTERNATIONAL VERSION

present the person to the priest, who will set the value for him according to what the man making the vow can afford.

9 " 'If what he vowed is an animal that is acceptable as an offering to the LORD, such an animal given to the LORD becomes holy. 10He must not exchange it or substitute a good one for a bad one, or a bad one for a good one; if he should substitute one animal for another, both it and the substitute become holy. 11If what he vowed is a ceremonially unclean animal—one that is not acceptable as an offering to the LORD—the animal must be presented to the priest, 12who will judge its quality as good or bad. Whatever value the priest then sets, that is what it will be. 13If the owner wishes to redeem the animal, he must add a fifth to its value.

14 " 'If a man dedicates his house as something holy to the LORD, the priest will judge its quality as good or bad. Whatever value the priest then sets, so it will remain. 15If the man who dedicates his house redeems it, he must add a fifth to its value, and the house will again become his.

16 " 'If a man dedicates to the LORD part of his family land, its value is to be set according to the amount of seed required for it—fifty shekels of silver to a homer*a* of barley seed. 17If he dedicates his field during the Year of Jubilee, the value that has been set remains. 18But if he dedicates his field after the Jubilee, the priest will determine the value according to the number of years that remain until the next Year of Jubilee, and its set value will be reduced. 19If the man who dedicates the field wishes to redeem it, he must add a fifth to its value, and the field will again become his. 20If, however, he does not redeem the field, or if he has sold it to someone else, it can never be redeemed. 21When the field is released in the Jubilee, it will become holy, like a field devoted to the LORD; it will become the property of the priests.*b*

22 " 'If a man dedicates to the LORD a field he has bought, which is not part of his family land, 23the priest will determine its value up to the Year of Jubilee, and the man must pay its value on that day as something holy to the LORD. 24In the Year of Jubilee the field will revert to the person from whom he bought it, the one whose land it was. 25Every value is to be set according to the sanctuary shekel, twenty gerahs to the shekel.

26 " 'No one, however, may dedicate the firstborn of an animal, since the firstborn already belongs to the LORD; whether an ox*c* or a sheep, it is the LORD's. 27If it is one of the unclean ani-

THE MESSAGE

the person to the priest, who will then set the value for him according to what the person making the vow can afford.

27.9-13   "If he vowed an animal that is acceptable as an offering to GOD, the animal is given to GOD and becomes the property of the Sanctuary. He must not exchange or substitute a good one for a bad one, or a bad one for a good one; if he should dishonestly substitute one animal for another, both the original and the substitute become property of the Sanctuary. If what he vowed is a ritually unclean animal, one that is not acceptable as an offering to GOD, the animal must be shown to the priest, who will set its value, either high or low. Whatever the priest sets will be its value. If the owner changes his mind and wants to redeem it, he must add twenty percent to its value.

27.14-15   "If a man dedicates his house to GOD, into the possession of the Sanctuary, the priest assesses its value, setting it either high or low. Whatever value the priest sets, that's what it is. If the man wants to buy it back, he must add twenty percent to its price and then it's his again.

27.16-21   "If a man dedicates to GOD part of his family land, its value is to be set according to the amount of seed that is needed for it at the rate of fifty shekels of silver to six bushels of barley seed. If he dedicates his field during the year of Jubilee, the set value stays. But if he dedicates it after the Jubilee, the priest will compute the value according to the years left until the next Jubilee, reducing the value proportionately. If the one dedicating it wants to buy it back, he must add twenty percent to its valuation, and then it's his again. But if he doesn't redeem it or sells the field to someone else, it can never be bought back. When the field is released in the Jubilee, it becomes holy to GOD, the possession of the Sanctuary, GOD's field. It goes into the hands of the priests.

27.22-25   "If a man dedicates to GOD a field he has bought, a field which is not part of the family land, the priest will compute its proportionate value in relation to the next year of Jubilee. The man must pay its value on the spot as something that is now holy to GOD, belonging to the Sanctuary. In the year of Jubilee it goes back to its original owner, the man from whom he bought it. The valuations will be reckoned by the Sanctuary shekel, at twenty gerahs to the shekel.

27.26-27   "No one is allowed to dedicate the firstborn of an animal; the firstborn, as firstborn, already belongs to GOD. No matter if it's cattle or sheep, it already belongs to GOD. If it's one of the ritu-

---

a 16 That is, probably about 6 bushels (about 220 liters)
b 21 Or *priest*   *c 26* The Hebrew word can include both male and female.

NEW INTERNATIONAL VERSION

mals, he may buy it back at its set value, adding a fifth of the value to it. If he does not redeem it, it is to be sold at its set value.

28 " 'But nothing that a man owns and devotes[a] to the LORD—whether man or animal or family land—may be sold or redeemed; everything so devoted is most holy to the LORD. 29 " 'No person devoted to destruction[b] may be ransomed; he must be put to death.

30 " 'A tithe of everything from the land, whether grain from the soil or fruit from the trees, belongs to the LORD; it is holy to the LORD. 31 If a man redeems any of his tithe, he must add a fifth of the value to it. 32 The entire tithe of the herd and flock—every tenth animal that passes under the shepherd's rod—will be holy to the LORD. 33 He must not pick out the good from the bad or make any substitution. If he does make a substitution, both the animal and its substitute become holy and cannot be redeemed.' "

34 These are the commands the LORD gave Moses on Mount Sinai for the Israelites.

THE MESSAGE

ally unclean animals, he can buy it back at its assessed value by adding twenty percent to it. If he doesn't redeem it, it is to be sold at its assessed value.

27.28 "But nothing that a man irrevocably devotes to GOD from what belongs to him, whether human or animal or family land, may be either sold or bought back. Everything devoted is holy to the highest degree; it's GOD's inalienable property.

27.29 "No human who has been devoted to destruction can be redeemed. He must be put to death.

✛

27.30-33 "A tenth of the land's produce, whether grain from the ground or fruit from the trees, is GOD's. It is holy to GOD. If a man buys back any of the tenth he has given, he must add twenty percent to it. A tenth of the entire herd and flock, every tenth animal that passes under the shepherd's rod, is holy to GOD. He is not permitted to pick out the good from the bad or make a substitution. If he dishonestly makes a substitution, both animals, the original and the substitute, become the possession of the Sanctuary and cannot be redeemed."

27.34 These are the commandments that GOD gave to Moses on Mount Sinai for the People of Israel.

a 28 The Hebrew term refers to the irrevocable giving over of things or persons to the LORD.   b 29 The Hebrew term refers to the irrevocable giving over of things or persons to the LORD, often by totally destroying them.

NUMBERS

NUMBERS

THE CENSUS

1 The LORD spoke to Moses in the Tent of Meeting in the Desert of Sinai on the first day of the second month of the second year after the Israelites came out of Egypt. He said: [2] "Take a census of the whole Israelite community by their clans and families, listing every man by name, one by one. [3] You and Aaron are to number by their divisions all the men in Israel twenty years old or more who are able to serve in the army. [4] One man from each tribe, each the head of his family, is to help you. [5] These are the names of the men who are to assist you:

from Reuben, Elizur son of Shedeur;
[6] from Simeon, Shelumiel son of Zurishaddai;
[7] from Judah, Nahshon son of Amminadab;
[8] from Issachar, Nethanel son of Zuar;
[9] from Zebulun, Eliab son of Helon;
[10] from the sons of Joseph:
   from Ephraim, Elishama son of Ammihud;
   from Manasseh, Gamaliel son of Pedahzur;
[11] from Benjamin, Abidan son of Gideoni;
[12] from Dan, Ahiezer son of Ammishaddai;
[13] from Asher, Pagiel son of Ocran;
[14] from Gad, Eliasaph son of Deuel;
[15] from Naphtali, Ahira son of Enan."

[16] These were the men appointed from the community, the leaders of their ancestral tribes. They were the heads of the clans of Israel.

[17] Moses and Aaron took these men whose names had been given, [18] and they called the whole community together on the first day of the second month. The people indicated their ancestry by their clans and families, and the men twenty years old or more were listed by name, one by one, [19] as the LORD commanded Moses. And so he counted them in the Desert of Sinai:

[20] From the descendants of Reuben the firstborn son of Israel:
   All the men twenty years old or more who were able to serve in the army were listed by name, one by one, according

CENSUS IN THE WILDERNESS OF SINAI

1 GOD spoke to Moses in the Wilderness of Sinai at the Tent of Meeting on the first day of the second month in the second year after they had left Egypt. He said, "Number the congregation of the People of Israel by clans and families, writing down the names of every male. You and Aaron are to register, company by company, every man who is twenty years and older who is able to fight in the army. Pick one man from each tribe who is head of his family to help you. These are the names of the men who will help you:

1.1-5

from Reuben: Elizur son of Shedeur
1.6   from Simeon: Shelumiel son of Zurishaddai
1.7   from Judah: Nahshon son of Amminadab
1.8   from Issachar: Nethanel son of Zuar
1.9   from Zebulun: Eliab son of Helon
1.10   from the sons of Joseph,
     from Ephraim: Elishama son of Ammihud
     from Manasseh: Gamaliel son of Pedahzur
1.11   from Benjamin: Abidan son of Gideoni
1.12   from Dan: Ahiezer son of Ammishaddai
1.13   from Asher: Pagiel son of Ocran
1.14   from Gad: Eliasaph son of Deuel
1.15   from Naphtali: Ahira son of Enan."

1.16   These were the men chosen from the congregation, leaders of their ancestral tribes, heads of Israel's military divisions.

1.17-19   Moses and Aaron took these men who had been named to help and gathered the whole congregation together on the first day of the second month. The people registered themselves in their tribes according to their ancestral families, putting down the names of those who were twenty years old and older, just as GOD commanded Moses. He numbered them in the Wilderness of Sinai.

1.20-21   The line of Reuben, Israel's firstborn: The men were counted off head by head, every male twenty years and older who was able to fight in the army, registered by tribes according to their

NEW INTERNATIONAL VERSION

to the records of their clans and families. ²¹The number from the tribe of Reuben was 46,500.

²²From the descendants of Simeon:

All the men twenty years old or more who were able to serve in the army were counted and listed by name, one by one, according to the records of their clans and families. ²³The number from the tribe of Simeon was 59,300.

²⁴From the descendants of Gad:

All the men twenty years old or more who were able to serve in the army were listed by name, according to the records of their clans and families. ²⁵The number from the tribe of Gad was 45,650.

²⁶From the descendants of Judah:

All the men twenty years old or more who were able to serve in the army were listed by name, according to the records of their clans and families. ²⁷The number from the tribe of Judah was 74,600.

²⁸From the descendants of Issachar:

All the men twenty years old or more who were able to serve in the army were listed by name, according to the records of their clans and families. ²⁹The number from the tribe of Issachar was 54,400.

³⁰From the descendants of Zebulun:

All the men twenty years old or more who were able to serve in the army were listed by name, according to the records of their clans and families. ³¹The number from the tribe of Zebulun was 57,400.

³²From the sons of Joseph:

From the descendants of Ephraim:

All the men twenty years old or more who were able to serve in the army were listed by name, according to the records of their clans and families. ³³The number from the tribe of Ephraim was 40,500.

³⁴From the descendants of Manasseh:

All the men twenty years old or more who were able to serve in the army were listed by name, according to the records of their clans and families. ³⁵The number from the tribe of Manasseh was 32,200.

³⁶From the descendants of Benjamin:

All the men twenty years old or more who were able to serve in the army were

THE MESSAGE

ancestral families. The tribe of Reuben numbered 46,500.

1.22-23   The line of Simeon: The men were counted off head by head, every male twenty years and older who was able to fight in the army, registered by clans and families. The tribe of Simeon numbered 59,300.

1.24-25   The line of Gad: The men were counted off head by head, every male twenty years and older who was able to fight in the army, registered by clans and families. The tribe of Gad numbered 45,650.

1.26-27   The line of Judah: The men were counted off head by head, every male twenty years and older who was able to fight in the army, registered by clans and families. The tribe of Judah numbered 74,600.

1.28-29   The line of Issachar: The men were counted off head by head, every male twenty years and older who was able to fight in the army, registered by clans and families. The tribe of Issachar numbered 54,400.

1.30-31   The line of Zebulun: The men were counted off head by head, every male twenty years and older who was able to fight in the army, registered by clans and families. The tribe of Zebulun numbered 57,400.

1.32-33   The line of Joseph: From son Ephraim the men were counted off head by head, every male twenty years and older who was able to fight in the army, registered by clans and families. The tribe of Ephraim numbered 40,500.

1.34-35   And from son Manasseh the men were counted off head by head, every male twenty years and older who was able to fight in the army, registered by clans and families. The tribe of Manasseh numbered 32,200.

1.36-37   The line of Benjamin: The men were counted off head by head, every male twenty years and older who was able to fight in the army,

NEW INTERNATIONAL VERSION

listed by name, according to the records of their clans and families. ³⁷The number from the tribe of Benjamin was 35,400.

³⁸From the descendants of Dan:
All the men twenty years old or more who were able to serve in the army were listed by name, according to the records of their clans and families. ³⁹The number from the tribe of Dan was 62,700.

⁴⁰From the descendants of Asher:
All the men twenty years old or more who were able to serve in the army were listed by name, according to the records of their clans and families. ⁴¹The number from the tribe of Asher was 41,500.

⁴²From the descendants of Naphtali:
All the men twenty years old or more who were able to serve in the army were listed by name, according to the records of their clans and families. ⁴³The number from the tribe of Naphtali was 53,400.

⁴⁴These were the men counted by Moses and Aaron and the twelve leaders of Israel, each one representing his family. ⁴⁵All the Israelites twenty years old or more who were able to serve in Israel's army were counted according to their families. ⁴⁶The total number was 603,550.

⁴⁷The families of the tribe of Levi, however, were not counted along with the others. ⁴⁸The LORD had said to Moses: ⁴⁹"You must not count the tribe of Levi or include them in the census of the other Israelites. ⁵⁰Instead, appoint the Levites to be in charge of the tabernacle of the Testimony—over all its furnishings and everything belonging to it. They are to carry the tabernacle and all its furnishings; they are to take care of it and encamp around it. ⁵¹Whenever the tabernacle is to move, the Levites are to take it down, and whenever the tabernacle is to be set up, the Levites shall do it. Anyone else who goes near it shall be put to death. ⁵²The Israelites are to set up their tents by divisions, each man in his own camp under his own standard. ⁵³The Levites, however, are to set up their tents around the tabernacle of the Testimony so that wrath will not fall on the Israelite community. The Levites are to be responsible for the care of the tabernacle of the Testimony."

⁵⁴The Israelites did all this just as the LORD commanded Moses.

THE MESSAGE

registered by clans and families. The tribe of Benjamin numbered 35,400.

1.38-39 The line of Dan: The men were counted off head by head, every male twenty years and older who was able to fight in the army, registered by clans and families. The tribe of Dan numbered 62,700.

1.40-41 The line of Asher: The men were counted off head by head, every male twenty years and older who was able to fight in the army, registered by clans and families. The tribe of Asher numbered 41,500.

1.42-43 The line of Naphtali: The men were counted off head by head, every male twenty years and older who was able to fight in the army, registered by clans and families. The tribe of Naphtali numbered 53,400.

1.44-46 These are the numbers of those registered by Moses and Aaron, registered with the help of the leaders of Israel, twelve men, each representing his ancestral family. The sum total of the People of Israel twenty years old and over who were able to fight in the army, counted by ancestral family, was 603,550.

1.47-51 The Levites, however, were not counted by their ancestral family along with the others. GOD had told Moses, "The tribe of Levi is an exception: Don't register them. Don't count the tribe of Levi; don't include them in the general census of the People of Israel. Instead, appoint the Levites to be in charge of The Dwelling of The Testimony—over all its furnishings and everything connected with it. Their job is to carry The Dwelling and all its furnishings, maintain it, and camp around it. When it's time to move The Dwelling, the Levites will take it down, and when it's time to set it up, the Levites will do it. Anyone else who even goes near it will be put to death.

1.52-53 "The rest of the People of Israel will set up their tents in companies, every man in his own camp under its own flag. But the Levites will set up camp around The Dwelling of The Testimony so that wrath will not fall on the community of Israel. The Levites are responsible for the security of The Dwelling of The Testimony."

1.54 The People of Israel did everything that God commanded Moses. They did it all.

NEW INTERNATIONAL VERSION

THE ARRANGEMENT OF THE TRIBAL CAMPS

2 The LORD said to Moses and Aaron: 2"The Israelites are to camp around the Tent of Meeting some distance from it, each man under his standard with the banners of his family."

3On the east, toward the sunrise, the divisions of the camp of Judah are to encamp under their standard. The leader of the people of Judah is Nahshon son of Amminadab. 4His division numbers 74,600.

5The tribe of Issachar will camp next to them. The leader of the people of Issachar is Nethanel son of Zuar. 6His division numbers 54,400.

7The tribe of Zebulun will be next. The leader of the people of Zebulun is Eliab son of Helon. 8His division numbers 57,400.

9All the men assigned to the camp of Judah, according to their divisions, number 186,400. They will set out first.

10On the south will be the divisions of the camp of Reuben under their standard. The leader of the people of Reuben is Elizur son of Shedeur. 11His division numbers 46,500.

12The tribe of Simeon will camp next to them. The leader of the people of Simeon is Shelumiel son of Zurishaddai. 13His division numbers 59,300.

14The tribe of Gad will be next. The leader of the people of Gad is Eliasaph son of Deuel.*a* 15His division numbers 45,650.

16All the men assigned to the camp of Reuben, according to their divisions, number 151,450. They will set out second.

17Then the Tent of Meeting and the camp of the Levites will set out in the middle of the camps. They will set out in the same order as they encamp, each in his own place under his standard.

18On the west will be the divisions of the camp of Ephraim under their standard. The leader of the people of Ephraim is Elishama son of Ammihud. 19His division numbers 40,500.

20The tribe of Manasseh will be next to them. The leader of the people of Manasseh is Gamaliel son of Pedahzur. 21His division numbers 32,200.

22The tribe of Benjamin will be next. The leader of the people of Benjamin is Abidan son of Gideoni. 23His division numbers 35,400.

---

a 14 Many manuscripts of the Masoretic Text, Samaritan Pentateuch and Vulgate (see also Num. 1:14); most manuscripts of the Masoretic Text *Reuel*

THE MESSAGE

MARCHING ORDERS

2 2.1-2 GOD spoke to Moses and Aaron. He said, "The People of Israel are to set up camp circling the Tent of Meeting and facing it. Each company is to camp under its distinctive tribal flag."

2.3-4 To the east toward the sunrise are the companies of the camp of Judah under its flag, led by Nahshon son of Amminadab. His troops number 74,600.

2.5-6 The tribe of Issachar will camp next to them, led by Nethanel son of Zuar. His troops number 54,400.

2.7-8 And the tribe of Zebulun is next to them, led by Eliab son of Helon. His troops number 57,400.

2.9 The total number of men assigned to Judah, troop by troop, is 186,400. They will lead the march.

2.10-11 To the south are the companies of the camp of Reuben under its flag, led by Elizur son of Shedeur. His troops number 46,500.

2.12-13 The tribe of Simeon will camp next to them, led by Shelumiel son of Zurishaddai. His troops number 59,300.

2.14-15 And the tribe of Gad is next to them, led by Eliasaph son of Deuel. His troops number 45,650.

2.16 The total number of men assigned to Reuben, troop by troop, is 151,450. They are second in the order of the march.

2.17 The Tent of Meeting with the camp of the Levites takes its place in the middle of the march. Each tribe will march in the same order in which they camped, each under its own flag.

2.18-19 To the west are the companies of the camp of Ephraim under its flag, led by Elishama son of Ammihud. His troops number 40,500.

2.20-21 The tribe of Manasseh will set up camp next to them, led by Gamaliel son of Pedahzur. His troops number 32,200.

2.22-23 And next to him is the camp of Benjamin, led by Abidan son of Gideoni. His troops number 35,400.

NEW INTERNATIONAL VERSION

²⁴All the men assigned to the camp of Ephraim, according to their divisions, number 108,100. They will set out third.

²⁵On the north will be the divisions of the camp of Dan, under their standard. The leader of the people of Dan is Ahiezer son of Ammishaddai. ²⁶His division numbers 62,700.

²⁷The tribe of Asher will camp next to them. The leader of the people of Asher is Pagiel son of Ocran. ²⁸His division numbers 41,500.

²⁹The tribe of Naphtali will be next. The leader of the people of Naphtali is Ahira son of Enan. ³⁰His division numbers 53,400.

³¹All the men assigned to the camp of Dan number 157,600. They will set out last, under their standards.

³²These are the Israelites, counted according to their families. All those in the camps, by their divisions, number 603,550. ³³The Levites, however, were not counted along with the other Israelites, as the LORD commanded Moses.

³⁴So the Israelites did everything the LORD commanded Moses; that is the way they encamped under their standards, and that is the way they set out, each with his clan and family.

THE LEVITES

3 This is the account of the family of Aaron and Moses at the time the LORD talked with Moses on Mount Sinai.

²The names of the sons of Aaron were Nadab the firstborn and Abihu, Eleazar and Ithamar. ³Those were the names of Aaron's sons, the anointed priests, who were ordained to serve as priests. ⁴Nadab and Abihu, however, fell dead before the LORD when they made an offering with unauthorized fire before him in the Desert of Sinai. They had no sons; so only Eleazar and Ithamar served as priests during the lifetime of their father Aaron.

⁵The LORD said to Moses, ⁶"Bring the tribe of Levi and present them to Aaron the priest to assist him. ⁷They are to perform duties for him and for the whole community at the Tent of Meeting by doing the work of the tabernacle. ⁸They are to take care of all the furnishings of the Tent of Meeting, fulfilling the obligations of the Israelites by doing the work of the tabernacle. ⁹Give the Levites to Aaron and his sons; they are the Israelites who are to be given wholly to

THE MESSAGE

2.24 The total number of men assigned to the camp of Ephraim, troop by troop, is 108,100. They are third in the order of the march.

2.25-26 To the north are the companies of the camp of Dan under its flag, led by Ahiezer son of Ammishaddai. His troops number 62,700.

2.27-28 The tribe of Asher will camp next to them, led by Pagiel son of Ocran. His troops number 41,500.

2.29-30 And next to them is the tribe of Naphtali, led by Ahira son of Enan. His troops number 53,400.

2.31 The total number of men assigned to the camp of Dan number 157,600. They will set out, under their flags, last in the line of the march.

2.32-33 These are the People of Israel, counted according to their ancestral families. The total number in the camps, counted troop by troop, comes to 603,550. Following GOD's command to Moses, the Levites were not counted in with the rest of Israel.

2.34 The People of Israel did everything the way GOD commanded Moses: They camped under their respective flags; they marched by tribe with their ancestral families.

THE LEVITES

3 This is the family tree of Aaron and Moses at the time GOD spoke with Moses on Mount Sinai.

3.1

3.2-4 The names of the sons of Aaron: Nadab the firstborn, Abihu, Eleazar, and Ithamar—anointed priests ordained to serve as priests. But Nadab and Abihu fell dead in the presence of GOD when they offered unauthorized sacrifice to him in the Wilderness of Sinai. They left no sons, and so only Eleazar and Ithamar served as priests during the lifetime of their father, Aaron.

3.5-10 GOD spoke to Moses. He said, "Bring forward the tribe of Levi and present them to Aaron so they can help him. They shall work for him and the whole congregation at the Tent of Meeting by doing the work of The Dwelling. Their job is to be responsible for all the furnishings of The Dwelling, ministering to the affairs of The Dwelling as the People of Israel come to perform their duties. Turn the Levites over to Aaron and his sons; they are the ones assigned to work full time for him. Appoint

NEW INTERNATIONAL VERSION

him.ᵃ ¹⁰Appoint Aaron and his sons to serve as priests; anyone else who approaches the sanctuary must be put to death."

¹¹The LORD also said to Moses, ¹²"I have taken the Levites from among the Israelites in place of the first male offspring of every Israelite woman. The Levites are mine, ¹³for all the firstborn are mine. When I struck down all the firstborn in Egypt, I set apart for myself every firstborn in Israel, whether man or animal. They are to be mine. I am the LORD."

¹⁴The LORD said to Moses in the Desert of Sinai, ¹⁵"Count the Levites by their families and clans. Count every male a month old or more." ¹⁶So Moses counted them, as he was commanded by the word of the LORD.

¹⁷These were the names of the sons of Levi:
Gershon, Kohath and Merari.
¹⁸These were the names of the Gershonite clans:
Libni and Shimei.
¹⁹The Kohathite clans:
Amram, Izhar, Hebron and Uzziel.
²⁰The Merarite clans:
Mahli and Mushi.
These were the Levite clans, according to their families.

²¹To Gershon belonged the clans of the Libnites and Shimeites; these were the Gershonite clans. ²²The number of all the males a month old or more who were counted was 7,500. ²³The Gershonite clans were to camp on the west, behind the tabernacle. ²⁴The leader of the families of the Gershonites was Eliasaph son of Lael. ²⁵At the Tent of Meeting the Gershonites were responsible for the care of the tabernacle and tent, its coverings, the curtain at the entrance to the Tent of Meeting, ²⁶the curtains of the courtyard, the curtain at the entrance to the courtyard surrounding the tabernacle and altar, and the ropes—and everything related to their use.

²⁷To Kohath belonged the clans of the Amramites, Izharites, Hebronites and Uzzielites; these were the Kohathite clans. ²⁸The number of all the males a month old or more was 8,600.ᵇ The Kohathites were responsible for the care of the sanctuary. ²⁹The Kohathite clans were to camp on the south side of the tabernacle. ³⁰The leader of the families of the Kohathite clans was Elizaphan son of Uzziel. ³¹They were responsible for the care of the ark, the table, the lampstand,

THE MESSAGE

Aaron and his sons to minister as priests; anyone else who tries to elbow his way in will be put to death."

3.11-13 GOD spoke to Moses: "I have taken the Levites from among the People of Israel as a stand-in for every Israelite mother's firstborn son. The Levites belong to me. All the firstborn are mine—when I killed all the firstborn in Egypt, I consecrated for my own use every firstborn in Israel, whether human or animal. They belong to me. I am GOD."

3.14-16 GOD spoke to Moses in the Wilderness of Sinai: "Count the Levites by their ancestral families and clans. Count every male a month old and older." Moses counted them just as he was instructed by the mouth of GOD.

3.17 These are the names of the sons of Levi: Gershon, Kohath, and Merari.

3.18 These are the names of the Gershonite clans: Libni and Shimei.

3.19 The sons of Kohath by clan: Amram, Izhar, Hebron, and Uzziel.

3.20 The sons of Merari by clan: Mahli and Mushi.

These are the clans of Levi, family by family.

3.21-26 Gershon was ancestor to the clans of the Libnites and Shimeites, known as the Gershonite clans. All the males who were one month and older numbered 7,500. The Gershonite clans camped on the west, behind The Dwelling, led by Eliasaph son of Lael. At the Tent of Meeting the Gershonites were in charge of maintaining The Dwelling and its tent, its coverings, the screen at the entrance to the Tent of Meeting, the hangings of the Courtyard, the screen at the entrance to the Courtyard that surrounded The Dwelling and Altar, and the cords—in short, everything having to do with these things.

3.27-32 Kohath was ancestor to the clans of the Amramites, Izharites, Hebronites, and Uzzielites. These were known as the Kohathite clans. All the males who were one month and older numbered 8,600. The Kohathites were in charge of the Sanctuary. The Kohathite clans camped on the south side of The Dwelling, led by Elizaphan son of Uzziel. They were in charge of caring for the Chest, the Table, the Lampstand,

---

ᵃ 9 Most manuscripts of the Masoretic Text; some manuscripts of the Masoretic Text, Samaritan Pentateuch and Septuagint (see also Num. 8:16) to me   ᵇ 28 Hebrew; some Septuagint manuscripts 8,300

the altars, the articles of the sanctuary used in ministering, the curtain, and everything related to their use. ³²The chief leader of the Levites was Eleazar son of Aaron, the priest. He was appointed over those who were responsible for the care of the sanctuary.

³³To Merari belonged the clans of the Mahlites and the Mushites; these were the Merarite clans. ³⁴The number of all the males a month old or more who were counted was 6,200. ³⁵The leader of the families of the Merarite clans was Zuriel son of Abihail; they were to camp on the north side of the tabernacle. ³⁶The Merarites were appointed to take care of the frames of the tabernacle, its crossbars, posts, bases, all its equipment, and everything related to their use, ³⁷as well as the posts of the surrounding courtyard with their bases, tent pegs and ropes.

³⁸Moses and Aaron and his sons were to camp to the east of the tabernacle, toward the sunrise, in front of the Tent of Meeting. They were responsible for the care of the sanctuary on behalf of the Israelites. Anyone else who approached the sanctuary was to be put to death.

³⁹The total number of Levites counted at the Lord's command by Moses and Aaron according to their clans, including every male a month old or more, was 22,000.

⁴⁰The Lord said to Moses, "Count all the firstborn Israelite males who are a month old or more and make a list of their names. ⁴¹Take the Levites for me in place of all the firstborn of the Israelites, and the livestock of the Levites in place of all the firstborn of the livestock of the Israelites. I am the Lord."

⁴²So Moses counted all the firstborn of the Israelites, as the Lord commanded him. ⁴³The total number of firstborn males a month old or more, listed by name, was 22,273.

⁴⁴The Lord also said to Moses, ⁴⁵"Take the Levites in place of all the firstborn of Israel, and the livestock of the Levites in place of their livestock. The Levites are to be mine. I am the Lord. ⁴⁶To redeem the 273 firstborn Israelites who exceed the number of the Levites, ⁴⁷collect five shekels^a for each one, according to the sanctuary shekel, which weighs twenty gerahs. ⁴⁸Give the money for the redemption of the additional Israelites to Aaron and his sons."

⁴⁹So Moses collected the redemption money from those who exceeded the number redeemed by the Levites. ⁵⁰From the firstborn of the Isra-

the Altars, the articles of the Sanctuary used in worship, and the screen—everything having to do with these things. Eleazar, the son of Aaron the priest, supervised the leaders of the Levites and those in charge of the Sanctuary.

^{3.33-37} Merari was ancestor to the clans of the Mahlites and the Mushites, known as the Merarite clans. The males who were one month and older numbered 6,200. They were led by Zuriel son of Abihail and camped on the north side of The Dwelling. The Merarites were in charge of the frames of The Dwelling, its crossbars, posts, bases, and all its equipment—everything having to do with these things, as well as the posts of the surrounding Courtyard with their bases, tent pegs, and cords.

^{3.38} Moses and Aaron and his sons camped to the east of The Dwelling, toward the rising sun, in front of the Tent of Meeting. They were in charge of maintaining the Sanctuary for the People of Israel and the rituals of worship. Anyone else who tried to perform these duties was to be put to death.

^{3.39} The sum total of Levites counted at God's command by Moses and Aaron, clan by clan, all the males one month and older, numbered 22,000.

^{3.40-41} God spoke to Moses: "Count all the firstborn males of the People of Israel who are one month and older. List their names. Then set apart for me the Levites—remember, I am God—in place of all the firstborn among the People of Israel, also the livestock of the Levites in place of their livestock. I am God."

^{3.42-43} So, just as God commanded him, Moses counted all the firstborn of the People of Israel. The total of firstborn males one month and older, listed by name, numbered 22,273.

^{3.44-48} Again God spoke to Moses. He said, "Take the Levites in place of all the firstborn of Israel and the livestock of the Levites in place of their livestock. The Levites are mine, I am God. Redeem the 273 firstborn Israelites who exceed the number of Levites by collecting five shekels for each one, using the Sanctuary shekel (the shekel weighing twenty gerahs). Give that money to Aaron and his sons for the redemption of the excess number of Israelites."

^{3.49-51} So Moses collected the redemption money from those who exceeded the number redeemed by the Levites. From the 273 firstborn

NEW INTERNATIONAL VERSION

elites he collected silver weighing 1,365 shek-els,[a] according to the sanctuary shekel. [51]Moses gave the redemption money to Aaron and his sons, as he was commanded by the word of the LORD.

THE KOHATHITES

4 The LORD said to Moses and Aaron: [2]"Take a census of the Kohathite branch of the Levites by their clans and families. [3]Count all the men from thirty to fifty years of age who come to serve in the work in the Tent of Meeting.

[4]"This is the work of the Kohathites in the Tent of Meeting: the care of the most holy things. [5]When the camp is to move, Aaron and his sons are to go in and take down the shielding curtain and cover the ark of the Testimony with it. [6]Then they are to cover this with hides of sea cows,[b] spread a cloth of solid blue over that and put the poles in place.

[7]"Over the table of the Presence they are to spread a blue cloth and put on it the plates, dishes and bowls, and the jars for drink offerings; the bread that is continually there is to remain on it. [8]Over these they are to spread a scarlet cloth, cover that with hides of sea cows and put its poles in place.

[9]"They are to take a blue cloth and cover the lampstand that is for light, together with its lamps, its wick trimmers and trays, and all its jars for the oil used to supply it. [10]Then they are to wrap it and all its accessories in a covering of hides of sea cows and put it on a carrying frame.

[11]"Over the gold altar they are to spread a blue cloth and cover that with hides of sea cows and put its poles in place.

[12]"They are to take all the articles used for ministering in the sanctuary, wrap them in a blue cloth, cover that with hides of sea cows and put them on a carrying frame.

[13]"They are to remove the ashes from the bronze altar and spread a purple cloth over it. [14]Then they are to place on it all the utensils used for ministering at the altar, including the firepans, meat forks, shovels and sprinkling bowls. Over it they are to spread a covering of hides of sea cows and put its poles in place.

[15]"After Aaron and his sons have finished covering the holy furnishings and all the holy articles, and when the camp is ready to move, the Kohathites are to come to do the carrying. But they must not touch the holy things or they will die. The Kohathites are to carry those things that are in the Tent of Meeting.

[16]"Eleazar son of Aaron, the priest, is to have

THE MESSAGE

Israelites he collected silver weighing 1,365 shekels according to the Sanctuary shekel. Moses turned over the redemption money to Aaron and his sons, as he was commanded by the word of GOD.

DUTIES OF THE KOHATHITES

4.1-3 4 GOD spoke to Moses and Aaron. He said, "Number the Kohathite line of Levites by clan and family. Count all the men from thirty to fifty years of age, all who enter the ministry to work in the Tent of Meeting.

4.4 "This is the assigned work of the Kohathites in the Tent of Meeting: care of the most holy things.

4.5-6 "When the camp is ready to set out, Aaron and his sons are to go in and take down the covering curtain and cover the Chest of The Testimony with it. Then they are to cover this with a dolphin skin, spread a solid blue cloth on top, and insert the poles.

4.7-8 "Then they are to spread a blue cloth on the Table of the Presence and set the Table with plates, incense dishes, bowls, and jugs for drink offerings. The bread that is always there stays on the Table. They are to cover these with a scarlet cloth, and on top of that spread the dolphin skin, and insert the poles.

4.9-10 "They are to use a blue cloth to cover the light-giving Lampstand and the lamps, snuffers, trays, and the oil jars that go with it. Then they are to wrap it all in a covering of dolphin skin and place it on a carrying frame.

4.11 "They are to spread a blue cloth over the Gold Altar and cover it with dolphin skins and place it on a carrying frame.

4.12 "They are to take all the articles used in ministering in the Sanctuary, wrap them in a blue cloth, cover them with dolphin skins, and place them on a carrying frame.

4.13-14 "They are to remove the ashes from the Altar and spread a purple cloth over it. They are to place on it all the articles used in ministering at the Altar—firepans, forks, shovels, bowls; everything used at the Altar—place them on the Altar, cover it with the dolphin skins, and insert the poles.

4.15 "When Aaron and his sons have finished covering the holy furnishings and all the holy articles, and the camp is ready to set out, the Kohathites are to come and do the carrying. But they must not touch the holy things or they will die. The Kohathites are in charge of carrying all the things that are in the Tent of Meeting.

4.16 "Eleazar son of Aaron the priest, is to be in

---

[a] 50 That is, about 35 pounds (about 15.5 kilograms)
[b] 6 That is, dugongs; also in verses 8, 10, 11, 12, 14 and 25

NEW INTERNATIONAL VERSION	THE MESSAGE

NEW INTERNATIONAL VERSION

charge of the oil for the light, the fragrant incense, the regular grain offering and the anointing oil. He is to be in charge of the entire tabernacle and everything in it, including its holy furnishings and articles."

17The LORD said to Moses and Aaron, 18"See that the Kohathite tribal clans are not cut off from the Levites. 19So that they may live and not die when they come near the most holy things, do this for them: Aaron and his sons are to go into the sanctuary and assign to each man his work and what he is to carry. 20But the Kohathites must not go in to look at the holy things, even for a moment, or they will die."

THE GERSHONITES

21The LORD said to Moses, 22"Take a census also of the Gershonites by their families and clans. 23Count all the men from thirty to fifty years of age who come to serve in the work at the Tent of Meeting.

24"This is the service of the Gershonite clans as they work and carry burdens: 25They are to carry the curtains of the tabernacle, the Tent of Meeting, its covering and the outer covering of hides of sea cows, the curtains for the entrance to the Tent of Meeting, 26the curtains of the courtyard surrounding the tabernacle and altar, the curtain for the entrance, the ropes and all the equipment used in its service. The Gershonites are to do all that needs to be done with these things. 27All their service, whether carrying or doing other work, is to be done under the direction of Aaron and his sons. You shall assign to them as their responsibility all they are to carry. 28This is the service of the Gershonite clans at the Tent of Meeting. Their duties are to be under the direction of Ithamar son of Aaron, the priest.

THE MERARITES

29"Count the Merarites by their clans and families. 30Count all the men from thirty to fifty years of age who come to serve in the work at the Tent of Meeting. 31This is their duty as they perform service at the Tent of Meeting: to carry the frames of the tabernacle, its crossbars, posts and bases, 32as well as the posts of the surrounding courtyard with their bases, tent pegs, ropes, all their equipment and everything related to their use. Assign to each man the specific things he is to carry. 33This is the service of the Merarite clans as they work at the Tent of Meeting under the direction of Ithamar son of Aaron, the priest."

THE NUMBERING OF THE LEVITE CLANS

34Moses, Aaron and the leaders of the com-

THE MESSAGE

charge of the oil for the light, the fragrant incense, the regular Grain-Offering, and the anointing oil. He is to be in charge of the entire Dwelling and everything in it, including its holy furnishings and articles."

4.17-20 GOD spoke to Moses and Aaron, "Don't let the tribal families of the Kohathites be destroyed from among the Levites. Protect them so they will live and not die when they come near the most holy things. To protect them, Aaron and his sons are to precede them into the Sanctuary and assign each man his task and what he is to carry. But the Kohathites themselves must not go in to look at the holy things, not even a glance at them, or they will die."

DUTIES OF THE GERSHONITES

4.21-23 GOD spoke to Moses: "Number the Gershonites by tribes according to their ancestral families. Count all the men from thirty to fifty years of age who enter the ministry of work in the Tent of Meeting.

4.24-28 "The Gershonites by family and clan will serve by carrying heavy loads: the curtains of the Sanctuary and the Tent of Meeting; the covering of the Tent and the outer covering of dolphin skins; the screens for the entrance to the Tent; the cords; and all the equipment used in its ministries. The Gershonites have the job of doing the work connected with these things. All their work of lifting and carrying and moving is to be done under the supervision of Aaron and his sons. Assign them specifically what they are to carry. This is the work of the Gershonite clans at the Tent of Meeting. Ithamar son of Aaron the priest is to supervise their work.

DUTIES OF THE MERARITES

4.29-30 "Number the Merarites by their ancestral families. Count all the men from thirty to fifty years of age who enter the ministry of work at the Tent of Meeting.

4.31-33 "This is their assigned duty as they go to work at the Tent of Meeting: to carry the frames of The Dwelling, its crossbars, posts, and bases, as well as the posts of the surrounding Courtyard with their bases, tent pegs, cords, and all the equipment related to their use. Assign to each man exactly what he is to carry. This is the ministry of the Merarite clans as they work at the Tent of Meeting under the supervision of Ithamar son of Aaron the priest."

☩

4.34-37 Moses, Aaron, and the leaders of the congrega-

NEW INTERNATIONAL VERSION

munity counted the Kohathites by their clans and families. [35]All the men from thirty to fifty years of age who came to serve in the work in the Tent of Meeting, [36]counted by clans, were 2,750. [37]This was the total of all those in the Kohathite clans who served in the Tent of Meeting. Moses and Aaron counted them according to the LORD's command through Moses.

[38]The Gershonites were counted by their clans and families. [39]All the men from thirty to fifty years of age who came to serve in the work at the Tent of Meeting, [40]counted by their clans and families, were 2,630. [41]This was the total of those in the Gershonite clans who served at the Tent of Meeting. Moses and Aaron counted them according to the LORD's command.

[42]The Merarites were counted by their clans and families. [43]All the men from thirty to fifty years of age who came to serve in the work at the Tent of Meeting, [44]counted by their clans, were 3,200. [45]This was the total of those in the Merarite clans. Moses and Aaron counted them according to the LORD's command through Moses.

[46]So Moses, Aaron and the leaders of Israel counted all the Levites by their clans and families. [47]All the men from thirty to fifty years of age who came to do the work of serving and carrying the Tent of Meeting [48]numbered 8,580. [49]At the LORD's command through Moses, each was assigned his work and told what to carry.

Thus they were counted, as the LORD commanded Moses.

THE PURITY OF THE CAMP

5 The LORD said to Moses, [2]"Command the Israelites to send away from the camp anyone who has an infectious skin disease[a] or a discharge of any kind, or who is ceremonially unclean because of a dead body. [3]Send away male and female alike; send them outside the camp so they will not defile their camp, where I dwell among them." [4]The Israelites did this; they sent them outside the camp. They did just as the LORD had instructed Moses.

RESTITUTION FOR WRONGS

[5]The LORD said to Moses, [6]"Say to the Israelites: 'When a man or woman wrongs another in any way[b] and so is unfaithful to the LORD, that person is guilty [7]and must confess the sin he has committed. He must make full restitution for his wrong, add one fifth to it and give it all to the person he has wronged. [8]But if that person has

---

a 2 Traditionally *leprosy;* the Hebrew word was used for various diseases affecting the skin—not necessarily leprosy.
b 6 Or *woman commits any wrong common to mankind*

THE MESSAGE

tion counted the Kohathites by clan and family. All the men from thirty to fifty years of age who came to serve in the work in the Tent of Meeting, counted by clans, were 2,750. This was the total from the Kohathite clans who served in the Tent of Meeting. Moses and Aaron counted them just as GOD had commanded through Moses.

4.38-41 The Gershonites were counted by clan and family. All the men from thirty to fifty years of age who came to serve in the work in the Tent of Meeting, counted by clan and family, were 2,630. This was the total from the Gershonite clans who served in the Tent of Meeting. Moses and Aaron counted them just as GOD had commanded.

4.42-45 The Merarites were counted by clan and family. All the men from thirty to fifty years of age who came to serve in the work in the Tent of Meeting, counted by clan, were 3,200. This was the total from the Merarite clans. Moses and Aaron counted them just as GOD had commanded through Moses.

4.46-49 So Moses and Aaron and the leaders of Israel counted all the Levites by clan and family. All the men from thirty to fifty years of age who came to do the work of serving and carrying the Tent of Meeting numbered 8,580. At GOD's command through Moses, each man was assigned his work and told what to carry.

And that's the story of their numbering, as GOD commanded Moses.

SOME CAMP RULES

5.1-3 **5** GOD spoke to Moses: "Command the People of Israel to ban from the camp anyone who has an infectious skin disease, anyone who has a discharge, and anyone who is ritually unclean from contact with a dead body. Ban male and female alike; send them outside the camp so that they won't defile their camp, the place I live among them."

5.4 The People of Israel did this, banning them from the camp. They did exactly what GOD had commanded through Moses.

✠

5.5-10 GOD spoke to Moses: "Tell the People of Israel, When a man or woman commits any sin, the person has broken trust with GOD, is guilty, and must confess the sin. Full compensation plus twenty percent must be made to whoever was wronged. If the wronged person has no close

NEW INTERNATIONAL VERSION

no close relative to whom restitution can be made for the wrong, the restitution belongs to the LORD and must be given to the priest, along with the ram with which atonement is made for him. [9]All the sacred contributions the Israelites bring to a priest will belong to him. [10]Each man's sacred gifts are his own, but what he gives to the priest will belong to the priest.' "

THE TEST FOR AN UNFAITHFUL WIFE

[11]Then the LORD said to Moses, [12]"Speak to the Israelites and say to them: 'If a man's wife goes astray and is unfaithful to him [13]by sleeping with another man, and this is hidden from her husband and her impurity is undetected (since there is no witness against her and she has not been caught in the act), [14]and if feelings of jealousy come over her husband and he suspects his wife and she is impure—or if he is jealous and suspects her even though she is not impure— [15]then he is to take his wife to the priest. He must also take an offering of a tenth of an ephah[a] of barley flour on her behalf. He must not pour oil on it or put incense on it, because it is a grain offering for jealousy, a reminder offering to draw attention to guilt.

[16]" 'The priest shall bring her and have her stand before the LORD. [17]Then he shall take some holy water in a clay jar and put some dust from the tabernacle floor into the water. [18]After the priest has had the woman stand before the LORD, he shall loosen her hair and place in her hands the reminder offering, the grain offering for jealousy, while he himself holds the bitter water that brings a curse. [19]Then the priest shall put the woman under oath and say to her, "If no other man has slept with you and you have not gone astray and become impure while married to your husband, may this bitter water that brings a curse not harm you. [20]But if you have gone astray while married to your husband and you have defiled yourself by sleeping with a man other than your husband"— [21]here the priest is to put the woman under this curse of the oath— "may the LORD cause your people to curse and denounce you when he causes your thigh to waste away and your abdomen to swell.[b] [22]May this water that brings a curse enter your body so that your abdomen swells and your thigh wastes away.[c]"

" 'Then the woman is to say, "Amen. So be it."

[23]" 'The priest is to write these curses on a scroll and then wash them off into the bitter wa-

THE MESSAGE

relative who can receive the compensation, the compensation belongs to GOD and must be given to the priest, along with the ram by which atonement is made. All the sacred offerings that the People of Israel bring to a priest belong to the priest. Each person's sacred offerings are his own, but what one gives to the priest stays with the priest."

✝

5.11-15 GOD spoke to Moses: "Tell the People of Israel, Say a man's wife goes off and has an affair, is unfaithful to him by sleeping with another man, but her husband knows nothing about it even though she has defiled herself. And then, even though there was no witness and she wasn't caught in the act, feelings of jealousy come over the husband and he suspects that his wife is impure. Even if she is innocent and his jealousy and suspicions are groundless, he is to take his wife to the priest. He must also take an offering of two quarts of barley flour for her. He is to pour no oil on it or mix incense with it because it is a Grain-Offering for jealousy, a Grain-Offering for bringing the guilt out into the open.

5.16-22 "The priest then is to take her and have her stand in the presence of GOD. He is to take some holy water in a pottery jar and put some dust from the floor of The Dwelling in the water. After the priest has her stand in the presence of GOD he is to uncover her hair and place the exposure-offering in her hands, the Grain-Offering for jealousy, while he holds the bitter water that delivers a curse. Then the priest will put the woman under oath and say, 'If no man has slept with you and you have not had an adulterous affair and become impure while married to your husband, may this bitter water that delivers a curse not harm you. But if you have had an affair while married to your husband and have defiled yourself by sleeping with a man other than your husband'—here the priest puts the woman under this curse—'may GOD cause your people to curse and revile you when he makes your womb shrivel and your belly swell. Let this water that delivers a curse enter your body so that your belly swells and your womb shrivels.'

"Then the woman shall say, 'Amen. Amen.'

5.23-28 "The priest is to write these curses on a scroll and then wash the words off into the bit-

---

[a] 15 That is, probably about 2 quarts (about 2 liters)
[b] 21 Or causes you to have a miscarrying womb and barrenness   [c] 22 Or body and cause you to be barren and have a miscarrying womb

NEW INTERNATIONAL VERSION

ter. [24]He shall have the woman drink the bitter water that brings a curse, and this water will enter her and cause bitter suffering. [25]The priest is to take from her hands the grain offering for jealousy, wave it before the LORD and bring it to the altar. [26]The priest is then to take a handful of the grain offering as a memorial offering and burn it on the altar; after that, he is to have the woman drink the water. [27]If she has defiled herself and been unfaithful to her husband, then when she is made to drink the water that brings a curse, it will go into her and cause bitter suffering; her abdomen will swell and her thigh waste away,[a] and she will become accursed among her people. [28]If, however, the woman has not defiled herself and is free from impurity, she will be cleared of guilt and will be able to have children.

[29]" 'This, then, is the law of jealousy when a woman goes astray and defiles herself while married to her husband, [30]or when feelings of jealousy come over a man because he suspects his wife. The priest is to have her stand before the LORD and is to apply this entire law to her. [31]The husband will be innocent of any wrongdoing, but the woman will bear the consequences of her sin.' "

THE NAZIRITE

6 The LORD said to Moses, [2]"Speak to the Israelites and say to them: 'If a man or woman wants to make a special vow, a vow of separation to the LORD as a Nazirite, [3]he must abstain from wine and other fermented drink and must not drink vinegar made from wine or from other fermented drink. He must not drink grape juice or eat grapes or raisins. [4]As long as he is a Nazirite, he must not eat anything that comes from the grapevine, not even the seeds or skins.

[5]" 'During the entire period of his vow of separation no razor may be used on his head. He must be holy until the period of his separation to the LORD is over; he must let the hair of his head grow long. [6]Throughout the period of his separation to the LORD he must not go near a dead body. [7]Even if his own father or mother or brother or sister dies, he must not make himself ceremonially unclean on account of them, because the symbol of his separation to God is on his head. [8]Throughout the period of his separation he is consecrated to the LORD.

[9]" 'If someone dies suddenly in his presence, thus defiling the hair he has dedicated, he must shave his head on the day of his cleansing—the seventh day. [10]Then on the eighth day he must bring two doves or two young pigeons to the

[a] 27 Or suffering; she will have barrenness and a miscarrying womb

THE MESSAGE

ter water. He then is to give the woman the bitter water that delivers a curse. This water will enter her body and cause acute pain. The priest then is to take from her hands a handful of the Grain-Offering for jealousy, wave it before GOD, and bring it to the Altar. The priest then is to take a handful of the Grain-Offering, using it as an exposure-offering, and burn it on the Altar; after this he is to make her drink the water. If she has defiled herself in being unfaithful to her husband, when she drinks the water that delivers a curse, it will enter her body and cause acute pain; her belly will swell and her womb shrivel. She will be cursed among her people. But if she has not defiled herself and is innocent of impurity, her name will be cleared and she will be able to have children.

5.29-31 "This is the law of jealousy in a case where a woman goes off and has an affair and defiles herself while married to her husband, or a husband is tormented with feelings of jealousy because he suspects his wife. The priest is to have her stand in the presence of GOD and go through this entire procedure with her. The husband will be cleared of wrong, but the woman will pay for her wrong."

NAZIRITE VOWS

6.1-4 **6** GOD spoke to Moses: "Speak to the People of Israel; tell them, If any of you, man or woman, wants to make a special Nazirite vow, consecrating yourself totally to GOD, you must not drink any wine or beer, no intoxicating drink of any kind, not even the juice of grapes—in fact, you must not even eat grapes or raisins. For the duration of the consecration, nothing from the grapevine—not even the seeds, not even the skin—may be eaten.

6.5 "Also, for the duration of the consecration you must not have your hair cut. Your long hair will be a continuing sign of holy separation to GOD.

6.6-7 "Also, for the duration of the consecration to GOD, you must not go near a corpse. Even if it's the body of your father or mother, brother or sister, you must not ritually defile yourself because the sign of consecration to God is on your head.

6.8 "For the entire duration of your consecration you are holy to GOD.

6.9-12 "If someone should die suddenly in your presence, so that your consecrated head is ritually defiled, you must shave your head on the day of your purifying, that is, the seventh day. Then on the eighth day bring two doves or two

NEW INTERNATIONAL VERSION

priest at the entrance to the Tent of Meeting.
¹¹The priest is to offer one as a sin offering and
the other as a burnt offering to make atonement
for him because he sinned by being in the presence of the dead body. That same day he is to
consecrate his head. ¹²He must dedicate himself
to the LORD for the period of his separation and
must bring a year-old male lamb as a guilt offering. The previous days do not count, because he
became defiled during his separation.

¹³" 'Now this is the law for the Nazirite when
the period of his separation is over. He is to be
brought to the entrance to the Tent of Meeting.
¹⁴There he is to present his offerings to the LORD:
a year-old male lamb without defect for a burnt
offering, a year-old ewe lamb without defect for a
sin offering, a ram without defect for a fellowship offering,ᵃ ¹⁵together with their grain offerings and drink offerings, and a basket of bread
made without yeast—cakes made of fine flour
mixed with oil, and wafers spread with oil.

¹⁶" 'The priest is to present them before the
LORD and make the sin offering and the burnt offering. ¹⁷He is to present the basket of unleavened bread and is to sacrifice the ram as a fellowship offering to the LORD, together with its grain
offering and drink offering.

¹⁸" 'Then at the entrance to the Tent of Meeting, the Nazirite must shave off the hair that he
dedicated. He is to take the hair and put it in
the fire that is under the sacrifice of the fellowship offering.

¹⁹" 'After the Nazirite has shaved off the hair
of his dedication, the priest is to place in his
hands a boiled shoulder of the ram, and a cake
and a wafer from the basket, both made without
yeast. ²⁰The priest shall then wave them before
the LORD as a wave offering; they are holy and
belong to the priest, together with the breast that
was waved and the thigh that was presented. After that, the Nazirite may drink wine.

²¹" 'This is the law of the Nazirite who vows
his offering to the LORD in accordance with his
separation, in addition to whatever else he can
afford. He must fulfill the vow he has made, according to the law of the Nazirite.' "

THE PRIESTLY BLESSING

²²The LORD said to Moses, ²³"Tell Aaron and
his sons, 'This is how you are to bless the Israelites. Say to them:

²⁴" ' "The LORD bless you
    and keep you;
²⁵the LORD make his face shine upon you
    and be gracious to you;

THE MESSAGE

pigeons to the priest at the entrance to the Tent
of Meeting. The priest will offer one for the
Absolution-Offering and one for the Whole-
Burnt-Offering, purifying you from the ritual
contamination of the corpse. You resanctify
your hair on that day and reconsecrate your
Nazirite consecration to GOD by bringing a
yearling lamb for a Compensation-Offering.
You start over; the previous days don't count
because your consecration was ritually defiled.

6.13-17   "These are the instructions for the time
when your special consecration to GOD is up.
First, you are to be brought to the entrance to
the Tent of Meeting. Then you will present
your offerings to GOD: a healthy yearling lamb
for the Whole-Burnt-Offering, a healthy yearling ewe for an Absolution-Offering, a healthy
ram for a Peace-Offering, a basket of unraised
bread made of fine flour, loaves mixed with
oil, and crackers spread with oil, along with
your Grain-Offerings and Drink-Offerings. The
priest will approach GOD and offer up your Absolution-Offering and Whole-Burnt-Offering.
He will sacrifice the ram as a Peace-Offering to
GOD with the basket of unraised bread, and,
last of all, the Grain-Offering and Drink-Offering.

6.18   "At the entrance to the Tent of Meeting,
shave off the hair you consecrated and put it in
the fire that is burning under the Peace-Offering.

6.19-20   "After you have shaved the hair of your consecration, the priest will take a shoulder from
the ram, boiled, and a piece of unraised bread
and a cracker from the basket and place them
in your hands. The priest will then wave them
before GOD, a Wave-Offering. They are holy
and belong to the priest, along with the breast
that was waved and the thigh that was offered.

"Now you are free to drink wine.

6.21   "These are the instructions for Nazirites as
they bring offerings to GOD in their vow of consecration, beyond their other offerings. They
must carry out the vow they have vowed following the instructions for the Nazirite."

THE AARONIC BLESSING

6.22-23   GOD spoke to Moses: "Tell Aaron and his sons,
This is how you are to bless the People of Israel. Say to them,

6.24   GOD bless you and keep you,
6.25   GOD smile on you and gift you,

ᵃ 14 Traditionally *peace offering*; also in verses 17 and 18

NEW INTERNATIONAL VERSION

²⁶the LORD turn his face toward you
and give you peace.” ’

²⁷“So they will put my name on the Israelites,
and I will bless them.”

OFFERINGS AT THE DEDICATION
OF THE TABERNACLE

7 When Moses finished setting up the tabernacle, he anointed it and consecrated it and all its furnishings. He also anointed and consecrated the altar and all its utensils. ²Then the leaders of Israel, the heads of families who were the tribal leaders in charge of those who were counted, made offerings. ³They brought as their gifts before the LORD six covered carts and twelve oxen—an ox from each leader and a cart from every two. These they presented before the tabernacle.

⁴The LORD said to Moses, ⁵“Accept these from them, that they may be used in the work at the Tent of Meeting. Give them to the Levites as each man's work requires.”

⁶So Moses took the carts and oxen and gave them to the Levites. ⁷He gave two carts and four oxen to the Gershonites, as their work required, ⁸and he gave four carts and eight oxen to the Merarites, as their work required. They were all under the direction of Ithamar son of Aaron, the priest. ⁹But Moses did not give any to the Kohathites, because they were to carry on their shoulders the holy things, for which they were responsible.

¹⁰When the altar was anointed, the leaders brought their offerings for its dedication and presented them before the altar. ¹¹For the LORD had said to Moses, “Each day one leader is to bring his offering for the dedication of the altar.”

¹²The one who brought his offering on the first day was Nahshon son of Amminadab of the tribe of Judah.

¹³His offering was one silver plate weighing a hundred and thirty shekels,^a and one silver sprinkling bowl weighing seventy shekels,^b both according to the sanctuary shekel, each filled with fine flour mixed with oil as a grain offering; ¹⁴one gold dish weighing ten shekels,^c filled with incense; ¹⁵one young bull, one ram and one male lamb a year old, for a burnt offering; ¹⁶one male goat for a sin offering; ¹⁷and two oxen, five rams, five male goats and five male

^a 13 That is, about 3 1/4 pounds (about 1.5 kilograms); also elsewhere in this chapter   ^b 13 That is, about 1 3/4 pounds (about 0.8 kilogram); also elsewhere in this chapter   ^c 14 That is, about 4 ounces (about 110 grams); also elsewhere in this chapter

THE MESSAGE

6.26 GOD look you full in the face
and make you prosper.

6.27 In so doing, they will place my name on the People of Israel—
I will confirm it by blessing them.”

OFFERINGS FOR THE DEDICATION

7.1 **7** When Moses finished setting up The Dwelling, he anointed it and consecrated it along with all that went with it. At the same time he anointed and consecrated the Altar and its accessories.

7.2-3 The leaders of Israel, the heads of the ancestral tribes who had carried out the census, brought offerings. They presented before GOD six covered wagons and twelve oxen, a wagon from each pair of leaders and an ox from each leader.

7.4-5 GOD spoke to Moses: “Receive these so that they can be used to transport the Tent of Meeting. Give them to the Levites according to what they need for their work.”

7.6-9 Moses took the wagons and oxen and gave them to the Levites. He gave two wagons and four oxen to the Gershonites for their work and four wagons and eight oxen to the Merarites for their work. They were all under the direction of Ithamar son of Aaron the priest. Moses didn't give any to the Kohathites because they had to carry the holy things for which they were responsible on their shoulders.

7.10-11 When the Altar was anointed, the leaders brought their offerings for its dedication and presented them before the Altar because GOD had instructed Moses, “Each day one leader is to present his offering for the dedication of the Altar.”

7.12-13 On the first day, Nahshon son of Amminadab, of the tribe of Judah, brought his offering. His offering was:
a silver plate weighing three and a quarter pounds and a silver bowl weighing one and three-quarter pounds (according to the standard Sanctuary weights), each filled with fine flour mixed with oil as a Grain-Offering;

7.14 a gold vessel weighing four ounces, filled with incense;

7.15 a young bull, a ram, and a yearling lamb for a Whole-Burnt-Offering;

7.16 a he-goat for an Absolution-Offering;
two oxen, five rams, five he-goats, and five

NEW INTERNATIONAL VERSION

lambs a year old, to be sacrificed as a fellowship offering.[a] This was the offering of Nahshon son of Amminadab.

[18]On the second day Nethanel son of Zuar, the leader of Issachar, brought his offering. [19]The offering he brought was one silver plate weighing a hundred and thirty shekels, and one silver sprinkling bowl weighing seventy shekels, both according to the sanctuary shekel, each filled with fine flour mixed with oil as a grain offering; [20]one gold dish weighing ten shekels, filled with incense; [21]one young bull, one ram and one male lamb a year old, for a burnt offering; [22]one male goat for a sin offering; [23]and two oxen, five rams, five male goats and five male lambs a year old, to be sacrificed as a fellowship offering. This was the offering of Nethanel son of Zuar.

[24]On the third day, Eliab son of Helon, the leader of the people of Zebulun, brought his offering. [25]His offering was one silver plate weighing a hundred and thirty shekels, and one silver sprinkling bowl weighing seventy shekels, both according to the sanctuary shekel, each filled with fine flour mixed with oil as a grain offering; [26]one gold dish weighing ten shekels, filled with incense; [27]one young bull, one ram and one male lamb a year old, for a burnt offering; [28]one male goat for a sin offering; [29]and two oxen, five rams, five male goats and five male lambs a year old, to be sacrificed as a fellowship offering. This was the offering of Eliab son of Helon.

[30]On the fourth day Elizur son of Shedeur, the leader of the people of Reuben, brought his offering. [31]His offering was one silver plate weighing a hundred and thirty shekels, and one silver sprinkling bowl weighing seventy shekels, both according to the sanctuary shekel, each filled with fine flour mixed with oil as a grain offering; [32]one gold dish weighing ten shekels, filled with incense; [33]one young bull, one ram and one male lamb a year old, for a burnt offering; [34]one male goat for a sin offering; [35]and two oxen, five rams, five male goats and five male lambs a year old, to be sacrificed as a fellowship offering. This was the offering of Elizur son of Shedeur.

a 17 Traditionally *peace offering*; also elsewhere in this chapter

THE MESSAGE

yearling lambs to be sacrificed as a Peace-Offering.

7.17 This was the offering of Nahshon son of Amminadab.

7.18-22 On the second day, Nethanel son of Zuar, the leader of Issachar, brought his offering. His offering was:

a silver plate weighing three and a quarter pounds and a silver bowl weighing one and three-quarter pounds (according to the standard Sanctuary weights), each filled with fine flour mixed with oil as a Grain-Offering;

a gold vessel weighing four ounces, filled with incense;

a young bull, a ram, and a yearling lamb for a Whole-Burnt-Offering;

a he-goat for an Absolution-Offering;

two oxen, five rams, five he-goats, and five yearling lambs to be sacrificed as a Peace-Offering.

This was the offering of Nethanel son of Zuar.

7.24-29 On the third day, Eliab son of Helon, the leader of the people of Zebulun, brought his offering. His offering was:

a silver plate weighing three and a quarter pounds and a silver bowl weighing one and three-quarter pounds (according to the standard Sanctuary weights), each filled with fine flour mixed with oil as a Grain-Offering;

a gold vessel weighing four ounces, filled with incense;

a young bull, a ram, and a yearling lamb for a Whole-Burnt-Offering;

a he-goat for an Absolution-Offering;

two oxen, five rams, five he-goats, and five yearling lambs to be sacrificed as a Peace-Offering.

This was the offering of Eliab son of Helon.

7.30-35 On the fourth day, Elizur son of Shedeur, the leader of the people of Reuben, brought his offering. His offering was:

a silver plate weighing three and a quarter pounds and a silver bowl weighing one and three-quarter pounds (according to the standard Sanctuary weights), each filled with fine flour mixed with oil as a Grain-Offering;

a gold vessel weighing four ounces, filled with incense;

a young bull, a ram, and a yearling lamb for a Whole-Burnt-Offering;

a he-goat for an Absolution-Offering;

two oxen, five rams, five he-goats, and five yearling lambs to be sacrificed as a Peace-Offering.

This was the offering of Elizur son of Shedeur.

NEW INTERNATIONAL VERSION

³⁶On the fifth day Shelumiel son of Zurishaddai, the leader of the people of Simeon, brought his offering. ³⁷His offering was one silver plate weighing a hundred and thirty shekels, and one silver sprinkling bowl weighing seventy shekels, both according to the sanctuary shekel, each filled with fine flour mixed with oil as a grain offering; ³⁸one gold dish weighing ten shekels, filled with incense; ³⁹one young bull, one ram and one male lamb a year old, for a burnt offering; ⁴⁰one male goat for a sin offering; ⁴¹and two oxen, five rams, five male goats and five male lambs a year old, to be sacrificed as a fellowship offering. This was the offering of Shelumiel son of Zurishaddai.

⁴²On the sixth day Eliasaph son of Deuel, the leader of the people of Gad, brought his offering. ⁴³His offering was one silver plate weighing a hundred and thirty shekels, and one silver sprinkling bowl weighing seventy shekels, both according to the sanctuary shekel, each filled with fine flour mixed with oil as a grain offering; ⁴⁴one gold dish weighing ten shekels, filled with incense; ⁴⁵one young bull, one ram and one male lamb a year old, for a burnt offering; ⁴⁶one male goat for a sin offering; ⁴⁷and two oxen, five rams, five male goats and five male lambs a year old, to be sacrificed as a fellowship offering. This was the offering of Eliasaph son of Deuel.

⁴⁸On the seventh day Elishama son of Ammihud, the leader of the people of Ephraim, brought his offering. ⁴⁹His offering was one silver plate weighing a hundred and thirty shekels, and one silver sprinkling bowl weighing seventy shekels, both according to the sanctuary shekel, each filled with fine flour mixed with oil as a grain offering; ⁵⁰one gold dish weighing ten shekels, filled with incense; ⁵¹one young bull, one ram and one male lamb a year old, for a burnt offering; ⁵²one male goat for a sin offering; ⁵³and two oxen, five rams, five male goats and five male lambs a year old, to be sacrificed as a fellowship offering. This was the offering of Elishama son of Ammihud.

⁵⁴On the eighth day Gamaliel son of Pedahzur, the leader of the people of Manasseh, brought his offering.

THE MESSAGE

7.36-41 On the fifth day, Shelumiel son of Zurishaddai, the leader of the people of Simeon, brought his offering. His offering was:
   a silver plate weighing three and a quarter pounds and a silver bowl weighing one and three-quarter pounds (according to the standard Sanctuary weights), each filled with fine flour mixed with oil as a Grain-Offering;
   a gold vessel weighing four ounces, filled with incense;
   a young bull, a ram, and a yearling lamb for a Whole-Burnt-Offering;
   a he-goat for an Absolution-Offering;
   two oxen, five rams, five he-goats, and five yearling lambs to be sacrificed as a Peace-Offering.
   This was the offering of Shelumiel son of Zurishaddai.

7.42-47 On the sixth day, Eliasaph son of Deuel, the leader of the people of Gad, brought his offering. His offering was:
   a silver plate weighing three and a quarter pounds and a silver bowl weighing one and three-quarter pounds (according to the standard Sanctuary weights), each filled with fine flour mixed with oil as a Grain-Offering;
   a gold vessel weighing four ounces, filled with incense;
   a young bull, a ram, and a yearling lamb for a Whole-Burnt-Offering;
   a he-goat for an Absolution-Offering;
   two oxen, five rams, five he-goats, and five yearling lambs to be sacrificed as a Peace-Offering.
   This was the offering of Eliasaph son of Deuel.

7.48-53 On the seventh day, Elishama son of Ammihud, the leader of the people of Ephraim, brought his offering. His offering was:
   a silver plate weighing three and a quarter pounds and a silver bowl weighing one and three-quarter pounds (according to the standard Sanctuary weights), each filled with fine flour mixed with oil as a Grain-Offering;
   a gold vessel weighing four ounces, filled with incense;
   a young bull, a ram, and a yearling lamb for a Whole-Burnt-Offering;
   a he-goat for an Absolution-Offering;
   two oxen, five rams, five he-goats, and five yearling lambs to be sacrificed as a Peace-Offering.
   This was the offering of Elishama son of Ammihud.

7.54-59 On the eighth day, Gamaliel son of Pedahzur, the leader of the people of Manasseh, brought his offering. His offering was:

NEW INTERNATIONAL VERSION

⁵⁵His offering was one silver plate weighing a hundred and thirty shekels, and one silver sprinkling bowl weighing seventy shekels, both according to the sanctuary shekel, each filled with fine flour mixed with oil as a grain offering; ⁵⁶one gold dish weighing ten shekels, filled with incense; ⁵⁷one young bull, one ram and one male lamb a year old, for a burnt offering; ⁵⁸one male goat for a sin offering; ⁵⁹and two oxen, five rams, five male goats and five male lambs a year old, to be sacrificed as a fellowship offering. This was the offering of Gamaliel son of Pedahzur.

⁶⁰On the ninth day Abidan son of Gideoni, the leader of the people of Benjamin, brought his offering.

⁶¹His offering was one silver plate weighing a hundred and thirty shekels, and one silver sprinkling bowl weighing seventy shekels, both according to the sanctuary shekel, each filled with fine flour mixed with oil as a grain offering; ⁶²one gold dish weighing ten shekels, filled with incense; ⁶³one young bull, one ram and one male lamb a year old, for a burnt offering; ⁶⁴one male goat for a sin offering; ⁶⁵and two oxen, five rams, five male goats and five male lambs a year old, to be sacrificed as a fellowship offering. This was the offering of Abidan son of Gideoni.

⁶⁶On the tenth day Ahiezer son of Ammishaddai, the leader of the people of Dan, brought his offering.

⁶⁷His offering was one silver plate weighing a hundred and thirty shekels, and one silver sprinkling bowl weighing seventy shekels, both according to the sanctuary shekel, each filled with fine flour mixed with oil as a grain offering; ⁶⁸one gold dish weighing ten shekels, filled with incense; ⁶⁹one young bull, one ram and one male lamb a year old, for a burnt offering; ⁷⁰one male goat for a sin offering; ⁷¹and two oxen, five rams, five male goats and five male lambs a year old, to be sacrificed as a fellowship offering. This was the offering of Ahiezer son of Ammishaddai.

⁷²On the eleventh day Pagiel son of Ocran, the leader of the people of Asher, brought his offering.

⁷³His offering was one silver plate weighing a hundred and thirty shekels, and one silver sprinkling bowl weighing seventy

THE MESSAGE

a silver plate weighing three and a quarter pounds and a silver bowl weighing one and three-quarter pounds (according to the standard Sanctuary weights), each filled with fine flour mixed with oil as a Grain-Offering; a gold vessel weighing four ounces, filled with incense; a young bull, a ram, and a yearling lamb for a Whole-Burnt-Offering; a he-goat for an Absolution-Offering; two oxen, five rams, five he-goats, and five yearling lambs to be sacrificed as a Peace-Offering.

This was the offering of Gamaliel son of Pedahzur.

7.60-65   On the ninth day, Abidan son of Gideoni, the leader of the people of Benjamin, brought his offering. His offering was:

a silver plate weighing three and a quarter pounds and a silver bowl weighing one and three-quarter pounds (according to the standard Sanctuary weights), each filled with fine flour mixed with oil as a Grain-Offering; a gold vessel weighing four ounces, filled with incense; a young bull, a ram, and a yearling lamb for a Whole-Burnt-Offering; a he-goat for an Absolution-Offering; two oxen, five rams, five he-goats, and five yearling lambs to be sacrificed as a Peace-Offering.

This was the offering of Abidan son of Gideoni.

7.66-71   On the tenth day, Ahiezer son of Ammishaddai, the leader of the people of Dan, brought his offering. His offering was:

a silver plate weighing three and a quarter pounds and a silver bowl weighing one and three-quarter pounds (according to the standard Sanctuary weights), each filled with fine flour mixed with oil as a Grain-Offering; a gold vessel weighing four ounces, filled with incense; a young bull, a ram, and a yearling lamb for a Whole-Burnt-Offering; a he-goat for an Absolution-Offering; two oxen, five rams, five he-goats, and five yearling lambs to be sacrificed as a Peace-Offering.

This was the offering of Ahiezer son of Ammishaddai.

7.72-77   On the eleventh day, Pagiel son of Ocran, the leader of the people of Asher, brought his offering. His offering was:

a silver plate weighing three and a quarter pounds and a silver bowl weighing one and

NEW INTERNATIONAL VERSION	THE MESSAGE

shekels, both according to the sanctuary shekel, each filled with fine flour mixed with oil as a grain offering; ⁷⁴one gold dish weighing ten shekels, filled with incense; ⁷⁵one young bull, one ram and one male lamb a year old, for a burnt offering; ⁷⁶one male goat for a sin offering; ⁷⁷and two oxen, five rams, five male goats and five male lambs a year old, to be sacrificed as a fellowship offering. This was the offering of Pagiel son of Ocran.

⁷⁸On the twelfth day Ahira son of Enan, the leader of the people of Naphtali, brought his offering.

⁷⁹His offering was one silver plate weighing a hundred and thirty shekels, and one silver sprinkling bowl weighing seventy shekels, both according to the sanctuary shekel, each filled with fine flour mixed with oil as a grain offering; ⁸⁰one gold dish weighing ten shekels, filled with incense; ⁸¹one young bull, one ram and one male lamb a year old, for a burnt offering; ⁸²one male goat for a sin offering; ⁸³and two oxen, five rams, five male goats and five male lambs a year old, to be sacrificed as a fellowship offering. This was the offering of Ahira son of Enan.

⁸⁴These were the offerings of the Israelite leaders for the dedication of the altar when it was anointed: twelve silver plates, twelve silver sprinkling bowls and twelve gold dishes. ⁸⁵Each silver plate weighed a hundred and thirty shekels, and each sprinkling bowl seventy shekels. Altogether, the silver dishes weighed two thousand four hundred shekels,ᵃ according to the sanctuary shekel. ⁸⁶The twelve gold dishes filled with incense weighed ten shekels each, according to the sanctuary shekel. Altogether, the gold dishes weighed a hundred and twenty shekels.ᵇ ⁸⁷The total number of animals for the burnt offering came to twelve young bulls, twelve rams and twelve male lambs a year old, together with their grain offering. Twelve male goats were used

---

three-quarter pounds (according to the standard Sanctuary weights), each filled with fine flour mixed with oil as a Grain-Offering;

a gold vessel weighing four ounces, filled with incense;

a young bull, a ram, and a yearling lamb for a Whole-Burnt-Offering;

a he-goat for an Absolution-Offering;

two oxen, five rams, five he-goats, and five yearling lambs to be sacrificed as a Peace-Offering.

This was the offering of Pagiel son of Ocran.

7.78-83 On the twelfth day, Ahira son of Enan, the leader of the people of Naphtali, brought his offering. His offering was:

a silver plate weighing three and a quarter pounds and a silver bowl weighing one and three-quarter pounds (according to the standard Sanctuary weights), each filled with fine flour mixed with oil as a Grain-Offering;

a gold vessel weighing four ounces, filled with incense;

a young bull, a ram, and a yearling lamb for a Whole-Burnt-Offering;

a he-goat for an Absolution-Offering;

two oxen, five rams, five he-goats, and five yearling lambs to be sacrificed as a Peace-Offering.

This was the offering of Ahira son of Enan.

7.84 These were the dedication offerings of the leaders of Israel for the anointing of the Altar:

twelve silver plates,
twelve silver bowls,
twelve gold vessels.

7.85-86 Each plate weighed three and a quarter pounds and each bowl one and three-quarter pounds. All the plates and bowls together weighed about sixty pounds (using the official Sanctuary weight). The twelve gold vessels filled with incense weighed four ounces each (using the official Sanctuary weight). Altogether the gold vessels weighed about three pounds.

7.87 The sum total of animals used for the Whole-Burnt-Offering together with the Grain-Offering:

twelve bulls,
twelve rams,
twelve yearling lambs.

For the Absolution-Offering:

twelve he-goats.

ᵃ 85 That is, about 60 pounds (about 28 kilograms)
ᵇ 86 That is, about 3 pounds (about 1.4 kilograms)

NEW INTERNATIONAL VERSION

for the sin offering. 88The total number of animals for the sacrifice of the fellowship offering came to twenty-four oxen, sixty rams, sixty male goats and sixty male lambs a year old. These were the offerings for the dedication of the altar after it was anointed.

89When Moses entered the Tent of Meeting to speak with the LORD, he heard the voice speaking to him from between the two cherubim above the atonement cover on the ark of the Testimony. And he spoke with him.

SETTING UP THE LAMPS

8 The LORD said to Moses, 2"Speak to Aaron and say to him, 'When you set up the seven lamps, they are to light the area in front of the lampstand.' "

3Aaron did so; he set up the lamps so that they faced forward on the lampstand, just as the LORD commanded Moses. 4This is how the lampstand was made: It was made of hammered gold—from its base to its blossoms. The lampstand was made exactly like the pattern the LORD had shown Moses.

THE SETTING APART OF THE LEVITES

5The LORD said to Moses: 6"Take the Levites from among the other Israelites and make them ceremonially clean. 7To purify them, do this: Sprinkle the water of cleansing on them; then have them shave their whole bodies and wash their clothes, and so purify themselves. 8Have them take a young bull with its grain offering of fine flour mixed with oil; then you are to take a second young bull for a sin offering. 9Bring the Levites to the front of the Tent of Meeting and assemble the whole Israelite community. 10You are to bring the Levites before the LORD, and the Israelites are to lay their hands on them. 11Aaron is to present the Levites before the LORD as a wave offering from the Israelites, so that they may be ready to do the work of the LORD.

12"After the Levites lay their hands on the heads of the bulls, use the one for a sin offering to the LORD and the other for a burnt offering, to make atonement for the Levites. 13Have the Levites stand in front of Aaron and his sons and then present them as a wave offering to the LORD. 14In this way you are to set the Levites apart from the other Israelites, and the Levites will be mine.

15"After you have purified the Levites and presented them as a wave offering, they are to come to do their work at the Tent of Meeting.

THE MESSAGE

7.88 The sum total of animals used for the sacrifice of the Peace-Offering:

> twenty-four bulls,
> sixty rams,
> sixty he-goats,
> sixty yearling lambs.

These were the offerings for the dedication of the Altar after it was anointed.

7.89 When Moses entered the Tent of Meeting to speak with GOD, he heard the Voice speaking to him from between the two angel-cherubim above the Atonement-Cover on the Chest of The Testimony. He spoke with him.

THE LIGHTS

8.1-2 **8** GOD spoke to Moses: "Tell Aaron, Install the seven lamps so they will throw light in front of the Lampstand."

8.3-4 Aaron did just that. He installed the lamps so they threw light in front of the Lampstand, as GOD had instructed Moses. The Lampstand was made of hammered gold from its stem to its petals. It was made precisely to the design GOD had shown Moses.

PURIFYING THE LEVITES

8.5-7 GOD spoke to Moses: "Take the Levites from the midst of the People of Israel and purify them for doing GOD's work. This is the way you will do it: Sprinkle water of absolution on them; have them shave their entire bodies; have them scrub their clothes. Then they will have purified themselves.

8.9-11 "Have them take a young bull with its accompanying Grain-Offering of fine flour mixed with oil, plus a second young bull for an Absolution-Offering. Bring the Levites to the front of the Tent of Meeting and gather the entire community of Israel. Present the Levites before GOD as the People of Israel lay their hands on them. Aaron will present the Levites before GOD as a Wave-Offering from the People of Israel so that they will be ready to do GOD's work.

8.12-14 "Have the Levites place their hands on the heads of the bulls, selecting one for the Absolution-Offering and another for the Whole-Burnt-Offering to GOD to make atonement for the Levites. Then have the Levites stand in front of Aaron and his sons and present them as a Wave-Offering to GOD. This is the procedure for setting apart the Levites from the rest of the People of Israel; the Levites are exclusively for my use.

8.15-19 "After you have purified the Levites and presented them as a Wave-Offering to GOD, they can go to work in the Tent of Meeting. The Le-

NEW INTERNATIONAL VERSION

16They are the Israelites who are to be given wholly to me. I have taken them as my own in place of the firstborn, the first male offspring from every Israelite woman. 17Every firstborn male in Israel, whether man or animal, is mine. When I struck down all the firstborn in Egypt, I set them apart for myself. 18And I have taken the Levites in place of all the firstborn sons in Israel. 19Of all the Israelites, I have given the Levites as gifts to Aaron and his sons to do the work at the Tent of Meeting on behalf of the Israelites and to make atonement for them so that no plague will strike the Israelites when they go near the sanctuary."

20Moses, Aaron and the whole Israelite community did with the Levites just as the LORD commanded Moses. 21The Levites purified themselves and washed their clothes. Then Aaron presented them as a wave offering before the LORD and made atonement for them to purify them. 22After that, the Levites came to do their work at the Tent of Meeting under the supervision of Aaron and his sons. They did with the Levites just as the LORD commanded Moses.

23The LORD said to Moses, 24"This applies to the Levites: Men twenty-five years old or more shall come to take part in the work at the Tent of Meeting, 25but at the age of fifty, they must retire from their regular service and work no longer. 26They may assist their brothers in performing their duties at the Tent of Meeting, but they themselves must not do the work. This, then, is how you are to assign the responsibilities of the Levites."

THE PASSOVER

9 The LORD spoke to Moses in the Desert of Sinai in the first month of the second year after they came out of Egypt. He said, 2"Have the Israelites celebrate the Passover at the appointed time. 3Celebrate it at the appointed time, at twilight on the fourteenth day of this month, in accordance with all its rules and regulations."

4So Moses told the Israelites to celebrate the Passover, 5and they did so in the Desert of Sinai at twilight on the fourteenth day of the first month. The Israelites did everything just as the LORD commanded Moses.

6But some of them could not celebrate the Passover on that day because they were ceremonially unclean on account of a dead body. So they came to Moses and Aaron that same day 7and said to Moses, "We have become unclean because of a dead body, but why should we be kept from presenting the LORD's offering with the other Israelites at the appointed time?"

THE MESSAGE

vites have been selected out of the People of Israel for my exclusive use; they function in place of every firstborn male born to an Israelite woman. Every firstborn male in Israel, animal or human, is set apart for my use. When I struck down all the firstborn of Egypt, I consecrated them for my holy uses. But now I take the Levites as stand-ins in place of every firstborn son in Israel, selected out of the People of Israel, and I have given the Levites to Aaron and his sons to do all the work involved in the Tent of Meeting on behalf of all the People of Israel and to make atonement for them so that nothing bad will happen to them when they approach the Sanctuary."

8.20-22 Moses, Aaron, and the entire community of the People of Israel carried out these procedures with the Levites, just as GOD had commanded Moses. The Levites purified themselves and scrubbed their clothes. Then Aaron presented them as a Wave-Offering before GOD and made atonement for them to purify them. Only then did the Levites go to work at the Tent of Meeting. Aaron and his sons supervised them following the directions GOD had given.

8.23-26 GOD spoke to Moses: "These are your instructions regarding the Levites: At the age of twenty-five they will join the work force in the Tent of Meeting; at the age of fifty they must retire from the work. They can assist their brothers in the tasks in the Tent of Meeting, but they are not permitted to do the actual work themselves. These are the ground rules for the work of the Levites."

PASSOVER

9.1-3 9 GOD spoke to Moses in the Wilderness of Sinai in the first month of the second year after leaving Egypt: "Have the People of Israel celebrate Passover at the set time. Celebrate it on schedule, on the evening of the fourteenth day of this month, following all the rules and procedures."

9.4-5 Moses told the People of Israel to celebrate the Passover and they did—in the Wilderness of Sinai at evening of the fourteenth day of the first month. The People of Israel did it all just as GOD had commanded Moses.

9.6-7 But some of them couldn't celebrate the Passover on the assigned day because they were ritually unclean on account of a corpse. So they presented themselves before Moses and Aaron on Passover and told Moses, "We have become ritually unclean because of a corpse, but why should we be barred from bringing GOD's offering along with other Israelites on the day set for Passover?"

NEW INTERNATIONAL VERSION

⁸Moses answered them, "Wait until I find out what the LORD commands concerning you."

⁹Then the LORD said to Moses, ¹⁰"Tell the Israelites: 'When any of you or your descendants are unclean because of a dead body or are away on a journey, they may still celebrate the LORD's Passover. ¹¹They are to celebrate it on the fourteenth day of the second month at twilight. They are to eat the lamb, together with unleavened bread and bitter herbs. ¹²They must not leave any of it till morning or break any of its bones. When they celebrate the Passover, they must follow all the regulations. ¹³But if a man who is ceremonially clean and not on a journey fails to celebrate the Passover, that person must be cut off from his people because he did not present the LORD's offering at the appointed time. That man will bear the consequences of his sin.

¹⁴" 'An alien living among you who wants to celebrate the LORD's Passover must do so in accordance with its rules and regulations. You must have the same regulations for the alien and the native-born.' "

THE CLOUD ABOVE THE TABERNACLE

¹⁵On the day the tabernacle, the Tent of the Testimony, was set up, the cloud covered it. From evening till morning the cloud above the tabernacle looked like fire. ¹⁶That is how it continued to be; the cloud covered it, and at night it looked like fire. ¹⁷Whenever the cloud lifted from above the Tent, the Israelites set out; wherever the cloud settled, the Israelites encamped. ¹⁸At the LORD's command the Israelites set out, and at his command they encamped. As long as the cloud stayed over the tabernacle, they remained in camp. ¹⁹When the cloud remained over the tabernacle a long time, the Israelites obeyed the LORD's order and did not set out. ²⁰Sometimes the cloud was over the tabernacle only a few days; at the LORD's command they would encamp, and then at his command they would set out. ²¹Sometimes the cloud stayed only from evening till morning, and when it lifted in the morning, they set out. Whether by day or by night, whenever the cloud lifted, they set out. ²²Whether the cloud stayed over the tabernacle for two days or a month or a year, the Israelites would remain in camp and not set out; but when it lifted, they would set out. ²³At the LORD's command they encamped, and at the LORD's command they set out. They obeyed the LORD's order, in accordance with his command through Moses.

THE MESSAGE

9.8 Moses said, "Give me some time; I'll find out what GOD says in your circumstances."

9.9-12 GOD spoke to Moses: "Tell the People of Israel, If one or another of you is ritually unclean because of a corpse, or you happen to be off on a long trip, you may still celebrate GOD's Passover. But celebrate it on the fourteenth day of the second month at evening. Eat the lamb together with unraised bread and bitter herbs. Don't leave any of it until morning. Don't break any of its bones. Follow all the procedures.

9.13 "But a man who is ritually clean and is not off on a trip and still fails to celebrate the Passover must be cut off from his people because he did not present GOD's offering at the set time. That man will pay for his sin.

9.14 "Any foreigner living among you who wants to celebrate GOD's Passover is welcome to do it, but he must follow all the rules and procedures. The same procedures go for both foreigner and native-born."

THE CLOUD

9.15-16 The day The Dwelling was set up, the Cloud covered The Dwelling of the Tent of Testimony. From sunset until daybreak it was over The Dwelling. It looked like fire. It was like that all the time, the Cloud over The Dwelling and at night looking like fire.

9.17-23 When the Cloud lifted above the Tent, the People of Israel marched out; and when the Cloud descended the people camped. The People of Israel marched at GOD's command and they camped at his command. As long as the Cloud was over The Dwelling, they camped. Even when the Cloud hovered over The Dwelling for many days, they honored GOD's command and wouldn't march. They stayed in camp, obedient to GOD's command, as long as the Cloud was over The Dwelling, but the moment GOD issued orders they marched. If the Cloud stayed only from sunset to daybreak and then lifted at daybreak, they marched. Night or day, it made no difference—when the Cloud lifted, they marched. It made no difference whether the Cloud hovered over The Dwelling for two days or a month or a year, as long as the Cloud was there, they were there. And when the Cloud went up, they got up and marched. They camped at GOD's command and they marched at GOD's command. They lived obediently by GOD's orders as delivered by Moses.

NEW INTERNATIONAL VERSION	THE MESSAGE

THE SILVER TRUMPETS

10 The LORD said to Moses: [2]"Make two trumpets of hammered silver, and use them for calling the community together and for having the camps set out. [3]When both are sounded, the whole community is to assemble before you at the entrance to the Tent of Meeting. [4]If only one is sounded, the leaders—the heads of the clans of Israel—are to assemble before you. [5]When a trumpet blast is sounded, the tribes camping on the east are to set out. [6]At the sounding of a second blast, the camps on the south are to set out. The blast will be the signal for setting out. [7]To gather the assembly, blow the trumpets, but not with the same signal.

[8]"The sons of Aaron, the priests, are to blow the trumpets. This is to be a lasting ordinance for you and the generations to come. [9]When you go into battle in your own land against an enemy who is oppressing you, sound a blast on the trumpets. Then you will be remembered by the LORD your God and rescued from your enemies. [10]Also at your times of rejoicing—your appointed feasts and New Moon festivals—you are to sound the trumpets over your burnt offerings and fellowship offerings,[a] and they will be a memorial for you before your God. I am the LORD your God."

THE ISRAELITES LEAVE SINAI

[11]On the twentieth day of the second month of the second year, the cloud lifted from above the tabernacle of the Testimony. [12]Then the Israelites set out from the Desert of Sinai and traveled from place to place until the cloud came to rest in the Desert of Paran. [13]They set out, this first time, at the LORD's command through Moses.

[14]The divisions of the camp of Judah went first, under their standard. Nahshon son of Amminadab was in command. [15]Nethanel son of Zuar was over the division of the tribe of Issachar, [16]and Eliab son of Helon was over the division of the tribe of Zebulun. [17]Then the tabernacle was taken down, and the Gershonites and Merarites, who carried it, set out.

[18]The divisions of the camp of Reuben went next, under their standard. Elizur son of Shedeur was in command. [19]Shelumiel son of Zurishaddai was over the division of the tribe of Simeon, [20]and Eliasaph son of Deuel was over the division of the tribe of Gad. [21]Then the Kohathites set out, carrying the holy things. The tabernacle was to be set up before they arrived.

[22]The divisions of the camp of Ephraim went next, under their standard. Elishama son of Am-

THE TWO BUGLES

10.1-3 **10** GOD spoke to Moses: "Make two bugles of hammered silver. Use them to call the congregation together and give marching orders to the camps. When you blow them, the whole community will meet you at the entrance of the Tent of Meeting.

10.4-7 "When a bugle gives a single, short blast, that's the signal for the leaders, the heads of the clans, to assemble. When it gives a long blast, that's the signal to march. At the first blast the tribes who were camped on the east set out. At the second blast the camps on the south set out. The long blasts are the signals to march. The bugle call that gathers the assembly is different from the signal to march.

10.8-10 "The sons of Aaron, the priests, are in charge of blowing the bugles; it's their assigned duty down through the generations. When you go to war against an aggressor, blow a long blast on the bugle so that GOD will notice you and deliver you from your enemies. Also at times of celebration, at the appointed feasts and New Moon festivals, blow the bugles over your Whole-Burnt-Offerings and Peace-Offerings: they will keep your attention on God. I am GOD, *your* God."

THE MARCH FROM SINAI TO PARAN

10.11-13 In the second year, on the twentieth day of the second month, the Cloud went up from over The Dwelling of The Testimony. At that the People of Israel set out on their travels from the Wilderness of Sinai until the Cloud finally settled in the Wilderness of Paran. They began their march at the command of GOD through Moses.

10.14-17 The flag of the camp of Judah led the way, rank after rank under the command of Nahshon son of Amminadab. Nethanel son of Zuar commanded the forces of the tribe of Issachar, and Eliab son of Helon commanded the forces of the tribe of Zebulun. As soon as The Dwelling was taken down, the Gershonites and the Merarites set out, carrying The Dwelling.

10.18-21 The flag of the camp of Reuben was next with Elizur son of Shedeur in command. Shelumiel son of Zurishaddai commanded the forces of the tribe of Simeon; Eliasaph son of Deuel commanded the forces of the tribe of Gad. Then the Kohathites left, carrying the holy things. By the time they arrived The Dwelling would be set up.

10.22-24 The flag of the tribe of Ephraim moved out next, commanded by Elishama son of Ammi-

---

[a] 10 Traditionally *peace offerings*

NEW INTERNATIONAL VERSION

mihud was in command. ²³Gamaliel son of Pedahzur was over the division of the tribe of Manasseh, ²⁴and Abidan son of Gideoni was over the division of the tribe of Benjamin.

²⁵Finally, as the rear guard for all the units, the divisions of the camp of Dan set out, under their standard. Ahiezer son of Ammishaddai was in command. ²⁶Pagiel son of Ocran was over the division of the tribe of Asher, ²⁷and Ahira son of Enan was over the division of the tribe of Naphtali. ²⁸This was the order of march for the Israelite divisions as they set out.

²⁹Now Moses said to Hobab son of Reuel the Midianite, Moses' father-in-law, "We are setting out for the place about which the LORD said, 'I will give it to you.' Come with us and we will treat you well, for the LORD has promised good things to Israel."

³⁰He answered, "No, I will not go; I am going back to my own land and my own people."

³¹But Moses said, "Please do not leave us. You know where we should camp in the desert, and you can be our eyes. ³²If you come with us, we will share with you whatever good things the LORD gives us."

³³So they set out from the mountain of the LORD and traveled for three days. The ark of the covenant of the LORD went before them during those three days to find them a place to rest. ³⁴The cloud of the LORD was over them by day when they set out from the camp.

³⁵Whenever the ark set out, Moses said,

"Rise up, O LORD!
May your enemies be scattered;
may your foes flee before you."

³⁶Whenever it came to rest, he said,

"Return, O LORD,
to the countless thousands of Israel."

FIRE FROM THE LORD

11 Now the people complained about their hardships in the hearing of the LORD, and when he heard them his anger was aroused. Then fire from the LORD burned among them and consumed some of the outskirts of the camp. ²When the people cried out to Moses, he prayed to the LORD and the fire died down. ³So that place was called Taberah,ᵃ because fire from the LORD had burned among them.

THE MESSAGE

hud. Gamaliel son of Pedahzur commanded the forces of the tribe of Manasseh; Abidan son of Gideoni commanded the forces of the tribe of Benjamin.

10.25-27 Finally, under the flag of the tribe of Dan, the rear guard of all the camps marched out with Ahiezer son of Ammishaddai in command. Pagiel son of Ocran commanded the forces of the tribe of Asher; Ahira son of Enan commanded the forces of the tribe of Naphtali.

10.28 These were the marching units of the People of Israel. They were on their way.

10.29 Moses said to his brother-in-law Hobab son of Reuel the Midianite, Moses' father-in-law, "We're marching to the place about which GOD promised, 'I'll give it to you.' Come with us; we'll treat you well. GOD has promised good things for Israel."

10.30 But Hobab said, "I'm not coming; I'm going back home to my own country, to my own family."

10.31-32 Moses countered, "Don't leave us. You know all the best places to camp in the wilderness. We need your eyes. If you come with us, we'll make sure that you share in all the good things GOD will do for us."

10.33-36 And so off they marched. From the Mountain of GOD they marched three days with the Chest of the Covenant of GOD in the lead to scout out a campsite. The Cloud of GOD was above them by day when they marched from the camp. With the Chest leading the way, Moses would say,

Get up, GOD!
Put down your enemies!
Chase those who hate you to the hills!

And when the Chest was set down, he would say,

Rest with us, GOD,
Stay with the many,
Many thousands of Israel.

CAMP TABERAH

11.1-3 **11** The people fell to grumbling over their hard life. GOD heard. When he heard his anger flared; then fire blazed up and burned the outer boundaries of the camp. The people cried out for help to Moses; Moses prayed to GOD and the fire died down. They named the place Taberah (Blaze) because fire from GOD had blazed up against them.

ᵃ 3 *Taberah* means *burning*.

NEW INTERNATIONAL VERSION

QUAIL FROM THE LORD

⁴The rabble with them began to crave other food, and again the Israelites started wailing and said, "If only we had meat to eat! ⁵We remember the fish we ate in Egypt at no cost—also the cucumbers, melons, leeks, onions and garlic. ⁶But now we have lost our appetite; we never see anything but this manna!"

⁷The manna was like coriander seed and looked like resin. ⁸The people went around gathering it, and then ground it in a handmill or crushed it in a mortar. They cooked it in a pot or made it into cakes. And it tasted like something made with olive oil. ⁹When the dew settled on the camp at night, the manna also came down.

¹⁰Moses heard the people of every family wailing, each at the entrance to his tent. The LORD became exceedingly angry, and Moses was troubled. ¹¹He asked the LORD, "Why have you brought this trouble on your servant? What have I done to displease you that you put the burden of all these people on me? ¹²Did I conceive all these people? Did I give them birth? Why do you tell me to carry them in my arms, as a nurse carries an infant, to the land you promised on oath to their forefathers? ¹³Where can I get meat for all these people? They keep wailing to me, 'Give us meat to eat!' ¹⁴I cannot carry all these people by myself; the burden is too heavy for me. ¹⁵If this is how you are going to treat me, put me to death right now—if I have found favor in your eyes—and do not let me face my own ruin."

¹⁶The LORD said to Moses: "Bring me seventy of Israel's elders who are known to you as leaders and officials among the people. Have them come to the Tent of Meeting, that they may stand there with you. ¹⁷I will come down and speak with you there, and I will take of the Spirit that is on you and put the Spirit on them. They will help you carry the burden of the people so that you will not have to carry it alone.

¹⁸"Tell the people: 'Consecrate yourselves in preparation for tomorrow, when you will eat meat. The LORD heard you when you wailed, "If only we had meat to eat! We were better off in Egypt!" Now the LORD will give you meat, and you will eat it. ¹⁹You will not eat it for just one day, or two days, or five, ten or twenty days, ²⁰but for a whole month—until it comes out of your nostrils and you loathe it—because you have rejected the LORD, who is among you, and have wailed before him, saying, "Why did we ever leave Egypt?" '"

THE MESSAGE

CAMP KIBROTH HATTAAVAH

¹¹.⁴⁻⁶ The riff-raff among the people had a craving and soon they had the People of Israel whining, "Why can't we have meat? We ate fish in Egypt—and got it free!—to say nothing of the cucumbers and melons, the leeks and onions and garlic. But nothing tastes good out here; all we get is manna, manna, manna."

¹¹.⁷⁻⁹ Manna was a seedlike substance with a shiny appearance like resin. The people went around collecting it and ground it between stones or pounded it fine in a mortar. Then they boiled it in a pot and shaped it into cakes. It tasted like a delicacy cooked in olive oil. When the dew fell on the camp at night, the manna was right there with it.

¹¹.¹⁰ Moses heard the whining, all those families whining in front of their tents. GOD's anger blazed up. Moses saw that things were in a bad way.

¹¹.¹¹⁻¹⁵ Moses said to GOD, "Why are you treating me this way? What did I ever do to you to deserve this? Did I conceive them? Was I their mother? So why dump the responsibility of this people on me? Why tell me to carry them around like a nursing mother, carry them all the way to the land you promised to their ancestors? Where am I supposed to get meat for all these people who are whining to me, 'Give us meat; we want meat.' I can't do this by myself—it's too much, all these people. If this is how you intend to treat me, do me a favor and kill me. I've seen enough; I've had enough. Let me out of here."

¹¹.¹⁶⁻¹⁷ GOD said to Moses, "Gather together seventy men from among the leaders of Israel, men whom you know to be respected and responsible. Take them to the Tent of Meeting. I'll meet you there. I'll come down and speak with you. I'll take some of the Spirit that is on you and place it on them; they'll then be able to take some of the load of this people—you won't have to carry the whole thing alone.

¹¹.¹⁸⁻²⁰ "Tell the people, Consecrate yourselves. Get ready for tomorrow when you're going to eat meat. You've been whining to GOD, 'We want meat; give us meat. We had a better life in Egypt.' GOD has heard your whining and he's going to give you meat. You're going to eat meat. And it's not just for a day that you'll eat meat, and not two days, or five or ten or twenty, but for a whole month. You're going to eat meat until it's coming out your nostrils. You're going to be so sick of meat that you'll throw up at the mere mention of it. And here's why: Because you have rejected GOD who is right here among you, whining to his face, 'Oh, why did we ever have to leave Egypt?' "

NEW INTERNATIONAL VERSION

²¹But Moses said, "Here I am among six hundred thousand men on foot, and you say, 'I will give them meat to eat for a whole month!' ²²Would they have enough if flocks and herds were slaughtered for them? Would they have enough if all the fish in the sea were caught for them?"

²³The LORD answered Moses, "Is the LORD's arm too short? You will now see whether or not what I say will come true for you."

²⁴So Moses went out and told the people what the LORD had said. He brought together seventy of their elders and had them stand around the Tent. ²⁵Then the LORD came down in the cloud and spoke with him, and he took of the Spirit that was on him and put the Spirit on the seventy elders. When the Spirit rested on them, they prophesied, but they did not do so again.ᵃ

²⁶However, two men, whose names were Eldad and Medad, had remained in the camp. They were listed among the elders, but did not go out to the Tent. Yet the Spirit also rested on them, and they prophesied in the camp. ²⁷A young man ran and told Moses, "Eldad and Medad are prophesying in the camp."

²⁸Joshua son of Nun, who had been Moses' aide since youth, spoke up and said, "Moses, my lord, stop them!"

²⁹But Moses replied, "Are you jealous for my sake? I wish that all the LORD's people were prophets and that the LORD would put his Spirit on them!" ³⁰Then Moses and the elders of Israel returned to the camp.

³¹Now a wind went out from the LORD and drove quail in from the sea. It brought themᵇ down all around the camp to about three feetᶜ above the ground, as far as a day's walk in any direction. ³²All that day and night and all the next day the people went out and gathered quail. No one gathered less than ten homers.ᵈ Then they spread them out all around the camp. ³³But while the meat was still between their teeth and before it could be consumed, the anger of the LORD burned against the people, and he struck them with a severe plague. ³⁴Therefore the place was named Kibroth Hattaavah,ᵉ because there they buried the people who had craved other food.

³⁵From Kibroth Hattaavah the people traveled to Hazeroth and stayed there.

THE MESSAGE

11.21-22 Moses said, "I'm standing here surrounded by 600,000 men on foot and you say, 'I'll give them meat, meat every day for a month.' So where's it coming from? Even if all the flocks and herds were butchered, would that be enough? Even if all the fish in the sea were caught, would that be enough?"

11.23 GOD answered Moses, "So, do you think I can't take care of you? You'll see soon enough whether what I say happens for you or not."

11.24-25 So Moses went out and told the people what GOD had said. He called together seventy of the leaders and had them stand around the Tent. GOD came down in a cloud and spoke to Moses and took some of the Spirit that was on him and put it on the seventy leaders. When the Spirit rested on them they prophesied. But they didn't continue; it was a onetime event.

⊹

11.26 Meanwhile two men, Eldad and Medad, had stayed in the camp. They were listed as leaders but they didn't leave camp to go to the Tent. Still, the Spirit also rested on them and they prophesied in the camp.

11.27 A young man ran and told Moses, "Eldad and Medad are prophesying in the camp!"

11.28 Joshua son of Nun, who had been Moses' right-hand man since his youth, said, "Moses, master! Stop them!"

11.29 But Moses said, "Are you jealous for me? Would that all GOD's people were prophets. Would that GOD would put his Spirit on all of them."

⊹

11.30-34 Then Moses and the leaders of Israel went back to the camp. A wind set in motion by GOD swept quails in from the sea. They piled up to a depth of about three feet in the camp and as far out as a day's walk in every direction. All that day and night and into the next day the people were out gathering the quail—huge amounts of quail; even the slowest person among them gathered at least sixty bushels. They spread them out all over the camp for drying. But while they were still chewing the quail and had hardly swallowed the first bites, GOD's anger blazed out against the people. He hit them with a terrible plague. They ended up calling the place Kibroth Hattaavah (Graves-of-the-Craving). There they buried the people who craved meat.

11.35 From Kibroth Hattaavah they marched on to Hazeroth. They remained at Hazeroth.

ᵃ 25 Or prophesied and continued to do so   ᵇ 31 Or They flew   ᶜ 31 Hebrew two cubits (about 1 meter)   ᵈ 32 That is, probably about 60 bushels (about 2.2 kiloliters)   ᵉ 34 Kibroth Hattaavah means graves of craving.

NEW INTERNATIONAL VERSION

MIRIAM AND AARON OPPOSE MOSES

12 Miriam and Aaron began to talk against Moses because of his Cushite wife, for he had married a Cushite. ²"Has the LORD spoken only through Moses?" they asked. "Hasn't he also spoken through us?" And the LORD heard this.

³(Now Moses was a very humble man, more humble than anyone else on the face of the earth.)

⁴At once the LORD said to Moses, Aaron and Miriam, "Come out to the Tent of Meeting, all three of you." So the three of them came out. ⁵Then the LORD came down in a pillar of cloud; he stood at the entrance to the Tent and summoned Aaron and Miriam. When both of them stepped forward, ⁶he said, "Listen to my words:

"When a prophet of the LORD is among you,
  I reveal myself to him in visions,
  I speak to him in dreams.
⁷But this is not true of my servant Moses;
  he is faithful in all my house.
⁸With him I speak face to face,
  clearly and not in riddles;
  he sees the form of the LORD.
Why then were you not afraid
  to speak against my servant Moses?"

⁹The anger of the LORD burned against them, and he left them.

¹⁰When the cloud lifted from above the Tent, there stood Miriam—leprous,ᵃ like snow. Aaron turned toward her and saw that she had leprosy; ¹¹and he said to Moses, "Please, my lord, do not hold against us the sin we have so foolishly committed. ¹²Do not let her be like a stillborn infant coming from its mother's womb with its flesh half eaten away."

¹³So Moses cried out to the LORD, "O God, please heal her!"

¹⁴The LORD replied to Moses, "If her father had spit in her face, would she not have been in disgrace for seven days? Confine her outside the camp for seven days; after that she can be brought back." ¹⁵So Miriam was confined outside the camp for seven days, and the people did not move on till she was brought back.

¹⁶After that, the people left Hazeroth and encamped in the Desert of Paran.

THE MESSAGE

CAMP HAZEROTH

12.1-2 **12** Miriam and Aaron talked against Moses behind his back because of his Cushite wife (he had married a Cushite woman). They said, "Is it only through Moses that GOD speaks? Doesn't he also speak through us?"

GOD overheard their talk.

12.3-8 Now the man Moses was a quietly humble man, more so than anyone living on Earth. GOD broke in suddenly on Moses and Aaron and Miriam saying, "Come out, you three, to the Tent of Meeting." The three went out. GOD descended in a Pillar of Cloud and stood at the entrance to the Tent. He called Aaron and Miriam to him. When they stepped out, he said,

Listen carefully to what I'm telling you.
  If there is a prophet of GOD among you,
I make myself known to him in visions,
  I speak to him in dreams.
But I don't do it that way with my servant
    Moses;
  he has the run of my entire house;
I speak to him intimately, in person,
  in plain talk without riddles:
He ponders the very form of GOD.
So why did you show no reverence or
    respect
  in speaking against my servant, against
    Moses?

12.9 The anger of GOD blazed out against them. And then he left.

12.10 When the Cloud moved off from the Tent, oh! Miriam had turned leprous, her skin like snow. Aaron took one look at Miriam—a leper!

12.11-12 He said to Moses, "Please, my master, please don't come down so hard on us for this foolish and thoughtless sin. Please don't make her like a stillborn baby coming out of its mother's womb with half its body decomposed."

12.13 And Moses prayed to GOD:

Please, God, heal her,
  please heal her.

12.14-16 GOD answered Moses, "If her father had spat in her face, wouldn't she be ostracized for seven days? Quarantine her outside the camp for seven days. Then she can be readmitted to the camp." So Miriam was in quarantine outside the camp for seven days. The people didn't march on until she was readmitted. Only then did the people march from Hazeroth and set up camp in the Wilderness of Paran.

ᵃ 10 The Hebrew word was used for various diseases affecting the skin—not necessarily leprosy.

NEW INTERNATIONAL VERSION

Exploring Canaan

13 The LORD said to Moses, ²"Send some men to explore the land of Canaan, which I am giving to the Israelites. From each ancestral tribe send one of its leaders."

³So at the LORD's command Moses sent them out from the Desert of Paran. All of them were leaders of the Israelites. ⁴These are their names:

from the tribe of Reuben, Shammua son of Zaccur;

⁵from the tribe of Simeon, Shaphat son of Hori;

⁶from the tribe of Judah, Caleb son of Jephunneh;

⁷from the tribe of Issachar, Igal son of Joseph;

⁸from the tribe of Ephraim, Hoshea son of Nun;

⁹from the tribe of Benjamin, Palti son of Raphu;

¹⁰from the tribe of Zebulun, Gaddiel son of Sodi;

¹¹from the tribe of Manasseh (a tribe of Joseph), Gaddi son of Susi;

¹²from the tribe of Dan, Ammiel son of Gemalli;

¹³from the tribe of Asher, Sethur son of Michael;

¹⁴from the tribe of Naphtali, Nahbi son of Vophsi;

¹⁵from the tribe of Gad, Geuel son of Maki.

¹⁶These are the names of the men Moses sent to explore the land. (Moses gave Hoshea son of Nun the name Joshua.)

¹⁷When Moses sent them to explore Canaan, he said, "Go up through the Negev and on into the hill country. ¹⁸See what the land is like and whether the people who live there are strong or weak, few or many. ¹⁹What kind of land do they live in? Is it good or bad? What kind of towns do they live in? Are they unwalled or fortified? ²⁰How is the soil? Is it fertile or poor? Are there trees on it or not? Do your best to bring back some of the fruit of the land." (It was the season for the first ripe grapes.)

²¹So they went up and explored the land from the Desert of Zin as far as Rehob, toward Lebo*ᵃ* Hamath. ²²They went up through the Negev and came to Hebron, where Ahiman, Sheshai and Talmai, the descendants of Anak, lived. (Hebron had been built seven years before Zoan in Egypt.) ²³When they reached the Valley of Eshcol,*ᵇ* they cut off a branch bearing a single cluster of grapes. Two of them carried it on a pole

---

THE MESSAGE

Scouting Out Canaan

13 ¹³·¹⁻² GOD spoke to Moses: "Send men to scout out the country of Canaan that I am giving to the People of Israel. Send one man from each ancestral tribe, each one a tried-and-true leader in the tribe."

¹³·³⁻¹⁵ So Moses sent them off from the Wilderness of Paran at the command of GOD. All of them were leaders in Israel, one from each tribe. These were their names:

from Reuben: Shammua son of Zaccur
from Simeon: Shaphat son of Hori
from Judah: Caleb son of Jephunneh
from Issachar: Igal son of Joseph
from Ephraim: Hoshea son of Nun
from Benjamin: Palti son of Raphu
from Zebulun: Gaddiel son of Sodi
from Manasseh (a Joseph tribe): Gaddi son of Susi
from Dan: Ammiel son of Gemalli
from Asher: Sethur son of Michael
from Naphtali: Nahbi son of Vophsi
from Gad: Geuel son of Maki

¹³·¹⁶ These are the names of the men Moses sent to scout out the land. Moses gave Hoshea (Salvation) son of Nun a new name—Joshua (GOD-Saves).

¹³·¹⁷⁻²⁰ When Moses sent them off to scout out Canaan, he said, "Go up through the Negev and then into the hill country. Look the land over, see what it is like. Assess the people: Are they strong or weak? Are there few or many? Observe the land: Is it pleasant or harsh? Describe the towns where they live: Are they open camps or fortified with walls? And the soil: Is it fertile or barren? Are there forests? And try to bring back a sample of the produce that grows there—this is the season for the first ripe grapes."

¹³·²¹⁻²⁵ With that they were on their way. They scouted out the land from the Wilderness of Zin as far as Rehob toward Lebo Hamath. Their route went through the Negev Desert to the town of Hebron. Ahiman, Sheshai, and Talmai, descendants of the giant Anak, lived there. Hebron had been built seven years before Zoan in Egypt. When they arrived at the Eshcol Valley they cut off a branch with a single cluster of grapes—it took two men to carry it—slung on

---

ᵃ 21 Or *toward the entrance to*   *ᵇ 23 Eshcol* means *cluster;* also in verse 24.

NEW INTERNATIONAL VERSION

between them, along with some pomegranates and figs. 24That place was called the Valley of Eshcol because of the cluster of grapes the Israelites cut off there. 25At the end of forty days they returned from exploring the land.

REPORT ON THE EXPLORATION

26They came back to Moses and Aaron and the whole Israelite community at Kadesh in the Desert of Paran. There they reported to them and to the whole assembly and showed them the fruit of the land. 27They gave Moses this account: "We went into the land to which you sent us, and it does flow with milk and honey! Here is its fruit. 28But the people who live there are powerful, and the cities are fortified and very large. We even saw descendants of Anak there. 29The Amalekites live in the Negev; the Hittites, Jebusites and Amorites live in the hill country; and the Canaanites live near the sea and along the Jordan."

30Then Caleb silenced the people before Moses and said, "We should go up and take possession of the land, for we can certainly do it."

31But the men who had gone up with him said, "We can't attack those people; they are stronger than we are." 32And they spread among the Israelites a bad report about the land they had explored. They said, "The land we explored devours those living in it. All the people we saw there are of great size. 33We saw the Nephilim there (the descendants of Anak come from the Nephilim). We seemed like grasshoppers in our own eyes, and we looked the same to them."

THE PEOPLE REBEL

14 That night all the people of the community raised their voices and wept aloud. 2All the Israelites grumbled against Moses and Aaron, and the whole assembly said to them, "If only we had died in Egypt! Or in this desert! 3Why is the LORD bringing us to this land only to let us fall by the sword? Our wives and children will be taken as plunder. Wouldn't it be better for us to go back to Egypt?" 4And they said to each other, "We should choose a leader and go back to Egypt."

5Then Moses and Aaron fell facedown in front of the whole Israelite assembly gathered there. 6Joshua son of Nun and Caleb son of Jephunneh, who were among those who had explored the land, tore their clothes 7and said to the entire Israelite assembly, "The land we passed through and explored is exceedingly good. 8If the LORD is

THE MESSAGE

a pole. They also picked some pomegranates and figs. They named the place Eshcol Valley (Grape-Cluster-Valley) because of the huge cluster of grapes they had cut down there. After forty days of scouting out the land, they returned home.

13.26-27   They presented themselves before Moses and Aaron and the whole congregation of the People of Israel in the Wilderness of Paran at Kadesh. They reported to the whole congregation and showed them the fruit of the land. Then they told the story of their trip:

13.27-29   "We went to the land to which you sent us and, oh! It *does* flow with milk and honey! Just look at this fruit! The only thing is that the people who live there are fierce, their cities are huge and well fortified. Worse yet, we saw descendants of the giant Anak. Amalekites are spread out in the Negev; Hittites, Jebusites, and Amorites hold the hill country; and the Canaanites are established on the Mediterranean Sea and along the Jordan."

13.30   Caleb interrupted, called for silence before Moses and said, "Let's go up and take the land—now. We can do it."

13.31-33   But the others said, "We can't attack those people; they're way stronger than we are." They spread scary rumors among the People of Israel. They said, "We scouted out the land from one end to the other—it's a land that swallows people whole. Everybody we saw was huge. Why, we even saw the Nephilim giants (the Anak giants come from the Nephilim). Alongside them we felt like grasshoppers. And they looked down on us as if we were grasshoppers."

⊹

14.1-3   **14** The whole community was in an uproar, wailing all night long. All the People of Israel grumbled against Moses and Aaron. The entire community was in on it: "Why didn't we die in Egypt? Or in this wilderness? Why has GOD brought us to this country to kill us? Our wives and children are about to become plunder. Why don't we just head back to Egypt? And right now!"

14.4   Soon they were all saying it to one another: "Let's pick a new leader; let's head back to Egypt."

14.5   Moses and Aaron fell on their faces in front of the entire community, gathered in emergency session.

14.6-9   Joshua son of Nun and Caleb son of Jephunneh, members of the scouting party, ripped their clothes and addressed the assembled People of Israel: "The land we walked through and scouted out is a very good land—very good in-

NEW INTERNATIONAL VERSION

pleased with us, he will lead us into that land, a land flowing with milk and honey, and will give it to us. ⁹Only do not rebel against the LORD. And do not be afraid of the people of the land, because we will swallow them up. Their protection is gone, but the LORD is with us. Do not be afraid of them."

¹⁰But the whole assembly talked about stoning them. Then the glory of the LORD appeared at the Tent of Meeting to all the Israelites. ¹¹The LORD said to Moses, "How long will these people treat me with contempt? How long will they refuse to believe in me, in spite of all the miraculous signs I have performed among them? ¹²I will strike them down with a plague and destroy them, but I will make you into a nation greater and stronger than they."

¹³Moses said to the LORD, "Then the Egyptians will hear about it! By your power you brought these people up from among them. ¹⁴And they will tell the inhabitants of this land about it. They have already heard that you, O LORD, are with these people and that you, O LORD, have been seen face to face, that your cloud stays over them, and that you go before them in a pillar of cloud by day and a pillar of fire by night. ¹⁵If you put these people to death all at one time, the nations who have heard this report about you will say, ¹⁶'The LORD was not able to bring these people into the land he promised them on oath; so he slaughtered them in the desert.'

¹⁷"Now may the Lord's strength be displayed, just as you have declared: ¹⁸'The LORD is slow to anger, abounding in love and forgiving sin and rebellion. Yet he does not leave the guilty unpunished; he punishes the children for the sin of the fathers to the third and fourth generation.' ¹⁹In accordance with your great love, forgive the sin of these people, just as you have pardoned them from the time they left Egypt until now."

²⁰The LORD replied, "I have forgiven them, as you asked. ²¹Nevertheless, as surely as I live and as surely as the glory of the LORD fills the whole earth, ²²not one of the men who saw my glory and the miraculous signs I performed in Egypt and in the desert but who disobeyed me and tested me ten times— ²³not one of them will ever see the land I promised on oath to their

THE MESSAGE

deed. If GOD is pleased with us, he will lead us into that land, a land that flows, as they say, with milk and honey. And he'll give it to us. Just don't rebel against GOD! And don't be afraid of those people. Why, we'll have them for lunch! They have no protection and GOD is on our side. Don't be afraid of them!"

14.10-12   But, up in arms now, the entire community was talking of hurling stones at them.

Just then the bright Glory of GOD appeared at the Tent of Meeting. Every Israelite saw it. GOD said to Moses, "How long will these people treat me like dirt? How long refuse to trust me? And with all these signs I've done among them! I've had enough—I'm going to hit them with a plague and kill them. But I'll make you into a nation bigger and stronger than they ever were."

14.13-16   But Moses said to GOD, "The Egyptians are going to hear about this! You delivered this people from Egypt with a great show of strength, and now this? The Egyptians will tell everyone. They've already heard that you are GOD, that you are on the side of this people, that you are present among them, that they see you with their own eyes in your Cloud that hovers over them, in the Pillar of Cloud that leads them by day and the Pillar of Fire at night. If you kill this entire people in one stroke, all the nations that have heard what has been going on will say, 'Since GOD couldn't get these people into the land which he had promised to give them, he slaughtered them out in the wilderness.'

14.17   "Now, please, let the power of the Master expand, enlarge itself greatly, along the lines you have laid out earlier when you said,

14.18   GOD, slow to get angry and huge in loyal
                love,
            forgiving iniquity and rebellion and sin;
            Still, never just whitewashing sin.
            But extending the fallout of parents' sins
                to children into the third,
                even the fourth generation.

14.19   "Please forgive the wrongdoing of this people out of the extravagance of your loyal love just as all along, from the time they left Egypt, you have been forgiving this people."

14.20-23   GOD said, "I forgive them, honoring your words. But as I live and as the Glory of GOD fills the whole Earth—not a single person of those who saw my Glory, saw the miracle signs I did in Egypt and the wilderness, and who have tested me over and over and over again, turning a deaf ear to me—not one of them will set eyes on the land I so solemnly promised to

NEW INTERNATIONAL VERSION

forefathers. No one who has treated me with contempt will ever see it. ²⁴But because my servant Caleb has a different spirit and follows me wholeheartedly, I will bring him into the land he went to, and his descendants will inherit it. ²⁵Since the Amalekites and Canaanites are living in the valleys, turn back tomorrow and set out toward the desert along the route to the Red Sea. ^a"

²⁶The LORD said to Moses and Aaron: ²⁷"How long will this wicked community grumble against me? I have heard the complaints of these grumbling Israelites. ²⁸So tell them, 'As surely as I live, declares the LORD, I will do to you the very things I heard you say: ²⁹In this desert your bodies will fall—every one of you twenty years old or more who was counted in the census and who has grumbled against me. ³⁰Not one of you will enter the land I swore with uplifted hand to make your home, except Caleb son of Jephunneh and Joshua son of Nun. ³¹As for your children that you said would be taken as plunder, I will bring them in to enjoy the land you have rejected. ³²But you—your bodies will fall in this desert. ³³Your children will be shepherds here for forty years, suffering for your unfaithfulness, until the last of your bodies lies in the desert. ³⁴For forty years—one year for each of the forty days you explored the land—you will suffer for your sins and know what it is like to have me against you.' ³⁵I, the LORD, have spoken, and I will surely do these things to this whole wicked community, which has banded together against me. They will meet their end in this desert; here they will die."

³⁶So the men Moses had sent to explore the land, who returned and made the whole community grumble against him by spreading a bad report about it— ³⁷these men responsible for spreading the bad report about the land were struck down and died of a plague before the LORD. ³⁸Of the men who went to explore the land, only Joshua son of Nun and Caleb son of Jephunneh survived.

³⁹When Moses reported this to all the Israelites, they mourned bitterly. ⁴⁰Early the next morning they went up toward the high hill country. "We have sinned," they said. "We will go up to the place the LORD promised."

⁴¹But Moses said, "Why are you disobeying

^a 25 Hebrew *Yam Suph*; that is, Sea of Reeds

THE MESSAGE

their ancestors. No one who has treated me with such repeated contempt will see it.

14.24   "But my servant Caleb—this is a different story. He has a different spirit; he follows me passionately. I'll bring him into the land that he scouted and his children will inherit it.

14.25   "Since the Amalekites and Canaanites are so well established in the valleys, for right now change course and head back into the wilderness following the route to the Red Sea."

14.26-30   GOD spoke to Moses and Aaron: "How long is this going to go on, all this grumbling against me by this evil-infested community? I've had my fill of complaints from these grumbling Israelites. Tell them, As I live—GOD's decree—here's what I'm going to do: Your corpses are going to litter the wilderness—every one of you twenty years and older who was counted in the census, this whole generation of grumblers and grousers. Not one of you will enter the land and make your home there, the firmly and solemnly promised land, except for Caleb son of Jephunneh and Joshua son of Nun.

14.31-34   "Your children, the very ones that you said would be taken for plunder, I'll bring in to enjoy the land you rejected while your corpses will be rotting in the wilderness. These children of yours will live as shepherds in the wilderness for forty years, living with the fallout of your whoring unfaithfulness until the last of your generation lies a corpse in the wilderness. You scouted out the land for forty days; your punishment will be a year for each day, a forty-year sentence to serve for your sins—a long schooling in my displeasure.

14.35   "I, GOD, have spoken. I will most certainly carry out these things against this entire evil-infested community which has banded together against me. In this wilderness they will come to their end. There they will die."

14.36-38   So it happened that the men Moses sent to scout out the land returned to circulate false rumors about the land causing the entire community to grumble against Moses—all these men died. Having spread false rumors of the land, they died in a plague, confronted by GOD. Only Joshua son of Nun and Caleb son of Jephunneh were left alive of the men who went to scout out the land.

14.39-40   When Moses told all of this to the People of Israel, they mourned long and hard. But early the next morning they started out for the high hill country, saying, "We're here; we're ready— let's go up and attack the land that GOD promised us. We sinned, but now we're ready."

14.41-43   But Moses said, "Why are you crossing GOD's

NEW INTERNATIONAL VERSION

the LORD's command? This will not succeed! 42Do not go up, because the LORD is not with you. You will be defeated by your enemies, 43for the Amalekites and Canaanites will face you there. Because you have turned away from the LORD, he will not be with you and you will fall by the sword."

44Nevertheless, in their presumption they went up toward the high hill country, though neither Moses nor the ark of the LORD's covenant moved from the camp. 45Then the Amalekites and Canaanites who lived in that hill country came down and attacked them and beat them down all the way to Hormah.

SUPPLEMENTARY OFFERINGS

15 The LORD said to Moses, 2"Speak to the Israelites and say to them: 'After you enter the land I am giving you as a home 3and you present to the LORD offerings made by fire, from the herd or the flock, as an aroma pleasing to the LORD—whether burnt offerings or sacrifices, for special vows or freewill offerings or festival offerings— 4then the one who brings his offering shall present to the LORD a grain offering of a tenth of an ephah*a* of fine flour mixed with a quarter of a hin*b* of oil. 5With each lamb for the burnt offering or the sacrifice, prepare a quarter of a hin of wine as a drink offering.

6" 'With a ram prepare a grain offering of two-tenths of an ephah*c* of fine flour mixed with a third of a hin*d* of oil, 7and a third of a hin of wine as a drink offering. Offer it as an aroma pleasing to the LORD.

8" 'When you prepare a young bull as a burnt offering or sacrifice, for a special vow or a fellowship offering*e* to the LORD, 9bring with the bull a grain offering of three-tenths of an ephah*f* of fine flour mixed with half a hin*g* of oil. 10Also bring half a hin of wine as a drink offering. It will be an offering made by fire, an aroma pleasing to the LORD. 11Each bull or ram, each lamb or young goat, is to be prepared in this manner. 12Do this for each one, for as many as you prepare.

13" 'Everyone who is native-born must do these things in this way when he brings an offering made by fire as an aroma pleasing to the LORD. 14For the generations to come, whenever an alien or anyone else living among you pre-

a 4 That is, probably about 2 quarts (about 2 liters)
b 4 That is, probably about 1 quart (about 1 liter); also in verse 5   *c 6* That is, probably about 4 quarts (about 4.5 liters)   *d 6* That is, probably about 1 1/4 quarts (about 1.2 liters); also in verse 7   *e 8* Traditionally *peace offering*
f 9 That is, probably about 6 quarts (about 6.5 liters)
g 9 That is, probably about 2 quarts (about 2 liters); also in verse 10

THE MESSAGE

command yet again? This won't work. Don't attack. GOD isn't with you in this—you'll be beaten badly by your enemies. The Amalekites and Canaanites are ready for you and they'll kill you. Because you have left off obediently following GOD, GOD is not going to be with you in this."

14.44-45   But they went anyway; recklessly and arrogantly they climbed to the high hill country. But the Chest of the Covenant and Moses didn't budge from the camp. The Amalekites and the Canaanites who lived in the hill country came out of the hills and attacked and beat them, a rout all the way down to Hormah.

MATTERS OF WORSHIP

15.1-5   **15** GOD spoke to Moses: "Speak to the People of Israel. Tell them, When you enter your homeland that I am giving to you and sacrifice a Fire-Gift to GOD, a Whole-Burnt-Offering or any sacrifice from the herd or flock for a Vow-Offering or Freewill-Offering at one of the appointed feasts, as a pleasing fragrance for GOD, the one bringing the offering shall present to GOD a Grain-Offering of two quarts of fine flour mixed with a quart of oil. With each lamb for the Whole-Burnt-Offering or other sacrifice, prepare a quart of oil and a quart of wine as a Drink-Offering.

15.6-7   "For a ram prepare a Grain-Offering of four quarts of fine flour mixed with one and a quarter quarts of oil and one and a quarter quarts of wine as a Drink-Offering. Present it as a pleasing fragrance to GOD.

15.8-10   "When you prepare a young bull as a Whole-Burnt-Offering or sacrifice for a special vow or a Peace-Offering to GOD, bring with the bull a Grain-Offering of six quarts of fine flour and two quarts of oil. Also bring two quarts of wine as a Drink-Offering. It will be a Fire-Gift, a pleasing fragrance to GOD.

15.11-12   "Each bull or ram, each lamb or young goat, is to be prepared in this same way. Carry out this procedure for each one, no matter how many you have to prepare.

15.13-16   "Every native-born Israelite is to follow this procedure when he brings a Fire-Gift as a pleasing fragrance to GOD. In future generations, when a foreigner or visitor living at

NEW INTERNATIONAL VERSION

sents an offering made by fire as an aroma pleasing to the LORD, he must do exactly as you do. ¹⁵The community is to have the same rules for you and for the alien living among you; this is a lasting ordinance for the generations to come. You and the alien shall be the same before the LORD: ¹⁶The same laws and regulations will apply both to you and to the alien living among you.' "

¹⁷The LORD said to Moses, ¹⁸"Speak to the Israelites and say to them: 'When you enter the land to which I am taking you ¹⁹and you eat the food of the land, present a portion as an offering to the LORD. ²⁰Present a cake from the first of your ground meal and present it as an offering from the threshing floor. ²¹Throughout the generations to come you are to give this offering to the LORD from the first of your ground meal.

OFFERINGS FOR UNINTENTIONAL SINS

²²" 'Now if you unintentionally fail to keep any of these commands the LORD gave Moses— ²³any of the LORD's commands to you through him, from the day the LORD gave them and continuing through the generations to come— ²⁴and if this is done unintentionally without the community being aware of it, then the whole community is to offer a young bull for a burnt offering as an aroma pleasing to the LORD, along with its prescribed grain offering and drink offering, and a male goat for a sin offering. ²⁵The priest is to make atonement for the whole Israelite community, and they will be forgiven, for it was not intentional and they have brought to the LORD for their wrong an offering made by fire and a sin offering. ²⁶The whole Israelite community and the aliens living among them will be forgiven, because all the people were involved in the unintentional wrong.

²⁷" 'But if just one person sins unintentionally, he must bring a year-old female goat for a sin offering. ²⁸The priest is to make atonement before the LORD for the one who erred by sinning unintentionally, and when atonement has been made for him, he will be forgiven. ²⁹One and the same law applies to everyone who sins unintentionally, whether he is a native-born Israelite or an alien.

³⁰" 'But anyone who sins defiantly, whether native-born or alien, blasphemes the LORD, and that person must be cut off from his people. ³¹Because he has despised the LORD's word and broken his commands, that person must surely be cut off; his guilt remains on him.' "

THE MESSAGE

length among you presents a Fire-Gift as a pleasing fragrance to GOD, the same procedures must be followed. The community has the same rules for you and the foreigner living among you. This is the regular rule for future generations. You and the foreigner are the same before GOD. The same laws and regulations apply to both you and the foreigner who lives with you."

15.17-21 GOD spoke to Moses: "Speak to the People of Israel. Tell them, When you enter the land into which I'm bringing you, and you eat the food of that country, set some aside as an offering for GOD. From the first batch of bread dough make a round loaf for an offering—an offering from the threshing floor. Down through the future generations make this offering to GOD from each first batch of dough.

✝

15.22-26 "But if you should get off the beaten track and not keep the commands which GOD spoke to Moses, any of the things that GOD commanded you under the authority of Moses from the time that GOD first commanded you right up to this present time, and if it happened more or less by mistake, with the congregation unaware of it, then the whole congregation is to sacrifice one young bull as a Whole-Burnt-Offering, a pleasing fragrance to GOD, accompanied by its Grain-Offering and Drink-Offering as stipulated in the rules, and a he-goat as an Absolution-Offering. The priest is to atone for the entire community of the People of Israel and they will stand forgiven. The sin was not deliberate, and they offered to GOD the Fire-Gift and Absolution-Offering for their inadvertence. The whole community of Israel including the foreigners living there will be absolved, because everyone was involved in the error.

15.27-28 "But if it's just one person who sins by mistake, not realizing what he's doing, he is to bring a yearling she-goat as an Absolution-Offering. The priest then is to atone for the person who accidentally sinned, to make atonement before GOD so that it won't be held against him.

15.29 "The same standard holds for everyone who sins by mistake; the native-born Israelites and the foreigners go by the same rules.

15.30-31 "But the person, native or foreigner, who sins defiantly, deliberately blaspheming GOD, must be cut off from his people: He has despised GOD's word, he has violated GOD's command; that person must be kicked out of the community, ostracized, left alone in his wrongdoing."

✝

NEW INTERNATIONAL VERSION

THE SABBATH-BREAKER PUT TO DEATH

³²While the Israelites were in the desert, a man was found gathering wood on the Sabbath day. ³³Those who found him gathering wood brought him to Moses and Aaron and the whole assembly, ³⁴and they kept him in custody, because it was not clear what should be done to him. ³⁵Then the LORD said to Moses, "The man must die. The whole assembly must stone him outside the camp." ³⁶So the assembly took him outside the camp and stoned him to death, as the LORD commanded Moses.

TASSELS ON GARMENTS

³⁷The LORD said to Moses, ³⁸"Speak to the Israelites and say to them: 'Throughout the generations to come you are to make tassels on the corners of your garments, with a blue cord on each tassel. ³⁹You will have these tassels to look at and so you will remember all the commands of the LORD, that you may obey them and not prostitute yourselves by going after the lusts of your own hearts and eyes. ⁴⁰Then you will remember to obey all my commands and will be consecrated to your God. ⁴¹I am the LORD your God, who brought you out of Egypt to be your God. I am the LORD your God.' "

KORAH, DATHAN AND ABIRAM

16 Korah son of Izhar, the son of Kohath, the son of Levi, and certain Reubenites— Dathan and Abiram, sons of Eliab, and On son of Peleth—became insolent*a* ²and rose up against Moses. With them were 250 Israelite men, well-known community leaders who had been appointed members of the council. ³They came as a group to oppose Moses and Aaron and said to them, "You have gone too far! The whole community is holy, every one of them, and the LORD is with them. Why then do you set yourselves above the LORD's assembly?"

⁴When Moses heard this, he fell facedown. ⁵Then he said to Korah and all his followers: "In the morning the LORD will show who belongs to him and who is holy, and he will have that person come near him. The man he chooses he will cause to come near him. ⁶You, Korah, and all your followers are to do this: Take censers ⁷and tomorrow put fire and incense in them before the LORD. The man the LORD chooses will be the one who is holy. You Levites have gone too far!"

⁸Moses also said to Korah, "Now listen, you Levites! ⁹Isn't it enough for you that the God of

a 1 Or Peleth—took ⟨men⟩

THE MESSAGE

¹⁵·³²⁻³⁵ Once, during those wilderness years of the People of Israel, a man was caught gathering wood on the Sabbath. The ones who caught him hauled him before Moses and Aaron and the entire congregation. They put him in custody until it became clear what to do with him. Then GOD spoke to Moses: "Give the man the death penalty. Yes, kill him, the whole community hurling stones at him outside the camp."

¹⁵·³⁶ So the whole community took him outside the camp and threw stones at him, an execution commanded by GOD and given through Moses.

✜

¹⁵·³⁷⁻⁴¹ GOD spoke to Moses: "Speak to the People of Israel. Tell them that from now on they are to make tassels on the corners of their garments and to mark each corner tassel with a blue thread. When you look at these tassels you'll remember and keep all the commandments of GOD, and not get distracted by everything you feel or see that seduces you into infidelities. The tassels will signal remembrance and observance of all my commandments, to live a holy life to GOD. I am your GOD who rescued you from the land of Egypt to be your personal God. Yes, I am GOD, *your* God."

THE REBELS

¹⁶·¹⁻³ **16** Getting on his high horse one day, Korah son of Izhar, the son of Kohath, the son of Levi, along with a few Reubenites—Dathan and Abiram sons of Eliab, and On son of Peleth—rebelled against Moses. He had with him 250 leaders of the congregation of Israel, prominent men with positions in the Council. They came as a group and confronted Moses and Aaron, saying, "You've overstepped yourself. This entire community is holy and GOD is in their midst. So why do you act like you're running the whole show?"

¹⁶·⁴ On hearing this, Moses threw himself facedown on the ground.

¹⁶·⁵ Then he addressed Korah and his gang: "In the morning GOD will make clear who is on his side, who is holy. GOD will take his stand with the one he chooses.

¹⁶·⁶⁻⁷ "Now, Korah, here's what I want you, you and your gang, to do: Tomorrow, take censers. In the presence of GOD, put fire in them and then incense. Then we'll see who is holy, see whom GOD chooses. Sons of Levi, you've overstepped *yourselves!*"

¹⁶·⁸⁻¹¹ Moses continued with Korah, "Listen well now, sons of Levi. Isn't it enough for you that

NEW INTERNATIONAL VERSION

Israel has separated you from the rest of the Israelite community and brought you near himself to do the work at the LORD's tabernacle and to stand before the community and minister to them? ¹⁰He has brought you and all your fellow Levites near himself, but now you are trying to get the priesthood too. ¹¹It is against the LORD that you and all your followers have banded together. Who is Aaron that you should grumble against him?"

¹²Then Moses summoned Dathan and Abiram, the sons of Eliab. But they said, "We will not come! ¹³Isn't it enough that you have brought us up out of a land flowing with milk and honey to kill us in the desert? And now you also want to lord it over us? ¹⁴Moreover, you haven't brought us into a land flowing with milk and honey or given us an inheritance of fields and vineyards. Will you gouge out the eyes of^a these men? No, we will not come!"

¹⁵Then Moses became very angry and said to the LORD, "Do not accept their offering. I have not taken so much as a donkey from them, nor have I wronged any of them."

¹⁶Moses said to Korah, "You and all your followers are to appear before the LORD tomorrow—you and they and Aaron. ¹⁷Each man is to take his censer and put incense in it—250 censers in all—and present it before the LORD. You and Aaron are to present your censers also." ¹⁸So each man took his censer, put fire and incense in it, and stood with Moses and Aaron at the entrance to the Tent of Meeting. ¹⁹When Korah had gathered all his followers in opposition to them at the entrance to the Tent of Meeting, the glory of the LORD appeared to the entire assembly. ²⁰The LORD said to Moses and Aaron, ²¹"Separate yourselves from this assembly so I can put an end to them at once."

²²But Moses and Aaron fell facedown and cried out, "O God, God of the spirits of all mankind, will you be angry with the entire assembly when only one man sins?"

²³Then the LORD said to Moses, ²⁴"Say to the assembly, 'Move away from the tents of Korah, Dathan and Abiram.' "

²⁵Moses got up and went to Dathan and Abiram, and the elders of Israel followed him. ²⁶He warned the assembly, "Move back from the tents of these wicked men! Do not touch anything belonging to them, or you will be swept away because of all their sins." ²⁷So they moved away

THE MESSAGE

the God of Israel has selected you out of the congregation of Israel to bring you near him to serve in the ministries of The Dwelling of GOD, and to stand before the congregation to minister to them? He has brought you and all your brother Levites into his inner circle, and now you're grasping for the priesthood too. It's GOD you've ganged up against, not us. What do you have against Aaron that you're bad-mouthing him?"

16.12-14 Moses then ordered Dathan and Abiram, sons of Eliab, to appear, but they said, "We're not coming. Isn't it enough that you yanked us out of a land flowing with milk and honey to kill us in the wilderness? And now you keep trying to boss us around! Face it, you haven't produced: You haven't brought us into a land flowing with milk and honey, you haven't given us the promised inheritance of fields and vineyards. You'd have to poke our eyes out to keep us from seeing what's going on. Forget it, we're not coming."

16.15 Moses' temper blazed white-hot. He said to GOD, "Don't accept their Grain-Offering. I haven't taken so much as a single donkey from them; I haven't hurt a single hair of their heads."

16.16-17 Moses said to Korah, "Bring your people before GOD tomorrow. Appear there with them and Aaron. Have each man bring his censer filled with incense and present it to GOD—all 250 censers. And you and Aaron do the same, bring your censers."

16.18 So they all did it. They brought their censers filled with fire and incense and stood at the entrance of the Tent of Meeting. Moses and Aaron did the same.

16.19 It was Korah and his gang against Moses and Aaron at the entrance of the Tent of Meeting. The entire community could see the Glory of GOD.

16.20-21 GOD said to Moses and Aaron, "Separate yourselves from this congregation so that I can finish them off and be done with them."

16.22 They threw themselves on their faces and said, "O God, God of everything living, when one man sins are you going to take it out on the whole community?"

16.23-24 GOD spoke to Moses: "Speak to the community. Tell them, Back off from the tents of Korah, Dathan, and Abiram."

16.25-26 Moses got up and went to Dathan and Abiram. The leaders of Israel followed him. He then spoke to the community: "Back off from the tents of these bad men; don't touch a thing that belongs to them lest you be carried off on the flood of their sins."

---

^a 14 Or you make slaves of; or you deceive

NEW INTERNATIONAL VERSION

from the tents of Korah, Dathan and Abiram. Dathan and Abiram had come out and were standing with their wives, children and little ones at the entrances to their tents.

²⁸Then Moses said, "This is how you will know that the LORD has sent me to do all these things and that it was not my idea: ²⁹If these men die a natural death and experience only what usually happens to men, then the LORD has not sent me. ³⁰But if the LORD brings about something totally new, and the earth opens its mouth and swallows them, with everything that belongs to them, and they go down alive into the grave,ᵃ then you will know that these men have treated the LORD with contempt."

³¹As soon as he finished saying all this, the ground under them split apart ³²and the earth opened its mouth and swallowed them, with their households and all Korah's men and all their possessions. ³³They went down alive into the grave, with everything they owned; the earth closed over them, and they perished and were gone from the community. ³⁴At their cries, all the Israelites around them fled, shouting, "The earth is going to swallow us too!"

³⁵And fire came out from the LORD and consumed the 250 men who were offering the incense.

³⁶The LORD said to Moses, ³⁷"Tell Eleazar son of Aaron, the priest, to take the censers out of the smoldering remains and scatter the coals some distance away, for the censers are holy— ³⁸the censers of the men who sinned at the cost of their lives. Hammer the censers into sheets to overlay the altar, for they were presented before the LORD and have become holy. Let them be a sign to the Israelites."

³⁹So Eleazar the priest collected the bronze censers brought by those who had been burned up, and he had them hammered out to overlay the altar, ⁴⁰as the LORD directed him through Moses. This was to remind the Israelites that no one except a descendant of Aaron should come to burn incense before the LORD, or he would become like Korah and his followers.

⁴¹The next day the whole Israelite community grumbled against Moses and Aaron. "You have killed the LORD's people," they said.

⁴²But when the assembly gathered in opposition to Moses and Aaron and turned toward the Tent of Meeting, suddenly the cloud covered it and the glory of the LORD appeared. ⁴³Then Moses and Aaron went to the front of the Tent of Meeting, ⁴⁴and the LORD said to Moses, ⁴⁵"Get

ᵃ 30 Hebrew *Sheol*; also in verse 33

THE MESSAGE

16.27 So they all backed away from the tents of Korah, Dathan, and Abiram. Dathan and Abiram by now had come out and were standing at the entrance to their tents with their wives, children, and babies.

16.28-30 Moses continued to address the community: "This is how you'll know that it was GOD who sent me to do all these things and that it wasn't anything I cooked up on my own. If these men die a natural death like all the rest of us, you'll know that it wasn't GOD who sent me. But if GOD does something unprecedented—if the ground opens up and swallows the lot of them and they are pitched alive into Sheol—then you'll know that these men have been insolent with GOD."

16.31-33 The words were hardly out of his mouth when the Earth split open. Earth opened its mouth and in one gulp swallowed them down, the men and their families, all the human beings connected with Korah, along with everything they owned. And that was the end of them, pitched alive into Sheol. The Earth closed up over them and that was the last the community heard of them.

16.34 At the sound of their cries everyone around ran for dear life, shouting, "We're about to be swallowed up alive!"

16.35 Then GOD sent lightning. The fire cremated the 250 men who were offering the incense.

16.36-38 GOD spoke to Moses: "Tell Eleazar son of Aaron the priest, Gather up the censers from the smoldering cinders and scatter the coals a distance away for these censers have become holy. Take the censers of the men who have sinned and are now dead and hammer them into thin sheets for covering the Altar. They have been offered to GOD and are holy to GOD. Let them serve as a sign to Israel, evidence of what happened this day."

16.39-40 So Eleazar gathered all the bronze censers that belonged to those who had been burned up and had them hammered flat and used to overlay the Altar, just as GOD had instructed him by Moses. This was to serve as a sign to Israel that only descendants of Aaron were allowed to burn incense before GOD; anyone else trying it would end up like Korah and his gang.

16.41 Grumbling broke out the next day in the community of Israel, grumbling against Moses and Aaron: "You have killed GOD's people!"

16.42 But it so happened that when the community got together against Moses and Aaron, they looked over at the Tent of Meeting and there was the Cloud—the Glory of GOD for all to see.

16.43-45 Moses and Aaron stood at the front of the Tent of Meeting. GOD spoke to Moses: "Back

NEW INTERNATIONAL VERSION

away from this assembly so I can put an end to them at once." And they fell facedown.

⁴⁶Then Moses said to Aaron, "Take your censer and put incense in it, along with fire from the altar, and hurry to the assembly to make atonement for them. Wrath has come out from the LORD; the plague has started." ⁴⁷So Aaron did as Moses said, and ran into the midst of the assembly. The plague had already started among the people, but Aaron offered the incense and made atonement for them. ⁴⁸He stood between the living and the dead, and the plague stopped. ⁴⁹But 14,700 people died from the plague, in addition to those who had died because of Korah. ⁵⁰Then Aaron returned to Moses at the entrance to the Tent of Meeting, for the plague had stopped.

THE BUDDING OF AARON'S STAFF

17 The LORD said to Moses, ²"Speak to the Israelites and get twelve staffs from them, one from the leader of each of their ancestral tribes. Write the name of each man on his staff. ³On the staff of Levi write Aaron's name, for there must be one staff for the head of each ancestral tribe. ⁴Place them in the Tent of Meeting in front of the Testimony, where I meet with you. ⁵The staff belonging to the man I choose will sprout, and I will rid myself of this constant grumbling against you by the Israelites."

⁶So Moses spoke to the Israelites, and their leaders gave him twelve staffs, one for the leader of each of their ancestral tribes, and Aaron's staff was among them. ⁷Moses placed the staffs before the LORD in the Tent of the Testimony.

⁸The next day Moses entered the Tent of the Testimony and saw that Aaron's staff, which represented the house of Levi, had not only sprouted but had budded, blossomed and produced almonds. ⁹Then Moses brought out all the staffs from the LORD'S presence to all the Israelites. They looked at them, and each man took his own staff.

¹⁰The LORD said to Moses, "Put back Aaron's staff in front of the Testimony, to be kept as a sign to the rebellious. This will put an end to their grumbling against me, so that they will not die." ¹¹Moses did just as the LORD commanded him.

¹²The Israelites said to Moses, "We will die! We are lost, we are all lost! ¹³Anyone who even comes near the tabernacle of the LORD will die. Are we all going to die?"

THE MESSAGE

away from this congregation so that I can do away with them this very minute."

They threw themselves facedown on the ground.

16.46 Moses said to Aaron, "Take your censer and fill it with incense, along with fire from the Altar. Get to the congregation as fast as you can: make atonement for them. Anger is pouring out from GOD—the plague has started!"

16.47-48 Aaron grabbed the censer, as directed by Moses, and ran into the midst of the congregation. The plague had already begun. He put burning incense into the censer and atoned for the people. He stood there between the living and the dead and stopped the plague.

16.49-50 Fourteen thousand seven hundred people died from the plague, not counting those who died in the affair of Korah. Aaron then went back to join Moses at the entrance to the Tent of Meeting. The plague was stopped.

AARON'S STAFF

17 GOD spoke to Moses: "Speak to the People of Israel. Get staffs from them—twelve staffs in all, one from the leader of each of their ancestral tribes. Write each man's name on his staff. Start with Aaron; write Aaron's name on the staff of Levi and then proceed with the rest, a staff for the leader of each ancestral tribe. Now lay them out in the Tent of Meeting in front of The Testimony where I keep appointments with you. What will happen next is this: The staff of the man I choose will sprout. I'm going to put a stop to this endless grumbling by the People of Israel against you."

17.6-7 Moses spoke to the People of Israel. Their leaders handed over twelve staffs, one for the leader of each tribe. And Aaron's staff was one of them. Moses laid out the staffs before GOD in the Tent of Testimony.

17.8-9 Moses walked into the Tent of Testimony the next day and saw that Aaron's staff, the staff of the tribe of Levi, had in fact sprouted—buds, blossoms, and even ripe almonds! Moses brought out all the staffs from GOD's presence and presented them to the People of Israel. They took a good look. Each leader took the staff with his name on it.

17.10 GOD said to Moses, "Return Aaron's staff to the front of The Testimony. Keep it there as a sign to rebels. This will put a stop to the grumbling against me and save their lives."

17.11 Moses did just as GOD commanded him.

17.12-13 The People of Israel said to Moses, "We're as good as dead. This is our death sentence. Anyone who even gets close to The Dwelling of GOD is as good as dead. Are we all doomed?"

NEW INTERNATIONAL VERSION

DUTIES OF PRIESTS AND LEVITES

18 The LORD said to Aaron, "You, your sons and your father's family are to bear the responsibility for offenses against the sanctuary, and you and your sons alone are to bear the responsibility for offenses against the priesthood. ²Bring your fellow Levites from your ancestral tribe to join you and assist you when you and your sons minister before the Tent of the Testimony. ³They are to be responsible to you and are to perform all the duties of the Tent, but they must not go near the furnishings of the sanctuary or the altar, or both they and you will die. ⁴They are to join you and be responsible for the care of the Tent of Meeting—all the work at the Tent—and no one else may come near where you are.

⁵"You are to be responsible for the care of the sanctuary and the altar, so that wrath will not fall on the Israelites again. ⁶I myself have selected your fellow Levites from among the Israelites as a gift to you, dedicated to the LORD to do the work at the Tent of Meeting. ⁷But only you and your sons may serve as priests in connection with everything at the altar and inside the curtain. I am giving you the service of the priesthood as a gift. Anyone else who comes near the sanctuary must be put to death."

OFFERINGS FOR PRIESTS AND LEVITES

⁸Then the LORD said to Aaron, "I myself have put you in charge of the offerings presented to me; all the holy offerings the Israelites give me I give to you and your sons as your portion and regular share. ⁹You are to have the part of the most holy offerings that is kept from the fire. From all the gifts they bring me as most holy offerings, whether grain or sin or guilt offerings, that part belongs to you and your sons. ¹⁰Eat it as something most holy; every male shall eat it. You must regard it as holy.

¹¹"This also is yours: whatever is set aside from the gifts of all the wave offerings of the Israelites. I give this to you and your sons and daughters as your regular share. Everyone in your household who is ceremonially clean may eat it.

¹²"I give you all the finest olive oil and all the finest new wine and grain they give the LORD as the firstfruits of their harvest. ¹³All the land's firstfruits that they bring to the LORD will be yours. Everyone in your household who is ceremonially clean may eat it.

¹⁴"Everything in Israel that is devoted*a* to the LORD is yours. ¹⁵The first offspring of every

---

a 14 The Hebrew term refers to the irrevocable giving over of things or persons to the LORD.

THE MESSAGE

DUTIES IN THE TENT OF TESTIMONY

18.1-4 **18** GOD said to Aaron, "You and your sons, along with your father's family, are responsible for taking care of sins having to do with the Sanctuary; you and your sons are also responsible for sins involving the priesthood. So enlist your brothers of the tribe of Levi to join you and assist you and your sons in your duties in the Tent of Testimony. They will report to you as they go about their duties related to the Tent, but they must not have anything to do with the holy things of the Altar under penalty of death—both they and you will die! They are to work with you in taking care of the Tent of Meeting, whatever work is involved in the Tent. Outsiders are not allowed to help you.

18.5-7 "Your job is to take care of the Sanctuary and the Altar so that there will be no more outbreaks of anger on the People of Israel. I personally have picked your brothers, the Levites, from Israel as a whole. I'm giving them to you as a gift, a gift of GOD, to help with the work of the Tent of Meeting. But only you and your sons may serve as priests, working around the Altar and inside the curtain. The work of the priesthood is my exclusive gift to you; it cannot be delegated—anyone else who invades the Sanctuary will be executed."

18.8-10 GOD spoke to Aaron, "I am personally putting you in charge of my contributions, all the holy gifts I get from the People of Israel. I am turning them over to you and your children for your personal use. This is the standing rule. You and your sons get what's left from the offerings, whatever hasn't been totally burned up on the Altar—the leftovers from Grain-Offerings, Absolution-Offerings, and Compensation-Offerings. Eat it reverently; it is most holy; every male may eat it. Treat it as holy.

18.11-13 "You also get the Wave-Offerings from the People of Israel. I present them to you and your sons and daughters as a gift. This is the standing rule. Anyone in your household who is ritually clean may eat it. I also give you all the best olive oil, the best new wine, and the grain that is offered to GOD as the firstfruits of their harvest—all the firstfruits they offer to GOD are yours. Anyone in your household who is ritually clean may eat it.

18.14-16 "You get every Totally-Devoted gift. Every firstborn that is offered to GOD, whether animal

NEW INTERNATIONAL VERSION

womb, both man and animal, that is offered to the LORD is yours. But you must redeem every firstborn son and every firstborn male of unclean animals. [16]When they are a month old, you must redeem them at the redemption price set at five shekels[a] of silver, according to the sanctuary shekel, which weighs twenty gerahs.

[17]"But you must not redeem the firstborn of an ox, a sheep or a goat; they are holy. Sprinkle their blood on the altar and burn their fat as an offering made by fire, an aroma pleasing to the LORD. [18]Their meat is to be yours, just as the breast of the wave offering and the right thigh are yours. [19]Whatever is set aside from the holy offerings the Israelites present to the LORD I give to you and your sons and daughters as your regular share. It is an everlasting covenant of salt before the LORD for both you and your offspring."

[20]The LORD said to Aaron, "You will have no inheritance in their land, nor will you have any share among them; I am your share and your inheritance among the Israelites.

[21]"I give to the Levites all the tithes in Israel as their inheritance in return for the work they do while serving at the Tent of Meeting. [22]From now on the Israelites must not go near the Tent of Meeting, or they will bear the consequences of their sin and will die. [23]It is the Levites who are to do the work at the Tent of Meeting and bear the responsibility for offenses against it. This is a lasting ordinance for the generations to come. They will receive no inheritance among the Israelites. [24]Instead, I give to the Levites as their inheritance the tithes that the Israelites present as an offering to the LORD. That is why I said concerning them: 'They will have no inheritance among the Israelites.' "

[25]The LORD said to Moses, [26]"Speak to the Levites and say to them: 'When you receive from the Israelites the tithe I give you as your inheritance, you must present a tenth of that tithe as the LORD's offering. [27]Your offering will be reckoned to you as grain from the threshing floor or juice from the winepress. [28]In this way you also will present an offering to the LORD from all the tithes you receive from the Israelites. From these tithes you must give the LORD's portion to Aaron the priest. [29]You must present as the LORD's portion the best and holiest part of everything given to you.'

[30]"Say to the Levites: 'When you present the best part, it will be reckoned to you as the product of the threshing floor or the winepress. [31]You and your households may eat the rest of it any-

[a]16 That is, about 2 ounces (about 55 grams)

THE MESSAGE

or person, is yours. Except you don't get the firstborn itself, but its redemption price; firstborn humans and ritually clean animals are bought back and you get the redemption price. When the firstborn is a month old it must be redeemed at the redemption price of five shekels of silver, using the standard of the Sanctuary shekel, which weighs twenty gerahs.

18.17-19 "On the other hand, you don't redeem a firstborn ox, sheep, or goat—they are holy. Instead splash their blood on the Altar and burn their fat as a Fire-Gift, a pleasing fragrance to GOD. But you get the meat, just as you get the breast from the Wave-Offering and the right thigh. All the holy offerings that the People of Israel set aside for GOD, I'm turning over to you and your children. That's the standard rule and includes both you and your children—a Covenant-of-Salt, eternal and unchangeable before GOD."

18.20 GOD said to Aaron, "You won't get any inheritance in land, not so much as a small plot of ground: I am your plot of ground, I am your inheritance among the People of Israel.

18.21-24 "I'm giving the Levites all the tithes of Israel as their pay for the work they do in the Tent of Meeting. Starting now, the rest of the People of Israel cannot wander in and out of the Tent of Meeting; they'll be penalized for their sin and the penalty is death. It's the Levites and only the Levites who are to work in the Tent of Meeting and they are responsible for anything that goes wrong. This is the regular rule for all time. They get no inheritance among the People of Israel; instead I turn over to them the tithes that the People of Israel present as an offering to GOD. That's why I give the ruling: They are to receive no land-inheritance among the People of Israel."

✝

18.25-29 GOD spoke to Moses: "Speak to the Levites. Tell them, When you get the tithe from the People of Israel, the inheritance that I have assigned to you, you must tithe that tithe and present it as an offering to GOD. Your offerings will be treated the same as other people's gifts of grain from the threshing floor or wine from the wine vat. This is your procedure for making offerings to GOD from all the tithes you get from the People of Israel: give GOD's portion from these tithes to Aaron the priest. Make sure that GOD's portion is the best and holiest of everything you get.

18.30-32 "Tell the Levites, When you offer the best part, the rest will be treated the same as grain from the threshing floor or wine from the wine vat that others give. You and your households

NEW INTERNATIONAL VERSION

where, for it is your wages for your work at the Tent of Meeting. ³²By presenting the best part of it you will not be guilty in this matter; then you will not defile the holy offerings of the Israelites, and you will not die.' "

THE WATER OF CLEANSING

19 The LORD said to Moses and Aaron: ²"This is a requirement of the law that the LORD has commanded: Tell the Israelites to bring you a red heifer without defect or blemish and that has never been under a yoke. ³Give it to Eleazar the priest; it is to be taken outside the camp and slaughtered in his presence. ⁴Then Eleazar the priest is to take some of its blood on his finger and sprinkle it seven times toward the front of the Tent of Meeting. ⁵While he watches, the heifer is to be burned—its hide, flesh, blood and offal. ⁶The priest is to take some cedar wood, hyssop and scarlet wool and throw them onto the burning heifer. ⁷After that, the priest must wash his clothes and bathe himself with water. He may then come into the camp, but he will be ceremonially unclean till evening. ⁸The man who burns it must also wash his clothes and bathe with water, and he too will be unclean till evening.

⁹"A man who is clean shall gather up the ashes of the heifer and put them in a ceremonially clean place outside the camp. They shall be kept by the Israelite community for use in the water of cleansing; it is for purification from sin. ¹⁰The man who gathers up the ashes of the heifer must also wash his clothes, and he too will be unclean till evening. This will be a lasting ordinance both for the Israelites and for the aliens living among them.

¹¹"Whoever touches the dead body of anyone will be unclean for seven days. ¹²He must purify himself with the water on the third day and on the seventh day; then he will be clean. But if he does not purify himself on the third and seventh days, he will not be clean. ¹³Whoever touches the dead body of anyone and fails to purify himself defiles the LORD's tabernacle. That person must be cut off from Israel. Because the water of cleansing has not been sprinkled on him, he is unclean; his uncleanness remains on him.

¹⁴"This is the law that applies when a person dies in a tent: Anyone who enters the tent and anyone who is in it will be unclean for seven days, ¹⁵and every open container without a lid fastened on it will be unclean.

¹⁶"Anyone out in the open who touches someone who has been killed with a sword or someone who has died a natural death, or any-

THE MESSAGE

are free to eat the rest of it anytime and anyplace—it's your wages for your work at the Tent of Meeting. By offering the best part, you'll avoid guilt, you won't desecrate the holy offerings of the People of Israel, and you won't die."

THE RED COW

^{19.1-4} **19** GOD spoke to Moses and Aaron: "This is the rule from the Revelation that GOD commands: Tell the People of Israel to get a red cow, a healthy specimen, ritually clean, that has never been in harness. Present it to Eleazar the priest, then take it outside the camp and butcher it while he looks on. Eleazar will take some of the blood on his finger and splash it seven times in the direction of the Tent of Meeting.

^{19.5-8}   "Then under Eleazar's supervision burn the cow, the whole thing—hide, meat, blood, even its dung. The priest then will take a stick of cedar, some sprigs of hyssop, and a piece of scarlet material and throw them on the burning cow. Afterwards the priest must wash his clothes and bathe well with water. He can then come into the camp but he remains ritually unclean until evening. The man who burns the cow must also wash his clothes and bathe with water. He also is unclean until evening.

^{19.9}   "Then a man who is ritually clean will gather the ashes of the cow and place them in a ritually clean place outside the camp. The congregation of Israel will keep them to use in the Water-of-Cleansing, an Absolution-Offering.

^{19.10}   "The man who gathered up the ashes must scrub his clothes; he is ritually unclean until evening. This is to be a standing rule for both native-born Israelites and foreigners living among them.

^{19.11-13}   "Anyone who touches a dead body is ritually unclean for seven days. He must purify himself with the Water-of-Cleansing on the third day; on the seventh day he will be clean. But if he doesn't follow the procedures for the third and seventh days, he won't be clean. Anyone who touches the dead body of anyone and doesn't get cleansed desecrates GOD's Dwelling and is to be excommunicated. For as long as the Water-of-Cleansing has not been sprinkled on him, he remains ritually unclean.

^{19.14-15}   "This is the rule for someone who dies in his tent: Anyone who enters the tent or is already in the tent is ritually unclean for seven days, and every open container without a lid is unclean.

^{19.16-21}   "Anyone out in the open field who touches a corpse, whether dead from violent or natural

NEW INTERNATIONAL VERSION

one who touches a human bone or a grave, will be unclean for seven days.

17 "For the unclean person, put some ashes from the burned purification offering into a jar and pour fresh water over them. 18 Then a man who is ceremonially clean is to take some hyssop, dip it in the water and sprinkle the tent and all the furnishings and the people who were there. He must also sprinkle anyone who has touched a human bone or a grave or someone who has been killed or someone who has died a natural death. 19 The man who is clean is to sprinkle the unclean person on the third and seventh days, and on the seventh day he is to purify him. The person being cleansed must wash his clothes and bathe with water, and that evening he will be clean. 20 But if a person who is unclean does not purify himself, he must be cut off from the community, because he has defiled the sanctuary of the LORD. The water of cleansing has not been sprinkled on him, and he is unclean. 21 This is a lasting ordinance for them.

"The man who sprinkles the water of cleansing must also wash his clothes, and anyone who touches the water of cleansing will be unclean till evening. 22 Anything that an unclean person touches becomes unclean, and anyone who touches it becomes unclean till evening."

WATER FROM THE ROCK

20 In the first month the whole Israelite community arrived at the Desert of Zin, and they stayed at Kadesh. There Miriam died and was buried.

2 Now there was no water for the community, and the people gathered in opposition to Moses and Aaron. 3 They quarreled with Moses and said, "If only we had died when our brothers fell dead before the LORD! 4 Why did you bring the LORD's community into this desert, that we and our livestock should die here? 5 Why did you bring us up out of Egypt to this terrible place? It has no grain or figs, grapevines or pomegranates. And there is no water to drink!"

6 Moses and Aaron went from the assembly to the entrance to the Tent of Meeting and fell facedown, and the glory of the LORD appeared to them. 7 The LORD said to Moses, 8 "Take the staff, and you and your brother Aaron gather the assembly together. Speak to that rock before their eyes and it will pour out its water. You will bring water out of the rock for the community so they and their livestock can drink."

9 So Moses took the staff from the LORD's pres-

THE MESSAGE

causes, or a human bone or a grave is unclean for seven days. For this unclean person, take some ashes from the burned Absolution-Offering and add some fresh water to it in a bowl. Find a ritually clean man to dip a sprig of hyssop into the water and sprinkle the tent and all its furnishings, the persons who were in the tent, the one who touched the bones of the person who was killed or died a natural death, and whoever may have touched a grave. Then he is to sprinkle the unclean person on the third and seventh days. On the seventh day he is considered cleansed. The cleansed person must then scrub his clothes and take a bath; by evening he is clean. But if an unclean person does not go through these cleansing procedures, he must be excommunicated from the community; he has desecrated the Sanctuary of GOD. The Water-of-Cleansing has not been sprinkled on him and he is ritually unclean. This is the standing rule for these cases.

"The man who sprinkles the Water-of-Cleansing has to scrub his clothes; anyone else who touched the Water-of-Cleansing is also ritually unclean until evening.

19.22   "Anything the ritually unclean man touches becomes unclean, and the person who touches what he touched is unclean until evening."

CAMP KADESH

20.1 **20** In the first month, the entire company of the People of Israel arrived in the Wilderness of Zin. The people stayed in Kadesh.

Miriam died there, and she was buried.

20.2-5   There was no water there for the community, so they ganged up on Moses and Aaron. They attacked Moses: "We wish we'd died when the rest of our brothers died before GOD. Why did you haul this congregation of GOD out here into this wilderness to die, people and cattle alike? And why did you take us out of Egypt in the first place, dragging us into this miserable country? No grain, no figs, no grapevines, no pomegranates—and now not even any water!"

20.6   Moses and Aaron walked from the assembled congregation to the Tent of Meeting and threw themselves facedown on the ground. And they saw the Glory of GOD.

20.7-8   GOD spoke to Moses: "Take the staff. Assemble the community, you and your brother Aaron. Speak to that rock that's right in front of them and it will give water. You will bring water out of the rock for them; congregation and cattle will both drink."

20.9-10   Moses took the staff away from GOD's pres-

NEW INTERNATIONAL VERSION

ence, just as he commanded him. ¹⁰He and Aaron gathered the assembly together in front of the rock and Moses said to them, "Listen, you rebels, must we bring you water out of this rock?" ¹¹Then Moses raised his arm and struck the rock twice with his staff. Water gushed out, and the community and their livestock drank.

¹²But the LORD said to Moses and Aaron, "Because you did not trust in me enough to honor me as holy in the sight of the Israelites, you will not bring this community into the land I give them."

¹³These were the waters of Meribah,ᵃ where the Israelites quarreled with the LORD and where he showed himself holy among them.

EDOM DENIES ISRAEL PASSAGE

¹⁴Moses sent messengers from Kadesh to the king of Edom, saying:

"This is what your brother Israel says: You know about all the hardships that have come upon us. ¹⁵Our forefathers went down into Egypt, and we lived there many years. The Egyptians mistreated us and our fathers, ¹⁶but when we cried out to the LORD, he heard our cry and sent an angel and brought us out of Egypt.

"Now we are here at Kadesh, a town on the edge of your territory. ¹⁷Please let us pass through your country. We will not go through any field or vineyard, or drink water from any well. We will travel along the king's highway and not turn to the right or to the left until we have passed through your territory."

¹⁸But Edom answered:

"You may not pass through here; if you try, we will march out and attack you with the sword."

¹⁹The Israelites replied:

"We will go along the main road, and if we or our livestock drink any of your water, we will pay for it. We only want to pass through on foot—nothing else."

²⁰Again they answered:

"You may not pass through."

Then Edom came out against them with a large and powerful army. ²¹Since Edom refused to let them go through their territory, Israel turned away from them.

ᵃ 13 Meribah means quarreling.

THE MESSAGE

ence, as commanded. He and Aaron rounded up the whole congregation in front of the rock. Moses spoke: "Listen, rebels! Do we have to bring water out of this rock for you?"

20.11 With that Moses raised his arm and slammed his staff against the rock—once, twice. Water poured out. Congregation and cattle drank.

20.12 GOD said to Moses and Aaron, "Because you didn't trust me, didn't treat me with holy reverence in front of the People of Israel, you two aren't going to lead this company into the land that I am giving them."

20.13 These were the Waters of Meribah (Bickering) where the People of Israel bickered with GOD, and he revealed himself as holy.

✝

20.14-16 Moses sent emissaries from Kadesh to the king of Edom with this message: "A message from your brother Israel: You are familiar with all the trouble we've run into. Our ancestors went down to Egypt and lived there a long time. The Egyptians viciously abused both us and our ancestors. But when we cried out for help to GOD, he heard our cry. He sent an angel and got us out of Egypt. And now here we are at Kadesh, a town at the border of your land.

20.17 "Will you give us permission to cut across your land? We won't trespass through your fields or orchards and we won't drink out of your wells; we'll keep to the main road, the King's Road, straying neither right nor left until we've crossed your border."

20.18 The king of Edom answered, "Not on your life. If you so much as set a foot on my land, I'll kill you."

20.19 The People of Israel said, "Look, we'll stay on the main road. If we or our animals drink any water, we'll pay you for it. We're harmless—just a company of footsore travelers."

20.20-21 He answered again: "No. You may not come through." And Edom came out and blocked the way with a crowd of people brandishing weapons. Edom refused to let them cross through his land. So Israel had to detour around him.

NEW INTERNATIONAL VERSION

THE DEATH OF AARON

22The whole Israelite community set out from Kadesh and came to Mount Hor. 23At Mount Hor, near the border of Edom, the LORD said to Moses and Aaron, 24"Aaron will be gathered to his people. He will not enter the land I give the Israelites, because both of you rebelled against my command at the waters of Meribah. 25Get Aaron and his son Eleazar and take them up Mount Hor. 26Remove Aaron's garments and put them on his son Eleazar, for Aaron will be gathered to his people; he will die there."

27Moses did as the LORD commanded: They went up Mount Hor in the sight of the whole community. 28Moses removed Aaron's garments and put them on his son Eleazar. And Aaron died there on top of the mountain. Then Moses and Eleazar came down from the mountain, 29and when the whole community learned that Aaron had died, the entire house of Israel mourned for him thirty days.

ARAD DESTROYED

21 When the Canaanite king of Arad, who lived in the Negev, heard that Israel was coming along the road to Atharim, he attacked the Israelites and captured some of them. 2Then Israel made this vow to the LORD: "If you will deliver these people into our hands, we will totally destroy*a* their cities." 3The LORD listened to Israel's plea and gave the Canaanites over to them. They completely destroyed them and their towns; so the place was named Hormah.*b*

THE BRONZE SNAKE

4They traveled from Mount Hor along the route to the Red Sea,*c* to go around Edom. But the people grew impatient on the way; 5they spoke against God and against Moses, and said, "Why have you brought us up out of Egypt to die in the desert? There is no bread! There is no water! And we detest this miserable food!"

6Then the LORD sent venomous snakes among them; they bit the people and many Israelites died. 7The people came to Moses and said, "We sinned when we spoke against the LORD and against you. Pray that the LORD will take the snakes away from us." So Moses prayed for the people.

8The LORD said to Moses, "Make a snake and put it up on a pole; anyone who is bitten can look at it and live." 9So Moses made a bronze snake and put it up on a pole. Then when any-

---

a 2 The Hebrew term refers to the irrevocable giving over of things or persons to the LORD, often by totally destroying them; also in verse 3.   *b 3 Hormah* means *destruction.*
c 4 Hebrew *Yam Suph;* that is, Sea of Reeds

THE MESSAGE

CAMP HOR

20.22 The People of Israel, the entire company, set out from Kadesh and traveled to Mount Hor.

20.23-26 GOD said to Moses and Aaron at Mount Hor at the border of Edom, "It's time for Aaron to be gathered into the company of his ancestors. He will not enter the land I am giving to the People of Israel because you both rebelled against my orders at the Waters of Meribah. So take Aaron and his son Eleazar and lead them up Mount Hor. Remove Aaron's clothes from him and put them on his son Eleazar. Aaron will be gathered there; Aaron will die."

20.27-29 Moses obeyed GOD's command. They climbed Mount Hor as the whole congregation watched. Moses took off Aaron's clothes and put them on his son Eleazar. Aaron died on top of the mountain. Then Moses and Eleazar came down from the mountain. The whole congregation, getting the news that Aaron had died, went into thirty days of mourning for him.

HORMAH

21.1 **21** The Canaanite king of Arad, ruling in the Negev, heard that Israel was advancing up the road to Atharim. He attacked Israel and took prisoners of war.

21.2 Israel vowed a vow to GOD: "If you will give this people into our power, we'll destroy their towns and present the ruins to you as a holy destruction."

21.3 GOD listened to Israel's prayer and gave them the Canaanites. They destroyed both them and their towns, a holy destruction. They named the place Hormah (Holy Destruction).

THE SNAKE OF FIERY COPPER

21.4-5 They set out from Mount Hor along the Red Sea Road, a detour around the land of Edom. The people became irritable and cross as they traveled. They spoke out against God and Moses: "Why did you drag us out of Egypt to die in this godforsaken country? No decent food; no water—we can't stomach this stuff any longer."

21.6-7 So GOD sent poisonous snakes among the people; they bit them and many in Israel died. The people came to Moses and said, "We sinned when we spoke out against GOD and you. Pray to GOD; ask him to take these snakes from us."

Moses prayed for the people.

21.8 GOD said to Moses, "Make a snake and put it on a flagpole: Whoever is bitten and looks at it will live."

21.9 So Moses made a snake of fiery copper and put it on top of a flagpole. Anyone bitten by a

NEW INTERNATIONAL VERSION

one was bitten by a snake and looked at the bronze snake, he lived.

THE JOURNEY TO MOAB

¹⁰The Israelites moved on and camped at Oboth. ¹¹Then they set out from Oboth and camped in Iye Abarim, in the desert that faces Moab toward the sunrise. ¹²From there they moved on and camped in the Zered Valley. ¹³They set out from there and camped alongside the Arnon, which is in the desert extending into Amorite territory. The Arnon is the border of Moab, between Moab and the Amorites. ¹⁴That is why the Book of the Wars of the LORD says:

> ". . . Waheb in Suphah*a* and the ravines,
>   the Arnon ¹⁵and*b* the slopes of the ravines
> that lead to the site of Ar
>   and lie along the border of Moab."

¹⁶From there they continued on to Beer, the well where the LORD said to Moses, "Gather the people together and I will give them water."

¹⁷Then Israel sang this song:

> "Spring up, O well!
>   Sing about it,
> ¹⁸about the well that the princes dug,
>   that the nobles of the people sank—
>   the nobles with scepters and staffs."

Then they went from the desert to Mattanah, ¹⁹from Mattanah to Nahaliel, from Nahaliel to Bamoth, ²⁰and from Bamoth to the valley in Moab where the top of Pisgah overlooks the wasteland.

DEFEAT OF SIHON AND OG

²¹Israel sent messengers to say to Sihon king of the Amorites:

²²"Let us pass through your country. We will not turn aside into any field or vineyard, or drink water from any well. We will travel along the king's highway until we have passed through your territory."

²³But Sihon would not let Israel pass through his territory. He mustered his entire army and marched out into the desert against Israel. When he reached Jahaz, he fought with Israel. ²⁴Israel, however, put him to the sword and took over his land from the Arnon to the Jabbok, but only as far as the Ammonites, because their border was fortified. ²⁵Israel captured all the cities of the Amorites and occupied them, including Heshbon and all its surrounding settlements.

a 14 The meaning of the Hebrew for this phrase is uncertain. b 14,15 Or "I have been given from Suphah and the ravines / of the Arnon ¹⁵to

THE MESSAGE

snake who then looked at the copper snake lived.

CAMPING ON THE WAY TO MOAB

21:10-15 The People of Israel set out and camped at Oboth. They left Oboth and camped at Iye Abarim in the wilderness that faces Moab on the east. They went from there and pitched camp in the Zered Valley. Their next camp was alongside the Arnon River, which marks the border between Amorite country and Moab. The Book of the Wars of GOD refers to this place:

> Waheb in Suphah,
>   the canyons of Arnon;
> Along the canyon ravines
>   that lead to the village Ar
> And lean hard against
>   the border of Moab.

21:16-18 They went on to Beer (The Well), where GOD said to Moses, "Gather the people; I'll give them water." That's where Israel sang this song:

> Erupt, Well!
> Sing the Song of the Well,
>   the well sunk by princes,
> Dug out by the peoples' leaders
>   digging with their scepters and staffs.

21:19-20 From the wilderness their route went from Mattanah to Nahaliel to Bamoth (The Heights) to the valley that opens into the fields of Moab from where Pisgah (The Summit) rises and overlooks Jeshimon (Wasteland).

21:21-22 Israel sent emissaries to Sihon, king of the Amorites, saying, "Let us cross your land. We won't trespass into your fields or drink water in your vineyards. We'll keep to the main road, the King's Road, until we're through your land."

21:23-27 But Sihon wouldn't let Israel go through. Instead he got his army together and marched into the wilderness to fight Israel. At Jahaz he attacked Israel. But Israel fought hard, beat him soundly, and took possession of his land from the Arnon all the way to the Jabbok right up to the Ammonite border. They stopped there because the Ammonite border was fortified. Israel took and occupied all the Amorite cities, including Heshbon and all its surrounding vil-

NEW INTERNATIONAL VERSION

26Heshbon was the city of Sihon king of the Amorites, who had fought against the former king of Moab and had taken from him all his land as far as the Arnon. 27That is why the poets say:

"Come to Heshbon and let it be rebuilt;
  let Sihon's city be restored.

28 "Fire went out from Heshbon,
  a blaze from the city of Sihon.
It consumed Ar of Moab,
  the citizens of Arnon's heights.
29Woe to you, O Moab!
  You are destroyed, O people of Chemosh!
He has given up his sons as fugitives
  and his daughters as captives
to Sihon king of the Amorites.

30 "But we have overthrown them;
  Heshbon is destroyed all the way to
    Dibon.
We have demolished them as far as Nophah,
  which extends to Medeba."

31So Israel settled in the land of the Amorites.
32After Moses had sent spies to Jazer, the Israelites captured its surrounding settlements and drove out the Amorites who were there. 33Then they turned and went up along the road toward Bashan, and Og king of Bashan and his whole army marched out to meet them in battle at Edrei. 34The LORD said to Moses, "Do not be afraid of him, for I have handed him over to you, with his whole army and his land. Do to him what you did to Sihon king of the Amorites, who reigned in Heshbon."

35So they struck him down, together with his sons and his whole army, leaving them no survivors. And they took possession of his land.

BALAK SUMMONS BALAAM

22 Then the Israelites traveled to the plains of Moab and camped along the Jordan across from Jericho.[a]

2Now Balak son of Zippor saw all that Israel had done to the Amorites, 3and Moab was terrified because there were so many people. Indeed, Moab was filled with dread because of the Israelites.

4The Moabites said to the elders of Midian, "This horde is going to lick up everything around us, as an ox licks up the grass of the field."

So Balak son of Zippor, who was king of Moab at that time, 5sent messengers to summon Balaam son of Beor, who was at Pethor, near the River,[b] in his native land. Balak said:

---

a 1 Hebrew *Jordan of Jericho*; possibly an ancient name for the Jordan River   b 5 That is, the Euphrates

THE MESSAGE

lages. Heshbon was the capital city of Sihon king of the Amorites. He had attacked the former king of Moab and captured all his land as far north as the river Arnon. That is why the folk singers sing,

Come to Heshbon to rebuild the city,
  restore Sihon's town.

21.28-29   Fire once poured out of Heshbon,
  flames from the city of Sihon;
Burning up Ar of Moab,
  the natives of Arnon's heights.
Doom, Moab!
  The people of Chemosh, done for!
Sons turned out as fugitives, daughters
      abandoned as captives
  to the king of the Amorites, to Sihon.

21.30   Oh, but we finished them off:
  Nothing left of Heshbon as far as Dibon;
Devastation as far off as Nophah,
  scorched earth all the way to Medeba.

21.31-32   Israel moved in and lived in Amorite country. Moses sent men to scout out Jazer. They captured its villages and drove away the Amorites who lived there.

21.33   Then they turned north on the road to Bashan. Og king of Bashan marched out with his entire army to meet Moses in battle at Edrei.

21.34   GOD said to Moses, "Don't be afraid of him. I'm making a present of him to you, him and all his people and his land. Treat him the same as Sihon king of the Amorites who ruled in Heshbon."

21.35   So they attacked him, his sons, and all the people—there was not a single survivor. Israel took the land.

BALAAM

22.1   **22** The People of Israel marched on and camped on the Plains of Moab at Jordan-Jericho.

22.2-3   Balak son of Zippor learned of all that Israel had done to the Amorites. The people of Moab were in a total panic because of Israel. There were so many of them! They were terrorized.

22.4-5   Moab spoke to the leaders of Midian: "Look, this mob is going to clean us out—a bunch of crows picking a carcass clean."

Balak son of Zippor, who was king of Moab at that time, sent emissaries to get Balaam son of Beor, who lived at Pethor on the banks of the Euphrates River, his homeland.

NEW INTERNATIONAL VERSION

"A people has come out of Egypt; they cover the face of the land and have settled next to me. 6Now come and put a curse on these people, because they are too powerful for me. Perhaps then I will be able to defeat them and drive them out of the country. For I know that those you bless are blessed, and those you curse are cursed."

7The elders of Moab and Midian left, taking with them the fee for divination. When they came to Balaam, they told him what Balak had said.

8"Spend the night here," Balaam said to them, "and I will bring you back the answer the LORD gives me." So the Moabite princes stayed with him.

9God came to Balaam and asked, "Who are these men with you?"

10Balaam said to God, "Balak son of Zippor, king of Moab, sent me this message: 11'A people that has come out of Egypt covers the face of the land. Now come and put a curse on them for me. Perhaps then I will be able to fight them and drive them away.'"

12But God said to Balaam, "Do not go with them. You must not put a curse on those people, because they are blessed."

13The next morning Balaam got up and said to Balak's princes, "Go back to your own country, for the LORD has refused to let me go with you."

14So the Moabite princes returned to Balak and said, "Balaam refused to come with us."

15Then Balak sent other princes, more numerous and more distinguished than the first. 16They came to Balaam and said:

"This is what Balak son of Zippor says: Do not let anything keep you from coming to me, 17because I will reward you handsomely and do whatever you say. Come and put a curse on these people for me."

18But Balaam answered them, "Even if Balak gave me his palace filled with silver and gold, I could not do anything great or small to go beyond the command of the LORD my God. 19Now stay here tonight as the others did, and I will find out what else the LORD will tell me."

20That night God came to Balaam and said, "Since these men have come to summon you, go with them, but do only what I tell you."

BALAAM'S DONKEY

21Balaam got up in the morning, saddled his donkey and went with the princes of Moab. 22But God was very angry when he went, and

THE MESSAGE

22.5-6 Balak's emissaries said, "Look. A people has come up out of Egypt, and they're all over the place! And they're pressing hard on me. Come and curse them for me—they're too much for me. Maybe then I can beat them; we'll attack and drive them out of the country. You have a reputation: Those you bless stay blessed; those you curse stay cursed."

22.7-8 The leaders of Moab and Midian were soon on their way, with the fee for the cursing tucked safely in their wallets. When they got to Balaam, they gave him Balak's message.

"Stay here for the night," Balaam said. "In the morning I'll deliver the answer that GOD gives me."

22.9 The Moabite nobles stayed with him.

22.10-11 Then God came to Balaam. He asked, "So who are these men here with you?"

Balaam answered, "Balak son of Zippor, king of Moab, sent them with a message: 'Look, the people that came up out of Egypt are all over the place! Come and curse them for me. Maybe then I'll be able to attack and drive them out of the country.'"

22.12 God said to Balaam, "Don't go with them. And don't curse the others—they are a blessed people."

22.13 The next morning Balaam got up and told Balak's nobles, "Go back home; GOD refuses to give me permission to go with you."

22.14 So the Moabite nobles left, came back to Balak, and said, "Balaam wouldn't come with us."

22.15-17 Balak sent another group of nobles, higher ranking and more distinguished. They came to Balaam and said, "Balak son of Zippor says, 'Please, don't refuse to come to me. I will honor and reward you lavishly—anything you tell me to do, I'll do; I'll pay anything—only come and curse this people.'"

22.18-19 Balaam answered Balak's servants: "Even if Balak gave me his house stuffed with silver and gold, I wouldn't be able to defy the orders of my GOD to do anything, whether big or little. But come along and stay with me tonight as the others did; I'll see what GOD will say to me this time."

22.20 God came to Balaam that night and said, "Since these men have come all this way to see you, go ahead and go with them. But make sure you do absolutely nothing other than what I tell you."

22.21-23 Balaam got up in the morning, saddled his donkey, and went off with the noblemen from Moab. As he was going, though, God's anger

NEW INTERNATIONAL VERSION

the angel of the LORD stood in the road to oppose him. Balaam was riding on his donkey, and his two servants were with him. ²³When the donkey saw the angel of the LORD standing in the road with a drawn sword in his hand, she turned off the road into a field. Balaam beat her to get her back on the road.

²⁴Then the angel of the LORD stood in a narrow path between two vineyards, with walls on both sides. ²⁵When the donkey saw the angel of the LORD, she pressed close to the wall, crushing Balaam's foot against it. So he beat her again.

²⁶Then the angel of the LORD moved on ahead and stood in a narrow place where there was no room to turn, either to the right or to the left. ²⁷When the donkey saw the angel of the LORD, she lay down under Balaam, and he was angry and beat her with his staff. ²⁸Then the LORD opened the donkey's mouth, and she said to Balaam, "What have I done to you to make you beat me these three times?"

²⁹Balaam answered the donkey, "You have made a fool of me! If I had a sword in my hand, I would kill you right now."

³⁰The donkey said to Balaam, "Am I not your own donkey, which you have always ridden, to this day? Have I been in the habit of doing this to you?"

"No," he said.

³¹Then the LORD opened Balaam's eyes, and he saw the angel of the LORD standing in the road with his sword drawn. So he bowed low and fell facedown.

³²The angel of the LORD asked him, "Why have you beaten your donkey these three times? I have come here to oppose you because your path is a reckless one before me. *ᵃ* ³³The donkey saw me and turned away from me these three times. If she had not turned away, I would certainly have killed you by now, but I would have spared her."

³⁴Balaam said to the angel of the LORD, "I have sinned. I did not realize you were standing in the road to oppose me. Now if you are displeased, I will go back."

³⁵The angel of the LORD said to Balaam, "Go with the men, but speak only what I tell you." So Balaam went with the princes of Balak.

³⁶When Balak heard that Balaam was coming, he went out to meet him at the Moabite town on the Arnon border, at the edge of his territory. ³⁷Balak said to Balaam, "Did I not send you an urgent summons? Why didn't you come to me? Am I really not able to reward you?"

ᵃ 32 The meaning of the Hebrew for this clause is uncertain.

THE MESSAGE

flared. The angel of GOD stood in the road to block his way. Balaam was riding his donkey, accompanied by his two servants. When the donkey saw the angel blocking the road and brandishing a sword, she veered off the road into the ditch. Balaam beat the donkey and got her back on the road.

22.24-25 But as they were going through a vineyard, with a fence on either side, the donkey again saw GOD's angel blocking the way and veered into the fence, crushing Balaam's foot against the fence. Balaam hit her again.

22.26-27 GOD's angel blocked the way yet again—a very narrow passage this time; there was no getting through on the right or left. Seeing the angel, Balaam's donkey sat down under him. Balaam lost his temper; he beat the donkey with his stick.

22.28 Then GOD gave speech to the donkey. She said to Balaam: "What have I ever done to you that you have beat me these three times?"

22.29 Balaam said, "Because you've been playing games with me! If I had a sword I would have killed you by now."

22.30 The donkey said to Balaam, "Am I not your trusty donkey on whom you've ridden for years right up until now? Have I ever done anything like this to you before? Have I?"

He said, "No."

22.31 Then GOD helped Balaam see what was going on: He saw GOD's angel blocking the way, brandishing a sword. Balaam fell to the ground, his face in the dirt.

22.32-33 GOD's angel said to him: "Why have you beaten your poor donkey these three times? I have come here to block your way because you're getting way ahead of yourself. The donkey saw me and turned away from me these three times. If she hadn't, I would have killed you by this time, but not the donkey. I would have let her off."

22.34 Balaam said to GOD's angel, "I have sinned. I had no idea you were standing in the road blocking my way. If you don't like what I'm doing, I'll head back."

22.35 But GOD's angel said to Balaam, "Go ahead and go with them. But only say what I tell you to say—absolutely no other word."

And so Balaam continued to go with Balak's nobles.

22.36 When Balak heard that Balaam was coming, he went out to meet him in the Moabite town that was on the banks of the Arnon, right on the boundary of his land.

22.37 Balak said to Balaam, "Didn't I send an urgent message for help? Why didn't you come when I called? Do you think I can't pay you enough?"

NEW INTERNATIONAL VERSION

³⁸"Well, I have come to you now," Balaam replied. "But can I say just anything? I must speak only what God puts in my mouth."

³⁹Then Balaam went with Balak to Kiriath Huzoth. ⁴⁰Balak sacrificed cattle and sheep, and gave some to Balaam and the princes who were with him. ⁴¹The next morning Balak took Balaam up to Bamoth Baal, and from there he saw part of the people.

BALAAM'S FIRST ORACLE

23 Balaam said, "Build me seven altars here, and prepare seven bulls and seven rams for me." ²Balak did as Balaam said, and the two of them offered a bull and a ram on each altar.

³Then Balaam said to Balak, "Stay here beside your offering while I go aside. Perhaps the LORD will come to meet with me. Whatever he reveals to me I will tell you." Then he went off to a barren height.

⁴God met with him, and Balaam said, "I have prepared seven altars, and on each altar I have offered a bull and a ram."

⁵The LORD put a message in Balaam's mouth and said, "Go back to Balak and give him this message."

⁶So he went back to him and found him standing beside his offering, with all the princes of Moab. ⁷Then Balaam uttered his oracle:

"Balak brought me from Aram,
   the king of Moab from the eastern
      mountains.
'Come,' he said, 'curse Jacob for me;
   come, denounce Israel.'
⁸How can I curse
   those whom God has not cursed?
How can I denounce
   those whom the LORD has not denounced?
⁹From the rocky peaks I see them,
   from the heights I view them.
I see a people who live apart
   and do not consider themselves one of the
      nations.
¹⁰Who can count the dust of Jacob
   or number the fourth part of Israel?
Let me die the death of the righteous,
   and may my end be like theirs!"

¹¹Balak said to Balaam, "What have you done to me? I brought you to curse my enemies, but you have done nothing but bless them!"

¹²He answered, "Must I not speak what the LORD puts in my mouth?"

THE MESSAGE

22.38   Balaam said to Balak, "Well, I'm here now. But I can't tell you just anything. I can speak only words that God gives me—no others."

22.39-40   Balaam then accompanied Balak to Kiriath Huzoth (Street-Town). Balak slaughtered cattle and sheep for sacrifices and presented them to Balaam and the nobles who were with him.

22.41   At daybreak Balak took Balaam up to Bamoth Baal (The Heights of Baal) so that he could get a good view of some of the people.

23.1   **23** Balaam said, "Build me seven altars here, and then prepare seven bulls and seven rams."

23.2   Balak did it. Then Balaam and Balak sacrificed a bull and a ram on each of the altars.

23.3   Balaam instructed Balak: "Stand watch here beside your Whole-Burnt-Offering while I go off by myself. Maybe GOD will come and meet with me. Whatever he shows or tells me, I'll report to you." Then he went off by himself.

23.4   God did meet with Balaam. Balaam said, "I've set up seven altars and offered a bull and a ram on each altar."

23.5   Then GOD gave Balaam a message: "Return to Balak and give him this message."

23.6-10   He went back and found him stationed beside his Whole-Burnt-Offering and with him all the nobles of Moab. Then Balaam spoke his message-oracle:

Balak led me here from Aram,
   the king of Moab all the way from the
      eastern mountains.
"Go, curse Jacob for me;
   go, damn Israel."
How can I curse whom God has not
      cursed?
   How can I damn whom GOD has not
      damned?
From rock pinnacles I see them,
   from hilltops I survey them:
Look! a people camping off by themselves,
   thinking themselves outsiders among
      nations.
But who could ever count the dust of Jacob
   or take a census of cloud-of-dust Israel?
I want to die like these right-living people!
   I want an end just like theirs!

23.11   Balak said to Balaam, "What's this? I brought you here to curse my enemies, and all you've done is bless them."

23.12   Balaam answered, "Don't I have to be careful to say what GOD gives me to say?"

✠

NEW INTERNATIONAL VERSION

BALAAM'S SECOND ORACLE

¹³Then Balak said to him, "Come with me to another place where you can see them; you will see only a part but not all of them. And from there, curse them for me." ¹⁴So he took him to the field of Zophim on the top of Pisgah, and there he built seven altars and offered a bull and a ram on each altar.

¹⁵Balaam said to Balak, "Stay here beside your offering while I meet with him over there."

¹⁶The LORD met with Balaam and put a message in his mouth and said, "Go back to Balak and give him this message."

¹⁷So he went to him and found him standing beside his offering, with the princes of Moab. Balak asked him, "What did the LORD say?"

¹⁸Then he uttered his oracle:

"Arise, Balak, and listen;
  hear me, son of Zippor.
¹⁹God is not a man, that he should lie,
  nor a son of man, that he should change
    his mind.
Does he speak and then not act?
  Does he promise and not fulfill?
²⁰I have received a command to bless;
  he has blessed, and I cannot change it.

²¹"No misfortune is seen in Jacob,
  no misery observed in Israel. ^a
The LORD their God is with them;
  the shout of the King is among them.
²²God brought them out of Egypt;
  they have the strength of a wild ox.
²³There is no sorcery against Jacob,
  no divination against Israel.
It will now be said of Jacob
  and of Israel, 'See what God has done!'
²⁴The people rise like a lioness;
  they rouse themselves like a lion
that does not rest till he devours his prey
  and drinks the blood of his victims."

²⁵Then Balak said to Balaam, "Neither curse them at all nor bless them at all!"

²⁶Balaam answered, "Did I not tell you I must do whatever the LORD says?"

BALAAM'S THIRD ORACLE

²⁷Then Balak said to Balaam, "Come, let me take you to another place. Perhaps it will please God to let you curse them for me from there."

THE MESSAGE

23.13 Balak said to him, "Go with me to another place from which you can only see the outskirts of their camp—you won't be able to see the whole camp. From there, curse them for my sake."

23.14 So he took him to Watchmen's Meadow at the top of Pisgah. He built seven altars there and offered a bull and a ram on each altar.

23.15 Balaam said to Balak, "Take up your station here beside your Whole-Burnt-Offering while I meet with him over there."

23.16 GOD met with Balaam and gave him a message. He said, "Return to Balak and give him the message."

23.17-24 Balaam returned and found him stationed beside his Whole-Burnt-Offering and the nobles of Moab with him. Balak said to him, "What did GOD say?" Then Balaam spoke his message-oracle:

On your feet, Balak. Listen,
  listen carefully son of Zippor:
God is not man, one given to lies,
  and not a son of man changing his mind.
Does he speak and not do what he says?
  Does he promise and not come through?
I was brought here to bless;
  and now he's blessed—how can I change
    that?
He has no bone to pick with Jacob,
  he sees nothing wrong with Israel.
GOD is with them,
  and they're with him, shouting praises to
    their King.
God brought them out of Egypt,
  rampaging like a wild ox.
No magic spells can bind Jacob,
  no incantations can hold back Israel.
People will look at Jacob and Israel and say,
  "What a great thing has God done!"
Look, a people rising to its feet, stretching
    like a lion,
  a king-of-the-beasts, aroused,
Unsleeping, unresting until its hunt is over
  and it's eaten and drunk its fill.

23.25 Balak said to Balaam, "Well, if you can't curse them, at least don't bless them."

23.26 Balaam replied to Balak, "Didn't I tell you earlier: 'All God speaks, and only what he speaks, I speak'?"

☩

23.27-28 Balak said to Balaam, "Please, let me take you to another place; maybe we can find the right place in God's eyes where you'll be able to curse them

---

^a 21 Or *He has not looked on Jacob's offenses / or on the wrongs found in Israel.*

NEW INTERNATIONAL VERSION

²⁸And Balak took Balaam to the top of Peor, overlooking the wasteland.

²⁹Balaam said, "Build me seven altars here, and prepare seven bulls and seven rams for me." ³⁰Balak did as Balaam had said, and offered a bull and a ram on each altar.

24 Now when Balaam saw that it pleased the LORD to bless Israel, he did not resort to sorcery as at other times, but turned his face toward the desert. ²When Balaam looked out and saw Israel encamped tribe by tribe, the Spirit of God came upon him ³and he uttered his oracle:

"The oracle of Balaam son of Beor,
    the oracle of one whose eye sees clearly,
⁴the oracle of one who hears the words of
        God,
    who sees a vision from the Almighty,ᵃ
    who falls prostrate, and whose eyes are
        opened:

⁵"How beautiful are your tents, O Jacob,
    your dwelling places, O Israel!

⁶"Like valleys they spread out,
    like gardens beside a river,
    like aloes planted by the LORD,
    like cedars beside the waters.
⁷Water will flow from their buckets;
    their seed will have abundant water.

"Their king will be greater than Agag;
    their kingdom will be exalted.

⁸"God brought them out of Egypt;
    they have the strength of a wild ox.
They devour hostile nations
    and break their bones in pieces;
    with their arrows they pierce them.
⁹Like a lion they crouch and lie down,
    like a lioness—who dares to rouse them?

"May those who bless you be blessed
    and those who curse you be cursed!"

¹⁰Then Balak's anger burned against Balaam. He struck his hands together and said to him, "I summoned you to curse my enemies, but you have blessed them these three times. ¹¹Now leave at once and go home! I said I would reward you handsomely, but the LORD has kept you from being rewarded."

¹²Balaam answered Balak, "Did I not tell the messengers you sent me, ¹³'Even if Balak gave me his palace filled with silver and gold, I could not do anything of my own accord, good or bad,

THE MESSAGE

for me." So Balak took Balaam to the top of Peor, with a vista over the Jeshimon (Wasteland).

23.29   Balaam said to Balak, "Build seven altars for me here and prepare seven bulls and seven rams for sacrifice."

23.30   Balak did it and presented an offering of a bull and a ram on each of the altars.

24 By now Balaam realized that GOD wanted to bless Israel. So he didn't work in any sorcery as he had done earlier. He turned and looked out over the wilderness. As Balaam looked, he saw Israel camped tribe by tribe. The Spirit of God came on him, and he spoke his oracle-message:

24.3-9   Decree of Balaam son of Beor,
        yes, decree of a man with 20/20 vision;
    Decree of a man who hears God speak,
        who sees what The Strong God shows
            him,
    Who falls on his face in worship,
        who sees what's really going on.

    What beautiful tents, Jacob,
        oh, your homes, Israel!
    Like valleys stretching out in the distance,
        like gardens planted by rivers,
    Like sweet herbs planted by the gardener
            GOD,
        like red cedars by pools and springs,
    Their buckets will brim with water,
        their seed will spread life everywhere.
    Their king will tower over Agag and his ilk,
        their kingdom surpassingly majestic.
    God brought them out of Egypt,
        rampaging like a wild ox,
    Gulping enemies like morsels of meat,
        crushing their bones, snapping their
            arrows.
    Israel crouches like a lion and naps,
        king-of-the-beasts—who dares disturb
            him?
    Whoever blesses you is blessed,
        whoever curses you is cursed.

24.10-11   Balak lost his temper with Balaam. He shook his fist. He said to Balaam: "I got you in here to curse my enemies and what have you done? Blessed them! Blessed them three times! Get out of here! Go home! I told you I would pay you well, but you're getting nothing. You can blame GOD."

24.12-15   Balaam said to Balak, "Didn't I tell you up front when you sent your emissaries, 'Even if Balak gave me his palace stuffed with silver and gold, I couldn't do anything on my own,

---

ᵃ 4 Hebrew *Shaddai*; also in verse 16

NEW INTERNATIONAL VERSION	THE MESSAGE

NEW INTERNATIONAL VERSION

to go beyond the command of the LORD—and I must say only what the LORD says'? ¹⁴Now I am going back to my people, but come, let me warn you of what this people will do to your people in days to come."

BALAAM'S FOURTH ORACLE

¹⁵Then he uttered his oracle:

"The oracle of Balaam son of Beor,
  the oracle of one whose eye sees clearly,
¹⁶the oracle of one who hears the words of
    God,
  who has knowledge from the Most High,
who sees a vision from the Almighty,
  who falls prostrate, and whose eyes are
    opened:

¹⁷"I see him, but not now;
  I behold him, but not near.
A star will come out of Jacob;
  a scepter will rise out of Israel.
He will crush the foreheads of Moab,
  the skulls*ᵃ* of*ᵇ* all the sons of Sheth.*ᶜ*
¹⁸Edom will be conquered;
  Seir, his enemy, will be conquered,
  but Israel will grow strong.
¹⁹A ruler will come out of Jacob
  and destroy the survivors of the city."

BALAAM'S FINAL ORACLES

²⁰Then Balaam saw Amalek and uttered his oracle:

"Amalek was first among the nations,
  but he will come to ruin at last."

²¹Then he saw the Kenites and uttered his oracle:

"Your dwelling place is secure,
  your nest is set in a rock;
²²yet you Kenites will be destroyed
  when Asshur takes you captive."

²³Then he uttered his oracle:

"Ah, who can live when God does this?*ᵈ*
²⁴ Ships will come from the shores of Kittim;
they will subdue Asshur and Eber,
  but they too will come to ruin."

²⁵Then Balaam got up and returned home and Balak went his own way.

ᵃ 17 Samaritan Pentateuch (see also Jer. 48:45); the meaning of the word in the Masoretic Text is uncertain. *ᵇ 17* Or possibly *Moab, / batter*   *ᶜ 17* Or *all the noisy boasters*   *ᵈ 23* Masoretic Text; with a different word division of the Hebrew *A people will gather from the north.*

THE MESSAGE

whether good or bad, that went against GOD's command'? I'm leaving for home and my people, but I warn you of what this people will do to your people in the days to come." Then he spoke his oracle-message:

24.15-19 Decree of Balaam son of Beor,
  decree of the man with 20/20 vision,
Decree of the man who hears godly speech,
  who knows what's going on with the
    High God,
Who sees what The Strong God reveals,
  who bows in worship and sees what's
    real.
I see him, but not right now,
  I perceive him, but not right here;
A star rises from Jacob
  a scepter from Israel,
Crushing the heads of Moab,
  the skulls of all the noisy windbags;
I see Edom sold off at auction,
  enemy Seir marked down at the flea
    market,
  while Israel walks off with the trophies.
A ruler is coming from Jacob
  who'll destroy what's left in the city.

                    ✝

24.20 Then Balaam spotted Amalek and delivered an oracle-message. He said,

Amalek, you're in first place among nations
    right now,
  but you're going to come in last, ruined.

                    ✝

24.21-22 He saw the Kenites and delivered his oracle-message to them:

Your home is in a nice secure place,
  like a nest high on the face of a cliff.
Still, you Kenites will look stupid
  when Asshur takes you prisoner.

                    ✝

24.23-24 Balaam spoke his final oracle-message:

Doom! Who stands a chance
  when God starts in?
Sea-Peoples, raiders from across the sea,
  will harass Asshur and Eber,
But they'll also come to nothing,
  just like all the rest.

Balaam got up and went home. Balak also went on his way.

NEW INTERNATIONAL VERSION

MOAB SEDUCES ISRAEL

25 While Israel was staying in Shittim, the men began to indulge in sexual immorality with Moabite women, 2who invited them to the sacrifices to their gods. The people ate and bowed down before these gods. 3So Israel joined in worshiping the Baal of Peor. And the LORD's anger burned against them.

4The LORD said to Moses, "Take all the leaders of these people, kill them and expose them in broad daylight before the LORD, so that the LORD's fierce anger may turn away from Israel."

5So Moses said to Israel's judges, "Each of you must put to death those of your men who have joined in worshiping the Baal of Peor."

6Then an Israelite man brought to his family a Midianite woman right before the eyes of Moses and the whole assembly of Israel while they were weeping at the entrance to the Tent of Meeting. 7When Phinehas son of Eleazar, the son of Aaron, the priest, saw this, he left the assembly, took a spear in his hand 8and followed the Israelite into the tent. He drove the spear through both of them—through the Israelite and into the woman's body. Then the plague against the Israelites was stopped; 9but those who died in the plague numbered 24,000.

10The LORD said to Moses, 11"Phinehas son of Eleazar, the son of Aaron, the priest, has turned my anger away from the Israelites; for he was as zealous as I am for my honor among them, so that in my zeal I did not put an end to them. 12Therefore tell him I am making my covenant of peace with him. 13He and his descendants will have a covenant of a lasting priesthood, because he was zealous for the honor of his God and made atonement for the Israelites."

14The name of the Israelite who was killed with the Midianite woman was Zimri son of Salu, the leader of a Simeonite family. 15And the name of the Midianite woman who was put to death was Cozbi daughter of Zur, a tribal chief of a Midianite family.

16The LORD said to Moses, 17"Treat the Midianites as enemies and kill them, 18because they treated you as enemies when they deceived you in the affair of Peor and their sister Cozbi, the daughter of a Midianite leader, the woman who was killed when the plague came as a result of Peor."

THE MESSAGE

THE ORGY AT SHITTIM

25.1-3 **25** While Israel was camped at Shittim (Acacia Grove), the men began to have sex with the Moabite women. It started when the women invited the men to their sex-and-religion worship. They ate together and then worshiped their gods. Israel ended up joining in the worship of the Baal of Peor. GOD was furious, his anger blazing out against Israel.

25.4 GOD said to Moses, "Take all the leaders of Israel and kill them by hanging, leaving them publicly exposed in order to turn GOD's anger away from Israel."

25.5 Moses issued orders to the judges of Israel: "Each of you must execute the men under your jurisdiction who joined in the worship of Baal Peor."

25.6-9 Just then, while everyone was weeping in penitence at the entrance of the Tent of Meeting, an Israelite man, flaunting his behavior in front of Moses and the whole assembly, paraded a Midianite woman into his family tent. Phinehas son of Eleazar, the son of Aaron the priest, saw what he was doing, grabbed his spear, and followed them into the tent. With one thrust he drove the spear through the two of them, the man of Israel and the woman, right through their private parts. That stopped the plague from continuing among the People of Israel. But 24,000 had already died.

25.10-13 GOD spoke to Moses: "Phinehas son of Eleazar, son of Aaron the priest, has stopped my anger against the People of Israel. Because he was as zealous for my honor as I myself am, I didn't kill all the People of Israel in my zeal. So tell him that I am making a Covenant-of-Peace with him. He and his descendants are joined in a covenant of eternal priesthood, because he was zealous for his God and made atonement for the People of Israel."

25.14-15 The name of the man of Israel who was killed with the Midianite woman was Zimri son of Salu, the head of the Simeonite family. And the name of the Midianite woman who was killed was Cozbi daughter of Zur, a tribal chief of a Midianite family.

25.16-18 GOD spoke to Moses: "From here on make the Midianites your enemies. Fight them tooth and nail. They turned out to be your enemies when they seduced you in the business of Peor and that woman Cozbi, daughter of a Midianite leader, the woman who was killed at the time of the plague in the matter of Peor."

NEW INTERNATIONAL VERSION

THE SECOND CENSUS

26 After the plague the LORD said to Moses and Eleazar son of Aaron, the priest, [2] "Take a census of the whole Israelite community by families—all those twenty years old or more who are able to serve in the army of Israel." [3] So on the plains of Moab by the Jordan across from Jericho,[a] Moses and Eleazar the priest spoke with them and said, [4] "Take a census of the men twenty years old or more, as the LORD commanded Moses."

These were the Israelites who came out of Egypt:

[5] The descendants of Reuben, the firstborn son of Israel, were:
    through Hanoch, the Hanochite clan;
    through Pallu, the Palluite clan;
    [6] through Hezron, the Hezronite clan;
    through Carmi, the Carmite clan.
[7] These were the clans of Reuben; those numbered were 43,730.

[8] The son of Pallu was Eliab, [9] and the sons of Eliab were Nemuel, Dathan and Abiram. The same Dathan and Abiram were the community officials who rebelled against Moses and Aaron and were among Korah's followers when they rebelled against the LORD. [10] The earth opened its mouth and swallowed them along with Korah, whose followers died when the fire devoured the 250 men. And they served as a warning sign. [11] The line of Korah, however, did not die out.

[12] The descendants of Simeon by their clans were:
    through Nemuel, the Nemuelite clan;
    through Jamin, the Jaminite clan;
    through Jakin, the Jakinite clan;
    [13] through Zerah, the Zerahite clan;
    through Shaul, the Shaulite clan.
[14] These were the clans of Simeon; there were 22,200 men.

[15] The descendants of Gad by their clans were:
    through Zephon, the Zephonite clan;
    through Haggi, the Haggite clan;
    through Shuni, the Shunite clan;
    [16] through Ozni, the Oznite clan;
    through Eri, the Erite clan;
    [17] through Arodi,[b] the Arodite clan;
    through Areli, the Arelite clan.
[18] These were the clans of Gad; those numbered were 40,500.

---

[a] 3 Hebrew *Jordan of Jericho*; possibly an ancient name for the Jordan River; also in verse 63   [b] 17 Samaritan Pentateuch and Syriac (see also Gen. 46:16); Masoretic Text *Arod*

THE MESSAGE

CENSUS ON THE PLAINS OF MOAB

26.1-2 **26** After the plague GOD said to Moses and Eleazar son of Aaron the priest, "Number the entire community of Israel by families—count every person who is twenty years and older who is able to serve in the army of Israel."

26.3-4   Obeying GOD's command, Moses and Eleazar the priest addressed them on the Plains of Moab at Jordan-Jericho: "Count off from age twenty and older."

26.4-7   The People of Israel who came out of the land of Egypt:
  Reuben, Israel's firstborn. The sons of Reuben were:
    Hanoch and the Hanochite clan,
    Pallu and the Palluite clan,
    Hezron and the Hezronite clan,
    Carmi and the Carmite clan.
These made up the Reubenite clans. They numbered 43,730.

26.8   The son of Pallu: Eliab.

26.9-11   The sons of Eliab: Nemuel, Dathan, and Abiram. (These were the same Dathan and Abiram, community leaders from Korah's gang, who rebelled against Moses and Aaron in the Korah Rebellion against GOD. The Earth opened its jaws and swallowed them along with Korah's gang who died when the fire ate them up, all 250 of them. After all these years, they're still a warning sign. But the line of Korah did not die out.)

26.12-14 The sons of Simeon by clans:
    Nemuel and the Nemuelite clan,
    Jamin and the Jaminite clan,
    Jakin and the Jakinite clan,
    Zerah and the Zerahite clan,
    Shaul and the Shaulite clan.
These were the clans of Simeon. They numbered 22,200 men.

26.15-18 The sons of Gad by clans:
    Zephon and the Zephonite clan,
    Haggi and the Haggite clan,
    Shuni and the Shunite clan,
    Ozni and the Oznite clan,
    Eri and the Erite clan,
    Arodi and the Arodite clan,
    Areli and the Arelite clan.
These were the clans of Gad. They numbered 40,500 men.

NEW INTERNATIONAL VERSION

¹⁹Er and Onan were sons of Judah, but they died in Canaan. ²⁰The descendants of Judah by their clans were:

through Shelah, the Shelanite clan;
through Perez, the Perezite clan;
through Zerah, the Zerahite clan.
²¹The descendants of Perez were:
through Hezron, the Hezronite clan;
through Hamul, the Hamulite clan.
²²These were the clans of Judah; those numbered were 76,500.

²³The descendants of Issachar by their clans were:

through Tola, the Tolaite clan;
through Puah, the Puite^a clan;
²⁴through Jashub, the Jashubite clan;
through Shimron, the Shimronite clan.
²⁵These were the clans of Issachar; those numbered were 64,300.

²⁶The descendants of Zebulun by their clans were:

through Sered, the Seredite clan;
through Elon, the Elonite clan;
through Jahleel, the Jahleelite clan.
²⁷These were the clans of Zebulun; those numbered were 60,500.

²⁸The descendants of Joseph by their clans through Manasseh and Ephraim were:

²⁹The descendants of Manasseh:

through Makir, the Makirite clan (Makir was the father of Gilead);
through Gilead, the Gileadite clan.
³⁰These were the descendants of Gilead:
through Iezer, the Iezerite clan;
through Helek, the Helekite clan;
³¹through Asriel, the Asrielite clan;
through Shechem, the Shechemite clan;
³²through Shemida, the Shemidaite clan;
through Hepher, the Hepherite clan.
³³(Zelophehad son of Hepher had no sons; he had only daughters, whose names were Mahlah, Noah, Hoglah, Milcah and Tirzah.)
³⁴These were the clans of Manasseh; those numbered were 52,700.

³⁵These were the descendants of Ephraim by their clans:

through Shuthelah, the Shuthelahite clan;
through Beker, the Bekerite clan;
through Tahan, the Tahanite clan.
³⁶These were the descendants of Shuthelah:
through Eran, the Eranite clan.

---

^a 23 Samaritan Pentateuch, Septuagint, Vulgate and Syriac (see also 1 Chron. 7:1); Masoretic Text *through Puvah, the Punite*

THE MESSAGE

26.19-22 Er and Onan were sons of Judah who died early on in Canaan. The sons of Judah by clans:

Shelah and the Shelanite clan,
Perez and the Perezite clan,
Zerah and the Zerahite clan.
The sons of Perez:
Hezron and the Hezronite clan,
Hamul and the Hamulite clan.
These were the clans of Judah. They numbered 76,500.

26.23-25 The sons of Issachar by clans:

Tola and the Tolaite clan,
Puah and the Puite clan,
Jashub and the Jashubite clan,
Shimron and the Shimronite clan.
These were the clans of Issachar. They numbered 64,300.

26.26-27 The sons of Zebulun by clans:

Sered and the Seredite clan,
Elon and the Elonite clan,
Jahleel and the Jahleelite clan.
These were the clans of Zebulun. They numbered 60,500.

26.28-34 The sons of Joseph by clans through Manasseh and Ephraim. Through Manasseh:

Makir and the Makirite clan
(now Makir was the father of Gilead),
Gilead and the Gileadite clan.
The sons of Gilead:
Iezer and the Iezerite clan,
Helek and the Helekite clan,
Asriel and the Asrielite clan,
Shechem and the Shechemite clan,
Shemida and the Shemidaite clan,
Hepher and the Hepherite clan.
Zelophehad son of Hepher had no sons, only daughters.
Their names were Mahlah, Noah, Hoglah, Milcah, and Tirzah.
These were the clans of Manasseh. They numbered 52,700.

26.35-37 The sons of Ephraim by clans:

Shuthelah and the Shuthelahite clan,
Beker and the Bekerite clan,
Tahan and the Tahanite clan.
The sons of Shuthelah:
Eran and the Eranite clan.

NEW INTERNATIONAL VERSION

³⁷These were the clans of Ephraim; those numbered were 32,500.

These were the descendants of Joseph by their clans.

³⁸The descendants of Benjamin by their clans were:
    through Bela, the Belaite clan;
    through Ashbel, the Ashbelite clan;
    through Ahiram, the Ahiramite clan;
 ³⁹through Shupham,ᵃ the Shuphamite clan;
    through Hupham, the Huphamite clan.
 ⁴⁰The descendants of Bela through Ard and
        Naaman were:
    through Ard,ᵇ the Ardite clan;
    through Naaman, the Naamite clan.
⁴¹These were the clans of Benjamin; those numbered were 45,600.

⁴²These were the descendants of Dan by their clans:
    through Shuham, the Shuhamite clan.
These were the clans of Dan: ⁴³All of them were Shuhamite clans; and those numbered were 64,400.

⁴⁴The descendants of Asher by their clans were:
    through Imnah, the Imnite clan;
    through Ishvi, the Ishvite clan;
    through Beriah, the Beriite clan;
 ⁴⁵and through the descendants of Beriah:
        through Heber, the Heberite clan;
        through Malkiel, the Malkielite clan.
 ⁴⁶(Asher had a daughter named Serah.)
⁴⁷These were the clans of Asher; those numbered were 53,400.

⁴⁸The descendants of Naphtali by their clans were:
    through Jahzeel, the Jahzeelite clan;
    through Guni, the Gunite clan;
 ⁴⁹through Jezer, the Jezerite clan;
    through Shillem, the Shillemite clan.
⁵⁰These were the clans of Naphtali; those numbered were 45,400.

⁵¹The total number of the men of Israel was 601,730.

⁵²The LORD said to Moses, ⁵³"The land is to be allotted to them as an inheritance based on the number of names. ⁵⁴To a larger group give a larger inheritance, and to a smaller group a smaller one; each is to receive its inheritance according

---

ᵃ 39 A few manuscripts of the Masoretic Text, Samaritan
Pentateuch, Vulgate and Syriac (see also Septuagint); most
manuscripts of the Masoretic Text *Shephupham*
ᵇ 40 Samaritan Pentateuch and Vulgate (see also
Septuagint); Masoretic Text does not have *through Ard*.

THE MESSAGE

These were the clans of Ephraim. They numbered 32,500.

These are all the sons of Joseph by their clans.

²⁶·³⁸⁻⁴¹ The sons of Benjamin by clans:
    Bela and the Belaite clan,
    Ashbel and the Ashbelite clan,
    Ahiram and the Ahiramite clan,
    Shupham and the Shuphamite clan,
    Hupham and the Huphamite clan.
The sons of Bela through Ard and Naaman:
    Ard and the Ardite clan,
    Naaman and the Naamite clan.
These were the clans of Benjamin. They numbered 45,600.

²⁶·⁴²⁻⁴³ The sons of Dan by clan:
    Shuham and the Shuhamite clan.
These are the clans of Dan, all Shuhamite clans. They numbered 64,400.

²⁶·⁴⁴⁻⁴⁷ The sons of Asher by clan:
    Imnah and the Imnite clan,
    Ishvi and the Ishvite clan,
    Beriah and the Beriite clan.
The sons of Beriah:
    Heber and the Heberite clan,
    Malkiel and the Malkielite clan.
Asher also had a daughter, Serah.
These were the clans of Asher. They numbered 53,400.

²⁶·⁴⁸⁻⁵⁰ The sons of Naphtali by clans:
    Jahzeel and the Jahzeelite clan,
    Guni and the Gunite clan,
    Jezer and the Jezerite clan,
    Shillem and the Shillemite clan.
These were the clans of Naphtali. They numbered 45,400.

²⁶·⁵¹   The total number of the People of Israel: 601,730.

✝

²⁶·⁵²⁻⁵⁴ GOD spoke to Moses: "Divide up the inheritance of the land based on population. A larger group gets a larger inheritance; a smaller group gets a smaller inheritance—each gets its inheritance based on the population count.

NEW INTERNATIONAL VERSION

to the number of those listed. ⁵⁵Be sure that the land is distributed by lot. What each group inherits will be according to the names for its ancestral tribe. ⁵⁶Each inheritance is to be distributed by lot among the larger and smaller groups."

⁵⁷These were the Levites who were counted by their clans:

through Gershon, the Gershonite clan;
through Kohath, the Kohathite clan;
through Merari, the Merarite clan.

⁵⁸These also were Levite clans:

the Libnite clan,
the Hebronite clan,
the Mahlite clan,
the Mushite clan,
the Korahite clan.

(Kohath was the forefather of Amram; ⁵⁹the name of Amram's wife was Jochebed, a descendant of Levi, who was born to the Levites*a* in Egypt. To Amram she bore Aaron, Moses and their sister Miriam. ⁶⁰Aaron was the father of Nadab and Abihu, Eleazar and Ithamar. ⁶¹But Nadab and Abihu died when they made an offering before the LORD with unauthorized fire.)

⁶²All the male Levites a month old or more numbered 23,000. They were not counted along with the other Israelites because they received no inheritance among them.

⁶³These are the ones counted by Moses and Eleazar the priest when they counted the Israelites on the plains of Moab by the Jordan across from Jericho. ⁶⁴Not one of them was among those counted by Moses and Aaron the priest when they counted the Israelites in the Desert of Sinai. ⁶⁵For the LORD had told those Israelites they would surely die in the desert, and not one of them was left except Caleb son of Jephunneh and Joshua son of Nun.

ZELOPHEHAD'S DAUGHTERS

27 The daughters of Zelophehad son of Hepher, the son of Gilead, the son of Makir, the son of Manasseh, belonged to the clans of Manasseh son of Joseph. The names of the daughters were Mahlah, Noah, Hoglah, Milcah and Tirzah. They approached ²the entrance to the Tent of Meeting and stood before Moses, Eleazar the priest, the leaders and the whole assembly, and said, ³"Our father died in the desert. He was not among Korah's followers, who banded together against the LORD, but he died for his own sin and left no sons. ⁴Why should our father's

a 59 Or Jochebed, a daughter of Levi, who was born to Levi

THE MESSAGE

26.55-56   "Make sure that the land is assigned by lot.

"Each group's inheritance is based on population, the number of names listed in its ancestral tribe, divided among the many and the few by lot."

✝

26.57-58 These are the numberings of the Levites by clan:

Gershon and the Gershonite clan,
Kohath and the Kohathite clan,
Merari and the Merarite clan.

The Levite clans also included:

the Libnite clan,
the Hebronite clan,
the Mahlite clan,
the Mushite clan,
the Korahite clan.

26.59-61   Kohath was the father of Amram. Amram's wife was Jochebed, a descendant of Levi, born into the Levite family during the Egyptian years. Jochebed bore Aaron, Moses, and their sister Miriam to Amram. Aaron was the father of Nadab and Abihu, Eleazar and Ithamar; however, Nadab and Abihu died when they offered unauthorized sacrifice in the presence of GOD.

26.62   The numbering of Levite males one month and older came to 23,000. They hadn't been counted in with the rest of the People of Israel because they didn't inherit any land.

26.63-65   These are the ones numbered by Moses and Eleazar the priest, the People of Israel counted in the Plains of Moab at Jordan-Jericho. Not one of them had been among those counted by Moses and Aaron the priest in the census of the People of Israel taken in the Wilderness of Sinai. For GOD had said of them, "They'll die, die in the wilderness—not one of them will be left except for Caleb son of Jephunneh, and Joshua son of Nun."

THE DAUGHTERS OF ZELOPHEHAD

27.1   **27** The daughters of Zelophehad showed up. Their father was the son of Hepher son of Gilead son of Makir son of Manasseh, belonging to the clans of Manasseh son of Joseph. The daughters were Mahlah, Noah, Hoglah, Milcah, and Tirzah.

27.2-4   They came to the entrance of the Tent of Meeting. They stood before Moses and Eleazar the priest and before the leaders and the congregation and said, "Our father died in the wilderness. He wasn't part of Korah's rebel anti-GOD gang. He died for his own sins. And he left no sons. But why should our father's name

NEW INTERNATIONAL VERSION

name disappear from his clan because he had no son? Give us property among our father's relatives."

⁵So Moses brought their case before the LORD ⁶and the LORD said to him, ⁷"What Zelophehad's daughters are saying is right. You must certainly give them property as an inheritance among their father's relatives and turn their father's inheritance over to them.

⁸"Say to the Israelites, 'If a man dies and leaves no son, turn his inheritance over to his daughter. ⁹If he has no daughter, give his inheritance to his brothers. ¹⁰If he has no brothers, give his inheritance to his father's brothers. ¹¹If his father had no brothers, give his inheritance to the nearest relative in his clan, that he may possess it. This is to be a legal requirement for the Israelites, as the LORD commanded Moses.' "

JOSHUA TO SUCCEED MOSES

¹²Then the LORD said to Moses, "Go up this mountain in the Abarim range and see the land I have given the Israelites. ¹³After you have seen it, you too will be gathered to your people, as your brother Aaron was, ¹⁴for when the community rebelled at the waters in the Desert of Zin, both of you disobeyed my command to honor me as holy before their eyes." (These were the waters of Meribah Kadesh, in the Desert of Zin.)

¹⁵Moses said to the LORD, ¹⁶"May the LORD, the God of the spirits of all mankind, appoint a man over this community ¹⁷to go out and come in before them, one who will lead them out and bring them in, so the LORD's people will not be like sheep without a shepherd."

¹⁸So the LORD said to Moses, "Take Joshua son of Nun, a man in whom is the spirit,ᵃ and lay your hand on him. ¹⁹Have him stand before Eleazar the priest and the entire assembly and commission him in their presence. ²⁰Give him some of your authority so the whole Israelite community will obey him. ²¹He is to stand before Eleazar the priest, who will obtain decisions for him by inquiring of the Urim before the LORD. At his command he and the entire community of the Israelites will go out, and at his command they will come in."

²²Moses did as the LORD commanded him. He took Joshua and had him stand before Eleazar the priest and the whole assembly. ²³Then he laid his hands on him and commissioned him, as the LORD instructed through Moses.

THE MESSAGE

die out from his clan just because he had no sons? So give us an inheritance among our father's relatives."

27.5 Moses brought their case to GOD.

27.6-7 GOD ruled: "Zelophehad's daughters are right. Give them land as an inheritance among their father's relatives. Give them their father's inheritance.

27.8-11 "Then tell the People of Israel, If a man dies and leaves no son, give his inheritance to his daughter. If he has no daughter, give it to his brothers. If he has no brothers, give it to his father's brothers. If his father had no brothers, give it to the nearest relative so that the inheritance stays in the family. This is the standard procedure for the People of Israel, as commanded by GOD through Moses."

JOSHUA

27.12-14 GOD said to Moses, "Climb up into the Abarim Mountains and look over at the land that I am giving to the People of Israel. When you've had a good look you'll be joined to your ancestors in the grave—yes, you also along with Aaron your brother. This goes back to the day when the congregation quarreled in the Wilderness of Zin and you didn't honor me in holy reverence before them in the matter of the waters, the Waters of Meribah (Quarreling) at Kadesh in the Wilderness of Zin."

27.15-17 Moses responded to GOD: "Let GOD, the God of the spirits of everyone living, set a man over this community to lead them, to show the way ahead and bring them back home so GOD's community will not be like sheep without a shepherd."

27.18-21 GOD said to Moses, "Take Joshua the son of Nun—the Spirit is in him!—and place your hand on him. Stand him before Eleazar the priest in front of the entire congregation and commission him with everyone watching. Pass your magisterial authority over to him so that the whole congregation of the People of Israel will listen obediently to him. He is to consult with Eleazar the priest who, using the oracle-Urim, will prayerfully advise him in the presence of GOD. He will command the People of Israel, the entire community, in all their comings and goings."

27.22-23 Moses followed GOD's orders. He took Joshua and stood him before Eleazar the priest in front of the entire community. He laid his hands on him and commissioned him, following the procedures GOD had given Moses.

ᵃ 18 Or *Spirit*

NEW INTERNATIONAL VERSION

DAILY OFFERINGS

28 The LORD said to Moses, ²"Give this command to the Israelites and say to them: 'See that you present to me at the appointed time the food for my offerings made by fire, as an aroma pleasing to me.' ³Say to them: 'This is the offering made by fire that you are to present to the LORD: two lambs a year old without defect, as a regular burnt offering each day. ⁴Prepare one lamb in the morning and the other at twilight, ⁵together with a grain offering of a tenth of an ephah*ᵃ* of fine flour mixed with a quarter of a hin*ᵇ* of oil from pressed olives. ⁶This is the regular burnt offering instituted at Mount Sinai as a pleasing aroma, an offering made to the LORD by fire. ⁷The accompanying drink offering is to be a quarter of a hin of fermented drink with each lamb. Pour out the drink offering to the LORD at the sanctuary. ⁸Prepare the second lamb at twilight, along with the same kind of grain offering and drink offering that you prepare in the morning. This is an offering made by fire, an aroma pleasing to the LORD.

SABBATH OFFERINGS

⁹" 'On the Sabbath day, make an offering of two lambs a year old without defect, together with its drink offering and a grain offering of two-tenths of an ephah*ᶜ* of fine flour mixed with oil. ¹⁰This is the burnt offering for every Sabbath, in addition to the regular burnt offering and its drink offering.

MONTHLY OFFERINGS

¹¹" 'On the first of every month, present to the LORD a burnt offering of two young bulls, one ram and seven male lambs a year old, all without defect. ¹²With each bull there is to be a grain offering of three-tenths of an ephah*ᵈ* of fine flour mixed with oil; with the ram, a grain offering of two-tenths of an ephah of fine flour mixed with oil; ¹³and with each lamb, a grain offering of a tenth of an ephah of fine flour mixed with oil. This is for a burnt offering, a pleasing aroma, an offering made to the LORD by fire. ¹⁴With each bull there is to be a drink offering of half a hin*ᵉ* of wine; with the ram, a third of a hin*ᶠ*; and with each lamb, a quarter of a hin. This is the monthly burnt offering to be made at each new moon during the year. ¹⁵Besides the

---

THE MESSAGE

OFFERINGS

28 GOD spoke to Moses: "Command the People of Israel. Tell them, You're in charge of presenting my food, my Fire-Gifts of pleasing fragrance, at the set times. Tell them, This is the Fire-Gift that you are to present to GOD: two healthy yearling lambs each day as a regular Whole-Burnt-Offering. Sacrifice one lamb in the morning, the other in the evening, together with two quarts of fine flour mixed with a quart of olive oil for a Grain-Offering. This is the standard Whole-Burnt-Offering instituted at Mount Sinai as a pleasing fragrance, a Fire-Gift to GOD. The Drink-Offering that goes with it is a quart of strong beer with each lamb. Pour out the Drink-Offering before GOD in the Sanctuary. Sacrifice the second lamb in the evening with the Grain-Offering and Drink-Offering the same as in the morning—a Fire-Gift of pleasing fragrance for GOD.

✝

28.9-10 "On the Sabbath, sacrifice two healthy yearling lambs, together with the Drink-Offering and the Grain-Offering of four quarts of fine flour mixed with oil. This is the regular Sabbath Whole-Burnt-Offering, in addition to the regular Whole-Burnt-Offering and its Drink-Offering.

✝

28.11 "On the first of the month offer a Whole-Burnt-Offering to GOD: two young bulls, one ram, and seven male yearling lambs—all healthy.

28.12-14 "A Grain-Offering of six quarts of fine flour mixed with oil goes with each bull, four quarts of fine flour mixed with oil with the ram, and two quarts of fine flour mixed with oil with each lamb. This is for a Whole-Burnt-Offering, a pleasing fragrance, a Fire-Gift to GOD. Also, Drink-Offerings of two quarts of wine for each bull, one and a quarter quarts of wine for the ram, and a quart of wine for each lamb are to be poured out.

28.14-15 "This is the first of the month Whole-Burnt-Offering to be made throughout the year. In

---

ᵃ 5 That is, probably about 2 quarts (about 2 liters); also in verses 13, 21 and 29   *ᵇ 5* That is, probably about 1 quart (about 1 liter); also in verses 7 and 14   *ᶜ 9* That is, probably about 4 quarts (about 4.5 liters); also in verses 12, 20 and 28   *ᵈ 12* That is, probably about 6 quarts (about 6.5 liters); also in verses 20 and 28   *ᵉ 14* That is, probably about 2 quarts (about 2 liters)   *ᶠ 14* That is, probably about 1 1/4 quarts (about 1.2 liters)

NEW INTERNATIONAL VERSION

regular burnt offering with its drink offering, one male goat is to be presented to the LORD as a sin offering.

THE PASSOVER

16" 'On the fourteenth day of the first month the LORD's Passover is to be held. 17On the fifteenth day of this month there is to be a festival; for seven days eat bread made without yeast. 18On the first day hold a sacred assembly and do no regular work. 19Present to the LORD an offering made by fire, a burnt offering of two young bulls, one ram and seven male lambs a year old, all without defect. 20With each bull prepare a grain offering of three-tenths of an ephah of fine flour mixed with oil; with the ram, two-tenths; 21and with each of the seven lambs, one-tenth. 22Include one male goat as a sin offering to make atonement for you. 23Prepare these in addition to the regular morning burnt offering. 24In this way prepare the food for the offering made by fire every day for seven days as an aroma pleasing to the LORD; it is to be prepared in addition to the regular burnt offering and its drink offering. 25On the seventh day hold a sacred assembly and do no regular work.

FEAST OF WEEKS

26" 'On the day of firstfruits, when you present to the LORD an offering of new grain during the Feast of Weeks, hold a sacred assembly and do no regular work. 27Present a burnt offering of two young bulls, one ram and seven male lambs a year old as an aroma pleasing to the LORD. 28With each bull there is to be a grain offering of three-tenths of an ephah of fine flour mixed with oil; with the ram, two-tenths; 29and with each of the seven lambs, one-tenth. 30Include one male goat to make atonement for you. 31Prepare these together with their drink offerings, in addition to the regular burnt offering and its grain offering. Be sure the animals are without defect.

FEAST OF TRUMPETS

29 " 'On the first day of the seventh month hold a sacred assembly and do no regular work. It is a day for you to sound the trumpets. 2As an aroma pleasing to the LORD, prepare a burnt offering of one young bull, one ram and seven male lambs a year old, all without defect. 3With the bull prepare a grain offering of three-tenths of an ephah*a* of fine flour mixed with oil;

THE MESSAGE

addition to the regular Whole-Burnt-Offering with its accompanying Drink-Offering, a he-goat is to be offered to GOD as an Absolution-Offering.

✝

28.16-17 "GOD's Passover is to be held on the fourteenth day of the first month. On the fifteenth day of this month hold a festival.

28.18-22 "For seven days, eat only unraised bread: Begin the first day in holy worship; don't do any regular work that day. Bring a Fire-Gift to GOD, a Whole-Burnt-Offering: two young bulls, one ram, and seven male yearling lambs—all healthy. Prepare a Grain-Offering of six quarts of fine flour mixed with oil for each bull, four quarts for the ram, and two quarts for each lamb, plus a goat as an Absolution-Offering to atone for you.

28.23-24 "Sacrifice these in addition to the regular morning Whole-Burnt-Offering. Prepare the food this way for the Fire-Gift, a pleasing fragrance to GOD, every day for seven days. Prepare it in addition to the regular Whole-Burnt-Offering and Drink-Offering.

28.25 "Conclude the seventh day in holy worship; don't do any regular work on that day.

✝

28.26-30 "On the Day of Firstfruits when you bring an offering of new grain to GOD on your Feast-of-Weeks, gather in holy worship and don't do any regular work. Bring a Whole-Burnt-Offering of two young bulls, one ram, and seven male yearling lambs as a pleasing fragrance to GOD. Prepare a Grain-Offering of six quarts of fine flour mixed with oil for each bull, four quarts for the ram, and two quarts for each lamb, plus a he-goat as an Absolution-Offering to atone for you.

28.31 "These are all over and above the daily Whole-Burnt-Offering and its Grain-Offering and the Drink-Offering. Remember, the animals must be healthy.

✝

29.1-5 **29** "On the first day of the seventh month, gather in holy worship and do no regular work. This is your Day-of-Trumpet-Blasts. Sacrifice a Whole-Burnt-Offering: one young bull, one ram, and seven male yearling lambs— all healthy—as a pleasing fragrance to GOD. Prepare a Grain-Offering of six quarts of fine

---

a 3 That is, probably about 6 quarts (about 6.5 liters); also in verses 9 and 14

NEW INTERNATIONAL VERSION

with the ram, two-tenths*a*; [4]and with each of the seven lambs, one-tenth.*b* [5]Include one male goat as a sin offering to make atonement for you. [6]These are in addition to the monthly and daily burnt offerings with their grain offerings and drink offerings as specified. They are offerings made to the LORD by fire—a pleasing aroma.

DAY OF ATONEMENT

[7]" 'On the tenth day of this seventh month hold a sacred assembly. You must deny yourselves*c* and do no work. [8]Present as an aroma pleasing to the LORD a burnt offering of one young bull, one ram and seven male lambs a year old, all without defect. [9]With the bull prepare a grain offering of three-tenths of an ephah of fine flour mixed with oil; with the ram, two-tenths; [10]and with each of the seven lambs, one-tenth. [11]Include one male goat as a sin offering, in addition to the sin offering for atonement and the regular burnt offering with its grain offering, and their drink offerings.

FEAST OF TABERNACLES

[12]" 'On the fifteenth day of the seventh month, hold a sacred assembly and do no regular work. Celebrate a festival to the LORD for seven days. [13]Present an offering made by fire as an aroma pleasing to the LORD, a burnt offering of thirteen young bulls, two rams and fourteen male lambs a year old, all without defect. [14]With each of the thirteen bulls prepare a grain offering of three-tenths of an ephah of fine flour mixed with oil; with each of the two rams, two-tenths; [15]and with each of the fourteen lambs, one-tenth. [16]Include one male goat as a sin offering, in addition to the regular burnt offering with its grain offering and drink offering.

[17]" 'On the second day prepare twelve young bulls, two rams and fourteen male lambs a year old, all without defect. [18]With the bulls, rams and lambs, prepare their grain offerings and drink offerings according to the number specified. [19]Include one male goat as a sin offering, in addition to the regular burnt offering with its grain offering, and their drink offerings.

[20]" 'On the third day prepare eleven bulls, two rams and fourteen male lambs a year old, all without defect. [21]With the bulls, rams and lambs, prepare their grain offerings and drink offerings according to the number specified. [22]Include one male goat as a sin offering, in addition to the regular burnt offering with its grain offering and drink offering.

a 3 That is, probably about 4 quarts (about 4.5 liters); also in verses 9 and 14   *b* 4 That is, probably about 2 quarts (about 2 liters); also in verses 10 and 15   *c* 7 Or *must fast*

THE MESSAGE

flour mixed with oil for the bull, four quarts for the ram, and two quarts for each lamb, plus a he-goat as an Absolution-Offering to atone for you.

29.6   "These are all over and above the monthly and daily Whole-Burnt-Offerings with their Grain-Offerings and Drink-Offerings as prescribed, a pleasing fragrance, a Fire-Gift to GOD.

✝

29.7   "On the tenth day of this seventh month, gather in holy worship, humble yourselves, and do no work.

29.8-11   "Bring a Whole-Burnt-Offering to GOD as a pleasing fragrance: one young bull, one ram, and seven yearling male lambs—all healthy. Prepare a Grain-Offering of six quarts of fine flour mixed with oil for the bull, four quarts for the ram, and two quarts for each of the seven lambs. Also bring a he-goat as an Absolution-Offering to atone for you in addition to the regular Whole-Burnt-Offering with its Grain-Offering and Drink-Offering.

✝

29.12-16   "Gather in holy worship on the fifteenth day of the seventh month; do no regular work. Celebrate a Festival to GOD for seven days. Bring a Whole-Burnt-Offering, a Fire-Gift of pleasing fragrance to GOD: thirteen young bulls, two rams, and fourteen yearling male lambs—all healthy. Prepare a Grain-Offering of six quarts of fine flour mixed with oil for each of the bulls, four quarts for each ram, and two quarts for each of the fourteen lambs. Also bring a he-goat as an Absolution-Offering in addition to the regular Whole-Burnt-Offering with its Grain-Offering and Drink-Offering.

29.17-19   "On the second day: twelve young bulls, two rams, and fourteen yearling male lambs—all healthy. Prepare Grain-Offerings and Drink-Offerings to go with the bulls, rams, and lambs following the prescribed recipes. And bring a he-goat as an Absolution-Offering in addition to the regular Whole-Burnt-Offering with its Grain-Offering and Drink-Offering.

29.20-22   "On the third day: eleven bulls, two rams, and fourteen male yearling lambs—all healthy. Prepare Grain-Offerings and Drink-Offerings to go with the bulls, rams, and lambs following the prescribed recipes. And bring a he-goat as an Absolution-Offering in addition to the regular Whole-Burnt-Offering with its Grain-Offering and Drink-Offering.

NEW INTERNATIONAL VERSION

23" 'On the fourth day prepare ten bulls, two rams and fourteen male lambs a year old, all without defect. 24With the bulls, rams and lambs, prepare their grain offerings and drink offerings according to the number specified. 25Include one male goat as a sin offering, in addition to the regular burnt offering with its grain offering and drink offering.

26" 'On the fifth day prepare nine bulls, two rams and fourteen male lambs a year old, all without defect. 27With the bulls, rams and lambs, prepare their grain offerings and drink offerings according to the number specified. 28Include one male goat as a sin offering, in addition to the regular burnt offering with its grain offering and drink offering.

29" 'On the sixth day prepare eight bulls, two rams and fourteen male lambs a year old, all without defect. 30With the bulls, rams and lambs, prepare their grain offerings and drink offerings according to the number specified. 31Include one male goat as a sin offering, in addition to the regular burnt offering with its grain offering and drink offering.

32" 'On the seventh day prepare seven bulls, two rams and fourteen male lambs a year old, all without defect. 33With the bulls, rams and lambs, prepare their grain offerings and drink offerings according to the number specified. 34Include one male goat as a sin offering, in addition to the regular burnt offering with its grain offering and drink offering.

35" 'On the eighth day hold an assembly and do no regular work. 36Present an offering made by fire as an aroma pleasing to the LORD, a burnt offering of one bull, one ram and seven male lambs a year old, all without defect. 37With the bull, the ram and the lambs, prepare their grain offerings and drink offerings according to the number specified. 38Include one male goat as a sin offering, in addition to the regular burnt offering with its grain offering and drink offering.

39" 'In addition to what you vow and your freewill offerings, prepare these for the LORD at your appointed feasts: your burnt offerings, grain offerings, drink offerings and fellowship offerings.*a* "

40Moses told the Israelites all that the LORD commanded him.

Vows

30 Moses said to the heads of the tribes of Israel: "This is what the LORD commands: 2When a man makes a vow to the LORD or takes an oath to obligate himself by a pledge,

---

THE MESSAGE

29.23-25 "On the fourth day: ten bulls, two rams, and fourteen male yearling lambs—all healthy. Prepare Grain-Offerings and Drink-Offerings to go with the bulls, rams, and lambs following the prescribed recipes. And bring a he-goat as an Absolution-Offering in addition to the regular Whole-Burnt-Offering with its Grain-Offering and Drink-Offering.

29.26-28 "On the fifth day: nine bulls, two rams, and fourteen male yearling lambs—all healthy. Prepare Grain-Offerings and Drink-Offerings to go with the bulls, rams, and lambs following the prescribed recipes. And bring a he-goat as an Absolution-Offering in addition to the regular Whole-Burnt-Offering with its Grain-Offering and Drink-Offering.

29.29-31 "On the sixth day: eight bulls, two rams, and fourteen male yearling lambs—all healthy. Prepare Grain-Offerings and Drink-Offerings to go with the bulls, rams, and lambs following the prescribed recipes. And bring a he-goat as an Absolution-Offering in addition to the regular Whole-Burnt-Offering with its Grain-Offering and Drink-Offering.

29.32-34 "On the seventh day: seven bulls, two rams, and fourteen male yearling lambs—all healthy. Prepare Grain-Offerings and Drink-Offerings to go with the bulls, rams, and lambs following the prescribed recipes. And bring a he-goat as an Absolution-Offering in addition to the regular Whole-Burnt-Offering with its Grain-Offering and Drink-Offering.

29.35-38 "On the eighth day: Gather in holy worship; do no regular work. Bring a Fire-Gift of pleasing fragrance to GOD, a Whole-Burnt-Offering: one bull, one ram, and seven male yearling lambs—all healthy. Prepare Grain-Offerings and Drink-Offerings to go with the bulls, rams, and lambs following the prescribed recipes. And bring a he-goat as an Absolution-Offering in addition to the regular Whole-Burnt-Offering with its Grain-Offering and Drink-Offering.

29.39 "Sacrifice these to GOD as a congregation at your set feasts: your Whole-Burnt-Offerings, Grain-Offerings, Drink-Offerings, and Peace-Offerings. These are all over and above your personal Vow-Offerings and Freewill-Offerings."

29.40 Moses instructed the People of Israel in all that GOD commanded him.

Vows

30.1-2 **30** Moses spoke to the heads of the tribes of the People of Israel: "This is what GOD commands: When a man makes a vow to GOD or binds himself by an oath to do some-

---

NEW INTERNATIONAL VERSION

he must not break his word but must do everything he said.

³"When a young woman still living in her father's house makes a vow to the LORD or obligates herself by a pledge ⁴and her father hears about her vow or pledge but says nothing to her, then all her vows and every pledge by which she obligated herself will stand. ⁵But if her father forbids her when he hears about it, none of her vows or the pledges by which she obligated herself will stand; the LORD will release her because her father has forbidden her.

⁶"If she marries after she makes a vow or after her lips utter a rash promise by which she obligates herself ⁷and her husband hears about it but says nothing to her, then her vows or the pledges by which she obligated herself will stand. ⁸But if her husband forbids her when he hears about it, he nullifies the vow that obligates her or the rash promise by which she obligates herself, and the LORD will release her.

⁹"Any vow or obligation taken by a widow or divorced woman will be binding on her.

¹⁰"If a woman living with her husband makes a vow or obligates herself by a pledge under oath ¹¹and her husband hears about it but says nothing to her and does not forbid her, then all her vows or the pledges by which she obligated herself will stand. ¹²But if her husband nullifies them when he hears about them, then none of the vows or pledges that came from her lips will stand. Her husband has nullified them, and the LORD will release her. ¹³Her husband may confirm or nullify any vow she makes or any sworn pledge to deny herself. ¹⁴But if her husband says nothing to her about it from day to day, then he confirms all her vows or the pledges binding on her. He confirms them by saying nothing to her when he hears about them. ¹⁵If, however, he nullifies them some time after he hears about them, then he is responsible for her guilt."

¹⁶These are the regulations the LORD gave Moses concerning relationships between a man and his wife, and between a father and his young daughter still living in his house.

VENGEANCE ON THE MIDIANITES

31 The LORD said to Moses, ²"Take vengeance on the Midianites for the Israelites. After that, you will be gathered to your people."

³So Moses said to the people, "Arm some of your men to go to war against the Midianites and to carry out the LORD's vengeance on them. ⁴Send into battle a thousand men from each of the tribes of Israel." ⁵So twelve thousand men armed for battle, a thousand from each tribe,

THE MESSAGE

thing, he must not break his word; he must do exactly what he has said.

30.3-5 "When a woman makes a vow to GOD and binds herself by a pledge as a young girl still living in her father's house, and her father hears of her vow or pledge but says nothing to her, then she has to make good on all her vows and pledges. But if her father holds her back when he hears of what she has done, none of her vows and pledges are valid. GOD will release her since her father held her back.

30.6-8 "If she marries after she makes a vow or has made some rash promise or pledge, and her husband hears of it but says nothing to her, then she has to make good on whatever she vowed or pledged. But if her husband intervenes when he hears of it, he cancels the vow or rash promise that binds her. And GOD will release her.

30.9 "Any vow or pledge taken by a widow or divorced woman is binding on her.

30.10-15 "When a woman who is living with her husband makes a vow or takes a pledge under oath and her husband hears about it but says nothing and doesn't say she can't do it, then all her vows and pledges are valid. But if her husband cancels them when he hears about them, then none of the vows and pledges that she made are binding. Her husband has canceled them and GOD will release her. Any vow and pledge that she makes that may be to her detriment can be either affirmed or annulled by her husband. But if her husband is silent and doesn't speak up day after day, he confirms her vows and pledges—she has to make good on them. By saying nothing to her when he hears of them, he binds her to them. If, however, he cancels them sometime after he hears of them, he takes her guilt on himself."

30.16 These are the rules that GOD gave Moses regarding conduct between a man and his wife and between a father and his young daughter who is still living at home.

THE MIDIANITE WAR

31.1-2 **31** GOD spoke to Moses: "Avenge the People of Israel on the Midianites. Afterward you will go to be with your dead ancestors."

31.3-4 Moses addressed the people: "Recruit men for a campaign against Midian, to exact GOD's vengeance on Midian, a thousand from each tribe of Israel to go to war."

31.5-6 A fighting force of a thousand from each tribe of Israel—twelve thousand in all—was re-

NEW INTERNATIONAL VERSION

were supplied from the clans of Israel. ⁶Moses sent them into battle, a thousand from each tribe, along with Phinehas son of Eleazar, the priest, who took with him articles from the sanctuary and the trumpets for signaling.

⁷They fought against Midian, as the LORD commanded Moses, and killed every man. ⁸Among their victims were Evi, Rekem, Zur, Hur and Reba—the five kings of Midian. They also killed Balaam son of Beor with the sword. ⁹The Israelites captured the Midianite women and children and took all the Midianite herds, flocks and goods as plunder. ¹⁰They burned all the towns where the Midianites had settled, as well as all their camps. ¹¹They took all the plunder and spoils, including the people and animals, ¹²and brought the captives, spoils and plunder to Moses and Eleazar the priest and the Israelite assembly at their camp on the plains of Moab, by the Jordan across from Jericho.ᵃ

¹³Moses, Eleazar the priest and all the leaders of the community went to meet them outside the camp. ¹⁴Moses was angry with the officers of the army—the commanders of thousands and commanders of hundreds—who returned from the battle.

¹⁵"Have you allowed all the women to live?" he asked them. ¹⁶"They were the ones who followed Balaam's advice and were the means of turning the Israelites away from the LORD in what happened at Peor, so that a plague struck the LORD's people. ¹⁷Now kill all the boys. And kill every woman who has slept with a man, ¹⁸but save for yourselves every girl who has never slept with a man.

¹⁹"All of you who have killed anyone or touched anyone who was killed must stay outside the camp seven days. On the third and seventh days you must purify yourselves and your captives. ²⁰Purify every garment as well as everything made of leather, goat hair or wood."

²¹Then Eleazar the priest said to the soldiers who had gone into battle, "This is the requirement of the law that the LORD gave Moses: ²²Gold, silver, bronze, iron, tin, lead ²³and anything else that can withstand fire must be put through the fire, and then it will be clean. But it must also be purified with the water of cleansing. And whatever cannot withstand fire must be put through that water. ²⁴On the seventh day wash your clothes and you will be clean. Then you may come into the camp."

DIVIDING THE SPOILS

²⁵The LORD said to Moses, ²⁶"You and Eleazar

THE MESSAGE

cruited. Moses sent them off to war, a thousand from each tribe, and also Phinehas son of Eleazar, who went as priest to the army, in charge of holy vessels and the signaling bugles.

31.7-12   They attacked Midian, just as GOD had commanded Moses, and killed every last man. Among the fallen were Evi, Rekem, Zur, Hur, and Reba—the five kings of Midian. They also killed Balaam son of Beor with the sword. The People of Israel took the Midianite women and children captive and took all their animals and herds and goods as plunder. They burned to the ground all the towns in which Midianites lived and also their tent camps. They looted and plundered everything and everyone—stuff and people and animals. They took it all—captives and booty and plunder—back to Moses and Eleazar the priest and the company of Israel where they were camped on the Plains of Moab, at Jordan-Jericho.

31.13-18   Moses, Eleazar, and all the leaders of the congregation went to meet the returning army outside the camp. Moses was furious with the army officers—the commanders of thousands and commanders of hundreds—as they came back from the battlefield: "What's this! You've let these women live! They're the ones who, under Balaam's direction, seduced the People of Israel away from GOD in that mess at Peor, causing the plague that hit GOD's people. Finish your job: kill all the boys. Kill every woman who has slept with a man. The younger women who are virgins you can keep alive for yourselves.

31.19-20   "Now here's what you are to do: Pitch tents outside the camp. All who have killed anyone or touched a corpse must stay outside the camp for seven days. Purify yourselves and your captives on the third and seventh days. Purify every piece of clothing and every utensil—everything made of leather, goat hair, or wood."

31.21-24   Eleazar the priest then spoke to the soldiers who had fought in the battle: "This is the ruling from the Revelation that GOD gave Moses: Gold, silver, bronze, iron, tin, and lead—and anything else that can survive fire—must be passed through the fire; then it will be ritually purified. It must also be ritually washed in the Water-of-Cleansing. Further, whatever cannot survive fire must be put through that water. On the seventh day scrub your clothes; you will be ritually clean. Then you can return to camp."

☩

31.25-27   GOD said to Moses, "I want you and Eleazar

NEW INTERNATIONAL VERSION

the priest and the family heads of the community are to count all the people and animals that were captured. ²⁷Divide the spoils between the soldiers who took part in the battle and the rest of the community. ²⁸From the soldiers who fought in the battle, set apart as tribute for the LORD one out of every five hundred, whether persons, cattle, donkeys, sheep or goats. ²⁹Take this tribute from their half share and give it to Eleazar the priest as the LORD's part. ³⁰From the Israelites' half, select one out of every fifty, whether persons, cattle, donkeys, sheep, goats or other animals. Give them to the Levites, who are responsible for the care of the LORD's tabernacle." ³¹So Moses and Eleazar the priest did as the LORD commanded Moses.

³²The plunder remaining from the spoils that the soldiers took was 675,000 sheep, ³³72,000 cattle, ³⁴61,000 donkeys ³⁵and 32,000 women who had never slept with a man.

³⁶The half share of those who fought in the battle was:

337,500 sheep, ³⁷of which the tribute for the LORD was 675;
³⁸36,000 cattle, of which the tribute for the LORD was 72;
³⁹30,500 donkeys, of which the tribute for the LORD was 61;
⁴⁰16,000 people, of which the tribute for the LORD was 32.

⁴¹Moses gave the tribute to Eleazar the priest as the LORD's part, as the LORD commanded Moses.

⁴²The half belonging to the Israelites, which Moses set apart from that of the fighting men— ⁴³the community's half—was 337,500 sheep, ⁴⁴36,000 cattle, ⁴⁵30,500 donkeys ⁴⁶and 16,000 people. ⁴⁷From the Israelites' half, Moses selected one out of every fifty persons and animals, as the LORD commanded him, and gave them to the Levites, who were responsible for the care of the LORD's tabernacle.

⁴⁸Then the officers who were over the units of the army—the commanders of thousands and commanders of hundreds—went to Moses ⁴⁹and said to him, "Your servants have counted the soldiers under our command, and not one is missing. ⁵⁰So we have brought as an offering to the LORD the gold articles each of us acquired—armlets, bracelets, signet rings, earrings and necklaces—to make atonement for ourselves before the LORD."

⁵¹Moses and Eleazar the priest accepted from them the gold—all the crafted articles. ⁵²All the gold from the commanders of thousands and commanders of hundreds that Moses and Elea-

THE MESSAGE

the priest and the family leaders in the community to count the captives, people and animals. Split the plunder between the soldiers who fought the battle and the rest of the congregation.

^{31.28-30} "Then tax the booty that goes to the soldiers at the rate of one life out of five hundred, whether humans, cattle, donkeys, or sheep. It's a GOD-tax taken from their half-share to be turned over to Eleazar the priest on behalf of GOD. Tax the congregation's half-share at the rate of one life out of fifty, whether persons, cattle, donkeys, sheep, goats, or other animals. Give this to the Levites who are in charge of the care of GOD's Dwelling."

^{31.31} Moses and Eleazar followed through with what GOD had commanded Moses.

^{31.32-35} The rest of the plunder taken by the army:
675,000 sheep
72,000 cattle
61,000 donkeys
32,000 women who were virgins
^{31.36-40} The half-share for those who had fought in the war:
337,500 sheep, with a tax of 675 for GOD
36,000 cattle, with a tax of 72 for GOD
30,500 donkeys, with a tax of 61 for GOD
16,000 people, with a tax of 32 for GOD
^{31.41} Moses turned the tax over to Eleazar the priest as GOD's part, following GOD's instructions to Moses.

^{31.42-46} The other half-share for the Israelite community that Moses set apart from what was given to the men who fought the war was:
337,500 sheep
36,000 cattle
30,500 donkeys
16,000 people
^{31.47} From the half-share going to the People of Israel, Moses, just as GOD had instructed him, picked one out of every fifty persons and animals and gave them to the Levites, who were in charge of maintaining GOD's Dwelling.

^{31.48-50} The military officers—commanders of thousands and commanders of hundreds—came to Moses and said, "We have counted the soldiers under our command and not a man is missing. We've brought offerings to GOD from the gold jewelry we got—armlets, bracelets, rings, earrings, ornaments—to make atonement for our lives before GOD."

^{31.51-54} Moses and Eleazar the priest received the gold from them, all that fine-crafted jewelry. In total, the gold from the commanders of thousands and hundreds that Moses and Eleazar of-

NEW INTERNATIONAL VERSION

zar presented as a gift to the LORD weighed 16,750 shekels. *a* 53Each soldier had taken plunder for himself. 54Moses and Eleazar the priest accepted the gold from the commanders of thousands and commanders of hundreds and brought it into the Tent of Meeting as a memorial for the Israelites before the LORD.

THE TRANSJORDAN TRIBES

32 The Reubenites and Gadites, who had very large herds and flocks, saw that the lands of Jazer and Gilead were suitable for livestock. 2So they came to Moses and Eleazar the priest and to the leaders of the community, and said, 3"Ataroth, Dibon, Jazer, Nimrah, Heshbon, Elealeh, Sebam, Nebo and Beon— 4the land the LORD subdued before the people of Israel—are suitable for livestock, and your servants have livestock. 5If we have found favor in your eyes," they said, "let this land be given to your servants as our possession. Do not make us cross the Jordan."

6Moses said to the Gadites and Reubenites, "Shall your countrymen go to war while you sit here? 7Why do you discourage the Israelites from going over into the land the LORD has given them? 8This is what your fathers did when I sent them from Kadesh Barnea to look over the land. 9After they went up to the Valley of Eshcol and viewed the land, they discouraged the Israelites from entering the land the LORD had given them. 10The LORD's anger was aroused that day and he swore this oath: 11'Because they have not followed me wholeheartedly, not one of the men twenty years old or more who came up out of Egypt will see the land I promised on oath to Abraham, Isaac and Jacob— 12not one except Caleb son of Jephunneh the Kenizzite and Joshua son of Nun, for they followed the LORD wholeheartedly.' 13The LORD's anger burned against Israel and he made them wander in the desert forty years, until the whole generation of those who had done evil in his sight was gone.

14"And here you are, a brood of sinners, standing in the place of your fathers and making the LORD even more angry with Israel. 15If you turn away from following him, he will again leave all this people in the desert, and you will be the cause of their destruction."

16Then they came up to him and said, "We would like to build pens here for our livestock

THE MESSAGE

fered as a gift to GOD weighed about six hundred pounds, all donated by the soldiers who had taken the booty. Moses and Eleazar took the gold from the commanders of thousands and hundreds and brought it to the Tent of Meeting, to serve as a reminder for the People of Israel before GOD.

TRIBES EAST OF THE JORDAN

32.1-4 **32** The families of Reuben and Gad had huge herds of livestock. They saw that the country of Jazer and Gilead was just the place for grazing livestock. And so they came, the families of Gad and of Reuben, and spoke to Moses and Eleazar the priest and the leaders of the congregation, saying, "Ataroth, Dibon, Jazer, Nimrah, Heshbon, Elealeh, Sebam, Nebo, and Beon—the country that GOD laid low before the community of Israel—is a country just right for livestock, and we have livestock."

32.5 They continued, "If you think we've done a good job so far, give us this country for our inheritance. Don't make us go across the Jordan."

32.6-12 Moses answered the families of Gad and Reuben: "Do you mean that you are going to leave the fighting that's ahead to your brothers while you settle down here? Why would you even think of letting the People of Israel down, demoralizing them just as they're about to move into the land GOD gave them? That's exactly what your ancestors did when I sent them from Kadesh Barnea to survey the country. They went as far as the Valley of Eshcol, took one look and quit. They completely demoralized the People of Israel from entering the land GOD had given them. And GOD got angry—oh, did he get angry! He swore: 'They'll never get to see it; none of those who came up out of Egypt who are twenty years and older will ever get to see the land that I promised to Abraham, Isaac, and Jacob. They weren't interested in following me—their hearts weren't in it. None, except for Caleb son of Jephunneh the Kenizzite, and Joshua son of Nun; they followed me—their hearts were in it.'

32.13 "GOD's anger smoked against Israel. He made them wander in the wilderness for forty years, until that entire generation that acted out evil in his sight had died out.

32.14-15 "And now here you are, just one more mob of sinners stepping up to replace your ancestors, throwing fuel on the already blazing anger of GOD against Israel. If you won't follow him, he'll do it again. He'll dump them in the desert and the disaster will be all your fault."

32.16-19 They came close to him and said, "All we want to do is build corrals for our livestock and

---

a 52 That is, about 420 pounds (about 190 kilograms)

NEW INTERNATIONAL VERSION

and cities for our women and children. ¹⁷But we are ready to arm ourselves and go ahead of the Israelites until we have brought them to their place. Meanwhile our women and children will live in fortified cities, for protection from the inhabitants of the land. ¹⁸We will not return to our homes until every Israelite has received his inheritance. ¹⁹We will not receive any inheritance with them on the other side of the Jordan, because our inheritance has come to us on the east side of the Jordan."

²⁰Then Moses said to them, "If you will do this—if you will arm yourselves before the LORD for battle, ²¹and if all of you will go armed over the Jordan before the LORD until he has driven his enemies out before him— ²²then when the land is subdued before the LORD, you may return and be free from your obligation to the LORD and to Israel. And this land will be your possession before the LORD.

²³"But if you fail to do this, you will be sinning against the LORD; and you may be sure that your sin will find you out. ²⁴Build cities for your women and children, and pens for your flocks, but do what you have promised."

²⁵The Gadites and Reubenites said to Moses, "We your servants will do as our lord commands. ²⁶Our children and wives, our flocks and herds will remain here in the cities of Gilead. ²⁷But your servants, every man armed for battle, will cross over to fight before the LORD, just as our lord says."

²⁸Then Moses gave orders about them to Eleazar the priest and Joshua son of Nun and to the family heads of the Israelite tribes. ²⁹He said to them, "If the Gadites and Reubenites, every man armed for battle, cross over the Jordan with you before the LORD, then when the land is subdued before you, give them the land of Gilead as their possession. ³⁰But if they do not cross over with you armed, they must accept their possession with you in Canaan."

³¹The Gadites and Reubenites answered, "Your servants will do what the LORD has said. ³²We will cross over before the LORD into Canaan armed, but the property we inherit will be on this side of the Jordan."

³³Then Moses gave to the Gadites, the Reubenites and the half-tribe of Manasseh son of Joseph the kingdom of Sihon king of the Amorites and the kingdom of Og king of Bashan—the whole land with its cities and the territory around them.

³⁴The Gadites built up Dibon, Ataroth, Aroer, ³⁵Atroth Shophan, Jazer, Jogbehah, ³⁶Beth Nimrah and Beth Haran as fortified cities, and built pens for their flocks. ³⁷And the Reubenites re-

THE MESSAGE

towns for our families. Then we'll take up arms and take the front lines, leading the People of Israel to their place. We'll be able to leave our families behind, secure in fortified towns, safe from those who live in the land. But we won't go back home until every Israelite is in full possession of his inheritance. We won't expect any inheritance west of the Jordan; we are claiming all our inheritance east of the Jordan."

32.20-22 Moses said, "If you do what you say, take up arms before GOD for battle and together go across the Jordan ready, before GOD, to fight until GOD has cleaned his enemies out of the land, then when the land is secure you will have fulfilled your duty to GOD and Israel. Then this land will be yours to keep before GOD.

32.23-24 "But if you don't do what you say, you will be sinning against GOD; you can be sure that your sin will track you down. So, go ahead. Build towns for your families and corrals for your livestock. Do what you said you'd do."

32.25-27 The families of Gad and Reuben told Moses: "We will do as our master commands. Our children and wives, our flocks and herds will stay behind here in the towns of Gilead. But we, every one of us fully armed, will cross the river to fight for GOD, just as our master has said."

32.28-30 So Moses issued orders for them to Eleazar the priest, Joshua the son of Nun, and the heads of the ancestral tribes of the People of Israel. Moses said, "If the families of Gad and Reuben cross the Jordan River with you and before GOD, all armed and ready to fight, then after the land is secure, you may give them the land of Gilead as their inheritance. But if they don't cross over with you, they'll have to settle up with you in Canaan."

32.31-32 The families of Gad and Reuben responded: "We will do what GOD has said. We will cross the Jordan before GOD, ready and willing to fight. But the land we inherit will be here, to the east of the Jordan."

32.33 Moses gave the families of Gad, Reuben, and the half-tribe of Manasseh son of Joseph the kingdom of Sihon, king of the Amorites, and the kingdom of Og, king of Bashan—the land, its towns, and all the territories connected with them—the works.

32.34-36 The Gadites rebuilt Dibon, Ataroth, Aroer, Atroth Shophan, Jazer, Jogbehah, Beth Nimrah, and Beth Haran as fortified cities; they also built corrals for their animals.

32.37-38 The Reubenites rebuilt Heshbon, Elealeh,

NEW INTERNATIONAL VERSION

built Heshbon, Elealeh and Kiriathaim, ³⁸as well as Nebo and Baal Meon (these names were changed) and Sibmah. They gave names to the cities they rebuilt.

³⁹The descendants of Makir son of Manasseh went to Gilead, captured it and drove out the Amorites who were there. ⁴⁰So Moses gave Gilead to the Makirites, the descendants of Manasseh, and they settled there. ⁴¹Jair, a descendant of Manasseh, captured their settlements and called them Havvoth Jair.[a] ⁴²And Nobah captured Kenath and its surrounding settlements and called it Nobah after himself.

STAGES IN ISRAEL'S JOURNEY

33 Here are the stages in the journey of the Israelites when they came out of Egypt by divisions under the leadership of Moses and Aaron. ²At the LORD's command Moses recorded the stages in their journey. This is their journey by stages:

³The Israelites set out from Rameses on the fifteenth day of the first month, the day after the Passover. They marched out boldly in full view of all the Egyptians, ⁴who were burying all their firstborn, whom the LORD had struck down among them; for the LORD had brought judgment on their gods.

⁵The Israelites left Rameses and camped at Succoth.

⁶They left Succoth and camped at Etham, on the edge of the desert.

⁷They left Etham, turned back to Pi Hahiroth, to the east of Baal Zephon, and camped near Migdol.

⁸They left Pi Hahiroth[b] and passed through the sea into the desert, and when they had traveled for three days in the Desert of Etham, they camped at Marah.

⁹They left Marah and went to Elim, where there were twelve springs and seventy palm trees, and they camped there.

¹⁰They left Elim and camped by the Red Sea.[c]

¹¹They left the Red Sea and camped in the Desert of Sin.

¹²They left the Desert of Sin and camped at Dophkah.

¹³They left Dophkah and camped at Alush.

THE MESSAGE

and Kiriathaim, also Nebo and Baal Meon and Sibmah. They renamed the cities that they rebuilt.

32.39-40 The family of Makir son of Manasseh went to Gilead, captured it, and drove out the Amorites who lived there. Moses then gave Gilead to the Makirites, the descendants of Manasseh. They moved in and settled there.

32.41 Jair, another son of Manasseh, captured some villages and named them Havvoth Jair (Jair's Tent-Camps).

32.42 Nobah captured Kenath and its surrounding camps. He renamed it after himself, Nobah.

CAMPSITES FROM RAMESES TO JORDAN-JERICHO

33.1-2 **33** These are the camping sites in the journey of the People of Israel after they left Egypt, deployed militarily under the command of Moses and Aaron. Under GOD's instruction Moses kept a log of every time they moved, camp by camp:

33.3-4 They marched out of Rameses the day after the Passover. It was the fifteenth day of the first month. They marched out heads high and confident. The Egyptians, busy burying their firstborn whom GOD had killed, watched them go. GOD had exposed the nonsense of their gods.

33.5-36 The People of Israel:
left Rameses and camped at Succoth;
left Succoth and camped at Etham at the edge of the wilderness;
left Etham, circled back to Pi Hahiroth east of Baal Zephon, and camped near Migdol;
left Pi Hahiroth and crossed through the Sea into the wilderness; three days into the Wilderness of Etham they camped at Marah;
left Marah and came to Elim where there were twelve springs and seventy palm trees; they camped there;
left Elim and camped by the Red Sea;
left the Red Sea and camped in the Wilderness of Sin;
left the Wilderness of Sin and camped at Dophkah;
left Dophkah and camped at Alush;

---

^a 41 Or *them the settlements of Jair*   ^b 8 Many manuscripts of the Masoretic Text, Samaritan Pentateuch and Vulgate; most manuscripts of the Masoretic Text *left from before Hahiroth*   ^c 10 Hebrew *Yam Suph*; that is, Sea of Reeds; also in verse 11

NEW INTERNATIONAL VERSION

¹⁴They left Alush and camped at Rephidim, where there was no water for the people to drink.

¹⁵They left Rephidim and camped in the Desert of Sinai.

¹⁶They left the Desert of Sinai and camped at Kibroth Hattaavah.

¹⁷They left Kibroth Hattaavah and camped at Hazeroth.

¹⁸They left Hazeroth and camped at Rithmah.

¹⁹They left Rithmah and camped at Rimmon Perez.

²⁰They left Rimmon Perez and camped at Libnah.

²¹They left Libnah and camped at Rissah.

²²They left Rissah and camped at Kehelathah.

²³They left Kehelathah and camped at Mount Shepher.

²⁴They left Mount Shepher and camped at Haradah.

²⁵They left Haradah and camped at Makheloth.

²⁶They left Makheloth and camped at Tahath.

²⁷They left Tahath and camped at Terah.

²⁸They left Terah and camped at Mithcah.

²⁹They left Mithcah and camped at Hashmonah.

³⁰They left Hashmonah and camped at Moseroth.

³¹They left Moseroth and camped at Bene Jaakan.

³²They left Bene Jaakan and camped at Hor Haggidgad.

³³They left Hor Haggidgad and camped at Jotbathah.

³⁴They left Jotbathah and camped at Abronah.

³⁵They left Abronah and camped at Ezion Geber.

³⁶They left Ezion Geber and camped at Kadesh, in the Desert of Zin.

³⁷They left Kadesh and camped at Mount Hor, on the border of Edom. ³⁸At the LORD's command Aaron the priest went up Mount Hor, where he died on the first day of the fifth month of the fortieth year after the Israelites came out of Egypt. ³⁹Aaron was a hundred and twenty-three years old when he died on Mount Hor.

⁴⁰The Canaanite king of Arad, who lived in the Negev of Canaan, heard that the Israelites were coming.

THE MESSAGE

left Alush and camped at Rephidim where there was no water for the people to drink;

left Rephidim and camped in the Wilderness of Sinai;

left the Wilderness of Sinai and camped at Kibroth Hattaavah;

left Kibroth Hattaavah and camped at Hazeroth;

left Hazeroth and camped at Rithmah;

left Rithmah and camped at Rimmon Perez;

left Rimmon Perez and camped at Libnah;

left Libnah and camped at Rissah;

left Rissah and camped at Kehelathah;

left Kehelathah and camped at Mount Shepher;

left Mount Shepher and camped at Haradah;

left Haradah and camped at Makheloth;

left Makheloth and camped at Tahath;

left Tahath and camped at Terah;

left Terah and camped at Mithcah;

left Mithcah and camped at Hashmonah;

left Hashmonah and camped at Moseroth;

left Moseroth and camped at Bene Jaakan;

left Bene Jaakan and camped at Hor Haggidgad;

left Hor Haggidgad and camped at Jotbathah;

left Jotbathah and camped at Abronah;

left Abronah and camped at Ezion Geber;

left Ezion Geber and camped at Kadesh in the Wilderness of Zin.

33.37-39 After they left Kadesh and camped at Mount Hor at the border of Edom, Aaron the priest climbed Mount Hor at GOD's command and died there. It was the first day of the fifth month in the fortieth year after the People of Israel had left Egypt. Aaron was 123 years old when he died on Mount Hor.

✠

33.40 The Canaanite king of Arad—he ruled in the Negev of Canaan—heard that the People of Israel had arrived.

NEW INTERNATIONAL VERSION

[41] They left Mount Hor and camped at Zalmonah.

[42] They left Zalmonah and camped at Punon.

[43] They left Punon and camped at Oboth.

[44] They left Oboth and camped at Iye Abarim, on the border of Moab.

[45] They left Iyim[a] and camped at Dibon Gad.

[46] They left Dibon Gad and camped at Almon Diblathaim.

[47] They left Almon Diblathaim and camped in the mountains of Abarim, near Nebo.

[48] They left the mountains of Abarim and camped on the plains of Moab by the Jordan across from Jericho.[b] [49] There on the plains of Moab they camped along the Jordan from Beth Jeshimoth to Abel Shittim.

[50] On the plains of Moab by the Jordan across from Jericho the LORD said to Moses, [51] "Speak to the Israelites and say to them: 'When you cross the Jordan into Canaan, [52] drive out all the inhabitants of the land before you. Destroy all their carved images and their cast idols, and demolish all their high places. [53] Take possession of the land and settle in it, for I have given you the land to possess. [54] Distribute the land by lot, according to your clans. To a larger group give a larger inheritance, and to a smaller group a smaller one. Whatever falls to them by lot will be theirs. Distribute it according to your ancestral tribes.

[55] "But if you do not drive out the inhabitants of the land, those you allow to remain will become barbs in your eyes and thorns in your sides. They will give you trouble in the land where you will live. [56] And then I will do to you what I plan to do to them.' "

BOUNDARIES OF CANAAN

34 The LORD said to Moses, [2] "Command the Israelites and say to them: 'When you enter Canaan, the land that will be allotted to you as an inheritance will have these boundaries:

[3] " 'Your southern side will include some of the Desert of Zin along the border of Edom. On the east, your southern boundary will start from the end of the Salt Sea,[c] [4] cross south of Scorpion[d] Pass, continue on to Zin and go south of Kadesh Barnea. Then it will go to Hazar Addar

THE MESSAGE

33.41-47 They left Mount Hor and camped at Zalmonah;

left Zalmonah and camped at Punon;

left Punon and camped at Oboth;

left Oboth and camped at Iye Abarim on the border of Moab;

left Iyim and camped at Dibon Gad;

left Dibon Gad and camped at Almon Diblathaim;

left Almon Diblathaim and camped in the mountains of Abarim (Across-the-River), within sight of Nebo.

33.48-49 After they left the mountains of Abarim they camped on the Plains of Moab at Jordan-Jericho. On the Plains of Moab their camp stretched along the banks of the Jordan from Beth Jeshimoth to Abel Shittim (Acacia Meadow).

33.50-53 GOD spoke to Moses on the Plains of Moab at Jordan-Jericho: "Tell the People of Israel, When you cross the Jordan into the country of Canaan, drive out the native population before you, destroy their carved idols, destroy their cast images, level their worship-mounds so that you take over the land and make yourself at home in it; I've given it to you. It's yours.

33.54 "Divide up the land by lot according to the size of your clans: Large clans will get large tracts of land, small clans will get smaller tracts of land. However the lot falls, that's it. Divide it up according to your ancestral tribes.

33.55-56 "But if you don't drive out the native population, everyone you let stay there will become a cinder in your eye and a splinter in your foot. They'll give you endless trouble right in your own backyards. And I'll start treating you the way I planned to treat them."

LAND INHERITANCE

34 GOD spoke to Moses: "Command the People of Israel. Tell them: When you 34.1-2 enter Canaan, these are the borders of the land you are getting as an inheritance:

34.3-5 "Your southern border will take in some of the Wilderness of Zin where it touches Edom. It starts in the east at the Dead Sea, curves south of Scorpion Pass and on to Zin, continues south of Kadesh Barnea, then to Hazar Ad-

---

[a] 45 That is, Iye Abarim   [b] 48 Hebrew *Jordan of Jericho*; possibly an ancient name for the Jordan River; also in verse 50   [c] 3 That is, the Dead Sea; also in verse 12
[d] 4 Hebrew *Akrabbim*

NEW INTERNATIONAL VERSION

and over to Azmon, [5]where it will turn, join the Wadi of Egypt and end at the Sea. [a]

[6]" 'Your western boundary will be the coast of the Great Sea. This will be your boundary on the west.

[7]" 'For your northern boundary, run a line from the Great Sea to Mount Hor [8]and from Mount Hor to Lebo[b] Hamath. Then the boundary will go to Zedad, [9]continue to Ziphron and end at Hazar Enan. This will be your boundary on the north.

[10]" 'For your eastern boundary, run a line from Hazar Enan to Shepham. [11]The boundary will go down from Shepham to Riblah on the east side of Ain and continue along the slopes east of the Sea of Kinnereth.[c] [12]Then the boundary will go down along the Jordan and end at the Salt Sea.

" 'This will be your land, with its boundaries on every side.' "

[13]Moses commanded the Israelites: "Assign this land by lot as an inheritance. The LORD has ordered that it be given to the nine and a half tribes, [14]because the families of the tribe of Reuben, the tribe of Gad and the half-tribe of Manasseh have received their inheritance. [15]These two and a half tribes have received their inheritance on the east side of the Jordan of Jericho,[d] toward the sunrise."

[16]The LORD said to Moses, [17]"These are the names of the men who are to assign the land for you as an inheritance: Eleazar the priest and Joshua son of Nun. [18]And appoint one leader from each tribe to help assign the land. [19]These are their names:

Caleb son of Jephunneh,
      from the tribe of Judah;
[20]Shemuel son of Ammihud,
      from the tribe of Simeon;
[21]Elidad son of Kislon,
      from the tribe of Benjamin;
[22]Bukki son of Jogli,
      the leader from the tribe of Dan;
[23]Hanniel son of Ephod,
      the leader from the tribe of Manasseh
      son of Joseph;
[24]Kemuel son of Shiphtan,
      the leader from the tribe of Ephraim son
      of Joseph;
[25]Elizaphan son of Parnach,
      the leader from the tribe of Zebulun;
[26]Paltiel son of Azzan,
      the leader from the tribe of Issachar;

THE MESSAGE

dar and on to Azmon, where it takes a turn to the northwest to the Brook of Egypt and on to the Mediterranean Sea.

34.6   "Your western border will be the Mediterranean Sea.

34.7-9   "Your northern border runs on a line from the Mediterranean Sea to Mount Hor, and from Mount Hor to Lebo Hamath, connects to Zedad, continues to Ziphron, and ends at Hazar Enan. This is your northern border.

34.10-12   "Your eastern border runs on a line from Hazar Enan to Shepham. The border goes south from Shepham to Riblah to the east of Ain, and continues along the slopes east of the Sea of Galilee. The border then follows the Jordan River and ends at the Dead Sea.

"This is your land with its four borders."

34.13-15   Moses then commanded the People of Israel: "This is the land: Divide up the inheritance by lot. GOD has ordered it to be given to the nine and a half tribes. The tribe of Reuben, the tribe of Gad, and the half-tribe of Manasseh have already received their inheritance; the two tribes and the half-tribe got their inheritance east of Jordan-Jericho, facing the sunrise."

✝

34.16-19   GOD spoke to Moses: "These are the men who will be in charge of distributing the inheritance of the land: Eleazar the priest and Joshua son of Nun. Assign one leader from each tribe to help them in distributing the land. Assign these:

34.19-28   Caleb son of Jephunneh from the tribe of Judah;

Shemuel son of Ammihud from the tribe of Simeon;

Elidad son of Kislon from the tribe of Benjamin;

Bukki son of Jogli, leader from the tribe of Dan;

Hanniel son of Ephod, leader from the tribe of Manasseh son of Joseph;

Kemuel son of Shiphtan, leader from the tribe of Ephraim son of Joseph;

Elizaphan son of Parnach, leader from the tribe of Zebulun;

Paltiel son of Azzan, leader from the tribe of Issachar;

---

[a] 5 That is, the Mediterranean; also in verses 6 and 7
[b] 8 Or to the entrance to   [c] 11 That is, Galilee
[d] 15 Jordan of Jericho was possibly an ancient name for the Jordan River.

NEW INTERNATIONAL VERSION

²⁷Ahihud son of Shelomi,
the leader from the tribe of Asher;
²⁸Pedahel son of Ammihud,
the leader from the tribe of Naphtali."

²⁹These are the men the LORD commanded to assign the inheritance to the Israelites in the land of Canaan.

TOWNS FOR THE LEVITES

35 On the plains of Moab by the Jordan across from Jericho,ª the LORD said to Moses, ²"Command the Israelites to give the Levites towns to live in from the inheritance the Israelites will possess. And give them pasturelands around the towns. ³Then they will have towns to live in and pasturelands for their cattle, flocks and all their other livestock.

⁴"The pasturelands around the towns that you give the Levites will extend out fifteen hundred feetᵇ from the town wall. ⁵Outside the town, measure three thousand feetᶜ on the east side, three thousand on the south side, three thousand on the west and three thousand on the north, with the town in the center. They will have this area as pastureland for the towns.

CITIES OF REFUGE

⁶"Six of the towns you give the Levites will be cities of refuge, to which a person who has killed someone may flee. In addition, give them forty-two other towns. ⁷In all you must give the Levites forty-eight towns, together with their pasturelands. ⁸The towns you give the Levites from the land the Israelites possess are to be given in proportion to the inheritance of each tribe: Take many towns from a tribe that has many, but few from one that has few."

⁹Then the LORD said to Moses: ¹⁰"Speak to the Israelites and say to them: 'When you cross the Jordan into Canaan, ¹¹select some towns to be your cities of refuge, to which a person who has killed someone accidentally may flee. ¹²They will be places of refuge from the avenger, so that a person accused of murder may not die before he stands trial before the assembly. ¹³These six towns you give will be your cities of refuge. ¹⁴Give three on this side of the Jordan and three in Canaan as cities of refuge. ¹⁵These six towns will be a place of refuge for Israelites, aliens and any other people living among them, so that anyone who has killed another accidentally can flee there.

¹⁶"'If a man strikes someone with an iron ob-

ª 1 Hebrew *Jordan of Jericho*; possibly an ancient name for the Jordan River   ᵇ 4 Hebrew *a thousand cubits* (about 450 meters)   ᶜ 5 Hebrew *two thousand cubits* (about 900 meters)

THE MESSAGE

Ahihud son of Shelomi, leader from the tribe of Asher;
Pedahel son of Ammihud, leader from the tribe of Naphtali."

³⁴.²⁹ These are the men GOD commanded to hand out the assignments of land-inheritance to the People of Israel in the country of Canaan.

CITIES FOR LEVITES AND ASYLUM-CITIES

³⁵.¹⁻³ **35** Then GOD spoke to Moses on the Plains of Moab at Jordan-Jericho: "Command the People of Israel to give the Levites as their part of the total inheritance towns to live in. Make sure there is plenty of pasture around the towns. Then they will be well taken care of with towns to live in and pastures for their cattle, flocks, and other livestock.

³⁵.⁴⁻⁵ "The pasture surrounding the Levites' towns is to extend 1,500 feet in each direction from the city wall. The outside borders of the pasture are to measure three thousand feet on each of the four sides—east, south, west, and north— with the town at the center. Each city will be supplied with pasture.

³⁵.⁶⁻⁸ "Six of these towns that you give the Levites will be asylum-cities to which anyone who accidentally kills another person may flee for asylum. In addition, you will give them forty-two other towns—forty-eight towns in all, together with their pastures. The towns that you give the Levites from the common inheritance of the People of Israel are to be taken in proportion to the size of each tribe—many towns from a tribe that has many, few from a tribe that has few."

³⁵.⁹⁻¹⁵ GOD spoke to Moses: "Speak to the People of Israel. Tell them, When you cross the River Jordan into the country of Canaan, designate your asylum-cities, towns to which a person who accidentally kills someone can flee for asylum. They will be places of refuge from the avenger so that the alleged murderer won't be killed until he can appear before the community in court. Provide six asylum-cities. Designate three of the towns to the east side of the Jordan, the other three in Canaan proper—asylum-cities for the People of Israel, for the foreigner, and for any occasional visitors or guests—six asylum-cities to run to for anyone who accidentally kills another.

³⁵.¹⁶ "But if the killer has used an iron object,

NEW INTERNATIONAL VERSION

ject so that he dies, he is a murderer; the murderer shall be put to death. ¹⁷Or if anyone has a stone in his hand that could kill, and he strikes someone so that he dies, he is a murderer; the murderer shall be put to death. ¹⁸Or if anyone has a wooden object in his hand that could kill, and he hits someone so that he dies, he is a murderer; the murderer shall be put to death. ¹⁹The avenger of blood shall put the murderer to death; when he meets him, he shall put him to death. ²⁰If anyone with malice aforethought shoves another or throws something at him intentionally so that he dies ²¹or if in hostility he hits him with his fist so that he dies, that person shall be put to death; he is a murderer. The avenger of blood shall put the murderer to death when he meets him.

²²" 'But if without hostility someone suddenly shoves another or throws something at him unintentionally ²³or, without seeing him, drops a stone on him that could kill him, and he dies, then since he was not his enemy and he did not intend to harm him, ²⁴the assembly must judge between him and the avenger of blood according to these regulations. ²⁵The assembly must protect the one accused of murder from the avenger of blood and send him back to the city of refuge to which he fled. He must stay there until the death of the high priest, who was anointed with the holy oil.

²⁶" 'But if the accused ever goes outside the limits of the city of refuge to which he has fled ²⁷and the avenger of blood finds him outside the city, the avenger of blood may kill the accused without being guilty of murder. ²⁸The accused must stay in his city of refuge until the death of the high priest; only after the death of the high priest may he return to his own property.

²⁹" 'These are to be legal requirements for you throughout the generations to come, wherever you live.

³⁰" 'Anyone who kills a person is to be put to death as a murderer only on the testimony of witnesses. But no one is to be put to death on the testimony of only one witness.

³¹" 'Do not accept a ransom for the life of a murderer, who deserves to die. He must surely be put to death.

³²" 'Do not accept a ransom for anyone who has fled to a city of refuge and so allow him to go back and live on his own land before the death of the high priest.

³³" 'Do not pollute the land where you are.

THE MESSAGE

that's just plain murder; he's obviously a murderer and must be put to death.

35.17 "Or if he has a rock in his hand big enough to kill and the man dies, that's murder; he's a murderer and must be put to death.

35.18 "Or if he's carrying a wooden club heavy enough to kill and the man dies, that's murder; he's a murderer and must be put to death.

35.19 "In such cases the avenger has a right to kill the murderer when he meets him—he can kill him on the spot.

35.20-21 "And if out of sheer hatred a man pushes another or from ambush throws something at him and he dies, or angrily hits him with his fist and kills him, that's murder—he must be put to death. The avenger has a right to kill him when he gets him.

35.22-27 "If, however, he impulsively pushes someone and there is no history of hard feelings, or he impetuously picks up something and throws it, or he accidentally drops a stone tool—a maul or hammer, say—and it hits and kills someone he didn't even know was there, and there's no suspicion that there was bad blood between them, the community is to judge between the killer and the avenger following these guidelines. It's the task of the community to save the killer from the hand of the avenger—the community is to return him to his asylum-city to which he fled. He must stay there until the death of the High Priest who was anointed with the holy oil. But if the murderer leaves the asylum-city to which he has fled, and the avenger finds him outside the borders of his asylum-city, the avenger has a right to kill the murderer. And he's not considered guilty of murder.

35.28 "So it's important that he stay in his asylum-city until the death of the High Priest. After the death of the High Priest he is free to return to his own place.

✝

35.29 "These are the procedures for making judgments from now on, wherever you live.

35.30 "Anyone who kills another may be executed only on the testimony of eyewitnesses. But no one can be executed on the testimony of only one witness.

35.31 "Don't accept bribe money in exchange for the life of a murderer. He's guilty and deserves the death penalty. Put him to death.

35.32 "And don't accept bribe money for anyone who has fled to an asylum-city so as to permit him to go back and live in his own place before the death of the High Priest.

35.33 "Don't pollute the land in which you live.

NEW INTERNATIONAL VERSION

Bloodshed pollutes the land, and atonement cannot be made for the land on which blood has been shed, except by the blood of the one who shed it. ³⁴Do not defile the land where you live and where I dwell, for I, the LORD, dwell among the Israelites.' "

INHERITANCE OF ZELOPHEHAD'S DAUGHTERS

36 The family heads of the clan of Gilead son of Makir, the son of Manasseh, who were from the clans of the descendants of Joseph, came and spoke before Moses and the leaders, the heads of the Israelite families. ²They said, "When the LORD commanded my lord to give the land as an inheritance to the Israelites by lot, he ordered you to give the inheritance of our brother Zelophehad to his daughters. ³Now suppose they marry men from other Israelite tribes; then their inheritance will be taken from our ancestral inheritance and added to that of the tribe they marry into. And so part of the inheritance allotted to us will be taken away. ⁴When the Year of Jubilee for the Israelites comes, their inheritance will be added to that of the tribe into which they marry, and their property will be taken from the tribal inheritance of our forefathers."

⁵Then at the LORD's command Moses gave this order to the Israelites: "What the tribe of the descendants of Joseph is saying is right. ⁶This is what the LORD commands for Zelophehad's daughters: They may marry anyone they please as long as they marry within the tribal clan of their father. ⁷No inheritance in Israel is to pass from tribe to tribe, for every Israelite shall keep the tribal land inherited from his forefathers. ⁸Every daughter who inherits land in any Israelite tribe must marry someone in her father's tribal clan, so that every Israelite will possess the inheritance of his fathers. ⁹No inheritance may pass from tribe to tribe, for each Israelite tribe is to keep the land it inherits."

¹⁰So Zelophehad's daughters did as the LORD commanded Moses. ¹¹Zelophehad's daughters—Mahlah, Tirzah, Hoglah, Milcah and Noah—married their cousins on their father's side. ¹²They married within the clans of the descendants of Manasseh son of Joseph, and their inheritance remained in their father's clan and tribe.

¹³These are the commands and regulations the LORD gave through Moses to the Israelites on the plains of Moab by the Jordan across from Jericho.ᵃ

ᵃ 13 Hebrew *Jordan of Jericho*; possibly an ancient name for the Jordan River

THE MESSAGE

Murder pollutes the land. The land can't be cleaned up of the blood of murder except through the blood of the murderer.

35.34 "Don't desecrate the land in which you live. I live here too—I, GOD, live in the same neighborhood with the People of Israel."

THE DAUGHTERS OF ZELOPHEHAD

36.1 **36** The heads of the ancestral clan of Gilead son of Makir, the son of Manasseh—they were from the clans of the descendants of Joseph—approached Moses and the leaders who were heads of the families in the People of Israel.

36.2-4 They said, "When GOD commanded my master to hand over the inheritance-lands by lot to the People of Israel, my master was also commanded by GOD to hand over the inheritance-land of Zelophehad our brother to his daughters. But what happens if they marry into another tribe in the People of Israel? Their inheritance-land will be taken out of our ancestral tribe and get added into the tribe into which they married. And then when the Year of Jubilee comes for the People of Israel their inheritance will be lumped in with the inheritance of the tribe into which they married—their land will be removed from our ancestors' inheritance!"

36.5-9 Moses, at GOD's command, issued this order to the People of Israel: "What the tribe of the sons of Joseph says is right. This is GOD's command to Zelophehad's daughters: They are free to marry anyone they choose as long as they marry within their ancestral clan. The inheritance-land of the People of Israel must not get passed around from tribe to tribe. No, keep the tribal inheritance-land in the family. Every daughter who inherits land, regardless of the tribe she is in, must marry a man from within her father's tribal clan. Every Israelite is responsible for making sure the inheritance stays within the ancestral tribe. No inheritance-land may be passed from tribe to tribe; each tribe of the People of Israel must hold tight to its own land."

36.10-12 Zelophehad's daughters did just as GOD commanded Moses. Mahlah, Tirzah, Hoglah, Milcah, and Noah, Zelophehad's daughters, all married their cousins on their father's side. They married within the families of Manasseh son of Joseph and their inheritance-lands stayed in their father's family.

36.13 These are the commands and regulations that GOD commanded through the authority of Moses to the People of Israel on the Plains of Moab at Jordan-Jericho.

DEUTERONOMY

DEUTERONOMY

THE COMMAND TO LEAVE HOREB

1 These are the words Moses spoke to all Israel in the desert east of the Jordan—that is, in the Arabah—opposite Suph, between Paran and Tophel, Laban, Hazeroth and Dizahab. ²(It takes eleven days to go from Horeb to Kadesh Barnea by the Mount Seir road.)

³In the fortieth year, on the first day of the eleventh month, Moses proclaimed to the Israelites all that the LORD had commanded him concerning them. ⁴This was after he had defeated Sihon king of the Amorites, who reigned in Heshbon, and at Edrei had defeated Og king of Bashan, who reigned in Ashtaroth.

⁵East of the Jordan in the territory of Moab, Moses began to expound this law, saying:

⁶The LORD our God said to us at Horeb, "You have stayed long enough at this mountain. ⁷Break camp and advance into the hill country of the Amorites; go to all the neighboring peoples in the Arabah, in the mountains, in the western foothills, in the Negev and along the coast, to the land of the Canaanites and to Lebanon, as far as the great river, the Euphrates. ⁸See, I have given you this land. Go in and take possession of the land that the LORD swore he would give to your fathers—to Abraham, Isaac and Jacob—and to their descendants after them."

THE APPOINTMENT OF LEADERS

⁹At that time I said to you, "You are too heavy a burden for me to carry alone. ¹⁰The LORD your God has increased your numbers so that today you are as many as the stars in the sky. ¹¹May the LORD, the God of your fathers, increase you a thousand times and bless you as he has promised! ¹²But how can I bear your problems and your burdens and your disputes all by myself? ¹³Choose some wise, understanding and respected men from each of your tribes, and I will set them over you."

1.1-2 **1** These are the sermons Moses preached to all Israel when they were east of the Jordan River in the Arabah Wilderness, opposite Suph, in the vicinity of Paran, Tophel, Laban, Hazeroth, and Dizahab. It takes eleven days to travel from Horeb to Kadesh Barnea following the Mount Seir route.

✝

1.3-4 It was on the first day of the eleventh month of the fortieth year when Moses addressed the People of Israel, telling them everything GOD had commanded him concerning them. This came after he had defeated Sihon king of the Amorites, who ruled from Heshbon, and Og king of Bashan, who ruled from Ashtaroth in Edrei. It was east of the Jordan in the land of Moab that Moses set out to explain this Revelation.

MOSES PREACHES TO ISRAEL ON THE PLAINS OF MOAB

1.5 He said:

1.6-8 Back at Horeb, GOD, our God, spoke to us: "You've stayed long enough at this mountain. On your way now. Get moving. Head for the Amorite hills, wherever people are living in the Arabah, the mountains, the foothills, the Negev, the seashore—the Canaanite country and the Lebanon all the way to the big river, the Euphrates. Look, I've given you this land. Now go in and take it. It's the land GOD promised to give your ancestors Abraham, Isaac, and Jacob and their children after them."

1.9-13 At the time I told you, "I can't do this, can't carry you all by myself. GOD, your God, has multiplied your numbers. Why, look at you—you rival the stars in the sky! And may GOD, the God-of-Your-Fathers, keep it up and multiply you another thousand times, bless you just as he promised. But how can I carry, all by myself, your troubles and burdens and quarrels? So select some wise, understanding, and seasoned men from your tribes, and I will commission them as your leaders."

NEW INTERNATIONAL VERSION

¹⁴You answered me, "What you propose to do is good."

¹⁵So I took the leading men of your tribes, wise and respected men, and appointed them to have authority over you—as commanders of thousands, of hundreds, of fifties and of tens and as tribal officials. ¹⁶And I charged your judges at that time: Hear the disputes between your brothers and judge fairly, whether the case is between brother Israelites or between one of them and an alien. ¹⁷Do not show partiality in judging; hear both small and great alike. Do not be afraid of any man, for judgment belongs to God. Bring me any case too hard for you, and I will hear it. ¹⁸And at that time I told you everything you were to do.

Spies Sent Out

¹⁹Then, as the LORD our God commanded us, we set out from Horeb and went toward the hill country of the Amorites through all that vast and dreadful desert that you have seen, and so we reached Kadesh Barnea. ²⁰Then I said to you, "You have reached the hill country of the Amorites, which the LORD our God is giving us. ²¹See, the LORD your God has given you the land. Go up and take possession of it as the LORD, the God of your fathers, told you. Do not be afraid; do not be discouraged."

²²Then all of you came to me and said, "Let us send men ahead to spy out the land for us and bring back a report about the route we are to take and the towns we will come to."

²³The idea seemed good to me; so I selected twelve of you, one man from each tribe. ²⁴They left and went up into the hill country, and came to the Valley of Eshcol and explored it. ²⁵Taking with them some of the fruit of the land, they brought it down to us and reported, "It is a good land that the LORD our God is giving us."

Rebellion Against the Lord

²⁶But you were unwilling to go up; you rebelled against the command of the LORD your God. ²⁷You grumbled in your tents and said, "The LORD hates us; so he brought us out of Egypt to deliver us into the hands of the Amorites to destroy us. ²⁸Where can we go? Our brothers have made us lose heart. They say, 'The people are stronger and taller than we are; the cities are large, with walls up to the sky. We even saw the Anakites there.' "

²⁹Then I said to you, "Do not be terrified; do not be afraid of them. ³⁰The LORD your God, who is going before you, will fight for you, as he did for you in Egypt, before your very eyes, ³¹and in the desert. There you saw how the LORD

THE MESSAGE

1.14 You answered me, "Good! A good solution."

1.15 So I went ahead and took the top men of your tribes, wise and seasoned, and made them your leaders—leaders of thousands, of hundreds, of fifties, and of tens, officials adequate for each of your tribes.

1.16-17 At the same time I gave orders to your judges: "Listen carefully to complaints and accusations between your fellow Israelites. Judge fairly between each person and his fellow or foreigner. Don't play favorites; treat the little and the big alike; listen carefully to each. Don't be impressed by big names. This is *God's* judgment you're dealing with. Hard cases you can bring to me; I'll deal with them."

1.18 I issued orders to you at that time regarding everything you would have to deal with.

1.19-21 Then we set out from Horeb and headed for the Amorite hill country, going through that huge and frightening wilderness that you've had more than an eyeful of by now—all under the command of GOD, our God—and finally arrived at Kadesh Barnea. There I told you, "You've made it to the Amorite hill country that GOD, our God, is giving us. Look, GOD, your God, has placed this land as a gift before you. Go ahead and take it now. GOD, the God-of-Your-Fathers, promised it to you. Don't be afraid. Don't lose heart."

1.22 But then you all came to me and said, "Let's send some men on ahead to scout out the land for us and bring back a report on the best route to take and the kinds of towns we can expect to find."

1.23-25 That seemed like a good idea to me, so I picked twelve men, one from each tribe. They set out, climbing through the hills. They came to the Eshcol Valley and looked it over. They took samples of the produce of the land and brought them back to us, saying, "It's a good land that GOD, our God, is giving us!"

1.26-28 But then you weren't willing to go up. You rebelled against GOD, your God's plain word. You complained in your tents: "GOD hates us. He hauled us out of Egypt in order to dump us among the Amorites—a death sentence for sure! How can we go up? We're trapped in a dead end. Our brothers took all the wind out of our sails, telling us, 'The people are bigger and stronger than we are; their cities are huge, their defenses massive—we even saw Anakite giants there!' "

1.29-33 I tried to relieve your fears: "Don't be terrified of them. GOD, your God, is leading the way; he's fighting for you. You saw with your own eyes what he did for you in Egypt; you saw what he did in the wilderness, how GOD,

NEW INTERNATIONAL VERSION

your God carried you, as a father carries his son, all the way you went until you reached this place."

³²In spite of this, you did not trust in the LORD your God, ³³who went ahead of you on your journey, in fire by night and in a cloud by day, to search out places for you to camp and to show you the way you should go.

³⁴When the LORD heard what you said, he was angry and solemnly swore: ³⁵"Not a man of this evil generation shall see the good land I swore to give your forefathers, ³⁶except Caleb son of Jephunneh. He will see it, and I will give him and his descendants the land he set his feet on, because he followed the LORD wholeheartedly."

³⁷Because of you the LORD became angry with me also and said, "You shall not enter it, either. ³⁸But your assistant, Joshua son of Nun, will enter it. Encourage him, because he will lead Israel to inherit it. ³⁹And the little ones that you said would be taken captive, your children who do not yet know good from bad—they will enter the land. I will give it to them and they will take possession of it. ⁴⁰But as for you, turn around and set out toward the desert along the route to the Red Sea.^a"

⁴¹Then you replied, "We have sinned against the LORD. We will go up and fight, as the LORD our God commanded us." So every one of you put on his weapons, thinking it easy to go up into the hill country.

⁴²But the LORD said to me, "Tell them, 'Do not go up and fight, because I will not be with you. You will be defeated by your enemies.' "

⁴³So I told you, but you would not listen. You rebelled against the LORD's command and in your arrogance you marched up into the hill country. ⁴⁴The Amorites who lived in those hills came out against you; they chased you like a swarm of bees and beat you down from Seir all the way to Hormah. ⁴⁵You came back and wept before the LORD, but he paid no attention to your weeping and turned a deaf ear to you. ⁴⁶And so you stayed in Kadesh many days—all the time you spent there.

WANDERINGS IN THE DESERT

2 Then we turned back and set out toward the desert along the route to the Red Sea,^a as the LORD had directed me. For a long time we made our way around the hill country of Seir.

^a 40, 1 Hebrew *Yam Suph*; that is, Sea of Reeds

THE MESSAGE

your God, carried you as a father carries his child, carried you the whole way until you arrived here. But now that you're here, you won't trust GOD, your God—this same GOD who goes ahead of you in your travels to scout out a place to pitch camp, a fire by night and a cloud by day to show you the way to go."

1.34-36   When GOD heard what you said, he exploded in anger. He swore, "Not a single person of this evil generation is going to get so much as a look at the good land that I promised to give to your parents. Not one—except for Caleb son of Jephunneh. He'll see it. I'll give him and his descendants the land he walked on because he was all for following GOD, heart and soul."

1.37-40   But I also got it. Because of you GOD's anger spilled over onto me. He said, "You aren't getting in either. Your assistant, Joshua son of Nun, will go in. Build up his courage. He's the one who will claim the inheritance for Israel. And your babies of whom you said, 'They'll be grabbed for plunder,' and all these little kids who right now don't even know right from wrong—they'll get in. I'll give it to them. Yes, they'll be the new owners. But not you. Turn around and head back into the wilderness following the route to the Red Sea."

1.41   You spoke up, "We've sinned against GOD. We'll go up and fight, following all the orders that GOD, our God, has commanded." You took your weapons and dressed for battle—you thought it would be so easy going into those hills!

1.42   But GOD told me, "Tell them, 'Don't do it; don't go up to fight—I'm not with you in this. Your enemies will waste you.' "

1.43-46   I told you but you wouldn't listen. You rebelled at the plain word of GOD. You threw out your chests and strutted into the hills. And those Amorites, who had lived in those hills all their lives, swarmed all over you like a hive of bees, chasing you from Seir all the way to Hormah, a stinging defeat. You came back and wept in the presence of GOD, but he didn't pay a bit of attention to you; GOD didn't give you the time of day. You stayed there in Kadesh a long time, about as long as you had stayed there earlier.

2.1   **2** Then we turned around and went back into the wilderness following the route to the Red Sea, as GOD had instructed me. We worked our way in and around the hills of Seir for a long, long time.

✠

NEW INTERNATIONAL VERSION

²Then the LORD said to me, ³"You have made your way around this hill country long enough; now turn north. ⁴Give the people these orders: 'You are about to pass through the territory of your brothers the descendants of Esau, who live in Seir. They will be afraid of you, but be very careful. ⁵Do not provoke them to war, for I will not give you any of their land, not even enough to put your foot on. I have given Esau the hill country of Seir as his own. ⁶You are to pay them in silver for the food you eat and the water you drink.' "

⁷The LORD your God has blessed you in all the work of your hands. He has watched over your journey through this vast desert. These forty years the LORD your God has been with you, and you have not lacked anything.

⁸So we went on past our brothers the descendants of Esau, who live in Seir. We turned from the Arabah road, which comes up from Elath and Ezion Geber, and traveled along the desert road of Moab.

⁹Then the LORD said to me, "Do not harass the Moabites or provoke them to war, for I will not give you any part of their land. I have given Ar to the descendants of Lot as a possession."

¹⁰(The Emites used to live there—a people strong and numerous, and as tall as the Anakites. ¹¹Like the Anakites, they too were considered Rephaites, but the Moabites called them Emites. ¹²Horites used to live in Seir, but the descendants of Esau drove them out. They destroyed the Horites from before them and settled in their place, just as Israel did in the land the LORD gave them as their possession.)

¹³And the LORD said, "Now get up and cross the Zered Valley." So we crossed the valley.

¹⁴Thirty-eight years passed from the time we left Kadesh Barnea until we crossed the Zered Valley. By then, that entire generation of fighting men had perished from the camp, as the LORD had sworn to them. ¹⁵The LORD's hand was against them until he had completely eliminated them from the camp.

¹⁶Now when the last of these fighting men among the people had died, ¹⁷the LORD said to me, ¹⁸"Today you are to pass by the region of Moab at Ar. ¹⁹When you come to the Ammonites, do not harass them or provoke them to war, for I will not give you possession of any land belonging to the Ammonites. I have given it as a possession to the descendants of Lot."

²⁰(That too was considered a land of the Rephaites, who used to live there; but the Ammonites called them Zamzummites. ²¹They were a people strong and numerous, and as tall as the Anakites. The LORD destroyed them from before

THE MESSAGE

2.2-6 Then GOD said, "You've been going around in circles in these hills long enough; go north. Command the people, You're about to cut through the land belonging to your relatives, the People of Esau who settled in Seir. They are terrified of you, but restrain yourselves. Don't try and start a fight. I am not giving you so much as a square inch of their land. I've already given all the hill country of Seir to Esau—he owns it all. Pay them up front for any food or water you get from them."

2.7 GOD, your God, has blessed you in everything you have done. He has guarded you in your travels through this immense wilderness. For forty years now, GOD, your God, has been right here with you. You haven't lacked one thing.

2.8 So we detoured around our brothers, the People of Esau who live in Seir, avoiding the Arabah Road that comes up from Elath and Ezion Geber; instead we used the road through the Wilderness of Moab.

2.9 GOD told me, "And don't try to pick a fight with the Moabites. I am not giving you any of their land. I've given ownership of Ar to the People of Lot."

2.10-12 The Emites (Monsters) used to live there—mobs of hulking giants, like Anakites. Along with the Anakites they were lumped in with the Rephaites (Ghosts) but in Moab they were called Emites. Horites also used to live in Seir, but the descendants of Esau took over and destroyed them, the same as Israel did in the land GOD gave them to possess.

2.13 GOD said, "It's time now to cross the Brook Zered." So we crossed the Brook Zered.

2.14-15 It took us thirty-eight years to get from Kadesh Barnea to the Brook Zered. That's how long it took for the entire generation of soldiers from the camp to die off, as GOD had sworn they would. GOD was relentless against them until the last one was gone from the camp.

2.16-23 When the last of these soldiers had died, GOD said to me, "This is the day you cut across the territory of Moab, at Ar. When you approach the People of Ammon, don't try and pick a fight with them because I'm not giving you any of the land of the People of Ammon for yourselves—I've already given it to the People of Lot." It is also considered to have once been the land of the Rephaites. Rephaites lived there long ago—the Ammonites called them Zamzummites (Barbarians)—huge mobs of them, giants like the Anakites. GOD destroyed

NEW INTERNATIONAL VERSION

the Ammonites, who drove them out and settled in their place. [22]The LORD had done the same for the descendants of Esau, who lived in Seir, when he destroyed the Horites from before them. They drove them out and have lived in their place to this day. [23]And as for the Avvites who lived in villages as far as Gaza, the Caphtorites coming out from Caphtor*a* destroyed them and settled in their place.)

DEFEAT OF SIHON KING OF HESHBON

[24]"Set out now and cross the Arnon Gorge. See, I have given into your hand Sihon the Amorite, king of Heshbon, and his country. Begin to take possession of it and engage him in battle. [25]This very day I will begin to put the terror and fear of you on all the nations under heaven. They will hear reports of you and will tremble and be in anguish because of you."

[26]From the desert of Kedemoth I sent messengers to Sihon king of Heshbon offering peace and saying, [27]"Let us pass through your country. We will stay on the main road; we will not turn aside to the right or to the left. [28]Sell us food to eat and water to drink for their price in silver. Only let us pass through on foot— [29]as the descendants of Esau, who live in Seir, and the Moabites, who live in Ar, did for us—until we cross the Jordan into the land the LORD our God is giving us." [30]But Sihon king of Heshbon refused to let us pass through. For the LORD your God had made his spirit stubborn and his heart obstinate in order to give him into your hands, as he has now done.

[31]The LORD said to me, "See, I have begun to deliver Sihon and his country over to you. Now begin to conquer and possess his land."

[32]When Sihon and all his army came out to meet us in battle at Jahaz, [33]the LORD our God delivered him over to us and we struck him down, together with his sons and his whole army. [34]At that time we took all his towns and completely destroyed*b* them—men, women and children. We left no survivors. [35]But the livestock and the plunder from the towns we had captured we carried off for ourselves. [36]From Aroer on the rim of the Arnon Gorge, and from the town in the gorge, even as far as Gilead, not one town was too strong for us. The LORD our God gave us all of them. [37]But in accordance with the command of the LORD our God, you did not encroach on any of the land of the Ammonites, neither the land along the course of the Jabbok nor that around the towns in the hills.

a 23 That is, Crete   b 34 The Hebrew term refers to the irrevocable giving over of things or persons to the LORD, often by totally destroying them.

THE MESSAGE

them and the Ammonites moved in and took over. It was the same with the People of Esau who live in Seir—GOD got rid of the Horites who lived there earlier and they moved in and took over, as you can see. Regarding the Avvites who lived in villages as far as Gaza, the Caphtorites who came from Caphtor (Crete) wiped them out and moved in.

✠

2.24-25 "On your feet now. Get started. Cross the Brook Arnon. Look: Here's Sihon the Amorite king of Heshbon and his land. I'm handing it over to you—it's all yours. Go ahead take it. Go to war with him. Before the day is out, I'll make sure that all the people around here are thoroughly terrified. Rumors of you are going to spread like wildfire; they'll totally panic."

2.26-28 From the Wilderness of Kedemoth, I sent messengers to Sihon, king of Heshbon. They carried a friendly message: "Let me cross through your land on the highway. I'll stay right on the highway; I won't trespass right or left. I'll pay you for any food or water we might need. Let me walk through.

2.29 "The People of Esau who live in Seir and the Moabites who live in Ar did this, helping me on my way until I can cross the Jordan and enter the land that GOD, our God, is giving us."

2.30 But Sihon king of Heshbon wouldn't let us cross his land. GOD, your God, turned his spirit mean and his heart hard so he could hand him over to you, as you can see that he has done.

2.31 Then GOD said to me, "Look, I've got the ball rolling—Sihon and his land are soon yours. Go ahead. Take it. It's practically yours!"

2.32-36 So Sihon and his entire army confronted us in battle at Jahaz. GOD handed him, his sons, and his entire army over to us and we utterly crushed them. While we were at it we captured all his towns and totally destroyed them, a holy destruction—men, women, and children. No survivors. We took the livestock and the plunder from the towns we had captured and carried them off for ourselves. From Aroer on the edge of the Brook Arnon and the town in the gorge, as far as Gilead, not a single town proved too much for us; GOD, our God, gave every last one of them to us.

2.37 The only land you didn't take, obeying GOD's command, was the land of the People of Ammon, the land along the Jabbok and around the cities in the hills.

✠

NEW INTERNATIONAL VERSION

Defeat of Og King of Bashan

3 Next we turned and went up along the road toward Bashan, and Og king of Bashan with his whole army marched out to meet us in battle at Edrei. ²The LORD said to me, "Do not be afraid of him, for I have handed him over to you with his whole army and his land. Do to him what you did to Sihon king of the Amorites, who reigned in Heshbon."

³So the LORD our God also gave into our hands Og king of Bashan and all his army. We struck them down, leaving no survivors. ⁴At that time we took all his cities. There was not one of the sixty cities that we did not take from them— the whole region of Argob, Og's kingdom in Bashan. ⁵All these cities were fortified with high walls and with gates and bars, and there were also a great many unwalled villages. ⁶We completely destroyed *a* them, as we had done with Sihon king of Heshbon, destroying *a* every city— men, women and children. ⁷But all the livestock and the plunder from their cities we carried off for ourselves.

⁸So at that time we took from these two kings of the Amorites the territory east of the Jordan, from the Arnon Gorge as far as Mount Hermon. ⁹(Hermon is called Sirion by the Sidonians; the Amorites call it Senir.) ¹⁰We took all the towns on the plateau, and all Gilead, and all Bashan as far as Salecah and Edrei, towns of Og's kingdom in Bashan. ¹¹(Only Og king of Bashan was left of the remnant of the Rephaites. His bed *b* was made of iron and was more than thirteen feet long and six feet wide. *c* It is still in Rabbah of the Ammonites.)

Division of the Land

¹²Of the land that we took over at that time, I gave the Reubenites and the Gadites the territory north of Aroer by the Arnon Gorge, including half the hill country of Gilead, together with its towns. ¹³The rest of Gilead and also all of Bashan, the kingdom of Og, I gave to the half-tribe of Manasseh. (The whole region of Argob in Bashan used to be known as a land of the Rephaites. ¹⁴Jair, a descendant of Manasseh, took the whole region of Argob as far as the border of the Geshurites and the Maacathites; it was named after him, so that to this day Bashan is called Havvoth Jair. *d*) ¹⁵And I gave Gilead to Makir. ¹⁶But to the Reubenites and the Gadites I gave the territory extending from Gilead down to the

a 6 The Hebrew term refers to the irrevocable giving over of things or persons to the LORD, often by totally destroying them. *b 11 Or sarcophagus* *c 11 Hebrew nine cubits long and four cubits wide (about 4 meters long and 1.8 meters wide)* *d 14 Or called the settlements of Jair*

THE MESSAGE

3.1 **3** Then we turned north and took the road to Bashan. Og king of Bashan, he and all his people, came out to meet us in battle at Edrei.

3.2 GOD said to me, "Don't be afraid of him; I'm turning him over to you, along with his whole army and his land. Treat him the way you treated Sihon king of the Amorites who ruled from Heshbon."

3.3-7 So GOD, our God, also handed Og king of Bashan over to us—Og and all his people—and we utterly crushed them. Again, no survivors. At the same time we took all his cities. There wasn't one of the sixty cities that we didn't take—the whole region of Argob, Og's kingdom in Bashan. All these cities were fortress cities with high walls and barred gates. There were also numerous unwalled villages. We totally destroyed them—a holy destruction. It was the same treatment we gave to Sihon king of Heshbon, a holy destruction of every city, man, woman, and child. But all the livestock and plunder from the cities we took for ourselves.

3.8-10 Throughout that time we took the land from under the control of the two kings of the Amorites who ruled the country east of the Jordan, all the way from the Brook Arnon to Mount Hermon. (Sirion is the name given Hermon by the Sidonians; the Amorites call it Senir.) We took all the towns of the plateau, everything in Gilead, everything in Bashan, as far as Salecah and Edrei, the border towns of Bashan, Og's kingdom.

3.11 Og king of Bashan was the last remaining Rephaite. His bed, made of iron, was over thirteen feet long and six wide. You can still see it on display in Rabbah of the People of Ammon.

3.12 Of the land that we possessed at that time, I gave the Reubenites and the Gadites the territory north of Aroer along the Brook Arnon and half the hill country of Gilead with its towns.

3.13 I gave the half-tribe of Manasseh the rest of Gilead and all of Bashan, Og's kingdom—all the region of Argob, which takes in all of Bashan. This used to be known as the Land of the Rephaites.

3.14 Jair, a son of Manasseh, got the region of Argob to the borders of the Geshurites and Maacathites. He named the Bashan villages after himself, Havvoth Jair (Jair's Tent-Villages). They're still called that.

3.15 I gave Gilead to Makir.

3.16-17 I gave the Reubenites and Gadites the land from Gilead down to the Brook Arnon, whose

NEW INTERNATIONAL VERSION

Arnon Gorge (the middle of the gorge being the border) and out to the Jabbok River, which is the border of the Ammonites. [17]Its western border was the Jordan in the Arabah, from Kinnereth to the Sea of the Arabah (the Salt Sea[a]), below the slopes of Pisgah.

[18]I commanded you at that time: "The LORD your God has given you this land to take possession of it. But all your able-bodied men, armed for battle, must cross over ahead of your brother Israelites. [19]However, your wives, your children and your livestock (I know you have much livestock) may stay in the towns I have given you, [20]until the LORD gives rest to your brothers as he has to you, and they too have taken over the land that the LORD your God is giving them, across the Jordan. After that, each of you may go back to the possession I have given you."

MOSES FORBIDDEN TO CROSS THE JORDAN

[21]At that time I commanded Joshua: "You have seen with your own eyes all that the LORD your God has done to these two kings. The LORD will do the same to all the kingdoms over there where you are going. [22]Do not be afraid of them; the LORD your God himself will fight for you."

[23]At that time I pleaded with the LORD: [24]"O Sovereign LORD, you have begun to show to your servant your greatness and your strong hand. For what god is there in heaven or on earth who can do the deeds and mighty works you do? [25]Let me go over and see the good land beyond the Jordan—that fine hill country and Lebanon."

[26]But because of you the LORD was angry with me and would not listen to me. "That is enough," the LORD said. "Do not speak to me anymore about this matter. [27]Go up to the top of Pisgah and look west and north and south and east. Look at the land with your own eyes, since you are not going to cross this Jordan. [28]But commission Joshua, and encourage and strengthen him, for he will lead this people across and will cause them to inherit the land that you will see." [29]So we stayed in the valley near Beth Peor.

THE MESSAGE

middle was the boundary, and as far as the Jabbok River, the boundary line of the People of Ammon. The western boundary was the Jordan River in the Arabah all the way from the Kinnereth (the Sea of Galilee) to the Sea of the Arabah (the Salt Sea or Dead Sea) at the base of the slopes of Mount Pisgah on the east.

☩

3.18-20 I commanded you at that time, "GOD, your God, has given you this land to possess. Your men, fit and armed for the fight, are to cross the river in advance of their brothers, the People of Israel. Only your wives, children, and livestock (I know you have much livestock) may go ahead and settle down in the towns I have already given you until GOD secures living space for your brothers as he has for you and they have taken possession of the country west of the Jordan that GOD, your God, is giving them. After that, each man may return to the land I've given you here."

☩

3.21-22 I commanded Joshua at that time, "You've seen with your own two eyes everything GOD, your God, has done to these two kings. GOD is going to do the same thing to all the kingdoms over there across the river where you're headed. Don't be afraid of them. GOD, your God—he's fighting for you."

3.23-25 At that same time, I begged GOD: "GOD, my Master, you let me in on the beginnings, you let me see your greatness, you let me see your might—what god in Heaven or Earth can do anything like what you've done! Please, let me in also on the endings, let me cross the river and see the good land over the Jordan, the lush hills, the Lebanon mountains."

3.26-27 But GOD was still angry with me because of you. He wouldn't listen. He said, "Enough of that. Not another word from you on this. Climb to the top of Mount Pisgah and look around: look west, north, south, east. Take in the land with your own eyes. Take a good look because you're not going to cross this Jordan.

3.28 "Then command Joshua: Give him courage. Give him strength. Single-handed he will lead this people across the river. Single-handed he'll cause them to inherit the land at which you can only look."

3.29 That's why we have stayed in this valley near Beth Peor.

☩

a 17 That is, the Dead Sea

NEW INTERNATIONAL VERSION	THE MESSAGE

OBEDIENCE COMMANDED

4 Hear now, O Israel, the decrees and laws I am about to teach you. Follow them so that you may live and may go in and take possession of the land that the LORD, the God of your fathers, is giving you. ²Do not add to what I command you and do not subtract from it, but keep the commands of the LORD your God that I give you.

³You saw with your own eyes what the LORD did at Baal Peor. The LORD your God destroyed from among you everyone who followed the Baal of Peor, ⁴but all of you who held fast to the LORD your God are still alive today.

⁵See, I have taught you decrees and laws as the LORD my God commanded me, so that you may follow them in the land you are entering to take possession of it. ⁶Observe them carefully, for this will show your wisdom and understanding to the nations, who will hear about all these decrees and say, "Surely this great nation is a wise and understanding people." ⁷What other nation is so great as to have their gods near them the way the LORD our God is near us whenever we pray to him? ⁸And what other nation is so great as to have such righteous decrees and laws as this body of laws I am setting before you today?

⁹Only be careful, and watch yourselves closely so that you do not forget the things your eyes have seen or let them slip from your heart as long as you live. Teach them to your children and to their children after them. ¹⁰Remember the day you stood before the LORD your God at Horeb, when he said to me, "Assemble the people before me to hear my words so that they may learn to revere me as long as they live in the land and may teach them to their children." ¹¹You came near and stood at the foot of the mountain while it blazed with fire to the very heavens, with black clouds and deep darkness. ¹²Then the LORD spoke to you out of the fire. You heard the sound of words but saw no form; there was only a voice. ¹³He declared to you his covenant, the Ten Commandments, which he commanded you to follow and then wrote them on two stone tablets. ¹⁴And the LORD directed me at that time to teach you the decrees and laws you are to follow in the land that you are crossing the Jordan to possess.

IDOLATRY FORBIDDEN

¹⁵You saw no form of any kind the day the

4.1-2 4 Now listen, Israel, listen carefully to the rules and regulations that I am teaching you to follow so that you may live and enter and take possession of the land that GOD, the God-of-Your-Fathers, is giving to you. Don't add a word to what I command you, and don't remove a word from it. Keep the commands of GOD, your God, that I am commanding you.

4.3-4 You saw with your own eyes what GOD did at Baal Peor, how GOD destroyed from among you every man who joined in the Baal Peor orgies. But you, the ones who held tight to GOD, your God, are alive and well, every one of you, today.

4.5-6 Pay attention: I'm teaching you the rules and regulations that GOD commanded me, so that you may live by them in the land you are entering to take up ownership. Keep them. Practice them. You'll become wise and understanding. When people hear and see what's going on, they'll say, "What a great nation! So wise, so understanding! We've never seen anything like it."

4.7-8 Yes. What other great nation has gods that are intimate with them the way GOD, our God, is with us, always ready to listen to us? And what other great nation has rules and regulations as good and fair as this Revelation that I'm setting before you today?

4.9 Just make sure you stay alert. Keep close watch over yourselves. Don't forget anything of what you've seen. Don't let your heart wander off. Stay vigilant as long as you live. Teach what you've seen and heard to your children and grandchildren.

4.10 That day when you stood before GOD, your God, at Horeb, GOD said to me, "Assemble the people in my presence to listen to my words so that they will learn to fear me in holy fear for as long as they live on the land, and then they will teach these same words to their children."

4.11-13 You gathered. You stood in the shadow of the mountain. The mountain was ablaze with fire, blazing high into the very heart of Heaven. You stood in deep darkness and thick clouds. GOD spoke to you out of the fire. You heard the sound of words but you saw nothing—no form, only a voice. He announced his covenant, the Ten Words, by which he commanded you to live. Then he wrote them down on two slabs of stone.

4.14 And GOD commanded me at that time to teach you the rules and regulations that you are to live by in the land which you are crossing over the Jordan to possess.

4.15-20 You saw no form on the day GOD spoke to

NEW INTERNATIONAL VERSION

LORD spoke to you at Horeb out of the fire. Therefore watch yourselves very carefully, ¹⁶so that you do not become corrupt and make for yourselves an idol, an image of any shape, whether formed like a man or a woman, ¹⁷or like any animal on earth or any bird that flies in the air, ¹⁸or like any creature that moves along the ground or any fish in the waters below. ¹⁹And when you look up to the sky and see the sun, the moon and the stars—all the heavenly array—do not be enticed into bowing down to them and worshiping things the LORD your God has apportioned to all the nations under heaven. ²⁰But as for you, the LORD took you and brought you out of the iron-smelting furnace, out of Egypt, to be the people of his inheritance, as you now are.

²¹The LORD was angry with me because of you, and he solemnly swore that I would not cross the Jordan and enter the good land the LORD your God is giving you as your inheritance. ²²I will die in this land; I will not cross the Jordan; but you are about to cross over and take possession of that good land. ²³Be careful not to forget the covenant with the LORD your God that he made with you; do not make for yourselves an idol in the form of anything the LORD your God has forbidden. ²⁴For the LORD your God is a consuming fire, a jealous God.

²⁵After you have had children and grandchildren and have lived in the land a long time—if you then become corrupt and make any kind of idol, doing evil in the eyes of the LORD your God and provoking him to anger, ²⁶I call heaven and earth as witnesses against you this day that you will quickly perish from the land that you are crossing the Jordan to possess. You will not live there long but will certainly be destroyed. ²⁷The LORD will scatter you among the peoples, and only a few of you will survive among the nations to which the LORD will drive you. ²⁸There you will worship man-made gods of wood and stone, which cannot see or hear or eat or smell. ²⁹But if from there you seek the LORD your God, you will find him if you look for him with all your heart and with all your soul. ³⁰When you are in distress and all these things have happened to you, then in later days you will return to the LORD your God and obey him. ³¹For the LORD your God is a merciful God; he will not abandon or destroy you or forget the covenant with your forefathers, which he confirmed to them by oath.

THE MESSAGE

you at Horeb from out of the fire. Remember that. Carefully guard yourselves so that you don't turn corrupt and make a form, carving a figure that looks male or female, or looks like a prowling animal or a flying bird or a slithering snake or a fish in a stream. And also carefully guard yourselves so that you don't look up into the skies and see the sun and moon and stars, all the constellations of the skies, and be seduced into worshiping and serving them. GOD set them out for everybody's benefit, everywhere. But you—GOD took you right out of the iron furnace, out of Egypt, to become the people of his inheritance—and that's what you are this very day.

4.21-22 But GOD was angry with me because of you and the things you said. He swore that I'd never cross the Jordan, never get to enter the good land that GOD, your God, is giving you as an inheritance. This means that I am going to die here. I'm not crossing the Jordan. But you will cross; you'll possess the good land.

4.23-24 So stay alert. Don't for a minute forget the covenant which GOD, your God, made with you. And don't take up with any carved images, no forms of any kind—GOD, your God, issued clear commands on that. GOD, your God, is not to be trifled with—he's a consuming fire, a jealous God.

4.25-28 When the time comes that you have children and grandchildren, put on years, and start taking things for granted, if you then become corrupt and make any carved images, no matter what their form, by doing what is sheer evil in GOD's eyes and provoking his anger—I can tell you right now, with Heaven and Earth as witnesses, that it will be all over for you. You'll be kicked off the land that you're about to cross over the Jordan to possess. Believe me, you'll have a very short stay there. You'll be ruined, completely ruined. GOD will scatter you far and wide; a few of you will survive here and there in the nations where GOD will drive you. There you can worship your homemade gods to your hearts' content, your wonderful gods of wood and stone that can't see or hear or eat or smell.

4.29-31 But even there, if you seek GOD, your God, you'll be able to find him if you're serious, looking for him with your whole heart and soul. When troubles come and all these awful things happen to you, in future days you will come back to GOD, your God, and listen obediently to what he says. GOD, your God, is above all a compassionate God. In the end he will not abandon you, he won't bring you to ruin, he won't forget the covenant with your ancestors which he swore to them.

NEW INTERNATIONAL VERSION

THE LORD IS GOD

³²Ask now about the former days, long before your time, from the day God created man on the earth; ask from one end of the heavens to the other. Has anything so great as this ever happened, or has anything like it ever been heard of? ³³Has any other people heard the voice of God^a speaking out of fire, as you have, and lived? ³⁴Has any god ever tried to take for himself one nation out of another nation, by testings, by miraculous signs and wonders, by war, by a mighty hand and an outstretched arm, or by great and awesome deeds, like all the things the LORD your God did for you in Egypt before your very eyes?

³⁵You were shown these things so that you might know that the LORD is God; besides him there is no other. ³⁶From heaven he made you hear his voice to discipline you. On earth he showed you his great fire, and you heard his words from out of the fire. ³⁷Because he loved your forefathers and chose their descendants after them, he brought you out of Egypt by his Presence and his great strength, ³⁸to drive out before you nations greater and stronger than you and to bring you into their land to give it to you for your inheritance, as it is today.

³⁹Acknowledge and take to heart this day that the LORD is God in heaven above and on the earth below. There is no other. ⁴⁰Keep his decrees and commands, which I am giving you today, so that it may go well with you and your children after you and that you may live long in the land the LORD your God gives you for all time.

CITIES OF REFUGE

⁴¹Then Moses set aside three cities east of the Jordan, ⁴²to which anyone who had killed a person could flee if he had unintentionally killed his neighbor without malice aforethought. He could flee into one of these cities and save his life. ⁴³The cities were these: Bezer in the desert plateau, for the Reubenites; Ramoth in Gilead, for the Gadites; and Golan in Bashan, for the Manassites.

INTRODUCTION TO THE LAW

⁴⁴This is the law Moses set before the Israelites. ⁴⁵These are the stipulations, decrees and laws Moses gave them when they came out of

^a 33 Or *of a god*

THE MESSAGE

4.32-33   Ask questions. Find out what has been going on all these years before you were born. From the day God created man and woman on this Earth, and from the horizon in the east to the horizon in the west—as far back as you can imagine and as far away as you can imagine—has as great a thing as this ever happened? Has anyone ever heard of such a thing? Has a people ever heard, as you did, a god speaking out of the middle of the fire and lived to tell the story?

4.34   Or has a god ever tried to select for himself a nation from within a nation using trials, miracles, and war, putting his strong hand in, reaching his long arm out, a spectacle awesome and staggering, the way GOD, your God, did it for you in Egypt while you stood right there and watched?

4.35-38   You were shown all this so that you would know that GOD is, well, God. He's the only God there is. He's it. He made it possible for you to hear his voice out of Heaven to discipline you. Down on Earth, he showed you the big fire and again you heard his words, this time out of the fire. He loved your ancestors and chose to work with their children. He personally and powerfully brought you out of Egypt in order to displace bigger and stronger and older nations with you, bringing you out and turning their land over to you as an inheritance. And now it's happening. This very day.

4.39-40   Know this well, then. Take it to heart right now: GOD is in Heaven above; GOD is on Earth below. He's the only God there is. Obediently live by his rules and commands which I'm giving you today so that you'll live well and your children after you—oh, you'll live a long time in the land that GOD, your God, is giving you.

4.41-42   Then Moses set aside three towns in the country on the east side of the Jordan to which someone who had unintentionally killed a person could flee and find refuge. If the murder was unintentional and there was no history of bad blood, the murderer could flee to one of these cities and save his life:

4.43   Bezer in the wilderness on the tableland for the Reubenites, Ramoth in Gilead for the Gadites, and Golan in Bashan for the Manassites.

4.44-49   This is the Revelation that Moses presented to the People of Israel. These are the testimonies, the rules and regulations Moses spoke to the People of Israel after their exodus from Egypt

NEW INTERNATIONAL VERSION

Egypt [46]and were in the valley near Beth Peor east of the Jordan, in the land of Sihon king of the Amorites, who reigned in Heshbon and was defeated by Moses and the Israelites as they came out of Egypt. [47]They took possession of his land and the land of Og king of Bashan, the two Amorite kings east of the Jordan. [48]This land extended from Aroer on the rim of the Arnon Gorge to Mount Siyon[a] (that is, Hermon), [49]and included all the Arabah east of the Jordan, as far as the Sea of the Arabah,[b] below the slopes of Pisgah.

THE TEN COMMANDMENTS

5 Moses summoned all Israel and said:
Hear, O Israel, the decrees and laws I declare in your hearing today. Learn them and be sure to follow them. [2]The LORD our God made a covenant with us at Horeb. [3]It was not with our fathers that the LORD made this covenant, but with us, with all of us who are alive here today. [4]The LORD spoke to you face to face out of the fire on the mountain. [5](At that time I stood between the LORD and you to declare to you the word of the LORD, because you were afraid of the fire and did not go up the mountain.) And he said:

[6]"I am the LORD your God, who brought you out of Egypt, out of the land of slavery.

[7]"You shall have no other gods before[c] me.

[8]"You shall not make for yourself an idol in the form of anything in heaven above or on the earth beneath or in the waters below. [9]You shall not bow down to them or worship them; for I, the LORD your God, am a jealous God, punishing the children for the sin of the fathers to the third and fourth generation of those who hate me, [10]but showing love to a thousand ⌊generations⌋ of those who love me and keep my commandments.

[11]"You shall not misuse the name of the LORD your God, for the LORD will not hold anyone guiltless who misuses his name.

[12]"Observe the Sabbath day by keeping it holy, as the LORD your God has commanded you. [13]Six days you shall labor and do all your work, [14]but the seventh day is a Sabbath to the LORD your God. On it you shall not do any work, neither you, nor your son or daughter, nor your manservant or

THE MESSAGE

and arrival on the east side of the Jordan in the valley near Beth Peor. It was the country of Sihon king of the Amorites who ruled from Heshbon. Moses and the People of Israel fought and beat him after they left Egypt and took his land. They also took the land of Og king of Bashan. The two Amorite kings held the country on the east of the Jordan from Aroer on the bank of the Brook Arnon as far north as Mount Siyon, that is, Mount Hermon, all the Arabah plain east of the Jordan, and as far south as the Sea of the Arabah (the Dead Sea) beneath the slopes of Mount Pisgah.

MOSES TEACHES ISRAEL ON THE PLAINS OF MOAB

5.1 5 Moses called all Israel together. He said to them,
Attention, Israel. Listen obediently to the rules and regulations I am delivering to your listening ears today. Learn them. Live them.

5.2-5 GOD, our God, made a covenant with us at Horeb. GOD didn't just make this covenant with our parents; he made it also with us, with all of us who are alive right now. GOD spoke to you personally out of the fire on the mountain. At the time I stood between GOD and you, to tell you what GOD said. You were afraid, remember, of the fire and wouldn't climb the mountain. He said:

5.6 I am GOD, your God,
who brought you out of the land of Egypt,
out of a house of slaves.

5.7 No other gods, only me.

5.8-10 No carved gods of any size, shape, or form of anything whatever, whether of things that fly or walk or swim. Don't bow down to them and don't serve them because I am GOD, your God, and I'm a most jealous God. I hold parents responsible for any sins they pass on to their children to the third, and yes, even to the fourth generation. But I'm lovingly loyal to the thousands who love me and keep my commandments.

5.11 No using the name of GOD, your God, in curses or silly banter; GOD won't put up with the irreverent use of his name.

5.12-15 No working on the Sabbath; keep it holy just as GOD, your God, commanded you. Work six days, doing everything you have to do, but the seventh day is a Sabbath, a Rest Day—no work: not you, your son, your daughter, your servant, your maid, your ox, your don-

---

[a] 48 Hebrew; Syriac (see also Deut. 3:9) *Sirion*   [b] 49 That is, the Dead Sea   [c] 7 Or *besides*

NEW INTERNATIONAL VERSION

maidservant, nor your ox, your donkey or any of your animals, nor the alien within your gates, so that your manservant and maidservant may rest, as you do. ¹⁵Remember that you were slaves in Egypt and that the Lord your God brought you out of there with a mighty hand and an outstretched arm. Therefore the Lord your God has commanded you to observe the Sabbath day.

¹⁶"Honor your father and your mother, as the Lord your God has commanded you, so that you may live long and that it may go well with you in the land the Lord your God is giving you.

¹⁷"You shall not murder.

¹⁸"You shall not commit adultery.

¹⁹"You shall not steal.

²⁰"You shall not give false testimony against your neighbor.

²¹"You shall not covet your neighbor's wife. You shall not set your desire on your neighbor's house or land, his manservant or maidservant, his ox or donkey, or anything that belongs to your neighbor."

²²These are the commandments the Lord proclaimed in a loud voice to your whole assembly there on the mountain from out of the fire, the cloud and the deep darkness; and he added nothing more. Then he wrote them on two stone tablets and gave them to me.

²³When you heard the voice out of the darkness, while the mountain was ablaze with fire, all the leading men of your tribes and your elders came to me. ²⁴And you said, "The Lord our God has shown us his glory and his majesty, and we have heard his voice from the fire. Today we have seen that a man can live even if God speaks with him. ²⁵But now, why should we die? This great fire will consume us, and we will die if we hear the voice of the Lord our God any longer. ²⁶For what mortal man has ever heard the voice of the living God speaking out of fire, as we have, and survived? ²⁷Go near and listen to all that the Lord our God says. Then tell us whatever the Lord our God tells you. We will listen and obey."

²⁸The Lord heard you when you spoke to me and the Lord said to me, "I have heard what this people said to you. Everything they said was good. ²⁹Oh, that their hearts would be inclined to fear me and keep all my commands always, so that it might go well with them and their children forever!

THE MESSAGE

key (or any of your animals), and not even the foreigner visiting your town. That way your servants and maids will get the same rest as you. Don't ever forget that you were slaves in Egypt and God, your God, got you out of there in a powerful show of strength. That's why God, your God, commands you to observe the day of Sabbath rest.

5.16 Respect your father and mother—God, your God, commands it! You'll have a long life; the land that God is giving you will treat you well.

5.17 No murder.

5.18 No adultery.

5.19 No stealing.

5.20 No lies about your neighbor.

5.21 No coveting your neighbor's wife. And no lusting for his house, field, servant, maid, ox, or donkey either—nothing that belongs to your neighbor!

5.22 These are the words that God spoke to the whole congregation at the mountain. He spoke in a tremendous voice from the fire and cloud and dark mist. And that was it. No more words. Then he wrote them on two slabs of stone and gave them to me.

5.23-24 As it turned out, when you heard the Voice out of that dark cloud and saw the mountain on fire, you approached me, all the heads of your tribes and your leaders, and said,

5.24-26 "Our God has revealed to us his glory and greatness. We've heard him speak from the fire today! We've seen that God can speak to humans and they can still live. But why risk it further? This huge fire will devour us if we stay around any longer. If we hear God's voice anymore, we'll die for sure. Has anyone ever known of anyone who has heard the Voice of God the way we have and lived to tell the story?

5.27 "From now on, *you* go and listen to what God, our God, says and then tell us what God tells you. We'll listen and we'll do it."

5.28-29 God heard what you said to me and told me, "I've heard what the people said to you. They're right—good and true words. What I wouldn't give if they'd always feel this way, continuing to revere me and always keep all my commands; they'd have a good life forever, they and their children!

NEW INTERNATIONAL VERSION

30"Go, tell them to return to their tents. 31But you stay here with me so that I may give you all the commands, decrees and laws you are to teach them to follow in the land I am giving them to possess."

32So be careful to do what the LORD your God has commanded you; do not turn aside to the right or to the left. 33Walk in all the way that the LORD your God has commanded you, so that you may live and prosper and prolong your days in the land that you will possess.

LOVE THE LORD YOUR GOD

6 These are the commands, decrees and laws the LORD your God directed me to teach you to observe in the land that you are crossing the Jordan to possess, 2so that you, your children and their children after them may fear the LORD your God as long as you live by keeping all his decrees and commands that I give you, and so that you may enjoy long life. 3Hear, O Israel, and be careful to obey so that it may go well with you and that you may increase greatly in a land flowing with milk and honey, just as the LORD, the God of your fathers, promised you.

4Hear, O Israel: The LORD our God, the LORD is one. *a* 5Love the LORD your God with all your heart and with all your soul and with all your strength. 6These commandments that I give you today are to be upon your hearts. 7Impress them on your children. Talk about them when you sit at home and when you walk along the road, when you lie down and when you get up. 8Tie them as symbols on your hands and bind them on your foreheads. 9Write them on the doorframes of your houses and on your gates.

10When the LORD your God brings you into the land he swore to your fathers, to Abraham, Isaac and Jacob, to give you—a land with large, flourishing cities you did not build, 11houses filled with all kinds of good things you did not provide, wells you did not dig, and vineyards and olive groves you did not plant—then when you eat and are satisfied, 12be careful that you do not forget the LORD, who brought you out of Egypt, out of the land of slavery.

13Fear the LORD your God, serve him only and take your oaths in his name. 14Do not follow other gods, the gods of the peoples around you; 15for the LORD your God, who is among you, is a

THE MESSAGE

5.30-31   "Go ahead and tell them to go home to their tents. But you, you stay here with me so I can tell you every commandment and all the rules and regulations that you must teach them so they'll know how to live in the land that I'm giving them as their own."

5.32-33   So be very careful to act exactly as GOD commands you. Don't veer off to the right or the left. Walk straight down the road GOD commands so that you'll have a good life and live a long time in the land that you're about to possess.

6.1-2   6 This is the commandment, the rules and regulations, that GOD, your God, commanded me to teach you to live out in the land you're about to cross into to possess. This is so that you'll live in deep reverence before GOD lifelong, observing all his rules and regulations that I'm commanding you, you and your children and your grandchildren, living good long lives.

6.3   Listen obediently, Israel. Do what you're told so that you'll have a good life, a life of abundance and bounty, just as GOD promised, in a land abounding in milk and honey.

6.4   Attention, Israel!
GOD, our God! GOD the one and only!

6.5   Love GOD, your God, with your whole heart: love him with all that's in you, love him with all you've got!

6.6-9   Write these commandments that I've given you today on your hearts. Get them inside of you and then get them inside your children. Talk about them wherever you are, sitting at home or walking in the street; talk about them from the time you get up in the morning to when you fall into bed at night. Tie them on your hands and foreheads as a reminder; inscribe them on the doorposts of your homes and on your city gates.

6.10-12   When GOD, your God, ushers you into the land he promised through your ancestors Abraham, Isaac, and Jacob to give you, you're going to walk into large, bustling cities you didn't build, well-furnished houses you didn't buy, come upon wells you didn't dig, vineyards and olive orchards you didn't plant. When you take it all in and settle down, pleased and content, make sure you don't forget how you got there—GOD brought you out of slavery in Egypt.

6.13-19   Deeply respect GOD, your God. Serve and worship him exclusively. Back up your promises with his name only. Don't fool around with other gods, the gods of your neighbors, because GOD, your God, who is alive among you is a

---

a 4 Or The LORD our God is one LORD; or The LORD is our God, the LORD is one; or The LORD is our God, the LORD alone

NEW INTERNATIONAL VERSION

jealous God and his anger will burn against you, and he will destroy you from the face of the land. [16]Do not test the LORD your God as you did at Massah. [17]Be sure to keep the commands of the LORD your God and the stipulations and decrees he has given you. [18]Do what is right and good in the LORD's sight, so that it may go well with you and you may go in and take over the good land that the LORD promised on oath to your forefathers, [19]thrusting out all your enemies before you, as the LORD said.

[20]In the future, when your son asks you, "What is the meaning of the stipulations, decrees and laws the LORD our God has commanded you?" [21]tell him: "We were slaves of Pharaoh in Egypt, but the LORD brought us out of Egypt with a mighty hand. [22]Before our eyes the LORD sent miraculous signs and wonders—great and terrible—upon Egypt and Pharaoh and his whole household. [23]But he brought us out from there to bring us in and give us the land that he promised on oath to our forefathers. [24]The LORD commanded us to obey all these decrees and to fear the LORD our God, so that we might always prosper and be kept alive, as is the case today. [25]And if we are careful to obey all this law before the LORD our God, as he has commanded us, that will be our righteousness."

DRIVING OUT THE NATIONS

7 When the LORD your God brings you into the land you are entering to possess and drives out before you many nations—the Hittites, Girgashites, Amorites, Canaanites, Perizzites, Hivites and Jebusites, seven nations larger and stronger than you— [2]and when the LORD your God has delivered them over to you and you have defeated them, then you must destroy them totally.[a] Make no treaty with them, and show them no mercy. [3]Do not intermarry with them. Do not give your daughters to their sons or take their daughters for your sons, [4]for they will turn your sons away from following me to serve other gods, and the LORD's anger will burn against you and will quickly destroy you. [5]This is what you are to do to them: Break down their altars, smash their sacred stones, cut down their

[a] 2 The Hebrew term refers to the irrevocable giving over of things or persons to the LORD, often by totally destroying them; also in verse 26.

THE MESSAGE

jealous God. Don't provoke him, igniting his hot anger that would burn you right off the face of the Earth. Don't push GOD, your God, to the wall as you did that day at Massah, the Testing-Place. Carefully keep the commands of GOD, your God, all the requirements and regulations he gave you. Do what is right; do what is good in GOD's sight so you'll live a good life and be able to march in and take this pleasant land that GOD so solemnly promised through your ancestors, throwing out your enemies left and right—exactly as GOD said.

6.20-24 The next time your child asks you, "What do these requirements and regulations and rules that GOD, our God, has commanded mean?" tell your child, "We were slaves to Pharaoh in Egypt and GOD powerfully intervened and got us out of that country. We stood there and watched as GOD delivered miracle-signs, great wonders, and evil-visitations on Egypt, on Pharaoh and his household. He pulled us out of there so he could bring us here and give us the land he so solemnly promised to our ancestors. That's why GOD commanded us to follow all these rules, so that we would live reverently before GOD, our God, as he gives us this good life, keeping us alive for a long time to come.

6.25 "It will be a set-right and put-together life for us if we make sure that we do this entire commandment in the Presence of GOD, our God, just as he commanded us to do."

✣

7.1-2 7 When GOD, your God, brings you into the country that you are about to enter and take over, he will clear out the superpowers that were there before you: the Hittite, the Girgashite, the Amorite, the Canaanite, the Perizzite, the Hivite, and the Jebusite. Those seven nations are all bigger and stronger than you are. GOD, your God, will turn them over to you and you will conquer them. You must completely destroy them, offering them up as a holy destruction to GOD.

Don't make a treaty with them.
Don't let them off in any way.

7.3-4 Don't marry them: Don't give your daughters to their sons and don't take their daughters for your sons—before you know it they'd involve you in worshiping their gods, and GOD would explode in anger, putting a quick end to you.

7.5 Here's what you are to do:

Tear apart their altars stone by stone,
smash their phallic pillars,

NEW INTERNATIONAL VERSION

Asherah poles[a] and burn their idols in the fire. [6]For you are a people holy to the LORD your God. The LORD your God has chosen you out of all the peoples on the face of the earth to be his people, his treasured possession.

[7]The LORD did not set his affection on you and choose you because you were more numerous than other peoples, for you were the fewest of all peoples. [8]But it was because the LORD loved you and kept the oath he swore to your forefathers that he brought you out with a mighty hand and redeemed you from the land of slavery, from the power of Pharaoh king of Egypt. [9]Know therefore that the LORD your God is God; he is the faithful God, keeping his covenant of love to a thousand generations of those who love him and keep his commands. [10]But

those who hate him he will repay to their
face by destruction;
he will not be slow to repay to their face
those who hate him.

[11]Therefore, take care to follow the commands, decrees and laws I give you today.

[12]If you pay attention to these laws and are careful to follow them, then the LORD your God will keep his covenant of love with you, as he swore to your forefathers. [13]He will love you and bless you and increase your numbers. He will bless the fruit of your womb, the crops of your land—your grain, new wine and oil—the calves of your herds and the lambs of your flocks in the land that he swore to your forefathers to give you. [14]You will be blessed more than any other people; none of your men or women will be childless, nor any of your livestock without young. [15]The LORD will keep you free from every disease. He will not inflict on you the horrible diseases you knew in Egypt, but he will inflict them on all who hate you. [16]You must destroy all the peoples the LORD your God gives over to you. Do not look on them with pity and do not serve their gods, for that will be a snare to you.

[17]You may say to yourselves, "These nations are stronger than we are. How can we drive them out?" [18]But do not be afraid of them; remember well what the LORD your God did to Pharaoh and to all Egypt. [19]You saw with your own eyes the great trials, the miraculous signs and won-

[a] 5 That is, symbols of the goddess Asherah; here and elsewhere in Deuteronomy

THE MESSAGE

chop down their sex-and-religion
Asherah groves,
set fire to their carved god-images.

7.6 Do this because you are a people set apart as holy to GOD, your God. GOD, your God, chose you out of all the people on Earth for himself as a cherished, personal treasure.

7.7-10 GOD wasn't attracted to you and didn't choose you because you were big and important—the fact is, there was almost nothing to you. He did it out of sheer love, keeping the promise he made to your ancestors. GOD stepped in and mightily bought you back out of that world of slavery, freed you from the iron grip of Pharaoh king of Egypt. Know this: GOD, your God, is God indeed, a God you can depend upon. He keeps his covenant of loyal love with those who love him and observe his commandments for a thousand generations. But he also pays back those who hate him, pays them the wages of death; he isn't slow to pay them off—those who hate him, he pays right on time.

7.11 So keep the command and the rules and regulations that I command you today. Do them.

7.12-13 And this is what will happen: When you, on your part, will obey these directives, keeping and following them, GOD, on his part, will keep the covenant of loyal love that he made with your ancestors:

He will love you,
he will bless you,
he will increase you.

7.13-15 He will bless the babies from your womb and the harvest of grain, new wine, and oil from your fields; he'll bless the calves from your herds and lambs from your flocks in the country he promised your ancestors that he'd give you. You'll be blessed beyond all other peoples: no sterility or barrenness in you or your animals. GOD will get rid of all sickness. And all the evil afflictions you experienced in Egypt he'll put not on you but on those who hate you.

7.16 You'll make mincemeat of all the peoples that GOD, your God, hands over to you. Don't feel sorry for them. And don't worship their gods—they'll trap you for sure.

7.17-19 You're going to think to yourselves, "Oh! We're outnumbered ten to one by these nations! We'll never even make a dent in them!" But I'm telling you, Don't be afraid. Remember, yes, remember in detail what GOD, your God, did to Pharaoh and all Egypt. Remember the great contests to which you were eyewitnesses: the miracle-signs, the wonders, GOD's mighty hand

NEW INTERNATIONAL VERSION

ders, the mighty hand and outstretched arm, with which the LORD your God brought you out. The LORD your God will do the same to all the peoples you now fear. ²⁰Moreover, the LORD your God will send the hornet among them until even the survivors who hide from you have perished. ²¹Do not be terrified by them, for the LORD your God, who is among you, is a great and awesome God. ²²The LORD your God will drive out those nations before you, little by little. You will not be allowed to eliminate them all at once, or the wild animals will multiply around you. ²³But the LORD your God will deliver them over to you, throwing them into great confusion until they are destroyed. ²⁴He will give their kings into your hand, and you will wipe out their names from under heaven. No one will be able to stand up against you; you will destroy them. ²⁵The images of their gods you are to burn in the fire. Do not covet the silver and gold on them, and do not take it for yourselves, or you will be ensnared by it, for it is detestable to the LORD your God. ²⁶Do not bring a detestable thing into your house or you, like it, will be set apart for destruction. Utterly abhor and detest it, for it is set apart for destruction.

DO NOT FORGET THE LORD

8 Be careful to follow every command I am giving you today, so that you may live and increase and may enter and possess the land that the LORD promised on oath to your forefathers. ²Remember how the LORD your God led you all the way in the desert these forty years, to humble you and to test you in order to know what was in your heart, whether or not you would keep his commands. ³He humbled you, causing you to hunger and then feeding you with manna, which neither you nor your fathers had known, to teach you that man does not live on bread alone but on every word that comes from the mouth of the LORD. ⁴Your clothes did not wear out and your feet did not swell during these forty years. ⁵Know then in your heart that as a man disciplines his son, so the LORD your God disciplines you.

⁶Observe the commands of the LORD your God, walking in his ways and revering him. ⁷For the LORD your God is bringing you into a good land—a land with streams and pools of water, with springs flowing in the valleys and hills; ⁸a land with wheat and barley, vines and fig trees, pomegranates, olive oil and honey; ⁹a land

THE MESSAGE

as he stretched out his arm and took you out of there. GOD, your God, is going to do the same thing to these people you're now so afraid of.

7.20 And to top it off, the Hornet. GOD will unleash the Hornet on them until every survivor-in-hiding is dead.

7.21-24 So don't be intimidated by them. GOD, your God, is among you—GOD majestic, GOD awesome. GOD, your God, will get rid of these nations, bit by bit. You won't be permitted to wipe them out all at once lest the wild animals take over and overwhelm you. But GOD, your God, will move them out of your way—he'll throw them into a huge panic until there's nothing left of them. He'll turn their kings over to you and you'll remove all trace of them under Heaven. Not one person will be able to stand up to you; you'll put an end to them all.

7.25-26 Make sure you set fire to their carved gods. Don't get greedy for the veneer of silver and gold on them and take it for yourselves—you'll get trapped by it for sure. GOD hates it; it's an abomination to GOD, your God. And don't dare bring one of these abominations home or you'll end up just like it, burned up as a holy destruction. No: It is forbidden! Hate it. Abominate it. Destroy it and preserve GOD's holiness.

⊹

8.1-5 **8** Keep and live out the entire commandment that I'm commanding you today so that you'll live and prosper and enter and own the land that GOD promised to your ancestors. Remember every road that GOD led you on for those forty years in the wilderness, pushing you to your limits, testing you so that he would know what you were made of, whether you would keep his commandments or not. He put you through hard times. He made you go hungry. Then he fed you with manna, something neither you nor your parents knew anything about, so you would learn that men and women don't live by bread only; we live by every word that comes from GOD's mouth. Your clothes didn't wear out and your feet didn't blister those forty years. You learned deep in your heart that GOD disciplines you in the same ways a father disciplines his child.

8.6-9 So it's paramount that you keep the commandments of GOD, your God, walk down the roads he shows you and reverently respect him. GOD is about to bring you into a good land, a land with brooks and rivers, springs and lakes, streams out of the hills and through the valleys. It's a land of wheat and barley, of vines and figs and pomegranates, of olives, oil, and

NEW INTERNATIONAL VERSION

where bread will not be scarce and you will lack nothing; a land where the rocks are iron and you can dig copper out of the hills.

¹⁰When you have eaten and are satisfied, praise the Lord your God for the good land he has given you. ¹¹Be careful that you do not forget the Lord your God, failing to observe his commands, his laws and his decrees that I am giving you this day. ¹²Otherwise, when you eat and are satisfied, when you build fine houses and settle down, ¹³and when your herds and flocks grow large and your silver and gold increase and all you have is multiplied, ¹⁴then your heart will become proud and you will forget the Lord your God, who brought you out of Egypt, out of the land of slavery. ¹⁵He led you through the vast and dreadful desert, that thirsty and waterless land, with its venomous snakes and scorpions. He brought you water out of hard rock. ¹⁶He gave you manna to eat in the desert, something your fathers had never known, to humble and to test you so that in the end it might go well with you. ¹⁷You may say to yourself, "My power and the strength of my hands have produced this wealth for me." ¹⁸But remember the Lord your God, for it is he who gives you the ability to produce wealth, and so confirms his covenant, which he swore to your forefathers, as it is today.

¹⁹If you ever forget the Lord your God and follow other gods and worship and bow down to them, I testify against you today that you will surely be destroyed. ²⁰Like the nations the Lord destroyed before you, so you will be destroyed for not obeying the Lord your God.

NOT BECAUSE OF ISRAEL'S RIGHTEOUSNESS

9 Hear, O Israel. You are now about to cross the Jordan to go in and dispossess nations greater and stronger than you, with large cities that have walls up to the sky. ²The people are strong and tall—Anakites! You know about them

THE MESSAGE

honey. It's land where you'll never go hungry—always food on the table and a roof over your head. It's a land where you'll get iron out of rocks and mine copper from the hills.

8.10 After a meal, satisfied, bless God, your God, for the good land he has given you.

8.11-16 Make sure you don't forget God, your God, by not keeping his commandments, his rules and regulations that I command you today. Make sure that when you eat and are satisfied, build pleasant houses and settle in, see your herds and flocks flourish and more and more money come in, watch your standard of living going up and up—make sure you don't become so full of yourself and your things that you forget God, your God,

the God who delivered you from Egyptian slavery;
the God who led you through that huge and fearsome wilderness, those desolate, arid badlands crawling with fiery snakes and scorpions;
the God who gave you water gushing from hard rock;
the God who gave you manna to eat in the wilderness, something your ancestors had never heard of, in order to give you a taste of the hard life, to test you so that you would be prepared to live well in the days ahead of you.

8.17-18 If you start thinking to yourselves, "I did all this. And all by myself. I'm rich. It's all mine!"—well, think again. Remember that God, your God, gave you the strength to produce all this wealth so as to confirm the covenant that he promised to your ancestors—as it is today.

8.19-20 If you forget, forget God, your God, and start taking up with other gods, serving and worshiping them, I'm on record right now as giving you firm warning: that will be the end of you; I mean it—destruction. You'll go to your doom—the same as the nations God is destroying before you; doom because you wouldn't obey the Voice of God, your God.

✝

9.1-2 **9** Attention, Israel!
This very day you are crossing the Jordan to enter the land and dispossess nations that are much bigger and stronger than you are. You're going to find huge cities with sky-high fortress-walls and gigantic people, descendants of the Anakites—you've heard all about them;

NEW INTERNATIONAL VERSION

and have heard it said: "Who can stand up against the Anakites?" ³But be assured today that the LORD your God is the one who goes across ahead of you like a devouring fire. He will destroy them; he will subdue them before you. And you will drive them out and annihilate them quickly, as the LORD has promised you.

⁴After the LORD your God has driven them out before you, do not say to yourself, "The LORD has brought me here to take possession of this land because of my righteousness." No, it is on account of the wickedness of these nations that the LORD is going to drive them out before you. ⁵It is not because of your righteousness or your integrity that you are going in to take possession of their land; but on account of the wickedness of these nations, the LORD your God will drive them out before you, to accomplish what he swore to your fathers, to Abraham, Isaac and Jacob. ⁶Understand, then, that it is not because of your righteousness that the LORD your God is giving you this good land to possess, for you are a stiff-necked people.

THE GOLDEN CALF

⁷Remember this and never forget how you provoked the LORD your God to anger in the desert. From the day you left Egypt until you arrived here, you have been rebellious against the LORD. ⁸At Horeb you aroused the LORD's wrath so that he was angry enough to destroy you. ⁹When I went up on the mountain to receive the tablets of stone, the tablets of the covenant that the LORD had made with you, I stayed on the mountain forty days and forty nights; I ate no bread and drank no water. ¹⁰The LORD gave me two stone tablets inscribed by the finger of God. On them were all the commandments the LORD proclaimed to you on the mountain out of the fire, on the day of the assembly.

¹¹At the end of the forty days and forty nights, the LORD gave me the two stone tablets, the tablets of the covenant. ¹²Then the LORD told me, "Go down from here at once, because your people whom you brought out of Egypt have become corrupt. They have turned away quickly from what I commanded them and have made a cast idol for themselves."

¹³And the LORD said to me, "I have seen this people, and they are a stiff-necked people indeed! ¹⁴Let me alone, so that I may destroy them and blot out their name from under heaven. And I will make you into a nation stronger and more numerous than they."

¹⁵So I turned and went down from the mountain while it was ablaze with fire. And the two

THE MESSAGE

you've heard the saying, "No one can stand up to an Anakite."

9.3 Today know this: GOD, your God, is crossing the river ahead of you—he's a consuming fire. He will destroy the nations, he will put them under your power. You will dispossess them and very quickly wipe them out, just as GOD promised you would.

9.4-5 But when GOD pushes them out ahead of you, don't start thinking to yourselves, "It's because of all the good I've done that GOD has brought me in here to dispossess these nations." Actually it's because of all the evil these nations have done. No, it's nothing good that you've done, no record for decency that you've built up, that got you here; it's because of the vile wickedness of these nations that GOD, your God, is dispossessing them before you so that he can keep his promised word to your ancestors, to Abraham, Isaac, and Jacob.

9.6-10 Know this and don't ever forget it: It's not because of any good that you've done that GOD is giving you this good land to own. Anything but! You're stubborn as mules. Keep in mind and don't ever forget how angry you made GOD, your God, in the wilderness. You've kicked and screamed against GOD from the day you left Egypt until you got to this place, rebels all the way. You made GOD angry at Horeb, made him so angry that he wanted to destroy you. When I climbed the mountain to receive the slabs of stone, the tablets of the covenant that GOD made with you, I stayed there on the mountain forty days and nights: I ate no food; I drank no water. Then GOD gave me the two slabs of stone, engraved with the finger of God. They contained word for word everything that GOD spoke to you on the mountain out of the fire, on the day of the assembly.

9.11-12 It was at the end of the forty days and nights that GOD gave me the two slabs of stone, the tablets of the covenant. GOD said to me, "Get going, and quickly. Get down there, because your people whom you led out of Egypt have ruined everything. In almost no time at all they have left the road that I laid out for them and gone off and made for themselves a cast god."

9.13-14 GOD said, "I look at this people and all I see are hardheaded, hardhearted rebels. Get out of my way now so I can destroy them. I'm going to wipe them off the face of the map. Then I'll start over with you to make a nation far better and bigger than they could ever be."

9.15-17 I turned around and started down the mountain—by now the mountain was blazing with fire—carrying the two tablets of the cov-

NEW INTERNATIONAL VERSION

tablets of the covenant were in my hands. *a* ¹⁶When I looked, I saw that you had sinned against the LORD your God; you had made for yourselves an idol cast in the shape of a calf. You had turned aside quickly from the way that the LORD had commanded you. ¹⁷So I took the two tablets and threw them out of my hands, breaking them to pieces before your eyes.

¹⁸Then once again I fell prostrate before the LORD for forty days and forty nights; I ate no bread and drank no water, because of all the sin you had committed, doing what was evil in the LORD's sight and so provoking him to anger. ¹⁹I feared the anger and wrath of the LORD, for he was angry enough with you to destroy you. But again the LORD listened to me. ²⁰And the LORD was angry enough with Aaron to destroy him, but at that time I prayed for Aaron too. ²¹Also I took that sinful thing of yours, the calf you had made, and burned it in the fire. Then I crushed it and ground it to powder as fine as dust and threw the dust into a stream that flowed down the mountain.

²²You also made the LORD angry at Taberah, at Massah and at Kibroth Hattaavah.

²³And when the LORD sent you out from Kadesh Barnea, he said, "Go up and take possession of the land I have given you." But you rebelled against the command of the LORD your God. You did not trust him or obey him. ²⁴You have been rebellious against the LORD ever since I have known you.

²⁵I lay prostrate before the LORD those forty days and forty nights because the LORD had said he would destroy you. ²⁶I prayed to the LORD and said, "O Sovereign LORD, do not destroy your people, your own inheritance that you redeemed by your great power and brought out of Egypt with a mighty hand. ²⁷Remember your servants Abraham, Isaac and Jacob. Overlook the stubbornness of this people, their wickedness and their sin. ²⁸Otherwise, the country from which you brought us will say, 'Because the LORD was not able to take them into the land he had promised them, and because he hated them, he brought them out to put them to death in the desert.' ²⁹But they are your people, your inheritance that you brought out by your great power and your outstretched arm."

a 15 Or And I had the two tablets of the covenant with me, one in each hand

THE MESSAGE

enant in my two arms. That's when I saw it: There you were, sinning against GOD, your God—you had made yourselves a cast god in the shape of a calf! So soon you had left the road that GOD had commanded you to walk on. I held the two stone slabs high and threw them down, smashing them to bits as you watched.

9.18-20 Then I prostrated myself before GOD, just as I had at the beginning of the forty days and nights. I ate no food; I drank no water. I did this because of you, all your sins, sinning against GOD, doing what is evil in GOD's eyes and making him angry. I was terrified of GOD's furious anger, his blazing anger. I was sure he would destroy you. But once again GOD listened to me. And Aaron! How furious he was with Aaron—ready to destroy him. But I prayed also for Aaron at that same time.

9.21 But that sin-thing that you made, that calf-god, I took and burned in the fire, pounded and ground it until it was crushed into a fine powder, then threw it into the stream that comes down the mountain.

9.22 And then there was Camp Taberah (Blaze), Massah (Testing-Place), and Camp Kibroth Hattaavah (Graves-of-the-Craving)—more occasions when you made God furious with you.

9.23-24 The most recent was when GOD sent you out from Kadesh Barnea, ordering you: "Go. Possess the land that I'm giving you." And what did you do? You rebelled. Rebelled against the clear orders of GOD, your God. Refused to trust him. Wouldn't obey him. You've been rebels against GOD from the first day I knew you.

9.25-26 When I was on my face, prostrate before God those forty days and nights after GOD said he would destroy you, I prayed to GOD for you, "My Master, GOD, don't destroy your people, your inheritance whom, in your immense generosity, you redeemed, using your enormous strength to get them out of Egypt.

9.27-28 "Remember your servants Abraham, Isaac, and Jacob; don't make too much of the stubbornness of this people, their evil and their sin, lest the Egyptians from whom you rescued them say, 'GOD couldn't do it; he got tired and wasn't able to take them to the land he promised them. He ended up hating them and dumped them in the wilderness to die.'

9.29 "They are your people still, your inheritance whom you powerfully and sovereignly rescued."

NEW INTERNATIONAL VERSION

TABLETS LIKE THE FIRST ONES

10 At that time the LORD said to me, "Chisel out two stone tablets like the first ones and come up to me on the mountain. Also make a wooden chest.*a* ²I will write on the tablets the words that were on the first tablets, which you broke. Then you are to put them in the chest."

³So I made the ark out of acacia wood and chiseled out two stone tablets like the first ones, and I went up on the mountain with the two tablets in my hands. ⁴The LORD wrote on these tablets what he had written before, the Ten Commandments he had proclaimed to you on the mountain, out of the fire, on the day of the assembly. And the LORD gave them to me. ⁵Then I came back down the mountain and put the tablets in the ark I had made, as the LORD commanded me, and they are there now.

⁶(The Israelites traveled from the wells of the Jaakanites to Moserah. There Aaron died and was buried, and Eleazar his son succeeded him as priest. ⁷From there they traveled to Gudgodah and on to Jotbathah, a land with streams of water. ⁸At that time the LORD set apart the tribe of Levi to carry the ark of the covenant of the LORD, to stand before the LORD to minister and to pronounce blessings in his name, as they still do today. ⁹That is why the Levites have no share or inheritance among their brothers; the LORD is their inheritance, as the LORD your God told them.)

¹⁰Now I had stayed on the mountain forty days and nights, as I did the first time, and the LORD listened to me at this time also. It was not his will to destroy you. ¹¹"Go," the LORD said to me, "and lead the people on their way, so that they may enter and possess the land that I swore to their fathers to give them."

FEAR THE LORD

¹²And now, O Israel, what does the LORD your God ask of you but to fear the LORD your God, to walk in all his ways, to love him, to serve the LORD your God with all your heart and with all your soul, ¹³and to observe the LORD's commands and decrees that I am giving you today for your own good?

¹⁴To the LORD your God belong the heavens, even the highest heavens, the earth and everything in it. ¹⁵Yet the LORD set his affection on your forefathers and loved them, and he chose you, their descendants, above all the nations, as it is today. ¹⁶Circumcise your hearts, therefore, and do not be stiff-necked any longer. ¹⁷For the LORD your God is God of gods and Lord of lords,

a 1 That is, an ark

THE MESSAGE

10 GOD responded. He said, "Shape two slabs of stone similar to the first ones. Climb the mountain and meet me. Also make yourself a wooden chest. I will engrave the stone slabs with the words that were on the first ones, the ones you smashed. Then you will put them in the Chest."

10.3-5 So I made a chest out of acacia wood, shaped two slabs of stone, just like the first ones, and climbed the mountain with the two slabs in my arms. He engraved the stone slabs the same as he had the first ones, the Ten Words that he addressed to you on the mountain out of the fire on the day of the assembly. Then GOD gave them to me. I turned around and came down the mountain. I put the stone slabs in the Chest that I made and they've been there ever since, just as GOD commanded me.

✝

10.6-7 The People of Israel went from the wells of the Jaakanites to Moserah. Aaron died there and was buried. His son Eleazar succeeded him as priest. From there they went to Gudgodah, and then to Jotbathah, a land of streams of water.

10.8-9 That's when GOD set apart the tribe of Levi to carry GOD's Covenant Chest, to be on duty in the Presence of GOD, to serve him, and to bless in his name, as they continue to do today. And that's why Levites don't have a piece of inherited land as their kinsmen do. GOD is their inheritance, as GOD, your God, promised them.

10.10 I stayed there on the mountain forty days and nights, just as I did the first time. And GOD listened to me, just as he did the first time: GOD decided not to destroy you.

10.11 GOD told me, "Now get going. Lead your people as they resume the journey to take possession of the land that I promised their ancestors that I'd give to them."

10.12-13 So now Israel, what do you think GOD expects from you? Just this: Live in his presence in holy reverence, follow the road he sets out for you, love him, serve GOD, your God, with everything you have in you, obey the commandments and regulations of GOD that I'm commanding you today—live a good life.

10.14-18 Look around you: Everything you see is GOD's—the heavens above and beyond, the Earth, and everything on it. But it was your ancestors who GOD fell in love with; he picked their children—that's you!—out of all the other peoples. That's where we are right now. So cut away the thick calluses from your heart and stop being so willfully hardheaded. GOD, your God, is the God of all gods, he's the Master of

NEW INTERNATIONAL VERSION

the great God, mighty and awesome, who shows no partiality and accepts no bribes. ¹⁸He defends the cause of the fatherless and the widow, and loves the alien, giving him food and clothing. ¹⁹And you are to love those who are aliens, for you yourselves were aliens in Egypt. ²⁰Fear the LORD your God and serve him. Hold fast to him and take your oaths in his name. ²¹He is your praise; he is your God, who performed for you those great and awesome wonders you saw with your own eyes. ²²Your forefathers who went down into Egypt were seventy in all, and now the LORD your God has made you as numerous as the stars in the sky.

LOVE AND OBEY THE LORD

11 Love the LORD your God and keep his requirements, his decrees, his laws and his commands always. ²Remember today that your children were not the ones who saw and experienced the discipline of the LORD your God: his majesty, his mighty hand, his outstretched arm; ³the signs he performed and the things he did in the heart of Egypt, both to Pharaoh king of Egypt and to his whole country; ⁴what he did to the Egyptian army, to its horses and chariots, how he overwhelmed them with the waters of the Red Sea*a* as they were pursuing you, and how the LORD brought lasting ruin on them. ⁵It was not your children who saw what he did for you in the desert until you arrived at this place, ⁶and what he did to Dathan and Abiram, sons of Eliab the Reubenite, when the earth opened its mouth right in the middle of all Israel and swallowed them up with their households, their tents and every living thing that belonged to them. ⁷But it was your own eyes that saw all these great things the LORD has done.

⁸Observe therefore all the commands I am giving you today, so that you may have the strength to go in and take over the land that you are crossing the Jordan to possess, ⁹and so that you may live long in the land that the LORD swore to your forefathers to give to them and their descendants, a land flowing with milk and honey. ¹⁰The land you are entering to take over

---

a 4 Hebrew Yam Suph; *that is, Sea of Reeds*

THE MESSAGE

all masters, a God immense and powerful and awesome. He doesn't play favorites, takes no bribes, makes sure orphans and widows are treated fairly, takes loving care of foreigners by seeing that they get food and clothing.

10.19-21 You must treat foreigners with the same
    loving care—
  remember, you were once foreigners in
    Egypt.
Reverently respect GOD, your God, serve
    him, hold tight to him,
  back up your promises with the
    authority of his name.
He's your praise! He's your God!
He did all these tremendous, these
    staggering things
  that you saw with your own eyes.

10.22 When your ancestors entered Egypt, they numbered a mere seventy souls. And now look at you—you look more like the stars in the night skies in number. And your GOD did it.

✠

11.1 **11** So love GOD, your God;
  guard well his rules and regulations;
    obey his commandments for the rest of
    time.

11.2-7 Today it's very clear that it isn't your children who are front and center here: They weren't in on what GOD did, didn't see the acts, didn't experience the discipline, didn't marvel at his greatness, the way he displayed his power in the miracle-signs and deeds that he let loose in Egypt on Pharaoh king of Egypt and all his land, the way he took care of the Egyptian army, its horses and chariots, burying them in the waters of the Red Sea as they pursued you. GOD drowned them. And you're standing here today alive. Nor was it your children who saw how GOD took care of you in the wilderness up until the time you arrived here, what he did to Dathan and Abiram, the sons of Eliab son of Reuben, how the Earth opened its jaws and swallowed them with their families—their tents, and everything around them—right out of the middle of Israel. Yes, it was you—your eyes—that saw every great thing that GOD did.

11.8-9 So it's you who are in charge of keeping the entire commandment that I command you today so that you'll have the strength to invade and possess the land that you are crossing the river to make your own. Your obedience will give you a long life on the soil that GOD promised to give to your ancestors and their children, a land flowing with milk and honey.

11.10-12 The land you are entering to take up owner-

NEW INTERNATIONAL VERSION

is not like the land of Egypt, from which you have come, where you planted your seed and irrigated it by foot as in a vegetable garden. ¹¹But the land you are crossing the Jordan to take possession of is a land of mountains and valleys that drinks rain from heaven. ¹²It is a land the LORD your God cares for; the eyes of the LORD your God are continually on it from the beginning of the year to its end.

¹³So if you faithfully obey the commands I am giving you today—to love the LORD your God and to serve him with all your heart and with all your soul— ¹⁴then I will send rain on your land in its season, both autumn and spring rains, so that you may gather in your grain, new wine and oil. ¹⁵I will provide grass in the fields for your cattle, and you will eat and be satisfied.

¹⁶Be careful, or you will be enticed to turn away and worship other gods and bow down to them. ¹⁷Then the LORD's anger will burn against you, and he will shut the heavens so that it will not rain and the ground will yield no produce, and you will soon perish from the good land the LORD is giving you. ¹⁸Fix these words of mine in your hearts and minds; tie them as symbols on your hands and bind them on your foreheads. ¹⁹Teach them to your children, talking about them when you sit at home and when you walk along the road, when you lie down and when you get up. ²⁰Write them on the doorframes of your houses and on your gates, ²¹so that your days and the days of your children may be many in the land that the LORD swore to give your forefathers, as many as the days that the heavens are above the earth.

²²If you carefully observe all these commands I am giving you to follow—to love the LORD your God, to walk in all his ways and to hold fast to him— ²³then the LORD will drive out all these nations before you, and you will dispossess nations larger and stronger than you. ²⁴Every place where you set your foot will be yours: Your territory will extend from the desert to Lebanon, and from the Euphrates River to the western sea.ᵃ ²⁵No man will be able to stand against you. The LORD your God, as he promised you, will put the terror and fear of you on the whole land, wherever you go.

²⁶See, I am setting before you today a blessing and a curse— ²⁷the blessing if you obey the commands of the LORD your God that I am giving you today; ²⁸the curse if you disobey the

THE MESSAGE

ship isn't like Egypt, the land you left, where you had to plant your own seed and water it yourselves as in a vegetable garden. But the land you are about to cross the river and take for your own is a land of mountains and valleys; it drinks water that rains from the sky. It's a land that GOD, your God, personally tends—he's the gardener—he alone keeps his eye on it all year long.

11.13-15 From now on if you listen obediently to the commandments that I am commanding you today, love GOD, your God, and serve him with everything you have within you, he'll take charge of sending the rain at the right time, both autumn and spring rains, so that you'll be able to harvest your grain, your grapes, your olives. He'll make sure there's plenty of grass for your animals. You'll have plenty to eat.

11.16-17 But be vigilant, lest you be seduced away and end up serving and worshiping other gods and GOD erupts in anger and shuts down Heaven so there's no rain and nothing grows in the fields, and in no time at all you're starved out—not a trace of you left on the good land that GOD is giving you.

11.18-21 Place these words on your hearts. Get them deep inside you. Tie them on your hands and foreheads as a reminder. Teach them to your children. Talk about them wherever you are, sitting at home or walking in the street; talk about them from the time you get up in the morning until you fall into bed at night. Inscribe them on the doorposts and gates of your cities so that you'll live a long time, and your children with you, on the soil that GOD promised to give your ancestors for as long as there is a sky over the Earth.

11.22-25 That's right. If you diligently keep all this commandment that I command you to obey—love GOD, your God, do what he tells you, stick close to him—GOD on his part will drive out all these nations that stand in your way. Yes, he'll drive out nations much bigger and stronger than you. Every square inch on which you place your foot will be yours. Your borders will stretch from the wilderness to the mountains of Lebanon, from the Euphrates River to the Mediterranean Sea. No one will be able to stand in your way. Everywhere you go, GOD-sent fear and trembling will precede you, just as he promised.

11.26 I've brought you today to the crossroads of Blessing and Curse.

11.27 The Blessing: if you listen obediently to the commandments of GOD, your God, which I command you today.

11.28 The Curse: if you don't pay attention to the

ᵃ 24 That is, the Mediterranean

NEW INTERNATIONAL VERSION

commands of the LORD your God and turn from the way that I command you today by following other gods, which you have not known. ²⁹When the LORD your God has brought you into the land you are entering to possess, you are to proclaim on Mount Gerizim the blessings, and on Mount Ebal the curses. ³⁰As you know, these mountains are across the Jordan, west of the road,^a toward the setting sun, near the great trees of Moreh, in the territory of those Canaanites living in the Arabah in the vicinity of Gilgal. ³¹You are about to cross the Jordan to enter and take possession of the land the LORD your God is giving you. When you have taken it over and are living there, ³²be sure that you obey all the decrees and laws I am setting before you today.

THE ONE PLACE OF WORSHIP

12 These are the decrees and laws you must be careful to follow in the land that the LORD, the God of your fathers, has given you to possess—as long as you live in the land. ²Destroy completely all the places on the high mountains and on the hills and under every spreading tree where the nations you are dispossessing worship their gods. ³Break down their altars, smash their sacred stones and burn their Asherah poles in the fire; cut down the idols of their gods and wipe out their names from those places.

⁴You must not worship the LORD your God in their way. ⁵But you are to seek the place the LORD your God will choose from among all your tribes to put his Name there for his dwelling. To that place you must go; ⁶there bring your burnt offerings and sacrifices, your tithes and special gifts, what you have vowed to give and your freewill offerings, and the firstborn of your herds and flocks. ⁷There, in the presence of the LORD your God, you and your families shall eat and shall rejoice in everything you have put your hand to, because the LORD your God has blessed you.

⁸You are not to do as we do here today, everyone as he sees fit, ⁹since you have not yet reached the resting place and the inheritance the LORD your God is giving you. ¹⁰But you will cross the Jordan and settle in the land the LORD your God is giving you as an inheritance, and he will give you rest from all your enemies around you so that you will live in safety. ¹¹Then to the place the LORD your God will choose as a dwelling for his Name—there you are to bring every-

THE MESSAGE

commandments of GOD, your God, but leave the road that I command you today, following other gods of which you know nothing.

11.29-30 Here's what comes next: When GOD, your God, brings you into the land you are going into to make your own, you are to give out the Blessing from Mount Gerizim and the Curse from Mount Ebal. After you cross the Jordan River, follow the road to the west through Canaanite settlements in the valley near Gilgal and the Oaks of Moreh.

11.31-32 You are crossing the Jordan River to invade and take the land that GOD, your God, is giving you. Be vigilant. Observe all the regulations and rules I am setting before you today.

✝

12.1 **12** These are the rules and regulations that you must diligently observe for as long as you live in this country that GOD, the God-of-Your-Fathers, has given you to possess.

12.2-3 Ruthlessly demolish all the sacred shrines where the nations that you're driving out worship their gods—wherever you find them, on hills and mountains or in groves of green trees. Tear apart their altars. Smash their phallic pillars. Burn their sex-and-religion Asherah shrines. Break up their carved gods. Obliterate the names of those god sites.

12.4 Stay clear of those places—don't let what went on there contaminate the worship of GOD, your God.

12.5-7 Instead find the site that GOD, your God, will choose and mark it with his name as a common center for all the tribes of Israel. Assemble there. Bring to that place your Absolution-Offerings and sacrifices, your tithes and Tribute-Offerings, your Vow-Offerings, your Freewill-Offerings, and the firstborn of your herds and flocks. Feast there in the Presence of GOD, your God. Celebrate everything that you and your families have accomplished under the blessing of GOD, your God.

12.8-10 Don't continue doing things the way we're doing them at present, each of us doing as we wish. Until now you haven't arrived at the goal, the resting place, the inheritance that GOD, your God, is giving you. But the minute you cross the Jordan River and settle into the land GOD, your God, is enabling you to inherit, he'll give you rest from all your surrounding enemies. You'll be able to settle down and live in safety.

12.11-12 From then on, at the place that GOD, your God, chooses to mark with his name as the place where you can meet him, bring every-

---

^a *30* Or *Jordan, westward*

NEW INTERNATIONAL VERSION

thing I command you: your burnt offerings and sacrifices, your tithes and special gifts, and all the choice possessions you have vowed to the LORD. [12]And there rejoice before the LORD your God, you, your sons and daughters, your menservants and maidservants, and the Levites from your towns, who have no allotment or inheritance of their own. [13]Be careful not to sacrifice your burnt offerings anywhere you please. [14]Offer them only at the place the LORD will choose in one of your tribes, and there observe everything I command you.

[15]Nevertheless, you may slaughter your animals in any of your towns and eat as much of the meat as you want, as if it were gazelle or deer, according to the blessing the LORD your God gives you. Both the ceremonially unclean and the clean may eat it. [16]But you must not eat the blood; pour it out on the ground like water. [17]You must not eat in your own towns the tithe of your grain and new wine and oil, or the firstborn of your herds and flocks, or whatever you have vowed to give, or your freewill offerings or special gifts. [18]Instead, you are to eat them in the presence of the LORD your God at the place the LORD your God will choose—you, your sons and daughters, your menservants and maidservants, and the Levites from your towns—and you are to rejoice before the LORD your God in everything you put your hand to. [19]Be careful not to neglect the Levites as long as you live in your land.

[20]When the LORD your God has enlarged your territory as he promised you, and you crave meat and say, "I would like some meat," then you may eat as much of it as you want. [21]If the place where the LORD your God chooses to put his Name is too far away from you, you may slaughter animals from the herds and flocks the LORD has given you, as I have commanded you, and in your own towns you may eat as much of them as you want. [22]Eat them as you would gazelle or deer. Both the ceremonially unclean and the clean may eat. [23]But be sure you do not eat the blood, because the blood is the life, and you must not eat the life with the meat. [24]You must not eat the blood; pour it out on the ground like water. [25]Do not eat it, so that it may go well with you and your children after you, because you will be doing what is right in the eyes of the LORD.

[26]But take your consecrated things and whatever you have vowed to give, and go to the place

THE MESSAGE

thing that I command you: your Absolution-Offerings and sacrifices, tithes and Tribute-Offerings, and the best of your Vow-Offerings that you vow to GOD. Celebrate there in the Presence of GOD, your God, you and your sons and daughters, your servants and maids, including the Levite living in your neighborhood because he has no place of his own in your inheritance.

12.13-14 Be extra careful: Don't offer your Absolution-Offerings just any place that strikes your fancy. Offer your Absolution-Offerings only in the place that GOD chooses in one of your tribal regions. There and only there are you to bring all that I command you.

12.15 It's permissible to slaughter your nonsacrificial animals like gazelle and deer in your towns and eat all you want from them with the blessing of GOD, your God. Both the ritually clean and unclean may eat.

12.16-18 But you may not eat the blood. Pour the blood out on the ground like water. Nor may you eat there the tithe of your grain, new wine, or olive oil; nor the firstborn of your herds and flocks; nor any of the Vow-Offerings that you vow; nor your Freewill-Offerings and Tribute-Offerings. All these you must eat in the Presence of GOD, your God, in the place GOD, your God, chooses—you, your son and daughter, your servant and maid, and the Levite who lives in your neighborhood. You are to celebrate in the Presence of GOD, your God, all the things you've been able to accomplish.

12.19 And make sure that for as long as you live on your land you never, never neglect the Levite.

12.20-22 When GOD, your God, expands your territory as he promised he would do, and you say, "I'm hungry for meat," because you happen to be craving meat at the time, go ahead and eat as much meat as you want. If you're too far away from the place that GOD, your God, has marked with his name, it's all right to slaughter animals from your herds and flocks that GOD has given you, as I've commanded you. In your own towns you may eat as much of them as you want. Just as the nonsacrificial animals like the gazelle and deer are eaten, you may eat them; the ritually unclean and clean may eat them at the same table.

12.23-25 Only this: Absolutely no blood. Don't eat the blood. Blood is life; don't eat the life with the meat. Don't eat it; pour it out on the ground like water. Don't eat it; then you'll have a good life, you and your children after you. By all means, do the right thing in GOD's eyes.

12.26-27 And this: Lift high your Holy-Offerings and your Vow-Offerings and bring them to the

NEW INTERNATIONAL VERSION

the LORD will choose. ²⁷Present your burnt offerings on the altar of the LORD your God, both the meat and the blood. The blood of your sacrifices must be poured beside the altar of the LORD your God, but you may eat the meat. ²⁸Be careful to obey all these regulations I am giving you, so that it may always go well with you and your children after you, because you will be doing what is good and right in the eyes of the LORD your God.

²⁹The LORD your God will cut off before you the nations you are about to invade and dispossess. But when you have driven them out and settled in their land, ³⁰and after they have been destroyed before you, be careful not to be ensnared by inquiring about their gods, saying, "How do these nations serve their gods? We will do the same." ³¹You must not worship the LORD your God in their way, because in worshiping their gods, they do all kinds of detestable things the LORD hates. They even burn their sons and daughters in the fire as sacrifices to their gods.

³²See that you do all I command you; do not add to it or take away from it.

WORSHIPING OTHER GODS

13 If a prophet, or one who foretells by dreams, appears among you and announces to you a miraculous sign or wonder, ²and if the sign or wonder of which he has spoken takes place, and he says, "Let us follow other gods" (gods you have not known) "and let us worship them," ³you must not listen to the words of that prophet or dreamer. The LORD your God is testing you to find out whether you love him with all your heart and with all your soul. ⁴It is the LORD your God you must follow, and him you must revere. Keep his commands and obey him; serve him and hold fast to him. ⁵That prophet or dreamer must be put to death, because he preached rebellion against the LORD your God, who brought you out of Egypt and redeemed you from the land of slavery; he has tried to turn you from the way the LORD your God commanded you to follow. You must purge the evil from among you.

⁶If your very own brother, or your son or daughter, or the wife you love, or your closest friend secretly entices you, saying, "Let us go and worship other gods" (gods that neither you nor your fathers have known, ⁷gods of the peoples around you, whether near or far, from one end of the land to the other), ⁸do not yield to him or listen to him. Show him no pity. Do not

THE MESSAGE

place GOD designates. Sacrifice your Absolution-Offerings, the meat and blood, on the Altar of GOD, your God; pour out the blood of the Absolution-Offering on the Altar of GOD, your God; then you can go ahead and eat the meat.

12.28   Be vigilant, listen obediently to these words that I command you so that you'll have a good life, you and your children, for a long, long time, doing what is good and right in the eyes of GOD, your God.

12.29-31   When GOD, your God, cuts off the nations whose land you are invading, shoves them out of your way so that you displace them and settle in their land, be careful that you don't get curious about them after they've been destroyed before you. Don't get fascinated with their gods, thinking, "I wonder what it was like for them, worshiping their gods. I'd like to try that myself." Don't do this to GOD, your God. They commit every imaginable abomination with their gods. GOD hates it all with a passion. Why, they even set their children on fire as offerings to their gods!

12.32   Diligently do everything I command you, the way I command you: don't add to it; don't subtract from it.

✝

13.1-4   **13** When a prophet or visionary gets up in your community and gives out a miracle-sign or wonder, and the miracle-sign or wonder that he gave out happens and he says, "Let's follow other gods" (these are gods you know nothing about), "let's worship them," don't pay any attention to what that prophet or visionary says. GOD, your God, is testing you to find out if you totally love him with everything you have in you. You are to follow only GOD, your God, hold him in deep reverence, keep his commandments, listen obediently to what he says, serve him—hold on to him for dear life!

13.5   And that prophet or visionary must be put to death. He has urged mutiny against GOD, your God, who rescued you from Egypt, who redeemed you from a world of slavery and put you on the road on which GOD, your God, has commanded you to walk. Purge the evil from your company.

13.6-10   And when your brother or son or daughter, or even your dear wife or lifelong friend, comes to you in secret and whispers, "Let's go and worship some other gods" (gods that you know nothing about, neither you nor your ancestors, the gods of the peoples around you near and far, from one end of the Earth to the other), don't go along with him; shut your ears. Don't

NEW INTERNATIONAL VERSION

spare him or shield him. ⁹You must certainly put him to death. Your hand must be the first in putting him to death, and then the hands of all the people. ¹⁰Stone him to death, because he tried to turn you away from the LORD your God, who brought you out of Egypt, out of the land of slavery. ¹¹Then all Israel will hear and be afraid, and no one among you will do such an evil thing again.

¹²If you hear it said about one of the towns the LORD your God is giving you to live in ¹³that wicked men have arisen among you and have led the people of their town astray, saying, "Let us go and worship other gods" (gods you have not known), ¹⁴then you must inquire, probe and investigate it thoroughly. And if it is true and it has been proved that this detestable thing has been done among you, ¹⁵you must certainly put to the sword all who live in that town. Destroy it completely,ᵃ both its people and its livestock. ¹⁶Gather all the plunder of the town into the middle of the public square and completely burn the town and all its plunder as a whole burnt offering to the LORD your God. It is to remain a ruin forever, never to be rebuilt. ¹⁷None of those condemned thingsᵃ shall be found in your hands, so that the LORD will turn from his fierce anger; he will show you mercy, have compassion on you, and increase your numbers, as he promised on oath to your forefathers, ¹⁸because you obey the LORD your God, keeping all his commands that I am giving you today and doing what is right in his eyes.

CLEAN AND UNCLEAN FOOD

14 You are the children of the LORD your God. Do not cut yourselves or shave the front of your heads for the dead, ²for you are a people holy to the LORD your God. Out of all the peoples on the face of the earth, the LORD has chosen you to be his treasured possession.

³Do not eat any detestable thing. ⁴These are the animals you may eat: the ox, the sheep, the goat, ⁵the deer, the gazelle, the roe deer, the wild goat, the ibex, the antelope and the mountain sheep.ᵇ ⁶You may eat any animal that has a split hoof divided in two and that chews the cud.

ᵃ *15, 17* The Hebrew term refers to the irrevocable giving over of things or persons to the LORD, often by totally destroying them.   ᵇ *5* The precise identification of some of the birds and animals in this chapter is uncertain.

THE MESSAGE

feel sorry for him and don't make excuses for him. Kill him. That's right, kill him. You throw the first stone. Take action at once and swiftly with everybody in the community getting in on it at the end. Stone him with stones so that he dies. He tried to turn you traitor against GOD, your God, the one who got you out of Egypt and the world of slavery.

13.11 Every man, woman, and child in Israel will hear what's been done and be in awe. No one will dare to do an evil thing like this again.

13.12-17 When word comes in from one of your cities that GOD, your God, is giving you to live in, reporting that evil men have gotten together with some of the citizens of the city and have broken away, saying, "Let's go and worship other gods" (gods you know nothing about), then you must conduct a careful examination. Ask questions, investigate. If it turns out that the report is true and this abomination did in fact take place in your community, you must execute the citizens of that town. Kill them, setting that city apart for holy destruction: the city and everything in it including its animals. Gather the plunder in the middle of the town square and burn it all—town and plunder together up in smoke, a holy sacrifice to GOD, your God. Leave it there, ashes and ruins. Don't build on that site again. And don't let any of the plunder devoted to holy destruction stick to your fingers. Get rid of it so that GOD may turn from anger to compassion, generously making you prosper, just as he promised your ancestors.

13.18 Yes. Obediently listen to GOD, your God. Keep all his commands that I am giving you today. Do the right thing in the eyes of GOD, your God.

✝

14.1-2 **14** You are children of GOD, your God, so don't mutilate your bodies or shave your heads in funeral rites for the dead. You only are a people holy to GOD, your God; GOD chose you out of all the people on Earth as his cherished personal treasure.

14.3-8 Don't eat anything abominable. These are the animals you may eat: ox, sheep, goat, deer, gazelle, roebuck, wild goat, ibex, antelope, mountain sheep—any animal that has a cloven hoof and chews the cud. But you may not eat

NEW INTERNATIONAL VERSION

7However, of those that chew the cud or that have a split hoof completely divided you may not eat the camel, the rabbit or the coney.*a* Although they chew the cud, they do not have a split hoof; they are ceremonially unclean for you. 8The pig is also unclean; although it has a split hoof, it does not chew the cud. You are not to eat their meat or touch their carcasses.

9Of all the creatures living in the water, you may eat any that has fins and scales. 10But anything that does not have fins and scales you may not eat; for you it is unclean.

11You may eat any clean bird. 12But these you may not eat: the eagle, the vulture, the black vulture, 13the red kite, the black kite, any kind of falcon, 14any kind of raven, 15the horned owl, the screech owl, the gull, any kind of hawk, 16the little owl, the great owl, the white owl, 17the desert owl, the osprey, the cormorant, 18the stork, any kind of heron, the hoopoe and the bat.

19All flying insects that swarm are unclean to you; do not eat them. 20But any winged creature that is clean you may eat.

21Do not eat anything you find already dead. You may give it to an alien living in any of your towns, and he may eat it, or you may sell it to a foreigner. But you are a people holy to the LORD your God.

Do not cook a young goat in its mother's milk.

TITHES

22Be sure to set aside a tenth of all that your fields produce each year. 23Eat the tithe of your grain, new wine and oil, and the firstborn of your herds and flocks in the presence of the LORD your God at the place he will choose as a dwelling for his Name, so that you may learn to revere the LORD your God always. 24But if that place is too distant and you have been blessed by the LORD your God and cannot carry your tithe (because the place where the LORD will choose to put his Name is so far away), 25then exchange your tithe for silver, and take the silver with you and go to the place the LORD your God will choose. 26Use the silver to buy whatever you like: cattle, sheep, wine or other fermented drink, or anything you wish. Then you and your household shall eat there in the presence of the LORD your God and rejoice. 27And do not neglect the Levites living in your towns, for they have no allotment or inheritance of their own.

28At the end of every three years, bring all the tithes of that year's produce and store it in your towns, 29so that the Levites (who have no allot-

a 7 That is, the hyrax or rock badger

THE MESSAGE

camels, rabbits, and rock badgers because they chew the cud but they don't have a cloven hoof—that makes them ritually unclean. And pigs: Don't eat pigs—they have a cloven hoof but don't chew the cud, which makes them ritually unclean. Don't even touch a pig's carcass.

14.9-10 This is what you may eat from the water: anything that has fins and scales. But if it doesn't have fins or scales, you may not eat it. It's ritually unclean.

14.11-18 You may eat any ritually clean bird. These are the exceptions, so don't eat these: eagle, vulture, black vulture, kite, falcon, the buzzard family, the raven family, ostrich, nighthawk, the hawk family, little owl, great owl, white owl, pelican, osprey, cormorant, stork, the heron family, hoopoe, bat.

14.19-20 Winged insects are ritually unclean; don't eat them. But ritually clean winged creatures are permitted.

14.21 Because you are a people holy to GOD, your God, don't eat anything that you find dead. You can, though, give it to a foreigner in your neighborhood for a meal or sell it to a foreigner. Don't boil a kid in its mother's milk.

14.22-26 Make an offering of ten percent, a tithe, of all the produce which grows in your fields year after year. Bring this into the Presence of GOD, your God, at the place he designates for worship and there eat the tithe from your grain, wine, and oil and the firstborn from your herds and flocks. In this way you will learn to live in deep reverence before GOD, your God, as long as you live. But if the place GOD, your God, designates for worship is too far away and you can't carry your tithe that far, GOD, your God, will still bless you: exchange your tithe for money and take the money to the place GOD, your God, has chosen to be worshiped. Use the money to buy anything you want: cattle, sheep, wine, or beer—anything that looks good to you. You and your family can then feast in the Presence of GOD, your God, and have a good time.

14.27 Meanwhile, don't forget to take good care of the Levites who live in your towns; they won't get any property or inheritance of their own as you will.

14.28-29 At the end of every third year, gather the tithe from all your produce of that year and put it aside in storage. Keep it in reserve for the Levite who won't get any property or inheri-

NEW INTERNATIONAL VERSION	THE MESSAGE

NEW INTERNATIONAL VERSION

ment or inheritance of their own) and the aliens, the fatherless and the widows who live in your towns may come and eat and be satisfied, and so that the LORD your God may bless you in all the work of your hands.

THE YEAR FOR CANCELING DEBTS

15 At the end of every seven years you must cancel debts. ²This is how it is to be done: Every creditor shall cancel the loan he has made to his fellow Israelite. He shall not require payment from his fellow Israelite or brother, because the LORD's time for canceling debts has been proclaimed. ³You may require payment from a foreigner, but you must cancel any debt your brother owes you. ⁴However, there should be no poor among you, for in the land the LORD your God is giving you to possess as your inheritance, he will richly bless you, ⁵if only you fully obey the LORD your God and are careful to follow all these commands I am giving you today. ⁶For the LORD your God will bless you as he has promised, and you will lend to many nations but will borrow from none. You will rule over many nations but none will rule over you.

⁷If there is a poor man among your brothers in any of the towns of the land that the LORD your God is giving you, do not be hardhearted or tightfisted toward your poor brother. ⁸Rather be openhanded and freely lend him whatever he needs. ⁹Be careful not to harbor this wicked thought: "The seventh year, the year for canceling debts, is near," so that you do not show ill will toward your needy brother and give him nothing. He may then appeal to the LORD against you, and you will be found guilty of sin. ¹⁰Give generously to him and do so without a grudging heart; then because of this the LORD your God will bless you in all your work and in everything you put your hand to. ¹¹There will always be poor people in the land. Therefore I command you to be openhanded toward your brothers and toward the poor and needy in your land.

FREEING SERVANTS

¹²If a fellow Hebrew, a man or a woman, sells himself to you and serves you six years, in the seventh year you must let him go free. ¹³And when you release him, do not send him away empty-handed. ¹⁴Supply him liberally from your flock, your threshing floor and your winepress. Give to him as the LORD your God has blessed

THE MESSAGE

tance as you will, and for the foreigner, the orphan, and the widow who live in your neighborhood. That way they'll have plenty to eat and GOD, your God, will bless you in all your work.

15.1-3 **15** At the end of every seventh year, cancel all debts. This is the procedure: Everyone who has lent money to a neighbor writes it off. You must not press your neighbor or his brother for payment: All-Debts-Are-Canceled— GOD says so. You may collect payment from foreigners, but whatever you have lent to your fellow Israelite you must write off.

15.4-6 There must be no poor people among you because GOD is going to bless you lavishly in this land that GOD, your God, is giving you as an inheritance, your very own land. But only if you listen obediently to the Voice of GOD, your God, diligently observing every commandment that I command you today. Oh yes—GOD, your God, will bless you just as he promised. You will lend to many nations but won't borrow from any; you'll rule over many nations but none will rule over you.

15.7-9 When you happen on someone who's in trouble or needs help among your people with whom you live in this land that GOD, your God, is giving you, don't look the other way pretending you don't see him. Don't keep a tight grip on your purse. No. Look at him, open your purse, lend whatever and as much as he needs. Don't count the cost. Don't listen to that selfish voice saying, "It's almost the seventh year, the year of All-Debts-Are-Canceled," and turn aside and leave your needy neighbor in the lurch, refusing to help him. He'll call GOD's attention to you and your blatant sin.

15.10-11 Give freely and spontaneously. Don't have a stingy heart. The way you handle matters like this triggers GOD, your God's, blessing in everything you do, all your work and ventures. There are always going to be poor and needy people among you. So I command you: Always be generous, open purse and hands, give to your neighbors in trouble, your poor and hurting neighbors.

15.12-15 If a Hebrew man or Hebrew woman was sold to you and has served you for six years, in the seventh year you must set him or her free, released into a free life. And when you set them free don't send them off empty-handed. Provide them with some animals, plenty of bread and wine and oil. Load them with provisions from all the blessings with which GOD, your God, has blessed you. Don't for a minute forget

NEW INTERNATIONAL VERSION

you. [15]Remember that you were slaves in Egypt and the LORD your God redeemed you. That is why I give you this command today.

[16]But if your servant says to you, "I do not want to leave you," because he loves you and your family and is well off with you, [17]then take an awl and push it through his ear lobe into the door, and he will become your servant for life. Do the same for your maidservant.

[18]Do not consider it a hardship to set your servant free, because his service to you these six years has been worth twice as much as that of a hired hand. And the LORD your God will bless you in everything you do.

THE FIRSTBORN ANIMALS

[19]Set apart for the LORD your God every firstborn male of your herds and flocks. Do not put the firstborn of your oxen to work, and do not shear the firstborn of your sheep. [20]Each year you and your family are to eat them in the presence of the LORD your God at the place he will choose. [21]If an animal has a defect, is lame or blind, or has any serious flaw, you must not sacrifice it to the LORD your God. [22]You are to eat it in your own towns. Both the ceremonially unclean and the clean may eat it, as if it were gazelle or deer. [23]But you must not eat the blood; pour it out on the ground like water.

PASSOVER

16 Observe the month of Abib and celebrate the Passover of the LORD your God, because in the month of Abib he brought you out of Egypt by night. [2]Sacrifice as the Passover to the LORD your God an animal from your flock or herd at the place the LORD will choose as a dwelling for his Name. [3]Do not eat it with bread made with yeast, but for seven days eat unleavened bread, the bread of affliction, because you left Egypt in haste—so that all the days of your life you may remember the time of your departure from Egypt. [4]Let no yeast be found in your possession in all your land for seven days. Do not let any of the meat you sacrifice on the evening of the first day remain until morning.

[5]You must not sacrifice the Passover in any town the LORD your God gives you [6]except in the place he will choose as a dwelling for his Name. There you must sacrifice the Passover in the evening, when the sun goes down, on the anniversary[a] of your departure from Egypt.

a 6 Or down, at the time of day

THE MESSAGE

that you were once slaves in Egypt and GOD, your God, redeemed you from that slave world.

For that reason, this day I command you to do this.

15.16-17 But if your slave, because he loves you and your family and has a good life with you, says, "I don't want to leave you," then take an awl and pierce through his earlobe into the doorpost, marking him as your slave forever. Do the same with your women slaves who want to stay with you.

15.18 Don't consider this an unreasonable hardship, this setting your slave free. After all, he's worked six years for you at half the cost of a hired hand.

Believe me, GOD, your God, will bless you in everything you do.

✛

15.19-23 Consecrate to GOD, your God, all the firstborn males in your herds and flocks. Don't use the firstborn from your herds as work animals; don't shear the firstborn from your flocks. These are for you to eat every year, you and your family, in the Presence of GOD, your God, at the place that GOD designates for worship. If the animal is defective, lame, say, or blind—anything wrong with it—don't slaughter it as a sacrifice to GOD, your God. Stay at home and eat it there. Both the ritually clean and unclean may eat it, the same as with a gazelle or a deer. Only you must not eat its blood. Pour the blood out on the ground like water.

✛

16.1-4 **16** Observe the month of Abib by celebrating the Passover to GOD, your God. It was in the month of Abib that GOD, your God, delivered you by night from Egypt. Offer the Passover-Sacrifice to GOD, your God, at the place GOD chooses to be worshiped by establishing his name there. Don't eat yeast bread with it; for seven days eat it with unraised bread, hard-times bread, because you left Egypt in a hurry—that bread will keep the memory fresh of how you left Egypt for as long as you live. There is to be no sign of yeast anywhere for seven days. And don't let any of the meat that you sacrifice in the evening be left over until morning.

16.5-7 Don't sacrifice the Passover in any of the towns that GOD, your God, gives you other than the one GOD, your God, designates for worship; there and there only you will offer the Passover-Sacrifice at evening as the sun goes down, marking the time that you left Egypt.

NEW INTERNATIONAL VERSION

⁷Roast it and eat it at the place the LORD your God will choose. Then in the morning return to your tents. ⁸For six days eat unleavened bread and on the seventh day hold an assembly to the LORD your God and do no work.

FEAST OF WEEKS

⁹Count off seven weeks from the time you begin to put the sickle to the standing grain. ¹⁰Then celebrate the Feast of Weeks to the LORD your God by giving a freewill offering in proportion to the blessings the LORD your God has given you. ¹¹And rejoice before the LORD your God at the place he will choose as a dwelling for his Name—you, your sons and daughters, your menservants and maidservants, the Levites in your towns, and the aliens, the fatherless and the widows living among you. ¹²Remember that you were slaves in Egypt, and follow carefully these decrees.

FEAST OF TABERNACLES

¹³Celebrate the Feast of Tabernacles for seven days after you have gathered the produce of your threshing floor and your winepress. ¹⁴Be joyful at your Feast—you, your sons and daughters, your menservants and maidservants, and the Levites, the aliens, the fatherless and the widows who live in your towns. ¹⁵For seven days celebrate the Feast to the LORD your God at the place the LORD will choose. For the LORD your God will bless you in all your harvest and in all the work of your hands, and your joy will be complete.

¹⁶Three times a year all your men must appear before the LORD your God at the place he will choose: at the Feast of Unleavened Bread, the Feast of Weeks and the Feast of Tabernacles. No man should appear before the LORD empty-handed: ¹⁷Each of you must bring a gift in proportion to the way the LORD your God has blessed you.

JUDGES

¹⁸Appoint judges and officials for each of your tribes in every town the LORD your God is giving you, and they shall judge the people fairly. ¹⁹Do not pervert justice or show partiality. Do not accept a bribe, for a bribe blinds the eyes of the wise and twists the words of the righteous. ²⁰Follow justice and justice alone, so that you may live and possess the land the LORD your God is giving you.

THE MESSAGE

Boil and eat it at the place designated by GOD, your God. Then, at daybreak, turn around and go home.

16.8 Eat unraised bread for six days. Set aside the seventh day as a holiday; don't do any work.

16.9-11 Starting from the day you put the sickle to the ripe grain, count out seven weeks. Celebrate the Feast-of-Weeks to GOD, your God, by bringing your Freewill-Offering—give as generously as GOD, your God, has blessed you. Rejoice in the Presence of GOD, your God: you, your son, your daughter, your servant, your maid, the Levite who lives in your neighborhood, the foreigner, the orphan and widow among you; rejoice at the place GOD, your God, will set aside to be worshiped.

16.12 Don't forget that you were once a slave in Egypt. So be diligent in observing these regulations.

16.13-15 Observe the Feast-of-Booths for seven days when you gather the harvest from your threshing-floor and your wine-vat. Rejoice at your festival: you, your son, your daughter, your servant, your maid, the Levite, the foreigner, and the orphans and widows who live in your neighborhood. Celebrate the Feast to GOD, your God, for seven days at the place GOD designates. GOD, your God, has been blessing you in your harvest and in all your work, so make a day of it—really celebrate!

16.16-17 All your men must appear before GOD, your God, three times each year at the place he designates: at the Feast-of-Unraised-Bread (Passover), at the Feast-of-Weeks, and at the Feast-of-Booths. No one is to show up in the Presence of GOD empty-handed; each man must bring as much as he can manage, giving generously in response to the blessings of GOD, your God.

16.18-19 Appoint judges and officers, organized by tribes, in all the towns that GOD, your God, is giving you. They are to judge the people fairly and honestly. Don't twist the law. Don't play favorites. Don't take a bribe—a bribe blinds even a wise person; it undermines the intentions of the best of people.

16.20 The right! The right! Pursue only what's right! It's the only way you can really live and possess the land that GOD, your God, is giving you.

NEW INTERNATIONAL VERSION

Worshiping Other Gods

²¹Do not set up any wooden Asherah pole^a beside the altar you build to the LORD your God, ²²and do not erect a sacred stone, for these the LORD your God hates.

17 Do not sacrifice to the LORD your God an ox or a sheep that has any defect or flaw in it, for that would be detestable to him. ²If a man or woman living among you in one of the towns the LORD gives you is found doing evil in the eyes of the LORD your God in violation of his covenant, ³and contrary to my command has worshiped other gods, bowing down to them or to the sun or the moon or the stars of the sky, ⁴and this has been brought to your attention, then you must investigate it thoroughly. If it is true and it has been proved that this detestable thing has been done in Israel, ⁵take the man or woman who has done this evil deed to your city gate and stone that person to death. ⁶On the testimony of two or three witnesses a man shall be put to death, but no one shall be put to death on the testimony of only one witness. ⁷The hands of the witnesses must be the first in putting him to death, and then the hands of all the people. You must purge the evil from among you.

Law Courts

⁸If cases come before your courts that are too difficult for you to judge—whether bloodshed, lawsuits or assaults—take them to the place the LORD your God will choose. ⁹Go to the priests, who are Levites, and to the judge who is in office at that time. Inquire of them and they will give you the verdict. ¹⁰You must act according to the decisions they give you at the place the LORD will choose. Be careful to do everything they direct you to do. ¹¹Act according to the law they teach you and the decisions they give you. Do not turn aside from what they tell you, to the right or to the left. ¹²The man who shows contempt for the judge or for the priest who stands ministering there to the LORD your God must be put to death. You must purge the evil from Israel. ¹³All the people will hear and be afraid, and will not be contemptuous again.

The King

¹⁴When you enter the land the LORD your God is giving you and have taken possession of it and settled in it, and you say, "Let us set a king

^a 21 Or *Do not plant any tree dedicated to Asherah*

THE MESSAGE

16.21-22 Don't plant fertility Asherah trees alongside the Altar of GOD, your God, that you build. Don't set up phallic sex pillars—GOD, your God, hates them.

✝

17 And don't sacrifice to GOD, your God, an ox or sheep that is defective or has anything at all wrong with it. That's an abomination, an insult to GOD, your God.

17.1

17.2-5 If you find anyone within the towns that GOD, your God, is giving you doing what is wrong in GOD's eyes, breaking his covenant by going off to worship other gods, bowing down to them—the sun, say, or the moon, or any rebel sky-gods—look at the evidence and investigate carefully. If you find that it is true, that, in fact, an abomination has been committed in Israel, then you are to take the man or woman who did this evil thing outside your city gates and stone the man or the woman. Hurl stones at the person until dead.

17.6-7 But only on the testimony of two or three witnesses may a person be put to death. No one may be put to death on the testimony of one witness. The witnesses must throw the first stones in the execution, then the rest of the community joins in. You have to purge the evil from your community.

17.8-9 When matters of justice come up that are too much for you—hard cases regarding homicides, legal disputes, fights—take them up to the central place of worship that GOD, your God, has designated. Bring them to the Levitical priests and the judge who is in office at the time. Consult them and they will hand down the decision for you.

17.10-13 Then carry out their verdict at the place designated by GOD, your God. Do what they tell you, in exactly the way they tell you. Follow their instructions precisely: Don't leave out anything; don't add anything. Anyone who presumes to override or twist the decision handed down by the priest or judge who was acting in the Presence of GOD, your God, is as good as dead—root him out, rid Israel of the evil. Everyone will take notice and be impressed. That will put an end to presumptuous behavior.

✝

17.14-17 When you enter the land that GOD, your God, is giving you and take it over and settle down, and then say, "I'm going to get me a king, a

NEW INTERNATIONAL VERSION

over us like all the nations around us," ¹⁵be sure to appoint over you the king the LORD your God chooses. He must be from among your own brothers. Do not place a foreigner over you, one who is not a brother Israelite. ¹⁶The king, moreover, must not acquire great numbers of horses for himself or make the people return to Egypt to get more of them, for the LORD has told you, "You are not to go back that way again." ¹⁷He must not take many wives, or his heart will be led astray. He must not accumulate large amounts of silver and gold.

¹⁸When he takes the throne of his kingdom, he is to write for himself on a scroll a copy of this law, taken from that of the priests, who are Levites. ¹⁹It is to be with him, and he is to read it all the days of his life so that he may learn to revere the LORD his God and follow carefully all the words of this law and these decrees ²⁰and not consider himself better than his brothers and turn from the law to the right or to the left. Then he and his descendants will reign a long time over his kingdom in Israel.

OFFERINGS FOR PRIESTS AND LEVITES

18 The priests, who are Levites—indeed the whole tribe of Levi—are to have no allotment or inheritance with Israel. They shall live on the offerings made to the LORD by fire, for that is their inheritance. ²They shall have no inheritance among their brothers; the LORD is their inheritance, as he promised them.

³This is the share due the priests from the people who sacrifice a bull or a sheep: the shoulder, the jowls and the inner parts. ⁴You are to give them the firstfruits of your grain, new wine and oil, and the first wool from the shearing of your sheep, ⁵for the LORD your God has chosen them and their descendants out of all your tribes to stand and minister in the LORD's name always.

⁶If a Levite moves from one of your towns anywhere in Israel where he is living, and comes in all earnestness to the place the LORD will choose, ⁷he may minister in the name of the LORD his God like all his fellow Levites who serve there in the presence of the LORD. ⁸He is to share equally in their benefits, even though he has received money from the sale of family possessions.

DETESTABLE PRACTICES

⁹When you enter the land the LORD your God

THE MESSAGE

king like all the nations around me," make sure you get yourself a king whom GOD, your God, chooses. Choose your king from among your kinsmen; don't take a foreigner—only a kinsman. And make sure he doesn't build up a war machine, amassing military horses and chariots. He must not send people to Egypt to get more horses, because GOD told you, "You'll never go back there again!" And make sure he doesn't build up a harem, collecting wives who will divert him from the straight and narrow. And make sure he doesn't pile up a lot of silver and gold.

17.18-20   This is what must be done: When he sits down on the throne of his kingdom, the first thing he must do is make himself a copy of this Revelation on a scroll, copied under the supervision of the Levitical priests. That scroll is to remain at his side at all times; he is to study it every day so that he may learn what it means to fear his GOD, living in reverent obedience before these rules and regulations by following them. He must not become proud and arrogant, changing the commands at whim to suit himself or making up his own versions. If he reads and learns, he will have a long reign as king in Israel, he and his sons.

☩

18.1-2   **18** The Levitical priests—that's the entire tribe of Levi—don't get any land-inheritance with the rest of Israel. They get the Fire-Gift-Offerings of GOD—they will live on that inheritance. But they don't get land-inheritance like the rest of their kinsmen. GOD is their inheritance.

18.3-5   This is what the priests get from the people from any offering of an ox or a sheep: the shoulder, the two cheeks, and the stomach. You must also give them the firstfruits of your grain, wine, and oil and the first fleece of your sheep, because GOD, your God, has chosen only them and their children out of all your tribes to be present and serve always in the name of GOD, your God.

18.6-8   If a Levite moves from any town in Israel— and he is quite free to move wherever he desires—and comes to the place GOD designates for worship, he may serve there in the name of GOD along with all his brother Levites who are present and serving in the Presence of GOD. And he will get an equal share to eat, even though he has money from the sale of his parents' possessions.

☩

18.9-12   When you enter the land that GOD, your God,

NEW INTERNATIONAL VERSION

is giving you, do not learn to imitate the detestable ways of the nations there. [10]Let no one be found among you who sacrifices his son or daughter in[a] the fire, who practices divination or sorcery, interprets omens, engages in witchcraft, [11]or casts spells, or who is a medium or spiritist or who consults the dead. [12]Anyone who does these things is detestable to the LORD, and because of these detestable practices the LORD your God will drive out those nations before you. [13]You must be blameless before the LORD your God.

THE PROPHET

[14]The nations you will dispossess listen to those who practice sorcery or divination. But as for you, the LORD your God has not permitted you to do so. [15]The LORD your God will raise up for you a prophet like me from among your own brothers. You must listen to him. [16]For this is what you asked of the LORD your God at Horeb on the day of the assembly when you said, "Let us not hear the voice of the LORD our God nor see this great fire anymore, or we will die."

[17]The LORD said to me: "What they say is good. [18]I will raise up for them a prophet like you from among their brothers; I will put my words in his mouth, and he will tell them everything I command him. [19]If anyone does not listen to my words that the prophet speaks in my name, I myself will call him to account. [20]But a prophet who presumes to speak in my name anything I have not commanded him to say, or a prophet who speaks in the name of other gods, must be put to death."

[21]You may say to yourselves, "How can we know when a message has not been spoken by the LORD?" [22]If what a prophet proclaims in the name of the LORD does not take place or come true, that is a message the LORD has not spoken. That prophet has spoken presumptuously. Do not be afraid of him.

CITIES OF REFUGE

19 When the LORD your God has destroyed the nations whose land he is giving you, and when you have driven them out and settled in their towns and houses, [2]then set aside for yourselves three cities centrally located in the land the LORD your God is giving you to possess. [3]Build roads to them and divide into three parts the land the LORD your God is giving you as an inheritance, so that anyone who kills a man may flee there.

[4]This is the rule concerning the man who kills another and flees there to save his life—one

[a] 10 Or *who makes his son or daughter pass through*

THE MESSAGE

is giving you, don't take on the abominable ways of life of the nations there. Don't you dare sacrifice your son or daughter in the fire. Don't practice divination, sorcery, fortunetelling, witchery, casting spells, holding séances, or channeling with the dead. People who do these things are an abomination to GOD. It's because of just such abominable practices that GOD, your God, is driving these nations out before you.

18.13-14   Be completely loyal to GOD, your God. These nations that you're about to run out of the country consort with sorcerers and witches. But not you. GOD, your God, forbids it.

18.15-16   GOD, your God, is going to raise up a prophet for you. GOD will raise him up from among your kinsmen, a prophet like me. Listen obediently to him. This is what you asked GOD, your God, for at Horeb on the day you were all gathered at the mountain and said, "We can't hear any more from GOD, our God; we can't stand seeing any more fire. We'll die!"

18.17-19   And GOD said to me, "They're right; they've spoken the truth. I'll raise up for them a prophet like you from their kinsmen. I'll tell him what to say and he will pass on to them everything I command him. And anyone who won't listen to my words spoken by him, I will personally hold responsible.

18.20   "But any prophet who fakes it, who claims to speak in my name something I haven't commanded him to say, or speaks in the name of other gods, that prophet must die."

18.21-22   You may be wondering among yourselves, "How can we tell the difference, whether it was GOD who spoke or not?" Here's how: If what the prophet spoke in GOD's name doesn't happen, then obviously GOD wasn't behind it; the prophet made it up. Forget about him.

✝

19.1-3   **19** When GOD, your God, throws the nations out of the country that GOD, your God, is giving you and you settle down in their cities and houses, you are to set aside three easily accessible cities in the land that GOD, your God, is giving you as your very own. Divide your land into thirds, this land that GOD, your God, is giving you to possess, and build roads to the towns so that anyone who accidentally kills another can flee there.

19.4-7   This is the guideline for the murderer who flees there to take refuge: He has to have killed

NEW INTERNATIONAL VERSION

who kills his neighbor unintentionally, without malice aforethought. [5]For instance, a man may go into the forest with his neighbor to cut wood, and as he swings his ax to fell a tree, the head may fly off and hit his neighbor and kill him. That man may flee to one of these cities and save his life. [6]Otherwise, the avenger of blood might pursue him in a rage, overtake him if the distance is too great, and kill him even though he is not deserving of death, since he did it to his neighbor without malice aforethought. [7]This is why I command you to set aside for yourselves three cities.

[8]If the LORD your God enlarges your territory, as he promised on oath to your forefathers, and gives you the whole land he promised them, [9]because you carefully follow all these laws I command you today—to love the LORD your God and to walk always in his ways—then you are to set aside three more cities. [10]Do this so that innocent blood will not be shed in your land, which the LORD your God is giving you as your inheritance, and so that you will not be guilty of bloodshed.

[11]But if a man hates his neighbor and lies in wait for him, assaults and kills him, and then flees to one of these cities, [12]the elders of his town shall send for him, bring him back from the city, and hand him over to the avenger of blood to die. [13]Show him no pity. You must purge from Israel the guilt of shedding innocent blood, so that it may go well with you.

[14]Do not move your neighbor's boundary stone set up by your predecessors in the inheritance you receive in the land the LORD your God is giving you to possess.

WITNESSES

[15]One witness is not enough to convict a man accused of any crime or offense he may have committed. A matter must be established by the testimony of two or three witnesses.

[16]If a malicious witness takes the stand to accuse a man of a crime, [17]the two men involved in the dispute must stand in the presence of the LORD before the priests and the judges who are in office at the time. [18]The judges must make a thorough investigation, and if the witness proves to be a liar, giving false testimony against his brother, [19]then do to him as he intended to do to his brother. You must purge the evil from among

THE MESSAGE

his neighbor without premeditation and with no history of bad blood between them. For instance, a man goes with his neighbor into the woods to cut a tree; he swings the ax, the head slips off the handle and hits his neighbor, killing him. He may then flee to one of these cities and save his life. If the city is too far away, the avenger of blood racing in hot-blooded pursuit might catch him since it's such a long distance, and kill him even though he didn't deserve it. It wasn't his fault. There was no history of hatred between them. Therefore I command you: Set aside the three cities for yourselves.

19.8-10 When GOD, your God, enlarges your land, extending its borders as he solemnly promised your ancestors, by giving you the whole land he promised them because you are diligently living the way I'm commanding you today, namely, to love GOD, your God, and do what he tells you all your life; and when that happens, then add three more to these three cities so that there is no chance of innocent blood being spilled in your land. GOD, your God, is giving you this land as an inheritance—you don't want to pollute it with innocent blood and bring bloodguilt upon yourselves.

19.11-13 On the other hand, if a man with a history of hatred toward his neighbor waits in ambush, then jumps him, mauls and kills him, and then runs to one of these cities, that's a different story. The elders of his own city are to send for him and have him brought back. They are to hand him over to the avenger of blood for execution. Don't feel sorry for him. Clean out the pollution of wrongful murder from Israel so that you'll be able to live well and breathe clean air.

✛

19.14 Don't move your neighbor's boundary markers, the longstanding landmarks set up by your pioneer ancestors defining their property.

✛

19.15 You cannot convict anyone of a crime or sin on the word of one witness. You need two or three witnesses to make a case.

19.16-21 If a hostile witness stands to accuse someone of a wrong, then both parties involved in the quarrel must stand in the Presence of GOD before the priests and judges who are in office at that time. The judges must conduct a careful investigation; if the witness turns out to be a false witness and has lied against his fellow Israelite, give him the same medicine he intended for the other party. Clean the polluting evil

NEW INTERNATIONAL VERSION

you. ²⁰The rest of the people will hear of this and be afraid, and never again will such an evil thing be done among you. ²¹Show no pity: life for life, eye for eye, tooth for tooth, hand for hand, foot for foot.

GOING TO WAR

20 When you go to war against your enemies and see horses and chariots and an army greater than yours, do not be afraid of them, because the LORD your God, who brought you up out of Egypt, will be with you. ²When you are about to go into battle, the priest shall come forward and address the army. ³He shall say: "Hear, O Israel, today you are going into battle against your enemies. Do not be faint-hearted or afraid; do not be terrified or give way to panic before them. ⁴For the LORD your God is the one who goes with you to fight for you against your enemies to give you victory."

⁵The officers shall say to the army: "Has anyone built a new house and not dedicated it? Let him go home, or he may die in battle and someone else may dedicate it. ⁶Has anyone planted a vineyard and not begun to enjoy it? Let him go home, or he may die in battle and someone else enjoy it. ⁷Has anyone become pledged to a woman and not married her? Let him go home, or he may die in battle and someone else marry her." ⁸Then the officers shall add, "Is any man afraid or fainthearted? Let him go home so that his brothers will not become disheartened too." ⁹When the officers have finished speaking to the army, they shall appoint commanders over it.

¹⁰When you march up to attack a city, make its people an offer of peace. ¹¹If they accept and open their gates, all the people in it shall be subject to forced labor and shall work for you. ¹²If they refuse to make peace and they engage you in battle, lay siege to that city. ¹³When the LORD your God delivers it into your hand, put to the sword all the men in it. ¹⁴As for the women, the children, the livestock and everything else in the city, you may take these as plunder for yourselves. And you may use the plunder the LORD your God gives you from your enemies. ¹⁵This is how you are to treat all the cities that are at a distance from you and do not belong to the nations nearby.

¹⁶However, in the cities of the nations the LORD your God is giving you as an inheritance, do not leave alive anything that breathes. ¹⁷Completely destroy*a* them—the Hittites, Amorites,

a 17 The Hebrew term refers to the irrevocable giving over of things or persons to the LORD, often by totally destroying them.

THE MESSAGE

from your company. People will hear of what you've done and be impressed; that will put a stop to this kind of evil among you. Don't feel sorry for the person: It's life for life, eye for eye, tooth for tooth, hand for hand, foot for foot.

✛

20.1-4 **20** When you go to war against your enemy and see horses and chariots and soldiers far outnumbering you, do not recoil in fear of them; GOD, your God, who brought you up out of Egypt is with you. When the battle is about to begin, let the priest come forward and speak to the troops. He'll say, "Attention, Israel. In a few minutes you're going to do battle with your enemies. Don't waver in resolve. Don't fear. Don't hesitate. Don't panic. GOD, your God, is right there with you, fighting with you against your enemies, fighting to win."

20.5-7 Then let the officers step up and speak to the troops: "Is there a man here who has built a new house but hasn't yet dedicated it? Let him go home right now lest he die in battle and another man dedicate it. And is there a man here who has planted a vineyard but hasn't yet enjoyed the grapes? Let him go home right now lest he die in battle and another man enjoy the grapes. Is there a man here engaged to marry who hasn't yet taken his wife? Let him go home right now lest he die in battle and another man take her."

20.8 The officers will then continue, "And is there a man here who is wavering in resolve and afraid? Let him go home right now so that he doesn't infect his fellows with his timidity and cowardly spirit."

20.9 When the officers have finished speaking to the troops, let them appoint commanders of the troops who shall muster them by units.

20.10-15 When you come up against a city to attack it, call out, "Peace?" If they answer, "Yes, peace!" and open the city to you, then everyone found there will be conscripted as forced laborers and work for you. But if they don't settle for peace and insist on war, then go ahead and attack. GOD, your God, will give them to you. Kill all the men with your swords. But don't kill the women and children and animals. Everything inside the town you can take as plunder for you to use and eat—GOD, your God, gives it to you. This is the way you deal with the distant towns, the towns that don't belong to the nations at hand.

20.16-18 But with the towns of the people that GOD, your God, is giving you as an inheritance, it's different: don't leave anyone alive. Consign them to holy destruction: the Hittites, Amo-

NEW INTERNATIONAL VERSION

Canaanites, Perizzites, Hivites and Jebusites—as the LORD your God has commanded you. [18]Otherwise, they will teach you to follow all the detestable things they do in worshiping their gods, and you will sin against the LORD your God.

[19]When you lay siege to a city for a long time, fighting against it to capture it, do not destroy its trees by putting an ax to them, because you can eat their fruit. Do not cut them down. Are the trees of the field people, that you should besiege them?[a] [20]However, you may cut down trees that you know are not fruit trees and use them to build siege works until the city at war with you falls.

ATONEMENT FOR AN UNSOLVED MURDER

21 If a man is found slain, lying in a field in the land the LORD your God is giving you to possess, and it is not known who killed him, [2]your elders and judges shall go out and measure the distance from the body to the neighboring towns. [3]Then the elders of the town nearest the body shall take a heifer that has never been worked and has never worn a yoke [4]and lead her down to a valley that has not been plowed or planted and where there is a flowing stream. There in the valley they are to break the heifer's neck. [5]The priests, the sons of Levi, shall step forward, for the LORD your God has chosen them to minister and to pronounce blessings in the name of the LORD and to decide all cases of dispute and assault. [6]Then all the elders of the town nearest the body shall wash their hands over the heifer whose neck was broken in the valley, [7]and they shall declare: "Our hands did not shed this blood, nor did our eyes see it done. [8]Accept this atonement for your people Israel, whom you have redeemed, O LORD, and do not hold your people guilty of the blood of an innocent man." And the bloodshed will be atoned for. [9]So you will purge from yourselves the guilt of shedding innocent blood, since you have done what is right in the eyes of the LORD.

MARRYING A CAPTIVE WOMAN

[10]When you go to war against your enemies and the LORD your God delivers them into your hands and you take captives, [11]if you notice among the captives a beautiful woman and are attracted to her, you may take her as your wife. [12]Bring her into your home and have her shave her head, trim her nails [13]and put aside the clothes she was wearing when captured. After

---

[a] 19 Or *down to use in the siege, for the fruit trees are for the benefit of man.*

THE MESSAGE

rites, Canaanites, Perizzites, Hivites, and Jebusites, obeying the command of GOD, your God. This is so there won't be any of them left to teach you to practice the abominations that they engage in with their gods and you end up sinning against GOD, your God.

20.19-20 When you mount an attack on a town and the siege goes on a long time, don't start cutting down the trees, swinging your axes against them. Those trees are your future food; don't cut them down. Are trees soldiers who come against you with weapons? The exception can be those trees which don't produce food; you can chop them down and use the timbers to build siege engines against the town that is resisting you until it falls.

✝

21.1-8 **21** If a dead body is found on the ground, this ground that GOD, your God, has given you, lying out in the open, and no one knows who killed him, your leaders and judges are to go out and measure the distance from the body to the nearest cities. The leaders and judges of the city that is nearest the corpse will then take a heifer that has never been used for work, never had a yoke on it. The leaders will take the heifer to a valley with a stream, a valley that has never been plowed or planted, and there break the neck of the heifer. The Levitical priests will then step up. GOD has chosen them to serve him in these matters by settling legal disputes and violent crimes and by pronouncing blessings in GOD's name. Finally, all the leaders of that town that is nearest the body will wash their hands over the heifer that had its neck broken at the stream and say, "We didn't kill this man and we didn't see who did it. Purify your people Israel whom you redeemed, O GOD. Clear your people Israel from any guilt in this murder."

21.8-9 That will clear them from any responsibility in the murder. By following these procedures you will have absolved yourselves of any part in the murder because you will have done what is right in GOD's sight.

✝

21.10-14 When you go to war against your enemies and GOD, your God, gives you victory and you take prisoners, and then you notice among the prisoners of war a good-looking woman whom you find attractive and would like to marry, this is what you do: Take her home; have her trim her hair, cut her nails, and discard the clothes she was wearing when captured. She is then to stay

NEW INTERNATIONAL VERSION

she has lived in your house and mourned her father and mother for a full month, then you may go to her and be her husband and she shall be your wife. [14]If you are not pleased with her, let her go wherever she wishes. You must not sell her or treat her as a slave, since you have dishonored her.

THE RIGHT OF THE FIRSTBORN

[15]If a man has two wives, and he loves one but not the other, and both bear him sons but the firstborn is the son of the wife he does not love, [16]when he wills his property to his sons, he must not give the rights of the firstborn to the son of the wife he loves in preference to his actual firstborn, the son of the wife he does not love. [17]He must acknowledge the son of his unloved wife as the firstborn by giving him a double share of all he has. That son is the first sign of his father's strength. The right of the firstborn belongs to him.

A REBELLIOUS SON

[18]If a man has a stubborn and rebellious son who does not obey his father and mother and will not listen to them when they discipline him, [19]his father and mother shall take hold of him and bring him to the elders at the gate of his town. [20]They shall say to the elders, "This son of ours is stubborn and rebellious. He will not obey us. He is a profligate and a drunkard." [21]Then all the men of his town shall stone him to death. You must purge the evil from among you. All Israel will hear of it and be afraid.

VARIOUS LAWS

[22]If a man guilty of a capital offense is put to death and his body is hung on a tree, [23]you must not leave his body on the tree overnight. Be sure to bury him that same day, because anyone who is hung on a tree is under God's curse. You must not desecrate the land the LORD your God is giving you as an inheritance.

22 If you see your brother's ox or sheep straying, do not ignore it but be sure to take it back to him. [2]If the brother does not live near you or if you do not know who he is, take it home with you and keep it until he comes looking for it. Then give it back to him. [3]Do the same if you find your brother's donkey or his cloak or anything he loses. Do not ignore it.

[4]If you see your brother's donkey or his ox

THE MESSAGE

in your home for a full month, mourning her father and mother. Then you may go to bed with her as husband and wife. If it turns out you don't like her, you must let her go and live wherever she wishes. But you can't sell her or use her as a slave since you've humiliated her.

✛

21.15-17 When a man has two wives, one loved and the other hated, and they both give him sons, but the firstborn is from the hated wife, at the time he divides the inheritance with his sons he must not treat the son of the loved wife as the firstborn, cutting out the son of the hated wife, who is the actual firstborn. No, he must acknowledge the inheritance rights of the real firstborn, the son of the hated wife, by giving him a double share of the inheritance: that son is the first proof of his virility; the rights of the firstborn belong to him.

✛

21.18-20 When a man has a stubborn son, a real rebel who won't do a thing his mother and father tell him, and even though they discipline him he still won't obey, his father and mother shall forcibly bring him before the leaders at the city gate and say to the city fathers, "This son of ours is a stubborn rebel; he won't listen to a thing we say. He's a glutton and a drunk."

21.21 Then all the men of the town are to throw rocks at him until he's dead. You will have purged the evil pollution from among you. All Israel will hear what's happened and be in awe.

✛

21.22-23 When a man has committed a capital crime, been given the death sentence, executed and hung from a tree, don't leave his dead body hanging overnight from the tree. Give him a decent burial that same day so that you don't desecrate your GOD-given land—a hanged man is an insult to God.

22.1-3 **22** If you see your kinsman's ox or sheep wandering off loose, don't look the other way as if you didn't see it. Return it promptly. If your fellow Israelite is not close by or you don't know whose it is, take the animal home with you and take care of it until your fellow asks about it. Then return it to him. Do the same if it's his donkey or a piece of clothing or anything else your fellow Israelite loses. Don't look the other way as if you didn't see it.

22.4 If you see your fellow's donkey or ox injured

NEW INTERNATIONAL VERSION	THE MESSAGE

NEW INTERNATIONAL VERSION

fallen on the road, do not ignore it. Help him get it to its feet.

⁵A woman must not wear men's clothing, nor a man wear women's clothing, for the LORD your God detests anyone who does this.

⁶If you come across a bird's nest beside the road, either in a tree or on the ground, and the mother is sitting on the young or on the eggs, do not take the mother with the young. ⁷You may take the young, but be sure to let the mother go, so that it may go well with you and you may have a long life.

⁸When you build a new house, make a parapet around your roof so that you may not bring the guilt of bloodshed on your house if someone falls from the roof.

⁹Do not plant two kinds of seed in your vineyard; if you do, not only the crops you plant but also the fruit of the vineyard will be defiled. ᵃ

¹⁰Do not plow with an ox and a donkey yoked together.

¹¹Do not wear clothes of wool and linen woven together.

¹²Make tassels on the four corners of the cloak you wear.

MARRIAGE VIOLATIONS

¹³If a man takes a wife and, after lying with her, dislikes her ¹⁴and slanders her and gives her a bad name, saying, "I married this woman, but when I approached her, I did not find proof of her virginity," ¹⁵then the girl's father and mother shall bring proof that she was a virgin to the town elders at the gate. ¹⁶The girl's father will say to the elders, "I gave my daughter in marriage to this man, but he dislikes her. ¹⁷Now he has slandered her and said, 'I did not find your daughter to be a virgin.' But here is the proof of my daughter's virginity." Then her parents shall display the cloth before the elders of the town, ¹⁸and the elders shall take the man and punish him. ¹⁹They shall fine him a hundred shekels of silver ᵇ and give them to the girl's father, because this man has given an Israelite virgin a bad name. She shall continue to be his wife; he must not divorce her as long as he lives.

²⁰If, however, the charge is true and no proof of the girl's virginity can be found, ²¹she shall be brought to the door of her father's house and there the men of her town shall stone her to death. She has done a disgraceful thing in Israel by being promiscuous while still in her father's house. You must purge the evil from among you.

²²If a man is found sleeping with another

THE MESSAGE

along the road, don't look the other way. Help him get it up and on its way.

22.5   A woman must not wear a man's clothing, nor a man wear women's clothing. This kind of thing is an abomination to GOD, your God.

22.6-7   When you come across a bird's nest alongside the road, whether in a tree or on the ground, and the mother is sitting on the young or on the eggs, don't take the mother with the young. You may take the babies, but let the mother go so that you will live a good and long life.

22.8   When you build a new house, make a parapet around your roof to make it safe so that someone doesn't fall off and die and your family become responsible for the death.

22.9   Don't plant two kinds of seed in your vineyard. If you do, you will forfeit what you've sown, the total production of the vineyard.

22.10   Don't plow with an ox and a donkey yoked together.

22.11   Don't wear clothes of mixed fabrics, wool and linen together.

22.12   Make tassels on the four corners of the cloak you use to cover yourself.

22.13-19   If a man marries a woman, sleeps with her, and then turns on her, calling her a slut, giving her a bad name, saying, "I married this woman, but when I slept with her I discovered she wasn't a virgin," then the father and mother of the girl are to take her with the proof of her virginity to the town leaders at the gate. The father is to tell the leaders, "I gave my daughter to this man as wife and he turned on her, rejecting her. And now he has slanderously accused her, claiming that she wasn't a virgin. But look at this, here is the proof of my daughter's virginity." And then he is to spread out her blood-stained wedding garment before the leaders for their examination. The town leaders then are to take the husband, whip him, fine him a hundred pieces of silver, and give it to the father of the girl. The man gave a virgin girl of Israel a bad name. He has to keep her as his wife and can never divorce her.

22.20-21   But if it turns out that the accusation is true and there is no evidence of the girl's virginity, the men of the town are to take her to the door of her father's house and stone her to death. She acted disgracefully in Israel. She lived like a whore while still in her parents' home. Purge the evil from among you.

22.22   If a man is found sleeping with another

ᵃ 9 Or *be forfeited to the sanctuary*   ᵇ 19 That is, about 2 1/2 pounds (about 1 kilogram)

NEW INTERNATIONAL VERSION

man's wife, both the man who slept with her and the woman must die. You must purge the evil from Israel.

23If a man happens to meet in a town a virgin pledged to be married and he sleeps with her, 24you shall take both of them to the gate of that town and stone them to death—the girl because she was in a town and did not scream for help, and the man because he violated another man's wife. You must purge the evil from among you.

25But if out in the country a man happens to meet a girl pledged to be married and rapes her, only the man who has done this shall die. 26Do nothing to the girl; she has committed no sin deserving death. This case is like that of someone who attacks and murders his neighbor, 27for the man found the girl out in the country, and though the betrothed girl screamed, there was no one to rescue her.

28If a man happens to meet a virgin who is not pledged to be married and rapes her and they are discovered, 29he shall pay the girl's father fifty shekels of silver.*a* He must marry the girl, for he has violated her. He can never divorce her as long as he lives.

30A man is not to marry his father's wife; he must not dishonor his father's bed.

EXCLUSION FROM THE ASSEMBLY

23 No one who has been emasculated by crushing or cutting may enter the assembly of the LORD.

2No one born of a forbidden marriage*b* nor any of his descendants may enter the assembly of the LORD, even down to the tenth generation.

3No Ammonite or Moabite or any of his descendants may enter the assembly of the LORD, even down to the tenth generation. 4For they did not come to meet you with bread and water on your way when you came out of Egypt, and they hired Balaam son of Beor from Pethor in Aram Naharaim*c* to pronounce a curse on you. 5However, the LORD your God would not listen to Balaam but turned the curse into a blessing for you, because the LORD your God loves you. 6Do not seek a treaty of friendship with them as long as you live.

7Do not abhor an Edomite, for he is your brother. Do not abhor an Egyptian, because you lived as an alien in his country. 8The third generation of children born to them may enter the assembly of the LORD.

THE MESSAGE

man's wife, both must die. Purge that evil from Israel.

22.23-24 If a man comes upon a virgin in town, a girl who is engaged to another man, and sleeps with her, take both of them to the town gate and stone them until they die—the girl because she didn't yell out for help in the town and the man because he raped her, violating the fiancée of his neighbor. You must purge the evil from among you.

22.25-27 But if it was out in the country that the man found the engaged girl and grabbed and raped her, only the man is to die, the man who raped her. Don't do anything to the girl; she did nothing wrong. This is similar to the case of a man who comes across his neighbor out in the country and murders him; when the engaged girl yelled out for help, there was no one around to hear or help her.

22.28-29 When a man comes upon a virgin who has never been engaged and grabs and rapes her and they are found out, the man who raped her has to give her father fifty pieces of silver. He has to marry her because he took advantage of her. And he can never divorce her.

22.30 A man may not marry his father's ex-wife—that would violate his father's rights.

✝

23.1 **23** No eunuch is to enter the congregation of GOD.

23.2 No bastard is to enter the congregation of GOD, even to the tenth generation, nor any of his children.

23.3-6 No Ammonite or Moabite is to enter the congregation of GOD, even to the tenth generation, nor any of his children, ever. Those nations didn't treat you with hospitality on your travels out of Egypt, and on top of that they also hired Balaam son of Beor from Pethor in Mesopotamia to curse you. GOD, your God, refused to listen to Balaam but turned the curse into a blessing—how GOD, your God, loves you! Don't even try to get along with them or do anything for them, ever.

23.7 But don't spurn an Edomite; he's your kin.

And don't spurn an Egyptian; you were a foreigner in his land.

23.8 Children born to Edomites and Egyptians may enter the congregation of GOD in the third generation.

✝

---

a 29 That is, about 1 1/4 pounds (about 0.6 kilogram)
b 2 Or *one of illegitimate birth*   *c* 4 That is, Northwest Mesopotamia

NEW INTERNATIONAL VERSION

UNCLEANNESS IN THE CAMP

⁹When you are encamped against your enemies, keep away from everything impure. ¹⁰If one of your men is unclean because of a nocturnal emission, he is to go outside the camp and stay there. ¹¹But as evening approaches he is to wash himself, and at sunset he may return to the camp.

¹²Designate a place outside the camp where you can go to relieve yourself. ¹³As part of your equipment have something to dig with, and when you relieve yourself, dig a hole and cover up your excrement. ¹⁴For the LORD your God moves about in your camp to protect you and to deliver your enemies to you. Your camp must be holy, so that he will not see among you anything indecent and turn away from you.

MISCELLANEOUS LAWS

¹⁵If a slave has taken refuge with you, do not hand him over to his master. ¹⁶Let him live among you wherever he likes and in whatever town he chooses. Do not oppress him.

¹⁷No Israelite man or woman is to become a shrine prostitute. ¹⁸You must not bring the earnings of a female prostitute or of a male prostitute^a into the house of the LORD your God to pay any vow, because the LORD your God detests them both.

¹⁹Do not charge your brother interest, whether on money or food or anything else that may earn interest. ²⁰You may charge a foreigner interest, but not a brother Israelite, so that the LORD your God may bless you in everything you put your hand to in the land you are entering to possess.

²¹If you make a vow to the LORD your God, do not be slow to pay it, for the LORD your God will certainly demand it of you and you will be guilty of sin. ²²But if you refrain from making a vow, you will not be guilty. ²³Whatever your lips utter you must be sure to do, because you made your vow freely to the LORD your God with your own mouth.

²⁴If you enter your neighbor's vineyard, you may eat all the grapes you want, but do not put any in your basket. ²⁵If you enter your neighbor's grainfield, you may pick kernels with your hands, but you must not put a sickle to his standing grain.

THE MESSAGE

23:9-11 When you are camped out, at war with your enemies, be careful to keep yourself from anything ritually defiling. If one of your men has become ritually unclean because of a nocturnal emission, he must go outside the camp and stay there until evening when he can wash himself, returning to the camp at sunset.

23:12-14 Mark out an area outside the camp where you can go to relieve yourselves. Along with your weapons have a stick with you. After you relieve yourself, dig a hole with the stick and cover your excrement. GOD, your God, strolls through your camp; he's present to deliver you and give you victory over your enemies. Keep your camp holy; don't permit anything indecent or offensive in GOD's eyes.

✠

23:15-16 Don't return a runaway slave to his master; he's come to you for refuge. Let him live wherever he wishes within the protective gates of your city. Don't take advantage of him.

23:17-18 No daughter of Israel is to become a sacred prostitute; and no son of Israel is to become a sacred prostitute. And don't bring the fee of a sacred whore or the earnings of a priest-pimp to the house of GOD, your God, to pay for any vow—they are both an abomination to GOD, your God.

23:19-20 Don't charge interest to your kinsmen on any loan: not for money or food or clothing or anything else that could earn interest. You may charge foreigners interest, but you may not charge your brothers interest; that way GOD, your God, will bless all the work that you take up and the land that you are entering to possess.

23:21-23 When you make a vow to GOD, your God, don't put off keeping it; GOD, your God, expects you to keep it and if you don't you're guilty. But if you don't make a vow in the first place, there's no sin. If you say you're going to do something, do it. Keep the vow you willingly vowed to GOD, your God. You promised it, so do it.

23:24-25 When you enter your neighbor's vineyard, you may eat all the grapes you want until you're full, but you may not put any in your bucket or bag. And when you walk through the ripe grain of your neighbor, you may pick the heads of grain, but you may not swing your sickle there.

a 18 Hebrew of a dog

NEW INTERNATIONAL VERSION

24 If a man marries a woman who becomes displeasing to him because he finds something indecent about her, and he writes her a certificate of divorce, gives it to her and sends her from his house, ²and if after she leaves his house she becomes the wife of another man, ³and her second husband dislikes her and writes her a certificate of divorce, gives it to her and sends her from his house, or if he dies, ⁴then her first husband, who divorced her, is not allowed to marry her again after she has been defiled. That would be detestable in the eyes of the LORD. Do not bring sin upon the land the LORD your God is giving you as an inheritance.

⁵If a man has recently married, he must not be sent to war or have any other duty laid on him. For one year he is to be free to stay at home and bring happiness to the wife he has married.

⁶Do not take a pair of millstones—not even the upper one—as security for a debt, because that would be taking a man's livelihood as security.

⁷If a man is caught kidnapping one of his brother Israelites and treats him as a slave or sells him, the kidnapper must die. You must purge the evil from among you.

⁸In cases of leprous*ᵃ* diseases be very careful to do exactly as the priests, who are Levites, instruct you. You must follow carefully what I have commanded them. ⁹Remember what the LORD your God did to Miriam along the way after you came out of Egypt.

¹⁰When you make a loan of any kind to your neighbor, do not go into his house to get what he is offering as a pledge. ¹¹Stay outside and let the man to whom you are making the loan bring the pledge out to you. ¹²If the man is poor, do not go to sleep with his pledge in your possession. ¹³Return his cloak to him by sunset so that he may sleep in it. Then he will thank you, and it will be regarded as a righteous act in the sight of the LORD your God.

¹⁴Do not take advantage of a hired man who is poor and needy, whether he is a brother Israelite or an alien living in one of your towns. ¹⁵Pay him his wages each day before sunset, because he is poor and is counting on it. Otherwise he may cry to the LORD against you, and you will be guilty of sin.

¹⁶Fathers shall not be put to death for their children, nor children put to death for their fathers; each is to die for his own sin.

¹⁷Do not deprive the alien or the fatherless of justice, or take the cloak of the widow as a pledge. ¹⁸Remember that you were slaves in

ᵃ 8 The Hebrew word was used for various diseases affecting the skin—not necessarily leprosy.

THE MESSAGE

24 ²⁴·¹⁻⁴ If a man marries a woman and then it happens that he no longer likes her because he has found something wrong with her, he may give her divorce papers, put them in her hand, and send her off. After she leaves, if she becomes another man's wife and he also comes to hate her and this second husband also gives her divorce papers, puts them in her hand, and sends her off, or if he should die, then the first husband who divorced her can't marry her again. She has made herself ritually unclean, and her remarriage would be an abomination in the Presence of GOD and defile the land with sin, this land that GOD, your God, is giving you as an inheritance.

²⁴·⁵ When a man takes a new wife, he is not to go out with the army or be given any business or work duties. He gets one year off simply to be at home making his wife happy.

²⁴·⁶ Don't seize a handmill or an upper millstone as collateral for a loan. You'd be seizing someone's very life.

²⁴·⁷ If a man is caught kidnapping one of his kinsmen, someone of the People of Israel, to enslave or sell him, the kidnapper must die. Purge that evil from among you.

²⁴·⁸⁻⁹ Warning! If a serious skin disease breaks out, follow exactly the rules set down by the Levitical priests. Follow them precisely as I commanded them. Don't forget what GOD, your God, did to Miriam on your way out of Egypt.

²⁴·¹⁰⁻¹³ When you make a loan of any kind to your neighbor, don't enter his house to claim his pledge. Wait outside. Let the man to whom you made the pledge bring the pledge to you outside. And if he is destitute, don't use his cloak as a bedroll; return it to him at nightfall so that he can sleep in his cloak and bless you. In the sight of GOD, your God, that will be viewed as a righteous act.

²⁴·¹⁴⁻¹⁵ Don't abuse a laborer who is destitute and needy, whether he is a fellow Israelite living in your land and in your city. Pay him at the end of each workday; he's living from hand to mouth and needs it now. If you hold back his pay, he'll protest to GOD and you'll have sin on your books.

²⁴·¹⁶ Parents shall not be put to death for their children, nor children for their parents. Each person shall be put to death for his own sin.

²⁴·¹⁷⁻¹⁸ Make sure foreigners and orphans get their just rights. Don't take the cloak of a widow as security for a loan. Don't ever forget that you

NEW INTERNATIONAL VERSION

Egypt and the LORD your God redeemed you from there. That is why I command you to do this. ¹⁹When you are harvesting in your field and you overlook a sheaf, do not go back to get it. Leave it for the alien, the fatherless and the widow, so that the LORD your God may bless you in all the work of your hands. ²⁰When you beat the olives from your trees, do not go over the branches a second time. Leave what remains for the alien, the fatherless and the widow. ²¹When you harvest the grapes in your vineyard, do not go over the vines again. Leave what remains for the alien, the fatherless and the widow. ²²Remember that you were slaves in Egypt. That is why I command you to do this.

25 When men have a dispute, they are to take it to court and the judges will decide the case, acquitting the innocent and condemning the guilty. ²If the guilty man deserves to be beaten, the judge shall make him lie down and have him flogged in his presence with the number of lashes his crime deserves, ³but he must not give him more than forty lashes. If he is flogged more than that, your brother will be degraded in your eyes.

⁴Do not muzzle an ox while it is treading out the grain.

⁵If brothers are living together and one of them dies without a son, his widow must not marry outside the family. Her husband's brother shall take her and marry her and fulfill the duty of a brother-in-law to her. ⁶The first son she bears shall carry on the name of the dead brother so that his name will not be blotted out from Israel.

⁷However, if a man does not want to marry his brother's wife, she shall go to the elders at the town gate and say, "My husband's brother refuses to carry on his brother's name in Israel. He will not fulfill the duty of a brother-in-law to me." ⁸Then the elders of his town shall summon him and talk to him. If he persists in saying, "I do not want to marry her," ⁹his brother's widow shall go up to him in the presence of the elders, take off one of his sandals, spit in his face and say, "This is what is done to the man who will not build up his brother's family line." ¹⁰That man's line shall be known in Israel as The Family of the Unsandaled.

¹¹If two men are fighting and the wife of one of them comes to rescue her husband from his assailant, and she reaches out and seizes him by his private parts, ¹²you shall cut off her hand. Show her no pity.

THE MESSAGE

were once slaves in Egypt and GOD, your God, got you out of there. I command you: Do what I'm telling you.

24.19-22 When you harvest your grain and forget a sheaf back in the field, don't go back and get it; leave it for the foreigner, the orphan, and the widow so that GOD, your God, will bless you in all your work. When you shake the olives off your trees, don't go back over the branches and strip them bare—what's left is for the foreigner, the orphan, and the widow. And when you cut the grapes in your vineyard, don't take every last grape—leave a few for the foreigner, the orphan, and the widow. Don't ever forget that you were a slave in Egypt. I command you: Do what I'm telling you.

25.1-3 **25** When men have a legal dispute, let them go to court; the judges will decide between them, declaring one innocent and the other guilty. If the guilty one deserves punishment, the judge will have him prostrate himself before him and lashed as many times as his crime deserves, but not more than forty. If you hit him more than forty times, you will degrade him to something less than human.

25.4 Don't muzzle an ox while it is threshing.

25.5-6 When brothers are living together and one of them dies without having had a son, the widow of the dead brother shall not marry a stranger from outside the family; her husband's brother is to come to her and marry her and do the brother-in-law's duty by her. The first son that she bears shall be named after her dead husband so his name won't die out in Israel.

25.7-10 But if the brother doesn't want to marry his sister-in-law, she is to go to the leaders at the city gate and say, "My brother-in-law refuses to keep his brother's name alive in Israel; he won't agree to do the brother-in-law's duty by me." Then the leaders will call for the brother and confront him. If he stands there defiant and says, "I don't want her," his sister-in-law is to pull his sandal off his foot, spit in his face, and say, "This is what happens to the man who refuses to build up the family of his brother—his name in Israel will be Family-No-Sandal."

25.11-12 When two men are in a fight and the wife of the one man, trying to rescue her husband, grabs the genitals of the man hitting him, you are to cut off her hand. Show no pity.

NEW INTERNATIONAL VERSION

¹³Do not have two differing weights in your bag—one heavy, one light. ¹⁴Do not have two differing measures in your house—one large, one small. ¹⁵You must have accurate and honest weights and measures, so that you may live long in the land the LORD your God is giving you. ¹⁶For the LORD your God detests anyone who does these things, anyone who deals dishonestly.

¹⁷Remember what the Amalekites did to you along the way when you came out of Egypt. ¹⁸When you were weary and worn out, they met you on your journey and cut off all who were lagging behind; they had no fear of God. ¹⁹When the LORD your God gives you rest from all the enemies around you in the land he is giving you to possess as an inheritance, you shall blot out the memory of Amalek from under heaven. Do not forget!

FIRSTFRUITS AND TITHES

26 When you have entered the land the LORD your God is giving you as an inheritance and have taken possession of it and settled in it, ²take some of the firstfruits of all that you produce from the soil of the land the LORD your God is giving you and put them in a basket. Then go to the place the LORD your God will choose as a dwelling for his Name ³and say to the priest in office at the time, "I declare today to the LORD your God that I have come to the land the LORD swore to our forefathers to give us." ⁴The priest shall take the basket from your hands and set it down in front of the altar of the LORD your God. ⁵Then you shall declare before the LORD your God: "My father was a wandering Aramean, and he went down into Egypt with a few people and lived there and became a great nation, powerful and numerous. ⁶But the Egyptians mistreated us and made us suffer, putting us to hard labor. ⁷Then we cried out to the LORD, the God of our fathers, and the LORD heard our voice and saw our misery, toil and oppression. ⁸So the LORD brought us out of Egypt with a mighty hand and an outstretched arm, with great terror and with miraculous signs and wonders. ⁹He brought us to this place and gave us this land, a land flowing with milk and honey; ¹⁰and

THE MESSAGE

25.13-16   Don't carry around with you two weights, one heavy and the other light, and don't keep two measures at hand, one large and the other small. Use only one weight, a true and honest weight, and one measure, a true and honest measure, so that you will live a long time on the land that GOD, your God, is giving you. Dishonest weights and measures are an abomination to GOD, your God—all this corruption in business deals!

25.17-19   Don't forget what Amalek did to you on the road after you left Egypt, how he attacked you when you were tired, barely able to put one foot in front of another, mercilessly cut off your stragglers, and had no regard for God. When GOD, your God, gives you rest from all the enemies that surround you in the inheritance-land GOD, your God, is giving you to possess, you are to wipe the name of Amalek from off the Earth. Don't forget!

26.1-5   **26** Once you enter the land that GOD, your God, is giving you as an inheritance and take it over and settle down, you are to take some of all the firstfruits of what you grow in the land that GOD, your God, is giving you, put them in a basket and go to the place GOD, your God, sets apart for you to worship him. At that time, go to the priest who is there and say, "I announce to GOD, your God, today that I have entered the land that GOD promised our ancestors that he'd give to us." The priest will take the basket from you and place it on the Altar of GOD, your God. And there in the Presence of GOD, your God, you will recite,

26.5-10
A wandering Aramean was my father,
    he went down to Egypt and sojourned there,
    he and just a handful of his brothers at first, but soon
    they became a great nation, mighty and many.
The Egyptians abused and battered us,
    in a cruel and savage slavery.
We cried out to GOD, the God-of-Our-Fathers:
He listened to our voice, he saw
    our destitution, our trouble, our cruel plight.
And GOD took us out of Egypt
    with his strong hand and long arm, terrible and great,
    with signs and miracle-wonders.
And he brought us to this place,

NEW INTERNATIONAL VERSION

now I bring the firstfruits of the soil that you, O LORD, have given me." Place the basket before the LORD your God and bow down before him. [11]And you and the Levites and the aliens among you shall rejoice in all the good things the LORD your God has given to you and your household.

[12]When you have finished setting aside a tenth of all your produce in the third year, the year of the tithe, you shall give it to the Levite, the alien, the fatherless and the widow, so that they may eat in your towns and be satisfied. [13]Then say to the LORD your God: "I have removed from my house the sacred portion and have given it to the Levite, the alien, the fatherless and the widow, according to all you commanded. I have not turned aside from your commands nor have I forgotten any of them. [14]I have not eaten any of the sacred portion while I was in mourning, nor have I removed any of it while I was unclean, nor have I offered any of it to the dead. I have obeyed the LORD my God; I have done everything you commanded me. [15]Look down from heaven, your holy dwelling place, and bless your people Israel and the land you have given us as you promised on oath to our forefathers, a land flowing with milk and honey."

FOLLOW THE LORD'S COMMANDS

[16]The LORD your God commands you this day to follow these decrees and laws; carefully observe them with all your heart and with all your soul. [17]You have declared this day that the LORD is your God and that you will walk in his ways, that you will keep his decrees, commands and laws, and that you will obey him. [18]And the LORD has declared this day that you are his people, his treasured possession as he promised, and that you are to keep all his commands. [19]He has declared that he will set you in praise, fame and honor high above all the nations he has made

THE MESSAGE

gave us this land flowing with milk and
    honey.
So here I am. I've brought the firstfruits
    of what I've grown on this ground you
    gave me, O GOD.

26.10-11   Then place it in the Presence of GOD, your God. Prostrate yourselves in the Presence of GOD, your God. And rejoice! Celebrate all the good things that GOD, your God, has given you and your family; you and the Levite and the foreigner who lives with you.

✝

26.12-14 Every third year, the year of the tithe, give a tenth of your produce to the Levite, the foreigner, the orphan, and the widow so that they may eat their fill in your cities. And then, in the Presence of GOD, your God, say this:

I have brought the sacred share,
I've given it to the Levite, foreigner,
    orphan, and widow.
What you commanded, I've done.
I haven't detoured around your
    commands,
I haven't forgotten a single one.
I haven't eaten from the sacred share
    while mourning,
I haven't removed any of it while ritually
    unclean,
I haven't used it in funeral feasts,
I have listened obediently to the Voice of
    GOD, my God,
I have lived the way you commanded
    me.

26.15   Look down from your holy house in
    Heaven!
Bless your people Israel and the ground
    you gave us,
just as you promised our ancestors you
    would,
this land flowing with milk and honey.

✝

26.16-17 This very day GOD, your God, commands you to follow these rules and regulations, to live them out with everything you have in you. You've renewed your vows today that GOD is your God, that you'll live the way he shows you; do what he tells you in the rules, regulations, and commandments; and listen obediently to him.

26.18-19 And today GOD has reaffirmed that you are dearly held treasure just as he promised, a people entrusted with keeping his commandments, a people set high above all other nations that he's made, high in praise, fame, and honor:

NEW INTERNATIONAL VERSION

and that you will be a people holy to the LORD your God, as he promised.

THE ALTAR ON MOUNT EBAL

27 Moses and the elders of Israel command-ed the people: "Keep all these commands that I give you today. ²When you have crossed the Jordan into the land the LORD your God is giving you, set up some large stones and coat them with plaster. ³Write on them all the words of this law when you have crossed over to enter the land the LORD your God is giving you, a land flowing with milk and honey, just as the LORD, the God of your fathers, promised you. ⁴And when you have crossed the Jordan, set up these stones on Mount Ebal, as I command you today, and coat them with plaster. ⁵Build there an altar to the LORD your God, an altar of stones. Do not use any iron tool upon them. ⁶Build the altar of the LORD your God with fieldstones and offer burnt offerings on it to the LORD your God. ⁷Sac-rifice fellowship offerings*ᵃ* there, eating them and rejoicing in the presence of the LORD your God. ⁸And you shall write very clearly all the words of this law on these stones you have set up."

CURSES FROM MOUNT EBAL

⁹Then Moses and the priests, who are Levites, said to all Israel, "Be silent, O Israel, and listen! You have now become the people of the LORD your God. ¹⁰Obey the LORD your God and follow his commands and decrees that I give you to-day."

¹¹On the same day Moses commanded the people:

¹²When you have crossed the Jordan, these tribes shall stand on Mount Gerizim to bless the people: Simeon, Levi, Judah, Issachar, Joseph and Benjamin. ¹³And these tribes shall stand on Mount Ebal to pronounce curses: Reuben, Gad, Asher, Zebulun, Dan and Naphtali.

¹⁴The Levites shall recite to all the people of Israel in a loud voice:

¹⁵"Cursed is the man who carves an im-age or casts an idol—a thing detestable to the LORD, the work of the craftsman's hands—and sets it up in secret."

Then all the people shall say,
"Amen!"

¹⁶"Cursed is the man who dishonors his father or his mother."

Then all the people shall say,
"Amen!"

ᵃ 7 Traditionally peace offerings

THE MESSAGE

you're a people holy to GOD, your God. That's what he has promised.

✛

27.1-3 **27** Moses commanded the leaders of Israel and charged the people: Keep every commandment that I command you today. On the day you cross the Jordan into the land that GOD, your God, is giving you, erect large stones and coat them with plaster. As soon as you cross over the river, write on the stones all the words of this Revelation so that you'll enter the land that GOD, your God, is giving you, that land flowing with milk and honey that GOD, the God-of-Your-Fathers, promised you.

27.4-7 So when you've crossed the Jordan, erect these stones on Mount Ebal. Then coat them with plaster. Build an Altar of stones for GOD, your God, there on the mountain. Don't use an iron tool on the stones; build the Altar to GOD, your God, with uncut stones and offer your Whole-Burnt-Offerings on it to GOD, your God. When you sacrifice your Peace-Offerings you will also eat them there, rejoicing in the Pres-ence of GOD, your God.

27.8 Write all the words of this Revelation on the stones. Incise them sharply.

27.9-10 Moses and the Levitical priests addressed all Israel: Quiet. Listen obediently, Israel. This very day you have become the people of GOD, your God. Listen to the Voice of GOD, your God. Keep his commandments and regulations that I'm commanding you today.

27.11-13 That day Moses commanded: After you've crossed the Jordan, these tribes will stand on Mount Gerizim to bless the people: Simeon, Levi, Judah, Issachar, Joseph, and Benjamin. And these will stand on Mount Ebal for the curse: Reuben, Gad, Asher, Zebulun, Dan, and Naphtali.

27.14-26 The Levites, acting as spokesmen and speak-ing loudly, will address Israel:

GOD's curse on anyone who carves or casts a god-image—an abomination to GOD made by a craftsman—and sets it up in secret.

All respond: *Yes. Absolutely.*

GOD's curse on anyone who demeans a parent.

All respond: *Yes. Absolutely.*

<table>
<tr><td>

NEW INTERNATIONAL VERSION

¹⁷"Cursed is the man who moves his neighbor's boundary stone."

Then all the people shall say, "Amen!"

¹⁸"Cursed is the man who leads the blind astray on the road."

Then all the people shall say, "Amen!"

¹⁹"Cursed is the man who withholds justice from the alien, the fatherless or the widow."

Then all the people shall say, "Amen!"

²⁰"Cursed is the man who sleeps with his father's wife, for he dishonors his father's bed."

Then all the people shall say, "Amen!"

²¹"Cursed is the man who has sexual relations with any animal."

Then all the people shall say, "Amen!"

²²"Cursed is the man who sleeps with his sister, the daughter of his father or the daughter of his mother."

Then all the people shall say, "Amen!"

²³"Cursed is the man who sleeps with his mother-in-law."

Then all the people shall say, "Amen!"

²⁴"Cursed is the man who kills his neighbor secretly."

Then all the people shall say, "Amen!"

²⁵"Cursed is the man who accepts a bribe to kill an innocent person."

Then all the people shall say, "Amen!"

²⁶"Cursed is the man who does not uphold the words of this law by carrying them out."

Then all the people shall say, "Amen!"

BLESSINGS FOR OBEDIENCE

28 If you fully obey the LORD your God and carefully follow all his commands I give you today, the LORD your God will set you high above all the nations on earth. ²All these blessings will come upon you and accompany you if you obey the LORD your God:

³You will be blessed in the city and blessed in the country.

⁴The fruit of your womb will be blessed,

</td><td>

THE MESSAGE

GOD's curse on anyone who moves his neighbor's boundary marker.

All respond: *Yes. Absolutely.*

GOD's curse on anyone who misdirects a blind man on the road.

All respond: *Yes. Absolutely.*

GOD's curse on anyone who interferes with justice due the foreigner, orphan, or widow.

All respond: *Yes. Absolutely.*

GOD's curse on anyone who has sex with his father's wife; he has violated the woman who belongs to his father.

All respond: *Yes. Absolutely.*

GOD's curse on anyone who has sex with an animal.

All respond: *Yes. Absolutely.*

GOD's curse on anyone who has sex with his sister, the daughter of his father or mother.

All respond: *Yes. Absolutely.*

GOD's curse on anyone who has sex with his mother-in-law.

All respond: *Yes. Absolutely.*

GOD's curse on anyone who kills his neighbor in secret.

All respond: *Yes. Absolutely.*

GOD's curse on anyone who takes a bribe to kill an innocent person.

All respond: *Yes. Absolutely.*

GOD's curse on whoever does not give substance to the words of this Revelation by living them.

All respond: *Yes. Absolutely.*

✝

28 ²⁸.₁₋₆ If you listen obediently to the Voice of GOD, your God, and heartily obey all his commandments that I command you today, GOD, your God, will place you on high, high above all the nations of the world. All these blessings will come down on you and spread out beyond you because you have responded to the Voice of GOD, your God:

GOD's blessing inside the city,
GOD's blessing in the country;
GOD's blessing on your children,

</td></tr>
</table>

NEW INTERNATIONAL VERSION

and the crops of your land and the young of your livestock—the calves of your herds and the lambs of your flocks. ⁵Your basket and your kneading trough will be blessed. ⁶You will be blessed when you come in and blessed when you go out.

⁷The LORD will grant that the enemies who rise up against you will be defeated before you. They will come at you from one direction but flee from you in seven.

⁸The LORD will send a blessing on your barns and on everything you put your hand to. The LORD your God will bless you in the land he is giving you.

⁹The LORD will establish you as his holy people, as he promised you on oath, if you keep the commands of the LORD your God and walk in his ways. ¹⁰Then all the peoples on earth will see that you are called by the name of the LORD, and they will fear you. ¹¹The LORD will grant you abundant prosperity—in the fruit of your womb, the young of your livestock and the crops of your ground—in the land he swore to your forefathers to give you.

¹²The LORD will open the heavens, the storehouse of his bounty, to send rain on your land in season and to bless all the work of your hands. You will lend to many nations but will borrow from none. ¹³The LORD will make you the head, not the tail. If you pay attention to the commands of the LORD your God that I give you this day and carefully follow them, you will always be at the top, never at the bottom. ¹⁴Do not turn aside from any of the commands I give you today, to the right or to the left, following other gods and serving them.

CURSES FOR DISOBEDIENCE

¹⁵However, if you do not obey the LORD your God and do not carefully follow all his commands and decrees I am giving you today, all these curses will come upon you and overtake you:

¹⁶You will be cursed in the city and cursed in the country.

¹⁷Your basket and your kneading trough will be cursed.

¹⁸The fruit of your womb will be cursed, and the crops of your land, and the calves of your herds and the lambs of your flocks.

¹⁹You will be cursed when you come in and cursed when you go out.

²⁰The LORD will send on you curses, confusion and rebuke in everything you put your

THE MESSAGE

the crops of your land,
the young of your livestock,
the calves of your herds,
the lambs of your flocks.
GOD's blessing on your basket and bread bowl;
GOD's blessing in your coming in,
GOD's blessing in your going out.

28.7 GOD will defeat your enemies who attack you. They'll come at you on one road and run away on seven roads.

28.8 GOD will order a blessing on your barns and workplaces; he'll bless you in the land that GOD, your God, is giving you.

28.9 GOD will form you as a people holy to him, just as he promised you, if you keep the commandments of GOD, your God, and live the way he has shown you.

28.10 All the peoples on Earth will see you living under the Name of GOD and hold you in respectful awe.

28.11-14 GOD will lavish you with good things: children from your womb, offspring from your animals, and crops from your land, the land that GOD promised your ancestors that he would give you. GOD will throw open the doors of his sky vaults and pour rain on your land on schedule and bless the work you take in hand. You will lend to many nations but you yourself won't have to take out a loan. GOD will make you the head, not the tail; you'll always be the top dog, never the bottom dog, as you obediently listen to and diligently keep the commands of GOD, your God, that I am commanding you today. Don't swerve an inch to the right or left from the words that I command you today by going off following and worshiping other gods.

28.15-19 Here's what will happen if you don't obediently listen to the Voice of GOD, your God, and diligently keep all the commandments and guidelines that I'm commanding you today. All these curses will come down hard on you:

GOD's curse in the city,
GOD's curse in the country;
GOD's curse on your basket and bread bowl;
GOD's curse on your children,
the crops of your land,
the young of your livestock,
the calves of your herds,
the lambs of your flocks.
GOD's curse in your coming in,
GOD's curse in your going out.

28.20 GOD will send The Curse, The Confusion, The Contrariness down on everything you try

NEW INTERNATIONAL VERSION

hand to, until you are destroyed and come to sudden ruin because of the evil you have done in forsaking him. *a* 21 The LORD will plague you with diseases until he has destroyed you from the land you are entering to possess. 22 The LORD will strike you with wasting disease, with fever and inflammation, with scorching heat and drought, with blight and mildew, which will plague you until you perish. 23 The sky over your head will be bronze, the ground beneath you iron. 24 The LORD will turn the rain of your country into dust and powder; it will come down from the skies until you are destroyed.

25 The LORD will cause you to be defeated before your enemies. You will come at them from one direction but flee from them in seven, and you will become a thing of horror to all the kingdoms on earth. 26 Your carcasses will be food for all the birds of the air and the beasts of the earth, and there will be no one to frighten them away. 27 The LORD will afflict you with the boils of Egypt and with tumors, festering sores and the itch, from which you cannot be cured. 28 The LORD will afflict you with madness, blindness and confusion of mind. 29 At midday you will grope about like a blind man in the dark. You will be unsuccessful in everything you do; day after day you will be oppressed and robbed, with no one to rescue you.

30 You will be pledged to be married to a woman, but another will take her and ravish her. You will build a house, but you will not live in it. You will plant a vineyard, but you will not even begin to enjoy its fruit. 31 Your ox will be slaughtered before your eyes, but you will eat none of it. Your donkey will be forcibly taken from you and will not be returned. Your sheep will be given to your enemies, and no one will rescue them. 32 Your sons and daughters will be given to another nation, and you will wear out your eyes watching for them day after day, powerless to lift a hand. 33 A people that you do not know will eat what your land and labor produce, and you will have nothing but cruel oppression all your days. 34 The sights you see will drive you mad. 35 The LORD will afflict your knees and legs with painful boils that cannot be cured, spreading from the soles of your feet to the top of your head.

36 The LORD will drive you and the king you set over you to a nation unknown to you or your fathers. There you will worship other gods, gods of wood and stone. 37 You will become a thing of horror and an object of scorn and ridicule to all the nations where the LORD will drive you.

38 You will sow much seed in the field but you will harvest little, because locusts will devour it.

THE MESSAGE

to do until you've been destroyed and there's nothing left of you—all because of your evil pursuits that led you to abandon me.

28.21 GOD will infect you with The Disease, wiping you right off the land that you're going in to possess.

28.22 GOD will set consumption and fever and rash and seizures and dehydration and blight and jaundice on you. They'll hunt you down until they kill you.

28.23-24 The sky over your head will become an iron roof, the ground under your feet, a slab of concrete. From out of the skies GOD will rain ash and dust down on you until you suffocate.

28.25-26 GOD will defeat you by enemy attack. You'll come at your enemies on one road and run away on seven roads. All the kingdoms of Earth will see you as a horror. Carrion birds and animals will boldly feast on your dead body with no one to chase them away.

28.27-29 GOD will hit you hard with the boils of Egypt, hemorrhoids, scabs, and an incurable itch. He'll make you go crazy and blind and senile. You'll grope around in the middle of the day like a blind person feeling his way through a lifetime of darkness; you'll never get to where you're going. Not a day will go by that you're not abused and robbed. And no one is going to help you.

28.30-31 You'll get engaged to a woman and another man will take her for his mistress; you'll build a house and never live in it; you'll plant a garden and never eat so much as a carrot; you'll watch your ox get butchered and not get a single steak from it; your donkey will be stolen from in front of you and you'll never see it again; your sheep will be sent off to your enemies and no one will lift a hand to help you.

28.32-34 Your sons and daughters will be shipped off to foreigners; you'll wear your eyes out looking vainly for them, helpless to do a thing. Your crops and everything you work for will be eaten and used by foreigners; you'll spend the rest of your lives abused and knocked around. What you see will drive you crazy.

28.35 GOD will hit you with painful boils on your knees and legs and no healing or relief from head to foot.

28.36-37 GOD will lead you and the king you set over you to a country neither you nor your ancestors have heard of; there you'll worship other gods, no-gods of wood and stone. Among all the peoples where GOD will take you, you'll be treated as a lesson or a proverb—a horror!

28.38-42 You'll plant sacks and sacks of seed in the field but get almost nothing—the grasshoppers

NEW INTERNATIONAL VERSION

³⁹You will plant vineyards and cultivate them but you will not drink the wine or gather the grapes, because worms will eat them. ⁴⁰You will have olive trees throughout your country but you will not use the oil, because the olives will drop off. ⁴¹You will have sons and daughters but you will not keep them, because they will go into captivity. ⁴²Swarms of locusts will take over all your trees and the crops of your land.

⁴³The alien who lives among you will rise above you higher and higher, but you will sink lower and lower. ⁴⁴He will lend to you, but you will not lend to him. He will be the head, but you will be the tail.

⁴⁵All these curses will come upon you. They will pursue you and overtake you until you are destroyed, because you did not obey the LORD your God and observe the commands and decrees he gave you. ⁴⁶They will be a sign and a wonder to you and your descendants forever. ⁴⁷Because you did not serve the LORD your God joyfully and gladly in the time of prosperity, ⁴⁸therefore in hunger and thirst, in nakedness and dire poverty, you will serve the enemies the LORD sends against you. He will put an iron yoke on your neck until he has destroyed you.

⁴⁹The LORD will bring a nation against you from far away, from the ends of the earth, like an eagle swooping down, a nation whose language you will not understand, ⁵⁰a fierce-looking nation without respect for the old or pity for the young. ⁵¹They will devour the young of your livestock and the crops of your land until you are destroyed. They will leave you no grain, new wine or oil, nor any calves of your herds or lambs of your flocks until you are ruined. ⁵²They will lay siege to all the cities throughout your land until the high fortified walls in which you trust fall down. They will besiege all the cities throughout the land the LORD your God is giving you.

⁵³Because of the suffering that your enemy will inflict on you during the siege, you will eat the fruit of the womb, the flesh of the sons and daughters the LORD your God has given you. ⁵⁴Even the most gentle and sensitive man among you will have no compassion on his own brother or the wife he loves or his surviving children, ⁵⁵and he will not give to one of them any of the flesh of his children that he is eating. It will be all he has left because of the suffering your enemy will inflict on you during the siege of all your

THE MESSAGE

will devour it. You'll plant and hoe and prune vineyards but won't drink or put up any wine—the worms will devour them. You'll have groves of olive trees everywhere, but you'll have no oil to rub on your face or hands—the olives will have fallen off. You'll have sons and daughters but they won't be yours for long—they'll go off to captivity. Locusts will take over all your trees and crops.

28.43-44 The foreigner who lives among you will climb the ladder, higher and higher, while you go deeper and deeper into the hole. He'll lend to you; you won't lend to him. He'll be the head; you'll be the tail.

28.45-46 All these curses are going to come on you. They're going to hunt you down and get you until there's nothing left of you because you didn't obediently listen to the Voice of GOD, your God, and diligently keep his commandments and guidelines that I commanded you. The curses will serve as signposts, warnings to your children ever after.

28.47-48 Because you didn't serve GOD, your God, out of the joy and goodness of your heart in the great abundance, you'll have to serve your enemies whom GOD will send against you. Life will be famine and drought, rags and wretchedness; then he'll put an iron yoke on your neck until he's destroyed you.

28.49-52 Yes, GOD will raise up a faraway nation against you, swooping down on you like an eagle, a nation whose language you can't understand, a mean-faced people, cruel to grandmothers and babies alike. They'll ravage the young of your animals and the crops from your fields until you're destroyed. They'll leave nothing behind: no grain, no wine, no oil, no calves, no lambs—and finally, no *you*. They'll lay siege to you while you're huddled behind your town gates. They'll knock those high, proud walls flat, those walls behind which you felt so safe. They'll lay siege to your fortified cities all over the country, this country that GOD, your God, has given you.

28.53-55 And you'll end up cannibalizing your own sons and daughters that GOD, your God, has given you. When the suffering from the siege gets extreme, you're going to eat your own babies. The most gentle and caring man among you will turn hard, his eye evil, against his own brother, his cherished wife, and even the rest of his children who are still alive, refusing to share with them a scrap of meat from the cannibal child-stew he is eating. He's lost everything, even his humanity, in the suffering of the siege that your enemy mounts against your fortified towns.

NEW INTERNATIONAL VERSION

cities. 56The most gentle and sensitive woman among you—so sensitive and gentle that she would not venture to touch the ground with the sole of her foot—will begrudge the husband she loves and her own son or daughter 57the afterbirth from her womb and the children she bears. For she intends to eat them secretly during the siege and in the distress that your enemy will inflict on you in your cities.

58If you do not carefully follow all the words of this law, which are written in this book, and do not revere this glorious and awesome name— the LORD your God— 59the LORD will send fearful plagues on you and your descendants, harsh and prolonged disasters, and severe and lingering illnesses. 60He will bring upon you all the diseases of Egypt that you dreaded, and they will cling to you. 61The LORD will also bring on you every kind of sickness and disaster not recorded in this Book of the Law, until you are destroyed. 62You who were as numerous as the stars in the sky will be left but few in number, because you did not obey the LORD your God. 63Just as it pleased the LORD to make you prosper and increase in number, so it will please him to ruin and destroy you. You will be uprooted from the land you are entering to possess.

64Then the LORD will scatter you among all nations, from one end of the earth to the other. There you will worship other gods—gods of wood and stone, which neither you nor your fathers have known. 65Among those nations you will find no repose, no resting place for the sole of your foot. There the LORD will give you an anxious mind, eyes weary with longing, and a despairing heart. 66You will live in constant suspense, filled with dread both night and day, never sure of your life. 67In the morning you will say, "If only it were evening!" and in the evening, "If only it were morning!"—because of the terror that will fill your hearts and the sights that your eyes will see. 68The LORD will send you back in ships to Egypt on a journey I said you should never make again. There you will offer yourselves for sale to your enemies as male and female slaves, but no one will buy you.

THE MESSAGE

28.56-57 And the most gentle and caring woman among you, a woman who wouldn't step on a wildflower, will turn hard, her eye evil, against her cherished husband, against her son, against her daughter, against even the afterbirth of her newborn infants; she plans to eat them in secret—she does eat them!—because she has lost everything, even her humanity, in the suffering of the siege that your enemy mounts against your fortified towns.

28.58-61 If you don't diligently keep all the words of this Revelation written in this book, living in holy awe before This Name glorious and terrible, GOD, your God, then GOD will pound you with catastrophes, you and your children, huge interminable catastrophes, hideous interminable illnesses. He'll bring back and stick you with every old Egyptian malady that once terrorized you. And yes, every disease and catastrophe imaginable—things not even written in the Book of this Revelation—GOD will bring on you until you're destroyed.

28.62 Because you didn't listen obediently to the Voice of GOD, your God, you'll be left with a few pitiful stragglers in place of the dazzling stars-in-the-heavens multitude you had become.

28.63-66 And this is how things will end up: Just as GOD once enjoyed you, took pleasure in making life good for you, giving you many children, so GOD will enjoy getting rid of you, clearing you off the Earth. He'll weed you out of the very soil that you are entering in to possess. He'll scatter you to the four winds, from one end of the Earth to the other. You'll worship all kinds of other gods, gods neither you nor your parents ever heard of, wood and stone no-gods. But you won't find a home there, you'll not be able to settle down. GOD will give you a restless heart, longing eyes, a homesick soul. You will live in constant jeopardy, terrified of every shadow, never knowing what you'll meet around the next corner.

28.67 In the morning you'll say, "I wish it were evening." In the evening you'll say, "I wish it were morning." Afraid, terrorized at what's coming next, afraid of the unknown, because of the sights you've witnessed.

28.68 GOD will ship you back to Egypt by a road I promised you'd never see again. There you'll offer yourselves for sale, both men and women, as slaves to your enemies. And not a buyer to be found.

NEW INTERNATIONAL VERSION

RENEWAL OF THE COVENANT

29 These are the terms of the covenant the LORD commanded Moses to make with the Israelites in Moab, in addition to the covenant he had made with them at Horeb.

²Moses summoned all the Israelites and said to them:

Your eyes have seen all that the LORD did in Egypt to Pharaoh, to all his officials and to all his land. ³With your own eyes you saw those great trials, those miraculous signs and great wonders. ⁴But to this day the LORD has not given you a mind that understands or eyes that see or ears that hear. ⁵During the forty years that I led you through the desert, your clothes did not wear out, nor did the sandals on your feet. ⁶You ate no bread and drank no wine or other fermented drink. I did this so that you might know that I am the LORD your God.

⁷When you reached this place, Sihon king of Heshbon and Og king of Bashan came out to fight against us, but we defeated them. ⁸We took their land and gave it as an inheritance to the Reubenites, the Gadites and the half-tribe of Manasseh.

⁹Carefully follow the terms of this covenant, so that you may prosper in everything you do. ¹⁰All of you are standing today in the presence of the LORD your God—your leaders and chief men, your elders and officials, and all the other men of Israel, ¹¹together with your children and your wives, and the aliens living in your camps who chop your wood and carry your water. ¹²You are standing here in order to enter into a covenant with the LORD your God, a covenant the LORD is making with you this day and sealing with an oath, ¹³to confirm you this day as his people, that he may be your God as he promised you and as he swore to your fathers, Abraham, Isaac and Jacob. ¹⁴I am making this covenant, with its oath, not only with you ¹⁵who are standing here with us today in the presence of the LORD our God but also with those who are not here today.

¹⁶You yourselves know how we lived in Egypt and how we passed through the countries on the way here. ¹⁷You saw among them their detestable images and idols of wood and stone, of silver and gold. ¹⁸Make sure there is no man or woman, clan or tribe among you today whose heart turns away from the LORD our God to go and worship the gods of those nations; make sure there is no root among you that produces such bitter poison.

¹⁹When such a person hears the words of this oath, he invokes a blessing on himself and therefore thinks, "I will be safe, even though I persist

THE MESSAGE

29 These are the terms of the Covenant that GOD commanded Moses to make with the People of Israel in the land of Moab, renewing the Covenant he made with them at Horeb.

MOSES BLESSES ISRAEL ON THE PLAINS OF MOAB

29.2-4 Moses called all Israel together and said, You've seen with your own eyes everything that GOD did in Egypt to Pharaoh and his servants, and to the land itself—the massive trials to which you were eyewitnesses, the great signs and miracle-wonders. But GOD didn't give you an understanding heart or perceptive eyes or attentive ears until right now, this very day.

29.5-6 I took you through the wilderness for forty years and through all that time the clothes on your backs didn't wear out, the sandals on your feet didn't wear out, and you lived well without bread and wine and beer, proving to you that I am in fact GOD, your God.

29.7-8 When you arrived here in this place, Sihon king of Heshbon and Og king of Bashan met us primed for war but we beat them. We took their land and gave it as an inheritance to the Reubenites, the Gadites, and the half-tribe of Manasseh.

29.9 Diligently keep the words of this Covenant. Do what they say so that you will live well and wisely in every detail.

29.10-13 You are all standing here today in the Presence of GOD, your God—the heads of your tribes, your leaders, your officials, all Israel: your babies, your wives, the resident foreigners in your camps who fetch your firewood and water—ready to cross over into the solemnly sworn Covenant that GOD, your God, is making with you today, the Covenant that this day confirms that you are his people and he is GOD, your God, just as he promised you and your ancestors Abraham, Isaac, and Jacob.

29.14-21 I'm not making this Covenant and its oath with you alone. I *am* making it with you who are standing here today in the Presence of GOD, our God, yes, but also with those who are not here today. You know the conditions in which we lived in Egypt and how we crisscrossed through nations in our travels. You got an eyeful of their obscenities, their wood and stone, silver and gold junk-gods. Don't let down your guard lest even now, today, someone—man or woman, clan or tribe—gets sidetracked from GOD, our God, and gets involved with the no-gods of the nations; lest some poisonous weed sprout and spread among you, a person who hears the words of the Covenant-oath but exempts himself, thinking, "I'll live just the way I

NEW INTERNATIONAL VERSION

in going my own way." This will bring disaster on the watered land as well as the dry.[a] 20The Lord will never be willing to forgive him; his wrath and zeal will burn against that man. All the curses written in this book will fall upon him, and the Lord will blot out his name from under heaven. 21The Lord will single him out from all the tribes of Israel for disaster, according to all the curses of the covenant written in this Book of the Law.

22Your children who follow you in later generations and foreigners who come from distant lands will see the calamities that have fallen on the land and the diseases with which the Lord has afflicted it. 23The whole land will be a burning waste of salt and sulfur—nothing planted, nothing sprouting, no vegetation growing on it. It will be like the destruction of Sodom and Gomorrah, Admah and Zeboiim, which the Lord overthrew in fierce anger. 24All the nations will ask: "Why has the Lord done this to this land? Why this fierce, burning anger?"

25And the answer will be: "It is because this people abandoned the covenant of the Lord, the God of their fathers, the covenant he made with them when he brought them out of Egypt. 26They went off and worshiped other gods and bowed down to them, gods they did not know, gods he had not given them. 27Therefore the Lord's anger burned against this land, so that he brought on it all the curses written in this book. 28In furious anger and in great wrath the Lord uprooted them from their land and thrust them into another land, as it is now."

29The secret things belong to the Lord our God, but the things revealed belong to us and to our children forever, that we may follow all the words of this law.

PROSPERITY AFTER TURNING TO THE LORD

30 When all these blessings and curses I have set before you come upon you and you take them to heart wherever the Lord your God disperses you among the nations, 2and when you and your children return to the Lord your God and obey him with all your heart and with all your soul according to everything I command you today, 3then the Lord your God will restore your fortunes[b] and have compassion on you and gather you again from all the nations where he scattered you. 4Even if you have been banished to the most distant land under the heavens, from there the Lord your God will gather you and bring you back. 5He will bring

THE MESSAGE

please, thank you," and ends up ruining life for everybody. God won't let him off the hook. God's anger and jealousy will erupt like a volcano against that person. The curses written in this book will bury him. God will delete his name from the records. God will separate him out from all the tribes of Israel for special punishment, according to all the curses of the Covenant written in this Book of Revelation.

29.22-23 The next generation, your children who come after you and the foreigner who comes from a far country, will be appalled when they see the widespread devastation, how God made the whole land sick. They'll see a fire-blackened wasteland of brimstone and salt flats, nothing planted, nothing growing, not so much as a blade of grass anywhere—like the overthrow of Sodom and Gomorrah, Admah and Zeboiim, which God overthrew in fiery rage.

29.24 All the nations will ask, "Why did God do this to this country? What on earth could have made him this angry?"

29.25-28 Your children will answer, "Because they abandoned the Covenant of the God of their ancestors that he made with them after he got them out of Egypt; they went off and worshiped other gods, submitted to gods they'd never heard of before, gods they had no business dealing with. So God's anger erupted against that land and all the curses written in this book came down on it. God, furiously angry, pulled them, roots and all, out of their land and dumped them in another country, as you can see."

29.29 God, our God, will take care of the hidden things but the revealed things are our business. It's up to us and our children to attend to all the terms in this Revelation.

30 30.1-5 Here's what will happen. While you're out among the nations where God has dispersed you and the blessings and curses come in just the way I have set them before you, and you and your children take them seriously and come back to God, your God, and obey him with your whole heart and soul according to everything that I command you today, God, your God, will restore everything you lost; he'll have compassion on you; he'll come back and pick up the pieces from all the places where you were scattered. No matter how far away you end up, God, your God, will get you out of there and bring you back to the land

---

[a] 19 Or way, in order to add drunkenness to thirst."
[b] 3 Or will bring you back from captivity

you to the land that belonged to your fathers, and you will take possession of it. He will make you more prosperous and numerous than your fathers. ⁶The LORD your God will circumcise your hearts and the hearts of your descendants, so that you may love him with all your heart and with all your soul, and live. ⁷The LORD your God will put all these curses on your enemies who hate and persecute you. ⁸You will again obey the LORD and follow all his commands I am giving you today. ⁹Then the LORD your God will make you most prosperous in all the work of your hands and in the fruit of your womb, the young of your livestock and the crops of your land. The LORD will again delight in you and make you prosperous, just as he delighted in your fathers, ¹⁰if you obey the LORD your God and keep his commands and decrees that are written in this Book of the Law and turn to the LORD your God with all your heart and with all your soul.

THE OFFER OF LIFE OR DEATH

¹¹Now what I am commanding you today is not too difficult for you or beyond your reach. ¹²It is not up in heaven, so that you have to ask, "Who will ascend into heaven to get it and proclaim it to us so we may obey it?" ¹³Nor is it beyond the sea, so that you have to ask, "Who will cross the sea to get it and proclaim it to us so we may obey it?" ¹⁴No, the word is very near you; it is in your mouth and in your heart so you may obey it.

¹⁵See, I set before you today life and prosperity, death and destruction. ¹⁶For I command you today to love the LORD your God, to walk in his ways, and to keep his commands, decrees and laws; then you will live and increase, and the LORD your God will bless you in the land you are entering to possess.

¹⁷But if your heart turns away and you are not obedient, and if you are drawn away to bow down to other gods and worship them, ¹⁸I declare to you this day that you will certainly be destroyed. You will not live long in the land you are crossing the Jordan to enter and possess.

¹⁹This day I call heaven and earth as witnesses against you that I have set before you life and death, blessings and curses. Now choose life, so that you and your children may live ²⁰and that you may love the LORD your God, listen to his

your ancestors once possessed. It will be yours again. He will give you a good life and make you more numerous than your ancestors.

30.6-7 GOD, your God, will cut away the thick calluses on your heart and your children's hearts, freeing you to love GOD, your God, with your whole heart and soul and live, really live. GOD, your God, will put all these curses on your enemies who hated you and were out to get you.

30.8-9 And you will make a new start, listening obediently to GOD, keeping all his commandments that I'm commanding you today. GOD, your God, will outdo himself in making things go well for you: you'll have babies, get calves, grow crops, and enjoy an all-around good life. Yes, GOD will start enjoying you again, making things go well for you just as he enjoyed doing it for your ancestors.

30.10 But only if you listen obediently to GOD, your God, and keep the commandments and regulations written in this Book of Revelation. Nothing halfhearted here; you must return to GOD, your God, totally, heart and soul, holding nothing back.

30.11-14 This commandment that I'm commanding you today isn't too much for you, it's not out of your reach. It's not on a high mountain—you don't have to get mountaineers to climb the peak and bring it down to your level and explain it before you can live it. And it's not across the ocean—you don't have to send sailors out to get it, bring it back, and then explain it before you can live it. No. The word is right here and now—as near as the tongue in your mouth, as near as the heart in your chest. Just do it!

30.15 Look at what I've done for you today: I've
       placed in front of you
   Life and Good
   Death and Evil.

30.16 And I command you today: Love GOD, your God. Walk in his ways. Keep his commandments, regulations, and rules so that you will live, really live, live exuberantly, blessed by GOD, your God, in the land you are about to enter and possess.

30.17-18 But I warn you: If you have a change of heart, refuse to listen obediently, and willfully go off to serve and worship other gods, you will most certainly die. You won't last long in the land that you are crossing the Jordan to enter and possess.

30.19-20 I call Heaven and Earth to witness against you today: I place before you Life and Death, Blessing and Curse. Choose life so that you and your children will live. And love GOD, your God, listening obediently to him, firmly em-

NEW INTERNATIONAL VERSION

voice, and hold fast to him. For the LORD is your life, and he will give you many years in the land he swore to give to your fathers, Abraham, Isaac and Jacob.

JOSHUA TO SUCCEED MOSES

31 Then Moses went out and spoke these words to all Israel: ²"I am now a hundred and twenty years old and I am no longer able to lead you. The LORD has said to me, 'You shall not cross the Jordan.' ³The LORD your God himself will cross over ahead of you. He will destroy these nations before you, and you will take possession of their land. Joshua also will cross over ahead of you, as the LORD said. ⁴And the LORD will do to them what he did to Sihon and Og, the kings of the Amorites, whom he destroyed along with their land. ⁵The LORD will deliver them to you, and you must do to them all that I have commanded you. ⁶Be strong and courageous. Do not be afraid or terrified because of them, for the LORD your God goes with you; he will never leave you nor forsake you."

⁷Then Moses summoned Joshua and said to him in the presence of all Israel, "Be strong and courageous, for you must go with this people into the land that the LORD swore to their forefathers to give them, and you must divide it among them as their inheritance. ⁸The LORD himself goes before you and will be with you; he will never leave you nor forsake you. Do not be afraid; do not be discouraged."

THE READING OF THE LAW

⁹So Moses wrote down this law and gave it to the priests, the sons of Levi, who carried the ark of the covenant of the LORD, and to all the elders of Israel. ¹⁰Then Moses commanded them: "At the end of every seven years, in the year for canceling debts, during the Feast of Tabernacles, ¹¹when all Israel comes to appear before the LORD your God at the place he will choose, you shall read this law before them in their hearing. ¹²Assemble the people—men, women and children, and the aliens living in your towns—so they can listen and learn to fear the LORD your God and follow carefully all the words of this law. ¹³Their children, who do not know this law, must hear it and learn to fear the LORD your God as long as you live in the land you are crossing the Jordan to possess."

THE MESSAGE

bracing him. Oh yes, he is life itself, a long life settled on the soil that GOD, your God, promised to give your ancestors, Abraham, Isaac, and Jacob.

THE CHARGE

31.1-2 **31** Moses went on and addressed these words to all Israel. He said, "I'm 120 years old today. I can't get about as I used to. And GOD told me, 'You're not going to cross this Jordan River.'

31.3-5 "GOD, your God, will cross the river ahead of you and destroy the nations in your path so that you may dispossess them. (And Joshua will cross the river before you, as GOD said he would.) GOD will give the nations the same treatment he gave the kings of the Amorites, Sihon and Og, and their land; he'll destroy them. GOD will hand the nations over to you, and you'll treat them exactly as I have commanded you.

31.6 "Be strong. Take courage. Don't be intimidated. Don't give them a second thought because GOD, your God, is striding ahead of you. He's right there with you. He won't let you down; he won't leave you."

31.7-8 Then Moses summoned Joshua. He said to him with all Israel watching, "Be strong. Take courage. You will enter the land with this people, this land that GOD promised their ancestors that he'd give them. You will make them the proud possessors of it. GOD is striding ahead of you. He's right there with you. He won't let you down; he won't leave you. Don't be intimidated. Don't worry."

⊹

31.9-13 Moses wrote out this Revelation and gave it to the priests, the sons of Levi, who carried the Chest of the Covenant of GOD, and to all the leaders of Israel. And he gave these orders: "At the end of every seven years, the Year-All-Debts-Are-Canceled, during the pilgrim Festival of Booths when everyone in Israel comes to appear in the Presence of GOD, your God, at the place he designates, read out this Revelation to all Israel, with everyone listening. Gather the people together—men, women, children, and the foreigners living among you—so they can listen well, so they may learn to live in holy awe before GOD, your God, and diligently keep everything in this Revelation. And do this so that their children, who don't yet know all this, will also listen and learn to live in holy awe before GOD, your God, for as long as you live on the land that you are crossing over the Jordan to possess."

NEW INTERNATIONAL VERSION

ISRAEL'S REBELLION PREDICTED

14The LORD said to Moses, "Now the day of your death is near. Call Joshua and present yourselves at the Tent of Meeting, where I will commission him." So Moses and Joshua came and presented themselves at the Tent of Meeting.

15Then the LORD appeared at the Tent in a pillar of cloud, and the cloud stood over the entrance to the Tent. **16**And the LORD said to Moses: "You are going to rest with your fathers, and these people will soon prostitute themselves to the foreign gods of the land they are entering. They will forsake me and break the covenant I made with them. **17**On that day I will become angry with them and forsake them; I will hide my face from them, and they will be destroyed. Many disasters and difficulties will come upon them, and on that day they will ask, 'Have not these disasters come upon us because our God is not with us?' **18**And I will certainly hide my face on that day because of all their wickedness in turning to other gods.

19"Now write down for yourselves this song and teach it to the Israelites and have them sing it, so that it may be a witness for me against them. **20**When I have brought them into the land flowing with milk and honey, the land I promised on oath to their forefathers, and when they eat their fill and thrive, they will turn to other gods and worship them, rejecting me and breaking my covenant. **21**And when many disasters and difficulties come upon them, this song will testify against them, because it will not be forgotten by their descendants. I know what they are disposed to do, even before I bring them into the land I promised them on oath." **22**So Moses wrote down this song that day and taught it to the Israelites.

23The LORD gave this command to Joshua son of Nun: "Be strong and courageous, for you will bring the Israelites into the land I promised them on oath, and I myself will be with you."

24After Moses finished writing in a book the words of this law from beginning to end, **25**he gave this command to the Levites who carried the ark of the covenant of the LORD: **26**"Take this Book of the Law and place it beside the ark of the covenant of the LORD your God. There it will remain as a witness against you. **27**For I know how rebellious and stiff-necked you are. If you have been rebellious against the LORD while I am still alive and with you, how much more will

THE MESSAGE

31.14-15 GOD spoke to Moses: "You are about to die. So call Joshua. Meet me in the Tent of Meeting so that I can commission him."

So Moses and Joshua went and stationed themselves in the Tent of Meeting. GOD appeared in the Tent in a Pillar of Cloud. The Cloud was near the entrance of the Tent of Meeting.

31.16-18 GOD spoke to Moses: "You're about to die and be buried with your ancestors. You'll no sooner be in the grave than this people will be up and whoring after the foreign gods of this country that they are entering. They will abandon me and violate my Covenant that I've made with them. I'll get angry, oh so angry! I'll walk off and leave them on their own, won't so much as look back at them. Then many calamities and disasters will devastate them because they are defenseless. They'll say, 'Isn't it because our God wasn't here that all this evil has come upon us?' But I'll stay out of their lives, keep looking the other way because of all their evil: they took up with other gods!

31.19-21 "But for right now, copy down this song and teach the People of Israel to sing it by heart. They'll have it then as my witness against them. When I bring them into the land that I promised to their ancestors, a land flowing with milk and honey, and they eat and become full and get fat and then begin fooling around with other gods and worshiping them, and then things start falling apart, many terrible things happening, this song will be there with them as a witness to who they are and what went wrong. Their children won't forget this song; they'll be singing it. Don't think I don't know what they are already scheming to do, and they're not even in the land yet, this land I promised them."

31.22 So Moses wrote down this song that very day and taught it to the People of Israel.

31.23 Then GOD commanded Joshua son of Nun saying, "Be strong. Take courage. You will lead the People of Israel into the land I promised to give them. And I'll be right there with you."

31.24-26 After Moses had finished writing down the words of this Revelation in a book, right down to the last word, he ordered the Levites who were responsible for carrying the Chest of the Covenant of GOD, saying, "Take this Book of Revelation and place it alongside the Chest of the Covenant of GOD, your God. Keep it there as a witness.

31.27-29 "I know what rebels you are, how stubborn and willful you can be. Even today, while I'm still alive and present with you, you're rebel-

NEW INTERNATIONAL VERSION

you rebel after I die! [28]Assemble before me all the elders of your tribes and all your officials, so that I can speak these words in their hearing and call heaven and earth to testify against them. [29]For I know that after my death you are sure to become utterly corrupt and to turn from the way I have commanded you. In days to come, disaster will fall upon you because you will do evil in the sight of the LORD and provoke him to anger by what your hands have made."

THE SONG OF MOSES

[30]And Moses recited the words of this song from beginning to end in the hearing of the whole assembly of Israel:

32

Listen, O heavens, and I will speak;
 hear, O earth, the words of my mouth.
[2]Let my teaching fall like rain
 and my words descend like dew,
like showers on new grass,
 like abundant rain on tender plants.

[3]I will proclaim the name of the LORD.
 Oh, praise the greatness of our God!
[4]He is the Rock, his works are perfect,
 and all his ways are just.
A faithful God who does no wrong,
 upright and just is he.

[5]They have acted corruptly toward him;
 to their shame they are no longer his
  children,
 but a warped and crooked generation. [a]
[6]Is this the way you repay the LORD,
 O foolish and unwise people?
Is he not your Father, your Creator, [b]
 who made you and formed you?

[7]Remember the days of old;
 consider the generations long past.
Ask your father and he will tell you,
 your elders, and they will explain to you.
[8]When the Most High gave the nations their
  inheritance,
 when he divided all mankind,
he set up boundaries for the peoples
 according to the number of the sons of
  Israel. [c]
[9]For the LORD's portion is his people,
 Jacob his allotted inheritance.

---

[a] 5 Or *Corrupt are they and not his children, / a generation warped and twisted to their shame*   [b] 6 Or *Father, who bought you*   [c] 8 Masoretic Text; Dead Sea Scrolls (see also Septuagint) *sons of God*

THE MESSAGE

lious against GOD. How much worse when I've died! So gather the leaders of the tribes and the officials here. I have something I need to say directly to them with Heaven and Earth as witnesses. I know that after I die you're going to make a mess of things, abandoning the way I commanded, inviting all kinds of evil consequences in the days ahead. You're determined to do evil in defiance of GOD—I know you are—deliberately provoking his anger by what you do."

31.30   So with everyone in Israel gathered and listening, Moses taught them the words of this song, from start to finish.

THE SONG

32.1-5

32

Listen, Heavens, I have something to
 tell you.
Attention, Earth, I've got a mouth full of
 words.
My teaching, let it fall like a gentle rain,
 my words arrive like morning dew,
Like a sprinkling rain on new grass,
 like spring showers on the garden.
For it's GOD's Name I'm preaching—
 respond to the greatness of our God!
The Rock: His works are perfect,
 and the way he works is fair and just;
A God you can depend upon, no exceptions,
 a straight-arrow God.
His messed-up, mixed-up children, his
 non-children,
 throw mud at him but none of it sticks.

32.6-7   Don't you realize it is GOD you are treating
  like this?
 This is crazy; don't you have any sense
  of reverence?
Isn't this your father who created you,
 who made you and gave you a place on
  Earth?
Read up on what happened before you
  were born;
 dig into the past, understand your roots.
Ask your parents what it was like before
  you were born;
 ask the old-ones, they'll tell you a thing
  or two.

32.8-9   When the High God gave the nations their
  stake,
 gave them their place on Earth,
He put each of the peoples within
  boundaries
 under the care of divine guardians.
But GOD himself took charge of his people,
 took Jacob on as his personal concern.

NEW INTERNATIONAL VERSION

¹⁰ In a desert land he found him,
   in a barren and howling waste.
He shielded him and cared for him;
   he guarded him as the apple of his eye,
¹¹ like an eagle that stirs up its nest
   and hovers over its young,
that spreads its wings to catch them
   and carries them on its pinions.
¹² The LORD alone led him;
   no foreign god was with him.

¹³ He made him ride on the heights of the land
   and fed him with the fruit of the fields.
He nourished him with honey from the rock,
   and with oil from the flinty crag,
¹⁴ with curds and milk from herd and flock
   and with fattened lambs and goats,
with choice rams of Bashan
   and the finest kernels of wheat.
You drank the foaming blood of the grape.

¹⁵ Jeshurun^a grew fat and kicked;
   filled with food, he became heavy and
      sleek.
He abandoned the God who made him
   and rejected the Rock his Savior.
¹⁶ They made him jealous with their foreign
      gods
   and angered him with their detestable
      idols.
¹⁷ They sacrificed to demons, which are not
      God—
   gods they had not known,
   gods that recently appeared,
   gods your fathers did not fear.
¹⁸ You deserted the Rock, who fathered you;
   you forgot the God who gave you birth.

¹⁹ The LORD saw this and rejected them
   because he was angered by his sons and
      daughters.
²⁰ "I will hide my face from them," he said,
   "and see what their end will be;
for they are a perverse generation,
   children who are unfaithful.
²¹ They made me jealous by what is no god
   and angered me with their worthless
      idols.
I will make them envious by those who are
      not a people;
   I will make them angry by a nation that
      has no understanding.
²² For a fire has been kindled by my wrath,
   one that burns to the realm of death^b
      below.

---

a 15 *Jeshurun* means *the upright one*, that is, Israel.
b 22 Hebrew *to Sheol*

THE MESSAGE

32.10-14 He found him out in the wilderness,
   in an empty, windswept wasteland.
He threw his arms around him, lavished
      attention on him,
   guarding him as the apple of his eye.
He was like an eagle hovering over its nest,
   overshadowing its young,
Then spreading its wings, lifting them into
      the air,
   teaching them to fly.
GOD alone led him;
   there was not a foreign god in sight.
GOD lifted him on to the hilltops,
   so he could feast on the crops in the
      fields.
He fed him honey from the rock,
   oil from granite crags,
Curds of cattle and the milk of sheep,
   the choice cuts of lambs and goats,
Fine Bashan rams, high-quality wheat,
   and the blood of grapes: you drank good
      wine!

32.15-18 Jeshurun put on weight and bucked;
   you got fat, became obese, a tub of lard.
He abandoned the God who made him,
   he mocked the Rock of his salvation.
They made him jealous with their foreign
      newfangled gods,
   and with obscenities they vexed him no
      end.
They sacrificed to no-god demons,
   gods they knew nothing about,
The latest in gods, fresh from the market,
   gods your ancestors would never call
      "gods."
You walked out on the Rock who gave you
      your life,
   forgot the birth-God who brought you
      into the world.

32.19-25 GOD saw it and turned on his heel,
   angered and hurt by his sons and
      daughters.
He said, "From now on I'm looking the
      other way.
   Wait and see what happens to them.
Oh, they're a turned-around, upside-down
      generation!
   Who knows what they'll do from one
      moment to the next?
They've goaded me with their no-gods,
   infuriated me with their hot-air gods;
I'm going to goad them with a no-people,
   with a hollow nation incense them.
My anger started a fire,
   a wildfire burning deep down in Sheol,

NEW INTERNATIONAL VERSION

It will devour the earth and its harvests
  and set afire the foundations of the
    mountains.
23 "I will heap calamities upon them
  and spend my arrows against them.
24 I will send wasting famine against them,
  consuming pestilence and deadly plague;
I will send against them the fangs of wild
    beasts,
  the venom of vipers that glide in the dust.
25 In the street the sword will make them
    childless;
  in their homes terror will reign.
Young men and young women will perish,
  infants and gray-haired men.
26 I said I would scatter them
  and blot out their memory from mankind,
27 but I dreaded the taunt of the enemy,
  lest the adversary misunderstand
and say, 'Our hand has triumphed;
  the LORD has not done all this.' "

28 They are a nation without sense,
  there is no discernment in them.
29 If only they were wise and would understand
    this
  and discern what their end will be!
30 How could one man chase a thousand,
  or two put ten thousand to flight,
unless their Rock had sold them,
  unless the LORD had given them up?
31 For their rock is not like our Rock,
  as even our enemies concede.
32 Their vine comes from the vine of Sodom
  and from the fields of Gomorrah.
Their grapes are filled with poison,
  and their clusters with bitterness.
33 Their wine is the venom of serpents,
  the deadly poison of cobras.

34 "Have I not kept this in reserve
  and sealed it in my vaults?
35 It is mine to avenge; I will repay.
  In due time their foot will slip;
their day of disaster is near
  and their doom rushes upon them."

36 The LORD will judge his people
  and have compassion on his servants

THE MESSAGE

Then shooting up and devouring the Earth
    and its crops,
  setting all the mountains, from bottom
    to top, on fire.
I'll pile catastrophes on them,
  I'll shoot my arrows at them:
Starvation, blistering heat, killing disease;
  I'll send snarling wild animals to attack
    from the forest
  and venomous creatures to strike from
    the dust.
Killing in the streets,
  terror in the houses,
Young men and virgins alike struck down,
  and yes, breast-feeding babies and gray-
    haired old men."

32.26-27 I could have said, "I'll hack them to pieces,
  wipe out all trace of them from the
    Earth,"
Except that I feared the enemy would grab
    the chance
  to take credit for all of it,
Crowing, "Look what we did!
  GOD had nothing to do with this."

32.28-33 They are a nation of ninnies,
  they don't know enough to come in out
    of the rain.
If they had any sense at all, they'd know
    this;
  they would see what's coming down the
    road.
How could one soldier chase a thousand
    enemies off,
  or two men run off two thousand,
Unless their Rock had sold them,
  unless GOD had given them away?
For their rock is nothing compared to our
    Rock;
  even our enemies say that.
They're a vine that comes right out of
    Sodom,
  who they are is rooted in Gomorrah;
Their grapes are poison grapes,
  their grape-clusters bitter.
Their wine is rattlesnake venom,
  mixed with lethal cobra poison.

32.34-35 Don't you realize that I have my shelves
  well stocked, locked behind iron doors?
I'm in charge of vengeance and payback,
  just waiting for them to slip up;
And the day of their doom is just around
    the corner,
  sudden and swift and sure.

32.36-38 Yes, GOD will judge his people,
  but oh how compassionately he'll do it.

NEW INTERNATIONAL VERSION

when he sees their strength is gone
and no one is left, slave or free.
37 He will say: "Now where are their gods,
the rock they took refuge in,
38 the gods who ate the fat of their sacrifices
and drank the wine of their drink
offerings?
Let them rise up to help you!
Let them give you shelter!

39 "See now that I myself am He!
There is no god besides me.
I put to death and I bring to life,
I have wounded and I will heal,
and no one can deliver out of my hand.
40 I lift my hand to heaven and declare:
As surely as I live forever,
41 when I sharpen my flashing sword
and my hand grasps it in judgment,
I will take vengeance on my adversaries
and repay those who hate me.
42 I will make my arrows drunk with blood,
while my sword devours flesh:
the blood of the slain and the captives,
the heads of the enemy leaders."

43 Rejoice, O nations, with his people,*a, b*
for he will avenge the blood of his
servants;
he will take vengeance on his enemies
and make atonement for his land and
people.

44 Moses came with Joshua*c* son of Nun and
spoke all the words of this song in the hearing of
the people. 45 When Moses finished reciting all
these words to all Israel, 46 he said to them, "Take
to heart all the words I have solemnly declared
to you this day, so that you may command your
children to obey carefully all the words of this
law. 47 They are not just idle words for you—they
are your life. By them you will live long in the
land you are crossing the Jordan to possess."

MOSES TO DIE ON MOUNT NEBO

48 On that same day the LORD told Moses,
49 "Go up into the Abarim Range to Mount Nebo
in Moab, across from Jericho, and view Canaan,
the land I am giving the Israelites as their own
possession. 50 There on the mountain that you
have climbed you will die and be gathered to
your people, just as your brother Aaron died on
Mount Hor and was gathered to his people.
51 This is because both of you broke faith with
me in the presence of the Israelites at the waters

a 43 Or *Make his people rejoice, O nations*   *b* 43 Masoretic
Text; Dead Sea Scrolls (see also Septuagint) *people, / and let
all the angels worship him /*   *c* 44 Hebrew *Hoshea,* a variant
of *Joshua*

THE MESSAGE

When he sees their weakened plight
and there is no one left, slave or free,
He'll say, "So where are their gods,
the rock in which they sought refuge,
The gods who feasted on the fat of their
sacrifices
and drank the wine of their drink-
offerings?
Let them show their stuff and help you,
let them give you a hand!

32.39-42   "Do you see it now? Do you see that I'm
the one?
Do you see that there's no other god
beside me?
I bring death and I give life, I wound and I
heal—
there is no getting away from or around
me!
I raise my hand in solemn oath;
I say, 'I'm always around. By that very
life I promise:
When I sharpen my lightning sword
and execute judgment,
I take vengeance on my enemies
and pay back those who hate me.
I'll make my arrows drunk with blood,
my sword will gorge itself on flesh,
Feasting on slain and captive alike,
the proud and vain enemy corpses.' "

32.43   Celebrate, nations, join the praise of his
people.
He avenges the deaths of his servants,
Pays back his enemies with vengeance,
and cleanses his land for his people.

32.44-47   Moses came and recited all the words of this
song in the hearing of the people, he and Joshua son of Nun. When Moses had finished saying all these words to all Israel, he said, "Take
to heart all these words to which I give witness
today and urgently command your children to
put them into practice, every single word of
this Revelation. Yes. This is no small matter for
you; it's your life. In keeping this word you'll
have a good and long life in this land that
you're crossing the Jordan to possess."

32.48-50   That same day GOD spoke to Moses: "Climb
the Abarim Mountains to Mount Nebo in the
land of Moab, overlooking Jericho, and view
the land of Canaan that I'm giving the People
of Israel to have and hold. Die on the mountain
that you climb and join your people in the
ground, just as your brother Aaron died on
Mount Hor and joined his people.

32.51-52   "This is because you broke faith with me in
the company of the People of Israel at the Wa-

NEW INTERNATIONAL VERSION	THE MESSAGE

of Meribah Kadesh in the Desert of Zin and because you did not uphold my holiness among the Israelites. ⁵²Therefore, you will see the land only from a distance; you will not enter the land I am giving to the people of Israel."

ters of Meribah Kadesh in the Wilderness of Zin—you didn't honor my Holy Presence in the company of the People of Israel. You'll look at the land spread out before you but you won't enter it, this land that I am giving to the People of Israel."

MOSES BLESSES THE TRIBES

33 This is the blessing that Moses the man of God pronounced on the Israelites before his death. ²He said:

"The LORD came from Sinai
  and dawned over them from Seir;
  he shone forth from Mount Paran.
He came with*a* myriads of holy ones
  from the south, from his mountain
    slopes.*b*
³Surely it is you who love the people;
  all the holy ones are in your hand.
At your feet they all bow down,
  and from you receive instruction,
⁴the law that Moses gave us,
  the possession of the assembly of Jacob.
⁵He was king over Jeshurun*c*
  when the leaders of the people assembled,
  along with the tribes of Israel.

⁶"Let Reuben live and not die,
  nor*d* his men be few."

⁷And this he said about Judah:

"Hear, O LORD, the cry of Judah;
  bring him to his people.
With his own hands he defends his cause.
  Oh, be his help against his foes!"

⁸About Levi he said:

"Your Thummim and Urim belong
  to the man you favored.
You tested him at Massah;
  you contended with him at the waters of
    Meribah.
⁹He said of his father and mother,
  'I have no regard for them.'
He did not recognize his brothers
  or acknowledge his own children,
but he watched over your word
  and guarded your covenant.
¹⁰He teaches your precepts to Jacob
  and your law to Israel.
He offers incense before you
  and whole burnt offerings on your altar.
¹¹Bless all his skills, O LORD,

THE BLESSING

33 Moses, man of God, blessed the People of Israel with this blessing before his death. He said,

33.1-5

GOD came down from Sinai,
  he dawned from Seir upon them;
He radiated light from Mount Paran,
  coming with ten thousand holy angels
And tongues of fire
  streaming from his right hand.
Oh, how you love the people,
  all his holy ones are palmed in your left
    hand.
They sit at your feet,
  honoring your teaching,
The Revelation commanded by Moses,
  as the assembly of Jacob's inheritance.
Thus GOD became king in Jeshurun
  as the leaders and tribes of Israel
    gathered.

33.6 Reuben:
"Let Reuben live and not die,
  but just barely, in diminishing numbers."

33.7 Judah:
"Listen, GOD, to the Voice of Judah,
  bring him to his people;
Strengthen his grip,
  be his helper against his foes."

33.8-11 Levi:
"Let your Thummim and Urim
  belong to your loyal saint;
The one you tested at Massah,
  whom you fought with at the Waters of
    Meribah,
Who said of his father and mother,
  'I no longer recognize them.'
He turned his back on his brothers
  and neglected his children,
Because he was guarding your sayings
  and watching over your Covenant.
Let him teach your rules to Jacob
  and your Revelation to Israel,
Let him keep the incense rising to your
    nostrils
  and the Whole-Burnt-Offerings on your
    Altar.
GOD bless his commitment,

---

a 2 Or *from*   *b* 2 The meaning of the Hebrew for this phrase is uncertain.   *c* 5 *Jeshurun* means *the upright one,* that is, Israel; also in verse 26.   *d* 6 Or *but let*

NEW INTERNATIONAL VERSION

and be pleased with the work of his
hands.
Smite the loins of those who rise up against
him;
strike his foes till they rise no more."

12About Benjamin he said:

"Let the beloved of the LORD rest secure in
him,
for he shields him all day long,
and the one the LORD loves rests between
his shoulders."

13About Joseph he said:

"May the LORD bless his land
with the precious dew from heaven above
and with the deep waters that lie below;
14with the best the sun brings forth
and the finest the moon can yield;
15with the choicest gifts of the ancient
mountains
and the fruitfulness of the everlasting
hills;
16with the best gifts of the earth and its
fullness
and the favor of him who dwelt in the
burning bush.
Let all these rest on the head of Joseph,
on the brow of the prince among*a* his
brothers.
17In majesty he is like a firstborn bull;
his horns are the horns of a wild ox.
With them he will gore the nations,
even those at the ends of the earth.
Such are the ten thousands of Ephraim;
such are the thousands of Manasseh."

18About Zebulun he said:

"Rejoice, Zebulun, in your going out,
and you, Issachar, in your tents.
19They will summon peoples to the mountain
and there offer sacrifices of righteousness;
they will feast on the abundance of the seas,
on the treasures hidden in the sand."

20About Gad he said:

"Blessed is he who enlarges Gad's domain!
Gad lives there like a lion,
tearing at arm or head.
21He chose the best land for himself;
the leader's portion was kept for him.
When the heads of the people assembled,
he carried out the LORD's righteous will,
and his judgments concerning Israel."

a 16 Or of the one separated from

THE MESSAGE

stamp your seal of approval on what he
does;
Disable the loins of those who defy him,
make sure we've heard the last from
those who hate him."

33.12   Benjamin:
"GOD's beloved;
GOD's permanent residence.
Encircled by GOD all day long,
within whom GOD is at home."

33.13-17   Joseph:
"Blessed by GOD be his land:
The best fresh dew from high heaven,
and fountains springing from the depths;
The best radiance streaming from the sun
and the best the moon has to offer;
Beauty pouring off the tops of the
mountains
and the best from the everlasting hills;
The best of Earth's exuberant gifts,
the smile of the Burning-Bush Dweller.
All this on the head of Joseph,
on the brow of the consecrated one
among his brothers.
In splendor he's like a firstborn bull,
his horns the horns of a wild ox;
He'll gore the nations with those horns,
push them all to the ends of the Earth.
Ephraim by the ten thousands will do this,
Manasseh by the thousands will do this."

33.18-19   Zebulun and Issachar:
"Celebrate, Zebulun, as you go out,
and Issachar, as you stay home.
They'll invite people to the Mountain
and offer sacrifices of right worship,
For they will have hauled riches in from
the sea
and gleaned treasures from the beaches."

33.20-21   Gad:
"Blessed is he who makes Gad large.
Gad roams like a lion,
tears off an arm, rips open a skull.
He took one look and grabbed the best
place for himself,
the portion just made for someone in
charge.
He took his place at the head,
carried out GOD's right ways
and his rules for life in Israel."

NEW INTERNATIONAL VERSION

²²About Dan he said:

"Dan is a lion's cub,
    springing out of Bashan."

²³About Naphtali he said:

"Naphtali is abounding with the favor of the
    LORD
    and is full of his blessing;
    he will inherit southward to the lake."

²⁴About Asher he said:

"Most blessed of sons is Asher;
    let him be favored by his brothers,
    and let him bathe his feet in oil.
²⁵The bolts of your gates will be iron and
        bronze,
    and your strength will equal your days.

²⁶"There is no one like the God of Jeshurun,
    who rides on the heavens to help you
    and on the clouds in his majesty.
²⁷The eternal God is your refuge,
    and underneath are the everlasting arms.
He will drive out your enemy before you,
    saying, 'Destroy him!'
²⁸So Israel will live in safety alone;
    Jacob's spring is secure
in a land of grain and new wine,
    where the heavens drop dew.
²⁹Blessed are you, O Israel!
    Who is like you,
    a people saved by the LORD?
He is your shield and helper
    and your glorious sword.
Your enemies will cower before you,
    and you will trample down their high
        places. ^a"

THE DEATH OF MOSES

34 Then Moses climbed Mount Nebo from
the plains of Moab to the top of Pisgah,
across from Jericho. There the LORD showed him
the whole land—from Gilead to Dan, ²all of
Naphtali, the territory of Ephraim and Manasseh, all the land of Judah as far as the western
sea, ^b ³the Negev and the whole region from the
Valley of Jericho, the City of Palms, as far as
Zoar. ⁴Then the LORD said to him, "This is the
land I promised on oath to Abraham, Isaac and
Jacob when I said, 'I will give it to your descendants.' I have let you see it with your eyes, but
you will not cross over into it."

⁵And Moses the servant of the LORD died
there in Moab, as the LORD had said. ⁶He buried
him^c in Moab, in the valley opposite Beth Peor,

THE MESSAGE

33.22   Dan:
    "Dan is a lion's cub
        leaping out of Bashan."

33.23   Naphtali:
    "Naphtali brims with blessings,
        spills over with GOD's blessings
    As he takes possession
        of the sea and southland."

33.24-25   Asher:
    "Asher, best blessed of the sons!
        May he be the favorite of his brothers,
        his feet massaged in oil.
    Safe behind iron-clad doors and gates,
        your strength like iron as long as you
            live."

☩

33.26-28   There is none like God, Jeshurun,
        riding to your rescue through the skies,
        his dignity haloed by clouds.
    The ancient God is home
        on a foundation of everlasting arms.
    He drove out the enemy before you
        and commanded, "Destroy!"
    Israel lived securely,
        the fountain of Jacob undisturbed
    In grain and wine country
        and, oh yes, his heavens drip dew.

33.29   Lucky Israel! Who has it as good as you?
        A people *saved* by GOD!
    The Shield who defends you,
        the Sword who brings triumph.
    Your enemies will come crawling on their
            bellies
        and you'll march on their backs.

THE DEATH OF MOSES

34.1-3   **34** Moses climbed from the Plains of Moab
        to Mount Nebo, the peak of Pisgah fac-
ing Jericho. GOD showed him all the land from
Gilead to Dan, all Naphtali, Ephraim, and Ma-
nasseh; all Judah reaching to the Mediterranean
Sea; the Negev and the plains which encircle
Jericho, City of Palms, as far south as Zoar.

34.4   Then and there GOD said to him, "This is
the land I promised to your ancestors, to Abraham, Isaac, and Jacob with the words 'I will
give it to your descendants.' I've let you see it
with your own eyes. There it is. But you're not
going to go in."

34.5-6   Moses died there in the land of Moab, Moses
the servant of GOD, just as GOD said. God
buried him in the valley in the land of Moab

NEW INTERNATIONAL VERSION

but to this day no one knows where his grave is. [7]Moses was a hundred and twenty years old when he died, yet his eyes were not weak nor his strength gone. [8]The Israelites grieved for Moses in the plains of Moab thirty days, until the time of weeping and mourning was over.

[9]Now Joshua son of Nun was filled with the spirit[a] of wisdom because Moses had laid his hands on him. So the Israelites listened to him and did what the LORD had commanded Moses.

[10]Since then, no prophet has risen in Israel like Moses, whom the LORD knew face to face, [11]who did all those miraculous signs and wonders the LORD sent him to do in Egypt—to Pharaoh and to all his officials and to his whole land. [12]For no one has ever shown the mighty power or performed the awesome deeds that Moses did in the sight of all Israel.

THE MESSAGE

opposite Beth Peor. No one knows his burial site to this very day.

34.7-8   Moses was 120 years old when he died. His eyesight was sharp; he still walked with a spring in his step. The People of Israel wept for Moses in the Plains of Moab thirty days. Then the days of weeping and mourning for Moses came to an end.

34.9   Joshua son of Nun was filled with the spirit of wisdom because Moses had laid his hands on him. The People of Israel listened obediently to him and did the same as when GOD had commanded Moses.

34.10-12   No prophet has risen since in Israel like Moses, whom GOD knew face-to-face. Never since has there been anything like the signs and miracle-wonders that GOD sent him to do in Egypt, to Pharaoh, to all his servants, and to all his land—nothing to compare with that all-powerful hand of his and all the great and terrible things Moses did as every eye in Israel watched.

[a] 9 Or Spirit

JOSHUA

JOSHUA

THE LORD COMMANDS JOSHUA

1 After the death of Moses the servant of the LORD, the LORD said to Joshua son of Nun, Moses' aide: ²"Moses my servant is dead. Now then, you and all these people, get ready to cross the Jordan River into the land I am about to give to them—to the Israelites. ³I will give you every place where you set your foot, as I promised Moses. ⁴Your territory will extend from the desert to Lebanon, and from the great river, the Euphrates—all the Hittite country—to the Great Sea*a* on the west. ⁵No one will be able to stand up against you all the days of your life. As I was with Moses, so I will be with you; I will never leave you nor forsake you.

⁶"Be strong and courageous, because you will lead these people to inherit the land I swore to their forefathers to give them. ⁷Be strong and very courageous. Be careful to obey all the law my servant Moses gave you; do not turn from it to the right or to the left, that you may be successful wherever you go. ⁸Do not let this Book of the Law depart from your mouth; meditate on it day and night, so that you may be careful to do everything written in it. Then you will be prosperous and successful. ⁹Have I not commanded you? Be strong and courageous. Do not be terrified; do not be discouraged, for the LORD your God will be with you wherever you go."

¹⁰So Joshua ordered the officers of the people: ¹¹"Go through the camp and tell the people, 'Get your supplies ready. Three days from now you will cross the Jordan here to go in and take possession of the land the LORD your God is giving you for your own.' "

¹²But to the Reubenites, the Gadites and the half-tribe of Manasseh, Joshua said, ¹³"Remember the command that Moses the servant of the LORD gave you: 'The LORD your God is giving you rest and has granted you this land.' ¹⁴Your wives, your children and your livestock may stay in the land that Moses gave you east of the Jordan, but all your fighting men, fully armed, must

a 4 That is, the Mediterranean

1.1-9 **1** After the death of Moses the servant of GOD, GOD spoke to Joshua, Moses' assistant:

"Moses my servant is dead. Get going. Cross this Jordan River, you and all the people. Cross to the country I'm giving to the People of Israel. I'm giving you every square inch of the land you set your foot on—just as I promised Moses. From the wilderness and this Lebanon east to the Great River, the Euphrates River—all the Hittite country—and then west to the Great Sea. It's all yours. All your life, no one will be able to hold out against you. In the same way I was with Moses, I'll be with you. I won't give up on you; I won't leave you. Strength! Courage! You are going to lead this people to inherit the land that I promised to give their ancestors. Give it everything you have, heart and soul. Make sure you carry out The Revelation that Moses commanded you, every bit of it. Don't get off track, either left or right, so as to make sure you get to where you're going. And don't for a minute let this Book of The Revelation be out of mind. Ponder and meditate on it day and night, making sure you practice everything written in it. Then you'll get where you're going; then you'll succeed. Haven't I commanded you? Strength! Courage! Don't be timid; don't get discouraged. GOD, your God, is with you every step you take."

THE TAKING OF THE LAND

1.10-11 Then Joshua gave orders to the people's leaders: "Go through the camp and give this order to the people: 'Pack your bags. In three days you will cross this Jordan River to enter and take the land GOD, your God, is giving you to possess.' "

1.12-15 Then Joshua addressed the Reubenites, the Gadites, and the half-tribe of Manasseh. He said, "Remember what Moses the servant of GOD commanded you: GOD, your God, gives you rest and he gives you this land. Your wives, your children, and your livestock can stay here east of the Jordan, the country Moses gave you; but you, tough soldiers all, must cross the Riv-

NEW INTERNATIONAL VERSION

cross over ahead of your brothers. You are to help your brothers ¹⁵until the LORD gives them rest, as he has done for you, and until they too have taken possession of the land that the LORD your God is giving them. After that, you may go back and occupy your own land, which Moses the servant of the LORD gave you east of the Jordan toward the sunrise."

¹⁶Then they answered Joshua, "Whatever you have commanded us we will do, and wherever you send us we will go. ¹⁷Just as we fully obeyed Moses, so we will obey you. Only may the LORD your God be with you as he was with Moses. ¹⁸Whoever rebels against your word and does not obey your words, whatever you may command them, will be put to death. Only be strong and courageous!"

RAHAB AND THE SPIES

2 Then Joshua son of Nun secretly sent two spies from Shittim. "Go, look over the land," he said, "especially Jericho." So they went and entered the house of a prostitute ᵃ named Rahab and stayed there.

²The king of Jericho was told, "Look! Some of the Israelites have come here tonight to spy out the land." ³So the king of Jericho sent this message to Rahab: "Bring out the men who came to you and entered your house, because they have come to spy out the whole land."

⁴But the woman had taken the two men and hidden them. She said, "Yes, the men came to me, but I did not know where they had come from. ⁵At dusk, when it was time to close the city gate, the men left. I don't know which way they went. Go after them quickly. You may catch up with them." ⁶(But she had taken them up to the roof and hidden them under the stalks of flax she had laid out on the roof.) ⁷So the men set out in pursuit of the spies on the road that leads to the fords of the Jordan, and as soon as the pursuers had gone out, the gate was shut.

⁸Before the spies lay down for the night, she went up on the roof ⁹and said to them, "I know that the LORD has given this land to you and that a great fear of you has fallen on us, so that all who live in this country are melting in fear because of you. ¹⁰We have heard how the LORD dried up the water of the Red Sea ᵇ for you when you came out of Egypt, and what you did to Sihon and Og, the two kings of the Amorites east of the Jordan, whom you completely destroyed. ᶜ ¹¹When we heard of it, our hearts melted and

THE MESSAGE

er in battle formation, leading your brothers, helping them until GOD, your God, gives your brothers a place of rest just as he has done for you. They also will take possession of the land that GOD, your God, is giving them. Then you will be free to return to your possession, given to you by Moses the servant of GOD, across the Jordan to the east."

1.16-18　They answered Joshua: "Everything you commanded us, we'll do. Wherever you send us, we'll go. We obeyed Moses to the letter; we'll also obey you—we just pray that GOD, your God, will be with you as he was with Moses. Anyone who questions what you say and refuses to obey whatever you command him will be put to death. Strength! Courage!"

RAHAB

2.1　Joshua son of Nun secretly sent out from Shittim two men as spies: "Go. Look over the land. Check out Jericho." They left and arrived at the house of a harlot named Rahab and stayed there.

2.2　The king of Jericho was told, "We've just learned that men arrived tonight to spy out the land. They're from the People of Israel."

2.3　The king of Jericho sent word to Rahab: "Bring out the men who came to you to stay the night in your house. They're spies; they've come to spy out the whole country."

2.4-7　The woman had taken the two men and hidden them. She said, "Yes, two men did come to me, but I didn't know where they'd come from. At dark, when the gate was about to be shut, the men left. But I have no idea where they went. Hurry up! Chase them—you can still catch them!" (She had actually taken them up on the roof and hidden them under the stalks of flax that were spread out for her on the roof.) So the men set chase down the Jordan road toward the fords. As soon as they were gone, the gate was shut.

2.8-11　Before the spies were down for the night, the woman came up to them on the roof and said, "I know that GOD has given you the land. We're all afraid. Everyone in the country feels hopeless. We heard how GOD dried up the waters of the Red Sea before you when you left Egypt, and what he did to the two Amorite kings east of the Jordan, Sihon and Og, whom you put under a holy curse and destroyed. We heard it and our hearts sank. We all had the wind

---

ᵃ 1 Or possibly an innkeeper　　ᵇ 10 Hebrew Yam Suph; that is, Sea of Reeds　　ᶜ 10 The Hebrew term refers to the irrevocable giving over of things or persons to the LORD, often by totally destroying them.

NEW INTERNATIONAL VERSION

everyone's courage failed because of you, for the LORD your God is God in heaven above and on the earth below. [12]Now then, please swear to me by the LORD that you will show kindness to my family, because I have shown kindness to you. Give me a sure sign [13]that you will spare the lives of my father and mother, my brothers and sisters, and all who belong to them, and that you will save us from death."

[14]"Our lives for your lives!" the men assured her. "If you don't tell what we are doing, we will treat you kindly and faithfully when the LORD gives us the land."

[15]So she let them down by a rope through the window, for the house she lived in was part of the city wall. [16]Now she had said to them, "Go to the hills so the pursuers will not find you. Hide yourselves there three days until they return, and then go on your way."

[17]The men said to her, "This oath you made us swear will not be binding on us [18]unless, when we enter the land, you have tied this scarlet cord in the window through which you let us down, and unless you have brought your father and mother, your brothers and all your family into your house. [19]If anyone goes outside your house into the street, his blood will be on his own head; we will not be responsible. As for anyone who is in the house with you, his blood will be on our head if a hand is laid on him. [20]But if you tell what we are doing, we will be released from the oath you made us swear."

[21]"Agreed," she replied. "Let it be as you say." So she sent them away and they departed. And she tied the scarlet cord in the window.

[22]When they left, they went into the hills and stayed there three days, until the pursuers had searched all along the road and returned without finding them. [23]Then the two men started back. They went down out of the hills, forded the river and came to Joshua son of Nun and told him everything that had happened to them. [24]They said to Joshua, "The LORD has surely given the whole land into our hands; all the people are melting in fear because of us."

CROSSING THE JORDAN

3 Early in the morning Joshua and all the Israelites set out from Shittim and went to the Jordan, where they camped before crossing over. [2]After three days the officers went throughout the camp, [3]giving orders to the people: "When you see the ark of the covenant of the LORD your God, and the priests, who are Levites, carrying it, you are to move out from your positions and follow it. [4]Then you will know which way to go, since you have never been this way before. But

THE MESSAGE

knocked out of us. And all because of you, you and GOD, your God, God of the heavens above and God of the earth below.

[2.12-13] "Now promise me by GOD. I showed you mercy; now show my family mercy. And give me some tangible proof, a guarantee of life for my father and mother, my brothers and sisters—everyone connected with my family. Save our souls from death!"

[2.14] "Our lives for yours!" said the men. "But don't tell anyone our business. When GOD turns this land over to us, we'll do right by you in loyal mercy."

[2.15-16] She lowered them down out a window with a rope because her house was on the city wall to the outside. She told them, "Run for the hills so your pursuers won't find you. Hide out for three days and give your pursuers time to return. Then get on your way."

[2.17-20] The men told her, "In order to keep this oath you made us swear, here is what you must do: Hang this red rope out the window through which you let us down and gather your entire family with you in your house—father, mother, brothers, and sisters. Anyone who goes out the doors of your house into the street and is killed, it's his own fault—we aren't responsible. But for everyone within the house we take full responsibility. If anyone lays a hand on one of them, it's our fault. But if you tell anyone of our business here, the oath you made us swear is canceled—we're no longer responsible."

[2.21] She said, "If that's what you say, that's the way it is," and sent them off. They left and she hung the red rope out the window.

[2.22] They headed for the hills and stayed there for three days until the pursuers had returned. The pursuers had looked high and low but found nothing.

[2.23-24] The men headed back. They came down out of the hills, crossed the river, and returned to Joshua son of Nun and reported all their experiences. They told Joshua, "Yes! GOD has given the whole country to us. Everybody there is in a state of panic because of us."

THE JORDAN

3 Joshua was up early and on his way from Shittim with all the People of Israel with him. He arrived at the Jordan and camped before crossing over. After three days, leaders went through the camp and gave out orders to the people: "When you see the Covenant-Chest of GOD, your God, carried by the Levitical priests, start moving. Follow it. Make sure you keep a proper distance between you and it, about half a mile—be sure now to keep your

NEW INTERNATIONAL VERSION

keep a distance of about a thousand yards[a] between you and the ark; do not go near it."

⁵Joshua told the people, "Consecrate yourselves, for tomorrow the LORD will do amazing things among you."

⁶Joshua said to the priests, "Take up the ark of the covenant and pass on ahead of the people." So they took it up and went ahead of them.

⁷And the LORD said to Joshua, "Today I will begin to exalt you in the eyes of all Israel, so they may know that I am with you as I was with Moses. ⁸Tell the priests who carry the ark of the covenant: 'When you reach the edge of the Jordan's waters, go and stand in the river.' "

⁹Joshua said to the Israelites, "Come here and listen to the words of the LORD your God. ¹⁰This is how you will know that the living God is among you and that he will certainly drive out before you the Canaanites, Hittites, Hivites, Perizzites, Girgashites, Amorites and Jebusites. ¹¹See, the ark of the covenant of the Lord of all the earth will go into the Jordan ahead of you. ¹²Now then, choose twelve men from the tribes of Israel, one from each tribe. ¹³And as soon as the priests who carry the ark of the LORD—the Lord of all the earth—set foot in the Jordan, its waters flowing downstream will be cut off and stand up in a heap."

¹⁴So when the people broke camp to cross the Jordan, the priests carrying the ark of the covenant went ahead of them. ¹⁵Now the Jordan is at flood stage all during harvest. Yet as soon as the priests who carried the ark reached the Jordan and their feet touched the water's edge, ¹⁶the water from upstream stopped flowing. It piled up in a heap a great distance away, at a town called Adam in the vicinity of Zarethan, while the water flowing down to the Sea of the Arabah (the Salt Sea[b]) was completely cut off. So the people crossed over opposite Jericho. ¹⁷The priests who carried the ark of the covenant of the LORD stood firm on dry ground in the middle of the Jordan, while all Israel passed by until the whole nation had completed the crossing on dry ground.

4 When the whole nation had finished crossing the Jordan, the LORD said to Joshua, ²"Choose twelve men from among the people, one from each tribe, ³and tell them to take up twelve stones from the middle of the Jordan

THE MESSAGE

distance!—and you'll see clearly the route to take. You've never been on this road before."

3.5 Then Joshua addressed the people: "Sanctify yourselves. Tomorrow GOD will work miracle-wonders among you."

3.6 Joshua instructed the priests, "Take up the Chest of the Covenant and step out before the people." So they took it up and processed before the people.

3.7-8 GOD said to Joshua, "This very day I will begin to make you great in the eyes of all Israel. They'll see for themselves that I'm with you in the same way that I was with Moses. You will command the priests who are carrying the Chest of the Covenant: 'When you come to the edge of the Jordan's waters, stand there on the river bank.' "

3.9-13 Then Joshua addressed the People of Israel: "Attention! Listen to what GOD, your God, has to say. This is how you'll know that God is alive among you—he will completely dispossess before you the Canaanites, Hittites, Hivites, Perizzites, Girgashites, Amorites, and Jebusites. Look at what's before you: the Chest of the Covenant. Think of it—the Master of the entire earth is crossing the Jordan as you watch. Now take twelve men from the tribes of Israel, one man from each tribe. When the soles of the feet of the priests carrying the Chest of GOD, Master of all the earth, touch the Jordan's water, the flow of water will be stopped—the water coming from upstream will pile up in a heap."

3.14-16 And that's what happened. The people left their tents to cross the Jordan, led by the priests carrying the Chest of the Covenant. When the priests got to the Jordan and their feet touched the water at the edge (the Jordan overflows its banks throughout the harvest), the flow of water stopped. It piled up in a heap—a long way off—at Adam, which is near Zarethan. The river went dry all the way down to the Arabah Sea (the Salt Sea). And the people crossed, facing Jericho.

3.17 And there they stood; those priests carrying the Chest of the Covenant stood firmly planted on dry ground in the middle of the Jordan while all Israel crossed on dry ground. Finally the whole nation was across the Jordan, and not one wet foot.

4.1-3 **4** When the whole nation was finally across, GOD spoke to Joshua: "Select twelve men from the people, a man from each tribe, and tell them, 'From right here, the middle of the

---

[a] 4 Hebrew *about two thousand cubits* (about 900 meters)
[b] 16 That is, the Dead Sea

NEW INTERNATIONAL VERSION

from right where the priests stood and to carry them over with you and put them down at the place where you stay tonight."

⁴So Joshua called together the twelve men he had appointed from the Israelites, one from each tribe, ⁵and said to them, "Go over before the ark of the Lord your God into the middle of the Jordan. Each of you is to take up a stone on his shoulder, according to the number of the tribes of the Israelites, ⁶to serve as a sign among you. In the future, when your children ask you, 'What do these stones mean?' ⁷tell them that the flow of the Jordan was cut off before the ark of the covenant of the Lord. When it crossed the Jordan, the waters of the Jordan were cut off. These stones are to be a memorial to the people of Israel forever."

⁸So the Israelites did as Joshua commanded them. They took twelve stones from the middle of the Jordan, according to the number of the tribes of the Israelites, as the Lord had told Joshua; and they carried them over with them to their camp, where they put them down. ⁹Joshua set up the twelve stones that had been*ᵃ* in the middle of the Jordan at the spot where the priests who carried the ark of the covenant had stood. And they are there to this day.

¹⁰Now the priests who carried the ark remained standing in the middle of the Jordan until everything the Lord had commanded Joshua was done by the people, just as Moses had directed Joshua. The people hurried over, ¹¹and as soon as all of them had crossed, the ark of the Lord and the priests came to the other side while the people watched. ¹²The men of Reuben, Gad and the half-tribe of Manasseh crossed over, armed, in front of the Israelites, as Moses had directed them. ¹³About forty thousand armed for battle crossed over before the Lord to the plains of Jericho for war.

¹⁴That day the Lord exalted Joshua in the sight of all Israel; and they revered him all the days of his life, just as they had revered Moses.

¹⁵Then the Lord said to Joshua, ¹⁶"Command the priests carrying the ark of the Testimony to come up out of the Jordan."

¹⁷So Joshua commanded the priests, "Come up out of the Jordan."

¹⁸And the priests came up out of the river carrying the ark of the covenant of the Lord. No sooner had they set their feet on the dry ground than the waters of the Jordan returned to their place and ran at flood stage as before.

ᵃ 9 Or *Joshua also set up twelve stones*

THE MESSAGE

Jordan where the feet of the priests are standing firm, take twelve stones. Carry them across with you and set them down in the place where you camp tonight.' "

4.4-7 Joshua called out the twelve men whom he selected from the People of Israel, one man from each tribe. Joshua directed them, "Cross to the middle of the Jordan and take your place in front of the Chest of God, your God. Each of you heft a stone to your shoulder, a stone for each of the tribes of the People of Israel, so you'll have something later to mark the occasion. When your children ask you, 'What are these stones to you?' you'll say, 'The flow of the Jordan was stopped in front of the Chest of the Covenant of God as it crossed the Jordan—stopped in its tracks. These stones are a permanent memorial for the People of Israel.' "

4.8-9 The People of Israel did exactly as Joshua commanded: They took twelve stones from the middle of the Jordan—a stone for each of the twelve tribes, just as God had instructed Joshua—carried them across with them to the camp, and set them down there. Joshua set up the twelve stones taken from the middle of the Jordan that had marked the place where the priests who carried the Chest of the Covenant had stood. They are still there today.

4.10-11 The priests carrying the Chest continued standing in the middle of the Jordan until everything God had instructed Joshua to tell the people to do was done (confirming what Moses had instructed Joshua). The people crossed; no one dawdled. When the crossing of all the people was complete, they watched as the Chest of the Covenant and the priests crossed over.

4.12-13 The Reubenites, Gadites, and the half-tribe of Manasseh had crossed over in battle formation in front of the People of Israel, obedient to Moses' instructions. All told, about 40,000 armed soldiers crossed over before God to the plains of Jericho, ready for battle.

4.14 God made Joshua great that day in the sight of all Israel. They were in awe of him just as they had been in awe of Moses all his life.

✝

4.15-16 God told Joshua, "Command the priests carrying the Chest of the Testimony to come up from the Jordan."

4.17 Joshua commanded the priests, "Come up out of the Jordan."

4.18 They did it. The priests carrying God's Chest of the Covenant came up from the middle of the Jordan. As soon as the soles of the priests' feet touched dry land, the Jordan's waters resumed their flow within the banks, just as before.

NEW INTERNATIONAL VERSION

¹⁹On the tenth day of the first month the people went up from the Jordan and camped at Gilgal on the eastern border of Jericho. ²⁰And Joshua set up at Gilgal the twelve stones they had taken out of the Jordan. ²¹He said to the Israelites, "In the future when your descendants ask their fathers, 'What do these stones mean?' ²²tell them, 'Israel crossed the Jordan on dry ground.' ²³For the LORD your God dried up the Jordan before you until you had crossed over. The LORD your God did to the Jordan just what he had done to the Red Sea[a] when he dried it up before us until we had crossed over. ²⁴He did this so that all the peoples of the earth might know that the hand of the LORD is powerful and so that you might always fear the LORD your God."

CIRCUMCISION AT GILGAL

5 Now when all the Amorite kings west of the Jordan and all the Canaanite kings along the coast heard how the LORD had dried up the Jordan before the Israelites until we had crossed over, their hearts melted and they no longer had the courage to face the Israelites.

²At that time the LORD said to Joshua, "Make flint knives and circumcise the Israelites again." ³So Joshua made flint knives and circumcised the Israelites at Gibeath Haaraloth.[b]

⁴Now this is why he did so: All those who came out of Egypt—all the men of military age—died in the desert on the way after leaving Egypt. ⁵All the people that came out had been circumcised, but all the people born in the desert during the journey from Egypt had not. ⁶The Israelites had moved about in the desert forty years until all the men who were of military age when they left Egypt had died, since they had not obeyed the LORD. For the LORD had sworn to them that they would not see the land that he had solemnly promised their fathers to give us, a land flowing with milk and honey. ⁷So he raised up their sons in their place, and these were the ones Joshua circumcised. They were still uncircumcised because they had not been circumcised on the way. ⁸And after the whole nation had been circumcised, they remained where they were in camp until they were healed.

⁹Then the LORD said to Joshua, "Today I have rolled away the reproach of Egypt from you." So the place has been called Gilgal[c] to this day.

THE MESSAGE

4.19-22 The people came up out of the Jordan on the tenth day of the first month. They set up camp at The Gilgal (The Circle) to the east of Jericho. Joshua erected a monument at The Gilgal, using the twelve stones that they had taken from the Jordan. And then he told the People of Israel, "In the days to come, when your children ask their fathers, 'What are these stones doing here?' tell your children this: 'Israel crossed over this Jordan on dry ground.'

4.23-24 "Yes, GOD, your God, dried up the Jordan's waters for you until you had crossed, just as GOD, your God, did at the Red Sea, which had dried up before us until we had crossed. This was so that everybody on earth would recognize how strong GOD's rescuing hand is and so that you would hold GOD in solemn reverence always."

✛

5.1 **5** When all the Amorite kings west of the Jordan and the Canaanite kings along the seacoast heard how GOD had stopped the Jordan River before the People of Israel until they had crossed over, their hearts sank; the courage drained out of them just thinking about the People of Israel.

5.2-3 At that time GOD said to Joshua, "Make stone knives and circumcise the People of Israel a second time." So Joshua made stone knives and circumcised the People of Israel at Foreskins Hill.

5.4-7 This is why Joshua conducted the circumcision. All the males who had left Egypt, the soldiers, had died in the wilderness on the journey out of Egypt. All the people who had come out of Egypt, of course, had been circumcised, but all those born in the wilderness along the way since leaving Egypt had not been. The fact is that the People of Israel had walked through that wilderness for forty years until the entire nation died out, all the men of military age who had come out of Egypt but had disobeyed the call of GOD. GOD vowed that these would never lay eyes on the land GOD had solemnly promised their ancestors to give us, a land flowing with milk and honey. But their children had replaced them. These are the ones Joshua circumcised. They had never been circumcised; no one had circumcised them along the way.

5.8 When they had completed the circumcising of the whole nation, they stayed where they were in camp until they were healed.

5.9 GOD said to Joshua, "Today I have rolled away the reproach of Egypt." That's why the place is called The Gilgal. It's still called that.

✛

---

[a] 23 Hebrew *Yam Suph*; that is, Sea of Reeds   [b] 3 *Gibeath Haaraloth* means *hill of foreskins*.   [c] 9 *Gilgal* sounds like the Hebrew for *roll*.

NEW INTERNATIONAL VERSION

[10]On the evening of the fourteenth day of the month, while camped at Gilgal on the plains of Jericho, the Israelites celebrated the Passover. [11]The day after the Passover, that very day, they ate some of the produce of the land: unleavened bread and roasted grain. [12]The manna stopped the day after[a] they ate this food from the land; there was no longer any manna for the Israelites, but that year they ate of the produce of Canaan.

THE FALL OF JERICHO

[13]Now when Joshua was near Jericho, he looked up and saw a man standing in front of him with a drawn sword in his hand. Joshua went up to him and asked, "Are you for us or for our enemies?"

[14]"Neither," he replied, "but as commander of the army of the LORD I have now come." Then Joshua fell facedown to the ground in reverence, and asked him, "What message does my Lord[b] have for his servant?"

[15]The commander of the LORD's army replied, "Take off your sandals, for the place where you are standing is holy." And Joshua did so.

6 Now Jericho was tightly shut up because of the Israelites. No one went out and no one came in.

[2]Then the LORD said to Joshua, "See, I have delivered Jericho into your hands, along with its king and its fighting men. [3]March around the city once with all the armed men. Do this for six days. [4]Have seven priests carry trumpets of rams' horns in front of the ark. On the seventh day, march around the city seven times, with the priests blowing the trumpets. [5]When you hear them sound a long blast on the trumpets, have all the people give a loud shout; then the wall of the city will collapse and the people will go up, every man straight in."

[6]So Joshua son of Nun called the priests and said to them, "Take up the ark of the covenant of the LORD and have seven priests carry trumpets in front of it." [7]And he ordered the people, "Advance! March around the city, with the armed guard going ahead of the ark of the LORD."

[8]When Joshua had spoken to the people, the seven priests carrying the seven trumpets before the LORD went forward, blowing their trumpets, and the ark of the LORD's covenant followed them. [9]The armed guard marched ahead of the

THE MESSAGE

5.10 The People of Israel continued to camp at The Gilgal. They celebrated the Passover on the evening of the fourteenth day of the month on the plains of Jericho.

5.11-12 Right away, the day after the Passover, they started eating the produce of that country, unraised bread and roasted grain. And then no more manna; the manna stopped. As soon as they started eating food grown in the land, there was no more manna for the People of Israel. That year they ate from the crops of Canaan.

✠

5.13 And then this, while Joshua was there near Jericho: He looked up and saw right in front of him a man standing, holding his drawn sword. Joshua stepped up to him and said, "Whose side are you on—ours or our enemies'?"

5.14 He said, "Neither. I'm commander of GOD's army. I've just arrived." Joshua fell, face to the ground, and worshiped. He asked, "What orders does my Master have for his servant?"

5.15 GOD's army commander ordered Joshua, "Take your sandals off your feet. The place you are standing is holy."

Joshua did it.

JERICHO

6.1 **6** Jericho was shut up tight as a drum because of the People of Israel: no one going in, no one coming out.

6.2-5 GOD spoke to Joshua, "Look sharp now. I've already given Jericho to you, along with its king and its crack troops. Here's what you are to do: March around the city, all your soldiers. Circle the city once. Repeat this for six days. Have seven priests carry seven ram's horn trumpets in front of the Chest. On the seventh day march around the city seven times, the priests blowing away on the trumpets. And then, a long blast on the ram's horn—when you hear that, all the people are to shout at the top of their lungs. The city wall will collapse at once. All the people are to enter, every man straight on in."

6.6 So Joshua son of Nun called the priests and told them, "Take up the Chest of the Covenant. Seven priests are to carry seven ram's horn trumpets leading GOD's Chest."

6.7 Then he told the people, "Set out! March around the city. Have the armed guard march before the Chest of GOD."

6.8-9 And it happened. Joshua spoke, the people moved: Seven priests with their seven ram's horn trumpets set out before GOD. They blew the trumpets, leading GOD's Chest of the Covenant. The armed guard marched ahead of the

a 12 Or the day   *b 14 Or lord*

NEW INTERNATIONAL VERSION

priests who blew the trumpets, and the rear guard followed the ark. All this time the trumpets were sounding. ¹⁰But Joshua had commanded the people, "Do not give a war cry, do not raise your voices, do not say a word until the day I tell you to shout. Then shout!" ¹¹So he had the ark of the LORD carried around the city, circling it once. Then the people returned to camp and spent the night there.

¹²Joshua got up early the next morning and the priests took up the ark of the LORD. ¹³The seven priests carrying the seven trumpets went forward, marching before the ark of the LORD and blowing the trumpets. The armed men went ahead of them and the rear guard followed the ark of the LORD, while the trumpets kept sounding. ¹⁴So on the second day they marched around the city once and returned to the camp. They did this for six days.

¹⁵On the seventh day, they got up at daybreak and marched around the city seven times in the same manner, except that on that day they circled the city seven times. ¹⁶The seventh time around, when the priests sounded the trumpet blast, Joshua commanded the people, "Shout! For the LORD has given you the city! ¹⁷The city and all that is in it are to be devoted *ᵃ* to the LORD. Only Rahab the prostitute *ᵇ* and all who are with her in her house shall be spared, because she hid the spies we sent. ¹⁸But keep away from the devoted things, so that you will not bring about your own destruction by taking any of them. Otherwise you will make the camp of Israel liable to destruction and bring trouble on it. ¹⁹All the silver and gold and the articles of bronze and iron are sacred to the LORD and must go into his treasury."

²⁰When the trumpets sounded, the people shouted, and at the sound of the trumpet, when the people gave a loud shout, the wall collapsed; so every man charged straight in, and they took the city. ²¹They devoted the city to the LORD and destroyed with the sword every living thing in it—men and women, young and old, cattle, sheep and donkeys.

²²Joshua said to the two men who had spied out the land, "Go into the prostitute's house and bring her out and all who belong to her, in accordance with your oath to her." ²³So the young men who had done the spying went in and brought out Rahab, her father and mother and brothers and all who belonged to her. They brought out her entire family and put them in a place outside the camp of Israel.

THE MESSAGE

trumpet-blowing priests; the rear guard was marching after the Chest, marching and blowing their trumpets.

6.10 Joshua had given orders to the people, "Don't shout. In fact, don't even speak—not so much as a whisper until you hear me say, 'Shout!'—then shout away!"

6.11-13 He sent the Chest of GOD on its way around the city. It circled once, came back to camp, and stayed for the night. Joshua was up early the next morning and the priests took up the Chest of GOD. The seven priests carrying the seven ram's horn trumpets marched before the Chest of GOD, marching and blowing the trumpets, with the armed guard marching before and the rear guard marching after. Marching and blowing of trumpets!

6.14 On the second day they again circled the city once and returned to camp. They did this six days.

6.15-17 When the seventh day came, they got up early and marched around the city this same way but seven times—yes, this day they circled the city seven times. On the seventh time around the priests blew the trumpets and Joshua signaled the people, "Shout!—GOD has given you the city! The city and everything in it is under a holy curse and offered up to GOD.

"Except for Rahab the harlot—she is to live, she and everyone in her house with her, because she hid the agents we sent.

6.18-19 "As for you, watch yourselves in the city under holy curse. Be careful that you don't covet anything in it and take something that's cursed, endangering the camp of Israel with the curse and making trouble for everyone. All silver and gold, all vessels of bronze and iron are holy to GOD. Put them in GOD's treasury."

6.20 The priests blew the trumpets. When the people heard the blast of the trumpets, they gave a thunderclap shout. The wall fell at once. The people rushed straight into the city and took it.

6.21 They put everything in the city under the holy curse, killing man and woman, young and old, ox and sheep and donkey.

6.22-24 Joshua ordered the two men who had spied out the land, "Enter the house of the harlot and rescue the woman and everyone connected with her, just as you promised her." So the young spies went in and brought out Rahab, her father, mother, and brothers—everyone connected with her. They got the whole family out and gave them a place outside the camp of

---

ᵃ 17 The Hebrew term refers to the irrevocable giving over of things or persons to the LORD, often by totally destroying them; also in verses 18 and 21. *ᵇ* 17 Or possibly *innkeeper*; also in verses 22 and 25

NEW INTERNATIONAL VERSION

²⁴Then they burned the whole city and everything in it, but they put the silver and gold and the articles of bronze and iron into the treasury of the LORD's house. ²⁵But Joshua spared Rahab the prostitute, with her family and all who belonged to her, because she hid the men Joshua had sent as spies to Jericho—and she lives among the Israelites to this day.

²⁶At that time Joshua pronounced this solemn oath: "Cursed before the LORD is the man who undertakes to rebuild this city, Jericho:

"At the cost of his firstborn son
    will he lay its foundations;
at the cost of his youngest
    will he set up its gates."

²⁷So the LORD was with Joshua, and his fame spread throughout the land.

ACHAN'S SIN

7 But the Israelites acted unfaithfully in regard to the devoted things*ª*; Achan son of Carmi, the son of Zimri,*ᵇ* the son of Zerah, of the tribe of Judah, took some of them. So the LORD's anger burned against Israel.

²Now Joshua sent men from Jericho to Ai, which is near Beth Aven to the east of Bethel, and told them, "Go up and spy out the region." So the men went up and spied out Ai.

³When they returned to Joshua, they said, "Not all the people will have to go up against Ai. Send two or three thousand men to take it and do not weary all the people, for only a few men are there." ⁴So about three thousand men went up; but they were routed by the men of Ai, ⁵who killed about thirty-six of them. They chased the Israelites from the city gate as far as the stone quarries*ᶜ* and struck them down on the slopes. At this the hearts of the people melted and became like water.

⁶Then Joshua tore his clothes and fell facedown to the ground before the ark of the LORD, remaining there till evening. The elders of Israel did the same, and sprinkled dust on their heads. ⁷And Joshua said, "Ah, Sovereign LORD, why did you ever bring this people across the Jordan to deliver us into the hands of the Amorites to destroy us? If only we had been content to stay on the other side of the Jordan! ⁸O Lord, what can I say, now that Israel has been routed by its enemies? ⁹The Canaanites and the other people of

---

ª 1 The Hebrew term refers to the irrevocable giving over of things or persons to the LORD, often by totally destroying them; also in verses 11, 12, 13 and 15. ᵇ 1 See Septuagint and 1 Chron. 2:6; Hebrew Zabdi; also in verses 17 and 18. ᶜ 5 Or as far as Shebarim

THE MESSAGE

Israel. But they burned down the city and everything in it, except for the gold and silver and the bronze and iron vessels—all that they put in the treasury of GOD's house.

6.25 But Joshua let Rahab the harlot live—Rahab and her father's household and everyone connected to her. She is still alive and well in Israel because she hid the agents whom Joshua sent to spy out Jericho.

6.26 Joshua swore a solemn oath at that time:

Cursed before GOD is the man
    who sets out to rebuild this city Jericho.
He'll pay for the foundation with his
    firstborn son,
    he'll pay for the gates with his youngest
    son.

6.27 GOD was with Joshua. He became famous all over the land.

ACHAN

7.1 **7** Then the People of Israel violated the holy curse. Achan son of Carmi, the son of Zabdi, the son of Zerah of the tribe of Judah, took some of the cursed things. GOD became angry with the People of Israel.

7.2 Joshua sent men from Jericho to Ai (The Ruin), which is near Beth Aven just east of Bethel. He instructed them, "Go up and spy out the land." The men went up and spied out Ai.

7.3 They returned to Joshua and reported, "Don't bother sending a lot of people—two or three thousand men are enough to defeat Ai. Don't wear out the whole army; there aren't that many people there."

7.4-5 So three thousand men went up—and then fled in defeat before the men of Ai! The men of Ai killed thirty-six—chased them from the city gate as far as The Quarries, killing them at the descent. The heart of the people sank, all spirit knocked out of them.

7.6 Joshua ripped his clothes and fell on his face to the ground before the Chest of GOD, he and the leaders throwing dirt on their heads, prostrate until evening.

7.7-9 Joshua said, "Oh, oh, oh . . . Master, GOD. Why did you insist on bringing this people across the Jordan? To make us victims of the Amorites? To wipe us out? Why didn't we just settle down on the east side of the Jordan? Oh, Master, what can I say after this, after Israel has been run off by its enemies? When the Canaanites and all the others living here get wind of

NEW INTERNATIONAL VERSION

the country will hear about this and they will surround us and wipe out our name from the earth. What then will you do for your own great name?"

¹⁰The LORD said to Joshua, "Stand up! What are you doing down on your face? ¹¹Israel has sinned; they have violated my covenant, which I commanded them to keep. They have taken some of the devoted things; they have stolen, they have lied, they have put them with their own possessions. ¹²That is why the Israelites cannot stand against their enemies; they turn their backs and run because they have been made liable to destruction. I will not be with you anymore unless you destroy whatever among you is devoted to destruction.

¹³"Go, consecrate the people. Tell them, 'Consecrate yourselves in preparation for tomorrow; for this is what the LORD, the God of Israel, says: That which is devoted is among you, O Israel. You cannot stand against your enemies until you remove it.

¹⁴"'In the morning, present yourselves tribe by tribe. The tribe that the LORD takes shall come forward clan by clan; the clan that the LORD takes shall come forward family by family; and the family that the LORD takes shall come forward man by man. ¹⁵He who is caught with the devoted things shall be destroyed by fire, along with all that belongs to him. He has violated the covenant of the LORD and has done a disgraceful thing in Israel!' "

¹⁶Early the next morning Joshua had Israel come forward by tribes, and Judah was taken. ¹⁷The clans of Judah came forward, and he took the Zerahites. He had the clan of the Zerahites come forward by families, and Zimri was taken. ¹⁸Joshua had his family come forward man by man, and Achan son of Carmi, the son of Zimri, the son of Zerah, of the tribe of Judah, was taken.

¹⁹Then Joshua said to Achan, "My son, give glory to the LORD,ᵃ the God of Israel, and give him the praise.ᵇ Tell me what you have done; do not hide it from me."

²⁰Achan replied, "It is true! I have sinned against the LORD, the God of Israel. This is what I have done: ²¹When I saw in the plunder a beautiful robe from Babylonia,ᶜ two hundred shekelsᵈ of silver and a wedge of gold weighing fifty shekels,ᵉ I coveted them and took them. They are hidden in the ground inside my tent, with the silver underneath."

²²So Joshua sent messengers, and they ran to the tent, and there it was, hidden in his tent, with the silver underneath. ²³They took the

THE MESSAGE

this, they'll gang up on us and make short work of us—and then how will you keep up *your* reputation?"

7.10-12 GOD said to Joshua, "Get up. Why are you groveling? Israel has sinned: They've broken the covenant I commanded them; they've taken forbidden plunder—stolen and then covered up the theft, squirreling it away with their own stuff. The People of Israel can no longer look their enemies in the eye—they themselves are plunder. I can't continue with you if you don't rid yourselves of the cursed things.

7.13 "So get started. Purify the people. Tell them: Get ready for tomorrow by purifying yourselves. For this is what GOD, the God of Israel, says: There are cursed things in the camp. You won't be able to face your enemies until you have gotten rid of these cursed things.

7.14-15 "First thing in the morning you will be called up by tribes. The tribe GOD names will come up clan by clan; the clan GOD names will come up family by family; and the family GOD names will come up man by man. The person found with the cursed things will be burned, he and everything he has, because he broke GOD's covenant and did this despicable thing in Israel."

7.16-18 Joshua was up at the crack of dawn and called Israel up tribe by tribe. The tribe of Judah was singled out. Then he called up the clans and singled out the Zerahites. He called up the Zerahite families and singled out the Zabdi family. He called up the family members one by one and singled out Achan son of Carmi, the son of Zabdi, the son of Zerah of the tribe of Judah.

7.19 Joshua spoke to Achan, "My son, give glory to GOD, the God of Israel. Make your confession to him. Tell me what you did. Don't keep back anything from me."

7.20-21 Achan answered Joshua, "It's true. I sinned against GOD, the God of Israel. This is how I did it. In the plunder I spotted a beautiful Shinar robe, two hundred shekels of silver, and a fifty-shekel bar of gold, and I coveted and took them. They are buried in my tent with the silver at the bottom."

7.22-23 Joshua sent off messengers. They ran to the tent. And there it was, buried in the tent with the silver at the bottom. They took the stuff from

---

ᵃ 19 A solemn charge to tell the truth   ᵇ 19 Or *and confess to him*   ᶜ 21 Hebrew *Shinar*   ᵈ 21 That is, about 5 pounds (about 2.3 kilograms)   ᵉ 21 That is, about 1 1/4 pounds (about 0.6 kilogram)

NEW INTERNATIONAL VERSION

things from the tent, brought them to Joshua and all the Israelites and spread them out before the Lord. 24Then Joshua, together with all Israel, took Achan son of Zerah, the silver, the robe, the gold wedge, his sons and daughters, his cattle, donkeys and sheep, his tent and all that he had, to the Valley of Achor. 25Joshua said, "Why have you brought this trouble on us? The Lord will bring trouble on you today."

Then all Israel stoned him, and after they had stoned the rest, they burned them. 26Over Achan they heaped up a large pile of rocks, which remains to this day. Then the Lord turned from his fierce anger. Therefore that place has been called the Valley of Achor*a* ever since.

Ai Destroyed

8 Then the Lord said to Joshua, "Do not be afraid; do not be discouraged. Take the whole army with you, and go up and attack Ai. For I have delivered into your hands the king of Ai, his people, his city and his land. 2You shall do to Ai and its king as you did to Jericho and its king, except that you may carry off their plunder and livestock for yourselves. Set an ambush behind the city."

3So Joshua and the whole army moved out to attack Ai. He chose thirty thousand of his best fighting men and sent them out at night 4with these orders: "Listen carefully. You are to set an ambush behind the city. Don't go very far from it. All of you be on the alert. 5I and all those with me will advance on the city, and when the men come out against us, as they did before, we will flee from them. 6They will pursue us until we have lured them away from the city, for they will say, 'They are running away from us as they did before.' So when we flee from them, 7you are to rise up from ambush and take the city. The Lord your God will give it into your hand. 8When you have taken the city, set it on fire. Do what the Lord has commanded. See to it; you have my orders."

9Then Joshua sent them off, and they went to the place of ambush and lay in wait between Bethel and Ai, to the west of Ai—but Joshua spent that night with the people.

10Early the next morning Joshua mustered his men, and he and the leaders of Israel marched before them to Ai. 11The entire force that was with him marched up and approached the city and arrived in front of it. They set up camp north of Ai, with the valley between them and the city. 12Joshua had taken about five thousand men and set them in ambush between Bethel and Ai, to the

THE MESSAGE

the tent and brought it to Joshua and to all the People of Israel and spread it out before God.

7.24 Joshua took Achan son of Zerah, took the silver, the robe, the gold bar, his sons and daughters, his ox, donkey, sheep, and tent— everything connected with him. All Israel was there. They led them off to the Valley of Achor (Trouble Valley).

7.25-26 Joshua said, "Why have you troubled us? God will now trouble you. Today!" And all Israel stoned him—burned him with fire and stoned him with stones. They piled a huge pile of stones over him. It's still there. Only then did God turn from his hot anger. That's how the place came to be called Trouble Valley right up to the present time.

Ai

8.1 **8** God said to Joshua, "Don't be timid and don't so much as hesitate. Take all your soldiers with you and go back to Ai. I have turned the king of Ai over to you—his people, his city, and his land.

8.2 "Do to Ai and its king what you did to Jericho and its king. Only this time you may plunder its stuff and cattle to your heart's content. Set an ambush behind the city."

8.3-8 Joshua and all his soldiers got ready to march on Ai. Joshua chose thirty thousand men, tough, seasoned fighters, and sent them off at night with these orders: "Look sharp now. Lie in ambush behind the city. Get as close as you can. Stay alert. I and the troops with me will approach the city head-on. When they come out to meet us just as before, we'll turn and run. They'll come after us, leaving the city. As we are off and running, they'll say, 'They're running away just like the first time.' That's your signal to spring from your ambush and take the city. God, your God, will hand it to you on a platter. Once you have the city, burn it down. God says it, you do it. Go to it. I've given you your orders."

8.9 Joshua sent them off. They set their ambush and waited between Bethel and Ai, just west of Ai. Joshua spent the night with the people.

8.10-13 Joshua was up early in the morning and mustered his army. He and the leaders of Israel led the troops to Ai. The whole army, fighting men all, marched right up within sight of the city and set camp on the north side of Ai. There was a valley between them and Ai. He had taken about five thousand men and put them in ambush between Bethel and Ai, west of the

NEW INTERNATIONAL VERSION

west of the city. ¹³They had the soldiers take up their positions—all those in the camp to the north of the city and the ambush to the west of it. That night Joshua went into the valley.

¹⁴When the king of Ai saw this, he and all the men of the city hurried out early in the morning to meet Israel in battle, at a certain place overlooking the Arabah. But he did not know that an ambush had been set against him behind the city. ¹⁵Joshua and all Israel let themselves be driven back before them, and they fled toward the desert. ¹⁶All the men of Ai were called to pursue them, and they pursued Joshua and were lured away from the city. ¹⁷Not a man remained in Ai or Bethel who did not go after Israel. They left the city open and went in pursuit of Israel.

¹⁸Then the LORD said to Joshua, "Hold out toward Ai the javelin that is in your hand, for into your hand I will deliver the city." So Joshua held out his javelin toward Ai. ¹⁹As soon as he did this, the men in the ambush rose quickly from their position and rushed forward. They entered the city and captured it and quickly set it on fire.

²⁰The men of Ai looked back and saw the smoke of the city rising against the sky, but they had no chance to escape in any direction, for the Israelites who had been fleeing toward the desert had turned back against their pursuers. ²¹For when Joshua and all Israel saw that the ambush had taken the city and that smoke was going up from the city, they turned around and attacked the men of Ai. ²²The men of the ambush also came out of the city against them, so that they were caught in the middle, with Israelites on both sides. Israel cut them down, leaving them neither survivors nor fugitives. ²³But they took the king of Ai alive and brought him to Joshua.

²⁴When Israel had finished killing all the men of Ai in the fields and in the desert where they had chased them, and when every one of them had been put to the sword, all the Israelites returned to Ai and killed those who were in it. ²⁵Twelve thousand men and women fell that day—all the people of Ai. ²⁶For Joshua did not draw back the hand that held out his javelin until he had destroyed[a] all who lived in Ai. ²⁷But Israel did carry off for themselves the livestock and plunder of this city, as the LORD had instructed Joshua.

²⁸So Joshua burned Ai and made it a permanent heap of ruins, a desolate place to this day. ²⁹He hung the king of Ai on a tree and left him there until evening. At sunset, Joshua ordered them to take his body from the tree and throw it down at the entrance of the city gate. And they

THE MESSAGE

city. They were all deployed, the main army to the north of the city and the ambush to the west. Joshua spent the night in the valley.

8.14 So it happened that when the king of Ai saw all this, the men of the city lost no time; they were out of there at the crack of dawn to join Israel in battle, the king and his troops, at a field en route to the Arabah. The king didn't know of the ambush set against him behind the city.

8.15-17 Joshua and all Israel let themselves be chased; they ran toward the wilderness. Everybody in the city was called to the chase. They pursued Joshua and were led away from the city. There wasn't a soul left in Ai or Bethel who wasn't out there chasing after Israel. The city was left empty and undefended as they were chasing Israel down.

8.18-19 Then GOD spoke to Joshua: "Stretch out the javelin in your hand toward Ai—I'm giving it to you." Joshua stretched out the javelin in his hand toward Ai. At the signal the men in ambush sprang to their feet, ran to the city, took it, and quickly had it up in flames.

8.20-21 The men of Ai looked back and, oh! saw the city going up in smoke. They found themselves trapped with nowhere to run. The army on the run toward the wilderness did an about-face—Joshua and all Israel, seeing that the ambush had taken the city, saw it going up in smoke, turned and attacked the men of Ai.

8.22-23 Then the men in the ambush poured out of the city. The men of Ai were caught in the middle with Israelites on both sides—a real massacre. And not a single survivor. Except for the king of Ai; they took him alive and brought him to Joshua.

8.24-25 When it was all over, Israel had killed everyone in Ai, whether in the fields or in the wilderness where they had chased them. When the killing was complete, the Israelites returned to Ai and completed the devastation. The death toll that day came to 12,000 men and women—everyone in Ai.

8.26-27 Joshua didn't lower his outstretched javelin until the sacred destruction of Ai and all its people was completed. Israel did get to take the livestock and loot left in the city; GOD's instructions to Joshua allowed for that.

8.28-29 Joshua burned Ai to the ground. A "heap" of nothing forever, a "no-place"—go see for yourself. He hanged the king of Ai from a tree. At evening, with the sun going down, Joshua ordered the corpse cut down. They dumped it at

---

[a] 26 The Hebrew term refers to the irrevocable giving over of things or persons to the LORD, often by totally destroying them.

NEW INTERNATIONAL VERSION

raised a large pile of rocks over it, which remains to this day.

THE COVENANT RENEWED AT MOUNT EBAL

³⁰Then Joshua built on Mount Ebal an altar to the LORD, the God of Israel, ³¹as Moses the servant of the LORD had commanded the Israelites. He built it according to what is written in the Book of the Law of Moses—an altar of uncut stones, on which no iron tool had been used. On it they offered to the LORD burnt offerings and sacrificed fellowship offerings.ᵃ ³²There, in the presence of the Israelites, Joshua copied on stones the law of Moses, which he had written. ³³All Israel, aliens and citizens alike, with their elders, officials and judges, were standing on both sides of the ark of the covenant of the LORD, facing those who carried it—the priests, who were Levites. Half of the people stood in front of Mount Gerizim and half of them in front of Mount Ebal, as Moses the servant of the LORD had formerly commanded when he gave instructions to bless the people of Israel.

³⁴Afterward, Joshua read all the words of the law—the blessings and the curses—just as it is written in the Book of the Law. ³⁵There was not a word of all that Moses had commanded that Joshua did not read to the whole assembly of Israel, including the women and children, and the aliens who lived among them.

THE GIBEONITE DECEPTION

9 Now when all the kings west of the Jordan heard about these things—those in the hill country, in the western foothills, and along the entire coast of the Great Seaᵇ as far as Lebanon (the kings of the Hittites, Amorites, Canaanites, Perizzites, Hivites and Jebusites)— ²they came together to make war against Joshua and Israel.

³However, when the people of Gibeon heard what Joshua had done to Jericho and Ai, ⁴they resorted to a ruse: They went as a delegation whose donkeys were loadedᶜ with worn-out sacks and old wineskins, cracked and mended. ⁵The men put worn and patched sandals on their feet and wore old clothes. All the bread of their food supply was dry and moldy. ⁶Then they went to Joshua in the camp at Gilgal and said to him and the men of Israel, "We have come from a distant country; make a treaty with us."

⁷The men of Israel said to the Hivites, "But perhaps you live near us. How then can we make a treaty with you?"

ᵃ 31 Traditionally *peace offerings*   ᵇ 1 That is, the Mediterranean   ᶜ 4 Most Hebrew manuscripts; some Hebrew manuscripts, Vulgate and Syriac (see also Septuagint) *They prepared provisions and loaded their donkeys*

THE MESSAGE

the entrance to the city and piled it high with stones—you can go see that also.

☩

8.30-32 Then Joshua built an altar to the GOD of Israel on Mount Ebal. He built it following the instructions of Moses the servant of GOD to the People of Israel and written in the Book of The Revelation of Moses, an altar of whole stones that hadn't been chiseled or shaped by an iron tool. On it they offered to GOD Whole-Burnt-Offerings and sacrificed Peace-Offerings. He also wrote out a copy of The Revelation of Moses on the stones. He wrote it with the People of Israel looking on.

8.33 All Israel was there, foreigners and citizens alike, with their elders, officers, and judges, standing on opposite sides of the Chest, facing the Levitical priests who carry GOD's Covenant Chest. Half of the people stood with their backs to Mount Gerizim and half with their backs to Mount Ebal to bless the People of Israel, just as Moses the servant of GOD had instructed earlier.

8.34-35 After that, he read out everything written in The Revelation, the Blessing and the Curse, everything in the Book of The Revelation. There wasn't a word of all that Moses commanded that Joshua didn't read to the entire congregation—men, women, children, and foreigners who had been with them on the journey.

GIBEON

9 9.1-2 All the kings west of the Jordan in the hills and foothills and along the Mediterranean seacoast north toward Lebanon—the Hittites, Amorites, Canaanites, Perizzites, Hivites, Girgashites, and Jebusites—got the news. They came together in a coalition to fight against Joshua and Israel under a single command.

9.3-6 The people of Gibeon heard what Joshua had done to Jericho and Ai and cooked up a ruse. They posed as travelers: their donkeys loaded with patched sacks and mended wineskins, threadbare sandals on their feet, tattered clothes on their bodies, nothing but dry crusts and crumbs for food. They came to Joshua at Gilgal and spoke to the men of Israel, "We've come from a far-off country; make a covenant with us."

9.7 The men of Israel said to these Hivites, "How do we know you aren't local people? How could we then make a covenant with you?"

NEW INTERNATIONAL VERSION

8"We are your servants," they said to Joshua.
But Joshua asked, "Who are you and where do you come from?"

9They answered: "Your servants have come from a very distant country because of the fame of the LORD your God. For we have heard reports of him: all that he did in Egypt, 10and all that he did to the two kings of the Amorites east of the Jordan—Sihon king of Heshbon, and Og king of Bashan, who reigned in Ashtaroth. 11And our elders and all those living in our country said to us, 'Take provisions for your journey; go and meet them and say to them, "We are your servants; make a treaty with us." ' 12This bread of ours was warm when we packed it at home on the day we left to come to you. But now see how dry and moldy it is. 13And these wineskins that we filled were new, but see how cracked they are. And our clothes and sandals are worn out by the very long journey."

14The men of Israel sampled their provisions but did not inquire of the LORD. 15Then Joshua made a treaty of peace with them to let them live, and the leaders of the assembly ratified it by oath.

16Three days after they made the treaty with the Gibeonites, the Israelites heard that they were neighbors, living near them. 17So the Israelites set out and on the third day came to their cities: Gibeon, Kephirah, Beeroth and Kiriath Jearim. 18But the Israelites did not attack them, because the leaders of the assembly had sworn an oath to them by the LORD, the God of Israel.

The whole assembly grumbled against the leaders, 19but all the leaders answered, "We have given them our oath by the LORD, the God of Israel, and we cannot touch them now. 20This is what we will do to them: We will let them live, so that wrath will not fall on us for breaking the oath we swore to them." 21They continued, "Let them live, but let them be woodcutters and water carriers for the entire community." So the leaders' promise to them was kept.

22Then Joshua summoned the Gibeonites and said, "Why did you deceive us by saying, 'We live a long way from you,' while actually you live near us? 23You are now under a curse: You will never cease to serve as woodcutters and water carriers for the house of my God."

24They answered Joshua, "Your servants were clearly told how the LORD your God had commanded his servant Moses to give you the whole land and to wipe out all its inhabitants from be-

THE MESSAGE

9.8   They said to Joshua, "We'll be your servants."

Joshua said, "Who are you now? Where did you come from?"

9.9-11   They said, "From a far-off country, very far away. Your servants came because we'd heard such great things about GOD, your God—all those things he did in Egypt! And the two Amorite kings across the Jordan, King Sihon of Heshbon and King Og of Bashan, who ruled in Ashtaroth! Our leaders and everybody else in our country told us, 'Pack up some food for the road and go meet them. Tell them, We're your servants; make a covenant with us.'

9.12-13   "This bread was warm from the oven when we packed it and left to come and see you. Now look at it—crusts and crumbs. And our cracked and mended wineskins, good as new when we filled them. And our clothes and sandals, in tatters from the long, hard traveling."

9.14   The men of Israel looked them over and accepted the evidence. But they didn't ask GOD about it.

9.15   So Joshua made peace with them and formalized it with a covenant to guarantee their lives. The leaders of the congregation swore to it.

9.16-18   And then, three days after making this covenant, they learned that they were next-door neighbors who had been living there all along! The People of Israel broke camp and set out; three days later they reached their towns—Gibeon, Kephirah, Beeroth, and Kiriath Jearim. But the People of Israel didn't attack them; the leaders of the congregation had given their word before the GOD of Israel. But the congregation was up in arms over their leaders.

9.19-21   The leaders were united in their response to the congregation: "We promised them in the presence of the GOD of Israel. We can't lay a hand on them now. But we can do this: We will let them live so we don't get blamed for breaking our promise." Then the leaders continued, "We'll let them live, but they will be woodcutters and water carriers for the entire congregation."

And that's what happened; the leaders' promise was kept.

9.22-23   But Joshua called the Gibeonites together and said, "Why did you lie to us, telling us, 'We live far, far away from you,' when you're our next-door neighbors? For that you are cursed. From now on it's menial labor for you—woodcutters and water carriers for the house of my God."

9.24-25   They answered Joshua, "We got the message loud and clear that GOD, your God, commanded through his servant Moses: to give you the whole country and destroy everyone living in

NEW INTERNATIONAL VERSION

fore you. So we feared for our lives because of you, and that is why we did this. ²⁵We are now in your hands. Do to us whatever seems good and right to you."

²⁶So Joshua saved them from the Israelites, and they did not kill them. ²⁷That day he made the Gibeonites woodcutters and water carriers for the community and for the altar of the LORD at the place the LORD would choose. And that is what they are to this day.

THE SUN STANDS STILL

10 Now Adoni-Zedek king of Jerusalem heard that Joshua had taken Ai and totally destroyed*ᵃ* it, doing to Ai and its king as he had done to Jericho and its king, and that the people of Gibeon had made a treaty of peace with Israel and were living near them. ²He and his people were very much alarmed at this, because Gibeon was an important city, like one of the royal cities; it was larger than Ai, and all its men were good fighters. ³So Adoni-Zedek king of Jerusalem appealed to Hoham king of Hebron, Piram king of Jarmuth, Japhia king of Lachish and Debir king of Eglon. ⁴"Come up and help me attack Gibeon," he said, "because it has made peace with Joshua and the Israelites."

⁵Then the five kings of the Amorites—the kings of Jerusalem, Hebron, Jarmuth, Lachish and Eglon—joined forces. They moved up with all their troops and took up positions against Gibeon and attacked it.

⁶The Gibeonites then sent word to Joshua in the camp at Gilgal: "Do not abandon your servants. Come up to us quickly and save us! Help us, because all the Amorite kings from the hill country have joined forces against us."

⁷So Joshua marched up from Gilgal with his entire army, including all the best fighting men. ⁸The LORD said to Joshua, "Do not be afraid of them; I have given them into your hand. Not one of them will be able to withstand you."

⁹After an all-night march from Gilgal, Joshua took them by surprise. ¹⁰The LORD threw them into confusion before Israel, who defeated them in a great victory at Gibeon. Israel pursued them along the road going up to Beth Horon and cut them down all the way to Azekah and Makkedah. ¹¹As they fled before Israel on the road down from Beth Horon to Azekah, the LORD hurled large hailstones down on them from the sky, and more of them died from the hailstones than were killed by the swords of the Israelites.

ᵃ 1 The Hebrew term refers to the irrevocable giving over of things or persons to the LORD, often by totally destroying them; also in verses 28, 35, 37, 39 and 40.

THE MESSAGE

it. We were terrified because of you; that's why we did this. That's it. We're at your mercy. Whatever you decide is right for us, do it."

9.26-27 And that's what they did. Joshua delivered them from the power of the People of Israel so they didn't kill them. But he made them woodcutters and water carriers for the congregation and for the Altar of GOD at the place GOD chooses. They still are.

THE FIVE KINGS

10.1-2 **10** It wasn't long before My-Master-Zedek king of Jerusalem heard that Joshua had taken Ai and destroyed it and its king under a holy curse, just as he had done to Jericho and its king. He also learned that the people of Gibeon had come to terms with Israel and were living as neighbors. He and his people were alarmed: Gibeon was a big city—as big as any with a king and bigger than Ai—and all its men were seasoned fighters.

10.3-4 Adoni-Zedek king of Jerusalem sent word to Hoham king of Hebron, Piram king of Jarmuth, Japhia king of Lachish, and Debir king of Eglon: "Come and help me. Let's attack Gibeon; they've joined up with Joshua and the People of Israel."

10.5 So the five Amorite (Western) kings—the king of Jerusalem, the king of Hebron, the king of Jarmuth, the king of Lachish, and the king of Eglon—combined their armies and set out to attack Gibeon.

10.6 The men of Gibeon sent word to Joshua camped at Gilgal, "Don't let us down now! Come up here quickly! Save us! Help us! All the Amorite kings who live up in the hills have ganged up on us."

10.7-8 So Joshua set out from Gilgal, his whole army with him—all those tough soldiers! GOD told him, "Don't give them a second thought. I've put them under your thumb—not one of them will stand up to you."

10.9-11 Joshua marched all night from Gilgal and took them by total surprise. GOD threw them into total confusion before Israel, a major victory at Gibeon. Israel chased them along the ridge to Beth Horon and fought them all the way down to Azekah and Makkedah. As they ran from the People of Israel, down from the Beth Horon ridge and all the way to Azekah, GOD pitched huge stones on them out of the sky and many died. More died from the hailstones than the People of Israel killed with the sword.

NEW INTERNATIONAL VERSION

¹²On the day the LORD gave the Amorites over to Israel, Joshua said to the LORD in the presence of Israel:

"O sun, stand still over Gibeon,
O moon, over the Valley of Aijalon."
¹³So the sun stood still,
and the moon stopped,
till the nation avenged itself on^a its
enemies,

as it is written in the Book of Jashar.

The sun stopped in the middle of the sky and delayed going down about a full day. ¹⁴There has never been a day like it before or since, a day when the LORD listened to a man. Surely the LORD was fighting for Israel!

¹⁵Then Joshua returned with all Israel to the camp at Gilgal.

FIVE AMORITE KINGS KILLED

¹⁶Now the five kings had fled and hidden in the cave at Makkedah. ¹⁷When Joshua was told that the five kings had been found hiding in the cave at Makkedah, ¹⁸he said, "Roll large rocks up to the mouth of the cave, and post some men there to guard it. ¹⁹But don't stop! Pursue your enemies, attack them from the rear and don't let them reach their cities, for the LORD your God has given them into your hand."

²⁰So Joshua and the Israelites destroyed them completely—almost to a man—but the few who were left reached their fortified cities. ²¹The whole army then returned safely to Joshua in the camp at Makkedah, and no one uttered a word against the Israelites.

²²Joshua said, "Open the mouth of the cave and bring those five kings out to me." ²³So they brought the five kings out of the cave—the kings of Jerusalem, Hebron, Jarmuth, Lachish and Eglon. ²⁴When they had brought these kings to Joshua, he summoned all the men of Israel and said to the army commanders who had come with him, "Come here and put your feet on the necks of these kings." So they came forward and placed their feet on their necks.

²⁵Joshua said to them, "Do not be afraid; do not be discouraged. Be strong and courageous. This is what the LORD will do to all the enemies you are going to fight." ²⁶Then Joshua struck and killed the kings and hung them on five trees, and they were left hanging on the trees until evening. ²⁷At sunset Joshua gave the order and they took them down from the trees and threw them into the cave where they had been hiding. At the mouth of the cave they placed large rocks, which are there to this day.

---

^a 13 Or *nation triumphed over*

THE MESSAGE

10.12-13   The day GOD gave the Amorites up to Israel, Joshua spoke to GOD, with all Israel listening:

"Stop, Sun, over Gibeon;
Halt, Moon, over Aijalon Valley."
And Sun stopped,
Moon stood stock still
Until he defeated his enemies.

10.13-14   (You can find this written in the Book of Jashar.) The sun stopped in its tracks in mid sky; just sat there all day. There's never been a day like that before or since—GOD took orders from a human voice! Truly, GOD fought for Israel.

10.15   Then Joshua returned, all Israel with him, to the camp at Gilgal.

10.16-17   Meanwhile the five kings had hidden in the cave at Makkedah. Joshua was told, "The five kings have been found, hidden in the cave at Makkedah."

10.18-19   Joshua said, "Roll big stones against the mouth of the cave and post guards to keep watch. But don't you hang around—go after your enemies. Cut off their retreat. Don't let them back into their cities. GOD has given them to you."

10.20-21   Joshua and the People of Israel then finished them off, total devastation. Only a few got away to the fortified towns. The whole army then returned intact to the camp and to Joshua at Makkedah. There was no criticism that day from the People of Israel!

10.22   Then Joshua said, "Open the mouth of the cave and bring me those five kings."

10.23   They did it. They brought him the five kings from the cave: the king of Jerusalem, the king of Hebron, the king of Jarmuth, the king of Lachish, and the king of Eglon.

10.24   When they had them all there in front of Joshua, he called up the army and told the field commanders who had been with him, "Come here. Put your feet on the necks of these kings."

They stepped up and put their feet on their necks.

10.25   Joshua told them, "Don't hold back. Don't be timid. Be strong! Be confident! This is what GOD will do to all your enemies when you fight them."

10.26-27   Then Joshua struck and killed the kings. He hung them on five trees where they remained until evening. At sunset Joshua gave the command. They took them down from the trees and threw them into the cave where they had hidden. They put large stones at the mouth of the cave. The kings are still in there.

NEW INTERNATIONAL VERSION

²⁸That day Joshua took Makkedah. He put the city and its king to the sword and totally destroyed everyone in it. He left no survivors. And he did to the king of Makkedah as he had done to the king of Jericho.

SOUTHERN CITIES CONQUERED

²⁹Then Joshua and all Israel with him moved on from Makkedah to Libnah and attacked it. ³⁰The LORD also gave that city and its king into Israel's hand. The city and everyone in it Joshua put to the sword. He left no survivors there. And he did to its king as he had done to the king of Jericho.

³¹Then Joshua and all Israel with him moved on from Libnah to Lachish; he took up positions against it and attacked it. ³²The LORD handed Lachish over to Israel, and Joshua took it on the second day. The city and everyone in it he put to the sword, just as he had done to Libnah. ³³Meanwhile, Horam king of Gezer had come up to help Lachish, but Joshua defeated him and his army—until no survivors were left.

³⁴Then Joshua and all Israel with him moved on from Lachish to Eglon; they took up positions against it and attacked it. ³⁵They captured it that same day and put it to the sword and totally destroyed everyone in it, just as they had done to Lachish.

³⁶Then Joshua and all Israel with him went up from Eglon to Hebron and attacked it. ³⁷They took the city and put it to the sword, together with its king, its villages and everyone in it. They left no survivors. Just as at Eglon, they totally destroyed it and everyone in it.

³⁸Then Joshua and all Israel with him turned around and attacked Debir. ³⁹They took the city, its king and its villages, and put them to the sword. Everyone in it they totally destroyed. They left no survivors. They did to Debir and its king as they had done to Libnah and its king and to Hebron.

⁴⁰So Joshua subdued the whole region, including the hill country, the Negev, the western foothills and the mountain slopes, together with all their kings. He left no survivors. He totally destroyed all who breathed, just as the LORD, the God of Israel, had commanded. ⁴¹Joshua subdued them from Kadesh Barnea to Gaza and from the whole region of Goshen to Gibeon. ⁴²All these kings and their lands Joshua conquered in one campaign, because the LORD, the God of Israel, fought for Israel.

⁴³Then Joshua returned with all Israel to the camp at Gilgal.

THE MESSAGE

NO SURVIVORS

10.28 That same day Joshua captured Makkedah, a massacre that included the king. He carried out the holy curse. No survivors. Makkedah's king got the same treatment as Jericho's king.

10.29-30 Joshua, all Israel with him, moved on from Makkedah to Libnah and fought against Libnah. GOD gave Libnah to Israel. They captured city and king and massacred the lot. No survivors. Libnah's king got the same treatment as Jericho's king.

10.31-32 Joshua, all Israel with him, moved on from Libnah to Lachish. He set up camp nearby and attacked. GOD gave Lachish to Israel. Israel took it in two days and killed everyone. He carried out the holy curse, the same as with Libnah.

10.33 Horam, king of Gezer, arrived to help Lachish. Joshua attacked him and his army until there was nothing left of them. No survivors.

10.34-35 Joshua, all Israel with him, moved on from Lachish to Eglon. They set up camp and attacked. They captured it and killed everyone, carrying out the holy curse, the same as they had done with Lachish.

10.36-37 Joshua, all Israel with him, went up from Eglon to Hebron. He attacked and captured it. They killed everyone, including its king, its villages, and their people. No survivors, the same as with Eglon. They carried out the holy curse on city and people.

10.38-39 Then Joshua, all Israel with him, turned toward Debir and attacked it. He captured it, its king, and its villages. They killed everyone. They put everyone and everything under the holy curse. No survivors. Debir and its king got the same treatment as Hebron and its king, and Libnah and its king.

✝

10.40-42 Joshua took the whole country: hills, desert, foothills, and mountain slopes, including all kings. He left no survivors. He carried out the holy curse on everything that breathed, just as GOD, the God of Israel, had commanded. Joshua's conquest stretched from Kadesh Barnea to Gaza and from the entire region of Goshen to Gibeon. Joshua took all these kings and their lands in a single campaign because GOD, the God of Israel, fought for Israel.

10.43 Then Joshua, all Israel with him, went back to the camp at Gilgal.

✝

NEW INTERNATIONAL VERSION	THE MESSAGE

NORTHERN KINGS DEFEATED

11 When Jabin king of Hazor heard of this, he sent word to Jobab king of Madon, to the kings of Shimron and Acshaph, ²and to the northern kings who were in the mountains, in the Arabah south of Kinnereth, in the western foothills and in Naphoth Dor*ᵃ* on the west; ³to the Canaanites in the east and west; to the Amorites, Hittites, Perizzites and Jebusites in the hill country; and to the Hivites below Hermon in the region of Mizpah. ⁴They came out with all their troops and a large number of horses and chariots—a huge army, as numerous as the sand on the seashore. ⁵All these kings joined forces and made camp together at the Waters of Merom, to fight against Israel.

⁶The LORD said to Joshua, "Do not be afraid of them, because by this time tomorrow I will hand all of them over to Israel, slain. You are to hamstring their horses and burn their chariots."

⁷So Joshua and his whole army came against them suddenly at the Waters of Merom and attacked them, ⁸and the LORD gave them into the hand of Israel. They defeated them and pursued them all the way to Greater Sidon, to Misrephoth Maim, and to the Valley of Mizpah on the east, until no survivors were left. ⁹Joshua did to them as the LORD had directed: He hamstrung their horses and burned their chariots.

¹⁰At that time Joshua turned back and captured Hazor and put its king to the sword. (Hazor had been the head of all these kingdoms.) ¹¹Everyone in it they put to the sword. They totally destroyed*ᵇ* them, not sparing anything that breathed, and he burned up Hazor itself.

¹²Joshua took all these royal cities and their kings and put them to the sword. He totally destroyed them, as Moses the servant of the LORD had commanded. ¹³Yet Israel did not burn any of the cities built on their mounds—except Hazor, which Joshua burned. ¹⁴The Israelites carried off for themselves all the plunder and livestock of these cities, but all the people they put to the sword until they completely destroyed them, not sparing anyone that breathed. ¹⁵As the LORD commanded his servant Moses, so Moses commanded Joshua, and Joshua did it; he left nothing undone of all that the LORD commanded Moses.

¹⁶So Joshua took this entire land: the hill country, all the Negev, the whole region of Goshen, the western foothills, the Arabah and the mountains of Israel with their foothills, ¹⁷from Mount Halak, which rises toward Seir, to Baal

11.1-3 **11** When Jabin king of Hazor heard of all this, he sent word to Jobab king of Madon; to the king of Shimron; to the king of Acshaph; to all the kings in the northern mountains; to the kings in the valley south of Kinnereth; to the kings in the western foothills and Naphoth Dor; to the Canaanites both east and west; to the Amorites, Hittites, Perizzites, and Jebusites in the hill country; and to the Hivites below Hermon in the region of Mizpah.

11.4-5 They came out in full force, all their troops massed together—a huge army, in number like sand on an ocean beach—to say nothing of all the horses and chariots. All these kings met and set up camp together at the Waters of Merom, ready to fight against Israel.

11.6 GOD said to Joshua: "Don't worry about them. This time tomorrow I'll hand them over to Israel, all dead. You'll hamstring their horses. You'll set fire to their chariots."

11.7-9 Joshua, his entire army with him, took them by surprise, falling on them at the Waters of Merom. GOD gave them to Israel, who struck and chased them all the way to Greater Sidon, to Misrephoth Maim, and then to the Valley of Mizpah on the east. No survivors. Joshua treated them following GOD's instructions: he hamstrung their horses; he burned up their chariots.

11.10-11 Then Joshua came back and took Hazor, killing its king. Early on Hazor had been head of all these kingdoms. They killed every person there, carrying out the holy curse—not a breath of life left anywhere. Then he burned down Hazor.

11.12-14 Joshua captured and massacred all the royal towns with their kings, the holy curse commanded by Moses the servant of GOD. But Israel didn't burn the cities that were built on mounds, except for Hazor—Joshua did burn down Hazor. The People of Israel plundered all the loot, including the cattle, from these towns for themselves. But they killed the people—total destruction. They left nothing human that breathed.

11.15 Just as GOD commanded his servant Moses, so Moses commanded Joshua, and Joshua did it. He didn't leave incomplete one thing that GOD had commanded Moses.

✝

11.16-20 Joshua took the whole country: the mountains, the southern desert, all of Goshen, the foothills, the valley (the Arabah), and the Israel mountains with their foothills, from Mount Halak, which towers over the region of Seir, all the way

---

ᵃ2 Or in the heights of Dor ᵇ11 The Hebrew term refers to the irrevocable giving over of things or persons to the LORD, often by totally destroying them; also in verses 12, 20 and 21.

NEW INTERNATIONAL VERSION	THE MESSAGE

Gad in the Valley of Lebanon below Mount Hermon. He captured all their kings and struck them down, putting them to death. [18]Joshua waged war against all these kings for a long time. [19]Except for the Hivites living in Gibeon, not one city made a treaty of peace with the Israelites, who took them all in battle. [20]For it was the Lord himself who hardened their hearts to wage war against Israel, so that he might destroy them totally, exterminating them without mercy, as the Lord had commanded Moses.

[21]At that time Joshua went and destroyed the Anakites from the hill country: from Hebron, Debir and Anab, from all the hill country of Judah, and from all the hill country of Israel. Joshua totally destroyed them and their towns. [22]No Anakites were left in Israelite territory; only in Gaza, Gath and Ashdod did any survive. [23]So Joshua took the entire land, just as the Lord had directed Moses, and he gave it as an inheritance to Israel according to their tribal divisions.

Then the land had rest from war.

List of Defeated Kings

12 These are the kings of the land whom the Israelites had defeated and whose territory they took over east of the Jordan, from the Arnon Gorge to Mount Hermon, including all the eastern side of the Arabah:

[2]Sihon king of the Amorites,
who reigned in Heshbon. He ruled from Aroer on the rim of the Arnon Gorge— from the middle of the gorge—to the Jabbok River, which is the border of the Ammonites. This included half of Gilead. [3]He also ruled over the eastern Arabah from the Sea of Kinnereth[a] to the Sea of the Arabah (the Salt Sea[b]), to Beth Jeshimoth, and then southward below the slopes of Pisgah.

[4]And the territory of Og king of Bashan, one of the last of the Rephaites, who reigned in Ashtaroth and Edrei. [5]He ruled over Mount Hermon, Salecah, all of Bashan to the border of the people of Geshur and Maacah, and half of Gilead to the border of Sihon king of Heshbon.

[6]Moses, the servant of the Lord, and the Israelites conquered them. And Moses the servant of the Lord gave their land to the Reubenites, the

---

to Baal Gad in the Valley of Lebanon in the shadows of Mount Hermon. He captured their kings and then killed them. Joshua fought against these kings for a long time. Not one town made peace with the People of Israel, with the one exception of the Hivites who lived in Gibeon. Israel fought and took all the rest. It was God's idea that they all would stubbornly fight the Israelites so he could put them under the holy curse without mercy. That way he could destroy them just as God had commanded Moses.

✠

11.21-22 Joshua came out at that time also to root out the Anakim from the hills, from Hebron, from Debir, from Anab, from the mountains of Judah, from the mountains of Israel. Joshua carried out the holy curse on them and their cities. No Anakim were left in the land of the People of Israel, except in Gaza, Gath, and Ashdod— there were a few left there.

11.23 Joshua took the whole region. He did everything that God had told Moses. Then he parceled it out as an inheritance to Israel according to their tribes.

And Israel had rest from war.

The Defeated Kings

12.1 **12** These are the kings that the People of Israel defeated and whose land they took on the east of the Jordan, from the Arnon Gorge to Mount Hermon, with the whole eastern side of the Arabah Valley.

12.2-3 Sihon king of the Amorites, who reigned from Heshbon: His rule extended from Aroer, which sits at the edge of the Arnon Gorge, from the middle of the gorge and over half of Gilead to the Gorge of the Jabbok River, which is the border of the Ammonites. His rule included the eastern Arabah Valley from the Sea of Kinnereth to the Arabah Sea (the Salt Sea), eastward toward Beth Jeshimoth and southward to the slopes of Pisgah.

12.4-5 And Og king of Bashan, one of the last of the Rephaim who reigned from Ashtaroth and Edrei: His rule extended from Mount Hermon and Salecah over the whole of Bashan to the border of the Geshurites and the Maacathites (the other half of Gilead) to the border of Sihon king of Heshbon.

12.6 Moses the servant of God and the People of Israel defeated them. And Moses the servant of God gave this land as an inheritance to the

---

[a] 3 That is, Galilee   [b] 3 That is, the Dead Sea

NEW INTERNATIONAL VERSION

Gadites and the half-tribe of Manasseh to be their possession.

⁷These are the kings of the land that Joshua and the Israelites conquered on the west side of the Jordan, from Baal Gad in the Valley of Lebanon to Mount Halak, which rises toward Seir (their lands Joshua gave as an inheritance to the tribes of Israel according to their tribal divisions— ⁸the hill country, the western foothills, the Arabah, the mountain slopes, the desert and the Negev—the lands of the Hittites, Amorites, Canaanites, Perizzites, Hivites and Jebusites):

⁹the king of Jericho	one
the king of Ai (near Bethel)	one
¹⁰the king of Jerusalem	one
the king of Hebron	one
¹¹the king of Jarmuth	one
the king of Lachish	one
¹²the king of Eglon	one
the king of Gezer	one
¹³the king of Debir	one
the king of Geder	one
¹⁴the king of Hormah	one
the king of Arad	one
¹⁵the king of Libnah	one
the king of Adullam	one
¹⁶the king of Makkedah	one
the king of Bethel	one
¹⁷the king of Tappuah	one
the king of Hepher	one
¹⁸the king of Aphek	one
the king of Lasharon	one
¹⁹the king of Madon	one
the king of Hazor	one
²⁰the king of Shimron Meron	one
the king of Acshaph	one
²¹the king of Taanach	one
the king of Megiddo	one
²²the king of Kedesh	one
the king of Jokneam in Carmel	one
²³the king of Dor (in Naphoth Dor*ᵃ*)	one
the king of Goyim in Gilgal	one
²⁴the king of Tirzah	one

thirty-one kings in all.

LAND STILL TO BE TAKEN

13 When Joshua was old and well advanced in years, the LORD said to him, "You are very old, and there are still very large areas of land to be taken over.

THE MESSAGE

Reubenites, the Gadites, and half of the tribe of Manasseh.

⸶

¹²·⁷⁻²⁴ And these are the kings of the land that Joshua and the People of Israel defeated in the country west of the Jordan, from Baal Gad in the Valley of Lebanon south to Mount Halak, which towers over Seir. Joshua gave this land to the tribes of Israel as a possession, according to their divisions: lands in the mountains, the western foothills, and the Arabah Valley, on the slopes, and in the wilderness and the Negev desert (lands on which Hittites, Amorites and Canaanites, Perizzites, Hivites, and Jebusites had lived). The kings were:

The king of Jericho	one
The king of Ai (near Bethel)	one
The king of Jerusalem	one
The king of Hebron	one
The king of Jarmuth	one
The king of Lachish	one
The king of Eglon	one
The king of Gezer	one
The king of Debir	one
The king of Geder	one
The king of Hormah	one
The king of Arad	one
The king of Libnah	one
The king of Adullam	one
The king of Makkedah	one
The king of Bethel	one
The king of Tappuah	one
The king of Hepher	one
The king of Aphek	one
The king of Lasharon	one
The king of Madon	one
The king of Hazor	one
The king of Shimron Meron	one
The king of Acshaph	one
The king of Taanach	one
The king of Megiddo	one
The king of Kedesh	one
The king of Jokneam in Carmel	one
The king of Dor (Naphoth Dor)	one
The king of Goyim in Gilgal	one
The king of Tirzah	one

A total of thirty-one kings.

THE RECEIVING OF THE LAND

¹³·¹⁻⁶ **13** When Joshua had reached a venerable age, GOD said to him, "You've had a good, long life, but there is a lot of land still to be taken. This is the land that remains:

NEW INTERNATIONAL VERSION

2"This is the land that remains: all the regions of the Philistines and Geshurites: 3from the Shihor River on the east of Egypt to the territory of Ekron on the north, all of it counted as Canaanite (the territory of the five Philistine rulers in Gaza, Ashdod, Ashkelon, Gath and Ekron—that of the Avvites); 4from the south, all the land of the Canaanites, from Arah of the Sidonians as far as Aphek, the region of the Amorites, 5the area of the Gebalites*a*; and all Lebanon to the east, from Baal Gad below Mount Hermon to Lebo*b* Hamath.

6"As for all the inhabitants of the mountain regions from Lebanon to Misrephoth Maim, that is, all the Sidonians, I myself will drive them out before the Israelites. Be sure to allocate this land to Israel for an inheritance, as I have instructed you, 7and divide it as an inheritance among the nine tribes and half of the tribe of Manasseh."

DIVISION OF THE LAND EAST OF THE JORDAN

8The other half of Manasseh,*c* the Reubenites and the Gadites had received the inheritance that Moses had given them east of the Jordan, as he, the servant of the LORD, had assigned it to them.

9It extended from Aroer on the rim of the Arnon Gorge, and from the town in the middle of the gorge, and included the whole plateau of Medeba as far as Dibon, 10and all the towns of Sihon king of the Amorites, who ruled in Heshbon, out to the border of the Ammonites. 11It also included Gilead, the territory of the people of Geshur and Maacah, all of Mount Hermon and all Bashan as far as Salecah— 12that is, the whole kingdom of Og in Bashan, who had reigned in Ashtaroth and Edrei and had survived as one of the last of the Rephaites. Moses had defeated them and taken over their land. 13But the Israelites did not drive out the people of Geshur and Maacah, so they continue to live among the Israelites to this day.

14But to the tribe of Levi he gave no inheritance, since the offerings made by fire to the LORD, the God of Israel, are their inheritance, as he promised them.

15This is what Moses had given to the tribe of Reuben, clan by clan:

16The territory from Aroer on the rim of the Arnon Gorge, and from the town in the

---

THE MESSAGE

all the districts of the Philistines and Geshurites;
the land from the Shihor River east of Egypt to the border of Ekron up north, Canaanite country (there were five Philistine tyrants—in Gaza, in Ashdod, in Ashkelon, in Gath, in Ekron); also the Avvim from the south;
all the Canaanite land from Arah (belonging to the Sidonians) to Aphek at the Amorite border;
the country of the Gebalites;
all Lebanon eastward from Baal Gad in the shadow of Mount Hermon to the Entrance of Hamath;
all who live in the mountains, from Lebanon to Misrephoth Maim;
all the Sidonians.

13.6-7 "I myself will drive them out before the People of Israel. All you have to do is allot this land to Israel as an inheritance, as I have instructed you. Do it now: Allot this land as an inheritance to the nine tribes and the half-tribe of Manasseh."

LAND EAST OF THE JORDAN

13.8 The other half-tribe of Manasseh, with the Reubenites and Gadites, had been given their inheritance by Moses on the other side of the Jordan eastward. Moses the servant of GOD gave it to them.

13.9-13 This land extended from Aroer at the edge of the Arnon Gorge and the city in the middle of the valley, taking in the entire tableland of Medeba as far as Dibon, and all the towns of Sihon king of the Amorites, who ruled from Heshbon, and out to the border of the Ammonites. It also included Gilead, the country of the people of Geshur and Maacah, all of Mount Hermon, and all Bashan as far as Salecah—the whole kingdom of Og in Bashan, who reigned in Ashtaroth and Edrei. He was one of the last survivors of the Rephaim. Moses had defeated them and taken their land. The People of Israel never did drive out the Geshurites and the Maacathites—they're still there, living in Israel.

13.14 Levi was the only tribe that did not receive an inheritance. The Fire-Gift offerings to GOD, the God of Israel, are their inheritance, just as he told them.

REUBEN

13.15-22 To the tribe of Reuben, clan by clan, Moses gave:
the land from Aroer at the edge of the Arnon Gorge and the town in the middle of the

---

a 5 That is, the area of Byblos   *b* 5 Or *to the entrance to*
c 8 Hebrew *With it* (that is, with the other half of Manasseh)

NEW INTERNATIONAL VERSION

middle of the gorge, and the whole plateau past Medeba [17]to Heshbon and all its towns on the plateau, including Dibon, Bamoth Baal, Beth Baal Meon, [18]Jahaz, Kedemoth, Mephaath, [19]Kiriathaim, Sibmah, Zereth Shahar on the hill in the valley, [20]Beth Peor, the slopes of Pisgah, and Beth Jeshimoth— [21]all the towns on the plateau and the entire realm of Sihon king of the Amorites, who ruled at Heshbon. Moses had defeated him and the Midianite chiefs, Evi, Rekem, Zur, Hur and Reba—princes allied with Sihon—who lived in that country. [22]In addition to those slain in battle, the Israelites had put to the sword Balaam son of Beor, who practiced divination. [23]The boundary of the Reubenites was the bank of the Jordan. These towns and their villages were the inheritance of the Reubenites, clan by clan.

[24]This is what Moses had given to the tribe of Gad, clan by clan:

[25]The territory of Jazer, all the towns of Gilead and half the Ammonite country as far as Aroer, near Rabbah; [26]and from Heshbon to Ramath Mizpah and Betonim, and from Mahanaim to the territory of Debir; [27]and in the valley, Beth Haram, Beth Nimrah, Succoth and Zaphon with the rest of the realm of Sihon king of Heshbon (the east side of the Jordan, the territory up to the end of the Sea of Kinnereth[a]). [28]These towns and their villages were the inheritance of the Gadites, clan by clan.

[29]This is what Moses had given to the half-tribe of Manasseh, that is, to half the family of the descendants of Manasseh, clan by clan:

[30]The territory extending from Mahanaim and including all of Bashan, the entire realm of Og king of Bashan—all the settlements of Jair in Bashan, sixty towns, [31]half of Gilead, and Ashtaroth and Edrei (the royal cities of Og in Bashan). This was for the descendants of Makir son of Manasseh—for half of the sons of Makir, clan by clan.

[32]This is the inheritance Moses had given when he was in the plains of Moab across the Jordan east of Jericho. [33]But to the tribe of Levi, Moses had given no inheritance; the LORD, the God of Israel, is their inheritance, as he promised them.

THE MESSAGE

valley, including the tableland around Medeba;

Heshbon on the tableland with all its towns (Dibon, Bamoth Baal, Beth Baal Meon, Jahaz, Kedemoth, Mephaath, Kiriathaim, Sibmah, Zereth Shahar on Valley Mountain, Beth Peor, the slopes of Pisgah, Beth Jeshimoth);

and all the cities of the tableland, the whole kingdom of Sihon king of the Amorites, who ruled at Heshbon, whom Moses put to death along with the princes of Midian: Evi, Rekem, Zur, Hur, and Reba, who lived in that country, all puppets of Sihon. (In addition to those killed in battle, Balaam son of Beor, the soothsayer, was put to death by the People of Israel.)

13.23   The boundary for the Reubenites was the bank of the Jordan River. This was the inheritance of the Reubenites, their villages and cities, according to their clans.

GAD

13.24-27   To the tribe of Gad, clan by clan, Moses gave:

the territory of Jazer and all the towns of Gilead and half the Ammonite country as far as Aroer near Rabbah;

the land from Heshbon to Ramath Mizpah and Betonim, and from Mahanaim to the region of Debir;

in the valley: Beth Haram, Beth Nimrah, Succoth, and Zaphon, with the rest of the kingdom of Sihon king of Heshbon (the east side of the Jordan, north to the end of the Sea of Kinnereth).

13.28   This was the inheritance of the Gadites, their cities and villages, clan by clan.

HALF-TRIBE OF MANASSEH

13.29-31   To the half-tribe of Manasseh, clan by clan, Moses gave:

the land stretching out from Mahanaim;

all of Bashan, which is the entire kingdom of Og king of Bashan, and all the settlements of Jair in Bashan—sixty towns in all.

Half of Gilead with Ashtaroth and Edrei, the royal cities of Og in Bashan, belong to the descendants of Makir, a son of Manasseh (in other words, the half-tribe of the children of Makir) for their clans.

13.32-33   This is the inheritance that Moses gave out when he was on the plains of Moab across the Jordan east of Jericho. But Moses gave no inheritance to the tribe of Levi. GOD, the God of Israel, is their inheritance, just as he told them.

NEW INTERNATIONAL VERSION

DIVISION OF THE LAND WEST OF THE JORDAN

14 Now these are the areas the Israelites received as an inheritance in the land of Canaan, which Eleazar the priest, Joshua son of Nun and the heads of the tribal clans of Israel allotted to them. ²Their inheritances were assigned by lot to the nine-and-a-half tribes, as the LORD had commanded through Moses. ³Moses had granted the two-and-a-half tribes their inheritance east of the Jordan but had not granted the Levites an inheritance among the rest, ⁴for the sons of Joseph had become two tribes—Manasseh and Ephraim. The Levites received no share of the land but only towns to live in, with pasturelands for their flocks and herds. ⁵So the Israelites divided the land, just as the LORD had commanded Moses.

HEBRON GIVEN TO CALEB

⁶Now the men of Judah approached Joshua at Gilgal, and Caleb son of Jephunneh the Kenizzite said to him, "You know what the LORD said to Moses the man of God at Kadesh Barnea about you and me. ⁷I was forty years old when Moses the servant of the LORD sent me from Kadesh Barnea to explore the land. And I brought him back a report according to my convictions, ⁸but my brothers who went up with me made the hearts of the people melt with fear. I, however, followed the LORD my God wholeheartedly. ⁹So on that day Moses swore to me, 'The land on which your feet have walked will be your inheritance and that of your children forever, because you have followed the LORD my God wholeheartedly.'ᵃ

¹⁰"Now then, just as the LORD promised, he has kept me alive for forty-five years since the time he said this to Moses, while Israel moved about in the desert. So here I am today, eighty-five years old! ¹¹I am still as strong today as the day Moses sent me out; I'm just as vigorous to go out to battle now as I was then. ¹²Now give me this hill country that the LORD promised me that day. You yourself heard then that the Anakites were there and their cities were large and fortified, but, the LORD helping me, I will drive them out just as he said."

¹³Then Joshua blessed Caleb son of Jephunneh and gave him Hebron as his inheritance. ¹⁴So Hebron has belonged to Caleb son of Jephunneh the Kenizzite ever since, because he followed the LORD, the God of Israel, wholeheartedly. ¹⁵(Hebron used to be called Kiriath Arba after Arba, who was the greatest man among the Anakites.)

Then the land had rest from war.

ᵃ 9 Deut. 1:36

THE MESSAGE

LAND WEST OF THE JORDAN

14.1-2 **14** Here are the inheritance allotments that the People of Israel received in the land of Canaan. Eleazar the priest, Joshua son of Nun, and the heads of the family clans made the allotments. Each inheritance was assigned by lot to the nine and a half tribes, just as GOD had commanded Moses.

14.3-4 Moses had given the two and a half tribes their inheritance east of the Jordan, but hadn't given an inheritance to the Levites, as he had to the others. Because the sons of Joseph had become two tribes, Manasseh and Ephraim, they gave no allotment to the Levites; but they did give them cities to live in with pasture rights for their flocks and herds.

14.5 The People of Israel followed through exactly as GOD had commanded Moses. They apportioned the land.

CALEB

14.6-12 The people of Judah came to Joshua at Gilgal. Caleb son of Jephunneh the Kenizzite spoke: "You'll remember what GOD said to Moses the man of God concerning you and me back at Kadesh Barnea. I was forty years old when Moses the servant of GOD sent me from Kadesh Barnea to spy out the land. And I brought back an honest and accurate report. My companions who went with me discouraged the people, but I stuck to my guns, totally with GOD, my God. That was the day that Moses solemnly promised, 'The land on which your feet have walked will be your inheritance, you and your children's, forever. Yes, you have lived totally for GOD.' Now look at me: GOD has kept me alive, as he promised. It is now forty-five years since GOD spoke this word to Moses, years in which Israel wandered in the wilderness. And here I am today, eighty-five years old! I'm as strong as I was the day Moses sent me out. I'm as strong as ever in battle, whether coming or going. So give me this hill country that GOD promised me. You yourself heard the report, that the Anakim were there with their great fortress cities. If GOD goes with me, I will drive them out, just as GOD said."

14.13-14 Joshua blessed him. He gave Hebron to Caleb son of Jephunneh as an inheritance. Hebron belongs to Caleb son of Jephunneh the Kenizzite still today, because he gave himself totally to GOD, the God of Israel.

14.15 The name of Hebron used to be Kiriath Arba, named after Arba, the greatest man among the Anakim.

And the land had rest from war.

NEW INTERNATIONAL VERSION

ALLOTMENT FOR JUDAH

15 The allotment for the tribe of Judah, clan by clan, extended down to the territory of Edom, to the Desert of Zin in the extreme south. ²Their southern boundary started from the bay at the southern end of the Salt Sea,ᵃ ³crossed south of Scorpionᵇ Pass, continued on to Zin and went over to the south of Kadesh Barnea. Then it ran past Hezron up to Addar and curved around to Karka. ⁴It then passed along to Azmon and joined the Wadi of Egypt, ending at the sea. This is theirᶜ southern boundary.

⁵The eastern boundary is the Salt Sea as far as the mouth of the Jordan.

The northern boundary started from the bay of the sea at the mouth of the Jordan, ⁶went up to Beth Hoglah and continued north of Beth Arabah to the Stone of Bohan son of Reuben. ⁷The boundary then went up to Debir from the Valley of Achor and turned north to Gilgal, which faces the Pass of Adummim south of the gorge. It continued along to the waters of En Shemesh and came out at En Rogel. ⁸Then it ran up the Valley of Ben Hinnom along the southern slope of the Jebusite city (that is, Jerusalem). From there it climbed to the top of the hill west of the Hinnom Valley at the northern end of the Valley of Rephaim. ⁹From the hilltop the boundary headed toward the spring of the waters of Nephtoah, came out at the towns of Mount Ephron and went down toward Baalah (that is, Kiriath Jearim). ¹⁰Then it curved westward from Baalah to Mount Seir, ran along the northern slope of Mount Jearim (that is, Kesalon), continued down to Beth Shemesh and crossed to Timnah. ¹¹It went to the northern slope of Ekron, turned toward Shikkeron, passed along to Mount Baalah and reached Jabneel. The boundary ended at the sea.

¹²The western boundary is the coastline of the Great Sea.ᵈ

These are the boundaries around the people of Judah by their clans.

¹³In accordance with the LORD's command to him, Joshua gave to Caleb son of Jephunneh a portion in Judah—Kiriath Arba, that is, Hebron. (Arba was the forefather of Anak.) ¹⁴From Hebron Caleb drove out the three Anakites—Sheshai, Ahiman and Talmai—descendants of Anak. ¹⁵From there he marched against the people liv-

THE MESSAGE

JUDAH

15.1 **15** The lot for the people of Judah, their clans, extended south to the border of Edom, to the wilderness of Zin in the extreme south.

15.2-4 The southern border ran from the tip of the Salt Sea south of The Tongue; it ran southward from Scorpions Pass, went around Zin and just south of Kadesh Barnea; then it ran past Hezron, ascended to Addar, and curved around to Karka; from there it passed along to Azmon, came out at the Brook of Egypt, ending at the Sea. This is the southern boundary.

15.5-11 The eastern boundary: the Salt Sea up to the mouth of the Jordan.

The northern boundary started at the shallows of the Sea at the mouth of the Jordan, went up to Beth Hoglah and around to the north of Beth Arabah and to the Stone of Bohan son of Reuben. The border then ascended to Debir from Trouble Valley and turned north toward Gilgal, which lies opposite Red Pass, just south of the gorge. The border then followed the Waters of En Shemesh and ended at En Rogel. The border followed the Valley of Ben Hinnom along the southern slope of the Jebusite ridge (that is, Jerusalem). It ascended to the top of the mountain opposite Hinnom Valley on the west, at the northern end of Rephaim Valley; the border then took a turn at the top of the mountain to the spring, the Waters of Nephtoah, and followed the valley out to Mount Ephron, turned toward Baalah (that is, Kiriath Jearim), took another turn west of Baalah to Mount Seir, curved around to the northern shoulder of Mount Jearim (that is, Kesalon), descended to Beth Shemesh, and crossed to Timnah. The border then went north to the ridge of Ekron, turned toward Shikkeron, passed along to Mount Baalah, and came out at Jabneel. The border ended at the Sea.

15.12 The western border: the coastline of the Great Sea.

This is the boundary around the people of Judah for their clans.

15.13 Joshua gave Caleb son of Jephunneh a section among the people of Judah, according to GOD's command. He gave him Kiriath Arba, that is, Hebron. Arba was the ancestor of Anak.

15.14-15 Caleb drove out three Anakim from Hebron: Sheshai, Ahiman, and Talmai, all descendants of Anak. He marched up from there against the

---

ᵃ 2 That is, the Dead Sea; also in verse 5   ᵇ 3 Hebrew *Akrabbim*   ᶜ 4 Hebrew *your*   ᵈ 12 That is, the Mediterranean; also in verse 47

NEW INTERNATIONAL VERSION

ing in Debir (formerly called Kiriath Sepher). ¹⁶And Caleb said, "I will give my daughter Acsah in marriage to the man who attacks and captures Kiriath Sepher." ¹⁷Othniel son of Kenaz, Caleb's brother, took it; so Caleb gave his daughter Acsah to him in marriage.

¹⁸One day when she came to Othniel, she urged him*ᵃ* to ask her father for a field. When she got off her donkey, Caleb asked her, "What can I do for you?"

¹⁹She replied, "Do me a special favor. Since you have given me land in the Negev, give me also springs of water." So Caleb gave her the upper and lower springs.

²⁰This is the inheritance of the tribe of Judah, clan by clan:

²¹The southernmost towns of the tribe of Judah in the Negev toward the boundary of Edom were:

Kabzeel, Eder, Jagur, ²²Kinah, Dimonah, Adadah, ²³Kedesh, Hazor, Ithnan, ²⁴Ziph, Telem, Bealoth, ²⁵Hazor Hadattah, Kerioth Hezron (that is, Hazor), ²⁶Amam, Shema, Moladah, ²⁷Hazar Gaddah, Heshmon, Beth Pelet, ²⁸Hazar Shual, Beersheba, Biziothiah, ²⁹Baalah, Iim, Ezem, ³⁰Eltolad, Kesil, Hormah, ³¹Ziklag, Madmannah, Sansannah, ³²Lebaoth, Shilhim, Ain and Rimmon—a total of twenty-nine towns and their villages.

³³In the western foothills:

Eshtaol, Zorah, Ashnah, ³⁴Zanoah, En Gannim, Tappuah, Enam, ³⁵Jarmuth, Adullam, Socoh, Azekah, ³⁶Shaaraim, Adithaim and Gederah (or Gederothaim)*ᵇ*—fourteen towns and their villages.

³⁷Zenan, Hadashah, Migdal Gad, ³⁸Dilean, Mizpah, Joktheel, ³⁹Lachish, Bozkath, Eglon, ⁴⁰Cabbon, Lahmas, Kitlish, ⁴¹Gederoth, Beth Dagon, Naamah and Makkedah—sixteen towns and their villages.

⁴²Libnah, Ether, Ashan, ⁴³Iphtah, Ashnah, Nezib, ⁴⁴Keilah, Aczib and Mareshah—nine towns and their villages.

ᵃ 18 Hebrew and some Septuagint manuscripts; other Septuagint manuscripts (see also note at Judges 1:14) *Othniel, he urged her*   *ᵇ 36* Or *Gederah and Gederothaim*

THE MESSAGE

people of Debir. Debir used to be called Kiriath Sepher.

15.16-17   Caleb said, "Whoever attacks Kiriath Sepher and takes it, I'll give my daughter Acsah to him as his wife." Othniel son of Kenaz, Caleb's brother, took it; so Caleb gave him his daughter Acsah as his wife.

15.18-19   When she arrived she got him
to ask for farm land from her father.
As she dismounted from her donkey
Caleb asked her, "What would you like?"
She said, "Give me a marriage gift.
You've given me desert land;
Now give me pools of water!"
And he gave her the upper and the lower pools.

15.20-32   This is the inheritance of the tribe of the people of Judah, clan by clan.

The southern towns of the tribe of Judah in the Negev were near the boundary of Edom:

Kabzeel, Eder, Jagur,
Kinah, Dimonah, Adadah,
Kedesh, Hazor, Ithnan,
Ziph, Telem, Bealoth,
Hazor Hadattah, Kerioth Hezron (that is, Hazor),
Amam, Shema, Moladah,
Hazar Gaddah, Heshmon, Beth Pelet,
Hazar Shual, Beersheba, Biziothiah,
Baalah, Iim, Ezem,
Eltolad, Kesil, Hormah,
Ziklag, Madmannah, Sansannah,
Lebaoth, Shilhim, Ain, and Rimmon—
a total of twenty-nine towns and their villages.

15.33-47   In the Shephelah (the western foothills) there were:
Eshtaol, Zorah, Ashnah,
Zanoah, En Gannim, Tappuah, Enam,
Jarmuth, Adullam, Socoh, Azekah,
Shaaraim, Adithaim, and Gederah (or Gederothaim)—
fourteen towns and their villages.
Zenan, Hadashah, Migdal Gad,
Dilean, Mizpah, Joktheel,
Lachish, Bozkath, Eglon,
Cabbon, Lahmas, Kitlish,
Gederoth, Beth Dagon, Naamah, and Makkedah—
sixteen towns and their villages.
Libnah, Ether, Ashan,
Iphtah, Ashnah, Nezib,
Keilah, Aczib, and Mareshah—
nine towns and their villages.

NEW INTERNATIONAL VERSION	THE MESSAGE

NEW INTERNATIONAL VERSION

⁴⁵Ekron, with its surrounding settlements and villages; ⁴⁶west of Ekron, all that were in the vicinity of Ashdod, together with their villages; ⁴⁷Ashdod, its surrounding settlements and villages; and Gaza, its settlements and villages, as far as the Wadi of Egypt and the coastline of the Great Sea.

⁴⁸In the hill country:
Shamir, Jattir, Socoh, ⁴⁹Dannah, Kiriath Sannah (that is, Debir), ⁵⁰Anab, Eshtemoh, Anim, ⁵¹Goshen, Holon and Giloh—eleven towns and their villages.

⁵²Arab, Dumah, Eshan, ⁵³Janim, Beth Tappuah, Aphekah, ⁵⁴Humtah, Kiriath Arba (that is, Hebron) and Zior—nine towns and their villages.

⁵⁵Maon, Carmel, Ziph, Juttah, ⁵⁶Jezreel, Jokdeam, Zanoah, ⁵⁷Kain, Gibeah and Timnah—ten towns and their villages.

⁵⁸Halhul, Beth Zur, Gedor, ⁵⁹Maarath, Beth Anoth and Eltekon—six towns and their villages.

⁶⁰Kiriath Baal (that is, Kiriath Jearim) and Rabbah—two towns and their villages.

⁶¹In the desert:
Beth Arabah, Middin, Secacah, ⁶²Nibshan, the City of Salt and En Gedi—six towns and their villages.

⁶³Judah could not dislodge the Jebusites, who were living in Jerusalem; to this day the Jebusites live there with the people of Judah.

ALLOTMENT FOR EPHRAIM AND MANASSEH

16 The allotment for Joseph began at the Jordan of Jericho,ᵃ east of the waters of Jericho, and went up from there through the desert into the hill country of Bethel. ²It went on from Bethel (that is, Luz),ᵇ crossed over to the territory of the Arkites in Ataroth, ³descended westward to the territory of the Japhletites as far as the region of Lower Beth Horon and on to Gezer, ending at the sea.

⁴So Manasseh and Ephraim, the descendants of Joseph, received their inheritance.

⁵This was the territory of Ephraim, clan by clan:
The boundary of their inheritance went from Ataroth Addar in the east to Upper

THE MESSAGE

Ekron with its towns and villages;
From Ekron, west to the sea, all that bordered Ashdod with its villages;
Ashdod with its towns and villages;
Gaza with its towns and villages all the way to the Brook of Egypt.
The Great Sea is the western border.

15.48-60 In the hill country:
Shamir, Jattir, Socoh,
Dannah, Kiriath Sannah (that is, Debir),
Anab, Eshtemoh, Anim,
Goshen, Holon, and Giloh—
eleven towns and their villages.
Arab, Dumah, Eshan,
Janim, Beth Tappuah, Aphekah,
Humtah, Kiriath Arba (that is, Hebron), and Zior—
nine towns and their villages.
Maon, Carmel, Ziph, Juttah,
Jezreel, Jokdeam, Zanoah,
Kain, Gibeah, and Timnah—
ten towns and their villages.
Halhul, Beth Zur, Gedor,
Maarath, Beth Anoth, and Eltekon—
six towns and their villages.
Kiriath Baal (that is, Kiriath Jearim) and Rabbah—
two towns and their villages.

15.61-62 In the wilderness:
Beth Arabah, Middin, Secacah,
Nibshan, the City of Salt, and En Gedi—
six towns and their villages.

15.63 The people of Judah couldn't get rid of the Jebusites who lived in Jerusalem. The Jebusites stayed put, living alongside the people of Judah. They are still living there in Jerusalem.

JOSEPH

16.1-3 **16** The lot for the people of Joseph went from the Jordan near Jericho, east of the spring of Jericho, north through the desert mountains to Bethel. It went on from Bethel (that is, Luz) to the territory of the Arkites in Ataroth. It then descended westward to the territory of the Japhletites to the region of Lower Beth Horon and on to Gezer, ending at the Sea.

16.4 This is the region from which the people of Joseph—Manasseh and Ephraim—got their inheritance.

✝

16.5-9 Ephraim's territory by clans:
The boundary of their inheritance went from Ataroth Addar in the east to Upper Beth

---

ᵃ 1 *Jordan of Jericho* was possibly an ancient name for the Jordan River. ᵇ 2 Septuagint; Hebrew *Bethel to Luz*

NEW INTERNATIONAL VERSION

Beth Horon [6]and continued to the sea. From Micmethath on the north it curved eastward to Taanath Shiloh, passing by it to Janoah on the east. [7]Then it went down from Janoah to Ataroth and Naarah, touched Jericho and came out at the Jordan. [8]From Tappuah the border went west to the Kanah Ravine and ended at the sea. This was the inheritance of the tribe of the Ephraimites, clan by clan. [9]It also included all the towns and their villages that were set aside for the Ephraimites within the inheritance of the Manassites.

[10]They did not dislodge the Canaanites living in Gezer; to this day the Canaanites live among the people of Ephraim but are required to do forced labor.

17 This was the allotment for the tribe of Manasseh as Joseph's firstborn, that is, for Makir, Manasseh's firstborn. Makir was the ancestor of the Gileadites, who had received Gilead and Bashan because the Makirites were great soldiers. [2]So this allotment was for the rest of the people of Manasseh—the clans of Abiezer, Helek, Asriel, Shechem, Hepher and Shemida. These are the other male descendants of Manasseh son of Joseph by their clans.

[3]Now Zelophehad son of Hepher, the son of Gilead, the son of Makir, the son of Manasseh, had no sons but only daughters, whose names were Mahlah, Noah, Hoglah, Milcah and Tirzah. [4]They went to Eleazar the priest, Joshua son of Nun, and the leaders and said, "The LORD commanded Moses to give us an inheritance among our brothers." So Joshua gave them an inheritance along with the brothers of their father, according to the LORD's command. [5]Manasseh's share consisted of ten tracts of land besides Gilead and Bashan east of the Jordan, [6]because the daughters of the tribe of Manasseh received an inheritance among the sons. The land of Gilead belonged to the rest of the descendants of Manasseh.

[7]The territory of Manasseh extended from Asher to Micmethath east of Shechem. The boundary ran southward from there to include the people living at En Tappuah. [8](Manasseh had the land of Tappuah, but Tappuah itself, on the boundary of Manasseh, belonged to the Ephraimites.) [9]Then the boundary continued south to the Kanah Ravine. There were towns belonging to Ephraim lying among the towns of Manasseh, but the boundary of Manasseh was the northern side of the ravine and

THE MESSAGE

Horon and then west to the Sea. From Micmethath on the north it turned eastward to Taanath Shiloh and passed along, still eastward, to Janoah. The border then descended from Janoah to Ataroth and Naarah; it touched Jericho and came out at the Jordan. From Tappuah the border went westward to the Brook Kanah and ended at the Sea. This was the inheritance of the tribe of Ephraim by clans, including the cities set aside for Ephraim within the inheritance of Manasseh—all those towns and their villages.

16:10 But they didn't get rid of the Canaanites who were living in Gezer. Canaanites are still living among the people of Ephraim, but they are made to do forced labor.

✝

7:1-2 **17** This is the lot that fell to the people of Manasseh, Joseph's firstborn. (Gilead and Bashan had already been given to Makir, Manasseh's firstborn and father of Gilead, because he was an outstanding fighter.) So the lot that follows went to the rest of the people of Manasseh and their clans, the clans of Abiezer, Helek, Asriel, Shechem, Hepher, and Shemida. These are the male descendants of Manasseh son of Joseph by their clans.

17:3-4 Zelophehad son of Hepher, the son of Gilead, the son of Makir, the son of Manasseh, had no sons, only daughters. Their names were Mahlah, Noah, Hoglah, Milcah, and Tirzah. They went to Eleazar the priest, Joshua son of Nun, and the leaders and said, "GOD commanded Moses to give us an inheritance among our kinsmen." And Joshua did it; he gave them, as GOD commanded, an inheritance amid their father's brothers.

17:5-6 Manasseh's lot came to ten portions, in addition to the land of Gilead and Bashan on the other side of the Jordan, because Manasseh's daughters got an inheritance along with his sons. The land of Gilead belonged to the rest of the people of Manasseh.

17:7-10 The boundary of Manasseh went from Asher all the way to Micmethath, just opposite Shechem, then ran southward to the people living at En Tappuah. (The land of Tappuah belonged to Manasseh, but Tappuah itself on the border of Manasseh belonged to the Ephraimites.) The boundary continued south to the Brook Kanah. (The cities there belonged to Ephraim although they lay among the cities of Manasseh.) The boundary of Manasseh ran north of the brook

NEW INTERNATIONAL VERSION

ended at the sea. [10]On the south the land belonged to Ephraim, on the north to Manasseh. The territory of Manasseh reached the sea and bordered Asher on the north and Issachar on the east.

[11]Within Issachar and Asher, Manasseh also had Beth Shan, Ibleam and the people of Dor, Endor, Taanach and Megiddo, together with their surrounding settlements (the third in the list is Naphoth[a]).

[12]Yet the Manassites were not able to occupy these towns, for the Canaanites were determined to live in that region. [13]However, when the Israelites grew stronger, they subjected the Canaanites to forced labor but did not drive them out completely.

[14]The people of Joseph said to Joshua, "Why have you given us only one allotment and one portion for an inheritance? We are a numerous people and the LORD has blessed us abundantly."

[15]"If you are so numerous," Joshua answered, "and if the hill country of Ephraim is too small for you, go up into the forest and clear land for yourselves there in the land of the Perizzites and Rephaites."

[16]The people of Joseph replied, "The hill country is not enough for us, and all the Canaanites who live in the plain have iron chariots, both those in Beth Shan and its settlements and those in the Valley of Jezreel."

[17]But Joshua said to the house of Joseph—to Ephraim and Manasseh—"You are numerous and very powerful. You will have not only one allotment [18]but the forested hill country as well. Clear it, and its farthest limits will be yours; though the Canaanites have iron chariots and though they are strong, you can drive them out."

DIVISION OF THE REST OF THE LAND

18 The whole assembly of the Israelites gathered at Shiloh and set up the Tent of Meeting there. The country was brought under their control, [2]but there were still seven Israelite tribes who had not yet received their inheritance.

[3]So Joshua said to the Israelites: "How long will you wait before you begin to take possession of the land that the LORD, the God of your fathers, has given you? [4]Appoint three men from each tribe. I will send them out to make a survey of the land and to write a description of it, according to the inheritance of each. Then they will return to me. [5]You are to divide the land

THE MESSAGE

and ended at the Sea. The land to the south belonged to Ephraim; the land to the north to Manasseh, with the Sea as their western border; they meet Asher on the north and Issachar on the east.

17.11 Within Issachar and Asher, Manasseh also held Beth Shan, Ibleam, and the people of Dor, Endor, Taanach, and Megiddo, together with their villages, and the third in the list is Naphoth.

17.12-13 The people of Manasseh never were able to take over these towns—the Canaanites wouldn't budge. But later, when the Israelites got stronger, they put the Canaanites to forced labor. But they never did get rid of them.

✝

17.14 The people of Joseph spoke to Joshua: "Why did you give us just one allotment, one solitary share? There are a lot of us, and growing—GOD has extravagantly blessed us."

17.15 Joshua responded, "Since there are so many of you, and you find the hill country of Ephraim too confining, climb into the forest and clear ground there for yourselves in the land of the Perizzites and the Rephaim."

17.16 But the people of Joseph said, "There's not enough hill country for us; and the Canaanites who live down in the plain, both those in Beth Shan and its villages and in the Valley of Jezreel, have iron chariots."

17.17-18 Joshua said to the family of Joseph (to Ephraim and Manasseh): "Yes, there are a lot of you, and you are very strong. One lot is not enough for you. You also get the hill country. It's nothing but trees now, but you will clear the land and make it your own from one end to the other. The powerful Canaanites, even with their iron chariots, won't stand a chance against you."

THE SHILOH SURVEY

18.1-2 **18** Then the entire congregation of the People of Israel got together at Shiloh. They put up the Tent of Meeting.

The land was under their control but there were still seven Israelite tribes who had yet to receive their inheritance.

18.3-5 Joshua addressed the People of Israel: "How long are you going to sit around on your hands, putting off taking possession of the land that GOD, the God of your ancestors, has given you? Pick three men from each tribe so I can commission them. They will survey and map the land, showing the inheritance due each tribe, and report back to me. They will divide it into

---

[a] 11 That is, Naphoth Dor

NEW INTERNATIONAL VERSION

into seven parts. Judah is to remain in its territory on the south and the house of Joseph in its territory on the north. ⁶After you have written descriptions of the seven parts of the land, bring them here to me and I will cast lots for you in the presence of the LORD our God. ⁷The Levites, however, do not get a portion among you, because the priestly service of the LORD is their inheritance. And Gad, Reuben and the half-tribe of Manasseh have already received their inheritance on the east side of the Jordan. Moses the servant of the LORD gave it to them."

⁸As the men started on their way to map out the land, Joshua instructed them, "Go and make a survey of the land and write a description of it. Then return to me, and I will cast lots for you here at Shiloh in the presence of the LORD." ⁹So the men left and went through the land. They wrote its description on a scroll, town by town, in seven parts, and returned to Joshua in the camp at Shiloh. ¹⁰Joshua then cast lots for them in Shiloh in the presence of the LORD, and there he distributed the land to the Israelites according to their tribal divisions.

ALLOTMENT FOR BENJAMIN

¹¹The lot came up for the tribe of Benjamin, clan by clan. Their allotted territory lay between the tribes of Judah and Joseph:

¹²On the north side their boundary began at the Jordan, passed the northern slope of Jericho and headed west into the hill country, coming out at the desert of Beth Aven. ¹³From there it crossed to the south slope of Luz (that is, Bethel) and went down to Ataroth Addar on the hill south of Lower Beth Horon.

¹⁴From the hill facing Beth Horon on the south the boundary turned south along the western side and came out at Kiriath Baal (that is, Kiriath Jearim), a town of the people of Judah. This was the western side.

¹⁵The southern side began at the outskirts of Kiriath Jearim on the west, and the boundary came out at the spring of the waters of Nephtoah. ¹⁶The boundary went down to the foot of the hill facing the Valley of Ben Hinnom, north of the Valley of Rephaim. It continued down the Hinnom Valley along the southern slope of the Jebusite city and so to En Rogel. ¹⁷It then curved north, went to En Shemesh, continued to Geliloth, which faces the Pass of Adummim, and ran down to the Stone of Bohan son of Reuben. ¹⁸It continued to the northern slope of Beth Arabah*ᵃ* and on

THE MESSAGE

seven parts. Judah will stay in its territory in the south and the people of Joseph will keep to their place in the north.

18.6 "You are responsible for preparing a survey map showing seven portions. Then bring it to me so that I can cast lots for you here in the presence of our GOD.

18.7 "Only the Levites get no portion among you because the priesthood of GOD is their inheritance. And Gad, Reuben, and the half-tribe of Manasseh already have their inheritance on the east side of the Jordan, given to them by Moses the servant of GOD."

18.8 So the men set out. As they went out to survey the land, Joshua charged them: "Go. Survey the land and map it. Then come back to me and I will cast lots for you here at Shiloh in the presence of GOD."

18.9 So off the men went. They covered the ground and mapped the country by towns in a scroll. Then they reported back to Joshua at the camp at Shiloh.

18.10 Joshua cast the lots for them at Shiloh in the presence of GOD. That's where Joshua divided up the land to the People of Israel, according to their tribal divisions.

BENJAMIN

18.11 The first lot turned up for the tribe of Benjamin with its clans. The border of the allotment went between the peoples of Judah and Joseph.

18.12-13 The northern border began at the Jordan, then went up to the ridge north of Jericho, ascending west into the hill country into the wilderness of Beth Aven. From there the border went around to Luz, to its southern ridge (that is, Bethel), and then down from Ataroth Addar to the mountain to the south of Lower Beth Horon.

18.14 There the border took a turn on the west side and swung south from the mountain to the south of Beth Horon and ended at Kiriath Baal (that is, Kiriath Jearim), a town of the people of Judah. This was the west side.

18.15-19 The southern border began at the edge of Kiriath Jearim on the west, then ran west until it reached the spring, the Waters of Nephtoah. It then descended to the foot of the mountain opposite the Valley of Ben Hinnom (which flanks the Valley of Rephaim to the north), descended to the Hinnom Valley, just south of the Jebusite ridge, and went on to En Rogel. From there it curved north to En Shemesh and Geliloth, opposite the Red Pass (Adummim), down to the Stone of Bohan the son of Reuben, continued toward the north flank of Beth Arabah,

---

ᵃ 18 Septuagint; Hebrew *slope facing the Arabah*

down into the Arabah. ¹⁹It then went to the northern slope of Beth Hoglah and came out at the northern bay of the Salt Sea,ᵃ at the mouth of the Jordan in the south. This was the southern boundary.

²⁰The Jordan formed the boundary on the eastern side.

These were the boundaries that marked out the inheritance of the clans of Benjamin on all sides.

²¹The tribe of Benjamin, clan by clan, had the following cities:

Jericho, Beth Hoglah, Emek Keziz, ²²Beth Arabah, Zemaraim, Bethel, ²³Avvim, Parah, Ophrah, ²⁴Kephar Ammoni, Ophni and Geba—twelve towns and their villages.

²⁵Gibeon, Ramah, Beeroth, ²⁶Mizpah, Kephirah, Mozah, ²⁷Rekem, Irpeel, Taralah, ²⁸Zelah, Haeleph, the Jebusite city (that is, Jerusalem), Gibeah and Kiriath—fourteen towns and their villages.

This was the inheritance of Benjamin for its clans.

ALLOTMENT FOR SIMEON

19 The second lot came out for the tribe of Simeon, clan by clan. Their inheritance lay within the territory of Judah. ²It included:

Beersheba (or Sheba),ᵇ Moladah, ³Hazar Shual, Balah, Ezem, ⁴Eltolad, Bethul, Hormah, ⁵Ziklag, Beth Marcaboth, Hazar Susah, ⁶Beth Lebaoth and Sharuhen—thirteen towns and their villages;

⁷Ain, Rimmon, Ether and Ashan—four towns and their villages— ⁸and all the villages around these towns as far as Baalath Beer (Ramah in the Negev).

This was the inheritance of the tribe of the Simeonites, clan by clan. ⁹The inheritance of the Simeonites was taken from the share of Judah, because Judah's portion was more than they needed. So the Simeonites received their inheritance within the territory of Judah.

ALLOTMENT FOR ZEBULUN

¹⁰The third lot came up for Zebulun, clan by clan:

The boundary of their inheritance went as far as Sarid. ¹¹Going west it ran to Maralah, touched Dabbesheth, and extended to the ravine near Jokneam. ¹²It turned east from Sarid toward the sunrise to the territory of Kisloth Tabor and went on to Daberath and up to Japhia. ¹³Then it continued

ᵃ 19 That is, the Dead Sea   ᵇ 2 Or Beersheba, Sheba; 1 Chron. 4:28 does not have Sheba.

then plunged to the Arabah. It then followed the slope of Beth Hoglah north and came out at the northern bay of the Salt Sea—the south end of the Jordan. This was the southern border.

18.20 The east border was formed by the Jordan.

This was the inheritance of the people of Benjamin for their clans, marked by these borders on all sides.

18.21-28 The cities of the tribe of Benjamin, clan by clan, were:

Jericho, Beth Hoglah, Emek Keziz, Beth Arabah, Zemaraim, Bethel, Avvim, Parah, Ophrah, Kephar Ammoni, Ophni, and Geba—twelve towns with their villages. Gibeon, Ramah, Beeroth, Mizpah, Kephirah, Mozah, Rekem, Irpeel, Taralah, Zelah, Haeleph, the Jebusite city (that is, Jerusalem), Gibeah, and Kiriath Jearim—fourteen cities with their villages.

This was the inheritance for Benjamin, according to its clans.

SIMEON

19.1-8 **19** The second lot went to Simeon for its clans. Their inheritance was within the territory of Judah. In their inheritance they had:

Beersheba (or Sheba), Moladah, Hazar Shual, Balah, Ezem, Eltolad, Bethul, Hormah, Ziklag, Beth Marcaboth, Hazar Susah, Beth Lebaoth, and Sharuhen—thirteen towns and their villages. Ain, Rimmon, Ether, and Ashan—four towns and their villages—plus all the villages around these towns as far as Baalath Beer, the Ramah of the Negev.

19.8-9 This is the inheritance of the tribe of Simeon according to its clans. The inheritance of Simeon came out of the share of Judah, because Judah's portion turned out to be more than they needed. That's how the people of Simeon came to get their lot from within Judah's portion.

ZEBULUN

19.10-15 The third lot went to Zebulun, clan by clan:

The border of their inheritance went all the way to Sarid. It ran west to Maralah, met Dabbesheth, and then went to the brook opposite Jokneam. In the other direction from Sarid, the border ran east; it followed the sunrise to the border of Kisloth Tabor, on to Daberath and up to Japhia. It continued east to Gath Hepher

NEW INTERNATIONAL VERSION

eastward to Gath Hepher and Eth Kazin; it came out at Rimmon and turned toward Neah. ¹⁴There the boundary went around on the north to Hannathon and ended at the Valley of Iphtah El. ¹⁵Included were Kattath, Nahalal, Shimron, Idalah and Bethlehem. There were twelve towns and their villages.
¹⁶These towns and their villages were the inheritance of Zebulun, clan by clan.

ALLOTMENT FOR ISSACHAR
¹⁷The fourth lot came out for Issachar, clan by clan. ¹⁸Their territory included:

Jezreel, Kesulloth, Shunem, ¹⁹Hapharaim, Shion, Anaharath, ²⁰Rabbith, Kishion, Ebez, ²¹Remeth, En Gannim, En Haddah and Beth Pazzez. ²²The boundary touched Tabor, Shahazumah and Beth Shemesh, and ended at the Jordan. There were sixteen towns and their villages.
²³These towns and their villages were the inheritance of the tribe of Issachar, clan by clan.

ALLOTMENT FOR ASHER
²⁴The fifth lot came out for the tribe of Asher, clan by clan. ²⁵Their territory included:

Helkath, Hali, Beten, Acshaph, ²⁶Allammelech, Amad and Mishal. On the west the boundary touched Carmel and Shihor Libnath. ²⁷It then turned east toward Beth Dagon, touched Zebulun and the Valley of Iphtah El, and went north to Beth Emek and Neiel, passing Cabul on the left. ²⁸It went to Abdon,ᵃ Rehob, Hammon and Kanah, as far as Greater Sidon. ²⁹The boundary then turned back toward Ramah and went to the fortified city of Tyre, turned toward Hosah and came out at the sea in the region of Aczib, ³⁰Ummah, Aphek and Rehob. There were twenty-two towns and their villages.
³¹These towns and their villages were the inheritance of the tribe of Asher, clan by clan.

ALLOTMENT FOR NAPHTALI
³²The sixth lot came out for Naphtali, clan by clan:

³³Their boundary went from Heleph and the large tree in Zaanannim, passing Adami Nekeb and Jabneel to Lakkum and ending at the Jordan. ³⁴The boundary ran west through Aznoth Tabor and came out at Hukkok. It touched Zebulun on the south,

---

ᵃ 28 Some Hebrew manuscripts (see also Joshua 21:30); most Hebrew manuscripts *Ebron*

THE MESSAGE

and Eth Kazin, came out at Rimmon, and turned toward Neah. There the border went around on the north to Hannathon and ran out into the Valley of Iphtah El. It included Kattath, Nahalal, Shimron, Idalah, and Bethlehem—twelve cities with their villages.

19.16   This is the inheritance of the people of Zebulun for their clans—these towns and their villages.

ISSACHAR
19.17-21 The fourth lot went to Issachar, clan by clan. Their territory included:

Jezreel, Kesulloth, Shunem,
Hapharaim, Shion, Anaharath,
Rabbith, Kishion, Ebez,
Remeth, En Gannim, En Haddah, and Beth Pazzez.

19.22   The boundary touched Tabor, Shahazumah, and Beth Shemesh and ended at the Jordan—sixteen towns and their villages.
19.23   These towns with their villages were the inheritance of the tribe of Issachar, clan by clan.

ASHER
19.24 The fifth lot went to the tribe of Asher, clan by clan:
19.25-30   Their territory included Helkath, Hali, Beten, Acshaph, Allammelech, Amad, and Mishal. The western border touched Carmel and Shihor Libnath, then turned east toward Beth Dagon, touched Zebulun and the Valley of Iphtah El, and went north to Beth Emek and Neiel, skirting Cabul on the left. It went on to Abdon, Rehob, Hammon, and Kanah, all the way to Greater Sidon. The border circled back toward Ramah, extended to the fort city of Tyre, turned toward Hosah, and came out at the Sea in the region of Aczib, Ummah, Aphek, and Rehob—twenty-two towns and their villages.

19.31   These towns and villages were the inheritance of the tribe of Asher, clan by clan.

NAPHTALI
19.32 The sixth lot came to Naphtali and its clans.
19.33   Their border ran from Heleph, from the oak at Zaanannim, passing Adami Nekeb and Jabneel to Lakkum and ending at the Jordan.
19.34   The border returned on the west at Aznoth Tabor and came out at Hukkok, meeting Zebu-

NEW INTERNATIONAL VERSION

Asher on the west and the Jordan*a* on the east. ³⁵The fortified cities were Ziddim, Zer, Hammath, Rakkath, Kinnereth, ³⁶Adamah, Ramah, Hazor, ³⁷Kedesh, Edrei, En Hazor, ³⁸Iron, Migdal El, Horem, Beth Anath and Beth Shemesh. There were nineteen towns and their villages.

³⁹These towns and their villages were the inheritance of the tribe of Naphtali, clan by clan.

ALLOTMENT FOR DAN

⁴⁰The seventh lot came out for the tribe of Dan, clan by clan. ⁴¹The territory of their inheritance included:

Zorah, Eshtaol, Ir Shemesh, ⁴²Shaalabbin, Aijalon, Ithlah, ⁴³Elon, Timnah, Ekron, ⁴⁴Eltekeh, Gibbethon, Baalath, ⁴⁵Jehud, Bene Berak, Gath Rimmon, ⁴⁶Me Jarkon and Rakkon, with the area facing Joppa.

⁴⁷(But the Danites had difficulty taking possession of their territory, so they went up and attacked Leshem, took it, put it to the sword and occupied it. They settled in Leshem and named it Dan after their forefather.)

⁴⁸These towns and their villages were the inheritance of the tribe of Dan, clan by clan.

ALLOTMENT FOR JOSHUA

⁴⁹When they had finished dividing the land into its allotted portions, the Israelites gave Joshua son of Nun an inheritance among them, ⁵⁰as the LORD had commanded. They gave him the town he asked for—Timnath Serah*b* in the hill country of Ephraim. And he built up the town and settled there.

⁵¹These are the territories that Eleazar the priest, Joshua son of Nun and the heads of the tribal clans of Israel assigned by lot at Shiloh in the presence of the LORD at the entrance to the Tent of Meeting. And so they finished dividing the land.

CITIES OF REFUGE

20 Then the LORD said to Joshua: ²"Tell the Israelites to designate the cities of refuge, as I instructed you through Moses, ³so that any-

---

THE MESSAGE

lun on the south, Asher on the west, and the Jordan on the east.

19.35-38 The fort cities were:

Ziddim, Zer, Hammath, Rakkath, Kinnereth, Adamah, Ramah, Hazor,
Kedesh, Edrei, En Hazor,
Iron, Migdal El, Horem, Beth Anath, and Beth Shemesh—
nineteen towns and their villages.

19.39 This is the inheritance of the tribe of Naphtali, the cities and their villages, clan by clan.

DAN

19.40-46 The seventh lot fell to Dan. The territory of their inheritance included:

Zorah, Eshtaol, Ir Shemesh,
Shaalabbin, Aijalon, Ithlah,
Elon, Timnah, Ekron,
Eltekeh, Gibbethon, Baalath,
Jehud, Bene Berak, Gath Rimmon,
Me Jarkon, and Rakkon, with the region facing Joppa.

19.47 But the people of Dan failed to get rid of the Westerners (Amorites), who pushed them back into the hills. The Westerners kept them out of the plain and they didn't have enough room. So the people of Dan marched up and attacked Leshem. They took it, killed the inhabitants, and settled in. They renamed it Leshem Dan after the name of Dan their ancestor.

19.48 This is the inheritance of the tribe of Dan, according to its clans, these towns with their villages.

✝

19.49-50 They completed the dividing of the land as inheritance and the setting of its boundaries. The People of Israel then gave an inheritance among them to Joshua son of Nun. In obedience to GOD's word, they gave him the city which he had requested, Timnath Serah in the hill country of Ephraim. He rebuilt the city and settled there.

19.51 These are the inheritances which Eleazar the priest and Joshua son of Nun and the ancestral leaders assigned by lot to the tribes of Israel at Shiloh in the presence of GOD at the entrance of the Tent of Meeting. They completed the dividing of the land.

ASYLUM-CITIES

20.1-3 **20** Then GOD spoke to Joshua: "Tell the People of Israel: Designate the asylum-cities, as I instructed you through Moses, so

---

a 34 Septuagint; Hebrew *west, and Judah, the Jordan,*
b 50 Also known as *Timnath Heres* (see Judges 2:9)

NEW INTERNATIONAL VERSION	THE MESSAGE

one who kills a person accidentally and unintentionally may flee there and find protection from the avenger of blood.

⁴"When he flees to one of these cities, he is to stand in the entrance of the city gate and state his case before the elders of that city. Then they are to admit him into their city and give him a place to live with them. ⁵If the avenger of blood pursues him, they must not surrender the one accused, because he killed his neighbor unintentionally and without malice aforethought. ⁶He is to stay in that city until he has stood trial before the assembly and until the death of the high priest who is serving at that time. Then he may go back to his own home in the town from which he fled."

⁷So they set apart Kedesh in Galilee in the hill country of Naphtali, Shechem in the hill country of Ephraim, and Kiriath Arba (that is, Hebron) in the hill country of Judah. ⁸On the east side of the Jordan of Jericho*ᵃ* they designated Bezer in the desert on the plateau in the tribe of Reuben, Ramoth in Gilead in the tribe of Gad, and Golan in Bashan in the tribe of Manasseh. ⁹Any of the Israelites or any alien living among them who killed someone accidentally could flee to these designated cities and not be killed by the avenger of blood prior to standing trial before the assembly.

TOWNS FOR THE LEVITES

21 Now the family heads of the Levites approached Eleazar the priest, Joshua son of Nun, and the heads of the other tribal families of Israel ²at Shiloh in Canaan and said to them, "The LORD commanded through Moses that you give us towns to live in, with pasturelands for our livestock." ³So, as the LORD had commanded, the Israelites gave the Levites the following towns and pasturelands out of their own inheritance:

⁴The first lot came out for the Kohathites, clan by clan. The Levites who were descendants of Aaron the priest were allotted thirteen towns from the tribes of Judah, Simeon and Benjamin. ⁵The rest of Kohath's descendants were allotted ten towns from the clans of the tribes of Ephraim, Dan and half of Manasseh.

⁶The descendants of Gershon were allotted thirteen towns from the clans of the tribes of Issachar, Asher, Naphtali and the half-tribe of Manasseh in Bashan.

---

that anyone who kills a person accidentally— that is, unintentionally—may flee there as a safe place of asylum from the avenger of blood.

20.4 "A person shall escape for refuge to one of these cities, stand at the entrance to the city gate, and lay out his case before the city's leaders. The leaders must then take him into the city among them and give him a place to live with them.

20.5-6 "If the avenger of blood chases after him, they must not give him up—he didn't intend to kill the person; there was no history of ill-feeling. He may stay in that city until he has stood trial before the congregation and until the death of the current high priest. Then he may go back to his own home in his hometown from which he fled."

20.7 They set apart Kedesh in Galilee in the hills of Naphtali, Shechem in the hills of Ephraim, and Kiriath Arba (that is, Hebron) in the hills of Judah.

20.8-9 On the other side of the Jordan, east of Jericho, they designated Bezer on the desert plateau from the tribe of Reuben, Ramoth in Gilead from the tribe of Gad, and Golan in Bashan from the tribe of Manasseh. These were the designated cities for the People of Israel and any resident foreigner living among them, so that anyone who killed someone unintentionally could flee there and not die by the hand of the avenger of blood without a fair trial before the congregation.

CITIES FOR THE LEVITES

21.1-2 **21** The ancestral heads of the Levites came to Eleazar the priest and Joshua son of Nun and to the heads of the other tribes of the People of Israel. This took place at Shiloh in the land of Canaan. They said, "GOD commanded through Moses that you give us cities to live in with access to pastures for our cattle."

21.3 So the People of Israel, out of their own inheritance, gave the Levites, just as GOD commanded, the following cities and pastures:

21.4-5 The lot came out for the families of the Kohathites this way: Levites descended from Aaron the priest received by lot thirteen cities out of the tribes of Judah, Simeon, and Benjamin. The rest of the Kohathites received by lot ten cities from the families of the tribes of Ephraim, Dan, and the half-tribe of Manasseh.

21.6 The Gershonites received by lot thirteen cities from the families of the tribes of Issachar, Asher, Naphtali, and the half-tribe of Manasseh in Bashan.

ᵃ 8 Jordan of Jericho was possibly an ancient name for the Jordan River.

NEW INTERNATIONAL VERSION

⁷The descendants of Merari, clan by clan, received twelve towns from the tribes of Reuben, Gad and Zebulun.

⁸So the Israelites allotted to the Levites these towns and their pasturelands, as the LORD had commanded through Moses.

⁹From the tribes of Judah and Simeon they allotted the following towns by name ¹⁰(these towns were assigned to the descendants of Aaron who were from the Kohathite clans of the Levites, because the first lot fell to them):

¹¹They gave them Kiriath Arba (that is, Hebron), with its surrounding pastureland, in the hill country of Judah. (Arba was the forefather of Anak.) ¹²But the fields and villages around the city they had given to Caleb son of Jephunneh as his possession.

¹³So to the descendants of Aaron the priest they gave Hebron (a city of refuge for one accused of murder), Libnah, ¹⁴Jattir, Eshtemoa, ¹⁵Holon, Debir, ¹⁶Ain, Juttah and Beth Shemesh, together with their pasturelands—nine towns from these two tribes.

¹⁷And from the tribe of Benjamin they gave them Gibeon, Geba, ¹⁸Anathoth and Almon, together with their pasturelands—four towns.

¹⁹All the towns for the priests, the descendants of Aaron, were thirteen, together with their pasturelands.

²⁰The rest of the Kohathite clans of the Levites were allotted towns from the tribe of Ephraim:

²¹In the hill country of Ephraim they were given Shechem (a city of refuge for one accused of murder) and Gezer, ²²Kibzaim and Beth Horon, together with their pasturelands—four towns.

²³Also from the tribe of Dan they received Eltekeh, Gibbethon, ²⁴Aijalon and Gath Rimmon, together with their pasturelands—four towns.

²⁵From half the tribe of Manasseh they received Taanach and Gath Rimmon, together with their pasturelands—two towns.

²⁶All these ten towns and their pasturelands were given to the rest of the Kohathite clans.

²⁷The Levite clans of the Gershonites were given:
from the half-tribe of Manasseh,
Golan in Bashan (a city of refuge for one accused of murder) and Be Eshtarah, together with their pasturelands—two towns;
²⁸from the tribe of Issachar,
Kishion, Daberath, ²⁹Jarmuth and En Gan-

THE MESSAGE

21.7   The families of the Merarites received twelve towns from the tribes of Reuben, Gad, and Zebulun.

21.8   So the People of Israel gave these cities with their pastures to the Levites just as GOD had ordered through Moses, that is, by lot.

CITIES FOR THE DESCENDANTS OF AARON

21.9-10 They assigned from the tribes of Judah, Simeon, and Benjamin the following towns, here named individually (these were for the descendants of Aaron who were from the families of the Kohathite branch of Levi because the first lot fell to them):

21.11-12 Kiriath Arba (Arba was the ancestor of Anak), that is, Hebron, in the hills of Judah, with access to the pastures around it. The fields of the city and its open lands they had already given to Caleb son of Jephunneh as his possession.

21.13-16 To the descendants of Aaron the priest they gave Hebron (the asylum-city for the unconvicted killers), Libnah, Jattir, Eshtemoa, Holon, Debir, Ain, Juttah, and Beth Shemesh, all with their accompanying pastures—nine towns from these two tribes.

21.17-18 And from the tribe of Benjamin: Gibeon, Geba, Anathoth, and Almon, together with their pastures—four towns.

21.19   The total for the cities and pastures for the priests descended from Aaron came to thirteen.

21.20-22 The rest of the Kohathite families from the tribe of Levi were assigned their cities by lot from the tribe of Ephraim: Shechem (the asylum-city for the unconvicted killer) in the hills of Ephraim, Gezer, Kibzaim, and Beth Horon, with their pastures—four towns.

21.23-24 From the tribe of Dan they received Eltekeh, Gibbethon, Aijalon, and Gath Rimmon, all with their pastures—four towns.

21.25   And from the half-tribe of Manasseh they received Taanach and Gath Rimmon with their pastures—two towns.

21.26   All told, ten cities with their pastures went to the remaining Kohathite families.

21.27   The Gershonite families of the tribe of Levi were given from the half-tribe of Manasseh: Golan in Bashan (an asylum-city for the unconvicted killer), and Be Eshtarah, with their pastures—two cities.

21.28-29 And from the tribe of Issachar: Kishion,

NEW INTERNATIONAL VERSION

nim, together with their pasturelands—four towns;

30from the tribe of Asher,
Mishal, Abdon, 31Helkath and Rehob, together with their pasturelands—four towns;

32from the tribe of Naphtali,
Kedesh in Galilee (a city of refuge for one accused of murder), Hammoth Dor and Kartan, together with their pasturelands—three towns.

33All the towns of the Gershonite clans were thirteen, together with their pasturelands.

34The Merarite clans (the rest of the Levites) were given:
from the tribe of Zebulun,
Jokneam, Kartah, 35Dimnah and Nahalal, together with their pasturelands—four towns;

36from the tribe of Reuben,
Bezer, Jahaz, 37Kedemoth and Mephaath, together with their pasturelands—four towns;

38from the tribe of Gad,
Ramoth in Gilead (a city of refuge for one accused of murder), Mahanaim, 39Heshbon and Jazer, together with their pasturelands—four towns in all.

40All the towns allotted to the Merarite clans, who were the rest of the Levites, were twelve.

41The towns of the Levites in the territory held by the Israelites were forty-eight in all, together with their pasturelands. 42Each of these towns had pasturelands surrounding it; this was true for all these towns.

43So the LORD gave Israel all the land he had sworn to give their forefathers, and they took possession of it and settled there. 44The LORD gave them rest on every side, just as he had sworn to their forefathers. Not one of their enemies withstood them; the LORD handed all their enemies over to them. 45Not one of all the LORD's good promises to the house of Israel failed; every one was fulfilled.

EASTERN TRIBES RETURN HOME

22 Then Joshua summoned the Reubenites, the Gadites and the half-tribe of Manasseh 2and said to them, "You have done all that Moses the servant of the LORD commanded, and you have obeyed me in everything I commanded. 3For a long time now—to this very day—you have not deserted your brothers but have carried out the mission the LORD your God gave you. 4Now that the LORD your God has given

THE MESSAGE

Daberath, Jarmuth, and En Gannim, with their pastures—four towns.

21.30-31 From the tribe of Asher: Mishal, Abdon, Helkath, and Rehob, with their pastures—four towns.

21.32 From the tribe of Naphtali: Kedesh in Galilee (an asylum-city for the unconvicted killer), Hammoth Dor, and Kartan, with their pastures—three towns.

21.33 For the Gershonites and their families: thirteen towns with their pastures.

21.34-35 The Merari families, the remaining Levites, were given from the tribe of Zebulun: Jokneam, Kartah, Dimnah, and Nahalal, with their pastures—four cities.

21.36-37 From the tribe of Reuben: Bezer, Jahaz, Kedemoth, and Mephaath, with their pastures—four towns.

21.38-39 From the tribe of Gad: Ramoth in Gilead (an asylum-city for the unconvicted killer), Mahanaim, Heshbon, and Jazer, with their pastures—a total of four towns.

21.40 All these towns were assigned by lot to the Merarites, the remaining Levites—twelve towns.

21.41-42 The Levites held forty-eight towns with their accompanying pastures within the territory of the People of Israel. Each of these towns had pastures surrounding it—this was the case for all these towns.

✠

21.43-44 And so GOD gave Israel the entire land that he had solemnly vowed to give to their ancestors. They took possession of it and made themselves at home in it. And GOD gave them rest on all sides, as he had also solemnly vowed to their ancestors. Not a single one of their enemies was able to stand up to them—GOD handed over all their enemies to them.

21.45 Not one word failed from all the good words GOD spoke to the house of Israel. Everything came out right.

✠

22.1-5 **22** Then Joshua called together the Reubenites, Gadites, and the half-tribe of Manasseh. He said: "You have carried out everything Moses the servant of GOD commanded you, and you have obediently done everything I have commanded you. All this time and right down to this very day you have not abandoned your brothers; you've shouldered the task laid on you by GOD, your God. And now GOD, your God, has given rest to your

NEW INTERNATIONAL VERSION	THE MESSAGE

NEW INTERNATIONAL VERSION

your brothers rest as he promised, return to your homes in the land that Moses the servant of the Lord gave you on the other side of the Jordan. ⁵But be very careful to keep the commandment and the law that Moses the servant of the Lord gave you: to love the Lord your God, to walk in all his ways, to obey his commands, to hold fast to him and to serve him with all your heart and all your soul."

⁶Then Joshua blessed them and sent them away, and they went to their homes. ⁷(To the half-tribe of Manasseh Moses had given land in Bashan, and to the other half of the tribe Joshua gave land on the west side of the Jordan with their brothers.) When Joshua sent them home, he blessed them, ⁸saying, "Return to your homes with your great wealth—with large herds of livestock, with silver, gold, bronze and iron, and a great quantity of clothing—and divide with your brothers the plunder from your enemies."

⁹So the Reubenites, the Gadites and the half-tribe of Manasseh left the Israelites at Shiloh in Canaan to return to Gilead, their own land, which they had acquired in accordance with the command of the Lord through Moses.

¹⁰When they came to Geliloth near the Jordan in the land of Canaan, the Reubenites, the Gadites and the half-tribe of Manasseh built an imposing altar there by the Jordan. ¹¹And when the Israelites heard that they had built the altar on the border of Canaan at Geliloth near the Jordan on the Israelite side, ¹²the whole assembly of Israel gathered at Shiloh to go to war against them.

¹³So the Israelites sent Phinehas son of Eleazar, the priest, to the land of Gilead—to Reuben, Gad and the half-tribe of Manasseh. ¹⁴With him they sent ten of the chief men, one for each of the tribes of Israel, each the head of a family division among the Israelite clans.

¹⁵When they went to Gilead—to Reuben, Gad and the half-tribe of Manasseh—they said to them: ¹⁶"The whole assembly of the Lord says: 'How could you break faith with the God of Israel like this? How could you turn away from the Lord and build yourselves an altar in rebellion against him now? ¹⁷Was not the sin of Peor enough for us? Up to this very day we have not cleansed ourselves from that sin, even though a plague fell on the community of the Lord! ¹⁸And are you now turning away from the Lord?

THE MESSAGE

brothers just as he promised them. You're now free to go back to your homes, the country of your inheritance that Moses the servant of God gave you on the other side of the Jordan. Only this: Be vigilant in keeping the Commandment and The Revelation that Moses the servant of God laid on you: Love God, your God, walk in all his ways, do what he's commanded, embrace him, serve him with everything you are and have."

22.6-7 Then Joshua blessed them and sent them on their way. They went home. (To the half-tribe of Manasseh, Moses had assigned a share in Bashan. To the other half, Joshua assigned land with their brothers west of the Jordan.)

22.7-8 When Joshua sent them off to their homes, he blessed them. He said: "Go home. You're going home rich—great herds of cattle, silver and gold, bronze and iron, huge piles of clothing. Share the wealth with your friends and families—all this plunder from your enemies!"

✠

22.9 The Reubenites, Gadites, and the half-tribe of Manasseh left the People of Israel at Shiloh in the land of Canaan to return to Gilead, the land of their possession, which they had taken under the command of Moses as ordered by God.

22.10 They arrived at Geliloth on the Jordan (touching on Canaanite land). There the Reubenites, Gadites, and the half-tribe of Manasseh built an altar on the banks of the Jordan—a huge altar!

22.11 The People of Israel heard of it: "What's this? The Reubenites, Gadites, and the half-tribe of Manasseh have built an altar facing the land of Canaan at Geliloth on the Jordan, across from the People of Israel!"

22.12-14 When the People of Israel heard this, the entire congregation mustered at Shiloh to go to war against them. They sent Phinehas son of Eleazar the priest to the Reubenites, Gadites, and the half-tribe of Manasseh (that is, to the land of Gilead). Accompanying him were ten chiefs, one chief for each of the ten tribes, each the head of his ancestral family. They represented the military divisions of Israel.

22.15-18 They went to the Reubenites, Gadites, and the half-tribe of Manasseh and spoke to them: "The entire congregation of God wants to know: What is this violation against the God of Israel that you have committed, turning your back on God and building your own altar—a blatant act of rebellion against God? Wasn't the crime of Peor enough for us? Why, to this day we aren't rid of it, still living with the fallout of the plague on the congregation of God! Look at you—turn-

NEW INTERNATIONAL VERSION

" 'If you rebel against the LORD today, tomorrow he will be angry with the whole community of Israel. ¹⁹If the land you possess is defiled, come over to the LORD's land, where the LORD's tabernacle stands, and share the land with us. But do not rebel against the LORD or against us by building an altar for yourselves, other than the altar of the LORD our God. ²⁰When Achan son of Zerah acted unfaithfully regarding the devoted things,ᵃ did not wrath come upon the whole community of Israel? He was not the only one who died for his sin.' "

²¹Then Reuben, Gad and the half-tribe of Manasseh replied to the heads of the clans of Israel: ²²"The Mighty One, God, the LORD! The Mighty One, God, the LORD! He knows! And let Israel know! If this has been in rebellion or disobedience to the LORD, do not spare us this day. ²³If we have built our own altar to turn away from the LORD and to offer burnt offerings and grain offerings, or to sacrifice fellowship offeringsᵇ on it, may the LORD himself call us to account.

²⁴"No! We did it for fear that some day your descendants might say to ours, 'What do you have to do with the LORD, the God of Israel? ²⁵The LORD has made the Jordan a boundary between us and you—you Reubenites and Gadites! You have no share in the LORD.' So your descendants might cause ours to stop fearing the LORD.

²⁶"That is why we said, 'Let us get ready and build an altar—but not for burnt offerings or sacrifices.' ²⁷On the contrary, it is to be a witness between us and you and the generations that follow, that we will worship the LORD at his sanctuary with our burnt offerings, sacrifices and fellowship offerings. Then in the future your descendants will not be able to say to ours, 'You have no share in the LORD.'

²⁸"And we said, 'If they ever say this to us, or to our descendants, we will answer: Look at the replica of the LORD's altar, which our fathers built, not for burnt offerings and sacrifices, but as a witness between us and you.'

²⁹"Far be it from us to rebel against the LORD and turn away from him today by building an altar for burnt offerings, grain offerings and sacri-

---

ᵃ *20* The Hebrew term refers to the irrevocable giving over of things or persons to the LORD, often by totally destroying them.   ᵇ *23* Traditionally *peace offerings*; also in verse 27

THE MESSAGE

ing your back on GOD! If you rebel against GOD today, tomorrow he'll vent his anger on all of us, the entire congregation of Israel.

22:19-20 "If you think the land of your possession isn't holy enough but somehow contaminated, come back over to GOD's possession, where GOD's Dwelling is set up, and take your land there, but don't rebel against GOD. And don't rebel against us by building your own altar apart from the Altar of our GOD. When Achan son of Zerah violated the holy curse, didn't anger fall on the whole congregation of Israel? He wasn't the only one to die for his sin."

22:21-22 The Reubenites, Gadites, and the half-tribe of Manasseh replied to the heads of the tribes of Israel:

> The God of Gods is GOD,
> The God of Gods is GOD!

22:22-23 "He knows and he'll let Israel know if this is a rebellious betrayal of GOD. And if it is, don't bother saving us. If we built ourselves an altar in rebellion against GOD, if we did it to present on it Whole-Burnt-Offerings or Grain-Offerings or to enact there sacrificial Peace-Offerings, let GOD decide.

22:24-25 "But that's not it. We did it because we cared. We were anxious lest someday your children should say to our children, 'You're not connected with GOD, the God of Israel! GOD made the Jordan a boundary between us and you. You Reubenites and Gadites have no part in GOD.' And then your children might cause our children to quit worshiping GOD.

22:26 "So we said to ourselves, 'Let's do something. Let's build an altar—but not for Whole-Burnt-Offerings, not for sacrifices.'

22:27 "We built this altar as a witness between us and you and our children coming after us, a witness to the Altar where we worship GOD in his Sacred Dwelling with our Whole-Burnt-Offerings and our sacrifices and our Peace-Offerings.

"This way, your children won't be able to say to our children in the future, 'You have no part in GOD.'

22:28 "We said to ourselves, 'If anyone speaks disparagingly to us or to our children in the future, we'll say: Look at this model of GOD's Altar which our ancestors made. It's not for Whole-Burnt-Offerings, not for sacrifices. It's a witness connecting us with you.'

22:29 "Rebelling against or turning our backs on GOD is the last thing on our minds right now. We never dreamed of building an altar for Whole-Burnt-Offerings or Grain-Offerings to

NEW INTERNATIONAL VERSION

fices, other than the altar of the LORD our God that stands before his tabernacle."

³⁰When Phinehas the priest and the leaders of the community—the heads of the clans of the Israelites—heard what Reuben, Gad and Manasseh had to say, they were pleased. ³¹And Phinehas son of Eleazar, the priest, said to Reuben, Gad and Manasseh, "Today we know that the LORD is with us, because you have not acted unfaithfully toward the LORD in this matter. Now you have rescued the Israelites from the LORD's hand."

³²Then Phinehas son of Eleazar, the priest, and the leaders returned to Canaan from their meeting with the Reubenites and Gadites in Gilead and reported to the Israelites. ³³They were glad to hear the report and praised God. And they talked no more about going to war against them to devastate the country where the Reubenites and the Gadites lived.

³⁴And the Reubenites and the Gadites gave the altar this name: A Witness Between Us that the LORD is God.

JOSHUA'S FAREWELL TO THE LEADERS

23 After a long time had passed and the LORD had given Israel rest from all their enemies around them, Joshua, by then old and well advanced in years, ²summoned all Israel—their elders, leaders, judges and officials—and said to them: "I am old and well advanced in years. ³You yourselves have seen everything the LORD your God has done to all these nations for your sake; it was the LORD your God who fought for you. ⁴Remember how I have allotted as an inheritance for your tribes all the land of the nations that remain—the nations I conquered—between the Jordan and the Great Sea*ᵃ* in the west. ⁵The LORD your God himself will drive them out of your way. He will push them out before you, and you will take possession of their land, as the LORD your God promised you.

⁶"Be very strong; be careful to obey all that is written in the Book of the Law of Moses, without turning aside to the right or to the left. ⁷Do not associate with these nations that remain among you; do not invoke the names of their gods or swear by them. You must not serve them or bow down to them. ⁸But you are to hold fast to the LORD your God, as you have until now.

⁹"The LORD has driven out before you great and powerful nations; to this day no one has been able to withstand you. ¹⁰One of you routs a

THE MESSAGE

rival the Altar of our GOD in front of his Sacred Dwelling."

22.30 Phinehas the priest, all the heads of the congregation, and the heads of the military divisions of Israel who were also with him heard what the Reubenites, Gadites, and the half-tribe of Manasseh had to say. They were satisfied.

22.31 Priest Phinehas son of Eleazar said to Reuben, Gad, and Manasseh, "Now we're convinced that GOD is present with us since you haven't been disloyal to GOD in this matter. You saved the People of Israel from GOD's discipline."

22.32-33 Then Priest Phinehas son of Eleazar left the Reubenites, Gadites, and the half-tribe of Manasseh (from Gilead) and, with the chiefs, returned to the land of Canaan to the People of Israel and gave a full report. They were pleased with the report. The People of Israel blessed God—there was no more talk of attacking and destroying the land in which the Reubenites and Gadites were living.

22.34 Reuben and Gad named the altar:

> A Witness Between Us.
> GOD Alone Is God.

JOSHUA'S CHARGE

23.1-2 **23** A long time later, after GOD had given Israel rest from all their surrounding enemies, and Joshua was a venerable old man, Joshua called all Israel together—elders, chiefs, judges, and officers. Then he spoke to them:

23.2-3 "I'm an old man. I've lived a long time. You have seen everything that GOD has done to these nations because of you. He did it because he's GOD, your God. He fought for you.

23.4-5 "Stay alert: I have assigned to you by lot these nations that remain as an inheritance to your tribes—these in addition to the nations I have already cut down—from the Jordan to the Great Sea in the west. GOD, your God, will drive them out of your path until there's nothing left of them and you'll take over their land just as GOD, your God, promised you.

23.6-8 "Now, stay strong and steady. Obediently do everything written in the Book of The Revelation of Moses—don't miss a detail. Don't get mixed up with the nations that are still around. Don't so much as speak the names of their gods or swear by them. And by all means don't worship or pray to them. Hold tight to GOD, your God, just as you've done up to now.

23.9-10 "GOD has driven out superpower nations before you. And up to now, no one has been able to stand up to you. Think of it—one of you,

---

ᵃ 4 That is, the Mediterranean

NEW INTERNATIONAL VERSION

thousand, because the Lord your God fights for you, just as he promised. ¹¹So be very careful to love the Lord your God.

¹²"But if you turn away and ally yourselves with the survivors of these nations that remain among you and if you intermarry with them and associate with them, ¹³then you may be sure that the Lord your God will no longer drive out these nations before you. Instead, they will become snares and traps for you, whips on your backs and thorns in your eyes, until you perish from this good land, which the Lord your God has given you.

¹⁴"Now I am about to go the way of all the earth. You know with all your heart and soul that not one of all the good promises the Lord your God gave you has failed. Every promise has been fulfilled; not one has failed. ¹⁵But just as every good promise of the Lord your God has come true, so the Lord will bring on you all the evil he has threatened, until he has destroyed you from this good land he has given you. ¹⁶If you violate the covenant of the Lord your God, which he commanded you, and go and serve other gods and bow down to them, the Lord's anger will burn against you, and you will quickly perish from the good land he has given you."

The Covenant Renewed at Shechem

24 Then Joshua assembled all the tribes of Israel at Shechem. He summoned the elders, leaders, judges and officials of Israel, and they presented themselves before God.

²Joshua said to all the people, "This is what the Lord, the God of Israel, says: 'Long ago your forefathers, including Terah the father of Abraham and Nahor, lived beyond the River[a] and worshiped other gods. ³But I took your father Abraham from the land beyond the River and led him throughout Canaan and gave him many descendants. I gave him Isaac, ⁴and to Isaac I gave Jacob and Esau. I assigned the hill country of Seir to Esau, but Jacob and his sons went down to Egypt.

⁵"'Then I sent Moses and Aaron, and I afflicted the Egyptians by what I did there, and I brought you out. ⁶When I brought your fathers out of Egypt, you came to the sea, and the Egyptians pursued them with chariots and horsemen[b] as far as the Red Sea.[c] ⁷But they cried to the

---

THE MESSAGE

single-handedly, putting a thousand on the run! Because God is God, your God. Because he fights for you, just as he promised you.

23.11-13 "Now, vigilantly guard your souls: Love God, your God. Because if you wander off and start taking up with these remaining nations still among you (intermarry, say, and have other dealings with them), know for certain that God, your God, will not get rid of these nations for you. They'll be nothing but trouble to you—horsewhips on your backs and sand in your eyes—until you're the ones who will be driven out of this good land that God, your God, has given you.

23.14 "As you can see, I'm about to go the way we all end up going. Know this with all your heart, with everything in you, that not one detail has failed of all the good things God, your God, promised you. It has all happened. Nothing's left undone—not so much as a word.

23.15-16 "But just as sure as everything good that God, your God, has promised has come true, so also God will bring to pass every bad thing until there's nothing left of you in this good land that God has given you. If you leave the path of the Covenant of God, your God, that he commanded you, go off and serve and worship other gods, God's anger will blaze out against you. In no time at all there'll be nothing left of you, no sign that you've ever been in this good land he gave you."

The Covenant at Shechem

24.1-2 **24** Joshua called together all the tribes of Israel at Shechem. He called in the elders, chiefs, judges, and officers. They presented themselves before God. Then Joshua addressed all the people:

24.2-6 "This is what God, the God of Israel, says: A long time ago your ancestors, Terah and his sons Abraham and Nahor, lived to the east of the River Euphrates. They worshiped other gods. I took your ancestor Abraham from the far side of The River. I led him all over the land of Canaan and multiplied his descendants. I gave him Isaac. Then I gave Isaac Jacob and Esau. I let Esau have the mountains of Seir as home, but Jacob and his sons ended up in Egypt. I sent Moses and Aaron. I hit Egypt hard with plagues and then led you out of there. I brought your ancestors out of Egypt. You came to the sea, the Egyptians in hot pursuit with chariots and cavalry, to the very edge of the Red Sea!

"Then they cried out for help to God. He

---

a 2 That is, the Euphrates; also in verses 3, 14 and 15
b 6 Or *charioteers*   *c 6* Hebrew *Yam Suph*; that is, Sea of Reeds

NEW INTERNATIONAL VERSION

Lord for help, and he put darkness between you and the Egyptians; he brought the sea over them and covered them. You saw with your own eyes what I did to the Egyptians. Then you lived in the desert for a long time.

8 " 'I brought you to the land of the Amorites who lived east of the Jordan. They fought against you, but I gave them into your hands. I destroyed them from before you, and you took possession of their land. 9When Balak son of Zippor, the king of Moab, prepared to fight against Israel, he sent for Balaam son of Beor to put a curse on you. 10But I would not listen to Balaam, so he blessed you again and again, and I delivered you out of his hand.

11 " 'Then you crossed the Jordan and came to Jericho. The citizens of Jericho fought against you, as did also the Amorites, Perizzites, Canaanites, Hittites, Girgashites, Hivites and Jebusites, but I gave them into your hands. 12I sent the hornet ahead of you, which drove them out before you—also the two Amorite kings. You did not do it with your own sword and bow. 13So I gave you a land on which you did not toil and cities you did not build; and you live in them and eat from vineyards and olive groves that you did not plant.'

14"Now fear the Lord and serve him with all faithfulness. Throw away the gods your forefathers worshiped beyond the River and in Egypt, and serve the Lord. 15But if serving the Lord seems undesirable to you, then choose for yourselves this day whom you will serve, whether the gods your forefathers served beyond the River, or the gods of the Amorites, in whose land you are living. But as for me and my household, we will serve the Lord."

16Then the people answered, "Far be it from us to forsake the Lord to serve other gods! 17It was the Lord our God himself who brought us and our fathers up out of Egypt, from that land of slavery, and performed those great signs before our eyes. He protected us on our entire journey and among all the nations through which we traveled. 18And the Lord drove out before us all the nations, including the Amorites, who lived in the land. We too will serve the Lord, because he is our God."

19Joshua said to the people, "You are not able to serve the Lord. He is a holy God; he is a jealous God. He will not forgive your rebellion and your sins. 20If you forsake the Lord and serve

THE MESSAGE

put a cloud between you and the Egyptians and then let the sea loose on them. It drowned them.

24.7-10 "You watched the whole thing with your own eyes, what I did to Egypt. And then you lived in the wilderness for a long time. I brought you to the country of the Amorites, who lived east of the Jordan, and they fought you. But I fought for you and you took their land. I destroyed them for you. Then Balak son of Zippor made his appearance. He was the king of Moab. He got ready to fight Israel by sending for Balaam son of Beor to come and curse you. But I wouldn't listen to Balaam—he ended up blessing you over and over! I saved you from him.

24.11 "You then crossed the Jordan and came to Jericho. The Jericho leaders ganged up on you as well as the Amorites, Perizzites, Canaanites, Hittites, Girgashites, Hivites, and Jebusites, but I turned them over to you.

24.12 "I sent the Hornet ahead of you. It drove out the two Amorite kings—did your work for you. You didn't have to do a thing, not so much as raise a finger.

24.13 "I handed you a land for which you did not work, towns you did not build. And here you are now living in them and eating from vineyards and olive groves you did not plant.

24.14 "So now: Fear God. Worship him in total commitment. Get rid of the gods your ancestors worshiped on the far side of The River (the Euphrates) and in Egypt. You, worship God.

24.15 "If you decide that it's a bad thing to worship God, then choose a god you'd rather serve—and do it today. Choose one of the gods your ancestors worshiped from the country beyond The River, or one of the gods of the Amorites, on whose land you're now living. As for me and my family, we'll worship God."

24.16 The people answered, "We'd never forsake God! Never! We'd never leave God to worship other gods.

24.17-18 "God is our God! He brought us up our ancestors from Egypt and from slave conditions. He did all those great signs while we watched. He has kept his eye on us all along the roads we've traveled and among the nations we've passed through. Just for us he drove out all the nations, Amorites and all, who lived in the land.

"Count us in: We too are going to worship God. He's our God."

24.19-20 Then Joshua told the people: "You can't do it; you're not able to worship God. He is a holy God. He is a jealous God. He won't put up with your fooling around and sinning. When you leave God and take up the worship of foreign

NEW INTERNATIONAL VERSION

foreign gods, he will turn and bring disaster on you and make an end of you, after he has been good to you."

²¹But the people said to Joshua, "No! We will serve the LORD."

²²Then Joshua said, "You are witnesses against yourselves that you have chosen to serve the LORD."

"Yes, we are witnesses," they replied.

²³"Now then," said Joshua, "throw away the foreign gods that are among you and yield your hearts to the LORD, the God of Israel."

²⁴And the people said to Joshua, "We will serve the LORD our God and obey him."

²⁵On that day Joshua made a covenant for the people, and there at Shechem he drew up for them decrees and laws. ²⁶And Joshua recorded these things in the Book of the Law of God. Then he took a large stone and set it up there under the oak near the holy place of the LORD.

²⁷"See!" he said to all the people. "This stone will be a witness against us. It has heard all the words the LORD has said to us. It will be a witness against you if you are untrue to your God."

BURIED IN THE PROMISED LAND

²⁸Then Joshua sent the people away, each to his own inheritance.

²⁹After these things, Joshua son of Nun, the servant of the LORD, died at the age of a hundred and ten. ³⁰And they buried him in the land of his inheritance, at Timnath Serah[a] in the hill country of Ephraim, north of Mount Gaash.

³¹Israel served the LORD throughout the lifetime of Joshua and of the elders who outlived him and who had experienced everything the LORD had done for Israel.

³²And Joseph's bones, which the Israelites had brought up from Egypt, were buried at Shechem in the tract of land that Jacob bought for a hundred pieces of silver[b] from the sons of Hamor, the father of Shechem. This became the inheritance of Joseph's descendants.

³³And Eleazar son of Aaron died and was buried at Gibeah, which had been allotted to his son Phinehas in the hill country of Ephraim.

THE MESSAGE

gods, he'll turn right around and come down on you hard. He'll put an end to you—and after all the good he has done for you!"

24.21 But the people told Joshua: "No! No! We worship GOD!"

24.22 And so Joshua addressed the people: "You are witnesses against yourselves that you have chosen GOD for yourselves—to worship him."

And they said, "We are witnesses."

24.23 Joshua said, "Now get rid of all the foreign gods you have with you. Say an unqualified Yes to GOD, the God of Israel."

24.24 The people answered Joshua, "We will worship GOD. What he says, we'll do."

24.25-26 Joshua completed a Covenant for the people that day there at Shechem. He made it official, spelling it out in detail. Joshua wrote out all the directions and regulations into the Book of The Revelation of God. Then he took a large stone and set it up under the oak that was in the holy place of GOD.

24.27 Joshua spoke to all the people: "This stone is a witness against us. It has heard every word that GOD has said to us. It is a standing witness against you lest you cheat on your God."

24.28 Then Joshua dismissed the people, each to his own place of inheritance.

✠

24.29-30 After all this, Joshua son of Nun, the servant of GOD, died. He was 110 years old. They buried him in the land of his inheritance at Timnath Serah in the mountains of Ephraim, north of Mount Gaash.

24.31 Israel served GOD through the lifetime of Joshua and of the elders who outlived him, who had themselves experienced all that GOD had done for Israel.

24.32 Joseph's bones, which the People of Israel had brought from Egypt, they buried in Shechem in the plot of ground that Jacob had purchased from the sons of Hamor (who was the father of Shechem). He paid a hundred silver coins for it. It belongs to the inheritance of the family of Joseph.

24.33 Eleazar son of Aaron died. They buried him at Gibeah, which had been allotted to his son Phinehas in the mountains of Ephraim.

ᵃ 30 Also known as *Timnath Heres* (see Judges 2:9)
ᵇ 32 Hebrew *hundred kesitahs*; a kesitah was a unit of money of unknown weight and value.

JUDGES

JUDGES

ISRAEL FIGHTS THE REMAINING CANAANITES

1 After the death of Joshua, the Israelites asked the LORD, "Who will be the first to go up and fight for us against the Canaanites?"

²The LORD answered, "Judah is to go; I have given the land into their hands."

³Then the men of Judah said to the Simeonites their brothers, "Come up with us into the territory allotted to us, to fight against the Canaanites. We in turn will go with you into yours." So the Simeonites went with them.

⁴When Judah attacked, the LORD gave the Canaanites and Perizzites into their hands and they struck down ten thousand men at Bezek. ⁵It was there that they found Adoni-Bezek and fought against him, putting to rout the Canaanites and Perizzites. ⁶Adoni-Bezek fled, but they chased him and caught him, and cut off his thumbs and big toes.

⁷Then Adoni-Bezek said, "Seventy kings with their thumbs and big toes cut off have picked up scraps under my table. Now God has paid me back for what I did to them." They brought him to Jerusalem, and he died there.

⁸The men of Judah attacked Jerusalem also and took it. They put the city to the sword and set it on fire.

⁹After that, the men of Judah went down to fight against the Canaanites living in the hill country, the Negev and the western foothills. ¹⁰They advanced against the Canaanites living in Hebron (formerly called Kiriath Arba) and defeated Sheshai, Ahiman and Talmai.

¹¹From there they advanced against the people living in Debir (formerly called Kiriath Sepher). ¹²And Caleb said, "I will give my daughter Acsah in marriage to the man who attacks and captures Kiriath Sepher." ¹³Othniel son of Kenaz, Caleb's younger brother, took it; so Caleb gave his daughter Acsah to him in marriage.

¹⁴One day when she came to Othniel, she

1.1 **1** A time came after the death of Joshua when the People of Israel asked GOD, "Who will take the lead in going up against the Canaanites to fight them?"

1.2 And GOD said, "Judah will go. I've given the land to him."

1.3 The men of Judah said to those of their brother Simeon, "Go up with us to our territory and we'll fight the Canaanites. Then we'll go with you to your territory." And Simeon went with them.

1.4 So Judah went up. GOD gave them the Canaanites and the Perizzites. They defeated them at Bezek—ten military units!

1.5-7 They caught up with My-Master-Bezek there and fought him. They smashed the Canaanites and the Perizzites. My-Master-Bezek ran, but they gave chase and caught him. They cut off his thumbs and big toes. My-Master-Bezek said, "Seventy kings with their thumbs and big toes cut off used to crawl under my table, scavenging. Now God has done to me what I did to them."

They brought him to Jerusalem and he died there.

✝

1.8-10 The people of Judah attacked and captured Jerusalem, subduing the city by sword and then sending it up in flames. After that they had gone down to fight the Canaanites who were living in the hill country, the Negev, and the foothills. Judah had gone on to the Canaanites who lived in Hebron (Hebron used to be called Kiriath Arba) and brought Sheshai, Ahiman, and Talmai to their knees.

1.11-12 From there they had marched against the population of Debir (Debir used to be called Kiriath Sepher). Caleb had said, "Whoever attacks Kiriath Sepher and takes it, I'll give my daughter Acsah to him as his wife."

1.13 Othniel son of Kenaz, Caleb's brother, took it, so Caleb gave him his daughter Acsah as his wife.

1.14-15 When she arrived she got him

NEW INTERNATIONAL VERSION

urged him[a] to ask her father for a field. When she got off her donkey, Caleb asked her, "What can I do for you?"

¹⁵She replied, "Do me a special favor. Since you have given me land in the Negev, give me also springs of water." Then Caleb gave her the upper and lower springs.

¹⁶The descendants of Moses' father-in-law, the Kenite, went up from the City of Palms[b] with the men of Judah to live among the people of the Desert of Judah in the Negev near Arad.

¹⁷Then the men of Judah went with the Simeonites their brothers and attacked the Canaanites living in Zephath, and they totally destroyed[c] the city. Therefore it was called Hormah.[d] ¹⁸The men of Judah also took[e] Gaza, Ashkelon and Ekron—each city with its territory.

¹⁹The LORD was with the men of Judah. They took possession of the hill country, but they were unable to drive the people from the plains, because they had iron chariots. ²⁰As Moses had promised, Hebron was given to Caleb, who drove from it the three sons of Anak. ²¹The Benjamites, however, failed to dislodge the Jebusites, who were living in Jerusalem; to this day the Jebusites live there with the Benjamites.

²²Now the house of Joseph attacked Bethel, and the LORD was with them. ²³When they sent men to spy out Bethel (formerly called Luz), ²⁴the spies saw a man coming out of the city and they said to him, "Show us how to get into the city and we will see that you are treated well." ²⁵So he showed them, and they put the city to the sword but spared the man and his whole family. ²⁶He then went to the land of the Hittites, where he built a city and called it Luz, which is its name to this day.

²⁷But Manasseh did not drive out the people of Beth Shan or Taanach or Dor or Ibleam or Megiddo and their surrounding settlements, for the Canaanites were determined to live in that land. ²⁸When Israel became strong, they pressed the Canaanites into forced labor but never drove them out completely. ²⁹Nor did Ephraim drive out the Canaanites living in Gezer, but the Canaanites continued to live there among them. ³⁰Neither did Zebulun drive out the Canaanites living in Kitron or Nahalol, who remained among them; but they did subject them

---

a 14 Hebrew; Septuagint and Vulgate *Othniel, he urged her*
b 16 That is, Jericho   *c 17* The Hebrew term refers to the irrevocable giving over of things or persons to the LORD, often by totally destroying them.   *d 17 Hormah* means *destruction.*   *e 18* Hebrew; Septuagint *Judah did not take*

THE MESSAGE

to ask for farm land from her father.
As she dismounted from her donkey
Caleb asked her, "What would you
like?"
She said, "Give me a marriage gift.
You've given me desert land;
Now give me pools of water!"
And he gave her the upper and the lower
pools.

✛

1.16 The people of Hobab the Kenite, Moses' relative, went up with the people of Judah from the City of Palms to the wilderness of Judah at the descent of Arad. They settled down there with the Amalekites.

1.17 The people of Judah went with their kin the Simeonites and struck the Canaanites who lived in Zephath. They carried out the holy curse and named the city Curse-town.

1.18-19 But Judah didn't manage to capture Gaza, Ashkelon, and Ekron with their territories. GOD was certainly with Judah in that they took over the hill country. But they couldn't oust the people on the plain because they had iron chariots.

1.20 They gave Hebron to Caleb, as Moses had directed. Caleb drove out the three sons of Anak.

1.21 But the people of Benjamin couldn't get rid of the Jebusites living in Jerusalem. Benjaminites and Jebusites live side by side in Jerusalem to this day.

✛

1.22-26 The house of Joseph went up to attack Bethel. GOD was with them. Joseph sent out spies to look the place over. Bethel used to be known as Luz. The spies saw a man leaving the city and said to him, "Show us a way into the city and we'll treat you well." The man showed them a way in. They killed everyone in the city but the man and his family. The man went to Hittite country and built a city. He named it Luz; that's its name to this day.

1.27-28 But Manasseh never managed to drive out Beth Shan, Taanach, Dor, Ibleam, and Megiddo with their territories. The Canaanites dug in their heels and wouldn't budge. When Israel became stronger they put the Canaanites to forced labor, but they never got rid of them.

1.29 Neither did Ephraim drive out the Canaanites who lived in Gezer. The Canaanites stuck it out and lived there with them.

1.30 Nor did Zebulun drive out the Canaanites in Kitron or Nahalol. They kept living there, but they were put to forced labor.

NEW INTERNATIONAL VERSION

to forced labor. ³¹Nor did Asher drive out those living in Acco or Sidon or Ahlab or Aczib or Helbah or Aphek or Rehob, ³²and because of this the people of Asher lived among the Canaanite inhabitants of the land. ³³Neither did Naphtali drive out those living in Beth Shemesh or Beth Anath; but the Naphtalites too lived among the Canaanite inhabitants of the land, and those living in Beth Shemesh and Beth Anath became forced laborers for them. ³⁴The Amorites confined the Danites to the hill country, not allowing them to come down into the plain. ³⁵And the Amorites were determined also to hold out in Mount Heres, Aijalon and Shaalbim, but when the power of the house of Joseph increased, they too were pressed into forced labor. ³⁶The boundary of the Amorites was from Scorpion[a] Pass to Sela and beyond.

THE ANGEL OF THE LORD AT BOKIM

2 The angel of the LORD went up from Gilgal to Bokim and said, "I brought you up out of Egypt and led you into the land that I swore to give to your forefathers. I said, 'I will never break my covenant with you, ²and you shall not make a covenant with the people of this land, but you shall break down their altars.' Yet you have disobeyed me. Why have you done this? ³Now therefore I tell you that I will not drive them out before you; they will be ⌊thorns⌋ in your sides and their gods will be a snare to you."

⁴When the angel of the LORD had spoken these things to all the Israelites, the people wept aloud, ⁵and they called that place Bokim.[b] There they offered sacrifices to the LORD.

DISOBEDIENCE AND DEFEAT

⁶After Joshua had dismissed the Israelites, they went to take possession of the land, each to his own inheritance. ⁷The people served the LORD throughout the lifetime of Joshua and of the elders who outlived him and who had seen all the great things the LORD had done for Israel. ⁸Joshua son of Nun, the servant of the LORD, died at the age of a hundred and ten. ⁹And they buried him in the land of his inheritance, at Timnath Heres[c] in the hill country of Ephraim, north of Mount Gaash.

¹⁰After that whole generation had been gathered to their fathers, another generation grew up, who knew neither the LORD nor what he had done for Israel. ¹¹Then the Israelites did evil in the eyes of the LORD and served the Baals. ¹²They forsook the LORD, the God of their fathers, who

---

[a] 36 Hebrew Akrabbim   [b] 5 Bokim means weepers.
[c] 9 Also known as Timnath Serah (see Joshua 19:50 and 24:30)

THE MESSAGE

1.31-32   Nor did Asher drive out the people of Acco, Sidon, Ahlab, Aczib, Helbah, Aphek, and Rehob. Asher went ahead and settled down with the Canaanites since they could not get rid of them.

1.33   Naphtali fared no better. They couldn't drive out the people of Beth Shemesh or Beth Anath so they just moved in and lived with them. They did, though, put them to forced labor.

1.34-35   The Amorites pushed the people of Dan up into the hills and wouldn't let them down on the plains. The Amorites stubbornly continued to live in Mount Heres, Aijalon, and Shaalbim. But when the house of Joseph got the upper hand, they were put to forced labor.

1.36   The Amorite border extended from Scorpions' Pass and Sela upward.

✝

2.1-2   2 GOD's angel went up from Gilgal to Bokim and said, "I brought you out of Egypt; I led you to the land that I promised to your fathers; and I said, I'll never break my covenant with you—never! And you're never to make a covenant with the people who live in this land. Tear down their altars! But you haven't obeyed me! What's this that you're doing?

2.3   "So now I'm telling you that I won't drive them out before you. They'll trip you up and their gods will become a trap."

2.4-5   When GOD's angel had spoken these words to all the People of Israel, they cried out—oh! how they wept! They named the place Bokim (Weepers). And there they sacrificed to GOD.

✝

2.6-9   After Joshua had dismissed them, the People of Israel went off to claim their allotted territories and take possession of the land. The people worshiped GOD throughout the lifetime of Joshua and the time of the leaders who survived him, leaders who had been in on all of GOD's great work that he had done for Israel. Then Joshua son of Nun, the servant of GOD, died. He was 110 years old. They buried him in his allotted inheritance at Timnath Heres in the hills of Ephraim north of Mount Gaash.

2.10   Eventually that entire generation died and was buried. Then another generation grew up that didn't know anything of GOD or the work he had done for Israel.

✝

2.11-15   The People of Israel did evil in GOD's sight: they served Baal-gods; they deserted GOD, the God of their parents who had led them out of Egypt;

NEW INTERNATIONAL VERSION

had brought them out of Egypt. They followed and worshiped various gods of the peoples around them. They provoked the LORD to anger ¹³because they forsook him and served Baal and the Ashtoreths. ¹⁴In his anger against Israel the LORD handed them over to raiders who plundered them. He sold them to their enemies all around, whom they were no longer able to resist. ¹⁵Whenever Israel went out to fight, the hand of the LORD was against them to defeat them, just as he had sworn to them. They were in great distress.

¹⁶Then the LORD raised up judges,ᵃ who saved them out of the hands of these raiders. ¹⁷Yet they would not listen to their judges but prostituted themselves to other gods and worshiped them. Unlike their fathers, they quickly turned from the way in which their fathers had walked, the way of obedience to the LORD's commands. ¹⁸Whenever the LORD raised up a judge for them, he was with the judge and saved them out of the hands of their enemies as long as the judge lived; for the LORD had compassion on them as they groaned under those who oppressed and afflicted them. ¹⁹But when the judge died, the people returned to ways even more corrupt than those of their fathers, following other gods and serving and worshiping them. They refused to give up their evil practices and stubborn ways.

²⁰Therefore the LORD was very angry with Israel and said, "Because this nation has violated the covenant that I laid down for their forefathers and has not listened to me, ²¹I will no longer drive out before them any of the nations Joshua left when he died. ²²I will use them to test Israel and see whether they will keep the way of the LORD and walk in it as their forefathers did." ²³The LORD had allowed those nations to remain; he did not drive them out at once by giving them into the hands of Joshua.

3 These are the nations the LORD left to test all those Israelites who had not experienced any of the wars in Canaan ²(he did this only to teach warfare to the descendants of the Israelites who had not had previous battle experience): ³the five rulers of the Philistines, all the Canaanites, the Sidonians, and the Hivites living in the Lebanon mountains from Mount Baal Hermon to Leboᵇ Hamath. ⁴They were left to test the Israelites to see whether they would obey the LORD's commands, which he had given their forefathers through Moses.

⁵The Israelites lived among the Canaanites,

THE MESSAGE

they took up with other gods, gods of the peoples around them. They actually worshiped them! And oh, how they angered GOD as they worshiped god Baal and goddess Astarte! GOD's anger was hot against Israel: He handed them off to plunderers who stripped them; he sold them cheap to enemies on all sides. They were helpless before their enemies. Every time they walked out the door GOD was with them—but for evil, just as GOD had said, just as he had sworn he would do. They were in a bad way.

2.16-17 But then GOD raised up judges who saved them from their plunderers. But they wouldn't listen to their judges; they prostituted themselves to other gods—worshiped them! They lost no time leaving the road walked by their parents, the road of obedience to GOD's commands. They refused to have anything to do with it.

2.18-19 When GOD was setting up judges for them, he would be right there with the judge: He would save them from their enemies' oppression as long as the judge was alive, for GOD was moved to compassion when he heard their groaning because of those who afflicted and beat them. But when the judge died, the people went right back to their old ways—but even worse than their parents!—running after other gods, serving and worshiping them. Stubborn as mules, they didn't drop a single evil practice.

2.20-22 And GOD's anger blazed against Israel. He said, "Because these people have thrown out my covenant that I commanded their parents and haven't listened to me, I'm not driving out one more person from the nations that Joshua left behind when he died. I'll use them to test Israel and see whether they stay on GOD's road and walk down it as their parents did."

2.23 That's why GOD let those nations remain. He didn't drive them out or let Joshua get rid of them.

3 These are the nations that GOD left there, using them to test the Israelites who had no experience in the Canaanite wars. He did it to train the descendants of Israel, the ones who had no battle experience, in the art of war. He left the five Philistine tyrants, all the Canaanites, the Sidonians, and the Hivites living on Mount Lebanon from Mount Baal Hermon to Hamath's Pass. They were there to test Israel and see whether they would obey GOD's commands that were given to their parents through Moses.

3.5-6 But the People of Israel made themselves at

ᵃ 16 Or leaders; similarly in verses 17-19   ᵇ 3 Or to the entrance to

NEW INTERNATIONAL VERSION

Hittites, Amorites, Perizzites, Hivites and Jebusites. ⁶They took their daughters in marriage and gave their own daughters to their sons, and served their gods.

OTHNIEL

⁷The Israelites did evil in the eyes of the LORD; they forgot the LORD their God and served the Baals and the Asherahs. ⁸The anger of the LORD burned against Israel so that he sold them into the hands of Cushan-Rishathaim king of Aram Naharaim,ᵃ to whom the Israelites were subject for eight years. ⁹But when they cried out to the LORD, he raised up for them a deliverer, Othniel son of Kenaz, Caleb's younger brother, who saved them. ¹⁰The Spirit of the LORD came upon him, so that he became Israel's judgeᵇ and went to war. The LORD gave Cushan-Rishathaim king of Aram into the hands of Othniel, who overpowered him. ¹¹So the land had peace for forty years, until Othniel son of Kenaz died.

EHUD

¹²Once again the Israelites did evil in the eyes of the LORD, and because they did this evil the LORD gave Eglon king of Moab power over Israel. ¹³Getting the Ammonites and Amalekites to join him, Eglon came and attacked Israel, and they took possession of the City of Palms.ᶜ ¹⁴The Israelites were subject to Eglon king of Moab for eighteen years.

¹⁵Again the Israelites cried out to the LORD, and he gave them a deliverer—Ehud, a left-handed man, the son of Gera the Benjamite. The Israelites sent him with tribute to Eglon king of Moab. ¹⁶Now Ehud had made a double-edged sword about a foot and a halfᵈ long, which he strapped to his right thigh under his clothing. ¹⁷He presented the tribute to Eglon king of Moab, who was a very fat man. ¹⁸After Ehud had presented the tribute, he sent on their way the men who had carried it. ¹⁹At the idolsᵉ near Gilgal he himself turned back and said, "I have a secret message for you, O king."

The king said, "Quiet!" And all his attendants left him.

²⁰Ehud then approached him while he was sitting alone in the upper room of his summer palaceᶠ and said, "I have a message from God for you." As the king rose from his seat, ²¹Ehud reached with his left hand, drew the sword from his right thigh and plunged it into the king's belly. ²²Even the handle sank in after the blade,

ᵃ 8 That is, Northwest Mesopotamia   ᵇ 10 Or leader
ᶜ 13 That is, Jericho   ᵈ 16 Hebrew a cubit (about 0.5 meter)   ᵉ 19 Or the stone quarries; also in verse 26
ᶠ 20 The meaning of the Hebrew for this phrase is uncertain.

THE MESSAGE

home among the Canaanites, Hittites, Amorites, Perizzites, Hivites, and Jebusites. They married their daughters and gave their own daughters to their sons in marriage. And they worshiped their gods.

OTHNIEL

3.7-8 The People of Israel did evil in GOD's sight. They forgot their GOD and worshiped the Baal gods and Asherah goddesses. GOD's hot anger blazed against Israel. He sold them off to Cushan-Rishathaim king of Aram Naharaim. The People of Israel were in servitude to Cushan-Rishathaim for eight years.

3.9-10 The People of Israel cried out to GOD and GOD raised up a savior who rescued them: Caleb's nephew Othniel, son of his younger brother Kenaz. The Spirit of GOD came on him and he rallied Israel. He went out to war and GOD gave him Cushan-Rishathaim king of Aram Naharaim. Othniel made short work of him.

3.11 The land was quiet for forty years. Then Othniel son of Kenaz died.

EHUD

3.12-14 But the People of Israel went back to doing evil in GOD's sight. So GOD made Eglon king of Moab a power against Israel because they did evil in GOD's sight. He recruited the Ammonites and Amalekites and went out and struck Israel. They took the City of Palms. The People of Israel were in servitude to Eglon fourteen years.

3.15-19 The People of Israel cried out to GOD and GOD raised up for them a savior, Ehud son of Gera, a Benjaminite. He was left-handed. The People of Israel sent tribute by him to Eglon king of Moab. Ehud made himself a short two-edged sword and strapped it on his right thigh under his clothes. He presented the tribute to Eglon king of Moab. Eglon was grossly fat. After Ehud finished presenting the tribute, he went a little way with the men who had carried it. But when he got as far as the stone images near Gilgal, he went back and said, "I have a private message for you, O king."

The king told his servants, "Leave." They all left.

3.20-24 Ehud approached him—the king was now quite alone in his cool rooftop room—and said, "I have a word of God for you." Eglon stood up from his throne. Ehud reached with his left hand and took his sword from his right thigh and plunged it into the king's big belly. Not only the blade but the hilt went in. The fat

NEW INTERNATIONAL VERSION

which came out his back. Ehud did not pull the sword out, and the fat closed in over it. ²³Then Ehud went out to the porch[a]; he shut the doors of the upper room behind him and locked them.

²⁴After he had gone, the servants came and found the doors of the upper room locked. They said, "He must be relieving himself in the inner room of the house." ²⁵They waited to the point of embarrassment, but when he did not open the doors of the room, they took a key and unlocked them. There they saw their lord fallen to the floor, dead.

²⁶While they waited, Ehud got away. He passed by the idols and escaped to Seirah. ²⁷When he arrived there, he blew a trumpet in the hill country of Ephraim, and the Israelites went down with him from the hills, with him leading them.

²⁸"Follow me," he ordered, "for the LORD has given Moab, your enemy, into your hands." So they followed him down and, taking possession of the fords of the Jordan that led to Moab, they allowed no one to cross over. ²⁹At that time they struck down about ten thousand Moabites, all vigorous and strong; not a man escaped. ³⁰That day Moab was made subject to Israel, and the land had peace for eighty years.

SHAMGAR

³¹After Ehud came Shamgar son of Anath, who struck down six hundred Philistines with an oxgoad. He too saved Israel.

DEBORAH

4 After Ehud died, the Israelites once again did evil in the eyes of the LORD. ²So the LORD sold them into the hands of Jabin, a king of Canaan, who reigned in Hazor. The commander of his army was Sisera, who lived in Harosheth Haggoyim. ³Because he had nine hundred iron chariots and had cruelly oppressed the Israelites for twenty years, they cried to the LORD for help.

⁴Deborah, a prophetess, the wife of Lappidoth, was leading[b] Israel at that time. ⁵She held court under the Palm of Deborah between Ramah and Bethel in the hill country of Ephraim, and the Israelites came to her to have their disputes decided. ⁶She sent for Barak son of Abinoam from Kedesh in Naphtali and said to him, "The LORD, the God of Israel, commands you: 'Go, take with you ten thousand men of Naphtali and Zebulun and lead the way to Mount Tabor. ⁷I will lure Sisera, the commander of Jabin's army,

---

[a] 23 The meaning of the Hebrew for this word is uncertain.
[b] 4 Traditionally judging

THE MESSAGE

closed in over it so he couldn't pull it out. Ehud slipped out by way of the porch and shut and locked the doors of the rooftop room behind him. Then he was gone.

When the servants came, they saw with surprise that the doors to the rooftop room were locked. They said, "He's probably relieving himself in the restroom."

3.25 They waited. And then they worried—no one was coming out of those locked doors. Finally, they got a key and unlocked them. There was their master, fallen on the floor, dead!

3.26-27 While they were standing around wondering what to do, Ehud was long gone. He got past the stone images and escaped to Seirah. When he got there, he sounded the trumpet on Mount Ephraim. The People of Israel came down from the hills and joined him. He took his place at their head.

3.28 He said, "Follow me, for GOD has given your enemies—yes, Moab!—to you." They went down after him and secured the fords of the Jordan against the Moabites. They let no one cross over.

3.29-30 At that time, they struck down about ten companies of Moabites, all of them well-fed and robust. Not one escaped. That day Moab was subdued under the hand of Israel.

The land was quiet for eighty years.

SHAMGAR

3.31 Shamgar son of Anath came after Ehud. Using a cattle prod, he killed six hundred Philistines single-handed. He too saved Israel.

DEBORAH

4 4.1-3 The People of Israel kept right on doing evil in GOD's sight. With Ehud dead, GOD sold them off to Jabin king of Canaan who ruled from Hazor. Sisera, who lived in Harosheth Haggoyim, was the commander of his army. The People of Israel cried out to GOD because he had cruelly oppressed them with his nine hundred iron chariots for twenty years.

4.4-5 Deborah was a prophet, the wife of Lappidoth. She was judge over Israel at that time. She held court under Deborah's Palm between Ramah and Bethel in the hills of Ephraim. The People of Israel went to her in matters of justice.

4.6-7 She sent for Barak son of Abinoam from Kedesh in Naphtali and said to him, "It has become clear that GOD, the God of Israel, commands you: Go to Mount Tabor and prepare for battle. Take ten companies of soldiers from Naphtali and Zebulun. I'll take care of getting Sisera, the leader of Jabin's army, to the Kishon

NEW INTERNATIONAL VERSION

with his chariots and his troops to the Kishon River and give him into your hands.' "

⁸Barak said to her, "If you go with me, I will go; but if you don't go with me, I won't go."

⁹"Very well," Deborah said, "I will go with you. But because of the way you are going about this,ᵃ the honor will not be yours, for the LORD will hand Sisera over to a woman." So Deborah went with Barak to Kedesh, ¹⁰where he summoned Zebulun and Naphtali. Ten thousand men followed him, and Deborah also went with him.

¹¹Now Heber the Kenite had left the other Kenites, the descendants of Hobab, Moses' brother-in-law,ᵇ and pitched his tent by the great tree in Zaanannim near Kedesh.

¹²When they told Sisera that Barak son of Abinoam had gone up to Mount Tabor, ¹³Sisera gathered together his nine hundred iron chariots and all the men with him, from Harosheth Haggoyim to the Kishon River.

¹⁴Then Deborah said to Barak, "Go! This is the day the LORD has given Sisera into your hands. Has not the LORD gone ahead of you?" So Barak went down Mount Tabor, followed by ten thousand men. ¹⁵At Barak's advance, the LORD routed Sisera and all his chariots and army by the sword, and Sisera abandoned his chariot and fled on foot. ¹⁶But Barak pursued the chariots and army as far as Harosheth Haggoyim. All the troops of Sisera fell by the sword; not a man was left.

¹⁷Sisera, however, fled on foot to the tent of Jael, the wife of Heber the Kenite, because there were friendly relations between Jabin king of Hazor and the clan of Heber the Kenite.

¹⁸Jael went out to meet Sisera and said to him, "Come, my lord, come right in. Don't be afraid." So he entered her tent, and she put a covering over him.

¹⁹"I'm thirsty," he said. "Please give me some water." She opened a skin of milk, gave him a drink, and covered him up.

²⁰"Stand in the doorway of the tent," he told her. "If someone comes by and asks you, 'Is anyone here?' say 'No.' "

²¹But Jael, Heber's wife, picked up a tent peg and a hammer and went quietly to him while he lay fast asleep, exhausted. She drove the peg through his temple into the ground, and he died.

²²Barak came by in pursuit of Sisera, and Jael went out to meet him. "Come," she said, "I will show you the man you're looking for." So he

THE MESSAGE

River with all his chariots and troops. And I'll make sure you win the battle."

4.8 Barak said, "If you go with me, I'll go. But if you don't go with me, I won't go."

4.9-10 She said, "Of course I'll go with you. But understand that with an attitude like that, there'll be no glory in it for you. GOD will use a woman's hand to take care of Sisera."

Deborah got ready and went with Barak to Kedesh. Barak called Zebulun and Naphtali together at Kedesh. Ten companies of men followed him. And Deborah was with him.

4.11-13 It happened that Heber the Kenite had parted company with the other Kenites, the descendants of Hobab, Moses' in-law. He was now living at Zaanannim Oak near Kedesh. They told Sisera that Barak son of Abinoam had gone up to Mount Tabor. Sisera immediately called up all his chariots to the Kishon River—nine hundred iron chariots!—along with all his troops who were with him at Harosheth Haggoyim.

4.14 Deborah said to Barak, "Charge! This very day GOD has given you victory over Sisera. Isn't GOD marching before you?"

Barak charged down the slopes of Mount Tabor, his ten companies following him.

4.15-16 GOD routed Sisera—all those chariots, all those troops!—before Barak. Sisera jumped out of his chariot and ran. Barak chased the chariots and troops all the way to Harosheth Haggoyim. Sisera's entire fighting force was killed—not one man left.

4.17-18 Meanwhile Sisera, running for his life, headed for the tent of Jael, wife of Heber the Kenite. Jabin king of Hazor and Heber the Kenite were on good terms with one another. Jael stepped out to meet Sisera and said, "Come in, sir. Stay here with me. Don't be afraid."

So he went with her into her tent. She covered him with a blanket.

4.19 He said to her, "Please, a little water. I'm thirsty."

She opened a bottle of milk, gave him a drink, and then covered him up again.

4.20 He then said, "Stand at the tent flap. If anyone comes by and asks you, 'Is there anyone here?' tell him, 'No, not a soul.' "

4.21 Then while he was fast asleep from exhaustion, Jael wife of Heber took a tent peg and hammer, tiptoed toward him, and drove the tent peg through his temple and all the way into the ground. He convulsed and died.

4.22 Barak arrived in pursuit of Sisera. Jael went out to greet him. She said, "Come, I'll show you the man you're looking for." He went with

---

ᵃ 9 Or But on the expedition you are undertaking
ᵇ 11 Or father-in-law

NEW INTERNATIONAL VERSION

went in with her, and there lay Sisera with the tent peg through his temple—dead.

²³On that day God subdued Jabin, the Canaanite king, before the Israelites. ²⁴And the hand of the Israelites grew stronger and stronger against Jabin, the Canaanite king, until they destroyed him.

THE SONG OF DEBORAH

5 On that day Deborah and Barak son of Abinoam sang this song:

² "When the princes in Israel take the lead,
　when the people willingly offer
　　themselves—
　praise the LORD!

³ "Hear this, you kings! Listen, you rulers!
　I will sing to*ᵃ* the LORD, I will sing;
　I will make music to*ᵇ* the LORD, the God
　　of Israel.

⁴ "O LORD, when you went out from Seir,
　when you marched from the land of
　　Edom,
　the earth shook, the heavens poured,
　the clouds poured down water.
⁵ The mountains quaked before the LORD, the
　　One of Sinai,
　before the LORD, the God of Israel.

⁶ "In the days of Shamgar son of Anath,
　in the days of Jael, the roads were
　　abandoned;
　travelers took to winding paths.
⁷ Village life*ᶜ* in Israel ceased,
　ceased until I,*ᵈ* Deborah, arose,
　arose a mother in Israel.
⁸ When they chose new gods,
　war came to the city gates,
　and not a shield or spear was seen
　　among forty thousand in Israel.
⁹ My heart is with Israel's princes,
　with the willing volunteers among the
　　people.
　Praise the LORD!

¹⁰ "You who ride on white donkeys,
　sitting on your saddle blankets,
　and you who walk along the road,
　consider ¹¹the voice of the singers*ᵉ* at the
　　watering places.
　They recite the righteous acts of the LORD,
　the righteous acts of his warriors*ᶠ* in
　　Israel.

ᵃ 3 Or of　*ᵇ 3 Or / with song I will praise*
ᶜ 7 Or Warriors　*ᵈ 7 Or you*　*ᵉ 11 Or archers;* the
meaning of the Hebrew for this word is uncertain.
ᶠ 11 Or villagers

THE MESSAGE

her and there he was—Sisera, stretched out, dead, with a tent peg through his temple.

4.23-24　On that day God subdued Jabin king of Canaan before the People of Israel. The People of Israel pressed harder and harder on Jabin king of Canaan until there was nothing left of him.

✝

5.1　**5** That day Deborah and Barak son of Abinoam sang this song:

5.2　When they let down their hair in Israel,
　　they let it blow wild in the wind.
　The people volunteered with abandon,
　　bless GOD!

5.3　Hear O kings! Listen O princes!
　　To GOD, yes to GOD, I'll sing,
　Make music to GOD,
　　to the God of Israel.

5.4-5　GOD, when you left Seir,
　　marched across the fields of Edom,
　Earth quaked, yes, the skies poured rain,
　　oh, the clouds made rivers.
　Mountains leapt before GOD, the Sinai God,
　　before GOD, the God of Israel.

5.6-8　In the time of Shamgar son of Anath,
　　and in the time of Jael,
　Public roads were abandoned,
　　travelers went by backroads.
　Warriors became fat and sloppy,
　　no fight left in them.
　Then you, Deborah, rose up;
　　you got up, a mother in Israel.
　God chose new leaders,
　　who then fought at the gates.
　And not a shield or spear to be seen
　　among the forty companies of Israel.

5.9　Lift your hearts high, O Israel,
　　with abandon, volunteering yourselves
　　　with the people—bless GOD!

✝

5.10-11　You who ride on prize donkeys
　　comfortably mounted on blankets
　And you who walk down the roads,
　　ponder, attend!
　Gather at the town well
　　and listen to them sing,
　Chanting the tale of GOD's victories,
　　his victories accomplished in Israel.

NEW INTERNATIONAL VERSION

"Then the people of the LORD
    went down to the city gates.
12 'Wake up, wake up, Deborah!
    Wake up, wake up, break out in song!
Arise, O Barak!
    Take captive your captives, O son of
      Abinoam.'

13 "Then the men who were left
    came down to the nobles;
the people of the LORD
    came to me with the mighty.
14 Some came from Ephraim, whose roots were
    in Amalek;
    Benjamin was with the people who
      followed you.
From Makir captains came down,
    from Zebulun those who bear a
      commander's staff.
15 The princes of Issachar were with Deborah;
    yes, Issachar was with Barak,
    rushing after him into the valley.
In the districts of Reuben
    there was much searching of heart.
16 Why did you stay among the campfires[a]
    to hear the whistling for the flocks?
In the districts of Reuben
    there was much searching of heart.
17 Gilead stayed beyond the Jordan.
    And Dan, why did he linger by the ships?
Asher remained on the coast
    and stayed in his coves.
18 The people of Zebulun risked their very
    lives;
    so did Naphtali on the heights of the field.

19 "Kings came, they fought;
    the kings of Canaan fought
  at Taanach by the waters of Megiddo,
    but they carried off no silver, no plunder.
20 From the heavens the stars fought,
    from their courses they fought against
      Sisera.
21 The river Kishon swept them away,
    the age-old river, the river Kishon.
    March on, my soul; be strong!
22 Then thundered the horses' hoofs—
    galloping, galloping go his mighty steeds.
23 'Curse Meroz,' said the angel of the LORD.
    'Curse its people bitterly,
  because they did not come to help the LORD,
    to help the LORD against the mighty.'

[a] 16 Or saddlebags

THE MESSAGE

Then the people of GOD
    went down to the city gates.
5.12   Wake up, wake up, Deborah!
    Wake up, wake up, sing a song!
On your feet, Barak!
    Take your prisoners, son of Abinoam!

✠

5.13-18   Then the remnant went down to greet the
    brave ones.
    The people of GOD joined the mighty
      ones.
The captains from Ephraim came to the
    valley,
    behind you, Benjamin, with your troops.
Captains marched down from Makir,
    from Zebulun high-ranking leaders came
      down.
Issachar's princes rallied to Deborah,
    Issachar stood fast with Barak,
    backing him up on the field of battle.
But in Reuben's divisions there was much
    second-guessing.
    Why all those campfire discussions?
Diverted and distracted,
    Reuben's divisions couldn't make up
      their minds.
Gilead played it safe across the Jordan,
    and Dan, why did he go off sailing?
Asher kept his distance on the seacoast,
    safe and secure in his harbors.
But Zebulun risked life and limb, defied
    death,
    as did Naphtali on the battle heights.

5.19-23   The kings came, they fought,
    the kings of Canaan fought.
At Taanach they fought, at Megiddo's
    brook,
    but they took no silver, no plunder.
The stars in the sky joined the fight,
    from their courses they fought against
      Sisera.
The torrent Kishon swept them away,
    the torrent attacked them, the torrent
      Kishon.
    Oh, you'll stomp on the necks of the
      strong!
Then the hoofs of the horses pounded,
    charging, stampeding stallions.
"Curse Meroz," says GOD's angel.
    "Curse, double curse, its people,
Because they didn't come when GOD
    needed them,
    didn't rally to GOD's side with valiant
      fighters."

✠

NEW INTERNATIONAL VERSION

²⁴ "Most blessed of women be Jael,
    the wife of Heber the Kenite,
    most blessed of tent-dwelling women.
²⁵ He asked for water, and she gave him milk;
    in a bowl fit for nobles she brought him
        curdled milk.
²⁶ Her hand reached for the tent peg,
    her right hand for the workman's hammer.
She struck Sisera, she crushed his head,
    she shattered and pierced his temple.
²⁷ At her feet he sank,
    he fell; there he lay.
At her feet he sank, he fell;
    where he sank, there he fell—dead.

²⁸ "Through the window peered Sisera's
        mother;
    behind the lattice she cried out,
    'Why is his chariot so long in coming?
    Why is the clatter of his chariots delayed?'
²⁹ The wisest of her ladies answer her;
    indeed, she keeps saying to herself,
³⁰ 'Are they not finding and dividing the spoils:
    a girl or two for each man,
    colorful garments as plunder for Sisera,
    colorful garments embroidered,
    highly embroidered garments for my
        neck—
all this as plunder?'

³¹ "So may all your enemies perish, O Lord!
    But may they who love you be like the
        sun
    when it rises in its strength."

Then the land had peace forty years.

Gideon

6 Again the Israelites did evil in the eyes of the Lord, and for seven years he gave them into the hands of the Midianites. ²Because the power of Midian was so oppressive, the Israelites prepared shelters for themselves in mountain clefts, caves and strongholds. ³Whenever the Israelites planted their crops, the Midianites, Amalekites and other eastern peoples invaded the country. ⁴They camped on the land and ruined the crops all the way to Gaza and did not spare a living thing for Israel, neither sheep nor cattle nor donkeys. ⁵They came up with their livestock and their tents like swarms of locusts. It was impossible to count the men and their camels; they invaded the land to ravage it. ⁶Midian so impover-

THE MESSAGE

5.24-27   Most blessed of all women is Jael,
    wife of Heber the Kenite,
    most blessed of homemaking women.
He asked for water,
    she brought milk;
In a handsome bowl,
    she offered cream.
She grabbed a tent peg in her left hand,
    with her right hand she seized a
        hammer.
She hammered Sisera, she smashed his
        head,
    she drove a hole through his temple.
He slumped at her feet. He fell. He
        sprawled.
He slumped at her feet. He fell.
    Slumped. Fallen. Dead.

✠

5.28-30   Sisera's mother waited at the window,
    a weary, anxious watch.
"What's keeping his chariot?
    What delays his chariot's rumble?"
The wisest of her ladies-in-waiting answers
    with calm, reassuring words,
"Don't you think they're busy at plunder,
    dividing up the loot?
A girl, maybe two girls,
    for each man,
And for Sisera a bright silk shirt,
    a prize, fancy silk shirt!
And a colorful scarf—make it two
        scarves—
    to grace the neck of the plunderer."

✠

5.31   Thus may all God's enemies perish,
    while his lovers be like the unclouded
        sun.

The land was quiet for forty years.

Gideon

6.1-6   6 Yet again the People of Israel went back to doing evil in God's sight. God put them under the domination of Midian for seven years. Midian overpowered Israel. Because of Midian, the People of Israel made for themselves hideouts in the mountains—caves and forts. When Israel planted its crops, Midian and Amalek, the easterners, would invade them, camp in their fields, and destroy their crops all the way down to Gaza. They left nothing for them to live on, neither sheep nor ox nor donkey. Bringing their cattle and tents, they came in and took over, like an invasion of locusts. And their camels—past counting! They marched in and devastated the country. The People of Isra-

NEW INTERNATIONAL VERSION

ished the Israelites that they cried out to the LORD for help.

⁷When the Israelites cried to the LORD because of Midian, ⁸he sent them a prophet, who said, "This is what the LORD, the God of Israel, says: I brought you up out of Egypt, out of the land of slavery. ⁹I snatched you from the power of Egypt and from the hand of all your oppressors. I drove them from before you and gave you their land. ¹⁰I said to you, 'I am the LORD your God; do not worship the gods of the Amorites, in whose land you live.' But you have not listened to me."

¹¹The angel of the LORD came and sat down under the oak in Ophrah that belonged to Joash the Abiezrite, where his son Gideon was threshing wheat in a winepress to keep it from the Midianites. ¹²When the angel of the LORD appeared to Gideon, he said, "The LORD is with you, mighty warrior."

¹³"But sir," Gideon replied, "if the LORD is with us, why has all this happened to us? Where are all his wonders that our fathers told us about when they said, 'Did not the LORD bring us up out of Egypt?' But now the LORD has abandoned us and put us into the hand of Midian."

¹⁴The LORD turned to him and said, "Go in the strength you have and save Israel out of Midian's hand. Am I not sending you?"

¹⁵"But Lord,ᵃ" Gideon asked, "how can I save Israel? My clan is the weakest in Manasseh, and I am the least in my family."

¹⁶The LORD answered, "I will be with you, and you will strike down all the Midianites together."

¹⁷Gideon replied, "If now I have found favor in your eyes, give me a sign that it is really you talking to me. ¹⁸Please do not go away until I come back and bring my offering and set it before you."

And the LORD said, "I will wait until you return."

¹⁹Gideon went in, prepared a young goat, and from an ephahᵇ of flour he made bread without yeast. Putting the meat in a basket and its broth in a pot, he brought them out and offered them to him under the oak.

²⁰The angel of God said to him, "Take the meat and the unleavened bread, place them on this rock, and pour out the broth." And Gideon did so. ²¹With the tip of the staff that was in his hand, the angel of the LORD touched the meat

THE MESSAGE

el, reduced to grinding poverty by Midian, cried out to GOD for help.

6.7-10 One time when the People of Israel had cried out to GOD because of Midian, GOD sent them a prophet with this message: "GOD, the God of Israel, says,

I delivered you from Egypt,
   I freed you from a life of slavery;
I rescued you from Egypt's brutality
   and then from every oppressor;
I pushed them out of your way
   and gave you their land.

"And I said to you, 'I am GOD, your God. Don't for a minute be afraid of the gods of the Amorites in whose land you are living.' But you didn't listen to me."

6.11-12 One day the angel of GOD came and sat down under the oak in Ophrah that belonged to Joash the Abiezrite, whose son Gideon was threshing wheat in the winepress, out of sight of the Midianites. The angel of GOD appeared to him and said,

"GOD is with you,
   O mighty warrior!"

6.13 Gideon replied, "With *me*, my master? If GOD is with us, why has all this happened to us? Where are all the miracle-wonders our parents and grandparents told us about, telling us, 'Didn't GOD deliver us from Egypt?' The fact is, GOD has nothing to do with us—he has turned us over to Midian."

6.14 But GOD faced him directly: "Go in this strength that is yours. Save Israel from Midian. Haven't I just sent you?"

6.15 Gideon said to him, "*Me*, my master? How and with what could I ever save Israel? Look at me. My clan's the weakest in Manasseh and I'm the runt of the litter."

6.16 GOD said to him, "I'll be with you. Believe me, you'll defeat Midian as one man."

6.17-18 Gideon said, "If you're serious about this, do me a favor: Give me a sign to back up what you're telling me. Don't leave until I come back and bring you my gift."

He said, "I'll wait till you get back."

6.19 Gideon went and prepared a young goat and a huge amount of unraised bread (he used over half a bushel of flour!). He put the meat in a basket and the broth in a pot and took them back under the shade of the oak tree for a sacred meal.

6.20 The angel of God said to him, "Take the meat and unraised bread, place them on that rock, and pour the broth on them." Gideon did it.

6.21-22 The angel of GOD stretched out the tip of the stick he was holding and touched the meat

---

ᵃ 15 Or sir   ᵇ 19 That is, probably about 3/5 bushel (about 22 liters)

NEW INTERNATIONAL VERSION

and the unleavened bread. Fire flared from the rock, consuming the meat and the bread. And the angel of the LORD disappeared. ²²When Gideon realized that it was the angel of the LORD, he exclaimed, "Ah, Sovereign LORD! I have seen the angel of the LORD face to face!"

²³But the LORD said to him, "Peace! Do not be afraid. You are not going to die."

²⁴So Gideon built an altar to the LORD there and called it The LORD is Peace. To this day it stands in Ophrah of the Abiezrites.

²⁵That same night the LORD said to him, "Take the second bull from your father's herd, the one seven years old.ᵃ Tear down your father's altar to Baal and cut down the Asherah poleᵇ beside it. ²⁶Then build a proper kind ofᶜ altar to the LORD your God on the top of this height. Using the wood of the Asherah pole that you cut down, offer the secondᵈ bull as a burnt offering."

²⁷So Gideon took ten of his servants and did as the LORD told him. But because he was afraid of his family and the men of the town, he did it at night rather than in the daytime.

²⁸In the morning when the men of the town got up, there was Baal's altar, demolished, with the Asherah pole beside it cut down and the second bull sacrificed on the newly built altar!

²⁹They asked each other, "Who did this?"

When they carefully investigated, they were told, "Gideon son of Joash did it."

³⁰The men of the town demanded of Joash, "Bring out your son. He must die, because he has broken down Baal's altar and cut down the Asherah pole beside it."

³¹But Joash replied to the hostile crowd around him, "Are you going to plead Baal's cause? Are you trying to save him? Whoever fights for him shall be put to death by morning! If Baal really is a god, he can defend himself when someone breaks down his altar." ³²So that day they called Gideon "Jerub-Baal,ᵉ" saying, "Let Baal contend with him," because he broke down Baal's altar.

³³Now all the Midianites, Amalekites and other eastern peoples joined forces and crossed over the Jordan and camped in the Valley of Jezreel. ³⁴Then the Spirit of the LORD came upon Gideon, and he blew a trumpet, summoning the Abiezrites to follow him. ³⁵He sent messengers throughout Manasseh, calling them to arms, and also into Asher, Zebulun and Naphtali, so that they too went up to meet them.

ᵃ 25 Or *Take a full-grown, mature bull from your father's herd*
ᵇ 25 That is, a symbol of the goddess Asherah; here and elsewhere in Judges   ᶜ 26 Or *build with layers of stone an*
ᵈ 26 Or *full-grown*; also in verse 28   ᵉ 32 *Jerub-Baal* means *let Baal contend*.

THE MESSAGE

and the bread. Fire broke out of the rock and burned up the meat and bread while the angel of God slipped away out of sight. And Gideon knew it was the angel of God!

Gideon said, "Oh no! Master, GOD! I have seen the angel of God face to face!"

6.23 But GOD reassured him, "Easy now. Don't panic. You won't die."

6.24 Then Gideon built an altar there to GOD and named it "GOD's Peace." It's still called that at Ophrah of Abiezer.

6.25-26 That night this happened. GOD said to him, "Take your father's best seven-year-old bull, the prime one. Tear down your father's Baal altar and chop down the Asherah fertility pole beside it. Then build an altar to GOD, your God, on the top of this hill. Take the prime bull and present it as a Whole-Burnt-Offering, using firewood from the Asherah pole that you cut down."

6.27 Gideon selected ten men from his servants and did exactly what GOD had told him. But because of his family and the people in the neighborhood, he was afraid to do it openly, so he did it that night.

6.28 Early in the morning, the people in town were shocked to find Baal's altar torn down, the Asherah pole beside it chopped down, and the prime bull burning away on the altar that had been built.

6.29 They kept asking, "Who did this?"

Questions and more questions, and then the answer: "Gideon son of Joash did it."

6.30 The men of the town demanded of Joash: "Bring out your son! He must die! Why, he tore down the Baal altar and chopped down the Asherah tree!"

6.31 But Joash stood up to the crowd pressing in on him, "Are you going to fight Baal's battles for him? Are you going to save him? Anyone who takes Baal's side will be dead by morning. If Baal is a god in fact, let him fight his own battles and defend his own altar."

6.32 They nicknamed Gideon that day Jerub-Baal because after he had torn down the Baal altar, he had said, "Let Baal fight his own battles."

✛

6.33-35 All the Midianites and Amalekites (the easterners) got together, crossed the river, and made camp in the Valley of Jezreel. GOD's Spirit came over Gideon. He blew his ram's horn trumpet and the Abiezrites came out, ready to follow him. He dispatched messengers all through Manasseh, calling them to the battle; also to Asher, Zebulun, and Naphtali. They all came.

NEW INTERNATIONAL VERSION

³⁶Gideon said to God, "If you will save Israel by my hand as you have promised— ³⁷look, I will place a wool fleece on the threshing floor. If there is dew only on the fleece and all the ground is dry, then I will know that you will save Israel by my hand, as you said." ³⁸And that is what happened. Gideon rose early the next day; he squeezed the fleece and wrung out the dew— a bowlful of water.

³⁹Then Gideon said to God, "Do not be angry with me. Let me make just one more request. Allow me one more test with the fleece. This time make the fleece dry and the ground covered with dew." ⁴⁰That night God did so. Only the fleece was dry; all the ground was covered with dew.

GIDEON DEFEATS THE MIDIANITES

7 Early in the morning, Jerub-Baal (that is, Gideon) and all his men camped at the spring of Harod. The camp of Midian was north of them in the valley near the hill of Moreh. ²The LORD said to Gideon, "You have too many men for me to deliver Midian into their hands. In order that Israel may not boast against me that her own strength has saved her, ³announce now to the people, 'Anyone who trembles with fear may turn back and leave Mount Gilead.'" So twenty-two thousand men left, while ten thousand remained.

⁴But the LORD said to Gideon, "There are still too many men. Take them down to the water, and I will sift them for you there. If I say, 'This one shall go with you,' he shall go; but if I say, 'This one shall not go with you,' he shall not go."

⁵So Gideon took the men down to the water. There the LORD told him, "Separate those who lap the water with their tongues like a dog from those who kneel down to drink." ⁶Three hundred men lapped with their hands to their mouths. All the rest got down on their knees to drink.

⁷The LORD said to Gideon, "With the three hundred men that lapped I will save you and give the Midianites into your hands. Let all the other men go, each to his own place." ⁸So Gideon sent the rest of the Israelites to their tents but kept the three hundred, who took over the provisions and trumpets of the others.

Now the camp of Midian lay below him in the valley. ⁹During that night the LORD said to Gideon, "Get up, go down against the camp, because I am going to give it into your hands. ¹⁰If

THE MESSAGE

6.36-37 Gideon said to God, "If this is right, if you are using me to save Israel as you've said, then look: I'm placing a fleece of wool on the threshing floor. If dew is on the fleece only, but the floor is dry, then I know that you will use me to save Israel, as you said."

6.38 That's what happened. When he got up early the next morning, he wrung out the fleece— enough dew to fill a bowl with water!

6.39 Then Gideon said to God, "Don't be impatient with me, but let me say one more thing. I want to try another time with the fleece. But this time let the fleece stay dry, while the dew drenches the ground."

6.40 God made it happen that very night. Only the fleece was dry while the ground was wet with dew.

✝

7.1 **7** Jerub-Baal (Gideon) got up early the next morning, all his troops right there with him. They set up camp at Harod's Spring. The camp of Midian was in the plain, north of them near the Hill of Moreh.

7.2-3 GOD said to Gideon, "You have too large an army with you. I can't turn Midian over to them like this—they'll take all the credit, saying, 'I did it all myself,' and forget about me. Make a public announcement: 'Anyone afraid, anyone who has any qualms at all, may leave Mount Gilead now and go home.'" Twenty-two companies headed for home. Ten companies were left.

7.4-5 GOD said to Gideon: "There are still too many. Take them down to the stream and I'll make a final cut. When I say, 'This one goes with you,' he'll go. When I say, 'This one doesn't go,' he won't go." So Gideon took the troops down to the stream.

7.5-6 GOD said to Gideon: "Everyone who laps with his tongue, the way a dog laps, set on one side. And everyone who kneels to drink, drinking with his face to the water, set to the other side." Three hundred lapped with their tongues from their cupped hands. All the rest knelt to drink.

7.7 GOD said to Gideon: "I'll use the three hundred men who lapped at the stream to save you and give Midian into your hands. All the rest may go home."

7.8 After Gideon took all their provisions and trumpets, he sent all the Israelites home. He took up his position with the three hundred. The camp of Midian stretched out below him in the valley.

7.9-12 That night, GOD told Gideon: "Get up and go down to the camp. I've given it to you. If

NEW INTERNATIONAL VERSION

you are afraid to attack, go down to the camp with your servant Purah ¹¹and listen to what they are saying. Afterward, you will be encouraged to attack the camp." So he and Purah his servant went down to the outposts of the camp. ¹²The Midianites, the Amalekites and all the other eastern peoples had settled in the valley, thick as locusts. Their camels could no more be counted than the sand on the seashore.

¹³Gideon arrived just as a man was telling a friend his dream. "I had a dream," he was saying. "A round loaf of barley bread came tumbling into the Midianite camp. It struck the tent with such force that the tent overturned and collapsed."

¹⁴His friend responded, "This can be nothing other than the sword of Gideon son of Joash, the Israelite. God has given the Midianites and the whole camp into his hands."

¹⁵When Gideon heard the dream and its interpretation, he worshiped God. He returned to the camp of Israel and called out, "Get up! The LORD has given the Midianite camp into your hands." ¹⁶Dividing the three hundred men into three companies, he placed trumpets and empty jars in the hands of all of them, with torches inside.

¹⁷"Watch me," he told them. "Follow my lead. When I get to the edge of the camp, do exactly as I do. ¹⁸When I and all who are with me blow our trumpets, then from all around the camp blow yours and shout, 'For the LORD and for Gideon.' "

¹⁹Gideon and the hundred men with him reached the edge of the camp at the beginning of the middle watch, just after they had changed the guard. They blew their trumpets and broke the jars that were in their hands. ²⁰The three companies blew the trumpets and smashed the jars. Grasping the torches in their left hands and holding in their right hands the trumpets they were to blow, they shouted, "A sword for the LORD and for Gideon!" ²¹While each man held his position around the camp, all the Midianites ran, crying out as they fled.

²²When the three hundred trumpets sounded, the LORD caused the men throughout the camp to turn on each other with their swords. The army fled to Beth Shittah toward Zererah as far as the border of Abel Meholah near Tabbath. ²³Israelites from Naphtali, Asher and all Manasseh were called out, and they pursued the Midianites. ²⁴Gideon sent messengers throughout the hill country of Ephraim, saying, "Come down against the Midianites and seize the waters of the Jordan ahead of them as far as Beth Barah."

So all the men of Ephraim were called out and they took the waters of the Jordan as far as Beth

THE MESSAGE

you have any doubts about going down, go down with Purah your armor bearer; when you hear what they're saying, you'll be bold and confident." He and his armor bearer Purah went down near the place where sentries were posted. Midian and Amalek, all the easterners, were spread out on the plain like a swarm of locusts. And their camels! Past counting, like grains of sand on the seashore!

7.13 Gideon arrived just in time to hear a man tell his friend a dream. He said, "I had this dream: A loaf of barley bread tumbled into the Midian camp. It came to the tent and hit it so hard it collapsed. The tent fell!"

7.14 His friend said, "This has to be the sword of Gideon son of Joash, the Israelite! God has turned Midian—the whole camp!—over to him."

7.15 When Gideon heard the telling of the dream and its interpretation, he went to his knees before God in prayer. Then he went back to the Israelite camp and said, "Get up and get going! GOD has just given us the Midianite army!"

7.16-18 He divided the three hundred men into three companies. He gave each man a trumpet and an empty jar, with a torch in the jar. He said, "Watch me and do what I do. When I get to the edge of the camp, do exactly what I do. When I and those with me blow the trumpets, you also, all around the camp, blow your trumpets and shout, 'For GOD and for Gideon!' "

7.19-22 Gideon and his hundred men got to the edge of the camp at the beginning of the middle watch, just after the sentries had been posted. They blew the trumpets, at the same time smashing the jars they carried. All three companies blew the trumpets and broke the jars. They held the torches in their left hands and the trumpets in their right hands, ready to blow, and shouted, "A sword for GOD and for Gideon!" They were stationed all around the camp, each man at his post. The whole Midianite camp jumped to its feet. They yelled and fled. When the three hundred blew the trumpets, GOD aimed each Midianite's sword against his companion, all over the camp. They ran for their lives—to Beth Shittah, toward Zererah, to the border of Abel Meholah near Tabbath.

7.23 Israelites rallied from Naphtali, from Asher, and from all over Manasseh. They had Midian on the run.

7.24 Gideon then sent messengers through all the hill country of Ephraim, urging them, "Come down against Midian! Capture the fords of the Jordan at Beth Barah."

7.25 So all the men of Ephraim rallied and captured the fords of the Jordan at Beth Barah.

NEW INTERNATIONAL VERSION

Barah. ²⁵They also captured two of the Midianite leaders, Oreb and Zeeb. They killed Oreb at the rock of Oreb, and Zeeb at the winepress of Zeeb. They pursued the Midianites and brought the heads of Oreb and Zeeb to Gideon, who was by the Jordan.

ZEBAH AND ZALMUNNA

8 Now the Ephraimites asked Gideon, "Why have you treated us like this? Why didn't you call us when you went to fight Midian?" And they criticized him sharply.

²But he answered them, "What have I accomplished compared to you? Aren't the gleanings of Ephraim's grapes better than the full grape harvest of Abiezer? ³God gave Oreb and Zeeb, the Midianite leaders, into your hands. What was I able to do compared to you?" At this, their resentment against him subsided.

⁴Gideon and his three hundred men, exhausted yet keeping up the pursuit, came to the Jordan and crossed it. ⁵He said to the men of Succoth, "Give my troops some bread; they are worn out, and I am still pursuing Zebah and Zalmunna, the kings of Midian."

⁶But the officials of Succoth said, "Do you already have the hands of Zebah and Zalmunna in your possession? Why should we give bread to your troops?"

⁷Then Gideon replied, "Just for that, when the LORD has given Zebah and Zalmunna into my hand, I will tear your flesh with desert thorns and briers."

⁸From there he went up to Peniel[a] and made the same request of them, but they answered as the men of Succoth had. ⁹So he said to the men of Peniel, "When I return in triumph, I will tear down this tower."

¹⁰Now Zebah and Zalmunna were in Karkor with a force of about fifteen thousand men, all that was left of the armies of the eastern peoples; a hundred and twenty thousand swordsmen had fallen. ¹¹Gideon went up by the route of the nomads east of Nobah and Jogbehah and fell upon the unsuspecting army. ¹²Zebah and Zalmunna, the two kings of Midian, fled, but he pursued them and captured them, routing their entire army.

¹³Gideon son of Joash then returned from the battle by the Pass of Heres. ¹⁴He caught a young man of Succoth and questioned him, and the young man wrote down for him the names of the seventy-seven officials of Succoth, the elders of the town. ¹⁵Then Gideon came and said to the men of Succoth, "Here are Zebah and Zal-

---

a 8 Hebrew *Penuel*, a variant of *Peniel*; also in verses 9 and 17

THE MESSAGE

They also captured the two Midianite commanders Oreb (Raven) and Zeeb (Wolf). They killed Oreb at Raven Rock; Zeeb they killed at Wolf Winepress. And they pressed the pursuit of Midian. They brought the heads of Oreb and Zeeb to Gideon across the Jordan.

8.1 **8** Then the Ephraimites said to Gideon, "Why did you leave us out of this, not calling us when you went to fight Midian?" They were indignant and let him know it.

8.2-3 But Gideon replied, "What have I done compared to you? Why, even the gleanings of Ephraim are superior to the vintage of Abiezer. God gave you Midian's commanders, Oreb and Zeeb. What have I done compared with you?"

When they heard this, they calmed down and cooled off.

✣

8.4-5 Gideon and his three hundred arrived at the Jordan and crossed over. They were bone-tired but still pressing the pursuit. He asked the men of Succoth, "Please, give me some loaves of bread for my troops I have with me. They're worn out, and I'm hot on the trail of Zebah and Zalmunna, the Midianite kings."

8.6 But the leaders in Succoth said, "You're on a wild goose chase; why should we help you on a fool's errand?"

8.7 Gideon said, "If you say so. But when GOD gives me Zebah and Zalmunna, I'll give you a thrashing, whip your bare flesh with desert thorns and thistles!"

8.8-9 He went from there to Peniel and made the same request. The men of Peniel, like the men of Succoth, also refused. Gideon told them, "When I return safe and sound, I'll demolish this tower."

8.10 Zebah and Zalmunna were in Karkor with an army of about fifteen companies, all that was left of the fighting force of the easterners—they had lost 120 companies of soldiers.

8.11-12 Gideon went up the caravan trail east of Nobah and Jogbehah, found and attacked the undefended camp. Zebah and Zalmunna fled, but he chased and captured the two kings of Midian. The whole camp had panicked.

8.13-15 Gideon son of Joash returned from the battle by way of the Heres Pass. He captured a young man from Succoth and asked some questions. The young man wrote down the names of the officials and leaders of Succoth, seventy-seven men. Then Gideon went to the men of Succoth and said, "Here are the wild geese, Zebah and

NEW INTERNATIONAL VERSION

munna, about whom you taunted me by saying, 'Do you already have the hands of Zebah and Zalmunna in your possession? Why should we give bread to your exhausted men?' " ¹⁶He took the elders of the town and taught the men of Succoth a lesson by punishing them with desert thorns and briers. ¹⁷He also pulled down the tower of Peniel and killed the men of the town.

¹⁸Then he asked Zebah and Zalmunna, "What kind of men did you kill at Tabor?"

"Men like you," they answered, "each one with the bearing of a prince."

¹⁹Gideon replied, "Those were my brothers, the sons of my own mother. As surely as the LORD lives, if you had spared their lives, I would not kill you." ²⁰Turning to Jether, his oldest son, he said, "Kill them!" But Jether did not draw his sword, because he was only a boy and was afraid.

²¹Zebah and Zalmunna said, "Come, do it yourself. 'As is the man, so is his strength.' " So Gideon stepped forward and killed them, and took the ornaments off their camels' necks.

GIDEON'S EPHOD

²²The Israelites said to Gideon, "Rule over us—you, your son and your grandson—because you have saved us out of the hand of Midian."

²³But Gideon told them, "I will not rule over you, nor will my son rule over you. The LORD will rule over you." ²⁴And he said, "I do have one request, that each of you give me an earring from your share of the plunder." (It was the custom of the Ishmaelites to wear gold earrings.)

²⁵They answered, "We'll be glad to give them." So they spread out a garment, and each man threw a ring from his plunder onto it. ²⁶The weight of the gold rings he asked for came to seventeen hundred shekels,ᵃ not counting the ornaments, the pendants and the purple garments worn by the kings of Midian or the chains that were on their camels' necks. ²⁷Gideon made the gold into an ephod, which he placed in Ophrah, his town. All Israel prostituted themselves by worshiping it there, and it became a snare to Gideon and his family.

GIDEON'S DEATH

²⁸Thus Midian was subdued before the Israelites and did not raise its head again. During Gideon's lifetime, the land enjoyed peace forty years.

²⁹Jerub-Baal son of Joash went back home to live. ³⁰He had seventy sons of his own, for he

THE MESSAGE

Zalmunna, you said I'd never catch. You wouldn't give so much as a scrap of bread to my worn-out men; you taunted us, saying that we were on a fool's errand."

8.16-17 Then he took the seventy-seven leaders of Succoth and thrashed them with desert thorns and thistles. And he demolished the tower of Peniel and killed the men of the city.

8.18 He then addressed Zebah and Zalmunna: "Tell me about the men you killed at Tabor."

"They were men much like you," they said, "each one like a king's son."

8.19 Gideon said, "They were my brothers, my mother's sons. As GOD lives, if you had let them live, I would let you live."

8.20 Then he spoke to Jether, his firstborn: "Get up and kill them." But he couldn't do it, couldn't draw his sword. He was afraid—he was still just a boy.

8.21 Zebah and Zalmunna said, "Do it yourself— if you're man enough!" And Gideon did it. He stepped up and killed Zebah and Zalmunna. Then he took the crescents that hung on the necks of their camels.

✝

8.22 The Israelites said, "Rule over us, you and your son and your grandson. You have saved us from Midian's tyranny."

8.23 Gideon said, "I most certainly will not rule over you, nor will my son. GOD will reign over you."

8.24 Then Gideon said, "But I do have one request. Give me, each of you, an earring that you took as plunder." Ishmaelites wore gold earrings, and the men all had their pockets full of them.

8.25-26 They said, "Of course. They're yours!"

They spread out a blanket and each man threw his plundered earrings on it. The gold earrings that Gideon had asked for weighed about forty-three pounds—and that didn't include the crescents and pendants, the purple robes worn by the Midianite kings, and the ornaments hung around the necks of their camels.

8.27 Gideon made the gold into a sacred ephod and put it on display in his hometown, Ophrah. All Israel prostituted itself there. Gideon and his family, too, were seduced by it.

8.28 Midian's tyranny was broken by the Israelites; nothing more was heard from them. The land was quiet for forty years in Gideon's time.

✝

8.29-31 Jerub-Baal son of Joash went home and lived in his house. Gideon had seventy sons. He fa-

---

ᵃ 26 That is, about 43 pounds (about 19.5 kilograms)

NEW INTERNATIONAL VERSION

had many wives. [31]His concubine, who lived in Shechem, also bore him a son, whom he named Abimelech. [32]Gideon son of Joash died at a good old age and was buried in the tomb of his father Joash in Ophrah of the Abiezrites.

[33]No sooner had Gideon died than the Israelites again prostituted themselves to the Baals. They set up Baal-Berith as their god [34]and did not remember the LORD their God, who had rescued them from the hands of all their enemies on every side. [35]They also failed to show kindness to the family of Jerub-Baal (that is, Gideon) for all the good things he had done for them.

ABIMELECH

9 Abimelech son of Jerub-Baal went to his mother's brothers in Shechem and said to them and to all his mother's clan, [2]"Ask all the citizens of Shechem, 'Which is better for you: to have all seventy of Jerub-Baal's sons rule over you, or just one man?' Remember, I am your flesh and blood."

[3]When the brothers repeated all this to the citizens of Shechem, they were inclined to follow Abimelech, for they said, "He is our brother." [4]They gave him seventy shekels[a] of silver from the temple of Baal-Berith, and Abimelech used it to hire reckless adventurers, who became his followers. [5]He went to his father's home in Ophrah and on one stone murdered his seventy brothers, the sons of Jerub-Baal. But Jotham, the youngest son of Jerub-Baal, escaped by hiding. [6]Then all the citizens of Shechem and Beth Millo gathered beside the great tree at the pillar in Shechem to crown Abimelech king.

[7]When Jotham was told about this, he climbed up on the top of Mount Gerizim and shouted to them, "Listen to me, citizens of Shechem, so that God may listen to you. [8]One day the trees went out to anoint a king for themselves. They said to the olive tree, 'Be our king.'

[9]"But the olive tree answered, 'Should I give up my oil, by which both gods and men are honored, to hold sway over the trees?'

[10]"Next, the trees said to the fig tree, 'Come and be our king.'

[11]"But the fig tree replied, 'Should I give up my fruit, so good and sweet, to hold sway over the trees?'

[12]"Then the trees said to the vine, 'Come and be our king.'

[13]"But the vine answered, 'Should I give up

THE MESSAGE

thered them all—he had a lot of wives! His concubine, the one at Shechem, also bore him a son. He named him Abimelech.

8.32 Gideon son of Joash died at a good old age. He was buried in the tomb of his father Joash at Ophrah of the Abiezrites.

ABIMELECH

8.33-35 Gideon was hardly cool in the tomb when the People of Israel had gotten off track and were prostituting themselves to Baal—they made Baal-of-the-Covenant their god. The People of Israel forgot all about GOD, their God, who had saved them from all their enemies who had hemmed them in. And they didn't keep faith with the family of Jerub-Baal (Gideon), honoring all the good he had done for Israel.

✝

9.1-2 **9** Abimelech son of Jerub-Baal went to Shechem to his uncles and all his mother's relatives and said to them, "Ask all the leading men of Shechem, 'What do you think is best, that seventy men rule you—all those sons of Jerub-Baal—or that one man rule? You'll remember that I am your own flesh and blood.' "

9.3 His mother's relatives reported the proposal to the leaders of Shechem. They were inclined to take Abimelech. "Because," they said, "he is, after all, one of us."

9.4-5 They gave him seventy silver pieces from the shrine of Baal-of-the-Covenant. With the money he hired some reckless riff-raff soldiers and they followed along after him. He went to his father's house in Ophrah and killed his half brothers, the sons of Jerub-Baal—seventy men! And on one stone! The youngest, Jotham son of Jerub-Baal, managed to hide, the only survivor.

9.6 Then all the leaders of Shechem and Beth Millo gathered at the Oak by the Standing Stone at Shechem and crowned Abimelech king.

9.7-9 When this was all told to Jotham, he climbed to the top of Mount Gerizim, raised his voice, and shouted:

Listen to me, leaders of Shechem.
    And let God listen to you!

The trees set out one day
    to anoint a king for themselves.
They said to Olive Tree,
    "Rule over us."
But Olive Tree told them,
    "Am I no longer good for making oil

---

[a] 4 That is, about 1 3/4 pounds (about 0.8 kilogram)

NEW INTERNATIONAL VERSION

my wine, which cheers both gods and men, to hold sway over the trees?'

14"Finally all the trees said to the thornbush, 'Come and be our king.'

15"The thornbush said to the trees, 'If you really want to anoint me king over you, come and take refuge in my shade; but if not, then let fire come out of the thornbush and consume the cedars of Lebanon!'

16"Now if you have acted honorably and in good faith when you made Abimelech king, and if you have been fair to Jerub-Baal and his family, and if you have treated him as he deserves— 17and to think that my father fought for you, risked his life to rescue you from the hand of Midian 18(but today you have revolted against my father's family, murdered his seventy sons on a single stone, and made Abimelech, the son of his slave girl, king over the citizens of Shechem because he is your brother)— 19if then you have acted honorably and in good faith toward Jerub-Baal and his family today, may Abimelech be your joy, and may you be his, too! 20But if you have not, let fire come out from Abimelech and consume you, citizens of Shechem and Beth Millo, and let fire come out from you, citizens of Shechem and Beth Millo, and consume Abimelech!"

21Then Jotham fled, escaping to Beer, and he lived there because he was afraid of his brother Abimelech.

22After Abimelech had governed Israel three years, 23God sent an evil spirit between Abimelech and the citizens of Shechem, who acted treacherously against Abimelech. 24God did this in order that the crime against Jerub-Baal's sev-

THE MESSAGE

That gives glory to gods and men,
and to be demoted to waving over
trees?"

9.10-11 The trees then said to Fig Tree,
"You come and rule over us."
But Fig Tree said to them,
"Am I no longer good for making
sweets,
My mouthwatering sweet fruits,
and to be demoted to waving over
trees?"

9.12-13 The trees then said to Vine,
"You come and rule over us."
But Vine said to them,
"Am I no longer good for making wine,
Wine that cheers gods and men,
and to be demoted to waving over
trees?"

9.14-15 All the trees then said to Tumbleweed,
"You come and reign over us."
But Tumbleweed said to the trees:
"If you're serious about making me your
king,
Come and find shelter in my shade.
But if not, let fire shoot from
Tumbleweed
and burn down the cedars of Lebanon!"

9.16-20 "Now listen: Do you think you did a right and honorable thing when you made Abimelech king? Do you think you treated Jerub-Baal and his family well, did for him what he deserved? My father fought for you, risked his own life, and rescued you from Midian's tyranny, and you have, just now, betrayed him. You massacred his sons—seventy men on a single stone! You made Abimelech, the son by his maidservant, king over Shechem's leaders because he's your relative. If you think that this is an honest day's work, this way you have treated Jerub-Baal today, then enjoy Abimelech and let him enjoy you. But if not, let fire break from Abimelech and burn up the leaders of Shechem and Beth Millo. And let fire break from the leaders of Shechem and Beth Millo and burn up Abimelech."

9.21 And Jotham fled. He ran for his life. He went to Beer and settled down there, because he was afraid of his brother Abimelech.

☩

9.22-24 Abimelech ruled over Israel for three years. Then God brought bad blood between Abimelech and Shechem's leaders, who now worked treacherously behind his back. Violence boomeranged: The murderous violence that killed

NEW INTERNATIONAL VERSION

enty sons, the shedding of their blood, might be avenged on their brother Abimelech and on the citizens of Shechem, who had helped him murder his brothers. ²⁵In opposition to him these citizens of Shechem set men on the hilltops to ambush and rob everyone who passed by, and this was reported to Abimelech.

²⁶Now Gaal son of Ebed moved with his brothers into Shechem, and its citizens put their confidence in him. ²⁷After they had gone out into the fields and gathered the grapes and trodden them, they held a festival in the temple of their god. While they were eating and drinking, they cursed Abimelech. ²⁸Then Gaal son of Ebed said, "Who is Abimelech, and who is Shechem, that we should be subject to him? Isn't he Jerub-Baal's son, and isn't Zebul his deputy? Serve the men of Hamor, Shechem's father! Why should we serve Abimelech? ²⁹If only this people were under my command! Then I would get rid of him. I would say to Abimelech, 'Call out your whole army!' "ᵃ

³⁰When Zebul the governor of the city heard what Gaal son of Ebed said, he was very angry. ³¹Under cover he sent messengers to Abimelech, saying, "Gaal son of Ebed and his brothers have come to Shechem and are stirring up the city against you. ³²Now then, during the night you and your men should come and lie in wait in the fields. ³³In the morning at sunrise, advance against the city. When Gaal and his men come out against you, do whatever your hand finds to do."

³⁴So Abimelech and all his troops set out by night and took up concealed positions near Shechem in four companies. ³⁵Now Gaal son of Ebed had gone out and was standing at the entrance to the city gate just as Abimelech and his soldiers came out from their hiding place.

³⁶When Gaal saw them, he said to Zebul, "Look, people are coming down from the tops of the mountains!"

Zebul replied, "You mistake the shadows of the mountains for men."

³⁷But Gaal spoke up again: "Look, people are coming down from the center of the land, and a company is coming from the direction of the soothsayers' tree."

³⁸Then Zebul said to him, "Where is your big talk now, you who said, 'Who is Abimelech that we should be subject to him?' Aren't these the men you ridiculed? Go out and fight them!"

ᵃ 29 Septuagint; Hebrew him." Then he said to Abimelech, "Call out your whole army!"

THE MESSAGE

the seventy brothers, the sons of Jerub-Baal, was now loose among Abimelech and Shechem's leaders, who had supported the violence.

9.25 To undermine Abimelech, Shechem's leaders put men in ambush on the mountain passes who robbed travelers on those roads. And Abimelech was told.

9.26-27 At that time Gaal son of Ebed arrived with his relatives and moved into Shechem. The leaders of Shechem trusted him. One day they went out into the fields, gathered grapes in the vineyards, and trod them in the winepress. Then they held a celebration in their god's temple, a feast, eating and drinking. And then they started putting down Abimelech.

9.28-29 Gaal son of Ebed said, "Who is this Abimelech? And who are we Shechemites to take orders from him? Isn't he the son of Jerub-Baal, and isn't this his henchman Zebul? We belong to the race of Hamor and bear the noble name of Shechem. Why should we be toadies of Abimelech? If I were in charge of this people, the first thing I'd do is get rid of Abimelech! I'd say, 'Show me your stuff, Abimelech—let's see who's boss here!' "

9.30-33 Zebul, governor of the city, heard what Gaal son of Ebed was saying and got angry. Secretly he sent messengers to Abimelech with the message, "Gaal son of Ebed and his relatives have come to Shechem and are stirring up trouble against you. Here's what you do: Tonight bring your troops and wait in ambush in the field. In the morning, as soon as the sun breaks, get moving and charge the city. Gaal and his troops will come out to you, and you'll know what to do next."

9.34-36 Abimelech and his troops, four companies of them, went up that night and waited in ambush approaching Shechem. Gaal son of Ebed had gotten up and was standing in the city gate. Abimelech and his troops left their cover. When Gaal saw them he said to Zebul, "Look at that, people coming down from the tops of the mountains!"

Zebul said, "That's nothing but mountain shadows; they just look like men." Gaal kept chattering away.

9.37 Then he said again, "Look at the troops coming down off Tabbur-erez (the Navel of the World)—and one company coming straight from the Oracle Oak."

9.38 Zebul said, "Where is that big mouth of yours now? You who said, 'And who is Abimelech that we should take orders from him?' Well, there he is with the troops you ridiculed. Here's your chance. Fight away!"

NEW INTERNATIONAL VERSION

³⁹So Gaal led out*ᵃ* the citizens of Shechem and fought Abimelech. ⁴⁰Abimelech chased him, and many fell wounded in the flight—all the way to the entrance to the gate. ⁴¹Abimelech stayed in Arumah, and Zebul drove Gaal and his brothers out of Shechem.

⁴²The next day the people of Shechem went out to the fields, and this was reported to Abimelech. ⁴³So he took his men, divided them into three companies and set an ambush in the fields. When he saw the people coming out of the city, he rose to attack them. ⁴⁴Abimelech and the companies with him rushed forward to a position at the entrance to the city gate. Then two companies rushed upon those in the fields and struck them down. ⁴⁵All that day Abimelech pressed his attack against the city until he had captured it and killed its people. Then he destroyed the city and scattered salt over it.

⁴⁶On hearing this, the citizens in the tower of Shechem went into the stronghold of the temple of El-Berith. ⁴⁷When Abimelech heard that they had assembled there, ⁴⁸he and all his men went up Mount Zalmon. He took an ax and cut off some branches, which he lifted to his shoulders. He ordered the men with him, "Quick! Do what you have seen me do!" ⁴⁹So all the men cut branches and followed Abimelech. They piled them against the stronghold and set it on fire over the people inside. So all the people in the tower of Shechem, about a thousand men and women, also died.

⁵⁰Next Abimelech went to Thebez and besieged it and captured it. ⁵¹Inside the city, however, was a strong tower, to which all the men and women—all the people of the city—fled. They locked themselves in and climbed up on the tower roof. ⁵²Abimelech went to the tower and stormed it. But as he approached the entrance to the tower to set it on fire, ⁵³a woman dropped an upper millstone on his head and cracked his skull.

⁵⁴Hurriedly he called to his armor-bearer, "Draw your sword and kill me, so that they can't say, 'A woman killed him.'" So his servant ran him through, and he died. ⁵⁵When the Israelites saw that Abimelech was dead, they went home.

⁵⁶Thus God repaid the wickedness that Abimelech had done to his father by murdering his seventy brothers. ⁵⁷God also made the men of

THE MESSAGE

9.39-40 Gaal went out, backed by the leaders of Shechem, and did battle with Abimelech. Abimelech chased him, and Gaal turned tail and ran. Many fell wounded, right up to the city gate.

9.41 Abimelech set up his field headquarters at Arumah while Zebul kept Gaal and his relatives out of Shechem.

9.42-45 The next day the people went out to the fields. This was reported to Abimelech. He took his troops, divided them into three companies, and placed them in ambush in the fields. When he saw that the people were well out in the open, he sprang up and attacked them. Abimelech and the company with him charged ahead and took control of the entrance to the city gate; the other two companies chased down those who were in the open fields and killed them. Abimelech fought at the city all that day. He captured the city and massacred everyone in it. He leveled the city to the ground, then sowed it with salt.

9.46-49 When the leaders connected with Shechem's Tower heard this, they went into the fortified God-of-the-Covenant temple. This was reported to Abimelech that the Shechem's Tower bunch were gathered together. He and his troops climbed Mount Zalmon (Dark Mountain). Abimelech took his ax and chopped a bundle of firewood, picked it up, and put it on his shoulder. He said to his troops, "Do what you've seen me do, and quickly." So each of his men cut his own bundle. They followed Abimelech, piled their bundles against the Tower fortifications, and set the whole structure on fire. Everyone in Shechem's Tower died, about a thousand men and women.

9.50-54 Abimelech went on to Thebez. He camped at Thebez and captured it. The Tower-of-Strength stood in the middle of the city; all the men and women of the city along with the city's leaders had fled there and locked themselves in. They were up on the tower roof. Abimelech got as far as the tower and assaulted it. He came up to the tower door to set it on fire. Just then some woman dropped an upper millstone on his head and crushed his skull. He called urgently to his young armor-bearer and said, "Draw your sword and kill me so they can't say of me, 'A woman killed him.'" His armor bearer drove in his sword, and Abimelech died.

9.55 When the Israelites saw that Abimelech was dead, they went home.

9.56-57 God avenged the evil Abimelech had done to his father, murdering his seventy brothers. And

---

ᵃ 39 Or *Gaal went out in the sight of*

NEW INTERNATIONAL VERSION

Shechem pay for all their wickedness. The curse of Jotham son of Jerub-Baal came on them.

TOLA

10 After the time of Abimelech a man of Issachar, Tola son of Puah, the son of Dodo, rose to save Israel. He lived in Shamir, in the hill country of Ephraim. ²He led*a* Israel twenty-three years; then he died, and was buried in Shamir.

JAIR

³He was followed by Jair of Gilead, who led Israel twenty-two years. ⁴He had thirty sons, who rode thirty donkeys. They controlled thirty towns in Gilead, which to this day are called Havvoth Jair.*b* ⁵When Jair died, he was buried in Kamon.

JEPHTHAH

⁶Again the Israelites did evil in the eyes of the LORD. They served the Baals and the Ashtoreths, and the gods of Aram, the gods of Sidon, the gods of Moab, the gods of the Ammonites and the gods of the Philistines. And because the Israelites forsook the LORD and no longer served him, ⁷he became angry with them. He sold them into the hands of the Philistines and the Ammonites, ⁸who that year shattered and crushed them. For eighteen years they oppressed all the Israelites on the east side of the Jordan in Gilead, the land of the Amorites. ⁹The Ammonites also crossed the Jordan to fight against Judah, Benjamin and the house of Ephraim; and Israel was in great distress. ¹⁰Then the Israelites cried out to the LORD, "We have sinned against you, forsaking our God and serving the Baals."

¹¹The LORD replied, "When the Egyptians, the Amorites, the Ammonites, the Philistines, ¹²the Sidonians, the Amalekites and the Maonites*c* oppressed you and you cried to me for help, did I not save you from their hands? ¹³But you have forsaken me and served other gods, so I will no longer save you. ¹⁴Go and cry out to the gods you have chosen. Let them save you when you are in trouble!"

¹⁵But the Israelites said to the LORD, "We have sinned. Do with us whatever you think best, but please rescue us now." ¹⁶Then they got rid of the foreign gods among them and served the LORD. And he could bear Israel's misery no longer.

¹⁷When the Ammonites were called to arms

THE MESSAGE

God brought down on the heads of the men of Shechem all the evil that they had done, the curse of Jotham son of Jerub-Baal.

TOLA

10.1-2 **10** Tola son of Puah, the son of Dodo, was next after Abimelech. He rose to the occasion to save Israel. He was a man of Issachar. He lived in Shamir in the hill country of Ephraim. He judged Israel for twenty-three years and then died and was buried at Shamir.

JAIR

10.3-5 After him, Jair the Gileadite stepped into leadership. He judged Israel for twenty-two years. He had thirty sons who rode on thirty donkeys and had thirty towns in Gilead. The towns are still called Jair's Villages. Jair died and was buried in Kamon.

✝

10.6-8 And then the People of Israel went back to doing evil in GOD's sight. They worshiped the Baal gods and Ashtoreth goddesses: gods of Aram, Sidon, and Moab; gods of the Ammonites and the Philistines. They just walked off and left GOD, quit worshiping him. And GOD exploded in hot anger at Israel and sold them off to the Philistines and Ammonites, who, beginning that year, bullied and battered the People of Israel mercilessly. For eighteen years they had them under their thumb, all the People of Israel who lived east of the Jordan in the Amorite country of Gilead.

10.9 Then the Ammonites crossed the Jordan to go to war also against Judah, Benjamin, and Ephraim. Israel was in a bad way!

10.10 The People of Israel cried out to GOD for help: "We've sinned against you! We left our God and worshiped the Baal gods!"

10.11-14 GOD answered the People of Israel: "When the Egyptians, Amorites, Ammonites, Philistines, Sidonians—even Amalek and Midian!—oppressed you and you cried out to me for help, I saved you from them. And now you've gone off and betrayed me, worshiping other gods. I'm not saving you anymore. Go ahead! Cry out for help to the gods you've chosen—let them get you out of the mess you're in!"

10.15 The People of Israel said to GOD: "We've sinned. Do to us whatever you think best, but please, get us out of this!"

10.16 Then they cleaned house of the foreign gods and worshiped only GOD. And GOD took Israel's troubles to heart.

JEPHTHAH

10.17-18 The Ammonites prepared for war, setting camp

---

a 2 Traditionally *judged*; also in verse 3   *b* 4 Or *called the settlements of Jair*   *c* 12 Hebrew; some Septuagint manuscripts *Midianites*

NEW INTERNATIONAL VERSION

and camped in Gilead, the Israelites assembled and camped at Mizpah. ¹⁸The leaders of the people of Gilead said to each other, "Whoever will launch the attack against the Ammonites will be the head of all those living in Gilead."

11 Jephthah the Gileadite was a mighty warrior. His father was Gilead; his mother was a prostitute. ²Gilead's wife also bore him sons, and when they were grown up, they drove Jephthah away. "You are not going to get any inheritance in our family," they said, "because you are the son of another woman." ³So Jephthah fled from his brothers and settled in the land of Tob, where a group of adventurers gathered around him and followed him.

⁴Some time later, when the Ammonites made war on Israel, ⁵the elders of Gilead went to get Jephthah from the land of Tob. ⁶"Come," they said, "be our commander, so we can fight the Ammonites."

⁷Jephthah said to them, "Didn't you hate me and drive me from my father's house? Why do you come to me now, when you're in trouble?"

⁸The elders of Gilead said to him, "Nevertheless, we are turning to you now; come with us to fight the Ammonites, and you will be our head over all who live in Gilead."

⁹Jephthah answered, "Suppose you take me back to fight the Ammonites and the LORD gives them to me—will I really be your head?"

¹⁰The elders of Gilead replied, "The LORD is our witness; we will certainly do as you say." ¹¹So Jephthah went with the elders of Gilead, and the people made him head and commander over them. And he repeated all his words before the LORD in Mizpah.

¹²Then Jephthah sent messengers to the Ammonite king with the question: "What do you have against us that you have attacked our country?"

¹³The king of the Ammonites answered Jephthah's messengers, "When Israel came up out of Egypt, they took away my land from the Arnon to the Jabbok, all the way to the Jordan. Now give it back peaceably."

¹⁴Jephthah sent back messengers to the Ammonite king, ¹⁵saying:

"This is what Jephthah says: Israel did not take the land of Moab or the land of the Ammonites. ¹⁶But when they came up out of Egypt, Israel went through the desert to the Red Sea*ᵃ* and on to Kadesh. ¹⁷Then Israel sent messengers to the king of Edom,

---

ᵃ 16 Hebrew Yam Suph; that is, Sea of Reeds

THE MESSAGE

in Gilead. The People of Israel set their rival camp in Mizpah. The leaders in Gilead said, "Who will stand up for us against the Ammonites? We'll make him head over everyone in Gilead!"

11.1-3 **11** Jephthah the Gileadite was one tough warrior. He was the son of a whore, but Gilead was his father. Meanwhile Gilead's legal wife had given him other sons, and when they grew up, his wife's sons threw Jephthah out. They told him: "You're not getting any of our family inheritance—you're the son of another woman." So Jephthah fled from his brothers and went to live in the land of Tob. Some riffraff joined him and went around with him.

11.4-6 Some time passed. And then the Ammonites started fighting Israel. With the Ammonites at war with them, the elders of Gilead went to get Jephthah from the land of Tob. They said to Jephthah: "Come. Be our general and we'll fight the Ammonites."

11.7 But Jephthah said to the elders of Gilead: "But you hate me. You kicked me out of my family home. So why are you coming to me now? Because you are in trouble. Right?"

11.8 The elders of Gilead replied, "That's it exactly. We've come to you to get you to go with us and fight the Ammonites. You'll be the head of all of us, all the Gileadites."

11.9 Jephthah addressed the elders of Gilead, "So if you bring me back home to fight the Ammonites and GOD gives them to me, I'll be your head—is that right?"

11.10-11 They said, "GOD is witness between us; whatever you say, we'll do." Jephthah went along with the elders of Gilead. The people made him their top man and general. And Jephthah repeated what he had said before GOD at Mizpah.

11.12 Then Jephthah sent messengers to the king of the Ammonites with a message: "What's going on here that you have come into my country picking a fight?"

11.13 The king of the Ammonites told Jephthah's messengers: "Because Israel took my land when they came up out of Egypt—from the Arnon all the way to the Jabbok and to the Jordan. Give it back peaceably and I'll go."

11.14-27 Jephthah again sent messengers to the king of the Ammonites with the message: "Jephthah's word: Israel took no Moabite land and no Ammonite land. When they came up from Egypt, Israel went through the desert as far as the Red Sea, arriving at Kadesh. There Israel sent messengers to the king of Edom say-

saying, 'Give us permission to go through your country,' but the king of Edom would not listen. They sent also to the king of Moab, and he refused. So Israel stayed at Kadesh.

¹⁸"Next they traveled through the desert, skirted the lands of Edom and Moab, passed along the eastern side of the country of Moab, and camped on the other side of the Arnon. They did not enter the territory of Moab, for the Arnon was its border.

¹⁹"Then Israel sent messengers to Sihon king of the Amorites, who ruled in Heshbon, and said to him, 'Let us pass through your country to our own place.' ²⁰Sihon, however, did not trust Israel*a* to pass through his territory. He mustered all his men and encamped at Jahaz and fought with Israel.

²¹"Then the Lord, the God of Israel, gave Sihon and all his men into Israel's hands, and they defeated them. Israel took over all the land of the Amorites who lived in that country, ²²capturing all of it from the Arnon to the Jabbok and from the desert to the Jordan.

²³"Now since the Lord, the God of Israel, has driven the Amorites out before his people Israel, what right have you to take it over? ²⁴Will you not take what your god Chemosh gives you? Likewise, whatever the Lord our God has given us, we will possess. ²⁵Are you better than Balak son of Zippor, king of Moab? Did he ever quarrel with Israel or fight with them? ²⁶For three hundred years Israel occupied Heshbon, Aroer, the surrounding settlements and all the towns along the Arnon. Why didn't you retake them during that time? ²⁷I have not wronged you, but you are doing me wrong by waging war against me. Let the Lord, the Judge,*b* decide the dispute this day between the Israelites and the Ammonites."

²⁸The king of Ammon, however, paid no attention to the message Jephthah sent him.

²⁹Then the Spirit of the Lord came upon Jephthah. He crossed Gilead and Manasseh, passed through Mizpah of Gilead, and from there he advanced against the Ammonites. ³⁰And Jephthah made a vow to the Lord: "If you give the Ammonites into my hands, ³¹whatever comes out of the door of my house to meet me when I return in triumph from the Ammonites will be the Lord's, and I will sacrifice it as a burnt offering."

a 20 Or however, would not make an agreement for Israel
b 27 Or Ruler

ing, 'Let us pass through your land, please.' But the king of Edom wouldn't let them. Israel also requested permission from the king of Moab, but he wouldn't let them cross either. They were stopped in their tracks at Kadesh. So they traveled across the desert and circled around the lands of Edom and Moab. They came out east of the land of Moab and set camp on the other side of the Arnon—they didn't set foot in Moabite territory, for Arnon was the Moabite border. Israel then sent messengers to Sihon king of the Amorites at Heshbon the capital. Israel asked, 'Let us pass, please, through your land on the way to our country.' But Sihon didn't trust Israel to cut across his land; he got his entire army together, set up camp at Jahaz, and fought Israel. But God, the God of Israel, gave Sihon and all his troops to Israel. Israel defeated them. Israel took all the Amorite land, all Amorite land from Arnon to the Jabbok and from the desert to the Jordan. It was God, the God of Israel, who pushed out the Amorites in favor of Israel; so who do you think you are to try to take it over? Why don't you just be satisfied with what your god Chemosh gives you and we'll settle for what God, our God, gives us? Do you think you're going to come off better than Balak son of Zippor, the king of Moab? Did he get anywhere in opposing Israel? Did he risk war? All this time—it's been three hundred years now!—that Israel has lived in Heshbon and its villages, in Aroer and its villages, and in all the towns along the Arnon, why didn't you try to snatch them away then? No, I haven't wronged you. But this is an evil thing that you are doing to me by starting a fight. Today God the Judge will decide between the People of Israel and the people of Ammon."

11.28 But the king of the Ammonites refused to listen to a word that Jephthah had sent him.

11.29-31 God's Spirit came upon Jephthah. He went across Gilead and Manasseh, went through Mizpah of Gilead, and from there approached the Ammonites. Jephthah made a vow before God: "If you give me a clear victory over the Ammonites, then I'll give to God whatever comes out of the door of my house to meet me when I return in one piece from among the Ammonites—I'll offer it up in a sacrificial burnt offering."

NEW INTERNATIONAL VERSION

³²Then Jephthah went over to fight the Ammonites, and the LORD gave them into his hands. ³³He devastated twenty towns from Aroer to the vicinity of Minnith, as far as Abel Keramim. Thus Israel subdued Ammon.

³⁴When Jephthah returned to his home in Mizpah, who should come out to meet him but his daughter, dancing to the sound of tambourines! She was an only child. Except for her he had neither son nor daughter. ³⁵When he saw her, he tore his clothes and cried, "Oh! My daughter! You have made me miserable and wretched, because I have made a vow to the LORD that I cannot break."

³⁶"My father," she replied, "you have given your word to the LORD. Do to me just as you promised, now that the LORD has avenged you of your enemies, the Ammonites. ³⁷But grant me this one request," she said. "Give me two months to roam the hills and weep with my friends, because I will never marry."

³⁸"You may go," he said. And he let her go for two months. She and the girls went into the hills and wept because she would never marry. ³⁹After the two months, she returned to her father and he did to her as he had vowed. And she was a virgin.

From this comes the Israelite custom ⁴⁰that each year the young women of Israel go out for four days to commemorate the daughter of Jephthah the Gileadite.

JEPHTHAH AND EPHRAIM

12 The men of Ephraim called out their forces, crossed over to Zaphon and said to Jephthah, "Why did you go to fight the Ammonites without calling us to go with you? We're going to burn down your house over your head."

²Jephthah answered, "I and my people were engaged in a great struggle with the Ammonites, and although I called, you didn't save me out of their hands. ³When I saw that you wouldn't help, I took my life in my hands and crossed over to fight the Ammonites, and the LORD gave me the victory over them. Now why have you come up today to fight me?"

⁴Jephthah then called together the men of Gilead and fought against Ephraim. The Gileadites struck them down because the Ephraimites had said, "You Gileadites are renegades from Ephraim and Manasseh." ⁵The Gileadites captured the fords of the Jordan leading to Ephraim, and whenever a survivor of Ephraim said, "Let me cross over," the men of Gilead asked him, "Are you an Ephraimite?" If he replied, "No," ⁶they said, "All right, say 'Shibboleth.'" If he

THE MESSAGE

11.32-33 Then Jephthah was off to fight the Ammonites. And GOD gave them to him. He beat them soundly, all the way from Aroer to the area around Minnith as far as Abel Keramim—twenty cities! A massacre! Ammonites brought to their knees by the People of Israel.

11.34-35 Jephthah came home to Mizpah. His daughter ran from the house to welcome him home—dancing to tambourines! She was his only child. He had no son or daughter except her. When he realized who it was, he ripped his clothes, saying, "Ah, dearest daughter—I'm dirt. I'm despicable. My heart is torn to shreds. I made a vow to GOD and I can't take it back!"

11.36 She said, "Dear father, if you made a vow to GOD, do to me what you vowed; GOD did his part and saved you from your Ammonite enemies."

11.37 And then she said to her father, "But let this one thing be done for me. Give me two months to wander through the hills and lament my virginity since I will never marry, I and my dear friends."

11.38-39 "Oh yes, go," he said. He sent her off for two months. She and her dear girlfriends went among the hills, lamenting that she would never marry. At the end of the two months, she came back to her father. He fulfilled the vow with her that he had made. She had never slept with a man.

11.39-40 It became a custom in Israel that for four days every year the young women of Israel went out to mourn for the daughter of Jephthah the Gileadite.

⁜

12.1 **12** The men of Ephraim mustered their troops, crossed to Zaphon, and said to Jephthah, "Why did you go out to fight the Ammonites without letting us go with you? We're going to burn your house down on you!"

12.2-3 Jephthah said, "I and my people had our hands full negotiating with the Ammonites. And I did call to you for help but you ignored me. When I saw that you weren't coming, I took my life in my hands and confronted the Ammonites myself. And GOD gave them to me! So why did you show up here today? Are you spoiling for a fight with me?"

12.4 So Jephthah got his Gilead troops together and fought Ephraim. And the men of Gilead hit them hard because they were saying, "Gileadites are nothing but half-breeds and rejects from Ephraim and Manasseh."

12.5-6 Gilead captured the fords of the Jordan at the crossing to Ephraim. If an Ephraimite fugitive said, "Let me cross," the men of Gilead would ask, "Are you an Ephraimite?" and he would say, "No." And they would say, "Say,

NEW INTERNATIONAL VERSION

said, "Sibboleth," because he could not pronounce the word correctly, they seized him and killed him at the fords of the Jordan. Forty-two thousand Ephraimites were killed at that time.

⁷Jephthah led*ᵃ* Israel six years. Then Jephthah the Gileadite died, and was buried in a town in Gilead.

IBZAN, ELON AND ABDON

⁸After him, Ibzan of Bethlehem led Israel. ⁹He had thirty sons and thirty daughters. He gave his daughters away in marriage to those outside his clan, and for his sons he brought in thirty young women as wives from outside his clan. Ibzan led Israel seven years. ¹⁰Then Ibzan died, and was buried in Bethlehem.

¹¹After him, Elon the Zebulunite led Israel ten years. ¹²Then Elon died, and was buried in Aijalon in the land of Zebulun.

¹³After him, Abdon son of Hillel, from Pirathon, led Israel. ¹⁴He had forty sons and thirty grandsons, who rode on seventy donkeys. He led Israel eight years. ¹⁵Then Abdon son of Hillel died, and was buried at Pirathon in Ephraim, in the hill country of the Amalekites.

THE BIRTH OF SAMSON

13 Again the Israelites did evil in the eyes of the LORD, so the LORD delivered them into the hands of the Philistines for forty years.

²A certain man of Zorah, named Manoah, from the clan of the Danites, had a wife who was sterile and remained childless. ³The angel of the LORD appeared to her and said, "You are sterile and childless, but you are going to conceive and have a son. ⁴Now see to it that you drink no wine or other fermented drink and that you do not eat anything unclean, ⁵because you will conceive and give birth to a son. No razor may be used on his head, because the boy is to be a Nazirite, set apart to God from birth, and he will begin the deliverance of Israel from the hands of the Philistines."

⁶Then the woman went to her husband and told him, "A man of God came to me. He looked like an angel of God, very awesome. I didn't ask him where he came from, and he didn't tell me his name. ⁷But he said to me, 'You will conceive and give birth to a son. Now then, drink no wine or other fermented drink and do not eat anything

THE MESSAGE

'Shibboleth.' " But he would always say, "Sibboleth"—he couldn't say it right. Then they would grab him and kill him there at the fords of the Jordan. Forty-two Ephraimite divisions were killed on that occasion.

12.7   Jephthah judged Israel six years. Jephthah the Gileadite died and was buried in his city, Mizpah of Gilead.

IBZAN

12.8-9 After him, Ibzan of Bethlehem judged Israel. He had thirty sons and thirty daughters. He gave his daughters in marriage outside his clan and brought in thirty daughters-in-law from the outside for his sons.

12.10   He judged Israel seven years. Ibzan died and was buried in Bethlehem.

ELON

12.11-12 After him, Elon the Zebulunite judged Israel. He judged Israel ten years. Elon the Zebulunite died and was buried at Aijalon in the land of Zebulun.

ABDON

12.13-15 After him, Abdon son of Hillel the Pirathonite judged Israel. He had forty sons and thirty grandsons who rode on seventy donkeys. He judged Israel eight years. Abdon son of Hillel the Pirathonite died and was buried at Pirathon in the land of Ephraim in the Amalekite hill country.

SAMSON

13.1   **13** And then the People of Israel were back at it again, doing what was evil in GOD's sight. GOD put them under the domination of the Philistines for forty years.

13.2-5 At that time there was a man named Manoah from Zorah from the tribe of Dan. His wife was barren and childless. The angel of God appeared to her and told her, "I know that you are barren and childless, but you're going to become pregnant and bear a son. But take much care: Drink no wine or beer; eat nothing ritually unclean. You are, in fact, pregnant right now, carrying a son. No razor will touch his head—the boy will be God's Nazirite from the moment of his birth. He will launch the deliverance from Philistine oppression."

13.6-7 The woman went to her husband and said, "A man of God came to me. He looked like the angel of God—terror laced with glory! I didn't ask him where he was from and he didn't tell me his name, but he told me, 'You're pregnant. You're going to give birth to a son. Don't drink any wine or beer and eat nothing ritually un-

---

ᵃ 7 Traditionally judged; also in verses 8-14

NEW INTERNATIONAL VERSION

unclean, because the boy will be a Nazirite of God from birth until the day of his death.' "

⁸Then Manoah prayed to the LORD: "O Lord, I beg you, let the man of God you sent to us come again to teach us how to bring up the boy who is to be born."

⁹God heard Manoah, and the angel of God came again to the woman while she was out in the field; but her husband Manoah was not with her. ¹⁰The woman hurried to tell her husband, "He's here! The man who appeared to me the other day!"

¹¹Manoah got up and followed his wife. When he came to the man, he said, "Are you the one who talked to my wife?"

"I am," he said.

¹²So Manoah asked him, "When your words are fulfilled, what is to be the rule for the boy's life and work?"

¹³The angel of the LORD answered, "Your wife must do all that I have told her. ¹⁴She must not eat anything that comes from the grapevine, nor drink any wine or other fermented drink nor eat anything unclean. She must do everything I have commanded her."

¹⁵Manoah said to the angel of the LORD, "We would like you to stay until we prepare a young goat for you."

¹⁶The angel of the LORD replied, "Even though you detain me, I will not eat any of your food. But if you prepare a burnt offering, offer it to the LORD." (Manoah did not realize that it was the angel of the LORD.)

¹⁷Then Manoah inquired of the angel of the LORD, "What is your name, so that we may honor you when your word comes true?"

¹⁸He replied, "Why do you ask my name? It is beyond understanding. ᵃ" ¹⁹Then Manoah took a young goat, together with the grain offering, and sacrificed it on a rock to the LORD. And the LORD did an amazing thing while Manoah and his wife watched: ²⁰As the flame blazed up from the altar toward heaven, the angel of the LORD ascended in the flame. Seeing this, Manoah and his wife fell with their faces to the ground. ²¹When the angel of the LORD did not show himself again to Manoah and his wife, Manoah realized that it was the angel of the LORD.

²²"We are doomed to die!" he said to his wife. "We have seen God!"

²³But his wife answered, "If the LORD had meant to kill us, he would not have accepted a burnt offering and grain offering from our hands, nor shown us all these things or now told us this."

²⁴The woman gave birth to a boy and named

ᵃ 18 Or is wonderful

THE MESSAGE

clean. The boy will be God's Nazirite from the moment of birth to the day of his death.' "

13.8 Manoah prayed to GOD: "Master, let the man of God you sent come to us again and teach us how to raise this boy who is to be born."

13.9-10 God listened to Manoah. God's angel came again to the woman. She was sitting in the field; her husband Manoah wasn't there with her. She jumped to her feet and ran and told her husband: "He's back! The man who came to me that day!"

13.11 Manoah got up and, following his wife, came to the man. He said to him, "Are you the man who spoke to my wife?"

He said, "I am."

13.12 Manoah said, "So. When what you say comes true, what do you have to tell us about this boy and his work?"

13.13-14 The angel of God said to Manoah, "Keep in mind everything I told the woman. Eat nothing that comes from the vine: Drink no wine or beer; eat no ritually unclean foods. She's to observe everything I commanded her."

13.15 Manoah said to the angel of God, "Please, stay with us a little longer; we'll prepare a meal for you—a young goat."

13.16 GOD's angel said to Manoah, "Even if I stay, I won't eat your food. But if you want to prepare a Whole-Burnt-Offering for GOD, go ahead—offer it!" Manoah had no idea that he was talking to the angel of God.

13.17 Then Manoah asked the angel of God, "What's your name? When your words come true, we'd like to honor you."

13.18 The angel of GOD said, "What's this? You ask for my name? You wouldn't understand—it's sheer wonder."

13.19-21 So Manoah took the kid and the Grain-Offering and sacrificed them on a rock altar to GOD who works wonders. As the flames leapt up from the altar to heaven, GOD's angel also ascended in the altar flames. When Manoah and his wife saw this, they fell facedown to the ground. Manoah and his wife never saw the angel of GOD again.

13.21-22 Only then did Manoah realize that this was GOD's angel. He said to his wife, "We're as good as dead! We've looked on God!"

13.23 But his wife said, "If GOD were planning to kill us, he wouldn't have accepted our Whole-Burnt-Offering and Grain-Offering, or revealed all these things to us—given us this birth announcement."

13.24-25 The woman gave birth to a son. They named

NEW INTERNATIONAL VERSION

him Samson. He grew and the LORD blessed him, 25and the Spirit of the LORD began to stir him while he was in Mahaneh Dan, between Zorah and Eshtaol.

SAMSON'S MARRIAGE

14 Samson went down to Timnah and saw there a young Philistine woman. 2When he returned, he said to his father and mother, "I have seen a Philistine woman in Timnah; now get her for me as my wife."

3His father and mother replied, "Isn't there an acceptable woman among your relatives or among all our people? Must you go to the uncircumcised Philistines to get a wife?"

But Samson said to his father, "Get her for me. She's the right one for me." 4(His parents did not know that this was from the LORD, who was seeking an occasion to confront the Philistines; for at that time they were ruling over Israel.) 5Samson went down to Timnah together with his father and mother. As they approached the vineyards of Timnah, suddenly a young lion came roaring toward him. 6The Spirit of the LORD came upon him in power so that he tore the lion apart with his bare hands as he might have torn a young goat. But he told neither his father nor his mother what he had done. 7Then he went down and talked with the woman, and he liked her.

8Some time later, when he went back to marry her, he turned aside to look at the lion's carcass. In it was a swarm of bees and some honey, 9which he scooped out with his hands and ate as he went along. When he rejoined his parents, he gave them some, and they too ate it. But he did not tell them that he had taken the honey from the lion's carcass.

10Now his father went down to see the woman. And Samson made a feast there, as was customary for bridegrooms. 11When he appeared, he was given thirty companions.

12"Let me tell you a riddle," Samson said to them. "If you can give me the answer within the seven days of the feast, I will give you thirty linen garments and thirty sets of clothes. 13If you can't tell me the answer, you must give me thirty linen garments and thirty sets of clothes."

"Tell us your riddle," they said. "Let's hear it." 14He replied,

"Out of the eater, something to eat;
out of the strong, something sweet."

For three days they could not give the answer.

THE MESSAGE

him Samson. The boy grew and GOD blessed him. The Spirit of GOD began working in him while he was staying at a Danite camp between Zorah and Eshtaol.

✝

14.1-2 **14** Samson went down to Timnah. There in Timnah a woman caught his eye, a Philistine girl. He came back and told his father and mother, "I saw a woman in Timnah, a Philistine girl; get her for me as my wife."

14.3 His parents said to him, "Isn't there a woman among the girls in the neighborhood of our people? Do you have to go get a wife from the uncircumcised Philistines?"

But Samson said to his father, "Get her for me. She's the one I want—she's the right one."

14.4 (His father and mother had no idea that GOD was behind this, that he was arranging an opportunity against the Philistines. At the time the Philistines lorded it over Israel.)

14.5-6 Samson went down to Timnah with his father and mother. When he got to the vineyards of Timnah, a young lion came at him, roaring. The Spirit of GOD came on him powerfully and he ripped it open barehanded, like tearing a young goat. But he didn't tell his parents what he had done.

14.7 Then he went on down and spoke to the woman. In Samson's eyes, she was the one.

14.8-9 Some days later when he came back to get her, he made a little detour to look at what was left of the lion. And there a wonder: a swarm of bees in the lion's carcass—and honey! He scooped it up in his hands and kept going, eating as he went. He rejoined his father and mother and gave some to them and they ate. But he didn't tell them that he had scooped out the honey from the lion's carcass.

14.10-11 His father went on down to make arrangements with the woman, while Samson prepared a feast there. That's what the young men did in those days. Because the people were wary of him, they arranged for thirty friends to mingle with him.

14.12-13 Samson said to them: "Let me put a riddle to you. If you can figure it out during the seven days of the feast, I'll give you thirty linen garments and thirty changes of fine clothing. But if you can't figure it out then you'll give me thirty linen garments and thirty changes of fine clothing."

14.13-14 They said, "Put your riddle. Let's hear it." So he said,

From the eater came something to eat,
From the strong came something sweet.

14.14-15 They couldn't figure it out. After three days

NEW INTERNATIONAL VERSION

¹⁵On the fourth*ᵃ* day, they said to Samson's wife, "Coax your husband into explaining the riddle for us, or we will burn you and your father's household to death. Did you invite us here to rob us?"

¹⁶Then Samson's wife threw herself on him, sobbing, "You hate me! You don't really love me. You've given my people a riddle, but you haven't told me the answer."

"I haven't even explained it to my father or mother," he replied, "so why should I explain it to you?" ¹⁷She cried the whole seven days of the feast. So on the seventh day he finally told her, because she continued to press him. She in turn explained the riddle to her people.

¹⁸Before sunset on the seventh day the men of the town said to him,

"What is sweeter than honey?
  What is stronger than a lion?"

Samson said to them,

"If you had not plowed with my heifer,
  you would not have solved my riddle."

¹⁹Then the Spirit of the Lord came upon him in power. He went down to Ashkelon, struck down thirty of their men, stripped them of their belongings and gave their clothes to those who had explained the riddle. Burning with anger, he went up to his father's house. ²⁰And Samson's wife was given to the friend who had attended him at his wedding.

SAMSON'S VENGEANCE ON THE PHILISTINES

15 Later on, at the time of wheat harvest, Samson took a young goat and went to visit his wife. He said, "I'm going to my wife's room." But her father would not let him go in.

²"I was so sure you thoroughly hated her," he said, "that I gave her to your friend. Isn't her younger sister more attractive? Take her instead."

³Samson said to them, "This time I have a right to get even with the Philistines; I will really harm them." ⁴So he went out and caught three hundred foxes and tied them tail to tail in pairs. He then fastened a torch to every pair of tails, ⁵lit the torches and let the foxes loose in the standing grain of the Philistines. He burned up the shocks and standing grain, together with the vineyards and olive groves.

⁶When the Philistines asked, "Who did this?" they were told, "Samson, the Timnite's son-in-law, because his wife was given to his friend."

So the Philistines went up and burned her and her father to death. ⁷Samson said to them,

THE MESSAGE

they were still stumped. On the fourth day they said to Samson's bride, "Worm the answer out of your husband or we'll burn you and your father's household. Have you invited us here to bankrupt us?"

14.16 So Samson's bride turned on the tears, saying to him, "You hate me. You don't love me. You've told a riddle to my people but you won't even tell me the answer."

He said, "I haven't told my own parents—why would I tell you?"

14.17 But she turned on the tears all the seven days of the feast. On the seventh day, worn out by her nagging, he told her. Then she went and told it to her people.

14.18 The men of the town came to him on the seventh day, just before sunset and said,

What is sweeter than honey?
What is stronger than a lion?

And Samson said,

If you hadn't plowed with my heifer,
You wouldn't have found out my riddle.

14.19-20 Then the Spirit of God came powerfully on him. He went down to Ashkelon and killed thirty of their men, stripped them, and gave their clothing to those who had solved the riddle. Stalking out, smoking with anger, he went home to his father's house. Samson's bride became the wife of the best man at his wedding.

✠

15.1-2 **15** Later on—it was during the wheat harvest—Samson visited his bride, bringing a young goat. He said, "Let me see my wife—show me her bedroom."

But her father wouldn't let him in. He said, "I concluded that by now you hated her with a passion, so I gave her to your best man. But her little sister is even more beautiful. Why not take her instead?"

15.3 Samson said, "That does it. This time when I wreak havoc on the Philistines, I'm blameless."

15.4-5 Samson then went out and caught three hundred jackals. He lashed the jackals' tails together in pairs and tied a torch between each pair of tails. He then set fire to the torches and let them loose in the Philistine fields of ripe grain. Everything burned, both stacked and standing grain, vineyards and olive orchards—everything.

15.6 The Philistines said, "Who did this?"

They were told, "Samson, son-in-law of the Timnite who took his bride and gave her to his best man."

The Philistines went up and burned both her and her father to death.

NEW INTERNATIONAL VERSION

"Since you've acted like this, I won't stop until I get my revenge on you." ⁸He attacked them viciously and slaughtered many of them. Then he went down and stayed in a cave in the rock of Etam.

⁹The Philistines went up and camped in Judah, spreading out near Lehi. ¹⁰The men of Judah asked, "Why have you come to fight us?"

"We have come to take Samson prisoner," they answered, "to do to him as he did to us."

¹¹Then three thousand men from Judah went down to the cave in the rock of Etam and said to Samson, "Don't you realize that the Philistines are rulers over us? What have you done to us?"

He answered, "I merely did to them what they did to me."

¹²They said to him, "We've come to tie you up and hand you over to the Philistines."

Samson said, "Swear to me that you won't kill me yourselves."

¹³"Agreed," they answered. "We will only tie you up and hand you over to them. We will not kill you." So they bound him with two new ropes and led him up from the rock. ¹⁴As he approached Lehi, the Philistines came toward him shouting. The Spirit of the LORD came upon him in power. The ropes on his arms became like charred flax, and the bindings dropped from his hands. ¹⁵Finding a fresh jawbone of a donkey, he grabbed it and struck down a thousand men.

¹⁶Then Samson said,

"With a donkey's jawbone
   I have made donkeys of them.ᵃ
With a donkey's jawbone
   I have killed a thousand men."

¹⁷When he finished speaking, he threw away the jawbone; and the place was called Ramath Lehi.ᵇ

¹⁸Because he was very thirsty, he cried out to the LORD, "You have given your servant this great victory. Must I now die of thirst and fall into the hands of the uncircumcised?" ¹⁹Then God opened up the hollow place in Lehi, and water came out of it. When Samson drank, his strength returned and he revived. So the spring was called En Hakkore,ᶜ and it is still there in Lehi.

²⁰Samson ledᵈ Israel for twenty years in the days of the Philistines.

ᵃ 16 Or made a heap or two; the Hebrew for donkey sounds like the Hebrew for heap. ᵇ 17 Ramath Lehi means jawbone hill. ᶜ 19 En Hakkore means caller's spring. ᵈ 20 Traditionally judged

THE MESSAGE

15.7 Samson then said, "If this is the way you're going to act, I swear I'll get even with you. And I'm not quitting till the job's done!"

15.8 With that he tore into them, ripping them limb from limb—a huge slaughter. Then he went down and stayed in a cave at Etam Rock.

✝

15.9-10 The Philistines set out and made camp in Judah, preparing to attack Lehi (Jawbone). When the men of Judah asked, "Why have you come up against us?" they said, "We're out to get Samson. We're going after Samson to do to him what he did to us."

15.11 Three companies of men from Judah went down to the cave at Etam Rock and said to Samson, "Don't you realize that the Philistines already bully and lord it over us? So what's going on with you, making things even worse?"

He said, "It was tit for tat. I only did to them what they did to me."

15.12 They said, "Well, we've come down here to tie you up and turn you over to the Philistines." Samson said, "Just promise not to hurt me."

15.13 "We promise," they said. "We will tie you up and surrender you to them but, believe us, we won't kill you." They proceeded to tie him with new ropes and led him up from the Rock.

15.14-16 As he approached Lehi, the Philistines came to meet him, shouting in triumph. And then the Spirit of GOD came on him with great power. The ropes on his arms fell apart like flax on fire; the thongs slipped off his hands. He spotted a fresh donkey jawbone, reached down and grabbed it, and with it killed the whole company. And Samson said,

With a donkey's jawbone
   I made heaps of donkeys of them.
With a donkey's jawbone
   I killed an entire company.

15.17 When he finished speaking, he threw away the jawbone. He named that place Ramath Lehi (Jawbone Hill).

15.18-19 Now he was suddenly very thirsty. He called out to GOD, "You have given your servant this great victory. Are you going to abandon me to die of thirst and fall into the hands of the uncircumcised?" So God split open the rock basin in Lehi; water gushed out and Samson drank. His spirit revived—he was alive again! That's why it's called En Hakkore (Caller's Spring). It's still there at Lehi today.

15.20 Samson judged Israel for twenty years in the days of the Philistines.

✝

NEW INTERNATIONAL VERSION

SAMSON AND DELILAH

16 One day Samson went to Gaza, where he saw a prostitute. He went in to spend the night with her. ²The people of Gaza were told, "Samson is here!" So they surrounded the place and lay in wait for him all night at the city gate. They made no move during the night, saying, "At dawn we'll kill him."

³But Samson lay there only until the middle of the night. Then he got up and took hold of the doors of the city gate, together with the two posts, and tore them loose, bar and all. He lifted them to his shoulders and carried them to the top of the hill that faces Hebron.

⁴Some time later, he fell in love with a woman in the Valley of Sorek whose name was Delilah. ⁵The rulers of the Philistines went to her and said, "See if you can lure him into showing you the secret of his great strength and how we can overpower him so we may tie him up and subdue him. Each one of us will give you eleven hundred shekels*ᵃ* of silver."

⁶So Delilah said to Samson, "Tell me the secret of your great strength and how you can be tied up and subdued."

⁷Samson answered her, "If anyone ties me with seven fresh thongs*ᵇ* that have not been dried, I'll become as weak as any other man."

⁸Then the rulers of the Philistines brought her seven fresh thongs that had not been dried, and she tied him with them. ⁹With men hidden in the room, she called to him, "Samson, the Philistines are upon you!" But he snapped the thongs as easily as a piece of string snaps when it comes close to a flame. So the secret of his strength was not discovered.

¹⁰Then Delilah said to Samson, "You have made a fool of me; you lied to me. Come now, tell me how you can be tied."

¹¹He said, "If anyone ties me securely with new ropes that have never been used, I'll become as weak as any other man."

¹²So Delilah took new ropes and tied him with them. Then, with men hidden in the room, she called to him, "Samson, the Philistines are upon you!" But he snapped the ropes off his arms as if they were threads.

¹³Delilah then said to Samson, "Until now, you have been making a fool of me and lying to me. Tell me how you can be tied."

He replied, "If you weave the seven braids of my head into the fabric ⌊on the loom⌋ and tighten it with the pin, I'll become as weak as any other man." So while he was sleeping, Delilah

THE MESSAGE

16 Samson went to Gaza and saw a prostitute. He went to her. The news got around: "Samson's here." They gathered around in hiding, waiting all night for him at the city gate, quiet as mice, thinking, "At sunrise we'll kill him."

16.3 Samson was in bed with the woman until midnight. Then he got up, seized the doors of the city gate and the two gateposts, bolts and all, hefted them on his shoulder, and carried them to the top of the hill that faces Hebron.

16.4-5 Some time later he fell in love with a woman in the Valley of Sorek (Grapes). Her name was Delilah. The Philistine tyrants approached her and said, "Seduce him. Discover what's behind his great strength and how we can tie him up and humble him. Each man's company will give you a hundred shekels of silver."

16.6 So Delilah said to Samson, "Tell me, dear, the secret of your great strength, and how you can be tied up and humbled."

16.7 Samson told her, "If they were to tie me up with seven bowstrings—the kind made from fresh animal tendons, not dried out—then I would become weak, just like anyone else."

16.8-9 The Philistine tyrants brought her seven bowstrings, not dried out, and she tied him up with them. The men were waiting in ambush in her room. Then she said, "The Philistines are on you, Samson!" He snapped the cords as though they were mere threads. The secret of his strength was still a secret.

16.10 Delilah said, "Come now, Samson—you're playing with me, making up stories. Be serious; tell me how you can be tied up."

16.11 He told her, "If you were to tie me up tight with new ropes, ropes never used for work, then I would be helpless, just like anybody else."

16.12 So Delilah got some new ropes and tied him up. She said, "The Philistines are on you, Samson!" The men were hidden in the next room. He snapped the ropes from his arms like threads.

16.13-14 Delilah said to Samson, "You're still playing games with me, teasing me with lies. Tell me how you can be tied up."

He said to her, "If you wove the seven braids of my hair into the fabric on the loom and drew it tight, then I would be as helpless as any other mortal."

When she had him fast asleep, Delilah took

ᵃ 5 That is, about 28 pounds (about 13 kilograms)
ᵇ 7 Or *bowstrings*; also in verses 8 and 9

NEW INTERNATIONAL VERSION

took the seven braids of his head, wove them into the fabric ¹⁴and*ᵃ* tightened it with the pin.

Again she called to him, "Samson, the Philistines are upon you!" He awoke from his sleep and pulled up the pin and the loom, with the fabric.

¹⁵Then she said to him, "How can you say, 'I love you,' when you won't confide in me? This is the third time you have made a fool of me and haven't told me the secret of your great strength." ¹⁶With such nagging she prodded him day after day until he was tired to death.

¹⁷So he told her everything. "No razor has ever been used on my head," he said, "because I have been a Nazirite set apart to God since birth. If my head were shaved, my strength would leave me, and I would become as weak as any other man."

¹⁸When Delilah saw that he had told her everything, she sent word to the rulers of the Philistines, "Come back once more; he has told me everything." So the rulers of the Philistines returned with the silver in their hands. ¹⁹Having put him to sleep on her lap, she called a man to shave off the seven braids of his hair, and so began to subdue him.*ᵇ* And his strength left him.

²⁰Then she called, "Samson, the Philistines are upon you!"

He awoke from his sleep and thought, "I'll go out as before and shake myself free." But he did not know that the LORD had left him.

²¹Then the Philistines seized him, gouged out his eyes and took him down to Gaza. Binding him with bronze shackles, they set him to grinding in the prison. ²²But the hair on his head began to grow again after it had been shaved.

THE DEATH OF SAMSON

²³Now the rulers of the Philistines assembled to offer a great sacrifice to Dagon their god and to celebrate, saying, "Our god has delivered Samson, our enemy, into our hands."

²⁴When the people saw him, they praised their god, saying,

"Our god has delivered our enemy
    into our hands,
the one who laid waste our land
    and multiplied our slain."

²⁵While they were in high spirits, they shouted, "Bring out Samson to entertain us." So they called Samson out of the prison, and he performed for them.

When they stood him among the pillars, ²⁶Samson said to the servant who held his hand,

THE MESSAGE

the seven braids of his hair and wove them into the fabric on the loom and drew it tight. Then she said, "The Philistines are on you, Samson!" He woke from his sleep and ripped loose from both the loom and fabric!

16.15 She said, "How can you say 'I love you' when you won't even trust me? Three times now you've toyed with me, like a cat with a mouse, refusing to tell me the secret of your great strength."

16.16-17 She kept at it day after day, nagging and tormenting him. Finally, he was fed up—he couldn't take another minute of it. He spilled it.

He told her, "A razor has never touched my head. I've been God's Nazirite from conception. If I were shaved, my strength would leave me; I would be as helpless as any other mortal."

16.18 When Delilah realized that he had told her his secret, she sent for the Philistine tyrants, telling them, "Come quickly—this time he's told me the truth." They came, bringing the bribe money.

16.19 When she got him to sleep, his head on her lap, she motioned to a man to cut off the seven braids of his hair. Immediately he began to grow weak. His strength drained from him.

16.20 Then she said, "The Philistines are on you, Samson!" He woke up, thinking, "I'll go out, like always, and shake free." He didn't realize that GOD had abandoned him.

16.21-22 The Philistines grabbed him, gouged out his eyes, and took him down to Gaza. They shackled him in irons and put him to the work of grinding in the prison. But his hair, though cut off, began to grow again.

16.23-24 The Philistine tyrants got together to offer a great sacrifice to their god Dagon. They celebrated, saying,

Our god has given us
Samson our enemy!

And when the people saw him, they joined in, cheering their god,

Our god has given
Our enemy to us,
The one who ravaged our country,
Piling high the corpses among us.

16.25-27 Then this: Everyone was feeling high and someone said, "Get Samson! Let him show us his stuff!" They got Samson from the prison and he put on a show for them.

They had him standing between the pillars. Samson said to the young man who was acting

---

ᵃ 13,14 Some Septuagint manuscripts; Hebrew "*I can, if you weave the seven braids of my head into the fabric ⸤on the loom⸥.*" ¹⁴*So she*   *ᵇ* 19 Hebrew; some Septuagint manuscripts *and he began to weaken*

NEW INTERNATIONAL VERSION

"Put me where I can feel the pillars that support the temple, so that I may lean against them." ²⁷Now the temple was crowded with men and women; all the rulers of the Philistines were there, and on the roof were about three thousand men and women watching Samson perform. ²⁸Then Samson prayed to the LORD, "O Sovereign LORD, remember me. O God, please strengthen me just once more, and let me with one blow get revenge on the Philistines for my two eyes." ²⁹Then Samson reached toward the two central pillars on which the temple stood. Bracing himself against them, his right hand on the one and his left hand on the other, ³⁰Samson said, "Let me die with the Philistines!" Then he pushed with all his might, and down came the temple on the rulers and all the people in it. Thus he killed many more when he died than while he lived.

³¹Then his brothers and his father's whole family went down to get him. They brought him back and buried him between Zorah and Eshtaol in the tomb of Manoah his father. He had led*ª* Israel twenty years.

MICAH'S IDOLS

17 Now a man named Micah from the hill country of Ephraim ²said to his mother, "The eleven hundred shekels*ᵇ* of silver that were taken from you and about which I heard you utter a curse—I have that silver with me; I took it."

Then his mother said, "The LORD bless you, my son!"

³When he returned the eleven hundred shekels of silver to his mother, she said, "I solemnly consecrate my silver to the LORD for my son to make a carved image and a cast idol. I will give it back to you."

⁴So he returned the silver to his mother, and she took two hundred shekels*ᶜ* of silver and gave them to a silversmith, who made them into the image and the idol. And they were put in Micah's house.

⁵Now this man Micah had a shrine, and he made an ephod and some idols and installed one of his sons as his priest. ⁶In those days Israel had no king; everyone did as he saw fit.

⁷A young Levite from Bethlehem in Judah,

ª 31 Traditionally *judged*   *ᵇ 2* That is, about 28 pounds (about 13 kilograms)   *ᶜ 4* That is, about 5 pounds (about 2.3 kilograms)

THE MESSAGE

as his guide, "Put me where I can touch the pillars that hold up the temple so I can rest against them." The building was packed with men and women, including all the Philistine tyrants. And there were at least 3,000 in the stands watching Samson's performance.

16.28 And Samson cried out to GOD:

> Master, GOD!
>   Oh, please, look on me again,
>   Oh, please, give strength yet once more.
> God!
>   With one avenging blow let me be
>   avenged
>   On the Philistines for my two eyes!

16.29-30 Then Samson reached out to the two central pillars that held up the building and pushed against them, one with his right arm, the other with his left. Saying, "Let me die with the Philistines," Samson pushed hard with all his might. The building crashed on the tyrants and all the people in it. He killed more people in his death than he had killed in his life.

16.31 His brothers and all his relatives went down to get his body. They carried him back and buried him in the tomb of Manoah his father, between Zorah and Eshtaol.

He judged Israel for twenty years.

MICAH

17.1-2 **17** There was a man from the hill country of Ephraim named Micah. He said to his mother, "Remember that 1,100 pieces of silver that were taken from you? I overheard you when you pronounced your curse. Well, I have the money; I stole it. But now I've brought it back to you."

His mother said, "GOD bless you, my son!"

17.3-4 As he returned the 1,100 silver pieces to his mother, she said, "I had totally consecrated this money to GOD for my son to make a statue, a cast god." Then she took 200 pieces of the silver and gave it to a sculptor and he cast them into the form of a god.

17.5 This man, Micah, had a private chapel. He had made an ephod and some teraphim-idols and had ordained one of his sons to be his priest.

17.6 In those days there was no king in Israel. People did whatever they felt like doing.

17.7-8 Meanwhile there was a young man from Bethlehem in Judah and from a family of Judah. He

NEW INTERNATIONAL VERSION

who had been living within the clan of Judah, [8]left that town in search of some other place to stay. On his way[a] he came to Micah's house in the hill country of Ephraim.

[9]Micah asked him, "Where are you from?"

"I'm a Levite from Bethlehem in Judah," he said, "and I'm looking for a place to stay."

[10]Then Micah said to him, "Live with me and be my father and priest, and I'll give you ten shekels[b] of silver a year, your clothes and your food." [11]So the Levite agreed to live with him, and the young man was to him like one of his sons. [12]Then Micah installed the Levite, and the young man became his priest and lived in his house. [13]And Micah said, "Now I know that the LORD will be good to me, since this Levite has become my priest."

DANITES SETTLE IN LAISH

18 In those days Israel had no king.

And in those days the tribe of the Danites was seeking a place of their own where they might settle, because they had not yet come into an inheritance among the tribes of Israel. [2]So the Danites sent five warriors from Zorah and Eshtaol to spy out the land and explore it. These men represented all their clans. They told them, "Go, explore the land."

The men entered the hill country of Ephraim and came to the house of Micah, where they spent the night. [3]When they were near Micah's house, they recognized the voice of the young Levite; so they turned in there and asked him, "Who brought you here? What are you doing in this place? Why are you here?"

[4]He told them what Micah had done for him, and said, "He has hired me and I am his priest."

[5]Then they said to him, "Please inquire of God to learn whether our journey will be successful."

[6]The priest answered them, "Go in peace. Your journey has the LORD's approval."

[7]So the five men left and came to Laish, where they saw that the people were living in safety, like the Sidonians, unsuspecting and secure. And since their land lacked nothing, they were prosperous.[c] Also, they lived a long way from the Sidonians and had no relationship with anyone else.[d]

[8]When they returned to Zorah and Eshtaol, their brothers asked them, "How did you find things?"

[9]They answered, "Come on, let's attack them! We have seen that the land is very good. Aren't

THE MESSAGE

was a Levite but was a stranger there. He left that town, Bethlehem in Judah, seeking his fortune. He got as far as the hill country of Ephraim and showed up at Micah's house.

17.9   Micah asked him, "So where are you from?"

He said, "I'm a Levite from Bethlehem in Judah. I'm on the road, looking for a place to settle down."

17.10   Micah said, "Stay here with me. Be my father and priest. I'll pay you ten pieces of silver a year, whatever clothes you need, and your meals."

17.11-12   The Levite agreed and moved in with Micah. The young man fit right in and became one of the family. Micah appointed the young Levite as his priest. This all took place in Micah's home.

17.13   Micah said, "Now I know that GOD will make things go well for me—why, I've got a Levite for a priest!"

⊹

18.1   **18** In those days there was no king in Israel. But also in those days, the tribe of Dan was looking for a place to settle down. They hadn't yet occupied their plot among the tribes of Israel.

18.2   The Danites sent out five robust warriors from Zorah and Eshtaol to look over the land and see what was out there suitable for their families. They said, "Go and explore the land."

They went into the hill country of Ephraim and got as far as the house of Micah. They camped there for the night. As they neared Micah's house, they recognized the voice of the young Levite. They went over and said to him, "How on earth did you get here? What's going on? What are you doing here?"

18.4   He said, "One thing led to another: Micah hired me and I'm now his priest."

18.5   They said, "Oh, good—inquire of God for us. Find out whether our mission will be a success."

18.6   The priest said, "Go assured. GOD's looking out for you all the way."

18.7   The five men left and headed north to Laish. They saw that the people there were living in safety under the umbrella of the Sidonians, quiet and unsuspecting. They had everything going for them. But the people lived a long way from the Sidonians to the west and had no treaty with the Arameans to the east.

18.8   When they got back to Zorah and Eshtaol, their brothers asked, "So, how did you find things?"

18.9-10   They said, "Let's go for it! Let's attack. We've seen the land and it is excellent. Are you going

---

[a] 8 Or *To carry on his profession*   [b] 10 That is, about 4 ounces (about 110 grams)   [c] 7 The meaning of the Hebrew for this clause is uncertain.   [d] 7 Hebrew; some Septuagint manuscripts *with the Arameans*

NEW INTERNATIONAL VERSION

you going to do something? Don't hesitate to go there and take it over. ¹⁰When you get there, you will find an unsuspecting people and a spacious land that God has put into your hands, a land that lacks nothing whatever."

¹¹Then six hundred men from the clan of the Danites, armed for battle, set out from Zorah and Eshtaol. ¹²On their way they set up camp near Kiriath Jearim in Judah. This is why the place west of Kiriath Jearim is called Mahaneh Dan*ᵃ* to this day. ¹³From there they went on to the hill country of Ephraim and came to Micah's house.

¹⁴Then the five men who had spied out the land of Laish said to their brothers, "Do you know that one of these houses has an ephod, other household gods, a carved image and a cast idol? Now you know what to do." ¹⁵So they turned in there and went to the house of the young Levite at Micah's place and greeted him. ¹⁶The six hundred Danites, armed for battle, stood at the entrance to the gate. ¹⁷The five men who had spied out the land went inside and took the carved image, the ephod, the other household gods and the cast idol while the priest and the six hundred armed men stood at the entrance to the gate.

¹⁸When these men went into Micah's house and took the carved image, the ephod, the other household gods and the cast idol, the priest said to them, "What are you doing?"

¹⁹They answered him, "Be quiet! Don't say a word. Come with us, and be our father and priest. Isn't it better that you serve a tribe and clan in Israel as priest rather than just one man's household?" ²⁰Then the priest was glad. He took the ephod, the other household gods and the carved image and went along with the people. ²¹Putting their little children, their livestock and their possessions in front of them, they turned away and left.

²²When they had gone some distance from Micah's house, the men who lived near Micah were called together and overtook the Danites. ²³As they shouted after them, the Danites turned and said to Micah, "What's the matter with you that you called out your men to fight?"

²⁴He replied, "You took the gods I made, and my priest, and went away. What else do I have? How can you ask, 'What's the matter with you?' "

²⁵The Danites answered, "Don't argue with us, or some hot-tempered men will attack you, and you and your family will lose your lives." ²⁶So the Danites went their way, and Micah, seeing that they were too strong for him, turned around and went back home.

ᵃ 12 *Mahaneh Dan* means *Dan's camp.*

THE MESSAGE

to just sit on your hands? Don't dawdle! Invade and conquer! When you get there, you'll find they're sitting ducks, totally unsuspecting. Wide open land—God is handing it over to you, everything you could ever ask for."

18.11-13 So 600 Danite men set out from Zorah and Eshtaol, armed to the teeth. Along the way they made camp at Kiriath Jearim in Judah. That is why the place is still today called Dan's Camp—it's just west of Kiriath Jearim. From there they proceeded into the hill country of Ephraim and came to Micah's house.

18.14 The five men who earlier had explored the country of Laish told their companions, "Did you know there's an ephod, teraphim-idols, and a cast god-sculpture in these buildings? What do you think? Do you want to do something about it?"

18.15-18 So they turned off the road there, went to the house of the young Levite at Micah's place and asked how things had been with him. The 600 Danites, all well-armed, stood guard at the entrance to the gate while the five scouts who had gone to explore the land went in and took the carved idol, the ephod, the teraphim-idols, and the god-sculpture. The priest was standing at the gate entrance with the 600 armed men. When the five went into Micah's house and took the carved idol, the ephod, the teraphim-idols, and the sculpted god, the priest said to them, "What do you think you're doing?"

18.19 They said to him, "Hush! Don't make a sound. Come with us. Be our father and priest. Which is more important, that you be a priest to one man or that you become priest to a whole tribe and clan in Israel?"

18.20 The priest jumped at the chance. He took the ephod, the teraphim-idols, and the idol and fell in with the troops.

18.21-23 They turned away and set out, putting the children, the cattle, and the gear in the lead. They were well on their way from Micah's house before Micah and his neighbors got organized. But they soon overtook the Danites. They shouted at them. The Danites turned around and said, "So what's all the noise about?"

18.24 Micah said, "You took my god, the one I made, and you took my priest. And you marched off! What do I have left? How can you now say, 'What's the matter?' "

18.25 But the Danites answered, "Don't yell at us; you just might provoke some fierce, hot-tempered men to attack you, and you'll end up an army of dead men."

18.26 The Danites went on their way. Micah saw that he didn't stand a chance against their arms. He turned back and went home.

NEW INTERNATIONAL VERSION

²⁷Then they took what Micah had made, and his priest, and went on to Laish, against a peaceful and unsuspecting people. They attacked them with the sword and burned down their city. ²⁸There was no one to rescue them because they lived a long way from Sidon and had no relationship with anyone else. The city was in a valley near Beth Rehob.

The Danites rebuilt the city and settled there. ²⁹They named it Dan after their forefather Dan, who was born to Israel—though the city used to be called Laish. ³⁰There the Danites set up for themselves the idols, and Jonathan son of Gershom, the son of Moses,ᵃ and his sons were priests for the tribe of Dan until the time of the captivity of the land. ³¹They continued to use the idols Micah had made, all the time the house of God was in Shiloh.

A LEVITE AND HIS CONCUBINE

19 In those days Israel had no king.
Now a Levite who lived in a remote area in the hill country of Ephraim took a concubine from Bethlehem in Judah. ²But she was unfaithful to him. She left him and went back to her father's house in Bethlehem, Judah. After she had been there four months, ³her husband went to her to persuade her to return. He had with him his servant and two donkeys. She took him into her father's house, and when her father saw him, he gladly welcomed him. ⁴His father-in-law, the girl's father, prevailed upon him to stay; so he remained with him three days, eating and drinking, and sleeping there.

⁵On the fourth day they got up early and he prepared to leave, but the girl's father said to his son-in-law, "Refresh yourself with something to eat; then you can go." ⁶So the two of them sat down to eat and drink together. Afterward the girl's father said, "Please stay tonight and enjoy yourself." ⁷And when the man got up to go, his father-in-law persuaded him, so he stayed there that night. ⁸On the morning of the fifth day, when he rose to go, the girl's father said, "Refresh yourself. Wait till afternoon!" So the two of them ate together.

⁹Then when the man, with his concubine and his servant, got up to leave, his father-in-law, the girl's father, said, "Now look, it's almost evening. Spend the night here; the day is nearly over. Stay and enjoy yourself. Early tomorrow morning you can get up and be on your way home." ¹⁰But, unwilling to stay another night, the man left and went toward Jebus (that is, Jerusalem),

ᵃ 30 An ancient Hebrew scribal tradition, some Septuagint manuscripts and Vulgate; Masoretic Text *Manasseh*

THE MESSAGE

18.27 So they took the things that Micah had made, along with his priest, and they arrived at Laish, that city of quiet and unsuspecting people. They massacred the people and burned down the city.

18.28-29 There was no one around to help. They were a long way from Sidon and had no treaty with the Arameans. Laish was in the valley of Beth Rehob. When they rebuilt the city they renamed it Dan after their ancestor who was a son of Israel, but its original name was Laish.

18.30-31 The Danites set up the god-figure for themselves. Jonathan son of Gershom, the son of Moses, and his descendants were priests to the tribe of Dan down to the time of the land's captivity. All during the time that there was a sanctuary of God in Shiloh, they kept for their private use the god-figure that Micah had made.

THE LEVITE

19.1-4 **19** It was an era when there was no king in Israel. A Levite, living as a stranger in the backwoods hill country of Ephraim, got himself a concubine, a woman from Bethlehem in Judah. But she quarreled with him and left, returning to her father's house in Bethlehem in Judah. She was there four months. Then her husband decided to go after her and try to win her back. He had a servant and a pair of donkeys with him. When he arrived at her father's house, the girl's father saw him, welcomed him, and made him feel at home. His father-in-law, the girl's father, pressed him to stay. He stayed with him three days; they feasted and drank and slept.

19.5-6 On the fourth day, they got up at the crack of dawn and got ready to go. But the girl's father said to his son-in-law, "Strengthen yourself with a hearty breakfast and then you can go." So they sat down and ate breakfast together.

19.6-7 The girl's father said to the man, "Come now, be my guest. Stay the night—make it a holiday." The man got up to go, but his father-in-law kept after him, so he ended up spending another night.

19.8-9 On the fifth day, he was again up early, ready to go. The girl's father said, "You need some breakfast." They went back and forth, and the day slipped on as they ate and drank together. But the man and his concubine were finally ready to go. Then his father-in-law, the girl's father, said, "Look, the day's almost gone—why not stay the night? There's very little daylight left; stay another night and enjoy yourself. Tomorrow you can get an early start and set off for your own place."

19.10-11 But this time the man wasn't willing to spend another night. He got things ready, left, and went as far as Jebus (Jerusalem) with his

NEW INTERNATIONAL VERSION

with his two saddled donkeys and his concubine.

¹¹When they were near Jebus and the day was almost gone, the servant said to his master, "Come, let's stop at this city of the Jebusites and spend the night."

¹²His master replied, "No. We won't go into an alien city, whose people are not Israelites. We will go on to Gibeah." ¹³He added, "Come, let's try to reach Gibeah or Ramah and spend the night in one of those places." ¹⁴So they went on, and the sun set as they neared Gibeah in Benjamin. ¹⁵There they stopped to spend the night. They went and sat in the city square, but no one took them into his home for the night.

¹⁶That evening an old man from the hill country of Ephraim, who was living in Gibeah (the men of the place were Benjamites), came in from his work in the fields. ¹⁷When he looked and saw the traveler in the city square, the old man asked, "Where are you going? Where did you come from?"

¹⁸He answered, "We are on our way from Bethlehem in Judah to a remote area in the hill country of Ephraim where I live. I have been to Bethlehem in Judah and now I am going to the house of the Lord. No one has taken me into his house. ¹⁹We have both straw and fodder for our donkeys and bread and wine for ourselves your servants—me, your maidservant, and the young man with us. We don't need anything."

²⁰"You are welcome at my house," the old man said. "Let me supply whatever you need. Only don't spend the night in the square." ²¹So he took him into his house and fed his donkeys. After they had washed their feet, they had something to eat and drink.

²²While they were enjoying themselves, some of the wicked men of the city surrounded the house. Pounding on the door, they shouted to the old man who owned the house, "Bring out the man who came to your house so we can have sex with him."

²³The owner of the house went outside and said to them, "No, my friends, don't be so vile. Since this man is my guest, don't do this disgraceful thing. ²⁴Look, here is my virgin daughter, and his concubine. I will bring them out to you now, and you can use them and do to them whatever you wish. But to this man, don't do such a disgraceful thing."

²⁵But the men would not listen to him. So the man took his concubine and sent her outside to them, and they raped her and abused her throughout the night, and at dawn they let her go. ²⁶At daybreak the woman went back to the

THE MESSAGE

pair of saddled donkeys, his concubine, and his servant. At Jebus, though, the day was nearly gone. The servant said to his master, "It's late; let's go into this Jebusite city and spend the night."

19.12-13 But his master said, "We're not going into any city of foreigners. We'll go on to Gibeah." He directed his servant, "Keep going. Let's go on ahead. We'll spend the night either at Gibeah or Ramah."

19.14-15 So they kept going. As they pressed on, the sun finally left them in the vicinity of Gibeah, which belongs to Benjamin. They left the road there to spend the night at Gibeah.

19.15-17 The Levite went and sat down in the town square, but no one invited them in to spend the night. Then, late in the evening, an old man came in from his day's work in the fields. He was from the hill country of Ephraim and lived temporarily in Gibeah where all the local citizens were Benjaminites. When the old man looked up and saw the traveler in the town square, he said, "Where are you going? And where are you from?"

19.18-19 The Levite said, "We're just passing through. We're coming from Bethlehem on our way to a remote spot in the hills of Ephraim. I come from there. I've just made a trip to Bethlehem in Judah and I'm on my way back home, but no one has invited us in for the night. We wouldn't be any trouble: We have food and straw for the donkeys, and bread and wine for the woman, the young man, and me—we don't need anything."

19.20-21 The old man said, "It's going to be all right; I'll take care of you. You aren't going to spend the night in the town square." He took them home and fed the donkeys. They washed up and sat down to a good meal.

19.22 They were relaxed and enjoying themselves when the men of the city, a gang of local hellraisers all, surrounded the house and started pounding on the door. They yelled for the owner of the house, the old man, "Bring out the man who came to your house. We want to have sex with him."

19.23-24 He went out and told them, "No, brothers! Don't be obscene—this man is my guest. Don't commit this outrage. Look, my virgin daughter and his concubine are here. I'll bring them out for you. Abuse them if you must, but don't do anything so senselessly vile to this man."

19.25-26 But the men wouldn't listen to him. Finally, the Levite pushed his concubine out the door to them. They raped her repeatedly all night long. Just before dawn they let her go. The woman came back and fell at the door of the

NEW INTERNATIONAL VERSION

house where her master was staying, fell down at the door and lay there until daylight. ²⁷When her master got up in the morning and opened the door of the house and stepped out to continue on his way, there lay his concubine, fallen in the doorway of the house, with her hands on the threshold. ²⁸He said to her, "Get up; let's go." But there was no answer. Then the man put her on his donkey and set out for home.

²⁹When he reached home, he took a knife and cut up his concubine, limb by limb, into twelve parts and sent them into all the areas of Israel. ³⁰Everyone who saw it said, "Such a thing has never been seen or done, not since the day the Israelites came up out of Egypt. Think about it! Consider it! Tell us what to do!"

ISRAELITES FIGHT THE BENJAMITES

20 Then all the Israelites from Dan to Beersheba and from the land of Gilead came out as one man and assembled before the LORD in Mizpah. ²The leaders of all the people of the tribes of Israel took their places in the assembly of the people of God, four hundred thousand soldiers armed with swords. ³(The Benjamites heard that the Israelites had gone up to Mizpah.) Then the Israelites said, "Tell us how this awful thing happened."

⁴So the Levite, the husband of the murdered woman, said, "I and my concubine came to Gibeah in Benjamin to spend the night. ⁵During the night the men of Gibeah came after me and surrounded the house, intending to kill me. They raped my concubine, and she died. ⁶I took my concubine, cut her into pieces and sent one piece to each region of Israel's inheritance, because they committed this lewd and disgraceful act in Israel. ⁷Now, all you Israelites, speak up and give your verdict."

⁸All the people rose as one man, saying, "None of us will go home. No, not one of us will return to his house. ⁹But now this is what we'll do to Gibeah: We'll go up against it as the lot directs. ¹⁰We'll take ten men out of every hundred from all the tribes of Israel, and a hundred from a thousand, and a thousand from ten thousand, to get provisions for the army. Then, when the army arrives at Gibeah*ᵃ* in Benjamin, it can give them what they deserve for all this vileness done in Israel." ¹¹So all the men of Israel got together and united as one man against the city.

¹²The tribes of Israel sent men throughout the

ᵃ 10 One Hebrew manuscript; most Hebrew manuscripts Geba, a variant of Gibeah

THE MESSAGE

house where her master was sleeping. When the sun rose, there she was.

19.27   It was morning. Her master got up and opened the door to continue his journey. There she was, his concubine, crumpled in a heap at the door, her hands on the threshold.

19.28   "Get up," he said. "Let's get going." There was no answer.

19.29-30   He lifted her onto his donkey and set out for home. When he got home he took a knife and dismembered his concubine—cut her into twelve pieces. He sent her, piece by piece, throughout the country of Israel. And he ordered the men he sent out, "Say to every man in Israel: 'Has such a thing as this ever happened from the time the Israelites came up from the land of Egypt until now? Think about it! Talk it over. Do something!'"

✝

20.1-2   **20** Then all the People of Israel came out. The congregation met in the presence of GOD at Mizpah. They were all there, from Dan to Beersheba, as one person! The leaders of all the people, representing all the tribes of Israel, took their places in the gathering of God's people. There were 400 divisions of sword-wielding infantry.

20.3   Meanwhile the Benjaminites got wind that the Israelites were meeting at Mizpah.

The People of Israel said, "Now tell us. How did this outrageous evil happen?"

20.4-7   The Levite, the husband of the murdered woman, spoke: "My concubine and I came to spend the night at Gibeah, a Benjaminite town. That night the men of Gibeah came after me. They surrounded the house, intending to kill me. They gang-raped my concubine and she died. So I took my concubine, cut up her body, and sent her piece by piece—twelve pieces!— to every part of Israel's inheritance. This vile and outrageous crime was committed *in Israel*! So, Israelites, make up your minds. Decide on some action!"

20.8-11   All the people were at once and as one person on their feet. "None of us will go home; not a single one of us will go to his own house. Here's our plan for dealing with Gibeah: We'll march against it by drawing lots. We'll take ten of every hundred men from all the tribes of Israel (a hundred of every thousand, and a thousand of every ten thousand) to carry food for the army. When the troops arrive at Gibeah they will settle accounts for this outrageous and vile evil that was done in Israel." So all the men in Israel were gathered against the city, totally united.

20.12-13   The Israelite tribes sent messengers through-

NEW INTERNATIONAL VERSION

tribe of Benjamin, saying, "What about this awful crime that was committed among you? [13]Now surrender those wicked men of Gibeah so that we may put them to death and purge the evil from Israel."

But the Benjamites would not listen to their fellow Israelites. [14]From their towns they came together at Gibeah to fight against the Israelites. [15]At once the Benjamites mobilized twenty-six thousand swordsmen from their towns, in addition to seven hundred chosen men from those living in Gibeah. [16]Among all these soldiers there were seven hundred chosen men who were left-handed, each of whom could sling a stone at a hair and not miss.

[17]Israel, apart from Benjamin, mustered four hundred thousand swordsmen, all of them fighting men.

[18]The Israelites went up to Bethel[a] and inquired of God. They said, "Who of us shall go first to fight against the Benjamites?"

The Lord replied, "Judah shall go first."

[19]The next morning the Israelites got up and pitched camp near Gibeah. [20]The men of Israel went out to fight the Benjamites and took up battle positions against them at Gibeah. [21]The Benjamites came out of Gibeah and cut down twenty-two thousand Israelites on the battlefield that day. [22]But the men of Israel encouraged one another and again took up their positions where they had stationed themselves the first day. [23]The Israelites went up and wept before the Lord until evening, and they inquired of the Lord. They said, "Shall we go up again to battle against the Benjamites, our brothers?"

The Lord answered, "Go up against them."

[24]Then the Israelites drew near to Benjamin the second day. [25]This time, when the Benjamites came out from Gibeah to oppose them, they cut down another eighteen thousand Israelites, all of them armed with swords.

[26]Then the Israelites, all the people, went up to Bethel, and there they sat weeping before the Lord. They fasted that day until evening and presented burnt offerings and fellowship offerings[b] to the Lord. [27]And the Israelites inquired of the Lord. (In those days the ark of the covenant of God was there, [28]with Phinehas son of Eleazar, the son of Aaron, ministering before it.) They asked, "Shall we go up again to battle with Benjamin our brother, or not?"

THE MESSAGE

out the tribe of Benjamin saying, "What's the meaning of this outrage that took place among you? Surrender the men right here and now, these hell-raisers of Gibeah. We'll put them to death and burn the evil out of Israel."

20.13-16   But they wouldn't do it. The Benjaminites refused to listen to their brothers, the People of Israel. Instead they raised an army from all their cities and rallied at Gibeah to go to war against the People of Israel. In no time at all they had recruited from their cities twenty-six divisions of sword-wielding infantry. From Gibeah they got 700 hand-picked fighters, the best. There were another 700 super marksmen who were ambidextrous—they could sling a stone at a hair and not miss.

20.17   The men of Israel, excluding Benjamin, mobilized 400 divisions of sword-wielding fighting men.

20.18   They set out and went to Bethel to inquire of God. The People of Israel said, "Who of us shall be first to go into battle with the Benjaminites?"

20.18   God said, "Judah goes first."

20.19-21   The People of Israel got up the next morning and camped before Gibeah. The army of Israel marched out against Benjamin and took up their positions, ready to attack Gibeah. But the Benjaminites poured out of Gibeah and devastated twenty-two Israelite divisions on the ground.

20.22-23   The Israelites went back to the sanctuary and wept before God until evening. They again inquired of God, "Shall we again go into battle against the Benjaminites, our brothers?"

God said, "Yes. Attack."

The army took heart. The men of Israel took up the positions they had deployed on the first day.

20.24-25   On the second day, the Israelites again advanced against Benjamin. This time as the Benjaminites came out of the city, on this second day, they devastated another eighteen Israelite divisions, all swordsmen.

20.26   All the People of Israel, the whole army, were back at Bethel, weeping, sitting there in the presence of God. That day they fasted until evening. They sacrificed Whole-Burnt-Offerings and Peace-Offerings before God.

20.27-28   And they again inquired of God. The Chest of God's Covenant was there at that time with Phinehas son of Eleazar, the son of Aaron, as the ministering priest. They asked, "Shall we again march into battle against the Benjaminites, our brothers? Or should we call it quits?"

---

a 18 Or *to the house of God*; also in verse 26
b 26 Traditionally *peace offerings*

NEW INTERNATIONAL VERSION

The LORD responded, "Go, for tomorrow I will give them into your hands."

29 Then Israel set an ambush around Gibeah. 30 They went up against the Benjamites on the third day and took up positions against Gibeah as they had done before. 31 The Benjamites came out to meet them and were drawn away from the city. They began to inflict casualties on the Israelites as before, so that about thirty men fell in the open field and on the roads—the one leading to Bethel and the other to Gibeah.

32 While the Benjamites were saying, "We are defeating them as before," the Israelites were saying, "Let's retreat and draw them away from the city to the roads."

33 All the men of Israel moved from their places and took up positions at Baal Tamar, and the Israelite ambush charged out of its place on the west[a] of Gibeah.[b] 34 Then ten thousand of Israel's finest men made a frontal attack on Gibeah. The fighting was so heavy that the Benjamites did not realize how near disaster was. 35 The LORD defeated Benjamin before Israel, and on that day the Israelites struck down 25,100 Benjamites, all armed with swords. 36 Then the Benjamites saw that they were beaten.

Now the men of Israel had given way before Benjamin, because they relied on the ambush they had set near Gibeah. 37 The men who had been in ambush made a sudden dash into Gibeah, spread out and put the whole city to the sword. 38 The men of Israel had arranged with the ambush that they should send up a great cloud of smoke from the city, 39 and then the men of Israel would turn in the battle.

The Benjamites had begun to inflict casualties on the men of Israel (about thirty), and they said, "We are defeating them as in the first battle." 40 But when the column of smoke began to rise from the city, the Benjamites turned and saw the smoke of the whole city going up into the sky. 41 Then the men of Israel turned on them, and the men of Benjamin were terrified, because they realized that disaster had come upon them. 42 So they fled before the Israelites in the direction of the desert, but they could not escape the battle. And the men of Israel who came out of the towns cut them down there. 43 They surrounded the Benjamites, chased them and easily[c] overran them in the vicinity of Gibeah on the east. 44 Eighteen thousand Benjamites fell, all of them valiant fighters. 45 As they turned and fled

a 33 Some Septuagint manuscripts and Vulgate; the meaning of the Hebrew for this word is uncertain.
b 33 Hebrew Geba, a variant of Gibeah   c 43 The meaning of the Hebrew for this word is uncertain.

THE MESSAGE

And GOD said, "Attack. Tomorrow I'll give you victory."

20.29-31 This time Israel placed men in ambush all around Gibeah. On the third day when Israel set out, they took up the same positions before the Benjaminites as before. When the Benjaminites came out to meet the army, they moved out from the city. Benjaminites began to cut down some of the troops just as they had before. About thirty men fell in the field and on the roads to Bethel and Gibeah.

20.32 The Benjaminites started bragging, "We're dropping them like flies, just as before!"

20.33 But the Israelites strategized: "Now let's retreat and pull them out of the city onto the main roads." So every Israelite moved farther out to Baal Tamar; at the same time the Israelite ambush rushed from its place west of Gibeah.

20.34-36 Ten crack divisions from all over Israel now arrived at Gibeah—intense, bloody fighting! The Benjaminites had no idea that they were about to go down in defeat—GOD routed them before Israel. The Israelites decimated twenty-five divisions of Benjamin that day—25,100 killed. They were all swordsmen. The Benjaminites saw that they were beaten.

The men of Israel acted like they were retreating before Benjamin, knowing that they could depend on the ambush they had prepared for Gibeah.

20.37-40 The ambush erupted and made quick work of Gibeah. The ambush spread out and massacred the city. The strategy for the main body of the ambush was that they send up a smoke signal from the city. Then the men of Israel would turn in battle. When that happened, Benjamin had killed about thirty Israelites and thought they were on their way to victory, yelling out, "They're on the run, just as in the first battle!" But then the signal went up from the city—a huge column of smoke. When the Benjaminites looked back, there it was, the whole city going up in smoke.

20.41-43 By the time the men of Israel had turned back on them, the men of Benjamin fell apart—they could see that they were trapped. Confronted by the Israelites, they tried to get away down the wilderness road, but by now the battle was everywhere. The men of Israel poured out of the towns, killing them right and left, hot on their trail, picking them off east of Gibeah.

✝

20.44 Eighteen divisions of Benjaminites were wiped out, all their best fighters.

20.45 Five divisions turned to escape to the

NEW INTERNATIONAL VERSION

toward the desert to the rock of Rimmon, the Israelites cut down five thousand men along the roads. They kept pressing after the Benjamites as far as Gidom and struck down two thousand more.

⁴⁶On that day twenty-five thousand Benjamite swordsmen fell, all of them valiant fighters. ⁴⁷But six hundred men turned and fled into the desert to the rock of Rimmon, where they stayed four months. ⁴⁸The men of Israel went back to Benjamin and put all the towns to the sword, including the animals and everything else they found. All the towns they came across they set on fire.

WIVES FOR THE BENJAMITES

21 The men of Israel had taken an oath at Mizpah: "Not one of us will give his daughter in marriage to a Benjamite."

²The people went to Bethel,ᵃ where they sat before God until evening, raising their voices and weeping bitterly. ³"O LORD, the God of Israel," they cried, "why has this happened to Israel? Why should one tribe be missing from Israel today?"

⁴Early the next day the people built an altar and presented burnt offerings and fellowship offerings.ᵇ

⁵Then the Israelites asked, "Who from all the tribes of Israel has failed to assemble before the LORD?" For they had taken a solemn oath that anyone who failed to assemble before the LORD at Mizpah should certainly be put to death.

⁶Now the Israelites grieved for their brothers, the Benjamites. "Today one tribe is cut off from Israel," they said. ⁷"How can we provide wives for those who are left, since we have taken an oath by the LORD not to give them any of our daughters in marriage?" ⁸Then they asked, "Which one of the tribes of Israel failed to assemble before the LORD at Mizpah?" They discovered that no one from Jabesh Gilead had come to the camp for the assembly. ⁹For when they counted the people, they found that none of the people of Jabesh Gilead were there.

¹⁰So the assembly sent twelve thousand fighting men with instructions to go to Jabesh Gilead and put to the sword those living there, including the women and children. ¹¹"This is what you are to do," they said. "Kill every male and every woman who is not a virgin." ¹²They found among the people living in Jabesh Gilead four

THE MESSAGE

wilderness, to Rimmon Rock, but the Israelites caught and slaughtered them on roads. Keeping the pressure on, the Israelites brought down two more divisions.

20.46 The total of the Benjaminites killed that day came to twenty-five divisions of infantry, their best swordsmen.

20.47 Six hundred men got away. They made it to Rimmon Rock in the wilderness and held out there for four months.

20.48 The men of Israel came back and killed all the Benjaminites who were left, all the men and animals they found in every town, and then torched the towns, sending them up in flames.

WIVES

21 Back at Mizpah the men of Israel had taken an oath: "No man among us will give his daughter to a Benjaminite in marriage."

21.2-3 Now, back in Bethel, the people sat in the presence of God until evening. They cried loudly; there was widespread lamentation. They said, "Why, O GOD, God of Israel, has this happened? Why do we find ourselves today missing one whole tribe from Israel?"

21.4 Early the next morning, the people got busy and built an altar. They sacrificed Whole-Burnt-Offerings and Peace-Offerings.

21.5 Then the Israelites said, "Who from all the tribes of Israel didn't show up as we gathered in the presence of GOD?" For they had all taken a sacred oath that anyone who had not gathered in the presence of GOD at Mizpah had to be put to death.

✝

21.6-7 But the People of Israel were feeling sorry for Benjamin, their brothers. They said, "Today, one tribe is cut off from Israel. How can we get wives for those who are left? We have sworn by GOD not to give any of our daughters to them in marriage."

21.8-9 They said, "Which one of the tribes of Israel didn't gather before GOD at Mizpah?"

It turned out that no one had come to the gathering from Jabesh Gilead. When they took a roll call of the people, not a single person from Jabesh Gilead was there.

21.10-11 So the congregation sent twelve divisions of their top men there with the command, "Kill everyone of Jabesh Gilead, including women and children. These are your instructions: Every man and woman who has had sexual intercourse you must kill. But keep the virgins alive." And that's what they did.

21.12 And they found 400 virgins among those

ᵃ 2 Or to the house of God   ᵇ 4 Traditionally peace offerings

NEW INTERNATIONAL VERSION

hundred young women who had never slept with a man, and they took them to the camp at Shiloh in Canaan.

¹³Then the whole assembly sent an offer of peace to the Benjamites at the rock of Rimmon. ¹⁴So the Benjamites returned at that time and were given the women of Jabesh Gilead who had been spared. But there were not enough for all of them.

¹⁵The people grieved for Benjamin, because the LORD had made a gap in the tribes of Israel. ¹⁶And the elders of the assembly said, "With the women of Benjamin destroyed, how shall we provide wives for the men who are left? ¹⁷The Benjamite survivors must have heirs," they said, "so that a tribe of Israel will not be wiped out. ¹⁸We can't give them our daughters as wives, since we Israelites have taken this oath: 'Cursed be anyone who gives a wife to a Benjamite.' ¹⁹But look, there is the annual festival of the LORD in Shiloh, to the north of Bethel, and east of the road that goes from Bethel to Shechem, and to the south of Lebonah."

²⁰So they instructed the Benjamites, saying, "Go and hide in the vineyards ²¹and watch. When the girls of Shiloh come out to join in the dancing, then rush from the vineyards and each of you seize a wife from the girls of Shiloh and go to the land of Benjamin. ²²When their fathers or brothers complain to us, we will say to them, 'Do us a kindness by helping them, because we did not get wives for them during the war, and you are innocent, since you did not give your daughters to them.' "

²³So that is what the Benjamites did. While the girls were dancing, each man caught one and carried her off to be his wife. Then they returned to their inheritance and rebuilt the towns and settled in them.

²⁴At that time the Israelites left that place and went home to their tribes and clans, each to his own inheritance.

²⁵In those days Israel had no king; everyone did as he saw fit.

THE MESSAGE

who lived in Jabesh Gilead; they had never had sexual intercourse with a man. And they brought them to the camp at Shiloh, which is in the land of Canaan.

²¹.¹³⁻¹⁴ Then the congregation sent word to the Benjaminites who were at the Rimmon Rock and offered them peace. And Benjamin came. They gave them the women they had let live at Jabesh Gilead. But even then, there weren't enough for all the men.

²¹.¹⁵ The people felt bad for Benjamin; GOD had left out Benjamin—the missing piece from the Israelite tribes.

✝

²¹.¹⁶⁻¹⁸ The elders of the congregation said, "How can we get wives for the rest of the men, since all the Benjaminite women have been killed? How can we keep the inheritance alive for the Benjaminite survivors? How can we prevent an entire tribe from extinction? We certainly can't give our own daughters to them as wives." (Remember, the Israelites had taken the oath: "Cursed is anyone who provides a wife to Benjamin.")

²¹.¹⁹ Then they said, "There is that festival of GOD held every year in Shiloh. It's north of Bethel, just east of the main road that goes up from Bethel to Shechem and a little south of Lebonah."

²¹.²⁰⁻²² So they told the Benjaminites, "Go and hide in the vineyards. Stay alert—when you see the Shiloh girls come out to dance the dances, run out of the vineyards, grab one of the Shiloh girls for your wife, and then hightail it back to the country of Benjamin. When their fathers or brothers come to lay charges against us, we'll tell them, 'We did them a favor. After all we didn't go to war and kill to get wives for men. And it wasn't as if you were in on it by giving consent. But if you keep this up, you will incur blame.' "

²¹.²³ And that's what the Benjaminites did: They carried off girls from the dance, wives enough for their number, got away, and went home to their inheritance. They rebuilt their towns and settled down.

²¹.²⁴ From there the People of Israel dispersed, each man heading back to his own tribe and clan, each to his own plot of land.

²¹.²⁵ At that time there was no king in Israel. People did whatever they felt like doing.

RUTH

RUTH

NAOMI AND RUTH

1 In the days when the judges ruled,[a] there was a famine in the land, and a man from Bethlehem in Judah, together with his wife and two sons, went to live for a while in the country of Moab. ²The man's name was Elimelech, his wife's name Naomi, and the names of his two sons were Mahlon and Kilion. They were Ephrathites from Bethlehem, Judah. And they went to Moab and lived there.

³Now Elimelech, Naomi's husband, died, and she was left with her two sons. ⁴They married Moabite women, one named Orpah and the other Ruth. After they had lived there about ten years, ⁵both Mahlon and Kilion also died, and Naomi was left without her two sons and her husband.

⁶When she heard in Moab that the LORD had come to the aid of his people by providing food for them, Naomi and her daughters-in-law prepared to return home from there. ⁷With her two daughters-in-law she left the place where she had been living and set out on the road that would take them back to the land of Judah.

⁸Then Naomi said to her two daughters-in-law, "Go back, each of you, to your mother's home. May the LORD show kindness to you, as you have shown to your dead and to me. ⁹May the LORD grant that each of you will find rest in the home of another husband."

Then she kissed them and they wept aloud ¹⁰and said to her, "We will go back with you to your people."

¹¹But Naomi said, "Return home, my daughters. Why would you come with me? Am I going to have any more sons, who could become your husbands? ¹²Return home, my daughters; I am too old to have another husband. Even if I thought there was still hope for me—even if I had a husband tonight and then gave birth to sons— ¹³would you wait until they grew up? Would you remain unmarried for them? No, my

1.1-2 1 Once upon a time—it was back in the days when judges led Israel—there was a famine in the land. A man from Bethlehem in Judah left home to live in the country of Moab, he and his wife and his two sons. The man's name was Elimelech; his wife's name was Naomi; his sons were named Mahlon and Kilion—all Ephrathites from Bethlehem in Judah. They all went to the country of Moab and settled there.

1.3-5 Elimelech died and Naomi was left, she and her two sons. The sons took Moabite wives; the name of the first was Orpah, the second Ruth. They lived there in Moab for the next ten years. But then the two brothers, Mahlon and Kilion, died. Now the woman was left without either her young men or her husband.

✝

1.6-7 One day she got herself together, she and her two daughters-in-law, to leave the country of Moab and set out for home; she had heard that GOD had been pleased to visit his people and give them food. And so she started out from the place she had been living, she and her two daughters-in-law with her, on the road back to the land of Judah.

1.8-9 After a short while on the road, Naomi told her two daughters-in-law, "Go back. Go home and live with your mothers. And may GOD treat you as graciously as you treated your deceased husbands and me. May GOD give each of you a new home and a new husband!" She kissed them and they cried openly.

1.10 They said, "No, we're going on with you to your people."

1.11-13 But Naomi was firm: "Go back, my dear daughters. Why would you come with me? Do you suppose I still have sons in my womb who can become your future husbands? Go back, dear daughters—on your way, please! I'm too old to get a husband. Why, even if I said, 'There's still hope!' and this very night got a man and had sons, can you imagine being satisfied to wait until they were grown? Would you wait that long to get married again? No,

NEW INTERNATIONAL VERSION

daughters. It is more bitter for me than for you, because the LORD's hand has gone out against me!"

¹⁴At this they wept again. Then Orpah kissed her mother-in-law good-by, but Ruth clung to her.

¹⁵"Look," said Naomi, "your sister-in-law is going back to her people and her gods. Go back with her."

¹⁶But Ruth replied, "Don't urge me to leave you or to turn back from you. Where you go I will go, and where you stay I will stay. Your people will be my people and your God my God. ¹⁷Where you die I will die, and there I will be buried. May the LORD deal with me, be it ever so severely, if anything but death separates you and me." ¹⁸When Naomi realized that Ruth was determined to go with her, she stopped urging her.

¹⁹So the two women went on until they came to Bethlehem. When they arrived in Bethlehem, the whole town was stirred because of them, and the women exclaimed, "Can this be Naomi?"

²⁰"Don't call me Naomi,ᵃ" she told them. "Call me Mara,ᵇ because the Almightyᶜ has made my life very bitter. ²¹I went away full, but the LORD has brought me back empty. Why call me Naomi? The LORD has afflictedᵈ me; the Almighty has brought misfortune upon me."

²²So Naomi returned from Moab accompanied by Ruth the Moabitess, her daughter-in-law, arriving in Bethlehem as the barley harvest was beginning.

RUTH MEETS BOAZ

2 Now Naomi had a relative on her husband's side, from the clan of Elimelech, a man of standing, whose name was Boaz.

²And Ruth the Moabitess said to Naomi, "Let me go to the fields and pick up the leftover grain behind anyone in whose eyes I find favor."

Naomi said to her, "Go ahead, my daughter." ³So she went out and began to glean in the fields behind the harvesters. As it turned out, she found herself working in a field belonging to Boaz, who was from the clan of Elimelech.

⁴Just then Boaz arrived from Bethlehem and greeted the harvesters, "The LORD be with you!"

"The LORD bless you!" they called back.

⁵Boaz asked the foreman of his harvesters, "Whose young woman is that?"

⁶The foreman replied, "She is the Moabitess who came back from Moab with Naomi. ⁷She

THE MESSAGE

dear daughters; this is a bitter pill for me to swallow—more bitter for me than for you. GOD has dealt me a hard blow."

1.14 Again they cried openly. Orpah kissed her mother-in-law good-bye; but Ruth embraced her and held on.

1.15 Naomi said, "Look, your sister-in-law is going back home to live with her own people and gods; go with her."

1.16-17 But Ruth said, "Don't force me to leave you; don't make me go home. Where you go, I go; and where you live, I'll live. Your people are my people, your God is my god; where you die, I'll die, and that's where I'll be buried, so help me GOD—not even death itself is going to come between us!"

1.18-19 When Naomi saw that Ruth had her heart set on going with her, she gave in. And so the two of them traveled on together to Bethlehem.

When they arrived in Bethlehem the whole town was soon buzzing: "Is this really our Naomi? And after all this time!"

1.20-21 But she said, "Don't call me Naomi; call me Bitter. The Strong One has dealt me a bitter blow. I left here full of life, and GOD has brought me back with nothing but the clothes on my back. Why would you call me Naomi? God certainly doesn't. The Strong One ruined me."

1.22 And so Naomi was back, and Ruth the foreigner with her, back from the country of Moab. They arrived in Bethlehem at the beginning of the barley harvest.

2.1 2 It so happened that Naomi had a relative by marriage, a man prominent and rich, connected with Elimelech's family. His name was Boaz.

2.2 One day Ruth, the Moabite foreigner, said to Naomi, "I'm going to work; I'm going out to glean among the sheaves, following after some harvester who will treat me kindly."

Naomi said, "Go ahead, dear daughter."

2.3-4 And so she set out. She went and started gleaning in a field, following in the wake of the harvesters. Eventually she ended up in the part of the field owned by Boaz, her father-in-law Elimelech's relative. A little later Boaz came out from Bethlehem, greeting his harvesters, "GOD be with you!" They replied, "And GOD bless you!"

2.5 Boaz asked his young servant who was foreman over the farm hands, "Who is this young woman? Where did she come from?"

2.6-7 The foreman said, "Why, that's the Moabite girl, the one who came with Naomi from the

---

ᵃ 20 *Naomi* means *pleasant*; also in verse 21.   ᵇ 20 *Mara* means *bitter.*   ᶜ 20 Hebrew *Shaddai*; also in verse 21   ᵈ 21 Or *has testified against*

NEW INTERNATIONAL VERSION

said, 'Please let me glean and gather among the sheaves behind the harvesters.' She went into the field and has worked steadily from morning till now, except for a short rest in the shelter."

⁸So Boaz said to Ruth, "My daughter, listen to me. Don't go and glean in another field and don't go away from here. Stay here with my servant girls. ⁹Watch the field where the men are harvesting, and follow along after the girls. I have told the men not to touch you. And whenever you are thirsty, go and get a drink from the water jars the men have filled."

¹⁰At this, she bowed down with her face to the ground. She exclaimed, "Why have I found such favor in your eyes that you notice me—a foreigner?"

¹¹Boaz replied, "I've been told all about what you have done for your mother-in-law since the death of your husband—how you left your father and mother and your homeland and came to live with a people you did not know before. ¹²May the LORD repay you for what you have done. May you be richly rewarded by the LORD, the God of Israel, under whose wings you have come to take refuge."

¹³"May I continue to find favor in your eyes, my lord," she said. "You have given me comfort and have spoken kindly to your servant—though I do not have the standing of one of your servant girls."

¹⁴At mealtime Boaz said to her, "Come over here. Have some bread and dip it in the wine vinegar."

When she sat down with the harvesters, he offered her some roasted grain. She ate all she wanted and had some left over. ¹⁵As she got up to glean, Boaz gave orders to his men, "Even if she gathers among the sheaves, don't embarrass her. ¹⁶Rather, pull out some stalks for her from the bundles and leave them for her to pick up, and don't rebuke her."

¹⁷So Ruth gleaned in the field until evening. Then she threshed the barley she had gathered, and it amounted to about an ephah. *ª* ¹⁸She carried it back to town, and her mother-in-law saw how much she had gathered. Ruth also brought out and gave her what she had left over after she had eaten enough.

¹⁹Her mother-in-law asked her, "Where did you glean today? Where did you work? Blessed be the man who took notice of you!"

Then Ruth told her mother-in-law about the one at whose place she had been working. "The name of the man I worked with today is Boaz," she said.

²⁰"The LORD bless him!" Naomi said to her

ª 17 That is, probably about 3/5 bushel (about 22 liters)

THE MESSAGE

country of Moab. She asked permission. 'Let me glean,' she said, 'and gather among the sheaves following after your harvesters.' She's been at it steady ever since, from early morning until now, without so much as a break."

2.8-9 Then Boaz spoke to Ruth: "Listen, my daughter. From now on don't go to any other field to glean—stay right here in this one. And stay close to my young women. Watch where they are harvesting and follow them. And don't worry about a thing; I've given orders to my servants not to harass you. When you get thirsty, feel free to go and drink from the water buckets that the servants have filled."

2.10 She dropped to her knees, then bowed her face to the ground. "How does this happen that you should pick me out and treat me so kindly—*me*, a foreigner?"

2.11-12 Boaz answered her, "I've heard all about you—heard about the way you treated your mother-in-law after the death of her husband, and how you left your father and mother and the land of your birth and have come to live among a bunch of total strangers. GOD reward you well for what you've done—and with a generous bonus besides from GOD, to whom you've come seeking protection under his wings."

2.13 She said, "Oh sir, such grace, such kindness—I don't deserve it. You've touched my heart, treated me like one of your own. And I don't even belong here!"

2.14 At the lunch break, Boaz said to her, "Come over here; eat some bread. Dip it in the wine."

So she joined the harvesters. Boaz passed the roasted grain to her. She ate her fill and even had some left over.

2.15-16 When she got up to go back to work, Boaz ordered his servants: "Let her glean where there's still plenty of grain on the ground—make it easy for her. Better yet, pull some of the good stuff out and leave it for her to glean. Give her special treatment."

2.17-18 Ruth gleaned in the field until evening. When she threshed out what she had gathered, she ended up with nearly a full sack of barley! She gathered up her gleanings, went back to town, and showed her mother-in-law the results of her day's work; she also gave her the leftovers from her lunch.

2.19 Naomi asked her, "So where did you glean today? Whose field? GOD bless whoever it was who took such good care of you!"

Ruth told her mother-in-law, "The man with whom I worked today? His name is Boaz."

2.20 Naomi said to her daughter-in-law, "Why,

NEW INTERNATIONAL VERSION

daughter-in-law. "He has not stopped showing his kindness to the living and the dead." She added, "That man is our close relative; he is one of our kinsman-redeemers."

²¹Then Ruth the Moabitess said, "He even said to me, 'Stay with my workers until they finish harvesting all my grain.' "

²²Naomi said to Ruth her daughter-in-law, "It will be good for you, my daughter, to go with his girls, because in someone else's field you might be harmed."

²³So Ruth stayed close to the servant girls of Boaz to glean until the barley and wheat harvests were finished. And she lived with her mother-in-law.

RUTH AND BOAZ AT THE THRESHING FLOOR

3 One day Naomi her mother-in-law said to her, "My daughter, should I not try to find a home*a* for you, where you will be well provided for? ²Is not Boaz, with whose servant girls you have been, a kinsman of ours? Tonight he will be winnowing barley on the threshing floor. ³Wash and perfume yourself, and put on your best clothes. Then go down to the threshing floor, but don't let him know you are there until he has finished eating and drinking. ⁴When he lies down, note the place where he is lying. Then go and uncover his feet and lie down. He will tell you what to do."

⁵"I will do whatever you say," Ruth answered. ⁶So she went down to the threshing floor and did everything her mother-in-law told her to do.

⁷When Boaz had finished eating and drinking and was in good spirits, he went over to lie down at the far end of the grain pile. Ruth approached quietly, uncovered his feet and lay down. ⁸In the middle of the night something startled the man, and he turned and discovered a woman lying at his feet.

⁹"Who are you?" he asked.

"I am your servant Ruth," she said. "Spread the corner of your garment over me, since you are a kinsman-redeemer."

¹⁰"The LORD bless you, my daughter," he replied. "This kindness is greater than that which you showed earlier: You have not run after the

a 1 Hebrew find rest (see Ruth 1:9)

THE MESSAGE

GOD bless that man! GOD hasn't quite walked out on us after all! He still loves us, in bad times as well as good!"

Naomi went on, "That man, Ruth, is one of our circle of covenant redeemers, a close relative of ours!"

2.21 Ruth the Moabitess said, "Well, listen to this: He also told me, 'Stick with my workers until my harvesting is finished.' "

2.22 Naomi said to Ruth, "That's wonderful, dear daughter! Do that! You'll be safe in the company of his young women; no danger now of being raped in some stranger's field."

2.23 So Ruth did it—she stuck close to Boaz's young women, gleaning in the fields daily until both the barley and wheat harvesting were finished. And she continued living with her mother-in-law.

✝

3.1-2 **3** One day her mother-in-law Naomi said to Ruth, "My dear daughter, isn't it about time I arranged a good home for you so you can have a happy life? And isn't Boaz our close relative, the one with whose young women you've been working? Maybe it's time to make our move. Tonight is the night of Boaz's barley harvest at the threshing floor.

3.3-4 "Take a bath. Put on some perfume. Get all dressed up and go to the threshing floor. But don't let him know you're there until the party is well under way and he's had plenty of food and drink. When you see him slipping off to sleep, watch where he lies down and then go there. Lie at his feet to let him know that you are available to him for marriage. Then wait and see what he says. He'll tell you what to do."

3.5 Ruth said, "If you say so, I'll do it, just as you've told me."

3.6 She went down to the threshing floor and put her mother-in-law's plan into action.

3.7 Boaz had a good time, eating and drinking his fill—he felt great. Then he went off to get some sleep, lying down at the end of a stack of barley. Ruth quietly followed; she lay down to signal her availability for marriage.

3.8 In the middle of the night the man was suddenly startled and sat up. Surprise! This woman asleep at his feet!

3.9 He said, "And who are you?"

She said, "I am Ruth, your maiden; take me under your protecting wing. You're my close relative, you know, in the circle of covenant redeemers—you do have the right to marry me."

3.10-13 He said, "GOD bless you, my dear daughter! What a splendid expression of love! And when you could have had your pick of any of the

NEW INTERNATIONAL VERSION

younger men, whether rich or poor. ¹¹And now, my daughter, don't be afraid. I will do for you all you ask. All my fellow townsmen know that you are a woman of noble character. ¹²Although it is true that I am near of kin, there is a kinsman-redeemer nearer than I. ¹³Stay here for the night, and in the morning if he wants to redeem, good; let him redeem. But if he is not willing, as surely as the LORD lives I will do it. Lie here until morning."

¹⁴So she lay at his feet until morning, but got up before anyone could be recognized; and he said, "Don't let it be known that a woman came to the threshing floor."

¹⁵He also said, "Bring me the shawl you are wearing and hold it out." When she did so, he poured into it six measures of barley and put it on her. Then he^a went back to town.

¹⁶When Ruth came to her mother-in-law, Naomi asked, "How did it go, my daughter?"

Then she told her everything Boaz had done for her ¹⁷and added, "He gave me these six measures of barley, saying, 'Don't go back to your mother-in-law empty-handed.' "

¹⁸Then Naomi said, "Wait, my daughter, until you find out what happens. For the man will not rest until the matter is settled today."

BOAZ MARRIES RUTH

4 Meanwhile Boaz went up to the town gate and sat there. When the kinsman-redeemer he had mentioned came along, Boaz said, "Come over here, my friend, and sit down." So he went over and sat down.

²Boaz took ten of the elders of the town and said, "Sit here," and they did so. ³Then he said to the kinsman-redeemer, "Naomi, who has come back from Moab, is selling the piece of land that belonged to our brother Elimelech. ⁴I thought I should bring the matter to your attention and suggest that you buy it in the presence of these seated here and in the presence of the elders of my people. If you will redeem it, do so. But if you^b will not, tell me, so I will know. For no one has the right to do it except you, and I am next in line."

a 15 Most Hebrew manuscripts; many Hebrew manuscripts, Vulgate and Syriac *she*   *b 4* Many Hebrew manuscripts, Septuagint, Vulgate and Syriac; most Hebrew manuscripts *he*

THE MESSAGE

young men around. And now, my dear daughter, don't you worry about a thing; I'll do all you could want or ask. Everybody in town knows what a courageous woman you are—a real prize! You're right, I am a close relative to you, but there is one even closer than I am. So stay the rest of the night. In the morning, if he wants to exercise his customary rights and responsibilities as the closest covenant redeemer, he'll have his chance; but if he isn't interested, as GOD lives, I'll do it. Now go back to sleep until morning."

3.14 Ruth slept at his feet until dawn, but she got up while it was still dark and wouldn't be recognized. Then Boaz said to himself, "No one must know that Ruth came to the threshing floor."

3.15 So Boaz said, "Bring the shawl you're wearing and spread it out."

She spread it out and he poured it full of barley, six measures, and put it on her shoulders. Then she went back to town.

3.16-17 When she came to her mother-in-law, Naomi asked, "And how did things go, my dear daughter?"

Ruth told her everything that the man had done for her, adding, "And he gave me all this barley besides—six quarts! He told me, 'You can't go back empty-handed to your mother-in-law!' "

3.18 Naomi said, "Sit back and relax, my dear daughter, until we find out how things turn out; that man isn't going to fool around. Mark my words, he's going to get everything wrapped up today."

✝

4.1 **4** Boaz went straight to the public square and took his place there. Before long the "closer relative," the one mentioned earlier by Boaz, strolled by.

"Step aside, old friend," said Boaz. "Take a seat." The man sat down.

4.2 Boaz then gathered ten of the town elders together and said, "Sit down here with us; we've got some business to take care of." And they sat down.

4.3-4 Boaz then said to his relative, "The piece of property that belonged to our relative Elimelech is being sold by his widow Naomi, who has just returned from the country of Moab. I thought you ought to know about it. Buy it back if you want it—you can make it official in the presence of those sitting here and before the town elders. You have first redeemer rights. If you don't want it, tell me so I'll know where I stand. You're first in line to do this and I'm next after you."

NEW INTERNATIONAL VERSION

"I will redeem it," he said.

⁵Then Boaz said, "On the day you buy the land from Naomi and from Ruth the Moabitess, you acquireᵃ the dead man's widow, in order to maintain the name of the dead with his property."

⁶At this, the kinsman-redeemer said, "Then I cannot redeem it because I might endanger my own estate. You redeem it yourself. I cannot do it."

⁷(Now in earlier times in Israel, for the redemption and transfer of property to become final, one party took off his sandal and gave it to the other. This was the method of legalizing transactions in Israel.)

⁸So the kinsman-redeemer said to Boaz, "Buy it yourself." And he removed his sandal.

⁹Then Boaz announced to the elders and all the people, "Today you are witnesses that I have bought from Naomi all the property of Elimelech, Kilion and Mahlon. ¹⁰I have also acquired Ruth the Moabitess, Mahlon's widow, as my wife, in order to maintain the name of the dead with his property, so that his name will not disappear from among his family or from the town records. Today you are witnesses!"

¹¹Then the elders and all those at the gate said, "We are witnesses. May the LORD make the woman who is coming into your home like Rachel and Leah, who together built up the house of Israel. May you have standing in Ephrathah and be famous in Bethlehem. ¹²Through the offspring the LORD gives you by this young woman, may your family be like that of Perez, whom Tamar bore to Judah."

THE GENEALOGY OF DAVID

¹³So Boaz took Ruth and she became his wife. Then he went to her, and the LORD enabled her to conceive, and she gave birth to a son. ¹⁴The women said to Naomi: "Praise be to the LORD, who this day has not left you without a kinsman-redeemer. May he become famous throughout Israel! ¹⁵He will renew your life and sustain you in your old age. For your daughter-in-law, who loves you and who is better to you than seven sons, has given him birth."

ᵃ 5 Hebrew; Vulgate and Syriac *Naomi, you acquire Ruth the Moabitess,*

THE MESSAGE

He said, "I'll buy it."

4.5   Then Boaz added, "You realize, don't you, that when you buy the field from Naomi, you also get Ruth the Moabite, the widow of our dead relative, along with the redeemer responsibility to have children with her to carry on the family inheritance."

4.6   Then the relative said, "Oh, I can't do that—I'd jeopardize my own family's inheritance. You go ahead and buy it—you can have my rights—I can't do it."

✝

4.7   In the olden times in Israel, this is how they handled official business regarding matters of property and inheritance: a man would take off his shoe and give it to the other person. This was the same as an official seal or personal signature in Israel.

4.8   So when Boaz's "redeemer" relative said, "Go ahead and buy it," he signed the deal by pulling off his shoe.

4.9-10   Boaz then addressed the elders and all the people in the town square that day: "You are witnesses today that I have bought from Naomi everything that belonged to Elimelech and Kilion and Mahlon, including responsibility for Ruth the foreigner, the widow of Mahlon—I'll take her as my wife and keep the name of the deceased alive along with his inheritance. The memory and reputation of the deceased is not going to disappear out of this family or from his hometown. To all this you are witnesses this very day."

4.11-12   All the people in the town square that day, backing up the elders, said, "Yes, we are witnesses. May GOD make this woman who is coming into your household like Rachel and Leah, the two women who built the family of Israel. May GOD make you a pillar in Ephrathah and famous in Bethlehem! With the children GOD gives you from this young woman, may your family rival the family of Perez, the son Tamar bore to Judah."

✝

4.13   Boaz married Ruth. She became his wife. Boaz slept with her. By GOD's gracious gift she conceived and had a son.

4.14-15   The town women said to Naomi, "Blessed be GOD! He didn't leave you without family to carry on your life. May this baby grow up to be famous in Israel! He'll make you young again! He'll take care of you in old age. And this daughter-in-law who has brought him into the world and loves you so much, why, she's worth more to you than seven sons!"

NEW INTERNATIONAL VERSION

¹⁶Then Naomi took the child, laid him in her lap and cared for him. ¹⁷The women living there said, "Naomi has a son." And they named him Obed. He was the father of Jesse, the father of David.

¹⁸This, then, is the family line of Perez:

Perez was the father of Hezron,
¹⁹Hezron the father of Ram,
Ram the father of Amminadab,
²⁰Amminadab the father of Nahshon,
Nahshon the father of Salmon,^a
²¹Salmon the father of Boaz,
Boaz the father of Obed,
²²Obed the father of Jesse,
and Jesse the father of David.

THE MESSAGE

4.16   Naomi took the baby and held him in her arms, cuddling him, cooing over him, waiting on him hand and foot.

4.17   The neighborhood women started calling him "Naomi's baby boy!" But his real name was Obed. Obed was the father of Jesse, and Jesse the father of David.

✝

4.18-22 This is the family tree of Perez:
Perez had Hezron,
Hezron had Ram,
Ram had Amminadab,
Amminadab had Nahshon,
Nahshon had Salmon,
Salmon had Boaz,
Boaz had Obed,
Obed had Jesse,
and Jesse had David.

---

^a 20 A few Hebrew manuscripts, some Septuagint manuscripts and Vulgate (see also verse 21 and Septuagint of 1 Chron. 2:11); most Hebrew manuscripts *Salma*

1 SAMUEL

1 SAMUEL

THE BIRTH OF SAMUEL

1 There was a certain man from Ramathaim, a Zuphite[a] from the hill country of Ephraim, whose name was Elkanah son of Jeroham, the son of Elihu, the son of Tohu, the son of Zuph, an Ephraimite. ²He had two wives; one was called Hannah and the other Peninnah. Peninnah had children, but Hannah had none.

³Year after year this man went up from his town to worship and sacrifice to the LORD Almighty at Shiloh, where Hophni and Phinehas, the two sons of Eli, were priests of the LORD. ⁴Whenever the day came for Elkanah to sacrifice, he would give portions of the meat to his wife Peninnah and to all her sons and daughters. ⁵But to Hannah he gave a double portion because he loved her, and the LORD had closed her womb. ⁶And because the LORD had closed her womb, her rival kept provoking her in order to irritate her. ⁷This went on year after year. Whenever Hannah went up to the house of the LORD, her rival provoked her till she wept and would not eat. ⁸Elkanah her husband would say to her, "Hannah, why are you weeping? Why don't you eat? Why are you downhearted? Don't I mean more to you than ten sons?"

⁹Once when they had finished eating and drinking in Shiloh, Hannah stood up. Now Eli the priest was sitting on a chair by the doorpost of the LORD's temple.[b] ¹⁰In bitterness of soul Hannah wept much and prayed to the LORD. ¹¹And she made a vow, saying, "O LORD Almighty, if you will only look upon your servant's misery and remember me, and not forget your servant but give her a son, then I will give him to the LORD for all the days of his life, and no razor will ever be used on his head."

HANNAH POURS OUT HER HEART TO GOD

1.1-2 **1** There once was a man who lived in Ramathaim. He was descended from the old Zuph family in the Ephraim hills. His name was Elkanah. (He was connected with the Zuphs from Ephraim through his father Jeroham, his grandfather Elihu, and his great-grandfather Tohu.) He had two wives. The first was Hannah; the second was Peninnah. Peninnah had children; Hannah did not.

1.3-7 Every year this man went from his hometown up to Shiloh to worship and offer a sacrifice to GOD-of-the-Angel-Armies. Eli and his two sons, Hophni and Phinehas, served as the priests of GOD there. When Elkanah sacrificed, he passed helpings from the sacrificial meal around to his wife Peninnah and all her children, but he always gave an especially generous helping to Hannah because he loved her so much, and because GOD had not given her children. But her rival wife taunted her cruelly, rubbing it in and never letting her forget that GOD had not given her children. This went on year after year. Every time she went to the sanctuary of GOD she could expect to be taunted. Hannah was reduced to tears and had no appetite.

1.8 Her husband Elkanah said, "Oh, Hannah, why are you crying? Why aren't you eating? And why are you so upset? Am I not of more worth to you than ten sons?"

1.9-11 So Hannah ate. Then she pulled herself together, slipped away quietly, and entered the sanctuary. The priest Eli was on duty at the entrance to GOD's Temple in the customary seat. Crushed in soul, Hannah prayed to GOD and cried and cried—inconsolably. Then she made a vow:

> Oh, GOD-of-the-Angel-Armies,
> If you'll take a good, hard look at my pain,
> If you'll quit neglecting me and go into
>   action for me
> By giving me a son,
> I'll give him completely, unreservedly to
>   you.
> I'll set him apart for a life of holy discipline.

---

a 1 Or from Ramathaim Zuphim   *b 9 That is, tabernacle*

NEW INTERNATIONAL VERSION

¹²As she kept on praying to the LORD, Eli observed her mouth. ¹³Hannah was praying in her heart, and her lips were moving but her voice was not heard. Eli thought she was drunk ¹⁴and said to her, "How long will you keep on getting drunk? Get rid of your wine."

¹⁵"Not so, my lord," Hannah replied, "I am a woman who is deeply troubled. I have not been drinking wine or beer; I was pouring out my soul to the LORD. ¹⁶Do not take your servant for a wicked woman; I have been praying here out of my great anguish and grief."

¹⁷Eli answered, "Go in peace, and may the God of Israel grant you what you have asked of him."

¹⁸She said, "May your servant find favor in your eyes." Then she went her way and ate something, and her face was no longer downcast.

¹⁹Early the next morning they arose and worshiped before the LORD and then went back to their home at Ramah. Elkanah lay with Hannah his wife, and the LORD remembered her. ²⁰So in the course of time Hannah conceived and gave birth to a son. She named him Samuel,ᵃ saying, "Because I asked the LORD for him."

HANNAH DEDICATES SAMUEL

²¹When the man Elkanah went up with all his family to offer the annual sacrifice to the LORD and to fulfill his vow, ²²Hannah did not go. She said to her husband, "After the boy is weaned, I will take him and present him before the LORD, and he will live there always."

²³"Do what seems best to you," Elkanah her husband told her. "Stay here until you have weaned him; only may the LORD make good hisᵇ word." So the woman stayed at home and nursed her son until she had weaned him.

²⁴After he was weaned, she took the boy with her, young as he was, along with a three-year-old bull,ᶜ an ephahᵈ of flour and a skin of wine, and brought him to the house of the LORD at Shiloh. ²⁵When they had slaughtered the bull, they brought the boy to Eli, ²⁶and she said to him, "As surely as you live, my lord, I am the woman who stood here beside you praying to the LORD. ²⁷I prayed for this child, and the LORD has granted me what I asked of him. ²⁸So now I give him to the LORD. For his whole life he will be given over to the LORD." And he worshiped the LORD there.

ᵃ 20 Samuel sounds like the Hebrew for heard of God.
ᵇ 23 Masoretic Text; Dead Sea Scrolls, Septuagint and Syriac your   ᶜ 24 Dead Sea Scrolls, Septuagint and Syriac; Masoretic Text with three bulls   ᵈ 24 That is, probably about 3/5 bushel (about 22 liters)

THE MESSAGE

1.12-14   It so happened that as she continued in prayer before GOD, Eli was watching her closely. Hannah was praying in her heart, silently. Her lips moved, but no sound was heard. Eli jumped to the conclusion that she was drunk. He approached her and said, "You're drunk! How long do you plan to keep this up? Sober up, woman!"

1.15-16   Hannah said, "Oh no, sir—please! I'm a woman hard used. I haven't been drinking. Not a drop of wine or beer. The only thing I've been pouring out is my heart, pouring it out to GOD. Don't for a minute think I'm a bad woman. It's because I'm so desperately unhappy and in such pain that I've stayed here so long."

1.17   Eli answered her, "Go in peace. And may the God of Israel give you what you have asked of him."

1.18   "Think well of me—and pray for me!" she said, and went her way. Then she ate heartily, her face radiant.

1.19   Up before dawn, they worshiped GOD and returned home to Ramah. Elkanah slept with Hannah his wife, and GOD began making the necessary arrangements in response to what she had asked.

DEDICATING THE CHILD TO GOD

1.20   Before the year was out, Hannah had conceived and given birth to a son. She named him Samuel, explaining, "I asked GOD for him."

1.21-22   When Elkanah next took his family on their annual trip to Shiloh to worship GOD, offering sacrifices and keeping his vow, Hannah didn't go. She told her husband, "After the child is weaned, I'll bring him myself and present him before GOD—and that's where he'll stay, for good."

1.23-24   Elkanah said to his wife, "Do what you think is best. Stay home until you have weaned him. Yes! Let GOD complete what he has begun!"

So she did. She stayed home and nursed her son until she had weaned him. Then she took him up to Shiloh, bringing also the makings of a generous sacrificial meal—a prize bull, flour, and wine. The child was so young to be sent off!

1.25-28   They first butchered the bull, then brought the child to Eli. Hannah said, "Excuse me, sir. Would you believe that I'm the very woman who was standing before you at this very spot, praying to GOD? I prayed for this child, and GOD gave me what I asked for. And now I have dedicated him to GOD. He's dedicated to GOD for life."

Then and there, they worshiped GOD.

NEW INTERNATIONAL VERSION	THE MESSAGE

NEW INTERNATIONAL VERSION

HANNAH'S PRAYER

2 Then Hannah prayed and said:

"My heart rejoices in the LORD;
    in the LORD my horn[a] is lifted high.
My mouth boasts over my enemies,
    for I delight in your deliverance.

2 "There is no one holy[b] like the LORD;
    there is no one besides you;
    there is no Rock like our God.

3 "Do not keep talking so proudly
    or let your mouth speak such arrogance,
for the LORD is a God who knows,
    and by him deeds are weighed.

4 "The bows of the warriors are broken,
    but those who stumbled are armed with
        strength.
5 Those who were full hire themselves out for
        food,
    but those who were hungry hunger no
        more.
She who was barren has borne seven
        children,
    but she who has had many sons pines
        away.

6 "The LORD brings death and makes alive;
    he brings down to the grave[c] and
        raises up.
7 The LORD sends poverty and wealth;
    he humbles and he exalts.
8 He raises the poor from the dust
    and lifts the needy from the ash heap;
he seats them with princes
    and has them inherit a throne of honor.

"For the foundations of the earth are the
    LORD's;
    upon them he has set the world.
9 He will guard the feet of his saints,
    but the wicked will be silenced in
        darkness.

"It is not by strength that one prevails;
10   those who oppose the LORD will be
        shattered.
He will thunder against them from heaven;
    the LORD will judge the ends of the earth.

"He will give strength to his king
    and exalt the horn of his anointed."

11 Then Elkanah went home to Ramah, but the
boy ministered before the LORD under Eli the
priest.

THE MESSAGE

2.1 **2** Hannah prayed:
    I'm bursting with God-news!
    I'm walking on air.
I'm laughing at my rivals.
    I'm dancing my salvation.

2.2-5 Nothing and no one is holy like GOD,
    no rock mountain like our God.
Don't dare talk pretentiously—
    not a word of boasting, ever!
For GOD knows what's going on.
    He takes the measure of everything that
        happens.
The weapons of the strong are smashed to
        pieces,
    while the weak are infused with fresh
        strength.
The well-fed are out begging in the streets
        for crusts,
    while the hungry are getting second
        helpings.
The barren woman has a houseful of
        children,
    while the mother of many is bereft.

2.6-10 GOD brings death and GOD brings life,
    brings down to the grave and raises up.
GOD brings poverty and GOD brings wealth;
    he lowers, he also lifts up.
He puts poor people on their feet again;
    he rekindles burned-out lives with fresh
        hope,
Restoring dignity and respect to their
        lives—
    a place in the sun!
For the very structures of earth are GOD's;
    he has laid out his operations on a firm
        foundation.
He protectively cares for his faithful
        friends, step by step,
    but leaves the wicked to stumble in the
        dark.
No one makes it in this life by sheer
        muscle!
GOD's enemies will be blasted out of the
        sky,
    crashed in a heap and burned.
GOD will set things right all over the earth,
    he'll give strength to his king,
    he'll set his anointed on top of the
        world!

2.11 Elkanah went home to Ramah. The boy
stayed and served GOD in the company of Eli
the priest.

---

a 1 *Horn* here symbolizes strength; also in verse 10.
b 2 Or *no Holy One*   c 6 Hebrew *Sheol*

NEW INTERNATIONAL VERSION

ELI'S WICKED SONS

¹²Eli's sons were wicked men; they had no regard for the LORD. ¹³Now it was the practice of the priests with the people that whenever anyone offered a sacrifice and while the meat was being boiled, the servant of the priest would come with a three-pronged fork in his hand. ¹⁴He would plunge it into the pan or kettle or caldron or pot, and the priest would take for himself whatever the fork brought up. This is how they treated all the Israelites who came to Shiloh. ¹⁵But even before the fat was burned, the servant of the priest would come and say to the man who was sacrificing, "Give the priest some meat to roast; he won't accept boiled meat from you, but only raw."

¹⁶If the man said to him, "Let the fat be burned up first, and then take whatever you want," the servant would then answer, "No, hand it over now; if you don't, I'll take it by force."

¹⁷This sin of the young men was very great in the LORD's sight, for they*ᵃ* were treating the LORD's offering with contempt.

¹⁸But Samuel was ministering before the LORD—a boy wearing a linen ephod. ¹⁹Each year his mother made him a little robe and took it to him when she went up with her husband to offer the annual sacrifice. ²⁰Eli would bless Elkanah and his wife, saying, "May the LORD give you children by this woman to take the place of the one she prayed for and gave to the LORD." Then they would go home. ²¹And the LORD was gracious to Hannah; she conceived and gave birth to three sons and two daughters. Meanwhile, the boy Samuel grew up in the presence of the LORD.

²²Now Eli, who was very old, heard about everything his sons were doing to all Israel and how they slept with the women who served at the entrance to the Tent of Meeting. ²³So he said to them, "Why do you do such things? I hear from all the people about these wicked deeds of yours. ²⁴No, my sons; it is not a good report that I hear spreading among the LORD's people. ²⁵If a man sins against another man, God*ᵇ* may mediate for him; but if a man sins against the LORD, who will intercede for him?" His sons, however, did not listen to their father's rebuke, for it was the LORD's will to put them to death.

²⁶And the boy Samuel continued to grow in stature and in favor with the LORD and with men.

PROPHECY AGAINST THE HOUSE OF ELI

²⁷Now a man of God came to Eli and said to him, "This is what the LORD says: 'Did I not clear-

---

ᵃ 17 Or men   ᵇ 25 Or the judges

THE MESSAGE

SAMUEL SERVES GOD

2.12-17 Eli's own sons were a bad lot. They didn't know GOD and could not have cared less about the customs of priests among the people. Ordinarily, when someone offered a sacrifice, the priest's servant was supposed to come up and, while the meat was boiling, stab a three-pronged fork into the cooking pot. The priest then got whatever came up on the fork. But this is how Eli's sons treated all the Israelites who came to Shiloh to offer sacrifices to GOD. Before they had even burned the fat to GOD, the priest's servant would interrupt whoever was sacrificing and say, "Hand over some of that meat for the priest to roast. He doesn't like boiled meat; he likes his rare." If the man objected, "First let the fat be burned—God's portion!—then take all you want," the servant would demand, "No, I want it now. If you won't give it, I'll take it." It was a horrible sin these young servants were committing—and right in the presence of GOD!—desecrating the holy offerings to GOD.

2.18-20 In the midst of all this, Samuel, a boy dressed in a priestly linen tunic, served GOD. Additionally, every year his mother would make him a little robe cut to his size and bring it to him when she and her husband came for the annual sacrifice. Eli would bless Elkanah and his wife, saying, "GOD give you children to replace this child you have dedicated to GOD." Then they would go home.

2.21 GOD was most especially kind to Hannah. She had three more sons and two daughters! The boy Samuel stayed at the sanctuary and grew up with GOD.

A HARD LIFE WITH MANY TEARS

2.22-25 By this time Eli was very old. He kept getting reports on how his sons were ripping off the people and sleeping with the women who helped out at the sanctuary. Eli took them to task: "What's going on here? Why are you doing these things? I hear story after story of your corrupt and evil carrying on. Oh, my sons, this is not right! These are terrible reports I'm getting, stories spreading right and left among GOD's people! If you sin against another person, there's help—God's help. But if you sin against GOD, who is around to help?"

2.25-26 But they were far gone in disobedience and refused to listen to a thing their father said. So GOD, who was fed up with them, decreed their death. But the boy Samuel was very much alive, growing up, blessed by GOD and popular with the people.

2.27-30 A holy man came to Eli and said: "This is GOD's message: I revealed myself openly to your

NEW INTERNATIONAL VERSION

ly reveal myself to your father's house when they were in Egypt under Pharaoh? ²⁸I chose your father out of all the tribes of Israel to be my priest, to go up to my altar, to burn incense, and to wear an ephod in my presence. I also gave your father's house all the offerings made with fire by the Israelites. ²⁹Why do you*a* scorn my sacrifice and offering that I prescribed for my dwelling? Why do you honor your sons more than me by fattening yourselves on the choice parts of every offering made by my people Israel?'

³⁰"Therefore the LORD, the God of Israel, declares: 'I promised that your house and your father's house would minister before me forever.' But now the LORD declares: 'Far be it from me! Those who honor me I will honor, but those who despise me will be disdained. ³¹The time is coming when I will cut short your strength and the strength of your father's house, so that there will not be an old man in your family line ³²and you will see distress in my dwelling. Although good will be done to Israel, in your family line there will never be an old man. ³³Every one of you that I do not cut off from my altar will be spared only to blind your eyes with tears and to grieve your heart, and all your descendants will die in the prime of life.

³⁴"'And what happens to your two sons, Hophni and Phinehas, will be a sign to you— they will both die on the same day. ³⁵I will raise up for myself a faithful priest, who will do according to what is in my heart and mind. I will firmly establish his house, and he will minister before my anointed one always. ³⁶Then everyone left in your family line will come and bow down before him for a piece of silver and a crust of bread and plead, "Appoint me to some priestly office so I can have food to eat." ' "

THE LORD CALLS SAMUEL

3 The boy Samuel ministered before the LORD under Eli. In those days the word of the LORD was rare; there were not many visions.

²One night Eli, whose eyes were becoming so weak that he could barely see, was lying down in his usual place. ³The lamp of God had not yet gone out, and Samuel was lying down in the temple*b* of the LORD, where the ark of God was. ⁴Then the LORD called Samuel.

Samuel answered, "Here I am." ⁵And he ran to Eli and said, "Here I am; you called me."

But Eli said, "I did not call; go back and lie down." So he went and lay down.

⁶Again the LORD called, "Samuel!" And Samuel got up and went to Eli and said, "Here I am; you called me."

^a 29 The Hebrew is plural.   ^b 3 That is, tabernacle

THE MESSAGE

ancestors when they were Pharaoh's slaves in Egypt. Out of all the tribes of Israel, I chose your family to be my priests: to preside at the altar, to burn incense, to wear the priestly robes in my presence. I put your ancestral family in charge of all the sacrificial offerings of Israel. So why do you now treat as mere loot these very sacrificial offerings that I commanded for my worship? Why do you treat your sons better than me, turning them loose to get fat on these offerings, and ignoring me? Therefore—this is GOD's word, the God of Israel speaking—I once said that you and your ancestral family would be my priests indefinitely, but now—GOD's word, remember!—there is no way this can continue.

> I honor those who honor me;
> those who scorn me I demean.

2.31-36   "Be well warned: It won't be long before I wipe out both your family and your future family. No one in your family will make it to old age! You'll see good things that I'm doing in Israel, but you'll see it and weep, for no one in your family will live to enjoy it. I will leave one person to serve at my altar, but it will be a hard life, with many tears. Everyone else in your family will die before their time. What happens to your two sons, Hophni and Phinehas, will be the proof: Both will die the same day. Then I'll establish for myself a true priest. He'll do what I want him to do, be what I want him to be. I'll make his position secure and he'll do his work freely in the service of my anointed one. Survivors from your family will come to him begging for handouts, saying, 'Please, give me some priest work, just enough to put some food on the table.' "

"SPEAK, GOD. I'M READY TO LISTEN"

3.1-3   **3** The boy Samuel was serving GOD under Eli's direction. This was at a time when the revelation of GOD was rarely heard or seen. One night Eli was sound asleep (his eyesight was very bad—he could hardly see). It was well before dawn; the sanctuary lamp was still burning. Samuel was still in bed in the Temple of GOD, where the Chest of God rested.

3.4-5   Then GOD called out, "Samuel, Samuel!"

Samuel answered, "Yes? I'm here." Then he ran to Eli saying, "I heard you call. Here I am."

Eli said, "I didn't call you. Go back to bed." And so he did.

3.6-7   GOD called again, "Samuel, Samuel!"

Samuel got up and went to Eli, "I heard you call. Here I am."

NEW INTERNATIONAL VERSION

"My son," Eli said, "I did not call; go back and lie down."

7Now Samuel did not yet know the LORD: The word of the LORD had not yet been revealed to him.

8The LORD called Samuel a third time, and Samuel got up and went to Eli and said, "Here I am; you called me."

Then Eli realized that the LORD was calling the boy. 9So Eli told Samuel, "Go and lie down, and if he calls you, say, 'Speak, LORD, for your servant is listening.'" So Samuel went and lay down in his place.

10The LORD came and stood there, calling as at the other times, "Samuel! Samuel!"

Then Samuel said, "Speak, for your servant is listening."

11And the LORD said to Samuel: "See, I am about to do something in Israel that will make the ears of everyone who hears of it tingle. 12At that time I will carry out against Eli everything I spoke against his family—from beginning to end. 13For I told him that I would judge his family forever because of the sin he knew about; his sons made themselves contemptible,*a* and he failed to restrain them. 14Therefore, I swore to the house of Eli, 'The guilt of Eli's house will never be atoned for by sacrifice or offering.'"

15Samuel lay down until morning and then opened the doors of the house of the LORD. He was afraid to tell Eli the vision, 16but Eli called him and said, "Samuel, my son."

Samuel answered, "Here I am."

17"What was it he said to you?" Eli asked. "Do not hide it from me. May God deal with you, be it ever so severely, if you hide from me anything he told you." 18So Samuel told him everything, hiding nothing from him. Then Eli said, "He is the LORD; let him do what is good in his eyes."

19The LORD was with Samuel as he grew up, and he let none of his words fall to the ground. 20And all Israel from Dan to Beersheba recognized that Samuel was attested as a prophet of the LORD. 21The LORD continued to appear at Shiloh, and there he revealed himself to Samuel through his word.

THE MESSAGE

Again Eli said, "Son, I didn't call you. Go back to bed." (This all happened before Samuel knew GOD for himself. It was before the revelation of GOD had been given to him personally.)

3.8-9 GOD called again, "Samuel!"—the third time! Yet again Samuel got up and went to Eli, "Yes? I heard you call me. Here I am."

That's when it dawned on Eli that GOD was calling the boy. So Eli directed Samuel, "Go back and lie down. If the voice calls again, say, 'Speak, GOD. I'm your servant, ready to listen.'" Samuel returned to his bed.

3.10 Then GOD came and stood before him exactly as before, calling out, "Samuel! Samuel!"

Samuel answered, "Speak. I'm your servant, ready to listen."

3.11-14 GOD said to Samuel, "Listen carefully. I'm getting ready to do something in Israel that is going to shake everyone up and get their attention. The time has come for me to bring down on Eli's family everything I warned him of, every last word of it. I'm letting him know that the time's up. I'm bringing judgment on his family for good. He knew what was going on, that his sons were desecrating God's name and God's place, and he did nothing to stop them. This is my sentence on the family of Eli: The evil of Eli's family can never be wiped out by sacrifice or offering."

3.15 Samuel stayed in bed until morning, then rose early and went about his duties, opening the doors of the sanctuary, but he dreaded having to tell the vision to Eli.

3.16 But then Eli summoned Samuel: "Samuel, my son!"

Samuel came running: "Yes? What can I do for you?"

3.17 "What did he say? Tell it to me, all of it. Don't suppress or soften one word, as God is your judge! I want it all, word for word as he said it to you."

3.18 So Samuel told him, word for word. He held back nothing.

Eli said, "He is GOD. Let him do whatever he thinks best."

3.19-21 Samuel grew up. GOD was with him, and Samuel's prophetic record was flawless. Everyone in Israel, from Dan in the north to Beersheba in the south, recognized that Samuel was the real thing—a true prophet of GOD. GOD continued to show up at Shiloh, revealed through his word to Samuel at Shiloh.

---

a 13 Masoretic Text; an ancient Hebrew scribal tradition and Septuagint *sons blasphemed God*

NEW INTERNATIONAL VERSION

4 And Samuel's word came to all Israel.

THE PHILISTINES CAPTURE THE ARK

Now the Israelites went out to fight against the Philistines. The Israelites camped at Ebenezer, and the Philistines at Aphek. ²The Philistines deployed their forces to meet Israel, and as the battle spread, Israel was defeated by the Philistines, who killed about four thousand of them on the battlefield. ³When the soldiers returned to camp, the elders of Israel asked, "Why did the LORD bring defeat upon us today before the Philistines? Let us bring the ark of the LORD's covenant from Shiloh, so that it*a* may go with us and save us from the hand of our enemies."

⁴So the people sent men to Shiloh, and they brought back the ark of the covenant of the LORD Almighty, who is enthroned between the cherubim. And Eli's two sons, Hophni and Phinehas, were there with the ark of the covenant of God.

⁵When the ark of the LORD's covenant came into the camp, all Israel raised such a great shout that the ground shook. ⁶Hearing the uproar, the Philistines asked, "What's all this shouting in the Hebrew camp?"

When they learned that the ark of the LORD had come into the camp, ⁷the Philistines were afraid. "A god has come into the camp," they said. "We're in trouble! Nothing like this has happened before. ⁸Woe to us! Who will deliver us from the hand of these mighty gods? They are the gods who struck the Egyptians with all kinds of plagues in the desert. ⁹Be strong, Philistines! Be men, or you will be subject to the Hebrews, as they have been to you. Be men, and fight!"

¹⁰So the Philistines fought, and the Israelites were defeated and every man fled to his tent. The slaughter was very great; Israel lost thirty thousand foot soldiers. ¹¹The ark of God was captured, and Eli's two sons, Hophni and Phinehas, died.

DEATH OF ELI

¹²That same day a Benjamite ran from the battle line and went to Shiloh, his clothes torn and dust on his head. ¹³When he arrived, there was Eli sitting on his chair by the side of the road, watching, because his heart feared for the ark of God. When the man entered the town and told what had happened, the whole town sent up a cry.

¹⁴Eli heard the outcry and asked, "What is the meaning of this uproar?"

a 3 Or he

THE MESSAGE

THE CHEST OF GOD IS TAKEN

4.1-3 4 Whatever Samuel said was broadcast all through Israel. Israel went to war against the Philistines. Israel set up camp at Ebenezer, the Philistines at Aphek. The Philistines marched out to meet Israel, the fighting spread, and Israel was badly beaten—about 4,000 soldiers left dead on the field. When the troops returned to camp, Israel's elders said, "Why has GOD given us such a beating today by the Philistines? Let's go to Shiloh and get the Chest of GOD's Covenant. It will accompany us and save us from the grip of our enemies."

4.4 So the army sent orders to Shiloh. They brought the Chest of the Covenant of GOD, the GOD-of-the-Angel-Armies, the Cherubim-Enthroned-GOD. Eli's two sons, Hophni and Phinehas, accompanied the Chest of the Covenant of God.

4.5-6 When the Chest of the Covenant of GOD was brought into camp, everyone gave a huge cheer. The shouts were like thunderclaps shaking the very ground. The Philistines heard the shouting and wondered what on earth was going on: "What's all this shouting among the Hebrews?"

4.6-9 Then they learned that the Chest of GOD had entered the Hebrew camp. The Philistines panicked: "Their gods have come to their camp! Nothing like this has ever happened before. We're done for! Who can save us from the clutches of these supergods? These are the same gods who hit the Egyptians with all kinds of plagues out in the wilderness. On your feet, Philistines! Courage! We're about to become slaves to the Hebrews, just as they have been slaves to us. Show what you're made of! Fight for your lives!"

4.10-11 And did they ever fight! It turned into a rout. They thrashed Israel so mercilessly that the Israelite soldiers ran for their lives, leaving behind an incredible 30,000 dead. As if that wasn't bad enough, the Chest of God was taken and the two sons of Eli—Hophni and Phinehas—were killed.

GLORY IS EXILED FROM ISRAEL

4.12-16 Immediately, a Benjaminite raced from the front lines back to Shiloh. Shirt torn and face smeared with dirt, he entered the town. Eli was sitting on his stool beside the road keeping vigil, for he was extremely worried about the Chest of God. When the man ran straight into town to tell the bad news, everyone wept. They were appalled. Eli heard the loud wailing and asked, "Why this uproar?" The messenger hur-

NEW INTERNATIONAL VERSION

The man hurried over to Eli, [15]who was ninety-eight years old and whose eyes were set so that he could not see. [16]He told Eli, "I have just come from the battle line; I fled from it this very day."

Eli asked, "What happened, my son?"

[17]The man who brought the news replied, "Israel fled before the Philistines, and the army has suffered heavy losses. Also your two sons, Hophni and Phinehas, are dead, and the ark of God has been captured."

[18]When he mentioned the ark of God, Eli fell backward off his chair by the side of the gate. His neck was broken and he died, for he was an old man and heavy. He had led[a] Israel forty years.

[19]His daughter-in-law, the wife of Phinehas, was pregnant and near the time of delivery. When she heard the news that the ark of God had been captured and that her father-in-law and her husband were dead, she went into labor and gave birth, but was overcome by her labor pains. [20]As she was dying, the women attending her said, "Don't despair; you have given birth to a son." But she did not respond or pay any attention.

[21]She named the boy Ichabod,[b] saying, "The glory has departed from Israel"—because of the capture of the ark of God and the deaths of her father-in-law and her husband. [22]She said, "The glory has departed from Israel, for the ark of God has been captured."

THE ARK IN ASHDOD AND EKRON

5 After the Philistines had captured the ark of God, they took it from Ebenezer to Ashdod. [2]Then they carried the ark into Dagon's temple and set it beside Dagon. [3]When the people of Ashdod rose early the next day, there was Dagon, fallen on his face on the ground before the ark of the LORD! They took Dagon and put him back in his place. [4]But the following morning when they rose, there was Dagon, fallen on his face on the ground before the ark of the LORD! His head and hands had been broken off and were lying on the threshold; only his body remained. [5]That is why to this day neither the priests of Dagon nor any others who enter Dagon's temple at Ashdod step on the threshold.

[6]The LORD's hand was heavy upon the people of Ashdod and its vicinity; he brought devastation upon them and afflicted them with tumors.[c] [7]When the men of Ashdod saw what was happening, they said, "The ark of the god of Israel must not stay here with us, because his hand is

---

[a] 18 Traditionally *judged*   [b] 21 *Ichabod* means *no glory.*
[c] 6 Hebrew; Septuagint and Vulgate *tumors. And rats appeared in their land, and death and destruction were throughout the city*

THE MESSAGE

ried over and reported. Eli was ninety-eight years old then, and blind. The man said to Eli, "I've just come from the front, barely escaping with my life."

"And so, my son," said Eli, "what happened?"

4.17 The messenger answered, "Israel scattered before the Philistines. The defeat was catastrophic, with enormous losses. Your sons Hophni and Phinehas died, and the Chest of God was taken."

4.18 At the words, "Chest of God," Eli fell backwards off his stool where he sat next to the gate. Eli was an old man, and very fat. When he fell, he broke his neck and died. He had led Israel forty years.

4.19-20 His daughter-in-law, the wife of Phinehas, was pregnant and ready to deliver. When she heard that the Chest of God had been taken and that both her father-in-law and her husband were dead, she went to her knees to give birth, going into hard labor. As she was about to die, her midwife said, "Don't be afraid. You've given birth to a son!" But she gave no sign that she had heard.

4.21-22 The Chest of God gone, father-in-law dead, husband dead, she named the boy Ichabod (Glory's-Gone), saying, "Glory is exiled from Israel since the Chest of God was taken."

THREATENED WITH MASS DEATH

5.1-2 **5** Once the Philistines had seized the Chest of God, they took it from Ebenezer to Ashdod, brought it into the shrine of Dagon, and placed it alongside the idol of Dagon.

5.3-5 Next morning when the citizens of Ashdod got up, they were shocked to find Dagon toppled from his place, flat on his face before the Chest of GOD. They picked him up and put him back where he belonged. First thing the next morning they found him again, toppled and flat on his face before the Chest of GOD. Dagon's head and arms were broken off, strewn across the entrance. Only his torso was in one piece. (That's why even today, the priests of Dagon and visitors to the Dagon shrine in Ashdod avoid stepping on the threshold.)

5.6 GOD was hard on the citizens of Ashdod. He devastated them by hitting them with tumors. This happened in both the town and the surrounding neighborhoods. He let loose rats among them. Jumping from ships there, rats swarmed all over the city! And everyone was deathly afraid.

5.7-8 When the leaders of Ashdod saw what was going on, they decided, "The chest of the god of Israel has got to go. We can't handle this,

NEW INTERNATIONAL VERSION

heavy upon us and upon Dagon our god." ⁸So they called together all the rulers of the Philistines and asked them, "What shall we do with the ark of the god of Israel?"

They answered, "Have the ark of the god of Israel moved to Gath." So they moved the ark of the God of Israel.

⁹But after they had moved it, the LORD's hand was against that city, throwing it into a great panic. He afflicted the people of the city, both young and old, with an outbreak of tumors.ᵃ ¹⁰So they sent the ark of God to Ekron.

As the ark of God was entering Ekron, the people of Ekron cried out, "They have brought the ark of the god of Israel around to us to kill us and our people." ¹¹So they called together all the rulers of the Philistines and said, "Send the ark of the god of Israel away; let it go back to its own place, or itᵇ will kill us and our people." For death had filled the city with panic; God's hand was very heavy upon it. ¹²Those who did not die were afflicted with tumors, and the outcry of the city went up to heaven.

THE ARK RETURNED TO ISRAEL

6 When the ark of the LORD had been in Philistine territory seven months, ²the Philistines called for the priests and the diviners and said, "What shall we do with the ark of the LORD? Tell us how we should send it back to its place."

³They answered, "If you return the ark of the god of Israel, do not send it away empty, but by all means send a guilt offering to him. Then you will be healed, and you will know why his hand has not been lifted from you."

⁴The Philistines asked, "What guilt offering should we send to him?"

They replied, "Five gold tumors and five gold rats, according to the number of the Philistine rulers, because the same plague has struck both you and your rulers. ⁵Make models of the tumors and of the rats that are destroying the country, and pay honor to Israel's god. Perhaps he will lift his hand from you and your gods and your land. ⁶Why do you harden your hearts as the Egyptians and Pharaoh did? When heᶜ treated them harshly, did they not send the Israelites out so they could go on their way?

⁷"Now then, get a new cart ready, with two cows that have calved and have never been yoked. Hitch the cows to the cart, but take their calves away and pen them up. ⁸Take the ark of the LORD and put it on the cart, and in a chest beside it put the gold objects you are sending

THE MESSAGE

and neither can our god Dagon." They called together all the Philistine leaders and put it to them: "How can we get rid of the chest of the god of Israel?"

The leaders agreed: "Move it to Gath." So they moved the Chest of the God of Israel to Gath.

5.9 But as soon as they moved it there, GOD came down hard on that city, too. It was mass hysteria! He hit them with tumors. Tumors broke out on everyone in town, young and old.

5.10-12 So they sent the Chest of God on to Ekron, but as the Chest was being brought into town, the people shouted in protest, "You'll kill us all by bringing in this Chest of the God of Israel!" They called the Philistine leaders together and demanded, "Get it out of here, this Chest of the God of Israel. Send it back where it came from. We're threatened with mass death!" For everyone was scared to death when the Chest of God showed up. God was already coming down very hard on the place. Those who didn't die were hit with tumors. All over the city cries of pain and lament filled the air.

GOLD TUMORS AND RATS

6.1-2 **6** After the Chest of GOD had been among the Philistine people for seven months, the Philistine leaders called together their religious professionals, the priests, and experts on the supernatural for consultation: "How can we get rid of this Chest of GOD, get it off our hands without making things worse? Tell us!"

6.3 They said, "If you're going to send the Chest of the God of Israel back, don't just dump it on them. Pay compensation. Then you will be healed. After you're in the clear again, God will let up on you. Why wouldn't he?"

6.4-6 "And what exactly would make for adequate compensation?"

"Five gold tumors and five gold rats," they said, "to match the number of Philistine leaders. Since all of you—leaders and people—suffered the same plague, make replicas of the tumors and rats that are devastating the country and present them as an offering to the glory of the God of Israel. Then maybe he'll ease up and not be so hard on you and your gods, and on your country. Why be stubborn like the Egyptians and Pharaoh? God didn't quit pounding on them until they let the people go. Only then did he let up.

6.7-9 "So here's what you do: Take a brand-new oxcart and two cows that have never been in harness. Hitch the cows to the oxcart and send their calves back to the barn. Put the Chest of GOD on the cart. Secure the gold replicas of the tumors and rats that you are offering as com-

---

ᵃ 9 Or with tumors in the groin (see Septuagint)
ᵇ 11 Or he   ᶜ 6 That is, God

NEW INTERNATIONAL VERSION

back to him as a guilt offering. Send it on its way, [9]but keep watching it. If it goes up to its own territory, toward Beth Shemesh, then the LORD has brought this great disaster on us. But if it does not, then we will know that it was not his hand that struck us and that it happened to us by chance."

[10]So they did this. They took two such cows and hitched them to the cart and penned up their calves. [11]They placed the ark of the LORD on the cart and along with it the chest containing the gold rats and the models of the tumors. [12]Then the cows went straight up toward Beth Shemesh, keeping on the road and lowing all the way; they did not turn to the right or to the left. The rulers of the Philistines followed them as far as the border of Beth Shemesh.

[13]Now the people of Beth Shemesh were harvesting their wheat in the valley, and when they looked up and saw the ark, they rejoiced at the sight. [14]The cart came to the field of Joshua of Beth Shemesh, and there it stopped beside a large rock. The people chopped up the wood of the cart and sacrificed the cows as a burnt offering to the LORD. [15]The Levites took down the ark of the LORD, together with the chest containing the gold objects, and placed them on the large rock. On that day the people of Beth Shemesh offered burnt offerings and made sacrifices to the LORD. [16]The five rulers of the Philistines saw all this and then returned that same day to Ekron.

[17]These are the gold tumors the Philistines sent as a guilt offering to the LORD—one each for Ashdod, Gaza, Ashkelon, Gath and Ekron. [18]And the number of the gold rats was according to the number of Philistine towns belonging to the five rulers—the fortified towns with their country villages. The large rock, on which[a] they set the ark of the LORD, is a witness to this day in the field of Joshua of Beth Shemesh.

[19]But God struck down some of the men of Beth Shemesh, putting seventy[b] of them to death because they had looked into the ark of the LORD. The people mourned because of the heavy blow the LORD had dealt them, [20]and the men of Beth Shemesh asked, "Who can stand in the presence of the LORD, this holy God? To whom will the ark go up from here?"

[21]Then they sent messengers to the people of Kiriath Jearim, saying, "The Philistines have returned the ark of the LORD. Come down and take it up to your place."

---

[a] 18 A few Hebrew manuscripts (see also Septuagint); most Hebrew manuscripts *villages as far as Greater Abel, where*
[b] 19 A few Hebrew manuscripts; most Hebrew manuscripts and Septuagint *50,070*

THE MESSAGE

pensation in a sack and set them next to the Chest. Then send it off. But keep your eyes on it. If it heads straight back home to where it came from, toward Beth Shemesh, it is clear that this catastrophe is a divine judgment, but if not, we'll know that God had nothing to do with it—it was just an accident."

6.10-12 So that's what they did: They hitched two cows to the cart, put their calves in the barn, and placed the Chest of GOD and the sack of gold rats and tumors on the cart. The cows headed straight for home, down the road to Beth Shemesh, straying neither right nor left, mooing all the way. The Philistine leaders followed them to the outskirts of Beth Shemesh.

6.13-15 The people of Beth Shemesh were harvesting wheat in the valley. They looked up and saw the Chest. Jubilant, they ran to meet it. The cart came into the field of Joshua, a Beth Shemeshite, and stopped there beside a huge boulder. The harvesters tore the cart to pieces, then chopped up the wood and sacrificed the cows as a burnt offering to GOD. The Levites took charge of the Chest of GOD and the sack containing the gold offerings, placing them on the boulder. Offering the sacrifices, everyone in Beth Shemesh worshiped GOD most heartily that day.

6.16 When the five Philistine leaders saw what they came to see, they returned the same day to Ekron.

6.17-18 The five gold replicas of the tumors were offered by the Philistines in compensation for the cities of Ashdod, Gaza, Ashkelon, Gath, and Ekron. The five gold rats matched the number of Philistine towns, both large and small, ruled by the five leaders. The big boulder on which they placed the Chest of GOD is still there in the field of Joshua of Beth Shemesh, a landmark.

IF YOU ARE SERIOUS ABOUT COMING BACK TO GOD

6.19-20 God struck some of the men of Beth Shemesh who, out of curiosity, irreverently peeked into the Chest of GOD. Seventy died. The whole town was in mourning, reeling under the hard blow from GOD, and questioning, "Who can stand before GOD, this holy God? And who can we get to take this Chest off our hands?"

6.21 They sent emissaries to Kiriath Jearim, saying, "The Philistines have returned the Chest of GOD. Come down and get it."

NEW INTERNATIONAL VERSION

7 ¹So the men of Kiriath Jearim came and took up the ark of the LORD. They took it to Abinadab's house on the hill and consecrated Eleazar his son to guard the ark of the LORD.

SAMUEL SUBDUES THE PHILISTINES AT MIZPAH

²It was a long time, twenty years in all, that the ark remained at Kiriath Jearim, and all the people of Israel mourned and sought after the LORD. ³And Samuel said to the whole house of Israel, "If you are returning to the LORD with all your hearts, then rid yourselves of the foreign gods and the Ashtoreths and commit yourselves to the LORD and serve him only, and he will deliver you out of the hand of the Philistines." ⁴So the Israelites put away their Baals and Ashtoreths, and served the LORD only.

⁵Then Samuel said, "Assemble all Israel at Mizpah and I will intercede with the LORD for you." ⁶When they had assembled at Mizpah, they drew water and poured it out before the LORD. On that day they fasted and there they confessed, "We have sinned against the LORD." And Samuel was leader[a] of Israel at Mizpah.

⁷When the Philistines heard that Israel had assembled at Mizpah, the rulers of the Philistines came up to attack them. And when the Israelites heard of it, they were afraid because of the Philistines. ⁸They said to Samuel, "Do not stop crying out to the LORD our God for us, that he may rescue us from the hand of the Philistines." ⁹Then Samuel took a suckling lamb and offered it up as a whole burnt offering to the LORD. He cried out to the LORD on Israel's behalf, and the LORD answered him.

¹⁰While Samuel was sacrificing the burnt offering, the Philistines drew near to engage Israel in battle. But that day the LORD thundered with loud thunder against the Philistines and threw them into such a panic that they were routed before the Israelites. ¹¹The men of Israel rushed out of Mizpah and pursued the Philistines, slaughtering them along the way to a point below Beth Car.

¹²Then Samuel took a stone and set it up between Mizpah and Shen. He named it Ebenezer,[b] saying, "Thus far has the LORD helped us." ¹³So the Philistines were subdued and did not invade Israelite territory again.

Throughout Samuel's lifetime, the hand of the

THE MESSAGE

7 And they did. The men of Kiriath Jearim came and got the Chest of GOD and delivered it to the house of Abinadab on the hill. They ordained his son, Eleazar, to take responsibility for the Chest of GOD.

7.2 From the time that the Chest came to rest in Kiriath Jearim, a long time passed—twenty years it was—and throughout Israel there was a widespread, fearful movement toward GOD.

7.3 Then Samuel addressed the house of Israel: "If you are truly serious about coming back to GOD, clean house. Get rid of the foreign gods and fertility goddesses, ground yourselves firmly in GOD, worship him and him alone, and he'll save you from Philistine oppression."

7.4 They did it. They got rid of the gods and goddesses, the images of Baal and Ashtoreth, and gave their exclusive attention and service to GOD.

7.5 Next Samuel said, "Get everybody together at Mizpah and I'll pray for you."

7.6 So everyone assembled at Mizpah. They drew water from the wells and poured it out before GOD in a ritual of cleansing. They fasted all day and prayed, "We have sinned against GOD."

So Samuel prepared the Israelites for holy war there at Mizpah.

THE PLACE WHERE GOD HELPED US

7.7 When the Philistines heard that Israel was meeting at Mizpah, the Philistine leaders went on the offensive. Israel got the report and became frightened—Philistines on the move again!

7.8 They pleaded with Samuel, "Pray with all your might! And don't let up! Pray to GOD, our God, that he'll save us from the boot of the Philistines."

7.9 Samuel took a young lamb not yet weaned and offered it whole as a Whole-Burnt-Offering to GOD. He prayed fervently to GOD, interceding for Israel. And GOD answered.

7.10-12 While Samuel was offering the sacrifice, the Philistines came within range to fight Israel. Just then GOD thundered, a huge thunderclap exploding among the Philistines. They panicked—mass confusion!—and ran helter-skelter from Israel. Israel poured out of Mizpah and gave chase, killing Philistines right and left, to a point just beyond Beth Car. Samuel took a single rock and set it upright between Mizpah and Shen. He named it "Ebenezer" (Rock of Help), saying, "This marks the place where GOD helped us."

7.13-14 The Philistines learned their lesson and stayed home—no more border crossings. GOD was hard on the Philistines all through Samuel's

---

[a] 6 Traditionally *judge*   [b] 12 *Ebenezer* means *stone of help*.

NEW INTERNATIONAL VERSION

LORD was against the Philistines. ¹⁴The towns from Ekron to Gath that the Philistines had captured from Israel were restored to her, and Israel delivered the neighboring territory from the power of the Philistines. And there was peace between Israel and the Amorites.

¹⁵Samuel continued as judge over Israel all the days of his life. ¹⁶From year to year he went on a circuit from Bethel to Gilgal to Mizpah, judging Israel in all those places. ¹⁷But he always went back to Ramah, where his home was, and there he also judged Israel. And he built an altar there to the LORD.

ISRAEL ASKS FOR A KING

8 When Samuel grew old, he appointed his sons as judges for Israel. ²The name of his firstborn was Joel and the name of his second was Abijah, and they served at Beersheba. ³But his sons did not walk in his ways. They turned aside after dishonest gain and accepted bribes and perverted justice.

⁴So all the elders of Israel gathered together and came to Samuel at Ramah. ⁵They said to him, "You are old, and your sons do not walk in your ways; now appoint a king to lead*ᵃ* us, such as all the other nations have."

⁶But when they said, "Give us a king to lead us," this displeased Samuel; so he prayed to the LORD. ⁷And the LORD told him: "Listen to all that the people are saying to you; it is not you they have rejected, but they have rejected me as their king. ⁸As they have done from the day I brought them up out of Egypt until this day, forsaking me and serving other gods, so they are doing to you. ⁹Now listen to them; but warn them solemnly and let them know what the king who will reign over them will do."

¹⁰Samuel told all the words of the LORD to the people who were asking him for a king. ¹¹He said, "This is what the king who will reign over you will do: He will take your sons and make them serve with his chariots and horses, and they will run in front of his chariots. ¹²Some he will assign to be commanders of thousands and commanders of fifties, and others to plow his ground and reap his harvest, and still others to make weapons of war and equipment for his chariots. ¹³He will take your daughters to be perfumers and cooks and bakers. ¹⁴He will take the best of your fields and vineyards and olive groves and give them to his attendants. ¹⁵He will take a tenth of your grain and of your vintage and give it to his officials and attendants. ¹⁶Your menservants and maidservants and the best of your

ᵃ 5 Traditionally judge; also in verses 6 and 20

THE MESSAGE

lifetime. All the cities from Ekron to Gath that the Philistines had taken from Israel were restored. Israel also freed the surrounding countryside from Philistine control. And there was peace between Israel and the Amorites.

7.15-17 Samuel gave solid leadership to Israel his entire life. Every year he went on a circuit from Bethel to Gilgal to Mizpah. He gave leadership to Israel in each of these places. But always he would return to Ramah, where he lived, and preside from there. That is where he built an altar to GOD.

REJECTING GOD AS THE KING

8.1-3 8 When Samuel got to be an old man, he set his sons up as judges in Israel. His firstborn son was named Joel, the name of his second, Abijah. They were assigned duty in Beersheba. But his sons didn't take after him; they were out for what they could get for themselves, taking bribes, corrupting justice.

8.4-5 Fed up, all the elders of Israel got together and confronted Samuel at Ramah. They presented their case: "Look, you're an old man, and your sons aren't following in your footsteps. Here's what we want you to do: Appoint a king to rule us, just like everybody else."

8.6 When Samuel heard their demand—"Give us a king to rule us!"—he was crushed. How awful! Samuel prayed to GOD.

8.7-9 GOD answered Samuel, "Go ahead and do what they're asking. They are not rejecting you. They've rejected me as their King. From the day I brought them out of Egypt until this very day they've been behaving like this, leaving me for other gods. And now they're doing it to you. So let them have their own way. But warn them of what they're in for. Tell them the way kings operate, just what they're likely to get from a king."

8.10-18 So Samuel told them, delivered GOD's warning to the people who were asking him to give them a king. He said, "This is the way the kind of king you're talking about operates. He'll take your sons and make soldiers of them—chariotry, cavalry, infantry, regimented in battalions and squadrons. He'll put some to forced labor on his farms, plowing and harvesting, and others to making either weapons of war or chariots in which he can ride in luxury. He'll put your daughters to work as beauticians and waitresses and cooks. He'll conscript your best fields, vineyards, and orchards and hand them over to his special friends. He'll tax your harvests and vintage to support his extensive bureaucracy. Your prize workers and best animals he'll

NEW INTERNATIONAL VERSION

cattle[a] and donkeys he will take for his own use. [17]He will take a tenth of your flocks, and you yourselves will become his slaves. [18]When that day comes, you will cry out for relief from the king you have chosen, and the LORD will not answer you in that day."

[19]But the people refused to listen to Samuel. "No!" they said. "We want a king over us. [20]Then we will be like all the other nations, with a king to lead us and to go out before us and fight our battles."

[21]When Samuel heard all that the people said, he repeated it before the LORD. [22]The LORD answered, "Listen to them and give them a king."

Then Samuel said to the men of Israel, "Everyone go back to his town."

SAMUEL ANOINTS SAUL

9 There was a Benjamite, a man of standing, whose name was Kish son of Abiel, the son of Zeror, the son of Becorath, the son of Aphiah of Benjamin. [2]He had a son named Saul, an impressive young man without equal among the Israelites—a head taller than any of the others.

[3]Now the donkeys belonging to Saul's father Kish were lost, and Kish said to his son Saul, "Take one of the servants with you and go and look for the donkeys." [4]So he passed through the hill country of Ephraim and through the area around Shalisha, but they did not find them. They went on into the district of Shaalim, but the donkeys were not there. Then he passed through the territory of Benjamin, but they did not find them.

[5]When they reached the district of Zuph, Saul said to the servant who was with him, "Come, let's go back, or my father will stop thinking about the donkeys and start worrying about us."

[6]But the servant replied, "Look, in this town there is a man of God; he is highly respected, and everything he says comes true. Let's go there now. Perhaps he will tell us what way to take."

[7]Saul said to his servant, "If we go, what can we give the man? The food in our sacks is gone. We have no gift to take to the man of God. What do we have?"

[8]The servant answered him again. "Look," he said, "I have a quarter of a shekel[b] of silver. I will give it to the man of God so that he will tell us what way to take." [9](Formerly in Israel, if a man went to inquire of God, he would say, "Come, let us go to the seer," because the prophet of today used to be called a seer.)

THE MESSAGE

take for his own use. He'll lay a tax on your flocks and you'll end up no better than slaves. The day will come when you will cry in desperation because of this king you so much want for yourselves. But don't expect GOD to answer."

8.19-20 But the people wouldn't listen to Samuel. "No!" they said. "We will have a king to rule us! Then we'll be just like all the other nations. Our king will rule us and lead us and fight our battles."

8.21-22 Samuel took in what they said and rehearsed it with GOD. GOD told Samuel, "Do what they say. Make them a king."

Then Samuel dismissed the men of Israel: "Go home, each of you to your own city."

SAUL—HEAD AND SHOULDERS ABOVE THE CROWD

9 There was a man from the tribe of Benjamin named Kish. He was the son of Abiel, grandson of Zeror, great-grandson of Becorath, great-great-grandson of Aphiah—a Benjaminite of stalwart character. He had a son, Saul, a most handsome young man. There was none finer—he literally stood head and shoulders above the crowd!

9.3-4 Some of Kish's donkeys got lost. Kish said to his son, "Saul, take one of the servants with you and go look for the donkeys." Saul took one of the servants and went to find the donkeys. They went into the hill country of Ephraim around Shalisha, but didn't find them. Then they went over to Shaalim—no luck. Then to Jabin, and still nothing.

9.5 When they got to Zuph, Saul said to the young man with him, "Enough of this. Let's go back. Soon my father is going to forget about the donkeys and start worrying about us."

9.6 He replied, "Not so fast. There's a holy man in this town. He carries a lot of weight around here. What he says is always right on the mark. Maybe he can tell us where to go."

9.7 Saul said, "If we go, what do we have to give him? There's no more bread in our sacks. We've nothing to bring as a gift to the holy man. Do we have anything else?"

9.8-9 The servant spoke up, "Look, I just happen to have this silver coin! I'll give it to the holy man and he'll tell us how to proceed!" (In former times in Israel, a person who wanted to seek God's word on a matter would say, "Let's visit the Seer," because the one we now call "the Prophet" used to be called "the Seer.")

---

[a] 16 Septuagint; Hebrew *young men*   [b] 8 That is, about 1/10 ounce (about 3 grams)

NEW INTERNATIONAL VERSION

¹⁰"Good," Saul said to his servant. "Come, let's go." So they set out for the town where the man of God was.

¹¹As they were going up the hill to the town, they met some girls coming out to draw water, and they asked them, "Is the seer here?"

¹²"He is," they answered. "He's ahead of you. Hurry now; he has just come to our town today, for the people have a sacrifice at the high place. ¹³As soon as you enter the town, you will find him before he goes up to the high place to eat. The people will not begin eating until he comes, because he must bless the sacrifice; afterward, those who are invited will eat. Go up now; you should find him about this time."

¹⁴They went up to the town, and as they were entering it, there was Samuel, coming toward them on his way up to the high place.

¹⁵Now the day before Saul came, the LORD had revealed this to Samuel: ¹⁶"About this time tomorrow I will send you a man from the land of Benjamin. Anoint him leader over my people Israel; he will deliver my people from the hand of the Philistines. I have looked upon my people, for their cry has reached me."

¹⁷When Samuel caught sight of Saul, the LORD said to him, "This is the man I spoke to you about; he will govern my people."

¹⁸Saul approached Samuel in the gateway and asked, "Would you please tell me where the seer's house is?"

¹⁹"I am the seer," Samuel replied. "Go up ahead of me to the high place, for today you are to eat with me, and in the morning I will let you go and will tell you all that is in your heart. ²⁰As for the donkeys you lost three days ago, do not worry about them; they have been found. And to whom is all the desire of Israel turned, if not to you and all your father's family?"

²¹Saul answered, "But am I not a Benjamite, from the smallest tribe of Israel, and is not my clan the least of all the clans of the tribe of Benjamin? Why do you say such a thing to me?"

²²Then Samuel brought Saul and his servant into the hall and seated them at the head of those who were invited—about thirty in number. ²³Samuel said to the cook, "Bring the piece of meat I gave you, the one I told you to lay aside."

²⁴So the cook took up the leg with what was on it and set it in front of Saul. Samuel said, "Here is what has been kept for you. Eat, because it was set aside for you for this occasion, from the time I said, 'I have invited guests.' " And Saul dined with Samuel that day.

²⁵After they came down from the high place to the town, Samuel talked with Saul on the roof of

THE MESSAGE

9.10 "Good," said Saul, "let's go." And they set off for the town where the holy man lived.

9.11 As they were climbing up the hill into the town, they met some girls who were coming out to draw water. They said to them, "Is this where the Seer lives?"

9.12-13 They answered, "It sure is—just ahead. Hurry up. He's come today because the people have prepared a sacrifice at the shrine. As soon as you enter the town, you can catch him before he goes up to the shrine to eat. The people won't eat until he arrives, for he has to bless the sacrifice. Only then can everyone eat. So get going. You're sure to find him!"

9.14 They continued their climb and entered the city. And then there he was—Samuel!—coming straight toward them on his way to the shrine!

9.15-16 The very day before, GOD had confided in Samuel, "This time tomorrow, I'm sending a man from the land of Benjamin to meet you. You're to anoint him as prince over my people Israel. He will free my people from Philistine oppression. Yes, I know all about their hard circumstances. I've heard their cries for help."

9.17 The moment Samuel laid eyes on Saul, GOD said, "He's the one, the man I told you about. This is the one who will keep my people in check."

9.18 Saul came up to Samuel in the street and said, "Pardon me, but can you tell me where the Seer lives?"

9.19-20 "I'm the Seer," said Samuel. "Accompany me to the shrine and eat with me. In the morning I'll tell you all about what's on your mind, and send you on your way. And by the way, your lost donkeys—the ones you've been hunting for the last three days—have been found, so don't worry about them. At this moment, Israel's future is in your hands."

9.21 Saul answered, "But I'm only a Benjaminite, from the smallest of Israel's tribes, and from the most insignificant clan in the tribe at that. Why are you talking to me like this?"

9.22-23 Samuel took Saul and his servant and led them into the dining hall at the shrine and seated them at the head of the table. There were about thirty guests. Then Samuel directed the chef, "Bring the choice cut I pointed out to you, the one I told you to reserve."

9.24 The chef brought it and placed it before Saul with a flourish, saying, "This meal was kept aside just for you. Eat! It was especially prepared for this time and occasion with these guests."

Saul ate with Samuel—a memorable day!

9.25 Afterward they went down from the shrine into the city. A bed was prepared for Saul on the breeze-cooled roof of Samuel's house.

NEW INTERNATIONAL VERSION

his house. ²⁶They rose about daybreak and Samuel called to Saul on the roof, "Get ready, and I will send you on your way." When Saul got ready, he and Samuel went outside together. ²⁷As they were going down to the edge of the town, Samuel said to Saul, "Tell the servant to go on ahead of us"— and the servant did so—"but you stay here awhile, so that I may give you a message from God."

10 Then Samuel took a flask of oil and poured it on Saul's head and kissed him, saying, "Has not the LORD anointed you leader over his inheritance?ᵃ ²When you leave me today, you will meet two men near Rachel's tomb, at Zelzah on the border of Benjamin. They will say to you, 'The donkeys you set out to look for have been found. And now your father has stopped thinking about them and is worried about you. He is asking, "What shall I do about my son?"'

³"Then you will go on from there until you reach the great tree of Tabor. Three men going up to God at Bethel will meet you there. One will be carrying three young goats, another three loaves of bread, and another a skin of wine. ⁴They will greet you and offer you two loaves of bread, which you will accept from them.

⁵"After that you will go to Gibeah of God, where there is a Philistine outpost. As you approach the town, you will meet a procession of prophets coming down from the high place with lyres, tambourines, flutes and harps being played before them, and they will be prophesying. ⁶The Spirit of the LORD will come upon you in power, and you will prophesy with them; and you will be changed into a different person. ⁷Once these signs are fulfilled, do whatever your hand finds to do, for God is with you.

⁸"Go down ahead of me to Gilgal. I will surely come down to you to sacrifice burnt offerings and fellowship offerings,ᵇ but you must wait seven days until I come to you and tell you what you are to do."

SAUL MADE KING

⁹As Saul turned to leave Samuel, God changed Saul's heart, and all these signs were fulfilled that day. ¹⁰When they arrived at Gibeah, a procession of prophets met him; the Spirit of God came upon him in power, and he joined in

ᵃ *1* Hebrew; Septuagint and Vulgate *over his people Israel?* *You will reign over the LORD's people and save them from the power of their enemies round about. And this will be a sign to you that the LORD has anointed you leader over his inheritance:* ᵇ *8* Traditionally *peace offerings*

THE MESSAGE

9.26   They woke at the break of day. Samuel called to Saul on the roof, "Get up and I'll send you off." Saul got up and the two of them went out in the street.

9.27   As they approached the outskirts of town, Samuel said to Saul, "Tell your servant to go on ahead of us. You stay with me for a bit. I have a word of God to give you."

"YOU'LL BE A NEW PERSON"

10.1-2 **10** Then Samuel took a flask of oil, poured it on Saul's head, and kissed him. He said, "Do you see what this means? GOD has anointed you prince over his people.

"This sign will confirm GOD's anointing of you as prince over his inheritance: After you leave me today, as you get closer to your home country of Benjamin, you'll meet two men near Rachel's Tomb. They'll say, 'The donkeys you went to look for are found. Your father has forgotten about the donkeys and is worried about you, wringing his hands—quite beside himself!'

10.3-4 "Leaving there, you'll arrive at the Oak of Tabor. There you'll meet three men going up to worship God at Bethel. One will be carrying three young goats, another carrying three sacks of bread, and the third a jug of wine. They'll say, 'Hello, how are you?' and offer you two loaves of bread, which you will accept.

10.5-6 "Next, you'll come to Gibeah of God, where there's a Philistine garrison. As you approach the town, you'll run into a bunch of prophets coming down from the shrine, playing harps and tambourines, flutes and drums. And they'll be prophesying. Before you know it, the Spirit of GOD will come on you and you'll be prophesying right along with them. And you'll be transformed. You'll be a new person!

10.7   "When these confirming signs are accomplished, you'll know that you're ready: Whatever job you're given to do, do it. God is with you!

10.8   "Now, go down to Gilgal and I will follow. I'll come down and join you in worship by sacrificing burnt offerings and peace offerings. Wait seven days. Then I'll come and tell you what to do next."

10.9   Saul turned and left Samuel. At that very moment God transformed him—made him a new person! And all the confirming signs took place the same day.

SAUL AMONG THE PROPHETS

10.10-12 When Saul and his party got to Gibeah, there were the prophets, right in front of them! Before he knew it, the Spirit of God came on Saul

NEW INTERNATIONAL VERSION

their prophesying. 11When all those who had formerly known him saw him prophesying with the prophets, they asked each other, "What is this that has happened to the son of Kish? Is Saul also among the prophets?"

12A man who lived there answered, "And who is their father?" So it became a saying: "Is Saul also among the prophets?" 13After Saul stopped prophesying, he went to the high place.

14Now Saul's uncle asked him and his servant, "Where have you been?"

"Looking for the donkeys," he said. "But when we saw they were not to be found, we went to Samuel."

15Saul's uncle said, "Tell me what Samuel said to you."

16Saul replied, "He assured us that the donkeys had been found." But he did not tell his uncle what Samuel had said about the kingship.

17Samuel summoned the people of Israel to the LORD at Mizpah 18and said to them, "This is what the LORD, the God of Israel, says: 'I brought Israel up out of Egypt, and I delivered you from the power of Egypt and all the kingdoms that oppressed you.' 19But you have now rejected your God, who saves you out of all your calamities and distresses. And you have said, 'No, set a king over us.' So now present yourselves before the LORD by your tribes and clans."

20When Samuel brought all the tribes of Israel near, the tribe of Benjamin was chosen. 21Then he brought forward the tribe of Benjamin, clan by clan, and Matri's clan was chosen. Finally Saul son of Kish was chosen. But when they looked for him, he was not to be found. 22So they inquired further of the LORD, "Has the man come here yet?"

And the LORD said, "Yes, he has hidden himself among the baggage."

23They ran and brought him out, and as he stood among the people he was a head taller than any of the others. 24Samuel said to all the people, "Do you see the man the LORD has chosen? There is no one like him among all the people."

THE MESSAGE

and he was prophesying right along with them. When those who had previously known Saul saw him prophesying with the prophets, they were totally surprised. "What's going on here? What's come over the son of Kish? How on earth did Saul get to be a prophet?" One man spoke up and said, "Who started this? Where did these people ever come from?"

That's how the saying got started, "Saul among the prophets! Who would have guessed?!"

10.13-14 When Saul was done prophesying, he returned home. His uncle asked him and his servant, "So where have you two been all this time?"

"Out looking for the donkeys. We looked and looked and couldn't find them. And then we found Samuel!"

10.15 "So," said Saul's uncle, "what did Samuel tell you?"

10.16 Saul said, "He told us not to worry—the donkeys had been found." But Saul didn't breathe a word to his uncle of what Samuel said about the king business.

"WE WANT A KING!"

10.17-18 Samuel called the people to assemble before GOD at Mizpah. He addressed the children of Israel, "This is GOD's personal message to you:

10.18-19 "I brought Israel up out of Egypt. I delivered you from Egyptian oppression—yes, from all the bullying governments that made your life miserable. And now you want nothing to do with your God, the very God who has a history of getting you out of troubles of all sorts.

"And now you say, 'No! We want a king; give us a king!'

"Well, if that's what you want, that's what you'll get! Present yourselves formally before GOD, ranked in tribes and families."

10.20-21 After Samuel got all the tribes of Israel lined up, the Benjamin tribe was picked. Then he lined up the Benjamin tribe in family groups, and the family of Matri was picked. The family of Matri took its place in the lineup, and the name Saul, son of Kish, was picked. But when they went looking for him, he was nowhere to be found.

10.22 Samuel went back to GOD: "Is he anywhere around?"

GOD said, "Yes, he's right over there—hidden in that pile of baggage."

10.23 They ran and got him. He took his place before everyone, standing tall—head and shoulders above them.

10.24 Samuel then addressed the people, "Take a good look at whom GOD has chosen: the best! No one like him in the whole country!"

NEW INTERNATIONAL VERSION

Then the people shouted, "Long live the king!"

²⁵Samuel explained to the people the regulations of the kingship. He wrote them down on a scroll and deposited it before the LORD. Then Samuel dismissed the people, each to his own home.

²⁶Saul also went to his home in Gibeah, accompanied by valiant men whose hearts God had touched. ²⁷But some troublemakers said, "How can this fellow save us?" They despised him and brought him no gifts. But Saul kept silent.

SAUL RESCUES THE CITY OF JABESH

11 Nahash the Ammonite went up and besieged Jabesh Gilead. And all the men of Jabesh said to him, "Make a treaty with us, and we will be subject to you."

²But Nahash the Ammonite replied, "I will make a treaty with you only on the condition that I gouge out the right eye of every one of you and so bring disgrace on all Israel."

³The elders of Jabesh said to him, "Give us seven days so we can send messengers throughout Israel; if no one comes to rescue us, we will surrender to you."

⁴When the messengers came to Gibeah of Saul and reported these terms to the people, they all wept aloud. ⁵Just then Saul was returning from the fields, behind his oxen, and he asked, "What is wrong with the people? Why are they weeping?" Then they repeated to him what the men of Jabesh had said.

⁶When Saul heard their words, the Spirit of God came upon him in power, and he burned with anger. ⁷He took a pair of oxen, cut them into pieces, and sent the pieces by messengers throughout Israel, proclaiming, "This is what will be done to the oxen of anyone who does not follow Saul and Samuel." Then the terror of the LORD fell on the people, and they turned out as one man. ⁸When Saul mustered them at Bezek, the men of Israel numbered three hundred thousand and the men of Judah thirty thousand.

THE MESSAGE

Then a great shout went up from the people: "Long live the king!"

10.25   Samuel went on to instruct the people in the rules and regulations involved in a kingdom, wrote it all down in a book, and placed it before GOD. Then Samuel sent everyone home.

10.26-27   Saul also went home to Gibeah, and with him some true and brave men whom GOD moved to join him. But the riff-raff went off muttering, "Deliverer? Don't make me laugh!" They held him in contempt and refused to congratulate him. But Saul paid them no mind.

SAUL IS CROWNED KING

Nahash, king of the Ammonites, was brutalizing the tribes of Gad and Reuben, gouging out their right eyes and intimidating anyone who would come to Israel's help. There were very few Israelites living on the east side of the Jordan River who had not had their right eyes gouged out by Nahash. But seven thousand men had escaped from the Ammonites and were now living safely in Jabesh.

11.1   **11** So Nahash went after them and prepared to go to war against Jabesh Gilead. The men of Jabesh petitioned Nahash: "Make a treaty with us and we'll serve you."

11.2   Nahash said, "I'll make a treaty with you on one condition: that every right eye among you be gouged out! I'll humiliate every last man and woman in Israel before I'm done!"

11.3   The town leaders of Jabesh said, "Give us time to send messengers around Israel—seven days should do it. If no one shows up to help us, we'll accept your terms."

11.4-5   The messengers came to Saul's place at Gibeah and told the people what was going on. As the people broke out in loud wails, Saul showed up. He was coming back from the field with his oxen.

Saul asked, "What happened? Why is everyone crying?"

And they repeated the message that had come from Jabesh.

11.6-7   The Spirit of God came on Saul when he heard the report and he flew into a rage. He grabbed the yoke of oxen and butchered them on the spot. He sent the messengers throughout Israel distributing the bloody pieces with this message: "Anyone who refuses to join up with Saul and Samuel, let this be the fate of his oxen!"

11.7-8   The terror of GOD seized the people, and they came out, one and all, not a laggard among them. Saul took command of the people at Bezek. There were 300,000 men from Israel, another 30,000 from Judah.

NEW INTERNATIONAL VERSION

⁹They told the messengers who had come, "Say to the men of Jabesh Gilead, 'By the time the sun is hot tomorrow, you will be delivered.'" When the messengers went and reported this to the men of Jabesh, they were elated. ¹⁰They said to the Ammonites, "Tomorrow we will surrender to you, and you can do to us whatever seems good to you."

¹¹The next day Saul separated his men into three divisions; during the last watch of the night they broke into the camp of the Ammonites and slaughtered them until the heat of the day. Those who survived were scattered, so that no two of them were left together.

SAUL CONFIRMED AS KING

¹²The people then said to Samuel, "Who was it that asked, 'Shall Saul reign over us?' Bring these men to us and we will put them to death."

¹³But Saul said, "No one shall be put to death today, for this day the LORD has rescued Israel."

¹⁴Then Samuel said to the people, "Come, let us go to Gilgal and there reaffirm the kingship." ¹⁵So all the people went to Gilgal and confirmed Saul as king in the presence of the LORD. There they sacrificed fellowship offerings*ᵃ* before the LORD, and Saul and all the Israelites held a great celebration.

SAMUEL'S FAREWELL SPEECH

12 Samuel said to all Israel, "I have listened to everything you said to me and have set a king over you. ²Now you have a king as your leader. As for me, I am old and gray, and my sons are here with you. I have been your leader from my youth until this day. ³Here I stand. Testify against me in the presence of the LORD and his anointed. Whose ox have I taken? Whose donkey have I taken? Whom have I cheated? Whom have I oppressed? From whose hand have I accepted a bribe to make me shut my eyes? If I have done any of these, I will make it right."

⁴"You have not cheated or oppressed us," they replied. "You have not taken anything from anyone's hand."

⁵Samuel said to them, "The LORD is witness against you, and also his anointed is witness this day, that you have not found anything in my hand."

"He is witness," they said.

⁶Then Samuel said to the people, "It is the LORD who appointed Moses and Aaron and brought your forefathers up out of Egypt. ⁷Now then, stand here, because I am going to confront you with evidence before the LORD as to all the righteous acts performed by the LORD for you and your fathers.

ᵃ 15 Traditionally peace offerings

THE MESSAGE

11.9-11   Saul instructed the messengers, "Tell this to the folk in Jabesh Gilead: 'Help is on the way. Expect it by noon tomorrow.'"

The messengers set straight off and delivered their message. Elated, the people of Jabesh Gilead sent word to Nahash: "Tomorrow we'll give ourselves up. You can deal with us on your terms." Long before dawn the next day, Saul had strategically placed his army in three groups. At first light they broke into the enemy camp and slaughtered Ammonites until noon. Those who were left ran for their lives, scattering every which way.

11.12   The people came to Samuel then and said, "Where are those men who said, 'Saul is not fit to rule over us'? Hand them over. We'll kill them!"

11.13-14   But Saul said, "Nobody is going to be executed this day. This is the day GOD saved Israel! Come, let's go to Gilgal and there reconsecrate the kingship."

11.15   They all trooped out to Gilgal. Before GOD, they crowned Saul king at Gilgal. And there they worshiped, sacrificing peace offerings. Saul and all Israel celebrated magnificently.

"DON'T CHASE AFTER GHOST-GODS"

12.1-3   **12** Samuel addressed all Israel: "I've listened to everything you've said to me, listened carefully to every word, and I've given you a king. See for yourself: Your king among you, leading you! But now look at me: I'm old and gray, and my sons are still here. I've led you faithfully from my youth until this very day. Look at me! Do you have any complaints to bring before GOD and his anointed? Have I ever stolen so much as an ox or a donkey? Have I ever taken advantage of you or exploited you? Have I ever taken a bribe or played fast and loose with the law? Bring your complaint and I'll make it right."

12.4   "Oh no," they said, "never. You've never done any of that—never abused us, never lined your own pockets."

12.5   "That settles it then," said Samuel. "GOD is witness, and his anointed is witness that you find nothing against me—no faults, no complaints."

12.6-8   And the people said, "He is witness."

Samuel continued, "This is the GOD who made Moses and Aaron your leaders and brought your ancestors out of Egypt. Take your stand before him now as I review your case before GOD in the light of all the righteous ways in which GOD has worked with you and your

NEW INTERNATIONAL VERSION

8 "After Jacob entered Egypt, they cried to the LORD for help, and the LORD sent Moses and Aaron, who brought your forefathers out of Egypt and settled them in this place.

9 "But they forgot the LORD their God; so he sold them into the hand of Sisera, the commander of the army of Hazor, and into the hands of the Philistines and the king of Moab, who fought against them. 10 They cried out to the LORD and said, 'We have sinned; we have forsaken the LORD and served the Baals and the Ashtoreths. But now deliver us from the hands of our enemies, and we will serve you.' 11 Then the LORD sent Jerub-Baal,^a Barak,^b Jephthah and Samuel,^c and he delivered you from the hands of your enemies on every side, so that you lived securely.

12 "But when you saw that Nahash king of the Ammonites was moving against you, you said to me, 'No, we want a king to rule over us'—even though the LORD your God was your king. 13 Now here is the king you have chosen, the one you asked for; see, the LORD has set a king over you. 14 If you fear the LORD and serve and obey him and do not rebel against his commands, and if both you and the king who reigns over you follow the LORD your God—good! 15 But if you do not obey the LORD, and if you rebel against his commands, his hand will be against you, as it was against your fathers.

16 "Now then, stand still and see this great thing the LORD is about to do before your eyes! 17 Is it not wheat harvest now? I will call upon the LORD to send thunder and rain. And you will realize what an evil thing you did in the eyes of the LORD when you asked for a king."

18 Then Samuel called upon the LORD, and that same day the LORD sent thunder and rain. So all the people stood in awe of the LORD and of Samuel.

19 The people all said to Samuel, "Pray to the LORD your God for your servants so that we will not die, for we have added to all our other sins the evil of asking for a king."

20 "Do not be afraid," Samuel replied. "You have done all this evil; yet do not turn away from the LORD, but serve the LORD with all your heart. 21 Do not turn away after useless idols. They can do you no good, nor can they rescue you, because they are useless. 22 For the sake of his great name the LORD will not reject his people, because the LORD was pleased to make you his

---

^a 11 Also called Gideon   ^b 11 Some Septuagint manuscripts and Syriac; Hebrew Bedan   ^c 11 Hebrew; some Septuagint manuscripts and Syriac Samson

THE MESSAGE

ancestors. When Jacob's sons entered Egypt, the Egyptians made life hard for them and they cried for help to GOD. GOD sent Moses and Aaron, who led your ancestors out of Egypt and settled them here in this place.

12.9   "They soon forgot their GOD, so he sold them off to Sisera, commander of Hazor's army, later to a hard life under the Philistines, and still later to the king of Moab. They had to fight for their lives.

12.10   "Then they cried for help to GOD. They confessed, 'We've sinned! We've gone off and left GOD and worshiped the fertility gods and goddesses of Canaan. Oh, deliver us from the brutalities of our enemies and we'll worship you alone.'

12.11   "So GOD sent Jerub-Baal (Gideon), Bedan (Barak), Jephthah, and Samuel. He saved you from that hard life surrounded by enemies, and you lived in peace.

12.12   "But when you saw Nahash, king of the Ammonites, preparing to attack you, you said to me, 'No more of this. We want a king to lead us.' And GOD was already your king!

12.13-15   "So here's the king you wanted, the king you asked for. GOD has let you have your own way, given you a king. If you fear GOD, worship and obey him, and don't rebel against what he tells you. If both you and your king follow GOD, no problem. GOD will be sure to save you. But if you don't obey him and rebel against what he tells you, king or no king, you will fare no better than your fathers.

12.16-17   "Pay attention! Watch this wonder that GOD is going to perform before you now! It's summer, as you well know, and the rainy season is over. But I'm going to pray to GOD. He'll send thunder and rain, a sign to convince you of the great wrong you have done to GOD by asking for a king."

12.18   Samuel prayed to GOD, and GOD sent thunder and rain that same day. The people were greatly afraid and in awe of GOD and of Samuel.

12.19   Then all the people begged Samuel, "Pray to your GOD for us, your servants. Pray that we won't die! On top of all our other sins, we've piled on one more—asking for a king!"

12.20-22   Samuel said to them, "Don't be fearful. It's true that you have done something very wrong. All the same, don't turn your back on GOD. Worship and serve him heart and soul! Don't chase after ghost-gods. There's nothing to them. They can't help you. They're nothing but ghost-gods! GOD, simply because of who he is, is not going to walk off and leave his people. GOD took delight in making you into his very own people.

NEW INTERNATIONAL VERSION

own. ²³As for me, far be it from me that I should sin against the LORD by failing to pray for you. And I will teach you the way that is good and right. ²⁴But be sure to fear the LORD and serve him faithfully with all your heart; consider what great things he has done for you. ²⁵Yet if you persist in doing evil, both you and your king will be swept away."

SAMUEL REBUKES SAUL

13 Saul was ⌐thirty¬ᵃ years old when he became king, and he reigned over Israel ⌐forty-¬ᵇ two years.

²Saulᶜ chose three thousand men from Israel; two thousand were with him at Micmash and in the hill country of Bethel, and a thousand were with Jonathan at Gibeah in Benjamin. The rest of the men he sent back to their homes.

³Jonathan attacked the Philistine outpost at Geba, and the Philistines heard about it. Then Saul had the trumpet blown throughout the land and said, "Let the Hebrews hear!" ⁴So all Israel heard the news: "Saul has attacked the Philistine outpost, and now Israel has become a stench to the Philistines." And the people were summoned to join Saul at Gilgal.

⁵The Philistines assembled to fight Israel, with three thousandᵈ chariots, six thousand charioteers, and soldiers as numerous as the sand on the seashore. They went up and camped at Micmash, east of Beth Aven. ⁶When the men of Israel saw that their situation was critical and that their army was hard pressed, they hid in caves and thickets, among the rocks, and in pits and cisterns. ⁷Some Hebrews even crossed the Jordan to the land of Gad and Gilead.

Saul remained at Gilgal, and all the troops with him were quaking with fear. ⁸He waited seven days, the time set by Samuel; but Samuel did not come to Gilgal, and Saul's men began to scatter. ⁹So he said, "Bring me the burnt offering and the fellowship offerings.ᵉ" And Saul offered up the burnt offering. ¹⁰Just as he finished making the offering, Samuel arrived, and Saul went out to greet him.

¹¹"What have you done?" asked Samuel.

Saul replied, "When I saw that the men were scattering, and that you did not come at the set time, and that the Philistines were assembling at

---

ᵃ 1 A few late manuscripts of the Septuagint; Hebrew does not have *thirty*.   ᵇ 1 See the round number in Acts 13:21; Hebrew does not have *forty-*.   ᶜ 1,2 Or *and when he had reigned over Israel two years,* ²*he*   ᵈ 5 Some Septuagint manuscripts and Syriac; Hebrew *thirty thousand*   ᵉ 9 Traditionally *peace offerings*

THE MESSAGE

¹²·²³⁻²⁵ "And neither will I walk off and leave you. That would be a sin against GOD! I'm staying right here at my post praying for you and teaching you the good and right way to live. But I beg of you, fear GOD and worship him honestly and heartily. You've seen how greatly he has worked among you! Be warned: If you live badly, both you and your king will be thrown out."

"GOD IS OUT LOOKING FOR YOUR REPLACEMENT"

¹³·¹ **13** Saul was a young man when he began as king. He was king over Israel for many years.

¹³·² Saul conscripted enough men for three companies of soldiers. He kept two companies under his command at Micmash and in the Bethel hills. The other company was under Jonathan at Gibeah in Benjamin. He sent the rest of the men home.

¹³·³⁻⁴ Jonathan attacked and killed the Philistine governor stationed at Geba (Gibeah). When the Philistines heard the news, they raised the alarm: "The Hebrews are in revolt!" Saul ordered the reveille trumpets blown throughout the land. The word went out all over Israel, "Saul has killed the Philistine governor—drawn first blood! The Philistines are stirred up and mad as hornets!" Summoned, the army came to Saul at Gilgal.

¹³·⁵ The Philistines rallied their forces to fight Israel: three companies of chariots, six companies of cavalry, and so many infantry they looked like sand on the seashore. They went up into the hills and set up camp at Micmash, east of Beth Aven.

¹³·⁶⁻⁷ When the Israelites saw that they were way outnumbered and in deep trouble, they ran for cover, hiding in caves and pits, ravines and brambles and cisterns—wherever. They retreated across the Jordan River, refugees fleeing to the country of Gad and Gilead. But Saul held his ground in Gilgal, his soldiers still with him but scared to death.

¹³·⁸ He waited seven days, the time set by Samuel. Samuel failed to show up at Gilgal, and the soldiers were slipping away, right and left.

¹³·⁹⁻¹⁰ So Saul took charge: "Bring me the burnt offering and the peace offerings!" He went ahead and sacrificed the burnt offering. No sooner had he done it than Samuel showed up! Saul greeted him.

¹³·¹¹⁻¹² Samuel said, "What on earth are you doing?"

Saul answered, "When I saw I was losing my army from under me, and that you hadn't come when you said you would, and that the Philis-

NEW INTERNATIONAL VERSION

Micmash, [12]I thought, 'Now the Philistines will come down against me at Gilgal, and I have not sought the LORD's favor.' So I felt compelled to offer the burnt offering."

[13]"You acted foolishly," Samuel said. "You have not kept the command the LORD your God gave you; if you had, he would have established your kingdom over Israel for all time. [14]But now your kingdom will not endure; the LORD has sought out a man after his own heart and appointed him leader of his people, because you have not kept the LORD's command."

[15]Then Samuel left Gilgal[a] and went up to Gibeah in Benjamin, and Saul counted the men who were with him. They numbered about six hundred.

ISRAEL WITHOUT WEAPONS

[16]Saul and his son Jonathan and the men with them were staying in Gibeah[b] in Benjamin, while the Philistines camped at Micmash. [17]Raiding parties went out from the Philistine camp in three detachments. One turned toward Ophrah in the vicinity of Shual, [18]another toward Beth Horon, and the third toward the borderland overlooking the Valley of Zeboim facing the desert.

[19]Not a blacksmith could be found in the whole land of Israel, because the Philistines had said, "Otherwise the Hebrews will make swords or spears!" [20]So all Israel went down to the Philistines to have their plowshares, mattocks, axes and sickles[c] sharpened. [21]The price was two thirds of a shekel[d] for sharpening plowshares and mattocks, and a third of a shekel[e] for sharpening forks and axes and for repointing goads.

[22]So on the day of the battle not a soldier with Saul and Jonathan had a sword or spear in his hand; only Saul and his son Jonathan had them.

JONATHAN ATTACKS THE PHILISTINES

[23]Now a detachment of Philistines had gone out to the pass at Micmash.

14 [1]One day Jonathan son of Saul said to the young man bearing his armor, "Come, let's go over to the Philistine outpost on the other side." But he did not tell his father.

[a] 15 Hebrew; Septuagint Gilgal and went his way; the rest of the people went after Saul to meet the army, and they went out of Gilgal   [b] 16 Two Hebrew manuscripts; most Hebrew manuscripts Geba, a variant of Gibeah   [c] 20 Septuagint; Hebrew plowshares   [d] 21 Hebrew pim; that is, about 1/4 ounce (about 8 grams)   [e] 21 That is, about 1/8 ounce (about 4 grams)

THE MESSAGE

tines were poised at Micmash, I said, 'The Philistines are about to come down on me in Gilgal, and I haven't yet come before GOD asking for his help.' So I took things into my own hands, and sacrificed the burnt offering."

13.13-14 "That was a fool thing to do," Samuel said to Saul. "If you had kept the appointment that your GOD commanded, by now GOD would have set a firm and lasting foundation under your kingly rule over Israel. As it is, your kingly rule is already falling to pieces. GOD is out looking for your replacement right now. This time he'll do the choosing. When he finds him, he'll appoint him leader of his people. And all because you didn't keep your appointment with GOD!"

13.15 At that, Samuel got up and left Gilgal. What army there was left followed Saul into battle. They went into the hills from Gilgal toward Gibeah in Benjamin. Saul looked over and assessed the soldiers still with him—a mere six hundred!

JONATHAN AND HIS ARMOR BEARER

13.16-18 Saul, his son Jonathan, and the soldiers who had remained made camp at Geba (Gibeah) of Benjamin. The Philistines were camped at Micmash. Three squads of raiding parties were regularly sent out from the Philistine camp. One squadron was assigned to the Ophrah road going toward Shual country; another was assigned to the Beth Horon road; the third took the border road that rimmed the Valley of Hyenas.

13.19-22 There wasn't a blacksmith to be found anywhere in Israel. The Philistines made sure of that—"Lest those Hebrews start making swords and spears." That meant that the Israelites had to go down among the Philistines to keep their farm tools—plowshares and mattocks, axes and sickles—sharp and in good repair. They charged a silver coin for the plowshares and mattocks, and half that for the rest. So when the battle of Micmash was joined, there wasn't a sword or spear to be found anywhere in Israel—except for Saul and his son Jonathan; they were both well-armed.

13.23 A patrol of Philistines took up a position at Micmash Pass.

14 14.1-3 Later that day, Jonathan, Saul's son, said to his armor bearer, "Come on, let's go over to the Philistine garrison patrol on the other side of the pass." But he didn't tell his fa-

NEW INTERNATIONAL VERSION

²Saul was staying on the outskirts of Gibeah under a pomegranate tree in Migron. With him were about six hundred men, ³among whom was Ahijah, who was wearing an ephod. He was a son of Ichabod's brother Ahitub son of Phinehas, the son of Eli, the LORD's priest in Shiloh. No one was aware that Jonathan had left.

⁴On each side of the pass that Jonathan intended to cross to reach the Philistine outpost was a cliff; one was called Bozez, and the other Seneh. ⁵One cliff stood to the north toward Micmash, the other to the south toward Geba.

⁶Jonathan said to his young armor-bearer, "Come, let's go over to the outpost of those uncircumcised fellows. Perhaps the LORD will act in our behalf. Nothing can hinder the LORD from saving, whether by many or by few."

⁷"Do all that you have in mind," his armor-bearer said. "Go ahead; I am with you heart and soul."

⁸Jonathan said, "Come, then; we will cross over toward the men and let them see us. ⁹If they say to us, 'Wait there until we come to you,' we will stay where we are and not go up to them. ¹⁰But if they say, 'Come up to us,' we will climb up, because that will be our sign that the LORD has given them into our hands."

¹¹So both of them showed themselves to the Philistine outpost. "Look!" said the Philistines. "The Hebrews are crawling out of the holes they were hiding in." ¹²The men of the outpost shouted to Jonathan and his armor-bearer, "Come up to us and we'll teach you a lesson."

So Jonathan said to his armor-bearer, "Climb up after me; the LORD has given them into the hand of Israel."

¹³Jonathan climbed up, using his hands and feet, with his armor-bearer right behind him. The Philistines fell before Jonathan, and his armor-bearer followed and killed behind him. ¹⁴In that first attack Jonathan and his armor-bearer killed some twenty men in an area of about half an acre.ᵃ

ISRAEL ROUTS THE PHILISTINES

¹⁵Then panic struck the whole army—those in the camp and field, and those in the outposts and raiding parties—and the ground shook. It was a panic sent by God.ᵇ

¹⁶Saul's lookouts at Gibeah in Benjamin saw the army melting away in all directions. ¹⁷Then

---

ᵃ 14 Hebrew *half a yoke*; a "yoke" was the land plowed by a yoke of oxen in one day.   ᵇ 15 Or *a terrible panic*

THE MESSAGE

ther. Meanwhile, Saul was taking it easy under the pomegranate tree at the threshing floor on the edge of town at Geba (Gibeah). There were about six hundred men with him. Ahijah, wearing the priestly Ephod, was also there. (Ahijah was the son of Ahitub, brother of Ichabod, son of Phinehas, who was the son of Eli the priest of GOD at Shiloh.) No one there knew that Jonathan had gone off.

14.4-5   The pass that Jonathan was planning to cross over to the Philistine garrison was flanked on either side by sharp rock outcroppings, cliffs named Bozez and Seneh. The cliff to the north faced Micmash; the cliff to the south faced Geba (Gibeah).

14.6   Jonathan said to his armor bearer, "Come on now, let's go across to these uncircumcised pagans. Maybe GOD will work for us. There's no rule that says GOD can only deliver by using a big army. No one can stop GOD from saving when he sets his mind to it."

14.7   His armor bearer said, "Go ahead. Do what you think best. I'm with you all the way."

14.8-10   Jonathan said, "Here's what we'll do. We'll cross over the pass and let the men see we're there. If they say, 'Halt! Don't move until we check you out,' we'll stay put and not go up. But if they say, 'Come on up,' we'll go right up—and we'll know GOD has given them to us. That will be our sign."

14.11   So they did it, the two of them. They stepped into the open where they could be seen by the Philistine garrison. The Philistines shouted out, "Look at that! The Hebrews are crawling out of their holes!"

14.12   Then they yelled down to Jonathan and his armor bearer, "Come on up here! We've got a thing or two to show you!"

14.13   Jonathan shouted to his armor bearer, "Up! Follow me! GOD has turned them over to Israel!" Jonathan scrambled up on all fours, his armor bearer right on his heels. When the Philistines came running up to them, he knocked them flat, his armor bearer right behind finishing them off, bashing their heads in with stones.

14.14-15   In this first bloody encounter, Jonathan and his armor bearer killed about twenty men. That set off a terrific upheaval in both camp and field, the soldiers in the garrison and the raiding squad badly shaken up, the ground itself shuddering—panic like you've never seen before!

STRAIGHT TO THE BATTLE

14.16-18   Saul's sentries posted back at Geba (Gibeah) in Benjamin saw the confusion and turmoil raging

NEW INTERNATIONAL VERSION

Saul said to the men who were with him, "Muster the forces and see who has left us." When they did, it was Jonathan and his armor-bearer who were not there.

¹⁸Saul said to Ahijah, "Bring the ark of God." (At that time it was with the Israelites.)ᵃ ¹⁹While Saul was talking to the priest, the tumult in the Philistine camp increased more and more. So Saul said to the priest, "Withdraw your hand."

²⁰Then Saul and all his men assembled and went to the battle. They found the Philistines in total confusion, striking each other with their swords. ²¹Those Hebrews who had previously been with the Philistines and had gone up with them to their camp went over to the Israelites who were with Saul and Jonathan. ²²When all the Israelites who had hidden in the hill country of Ephraim heard that the Philistines were on the run, they joined the battle in hot pursuit. ²³So the LORD rescued Israel that day, and the battle moved on beyond Beth Aven.

JONATHAN EATS HONEY

²⁴Now the men of Israel were in distress that day, because Saul had bound the people under an oath, saying, "Cursed be any man who eats food before evening comes, before I have avenged myself on my enemies!" So none of the troops tasted food.

²⁵The entire armyᵇ entered the woods, and there was honey on the ground. ²⁶When they went into the woods, they saw the honey oozing out, yet no one put his hand to his mouth, because they feared the oath. ²⁷But Jonathan had not heard that his father had bound the people with the oath, so he reached out the end of the staff that was in his hand and dipped it into the honeycomb. He raised his hand to his mouth, and his eyes brightened.ᶜ ²⁸Then one of the soldiers told him, "Your father bound the army under a strict oath, saying, 'Cursed be any man who eats food today!' That is why the men are faint."

²⁹Jonathan said, "My father has made trouble for the country. See how my eyes brightenedᵈ when I tasted a little of this honey. ³⁰How much better it would have been if the men had eaten today some of the plunder they took from their enemies. Would not the slaughter of the Philistines have been even greater?"

³¹That day, after the Israelites had struck down the Philistines from Micmash to Aijalon, they were exhausted. ³²They pounced on the

---

ᵃ 18 Hebrew; Septuagint "Bring the ephod." (At that time he wore the ephod before the Israelites.) ᵇ 25 Or Now all the people of the land ᶜ 27 Or his strength was renewed ᵈ 29 Or my strength was renewed

THE MESSAGE

in the camp. Saul commanded, "Line up and take the roll. See who's here and who's missing." When they called the roll, Jonathan and his armor bearer turned up missing.

14:18-19 Saul ordered Ahijah, "Bring the priestly Ephod. Let's see what GOD has to say here." (Ahijah was responsible for the Ephod in those days.) While Saul was in conversation with the priest, the upheaval in the Philistine camp became greater and louder. Then Saul interrupted Ahijah: "Put the Ephod away."

14:20-23 Saul immediately called his army together and they went straight to the battle. When they got there they found total confusion—Philistines swinging their swords wildly, killing each other. Hebrews who had earlier defected to the Philistine camp came back. They now wanted to be with Israel under Saul and Jonathan. Not only that, but when all the Israelites who had been hiding out in the backwoods of Ephraim heard that the Philistines were running for their lives, they came out and joined the chase. GOD saved Israel! What a day!

The fighting moved on to Beth Aven. The whole army was behind Saul now—ten thousand strong!—with the fighting scattering into all the towns throughout the hills of Ephraim.

14:24 Saul did something really foolish that day. He addressed the army: "A curse on the man who eats anything before evening, before I've wreaked vengeance on my enemies!" None of them ate a thing all day.

14:25-27 There were honeycombs here and there in the fields. But no one so much as put his finger in the honey to taste it, for the soldiers to a man feared the curse. But Jonathan hadn't heard his father put the army under oath. He stuck the tip of his staff into some honey and ate it. Refreshed, his eyes lit up with renewed vigor.

14:28 A soldier spoke up, "Your father has put the army under solemn oath, saying, 'A curse on the man who eats anything before evening!' No wonder the soldiers are drooping!"

14:29-30 Jonathan said, "My father has imperiled the country. Just look how quickly my energy has returned since I ate a little of this honey! It would have been a lot better, believe me, if the soldiers had eaten their fill of whatever they took from the enemy. Who knows how much worse we could have whipped them!"

14:31-32 They killed Philistines that day all the way from Micmash to Aijalon, but the soldiers ended up totally exhausted. Then they started plundering. They grabbed anything in sight—

NEW INTERNATIONAL VERSION

plunder and, taking sheep, cattle and calves, they butchered them on the ground and ate them, together with the blood. 33Then someone said to Saul, "Look, the men are sinning against the LORD by eating meat that has blood in it."

"You have broken faith," he said. "Roll a large stone over here at once." 34Then he said, "Go out among the men and tell them, 'Each of you bring me your cattle and sheep, and slaughter them here and eat them. Do not sin against the LORD by eating meat with blood still in it.' "

So everyone brought his ox that night and slaughtered it there. 35Then Saul built an altar to the LORD; it was the first time he had done this.

36Saul said, "Let us go down after the Philistines by night and plunder them till dawn, and let us not leave one of them alive."

"Do whatever seems best to you," they replied.

But the priest said, "Let us inquire of God here."

37So Saul asked God, "Shall I go down after the Philistines? Will you give them into Israel's hand?" But God did not answer him that day.

38Saul therefore said, "Come here, all you who are leaders of the army, and let us find out what sin has been committed today. 39As surely as the LORD who rescues Israel lives, even if it lies with my son Jonathan, he must die." But not one of the men said a word.

40Saul then said to all the Israelites, "You stand over there; I and Jonathan my son will stand over here."

"Do what seems best to you," the men replied.

41Then Saul prayed to the LORD, the God of Israel, "Give me the right answer." [a] And Jonathan and Saul were taken by lot, and the men were cleared. 42Saul said, "Cast the lot between me and Jonathan my son." And Jonathan was taken.

---

[a] 41 Hebrew; Septuagint *"Why have you not answered your servant today? If the fault is in me or my son Jonathan, respond with Urim, but if the men of Israel are at fault, respond with Thummim."*

THE MESSAGE

sheep, cattle, calves—and butchered it where they found it. Then they glutted themselves—meat, blood, the works.

14:33-34 Saul was told, "Do something! The soldiers are sinning against GOD. They're eating meat with the blood still in it!"

Saul said, "You're biting the hand that feeds you! Roll a big rock over here—now!" He continued, "Disperse among the troops and tell them, 'Bring your oxen and sheep to me and butcher them properly here. Then you can feast to your heart's content. Please don't sin against GOD by eating meat with the blood still in it.' "

And so they did. That night each soldier, one after another, led his animal there to be butchered.

14:35 That's the story behind Saul's building an altar to GOD. It's the first altar to GOD that he built.

FIND OUT WHAT GOD THINKS

14:36 Saul said, "Let's go after the Philistines tonight! We can spend the night looting and plundering. We won't leave a single live Philistine!"

"Sounds good to us," said the troops. "Let's do it!"

But the priest slowed them down: "Let's find out what God thinks about this."

14:37 So Saul prayed to God, "Shall I go after the Philistines? Will you put them in Israel's hand?" God didn't answer him on that occasion.

14:38-39 Saul then said, "All army officers, step forward. Some sin has been committed this day. We're going to find out what it is and who did it! As GOD lives, Israel's Savior God, whoever sinned will die, even if it should turn out to be Jonathan, my son!"

Nobody said a word.

14:40 Saul said to the Israelites, "You line up over on that side, and I and Jonathan my son will stand on this side."

The army agreed, "Fine. Whatever you say."

14:41 Then Saul prayed to GOD, "O God of Israel, why haven't you answered me today? Show me the truth. If the sin is in me or Jonathan, then, O GOD, give the sign Urim. But if the sin is in the army of Israel, give the sign Thummim."

The Urim sign turned up and pointed to Saul and Jonathan. That cleared the army.

14:42 Next Saul said, "Cast the lots between me and Jonathan—and death to the one GOD points to!"

The soldiers protested, "No—this is not right. Stop this!" But Saul pushed on anyway. They cast the lots, Urim and Thummim, and the lot fell to Jonathan.

NEW INTERNATIONAL VERSION

⁴³Then Saul said to Jonathan, "Tell me what you have done."

So Jonathan told him, "I merely tasted a little honey with the end of my staff. And now must I die?"

⁴⁴Saul said, "May God deal with me, be it ever so severely, if you do not die, Jonathan."

⁴⁵But the men said to Saul, "Should Jonathan die—he who has brought about this great deliverance in Israel? Never! As surely as the LORD lives, not a hair of his head will fall to the ground, for he did this today with God's help." So the men rescued Jonathan, and he was not put to death.

⁴⁶Then Saul stopped pursuing the Philistines, and they withdrew to their own land.

⁴⁷After Saul had assumed rule over Israel, he fought against their enemies on every side: Moab, the Ammonites, Edom, the kings*a* of Zobah, and the Philistines. Wherever he turned, he inflicted punishment on them.*b* ⁴⁸He fought valiantly and defeated the Amalekites, delivering Israel from the hands of those who had plundered them.

SAUL'S FAMILY

⁴⁹Saul's sons were Jonathan, Ishvi and Malki-Shua. The name of his older daughter was Merab, and that of the younger was Michal. ⁵⁰His wife's name was Ahinoam daughter of Ahimaaz. The name of the commander of Saul's army was Abner son of Ner, and Ner was Saul's uncle. ⁵¹Saul's father Kish and Abner's father Ner were sons of Abiel.

⁵²All the days of Saul there was bitter war with the Philistines, and whenever Saul saw a mighty or brave man, he took him into his service.

THE LORD REJECTS SAUL AS KING

15 Samuel said to Saul, "I am the one the LORD sent to anoint you king over his people Israel; so listen now to the message from the LORD. ²This is what the LORD Almighty says: 'I will punish the Amalekites for what they did to Israel when they waylaid them as they came up from Egypt. ³Now go, attack the Amalekites and totally destroy*c* everything that belongs to them. Do not spare them; put to death men and women, children and infants, cattle and sheep, camels and donkeys.' "

⁴So Saul summoned the men and mustered them at Telaim—two hundred thousand foot soldiers and ten thousand men from Judah. ⁵Saul went to the city of Amalek and set an ambush in

---

a 47 Masoretic Text; Dead Sea Scrolls and Septuagint *king*
b 47 Hebrew; Septuagint *he was victorious*
c 3 The Hebrew term refers to the irrevocable giving over of things or persons to the LORD, often by totally destroying them; also in verses 8, 9, 15, 18, 20 and 21.

THE MESSAGE

14.43 Saul confronted Jonathan. "What did you do? Tell me!"

Jonathan said, "I licked a bit of honey off the tip of the staff I was carrying. That's it—and for that I'm to die?"

14.44 Saul said, "Yes. Jonathan most certainly will die. It's out of my hands—I can't go against God, can I?"

14.45 The soldiers rose up: "Jonathan—die? Never! He's just carried out this stunning salvation victory for Israel. As surely as GOD lives, not a hair on his head is going to be harmed. Why, he's been working hand-in-hand with God all day!" The soldiers rescued Jonathan and he didn't die.

14.46 Saul pulled back from chasing the Philistines, and the Philistines went home.

14.47-48 Saul extended his rule, capturing neighboring kingdoms. He fought enemies on every front—Moab, Ammon, Edom, the king of Zobah, the Philistines. Wherever he turned, he came up with a victory. He became invincible! He smashed Amalek, freeing Israel from the savagery and looting.

14.49-51 Saul's sons were Jonathan, Ishvi, and Malki-Shua. His daughters were Merab, the firstborn, and Michal, the younger. Saul's wife was Ahinoam, daughter of Ahimaaz. Abner son of Ner was commander of Saul's army (Ner was Saul's uncle). Kish, Saul's father, and Ner, Abner's father, were the sons of Abiel.

14.52 All through Saul's life there was war, bitter and relentless, with the Philistines. Saul conscripted every strong and brave man he laid eyes on.

15 15.1-2 Samuel said to Saul, "GOD sent me to anoint you king over his people, Israel. Now, listen again to what GOD says. This is the GOD-of-the-Angel-Armies speaking:

15.2-3 " 'I'm about to get even with Amalek for ambushing Israel when Israel came up out of Egypt. Here's what you are to do: Go to war against Amalek. Put everything connected with Amalek under a holy ban. And no exceptions! This is to be total destruction—men and women, children and infants, cattle and sheep, camels and donkeys—the works.' "

15.4-5 Saul called the army together at Telaim and prepared them to go to war—two hundred companies of infantry from Israel and another ten companies from Judah. Saul marched to Amalek City and hid in the canyon.

NEW INTERNATIONAL VERSION

the ravine. ⁶Then he said to the Kenites, "Go away, leave the Amalekites so that I do not destroy you along with them; for you showed kindness to all the Israelites when they came up out of Egypt." So the Kenites moved away from the Amalekites.

⁷Then Saul attacked the Amalekites all the way from Havilah to Shur, to the east of Egypt. ⁸He took Agag king of the Amalekites alive, and all his people he totally destroyed with the sword. ⁹But Saul and the army spared Agag and the best of the sheep and cattle, the fat calves*ᵃ* and lambs—everything that was good. These they were unwilling to destroy completely, but everything that was despised and weak they totally destroyed.

¹⁰Then the word of the LORD came to Samuel: ¹¹"I am grieved that I have made Saul king, because he has turned away from me and has not carried out my instructions." Samuel was troubled, and he cried out to the LORD all that night.

¹²Early in the morning Samuel got up and went to meet Saul, but he was told, "Saul has gone to Carmel. There he has set up a monument in his own honor and has turned and gone on down to Gilgal."

¹³When Samuel reached him, Saul said, "The LORD bless you! I have carried out the LORD's instructions."

¹⁴But Samuel said, "What then is this bleating of sheep in my ears? What is this lowing of cattle that I hear?"

¹⁵Saul answered, "The soldiers brought them from the Amalekites; they spared the best of the sheep and cattle to sacrifice to the LORD your God, but we totally destroyed the rest."

¹⁶"Stop!" Samuel said to Saul. "Let me tell you what the LORD said to me last night."

"Tell me," Saul replied.

¹⁷Samuel said, "Although you were once small in your own eyes, did you not become the head of the tribes of Israel? The LORD anointed you king over Israel. ¹⁸And he sent you on a mission, saying, 'Go and completely destroy those wicked people, the Amalekites; make war on them until you have wiped them out.' ¹⁹Why did you not obey the LORD? Why did you pounce on the plunder and do evil in the eyes of the LORD?"

²⁰"But I did obey the LORD," Saul said. "I went on the mission the LORD assigned me. I com-

---

ᵃ 9 Or the grown bulls; the meaning of the Hebrew for this phrase is uncertain.

THE MESSAGE

15.6   Then Saul got word to the Kenites: "Get out of here while you can. Evacuate the city right now or you'll get lumped in with the Amalekites. I'm warning you because you showed real kindness to the Israelites when they came up out of Egypt."

15.6   And they did. The Kenites evacuated the place.

15.7-9   Then Saul went after Amalek, from the canyon all the way to Shur near the Egyptian border. He captured Agag, king of Amalek, alive. Everyone else was killed under the terms of the holy ban. Saul and the army made an exception for Agag, and for the choice sheep and cattle. They didn't include them under the terms of the holy ban. But all the rest, which nobody wanted anyway, they destroyed as decreed by the holy ban.

15.10-11   Then GOD spoke to Samuel: "I'm sorry I ever made Saul king. He's turned his back on me. He refuses to do what I tell him."

15.11-12   Samuel was angry when he heard this. He prayed his anger and disappointment all through the night. He got up early in the morning to confront Saul but was told, "Saul's gone. He went to Carmel to set up a victory monument in his own honor, and then was headed for Gilgal."

By the time Samuel caught up with him, Saul had just finished an act of worship, having used Amalekite plunder for the burnt offerings sacrificed to GOD.

15.13   As Samuel came close, Saul called out, "GOD's blessings on you! I accomplished GOD's plan to the letter!"

15.14   Samuel said, "So what's this I'm hearing—this bleating of sheep, this mooing of cattle?"

15.15   "Only some Amalekite loot," said Saul. "The soldiers saved back a few of the choice cattle and sheep to offer up in sacrifice to GOD. But everything else we destroyed under the holy ban."

15.16   "Enough!" interrupted Samuel. "Let me tell you what GOD told me last night."

Saul said, "Go ahead. Tell me."

15.17-19   And Samuel told him. "When you started out in this, you were nothing—and you knew it. Then GOD put you at the head of Israel—made you king over Israel. Then GOD sent you off to do a job for him, ordering you, 'Go and put those sinners, the Amalekites, under a holy ban. Go to war against them until you have totally wiped them out.' So why did you not obey GOD? Why did you grab all this loot? Why, with GOD's eyes on you all the time, did you brazenly carry out this evil?"

15.20-21   Saul defended himself. "What are you talking about? I did obey GOD. I did the job GOD

NEW INTERNATIONAL VERSION

pletely destroyed the Amalekites and brought back Agag their king. [21] The soldiers took sheep and cattle from the plunder, the best of what was devoted to God, in order to sacrifice them to the LORD your God at Gilgal."

[22] But Samuel replied:

"Does the LORD delight in burnt offerings
    and sacrifices
    as much as in obeying the voice of the
        LORD?
To obey is better than sacrifice,
    and to heed is better than the fat of rams.
[23] For rebellion is like the sin of divination,
    and arrogance like the evil of idolatry.
Because you have rejected the word of the
        LORD,
    he has rejected you as king."

[24] Then Saul said to Samuel, "I have sinned. I violated the LORD's command and your instructions. I was afraid of the people and so I gave in to them. [25] Now I beg you, forgive my sin and come back with me, so that I may worship the LORD."

[26] But Samuel said to him, "I will not go back with you. You have rejected the word of the LORD, and the LORD has rejected you as king over Israel!"

[27] As Samuel turned to leave, Saul caught hold of the hem of his robe, and it tore. [28] Samuel said to him, "The LORD has torn the kingdom of Israel from you today and has given it to one of your neighbors—to one better than you. [29] He who is the Glory of Israel does not lie or change his mind; for he is not a man, that he should change his mind."

[30] Saul replied, "I have sinned. But please honor me before the elders of my people and before Israel; come back with me, so that I may worship the LORD your God." [31] So Samuel went back with Saul, and Saul worshiped the LORD.

[32] Then Samuel said, "Bring me Agag king of the Amalekites."

Agag came to him confidently,[a] thinking, "Surely the bitterness of death is past."

[33] But Samuel said,

"As your sword has made women childless,
    so will your mother be childless among
        women."

And Samuel put Agag to death before the LORD at Gilgal.

[34] Then Samuel left for Ramah, but Saul went up to his home in Gibeah of Saul. [35] Until the day Samuel died, he did not go to see Saul again, though Samuel mourned for him. And the LORD was grieved that he had made Saul king over Israel.

[a] 32 Or him trembling, yet

THE MESSAGE

set for me. I brought in King Agag and destroyed the Amalekites under the terms of the holy ban. So the soldiers saved back a few choice sheep and cattle from the holy ban for sacrifice to GOD at Gilgal—what's wrong with that?"

15.22-23 Then Samuel said,

Do you think all GOD wants are sacrifices—
    empty rituals just for show?
He wants you to listen to him!
Plain listening is the thing,
    not staging a lavish religious production.
Not doing what GOD tells you
    is far worse than fooling around in the
        occult.
Getting self-important around GOD
    is far worse than making deals with your
        dead ancestors.
Because you said No to GOD's command,
    he says No to your kingship.

15.24-25 Saul gave in and confessed, "I've sinned. I've trampled roughshod over GOD's Word and your instructions. I cared more about pleasing the people. I let them tell me what to do. Oh, absolve me of my sin! Take my hand and lead me to the altar so I can worship GOD!"

15.26 But Samuel refused: "No, I can't come alongside you in this. You rejected GOD's command. Now GOD has rejected you as king over Israel."

15.27-29 As Samuel turned to leave, Saul grabbed at his priestly robe and a piece tore off. Samuel said, "GOD has just now torn the kingdom from you, and handed it over to your neighbor, a better man than you are. Israel's God-of-Glory doesn't deceive and he doesn't dither. He says what he means and means what he says."

15.30 Saul tried again, "I have sinned. But don't abandon me! Support me with your presence before the leaders and the people. Come alongside me as I go back to worship GOD."

15.31 Samuel did. He went back with him. And Saul went to his knees before GOD and worshiped.

15.32 Then Samuel said, "Present King Agag of Amalek to me." Agag came, dragging his feet, muttering that he'd be better off dead.

15.33 Samuel said, "Just as your sword made many a woman childless, so your mother will be childless among those women!" And Samuel cut Agag down in the presence of GOD right there in Gilgal.

15.34-35 Samuel left immediately for Ramah and Saul went home to Gibeah. Samuel had nothing to do with Saul from then on, though he grieved long and deeply over him. But GOD was sorry he had ever made Saul king in the first place.

NEW INTERNATIONAL VERSION

SAMUEL ANOINTS DAVID

16 The LORD said to Samuel, "How long will you mourn for Saul, since I have rejected him as king over Israel? Fill your horn with oil and be on your way; I am sending you to Jesse of Bethlehem. I have chosen one of his sons to be king."

²But Samuel said, "How can I go? Saul will hear about it and kill me."

The LORD said, "Take a heifer with you and say, 'I have come to sacrifice to the LORD.' ³Invite Jesse to the sacrifice, and I will show you what to do. You are to anoint for me the one I indicate."

⁴Samuel did what the LORD said. When he arrived at Bethlehem, the elders of the town trembled when they met him. They asked, "Do you come in peace?"

⁵Samuel replied, "Yes, in peace; I have come to sacrifice to the LORD. Consecrate yourselves and come to the sacrifice with me." Then he consecrated Jesse and his sons and invited them to the sacrifice.

⁶When they arrived, Samuel saw Eliab and thought, "Surely the LORD's anointed stands here before the LORD."

⁷But the LORD said to Samuel, "Do not consider his appearance or his height, for I have rejected him. The LORD does not look at the things man looks at. Man looks at the outward appearance, but the LORD looks at the heart."

⁸Then Jesse called Abinadab and had him pass in front of Samuel. But Samuel said, "The LORD has not chosen this one either." ⁹Jesse then had Shammah pass by, but Samuel said, "Nor has the LORD chosen this one." ¹⁰Jesse had seven of his sons pass before Samuel, but Samuel said to him, "The LORD has not chosen these." ¹¹So he asked Jesse, "Are these all the sons you have?"

"There is still the youngest," Jesse answered, "but he is tending the sheep."

Samuel said, "Send for him; we will not sit down *a* until he arrives."

¹²So he sent and had him brought in. He was ruddy, with a fine appearance and handsome features.

Then the LORD said, "Rise and anoint him; he is the one."

¹³So Samuel took the horn of oil and anointed him in the presence of his brothers, and from that day on the Spirit of the LORD came upon David in power. Samuel then went to Ramah.

a 11 Some Septuagint manuscripts; Hebrew *not gather around*

THE MESSAGE

GOD LOOKS INTO THE HEART

16 ¹·¹ GOD addressed Samuel: "So, how long are you going to mope over Saul? You know I've rejected him as king over Israel. Fill your flask with anointing oil and get going. I'm sending you to Jesse of Bethlehem. I've spotted the very king I want among his sons."

¹⁶.²⁻³ "I can't do that," said Samuel. "Saul will hear about it and kill me."

GOD said, "Take a heifer with you and announce, 'I've come to lead you in worship of GOD, with this heifer as a sacrifice.' Make sure Jesse gets invited. I'll let you know what to do next. I'll point out the one you are to anoint."

¹⁶.⁴ Samuel did what GOD told him. When he arrived at Bethlehem, the town fathers greeted him, but apprehensively. "Is there something wrong?"

¹⁶.⁵ "Nothing's wrong. I've come to sacrifice this heifer and lead you in the worship of GOD. Prepare yourselves, be consecrated, and join me in worship." He made sure Jesse and his sons were also consecrated and called to worship.

¹⁶.⁶ When they arrived, Samuel took one look at Eliab and thought, "Here he is! GOD's anointed!"

¹⁶.⁷ But GOD told Samuel, "Looks aren't everything. Don't be impressed with his looks and stature. I've already eliminated him. GOD judges persons differently than humans do. Men and women look at the face; GOD looks into the heart."

¹⁶.⁸ Jesse then called up Abinadab and presented him to Samuel. Samuel said, "This man isn't GOD's choice either."

¹⁶.⁹ Next Jesse presented Shammah. Samuel said, "No, this man isn't either."

¹⁶.¹⁰ Jesse presented his seven sons to Samuel. Samuel was blunt with Jesse, "GOD hasn't chosen any of these."

¹⁶.¹¹ Then he asked Jesse, "Is this it? Are there no more sons?"

"Well, yes, there's the runt. But he's out tending the sheep."

Samuel ordered Jesse, "Go get him. We're not moving from this spot until he's here."

¹⁶.¹² Jesse sent for him. He was brought in, the very picture of health—bright-eyed, good-looking.

GOD said, "Up on your feet! Anoint him! This is the one."

¹⁶.¹³ Samuel took his flask of oil and anointed him, with his brothers standing around watching. The Spirit of GOD entered David like a rush of wind, God vitally empowering him for the rest of his life.

Samuel left and went home to Ramah.

NEW INTERNATIONAL VERSION

DAVID IN SAUL'S SERVICE

¹⁴Now the Spirit of the LORD had departed from Saul, and an evil*ᵃ* spirit from the LORD tormented him.

¹⁵Saul's attendants said to him, "See, an evil spirit from God is tormenting you. ¹⁶Let our lord command his servants here to search for someone who can play the harp. He will play when the evil spirit from God comes upon you, and you will feel better."

¹⁷So Saul said to his attendants, "Find someone who plays well and bring him to me."

¹⁸One of the servants answered, "I have seen a son of Jesse of Bethlehem who knows how to play the harp. He is a brave man and a warrior. He speaks well and is a fine-looking man. And the LORD is with him."

¹⁹Then Saul sent messengers to Jesse and said, "Send me your son David, who is with the sheep." ²⁰So Jesse took a donkey loaded with bread, a skin of wine and a young goat and sent them with his son David to Saul.

²¹David came to Saul and entered his service. Saul liked him very much, and David became one of his armor-bearers. ²²Then Saul sent word to Jesse, saying, "Allow David to remain in my service, for I am pleased with him."

²³Whenever the spirit from God came upon Saul, David would take his harp and play. Then relief would come to Saul; he would feel better, and the evil spirit would leave him.

DAVID AND GOLIATH

17 Now the Philistines gathered their forces for war and assembled at Socoh in Judah. They pitched camp at Ephes Dammim, between Socoh and Azekah. ²Saul and the Israelites assembled and camped in the Valley of Elah and drew up their battle line to meet the Philistines. ³The Philistines occupied one hill and the Israelites another, with the valley between them.

⁴A champion named Goliath, who was from Gath, came out of the Philistine camp. He was over nine feet*ᵇ* tall. ⁵He had a bronze helmet on his head and wore a coat of scale armor of bronze weighing five thousand shekels*ᶜ*; ⁶on his legs he wore bronze greaves, and a bronze javelin was slung on his back. ⁷His spear shaft was like a weaver's rod, and its iron point weighed six hundred shekels.*ᵈ* His shield bearer went ahead of him.

THE MESSAGE

DAVID—AN EXCELLENT MUSICIAN

16.14 At that very moment the Spirit of GOD left Saul and in its place a black mood sent by GOD settled on him. He was terrified.

16.15-16 Saul's advisors said, "This awful tormenting depression from God is making your life miserable. O master, let us help. Let us look for someone who can play the harp. When the black mood from God moves in, he'll play his music and you'll feel better."

16.17 Saul told his servants, "Go ahead. Find me someone who can play well and bring him to me."

16.18 One of the young men spoke up, "I know someone. I've seen him myself: the son of Jesse of Bethlehem, an excellent musician. He's also courageous, of age, well-spoken, and good-looking. And GOD is with him."

16.19 So Saul sent messengers to Jesse requesting, "Send your son David to me, the one who tends the sheep."

16.20-21 Jesse took a donkey, loaded it with a couple of loaves of bread, a flask of wine, and a young goat, and sent his son David with it to Saul. David came to Saul and stood before him. Saul liked him immediately and made him his right-hand man.

16.22 Saul sent word back to Jesse: "Thank you. David will stay here. He's just the one I was looking for. I'm very impressed by him."

16.23 After that, whenever the bad depression from God tormented Saul, David got out his harp and played. That would calm Saul down, and he would feel better as the moodiness lifted.

GOLIATH

17.1-3 **17** The Philistines drew up their troops for battle. They deployed them at Socoh in Judah, and set up camp between Socoh and Azekah at Ephes Dammim. Saul and the Israelites came together, camped at Oak Valley, and spread out their troops in battle readiness for the Philistines. The Philistines were on one hill, the Israelites on the opposing hill, with the valley between them.

17.4-7 A giant nearly ten feet tall stepped out from the Philistine line into the open, Goliath from Gath. He had a bronze helmet on his head and was dressed in armor—126 pounds of it! He wore bronze shin guards and carried a bronze sword. His spear was like a fence rail—the spear tip alone weighed over fifteen pounds. His shield bearer walked ahead of him.

ᵃ 14 Or *injurious*; also in verses 15, 16 and 23
ᵇ 4 Hebrew *was six cubits and a span* (about 3 meters)
ᶜ 5 That is, about 125 pounds (about 57 kilograms)
ᵈ 7 That is, about 15 pounds (about 7 kilograms)

NEW INTERNATIONAL VERSION

⁸Goliath stood and shouted to the ranks of Israel, "Why do you come out and line up for battle? Am I not a Philistine, and are you not the servants of Saul? Choose a man and have him come down to me. ⁹If he is able to fight and kill me, we will become your subjects; but if I overcome him and kill him, you will become our subjects and serve us." ¹⁰Then the Philistine said, "This day I defy the ranks of Israel! Give me a man and let us fight each other." ¹¹On hearing the Philistine's words, Saul and all the Israelites were dismayed and terrified.

¹²Now David was the son of an Ephrathite named Jesse, who was from Bethlehem in Judah. Jesse had eight sons, and in Saul's time he was old and well advanced in years. ¹³Jesse's three oldest sons had followed Saul to the war: The firstborn was Eliab; the second, Abinadab; and the third, Shammah. ¹⁴David was the youngest. The three oldest followed Saul, ¹⁵but David went back and forth from Saul to tend his father's sheep at Bethlehem.

¹⁶For forty days the Philistine came forward every morning and evening and took his stand.

¹⁷Now Jesse said to his son David, "Take this ephah*ᵃ* of roasted grain and these ten loaves of bread for your brothers and hurry to their camp. ¹⁸Take along these ten cheeses to the commander of their unit.*ᵇ* See how your brothers are and bring back some assurance*ᶜ* from them. ¹⁹They are with Saul and all the men of Israel in the Valley of Elah, fighting against the Philistines."

²⁰Early in the morning David left the flock with a shepherd, loaded up and set out, as Jesse had directed. He reached the camp as the army was going out to its battle positions, shouting the war cry. ²¹Israel and the Philistines were drawing up their lines facing each other. ²²David left his things with the keeper of supplies, ran to the battle lines and greeted his brothers. ²³As he was talking with them, Goliath, the Philistine champion from Gath, stepped out from his lines and shouted his usual defiance, and David heard it. ²⁴When the Israelites saw the man, they all ran from him in great fear.

²⁵Now the Israelites had been saying, "Do you see how this man keeps coming out? He comes out to defy Israel. The king will give great wealth to the man who kills him. He will also give him his daughter in marriage and will exempt his father's family from taxes in Israel."

ᵃ 17 That is, probably about 3/5 bushel (about 22 liters)
ᵇ 18 Hebrew *thousand*   *ᶜ 18* Or *some token*; or *some pledge of spoils*

THE MESSAGE

17.8-10   Goliath stood there and called out to the Israelite troops, "Why bother using your whole army? Am I not Philistine enough for you? And you're all committed to Saul, aren't you? So pick your best fighter and pit him against me. If he gets the upper hand and kills me, the Philistines will all become your slaves. But if I get the upper hand and kill him, you'll all become our slaves and serve us. I challenge the troops of Israel this day. Give me a man. Let us fight it out together!"

17.11   When Saul and his troops heard the Philistine's challenge, they were terrified and lost all hope.

17.12-15   Enter David. He was the son of Jesse the Ephrathite from Bethlehem in Judah. Jesse, the father of eight sons, was himself too old to join Saul's army. Jesse's three older sons had followed Saul to war. The names of the three sons who had joined up with Saul were Eliab, the firstborn; next, Abinadab; and third, Shammah. David was the youngest son. While his three oldest brothers went to war with Saul, David went back and forth from attending to Saul to tending his father's sheep in Bethlehem.

17.16   Each morning and evening for forty days, Goliath took his stand and made his speech.

17.17-19   One day, Jesse told David his son, "Take this sack of cracked wheat and these ten loaves of bread and run them down to your brothers in the camp. And take these ten wedges of cheese to the captain of their division. Check in on your brothers to see whether they are getting along all right, and let me know how they're doing—Saul and your brothers, and all the Israelites in their war with the Philistines in the Oak Valley."

17.20-23   David was up at the crack of dawn and, having arranged for someone to tend his flock, took the food and was on his way just as Jesse had directed him. He arrived at the camp just as the army was moving into battle formation, shouting the war cry. Israel and the Philistines moved into position, facing each other, battle-ready. David left his bundles of food in the care of a sentry, ran to the troops who were deployed, and greeted his brothers. While they were talking together, the Philistine champion, Goliath of Gath, stepped out from the front lines of the Philistines, and gave his usual challenge. David heard him.

17.24-25   The Israelites, to a man, fell back the moment they saw the giant—totally frightened. The talk among the troops was, "Have you ever seen anything like this, this man openly and defiantly challenging Israel? The man who kills the giant will have it made. The king will give him a huge reward, offer his daughter as a bride, and give his entire family a free ride."

NEW INTERNATIONAL VERSION

²⁶David asked the men standing near him, "What will be done for the man who kills this Philistine and removes this disgrace from Israel? Who is this uncircumcised Philistine that he should defy the armies of the living God?"

²⁷They repeated to him what they had been saying and told him, "This is what will be done for the man who kills him."

²⁸When Eliab, David's oldest brother, heard him speaking with the men, he burned with anger at him and asked, "Why have you come down here? And with whom did you leave those few sheep in the desert? I know how conceited you are and how wicked your heart is; you came down only to watch the battle."

²⁹"Now what have I done?" said David. "Can't I even speak?" ³⁰He then turned away to someone else and brought up the same matter, and the men answered him as before. ³¹What David said was overheard and reported to Saul, and Saul sent for him.

³²David said to Saul, "Let no one lose heart on account of this Philistine; your servant will go and fight him."

³³Saul replied, "You are not able to go out against this Philistine and fight him; you are only a boy, and he has been a fighting man from his youth."

³⁴But David said to Saul, "Your servant has been keeping his father's sheep. When a lion or a bear came and carried off a sheep from the flock, ³⁵I went after it, struck it and rescued the sheep from its mouth. When it turned on me, I seized it by its hair, struck it and killed it. ³⁶Your servant has killed both the lion and the bear; this uncircumcised Philistine will be like one of them, because he has defied the armies of the living God. ³⁷The LORD who delivered me from the paw of the lion and the paw of the bear will deliver me from the hand of this Philistine."

Saul said to David, "Go, and the LORD be with you."

³⁸Then Saul dressed David in his own tunic. He put a coat of armor on him and a bronze helmet on his head. ³⁹David fastened on his sword over the tunic and tried walking around, because he was not used to them.

"I cannot go in these," he said to Saul, "because I am not used to them." So he took them off. ⁴⁰Then he took his staff in his hand, chose five smooth stones from the stream, put them in the pouch of his shepherd's bag and, with his sling in his hand, approached the Philistine.

⁴¹Meanwhile, the Philistine, with his shield bearer in front of him, kept coming closer to David. ⁴²He looked David over and saw that he was

THE MESSAGE

FIVE SMOOTH STONES

17.26 David, who was talking to the men standing around him, asked, "What's in it for the man who kills that Philistine and gets rid of this ugly blot on Israel's honor? Who does he think he is, anyway, this uncircumcised Philistine, taunting the armies of God-Alive?"

17.27 They told him what everyone was saying about what the king would do for the man who killed the Philistine.

17.28 Eliab, his older brother, heard David fraternizing with the men and lost his temper: "What are you doing here! Why aren't you minding your own business, tending that scrawny flock of sheep? I know what you're up to. You've come down here to see the sights, hoping for a ringside seat at a bloody battle!"

17.29-30 "What is it with you?" replied David. "All I did was ask a question." Ignoring his brother, he turned to someone else, asked the same question, and got the same answer as before.

17.31 The things David was saying were picked up and reported to Saul. Saul sent for him.

17.32 "Master," said David, "don't give up hope. I'm ready to go and fight this Philistine."

17.33 Saul answered David, "You can't go and fight this Philistine. You're too young and inexperienced—and he's been at this fighting business since before you were born."

17.34-37 David said, "I've been a shepherd, tending sheep for my father. Whenever a lion or bear came and took a lamb from the flock, I'd go after it, knock it down, and rescue the lamb. If it turned on me, I'd grab it by the throat, wring its neck, and kill it. Lion or bear, it made no difference—I killed it. And I'll do the same to this Philistine pig who is taunting the troops of God-Alive. GOD, who delivered me from the teeth of the lion and the claws of the bear, will deliver me from this Philistine."

Saul said, "Go. And GOD help you!"

17.38-39 Then Saul outfitted David as a soldier in armor. He put his bronze helmet on his head and belted his sword on him over the armor. David tried to walk but he could hardly budge.

David told Saul, "I can't even move with all this stuff on me. I'm not used to this." And he took it all off.

17.40 Then David took his shepherd's staff, selected five smooth stones from the brook, and put them in the pocket of his shepherd's pack, and with his sling in his hand approached Goliath.

17.41-42 As the Philistine paced back and forth, his shield bearer in front of him, he noticed David. He took one look down on him and sneered—

NEW INTERNATIONAL VERSION

only a boy, ruddy and handsome, and he despised him. ⁴³He said to David, "Am I a dog, that you come at me with sticks?" And the Philistine cursed David by his gods. ⁴⁴"Come here," he said, "and I'll give your flesh to the birds of the air and the beasts of the field!"

⁴⁵David said to the Philistine, "You come against me with sword and spear and javelin, but I come against you in the name of the LORD Almighty, the God of the armies of Israel, whom you have defied. ⁴⁶This day the LORD will hand you over to me, and I'll strike you down and cut off your head. Today I will give the carcasses of the Philistine army to the birds of the air and the beasts of the earth, and the whole world will know that there is a God in Israel. ⁴⁷All those gathered here will know that it is not by sword or spear that the LORD saves; for the battle is the LORD's, and he will give all of you into our hands."

⁴⁸As the Philistine moved closer to attack him, David ran quickly toward the battle line to meet him. ⁴⁹Reaching into his bag and taking out a stone, he slung it and struck the Philistine on the forehead. The stone sank into his forehead, and he fell facedown on the ground.

⁵⁰So David triumphed over the Philistine with a sling and a stone; without a sword in his hand he struck down the Philistine and killed him.

⁵¹David ran and stood over him. He took hold of the Philistine's sword and drew it from the scabbard. After he killed him, he cut off his head with the sword.

When the Philistines saw that their hero was dead, they turned and ran. ⁵²Then the men of Israel and Judah surged forward with a shout and pursued the Philistines to the entrance of Gath*ᵃ* and to the gates of Ekron. Their dead were strewn along the Shaaraim road to Gath and Ekron. ⁵³When the Israelites returned from chasing the Philistines, they plundered their camp. ⁵⁴David took the Philistine's head and brought it to Jerusalem, and he put the Philistine's weapons in his own tent.

⁵⁵As Saul watched David going out to meet the Philistine, he said to Abner, commander of the army, "Abner, whose son is that young man?"

Abner replied, "As surely as you live, O king, I don't know."

⁵⁶The king said, "Find out whose son this young man is."

⁵⁷As soon as David returned from killing the

THE MESSAGE

a mere youngster, apple-cheeked and peach-fuzzed.

17.43   The Philistine ridiculed David. "Am I a dog that you come after me with a stick?" And he cursed him by his gods.

17.44   "Come on," said the Philistine. "I'll make roadkill of you for the buzzards. I'll turn you into a tasty morsel for the field mice."

17.45-47   David answered, "You come at me with sword and spear and battle-ax. I come at you in the name of GOD-of-the-Angel-Armies, the God of Israel's troops, whom you curse and mock. This very day GOD is handing you over to me. I'm about to kill you, cut off your head, and serve up your body and the bodies of your Philistine buddies to the crows and coyotes. The whole earth will know that there's an extraordinary God in Israel. And everyone gathered here will learn that GOD doesn't save by means of sword or spear. The battle belongs to GOD—he's handing you to us on a platter!"

17.48-49   That roused the Philistine, and he started toward David. David took off from the front line, running toward the Philistine. David reached into his pocket for a stone, slung it, and hit the Philistine hard in the forehead, embedding the stone deeply. The Philistine crashed, facedown in the dirt.

17.50   That's how David beat the Philistine—with a sling and a stone. He hit him and killed him. No sword for David!

17.51   Then David ran up to the Philistine and stood over him, pulled the giant's sword from its sheath, and finished the job by cutting off his head. When the Philistines saw that their great champion was dead, they scattered, running for their lives.

17.52-54   The men of Israel and Judah were up on their feet, shouting! They chased the Philistines all the way to the outskirts of Gath and the gates of Ekron. Wounded Philistines were strewn along the Shaaraim road all the way to Gath and Ekron. After chasing the Philistines, the Israelites came back and looted their camp. David took the Philistine's head and brought it to Jerusalem. But the giant's weapons he placed in his own tent.

✝

17.55   When Saul saw David go out to meet the Philistine, he said to Abner, commander of the army, "Tell me about this young man's family."

Abner said, "For the life of me, O King, I don't know."

17.56   The king said, "Well, find out the lineage of this raw youth."

17.57   As soon as David came back from killing the

ᵃ 52 Some Septuagint manuscripts; Hebrew *a valley*

NEW INTERNATIONAL VERSION

Philistine, Abner took him and brought him before Saul, with David still holding the Philistine's head. ⁵⁸"Whose son are you, young man?" Saul asked him.

David said, "I am the son of your servant Jesse of Bethlehem."

SAUL'S JEALOUSY OF DAVID

18 After David had finished talking with Saul, Jonathan became one in spirit with David, and he loved him as himself. ²From that day Saul kept David with him and did not let him return to his father's house. ³And Jonathan made a covenant with David because he loved him as himself. ⁴Jonathan took off the robe he was wearing and gave it to David, along with his tunic, and even his sword, his bow and his belt.

⁵Whatever Saul sent him to do, David did it so successfully[a] that Saul gave him a high rank in the army. This pleased all the people, and Saul's officers as well.

⁶When the men were returning home after David had killed the Philistine, the women came out from all the towns of Israel to meet King Saul with singing and dancing, with joyful songs and with tambourines and lutes. ⁷As they danced, they sang:

"Saul has slain his thousands,
and David his tens of thousands."

⁸Saul was very angry; this refrain galled him. "They have credited David with tens of thousands," he thought, "but me with only thousands. What more can he get but the kingdom?" ⁹And from that time on Saul kept a jealous eye on David.

¹⁰The next day an evil[b] spirit from God came forcefully upon Saul. He was prophesying in his house, while David was playing the harp, as he usually did. Saul had a spear in his hand ¹¹and he hurled it, saying to himself, "I'll pin David to the wall." But David eluded him twice.

¹²Saul was afraid of David, because the LORD was with David but had left Saul. ¹³So he sent David away from him and gave him command over a thousand men, and David led the troops in their campaigns. ¹⁴In everything he did he had great success,[c] because the LORD was with him. ¹⁵When Saul saw how successful[d] he was,

THE MESSAGE

Philistine, Abner brought him, the Philistine's head still in his hand, straight to Saul.

17.58 Saul asked him, "Young man, whose son are you?"

"I'm the son of your servant Jesse," said David, "the one who lives in Bethlehem."

JONATHAN AND DAVID—SOUL FRIENDS

18.1 **18** By the time David had finished reporting to Saul, Jonathan was deeply impressed with David—an immediate bond was forged between them. He became totally committed to David. From that point on he would be David's number-one advocate and friend.

18.2 Saul received David into his own household that day, no more to return to the home of his father.

18.3-4 Jonathan, out of his deep love for David, made a covenant with him. He formalized it with solemn gifts: his own royal robe and weapons—armor, sword, bow, and belt.

18.5 Whatever Saul gave David to do, he did it— and did it well. So well that Saul put him in charge of his military operations. Everybody, both the people in general and Saul's servants, approved of and admired David's leadership.

DAVID—THE NAME ON EVERYONE'S LIPS

18.6-9 As they returned home, after David had killed the Philistine, the women poured out of all the villages of Israel singing and dancing, welcoming King Saul with tambourines, festive songs, and lutes. In playful frolic the women sang,

Saul kills by the thousand,
David by the ten thousand!

This made Saul angry—very angry. He took it as a personal insult. He said, "They credit David with 'ten thousands' and me with only 'thousands.' Before you know it they'll be giving him the kingdom!" From that moment on, Saul kept his eye on David.

18.10-11 The next day an ugly mood was sent by God to afflict Saul, who became quite beside himself, raving. David played his harp, as he usually did at such times. Saul had a spear in his hand. Suddenly Saul threw the spear, thinking, "I'll nail David to the wall." David ducked, and the spear missed. This happened twice.

18.12-16 Now Saul feared David. It was clear that GOD was with David and had left Saul. So, Saul got David out of his sight by making him an officer in the army. David was in combat frequently. Everything David did turned out well. Yes, GOD was with him. As Saul saw David becoming more successful, he himself grew more

NEW INTERNATIONAL VERSION

he was afraid of him. ¹⁶But all Israel and Judah loved David, because he led them in their campaigns.

¹⁷Saul said to David, "Here is my older daughter Merab. I will give her to you in marriage; only serve me bravely and fight the battles of the LORD." For Saul said to himself, "I will not raise a hand against him. Let the Philistines do that!"

¹⁸But David said to Saul, "Who am I, and what is my family or my father's clan in Israel, that I should become the king's son-in-law?" ¹⁹So ᵃ when the time came for Merab, Saul's daughter, to be given to David, she was given in marriage to Adriel of Meholah.

²⁰Now Saul's daughter Michal was in love with David, and when they told Saul about it, he was pleased. ²¹"I will give her to him," he thought, "so that she may be a snare to him and so that the hand of the Philistines may be against him." So Saul said to David, "Now you have a second opportunity to become my son-in-law."

²²Then Saul ordered his attendants: "Speak to David privately and say, 'Look, the king is pleased with you, and his attendants all like you; now become his son-in-law.' "

²³They repeated these words to David. But David said, "Do you think it is a small matter to become the king's son-in-law? I'm only a poor man and little known."

²⁴When Saul's servants told him what David had said, ²⁵Saul replied, "Say to David, 'The king wants no other price for the bride than a hundred Philistine foreskins, to take revenge on his enemies.' " Saul's plan was to have David fall by the hands of the Philistines.

²⁶When the attendants told David these things, he was pleased to become the king's son-in-law. So before the allotted time elapsed, ²⁷David and his men went out and killed two hundred Philistines. He brought their foreskins and presented the full number to the king so that he might become the king's son-in-law. Then Saul gave him his daughter Michal in marriage.

²⁸When Saul realized that the LORD was with David and that his daughter Michal loved David, ²⁹Saul became still more afraid of him, and he remained his enemy the rest of his days.

³⁰The Philistine commanders continued to go out to battle, and as often as they did, David met with more success ᵇ than the rest of Saul's officers, and his name became well known.

THE MESSAGE

fearful. He could see the handwriting on the wall. But everyone else in Israel and Judah loved David. They loved watching him in action.

18.17 One day Saul said to David, "Here is Merab, my eldest daughter. I want to give her to you as your wife. Be brave and bold for my sake. Fight GOD's battles!" But all the time Saul was thinking, "The Philistines will kill him for me. I won't have to lift a hand against him."

18.18 David, embarrassed, answered, "Do you really mean that? I'm from a family of nobodies! I can't be son-in-law to the king."

18.19 The wedding day was set, but as the time neared for Merab and David to be married, Saul reneged and married his daughter off to Adriel the Meholathite.

18.20-21 Meanwhile, Saul's daughter Michal was in love with David. When Saul was told of this, he rubbed his hands in anticipation. "Ah, a second chance. I'll use Michal as bait to get David out where the Philistines will make short work of him." So again he said to David, "You're going to be my son-in-law."

18.22 Saul ordered his servants, "Get David off by himself and tell him, 'The king is very taken with you, and everyone at court loves you. Go ahead, become the king's son-in-law!' "

18.23 The king's servants told all this to David, but David held back. "What are you thinking of? I can't do that. I'm a nobody; I have nothing to offer."

18.24-25 When the servants reported David's response to Saul, he told them to tell David this: "The king isn't expecting any money from you; only this: Go kill a hundred Philistines and bring evidence of your vengeance on the king's behalf. Avenge the king on his enemies." (Saul expected David to be killed in action.)

18.26-27 On receiving this message, David was pleased. There was something he could do for the king that would qualify him to be his son-in-law! He lost no time but went right out, he and his men, killed the hundred Philistines, brought their evidence back in a sack, and counted it out before the king—mission completed! Saul gave Michal his daughter to David in marriage.

18.28-29 As Saul more and more realized that GOD was with David, and how much his own daughter, Michal, loved him, his fear of David increased and settled into hate. Saul hated David.

18.30 Whenever the Philistine warlords came out to battle, David was there to meet them—and beat them, upstaging Saul's men. David's name was on everyone's lips.

ᵃ 19 Or However, ᵇ 30 Or David acted more wisely

NEW INTERNATIONAL VERSION

SAUL TRIES TO KILL DAVID

19 Saul told his son Jonathan and all the attendants to kill David. But Jonathan was very fond of David ²and warned him, "My father Saul is looking for a chance to kill you. Be on your guard tomorrow morning; go into hiding and stay there. ³I will go out and stand with my father in the field where you are. I'll speak to him about you and will tell you what I find out."

⁴Jonathan spoke well of David to Saul his father and said to him, "Let not the king do wrong to his servant David; he has not wronged you, and what he has done has benefited you greatly. ⁵He took his life in his hands when he killed the Philistine. The LORD won a great victory for all Israel, and you saw it and were glad. Why then would you do wrong to an innocent man like David by killing him for no reason?"

⁶Saul listened to Jonathan and took this oath: "As surely as the LORD lives, David will not be put to death."

⁷So Jonathan called David and told him the whole conversation. He brought him to Saul, and David was with Saul as before.

⁸Once more war broke out, and David went out and fought the Philistines. He struck them with such force that they fled before him.

⁹But an evil*ᵃ* spirit from the LORD came upon Saul as he was sitting in his house with his spear in his hand. While David was playing the harp, ¹⁰Saul tried to pin him to the wall with his spear, but David eluded him as Saul drove the spear into the wall. That night David made good his escape.

¹¹Saul sent men to David's house to watch it and to kill him in the morning. But Michal, David's wife, warned him, "If you don't run for your life tonight, tomorrow you'll be killed." ¹²So Michal let David down through a window, and he fled and escaped. ¹³Then Michal took an idol*ᵇ* and laid it on the bed, covering it with a garment and putting some goats' hair at the head.

¹⁴When Saul sent the men to capture David, Michal said, "He is ill."

¹⁵Then Saul sent the men back to see David and told them, "Bring him up to me in his bed so that I may kill him." ¹⁶But when the men entered, there was the idol in the bed, and at the head was some goats' hair.

¹⁷Saul said to Michal, "Why did you deceive me like this and send my enemy away so that he escaped?"

Michal told him, "He said to me, 'Let me get away. Why should I kill you?'"

ᵃ 9 Or *injurious*   ᵇ 13 Hebrew *teraphim*; also in verse 16

THE MESSAGE

THE BLACK MOOD OF SAUL

19 Saul called his son Jonathan together with his servants and ordered them to kill David. But because Jonathan treasured David, he went and warned him: "My father is looking for a way to kill you. Here's what you are to do. Tomorrow morning, hide and stay hidden. I'll go out with my father into the field where you are hiding. I'll talk about you with my father and we'll see what he says. Then I'll report back to you."

¹⁹.⁴⁻⁵ Jonathan brought up David with his father, speaking well of him. "Please," he said to his father, "don't attack David. He hasn't wronged you, has he? And just look at all the good he has done! He put his life on the line when he killed the Philistine. What a great victory GOD gave Israel that day! You were there. You saw it and were on your feet applauding with everyone else. So why would you even think of sinning against an innocent person, killing David for no reason whatever?"

¹⁹.⁶ Saul listened to Jonathan and said, "You're right. As GOD lives, David lives. He will not be killed."

¹⁹.⁷ Jonathan sent for David and reported to him everything that was said. Then he brought David back to Saul and everything was as it was before.

¹⁹.⁸ War broke out again and David went out to fight Philistines. He beat them badly, and they ran for their lives.

¹⁹.⁹⁻¹⁰ But then a black mood from God settled over Saul and took control of him. He was sitting at home, his spear in his hand, while David was playing music. Suddenly, Saul tried to skewer David with his spear, but David ducked. The spear stuck in the wall and David got away. It was night.

¹⁹.¹¹⁻¹⁴ Saul sent men to David's house to stake it out and then, first thing in the morning, to kill him. But Michal, David's wife, told him what was going on. "Quickly now—make your escape tonight. If not, you'll be dead by morning!" She let him out of a window, and he made his escape. Then Michal took a dummy god and put it in the bed, placed a wig of goat's hair on its head, and threw a quilt over it. When Saul's men arrived to get David, she said, "He's sick in bed."

¹⁹.¹⁵⁻¹⁶ Saul sent his men back, ordering them, "Bring him, bed and all, so I can kill him." When the men entered the room, all they found in the bed was the dummy god with its goat-hair wig!

¹⁹.¹⁷ Saul stormed at Michal: "How could you play tricks on me like this? You sided with my enemy, and now he's gotten away!"

¹⁹.¹⁷ Michal said, "He threatened me. He said, 'Help me out of here or I'll kill you.'"

NEW INTERNATIONAL VERSION

¹⁸When David had fled and made his escape, he went to Samuel at Ramah and told him all that Saul had done to him. Then he and Samuel went to Naioth and stayed there. ¹⁹Word came to Saul: "David is in Naioth at Ramah"; ²⁰so he sent men to capture him. But when they saw a group of prophets prophesying, with Samuel standing there as their leader, the Spirit of God came upon Saul's men and they also prophesied. ²¹Saul was told about it, and he sent more men, and they prophesied too. Saul sent men a third time, and they also prophesied. ²²Finally, he himself left for Ramah and went to the great cistern at Secu. And he asked, "Where are Samuel and David?"

"Over in Naioth at Ramah," they said.

²³So Saul went to Naioth at Ramah. But the Spirit of God came even upon him, and he walked along prophesying until he came to Naioth. ²⁴He stripped off his robes and also prophesied in Samuel's presence. He lay that way all that day and night. This is why people say, "Is Saul also among the prophets?"

DAVID AND JONATHAN

20 Then David fled from Naioth at Ramah and went to Jonathan and asked, "What have I done? What is my crime? How have I wronged your father, that he is trying to take my life?"

²"Never!" Jonathan replied. "You are not going to die! Look, my father doesn't do anything, great or small, without confiding in me. Why would he hide this from me? It's not so!"

³But David took an oath and said, "Your father knows very well that I have found favor in your eyes, and he has said to himself, 'Jonathan must not know this or he will be grieved.' Yet as surely as the LORD lives and as you live, there is only a step between me and death."

⁴Jonathan said to David, "Whatever you want me to do, I'll do for you."

⁵So David said, "Look, tomorrow is the New Moon festival, and I am supposed to dine with the king; but let me go and hide in the field until the evening of the day after tomorrow. ⁶If your father misses me at all, tell him, 'David earnestly asked my permission to hurry to Bethlehem, his hometown, because an annual sacrifice is being made there for his whole clan.' ⁷If he says, 'Very well,' then your servant is safe. But if he loses his

THE MESSAGE

19.18   David made good his escape and went to Samuel at Ramah and told him everything Saul had done to him. Then he and Samuel withdrew to the privacy of Naioth.

19.19-20   Saul was told, "David's at Naioth in Ramah." He immediately sent his men to capture him. They saw a band of prophets prophesying with Samuel presiding over them. Before they knew it, the Spirit of God was on them, too, and they were ranting and raving right along with the prophets!

19.21   That was reported back to Saul, and he dispatched more men. They, too, were soon prophesying. So Saul tried a third time—a third set of men—and they ended up mindlessly raving as well!

19.22   Fed up, Saul went to Ramah himself. He came to the big cistern at Secu and inquired, "Where are Samuel and David?"

A bystander said, "Over at Naioth in Ramah."

19.23-24   As he headed out for Naioth in Ramah, the Spirit of God was on him, too. All the way to Naioth he was caught up in a babbling trance! He ripped off his clothes and lay there rambling gibberish before Samuel for a day and a night, stretched out naked. People are still talking about it: "Saul among the prophets! Who would have guessed?"

A COVENANT FRIENDSHIP IN GOD'S NAME

20.1   **20** David got out of Naioth in Ramah alive and went to Jonathan. "What do I do now? What wrong have I inflicted on your father that makes him so determined to kill me?"

20.2   "Nothing," said Jonathan. "You've done nothing wrong. And you're not going to die. Really, you're not! My father tells me everything. He does nothing, whether big or little, without confiding in me. So why would he do this behind my back? It can't be."

20.3   But David said, "Your father knows that we are the best of friends. So he says to himself, 'Jonathan must know nothing of this. If he does, he'll side with David.' But it's true—as sure as GOD lives, and as sure as you're alive before me right now—he's determined to kill me."

20.4   Jonathan said, "Tell me what you have in mind. I'll do anything for you."

20.5-8   David said, "Tomorrow marks the New Moon. I'm scheduled to eat dinner with the king. Instead, I'll go hide in the field until the evening of the third. If your father misses me, say, 'David asked if he could run down to Bethlehem, his hometown, for an anniversary reunion, and worship with his family.' If he says, 'Good!' then I'm safe. But if he gets angry, you'll

NEW INTERNATIONAL VERSION

temper, you can be sure that he is determined to harm me. ⁸As for you, show kindness to your servant, for you have brought him into a covenant with you before the LORD. If I am guilty, then kill me yourself! Why hand me over to your father?"

⁹"Never!" Jonathan said. "If I had the least inkling that my father was determined to harm you, wouldn't I tell you?"

¹⁰David asked, "Who will tell me if your father answers you harshly?"

¹¹"Come," Jonathan said, "let's go out into the field." So they went there together.

¹²Then Jonathan said to David: "By the LORD, the God of Israel, I will surely sound out my father by this time the day after tomorrow! If he is favorably disposed toward you, will I not send you word and let you know? ¹³But if my father is inclined to harm you, may the LORD deal with me, be it ever so severely, if I do not let you know and send you away safely. May the LORD be with you as he has been with my father. ¹⁴But show me unfailing kindness like that of the LORD as long as I live, so that I may not be killed, ¹⁵and do not ever cut off your kindness from my family—not even when the LORD has cut off every one of David's enemies from the face of the earth."

¹⁶So Jonathan made a covenant with the house of David, saying, "May the LORD call David's enemies to account." ¹⁷And Jonathan had David reaffirm his oath out of love for him, because he loved him as he loved himself.

¹⁸Then Jonathan said to David: "Tomorrow is the New Moon festival. You will be missed, because your seat will be empty. ¹⁹The day after tomorrow, toward evening, go to the place where you hid when this trouble began, and wait by the stone Ezel. ²⁰I will shoot three arrows to the side of it, as though I were shooting at a target. ²¹Then I will send a boy and say, 'Go, find the arrows.' If I say to him, 'Look, the arrows are on this side of you; bring them here,' then come, because, as surely as the LORD lives, you are safe; there is no danger. ²²But if I say to the boy, 'Look, the arrows are beyond you,' then you must go, because the LORD has sent you away. ²³And about the matter you and I discussed—remember, the LORD is witness between you and me forever."

²⁴So David hid in the field, and when the New Moon festival came, the king sat down to eat. ²⁵He sat in his customary place by the wall, opposite Jonathan,ᵃ and Abner sat next to Saul, but David's place was empty. ²⁶Saul said nothing that day, for he thought, "Something must have happened to David to make him ceremonially unclean—surely he is unclean." ²⁷But the next day,

ᵃ 25 Septuagint; Hebrew wall. Jonathan arose

THE MESSAGE

know for sure that he's made up his mind to kill me. Oh, stick with me in this. You've entered into a covenant of GOD with me, remember! If I'm in the wrong, go ahead and kill me yourself. Why bother giving me up to your father?"

20.9 "Never!" exclaimed Jonathan. "I'd never do that! If I get the slightest hint that my father is fixated on killing you, I'll tell you."

20.10 David asked, "And whom will you get to tell me if your father comes back with a harsh answer?"

20.11-17 "Come outside," said Jonathan. "Let's go to the field." When the two of them were out in the field, Jonathan said, "As GOD, the God of Israel, is my witness, by this time tomorrow I'll get it out of my father how he feels about you. Then I'll let you know what I learn. May GOD do his worst to me if I let you down! If my father still intends to kill you, I'll tell you and get you out of here in one piece. And GOD be with you as he's been with my father! If I make it through this alive, continue to be my covenant friend. And if I die, keep the covenant friendship with my family—forever. And when GOD finally rids the earth of David's enemies, stay loyal to Jonathan!" Jonathan repeated his pledge of love and friendship for David. He loved David more than his own soul!

20.18-23 Jonathan then laid out his plan: "Tomorrow is the New Moon, and you'll be missed when you don't show up for dinner. On the third day, when they've quit expecting you, come to the place where you hid before, and wait beside that big boulder. I'll shoot three arrows in the direction of the boulder. Then I'll send off my servant, 'Go find the arrows.' If I yell after the servant, 'The arrows are on this side! Retrieve them!' that's the signal that you can return safely—as GOD lives, not a thing to fear! But if I yell, 'The arrows are farther out!' then run for it—GOD wants you out of here! Regarding all the things we've discussed, remember that GOD's in on this with us to the very end!"

20.24-26 David hid in the field. On the holiday of the New Moon, the king came to the table to eat. He sat where he always sat, the place against the wall, with Jonathan across the table and Abner at Saul's side. But David's seat was empty. Saul didn't mention it at the time, thinking, "Something's happened that's made him unclean. That's it—he's probably unclean for the holy meal."

NEW INTERNATIONAL VERSION

the second day of the month, David's place was empty again. Then Saul said to his son Jonathan, "Why hasn't the son of Jesse come to the meal, either yesterday or today?"

²⁸Jonathan answered, "David earnestly asked me for permission to go to Bethlehem. ²⁹He said, 'Let me go, because our family is observing a sacrifice in the town and my brother has ordered me to be there. If I have found favor in your eyes, let me get away to see my brothers.' That is why he has not come to the king's table."

³⁰Saul's anger flared up at Jonathan and he said to him, "You son of a perverse and rebellious woman! Don't I know that you have sided with the son of Jesse to your own shame and to the shame of the mother who bore you? ³¹As long as the son of Jesse lives on this earth, neither you nor your kingdom will be established. Now send and bring him to me, for he must die!"

³²"Why should he be put to death? What has he done?" Jonathan asked his father. ³³But Saul hurled his spear at him to kill him. Then Jonathan knew that his father intended to kill David.

³⁴Jonathan got up from the table in fierce anger; on that second day of the month he did not eat, because he was grieved at his father's shameful treatment of David.

³⁵In the morning Jonathan went out to the field for his meeting with David. He had a small boy with him, ³⁶and he said to the boy, "Run and find the arrows I shoot." As the boy ran, he shot an arrow beyond him. ³⁷When the boy came to the place where Jonathan's arrow had fallen, Jonathan called out after him, "Isn't the arrow beyond you?" ³⁸Then he shouted, "Hurry! Go quickly! Don't stop!" The boy picked up the arrow and returned to his master. ³⁹(The boy knew nothing of all this; only Jonathan and David knew.) ⁴⁰Then Jonathan gave his weapons to the boy and said, "Go, carry them back to town."

⁴¹After the boy had gone, David got up from the south side ⌊of the stone⌋ and bowed down before Jonathan three times, with his face to the ground. Then they kissed each other and wept together—but David wept the most.

⁴²Jonathan said to David, "Go in peace, for we have sworn friendship with each other in the name of the LORD, saying, 'The LORD is witness between you and me, and between your descendants and my descendants forever.' " Then David left, and Jonathan went back to the town.

THE MESSAGE

20.27 But the day after the New Moon, day two of the holiday, David's seat was still empty. Saul asked Jonathan his son, "So where's that son of Jesse? He hasn't eaten with us either yesterday or today."

20.28-29 Jonathan said, "David asked my special permission to go to Bethlehem. He said, 'Give me leave to attend a family reunion back home. My brothers have ordered me to be there. If it seems all right to you, let me go and see my brothers.' That's why he's not here at the king's table."

20.30-31 Saul exploded in anger at Jonathan: "You son of a slut! Don't you think I know that you're in cahoots with the son of Jesse, disgracing both you and your mother? For as long as the son of Jesse is walking around free on this earth, your future in this kingdom is at risk. Now go get him. Bring him here. From this moment, he's as good as dead!"

20.32 Jonathan stood up to his father. "Why dead? What's he done?"

20.33 Saul threw his spear at him to kill him. That convinced Jonathan that his father was fixated on killing David.

20.34 Jonathan stormed from the table, furiously angry, and ate nothing the rest of the day, upset for David and smarting under the humiliation from his father.

20.35-39 In the morning, Jonathan went to the field for the appointment with David. He had his young servant with him. He told the servant, "Run and get the arrows I'm about to shoot." The boy started running and Jonathan shot an arrow way beyond him. As the boy came to the area where the arrow had been shot, Jonathan yelled out, "Isn't the arrow farther out?" He yelled again, "Hurry! Quickly! Don't just stand there!" Jonathan's servant then picked up the arrow and brought it to his master. The boy, of course, knew nothing of what was going on. Only Jonathan and David knew.

20.40-41 Jonathan gave his quiver and bow to the boy and sent him back to town. After the servant was gone, David got up from his hiding place beside the boulder, then fell on his face to the ground—three times prostrating himself! And then they kissed one another and wept, friend over friend, David weeping especially hard.

20.42 Jonathan said, "Go in peace! The two of us have vowed friendship in GOD's name, saying, 'GOD will be the bond between me and you, and between my children and your children forever!' "

NEW INTERNATIONAL VERSION

DAVID AT NOB

21 David went to Nob, to Ahimelech the priest. Ahimelech trembled when he met him, and asked, "Why are you alone? Why is no one with you?"

²David answered Ahimelech the priest, "The king charged me with a certain matter and said to me, 'No one is to know anything about your mission and your instructions.' As for my men, I have told them to meet me at a certain place. ³Now then, what do you have on hand? Give me five loaves of bread, or whatever you can find."

⁴But the priest answered David, "I don't have any ordinary bread on hand; however, there is some consecrated bread here—provided the men have kept themselves from women."

⁵David replied, "Indeed women have been kept from us, as usual whenever*ᵃ* I set out. The men's things*ᵇ* are holy even on missions that are not holy. How much more so today!" ⁶So the priest gave him the consecrated bread, since there was no bread there except the bread of the Presence that had been removed from before the LORD and replaced by hot bread on the day it was taken away.

⁷Now one of Saul's servants was there that day, detained before the LORD; he was Doeg the Edomite, Saul's head shepherd.

⁸David asked Ahimelech, "Don't you have a spear or a sword here? I haven't brought my sword or any other weapon, because the king's business was urgent."

⁹The priest replied, "The sword of Goliath the Philistine, whom you killed in the Valley of Elah, is here; it is wrapped in a cloth behind the ephod. If you want it, take it; there is no sword here but that one."

David said, "There is none like it; give it to me."

DAVID AT GATH

¹⁰That day David fled from Saul and went to Achish king of Gath. ¹¹But the servants of Achish said to him, "Isn't this David, the king of the land? Isn't he the one they sing about in their dances:

" 'Saul has slain his thousands,
   and David his tens of thousands'?"

¹²David took these words to heart and was very much afraid of Achish king of Gath. ¹³So he pretended to be insane in their presence; and while he was in their hands he acted like a madman, making marks on the doors of the gate and letting saliva run down his beard.

¹⁴Achish said to his servants, "Look at the

THE MESSAGE

DAVID PRETENDS TO GO CRAZY

21.1 **21** David went on his way and Jonathan returned to town.

David went to Nob, to Ahimelech the Priest. Ahimelech was alarmed as he went out to greet David: "What are you doing here all by yourself—and not a soul with you?"

21.2-3 David answered Ahimelech the Priest, "The king sent me on a mission and gave strict orders: 'This is top secret—not a word of this to a soul.' I've arranged to meet up with my men in a certain place. Now, what's there here to eat? Do you have five loaves of bread? Give me whatever you can scrounge up!"

21.4 "I don't have any regular bread on hand," said the priest. "I only have holy bread. If your men have not slept with women recently, it's yours."

21.5 David said, "None of us has touched a woman. I always do it this way when I'm on a mission: My men abstain from sex. Even when it is an ordinary mission we do that—how much more on this holy mission."

21.6 So the priest gave them the holy bread. It was the only bread he had, Bread of the Presence that had been removed from GOD's presence and replaced by fresh bread at the same time.

21.7 One of Saul's officials was present that day keeping a religious vow. His name was Doeg the Edomite. He was chief of Saul's shepherds.

21.8 David asked Ahimelech, "Do you have a spear or sword of any kind around here? I didn't have a chance to grab my weapons. The king's mission was urgent and I left in a hurry."

21.9 The priest said, "The sword of Goliath, the Philistine you killed at Oak Valley—that's here! It's behind the Ephod wrapped in a cloth. If you want it, take it. There's nothing else here."

21.10-11 "Oh," said David, "there's no sword like that! Give it to me!"

And at that, David shot out of there, running for his life from Saul. He went to Achish, king of Gath. When the servants of Achish saw him, they said, "Can this be David, the famous David? Is this the one they sing of at their dances?

Saul kills by the thousand,
   David by the ten thousand!"

21.12-15 When David realized that he had been recognized, he panicked, fearing the worst from Achish, king of Gath. So right there, while they were looking at him, he pretended to go crazy, pounding his head on the city gate and foaming at the mouth, spit dripping from his beard. Achish took one look at him and said to his

---

ᵃ 5 Or from us in the past few days since   ᵇ 5 Or bodies

NEW INTERNATIONAL VERSION

man! He is insane! Why bring him to me? ¹⁵Am I so short of madmen that you have to bring this fellow here to carry on like this in front of me? Must this man come into my house?"

DAVID AT ADULLAM AND MIZPAH

22 David left Gath and escaped to the cave of Adullam. When his brothers and his father's household heard about it, they went down to him there. ²All those who were in distress or in debt or discontented gathered around him, and he became their leader. About four hundred men were with him.

³From there David went to Mizpah in Moab and said to the king of Moab, "Would you let my father and mother come and stay with you until I learn what God will do for me?" ⁴So he left them with the king of Moab, and they stayed with him as long as David was in the stronghold.

⁵But the prophet Gad said to David, "Do not stay in the stronghold. Go into the land of Judah." So David left and went to the forest of Hereth.

SAUL KILLS THE PRIESTS OF NOB

⁶Now Saul heard that David and his men had been discovered. And Saul, spear in hand, was seated under the tamarisk tree on the hill at Gibeah, with all his officials standing around him. ⁷Saul said to them, "Listen, men of Benjamin! Will the son of Jesse give all of you fields and vineyards? Will he make all of you commanders of thousands and commanders of hundreds? ⁸Is that why you have all conspired against me? No one tells me when my son makes a covenant with the son of Jesse. None of you is concerned about me or tells me that my son has incited my servant to lie in wait for me, as he does today."

⁹But Doeg the Edomite, who was standing with Saul's officials, said, "I saw the son of Jesse come to Ahimelech son of Ahitub at Nob. ¹⁰Ahimelech inquired of the LORD for him; he also gave him provisions and the sword of Goliath the Philistine."

¹¹Then the king sent for the priest Ahimelech son of Ahitub and his father's whole family, who were the priests at Nob, and they all came to the king. ¹²Saul said, "Listen now, son of Ahitub."

"Yes, my lord," he answered.

¹³Saul said to him, "Why have you conspired against me, you and the son of Jesse, giving him bread and a sword and inquiring of God for him, so that he has rebelled against me and lies in wait for me, as he does today?"

¹⁴Ahimelech answered the king, "Who of all your servants is as loyal as David, the king's son-in-law, captain of your bodyguard and highly respected in your household? ¹⁵Was that day the

THE MESSAGE

servants, "Can't you see he's crazy? Why did you let him in here? Don't you think I have enough crazy people to put up with as it is without adding another? Get him out of here!"

SAUL MURDERS THE PRIESTS OF GOD

22.1-2 **22** So David got away and escaped to the Cave of Adullam. When his brothers and others associated with his family heard where he was, they came down and joined him. Not only that, but all who were down on their luck came around—losers and vagrants and misfits of all sorts. David became their leader. There were about four hundred in all.

22.3-4   Then David went to Mizpah in Moab. He petitioned the king of Moab, "Grant asylum to my father and mother until I find out what God has planned for me." David left his parents in the care of the king of Moab. They stayed there all through the time David was hiding out.

22.5   The prophet Gad told David, "Don't go back to the cave. Go to Judah." David did what he told him. He went to the forest of Hereth.

22.6-8   Saul got word of the whereabouts of David and his men. He was sitting under the big oak on the hill at Gibeah at the time, spear in hand, holding court surrounded by his officials. He said, "Listen here, you Benjaminites! Don't think for a minute that you have any future with the son of Jesse! Do you think he's going to hand over choice land, give you all influential jobs? Think again. Here you are, conspiring against me, whispering behind my back—not one of you is man enough to tell me that my own son is making deals with the son of Jesse, not one of you who cares enough to tell me that my son has taken the side of this, this . . . outlaw!"

22.9-10   Then Doeg the Edomite, who was standing with Saul's officials, spoke up: "I saw the son of Jesse meet with Ahimelech son of Ahitub, in Nob. I saw Ahimelech pray with him for God's guidance, give him food, and arm him with the sword of Goliath the Philistine."

22.11   Saul sent for the priest Ahimelech son of Ahitub, along with the whole family of priests at Nob. They all came to the king.

22.12   Saul said, "You listen to me, son of Ahitub!"
"Certainly, master," he said.

22.13   "Why have you ganged up against me with the son of Jesse, giving him bread and a sword, even praying with him for GOD's guidance, setting him up as an outlaw, out to get me?"

22.14-15   Ahimelech answered the king, "There's not an official in your administration as true to you as David, your own son-in-law and captain of your bodyguard. None more honorable either.

NEW INTERNATIONAL VERSION

first time I inquired of God for him? Of course not! Let not the king accuse your servant or any of his father's family, for your servant knows nothing at all about this whole affair."

¹⁶But the king said, "You will surely die, Ahimelech, you and your father's whole family."

¹⁷Then the king ordered the guards at his side: "Turn and kill the priests of the LORD, because they too have sided with David. They knew he was fleeing, yet they did not tell me."

But the king's officials were not willing to raise a hand to strike the priests of the LORD.

¹⁸The king then ordered Doeg, "You turn and strike down the priests." So Doeg the Edomite turned and struck them down. That day he killed eighty-five men who wore the linen ephod. ¹⁹He also put to the sword Nob, the town of the priests, with its men and women, its children and infants, and its cattle, donkeys and sheep.

²⁰But Abiathar, a son of Ahimelech son of Ahitub, escaped and fled to join David. ²¹He told David that Saul had killed the priests of the LORD. ²²Then David said to Abiathar: "That day, when Doeg the Edomite was there, I knew he would be sure to tell Saul. I am responsible for the death of your father's whole family. ²³Stay with me; don't be afraid; the man who is seeking your life is seeking mine also. You will be safe with me."

DAVID SAVES KEILAH

23 When David was told, "Look, the Philistines are fighting against Keilah and are looting the threshing floors," ²he inquired of the LORD, saying, "Shall I go and attack these Philistines?"

The LORD answered him, "Go, attack the Philistines and save Keilah."

³But David's men said to him, "Here in Judah we are afraid. How much more, then, if we go to Keilah against the Philistine forces!"

⁴Once again David inquired of the LORD, and the LORD answered him, "Go down to Keilah, for I am going to give the Philistines into your hand." ⁵So David and his men went to Keilah, fought the Philistines and carried off their livestock. He inflicted heavy losses on the Philistines and saved the people of Keilah. ⁶(Now Abiathar son of Ahimelech had brought the ephod down with him when he fled to David at Keilah.)

SAUL PURSUES DAVID

⁷Saul was told that David had gone to Keilah, and he said, "God has handed him over to me, for David has imprisoned himself by entering a town with gates and bars." ⁸And Saul called up

THE MESSAGE

Do you think that was the first time I prayed with him for God's guidance? Hardly! But don't accuse me of any wrongdoing, me or my family. I have no idea what you're trying to get at with this 'outlaw' talk."

22.16 The king said, "Death, Ahimelech! You're going to die—you and everyone in your family!"

22.17 The king ordered his henchmen, "Surround and kill the priests of GOD! They're hand in glove with David. They knew he was running away from me and didn't tell me." But the king's men wouldn't do it. They refused to lay a hand on the priests of GOD.

22.18-19 Then the king told Doeg, "You do it—massacre the priests!" Doeg the Edomite led the attack and slaughtered the priests, the eighty-five men who wore the sacred robes. He then carried the massacre into Nob, the city of priests, killing man and woman, child and baby, ox, donkey, and sheep—the works.

22.20-21 Only one son of Ahimelech son of Ahitub escaped: Abiathar. He got away and joined up with David. Abiathar reported to David that Saul had murdered the priests of GOD.

22.22-23 David said to Abiathar, "I knew it—that day I saw Doeg the Edomite there, I knew he'd tell Saul. I'm to blame for the death of everyone in your father's family. Stay here with me. Don't be afraid. The one out to kill you is out to kill me, too. Stick with me. I'll protect you."

LIVING IN DESERT HIDEOUTS

23 It was reported to David that the Philistines were raiding Keilah and looting the grain. David went in prayer to GOD: "Should I go after these Philistines and teach them a lesson?"

GOD said, "Go. Attack the Philistines and save Keilah."

23.3 But David's men said, "We live in fear of our lives right here in Judah. How can you think of going to Keilah in the thick of the Philistines?"

23.4 So David went back to GOD in prayer. GOD said, "Get going. Head for Keilah. I'm placing the Philistines in your hands."

23.5-6 David and his men went to Keilah and fought the Philistines. He scattered their cattle, beat them decisively, and saved the people of Keilah. After Abiathar took refuge with David, he joined David in the raid on Keilah, bringing the Ephod with him.

23.7-8 Saul learned that David had gone to Keilah and thought immediately, "Good! God has handed him to me on a platter! He's in a walled city with locked gates, trapped!" Saul mustered

NEW INTERNATIONAL VERSION

all his forces for battle, to go down to Keilah to besiege David and his men.

⁹When David learned that Saul was plotting against him, he said to Abiathar the priest, "Bring the ephod." ¹⁰David said, "O LORD, God of Israel, your servant has heard definitely that Saul plans to come to Keilah and destroy the town on account of me. ¹¹Will the citizens of Keilah surrender me to him? Will Saul come down, as your servant has heard? O LORD, God of Israel, tell your servant."

And the LORD said, "He will."

¹²Again David asked, "Will the citizens of Keilah surrender me and my men to Saul?"

And the LORD said, "They will."

¹³So David and his men, about six hundred in number, left Keilah and kept moving from place to place. When Saul was told that David had escaped from Keilah, he did not go there.

¹⁴David stayed in the desert strongholds and in the hills of the Desert of Ziph. Day after day Saul searched for him, but God did not give David into his hands.

¹⁵While David was at Horesh in the Desert of Ziph, he learned that Saul had come out to take his life. ¹⁶And Saul's son Jonathan went to David at Horesh and helped him find strength in God. ¹⁷"Don't be afraid," he said. "My father Saul will not lay a hand on you. You will be king over Israel, and I will be second to you. Even my father Saul knows this." ¹⁸The two of them made a covenant before the LORD. Then Jonathan went home, but David remained at Horesh.

¹⁹The Ziphites went up to Saul at Gibeah and said, "Is not David hiding among us in the strongholds at Horesh, on the hill of Hakilah, south of Jeshimon? ²⁰Now, O king, come down whenever it pleases you to do so, and we will be responsible for handing him over to the king."

²¹Saul replied, "The LORD bless you for your concern for me. ²²Go and make further preparation. Find out where David usually goes and who has seen him there. They tell me he is very crafty. ²³Find out about all the hiding places he uses and come back to me with definite information.ᵃ Then I will go with you; if he is in the area, I will track him down among all the clans of Judah."

²⁴So they set out and went to Ziph ahead of Saul. Now David and his men were in the Desert of Maon, in the Arabah south of Jeshimon. ²⁵Saul and his men began the search, and when David was told about it, he went down to the rock and stayed in the Desert of Maon. When

THE MESSAGE

his troops for battle and set out for Keilah to lay siege to David and his men.

23.9-11 But David got wind of Saul's strategy to destroy him and said to Abiathar the priest, "Get the Ephod." Then David prayed to GOD: "God of Israel, I've just heard that Saul plans to come to Keilah and destroy the city because of me. Will the city fathers of Keilah turn me over to him? Will Saul come down and do what I've heard? O GOD, God of Israel, tell me!"

GOD replied, "He's coming down."

23.12 "And will the head men of Keilah turn me and my men over to Saul?"

And GOD said, "They'll turn you over."

23.13 So David and his men got out of there. There were about six hundred of them. They left Keilah and kept moving, going here, there, wherever—always on the move.

When Saul was told that David had escaped from Keilah, he called off the raid.

23.14-15 David continued to live in desert hideouts and the backcountry wilderness hills of Ziph. Saul was out looking for him day after day, but God never turned David over to him. David kept out of the way in the wilderness of Ziph, secluded at Horesh, since it was plain that Saul was determined to hunt him down.

23.16-18 Jonathan, Saul's son, visited David at Horesh and encouraged him in God. He said, "Don't despair. My father, Saul, can't lay a hand on you. You will be Israel's king and I'll be right at your side to help. And my father knows it." Then the two of them made a covenant before GOD. David stayed at Horesh and Jonathan went home.

23.19-20 Some Ziphites went to Saul at Gibeah and said, "Did you know that David is hiding out near us in the caves and canyons of Horesh? Right now he's at Hakilah Hill just south of Jeshimon. So whenever you're ready to come down, we'd count it an honor to hand him over to the king."

23.21-23 Saul said, "GOD bless you for thinking about me! Now go back and check everything out. Learn his routines. Observe his movements—where he goes, who he's with. He's very shrewd, you know. Scout out all his hiding places. Then meet me at Nacon and I'll go with you. If he is anywhere to be found in all the thousands of Judah, I'll track him down!"

23.24-27 So the Ziphites set out on their reconnaissance for Saul.

Meanwhile, David and his men were in the wilderness of Maon, in the desert south of Jeshimon. Saul and his men arrived and began their search. When David heard of it, he went south to Rock Mountain, camping out in the

---

ᵃ 23 Or *me at Nacon*

NEW INTERNATIONAL VERSION

Saul heard this, he went into the Desert of Maon in pursuit of David.

²⁶Saul was going along one side of the mountain, and David and his men were on the other side, hurrying to get away from Saul. As Saul and his forces were closing in on David and his men to capture them, ²⁷a messenger came to Saul, saying, "Come quickly! The Philistines are raiding the land." ²⁸Then Saul broke off his pursuit of David and went to meet the Philistines. That is why they call this place Sela Hammahlekoth. ᵃ ²⁹And David went up from there and lived in the strongholds of En Gedi.

DAVID SPARES SAUL'S LIFE

24 After Saul returned from pursuing the Philistines, he was told, "David is in the Desert of En Gedi." ²So Saul took three thousand chosen men from all Israel and set out to look for David and his men near the Crags of the Wild Goats.

³He came to the sheep pens along the way; a cave was there, and Saul went in to relieve himself. David and his men were far back in the cave. ⁴The men said, "This is the day the LORD spoke of when he said ᵇ to you, 'I will give your enemy into your hands for you to deal with as you wish.' " Then David crept up unnoticed and cut off a corner of Saul's robe.

⁵Afterward, David was conscience-stricken for having cut off a corner of his robe. ⁶He said to his men, "The LORD forbid that I should do such a thing to my master, the LORD's anointed, or lift my hand against him; for he is the anointed of the LORD." ⁷With these words David rebuked his men and did not allow them to attack Saul. And Saul left the cave and went his way.

⁸Then David went out of the cave and called out to Saul, "My lord the king!" When Saul looked behind him, David bowed down and prostrated himself with his face to the ground. ⁹He said to Saul, "Why do you listen when men say, 'David is bent on harming you'? ¹⁰This day you have seen with your own eyes how the LORD delivered you into my hands in the cave. Some urged me to kill you, but I spared you; I said, 'I will not lift my hand against my master, because he is the LORD's anointed.' ¹¹See, my father, look at this piece of your robe in my hand! I cut off the corner of your robe but did not kill you. Now understand and recognize that I am not guilty of wrongdoing or rebellion. I have not wronged you, but you are hunting me down to take my life. ¹²May the LORD judge between you and me. And may the LORD avenge the wrongs you have

THE MESSAGE

wilderness of Maon. Saul heard where he was and set off for the wilderness of Maon in pursuit. Saul was on one side of the mountain, David and his men on the other. David was in full retreat, running, with Saul and his men closing in, about to get him. Just then a messenger came to Saul and said, "Hurry! Come back! The Philistines have just attacked the country!"

23.28-29 So Saul called off his pursuit of David and went back to deal with the Philistines. That's how that place got the name Narrow Escape. David left there and camped out in the caves and canyons of En Gedi.

"I'M NO REBEL."

24.1-4 **24** When Saul came back after dealing with the Philistines, he was told, "David is now in the wilderness of En Gedi." Saul took three companies—the best he could find in all Israel—and set out in search of David and his men in the region of Wild Goat Rocks. He came to some sheep pens along the road. There was a cave there and Saul went in to relieve himself. David and his men were huddled far back in the same cave. David's men whispered to him, "Can you believe it? This is the day GOD was talking about when he said, 'I'll put your enemy in your hands. You can do whatever you want with him.' " Quiet as a cat, David crept up and cut off a piece of Saul's royal robe.

24.5-7 Immediately, he felt guilty. He said to his men, "GOD forbid that I should have done this to my master, GOD's anointed, that I should so much as raise a finger against him. He's GOD's anointed!" David held his men in check with these words and wouldn't let them pounce on Saul. Saul got up, left the cave, and went on down the road.

24.8-13 Then David stood at the mouth of the cave and called to Saul, "My master! My king!" Saul looked back. David fell to his knees and bowed in reverence. He called out, "Why do you listen to those who say 'David is out to get you'? This very day with your very own eyes you have seen that just now in the cave GOD put you in my hands. My men wanted me to kill you, but I wouldn't do it. I told them that I won't lift a finger against my master—he's GOD's anointed. Oh, my father, look at this, look at this piece that I cut from your robe. I could have cut you—killed you!—but I didn't. Look at the evidence! I'm not against you. I'm no rebel. I haven't sinned against you, and yet you're hunting me down to kill me. Let's decide which of us is in the right. God may avenge me, but it

ᵃ 28 *Sela Hammahlekoth* means *rock of parting.*
ᵇ 4 Or *"Today the* LORD *is saying*

NEW INTERNATIONAL VERSION

done to me, but my hand will not touch you. 13As the old saying goes, 'From evildoers come evil deeds,' so my hand will not touch you.

14"Against whom has the king of Israel come out? Whom are you pursuing? A dead dog? A flea? 15May the LORD be our judge and decide between us. May he consider my cause and uphold it; may he vindicate me by delivering me from your hand."

16When David finished saying this, Saul asked, "Is that your voice, David my son?" And he wept aloud. 17"You are more righteous than I," he said. "You have treated me well, but I have treated you badly. 18You have just now told me of the good you did to me; the LORD delivered me into your hands, but you did not kill me. 19When a man finds his enemy, does he let him get away unharmed? May the LORD reward you well for the way you treated me today. 20I know that you will surely be king and that the kingdom of Israel will be established in your hands. 21Now swear to me by the LORD that you will not cut off my descendants or wipe out my name from my father's family."

22So David gave his oath to Saul. Then Saul returned home, but David and his men went up to the stronghold.

DAVID, NABAL AND ABIGAIL

25 Now Samuel died, and all Israel assembled and mourned for him; and they buried him at his home in Ramah.

Then David moved down into the Desert of Maon.[a] 2A certain man in Maon, who had property there at Carmel, was very wealthy. He had a thousand goats and three thousand sheep, which he was shearing in Carmel. 3His name was Nabal and his wife's name was Abigail. She was an intelligent and beautiful woman, but her husband, a Calebite, was surly and mean in his dealings.

4While David was in the desert, he heard that Nabal was shearing sheep. 5So he sent ten young men and said to them, "Go up to Nabal at Carmel and greet him in my name. 6Say to him: 'Long life to you! Good health to you and your household! And good health to all that is yours!

7"'Now I hear that it is sheep-shearing time. When your shepherds were with us, we did not mistreat them, and the whole time they were at Carmel nothing of theirs was missing. 8Ask your own servants and they will tell you. Therefore be favorable toward my young men, since we come at a festive time. Please give your servants and your son David whatever you can find for them.'"

THE MESSAGE

is in his hands, not mine. An old proverb says, 'Evil deeds come from evil people.' So be assured that my hand won't touch you.

24.14-15 "What does the king of Israel think he's doing? Who do you think you're chasing? A dead dog? A flea? GOD is our judge. He'll decide who is right. Oh, that he would look down right now, decide right now—and set me free of you!"

24.16-21 When David had finished saying all this, Saul said, "Can this be the voice of my son David?" and he wept in loud sobs. "You're the one in the right, not me," he continued. "You've heaped good on me; I've dumped evil on you. And now you've done it again—treated me generously. GOD put me in your hands and you didn't kill me. Why? When a man meets his enemy, does he send him down the road with a blessing? May GOD give you a bonus of blessings for what you've done for me today! I know now beyond doubt that you will rule as king. The kingdom of Israel is already in your grasp! Now promise me under GOD that you will not kill off my family or wipe my name off the books."

24.22 David promised Saul. Then Saul went home and David and his men went up to their wilderness refuge.

TO FIGHT GOD'S BATTLES

25.1 25 Samuel died. The whole country came to his funeral. Everyone grieved over his death, and he was buried in his hometown of Ramah. Meanwhile, David moved again, this time to the wilderness of Maon.

25.2-3 There was a certain man in Maon who carried on his business in the region of Carmel. He was very prosperous—three thousand sheep and a thousand goats, and it was sheep-shearing time in Carmel. The man's name was Nabal (Fool), a Calebite, and his wife's name was Abigail. The woman was intelligent and good-looking, the man brutish and mean.

25.4-8 David, out in the backcountry, heard that Nabal was shearing his sheep and sent ten of his young men off with these instructions: "Go to Carmel and approach Nabal. Greet him in my name, 'Peace! Life and peace to you. Peace to your household, peace to everyone here! I heard that it's sheep-shearing time. Here's the point: When your shepherds were camped near us we didn't take advantage of them. They didn't lose a thing all the time they were with us in Carmel. Ask your young men—they'll tell you. What I'm asking is that you be generous with my men—share the feast! Give whatever your heart tells you to your servants and to me, David your son.'"

NEW INTERNATIONAL VERSION

⁹When David's men arrived, they gave Nabal this message in David's name. Then they waited.

¹⁰Nabal answered David's servants, "Who is this David? Who is this son of Jesse? Many servants are breaking away from their masters these days. ¹¹Why should I take my bread and water, and the meat I have slaughtered for my shearers, and give it to men coming from who knows where?"

¹²David's men turned around and went back. When they arrived, they reported every word. ¹³David said to his men, "Put on your swords!" So they put on their swords, and David put on his. About four hundred men went up with David, while two hundred stayed with the supplies.

¹⁴One of the servants told Nabal's wife Abigail: "David sent messengers from the desert to give our master his greetings, but he hurled insults at them. ¹⁵Yet these men were very good to us. They did not mistreat us, and the whole time we were out in the fields near them nothing was missing. ¹⁶Night and day they were a wall around us all the time we were herding our sheep near them. ¹⁷Now think it over and see what you can do, because disaster is hanging over our master and his whole household. He is such a wicked man that no one can talk to him."

¹⁸Abigail lost no time. She took two hundred loaves of bread, two skins of wine, five dressed sheep, five seahs*ᵃ* of roasted grain, a hundred cakes of raisins and two hundred cakes of pressed figs, and loaded them on donkeys. ¹⁹Then she told her servants, "Go on ahead; I'll follow you." But she did not tell her husband Nabal.

²⁰As she came riding her donkey into a mountain ravine, there were David and his men descending toward her, and she met them. ²¹David had just said, "It's been useless—all my watching over this fellow's property in the desert so that nothing of his was missing. He has paid me back evil for good. ²²May God deal with David,*ᵇ* be it ever so severely, if by morning I leave alive one male of all who belong to him!"

²³When Abigail saw David, she quickly got off her donkey and bowed down before David with her face to the ground. ²⁴She fell at his feet and said: "My lord, let the blame be on me alone. Please let your servant speak to you; hear what your servant has to say. ²⁵May my lord pay no attention to that wicked man Nabal. He is just like his name—his name is Fool, and folly goes with him. But as for me, your servant, I did not see the men my master sent.

ᵃ 18 That is, probably about a bushel (about 37 liters)
ᵇ 22 Some Septuagint manuscripts; Hebrew *with David's enemies*

THE MESSAGE

25.9-11   David's young men went and delivered his message word for word to Nabal. Nabal tore into them, "Who is this David? Who is this son of Jesse? The country is full of runaway servants these days. Do you think I'm going to take good bread and wine and meat freshly butchered for my sheepshearers and give it to men I've never laid eyes on? Who knows where they've come from?"

25.12-13   David's men got out of there and went back and told David what he had said. David said, "Strap on your swords!" They all strapped on their swords, David and his men, and set out, four hundred of them. Two hundred stayed behind to guard the camp.

25.14-17   Meanwhile, one of the young shepherds told Abigail, Nabal's wife, what had happened: "David sent messengers from the backcountry to salute our master, but he tore into them with insults. Yet these men treated us very well. They took nothing from us and didn't take advantage of us all the time we were in the fields. They formed a wall around us, protecting us day and night all the time we were out tending the sheep. Do something quickly because big trouble is ahead for our master and all of us. Nobody can talk to him. He's impossible—a real brute!"

25.18-19   Abigail flew into action. She took two hundred loaves of bread, two skins of wine, five sheep dressed out and ready for cooking, a bushel of roasted grain, a hundred raisin cakes, and two hundred fig cakes, and she had it all loaded on some donkeys. Then she said to her young servants, "Go ahead and pave the way for me. I'm right behind you." But she said nothing to her husband Nabal.

25.20-22   As she was riding her donkey, descending into a ravine, David and his men were descending from the other end, so they met there on the road. David had just said, "That sure was a waste, guarding everything this man had out in the wild so that nothing he had was lost—and now he rewards me with insults. A real slap in the face! May God do his worst to me if Nabal and every cur in his misbegotten brood isn't dead meat by morning!"

25.23-25   As soon as Abigail saw David, she got off her donkey and fell on her knees at his feet, her face to the ground in homage, saying, "My master, let me take the blame! Let me speak to you. Listen to what I have to say. Don't dwell on what that brute Nabal did. He acts out the meaning of his name: Nabal, Fool. Foolishness oozes from him.

25.25-27   "I wasn't there when the young men my master sent arrived. I didn't see them. And now,

NEW INTERNATIONAL VERSION

26"Now since the LORD has kept you, my master, from bloodshed and from avenging yourself with your own hands, as surely as the LORD lives and as you live, may your enemies and all who intend to harm my master be like Nabal. 27And let this gift, which your servant has brought to my master, be given to the men who follow you. 28Please forgive your servant's offense, for the LORD will certainly make a lasting dynasty for my master, because he fights the LORD's battles. Let no wrongdoing be found in you as long as you live. 29Even though someone is pursuing you to take your life, the life of my master will be bound securely in the bundle of the living by the LORD your God. But the lives of your enemies he will hurl away as from the pocket of a sling. 30When the LORD has done for my master every good thing he promised concerning him and has appointed him leader over Israel, 31my master will not have on his conscience the staggering burden of needless bloodshed or of having avenged himself. And when the LORD has brought my master success, remember your servant."

32David said to Abigail, "Praise be to the LORD, the God of Israel, who has sent you today to meet me. 33May you be blessed for your good judgment and for keeping me from bloodshed this day and from avenging myself with my own hands. 34Otherwise, as surely as the LORD, the God of Israel, lives, who has kept me from harming you, if you had not come quickly to meet me, not one male belonging to Nabal would have been left alive by daybreak."

35Then David accepted from her hand what she had brought him and said, "Go home in peace. I have heard your words and granted your request."

36When Abigail went to Nabal, he was in the house holding a banquet like that of a king. He was in high spirits and very drunk. So she told him nothing until daybreak. 37Then in the morning, when Nabal was sober, his wife told him all these things, and his heart failed him and he became like a stone. 38About ten days later, the LORD struck Nabal and he died.

39When David heard that Nabal was dead, he said, "Praise be to the LORD, who has upheld my cause against Nabal for treating me with contempt. He has kept his servant from doing wrong and has brought Nabal's wrongdoing down on his own head."

Then David sent word to Abigail, asking her to become his wife. 40His servants went to Carmel and said to Abigail, "David has sent us to you to take you to become his wife."

THE MESSAGE

my master, as GOD lives and as you live, GOD has kept you from this avenging murder—and may your enemies, all who seek my master's harm, end up like Nabal! Now take this gift that I, your servant girl, have brought to my master, and give it to the young men who follow in the steps of my master.

25.28-29 "Forgive my presumption! But GOD is at work in my master, developing a rule solid and dependable. My master fights GOD's battles! As long as you live no evil will stick to you.

If anyone stands in your way,
    if anyone tries to get you out of the way,
Know this: Your God-honored life is tightly
    bound
    in the bundle of God-protected life;
But the lives of your enemies will be hurled
    aside
    as a stone is thrown from a sling.

25.30-31 "When GOD completes all the goodness he has promised my master and sets you up as prince over Israel, my master will not have this dead weight in his heart, the guilt of an avenging murder. And when GOD has worked things for good for my master, remember me."

25.32-34 And David said, "Blessed be GOD, the God of Israel. He sent you to meet me! And blessed be your good sense! Bless you for keeping me from murder and taking charge of looking out for me. A close call! As GOD lives, the God of Israel who kept me from hurting you, if you had not come as quickly as you did, stopping me in my tracks, by morning there would have been nothing left of Nabal but dead meat."

25.35 Then David accepted the gift she brought him and said, "Return home in peace. I've heard what you've said and I'll do what you've asked."

25.36-38 When Abigail got home she found Nabal presiding over a huge banquet. He was in high spirits—and very, very drunk. So she didn't tell him anything of what she'd done until morning. But in the morning, after Nabal had sobered up, she told him the whole story. Right then and there he had a heart attack and fell into a coma. About ten days later GOD finished him off and he died.

25.39-40 When David heard that Nabal was dead he said, "Blessed be GOD who has stood up for me against Nabal's insults, kept me from an evil act, and let Nabal's evil boomerang back on him."

Then David sent for Abigail to tell her that he wanted her for his wife. David's servants went to Abigail at Carmel with the message, "David sent us to bring you to marry him."

NEW INTERNATIONAL VERSION

⁴¹She bowed down with her face to the ground and said, "Here is your maidservant, ready to serve you and wash the feet of my master's servants." ⁴²Abigail quickly got on a donkey and, attended by her five maids, went with David's messengers and became his wife. ⁴³David had also married Ahinoam of Jezreel, and they both were his wives. ⁴⁴But Saul had given his daughter Michal, David's wife, to Paltiel[a] son of Laish, who was from Gallim.

DAVID AGAIN SPARES SAUL'S LIFE

26 The Ziphites went to Saul at Gibeah and said, "Is not David hiding on the hill of Hakilah, which faces Jeshimon?"

²So Saul went down to the Desert of Ziph, with his three thousand chosen men of Israel, to search there for David. ³Saul made his camp beside the road on the hill of Hakilah facing Jeshimon, but David stayed in the desert. When he saw that Saul had followed him there, ⁴he sent out scouts and learned that Saul had definitely arrived.[b]

⁵Then David set out and went to the place where Saul had camped. He saw where Saul and Abner son of Ner, the commander of the army, had lain down. Saul was lying inside the camp, with the army encamped around him.

⁶David then asked Ahimelech the Hittite and Abishai son of Zeruiah, Joab's brother, "Who will go down into the camp with me to Saul?"

"I'll go with you," said Abishai.

⁷So David and Abishai went to the army by night, and there was Saul, lying asleep inside the camp with his spear stuck in the ground near his head. Abner and the soldiers were lying around him.

⁸Abishai said to David, "Today God has delivered your enemy into your hands. Now let me pin him to the ground with one thrust of my spear; I won't strike him twice."

⁹But David said to Abishai, "Don't destroy him! Who can lay a hand on the LORD's anointed and be guiltless? ¹⁰As surely as the LORD lives," he said, "the LORD himself will strike him; either his time will come and he will die, or he will go into battle and perish. ¹¹But the LORD forbid that I should lay a hand on the LORD's anointed. Now get the spear and water jug that are near his head, and let's go."

¹²So David took the spear and water jug near

THE MESSAGE

25.41   She got up, and then bowed down, face to the ground, saying, "I'm your servant, ready to do anything you want. I'll even wash the feet of my master's servants!"

25.42   Abigail didn't linger. She got on her donkey and, with her five maids in attendance, went with the messengers to David and became his wife.

25.43-44   David also married Ahinoam of Jezreel. Both women were his wives. Saul had married off David's wife Michal to Palti (Paltiel) son of Laish, who was from Gallim.

OBSESSED WITH A SINGLE FLEA

26.1-3   **26** Some Ziphites came to Saul at Gibeah and said, "Did you know that David is hiding out on the Hakilah Hill just opposite Jeshimon?" Saul was on his feet in a minute and on his way to the wilderness of Ziph, taking three thousand of his best men, the pick of the crop, to hunt for David in that wild desert. He camped just off the road at the Hakilah Hill, opposite Jeshimon.

26.3-5   David, still out in the backcountry, knew Saul had come after him. He sent scouts to determine his precise location. Then David set out and came to the place where Saul had set up camp and saw for himself where Saul and Abner, son of Ner, his general, were staying. Saul was safely inside the camp, encircled by the army.

26.6   Taking charge, David spoke to Ahimelech the Hittite and to Abishai son of Zeruiah, Joab's brother: "Who will go down with me and enter Saul's camp?"

Abishai whispered, "I'll go with you."

26.7   So David and Abishai entered the encampment by night, and there he was—Saul, stretched out asleep at the center of the camp, his spear stuck in the ground near his head, with Abner and the troops sound asleep on all sides.

26.8   Abishai said, "This is the moment! God has put your enemy in your grasp. Let me nail him to the ground with his spear. One hit will do it, believe me; I won't need a second!"

26.9   But David said to Abishai, "Don't you dare hurt him! Who could lay a hand on GOD's anointed and even think of getting away with it?"

26.10-11   He went on, "As GOD lives, either GOD will strike him, or his time will come and he'll die in bed, or he'll fall in battle, but GOD forbid that I should lay a finger on GOD's anointed. Now, grab the spear at his head and the water jug and let's get out of here."

26.12   David took the spear and water jug that

---

[a] 44 Hebrew *Palti*, a variant of *Paltiel*   [b] 4 Or *had come to Nacon*

NEW INTERNATIONAL VERSION

Saul's head, and they left. No one saw or knew about it, nor did anyone wake up. They were all sleeping, because the LORD had put them into a deep sleep.

¹³Then David crossed over to the other side and stood on top of the hill some distance away; there was a wide space between them. ¹⁴He called out to the army and to Abner son of Ner, "Aren't you going to answer me, Abner?"

Abner replied, "Who are you who calls to the king?"

¹⁵David said, "You're a man, aren't you? And who is like you in Israel? Why didn't you guard your lord the king? Someone came to destroy your lord the king. ¹⁶What you have done is not good. As surely as the LORD lives, you and your men deserve to die, because you did not guard your master, the LORD's anointed. Look around you. Where are the king's spear and water jug that were near his head?"

¹⁷Saul recognized David's voice and said, "Is that your voice, David my son?"

David replied, "Yes it is, my lord the king." ¹⁸And he added, "Why is my lord pursuing his servant? What have I done, and what wrong am I guilty of? ¹⁹Now let my lord the king listen to his servant's words. If the LORD has incited you against me, then may he accept an offering. If, however, men have done it, may they be cursed before the LORD! They have now driven me from my share in the LORD's inheritance and have said, 'Go, serve other gods.' ²⁰Now do not let my blood fall to the ground far from the presence of the LORD. The king of Israel has come out to look for a flea—as one hunts a partridge in the mountains."

²¹Then Saul said, "I have sinned. Come back, David my son. Because you considered my life precious today, I will not try to harm you again. Surely I have acted like a fool and have erred greatly."

²²"Here is the king's spear," David answered. "Let one of your young men come over and get it. ²³The LORD rewards every man for his righteousness and faithfulness. The LORD delivered you into my hands today, but I would not lay a hand on the LORD's anointed. ²⁴As surely as I valued your life today, so may the LORD value my life and deliver me from all trouble."

²⁵Then Saul said to David, "May you be blessed, my son David; you will do great things and surely triumph."

So David went on his way, and Saul returned home.

THE MESSAGE

were right beside Saul's head, and they slipped away. Not a soul saw. Not a soul knew. No one woke up! They all slept through the whole thing. A blanket of deep sleep from GOD had fallen on them.

26.13-14 Then David went across to the opposite hill and stood far away on the top of the mountain. With this safe distance between them, he shouted across to the army and Abner son of Ner, "Hey Abner! How long do I have to wait for you to wake up and answer me?"

Abner said, "Who's calling?"

26.15-16 "Aren't you in charge there?" said David. "Why aren't you minding the store? Why weren't you standing guard over your master the king, when a soldier came to kill the king your master? Bad form! As GOD lives, your life should be forfeit, you and the entire bodyguard. Look what I have—the king's spear and water jug that were right beside his head!"

26.17-20 By now, Saul had recognized David's voice and said, "Is that you, my son David?"

David said, "Yes, it's me, O King, my master. Why are you after me, hunting me down? What have I done? What crime have I committed? Oh, my master, my king, listen to this from your servant: If GOD has stirred you up against me, then I gladly offer my life as a sacrifice. But if it's men who have done it, let them be banished from GOD's presence! They've expelled me from my rightful place in GOD's heritage, sneering, 'Out of here! Go get a job with some other god!' But you're not getting rid of me that easily; you'll not separate me from GOD in life or death. The absurdity! The king of Israel obsessed with a single flea! Hunting me down—a mere partridge—out in the hills!"

26.21 Saul confessed, "I've sinned! Oh, come back, my dear son David! I won't hurt you anymore. You've honored me this day, treating my life as most precious. And I've acted the fool—a moral dunce, a real clown."

26.22-24 David answered, "See what I have here? The king's spear. Let one of your servants come and get it. It's GOD's business to decide what to do with each of us in regard to what's right and who's loyal. GOD put your life in my hands today, but I wasn't willing to lift a finger against GOD's anointed. Just as I honored your life today, may GOD honor my life and rescue me from all trouble."

26.25 Saul said to David, "Bless you, dear son David! Yes, do what you have to do! And, yes, succeed in all you attempt!"

Then David went on his way, and Saul went home.

NEW INTERNATIONAL VERSION

DAVID AMONG THE PHILISTINES

27 But David thought to himself, "One of these days I will be destroyed by the hand of Saul. The best thing I can do is to escape to the land of the Philistines. Then Saul will give up searching for me anywhere in Israel, and I will slip out of his hand."

²So David and the six hundred men with him left and went over to Achish son of Maoch king of Gath. ³David and his men settled in Gath with Achish. Each man had his family with him, and David had his two wives: Ahinoam of Jezreel and Abigail of Carmel, the widow of Nabal. ⁴When Saul was told that David had fled to Gath, he no longer searched for him.

⁵Then David said to Achish, "If I have found favor in your eyes, let a place be assigned to me in one of the country towns, that I may live there. Why should your servant live in the royal city with you?"

⁶So on that day Achish gave him Ziklag, and it has belonged to the kings of Judah ever since. ⁷David lived in Philistine territory a year and four months.

⁸Now David and his men went up and raided the Geshurites, the Girzites and the Amalekites. (From ancient times these peoples had lived in the land extending to Shur and Egypt.) ⁹Whenever David attacked an area, he did not leave a man or woman alive, but took sheep and cattle, donkeys and camels, and clothes. Then he returned to Achish.

¹⁰When Achish asked, "Where did you go raiding today?" David would say, "Against the Negev of Judah" or "Against the Negev of Jerahmeel" or "Against the Negev of the Kenites." ¹¹He did not leave a man or woman alive to be brought to Gath, for he thought, "They might inform on us and say, 'This is what David did.' " And such was his practice as long as he lived in Philistine territory. ¹²Achish trusted David and said to himself, "He has become so odious to his people, the Israelites, that he will be my servant forever."

SAUL AND THE WITCH OF ENDOR

28 In those days the Philistines gathered their forces to fight against Israel. Achish said to David, "You must understand that you and your men will accompany me in the army."

²David said, "Then you will see for yourself what your servant can do."

Achish replied, "Very well, I will make you my bodyguard for life."

THE MESSAGE

27.1 **27** David thought to himself, "Sooner or later, Saul's going to get me. The best thing I can do is escape to Philistine country. Saul will count me a lost cause and quit hunting me down in every nook and cranny of Israel. I'll be out of his reach for good."

27.2-4 So David left; he and his six hundred men went to Achish son of Maoch, king of Gath. They moved in and settled down in Gath, with Achish. Each man brought his household; David brought his two wives, Ahinoam of Jezreel and Abigail, widow of Nabal of Carmel. When Saul was told that David had escaped to Gath, he called off the hunt.

27.5 Then David said to Achish, "If it's agreeable to you, assign me a place in one of the rural villages. It doesn't seem right that I, your mere servant, should be taking up space in the royal city."

27.6-7 So Achish assigned him Ziklag. (This is how Ziklag got to be what it is now, a city of the kings of Judah.) David lived in Philistine country a year and four months.

27.8-9 From time to time David and his men raided the Geshurites, the Girzites, and the Amalekites—these people were longtime inhabitants of the land stretching toward Shur and on to Egypt. When David raided an area he left no one alive, neither man nor woman, but took everything else: sheep, cattle, donkeys, camels, clothing—the works. Then he'd return to Achish.

Achish would ask, "And whom did you raid today?"

27.10-11 David would tell him, "Oh, the Negev of Judah," or "The Negev of Jerahmeel," or "The Negev of the Kenites." He never left a single person alive lest one show up in Gath and report what David had really been doing. This is the way David operated all the time he lived in Philistine country.

27.12 Achish came to trust David completely. He thought, "He's made himself so repugnant to his people that he'll be in my camp forever."

28.1 **28** During this time the Philistines mustered their troops to make war on Israel. Achish said to David, "You can count on this: You're marching with my troops, you and your men."

28.2 And David said, "Good! Now you'll see for yourself what I can do!"

"Great!" said Achish. "I'm making you my personal bodyguard—for life!"

NEW INTERNATIONAL VERSION

³Now Samuel was dead, and all Israel had mourned for him and buried him in his own town of Ramah. Saul had expelled the mediums and spiritists from the land.

⁴The Philistines assembled and came and set up camp at Shunem, while Saul gathered all the Israelites and set up camp at Gilboa. ⁵When Saul saw the Philistine army, he was afraid; terror filled his heart. ⁶He inquired of the LORD, but the LORD did not answer him by dreams or Urim or prophets. ⁷Saul then said to his attendants, "Find me a woman who is a medium, so I may go and inquire of her."

"There is one in Endor," they said.

⁸So Saul disguised himself, putting on other clothes, and at night he and two men went to the woman. "Consult a spirit for me," he said, "and bring up for me the one I name."

⁹But the woman said to him, "Surely you know what Saul has done. He has cut off the mediums and spiritists from the land. Why have you set a trap for my life to bring about my death?"

¹⁰Saul swore to her by the LORD, "As surely as the LORD lives, you will not be punished for this."

¹¹Then the woman asked, "Whom shall I bring up for you?"

"Bring up Samuel," he said.

¹²When the woman saw Samuel, she cried out at the top of her voice and said to Saul, "Why have you deceived me? You are Saul!"

¹³The king said to her, "Don't be afraid. What do you see?"

The woman said, "I see a spirit*a* coming up out of the ground."

¹⁴"What does he look like?" he asked.

"An old man wearing a robe is coming up," she said.

Then Saul knew it was Samuel, and he bowed down and prostrated himself with his face to the ground.

¹⁵Samuel said to Saul, "Why have you disturbed me by bringing me up?"

"I am in great distress," Saul said. "The Philistines are fighting against me, and God has turned away from me. He no longer answers me, either by prophets or by dreams. So I have called on you to tell me what to do."

¹⁶Samuel said, "Why do you consult me, now that the LORD has turned away from you and become your enemy? ¹⁷The LORD has done what he predicted through me. The LORD has torn the kingdom out of your hands and given it to one of your neighbors—to David. ¹⁸Because you did

---

a 13 Or see spirits; or see gods

THE MESSAGE

SAUL PRAYED, BUT GOD DIDN'T ANSWER

28.3 Samuel was now dead. All Israel had mourned his death and buried him in Ramah, his hometown. Saul had long since cleaned out all those who held seances with the dead.

28.4-5 The Philistines had mustered their troops and camped at Shunem. Saul had assembled all Israel and camped at Gilboa. But when Saul saw the Philistine troops, he shook in his boots, scared to death.

28.6 Saul prayed to GOD, but GOD didn't answer—neither by dream nor by sign nor by prophet.

28.7 So Saul ordered his officials, "Find me someone who can call up spirits so I may go and seek counsel from those spirits."

His servants said, "There's a witch at Endor."

28.8 Saul disguised himself by putting on different clothes. Then, taking two men with him, he went under the cover of night to the woman and said, "I want you to consult a ghost for me. Call up the person I name."

28.9 The woman said, "Just hold on now! You know what Saul did, how he swept the country clean of mediums. Why are you trying to trap me and get me killed?"

28.10 Saul swore solemnly, "As GOD lives, you won't get in any trouble for this."

28.11 The woman said, "So whom do you want me to bring up?"

"Samuel. Bring me Samuel."

28.12 When the woman saw Samuel, she cried out loudly to Saul, "Why did you lie to me? You're Saul!"

28.13 The king told her, "You have nothing to fear . . . but what do you see?"

"I see a spirit ascending from the underground."

28.14 "And what does he look like?" Saul asked.

"An old man ascending, robed like a priest."

Saul knew it was Samuel. He fell down, face to the ground, and worshiped.

28.15 Samuel said to Saul, "Why have you disturbed me by calling me up?"

"Because I'm in deep trouble," said Saul. "The Philistines are making war against me and God has deserted me—he doesn't answer me any more, either by prophet or by dream. And so I'm calling on you to tell me what to do."

28.16-19 "Why ask me?" said Samuel. "GOD has turned away from you and is now on the side of your neighbor. GOD has done exactly what he told you through me—ripped the kingdom right out of your hands and given it to your neighbor. It's because you did not obey GOD,

NEW INTERNATIONAL VERSION

not obey the LORD or carry out his fierce wrath against the Amalekites, the LORD has done this to you today. ¹⁹The LORD will hand over both Israel and you to the Philistines, and tomorrow you and your sons will be with me. The LORD will also hand over the army of Israel to the Philistines."

²⁰Immediately Saul fell full length on the ground, filled with fear because of Samuel's words. His strength was gone, for he had eaten nothing all that day and night.

²¹When the woman came to Saul and saw that he was greatly shaken, she said, "Look, your maidservant has obeyed you. I took my life in my hands and did what you told me to do. ²²Now please listen to your servant and let me give you some food so you may eat and have the strength to go on your way."

²³He refused and said, "I will not eat."

But his men joined the woman in urging him, and he listened to them. He got up from the ground and sat on the couch.

²⁴The woman had a fattened calf at the house, which she butchered at once. She took some flour, kneaded it and baked bread without yeast. ²⁵Then she set it before Saul and his men, and they ate. That same night they got up and left.

ACHISH SENDS DAVID BACK TO ZIKLAG

29 The Philistines gathered all their forces at Aphek, and Israel camped by the spring in Jezreel. ²As the Philistine rulers marched with their units of hundreds and thousands, David and his men were marching at the rear with Achish. ³The commanders of the Philistines asked, "What about these Hebrews?"

Achish replied, "Is this not David, who was an officer of Saul king of Israel? He has already been with me for over a year, and from the day he left Saul until now, I have found no fault in him."

⁴But the Philistine commanders were angry with him and said, "Send the man back, that he may return to the place you assigned him. He must not go with us into battle, or he will turn against us during the fighting. How better could he regain his master's favor than by taking the heads of our own men? ⁵Isn't this the David they sang about in their dances:

" 'Saul has slain his thousands,
    and David his tens of thousands'?"

⁶So Achish called David and said to him, "As surely as the LORD lives, you have been reliable,

THE MESSAGE

refused to carry out his seething judgment on Amalek, that GOD does to you what he is doing today. Worse yet, GOD is turning Israel, along with you, over to the Philistines. Tomorrow you and your sons will be with me. And, yes, indeed, GOD is giving Israel's army up to the Philistines."

28.20-22   Saul dropped to the ground, felled like a tree, terrified by Samuel's words. There wasn't an ounce of strength left in him—he'd eaten nothing all day and all night. The woman, realizing that he was in deep shock, said to him, "Listen to me. I did what you asked me to do, put my life in your hands in doing it, carried out your instructions to the letter. It's your turn to do what I tell you: Let me give you some food. Eat it. It will give you strength so you can get on your way."

28.23-25   He refused. "I'm not eating anything."

But when his servants joined the woman in urging him, he gave in to their pleas, picked himself up off the ground, and sat on the bed. The woman moved swiftly. She butchered a grain-fed calf she had, and took some flour, kneaded it, and baked some flat bread. Then she served it all up for Saul and his servants. After dining handsomely, they got up from the table and were on their way that same night.

29.1-2   **29** The Philistines mustered all their troops at Aphek. Meanwhile Israel had made camp at the spring at Jezreel. As the Philistine warlords marched forward by regiments and divisions, David and his men were bringing up the rear with Achish.

29.3   The Philistine officers said, "What business do these Hebrews have being here?"

Achish answered the officers, "Don't you recognize David, ex-servant of King Saul of Israel? He's been with me a long time. I've found nothing to be suspicious of, nothing to complain about, from the day he defected from Saul until now."

29.4-5   Angry with Achish, the Philistine officers said, "Send this man back to where he came from. Let him stick to his normal duties. He's not going into battle with us. He'd switch sides in the middle of the fight! What better chance to get back in favor with his master than by stabbing us in the back! Isn't this the same David they celebrate at their parties, singing,

Saul kills by the thousand,
    David by the ten thousand!"

29.6-7   So Achish had to send for David and tell him, "As GOD lives, you've been a trusty ally—

NEW INTERNATIONAL VERSION

and I would be pleased to have you serve with me in the army. From the day you came to me until now, I have found no fault in you, but the rulers don't approve of you. ⁷Turn back and go in peace; do nothing to displease the Philistine rulers."

⁸"But what have I done?" asked David. "What have you found against your servant from the day I came to you until now? Why can't I go and fight against the enemies of my lord the king?"

⁹Achish answered, "I know that you have been as pleasing in my eyes as an angel of God; nevertheless, the Philistine commanders have said, 'He must not go up with us into battle.' ¹⁰Now get up early, along with your master's servants who have come with you, and leave in the morning as soon as it is light."

¹¹So David and his men got up early in the morning to go back to the land of the Philistines, and the Philistines went up to Jezreel.

DAVID DESTROYS THE AMALEKITES

30 David and his men reached Ziklag on the third day. Now the Amalekites had raided the Negev and Ziklag. They had attacked Ziklag and burned it, ²and had taken captive the women and all who were in it, both young and old. They killed none of them, but carried them off as they went on their way.

³When David and his men came to Ziklag, they found it destroyed by fire and their wives and sons and daughters taken captive. ⁴So David and his men wept aloud until they had no strength left to weep. ⁵David's two wives had been captured—Ahinoam of Jezreel and Abigail, the widow of Nabal of Carmel. ⁶David was greatly distressed because the men were talking of stoning him; each one was bitter in spirit because of his sons and daughters. But David found strength in the LORD his God.

⁷Then David said to Abiathar the priest, the son of Ahimelech, "Bring me the ephod." Abiathar brought it to him, ⁸and David inquired of the LORD, "Shall I pursue this raiding party? Will I overtake them?"

"Pursue them," he answered. "You will certainly overtake them and succeed in the rescue."

⁹David and the six hundred men with him came to the Besor Ravine, where some stayed behind, ¹⁰for two hundred men were too exhausted to cross the ravine. But David and four hundred men continued the pursuit.

¹¹They found an Egyptian in a field and brought him to David. They gave him water to

THE MESSAGE

excellent in all the ways you have worked with me, beyond reproach in the ways you have conducted yourself. But the warlords don't see it that way. So it's best that you leave peacefully, now. It's not worth it, displeasing the Philistine warlords."

29.8 "But what have I done?" said David. "Have you had a single cause for complaint from the day I joined up with you until now? Why can't I fight against the enemies of my master the king?"

29.9-10 "I agree," said Achish. "You're a good man— as far as I'm concerned, God's angel! But the Philistine officers were emphatic: 'He's not to go with us into battle.' So get an early start, you and the men who came with you. As soon as you have light enough to travel, go."

29.11 David rose early, he and his men, and by daybreak they were on their way back to Philistine country. The Philistines went on to Jezreel.

DAVID'S STRENGTH WAS IN HIS GOD

30.1-3 **30** Three days later, David and his men arrived back in Ziklag. Amalekites had raided the Negev and Ziklag. They tore Ziklag to pieces and then burned it down. They captured all the women, young and old. They didn't kill anyone, but drove them like a herd of cattle. By the time David and his men entered the village, it had been burned to the ground, and their wives, sons, and daughters all taken prisoner.

30.4-6 David and his men burst out in loud wails— wept and wept until they were exhausted with weeping. David's two wives, Ahinoam of Jezreel and Abigail widow of Nabal of Carmel, had been taken prisoner along with the rest. And suddenly David was in even worse trouble. There was talk among the men, bitter over the loss of their families, of stoning him.

30.6-7 David strengthened himself with trust in his GOD. He ordered Abiathar the priest, son of Ahimelech, "Bring me the Ephod so I can consult God." Abiathar brought it to David.

30.8 Then David prayed to GOD, "Shall I go after these raiders? Can I catch them?"

The answer came, "Go after them! Yes, you'll catch them! Yes, you'll make the rescue!"

30.9-10 David went, he and the six hundred men with him. They arrived at the Brook Besor, where some of them dropped out. David and four hundred men kept up the pursuit, but two hundred of them were too fatigued to cross the Brook Besor, and stayed there.

30.11-12 Some who went on came across an Egyptian in a field and took him to David. They gave him bread and he ate. And he drank some wa-

NEW INTERNATIONAL VERSION

drink and food to eat— ¹²part of a cake of pressed figs and two cakes of raisins. He ate and was revived, for he had not eaten any food or drunk any water for three days and three nights.

¹³David asked him, "To whom do you belong, and where do you come from?"

He said, "I am an Egyptian, the slave of an Amalekite. My master abandoned me when I became ill three days ago. ¹⁴We raided the Negev of the Kerethites and the territory belonging to Judah and the Negev of Caleb. And we burned Ziklag."

¹⁵David asked him, "Can you lead me down to this raiding party?"

He answered, "Swear to me before God that you will not kill me or hand me over to my master, and I will take you down to them."

¹⁶He led David down, and there they were, scattered over the countryside, eating, drinking and reveling because of the great amount of plunder they had taken from the land of the Philistines and from Judah. ¹⁷David fought them from dusk until the evening of the next day, and none of them got away, except four hundred young men who rode off on camels and fled. ¹⁸David recovered everything the Amalekites had taken, including his two wives. ¹⁹Nothing was missing: young or old, boy or girl, plunder or anything else they had taken. David brought everything back. ²⁰He took all the flocks and herds, and his men drove them ahead of the other livestock, saying, "This is David's plunder."

²¹Then David came to the two hundred men who had been too exhausted to follow him and who were left behind at the Besor Ravine. They came out to meet David and the people with him. As David and his men approached, he greeted them. ²²But all the evil men and troublemakers among David's followers said, "Because they did not go out with us, we will not share with them the plunder we recovered. However, each man may take his wife and children and go."

²³David replied, "No, my brothers, you must not do that with what the LORD has given us. He has protected us and handed over to us the forces that came against us. ²⁴Who will listen to what you say? The share of the man who stayed with the supplies is to be the same as that of him who went down to the battle. All will share alike." ²⁵David made this a statute and ordinance for Israel from that day to this.

²⁶When David arrived in Ziklag, he sent some of the plunder to the elders of Judah, who were his friends, saying, "Here is a present for you from the plunder of the LORD's enemies."

²⁷He sent it to those who were in Bethel, Ra-

THE MESSAGE

ter. They gave him a piece of fig cake and a couple of raisin muffins. Life began to revive in him. He hadn't eaten or drunk a thing for three days and nights!

30.13-14 David said to him, "Who do you belong to? Where are you from?"

"I'm an Egyptian slave of an Amalekite," he said. "My master walked off and left me when I got sick—that was three days ago. We had raided the Negev of the Kerethites, of Judah, and of Caleb. Ziklag we burned."

30.15 David asked him, "Can you take us to the raiders?"

"Promise me by God," he said, "that you won't kill me or turn me over to my old master, and I'll take you straight to the raiders."

30.16 He led David to them. They were scattered all over the place, eating and drinking, gorging themselves on all the loot they had plundered from Philistia and Judah.

30.17-20 David pounced. He fought them from before sunrise until evening of the next day. None got away except for four hundred of the younger men who escaped by riding off on camels. David rescued everything the Amalekites had taken. And he rescued his two wives! Nothing and no one was missing—young or old, son or daughter, plunder or whatever. David recovered the whole lot. He herded the sheep and cattle before them, and they all shouted, "David's plunder!"

30.21 Then David came to the two hundred who had been too tired to continue with him and had dropped out at the Brook Besor. They came out to welcome David and his band. As he came near he called out, "Success!"

30.22 But all the mean-spirited men who had marched with David, the rabble element, objected: "They didn't help in the rescue, they don't get any of the plunder we recovered. Each man can have his wife and children, but that's it. Take them and go!"

30.23-25 "Families don't do this sort of thing! Oh no, my brothers!" said David as he broke up the argument. "You can't act this way with what GOD gave us! God kept us safe. He handed over the raiders who attacked us. Who would ever listen to this kind of talk? The share of the one who stays with the gear is the share of the one who fights—equal shares. Share and share alike!" From that day on, David made that the rule in Israel—and it still is.

30.26-31 On returning to Ziklag, David sent portions of the plunder to the elders of Judah, his neighbors, with a note saying, "A gift from the plunder of GOD's enemies!" He sent them to the elders in Bethel, Ramoth Negev, Jattir, Aroer,

NEW INTERNATIONAL VERSION

moth Negev and Jattir; ²⁸to those in Aroer, Siph-moth, Eshtemoa ²⁹and Racal; to those in the towns of the Jerahmeelites and the Kenites; ³⁰to those in Hormah, Bor Ashan, Athach ³¹and He-bron; and to those in all the other places where David and his men had roamed.

SAUL TAKES HIS LIFE

31 Now the Philistines fought against Isra-el; the Israelites fled before them, and many fell slain on Mount Gilboa. ²The Philis-tines pressed hard after Saul and his sons, and they killed his sons Jonathan, Abinadab and Malki-Shua. ³The fighting grew fierce around Saul, and when the archers overtook him, they wounded him critically.

⁴Saul said to his armor-bearer, "Draw your sword and run me through, or these uncircum-cised fellows will come and run me through and abuse me."

But his armor-bearer was terrified and would not do it; so Saul took his own sword and fell on it. ⁵When the armor-bearer saw that Saul was dead, he too fell on his sword and died with him. ⁶So Saul and his three sons and his armor-bearer and all his men died together that same day.

⁷When the Israelites along the valley and those across the Jordan saw that the Israelite army had fled and that Saul and his sons had died, they abandoned their towns and fled. And the Philistines came and occupied them.

⁸The next day, when the Philistines came to strip the dead, they found Saul and his three sons fallen on Mount Gilboa. ⁹They cut off his head and stripped off his armor, and they sent messengers throughout the land of the Philis-tines to proclaim the news in the temple of their idols and among their people. ¹⁰They put his ar-mor in the temple of the Ashtoreths and fastened his body to the wall of Beth Shan.

¹¹When the people of Jabesh Gilead heard of what the Philistines had done to Saul, ¹²all their valiant men journeyed through the night to Beth Shan. They took down the bodies of Saul and his sons from the wall of Beth Shan and went to Jabesh, where they burned them. ¹³Then they took their bones and buried them under a tama-risk tree at Jabesh, and they fasted seven days.

THE MESSAGE

Siphmoth, Eshtemoa, Racal, Jerahmeelite cit-ies, Kenite cities, Hormah, Bor Ashan, Athach, and Hebron, along with a number of other places David and his men went to from time to time.

SAUL AND JONATHAN, DEAD ON THE MOUNTAIN

31.1-2 **31** The Philistines made war on Israel. The men of Israel were in full retreat from the Philistines, falling left and right, wounded on Mount Gilboa. The Philistines caught up with Saul and his sons. They killed Jonathan, Abinadab, and Malki-Shua, Saul's sons.

31.3-4 The battle was hot and heavy around Saul. The archers got his range and wounded him badly. Saul said to his weapon bearer, "Draw your sword and put me out of my misery, lest these pagan pigs come and make a game out of killing me."

31.4-6 But his weapon bearer wouldn't do it. He was terrified. So Saul took the sword himself and fell on it. When the weapon bearer saw that Saul was dead, he too fell on his sword and died with him. So Saul, his three sons, and his weapon bearer—the men closest to him— died together that day.

31.7 When the Israelites in the valley opposite and those on the other side of the Jordan saw that their army was in full retreat and that Saul and his sons were dead, they left their cities and ran for their lives. The Philistines moved in and occupied the sites.

31.8-10 The next day, when the Philistines came to rob the dead, they found Saul and his three sons dead on Mount Gilboa. They cut off Saul's head and stripped off his armor. Then they spread the good news all through Philistine country in the shrines of their idols and among the people. They displayed his armor in the shrine of the Ashtoreth. They nailed his corpse to the wall at Beth Shan.

31.11-13 The people of Jabesh Gilead heard what the Philistines had done to Saul. Their valiant men sprang into action. They traveled all night, took the corpses of Saul and his three sons from the wall at Beth Shan, and carried them back to Ja-besh and burned off the flesh. They then buried the bones under the tamarisk tree in Jabesh and fasted in mourning for seven days.

NEW INTERNATIONAL VERSION	THE MESSAGE

2 SAMUEL

2 SAMUEL

DAVID HEARS OF SAUL'S DEATH

1 After the death of Saul, David returned from defeating the Amalekites and stayed in Ziklag two days. ²On the third day a man arrived from Saul's camp, with his clothes torn and with dust on his head. When he came to David, he fell to the ground to pay him honor.

³"Where have you come from?" David asked him.

He answered, "I have escaped from the Israelite camp."

⁴"What happened?" David asked. "Tell me."

He said, "The men fled from the battle. Many of them fell and died. And Saul and his son Jonathan are dead."

⁵Then David said to the young man who brought him the report, "How do you know that Saul and his son Jonathan are dead?"

⁶"I happened to be on Mount Gilboa," the young man said, "and there was Saul, leaning on his spear, with the chariots and riders almost upon him. ⁷When he turned around and saw me, he called out to me, and I said, 'What can I do?'

⁸"He asked me, 'Who are you?'

"'An Amalekite,' I answered.

⁹"Then he said to me, 'Stand over me and kill me! I am in the throes of death, but I'm still alive.'

¹⁰"So I stood over him and killed him, because I knew that after he had fallen he could not survive. And I took the crown that was on his head and the band on his arm and have brought them here to my lord."

¹¹Then David and all the men with him took hold of their clothes and tore them. ¹²They mourned and wept and fasted till evening for Saul and his son Jonathan, and for the army of the LORD and the house of Israel, because they had fallen by the sword.

¹³David said to the young man who brought him the report, "Where are you from?"

"I am the son of an alien, an Amalekite," he answered.

¹⁴David asked him, "Why were you not afraid to lift your hand to destroy the LORD's anointed?"

1 Shortly after Saul died, David returned to Ziklag from his rout of the Amalekites. Three days later a man showed up unannounced from Saul's army camp.

Disheveled and obviously in mourning, he fell to his knees in respect before David. David asked, "What brings you here?"

He answered, "I've just escaped from the camp of Israel."

"So what happened?" said David. "What's the news?"

He said, "The Israelites have fled the battlefield, leaving a lot of their dead comrades behind. And Saul and his son Jonathan are dead."

David pressed the young soldier for details: "How do you know for sure that Saul and Jonathan are dead?"

"I just happened by Mount Gilboa and came on Saul, badly wounded and leaning on his spear, with enemy chariots and horsemen bearing down hard on him. He looked behind him, saw me, and called me to him. 'Yes sir,' I said, 'at your service.' He asked me who I was, and I told him, 'I'm an Amalekite.'"

"Come here," he said, "and put me out of my misery. I'm nearly dead already, but my life hangs on."

"So I did what he asked—I killed him. I knew he wouldn't last much longer anyway. I removed his royal headband and bracelet, and have brought them to my master. Here they are."

In lament, David ripped his clothes to ribbons. All the men with him did the same. They wept and fasted the rest of the day, grieving the death of Saul and his son Jonathan, and also the army of GOD and the nation Israel, victims in a failed battle.

Then David spoke to the young soldier who had brought the report: "Who are you, anyway?"

"I'm from an immigrant family—an Amalekite."

"Do you mean to say," said David, "that you weren't afraid to up and kill GOD's anointed

Reference markers (The Message column): 1.1-2, 1.2-3, 1.4, 1.5, 1.6-8, 1.9, 1.10, 1.11-12, 1.13, 1.14-15

NEW INTERNATIONAL VERSION

¹⁵Then David called one of his men and said, "Go, strike him down!" So he struck him down, and he died. ¹⁶For David had said to him, "Your blood be on your own head. Your own mouth testified against you when you said, 'I killed the LORD's anointed.' "

DAVID'S LAMENT FOR SAUL AND JONATHAN

¹⁷David took up this lament concerning Saul and his son Jonathan, ¹⁸and ordered that the men of Judah be taught this lament of the bow (it is written in the Book of Jashar):

¹⁹ "Your glory, O Israel, lies slain on your
          heights.
     How the mighty have fallen!

²⁰ "Tell it not in Gath,
          proclaim it not in the streets of Ashkelon,
     lest the daughters of the Philistines be glad,
          lest the daughters of the uncircumcised
               rejoice.

²¹ "O mountains of Gilboa,
          may you have neither dew nor rain,
          nor fields that yield offerings of grain.
     For there the shield of the mighty was
          defiled,
          the shield of Saul—no longer rubbed with
               oil.

²²From the blood of the slain,
     from the flesh of the mighty,
     the bow of Jonathan did not turn back,
     the sword of Saul did not return
          unsatisfied.

²³ "Saul and Jonathan—
          in life they were loved and gracious,
          and in death they were not parted.
     They were swifter than eagles,
          they were stronger than lions.

²⁴ "O daughters of Israel,
          weep for Saul,
     who clothed you in scarlet and finery,
     who adorned your garments with
          ornaments of gold.

²⁵ "How the mighty have fallen in battle!
          Jonathan lies slain on your heights.
²⁶I grieve for you, Jonathan my brother;
          you were very dear to me.
     Your love for me was wonderful,
          more wonderful than that of women.

²⁷ "How the mighty have fallen!
          The weapons of war have perished!"

THE MESSAGE

king?" Right then he ordered one of his soldiers, "Strike him dead!" The soldier struck him, and he died.

¹·¹⁶ "You asked for it," David told him. "You sealed your death sentence when you said you killed GOD's anointed king."

¹·¹⁷⁻¹⁸ Then David sang this lament over Saul and his son Jonathan, and gave orders that everyone in Judah learn it by heart. Yes, it's even inscribed in The Book of Jashar.

¹·¹⁹⁻²¹ Oh, oh, Gazelles of Israel, struck down on
          your hills,
     the mighty warriors—fallen, fallen!
Don't announce it in the city of Gath,
     don't post the news in the streets of
          Ashkelon.
Don't give those coarse Philistine girls
     one more excuse for a drunken party!
No more dew or rain for you, hills of
          Gilboa,
     and not a drop from springs and wells,
For there the warriors' shields were
          dragged through the mud,
     Saul's shield left there to rot.

¹·²² Jonathan's bow was bold—
     the bigger they were the harder they fell.
Saul's sword was fearless—
     once out of the scabbard, nothing could
          stop it.

¹·²³ Saul and Jonathan—beloved, beautiful!
     Together in life, together in death.
Swifter than plummeting eagles,
     stronger than proud lions.

¹·²⁴⁻²⁵ Women of Israel, weep for Saul.
     He dressed you in finest cottons and
          silks,
     spared no expense in making you
          elegant.
The mighty warriors—fallen, fallen
     in the middle of the fight!
Jonathan—struck down on your hills!

¹·²⁶ O my dear brother Jonathan,
     I'm crushed by your death.
Your friendship was a miracle-wonder,
     love far exceeding anything I've
          known—
     or ever hope to know.

¹·²⁷ The mighty warriors—fallen, fallen.
     And the arms of war broken to bits.

NEW INTERNATIONAL VERSION

David Anointed King Over Judah

2 In the course of time, David inquired of the LORD. "Shall I go up to one of the towns of Judah?" he asked.

The LORD said, "Go up."

David asked, "Where shall I go?"

"To Hebron," the LORD answered.

²So David went up there with his two wives, Ahinoam of Jezreel and Abigail, the widow of Nabal of Carmel. ³David also took the men who were with him, each with his family, and they settled in Hebron and its towns. ⁴Then the men of Judah came to Hebron and there they anointed David king over the house of Judah.

When David was told that it was the men of Jabesh Gilead who had buried Saul, ⁵he sent messengers to the men of Jabesh Gilead to say to them, "The LORD bless you for showing this kindness to Saul your master by burying him. ⁶May the LORD now show you kindness and faithfulness, and I too will show you the same favor because you have done this. ⁷Now then, be strong and brave, for Saul your master is dead, and the house of Judah has anointed me king over them."

War Between the Houses of David and Saul

⁸Meanwhile, Abner son of Ner, the commander of Saul's army, had taken Ish-Bosheth son of Saul and brought him over to Mahanaim. ⁹He made him king over Gilead, Ashuri ᵃ and Jezreel, and also over Ephraim, Benjamin and all Israel.

¹⁰Ish-Bosheth son of Saul was forty years old when he became king over Israel, and he reigned two years. The house of Judah, however, followed David. ¹¹The length of time David was king in Hebron over the house of Judah was seven years and six months.

¹²Abner son of Ner, together with the men of Ish-Bosheth son of Saul, left Mahanaim and went to Gibeon. ¹³Joab son of Zeruiah and David's men went out and met them at the pool of Gibeon. One group sat down on one side of the pool and one group on the other side.

¹⁴Then Abner said to Joab, "Let's have some of the young men get up and fight hand to hand in front of us."

"All right, let them do it," Joab said.

¹⁵So they stood up and were counted off—twelve men for Benjamin and Ish-Bosheth son of Saul, and twelve for David. ¹⁶Then each man grabbed his opponent by the head and thrust his dagger into his opponent's side, and they fell down together. So that place in Gibeon was called Helkath Hazzurim. ᵇ

ᵃ 9 Or Asher   ᵇ 16 Helkath Hazzurim means field of daggers or field of hostilities.

THE MESSAGE

2 After all this, David prayed. He asked GOD, "Shall I move to one of the cities of Judah?"

GOD said, "Yes, move."

"And to which city?"

"To Hebron."

²⁻³ So David moved to Hebron, along with his two wives, Ahinoam of Jezreel and Abigail the widow of Nabal of Carmel. David's men, along with their families, also went with him and made their home in and around Hebron.

²⁻⁴⁻⁷ The citizens of Judah came to Hebron, and then and there made David king over the clans of Judah.

A report was brought to David that the men of Jabesh Gilead had given Saul a decent burial. David sent messengers to the men of Jabesh Gilead: "GOD bless you for this—for honoring your master, Saul, with a funeral. GOD honor you and be true to you—and I'll do the same, matching your generous act of goodness. Strengthen your resolve and do what must be done. Your master, Saul, is dead. The citizens of Judah have made me their king."

✝

²⁻⁸⁻¹¹ In the meantime, Abner son of Ner, commander of Saul's army, had taken Saul's son Ish-Bosheth to Mahanaim and made him king over Gilead, over Asher, over Jezreel, over Ephraim, over Benjamin—king, as it turns out, over all Israel. Ish-Bosheth, Saul's son, was forty years old when he was made king over Israel. He lasted only two years. But the people of Judah stuck with David. David ruled the people of Judah from Hebron for seven and a half years.

²⁻¹²⁻¹³ One day Abner son of Ner set out from Mahanaim with the soldiers of Ish-Bosheth son of Saul, headed for Gibeon. Joab son of Zeruiah, with David's soldiers, also set out. They met at the Pool of Gibeon, Abner's group on one side, Joab's on the other.

²⁻¹⁴ Abner challenged Joab, "Put up your best fighters. Let's see them do their stuff."

Joab said, "Good! Let them go at it!"

²⁻¹⁵⁻¹⁶ So they lined up for the fight, twelve Benjaminites from the side of Ish-Bosheth son of Saul, and twelve soldiers from David's side. The men from each side grabbed their opponents' heads and stabbed them with their daggers. They all fell dead—the whole bunch together. So, they called the place Slaughter Park. It's right there at Gibeon.

NEW INTERNATIONAL VERSION

¹⁷The battle that day was very fierce, and Abner and the men of Israel were defeated by David's men.

¹⁸The three sons of Zeruiah were there: Joab, Abishai and Asahel. Now Asahel was as fleet-footed as a wild gazelle. ¹⁹He chased Abner, turning neither to the right nor to the left as he pursued him. ²⁰Abner looked behind him and asked, "Is that you, Asahel?"

"It is," he answered.

²¹Then Abner said to him, "Turn aside to the right or to the left; take on one of the young men and strip him of his weapons." But Asahel would not stop chasing him.

²²Again Abner warned Asahel, "Stop chasing me! Why should I strike you down? How could I look your brother Joab in the face?"

²³But Asahel refused to give up the pursuit; so Abner thrust the butt of his spear into Asahel's stomach, and the spear came out through his back. He fell there and died on the spot. And every man stopped when he came to the place where Asahel had fallen and died.

²⁴But Joab and Abishai pursued Abner, and as the sun was setting, they came to the hill of Ammah, near Giah on the way to the wasteland of Gibeon. ²⁵Then the men of Benjamin rallied behind Abner. They formed themselves into a group and took their stand on top of a hill.

²⁶Abner called out to Joab, "Must the sword devour forever? Don't you realize that this will end in bitterness? How long before you order your men to stop pursuing their brothers?"

²⁷Joab answered, "As surely as God lives, if you had not spoken, the men would have continued the pursuit of their brothers until morning.ᵃ"

²⁸So Joab blew the trumpet, and all the men came to a halt; they no longer pursued Israel, nor did they fight anymore.

²⁹All that night Abner and his men marched through the Arabah. They crossed the Jordan, continued through the whole Bithronᵇ and came to Mahanaim.

³⁰Then Joab returned from pursuing Abner and assembled all his men. Besides Asahel, nineteen of David's men were found missing. ³¹But David's men had killed three hundred and sixty Benjamites who were with Abner. ³²They took Asahel and buried him in his father's tomb at Bethlehem. Then Joab and his men marched all night and arrived at Hebron by daybreak.

ᵃ 27 Or spoken this morning, the men would not have taken up the pursuit of their brothers; or spoken, the men would have given up the pursuit of their brothers by morning
ᵇ 29 Or morning; or ravine; the meaning of the Hebrew for this word is uncertain.

THE MESSAGE

2.17-19 The fighting went from bad to worse throughout the day. Abner and the men of Israel were beaten to a pulp by David's men. The three sons of Zeruiah were present: Joab, Abishai, and Asahel. Asahel, as fast as a wild antelope on the open plain, chased Abner, staying hard on his heels.

2.20 Abner turned and said, "Is that you, Asahel?"

"It surely is," he said.

2.21 Abner said, "Let up on me. Pick on someone you have a chance of beating and be content with those spoils!" But Asahel wouldn't let up.

2.22 Abner tried again, "Turn back. Don't force me to kill you. How would I face your brother Joab?"

2.23-25 When he refused to quit, Abner struck him in the belly with the blunt end of his spear so hard that it came out his back. Asahel fell to the ground and died at once. Everyone who arrived at the spot where Asahel fell and died stood and gaped—Asahel dead! But Joab and Abishai kept up the chase after Abner. As the sun began to set, they came to the hill of Ammah that faced Giah on the road to the backcountry of Gibeon. The Benjaminites had taken their stand with Abner there, deployed strategically on a hill.

2.26 Abner called out to Joab, "Are we going to keep killing each other till doomsday? Don't you know that nothing but bitterness will come from this? How long before you call off your men from chasing their brothers?"

2.27-28 "As God lives," said Joab, "if you hadn't spoken up, we'd have kept up the chase until morning!" Then he blew the ram's horn trumpet and the whole army of Judah stopped in its tracks. They quit chasing Israel and called off the fighting.

2.29 Abner and his soldiers marched all that night up the Arabah Valley. They crossed the Jordan and, after a long morning's march, arrived at Mahanaim.

2.30-32 After Joab returned from chasing Abner, he took a head count of the army. Nineteen of David's men (besides Asahel) were missing. David's men had cut down three hundred and sixty of Abner's men, all Benjaminites—all dead. They brought Asahel and buried him in the family tomb in Bethlehem. Joab and his men then marched all night, arriving in Hebron as the dawn broke.

NEW INTERNATIONAL VERSION

3 The war between the house of Saul and the house of David lasted a long time. David grew stronger and stronger, while the house of Saul grew weaker and weaker.

² Sons were born to David in Hebron:

His firstborn was Amnon the son of Ahinoam of Jezreel;

³ his second, Kileab the son of Abigail the widow of Nabal of Carmel;

the third, Absalom the son of Maacah daughter of Talmai king of Geshur;

⁴ the fourth, Adonijah the son of Haggith;

the fifth, Shephatiah the son of Abital;

⁵ and the sixth, Ithream the son of David's wife Eglah.

These were born to David in Hebron.

ABNER GOES OVER TO DAVID

⁶During the war between the house of Saul and the house of David, Abner had been strengthening his own position in the house of Saul. ⁷Now Saul had had a concubine named Rizpah daughter of Aiah. And Ish-Bosheth said to Abner, "Why did you sleep with my father's concubine?"

⁸Abner was very angry because of what Ish-Bosheth said and he answered, "Am I a dog's head—on Judah's side? This very day I am loyal to the house of your father Saul and to his family and friends. I haven't handed you over to David. Yet now you accuse me of an offense involving this woman! ⁹May God deal with Abner, be it ever so severely, if I do not do for David what the LORD promised him on oath ¹⁰and transfer the kingdom from the house of Saul and establish David's throne over Israel and Judah from Dan to Beersheba." ¹¹Ish-Bosheth did not dare to say another word to Abner, because he was afraid of him.

¹²Then Abner sent messengers on his behalf to say to David, "Whose land is it? Make an agreement with me, and I will help you bring all Israel over to you."

¹³"Good," said David. "I will make an agreement with you. But I demand one thing of you: Do not come into my presence unless you bring Michal daughter of Saul when you come to see me." ¹⁴Then David sent messengers to Ish-Bosheth son of Saul, demanding, "Give me my wife Michal, whom I betrothed to myself for the price of a hundred Philistine foreskins."

¹⁵So Ish-Bosheth gave orders and had her taken away from her husband Paltiel son of Laish. ¹⁶Her husband, however, went with her, weeping

THE MESSAGE

3 ^{3.1} The war between the house of Saul and the house of David dragged on and on. The longer it went on the stronger David became, with the house of Saul getting weaker.

✝

^{3.2-5} During the Hebron years, sons were born to David:

Amnon, born of Ahinoam of Jezreel—the firstborn;

Kileab, born of Abigail of Carmel, Nabal's widow—his second;

Absalom, born of Maacah, daughter of Talmai, king of Geshur—the third;

Adonijah, born of Haggith—the fourth;

Shephatiah, born of Abital—the fifth;

Ithream, born of Eglah—the sixth.

These six sons of David were born in Hebron.

✝

^{3.6-7} Abner took advantage of the continuing war between the house of Saul and the house of David to gain power for himself. Saul had had a concubine, Rizpah, the daughter of Aiah. One day Ish-Bosheth confronted Abner: "What business do you have sleeping with my father's concubine?"

^{3.8-10} Abner lost his temper with Ish-Bosheth, "Treat me like a dog, will you! Is this the thanks I get for sticking by the house of your father, Saul, and all his family and friends? I personally saved you from certain capture by David, and you make an issue out of my going to bed with a woman! What GOD promised David, I'll help accomplish—transfer the kingdom from the house of Saul and make David ruler over the whole country, both Israel and Judah, from Dan to Beersheba. If not, may God do his worst to me."

^{3.11} Ish-Bosheth, cowed by Abner's outburst, couldn't say another word.

^{3.12} Abner went ahead and sent personal messengers to David: "Make a deal with me and I'll help bring the whole country of Israel over to you."

^{3.13} "Great," said David. "It's a deal. But only on one condition: You're not welcome here unless you bring Michal, Saul's daughter, with you when you come to meet me."

^{3.14} David then sent messengers to Ish-Bosheth son of Saul: "Give me back Michal, whom I won as my wife at the cost of a hundred Philistine foreskins."

^{3.15-16} Ish-Bosheth ordered that she be taken from her husband Paltiel son of Laish. But Paltiel followed her, weeping all the way, to Bahurim.

NEW INTERNATIONAL VERSION

behind her all the way to Bahurim. Then Abner said to him, "Go back home!" So he went back.

17Abner conferred with the elders of Israel and said, "For some time you have wanted to make David your king. 18Now do it! For the LORD promised David, 'By my servant David I will rescue my people Israel from the hand of the Philistines and from the hand of all their enemies.'"

19Abner also spoke to the Benjamites in person. Then he went to Hebron to tell David everything that Israel and the whole house of Benjamin wanted to do. 20When Abner, who had twenty men with him, came to David at Hebron, David prepared a feast for him and his men. 21Then Abner said to David, "Let me go at once and assemble all Israel for my lord the king, so that they may make a compact with you, and that you may rule over all that your heart desires." So David sent Abner away, and he went in peace.

JOAB MURDERS ABNER

22Just then David's men and Joab returned from a raid and brought with them a great deal of plunder. But Abner was no longer with David in Hebron, because David had sent him away, and he had gone in peace. 23When Joab and all the soldiers with him arrived, he was told that Abner son of Ner had come to the king and that the king had sent him away and that he had gone in peace.

24So Joab went to the king and said, "What have you done? Look, Abner came to you. Why did you let him go? Now he is gone! 25You know Abner son of Ner; he came to deceive you and observe your movements and find out everything you are doing."

26Joab then left David and sent messengers after Abner, and they brought him back from the well of Sirah. But David did not know it. 27Now when Abner returned to Hebron, Joab took him aside into the gateway, as though to speak with him privately. And there, to avenge the blood of his brother Asahel, Joab stabbed him in the stomach, and he died.

28Later, when David heard about this, he said, "I and my kingdom are forever innocent before the LORD concerning the blood of Abner son of Ner. 29May his blood fall upon the head of Joab and upon all his father's house! May Joab's house never be without someone who has a running sore or leprosy*a* or who leans on a crutch or who falls by the sword or who lacks food."

30(Joab and his brother Abishai murdered Ab-

a 29 The Hebrew word was used for various diseases affecting the skin—not necessarily leprosy.

THE MESSAGE

There Abner told him, "Go home." And he went home.

3.17-18 Abner got the elders of Israel together and said, "Only yesterday, it seems, you were looking for a way to make David your king. So do it—now! For GOD has given the go-ahead on David: 'By my servant David's hand, I'll save my people Israel from the oppression of the Philistines and all their other enemies.'"

3.19 Abner took the Benjaminites aside and spoke to them. Then he went to Hebron for a private talk with David, telling him everything that Israel in general and Benjamin in particular were planning to do.

3.20 When Abner and the twenty men who were with him met with David in Hebron, David laid out a feast for them.

3.21 Abner then said, "I'm ready. Let me go now to rally everyone in Israel for my master, the king. They'll make a treaty with you, authorizing you to rule them however you see fit." Abner was sent off with David's blessing.

3.22-23 Soon after that, David's men, led by Joab, came back from a field assignment. Abner was no longer in Hebron with David, having just been dismissed with David's blessing. As Joab and his raiding party arrived, they were told that Abner the son of Ner had been there with David and had been sent off with David's blessing.

3.24-25 Joab went straight to the king: "What's this you've done? Abner shows up, and you let him walk away scot-free? You know Abner son of Ner better than that. This was no friendly visit. He was here to spy on you, figure out your comings and goings, find out what you're up to."

3.26-27 Joab left David and went into action. He sent messengers after Abner; they caught up with him at the well at Sirah and brought him back. David knew nothing of all this. When Abner got back to Hebron, Joab steered him aside at the gate for a personal word with him. There he stabbed him in the belly, killed him in cold blood for the murder of his brother Asahel.

3.28-30 Later on, when David heard what happened, he said, "Before GOD I and my kingdom are totally innocent of this murder of Abner son of Ner. Joab and his entire family will always be under the curse of this bloodguilt. May they forever be victims of crippling diseases, violence, and famine." (Joab and his brother,

NEW INTERNATIONAL VERSION

ner because he had killed their brother Asahel in the battle at Gibeon.)

31 Then David said to Joab and all the people with him, "Tear your clothes and put on sackcloth and walk in mourning in front of Abner." King David himself walked behind the bier. 32 They buried Abner in Hebron, and the king wept aloud at Abner's tomb. All the people wept also.

33 The king sang this lament for Abner:

"Should Abner have died as the lawless die?
34   Your hands were not bound,
      your feet were not fettered.
You fell as one falls before wicked men."

And all the people wept over him again.

35 Then they all came and urged David to eat something while it was still day; but David took an oath, saying, "May God deal with me, be it ever so severely, if I taste bread or anything else before the sun sets!"

36 All the people took note and were pleased; indeed, everything the king did pleased them. 37 So on that day all the people and all Israel knew that the king had no part in the murder of Abner son of Ner.

38 Then the king said to his men, "Do you not realize that a prince and a great man has fallen in Israel this day? 39 And today, though I am the anointed king, I am weak, and these sons of Zeruiah are too strong for me. May the LORD repay the evildoer according to his evil deeds!"

ISH-BOSHETH MURDERED

4 When Ish-Bosheth son of Saul heard that Abner had died in Hebron, he lost courage, and all Israel became alarmed. 2 Now Saul's son had two men who were leaders of raiding bands. One was named Baanah and the other Recab; they were sons of Rimmon the Beerothite from the tribe of Benjamin—Beeroth is considered part of Benjamin, 3 because the people of Beeroth fled to Gittaim and have lived there as aliens to this day.

4 (Jonathan son of Saul had a son who was lame in both feet. He was five years old when the news about Saul and Jonathan came from Jezreel. His nurse picked him up and fled, but as she hurried to leave, he fell and became crippled. His name was Mephibosheth.)

5 Now Recab and Baanah, the sons of Rimmon

THE MESSAGE

Abishai, murdered Abner because he had killed their brother Asahel at the battle of Gibeon.)

3.31-32 David ordered Joab and all the men under him, "Rip your cloaks into rags! Wear mourning clothes! Lead Abner's funeral procession with loud lament!" King David followed the coffin. They buried Abner in Hebron. The king's voice was loud in lament as he wept at the side of Abner's grave. All the people wept, too.

3.33-34 Then the king sang this tribute to Abner:

Can this be? Abner dead like a nameless
      bum?
You were a free man, free to go and do as
      you wished—
Yet you fell as a victim in a street brawl.

And all the people wept—a crescendo of crying!

3.35-37 They all came then to David, trying to get him to eat something before dark. But David solemnly swore, "I'll not so much as taste a piece of bread, or anything else for that matter, before sunset, so help me God!" Everyone at the funeral took notice—and liked what they saw. In fact everything the king did was applauded by the people. It was clear to everyone that day, including all Israel, that the king had nothing to do with the death of Abner son of Ner.

3.38-39 The king spoke to his servants: "You realize, don't you, that today a prince and hero fell victim of foul play in Israel? And I, though anointed king, was helpless to do anything about it. These sons of Zeruiah are too much for me. GOD, requite the criminal for his crime!"

THE MURDER OF ISH-BOSHETH

4.1 4 Saul's son, Ish-Bosheth, heard that Abner had died in Hebron. His heart sank. The whole country was shaken.

4.2-3 Ish-Bosheth had two men who were captains of raiding bands—one was named Baanah, the other Recab. They were sons of Rimmon the Beerothite, a Benjaminite. (The people of Beeroth had been assigned to Benjamin ever since they escaped to Gittaim. They still live there as resident aliens.)

4.4 It so happened that Saul's son, Jonathan, had a son who was maimed in both feet. When he was five years old, the report on Saul and Jonathan came from Jezreel. His nurse picked him up and ran, but in her hurry to get away she fell, and the boy was maimed. His name was Mephibosheth.

4.5-7 One day Baanah and Recab, the two sons of

NEW INTERNATIONAL VERSION

the Beerothite, set out for the house of Ish-Bosheth, and they arrived there in the heat of the day while he was taking his noonday rest. ⁶They went into the inner part of the house as if to get some wheat, and they stabbed him in the stomach. Then Recab and his brother Baanah slipped away.

⁷They had gone into the house while he was lying on the bed in his bedroom. After they stabbed and killed him, they cut off his head. Taking it with them, they traveled all night by way of the Arabah. ⁸They brought the head of Ish-Bosheth to David at Hebron and said to the king, "Here is the head of Ish-Bosheth son of Saul, your enemy, who tried to take your life. This day the LORD has avenged my lord the king against Saul and his offspring."

⁹David answered Recab and his brother Baanah, the sons of Rimmon the Beerothite, "As surely as the LORD lives, who has delivered me out of all trouble, ¹⁰when a man told me, 'Saul is dead,' and thought he was bringing good news, I seized him and put him to death in Ziklag. That was the reward I gave him for his news! ¹¹How much more—when wicked men have killed an innocent man in his own house and on his own bed—should I not now demand his blood from your hand and rid the earth of you!"

¹²So David gave an order to his men, and they killed them. They cut off their hands and feet and hung the bodies by the pool in Hebron. But they took the head of Ish-Bosheth and buried it in Abner's tomb at Hebron.

DAVID BECOMES KING OVER ISRAEL

5 All the tribes of Israel came to David at Hebron and said, "We are your own flesh and blood. ²In the past, while Saul was king over us, you were the one who led Israel on their military campaigns. And the LORD said to you, 'You will shepherd my people Israel, and you will become their ruler.' "

³When all the elders of Israel had come to King David at Hebron, the king made a compact with them at Hebron before the LORD, and they anointed David king over Israel.

⁴David was thirty years old when he became king, and he reigned forty years. ⁵In Hebron he reigned over Judah seven years and six months, and in Jerusalem he reigned over all Israel and Judah thirty-three years.

DAVID CONQUERS JERUSALEM

⁶The king and his men marched to Jerusalem to attack the Jebusites, who lived there. The Jebusites said to David, "You will not get in here;

THE MESSAGE

Rimmon, headed out for the house of Ish-Bosheth. They arrived at the hottest time of the day, just as he was taking his afternoon nap. They entered the house on a ruse, pretending official business. The maid guarding the bedroom had fallen asleep, so Recab and Baanah slipped by her and entered the room where Ish-Bosheth was asleep on his bed. They killed him and then cut off his head, carrying it off as a trophy. They traveled all night long, taking the route through the Arabah Valley.

⁴·⁸ They presented the head of Ish-Bosheth to David at Hebron, telling the king, "Here's the head of Ish-Bosheth, Saul's son, your enemy. He was out to kill you, but GOD has given vengeance to my master, the king—vengeance this very day on Saul and his children!"

⁴·⁹⁻¹¹ David answered the brothers Recab and Baanah, sons of Rimmon the Beerothite, "As surely as GOD lives—the One who got me out of every trouble I've ever been in—when the messenger told me, 'Good news! Saul is dead!' supposing I'd be delighted, I arrested him and killed him on the spot in Ziklag. That's what he got for his so-called good news! And now you show up—evil men who killed an innocent man in cold blood, a man asleep in his own house! Don't think I won't find you guilty of murder and rid the country of you!"

⁴·¹² David then issued orders to his soldiers. They killed the two—chopped off their hands and feet, and hung the corpses at the pool in Hebron. But Ish-Bosheth's head they took and buried in Abner's tomb in Hebron.

⁵·¹⁻² **5** Before long all the tribes of Israel approached David in Hebron and said, "Look at us—your own flesh and blood! In time past when Saul was our king, you were the one who really ran the country. Even then GOD said to you, 'You will shepherd my people Israel and you'll be the prince.' "

⁵·³ All the leaders of Israel met with King David at Hebron, and the king made a treaty with them in the presence of GOD. And so they anointed David king over Israel.

⁵·⁴⁻⁵ David was thirty years old when he became king, and ruled for forty years. In Hebron he ruled Judah for seven and a half years. In Jerusalem he ruled all Israel and Judah for thirty-three years.

⁵·⁶ David and his men immediately set out for Jerusalem to take on the Jebusites, who lived in that country. But they said, "You might as well

NEW INTERNATIONAL VERSION

even the blind and the lame can ward you off." They thought, "David cannot get in here." [7]Nevertheless, David captured the fortress of Zion, the City of David.

[8]On that day, David said, "Anyone who conquers the Jebusites will have to use the water shaft[a] to reach those 'lame and blind' who are David's enemies.[b]" That is why they say, "The 'blind and lame' will not enter the palace."

[9]David then took up residence in the fortress and called it the City of David. He built up the area around it, from the supporting terraces[c] inward. [10]And he became more and more powerful, because the LORD God Almighty was with him.

[11]Now Hiram king of Tyre sent messengers to David, along with cedar logs and carpenters and stonemasons, and they built a palace for David. [12]And David knew that the LORD had established him as king over Israel and had exalted his kingdom for the sake of his people Israel.

[13]After he left Hebron, David took more concubines and wives in Jerusalem, and more sons and daughters were born to him. [14]These are the names of the children born to him there: Shammua, Shobab, Nathan, Solomon, [15]Ibhar, Elishua, Nepheg, Japhia, [16]Elishama, Eliada and Eliphelet.

DAVID DEFEATS THE PHILISTINES

[17]When the Philistines heard that David had been anointed king over Israel, they went up in full force to search for him, but David heard about it and went down to the stronghold. [18]Now the Philistines had come and spread out in the Valley of Rephaim; [19]so David inquired of the LORD, "Shall I go and attack the Philistines? Will you hand them over to me?"

The LORD answered him, "Go, for I will surely hand the Philistines over to you."

[20]So David went to Baal Perazim, and there he defeated them. He said, "As waters break out, the LORD has broken out against my enemies be-

THE MESSAGE

go home! Even the blind and the lame could keep you out. You can't get in here!" They had convinced themselves that David couldn't break through.

5.7-8 But David went right ahead and captured the fortress of Zion, known ever since as the City of David. That day David said, "To get the best of these Jebusites, one must target the water system, not to mention this so-called lame and blind bunch that David hates." (In fact, he was so sick and tired of it, people coined the expression, "No lame and blind allowed in the palace.")

5.9-10 David made the fortress city his home and named it "City of David." He developed the city from the outside terraces inward. David proceeded with a longer stride, a larger embrace since the GOD-of-the-Angel-Armies was with him.

5.11-12 It was at this time that Hiram, king of Tyre, sent messengers to David, along with timbers of cedar. He also sent carpenters and masons to build a house for David. David took this as a sign that GOD had confirmed him as king of Israel, giving his kingship world prominence for the sake of Israel, his people.

5.13-16 David took on more concubines and wives from Jerusalem after he left Hebron. And more sons and daughters were born to him. These are the names of those born to him in Jerusalem:

> Shammua,
> Shobab,
> Nathan,
> Solomon,
> Ibhar,
> Elishua,
> Nepheg,
> Japhia,
> Elishama,
> Eliada,
> Eliphelet.

5.17-18 When the Philistines got word that David had been made king over all Israel, they came on the hunt for him. David heard of it and went down to the stronghold. When the Philistines arrived, they deployed their forces in Raphaim Valley.

5.19 Then David prayed to GOD: "Shall I go up and fight the Philistines? Will you help me beat them?"

"Go up," GOD replied. "Count on me. I'll help you beat them."

5.20-21 David then went straight to Baal Perazim, and smashed them to pieces. Afterward David said, "GOD exploded on my enemies like a gush

---

[a] 8 Or use scaling hooks   [b] 8 Or are hated by David
[c] 9 Or the Millo

NEW INTERNATIONAL VERSION

fore me." So that place was called Baal Perazim. *a* ²¹The Philistines abandoned their idols there, and David and his men carried them off.

²²Once more the Philistines came up and spread out in the Valley of Rephaim; ²³so David inquired of the LORD, and he answered, "Do not go straight up, but circle around behind them and attack them in front of the balsam trees. ²⁴As soon as you hear the sound of marching in the tops of the balsam trees, move quickly, because that will mean the LORD has gone out in front of you to strike the Philistine army." ²⁵So David did as the LORD commanded him, and he struck down the Philistines all the way from Gibeon *b* to Gezer.

THE ARK BROUGHT TO JERUSALEM

6 David again brought together out of Israel chosen men, thirty thousand in all. ²He and all his men set out from Baalah of Judah *c* to bring up from there the ark of God, which is called by the Name, *d* the name of the LORD Almighty, who is enthroned between the cherubim that are on the ark. ³They set the ark of God on a new cart and brought it from the house of Abinadab, which was on the hill. Uzzah and Ahio, sons of Abinadab, were guiding the new cart ⁴with the ark of God on it, *e* and Ahio was walking in front of it. ⁵David and the whole house of Israel were celebrating with all their might before the LORD, with songs *f* and with harps, lyres, tambourines, sistrums and cymbals.

⁶When they came to the threshing floor of Nacon, Uzzah reached out and took hold of the ark of God, because the oxen stumbled. ⁷The LORD's anger burned against Uzzah because of his irreverent act; therefore God struck him down and he died there beside the ark of God.

⁸Then David was angry because the LORD's wrath had broken out against Uzzah, and to this day that place is called Perez Uzzah. *g*

⁹David was afraid of the LORD that day and said, "How can the ark of the LORD ever come to me?" ¹⁰He was not willing to take the ark of the

---

a 20 Baal Perazim means *the lord who breaks out.*
b 25 Septuagint (see also 1 Chron. 14:16); Hebrew *Geba*
c 2 That is, Kiriath Jearim; Hebrew *Baale Judah,* a variant of *Baalah of Judah* *d 2* Hebrew; Septuagint and Vulgate do not have *the Name.* *e 3,4* Dead Sea Scrolls and some Septuagint manuscripts; Masoretic Text *cart* ⁴*and they brought it with the ark of God from the house of Abinadab, which was on the hill* *f 5* See Dead Sea Scrolls, Septuagint and 1 Chronicles 13:8; Masoretic Text *celebrating before the LORD with all kinds of instruments made of pine.* *g 8 Perez Uzzah* means *outbreak against Uzzah.*

THE MESSAGE

of water." That's why David named the place Baal Perazim (The-Master-Who-Explodes). The retreating Philistines dumped their idols, and David and his soldiers took them away.

5.22-23 Later there was a repeat performance. The Philistines came up again and deployed their troops in the Rephaim Valley. David again prayed to GOD.

5.23-24 This time GOD said, "Don't attack them head-on. Instead, circle around behind them and ambush them from the grove of sacred trees. When you hear the sound of shuffling in the trees, get ready to move out. It's a signal that GOD is going ahead of you to smash the Philistine camp."

5.25 David did exactly what GOD told him. He routed the Philistines all the way from Gibeon to Gezer.

6 David mustered the pick of the troops of Israel—thirty divisions of them. Together with his soldiers, David headed for Baalah to recover the Chest of God, which was called by the Name GOD-of-the-Angel-Armies, who was enthroned over the pair of angels on the Chest.

6.3-7 They placed the Chest of God on a brand-new oxcart and removed it from Abinadab's house on the hill. Uzzah and Ahio, Abinadab's sons, were driving the new cart loaded with the Chest of God, Ahio in the lead and Uzzah alongside the Chest. David and the whole company of Israel were in the parade, singing at the top of their lungs and playing mandolins, harps, tambourines, castanets, and cymbals. When they came to the threshing floor of Nacon, the oxen stumbled, so Uzzah reached out and grabbed the Chest of God. GOD blazed in anger against Uzzah and struck him hard because he had profaned the Chest. Uzzah died on the spot, right alongside the Chest.

6.8-11 Then David got angry because of GOD's deadly outburst against Uzzah. That place is still called Perez Uzzah (The-Explosion-Against-Uzzah). David became fearful of GOD that day and said, "This Chest is too hot to handle. How can I ever get it back to the City of David?" He refused to take the Chest of GOD

NEW INTERNATIONAL VERSION

LORD to be with him in the City of David. Instead, he took it aside to the house of Obed-Edom the Gittite. ¹¹The ark of the LORD remained in the house of Obed-Edom the Gittite for three months, and the LORD blessed him and his entire household.

¹²Now King David was told, "The LORD has blessed the household of Obed-Edom and everything he has, because of the ark of God." So David went down and brought up the ark of God from the house of Obed-Edom to the City of David with rejoicing. ¹³When those who were carrying the ark of the LORD had taken six steps, he sacrificed a bull and a fattened calf. ¹⁴David, wearing a linen ephod, danced before the LORD with all his might, ¹⁵while he and the entire house of Israel brought up the ark of the LORD with shouts and the sound of trumpets.

¹⁶As the ark of the LORD was entering the City of David, Michal daughter of Saul watched from a window. And when she saw King David leaping and dancing before the LORD, she despised him in her heart.

¹⁷They brought the ark of the LORD and set it in its place inside the tent that David had pitched for it, and David sacrificed burnt offerings and fellowship offerings*a* before the LORD. ¹⁸After he had finished sacrificing the burnt offerings and fellowship offerings, he blessed the people in the name of the LORD Almighty. ¹⁹Then he gave a loaf of bread, a cake of dates and a cake of raisins to each person in the whole crowd of Israelites, both men and women. And all the people went to their homes.

²⁰When David returned home to bless his household, Michal daughter of Saul came out to meet him and said, "How the king of Israel has distinguished himself today, disrobing in the sight of the slave girls of his servants as any vulgar fellow would!"

²¹David said to Michal, "It was before the LORD, who chose me rather than your father or anyone from his house when he appointed me ruler over the LORD's people Israel—I will celebrate before the LORD. ²²I will become even more undignified than this, and I will be humiliated in my own eyes. But by these slave girls you spoke of, I will be held in honor."

²³And Michal daughter of Saul had no children to the day of her death.

THE MESSAGE

a step farther. Instead, David removed it off the road and to the house of Obed-Edom the Gittite. The Chest of GOD stayed at the house of Obed-Edom the Gittite for three months. And GOD prospered Obed-Edom and his entire household.

6.12-16 It was reported to King David that GOD had prospered Obed-Edom and his entire household because of the Chest of God. So David thought, "I'll get that blessing for myself," and went and brought up the Chest of God from the house of Obed-Edom to the City of David, celebrating extravagantly all the way, with frequent sacrifices of choice bulls. David, ceremonially dressed in priest's linen, danced with great abandon before GOD. The whole country was with him as he accompanied the Chest of GOD with shouts and trumpet blasts. But as the Chest of GOD came into the City of David, Michal, Saul's daughter, happened to be looking out a window. When she saw King David leaping and dancing before GOD, her heart filled with scorn.

6.17-19 They brought the Chest of GOD and set it in the middle of the tent pavilion that David had pitched for it. Then and there David worshiped, offering burnt offerings and peace offerings. When David had completed the sacrifices of burnt and peace offerings, he blessed the people in the name of GOD-of-the-Angel-Armies and handed out to each person in the crowd, men and women alike, a loaf of bread, a date cake, and a raisin cake. Then everyone went home.

6.20-22 David returned home to bless his family. Michal, Saul's daughter, came out to greet him: "How wonderfully the king has distinguished himself today—exposing himself to the eyes of the servants' maids like some burlesque street dancer!" David replied to Michal, "In GOD's presence I'll dance all I want! He chose me over your father and the rest of our family and made me prince over GOD's people, over Israel. Oh yes, I'll dance to GOD's glory—more recklessly even than this. And as far as I'm concerned . . . I'll gladly look like a fool . . . but among these maids you're so worried about, I'll be honored no end."

6.23 Michal, Saul's daughter, was barren the rest of her life.

✝

---

a 17 Traditionally peace offerings; also in verse 18

NEW INTERNATIONAL VERSION

GOD'S PROMISE TO DAVID

7 After the king was settled in his palace and the LORD had given him rest from all his enemies around him, ²he said to Nathan the prophet, "Here I am, living in a palace of cedar, while the ark of God remains in a tent."

³Nathan replied to the king, "Whatever you have in mind, go ahead and do it, for the LORD is with you."

⁴That night the word of the LORD came to Nathan, saying:

⁵"Go and tell my servant David, 'This is what the LORD says: Are you the one to build me a house to dwell in? ⁶I have not dwelt in a house from the day I brought the Israelites up out of Egypt to this day. I have been moving from place to place with a tent as my dwelling. ⁷Wherever I have moved with all the Israelites, did I ever say to any of their rulers whom I commanded to shepherd my people Israel, "Why have you not built me a house of cedar?" '

⁸"Now then, tell my servant David, 'This is what the LORD Almighty says: I took you from the pasture and from following the flock to be ruler over my people Israel. ⁹I have been with you wherever you have gone, and I have cut off all your enemies from before you. Now I will make your name great, like the names of the greatest men of the earth. ¹⁰And I will provide a place for my people Israel and will plant them so that they can have a home of their own and no longer be disturbed. Wicked people will not oppress them anymore, as they did at the beginning ¹¹and have done ever since the time I appointed leaders[a] over my people Israel. I will also give you rest from all your enemies.

" 'The LORD declares to you that the LORD himself will establish a house for you: ¹²When your days are over and you rest with your fathers, I will raise up your offspring to succeed you, who will come from your own body, and I will establish his kingdom. ¹³He is the one who will build a house for my Name, and I will establish the throne of his kingdom forever. ¹⁴I will be his father, and he will be my son. When he does wrong, I will punish him with the rod of men, with floggings inflicted by men. ¹⁵But my love will never be taken away from him, as I took it away from Saul, whom I removed from before you. ¹⁶Your house and your kingdom will endure for-

---

THE MESSAGE

GOD'S COVENANT WITH DAVID

7 ^{7.1-2} Before long, the king made himself at home and GOD gave him peace from all his enemies. Then one day King David said to Nathan the prophet, "Look at this: Here I am, comfortable in a luxurious house of cedar, and the Chest of God sits in a plain tent."

^{7.3} Nathan told the king, "Whatever is on your heart, go and do it. GOD is with you."

^{7.4-7} But that night, the word of GOD came to Nathan saying, "Go and tell my servant David: This is GOD's word on the matter: You're going to build a 'house' for me to live in? Why, I haven't lived in a 'house' from the time I brought the children of Israel up from Egypt till now. All that time I've moved about with nothing but a tent. And in all my travels with Israel, did I ever say to any of the leaders I commanded to shepherd Israel, 'Why haven't you built me a house of cedar?'

^{7.8-11} "So here is what you are to tell my servant David: The GOD-of-the-Angel-Armies has this word for you: I took you from the pasture, tagging along after sheep, and made you prince over my people Israel. I was with you everywhere you went and mowed your enemies down before you. Now I'm making you famous, to be ranked with the great names on earth. And I'm going to set aside a place for my people Israel and plant them there so they'll have their own home and not be knocked around any more. Nor will evil men afflict you as they always have, even during the days I set judges over my people Israel. Finally, I'm going to give you peace from all your enemies.

^{7.11-16} "Furthermore, GOD has this message for you: GOD himself will build you a house! When your life is complete and you're buried with your ancestors, then I'll raise up your child, your own flesh and blood, to succeed you, and I'll firmly establish his rule. He will build a house to honor me, and I will guarantee his kingdom's rule permanently. I'll be a father to him, and he'll be a son to me. When he does wrong, I'll discipline him in the usual ways, the pitfalls and obstacles of this mortal life. But I'll never remove my gracious love from him, as I removed it from Saul, who preceded you and whom I most certainly did remove. Your family and your kingdom are permanently secured.

---

^a 11 Traditionally *judges*

NEW INTERNATIONAL VERSION

ever before me[a]; your throne will be established forever.' "

[17]Nathan reported to David all the words of this entire revelation.

DAVID'S PRAYER

[18]Then King David went in and sat before the LORD, and he said:

"Who am I, O Sovereign LORD, and what is my family, that you have brought me this far? [19]And as if this were not enough in your sight, O Sovereign LORD, you have also spoken about the future of the house of your servant. Is this your usual way of dealing with man, O Sovereign LORD?

[20]"What more can David say to you? For you know your servant, O Sovereign LORD. [21]For the sake of your word and according to your will, you have done this great thing and made it known to your servant.

[22]"How great you are, O Sovereign LORD! There is no one like you, and there is no God but you, as we have heard with our own ears. [23]And who is like your people Israel—the one nation on earth that God went out to redeem as a people for himself, and to make a name for himself, and to perform great and awesome wonders by driving out nations and their gods from before your people, whom you redeemed from Egypt?[b] [24]You have established your people Israel as your very own forever, and you, O LORD, have become their God.

[25]"And now, LORD God, keep forever the promise you have made concerning your servant and his house. Do as you promised, [26]so that your name will be great forever. Then men will say, 'The LORD Almighty is God over Israel!' And the house of your servant David will be established before you.

[27]"O LORD Almighty, God of Israel, you have revealed this to your servant, saying, 'I will build a house for you.' So your servant has found courage to offer you this prayer. [28]O Sovereign LORD, you are God! Your words are trustworthy, and you have promised these good things to your servant. [29]Now be pleased to bless the house

---

[a] 16 Some Hebrew manuscripts and Septuagint; most Hebrew manuscripts you   [b] 23 See Septuagint and 1 Chron. 17:21; Hebrew *wonders for your land and before your people, whom you redeemed from Egypt, from the nations and their gods.*

THE MESSAGE

I'm keeping my eye on them! And your royal throne will always be there, rock solid."

7.17   Nathan gave David a complete and accurate account of everything he heard and saw in the vision.

7.18-21   King David went in, took his place before GOD, and prayed: "Who am I, my Master GOD, and what is my family, that you have brought me to this place in life? But that's nothing compared to what's coming, for you've also spoken of my family far into the future, given me a glimpse into tomorrow, my Master GOD! What can I possibly say in the face of all this? You know me, Master GOD, just as I am. You've done all this not because of who I am but because of who you are—out of your very heart!—but you've let me in on it.

7.22-24   "This is what makes you so great, Master GOD! There is none like you, no God but you, nothing to compare with what we've heard with our own ears. And who is like your people, like Israel, a nation unique in the earth, whom God set out to redeem for himself (and became most famous for it), performing great and fearsome acts, throwing out nations and their gods left and right as you saved your people from Egypt? You established for yourself a people—your very own Israel!—your people permanently. And you, GOD, became their God.

7.25-27   "So now, great GOD, this word that you have spoken to me and my family, guarantee it permanently! Do exactly what you've promised! Then your reputation will flourish always as people exclaim, 'The GOD-of-the-Angel-Armies is God over Israel!' And the house of your servant David will remain sure and solid in your watchful presence. For you, GOD-of-the-Angel-Armies, Israel's God, told me plainly, 'I will build you a house.' That's how I was able to find the courage to pray this prayer to you.

7.28-29   "And now, Master GOD, being the God you are, speaking sure words as you do, and having just said this wonderful thing to me, please, just one more thing: Bless my family; keep your

NEW INTERNATIONAL VERSION

of your servant, that it may continue forever in your sight; for you, O Sovereign LORD, have spoken, and with your blessing the house of your servant will be blessed forever."

DAVID'S VICTORIES

8 In the course of time, David defeated the Philistines and subdued them, and he took Metheg Ammah from the control of the Philistines.

²David also defeated the Moabites. He made them lie down on the ground and measured them off with a length of cord. Every two lengths of them were put to death, and the third length was allowed to live. So the Moabites became subject to David and brought tribute.

³Moreover, David fought Hadadezer son of Rehob, king of Zobah, when he went to restore his control along the Euphrates River. ⁴David captured a thousand of his chariots, seven thousand charioteers [a] and twenty thousand foot soldiers. He hamstrung all but a hundred of the chariot horses.

⁵When the Arameans of Damascus came to help Hadadezer king of Zobah, David struck down twenty-two thousand of them. ⁶He put garrisons in the Aramean kingdom of Damascus, and the Arameans became subject to him and brought tribute. The LORD gave David victory wherever he went.

⁷David took the gold shields that belonged to the officers of Hadadezer and brought them to Jerusalem. ⁸From Tebah [b] and Berothai, towns that belonged to Hadadezer, King David took a great quantity of bronze.

⁹When Tou [c] king of Hamath heard that David had defeated the entire army of Hadadezer, ¹⁰he sent his son Joram [d] to King David to greet him and congratulate him on his victory in battle over Hadadezer, who had been at war with Tou. Joram brought with him articles of silver and gold and bronze.

¹¹King David dedicated these articles to the LORD, as he had done with the silver and gold from all the nations he had subdued: ¹²Edom [e] and Moab, the Ammonites and the Philistines, and Amalek. He also dedicated the plunder taken from Hadadezer son of Rehob, king of Zobah.

---

^a 4 Septuagint (see also Dead Sea Scrolls and 1 Chron. 18:4); Masoretic Text *captured seventeen hundred of his charioteers*   ^b 8 See some Septuagint manuscripts (see also 1 Chron. 18:8); Hebrew *Betah*.   ^c 9 Hebrew *Toi*, a variant of *Tou*; also in verse 10   ^d 10 A variant of *Hadoram*   ^e 12 Some Hebrew manuscripts, Septuagint and Syriac (see also 1 Chron. 18:11); most Hebrew manuscripts *Aram*

THE MESSAGE

eye on them always. You've already as much as said that you would, Master GOD! Oh, may your blessing be on my family permanently!"

8.1 **8** In the days that followed, David struck hard at the Philistines—brought them to their knees and took control of the countryside.

8.2   He also fought and defeated Moab. He chose two-thirds of them randomly and executed them. The other third he spared. So the Moabites fell under David's rule and were forced to bring tribute.

8.3-4   On his way to restore his sovereignty at the River Euphrates, David next defeated Hadadezer son of Rehob the king of Zobah. He captured from him a thousand chariots, seven thousand cavalry, and twenty thousand infantry. He hamstrung all the chariot horses, but saved back a hundred.

8.5-6   When the Arameans from Damascus came to the aid of Hadadezer king of Zobah, David killed twenty-two thousand of them. David set up a puppet government in Aram-Damascus. The Arameans became subjects of David and were forced to bring tribute. GOD gave victory to David wherever he marched.

8.7-8   David plundered the gold shields that belonged to the servants of Hadadezer and brought them to Jerusalem. He also looted a great quantity of bronze from Tebah and Berothai, cities of Hadadezer.

8.9-12   Toi, king of Hamath, heard that David had struck down the entire army of Hadadezer. So he sent his son Joram to King David to greet and congratulate him for fighting and defeating them, for Toi and Hadadezer were old enemies. He brought with him gifts of silver, gold, and bronze. King David consecrated these along with the silver and gold from all the nations he had conquered—from Aram, Moab, the Ammonites, the Philistines, and from Amalek, along with the plunder from Hadadezer son of Rehob king of Zobah.

NEW INTERNATIONAL VERSION

¹³And David became famous after he returned from striking down eighteen thousand Edomites*a* in the Valley of Salt.

¹⁴He put garrisons throughout Edom, and all the Edomites became subject to David. The LORD gave David victory wherever he went.

DAVID'S OFFICIALS

¹⁵David reigned over all Israel, doing what was just and right for all his people. ¹⁶Joab son of Zeruiah was over the army; Jehoshaphat son of Ahilud was recorder; ¹⁷Zadok son of Ahitub and Ahimelech son of Abiathar were priests; Seraiah was secretary; ¹⁸Benaiah son of Jehoiada was over the Kerethites and Pelethites; and David's sons were royal advisers.*b*

DAVID AND MEPHIBOSHETH

9 David asked, "Is there anyone still left of the house of Saul to whom I can show kindness for Jonathan's sake?"

²Now there was a servant of Saul's household named Ziba. They called him to appear before David, and the king said to him, "Are you Ziba?"

"Your servant," he replied.

³The king asked, "Is there no one still left of the house of Saul to whom I can show God's kindness?"

Ziba answered the king, "There is still a son of Jonathan; he is crippled in both feet."

⁴"Where is he?" the king asked.

Ziba answered, "He is at the house of Makir son of Ammiel in Lo Debar."

⁵So King David had him brought from Lo Debar, from the house of Makir son of Ammiel.

⁶When Mephibosheth son of Jonathan, the son of Saul, came to David, he bowed down to pay him honor.

David said, "Mephibosheth!"

"Your servant," he replied.

⁷"Don't be afraid," David said to him, "for I will surely show you kindness for the sake of your father Jonathan. I will restore to you all the land that belonged to your grandfather Saul, and you will always eat at my table."

⁸Mephibosheth bowed down and said, "What is your servant, that you should notice a dead dog like me?"

⁹Then the king summoned Ziba, Saul's ser-

---

a 13 A few Hebrew manuscripts, Septuagint and Syriac (see also 1 Chron. 18:12); most Hebrew manuscripts *Aram* (that is, Arameans) *b 18* Or *were priests*

THE MESSAGE

8.13-14 David built a victory monument on his return from defeating the Arameans.

Abishai son of Zeruiah fought and defeated the Edomites in the Salt Valley. Eighteen thousand of them were killed. David set up a puppet government in Edom, and the Edomites became subjects under David.

GOD gave David victory wherever he marched.

8.15 Thus David ruled over all of Israel. He ruled well—fair and evenhanded in all his duties and relationships.

8.16 Joab son of Zeruiah was head of the army;
Jehoshaphat son of Ahilud was clerk;

8.17 Zadok son of Ahitub and Ahimelech son of Abiathar were priests;
Seraiah was secretary;

8.18 Benaiah son of Jehoiada was over the Kerethites and Pelethites;
And David's sons were priests.

AN OPEN TABLE FOR MEPHIBOSHETH

9.1 **9** One day David asked, "Is there anyone left of Saul's family? If so, I'd like to show him some kindness in honor of Jonathan."

9.2 It happened that a servant from Saul's household named Ziba was there. They called him into David's presence. The king asked him, "Are you Ziba?"

"Yes sir," he replied.

9.3 The king asked, "Is there anyone left from the family of Saul to whom I can show some godly kindness?"

9.3 Ziba told the king, "Yes, there is Jonathan's son, lame in both feet."

9.4 "Where is he?"

"He's living at the home of Makir son of Ammiel in Lo Debar."

9.5 King David didn't lose a minute. He sent and got him from the home of Makir son of Ammiel in Lo Debar.

9.6 When Mephibosheth son of Jonathan (who was the son of Saul), came before David, he bowed deeply, abasing himself, honoring David.

David spoke his name: "Mephibosheth."

"Yes sir?"

9.7 "Don't be frightened," said David. "I'd like to do something special for you in memory of your father Jonathan. To begin with, I'm returning to you all the properties of your grandfather Saul. Furthermore, from now on you'll take all your meals at my table."

9.8 Shuffling and stammering, not looking him in the eye, Mephibosheth said, "Who am I that you pay attention to a stray dog like me?"

9.9-10 David then called in Ziba, Saul's right-hand

NEW INTERNATIONAL VERSION

vant, and said to him, "I have given your master's grandson everything that belonged to Saul and his family. ¹⁰You and your sons and your servants are to farm the land for him and bring in the crops, so that your master's grandson may be provided for. And Mephibosheth, grandson of your master, will always eat at my table." (Now Ziba had fifteen sons and twenty servants.)

¹¹Then Ziba said to the king, "Your servant will do whatever my lord the king commands his servant to do." So Mephibosheth ate at David's*ᵃ* table like one of the king's sons.

¹²Mephibosheth had a young son named Mica, and all the members of Ziba's household were servants of Mephibosheth. ¹³And Mephibosheth lived in Jerusalem, because he always ate at the king's table, and he was crippled in both feet.

DAVID DEFEATS THE AMMONITES

10 In the course of time, the king of the Ammonites died, and his son Hanun succeeded him as king. ²David thought, "I will show kindness to Hanun son of Nahash, just as his father showed kindness to me." So David sent a delegation to express his sympathy to Hanun concerning his father.

When David's men came to the land of the Ammonites, ³the Ammonite nobles said to Hanun their lord, "Do you think David is honoring your father by sending men to you to express sympathy? Hasn't David sent them to you to explore the city and spy it out and overthrow it?" ⁴So Hanun seized David's men, shaved off half of each man's beard, cut off their garments in the middle at the buttocks, and sent them away.

⁵When David was told about this, he sent messengers to meet the men, for they were greatly humiliated. The king said, "Stay at Jericho till your beards have grown, and then come back."

⁶When the Ammonites realized that they had become a stench in David's nostrils, they hired twenty thousand Aramean foot soldiers from Beth Rehob and Zobah, as well as the king of Maacah with a thousand men, and also twelve thousand men from Tob. ⁷On hearing this, David sent Joab out with the entire army of fighting men. ⁸The Ammonites came out and drew up in battle formation at the entrance to their city gate, while the Arameans of Zobah and Rehob and the men of Tob and Maacah were by themselves in the open country.

THE MESSAGE

man, and told him, "Everything that belonged to Saul and his family, I've handed over to your master's grandson. You and your sons and your servants will work his land and bring in the produce, provisions for your master's grandson. Mephibosheth himself, your master's grandson, from now on will take all his meals at my table." Ziba had fifteen sons and twenty servants.

9.11-12 "All that my master the king has ordered his servant," answered Ziba, "your servant will surely do."

And Mephibosheth ate at David's table, just like one of the royal family. Mephibosheth also had a small son named Mica. All who were part of Ziba's household were now the servants of Mephibosheth.

9.13 Mephibosheth lived in Jerusalem, taking all his meals at the king's table. He was lame in both feet.

10 10.1-2 Sometime after this, the king of the Ammonites died and Hanun, his son, succeeded him as king. David said, "I'd like to show some kindness to Hanun, the son of Nahash—treat him as well and as kindly as his father treated me." So David sent Hanun condolences regarding his father.

10.2-3 But when David's servants got to the land of the Ammonites, the Ammonite leaders warned Hanun, their head delegate, "Do you for a minute suppose that David is honoring your father by sending you comforters? Don't you think it's because he wants to snoop around the city and size it up that David has sent his emissaries to you?"

10.4 So Hanun seized David's men, shaved off half their beards, cut off their robes halfway up their buttocks, and sent them packing.

10.5 When all this was reported to David, he sent someone to meet them, for they were seriously humiliated. The king told them, "Stay in Jericho until your beards grow out. Only then come back."

10.6 When it dawned on the Ammonites that as far as David was concerned they stunk to high heaven, they hired Aramean soldiers from Beth-Rehob and Zobah—twenty thousand infantry—and a thousand men from the king of Maacah, and twelve thousand men from Tob.

10.7 When David heard of this, he dispatched Joab with his strongest fighters in full force.

10.8-12 The Ammonites marched out and arranged themselves in battle formation at the city gate. The Arameans of Zobah and Rehob and the men of Tob and Maacah took up a position out

---

ᵃ 11 Septuagint; Hebrew my

NEW INTERNATIONAL VERSION

⁹Joab saw that there were battle lines in front of him and behind him; so he selected some of the best troops in Israel and deployed them against the Arameans. ¹⁰He put the rest of the men under the command of Abishai his brother and deployed them against the Ammonites. ¹¹Joab said, "If the Arameans are too strong for me, then you are to come to my rescue; but if the Ammonites are too strong for you, then I will come to rescue you. ¹²Be strong and let us fight bravely for our people and the cities of our God. The LORD will do what is good in his sight."

¹³Then Joab and the troops with him advanced to fight the Arameans, and they fled before him. ¹⁴When the Ammonites saw that the Arameans were fleeing, they fled before Abishai and went inside the city. So Joab returned from fighting the Ammonites and came to Jerusalem.

¹⁵After the Arameans saw that they had been routed by Israel, they regrouped. ¹⁶Hadadezer had Arameans brought from beyond the River*ᵃ*; they went to Helam, with Shobach the commander of Hadadezer's army leading them. ¹⁷When David was told of this, he gathered all Israel, crossed the Jordan and went to Helam. The Arameans formed their battle lines to meet David and fought against him. ¹⁸But they fled before Israel, and David killed seven hundred of their charioteers and forty thousand of their foot soldiers.*ᵇ* He also struck down Shobach the commander of their army, and he died there. ¹⁹When all the kings who were vassals of Hadadezer saw that they had been defeated by Israel, they made peace with the Israelites and became subject to them.

So the Arameans were afraid to help the Ammonites anymore.

DAVID AND BATHSHEBA

11 In the spring, at the time when kings go off to war, David sent Joab out with the king's men and the whole Israelite army. They destroyed the Ammonites and besieged Rabbah. But David remained in Jerusalem.

²One evening David got up from his bed and walked around on the roof of the palace. From the roof he saw a woman bathing. The woman was very beautiful, ³and David sent someone to find out about her. The man said, "Isn't this Bathsheba, the daughter of Eliam and the wife of Uriah the Hittite?" ⁴Then David sent messengers to get her. She came to him, and he slept with her. (She had purified herself from her unclean-

ᵃ 16 That is, the Euphrates   *ᵇ 18* Some Septuagint manuscripts (see also 1 Chron. 19:18); Hebrew *horsemen*

THE MESSAGE

in the open fields. When Joab saw that he had two fronts to fight, before and behind, he took his pick of the best of Israel and deployed them to confront the Arameans. The rest of the army he put under the command of Abishai, his brother, and deployed them to confront the Ammonites. Then he said, "If the Arameans are too much for me, you help me. And if the Ammonites prove too much for you, I'll come and help you. Courage! We'll fight with might and main for our people and for the cities of our God. And GOD will do whatever he sees needs doing!"

10.13-14 But when Joab and his soldiers moved in to fight the Arameans, they ran off in full retreat. Then the Ammonites, seeing the Arameans run for dear life, took to their heels from Abishai and went into the city.

So Joab left off fighting the Ammonites and returned to Jerusalem.

10.15-17 When the Arameans saw how badly they'd been beaten by Israel, they picked up the pieces and regrouped. Hadadezer sent for the Arameans who were across the River. They came to Helam. Shobach, commander of Hadadezer's army, led them. All this was reported to David.

10.17-19 So David mustered Israel, crossed the Jordan, and came to Helam. The Arameans went into battle formation, ready for David, and the fight was on. But the Arameans again scattered before Israel. David killed seven hundred chariot drivers and forty thousand cavalry. And he mortally wounded Shobach, the army commander, who died on the battlefield. When all the kings who were vassals of Hadadezer saw that they had been routed by Israel, they made peace and became Israel's vassals. The Arameans were afraid to help the Ammonites ever again.

DAVID'S SIN AND SORROW

11.1 **11** When that time of year came around again, the anniversary of the Ammonite aggression, David dispatched Joab and his fighting men of Israel in full force to destroy the Ammonites for good. They laid siege to Rabbah, but David stayed in Jerusalem.

11.2-5 One late afternoon, David got up from taking his nap and was strolling on the roof of the palace. From his vantage point on the roof he saw a woman bathing. The woman was stunningly beautiful. David sent to ask about her, and was told, "Isn't this Bathsheba, daughter of Eliam and wife of Uriah the Hittite?" David sent his agents to get her. After she arrived, he went to bed with her. (This occurred during the time of "purification" following her peri-

NEW INTERNATIONAL VERSION

ness.) Then[a] she went back home. ⁵The woman conceived and sent word to David, saying, "I am pregnant."

⁶So David sent this word to Joab: "Send me Uriah the Hittite." And Joab sent him to David. ⁷When Uriah came to him, David asked him how Joab was, how the soldiers were and how the war was going. ⁸Then David said to Uriah, "Go down to your house and wash your feet." So Uriah left the palace, and a gift from the king was sent after him. ⁹But Uriah slept at the entrance to the palace with all his master's servants and did not go down to his house.

¹⁰When David was told, "Uriah did not go home," he asked him, "Haven't you just come from a distance? Why didn't you go home?" ¹¹Uriah said to David, "The ark and Israel and Judah are staying in tents, and my master Joab and my lord's men are camped in the open fields. How could I go to my house to eat and drink and lie with my wife? As surely as you live, I will not do such a thing!"

¹²Then David said to him, "Stay here one more day, and tomorrow I will send you back." So Uriah remained in Jerusalem that day and the next. ¹³At David's invitation, he ate and drank with him, and David made him drunk. But in the evening Uriah went out to sleep on his mat among his master's servants; he did not go home.

¹⁴In the morning David wrote a letter to Joab and sent it with Uriah. ¹⁵In it he wrote, "Put Uriah in the front line where the fighting is fiercest. Then withdraw from him so he will be struck down and die."

¹⁶So while Joab had the city under siege, he put Uriah at a place where he knew the strongest defenders were. ¹⁷When the men of the city came out and fought against Joab, some of the men in David's army fell; moreover, Uriah the Hittite died.

¹⁸Joab sent David a full account of the battle. ¹⁹He instructed the messenger: "When you have finished giving the king this account of the battle, ²⁰the king's anger may flare up, and he may ask you, 'Why did you get so close to the city to fight? Didn't you know they would shoot arrows from the wall? ²¹Who killed Abimelech son of Jerub-Besheth[b]? Didn't a woman throw an upper millstone on him from the wall, so that he died in Thebez? Why did you get so close to the wall?' If he asks you this, then say to him, 'Also, your servant Uriah the Hittite is dead.' "

²²The messenger set out, and when he arrived he told David everything Joab had sent him to

THE MESSAGE

od.) Then she returned home. Before long she realized she was pregnant.

Later she sent word to David: "I'm pregnant."

11.6 David then got in touch with Joab: "Send Uriah the Hittite to me." Joab sent him.

11.7-8 When he arrived, David asked him for news from the front—how things were going with Joab and the troops and with the fighting. Then he said to Uriah, "Go home. Have a refreshing bath and a good night's rest."

11.8-9 After Uriah left the palace, an informant of the king was sent after him. But Uriah didn't go home. He slept that night at the palace entrance, along with the king's servants.

11.10 David was told that Uriah had not gone home. He asked Uriah, "Didn't you just come off a hard trip? So why didn't you go home?"

11.11 Uriah replied to David, "The Chest is out there with the fighting men of Israel and Judah—in tents. My master Joab and his servants are roughing it out in the fields. So, how can I go home and eat and drink and enjoy my wife? On your life, I'll not do it!"

11.12-13 "All right," said David, "have it your way. Stay for the day and I'll send you back tomorrow." So Uriah stayed in Jerusalem the rest of the day.

The next day David invited him to eat and drink with him, and David got him drunk. But in the evening Uriah again went out and slept with his master's servants. He didn't go home.

11.14-15 In the morning David wrote a letter to Joab and sent it with Uriah. In the letter he wrote, "Put Uriah in the front lines where the fighting is the fiercest. Then pull back and leave him exposed so that he's sure to be killed."

11.16-17 So Joab, holding the city under siege, put Uriah in a place where he knew there were fierce enemy fighters. When the city's defenders came out to fight Joab, some of David's soldiers were killed, including Uriah the Hittite.

11.18-21 Joab sent David a full report on the battle. He instructed the messenger, "After you have given to the king a detailed report on the battle, if he flares in anger, say, 'And by the way, your servant Uriah the Hittite is dead.' "

11.22-24 Joab's messenger arrived in Jerusalem and

---

[a] 4 Or with her. When she purified herself from her uncleanness, [b] 21 Also known as Jerub-Baal (that is, Gideon)

NEW INTERNATIONAL VERSION

say. 23The messenger said to David, "The men overpowered us and came out against us in the open, but we drove them back to the entrance to the city gate. 24Then the archers shot arrows at your servants from the wall, and some of the king's men died. Moreover, your servant Uriah the Hittite is dead."

25David told the messenger, "Say this to Joab: 'Don't let this upset you; the sword devours one as well as another. Press the attack against the city and destroy it.' Say this to encourage Joab."

26When Uriah's wife heard that her husband was dead, she mourned for him. 27After the time of mourning was over, David had her brought to his house, and she became his wife and bore him a son. But the thing David had done displeased the LORD.

NATHAN REBUKES DAVID

12 The LORD sent Nathan to David. When he came to him, he said, "There were two men in a certain town, one rich and the other poor. 2The rich man had a very large number of sheep and cattle, 3but the poor man had nothing except one little ewe lamb he had bought. He raised it, and it grew up with him and his children. It shared his food, drank from his cup and even slept in his arms. It was like a daughter to him.

4"Now a traveler came to the rich man, but the rich man refrained from taking one of his own sheep or cattle to prepare a meal for the traveler who had come to him. Instead, he took the ewe lamb that belonged to the poor man and prepared it for the one who had come to him."

5David burned with anger against the man and said to Nathan, "As surely as the LORD lives, the man who did this deserves to die! 6He must pay for that lamb four times over, because he did such a thing and had no pity."

7Then Nathan said to David, "You are the man! This is what the LORD, the God of Israel, says: 'I anointed you king over Israel, and I delivered you from the hand of Saul. 8I gave your master's house to you, and your master's wives into your arms. I gave you the house of Israel and Judah. And if all this had been too little, I

THE MESSAGE

gave the king a full report. He said, "The enemy was too much for us. They advanced on us in the open field, and we pushed them back to the city gate. But then arrows came hot and heavy on us from the city wall, and eighteen of the king's soldiers died."

11.25 When the messenger completed his report of the battle, David got angry at Joab. He vented it on the messenger: "Why did you get so close to the city? Didn't you know you'd be attacked from the wall? Didn't you remember how Abimelech son of Jerub-Besheth got killed? Wasn't it a woman who dropped a millstone on him from the wall and crushed him at Thebez? Why did you go close to the wall!"

"By the way," said Joab's messenger, "your servant Uriah the Hittite is dead."

Then David told the messenger, "Oh. I see. Tell Joab, 'Don't trouble yourself over this. War kills—sometimes one, sometimes another—you never know who's next. Redouble your assault on the city and destroy it.' Encourage Joab."

11.26-27 When Uriah's wife heard that her husband was dead, she grieved for her husband. When the time of mourning was over, David sent someone to bring her to his house. She became his wife and bore him a son.

12 But GOD was not at all pleased with what David had done, and sent Nathan to David. Nathan said to him, "There were two men in the same city—one rich, the other poor. The rich man had huge flocks of sheep, herds of cattle. The poor man had nothing but one little female lamb, which he had bought and raised. It grew up with him and his children as a member of the family. It ate off his plate and drank from his cup and slept on his bed. It was like a daughter to him.

12.4 "One day a traveler dropped in on the rich man. He was too stingy to take an animal from his own herds or flocks to make a meal for his visitor, so he took the poor man's lamb and prepared a meal to set before his guest."

12.5-6 David exploded in anger. "As surely as GOD lives," he said to Nathan, "the man who did this ought to be lynched! He must repay for the lamb four times over for his crime and his stinginess!"

12.7-12 "You're the man!" said Nathan. "And here's what GOD, the God of Israel, has to say to you: I made you king over Israel. I freed you from the fist of Saul. I gave you your master's daughter and other wives to have and to hold. I gave you both Israel and Judah. And if that hadn't

NEW INTERNATIONAL VERSION

would have given you even more. ⁹Why did you despise the word of the LORD by doing what is evil in his eyes? You struck down Uriah the Hittite with the sword and took his wife to be your own. You killed him with the sword of the Ammonites. ¹⁰Now, therefore, the sword will never depart from your house, because you despised me and took the wife of Uriah the Hittite to be your own.'

¹¹"This is what the LORD says: 'Out of your own household I am going to bring calamity upon you. Before your very eyes I will take your wives and give them to one who is close to you, and he will lie with your wives in broad daylight. ¹²You did it in secret, but I will do this thing in broad daylight before all Israel.' "

¹³Then David said to Nathan, "I have sinned against the LORD."

Nathan replied, "The LORD has taken away your sin. You are not going to die. ¹⁴But because by doing this you have made the enemies of the LORD show utter contempt,ᵃ the son born to you will die."

¹⁵After Nathan had gone home, the LORD struck the child that Uriah's wife had borne to David, and he became ill. ¹⁶David pleaded with God for the child. He fasted and went into his house and spent the nights lying on the ground. ¹⁷The elders of his household stood beside him to get him up from the ground, but he refused, and he would not eat any food with them.

¹⁸On the seventh day the child died. David's servants were afraid to tell him that the child was dead, for they thought, "While the child was still living, we spoke to David but he would not listen to us. How can we tell him the child is dead? He may do something desperate."

¹⁹David noticed that his servants were whispering among themselves and he realized the child was dead. "Is the child dead?" he asked.

"Yes," they replied, "he is dead."

²⁰Then David got up from the ground. After he had washed, put on lotions and changed his clothes, he went into the house of the LORD and worshiped. Then he went to his own house, and at his request they served him food, and he ate.

²¹His servants asked him, "Why are you acting this way? While the child was alive, you fasted and wept, but now that the child is dead, you get up and eat!"

²²He answered, "While the child was still alive, I fasted and wept. I thought, 'Who knows? The LORD may be gracious to me and let the child live.' ²³But now that he is dead, why

THE MESSAGE

been enough, I'd have gladly thrown in much more. So why have you treated the word of GOD with brazen contempt, doing this great evil? You murdered Uriah the Hittite, then took his wife as your wife. Worse, you killed him with an Ammonite sword! And now, because you treated God with such contempt and took Uriah the Hittite's wife as your wife, killing and murder will continually plague your family. This is GOD speaking, remember! I'll make trouble for you out of your own family. I'll take your wives from right out in front of you. I'll give them to some neighbor, and he'll go to bed with them openly. You did your deed in secret; I'm doing mine with the whole country watching!"

12.13-14 Then David confessed to Nathan, "I've sinned against GOD."

Nathan pronounced, "Yes, but that's not the last word. GOD forgives your sin. You won't die for it. But because of your blasphemous behavior, the son born to you will die."

12.15-18 After Nathan went home, GOD afflicted the child that Uriah's wife bore to David, and he came down sick. David prayed desperately to God for the little boy. He fasted, wouldn't go out, and slept on the floor. The elders in his family came in and tried to get him off the floor, but he wouldn't budge. Nor could they get him to eat anything. On the seventh day the child died. David's servants were afraid to tell him. They said, "What do we do now? While the child was living he wouldn't listen to a word we said. Now, with the child dead, if we speak to him there's no telling what he'll do."

12.19 David noticed that the servants were whispering behind his back, and realized that the boy must have died.

He asked the servants, "Is the boy dead?"

"Yes," they answered. "He's dead."

12.20 David got up from the floor, washed his face and combed his hair, put on a fresh change of clothes, then went into the sanctuary and worshiped. Then he came home and asked for something to eat. They set it before him and he ate.

12.21 His servants asked him, "What's going on with you? While the child was alive you fasted and wept and stayed up all night. Now that he's dead, you get up and eat."

12.22-23 "While the child was alive," he said, "I fasted and wept, thinking GOD might have mercy on me and the child would live. But now that

ᵃ 14 Masoretic Text; an ancient Hebrew scribal tradition *this you have shown utter contempt for the LORD*

NEW INTERNATIONAL VERSION

should I fast? Can I bring him back again? I will go to him, but he will not return to me."

²⁴Then David comforted his wife Bathsheba, and he went to her and lay with her. She gave birth to a son, and they named him Solomon. The LORD loved him; ²⁵and because the LORD loved him, he sent word through Nathan the prophet to name him Jedidiah.ᵃ

²⁶Meanwhile Joab fought against Rabbah of the Ammonites and captured the royal citadel. ²⁷Joab then sent messengers to David, saying, "I have fought against Rabbah and taken its water supply. ²⁸Now muster the rest of the troops and besiege the city and capture it. Otherwise I will take the city, and it will be named after me."

²⁹So David mustered the entire army and went to Rabbah, and attacked and captured it. ³⁰He took the crown from the head of their kingᵇ—its weight was a talentᶜ of gold, and it was set with precious stones—and it was placed on David's head. He took a great quantity of plunder from the city ³¹and brought out the people who were there, consigning them to labor with saws and with iron picks and axes, and he made them work at brickmaking.ᵈ He did this to all the Ammonite towns. Then David and his entire army returned to Jerusalem.

AMNON AND TAMAR

13 In the course of time, Amnon son of David fell in love with Tamar, the beautiful sister of Absalom son of David.

²Amnon became frustrated to the point of illness on account of his sister Tamar, for she was a virgin, and it seemed impossible for him to do anything to her.

³Now Amnon had a friend named Jonadab son of Shimeah, David's brother. Jonadab was a very shrewd man. ⁴He asked Amnon, "Why do you, the king's son, look so haggard morning after morning? Won't you tell me?"

Amnon said to him, "I'm in love with Tamar, my brother Absalom's sister."

⁵"Go to bed and pretend to be ill," Jonadab said. "When your father comes to see you, say to him, 'I would like my sister Tamar to come and give me something to eat. Let her prepare the food in my sight so I may watch her and then eat it from her hand.' "

⁶So Amnon lay down and pretended to be ill. When the king came to see him, Amnon said to

THE MESSAGE

he's dead, why fast? Can I bring him back now? I can go to him, but he can't come to me."

¹²·²⁴⁻²⁵ David went and comforted his wife Bathsheba. And when he slept with her, they conceived a son. When he was born they named him Solomon. GOD had a special love for him and sent word by Nathan the prophet that GOD wanted him named Jedidiah (God's Beloved).

✛

¹²·²⁶⁻³⁰ Joab, at war in Rabbah against the Ammonites, captured the royal city. He sent messengers to David saying, "I'm fighting at Rabbah, and I've just captured the city's water supply. Hurry and get the rest of the troops together and set up camp here at the city and complete the capture yourself. Otherwise, I'll capture it and get all the credit instead of you." So David marshaled all the troops, went to Rabbah, and fought and captured it. He took the crown from their king's head—very heavy with gold, and with a precious stone in it. It ended up on David's head. And they plundered the city, carrying off a great quantity of loot.

¹²·³¹ David emptied the city of its people and put them to slave labor using saws, picks, and axes, and making bricks. He did this to all the Ammonite cities. Then David and the whole army returned to Jerusalem.

13 ¹³·¹⁻⁴ Some time later, this happened: Absalom, David's son, had a sister who was very attractive. Her name was Tamar. Amnon, also David's son, was in love with her. Amnon was obsessed with his sister Tamar to the point of making himself sick over her. She was a virgin, so he couldn't see how he could get his hands on her. Amnon had a good friend, Jonadab, the son of David's brother Shimeah. Jonadab was exceptionally streetwise. He said to Amnon, "Why are you moping around like this, day after day—you, the son of the king! Tell me what's eating at you."

"In a word, Tamar," said Amnon. "My brother Absalom's sister. I'm in love with her."

¹³·⁵ "Here's what you do," said Jonadab. "Go to bed and pretend you're sick. When your father comes to visit you, say, 'Have my sister Tamar come and prepare some supper for me here where I can watch her and she can feed me.' "

¹³·⁶ So Amnon took to his bed and acted sick. When the king came to visit, Amnon said,

---

ᵃ 25 Jedidiah means loved by the LORD.   ᵇ 30 Or of Milcom (that is, Molech)   ᶜ 30 That is, about 75 pounds (about 34 kilograms)   ᵈ 31 The meaning of the Hebrew for this clause is uncertain.

NEW INTERNATIONAL VERSION

him, "I would like my sister Tamar to come and make some special bread in my sight, so I may eat from her hand."

7David sent word to Tamar at the palace: "Go to the house of your brother Amnon and prepare some food for him." 8So Tamar went to the house of her brother Amnon, who was lying down. She took some dough, kneaded it, made the bread in his sight and baked it. 9Then she took the pan and served him the bread, but he refused to eat.

"Send everyone out of here," Amnon said. So everyone left him. 10Then Amnon said to Tamar, "Bring the food here into my bedroom so I may eat from your hand." And Tamar took the bread she had prepared and brought it to her brother Amnon in his bedroom. 11But when she took it to him to eat, he grabbed her and said, "Come to bed with me, my sister."

12"Don't, my brother!" she said to him. "Don't force me. Such a thing should not be done in Israel! Don't do this wicked thing. 13What about me? Where could I get rid of my disgrace? And what about you? You would be like one of the wicked fools in Israel. Please speak to the king; he will not keep me from being married to you." 14But he refused to listen to her, and since he was stronger than she, he raped her.

15Then Amnon hated her with intense hatred. In fact, he hated her more than he had loved her. Amnon said to her, "Get up and get out!"

16"No!" she said to him. "Sending me away would be a greater wrong than what you have already done to me."

But he refused to listen to her. 17He called his personal servant and said, "Get this woman out of here and bolt the door after her." 18So his servant put her out and bolted the door after her. She was wearing a richly ornamented*a* robe, for this was the kind of garment the virgin daughters of the king wore. 19Tamar put ashes on her head and tore the ornamented*b* robe she was wearing. She put her hand on her head and went away, weeping aloud as she went.

20Her brother Absalom said to her, "Has that Amnon, your brother, been with you? Be quiet now, my sister; he is your brother. Don't take this thing to heart." And Tamar lived in her brother Absalom's house, a desolate woman.

21When King David heard all this, he was furious. 22Absalom never said a word to Amnon, either good or bad; he hated Amnon because he had disgraced his sister Tamar.

---

a 18 The meaning of the Hebrew for this phrase is uncertain. *b 19* The meaning of the Hebrew for this word is uncertain.

THE MESSAGE

"Would you do me a favor? Have my sister Tamar come and make some nourishing dumplings here where I can watch her and be fed by her."

13.7 David sent word to Tamar who was home at the time: "Go to the house of your brother Amnon and prepare a meal for him."

13.8-9 So Tamar went to her brother Amnon's house. She took dough, kneaded it, formed it into dumplings, and cooked them while he watched from his bed. But when she took the cooking pot and served him, he wouldn't eat.

13.9-11 Amnon said, "Clear everyone out of the house," and they all cleared out. Then he said to Tamar, "Bring the food into my bedroom, where we can eat in privacy." She took the nourishing dumplings she had prepared and brought them to her brother Amnon in his bedroom. But when she got ready to feed him, he grabbed her and said, "Come to bed with me, sister!"

13.12-13 "No, brother!" she said, "Don't hurt me! This kind of thing isn't done in Israel! Don't do this terrible thing! Where could I ever show my face? And you—you'll be out on the street in disgrace. Oh, please! Speak to the king—he'll let you marry me."

13.14 But he wouldn't listen. Being much stronger than she, he raped her.

13.15 No sooner had Amnon raped her than he hated her—an immense hatred. The hatred that he felt for her was greater than the love he'd had for her. "Get up," he said, "and get out!"

13.16-18 "Oh no, brother," she said. "Please! This is an even worse evil than what you just did to me!"

But he wouldn't listen to her. He called for his valet. "Get rid of this woman. Get her out of my sight! And lock the door after her." The valet threw her out and locked the door behind her.

13.18-19 She was wearing a long-sleeved gown. (That's how virgin princesses used to dress from early adolescence on.) Tamar poured ashes on her head, then she ripped the long-sleeved gown, held her head in her hands, and walked away, sobbing as she went.

13.20 Her brother Absalom said to her, "Has your brother Amnon had his way with you? Now, my dear sister, let's keep it quiet—a family matter. He is, after all, your brother. Don't take this so hard." Tamar lived in her brother Absalom's home, bitter and desolate.

13.21-22 King David heard the whole story and was enraged, but he didn't discipline Amnon. David doted on him because he was his firstborn. Absalom quit speaking to Amnon—not a word, whether good or bad—because he hated him for violating his sister Tamar.

NEW INTERNATIONAL VERSION

ABSALOM KILLS AMNON

²³Two years later, when Absalom's sheepshearers were at Baal Hazor near the border of Ephraim, he invited all the king's sons to come there. ²⁴Absalom went to the king and said, "Your servant has had shearers come. Will the king and his officials please join me?"

²⁵"No, my son," the king replied. "All of us should not go; we would only be a burden to you." Although Absalom urged him, he still refused to go, but gave him his blessing.

²⁶Then Absalom said, "If not, please let my brother Amnon come with us."

The king asked him, "Why should he go with you?" ²⁷But Absalom urged him, so he sent with him Amnon and the rest of the king's sons.

²⁸Absalom ordered his men, "Listen! When Amnon is in high spirits from drinking wine and I say to you, 'Strike Amnon down,' then kill him. Don't be afraid. Have not I given you this order? Be strong and brave." ²⁹So Absalom's men did to Amnon what Absalom had ordered. Then all the king's sons got up, mounted their mules and fled.

³⁰While they were on their way, the report came to David: "Absalom has struck down all the king's sons; not one of them is left." ³¹The king stood up, tore his clothes and lay down on the ground; and all his servants stood by with their clothes torn.

³²But Jonadab son of Shimeah, David's brother, said, "My lord should not think that they killed all the princes; only Amnon is dead. This has been Absalom's expressed intention ever since the day Amnon raped his sister Tamar. ³³My lord the king should not be concerned about the report that all the king's sons are dead. Only Amnon is dead."

³⁴Meanwhile, Absalom had fled.

Now the man standing watch looked up and saw many people on the road west of him, coming down the side of the hill. The watchman went and told the king, "I see men in the direction of Horonaim, on the side of the hill."ᵃ

³⁵Jonadab said to the king, "See, the king's sons are here; it has happened just as your servant said."

³⁶As he finished speaking, the king's sons came in, wailing loudly. The king, too, and all his servants wept very bitterly.

³⁷Absalom fled and went to Talmai son of Ammihud, the king of Geshur. But King David mourned for his son every day.

³⁸After Absalom fled and went to Geshur, he stayed there three years. ³⁹And the spirit of the

---

ᵃ 34 Septuagint; Hebrew does not have this sentence.

THE MESSAGE

13.23-24 Two years went by. One day Absalom threw a sheep-shearing party in Baal Hazor in the vicinity of Ephraim and invited all the king's sons. He also went to the king and invited him. "Look, I'm throwing a sheep-shearing party. Come, and bring your servants."

13.25 But the king said, "No, son—not this time, and not the whole household. We'd just be a burden to you." Absalom pushed, but David wouldn't budge. But he did give him his blessing.

13.26-27 Then Absalom said, "Well, if you won't come, at least let my brother Amnon come."

"And why," said the king, "should he go with you?" But Absalom was so insistent that he gave in and let Amnon and all the rest of the king's sons go.

13.28 Absalom prepared a banquet fit for a king. Then he instructed his servants, "Look sharp, now. When Amnon is well into the sauce and feeling no pain, and I give the order 'Strike Amnon,' kill him. And don't be afraid—I'm the one giving the command. Courage! You can do it!"

13.29-31 Absalom's servants did to Amnon exactly what their master ordered. All the king's sons got out as fast as they could, jumped on their mules, and rode off. While they were still on the road, a rumor came to the king: "Absalom just killed all the king's sons—not one is left!" The king stood up, ripped his clothes to shreds, and threw himself on the floor. All his servants who were standing around at the time did the same.

13.32-33 Just then, Jonadab, his brother Shimeah's son, stepped up. "My master must not think that all the young men, the king's sons, are dead. Only Amnon is dead. This happened because of Absalom's outrage since the day that Amnon violated his sister Tamar. So my master, the king, mustn't make things worse than they are, thinking that all your sons are dead. Only Amnon is dead."

13.34 Absalom fled.

Just then the sentry on duty looked up and saw a cloud of dust on the road from Horonaim alongside the mountain. He came and told the king, "I've just seen a bunch of men on the Horonaim road, coming around the mountain."

13.35-37 Then Jonadab exclaimed to the king, "See! It's the king's sons coming, just as I said!" He had no sooner said the words than the king's sons burst in—loud laments and weeping! The king joined in, along with all the servants—loud weeping, many tears. David mourned the death of his son a long time.

13.37-39 When Absalom fled, he went to Talmai son of Ammihud, king of Geshur. He was there three years. The king finally gave up trying to

NEW INTERNATIONAL VERSION

king[a] longed to go to Absalom, for he was consoled concerning Amnon's death.

ABSALOM RETURNS TO JERUSALEM

14 Joab son of Zeruiah knew that the king's heart longed for Absalom. ²So Joab sent someone to Tekoa and had a wise woman brought from there. He said to her, "Pretend you are in mourning. Dress in mourning clothes, and don't use any cosmetic lotions. Act like a woman who has spent many days grieving for the dead. ³Then go to the king and speak these words to him." And Joab put the words in her mouth.

⁴When the woman from Tekoa went[b] to the king, she fell with her face to the ground to pay him honor, and she said, "Help me, O king!"

⁵The king asked her, "What is troubling you?"

She said, "I am indeed a widow; my husband is dead. ⁶I your servant had two sons. They got into a fight with each other in the field, and no one was there to separate them. One struck the other and killed him. ⁷Now the whole clan has risen up against your servant; they say, 'Hand over the one who struck his brother down, so that we may put him to death for the life of his brother whom he killed; then we will get rid of the heir as well.' They would put out the only burning coal I have left, leaving my husband neither name nor descendant on the face of the earth."

⁸The king said to the woman, "Go home, and I will issue an order in your behalf."

⁹But the woman from Tekoa said to him, "My lord the king, let the blame rest on me and on my father's family, and let the king and his throne be without guilt."

¹⁰The king replied, "If anyone says anything to you, bring him to me, and he will not bother you again."

¹¹She said, "Then let the king invoke the LORD his God to prevent the avenger of blood from adding to the destruction, so that my son will not be destroyed."

"As surely as the LORD lives," he said, "not one hair of your son's head will fall to the ground."

¹²Then the woman said, "Let your servant speak a word to my lord the king."

THE MESSAGE

get back at Absalom. He had come to terms with Amnon's death.

14.1-3 **14** Joab son of Zeruiah knew that the king, deep down, still cared for Absalom. So he sent to Tekoa for a wise woman who lived there and instructed her, "Pretend you are in mourning. Dress in black and don't comb your hair, so you'll look like you've been grieving over a dead loved one for a long time. Then go to the king and tell him this . . . ," Joab then told her exactly what to say.

14.4 The woman of Tekoa went to the king, bowed deeply before him in homage, and said, "O King, help!"

14.5-7 He said, "How can I help?"

"I'm a widow," she said. "My husband is dead. I had two sons. The two of them got into a fight out in the field and there was no one around to step between them. The one struck the other and killed him. Then the whole family ganged up against me and demanded, 'Hand over this murderer so we can kill him for the life of the brother he murdered!' They want to wipe out the heir and snuff out the one spark of life left to me. And then there would be nothing left of my husband—not so much as a name—on the face of the earth."

14.15-17 "So now I've dared come to the king, my master, about all this. They're making my life miserable, and I'm afraid. I said to myself, 'I'll go to the king. Maybe he'll do something! When the king hears what's going on, he'll step in and rescue me from the abuse of the man who would get rid of me and my son and God's inheritance—the works!' As your handmaid, I decided ahead of time, 'The word of my master, the king, will be the last word in this, for my master is like an angel of God in discerning good and evil.' GOD be with you!"

14.8 The king said, "Go home, and I'll take care of this for you."

14.9 "I'll take all responsibility for what happens," the woman of Tekoa said. "I don't want to compromise the king and his reputation."

14.10 "Bring the man who has been harassing you," the king continued. "I'll see to it that he doesn't bother you anymore."

14.11 "Let the king invoke the name of GOD," said the woman, "so this self-styled vigilante won't ruin everything, to say nothing of killing my son."

14.11 "As surely as GOD lives," he said, "not so much as a hair of your son's head will be lost."

14.12 Then she asked, "May I say one more thing to my master, the king?"

---

[a] 39 Dead Sea Scrolls and some Septuagint manuscripts; Masoretic Text *But the spirit of David the king*   [b] 4 Many Hebrew manuscripts, Septuagint, Vulgate and Syriac; most Hebrew manuscripts *spoke*

NEW INTERNATIONAL VERSION

"Speak," he replied.

¹³The woman said, "Why then have you devised a thing like this against the people of God? When the king says this, does he not convict himself, for the king has not brought back his banished son? ¹⁴Like water spilled on the ground, which cannot be recovered, so we must die. But God does not take away life; instead, he devises ways so that a banished person may not remain estranged from him.

¹⁵"And now I have come to say this to my lord the king because the people have made me afraid. Your servant thought, 'I will speak to the king; perhaps he will do what his servant asks. ¹⁶Perhaps the king will agree to deliver his servant from the hand of the man who is trying to cut off both me and my son from the inheritance God gave us.'

¹⁷"And now your servant says, 'May the word of my lord the king bring me rest, for my lord the king is like an angel of God in discerning good and evil. May the LORD your God be with you.' "

¹⁸Then the king said to the woman, "Do not keep from me the answer to what I am going to ask you."

"Let my lord the king speak," the woman said.

¹⁹The king asked, "Isn't the hand of Joab with you in all this?"

The woman answered, "As surely as you live, my lord the king, no one can turn to the right or to the left from anything my lord the king says. Yes, it was your servant Joab who instructed me to do this and who put all these words into the mouth of your servant. ²⁰Your servant Joab did this to change the present situation. My lord has wisdom like that of an angel of God—he knows everything that happens in the land."

²¹The king said to Joab, "Very well, I will do it. Go, bring back the young man Absalom."

²²Joab fell with his face to the ground to pay him honor, and he blessed the king. Joab said, "Today your servant knows that he has found favor in your eyes, my lord the king, because the king has granted his servant's request."

²³Then Joab went to Geshur and brought Absalom back to Jerusalem. ²⁴But the king said, "He must go to his own house; he must not see my face." So Absalom went to his own house and did not see the face of the king.

²⁵In all Israel there was not a man so highly praised for his handsome appearance as Absalom. From the top of his head to the sole of his foot there was no blemish in him. ²⁶Whenever he cut the hair of his head—he used to cut his hair from time to time when it became too heavy

THE MESSAGE

He said, "Go ahead."

14.13-14 "Why, then," the woman said, "have you done this very thing against God's people? In his verdict, the king convicts himself by not bringing home his exiled son. We all die sometime. Water spilled on the ground can't be gathered up again. But God does not take away life. He works out ways to get the exile back."

14.18 The king then said, "I'm going to ask you something. Answer me truthfully."

"Certainly," she said. "Let my master, the king, speak."

14.19-20 The king said, "Is the hand of Joab mixed up in this?"

"On your life, my master king, a body can't veer an inch right or left and get by with it in the royal presence! Yes, it was your servant Joab who put me up to this, and put these very words in my mouth. It was because he wanted to turn things around that your servant Joab did this. But my master is as wise as God's angels in knowing how to handle things on this earth."

14.21 The king spoke to Joab. "All right, I'll do it. Go and bring the young man Absalom back."

14.22 Joab bowed deeply in reverence and blessed the king. "I'm reassured to know that I'm still in your good graces and have your confidence, since the king is taking the counsel of his servant."

14.23-24 Joab got up, went to Geshur, and brought Absalom to Jerusalem. The king said, "He may return to his house, but he is not to see me face to face." So Absalom returned home, but was not permitted to see the king.

14.25-27 This Absalom! There wasn't a man in all Israel talked about so much for his handsome good looks—and not a blemish on him from head to toe! When he cut his hair—he always cut it short in the spring because it had grown

NEW INTERNATIONAL VERSION

for him—he would weigh it, and its weight was two hundred shekels*a* by the royal standard.

²⁷Three sons and a daughter were born to Absalom. The daughter's name was Tamar, and she became a beautiful woman.

²⁸Absalom lived two years in Jerusalem without seeing the king's face. ²⁹Then Absalom sent for Joab in order to send him to the king, but Joab refused to come to him. So he sent a second time, but he refused to come. ³⁰Then he said to his servants, "Look, Joab's field is next to mine, and he has barley there. Go and set it on fire." So Absalom's servants set the field on fire.

³¹Then Joab did go to Absalom's house and he said to him, "Why have your servants set my field on fire?"

³²Absalom said to Joab, "Look, I sent word to you and said, 'Come here so I can send you to the king to ask, "Why have I come from Geshur? It would be better for me if I were still there!"' Now then, I want to see the king's face, and if I am guilty of anything, let him put me to death."

³³So Joab went to the king and told him this. Then the king summoned Absalom, and he came in and bowed down with his face to the ground before the king. And the king kissed Absalom.

ABSALOM'S CONSPIRACY

15 In the course of time, Absalom provided himself with a chariot and horses and with fifty men to run ahead of him. ²He would get up early and stand by the side of the road leading to the city gate. Whenever anyone came with a complaint to be placed before the king for a decision, Absalom would call out to him, "What town are you from?" He would answer, "Your servant is from one of the tribes of Israel." ³Then Absalom would say to him, "Look, your claims are valid and proper, but there is no representative of the king to hear you." ⁴And Absalom would add, "If only I were appointed judge in the land! Then everyone who has a complaint or case could come to me and I would see that he gets justice."

⁵Also, whenever anyone approached him to bow down before him, Absalom would reach out his hand, take hold of him and kiss him. ⁶Absalom behaved in this way toward all the Israelites who came to the king asking for justice, and so he stole the hearts of the men of Israel.

⁷At the end of four*b* years, Absalom said to the king, "Let me go to Hebron and fulfill a vow I made to the LORD. ⁸While your servant was living at Geshur in Aram, I made this vow: 'If the

THE MESSAGE

so heavy—the weight of the hair from his head was over two pounds! Three sons were born to Absalom, and one daughter. Her name was Tamar—and she was a beauty.

14.28-31 Absalom lived in Jerusalem for two years, and not once did he see the king face to face. He sent for Joab to get him in to see the king, but Joab still wouldn't budge. He tried a second time and Joab still wouldn't. So he told his servants, "Listen. Joab's field adjoins mine, and he has a crop of barley in it. Go set fire to it." So Absalom's servants set fire to the field. That got him moving—Joab came to Absalom at home and said, "Why did your servants set my field on fire?"

14.32 Absalom answered him, "Listen, I sent for you saying, 'Come, and soon. I want to send you to the king to ask, "What's the point of my coming back from Geshur? I'd be better off still there!" Let me see the king face to face. If he finds me guilty, then he can put me to death.' "

14.33 Joab went to the king and told him what was going on. Absalom was then summoned—he came and bowed deeply in reverence before him. And the king kissed Absalom.

15.1-2 **15** As time went on, Absalom took to riding in a horse-drawn chariot, with fifty men running in front of him. Early each morning he would take up his post beside the road at the city gate. When anyone showed up with a case to bring to the king for a decision, Absalom would call him over and say, "Where do you hail from?"

And the answer would come, "Your servant is from one of the tribes of Israel."

15.3-6 Then Absalom would say, "Look, you've got a strong case; but the king isn't going to listen to you." Then he'd say, "Why doesn't someone make me a judge for this country? Anybody with a case could bring it to me and I'd settle things fair and square." Whenever someone would treat him with special honor, he'd shrug it off and treat him like an equal, making him feel important. Absalom did this to everyone who came to do business with the king and stole the hearts of everyone in Israel.

15.7-8 After four years of this, Absalom spoke to the king, "Let me go to Hebron to pay a vow that I made to GOD. Your servant made a vow

---

a 26 That is, about 5 pounds (about 2.3 kilograms)
b 7 Some Septuagint manuscripts, Syriac and Josephus; Hebrew *forty*

NEW INTERNATIONAL VERSION

LORD takes me back to Jerusalem, I will worship the LORD in Hebron.*a*' "

⁹The king said to him, "Go in peace." So he went to Hebron.

¹⁰Then Absalom sent secret messengers throughout the tribes of Israel to say, "As soon as you hear the sound of the trumpets, then say, 'Absalom is king in Hebron.' " ¹¹Two hundred men from Jerusalem had accompanied Absalom. They had been invited as guests and went quite innocently, knowing nothing about the matter. ¹²While Absalom was offering sacrifices, he also sent for Ahithophel the Gilonite, David's counselor, to come from Giloh, his hometown. And so the conspiracy gained strength, and Absalom's following kept on increasing.

DAVID FLEES

¹³A messenger came and told David, "The hearts of the men of Israel are with Absalom."

¹⁴Then David said to all his officials who were with him in Jerusalem, "Come! We must flee, or none of us will escape from Absalom. We must leave immediately, or he will move quickly to overtake us and bring ruin upon us and put the city to the sword."

¹⁵The king's officials answered him, "Your servants are ready to do whatever our lord the king chooses."

¹⁶The king set out, with his entire household following him; but he left ten concubines to take care of the palace. ¹⁷So the king set out, with all the people following him, and they halted at a place some distance away. ¹⁸All his men marched past him, along with all the Kerethites and Pelethites; and all the six hundred Gittites who had accompanied him from Gath marched before the king.

¹⁹The king said to Ittai the Gittite, "Why should you come along with us? Go back and stay with King Absalom. You are a foreigner, an exile from your homeland. ²⁰You came only yesterday. And today shall I make you wander about with us, when I do not know where I am going? Go back, and take your countrymen. May kindness and faithfulness be with you."

²¹But Ittai replied to the king, "As surely as the LORD lives, and as my lord the king lives, wherever my lord the king may be, whether it means life or death, there will your servant be."

²²David said to Ittai, "Go ahead, march on." So Ittai the Gittite marched on with all his men and the families that were with him.

²³The whole countryside wept aloud as all the people passed by. The king also crossed the Kid-

---

a 8 Some Septuagint manuscripts; Hebrew does not have *in Hebron.*

THE MESSAGE

when I was living in Geshur in Aram saying, 'If GOD will bring me back to Jerusalem, I'll serve him with my life.' "

15.9 The king said, "Go with my blessing." And he got up and set off for Hebron.

15.10-12 Then Absalom sent undercover agents to all the tribes of Israel with the message, "When you hear the blast of the ram's horn trumpet, that's your signal: Shout, 'Absalom is king in Hebron!' " Two hundred men went with Absalom from Jerusalem. But they had been called together knowing nothing of the plot and made the trip innocently. While Absalom was offering sacrifices, he managed also to involve Ahithophel the Gilonite, David's advisor, calling him away from his hometown of Giloh. The conspiracy grew powerful and Absalom's supporters multiplied.

15.13 Someone came to David with the report, "The whole country has taken up with Absalom!"

15.14 "Up and out of here!" called David to all his servants who were with him in Jerusalem. "We've got to run for our lives or none of us will escape Absalom! Hurry, he's about to pull the city down around our ears and slaughter us all!"

15.15 The king's servants said, "Whatever our master, the king, says, we'll do; we're with you all the way!"

15.16-18 So the king and his entire household escaped on foot. The king left ten concubines behind to tend to the palace. And so they left, step by step by step, and then paused at the last house as the whole army passed by him—all the Kerethites, all the Pelethites, and the six hundred Gittites who had marched with him from Gath, went past.

15.19-20 The king called out to Ittai the Gittite, "What are you doing here? Go back with King Absalom. You're a stranger here and freshly uprooted from your own country. You arrived only yesterday, and am I going to let you take your chances with us as I live on the road like a gypsy? Go back, and take your family with you. And God's grace and truth go with you!"

15.21 But Ittai answered, "As GOD lives and my master the king lives, where my master is, that's where I'll be—whether it means life or death."

15.22 "All right," said David, "go ahead." And they went on, Ittai the Gittite with all his men and all the children he had with him.

15.23-24 The whole country was weeping in loud lament as all the people passed by. As the king

NEW INTERNATIONAL VERSION

ron Valley, and all the people moved on toward the desert.

24Zadok was there, too, and all the Levites who were with him were carrying the ark of the covenant of God. They set down the ark of God, and Abiathar offered sacrifices[a] until all the people had finished leaving the city.

25Then the king said to Zadok, "Take the ark of God back into the city. If I find favor in the Lord's eyes, he will bring me back and let me see it and his dwelling place again. 26But if he says, 'I am not pleased with you,' then I am ready; let him do to me whatever seems good to him."

27The king also said to Zadok the priest, "Aren't you a seer? Go back to the city in peace, with your son Ahimaaz and Jonathan son of Abiathar. You and Abiathar take your two sons with you. 28I will wait at the fords in the desert until word comes from you to inform me." 29So Zadok and Abiathar took the ark of God back to Jerusalem and stayed there.

30But David continued up the Mount of Olives, weeping as he went; his head was covered and he was barefoot. All the people with him covered their heads too and were weeping as they went up. 31Now David had been told, "Ahithophel is among the conspirators with Absalom." So David prayed, "O Lord, turn Ahithophel's counsel into foolishness."

32When David arrived at the summit, where people used to worship God, Hushai the Arkite was there to meet him, his robe torn and dust on his head. 33David said to him, "If you go with me, you will be a burden to me. 34But if you return to the city and say to Absalom, 'I will be your servant, O king; I was your father's servant in the past, but now I will be your servant,' then you can help me by frustrating Ahithophel's advice. 35Won't the priests Zadok and Abiathar be there with you? Tell them anything you hear in the king's palace. 36Their two sons, Ahimaaz son of Zadok and Jonathan son of Abiathar, are there with them. Send them to me with anything you hear."

37So David's friend Hushai arrived at Jerusalem as Absalom was entering the city.

DAVID AND ZIBA

16 When David had gone a short distance beyond the summit, there was Ziba, the steward of Mephibosheth, waiting to meet him. He had a string of donkeys saddled and loaded with two hundred loaves of bread, a hundred cakes of raisins, a hundred cakes of figs and a skin of wine.

[a] 24 Or Abiathar went up

THE MESSAGE

crossed the Brook Kidron, the army headed for the road to the wilderness. Zadok was also there, the Levites with him, carrying God's Chest of the Covenant. They set the Chest of God down, Abiathar standing by, until all the people had evacuated the city.

15.25-26 Then the king ordered Zadok, "Take the Chest back to the city. If I get back in God's good graces, he'll bring me back and show me where the Chest has been set down. But if he says, 'I'm not pleased with you'—well, he can then do with me whatever he pleases."

15.27-30 The king directed Zadok the priest, "Here's the plan: Return to the city peacefully, with Ahimaaz your son and Jonathan, Abiathar's son, with you. I'll wait at a spot in the wilderness across the river, until I get word from you telling us what's up." So Zadok and Abiathar took the Chest of God back to Jerusalem and placed it there, while David went up the Mount of Olives weeping, head covered but barefooted, and the whole army was with him, heads covered and weeping as they ascended.

15.31 David was told, "Ahithophel has joined the conspirators with Absalom." He prayed, "Oh, God—turn Ahithophel's counsel to foolishness."

15.32-36 As David approached the top of the hill where God was worshiped, Hushai the Arkite, clothes ripped to shreds and dirt on his head, was there waiting for him. David said, "If you come with me, you'll be just one more piece of luggage. Go back to the city and say to Absalom, 'I'm ready to be your servant, O King; I used to be your father's servant, now I'm your servant.' Do that and you'll be able to confuse Ahithophel's counsel for me. The priests Zadok and Abiathar are already there; whatever information you pick up in the palace, tell them. Their two sons—Zadok's son Ahimaaz and Abiathar's son Jonathan—are there with them—anything you pick up can be sent to me by them."

15.37 Hushai, David's friend, arrived at the same time Absalom was entering Jerusalem.

16.1 **16** Shortly after David passed the crest of the hill, Mephibosheth's steward Ziba met him with a string of pack animals, saddled and loaded with a hundred loaves of bread, a hundred raisin cakes, a hundred baskets of fresh fruit, and a skin of wine.

NEW INTERNATIONAL VERSION

²The king asked Ziba, "Why have you brought these?"

Ziba answered, "The donkeys are for the king's household to ride on, the bread and fruit are for the men to eat, and the wine is to refresh those who become exhausted in the desert."

³The king then asked, "Where is your master's grandson?"

Ziba said to him, "He is staying in Jerusalem, because he thinks, 'Today the house of Israel will give me back my grandfather's kingdom.' "

⁴Then the king said to Ziba, "All that belonged to Mephibosheth is now yours."

"I humbly bow," Ziba said. "May I find favor in your eyes, my lord the king."

Shimei Curses David

⁵As King David approached Bahurim, a man from the same clan as Saul's family came out from there. His name was Shimei son of Gera, and he cursed as he came out. ⁶He pelted David and all the king's officials with stones, though all the troops and the special guard were on David's right and left. ⁷As he cursed, Shimei said, "Get out, get out, you man of blood, you scoundrel! ⁸The Lord has repaid you for all the blood you shed in the household of Saul, in whose place you have reigned. The Lord has handed the kingdom over to your son Absalom. You have come to ruin because you are a man of blood!"

⁹Then Abishai son of Zeruiah said to the king, "Why should this dead dog curse my lord the king? Let me go over and cut off his head."

¹⁰But the king said, "What do you and I have in common, you sons of Zeruiah? If he is cursing because the Lord said to him, 'Curse David,' who can ask, 'Why do you do this?' "

¹¹David then said to Abishai and all his officials, "My son, who is of my own flesh, is trying to take my life. How much more, then, this Benjamite! Leave him alone; let him curse, for the Lord has told him to. ¹²It may be that the Lord will see my distress and repay me with good for the cursing I am receiving today."

¹³So David and his men continued along the road while Shimei was going along the hillside opposite him, cursing as he went and throwing stones at him and showering him with dirt. ¹⁴The king and all the people with him arrived at their destination exhausted. And there he refreshed himself.

The Advice of Ahithophel and Hushai

¹⁵Meanwhile, Absalom and all the men of Israel came to Jerusalem, and Ahithophel was with him. ¹⁶Then Hushai the Arkite, David's friend,

THE MESSAGE

16.2   The king said to Ziba, "What's all this?"

"The donkeys," said Ziba, "are for the king's household to ride, the bread and fruit are for the servants to eat, and the wine is for drinking, especially for those overcome by fatigue in the wilderness."

16.3   The king said, "And where is your master's grandson?"

"He stayed in Jerusalem," said Ziba. "He said, 'This is the day Israel is going to restore my grandfather's kingdom to me.' "

16.4   "Everything that belonged to Mephibosheth," said the king, "is now yours."

Ziba said, "How can I ever thank you? I'll be forever in your debt, my master and king; may you always look on me with such kindness!"

16.5-8   When the king got to Bahurim, a man appeared who had connections with Saul's family. His name was Shimei son of Gera. As he followed along he shouted insults and threw rocks right and left at David and his company, servants and soldiers alike. To the accompaniment of curses he shouted, "Get lost, get lost, you butcher, you hellhound! God has paid you back for all your dirty work in the family of Saul and for stealing his kingdom. God has given the kingdom to your son Absalom. Look at you now—ruined! And good riddance, you pathetic old man!"

16.9   Abishai son of Zeruiah said, "This mangy dog can't insult my master the king this way— let me go over and cut off his head!"

16.10   But the king said, "Why are you sons of Zeruiah always interfering and getting in the way? If he's cursing, it's because God told him, 'Curse David.' So who dares raise questions?"

16.11-12   "Besides," continued David to Abishai and the rest of his servants, "my own son, my flesh and bone, is right now trying to kill me; compared to that this Benjaminite is small potatoes. Don't bother with him; let him curse; he's preaching God's word to me. And who knows, maybe God will see the trouble I'm in today and exchange the curses for something good."

16.13   David and his men went on down the road, while Shimei followed along on the ridge of the hill alongside, cursing, throwing stones down on them, and kicking up dirt.

16.14   By the time they reached the Jordan River, David and all the men of the company were exhausted. There they rested and were revived.

16.15   By this time Absalom and all his men were in Jerusalem.

And Ahithophel was with them.

16.16   Soon after, Hushai the Arkite, David's friend,

NEW INTERNATIONAL VERSION

went to Absalom and said to him, "Long live the king! Long live the king!"

[17]Absalom asked Hushai, "Is this the love you show your friend? Why didn't you go with your friend?"

[18]Hushai said to Absalom, "No, the one chosen by the LORD, by these people, and by all the men of Israel—his I will be, and I will remain with him. [19]Furthermore, whom should I serve? Should I not serve the son? Just as I served your father, so I will serve you."

[20]Absalom said to Ahithophel, "Give us your advice. What should we do?"

[21]Ahithophel answered, "Lie with your father's concubines whom he left to take care of the palace. Then all Israel will hear that you have made yourself a stench in your father's nostrils, and the hands of everyone with you will be strengthened." [22]So they pitched a tent for Absalom on the roof, and he lay with his father's concubines in the sight of all Israel.

[23]Now in those days the advice Ahithophel gave was like that of one who inquires of God. That was how both David and Absalom regarded all of Ahithophel's advice.

17 Ahithophel said to Absalom, "I would[a] choose twelve thousand men and set out tonight in pursuit of David. [2]I would[a] attack him while he is weary and weak. I would[a] strike him with terror, and then all the people with him will flee. I would[a] strike down only the king [3]and bring all the people back to you. The death of the man you seek will mean the return of all; all the people will be unharmed." [4]This plan seemed good to Absalom and to all the elders of Israel.

[5]But Absalom said, "Summon also Hushai the Arkite, so we can hear what he has to say." [6]When Hushai came to him, Absalom said, "Ahithophel has given this advice. Should we do what he says? If not, give us your opinion."

[7]Hushai replied to Absalom, "The advice Ahithophel has given is not good this time. [8]You know your father and his men; they are fighters, and as fierce as a wild bear robbed of her cubs. Besides, your father is an experienced fighter; he will not spend the night with the troops. [9]Even now, he is hidden in a cave or some other place. If he should attack your troops first,[b] whoever hears about it will say, 'There has been a slaughter among the troops who follow Absalom.' [10]Then even the bravest soldier, whose heart is like the heart of a lion, will melt with fear, for all

---

THE MESSAGE

came and greeted Absalom, "Long live the king! Long live the king!"

16.17   Absalom said to Hushai, "Is this the way you show devotion to your good friend? Why didn't you go with your friend David?"

16.18-19   "Because," said Hushai, "I want to be with the person that GOD and this people and all Israel have chosen. And I want to stay with him. Besides, who is there to serve other than the son? Just as I served your father, I'm now ready to serve you."

16.20   Then Absalom spoke to Ahithophel, "Are you ready to give counsel? What do we do next?"

16.21-22   Ahithophel told Absalom, "Go and sleep with your father's concubines, the ones he left to tend to the palace. Everyone will hear that you have openly disgraced your father, and the morale of everyone on your side will be strengthened." So Absalom pitched a tent up on the roof in public view, and went in and slept with his father's concubines.

16.23   The counsel that Ahithophel gave in those days was treated as if God himself had spoken. That was the reputation of Ahithophel's counsel to David; it was the same with Absalom.

17 Next Ahithophel advised Absalom, "Let me handpick twelve thousand men and go after David tonight. I'll come on him when he's bone tired and take him by complete surprise. The whole army will run off and I'll kill only David. Then I'll bring the army back to you—a bride brought back to her husband! You're only after one man, after all. Then everyone will be together in peace!"

17.4   Absalom thought it was an excellent strategy, and all the elders of Israel agreed.

17.5   But then Absalom said, "Call in Hushai the Arkite—let's hear what he has to say."

17.6   So Hushai came and Absalom put it to him, "This is what Ahithophel advised. Should we do it? What do you say?"

17.7-10   Hushai said, "The counsel that Ahithophel has given in this instance is not good. You know your father and his men, brave and bitterly angry—like a bear robbed of her cubs. And your father is an experienced fighter; you can be sure he won't be caught napping at a time like this. Even while we're talking, he's probably holed up in some cave or other. If he jumps your men from ambush, word will soon get back, 'A slaughter of Absalom's army!' Even if your men are valiant with hearts of lions, they'll fall apart at such news, for everyone in

---

[a] 1,2 Or *Let me*   [b] 9 Or *When some of the men fall at the first attack*

NEW INTERNATIONAL VERSION

Israel knows that your father is a fighter and that those with him are brave.

[11] "So I advise you: Let all Israel, from Dan to Beersheba—as numerous as the sand on the seashore—be gathered to you, with you yourself leading them into battle. [12] Then we will attack him wherever he may be found, and we will fall on him as dew settles on the ground. Neither he nor any of his men will be left alive. [13] If he withdraws into a city, then all Israel will bring ropes to that city, and we will drag it down to the valley until not even a piece of it can be found."

[14] Absalom and all the men of Israel said, "The advice of Hushai the Arkite is better than that of Ahithophel." For the LORD had determined to frustrate the good advice of Ahithophel in order to bring disaster on Absalom.

[15] Hushai told Zadok and Abiathar, the priests, "Ahithophel has advised Absalom and the elders of Israel to do such and such, but I have advised them to do so and so. [16] Now send a message immediately and tell David, 'Do not spend the night at the fords in the desert; cross over without fail, or the king and all the people with him will be swallowed up.' "

[17] Jonathan and Ahimaaz were staying at En Rogel. A servant girl was to go and inform them, and they were to go and tell King David, for they could not risk being seen entering the city. [18] But a young man saw them and told Absalom. So the two of them left quickly and went to the house of a man in Bahurim. He had a well in his courtyard, and they climbed down into it. [19] His wife took a covering and spread it out over the opening of the well and scattered grain over it. No one knew anything about it.

[20] When Absalom's men came to the woman at the house, they asked, "Where are Ahimaaz and Jonathan?"

The woman answered them, "They crossed over the brook." [a] The men searched but found no one, so they returned to Jerusalem.

[21] After the men had gone, the two climbed out of the well and went to inform King David. They said to him, "Set out and cross the river at once; Ahithophel has advised such and such against you." [22] So David and all the people with him set out and crossed the Jordan. By daybreak, no one was left who had not crossed the Jordan.

[23] When Ahithophel saw that his advice had not been followed, he saddled his donkey and set out for his house in his hometown. He put his house in order and then hanged himself. So he died and was buried in his father's tomb.

[24] David went to Mahanaim, and Absalom

---

^a 20 Or *"They passed by the sheep pen toward the water."*

THE MESSAGE

Israel knows the kind of fighting stuff your father's made of, and also the men with him.

[17.11-13] "Here's what I'd advise: Muster the whole country, from Dan to Beersheba, an army like the sand of the sea, and you personally lead them. We'll smoke him out wherever he is, fall on him like dew falls on the earth, and, believe me, there won't be a single survivor. If he hides out in a city, then the whole army will bring ropes to that city and pull it down and into a gully—not so much as a pebble left of it!"

[17.14] Absalom and all his company agreed that the counsel of Hushai the Arkite was better than the counsel of Ahithophel. (GOD had determined to discredit the counsel of Ahithophel so as to bring ruin on Absalom.)

[17.15-16] Then Hushai told the priests Zadok and Abiathar, "Ahithophel advised Absalom and the elders of Israel thus and thus, and I advised them thus and thus. Now send this message as quickly as possible to David: 'Don't spend the night on this side of the river; cross immediately or the king and everyone with him will be swallowed up alive.' "

[17.17-20] Jonathan and Ahimaaz were waiting around at En Rogel. A servant girl would come and give them messages and then they would go and tell King David, for it wasn't safe to be seen coming into the city. But a soldier spotted them and told Absalom, so the two of them got out of there fast and went to a man's house in Bahurim. He had a well in his yard and they climbed into it. The wife took a rug and covered the well, then spread grain on it so no one would notice anything out of the ordinary. Shortly, Absalom's servants came to the woman's house and asked her, "Have you seen Ahimaaz and Jonathan?"

The woman said, "They were headed toward the river."

They looked but didn't find them, and then went back to Jerusalem.

[17.21] When the coast was clear, Ahimaaz and Jonathan climbed out of the well and went on to make their report to King David, "Get up and cross the river quickly; Ahithophel has given counsel against you!"

[17.22] David and his whole army were soon up and moving and crossed the Jordan. As morning broke there was not a single person who had not made it across the Jordan.

[17.23] When Ahithophel realized that his counsel was not followed, he saddled his donkey and left for his hometown. After making out his will and putting his house in order, he hanged himself and died. He was buried in the family tomb.

[17.24-26] About the time David arrived at Mahanaim,

NEW INTERNATIONAL VERSION

crossed the Jordan with all the men of Israel. [25]Absalom had appointed Amasa over the army in place of Joab. Amasa was the son of a man named Jether,[a] an Israelite[b] who had married Abigail,[c] the daughter of Nahash and sister of Zeruiah the mother of Joab. [26]The Israelites and Absalom camped in the land of Gilead.

[27]When David came to Mahanaim, Shobi son of Nahash from Rabbah of the Ammonites, and Makir son of Ammiel from Lo Debar, and Barzillai the Gileadite from Rogelim [28]brought bedding and bowls and articles of pottery. They also brought wheat and barley, flour and roasted grain, beans and lentils,[d] [29]honey and curds, sheep, and cheese from cows' milk for David and his people to eat. For they said, "The people have become hungry and tired and thirsty in the desert."

ABSALOM'S DEATH

18 David mustered the men who were with him and appointed over them commanders of thousands and commanders of hundreds. [2]David sent the troops out—a third under the command of Joab, a third under Joab's brother Abishai son of Zeruiah, and a third under Ittai the Gittite. The king told the troops, "I myself will surely march out with you."

[3]But the men said, "You must not go out; if we are forced to flee, they won't care about us. Even if half of us die, they won't care; but you are worth ten thousand of us.[e] It would be better now for you to give us support from the city."

[4]The king answered, "I will do whatever seems best to you."

So the king stood beside the gate while all the men marched out in units of hundreds and of thousands. [5]The king commanded Joab, Abishai and Ittai, "Be gentle with the young man Absalom for my sake." And all the troops heard the king giving orders concerning Absalom to each of the commanders.

[6]The army marched into the field to fight Israel, and the battle took place in the forest of Ephraim. [7]There the army of Israel was defeated by David's men, and the casualties that day were great—twenty thousand men. [8]The battle spread out over the whole countryside, and the forest claimed more lives that day than the sword.

[9]Now Absalom happened to meet David's men.

---

[a] 25 Hebrew *Ithra*, a variant of *Jether*   [b] 25 Hebrew *and some Septuagint manuscripts; other Septuagint manuscripts* (see also 1 Chron. 2:17) *Ishmaelite* or *Jezreelite*   [c] 25 Hebrew *Abigal*, a variant of *Abigail*   [d] 28 Most Septuagint manuscripts and Syriac; Hebrew *lentils, and roasted grain*   [e] 3 Two Hebrew manuscripts, some Septuagint manuscripts and Vulgate; most Hebrew manuscripts *care; for now there are ten thousand like us*

THE MESSAGE

Absalom crossed the Jordan, and the whole army of Israel with him. Absalom had made Amasa head of the army, replacing Joab. (Amasa was the son of a man named Ithra, an Ishmaelite who had married Abigail, daughter of Nahash and sister of Zeruiah, the mother of Joab.) Israel and Absalom set camp in Gilead.

17:27-29 When David arrived at Mahanaim, Shobi son of Nahash from Ammonite Rabbah, and Makir son of Ammiel from Lo Debar, and Barzillai the Gileadite from Rogelim brought beds and blankets, bowls and jugs filled with wheat, barley, flour, roasted grain, beans and lentils, honey, and curds and cheese from the flocks and herds. They presented all this to David and his army to eat, "because," they said, "the army must be starved and exhausted and thirsty out in this wilderness."

18:1-2 **18** David organized his forces. He appointed captains of thousands and captains of hundreds. Then David deployed his troops, a third under Joab, a third under Abishai son of Zeruiah, Joab's brother, and a third under Ittai the Gittite.

The king then announced, "I'm marching with you."

18:3 They said, "No, you mustn't march with us. If we're forced to retreat, the enemy won't give it a second thought. And if half of us die, they won't do so either. But you are worth ten thousand of us. It will be better for us if you stay in the city and help from there."

18:4 "If you say so," said the king. "I'll do what you think is best." And so he stood beside the city gate as the whole army marched out by hundreds and by thousands.

18:5 Then the king ordered Joab and Abishai and Ittai, "Deal gently for my sake with the young man Absalom." The whole army heard what the king commanded the three captains regarding Absalom.

18:6-8 The army took the field to meet Israel. It turned out that the battle was joined in the Forest of Ephraim. The army of Israel was beaten badly there that day by David's men, a terrific slaughter—twenty thousand men! There was fighting helter-skelter all over the place—the forest claimed more lives that day than the sword!

18:9-10 Absalom ran into David's men, but was out

NEW INTERNATIONAL VERSION

He was riding his mule, and as the mule went under the thick branches of a large oak, Absalom's head got caught in the tree. He was left hanging in midair, while the mule he was riding kept on going."

¹⁰When one of the men saw this, he told Joab, "I just saw Absalom hanging in an oak tree."

¹¹Joab said to the man who had told him this, "What! You saw him? Why didn't you strike him to the ground right there? Then I would have had to give you ten shekels^a of silver and a warrior's belt."

¹²But the man replied, "Even if a thousand shekels^b were weighed out into my hands, I would not lift my hand against the king's son. In our hearing the king commanded you and Abishai and Ittai, 'Protect the young man Absalom for my sake.'^c ¹³And if I had put my life in jeopardy^d—and nothing is hidden from the king—you would have kept your distance from me."

¹⁴Joab said, "I'm not going to wait like this for you." So he took three javelins in his hand and plunged them into Absalom's heart while Absalom was still alive in the oak tree. ¹⁵And ten of Joab's armor-bearers surrounded Absalom, struck him and killed him.

¹⁶Then Joab sounded the trumpet, and the troops stopped pursuing Israel, for Joab halted them. ¹⁷They took Absalom, threw him into a big pit in the forest and piled up a large heap of rocks over him. Meanwhile, all the Israelites fled to their homes.

¹⁸During his lifetime Absalom had taken a pillar and erected it in the King's Valley as a monument to himself, for he thought, "I have no son to carry on the memory of my name." He named the pillar after himself, and it is called Absalom's Monument to this day.

DAVID MOURNS

¹⁹Now Ahimaaz son of Zadok said, "Let me run and take the news to the king that the LORD has delivered him from the hand of his enemies."

²⁰"You are not the one to take the news today," Joab told him. "You may take the news another time, but you must not do so today, because the king's son is dead."

²¹Then Joab said to a Cushite, "Go, tell the king what you have seen." The Cushite bowed down before Joab and ran off.

²²Ahimaaz son of Zadok again said to Joab,

---

a 11 That is, about 4 ounces (about 115 grams)
b 12 That is, about 25 pounds (about 11 kilograms)
c 12 A few Hebrew manuscripts, Septuagint, Vulgate and Syriac; most Hebrew manuscripts may be translated *Absalom, whoever you may be.* d 13 Or *Otherwise, if I had acted treacherously toward him*

THE MESSAGE

in front of them riding his mule, when the mule ran under the branches of a huge oak tree. Absalom's head was caught in the oak and he was left dangling between heaven and earth, the mule running right out from under him. A solitary soldier saw him and reported it to Joab, "I just saw Absalom hanging from an oak tree!"

18.11 Joab said to the man who told him, "If you saw him, why didn't you kill him then and there? I'd have rewarded you with ten pieces of silver and a fancy belt."

18.12-13 The man told Joab, "Even if I'd had a chance at a thousand pieces of silver, I wouldn't have laid a hand on the king's son. We all heard the king command you and Abishai and Ittai, 'For my sake, protect the young man Absalom.' Why, I'd be risking my life, for nothing is hidden from the king. And you would have just stood there!"

18.14-15 Joab said, "I can't waste my time with you." He then grabbed three knives and stabbed Absalom in the heart while he was still alive in the tree; by then Absalom was surrounded by ten of Joab's armor bearers; they hacked away at him and killed him.

18.16-17 Joab then blew the ram's horn trumpet, calling off the army in its pursuit of Israel. They took Absalom, dumped him into a huge pit in the forest, and piled an immense mound of rocks over him.

Meanwhile the whole army of Israel was in flight, each man making his own way home.

18.18 While alive, Absalom had erected for himself a pillar in the Valley of the King, "because," he said, "I have no son to carry on my name." He inscribed the pillar with his own name. To this day it is called "The Absalom Memorial."

18.19-20 Ahimaaz, Zadok's son, said, "Let me run to the king and bring him the good news that GOD has delivered him from his enemies." But Joab said, "You're not the one to deliver the good news today; some other day, maybe, but it's not 'good news' today." (This was because the king's son was dead.)

18.21 Then Joab ordered a Cushite, "You go. Tell the king what you've seen."

"Yes sir," said the Cushite, and ran off.

18.22 Ahimaaz son of Zadok kept at it, begging

NEW INTERNATIONAL VERSION

"Come what may, please let me run behind the Cushite."

But Joab replied, "My son, why do you want to go? You don't have any news that will bring you a reward."

²³He said, "Come what may, I want to run."

So Joab said, "Run!" Then Ahimaaz ran by way of the plain*ᵃ* and outran the Cushite.

²⁴While David was sitting between the inner and outer gates, the watchman went up to the roof of the gateway by the wall. As he looked out, he saw a man running alone. ²⁵The watchman called out to the king and reported it.

The king said, "If he is alone, he must have good news." And the man came closer and closer.

²⁶Then the watchman saw another man running, and he called down to the gatekeeper, "Look, another man running alone!"

The king said, "He must be bringing good news, too."

²⁷The watchman said, "It seems to me that the first one runs like Ahimaaz son of Zadok."

"He's a good man," the king said. "He comes with good news."

²⁸Then Ahimaaz called out to the king, "All is well!" He bowed down before the king with his face to the ground and said, "Praise be to the LORD your God! He has delivered up the men who lifted their hands against my lord the king."

²⁹The king asked, "Is the young man Absalom safe?"

Ahimaaz answered, "I saw great confusion just as Joab was about to send the king's servant and me, your servant, but I don't know what it was."

³⁰The king said, "Stand aside and wait here." So he stepped aside and stood there.

³¹Then the Cushite arrived and said, "My lord the king, hear the good news! The LORD has delivered you today from all who rose up against you."

³²The king asked the Cushite, "Is the young man Absalom safe?"

The Cushite replied, "May the enemies of my lord the king and all who rise up to harm you be like that young man."

³³The king was shaken. He went up to the room over the gateway and wept. As he went, he said: "O my son Absalom! My son, my son Absalom! If only I had died instead of you—O Absalom, my son, my son!"

THE MESSAGE

Joab, "What does it matter? Let me run too, following the Cushite."

Joab said, "Why all this 'Run, run'? You'll get no thanks for it, I can tell you."

18.23 "I don't care; let me run."

"Okay," said Joab, "run." So Ahimaaz ran, taking the lower valley road, and passed the Cushite.

18.24-25 David was sitting between the two gates. The sentry had gone up to the top of the gate on the wall and looked around. He saw a solitary runner. The sentry called down and told the king. The king said, "If he's alone, it must be good news!"

18.25-26 As the runner came closer, the sentry saw another runner and called down to the gate, "Another runner all by himself."

And the king said, "This also must be good news."

18.27 Then the sentry said, "I can see the first man now; he runs like Ahimaaz son of Zadok."

"He's a good man," said the king. "He's bringing good news for sure."

18.28 Then Ahimaaz called out and said to the king, "Peace!" Then he bowed deeply before the king, his face to the ground. "Blessed be your GOD; he has handed over the men who rebelled against my master the king."

18.29 The king asked, "But is the young man Absalom all right?"

Ahimaaz said, "I saw a huge ruckus just as Joab was sending me off, but I don't know what it was about."

18.30 The king said, "Step aside and stand over there." So he stepped aside.

18.31 Then the Cushite arrived and said, "Good news, my master and king! GOD has given victory today over all those who rebelled against you!"

18.32 "But," said the king, "is the young man Absalom all right?"

And the Cushite replied, "Would that all of the enemies of my master the king and all who maliciously rose against you end up like that young man."

18.33 The king was stunned. Heartbroken, he went up to the room over the gate and wept. As he wept he cried out,

O my son Absalom, my dear, dear son
    Absalom!
Why not me rather than you, my death and
    not yours,
O Absalom, my dear, dear son!

NEW INTERNATIONAL VERSION

19 Joab was told, "The king is weeping and mourning for Absalom." ²And for the whole army the victory that day was turned into mourning, because on that day the troops heard it said, "The king is grieving for his son." ³The men stole into the city that day as men steal in who are ashamed when they flee from battle. ⁴The king covered his face and cried aloud, "O my son Absalom! O Absalom, my son, my son!"

⁵Then Joab went into the house to the king and said, "Today you have humiliated all your men, who have just saved your life and the lives of your sons and daughters and the lives of your wives and concubines. ⁶You love those who hate you and hate those who love you. You have made it clear today that the commanders and their men mean nothing to you. I see that you would be pleased if Absalom were alive today and all of us were dead. ⁷Now go out and encourage your men. I swear by the LORD that if you don't go out, not a man will be left with you by nightfall. This will be worse for you than all the calamities that have come upon you from your youth till now."

⁸So the king got up and took his seat in the gateway. When the men were told, "The king is sitting in the gateway," they all came before him.

DAVID RETURNS TO JERUSALEM

Meanwhile, the Israelites had fled to their homes. ⁹Throughout the tribes of Israel, the people were all arguing with each other, saying, "The king delivered us from the hand of our enemies; he is the one who rescued us from the hand of the Philistines. But now he has fled the country because of Absalom; ¹⁰and Absalom, whom we anointed to rule over us, has died in battle. So why do you say nothing about bringing the king back?"

¹¹King David sent this message to Zadok and Abiathar, the priests: "Ask the elders of Judah, 'Why should you be the last to bring the king back to his palace, since what is being said throughout Israel has reached the king at his quarters? ¹²You are my brothers, my own flesh and blood. So why should you be the last to bring back the king?' ¹³And say to Amasa, 'Are you not my own flesh and blood? May God deal with me, be it ever so severely, if from now on you are not the commander of my army in place of Joab.' "

¹⁴He won over the hearts of all the men of Judah as though they were one man. They sent word to the king, "Return, you and all your men." ¹⁵Then the king returned and went as far as the Jordan.

THE MESSAGE

DAVID'S GRIEF FOR ABSALOM

19.1-4 **19** Joab was told that David was weeping and lamenting over Absalom. The day's victory turned into a day of mourning as word passed through the army, "David is grieving over his son." The army straggled back to the city that day demoralized, dragging their tails. And the king held his face in his hands and lamented loudly,

O my son Absalom,
Absalom my dear, dear son!

19.5-7 But in private Joab rebuked the king: "Now you've done it—knocked the wind out of your loyal servants who have just saved your life, to say nothing of the lives of your sons and daughters, wives and concubines. What is this—loving those who hate you and hating those who love you? Your actions give a clear message: officers and soldiers mean nothing to you. You know that if Absalom were alive right now, we'd all be dead—would that make you happy? Get hold of yourself; get out there and put some heart into your servants! I swear to GOD that if you don't go to them they'll desert; not a soldier will be left here by nightfall. And that will be the worst thing that has happened yet."

19.8 So the king came out and took his place at the city gate. Soon everyone knew: "Oh, look! The king has come out to receive us." And his whole army came and presented itself to the king. But the Israelites had fled the field of battle and gone home.

19.9-10 Meanwhile, the whole populace was now complaining to its leaders, "Wasn't it the king who saved us time and again from our enemies, and rescued us from the Philistines? And now he has had to flee the country on account of Absalom. And now this Absalom whom we made king is dead in battle. So what are you waiting for? Why don't you bring the king back?"

19.11-13 When David heard what was being said, he sent word to Zadok and Abiathar, the priests, "Ask the elders of Judah, 'Why are you so laggard in bringing the king back home? You're my brothers! You're my own flesh and blood! So why are you the last ones to bring the king back home?' And tell Amasa, 'You, too, are my flesh and blood. As God is my witness, I'm making you the permanent commander of the army in place of Joab.' "

19.14 He captured the hearts of everyone in Judah. They were unanimous in sending for the king: "Come back, you and all your servants."

19.15-18 So the king returned. He arrived at the Jor-

NEW INTERNATIONAL VERSION

Now the men of Judah had come to Gilgal to go out and meet the king and bring him across the Jordan. ¹⁶Shimei son of Gera, the Benjamite from Bahurim, hurried down with the men of Judah to meet King David. ¹⁷With him were a thousand Benjamites, along with Ziba, the steward of Saul's household, and his fifteen sons and twenty servants. They rushed to the Jordan, where the king was. ¹⁸They crossed at the ford to take the king's household over and to do whatever he wished.

When Shimei son of Gera crossed the Jordan, he fell prostrate before the king ¹⁹and said to him, "May my lord not hold me guilty. Do not remember how your servant did wrong on the day my lord the king left Jerusalem. May the king put it out of his mind. ²⁰For I your servant know that I have sinned, but today I have come here as the first of the whole house of Joseph to come down and meet my lord the king."

²¹Then Abishai son of Zeruiah said, "Shouldn't Shimei be put to death for this? He cursed the LORD's anointed."

²²David replied, "What do you and I have in common, you sons of Zeruiah? This day you have become my adversaries! Should anyone be put to death in Israel today? Do I not know that today I am king over Israel?" ²³So the king said to Shimei, "You shall not die." And the king promised him on oath.

²⁴Mephibosheth, Saul's grandson, also went down to meet the king. He had not taken care of his feet or trimmed his mustache or washed his clothes from the day the king left until the day he returned safely. ²⁵When he came from Jerusalem to meet the king, the king asked him, "Why didn't you go with me, Mephibosheth?"

²⁶He said, "My lord the king, since I your servant am lame, I said, 'I will have my donkey saddled and will ride on it, so I can go with the king.' But Ziba my servant betrayed me. ²⁷And he has slandered your servant to my lord the king. My lord the king is like an angel of God; so do whatever pleases you. ²⁸All my grandfather's descendants deserved nothing but death from my lord the king, but you gave your servant a place among those who eat at your table. So what right do I have to make any more appeals to the king?"

²⁹The king said to him, "Why say more? I order you and Ziba to divide the fields."

³⁰Mephibosheth said to the king, "Let him take everything, now that my lord the king has arrived home safely."

³¹Barzillai the Gileadite also came down from Rogelim to cross the Jordan with the king and to send him on his way from there. ³²Now Barzillai

THE MESSAGE

dan just as Judah reached Gilgal on their way to welcome the king and escort him across the Jordan. Even Shimei son of Gera, the Benjaminite from Bahurim, hurried down to join the men of Judah so he could welcome the king, a thousand Benjaminites with him. And Ziba, Saul's steward, with his fifteen sons and twenty servants, waded across the Jordan to meet the king and brought his entourage across, doing whatever they could to make the king comfortable.

19.18-20 Shimei son of Gera bowed deeply in homage to the king as soon as he was across the Jordan and said, "Don't think badly of me, my master! Overlook my irresponsible outburst on the day my master the king left Jerusalem—don't hold it against me! I know I sinned, but look at me now—the first of all the tribe of Joseph to come down and welcome back my master the king!"

19.21 Abishai son of Zeruiah interrupted, "Enough of this! Shouldn't we kill him outright? Why, he cursed GOD's anointed!"

19.22 But David said, "What is it with you sons of Zeruiah? Why do you insist on being so contentious? Nobody is going to be killed today. I am again king over Israel!"

19.23 Then the king turned to Shimei, "You're not going to die." And the king gave him his word.

19.24-25 Next Mephibosheth grandson of Saul arrived from Jerusalem to welcome the king. He hadn't combed his hair or trimmed his beard or washed his clothes from the day the king left until the day he returned safe and sound. The king said, "And why didn't you come with me, Mephibosheth?"

19.26-28 "My master the king," he said, "my servant betrayed me. I told him to saddle my donkey so I could ride it and go with the king, for, as you know, I am lame. And then he lied to you about me. But my master the king has been like one of God's angels: he knew what was right and did it. Wasn't everyone in my father's house doomed? But you took me in and gave me a place at your table. What more could I ever expect or ask?"

19.29 "That's enough," said the king. "Say no more. Here's my decision: You and Ziba divide the property between you."

19.30 Mephibosheth said, "Oh, let him have it all! All I care about is that my master the king is home safe and sound!"

19.31-32 Barzillai the Gileadite had come down from Rogelim. He crossed the Jordan with the king to give him a good send-off. Barzillai was a very

NEW INTERNATIONAL VERSION

was a very old man, eighty years of age. He had provided for the king during his stay in Mahanaim, for he was a very wealthy man. ³³The king said to Barzillai, "Cross over with me and stay with me in Jerusalem, and I will provide for you."

³⁴But Barzillai answered the king, "How many more years will I live, that I should go up to Jerusalem with the king? ³⁵I am now eighty years old. Can I tell the difference between what is good and what is not? Can your servant taste what he eats and drinks? Can I still hear the voices of men and women singers? Why should your servant be an added burden to my lord the king? ³⁶Your servant will cross over the Jordan with the king for a short distance, but why should the king reward me in this way? ³⁷Let your servant return, that I may die in my own town near the tomb of my father and mother. But here is your servant Kimham. Let him cross over with my lord the king. Do for him whatever pleases you."

³⁸The king said, "Kimham shall cross over with me, and I will do for him whatever pleases you. And anything you desire from me I will do for you."

³⁹So all the people crossed the Jordan, and then the king crossed over. The king kissed Barzillai and gave him his blessing, and Barzillai returned to his home.

⁴⁰When the king crossed over to Gilgal, Kimham crossed with him. All the troops of Judah and half the troops of Israel had taken the king over.

⁴¹Soon all the men of Israel were coming to the king and saying to him, "Why did our brothers, the men of Judah, steal the king away and bring him and his household across the Jordan, together with all his men?"

⁴²All the men of Judah answered the men of Israel, "We did this because the king is closely related to us. Why are you angry about it? Have we eaten any of the king's provisions? Have we taken anything for ourselves?"

⁴³Then the men of Israel answered the men of Judah, "We have ten shares in the king; and besides, we have a greater claim on David than you have. So why do you treat us with contempt? Were we not the first to speak of bringing back our king?"

But the men of Judah responded even more harshly than the men of Israel.

Sheba Rebels Against David

20 Now a troublemaker named Sheba son of Bicri, a Benjamite, happened to be there. He sounded the trumpet and shouted,

THE MESSAGE

old man—eighty years old! He had supplied the king's needs all the while he was in Mahanaim since he was very wealthy.

^{19.33} "Join me in Jerusalem," the king said to Barzillai. "Let me take care of you."

^{19.34-37} But Barzillai declined the offer, "How long do you think I'd live if I went with the king to Jerusalem? I'm eighty years old and not much good anymore to anyone. Can't taste food; can't hear music. So why add to the burdens of my master the king? I'll just go a little way across the Jordan with the king. But why would the king need to make a great thing of that? Let me go back and die in my hometown and be buried with my father and mother. But my servant Kimham here; let him go with you in my place. But treat him well!"

^{19.38} The king said, "That's settled; Kimham goes with me. And I will treat him well! If you think of anything else, I'll do that for you, too."

^{19.39-40} The army crossed the Jordan but the king stayed. The king kissed and blessed Barzillai, who then returned home. Then the king, Kimham with him, crossed over at Gilgal.

^{19.40-41} The whole army of Judah and half the army of Israel processed with the king. The men of Israel came to the king and said, "Why have our brothers, the men of Judah, taken over as if they owned the king, escorting the king and his family and close associates across the Jordan?"

^{19.42} The men of Judah retorted, "Because the king is related to us, that's why! But why make a scene? You don't see us getting treated special because of it, do you?"

^{19.43} The men of Israel shot back, "We have ten shares in the king to your one. Besides we're the firstborn—so why are we having to play second fiddle? It was our idea to bring him back."

But the men of Judah took a harder line than the men of Israel.

^{20.1} **20** Just then a good-for-nothing named Sheba son of Bicri the Benjaminite blew a blast on the ram's horn trumpet, calling out,

NEW INTERNATIONAL VERSION

"We have no share in David,
no part in Jesse's son!
Every man to his tent, O Israel!"

²So all the men of Israel deserted David to follow Sheba son of Bicri. But the men of Judah stayed by their king all the way from the Jordan to Jerusalem.

³When David returned to his palace in Jerusalem, he took the ten concubines he had left to take care of the palace and put them in a house under guard. He provided for them, but did not lie with them. They were kept in confinement till the day of their death, living as widows.

⁴Then the king said to Amasa, "Summon the men of Judah to come to me within three days, and be here yourself." ⁵But when Amasa went to summon Judah, he took longer than the time the king had set for him.

⁶David said to Abishai, "Now Sheba son of Bicri will do us more harm than Absalom did. Take your master's men and pursue him, or he will find fortified cities and escape from us." ⁷So Joab's men and the Kerethites and Pelethites and all the mighty warriors went out under the command of Abishai. They marched out from Jerusalem to pursue Sheba son of Bicri.

⁸While they were at the great rock in Gibeon, Amasa came to meet them. Joab was wearing his military tunic, and strapped over it at his waist was a belt with a dagger in its sheath. As he stepped forward, it dropped out of its sheath.

⁹Joab said to Amasa, "How are you, my brother?" Then Joab took Amasa by the beard with his right hand to kiss him. ¹⁰Amasa was not on his guard against the dagger in Joab's hand, and Joab plunged it into his belly, and his intestines spilled out on the ground. Without being stabbed again, Amasa died. Then Joab and his brother Abishai pursued Sheba son of Bicri.

¹¹One of Joab's men stood beside Amasa and said, "Whoever favors Joab, and whoever is for David, let him follow Joab!" ¹²Amasa lay wallowing in his blood in the middle of the road, and the man saw that all the troops came to a halt there. When he realized that everyone who came up to Amasa stopped, he dragged him from the road into a field and threw a garment over him. ¹³After Amasa had been removed from the road, all the men went on with Joab to pursue Sheba son of Bicri.

¹⁴Sheba passed through all the tribes of Israel to Abel Beth Maacah ᵃ and through the entire region of the Berites, who gathered together and followed him. ¹⁵All the troops with Joab came and besieged Sheba in Abel Beth Maacah. They

THE MESSAGE

We've got nothing to do with David,
there's no future for us with the son of Jesse!
Let's get out of here, Israel—head for your tents!

²⁰·²⁻³ So all the men of Israel deserted David and followed Sheba son of Bicri. But the men of Judah stayed committed, sticking with their king all the way from the Jordan to Jerusalem. When David arrived home in Jerusalem, the king took the ten concubines he had left to watch the palace and placed them in seclusion, under guard. He provided for their needs but didn't visit them. They were virtual prisoners until they died, widows as long as they lived.

²⁰·⁴⁻¹⁰ The king ordered Amasa, "Muster the men of Judah for me in three days; then report in." Amasa went to carry out his orders, but he was late reporting back. So David told Abishai, "Sheba son of Bicri is going to hurt us even worse than Absalom did. Take your master's servants and hunt him down before he gets holed up in some fortress city where we can't get to him." So under Abishai's command, all the best men—Joab's men and the Kerethites and Pelethites—left Jerusalem to hunt down Sheba son of Bicri. They were near the boulder at Gibeon when Amasa came their way. Joab was wearing a tunic with a sheathed sword strapped on his waist, but the sword slipped out and fell to the ground. Joab greeted Amasa, "How are you, brother?" and took Amasa's beard in his right hand as if to kiss him. Amasa didn't notice the sword in Joab's other hand. Joab stuck him in the belly and his guts spilled to the ground. A second blow wasn't needed; he was dead. Then Joab and his brother Abishai continued to chase Sheba son of Bicri.

²⁰·¹¹⁻¹⁴ One of Joab's soldiers took up his post over the body and called out, "Everyone who sides with Joab and supports David, follow Joab!" Amasa was lying in a pool of blood in the middle of the road; the man realized that the whole army was going to stop and take a look, so he pulled Amasa's corpse off the road into the field and threw a blanket over him so it wouldn't collect spectators. As soon as he'd gotten him off the road, the traffic flowed normally, following Joab in the chase after Sheba son of Bicri. Sheba passed through all the tribes of Israel as far as Abel Beth Maacah; all the Bicrites clustered and followed him into the city.

²⁰·¹⁵ Joab's army arrived and laid siege to Sheba in Abel Beth Maacah. They built a siege-ramp up

---

ᵃ 14 Or *Abel, even Beth Maacah*; also in verse 15

NEW INTERNATIONAL VERSION

built a siege ramp up to the city, and it stood against the outer fortifications. While they were battering the wall to bring it down, ¹⁶a wise woman called from the city, "Listen! Listen! Tell Joab to come here so I can speak to him." ¹⁷He went toward her, and she asked, "Are you Joab?"

"I am," he answered.

She said, "Listen to what your servant has to say."

"I'm listening," he said.

¹⁸She continued, "Long ago they used to say, 'Get your answer at Abel,' and that settled it. ¹⁹We are the peaceful and faithful in Israel. You are trying to destroy a city that is a mother in Israel. Why do you want to swallow up the LORD's inheritance?"

²⁰"Far be it from me!" Joab replied, "Far be it from me to swallow up or destroy! ²¹That is not the case. A man named Sheba son of Bicri, from the hill country of Ephraim, has lifted up his hand against the king, against David. Hand over this one man, and I'll withdraw from the city."

The woman said to Joab, "His head will be thrown to you from the wall."

²²Then the woman went to all the people with her wise advice, and they cut off the head of Sheba son of Bicri and threw it to Joab. So he sounded the trumpet, and his men dispersed from the city, each returning to his home. And Joab went back to the king in Jerusalem.

²³Joab was over Israel's entire army; Benaiah son of Jehoiada was over the Kerethites and Pelethites; ²⁴Adoniram^a was in charge of forced labor; Jehoshaphat son of Ahilud was recorder; ²⁵Sheva was secretary; Zadok and Abiathar were priests; ²⁶and Ira the Jairite was David's priest.

THE GIBEONITES AVENGED

21 During the reign of David, there was a famine for three successive years; so David sought the face of the LORD. The LORD said, "It is on account of Saul and his blood-stained house; it is because he put the Gibeonites to death."

²The king summoned the Gibeonites and spoke to them. (Now the Gibeonites were not a part of Israel but were survivors of the Amorites; the Israelites had sworn to ⌊spare⌋ them, but Saul in his zeal for Israel and Judah had tried to annihilate them.) ³David asked the Gibeonites, "What shall I do for you? How shall I make amends so that you will bless the LORD's inheritance?"

^a 24 Some Septuagint manuscripts (see also 1 Kings 4:6 and 5:14); Hebrew *Adoram*

THE MESSAGE

against the city's fortification. The plan was to knock down the wall.

^{20.16-17} But a shrewd woman called out from the city, "Listen, everybody! Please tell Joab to come close so I can talk to him." When he had come, the woman said, "Are you Joab?"

He said, "I am."

"Then," she said, "listen to what I have to say."

He said, "I'm listening."

^{20.18-19} "There's an old saying in these parts: 'If it's answers you want, come to Abel and get it straight.' We're a peaceful people here, and reliable. And here you are, trying to tear down one of Israel's mother cities. Why would you want to mess with GOD's legacy like that?"

^{20.20-21} Joab protested, "Believe me, you've got me all wrong. I'm not here to hurt anyone or destroy anything—not on your life! But a man from the hill country of Ephraim, Sheba son of Bicri by name, revolted against King David; hand him over, him only, and we'll get out of here."

^{20.22} The woman told Joab, "Sounds good. His head will be tossed to you from the wall."

The woman presented her strategy to the whole city and they did it: They cut off the head of Sheba son of Bicri and tossed it down to Joab. He then blew a blast on the ram's horn trumpet and the soldiers all went home. Joab returned to the king in Jerusalem.

^{20.23-26} Joab was again commander of the whole army of Israel. Benaiah son of Jehoiada was over the Kerethites and Pelethites; Adoniram over the work crews; Jehoshaphat son of Ahilud was clerk; Sheva was historian; Zadok and Abiathar were priests; Ira the Jairite was David's chaplain.

FAMINE AND WAR

^{21.1} **21** There was a famine in David's time. It went on year after year after year—three years. David went to GOD seeking the reason.

GOD said, "This is because there is blood on Saul and his house, from the time he massacred the Gibeonites."

^{21.2} So the king called the Gibeonites together for consultation. (The Gibeonites were not part of Israel; they were what was left of the Amorites, and protected by a treaty with Israel. But Saul, a fanatic for the honor of Israel and Judah, tried to kill them off.)

^{21.3} David addressed the Gibeonites: "What can I do for you? How can I compensate you so that you will bless GOD's legacy of land and people?"

NEW INTERNATIONAL VERSION

⁴The Gibeonites answered him, "We have no right to demand silver or gold from Saul or his family, nor do we have the right to put anyone in Israel to death."

"What do you want me to do for you?" David asked.

⁵They answered the king, "As for the man who destroyed us and plotted against us so that we have been decimated and have no place anywhere in Israel, ⁶let seven of his male descendants be given to us to be killed and exposed before the LORD at Gibeah of Saul—the LORD's chosen one."

So the king said, "I will give them to you."

⁷The king spared Mephibosheth son of Jonathan, the son of Saul, because of the oath before the LORD between David and Jonathan son of Saul. ⁸But the king took Armoni and Mephibosheth, the two sons of Aiah's daughter Rizpah, whom she had borne to Saul, together with the five sons of Saul's daughter Merab,ᵃ whom she had borne to Adriel son of Barzillai the Meholathite. ⁹He handed them over to the Gibeonites, who killed and exposed them on a hill before the LORD. All seven of them fell together; they were put to death during the first days of the harvest, just as the barley harvest was beginning.

¹⁰Rizpah daughter of Aiah took sackcloth and spread it out for herself on a rock. From the beginning of the harvest till the rain poured down from the heavens on the bodies, she did not let the birds of the air touch them by day or the wild animals by night. ¹¹When David was told what Aiah's daughter Rizpah, Saul's concubine, had done, ¹²he went and took the bones of Saul and his son Jonathan from the citizens of Jabesh Gilead. (They had taken them secretly from the public square at Beth Shan, where the Philistines had hung them after they struck Saul down on Gilboa.) ¹³David brought the bones of Saul and his son Jonathan from there, and the bones of those who had been killed and exposed were gathered up.

¹⁴They buried the bones of Saul and his son Jonathan in the tomb of Saul's father Kish, at Zela in Benjamin, and did everything the king commanded. After that, God answered prayer in behalf of the land.

WARS AGAINST THE PHILISTINES

¹⁵Once again there was a battle between the Philistines and Israel. David went down with his men to fight against the Philistines, and he became exhausted. ¹⁶And Ishbi-Benob, one of the

---

ᵃ 8 Two Hebrew manuscripts, some Septuagint manuscripts and Syriac (see also 1 Samuel 18:19); most Hebrew and Septuagint manuscripts *Michal*

THE MESSAGE

²¹.⁴ The Gibeonites replied, "We don't want any money from Saul and his family. And it's not up to us to put anyone in Israel to death."

But David persisted: "What are you saying I should do for you?"

²¹.⁵⁻⁶ Then they told the king, "The man who tried to get rid of us, who schemed to wipe us off the map of Israel—well, let seven of his sons be handed over to us to be executed—hanged before GOD at Gibeah of Saul, the holy mountain."

And David agreed, "I'll hand them over to you."

²¹.⁷⁻⁹ The king spared Mephibosheth son of Jonathan, the son of Saul, because of the promise David and Jonathan had spoken before GOD. But the king selected Armoni and Mephibosheth, the two sons that Rizpah daughter of Aiah had borne to Saul, plus the five sons that Saul's daughter Merab had borne to Adriel son of Barzillai the Meholathite. He turned them over to the Gibeonites who hanged them on the mountain before GOD—all seven died together. Harvest was just getting underway, the beginning of the barley harvest, when they were executed.

²¹.¹⁰ Rizpah daughter of Aiah took rough burlap and spread it out for herself on a rock from the beginning of the harvest until the heavy rains started. She kept the birds away from the bodies by day and the wild animals by night.

²¹.¹¹⁻¹⁴ David was told what she had done, this Rizpah daughter of Aiah and concubine of Saul. He then went and got the remains of Saul and Jonathan his son from the leaders at Jabesh Gilead (who had rescued them from the town square at Beth Shan where the Philistines had hung them after striking them down at Gilboa). He gathered up their remains and brought them together with the dead bodies of the seven who had just been hanged. The bodies were taken back to the land of Benjamin and given a decent burial in the tomb of Kish, Saul's father.

They did everything the king ordered to be done. That cleared things up: from then on God responded to Israel's prayers for the land.

²¹.¹⁵⁻¹⁷ War broke out again between the Philistines and Israel. David and his men went down to fight. David became exhausted. Ishbi-Benob, a

NEW INTERNATIONAL VERSION

descendants of Rapha, whose bronze spearhead weighed three hundred shekels[a] and who was armed with a new ⌊sword⌋, said he would kill David. [17]But Abishai son of Zeruiah came to David's rescue; he struck the Philistine down and killed him. Then David's men swore to him, saying, "Never again will you go out with us to battle, so that the lamp of Israel will not be extinguished."

[18]In the course of time, there was another battle with the Philistines, at Gob. At that time Sibbecai the Hushathite killed Saph, one of the descendants of Rapha.

[19]In another battle with the Philistines at Gob, Elhanan son of Jaare-Oregim[b] the Bethlehemite killed Goliath[c] the Gittite, who had a spear with a shaft like a weaver's rod.

[20]In still another battle, which took place at Gath, there was a huge man with six fingers on each hand and six toes on each foot—twenty-four in all. He also was descended from Rapha. [21]When he taunted Israel, Jonathan son of Shimeah, David's brother, killed him.

[22]These four were descendants of Rapha in Gath, and they fell at the hands of David and his men.

DAVID'S SONG OF PRAISE

22 David sang to the LORD the words of this song when the LORD delivered him from the hand of all his enemies and from the hand of Saul. [2]He said:

"The LORD is my rock, my fortress and my deliverer;
[3] my God is my rock, in whom I take refuge,
my shield and the horn[d] of my salvation.
He is my stronghold, my refuge and my savior—
from violent men you save me.
[4]I call to the LORD, who is worthy of praise,
and I am saved from my enemies.

[5]"The waves of death swirled about me;
the torrents of destruction overwhelmed me.
[6]The cords of the grave[e] coiled around me;
the snares of death confronted me.
[7]In my distress I called to the LORD;
I called out to my God.
From his temple he heard my voice;
my cry came to his ears.

THE MESSAGE

warrior descended from Rapha, with a spear weighing nearly eight pounds and outfitted in brand-new armor, announced that he'd kill David. But Abishai son of Zeruiah came to the rescue, struck the Philistine, and killed him.

Then David's men swore to him, "No more fighting on the front-lines for you! Don't snuff out the lamp of Israel!"

21.18 Later there was another skirmish with the Philistines at Gob. That time Sibbecai the Hushathite killed Saph, another of the warriors descended from Rapha.

21.19 At yet another battle with the Philistines at Gob, Elhanan son of Jaar, the weaver of Bethlehem, killed Goliath the Gittite whose spear was as big as a flagpole.

21.20-21 Still another fight broke out in Gath. There was a giant there with six fingers on his hands and six toes on his feet—twenty-four fingers and toes! He was another of those descended from Rapha. He insulted Israel, and Jonathan son of Shimeah, David's brother, killed him.

21.22 These four were descended from Rapha in Gath. And they all were killed by David and his soldiers.

22.1 **22** David prayed to GOD the words of this song after GOD saved him from all his enemies and from Saul.

22.2-3 GOD is bedrock under my feet,
the castle in which I live,
my rescuing knight.
My God—the high crag
where I run for dear life,
hiding behind the boulders,
safe in the granite hideout;
My mountaintop refuge,
he saves me from ruthless men.

22.4 I sing to GOD the Praise-Lofty,
and find myself safe and saved.

22.5-6 The waves of death crashed over me,
devil waters rushed over me.
Hell's ropes cinched me tight;
death traps barred every exit.

22.7 A hostile world! I called to GOD,
to my God I cried out.
From his palace he heard me call;
my cry brought me right into his presence—
a private audience!

---

[a] 16 That is, about 7 1/2 pounds (about 3.5 kilograms)
[b] 19 Or *son of Jair the weaver*   [c] 19 Hebrew and Septuagint; 1 Chron. 20:5 *son of Jair killed Lahmi the brother of Goliath*   [d] 3 *Horn* here symbolizes strength.
[e] 6 Hebrew *Sheol*

NEW INTERNATIONAL VERSION	THE MESSAGE

NEW INTERNATIONAL VERSION

8 "The earth trembled and quaked,
  the foundations of the heavens*a* shook;
  they trembled because he was angry.
9 Smoke rose from his nostrils;
  consuming fire came from his mouth,
  burning coals blazed out of it.
10 He parted the heavens and came down;
  dark clouds were under his feet.
11 He mounted the cherubim and flew;
  he soared*b* on the wings of the wind.
12 He made darkness his canopy around him—
  the dark*c* rain clouds of the sky.
13 Out of the brightness of his presence
  bolts of lightning blazed forth.
14 The LORD thundered from heaven;
  the voice of the Most High resounded.
15 He shot arrows and scattered ⌊the enemies⌋,
  bolts of lightning and routed them.
16 The valleys of the sea were exposed
  and the foundations of the earth laid bare
at the rebuke of the LORD,
  at the blast of breath from his nostrils.

17 "He reached down from on high and took
    hold of me;
  he drew me out of deep waters.
18 He rescued me from my powerful enemy,
  from my foes, who were too strong for
    me.
19 They confronted me in the day of my
    disaster,
  but the LORD was my support.
20 He brought me out into a spacious place;
  he rescued me because he delighted in me.

21 "The LORD has dealt with me according to
    my righteousness;
  according to the cleanness of my hands he
    has rewarded me.
22 For I have kept the ways of the LORD;
  I have not done evil by turning from my
    God.
23 All his laws are before me;
  I have not turned away from his decrees.
24 I have been blameless before him
  and have kept myself from sin.
25 The LORD has rewarded me according to my
    righteousness,
  according to my cleanness*d* in his sight.

26 "To the faithful you show yourself faithful,
  to the blameless you show yourself
    blameless,

THE MESSAGE

22.8-16 Earth wobbled and lurched;
  the very heavens shook like leaves,
Quaked like aspen leaves
  because of his rage.
His nostrils flared, billowing smoke;
  his mouth spit fire.
Tongues of fire darted in and out;
  he lowered the sky.
He stepped down;
  under his feet an abyss opened up.
He rode a winged creature,
  swift on wind-wings.
He wrapped himself
  in a trenchcoat of black rain-cloud
    darkness.
But his cloud-brightness burst through,
  a grand comet of fireworks.
Then GOD thundered out of heaven;
  the High God gave a great shout.
God shot his arrows—pandemonium!
  He hurled his lightnings—a rout!
The secret sources of ocean were exposed,
  the hidden depths of earth lay uncovered
The moment GOD roared in protest,
  let loose his hurricane anger.

22.17-20 But me he caught—reached all the way
  from sky to sea; he pulled me out
Of that ocean of hate, that enemy chaos,
  the void in which I was drowning.
They hit me when I was down,
  but GOD stuck by me.
He stood me up on a wide-open field;
  I stood there saved—surprised to be
    loved!

22.21-25 GOD made my life complete
  when I placed all the pieces before him.
When I cleaned up my act,
  he gave me a fresh start.
Indeed, I've kept alert to GOD's ways;
  I haven't taken God for granted.
Every day I review the ways he works,
  I try not to miss a trick.
I feel put back together,
  and I'm watching my step.
GOD rewrote the text of my life
  when I opened the book of my heart to
    his eyes.

22.26-28 You stick by people who stick with you,
  you're straight with people who're
    straight with you,

---

a 8 Hebrew; Vulgate and Syriac (see also Psalm 18:7)
mountains *b 11* Many Hebrew manuscripts (see also
Psalm 18:10); most Hebrew manuscripts *appeared*
c 12 Septuagint and Vulgate (see also Psalm 18:11); Hebrew
massed *d 25* Hebrew; Septuagint and Vulgate (see also
Psalm 18:24) *to the cleanness of my hands*

NEW INTERNATIONAL VERSION

²⁷to the pure you show yourself pure,
  but to the crooked you show yourself
    shrewd.
²⁸You save the humble,
  but your eyes are on the haughty to bring
    them low.
²⁹You are my lamp, O LORD;
  the LORD turns my darkness into light.
³⁰With your help I can advance against a
    troop^a;
  with my God I can scale a wall.

³¹"As for God, his way is perfect;
  the word of the LORD is flawless.
He is a shield
  for all who take refuge in him.
³²For who is God besides the LORD?
  And who is the Rock except our God?
³³It is God who arms me with strength^b
  and makes my way perfect.
³⁴He makes my feet like the feet of a deer;
  he enables me to stand on the heights.
³⁵He trains my hands for battle;
  my arms can bend a bow of bronze.
³⁶You give me your shield of victory;
  you stoop down to make me great.
³⁷You broaden the path beneath me,
  so that my ankles do not turn.

³⁸"I pursued my enemies and crushed them;
  I did not turn back till they were
    destroyed.
³⁹I crushed them completely, and they could
    not rise;
  they fell beneath my feet.
⁴⁰You armed me with strength for battle;
  you made my adversaries bow at my feet.
⁴¹You made my enemies turn their backs in
    flight,
  and I destroyed my foes.
⁴²They cried for help, but there was no one to
    save them—
  to the LORD, but he did not answer.
⁴³I beat them as fine as the dust of the earth;
  I pounded and trampled them like mud in
    the streets.

⁴⁴"You have delivered me from the attacks of
    my people;
  you have preserved me as the head of
    nations.
People I did not know are subject to me,
⁴⁵ and foreigners come cringing to me;
  as soon as they hear me, they obey me.

---

^a 30 Or can run through a barricade   ^b 33 Dead Sea
Scrolls, some Septuagint manuscripts, Vulgate and Syriac
(see also Psalm 18:32); Masoretic Text who is my strong
refuge

THE MESSAGE

You're good to good people,
  you shrewdly work around the bad ones.
You take the side of the down-and-out,
  but the stuck-up you take down a peg.

22.29-31 Suddenly, GOD, your light floods my path,
  GOD drives out the darkness.
I smash the bands of marauders,
  I vault the high fences.
What a God! His road
  stretches straight and smooth.
Every GOD-direction is road-tested.
  Everyone who runs toward him
Makes it.

22.32-46 Is there any god like GOD?
  Are we not at bedrock?
Is not this the God who armed me well,
  then aimed me in the right direction?
Now I run like a deer;
  I'm king of the mountain.
He shows me how to fight;
  I can bend a bronze bow!
You protect me with salvation-armor;
  you touch me and I feel ten feet tall.
You cleared the ground under me
  so my footing was firm.
When I chased my enemies I caught them;
  I didn't let go till they were dead men.
I nailed them; they were down for good;
  then I walked all over them.
You armed me well for this fight;
  you smashed the upstarts.
You made my enemies turn tail,
  and I wiped out the haters.
They cried "uncle"
  but Uncle didn't come;
They yelled for GOD
  and got no for an answer.
I ground them to dust; they gusted in the
    wind.
  I threw them out, like garbage in the
    gutter.
You rescued me from a squabbling people;
  you made me a leader of nations.
People I'd never heard of served me;
  the moment they got wind of me they
    submitted.

NEW INTERNATIONAL VERSION

46 They all lose heart;
   they come trembling[a] from their
      strongholds.
47 "The LORD lives! Praise be to my Rock!
   Exalted be God, the Rock, my Savior!
48 He is the God who avenges me,
   who puts the nations under me,
49   who sets me free from my enemies.
   You exalted me above my foes;
      from violent men you rescued me.
50 Therefore I will praise you, O LORD, among
      the nations;
   I will sing praises to your name.
51 He gives his king great victories;
   he shows unfailing kindness to his
      anointed,
   to David and his descendants forever."

THE LAST WORDS OF DAVID

23 These are the last words of David:

   "The oracle of David son of Jesse,
      the oracle of the man exalted by the Most
         High,
   the man anointed by the God of Jacob,
      Israel's singer of songs[b]:

2 "The Spirit of the LORD spoke through me;
   his word was on my tongue.
3 The God of Israel spoke,
   the Rock of Israel said to me:
'When one rules over men in
      righteousness,
   when he rules in the fear of God,
4 he is like the light of morning at sunrise
   on a cloudless morning,
like the brightness after rain
   that brings the grass from the earth.'

5 "Is not my house right with God?
   Has he not made with me an everlasting
      covenant,
   arranged and secured in every part?
Will he not bring to fruition my salvation
   and grant me my every desire?
6 But evil men are all to be cast aside like
      thorns,
   which are not gathered with the hand.
7 Whoever touches thorns
   uses a tool of iron or the shaft of a spear;
   they are burned up where they lie."

DAVID'S MIGHTY MEN

8 These are the names of David's mighty men:

THE MESSAGE

They gave up; they came trembling from
      their hideouts.
22.47-51 Live, GOD! Blessing to my Rock,
   my towering Salvation-God!
This God set things right for me
   and shut up the people who talked back.
He rescued me from enemy anger.
   You pulled me from the grip of upstarts,
You saved me from the bullies.
   That's why I'm thanking you, GOD,
   all over the world.
That's why I'm singing songs
   that rhyme your name.
God's king takes the trophy;
   God's chosen is beloved.
I mean David and all his children—
   always.

23.1 23 These are David's last words:
   The voice of the son of Jesse,
   the voice of the man God took to the
         top,
   Whom the God of Jacob made king,
   and Israel's most popular singer!

23.2-7 GOD's Spirit spoke through me,
   his words took shape on my tongue.
The God of Israel spoke to me,
   Israel's Rock-Mountain said,
"Whoever governs fairly and well,
   who rules in the Fear-of-God,
Is like first light at daybreak
   without a cloud in the sky,
Like green grass carpeting earth,
   glistening under fresh rain."
And this is just how my regime has been,
   for God guaranteed his covenant with
         me,
Spelled it out plainly
   and kept every promised word—
My entire salvation,
   my every desire.
But the devil's henchmen are like thorns
   culled and piled as trash;
Better not try to touch them;
   keep your distance with a rake or hoe.
They'll make a glorious bonfire!

✛

23.8 This is the listing of David's top men.

NEW INTERNATIONAL VERSION

Josheb-Basshebeth,ᵃ a Tahkemonite,ᵇ was chief of the Three; he raised his spear against eight hundred men, whom he killedᶜ in one encounter.

⁹Next to him was Eleazar son of Dodai the Ahohite. As one of the three mighty men, he was with David when they taunted the Philistines gathered ⌊at Pas Dammim⌋ᵈ for battle. Then the men of Israel retreated, ¹⁰but he stood his ground and struck down the Philistines till his hand grew tired and froze to the sword. The Lord brought about a great victory that day. The troops returned to Eleazar, but only to strip the dead.

¹¹Next to him was Shammah son of Agee the Hararite. When the Philistines banded together at a place where there was a field full of lentils, Israel's troops fled from them. ¹²But Shammah took his stand in the middle of the field. He defended it and struck the Philistines down, and the Lord brought about a great victory.

¹³During harvest time, three of the thirty chief men came down to David at the cave of Adullam, while a band of Philistines was encamped in the Valley of Rephaim. ¹⁴At that time David was in the stronghold, and the Philistine garrison was at Bethlehem. ¹⁵David longed for water and said, "Oh, that someone would get me a drink of water from the well near the gate of Bethlehem!" ¹⁶So the three mighty men broke through the Philistine lines, drew water from the well near the gate of Bethlehem and carried it back to David. But he refused to drink it; instead, he poured it out before the Lord. ¹⁷"Far be it from me, O Lord, to do this!" he said. "Is it not the blood of men who went at the risk of their lives?" And David would not drink it.

Such were the exploits of the three mighty men.

¹⁸Abishai the brother of Joab son of Zeruiah was chief of the Three.ᵉ He raised his spear against three hundred men, whom he killed, and so he became as famous as the Three. ¹⁹Was he not held in greater honor than the Three? He became their commander, even though he was not included among them.

²⁰Benaiah son of Jehoiada was a valiant fighter from Kabzeel, who performed great exploits. He struck down two of Moab's best men. He also

THE MESSAGE

Josheb-Basshebeth, the Tahkemonite. He was chief of the Three. He once put his spear to work against eight hundred—killed them all in a day.

23.9-10 Eleazar son of Dodai the Ahohite was the next of the elite Three. He was with David when the Philistines poked fun at them at Pas Dammim. When the Philistines drew up for battle, Israel retreated. But Eleazar stood his ground and killed Philistines right and left until he was exhausted—but he never let go of his sword! A big win for God that day. The army then rejoined Eleazar, but all there was left to do was the clean-up.

23.11-12 Shammah son of Agee the Hararite was the third of the Three. The Philistines had mustered for battle at Lehi, where there was a field full of lentils. Israel fled before the Philistines, but Shammah took his stand at the center of the field, successfully defended it, and routed the Philistines. Another great victory for God!

23.13-17 One day during harvest, the Three parted from the Thirty and joined David at the Cave of Adullam. A squad of Philistines had set up camp in the Valley of Rephaim. While David was holed up in the Cave, the Philistines had their base camp in Bethlehem. David had a sudden craving and said, "Would I ever like a drink of water from the well at the gate of Bethlehem!" So the Three penetrated the Philistine lines, drew water from the well at the gate of Bethlehem, and brought it back to David. But David wouldn't drink it; he poured it out as an offering to God, saying, "There is no way, God, that I'll drink this! This isn't mere water, it's their life-blood—they risked their very lives to bring it!" So David refused to drink it.

This is the sort of thing that the Three did.

23.18-19 Abishai brother of Joab and son of Zeruiah was the head of the Thirty. He once got credit for killing three hundred with his spear, but he was never named in the same breath as the Three. He was the most respected of the Thirty and was their captain, but never got included among the Three.

23.20-21 Benaiah son of Jehoiada from Kabzeel was a vigorous man who accomplished a great deal. He once killed two lion cubs in Moab. Another

---

ᵃ 8 Hebrew; some Septuagint manuscripts suggest *Ish-Bosheth,* that is, *Esh-Baal* (see also 1 Chron. 11:11 *Jashobeam*).   ᵇ 8 Probably a variant of *Hacmoni* (see 1 Chron. 11:11)   ᶜ 8 Some Septuagint manuscripts (see also 1 Chron. 11:11); Hebrew and other Septuagint manuscripts *Three; it was Adino the Eznite who killed eight hundred men*   ᵈ 9 See 1 Chron. 11:13; Hebrew *gathered there.*   ᵉ 18 Most Hebrew manuscripts (see also 1 Chron. 11:20); two Hebrew manuscripts and Syriac *Thirty*

NEW INTERNATIONAL VERSION	THE MESSAGE

NEW INTERNATIONAL VERSION

went down into a pit on a snowy day and killed a lion. 21And he struck down a huge Egyptian. Although the Egyptian had a spear in his hand, Benaiah went against him with a club. He snatched the spear from the Egyptian's hand and killed him with his own spear. 22Such were the exploits of Benaiah son of Jehoiada; he too was as famous as the three mighty men. 23He was held in greater honor than any of the Thirty, but he was not included among the Three. And David put him in charge of his bodyguard.

24Among the Thirty were:
   Asahel the brother of Joab,
   Elhanan son of Dodo from Bethlehem,
25Shammah the Harodite,
   Elika the Harodite,
26Helez the Paltite,
   Ira son of Ikkesh from Tekoa,
27Abiezer from Anathoth,
   Mebunnai*a* the Hushathite,
28Zalmon the Ahohite,
   Maharai the Netophathite,
29Heled*b* son of Baanah the Netophathite,
   Ithai son of Ribai from Gibeah in Benjamin,
30Benaiah the Pirathonite,
   Hiddai*c* from the ravines of Gaash,
31Abi-Albon the Arbathite,
   Azmaveth the Barhumite,
32Eliahba the Shaalbonite,
   the sons of Jashen,
   Jonathan 33son of*d* Shammah the Hararite,
   Ahiam son of Sharar*e* the Hararite,
34Eliphelet son of Ahasbai the Maacathite,
   Eliam son of Ahithophel the Gilonite,
35Hezro the Carmelite,
   Paarai the Arbite,
36Igal son of Nathan from Zobah,
   the son of Hagri,*f*
37Zelek the Ammonite,
   Naharai the Beerothite, the armor-bearer of Joab son of Zeruiah,
38Ira the Ithrite,
   Gareb the Ithrite
39and Uriah the Hittite.
   There were thirty-seven in all.

THE MESSAGE

time, on a snowy day, he climbed down into a pit and killed a lion. Another time he killed a formidable Egyptian. The Egyptian was armed with a spear and Benaiah went against him with nothing but a walking stick; he seized the spear from his grip and killed him with his own spear.

23.22-23   These are the things that Benaiah son of Jehoiada is famous for. But neither did he ever get ranked with the Three. He was held in greatest respect among the Thirty, but he never got included with the Three. David put him in charge of his bodyguard.

THE THIRTY

23.24-39   "The Thirty" consisted of:
   Asahel brother of Joab;
   Elhanan son of Dodo of Bethlehem;
   Shammah the Harodite;
   Elika the Harodite;
   Helez the Paltite;
   Ira son of Ikkesh the Tekoite;
   Abiezer the Anathothite;
   Sibbecai the Hushathite;
   Zalmon the Ahohite;
   Maharai the Netophathite;
   Heled son of Baanah the Netophathite;
   Ithai son of Ribai from Gibeah of the Benjaminites;
   Benaiah the Pirathonite;
   Hiddai from the badlands of Gaash;
   Abi-Albon the Arbathite;
   Azmaveth the Barhumite;
   Eliahba the Shaalbonite;
   Jashen the Gizonite;
   Jonathan son of Shammah the Hararite;
   Ahiam son of Sharar the Urite;
   Eliphelet son of Ahasbai the Maacathite;
   Eliam son of Ahithophel the Gilonite;
   Hezro the Carmelite;
   Paarai the Arbite;
   Igal son of Nathan, commander of the army of Hagrites;
   Zelek the Ammonite;
   Naharai the Beerothite, weapon bearer of Joab son of Zeruiah;
   Ira the Ithrite;
   Gareb the Ithrite;
   Uriah the Hittite.
Thirty-seven, all told.

---

a 27 Hebrew; some Septuagint manuscripts (see also 1 Chron. 11:29) *Sibbecai*   *b* 29 Some Hebrew manuscripts and Vulgate (see also 1 Chron. 11:30); most Hebrew manuscripts *Heleb*   *c* 30 Hebrew; some Septuagint manuscripts (see also 1 Chron. 11:32) *Hurai*   *d* 33 Some Septuagint manuscripts (see also 1 Chron. 11:34); Hebrew does not have *son of.*   *e* 33 Hebrew; some Septuagint manuscripts (see also 1 Chron. 11:35) *Sacar*   *f* 36 Some Septuagint manuscripts (see also 1 Chron. 11:38); Hebrew *Haggadi*

NEW INTERNATIONAL VERSION

DAVID COUNTS THE FIGHTING MEN

24 Again the anger of the LORD burned against Israel, and he incited David against them, saying, "Go and take a census of Israel and Judah."

²So the king said to Joab and the army commanders*a* with him, "Go throughout the tribes of Israel from Dan to Beersheba and enroll the fighting men, so that I may know how many there are."

³But Joab replied to the king, "May the LORD your God multiply the troops a hundred times over, and may the eyes of my lord the king see it. But why does my lord the king want to do such a thing?"

⁴The king's word, however, overruled Joab and the army commanders; so they left the presence of the king to enroll the fighting men of Israel.

⁵After crossing the Jordan, they camped near Aroer, south of the town in the gorge, and then went through Gad and on to Jazer. ⁶They went to Gilead and the region of Tahtim Hodshi, and on to Dan Jaan and around toward Sidon. ⁷Then they went toward the fortress of Tyre and all the towns of the Hivites and Canaanites. Finally, they went on to Beersheba in the Negev of Judah.

⁸After they had gone through the entire land, they came back to Jerusalem at the end of nine months and twenty days.

⁹Joab reported the number of the fighting men to the king: In Israel there were eight hundred thousand able-bodied men who could handle a sword, and in Judah five hundred thousand.

¹⁰David was conscience-stricken after he had counted the fighting men, and he said to the LORD, "I have sinned greatly in what I have done. Now, O LORD, I beg you, take away the guilt of your servant. I have done a very foolish thing."

¹¹Before David got up the next morning, the word of the LORD had come to Gad the prophet, David's seer: ¹²"Go and tell David, 'This is what the LORD says: I am giving you three options. Choose one of them for me to carry out against you.' "

¹³So Gad went to David and said to him, "Shall there come upon you three*b* years of famine in your land? Or three months of fleeing from your enemies while they pursue you? Or three days of plague in your land? Now then, think it over and decide how I should answer the one who sent me."

THE MESSAGE

24 Once again GOD's anger blazed out against Israel. He tested David by telling him, "Go and take a census of Israel and Judah." So David gave orders to Joab and the army officers under him, "Canvass all the tribes of Israel, from Dan to Beersheba, and get a count of the population. I want to know the number."

But Joab resisted the king: "May your GOD multiply people by the hundreds right before the eyes of my master the king, but why on earth would you do a thing like this?"

Nevertheless, the king insisted, and so Joab and the army officers left the king to take a census of Israel. They crossed the Jordan and began with Aroer and the town in the canyon of the Gadites near Jazer, proceeded through Gilead, passed Hermon, then on to Dan, but detoured Sidon. They covered Fort Tyre and all the Hivite and Canaanite cities, and finally reached the Negev of Judah at Beersheba. They canvassed the whole country and after nine months and twenty days arrived back in Jerusalem. Joab gave the results of the census to the king: 800,000 able-bodied fighting men in Israel; in Judah 500,000.

But when it was all done, David was overwhelmed with guilt because he had counted the people, replacing trust with statistics. And David prayed to GOD, "I have sinned badly in what I have just done. But now GOD forgive my guilt—I've been really stupid."

When David got up the next morning, the word of GOD had already come to Gad the prophet, David's spiritual advisor, "Go and give David this message: 'GOD has spoken thus: There are three things I can do to you; choose one out of the three and I'll see that it's done.' "

Gad came to deliver the message: "Do you want three years of famine in the land, or three months of running from your enemies while they chase you down, or three days of an epidemic on the country? Think it over and make up your mind. What shall I tell the one who sent me?"

a 2 Septuagint (see also verse 4 and 1 Chron. 21:2); Hebrew *Joab the army commander*   *b 13* Septuagint (see also 1 Chron. 21:12); Hebrew *seven*

NEW INTERNATIONAL VERSION

¹⁴David said to Gad, "I am in deep distress. Let us fall into the hands of the LORD, for his mercy is great; but do not let me fall into the hands of men."

¹⁵So the LORD sent a plague on Israel from that morning until the end of the time designated, and seventy thousand of the people from Dan to Beersheba died. ¹⁶When the angel stretched out his hand to destroy Jerusalem, the LORD was grieved because of the calamity and said to the angel who was afflicting the people, "Enough! Withdraw your hand." The angel of the LORD was then at the threshing floor of Araunah the Jebusite.

¹⁷When David saw the angel who was striking down the people, he said to the LORD, "I am the one who has sinned and done wrong. These are but sheep. What have they done? Let your hand fall upon me and my family."

DAVID BUILDS AN ALTAR

¹⁸On that day Gad went to David and said to him, "Go up and build an altar to the LORD on the threshing floor of Araunah the Jebusite." ¹⁹So David went up, as the LORD had commanded through Gad. ²⁰When Araunah looked and saw the king and his men coming toward him, he went out and bowed down before the king with his face to the ground.

²¹Araunah said, "Why has my lord the king come to his servant?"

"To buy your threshing floor," David answered, "so I can build an altar to the LORD, that the plague on the people may be stopped."

²²Araunah said to David, "Let my lord the king take whatever pleases him and offer it up. Here are oxen for the burnt offering, and here are threshing sledges and ox yokes for the wood. ²³O king, Araunah gives all this to the king." Araunah also said to him, "May the LORD your God accept you."

²⁴But the king replied to Araunah, "No, I insist on paying you for it. I will not sacrifice to the LORD my God burnt offerings that cost me nothing."

So David bought the threshing floor and the oxen and paid fifty shekels[a] of silver for them. ²⁵David built an altar to the LORD there and sacrificed burnt offerings and fellowship offerings.[b] Then the LORD answered prayer in behalf of the land, and the plague on Israel was stopped.

THE MESSAGE

24.14 David told Gad, "They're all terrible! But I'd rather be punished by GOD, whose mercy is great, than fall into human hands."

24.15-16 So GOD let loose an epidemic from morning until suppertime. From Dan to Beersheba seventy thousand people died. But when the angel reached out over Jerusalem to destroy it, GOD felt the pain of the terror and told the angel who was spreading death among the people, "Enough's enough! Pull back!"

The angel of GOD had just reached the threshing floor of Araunah the Jebusite. David looked up and saw the angel hovering between earth and sky, sword drawn and about to strike Jerusalem. David and the elders bowed in prayer and covered themselves with rough burlap.

24.17 When David saw the angel about to destroy the people, he prayed, "Please! I'm the one who sinned; I, the shepherd, did the wrong. But these sheep, what did they do wrong? Punish me and my family, not them."

24.18-19 That same day Gad came to David and said, "Go and build an altar on the threshing floor of Araunah the Jebusite." David did what Gad told him, what GOD commanded.

24.20-21 Araunah looked up and saw David and his men coming his way; he met them, bowing deeply, honoring the king and saying, "Why has my master the king come to see me?"

"To buy your threshing floor," said David, "so I can build an altar to GOD here and put an end to this disaster."

24.22-23 "Oh," said Araunah, "let my master the king take and sacrifice whatever he wants. Look, here's an ox for the burnt offering and threshing paddles and ox-yokes for fuel—Araunah gives it all to the king! And may GOD, your God, act in your favor."

24.24-25 But the king said to Araunah, "No. I've got to buy it from you for a good price; I'm not going to offer GOD, my God, sacrifices that are no sacrifice."

So David bought the threshing floor and the ox, paying out fifty shekels of silver. He built an altar to GOD there and sacrificed burnt offerings and peace offerings. GOD was moved by the prayers and that was the end of the disaster.

ᵃ 24 That is, about 1 1/4 pounds (about 0.6 kilogram)
ᵇ 25 Traditionally *peace offerings*

1 KINGS

1 KINGS

ADONIJAH SETS HIMSELF UP AS KING

1 When King David was old and well advanced in years, he could not keep warm even when they put covers over him. ²So his servants said to him, "Let us look for a young virgin to attend the king and take care of him. She can lie beside him so that our lord the king may keep warm."

³Then they searched throughout Israel for a beautiful girl and found Abishag, a Shunammite, and brought her to the king. ⁴The girl was very beautiful; she took care of the king and waited on him, but the king had no intimate relations with her.

⁵Now Adonijah, whose mother was Haggith, put himself forward and said, "I will be king." So he got chariots and horses[a] ready, with fifty men to run ahead of him. ⁶(His father had never interfered with him by asking, "Why do you behave as you do?" He was also very handsome and was born next after Absalom.)

⁷Adonijah conferred with Joab son of Zeruiah and with Abiathar the priest, and they gave him their support. ⁸But Zadok the priest, Benaiah son of Jehoiada, Nathan the prophet, Shimei and Rei[b] and David's special guard did not join Adonijah.

⁹Adonijah then sacrificed sheep, cattle and fattened calves at the Stone of Zoheleth near En Rogel. He invited all his brothers, the king's sons, and all the men of Judah who were royal officials, ¹⁰but he did not invite Nathan the prophet or Benaiah or the special guard or his brother Solomon.

¹¹Then Nathan asked Bathsheba, Solomon's mother, "Have you not heard that Adonijah, the son of Haggith, has become king without our lord David's knowing it? ¹²Now then, let me advise you how you can save your own life and the life of your son Solomon. ¹³Go in to King David and say to him, 'My lord the king, did you not swear to me your servant: "Surely Solomon your son shall be king after me, and he will sit on my throne"? Why then has Adonijah become king?' ¹⁴While you are still there talking to the king, I will come in and confirm what you have said."

DAVID

1 1.1-4 King David grew old. The years had caught up with him. Even though they piled blankets on him, he couldn't keep warm. So his servants said to him, "We're going to get a young virgin for our master the king to be at his side and look after him; she'll get in bed with you and arouse our master the king." So they searched the country of Israel for the most ravishing girl they could find; they found Abishag the Shunammite and brought her to the king. The girl was stunningly beautiful; she stayed at his side and looked after the king, but the king did not have sex with her.

1.5-6 At this time Adonijah, whose mother was Haggith, puffed himself up saying, "I'm the next king!" He made quite a splash, with chariots and riders and fifty men to run ahead of him. His father had spoiled him rotten as a child, never once reprimanding him. Besides that, he was very good-looking and the next in line after Absalom.

1.7-8 Adonijah talked with Joab son of Zeruiah and with Abiathar the priest, and they threw their weight on his side. But neither the priest Zadok, nor Benaiah son of Jehoiada, nor Nathan the prophet, nor Shimei and Rei, nor David's personal bodyguards supported Adonijah.

1.9-10 Next Adonijah held a coronation feast, sacrificing sheep, cattle, and grain-fed heifers at the Stone of Zoheleth near the Rogel Spring. He invited all his brothers, the king's sons, and everyone in Judah who had position and influence—but he did not invite the prophet Nathan, Benaiah, the bodyguards, or his brother Solomon.

1.11-14 Nathan went to Bathsheba, Solomon's mother, "Did you know that Adonijah, Haggith's son, has taken over as king, and our master David doesn't know a thing about it? Quickly now, let me tell you how you can save both your own life and Solomon's. Go immediately to King David. Speak up: 'Didn't you, my master the king, promise me, "Your son Solomon will be king after me and sit on my throne"? So why is Adonijah now king?' While you're there talking with the king, I'll come in and corroborate your story."

---

a 5 Or charioteers *b 8 Or and his friends*

NEW INTERNATIONAL VERSION

¹⁵So Bathsheba went to see the aged king in his room, where Abishag the Shunammite was attending him. ¹⁶Bathsheba bowed low and knelt before the king.

"What is it you want?" the king asked.

¹⁷She said to him, "My lord, you yourself swore to me your servant by the LORD your God: 'Solomon your son shall be king after me, and he will sit on my throne.' ¹⁸But now Adonijah has become king, and you, my lord the king, do not know about it. ¹⁹He has sacrificed great numbers of cattle, fattened calves, and sheep, and has invited all the king's sons, Abiathar the priest and Joab the commander of the army, but he has not invited Solomon your servant. ²⁰My lord the king, the eyes of all Israel are on you, to learn from you who will sit on the throne of my lord the king after him. ²¹Otherwise, as soon as my lord the king is laid to rest with his fathers, I and my son Solomon will be treated as criminals."

²²While she was still speaking with the king, Nathan the prophet arrived. ²³And they told the king, "Nathan the prophet is here." So he went before the king and bowed with his face to the ground.

²⁴Nathan said, "Have you, my lord the king, declared that Adonijah shall be king after you, and that he will sit on your throne? ²⁵Today he has gone down and sacrificed great numbers of cattle, fattened calves, and sheep. He has invited all the king's sons, the commanders of the army and Abiathar the priest. Right now they are eating and drinking with him and saying, 'Long live King Adonijah!' ²⁶But me your servant, and Zadok the priest, and Benaiah son of Jehoiada, and your servant Solomon he did not invite. ²⁷Is this something my lord the king has done without letting his servants know who should sit on the throne of my lord the king after him?"

DAVID MAKES SOLOMON KING

²⁸Then King David said, "Call in Bathsheba." So she came into the king's presence and stood before him.

²⁹The king then took an oath: "As surely as the LORD lives, who has delivered me out of every trouble, ³⁰I will surely carry out today what I swore to you by the LORD, the God of Israel: Solomon your son shall be king after me, and he will sit on my throne in my place."

³¹Then Bathsheba bowed low with her face to the ground and, kneeling before the king, said, "May my lord King David live forever!"

³²King David said, "Call in Zadok the priest, Nathan the prophet and Benaiah son of Jehoiada." When they came before the king, ³³he said

THE MESSAGE

1.15-16 Bathsheba went at once to the king in his palace bedroom. He was so old! Abishag was at his side making him comfortable. As Bathsheba bowed low, honoring the king, he said, "What do you want?"

1.17-21 "My master," she said, "you promised me in GOD's name, 'Your son Solomon will be king after me and sit on my throne.' And now look what's happened—Adonijah has taken over as king, and my master the king doesn't even know it! He has thrown a huge coronation feast—cattle and grain-fed heifers and sheep—inviting all the king's sons, the priest Abiathar, and Joab head of the army. But your servant Solomon was *not* invited. My master the king, every eye in Israel is watching you to see what you'll do—to see who will sit on the throne of my master the king after him. If you fail to act, the moment you're buried my son Solomon and I are as good as dead."

1.22-23 Abruptly, while she was telling the king all this, Nathan the prophet came in and was announced: "Nathan the prophet is here." He came before the king, honoring him by bowing deeply, his face touching the ground.

1.24-27 "My master the king," Nathan began, "did you say, 'Adonijah shall be king after me and sit on my throne'? Because that's what's happening. He's thrown a huge coronation feast—cattle, grain-fed heifers, sheep—inviting all the king's sons, the army officers, and Abiathar the priest. They're having a grand time, eating and drinking and shouting, 'Long live King Adonijah!' But I wasn't invited, nor was the priest Zadok, nor Benaiah son of Jehoiada, nor your servant Solomon. Is this something that my master the king has done behind our backs, not telling your servants who you intended to be king after you?"

1.28 King David took action: "Get Bathsheba back in here." She entered and stood before the king.

1.29-30 The king solemnly promised, "As GOD lives, the God who delivered me from every kind of trouble, I'll do exactly what I promised in GOD's name, the God of Israel: Your son Solomon will be king after me and take my place on the throne. And I'll make sure it happens this very day."

1.31 Bathsheba bowed low, her face to the ground. Kneeling in reverence before the king she said, "Oh, may my master, King David, live forever!"

1.32 King David said, "Call Zadok the priest, Nathan the prophet, and Benaiah son of Jehoiada." They came to the king.

NEW INTERNATIONAL VERSION

to them: "Take your lord's servants with you and set Solomon my son on my own mule and take him down to Gihon. ³⁴There have Zadok the priest and Nathan the prophet anoint him king over Israel. Blow the trumpet and shout, 'Long live King Solomon!' ³⁵Then you are to go up with him, and he is to come and sit on my throne and reign in my place. I have appointed him ruler over Israel and Judah."

³⁶Benaiah son of Jehoiada answered the king, "Amen! May the LORD, the God of my lord the king, so declare it. ³⁷As the LORD was with my lord the king, so may he be with Solomon to make his throne even greater than the throne of my lord King David!"

³⁸So Zadok the priest, Nathan the prophet, Benaiah son of Jehoiada, the Kerethites and the Pelethites went down and put Solomon on King David's mule and escorted him to Gihon. ³⁹Zadok the priest took the horn of oil from the sacred tent and anointed Solomon. Then they sounded the trumpet and all the people shouted, "Long live King Solomon!" ⁴⁰And all the people went up after him, playing flutes and rejoicing greatly, so that the ground shook with the sound.

⁴¹Adonijah and all the guests who were with him heard it as they were finishing their feast. On hearing the sound of the trumpet, Joab asked, "What's the meaning of all the noise in the city?"

⁴²Even as he was speaking, Jonathan son of Abiathar the priest arrived. Adonijah said, "Come in. A worthy man like you must be bringing good news."

⁴³"Not at all!" Jonathan answered. "Our lord King David has made Solomon king. ⁴⁴The king has sent with him Zadok the priest, Nathan the prophet, Benaiah son of Jehoiada, the Kerethites and the Pelethites, and they have put him on the king's mule, ⁴⁵and Zadok the priest and Nathan the prophet have anointed him king at Gihon. From there they have gone up cheering, and the city resounds with it. That's the noise you hear. ⁴⁶Moreover, Solomon has taken his seat on the royal throne. ⁴⁷Also, the royal officials have come to congratulate our lord King David, saying, 'May your God make Solomon's name more famous than yours and his throne greater than yours!' And the king bowed in worship on his bed ⁴⁸and said, 'Praise be to the LORD, the God of Israel, who has allowed my eyes to see a successor on my throne today.' "

THE MESSAGE

1.33-35   Then he ordered, "Gather my servants, then mount my son Solomon on my royal mule and lead him in procession down to Gihon. When you get there, Zadok the priest and Nathan the prophet will anoint him king over Israel. Then blow the ram's horn trumpet and shout, 'Long live King Solomon!' You will then accompany him as he enters and takes his place on my throne, succeeding me as king. I have named him ruler over Israel and Judah."

1.36-37   Benaiah son of Jehoiada backed the king: "Yes! And may GOD, the God of my master the king, confirm it! Just as GOD has been with my master the king, may he also be with Solomon and make his rule even greater than that of my master King David!"

1.38-40   Then Zadok the priest, Nathan the prophet, Benaiah son of Jehoiada, and the king's personal bodyguard (the Kerethites and Pelethites) went down, mounted Solomon on King David's mule, and paraded with him to Gihon. Zadok the priest brought a flask of oil from the sanctuary and anointed Solomon. They blew the ram's horn trumpet and everyone shouted, "Long live King Solomon!" Everyone joined the fanfare, the band playing and the people singing, the very earth reverberating to the sound.

1.41   Adonijah and his retinue of guests were just finishing their "coronation" feast when they heard it. When Joab heard the blast of the ram's horn trumpet he said, "What's going on here? What's all this uproar?"

1.42   Suddenly, in the midst of the questioning, Jonathan son of Abiathar the priest, showed up. Adonijah said, "Welcome! A brave and good man like you must have good news."

1.43-48   But Jonathan answered, "Hardly! Our master King David has just made Solomon king! And the king has surrounded him with Zadok the priest, Nathan the prophet, Benaiah son of Jehoiada, with the Kerethites and Pelethites; and they've mounted Solomon on the royal mule. Zadok the priest and Nathan the prophet have anointed him king at Gihon and the parade is headed up this way singing—a great fanfare! The city is rocking! That's what you're hearing. Here's the crowning touch—Solomon is seated on the throne of the kingdom! And that's not all: The king's servants have come to give their blessing to our master King David saying, 'God make Solomon's name even more honored than yours, and make his rule greater than yours!' On his death bed the king worshiped God and prayed, 'Blessed be GOD, Israel's God, who has provided a successor to my throne, and I've lived to see it!' "

NEW INTERNATIONAL VERSION

⁴⁹At this, all Adonijah's guests rose in alarm and dispersed. ⁵⁰But Adonijah, in fear of Solomon, went and took hold of the horns of the altar. ⁵¹Then Solomon was told, "Adonijah is afraid of King Solomon and is clinging to the horns of the altar. He says, 'Let King Solomon swear to me today that he will not put his servant to death with the sword.'"

⁵²Solomon replied, "If he shows himself to be a worthy man, not a hair of his head will fall to the ground; but if evil is found in him, he will die." ⁵³Then King Solomon sent men, and they brought him down from the altar. And Adonijah came and bowed down to King Solomon, and Solomon said, "Go to your home."

DAVID'S CHARGE TO SOLOMON

2 When the time drew near for David to die, he gave a charge to Solomon his son.

²"I am about to go the way of all the earth," he said. "So be strong, show yourself a man, ³and observe what the LORD your God requires: Walk in his ways, and keep his decrees and commands, his laws and requirements, as written in the Law of Moses, so that you may prosper in all you do and wherever you go, ⁴and that the LORD may keep his promise to me: 'If your descendants watch how they live, and if they walk faithfully before me with all their heart and soul, you will never fail to have a man on the throne of Israel.'

⁵"Now you yourself know what Joab son of Zeruiah did to me—what he did to the two commanders of Israel's armies, Abner son of Ner and Amasa son of Jether. He killed them, shedding their blood in peacetime as if in battle, and with that blood stained the belt around his waist and the sandals on his feet. ⁶Deal with him according to your wisdom, but do not let his gray head go down to the grave[a] in peace.

⁷"But show kindness to the sons of Barzillai of Gilead and let them be among those who eat at your table. They stood by me when I fled from your brother Absalom.

⁸"And remember, you have with you Shimei son of Gera, the Benjamite from Bahurim, who called down bitter curses on me the day I went to Mahanaim. When he came down to meet me at the Jordan, I swore to him by the LORD: 'I will not put you to death by the sword.' ⁹But now, do not consider him innocent. You are a man of wisdom; you will know what to do to him. Bring his gray head down to the grave in blood."

¹⁰Then David rested with his fathers and was buried in the City of David. ¹¹He had reigned forty years over Israel—seven years in Hebron

THE MESSAGE

1.49-50 Panicked, Adonijah's guests got out of there, scattering every which way. But Adonijah himself, afraid for his life because of Solomon, fled to the sanctuary and grabbed the horns of the Altar.

1.51 Solomon was told, "Adonijah, fearful of King Solomon, has taken sanctuary and seized the horns of the Altar and is saying, 'I'm not leaving until King Solomon promises that he won't kill me.'"

1.52-53 Solomon then said, "If he proves to be a man of honor, not a hair of his head will be hurt; but if there is evil in him, he'll die." Solomon summoned him and they brought him from the Altar. Adonijah came and bowed down, honoring the king. Solomon dismissed him, "Go home."

2.1-4 **2** When David's time to die approached, he charged his son Solomon, saying, "I'm about to go the way of all the earth, but you—be strong; show what you're made of! Do what GOD tells you. Walk in the paths he shows you: Follow the life-map absolutely, keep an eye out for the signposts, his course for life set out in the revelation to Moses; then you'll get on well in whatever you do and wherever you go. Then GOD will confirm what he promised me when he said, 'If your sons watch their step, staying true to me heart and soul, you'll always have a successor on Israel's throne.'

2.5-6 "And don't forget what Joab son of Zeruiah did to the two commanders of Israel's army, to Abner son of Ner and to Amasa son of Jether. He murdered them in cold blood, acting in peacetime as if he were at war, and has been stained with that blood ever since. Do what you think best with him, but by no means let him get off scot-free—make him pay.

2.7 "But be generous to the sons of Barzillai the Gileadite—extend every hospitality to them; that's the way they treated me when I was running for my life from Absalom your brother.

2.8-9 "You also will have to deal with Shimei son of Gera the Benjaminite from Bahurim, the one who cursed me so viciously when I was on my way to Mahanaim. Later, when he welcomed me back at the Jordan, I promised him under GOD, 'I won't put you to death.' But neither should you treat him as if nothing ever happened. You're wise, you know how to handle these things. You'll know what to do to make him pay before he dies."

⊹

2.10-12 Then David joined his ancestors. He was buried in the City of David. David ruled Israel for forty years—seven years in Hebron and an-

---

[a] 6 Hebrew *Sheol*; also in verse 9

NEW INTERNATIONAL VERSION

and thirty-three in Jerusalem. ¹²So Solomon sat on the throne of his father David, and his rule was firmly established.

SOLOMON'S THRONE ESTABLISHED

¹³Now Adonijah, the son of Haggith, went to Bathsheba, Solomon's mother. Bathsheba asked him, "Do you come peacefully?"

He answered, "Yes, peacefully." ¹⁴Then he added, "I have something to say to you."

"You may say it," she replied.

¹⁵"As you know," he said, "the kingdom was mine. All Israel looked to me as their king. But things changed, and the kingdom has gone to my brother; for it has come to him from the LORD. ¹⁶Now I have one request to make of you. Do not refuse me."

"You may make it," she said.

¹⁷So he continued, "Please ask King Solomon—he will not refuse you—to give me Abishag the Shunammite as my wife."

¹⁸"Very well," Bathsheba replied, "I will speak to the king for you."

¹⁹When Bathsheba went to King Solomon to speak to him for Adonijah, the king stood up to meet her, bowed down to her and sat down on his throne. He had a throne brought for the king's mother, and she sat down at his right hand.

²⁰"I have one small request to make of you," she said. "Do not refuse me."

The king replied, "Make it, my mother; I will not refuse you."

²¹So she said, "Let Abishag the Shunammite be given in marriage to your brother Adonijah."

²²King Solomon answered his mother, "Why do you request Abishag the Shunammite for Adonijah? You might as well request the kingdom for him—after all, he is my older brother—yes, for him and for Abiathar the priest and Joab son of Zeruiah!"

²³Then King Solomon swore by the LORD: "May God deal with me, be it ever so severely, if Adonijah does not pay with his life for this request! ²⁴And now, as surely as the LORD lives—he who has established me securely on the throne of my father David and has founded a dynasty for me as he promised—Adonijah shall be put to death today!" ²⁵So King Solomon gave orders to Benaiah son of Jehoiada, and he struck down Adonijah and he died.

²⁶To Abiathar the priest the king said, "Go back to your fields in Anathoth. You deserve to die, but I will not put you to death now, because you carried the ark of the Sovereign LORD before my father David and shared all my father's hard-

THE MESSAGE

other thirty-three in Jerusalem. Solomon took over on the throne of his father David; he had a firm grip on the kingdom.

SOLOMON

²·¹³⁻¹⁴ Adonijah son of Haggith came to Bathsheba, Solomon's mother. She said, "Do you come in peace?"

He said, "In peace." And then, "May I say something to you?"

"Go ahead," she said, "speak."

²·¹⁵⁻¹⁶ "You know that I had the kingdom right in my hands and everyone expected me to be king, and then the whole thing backfired and the kingdom landed in my brother's lap—GOD's doing. So now I have one request to ask of you; please don't refuse me."

"Go ahead, ask," she said.

²·¹⁷ "Ask King Solomon—he won't turn you down—to give me Abishag the Shunammite as my wife."

²·¹⁸ "Certainly," said Bathsheba. "I'll speak to the king for you."

²·¹⁹ Bathsheba went to King Solomon to present Adonijah's request. The king got up and welcomed her, bowing respectfully, and returned to his throne. Then he had a throne put in place for his mother, and she sat at his right hand.

²·²⁰ She said, "I have a small favor to ask of you. Don't refuse me."

The king replied, "Go ahead, Mother; of course I won't refuse you."

²·²¹ She said, "Give Abishag the Shunammite to your brother Adonijah as his wife."

²·²² King Solomon answered his mother, "What kind of favor is this, asking that Abishag the Shunammite be given to Adonijah? Why don't you just ask me to hand over the whole kingdom to him on a platter since he is my older brother and has Abiathar the priest and Joab son of Zeruiah on his side!"

²·²³⁻²⁴ Then King Solomon swore under GOD, "May God do his worst to me if Adonijah doesn't pay for this with his life! As surely as GOD lives, the God who has set me firmly on the throne of my father David and has put me in charge of the kingdom just as he promised, Adonijah will die for this—today!"

²·²⁵ King Solomon dispatched Benaiah son of Jehoiada; he struck Adonijah and he died.

²·²⁶ The king then told Abiathar the priest, "You're exiled to your place in Anathoth. You deserve death but I'm not going to kill you—for now anyway—because you were in charge of the Chest of our ruling GOD in the company of David my father, and because you shared all the hard times with my father."

NEW INTERNATIONAL VERSION

ships." ²⁷So Solomon removed Abiathar from the priesthood of the LORD, fulfilling the word the LORD had spoken at Shiloh about the house of Eli.

²⁸When the news reached Joab, who had conspired with Adonijah though not with Absalom, he fled to the tent of the LORD and took hold of the horns of the altar. ²⁹King Solomon was told that Joab had fled to the tent of the LORD and was beside the altar. Then Solomon ordered Benaiah son of Jehoiada, "Go, strike him down!"

³⁰So Benaiah entered the tent of the LORD and said to Joab, "The king says, 'Come out!' "

But he answered, "No, I will die here."

Benaiah reported to the king, "This is how Joab answered me."

³¹Then the king commanded Benaiah, "Do as he says. Strike him down and bury him, and so clear me and my father's house of the guilt of the innocent blood that Joab shed. ³²The LORD will repay him for the blood he shed, because without the knowledge of my father David he attacked two men and killed them with the sword. Both of them—Abner son of Ner, commander of Israel's army, and Amasa son of Jether, commander of Judah's army—were better men and more upright than he. ³³May the guilt of their blood rest on the head of Joab and his descendants forever. But on David and his descendants, his house and his throne, may there be the LORD's peace forever."

³⁴So Benaiah son of Jehoiada went up and struck down Joab and killed him, and he was buried on his own land^a in the desert. ³⁵The king put Benaiah son of Jehoiada over the army in Joab's position and replaced Abiathar with Zadok the priest.

³⁶Then the king sent for Shimei and said to him, "Build yourself a house in Jerusalem and live there, but do not go anywhere else. ³⁷The day you leave and cross the Kidron Valley, you can be sure you will die; your blood will be on your own head."

³⁸Shimei answered the king, "What you say is good. Your servant will do as my lord the king has said." And Shimei stayed in Jerusalem for a long time.

³⁹But three years later, two of Shimei's slaves ran off to Achish son of Maacah, king of Gath, and Shimei was told, "Your slaves are in Gath." ⁴⁰At this, he saddled his donkey and went to Achish at Gath in search of his slaves. So Shimei went away and brought the slaves back from Gath.

⁴¹When Solomon was told that Shimei had gone from Jerusalem to Gath and had returned, ⁴²the king summoned Shimei and said to him,

THE MESSAGE

2.27   Solomon stripped Abiathar of his priesthood, fulfilling GOD's word at Shiloh regarding the family of Eli.

2.28-29   When this news reached Joab, this Joab who had conspired with Adonijah (although he had remained loyal in the Absalom affair), he took refuge in the sanctuary of GOD, seizing the horns of the Altar and holding on for dear life. King Solomon was told that Joab had escaped to the sanctuary of GOD and was clinging to the Altar; he immediately sent Benaiah son of Jehoiada with orders, "Kill him."

2.30   Benaiah went to the sanctuary of GOD and said, "King's orders: Come out."

He said, "No—I'll die right here."

Benaiah went back to the king and reported, "This was Joab's answer."

2.31-33   The king said, "Go ahead then, do what he says: Kill him and bury him. Absolve me and my father's family of the guilt from Joab's senseless murders. GOD is avenging those bloody murders on Joab's head. Two men he murdered, men better by far than he ever was: Behind my father's back he brutally murdered Abner son of Ner, commander of Israel's army, and Amasa son of Jether, commander of Judah's army. Responsibility for their murders is forever fixed on Joab and his descendants; but for David and his descendants, his family and kingdom, the final verdict is GOD's peace."

2.34-35   So Benaiah son of Jehoiada went back, struck Joab, and killed him. He was buried in his family plot out in the desert. The king appointed Benaiah son of Jehoiada over the army in place of Joab, and replaced Abiathar with Zadok the priest.

2.36-37   The king next called in Shimei and told him, "Build yourself a house in Jerusalem and live there, but you are not to leave the area. If you so much as cross the Brook Kidron, you're as good as dead—you will have decreed your own death sentence."

2.38   Shimei answered the king, "Oh, thank you! Your servant will do exactly as my master the king says." Shimei lived in Jerusalem a long time.

2.39-40   But it so happened that three years later, two of Shimei's slaves ran away to Achish son of Maacah, king of Gath. Shimei was told, "Your slaves are in Gath." Shimei sprang into action, saddled his donkey, and went to Achish in Gath looking for his slaves. And then he came back, bringing his slaves.

2.41   Solomon was told, "Shimei left Jerusalem for Gath, and now he's back."

2.42-43   Solomon then called for Shimei and said,

^a 34 Or buried in his tomb

NEW INTERNATIONAL VERSION

"Did I not make you swear by the LORD and warn you, 'On the day you leave to go anywhere else, you can be sure you will die'? At that time you said to me, 'What you say is good. I will obey.' 43Why then did you not keep your oath to the LORD and obey the command I gave you?"

44The king also said to Shimei, "You know in your heart all the wrong you did to my father David. Now the LORD will repay you for your wrongdoing. 45But King Solomon will be blessed, and David's throne will remain secure before the LORD forever."

46Then the king gave the order to Benaiah son of Jehoiada, and he went out and struck Shimei down and killed him.

The kingdom was now firmly established in Solomon's hands.

SOLOMON ASKS FOR WISDOM

3 Solomon made an alliance with Pharaoh king of Egypt and married his daughter. He brought her to the City of David until he finished building his palace and the temple of the LORD, and the wall around Jerusalem. 2The people, however, were still sacrificing at the high places, because a temple had not yet been built for the Name of the LORD. 3Solomon showed his love for the LORD by walking according to the statutes of his father David, except that he offered sacrifices and burned incense on the high places.

4The king went to Gibeon to offer sacrifices, for that was the most important high place, and Solomon offered a thousand burnt offerings on that altar. 5At Gibeon the LORD appeared to Solomon during the night in a dream, and God said, "Ask for whatever you want me to give you."

6Solomon answered, "You have shown great kindness to your servant, my father David, because he was faithful to you and righteous and upright in heart. You have continued this great kindness to him and have given him a son to sit on his throne this very day.

7"Now, O LORD my God, you have made your servant king in place of my father David. But I am only a little child and do not know how to carry out my duties. 8Your servant is here among the people you have chosen, a great people, too numerous to count or number. 9So give your servant a discerning heart to govern your people and to distinguish between right and wrong. For who is able to govern this great people of yours?"

THE MESSAGE

"Didn't I make you promise me under GOD, and give you a good warning besides, that you would not leave this area? That if you left you would have decreed your own death sentence? And didn't you say, 'Oh, thank you—I'll do exactly as you say'? So why didn't you keep your sacred promise and do what I ordered?"

2.44-45 Then the king told Shimei, "Deep in your heart you know all the evil that you did to my father David; GOD will now avenge that evil on you. But King Solomon will be blessed and the rule of David will be a sure thing under GOD forever."

2.46 The king then gave orders to Benaiah son of Jehoiada; he went out and struck Shimei dead.

The kingdom was now securely in Solomon's grasp.

3.1-3 **3** Solomon arranged a marriage contract with Pharaoh, king of Egypt. He married Pharaoh's daughter and brought her to the City of David until he had completed building his royal palace and GOD's Temple and the wall around Jerusalem. Meanwhile, the people were worshiping at local shrines because at that time no temple had yet been built to the Name of GOD. Solomon loved GOD and continued to live in the God-honoring ways of David his father, except that he also worshiped at the local shrines, offering sacrifices and burning incense.

3.4-5 The king went to Gibeon, the most prestigious of the local shrines, to worship. He sacrificed a thousand Whole-Burnt-Offerings on that altar. That night, there in Gibeon, GOD appeared to Solomon in a dream: God said, "What can I give you? Ask."

3.6 Solomon said, "You were extravagantly generous in love with David my father, and he lived faithfully in your presence, his relationships were just and his heart right. And you have persisted in this great and generous love by giving him—and this very day!—a son to sit on his throne.

3.7-8 "And now here I am: GOD, my God, you have made me, your servant, ruler of the kingdom in place of David my father. I'm too young for this, a mere child! I don't know the ropes, hardly know the 'ins' and 'outs' of this job. And here I am, set down in the middle of the people you've chosen, a great people—far too many to ever count.

3.9 "Here's what I want: Give me a God-listening heart so I can lead your people well, discerning the difference between good and evil. For who on their own is capable of leading your glorious people?"

NEW INTERNATIONAL VERSION

¹⁰The Lord was pleased that Solomon had asked for this. ¹¹So God said to him, "Since you have asked for this and not for long life or wealth for yourself, nor have asked for the death of your enemies but for discernment in administering justice, ¹²I will do what you have asked. I will give you a wise and discerning heart, so that there will never have been anyone like you, nor will there ever be. ¹³Moreover, I will give you what you have not asked for—both riches and honor—so that in your lifetime you will have no equal among kings. ¹⁴And if you walk in my ways and obey my statutes and commands as David your father did, I will give you a long life." ¹⁵Then Solomon awoke—and he realized it had been a dream.

He returned to Jerusalem, stood before the ark of the Lord's covenant and sacrificed burnt offerings and fellowship offerings.*a* Then he gave a feast for all his court.

A Wise Ruling

¹⁶Now two prostitutes came to the king and stood before him. ¹⁷One of them said, "My lord, this woman and I live in the same house. I had a baby while she was there with me. ¹⁸The third day after my child was born, this woman also had a baby. We were alone; there was no one in the house but the two of us.

¹⁹"During the night this woman's son died because she lay on him. ²⁰So she got up in the middle of the night and took my son from my side while I your servant was asleep. She put him by her breast and put her dead son by my breast. ²¹The next morning, I got up to nurse my son—and he was dead! But when I looked at him closely in the morning light, I saw that it wasn't the son I had borne."

²²The other woman said, "No! The living one is my son; the dead one is yours."

But the first one insisted, "No! The dead one is yours; the living one is mine." And so they argued before the king.

²³The king said, "This one says, 'My son is alive and your son is dead,' while that one says, 'No! Your son is dead and mine is alive.' "

²⁴Then the king said, "Bring me a sword." So they brought a sword for the king. ²⁵He then gave an order: "Cut the living child in two and give half to one and half to the other."

²⁶The woman whose son was alive was filled with compassion for her son and said to the king, "Please, my lord, give her the living baby! Don't kill him!"

But the other said, "Neither I nor you shall have him. Cut him in two!"

a 15 Traditionally peace offerings

THE MESSAGE

3.10-14 God, the Master, was delighted with Solomon's response. And God said to him, "Because you have asked for this and haven't grasped after a long life, or riches, or the doom of your enemies, but you have asked for the ability to lead and govern well, I'll give you what you've asked for—I'm giving you a wise and mature heart. There's never been one like you before; and there'll be no one after. As a bonus, I'm giving you both the wealth and glory you didn't ask for—there's not a king anywhere who will come up to your mark. And if you stay on course, keeping your eye on the life-map and the God-signs as your father David did, I'll also give you a long life."

3.15 Solomon woke up—what a dream! He returned to Jerusalem, took his place before the Chest of the Covenant of God, and worshiped by sacrificing Whole-Burnt-Offerings and Peace-Offerings. Then he laid out a banquet for everyone in his service.

3.16-21 The very next thing, two prostitutes showed up before the king. The one woman said, "My master, this woman and I live in the same house. While we were living together, I had a baby. Three days after I gave birth, this woman also had a baby. We were alone—there wasn't anyone else in the house except for the two of us. The infant son of this woman died one night when she rolled over on him in her sleep. She got up in the middle of the night and took my son—I was sound asleep, mind you!—and put him at her breast and put her dead son at my breast. When I got up in the morning to nurse my son, here was this dead baby! But when I looked at him in the morning light, I saw immediately that he wasn't my baby."

3.22 "Not so!" said the other woman. "The living one's mine; the dead one's yours."

The first woman countered, "No! Your son's the dead one; mine's the living one."

They went back and forth this way in front of the king.

3.23 The king said, "What are we to do? This woman says, 'The living son is mine and the dead one is yours,' and this woman says, 'No, the dead one's yours and the living one's mine.' "

3.24 After a moment the king said, "Bring me a sword." They brought the sword to the king.

3.25 Then he said, "Cut the living baby in two—give half to one and half to the other."

3.26 The real mother of the living baby was overcome with emotion for her son and said, "Oh no, master! Give her the whole baby alive; don't kill him!"

But the other one said, "If I can't have him, you can't have him—cut away!"

NEW INTERNATIONAL VERSION

²⁷Then the king gave his ruling: "Give the living baby to the first woman. Do not kill him; she is his mother."

²⁸When all Israel heard the verdict the king had given, they held the king in awe, because they saw that he had wisdom from God to administer justice.

SOLOMON'S OFFICIALS AND GOVERNORS

4 So King Solomon ruled over all Israel. ²And these were his chief officials:

Azariah son of Zadok—the priest;
³Elihoreph and Ahijah, sons of Shisha—secretaries;
Jehoshaphat son of Ahilud—recorder;
⁴Benaiah son of Jehoiada—commander in chief;
Zadok and Abiathar—priests;
⁵Azariah son of Nathan—in charge of the district officers;
Zabud son of Nathan—a priest and personal adviser to the king;
⁶Ahishar—in charge of the palace;
Adoniram son of Abda—in charge of forced labor.

⁷Solomon also had twelve district governors over all Israel, who supplied provisions for the king and the royal household. Each one had to provide supplies for one month in the year. ⁸These are their names:

Ben-Hur—in the hill country of Ephraim;
⁹Ben-Deker—in Makaz, Shaalbim, Beth Shemesh and Elon Bethhanan;
¹⁰Ben-Hesed—in Arubboth (Socoh and all the land of Hepher were his);
¹¹Ben-Abinadab—in Naphoth Dor ᵃ (he was married to Taphath daughter of Solomon);
¹²Baana son of Ahilud—in Taanach and Megiddo, and in all of Beth Shan next to Zarethan below Jezreel, from Beth Shan to Abel Meholah across to Jokmeam;
¹³Ben-Geber—in Ramoth Gilead (the settlements of Jair son of Manasseh in Gilead were his, as well as the district of Argob in Bashan and its sixty large walled cities with bronze gate bars);
¹⁴Ahinadab son of Iddo—in Mahanaim;
¹⁵Ahimaaz—in Naphtali (he had married Basemath daughter of Solomon);
¹⁶Baana son of Hushai—in Asher and in Aloth;
¹⁷Jehoshaphat son of Paruah—in Issachar;
¹⁸Shimei son of Ela—in Benjamin;

THE MESSAGE

3.27 The king gave his decision: "Give the living baby to the first woman. Nobody is going to kill this baby. She is the real mother."

3.28 The word got around—everyone in Israel heard of the king's judgment. They were all in awe of the king, realizing that it was God's wisdom that enabled him to judge truly.

4.1-2 4 King Solomon was off to a good start ruling Israel.

These were the leaders in his government:

4.2-6 Azariah son of Zadok—the priest;
Elihoreph and Ahijah, sons of Shisha—secretaries;
Jehoshaphat son of Ahilud—historian;
Benaiah son of Jehoiada—commander of the army;
Zadok and Abiathar—priests;
Azariah son of Nathan—in charge of the regional managers;
Zabud son of Nathan—priest and friend to the king;
Ahishar—manager of the palace;
Adoniram son of Abda—manager of the slave labor.

4.7-19 Solomon had twelve regional managers distributed throughout Israel. They were responsible for supplying provisions for the king and his administration. Each was in charge of bringing supplies for one month of the year. These are the names:

Ben-Hur in the Ephraim hills;
Ben-Deker in Makaz, Shaalbim, Beth Shemesh, and Elon Bethhanan;
Ben-Hesed in Arubboth—this included Socoh and all of Hepher;
Ben-Abinadab in Naphoth Dor (he was married to Solomon's daughter Taphath);
Baana son of Ahilud in Taanach and Megiddo, all of Beth Shan next to Zarethan below Jezreel, and from Beth Shan to Abel Meholah over to Jokmeam;
Ben-Geber in Ramoth Gilead—this included the villages of Jair son of Manasseh in Gilead and the region of Argob in Bashan with its sixty large walled cities with bronze-studded gates;
Ahinadab son of Iddo in Mahanaim;
Ahimaaz in Naphtali (he was married to Solomon's daughter Basemath);
Baana son of Hushai in Asher and Aloth;
Jehoshaphat son of Paruah in Issachar;
Shimei son of Ela in Benjamin;

ᵃ 11 Or in the heights of Dor

NEW INTERNATIONAL VERSION	THE MESSAGE

NEW INTERNATIONAL VERSION

¹⁹Geber son of Uri—in Gilead (the country of Sihon king of the Amorites and the country of Og king of Bashan). He was the only governor over the district.

SOLOMON'S DAILY PROVISIONS

²⁰The people of Judah and Israel were as numerous as the sand on the seashore; they ate, they drank and they were happy. ²¹And Solomon ruled over all the kingdoms from the River*a* to the land of the Philistines, as far as the border of Egypt. These countries brought tribute and were Solomon's subjects all his life.

²²Solomon's daily provisions were thirty cors*b* of fine flour and sixty cors*c* of meal, ²³ten head of stall-fed cattle, twenty of pasture-fed cattle and a hundred sheep and goats, as well as deer, gazelles, roebucks and choice fowl. ²⁴For he ruled over all the kingdoms west of the River, from Tiphsah to Gaza, and had peace on all sides. ²⁵During Solomon's lifetime Judah and Israel, from Dan to Beersheba, lived in safety, each man under his own vine and fig tree.

²⁶Solomon had four*d* thousand stalls for chariot horses, and twelve thousand horses.*e*

²⁷The district officers, each in his month, supplied provisions for King Solomon and all who came to the king's table. They saw to it that nothing was lacking. ²⁸They also brought to the proper place their quotas of barley and straw for the chariot horses and the other horses.

SOLOMON'S WISDOM

²⁹God gave Solomon wisdom and very great insight, and a breadth of understanding as measureless as the sand on the seashore. ³⁰Solomon's wisdom was greater than the wisdom of all the men of the East, and greater than all the wisdom of Egypt. ³¹He was wiser than any other man, including Ethan the Ezrahite—wiser than Heman, Calcol and Darda, the sons of Mahol. And his fame spread to all the surrounding nations. ³²He spoke three thousand proverbs and his songs numbered a thousand and five. ³³He described plant life, from the cedar of Lebanon to the hyssop that grows out of walls. He also taught about animals and birds, reptiles and fish. ³⁴Men of all nations came to listen to Solomon's wisdom, sent by all the kings of the world, who had heard of his wisdom.

THE MESSAGE

Geber son of Uri in Gilead—this was the country of Sihon king of the Amorites and also of Og king of Bashan; he managed the whole district by himself.

SOLOMON'S PROSPERITY

4.20-21 Judah and Israel were densely populated—like sand on an ocean beach! All their needs were met; they ate and drank and were happy. Solomon was sovereign over all the kingdoms from the River Euphrates in the east to the country of the Philistines in the west, all the way to the border of Egypt. They brought tribute and were vassals of Solomon all his life.

4.22-23 One day's food supply for Solomon's household was:
185 bushels of fine flour
375 bushels of meal
10 grain-fed cattle
20 range cattle
100 sheep
and miscellaneous deer, gazelles, roebucks, and choice fowl.

4.24-25 Solomon was sovereign over everything, countries and kings, west of the River Euphrates from Tiphsah to Gaza. Peace reigned everywhere. Throughout Solomon's life, everyone in Israel and Judah lived safe and sound, all of them from Dan in the north to Beersheba in the south—content with what they had.

4.26-28 Solomon had forty thousand stalls for chariot horses and twelve thousand horsemen. The district managers, each according to his assigned month, delivered food supplies for King Solomon and all who sat at the king's table; there was always plenty. They also brought to the designated place their assigned quota of barley and straw for the horses.

4.29-34 God gave Solomon wisdom—the deepest of understanding and the largest of hearts. There was nothing beyond him, nothing he couldn't handle. Solomon's wisdom outclassed the vaunted wisdom of wise men of the East, outshone the famous wisdom of Egypt. He was wiser than anyone—wiser than Ethan the Ezrahite, wiser than Heman, wiser than Calcol and Darda the sons of Mahol. He became famous among all the surrounding nations. He created three thousand proverbs; his songs added up to 1,005. He knew all about plants, from the huge cedar that grows in Lebanon to the tiny hyssop that grows in the cracks of a wall. He understood everything about animals and birds, reptiles and fish. Sent by kings from all over the earth who had heard of his reputation, people came from far and near to listen to the wisdom of Solomon.

a 21 That is, the Euphrates; also in verse 24   *b 22* That is, probably about 185 bushels (about 6.6 kiloliters)
c 22 That is, probably about 375 bushels (about 13.2 kiloliters)   *d 26* Some Septuagint manuscripts (see also 2 Chron. 9:25); Hebrew *forty*   *e 26* Or *charioteers*

NEW INTERNATIONAL VERSION

PREPARATIONS FOR BUILDING THE TEMPLE

5 When Hiram king of Tyre heard that Solomon had been anointed king to succeed his father David, he sent his envoys to Solomon, because he had always been on friendly terms with David. ²Solomon sent back this message to Hiram:

³"You know that because of the wars waged against my father David from all sides, he could not build a temple for the Name of the LORD his God until the LORD put his enemies under his feet. ⁴But now the LORD my God has given me rest on every side, and there is no adversary or disaster. ⁵I intend, therefore, to build a temple for the Name of the LORD my God, as the LORD told my father David, when he said, 'Your son whom I will put on the throne in your place will build the temple for my Name.'

⁶"So give orders that cedars of Lebanon be cut for me. My men will work with yours, and I will pay you for your men whatever wages you set. You know that we have no one so skilled in felling timber as the Sidonians."

⁷When Hiram heard Solomon's message, he was greatly pleased and said, "Praise be to the LORD today, for he has given David a wise son to rule over this great nation."

⁸So Hiram sent word to Solomon:

"I have received the message you sent me and will do all you want in providing the cedar and pine logs. ⁹My men will haul them down from Lebanon to the sea, and I will float them in rafts by sea to the place you specify. There I will separate them and you can take them away. And you are to grant my wish by providing food for my royal household."

¹⁰In this way Hiram kept Solomon supplied with all the cedar and pine logs he wanted, ¹¹and Solomon gave Hiram twenty thousand cors*ᵃ* of wheat as food for his household, in addition to twenty thousand baths*ᵇ,ᶜ* of pressed olive oil. Solomon continued to do this for Hiram year after year. ¹²The LORD gave Solomon wisdom, just as he had promised him. There were peaceful relations between Hiram and Solomon, and the two of them made a treaty.

¹³King Solomon conscripted laborers from all Israel—thirty thousand men. ¹⁴He sent them off

---

THE MESSAGE

INTERNATIONAL FAME

5 5.1-4 Hiram king of Tyre sent ambassadors to Solomon when he heard that he had been crowned king in David's place. Hiram had loved David his whole life. Solomon responded, saying, "You know that David my father was not able to build a temple in honor of GOD because of the wars he had to fight on all sides, until GOD finally put them down. But now GOD has provided peace all around—no one against us, nothing at odds with us.

5.5-6 "Now here is what I want to do: Build a temple in honor of GOD, my God, following the promise that GOD gave to David my father, namely, 'Your son whom I will provide to succeed you as king, he will build a house in my honor.' And here is how you can help: Give orders for cedars to be cut from the Lebanon forest; my loggers will work alongside yours and I'll pay your men whatever wage you set. We both know that there is no one like you Sidonians for cutting timber."

5.7 When Hiram got Solomon's message, he was delighted, exclaiming, "Blessed be GOD for giving David such a wise son to rule this flourishing people!"

5.8-9 Then he sent this message to Solomon: "I received your request for the cedars and cypresses. It's as good as done—your wish is my command. My lumberjacks will haul the timbers from the Lebanon forest to the sea, assemble them into log rafts, float them to the place you set, then have them disassembled for you to haul away. All I want from you is that you feed my crew."

5.10-12 In this way Hiram supplied all the cedar and cypress timber that Solomon wanted. In his turn, Solomon gave Hiram 125,000 bushels of wheat and 115,000 gallons of virgin olive oil. He did this every year. And GOD, for his part, gave Solomon wisdom, just as he had promised. The healthy peace between Hiram and Solomon was formalized by a treaty.

THE TEMPLE WORK BEGINS

5.13-18 King Solomon raised a workforce of 30,000 men from all over Israel. He sent them in shifts

---

ᵃ 11 That is, probably about 125,000 bushels (about 4,400 kiloliters)   ᵇ 11 Septuagint (see also 2 Chron. 2:10); Hebrew *twenty cors*   ᶜ 11 That is, about 115,000 gallons (about 440 kiloliters)

NEW INTERNATIONAL VERSION

to Lebanon in shifts of ten thousand a month, so that they spent one month in Lebanon and two months at home. Adoniram was in charge of the forced labor. ¹⁵Solomon had seventy thousand carriers and eighty thousand stonecutters in the hills, ¹⁶as well as thirty-three hundred*a* foremen who supervised the project and directed the workmen. ¹⁷At the king's command they removed from the quarry large blocks of quality stone to provide a foundation of dressed stone for the temple. ¹⁸The craftsmen of Solomon and Hiram and the men of Gebal*b* cut and prepared the timber and stone for the building of the temple.

SOLOMON BUILDS THE TEMPLE

6 In the four hundred and eightieth*c* year after the Israelites had come out of Egypt, in the fourth year of Solomon's reign over Israel, in the month of Ziv, the second month, he began to build the temple of the LORD.

²The temple that King Solomon built for the LORD was sixty cubits long, twenty wide and thirty high.*d* ³The portico at the front of the main hall of the temple extended the width of the temple, that is twenty cubits,*e* and projected ten cubits*f* from the front of the temple. ⁴He made narrow clerestory windows in the temple. ⁵Against the walls of the main hall and inner sanctuary he built a structure around the building, in which there were side rooms. ⁶The lowest floor was five cubits*g* wide, the middle floor six cubits*h* and the third floor seven.*i* He made offset ledges around the outside of the temple so that nothing would be inserted into the temple walls.

⁷In building the temple, only blocks dressed at the quarry were used, and no hammer, chisel or any other iron tool was heard at the temple site while it was being built.

⁸The entrance to the lowest*j* floor was on the south side of the temple; a stairway led up to the middle level and from there to the third. ⁹So he built the temple and completed it, roofing it with beams and cedar planks. ¹⁰And he built the side rooms all along the temple. The height of each was five cubits, and they were attached to the temple by beams of cedar.

¹¹The word of the LORD came to Solomon:

---

a 16 Hebrew; some Septuagint manuscripts (see also 2 Chron. 2:2,18) *thirty-six hundred*   *b 18* That is, Byblos   *c 1* Hebrew; Septuagint *four hundred and fortieth*   *d 2* That is, about 90 feet (about 27 meters) long and 30 feet (about 9 meters) wide and 45 feet (about 13.5 meters) high   *e 3* That is, about 30 feet (about 9 meters)   *f 3* That is, about 15 feet (about 4.5 meters)   *g 6* That is, about 7 1/2 feet (about 2.3 meters); also in verses 10 and 24   *h 6* That is, about 9 feet (about 2.7 meters)   *i 6* That is, about 10 1/2 feet (about 3.1 meters)   *j 8* Septuagint; Hebrew *middle*

THE MESSAGE

of 10,000 each month to the Lebanon forest; they would work a month in Lebanon and then be at home two months. Adoniram was in charge of the work crew. Solomon also had 70,000 unskilled workers and another 80,000 stonecutters up in the hills—plus 3,300 foremen managing the project and supervising the work crews. Following the king's orders, they quarried huge blocks of the best stone—dressed stone for the foundation of The Temple. Solomon and Hiram's construction workers, assisted by the men of Gebal, cut and prepared the timber and stone for building The Temple.

6.1-6 **6** Four hundred and eighty years after the Israelites came out of Egypt, in the fourth year of Solomon's rule over Israel, in the month of Ziv, the second month, Solomon started building The Temple of GOD. The Temple that King Solomon built to GOD was ninety feet long, thirty feet wide, and forty-five feet high. There was a porch across the thirty-foot width of The Temple that extended out fifteen feet. Within The Temple he made narrow, deep-silled windows. Against the outside walls he built a supporting structure in which there were smaller rooms: The lower floor was seven and a half feet wide, the middle floor nine feet, and the third floor ten and a half feet. He had projecting ledges built into the outside Temple walls to support the buttressing beams.

6.7 The stone blocks for the building of The Temple were all dressed at the quarry so that the building site itself was reverently quiet—no noise from hammers and chisels and other iron tools.

6.8-10 The entrance to the ground floor was at the south end of The Temple; stairs led to the second floor and then to the third. Solomon built and completed The Temple, finishing it off with roof beams and planks of cedar. The supporting structure along the outside walls was attached to The Temple with cedar beams and the rooms in it were seven and a half feet tall.

6.11-13 The word of GOD came to Solomon saying,

NEW INTERNATIONAL VERSION

¹²"As for this temple you are building, if you follow my decrees, carry out my regulations and keep all my commands and obey them, I will fulfill through you the promise I gave to David your father. ¹³And I will live among the Israelites and will not abandon my people Israel."

¹⁴So Solomon built the temple and completed it. ¹⁵He lined its interior walls with cedar boards, paneling them from the floor of the temple to the ceiling, and covered the floor of the temple with planks of pine. ¹⁶He partitioned off twenty cubits*ᵃ* at the rear of the temple with cedar boards from floor to ceiling to form within the temple an inner sanctuary, the Most Holy Place. ¹⁷The main hall in front of this room was forty cubits*ᵇ* long. ¹⁸The inside of the temple was cedar, carved with gourds and open flowers. Everything was cedar; no stone was to be seen.

¹⁹He prepared the inner sanctuary within the temple to set the ark of the covenant of the LORD there. ²⁰The inner sanctuary was twenty cubits long, twenty wide and twenty high.*ᶜ* He overlaid the inside with pure gold, and he also overlaid the altar of cedar. ²¹Solomon covered the inside of the temple with pure gold, and he extended gold chains across the front of the inner sanctuary, which was overlaid with gold. ²²So he overlaid the whole interior with gold. He also overlaid with gold the altar that belonged to the inner sanctuary.

²³In the inner sanctuary he made a pair of cherubim of olive wood, each ten cubits*ᵈ* high. ²⁴One wing of the first cherub was five cubits long, and the other wing five cubits—ten cubits from wing tip to wing tip. ²⁵The second cherub also measured ten cubits, for the two cherubim were identical in size and shape. ²⁶The height of each cherub was ten cubits. ²⁷He placed the cherubim inside the innermost room of the temple, with their wings spread out. The wing of one cherub touched one wall, while the wing of the other touched the other wall, and their wings touched each other in the middle of the room. ²⁸He overlaid the cherubim with gold.

²⁹On the walls all around the temple, in both the inner and outer rooms, he carved cherubim, palm trees and open flowers. ³⁰He also covered the floors of both the inner and outer rooms of the temple with gold.

³¹For the entrance of the inner sanctuary he made doors of olive wood with five-sided jambs. ³²And on the two olive wood doors he carved cherubim, palm trees and open flowers, and overlaid the cherubim and palm trees with beat-

THE MESSAGE

"About this Temple you are building—what's important is that you *live* the way I've set out for you and *do* what I tell you, following my instructions carefully and obediently. Then I'll complete in you the promise I made to David your father. I'll personally take up my residence among the Israelites—I won't desert my people Israel."

6.14-18 Solomon built and completed The Temple. He paneled the interior walls from floor to ceiling with cedar planks; for flooring he used cypress. The thirty feet at the rear of The Temple he made into an Inner Sanctuary, cedar planks from floor to ceiling—the Holy of Holies. The Main Sanctuary area in front was sixty feet long. The entire interior of The Temple was cedar, with carvings of fruits and flowers. All cedar—none of the stone was exposed.

6.19-22 The Inner Sanctuary within The Temple was for housing the Chest of the Covenant of God. This Inner Sanctuary was a cube, thirty feet each way, all plated with gold. The Altar of cedar was also gold-plated. Everywhere you looked there was pure gold: gold chains strung in front of the gold-plated Inner Sanctuary—gold everywhere—walls, ceiling, floor, and Altar. Dazzling!

6.23-28 Then he made two cherubim, gigantic angel-like figures, from olivewood. Each was fifteen feet tall. The outstretched wings of the cherubim (they were identical in size and shape) measured another fifteen feet. He placed the two cherubim, their wings spread, in the Inner Sanctuary. The combined wingspread stretched the width of the room, the wing of one cherub touched one wall, the wing of the other the other wall, and the wings touched in the middle. The cherubim were gold plated.

6.29-30 He then carved engravings of cherubim, palm trees, and flower blossoms on all the walls of both the Inner and the Main Sanctuary. And all the floors of both inner and outer rooms were gold plated.

6.31-32 He constructed doors of olivewood for the entrance to the Inner Sanctuary; the lintel and doorposts were five-sided. The doors were also carved with cherubim, palm trees, and flowers, and then covered with gold leaf.

ᵃ 16 That is, about 30 feet (about 9 meters)   *ᵇ 17* That is, about 60 feet (about 18 meters)   *ᶜ 20* That is, about 30 feet (about 9 meters) long, wide and high   *ᵈ 23* That is, about 15 feet (about 4.5 meters)

NEW INTERNATIONAL VERSION

en gold. [33]In the same way he made four-sided jambs of olive wood for the entrance to the main hall. [34]He also made two pine doors, each having two leaves that turned in sockets. [35]He carved cherubim, palm trees and open flowers on them and overlaid them with gold hammered evenly over the carvings.

[36]And he built the inner courtyard of three courses of dressed stone and one course of trimmed cedar beams.

[37]The foundation of the temple of the LORD was laid in the fourth year, in the month of Ziv. [38]In the eleventh year in the month of Bul, the eighth month, the temple was finished in all its details according to its specifications. He had spent seven years building it.

SOLOMON BUILDS HIS PALACE

7 It took Solomon thirteen years, however, to complete the construction of his palace. [2]He built the Palace of the Forest of Lebanon a hundred cubits long, fifty wide and thirty high,[a] with four rows of cedar columns supporting trimmed cedar beams. [3]It was roofed with cedar above the beams that rested on the columns—forty-five beams, fifteen to a row. [4]Its windows were placed high in sets of three, facing each other. [5]All the doorways had rectangular frames; they were in the front part in sets of three, facing each other.[b]

[6]He made a colonnade fifty cubits long and thirty wide.[c] In front of it was a portico, and in front of that were pillars and an overhanging roof.

[7]He built the throne hall, the Hall of Justice, where he was to judge, and he covered it with cedar from floor to ceiling.[d] [8]And the palace in which he was to live, set farther back, was similar in design. Solomon also made a palace like this hall for Pharaoh's daughter, whom he had married.

[9]All these structures, from the outside to the great courtyard and from foundation to eaves, were made of blocks of high-grade stone cut to size and trimmed with a saw on their inner and outer faces. [10]The foundations were laid with large stones of good quality, some measuring ten cubits[e] and some eight.[f] [11]Above were high-grade stones, cut to size, and cedar beams. [12]The great courtyard was surrounded by a wall of

---

[a] 2 That is, about 150 feet (about 46 meters) long, 75 feet (about 23 meters) wide and 45 feet (about 13.5 meters) high   [b] 5 The meaning of the Hebrew for this verse is uncertain.   [c] 6 That is, about 75 feet (about 23 meters) long and 45 feet (about 13.5 meters) wide   [d] 7 Vulgate and Syriac; Hebrew *floor*   [e] 10 That is, about 15 feet (about 4.5 meters)   [f] 10 That is, about 12 feet (about 3.6 meters)

THE MESSAGE

6.33-35 Similarly, he built the entrance to the Main Sanctuary using olivewood for the doorposts but these doorposts were four-sided. The doors were of cypress, split into two panels, each panel swinging separately. These also were carved with cherubim, palm trees, and flowers, and plated with finely hammered gold leaf.

6.36 He built the inner court with three courses of dressed stones topped with a course of planed cedar timbers.

6.37-38 The foundation for GOD's Temple was laid in the fourth year in the month of Ziv. It was completed in the eleventh year in the month of Bul (the eighth month) down to the last detail, just as planned. It took Solomon seven years to build it.

7.1-5 **7** It took Solomon another thirteen years to finish building his own palace complex. He built the Palace of the Forest of Lebanon a hundred and fifty feet long, seventy-five feet wide, and forty-five feet high. There were four rows of cedar columns supporting forty-five cedar beams, fifteen in each row, and then roofed with cedar. Windows in groupings of three set high in the walls on either side. All the doors were rectangular and arranged symmetrically.

7.6 He built a colonnaded courtyard seventy-five feet long and forty-five wide. It had a roofed porch at the front with ample eaves.

7.7 He built a court room, the Hall of Justice, where he would decide judicial matters, and paneled it with cedar.

7.8 He built his personal residence behind the Hall on a similar plan. Solomon also built another one just like it for Pharaoh's daughter, whom he had married.

7.9-12 No expense was spared—everything here, inside and out, from foundation to roof was constructed using high-quality stone, accurately cut and shaped and polished. The foundation stones were huge, ranging in size from twelve to fifteen feet, and of the very best quality. The finest stone was used above the foundation, shaped to size and trimmed with cedar. The courtyard was enclosed with a wall made

NEW INTERNATIONAL VERSION

three courses of dressed stone and one course of trimmed cedar beams, as was the inner courtyard of the temple of the LORD with its portico.

THE TEMPLE'S FURNISHINGS

¹³King Solomon sent to Tyre and brought Huram,*a* ¹⁴whose mother was a widow from the tribe of Naphtali and whose father was a man of Tyre and a craftsman in bronze. Huram was highly skilled and experienced in all kinds of bronze work. He came to King Solomon and did all the work assigned to him.

¹⁵He cast two bronze pillars, each eighteen cubits high and twelve cubits around,*b* by line. ¹⁶He also made two capitals of cast bronze to set on the tops of the pillars; each capital was five cubits*c* high. ¹⁷A network of interwoven chains festooned the capitals on top of the pillars, seven for each capital. ¹⁸He made pomegranates in two rows*d* encircling each network to decorate the capitals on top of the pillars.*e* He did the same for each capital. ¹⁹The capitals on top of the pillars in the portico were in the shape of lilies, four cubits*f* high. ²⁰On the capitals of both pillars, above the bowl-shaped part next to the network, were the two hundred pomegranates in rows all around. ²¹He erected the pillars at the portico of the temple. The pillar to the south he named Jakin*g* and the one to the north Boaz.*h* ²²The capitals on top were in the shape of lilies. And so the work on the pillars was completed.

²³He made the Sea of cast metal, circular in shape, measuring ten cubits*i* from rim to rim and five cubits high. It took a line of thirty cubits*j* to measure around it. ²⁴Below the rim, gourds encircled it—ten to a cubit. The gourds were cast in two rows in one piece with the Sea.

²⁵The Sea stood on twelve bulls, three facing north, three facing west, three facing south and three facing east. The Sea rested on top of them, and their hindquarters were toward the center. ²⁶It was a handbreadth*k* in thickness, and its rim was like the rim of a cup, like a lily blossom. It held two thousand baths.*l*

---

a 13 Hebrew *Hiram*, a variant of *Huram*; also in verses 40 and 45   *b* 15 That is, about 27 feet (about 8.1 meters) high and 18 feet (about 5.4 meters) around   *c* 16 That is, about 7 1/2 feet (about 2.3 meters); also in verse 23   *d* 18 Two Hebrew manuscripts and Septuagint; most Hebrew manuscripts *made the pillars, and there were two rows*   *e* 18 Many Hebrew manuscripts and Syriac; most Hebrew manuscripts *pomegranates*   *f* 19 That is, about 6 feet (about 1.8 meters); also in verse 38   *g* 21 *Jakin* probably means *he establishes*.   *h* 21 *Boaz* probably means *in him is strength*.   *i* 23 That is, about 15 feet (about 4.5 meters)   *j* 23 That is, about 45 feet (about 13.5 meters)   *k* 26 That is, about 3 inches (about 8 centimeters)   *l* 26 That is, probably about 11,500 gallons (about 44 kiloliters); the Septuagint does not have this sentence.

THE MESSAGE

of three layers of stone and topped with cedar timbers, just like the one in the porch of The Temple of GOD.

⊹

7.13-14   King Solomon sent to Tyre and asked Hiram (not the king; another Hiram) to come. Hiram's mother was a widow from the tribe of Naphtali. His father was a Tyrian and a master worker in bronze. Hiram was a real artist—he could do anything with bronze. He came to King Solomon and did all the bronze work.

7.15-22   First he cast two pillars in bronze, each twenty-seven feet tall and eighteen feet in circumference. He then cast two capitals in bronze to set on the pillars; each capital was seven and a half feet high and flared at the top in the shape of a lily. Each capital was dressed with an elaborate filigree of seven braided chains and a double row of two hundred pomegranates, setting the pillars off magnificently. He set the pillars up in the entrance porch to The Temple; the pillar to the south he named Security (Jachin) and the pillar to the north Stability (Boaz). The capitals were in the shape of lilies.

7.22-24   When the pillars were finished, Hiram's next project was to make the Sea—an immense round basin of cast metal fifteen feet in diameter, seven and a half feet tall, and forty-five feet in circumference. Just under the rim there were two bands of decorative gourds, ten gourds to each foot and a half. The gourds were cast in one piece with the Sea.

7.25-26   The Sea was set on twelve bulls, three facing north, three facing west, three facing south, and three facing east; the bulls faced outward supporting the Sea on their hindquarters. The Sea was three inches thick and flared at the rim like a cup, or like a lily. It held about 11,500 gallons.

NEW INTERNATIONAL VERSION

²⁷He also made ten movable stands of bronze; each was four cubits long, four wide and three high.ᵃ ²⁸This is how the stands were made: They had side panels attached to uprights. ²⁹On the panels between the uprights were lions, bulls and cherubim—and on the uprights as well. Above and below the lions and bulls were wreaths of hammered work. ³⁰Each stand had four bronze wheels with bronze axles, and each had a basin resting on four supports, cast with wreaths on each side. ³¹On the inside of the stand there was an opening that had a circular frame one cubitᵇ deep. This opening was round, and with its basework it measured a cubit and a half.ᶜ Around its opening there was engraving. The panels of the stands were square, not round. ³²The four wheels were under the panels, and the axles of the wheels were attached to the stand. The diameter of each wheel was a cubit and a half. ³³The wheels were made like chariot wheels; the axles, rims, spokes and hubs were all of cast metal.

³⁴Each stand had four handles, one on each corner, projecting from the stand. ³⁵At the top of the stand there was a circular band half a cubitᵈ deep. The supports and panels were attached to the top of the stand. ³⁶He engraved cherubim, lions and palm trees on the surfaces of the supports and on the panels, in every available space, with wreaths all around. ³⁷This is the way he made the ten stands. They were all cast in the same molds and were identical in size and shape.

³⁸He then made ten bronze basins, each holding forty bathsᵉ and measuring four cubits across, one basin to go on each of the ten stands. ³⁹He placed five of the stands on the south side of the temple and five on the north. He placed the Sea on the south side, at the southeast corner of the temple. ⁴⁰He also made the basins and shovels and sprinkling bowls.

So Huram finished all the work he had undertaken for King Solomon in the temple of the LORD:

⁴¹the two pillars;

the two bowl-shaped capitals on top of the pillars;

the two sets of network decorating the two bowl-shaped capitals on top of the pillars;

⁴²the four hundred pomegranates for the two sets of network (two rows of pomegran-

---

ᵃ 27 That is, about 6 feet (about 1.8 meters) long and wide and about 4 1/2 feet (about 1.3 meters) high   ᵇ 31 That is, about 1 1/2 feet (about 0.5 meter)   ᶜ 31 That is, about 2 1/4 feet (about 0.7 meter); also in verse 32   ᵈ 35 That is, about 3/4 foot (about 0.2 meter)   ᵉ 38 That is, about 230 gallons (about 880 liters)

THE MESSAGE

7.27-33   Hiram also made ten washstands of bronze. Each was six feet square and four and a half feet tall. They were made like this: Panels were fastened to the uprights. Lions, bulls, and cherubim were represented on the panels and uprights. Beveled wreath-work bordered the lions and bulls above and below. Each stand was mounted on four bronze wheels with bronze axles. The uprights were cast with decorative relief work. Each stand held a basin on a circular engraved support a foot and a half deep set on a pedestal two and a quarter feet square. The washstand itself was square. The axles were attached under the stand and the wheels fixed to them. The wheels were twenty-seven inches in diameter; they were designed like chariot wheels. Everything—axles, rims, spokes, and hubs—was of cast metal.

7.34-37   There was a handle at the four corners of each washstand, the handles cast in one piece with the stand. At the top of the washstand there was a ring about nine inches deep. The uprights and handles were cast with the stand. Everything and every available surface was engraved with cherubim, lions, and palm trees, bordered by arabesques. The washstands were identical, all cast in the same mold.

7.38-40   He also made ten bronze washbasins, each six feet in diameter with a capacity of 230 gallons, one basin for each of the ten washstands. He arranged five stands on the south side of The Temple and five on the north. The Sea was placed at the southeast corner of The Temple. Hiram then fashioned the various utensils: buckets and shovels and bowls.

7.40-45   Hiram completed all the work he set out to do for King Solomon on The Temple of GOD:

two pillars;

two capitals on top of the pillars;

two decorative filigrees for the capitals;

four hundred pomegranates for the two filigrees

NEW INTERNATIONAL VERSION

ates for each network, decorating the bowl-shaped capitals on top of the pillars);
⁴³ the ten stands with their ten basins;
⁴⁴ the Sea and the twelve bulls under it;
⁴⁵ the pots, shovels and sprinkling bowls.

All these objects that Huram made for King Solomon for the temple of the LORD were of burnished bronze. ⁴⁶ The king had them cast in clay molds in the plain of the Jordan between Succoth and Zarethan. ⁴⁷ Solomon left all these things unweighed, because there were so many; the weight of the bronze was not determined.

⁴⁸ Solomon also made all the furnishings that were in the LORD's temple:

the golden altar;
the golden table on which was the bread of the Presence;
⁴⁹ the lampstands of pure gold (five on the right and five on the left, in front of the inner sanctuary);
the gold floral work and lamps and tongs;
⁵⁰ the pure gold basins, wick trimmers, sprinkling bowls, dishes and censers;
and the gold sockets for the doors of the innermost room, the Most Holy Place, and also for the doors of the main hall of the temple.

⁵¹ When all the work King Solomon had done for the temple of the LORD was finished, he brought in the things his father David had dedicated—the silver and gold and the furnishings—and he placed them in the treasuries of the LORD's temple.

THE ARK BROUGHT TO THE TEMPLE

8 Then King Solomon summoned into his presence at Jerusalem the elders of Israel, all the heads of the tribes and the chiefs of the Israelite families, to bring up the ark of the LORD's covenant from Zion, the City of David. ²All the men of Israel came together to King Solomon at the time of the festival in the month of Ethanim, the seventh month.

³ When all the elders of Israel had arrived, the priests took up the ark, ⁴ and they brought up the ark of the LORD and the Tent of Meeting and all the sacred furnishings in it. The priests and Levites carried them up, ⁵ and King Solomon and the entire assembly of Israel that had gathered about him were before the ark, sacrificing so many sheep and cattle that they could not be recorded or counted.

⁶ The priests then brought the ark of the LORD's

THE MESSAGE

(a double row of pomegranates for each filigree);
ten washstands each with its washbasin;
one Sea;
twelve bulls under the Sea;
miscellaneous buckets, shovels, and bowls.

7.45-47 All these artifacts that Hiram made for King Solomon for The Temple of GOD were of burnished bronze. He cast them in clay in a foundry on the Jordan plain between Succoth and Zarethan. These artifacts were never weighed—there were far too many! Nobody has any idea how much bronze was used.

7.48-50 Solomon was also responsible for all the furniture and accessories in The Temple of GOD:

the gold Altar;
the gold Table that held the Bread of the Presence;
the pure gold candelabras, five to the right and five to the left in front of the Inner Sanctuary;
the gold flowers, lamps, and tongs;
the pure gold dishes, wick trimmers, sprinkling bowls, ladles, and censers;
the gold sockets for the doors of the Inner Sanctuary, the Holy of Holies, used also for the doors of the Main Sanctuary.

7.51 That completed all the work King Solomon did on The Temple of GOD. He then brought in the items consecrated by his father David, the silver and the gold and the artifacts. He placed them all in the treasury of GOD's Temple.

✝

8.1-2 **8** Bringing all this to a climax, King Solomon called in the leaders of Israel, all the heads of the tribes and the family patriarchs, to bring up the Chest of the Covenant of GOD from Zion, the City of David. And they came, all Israel before King Solomon in the month of Ethanim, the seventh month, for the great autumn festival.

8.3-5 With all Israel's leaders present, the priests took up the Chest of GOD and carried up the Chest and the Tent of Meeting and all the holy vessels that went with the Tent. King Solomon and the entire congregation of Israel were there at the Chest worshiping and sacrificing huge numbers of sheep and cattle—so many that no one could keep track.

8.6-9 Then the priests brought the Chest of the

NEW INTERNATIONAL VERSION	THE MESSAGE

covenant to its place in the inner sanctuary of the temple, the Most Holy Place, and put it beneath the wings of the cherubim. [7]The cherubim spread their wings over the place of the ark and overshadowed the ark and its carrying poles. [8]These poles were so long that their ends could be seen from the Holy Place in front of the inner sanctuary, but not from outside the Holy Place; and they are still there today. [9]There was nothing in the ark except the two stone tablets that Moses had placed in it at Horeb, where the LORD made a covenant with the Israelites after they came out of Egypt.

[10]When the priests withdrew from the Holy Place, the cloud filled the temple of the LORD. [11]And the priests could not perform their service because of the cloud, for the glory of the LORD filled his temple.

[12]Then Solomon said, "The LORD has said that he would dwell in a dark cloud; [13]I have indeed built a magnificent temple for you, a place for you to dwell forever."

[14]While the whole assembly of Israel was standing there, the king turned around and blessed them. [15]Then he said:

"Praise be to the LORD, the God of Israel, who with his own hand has fulfilled what he promised with his own mouth to my father David. For he said, [16]'Since the day I brought my people Israel out of Egypt, I have not chosen a city in any tribe of Israel to have a temple built for my Name to be there, but I have chosen David to rule my people Israel.'

[17]"My father David had it in his heart to build a temple for the Name of the LORD, the God of Israel. [18]But the LORD said to my father David, 'Because it was in your heart to build a temple for my name, you did well to have this in your heart. [19]Nevertheless, you are not the one to build the temple, but your son, who is your own flesh and blood—he is the one who will build the temple for my Name.'

[20]"The LORD has kept the promise he made: I have succeeded David my father and now I sit on the throne of Israel, just as the LORD promised, and I have built the temple for the Name of the LORD, the God of Israel. [21]I have provided a place there for the ark, in which is the covenant of the LORD that he made with our fathers when he brought them out of Egypt."

SOLOMON'S PRAYER OF DEDICATION

[22]Then Solomon stood before the altar of the LORD in front of the whole assembly of Israel, spread out his hands toward heaven [23]and said:

Covenant of GOD to its place in the Inner Sanctuary, the Holy of Holies, under the wings of the cherubim. The outspread wings of the cherubim stretched over the Chest and its poles. The poles were so long that their ends could be seen from the entrance to the Inner Sanctuary, but were not noticeable farther out. They're still there today. There was nothing in the Chest but the two stone tablets that Moses had placed in it at Horeb where GOD made a covenant with Israel after bringing them up from Egypt.

THE TEMPLE FINISHED, DEDICATED, FILLED

8.10-11 When the priests left the Holy Place, a cloud filled The Temple of GOD. The priests couldn't carry out their priestly duties because of the cloud—the glory of GOD filled The Temple of GOD!

8.12-13 Then Solomon spoke:

GOD has told us that he lives in the dark
where no one can see him;
I've built this splendid Temple, O God,
to mark your invisible presence forever.

8.14 The king then turned to face the congregation and blessed them:

8.15-16 "Blessed be GOD, the God of Israel, who spoke personally to my father David. Now he has kept the promise he made when he said, 'From the day I brought my people Israel from Egypt, I haven't set apart one city among the tribes of Israel to build a Temple to fix my Name there. But I did choose David to rule my people Israel.'

8.17-19 "My father David had it in his heart to build a Temple honoring the Name of GOD, the God of Israel. But GOD told him 'It was good that you wanted to build a Temple in my honor—most commendable! But you are not the one to do it—your son will build it to honor my Name.'

8.20-21 "GOD has done what he said he would do: I have succeeded David my father and ruled over Israel just as GOD promised; and now I've built a Temple to honor GOD, the God of Israel, and I've secured a place for the Chest that holds the covenant of GOD, the covenant that he made with our ancestors when he brought them up from the land of Egypt."

✜

8.22-25 Before the entire congregation of Israel, Solomon took a position before the Altar, spread his hands out before heaven, and prayed,

NEW INTERNATIONAL VERSION

"O LORD, God of Israel, there is no God like you in heaven above or on earth below—you who keep your covenant of love with your servants who continue wholeheartedly in your way. 24You have kept your promise to your servant David my father; with your mouth you have promised and with your hand you have fulfilled it—as it is today.

25"Now LORD, God of Israel, keep for your servant David my father the promises you made to him when you said, 'You shall never fail to have a man to sit before me on the throne of Israel, if only your sons are careful in all they do to walk before me as you have done.' 26And now, O God of Israel, let your word that you promised your servant David my father come true.

27"But will God really dwell on earth? The heavens, even the highest heaven, cannot contain you. How much less this temple I have built! 28Yet give attention to your servant's prayer and his plea for mercy, O LORD my God. Hear the cry and the prayer that your servant is praying in your presence this day. 29May your eyes be open toward this temple night and day, this place of which you said, 'My Name shall be there,' so that you will hear the prayer your servant prays toward this place. 30Hear the supplication of your servant and of your people Israel when they pray toward this place. Hear from heaven, your dwelling place, and when you hear, forgive.

31"When a man wrongs his neighbor and is required to take an oath and he comes and swears the oath before your altar in this temple, 32then hear from heaven and act. Judge between your servants, condemning the guilty and bringing down on his own head what he has done. Declare the innocent not guilty, and so establish his innocence.

33"When your people Israel have been defeated by an enemy because they have sinned against you, and when they turn back to you and confess your name, praying and making supplication to you in this temple, 34then hear from heaven and forgive the sin of your people Israel and bring them back to the land you gave to their fathers.

35"When the heavens are shut up and there is no rain because your people have sinned against you, and when they pray toward this place and confess your name and

THE MESSAGE

O GOD, God of Israel, there is no God like you in the skies above or on the earth below who unswervingly keeps covenant with his servants and relentlessly loves them as they sincerely live in obedience to your way. You kept your word to David my father, your personal word. You did exactly what you promised—every detail. The proof is before us today!

8.26 Keep it up, GOD, O God of Israel! Continue to keep the promises you made to David my father when you said, "You'll always have a descendant to represent my rule on Israel's throne, on the condition that your sons are as careful to live obediently in my presence as you have."

O God of Israel, let this all happen;
confirm and establish it!

8.27-32 Can it be that God will actually move into our neighborhood? Why, the cosmos itself isn't large enough to give you breathing room, let alone this Temple I've built. Even so, I'm bold to ask: Pay attention to these my prayers, both intercessory and personal, O GOD, my God. Listen to my prayers, energetic and devout, that I'm setting before you right now. Keep your eyes open to this Temple night and day, this place of which you said, "My Name will be honored there," and listen to the prayers that I pray at this place.

Listen from your home in heaven
and when you hear, forgive.

When someone hurts a neighbor and promises to make things right, and then comes and repeats the promise before your Altar in this Temple, listen from heaven and act accordingly: Judge your servants, making the offender pay for his offense and setting the offended free of any charges.

8.33-34 When your people Israel are beaten by an enemy because they've sinned against you, but then turn to you and acknowledge your rule in prayers desperate and devout in this Temple,

Listen from your home in heaven,
forgive the sin of your people Israel,
return them to the land you gave their
ancestors.

8.35-36 When the skies shrivel up and there is no rain because your people have sinned against you, but then they pray at this place, acknowledging your rule and quit-

turn from their sin because you have afflicted them, [36]then hear from heaven and forgive the sin of your servants, your people Israel. Teach them the right way to live, and send rain on the land you gave your people for an inheritance.

[37]"When famine or plague comes to the land, or blight or mildew, locusts or grasshoppers, or when an enemy besieges them in any of their cities, whatever disaster or disease may come, [38]and when a prayer or plea is made by any of your people Israel—each one aware of the afflictions of his own heart, and spreading out his hands toward this temple— [39]then hear from heaven, your dwelling place. Forgive and act; deal with each man according to all he does, since you know his heart (for you alone know the hearts of all men), [40]so that they will fear you all the time they live in the land you gave our fathers.

[41]"As for the foreigner who does not belong to your people Israel but has come from a distant land because of your name— [42]for men will hear of your great name and your mighty hand and your outstretched arm—when he comes and prays toward this temple, [43]then hear from heaven, your dwelling place, and do whatever the foreigner asks of you, so that all the peoples of the earth may know your name and fear you, as do your own people Israel, and may know that this house I have built bears your Name.

[44]"When your people go to war against their enemies, wherever you send them, and when they pray to the LORD toward the city you have chosen and the temple I have built for your Name, [45]then hear from heaven their prayer and their plea, and uphold their cause.

[46]"When they sin against you—for there is no one who does not sin—and you become angry with them and give them over to the enemy, who takes them captive to his own land, far away or near; [47]and if they have a change of heart in the land where they are held captive, and repent

ting their sins because you have scourged them,

> Listen from your home in heaven,
> forgive the sins of your servants, your
> people Israel.

Then start over with them: Train them to live right and well; send rain on the land you gave your people as an inheritance.

8.37-40 When disasters strike, famine or catastrophe, crop failure or disease, locust or beetle, or when an enemy attacks their defenses—calamity of any sort—any prayer that's prayed from anyone at all among your people Israel, hearts penetrated by the disaster, hands and arms thrown out to this Temple for help,

> Listen from your home in heaven.

Forgive and go to work on us. Give what each deserves, for you know each life from the inside (you're the only one with such "inside knowledge"!) so that they'll live before you in lifelong reverent and believing obedience on this land you gave our ancestors.

8.41-43 And don't forget the foreigner who is not a member of your people Israel but has come from a far country because of your reputation. People *are* going to be attracted here by your great reputation, your wonder-working power, who come to pray at this Temple.

> Listen from your home in heaven.

Honor the prayers of the foreigner so that people all over the world will know who you are and what you're like and will live in reverent obedience before you, just as your own people Israel do; so they'll know that you personally make this Temple that I've built what it is.

8.44-51 When your people go to war against their enemies at the time and place you send them and they pray to GOD toward the city you chose and this Temple I've built to honor your Name,

> Listen from heaven to what they pray
> and ask for,
> and do what's right for them.

When they sin against you—and they certainly will; there's no one without sin!—and in anger you turn them over to the enemy and they are taken captive to the enemy's land, whether far or near, but repent in the country of their captivity

NEW INTERNATIONAL VERSION

and plead with you in the land of their conquerors and say, 'We have sinned, we have done wrong, we have acted wickedly'; ⁴⁸and if they turn back to you with all their heart and soul in the land of their enemies who took them captive, and pray to you toward the land you gave their fathers, toward the city you have chosen and the temple I have built for your Name; ⁴⁹then from heaven, your dwelling place, hear their prayer and their plea, and uphold their cause. ⁵⁰And forgive your people, who have sinned against you; forgive all the offenses they have committed against you, and cause their conquerors to show them mercy; ⁵¹for they are your people and your inheritance, whom you brought out of Egypt, out of that iron-smelting furnace.

⁵²"May your eyes be open to your servant's plea and to the plea of your people Israel, and may you listen to them whenever they cry out to you. ⁵³For you singled them out from all the nations of the world to be your own inheritance, just as you declared through your servant Moses when you, O Sovereign Lord, brought our fathers out of Egypt."

⁵⁴When Solomon had finished all these prayers and supplications to the Lord, he rose from before the altar of the Lord, where he had been kneeling with his hands spread out toward heaven. ⁵⁵He stood and blessed the whole assembly of Israel in a loud voice, saying:

⁵⁶"Praise be to the Lord, who has given rest to his people Israel just as he promised. Not one word has failed of all the good promises he gave through his servant Moses. ⁵⁷May the Lord our God be with us as he was with our fathers; may he never leave us nor forsake us. ⁵⁸May he turn our hearts to him, to walk in all his ways and to keep the commands, decrees and regulations he gave our fathers. ⁵⁹And may these words of mine, which I have prayed before the Lord, be near to the Lord our God day and night, that he may uphold the cause of his servant and the cause of his people Israel according to each day's need, ⁶⁰so that all the peoples of the earth may know that the Lord is God and that there is no other. ⁶¹But your hearts must be fully

THE MESSAGE

and pray with changed hearts in their exile, "We've sinned; we've done wrong; we've been most wicked," and turn back to you heart and soul in the land of the enemy who conquered them, and pray to you toward their homeland, the land you gave their ancestors, toward the city you chose, and this Temple I have built to the honor of your Name,

> Listen from your home in heaven
> to their prayers desperate and devout
> and do what is best for them.

Forgive your people who have sinned against you; forgive their gross rebellions and move their captors to treat them with compassion. They are, after all, your people and your precious inheritance whom you rescued from the heart of that iron-smelting furnace, Egypt!

8.52-53   O be alert and attentive to the needy prayers of me, your servant, and your dear people Israel; listen every time they cry out to you! You handpicked them from all the peoples on earth to be your very own people, as you announced through your servant Moses when you, O God, in your masterful rule, delivered our ancestors from Egypt.

✝

8.54-55 Having finished praying to God—all these bold and passionate prayers—Solomon stood up before God's Altar where he had been kneeling all this time, his arms stretched upward to heaven. Standing, he blessed the whole congregation of Israel, blessing them at the top of his lungs:

8.56-58   "Blessed be God, who has given peace to his people Israel just as he said he'd do. Not one of all those good and wonderful words that he spoke through Moses has misfired. May God, our very own God, continue to be with us just as he was with our ancestors—may he never give up and walk out on us. May he keep us centered and devoted to him, following the life path he has cleared, watching the signposts, walking at the pace and rhythms he laid down for our ancestors.

8.59-61   "And let these words that I've prayed in the presence of God be always right there before him, day and night, so that he'll do what is right for me, to guarantee justice for his people Israel day after day after day. Then all the people on earth will know God is the true God; there is no other God. And you, your lives must be totally obedient to God, our personal God,

NEW INTERNATIONAL VERSION

committed to the LORD our God, to live by his decrees and obey his commands, as at this time."

THE DEDICATION OF THE TEMPLE

62Then the king and all Israel with him offered sacrifices before the LORD. 63Solomon offered a sacrifice of fellowship offerings*a* to the LORD: twenty-two thousand cattle and a hundred and twenty thousand sheep and goats. So the king and all the Israelites dedicated the temple of the LORD.

64On that same day the king consecrated the middle part of the courtyard in front of the temple of the LORD, and there he offered burnt offerings, grain offerings and the fat of the fellowship offerings, because the bronze altar before the LORD was too small to hold the burnt offerings, the grain offerings and the fat of the fellowship offerings.

65So Solomon observed the festival at that time, and all Israel with him—a vast assembly, people from Lebo*b* Hamath to the Wadi of Egypt. They celebrated it before the LORD our God for seven days and seven days more, fourteen days in all. 66On the following day he sent the people away. They blessed the king and then went home, joyful and glad in heart for all the good things the LORD had done for his servant David and his people Israel.

THE LORD APPEARS TO SOLOMON

9 When Solomon had finished building the temple of the LORD and the royal palace, and had achieved all he had desired to do, 2the LORD appeared to him a second time, as he had appeared to him at Gibeon. 3The LORD said to him:

"I have heard the prayer and plea you have made before me; I have consecrated this temple, which you have built, by putting my Name there forever. My eyes and my heart will always be there.

4"As for you, if you walk before me in integrity of heart and uprightness, as David your father did, and do all I command and observe my decrees and laws, 5I will establish your royal throne over Israel forever, as I promised David your father when I said, 'You shall never fail to have a man on the throne of Israel.'

6"But if you*c* or your sons turn away from me and do not observe the commands and decrees I have given you*c* and go off to serve other gods and worship them, 7then I will cut off Israel from the land I have given them and will reject this

THE MESSAGE

following the life path he has cleared, alert and attentive to everything he has made plain this day."

✠

8.62-63 The king and all Israel with him then worshiped, offering sacrifices to GOD. Solomon offered Peace-Offerings, sacrificing to GOD twenty-two thousand cattle, a hundred and twenty thousand sheep. This is how the king and all Israel dedicated The Temple of GOD.

8.64 That same day, the king set apart the central area of the Courtyard in front of GOD's Temple for sacred use and there sacrificed the Whole-Burnt-Offerings, Grain-Offerings, and fat from the Peace-Offerings—the bronze Altar was too small to handle all these offerings.

8.65-66 This is how Solomon kept the great autumn feast, and all Israel with him, people there all the way from the far northeast (the Entrance to Hamath) to the far southwest (the Brook of Egypt)—a huge congregation. They started out celebrating for seven days—and then did it another seven days! Two solid weeks of celebration! Then he dismissed them. They blessed the king and went home, exuberant with heartfelt gratitude for all the good GOD had done for his servant David and for his people Israel.

✠

9.1-2 **9** After Solomon had completed building The Temple of GOD and his own palace, all the projects he had set his heart on doing, GOD appeared to Solomon again, just as he had appeared to him at Gibeon.

9.3-5 And GOD said to him, "I've listened to and received all your prayers, your ever-so-passionate prayers. I've sanctified this Temple that you have built: My Name is stamped on it forever; my eyes are on it and my heart in it always. As for you, if you live in my presence as your father David lived, pure in heart and action, living the life I've set out for you, attentively obedient to my guidance and judgments, then I'll back your kingly rule over Israel, make it a sure thing on a solid foundation. The same guarantee I gave David your father I'm giving you: 'You can count on always having a descendant on Israel's throne.'

9.6-9 "But if you or your sons betray me, ignoring my guidance and judgments, taking up with alien gods by serving and worshiping them, then the guarantee is off: I'll wipe Israel right off the map and repudiate this Temple I've just

---

a 63 Traditionally *peace offerings*; also in verse 64
b 65 Or *from the entrance to*   *c* 6 The Hebrew is plural.

NEW INTERNATIONAL VERSION

temple I have consecrated for my Name. Israel will then become a byword and an object of ridicule among all peoples. **8**And though this temple is now imposing, all who pass by will be appalled and will scoff and say, 'Why has the LORD done such a thing to this land and to this temple?' **9**People will answer, 'Because they have forsaken the LORD their God, who brought their fathers out of Egypt, and have embraced other gods, worshiping and serving them—that is why the LORD brought all this disaster on them.' "

SOLOMON'S OTHER ACTIVITIES

10At the end of twenty years, during which Solomon built these two buildings—the temple of the LORD and the royal palace— **11**King Solomon gave twenty towns in Galilee to Hiram king of Tyre, because Hiram had supplied him with all the cedar and pine and gold he wanted. **12**But when Hiram went from Tyre to see the towns that Solomon had given him, he was not pleased with them. **13**"What kind of towns are these you have given me, my brother?" he asked. And he called them the Land of Cabul,*a* a name they have to this day. **14**Now Hiram had sent to the king 120 talents*b* of gold.

15Here is the account of the forced labor King Solomon conscripted to build the LORD's temple, his own palace, the supporting terraces,*c* the wall of Jerusalem, and Hazor, Megiddo and Gezer. **16**(Pharaoh king of Egypt had attacked and captured Gezer. He had set it on fire. He killed its Canaanite inhabitants and then gave it as a wedding gift to his daughter, Solomon's wife. **17**And Solomon rebuilt Gezer.) He built up Lower Beth Horon, **18**Baalath, and Tadmor*d* in the desert, within his land, **19**as well as all his store cities and the towns for his chariots and for his horses*e*—whatever he desired to build in Jerusalem, in Lebanon and throughout all the territory he ruled. **20**All the people left from the Amorites, Hittites, Perizzites, Hivites and Jebusites (these peoples were not Israelites), **21**that is, their descendants remaining in the land, whom the Israelites could not exterminate*f*—these Solomon conscripted for his slave labor force, as it is to this day. **22**But Solomon did not make slaves of any of the Israelites; they were his fighting men, his

a 13 Cabul sounds like the Hebrew for *good-for-nothing.*
b 14 That is, about 4 1/2 tons (about 4 metric tons)
c 15 Or *the Millo;* also in verse 24   *d 18* The Hebrew may also be read *Tamar.*   *e 19* Or *charioteers*
f 21 The Hebrew term refers to the irrevocable giving over of things or persons to the LORD, often by totally destroying them.

THE MESSAGE

sanctified to honor my Name. And Israel will become nothing but a bad joke among the peoples of the world. And this Temple, splendid as it now is, will become an object of contempt; visitors will shake their heads, saying, 'Whatever happened here? What's the story behind these ruins?' Then they'll be told, 'The people who used to live here betrayed their GOD, the very God who rescued their ancestors from Egypt; they took up with alien gods, worshiping and serving them. That's what's behind this GOD-visited devastation.' "

✝

9.10-12 At the end of twenty years, having built the two buildings, The Temple of GOD and his personal palace, Solomon rewarded Hiram king of Tyre with a gift of twenty villages in the district of Galilee. Hiram had provided him with all the cedar and cypress and gold that he had wanted. But when Hiram left Tyre to look over the villages that Solomon had given him, he didn't like what he saw.

9.13-14 He said, "What kind of reward is this, my friend? Twenty backwoods hick towns!" People still refer to them that way. This is all Hiram got from Solomon in exchange for four and a half tons of gold!

✝

9.15 This is the work record of the labor force that King Solomon raised to build The Temple of GOD, his palace, the defense complex (the Millo), the Jerusalem wall, and the fortified cities of Hazor, Megiddo, and Gezer.

9.16-17 Pharaoh king of Egypt had come up and captured Gezer, torched it, and killed all the Canaanites who lived there. He gave it as a wedding present to his daughter, Solomon's wife. So Solomon rebuilt Gezer.

9.17-19 He also built Lower Beth Horon, Baalath, and Tamar in the desert, back-country storehouse villages, and villages for chariots and horses. Solomon built widely and extravagantly in Jerusalem, in Lebanon, and wherever he fancied.

9.20-23 The remnants from the original inhabitants of the land (Amorites, Hittites, Perizzites, Hivites, and Jebusites—all non-Israelites), survivors of the holy wars, were rounded up by Solomon for his gangs of slave labor, a policy still in effect. But true Israelites were not treated this way; they were used in his army and

NEW INTERNATIONAL VERSION

government officials, his officers, his captains, and the commanders of his chariots and charioteers. [23]They were also the chief officials in charge of Solomon's projects—550 officials supervising the men who did the work.

[24]After Pharaoh's daughter had come up from the City of David to the palace Solomon had built for her, he constructed the supporting terraces.

[25]Three times a year Solomon sacrificed burnt offerings and fellowship offerings[a] on the altar he had built for the LORD, burning incense before the LORD along with them, and so fulfilled the temple obligations.

[26]King Solomon also built ships at Ezion Geber, which is near Elath in Edom, on the shore of the Red Sea.[b] [27]And Hiram sent his men—sailors who knew the sea—to serve in the fleet with Solomon's men. [28]They sailed to Ophir and brought back 420 talents[c] of gold, which they delivered to King Solomon.

THE QUEEN OF SHEBA VISITS SOLOMON

10 When the queen of Sheba heard about the fame of Solomon and his relation to the name of the LORD, she came to test him with hard questions. [2]Arriving at Jerusalem with a very great caravan—with camels carrying spices, large quantities of gold, and precious stones—she came to Solomon and talked with him about all that she had on her mind. [3]Solomon answered all her questions; nothing was too hard for the king to explain to her. [4]When the queen of Sheba saw all the wisdom of Solomon and the palace he had built, [5]the food on his table, the seating of his officials, the attending servants in their robes, his cupbearers, and the burnt offerings he made at[d] the temple of the LORD, she was overwhelmed.

[6]She said to the king, "The report I heard in my own country about your achievements and your wisdom is true. [7]But I did not believe these things until I came and saw with my own eyes. Indeed, not even half was told me; in wisdom and wealth you have far exceeded the report I heard. [8]How happy your men must be! How happy your officials, who continually stand before you and hear your wisdom! [9]Praise be to the LORD your God, who has delighted in you and placed you on the throne of Israel. Because

---

a 25 Traditionally *peace offerings*   *b* 26 Hebrew *Yam Suph*; that is, Sea of Reeds   *c* 28 That is, about 16 tons (about 14.5 metric tons)   *d* 5 Or *the ascent by which he went up to*

THE MESSAGE

administration—government leaders and commanders of his chariots and charioteers. They were also the project managers responsible for Solomon's building operations—550 of them in charge of the workforce.

9.24   It was after Pharaoh's daughter ceremonially ascended from the City of David and took up residence in the house built especially for her that Solomon built the defense complex (the Millo).

9.25   Three times a year Solomon worshiped at the Altar of GOD, sacrificing Whole-Burnt-Offerings and Peace-Offerings, and burning incense in the presence of GOD. Everything that had to do with The Temple he did generously and well; he didn't skimp.

9.26-28   And ships! King Solomon also built ships at Ezion Geber, located near Elath in Edom on the Red Sea. Hiram sent seaworthy sailors to assist Solomon's men with the fleet. They embarked for Ophir, brought back sixteen tons of gold, and presented it to King Solomon.

✝

THE QUEEN OF SHEBA VISITS

10.1-5   **10** The Queen of Sheba heard about Solomon and his connection with the Name of GOD. She came to put his reputation to the test by asking tough questions. She made a grand and showy entrance into Jerusalem—camels loaded with spices, a huge amount of gold, and precious gems. She came to Solomon and talked about all the things that she cared about, emptying her heart to him. Solomon answered everything she put to him—nothing stumped him. When the Queen of Sheba experienced for herself Solomon's wisdom and saw with her own eyes the palace he had built, the meals that were served, the impressive array of court officials and sharply dressed waiters, the lavish crystal, and the elaborate worship extravagant with Whole-Burnt-Offerings at the steps leading up to The Temple of GOD, it took her breath away.

10.6-9   She said to the king, "It's all true! Your reputation for accomplishment and wisdom that reached all the way to my country is confirmed. I wouldn't have believed it if I hadn't seen it for myself; they didn't exaggerate! Such wisdom and elegance—far more than I could ever have imagined. Lucky the men and women who work for you, getting to be around you every day and hear your wise words firsthand! And blessed be GOD, your God, who took such a liking to you and made you king. Clearly,

NEW INTERNATIONAL VERSION

of the LORD's eternal love for Israel, he has made you king, to maintain justice and righteousness."

¹⁰And she gave the king 120 talents*a* of gold, large quantities of spices, and precious stones. Never again were so many spices brought in as those the queen of Sheba gave to King Solomon.

¹¹(Hiram's ships brought gold from Ophir; and from there they brought great cargoes of almugwood*b* and precious stones. ¹²The king used the almugwood to make supports for the temple of the LORD and for the royal palace, and to make harps and lyres for the musicians. So much almugwood has never been imported or seen since that day.)

¹³King Solomon gave the queen of Sheba all she desired and asked for, besides what he had given her out of his royal bounty. Then she left and returned with her retinue to her own country.

SOLOMON'S SPLENDOR

¹⁴The weight of the gold that Solomon received yearly was 666 talents,*c* ¹⁵not including the revenues from merchants and traders and from all the Arabian kings and the governors of the land.

¹⁶King Solomon made two hundred large shields of hammered gold; six hundred bekas*d* of gold went into each shield. ¹⁷He also made three hundred small shields of hammered gold, with three minas*e* of gold in each shield. The king put them in the Palace of the Forest of Lebanon.

¹⁸Then the king made a great throne inlaid with ivory and overlaid with fine gold. ¹⁹The throne had six steps, and its back had a rounded top. On both sides of the seat were armrests, with a lion standing beside each of them. ²⁰Twelve lions stood on the six steps, one at either end of each step. Nothing like it had ever been made for any other kingdom. ²¹All King Solomon's goblets were gold, and all the household articles in the Palace of the Forest of Lebanon were pure gold. Nothing was made of silver, because silver was considered of little value in Solomon's days. ²²The king had a fleet of trading ships*f* at sea along with the ships of Hiram. Once every three years it returned, carrying gold, silver and ivory, and apes and baboons.

²³King Solomon was greater in riches and wisdom than all the other kings of the earth. ²⁴The whole world sought audience with Solomon to hear the wisdom God had put in his heart. ²⁵Year

a 10 That is, about 4 1/2 tons (about 4 metric tons)
b 11 Probably a variant of *algumwood*; also in verse 12
c 14 That is, about 25 tons (about 23 metric tons)
d 16 That is, about 7 1/2 pounds (about 3.5 kilograms)
e 17 That is, about 3 3/4 pounds (about 1.7 kilograms)
f 22 Hebrew *of ships of Tarshish*

THE MESSAGE

GOD's love for Israel is behind this, making you king to keep a just order and nurture a God-pleasing people."

10.10 She then gave the king four and a half tons of gold, and also sack after sack of spices and expensive gems. There hasn't been a cargo of spices like that since that shipload the Queen of Sheba brought to King Solomon.

10.11-12 The ships of Hiram also imported gold from Ophir along with tremendous loads of fragrant sandalwood and expensive gems. The king used the sandalwood for fine cabinetry in The Temple of GOD and the palace complex, and for making harps and dulcimers for the musicians. Nothing like that shipment of sandalwood has been seen since.

10.13 King Solomon for his part gave the Queen of Sheba all her heart's desire—everything she asked for, on top of what he had already so generously given her. Satisfied, she returned home with her train of servants.

⊹

10.14-15 Solomon received twenty-five tons of gold in tribute annually. This was above and beyond the taxes and profit on trade with merchants and assorted kings and governors.

10.16-17 King Solomon crafted two hundred body-length shields of hammered gold—seven and a half pounds of gold to each shield—and three hundred smaller shields about half that size. He stored the shields in the House of the Forest of Lebanon.

10.18-20 The king built a massive throne of ivory accented with a veneer of gold. The throne had six steps leading up to it, its back shaped like an arch. The armrests on each side were flanked by lions. Lions, twelve of them, were placed at either end of the six steps. There was no throne like it in any of the surrounding kingdoms.

10.21 King Solomon's chalices and tankards were made of gold and all the dinnerware and serving utensils in the House of the Forest of Lebanon were pure gold—nothing was made of silver; silver was considered common and cheap.

10.22 The king had a fleet of ocean-going ships at sea with Hiram's ships. Every three years the fleet would bring in a cargo of gold, silver, and ivory, and apes and peacocks.

10.23-25 King Solomon was wiser and richer than all the kings of the earth—he surpassed them all. People came from all over the world to be with Solomon and drink in the wisdom God had

NEW INTERNATIONAL VERSION

after year, everyone who came brought a gift—articles of silver and gold, robes, weapons and spices, and horses and mules.

²⁶Solomon accumulated chariots and horses; he had fourteen hundred chariots and twelve thousand horses,*ᵃ* which he kept in the chariot cities and also with him in Jerusalem. ²⁷The king made silver as common in Jerusalem as stones, and cedar as plentiful as sycamore-fig trees in the foothills. ²⁸Solomon's horses were imported from Egypt*ᵇ* and from Kue*ᶜ*—the royal merchants purchased them from Kue. ²⁹They imported a chariot from Egypt for six hundred shekels*ᵈ* of silver, and a horse for a hundred and fifty.*ᵉ* They also exported them to all the kings of the Hittites and of the Arameans.

SOLOMON'S WIVES

11 King Solomon, however, loved many foreign women besides Pharaoh's daughter—Moabites, Ammonites, Edomites, Sidonians and Hittites. ²They were from nations about which the LORD had told the Israelites, "You must not intermarry with them, because they will surely turn your hearts after their gods." Nevertheless, Solomon held fast to them in love. ³He had seven hundred wives of royal birth and three hundred concubines, and his wives led him astray. ⁴As Solomon grew old, his wives turned his heart after other gods, and his heart was not fully devoted to the LORD his God, as the heart of David his father had been. ⁵He followed Ashtoreth the goddess of the Sidonians, and Molech*ᶠ* the detestable god of the Ammonites. ⁶So Solomon did evil in the eyes of the LORD; he did not follow the LORD completely, as David his father had done.

⁷On a hill east of Jerusalem, Solomon built a high place for Chemosh the detestable god of Moab, and for Molech the detestable god of the Ammonites. ⁸He did the same for all his foreign wives, who burned incense and offered sacrifices to their gods.

⁹The LORD became angry with Solomon because his heart had turned away from the LORD, the God of Israel, who had appeared to him twice. ¹⁰Although he had forbidden Solomon to follow other gods, Solomon did not keep the LORD's command. ¹¹So the LORD said to Solomon, "Since this is your attitude and you have not kept my covenant and my decrees, which I commanded you, I will most certainly tear the king-

ᵃ 26 Or *charioteers*   *ᵇ 28* Or possibly *Muzur,* a region in Cilicia; also in verse 29   *ᶜ 28* Probably *Cilicia*
ᵈ 29 That is, about 15 pounds (about 7 kilograms)
ᵉ 29 That is, about 3 3/4 pounds (about 1.7 kilograms)
ᶠ 5 Hebrew *Milcom;* also in verse 33

THE MESSAGE

given him. And everyone who came brought gifts—artifacts of gold and silver, fashionable robes and gowns, the latest in weapons, exotic spices, and horses and mules—parades of visitors, year after year.

10.26-29   Solomon collected chariots and horses: fourteen hundred chariots and twelve thousand horses! He stabled them in the special chariot cities as well as in Jerusalem. The king made silver as common as rocks and cedar as common as the fig trees in the lowland hills. His horses were brought in from Egypt and Cilicia, specially acquired by the king's agents. Chariots from Egypt went for fifteen pounds of silver and a horse for about three and three-quarter pounds of silver. Solomon carried on a brisk horse-trading business with the Hittite and Aramean royal houses.

11.1-5   **11** King Solomon was obsessed with women. Pharaoh's daughter was only the first of the many foreign women he loved—Moabite, Ammonite, Edomite, Sidonian, and Hittite. He took them from the surrounding pagan nations of which GOD had clearly warned Israel, "You must not marry them; they'll seduce you into infatuations with their gods." Solomon fell in love with them anyway, refusing to give them up. He had seven hundred royal wives and three hundred concubines—a thousand women in all! And they did seduce him away from God. As Solomon grew older, his wives beguiled him with their alien gods and he became unfaithful—he didn't stay true to his GOD as his father David had done. Solomon took up with Ashtoreth, the whore goddess of the Sidonians, and Molech, the horrible god of the Ammonites.

11.6-8   Solomon openly defied GOD; he did not follow in his father David's footsteps. He went on to build a sacred shrine to Chemosh, the horrible god of Moab, and to Molech, the horrible god of the Ammonites, on a hill just east of Jerusalem. He built similar shrines for all his foreign wives, who then polluted the countryside with the smoke and stench of their sacrifices.

11.9-10   GOD was furious with Solomon for abandoning the GOD of Israel, the God who had twice appeared to him and had so clearly commanded him not to fool around with other gods. Solomon faithlessly disobeyed GOD's orders.

11.11-13   GOD said to Solomon, "Since this is the way it is with you, that you have no intention of keeping faith with me and doing what I have commanded, I'm going to rip the kingdom

NEW INTERNATIONAL VERSION	THE MESSAGE

dom away from you and give it to one of your subordinates. ¹²Nevertheless, for the sake of David your father, I will not do it during your lifetime. I will tear it out of the hand of your son. ¹³Yet I will not tear the whole kingdom from him, but will give him one tribe for the sake of David my servant and for the sake of Jerusalem, which I have chosen."

Solomon's Adversaries

¹⁴Then the LORD raised up against Solomon an adversary, Hadad the Edomite, from the royal line of Edom. ¹⁵Earlier when David was fighting with Edom, Joab the commander of the army, who had gone up to bury the dead, had struck down all the men in Edom. ¹⁶Joab and all the Israelites stayed there for six months, until they had destroyed all the men in Edom. ¹⁷But Hadad, still only a boy, fled to Egypt with some Edomite officials who had served his father. ¹⁸They set out from Midian and went to Paran. Then taking men from Paran with them, they went to Egypt, to Pharaoh king of Egypt, who gave Hadad a house and land and provided him with food.

¹⁹Pharaoh was so pleased with Hadad that he gave him a sister of his own wife, Queen Tahpenes, in marriage. ²⁰The sister of Tahpenes bore him a son named Genubath, whom Tahpenes brought up in the royal palace. There Genubath lived with Pharaoh's own children.

²¹While he was in Egypt, Hadad heard that David rested with his fathers and that Joab the commander of the army was also dead. Then Hadad said to Pharaoh, "Let me go, that I may return to my own country."

²²"What have you lacked here that you want to go back to your own country?" Pharaoh asked.

"Nothing," Hadad replied, "but do let me go!"

²³And God raised up against Solomon another adversary, Rezon son of Eliada, who had fled from his master, Hadadezer king of Zobah. ²⁴He gathered men around him and became the leader of a band of rebels when David destroyed the forces[a] ⌊of Zobah⌋; the rebels went to Damascus, where they settled and took control. ²⁵Rezon was Israel's adversary as long as Solomon lived, adding to the trouble caused by Hadad. So Rezon ruled in Aram and was hostile toward Israel.

Jeroboam Rebels Against Solomon

²⁶Also, Jeroboam son of Nebat rebelled against the king. He was one of Solomon's officials, an Ephraimite from Zeredah, and his mother was a widow named Zeruah.

---

from you and hand it over to someone else. But out of respect for your father David I won't do it in your lifetime. It's your son who will pay— I'll rip it right out of his grasp. Even then I won't take it all; I'll leave him one tribe in honor of my servant David and out of respect for my chosen city Jerusalem."

11.14-20   GOD incited Hadad, a descendant of the king of Edom, into hostile actions against Solomon. Years earlier, when David devastated Edom, Joab, commander of the army, on his way to bury the dead, massacred all the men of Edom. Joab and his army stayed there for six months, making sure they had killed every man in Edom. Hadad, just a boy at the time, had escaped with some of the Edomites who had worked for his father. Their escape route took them through Midian to Paran. They picked up some men in Paran and went on to Egypt and to Pharaoh king of Egypt, who gave Hadad a house, food, and even land. Pharaoh liked him so well that he gave him the sister of his wife, Queen Tahpenes, in marriage. She bore Hadad a son named Genubath who was raised like one of the royal family. Genubath grew up in the palace with Pharaoh's children.

11.21   While living in Egypt, Hadad heard that both David and Joab, commander of the army, were dead. He approached Pharaoh and said, "Send me off with your blessing—I want to return to my own country."

11.22   "But why?" said Pharaoh. "Why would you want to leave? Hasn't everything been to your liking?"

"Everything has been just fine," said Hadad, "but I want to go home—give me a good sendoff!"

✝

11.23-25   Then God incited another adversary against Solomon, Rezon son of Eliada, who had deserted from his master, Hadadezer king of Zobah. After David's slaughter of the Arameans, Rezon collected a band of outlaws and became their leader. They later settled in Damascus, where Rezon eventually took over as king. Like Hadad, Rezon was a thorn in Israel's side all of Solomon's life. He was king over Aram, and he hated Israel.

Adversaries Arise

11.26   And then, the last straw: Jeroboam son of Nebat rebelled against the king. He was an Ephraimite from Zeredah, his mother a widow named Zeruah. He served in Solomon's administration.

ᵃ 24 Hebrew *destroyed them*

NEW INTERNATIONAL VERSION

²⁷Here is the account of how he rebelled against the king: Solomon had built the supporting terraces^a and had filled in the gap in the wall of the city of David his father. ²⁸Now Jeroboam was a man of standing, and when Solomon saw how well the young man did his work, he put him in charge of the whole labor force of the house of Joseph.

²⁹About that time Jeroboam was going out of Jerusalem, and Ahijah the prophet of Shiloh met him on the way, wearing a new cloak. The two of them were alone out in the country, ³⁰and Ahijah took hold of the new cloak he was wearing and tore it into twelve pieces. ³¹Then he said to Jeroboam, "Take ten pieces for yourself, for this is what the LORD, the God of Israel, says: 'See, I am going to tear the kingdom out of Solomon's hand and give you ten tribes. ³²But for the sake of my servant David and the city of Jerusalem, which I have chosen out of all the tribes of Israel, he will have one tribe. ³³I will do this because they have^b forsaken me and worshiped Ashtoreth the goddess of the Sidonians, Chemosh the god of the Moabites, and Molech the god of the Ammonites, and have not walked in my ways, nor done what is right in my eyes, nor kept my statutes and laws as David, Solomon's father, did.

³⁴" 'But I will not take the whole kingdom out of Solomon's hand; I have made him ruler all the days of his life for the sake of David my servant, whom I chose and who observed my commands and statutes. ³⁵I will take the kingdom from his son's hands and give you ten tribes. ³⁶I will give one tribe to his son so that David my servant may always have a lamp before me in Jerusalem, the city where I chose to put my Name. ³⁷However, as for you, I will take you, and you will rule over all that your heart desires; you will be king over Israel. ³⁸If you do whatever I command you and walk in my ways and do what is right in my eyes by keeping my statutes and commands, as David my servant did, I will be with you. I will build you a dynasty as enduring as the one I built for David and will give Israel to you. ³⁹I will humble David's descendants because of this, but not forever.' "

⁴⁰Solomon tried to kill Jeroboam, but Jeroboam fled to Egypt, to Shishak the king, and stayed there until Solomon's death.

SOLOMON'S DEATH

⁴¹As for the other events of Solomon's reign— all he did and the wisdom he displayed—are they not written in the book of the annals of Solomon? ⁴²Solomon reigned in Jerusalem over all Israel forty years. ⁴³Then he rested with his fathers

^a 27 Or the Millo ^b 33 Hebrew; Septuagint, Vulgate and Syriac because he has

THE MESSAGE

^{11.27-28} This is why he rebelled. Solomon had built the outer defense system (the Millo) and had restored the fortifications that were in disrepair from the time of his father David. Jeroboam stood out during the construction as strong and able. When Solomon observed what a good worker he was, he put the young man in charge of the entire workforce of the tribe of Joseph.

^{11.29-30} One day Jeroboam was walking down the road out of Jerusalem. Ahijah the prophet of Shiloh, wearing a brand-new cloak, met him. The two of them were alone on that remote stretch of road. Ahijah took off the new cloak that he was wearing and ripped it into twelve pieces.

^{11.31-33} Then he said to Jeroboam, "Take ten of these pieces for yourself; this is by order of the GOD of Israel: See what I'm doing—I'm ripping the kingdom out of Solomon's hands and giving you ten of the tribes. In honor of my servant David and out of respect for Jerusalem, the city I especially chose, he will get one tribe. And here's the reason: He faithlessly abandoned me and went off worshiping Ashtoreth goddess of the Sidonians, Chemosh god of the Moabites, and Molech god of the Ammonites. He hasn't lived the way I have shown him, hasn't done what I have wanted, and hasn't followed directions or obeyed orders as his father David did.

^{11.34-36} "Still, I won't take the whole kingdom away from him. I'll stick with him through his lifetime because of my servant David whom I chose and who did follow my directions and obey my orders. But after that I'll remove the kingdom from his son's control and give you ten tribes. I'll leave one tribe to his son, to maintain a witness to my servant David in Jerusalem, the city I chose as a memorial to my Name.

^{11.37-39} "But I have taken you in hand. Rule to your heart's content! You are to be the king of Israel. If you listen to what I tell you and live the way I show you and do what pleases me, following directions and obeying orders as my servant David did, I'll stick with you no matter what. I'll build you a kingdom as solid as the one I built for David. Israel will be yours! I am bringing pain and trouble on David's descendants, but the trials won't last forever."

^{11.40} Solomon ordered the assassination of Jeroboam, but he got away to Egypt and found asylum there with King Shishak. He remained in exile there until Solomon died.

^{11.41-43} The rest of Solomon's life and rule, his work and his wisdom, you can read for yourself in *The Chronicles of Solomon*. Solomon ruled in Jerusalem over all Israel for forty years. He died

and was buried in the city of David his father. And Rehoboam his son succeeded him as king.

ISRAEL REBELS AGAINST REHOBOAM

12 Rehoboam went to Shechem, for all the Israelites had gone there to make him king. ²When Jeroboam son of Nebat heard this (he was still in Egypt, where he had fled from King Solomon), he returned from*ᵃ* Egypt. ³So they sent for Jeroboam, and he and the whole assembly of Israel went to Rehoboam and said to him: ⁴"Your father put a heavy yoke on us, but now lighten the harsh labor and the heavy yoke he put on us, and we will serve you."

⁵Rehoboam answered, "Go away for three days and then come back to me." So the people went away.

⁶Then King Rehoboam consulted the elders who had served his father Solomon during his lifetime. "How would you advise me to answer these people?" he asked.

⁷They replied, "If today you will be a servant to these people and serve them and give them a favorable answer, they will always be your servants."

⁸But Rehoboam rejected the advice the elders gave him and consulted the young men who had grown up with him and were serving him. ⁹He asked, "What is your advice? How should we answer these people who say to me, 'Lighten the yoke your father put on us'?"

¹⁰The young men who had grown up with him replied, "Tell these people who have said to you, 'Your father put a heavy yoke on us, but make our yoke lighter'—tell them, 'My little finger is thicker than my father's waist. ¹¹My father laid on you a heavy yoke; I will make it even heavier. My father scourged you with whips; I will scourge you with scorpions.'"

¹²Three days later Jeroboam and all the people returned to Rehoboam, as the king had said, "Come back to me in three days." ¹³The king answered the people harshly. Rejecting the advice given him by the elders, ¹⁴he followed the advice of the young men and said, "My father made your yoke heavy; I will make it even heavier. My father scourged you with whips; I will scourge you with scorpions." ¹⁵So the king did not listen to the people, for this turn of events was from the LORD, to fulfill the word the LORD had spoken to Jeroboam son of Nebat through Ahijah the Shilonite.

¹⁶When all Israel saw that the king refused to listen to them, they answered the king:

"What share do we have in David,

ᵃ 2 Or he remained in

and was buried in the City of David his father. His son Rehoboam was the next king.

REHOBOAM

12 Rehoboam traveled to Shechem where all Israel had gathered to inaugurate him as king. Jeroboam had been in Egypt, where he had taken asylum from King Solomon; when he got the report of Solomon's death he had come back.

Rehoboam assembled Jeroboam and all the people. They said to Rehoboam, "Your father made life hard for us—worked our fingers to the bone. Give us a break; lighten up on us and we'll willingly serve you."

"Give me three days to think it over, then come back," Rehoboam said.

King Rehoboam talked it over with the elders who had advised his father when he was alive: "What's your counsel? How do you suggest that I answer the people?"

They said, "If you will be a servant to this people, be considerate of their needs and respond with compassion, work things out with them, they'll end up doing anything for you."

But he rejected the counsel of the elders and asked the young men he'd grown up with who were now currying his favor, "What do you think? What should I say to these people who are saying, 'Give us a break from your father's harsh ways—lighten up on us'?"

The young turks he'd grown up with said, "These people who complain, 'Your father was too hard on us; lighten up'—well, tell them this: 'My little finger is thicker than my father's waist.' If you think life under my father was hard, you haven't seen the half of it. My father thrashed you with whips; I'll beat you bloody with chains!'"

Three days later Jeroboam and the people showed up, just as Rehoboam had directed when he said, "Give me three days to think it over, then come back." The king's answer was harsh and rude. He spurned the counsel of the elders and went with the advice of the younger set, "If you think life under my father was hard, you haven't seen the half of it. My father thrashed you with whips; I'll beat you bloody with chains!"

Rehoboam turned a deaf ear to the people. GOD was behind all this, confirming the message that he had given to Jeroboam son of Nebat through Ahijah of Shiloh.

When all Israel realized that the king hadn't listened to a word they'd said, they stood up to him and said,

Get lost, David!

NEW INTERNATIONAL VERSION

what part in Jesse's son?
To your tents, O Israel!
    Look after your own house, O David!"

So the Israelites went home. [17]But as for the Israelites who were living in the towns of Judah, Rehoboam still ruled over them.

[18]King Rehoboam sent out Adoniram,[a] who was in charge of forced labor, but all Israel stoned him to death. King Rehoboam, however, managed to get into his chariot and escape to Jerusalem. [19]So Israel has been in rebellion against the house of David to this day.

[20]When all the Israelites heard that Jeroboam had returned, they sent and called him to the assembly and made him king over all Israel. Only the tribe of Judah remained loyal to the house of David.

[21]When Rehoboam arrived in Jerusalem, he mustered the whole house of Judah and the tribe of Benjamin—a hundred and eighty thousand fighting men—to make war against the house of Israel and to regain the kingdom for Rehoboam son of Solomon.

[22]But this word of God came to Shemaiah the man of God: [23]"Say to Rehoboam son of Solomon king of Judah, to the whole house of Judah and Benjamin, and to the rest of the people, [24]'This is what the LORD says: Do not go up to fight against your brothers, the Israelites. Go home, every one of you, for this is my doing.' " So they obeyed the word of the LORD and went home again, as the LORD had ordered.

GOLDEN CALVES AT BETHEL AND DAN

[25]Then Jeroboam fortified Shechem in the hill country of Ephraim and lived there. From there he went out and built up Peniel.[b]

[26]Jeroboam thought to himself, "The kingdom will now likely revert to the house of David. [27]If these people go up to offer sacrifices at the temple of the LORD in Jerusalem, they will again give their allegiance to their lord, Rehoboam king of Judah. They will kill me and return to King Rehoboam."

[28]After seeking advice, the king made two golden calves. He said to the people, "It is too much for you to go up to Jerusalem. Here are your gods, O Israel, who brought you up out of Egypt." [29]One he set up in Bethel, and the other in Dan. [30]And this thing became a sin; the people went even as far as Dan to worship the one there.

---

[a] 18 Some Septuagint manuscripts and Syriac (see also 1 Kings 4:6 and 5:14); Hebrew *Adoram*   [b] 25 Hebrew *Penuel*, a variant of *Peniel*

THE MESSAGE

We've had it with you, son of Jesse!
Let's get out of here, Israel, and fast!
From now on, David, mind your own
    business.

And with that, they left. But Rehoboam continued to rule those who lived in the towns of Judah.

12.18-19 When King Rehoboam next sent out Adoniram, head of the workforce, the Israelites ganged up on him, pelted him with stones, and killed him. King Rehoboam jumped in his chariot and fled to Jerusalem as fast as he could. Israel has been in rebellion against the Davidic regime ever since.

JEROBOAM OF ISRAEL

12.20 When the word was out that Jeroboam was back and available, the assembled people invited him and inaugurated him king over all Israel. The only tribe left to the Davidic dynasty was Judah.

12.21 When Rehoboam got back to Jerusalem, he called up the men of Judah and the tribe of Benjamin, a hundred and eighty thousand of their best soldiers, to go to war against Israel and recover the kingdom for Rehoboam son of Solomon.

12.22-24 At this time the word of God came to Shemaiah, a man of God: "Tell this to Rehoboam son of Solomon king of Judah, along with everyone in Judah and Benjamin and anyone else who is around: This is GOD's word: Don't march out; don't fight against your brothers the Israelites; go back home, every last one of you; *I'm* in charge here." And they did it; they did what GOD said and went home.

12.25 Jeroboam made a fort at Shechem in the hills of Ephraim, and made that his headquarters. He also built a fort at Penuel.

12.26-27 But then Jeroboam thought, "It won't be long before the kingdom is reunited under David. As soon as these people resume worship at The Temple of GOD in Jerusalem, they'll start thinking of Rehoboam king of Judah as their ruler. They'll then kill me and go back to King Rehoboam."

12.28-30 So the king came up with a plan: He made two golden calves. Then he announced, "It's too much trouble for you to go to Jerusalem to worship. Look at these—the gods who brought you out of Egypt!" He put one calf in Bethel; the other he placed in Dan. This was blatant sin. Think of it—people traveling all the way to Dan to worship a calf!

NEW INTERNATIONAL VERSION

³¹Jeroboam built shrines on high places and appointed priests from all sorts of people, even though they were not Levites. ³²He instituted a festival on the fifteenth day of the eighth month, like the festival held in Judah, and offered sacrifices on the altar. This he did in Bethel, sacrificing to the calves he had made. And at Bethel he also installed priests at the high places he had made. ³³On the fifteenth day of the eighth month, a month of his own choosing, he offered sacrifices on the altar he had built at Bethel. So he instituted the festival for the Israelites and went up to the altar to make offerings.

THE MAN OF GOD FROM JUDAH

13 By the word of the LORD a man of God came from Judah to Bethel, as Jeroboam was standing by the altar to make an offering. ²He cried out against the altar by the word of the LORD: "O altar, altar! This is what the LORD says: 'A son named Josiah will be born to the house of David. On you he will sacrifice the priests of the high places who now make offerings here, and human bones will be burned on you.'" ³That same day the man of God gave a sign: "This is the sign the LORD has declared: The altar will be split apart and the ashes on it will be poured out."

⁴When King Jeroboam heard what the man of God cried out against the altar at Bethel, he stretched out his hand from the altar and said, "Seize him!" But the hand he stretched out toward the man shriveled up, so that he could not pull it back. ⁵Also, the altar was split apart and its ashes poured out according to the sign given by the man of God by the word of the LORD.

⁶Then the king said to the man of God, "Intercede with the LORD your God and pray for me that my hand may be restored." So the man of God interceded with the LORD, and the king's hand was restored and became as it was before.

⁷The king said to the man of God, "Come home with me and have something to eat, and I will give you a gift."

⁸But the man of God answered the king, "Even if you were to give me half your possessions, I would not go with you, nor would I eat bread or drink water here. ⁹For I was commanded by the word of the LORD: 'You must not eat bread or drink water or return by the way you came.'" ¹⁰So he took another road and did not return by the way he had come to Bethel.

¹¹Now there was a certain old prophet living in Bethel, whose sons came and told him all that the man of God had done there that day. They

THE MESSAGE

12.31-33 And that wasn't the end of it. Jeroboam built forbidden shrines all over the place and recruited priests from wherever he could find them, regardless of whether they were fit for the job or not. To top it off, he created a holy New Year festival to be held on the fifteenth day of the eighth month to replace the one in Judah, complete with worship offered on the Altar at Bethel and sacrificing before the calves he had set up there. He staffed Bethel with priests from the local shrines he had made. This was strictly his own idea to compete with the feast in Judah; and he carried it off with flair, a festival exclusively for Israel, Jeroboam himself leading the worship at the Altar.

13.1-3 **13** And then this happened: Just as Jeroboam was at the Altar, about to make an offering, a holy man came from Judah by GOD's command and preached (these were GOD's orders) to the Altar: "Altar, Altar! GOD's message! 'A son will be born into David's family named Josiah. The priests from the shrines who are making offerings on you, he will sacrifice—on you! Human bones burned on you!'" At the same time he announced a sign: "This is the proof GOD gives—the Altar will split into pieces and the holy offerings spill into the dirt."

13.4-5 When the king heard the message the holy man preached against the Altar at Bethel, he reached out to grab him, yelling, "Arrest him!" But his arm was paralyzed and hung useless. At the same time the Altar broke apart and the holy offerings all spilled into the dirt—the very sign the holy man had announced by GOD's command.

13.6 The king pleaded with the holy man, "Help me! Pray to your GOD for the healing of my arm." The holy man prayed for him and the king's arm was healed—as good as new!

13.7 Then the king invited the holy man, "Join me for a meal; I have a gift for you."

13.8-10 The holy man told the king, "Not on your life! You couldn't pay me enough to get me to sit down with you at a meal in this place. I'm here under GOD's orders, and he commanded, 'Don't eat a crumb, don't drink a drop, and don't go back the way you came.'" Then he left by a different road than the one on which he had walked to Bethel.

13.11 There was an old prophet who lived in Bethel. His sons came and told him the story of what the holy man had done that day in Bethel,

NEW INTERNATIONAL VERSION

also told their father what he had said to the king. [12]Their father asked them, "Which way did he go?" And his sons showed him which road the man of God from Judah had taken. [13]So he said to his sons, "Saddle the donkey for me." And when they had saddled the donkey for him, he mounted it [14]and rode after the man of God. He found him sitting under an oak tree and asked, "Are you the man of God who came from Judah?"

"I am," he replied.

[15]So the prophet said to him, "Come home with me and eat."

[16]The man of God said, "I cannot turn back and go with you, nor can I eat bread or drink water with you in this place. [17]I have been told by the word of the LORD: 'You must not eat bread or drink water there or return by the way you came.' "

[18]The old prophet answered, "I too am a prophet, as you are. And an angel said to me by the word of the LORD: 'Bring him back with you to your house so that he may eat bread and drink water.' " (But he was lying to him.) [19]So the man of God returned with him and ate and drank in his house.

[20]While they were sitting at the table, the word of the LORD came to the old prophet who had brought him back. [21]He cried out to the man of God who had come from Judah, "This is what the LORD says: 'You have defied the word of the LORD and have not kept the command the LORD your God gave you. [22]You came back and ate bread and drank water in the place where he told you not to eat or drink. Therefore your body will not be buried in the tomb of your fathers.' "

[23]When the man of God had finished eating and drinking, the prophet who had brought him back saddled his donkey for him. [24]As he went on his way, a lion met him on the road and killed him, and his body was thrown down on the road, with both the donkey and the lion standing beside it. [25]Some people who passed by saw the body thrown down there, with the lion standing beside the body, and they went and reported it in the city where the old prophet lived.

[26]When the prophet who had brought him back from his journey heard of it, he said, "It is the man of God who defied the word of the LORD. The LORD has given him over to the lion, which has mauled him and killed him, as the word of the LORD had warned him."

[27]The prophet said to his sons, "Saddle the donkey for me," and they did so. [28]Then he went out and found the body thrown down on the road, with the donkey and the lion standing beside it. The lion had neither eaten the body nor mauled the donkey. [29]So the prophet picked up

THE MESSAGE

told him everything that had happened and what the holy man had said to the king.

13.12   Their father said, "Which way did he go?" His sons pointed out the road that the holy man from Judah had taken.

13.13-14   He told his sons, "Saddle my donkey." When they had saddled it, he got on and rode after the holy man. He found him sitting under an oak tree.

He asked him, "Are you the holy man who came from Judah?"

"Yes, I am," he said.

13.15   "Well, come home with me and have a meal."

13.16-17   "Sorry, I can't do that," the holy man said. "I can neither go back with you nor eat with you in this country. I'm under strict orders from GOD: 'Don't eat a crumb; don't drink a drop; and don't come back the way you came.' "

13.18-19   But he said, "I am also a prophet, just like you. And an angel came to me with a message from GOD: 'Bring him home with you, and give him a good meal!' " But the man was lying. So the holy man went home with him and they had a meal together.

13.20-22   There they were, sitting at the table together, when the word of GOD came to the prophet who had brought him back. He confronted the holy man who had come from Judah: "GOD's word to you: You disobeyed GOD's command; you didn't keep the strict orders your GOD gave you; you came back and sat down to a good meal in the very place GOD told you, 'Don't eat a crumb; don't drink a drop.' For that you're going to die far from home and not be buried in your ancestral tomb."

13.23-25   When the meal was over, the prophet who had brought him back saddled his donkey for him. Down the road a way, a lion met him and killed him. His corpse lay crumpled on the road, the lion on one side and the donkey on the other. Some passersby saw the corpse in a heap on the road, with the lion standing guard beside it. They went to the village where the old prophet lived and told what they had seen.

13.26   When the prophet who had gotten him off track heard it, he said, "It's the holy man who disobeyed GOD's strict orders. GOD turned him over to the lion who knocked him around and killed him, just as GOD had told him."

13.27-30   The prophet told his sons, "Saddle my donkey." They did it. He rode out and found the corpse in a heap in the road, with the lion and the donkey standing there. The lion hadn't bothered either the corpse or the donkey. The

the body of the man of God, laid it on the donkey, and brought it back to his own city to mourn for him and bury him. ³⁰Then he laid the body in his own tomb, and they mourned over him and said, "Oh, my brother!"

³¹After burying him, he said to his sons, "When I die, bury me in the grave where the man of God is buried; lay my bones beside his bones. ³²For the message he declared by the word of the LORD against the altar in Bethel and against all the shrines on the high places in the towns of Samaria will certainly come true."

³³Even after this, Jeroboam did not change his evil ways, but once more appointed priests for the high places from all sorts of people. Anyone who wanted to become a priest he consecrated for the high places. ³⁴This was the sin of the house of Jeroboam that led to its downfall and to its destruction from the face of the earth.

AHIJAH'S PROPHECY AGAINST JEROBOAM

14 At that time Abijah son of Jeroboam became ill, ²and Jeroboam said to his wife, "Go, disguise yourself, so you won't be recognized as the wife of Jeroboam. Then go to Shiloh. Ahijah the prophet is there—the one who told me I would be king over this people. ³Take ten loaves of bread with you, some cakes and a jar of honey, and go to him. He will tell you what will happen to the boy." ⁴So Jeroboam's wife did what he said and went to Ahijah's house in Shiloh.

Now Ahijah could not see; his sight was gone because of his age. ⁵But the LORD had told Ahijah, "Jeroboam's wife is coming to ask you about her son, for he is ill, and you are to give her such and such an answer. When she arrives, she will pretend to be someone else."

⁶So when Ahijah heard the sound of her footsteps at the door, he said, "Come in, wife of Jeroboam. Why this pretense? I have been sent to you with bad news. ⁷Go, tell Jeroboam that this is what the LORD, the God of Israel, says: 'I raised you up from among the people and made you a leader over my people Israel. ⁸I tore the kingdom away from the house of David and gave it to you, but you have not been like my servant David, who kept my commands and followed me with all his heart, doing only what was right in my eyes. ⁹You have done more evil than all who lived before you. You have made for yourself other gods, idols made of metal; you have provoked me to anger and thrust me behind your back.

¹⁰"Because of this, I am going to bring disaster on the house of Jeroboam. I will cut off from Jeroboam every last male in Israel—slave or free.

old prophet loaded the corpse of the holy man on his donkey and returned it to his own town to give it a decent burial. He placed the body in his own tomb. The people mourned, saying, "A sad day, brother!"

13.31-32 After the funeral, the prophet said to his sons, "When I die, bury me in the same tomb where the holy man is buried, my bones alongside his bones. The message that he preached by GOD's command against the Altar at Bethel and against all the sex-and-religion shrines in the towns of Samaria will come true."

13.33-34 After this happened, Jeroboam kept right on doing evil, recruiting priests for the forbidden shrines indiscriminately—anyone who wanted to could be a priest at one of the local shrines. This was the root sin of Jeroboam's government. And it was this that ruined him.

✠

14.1-3 **14** At about this time Jeroboam's son Abijah came down sick. Jeroboam said to his wife, "Do something. Disguise yourself so no one will know you are the queen and go to Shiloh. Ahijah the prophet lives there, the same Ahijah who told me I'd be king over this people. Take along ten loaves of bread, some sweet rolls, and a jug of honey. Make a visit to him and he'll tell you what's going on with our boy."

14.4-5 Jeroboam's wife did as she was told; she went straight to Shiloh and to Ahijah's house. Ahijah was an old man at this time, and blind, but GOD had warned Ahijah, "Jeroboam's wife is on her way to consult with you regarding her sick son; tell her this and this and this."

14.5-9 When she came in she was disguised. Ahijah heard her come through the door and said, "Welcome, wife of Jeroboam! But why the deception? I've got bad news for you. Go and deliver this message I received firsthand from GOD, the God of Israel, to Jeroboam: I raised you up from obscurity and made you the leader of my people Israel. I ripped the kingdom from the hands of David's family and gave it to you, but you weren't at all like my servant David who did what I told him and lived from his undivided heart, pleasing me. Instead you've set a new record in works of evil by making alien gods—tin gods! Pushing me aside and turning your back—you've made me mighty angry.

14.10-11 "And I'll not put up with it: I'm bringing doom on the household of Jeroboam, killing the lot of them right down to the last male wretch in Israel, whether slave or free. They've

NEW INTERNATIONAL VERSION

I will burn up the house of Jeroboam as one burns dung, until it is all gone. ¹¹Dogs will eat those belonging to Jeroboam who die in the city, and the birds of the air will feed on those who die in the country. The LORD has spoken!'

¹²"As for you, go back home. When you set foot in your city, the boy will die. ¹³All Israel will mourn for him and bury him. He is the only one belonging to Jeroboam who will be buried, because he is the only one in the house of Jeroboam in whom the LORD, the God of Israel, has found anything good.

¹⁴"The LORD will raise up for himself a king over Israel who will cut off the family of Jeroboam. This is the day! What? Yes, even now.ᵃ ¹⁵And the LORD will strike Israel, so that it will be like a reed swaying in the water. He will uproot Israel from this good land that he gave to their forefathers and scatter them beyond the River,ᵇ because they provoked the LORD to anger by making Asherah poles.ᶜ ¹⁶And he will give Israel up because of the sins Jeroboam has committed and has caused Israel to commit."

¹⁷Then Jeroboam's wife got up and left and went to Tirzah. As soon as she stepped over the threshold of the house, the boy died. ¹⁸They buried him, and all Israel mourned for him, as the LORD had said through his servant the prophet Ahijah.

¹⁹The other events of Jeroboam's reign, his wars and how he ruled, are written in the book of the annals of the kings of Israel. ²⁰He reigned for twenty-two years and then rested with his fathers. And Nadab his son succeeded him as king.

REHOBOAM KING OF JUDAH

²¹Rehoboam son of Solomon was king in Judah. He was forty-one years old when he became king, and he reigned seventeen years in Jerusalem, the city the LORD had chosen out of all the tribes of Israel in which to put his Name. His mother's name was Naamah; she was an Ammonite.

²²Judah did evil in the eyes of the LORD. By the sins they committed they stirred up his jealous anger more than their fathers had done. ²³They also set up for themselves high places, sacred stones and Asherah poles on every high hill and under every spreading tree. ²⁴There were even male shrine prostitutes in the land; the people engaged in all the detestable practices of the nations the LORD had driven out before the Israelites.

²⁵In the fifth year of King Rehoboam, Shishak king of Egypt attacked Jerusalem. ²⁶He carried off

THE MESSAGE

become nothing but garbage and I'm getting rid of them. The ones who die in the city will be eaten by stray dogs; the ones who die out in the country will be eaten by carrion crows. GOD's decree!

14:12-13 "And that's it. Go on home—the minute you step foot in town, the boy will die. Everyone will come to his burial, mourning his death. He is the only one in Jeroboam's family who will get a decent burial; he's the only one for whom GOD, the God of Israel, has a good word to say.

14:14-16 "Then GOD will appoint a king over Israel who will wipe out Jeroboam's family, wipe them right off the map—doomsday for Jeroboam! He will hit Israel hard, as a storm slaps reeds about; he'll pull them up by the roots from this good land of their inheritance, weeding them out, and then scatter them to the four winds. And why? Because they made GOD so angry with Asherah sex-and-religion shrines. He'll wash his hands of Israel because of Jeroboam's sins, which have led Israel into a life of sin."

14:17-18 Jeroboam's wife left and went home to Tirzah. The moment she stepped through the door, the boy died. They buried him and everyone mourned his death, just as GOD had said through his servant the prophet Ahijah.

14:19-20 The rest of Jeroboam's life, the wars he fought and the way he ruled, is written in *The Chronicles of the Kings of Israel*. He ruled for twenty-two years. He died and was buried with his ancestors. Nadab his son was king after him.

⊹

14:21-24 Rehoboam son of Solomon was king in Judah. He was forty-one years old when he took the throne and was king for seventeen years in Jerusalem, the city GOD selected from all the tribes of Israel for the worship of his Name. Rehoboam's mother was Naamah, an Ammonite. Judah was openly wicked before GOD, making him very angry. They set new records in sin, surpassing anything their ancestors had done. They built Asherah sex-and-religion shrines and set up sacred stones all over the place—on hills, under trees, wherever you looked. Worse, they had male sacred prostitutes, polluting the country outrageously—all the stuff that GOD had gotten rid of when he brought Israel into the land.

14:25-28 In the fifth year of King Rehoboam's rule, Shishak king of Egypt made war against Jerusa-

NEW INTERNATIONAL VERSION

the treasures of the temple of the LORD and the treasures of the royal palace. He took everything, including all the gold shields Solomon had made. 27So King Rehoboam made bronze shields to replace them and assigned these to the commanders of the guard on duty at the entrance to the royal palace. 28Whenever the king went to the LORD's temple, the guards bore the shields, and afterward they returned them to the guardroom.

29As for the other events of Rehoboam's reign, and all he did, are they not written in the book of the annals of the kings of Judah? 30There was continual warfare between Rehoboam and Jeroboam. 31And Rehoboam rested with his fathers and was buried with them in the City of David. His mother's name was Naamah; she was an Ammonite. And Abijah*a* his son succeeded him as king.

ABIJAH KING OF JUDAH

15 In the eighteenth year of the reign of Jeroboam son of Nebat, Abijah*b* became king of Judah, 2and he reigned in Jerusalem three years. His mother's name was Maacah daughter of Abishalom.*c*

3He committed all the sins his father had done before him; his heart was not fully devoted to the LORD his God, as the heart of David his forefather had been. 4Nevertheless, for David's sake the LORD his God gave him a lamp in Jerusalem by raising up a son to succeed him and by making Jerusalem strong. 5For David had done what was right in the eyes of the LORD and had not failed to keep any of the LORD's commands all the days of his life—except in the case of Uriah the Hittite.

6There was war between Rehoboam*d* and Jeroboam throughout ⌐Abijah's⌐ lifetime. 7As for the other events of Abijah's reign, and all he did, are they not written in the book of the annals of the kings of Judah? There was war between Abijah and Jeroboam. 8And Abijah rested with his fathers and was buried in the City of David. And Asa his son succeeded him as king.

ASA KING OF JUDAH

9In the twentieth year of Jeroboam king of Israel, Asa became king of Judah, 10and he reigned in Jerusalem forty-one years. His grandmother's name was Maacah daughter of Abishalom.

11Asa did what was right in the eyes of the LORD, as his father David had done. 12He ex-

---

a 31 Some Hebrew manuscripts and Septuagint (see also
2 Chron. 12:16); most Hebrew manuscripts *Abijam*
b 1 Some Hebrew manuscripts and Septuagint (see also
2 Chron. 12:16); most Hebrew manuscripts *Abijam*; also in
verses 7 and 8   *c 2* A variant of *Absalom*; also in verse 10
d 6 Most Hebrew manuscripts; some Hebrew manuscripts
and Syriac *Abijam* (that is, Abijah)

THE MESSAGE

lem. He plundered The Temple of GOD and the royal palace of their treasures, cleaned them out—even the gold shields that Solomon had made. King Rehoboam replaced them with bronze shields and outfitted the royal palace guards with them. Whenever the king went to GOD's Temple, the guards carried the shields but always returned them to the guardroom.

14.29-31 The rest of Rehoboam's life, what he said and did, is all written in *The Chronicles of the Kings of Judah*. There was war between Rehoboam and Jeroboam the whole time. Rehoboam died and was buried with his ancestors in the City of David. His mother was Naamah, an Ammonite. His son Abijah ruled after him.

ABIJAH OF JUDAH

15.1-6 **15** In the eighteenth year of the rule of Jeroboam son of Nebat, Abijah took over the throne of Judah. He ruled in Jerusalem three years. His mother was Maacah daughter of Absalom. He continued to sin just like his father before him. He was not truehearted to GOD as his great-grandfather David had been. But despite that, out of respect for David, his GOD graciously gave him a lamp, a son to follow him and keep Jerusalem secure. For David had lived an exemplary life before GOD all his days, not going off on his own in willful defiance of GOD's clear directions (except for that time with Uriah the Hittite). But war continued between Abijah and Jeroboam the whole time.

15.7-8 The rest of Abijah's life, everything he did, is written in *The Chronicles of the Kings of Judah*. But the war with Jeroboam was the dominant theme. Abijah died and was buried with his ancestors in the City of David. His son Asa was king after him.

ASA OF JUDAH

15.9-10 In the twentieth year of Jeroboam king of Israel, Asa began his rule over Judah. He ruled for forty-one years in Jerusalem. His grandmother's name was Maacah.

15.11-15 Asa conducted himself well before GOD, reviving the ways of his ancestor David. He

NEW INTERNATIONAL VERSION

pelled the male shrine prostitutes from the land and got rid of all the idols his fathers had made. [13]He even deposed his grandmother Maacah from her position as queen mother, because she had made a repulsive Asherah pole. Asa cut the pole down and burned it in the Kidron Valley. [14]Although he did not remove the high places, Asa's heart was fully committed to the LORD all his life. [15]He brought into the temple of the LORD the silver and gold and the articles that he and his father had dedicated.

[16]There was war between Asa and Baasha king of Israel throughout their reigns. [17]Baasha king of Israel went up against Judah and fortified Ramah to prevent anyone from leaving or entering the territory of Asa king of Judah.

[18]Asa then took all the silver and gold that was left in the treasuries of the LORD's temple and of his own palace. He entrusted it to his officials and sent them to Ben-Hadad son of Tabrimmon, the son of Hezion, the king of Aram, who was ruling in Damascus. [19]"Let there be a treaty between me and you," he said, "as there was between my father and your father. See, I am sending you a gift of silver and gold. Now break your treaty with Baasha king of Israel so he will withdraw from me."

[20]Ben-Hadad agreed with King Asa and sent the commanders of his forces against the towns of Israel. He conquered Ijon, Dan, Abel Beth Maacah and all Kinnereth in addition to Naphtali. [21]When Baasha heard this, he stopped building Ramah and withdrew to Tirzah. [22]Then King Asa issued an order to all Judah—no one was exempt—and they carried away from Ramah the stones and timber Baasha had been using there. With them King Asa built up Geba in Benjamin, and also Mizpah.

[23]As for all the other events of Asa's reign, all his achievements, all he did and the cities he built, are they not written in the book of the annals of the kings of Judah? In his old age, however, his feet became diseased. [24]Then Asa rested with his fathers and was buried with them in the city of his father David. And Jehoshaphat his son succeeded him as king.

NADAB KING OF ISRAEL

[25]Nadab son of Jeroboam became king of Israel in the second year of Asa king of Judah, and he reigned over Israel two years. [26]He did evil in the eyes of the LORD, walking in the ways of his father and in his sin, which he had caused Israel to commit.

[27]Baasha son of Ahijah of the house of Issachar plotted against him, and he struck him down at Gibbethon, a Philistine town, while Na-

THE MESSAGE

cleaned house: He got rid of the sacred prostitutes and threw out all the idols his predecessors had made. Asa spared nothing and no one; he went so far as to remove Queen Maacah from her position because she had built a shockingly obscene memorial to the whore goddess Asherah. Asa tore it down and burned it up in the Kidron Valley. Unfortunately, he didn't get rid of the local sex-and-religion shrines. But he was well-intentioned—his heart was in the right place, in tune with GOD. All the gold and silver vessels and artifacts that he and his father had consecrated for holy use he installed in The Temple.

15.16-17 But through much of his reign there was war between Asa and Baasha king of Israel. Baasha king of Israel started it by building a fort at Ramah and closing the border between Israel and Judah so no one could enter or leave Judah.

15.18-19 Asa took all the silver and gold that was left in the treasuries of The Temple of GOD and the royal palace, gave it to his servants, and sent them to Ben-Hadad son of Tabrimmon, the son of Hezion king of Aram, who was ruling in Damascus, with this message: "Let's make a treaty like the one between our fathers. I'm showing my good faith with this gift of silver and gold. Break your deal with Baasha king of Israel so he'll quit fighting against me."

15.20-21 Ben-Hadad went along with King Asa and sent out his troops against the towns of Israel. He attacked Ijon, Dan, Abel Beth Maacah, and the entire region of Kinnereth, including Naphtali. When Baasha got the report he quit fortifying Ramah and pulled back to Tirzah.

15.22 Then King Asa issued orders to everyone in Judah—no exemptions—to haul away the logs and stones Baasha had used in the fortification of Ramah and use them to fortify Geba in Benjamin and Mizpah.

15.23-24 A full account of Asa's life, all the great things he did and the fortifications he constructed, is written in *The Chronicles of the Kings of Judah*. In his old age he developed severe gout. Then Asa died and was buried with his ancestors in the City of David. His son Jehoshaphat became king after him.

NADAB OF ISRAEL

15.25-26 Nadab son of Jeroboam became king over Israel in the second year of Asa's rule in Judah. He was king of Israel two years. He was openly evil before GOD—he followed in the footsteps of his father who both sinned and made Israel sin.

15.27-28 Baasha son of Ahijah of the tribe of Issachar ganged up on him and attacked him at the Philistine town of Gibbethon while Nadab and

NEW INTERNATIONAL VERSION

dab and all Israel were besieging it. ²⁸Baasha killed Nadab in the third year of Asa king of Judah and succeeded him as king.

²⁹As soon as he began to reign, he killed Jeroboam's whole family. He did not leave Jeroboam anyone that breathed, but destroyed them all, according to the word of the LORD given through his servant Ahijah the Shilonite— ³⁰because of the sins Jeroboam had committed and had caused Israel to commit, and because he provoked the LORD, the God of Israel, to anger.

³¹As for the other events of Nadab's reign, and all he did, are they not written in the book of the annals of the kings of Israel? ³²There was war between Asa and Baasha king of Israel throughout their reigns.

BAASHA KING OF ISRAEL

³³In the third year of Asa king of Judah, Baasha son of Ahijah became king of all Israel in Tirzah, and he reigned twenty-four years. ³⁴He did evil in the eyes of the LORD, walking in the ways of Jeroboam and in his sin, which he had caused Israel to commit.

16 Then the word of the LORD came to Jehu son of Hanani against Baasha: ²"I lifted you up from the dust and made you leader of my people Israel, but you walked in the ways of Jeroboam and caused my people Israel to sin and to provoke me to anger by their sins. ³So I am about to consume Baasha and his house, and I will make your house like that of Jeroboam son of Nebat. ⁴Dogs will eat those belonging to Baasha who die in the city, and the birds of the air will feed on those who die in the country."

⁵As for the other events of Baasha's reign, what he did and his achievements, are they not written in the book of the annals of the kings of Israel? ⁶Baasha rested with his fathers and was buried in Tirzah. And Elah his son succeeded him as king.

⁷Moreover, the word of the LORD came through the prophet Jehu son of Hanani to Baasha and his house, because of all the evil he had done in the eyes of the LORD, provoking him to anger by the things he did, and becoming like the house of Jeroboam—and also because he destroyed it.

ELAH KING OF ISRAEL

⁸In the twenty-sixth year of Asa king of Judah, Elah son of Baasha became king of Israel, and he reigned in Tirzah two years.

⁹Zimri, one of his officials, who had command of half his chariots, plotted against him.

THE MESSAGE

the Israelites were doing battle there. Baasha killed Nadab in the third year of Asa king of Judah and became Israel's next king.

15.29-30 As soon as he was king he killed everyone in Jeroboam's family. There wasn't a living soul left to the name of Jeroboam; Baasha wiped them out totally, just as GOD's servant Ahijah of Shiloh had prophesied—punishment for Jeroboam's sins and for making Israel sin, for making the GOD of Israel thoroughly angry.

15.31-32 The rest of Nadab's life, everything else he did, is written in *The Chronicles of the Kings of Israel*. There was continuous war between Asa and Baasha king of Israel.

BAASHA OF ISRAEL

15.33-34 In the third year of Asa king of Judah, Baasha son of Ahijah became king in Tirzah over all Israel. He ruled twenty-four years. He was openly evil before GOD, walking in the footsteps of Jeroboam, who both sinned and made Israel sin.

16.1-4 **16** The word of GOD came to Jehu son of Hanani with this message for Baasha: "I took you from nothing—a complete nobody—and set you up as the leader of my people Israel, but you plodded along in the rut of Jeroboam, making my people Israel sin and making me seethe over their sin. And now the consequences—I will burn Baasha and his regime to cinders, the identical fate of Jeroboam son of Nebat. Baasha's people who die in the city will be eaten by scavenger dogs; carrion crows will eat the ones who die in the country."

16.5-6 The rest of Baasha's life, the record of his regime, is written in *The Chronicles of the Kings of Israel*. Baasha died and was buried with his ancestors in Tirzah. His son Elah was king after him.

16.7 That's the way it was with Baasha: Through the prophet Jehu son of Hanani, GOD's word came to him and his regime because of his life of open evil before GOD and his making GOD so angry—a chip off the block of Jeroboam, even though GOD had destroyed him.

ELAH OF ISRAEL

16.8-10 In the twenty-sixth year of Asa king of Judah, Elah son of Baasha began his rule. He was king in Tirzah only two years. One day when he was at the house of Arza the palace manager, drinking himself drunk, Zimri, captain of half his chariot-force, conspired against him. Zimri

NEW INTERNATIONAL VERSION

Elah was in Tirzah at the time, getting drunk in the home of Arza, the man in charge of the palace at Tirzah. ¹⁰Zimri came in, struck him down and killed him in the twenty-seventh year of Asa king of Judah. Then he succeeded him as king.

¹¹As soon as he began to reign and was seated on the throne, he killed off Baasha's whole family. He did not spare a single male, whether relative or friend. ¹²So Zimri destroyed the whole family of Baasha, in accordance with the word of the LORD spoken against Baasha through the prophet Jehu— ¹³because of all the sins Baasha and his son Elah had committed and had caused Israel to commit, so that they provoked the LORD, the God of Israel, to anger by their worthless idols.

¹⁴As for the other events of Elah's reign, and all he did, are they not written in the book of the annals of the kings of Israel?

ZIMRI KING OF ISRAEL

¹⁵In the twenty-seventh year of Asa king of Judah, Zimri reigned in Tirzah seven days. The army was encamped near Gibbethon, a Philistine town. ¹⁶When the Israelites in the camp heard that Zimri had plotted against the king and murdered him, they proclaimed Omri, the commander of the army, king over Israel that very day there in the camp. ¹⁷Then Omri and all the Israelites with him withdrew from Gibbethon and laid siege to Tirzah. ¹⁸When Zimri saw that the city was taken, he went into the citadel of the royal palace and set the palace on fire around him. So he died, ¹⁹because of the sins he had committed, doing evil in the eyes of the LORD and walking in the ways of Jeroboam and in the sin he had committed and had caused Israel to commit.

²⁰As for the other events of Zimri's reign, and the rebellion he carried out, are they not written in the book of the annals of the kings of Israel?

OMRI KING OF ISRAEL

²¹Then the people of Israel were split into two factions; half supported Tibni son of Ginath for king, and the other half supported Omri. ²²But Omri's followers proved stronger than those of Tibni son of Ginath. So Tibni died and Omri became king.

²³In the thirty-first year of Asa king of Judah, Omri became king of Israel, and he reigned twelve years, six of them in Tirzah. ²⁴He bought the hill of Samaria from Shemer for two talents[a] of silver and built a city on the hill, calling it Samaria, after Shemer, the name of the former owner of the hill.

[a] 24 That is, about 150 pounds (about 70 kilograms)

THE MESSAGE

slipped in, knocked Elah to the ground, and killed him. This happened in the twenty-seventh year of Asa king of Judah. Zimri then became the king.

16.11-13 Zimri had no sooner become king than he killed everyone connected with Baasha, got rid of them all like so many stray dogs—relatives and friends alike. Zimri totally wiped out the family of Baasha, just as GOD's word delivered by the prophet Jehu had said—wages for the sins of Baasha and his son Elah; not only for their sins but for dragging Israel into their sins and making the GOD of Israel angry with their stupid idols.

16.14 The rest of Elah's life, what he said and did, is written in *The Chronicles of the Kings of Israel*.

ZIMRI OF ISRAEL

16.15-19 Zimri was king in Tirzah for all of seven days during the twenty-seventh year of the reign of Asa king of Judah. The Israelite army was on maneuvers near the Philistine town of Gibbethon at the time. When they got the report, "Zimri has conspired against the king and killed him," right there in the camp they made Omri, commander of the army, king. Omri and the army immediately left Gibbethon and attacked Tirzah. When Zimri saw that he was surrounded and as good as dead, he entered the palace citadel, set the place on fire, and died. It was a fit end for his sins, for living a flagrantly evil life before GOD, walking in the footsteps of Jeroboam, sinning and then dragging Israel into his sins.

16.20 As for the rest of Zimri's life, along with his infamous conspiracy, it's all written in *The Chronicles of the Kings of Israel*.

OMRI OF ISRAEL

16.21-22 After that the people of Israel were split right down the middle: Half favored Tibni son of Ginath as king, and half wanted Omri. Eventually the Omri side proved stronger than the Tibni side. Tibni ended up dead and Omri king.

16.23-24 Omri took over as king of Israel in the thirty-first year of the reign of Asa king of Judah. He ruled for twelve years, the first six in Tirzah. He then bought the hill Samaria from Shemer for 150 pounds of silver. He developed the hill and named the city that he built Samaria, after its original owner Shemer.

NEW INTERNATIONAL VERSION

²⁵But Omri did evil in the eyes of the LORD and sinned more than all those before him. ²⁶He walked in all the ways of Jeroboam son of Nebat and in his sin, which he had caused Israel to commit, so that they provoked the LORD, the God of Israel, to anger by their worthless idols.

²⁷As for the other events of Omri's reign, what he did and the things he achieved, are they not written in the book of the annals of the kings of Israel? ²⁸Omri rested with his fathers and was buried in Samaria. And Ahab his son succeeded him as king.

AHAB BECOMES KING OF ISRAEL

²⁹In the thirty-eighth year of Asa king of Judah, Ahab son of Omri became king of Israel, and he reigned in Samaria over Israel twenty-two years. ³⁰Ahab son of Omri did more evil in the eyes of the LORD than any of those before him. ³¹He not only considered it trivial to commit the sins of Jeroboam son of Nebat, but he also married Jezebel daughter of Ethbaal king of the Sidonians, and began to serve Baal and worship him. ³²He set up an altar for Baal in the temple of Baal that he built in Samaria. ³³Ahab also made an Asherah pole and did more to provoke the LORD, the God of Israel, to anger than did all the kings of Israel before him.

³⁴In Ahab's time, Hiel of Bethel rebuilt Jericho. He laid its foundations at the cost of his firstborn son Abiram, and he set up its gates at the cost of his youngest son Segub, in accordance with the word of the LORD spoken by Joshua son of Nun.

ELIJAH FED BY RAVENS

17 Now Elijah the Tishbite, from Tishbe[a] in Gilead, said to Ahab, "As the LORD, the God of Israel, lives, whom I serve, there will be neither dew nor rain in the next few years except at my word."

²Then the word of the LORD came to Elijah: ³"Leave here, turn eastward and hide in the Kerith Ravine, east of the Jordan. ⁴You will drink from the brook, and I have ordered the ravens to feed you there."

⁵So he did what the LORD had told him. He went to the Kerith Ravine, east of the Jordan, and stayed there. ⁶The ravens brought him bread and meat in the morning and bread and meat in the evening, and he drank from the brook.

THE WIDOW AT ZAREPHATH

⁷Some time later the brook dried up because there had been no rain in the land. ⁸Then the word of the LORD came to him: ⁹"Go at once to

THE MESSAGE

16.25-26 But as far as GOD was concerned, Omri lived an evil life—set new records in evil. He walked in the footsteps of Jeroboam son of Nebat, who not only sinned but dragged Israel into his sins, making GOD angry—such an empty-headed, empty-hearted life!

16.27-28 The rest of Omri's life, the mark he made on his times, is written in *The Chronicles of the Kings of Israel.* Omri died and was buried in Samaria. His son Ahab was the next king after him.

AHAB OF ISRAEL

16.29-33 Ahab son of Omri became king of Israel in the thirty-eighth year of Asa king of Judah. Ahab son of Omri was king over Israel for twenty-two years. He ruled from Samaria. Ahab son of Omri did even more open evil before GOD than anyone yet—a new champion in evil! It wasn't enough for him to copy the sins of Jeroboam son of Nebat; no, he went all out, first by marrying Jezebel daughter of Ethbaal king of the Sidonians, and then by serving and worshiping the god Baal. He built a temple for Baal in Samaria, and then furnished it with an altar for Baal. Worse, he went on and built a shrine to the sacred whore Asherah. He made the GOD of Israel angrier than all the previous kings of Israel put together.

16.34 It was under Ahab's rule that Hiel of Bethel refortified Jericho, but at a terrible cost: He ritually sacrificed his firstborn son Abiram at the laying of the foundation, and his youngest son Segub at the setting up of the gates. This is exactly what Joshua son of Nun said would happen.

17.1 **17** And then this happened: Elijah the Tishbite, from among the settlers of Gilead, confronted Ahab: "As surely as GOD lives, the God of Israel before whom I stand in obedient service, the next years are going to see a total drought—not a drop of dew or rain unless I say otherwise."

17.2-4 GOD then told Elijah, "Get out of here, and fast. Head east and hide out at the Kerith Ravine on the other side of the Jordan River. You can drink fresh water from the brook; I've ordered the ravens to feed you."

17.5-6 Elijah obeyed GOD's orders. He went and camped in the Kerith canyon on the other side of the Jordan. And sure enough, ravens brought him his meals, both breakfast and supper, and he drank from the brook.

17.7-9 Eventually the brook dried up because of the drought. Then GOD spoke to him: "Get up and

---

ᵃ 1 Or *Tishbite, of the settlers*

NEW INTERNATIONAL VERSION

Zarephath of Sidon and stay there. I have commanded a widow in that place to supply you with food." 10So he went to Zarephath. When he came to the town gate, a widow was there gathering sticks. He called to her and asked, "Would you bring me a little water in a jar so I may have a drink?" 11As she was going to get it, he called, "And bring me, please, a piece of bread."

12"As surely as the LORD your God lives," she replied, "I don't have any bread—only a handful of flour in a jar and a little oil in a jug. I am gathering a few sticks to take home and make a meal for myself and my son, that we may eat it—and die."

13Elijah said to her, "Don't be afraid. Go home and do as you have said. But first make a small cake of bread for me from what you have and bring it to me, and then make something for yourself and your son. 14For this is what the LORD, the God of Israel, says: 'The jar of flour will not be used up and the jug of oil will not run dry until the day the LORD gives rain on the land.'"

15She went away and did as Elijah had told her. So there was food every day for Elijah and for the woman and her family. 16For the jar of flour was not used up and the jug of oil did not run dry, in keeping with the word of the LORD spoken by Elijah.

17Some time later the son of the woman who owned the house became ill. He grew worse and worse, and finally stopped breathing. 18She said to Elijah, "What do you have against me, man of God? Did you come to remind me of my sin and kill my son?"

19"Give me your son," Elijah replied. He took him from her arms, carried him to the upper room where he was staying, and laid him on his bed. 20Then he cried out to the LORD, "O LORD my God, have you brought tragedy also upon this widow I am staying with, by causing her son to die?" 21Then he stretched himself out on the boy three times and cried to the LORD, "O LORD my God, let this boy's life return to him!"

22The LORD heard Elijah's cry, and the boy's life returned to him, and he lived. 23Elijah picked up the child and carried him down from the room into the house. He gave him to his mother and said, "Look, your son is alive!"

24Then the woman said to Elijah, "Now I know that you are a man of God and that the word of the LORD from your mouth is the truth."

THE MESSAGE

go to Zarephath in Sidon and live there. I've instructed a woman who lives there, a widow, to feed you."

17.10-11   So he got up and went to Zarephath. As he came to the entrance of the village he met a woman, a widow, gathering firewood. He asked her, "Please, would you bring me a little water in a jug? I need a drink." As she went to get it, he called out, "And while you're at it, would you bring me something to eat?"

17.12   She said, "I swear, as surely as your GOD lives, I don't have so much as a biscuit. I have a handful of flour in a jar and a little oil in a bottle; you found me scratching together just enough firewood to make a last meal for my son and me. After we eat it, we'll die."

17.13-14   Elijah said to her, "Don't worry about a thing. Go ahead and do what you've said. But first make a small biscuit for me and bring it back here. Then go ahead and make a meal from what's left for you and your son. This is the word of the GOD of Israel: 'The jar of flour will not run out and the bottle of oil will not become empty before GOD sends rain on the land and ends this drought.'"

17.15-16   And she went right off and did it, did just as Elijah asked. And it turned out as he said—daily food for her and her family. The jar of meal didn't run out and the bottle of oil didn't become empty: GOD's promise fulfilled to the letter, exactly as Elijah had delivered it!

17.17   Later on the woman's son became sick. The sickness took a turn for the worse—and then he stopped breathing.

17.18   The woman said to Elijah, "Why did you ever show up here in the first place—a holy man barging in, exposing my sins, and killing my son?"

17.19-20   Elijah said, "Hand me your son."
He then took him from her bosom, carried him up to the loft where he was staying, and laid him on his bed. Then he prayed, "O GOD, my God, why have you brought this terrible thing on this widow who has opened her home to me? Why have you killed her son?"

17.21-23   Three times he stretched himself out full-length on the boy, praying with all his might, "GOD, my God, put breath back into this boy's body!" GOD listened to Elijah's prayer and put breath back into his body—he was alive! Elijah picked the boy up, carried him downstairs from the loft, and gave him to his mother. "Here's your son," said Elijah, "alive!"

17.24   The woman said to Elijah, "I see it all now—you are a holy man. When you speak, GOD speaks—a true word!"

NEW INTERNATIONAL VERSION

ELIJAH AND OBADIAH

18 After a long time, in the third year, the word of the LORD came to Elijah: "Go and present yourself to Ahab, and I will send rain on the land." ²So Elijah went to present himself to Ahab.

Now the famine was severe in Samaria, ³and Ahab had summoned Obadiah, who was in charge of his palace. (Obadiah was a devout believer in the LORD. ⁴While Jezebel was killing off the LORD's prophets, Obadiah had taken a hundred prophets and hidden them in two caves, fifty in each, and had supplied them with food and water.) ⁵Ahab had said to Obadiah, "Go through the land to all the springs and valleys. Maybe we can find some grass to keep the horses and mules alive so we will not have to kill any of our animals." ⁶So they divided the land they were to cover, Ahab going in one direction and Obadiah in another.

⁷As Obadiah was walking along, Elijah met him. Obadiah recognized him, bowed down to the ground, and said, "Is it really you, my lord Elijah?"

⁸"Yes," he replied. "Go tell your master, 'Elijah is here.' "

⁹"What have I done wrong," asked Obadiah, "that you are handing your servant over to Ahab to be put to death? ¹⁰As surely as the LORD your God lives, there is not a nation or kingdom where my master has not sent someone to look for you. And whenever a nation or kingdom claimed you were not there, he made them swear they could not find you. ¹¹But now you tell me to go to my master and say, 'Elijah is here.' ¹²I don't know where the Spirit of the LORD may carry you when I leave you. If I go and tell Ahab and he doesn't find you, he will kill me. Yet I your servant have worshiped the LORD since my youth. ¹³Haven't you heard, my lord, what I did while Jezebel was killing the prophets of the LORD? I hid a hundred of the LORD's prophets in two caves, fifty in each, and supplied them with food and water. ¹⁴And now you tell me to go to my master and say, 'Elijah is here.' He will kill me!"

¹⁵Elijah said, "As the LORD Almighty lives, whom I serve, I will surely present myself to Ahab today."

ELIJAH ON MOUNT CARMEL

¹⁶So Obadiah went to meet Ahab and told him, and Ahab went to meet Elijah. ¹⁷When he saw Elijah, he said to him, "Is that you, you troubler of Israel?"

THE MESSAGE

18.1-2 **18** A long time passed. Then GOD's word came to Elijah. The drought was now in its third year. The message: "Go and present yourself to Ahab; I'm about to make it rain on the country." Elijah set out to present himself to Ahab. The drought in Samaria at the time was most severe.

18.3-4 Ahab called for Obadiah, who was in charge of the palace. Obadiah feared GOD—he was very devout. Earlier, when Jezebel had tried to kill off all the prophets of GOD, Obadiah had hidden away a hundred of them in two caves, fifty in a cave, and then supplied them with food and water.

18.5-6 Ahab ordered Obadiah, "Go through the country; locate every spring and every stream. Let's see if we can find enough grass to keep our horses and mules from dying." So they divided the country between them for the search—Ahab went one way, Obadiah the other.

18.7 Obadiah went his way and suddenly there he was—Elijah! Obadiah fell on his knees, bowing in reverence, and exclaimed, "Is it really you—my master Elijah?"

18.8 "Yes," said Elijah, "the real me. Now go and tell your boss, 'I've seen Elijah.' "

18.9-14 Obadiah said, "But what have I done to deserve this? Ahab will kill me. As surely as your GOD lives, there isn't a country or kingdom where my master hasn't sent out search parties looking for you. And if they said, 'We can't find him; we've looked high and low,' he would make that country or kingdom swear that you were not to be found. And now you're telling me, 'Go and tell your master Elijah's found!' The minute I leave you the Spirit of GOD will whisk you away to who knows where. Then when I report to Ahab, you'll have disappeared and Ahab will kill me. And I've served GOD devoutly since I was a boy! Hasn't anyone told you what I did when Jezebel was out to kill the prophets of GOD, how I risked my life by hiding a hundred of them, fifty to a cave, and made sure they got food and water? And now you're telling me to draw attention to myself by announcing to my master, 'Elijah's been found.' Why, he'll kill me for sure."

18.15 Elijah said, "As surely as GOD-of-the-Angel-Armies lives, and before whom I take my stand, I'll meet with your master face to face this very day."

18.16 So Obadiah went straight to Ahab and told him. And Ahab went out to meet Elijah.

18.17-19 The moment Ahab saw Elijah he said, "So it's you, old troublemaker!"

NEW INTERNATIONAL VERSION

¹⁸"I have not made trouble for Israel," Elijah replied. "But you and your father's family have. You have abandoned the LORD's commands and have followed the Baals. ¹⁹Now summon the people from all over Israel to meet me on Mount Carmel. And bring the four hundred and fifty prophets of Baal and the four hundred prophets of Asherah, who eat at Jezebel's table."

²⁰So Ahab sent word throughout all Israel and assembled the prophets on Mount Carmel. ²¹Elijah went before the people and said, "How long will you waver between two opinions? If the LORD is God, follow him; but if Baal is God, follow him."

But the people said nothing.

²²Then Elijah said to them, "I am the only one of the LORD's prophets left, but Baal has four hundred and fifty prophets. ²³Get two bulls for us. Let them choose one for themselves, and let them cut it into pieces and put it on the wood but not set fire to it. I will prepare the other bull and put it on the wood but not set fire to it. ²⁴Then you call on the name of your god, and I will call on the name of the LORD. The god who answers by fire—he is God."

Then all the people said, "What you say is good."

²⁵Elijah said to the prophets of Baal, "Choose one of the bulls and prepare it first, since there are so many of you. Call on the name of your god, but do not light the fire." ²⁶So they took the bull given them and prepared it.

Then they called on the name of Baal from morning till noon. "O Baal, answer us!" they shouted. But there was no response; no one answered. And they danced around the altar they had made.

²⁷At noon Elijah began to taunt them. "Shout louder!" he said. "Surely he is a god! Perhaps he is deep in thought, or busy, or traveling. Maybe he is sleeping and must be awakened." ²⁸So they shouted louder and slashed themselves with swords and spears, as was their custom, until their blood flowed. ²⁹Midday passed, and they continued their frantic prophesying until the time for the evening sacrifice. But there was no response, no one answered, no one paid attention.

³⁰Then Elijah said to all the people, "Come here to me." They came to him, and he repaired the altar of the LORD, which was in ruins. ³¹Elijah took twelve stones, one for each of the tribes

THE MESSAGE

"It's not I who has caused trouble in Israel," said Elijah, "but you and your government—you've dumped GOD's ways and commands and run off after the local gods, the Baals. Here's what I want you to do: Assemble everyone in Israel at Mount Carmel. And make sure that the special pets of Jezebel, the four hundred and fifty prophets of the local gods, the Baals, and the four hundred prophets of the whore goddess Asherah, are there."

¹⁸·²⁰ So Ahab summoned everyone in Israel, particularly the prophets, to Mount Carmel.

¹⁸·²¹ Elijah challenged the people: "How long are you going to sit on the fence? If GOD is the real God, follow him; if it's Baal, follow him. Make up your minds!"

Nobody said a word; nobody made a move.

¹⁸·²²⁻²⁴ Then Elijah said, "I'm the only prophet of GOD left in Israel; and there are four hundred and fifty prophets of Baal. Let the Baal prophets bring up two oxen; let them pick one, butcher it, and lay it out on an altar on firewood—but don't ignite it. I'll take the other ox, cut it up, and lay it on the wood. But neither will I light the fire. Then you pray to your gods and I'll pray to GOD. The god who answers with fire will prove to be, in fact, God."

All the people agreed: "A good plan—do it!"

¹⁸·²⁵ Elijah told the Baal prophets, "Choose your ox and prepare it. You go first, you're the majority. Then pray to your god, but don't light the fire."

¹⁸·²⁶ So they took the ox he had given them, prepared it for the altar, then prayed to Baal. They prayed all morning long, "O Baal, answer us!" But nothing happened—not so much as a whisper of breeze. Desperate, they jumped and stomped on the altar they had made.

¹⁸·²⁷⁻²⁸ By noon, Elijah had started making fun of them, taunting, "Call a little louder—he is a god, after all. Maybe he's off meditating somewhere or other, or maybe he's gotten involved in a project, or maybe he's on vacation. You don't suppose he's overslept, do you, and needs to be waked up?" They prayed louder and louder, cutting themselves with swords and knives—a ritual common to them—until they were covered with blood.

¹⁸·²⁹ This went on until well past noon. They used every religious trick and strategy they knew to make something happen on the altar, but nothing happened—not so much as a whisper, not a flicker of response.

¹⁸·³⁰⁻³⁵ Then Elijah told the people, "Enough of that—it's my turn. Gather around." And they gathered. He then put the altar back together for by now it was in ruins. Elijah took twelve

NEW INTERNATIONAL VERSION

descended from Jacob, to whom the word of the LORD had come, saying, "Your name shall be Israel." ³²With the stones he built an altar in the name of the LORD, and he dug a trench around it large enough to hold two seahs*a* of seed. ³³He arranged the wood, cut the bull into pieces and laid it on the wood. Then he said to them, "Fill four large jars with water and pour it on the offering and on the wood."

³⁴"Do it again," he said, and they did it again.

"Do it a third time," he ordered, and they did it the third time. ³⁵The water ran down around the altar and even filled the trench.

³⁶At the time of sacrifice, the prophet Elijah stepped forward and prayed: "O LORD, God of Abraham, Isaac and Israel, let it be known today that you are God in Israel and that I am your servant and have done all these things at your command. ³⁷Answer me, O LORD, answer me, so these people will know that you, O LORD, are God, and that you are turning their hearts back again."

³⁸Then the fire of the LORD fell and burned up the sacrifice, the wood, the stones and the soil, and also licked up the water in the trench.

³⁹When all the people saw this, they fell prostrate and cried, "The LORD—he is God! The LORD—he is God!"

⁴⁰Then Elijah commanded them, "Seize the prophets of Baal. Don't let anyone get away!" They seized them, and Elijah had them brought down to the Kishon Valley and slaughtered there.

⁴¹And Elijah said to Ahab, "Go, eat and drink, for there is the sound of a heavy rain." ⁴²So Ahab went off to eat and drink, but Elijah climbed to the top of Carmel, bent down to the ground and put his face between his knees.

⁴³"Go and look toward the sea," he told his servant. And he went up and looked.

"There is nothing there," he said.

Seven times Elijah said, "Go back."

⁴⁴The seventh time the servant reported, "A cloud as small as a man's hand is rising from the sea."

So Elijah said, "Go and tell Ahab, 'Hitch up your chariot and go down before the rain stops you.'"

⁴⁵Meanwhile, the sky grew black with clouds, the wind rose, a heavy rain came on and Ahab rode off to Jezreel. ⁴⁶The power of the LORD came upon Elijah and, tucking his cloak into his belt, he ran ahead of Ahab all the way to Jezreel.

---

a 32 That is, probably about 13 quarts (about 15 liters)

THE MESSAGE

stones, one for each of the tribes of Jacob, the same Jacob to whom GOD had said, "From now on your name is Israel." He built the stones into the altar in honor of GOD. Then Elijah dug a fairly wide trench around the altar. He laid firewood on the altar, cut up the ox, put it on the wood, and said, "Fill four buckets with water and drench both the ox and the firewood." Then he said, "Do it again," and they did it. Then he said, "Do it a third time," and they did it a third time. The altar was drenched and the trench was filled with water.

18.36-37 When it was time for the sacrifice to be offered, Elijah the prophet came up and prayed, "O GOD, God of Abraham, Isaac, and Israel, make it known right now that you are God in Israel, that I am your servant, and that I'm doing what I'm doing under your orders. Answer me, GOD; O answer me and reveal to this people that you are GOD, the true God, and that you are giving these people another chance at repentance."

18.38 Immediately the fire of GOD fell and burned up the offering, the wood, the stones, the dirt, and even the water in the trench.

18.39 All the people saw it happen and fell on their faces in awed worship, exclaiming, "GOD is the true God! GOD is the true God!"

18.40 Elijah told them, "Grab the Baal prophets! Don't let one get away!"

They grabbed them. Elijah had them taken down to the Brook Kishon and they massacred the lot.

18.41 Elijah said to Ahab, "Up on your feet! Eat and drink—celebrate! Rain is on the way; I hear it coming."

18.42-43 Ahab did it: got up and ate and drank. Meanwhile, Elijah climbed to the top of Carmel, bowed deeply in prayer, his face between his knees. Then he said to his young servant, "On your feet now! Look toward the sea."

He went, looked, and reported back, "I don't see a thing."

"Keep looking," said Elijah, "seven times if necessary."

18.44 And sure enough, the seventh time he said, "Oh yes, a cloud! But very small, no bigger than someone's hand, rising out of the sea."

"Quickly then, on your way. Tell Ahab, 'Saddle up and get down from the mountain before the rain stops you.'"

18.45-46 Things happened fast. The sky grew black with wind-driven clouds, and then a huge cloudburst of rain, with Ahab hightailing it in his chariot for Jezreel. And GOD strengthened Elijah mightily. Pulling up his robe and tying it around his waist, Elijah ran in front of Ahab's chariot until they reached Jezreel.

NEW INTERNATIONAL VERSION

ELIJAH FLEES TO HOREB

19 Now Ahab told Jezebel everything Elijah had done and how he had killed all the prophets with the sword. ²So Jezebel sent a messenger to Elijah to say, "May the gods deal with me, be it ever so severely, if by this time tomorrow I do not make your life like that of one of them."

³Elijah was afraid[a] and ran for his life. When he came to Beersheba in Judah, he left his servant there, ⁴while he himself went a day's journey into the desert. He came to a broom tree, sat down under it and prayed that he might die. "I have had enough, LORD," he said. "Take my life; I am no better than my ancestors." ⁵Then he lay down under the tree and fell asleep.

All at once an angel touched him and said, "Get up and eat." ⁶He looked around, and there by his head was a cake of bread baked over hot coals, and a jar of water. He ate and drank and then lay down again.

⁷The angel of the LORD came back a second time and touched him and said, "Get up and eat, for the journey is too much for you." ⁸So he got up and ate and drank. Strengthened by that food, he traveled forty days and forty nights until he reached Horeb, the mountain of God. ⁹There he went into a cave and spent the night.

THE LORD APPEARS TO ELIJAH

And the word of the LORD came to him: "What are you doing here, Elijah?"

¹⁰He replied, "I have been very zealous for the LORD God Almighty. The Israelites have rejected your covenant, broken down your altars, and put your prophets to death with the sword. I am the only one left, and now they are trying to kill me too."

¹¹The LORD said, "Go out and stand on the mountain in the presence of the LORD, for the LORD is about to pass by."

Then a great and powerful wind tore the mountains apart and shattered the rocks before the LORD, but the LORD was not in the wind. After the wind there was an earthquake, but the LORD was not in the earthquake. ¹²After the earthquake came a fire, but the LORD was not in the fire. And after the fire came a gentle whisper. ¹³When Elijah heard it, he pulled his cloak over his face and went out and stood at the mouth of the cave.

Then a voice said to him, "What are you doing here, Elijah?"

¹⁴He replied, "I have been very zealous for the LORD God Almighty. The Israelites have rejected

---

a 3 Or Elijah saw

THE MESSAGE

REVENGE FROM JEZEBEL

19 Ahab reported to Jezebel everything that Elijah had done, including the massacre of the prophets. Jezebel immediately sent a messenger to Elijah with her threat: "The gods will get you for this and I'll get even with you! By this time tomorrow you'll be as dead as any one of those prophets."

19.3-5 When Elijah saw how things were, he ran for dear life to Beersheba, far in the south of Judah. He left his young servant there and then went on into the desert another day's journey. He came to a lone broom bush and collapsed in its shade, wanting in the worst way to be done with it all—to just die: "Enough of this, GOD! Take my life—I'm ready to join my ancestors in the grave!" Exhausted, he fell asleep under the lone broom bush.

Suddenly an angel shook him awake and said, "Get up and eat!"

19.6 He looked around and, to his surprise, right by his head were a loaf of bread baked on some coals and a jug of water. He ate the meal and went back to sleep.

19.7 The angel of GOD came back, shook him awake again, and said, "Get up and eat some more—you've got a long journey ahead of you."

19.8-9 He got up, ate and drank his fill, and set out. Nourished by that meal, he walked forty days and nights, all the way to the mountain of God, to Horeb. When he got there, he crawled into a cave and went to sleep.

Then the word of GOD came to him: "So Elijah, what are you doing here?"

19.10 "I've been working my heart out for the GOD-of-the-Angel-Armies," said Elijah. "The people of Israel have abandoned your covenant, destroyed the places of worship, and murdered your prophets. I'm the only one left, and now they're trying to kill me."

19.11-12 Then he was told, "Go, stand on the mountain at attention before GOD. GOD will pass by."

A hurricane wind ripped through the mountains and shattered the rocks before GOD, but GOD wasn't to be found in the wind; after the wind an earthquake, but GOD wasn't in the earthquake; and after the earthquake fire, but GOD wasn't in the fire; and after the fire a gentle and quiet whisper.

19.13-14 When Elijah heard the quiet voice, he muffled his face with his great cloak, went to the mouth of the cave, and stood there. A quiet voice asked, "So Elijah, now tell me, what are you doing here?" Elijah said it again, "I've been working my heart out for GOD, the GOD-of-the-Angel-Armies, because the people of Israel

NEW INTERNATIONAL VERSION

your covenant, broken down your altars, and put your prophets to death with the sword. I am the only one left, and now they are trying to kill me too."

¹⁵The LORD said to him, "Go back the way you came, and go to the Desert of Damascus. When you get there, anoint Hazael king over Aram. ¹⁶Also, anoint Jehu son of Nimshi king over Israel, and anoint Elisha son of Shaphat from Abel Meholah to succeed you as prophet. ¹⁷Jehu will put to death any who escape the sword of Hazael, and Elisha will put to death any who escape the sword of Jehu. ¹⁸Yet I reserve seven thousand in Israel—all whose knees have not bowed down to Baal and all whose mouths have not kissed him."

THE CALL OF ELISHA

¹⁹So Elijah went from there and found Elisha son of Shaphat. He was plowing with twelve yoke of oxen, and he himself was driving the twelfth pair. Elijah went up to him and threw his cloak around him. ²⁰Elisha then left his oxen and ran after Elijah. "Let me kiss my father and mother good-by," he said, "and then I will come with you."

"Go back," Elijah replied. "What have I done to you?"

²¹So Elisha left him and went back. He took his yoke of oxen and slaughtered them. He burned the plowing equipment to cook the meat and gave it to the people, and they ate. Then he set out to follow Elijah and became his attendant.

BEN-HADAD ATTACKS SAMARIA

20 Now Ben-Hadad king of Aram mustered his entire army. Accompanied by thirty-two kings with their horses and chariots, he went up and besieged Samaria and attacked it. ²He sent messengers into the city to Ahab king of Israel, saying, "This is what Ben-Hadad says: ³'Your silver and gold are mine, and the best of your wives and children are mine.' "

⁴The king of Israel answered, "Just as you say, my lord the king. I and all I have are yours."

⁵The messengers came again and said, "This is what Ben-Hadad says: 'I sent to demand your silver and gold, your wives and your children. ⁶But about this time tomorrow I am going to send my officials to search your palace and the houses of your officials. They will seize everything you value and carry it away.' "

⁷The king of Israel summoned all the elders of the land and said to them, "See how this man is

THE MESSAGE

have abandoned your covenant, destroyed your places of worship, and murdered your prophets. I'm the only one left, and now they're trying to kill me."

19.15-18 GOD said, "Go back the way you came through the desert to Damascus. When you get there anoint Hazael; make him king over Aram. Then anoint Jehu son of Nimshi; make him king over Israel. Finally, anoint Elisha son of Shaphat from Abel Meholah to succeed you as prophet. Anyone who escapes death by Hazael will be killed by Jehu; and anyone who escapes death by Jehu will be killed by Elisha. Meanwhile, I'm preserving for myself seven thousand souls: the knees that haven't bowed to the god Baal, the mouths that haven't kissed his image."

19.19 Elijah went straight out and found Elisha son of Shaphat in a field where there were twelve pairs of yoked oxen at work plowing; Elisha was in charge of the twelfth pair. Elijah went up to him and threw his cloak over him.

19.20 Elisha deserted the oxen, ran after Elijah, and said, "Please! Let me kiss my father and mother good-bye—then I'll follow you."

"Go ahead," said Elijah, "but, mind you, don't forget what I've just done to you."

19.21 So Elisha left; he took his yoke of oxen and butchered them. He made a fire with the plow and tackle and then boiled the meat—a true farewell meal for the family. Then he left and followed Elijah, becoming his right-hand man.

20 At about this same time Ben-Hadad king of Aram mustered his troops. He recruited in addition thirty-two local sheiks, all outfitted with horses and chariots. He set out in force and surrounded Samaria, ready to make war. He sent an envoy into the city to set his terms before Ahab king of Israel: "Ben-Hadad lays claim to your silver and gold, and to the pick of your wives and sons."

20.4 The king of Israel accepted the terms: "As you say, distinguished lord; I and everything I have is yours."

20.5-6 But then the envoy returned a second time, saying, "On second thought, I want it all—your silver and gold and *all* your wives and sons. Hand them over—the whole works. I'll give you twenty-four hours; then my servants will arrive to search your palace and the houses of your officials and loot them; anything that strikes their fancy, they'll take."

20.7 The king of Israel called a meeting of all his tribal elders. He said, "Look at this—outra-

NEW INTERNATIONAL VERSION

looking for trouble! When he sent for my wives and my children, my silver and my gold, I did not refuse him."

⁸The elders and the people all answered, "Don't listen to him or agree to his demands."

⁹So he replied to Ben-Hadad's messengers, "Tell my lord the king, 'Your servant will do all you demanded the first time, but this demand I cannot meet.' " They left and took the answer back to Ben-Hadad.

¹⁰Then Ben-Hadad sent another message to Ahab: "May the gods deal with me, be it ever so severely, if enough dust remains in Samaria to give each of my men a handful."

¹¹The king of Israel answered, "Tell him: 'One who puts on his armor should not boast like one who takes it off.' "

¹²Ben-Hadad heard this message while he and the kings were drinking in their tents,ᵃ and he ordered his men: "Prepare to attack." So they prepared to attack the city.

AHAB DEFEATS BEN-HADAD

¹³Meanwhile a prophet came to Ahab king of Israel and announced, "This is what the LORD says: 'Do you see this vast army? I will give it into your hand today, and then you will know that I am the LORD.' "

¹⁴"But who will do this?" asked Ahab.

The prophet replied, "This is what the LORD says: 'The young officers of the provincial commanders will do it.' "

"And who will start the battle?" he asked.

The prophet answered, "You will."

¹⁵So Ahab summoned the young officers of the provincial commanders, 232 men. Then he assembled the rest of the Israelites, 7,000 in all. ¹⁶They set out at noon while Ben-Hadad and the 32 kings allied with him were in their tents getting drunk. ¹⁷The young officers of the provincial commanders went out first.

Now Ben-Hadad had dispatched scouts, who reported, "Men are advancing from Samaria."

¹⁸He said, "If they have come out for peace, take them alive; if they have come out for war, take them alive."

¹⁹The young officers of the provincial commanders marched out of the city with the army behind them ²⁰and each one struck down his opponent. At that, the Arameans fled, with the Israelites in pursuit. But Ben-Hadad king of Aram escaped on horseback with some of his horsemen. ²¹The king of Israel advanced and overpowered the horses and chariots and inflicted heavy losses on the Arameans.

ᵃ 12 Or in Succoth; also in verse 16

THE MESSAGE

geous! He's just looking for trouble. He means to clean me out, demanding all my women and children. And after I already agreed to pay him off handsomely!"

20.8 The elders, backed by the people, said, "Don't cave in to him. Don't give an inch."

20.9 So he sent an envoy to Ben-Hadad, "Tell my distinguished lord, 'I agreed to the terms you delivered the first time, but this I can't do—this I won't do!' "

The envoy went back and delivered the answer.

20.10 Ben-Hadad shot back his response: "May the gods do their worst to me, and then worse again, if there'll be anything left of Samaria but rubble."

20.11 The king of Israel countered, "Think about it—it's easier to start a fight than end one."

20.12 It happened that when Ben-Hadad heard this retort he was into some heavy drinking, boozing it up with the sheiks in their field shelters. Drunkenly, he ordered his henchmen, "Go after them!" And they attacked the city.

20.13 Just then a lone prophet approached Ahab king of Israel and said, "GOD's word: Have you taken a good look at this mob? Well, look again—I'm turning it over to you this very day. And you'll know, beyond the shadow of a doubt, that I am GOD."

20.14 Ahab said, "Really? And who is going to make this happen?"

GOD said, "The young commandos of the regional chiefs."

"And who," said Ahab, "will strike the first blow?"

GOD said, "You."

20.15 Ahab looked over the commandos of the regional chiefs; he counted 232. Then he assessed the available troops—7,000.

20.16-17 At noon they set out after Ben-Hadad who, with his allies, the thirty-two sheiks, was busy at serious drinking in the field shelters. The commandos of the regional chiefs made up the vanguard.

A report was brought to Ben-Hadad: "Men are on their way from Samaria."

20.18 He said, "If they've come in peace, take them alive as hostages; if they've come to fight, the same—take them alive as hostages."

20.19-20 The commandos poured out of the city with the full army behind them. They hit hard in hand-to-hand combat. The Arameans scattered from the field, with Israel hard on their heels. But Ben-Hadad king of Aram got away on horseback, along with his cavalry.

20.21 The king of Israel cut down both horses and chariots—an enormous defeat for Aram.

NEW INTERNATIONAL VERSION

²²Afterward, the prophet came to the king of Israel and said, "Strengthen your position and see what must be done, because next spring the king of Aram will attack you again."

²³Meanwhile, the officials of the king of Aram advised him, "Their gods are gods of the hills. That is why they were too strong for us. But if we fight them on the plains, surely we will be stronger than they. ²⁴Do this: Remove all the kings from their commands and replace them with other officers. ²⁵You must also raise an army like the one you lost—horse for horse and chariot for chariot—so we can fight Israel on the plains. Then surely we will be stronger than they." He agreed with them and acted accordingly.

²⁶The next spring Ben-Hadad mustered the Arameans and went up to Aphek to fight against Israel. ²⁷When the Israelites were also mustered and given provisions, they marched out to meet them. The Israelites camped opposite them like two small flocks of goats, while the Arameans covered the countryside.

²⁸The man of God came up and told the king of Israel, "This is what the LORD says: 'Because the Arameans think the LORD is a god of the hills and not a god of the valleys, I will deliver this vast army into your hands, and you will know that I am the LORD.' "

²⁹For seven days they camped opposite each other, and on the seventh day the battle was joined. The Israelites inflicted a hundred thousand casualties on the Aramean foot soldiers in one day. ³⁰The rest of them escaped to the city of Aphek, where the wall collapsed on twenty-seven thousand of them. And Ben-Hadad fled to the city and hid in an inner room.

³¹His officials said to him, "Look, we have heard that the kings of the house of Israel are merciful. Let us go to the king of Israel with sackcloth around our waists and ropes around our heads. Perhaps he will spare your life."

³²Wearing sackcloth around their waists and ropes around their heads, they went to the king of Israel and said, "Your servant Ben-Hadad says: 'Please let me live.' "

The king answered, "Is he still alive? He is my brother."

³³The men took this as a good sign and were quick to pick up his word. "Yes, your brother Ben-Hadad!" they said.

"Go and get him," the king said. When Ben-Hadad came out, Ahab had him come up into his chariot.

THE MESSAGE

20.22 Sometime later the prophet came to the king of Israel and said, "On the alert now—build up your army, assess your capabilities, and see what has to be done. Before the year is out, the king of Aram will be back in force."

20.23-25 Meanwhile the advisors to the king of Aram said, "Their god is a god of the mountains—we don't stand a chance against them there. So let's engage them on the plain where we'll have the advantage. Here's the strategy: Remove each sheik from his place of leadership and replace him with a seasoned officer. Then recruit a fighting force equivalent in size to the army that deserted earlier—horse for horse, chariot for chariot. And we'll fight them on the plain— we're sure to prove stronger than they are."

20.25 It sounded good to the king; he did what they advised.

20.26-27 As the new year approached, Ben-Hadad rallied Aram and they went up to Aphek to make war on Israel. The Israelite army prepared to fight and took the field to meet Aram. They moved into battle formation before Aram in two camps, like two flocks of goats. The plain was seething with Arameans.

20.28 Just then a holy man approached the king of Israel saying, "This is GOD's word: Because Aram said, 'GOD is a god of the mountains and not a god of the valleys,' I'll hand over this huge mob of an army to you. Then you'll know that I am GOD."

20.29-30 The two armies were poised in a standoff for seven days. On the seventh day fighting broke out. The Israelites killed 100,000 of the Aramean infantry in one day. The rest of the army ran for their lives back to the city, Aphek, only to have the city wall fall on 27,000 of the survivors.

20.30-31 Ben-Hadad escaped into the city and hid in a closet. Then his advisors told him, "Look, we've heard that the kings of Israel play by the rules; let's dress in old gunnysacks, carry a white flag of truce, and present ourselves to the king of Israel on the chance that he'll let you live."

20.32 So that's what they did. They dressed in old gunnysacks and carried a white flag, and came to the king of Israel saying, "Your servant Ben-Hadad said, 'Please let me live.' "

Ahab said, "You mean to tell me that he's still alive? If he's alive, he's my brother."

20.33 The men took this as a good sign and concluded that everything was going to be all right: "Ben-Hadad is most certainly your brother!"

20.33 The king said, "Go and get him." They went and brought him back by chariot.

NEW INTERNATIONAL VERSION

³⁴"I will return the cities my father took from your father," Ben-Hadad offered. "You may set up your own market areas in Damascus, as my father did in Samaria."

⌊Ahab said,⌋ "On the basis of a treaty I will set you free." So he made a treaty with him, and let him go.

A Prophet Condemns Ahab

³⁵By the word of the LORD one of the sons of the prophets said to his companion, "Strike me with your weapon," but the man refused.

³⁶So the prophet said, "Because you have not obeyed the LORD, as soon as you leave me a lion will kill you." And after the man went away, a lion found him and killed him.

³⁷The prophet found another man and said, "Strike me, please." So the man struck him and wounded him. ³⁸Then the prophet went and stood by the road waiting for the king. He disguised himself with his headband down over his eyes. ³⁹As the king passed by, the prophet called out to him, "Your servant went into the thick of the battle, and someone came to me with a captive and said, 'Guard this man. If he is missing, it will be your life for his life, or you must pay a talent*a* of silver.' ⁴⁰While your servant was busy here and there, the man disappeared."

"That is your sentence," the king of Israel said. "You have pronounced it yourself."

⁴¹Then the prophet quickly removed the headband from his eyes, and the king of Israel recognized him as one of the prophets. ⁴²He said to the king, "This is what the LORD says: 'You have set free a man I had determined should die.*b* Therefore it is your life for his life, your people for his people.' " ⁴³Sullen and angry, the king of Israel went to his palace in Samaria.

Naboth's Vineyard

21 Some time later there was an incident involving a vineyard belonging to Naboth the Jezreelite. The vineyard was in Jezreel, close to the palace of Ahab king of Samaria. ²Ahab said to Naboth, "Let me have your vineyard to use for a vegetable garden, since it is close to my palace. In exchange I will give you a better vineyard or, if you prefer, I will pay you whatever it is worth."

³But Naboth replied, "The LORD forbid that I should give you the inheritance of my fathers."

⁴So Ahab went home, sullen and angry because Naboth the Jezreelite had said, "I will not

---

^a 39 That is, about 75 pounds (about 34 kilograms)
^b 42 The Hebrew term refers to the irrevocable giving over of things or persons to the LORD, often by totally destroying them.

THE MESSAGE

20.34 Ahab said, "I am prepared to return the cities that my father took from your father. And you can set up your headquarters in Damascus just as my father did in Samaria; I'll send you home under safe conduct." Then he made a covenant with him and sent him off.

20.35 A man who was one of the prophets said to a bystander, "Hit me; wound me. Do it for GOD's sake—it's his command. Hit me; wound me." But the man wouldn't do it.

20.36 So he told him, "Because you wouldn't obey GOD's orders, as soon as you leave me a lion will attack you." No sooner had the man left his side than a lion met him and attacked.

20.37 He then found another man and said, "Hit me; wound me." That man did it—hit him hard in the face, drawing blood.

20.38-40 Then the prophet went and took a position along the road, with a bandage over his eyes, waiting for the king. It wasn't long before the king happened by. The man cried out to the king, "Your servant was in the thick of the battle when a man showed up and turned over a prisoner to me, saying, 'Guard this man with your life; if he turns up missing you'll pay dearly.' But I got busy doing one thing after another and the next time I looked he was gone."

The king of Israel said, "You've just pronounced your own verdict."

20.41 At that, the man ripped the bandage off his eyes and the king recognized who he was—one of the prophets!

20.42 The man said to the king, "GOD's word: Because you let a man go who was under sentence by GOD, it's now your life for his, your people for his."

20.43 The king of Israel went home in a sulk. He arrived in Samaria in a very bad mood.

21 And then, to top it off, came this: Naboth the Jezreelite owned a vineyard in Jezreel that bordered the palace of Ahab king of Samaria. One day Ahab spoke to Naboth, saying, "Give me your vineyard so I can use it as a kitchen garden; it's right next to my house—so convenient. In exchange I'll give you a far better vineyard, or if you'd prefer I'll pay you money for it."

21.3-4 But Naboth told Ahab, "Not on your life! So help me GOD, I'd never sell the family farm to you!" Ahab went home in a black mood, sulking over Naboth the Jezreelite's words, "I'll nev-

NEW INTERNATIONAL VERSION

give you the inheritance of my fathers." He lay on his bed sulking and refused to eat.

⁵His wife Jezebel came in and asked him, "Why are you so sullen? Why won't you eat?"

⁶He answered her, "Because I said to Naboth the Jezreelite, 'Sell me your vineyard; or if you prefer, I will give you another vineyard in its place.' But he said, 'I will not give you my vineyard.' "

⁷Jezebel his wife said, "Is this how you act as king over Israel? Get up and eat! Cheer up. I'll get you the vineyard of Naboth the Jezreelite."

⁸So she wrote letters in Ahab's name, placed his seal on them, and sent them to the elders and nobles who lived in Naboth's city with him. ⁹In those letters she wrote:

> "Proclaim a day of fasting and seat Naboth in a prominent place among the people. ¹⁰But seat two scoundrels opposite him and have them testify that he has cursed both God and the king. Then take him out and stone him to death."

¹¹So the elders and nobles who lived in Naboth's city did as Jezebel directed in the letters she had written to them. ¹²They proclaimed a fast and seated Naboth in a prominent place among the people. ¹³Then two scoundrels came and sat opposite him and brought charges against Naboth before the people, saying, "Naboth has cursed both God and the king." So they took him outside the city and stoned him to death. ¹⁴Then they sent word to Jezebel: "Naboth has been stoned and is dead."

¹⁵As soon as Jezebel heard that Naboth had been stoned to death, she said to Ahab, "Get up and take possession of the vineyard of Naboth the Jezreelite that he refused to sell you. He is no longer alive, but dead." ¹⁶When Ahab heard that Naboth was dead, he got up and went down to take possession of Naboth's vineyard.

¹⁷Then the word of the LORD came to Elijah the Tishbite: ¹⁸"Go down to meet Ahab king of Israel, who rules in Samaria. He is now in Naboth's vineyard, where he has gone to take possession of it. ¹⁹Say to him, 'This is what the LORD says: Have you not murdered a man and seized his property?' Then say to him, 'This is what the LORD says: In the place where dogs licked up Naboth's blood, dogs will lick up your blood—yes, yours!' "

²⁰Ahab said to Elijah, "So you have found me, my enemy!"

"I have found you," he answered, "because you have sold yourself to do evil in the eyes of the LORD. ²¹I am going to bring disaster on you.

THE MESSAGE

er turn over my family inheritance to you." He went to bed, stuffed his face in his pillow, and refused to eat.

21.5 Jezebel his wife came to him. She said, "What's going on? Why are you so out of sorts and refusing to eat?"

21.6 He told her, "Because I spoke to Naboth the Jezreelite. I said, 'Give me your vineyard—I'll pay you for it or, if you'd rather, I'll give you another vineyard in exchange.' And he said, 'I'll never give you my vineyard.' "

21.7 Jezebel said, "Is this any way for a king of Israel to act? Aren't you the boss? On your feet! Eat! Cheer up! I'll take care of this; I'll get the vineyard of this Naboth the Jezreelite for you."

21.8-10 She wrote letters over Ahab's signature, stamped them with his official seal, and sent them to the elders in Naboth's city and to the civic leaders. She wrote "Call for a fast day and put Naboth at the head table. Then seat a couple of stool pigeons across from him who, in front of everybody will say, 'You! You blasphemed God and the king!' Then they'll throw him out and stone him to death."

21.11-14 And they did it. The men of the city—the elders and civic leaders—followed Jezebel's instructions that she wrote in the letters sent to them. They called for a fast day and seated Naboth at the head table. Then they brought in two stool pigeons and seated them opposite Naboth. In front of everybody the two degenerates accused him, "He blasphemed God and the king!" The company threw him out in the street, stoned him mercilessly, and he died.

21.15 When Jezebel got word that Naboth had been stoned to death, she told Ahab, "Go for it, Ahab—take the vineyard of Naboth the Jezreelite for your own, the vineyard he refused to sell you. Naboth is no more; Naboth is dead."

21.16 The minute Ahab heard that Naboth was dead, he set out for the vineyard of Naboth the Jezreelite and claimed it for his own.

21.17-19 Then GOD stepped in and spoke to Elijah the Tishbite, "On your feet; go down and confront Ahab of Samaria, king of Israel. You'll find him in the vineyard of Naboth; he's gone there to claim it as his own. Say this to him: 'GOD's word: What's going on here? First murder, then theft?' Then tell him, 'GOD's verdict: The very spot where the dogs lapped up Naboth's blood, they'll lap up your blood—that's right, *your* blood.' "

21.20-22 Ahab answered Elijah, "My enemy! So, you've run me down!"

"Yes, I've found you out," said Elijah. "And because you've bought into the business of evil, defying GOD. 'I will most certainly bring doom

NEW INTERNATIONAL VERSION

I will consume your descendants and cut off from Ahab every last male in Israel—slave or free. ²²I will make your house like that of Jeroboam son of Nebat and that of Baasha son of Ahijah, because you have provoked me to anger and have caused Israel to sin.'

²³"And also concerning Jezebel the LORD says: 'Dogs will devour Jezebel by the wall of*ᵃ* Jezreel.'

²⁴"Dogs will eat those belonging to Ahab who die in the city, and the birds of the air will feed on those who die in the country."

²⁵(There was never a man like Ahab, who sold himself to do evil in the eyes of the LORD, urged on by Jezebel his wife. ²⁶He behaved in the vilest manner by going after idols, like the Amorites the LORD drove out before Israel.)

²⁷When Ahab heard these words, he tore his clothes, put on sackcloth and fasted. He lay in sackcloth and went around meekly.

²⁸Then the word of the LORD came to Elijah the Tishbite: ²⁹"Have you noticed how Ahab has humbled himself before me? Because he has humbled himself, I will not bring this disaster in his day, but I will bring it on his house in the days of his son."

MICAIAH PROPHESIES AGAINST AHAB

22 For three years there was no war between Aram and Israel. ²But in the third year Jehoshaphat king of Judah went down to see the king of Israel. ³The king of Israel had said to his officials, "Don't you know that Ramoth Gilead belongs to us and yet we are doing nothing to retake it from the king of Aram?"

⁴So he asked Jehoshaphat, "Will you go with me to fight against Ramoth Gilead?"

Jehoshaphat replied to the king of Israel, "I am as you are, my people as your people, my horses as your horses." ⁵But Jehoshaphat also said to the king of Israel, "First seek the counsel of the LORD."

⁶So the king of Israel brought together the prophets—about four hundred men—and asked them, "Shall I go to war against Ramoth Gilead, or shall I refrain?"

"Go," they answered, "for the Lord will give it into the king's hand."

⁷But Jehoshaphat asked, "Is there not a prophet of the LORD here whom we can inquire of?"

⁸The king of Israel answered Jehoshaphat, "There is still one man through whom we can

THE MESSAGE

upon you, make mincemeat of your descendants, kill off every sorry male wretch who's even remotely connected with the name Ahab. And I'll bring down on you the same fate that fell on Jeroboam son of Nebat and Baasha son of Ahijah—you've made me *that* angry by making Israel sin.' "

21.23-24 As for Jezebel, GOD said, "Dogs will fight over the flesh of Jezebel all over Jezreel. Anyone tainted by Ahab who dies in the city will be eaten by stray dogs; corpses in the country will be eaten by carrion crows."

21.25-26 Ahab, pushed by his wife Jezebel and in open defiance of GOD, set an all-time record in making big business of evil. He indulged in outrageous obscenities in the world of idols, copying the Amorites whom GOD had earlier kicked out of Israelite territory.

21.27 When Ahab heard what Elijah had to say, he ripped his clothes to shreds, dressed in penitential rough burlap, and fasted. He even slept in coarse burlap pajamas. He tiptoed around, quiet as a mouse.

21.28-29 Then GOD spoke to Elijah the Tishbite: "Do you see how penitently submissive Ahab has become to me? Because of his repentance I'll not bring the doom during his lifetime; Ahab's son, though, will get it."

22.1-3 **22** They enjoyed three years of peace—no fighting between Aram and Israel. In the third year, Jehoshaphat king of Judah had a meeting with the king of Israel. Israel's king remarked to his aides, "Do you realize that Ramoth Gilead belongs to us, and we're sitting around on our hands instead of taking it back from the king of Aram?"

22.4-5 He turned to Jehoshaphat and said, "Will you join me in fighting for Ramoth Gilead?"

Jehoshaphat said, "You bet. I'm with you all the way—my troops are your troops, my horses are your horses." He then continued, "But before you do anything, ask GOD for guidance."

22.6 The king of Israel got the prophets together—all four hundred of them—and put the question to them: "Should I attack Ramoth Gilead? Or should I hold back?"

22.6 "Go for it," they said. "GOD will hand it over to the king."

22.7 But Jehoshaphat dragged his heels: "Is there still another prophet of GOD around here we can consult?"

22.8 The king of Israel told Jehoshaphat, "As a matter of fact, there is still one such man. But I

ᵃ 23 Most Hebrew manuscripts; a few Hebrew manuscripts, Vulgate and Syriac (see also 2 Kings 9:26) *the plot of ground at*

NEW INTERNATIONAL VERSION

inquire of the LORD, but I hate him because he never prophesies anything good about me, but always bad. He is Micaiah son of Imlah."

"The king should not say that," Jehoshaphat replied.

⁹So the king of Israel called one of his officials and said, "Bring Micaiah son of Imlah at once."

¹⁰Dressed in their royal robes, the king of Israel and Jehoshaphat king of Judah were sitting on their thrones at the threshing floor by the entrance of the gate of Samaria, with all the prophets prophesying before them. ¹¹Now Zedekiah son of Kenaanah had made iron horns and he declared, "This is what the LORD says: 'With these you will gore the Arameans until they are destroyed.'"

¹²All the other prophets were prophesying the same thing. "Attack Ramoth Gilead and be victorious," they said, "for the LORD will give it into the king's hand."

¹³The messenger who had gone to summon Micaiah said to him, "Look, as one man the other prophets are predicting success for the king. Let your word agree with theirs, and speak favorably."

¹⁴But Micaiah said, "As surely as the LORD lives, I can tell him only what the LORD tells me."

¹⁵When he arrived, the king asked him, "Micaiah, shall we go to war against Ramoth Gilead, or shall I refrain?"

"Attack and be victorious," he answered, "for the LORD will give it into the king's hand."

¹⁶The king said to him, "How many times must I make you swear to tell me nothing but the truth in the name of the LORD?"

¹⁷Then Micaiah answered, "I saw all Israel scattered on the hills like sheep without a shepherd, and the LORD said, 'These people have no master. Let each one go home in peace.'"

¹⁸The king of Israel said to Jehoshaphat, "Didn't I tell you that he never prophesies anything good about me, but only bad?"

¹⁹Micaiah continued, "Therefore hear the word of the LORD: I saw the LORD sitting on his throne with all the host of heaven standing around him on his right and on his left. ²⁰And the LORD said, 'Who will entice Ahab into attacking Ramoth Gilead and going to his death there?'

"One suggested this, and another that. ²¹Finally, a spirit came forward, stood before the LORD and said, 'I will entice him.'

²²"'By what means?' the LORD asked.

THE MESSAGE

hate him. He never preaches anything good to me, only doom, doom, doom—Micaiah son of Imlah."

22.9 "The king shouldn't talk about a prophet like that," said Jehoshaphat.

So the king of Israel ordered one of his men, "On the double! Get Micaiah son of Imlah."

22.10-12 Meanwhile, the king of Israel and Jehoshaphat were seated on their thrones, dressed in their royal robes, resplendent in front of the Samaria city gates. All the prophets were staging a prophecy-performance for their benefit. Zedekiah son of Kenaanah had even made a set of iron horns, and brandishing them called out, "GOD's word! With these horns you'll gore Aram until there's nothing left of him!" All the prophets chimed in, "Yes! Go for Ramoth Gilead! An easy victory! GOD's gift to the king!"

22.13 The messenger who went to get Micaiah said, "The prophets have all said Yes to the king. Make it unanimous—vote Yes!"

22.14 But Micaiah said, "As surely as GOD lives, what GOD says, I'll say."

22.15 With Micaiah before him, the king asked him, "So Micaiah—do we attack Ramoth Gilead, or do we hold back?"

"Go ahead," he said. "An easy victory. GOD's gift to the king."

22.16 "Not so fast," said the king. "How many times have I made you promise under oath to tell me the truth and nothing but the truth?"

22.17 "All right," said Micaiah, "since you insist.

I saw all of Israel scattered over the hills,
    sheep with no shepherd.
Then GOD spoke: 'These poor people
    have no one to tell them what to do.
Let them go home and do
    the best they can for themselves.'"

22.18 Then the king of Israel turned to Jehoshaphat, "See! What did I tell you? He never has a good word for me from GOD, only doom."

22.19-23 Micaiah kept on: "I'm not done yet; listen to GOD's word:

I saw GOD enthroned,
    and all the angel armies of heaven
Standing at attention
    ranged on his right and his left.
And GOD said, 'How can we seduce Ahab
    into attacking Ramoth Gilead?'
Some said this,
    and some said that.
Then a bold angel stepped out,
    stood before GOD, and said,
'I'll seduce him.'
    'And how will you do it?' said GOD.
'Easy,' said the angel,

NEW INTERNATIONAL VERSION

" 'I will go out and be a lying spirit in the mouths of all his prophets,' he said.

" 'You will succeed in enticing him,' said the Lord. 'Go and do it.'

²³"So now the Lord has put a lying spirit in the mouths of all these prophets of yours. The Lord has decreed disaster for you."

²⁴Then Zedekiah son of Kenaanah went up and slapped Micaiah in the face. "Which way did the spirit from*ᵃ* the Lord go when he went from me to speak to you?" he asked.

²⁵Micaiah replied, "You will find out on the day you go to hide in an inner room."

²⁶The king of Israel then ordered, "Take Micaiah and send him back to Amon the ruler of the city and to Joash the king's son ²⁷and say, 'This is what the king says: Put this fellow in prison and give him nothing but bread and water until I return safely.' "

²⁸Micaiah declared, "If you ever return safely, the Lord has not spoken through me." Then he added, "Mark my words, all you people!"

Ahab Killed at Ramoth Gilead

²⁹So the king of Israel and Jehoshaphat king of Judah went up to Ramoth Gilead. ³⁰The king of Israel said to Jehoshaphat, "I will enter the bat-tle in disguise, but you wear your royal robes." So the king of Israel disguised himself and went into battle.

³¹Now the king of Aram had ordered his thirty-two chariot commanders, "Do not fight with anyone, small or great, except the king of Israel." ³²When the chariot commanders saw Jehoshaphat, they thought, "Surely this is the king of Israel." So they turned to attack him, but when Jehoshaphat cried out, ³³the chariot commanders saw that he was not the king of Israel and stopped pursuing him.

³⁴But someone drew his bow at random and hit the king of Israel between the sections of his armor. The king told his chariot driver, "Wheel around and get me out of the fighting. I've been wounded." ³⁵All day long the battle raged, and the king was propped up in his chariot facing the Arameans. The blood from his wound ran onto the floor of the chariot, and that evening he died. ³⁶As the sun was setting, a cry spread through the army: "Every man to his town; everyone to his land!"

³⁷So the king died and was brought to Samaria, and they buried him there. ³⁸They washed the chariot at a pool in Samaria (where the prostitutes bathed),*ᵇ* and the dogs licked up his blood, as the word of the Lord had declared.

THE MESSAGE

'I'll get all the prophets to lie.'
'That should do it,' said God.
'On your way—seduce him!'

"And that's what has happened. God filled the mouths of your puppet prophets with seductive lies. God has pronounced your doom."

22.24 Just then Zedekiah son of Kenaanah came up and punched Micaiah in the nose, saying, "Since when did the Spirit of God leave me and take up with you?"

22.25 Micaiah said, "You'll know soon enough; you'll know it when you're frantically and futilely looking for a place to hide."

22.26-27 The king of Israel had heard enough: "Get Micaiah out of here! Turn him over to Amon the city magistrate and to Joash the king's son with this message, 'King's orders: Lock him up in jail; keep him on bread and water until I'm back in one piece.' "

22.28 Micaiah said, "If you ever get back in one piece, I'm no prophet of God."

He added, "When it happens, O people, remember where you heard it!"

22.29-30 The king of Israel and Jehoshaphat king of Judah attacked Ramoth Gilead. The king of Israel said to Jehoshaphat, "Wear my kingly robe; I'm going into battle disguised." So the king of Israel entered the battle in disguise.

22.31 Meanwhile, the king of Aram had ordered his chariot commanders (there were thirty-two of them): "Don't bother with anyone, whether small or great; go after the king of Israel and him only."

22.32-33 When the chariot commanders saw Jehoshaphat they said, "There he is! The king of Israel!" and took after him. Jehoshaphat yelled out, and the chariot commanders realized they had the wrong man—it wasn't the king of Israel after all. They let him go.

22.34 Just then someone, without aiming, shot an arrow randomly into the crowd and hit the king of Israel in the chink of his armor. The king told his charioteer, "Turn back! Get me out of here—I'm wounded."

22.35-37 All day the fighting continued, hot and heavy. Propped up in his chariot, the king watched from the sidelines. He died that evening. Blood from his wound pooled in the chariot. As the sun went down, shouts reverberated through the ranks, "Abandon camp! Head for home! The king is dead!"

22.37-38 The king was brought to Samaria and there they buried him. They washed down the chariot at the pool of Samaria where the town whores bathed, and the dogs lapped up the blood, just as God's word had said.

ᵃ 24 Or *Spirit of*   *ᵇ* 38 Or *Samaria and cleaned the weapons*

NEW INTERNATIONAL VERSION

³⁹As for the other events of Ahab's reign, including all he did, the palace he built and inlaid with ivory, and the cities he fortified, are they not written in the book of the annals of the kings of Israel? ⁴⁰Ahab rested with his fathers. And Ahaziah his son succeeded him as king.

JEHOSHAPHAT KING OF JUDAH

⁴¹Jehoshaphat son of Asa became king of Judah in the fourth year of Ahab king of Israel. ⁴²Jehoshaphat was thirty-five years old when he became king, and he reigned in Jerusalem twenty-five years. His mother's name was Azubah daughter of Shilhi. ⁴³In everything he walked in the ways of his father Asa and did not stray from them; he did what was right in the eyes of the LORD. The high places, however, were not removed, and the people continued to offer sacrifices and burn incense there. ⁴⁴Jehoshaphat was also at peace with the king of Israel.

⁴⁵As for the other events of Jehoshaphat's reign, the things he achieved and his military exploits, are they not written in the book of the annals of the kings of Judah? ⁴⁶He rid the land of the rest of the male shrine prostitutes who remained there even after the reign of his father Asa. ⁴⁷There was then no king in Edom; a deputy ruled.

⁴⁸Now Jehoshaphat built a fleet of trading ships*a* to go to Ophir for gold, but they never set sail—they were wrecked at Ezion Geber. ⁴⁹At that time Ahaziah son of Ahab said to Jehoshaphat, "Let my men sail with your men," but Jehoshaphat refused.

⁵⁰Then Jehoshaphat rested with his fathers and was buried with them in the city of David his father. And Jehoram his son succeeded him.

AHAZIAH KING OF ISRAEL

⁵¹Ahaziah son of Ahab became king of Israel in Samaria in the seventeenth year of Jehoshaphat king of Judah, and he reigned over Israel two years. ⁵²He did evil in the eyes of the LORD, because he walked in the ways of his father and mother and in the ways of Jeroboam son of Nebat, who caused Israel to sin. ⁵³He served and worshiped Baal and provoked the LORD, the God of Israel, to anger, just as his father had done.

THE MESSAGE

22.39-40 The rest of Ahab's life—everything he did, the ivory palace he built, the towns he founded, and the defense system he built up—is all written up in *The Chronicles of the Kings of Israel.* He was buried in the family cemetery and his son Ahaziah was the next king.

JEHOSHAPHAT OF JUDAH

22.41-44 Jehoshaphat son of Asa became king of Judah in the fourth year of Ahab king of Israel. Jehoshaphat was thirty-five years old when he became king and he ruled for twenty-five years in Jerusalem. His mother was Azubah daughter of Shilhi. He continued the kind of life characteristic of his father Asa—no detours, no dead ends—pleasing GOD with his life. But he failed to get rid of the neighborhood sex-and-religion shrines. People continued to pray and worship at these idolatrous shrines. And he kept on good terms with the king of Israel.

22.45-46 The rest of Jehoshaphat's life, his achievements and his battles, is all written in *The Chronicles of the Kings of Judah.* Also, he got rid of the sacred prostitutes left over from the days of his father Asa.

22.47 Edom was kingless during his reign; a deputy was in charge.

22.48-49 Jehoshaphat built ocean-going ships to sail to Ophir for gold. But they never made it; they shipwrecked at Ezion Geber. During that time Ahaziah son of Ahab proposed a joint shipping venture, but Jehoshaphat wouldn't go in with him.

22.50 Then Jehoshaphat died and was buried in the family cemetery in the City of David his ancestor. Jehoram his son was the next king.

AHAZIAH OF ISRAEL

22.51-53 Ahaziah son of Ahab became king over Israel in Samaria in the seventeenth year of Jehoshaphat king of Judah. He ruled Israel for two years. As far as GOD was concerned, he lived an evil life, reproducing the bad life of his father and mother, repeating the pattern set down by Jeroboam son of Nebat, who led Israel into a life of sin. Worshiping at the Baal shrines, he made GOD, the God of Israel, angry, oh, so angry. If anything, he was worse than his father.

---

a 48 Hebrew *of ships of Tarshish*

2 KINGS

2 KINGS

THE LORD'S JUDGMENT ON AHAZIAH

1 After Ahab's death, Moab rebelled against Israel. ²Now Ahaziah had fallen through the lattice of his upper room in Samaria and injured himself. So he sent messengers, saying to them, "Go and consult Baal-Zebub, the god of Ekron, to see if I will recover from this injury."

³But the angel of the LORD said to Elijah the Tishbite, "Go up and meet the messengers of the king of Samaria and ask them, 'Is it because there is no God in Israel that you are going off to consult Baal-Zebub, the god of Ekron?' ⁴Therefore this is what the LORD says: 'You will not leave the bed you are lying on. You will certainly die!' " So Elijah went.

⁵When the messengers returned to the king, he asked them, "Why have you come back?"

⁶"A man came to meet us," they replied. "And he said to us, 'Go back to the king who sent you and tell him, "This is what the LORD says: Is it because there is no God in Israel that you are sending men to consult Baal-Zebub, the god of Ekron? Therefore you will not leave the bed you are lying on. You will certainly die!" ' "

⁷The king asked them, "What kind of man was it who came to meet you and told you this?"

⁸They replied, "He was a man with a garment of hair and with a leather belt around his waist."

The king said, "That was Elijah the Tishbite."

⁹Then he sent to Elijah a captain with his company of fifty men. The captain went up to Elijah, who was sitting on the top of a hill, and said to him, "Man of God, the king says, 'Come down!' "

¹⁰Elijah answered the captain, "If I am a man of God, may fire come down from heaven and consume you and your fifty men!" Then fire fell from heaven and consumed the captain and his men.

¹¹At this the king sent to Elijah another captain with his fifty men. The captain said to him, "Man of God, this is what the king says, 'Come down at once!' "

¹²"If I am a man of God," Elijah replied, "may

1 After Ahab died, Moab rebelled against Israel.

1.1

1.2 One day Ahaziah fell through the balcony railing on the rooftop of his house in Samaria and was injured. He sent messengers off to consult Baal-Zebub, the god of Ekron, "Am I going to recover from this accident?"

1.3-4 GOD's angel spoke to Elijah the Tishbite: "Up on your feet! Go out and meet the messengers of the king of Samaria with this word, 'Is it because there's no God in Israel that you're running off to consult Baal-Zebub god of Ekron?' Here's a message from the GOD you've tried to bypass: 'You're not going to get out of that bed you're in—you're as good as dead already.' " Elijah delivered the message and was gone.

1.5 The messengers went back. The king said, "So why are you back so soon—what's going on?"

1.6 They told him, "A man met us and said, 'Turn around and go back to the king who sent you; tell him, GOD's message: Is it because there's no God in Israel that you're running off to consult Baal-Zebub god of Ekron? You needn't bother. You're not going to get out of that bed you're in—you're as good as dead already.' "

1.7 The king said, "Tell me more about this man who met you and said these things to you. What was he like?"

1.8 "Shaggy," they said, "and wearing a leather belt."

He said, "That has to be Elijah the Tishbite!"

1.9 The king sent a captain with fifty men to Elijah. Meanwhile Elijah was sitting, big as life, on top of a hill. The captain said, "O Holy Man! King's orders: Come down!"

1.10 Elijah answered the captain of the fifty, "If it's true that I'm a 'holy man,' lightning strike you and your fifty men!" Out of the blue lightning struck and incinerated the captain and his fifty.

1.11 The king sent another captain with his fifty men, "O Holy Man! King's orders: Come down. And right now!"

1.12 Elijah answered, "If it's true that I'm a 'holy

NEW INTERNATIONAL VERSION

fire come down from heaven and consume you and your fifty men!" Then the fire of God fell from heaven and consumed him and his fifty men.

¹³So the king sent a third captain with his fifty men. This third captain went up and fell on his knees before Elijah. "Man of God," he begged, "please have respect for my life and the lives of these fifty men, your servants! ¹⁴See, fire has fallen from heaven and consumed the first two captains and all their men. But now have respect for my life!"

¹⁵The angel of the LORD said to Elijah, "Go down with him; do not be afraid of him." So Elijah got up and went down with him to the king.

¹⁶He told the king, "This is what the LORD says: Is it because there is no God in Israel for you to consult that you have sent messengers to consult Baal-Zebub, the god of Ekron? Because you have done this, you will never leave the bed you are lying on. You will certainly die!" ¹⁷So he died, according to the word of the LORD that Elijah had spoken.

Because Ahaziah had no son, Joram ᵃ succeeded him as king in the second year of Jehoram son of Jehoshaphat king of Judah. ¹⁸As for all the other events of Ahaziah's reign, and what he did, are they not written in the book of the annals of the kings of Israel?

ELIJAH TAKEN UP TO HEAVEN

2 When the LORD was about to take Elijah up to heaven in a whirlwind, Elijah and Elisha were on their way from Gilgal. ²Elijah said to Elisha, "Stay here; the LORD has sent me to Bethel."

But Elisha said, "As surely as the LORD lives and as you live, I will not leave you." So they went down to Bethel.

³The company of the prophets at Bethel came out to Elisha and asked, "Do you know that the LORD is going to take your master from you today?"

"Yes, I know," Elisha replied, "but do not speak of it."

⁴Then Elijah said to him, "Stay here, Elisha; the LORD has sent me to Jericho."

And he replied, "As surely as the LORD lives and as you live, I will not leave you." So they went to Jericho.

⁵The company of the prophets at Jericho went up to Elisha and asked him, "Do you know that the LORD is going to take your master from you today?"

"Yes, I know," he replied, "but do not speak of it."

⁶Then Elijah said to him, "Stay here; the LORD has sent me to the Jordan."

THE MESSAGE

man,' lightning strike you and your fifty men!" Immediately a divine lightning bolt struck and incinerated the captain and his fifty.

1.13-14 The king then sent a third captain with his fifty men. For a third time, a captain with his fifty approached Elijah. This one fell on his knees in supplication: "O Holy Man, have respect for my life and the souls of these fifty men! Twice now lightning from out of the blue has struck and incinerated captains with their fifty men; please, I beg you, respect my life!"

1.15 The angel of GOD told Elijah, "Go ahead; and don't be afraid." Elijah got up and went down with him to the king.

1.16 Elijah told him, "GOD's word: Because you sent messengers to consult Baal-Zebub the god of Ekron, as if there were no God in Israel to whom you could pray, you'll never get out of that bed alive—already you're as good as dead."

1.17 And he died, exactly as GOD's word spoken by Elijah had said.

1.17 Because Ahaziah had no son, his brother Joram became the next king. The succession took place in the second year of the reign of Jehoram son of Jehoshaphat king of Judah.

1.18 The rest of Ahaziah's life is recorded in *The Chronicles of the Kings of Israel.*

2.1-2 **2** Just before GOD took Elijah to heaven in a whirlwind, Elijah and Elisha were on a walk out of Gilgal. Elijah said to Elisha, "Stay here. GOD has sent me on an errand to Bethel."

Elisha said, "Not on your life! I'm not letting you out of my sight!" So they both went to Bethel.

2.3 The guild of prophets at Bethel met Elisha and said, "Did you know that GOD is going to take your master away from you today?"

"Yes," he said, "I know it. But keep it quiet."

2.4 Then Elijah said to Elisha, "Stay here. GOD has sent me on an errand to Jericho."

Elisha said, "Not on your life! I'm not letting you out of my sight!" So they both went to Jericho.

2.5 The guild of prophets at Jericho came to Elisha and said, "Did you know that GOD is going to take your master away from you today?"

"Yes," he said, "I know it. But keep it quiet."

2.6 Then Elijah said to Elisha, "Stay here. GOD has sent me on an errand to the Jordan."

ᵃ 17 Hebrew *Jehoram,* a variant of *Joram*

NEW INTERNATIONAL VERSION

And he replied, "As surely as the LORD lives and as you live, I will not leave you." So the two of them walked on.

⁷Fifty men of the company of the prophets went and stood at a distance, facing the place where Elijah and Elisha had stopped at the Jordan. ⁸Elijah took his cloak, rolled it up and struck the water with it. The water divided to the right and to the left, and the two of them crossed over on dry ground.

⁹When they had crossed, Elijah said to Elisha, "Tell me, what can I do for you before I am taken from you?"

"Let me inherit a double portion of your spirit," Elisha replied.

¹⁰"You have asked a difficult thing," Elijah said, "yet if you see me when I am taken from you, it will be yours—otherwise not."

¹¹As they were walking along and talking together, suddenly a chariot of fire and horses of fire appeared and separated the two of them, and Elijah went up to heaven in a whirlwind. ¹²Elisha saw this and cried out, "My father! My father! The chariots and horsemen of Israel!" And Elisha saw him no more. Then he took hold of his own clothes and tore them apart.

¹³He picked up the cloak that had fallen from Elijah and went back and stood on the bank of the Jordan. ¹⁴Then he took the cloak that had fallen from him and struck the water with it. "Where now is the LORD, the God of Elijah?" he asked. When he struck the water, it divided to the right and to the left, and he crossed over.

¹⁵The company of the prophets from Jericho, who were watching, said, "The spirit of Elijah is resting on Elisha." And they went to meet him and bowed to the ground before him. ¹⁶"Look," they said, "we your servants have fifty able men. Let them go and look for your master. Perhaps the Spirit of the LORD has picked him up and set him down on some mountain or in some valley."

"No," Elisha replied, "do not send them."

¹⁷But they persisted until he was too ashamed to refuse. So he said, "Send them." And they sent fifty men, who searched for three days but did not find him. ¹⁸When they returned to Elisha, who was staying in Jericho, he said to them, "Didn't I tell you not to go?"

HEALING OF THE WATER

¹⁹The men of the city said to Elisha, "Look, our lord, this town is well situated, as you can see, but the water is bad and the land is unproductive."

²⁰"Bring me a new bowl," he said, "and put salt in it." So they brought it to him.

²¹Then he went out to the spring and threw

THE MESSAGE

Elisha said, "Not on your life! I'm not letting you out of my sight!" And so the two of them went their way together.

2.7 Meanwhile, fifty men from the guild of prophets gathered some distance away while the two of them stood at the Jordan.

2.8 Elijah took his cloak, rolled it up, and hit the water with it. The river divided and the two men walked through on dry land.

2.9 When they reached the other side, Elijah said to Elisha, "What can I do for you before I'm taken from you? Ask anything."

Elisha said, "Your life repeated in my life. I want to be a holy man just like you."

2.10 "That's a hard one!" said Elijah. "But if you're watching when I'm taken from you, you'll get what you've asked for. But only if you're watching."

2.11-14 And so it happened. They were walking along and talking. Suddenly a chariot and horses of fire came between them and Elijah went up in a whirlwind to heaven. Elisha saw it all and shouted, "My father, my father! You—the chariot and cavalry of Israel!" When he could no longer see anything, he grabbed his robe and ripped it to pieces. Then he picked up Elijah's cloak that had fallen from him, returned to the shore of the Jordan, and stood there. He took Elijah's cloak—all that was left of Elijah!—and hit the river with it, saying, "Now where is the GOD of Elijah? Where is he?"

When he struck the water, the river divided and Elisha walked through.

2.15 The guild of prophets from Jericho saw the whole thing from where they were standing. They said, "The spirit of Elijah lives in Elisha!" They welcomed and honored him.

2.16 They then said, "We're at your service. We have fifty reliable men here; let's send them out to look for your master. Maybe GOD's spirit has swept him off to some mountain or dropped him into a remote ravine."

Elisha said, "No. Don't send them."

2.17 But they pestered him until he caved in: "Go ahead then. Send them."

So they sent the fifty men off. For three days they looked, searching high and low. Nothing.

2.18 Finally, they returned to Elisha in Jericho. He told them, "So there—didn't I tell you?"

2.19 One day the men of the city said to Elisha, "You can see for yourself, master, how well our city is located. But the water is polluted and nothing grows."

2.20 He said, "Bring me a brand-new bowl and put some salt in it." They brought it to him.

2.21-22 He then went to the spring, sprinkled the

NEW INTERNATIONAL VERSION

the salt into it, saying, "This is what the LORD says: 'I have healed this water. Never again will it cause death or make the land unproductive.' " ²²And the water has remained wholesome to this day, according to the word Elisha had spoken.

ELISHA IS JEERED

²³From there Elisha went up to Bethel. As he was walking along the road, some youths came out of the town and jeered at him. "Go on up, you baldhead!" they said. "Go on up, you baldhead!" ²⁴He turned around, looked at them and called down a curse on them in the name of the LORD. Then two bears came out of the woods and mauled forty-two of the youths. ²⁵And he went on to Mount Carmel and from there returned to Samaria.

MOAB REVOLTS

3 Joram^a son of Ahab became king of Israel in Samaria in the eighteenth year of Jehoshaphat king of Judah, and he reigned twelve years. ²He did evil in the eyes of the LORD, but not as his father and mother had done. He got rid of the sacred stone of Baal that his father had made. ³Nevertheless he clung to the sins of Jeroboam son of Nebat, which he had caused Israel to commit; he did not turn away from them.

⁴Now Mesha king of Moab raised sheep, and he had to supply the king of Israel with a hundred thousand lambs and with the wool of a hundred thousand rams. ⁵But after Ahab died, the king of Moab rebelled against the king of Israel. ⁶So at that time King Joram set out from Samaria and mobilized all Israel. ⁷He also sent this message to Jehoshaphat king of Judah: "The king of Moab has rebelled against me. Will you go with me to fight against Moab?"

"I will go with you," he replied. "I am as you are, my people as your people, my horses as your horses."

⁸"By what route shall we attack?" he asked.

"Through the Desert of Edom," he answered.

⁹So the king of Israel set out with the king of Judah and the king of Edom. After a roundabout march of seven days, the army had no more water for themselves or for the animals with them.

¹⁰"What!" exclaimed the king of Israel. "Has the LORD called us three kings together only to hand us over to Moab?"

¹¹But Jehoshaphat asked, "Is there no prophet of the LORD here, that we may inquire of the LORD through him?"

An officer of the king of Israel answered, "Eli-

^a 1 Hebrew *Jehoram*, a variant of *Joram*; also in verse 6

THE MESSAGE

salt into it, and proclaimed, "GOD's word: I've healed this water. It will no longer kill you or poison your land." And sure enough, the water was healed—and remains so to this day, just as Elisha said.

2.23 Another time, Elisha was on his way to Bethel and some little kids came out from the town and taunted him, "What's up, old baldhead! Out of our way, skinhead!"

2.24 Elisha turned, took one look at them, and cursed them in the name of GOD. Two bears charged out of the underbrush and knocked them about, ripping them limb from limb—forty-two children in all!

2.25 Elisha went on to Mount Carmel, and then returned to Samaria.

JORAM OF ISRAEL

3.1-3 **3** Joram son of Ahab began his rule over Israel in Samaria in the eighteenth year of Jehoshaphat king of Judah. He was king for twelve years. In GOD's sight he was a bad king. But he wasn't as bad as his father and mother—to his credit he destroyed the obscene Baal stone that his father had made. But he hung on to the sinful practices of Jeroboam son of Nebat, the ones that had corrupted Israel for so long. He wasn't about to give them up.

3.4-7 King Mesha of Moab raised sheep. He was forced to give the king of Israel one hundred thousand lambs and another hundred thousand rams. When Ahab died, the king of Moab rebelled against the king of Israel. So King Joram set out from Samaria and prepared Israel for war. His first move was to send a message to Jehoshaphat king of Judah: "The king of Moab has rebelled against me. Would you join me and fight him?"

3.7-8 "I'm with you all the way," said Jehoshaphat. "My troops are your troops, my horses are your horses. Which route shall we take?"

"Through the badlands of Edom."

3.9 The king of Israel, the king of Judah, and the king of Edom started out on what proved to be a looping detour. After seven days they had run out of water for both army and animals.

3.10 The king of Israel said, "Bad news! GOD has gotten us three kings out here to dump us into the hand of Moab."

3.11 But Jehoshaphat said, "Isn't there a prophet of GOD anywhere around through whom we can consult GOD?"

One of the servants of the king of Israel said,

NEW INTERNATIONAL VERSION

sha son of Shaphat is here. He used to pour water on the hands of Elijah. *a*"

¹²Jehoshaphat said, "The word of the LORD is with him." So the king of Israel and Jehoshaphat and the king of Edom went down to him.

¹³Elisha said to the king of Israel, "What do we have to do with each other? Go to the prophets of your father and the prophets of your mother."

"No," the king of Israel answered, "because it was the LORD who called us three kings together to hand us over to Moab."

¹⁴Elisha said, "As surely as the LORD Almighty lives, whom I serve, if I did not have respect for the presence of Jehoshaphat king of Judah, I would not look at you or even notice you. ¹⁵But now bring me a harpist."

While the harpist was playing, the hand of the LORD came upon Elisha ¹⁶and he said, "This is what the LORD says: Make this valley full of ditches. ¹⁷For this is what the LORD says: You will see neither wind nor rain, yet this valley will be filled with water, and you, your cattle and your other animals will drink. ¹⁸This is an easy thing in the eyes of the LORD; he will also hand Moab over to you. ¹⁹You will overthrow every fortified city and every major town. You will cut down every good tree, stop up all the springs, and ruin every good field with stones."

²⁰The next morning, about the time for offering the sacrifice, there it was—water flowing from the direction of Edom! And the land was filled with water.

²¹Now all the Moabites had heard that the kings had come to fight against them; so every man, young and old, who could bear arms was called up and stationed on the border. ²²When they got up early in the morning, the sun was shining on the water. To the Moabites across the way, the water looked red—like blood. ²³"That's blood!" they said. "Those kings must have fought and slaughtered each other. Now to the plunder, Moab!"

²⁴But when the Moabites came to the camp of Israel, the Israelites rose up and fought them until they fled. And the Israelites invaded the land and slaughtered the Moabites. ²⁵They destroyed the towns, and each man threw a stone on every good field until it was covered. They stopped up all the springs and cut down every good tree. Only Kir Hareseth was left with its stones in place, but men armed with slings surrounded it and attacked it as well.

²⁶When the king of Moab saw that the battle had gone against him, he took with him seven hundred swordsmen to break through to the

---

a 11 That is, he was Elijah's personal servant.

THE MESSAGE

"Elisha son of Shaphat is around somewhere— the one who was Elijah's right-hand man."

3.12   Jehoshaphat said, "Good! A man we can trust!" So the three of them—the king of Israel, Jehoshaphat, and the king of Edom—went to meet him.

3.13   Elisha addressed the king of Israel, "What do you and I have in common? Go consult the puppet-prophets of your father and mother."

"Never!" said the king of Israel. "It's GOD who has gotten us into this fix, dumping all three of us kings into the hand of Moab."

3.14-15   Elisha said, "As GOD-of-the-Angel-Armies lives, and before whom I stand ready to serve, if it weren't for the respect I have for Jehoshaphat king of Judah, I wouldn't give you the time of day. But considering—bring me a minstrel." (When a minstrel played, the power of GOD came on Elisha.)

3.16-19   He then said, "GOD's word: Dig ditches all over this valley. Here's what will happen—you won't hear the wind, you won't see the rain, but this valley is going to fill up with water and your army and your animals will drink their fill. This is easy for GOD to do; he will also hand over Moab to you. You will ravage the country: Knock out its fortifications, level the key villages, clear-cut the orchards, clog the springs, and litter the cultivated fields with stones."

3.20   In the morning—it was at the hour of morning sacrifice—the water had arrived, water pouring in from the west, from Edom, a flash-flood filling the valley with water.

3.21-22   By this time everyone in Moab had heard that the kings had come up to make war against them. Everyone who was able to handle a sword was called into service and took a stand at the border. They were up and ready early in the morning when the sun rose over the water. From where the Moabites stood, the water reflecting the sun looked red, like blood.

3.23   "Blood! Look at the blood!" they said. "The kings must have fought each other—a bloody massacre! Go for the loot, Moab!"

3.24-25   When Moab entered the camp of Israel, the Israelites were up on their feet killing Moabites right and left, the Moabites running for their lives, Israelites relentless in pursuit—a slaughter. They leveled the towns, littered the cultivated fields with rocks, clogged the springs, and clear-cut the orchards. Only the capital, Kir Hareseth, was left intact, and that not for long; it too was surrounded and attacked with thrown and flung rocks.

3.26-27   When the king of Moab realized that he was fighting a losing battle, he took seven hundred swordsmen to hack a corridor past the king of

NEW INTERNATIONAL VERSION

king of Edom, but they failed. ²⁷Then he took his firstborn son, who was to succeed him as king, and offered him as a sacrifice on the city wall. The fury against Israel was great; they withdrew and returned to their own land.

THE WIDOW'S OIL

4 The wife of a man from the company of the prophets cried out to Elisha, "Your servant my husband is dead, and you know that he revered the LORD. But now his creditor is coming to take my two boys as his slaves."

²Elisha replied to her, "How can I help you? Tell me, what do you have in your house?"

"Your servant has nothing there at all," she said, "except a little oil."

³Elisha said, "Go around and ask all your neighbors for empty jars. Don't ask for just a few. ⁴Then go inside and shut the door behind you and your sons. Pour oil into all the jars, and as each is filled, put it to one side."

⁵She left him and afterward shut the door behind her and her sons. They brought the jars to her and she kept pouring. ⁶When all the jars were full, she said to her son, "Bring me another one."

But he replied, "There is not a jar left." Then the oil stopped flowing.

⁷She went and told the man of God, and he said, "Go, sell the oil and pay your debts. You and your sons can live on what is left."

THE SHUNAMMITE'S SON RESTORED TO LIFE

⁸One day Elisha went to Shunem. And a well-to-do woman was there, who urged him to stay for a meal. So whenever he came by, he stopped there to eat. ⁹She said to her husband, "I know that this man who often comes our way is a holy man of God. ¹⁰Let's make a small room on the roof and put in it a bed and a table, a chair and a lamp for him. Then he can stay there whenever he comes to us."

¹¹One day when Elisha came, he went up to his room and lay down there. ¹²He said to his servant Gehazi, "Call the Shunammite." So he called her, and she stood before him. ¹³Elisha said to him, "Tell her, 'You have gone to all this trouble for us. Now what can be done for you? Can we speak on your behalf to the king or the commander of the army?'"

THE MESSAGE

Edom, but they didn't make it. Then he took his son, his firstborn who would succeed him as king, and sacrificed him on the city wall. That set off furious anger against Israel. Israel pulled back and returned home.

4.1 4 One day the wife of a man from the guild of prophets called out to Elisha, "Your servant my husband is dead. You well know what a good man he was, devoted to GOD. And now the man to whom he was in debt is on his way to collect by taking my two children as slaves."

4.2 Elisha said, "I wonder how I can be of help. Tell me, what do you have in your house?"

"Nothing," she said. "Well, I do have a little oil."

4.3-4 "Here's what you do," said Elisha. "Go up and down the street and borrow jugs and bowls from all your neighbors. And not just a few—all you can get. Then come home and lock the door behind you, you and your sons. Pour oil into each container; when each is full, set it aside."

4.5-6 She did what he said. She locked the door behind her and her sons; as they brought the containers to her, she filled them. When all the jugs and bowls were full, she said to one of her sons, "Another jug, please."

He said, "That's it. There are no more jugs." Then the oil stopped.

4.7 She went and told the story to the man of God. He said, "Go sell the oil and make good on your debts. Live, both you and your sons, on what's left."

⁜

4.8 One day Elisha passed through Shunem. A leading lady of the town talked him into stopping for a meal. And then it became his custom: Whenever he passed through, he stopped by for a meal.

4.9-10 "I'm certain," said the woman to her husband, "that this man who stops by with us all the time is a holy man of God. Why don't we add on a small room upstairs and furnish it with a bed and desk, chair and lamp, so that when he comes by he can stay with us?"

4.11 And so it happened that the next time Elisha came by he went to the room and lay down for a nap.

4.12 Then he said to his servant Gehazi, "Tell the Shunammite woman I want to see her." He called her and she came to him.

4.13 Through Gehazi Elisha said, "You've gone far beyond the call of duty in taking care of us; what can we do for you? Do you have a request we can bring to the king or to the commander of the army?"

NEW INTERNATIONAL VERSION	THE MESSAGE

NEW INTERNATIONAL VERSION

She replied, "I have a home among my own people."

¹⁴"What can be done for her?" Elisha asked.

Gehazi said, "Well, she has no son and her husband is old."

¹⁵Then Elisha said, "Call her." So he called her, and she stood in the doorway. ¹⁶"About this time next year," Elisha said, "you will hold a son in your arms."

"No, my lord," she objected. "Don't mislead your servant, O man of God!"

¹⁷But the woman became pregnant, and the next year about that same time she gave birth to a son, just as Elisha had told her.

¹⁸The child grew, and one day he went out to his father, who was with the reapers. ¹⁹"My head! My head!" he said to his father.

His father told a servant, "Carry him to his mother." ²⁰After the servant had lifted him up and carried him to his mother, the boy sat on her lap until noon, and then he died. ²¹She went up and laid him on the bed of the man of God, then shut the door and went out.

²²She called her husband and said, "Please send me one of the servants and a donkey so I can go to the man of God quickly and return."

²³"Why go to him today?" he asked. "It's not the New Moon or the Sabbath."

"It's all right," she said.

²⁴She saddled the donkey and said to her servant, "Lead on; don't slow down for me unless I tell you." ²⁵So she set out and came to the man of God at Mount Carmel.

When he saw her in the distance, the man of God said to his servant Gehazi, "Look! There's the Shunammite! ²⁶Run to meet her and ask her, 'Are you all right? Is your husband all right? Is your child all right?' "

"Everything is all right," she said.

²⁷When she reached the man of God at the mountain, she took hold of his feet. Gehazi came over to push her away, but the man of God said, "Leave her alone! She is in bitter distress, but the LORD has hidden it from me and has not told me why."

²⁸"Did I ask you for a son, my lord?" she said. "Didn't I tell you, 'Don't raise my hopes'?"

²⁹Elisha said to Gehazi, "Tuck your cloak into your belt, take my staff in your hand and run. If you meet anyone, do not greet him, and if any-

THE MESSAGE

She replied, "Nothing. I'm secure and satisfied in my family."

4.14 Elisha conferred with Gehazi: "There's got to be something we can do for her. But what?"

Gehazi said, "Well, she has no son, and her husband is an old man."

4.15 "Call her in," said Elisha. He called her and she stood at the open door.

4.16 Elisha said to her, "This time next year you're going to be nursing an infant son."

"O my master, O Holy Man," she said, "don't play games with me, teasing me with such fantasies!"

4.17 The woman conceived. A year later, just as Elisha had said, she had a son.

4.18-19 The child grew up. One day he went to his father, who was working with the harvest hands, complaining, "My head, my head!"

His father ordered a servant, "Carry him to his mother."

4.20 The servant took him in his arms and carried him to his mother. He lay on her lap until noon and died.

4.21 She took him up and laid him on the bed of the man of God, shut him in alone, and left.

4.22 She then called her husband, "Get me a servant and a donkey so I can go to the Holy Man; I'll be back as soon as I can."

4.23 "But why today? This isn't a holy day—it's neither New Moon nor Sabbath."

She said, "Don't ask questions; I need to go right now. Trust me."

4.24-25 She went ahead and saddled the donkey, ordering her servant, "Take the lead—and go as fast as you can; I'll tell you if you're going too fast." And so off she went. She came to the Holy Man at Mount Carmel.

4.25-26 The Holy Man, spotting her while she was still a long way off, said to his servant Gehazi, "Look out there; why, it's the Shunammite woman! Quickly now. Ask her, 'Is something wrong? Are you all right? Your husband? Your child?' "

She said, "Everything's fine."

4.27 But when she reached the Holy Man at the mountain, she threw herself at his feet and held tightly to him.

4.27 Gehazi came up to pull her away, but the Holy Man said, "Leave her alone—can't you see that she's in distress? But GOD hasn't let me in on why; I'm completely in the dark."

4.28 Then she spoke up: "Did I ask for a son, master? Didn't I tell you, 'Don't tease me with false hopes'?"

4.29 He ordered Gehazi, "Don't lose a minute—grab my staff and run as fast as you can. If you meet anyone, don't even take time to greet him,

NEW INTERNATIONAL VERSION

one greets you, do not answer. Lay my staff on the boy's face."

³⁰But the child's mother said, "As surely as the LORD lives and as you live, I will not leave you." So he got up and followed her.

³¹Gehazi went on ahead and laid the staff on the boy's face, but there was no sound or response. So Gehazi went back to meet Elisha and told him, "The boy has not awakened."

³²When Elisha reached the house, there was the boy lying dead on his couch. ³³He went in, shut the door on the two of them and prayed to the LORD. ³⁴Then he got on the bed and lay upon the boy, mouth to mouth, eyes to eyes, hands to hands. As he stretched himself out upon him, the boy's body grew warm. ³⁵Elisha turned away and walked back and forth in the room and then got on the bed and stretched out upon him once more. The boy sneezed seven times and opened his eyes.

³⁶Elisha summoned Gehazi and said, "Call the Shunammite." And he did. When she came, he said, "Take your son." ³⁷She came in, fell at his feet and bowed to the ground. Then she took her son and went out.

DEATH IN THE POT

³⁸Elisha returned to Gilgal and there was a famine in that region. While the company of the prophets was meeting with him, he said to his servant, "Put on the large pot and cook some stew for these men."

³⁹One of them went out into the fields to gather herbs and found a wild vine. He gathered some of its gourds and filled the fold of his cloak. When he returned, he cut them up into the pot of stew, though no one knew what they were. ⁴⁰The stew was poured out for the men, but as they began to eat it, they cried out, "O man of God, there is death in the pot!" And they could not eat it.

⁴¹Elisha said, "Get some flour." He put it into the pot and said, "Serve it to the people to eat." And there was nothing harmful in the pot.

FEEDING OF A HUNDRED

⁴²A man came from Baal Shalishah, bringing the man of God twenty loaves of barley bread baked from the first ripe grain, along with some heads of new grain. "Give it to the people to eat," Elisha said.

⁴³"How can I set this before a hundred men?" his servant asked.

But Elisha answered, "Give it to the people to eat. For this is what the LORD says: 'They will

THE MESSAGE

and if anyone greets you, don't even answer. Lay my staff across the boy's face."

4.30 The boy's mother said, "As sure as GOD lives and you live, you're not leaving me behind." And so Gehazi let her take the lead, and followed behind.

4.31 But Gehazi arrived first and laid the staff across the boy's face. But there was no sound—no sign of life. Gehazi went back to meet Elisha and said, "The boy hasn't stirred."

4.32-35 Elisha entered the house and found the boy stretched out on the bed dead. He went into the room and locked the door—just the two of them in the room—and prayed to GOD. He then got into bed with the boy and covered him with his body, mouth on mouth, eyes on eyes, hands on hands. As he was stretched out over him like that, the boy's body became warm. Elisha got up and paced back and forth in the room. Then he went back and stretched himself upon the boy again. The boy started sneezing—seven times he sneezed!—and opened his eyes.

4.36 He called Gehazi and said, "Get the Shunammite woman in here!" He called her and she came in.

Elisha said, "Embrace your son!"

4.37 She fell at Elisha's feet, face to the ground in reverent awe. Then she embraced her son and went out with him.

4.38 Elisha went back down to Gilgal. There was a famine there. While he was consulting with the guild of prophets, he told his servant, "Put a large pot on the fire and cook up some stew for the prophets."

4.39-40 One of the men went out into the field to get some herbs; he came across a wild vine and picked gourds from it, filling his gunnysack. He brought them back, sliced them up, and put them in the stew, even though no one knew what kind of plant it was. The stew was then served up for the men to eat. They started to eat, and then exclaimed, "Death in the pot, O man of God! Death in the pot!" Nobody could eat it.

4.41 Elisha ordered, "Get me some meal." Then he sprinkled it into the stew pot.

"Now serve it up to the men," he said. They ate it, and it was just fine—nothing wrong with *that* stew!

4.42 One day a man arrived from Baal Shalishah. He brought the man of God twenty loaves of fresh baked bread from the early harvest, along with a few apples from the orchard.

Elisha said, "Pass it around to the people to eat."

4.43 His servant said, "For a hundred men? There's not nearly enough!"

4.43 Elisha said, "Just go ahead and do it. GOD says there's plenty."

NEW INTERNATIONAL VERSION

eat and have some left over.' " ⁴⁴Then he set it before them, and they ate and had some left over, according to the word of the LORD.

NAAMAN HEALED OF LEPROSY

5 Now Naaman was commander of the army of the king of Aram. He was a great man in the sight of his master and highly regarded, because through him the LORD had given victory to Aram. He was a valiant soldier, but he had leprosy.ᵃ

²Now bands from Aram had gone out and had taken captive a young girl from Israel, and she served Naaman's wife. ³She said to her mistress, "If only my master would see the prophet who is in Samaria! He would cure him of his leprosy."

⁴Naaman went to his master and told him what the girl from Israel had said. ⁵"By all means, go," the king of Aram replied. "I will send a letter to the king of Israel." So Naaman left, taking with him ten talentsᵇ of silver, six thousand shekelsᶜ of gold and ten sets of clothing. ⁶The letter that he took to the king of Israel read: "With this letter I am sending my servant Naaman to you so that you may cure him of his leprosy."

⁷As soon as the king of Israel read the letter, he tore his robes and said, "Am I God? Can I kill and bring back to life? Why does this fellow send someone to me to be cured of his leprosy? See how he is trying to pick a quarrel with me!"

⁸When Elisha the man of God heard that the king of Israel had torn his robes, he sent him this message: "Why have you torn your robes? Have the man come to me and he will know that there is a prophet in Israel." ⁹So Naaman went with his horses and chariots and stopped at the door of Elisha's house. ¹⁰Elisha sent a messenger to say to him, "Go, wash yourself seven times in the Jordan, and your flesh will be restored and you will be cleansed."

¹¹But Naaman went away angry and said, "I thought that he would surely come out to me and stand and call on the name of the LORD his God, wave his hand over the spot and cure me of my leprosy. ¹²Are not Abana and Pharpar, the rivers of Damascus, better than any of the waters of Israel? Couldn't I wash in them and be cleansed?" So he turned and went off in a rage.

¹³Naaman's servants went to him and said, "My father, if the prophet had told you to do

---

ᵃ 1 The Hebrew word was used for various diseases affecting the skin—not necessarily leprosy; also in verses 3, 6, 7, 11 and 27.   ᵇ 5 That is, about 750 pounds (about 340 kilograms)   ᶜ 5 That is, about 150 pounds (about 70 kilograms)

THE MESSAGE

4.44 And sure enough, there was. He passed around what he had—they not only ate, but had leftovers.

5.1-3 **5** Naaman was general of the army under the king of Aram. He was important to his master, who held him in the highest esteem because it was by him that GOD had given victory to Aram: a truly great man, but afflicted with a grievous skin disease. It so happened that Aram, on one of its raiding expeditions against Israel, captured a young girl who became a maid to Naaman's wife. One day she said to her mistress, "Oh, if only my master could meet the prophet of Samaria, he would be healed of his skin disease."

5.4 Naaman went straight to his master and reported what the girl from Israel had said.

5.5 "Well then, go," said the king of Aram. "And I'll send a letter of introduction to the king of Israel."

So he went off, taking with him about 750 pounds of silver, 150 pounds of gold, and ten sets of clothes.

5.6 Naaman delivered the letter to the king of Israel. The letter read, "When you get this letter, you'll know that I've personally sent my servant Naaman to you; heal him of his skin disease."

5.7 When the king of Israel read the letter, he was terribly upset, ripping his robe to pieces. He said, "Am I a god with the power to bring death or life that I get orders to heal this man from his disease? What's going on here? That king's trying to pick a fight, that's what!"

5.8 Elisha the man of God heard what had happened, that the king of Israel was so distressed that he'd ripped his robe to shreds. He sent word to the king, "Why are you so upset, ripping your robe like this? Send him to me so he'll learn that there's a prophet in Israel."

5.9 So Naaman with his horses and chariots arrived in style and stopped at Elisha's door.

5.10 Elisha sent out a servant to meet him with this message: "Go to the River Jordan and immerse yourself seven times. Your skin will be healed and you'll be as good as new."

5.11-12 Naaman lost his temper. He turned on his heel saying, "I thought he'd personally come out and meet me, call on the name of GOD, wave his hand over the diseased spot, and get rid of the disease. The Damascus rivers, Abana and Pharpar, are cleaner by far than any of the rivers in Israel. Why not bathe in them? I'd at least get clean." He stomped off, mad as a hornet.

5.13 But his servants caught up with him and said, "Father, if the prophet had asked you to

NEW INTERNATIONAL VERSION

some great thing, would you not have done it? How much more, then, when he tells you, 'Wash and be cleansed'!" ¹⁴So he went down and dipped himself in the Jordan seven times, as the man of God had told him, and his flesh was restored and became clean like that of a young boy.

¹⁵Then Naaman and all his attendants went back to the man of God. He stood before him and said, "Now I know that there is no God in all the world except in Israel. Please accept now a gift from your servant."

¹⁶The prophet answered, "As surely as the LORD lives, whom I serve, I will not accept a thing." And even though Naaman urged him, he refused.

¹⁷"If you will not," said Naaman, "please let me, your servant, be given as much earth as a pair of mules can carry, for your servant will never again make burnt offerings and sacrifices to any other god but the LORD. ¹⁸But may the LORD forgive your servant for this one thing: When my master enters the temple of Rimmon to bow down and he is leaning on my arm and I bow there also—when I bow down in the temple of Rimmon, may the LORD forgive your servant for this."

¹⁹"Go in peace," Elisha said.

After Naaman had traveled some distance, ²⁰Gehazi, the servant of Elisha the man of God, said to himself, "My master was too easy on Naaman, this Aramean, by not accepting from him what he brought. As surely as the LORD lives, I will run after him and get something from him."

²¹So Gehazi hurried after Naaman. When Naaman saw him running toward him, he got down from the chariot to meet him. "Is everything all right?" he asked.

²²"Everything is all right," Gehazi answered. "My master sent me to say, 'Two young men from the company of the prophets have just come to me from the hill country of Ephraim. Please give them a talent[a] of silver and two sets of clothing.'"

²³"By all means, take two talents," said Naaman. He urged Gehazi to accept them, and then tied up the two talents of silver in two bags, with two sets of clothing. He gave them to two of his servants, and they carried them ahead of Gehazi. ²⁴When Gehazi came to the hill, he took the things from the servants and put them away in the house. He sent the men away and they left. ²⁵Then he went in and stood before his master Elisha.

"Where have you been, Gehazi?" Elisha asked.

"Your servant didn't go anywhere," Gehazi answered.

a 22 That is, about 75 pounds (about 34 kilograms)

THE MESSAGE

do something hard and heroic, wouldn't you have done it? So why not this simple 'wash and be clean'?"

⁵.¹⁴ So he did it. He went down and immersed himself in the Jordan seven times, following the orders of the Holy Man. His skin was healed; it was like the skin of a little baby. He was as good as new.

⁵.¹⁵ He then went back to the Holy Man, he and his entourage, stood before him, and said, "I now know beyond a shadow of a doubt that there is no God anywhere on earth other than the God of Israel. In gratitude let me give you a gift."

⁵.¹⁶ "As GOD lives," Elisha replied, "the God whom I serve, I'll take nothing from you." Naaman tried his best to get him to take something, but he wouldn't do it.

⁵.¹⁷⁻¹⁸ "If you won't take anything," said Naaman, "let me ask you for something: Give me a load of dirt, as much as a team of donkeys can carry, because I'm never again going to worship any god other than GOD. But there's one thing for which I need GOD's pardon: When my master, leaning on my arm, enters the shrine of Rimmon and worships there, and I'm with him there, worshiping Rimmon, may you see to it that GOD forgive me for this."

⁵.¹⁹⁻²¹ Elisha said, "Everything will be all right. Go in peace."

But he hadn't gone far when Gehazi, servant to Elisha the Holy Man, said to himself, "My master has let this Aramean Naaman slip through his fingers without so much as a thank-you. By the living GOD, I'm going after him to get something or other from him!" And Gehazi took off after Naaman.

Naaman saw him running after him and jumped down from his chariot to greet him, "Is something wrong?"

⁵.²² "Nothing's wrong, but something's come up. My master sent me to tell you: 'Two young men just showed up from the hill country of Ephraim, brothers from the guild of the prophets. Supply their needs with a gift of seventy-five pounds of silver and a couple of sets of clothes.'"

⁵.²³ Naaman said, "Of course, how about a hundred and fifty pounds?" Naaman insisted. He tied up the money in two sacks and gave him the two sets of clothes; he even gave him two servants to carry the gifts back with him.

⁵.²⁴ When they got to the fort on the hill, Gehazi took the gifts from the servants, stored them inside, then sent the servants back.

⁵.²⁵ He returned and stood before his master. Elisha said, "So what have you been up to, Gehazi?"

"Nothing much," he said.

NEW INTERNATIONAL VERSION

²⁶But Elisha said to him, "Was not my spirit with you when the man got down from his chariot to meet you? Is this the time to take money, or to accept clothes, olive groves, vineyards, flocks, herds, or menservants and maidservants? ²⁷Naaman's leprosy will cling to you and to your descendants forever." Then Gehazi went from Elisha's presence and he was leprous, as white as snow.

AN AXHEAD FLOATS

6 The company of the prophets said to Elisha, "Look, the place where we meet with you is too small for us. ²Let us go to the Jordan, where each of us can get a pole; and let us build a place there for us to live."

And he said, "Go."

³Then one of them said, "Won't you please come with your servants?"

"I will," Elisha replied. ⁴And he went with them.

They went to the Jordan and began to cut down trees. ⁵As one of them was cutting down a tree, the iron axhead fell into the water. "Oh, my lord," he cried out, "it was borrowed!"

⁶The man of God asked, "Where did it fall?" When he showed him the place, Elisha cut a stick and threw it there, and made the iron float. ⁷"Lift it out," he said. Then the man reached out his hand and took it.

ELISHA TRAPS BLINDED ARAMEANS

⁸Now the king of Aram was at war with Israel. After conferring with his officers, he said, "I will set up my camp in such and such a place."

⁹The man of God sent word to the king of Israel: "Beware of passing that place, because the Arameans are going down there." ¹⁰So the king of Israel checked on the place indicated by the man of God. Time and again Elisha warned the king, so that he was on his guard in such places.

¹¹This enraged the king of Aram. He summoned his officers and demanded of them, "Will you not tell me which of us is on the side of the king of Israel?"

¹²"None of us, my lord the king," said one of his officers, "but Elisha, the prophet who is in Israel, tells the king of Israel the very words you speak in your bedroom."

¹³"Go, find out where he is," the king ordered, "so I can send men and capture him." The report came back: "He is in Dothan." ¹⁴Then he sent horses and chariots and a strong force there. They went by night and surrounded the city.

THE MESSAGE

5.26-27 Elisha said, "Didn't you know I was with you in spirit when that man stepped down from his chariot to greet you? Tell me, is this a time to look after yourself, lining your pockets with gifts? Naaman's skin disease will now infect you and your family, with no relief in sight."

Gehazi walked away, his skin flaky and white like snow.

6.1-2 **6** One day the guild of prophets came to Elisha and said, "You can see that this place where we're living under your leadership is getting cramped—we have no elbow room. Give us permission to go down to the Jordan where each of us will get a log. We'll build a roomier place."

Elisha said, "Go ahead."

6.3 One of them then said, "Please! Come along with us!"

He said, "Certainly."

6.4-5 He went with them. They came to the Jordan and started chopping down trees. As one of them was felling a timber, his axhead flew off and sank in the river.

"Oh no, master!" he cried out. "And it was borrowed!"

6.6 The Holy Man said, "Where did it sink?"

The man showed him the place.

He cut off a branch and tossed it at the spot. The axhead floated up.

6.7 "Grab it," he said. The man reached out and took it.

6.8 One time when the king of Aram was at war with Israel, after consulting with his officers, he said, "At such and such a place I want an ambush set."

6.9 The Holy Man sent a message to the king of Israel: "Watch out when you're passing this place, because Aram has set an ambush there."

6.10 So the king of Israel sent word concerning the place of which the Holy Man had warned him.

This kind of thing happened all the time.

6.11 The king of Aram was furious over all this. He called his officers together and said, "Tell me, who is leaking information to the king of Israel? Who is the spy in our ranks?"

6.12 But one of his men said, "No, my master, dear king. It's not any of us. It's Elisha the prophet in Israel. He tells the king of Israel everything you say, even what you whisper in your bedroom."

6.13 The king said, "Go and find out where he is. I'll send someone and capture him."

The report came back, "He's in Dothan."

6.14 Then he dispatched horses and chariots, an impressive fighting force. They came by night and surrounded the city.

NEW INTERNATIONAL VERSION

¹⁵When the servant of the man of God got up and went out early the next morning, an army with horses and chariots had surrounded the city. "Oh, my lord, what shall we do?" the servant asked.

¹⁶"Don't be afraid," the prophet answered. "Those who are with us are more than those who are with them."

¹⁷And Elisha prayed, "O LORD, open his eyes so he may see." Then the LORD opened the servant's eyes, and he looked and saw the hills full of horses and chariots of fire all around Elisha.

¹⁸As the enemy came down toward him, Elisha prayed to the LORD, "Strike these people with blindness." So he struck them with blindness, as Elisha had asked.

¹⁹Elisha told them, "This is not the road and this is not the city. Follow me, and I will lead you to the man you are looking for." And he led them to Samaria.

²⁰After they entered the city, Elisha said, "LORD, open the eyes of these men so they can see." Then the LORD opened their eyes and they looked, and there they were, inside Samaria.

²¹When the king of Israel saw them, he asked Elisha, "Shall I kill them, my father? Shall I kill them?"

²²"Do not kill them," he answered. "Would you kill men you have captured with your own sword or bow? Set food and water before them so that they may eat and drink and then go back to their master." ²³So he prepared a great feast for them, and after they had finished eating and drinking, he sent them away, and they returned to their master. So the bands from Aram stopped raiding Israel's territory.

FAMINE IN BESIEGED SAMARIA

²⁴Some time later, Ben-Hadad king of Aram mobilized his entire army and marched up and laid siege to Samaria. ²⁵There was a great famine in the city; the siege lasted so long that a donkey's head sold for eighty shekels*a* of silver, and a quarter of a cab*b* of seed pods*c* for five shekels.*d*

²⁶As the king of Israel was passing by on the wall, a woman cried to him, "Help me, my lord the king!"

²⁷The king replied, "If the LORD does not help you, where can I get help for you? From the threshing floor? From the winepress?" ²⁸Then he asked her, "What's the matter?"

She answered, "This woman said to me, 'Give up your son so we may eat him today, and to-

THE MESSAGE

6.15 Early in the morning a servant of the Holy Man got up and went out. Surprise! Horses and chariots surrounding the city! The young man exclaimed, "Oh, master! What shall we do?"

6.16 He said, "Don't worry about it—there are more on our side than on their side."

6.17 Then Elisha prayed, "O GOD, open his eyes and let him see."

The eyes of the young man were opened and he saw. A wonder! The whole mountainside full of horses and chariots of fire surrounding Elisha!

6.18 When the Arameans attacked, Elisha prayed to GOD, "Strike these people blind!" And GOD struck them blind, just as Elisha said.

6.19 Then Elisha called out to them, "Not that way! Not this city! Follow me and I'll lead you to the man you're looking for." And he led them into Samaria.

6.20 As they entered the city, Elisha prayed, "O GOD, open their eyes so they can see where they are." GOD opened their eyes. They looked around—they were trapped in Samaria!

6.21 When the king of Israel saw them, he said to Elisha, "Father, shall I massacre the lot?"

6.22 "Not on your life!" said Elisha. "You didn't lift a hand to capture them, and now you're going to kill them? No sir, make a feast for them and send them back to their master."

6.23 So he prepared a huge feast for them. After they ate and drank their fill he dismissed them. Then they returned home to their master. The raiding bands of Aram didn't bother Israel anymore.

6.24-25 At a later time, this: Ben-Hadad king of Aram pulled together his troops and launched a siege on Samaria. This brought on a terrible famine, so bad that food prices soared astronomically. Eighty shekels for a donkey's head! Five shekels for a bowl of field greens!

6.26 One day the king of Israel was walking along the city wall. A woman cried out, "Help! Your majesty!"

6.27 He answered, "If GOD won't help you, where on earth can *I* go for help? To the granary? To the dairy?"

6.28-29 The king continued, "Tell me your story."

She said, "This woman came to me and said, 'Give up your son and we'll have him for to-

---

a 25 That is, about 2 pounds (about 1 kilogram)
b 25 That is, probably about 1/2 pint (about 0.3 liter)
c 25 Or *of doves' dung*   *d 25* That is, about 2 ounces (about 55 grams)

NEW INTERNATIONAL VERSION

morrow we'll eat my son.' ²⁹So we cooked my son and ate him. The next day I said to her, 'Give up your son so we may eat him,' but she had hidden him."

³⁰When the king heard the woman's words, he tore his robes. As he went along the wall, the people looked, and there, underneath, he had sackcloth on his body. ³¹He said, "May God deal with me, be it ever so severely, if the head of Elisha son of Shaphat remains on his shoulders today!"

³²Now Elisha was sitting in his house, and the elders were sitting with him. The king sent a messenger ahead, but before he arrived, Elisha said to the elders, "Don't you see how this murderer is sending someone to cut off my head? Look, when the messenger comes, shut the door and hold it shut against him. Is not the sound of his master's footsteps behind him?"

³³While he was still talking to them, the messenger came down to him. And ⌊the king⌋ said, "This disaster is from the LORD. Why should I wait for the LORD any longer?"

7 Elisha said, "Hear the word of the LORD. This is what the LORD says: About this time tomorrow, a seah*ᵃ* of flour will sell for a shekel*ᵇ* and two seahs*ᶜ* of barley for a shekel at the gate of Samaria."

²The officer on whose arm the king was leaning said to the man of God, "Look, even if the LORD should open the floodgates of the heavens, could this happen?"

"You will see it with your own eyes," answered Elisha, "but you will not eat any of it!"

THE SIEGE LIFTED

³Now there were four men with leprosy*ᵈ* at the entrance of the city gate. They said to each other, "Why stay here until we die? ⁴If we say, 'We'll go into the city'—the famine is there, and we will die. And if we stay here, we will die. So let's go over to the camp of the Arameans and surrender. If they spare us, we live; if they kill us, then we die."

⁵At dusk they got up and went to the camp of the Arameans. When they reached the edge of the camp, not a man was there, ⁶for the Lord had caused the Arameans to hear the sound of chariots and horses and a great army, so that

THE MESSAGE

day's supper; tomorrow we'll eat my son.' So we cooked my son. The next day I told her, 'Your turn—bring your son so we can have him for supper.' But she had hidden her son away."

6.30-31 When the king heard the woman's story he ripped apart his robe. Since he was walking on the city wall, everyone saw that next to his skin he was wearing coarse burlap. And he called out, "God do his worst to me—and more—if Elisha son of Shaphat still has a head on his shoulders at this day's end."

6.32 Elisha was sitting at home, the elders sitting with him. The king had already dispatched an executioner, but before the man arrived Elisha spoke to the elders: "Do you know that this murderer has just now sent a man to take off my head? Look, when the executioner arrives, shut the door and lock it. Don't I even now hear the footsteps of his master behind him?"

6.33 While he was giving his instructions, the king showed up, accusing, "This trouble is directly from GOD! And what's next? I'm fed up with GOD!"

7.1 **7** Elisha said, "Listen! GOD's word! The famine's over. This time tomorrow food will be plentiful—a handful of meal for a shekel; two handfuls of grain for a shekel. The market at the city gate will be buzzing."

7.2 The attendant on whom the king leaned for support said to the Holy Man, "You expect us to believe that? Trapdoors opening in the sky and food tumbling out?"

"You'll watch it with your own eyes," he said, "but *you* will not eat so much as a mouthful!"

7.3-4 It happened that four lepers were sitting just outside the city gate. They said to one another, "What are we doing sitting here at death's door? If we enter the famine-struck city we'll die; if we stay here we'll die. So let's take our chances in the camp of Aram and throw ourselves on their mercy. If they receive us we'll live, if they kill us we'll die. We've got nothing to lose."

7.5-8 So after the sun went down they got up and went to the camp of Aram. When they got to the edge of the camp, surprise! Not a man in the camp! The Master had made the army of Aram hear the sound of horses and a mighty army on the march. They told one another, "The king of

---

ᵃ 1 That is, probably about 7 quarts (about 7.3 liters); also in verses 16 and 18   *ᵇ 1* That is, about 2/5 ounce (about 11 grams); also in verses 16 and 18   *ᶜ 1* That is, probably about 13 quarts (about 15 liters); also in verses 16 and 18
ᵈ 3 The Hebrew word is used for various diseases affecting the skin—not necessarily leprosy; also in verse 8.

NEW INTERNATIONAL VERSION

they said to one another, "Look, the king of Israel has hired the Hittite and Egyptian kings to attack us!" ⁷So they got up and fled in the dusk and abandoned their tents and their horses and donkeys. They left the camp as it was and ran for their lives.

⁸The men who had leprosy reached the edge of the camp and entered one of the tents. They ate and drank, and carried away silver, gold and clothes, and went off and hid them. They returned and entered another tent and took some things from it and hid them also.

⁹Then they said to each other, "We're not doing right. This is a day of good news and we are keeping it to ourselves. If we wait until daylight, punishment will overtake us. Let's go at once and report this to the royal palace."

¹⁰So they went and called out to the city gatekeepers and told them, "We went into the Aramean camp and not a man was there—not a sound of anyone—only tethered horses and donkeys, and the tents left just as they were." ¹¹The gatekeepers shouted the news, and it was reported within the palace.

¹²The king got up in the night and said to his officers, "I will tell you what the Arameans have done to us. They know we are starving; so they have left the camp to hide in the countryside, thinking, 'They will surely come out, and then we will take them alive and get into the city.' "

¹³One of his officers answered, "Have some men take five of the horses that are left in the city. Their plight will be like that of all the Israelites left here—yes, they will only be like all these Israelites who are doomed. So let us send them to find out what happened."

¹⁴So they selected two chariots with their horses, and the king sent them after the Aramean army. He commanded the drivers, "Go and find out what has happened." ¹⁵They followed them as far as the Jordan, and they found the whole road strewn with the clothing and equipment the Arameans had thrown away in their headlong flight. So the messengers returned and reported to the king. ¹⁶Then the people went out and plundered the camp of the Arameans. So a seah of flour sold for a shekel, and two seahs of barley sold for a shekel, as the Lord had said.

¹⁷Now the king had put the officer on whose arm he leaned in charge of the gate, and the people trampled him in the gateway, and he died, just as the man of God had foretold when the king came down to his house. ¹⁸It happened as the man of God had said to the king: "About this time tomorrow, a seah of flour will sell for a shekel and two seahs of barley for a shekel at the gate of Samaria."

THE MESSAGE

Israel hired the kings of the Hittites and the kings of Egypt to attack us!" Panicked, they ran for their lives through the darkness, abandoning tents, horses, donkeys—the whole camp just as it was—running for dear life. These four lepers entered the camp and went into a tent. First they ate and drank. Then they grabbed silver, gold, and clothing, and went off and hid it. They came back, entered another tent, and looted it, again hiding their plunder.

7.9 Finally they said to one another, "We shouldn't be doing this! This is a day of good news and we're making it into a private party! If we wait around until morning we'll get caught and punished. Come on! Let's go tell the news to the king's palace!"

7.10 So they went and called out at the city gate, telling what had happened: "We went to the camp of Aram and, surprise!—the place was deserted. Not a soul, not a sound! Horses and donkeys left tethered and tents abandoned just as they were."

7.11-12 The gatekeepers got the word to the royal palace, giving them the whole story. Roused in the middle of the night, the king told his servants, "Let me tell you what Aram has done. They knew that we were starving, so they left camp and have hid in the field, thinking, 'When they come out of the city, we'll capture them alive and take the city.' "

7.13 One of his advisors answered, "Let some men go and take five of the horses left behind. The worst that can happen is no worse than what could happen to the whole city. Let's send them and find out what's happened."

7.14 They took two chariots with horses. The king sent them after the army of Aram with the orders, "Scout them out; find out what happened."

7.15 They went after them all the way to the Jordan. The whole way was strewn with clothes and equipment that Aram had dumped in their panicked flight. The scouts came back and reported to the king.

7.16 The people then looted the camp of Aram. Food prices dropped overnight—a handful of meal for a shekel; two handfuls of grain for a shekel—God's word to the letter!

7.17 The king ordered his attendant, the one he leaned on for support, to be in charge of the city gate. The people, turned into a mob, poured through the gate, trampling him to death. It was exactly what the Holy Man had said when the king had come to see him.

7.18-20 Every word of the Holy Man to the king— "A handful of meal for a shekel, two handfuls of grain for a shekel this time tomorrow in the gate of Samaria," with the attendant's sarcastic

NEW INTERNATIONAL VERSION

¹⁹The officer had said to the man of God, "Look, even if the Lord should open the floodgates of the heavens, could this happen?" The man of God had replied, "You will see it with your own eyes, but you will not eat any of it!" ²⁰And that is exactly what happened to him, for the people trampled him in the gateway, and he died.

The Shunammite's Land Restored

8 Now Elisha had said to the woman whose son he had restored to life, "Go away with your family and stay for a while wherever you can, because the Lord has decreed a famine in the land that will last seven years." ²The woman proceeded to do as the man of God said. She and her family went away and stayed in the land of the Philistines seven years.

³At the end of the seven years she came back from the land of the Philistines and went to the king to beg for her house and land. ⁴The king was talking to Gehazi, the servant of the man of God, and had said, "Tell me about all the great things Elisha has done." ⁵Just as Gehazi was telling the king how Elisha had restored the dead to life, the woman whose son Elisha had brought back to life came to beg the king for her house and land.

Gehazi said, "This is the woman, my lord the king, and this is her son whom Elisha restored to life." ⁶The king asked the woman about it, and she told him.

Then he assigned an official to her case and said to him, "Give back everything that belonged to her, including all the income from her land from the day she left the country until now."

Hazael Murders Ben-Hadad

⁷Elisha went to Damascus, and Ben-Hadad king of Aram was ill. When the king was told, "The man of God has come all the way up here," ⁸he said to Hazael, "Take a gift with you and go to meet the man of God. Consult the Lord through him; ask him, 'Will I recover from this illness?'"

⁹Hazael went to meet Elisha, taking with him as a gift forty camel-loads of all the finest wares of Damascus. He went in and stood before him, and said, "Your son Ben-Hadad king of Aram has sent me to ask, 'Will I recover from this illness?'"

¹⁰Elisha answered, "Go and say to him, 'You will certainly recover'; but ᵃ the Lord has revealed to me that he will in fact die." ¹¹He stared at him with a fixed gaze until Hazael felt ashamed. Then the man of God began to weep.

¹²"Why is my lord weeping?" asked Hazael.

ᵃ 10 The Hebrew may also be read *Go and say, 'You will certainly not recover,' for.*

THE MESSAGE

reply to the Holy Man, "You expect us to believe that? Trapdoors opening in the sky and food tumbling out?" followed by the response, "You'll watch it with your own eyes, but you won't eat so much as a mouthful"—proved true. The final stroke came when the people trampled the man to death at the city gate.

8 8.1-3 Years before, Elisha had told the woman whose son he had brought to life, "Leave here and go, you and your family, and live someplace else. God has ordered a famine in the land; it will last for seven years." The woman did what the Holy Man told her and left. She and her family lived as aliens in the country of Philistia for seven years. Then, when the seven years were up, the woman and her family came back. She went directly to the king and asked for her home and farm.

8.4-5 The king was talking with Gehazi, servant to the Holy Man, saying, "Tell me some stories of the great things Elisha did." It so happened that as he was telling the king the story of the dead person brought back to life, the woman whose son was brought to life showed up asking for her home and farm.

Gehazi said, "My master the king, this is the woman! And this is her son whom Elisha brought back to life!"

8.6 The king wanted to know all about it, and so she told him the story. The king assigned an officer to take care of her, saying, "Make sure she gets everything back that's hers, plus all profits from the farm from the time she left until now."

8.7 Elisha traveled to Damascus. Ben-Hadad, king of Aram, was sick at the time. He was told, "The Holy Man is in town."

8.8 The king ordered Hazael, "Take a gift with you and go meet the Holy Man. Ask God through him, 'Am I going to recover from this sickness?'"

8.9 Hazael went and met with Elisha. He brought with him every choice thing he could think of from Damascus—forty camel-loads of items! When he arrived he stood before Elisha and said, "Your son Ben-Hadad, king of Aram, sent me here to ask you, 'Am I going to recover from this sickness?'"

8.10-11 Elisha answered, "Go and tell him, 'Don't worry; you'll live.' The fact is, though—God showed me—that he's doomed to die." Elisha then stared hard at Hazael, reading his heart. Hazael felt exposed and dropped his eyes. Then the Holy Man wept.

8.12 Hazael said, "Why does my master weep?"

NEW INTERNATIONAL VERSION

"Because I know the harm you will do to the Israelites," he answered. "You will set fire to their fortified places, kill their young men with the sword, dash their little children to the ground, and rip open their pregnant women."

¹³Hazael said, "How could your servant, a mere dog, accomplish such a feat?"

"The LORD has shown me that you will become king of Aram," answered Elisha.

¹⁴Then Hazael left Elisha and returned to his master. When Ben-Hadad asked, "What did Elisha say to you?" Hazael replied, "He told me that you would certainly recover." ¹⁵But the next day he took a thick cloth, soaked it in water and spread it over the king's face, so that he died. Then Hazael succeeded him as king.

JEHORAM KING OF JUDAH

¹⁶In the fifth year of Joram son of Ahab king of Israel, when Jehoshaphat was king of Judah, Jehoram son of Jehoshaphat began his reign as king of Judah. ¹⁷He was thirty-two years old when he became king, and he reigned in Jerusalem eight years. ¹⁸He walked in the ways of the kings of Israel, as the house of Ahab had done, for he married a daughter of Ahab. He did evil in the eyes of the LORD. ¹⁹Nevertheless, for the sake of his servant David, the LORD was not willing to destroy Judah. He had promised to maintain a lamp for David and his descendants forever.

²⁰In the time of Jehoram, Edom rebelled against Judah and set up its own king. ²¹So Jehoram[a] went to Zair with all his chariots. The Edomites surrounded him and his chariot commanders, but he rose up and broke through by night; his army, however, fled back home. ²²To this day Edom has been in rebellion against Judah. Libnah revolted at the same time.

²³As for the other events of Jehoram's reign, and all he did, are they not written in the book of the annals of the kings of Judah? ²⁴Jehoram rested with his fathers and was buried with them in the City of David. And Ahaziah his son succeeded him as king.

AHAZIAH KING OF JUDAH

²⁵In the twelfth year of Joram son of Ahab king of Israel, Ahaziah son of Jehoram king of Judah began to reign. ²⁶Ahaziah was twenty-two years old when he became king, and he reigned in Jerusalem one year. His mother's name was Athaliah, a granddaughter of Omri king of Israel. ²⁷He walked in the ways of the house of Ahab and did evil in the eyes of the LORD, as the house

---

a 21 Hebrew *Joram*, a variant of *Jehoram*; also in verses 23 and 24

THE MESSAGE

"Because," said Elisha, "I know what you're going to do to the children of Israel:

burn down their forts,
murder their youth,
smash their babies,
rip open their pregnant women."

8.13 Hazael said, "Am I a mongrel dog that I'd do such a horrible thing?"

"GOD showed me," said Elisha, "that you'll be king of Aram."

8.14 Hazael left Elisha and returned to his master, who asked, "So, what did Elisha tell you?"

"He told me, 'Don't worry; you'll live.' "

8.15 But the very next day, someone took a heavy quilt, soaked it in water, covered the king's face, and suffocated him.

Now Hazael was king.

JEHORAM OF JUDAH

8.16-19 In the fifth year of the reign of Joram son of Ahab king of Israel, Jehoram son of Jehoshaphat king of Judah became king. He was thirty-two years old when he began his rule, and was king for eight years in Jerusalem. He copied the way of life of the kings of Israel, marrying into the Ahab family and continuing the Ahab line of sin—from GOD's point of view, an evil man living an evil life. But despite that, because of his servant David, GOD was not ready to destroy Judah. He had, after all, promised to keep a lamp burning through David's descendants.

8.20-21 During Jehoram's reign, Edom revolted against Judah's rule and set up their own king. Jehoram responded by taking his army of chariots to Zair. Edom surrounded him, but in the middle of the night he and his charioteers broke through the lines and hit Edom hard. But his infantry deserted him.

8.22 Edom continues in revolt against Judah right up to the present. Even little Libnah revolted at that time.

8.23-24 The rest of the life and times of Jehoram, the record of his rule, is written in *The Chronicles of the Kings of Judah*. Jehoram died and was buried in the family grave in the City of David. His son Ahaziah succeeded him as king.

AHAZIAH OF JUDAH

8.25-27 In the twelfth year of the reign of Joram son of Ahab king of Israel, Ahaziah son of Jehoram king of Judah began his reign. Ahaziah was twenty-two years old when he became king; he ruled only a year in Jerusalem. His mother was Athaliah, granddaughter of Omri king of Israel. He lived and ruled just like the Ahab family had done, continuing the same evil-in-GOD's-

NEW INTERNATIONAL VERSION

of Ahab had done, for he was related by marriage to Ahab's family.

²⁸Ahaziah went with Joram son of Ahab to war against Hazael king of Aram at Ramoth Gilead. The Arameans wounded Joram; ²⁹so King Joram returned to Jezreel to recover from the wounds the Arameans had inflicted on him at Ramoth*ᵃ* in his battle with Hazael king of Aram.

Then Ahaziah son of Jehoram king of Judah went down to Jezreel to see Joram son of Ahab, because he had been wounded.

JEHU ANOINTED KING OF ISRAEL

9 The prophet Elisha summoned a man from the company of the prophets and said to him, "Tuck your cloak into your belt, take this flask of oil with you and go to Ramoth Gilead. ²When you get there, look for Jehu son of Jehoshaphat, the son of Nimshi. Go to him, get him away from his companions and take him into an inner room. ³Then take the flask and pour the oil on his head and declare, 'This is what the LORD says: I anoint you king over Israel.' Then open the door and run; don't delay!"

⁴So the young man, the prophet, went to Ramoth Gilead. ⁵When he arrived, he found the army officers sitting together. "I have a message for you, commander," he said.

"For which of us?" asked Jehu.

"For you, commander," he replied.

⁶Jehu got up and went into the house. Then the prophet poured the oil on Jehu's head and declared, "This is what the LORD, the God of Israel, says: 'I anoint you king over the LORD's people Israel. ⁷You are to destroy the house of Ahab your master, and I will avenge the blood of my servants the prophets and the blood of all the LORD's servants shed by Jezebel. ⁸The whole house of Ahab will perish. I will cut off from Ahab every last male in Israel—slave or free. ⁹I will make the house of Ahab like the house of Jeroboam son of Nebat and like the house of Baasha son of Ahijah. ¹⁰As for Jezebel, dogs will devour her on the plot of ground at Jezreel, and no one will bury her.' " Then he opened the door and ran.

¹¹When Jehu went out to his fellow officers, one of them asked him, "Is everything all right? Why did this madman come to you?"

"You know the man and the sort of things he says," Jehu replied.

¹²"That's not true!" they said. "Tell us."

Jehu said, "Here is what he told me: 'This is what the LORD says: I anoint you king over Israel.' "

¹³They hurried and took their cloaks and spread them under him on the bare steps. Then

THE MESSAGE

sight line of sin, related by both marriage and sin to the Ahab clan.

8.28-29 He joined Joram son of Ahab king of Israel in a war against Hazael king of Aram at Ramoth Gilead. The archers wounded Joram. Joram pulled back to Jezreel to convalesce from the injuries he had received in the fight with Hazael. Ahaziah son of Jehoram king of Judah paid a visit to Joram son of Ahab on his sickbed in Jezreel.

JEHU OF ISRAEL

9.1-3 **9** One day Elisha the prophet ordered a member of the guild of prophets, "Get yourself ready, take a flask of oil, and go to Ramoth Gilead. Look for Jehu son of Jehoshaphat son of Nimshi. When you find him, get him away from his companions and take him to a back room. Take your flask of oil and pour it over his head and say, 'GOD's word: I anoint you king over Israel.' Then open the door and get out of there as fast as you can. Don't wait around."

9.4-5 The young prophet went to Ramoth Gilead. On arrival he found the army officers all sitting around. He said, "I have a matter of business with you, officer."

Jehu said, "Which one of us?"

"With you, officer."

9.6-10 He got up and went inside the building. The young prophet poured the oil on his head and said, "GOD's word, the God of Israel: I've anointed you to be king over the people of GOD, over Israel. Your assignment is to attack the regime of Ahab your master. I am avenging the massacre of my servants the prophets—yes, the Jezebel-massacre of all the prophets of GOD. The entire line of Ahab is doomed. I'm wiping out the entire bunch of that sad lot. I'll see to it that the family of Ahab experiences the same fate as the family of Jeroboam son of Nebat and the family of Baasha son of Ahijah. As for Jezebel, the dogs will eat her carcass in the open fields of Jezreel. No burial for her!" Then he opened the door and made a run for it.

9.11 Jehu went back out to his master's officers. They asked, "Is everything all right? What did that crazy fool want with you?"

He said, "You know that kind of man—all talk."

9.12 "That's a lie!" they said. "Tell us what's going on."

He said, "He told me this and this and this—in effect, 'GOD's word: I anoint you king of Israel!' "

9.13 They sprang into action. Each man grabbed his robe; they piled them at the top of the steps

---

ᵃ 29 Hebrew *Ramah,* a variant of *Ramoth*

NEW INTERNATIONAL VERSION

they blew the trumpet and shouted, "Jehu is king!"

JEHU KILLS JORAM AND AHAZIAH

¹⁴So Jehu son of Jehoshaphat, the son of Nimshi, conspired against Joram. (Now Joram and all Israel had been defending Ramoth Gilead against Hazael king of Aram, ¹⁵but King Joram*ᵃ* had returned to Jezreel to recover from the wounds the Arameans had inflicted on him in the battle with Hazael king of Aram.) Jehu said, "If this is the way you feel, don't let anyone slip out of the city to go and tell the news in Jezreel." ¹⁶Then he got into his chariot and rode to Jezreel, because Joram was resting there and Ahaziah king of Judah had gone down to see him.

¹⁷When the lookout standing on the tower in Jezreel saw Jehu's troops approaching, he called out, "I see some troops coming."

"Get a horseman," Joram ordered. "Send him to meet them and ask, 'Do you come in peace?' "

¹⁸The horseman rode off to meet Jehu and said, "This is what the king says: 'Do you come in peace?' "

"What do you have to do with peace?" Jehu replied. "Fall in behind me."

The lookout reported, "The messenger has reached them, but he isn't coming back."

¹⁹So the king sent out a second horseman. When he came to them he said, "This is what the king says: 'Do you come in peace?' "

Jehu replied, "What do you have to do with peace? Fall in behind me."

²⁰The lookout reported, "He has reached them, but he isn't coming back either. The driving is like that of Jehu son of Nimshi—he drives like a madman."

²¹"Hitch up my chariot," Joram ordered. And when it was hitched up, Joram king of Israel and Ahaziah king of Judah rode out, each in his own chariot, to meet Jehu. They met him at the plot of ground that had belonged to Naboth the Jezreelite. ²²When Joram saw Jehu he asked, "Have you come in peace, Jehu?"

"How can there be peace," Jehu replied, "as long as all the idolatry and witchcraft of your mother Jezebel abound?"

²³Joram turned about and fled, calling out to Ahaziah, "Treachery, Ahaziah!"

²⁴Then Jehu drew his bow and shot Joram between the shoulders. The arrow pierced his heart and he slumped down in his chariot. ²⁵Jehu said to Bidkar, his chariot officer, "Pick him up and throw him on the field that belonged to Naboth

---

THE MESSAGE

for a makeshift throne. Then they blew the trumpet and declared, "Jehu is king!"

9.14-15 That ignited the conspiracy of Jehu son of Jehoshaphat son of Nimshi against Joram.

Meanwhile, Joram and the entire army were defending Ramoth Gilead against Hazael king of Aram. Except that Joram had pulled back to Jezreel to convalesce from the injuries he got from the Arameans in the battle with Hazael king of Aram.

Jehu said, "If you really want me as king, don't let anyone sneak out of the city and blab the news in Jezreel."

9.16 Then Jehu mounted a chariot and rode to Jezreel, where Joram was in bed, resting. King Ahaziah of Judah had come down to visit Joram.

9.17 A sentry standing duty on the watchtower in Jezreel saw the company of Jehu arrive. He said, "I see a band of men."

Joram said, "Get a horseman and send him out to meet them and inquire, 'Is anything wrong?' "

9.18 The horseman rode out to meet Jehu and said, "The king wants to know if there's anything wrong."

Jehu said, "What's it to you whether things are right or wrong? Fall in behind me."

The sentry said, "The messenger reached them, but he's not returning."

9.19 The king then sent a second horseman. When he reached them he said, "The king wants to know if there's anything wrong."

Jehu said, "What's it to you whether things are right or wrong? Fall in behind me."

9.20 The sentry said, "The messenger reached them, but he's not returning. The driving is like the driving of Jehu son of Nimshi—crazy!"

9.21 Joram ordered, "Get my chariot ready!" They hitched up his chariot. Joram king of Israel and Ahaziah king of Judah, each in his own chariot, drove out to meet Jehu. They met in the field of Naboth of Jezreel.

9.22 When Joram saw Jehu he called out, "Good day, Jehu!"

Jehu answered, "What's good about it? How can there be anything good about it as long as the promiscuous whoring and sorceries of your mother Jezebel pollute the country?"

9.23 Joram wheeled his chariot around and fled, yelling to Ahaziah, "It's a trap, Ahaziah!"

9.24 Jehu pulled on his bow and released an arrow; it hit Joram between the shoulder blades and went right through his heart. He slumped to his knees in his chariot.

9.25-26 Jehu ordered Bidkar, his lieutenant, "Quick—throw him into the field of Naboth of Jezreel.

ᵃ 15 Hebrew Jehoram, a variant of Joram; also in verses 17 and 21-24

NEW INTERNATIONAL VERSION

the Jezreelite. Remember how you and I were riding together in chariots behind Ahab his father when the LORD made this prophecy about him: 26'Yesterday I saw the blood of Naboth and the blood of his sons, declares the LORD, and I will surely make you pay for it on this plot of ground, declares the LORD.'*a* Now then, pick him up and throw him on that plot, in accordance with the word of the LORD."

27When Ahaziah king of Judah saw what had happened, he fled up the road to Beth Haggan.*b* Jehu chased him, shouting, "Kill him too!" They wounded him in his chariot on the way up to Gur near Ibleam, but he escaped to Megiddo and died there. 28His servants took him by chariot to Jerusalem and buried him with his fathers in his tomb in the City of David. 29(In the eleventh year of Joram son of Ahab, Ahaziah had become king of Judah.)

JEZEBEL KILLED

30Then Jehu went to Jezreel. When Jezebel heard about it, she painted her eyes, arranged her hair and looked out of a window. 31As Jehu entered the gate, she asked, "Have you come in peace, Zimri, you murderer of your master?"*c*

32He looked up at the window and called out, "Who is on my side? Who?" Two or three eunuchs looked down at him. 33"Throw her down!" Jehu said. So they threw her down, and some of her blood spattered the wall and the horses as they trampled her underfoot.

34Jehu went in and ate and drank. "Take care of that cursed woman," he said, "and bury her, for she was a king's daughter." 35But when they went out to bury her, they found nothing except her skull, her feet and her hands. 36They went back and told Jehu, who said, "This is the word of the LORD that he spoke through his servant Elijah the Tishbite: On the plot of ground at Jezreel dogs will devour Jezebel's flesh.*d* 37Jezebel's body will be like refuse on the ground in the plot at Jezreel, so that no one will be able to say, 'This is Jezebel.' "

AHAB'S FAMILY KILLED

10 Now there were in Samaria seventy sons of the house of Ahab. So Jehu wrote letters and sent them to Samaria: to the officials of

THE MESSAGE

Remember when you and I were driving our chariots behind Ahab his father? That's when GOD pronounced this doom upon him: 'As surely as I saw the blood of murdered Naboth and his sons yesterday, you'll pay for it on this exact piece of ground. GOD's word!' So take him and throw him out in the field. GOD's instructions carried out to the letter!"

9.27   Ahaziah king of Judah saw what was going on and made his escape on the road toward Beth Haggan. Jehu chased him, yelling out, "Get him, too!" Jehu's troops shot and wounded him in his chariot on the hill up to Gur, near Ibleam. He was able to make it as far as Megiddo; there he died.

9.28   His aides drove on to Jerusalem. They buried him in the family plot in the City of David.

9.29   In the eleventh year of the reign of Joram son of Ahab, Ahaziah had become king of Judah.

9.30-31   When Jezebel heard that Jehu had arrived in Jezreel, she made herself up—put on eyeshadow and arranged her hair—and posed seductively at the window. When Jehu came through the city gate, she called down, "So, how are things, 'Zimri,' you dashing king-killer?"

9.32   Jehu looked up at the window and called, "Is there anybody up there on my side?" Two or three palace eunuchs looked out.

9.33   He ordered, "Throw her down!" They threw her out the window. Her blood spattered the wall and the horses, and Jehu trampled her under his horse's hooves.

9.34   Then Jehu went inside and ate his lunch. During lunch he gave orders, "Take care of that damned woman; give her a decent burial—she is, after all, a king's daughter."

9.35-36   They went out to bury her, but there was nothing left of her but skull, feet, and hands. They came back and told Jehu. He said, "It's GOD's word, the word spoken by Elijah the Tishbite:

In the field of Jezreel,
   dogs will eat Jezebel;

9.37   The body of Jezebel will be like
   dog-droppings on the ground in Jezreel.
Old friends and lovers will say,
   'I wonder, is *this* Jezebel?' "

10.1-2   **10** Ahab had seventy sons still living in Samaria. Jehu wrote letters addressed to the officers of Jezreel, the city elders, and those

---

a 26 See 1 Kings 21:19.   *b* 27 Or *fled by way of the garden house*   *c* 31 Or *"Did Zimri have peace, who murdered his master?"*   *d* 36 See 1 Kings 21:23.

NEW INTERNATIONAL VERSION

Jezreel,[a] to the elders and to the guardians of Ahab's children. He said, 2"As soon as this letter reaches you, since your master's sons are with you and you have chariots and horses, a fortified city and weapons, 3choose the best and most worthy of your master's sons and set him on his father's throne. Then fight for your master's house."

4But they were terrified and said, "If two kings could not resist him, how can we?"

5So the palace administrator, the city governor, the elders and the guardians sent this message to Jehu: "We are your servants and we will do anything you say. We will not appoint anyone as king; you do whatever you think best."

6Then Jehu wrote them a second letter, saying, "If you are on my side and will obey me, take the heads of your master's sons and come to me in Jezreel by this time tomorrow."

Now the royal princes, seventy of them, were with the leading men of the city, who were rearing them. 7When the letter arrived, these men took the princes and slaughtered all seventy of them. They put their heads in baskets and sent them to Jehu in Jezreel. 8When the messenger arrived, he told Jehu, "They have brought the heads of the princes."

Then Jehu ordered, "Put them in two piles at the entrance of the city gate until morning."

9The next morning Jehu went out. He stood before all the people and said, "You are innocent. It was I who conspired against my master and killed him, but who killed all these? 10Know then, that not a word the LORD has spoken against the house of Ahab will fail. The LORD has done what he promised through his servant Elijah." 11So Jehu killed everyone in Jezreel who remained of the house of Ahab, as well as all his chief men, his close friends and his priests, leaving him no survivor.

12Jehu then set out and went toward Samaria. At Beth Eked of the Shepherds, 13he met some relatives of Ahaziah king of Judah and asked, "Who are you?"

They said, "We are relatives of Ahaziah, and we have come down to greet the families of the king and of the queen mother."

---

a 1 Hebrew; some Septuagint manuscripts and Vulgate *of the city*

THE MESSAGE

in charge of Ahab's sons, and posted them to Samaria. The letters read:

10.2-3 This letter is fair warning. You're in charge of your master's children, chariots, horses, fortifications, and weapons. Pick the best and most capable of your master's sons and put him on the throne. Prepare to fight for your master's position.

10.4 They were absolutely terrified at the letter. They said, "Two kings have already been wiped out by him; what hope do we have?"

10.5 So they sent the warden of the palace, the mayor of the city, the elders, and the guardians to Jehu with this message: "We are your servants. Whatever you say, we'll do. We're not making anyone king here. You're in charge—do what you think best."

10.6-7 Then Jehu wrote a second letter:

If you are on my side and are willing to follow my orders, here's what you do: Decapitate the sons of your master and bring the heads to me by this time tomorrow in Jezreel.

The king's sons numbered seventy. The leaders of the city had taken responsibility for them. When they got the letter, they took the king's sons and killed all seventy. Then they put the heads in baskets and sent them to Jehu in Jezreel.

10.8 A messenger reported to Jehu: "They've delivered the heads of the king's sons."

He said, "Stack them in two piles at the city gate until morning."

10.9-10 In the morning Jehu came out, stood before the people, and addressed them formally: "Do you realize that this very day you are participants in GOD's righteous workings? True, I am the one who conspired against my master and assassinated him. But who, do you suppose, is responsible for this pile of skulls? Know this for certain: Not a single syllable that GOD spoke in judgment on the family of Ahab is canceled; you're seeing it with your own eyes—GOD doing what, through Elijah, he said he'd do."

10.11 Then Jehu proceeded to kill everyone who had anything to do with Ahab's family in Jezreel—leaders, friends, priests. He wiped out the entire lot.

10.12-13 That done, he brushed himself off and set out for Samaria. Along the way, at Beth Eked (Binding House) of the Shepherds, he met up with some relatives of Ahaziah king of Judah. Jehu said, "Who are you?"

They said, "We're relatives of Ahaziah and we've come down to a reunion of the royal family."

NEW INTERNATIONAL VERSION

¹⁴"Take them alive!" he ordered. So they took them alive and slaughtered them by the well of Beth Eked—forty-two men. He left no survivor.

¹⁵After he left there, he came upon Jehonadab son of Recab, who was on his way to meet him. Jehu greeted him and said, "Are you in accord with me, as I am with you?"

"I am," Jehonadab answered.

"If so," said Jehu, "give me your hand." So he did, and Jehu helped him up into the chariot. ¹⁶Jehu said, "Come with me and see my zeal for the LORD." Then he had him ride along in his chariot.

¹⁷When Jehu came to Samaria, he killed all who were left there of Ahab's family; he destroyed them, according to the word of the LORD spoken to Elijah.

MINISTERS OF BAAL KILLED

¹⁸Then Jehu brought all the people together and said to them, "Ahab served Baal a little; Jehu will serve him much. ¹⁹Now summon all the prophets of Baal, all his ministers and all his priests. See that no one is missing, because I am going to hold a great sacrifice for Baal. Anyone who fails to come will no longer live." But Jehu was acting deceptively in order to destroy the ministers of Baal.

²⁰Jehu said, "Call an assembly in honor of Baal." So they proclaimed it. ²¹Then he sent word throughout Israel, and all the ministers of Baal came; not one stayed away. They crowded into the temple of Baal until it was full from one end to the other. ²²And Jehu said to the keeper of the wardrobe, "Bring robes for all the ministers of Baal." So he brought out robes for them.

²³Then Jehu and Jehonadab son of Recab went into the temple of Baal. Jehu said to the ministers of Baal, "Look around and see that no servants of the LORD are here with you—only ministers of Baal." ²⁴So they went in to make sacrifices and burnt offerings. Now Jehu had posted eighty men outside with this warning: "If one of you lets any of the men I am placing in your hands escape, it will be your life for his life."

²⁵As soon as Jehu had finished making the burnt offering, he ordered the guards and officers: "Go in and kill them; let no one escape." So they cut them down with the sword. The guards and officers threw the bodies out and then entered the inner shrine of the temple of Baal. ²⁶They brought the sacred stone out of the temple of Baal and burned it. ²⁷They demolished the sacred stone of Baal and tore down the temple of

THE MESSAGE

10.14 "Grab them!" ordered Jehu. They were taken and then massacred at the well of Beth Eked. Forty-two of them—no survivors.

10.15 He went on from there and came upon Jehonadab the Recabite who was on his way to meet him. Greeting him, he said, "Are we together and of one mind in this?"

Jehonadab said, "We are—count on me."

"Then give me your hand," said Jehu.

They shook hands on it and Jehonadab stepped up into the chariot with Jehu.

10.16 "Come along with me," said Jehu, "and witness my zeal for GOD." Together they proceeded in the chariot.

10.17 When they arrived in Samaria, Jehu massacred everyone left in Samaria who was in any way connected with Ahab—a mass execution, just as GOD had told Elijah.

10.18-19 Next, Jehu got all the people together and addressed them:

Ahab served Baal small-time;
Jehu will serve him big-time.

"Get all the prophets of Baal here—everyone who served him, all his priests. Get everyone here; don't leave anyone out. I have a great sacrifice to offer Baal. If you don't show up, you won't live to tell about it." (Jehu was lying, of course. He planned to destroy all the worshipers of Baal.)

10.20 Jehu ordered, "Make preparation for a holy convocation for Baal." They did and posted the date.

10.21 Jehu then summoned everyone in Israel. They came in droves—every worshiper of Baal in the country. Nobody stayed home. They came and packed the temple of Baal to capacity.

10.22 Jehu directed the keeper of the wardrobe, "Get robes for all the servants of Baal." He brought out their robes.

10.23-24 Jehu and Jehonadab the Recabite now entered the temple of Baal and said, "Double-check and make sure that there are no worshipers of GOD in here; only Baal-worshipers are allowed." Then they launched the worship, making the sacrifices and burnt offerings.

Meanwhile, Jehu had stationed eighty men outside with orders: "Don't let a single person escape; if you do, it's your life for his life."

10.25-27 When Jehu had finished with the sacrificial solemnities, he signaled to the officers and guards, "Enter and kill! No survivors!"

And the bloody slaughter began. The officers and guards threw the corpses outside and cleared the way to enter the inner shrine of Baal. They hauled out the sacred phallic stone from the temple of Baal and pulverized it. They

NEW INTERNATIONAL VERSION

Baal, and people have used it for a latrine to this day.

²⁸So Jehu destroyed Baal worship in Israel. ²⁹However, he did not turn away from the sins of Jeroboam son of Nebat, which he had caused Israel to commit—the worship of the golden calves at Bethel and Dan.

³⁰The LORD said to Jehu, "Because you have done well in accomplishing what is right in my eyes and have done to the house of Ahab all I had in mind to do, your descendants will sit on the throne of Israel to the fourth generation." ³¹Yet Jehu was not careful to keep the law of the LORD, the God of Israel, with all his heart. He did not turn away from the sins of Jeroboam, which he had caused Israel to commit.

³²In those days the LORD began to reduce the size of Israel. Hazael overpowered the Israelites throughout their territory ³³east of the Jordan in all the land of Gilead (the region of Gad, Reuben and Manasseh), from Aroer by the Arnon Gorge through Gilead to Bashan.

³⁴As for the other events of Jehu's reign, all he did, and all his achievements, are they not written in the book of the annals of the kings of Israel?

³⁵Jehu rested with his fathers and was buried in Samaria. And Jehoahaz his son succeeded him as king. ³⁶The time that Jehu reigned over Israel in Samaria was twenty-eight years.

ATHALIAH AND JOASH

11 When Athaliah the mother of Ahaziah saw that her son was dead, she proceeded to destroy the whole royal family. ²But Jehosheba, the daughter of King Jehoram*a* and sister of Ahaziah, took Joash son of Ahaziah and stole him away from among the royal princes, who were about to be murdered. She put him and his nurse in a bedroom to hide him from Athaliah; so he was not killed. ³He remained hidden with his nurse at the temple of the LORD for six years while Athaliah ruled the land.

⁴In the seventh year Jehoiada sent for the commanders of units of a hundred, the Carites and the guards and had them brought to him at the temple of the LORD. He made a covenant with them and put them under oath at the temple of the LORD. Then he showed them the king's son. ⁵He commanded them, saying, "This is what you are to do: You who are in the three companies that are going on duty on the Sabbath—a third of you guarding the royal palace, ⁶a third at the Sur Gate, and a third at the gate behind the guard, who take turns guarding the temple— ⁷and you

a 2 Hebrew Joram, a variant of Jehoram

THE MESSAGE

smashed the Baal altars and tore down the Baal temple. It's been a public toilet ever since.

10.28 And that's the story of Jehu's wasting of Baal in Israel.

10.29 But for all that, Jehu didn't turn back from the sins of Jeroboam son of Nebat, the sins that had dragged Israel into a life of sin—the golden calves in Bethel and Dan stayed.

10.30 GOD commended Jehu: "You did well to do what I saw was best. You did what I ordered against the family of Ahab. As reward, your sons will occupy the throne of Israel for four generations."

10.31 Even then, though, Jehu wasn't careful to walk in GOD's ways and honor the God of Israel from an undivided heart. He didn't turn back from the sins of Jeroboam son of Nebat, who led Israel into a life of sin.

10.32-33 It was about this time that GOD began to shrink Israel. Hazael hacked away at the borders of Israel from the Jordan to the east—all the territory of Gilead, Gad, Reuben, and Manasseh from Aroer near the Brook Arnon. In effect, all Gilead and Bashan.

10.34-36 The rest of the life and times of Jehu, his accomplishments and fame, are written in *The Chronicles of the Kings of Israel.* Jehu died and was buried in the family plot in Samaria. His son Jehoahaz was the next king. Jehu ruled Israel from Samaria for twenty-eight years.

ATHALIAH OF JUDAH

11.1-3 **11** Athaliah was the mother of Ahaziah. When she saw that her son was dead, she took over. She began by massacring the entire royal family. But Jehosheba, daughter of King Joram and sister of Ahaziah, took Ahaziah's son Joash and kidnapped him from among the king's sons slated for slaughter. She hid him and his nurse in a private room away from Athaliah. He didn't get killed. He was there with her, hidden away for six years in The Temple of GOD. Athaliah, oblivious to his existence, ruled the country.

11.4 In the seventh year Jehoiada sent for the captains of the bodyguards and the Palace Security Force. They met him in The Temple of GOD. He made a covenant with them, swore them to secrecy, and only then showed them the young prince.

11.5-8 Then he commanded them, "These are your instructions: Those of you who come on duty on the Sabbath and guard the palace, and those of you who go off duty on the Sabbath and

NEW INTERNATIONAL VERSION

who are in the other two companies that normally go off Sabbath duty are all to guard the temple for the king. [8]Station yourselves around the king, each man with his weapon in his hand. Anyone who approaches your ranks[a] must be put to death. Stay close to the king wherever he goes."

[9]The commanders of units of a hundred did just as Jehoiada the priest ordered. Each one took his men—those who were going on duty on the Sabbath and those who were going off duty—and came to Jehoiada the priest. [10]Then he gave the commanders the spears and shields that had belonged to King David and that were in the temple of the LORD. [11]The guards, each with his weapon in his hand, stationed themselves around the king—near the altar and the temple, from the south side to the north side of the temple.

[12]Jehoiada brought out the king's son and put the crown on him; he presented him with a copy of the covenant and proclaimed him king. They anointed him, and the people clapped their hands and shouted, "Long live the king!"

[13]When Athaliah heard the noise made by the guards and the people, she went to the people at the temple of the LORD. [14]She looked and there was the king, standing by the pillar, as the custom was. The officers and the trumpeters were beside the king, and all the people of the land were rejoicing and blowing trumpets. Then Athaliah tore her robes and called out, "Treason! Treason!"

[15]Jehoiada the priest ordered the commanders of units of a hundred, who were in charge of the troops: "Bring her out between the ranks[b] and put to the sword anyone who follows her." For the priest had said, "She must not be put to death in the temple of the LORD." [16]So they seized her as she reached the place where the horses enter the palace grounds, and there she was put to death.

[17]Jehoiada then made a covenant between the LORD and the king and people that they would be the LORD's people. He also made a covenant between the king and the people. [18]All the people of the land went to the temple of Baal and tore it down. They smashed the altars and idols to pieces and killed Mattan the priest of Baal in front of the altars.

Then Jehoiada the priest posted guards at the temple of the LORD. [19]He took with him the commanders of hundreds, the Carites, the guards and all the people of the land, and together they brought the king down from the temple of the LORD and went into the palace, entering by way of the gate of the guards. The king then took his place on the royal throne, [20]and all the people of the land rejoiced. And the city was quiet, because Athaliah had been slain with the sword at the palace.

THE MESSAGE

guard The Temple of GOD, are to join forces at the time of the changing of the guard and form a ring around the young king, weapons at the ready. Kill anyone who tries to break through your ranks. Your job is to stay with the king at all times and places, coming and going."

11.9-11 The captains obeyed the orders of Jehoiada the priest. Each took his men, those who came on duty on the Sabbath and those who went off duty on the Sabbath, and presented them to Jehoiada the priest. The priest armed the officers with spears and shields originally belonging to King David, stored in The Temple of GOD. Well-armed, the guards took up their assigned positions for protecting the king, from one end of The Temple to the other, surrounding both Altar and Temple.

11.12 Then the priest brought the prince into view, crowned him, handed him the scroll of God's covenant, and made him king. As they anointed him, everyone applauded and shouted, "Long live the king!"

11.13-14 Athaliah heard the shouting of guards and people and came to the crowd gathered at The Temple of GOD. Astonished, she saw the king standing beside the throne, flanked by the captains and heralds, with everybody beside themselves with joy, trumpets blaring. Athaliah ripped her robes in dismay and shouted, "Treason! Treason!"

11.15-16 Jehoiada the priest ordered the military officers, "Drag her outside and kill anyone who tries to follow her!" (The priest had said, "Don't kill her inside The Temple of GOD.") So they dragged her out to the palace's horse corral; there they killed her.

11.17 Jehoiada now made a covenant between GOD and the king and the people: They were GOD's people. Another covenant was made between the king and the people.

11.18-20 The people poured into the temple of Baal and tore it down, smashing altar and images to smithereens. They killed Mattan the priest in front of the altar.

Jehoiada then stationed sentries in The Temple of GOD. He arranged for the officers of the bodyguard and the palace security, along with the people themselves, to escort the king down from The Temple of GOD through the Gate of the Guards and into the palace. There he sat on the royal throne. Everybody celebrated the event. And the city was safe and undisturbed—they had killed Athaliah with the royal sword.

---

[a] 8 Or approaches the precincts   [b] 15 Or out from the precincts

NEW INTERNATIONAL VERSION

²¹Joash*ᵃ* was seven years old when he began to reign.

JOASH REPAIRS THE TEMPLE

12 In the seventh year of Jehu, Joash*ᵇ* became king, and he reigned in Jerusalem forty years. His mother's name was Zibiah; she was from Beersheba. ²Joash did what was right in the eyes of the LORD all the years Jehoiada the priest instructed him. ³The high places, however, were not removed; the people continued to offer sacrifices and burn incense there.

⁴Joash said to the priests, "Collect all the money that is brought as sacred offerings to the temple of the LORD—the money collected in the census, the money received from personal vows and the money brought voluntarily to the temple. ⁵Let every priest receive the money from one of the treasurers, and let it be used to repair whatever damage is found in the temple."

⁶But by the twenty-third year of King Joash the priests still had not repaired the temple. ⁷Therefore King Joash summoned Jehoiada the priest and the other priests and asked them, "Why aren't you repairing the damage done to the temple? Take no more money from your treasurers, but hand it over for repairing the temple." ⁸The priests agreed that they would not collect any more money from the people and that they would not repair the temple themselves.

⁹Jehoiada the priest took a chest and bored a hole in its lid. He placed it beside the altar, on the right side as one enters the temple of the LORD. The priests who guarded the entrance put into the chest all the money that was brought to the temple of the LORD. ¹⁰Whenever they saw that there was a large amount of money in the chest, the royal secretary and the high priest came, counted the money that had been brought into the temple of the LORD and put it into bags. ¹¹When the amount had been determined, they gave the money to the men appointed to supervise the work on the temple. With it they paid those who worked on the temple of the LORD—the carpenters and builders, ¹²the masons and stonecutters. They purchased timber and dressed stone for the repair of the temple of the LORD, and met all the other expenses of restoring the temple.

¹³The money brought into the temple was not spent for making silver basins, wick trimmers, sprinkling bowls, trumpets or any other articles of gold or silver for the temple of the LORD; ¹⁴it was paid to the workmen, who used it to repair the temple. ¹⁵They did not require an accounting from those to whom they gave the money to pay

THE MESSAGE

11.21 Joash was seven years old when he became king.

JOASH OF JUDAH

12 12.1 In the seventh year of Jehu, Joash began his kingly rule. He was king for forty years in Jerusalem. His mother's name was Gazelle. She was from Beersheba.

12.2-3 Taught and trained by Jehoiada the priest, Joash did what pleased GOD for as long as he lived. (Even so, he didn't get rid of the sacred fertility shrines—people still frequented them, sacrificing and burning incense.)

12.4-5 Joash instructed the priests: "Take the money that is brought into The Temple of GOD for holy offerings—both mandatory offerings and freewill offerings—and, keeping a careful accounting, use them to renovate The Temple wherever it has fallen into disrepair."

12.6 But by the twenty-third year of Joash's rule, the priests hadn't done one thing—The Temple was as dilapidated as ever.

12.7 King Joash called Jehoiada the priest and the company of priests and said, "Why haven't you renovated this sorry-looking Temple? You are forbidden to take any more money for Temple repairs—from now on, hand over everything you get."

12.8 The priests agreed not to take any more money or to be involved in The Temple renovation.

12.9-16 Then Jehoiada took a single chest and bored a hole in the lid and placed it to the right of the main entrance into The Temple of GOD. All the offerings that were brought to The Temple of GOD were placed in the chest by the priests who guarded the entrance. When they saw that a large sum of money had accumulated in the chest, the king's secretary and the chief priest would empty the chest and count the offerings. They would give the money accounted for to the managers of The Temple project; they in turn would pay the carpenters, construction workers, masons, stoneworkers, and the buyers of timber and quarried stone for the repair and renovation of The Temple of GOD—any expenses connected with fixing up The Temple. But none of the money brought into The Temple of GOD was used for liturgical "extras" (silver chalices, candle snuffers, trumpets, various gold and silver vessels, etc.). It was given to the workmen to pay for their repairing GOD's Temple. And no one even had to check on the men who handled the money given for the

---

*ᵃ 21 Hebrew Jehoash, a variant of Joash   ᵇ 1 Hebrew
Jehoash, a variant of Joash; also in verses 2, 4, 6, 7 and 18*

NEW INTERNATIONAL VERSION

the workers, because they acted with complete honesty. ¹⁶The money from the guilt offerings and sin offerings was not brought into the temple of the LORD; it belonged to the priests.

¹⁷About this time Hazael king of Aram went up and attacked Gath and captured it. Then he turned to attack Jerusalem. ¹⁸But Joash king of Judah took all the sacred objects dedicated by his fathers—Jehoshaphat, Jehoram and Ahaziah, the kings of Judah—and the gifts he himself had dedicated and all the gold found in the treasuries of the temple of the LORD and of the royal palace, and he sent them to Hazael king of Aram, who then withdrew from Jerusalem.

¹⁹As for the other events of the reign of Joash, and all he did, are they not written in the book of the annals of the kings of Judah? ²⁰His officials conspired against him and assassinated him at Beth Millo, on the road down to Silla. ²¹The officials who murdered him were Jozabad son of Shimeath and Jehozabad son of Shomer. He died and was buried with his fathers in the City of David. And Amaziah his son succeeded him as king.

JEHOAHAZ KING OF ISRAEL

13 In the twenty-third year of Joash son of Ahaziah king of Judah, Jehoahaz son of Jehu became king of Israel in Samaria, and he reigned seventeen years. ²He did evil in the eyes of the LORD by following the sins of Jeroboam son of Nebat, which he had caused Israel to commit, and he did not turn away from them. ³So the LORD's anger burned against Israel, and for a long time he kept them under the power of Hazael king of Aram and Ben-Hadad his son.

⁴Then Jehoahaz sought the LORD's favor, and the LORD listened to him, for he saw how severely the king of Aram was oppressing Israel. ⁵The LORD provided a deliverer for Israel, and they escaped from the power of Aram. So the Israelites lived in their own homes as they had before. ⁶But they did not turn away from the sins of the house of Jeroboam, which he had caused Israel to commit; they continued in them. Also, the Asherah pole[a] remained standing in Samaria.

⁷Nothing had been left of the army of Jehoahaz except fifty horsemen, ten chariots and ten thousand foot soldiers, for the king of Aram had destroyed the rest and made them like the dust at threshing time.

⁸As for the other events of the reign of Jehoahaz, all he did and his achievements, are they not written in the book of the annals of the kings

[a] 6 That is, a symbol of the goddess Asherah; here and elsewhere in 2 Kings

THE MESSAGE

project—they were honest men. Offerings designated for Compensation Offerings and Absolution Offerings didn't go into the building project—those went directly to the priests.

^{12.17-18} Around this time Hazael king of Aram ventured out and attacked Gath, and he captured it. Then he decided to try for Jerusalem. Joash king of Judah countered by gathering up all the sacred memorials—gifts dedicated for holy use by his ancestors, the kings of Judah, Jehoshaphat, Jehoram, and Ahaziah, along with the holy memorials he himself had received, plus all the gold that he could find in the temple and palace storerooms—and sent it to Hazael king of Aram. Appeased, Hazael went on his way and didn't bother Jerusalem.

^{12.19-21} The rest of the life and times of Joash and all that he did are written in *The Chronicles of the Kings of Judah*. At the last his palace staff formed a conspiracy and assassinated Joash as he was strolling along the ramp of the fortified outside city wall. Jozabad son of Shimeath and Jehozabad son of Shomer were the assassins. And so Joash died and was buried in the family plot in the City of David. His son Amaziah was king after him.

JEHOAHAZ OF ISRAEL

^{13.1-3} **13** In the twenty-third year of Joash son of Ahaziah king of Judah, Jehoahaz son of Jehu became king of Israel in Samaria—a rule of seventeen years. He lived an evil life before GOD, walking step for step in the tracks of Jeroboam son of Nebat who led Israel into a life of sin, swerving neither left or right. Exasperated, GOD was furious with Israel and turned them over to Hazael king of Aram and Ben-Hadad son of Hazael. This domination went on for a long time.

^{13.4-6} Then Jehoahaz prayed for a softening of GOD's anger, and GOD listened. He realized how wretched Israel had become under the brutalities of the king of Aram. So GOD provided a savior for Israel who brought them out from under Aram's oppression. The children of Israel were again able to live at peace in their own homes. But it didn't make any difference: They didn't change their lives, didn't turn away from the Jeroboam-sins that now characterized Israel, including the sex-and-religion shrines of Asherah still flourishing in Samaria.

^{13.7} Nothing was left of Jehoahaz's army after Hazael's oppression except for fifty cavalry, ten chariots, and ten thousand infantry. The king of Aram had decimated the rest, leaving behind him mostly chaff.

^{13.8-9} The rest of the life and times of Jehoahaz, the record of his accomplishments, are written in *The Chronicles of the Kings of Israel*. Jehoahaz

NEW INTERNATIONAL VERSION

of Israel? ⁹Jehoahaz rested with his fathers and was buried in Samaria. And Jehoash*a* his son succeeded him as king.

JEHOASH KING OF ISRAEL

¹⁰In the thirty-seventh year of Joash king of Judah, Jehoash son of Jehoahaz became king of Israel in Samaria, and he reigned sixteen years. ¹¹He did evil in the eyes of the LORD and did not turn away from any of the sins of Jeroboam son of Nebat, which he had caused Israel to commit; he continued in them.

¹²As for the other events of the reign of Jehoash, all he did and his achievements, including his war against Amaziah king of Judah, are they not written in the book of the annals of the kings of Israel? ¹³Jehoash rested with his fathers, and Jeroboam succeeded him on the throne. Jehoash was buried in Samaria with the kings of Israel.

¹⁴Now Elisha was suffering from the illness from which he died. Jehoash king of Israel went down to see him and wept over him. "My father! My father!" he cried. "The chariots and horsemen of Israel!"

¹⁵Elisha said, "Get a bow and some arrows," and he did so. ¹⁶"Take the bow in your hands," he said to the king of Israel. When he had taken it, Elisha put his hands on the king's hands.

¹⁷"Open the east window," he said, and he opened it. "Shoot!" Elisha said, and he shot. "The LORD's arrow of victory, the arrow of victory over Aram!" Elisha declared. "You will completely destroy the Arameans at Aphek."

¹⁸Then he said, "Take the arrows," and the king took them. Elisha told him, "Strike the ground." He struck it three times and stopped. ¹⁹The man of God was angry with him and said, "You should have struck the ground five or six times; then you would have defeated Aram and completely destroyed it. But now you will defeat it only three times."

²⁰Elisha died and was buried.

Now Moabite raiders used to enter the country every spring. ²¹Once while some Israelites were burying a man, suddenly they saw a band of raiders; so they threw the man's body into Elisha's tomb. When the body touched Elisha's bones, the man came to life and stood up on his feet.

²²Hazael king of Aram oppressed Israel

a 9 Hebrew *Joash,* a variant of *Jehoash;* also in verses 12-14 and 25

THE MESSAGE

died and was buried with his ancestors in Samaria. His son Jehoash succeeded him as king.

JEHOASH OF ISRAEL

13.10-11 In the thirty-seventh year of Joash king of Judah, Jehoash son of Jehoahaz became king of Israel in Samaria—a reign of sixteen years. In GOD's eyes he lived an evil life. He didn't deviate one bit from the sins of Jeroboam son of Nebat, who led Israel into a life of sin. He plodded along in the same tracks, step after step.

13.12-13 The rest of the life and times of Jehoash, the record of his accomplishments and his war against Amaziah king of Judah, are written in *The Chronicles of the Kings of Israel.* Jehoash died and joined his ancestors. Jeroboam took over his throne. Jehoash was buried in Samaria in the royal cemetery.

13.14 Elisha came down sick. It was the sickness of which he would soon die. Jehoash king of Israel paid him a visit. When he saw him he wept openly, crying, "My father, my father! Chariot and horsemen of Israel!"

13.15 Elisha told him, "Go and get a bow and some arrows." The king brought him the bow and arrows.

13.16 Then he told the king, "Put your hand on the bow." He put his hand on the bow. Then Elisha put his hand over the hand of the king.

13.17 Elisha said, "Now open the east window." He opened it.

Then he said, "Shoot!" And he shot.

"The arrow of GOD's salvation!" exclaimed Elisha. "The arrow of deliverance from Aram! You will do battle against Aram until there's nothing left of it."

13.18 "Now pick up the other arrows," said Elisha. He picked them up.

Then he said to the king of Israel, "Strike the ground."

The king struck the ground three times and then quit.

13.19 The Holy Man became angry with him: "Why didn't you hit the ground five or six times? Then you would beat Aram until he was finished. As it is, you'll defeat him three times only."

13.20-21 Then Elisha died and they buried him.

Some time later, raiding bands of Moabites, as they often did, invaded the country. One day, some men were burying a man and spotted the raiders. They threw the man into Elisha's tomb and got away. When the body touched Elisha's bones, the man came alive, stood up, and walked out on his own two feet.

13.22-24 Hazael king of Aram badgered and bedeviled

NEW INTERNATIONAL VERSION

throughout the reign of Jehoahaz. ²³But the LORD was gracious to them and had compassion and showed concern for them because of his covenant with Abraham, Isaac and Jacob. To this day he has been unwilling to destroy them or banish them from his presence.

²⁴Hazael king of Aram died, and Ben-Hadad his son succeeded him as king. ²⁵Then Jehoash son of Jehoahaz recaptured from Ben-Hadad son of Hazael the towns he had taken in battle from his father Jehoahaz. Three times Jehoash defeated him, and so he recovered the Israelite towns.

AMAZIAH KING OF JUDAH

14 In the second year of Jehoash[a] son of Jehoahaz king of Israel, Amaziah son of Joash king of Judah began to reign. ²He was twenty-five years old when he became king, and he reigned in Jerusalem twenty-nine years. His mother's name was Jehoaddin; she was from Jerusalem. ³He did what was right in the eyes of the LORD, but not as his father David had done. In everything he followed the example of his father Joash. ⁴The high places, however, were not removed; the people continued to offer sacrifices and burn incense there.

⁵After the kingdom was firmly in his grasp, he executed the officials who had murdered his father the king. ⁶Yet he did not put the sons of the assassins to death, in accordance with what is written in the Book of the Law of Moses where the LORD commanded: "Fathers shall not be put to death for their children, nor children put to death for their fathers; each is to die for his own sins."[b]

⁷He was the one who defeated ten thousand Edomites in the Valley of Salt and captured Sela in battle, calling it Joktheel, the name it has to this day.

⁸Then Amaziah sent messengers to Jehoash son of Jehoahaz, the son of Jehu, king of Israel, with the challenge: "Come, meet me face to face."

⁹But Jehoash king of Israel replied to Amaziah king of Judah: "A thistle in Lebanon sent a message to a cedar in Lebanon, 'Give your daughter to my son in marriage.' Then a wild beast in Lebanon came along and trampled the thistle underfoot. ¹⁰You have indeed defeated Edom and now you are arrogant. Glory in your victory, but stay at home! Why ask for trouble and cause your own downfall and that of Judah also?"

¹¹Amaziah, however, would not listen, so Jehoash king of Israel attacked. He and Amaziah king of Judah faced each other at Beth Shemesh

^a 1 Hebrew *Joash*, a variant of *Jehoash*; also in verses 13, 23 and 27   ^b 6 Deut. 24:16

THE MESSAGE

Israel all through the reign of Jehoahaz. But GOD was gracious and showed mercy to them. He stuck with them out of respect for his covenant with Abraham, Isaac, and Jacob. He never gave up on them, never even considered discarding them, even to this day. Hazael king of Aram died. His son Ben-Hadad was the next king.

13.25   Jehoash son of Jehoahaz turned things around and took back the cities that Ben-Hadad son of Hazael had taken from his father Jehoahaz. Jehoash went to war three times and defeated him each time, recapturing the cities of Israel.

AMAZIAH OF JUDAH

14.1-2 **14** In the second year of Jehoash son of Jehoahaz king of Israel, Amaziah son of Joash became king of Judah. He was twenty-five years old when he became king and he reigned for twenty-nine years in Jerusalem. His mother's name was Jehoaddin. She was from Jerusalem.

14.3-4 He lived the way GOD wanted and did the right thing. But he didn't come up to the standards of his ancestor David; instead he lived pretty much as his father Joash had; the local sex-and-religion shrines continued to stay in business with people frequenting them.

14.5-6 When he had the affairs of the kingdom well in hand, he executed the palace guard that had assassinated his father the king. But he didn't kill the sons of the assassins. He was obedient to what GOD commanded, written in the Word revealed to Moses, that parents shouldn't be executed for their children's sins, nor children for those of their parents. We each pay personally for our sins.

14.7   Amaziah roundly defeated Edom in the Valley of Salt to the tune of ten thousand dead. In another battle he took The Rock and renamed it Joktheel, the name it still bears.

14.8   One day Amaziah sent envoys to Jehoash son of Jehoahaz, the son of Jehu, king of Israel, challenging him to a fight: "Come and meet with me—I dare you. Let's have it out face to face!"

14.9-10 Jehoash king of Israel replied to Amaziah king of Judah, "One day a thistle in Lebanon sent word to a cedar in Lebanon, 'Give your daughter to my son in marriage.' But then a wild animal of Lebanon passed by and stepped on the thistle, crushing it. Just because you've defeated Edom in battle, you now think you're a big shot. Go ahead and be proud, but stay home. Why press your luck? Why bring defeat on yourself and Judah?"

14.11 Amaziah wouldn't take No for an answer. So Jehoash king of Israel gave in and agreed to a battle between him and Amaziah king of Judah. They met at Beth Shemesh, a town of Judah.

NEW INTERNATIONAL VERSION

in Judah. 12Judah was routed by Israel, and every man fled to his home. 13Jehoash king of Israel captured Amaziah king of Judah, the son of Joash, the son of Ahaziah, at Beth Shemesh. Then Jehoash went to Jerusalem and broke down the wall of Jerusalem from the Ephraim Gate to the Corner Gate—a section about six hundred feet long.*a* 14He took all the gold and silver and all the articles found in the temple of the LORD and in the treasuries of the royal palace. He also took hostages and returned to Samaria.

15As for the other events of the reign of Jehoash, what he did and his achievements, including his war against Amaziah king of Judah, are they not written in the book of the annals of the kings of Israel? 16Jehoash rested with his fathers and was buried in Samaria with the kings of Israel. And Jeroboam his son succeeded him as king.

17Amaziah son of Joash king of Judah lived for fifteen years after the death of Jehoash son of Jehoahaz king of Israel. 18As for the other events of Amaziah's reign, are they not written in the book of the annals of the kings of Judah?

19They conspired against him in Jerusalem, and he fled to Lachish, but they sent men after him to Lachish and killed him there. 20He was brought back by horse and was buried in Jerusalem with his fathers, in the City of David.

21Then all the people of Judah took Azariah,*b* who was sixteen years old, and made him king in place of his father Amaziah. 22He was the one who rebuilt Elath and restored it to Judah after Amaziah rested with his fathers.

JEROBOAM II KING OF ISRAEL

23In the fifteenth year of Amaziah son of Joash king of Judah, Jeroboam son of Jehoash king of Israel became king in Samaria, and he reigned forty-one years. 24He did evil in the eyes of the LORD and did not turn away from any of the sins of Jeroboam son of Nebat, which he had caused Israel to commit. 25He was the one who restored the boundaries of Israel from Lebo*c* Hamath to the Sea of the Arabah,*d* in accordance with the word of the LORD, the God of Israel, spoken through his servant Jonah son of Amittai, the prophet from Gath Hepher.

26The LORD had seen how bitterly everyone in Israel, whether slave or free, was suffering; there was no one to help them. 27And since the LORD had not said he would blot out the name of Israel from under heaven, he saved them by the hand of Jeroboam son of Jehoash.

a 13 Hebrew *four hundred cubits* (about 180 meters)
b 21 Also called *Uzziah*   *c* 25 Or *from the entrance to*
d 25 That is, the Dead Sea

THE MESSAGE

14.12   Judah was thoroughly beaten by Israel—all their soldiers ran home in defeat.

14.13-14   Jehoash king of Israel captured Amaziah king of Judah, the son of Joash, the son of Ahaziah, at Beth Shemesh. But Jehoash didn't stop there; he went on to attack Jerusalem. He demolished the wall of Jerusalem all the way from the Ephraim Gate to the Corner Gate—a stretch of about 600 feet. He looted the gold, silver, and furnishings—anything he found that was worth taking—from both the palace and The Temple of GOD. And, for good measure, he took hostages. Then he returned to Samaria.

14.15-16   The rest of the life and times of Jehoash, his significant accomplishments and the fight with Amaziah king of Judah, are all written in *The Chronicles of the Kings of Israel*. Jehoash died and was buried in Samaria in the cemetery of the kings of Israel. His son Jeroboam became the next king.

14.17-18   Amaziah son of Joash king of Judah continued as king fifteen years after the death of Jehoash son of Jehoahaz king of Israel. The rest of the life and times of Amaziah is written in *The Chronicles of the Kings of Judah*.

14.19-20   At the last they cooked up a plot against Amaziah in Jerusalem and he had to flee to Lachish. But they tracked him down in Lachish and killed him there. They brought him back on horseback and buried him in Jerusalem, with his ancestors in the City of David.

14.21-22   Azariah—he was only sixteen years old at the time—was the unanimous choice of the people of Judah to succeed his father Amaziah as king. Following his father's death, he rebuilt and restored Elath to Judah.

JEROBOAM II OF ISRAEL

14.23-25 In the fifteenth year of Amaziah son of Joash king of Judah, Jeroboam son of Jehoash became king of Israel in Samaria. He ruled for forty-one years. As far as GOD was concerned he lived an evil life, never deviating an inch from all the sin of Jeroboam son of Nebat, who led Israel into a life of sin. But he did restore the borders of Israel to Lebo Hamath in the far north and to the Dead Sea in the south, matching what GOD, the God of Israel, had pronounced through his servant Jonah son of Amittai, the prophet from Gath Hepher.

14.26-27   GOD was fully aware of the trouble in Israel, its bitterly hard times. No one was exempt, whether slave or citizen, and no hope of help anywhere was in sight. But GOD wasn't yet ready to blot out the name of Israel from history, so he used Jeroboam son of Jehoash to save them.

NEW INTERNATIONAL VERSION

²⁸As for the other events of Jeroboam's reign, all he did, and his military achievements, including how he recovered for Israel both Damascus and Hamath, which had belonged to Yaudi,ᵃ are they not written in the book of the annals of the kings of Israel? ²⁹Jeroboam rested with his fathers, the kings of Israel. And Zechariah his son succeeded him as king.

AZARIAH KING OF JUDAH

15 In the twenty-seventh year of Jeroboam king of Israel, Azariah son of Amaziah king of Judah began to reign. ²He was sixteen years old when he became king, and he reigned in Jerusalem fifty-two years. His mother's name was Jecoliah; she was from Jerusalem. ³He did what was right in the eyes of the LORD, just as his father Amaziah had done. ⁴The high places, however, were not removed; the people continued to offer sacrifices and burn incense there.

⁵The LORD afflicted the king with leprosyᵇ until the day he died, and he lived in a separate house.ᶜ Jotham the king's son had charge of the palace and governed the people of the land.

⁶As for the other events of Azariah's reign, and all he did, are they not written in the book of the annals of the kings of Judah? ⁷Azariah rested with his fathers and was buried near them in the City of David. And Jotham his son succeeded him as king.

ZECHARIAH KING OF ISRAEL

⁸In the thirty-eighth year of Azariah king of Judah, Zechariah son of Jeroboam became king of Israel in Samaria, and he reigned six months. ⁹He did evil in the eyes of the LORD, as his fathers had done. He did not turn away from the sins of Jeroboam son of Nebat, which he had caused Israel to commit.

¹⁰Shallum son of Jabesh conspired against Zechariah. He attacked him in front of the people,ᵈ assassinated him and succeeded him as king. ¹¹The other events of Zechariah's reign are written in the book of the annals of the kings of Israel. ¹²So the word of the LORD spoken to Jehu was fulfilled: "Your descendants will sit on the throne of Israel to the fourth generation."ᵉ

SHALLUM KING OF ISRAEL

¹³Shallum son of Jabesh became king in the thirty-ninth year of Uzziah king of Judah, and he reigned in Samaria one month. ¹⁴Then Menahem son of Gadi went from Tirzah up to Samar-

---

ᵃ 28 Or *Judah*   ᵇ 5 The Hebrew word was used for various diseases affecting the skin—not necessarily leprosy.
ᶜ 5 Or *in a house where he was relieved of responsibility*
ᵈ 10 Hebrew; some Septuagint manuscripts *in Ibleam*
ᵉ 12 2 Kings 10:30

THE MESSAGE

14.28-29 The rest of the life and times of Jeroboam, his victories in battle and how he recovered for Israel both Damascus and Hamath which had belonged to Judah, these are all written in *The Chronicles of the Kings of Israel*. Jeroboam died and was buried with his ancestors in the royal cemetery. His son Zechariah became the next king.

AZARIAH (UZZIAH) OF JUDAH

15 In the twenty-seventh year of Jeroboam king of Israel, Azariah son of Amaziah became king in Judah. He was sixteen years old when he began his rule and he was king for fifty-two years in Jerusalem. His mother's name was Jecoliah. She was from Jerusalem. He did well in the eyes of GOD, following in the footsteps of his father Amaziah. But he also failed to get rid of the local sex-and-religion shrines; they continued to be popular with the people. GOD afflicted the king with a bad skin disease until the day of his death. He lived in the palace but no longer acted as king; his son Jotham ran the government and ruled the country.

15.6-7 The rest of the life and times of Azariah, everything he accomplished, is written in *The Chronicles of the Kings of Judah*. Azariah died and was buried with his ancestors in the City of David. Jotham his son was king after him.

ZECHARIAH OF ISRAEL

15.8-9 In the thirty-eighth year of Azariah king of Judah, Zechariah son of Jeroboam became king over Israel in Samaria. He lasted only six months. He lived a bad life before GOD, no different from his ancestors. He continued in the line of Jeroboam son of Nebat who led Israel into a life of sin.

15.10 Shallum son of Jabesh conspired against him, assassinated him in public view, and took over as king.

15.11-12 The rest of the life and times of Zechariah is written plainly in *The Chronicles of the Kings of Israel*. That completed the word of GOD that was given to Jehu, namely, "For four generations your sons will sit on the throne of Israel." Zechariah was the fourth.

SHALLUM OF ISRAEL

15.13 Shallum son of Jabesh became king in the thirty-ninth year of Azariah king of Judah. He was king in Samaria for only a month.

15.14 Menahem son of Gadi came up from Tirzah

NEW INTERNATIONAL VERSION

ia. He attacked Shallum son of Jabesh in Samaria, assassinated him and succeeded him as king.

¹⁵The other events of Shallum's reign, and the conspiracy he led, are written in the book of the annals of the kings of Israel.

¹⁶At that time Menahem, starting out from Tirzah, attacked Tiphsah and everyone in the city and its vicinity, because they refused to open their gates. He sacked Tiphsah and ripped open all the pregnant women.

MENAHEM KING OF ISRAEL

¹⁷In the thirty-ninth year of Azariah king of Judah, Menahem son of Gadi became king of Israel, and he reigned in Samaria ten years. ¹⁸He did evil in the eyes of the LORD. During his entire reign he did not turn away from the sins of Jeroboam son of Nebat, which he had caused Israel to commit.

¹⁹Then Pul*a* king of Assyria invaded the land, and Menahem gave him a thousand talents*b* of silver to gain his support and strengthen his own hold on the kingdom. ²⁰Menahem exacted this money from Israel. Every wealthy man had to contribute fifty shekels*c* of silver to be given to the king of Assyria. So the king of Assyria withdrew and stayed in the land no longer.

²¹As for the other events of Menahem's reign, and all he did, are they not written in the book of the annals of the kings of Israel? ²²Menahem rested with his fathers. And Pekahiah his son succeeded him as king.

PEKAHIAH KING OF ISRAEL

²³In the fiftieth year of Azariah king of Judah, Pekahiah son of Menahem became king of Israel in Samaria, and he reigned two years. ²⁴Pekahiah did evil in the eyes of the LORD. He did not turn away from the sins of Jeroboam son of Nebat, which he had caused Israel to commit. ²⁵One of his chief officers, Pekah son of Remaliah, conspired against him. Taking fifty men of Gilead with him, he assassinated Pekahiah, along with Argob and Arieh, in the citadel of the royal palace at Samaria. So Pekah killed Pekahiah and succeeded him as king.

²⁶The other events of Pekahiah's reign, and all he did, are written in the book of the annals of the kings of Israel.

PEKAH KING OF ISRAEL

²⁷In the fifty-second year of Azariah king of Judah, Pekah son of Remaliah became king of Israel in Samaria, and he reigned twenty years. ²⁸He did evil in the eyes of the LORD. He did not

THE MESSAGE

to Samaria. He attacked Shallum son of Jabesh and killed him. He then became king.

15.15 The rest of the life and times of Shallum and the account of the conspiracy are written in *The Chronicles of the Kings of Israel.*

MENAHEM OF ISRAEL

15.16 Using Tirzah as his base, Menahem opened his reign by smashing Tiphsah, devastating both the town and its suburbs because they didn't welcome him with open arms. He savagely ripped open all the pregnant women.

15.17-18 In the thirty-ninth year of Azariah king of Judah, Menahem son of Gadi became king over Israel. He ruled from Samaria for ten years. As far as GOD was concerned he lived an evil life. Sin for sin, he repeated the sins of Jeroboam son of Nebat, who led Israel into a life of sin.

15.19-20 Then Tiglath-Pileser III king of Assyria showed up and attacked the country. But Menahem made a deal with him: He bought his support by handing over about thirty-seven tons of silver. He raised the money by making every landowner in Israel pay fifty shekels to the king of Assyria. That satisfied the king of Assyria, and he left the country.

15.21-22 The rest of the life and times of Menahem, everything he did, is written in *The Chronicles of the Kings of Israel.* Menahem died and joined his ancestors. His son Pekahiah became the next king.

PEKAHIAH OF ISRAEL

15.23-24 In the fiftieth year of Azariah king of Judah, Pekahiah son of Menahem became king of Israel. He ruled in Samaria for two years. In GOD's eyes he lived an evil life. He stuck to the old sin tracks of Jeroboam son of Nebat, who led Israel into a life of sin.

15.25 And then his military aide Pekah son of Remaliah conspired against him—killed him in cold blood while he was in his private quarters in the royal palace in Samaria. He also killed Argob and Arieh. Fifty Gadites were in on the conspiracy with him. After the murder he became the next king.

15.26 The rest of the life and times of Pekahiah, everything he did, is written in *The Chronicles of the Kings of Israel.*

PEKAH OF ISRAEL

15.27-28 In the fifty-second year of Azariah king of Judah, Pekah son of Remaliah became king of Israel in Samaria. He ruled for twenty years. In GOD's view he lived an evil life; he didn't devi-

---

a 19 Also called *Tiglath-Pileser*   *b 19* That is, about 37 tons (about 34 metric tons)   *c 20* That is, about 1 1/4 pounds (about 0.6 kilogram)

NEW INTERNATIONAL VERSION

turn away from the sins of Jeroboam son of Nebat, which he had caused Israel to commit.

²⁹In the time of Pekah king of Israel, Tiglath-Pileser king of Assyria came and took Ijon, Abel Beth Maacah, Janoah, Kedesh and Hazor. He took Gilead and Galilee, including all the land of Naphtali, and deported the people to Assyria. ³⁰Then Hoshea son of Elah conspired against Pekah son of Remaliah. He attacked and assassinated him, and then succeeded him as king in the twentieth year of Jotham son of Uzziah.

³¹As for the other events of Pekah's reign, and all he did, are they not written in the book of the annals of the kings of Israel?

JOTHAM KING OF JUDAH

³²In the second year of Pekah son of Remaliah king of Israel, Jotham son of Uzziah king of Judah began to reign. ³³He was twenty-five years old when he became king, and he reigned in Jerusalem sixteen years. His mother's name was Jerusha daughter of Zadok. ³⁴He did what was right in the eyes of the LORD, just as his father Uzziah had done. ³⁵The high places, however, were not removed; the people continued to offer sacrifices and burn incense there. Jotham rebuilt the Upper Gate of the temple of the LORD.

³⁶As for the other events of Jotham's reign, and what he did, are they not written in the book of the annals of the kings of Judah? ³⁷(In those days the LORD began to send Rezin king of Aram and Pekah son of Remaliah against Judah.) ³⁸Jotham rested with his fathers and was buried with them in the City of David, the city of his father. And Ahaz his son succeeded him as king.

AHAZ KING OF JUDAH

16 In the seventeenth year of Pekah son of Remaliah, Ahaz son of Jotham king of Judah began to reign. ²Ahaz was twenty years old when he became king, and he reigned in Jerusalem sixteen years. Unlike David his father, he did not do what was right in the eyes of the LORD his God. ³He walked in the ways of the kings of Israel and even sacrificed his son in ᵃ the fire, following the detestable ways of the nations the LORD had driven out before the Israelites. ⁴He offered sacrifices and burned incense at the high places, on the hilltops and under every spreading tree.

⁵Then Rezin king of Aram and Pekah son of Remaliah king of Israel marched up to fight against Jerusalem and besieged Ahaz, but they

ᵃ 3 Or even made his son pass through

THE MESSAGE

ate so much as a hair's breadth from the path laid down by Jeroboam son of Nebat, who led Israel into a life of sin.

15.29 During the reign of Pekah king of Israel, Tiglath-Pileser III king of Assyria invaded the country. He captured Ijon, Abel Beth Maacah, Janoah, Kedesh, Hazor, Gilead, Galilee—the whole country of Naphtali—and took everyone captive to Assyria.

15.30 But then Hoshea son of Elah mounted a conspiracy against Pekah son of Remaliah. He assassinated him and took over as king. This was in the twentieth year of Jotham son of Uzziah.

15.31 The rest of the life and times of Pekah, everything he did, is written in *The Chronicles of the Kings of Israel.*

JOTHAM OF JUDAH

15.32-35 In the second year of Pekah son of Remaliah king of Israel, Jotham son of Uzziah became king in Judah. He was twenty-five years old when he became king and reigned sixteen years in Jerusalem. His mother's name was Jerusha daughter of Zadok. He acted well in GOD's eyes, following in the steps of his father Uzziah. But he didn't interfere with the traffic to the neighborhood sex-and-religion shrines; they continued, as popular as ever. The construction of the High Gate to The Temple of GOD was his work.

15.36-38 The rest of the life and times of Jotham, the record of his work, is written in *The Chronicles of the Kings of Judah.* It was during these years that GOD began sending Rezin king of Aram and Pekah son of Remaliah to attack Judah. Jotham died and joined his ancestors. They buried him in the family cemetery in the City of David. His son Ahaz was the next king.

AHAZ OF JUDAH

16 In the seventeenth year of Pekah son of Remaliah, Ahaz son of Jotham became king of Judah. Ahaz was twenty years old when he became king and he ruled for sixteen years in Jerusalem. He didn't behave in the eyes of his GOD; he wasn't at all like his ancestor David. Instead he followed in the track of the kings of Israel. He even indulged in the outrageous practice of "passing his son through the fire"—a truly abominable act he picked up from the pagans GOD had earlier thrown out of the country. He also participated in the activities of the neighborhood sex-and-religion shrines that flourished all over the place.

16.5 Then Rezin king of Aram and Pekah son of Remaliah king of Israel ganged up against Jerusalem, throwing a siege around the city, but they couldn't make further headway against Ahaz.

NEW INTERNATIONAL VERSION

could not overpower him. ⁶At that time, Rezin king of Aram recovered Elath for Aram by driving out the men of Judah. Edomites then moved into Elath and have lived there to this day.

⁷Ahaz sent messengers to say to Tiglath-Pileser king of Assyria, "I am your servant and vassal. Come up and save me out of the hand of the king of Aram and of the king of Israel, who are attacking me." ⁸And Ahaz took the silver and gold found in the temple of the LORD and in the treasuries of the royal palace and sent it as a gift to the king of Assyria. ⁹The king of Assyria complied by attacking Damascus and capturing it. He deported its inhabitants to Kir and put Rezin to death.

¹⁰Then King Ahaz went to Damascus to meet Tiglath-Pileser king of Assyria. He saw an altar in Damascus and sent to Uriah the priest a sketch of the altar, with detailed plans for its construction. ¹¹So Uriah the priest built an altar in accordance with all the plans that King Ahaz had sent from Damascus and finished it before King Ahaz returned. ¹²When the king came back from Damascus and saw the altar, he approached it and presented offerings*a* on it. ¹³He offered up his burnt offering and grain offering, poured out his drink offering, and sprinkled the blood of his fellowship offerings*b* on the altar. ¹⁴The bronze altar that stood before the LORD he brought from the front of the temple—from between the new altar and the temple of the LORD—and put it on the north side of the new altar.

¹⁵King Ahaz then gave these orders to Uriah the priest: "On the large new altar, offer the morning burnt offering and the evening grain offering, the king's burnt offering and his grain offering, and the burnt offering of all the people of the land, and their grain offering and their drink offering. Sprinkle on the altar all the blood of the burnt offerings and sacrifices. But I will use the bronze altar for seeking guidance." ¹⁶And Uriah the priest did just as King Ahaz had ordered.

¹⁷King Ahaz took away the side panels and removed the basins from the movable stands. He removed the Sea from the bronze bulls that supported it and set it on a stone base. ¹⁸He took away the Sabbath canopy*c* that had been built at the temple and removed the royal entryway outside the temple of the LORD, in deference to the king of Assyria.

¹⁹As for the other events of the reign of Ahaz, and what he did, are they not written in the book of the annals of the kings of Judah? ²⁰Ahaz rested with his fathers and was buried with them

THE MESSAGE

16.6 At about this same time and on another front, the king of Edom recovered the port of Elath and expelled the men of Judah. The Edomites occupied Elath and have been there ever since.

16.7-8 Ahaz sent envoys to Tiglath-Pileser king of Assyria with this message: "I'm your servant and your son. Come and save me from the heavy-handed invasion of the king of Aram and the king of Israel. They're attacking me right now." Then Ahaz robbed the treasuries of the palace and The Temple of GOD of their gold and silver and sent them to the king of Assyria as a bribe.

16.9 The king of Assyria responded to him. He attacked and captured Damascus. He deported the people to Nineveh as exiles. Rezin he killed.

16.10-11 King Ahaz went to meet Tiglath-Pileser king of Assyria in Damascus. The altar in Damascus made a great impression on him. He sent back to Uriah the priest a drawing and set of blueprints of the altar. Uriah the priest built the altar to the specifications that King Ahaz had sent from Damascus. By the time the king returned from Damascus, Uriah had completed the altar.

16.12-14 The minute the king saw the altar he approached it with reverence and arranged a service of worship with a full course of offerings: Whole-Burnt-Offerings with billows of smoke, Grain-Offerings, libations of Drink-Offerings, the sprinkling of blood from the Peace-Offerings—the works. But the old bronze Altar that signaled the presence of GOD he displaced from its central place and pushed it off to the side of his new altar.

16.15 Then King Ahaz ordered Uriah the priest: "From now on offer all the sacrifices on the new altar, the great altar: morning Whole-Burnt-Offerings, evening Grain-Offerings, the king's Whole-Burnt-Offerings and Grain-Offerings, the people's Whole-Burnt-Offerings and Grain-Offerings, and also their Drink-Offerings. Splash all the blood from the burnt offerings and sacrifices against this altar. The old bronze Altar will be for my personal use."

16.16 The priest Uriah followed King Ahaz's orders to the letter.

16.17-18 Then King Ahaz proceeded to plunder The Temple furniture of all its bronze. He stripped the bronze from The Temple furnishings, even salvaged the four bronze oxen that supported the huge basin, The Sea, and set The Sea unceremoniously on the stone pavement. Finally, he removed any distinctive features from within The Temple that were offensive to the king of Assyria.

16.19-20 The rest of the life and times of Ahaz is written in *The Chronicles of the Kings of Judah.* Ahaz died and was buried with his ancestors in the

---

a 12 Or *and went up*   *b* 13 Traditionally *peace offerings*
c 18 Or *the dais of his throne* (see Septuagint)

NEW INTERNATIONAL VERSION

in the City of David. And Hezekiah his son succeeded him as king.

HOSHEA LAST KING OF ISRAEL

17 In the twelfth year of Ahaz king of Judah, Hoshea son of Elah became king of Israel in Samaria, and he reigned nine years. ²He did evil in the eyes of the LORD, but not like the kings of Israel who preceded him.

³Shalmaneser king of Assyria came up to attack Hoshea, who had been Shalmaneser's vassal and had paid him tribute. ⁴But the king of Assyria discovered that Hoshea was a traitor, for he had sent envoys to So*ᵃ* king of Egypt, and he no longer paid tribute to the king of Assyria, as he had done year by year. Therefore Shalmaneser seized him and put him in prison. ⁵The king of Assyria invaded the entire land, marched against Samaria and laid siege to it for three years. ⁶In the ninth year of Hoshea, the king of Assyria captured Samaria and deported the Israelites to Assyria. He settled them in Halah, in Gozan on the Habor River and in the towns of the Medes.

ISRAEL EXILED BECAUSE OF SIN

⁷All this took place because the Israelites had sinned against the LORD their God, who had brought them up out of Egypt from under the power of Pharaoh king of Egypt. They worshiped other gods ⁸and followed the practices of the nations the LORD had driven out before them, as well as the practices that the kings of Israel had introduced. ⁹The Israelites secretly did things against the LORD their God that were not right. From watchtower to fortified city they built themselves high places in all their towns. ¹⁰They set up sacred stones and Asherah poles on every high hill and under every spreading tree. ¹¹At every high place they burned incense, as the nations whom the LORD had driven out before them had done. They did wicked things that provoked the LORD to anger. ¹²They worshiped idols, though the LORD had said, "You shall not do this."*ᵇ* ¹³The LORD warned Israel and Judah through all his prophets and seers: "Turn from your evil ways. Observe my commands and decrees, in accordance with the entire Law that I commanded your fathers to obey and that I delivered to you through my servants the prophets."

¹⁴But they would not listen and were as stiffnecked as their fathers, who did not trust in the

---

ᵃ 4 Or *to Sais, to the;* So is possibly an abbreviation for *Osorkon.* *ᵇ 12* Exodus 20:4,5

THE MESSAGE

City of David. His son Hezekiah became the next king.

HOSHEA OF ISRAEL

17.1-2 **17** In the twelfth year of Ahaz king of Judah, Hoshea son of Elah became king of Israel. He ruled in Samaria for nine years. As far as GOD was concerned, he lived a bad life, but not nearly as bad as the kings who had preceded him.

17.3-5 Then Shalmaneser king of Assyria attacked. Hoshea was already a puppet of the Assyrian king and regularly sent him tribute, but Shalmaneser discovered that Hoshea had been operating traitorously behind his back—having worked out a deal with King So of Egypt. And, adding insult to injury, Hoshea was way behind on his annual payments of tribute to Assyria. So the king of Assyria arrested him and threw him in prison, then proceeded to invade the entire country. He attacked Samaria and threw up a siege against it. The siege lasted three years.

17.6 In the ninth year of Hoshea's reign the king of Assyria captured Samaria and took the people into exile in Assyria. He relocated them in Halah, in Gozan along the Habor River, and in the towns of the Medes.

17.7-12 The exile came about because of sin: The children of Israel sinned against GOD, their God, who had delivered them from Egypt and the brutal oppression of Pharaoh king of Egypt. They took up with other gods, fell in with the ways of life of the pagan nations GOD had chased off, and went along with whatever their kings did. They did all kinds of things on the sly, things offensive to their GOD, then openly and shamelessly built local sex-and-religion shrines at every available site. They set up their sex-and-religion symbols at practically every crossroads. Everywhere you looked there was smoke from their pagan offerings to the deities—the identical offerings that had gotten the pagan nations off into exile. They had accumulated a long list of evil actions and GOD was fed up, fed up with their persistent worship of gods carved out of deadwood or shaped out of clay, even though GOD had plainly said, "Don't do this—ever!"

17.13 GOD had taken a stand against Israel and Judah, speaking clearly through countless holy prophets and seers time and time again, "Turn away from your evil way of life. Do what I tell you and have been telling you in The Revelation I gave your ancestors and of which I've kept reminding you ever since through my servants the prophets."

17.14-15 But they wouldn't listen. If anything, they were even more bullheaded than their stubborn

LORD their God. 15They rejected his decrees and the covenant he had made with their fathers and the warnings he had given them. They followed worthless idols and themselves became worthless. They imitated the nations around them although the LORD had ordered them, "Do not do as they do," and they did the things the LORD had forbidden them to do.

16They forsook all the commands of the LORD their God and made for themselves two idols cast in the shape of calves, and an Asherah pole. They bowed down to all the starry hosts, and they worshiped Baal. 17They sacrificed their sons and daughters in*a* the fire. They practiced divination and sorcery and sold themselves to do evil in the eyes of the LORD, provoking him to anger.

18So the LORD was very angry with Israel and removed them from his presence. Only the tribe of Judah was left, 19and even Judah did not keep the commands of the LORD their God. They followed the practices Israel had introduced. 20Therefore the LORD rejected all the people of Israel; he afflicted them and gave them into the hands of plunderers, until he thrust them from his presence.

21When he tore Israel away from the house of David, they made Jeroboam son of Nebat their king. Jeroboam enticed Israel away from following the LORD and caused them to commit a great sin. 22The Israelites persisted in all the sins of Jeroboam and did not turn away from them 23until the LORD removed them from his presence, as he had warned through all his servants the prophets. So the people of Israel were taken from their homeland into exile in Assyria, and they are still there.

SAMARIA RESETTLED

24The king of Assyria brought people from Babylon, Cuthah, Avva, Hamath and Sepharvaim and settled them in the towns of Samaria to replace the Israelites. They took over Samaria and lived in its towns. 25When they first lived there, they did not worship the LORD; so he sent lions among them and they killed some of the people. 26It was reported to the king of Assyria: "The people you deported and resettled in the towns of Samaria do not know what the god of that

---

a 17 Or They made their sons and daughters pass through

ancestors, if that's possible. They were contemptuous of his instructions, the solemn and holy covenant he had made with their ancestors, and of his repeated reminders and warnings. They lived a "nothing" life and became "nothings"—just like the pagan peoples all around them. They were well-warned: GOD said, "Don't!" but they did it anyway.

17.16-17 They threw out everything GOD, their God, had told them, and replaced him with two statue-gods shaped like bull-calves and then a phallic pole for the whore goddess Asherah. They worshiped cosmic forces—sky gods and goddesses—and frequented the sex-and-religion shrines of Baal. They even sank so low as to offer their own sons and daughters as sacrificial burnt offerings! They indulged in all the black arts of magic and sorcery. In short, they prostituted themselves to every kind of evil available to them. And GOD had had enough.

17.18-20 GOD was so thoroughly angry that he got rid of them, got them out of the country for good until only one tribe was left—Judah. (Judah, actually, wasn't much better, for Judah also failed to keep GOD's commands, falling into the same way of life that Israel had adopted.) GOD rejected everyone connected with Israel, made life hard for them, and permitted anyone with a mind to exploit them to do so. And then this final No as he threw them out of his sight.

17.21-23 Back at the time that God ripped Israel out of their place in the family of David, they had made Jeroboam son of Nebat king. Jeroboam debauched Israel—turned them away from serving GOD and led them into a life of total sin. The children of Israel went along with all the sins that Jeroboam did, never murmured so much as a word of protest. In the end, GOD spoke a final No to Israel and turned his back on them. He had given them fair warning, and plenty of time, through the preaching of all his servants the prophets. Then he exiled Israel from her land to Assyria. And that's where they are now.

17.24-25 The king of Assyria brought in people from Babylon, Cuthah, Avva, Hamath, and Sepharvaim, and relocated them in the towns of Samaria, replacing the exiled Israelites. They moved in as if they owned the place and made themselves at home. When the Assyrians first moved in, GOD was just another god to them; they neither honored nor worshiped him. Then GOD sent lions among them and people were mauled and killed.

17.26 This message was then sent back to the king of Assyria: "The people you brought in to occupy the towns of Samaria don't know what's expected of them from the god of the land, and

NEW INTERNATIONAL VERSION

country requires. He has sent lions among them, which are killing them off, because the people do not know what he requires."

²⁷Then the king of Assyria gave this order: "Have one of the priests you took captive from Samaria go back to live there and teach the people what the god of the land requires." ²⁸So one of the priests who had been exiled from Samaria came to live in Bethel and taught them how to worship the LORD.

²⁹Nevertheless, each national group made its own gods in the several towns where they settled, and set them up in the shrines the people of Samaria had made at the high places. ³⁰The men from Babylon made Succoth Benoth, the men from Cuthah made Nergal, and the men from Hamath made Ashima; ³¹the Avvites made Nibhaz and Tartak, and the Sepharvites burned their children in the fire as sacrifices to Adrammelech and Anammelech, the gods of Sepharvaim. ³²They worshiped the LORD, but they also appointed all sorts of their own people to officiate for them as priests in the shrines at the high places. ³³They worshiped the LORD, but they also served their own gods in accordance with the customs of the nations from which they had been brought.

³⁴To this day they persist in their former practices. They neither worship the LORD nor adhere to the decrees and ordinances, the laws and commands that the LORD gave the descendants of Jacob, whom he named Israel. ³⁵When the LORD made a covenant with the Israelites, he commanded them: "Do not worship any other gods or bow down to them, serve them or sacrifice to them. ³⁶But the LORD, who brought you up out of Egypt with mighty power and outstretched arm, is the one you must worship. To him you shall bow down and to him offer sacrifices. ³⁷You must always be careful to keep the decrees and ordinances, the laws and commands he wrote for you. Do not worship other gods. ³⁸Do not forget the covenant I have made with you, and do not worship other gods. ³⁹Rather, worship the LORD your God; it is he who will deliver you from the hand of all your enemies."

⁴⁰They would not listen, however, but persisted in their former practices. ⁴¹Even while these people were worshiping the LORD, they were serving their idols. To this day their children and grandchildren continue to do as their fathers did.

THE MESSAGE

now he's sent lions and they're killing people right and left because nobody knows what the god of the land expects of them."

17.27 The king of Assyria ordered, "Send back some priests who were taken into exile from there. They can go back and live there and instruct the people in what the god of the land expects of them."

17.28 One of the priests who had been exiled from Samaria came back and moved into Bethel. He taught them how to honor and worship GOD.

17.29-31 But each people that Assyria had settled went ahead anyway making its own gods and setting them up in the neighborhood sex-and-religion shrines that the citizens of Samaria had left behind—a local custom-made god for each people:

for Babylon, Succoth Benoth;
for Cuthah, Nergal;
for Hamath, Ashima;
for Avva, Nibhaz and Tartak;
for Sepharvaim, Adrammelech and Anammelech (people burned their children in sacrificial offerings to these gods!).

17.32-33 They honored and worshiped GOD, but not exclusively—they also appointed all sorts of priests, regardless of qualification, to conduct a variety of rites at the local fertility shrines. They honored and worshiped GOD, but they also kept up their devotions to the old gods of the places they had come from.

17.34-39 And they're still doing it, still worshiping any old god that has nostalgic appeal to them. They don't really worship GOD—they don't take seriously what he says regarding how to behave and what to believe, what he revealed to the children of Jacob whom he named Israel. GOD made a covenant with his people and ordered them, "Don't honor other gods: Don't worship them, don't serve them, don't offer sacrifices to them. Worship GOD, the God who delivered you from Egypt in great and personal power. Reverence and fear him. Worship him. Sacrifice to him. And only him! All the things he had written down for you, directing you in what to believe and how to behave—well, do them for as long as you live. And whatever you do, *don't worship other gods!* And the covenant he made with you, don't forget your part in that. *And don't worship other gods!* Worship GOD, and GOD only—he's the one who will save you from enemy oppression."

17.40-41 But they didn't pay any attention. They kept doing what they'd always done. As it turned out, all the time these people were putting on a front of worshiping GOD, they were at the same time involved with their local idols. And they're still doing it. Like father, like son.

NEW INTERNATIONAL VERSION

Hezekiah King of Judah

18 In the third year of Hoshea son of Elah king of Israel, Hezekiah son of Ahaz king of Judah began to reign. ²He was twenty-five years old when he became king, and he reigned in Jerusalem twenty-nine years. His mother's name was Abijah*ᵃ* daughter of Zechariah. ³He did what was right in the eyes of the LORD, just as his father David had done. ⁴He removed the high places, smashed the sacred stones and cut down the Asherah poles. He broke into pieces the bronze snake Moses had made, for up to that time the Israelites had been burning incense to it. (It was called*ᵇ* Nehushtan.*ᶜ*)

⁵Hezekiah trusted in the LORD, the God of Israel. There was no one like him among all the kings of Judah, either before him or after him. ⁶He held fast to the LORD and did not cease to follow him; he kept the commands the LORD had given Moses. ⁷And the LORD was with him; he was successful in whatever he undertook. He rebelled against the king of Assyria and did not serve him. ⁸From watchtower to fortified city, he defeated the Philistines, as far as Gaza and its territory.

⁹In King Hezekiah's fourth year, which was the seventh year of Hoshea son of Elah king of Israel, Shalmaneser king of Assyria marched against Samaria and laid siege to it. ¹⁰At the end of three years the Assyrians took it. So Samaria was captured in Hezekiah's sixth year, which was the ninth year of Hoshea king of Israel. ¹¹The king of Assyria deported Israel to Assyria and settled them in Halah, in Gozan on the Habor River and in towns of the Medes. ¹²This happened because they had not obeyed the LORD their God, but had violated his covenant—all that Moses the servant of the LORD commanded. They neither listened to the commands nor carried them out.

¹³In the fourteenth year of King Hezekiah's reign, Sennacherib king of Assyria attacked all the fortified cities of Judah and captured them. ¹⁴So Hezekiah king of Judah sent this message to the king of Assyria at Lachish: "I have done wrong. Withdraw from me, and I will pay whatever you demand of me." The king of Assyria exacted from Hezekiah king of Judah three hundred talents*ᵈ* of silver and thirty talents*ᵉ* of gold. ¹⁵So Hezekiah gave him all the silver that was found in the temple of the LORD and in the treasuries of the royal palace.

¹⁶At this time Hezekiah king of Judah stripped off the gold with which he had covered the doors and doorposts of the temple of the LORD, and gave it to the king of Assyria.

ᵃ 2 Hebrew Abi, a variant of Abijah   *ᵇ 4 Or He called it*
ᶜ 4 Nehushtan sounds like the Hebrew for bronze and snake
and unclean thing.   *ᵈ 14 That is, about 11 tons (about 10*
metric tons)   *ᵉ 14 That is, about 1 ton (about 1 metric ton)*

THE MESSAGE

Hezekiah of Judah

18.1-4 **18** In the third year of Hoshea son of Elah king of Israel, Hezekiah son of Ahaz began his rule over Judah. He was twenty-five years old when he became king and he ruled for twenty-nine years in Jerusalem. His mother's name was Abijah daughter of Zechariah. In GOD's opinion he was a good king; he kept to the standards of his ancestor David. He got rid of the local fertility shrines, smashed the phallic stone monuments, and cut down the sex-and-religion Asherah groves. As a final stroke he pulverized the ancient bronze serpent that Moses had made; at that time the Israelites had taken up the practice of sacrificing to it—they had even dignified it with a name, Nehushtan (The Old Serpent).

18.5-6 Hezekiah put his whole trust in the GOD of Israel. There was no king quite like him, either before or after. He held fast to GOD—never loosened his grip—and obeyed to the letter everything GOD had commanded Moses. And GOD, for his part, held fast to him through all his adventures.

18.7-8 He revolted against the king of Assyria; he refused to serve him one more day. And he drove back the Philistines, whether in sentry outposts or fortress cities, all the way to Gaza and its borders.

18.9-11 In the fourth year of Hezekiah and the seventh year of Hoshea son of Elah king of Israel, Shalmaneser king of Assyria attacked Samaria. He threw a siege around it and after three years captured it. It was in the sixth year of Hezekiah and the ninth year of Hoshea that Samaria fell to Assyria. The king of Assyria took Israel into exile and relocated them in Halah, in Gozan on the Habor River, and in towns of the Medes.

18.12 All this happened because they wouldn't listen to the voice of their GOD and treated his covenant with careless contempt. They refused either to listen or do a word of what Moses, the servant of GOD, commanded.

18.13-14 In the fourteenth year of King Hezekiah, Sennacherib king of Assyria attacked all the outlying fortress cities of Judah and captured them. King Hezekiah sent a message to the king of Assyria at his headquarters in Lachish: "I've done wrong; I admit it. Pull back your army; I'll pay whatever tribute you set."

18.14-16 The king of Assyria demanded tribute from Hezekiah king of Judah—eleven tons of silver and a ton of gold. Hezekiah turned over all the silver he could find in The Temple of GOD and in the palace treasuries. Hezekiah even took down the doors of The Temple of GOD and the doorposts that he had overlaid with gold and gave them to the king of Assyria.

NEW INTERNATIONAL VERSION

Sennacherib Threatens Jerusalem

17The king of Assyria sent his supreme commander, his chief officer and his field commander with a large army, from Lachish to King Hezekiah at Jerusalem. They came up to Jerusalem and stopped at the aqueduct of the Upper Pool, on the road to the Washerman's Field. **18**They called for the king; and Eliakim son of Hilkiah the palace administrator, Shebna the secretary, and Joah son of Asaph the recorder went out to them.

19The field commander said to them, "Tell Hezekiah:

" 'This is what the great king, the king of Assyria, says: On what are you basing this confidence of yours? **20**You say you have strategy and military strength—but you speak only empty words. On whom are you depending, that you rebel against me? **21**Look now, you are depending on Egypt, that splintered reed of a staff, which pierces a man's hand and wounds him if he leans on it! Such is Pharaoh king of Egypt to all who depend on him. **22**And if you say to me, "We are depending on the LORD our God"—isn't he the one whose high places and altars Hezekiah removed, saying to Judah and Jerusalem, "You must worship before this altar in Jerusalem"?

23" 'Come now, make a bargain with my master, the king of Assyria: I will give you two thousand horses—if you can put riders on them! **24**How can you repulse one officer of the least of my master's officials, even though you are depending on Egypt for chariots and horsemen*a*? **25**Furthermore, have I come to attack and destroy this place without word from the LORD? The LORD himself told me to march against this country and destroy it.' "

26Then Eliakim son of Hilkiah, and Shebna and Joah said to the field commander, "Please speak to your servants in Aramaic, since we understand it. Don't speak to us in Hebrew in the hearing of the people on the wall."

27But the commander replied, "Was it only to your master and you that my master sent me to say these things, and not to the men sitting on the wall—who, like you, will have to eat their own filth and drink their own urine?"

28Then the commander stood and called out in Hebrew: "Hear the word of the great king, the

a 24 Or charioteers

THE MESSAGE

18.17 So the king of Assyria sent his top three military chiefs (the Tartan, the Rabsaris, and the Rabshakeh) from Lachish with a strong military force to King Hezekiah in Jerusalem. When they arrived at Jerusalem, they stopped at the aqueduct of the Upper Pool on the road to the laundry commons.

18.18 They called loudly for the king. Eliakim son of Hilkiah who was in charge of the palace, Shebna the royal secretary, and Joah son of Asaph the court historian went out to meet them.

18.19-22 The third officer, the Rabshakeh, was spokesman. He said, "Tell Hezekiah: A message from The Great King, the king of Assyria: You're living in a world of make-believe, of pious fantasy. Do you think that mere words are any substitute for military strategy and troops? Now that you've revolted against me, who can you expect to help you? You thought Egypt would, but Egypt's nothing but a paper tiger—one puff of wind and she collapses; Pharaoh king of Egypt is nothing but bluff and bluster. Or are you going to tell me, 'We rely on GOD'? But Hezekiah has just eliminated most of the people's access to God by getting rid of all the local God-shrines, ordering everyone in Judah and Jerusalem, 'You must worship at the Jerusalem altar only.'

18.23-24 "So be reasonable. Make a deal with my master, the king of Assyria. I'll give you two thousand horses if you think you can provide riders for them. You can't do it? Well, then, how do you think you're going to turn back even one raw buck private from my master's troops? How long are you going to hold on to that figment of your imagination, these hoped-for Egyptian chariots and horses?

18.25 "Do you think I've come up here to destroy this country without the express approval of GOD? The fact is that GOD expressly ordered me, 'Attack and destroy this country!' "

18.26 Eliakim son of Hilkiah and Shebna and Joah said to the Rabshakeh, "Please, speak to us in the Aramaic language. We understand Aramaic. Don't speak in Hebrew—everyone crowded on the city wall can hear you."

18.27 But the Rabshakeh said, "We weren't sent with a private message to your master and you; this is public—a message to everyone within earshot. After all, they're involved in this as well as you; if you don't come to terms, they'll be eating their own turds and drinking their own pee right along with you."

18.28-32 Then he stepped forward and spoke in Hebrew loud enough for everyone to hear, "Listen carefully to the words of The Great King, the

NEW INTERNATIONAL VERSION

king of Assyria! ²⁹This is what the king says: Do not let Hezekiah deceive you. He cannot deliver you from my hand. ³⁰Do not let Hezekiah persuade you to trust in the LORD when he says, 'The LORD will surely deliver us; this city will not be given into the hand of the king of Assyria.'

³¹"Do not listen to Hezekiah. This is what the king of Assyria says: Make peace with me and come out to me. Then every one of you will eat from his own vine and fig tree and drink water from his own cistern, ³²until I come and take you to a land like your own, a land of grain and new wine, a land of bread and vineyards, a land of olive trees and honey. Choose life and not death!

"Do not listen to Hezekiah, for he is misleading you when he says, 'The LORD will deliver us.' ³³Has the god of any nation ever delivered his land from the hand of the king of Assyria? ³⁴Where are the gods of Hamath and Arpad? Where are the gods of Sepharvaim, Hena and Ivvah? Have they rescued Samaria from my hand? ³⁵Who of all the gods of these countries has been able to save his land from me? How then can the LORD deliver Jerusalem from my hand?"

³⁶But the people remained silent and said nothing in reply, because the king had commanded, "Do not answer him."

³⁷Then Eliakim son of Hilkiah the palace administrator, Shebna the secretary and Joah son of Asaph the recorder went to Hezekiah, with their clothes torn, and told him what the field commander had said.

JERUSALEM'S DELIVERANCE FORETOLD

19 When King Hezekiah heard this, he tore his clothes and put on sackcloth and went into the temple of the LORD. ²He sent Eliakim the palace administrator, Shebna the secretary and the leading priests, all wearing sackcloth, to the prophet Isaiah son of Amoz. ³They told him, "This is what Hezekiah says: This day is a day of distress and rebuke and disgrace, as when children come to the point of birth and there is no strength to deliver them. ⁴It may be that the LORD your God will hear all the words of the field commander, whom his master, the king of Assyria, has sent to ridicule the living God, and that he will rebuke him for the words the LORD your God has heard. Therefore pray for the remnant that still survives."

⁵When King Hezekiah's officials came to Isaiah, ⁶Isaiah said to them, "Tell your master, 'This is what the LORD says: Do not be afraid of what

THE MESSAGE

king of Assyria: Don't let Hezekiah fool you; he can't save you. And don't let Hezekiah give you that line about trusting in GOD, telling you, 'GOD will save us—this city will never be abandoned to the king of Assyria.' Don't listen to Hezekiah—he doesn't know what he's talking about. Listen to the king of Assyria—deal with me and live the good life; I'll guarantee everyone your own plot of ground—a garden and a well! I'll take you to a land sweeter by far than this one, a land of grain and wine, bread and vineyards, olive orchards and honey. You only live once—so live, really live!

18.32-35 "No. Don't listen to Hezekiah. Don't listen to his lies, telling you 'GOD will save us.' Has there ever been a god anywhere who delivered anyone from the king of Assyria? Where are the gods of Hamath and Arpad? Where are the gods of Sepharvaim, Hena, and Ivvah? And Samaria—did their gods save them? Can you name a god who saved anyone anywhere from me, the king of Assyria? So what makes you think that GOD can save Jerusalem from me?"

18.36 The people were silent. No one spoke a word for the king had ordered, "Don't anyone say a word—not one word!"

18.37 Then Eliakim son of Hilkiah, the palace administrator, and Shebna the royal secretary, and Joah son of Asaph the court historian went back to Hezekiah. They had ripped their robes in despair; they reported to Hezekiah the speech of the Rabshakeh.

19.1-3 **19** When Hezekiah heard it all, he too ripped his robes apart and dressed himself in rough burlap. Then he went into The Temple of GOD. He sent Eliakim, who was in charge of the palace, Shebna the secretary, and the senior priests, all of them dressed in rough burlap, to the prophet Isaiah son of Amoz. They said to him, "A message from Hezekiah: 'This is a black day, a terrible day—doomsday!

> Babies poised to be born,
> No strength to birth them.

19.4 "'Maybe GOD, your God, has been listening to the blasphemous speech of the Rabshakeh who was sent by the king of Assyria, his master, to humiliate the living God; maybe GOD, your God, won't let him get by with such talk; and you, maybe you will lift up prayers for what's left of these people.'"

19.5 That's the message King Hezekiah's servants delivered to Isaiah.

19.6-7 Isaiah answered them, "Tell your master, 'GOD's word: Don't be at all concerned about

NEW INTERNATIONAL VERSION

you have heard—those words with which the underlings of the king of Assyria have blasphemed me. [7]Listen! I am going to put such a spirit in him that when he hears a certain report, he will return to his own country, and there I will have him cut down with the sword.' "

[8]When the field commander heard that the king of Assyria had left Lachish, he withdrew and found the king fighting against Libnah.

[9]Now Sennacherib received a report that Tirhakah, the Cushite[a] king ⌊of Egypt⌋, was marching out to fight against him. So he again sent messengers to Hezekiah with this word: [10]"Say to Hezekiah king of Judah: Do not let the god you depend on deceive you when he says, 'Jerusalem will not be handed over to the king of Assyria.' [11]Surely you have heard what the kings of Assyria have done to all the countries, destroying them completely. And will you be delivered? [12]Did the gods of the nations that were destroyed by my forefathers deliver them: the gods of Gozan, Haran, Rezeph and the people of Eden who were in Tel Assar? [13]Where is the king of Hamath, the king of Arpad, the king of the city of Sepharvaim, or of Hena or Ivvah?"

HEZEKIAH'S PRAYER

[14]Hezekiah received the letter from the messengers and read it. Then he went up to the temple of the LORD and spread it out before the LORD. [15]And Hezekiah prayed to the LORD: "O LORD, God of Israel, enthroned between the cherubim, you alone are God over all the kingdoms of the earth. You have made heaven and earth. [16]Give ear, O LORD, and hear; open your eyes, O LORD, and see; listen to the words Sennacherib has sent to insult the living God.

[17]"It is true, O LORD, that the Assyrian kings have laid waste these nations and their lands. [18]They have thrown their gods into the fire and destroyed them, for they were not gods but only wood and stone, fashioned by men's hands. [19]Now, O LORD our God, deliver us from his hand, so that all kingdoms on earth may know that you alone, O LORD, are God."

ISAIAH PROPHESIES SENNACHERIB'S FALL

[20]Then Isaiah son of Amoz sent a message to Hezekiah: "This is what the LORD, the God of Israel, says: I have heard your prayer concerning

THE MESSAGE

what you've heard from the king of Assyria's bootlicking errand boys—these outrageous blasphemies. Here's what I'm going to do: Afflict him with self-doubt. He's going to hear a rumor and, frightened for his life, retreat to his own country. Once there, I'll see to it that he gets killed.' "

19.8-13 The Rabshakeh left and found that the king of Assyria had pulled up stakes from Lachish and was now fighting against Libnah. Then Sennacherib heard that Tirhakah king of Cush was on his way to fight against him. So he sent another envoy with orders to deliver this message to Hezekiah king of Judah: "Don't let that god that you think so much of keep stringing you along with the line, 'Jerusalem will never fall to the king of Assyria.' That's a barefaced lie. You know the track record of the kings of Assyria—country after country laid waste, devastated. And what makes you think you'll be an exception? Take a good look at these wasted nations, destroyed by my ancestors; did their gods do them any good? Look at Gozan, Haran, Rezeph, the people of Eden at Tel Assar. Ruins. And what's left of the king of Hamath, the king of Arpad, the king of Sepharvaim, of Hena, of Ivvah? Bones."

19.14-15 Hezekiah took the letter from the envoy and read it. He went to The Temple of GOD and spread it out before GOD. And Hezekiah prayed—oh, how he prayed!

GOD, God of Israel, seated
   in majesty on the cherubim-throne.
You are the one and only God,
   sovereign over all kingdoms on earth,
Maker of heaven,
   maker of earth.

19.16 Open your ears, GOD, and listen,
   open your eyes and look.
Look at this letter Sennacherib has sent,
   a brazen insult to the living God!

19.17 The facts are true, O GOD: The kings of
      Assyria
   have laid waste countries and kingdoms.

19.18 Huge bonfires they made of their gods,
      their
   no-gods hand-made from wood and
      stone.

19.19 But now O GOD, *our* God,
   save us from raw Assyrian power;
Make all the kingdoms on earth know
   that you are GOD, the one and only God.

19.20-21 It wasn't long before Isaiah son of Amoz sent word to Hezekiah:

GOD'S word: You've prayed to me regarding Sennacherib king of Assyria; I've

---

[a] 9 That is, from the upper Nile region

NEW INTERNATIONAL VERSION

Sennacherib king of Assyria. ²¹This is the word
that the LORD has spoken against him:

" 'The Virgin Daughter of Zion
    despises you and mocks you.
The Daughter of Jerusalem
    tosses her head as you flee.
²²Who is it you have insulted and
        blasphemed?
    Against whom have you raised your voice
and lifted your eyes in pride?
    Against the Holy One of Israel!
²³By your messengers
    you have heaped insults on the Lord.
And you have said,
    "With my many chariots
I have ascended the heights of the
        mountains,
    the utmost heights of Lebanon.
I have cut down its tallest cedars,
    the choicest of its pines.
I have reached its remotest parts,
    the finest of its forests.
²⁴I have dug wells in foreign lands
    and drunk the water there.
With the soles of my feet
    I have dried up all the streams of Egypt."

²⁵" 'Have you not heard?
    Long ago I ordained it.
In days of old I planned it;
    now I have brought it to pass,
that you have turned fortified cities
    into piles of stone.
²⁶Their people, drained of power,
    are dismayed and put to shame.
They are like plants in the field,
    like tender green shoots,
like grass sprouting on the roof,
    scorched before it grows up.

²⁷" 'But I know where you stay
    and when you come and go
    and how you rage against me.
²⁸Because you rage against me
    and your insolence has reached my ears,
I will put my hook in your nose
    and my bit in your mouth,
and I will make you return
    by the way you came.'

²⁹"This will be the sign for you, O Hezekiah:

"This year you will eat what grows by itself,
    and the second year what springs from that.
But in the third year sow and reap,
    plant vineyards and eat their fruit.
³⁰Once more a remnant of the house of Judah
    will take root below and bear fruit above.

THE MESSAGE

heard your prayer. This is my response to
him:

The Virgin Daughter of Zion
    holds you in utter contempt;
Daughter Jerusalem
    thinks you're nothing but scum.
19.22   Who do you think it is you've insulted?
    Who do you think you've been
        bad-mouthing?
    Before whom do you suppose you've been
        strutting?
    The Holy One of Israel, that's who!
19.23   You dispatched your errand boys
        to humiliate the Master.
    You bragged, "With my army of chariots
        I've climbed the highest mountains,
        snow-peaked alpine Lebanon
            mountains!
    I've cut down its giant cedars,
        chopped down its prize pine trees.
    I've traveled the world,
        visited the finest forest retreats.
19.24   I've dug wells in faraway places
        and drunk their exotic waters;
    I've waded and splashed barefoot
        in the rivers of Egypt."

19.25   Did it never occur to you
        that I'm behind all this?
    Long, long ago I drew up the plans,
        and now I've gone into action,
    Using you as a doomsday weapon,
        reducing proud cities to piles of rubble,
19.26   Leaving their people dispirited,
        slumped shoulders, limp souls.
    Useless as weeds, fragile as grass,
        insubstantial as wind-blown chaff.
19.27   I know when you sit down, when you
        come
        and when you go;
    And, yes, I've marked every one
        of your temper tantrums against me.
19.28   It's because of your temper,
        your blasphemous foul temper,
    That I'm putting my hook in your nose
        and my bit in your mouth
    And turning you back
        to where you came from.

19.29   And this, Hezekiah, will be for you the confirming sign:

    This year you'll eat the gleanings, next year
        whatever you can beg, borrow, or steal;
    But the third year you'll sow and harvest,
        plant vineyards and eat grapes.
19.30   A remnant of the family of Judah yet again
        will sink down roots and raise up fruit.

NEW INTERNATIONAL VERSION

31 For out of Jerusalem will come a remnant,
and out of Mount Zion a band of survivors.

The zeal of the LORD Almighty will accomplish this.

32 "Therefore this is what the LORD says concerning the king of Assyria:

"He will not enter this city
or shoot an arrow here.
He will not come before it with shield
or build a siege ramp against it.
33 By the way that he came he will return;
he will not enter this city,
declares the LORD.
34 I will defend this city and save it,
for my sake and for the sake of David my
servant."

35 That night the angel of the LORD went out and put to death a hundred and eighty-five thousand men in the Assyrian camp. When the people got up the next morning—there were all the dead bodies! 36 So Sennacherib king of Assyria broke camp and withdrew. He returned to Nineveh and stayed there.

37 One day, while he was worshiping in the temple of his god Nisroch, his sons Adrammelech and Sharezer cut him down with the sword, and they escaped to the land of Ararat. And Esarhaddon his son succeeded him as king.

HEZEKIAH'S ILLNESS

20 In those days Hezekiah became ill and was at the point of death. The prophet Isaiah son of Amoz went to him and said, "This is what the LORD says: Put your house in order, because you are going to die; you will not recover."

2 Hezekiah turned his face to the wall and prayed to the LORD, 3 "Remember, O LORD, how I have walked before you faithfully and with wholehearted devotion and have done what is good in your eyes." And Hezekiah wept bitterly.

4 Before Isaiah had left the middle court, the word of the LORD came to him: 5 "Go back and tell Hezekiah, the leader of my people, 'This is what the LORD, the God of your father David, says: I have heard your prayer and seen your tears; I will heal you. On the third day from now you will go up to the temple of the LORD. 6 I will add fifteen years to your life. And I will deliver

THE MESSAGE

19.31 The remnant will come from Jerusalem,
the survivors from Mount Zion.
The Zeal of GOD
will make it happen.

19.32 To sum up, this is what GOD says regarding the king of Assyria:

He won't enter this city,
nor shoot so much as a single arrow
there;
Won't brandish a shield,
won't even begin to set siege;
19.33 He'll go home by the same road he came;
he won't enter this city. GOD's word!
19.34 I'll shield this city, I'll save this city,
for my sake and for David's sake.

19.35 And it so happened that that very night an angel of GOD came and massacred a hundred and eighty-five thousand Assyrians. When the people of Jerusalem got up next morning, there it was—a whole camp of corpses!

19.36-37 Sennacherib king of Assyria got out of there fast, headed straight home for Nineveh, and stayed put. One day when he was worshiping in the temple of his god Nisroch, his sons Adrammelech and Sharezer murdered him and then escaped to the land of Ararat. His son Esarhaddon became the next king.

20.1 **20** Some time later Hezekiah became deathly sick. The prophet Isaiah son of Amoz paid him a visit and said, "Put your affairs in order; you're about to die—you haven't long to live."

20.2-3 Hezekiah turned from Isaiah and faced GOD, praying:

Remember, O GOD, who I am, what I've
done!
I've lived an honest life before you,
My heart's been true and steady,
I've lived to please you; lived for your
approval.

And then the tears flowed. Hezekiah wept.

20.4-6 Isaiah, leaving, was not halfway across the courtyard when the word of GOD stopped him: "Go back and tell Hezekiah, prince of my people, 'GOD's word, Hezekiah! From the God of your ancestor David: I've listened to your prayer and I've observed your tears. I'm going to heal you. In three days you will walk on your own legs into The Temple of GOD. I've just added fifteen years to your life; I'm saving

NEW INTERNATIONAL VERSION

you and this city from the hand of the king of Assyria. I will defend this city for my sake and for the sake of my servant David.' "

⁷Then Isaiah said, "Prepare a poultice of figs." They did so and applied it to the boil, and he recovered.

⁸Hezekiah had asked Isaiah, "What will be the sign that the LORD will heal me and that I will go up to the temple of the LORD on the third day from now?"

⁹Isaiah answered, "This is the LORD's sign to you that the LORD will do what he has promised: Shall the shadow go forward ten steps, or shall it go back ten steps?"

¹⁰"It is a simple matter for the shadow to go forward ten steps," said Hezekiah. "Rather, have it go back ten steps."

¹¹Then the prophet Isaiah called upon the LORD, and the LORD made the shadow go back the ten steps it had gone down on the stairway of Ahaz.

ENVOYS FROM BABYLON

¹²At that time Merodach-Baladan son of Baladan king of Babylon sent Hezekiah letters and a gift, because he had heard of Hezekiah's illness. ¹³Hezekiah received the messengers and showed them all that was in his storehouses—the silver, the gold, the spices and the fine oil—his armory and everything found among his treasures. There was nothing in his palace or in all his kingdom that Hezekiah did not show them.

¹⁴Then Isaiah the prophet went to King Hezekiah and asked, "What did those men say, and where did they come from?"

"From a distant land," Hezekiah replied. "They came from Babylon."

¹⁵The prophet asked, "What did they see in your palace?"

"They saw everything in my palace," Hezekiah said. "There is nothing among my treasures that I did not show them."

¹⁶Then Isaiah said to Hezekiah, "Hear the word of the LORD: ¹⁷The time will surely come when everything in your palace, and all that your fathers have stored up until this day, will be carried off to Babylon. Nothing will be left, says the LORD. ¹⁸And some of your descendants, your own flesh and blood, that will be born to you, will be taken away, and they will become eunuchs in the palace of the king of Babylon."

¹⁹"The word of the LORD you have spoken is good," Hezekiah replied. For he thought, "Will there not be peace and security in my lifetime?"

²⁰As for the other events of Hezekiah's reign, all his achievements and how he made the pool and the tunnel by which he brought water into

THE MESSAGE

you from the king of Assyria, and I'm covering this city with my shield—for my sake and my servant David's sake.' "

²⁰·⁷ Isaiah then said, "Prepare a plaster of figs."

They prepared the plaster, applied it to the boil, and Hezekiah was on his way to recovery.

²⁰·⁸ Hezekiah said to Isaiah, "How do I know whether this is of GOD and not just the fig plaster? What confirming sign is there that GOD is healing me and that in three days I'll walk into The Temple of GOD on my own legs?"

²⁰·⁹ "This will be your sign from GOD," said Isaiah, "that GOD is doing what he said he'd do: Do you want the shadow to advance ten degrees on the sundial or go back ten degrees? You choose."

²⁰·¹⁰ Hezekiah said, "It would be easy to make the sun's shadow advance ten degrees. Make it go back ten degrees."

²⁰·¹¹ So Isaiah called out in prayer to GOD, and the shadow went back ten degrees on Ahaz's sundial.

²⁰·¹²⁻¹³ Shortly after this, Merodach-Baladan, the son of Baladan king of Babylon, having heard that the king was sick, sent a get-well card and a gift to Hezekiah. Hezekiah was pleased and showed the messengers around the place—silver, gold, spices, aromatic oils, his stockpile of weapons—a guided tour of all his prized possessions. There wasn't a thing in his palace or kingdom that Hezekiah didn't show them.

²⁰·¹⁴ And then Isaiah the prophet showed up: "And just what were these men doing here? Where did they come from and why?"

²⁰·¹⁵ Hezekiah said, "They came from far away—from Babylon."

"And what did they see in your palace?"

"Everything," said Hezekiah. "There isn't anything I didn't show them—I gave them the grand tour."

²⁰·¹⁶⁻¹⁸ Then Isaiah spoke to Hezekiah, "Listen to what GOD has to say about this: The day is coming when everything you own and everything your ancestors have passed down to you, right down to the last cup and saucer, will be cleaned out of here—plundered and packed off to Babylon. GOD's word! Worse yet, your sons, the progeny of sons you've begotten, will end up as eunuchs in the palace of the king of Babylon."

²⁰·¹⁹ Hezekiah said to Isaiah, "If GOD says it, it must be good." But he was thinking to himself, "It won't happen during my lifetime—I'll enjoy peace and security as long as I live."

²⁰·²⁰⁻²¹ The rest of the life and times of Hezekiah, along with his projects, especially the way he engineered the Upper Pool and brought water

NEW INTERNATIONAL VERSION

the city, are they not written in the book of the annals of the kings of Judah? [21]Hezekiah rested with his fathers. And Manasseh his son succeeded him as king.

MANASSEH KING OF JUDAH

21 Manasseh was twelve years old when he became king, and he reigned in Jerusalem fifty-five years. His mother's name was Hephzibah. [2]He did evil in the eyes of the LORD, following the detestable practices of the nations the LORD had driven out before the Israelites. [3]He rebuilt the high places his father Hezekiah had destroyed; he also erected altars to Baal and made an Asherah pole, as Ahab king of Israel had done. He bowed down to all the starry hosts and worshiped them. [4]He built altars in the temple of the LORD, of which the LORD had said, "In Jerusalem I will put my Name." [5]In both courts of the temple of the LORD, he built altars to all the starry hosts. [6]He sacrificed his own son in[a] the fire, practiced sorcery and divination, and consulted mediums and spiritists. He did much evil in the eyes of the LORD, provoking him to anger.

[7]He took the carved Asherah pole he had made and put it in the temple, of which the LORD had said to David and to his son Solomon, "In this temple and in Jerusalem, which I have chosen out of all the tribes of Israel, I will put my Name forever. [8]I will not again make the feet of the Israelites wander from the land I gave their forefathers, if only they will be careful to do everything I commanded them and will keep the whole Law that my servant Moses gave them." [9]But the people did not listen. Manasseh led them astray, so that they did more evil than the nations the LORD had destroyed before the Israelites.

[10]The LORD said through his servants the prophets: [11]"Manasseh king of Judah has committed these detestable sins. He has done more evil than the Amorites who preceded him and has led Judah into sin with his idols. [12]Therefore this is what the LORD, the God of Israel, says: I am going to bring such disaster on Jerusalem

---

THE MESSAGE

into the city, are written in *The Chronicles of the Kings of Judah*. Hezekiah died and was buried with his ancestors. His son Manasseh became the next king.

MANASSEH OF JUDAH

21.1-6 **21** Manasseh was twelve years old when he became king. He ruled for fifty-five years in Jerusalem. His mother's name was Hephzibah. In GOD's judgment he was a bad king—an evil king. He reintroduced all the moral rot and spiritual corruption that had been scoured from the country when GOD dispossessed the pagan nations in favor of the children of Israel. He rebuilt all the sex-and-religion shrines that his father Hezekiah had torn down, and he built altars and phallic images for the sex god Baal and sex goddess Asherah, exactly what Ahaz king of Israel had done. He worshiped the cosmic powers, taking orders from the constellations. He even built these pagan altars in The Temple of GOD, the very Jerusalem Temple dedicated exclusively by GOD's decree ("in Jerusalem I place my Name") to GOD's Name. And he built shrines to the cosmic powers and placed them in both courtyards of The Temple of GOD. He burned his own son in a sacrificial offering. He practiced black magic and fortunetelling. He held séances and consulted spirits from the underworld. Much evil—in GOD's judgment, a career in evil. And GOD was angry.

21.7-8 As a last straw he placed the carved image of the sex goddess Asherah in The Temple of GOD, a flagrant and provocative violation of GOD's well-known statement to both David and Solomon, "In this Temple and in this city Jerusalem, my choice out of all the tribes of Israel, I place my Name—exclusively and forever. Never again will I let my people Israel wander off from this land I gave to their ancestors. But here's the condition: They must keep everything I've commanded in the instructions my servant Moses passed on to them."

21.9 But the people didn't listen. Manasseh led them off the beaten path into practices of evil even exceeding the evil of the pagan nations that GOD had earlier destroyed.

21.10-12 GOD, thoroughly fed up, sent word through his servants the prophets: "Because Manasseh king of Judah has committed these outrageous sins, eclipsing the sin-performance of the Amorites before him, setting new records in evil, using foul idols to debase Judah into a nation of sinners, this is my judgment, GOD's verdict: I, the God of Israel, will visit catastrophe on Jerusalem and Judah, a doom so terrible that

---

[a] 6 Or *He made his own son pass through*

NEW INTERNATIONAL VERSION

and Judah that the ears of everyone who hears of it will tingle. ¹³I will stretch out over Jerusalem the measuring line used against Samaria and the plumb line used against the house of Ahab. I will wipe out Jerusalem as one wipes a dish, wiping it and turning it upside down. ¹⁴I will forsake the remnant of my inheritance and hand them over to their enemies. They will be looted and plundered by all their foes, ¹⁵because they have done evil in my eyes and have provoked me to anger from the day their forefathers came out of Egypt until this day."

¹⁶Moreover, Manasseh also shed so much innocent blood that he filled Jerusalem from end to end—besides the sin that he had caused Judah to commit, so that they did evil in the eyes of the LORD.

¹⁷As for the other events of Manasseh's reign, and all he did, including the sin he committed, are they not written in the book of the annals of the kings of Judah? ¹⁸Manasseh rested with his fathers and was buried in his palace garden, the garden of Uzza. And Amon his son succeeded him as king.

AMON KING OF JUDAH

¹⁹Amon was twenty-two years old when he became king, and he reigned in Jerusalem two years. His mother's name was Meshullemeth daughter of Haruz; she was from Jotbah. ²⁰He did evil in the eyes of the LORD, as his father Manasseh had done. ²¹He walked in all the ways of his father; he worshiped the idols his father had worshiped, and bowed down to them. ²²He forsook the LORD, the God of his fathers, and did not walk in the way of the LORD.

²³Amon's officials conspired against him and assassinated the king in his palace. ²⁴Then the people of the land killed all who had plotted against King Amon, and they made Josiah his son king in his place.

²⁵As for the other events of Amon's reign, and what he did, are they not written in the book of the annals of the kings of Judah? ²⁶He was buried in his grave in the garden of Uzza. And Josiah his son succeeded him as king.

THE BOOK OF THE LAW FOUND

22 Josiah was eight years old when he became king, and he reigned in Jerusalem thirty-one years. His mother's name was Jedidah daughter of Adaiah; she was from Bozkath. ²He did what was right in the eyes of the LORD and walked in all the ways of his father David, not turning aside to the right or to the left.

³In the eighteenth year of his reign, King Josiah sent the secretary, Shaphan son of Azaliah,

THE MESSAGE

when people hear of it they'll shake their heads in disbelief, saying, 'I can't believe it!'

21.13-15 "I'll visit the fate of Samaria on Jerusalem, a rerun of Ahab's doom. I'll wipe out Jerusalem as you would wipe out a dish, wiping it out and turning it over to dry. I'll get rid of what's left of my inheritance, dumping them on their enemies. If their enemies can salvage anything from them, they're welcome to it. They've been nothing but trouble to me from the day their ancestors left Egypt until now. They pushed me to my limit; I won't put up with their evil any longer."

21.16   The final word on Manasseh was that he was an indiscriminate murderer. He drenched Jerusalem with the innocent blood of his victims. That's on top of all the sins in which he involved his people. As far as GOD was concerned, he'd turned them into a nation of sinners.

21.17-18   The rest of the life and times of Manasseh, everything he did and his sorry record of sin, is written in *The Chronicles of the Kings of Judah*. Manasseh died and joined his ancestors. He was buried in the palace garden, the Garden of Uzza. His son Amon became the next king.

AMON OF JUDAH

21.19-22 Amon was twenty-two years old when he became king. He was king for two years in Jerusalem. His mother's name was Meshullemeth, the daughter of Haruz. She was from Jotbah. In GOD's opinion he lived an evil life, just like his father Manasseh. He followed in the footsteps of his father, serving and worshiping the same foul gods his father had served. He totally deserted the GOD of his ancestors; he did not live GOD's way.

21.23-24   Amon's servants revolted and assassinated him, killing the king right in his own palace. But the people, in their turn, killed the conspirators against King Amon and then crowned Josiah, Amon's son, as king.

21.25-26   The rest of the life and times of Amon is written in *The Chronicles of the Kings of Judah*. They buried Amon in his burial plot in the Garden of Uzza. His son Josiah became the next king.

JOSIAH OF JUDAH

22.1-2 **22** Josiah was eight years old when he became king. He ruled for thirty-one years in Jerusalem. His mother's name was Jedidah daughter of Adaiah; she was from Bozkath. He lived the way GOD wanted. He kept straight on the path blazed by his ancestor David, not one step to either left or right.

22.3-7   One day in the eighteenth year of his kingship, King Josiah sent the royal secretary Sha-

NEW INTERNATIONAL VERSION

the son of Meshullam, to the temple of the LORD. He said: [4]"Go up to Hilkiah the high priest and have him get ready the money that has been brought into the temple of the LORD, which the doorkeepers have collected from the people. [5]Have them entrust it to the men appointed to supervise the work on the temple. And have these men pay the workers who repair the temple of the LORD— [6]the carpenters, the builders and the masons. Also have them purchase timber and dressed stone to repair the temple. [7]But they need not account for the money entrusted to them, because they are acting faithfully."

[8]Hilkiah the high priest said to Shaphan the secretary, "I have found the Book of the Law in the temple of the LORD." He gave it to Shaphan, who read it. [9]Then Shaphan the secretary went to the king and reported to him: "Your officials have paid out the money that was in the temple of the LORD and have entrusted it to the workers and supervisors at the temple." [10]Then Shaphan the secretary informed the king, "Hilkiah the priest has given me a book." And Shaphan read from it in the presence of the king.

[11]When the king heard the words of the Book of the Law, he tore his robes. [12]He gave these orders to Hilkiah the priest, Ahikam son of Shaphan, Acbor son of Micaiah, Shaphan the secretary and Asaiah the king's attendant: [13]"Go and inquire of the LORD for me and for the people and for all Judah about what is written in this book that has been found. Great is the LORD's anger that burns against us because our fathers have not obeyed the words of this book; they have not acted in accordance with all that is written there concerning us."

[14]Hilkiah the priest, Ahikam, Acbor, Shaphan and Asaiah went to speak to the prophetess Huldah, who was the wife of Shallum son of Tikvah, the son of Harhas, keeper of the wardrobe. She lived in Jerusalem, in the Second District.

[15]She said to them, "This is what the LORD, the God of Israel, says: Tell the man who sent you to me, [16]'This is what the LORD says: I am going to bring disaster on this place and its people, according to everything written in the book the king of Judah has read. [17]Because they have forsaken me and burned incense to other gods and provoked me to anger by all the idols their hands have made,[a] my anger will burn against this place and will not be quenched.' [18]Tell the king of

THE MESSAGE

phan son of Azaliah, the son of Meshullam, to The Temple of GOD with instructions: "Go to Hilkiah the high priest and have him count the money that has been brought to The Temple of GOD that the doormen have collected from the people. Have them turn it over to the foremen who are managing the work on The Temple of GOD so they can pay the workers who are repairing GOD's Temple, all the carpenters, construction workers, and masons. Also, authorize them to buy the lumber and dressed stone for The Temple repairs. You don't need to get a receipt for the money you give them—they're all honest men."

22.8 The high priest Hilkiah reported to Shaphan the royal secretary, "I've just found the Book of GOD's Revelation, instructing us in GOD's ways. I found it in The Temple!" He gave it to Shaphan and Shaphan read it.

22.9 Then Shaphan the royal secretary came back to the king and gave him an account of what had gone on: "Your servants have bagged up the money that has been collected for The Temple; they have given it to the foremen to pay The Temple workers."

22.10 Then Shaphan the royal secretary told the king, "Hilkiah the priest gave me a book." Shaphan proceeded to read it to the king.

22.11-13 When the king heard what was written in the book, God's Revelation, he ripped his robes in dismay. And then he called for Hilkiah the priest, Ahikam son of Shaphan, Acbor son of Micaiah, Shaphan the royal secretary, and Asaiah the king's personal aide. He ordered them all: "Go and pray to GOD for me and for this people—for all Judah! Find out what we must do in response to what is written in this book that has just been found! GOD's anger must be burning furiously against us—our ancestors haven't obeyed a thing written in this book, followed none of the instructions directed to us."

22.14-17 Hilkiah the priest, Ahikam, Acbor, Shaphan, and Asaiah went straight to Huldah the prophetess. She was the wife of Shallum son of Tikvah, the son of Harhas, who was in charge of the palace wardrobe. She lived in Jerusalem in the Second Quarter. The five men consulted with her. In response to them she said, "GOD's word, the God of Israel: Tell the man who sent you here that I'm on my way to bring the doom of judgment on this place and this people. Every word written in the book read by the king of Judah will happen. And why? Because they've deserted me and taken up with other gods, made me thoroughly angry by setting up their god-making businesses. My anger is raging white-hot against this place and nobody is going to put it out.

---

[a] 17 Or by everything they have done

NEW INTERNATIONAL VERSION

Judah, who sent you to inquire of the LORD, 'This is what the LORD, the God of Israel, says concerning the words you heard: ¹⁹Because your heart was responsive and you humbled yourself before the LORD when you heard what I have spoken against this place and its people, that they would become accursed and laid waste, and because you tore your robes and wept in my presence, I have heard you, declares the LORD. ²⁰Therefore I will gather you to your fathers, and you will be buried in peace. Your eyes will not see all the disaster I am going to bring on this place.' "

So they took her answer back to the king.

JOSIAH RENEWS THE COVENANT

23 Then the king called together all the elders of Judah and Jerusalem. ²He went up to the temple of the LORD with the men of Judah, the people of Jerusalem, the priests and the prophets—all the people from the least to the greatest. He read in their hearing all the words of the Book of the Covenant, which had been found in the temple of the LORD. ³The king stood by the pillar and renewed the covenant in the presence of the LORD—to follow the LORD and keep his commands, regulations and decrees with all his heart and all his soul, thus confirming the words of the covenant written in this book. Then all the people pledged themselves to the covenant.

⁴The king ordered Hilkiah the high priest, the priests next in rank and the doorkeepers to remove from the temple of the LORD all the articles made for Baal and Asherah and all the starry hosts. He burned them outside Jerusalem in the fields of the Kidron Valley and took the ashes to Bethel. ⁵He did away with the pagan priests appointed by the kings of Judah to burn incense on the high places of the towns of Judah and on those around Jerusalem—those who burned incense to Baal, to the sun and moon, to the constellations and to all the starry hosts. ⁶He took the Asherah pole from the temple of the LORD to the Kidron Valley outside Jerusalem and burned it there. He ground it to powder and scattered the dust over the graves of the common people. ⁷He also tore down the quarters of the male shrine prostitutes, which were in the temple of the LORD and where women did weaving for Asherah.

⁸Josiah brought all the priests from the towns of Judah and desecrated the high places, from

THE MESSAGE

²²·¹⁸⁻¹⁹ "And also tell the king of Judah, since he sent you to ask GOD for direction; tell him this, GOD's comment on what he read in the book: 'Because you took seriously the doom of judgment I spoke against this place and people, and because you responded in humble repentance, tearing your robe in dismay and weeping before me, I'm taking you seriously. GOD's word: I'll take care of you. You'll have a quiet death and be buried in peace. You won't be around to see the doom that I'm going to bring upon this place.' "

The men took her message back to the king.

²³·¹⁻³ **23** The king acted immediately, assembling all the elders of Judah and Jerusalem. Then the king proceeded to The Temple of GOD, bringing everyone in his train—priests and prophets and people ranging from the famous to the unknown. Then he read out publicly everything written in the Book of the Covenant that was found in The Temple of GOD. The king stood by the pillar and before GOD solemnly committed them all to the covenant: to follow GOD believingly and obediently; to follow his instructions, heart and soul, on what to believe and do; to put into practice the entire covenant, all that was written in the book. The people stood in affirmation; their commitment was unanimous.

²³·⁴⁻⁹ Then the king ordered Hilkiah the high priest, his associate priest, and The Temple sentries to clean house—to get rid of everything in The Temple of GOD that had been made for worshiping Baal and Asherah and the cosmic powers. He had them burned outside Jerusalem in the fields of Kidron and then disposed of the ashes in Bethel. He fired the pagan priests whom the kings of Judah had hired to supervise the local sex-and-religion shrines in the towns of Judah and neighborhoods of Jerusalem. In a stroke he swept the country clean of the polluting stench of the round-the-clock worship of Baal, sun and moon, stars—all the so-called cosmic powers. He took the obscene phallic Asherah pole from The Temple of GOD to the Valley of Kidron outside Jerusalem, burned it up, then ground up the ashes and scattered them in the cemetery. He tore out the rooms of the male sacred prostitutes that had been set up in The Temple of GOD; women also used these rooms for weavings for Asherah. He swept the outlying towns of Judah clean of priests and smashed the sex-and-religion shrines where they worked their trade from one end of the country to the other—all the

NEW INTERNATIONAL VERSION

Geba to Beersheba, where the priests had burned incense. He broke down the shrines *a* at the gates—at the entrance to the Gate of Joshua, the city governor, which is on the left of the city gate. 9Although the priests of the high places did not serve at the altar of the Lord in Jerusalem, they ate unleavened bread with their fellow priests.

10He desecrated Topheth, which was in the Valley of Ben Hinnom, so no one could use it to sacrifice his son or daughter in *b* the fire to Molech. 11He removed from the entrance to the temple of the Lord the horses that the kings of Judah had dedicated to the sun. They were in the court near the room of an official named Nathan-Melech. Josiah then burned the chariots dedicated to the sun.

12He pulled down the altars the kings of Judah had erected on the roof near the upper room of Ahaz, and the altars Manasseh had built in the two courts of the temple of the Lord. He removed them from there, smashed them to pieces and threw the rubble into the Kidron Valley. 13The king also desecrated the high places that were east of Jerusalem on the south of the Hill of Corruption—the ones Solomon king of Israel had built for Ashtoreth the vile goddess of the Sidonians, for Chemosh the vile god of Moab, and for Molech *c* the detestable god of the people of Ammon. 14Josiah smashed the sacred stones and cut down the Asherah poles and covered the sites with human bones.

15Even the altar at Bethel, the high place made by Jeroboam son of Nebat, who had caused Israel to sin—even that altar and high place he demolished. He burned the high place and ground it to powder, and burned the Asherah pole also. 16Then Josiah looked around, and when he saw the tombs that were there on the hillside, he had the bones removed from them and burned on the altar to defile it, in accordance with the word of the Lord proclaimed by the man of God who foretold these things.

17The king asked, "What is that tombstone I see?"

The men of the city said, "It marks the tomb of the man of God who came from Judah and pronounced against the altar of Bethel the very things you have done to it."

18"Leave it alone," he said. "Don't let anyone disturb his bones." So they spared his bones and those of the prophet who had come from Samaria.

a 8 Or high places *b 10 Or to make his son or daughter pass through* *c 13 Hebrew Milcom*

THE MESSAGE

way from Geba to Beersheba. He smashed the sex-and-religion shrine that had been set up just to the left of the city gate for the private use of Joshua, the city mayor. Even though these sex-and-religion priests did not defile the Altar in The Temple itself, they were part of the general priestly corruption and had to go.

23:10-11 Then Josiah demolished the Topheth, the iron furnace griddle set up in the Valley of Ben Hinnom for sacrificing children in the fire. No longer could anyone burn son or daughter to the god Molech. He hauled off the horse statues honoring the sun god that the kings of Judah had set up near the entrance to The Temple. They were in the courtyard next to the office of Nathan-Melech, the warden. He burned up the sun-chariots as so much rubbish.

23:12-15 The king smashed all the altars to smithereens—the altar on the roof shrine of Ahaz, the various altars the kings of Judah had made, the altars of Manasseh that littered the courtyard of The Temple—he smashed them all, pulverized the fragments, and scattered their dust in the Valley of Kidron. The king proceeded to make a clean sweep of all the sex-and-religion shrines that had proliferated east of Jerusalem on the south slope of Abomination Hill, the ones Solomon king of Israel had built to the obscene Sidonian sex goddess Ashtoreth, to Chemosh the dirty-old-god of the Moabites, and to Milcom the depraved god of the Ammonites. He tore apart the altars, chopped down the phallic Asherah-poles, and scattered old bones over the sites. Next, he took care of the altar at the shrine in Bethel that Jeroboam son of Nebat had built—the same Jeroboam who had led Israel into a life of sin. He tore apart the altar, burned down the shrine leaving it in ashes, and then lit fire to the phallic Asherah-pole.

23:16 As Josiah looked over the scene, he noticed the tombs on the hillside. He ordered the bones removed from the tombs and had them cremated on the ruined altars, desacralizing the evil altars. This was a fulfillment of the word of God spoken by the Holy Man years before when Jeroboam had stood by the altar at the sacred convocation.

23:17 Then the king said, "And *that* memorial stone—whose is that?"

The men from the city said, "That's the grave of the Holy Man who spoke the message against the altar at Bethel that you have just fulfilled."

23:18 Josiah said, "Don't trouble his bones." So they left his bones undisturbed, along with the bones of the prophet from Samaria.

NEW INTERNATIONAL VERSION

¹⁹Just as he had done at Bethel, Josiah removed and defiled all the shrines at the high places that the kings of Israel had built in the towns of Samaria that had provoked the LORD to anger. ²⁰Josiah slaughtered all the priests of those high places on the altars and burned human bones on them. Then he went back to Jerusalem.

²¹The king gave this order to all the people: "Celebrate the Passover to the LORD your God, as it is written in this Book of the Covenant." ²²Not since the days of the judges who led Israel, nor throughout the days of the kings of Israel and the kings of Judah, had any such Passover been observed. ²³But in the eighteenth year of King Josiah, this Passover was celebrated to the LORD in Jerusalem.

²⁴Furthermore, Josiah got rid of the mediums and spiritists, the household gods, the idols and all the other detestable things seen in Judah and Jerusalem. This he did to fulfill the requirements of the law written in the book that Hilkiah the priest had discovered in the temple of the LORD. ²⁵Neither before nor after Josiah was there a king like him who turned to the LORD as he did—with all his heart and with all his soul and with all his strength, in accordance with all the Law of Moses.

²⁶Nevertheless, the LORD did not turn away from the heat of his fierce anger, which burned against Judah because of all that Manasseh had done to provoke him to anger. ²⁷So the LORD said, "I will remove Judah also from my presence as I removed Israel, and I will reject Jerusalem, the city I chose, and this temple, about which I said, 'There shall my Name be.'ᵃ"

²⁸As for the other events of Josiah's reign, and all he did, are they not written in the book of the annals of the kings of Judah?

²⁹While Josiah was king, Pharaoh Neco king of Egypt went up to the Euphrates River to help the king of Assyria. King Josiah marched out to meet him in battle, but Neco faced him and killed him at Megiddo. ³⁰Josiah's servants brought his body in a chariot from Megiddo to Jerusalem and buried him in his own tomb. And the people of the land took Jehoahaz son of Josiah and anointed him and made him king in place of his father.

JEHOAHAZ KING OF JUDAH

³¹Jehoahaz was twenty-three years old when he became king, and he reigned in Jerusalem three months. His mother's name was Hamutal

ᵃ 27 1 Kings 8:29

THE MESSAGE

23.19-20   But Josiah hadn't finished. He now moved through all the towns of Samaria where the kings of Israel had built neighborhood sex-and-religion shrines, shrines that had so angered GOD. He tore the shrines down and left them in ruins—just as at Bethel. He killed all the priests who had conducted the sacrifices and cremated them on their own altars, thus desacralizing the altars. Only then did Josiah return to Jerusalem.

23.21   The king now commanded the people, "Celebrate the Passover to GOD, your God, exactly as directed in this Book of the Covenant."

23.22-23   This commanded Passover had not been celebrated since the days that the judges judged Israel—none of the kings of Israel and Judah had celebrated it. But in the eighteenth year of the rule of King Josiah this very Passover was celebrated to GOD in Jerusalem.

23.24   Josiah scrubbed the place clean and trashed spirit-mediums, sorcerers, domestic gods, and carved figures—all the vast accumulation of foul and obscene relics and images on display everywhere you looked in Judah and Jerusalem. Josiah did this in obedience to the words of GOD's Revelation written in the book that Hilkiah the priest found in The Temple of GOD.

23.25   There was no king to compare with Josiah—neither before nor after—a king who turned in total and repentant obedience to GOD, heart and mind and strength, following the instructions revealed to and written by Moses. The world would never again see a king like Josiah.

23.26-27   But despite Josiah, GOD's hot anger did not cool; the raging anger ignited by Manasseh burned unchecked. And GOD, not swerving in his judgment, gave sentence: "I'll remove Judah from my presence in the same way I removed Israel. I'll turn my back on this city, Jerusalem, that I chose, and even from this Temple of which I said, 'My Name lives here.'"

23.28-30   The rest of the life and times of Josiah is written in The Chronicles of the Kings of Judah. Josiah's death came about when Pharaoh Neco king of Egypt marched out to join forces with the king of Assyria at the Euphrates River. When King Josiah intercepted him at the Plain of Megiddo, Neco killed him. Josiah's servants took his body in a chariot, returned him to Jerusalem, and buried him in his own tomb. By popular choice Jehoahaz son of Josiah was anointed and succeeded his father as king.

JEHOAHAZ OF JUDAH

23.31   Jehoahaz was twenty-three years old when he began to rule. He was king in Jerusalem for a mere three months. His mother's name was Ha-

NEW INTERNATIONAL VERSION

daughter of Jeremiah; she was from Libnah. ³²He did evil in the eyes of the LORD, just as his fathers had done. ³³Pharaoh Neco put him in chains at Riblah in the land of Hamath*a* so that he might not reign in Jerusalem, and he imposed on Judah a levy of a hundred talents*b* of silver and a talent*c* of gold. ³⁴Pharaoh Neco made Eliakim son of Josiah king in place of his father Josiah and changed Eliakim's name to Jehoiakim. But he took Jehoahaz and carried him off to Egypt, and there he died. ³⁵Jehoiakim paid Pharaoh Neco the silver and gold he demanded. In order to do so, he taxed the land and exacted the silver and gold from the people of the land according to their assessments.

JEHOIAKIM KING OF JUDAH

³⁶Jehoiakim was twenty-five years old when he became king, and he reigned in Jerusalem eleven years. His mother's name was Zebidah daughter of Pedaiah; she was from Rumah. ³⁷And he did evil in the eyes of the LORD, just as his fathers had done.

24 During Jehoiakim's reign, Nebuchadnezzar king of Babylon invaded the land, and Jehoiakim became his vassal for three years. But then he changed his mind and rebelled against Nebuchadnezzar. ²The LORD sent Babylonian,*d* Aramean, Moabite and Ammonite raiders against him. He sent them to destroy Judah, in accordance with the word of the LORD proclaimed by his servants the prophets. ³Surely these things happened to Judah according to the LORD's command, in order to remove them from his presence because of the sins of Manasseh and all he had done, ⁴including the shedding of innocent blood. For he had filled Jerusalem with innocent blood, and the LORD was not willing to forgive.

⁵As for the other events of Jehoiakim's reign, and all he did, are they not written in the book of the annals of the kings of Judah? ⁶Jehoiakim rested with his fathers. And Jehoiachin his son succeeded him as king.

⁷The king of Egypt did not march out from his own country again, because the king of Babylon had taken all his territory, from the Wadi of Egypt to the Euphrates River.

---

a 33 Hebrew; Septuagint (see also 2 Chron. 36:3) *Neco at Riblah in Hamath removed him*   *b 33* That is, about 3 3/4 tons (about 3.4 metric tons)   *c 33* That is, about 75 pounds (about 34 kilograms)   *d 2* Or *Chaldean*

THE MESSAGE

mutal daughter of Jeremiah. She came from Libnah.

23.32   In GOD's opinion, he was an evil king, reverting to the evil ways of his ancestors.

23.33-34   Pharaoh Neco captured Jehoahaz at Riblah in the country of Hamath and put him in chains, preventing him from ruling in Jerusalem. He demanded that Judah pay tribute of nearly four tons of silver and seventy-five pounds of gold. Then Pharaoh Neco made Eliakim son of Josiah the successor to Josiah, but changed his name to Jehoiakim. Jehoahaz was carted off to Egypt and eventually died there.

23.35   Meanwhile Jehoiakim, like a good puppet, dutifully paid out the silver and gold demanded by Pharaoh. He scraped up the money by gouging the people, making everyone pay an assessed tax.

JEHOIAKIM OF JUDAH

23.36-37 Jehoiakim was twenty-five years old when he began to rule; he was king for eleven years in Jerusalem. His mother's name was Zebidah daughter of Pedaiah. She had come from Rumah. In GOD's opinion he was an evil king, picking up on the evil ways of his ancestors.

24 It was during his reign that Nebuchadnezzar king of Babylon invaded the country. Jehoiakim became his puppet. But after three years he had had enough and revolted.

24.2-4   GOD dispatched a succession of raiding bands against him: Babylonian, Aramean, Moabite, and Ammonite. The strategy was to destroy Judah. Through the preaching of his servants and prophets, GOD had said he would do this, and now he was doing it. None of this was by chance—it was GOD's judgment as he turned his back on Judah because of the enormity of the sins of Manasseh—Manasseh, the killer-king, who made the Jerusalem streets flow with the innocent blood of his victims. GOD wasn't about to overlook such crimes.

24.5-6   The rest of the life and times of Jehoiakim is written in *The Chronicles of the Kings of Judah*. Jehoiakim died and was buried with his ancestors. His son Jehoiachin became the next king.

24.7   The threat from Egypt was now over—no more invasions by the king of Egypt—for by this time the king of Babylon had captured all the land between the Brook of Egypt and the Euphrates River, land formerly controlled by the king of Egypt.

NEW INTERNATIONAL VERSION

JEHOIACHIN KING OF JUDAH

⁸Jehoiachin was eighteen years old when he became king, and he reigned in Jerusalem three months. His mother's name was Nehushta daughter of Elnathan; she was from Jerusalem. ⁹He did evil in the eyes of the LORD, just as his father had done.

¹⁰At that time the officers of Nebuchadnezzar king of Babylon advanced on Jerusalem and laid siege to it, ¹¹and Nebuchadnezzar himself came up to the city while his officers were besieging it. ¹²Jehoiachin king of Judah, his mother, his attendants, his nobles and his officials all surrendered to him.

In the eighth year of the reign of the king of Babylon, he took Jehoiachin prisoner. ¹³As the LORD had declared, Nebuchadnezzar removed all the treasures from the temple of the LORD and from the royal palace, and took away all the gold articles that Solomon king of Israel had made for the temple of the LORD. ¹⁴He carried into exile all Jerusalem: all the officers and fighting men, and all the craftsmen and artisans—a total of ten thousand. Only the poorest people of the land were left.

¹⁵Nebuchadnezzar took Jehoiachin captive to Babylon. He also took from Jerusalem to Babylon the king's mother, his wives, his officials and the leading men of the land. ¹⁶The king of Babylon also deported to Babylon the entire force of seven thousand fighting men, strong and fit for war, and a thousand craftsmen and artisans. ¹⁷He made Mattaniah, Jehoiachin's uncle, king in his place and changed his name to Zedekiah.

ZEDEKIAH KING OF JUDAH

¹⁸Zedekiah was twenty-one years old when he became king, and he reigned in Jerusalem eleven years. His mother's name was Hamutal daughter of Jeremiah; she was from Libnah. ¹⁹He did evil in the eyes of the LORD, just as Jehoiakim had done. ²⁰It was because of the LORD's anger that all this happened to Jerusalem and Judah, and in the end he thrust them from his presence.

THE FALL OF JERUSALEM

Now Zedekiah rebelled against the king of Babylon.

25 So in the ninth year of Zedekiah's reign, on the tenth day of the tenth month, Nebuchadnezzar king of Babylon marched against Jerusalem with his whole army. He en-

THE MESSAGE

JEHOIACHIN OF JUDAH

24.8-9 Jehoiachin was eighteen years old when he became king. His rule in Jerusalem lasted only three months. His mother's name was Nehushta daughter of Elnathan; she was from Jerusalem. In GOD's opinion he also was an evil king, no different from his father.

24.10-12 The next thing to happen was that the officers of Nebuchadnezzar king of Babylon attacked Jerusalem and put it under siege. While his officers were laying siege to the city, Nebuchadnezzar king of Babylon paid a personal visit. And Jehoiachin king of Judah, along with his mother, officers, advisors, and government leaders, surrendered.

24.12-14 In the eighth year of his reign Jehoiachin was taken prisoner by the king of Babylon. Nebuchadnezzar emptied the treasuries of both The Temple of GOD and the royal palace and confiscated all the gold furnishings that Solomon king of Israel had made for The Temple of GOD. This should have been no surprise—GOD had said it would happen. And then he emptied Jerusalem of people—all its leaders and soldiers, all its craftsmen and artisans. He took them into exile, something like ten thousand of them! The only ones he left were the very poor.

24.15-16 He took Jehoiachin into exile to Babylon. With him he took the king's mother, his wives, his chief officers, the community leaders, anyone who was anybody—in round numbers, seven thousand soldiers plus another thousand or so craftsmen and artisans, all herded off into exile in Babylon.

24.17 Then the king of Babylon made Jehoiachin's uncle, Mattaniah, his puppet king, but changed his name to Zedekiah.

ZEDEKIAH OF JUDAH

24.18 Zedekiah was twenty-one years old when he started out as king. He was king in Jerusalem for eleven years. His mother's name was Hamutal the daughter of Jeremiah. Her hometown was Libnah.

24.19 As far as GOD was concerned Zedekiah was just one more evil king, a carbon copy of Jehoiakim.

24.20 The source of all this doom to Jerusalem and Judah was GOD's anger—GOD turned his back on them as an act of judgment. And then Zedekiah revolted against the king of Babylon.

25.1-7 **25** The revolt dates from the ninth year and tenth month of Zedekiah's reign. Nebuchadnezzar set out for Jerusalem immediately with a full army. He set up camp and

NEW INTERNATIONAL VERSION

camped outside the city and built siege works all around it. ²The city was kept under siege until the eleventh year of King Zedekiah. ³By the ninth day of the ⌊fourth⌋ᵃ month the famine in the city had become so severe that there was no food for the people to eat. ⁴Then the city wall was broken through, and the whole army fled at night through the gate between the two walls near the king's garden, though the Babyloniansᵇ were surrounding the city. They fled toward the Arabah,ᶜ ⁵but the Babylonianᵈ army pursued the king and overtook him in the plains of Jericho. All his soldiers were separated from him and scattered, ⁶and he was captured. He was taken to the king of Babylon at Riblah, where sentence was pronounced on him. ⁷They killed the sons of Zedekiah before his eyes. Then they put out his eyes, bound him with bronze shackles and took him to Babylon.

⁸On the seventh day of the fifth month, in the nineteenth year of Nebuchadnezzar king of Babylon, Nebuzaradan commander of the imperial guard, an official of the king of Babylon, came to Jerusalem. ⁹He set fire to the temple of the LORD, the royal palace and all the houses of Jerusalem. Every important building he burned down. ¹⁰The whole Babylonian army, under the commander of the imperial guard, broke down the walls around Jerusalem. ¹¹Nebuzaradan the commander of the guard carried into exile the people who remained in the city, along with the rest of the populace and those who had gone over to the king of Babylon. ¹²But the commander left behind some of the poorest people of the land to work the vineyards and fields.

¹³The Babylonians broke up the bronze pillars, the movable stands and the bronze Sea that were at the temple of the LORD and they carried the bronze to Babylon. ¹⁴They also took away the pots, shovels, wick trimmers, dishes and all the bronze articles used in the temple service. ¹⁵The commander of the imperial guard took away the censers and sprinkling bowls—all that were made of pure gold or silver.

¹⁶The bronze from the two pillars, the Sea and the movable stands, which Solomon had made for the temple of the LORD, was more than could be weighed. ¹⁷Each pillar was twenty-seven feetᵉ high. The bronze capital on top of one pillar was four and a half feetᶠ high and was decorated with a network and pomegranates of bronze all around. The other pillar, with its network, was similar.

ᵃ 3 See Jer. 52:6.   ᵇ 4 Or *Chaldeans*; also in verses 13, 25 and 26   ᶜ 4 Or *the Jordan Valley*   ᵈ 5 Or *Chaldean*; also in verses 10 and 24   ᵉ 17 Hebrew *eighteen cubits* (about 8.1 meters)   ᶠ 17 Hebrew *three cubits* (about 1.3 meters)

THE MESSAGE

sealed off the city by building siege mounds around it. The city was under siege for nineteen months (until the eleventh year of Zedekiah). By the fourth month of Zedekiah's eleventh year, on the ninth day of the month, the famine was so bad that there wasn't so much as a crumb of bread for anyone. Then there was a breakthrough. At night, under cover of darkness, the entire army escaped through an opening in the wall (it was the gate between the two walls above the King's Garden). They slipped through the lines of the Babylonians who surrounded the city and headed for the Jordan on the Arabah Valley road. But the Babylonians were in pursuit of the king and they caught up with him in the Plains of Jericho. By then Zedekiah's army had deserted and was scattered. The Babylonians took Zedekiah prisoner and marched him off to the king of Babylon at Riblah, then tried and sentenced him on the spot. Zedekiah's sons were executed right before his eyes; the summary murder of his sons was the last thing he saw, for they then blinded him. Securely handcuffed, he was hauled off to Babylon.

25.8-12   In the nineteenth year of Nebuchadnezzar king of Babylon, on the seventh day of the fifth month, Nebuzaradan, the king of Babylon's chief deputy, arrived in Jerusalem. He burned The Temple of GOD to the ground, went on to the royal palace, and then finished off the city—burned the whole place down. He put the Babylonian troops he had with him to work knocking down the city walls. Finally, he rounded up everyone left in the city, including those who had earlier deserted to the king of Babylon, and took them off into exile. He left a few poor dirt farmers behind to tend the vineyards and what was left of the fields.

25.13-15   The Babylonians broke up the bronze pillars, the bronze washstands, and the huge bronze basin (the Sea) that were in The Temple of GOD and hauled the bronze off to Babylon. They also took the various bronze-crafted liturgical accessories used in the services of Temple worship, as well as the gold and silver censers and sprinkling bowls. The king's deputy didn't miss a thing—he took every scrap of precious metal he could find.

25.16-17   The amount of bronze they got from the two pillars, the Sea, and all the washstands that Solomon had made for The Temple of GOD was enormous—they couldn't weigh it all! Each pillar stood twenty-seven feet high, plus another four and a half feet for an ornate capital of bronze filigree and decorative fruit.

NEW INTERNATIONAL VERSION

¹⁸The commander of the guard took as prisoners Seraiah the chief priest, Zephaniah the priest next in rank and the three doorkeepers. ¹⁹Of those still in the city, he took the officer in charge of the fighting men and five royal advisers. He also took the secretary who was chief officer in charge of conscripting the people of the land and sixty of his men who were found in the city. ²⁰Nebuzaradan the commander took them all and brought them to the king of Babylon at Riblah. ²¹There at Riblah, in the land of Hamath, the king had them executed.

So Judah went into captivity, away from her land.

²²Nebuchadnezzar king of Babylon appointed Gedaliah son of Ahikam, the son of Shaphan, to be over the people he had left behind in Judah. ²³When all the army officers and their men heard that the king of Babylon had appointed Gedaliah as governor, they came to Gedaliah at Mizpah—Ishmael son of Nethaniah, Johanan son of Kareah, Seraiah son of Tanhumeth the Netophathite, Jaazaniah the son of the Maacathite, and their men. ²⁴Gedaliah took an oath to reassure them and their men. "Do not be afraid of the Babylonian officials," he said. "Settle down in the land and serve the king of Babylon, and it will go well with you."

²⁵In the seventh month, however, Ishmael son of Nethaniah, the son of Elishama, who was of royal blood, came with ten men and assassinated Gedaliah and also the men of Judah and the Babylonians who were with him at Mizpah. ²⁶At this, all the people from the least to the greatest, together with the army officers, fled to Egypt for fear of the Babylonians.

JEHOIACHIN RELEASED

²⁷In the thirty-seventh year of the exile of Jehoiachin king of Judah, in the year Evil-Merodach*ᵃ* became king of Babylon, he released Jehoiachin from prison on the twenty-seventh day of the twelfth month. ²⁸He spoke kindly to him and gave him a seat of honor higher than those of the other kings who were with him in Babylon. ²⁹So Jehoiachin put aside his prison clothes and for the rest of his life ate regularly at the king's table. ³⁰Day by day the king gave Jehoiachin a regular allowance as long as he lived.

ᵃ 27 Also called *Amel-Marduk*

THE MESSAGE

25.18-21 The king's deputy took a number of special prisoners: Seraiah the chief priest, Zephaniah the associate priest, three wardens, the chief remaining army officer, five of the king's counselors, the accountant, the chief recruiting officer for the army, and sixty men of standing from among the people. Nebuzaradan the king's deputy marched them all off to the king of Babylon at Riblah. And there at Riblah, in the land of Hamath, the king of Babylon killed the lot of them in cold blood.

Judah went into exile, orphaned from her land.

25.22-23 Regarding the common people who were left behind in Judah, this: Nebuchadnezzar king of Babylon appointed Gedaliah son of Ahikam, the son of Shaphan, as their governor. When veteran army officers among the people heard that the king of Babylon had appointed Gedaliah, they came to Gedaliah at Mizpah. Among them were Ishmael son of Nethaniah, Johanan son of Kareah, Seraiah son of Tanhumeth the Netophathite, Jaazaniah the son of the Maacathite, and some of their followers.

25.24 Gedaliah assured the officers and their men, giving them his word, "Don't be afraid of the Babylonian officials. Go back to your farms and families and respect the king of Babylon. Trust me, everything is going to be all right."

25.25 Some time later—it was in the seventh month—Ishmael son of Nethaniah, the son of Elishama (he had royal blood in him), came back with ten men and killed Gedaliah, the traitor Jews, and the Babylonian officials who were stationed at Mizpah—a bloody massacre.

25.26 But then, afraid of what the Babylonians would do, they all took off for Egypt, leaders and people, small and great.

25.27-30 When Jehoiachin king of Judah had been in exile for thirty-seven years, Evil-Merodach became king in Babylon and let Jehoiachin out of prison. This release took place on the twenty-seventh day of the twelfth month. The king treated him most courteously and gave him preferential treatment beyond anything experienced by the other political prisoners held in Babylon. Jehoiachin took off his prison garb and for the rest of his life ate his meals in company with the king. The king provided everything he needed to live comfortably.

1 CHRONICLES

1 CHRONICLES

HISTORICAL RECORDS FROM ADAM TO ABRAHAM

TO NOAH'S SONS

1 Adam, Seth, Enosh, ²Kenan, Mahalalel, Jared, ³Enoch, Methuselah, Lamech, Noah.

⁴ The sons of Noah:ᵃ
  Shem, Ham and Japheth.

THE JAPHETHITES

⁵ The sonsᵇ of Japheth:
  Gomer, Magog, Madai, Javan, Tubal, Meshech and Tiras.
⁶ The sons of Gomer:
  Ashkenaz, Riphathᶜ and Togarmah.
⁷ The sons of Javan:
  Elishah, Tarshish, the Kittim and the Rodanim.

THE HAMITES

⁸ The sons of Ham:
  Cush, Mizraim,ᵈ Put and Canaan.
⁹ The sons of Cush:
  Seba, Havilah, Sabta, Raamah and Sabteca.
  The sons of Raamah:
  Sheba and Dedan.
¹⁰ Cush was the fatherᵉ of
  Nimrod, who grew to be a mighty warrior on earth.
¹¹ Mizraim was the father of
  the Ludites, Anamites, Lehabites, Naphtuhites, ¹²Pathrusites, Casluhites (from whom the Philistines came) and Caphtorites.
¹³ Canaan was the father of
  Sidon his firstborn,ᶠ and of the Hittites, ¹⁴Jebusites, Amorites, Girgashites, ¹⁵Hivites, Arkites, Sinites, ¹⁶Arvadites, Zemarites and Hamathites.

ISRAEL'S FAMILY TREE: THE TRUNK

1.1-4 **1** Adam
  Seth
  Enosh
  Kenan
  Mahalalel
  Jared
  Enoch
  Methuselah
  Lamech
  Noah
  Shem, Ham, and Japheth.

THE JAPHETH BRANCH

1.5 Japheth had Gomer, Magog, Madai, Javan, Tubal, Meshech, and Tiras.
1.6   Gomer had Ashkenaz, Riphath, and Togarmah.
1.7   Javan had Elisha, Tarshish, Kittim, and Rodanim.

THE HAM BRANCH

1.8 Ham had Cush, Mizraim, Put, and Canaan.
1.9   Cush had Seba, Havilah, Sabta, Raamah, and Sabteca.
  Raamah had Sheba and Dedan.
1.10   Cush had Nimrod, the first great hero on earth.
1.11-12   Mizraim was ancestor to the Ludim, the Anamim, the Lehabim, the Naphtuhim, the Pathrusim, the Casluhim, and the Caphtorim from whom the Philistines descended.
1.13-16   Canaan had Sidon (his firstborn) and Heth, and was ancestor to the Jebusites, the Amorites, the Girgashites, the Hivites, the Arkites, the Sinites, the Arvadites, the Zemarites, and the Hamathites.

ᵃ 4 Septuagint; Hebrew does not have this line.   ᵇ 5 *Sons* may mean *descendants* or *successors* or *nations*; also in verses 6-10, 17 and 20.   ᶜ 6 Many Hebrew manuscripts and Vulgate (see also Septuagint and Gen. 10:3); most Hebrew manuscripts *Diphath*   ᵈ 8 That is, Egypt; also in verse 11   ᵉ 10 *Father* may mean *ancestor* or *predecessor* or *founder*; also in verses 11, 13, 18 and 20.   ᶠ 13 Or *of the Sidonians, the foremost*

NEW INTERNATIONAL VERSION	THE MESSAGE

NEW INTERNATIONAL VERSION

THE SEMITES

17 The sons of Shem:

Elam, Asshur, Arphaxad, Lud and Aram.

The sons of Aram:*a*

Uz, Hul, Gether and Meshech.

18 Arphaxad was the father of Shelah,
and Shelah the father of Eber.

19 Two sons were born to Eber:

One was named Peleg,*b* because in his
time the earth was divided; his brother
was named Joktan.

20 Joktan was the father of

Almodad, Sheleph, Hazarmaveth, Je-
rah, 21 Hadoram, Uzal, Diklah, 22 Obal,*c*
Abimael, Sheba, 23 Ophir, Havilah and
Jobab. All these were sons of Joktan.

24 Shem, Arphaxad,*d* Shelah,
25 Eber, Peleg, Reu,
26 Serug, Nahor, Terah
27 and Abram (that is, Abraham).

THE FAMILY OF ABRAHAM

28 The sons of Abraham:

Isaac and Ishmael.

DESCENDANTS OF HAGAR

29 These were their descendants:

Nebaioth the firstborn of Ishmael, Kedar,
Adbeel, Mibsam, 30 Mishma, Dumah, Mas-
sa, Hadad, Tema, 31 Jetur, Naphish and
Kedemah. These were the sons of Ishmael.

DESCENDANTS OF KETURAH

32 The sons born to Keturah, Abraham's concubine:

Zimran, Jokshan, Medan, Midian, Ishbak and Shuah.

The sons of Jokshan:

Sheba and Dedan.

33 The sons of Midian:

Ephah, Epher, Hanoch, Abida and Eldaah.

All these were descendants of Keturah.

DESCENDANTS OF SARAH

34 Abraham was the father of Isaac.

The sons of Isaac:

Esau and Israel.

ESAU'S SONS

35 The sons of Esau:

a 17 One Hebrew manuscript and some Septuagint
manuscripts (see also Gen. 10:23); most Hebrew
manuscripts do not have this line.   *b 19 Peleg* means
division.   *c 22* Some Hebrew manuscripts and Syriac (see
also Gen. 10:28); most Hebrew manuscripts *Ebal*
d 24 Hebrew; some Septuagint manuscripts *Arphaxad,*
Cainan (see also note at Gen. 11:10)

THE MESSAGE

THE SHEM BRANCH

1.17 Shem had Elam, Asshur, Arphaxad, Lud, Aram,
Uz, Hul, Gether, and Meshech.

1.18-19 Arphaxad had Shelah and Shelah had Eber.
Eber had two sons: Peleg (Division) because in
his time the earth was divided up; his brother
was Joktan.

1.20-23 Joktan had Almodad, Sheleph, Hazarmaveth, Jerah, Hadoram, Uzal, Diklah, Ebal,
Abimael, Sheba, Ophir, Havilah, and Jobab—all
sons of Joktan.

1.24-28 The three main branches in summary:
Shem, Arphaxad, Shelah, Eber, Peleg, Reu, Se-
rug, Nahor, Terah, and Abram (Abraham). And
Abraham had Isaac and Ishmael.

THE FAMILY OF ABRAHAM

1.29-31 Abraham's family tree developed along these
lines: Ishmael had Nebaioth (his firstborn),
then Kedar, Adbeel, Mibsam, Mishma, Dumah,
Massa, Hadad, Tema, Jetur, Naphish, and Kedemah—the Ishmael branch.

1.32-33 Keturah, Abraham's concubine, gave birth to
Zimran, Jokshan, Medan, Midian, Ishbak, and
Shuah. Then Jokshan had Sheba and Dedan.
And Midian had Ephah, Epher, Hanoch, Abida,
and Eldaah. These made up the Keturah
branch.

1.34-37 Abraham had Isaac, and Isaac had Esau and
Israel (Jacob). Esau had Eliphaz, Reuel, Jeush,

NEW INTERNATIONAL VERSION	THE MESSAGE

NEW INTERNATIONAL VERSION

Eliphaz, Reuel, Jeush, Jalam and Korah.
36 The sons of Eliphaz:
Teman, Omar, Zepho,*a* Gatam and Kenaz;
by Timna: Amalek.*b*
37 The sons of Reuel:
Nahath, Zerah, Shammah and Mizzah.

THE PEOPLE OF SEIR IN EDOM

38 The sons of Seir:
Lotan, Shobal, Zibeon, Anah, Dishon, Ezer and Dishan.
39 The sons of Lotan:
Hori and Homam. Timna was Lotan's sister.
40 The sons of Shobal:
Alvan,*c* Manahath, Ebal, Shepho and Onam.
The sons of Zibeon:
Aiah and Anah.
41 The son of Anah:
Dishon.
The sons of Dishon:
Hemdan,*d* Eshban, Ithran and Keran.
42 The sons of Ezer:
Bilhan, Zaavan and Akan.*e*
The sons of Dishan*f*:
Uz and Aran.

THE RULERS OF EDOM

43 These were the kings who reigned in Edom before any Israelite king reigned*g*:
Bela son of Beor, whose city was named Dinhabah.
44 When Bela died, Jobab son of Zerah from Bozrah succeeded him as king.
45 When Jobab died, Husham from the land of the Temanites succeeded him as king.
46 When Husham died, Hadad son of Bedad, who defeated Midian in the country of Moab, succeeded him as king. His city was named Avith.
47 When Hadad died, Samlah from Masrekah succeeded him as king.
48 When Samlah died, Shaul from Rehoboth on the river*h* succeeded him as king.

a 36 Many Hebrew manuscripts, some Septuagint manuscripts and Syriac (see also Gen. 36:11); most Hebrew manuscripts *Zephi*   *b 36* Some Septuagint manuscripts (see also Gen. 36:12); Hebrew *Gatam, Kenaz, Timna and Amalek*   *c 40* Many Hebrew manuscripts and some Septuagint manuscripts (see also Gen. 36:23); most Hebrew manuscripts *Alian*   *d 41* Many Hebrew manuscripts and some Septuagint manuscripts (see also Gen. 36:26); most Hebrew manuscripts *Hamran*   *e 42* Many Hebrew and Septuagint manuscripts (see also Gen. 36:27); most Hebrew manuscripts *Zaavan, Jaakan*   *f 42* Hebrew *Dishon*, a variant of *Dishan*   *g 43* Or *before an Israelite king reigned over them*   *h 48* Possibly the Euphrates

THE MESSAGE

Jalam, and Korah. Eliphaz had Teman, Omar, Zepho, Gatam, Kenaz, Timna, and Amalek. And Reuel had Nahath, Zerah, Shammah, and Mizzah.

1.38-42 Seir then had Lotan, Shobal, Zibeon, Anah, Dishon, Ezer, and Dishan. Lotan had Hori and Homam. Timna was Lotan's sister. Shobal had Alian, Manahath, Ebal, Shepho, and Onam. Zibeon had Aiah and Anah. Anah had Dishon. Dishon had Hemdan, Eshban, Ithran, and Keran. Ezer had Bilhan, Zaavan, and Akan. And Dishan had Uz and Aran.

THE EDOMITE KING LIST

1.43-51 A list of the kings who ruled in the country of Edom before Israel had a king:
Bela son of Beor; his city was Dinhabah.
Bela died; Jobab son of Zerah from Bozrah was the next king.
Jobab died; Husham from the country of the Temanites was the next king.
Husham died; Hadad son of Bedad, who defeated Midian in the country of Moab, was the next king; his city was Avith.
Hadad died; Samlah from Masrekah was the next king.
Samlah died; Shaul from Rehoboth-by-the-River was the next king.

NEW INTERNATIONAL VERSION	THE MESSAGE

NEW INTERNATIONAL VERSION

[49] When Shaul died, Baal-Hanan son of Acbor succeeded him as king.
[50] When Baal-Hanan died, Hadad succeeded him as king. His city was named Pau,[a] and his wife's name was Mehetabel daughter of Matred, the daughter of Me-Zahab. [51] Hadad also died.

The chiefs of Edom were:

Timna, Alvah, Jetheth, [52] Oholibamah, Elah, Pinon, [53] Kenaz, Teman, Mibzar, [54] Magdiel and Iram. These were the chiefs of Edom.

ISRAEL'S SONS

2 These were the sons of Israel:
Reuben, Simeon, Levi, Judah, Issachar, Zebulun, [2] Dan, Joseph, Benjamin, Naphtali, Gad and Asher.

JUDAH

TO HEZRON'S SONS

[3] The sons of Judah:

Er, Onan and Shelah. These three were born to him by a Canaanite woman, the daughter of Shua. Er, Judah's firstborn, was wicked in the LORD's sight; so the LORD put him to death. [4] Tamar, Judah's daughter-in-law, bore him Perez and Zerah. Judah had five sons in all.

[5] The sons of Perez:
Hezron and Hamul.
[6] The sons of Zerah:
Zimri, Ethan, Heman, Calcol and Darda[b]—five in all.
[7] The son of Carmi:
Achar,[c] who brought trouble on Israel by violating the ban on taking devoted things.[d]
[8] The son of Ethan:
Azariah.
[9] The sons born to Hezron were:
Jerahmeel, Ram and Caleb.[e]

FROM RAM SON OF HEZRON

[10] Ram was the father of
Amminadab, and Amminadab the father of Nahshon, the leader of the people of

---

a 50 Many Hebrew manuscripts, some Septuagint manuscripts, Vulgate and Syriac (see also Gen. 36:39); most Hebrew manuscripts *Pai*   *b 6* Many Hebrew manuscripts, some Septuagint manuscripts and Syriac (see also 1 Kings 4:31); most Hebrew manuscripts *Dara*   *c 7 Achar* means *trouble; Achar* is called *Achan* in Joshua.   *d 7* The Hebrew term refers to the irrevocable giving over of things or persons to the LORD, often by totally destroying them.
e 9 Hebrew *Kelubai*, a variant of *Caleb*

THE MESSAGE

Shaul died; Baal-Hanan son of Acbor was the next king.

Baal-Hanan died; Hadad was the next king; his city was Pau and his wife was Mehetabel daughter of Matred, the daughter of Me-Zahab. Last of all Hadad died.

1.51-54   The chieftains of Edom after that were Chief Timna, Chief Alvah, Chief Jetheth, Chief Oholibamah, Chief Elah, Chief Pinon, Chief Kenaz, Chief Teman, Chief Mibzar, Chief Magdiel, and Chief Iram. These were the chieftains of Edom.

THE FAMILY OF ISRAEL (JACOB)

2.1-2   **2** Israel's (that is, Jacob's) sons: Reuben, Simeon, Levi, Judah, Issachar, Zebulun, Dan, Joseph, Benjamin, Naphtali, Gad, and Asher.

2.3-9   Judah had Er, Onan, and Shelah; their mother was Bathshua the Canaanite. Er, Judah's firstborn, was so bad before GOD that GOD killed him. Judah also had Perez and Zerah by his daughter-in-law Tamar—a total of five sons. Perez had Hezron and Hamul; Zerah had Zimri, Ethan, Heman, Calcol, and Darda—five sons. Carmi had Achar, who brought doom on Israel when he violated a holy ban. Ethan's son was Azariah. And Hezron had Jerahmeel, Ram, and Chelubai.

2.10-17   Ram had Amminadab and Amminadab had Nahshon, a prominent leader in the Judah fam-

NEW INTERNATIONAL VERSION

Judah. [11]Nahshon was the father of Salmon,[a] Salmon the father of Boaz, [12]Boaz the father of Obed and Obed the father of Jesse.

[13]Jesse was the father of

Eliab his firstborn; the second son was Abinadab, the third Shimea, [14]the fourth Nethanel, the fifth Raddai, [15]the sixth Ozem and the seventh David. [16]Their sisters were Zeruiah and Abigail. Zeruiah's three sons were Abishai, Joab and Asahel. [17]Abigail was the mother of Amasa, whose father was Jether the Ishmaelite.

CALEB SON OF HEZRON

[18]Caleb son of Hezron had children by his wife Azubah (and by Jerioth). These were her sons: Jesher, Shobab and Ardon. [19]When Azubah died, Caleb married Ephrath, who bore him Hur. [20]Hur was the father of Uri, and Uri the father of Bezalel.

[21]Later, Hezron lay with the daughter of Makir the father of Gilead (he had married her when he was sixty years old), and she bore him Segub. [22]Segub was the father of Jair, who controlled twenty-three towns in Gilead. [23](But Geshur and Aram captured Havvoth Jair,[b] as well as Kenath with its surrounding settlements—sixty towns.) All these were descendants of Makir the father of Gilead.

[24]After Hezron died in Caleb Ephrathah, Abijah the wife of Hezron bore him Ashhur the father[c] of Tekoa.

JERAHMEEL SON OF HEZRON

[25]The sons of Jerahmeel the firstborn of Hezron:

Ram his firstborn, Bunah, Oren, Ozem and[d] Ahijah. [26]Jerahmeel had another wife, whose name was Atarah; she was the mother of Onam.

[27]The sons of Ram the firstborn of Jerahmeel:

Maaz, Jamin and Eker.

[28]The sons of Onam:

Shammai and Jada.

The sons of Shammai:

Nadab and Abishur.

[29]Abishur's wife was named Abihail, who bore him Ahban and Molid.

---

a 11 Septuagint (see also Ruth 4:21); Hebrew *Salma*
b 23 Or *captured the settlements of Jair*   *c 24 Father* may mean *civic leader* or *military leader*; also in verses 42, 45, 49-52 and possibly elsewhere.   *d 25* Or *Oren and Ozem,* by

THE MESSAGE

ily. Nahshon had Salmon and Salmon had Boaz. Boaz had Obed and Obed had Jesse. Jesse's firstborn was Eliab, followed by Abinadab, Shimea, Nethanel, Raddai, Ozem, and finally David; David was the seventh. Their sisters were Zeruiah and Abigail. Zeruiah gave birth to three sons: Abishai, Joab, and Asahel; Abigail was the mother of Amasa (the father was Jether the Ishmaelite).

THE FAMILY OF CALEB

2.18-24 Caleb son of Hezron had children by his wife Azubah and also by Jerioth. Azubah's sons were Jesher, Shobab, and Ardon. After Azubah died, Caleb married Ephrath, who gave birth to Hur. Hur had Uri and Uri had Bezalel. Some time later Hezron married the daughter of Makir the father of Gilead; he was sixty years old when he married her; she gave birth to Segub. Then Segub had Jair who owned twenty-three cities in the land of Gilead. Geshur and Aram captured the nomadic villages of Jair and Kenath and their satellite settlements—sixty towns. These all belonged to Makir the father of Gilead. After the death of Hezron, Caleb married Ephrathah the wife of his father Hezron; she then gave birth to Ashhur the father of Tekoa.

THE FAMILY OF JERAHMEEL

2.25-26 The sons of Jerahmeel, Hezron's firstborn: Ram his firstborn, followed by Bunah, Oren, Ozem, and Ahijah. Jerahmeel had another wife whose name was Atarah; she gave birth to Onam.

2.27   The sons of Ram, Jerahmeel's firstborn: Maaz, Jamin, and Eker.

2.28-29   The sons of Onam: Shammai and Jada.

The sons of Shammai: Nadab and Abishur. Abishur's wife was Abihail; she gave birth to Ahban and Molid.

NEW INTERNATIONAL VERSION

³⁰ The sons of Nadab:
   Seled and Appaim. Seled died without
   children.
³¹ The son of Appaim:
   Ishi, who was the father of Sheshan.
   Sheshan was the father of Ahlai.
³² The sons of Jada, Shammai's brother:
   Jether and Jonathan. Jether died without children.
³³ The sons of Jonathan:
   Peleth and Zaza.
   These were the descendants of Jerahmeel.
³⁴ Sheshan had no sons—only daughters.
   He had an Egyptian servant named Jarha. ³⁵ Sheshan gave his daughter in marriage to his servant Jarha, and she bore
   him Attai.
³⁶ Attai was the father of Nathan,
   Nathan the father of Zabad,
   ³⁷ Zabad the father of Ephlal,
   Ephlal the father of Obed,
   ³⁸ Obed the father of Jehu,
   Jehu the father of Azariah,
   ³⁹ Azariah the father of Helez,
   Helez the father of Eleasah,
   ⁴⁰ Eleasah the father of Sismai,
   Sismai the father of Shallum,
   ⁴¹ Shallum the father of Jekamiah,
   and Jekamiah the father of Elishama.

THE CLANS OF CALEB

⁴² The sons of Caleb the brother of Jerahmeel:
   Mesha his firstborn, who was the father
   of Ziph, and his son Mareshah,ᵃ who
   was the father of Hebron.
⁴³ The sons of Hebron:
   Korah, Tappuah, Rekem and Shema.
   ⁴⁴ Shema was the father of Raham, and
   Raham the father of Jorkeam. Rekem
   was the father of Shammai. ⁴⁵ The son of
   Shammai was Maon, and Maon was the
   father of Beth Zur.
⁴⁶ Caleb's concubine Ephah was the mother
   of Haran, Moza and Gazez. Haran was
   the father of Gazez.
⁴⁷ The sons of Jahdai:
   Regem, Jotham, Geshan, Pelet, Ephah
   and Shaaph.
⁴⁸ Caleb's concubine Maacah was the mother
   of Sheber and Tirhanah. ⁴⁹ She also gave
   birth to Shaaph the father of Madmannah and to Sheva the father of Macbenah and Gibea. Caleb's daughter was Acsah. ⁵⁰ These were the descendants of
   Caleb.

ᵃ 42 The meaning of the Hebrew for this phrase is
uncertain.

THE MESSAGE

2.30   Nadab had Seled and Appaim. Seled died
leaving no sons.

2.31   Appaim had Ishi; Ishi had Sheshan; and Sheshan had Ahlai.

2.32   Jada, Shammai's brother, had Jether and Jonathan. Jether died leaving no sons.

2.33   Jonathan had Peleth and Zaza.
   This is the family tree of the sons of Jerahmeel.

✝

2.34-41   Sheshan had no sons, only daughters. But Sheshan had an Egyptian servant, Jarha. Sheshan
married his daughter to Jarha and she gave
birth to Attai. Attai had Nathan, Nathan had
Zabad, Zabad had Ephlal, Ephlal had Obed,
Obed had Jehu, Jehu had Azariah, Azariah had
Helez, Helez had Eleasah, Eleasah had Sismai,
Sismai had Shallum, Shallum had Jekamiah,
and Jekamiah had Elishama.

✝

2.42   Jerahmeel's brother Caleb had a son, his firstborn, named Mesha; Mesha had Ziph; Ziph's
son was Mareshah the father of Hebron.

2.43-44   The sons of Hebron: Korah, Tappuah, Rekem, and Shema. Shema had Raham the father
of Jorkeam; Rekem had Shammai.

2.45   Shammai's son was Maon and Maon was the
father of Beth Zur.

2.46   Caleb's concubine Ephah gave birth to Haran, Moza, and Gazez; Haran had Gazez.

2.47   The sons of Jahdai: Regem, Jotham, Geshan,
Pelet, Ephah, and Shaaph.

2.48-50   Another concubine of Caleb, Maacah, gave
birth to Sheber and Tirhanah. She also bore
Shaaph the father of Madmannah and Sheva
the father of Macbenah and Gibea. Caleb's
daughter was Acsah. These made up the Caleb
branch of the family tree.

NEW INTERNATIONAL VERSION

The sons of Hur the firstborn of Ephrathah:

Shobal the father of Kiriath Jearim, [51]Salma the father of Bethlehem, and Hareph the father of Beth Gader.

[52] The descendants of Shobal the father of Kiriath Jearim were:

Haroeh, half the Manahathites, [53]and the clans of Kiriath Jearim: the Ithrites, Puthites, Shumathites and Mishraites. From these descended the Zorathites and Eshtaolites.

[54] The descendants of Salma:

Bethlehem, the Netophathites, Atroth Beth Joab, half the Manahathites, the Zorites, [55]and the clans of scribes[a] who lived at Jabez: the Tirathites, Shimeathites and Sucathites. These are the Kenites who came from Hammath, the father of the house of Recab.[b]

THE SONS OF DAVID

3 These were the sons of David born to him in Hebron:

The firstborn was Amnon the son of Ahinoam of Jezreel;

the second, Daniel the son of Abigail of Carmel;

[2] the third, Absalom the son of Maacah daughter of Talmai king of Geshur;

the fourth, Adonijah the son of Haggith;

[3] the fifth, Shephatiah the son of Abital;

and the sixth, Ithream, by his wife Eglah.

[4] These six were born to David in Hebron, where he reigned seven years and six months.

David reigned in Jerusalem thirty-three years, [5]and these were the children born to him there:

Shammua,[c] Shobab, Nathan and Solomon. These four were by Bathsheba[d] daughter of Ammiel. [6]There were also Ibhar, Elishua,[e] Eliphelet, [7]Nogah, Nepheg, Japhia, [8]Elishama, Eliada and Eliphelet—nine in all. [9]All these were the sons of David, besides his sons by his concubines. And Tamar was their sister.

THE KINGS OF JUDAH

[10] Solomon's son was Rehoboam,

---

[a] 55 Or *of the Sopherites*   [b] 55 Or *father of Beth Recab*
[c] 5 Hebrew *Shimea*, a variant of *Shammua*
[d] 5 One Hebrew manuscript and Vulgate (see also Septuagint and 2 Samuel 11:3); most Hebrew manuscripts *Bathshua*   [e] 6 Two Hebrew manuscripts (see also 2 Samuel 5:15 and 1 Chron. 14:5); most Hebrew manuscripts *Elishama*

THE MESSAGE

[2.50-51] The sons of Hur, Ephrathah's firstborn: Shobal who had Kiriath Jearim, Salma who had Bethlehem, and Hareph father of Beth Gader.

[2.52-53] The family of Shobal, father of Kiriath Jearim: Haroeh, half of the population of Manahath, the families of Kiriath Jearim, the Ithrites, the Puthites, the Shumathites, and the Mishraites. The Zorathites and Eshtaolites also came from this line.

[2.54-55] The sons of Salma: Bethlehem, the Netophathites, Atroth Beth Joab, half of the Manahathites, the Zorites, and the families of Sopherim who lived at Jabez—the Tirathites, the Shimeathites, and the Sucathites. They made up the Kenites who came from Hammath the father of the house of Recab.

THE FAMILY OF DAVID

[3.1-3] **3** These are the sons that David had while he lived at Hebron:

His firstborn was Amnon by Ahinoam of Jezreel;

second, Daniel by Abigail of Carmel;

third, Absalom born of Maacah, daughter of Talmai king of Geshur;

fourth, Adonijah born of Haggith;

fifth, Shephatiah born of Abital;

sixth, Ithream born of his wife Eglah.

[3.4-9] He had these six sons while he was in Hebron; he was king there for seven years and six months.

He went on to be king in Jerusalem for another thirty-three years. These are the sons he had in Jerusalem: first Shammua, then Shobab, Nathan, and Solomon. Bathsheba daughter of Ammiel was the mother of these four. And then there were another nine sons: Ibhar, Elishua, Eliphelet, Nogah, Nepheg, Japhia, Elishama, Eliada, Eliphelet—David's sons, plus Tamar their sister. There were other sons by his concubines.

[3.10-14] In the next generation Solomon had Reho-

NEW INTERNATIONAL VERSION	THE MESSAGE

NEW INTERNATIONAL VERSION

Abijah his son,
Asa his son,
Jehoshaphat his son,
11 Jehoram[a] his son,
Ahaziah his son,
Joash his son,
12 Amaziah his son,
Azariah his son,
Jotham his son,
13 Ahaz his son,
Hezekiah his son,
Manasseh his son,
14 Amon his son,
Josiah his son.
15 The sons of Josiah:
Johanan the firstborn,
Jehoiakim the second son,
Zedekiah the third,
Shallum the fourth.
16 The successors of Jehoiakim:
Jehoiachin[b] his son,
and Zedekiah.

THE ROYAL LINE AFTER THE EXILE
17 The descendants of Jehoiachin the captive:
Shealtiel his son, 18 Malkiram, Pedaiah,
Shenazzar, Jekamiah, Hoshama and
Nedabiah.
19 The sons of Pedaiah:
Zerubbabel and Shimei.
The sons of Zerubbabel:
Meshullam and Hananiah.
Shelomith was their sister.
20 There were also five others:
Hashubah, Ohel, Berekiah, Hasadiah
and Jushab-Hesed.
21 The descendants of Hananiah:
Pelatiah and Jeshaiah, and the sons of
Rephaiah, of Arnan, of Obadiah and of
Shecaniah.
22 The descendants of Shecaniah:
Shemaiah and his sons:
Hattush, Igal, Bariah, Neariah and Sha-
phat—six in all.
23 The sons of Neariah:
Elioenai, Hizkiah and Azrikam—three
in all.
24 The sons of Elioenai:
Hodaviah, Eliashib, Pelaiah, Akkub, Johanan, Delaiah and Anani—seven in all.

OTHER CLANS OF JUDAH
4 The descendants of Judah:
Perez, Hezron, Carmi, Hur and Shobal.
2 Reaiah son of Shobal was the father of Ja-

THE MESSAGE

boam, who had Abijah, who had Asa, who had
Jehoshaphat, who had Jehoram, who had Ahaziah, who had Joash, who had Amaziah, who
had Azariah, who had Jotham, who had Ahaz,
who had Hezekiah, who had Manasseh, who
had Amon, who had Josiah.

3.15   Josiah's firstborn was Johanan, followed by
Jehoiakim, then Zedekiah, and finally Shallum.

3.16   Jehoiakim's sons were Jeconiah (Jehoiachin)
and Zedekiah.

3.17-18   The sons of Jeconiah born while he was captive in Babylon: Shealtiel, Malkiram, Pedaiah,
Shenazzar, Jekamiah, Hoshama, and Nedabiah.

3.19-20   Pedaiah had Zerubbabel and Shimei; Zerubbabel had Meshullam and Hananiah. Shelomith
was their sister. And then five more—Hashubah, Ohel, Berekiah, Hasadiah, and Jushab-Hesed.

3.21   Hananiah's sons were Pelatiah and Jeshaiah.
There were also sons of Rephaiah, sons of Arnan, sons of Obadiah, and sons of Shecaniah.

3.22   Shecaniah had Shemaiah who in his turn
had Hattush, Igal, Bariah, Neariah, and Shaphat—six of them.

3.23   Neariah had three sons: Elioenai, Hizkiah,
and Azrikam.

3.24   And Elioenai had seven sons: Hodaviah, Eliashib, Pelaiah, Akkub, Johanan, Delaiah, and
Anani.

AN APPENDIX TO THE FAMILY OF JUDAH
4.1-2   Sons of Judah: Perez, Hezron, Carmi, Hur,
and Shobal. Reaiah, Shobal's son, had Ja-

---

a 11 Hebrew Joram, a variant of Jehoram   b 16 Hebrew
Jeconiah, a variant of Jehoiachin; also in verse 17

NEW INTERNATIONAL VERSION

hath, and Jahath the father of Ahumai and Lahad. These were the clans of the Zorathites.

³ These were the sons*ᵃ* of Etam:

Jezreel, Ishma and Idbash. Their sister was named Hazzelelponi. ⁴Penuel was the father of Gedor, and Ezer the father of Hushah.

These were the descendants of Hur, the firstborn of Ephrathah and father*ᵇ* of Bethlehem.

⁵ Ashhur the father of Tekoa had two wives, Helah and Naarah.

⁶ Naarah bore him Ahuzzam, Hepher, Temeni and Haahashtari. These were the descendants of Naarah.

⁷ The sons of Helah:

Zereth, Zohar, Ethnan, ⁸and Koz, who was the father of Anub and Hazzobebah and of the clans of Aharhel son of Harum.

⁹Jabez was more honorable than his brothers. His mother had named him Jabez,*ᶜ* saying, "I gave birth to him in pain." ¹⁰Jabez cried out to the God of Israel, "Oh, that you would bless me and enlarge my territory! Let your hand be with me, and keep me from harm so that I will be free from pain." And God granted his request.

¹¹ Kelub, Shuhah's brother, was the father of Mehir, who was the father of Eshton. ¹²Eshton was the father of Beth Rapha, Paseah and Tehinnah the father of Ir Nahash.*ᵈ* These were the men of Recah.

¹³ The sons of Kenaz:

Othniel and Seraiah.

The sons of Othniel:

Hathath and Meonothai.*ᵉ* ¹⁴Meonothai was the father of Ophrah.

Seraiah was the father of Joab,

the father of Ge Harashim.*ᶠ* It was called this because its people were craftsmen.

¹⁵ The sons of Caleb son of Jephunneh:

Iru, Elah and Naam.

The son of Elah:

Kenaz.

¹⁶ The sons of Jehallelel:

Ziph, Ziphah, Tiria and Asarel.

¹⁷ The sons of Ezrah:

Jether, Mered, Epher and Jalon. One of Mered's wives gave birth to Miriam,

THE MESSAGE

hath; and Jahath had Ahumai and Lahad. These made up the families of the Zorathites.

4.3-4   Sons of Etam: Jezreel, Ishma, and Idbash. Their sister was named Hazzelelponi. Penuel had Gedor and Ezer had Hushah. These were the sons of Hur, firstborn son of Ephrathah, who was the father of Bethlehem.

4.5-8   Ashhur the father of Tekoa had two wives, Helah and Naarah. Naarah gave birth to Ahuzzam, Hepher, Temeni, and Haahashtari—Naarah's children. Helah's sons were Zereth, Zohar, Ethnan, and Koz, who had Anub, Hazzobebah, and the families of Aharhel son of Harum.

4.9-10 Jabez was a better man than his brothers, a man of honor. His mother had named him Jabez (Oh, the pain!), saying, "A painful birth! I bore him in great pain!" Jabez prayed to the God of Israel: "Bless me, O bless me! Give me land, large tracts of land. And provide your personal protection—don't let evil hurt me." God gave him what he asked.

4.11-12 Kelub, Shuhah's brother, had Mehir; Mehir had Eshton; Eshton had Beth Rapha, Paseah, and Tehinnah, who founded Ir Nahash (City of Smiths). These were known as the men of Recah.

4.13   The sons of Kenaz: Othniel and Seraiah.

The sons of Othniel: Hathath and Meonothai.

4.14   Meonothai had Ophrah; Seraiah had Joab, the founder of Ge Harashim (Colony of Artisans).

4.15   The sons of Caleb son of Jephunneh: Iru, Elah, and Naam.

The son of Elah: Kenaz.

4.16   The sons of Jehallelel: Ziph, Ziphah, Tiria, and Asarel.

4.17-18 The sons of Ezrah: Jether, Mered, Epher, and Jalon. One of Mered's wives, Pharaoh's daugh-

---

ᵃ 3 Some Septuagint manuscripts (see also Vulgate); Hebrew *father*   *ᵇ 4 Father* may mean *civic leader* or *military leader*; also in verses 12, 14, 17, 18 and possibly elsewhere.   *ᶜ 9 Jabez* sounds like the Hebrew for *pain*.   *ᵈ 12* Or *of the city of Nahash*   *ᵉ 13* Some Septuagint manuscripts and Vulgate; Hebrew does not have *and Meonothai*.   *ᶠ 14 Ge Harashim* means *valley of craftsmen*.

NEW INTERNATIONAL VERSION

Shammai and Ishbah the father of Eshtemoa. ¹⁸(His Judean wife gave birth to
Jered the father of Gedor, Heber the father of Soco, and Jekuthiel the father
of Zanoah.) These were the children of
Pharaoh's daughter Bithiah, whom Mered had married.

¹⁹ The sons of Hodiah's wife, the sister of Naham:
    the father of Keilah the Garmite, and
    Eshtemoa the Maacathite.

²⁰ The sons of Shimon:
    Amnon, Rinnah, Ben-Hanan and Tilon.
    The descendants of Ishi:
    Zoheth and Ben-Zoheth.

²¹ The sons of Shelah son of Judah:
    Er the father of Lecah, Laadah the father
    of Mareshah and the clans of the linen
    workers at Beth Ashbea, ²²Jokim, the
    men of Cozeba, and Joash and Saraph,
    who ruled in Moab and Jashubi Lehem.
    (These records are from ancient times.)
    ²³They were the potters who lived at
    Netaim and Gederah; they stayed there
    and worked for the king.

SIMEON

²⁴ The descendants of Simeon:
    Nemuel, Jamin, Jarib, Zerah and Shaul;
    ²⁵Shallum was Shaul's son, Mibsam his
    son and Mishma his son.

²⁶ The descendants of Mishma:
    Hammuel his son, Zaccur his son and
    Shimei his son.

²⁷Shimei had sixteen sons and six daughters,
but his brothers did not have many children; so
their entire clan did not become as numerous as
the people of Judah. ²⁸They lived in Beersheba,
Moladah, Hazar Shual, ²⁹Bilhah, Ezem, Tolad,
³⁰Bethuel, Hormah, Ziklag, ³¹Beth Marcaboth,
Hazar Susim, Beth Biri and Shaaraim. These
were their towns until the reign of David.
³²Their surrounding villages were Etam, Ain,
Rimmon, Token and Ashan—five towns— ³³and
all the villages around these towns as far as Baal-
ath.ᵃ These were their settlements. And they
kept a genealogical record.

³⁴Meshobab, Jamlech, Joshah son of Amaziah, ³⁵Joel, Jehu son of Joshibiah, the son
of Seraiah, the son of Asiel, ³⁶also Elioenai,
Jaakobah, Jeshohaiah, Asaiah, Adiel, Jesimiel, Benaiah, ³⁷and Ziza son of Shiphi, the
son of Allon, the son of Jedaiah, the son of
Shimri, the son of Shemaiah.

ᵃ 33 Some Septuagint manuscripts (see also Joshua 19:8);
Hebrew Baal

THE MESSAGE

ter Bithiah, gave birth to Miriam, Shammai,
and Ishbah the father of Eshtemoa. His Judean
wife gave birth to Jered father of Gedor, Heber
father of Soco, and Jekuthiel father of Zanoah.

4.19 The sons of Hodiah's wife, Naham's sister:
the father of Keilah the Garmite, and Eshtemoa
the Maacathite.

4.20 The sons of Shimon: Amnon, Rinnah, Ben-
Hanan, and Tilon.

4.20 The sons of Ishi: Zoheth and Ben-Zoheth.

4.21-23 The sons of Shelah son of Judah: Er the father of Lecah, Laadah the father of Mareshah
and the family of linen workers at Beth Ashbea,
Jokim, the men of Cozeba, and Joash and Sa-
raph, who ruled in Moab and Jashubi Lehem.
(These records are from very old traditions.)
They were the potters who lived at Netaim and
Gederah, resident potters who worked for the
king.

THE FAMILY OF SIMEON

4.24-25 The Simeon family tree: Nemuel, Jamin, Jarib,
Zerah, and Shaul; Shaul had Shallum, Shallum
had Mibsam, and Mibsam had Mishma.

4.26 The sons of Mishma: Hammuel had Zaccur
and Zaccur had Shimei.

4.27-33 Shimei had sixteen sons and six daughters,
but his brothers were not nearly as prolific and
never became a large family like Judah. They
lived in Beersheba, Moladah, Hazar Shual, Bilhah, Ezem, Tolad, Bethuel, Hormah, Ziklag,
Beth Marcaboth, Hazar Susim, Beth Biri, and
Shaaraim. They lived in these towns until David became king. Other settlements in the
vicinity were the five towns of Etam, Ain, Rimmon, Token, and Ashan, and all the villages
around these towns as far as Baalath. These
were their settlements. And they kept good
family records.

4.34-40 Meshobab; Jamlech; Joshah the son of Amaziah; Joel; Jehu the son of Joshibiah, the son of
Seraiah, the son of Asiel; Elioenai; Jaakobah;
Jeshohaiah; Asaiah; Adiel; Jesimiel; Benaiah;
and Ziza the son of Shiphi, the son of Allon,
the son of Jedaiah, the son of Shimri, the son of

NEW INTERNATIONAL VERSION

[38]The men listed above by name were leaders of their clans. Their families increased greatly, [39]and they went to the outskirts of Gedor to the east of the valley in search of pasture for their flocks. [40]They found rich, good pasture, and the land was spacious, peaceful and quiet. Some Hamites had lived there formerly.

[41]The men whose names were listed came in the days of Hezekiah king of Judah. They attacked the Hamites in their dwellings and also the Meunites who were there and completely destroyed[a] them, as is evident to this day. Then they settled in their place, because there was pasture for their flocks. [42]And five hundred of these Simeonites, led by Pelatiah, Neariah, Rephaiah and Uzziel, the sons of Ishi, invaded the hill country of Seir. [43]They killed the remaining Amalekites who had escaped, and they have lived there to this day.

REUBEN

5 The sons of Reuben the firstborn of Israel (he was the firstborn, but when he defiled his father's marriage bed, his rights as firstborn were given to the sons of Joseph son of Israel; so he could not be listed in the genealogical record in accordance with his birthright, [2]and though Judah was the strongest of his brothers and a ruler came from him, the rights of the firstborn belonged to Joseph)— [3]the sons of Reuben the firstborn of Israel:

Hanoch, Pallu, Hezron and Carmi.
[4]The descendants of Joel:
Shemaiah his son, Gog his son,
Shimei his son, [5]Micah his son,
Reaiah his son, Baal his son,
[6]and Beerah his son, whom Tiglath-Pileser[b] king of Assyria took into exile. Beerah was a leader of the Reubenites.
[7]Their relatives by clans, listed according to their genealogical records:
Jeiel the chief, Zechariah, [8]and Bela son of Azaz, the son of Shema, the son of Joel. They settled in the area from Aroer to Nebo and Baal Meon. [9]To the east they occupied the land up to the edge of the desert that extends to the Euphrates River, because their livestock had increased in Gilead.
[10]During Saul's reign they waged war against the Hagrites, who were defeated at their hands; they occupied the dwellings of the Hagrites throughout the entire region east of Gilead.

---

a 41 The Hebrew term refers to the irrevocable giving over of things or persons to the LORD, often by totally destroying them. *b 6* Hebrew *Tilgath-Pilneser,* a variant of *Tiglath-Pileser;* also in verse 26

THE MESSAGE

Shemaiah—all these were the leaders in their families. They prospered and increased in numbers so that they had to go as far as Gedor (Gerar) to the east of the valley looking for pasture for their flocks. And they found it—lush pasture, lots of elbow room, peaceful and quiet.

4.40-43 Some Hamites had lived there in former times. But the men in these family trees came when Hezekiah was king of Judah and attacked the Hamites, tearing down their tents and houses. There was nothing left of them, as you can see today. Then they moved in and took over because of the great pastureland. Five hundred of these Simeonites went on and invaded the hill country of Seir, led by Pelatiah, Neariah, Rephaiah, and Uzziel, the sons of Ishi. They killed all the escaped Amalekites who were still around. And they still live there.

THE FAMILY OF REUBEN

5.1-2 5 The family of Reuben the firstborn of Israel: Though Reuben was Israel's firstborn, after he slept with his father's concubine, a defiling act, his rights as the firstborn were passed on to the sons of Joseph son of Israel. He lost his "firstborn" place in the family tree. And even though Judah became the strongest of his brothers and King David eventually came from that family, the firstborn rights stayed with Joseph.

5.3 The sons of Reuben, firstborn of Israel: Hanoch, Pallu, Hezron, and Carmi.

5.4-6 The descendants of Joel: Shemaiah his son, Gog his son, Shimei his son, Micah his son, Reaiah his son, Baal his son, and Beerah his son, whom Tiglath-Pileser king of Assyria took into exile. Beerah was the prince of the Reubenites.

5.7-10 Beerah's brothers are listed in the family tree by families: first Jeiel, followed by Zechariah: then Bela son of Azaz, the son of Shema, the son of Joel. Joel lived in the area from Aroer to Nebo and Baal Meon. His family occupied the land up to the edge of the desert that goes all the way to the Euphrates River, since their growing herds of livestock spilled out of Gilead. During Saul's reign they fought and defeated the Hagrites; they then took over their tents and lived in them on the eastern frontier of Gilead.

NEW INTERNATIONAL VERSION

GAD

11 The Gadites lived next to them in Bashan, as far as Salecah:

12 Joel was the chief, Shapham the second, then Janai and Shaphat, in Bashan.

13 Their relatives, by families, were:
Michael, Meshullam, Sheba, Jorai, Jacan, Zia and Eber—seven in all.

14 These were the sons of Abihail son of Huri, the son of Jaroah, the son of Gilead, the son of Michael, the son of Jeshishai, the son of Jahdo, the son of Buz.

15 Ahi son of Abdiel, the son of Guni, was head of their family.

16 The Gadites lived in Gilead, in Bashan and its outlying villages, and on all the pasturelands of Sharon as far as they extended.

17 All these were entered in the genealogical records during the reigns of Jotham king of Judah and Jeroboam king of Israel.

18 The Reubenites, the Gadites and the half-tribe of Manasseh had 44,760 men ready for military service—able-bodied men who could handle shield and sword, who could use a bow, and who were trained for battle. 19 They waged war against the Hagrites, Jetur, Naphish and Nodab. 20 They were helped in fighting them, and God handed the Hagrites and all their allies over to them, because they cried out to him during the battle. He answered their prayers, because they trusted in him. 21 They seized the livestock of the Hagrites—fifty thousand camels, two hundred fifty thousand sheep and two thousand donkeys. They also took one hundred thousand people captive, 22 and many others fell slain, because the battle was God's. And they occupied the land until the exile.

THE HALF-TRIBE OF MANASSEH

23 The people of the half-tribe of Manasseh were numerous; they settled in the land from Bashan to Baal Hermon, that is, to Senir (Mount Hermon).

24 These were the heads of their families: Epher, Ishi, Eliel, Azriel, Jeremiah, Hodaviah and Jahdiel. They were brave warriors, famous men, and heads of their families. 25 But they were unfaithful to the God of their fathers and prostituted themselves to the gods of the peoples of the land, whom God had destroyed before them. 26 So the God of Israel stirred up the spirit of Pul king of Assyria (that is, Tiglath-Pileser king of Assyria), who took the Reubenites, the Gadites and the half-tribe of Manasseh into exile. He took them to Halah, Habor, Hara and the river of Gozan, where they are to this day.

THE MESSAGE

5.11-12 The family of Gad were their neighbors in Bashan, as far as Salecah: Joel was the chief, Shapham the second-in-command, and then Janai, the judge in Bashan.

5.13-15 Their brothers, by families, were Michael, Meshullam, Sheba, Jorai, Jacan, Zia, and Eber—seven in all. These were the sons of Abihail son of Huri, the son of Jaroah, the son of Gilead, the son of Michael, the son of Jeshishai, the son of Jahdo, the son of Buz. Ahi son of Abdiel, the son of Guni, was head of their family.

5.16 The family of Gad lived in Gilead and Bashan, including the outlying villages and extending as far as the pastures of Sharon.

5.17 They were all written into the official family tree during the reigns of Jotham king of Judah and Jeroboam king of Israel.

✠

5.18-22 The families of Reuben, Gad, and the half-tribe of Manasseh had 44,760 men trained for war—physically fit and skilled in handling shield, sword, and bow. They fought against the Hagrites, Jetur, Naphish, and Nodab. God helped them as they fought. God handed the Hagrites and all their allies over to them, because they cried out to him during the battle. God answered their prayers because they trusted him. They plundered the Hagrite herds and flocks: 50,000 camels, 250,000 sheep, and 2,000 donkeys. They also captured 100,000 people. Many were killed, because the battle was God's. They lived in that country until the exile.

✠

5.23-26 The half-tribe of Manasseh had a large population. They occupied the land from Bashan to Baal Hermon, that is, to Senir (Mount Hermon). The heads of their families were Epher, Ishi, Eliel, Azriel, Jeremiah, Hodaviah, and Jahdiel—brave warriors, famous, and heads of their families. But they were not faithful to the God of their ancestors. They took up with the ungodly gods of the peoples of the land whom God had gotten rid of before they arrived. So the God of Israel stirred up the spirit of Pul king of Assyria (Tiglath-Pileser king of Assyria) to take the families of Reuben, Gad, and the half-tribe of Manasseh into exile. He deported them to Halah, Habor, Hara, and the river of Gozan. They've been there ever since.

NEW INTERNATIONAL VERSION

LEVI

6 The sons of Levi:
 Gershon, Kohath and Merari.
² The sons of Kohath:
 Amram, Izhar, Hebron and Uzziel.
³ The children of Amram:
 Aaron, Moses and Miriam.
 The sons of Aaron:
 Nadab, Abihu, Eleazar and Ithamar.
⁴ Eleazar was the father of Phinehas,
 Phinehas the father of Abishua,
⁵ Abishua the father of Bukki,
 Bukki the father of Uzzi,
⁶ Uzzi the father of Zerahiah,
 Zerahiah the father of Meraioth,
⁷ Meraioth the father of Amariah,
 Amariah the father of Ahitub,
⁸ Ahitub the father of Zadok,
 Zadok the father of Ahimaaz,
⁹ Ahimaaz the father of Azariah,
 Azariah the father of Johanan,
¹⁰ Johanan the father of Azariah (it was he
 who served as priest in the temple Solomon built in Jerusalem),
¹¹ Azariah the father of Amariah,
 Amariah the father of Ahitub,
¹² Ahitub the father of Zadok,
 Zadok the father of Shallum,
¹³ Shallum the father of Hilkiah,
 Hilkiah the father of Azariah,
¹⁴ Azariah the father of Seraiah,
 and Seraiah the father of Jehozadak.

¹⁵ Jehozadak was deported when the LORD
 sent Judah and Jerusalem into exile by the
 hand of Nebuchadnezzar.

¹⁶ The sons of Levi:
 Gershon,ᵃ Kohath and Merari.
¹⁷ These are the names of the sons of Ger-
 shon:
 Libni and Shimei.
¹⁸ The sons of Kohath:
 Amram, Izhar, Hebron and Uzziel.
¹⁹ The sons of Merari:
 Mahli and Mushi.
 These are the clans of the Levites listed ac-
 cording to their fathers:
²⁰ Of Gershon:
 Libni his son, Jehath his son,
 Zimmah his son, ²¹ Joah his son,
 Iddo his son, Zerah his son
 and Jeatherai his son.
²² The descendants of Kohath:
 Amminadab his son, Korah his son,
 Assir his son, ²³ Elkanah his son,

ᵃ 16 Hebrew *Gershom,* a variant of *Gershon*; also in verses
17, 20, 43, 62 and 71

THE MESSAGE

THE FAMILY OF LEVI

6.1-14 6 The sons of Levi were Gershon, Kohath,
 and Merari. The sons of Kohath were Amram, Izhar, Hebron, and Uzziel. The children of
Amram were Aaron, Moses, and Miriam. The
sons of Aaron were Nadab, Abihu, Eleazar, and
Ithamar. Eleazar had Phinehas, Phinehas had
Abishua, Abishua had Bukki, Bukki had Uzzi,
Uzzi had Zerahiah, Zerahiah had Meraioth,
Meraioth had Amariah, Amariah had Ahitub,
Ahitub had Zadok, Zadok had Ahimaaz, Ahimaaz had Azariah, Azariah had Johanan, and Johanan had Azariah (who served as priest in the
temple Solomon built in Jerusalem). Azariah
had Amariah, Amariah had Ahitub, Ahitub had
Zadok, Zadok had Shallum, Shallum had Hilkiah, Hilkiah had Azariah, Azariah had Seraiah,
and Seraiah had Jehozadak.

6.15 Jehozadak went off to exile when GOD used
 Nebuchadnezzar to take Judah and Jerusalem
into exile.

✝

6.16-30 The sons of Levi were Gershon, Kohath, and
 Merari. These are the names of the sons of Gershon: Libni and Shimei. The sons of Kohath
were Amram, Izhar, Hebron, and Uzziel. The
sons of Merari were Mahli and Mushi. These
are the Levitical clans according to families: the
sons of Gershon were Libni his son, Jehath
his son, Zimmah his son, Joah his son, Iddo his
son, Zerah his son, and Jeatherai his son. The
sons of Kohath were Amminadab his son, Korah his son, Assir his son, Elkanah his son,

NEW INTERNATIONAL VERSION

Ebiasaph his son, Assir his son,
24 Tahath his son, Uriel his son,
Uzziah his son and Shaul his son.
25 The descendants of Elkanah:
Amasai, Ahimoth,
26 Elkanah his son,[a] Zophai his son,
Nahath his son, 27 Eliab his son,
Jeroham his son, Elkanah his son
and Samuel his son.[b]
28 The sons of Samuel:
Joel[c] the firstborn
and Abijah the second son.
29 The descendants of Merari:
Mahli, Libni his son,
Shimei his son, Uzzah his son,
30 Shimea his son, Haggiah his son
and Asaiah his son.

THE TEMPLE MUSICIANS

31 These are the men David put in charge of
the music in the house of the LORD after the ark
came to rest there. 32 They ministered with music
before the tabernacle, the Tent of Meeting, until
Solomon built the temple of the LORD in Jerusalem. They performed their duties according to
the regulations laid down for them.

33 Here are the men who served, together with
their sons:

From the Kohathites:
Heman, the musician,
the son of Joel, the son of Samuel,
34 the son of Elkanah, the son of Jeroham,
the son of Eliel, the son of Toah,
35 the son of Zuph, the son of Elkanah,
the son of Mahath, the son of Amasai,
36 the son of Elkanah, the son of Joel,
the son of Azariah, the son of Zephaniah,
37 the son of Tahath, the son of Assir,
the son of Ebiasaph, the son of Korah,
38 the son of Izhar, the son of Kohath,
the son of Levi, the son of Israel;
39 and Heman's associate Asaph, who served
at his right hand:
Asaph son of Berekiah, the son of Shimea,
40 the son of Michael, the son of Baaseiah,[d]
the son of Malkijah, 41 the son of Ethni,
the son of Zerah, the son of Adaiah,

THE MESSAGE

Ebiasaph his son, Assir his son, Tahath his son,
Uriel his son, Uzziah his son, and Shaul his
son. The sons of Elkanah were Amasai and
Ahimoth, Elkanah his son, Zophai his son, Na-
hath his son, Eliab his son, Jeroham his son,
and Elkanah his son. The sons of Samuel were
Joel his firstborn son and Abijah his second.
The sons of Merari were Mahli, Libni his son,
Shimei his son, Uzzah his son, Shimea his son,
Haggiah his son, and Asaiah his son.

DAVID'S WORSHIP LEADERS

6.31-32   These are the persons David appointed to lead
the singing in the house of GOD after the Chest
was placed there. They were the ministers of
music in the place of worship, which was the
Tent of Meeting until Solomon built The Temple of GOD in Jerusalem. As they carried out
their work, they followed the instructions giv-
en to them.

6.33-38   These are the persons, together with their
sons, who served by preparing for and directing
worship: from the family of the Kohathites was
Heman the choirmaster, the son of Joel, the son
of Samuel, the son of Elkanah, the son of Jeroham, the son of Eliel, the son of Toah, the son
of Zuph, the son of Elkanah, the son of Mahath, the son of Amasai, the son of Elkanah,
the son of Joel, the son of Azariah, the son of
Zephaniah, the son of Tahath, the son of Assir,
the son of Ebiasaph, the son of Korah, the son
of Izhar, the son of Kohath, the son of Levi, the
son of Israel.

6.39-43   Heman's associate Asaph stood at his right
hand. Asaph was the son of Berekiah, the son
of Shimea, the son of Michael, the son of Baaseiah, the son of Malkijah, the son of Ethni,
the son of Zerah, the son of Adaiah, the son of

---

a 26 Some Hebrew manuscripts, Septuagint and Syriac;
most Hebrew manuscripts *Ahimoth* 26*and Elkanah. The sons
of Elkanah:*   *b 27* Some Septuagint manuscripts (see also
1 Samuel 1:19,20 and 1 Chron. 6:33,34); Hebrew does not
have *and Samuel his son.*   *c 28* Some Septuagint
manuscripts and Syriac (see also 1 Samuel 8:2 and 1 Chron.
6:33); Hebrew does not have *Joel.*   *d 40* Most Hebrew
manuscripts; some Hebrew manuscripts, one Septuagint
manuscript and Syriac *Maaseiah*

NEW INTERNATIONAL VERSION

⁴²the son of Ethan, the son of Zimmah,
the son of Shimei, ⁴³the son of Jahath,
the son of Gershon, the son of Levi;
⁴⁴and from their associates, the Merarites, at
his left hand:
Ethan son of Kishi, the son of Abdi,
the son of Malluch, ⁴⁵the son of Hashabiah,
the son of Amaziah, the son of Hilkiah,
⁴⁶the son of Amzi, the son of Bani,
the son of Shemer, ⁴⁷the son of Mahli,
the son of Mushi, the son of Merari,
the son of Levi.

⁴⁸Their fellow Levites were assigned to all the
other duties of the tabernacle, the house of God.
⁴⁹But Aaron and his descendants were the ones
who presented offerings on the altar of burnt offering and on the altar of incense in connection
with all that was done in the Most Holy Place,
making atonement for Israel, in accordance with
all that Moses the servant of God had commanded.

⁵⁰These were the descendants of Aaron:
Eleazar his son, Phinehas his son,
Abishua his son, ⁵¹Bukki his son,
Uzzi his son, Zerahiah his son,
⁵²Meraioth his son, Amariah his son,
Ahitub his son, ⁵³Zadok his son
and Ahimaaz his son.

⁵⁴These were the locations of their settlements
allotted as their territory (they were assigned to
the descendants of Aaron who were from the Kohathite clan, because the first lot was for them):
⁵⁵They were given Hebron in Judah with
its surrounding pasturelands. ⁵⁶But the
fields and villages around the city were giv-
en to Caleb son of Jephunneh.
⁵⁷So the descendants of Aaron were giv-
en Hebron (a city of refuge), and Libnah, ᵃ
Jattir, Eshtemoa, ⁵⁸Hilen, Debir, ⁵⁹Ashan,
Juttah ᵇ and Beth Shemesh, together with
their pasturelands. ⁶⁰And from the tribe of
Benjamin they were given Gibeon, ᶜ Geba,
Alemeth and Anathoth, together with their
pasturelands.
These towns, which were distributed
among the Kohathite clans, were thirteen
in all.
⁶¹The rest of Kohath's descendants were allotted ten towns from the clans of half the tribe of
Manasseh.
⁶²The descendants of Gershon, clan by clan,

THE MESSAGE

Ethan, the son of Zimmah, the son of Shimei,
the son of Jahath, the son of Gershon, the son
of Levi.

6.44-47 Of the sons of Merari, the associates who
stood at his left hand, was Ethan the son of
Kishi, the son of Abdi, the son of Malluch, the
son of Hashabiah, the son of Amaziah, the son
of Hilkiah, the son of Amzi, the son of Bani, the
son of Shemer, the son of Mahli, the son of Mushi, the son of Merari, the son of Levi.

6.48 The rest of the Levites were assigned to all
the other work in the place of worship, the
house of God.

✣

6.49 Aaron and his sons offered the sacrifices on the
Altar of Burnt Offering and the Altar of Incense; they were in charge of all the work surrounding the Holy of Holies. They made atonement for Israel following the instructions
commanded by Moses, servant of God.

6.50-53 These are the sons of Aaron: Eleazar his son,
Phinehas his son, Abishua his son, Bukki his
son, Uzzi his son, Zerahiah his son, Meraioth
his son, Amariah his son, Ahitub his son, Zadok his son, and Ahimaaz his son.

THE PRIESTLY CITIES

6.54-81 And these are the places where the priestly
families were assigned to live. The first assignment went by lot to the sons of Aaron of the
Kohathite family; they were given Hebron in
the land of Judah and all the neighboring pastures. Caleb the son of Jephunneh got the fields
and villages around the city. The family of Aaron was also given the cities of refuge, with pastures included: Hebron, Libnah, Jattir, Eshtemoa, Hilen, Debir, Ashan, and Beth Shemesh.
They were also given Geba from the tribe of
Benjamin, Alemeth, and Anathoth, all with pastures included. In all, thirteen cities were distributed among the Kohathite families. The rest
of the Kohathites were given another ten cities,
distributed by lot from the half-tribe of Manasseh. The sons of Gershon were given, family

---

ᵃ 57 See Joshua 21:13; Hebrew *given the cities of refuge:
Hebron, Libnah.*   ᵇ 59 Syriac (see also Septuagint and
Joshua 21:16); Hebrew does not have *Juttah.*
ᶜ 60 See Joshua 21:17; Hebrew does not have *Gibeon.*

NEW INTERNATIONAL VERSION

were allotted thirteen towns from the tribes of Issachar, Asher and Naphtali, and from the part of the tribe of Manasseh that is in Bashan.

⁶³The descendants of Merari, clan by clan, were allotted twelve towns from the tribes of Reuben, Gad and Zebulun.

⁶⁴So the Israelites gave the Levites these towns and their pasturelands. ⁶⁵From the tribes of Judah, Simeon and Benjamin they allotted the previously named towns.

⁶⁶Some of the Kohathite clans were given as their territory towns from the tribe of Ephraim.

⁶⁷In the hill country of Ephraim they were given Shechem (a city of refuge), and Gezer,ᵃ ⁶⁸Jokmeam, Beth Horon, ⁶⁹Aijalon and Gath Rimmon, together with their pasturelands.

⁷⁰And from half the tribe of Manasseh the Israelites gave Aner and Bileam, together with their pasturelands, to the rest of the Kohathite clans.

⁷¹The Gershonites received the following:

From the clan of the half-tribe of Manasseh they received Golan in Bashan and also Ashtaroth, together with their pasturelands;

⁷²from the tribe of Issachar
they received Kedesh, Daberath, ⁷³Ramoth and Anem, together with their pasturelands;

⁷⁴from the tribe of Asher
they received Mashal, Abdon, ⁷⁵Hukok and Rehob, together with their pasturelands;

⁷⁶and from the tribe of Naphtali
they received Kedesh in Galilee, Hammon and Kiriathaim, together with their pasturelands.

⁷⁷The Merarites (the rest of the Levites) received the following:

From the tribe of Zebulun
they received Jokneam, Kartah,ᵇ Rimmono and Tabor, together with their pasturelands;

⁷⁸from the tribe of Reuben across the Jordan east of Jericho
they received Bezer in the desert, Jahzah, ⁷⁹Kedemoth and Mephaath, together with their pasturelands;

⁸⁰and from the tribe of Gad
they received Ramoth in Gilead, Mahanaim, ⁸¹Heshbon and Jazer, together with their pasturelands.

ᵃ 67 See Joshua 21:21; Hebrew *given the cities of refuge: Shechem, Gezer.*   ᵇ 77 See Septuagint and Joshua 21:34; Hebrew does not have *Jokneam, Kartah.*

THE MESSAGE

by family, thirteen cities from the tribes of Issachar, Asher, Naphtali, and Manasseh in Bashan. The sons of Merari, family by family, were assigned by lot twelve cities from the tribes of Reuben, Gad, and Zebulun. The sons of Israel gave the Levites both the cities and their pastures. They also distributed by lot cities from the tribes of Judah, Simeon, and Benjamin. Some of the Kohath families were given their cities from the tribe of Ephraim, cities of refuge: Shechem in the hill country of Ephraim, Gezer, Jokmeam, Beth Horon, Aijalon, and Gath Rimmon—all with their pastures. The rest of the sons of Kohath were given Aner and Bileam with their pastures from the half-tribe of Manasseh. The sons of Gershon were given, family by family, from the half-tribe of Manasseh, Golan in Bashan and Ashtaroth; from the tribe of Issachar, Kedesh, Daberath, Ramoth, and Anem; from the tribe of Asher, Mashal, Abdon, Hukok, and Rehob; from the tribe of Naphtali, Kedesh in Galilee, Hammon, and Kiriathaim. The rest of the sons of Merari got Rimmono and Tabor from the tribe of Zebulun; Bezer in the desert, Jahzah, Kedemoth, and Mephaath from the tribe of Reuben to the east of the Jordan; and Ramoth in Gilead, Mahanaim, Heshbon, and Jazer from the tribe of Gad. Pastures were included in all these towns.

NEW INTERNATIONAL VERSION

ISSACHAR

7 The sons of Issachar:
Tola, Puah, Jashub and Shimron—four in all.
² The sons of Tola:
Uzzi, Rephaiah, Jeriel, Jahmai, Ibsam and Samuel—heads of their families. During the reign of David, the descendants of Tola listed as fighting men in their genealogy numbered 22,600.
³ The son of Uzzi:
Izrahiah.

The sons of Izrahiah:
Michael, Obadiah, Joel and Isshiah. All five of them were chiefs. ⁴According to their family genealogy, they had 36,000 men ready for battle, for they had many wives and children.
⁵ The relatives who were fighting men belonging to all the clans of Issachar, as listed in their genealogy, were 87,000 in all.

BENJAMIN

⁶ Three sons of Benjamin:
Bela, Beker and Jediael.
⁷ The sons of Bela:
Ezbon, Uzzi, Uzziel, Jerimoth and Iri, heads of families—five in all. Their genealogical record listed 22,034 fighting men.
⁸ The sons of Beker:
Zemirah, Joash, Eliezer, Elioenai, Omri, Jeremoth, Abijah, Anathoth and Alemeth. All these were the sons of Beker.
⁹ Their genealogical record listed the heads of families and 20,200 fighting men.
¹⁰ The son of Jediael:
Bilhan.

The sons of Bilhan:
Jeush, Benjamin, Ehud, Kenaanah, Zethan, Tarshish and Ahishahar. ¹¹All these sons of Jediael were heads of families. There were 17,200 fighting men ready to go out to war.
¹² The Shuppites and Huppites were the descendants of Ir, and the Hushites the descendants of Aher.

NAPHTALI

¹³ The sons of Naphtali:
Jahziel, Guni, Jezer and Shillem ᵃ—the descendants of Bilhah.

ᵃ 13 Some Hebrew and Septuagint manuscripts (see also Gen. 46:24 and Num. 26:49); most Hebrew manuscripts *Shallum*

THE MESSAGE

THE FAMILY OF ISSACHAR

7.1-5 **7** The sons of Issachar were Tola, Puah, Jashub, and Shimron—four sons. The sons of Tola were Uzzi, Rephaiah, Jeriel, Jahmai, Ibsam, and Samuel—the chiefs of their families. During David's reign, the Tola family counted 22,600 warriors in their lineage. The son of Uzzi was Izrahiah; the sons of Izrahiah were Michael, Obadiah, Joel, and Isshiah—five sons and all of them chiefs. They counted 36,000 warriors in their lineage because they had more wives and sons than their brothers. The extended families of Issachar accounted for 87,000 warriors—all of them listed in the family tree.

THE FAMILY OF BENJAMIN

7.6-12 Benjamin had three sons: Bela, Beker, and Jediael. Bela had five: Ezbon, Uzzi, Uzziel, Jerimoth, and Iri, all of them chiefs and warriors. They counted 22,034 names in their family tree. Beker's sons were Zemirah, Joash, Eliezer, Elioenai, Omri, Jeremoth, Abijah, Anathoth, and Alemeth. Through these chiefs their family tree listed 20,200 warriors. Jediael's son was Bilhan and the sons of Bilhan were Jeush, Benjamin, Ehud, Kenaanah, Zethan, Tarshish, and Ahishahar—all sons of Jediael and family chiefs; they counted 17,200 combat-ready warriors. Shuppim and Huppim were the sons of Ir; Hushim were from the family of Aher.

THE FAMILY OF NAPHTALI

7.13 The sons of Naphtali were Jahziel, Guni, Jezer, and Shallum; they are listed under the maternal line of Bilhah, their grandfather's concubine.

NEW INTERNATIONAL VERSION

MANASSEH

14 The descendants of Manasseh:

Asriel was his descendant through his Aramean concubine. She gave birth to Makir the father of Gilead. 15 Makir took a wife from among the Huppites and Shuppites. His sister's name was Maacah.

Another descendant was named Zelophehad, who had only daughters.

16 Makir's wife Maacah gave birth to a son and named him Peresh. His brother was named Sheresh, and his sons were Ulam and Rakem.

17 The son of Ulam:

Bedan.

These were the sons of Gilead son of Makir, the son of Manasseh. 18 His sister Hammoleketh gave birth to Ishhod, Abiezer and Mahlah.

19 The sons of Shemida were:

Ahian, Shechem, Likhi and Aniam.

EPHRAIM

20 The descendants of Ephraim:

Shuthelah, Bered his son,
Tahath his son, Eleadah his son,
Tahath his son, 21 Zabad his son
and Shuthelah his son.

Ezer and Elead were killed by the native-born men of Gath, when they went down to seize their livestock. 22 Their father Ephraim mourned for them many days, and his relatives came to comfort him. 23 Then he lay with his wife again, and she became pregnant and gave birth to a son. He named him Beriah,[a] because there had been misfortune in his family. 24 His daughter was Sheerah, who built Lower and Upper Beth Horon as well as Uzzen Sheerah.

25 Rephah was his son, Resheph his son,[b]
Telah his son, Tahan his son,
26 Ladan his son, Ammihud his son,
Elishama his son, 27 Nun his son
and Joshua his son.

28 Their lands and settlements included Bethel and its surrounding villages, Naaran to the east, Gezer and its villages to the west, and Shechem and its villages all the way to Ayyah and its villages. 29 Along the borders of Manasseh were Beth Shan, Taanach, Megiddo and Dor, together with their villages. The descendants of Joseph son of Israel lived in these towns.

a 23 Beriah sounds like the Hebrew for misfortune.
b 25 Some Septuagint manuscripts; Hebrew does not have his son.

THE MESSAGE

THE FAMILY OF MANASSEH

7.14-19 Manasseh's sons, born of his Aramean concubine, were Asriel and Makir the father of Gilead. Makir got his wife from the Huppites and Shuppites. His sister's name was Maacah. Another son, Zelophehad, had only daughters. Makir's wife Maacah bore a son whom she named Peresh; his brother's name was Sheresh and his sons were Ulam and Rakem. Ulam's son was Bedan. This accounts for the sons of Gilead son of Makir, the son of Manasseh. His sister Hammoleketh gave birth to Ishdod, Abiezer, and Mahlah. The sons of Shemida were Ahian, Shechem, Likhi, and Aniam.

THE FAMILY OF EPHRAIM

7.20-24 The sons of Ephraim were Shuthelah, Bered his son, Tahath his son, Eleadah his son, Tahath his son, Zabad his son, Shuthelah his son, and Ezer and Elead, cattle-rustlers, killed on one of their raids by the natives of Gath. Their father Ephraim grieved a long time and his family gathered to give him comfort. Then he slept with his wife again. She conceived and produced a son. He named him Beriah (Unlucky), because of the bad luck that had come to his family. His daughter was Sheerah. She built Lower and Upper Beth Horon and Uzzen Sheerah.

7.25-29 Rephah was Ephraim's son and also Resheph; Telah was his son, Tahan his son, Ladan his son, Ammihud his son, Elishama his son, Nun his son, and Joshua his son. They occupied Bethel and the neighboring country from Naaran on the east to Gezer and its villages on the west, along with Shechem and its villages, and extending as far as Ayyah and its villages. Stretched along the borders of Manasseh were Beth Shan, Taanach, Megiddo, and Dor, together with their satellite villages. The families descended from Joseph son of Israel lived in all these places.

NEW INTERNATIONAL VERSION

ASHER

30 The sons of Asher:
    Imnah, Ishvah, Ishvi and Beriah. Their
    sister was Serah.
31 The sons of Beriah:
    Heber and Malkiel, who was the father
    of Birzaith.
32 Heber was the father of Japhlet, Shomer
    and Hotham and of their sister Shua.
33 The sons of Japhlet:
    Pasach, Bimhal and Ashvath.
    These were Japhlet's sons.
34 The sons of Shomer:
    Ahi, Rohgah,*a* Hubbah and Aram.
35 The sons of his brother Helem:
    Zophah, Imna, Shelesh and Amal.
36 The sons of Zophah:
    Suah, Harnepher, Shual, Beri, Imrah,
    37 Bezer, Hod, Shamma, Shilshah, Ithran*b*
    and Beera.
38 The sons of Jether:
    Jephunneh, Pispah and Ara.
39 The sons of Ulla:
    Arah, Hanniel and Rizia.
40 All these were descendants of Asher—heads
of families, choice men, brave warriors and outstanding leaders. The number of men ready for
battle, as listed in their genealogy, was 26,000.

THE GENEALOGY OF SAUL THE BENJAMITE

8 Benjamin was the father of Bela his firstborn,
    Ashbel the second son, Aharah the
    third,
    2 Nohah the fourth and Rapha the fifth.
3 The sons of Bela were:
    Addar, Gera, Abihud,*c* 4 Abishua, Naa-
    man, Ahoah, 5 Gera, Shephuphan and
    Huram.
6 These were the descendants of Ehud, who
    were heads of families of those living in
    Geba and were deported to Manahath:
    7 Naaman, Ahijah, and Gera, who deport-
    ed them and who was the father of Uzza
    and Ahihud.
8 Sons were born to Shaharaim in Moab after
    he had divorced his wives Hushim and
    Baara. 9 By his wife Hodesh he had Jo-
    bab, Zibia, Mesha, Malcam, 10 Jeuz, Sakia
    and Mirmah. These were his sons, heads
    of families. 11 By Hushim he had Abitub
    and Elpaal.
12 The sons of Elpaal:
    Eber, Misham, Shemed (who built Ono
    and Lod with its surrounding villages),

a 34 Or *of his brother Shomer: Rohgah*   *b 37* Possibly a
variant of *Jether*   *c 3* Or *Gera the father of Ehud*

THE MESSAGE

THE FAMILY OF ASHER

7.30-32 The sons of Asher were Imnah, Ishvah, Ishvi,
and Beriah; Serah was their sister. The sons of
Beriah were Heber and Malkiel, who had Birza-
ith. Heber had Japhlet, Shomer, Hotham, and
Shua their sister.

7.33-40   Japhlet had Pasach, Bimhal, and Ashvath.
His brother Shomer had Rohgah, Hubbah, and
Aram. His brother Helem had Zophah, Imna,
Shelesh, and Amal. Zophah had Suah,
Harnepher, Shual, Beri, Imrah, Bezer, Hod,
Shamma, Shilshah, Ithran, and Beera. Jether
had Jephunneh, Pispah, and Ara. Ulla had
Arah, Hanniel, and Rizia. These were Asher's
sons, all of them responsible, excellent in char-
acter, and brave in battle—good leaders. They
listed 26,000 combat-ready men in their family
tree.

THE FAMILY OF BENJAMIN (CONTINUED)

8.1-5   **8** Benjamin's firstborn son was Bela, followed
by Ashbel, Aharah, Nohah, and Rapha—
five in all. Bela's sons were Addar, Gera, Abi-
hud, Abishua, Naaman, Ahoah, Gera, She-
phuphan, and Huram.

8.6-7   These are the families of Ehud that lived in
Geba and were exiled to Manahath: Naaman,
Ahijah, and Gera, who led them to exile and
had Uzza and Ahihud.

8.8-12   In the land of Moab, Shaharaim had children after he divorced his wives Hushim and
Baara. From his new wife Hodesh he had Jobab, Zibia, Mesha, Malcam, Jeuz, Sakia, and
Mirmah—sons who became heads of families.
From his earlier wife Hushim he had Abitub
and Elpaal. Elpaal's sons were Eber, Misham,
and Shemed, who built Ono and Lod with all
their villages.

NEW INTERNATIONAL VERSION

¹³and Beriah and Shema, who were heads of families of those living in Aijalon and who drove out the inhabitants of Gath.

¹⁴Ahio, Shashak, Jeremoth, ¹⁵Zebadiah, Arad, Eder, ¹⁶Michael, Ishpah and Joha were the sons of Beriah.

¹⁷Zebadiah, Meshullam, Hizki, Heber, ¹⁸Ishmerai, Izliah and Jobab were the sons of Elpaal.

¹⁹Jakim, Zicri, Zabdi, ²⁰Elienai, Zillethai, Eliel, ²¹Adaiah, Beraiah and Shimrath were the sons of Shimei.

²²Ishpan, Eber, Eliel, ²³Abdon, Zicri, Hanan, ²⁴Hananiah, Elam, Anthothijah, ²⁵Iphdeiah and Penuel were the sons of Shashak.

²⁶Shamsherai, Shehariah, Athaliah, ²⁷Jaareshiah, Elijah and Zicri were the sons of Jeroham.

²⁸All these were heads of families, chiefs as listed in their genealogy, and they lived in Jerusalem.

²⁹Jeielᵃ the fatherᵇ of Gibeon lived in Gibeon.

His wife's name was Maacah, ³⁰and his firstborn son was Abdon, followed by Zur, Kish, Baal, Ner,ᶜ Nadab, ³¹Gedor, Ahio, Zeker ³²and Mikloth, who was the father of Shimeah. They too lived near their relatives in Jerusalem.

³³Ner was the father of Kish, Kish the father of Saul, and Saul the father of Jonathan, Malki-Shua, Abinadab and Esh-Baal.ᵈ

³⁴The son of Jonathan:

Merib-Baal,ᵉ who was the father of Micah.

³⁵The sons of Micah:

Pithon, Melech, Tarea and Ahaz.

³⁶Ahaz was the father of Jehoaddah, Jehoaddah was the father of Alemeth, Azmaveth and Zimri, and Zimri was the father of Moza. ³⁷Moza was the father of Binea; Raphah was his son, Eleasah his son and Azel his son.

³⁸Azel had six sons, and these were their names:

Azrikam, Bokeru, Ishmael, Sheariah, Obadiah and Hanan. All these were the sons of Azel.

³⁹The sons of his brother Eshek:

THE MESSAGE

8.13-28   Beriah and Shema were family chiefs who lived at Aijalon. They drove out the citizens of Gath. Their brothers were Shashak and Jeremoth. The sons of Beriah were Zebadiah, Arad, Eder, Michael, Ishpah, and Joha. The sons of Elpaal were Zebadiah, Meshullam, Hizki, Heber, Ishmerai, Izliah, and Jobab. The sons of Shimei were Jakim, Zicri, Zabdi, Elienai, Zillethai, Eliel, Adaiah, Beraiah, and Shimrath. The sons of Shashak were Ishpan, Eber, Eliel, Abdon, Zicri, Hanan, Hananiah, Elam, Anthothijah, Iphdeiah, and Penuel. The sons of Jeroham were Shamsherai, Shehariah, Athaliah, Jaareshiah, Elijah, and Zicri. These were the chiefs of the families as listed in their family tree. They lived in Jerusalem.

8.29-32   Jeiel the father of Gibeon lived in Gibeon. His wife's name was Maacah. Abdon was his firstborn son, followed by Zur, Kish, Baal, Nadab, Gedor, Ahio, Zeker, and Mikloth. Mikloth had Shimeah. They lived in the neighborhood of their extended families in Jerusalem.

8.33-40   Ner had Kish, Kish had Saul, and Saul had Jonathan, Malki-Shua, Abinadab, and Esh-Baal. Jonathan had Merib-Baal, and Merib-Baal had Micah. Micah's sons were Pithon, Melech, Tarea, and Ahaz. Ahaz had Jehoaddah and Jehoaddah had Alemeth, Azmaveth, and Zimri. Zimri had Moza and Moza had Binea. Raphah was his son, Eleasah his son, and Azel his son. Azel had six sons named Azrikam, Bokeru, Ishmael, Sheariah, Obadiah, and Hanan. His brother Eshek's sons were Ulam his firstborn,

ᵃ 29 Some Septuagint manuscripts (see also 1 Chron. 9:35); Hebrew does not have Jeiel.   ᵇ 29 Father may mean civic leader or military leader.   ᶜ 30 Some Septuagint manuscripts (see also 1 Chron. 9:36); Hebrew does not have Ner.   ᵈ 33 Also known as Ish-Bosheth   ᵉ 34 Also known as Mephibosheth

NEW INTERNATIONAL VERSION

Ulam his firstborn, Jeush the second son and Eliphelet the third. ⁴⁰The sons of Ulam were brave warriors who could handle the bow. They had many sons and grandsons—150 in all.

All these were the descendants of Benjamin.

9 All Israel was listed in the genealogies recorded in the book of the kings of Israel.

THE PEOPLE IN JERUSALEM

The people of Judah were taken captive to Babylon because of their unfaithfulness. ²Now the first to resettle on their own property in their own towns were some Israelites, priests, Levites and temple servants.

³Those from Judah, from Benjamin, and from Ephraim and Manasseh who lived in Jerusalem were:

⁴Uthai son of Ammihud, the son of Omri, the son of Imri, the son of Bani, a descendant of Perez son of Judah.

⁵Of the Shilonites:

Asaiah the firstborn and his sons.

⁶Of the Zerahites:

Jeuel.

The people from Judah numbered 690.

⁷Of the Benjamites:

Sallu son of Meshullam, the son of Hodaviah, the son of Hassenuah;

⁸Ibneiah son of Jeroham; Elah son of Uzzi, the son of Micri; and Meshullam son of Shephatiah, the son of Reuel, the son of Ibnijah.

⁹The people from Benjamin, as listed in their genealogy, numbered 956. All these men were heads of their families.

¹⁰Of the priests:

Jedaiah; Jehoiarib; Jakin;

¹¹Azariah son of Hilkiah, the son of Meshullam, the son of Zadok, the son of Meraioth, the son of Ahitub, the official in charge of the house of God;

¹²Adaiah son of Jeroham, the son of Pashhur, the son of Malkijah; and Maasai son of Adiel, the son of Jahzerah, the son of Meshullam, the son of Meshillemith, the son of Immer.

¹³The priests, who were heads of families, numbered 1,760. They were able men, responsible for ministering in the house of God.

¹⁴Of the Levites:

Shemaiah son of Hasshub, the son of Azrikam, the son of Hashabiah, a Mera-

THE MESSAGE

followed by Jeush and Eliphelet. Ulam's sons were warriors well known as archers. They had lots of sons and grandsons—at least 150. These were all in Benjamin's family tree.

^{9.1} **9** This is the complete family tree for all Israel, recorded in the *Royal Annals of the Kings of Israel and Judah* at the time they were exiled to Babylon because of their unbelieving and disobedient lives.

THE BACK-FROM-EXILE COMMUNITY IN JERUSALEM

^{9.2} The first Israelites to return from exile to their homes and cities were the priests, the Levites, and the temple support staff.

^{9.3-6} Returning to Jerusalem from the families of Judah, Benjamin, Ephraim, and Manasseh were the following: Uthai son of Ammihud, the son of Omri, the son of Imri, the son of Bani, from the line of Perez son of Judah; from the Shilonites were Asaiah the firstborn and his sons; from the family of Zerah there was Jeuel. There were 690 in the Judah group.

^{9.7-9} From the family of Benjamin were Sallu son of Meshullam, the son of Hodaviah, the son of Hassenuah, and Ibneiah son of Jeroham, and Elah son of Uzzi, the son of Micri, and Meshullam son of Shephatiah, the son of Reuel, the son of Ibnijah. There were 956 in the Benjamin group. All these named were heads of families.

^{9.10-13} From the company of priests there were Jedaiah; Jehoiarib; Jakin; Azariah son of Hilkiah, the son of Meshullam, the son of Zadok, the son of Meraioth, the son of Ahitub, who was in charge of taking care of the house of God; Adaiah son of Jeroham, the son of Pashhur, the son of Malkijah; also Maasai son of Adiel, the son of Jahzerah, the son of Meshullam, the son of Meshillemith, the son of Immer. The priests, all of them heads of families, numbered 1,760, skilled and seasoned servants in the work of worshiping God.

^{9.14-16} From the Levites were Shemaiah son of Hasshub, the son of Azrikam, the son of Hashabi-

NEW INTERNATIONAL VERSION

rite; [15]Bakbakkar, Heresh, Galal and Mattaniah son of Mica, the son of Zicri, the son of Asaph; [16]Obadiah son of Shemaiah, the son of Galal, the son of Jeduthun; and Berekiah son of Asa, the son of Elkanah, who lived in the villages of the Netophathites.

[17] The gatekeepers:

Shallum, Akkub, Talmon, Ahiman and their brothers, Shallum their chief [18]being stationed at the King's Gate on the east, up to the present time. These were the gatekeepers belonging to the camp of the Levites. [19]Shallum son of Kore, the son of Ebiasaph, the son of Korah, and his fellow gatekeepers from his family (the Korahites) were responsible for guarding the thresholds of the Tent[a] just as their fathers had been responsible for guarding the entrance to the dwelling of the LORD. [20]In earlier times Phinehas son of Eleazar was in charge of the gatekeepers, and the LORD was with him. [21]Zechariah son of Meshelemiah was the gatekeeper at the entrance to the Tent of Meeting.

[22]Altogether, those chosen to be gatekeepers at the thresholds numbered 212. They were registered by genealogy in their villages. The gatekeepers had been assigned to their positions of trust by David and Samuel the seer. [23]They and their descendants were in charge of guarding the gates of the house of the LORD—the house called the Tent. [24]The gatekeepers were on the four sides: east, west, north and south. [25]Their brothers in their villages had to come from time to time and share their duties for seven-day periods. [26]But the four principal gatekeepers, who were Levites, were entrusted with the responsibility for the rooms and treasuries in the house of God. [27]They would spend the night stationed around the house of God, because they had to guard it; and they had charge of the key for opening it each morning.

[28]Some of them were in charge of the articles used in the temple service; they counted them when they were brought in and when they were taken out. [29]Others were assigned to take care of the furnishings and all the other articles of the sanctuary, as well as the flour and wine, and the oil, incense and spices. [30]But some of the priests took care of mixing the spices. [31]A Levite named Mattithiah, the firstborn son of Shallum the Korahite, was entrusted with the responsibility for baking the offering bread. [32]Some of their Kohathite brothers were in charge of preparing for every Sabbath the bread set out on the table.

[a] 19 That is, the temple; also in verses 21 and 23

THE MESSAGE

ah, a Merarite; then Bakbakkar, Heresh, Galal, Mattaniah son of Mica, the son of Zicri, the son of Asaph; also Obadiah son of Shemaiah, the son of Galal, the son of Jeduthun; and finally Berekiah son of Asa, the son of Elkanah, who lived in the villages of the Netophathites.

9.17-18 The security guards were Shallum, Akkub, Talmon, Ahiman, and their brothers. Shallum was the chief and up to now the security guard at the King's Gate on the east. They also served as security guards at the camps of Levite families.

9.19-25 Shallum son of Kore, the son of Ebiasaph, the son of Korah, along with his brothers in the Korahite family, were in charge of the services of worship as doorkeepers of the Tent, as their ancestors had guarded the entrance to the camp of God. In the early days, Phinehas son of Eleazar was in charge of the security guards—God be with him! Now Zechariah son of Meshelemiah was the security guard at the entrance of the Tent of Meeting. The number of those who had been chosen to be security guards was 212—they were officially registered in their own camps. David and Samuel the seer handpicked them for their dependability. They and their sons had the permanent responsibility for guarding the gates of God's house, the house of worship; the main security guards were posted at the four entrances, east, west, north, and south; their brothers in the villages were scheduled to give them relief weekly— the four main security guards were responsible for round-the-clock surveillance.

9.26-32 Being Levites, they were responsible for the security of all supplies and valuables in the house of God. They kept watch all through the night and had the key to open the doors each morning. Some were in charge of the articles used in The Temple worship—they counted them both when they brought them in and when they took them out. Others were in charge of supplies in the sanctuary—flour, wine, oil, incense, and spices. And some of the priests were assigned to mixing the oils for the perfume. The Levite Mattithiah, the firstborn son of Shallum the Korahite, was responsible for baking the bread for the services of worship. Some of the brothers, sons of the Kohathites, were assigned to preparing the bread set out on the table each Sabbath.

NEW INTERNATIONAL VERSION

33Those who were musicians, heads of Levite families, stayed in the rooms of the temple and were exempt from other duties because they were responsible for the work day and night.

34All these were heads of Levite families, chiefs as listed in their genealogy, and they lived in Jerusalem.

THE GENEALOGY OF SAUL

35Jeiel the father[a] of Gibeon lived in Gibeon. His wife's name was Maacah, 36and his firstborn son was Abdon, followed by Zur, Kish, Baal, Ner, Nadab, 37Gedor, Ahio, Zechariah and Mikloth. 38Mikloth was the father of Shimeam. They too lived near their relatives in Jerusalem.

39Ner was the father of Kish, Kish the father of Saul, and Saul the father of Jonathan, Malki-Shua, Abinadab and Esh-Baal.[b]

40The son of Jonathan:

Merib-Baal,[c] who was the father of Micah.

41The sons of Micah:

Pithon, Melech, Tahrea and Ahaz.[d]

42Ahaz was the father of Jadah, Jadah[e] was the father of Alemeth, Azmaveth and Zimri, and Zimri was the father of Moza. 43Moza was the father of Binea; Rephaiah was his son, Eleasah his son and Azel his son.

44Azel had six sons, and these were their names:

Azrikam, Bokeru, Ishmael, Sheariah, Obadiah and Hanan. These were the sons of Azel.

SAUL TAKES HIS LIFE

10 Now the Philistines fought against Israel; the Israelites fled before them, and many fell slain on Mount Gilboa. 2The Philistines pressed hard after Saul and his sons, and they killed his sons Jonathan, Abinadab and Malki-Shua. 3The fighting grew fierce around Saul, and when the archers overtook him, they wounded him.

4Saul said to his armor-bearer, "Draw your sword and run me through, or these uncircumcised fellows will come and abuse me."

But his armor-bearer was terrified and would not do it; so Saul took his own sword and fell on it. 5When the armor-bearer saw that Saul was dead, he too fell on his sword and died. 6So Saul

THE MESSAGE

9.33-34 And then there were the musicians, all heads of Levite families. They had permanent living quarters in The Temple; because they were on twenty-four-hour duty, they were exempt from all other duties. These were the heads of Levite families as designated in their family tree. They lived in Jerusalem.

THE FAMILY OF SAUL

9.35-38 Jeiel the father of Gibeon lived at Gibeon; his wife was Maacah. His firstborn son was Abdon, followed by Zur, Kish, Baal, Ner, Nadab, Gedor, Ahio, Zechariah, and Mikloth. Mikloth had Shimeam. They lived in the same neighborhood as their relatives in Jerusalem.

9.39-44 Ner had Kish, Kish had Saul, Saul had Jonathan, Malki-Shua, Abinadab, and Esh-Baal. Merib-Baal was the son of Jonathan and Merib-Baal had Micah. Micah's sons were Pithon, Melech, and Tahrea. Ahaz had Jarah, Jarah had Alemeth, Azmaveth, and Zimri; Zimri had Moza, Moza had Binea, Rephaiah was his son, Eleasah was his son, and Azel was his son. Azel had six sons: Azrikam, Bokeru, Ishmael, Sheariah, Obadiah, and Hanan—the sons of Azel.

✝

10.1-5 **10** The Philistines went to war against Israel; the Israelites ran for their lives from the Philistines but fell, slaughtered on Mount Gilboa. The Philistines zeroed in on Saul and his sons and killed his sons Jonathan, Abinadab, and Malki-Shua. The battle went hard against Saul—the archers found him and wounded him. Saul said to his armor bearer, "Draw your sword and finish me off before these pagan pigs get to me and make a sport of my body." But his armor bearer, restrained by both reverence and fear, wouldn't do it. So Saul took his own sword and killed himself. The armor bearer, panicked because Saul was dead, then killed himself.

---

a 35 Father may mean *civic leader* or *military leader.*
b 39 Also known as *Ish-Bosheth*   *c 40* Also known as *Mephibosheth*   *d 41* Vulgate and Syriac (see also Septuagint and 1 Chron. 8:35); Hebrew does not have *and Ahaz.*
e 42 Some Hebrew manuscripts and Septuagint (see also 1 Chron. 8:36); most Hebrew manuscripts *Jarah, Jarah*

NEW INTERNATIONAL VERSION

and his three sons died, and all his house died together.

7When all the Israelites in the valley saw that the army had fled and that Saul and his sons had died, they abandoned their towns and fled. And the Philistines came and occupied them.

8The next day, when the Philistines came to strip the dead, they found Saul and his sons fallen on Mount Gilboa. 9They stripped him and took his head and his armor, and sent messengers throughout the land of the Philistines to proclaim the news among their idols and their people. 10They put his armor in the temple of their gods and hung up his head in the temple of Dagon.

11When all the inhabitants of Jabesh Gilead heard of everything the Philistines had done to Saul, 12all their valiant men went and took the bodies of Saul and his sons and brought them to Jabesh. Then they buried their bones under the great tree in Jabesh, and they fasted seven days.

13Saul died because he was unfaithful to the LORD; he did not keep the word of the LORD and even consulted a medium for guidance, 14and did not inquire of the LORD. So the LORD put him to death and turned the kingdom over to David son of Jesse.

DAVID BECOMES KING OVER ISRAEL

11 All Israel came together to David at Hebron and said, "We are your own flesh and blood. 2In the past, even while Saul was king, you were the one who led Israel on their military campaigns. And the LORD your God said to you, 'You will shepherd my people Israel, and you will become their ruler.' "

3When all the elders of Israel had come to King David at Hebron, he made a compact with them at Hebron before the LORD, and they anointed David king over Israel, as the LORD had promised through Samuel.

DAVID CONQUERS JERUSALEM

4David and all the Israelites marched to Jerusalem (that is, Jebus). The Jebusites who lived there 5said to David, "You will not get in here." Nevertheless, David captured the fortress of Zion, the City of David.

6David had said, "Whoever leads the attack on the Jebusites will become commander-in-chief." Joab son of Zeruiah went up first, and so he received the command.

7David then took up residence in the fortress, and so it was called the City of David. 8He built up the city around it, from the supporting ter-

THE MESSAGE

10.6-7 So Saul and his three sons—all four the same day—died. When all the Israelites in the valley saw that the army had fled and that Saul and his sons were dead, they abandoned their cities and ran off; the Philistines came and moved in.

10.8-10 The next day the Philistines came to plunder the dead bodies and found Saul and his sons dead on Mount Gilboa. They stripped Saul, removed his head and his armor, and put them on exhibit throughout Philistia, reporting the victory news to their idols and the people. Then they put Saul's armor on display in the temple of their gods and placed his skull as a trophy in the temple of their god Dagon.

10.11-12 The people of Jabesh Gilead heard what the Philistines had done to Saul. All of their fighting men went into action—retrieved the bodies of Saul and his sons and brought them to Jabesh, gave them a dignified burial under the oak at Jabesh, and mourned their deaths for seven days.

10.13-14 Saul died in disobedience, disobedient to GOD. He didn't obey GOD's words. Instead of praying, he went to a witch to seek guidance. Because he didn't go to GOD for help, GOD took his life and turned the kingdom over to David son of Jesse.

KING DAVID

11 Then all Israel assembled before David at Hebron. "Look at us," they said. "We're your very flesh and blood. In the past, yes, even while Saul was king, you were the real leader of Israel. GOD told you, 'You will shepherd my people Israel; you are to be the ruler of my people Israel.' " When all the elders of Israel came to the king at Hebron, David made a covenant with them in the presence of GOD at Hebron. Then they anointed David king over Israel exactly as GOD had commanded through Samuel.

11.4-6 David and all Israel went to Jerusalem (it was the old Jebus, where the Jebusites lived). The citizens of Jebus told David, "No trespassing—you can't come here." David came on anyway and captured the fortress of Zion, the City of David. David had said, "The first person to kill a Jebusite will be commander-in-chief." Joab son of Zeruiah was the first; and he became the chief.

11.7-9 David took up residence in the fortress city; that's how it got its name, "City of David." David fortified the city all the way around, both

NEW INTERNATIONAL VERSION

races*a* to the surrounding wall, while Joab restored the rest of the city. 9And David became more and more powerful, because the LORD Almighty was with him.

DAVID'S MIGHTY MEN

10These were the chiefs of David's mighty men—they, together with all Israel, gave his kingship strong support to extend it over the whole land, as the LORD had promised— 11this is the list of David's mighty men:

Jashobeam,*b* a Hacmonite, was chief of the officers*c*; he raised his spear against three hundred men, whom he killed in one encounter.

12Next to him was Eleazar son of Dodai the Ahohite, one of the three mighty men. 13He was with David at Pas Dammim when the Philistines gathered there for battle. At a place where there was a field full of barley, the troops fled from the Philistines. 14But they took their stand in the middle of the field. They defended it and struck the Philistines down, and the LORD brought about a great victory.

15Three of the thirty chiefs came down to David to the rock at the cave of Adullam, while a band of Philistines was encamped in the Valley of Rephaim. 16At that time David was in the stronghold, and the Philistine garrison was at Bethlehem. 17David longed for water and said, "Oh, that someone would get me a drink of water from the well near the gate of Bethlehem!" 18So the Three broke through the Philistine lines, drew water from the well near the gate of Bethlehem and carried it back to David. But he refused to drink it; instead, he poured it out before the LORD. 19"God forbid that I should do this!" he said. "Should I drink the blood of these men who went at the risk of their lives?" Because they risked their lives to bring it back, David would not drink it.

Such were the exploits of the three mighty men.

20Abishai the brother of Joab was chief of the Three. He raised his spear against three hundred men, whom he killed, and so he became as famous as the Three. 21He was doubly honored above the Three and became their commander, even though he was not included among them.

22Benaiah son of Jehoiada was a valiant fighter from Kabzeel, who performed great exploits. He struck down two of Moab's best men. He also went down into a pit on a snowy day and killed a lion. 23And he struck down an Egyptian who was seven and a half feet*d* tall. Although the

THE MESSAGE

the outer bulwarks (the Millo) and the outside wall. Joab rebuilt the city gates. David's stride became longer, his embrace larger—yes, GOD-of-the-Angel-Armies was with him!

DAVID'S MIGHTY MEN

11.10-11 These are the chiefs of David's Mighty Men, the ones who linked arms with him as he took up his kingship, with all Israel joining in, helping him become king in just the way GOD had spoken regarding Israel. The list of David's Mighty Men:

Jashobeam son of Hacmoni was chief of the Thirty. Singlehandedly he killed three hundred men, killed them all in one skirmish.

11.12-14 Next was Eleazar son of Dodai the Ahohite, one of the Big Three of the Mighty Men. He was with David at Pas Dammim, where the Philistines had mustered their troops for battle. It was an area where there was a field of barley. The army started to flee from the Philistines and then took its stand right in that field—and turned the tide! They slaughtered the Philistines, GOD helping them—a huge victory.

11.15-19 The Big Three from the Thirty made a rocky descent to David at the Cave of Adullam while a company of Philistines was camped in the Valley of Rephaim. David was holed up in the Cave while the Philistines were prepared for battle at Bethlehem. David had a sudden craving: "What I wouldn't give for a drink of water from the well in Bethlehem, the one at the gate!" The Three penetrated the Philistine camp, drew water from the well at the Bethlehem gate, shouldered it, and brought it to David. And then David wouldn't drink it! He poured it out as a sacred offering to GOD, saying, "I'd rather be damned by God than drink this! It would be like drinking the lifeblood of these men—they risked their lives to bring it." So he refused to drink it. These are the kinds of things that the Big Three of the Mighty Men did.

11.20-21 Abishai brother of Joab was the chief of the Thirty. Singlehandedly he fought three hundred men, and killed the lot, but he never made it into the circle of the Three. He was highly honored by the Thirty—he was their chief—still, he didn't measure up to the Three.

11.22-25 Benaiah son of Jehoiada was a Mighty Man from Kabzeel with many exploits to his credit: he killed two famous Moabites; he climbed down into a pit and killed a lion on a snowy day; and he killed an Egyptian, a giant seven and a half feet tall. The Egyptian had a spear

---

a 8 Or the Millo b 11 Possibly a variant of Jashob-Baal c 11 Or Thirty; some Septuagint manuscripts Three (see also 2 Samuel 23:8) d 23 Hebrew five cubits (about 2.3 meters)

NEW INTERNATIONAL VERSION

Egyptian had a spear like a weaver's rod in his hand, Benaiah went against him with a club. He snatched the spear from the Egyptian's hand and killed him with his own spear. ²⁴Such were the exploits of Benaiah son of Jehoiada; he too was as famous as the three mighty men. ²⁵He was held in greater honor than any of the Thirty, but he was not included among the Three. And David put him in charge of his bodyguard.

²⁶The mighty men were:

Asahel the brother of Joab,
Elhanan son of Dodo from Bethlehem,
²⁷Shammoth the Harorite,
Helez the Pelonite,
²⁸Ira son of Ikkesh from Tekoa,
Abiezer from Anathoth,
²⁹Sibbecai the Hushathite,
Ilai the Ahohite,
³⁰Maharai the Netophathite,
Heled son of Baanah the Netophathite,
³¹Ithai son of Ribai from Gibeah in Benjamin,
Benaiah the Pirathonite,
³²Hurai from the ravines of Gaash,
Abiel the Arbathite,
³³Azmaveth the Baharumite,
Eliahba the Shaalbonite,
³⁴the sons of Hashem the Gizonite,
Jonathan son of Shagee the Hararite,
³⁵Ahiam son of Sacar the Hararite,
Eliphal son of Ur,
³⁶Hepher the Mekerathite,
Ahijah the Pelonite,
³⁷Hezro the Carmelite,
Naarai son of Ezbai,
³⁸Joel the brother of Nathan,
Mibhar son of Hagri,
³⁹Zelek the Ammonite,
Naharai the Berothite, the armor-bearer of Joab son of Zeruiah,
⁴⁰Ira the Ithrite,
Gareb the Ithrite,
⁴¹Uriah the Hittite,
Zabad son of Ahlai,
⁴²Adina son of Shiza the Reubenite, who was chief of the Reubenites, and the thirty with him,
⁴³Hanan son of Maacah,
Joshaphat the Mithnite,
⁴⁴Uzzia the Ashterathite,
Shama and Jeiel the sons of Hotham the Aroerite,
⁴⁵Jediael son of Shimri,
his brother Joha the Tizite,
⁴⁶Eliel the Mahavite,
Jeribai and Joshaviah the sons of Elnaam,

THE MESSAGE

like a ship's boom but Benaiah went at him with a mere club, tore the spear from the Egyptian's hand, and killed him with it. These are some of the things Benaiah son of Jehoiada did. But he was never included with the Three. He was highly honored among the Thirty, but didn't measure up to the Three. David put him in charge of his personal bodyguard.

11.26-47   The Mighty Men of the military were Asahel brother of Joab, Elhanan son of Dodo of Bethlehem, Shammoth the Harorite, Helez the Pelonite, Ira son of Ikkesh the Tekoite, Abiezer the Anathothite, Sibbecai the Hushathite, Ilai the Ahohite, Maharai the Netophathite, Heled son of Baanah the Netophathite, Ithai son of Ribai from Gibeah of the Benjaminite, Benaiah the Pirathonite, Hurai from the ravines of Gaash, Abiel the Arbathite, Azmaveth the Baharumite, Eliahba the Shaalbonite, the sons of Hashem the Gizonite, Jonathan son of Shagee the Hararite, Ahiam son of Sacar the Haranite, Eliphal son of Ur, Hepher the Mekerathite, Ahijah the Pelonite, Hezro the Carmelite, Naarai son of Ezbai, Joel brother of Nathan, Mibhar son of Hagri, Zelek the Ammonite, Naharai the Berothite, the armor bearer of Joab son of Zeruiah, Ira the Ithrite, Gareb the Ithrite, Uriah the Hittite, Zabad son of Ahlai, Adina son of Shiza the Reubenite chief of the Thirty, Hanan son of Maacah, Joshaphat the Mithnite, Uzzia the Ashterathite, Shama and Jeiel the sons of Hotham the Aroerite, Jediael son of Shimri, Joha the Tizite his brother, Eliel the Mahavite, Jeribai and Joshaviah the sons of

NEW INTERNATIONAL VERSION	THE MESSAGE

NEW INTERNATIONAL VERSION

Ithmah the Moabite,
⁴⁷Eliel, Obed and Jaasiel the Mezobaite.

WARRIORS JOIN DAVID

12 These were the men who came to David at Ziklag, while he was banished from the presence of Saul son of Kish (they were among the warriors who helped him in battle; ²they were armed with bows and were able to shoot arrows or to sling stones right-handed or left-handed; they were kinsmen of Saul from the tribe of Benjamin):

³Ahiezer their chief and Joash the sons of Shemaah the Gibeathite; Jeziel and Pelet the sons of Azmaveth; Beracah, Jehu the Anathothite, ⁴and Ishmaiah the Gibeonite, a mighty man among the Thirty, who was a leader of the Thirty; Jeremiah, Jahaziel, Johanan, Jozabad the Gederathite, ⁵Eluzai, Jerimoth, Bealiah, Shemariah and Shephatiah the Haruphite; ⁶Elkanah, Isshiah, Azarel, Joezer and Jashobeam the Korahites; ⁷and Joelah and Zebadiah the sons of Jeroham from Gedor.

⁸Some Gadites defected to David at his stronghold in the desert. They were brave warriors, ready for battle and able to handle the shield and spear. Their faces were the faces of lions, and they were as swift as gazelles in the mountains.

⁹Ezer was the chief,
Obadiah the second in command, Eliab the third,
¹⁰Mishmannah the fourth, Jeremiah the fifth,
¹¹Attai the sixth, Eliel the seventh,
¹²Johanan the eighth, Elzabad the ninth,
¹³Jeremiah the tenth and Macbannai the eleventh.

¹⁴These Gadites were army commanders; the least was a match for a hundred, and the greatest for a thousand. ¹⁵It was they who crossed the Jordan in the first month when it was overflowing all its banks, and they put to flight everyone living in the valleys, to the east and to the west.

¹⁶Other Benjamites and some men from Judah also came to David in his stronghold. ¹⁷David went out to meet them and said to them, "If you have come to me in peace, to help me, I am ready to have you unite with me. But if you have come to betray me to my enemies when my hands are free from violence, may the God of our fathers see it and judge you."

¹⁸Then the Spirit came upon Amasai, chief of the Thirty, and he said:

"We are yours, O David!
    We are with you, O son of Jesse!

THE MESSAGE

Elnaam, Ithmah the Moabite, Eliel, Obed, and Jaasiel the Mezobaite.

¹²·¹⁻² **12** These are the men who joined David in Ziklag; it was during the time he was banished by Saul the son of Kish; they were among the Mighty Men, good fighters. They were armed with bows and could sling stones and shoot arrows either right- or left-handed. They hailed from Saul's tribe, Benjamin.

¹²·³⁻⁷ The first was Ahiezer; then Joash son of Shemaah the Gibeathite; Jeziel and Pelet the sons of Azmaveth; Beracah; Jehu the Anathothite; Ishmaiah the Gibeonite, a Mighty Man among the Thirty, a leader of the Thirty; Jeremiah; Jahaziel; Johanan; Jozabad the Gederathite; Eluzai; Jerimoth; Bealiah; Shemariah; Shephatiah the Haruphite; Elkanah; Isshiah; Azarel; Joezer; Jashobeam; the Korahites; and Joelah and Zebadiah, the sons of Jeroham from Gedor.

¹²·⁸⁻¹⁵ There were some Gadites there who had defected to David at his wilderness fortress; they were seasoned and eager fighters who knew how to handle shield and spear. They were wild in appearance, like lions, but as agile as gazelles racing across the hills. Ezer was the first, then Obadiah, Eliab, Mishmannah, Jeremiah, Attai, Eliel, Johanan, Elzabad, Jeremiah, and Macbannai—eleven of them. These Gadites were the cream of the crop—any one of them was worth a hundred lesser men, and the best of them were worth a thousand. They were the ones who crossed the Jordan when it was at flood stage in the first month, and put everyone in the lowlands to flight, both east and west.

¹²·¹⁶⁻¹⁷ There were also men from the tribes of Benjamin and Judah who joined David in his wilderness fortress. When David went out to meet them, this is what he said: "If you have come in peace and to help me, you are most welcome to join this company; but if you have come to betray me to my enemies, innocent as I am, the God of our ancestors will see through you and bring judgment on you."

¹²·¹⁸ Just then Amasai chief of the Thirty, moved by God's Spirit, said,

We're on your side, O David,
    We're committed, O son of Jesse;

NEW INTERNATIONAL VERSION

Success, success to you,
  and success to those who help you,
    for your God will help you."

So David received them and made them leaders of his raiding bands.

[19]Some of the men of Manasseh defected to David when he went with the Philistines to fight against Saul. (He and his men did not help the Philistines because, after consultation, their rulers sent him away. They said, "It will cost us our heads if he deserts to his master Saul.") [20]When David went to Ziklag, these were the men of Manasseh who defected to him: Adnah, Jozabad, Jediael, Michael, Jozabad, Elihu and Zillethai, leaders of units of a thousand in Manasseh. [21]They helped David against raiding bands, for all of them were brave warriors, and they were commanders in his army. [22]Day after day men came to help David, until he had a great army, like the army of God.[a]

OTHERS JOIN DAVID AT HEBRON

[23]These are the numbers of the men armed for battle who came to David at Hebron to turn Saul's kingdom over to him, as the LORD had said:

[24]men of Judah, carrying shield and spear— 6,800 armed for battle;

[25]men of Simeon, warriors ready for battle— 7,100;

[26]men of Levi—4,600, [27]including Jehoiada, leader of the family of Aaron, with 3,700 men, [28]and Zadok, a brave young warrior, with 22 officers from his family;

[29]men of Benjamin, Saul's kinsmen—3,000, most of whom had remained loyal to Saul's house until then;

[30]men of Ephraim, brave warriors, famous in their own clans—20,800;

[31]men of half the tribe of Manasseh, designated by name to come and make David king—18,000;

[32]men of Issachar, who understood the times and knew what Israel should do—200 chiefs, with all their relatives under their command;

[33]men of Zebulun, experienced soldiers prepared for battle with every type of weapon, to help David with undivided loyalty—50,000;

[34]men of Naphtali—1,000 officers, together with 37,000 men carrying shields and spears;

[35]men of Dan, ready for battle—28,600;

[36]men of Asher, experienced soldiers prepared for battle—40,000;

[a] 22 Or a great and mighty army

THE MESSAGE

All is well, yes, all is well with you,
  And all's well with whoever helps you.
Yes, for your God has helped and does help you.

So David took them on and assigned them a place under the chiefs of the raiders.

12.19 Some from the tribe of Manasseh also defected to David when he started out with the Philistines to go to war against Saul. In the end, they didn't actually fight because the Philistine leaders, after talking it over, sent them home, saying, "We can't trust them with our lives— they'll betray us to their master Saul."

12.20-22 The men from Manasseh who defected to David at Ziklag were Adnah, Jozabad, Jediael, Michael, Jozabad, Elihu, and Zillethai, all leaders among the families of Manasseh. They helped David in his raids against the desert bandits; they were all stalwart fighters and good leaders among his raiders. Hardly a day went by without men showing up to help—it wasn't long before his band seemed as large as God's own army!

⊹

12.23-37 Here are the statistics on the battle-seasoned warriors who came down from the north to David at Hebron to hand over Saul's kingdom, in accord with GOD's word: from Judah, carrying shield and spear, 6,800 battle-ready; from Simeon, 7,100 stalwart fighters; from Levi, 4,600, which included Jehoiada leader of the family of Aaron, bringing 3,700 men and the young and stalwart Zadok with twenty-two leaders from his family; from Benjamin, Saul's family, 3,000, most of whom had stuck it out with Saul until now; from Ephraim, 20,800, fierce fighters and famous in their hometowns; from the half-tribe of Manasseh, 18,000 elected to come and make David king; from Issachar, men who understood both the times and Israel's duties, 200 leaders with their families; from Zebulun, 50,000 well-equipped veteran warriors, unswervingly loyal; from Naphtali, 1,000 chiefs leading 37,000 men heavily armed; from Dan, 28,600 battle-ready men; from Asher, 40,000 veterans, battle-ready;

NEW INTERNATIONAL VERSION

37and from east of the Jordan, men of Reuben, Gad and the half-tribe of Manasseh, armed with every type of weapon—120,000.

38All these were fighting men who volunteered to serve in the ranks. They came to Hebron fully determined to make David king over all Israel. All the rest of the Israelites were also of one mind to make David king. 39The men spent three days there with David, eating and drinking, for their families had supplied provisions for them. 40Also, their neighbors from as far away as Issachar, Zebulun and Naphtali came bringing food on donkeys, camels, mules and oxen. There were plentiful supplies of flour, fig cakes, raisin cakes, wine, oil, cattle and sheep, for there was joy in Israel.

BRINGING BACK THE ARK

13 David conferred with each of his officers, the commanders of thousands and commanders of hundreds. 2He then said to the whole assembly of Israel, "If it seems good to you and if it is the will of the LORD our God, let us send word far and wide to the rest of our brothers throughout the territories of Israel, and also to the priests and Levites who are with them in their towns and pasturelands, to come and join us. 3Let us bring the ark of our God back to us, for we did not inquire of*a* it*b* during the reign of Saul." 4The whole assembly agreed to do this, because it seemed right to all the people.

5So David assembled all the Israelites, from the Shihor River in Egypt to Lebo*c* Hamath, to bring the ark of God from Kiriath Jearim. 6David and all the Israelites with him went to Baalah of Judah (Kiriath Jearim) to bring up from there the ark of God the LORD, who is enthroned between the cherubim—the ark that is called by the Name.

7They moved the ark of God from Abinadab's house on a new cart, with Uzzah and Ahio guiding it. 8David and all the Israelites were celebrating with all their might before God, with songs and with harps, lyres, tambourines, cymbals and trumpets.

9When they came to the threshing floor of Kidon, Uzzah reached out his hand to steady the ark, because the oxen stumbled. 10The LORD's anger burned against Uzzah, and he struck him down because he had put his hand on the ark. So he died there before God.

11Then David was angry because the LORD's wrath had broken out against Uzzah, and to this day that place is called Perez Uzzah.*d*

THE MESSAGE

and from East of Jordan, men from Reuben, Gad, and the half-tribe of Manasseh, heavily armed, 120,000.

12.38-40 All these soldiers came to David at Hebron, ready to fight if necessary; they were both united and determined to make David king over all Israel. And everyone else in Israel was of the same mind—"Make David king!" They were with David for three days of feasting celebration, with food and drink supplied by their families. Neighbors ranging from as far north as Issachar, Zebulun, and Naphtali arrived with donkeys, camels, mules, and oxen loaded down with food for the party: flour, fig cakes, raisin cakes, wine, oil, cattle, and sheep—joy in Israel!

DAVID GOES TO GET THE CHEST OF GOD

13.1-14 **13** David consulted with all of his leaders, the commanders of thousands and of hundreds. Then David addressed the entire assembly of Israel, "If it seems right to you, and it is GOD's will, let's invite all our relatives wherever they are throughout Israel, along with their relatives, including their priests and Levites from their cities and surrounding pastures, to join us. And let's bring the Chest of our God back—the Chest that was out of sight, out of mind during the days of Saul." The entire assembly of Israel agreed—everybody agreed that it was the right thing to do. So David gathered all Israel together, from Egypt's Pond of Horus in the southwest to the Pass of Hamath in the northeast, to go and get the Chest of God from Kiriath Jearim. Then David and all Israel went to Baalah (Kiriath Jearim) in Judah to bring back the Chest of God, the "Cherubim-Throne-of-GOD," where GOD's Name is invoked. They moved the Chest of God on a brand-new cart from the house of Abinadab with Uzzah and Ahio in charge. In procession with the Chest of God, David and all Israel worshiped exuberantly in song and dance, with a marching band of all kinds of instruments. When they were at the threshing floor of Kidon, the oxen stumbled and Uzzah grabbed the Chest to keep it from falling off. GOD erupted in anger against Uzzah and killed him because he grabbed the Chest. He died on the spot—in the presence of God. David lost his temper, angry because GOD exploded against Uzzah; the place is still called Perez Uz-

---

a 3 Or *we neglected*   *b* 3 Or *him*   *c* 5 Or *to the entrance to*   *d* 11 *Perez Uzzah* means *outbreak against Uzzah.*

NEW INTERNATIONAL VERSION

¹²David was afraid of God that day and asked, "How can I ever bring the ark of God to me?" ¹³He did not take the ark to be with him in the City of David. Instead, he took it aside to the house of Obed-Edom the Gittite. ¹⁴The ark of God remained with the family of Obed-Edom in his house for three months, and the LORD blessed his household and everything he had.

DAVID'S HOUSE AND FAMILY

14 Now Hiram king of Tyre sent messengers to David, along with cedar logs, stonemasons and carpenters to build a palace for him. ²And David knew that the LORD had established him as king over Israel and that his kingdom had been highly exalted for the sake of his people Israel.

³In Jerusalem David took more wives and became the father of more sons and daughters. ⁴These are the names of the children born to him there: Shammua, Shobab, Nathan, Solomon, ⁵Ibhar, Elishua, Elpelet, ⁶Nogah, Nepheg, Japhia, ⁷Elishama, Beeliada ᵃ and Eliphelet.

DAVID DEFEATS THE PHILISTINES

⁸When the Philistines heard that David had been anointed king over all Israel, they went up in full force to search for him, but David heard about it and went out to meet them. ⁹Now the Philistines had come and raided the Valley of Rephaim; ¹⁰so David inquired of God: "Shall I go and attack the Philistines? Will you hand them over to me?"

The LORD answered him, "Go, I will hand them over to you."

¹¹So David and his men went up to Baal Perazim, and there he defeated them. He said, "As waters break out, God has broken out against my enemies by my hand." So that place was called Baal Perazim. ᵇ ¹²The Philistines had abandoned their gods there, and David gave orders to burn them in the fire.

¹³Once more the Philistines raided the valley; ¹⁴so David inquired of God again, and God answered him, "Do not go straight up, but circle around them and attack them in front of the balsam trees. ¹⁵As soon as you hear the sound of marching in the tops of the balsam trees, move out to battle, because that will mean God has gone out in front of you to strike the Philistine army." ¹⁶So David did as God commanded him, and they struck down the Philistine army, all the way from Gibeon to Gezer.

¹⁷So David's fame spread throughout every land, and the LORD made all the nations fear him.

ᵃ 7 A variant of *Eliada*   ᵇ 11 *Baal Perazim* means *the lord who breaks out.*

THE MESSAGE

zah (Exploded Uzzah). David was terrified of God that day; he said, "How can I possibly continue this parade with the Chest of God?" So David called off the parade of the Chest to the City of David; instead he stored it in the house of Obed-Edom the Gittite. The Chest of God was in storage in the house of Obed-Edom for three months. GOD blessed the family of Obed-Edom and everything around him.

DAVID BUILDS

14.1-7 **14** King Hiram of Tyre sent an envoy to David, along with cedar lumber, masons, and carpenters to build him a royal palace. Then David knew for sure that GOD had confirmed him as king over Israel, because of the rising reputation that GOD was giving his kingdom for the benefit of his people Israel. David married more wives and had more children in Jerusalem. His children born in Jerusalem were Shammua, Shobab, Nathan, Solomon, Ibhar, Elishua, Elpelet, Nogah, Nepheg, Japhia, Elishama, Beeliada, and Eliphelet.

✢

14.8-9 The minute the Philistines heard that David had been made king over a united Israel, they went out in force to capture David. When David got the report, he marched out to confront them. On their way, the Philistines stopped off to plunder the Valley of Rephaim.

14.10 David prayed to God: "Is this the right time to attack the Philistines? Will you give me the victory?"

GOD answered, "Attack; I'll give you the victory."

14.11-12 David attacked at Baal Perazim and slaughtered them. David said, "God exploded my enemies, as water explodes from a burst pipe." That's how the place got its name, Baal Perazim (Baal-Explosion). The Philistines left their gods behind and David ordered that they be burned up.

14.13-15 And then the Philistines were back at it again, plundering in the valley. David again prayed to God. God answered, "This time don't attack head-on; circle around and come at them out of the balsam grove. When you hear a sound like shuffling feet in the tops of the balsams, attack; God will be two steps ahead of you, slaughtering the Philistines."

14.16 David did exactly as God commanded, slaughtering Philistines all the way from Gibeon to Gezer.

14.17 David was soon famous all over the place, far and near; and GOD put the fear of God into the godless nations.

NEW INTERNATIONAL VERSION

THE ARK BROUGHT TO JERUSALEM

15 After David had constructed buildings for himself in the City of David, he prepared a place for the ark of God and pitched a tent for it. ²Then David said, "No one but the Levites may carry the ark of God, because the LORD chose them to carry the ark of the LORD and to minister before him forever."

³David assembled all Israel in Jerusalem to bring up the ark of the LORD to the place he had prepared for it. ⁴He called together the descendants of Aaron and the Levites:

⁵From the descendants of Kohath,
  Uriel the leader and 120 relatives;
⁶from the descendants of Merari,
  Asaiah the leader and 220 relatives;
⁷from the descendants of Gershon, ᵃ
  Joel the leader and 130 relatives;
⁸from the descendants of Elizaphan,
  Shemaiah the leader and 200 relatives;
⁹from the descendants of Hebron,
  Eliel the leader and 80 relatives;
¹⁰from the descendants of Uzziel,
  Amminadab the leader and 112 relatives.

¹¹Then David summoned Zadok and Abiathar the priests, and Uriel, Asaiah, Joel, Shemaiah, Eliel and Amminadab the Levites. ¹²He said to them, "You are the heads of the Levitical families; you and your fellow Levites are to consecrate yourselves and bring up the ark of the LORD, the God of Israel, to the place I have prepared for it. ¹³It was because you, the Levites, did not bring it up the first time that the LORD our God broke out in anger against us. We did not inquire of him about how to do it in the prescribed way." ¹⁴So the priests and Levites consecrated themselves in order to bring up the ark of the LORD, the God of Israel. ¹⁵And the Levites carried the ark of God with the poles on their shoulders, as Moses had commanded in accordance with the word of the LORD.

¹⁶David told the leaders of the Levites to appoint their brothers as singers to sing joyful songs, accompanied by musical instruments: lyres, harps and cymbals.

¹⁷So the Levites appointed Heman son of Joel; from his brothers, Asaph son of Berekiah; and from their brothers the Merarites, Ethan son of Kushaiah; ¹⁸and with them their brothers next in rank: Zechariah, ᵇ Jaaziel, Shemiramoth, Jehiel, Unni, Eliab, Benaiah, Maaseiah, Mattithiah, Eliphelehu, Mikneiah, Obed-Edom and Jeiel, ᶜ the gatekeepers.

ᵃ *7 Hebrew Gershom, a variant of Gershon*   ᵇ *18 Three Hebrew manuscripts and most Septuagint manuscripts (see also verse 20 and 1 Chron. 16:5); most Hebrew manuscripts Zechariah son and or Zechariah, Ben and*   ᶜ *18 Hebrew; Septuagint (see also verse 21) Jeiel and Azaziah*

THE MESSAGE

DAVID WORSHIPS

15.1-2 **15** After David built houses for himself in the City of David, he cleared a place for the Chest and pitched a tent for it. Then David gave orders: "No one carries the Chest of God except the Levites; GOD designated them and them only to carry the Chest of GOD and be available full time for service in the work of worship."

15.3-10 David then called everyone in Israel to assemble in Jerusalem to bring up the Chest of GOD to its specially prepared place. David also called in the family of Aaron and the Levites. From the family of Kohath, Uriel the head with 120 relatives; from the family of Merari, Asaiah the head with 220 relatives; from the family of Gershon, Joel the head with 130 relatives; from the family of Elizaphan, Shemaiah the head with 200 relatives; from the family of Hebron, Eliel the head with 80 relatives; from the family of Uzziel, Amminadab the head with 112 relatives.

15.11-13 Then David called in Zadok and Abiathar the priests, and Uriel, Asaiah, Joel, Shemaiah, Eliel, and Amminadab the Levites. He said, "You are responsible for the Levitical families; now consecrate yourselves, both you and your relatives, and bring up the Chest of the GOD of Israel to the place I have set aside for it. The first time we did this, you Levites did not carry it properly, and GOD exploded in anger at us because we didn't make proper preparation and follow instructions."

15.14-15 So the priests and Levites consecrated themselves to bring up the Chest of the GOD of Israel. The Levites carried the Chest of God exactly as Moses, instructed by GOD, commanded—carried it with poles on their shoulders, careful not to touch it with their hands.

15.16 David ordered the heads of the Levites to assign their relatives to sing in the choir, accompanied by a well-equipped marching band, and fill the air with joyful sound.

15.17-18 The Levites assigned Heman son of Joel, and from his family, Asaph son of Berekiah, then Ethan son of Kushaiah from the family of Merari, and after them in the second rank their brothers Zechariah, Jaaziel, Shemiramoth, Jehiel, Unni, Eliab, Benaiah, Maaseiah, Mattithiah, Eliphelehu, Mikneiah, Obed-Edom, and Jeiel as security guards.

NEW INTERNATIONAL VERSION

¹⁹The musicians Heman, Asaph and Ethan were to sound the bronze cymbals; ²⁰Zechariah, Aziel, Shemiramoth, Jehiel, Unni, Eliab, Maaseiah and Benaiah were to play the lyres according to *alamoth*,ᵃ ²¹and Mattithiah, Eliphelehu, Mikneiah, Obed-Edom, Jeiel and Azaziah were to play the harps, directing according to *sheminith*.ᵃ ²²Kenaniah the head Levite was in charge of the singing; that was his responsibility because he was skillful at it.

²³Berekiah and Elkanah were to be doorkeepers for the ark. ²⁴Shebaniah, Joshaphat, Nethanel, Amasai, Zechariah, Benaiah and Eliezer the priests were to blow trumpets before the ark of God. Obed-Edom and Jehiah were also to be doorkeepers for the ark.

²⁵So David and the elders of Israel and the commanders of units of a thousand went to bring up the ark of the covenant of the LORD from the house of Obed-Edom, with rejoicing. ²⁶Because God had helped the Levites who were carrying the ark of the covenant of the LORD, seven bulls and seven rams were sacrificed. ²⁷Now David was clothed in a robe of fine linen, as were all the Levites who were carrying the ark, and as were the singers, and Kenaniah, who was in charge of the singing of the choirs. David also wore a linen ephod. ²⁸So all Israel brought up the ark of the covenant of the LORD with shouts, with the sounding of rams' horns and trumpets, and of cymbals, and the playing of lyres and harps.

²⁹As the ark of the covenant of the LORD was entering the City of David, Michal daughter of Saul watched from a window. And when she saw King David dancing and celebrating, she despised him in her heart.

16 They brought the ark of God and set it inside the tent that David had pitched for it, and they presented burnt offerings and fellowship offeringsᵇ before God. ²After David had finished sacrificing the burnt offerings and fellowship offerings, he blessed the people in the name of the LORD. ³Then he gave a loaf of bread, a cake of dates and a cake of raisins to each Israelite man and woman.

⁴He appointed some of the Levites to minister before the ark of the LORD, to make petition, to give thanks, and to praise the LORD, the God of Israel: ⁵Asaph was the chief, Zechariah second, then Jeiel, Shemiramoth, Jehiel, Mattithiah, Eliab, Benaiah, Obed-Edom and Jeiel. They were to play the lyres and harps, Asaph was to sound

ᵃ 20, 21 Probably a musical term   ᵇ 1 Traditionally *peace offerings*; also in verse 2

THE MESSAGE

15.19-22 The members of the choir and marching band were: Heman, Asaph, and Ethan with bronze cymbals; Zechariah, Aziel, Shemiramoth, Jehiel, Unni, Eliab, Maaseiah, and Benaiah with lyres carrying the melody; Mattithiah, Eliphelehu, Mikneiah, Obed-Edom, Jeiel, and Azaziah with harps filling in the harmony; Kenaniah, the Levite in charge of music, a very gifted musician, was music director.

15.23-24 Berekiah and Elkanah were porters for the Chest. The priests Shebaniah, Joshaphat, Nethanel, Amasai, Zechariah, Benaiah, and Eliezer blew the trumpets before the Chest of God. Obed-Edom and Jehiah were also porters for the Chest.

15.25-28 Now they were ready. David, the elders of Israel, and the commanders of thousands started out to get the Chest of the Covenant of GOD and bring it up from the house of Obed-Edom. And they went rejoicing. Because God helped the Levites, strengthening them as they carried the Chest of the Covenant of GOD, they paused to worship by sacrificing seven bulls and seven rams. They were all dressed in elegant linen—David, the Levites carrying the Chest, the choir and band, and Kenaniah who was directing the music. David also wore a linen prayer shawl (called an ephod). On they came, all Israel on parade bringing up the Chest of the Covenant of GOD, shouting and cheering, playing every kind of brass and percussion and string instrument.

15.29 When the Chest of the Covenant of GOD entered the City of David, Michal, Saul's daughter, was watching from a window. When she saw King David dancing ecstatically she was filled with contempt.

✠

16.1-3 **16** They brought the Chest of God and placed it right in the center of the tent that David had pitched for it; then they worshiped by presenting burnt offerings and peace offerings to God. When David had completed the offerings of worship, he blessed the people in the name of GOD. Then he passed around to every one there, men and women alike, a loaf of bread, a slice of barbecue, and a raisin cake.

16.4-6 Then David assigned some of the Levites to the Chest of GOD to lead worship—to intercede, give thanks, and praise the GOD of Israel. Asaph was in charge; under him were Zechariah, Jeiel, Shemiramoth, Jehiel, Mattithiah, Eliab, Benaiah, Obed-Edom, and Jeiel, who played the musical instruments. Asaph was on percus-

NEW INTERNATIONAL VERSION

the cymbals, [6]and Benaiah and Jahaziel the priests were to blow the trumpets regularly before the ark of the covenant of God.

DAVID'S PSALM OF THANKS

[7]That day David first committed to Asaph and his associates this psalm of thanks to the LORD:

[8]Give thanks to the LORD, call on his name;
　　make known among the nations what he
　　　has done.
[9]Sing to him, sing praise to him;
　　tell of all his wonderful acts.
[10]Glory in his holy name;
　　let the hearts of those who seek the LORD
　　　rejoice.
[11]Look to the LORD and his strength;
　　seek his face always.
[12]Remember the wonders he has done,
　　his miracles, and the judgments he
　　　pronounced,
[13]O descendants of Israel his servant,
　　O sons of Jacob, his chosen ones.

[14]He is the LORD our God;
　　his judgments are in all the earth.
[15]He remembers[a] his covenant forever,
　　the word he commanded, for a thousand
　　　generations,
[16]the covenant he made with Abraham,
　　the oath he swore to Isaac.
[17]He confirmed it to Jacob as a decree,
　　to Israel as an everlasting covenant:
[18]"To you I will give the land of Canaan
　　as the portion you will inherit."

[19]When they were but few in number,
　　few indeed, and strangers in it,
[20]they[b] wandered from nation to nation,
　　from one kingdom to another.
[21]He allowed no man to oppress them;
　　for their sake he rebuked kings:
[22]"Do not touch my anointed ones;
　　do my prophets no harm."

[23]Sing to the LORD, all the earth;
　　proclaim his salvation day after day.
[24]Declare his glory among the nations,
　　his marvelous deeds among all peoples.
[25]For great is the LORD and most worthy of
　　　praise;
　　he is to be feared above all gods.
[26]For all the gods of the nations are idols,
　　but the LORD made the heavens.

[a] 15 Some Septuagint manuscripts (see also Psalm 105:8); Hebrew *Remember*　[b] 18-20 One Hebrew manuscript, Septuagint and Vulgate (see also Psalm 105:12); most Hebrew manuscripts *inherit*, / [19]*though you are but few in number, / few indeed, and strangers in it." /* [20]*They*

THE MESSAGE

sion. The priests Benaiah and Jahaziel blew the trumpets before the Chest of the Covenant of God at set times through the day.

16.7　That was the day that David inaugurated regular worship of praise to GOD, led by Asaph and his company.

16.8-19　Thank GOD! Call out his Name!
　　Tell the whole world who he is and what
　　　he's done!
Sing to him! Play songs for him!
　　Broadcast all his wonders!
Revel in his holy Name,
　　GOD-seekers, be jubilant!
Study GOD and his strength,
　　seek his presence day and night;
Remember all the wonders he performed,
　　the miracles and judgments that came
　　　out of his mouth.
Seed of Israel his servant!
　　Children of Jacob, his first choice!
He is GOD, *our* God;
　　wherever you go you come on his
　　　judgments and decisions.
He keeps his commitments across
　　　thousands
　　of generations, the covenant he
　　　commanded,
The same one he made with Abraham,
　　the very one he swore to Isaac;
He posted it in big block letters to Jacob,
　　this eternal covenant with Israel:
"I give you the land of Canaan,
　　this is your inheritance;
Even though you're not much to look at,
　　a few straggling strangers."

16.20-22　They wandered from country to country,
　　camped out in one kingdom after
　　　another;
But he didn't let anyone push them around,
　　he stood up for them against bully-
　　　kings:
"Don't you dare touch my anointed ones,
　　don't lay a hand on my prophets."

16.23-27　Sing to GOD, everyone and everything!
　　Get out his salvation news every day!
Publish his glory among the godless
　　　nations,
　　his wonders to all races and religions.
And why? Because GOD is great—well
　　　worth praising!
　　No god or goddess comes close in honor.
All the popular gods are stuff and
　　　nonsense,
　　but GOD made the cosmos!

NEW INTERNATIONAL VERSION

²⁷Splendor and majesty are before him;
　　strength and joy in his dwelling place.
²⁸Ascribe to the LORD, O families of nations,
　　ascribe to the LORD glory and strength,
²⁹　ascribe to the LORD the glory due his
　　　name.
　Bring an offering and come before him;
　　worship the LORD in the splendor of his*
　　holiness.
³⁰Tremble before him, all the earth!
　　The world is firmly established; it cannot
　　be moved.
³¹Let the heavens rejoice, let the earth be glad;
　　let them say among the nations, "The
　　LORD reigns!"
³²Let the sea resound, and all that is in it;
　　let the fields be jubilant, and everything in
　　them!
³³Then the trees of the forest will sing,
　　they will sing for joy before the LORD,
　　for he comes to judge the earth.

³⁴Give thanks to the LORD, for he is good;
　　his love endures forever.
³⁵Cry out, "Save us, O God our Savior;
　　gather us and deliver us from the nations,
　that we may give thanks to your holy name,
　　that we may glory in your praise."
³⁶Praise be to the LORD, the God of Israel,
　　from everlasting to everlasting.

Then all the people said "Amen" and "Praise the
LORD."

³⁷David left Asaph and his associates before
the ark of the covenant of the LORD to minister
there regularly, according to each day's requirements. ³⁸He also left Obed-Edom and his sixty-
eight associates to minister with them. Obed-
Edom son of Jeduthun, and also Hosah, were
gatekeepers.

³⁹David left Zadok the priest and his fellow
priests before the tabernacle of the LORD at the
high place in Gibeon ⁴⁰to present burnt offerings to the LORD on the altar of burnt offering
regularly, morning and evening, in accordance
with everything written in the Law of the LORD,
which he had given Israel. ⁴¹With them were Heman and Jeduthun and the rest of those chosen
and designated by name to give thanks to the
LORD, "for his love endures forever." ⁴²Heman

a 29 Or LORD *with the splendor of*

THE MESSAGE

Splendor and majesty flow out of him,
　　strength and joy fill his place.

Shout Bravo! to GOD, families of the
　　peoples,
　　in awe of the Glory, in awe of the
　　Strength: Bravo!
16.28-29　Shout Bravo! to his famous Name,
　　lift high an offering and enter his
　　presence!
Stand resplendent in his robes of holiness!

16.30-33　God is serious business, take him seriously;
　　he's put the earth in place and it's not
　　moving.
So let heaven rejoice, let earth be jubilant,
　　and pass the word among the nations,
　　"GOD reigns!"
Let Ocean, all teeming with life, bellow,
　　let Field and all its creatures shake the
　　rafters;
Then the trees in the forest will add their
　　applause
　　to all who are pleased and present before
　　GOD
　　—he's on his way to set things right!

16.34-36　Give thanks to GOD—he is good
　　and his love never quits.
Say, "Save us, Savior God,
　　round us up and get us out of these
　　godless places,
So we can give thanks to your holy Name,
　　and bask in your life of praise."
Blessed be GOD, the God of Israel,
　　from everlasting to everlasting.

Then everybody said, "Yes! Amen!" and
"Praise GOD!"

✝

16.37-42　David left Asaph and his coworkers with the
Chest of the Covenant of GOD and in charge of
the work of worship; they were responsible for
the needs of worship around the clock. He also
assigned Obed-Edom and his sixty-eight relatives to help them. Obed-Edom son of Jeduthun and Hosah were in charge of the security
guards. The priest Zadok and his family of
priests were assigned to the Tent of GOD at the
sacred mound at Gibeon to make sure that the
services of morning and evening worship were
conducted daily, complete with Whole-Burnt-
Offerings offered on the Altar of Burnt Offering, as ordered in the Law of GOD, which was
the norm for Israel. With them were Heman,
Jeduthun, and others specifically named, with
the job description: "Give thanks to GOD, for
his love never quits!" Heman and Jeduthun

NEW INTERNATIONAL VERSION

and Jeduthun were responsible for the sounding of the trumpets and cymbals and for the playing of the other instruments for sacred song. The sons of Jeduthun were stationed at the gate.

⁴³Then all the people left, each for his own home, and David returned home to bless his family.

GOD'S PROMISE TO DAVID

17 After David was settled in his palace, he said to Nathan the prophet, "Here I am, living in a palace of cedar, while the ark of the covenant of the LORD is under a tent."

²Nathan replied to David, "Whatever you have in mind, do it, for God is with you."

³That night the word of God came to Nathan, saying:

⁴"Go and tell my servant David, 'This is what the LORD says: You are not the one to build me a house to dwell in. ⁵I have not dwelt in a house from the day I brought Israel up out of Egypt to this day. I have moved from one tent site to another, from one dwelling place to another. ⁶Wherever I have moved with all the Israelites, did I ever say to any of their leaders*ᵃ* whom I commanded to shepherd my people, "Why have you not built me a house of cedar?" '

⁷"Now then, tell my servant David, 'This is what the LORD Almighty says: I took you from the pasture and from following the flock, to be ruler over my people Israel. ⁸I have been with you wherever you have gone, and I have cut off all your enemies from before you. Now I will make your name like the names of the greatest men of the earth. ⁹And I will provide a place for my people Israel and will plant them so that they can have a home of their own and no longer be disturbed. Wicked people will not oppress them anymore, as they did at the beginning ¹⁰and have done ever since the time I appointed leaders over my people Israel. I will also subdue all your enemies.

" 'I declare to you that the LORD will build a house for you: ¹¹When your days are over and you go to be with your fathers, I will raise up your offspring to succeed you, one of your own sons, and I will establish his kingdom. ¹²He is the one who will build a house for me, and I will establish his throne forever. ¹³I will be his father, and he will be my son. I will never take my love away from him, as I took it

THE MESSAGE

were also well equipped with trumpets, cymbals, and other instruments for accompanying sacred songs. The sons of Jeduthun formed the security guard.

16.43 Arrangements completed, the people all left for home. And David went home to bless his family.

DAVID SUBMITS AND PRAYS

17.1 **17** After the king had made himself at home, he said to Nathan the prophet, "Look at this: Here I am comfortable in a luxurious palace of cedar and the Chest of the Covenant of GOD sits under a tent."

17.2 Nathan told David, "Whatever is on your heart, go and do it; God is with you."

17.3-6 But that night, the word of God came to Nathan, saying, "Go and tell my servant David, This is GOD's word on the matter: You will not build me a 'house' to live in. Why, I haven't lived in a 'house' from the time I brought up the children of Israel from Egypt till now; I've gone from one tent and makeshift shelter to another. In all my travels with all Israel, did I ever say to any of the leaders I commanded to shepherd Israel, 'Why haven't you built me a house of cedar?'

17.7-10 "So here is what you are to tell my servant David: The GOD-of-the-Angel-Armies has this word for you: I took you from the pasture, tagging after sheep, and made you prince over my people Israel. I was with you everywhere you went and mowed your enemies down before you; and now I'm about to make you famous, ranked with the great names on earth. I'm going to set aside a place for my people Israel and plant them there so they'll have their own home and not be knocked around anymore; nor will evil nations afflict them as they always have, even during the days I set judges over my people Israel. And finally, I'm going to conquer all your enemies.

17.10-14 "And now I'm telling you this: GOD himself will build *you* a house! When your life is complete and you're buried with your ancestors, then I'll raise up your child to succeed you, a child from your own body, and I'll firmly establish his rule. *He* will build a house to honor me, and I will guarantee his kingdom's rule forever. I'll be a father to him, and he'll be a son to me. I will never remove my gracious love from

---

ᵃ 6 Traditionally *judges*; also in verse 10

NEW INTERNATIONAL VERSION

away from your predecessor. ¹⁴I will set him over my house and my kingdom forever; his throne will be established forever.' "

¹⁵Nathan reported to David all the words of this entire revelation.

DAVID'S PRAYER

¹⁶Then King David went in and sat before the LORD, and he said:

"Who am I, O LORD God, and what is my family, that you have brought me this far? ¹⁷And as if this were not enough in your sight, O God, you have spoken about the future of the house of your servant. You have looked on me as though I were the most exalted of men, O LORD God.

¹⁸"What more can David say to you for honoring your servant? For you know your servant, ¹⁹O LORD. For the sake of your servant and according to your will, you have done this great thing and made known all these great promises.

²⁰"There is no one like you, O LORD, and there is no God but you, as we have heard with our own ears. ²¹And who is like your people Israel—the one nation on earth whose God went out to redeem a people for himself, and to make a name for yourself, and to perform great and awesome wonders by driving out nations from before your people, whom you redeemed from Egypt? ²²You made your people Israel your very own forever, and you, O LORD, have become their God.

²³"And now, LORD, let the promise you have made concerning your servant and his house be established forever. Do as you promised, ²⁴so that it will be established and that your name will be great forever. Then men will say, 'The LORD Almighty, the God over Israel, is Israel's God!' And the house of your servant David will be established before you.

²⁵"You, my God, have revealed to your servant that you will build a house for him. So your servant has found courage to pray to you. ²⁶O LORD, you are God! You have promised these good things to your servant. ²⁷Now you have been pleased to bless the house of your servant, that it may continue forever in your sight; for you, O LORD, have blessed it, and it will be blessed forever."

THE MESSAGE

him as I did from the one who preceded you. I will set him over my house and my kingdom forever; his throne will always be there, rock solid."

17.15 Nathan gave David a complete and accurate report of everything he heard and saw in the vision.

17.16-27 King David went in, took his place before GOD, and prayed:

Who am I, my Master GOD, and what is my family, that you have brought me to this place in life? But that's nothing compared to what's coming, for you've also spoken of my family far into the future, given me a glimpse into tomorrow and looked on me, Master GOD, as a Somebody. What's left for David to say to this—to your honoring your servant, even though you know me, just as I am? O GOD, out of the goodness of your heart, you've taken your servant to do this great thing and put your great work on display. There's none like you, GOD, no *God* but you, nothing to compare with what we've heard with our own ears. And who is like your people, like Israel, a nation unique on earth, whom God set out to redeem as his own people (and became most famous for it), performing great and fearsome acts, throwing out nations and their gods left and right as you saved your people from Egypt? You established for yourself a people—your very own Israel!—your people forever. And you, GOD, became their God.

So now, great GOD, this word that you have spoken to me and my family, guarantee it forever! Do exactly what you've promised! Then your reputation will be confirmed and flourish always as people exclaim, "The GOD-of-the-Angel-Armies, the God over Israel, is Israel's God!" And the house of your servant David will remain rock solid under your watchful presence. You, my God, have told me plainly, "I will build you a house." That's how I was able to find the courage to pray this prayer to you. GOD, being the God you are, you have spoken all these wonderful words to me. As if that weren't enough, you've blessed my family so that it will continue in your presence always. Because you have blessed it, GOD, it's *really* blessed—blessed for good!

NEW INTERNATIONAL VERSION

DAVID'S VICTORIES

18 In the course of time, David defeated the Philistines and subdued them, and he took Gath and its surrounding villages from the control of the Philistines.

²David also defeated the Moabites, and they became subject to him and brought tribute.

³Moreover, David fought Hadadezer king of Zobah, as far as Hamath, when he went to establish his control along the Euphrates River. ⁴David captured a thousand of his chariots, seven thousand charioteers and twenty thousand foot soldiers. He hamstrung all but a hundred of the chariot horses.

⁵When the Arameans of Damascus came to help Hadadezer king of Zobah, David struck down twenty-two thousand of them. ⁶He put garrisons in the Aramean kingdom of Damascus, and the Arameans became subject to him and brought tribute. The LORD gave David victory everywhere he went.

⁷David took the gold shields carried by the officers of Hadadezer and brought them to Jerusalem. ⁸From Tebah*ᵃ* and Cun, towns that belonged to Hadadezer, David took a great quantity of bronze, which Solomon used to make the bronze Sea, the pillars and various bronze articles.

⁹When Tou king of Hamath heard that David had defeated the entire army of Hadadezer king of Zobah, ¹⁰he sent his son Hadoram to King David to greet him and congratulate him on his victory in battle over Hadadezer, who had been at war with Tou. Hadoram brought all kinds of articles of gold and silver and bronze.

¹¹King David dedicated these articles to the LORD, as he had done with the silver and gold he had taken from all these nations: Edom and Moab, the Ammonites and the Philistines, and Amalek.

¹²Abishai son of Zeruiah struck down eighteen thousand Edomites in the Valley of Salt. ¹³He put garrisons in Edom, and all the Edomites became subject to David. The LORD gave David victory everywhere he went.

DAVID'S OFFICIALS

¹⁴David reigned over all Israel, doing what was just and right for all his people. ¹⁵Joab son of Zeruiah was over the army; Jehoshaphat son of Ahilud was recorder; ¹⁶Zadok son of Ahitub and Ahimelech*ᵇ* son of Abiathar were priests;

ᵃ 8 Hebrew *Tibhath*, a variant of *Tebah*   *ᵇ 16* Some Hebrew manuscripts, Vulgate and Syriac (see also 2 Samuel 8:17); most Hebrew manuscripts *Abimelech*

THE MESSAGE

DAVID FIGHTS

18.1 **18** In the days that followed, David struck hard at the Philistines, bringing them to their knees, captured Gath, and took control of the surrounding countryside.

18.2 He also fought and defeated Moab. The Moabites came under David's rule and paid regular tribute.

18.3-4 On his way to restore his sovereignty at the Euphrates River, David defeated Hadadezer king of Zobah (over toward Hamath). David captured a thousand chariots, 7,000 cavalry, and 20,000 infantry from him. He hamstrung all the chariot horses, but saved back a hundred.

18.5-6 When the Arameans from Damascus came to the aid of Hadadezer king of Zobah, David killed 22,000 of them. David set up a puppet government in Aram-Damascus. The Arameans became subjects of David and were forced to bring tribute. GOD gave victory to David wherever he marched.

18.7-8 David plundered the gold shields that belonged to the servants of Hadadezer and brought them to Jerusalem. He also looted Tebah and Cun, cities of Hadadezer, of a huge quantity of bronze that Solomon later used to make the Great Bronze Sea, the Pillars, and bronze equipment in The Temple.

18.9-11 Tou king of Hamath heard that David had struck down the entire army of Hadadezer king of Zobah. He sent his son Hadoram to King David to greet and congratulate him for fighting and defeating Hadadezer. Tou and Hadadezer were old enemies. Hadoram brought David various things made of silver, gold, and bronze. King David consecrated these things along with the silver and gold that he had plundered from other nations: Edom, Moab, the Ammonites, the Philistines, and Amalek.

18.12-13 Abishai son of Zeruiah fought and defeated the Edomites in the Valley of Salt—18,000 of them. He set up a puppet government in Edom and the Edomites became subjects under David.

GOD gave David victory wherever he marched.

18.14-17 Thus David ruled over all of Israel. He ruled well, fair and evenhanded in all his duties and relationships.

Joab son of Zeruiah was head of the army;

Jehoshaphat son of Ahilud was in charge of public records;

Zadok son of Ahitub and Abimelech son of Abiathar were priests;

NEW INTERNATIONAL VERSION

Shavsha was secretary; [17]Benaiah son of Jehoiada was over the Kerethites and Pelethites; and David's sons were chief officials at the king's side.

THE BATTLE AGAINST THE AMMONITES

19 In the course of time, Nahash king of the Ammonites died, and his son succeeded him as king. [2]David thought, "I will show kindness to Hanun son of Nahash, because his father showed kindness to me." So David sent a delegation to express his sympathy to Hanun concerning his father.

When David's men came to Hanun in the land of the Ammonites to express sympathy to him, [3]the Ammonite nobles said to Hanun, "Do you think David is honoring your father by sending men to you to express sympathy? Haven't his men come to you to explore and spy out the country and overthrow it?" [4]So Hanun seized David's men, shaved them, cut off their garments in the middle at the buttocks, and sent them away.

[5]When someone came and told David about the men, he sent messengers to meet them, for they were greatly humiliated. The king said, "Stay at Jericho till your beards have grown, and then come back."

[6]When the Ammonites realized that they had become a stench in David's nostrils, Hanun and the Ammonites sent a thousand talents[a] of silver to hire chariots and charioteers from Aram Naharaim,[b] Aram Maacah and Zobah. [7]They hired thirty-two thousand chariots and charioteers, as well as the king of Maacah with his troops, who came and camped near Medeba, while the Ammonites were mustered from their towns and moved out for battle.

[8]On hearing this, David sent Joab out with the entire army of fighting men. [9]The Ammonites came out and drew up in battle formation at the entrance to their city, while the kings who had come were by themselves in the open country.

[10]Joab saw that there were battle lines in front of him and behind him; so he selected some of the best troops in Israel and deployed them against the Arameans. [11]He put the rest of the men under the command of Abishai his brother, and they were deployed against the Ammonites. [12]Joab said, "If the Arameans are too strong for me, then you are to rescue me; but if the Ammonites are too strong for you, then I will rescue you. [13]Be strong and let us fight bravely for our

---

[a] 6 That is, about 37 tons (about 34 metric tons)
[b] 6 That is, Northwest Mesopotamia

THE MESSAGE

Shavsha was secretary;

Benaiah son of Jehoiada was over the special forces, the Kerethites and Pelethites;

And David's sons held high positions, close to the king.

☩

19.1-2 **19** Some time after this Nahash king of the Ammonites died and his son succeeded him as king. David said, "I'd like to show some kindness to Hanun son of Nahash—treat him as well and as kindly as his father treated me." So David sent condolences about his father's death.

19.2-3 But when David's servants arrived in Ammonite country and came to Hanun to bring condolences, the Ammonite leaders warned Hanun, "Do you for a minute suppose that David is honoring your father by sending you comforters? Don't you know that he's sent these men to snoop around the city and size it up so that he can capture it?"

19.4 So Hanun seized David's men, shaved them clean, cut off their robes half way up their buttocks, and sent them packing.

19.5 When this was all reported to David, he sent someone to meet them, for they were seriously humiliated. The king told them, "Stay in Jericho until your beards grow out; only then come back."

19.6-7 When it dawned on the Ammonites that as far as David was concerned, they stank to high heaven, they hired, at a cost of a thousand talents of silver (thirty-seven and a half tons!), chariots and horsemen from the Arameans of Naharaim, Maacah, and Zobah—32,000 chariots and drivers; plus the king of Maacah with his troops who came and set up camp at Medeba; the Ammonites, too, were mobilized from their cities and got ready for battle.

19.8 When David heard this, he dispatched Joab with his strongest fighters in full force.

19.9-13 The Ammonites marched out and spread out in battle formation at the city gate; the kings who had come as allies took up a position in the open fields. When Joab saw that he had two fronts to fight, before and behind, he took his pick of the best of Israel and deployed them to confront the Arameans. The rest of the army he put under the command of Abishai, his brother, and deployed them to deal with the Ammonites. Then he said, "If the Arameans are too much for me, you help me; and if the Ammonites prove too much for you, I'll come and help you. Courage! We'll fight might and main for our

NEW INTERNATIONAL VERSION

people and the cities of our God. The LORD will do what is good in his sight."

¹⁴Then Joab and the troops with him advanced to fight the Arameans, and they fled before him. ¹⁵When the Ammonites saw that the Arameans were fleeing, they too fled before his brother Abishai and went inside the city. So Joab went back to Jerusalem.

¹⁶After the Arameans saw that they had been routed by Israel, they sent messengers and had Arameans brought from beyond the River,ᵃ with Shophach the commander of Hadadezer's army leading them.

¹⁷When David was told of this, he gathered all Israel and crossed the Jordan; he advanced against them and formed his battle lines opposite them. David formed his lines to meet the Arameans in battle, and they fought against him. ¹⁸But they fled before Israel, and David killed seven thousand of their charioteers and forty thousand of their foot soldiers. He also killed Shophach the commander of their army.

¹⁹When the vassals of Hadadezer saw that they had been defeated by Israel, they made peace with David and became subject to him.

So the Arameans were not willing to help the Ammonites anymore.

THE CAPTURE OF RABBAH

20 In the spring, at the time when kings go off to war, Joab led out the armed forces. He laid waste the land of the Ammonites and went to Rabbah and besieged it, but David remained in Jerusalem. Joab attacked Rabbah and left it in ruins. ²David took the crown from the head of their kingᵇ—its weight was found to be a talentᶜ of gold, and it was set with precious stones—and it was placed on David's head. He took a great quantity of plunder from the city ³and brought out the people who were there, consigning them to labor with saws and with iron picks and axes. David did this to all the Ammonite towns. Then David and his entire army returned to Jerusalem.

WAR WITH THE PHILISTINES

⁴In the course of time, war broke out with the Philistines, at Gezer. At that time Sibbecai the Hushathite killed Sippai, one of the descendants of the Rephaites, and the Philistines were subjugated.

⁵In another battle with the Philistines, Elhanan son of Jair killed Lahmi the brother of Goliath the Gittite, who had a spear with a shaft like a weaver's rod.

THE MESSAGE

people and for the cities of our God. And GOD will do whatever he sees needs doing!"

19.14-15 But when Joab and his soldiers moved in to fight the Arameans, they ran off in full retreat. Then the Ammonites, seeing the Arameans run for dear life, took to their heels and ran from Abishai into the city.

So Joab withdrew from the Ammonites and returned to Jerusalem.

19.16 When the Arameans saw how badly they'd been beaten by Israel, they picked up the pieces and regrouped; they sent for the Arameans who were across the river; Shophach, commander of Hadadezer's army, led them.

19.17-19 When all this was reported to David, he mustered all Israel, crossed the Jordan, advanced, and prepared to fight. The Arameans went into battle formation, ready for David, and the fight was on. But the Arameans again scattered before Israel. David killed 7,000 chariot drivers and 40,000 infantry. He also killed Shophach, the army commander. When all the kings who were vassals of Hadadezer saw that they had been routed by Israel, they made peace with David and served him. The Arameans were afraid to help the Ammonites ever again.

✟

20.1-3 That spring, the time when kings usually go off to war, Joab led the army out and ravaged the Ammonites. He then set siege to Rabbah. David meanwhile was back in Jerusalem. Joab hit Rabbah hard and left it in ruins. David took the crown off the head of their king. Its weight was found to be a talent of gold and set with a precious stone. It was placed on David's head. He hauled great quantities of loot from the city and put the people to hard labor with saws and picks and axes. This is what he did to all the Ammonites. Then David and his army returned to Jerusalem.

20.4-8 Later war broke out with the Philistines at Gezer. That was the time Sibbecai the Hushathite killed Sippai of the clan of giants. The Philistines had to eat crow. In another war with the Philistines, Elhanan son of Jair killed Lahmi, the brother of Goliath the Gittite whose spear was like a ship's boom. And then there

---

ᵃ 16 That is, the Euphrates   ᵇ 2 Or of Milcom, that is, Molech   ᶜ 2 That is, about 75 pounds (about 34 kilograms)

| NEW INTERNATIONAL VERSION | THE MESSAGE |

NEW INTERNATIONAL VERSION

⁶In still another battle, which took place at Gath, there was a huge man with six fingers on each hand and six toes on each foot—twenty-four in all. He also was descended from Rapha. ⁷When he taunted Israel, Jonathan son of Shimea, David's brother, killed him.

⁸These were descendants of Rapha in Gath, and they fell at the hands of David and his men.

DAVID NUMBERS THE FIGHTING MEN

21 Satan rose up against Israel and incited David to take a census of Israel. ²So David said to Joab and the commanders of the troops, "Go and count the Israelites from Beersheba to Dan. Then report back to me so that I may know how many there are."

³But Joab replied, "May the LORD multiply his troops a hundred times over. My lord the king, are they not all my lord's subjects? Why does my lord want to do this? Why should he bring guilt on Israel?"

⁴The king's word, however, overruled Joab; so Joab left and went throughout Israel and then came back to Jerusalem. ⁵Joab reported the number of the fighting men to David: In all Israel there were one million one hundred thousand men who could handle a sword, including four hundred and seventy thousand in Judah.

⁶But Joab did not include Levi and Benjamin in the numbering, because the king's command was repulsive to him. ⁷This command was also evil in the sight of God; so he punished Israel.

⁸Then David said to God, "I have sinned greatly by doing this. Now, I beg you, take away the guilt of your servant. I have done a very foolish thing."

⁹The LORD said to Gad, David's seer, ¹⁰"Go and tell David, 'This is what the LORD says: I am giving you three options. Choose one of them for me to carry out against you.'"

¹¹So Gad went to David and said to him, "This is what the LORD says: 'Take your choice: ¹²three years of famine, three months of being swept awayᵃ before your enemies, with their swords overtaking you, or three days of the sword of the LORD—days of plague in the land, with the angel of the LORD ravaging every part of Israel.' Now then, decide how I should answer the one who sent me."

¹³David said to Gad, "I am in deep distress. Let me fall into the hands of the LORD, for his mercy is very great; but do not let me fall into the hands of men."

¹⁴So the LORD sent a plague on Israel, and seventy thousand men of Israel fell dead. ¹⁵And

ᵃ 12 Hebrew; Septuagint and Vulgate (see also 2 Samuel 24:13) of fleeing

THE MESSAGE

was the war at Gath that featured a hulking giant who had twenty-four fingers and toes, six on each hand and foot—yet another from the clan of giants. When he mocked Israel, Jonathan son of Shimea, David's brother, killed him. These came from the clan of giants and were killed by David and his men.

DAVID, SATAN, AND ARAUNAH

21.1-2 **21** Now Satan entered the scene and seduced David into taking a census of Israel. David gave orders to Joab and the army officers under him, "Canvass all the tribes of Israel, from Dan to Beersheba, and get a count of the population. I want to know the number."

21.3 Joab resisted: "May GOD multiply his people by hundreds! Don't they all belong to my master the king? But why on earth would you do a thing like this—why risk getting Israel into trouble with God?"

21.4-7 But David wouldn't take no for an answer, so Joab went off and did it—canvassed the country and then came back to Jerusalem and reported the results of the census: There were 1,100,000 fighting men; of that total, Judah accounted for 470,000. Joab, disgusted by the command—it, in fact, turned his stomach!—protested by leaving Levi and Benjamin out of the census-taking. And God, offended by the whole thing, punished Israel.

21.8 Then David prayed, "I have sinned badly in what I have just done, substituting statistics for trust; forgive my sin—I've been really stupid."

21.9-10 GOD answered by speaking to Gad, David's pastor: "Go and give David this message: 'GOD's word: You have your choice of three punishments; choose one and I'll do the rest.'"

21.11-12 Gad delivered the message to David: "Do you want three years of famine, three months of running from your enemies while they chase you down, or three days of the sword of GOD—an epidemic unleashed on the country by an angel of GOD? Think it over and make up your mind. What shall I tell the One who sent me?"

21.13 David told Gad, "They're all terrible! But I'd rather be punished by GOD whose mercy is great, than fall into human hands."

21.14-15 So GOD unleashed an epidemic in Israel—70,000 Israelites died. God then sent the angel

NEW INTERNATIONAL VERSION	THE MESSAGE

NEW INTERNATIONAL VERSION

God sent an angel to destroy Jerusalem. But as the angel was doing so, the LORD saw it and was grieved because of the calamity and said to the angel who was destroying the people, "Enough! Withdraw your hand." The angel of the LORD was then standing at the threshing floor of Araunah *a* the Jebusite.

¹⁶David looked up and saw the angel of the LORD standing between heaven and earth, with a drawn sword in his hand extended over Jerusalem. Then David and the elders, clothed in sackcloth, fell facedown.

¹⁷David said to God, "Was it not I who ordered the fighting men to be counted? I am the one who has sinned and done wrong. These are but sheep. What have they done? O LORD my God, let your hand fall upon me and my family, but do not let this plague remain on your people."

¹⁸Then the angel of the LORD ordered Gad to tell David to go up and build an altar to the LORD on the threshing floor of Araunah the Jebusite. ¹⁹So David went up in obedience to the word that Gad had spoken in the name of the LORD.

²⁰While Araunah was threshing wheat, he turned and saw the angel; his four sons who were with him hid themselves. ²¹Then David approached, and when Araunah looked and saw him, he left the threshing floor and bowed down before David with his face to the ground.

²²David said to him, "Let me have the site of your threshing floor so I can build an altar to the LORD, that the plague on the people may be stopped. Sell it to me at the full price."

²³Araunah said to David, "Take it! Let my lord the king do whatever pleases him. Look, I will give the oxen for the burnt offerings, the threshing sledges for the wood, and the wheat for the grain offering. I will give all this."

²⁴But King David replied to Araunah, "No, I insist on paying the full price. I will not take for the LORD what is yours, or sacrifice a burnt offering that costs me nothing."

²⁵So David paid Araunah six hundred shekels *b* of gold for the site. ²⁶David built an altar to the LORD there and sacrificed burnt offerings and fellowship offerings. *c* He called on the LORD, and the LORD answered him with fire from heaven on the altar of burnt offering.

²⁷Then the LORD spoke to the angel, and he put his sword back into its sheath. ²⁸At that time, when David saw that the LORD had answered him on the threshing floor of Araunah the Jebusite, he offered sacrifices there. ²⁹The

---

a 15 Hebrew *Ornan*, a variant of *Araunah*; also in verses 18-28   *b 25* That is, about 15 pounds (about 7 kilograms)
c 26 Traditionally *peace offerings*

THE MESSAGE

to Jerusalem but when he saw the destruction about to begin, he compassionately changed his mind and ordered the death angel, "Enough's enough! Pull back!"

21.15-16 The angel of GOD had just reached the threshing floor of Araunah the Jebusite. David looked up and saw the angel hovering between earth and sky, sword drawn and about to strike Jerusalem. David and the elders bowed in prayer and covered themselves with rough burlap.

21.17 David prayed, "Please! I'm the one who sinned; I'm the one at fault. But these sheep, what did they do wrong? Punish me, not them, me and my family; don't take it out on them."

21.18-19 The angel of GOD ordered Gad to tell David to go and build an altar to GOD on the threshing floor of Araunah the Jebusite. David did what Gad told him in obedience to GOD's command.

21.20-21 Meanwhile Araunah had quit threshing the wheat and was watching the angel; his four sons took cover and hid. David came up to Araunah. When Araunah saw David, he left the threshing floor and bowed deeply before David, honoring the king.

21.22 David said to Araunah, "Give me the site of the threshing floor so I can build an altar to GOD. Charge me the market price; we're going to put an end to this disaster."

21.23 "O master, my king," said Araunah, "just take it; do whatever you want with it! Look, here's an ox for the burnt offering and threshing paddles for the fuel and wheat for the meal offering—it's all yours!"

21.24-27 David replied to Araunah, "No. I'm *buying* it from you, and at the full market price. I'm not going to offer GOD sacrifices that are no sacrifice." So David bought the place from Araunah for 600 shekels of gold. He built an altar to GOD there and sacrificed Whole-Burnt-Offerings and Peace-Offerings. He called out to GOD and GOD answered by striking the altar of Whole-Burnt-Offering with lightning. Then GOD told the angel to put his sword back into its scabbard.

21.28 And that's the story of what happened when David saw that GOD answered him on the threshing floor of Araunah the Jebusite at the time he offered the sacrifice.

✠

NEW INTERNATIONAL VERSION

tabernacle of the LORD, which Moses had made in the desert, and the altar of burnt offering were at that time on the high place at Gibeon. ³⁰But David could not go before it to inquire of God, because he was afraid of the sword of the angel of the LORD.

22 Then David said, "The house of the LORD God is to be here, and also the altar of burnt offering for Israel."

PREPARATIONS FOR THE TEMPLE

²So David gave orders to assemble the aliens living in Israel, and from among them he appointed stonecutters to prepare dressed stone for building the house of God. ³He provided a large amount of iron to make nails for the doors of the gateways and for the fittings, and more bronze than could be weighed. ⁴He also provided more cedar logs than could be counted, for the Sidonians and Tyrians had brought large numbers of them to David.

⁵David said, "My son Solomon is young and inexperienced, and the house to be built for the LORD should be of great magnificence and fame and splendor in the sight of all the nations. Therefore I will make preparations for it." So David made extensive preparations before his death.

⁶Then he called for his son Solomon and charged him to build a house for the LORD, the God of Israel. ⁷David said to Solomon: "My son, I had it in my heart to build a house for the Name of the LORD my God. ⁸But this word of the LORD came to me: 'You have shed much blood and have fought many wars. You are not to build a house for my Name, because you have shed much blood on the earth in my sight. ⁹But you will have a son who will be a man of peace and rest, and I will give him rest from all his enemies on every side. His name will be Solomon,ᵃ and I will grant Israel peace and quiet during his reign. ¹⁰He is the one who will build a house for my Name. He will be my son, and I will be his father. And I will establish the throne of his kingdom over Israel forever.'

¹¹"Now, my son, the LORD be with you, and may you have success and build the house of the LORD your God, as he said you would. ¹²May the LORD give you discretion and understanding when he puts you in command over Israel, so

ᵃ *9 Solomon sounds like and may be derived from the Hebrew for peace.*

THE MESSAGE

²¹.²⁹⁻³⁰ At this time the Tabernacle that Moses had constructed in the desert, and with it the Altar of Burnt Offering, were set up at the worship center at Gibeon. But David, terrified by the angel's sword, wouldn't go there to pray to God anymore.

²².¹ So David declared, "From now on, *this* is the site for the worship of GOD; *this* is the place for Israel's Altar of Burnt Offering."

DAVID CHARGES SOLOMON TO BUILD THE TEMPLE

²².²⁻⁴ **22** David ordered all the resident aliens in the land to come together; he sent them to the stone quarries to cut dressed stone to build The Temple of God. He also stockpiled a huge quantity of iron for nails and bracings for the doors of the gates, more bronze than could be weighed, and cedar logs past counting (the Sidonians and Tyrians shipped in huge loads of cedar logs for David).

²².⁵⁻⁶ David was thinking, "My son Solomon is too young to plan ahead for this. But the sanctuary that is to be built for GOD has to be the greatest, the talk of all the nations; so I'll get the construction materials together." That's why David prepared this huge stockpile of building materials before he died. Then he called in Solomon his son and commanded him to build a sanctuary for the GOD of Israel.

²².⁷⁻¹⁰ David said to Solomon, "I wanted in the worst way to build a sanctuary to honor my GOD. But GOD prevented me, saying, 'You've killed too many people, fought too many wars. You are not the one to honor me by building a sanctuary—you've been responsible for too much killing, too much bloodshed. But you are going to have a son and he will be a quiet and peaceful man, and I will calm his enemies down on all sides. His very name will speak peace—that is, Solomon, which means Peace—and I'll give peace and rest under his rule. He will be the one to build a sanctuary in my honor. He'll be my royal adopted son and I'll be his father; and I'll make sure that the authority of his kingdom over Israel lasts forever.'

²².¹¹⁻¹⁶ "So now, son, GOD be with you. GOD-speed as you build the sanctuary for your GOD, the job God has given you. And may GOD also give you discernment and understanding when he puts you in charge of Israel so that you will

NEW INTERNATIONAL VERSION

that you may keep the law of the LORD your God. [13]Then you will have success if you are careful to observe the decrees and laws that the LORD gave Moses for Israel. Be strong and courageous. Do not be afraid or discouraged.

[14]"I have taken great pains to provide for the temple of the LORD a hundred thousand talents[a] of gold, a million talents[b] of silver, quantities of bronze and iron too great to be weighed, and wood and stone. And you may add to them. [15]You have many workmen: stonecutters, masons and carpenters, as well as men skilled in every kind of work [16]in gold and silver, bronze and iron—craftsmen beyond number. Now begin the work, and the LORD be with you."

[17]Then David ordered all the leaders of Israel to help his son Solomon. [18]He said to them, "Is not the LORD your God with you? And has he not granted you rest on every side? For he has handed the inhabitants of the land over to me, and the land is subject to the LORD and to his people. [19]Now devote your heart and soul to seeking the LORD your God. Begin to build the sanctuary of the LORD God, so that you may bring the ark of the covenant of the LORD and the sacred articles belonging to God into the temple that will be built for the Name of the LORD."

THE LEVITES

23 When David was old and full of years, he made his son Solomon king over Israel.

[2]He also gathered together all the leaders of Israel, as well as the priests and Levites. [3]The Levites thirty years old or more were counted, and the total number of men was thirty-eight thousand. [4]David said, "Of these, twenty-four thousand are to supervise the work of the temple of the LORD and six thousand are to be officials and judges. [5]Four thousand are to be gatekeepers and four thousand are to praise the LORD with the musical instruments I have provided for that purpose."

[6]David divided the Levites into groups corresponding to the sons of Levi: Gershon, Kohath and Merari.

GERSHONITES

[7]Belonging to the Gershonites:
    Ladan and Shimei.
  [8]The sons of Ladan:
    Jehiel the first, Zetham and Joel—three in all.
  [9]The sons of Shimei:
    Shelomoth, Haziel and Haran—three in all.

THE MESSAGE

rule in reverent obedience under GOD's Revelation. That's what will make you successful, following the directions and doing the things that GOD commanded Moses for Israel. Courage! Take charge! Don't be timid; don't hold back. Look at this—I've gone to a lot of trouble to stockpile materials for the sanctuary of GOD: 100,000 talents (3,775 tons) of gold, a million talents (37,750 tons) of silver, tons of bronze and iron—too much to weigh—and all this timber and stone. And you're free to add more. And workers both plentiful and prepared: stonecutters, masons, carpenters, artisans in gold and silver, bronze and iron. You're all set—get to work! And GOD-speed!"

22.17-19 David gave orders to all of Israel's leaders to help his son Solomon, saying, "Isn't it obvious that your GOD is present with you; that he has given you peaceful relations with everyone around? My part in this was to put down the enemies, subdue the land to GOD and his people; your part is to give yourselves, heart and soul, to praying to your GOD. So get moving—build the sacred house of worship to GOD! Then bring the Chest of the Covenant of GOD and all the holy furnishings for the worship of God into the sanctuary built in honor of GOD."

PREPARATIONS FOR WORSHIP

23.1 **23** When David got to be an old man, he made his son Solomon king over Israel.

23.2-5 At the same time he brought together all the leaders of Israel, the priests, and the Levites. The Levites thirty years and older were counted; the total was 38,000. David sorted them into work groups: "24,000 are in charge of administering worship in the sanctuary; 6,000 are officials and judges; 4,000 are security guards; and 4,000 are to serve in the orchestra, praising GOD with instruments that I have provided for praise."

23.6 David then divided the Levites into groupings named after the sons of Levi: Gershon, Kohath, and Merari.

23.7-11 The Gershonites: Ladan and Shimei. The three sons of Ladan: Jehiel, Zetham, and Joel. The three sons of Shimei: Shelomoth, Haziel,

---

[a] 14 That is, about 3,750 tons (about 3,450 metric tons)
[b] 14 That is, about 37,500 tons (about 34,500 metric tons)

NEW INTERNATIONAL VERSION

These were the heads of the families of Ladan.

¹⁰And the sons of Shimei:

Jahath, Ziza,^a Jeush and Beriah.

These were the sons of Shimei—four in all.

¹¹Jahath was the first and Ziza the second, but Jeush and Beriah did not have many sons; so they were counted as one family with one assignment.

KOHATHITES

¹²The sons of Kohath:

Amram, Izhar, Hebron and Uzziel—four in all.

¹³The sons of Amram:

Aaron and Moses.

Aaron was set apart, he and his descendants forever, to consecrate the most holy things, to offer sacrifices before the LORD, to minister before him and to pronounce blessings in his name forever. ¹⁴The sons of Moses the man of God were counted as part of the tribe of Levi.

¹⁵The sons of Moses:

Gershom and Eliezer.

¹⁶The descendants of Gershom:

Shubael was the first.

¹⁷The descendants of Eliezer:

Rehabiah was the first.

Eliezer had no other sons, but the sons of Rehabiah were very numerous.

¹⁸The sons of Izhar:

Shelomith was the first.

¹⁹The sons of Hebron:

Jeriah the first, Amariah the second, Jahaziel the third and Jekameam the fourth.

²⁰The sons of Uzziel:

Micah the first and Isshiah the second.

MERARITES

²¹The sons of Merari:

Mahli and Mushi.

The sons of Mahli:

Eleazar and Kish.

²²Eleazar died without having sons: he had only daughters. Their cousins, the sons of Kish, married them.

²³The sons of Mushi:

Mahli, Eder and Jerimoth—three in all.

²⁴These were the descendants of Levi by their families—the heads of families as they were registered under their names and counted individually, that is, the workers twenty years old or more who served in the temple of the LORD. ²⁵For

^a 10 One Hebrew manuscript, Septuagint and Vulgate (see also verse 11); most Hebrew manuscripts Zina

THE MESSAGE

and Haran, all heads of the families of Ladan. The four sons of Shimei: Jahath, Ziza, Jeush, and Beriah. Jahath came first, followed by Ziza. Jeush and Beriah did not have many sons so they were counted as one family with one task.

^{23.12-14} The four sons of Kohath: Amram, Izhar, Hebron, and Uzziel. The sons of Amram: Aaron and Moses. Aaron was especially ordained to work in the Holy of Holies, to burn incense before GOD, to serve God and bless his Name always. This was a permanent appointment for Aaron and his sons. Moses and his sons were counted in the tribe of Levi.

^{23.15-17} The sons of Moses: Gershom and Eliezer. Shubael was the first son of Gershom. Rehabiah was the first and only son of Eliezer; but though Eliezer had no other sons, Rehabiah had many sons.

^{23.18-23} Shelomith was the first son of Izhar. Hebron had four sons: Jeriah, Amariah, Jahaziel, and Jekameam. Uzziel had two sons: Micah and Isshiah. The sons of Merari: Mahli and Mushi. The sons of Mahli: Eleazar and Kish. Eleazar died without any sons, only daughters. Their cousins, the sons of Kish, married the daughters. Mushi had three sons: Mahli, Eder, and Jerimoth.

^{23.24} These are the sons of Levi twenty years and older, divided up according to families and heads of families and listed in the work groups that took care of the worship in the sanctuary of GOD.

NEW INTERNATIONAL VERSION

David had said, "Since the LORD, the God of Israel, has granted rest to his people and has come to dwell in Jerusalem forever, ²⁶the Levites no longer need to carry the tabernacle or any of the articles used in its service." ²⁷According to the last instructions of David, the Levites were counted from those twenty years old or more.

²⁸The duty of the Levites was to help Aaron's descendants in the service of the temple of the LORD: to be in charge of the courtyards, the side rooms, the purification of all sacred things and the performance of other duties at the house of God. ²⁹They were in charge of the bread set out on the table, the flour for the grain offerings, the unleavened wafers, the baking and the mixing, and all measurements of quantity and size. ³⁰They were also to stand every morning to thank and praise the LORD. They were to do the same in the evening ³¹and whenever burnt offerings were presented to the LORD on Sabbaths and at New Moon festivals and at appointed feasts. They were to serve before the LORD regularly in the proper number and in the way prescribed for them.

³²And so the Levites carried out their responsibilities for the Tent of Meeting, for the Holy Place and, under their brothers the descendants of Aaron, for the service of the temple of the LORD.

THE DIVISIONS OF PRIESTS

24 These were the divisions of the sons of Aaron:

The sons of Aaron were Nadab, Abihu, Eleazar and Ithamar. ²But Nadab and Abihu died before their father did, and they had no sons; so Eleazar and Ithamar served as the priests. ³With the help of Zadok a descendant of Eleazar and Ahimelech a descendant of Ithamar, David separated them into divisions for their appointed order of ministering. ⁴A larger number of leaders were found among Eleazar's descendants than among Ithamar's, and they were divided accordingly: sixteen heads of families from Eleazar's descendants and eight heads of families from Ithamar's descendants. ⁵They divided them impartially by drawing lots, for there were officials of the sanctuary and officials of God among the descendants of both Eleazar and Ithamar.

⁶The scribe Shemaiah son of Nethanel, a Levite, recorded their names in the presence of the king and of the officials: Zadok the priest, Ahimelech son of Abiathar and the heads of families of the priests and of the Levites—one family being taken from Eleazar and then one from Ithamar.

⁷The first lot fell to Jehoiarib,
the second to Jedaiah,

THE MESSAGE

23.25-27 David said, "Now that the GOD of Israel has given rest to his people and made Jerusalem his permanent home, the Levites no longer have to carry the Tabernacle and all the furniture required for the work of worship." These last words of David referred only to Levites twenty years old and above.

23.28-31 From now on the assigned work of the Levites was to assist Aaron's sons in the work of worship in GOD's house: maintain courtyards and closets, keep the furniture and utensils of worship clean, take care of any extra work needed in the work of worship, and provide bread for the table and flour for the Meal Offerings and the unraised wafers—all baking and mixing, all measuring and weighing. Also they were to be present for morning prayers, thanking and praising GOD, for evening prayers, and at the service of Whole-Burnt-Offerings to GOD on Sabbath, at New Moons, and at all festivals. They were on regular duty to serve GOD according to their assignment and the required number.

23.32 In short, the Levites, with the sons of Aaron as their companions in the ministry of holy worship, were responsible for everything that had to do with worship: the place and times and ordering of worship.

24 24.1-5 The family of Aaron was grouped as follows: Aaron's sons were Nadab, Abihu, Eleazar, and Ithamar. Nadab and Abihu died before their father and left no sons. So Eleazar and Ithamar filled the office of priest. David assigned Zadok from the family of Eleazar and Ahimelech from the family of Ithamar and assigned them to separate divisions for carrying out their appointed ministries. It turned out that there were more leaders in Eleazar's family than in Ithamar's and so they divided them proportionately: sixteen clan leaders from Eleazar's family and eight clan leaders from Ithamar's family. They assigned the leaders by lot, treating both families alike, for there were officials of the sanctuary and officials of God among both the Eleazar and Ithamar families.

24.6 The secretary Shemaiah son of Nethanel, a Levite, wrote down their names in the presence of the king, the officials, Zadok the priest, Ahimelech son of Abiathar, and the leaders of the priestly and Levitical families. They took turns: One family was selected from Eleazar and then one from Ithamar.

24.7-18 The first lot fell to Jehoiarib,
the second to Jedaiah,

NEW INTERNATIONAL VERSION

8 the third to Harim,
the fourth to Seorim,
9 the fifth to Malkijah,
the sixth to Mijamin,
10 the seventh to Hakkoz,
the eighth to Abijah,
11 the ninth to Jeshua,
the tenth to Shecaniah,
12 the eleventh to Eliashib,
the twelfth to Jakim,
13 the thirteenth to Huppah,
the fourteenth to Jeshebeab,
14 the fifteenth to Bilgah,
the sixteenth to Immer,
15 the seventeenth to Hezir,
the eighteenth to Happizzez,
16 the nineteenth to Pethahiah,
the twentieth to Jehezkel,
17 the twenty-first to Jakin,
the twenty-second to Gamul,
18 the twenty-third to Delaiah
and the twenty-fourth to Maaziah.

19 This was their appointed order of ministering when they entered the temple of the LORD, according to the regulations prescribed for them by their forefather Aaron, as the LORD, the God of Israel, had commanded him.

THE REST OF THE LEVITES

20 As for the rest of the descendants of Levi:
from the sons of Amram: Shubael;
from the sons of Shubael: Jehdeiah.
21 As for Rehabiah, from his sons:
Isshiah was the first.
22 From the Izharites: Shelomoth;
from the sons of Shelomoth: Jahath.
23 The sons of Hebron: Jeriah the first,[a] Amariah the second, Jahaziel the third and Jekameam the fourth.
24 The son of Uzziel: Micah;
from the sons of Micah: Shamir.
25 The brother of Micah: Isshiah;
from the sons of Isshiah: Zechariah.
26 The sons of Merari: Mahli and Mushi.
The son of Jaaziah: Beno.
27 The sons of Merari:
from Jaaziah: Beno, Shoham, Zaccur and Ibri.
28 From Mahli: Eleazar, who had no sons.
29 From Kish: the son of Kish:
Jerahmeel.
30 And the sons of Mushi: Mahli, Eder and Jerimoth.

a 23 Two Hebrew manuscripts and some Septuagint manuscripts (see also 1 Chron. 23:19); most Hebrew manuscripts The sons of Jeriah:

THE MESSAGE

the third to Harim,
the fourth to Seorim,
the fifth to Malkijah,
the sixth to Mijamin,
the seventh to Hakkoz,
the eighth to Abijah,
the ninth to Jeshua,
the tenth to Shecaniah,
the eleventh to Eliashib,
the twelfth to Jakim,
the thirteenth to Huppah,
the fourteenth to Jeshebeab,
the fifteenth to Bilgah,
the sixteenth to Immer,
the seventeenth to Hezir,
the eighteenth to Happizzez,
the nineteenth to Pethahiah,
the twentieth to Jehezkel,
the twenty-first to Jakin,
the twenty-second to Gamul,
the twenty-third to Delaiah,
and the twenty-fourth to Maaziah.

24.19 They served in this appointed order when they entered The Temple of GOD, following the procedures laid down by their ancestor Aaron as GOD, the God of Israel, had commanded him.

24.20 The rest of the Levites are as follows:
From the sons of Amram: Shubael; from the sons of Shubael: Jehdeiah.
24.21 Concerning Rehabiah: from his sons, Isshiah was the first.
24.22 From the Izharites: Shelomoth; from the sons of Shelomoth: Jahath.
24.23 The sons of Hebron: Jeriah the first, Amariah the second, Jahaziel the third, and Jekameam the fourth.
24.24-25 The son of Uzziel: Micah, and from the sons of Micah: Shamir. The brother of Micah was Isshiah, and from the sons of Isshiah: Zechariah.
24.26-27 The sons of Merari: Mahli and Mushi. The son of Jaaziah: Beno. The sons of Merari from Jaaziah: Beno, Shoham, Zaccur, and Ibri.
24.28 From Mahli: Eleazar, who had no sons.
24.29 From Kish: Jerahmeel, the son of Kish.
24.30-31 And from the sons of Mushi: Mahli, Eder, and Jerimoth.

NEW INTERNATIONAL VERSION

These were the Levites, according to their families. [31] They also cast lots, just as their brothers the descendants of Aaron did, in the presence of King David and of Zadok, Ahimelech, and the heads of families of the priests and of the Levites. The families of the oldest brother were treated the same as those of the youngest.

THE SINGERS

25 David, together with the commanders of the army, set apart some of the sons of Asaph, Heman and Jeduthun for the ministry of prophesying, accompanied by harps, lyres and cymbals. Here is the list of the men who performed this service:

[2] From the sons of Asaph:

Zaccur, Joseph, Nethaniah and Asarelah. The sons of Asaph were under the supervision of Asaph, who prophesied under the king's supervision.

[3] As for Jeduthun, from his sons:

Gedaliah, Zeri, Jeshaiah, Shimei,[a] Hashabiah and Mattithiah, six in all, under the supervision of their father Jeduthun, who prophesied, using the harp in thanking and praising the LORD.

[4] As for Heman, from his sons:

Bukkiah, Mattaniah, Uzziel, Shubael and Jerimoth; Hananiah, Hanani, Eliathah, Giddalti and Romamti-Ezer; Joshbekashah, Mallothi, Hothir and Mahazioth. [5] All these were sons of Heman the king's seer. They were given him through the promises of God to exalt him.[b] God gave Heman fourteen sons and three daughters.

[6] All these men were under the supervision of their fathers for the music of the temple of the LORD, with cymbals, lyres and harps, for the ministry at the house of God. Asaph, Jeduthun and Heman were under the supervision of the king. [7] Along with their relatives—all of them trained and skilled in music for the LORD—they numbered 288. [8] Young and old alike, teacher as well as student, cast lots for their duties.

[9] The first lot, which was for Asaph, fell to Joseph,

his sons and relatives,[c]	12[d]
the second to Gedaliah,	
he and his relatives and sons,	12

THE MESSAGE

These were the Levites by their families. They also cast lots, the same as their kindred the sons of Aaron had done, in the presence of David the king, Zadok, Ahimelech, and the leaders of the priestly and Levitical families. The families of the oldest and youngest brothers were treated the same.

THE MUSICIANS FOR WORSHIP

25.1-7 **25** Next David and the worship leaders selected some from the family of Asaph, Heman, and Jeduthun for special service in preaching and music. Here is the roster of names and assignments: From the family of Asaph: Zaccur, Joseph, Nethaniah, and Asarelah; they were supervised by Asaph, who spoke for GOD backed up by the king's authority. From the family of Jeduthun there were six sons: Gedaliah, Zeri, Jeshaiah, Shimei, Hashabiah, and Mattithiah; they were supervised by their father Jeduthun, who preached and accompanied himself with the zither—he was responsible for leading the thanks and praise to GOD. From the family of Heman: Bukkiah, Mattaniah, Uzziel, Shubael, Jerimoth, Hananiah, Hanani, Eliathah, Giddalti, Romamti-Ezer, Joshbekashah, Mallothi, Hothir, and Mahazioth. These were the sons of Heman the king's seer; they supported and assisted him in his divinely appointed work. God gave Heman fourteen sons and three daughters. Under their father's supervision they were in charge of leading the singing and providing musical accompaniment in the work of worship in the sanctuary of God (Asaph, Jeduthun, and Heman took their orders directly from the king). They were well-trained in the sacred music, all of them masters. There were 288 of them.

25.8 They drew names at random to see who would do what. Nobody, whether young or old, teacher or student, was given preference or advantage over another.

25.9-31 The first name from Asaph's family was Joseph and his twelve sons and brothers; second, Gedaliah and his twelve sons and brothers;

[a] 3 One Hebrew manuscript and some Septuagint manuscripts (see also verse 17); most Hebrew manuscripts do not have *Shimei.* [b] 5 Hebrew *exalt the horn*
[c] 9 See Septuagint; Hebrew does not have *his sons and relatives.* [d] 9 See the total in verse 7; Hebrew does not have *twelve.*

NEW INTERNATIONAL VERSION

[10] the third to Zaccur,
    his sons and relatives,   12
[11] the fourth to Izri,[a]
    his sons and relatives,   12
[12] the fifth to Nethaniah,
    his sons and relatives,   12
[13] the sixth to Bukkiah,
    his sons and relatives,   12
[14] the seventh to Jesarelah,[b]
    his sons and relatives,   12
[15] the eighth to Jeshaiah,
    his sons and relatives,   12
[16] the ninth to Mattaniah,
    his sons and relatives,   12
[17] the tenth to Shimei,
    his sons and relatives,   12
[18] the eleventh to Azarel,[c]
    his sons and relatives,   12
[19] the twelfth to Hashabiah,
    his sons and relatives,   12
[20] the thirteenth to Shubael,
    his sons and relatives,   12
[21] the fourteenth to Mattithiah,
    his sons and relatives,   12
[22] the fifteenth to Jerimoth,
    his sons and relatives,   12
[23] the sixteenth to Hananiah,
    his sons and relatives,   12
[24] the seventeenth to Joshbekashah,
    his sons and relatives,   12
[25] the eighteenth to Hanani,
    his sons and relatives,   12
[26] the nineteenth to Mallothi,
    his sons and relatives,   12
[27] the twentieth to Eliathah,
    his sons and relatives,   12
[28] the twenty-first to Hothir,
    his sons and relatives,   12
[29] the twenty-second to Giddalti,
    his sons and relatives,   12
[30] the twenty-third to Mahazioth,
    his sons and relatives,   12
[31] the twenty-fourth to Romamti-Ezer,
    his sons and relatives,   12

THE GATEKEEPERS

26 The divisions of the gatekeepers:

From the Korahites: Meshelemiah son of
  Kore, one of the sons of Asaph.
[2] Meshelemiah had sons:
  Zechariah the firstborn,
  Jediael the second,
  Zebadiah the third,
  Jathniel the fourth,

[a] 11 A variant of Zeri   [b] 14 A variant of Asarelah
[c] 18 A variant of Uzziel

THE MESSAGE

third, Zaccur and his twelve sons and brothers; fourth, Izri and his twelve sons and brothers; fifth, Nethaniah and his twelve sons and
brothers; sixth, Bukkiah and his twelve sons
and brothers; seventh, Jesarelah and his twelve
sons and brothers; eighth, Jeshaiah and his
twelve sons and brothers; ninth, Mattaniah and
his twelve sons and brothers; tenth, Shimei and
his twelve sons and brothers; eleventh, Azarel
and his twelve sons and brothers; twelfth,
Hashabiah and his twelve sons and brothers;
thirteenth, Shubael and his twelve sons and
brothers; fourteenth, Mattithiah and his twelve
sons and brothers; fifteenth, Jerimoth and his
twelve sons and brothers; sixteenth, Hananiah
and his twelve sons and brothers; seventeenth,
Joshbekashah and his twelve sons and brothers; eighteenth, Hanani and his twelve sons and
brothers; nineteenth, Mallothi and his twelve
sons and brothers; twentieth, Eliathah and his
twelve sons and brothers; twenty-first, Hothir
and his twelve sons and brothers; twenty-second, Giddalti and his twelve sons and brothers;
twenty-third, Mahazioth and his twelve sons
and brothers; twenty-fourth, Romamti-Ezer
and his twelve sons and brothers.

THE SECURITY GUARDS

26.1-11 **26** The teams of security guards were from
the family of Korah: Meshelemiah son
of Kore (one of the sons of Asaph). Meshelemiah's sons were Zechariah, the firstborn, followed by Jediael, Zebadiah, Jathniel, Elam, Je-

NEW INTERNATIONAL VERSION

³Elam the fifth,
Jehohanan the sixth
and Eliehoenai the seventh.
⁴Obed-Edom also had sons:
Shemaiah the firstborn,
Jehozabad the second,
Joah the third,
Sacar the fourth,
Nethanel the fifth,
⁵Ammiel the sixth,
Issachar the seventh
and Peullethai the eighth.
(For God had blessed Obed-Edom.)

⁶His son Shemaiah also had sons, who were leaders in their father's family because they were very capable men. ⁷The sons of Shemaiah: Othni, Rephael, Obed and Elzabad; his relatives Elihu and Semakiah were also able men. ⁸All these were descendants of Obed-Edom; they and their sons and their relatives were capable men with the strength to do the work—descendants of Obed-Edom, 62 in all.

⁹Meshelemiah had sons and relatives, who were able men—18 in all.

¹⁰Hosah the Merarite had sons: Shimri the first (although he was not the firstborn, his father had appointed him the first), ¹¹Hilkiah the second, Tabaliah the third and Zechariah the fourth. The sons and relatives of Hosah were 13 in all.

¹²These divisions of the gatekeepers, through their chief men, had duties for ministering in the temple of the Lord, just as their relatives had. ¹³Lots were cast for each gate, according to their families, young and old alike.

¹⁴The lot for the East Gate fell to Shelemiah.^a Then lots were cast for his son Zechariah, a wise counselor, and the lot for the North Gate fell to him. ¹⁵The lot for the South Gate fell to Obed-Edom, and the lot for the storehouse fell to his sons. ¹⁶The lots for the West Gate and the Shalleketh Gate on the upper road fell to Shuppim and Hosah.

Guard was alongside of guard: ¹⁷There were six Levites a day on the east, four a day on the north, four a day on the south and two at a time at the storehouse. ¹⁸As for the court to the west, there were four at the road and two at the court itself.

¹⁹These were the divisions of the gatekeepers who were descendants of Korah and Merari.

---

^a *14* A variant of *Meshelemiah*

THE MESSAGE

hohanan, and Eliehoenai—seven sons. Obed-Edom's sons were Shemaiah, the firstborn, followed by Jehozabad, Joah, Sacar, Nethanel, Ammiel, Issachar, and Peullethai—God blessed him with eight sons. His son Shemaiah had sons who provided outstanding leadership in the family: Othni, Rephael, Obed, and Elzabad; his relatives Elihu and Semakiah were also exceptional. These all came from the line of Obed-Edom—all of them outstanding and strong. There were sixty-two of them. Meshelemiah had eighteen sons and relatives who were outstanding. The sons of Hosah the Merarite were Shimri (he was not the firstborn but his father made him first), then Hilkiah, followed by Tabaliah and Zechariah. Hosah accounted for thirteen.

^{26.12-16} These teams of security guards, supervised by their leaders, kept order in The Temple of God, keeping up the traditions of their ancestors. They were all assigned to their posts by the same method regardless of the prominence of their families—each picked his gate assignment from a hat. Shelemiah was assigned to the East Gate; his son Zechariah, a shrewd counselor, got the North Gate. Obed-Edom got the South Gate; and his sons pulled duty at the storehouse. Shuppim and Hosah were posted to the West Gate and the Shalleketh Gate on the high road.

^{26.16-18} The guards stood shoulder to shoulder: six Levites per day on the east, four per day on the north and on the south, and two at a time at the storehouse. At the open court to the west, four guards were posted on the road and two at the court.

^{26.19} These are the teams of security guards from the sons of Korah and Merari.

NEW INTERNATIONAL VERSION

THE TREASURERS AND OTHER OFFICIALS

²⁰Their fellow Levites were *a* in charge of the treasuries of the house of God and the treasuries for the dedicated things.

²¹The descendants of Ladan, who were Gershonites through Ladan and who were heads of families belonging to Ladan the Gershonite, were Jehieli, ²²the sons of Jehieli, Zetham and his brother Joel. They were in charge of the treasuries of the temple of the LORD.

²³From the Amramites, the Izharites, the Hebronites and the Uzzielites:

²⁴Shubael, a descendant of Gershom son of Moses, was the officer in charge of the treasuries. ²⁵His relatives through Eliezer: Rehabiah his son, Jeshaiah his son, Joram his son, Zicri his son and Shelomith his son. ²⁶Shelomith and his relatives were in charge of all the treasuries for the things dedicated by King David, by the heads of families who were the commanders of thousands and commanders of hundreds, and by the other army commanders. ²⁷Some of the plunder taken in battle they dedicated for the repair of the temple of the LORD. ²⁸And everything dedicated by Samuel the seer and by Saul son of Kish, Abner son of Ner and Joab son of Zeruiah, and all the other dedicated things were in the care of Shelomith and his relatives.

²⁹From the Izharites: Kenaniah and his sons were assigned duties away from the temple, as officials and judges over Israel.

³⁰From the Hebronites: Hashabiah and his relatives—seventeen hundred able men—were responsible in Israel west of the Jordan for all the work of the LORD and for the king's service. ³¹As for the Hebronites, Jeriah was their chief according to the genealogical records of their families. In the fortieth year of David's reign a search was made in the records, and capable men among the Hebronites were found at Jazer in Gilead. ³²Jeriah had twenty-seven hundred relatives, who were able men and heads of families, and King David put them in charge of the Reubenites, the Gadites and the half-tribe of Manasseh for every matter pertaining to God and for the affairs of the king.

THE MESSAGE

FINANCIAL AFFAIRS: ACCOUNTANTS AND BOOKKEEPERS

26.20-22 Other Levites were put in charge of the financial affairs of The Temple of God. From the family of Ladan (all Gershonites) came Jehieli, and the sons of Jehieli, Zetham and his brother Joel. They supervised the finances of the sanctuary of GOD.

26.23-28 From the Amramites, the Izharites, the Hebronites, and the Uzzielites: Shubael, descended from Gershom the son of Moses, was the chief financial officer. His relatives through Eliezer: his son Rehabiah, his son Jeshaiah, his son Joram, his son Zicri, and his son Shelomith. Shelomith and his relatives were in charge of valuables consecrated by David the king, family heads, and various generals and commanders from the army. They dedicated the plunder that they had gotten in war to the work of the worship of GOD. In addition, everything that had been dedicated by Samuel the seer, Saul son of Kish, Abner son of Ner, and Joab son of Zeruiah—anything that had been dedicated, ever, was the responsibility of Shelomith and his family.

26.29-30 From the family of the Izharites, Kenaniah and sons were appointed as officials and judges responsible for affairs outside the work of worship and sanctuary. From the family of the Hebronites, Hashabiah and his relatives—1,700 well-qualified men—were responsible for administration of matters related to the worship of GOD and the king's work in the territory west of the Jordan.

26.31-32 According to the family tree of the Hebronites, Jeriah held pride of place. In the fortieth year of David's reign (his last), the Hebron family tree was researched and outstanding men were found at Jazer in Gilead, namely, Jeriah and 2,700 men of his extended family: David the king made them responsible for administration of matters related to the worship of God and the work of the king in the territory east of the Jordan—the Reubenites, the Gadites, and the half-tribe of Manasseh.

---

a 20 Septuagint; Hebrew *As for the Levites, Ahijah was*

NEW INTERNATIONAL VERSION

ARMY DIVISIONS

27 This is the list of the Israelites—heads of families, commanders of thousands and commanders of hundreds, and their officers, who served the king in all that concerned the army divisions that were on duty month by month throughout the year. Each division consisted of 24,000 men.

2 In charge of the first division, for the first month, was Jashobeam son of Zabdiel. There were 24,000 men in his division. 3 He was a descendant of Perez and chief of all the army officers for the first month.

4 In charge of the division for the second month was Dodai the Ahohite; Mikloth was the leader of his division. There were 24,000 men in his division.

5 The third army commander, for the third month, was Benaiah son of Jehoiada the priest. He was chief and there were 24,000 men in his division. 6 This was the Benaiah who was a mighty man among the Thirty and was over the Thirty. His son Ammizabad was in charge of his division.

7 The fourth, for the fourth month, was Asahel the brother of Joab; his son Zebadiah was his successor. There were 24,000 men in his division.

8 The fifth, for the fifth month, was the commander Shamhuth the Izrahite. There were 24,000 men in his division.

9 The sixth, for the sixth month, was Ira the son of Ikkesh the Tekoite. There were 24,000 men in his division.

10 The seventh, for the seventh month, was Helez the Pelonite, an Ephraimite. There were 24,000 men in his division.

11 The eighth, for the eighth month, was Sibbecai the Hushathite, a Zerahite. There were 24,000 men in his division.

12 The ninth, for the ninth month, was Abiezer the Anathothite, a Benjamite. There were 24,000 men in his division.

13 The tenth, for the tenth month, was Maharai the Netophathite, a Zerahite. There were 24,000 men in his division.

14 The eleventh, for the eleventh month, was Benaiah the Pirathonite, an Ephraimite. There were 24,000 men in his division.

15 The twelfth, for the twelfth month, was Heldai the Netophathite, from the family of Othniel. There were 24,000 men in his division.

THE MESSAGE

MILITARY ORGANIZATION

27.1 **27** Here is the listing of the sons of Israel by family heads, commanders and captains, and other officers who served the king in everything military. Army divisions were on duty a month at a time for the twelve months of the year. Each division comprised 24,000 men.

27.2-3 First division, first month: Jashobeam son of Zabdiel was in charge with 24,000 men. He came from the line of Perez. He was over all the army officers during the first month.

27.4 The division for the second month: Dodai the Ahohite was in charge: 24,000 men; Mikloth was the leader of his division.

27.5-6 Commander for the third month: Benaiah son of Jehoiada the priest with 24,000 men. This was the same Benaiah who was a Mighty Man among the Thirty and their chief. His son Ammizabad was in charge of the division.

27.7 Fourth division for the fourth month: Asahel brother of Joab; his son Zebadiah succeeded him: 24,000 men.

27.8 Fifth division, fifth month: commander Shamhuth the Izrahite: 24,000 men.

27.9 Sixth division, sixth month: Ira son of Ikkesh the Tekoite: 24,000 men.

27.10 Seventh division, seventh month: Helez the Pelonite, an Ephraimite: 24,000 men.

27.11 Eighth division, eighth month: Sibbecai the Hushathite, a Zerahite: 24,000 men.

27.12 Ninth division, ninth month: Abiezer the Anathothite, a Benjaminite: 24,000 men.

27.13 Tenth division, tenth month: Maharai the Netophathite, a Zerahite: 24,000 men.

27.14 Eleventh division, eleventh month: Benaiah the Pirathomite, an Ephraimite: 24,000 men.

27.15 Twelfth division, twelfth month: Heldai the Netophathite from the family of Othniel: 24,000 men.

NEW INTERNATIONAL VERSION

OFFICERS OF THE TRIBES

¹⁶The officers over the tribes of Israel:

over the Reubenites: Eliezer son of Zicri;
over the Simeonites: Shephatiah son of Maacah;
¹⁷over Levi: Hashabiah son of Kemuel;
over Aaron: Zadok;
¹⁸over Judah: Elihu, a brother of David;
over Issachar: Omri son of Michael;
¹⁹over Zebulun: Ishmaiah son of Obadiah;
over Naphtali: Jerimoth son of Azriel;
²⁰over the Ephraimites: Hoshea son of Azaziah;
over half the tribe of Manasseh: Joel son of Pedaiah;
²¹over the half-tribe of Manasseh in Gilead: Iddo son of Zechariah;
over Benjamin: Jaasiel son of Abner;
²²over Dan: Azarel son of Jeroham.

These were the officers over the tribes of Israel.

²³David did not take the number of the men twenty years old or less, because the LORD had promised to make Israel as numerous as the stars in the sky. ²⁴Joab son of Zeruiah began to count the men but did not finish. Wrath came on Israel on account of this numbering, and the number was not entered in the book^a of the annals of King David.

THE KING'S OVERSEERS

²⁵Azmaveth son of Adiel was in charge of the royal storehouses.

Jonathan son of Uzziah was in charge of the storehouses in the outlying districts, in the towns, the villages and the watchtowers.
²⁶Ezri son of Kelub was in charge of the field workers who farmed the land.
²⁷Shimei the Ramathite was in charge of the vineyards.

Zabdi the Shiphmite was in charge of the produce of the vineyards for the wine vats.
²⁸Baal-Hanan the Gederite was in charge of the olive and sycamore-fig trees in the western foothills.

Joash was in charge of the supplies of olive oil.
²⁹Shitrai the Sharonite was in charge of the herds grazing in Sharon.

Shaphat son of Adlai was in charge of the herds in the valleys.
³⁰Obil the Ishmaelite was in charge of the camels.

Jehdeiah the Meronothite was in charge of the donkeys.

^a 24 Septuagint; Hebrew *number*

THE MESSAGE

TRIBAL ADMINISTRATORS

27.16-22 Administrators of the affairs of the tribes:

for Reuben: Eliezer son of Zicri;
for Simeon: Shephatiah son of Maacah;
for Levi: Hashabiah son of Kemuel;
for Aaron: Zadok;
for Judah: Elihu, David's brother;
for Issachar: Omri son of Michael;
for Zebulun: Ishmaiah son of Obadiah;
for Naphtali: Jerimoth son of Azriel;
for Ephraim: Hoshea son of Azariah;
for one half-tribe of Manasseh: Joel son of Pedaiah;
for the half-tribe of Manasseh in Gilead: Iddo son of Zechariah;
for Benjamin: Jaasiel son of Abner;
for Dan: Azarel son of Jeroham.

These are the administrative officers assigned to the tribes of Israel.

27.23-24 David didn't keep a count of men under the age of twenty, because GOD had promised to give Israel a population as numerous as the stars in the sky. Joab son of Zeruiah started out counting the men, but he never finished. God's anger broke out on Israel because of the counting. As it turned out, the numbers were never entered into the court records of King David.

SUPPLY OFFICERS

27.25 The king's storage facilities were supervised by Azmaveth son of Adiel. Jonathan son of Uzziah was responsible for the warehouses in the outlying areas.

27.26 Ezri son of Kelub was in charge of the field workers on the farms.

27.27 Shimei the Ramathite was in charge of the vineyards and Zabdi the Shiphmite was in charge of grapes for the wine vats.

27.28 Baal-Hanan the Gederite was in charge of the olive and sycamore-fig trees in the western hills, and Joash was in charge of the olive oil.

27.29 Shitrai the Sharonite was in charge of herds grazing in Sharon and Shaphat son of Adlai was in charge of herds in the valley.

27.30-31 Obil the Ismaelite was in charge of the camels, Jehdeiah the Meronothite was in charge

NEW INTERNATIONAL VERSION	THE MESSAGE

NEW INTERNATIONAL VERSION

³¹Jaziz the Hagrite was in charge of the flocks.

All these were the officials in charge of King David's property.

³²Jonathan, David's uncle, was a counselor, a man of insight and a scribe. Jehiel son of Hacmoni took care of the king's sons.

³³Ahithophel was the king's counselor.

Hushai the Arkite was the king's friend. ³⁴Ahithophel was succeeded by Jehoiada son of Benaiah and by Abiathar.

Joab was the commander of the royal army.

DAVID'S PLANS FOR THE TEMPLE

28 David summoned all the officials of Israel to assemble at Jerusalem: the officers over the tribes, the commanders of the divisions in the service of the king, the commanders of thousands and commanders of hundreds, and the officials in charge of all the property and livestock belonging to the king and his sons, together with the palace officials, the mighty men and all the brave warriors.

²King David rose to his feet and said: "Listen to me, my brothers and my people. I had it in my heart to build a house as a place of rest for the ark of the covenant of the LORD, for the footstool of our God, and I made plans to build it. ³But God said to me, 'You are not to build a house for my Name, because you are a warrior and have shed blood.'

⁴"Yet the LORD, the God of Israel, chose me from my whole family to be king over Israel forever. He chose Judah as leader, and from the house of Judah he chose my family, and from my father's sons he was pleased to make me king over all Israel. ⁵Of all my sons—and the LORD has given me many—he has chosen my son Solomon to sit on the throne of the kingdom of the LORD over Israel. ⁶He said to me: 'Solomon your son is the one who will build my house and my courts, for I have chosen him to be my son, and I will be his father. ⁷I will establish his kingdom forever if he is unswerving in carrying out my commands and laws, as is being done at this time.'

⁸"So now I charge you in the sight of all Israel and of the assembly of the LORD, and in the hearing of our God: Be careful to follow all the commands of the LORD your God, that you may possess this good land and pass it on as an inheritance to your descendants forever.

⁹"And you, my son Solomon, acknowledge the God of your father, and serve him with wholehearted devotion and with a willing mind, for the LORD searches every heart and under-

THE MESSAGE

of the donkeys, and Jaziz the Hagrite was in charge of the flocks.

These were the ones responsible for taking care of King David's property.

DAVID'S COUNSELORS

27.32 Jonathan, David's uncle, a wise and literate counselor, and Jehiel son of Hacmoni, were responsible for rearing the king's sons.

27.33-34 Ahithophel was the king's counselor; Hushai the Arkite was the king's friend. Ahithophel was later replaced by Jehoiada son of Benaiah and by Abiathar.

Joab was commander of the king's army.

DAVID'S VALEDICTORY ADDRESS

28.1 **28** David called together all the leaders of Israel—tribal administrators, heads of various governmental operations, military commanders and captains, stewards in charge of the property and livestock belonging to the king and his sons—everyone who held responsible positions in the kingdom.

28.2-7 King David stood tall and spoke: "Listen to me, my people: I fully intended to build a permanent structure for the Chest of the Covenant of GOD, God's footstool. But when I got ready to build it, God said to me, 'You may not build a house to honor me—you've done too much fighting—killed too many people.' GOD chose me out of my family to be king over Israel forever. First he chose Judah as the lead tribe, then he narrowed it down to my family, and finally he picked me from my father's sons, pleased to make me the king over all Israel. And then from all my sons—and GOD gave me many!—he chose my son Solomon to sit on the throne of GOD's rule over Israel. He went on to say, 'Your son Solomon will build my house and my courts: I have chosen him to be my royal adopted son; and I will be to him a father. I will guarantee that his kingdom will last if he continues to be as strong-minded in doing what I command and carrying out my decisions as he is doing now.'

28.8 "And now, in this public place, all Israel looking on and God listening in, as GOD's people, obey and study every last one of the commandments of your GOD so that you can make the most of living in this good land and pass it on intact to your children, insuring a good future.

28.9-10 "And you, Solomon my son, get to know well your father's God; serve him with a whole heart and eager mind, for GOD examines every heart

NEW INTERNATIONAL VERSION

stands every motive behind the thoughts. If you seek him, he will be found by you; but if you forsake him, he will reject you forever. ¹⁰Consider now, for the LORD has chosen you to build a temple as a sanctuary. Be strong and do the work."

¹¹Then David gave his son Solomon the plans for the portico of the temple, its buildings, its storerooms, its upper parts, its inner rooms and the place of atonement. ¹²He gave him the plans of all that the Spirit had put in his mind for the courts of the temple of the LORD and all the surrounding rooms, for the treasuries of the temple of God and for the treasuries for the dedicated things. ¹³He gave him instructions for the divisions of the priests and Levites, and for all the work of serving in the temple of the LORD, as well as for all the articles to be used in its service. ¹⁴He designated the weight of gold for all the gold articles to be used in various kinds of service, and the weight of silver for all the silver articles to be used in various kinds of service: ¹⁵the weight of gold for the gold lampstands and their lamps, with the weight for each lampstand and its lamps; and the weight of silver for each silver lampstand and its lamps, according to the use of each lampstand; ¹⁶the weight of gold for each table for consecrated bread; the weight of silver for the silver tables; ¹⁷the weight of pure gold for the forks, sprinkling bowls and pitchers; the weight of gold for each gold dish; the weight of silver for each silver dish; ¹⁸and the weight of the refined gold for the altar of incense. He also gave him the plan for the chariot, that is, the cherubim of gold that spread their wings and shelter the ark of the covenant of the LORD.

¹⁹"All this," David said, "I have in writing from the hand of the LORD upon me, and he gave me understanding in all the details of the plan."

²⁰David also said to Solomon his son, "Be strong and courageous, and do the work. Do not be afraid or discouraged, for the LORD God, my God, is with you. He will not fail you or forsake you until all the work for the service of the temple of the LORD is finished. ²¹The divisions of the priests and Levites are ready for all the work on the temple of God, and every willing man skilled in any craft will help you in all the work. The officials and all the people will obey your every command."

GIFTS FOR BUILDING THE TEMPLE

29 Then King David said to the whole assembly: "My son Solomon, the one whom God has chosen, is young and inexperienced. The task is great, because this palatial structure is not for man but for the LORD God.

THE MESSAGE

and sees through every motive. If you seek him, he'll make sure you find him, but if you abandon him, he'll leave you for good. Look sharp now! GOD has chosen you to build his holy house. Be brave, determined! And do it!"

28.11-19 Then David presented his son Solomon with the plans for The Temple complex: porch, storerooms, meeting rooms, and the place for atoning sacrifice. He turned over the plans for everything that God's Spirit had brought to his mind: the design of the courtyards, the arrangements of rooms, and the closets for storing all the holy things. He gave him his plan for organizing the Levites and priests in their work of leading and ordering worship in the house of God, and for caring for the liturgical furnishings. He provided exact specifications for how much gold and silver was needed for each article used in the services of worship: the gold and silver Lampstands and lamps, the gold tables for consecrated bread, the silver tables, the gold forks, the bowls and the jars, and the incense altar. And he gave him the plan for sculpting the cherubs with their wings outstretched over the Chest of the Covenant of GOD—the cherubim throne. "Here are the blueprints for the whole project as GOD gave me to understand it," David said.

28.20-21 David continued to address Solomon: "Take charge! Take heart! Don't be anxious or get discouraged. GOD, my God, is with you in this; he won't walk off and leave you in the lurch. He's at your side until every last detail is completed for conducting the worship of GOD. You have all the priests and Levites standing ready to pitch in, and skillful craftsmen and artisans of every kind ready to go to work. Both leaders and people are ready. Just say the word."

THEY GET READY TO BUILD

29.1-5 **29** Then David the king addressed the congregation: "My son Solomon was singled out and chosen by God to do this. But he's young and untested and the work is huge—this is not just a place for people to meet each other, but a house for GOD to meet us. I've done my

NEW INTERNATIONAL VERSION

²With all my resources I have provided for the temple of my God—gold for the gold work, silver for the silver, bronze for the bronze, iron for the iron and wood for the wood, as well as onyx for the settings, turquoise,ᵃ stones of various colors, and all kinds of fine stone and marble—all of these in large quantities. ³Besides, in my devotion to the temple of my God I now give my personal treasures of gold and silver for the temple of my God, over and above everything I have provided for this holy temple: ⁴three thousand talentsᵇ of gold (gold of Ophir) and seven thousand talentsᶜ of refined silver, for the overlaying of the walls of the buildings, ⁵for the gold work and the silver work, and for all the work to be done by the craftsmen. Now, who is willing to consecrate himself today to the LORD?"

⁶Then the leaders of families, the officers of the tribes of Israel, the commanders of thousands and commanders of hundreds, and the officials in charge of the king's work gave willingly. ⁷They gave toward the work on the temple of God five thousand talentsᵈ and ten thousand daricsᵉ of gold, ten thousand talentsᶠ of silver, eighteen thousand talentsᵍ of bronze and a hundred thousand talentsʰ of iron. ⁸Any who had precious stones gave them to the treasury of the temple of the LORD in the custody of Jehiel the Gershonite. ⁹The people rejoiced at the willing response of their leaders, for they had given freely and wholeheartedly to the LORD. David the king also rejoiced greatly.

DAVID'S PRAYER

¹⁰David praised the LORD in the presence of the whole assembly, saying,

"Praise be to you, O LORD,
   God of our father Israel,
   from everlasting to everlasting.
¹¹Yours, O LORD, is the greatness and the
      power
   and the glory and the majesty and the
      splendor,
   for everything in heaven and earth is
      yours.
Yours, O LORD, is the kingdom;
   you are exalted as head over all.
¹²Wealth and honor come from you;
   you are the ruler of all things.

ᵃ 2 The meaning of the Hebrew for this word is uncertain.
ᵇ 4 That is, about 110 tons (about 100 metric tons)
ᶜ 4 That is, about 260 tons (about 240 metric tons)
ᵈ 7 That is, about 190 tons (about 170 metric tons)
ᵉ 7 That is, about 185 pounds (about 84 kilograms)
ᶠ 7 That is, about 375 tons (about 345 metric tons)
ᵍ 7 That is, about 675 tons (about 610 metric tons)
ʰ 7 That is, about 3,750 tons (about 3,450 metric tons)

THE MESSAGE

best to get everything together for building this house for my God, all the materials necessary: gold, silver, bronze, iron, lumber, precious and varicolored stones, and building stones—vast stockpiles. Furthermore, because my heart is in this, in addition to and beyond what I have gathered, I'm turning over my personal fortune of gold and silver for making this place of worship for my God: 3,000 talents (about 113 tons) of gold—all from Ophir, the best—and 7,000 talents (214 tons) of silver for covering the walls of the buildings, and for the gold and silver work by craftsmen and artisans.

"And now, how about you? Who among you is ready and willing to join in the giving?"

29:6-8   Ready and willing, the heads of families, leaders of the tribes of Israel, commanders and captains in the army, stewards of the king's affairs, stepped forward and gave willingly. They gave 5,000 talents (188 tons) and 10,000 darics (185 pounds) of gold, 10,000 talents of silver (377 tons), 18,000 talents of bronze (679 tons), and 100,000 talents (3,775 tons) of iron. Anyone who had precious jewels put them in the treasury for the building of The Temple of GOD in the custody of Jehiel the Gershonite.

29:9   And the people were full of a sense of celebration—all that giving! And all given willingly, freely! King David was exuberant.

29:10-13   David blessed GOD in full view of the entire congregation:

Blessed are you, GOD of Israel, our father
      from of old and forever.
To you, O GOD, belong the greatness and
      the might,
   the glory, the victory, the majesty, the
      splendor;
Yes! Everything in heaven, everything on
      earth;
   the kingdom all yours! You've raised
      yourself high over all.
Riches and glory come from you,
   you're ruler over all;

NEW INTERNATIONAL VERSION

In your hands are strength and power
   to exalt and give strength to all.
¹³Now, our God, we give you thanks,
   and praise your glorious name.

¹⁴"But who am I, and who are my people, that
we should be able to give as generously as this?
Everything comes from you, and we have given
you only what comes from your hand. ¹⁵We are
aliens and strangers in your sight, as were all our
forefathers. Our days on earth are like a shadow,
without hope. ¹⁶O LORD our God, as for all this
abundance that we have provided for building
you a temple for your Holy Name, it comes from
your hand, and all of it belongs to you. ¹⁷I know,
my God, that you test the heart and are pleased
with integrity. All these things have I given willingly and with honest intent. And now I have
seen with joy how willingly your people who are
here have given to you. ¹⁸O LORD, God of our fathers Abraham, Isaac and Israel, keep this desire
in the hearts of your people forever, and keep
their hearts loyal to you. ¹⁹And give my son Solomon the wholehearted devotion to keep your
commands, requirements and decrees and to do
everything to build the palatial structure for
which I have provided."

²⁰Then David said to the whole assembly,
"Praise the LORD your God." So they all praised
the LORD, the God of their fathers; they bowed
low and fell prostrate before the LORD and the
king.

SOLOMON ACKNOWLEDGED AS KING

²¹The next day they made sacrifices to the
LORD and presented burnt offerings to him: a
thousand bulls, a thousand rams and a thousand
male lambs, together with their drink offerings,
and other sacrifices in abundance for all Israel.
²²They ate and drank with great joy in the presence of the LORD that day.

Then they acknowledged Solomon son of David as king a second time, anointing him before
the LORD to be ruler and Zadok to be priest. ²³So
Solomon sat on the throne of the LORD as king in
place of his father David. He prospered and all
Israel obeyed him. ²⁴All the officers and mighty
men, as well as all of King David's sons, pledged
their submission to King Solomon.

²⁵The LORD highly exalted Solomon in the
sight of all Israel and bestowed on him royal
splendor such as no king over Israel ever had
before.

THE MESSAGE

You hold strength and power in the palm of
      your hand
   to build up and strengthen all.
And here we are, O God, our God, giving
      thanks to you,
   praising your splendid Name.

29.14-19   "But me—who am I, and who are these my
people, that we should presume to be giving
something to you? Everything comes from you;
all we're doing is giving back what we've been
given from your generous hand. As far as
you're concerned, we're homeless, shiftless
wanderers like our ancestors, our lives mere
shadows, hardly anything to us. GOD, our God,
all these materials—these piles of stuff for
building a house of worship for you, honoring
your Holy Name—it all came from you! It was
all yours in the first place! I know, dear God,
that you care nothing for the surface—you
want *us*, our true selves—and so I have given
from the heart, honestly and happily. And now
see all these people doing the same, giving
freely, willingly—what a joy! O GOD, God of
our fathers Abraham, Isaac, and Israel, keep
this generous spirit alive forever in these people
always, keep their hearts set firmly in you. And
give my son Solomon an uncluttered and focused heart so that he can obey what you command, live by your directions and counsel, and
carry through with building The Temple for
which I have provided."

29.20   David then addressed the congregation:
"Bless GOD, your God!" And they did it,
blessed GOD, the God of their ancestors, and
worshiped reverently in the presence of GOD
and the king.

29.21-22   The very next day they butchered the sacrificial animals and offered in the worship of Israel to GOD a thousand bulls, a thousand rams,
a thousand sheep, and in addition drink offerings and many other sacrifices. They feasted all
day, eating and drinking before GOD, exuberant
with joy.

29.22-25   Then they ceremonially reenacted Solomon's
coronation, anointing David's son before GOD
as their leader, and Zadok as priest. Solomon
sat on the throne of GOD as king in place of
David his father. And everything went well; all
Israel obeyed him. All the leaders of the people,
including all the sons of King David, accepted
Solomon as their king and promised their loyalty. Solomon rode high on a crest of popular
acclaim—it was all GOD's doing. GOD gave him
position and honor beyond any king in Israel
before him.

✠

NEW INTERNATIONAL VERSION

THE DEATH OF DAVID

26David son of Jesse was king over all Israel. 27He ruled over Israel forty years—seven in Hebron and thirty-three in Jerusalem. 28He died at a good old age, having enjoyed long life, wealth and honor. His son Solomon succeeded him as king.

29As for the events of King David's reign, from beginning to end, they are written in the records of Samuel the seer, the records of Nathan the prophet and the records of Gad the seer, 30together with the details of his reign and power, and the circumstances that surrounded him and Israel and the kingdoms of all the other lands.

THE MESSAGE

29.26-30 David son of Jesse ruled over all Israel. He was king for forty years. He ruled from Hebron seven years and from Jerusalem thirty-three. He died at a ripe old age, full of days, wealth, and glory. His son Solomon ruled after him. The history of David the king, from start to finish, is written in the chronicles of Samuel the seer, Nathan the prophet, and Gad the seer, including a full account of his rule, his exploits, and the times through which he and Israel and the surrounding kingdoms passed.

2 CHRONICLES

2 CHRONICLES

SOLOMON ASKS FOR WISDOM

1 Solomon son of David established himself firmly over his kingdom, for the LORD his God was with him and made him exceedingly great.

² Then Solomon spoke to all Israel—to the commanders of thousands and commanders of hundreds, to the judges and to all the leaders in Israel, the heads of families— ³ and Solomon and the whole assembly went to the high place at Gibeon, for God's Tent of Meeting was there, which Moses the LORD's servant had made in the desert. ⁴ Now David had brought up the ark of God from Kiriath Jearim to the place he had prepared for it, because he had pitched a tent for it in Jerusalem. ⁵ But the bronze altar that Bezalel son of Uri, the son of Hur, had made was in Gibeon in front of the tabernacle of the LORD; so Solomon and the assembly inquired of him there. ⁶ Solomon went up to the bronze altar before the LORD in the Tent of Meeting and offered a thousand burnt offerings on it.

⁷ That night God appeared to Solomon and said to him, "Ask for whatever you want me to give you."

⁸ Solomon answered God, "You have shown great kindness to David my father and have made me king in his place. ⁹ Now, LORD God, let your promise to my father David be confirmed, for you have made me king over a people who are as numerous as the dust of the earth. ¹⁰ Give me wisdom and knowledge, that I may lead this people, for who is able to govern this great people of yours?"

¹¹ God said to Solomon, "Since this is your heart's desire and you have not asked for wealth, riches or honor, nor for the death of your enemies, and since you have not asked for a long life but for wisdom and knowledge to govern my people over whom I have made you king, ¹² therefore wisdom and knowledge will be given you. And I will also give you wealth, riches and honor, such as no king who was before you ever had and none after you will have."

¹³ Then Solomon went to Jerusalem from the high place at Gibeon, from before the Tent of Meeting. And he reigned over Israel.

KING SOLOMON

1.1-6 **1** Solomon son of David took a firm grip on the reins of his kingdom. GOD was with him and gave him much help. Solomon addressed all Israel—the commanders and captains, the judges, every leader, and all the heads of families. Then Solomon and the entire company went to the worship center at Gibeon— that's where the Tent of Meeting of God was, the one that Moses the servant of GOD had made in the wilderness. The Chest of God, though, was in Jerusalem—David had brought it up from Kiriath Jearim, prepared a special place for it, and pitched a tent for it. But the Bronze Altar that Bezalel son of Uri, the son of Hur, had made was in Gibeon, in its place before the Tabernacle of GOD; and that is where Solomon and the congregation gathered to pray. Solomon worshiped GOD at the Bronze Altar in front of the Tent of Meeting; he sacrificed a thousand Whole-Burnt-Offerings on it.

1.7 That night God appeared to Solomon. God said, "What do you want from me? Ask."

1.8-10 Solomon answered, "You were extravagantly generous with David my father, and now you have made me king in his place. Establish, GOD, the words you spoke to my father, for you've given me a staggering task, ruling this mob of people. Yes, give me wisdom and knowledge as I come and go among this people—for who on his own is capable of leading these, your glorious people?"

1.11-12 God answered Solomon, "This is what has come out of your heart: You didn't grasp for money, wealth, fame, and the doom of your enemies; you didn't even ask for a long life. You asked for wisdom and knowledge so you could govern well my people over whom I've made you king. Because of this, you get what you asked for—wisdom and knowledge. And I'm presenting you the rest as a bonus—money, wealth, and fame beyond anything the kings before or after you had or will have."

1.13 Then Solomon left the worship center at Gibeon and the Tent of Meeting and went to Jerusalem. He set to work as king of Israel.

NEW INTERNATIONAL VERSION

¹⁴Solomon accumulated chariots and horses; he had fourteen hundred chariots and twelve thousand horses,ᵃ which he kept in the chariot cities and also with him in Jerusalem. ¹⁵The king made silver and gold as common in Jerusalem as stones, and cedar as plentiful as sycamore-fig trees in the foothills. ¹⁶Solomon's horses were imported from Egyptᵇ and from Kueᶜ—the royal merchants purchased them from Kue. ¹⁷They imported a chariot from Egypt for six hundred shekelsᵈ of silver, and a horse for a hundred and fifty.ᵉ They also exported them to all the kings of the Hittites and of the Arameans.

PREPARATIONS FOR BUILDING THE TEMPLE

2 Solomon gave orders to build a temple for the Name of the Lᴏʀᴅ and a royal palace for himself. ²He conscripted seventy thousand men as carriers and eighty thousand as stonecutters in the hills and thirty-six hundred as foremen over them.

³Solomon sent this message to Hiramᶠ king of Tyre:

"Send me cedar logs as you did for my father David when you sent him cedar to build a palace to live in. ⁴Now I am about to build a temple for the Name of the Lᴏʀᴅ my God and to dedicate it to him for burning fragrant incense before him, for setting out the consecrated bread regularly, and for making burnt offerings every morning and evening and on Sabbaths and New Moons and at the appointed feasts of the Lᴏʀᴅ our God. This is a lasting ordinance for Israel.

⁵"The temple I am going to build will be great, because our God is greater than all other gods. ⁶But who is able to build a temple for him, since the heavens, even the highest heavens, cannot contain him? Who then am I to build a temple for him, except as a place to burn sacrifices before him?

⁷"Send me, therefore, a man skilled to work in gold and silver, bronze and iron, and in purple, crimson and blue yarn, and experienced in the art of engraving, to work in Judah and Jerusalem with my skilled craftsmen, whom my father David provided.

⁸"Send me also cedar, pine and algumᵍ logs from Lebanon, for I know that your men are skilled in cutting timber there. My

THE MESSAGE

1.14-17 Solomon collected chariots and horses: 1,400 chariots and 12,000 horses! He stabled them in the special chariot-cities as well as in Jerusalem. The king made silver and gold as common as rocks, and cedar as common as the fig trees in the lowland hills. His horses were brought in from Egypt and Cilicia, specially acquired by the king's agents. Chariots from Egypt went for fifteen pounds of silver and a horse for about three and three-quarters of a pound of silver. Solomon carried on a brisk horse-trading business with the Hittite and Aramean royal houses.

THE TEMPLE CONSTRUCTION BEGINS

2.1 **2** Solomon gave orders to begin construction on the house of worship in honor of Gᴏᴅ and a palace for himself.

2.2 Solomon assigned 70,000 common laborers, 80,000 to work the quarries in the mountains, and 3,600 foremen to manage the workforce.

2.3-4 Then Solomon sent this message to King Hiram of Tyre: "Send me cedar logs, the same kind you sent David my father for building his palace. I'm about to build a house of worship in honor of Gᴏᴅ, a holy place for burning perfumed incense, for setting out holy bread, for making Whole-Burnt-Offerings at morning and evening worship, and for Sabbath, New Moon, and Holy Day services of worship—the acts of worship required of Israel.

2.5-10 "The house I am building has to be the best, for our God is the best, far better than competing gods. But who is capable of building such a structure? Why, the skies—the entire cosmos!—can't begin to contain him. And me, who am I to think I can build a house adequate for God—burning incense to him is about all I'm good for! I need your help: Send me a master artisan in gold, silver, bronze, iron, textiles of purple, crimson, and violet, and who knows the craft of engraving; he will supervise the trained craftsmen in Judah and Jerusalem that my father provided. Also send cedar, cypress, and algum logs from Lebanon; I know you have lumberjacks experienced in the Lebanon forests. I'll send work-

---

ᵃ 14 Or *charioteers*   ᵇ 16 Or possibly *Muzur,* a region in Cilicia; also in verse 17   ᶜ 16 Probably Cilicia
ᵈ 17 That is, about 15 pounds (about 7 kilograms)
ᵉ 17 That is, about 3 3/4 pounds (about 1.7 kilograms)
ᶠ 3 Hebrew *Huram,* a variant of *Hiram;* also in verses 11 and 12   ᵍ 8 Probably a variant of *almug;* possibly juniper

NEW INTERNATIONAL VERSION

men will work with yours ⁹to provide me with plenty of lumber, because the temple I build must be large and magnificent. ¹⁰I will give your servants, the woodsmen who cut the timber, twenty thousand cors*a* of ground wheat, twenty thousand cors of barley, twenty thousand baths*b* of wine and twenty thousand baths of olive oil."

¹¹Hiram king of Tyre replied by letter to Solomon:

"Because the LORD loves his people, he has made you their king."

¹²And Hiram added:

"Praise be to the LORD, the God of Israel, who made heaven and earth! He has given King David a wise son, endowed with intelligence and discernment, who will build a temple for the LORD and a palace for himself.

¹³"I am sending you Huram-Abi, a man of great skill, ¹⁴whose mother was from Dan and whose father was from Tyre. He is trained to work in gold and silver, bronze and iron, stone and wood, and with purple and blue and crimson yarn and fine linen. He is experienced in all kinds of engraving and can execute any design given to him. He will work with your craftsmen and with those of my lord, David your father.

¹⁵"Now let my lord send his servants the wheat and barley and the olive oil and wine he promised, ¹⁶and we will cut all the logs from Lebanon that you need and will float them in rafts by sea down to Joppa. You can then take them up to Jerusalem."

¹⁷Solomon took a census of all the aliens who were in Israel, after the census his father David had taken; and they were found to be 153,600. ¹⁸He assigned 70,000 of them to be carriers and 80,000 to be stonecutters in the hills, with 3,600 foremen over them to keep the people working.

SOLOMON BUILDS THE TEMPLE

3 Then Solomon began to build the temple of the LORD in Jerusalem on Mount Moriah, where the LORD had appeared to his father David. It was on the threshing floor of Araunah*c* the Jebusite, the place provided by David. ²He began building on the second day of the second month in the fourth year of his reign.

³The foundation Solomon laid for building

---

a 10 That is, probably about 125,000 bushels (about 4,400 kiloliters)   *b 10* That is, probably about 115,000 gallons (about 440 kiloliters)   *c 1* Hebrew *Ornan,* a variant of *Araunah*

THE MESSAGE

ers to join your crews to cut plenty of timber—I'm going to need a lot, for this house I'm building is going to be absolutely stunning—a showcase temple! I'll provide all the food necessary for your crew of lumberjacks and loggers: 130,000 bushels of wheat, 120,000 gallons of wine, and 120,000 gallons of olive oil."

2.11   Hiram king of Tyre wrote Solomon in reply: "It's plain that GOD loves his people—he made you king over them!"

2.12-14   He wrote on, "Blessed be the GOD of Israel, who made heaven and earth, and who gave King David a son so wise, so knowledgeable and shrewd, to build a temple for GOD and a palace for himself. I've sent you Huram-Abi—he's already on his way—he knows the construction business inside and out. His mother is from Dan and his father from Tyre. He knows how to work in gold, silver, bronze, iron, stone, and wood, in purple, violet, linen, and crimson textiles; he is also an expert engraver and competent to work out designs with your artists and architects, and those of my master David, your father.

2.15-16   "Go ahead and send the wheat, barley, olive oil, and wine you promised for my work crews. We'll log the trees you need from the Lebanon forests and raft them down to Joppa. You'll have to get the timber up to Jerusalem yourself."

2.17-18   Solomon then took a census of all the foreigners living in Israel, using the same census-taking method employed by his father. They numbered 153,600. He assigned 70,000 of them as common laborers, 80,000 to work the quarries in the mountains, and 3,600 as foremen to manage the work crews.

3.1-4   **3** So Solomon broke ground, launched construction of the house of GOD in Jerusalem on Mount Moriah, the place where GOD had appeared to his father David. The precise site, the threshing floor of Araunah the Jebusite, had been designated by David. He broke ground on the second day in the second month of the fourth year of his rule. These are the dimensions that Solomon set for the construction of

NEW INTERNATIONAL VERSION

the temple of God was sixty cubits long and twenty cubits wide*a* (using the cubit of the old standard). 4The portico at the front of the temple was twenty cubits*b* long across the width of the building and twenty cubits*c* high.

He overlaid the inside with pure gold. 5He paneled the main hall with pine and covered it with fine gold and decorated it with palm tree and chain designs. 6He adorned the temple with precious stones. And the gold he used was gold of Parvaim. 7He overlaid the ceiling beams, doorframes, walls and doors of the temple with gold, and he carved cherubim on the walls.

8He built the Most Holy Place, its length corresponding to the width of the temple—twenty cubits long and twenty cubits wide. He overlaid the inside with six hundred talents*d* of fine gold. 9The gold nails weighed fifty shekels.*e* He also overlaid the upper parts with gold.

10In the Most Holy Place he made a pair of sculptured cherubim and overlaid them with gold. 11The total wingspan of the cherubim was twenty cubits. One wing of the first cherub was five cubits*f* long and touched the temple wall, while its other wing, also five cubits long, touched the wing of the other cherub. 12Similarly one wing of the second cherub was five cubits long and touched the other temple wall, and its other wing, also five cubits long, touched the wing of the first cherub. 13The wings of these cherubim extended twenty cubits. They stood on their feet, facing the main hall.*g*

14He made the curtain of blue, purple and crimson yarn and fine linen, with cherubim worked into it.

15In the front of the temple he made two pillars, which ⌊together⌋ were thirty-five cubits*h* long, each with a capital on top measuring five cubits. 16He made interwoven chains*i* and put them on top of the pillars. He also made a hundred pomegranates and attached them to the chains. 17He erected the pillars in the front of the temple, one to the south and one to the north. The one to the south he named Jakin*j* and the one to the north Boaz.*k*

THE MESSAGE

the house of God: ninety feet long and thirty feet wide. The porch in front stretched the width of the building, that is, thirty feet; and it was thirty feet high.

3.4-7 The interior was gold-plated. He paneled the main hall with cypress and veneered it with fine gold engraved with palm tree and chain designs. He decorated the building with precious stones and gold from Parvaim. Everything was coated with gold veneer: rafters, doorframes, walls, and doors. Cherubim were engraved on the walls.

3.8-9 He made the Holy of Holies a cube, thirty feet wide, long, and high. It was veneered with 600 talents (something over twenty-two tons) of gold. The gold nails weighed fifty shekels (a little over a pound). The upper rooms were also veneered in gold.

3.10-13 He made two sculptures of cherubim, gigantic angel-like figures, for the Holy of Holies, both veneered with gold. The combined wing-spread of the side-by-side cherubim (each wing measuring seven and a half feet) stretched from wall to wall, thirty feet. They stood erect facing the main hall.

3.14 He fashioned the curtain of violet, purple, and crimson fabric and worked a cherub design into it.

3.15-17 He made two huge free-standing pillars, each fifty-two feet tall, their capitals extending another seven and a half feet. The top of each pillar was set off with an elaborate filigree of chains, like necklaces, from which hung a hundred pomegranates. He placed the pillars in front of The Temple, one on the right, and the other on the left. The right pillar he named Jakin (Security) and the left pillar he named Boaz (Stability).

---

a 3 That is, about 90 feet (about 27 meters) long and 30 feet (about 9 meters) wide   *b 4* That is, about 30 feet (about 9 meters); also in verses 8, 11 and 13   *c 4* Some Septuagint and Syriac manuscripts; Hebrew *and a hundred and twenty*   *d 8* That is, about 23 tons (about 21 metric tons)   *e 9* That is, about 1 1/4 pounds (about 0.6 kilogram)   *f 11* That is, about 7 1/2 feet (about 2.3 meters); also in verse 15   *g 13* Or *facing inward*   *h 15* That is, about 52 feet (about 16 meters)   *i 16* Or possibly *made chains in the inner sanctuary*; the meaning of the Hebrew for this phrase is uncertain.   *j 17* Jakin probably means *he establishes.*   *k 17* Boaz probably means *in him is strength.*

NEW INTERNATIONAL VERSION

THE TEMPLE'S FURNISHINGS

4 He made a bronze altar twenty cubits long, twenty cubits wide and ten cubits high. *a* ²He made the Sea of cast metal, circular in shape, measuring ten cubits from rim to rim and five cubits *b* high. It took a line of thirty cubits *c* to measure around it. ³Below the rim, figures of bulls encircled it—ten to a cubit. *d* The bulls were cast in two rows in one piece with the Sea.

⁴The Sea stood on twelve bulls, three facing north, three facing west, three facing south and three facing east. The Sea rested on top of them, and their hindquarters were toward the center. ⁵It was a handbreadth *e* in thickness, and its rim was like the rim of a cup, like a lily blossom. It held three thousand baths. *f*

⁶He then made ten basins for washing and placed five on the south side and five on the north. In them the things to be used for the burnt offerings were rinsed, but the Sea was to be used by the priests for washing.

⁷He made ten gold lampstands according to the specifications for them and placed them in the temple, five on the south side and five on the north.

⁸He made ten tables and placed them in the temple, five on the south side and five on the north. He also made a hundred gold sprinkling bowls.

⁹He made the courtyard of the priests, and the large court and the doors for the court, and overlaid the doors with bronze. ¹⁰He placed the Sea on the south side, at the southeast corner.

¹¹He also made the pots and shovels and sprinkling bowls.

So Huram finished the work he had undertaken for King Solomon in the temple of God:

¹² the two pillars;

the two bowl-shaped capitals on top of the pillars;

the two sets of network decorating the two bowl-shaped capitals on top of the pillars;

¹³ the four hundred pomegranates for the two sets of network (two rows of pomegranates for each network, decorating the bowl-shaped capitals on top of the pillars);

¹⁴ the stands with their basins;

¹⁵ the Sea and the twelve bulls under it;

THE MESSAGE

TEMPLE FURNISHINGS

4.1 **4** He made the Bronze Altar thirty feet long, thirty feet wide, and ten feet high.

4.2-5 He made a Sea—an immense round basin of cast metal fifteen feet in diameter, seven and a half feet high, and forty-five feet in circumference. Just under the rim, there were two parallel bands of something like bulls, ten to each foot and a half. The figures were cast in one piece with the Sea. The Sea was set on twelve bulls, three facing north, three facing west, three facing south, and three facing east. All the bulls faced outward and supported the Sea on their hindquarters. The Sea was three inches thick and flared at the rim like a cup, or a lily. It held about 18,000 gallons.

4.6 He made ten Washbasins, five set on the right and five on the left, for rinsing the things used for the Whole-Burnt-Offerings. The priests washed themselves in the Sea.

4.7 He made ten gold Lampstands, following the specified pattern, and placed five on the right and five on the left.

4.8 He made ten tables and set five on the right and five on the left. He also made a hundred gold bowls.

4.9 He built a Courtyard especially for the priests and then the great court and doors for the court. The doors were covered with bronze.

4.10 He placed the Sea on the right side of The Temple at the southeast corner.

4.11-16 He also made ash buckets, shovels, and bowls.

And that about wrapped it up: Huram completed the work he had contracted to do for King Solomon:

two pillars;

two bowl-shaped capitals for the tops of the pillars;

two decorative filigrees for the capitals;

four hundred pomegranates for the filigrees (a double row of pomegranates for each filigree);

ten washstands with their basins;

one Sea and the twelve bulls under it;

---

a 1 That is, about 30 feet (about 9 meters) long and wide, and about 15 feet (about 4.5 meters) high   *b 2* That is, about 7 1/2 feet (about 2.3 meters)   *c 2* That is, about 45 feet (about 13.5 meters)   *d 3* That is, about 1 1/2 feet (about 0.5 meter)   *e 5* That is, about 3 inches (about 8 centimeters)   *f 5* That is, about 17,500 gallons (about 66 kiloliters)

NEW INTERNATIONAL VERSION

¹⁶the pots, shovels, meat forks and all related articles.

All the objects that Huram-Abi made for King Solomon for the temple of the LORD were of polished bronze. ¹⁷The king had them cast in clay molds in the plain of the Jordan between Succoth and Zarethan.ᵃ ¹⁸All these things that Solomon made amounted to so much that the weight of the bronze was not determined.

¹⁹Solomon also made all the furnishings that were in God's temple:

the golden altar;
the tables on which was the bread of the Presence;
²⁰the lampstands of pure gold with their lamps, to burn in front of the inner sanctuary as prescribed;
²¹the gold floral work and lamps and tongs (they were solid gold);
²²the pure gold wick trimmers, sprinkling bowls, dishes and censers; and the gold doors of the temple: the inner doors to the Most Holy Place and the doors of the main hall.

5 When all the work Solomon had done for the temple of the LORD was finished, he brought in the things his father David had dedicated—the silver and gold and all the furnishings—and he placed them in the treasuries of God's temple.

THE ARK BROUGHT TO THE TEMPLE

²Then Solomon summoned to Jerusalem the elders of Israel, all the heads of the tribes and the chiefs of the Israelite families, to bring up the ark of the LORD's covenant from Zion, the City of David. ³And all the men of Israel came together to the king at the time of the festival in the seventh month.

⁴When all the elders of Israel had arrived, the Levites took up the ark, ⁵and they brought up the ark and the Tent of Meeting and all the sacred furnishings in it. The priests, who were Levites, carried them up; ⁶and King Solomon and the entire assembly of Israel that had gathered about him were before the ark, sacrificing so many sheep and cattle that they could not be recorded or counted.

⁷The priests then brought the ark of the LORD's covenant to its place in the inner sanctuary of the temple, the Most Holy Place, and put

THE MESSAGE

miscellaneous buckets, forks, shovels, and bowls.

4.16-18 All these artifacts that Huram-Abi made for King Solomon for The Temple of GOD were made of burnished bronze. The king had them cast in clay in a foundry on the Jordan plain between Succoth and Zarethan. These artifacts were never weighed—there were far too many! Nobody has any idea how much bronze was used.

4.19-22 Solomon was also responsible for the furniture and accessories in The Temple of God:

the gold Altar;
the tables that held the Bread of the Presence;
the Lampstands of pure gold with their lamps, to be lighted before the Inner Sanctuary, the Holy of Holies;
the gold flowers, lamps, and tongs (all solid gold);
the gold wick trimmers, bowls, ladles, and censers;
the gold doors of The Temple, doors to the Holy of Holies, and the doors to the main sanctuary.

5.1 **5** That completed the work King Solomon did on The Temple of GOD. He then brought in the holy offerings of his father David, the silver and the gold and the artifacts. He placed them all in the treasury of God's Temple.

INSTALLING THE CHEST

5.2-3 Bringing all this to a climax, Solomon got all the leaders together in Jerusalem—all the chiefs of tribes and the family patriarchs—to move the Chest of the Covenant of GOD from Zion and install it in The Temple. All the men of Israel assembled before the king on the feast day of the seventh month, the Feast of Booths.

5.4-6 When all the leaders of Israel were ready, the Levites took up the Chest. They carried the Chest, the Tent of Meeting, and all the sacred things in the Tent used in worship. The priests, all Levites, carried them. King Solomon and the entire congregation of Israel were there before the Chest, worshiping and sacrificing huge numbers of sheep and cattle—so many that no one could keep track.

5.7-10 The priests brought the Chest of the Covenant of GOD to its place in the Inner Sanctuary, the Holy of Holies, under the wings of the

---

ᵃ 17 Hebrew *Zeredatha*, a variant of *Zarethan*

NEW INTERNATIONAL VERSION

it beneath the wings of the cherubim. 8The cherubim spread their wings over the place of the ark and covered the ark and its carrying poles. 9These poles were so long that their ends, extending from the ark, could be seen from in front of the inner sanctuary, but not from outside the Holy Place; and they are still there today. 10There was nothing in the ark except the two tablets that Moses had placed in it at Horeb, where the LORD made a covenant with the Israelites after they came out of Egypt.

11The priests then withdrew from the Holy Place. All the priests who were there had consecrated themselves, regardless of their divisions. 12All the Levites who were musicians—Asaph, Heman, Jeduthun and their sons and relatives—stood on the east side of the altar, dressed in fine linen and playing cymbals, harps and lyres. They were accompanied by 120 priests sounding trumpets. 13The trumpeters and singers joined in unison, as with one voice, to give praise and thanks to the LORD. Accompanied by trumpets, cymbals and other instruments, they raised their voices in praise to the LORD and sang:

"He is good;
his love endures forever."

Then the temple of the LORD was filled with a cloud, 14and the priests could not perform their service because of the cloud, for the glory of the LORD filled the temple of God.

6 Then Solomon said, "The LORD has said that he would dwell in a dark cloud; 2I have built a magnificent temple for you, a place for you to dwell forever."

3While the whole assembly of Israel was standing there, the king turned around and blessed them. 4Then he said:

"Praise be to the LORD, the God of Israel, who with his hands has fulfilled what he promised with his mouth to my father David. For he said, 5'Since the day I brought my people out of Egypt, I have not chosen a city in any tribe of Israel to have a temple built for my Name to be there, nor have I chosen anyone to be the leader over my people Israel. 6But now I have chosen Jerusalem for my Name to be there, and I have chosen David to rule my people Israel.'

7"My father David had it in his heart to build a temple for the Name of the LORD, the God of Israel. 8But the LORD said to my father David, 'Because it was in your heart to build a temple for my Name, you did well to have this in your heart. 9Neverthe-

THE MESSAGE

cherubim. The outspread wings of the cherubim formed a canopy over the Chest and its poles. The ends of the poles were so long that they stuck out from the entrance of the Inner Sanctuary, but were not noticeable further out—they're still there today. There was nothing in the Chest itself but the two stone tablets that Moses had placed in it at Horeb where GOD made a covenant with Israel after bringing them up from Egypt.

5.11-13 The priests then left the Holy Place. All the priests there were consecrated, regardless of rank or assignment; and all the Levites who were musicians were there—Asaph, Heman, Jeduthun, and their families, dressed in their worship robes; the choir and orchestra assembled on the east side of the Altar and were joined by 120 priests blowing trumpets. The choir and trumpets made one voice of praise and thanks to GOD—orchestra and choir in perfect harmony singing and playing praise to GOD:

Yes! God is good!
His loyal love goes on forever!

5.13-14 Then a billowing cloud filled The Temple of GOD. The priests couldn't even carry out their duties because of the cloud—the glory of GOD!—that filled The Temple of God.

SOLOMON'S DEDICATION AND PRAYER

6.1-2 6 Then Solomon said,
GOD said he would dwell in a cloud,
But I've built a temple most splendid,
A place for you to live in forever.

6.3 The king then turned to face the congregation that had come together and blessed them:

6.4-6 "Blessed be GOD, the God of Israel, who spoke personally to my father David. Now he has done what he promised when he said, 'From the day I brought my people Israel up from Egypt, I haven't set apart one city among the tribes of Israel in which to build a temple to honor my Name, or chosen one person to be the leader. But now I have chosen both a city and a person: Jerusalem for honoring my Name and David to lead my people Israel.'

6.7-9 "My father David very much wanted to build a temple honoring the Name of GOD, the God of Israel, but GOD told him, 'It was good that you wanted to build a temple in my honor—most commendable! But you are not the one to

NEW INTERNATIONAL VERSION

less, you are not the one to build the temple, but your son, who is your own flesh and blood—he is the one who will build the temple for my Name.'

10 "The LORD has kept the promise he made. I have succeeded David my father and now I sit on the throne of Israel, just as the LORD promised, and I have built the temple for the Name of the LORD, the God of Israel. 11 There I have placed the ark, in which is the covenant of the LORD that he made with the people of Israel."

SOLOMON'S PRAYER OF DEDICATION

12 Then Solomon stood before the altar of the LORD in front of the whole assembly of Israel and spread out his hands. 13 Now he had made a bronze platform, five cubits*a* long, five cubits wide and three cubits*b* high, and had placed it in the center of the outer court. He stood on the platform and then knelt down before the whole assembly of Israel and spread out his hands toward heaven. 14 He said:

"O LORD, God of Israel, there is no God like you in heaven or on earth—you who keep your covenant of love with your servants who continue wholeheartedly in your way. 15 You have kept your promise to your servant David my father; with your mouth you have promised and with your hand you have fulfilled it—as it is today.

16 "Now LORD, God of Israel, keep for your servant David my father the promises you made to him when you said, 'You shall never fail to have a man to sit before me on the throne of Israel, if only your sons are careful in all they do to walk before me according to my law, as you have done.' 17 And now, O LORD, God of Israel, let your word that you promised your servant David come true.

18 "But will God really dwell on earth with men? The heavens, even the highest heavens, cannot contain you. How much less this temple I have built! 19 Yet give attention to your servant's prayer and his plea for mercy, O LORD my God. Hear the cry and the prayer that your servant is praying in your presence. 20 May your eyes be open toward this temple day and night, this place of which you said you would put your Name there. May you hear the prayer your servant prays toward this place. 21 Hear the supplications of your servant and of your people Israel when they pray

---

THE MESSAGE

do it. Your son, who will carry on your dynasty, will build it for my Name.'

6.10-11 "And now you see the promise completed. GOD has done what he said he would do; I have succeeded David my father and now rule Israel; and I have built a temple to honor GOD, the God of Israel, and have secured a place for the Chest that holds the Covenant of GOD, the covenant he made with the people of Israel."

6.12-16 Before the entire congregation of Israel, Solomon took his position at the Altar of GOD and stretched out his hands. Solomon had made a bronze dais seven and a half feet square and four and a half feet high and placed it inside the court; that's where he now stood. Then he knelt in full view of the whole congregation, stretched his hands to heaven, and prayed:

6.17 GOD, O God of Israel, there is no God like you in the skies above or on the earth below, who unswervingly keeps covenant with his servants and unfailingly loves them while they sincerely live in obedience to your way. You kept your word to David my father, your promise. You did exactly what you promised—every detail. The proof is before us today!

Keep it up, GOD, O God of Israel! Continue to keep the promises you made to David my father when you said, "You'll always have a descendant to represent my rule on Israel's throne, on the one condition that your sons are as careful to live obediently in my presence as you have."

O GOD, God of Israel, let this all happen— confirm and establish it!

6.18-21 Can it be that God will actually move into our neighborhood? Why, the cosmos itself isn't large enough to give you breathing room, let alone this Temple I've built. Even so, I'm bold to ask: Pay attention to these my prayers, both intercessory and personal, O GOD, my God. Listen to my prayers, energetic and devout, that I'm setting before you right now. Keep your eyes open to this Temple day and night, this place you promised to dignify with your Name. And listen to the prayers that I pray in this place. And listen to your people Israel when they pray at this place.

---

a 13 That is, about 7 1/2 feet (about 2.3 meters)
b 13 That is, about 4 1/2 feet (about 1.3 meters)

NEW INTERNATIONAL VERSION

toward this place. Hear from heaven, your dwelling place; and when you hear, forgive.

22"When a man wrongs his neighbor and is required to take an oath and he comes and swears the oath before your altar in this temple, 23then hear from heaven and act. Judge between your servants, repaying the guilty by bringing down on his own head what he has done. Declare the innocent not guilty and so establish his innocence.

24"When your people Israel have been defeated by an enemy because they have sinned against you and when they turn back and confess your name, praying and making supplication before you in this temple, 25then hear from heaven and forgive the sin of your people Israel and bring them back to the land you gave to them and their fathers.

26"When the heavens are shut up and there is no rain because your people have sinned against you, and when they pray toward this place and confess your name and turn from their sin because you have afflicted them, 27then hear from heaven and forgive the sin of your servants, your people Israel. Teach them the right way to live, and send rain on the land you gave your people for an inheritance.

28"When famine or plague comes to the land, or blight or mildew, locusts or grasshoppers, or when enemies besiege them in any of their cities, whatever disaster or disease may come, 29and when a prayer or plea is made by any of your people Israel—each one aware of his afflictions and pains, and spreading out his hands toward this temple— 30then hear from heaven, your dwelling place. Forgive, and deal with each man according to all he does, since you know his heart (for you alone know the hearts of men), 31so that they will fear you and walk in your ways all the time they live in the land you gave our fathers.

32"As for the foreigner who does not belong to your people Israel but has come

THE MESSAGE

Listen from your home in heaven
    and when you hear, forgive.

6.22   When someone hurts a neighbor and promises to make things right, and then comes and repeats the promise before your Altar in this Temple,

6.23   Listen from heaven and act;
        judge your servants, making the
            offender pay for the offense
And set the offended free,
        dismissing all charges.

6.24-25   When your people Israel are beaten by an enemy because they've sinned against you, but then turn to you and acknowledge your rule in prayers desperate and devout in this Temple,

Listen from your home in heaven;
        forgive the sin of your people Israel,
        return them to the land you gave to
            them and their ancestors.

6.26-27   When the skies shrivel up and there is no rain because your people have sinned against you, but then they pray at this place, acknowledging your rule and quit their sins because you have scourged them,

Listen from your home in heaven,
        forgive the sins of your servants, your
            people Israel.
Then start over with them;
        train them to live right and well;
Send rain on the land
        you gave as inheritance to your people.

6.28-31   When disasters strike, famine or catastrophe, crop failure or disease, locust or beetle, or when an enemy attacks their defenses—calamity of any sort—any prayer that's prayed from anyone at all among your people Israel, their hearts penetrated by disaster, hands and arms thrown out for help to this Temple,

Listen from your home in heaven, forgive
        and reward us:
    reward each life and circumstance,
For you know each life from the inside,
        (you're the only one with such inside
            knowledge!),
So they'll live before you in lifelong
        reverence and believing
        obedience on this land you gave our
            ancestors.

6.32   And don't forget the foreigner who is not a member of your people Israel but

NEW INTERNATIONAL VERSION

from a distant land because of your great name and your mighty hand and your outstretched arm—when he comes and prays toward this temple, [33]then hear from heaven, your dwelling place, and do whatever the foreigner asks of you, so that all the peoples of the earth may know your name and fear you, as do your own people Israel, and may know that this house I have built bears your Name.

[34]"When your people go to war against their enemies, wherever you send them, and when they pray to you toward this city you have chosen and the temple I have built for your Name, [35]then hear from heaven their prayer and their plea, and uphold their cause.

[36]"When they sin against you—for there is no one who does not sin—and you become angry with them and give them over to the enemy, who takes them captive to a land far away or near; [37]and if they have a change of heart in the land where they are held captive, and repent and plead with you in the land of their captivity and say, 'We have sinned, we have done wrong and acted wickedly'; [38]and if they turn back to you with all their heart and soul in the land of their captivity where they were taken, and pray toward the land you gave their fathers, toward the city you have chosen and toward the temple I have built for your Name; [39]then from heaven, your dwelling place, hear their prayer and their pleas, and uphold their cause. And forgive your people, who have sinned against you.

[40]"Now, my God, may your eyes be open and your ears attentive to the prayers offered in this place.

[41]"Now arise, O LORD God, and come to
    your resting place,
  you and the ark of your might.
May your priests, O LORD God, be
    clothed with salvation,
  may your saints rejoice in your
    goodness.
[42]O LORD God, do not reject your
    anointed one.
  Remember the great love promised to
    David your servant."

THE MESSAGE

has come from a far country because of your reputation—people *are* going to be attracted here by your great reputation, your wonderworking power—and who come to pray to this Temple.

6.33
Listen from your home in heaven
  and honor the prayers of the foreigner,
So that people all over the world
  will know who you are and what you're
    like,
And live in reverent obedience before you,
  just as your own people Israel do,
So they'll know that you personally
  make this Temple that I've built what it is.

6.34-35
When your people go to war against their enemies at the time and place you send them and they pray to GOD toward the city you chose and The Temple I've built to honor your Name,

Listen from heaven to what they pray and
  ask for
  and do what is right for them.

6.36-39
When they sin against you—and they certainly will; there's no one without sin!—and in anger you turn them over to the enemy and they are taken off captive to the enemy's land, whether far or near, but then repent in the country of their captivity and pray with changed hearts in their exile, "We've sinned; we've done wrong; we've been most wicked," and they turn back to you heart and soul in the land of the enemy who conquered them, and pray to you toward their homeland, the land you gave their ancestors, toward the city you chose, and this Temple I have built to the honor of your Name,

Listen from your home in heaven
  to their prayers desperate and devout;
Do what is best for them.
  Forgive your people who have sinned
    against you.

6.40
And now, dear God, be alert and attentive to prayer, all prayer, offered in this place.

6.41-42
Up, GOD, enjoy your new place of quiet
  repose,
  you and your mighty covenant Chest;
Dress your priests up in salvation clothes,
  let your holy people celebrate goodness.
And don't, GOD, back out on your anointed
  ones,
  keep in mind the love promised to David
    your servant.

NEW INTERNATIONAL VERSION

THE DEDICATION OF THE TEMPLE

7 When Solomon finished praying, fire came down from heaven and consumed the burnt offering and the sacrifices, and the glory of the LORD filled the temple. ²The priests could not enter the temple of the LORD because the glory of the LORD filled it. ³When all the Israelites saw the fire coming down and the glory of the LORD above the temple, they knelt on the pavement with their faces to the ground, and they worshiped and gave thanks to the LORD, saying,

"He is good;
his love endures forever."

⁴Then the king and all the people offered sacrifices before the LORD. ⁵And King Solomon offered a sacrifice of twenty-two thousand head of cattle and a hundred and twenty thousand sheep and goats. So the king and all the people dedicated the temple of God. ⁶The priests took their positions, as did the Levites with the LORD's musical instruments, which King David had made for praising the LORD and which were used when he gave thanks, saying, "His love endures forever." Opposite the Levites, the priests blew their trumpets, and all the Israelites were standing.

⁷Solomon consecrated the middle part of the courtyard in front of the temple of the LORD, and there he offered burnt offerings and the fat of the fellowship offerings,ᵃ because the bronze altar he had made could not hold the burnt offerings, the grain offerings and the fat portions.

⁸So Solomon observed the festival at that time for seven days, and all Israel with him—a vast assembly, people from Leboᵇ Hamath to the Wadi of Egypt. ⁹On the eighth day they held an assembly, for they had celebrated the dedication of the altar for seven days and the festival for seven days more. ¹⁰On the twenty-third day of the seventh month he sent the people to their homes, joyful and glad in heart for the good things the LORD had done for David and Solomon and for his people Israel.

THE LORD APPEARS TO SOLOMON

¹¹When Solomon had finished the temple of the LORD and the royal palace, and had succeeded in carrying out all he had in mind to do in the temple of the LORD and in his own palace, ¹²the LORD appeared to him at night and said:

"I have heard your prayer and have chosen this place for myself as a temple for sacrifices.

¹³"When I shut up the heavens so that there is no rain, or command locusts to de-

THE MESSAGE

THE TEMPLE DEDICATION

7.1-3 **7** When Solomon finished praying, a bolt of lightning out of heaven struck the Whole-Burnt-Offering and sacrifices and the Glory of GOD filled The Temple. The Glory was so dense that the priests couldn't get in—GOD so filled The Temple that there was no room for the priests! When all Israel saw the fire fall from heaven and the Glory of GOD fill The Temple, they fell on their knees, bowed their heads, and worshiped, thanking GOD:

Yes! God is good!
His love never quits!

7.4-6 Then the king and all Israel worshiped, offering sacrifices to GOD. King Solomon worshiped by sacrificing 22,000 cattle and 120,000 sheep at the dedication of The Temple. The priests were all on duty; the choir and orchestra of Levites that David had provided for singing and playing anthems to the praise and love of GOD were all there; across the courtyard the priests blew trumpets. All Israelites were on their feet.

7.7-10 Solomon set apart the central area of the courtyard in front of GOD's Temple for sacred use and there sacrificed the Whole-Burnt-Offerings, Grain-Offerings, and fat from the Peace-Offerings—the Bronze Altar was too small to handle all these offerings. This is how Solomon kept the great autumn Feast of Booths. For seven days there were people there all the way from the far northeast (the Entrance to Hamath) to the far southwest (the Brook of Egypt)—a huge congregation. They started out celebrating for seven days, and then did it for another seven days, a week for dedicating the Altar and another for the Feast itself—two solid weeks of celebration! On the twenty-third day of the seventh month Solomon dismissed his congregation. They left rejoicing, exuberant over all the good GOD had done for David and Solomon and his people Israel.

GOD'S CONFIRMATION

7.11 Solomon completed building The Temple of GOD and the royal palace—the projects he had set his heart on doing. Everything was done—success! Satisfaction!

7.12-18 GOD appeared to Solomon that very night and said, "I accept your prayer; yes, I have chosen this place as a temple for sacrifice, a house of worship. If I ever shut off the supply of rain from the skies or order the locusts to eat the

---

ᵃ 7 Traditionally *peace offerings*   ᵇ 8 Or *from the entrance to*

NEW INTERNATIONAL VERSION

vour the land or send a plague among my people, 14if my people, who are called by my name, will humble themselves and pray and seek my face and turn from their wicked ways, then will I hear from heaven and will forgive their sin and will heal their land. 15Now my eyes will be open and my ears attentive to the prayers offered in this place. 16I have chosen and consecrated this temple so that my Name may be there forever. My eyes and my heart will always be there.

17"As for you, if you walk before me as David your father did, and do all I command, and observe my decrees and laws, 18I will establish your royal throne, as I covenanted with David your father when I said, 'You shall never fail to have a man to rule over Israel.'

19"But if you*a* turn away and forsake the decrees and commands I have given you*a* and go off to serve other gods and worship them, 20then I will uproot Israel from my land, which I have given them, and will reject this temple I have consecrated for my Name. I will make it a byword and an object of ridicule among all peoples. 21And though this temple is now so imposing, all who pass by will be appalled and say, 'Why has the LORD done such a thing to this land and to this temple?' 22People will answer, 'Because they have forsaken the LORD, the God of their fathers, who brought them out of Egypt, and have embraced other gods, worshiping and serving them—that is why he brought all this disaster on them.' "

SOLOMON'S OTHER ACTIVITIES

8 At the end of twenty years, during which Solomon built the temple of the LORD and his own palace, 2Solomon rebuilt the villages that Hiram*b* had given him, and settled Israelites in them. 3Solomon then went to Hamath Zobah and captured it. 4He also built up Tadmor in the desert and all the store cities he had built in Hamath. 5He rebuilt Upper Beth Horon and Lower Beth Horon as fortified cities, with walls and with gates and bars, 6as well as Baalath and all his store cities, and all the cities for his chariots and for his horses*c*—whatever he desired to

THE MESSAGE

crops or send a plague on my people, and my people, my God-defined people, respond by humbling themselves, praying, seeking my presence, and turning their backs on their wicked lives, I'll be there ready for you: I'll listen from heaven, forgive their sins, and restore their land to health. From now on I'm alert day and night to the prayers offered at this place. Believe me, I've chosen and sanctified this Temple that you have built: My Name is stamped on it forever; my eyes are on it and my heart in it always. As for you, if you live in my presence as your father David lived, pure in heart and action, living the life I've set out for you, attentively obedient to my guidance and judgments, then I'll back your kingly rule over Israel—make it a sure thing on a sure foundation. The same covenant guarantee I gave to David your father I'm giving to you, namely, 'You can count on always having a descendant on Israel's throne.'

7.19-22 "But if you or your sons betray me, ignoring my guidance and judgments, taking up with alien gods by serving and worshiping them, then the guarantee is off: I'll wipe Israel right off the map and repudiate this Temple I've just sanctified to honor my Name. And Israel will be nothing but a bad joke among the peoples of the world. And this Temple, splendid as it now is, will become an object of contempt; tourists will shake their heads, saying, 'What happened here? What's the story behind these ruins?' Then they'll be told, 'The people who used to live here betrayed their GOD, the very God who rescued their ancestors from Egypt; they took up with alien gods, worshiping and serving them. That's what's behind this God-visited devastation.' "

MORE ON SOLOMON

8.1-6 **8** At the end of twenty years, Solomon had quite a list of accomplishments. He had:

built The Temple of GOD and his own palace;
rebuilt the cities that Hiram had given him and colonized them with Israelites;
marched on Hamath Zobah and took it;
fortified Tadmor in the desert and all the store-cities he had founded in Hamath;
built the fortress cities Upper Beth Horon and Lower Beth Horon, complete with walls, gates, and bars;
built Baalath and store-cities;
built chariot-cities for his horses.

---

a 19 The Hebrew is plural.   *b 2* Hebrew *Huram*, a variant of *Hiram*; also in verse 18   *c 6* Or *charioteers*

NEW INTERNATIONAL VERSION

build in Jerusalem, in Lebanon and throughout all the territory he ruled.

⁷All the people left from the Hittites, Amorites, Perizzites, Hivites and Jebusites (these peoples were not Israelites), ⁸that is, their descendants remaining in the land, whom the Israelites had not destroyed—these Solomon conscripted for his slave labor force, as it is to this day. ⁹But Solomon did not make slaves of the Israelites for his work; they were his fighting men, commanders of his captains, and commanders of his chariots and charioteers. ¹⁰They were also King Solomon's chief officials—two hundred and fifty officials supervising the men.

¹¹Solomon brought Pharaoh's daughter up from the City of David to the palace he had built for her, for he said, "My wife must not live in the palace of David king of Israel, because the places the ark of the LORD has entered are holy."

¹²On the altar of the LORD that he had built in front of the portico, Solomon sacrificed burnt offerings to the LORD, ¹³according to the daily requirement for offerings commanded by Moses for Sabbaths, New Moons and the three annual feasts—the Feast of Unleavened Bread, the Feast of Weeks and the Feast of Tabernacles. ¹⁴In keeping with the ordinance of his father David, he appointed the divisions of the priests for their duties, and the Levites to lead the praise and to assist the priests according to each day's requirement. He also appointed the gatekeepers by divisions for the various gates, because this was what David the man of God had ordered. ¹⁵They did not deviate from the king's commands to the priests or to the Levites in any matter, including that of the treasuries.

¹⁶All Solomon's work was carried out, from the day the foundation of the temple of the LORD was laid until its completion. So the temple of the LORD was finished.

¹⁷Then Solomon went to Ezion Geber and Elath on the coast of Edom. ¹⁸And Hiram sent him ships commanded by his own officers, men who knew the sea. These, with Solomon's men, sailed to Ophir and brought back four hundred and fifty talents*a* of gold, which they delivered to King Solomon.

THE QUEEN OF SHEBA VISITS SOLOMON

9 When the queen of Sheba heard of Solomon's fame, she came to Jerusalem to test him with hard questions. Arriving with a very great caravan—with camels carrying spices, large quantities of gold, and precious stones—she came to Solomon and talked with him about all she had

a 18 That is, about 17 tons (about 16 metric tons)

THE MESSAGE

8.6   Solomon built impulsively and extravagantly—whenever a whim took him. And in Jerusalem, in Lebanon—wherever he fancied.

8.7-10   The remnants from the original inhabitants of the land (Hittites, Amorites, Perizzites, Hivites, Jebusites—all non-Israelites), survivors of the holy wars, were rounded up by Solomon for his gangs of slave labor. The policy is in effect today. But true Israelites were not treated this way; they were used in his army and administration—government leaders and commanders of his chariots and charioteers. They were also the project managers responsible for Solomon's building operations—250 in all in charge of the workforce.

8.11   Solomon brought Pharaoh's daughter from the City of David to a house built especially for her, "Because," he said, "my wife cannot live in the house of David king of Israel, for the areas in which the Chest of GOD has entered are sacred."

8.12-13   Then Solomon offered Whole-Burnt-Offerings to GOD on the Altar of GOD that he had built in front of The Temple porch. He kept to the regular schedule of worship set down by Moses: Sabbaths, New Moons, and the three annual feasts of Unraised Bread (Passover), Weeks (Pentecost), and Booths.

8.14-15   He followed the practice of his father David in setting up groups of priests carrying out the work of worship, with the Levites assigned to lead the sacred music for praising God and to assist the priests in the daily worship; he assigned security guards to be on duty at each gate—that's what David the man of God had ordered. The king's directions to the priests and Levites and financial stewards were kept right down to the fine print—no innovations—including the treasuries.

8.16   All that Solomon set out to do, from the groundbreaking of The Temple of GOD to its finish, was now complete.

8.17-18   Then Solomon went to Ezion Geber and Elath on the coast of Edom. Hiram sent him ships and with them veteran sailors. Joined by Solomon's men they sailed to Ophir (in east Africa), loaded on fifteen tons of gold, and brought it back to King Solomon.

⊹

9.1-4   9 The Queen of Sheba heard of Solomon's reputation and came to Jerusalem to put his reputation to the test, asking all the tough questions. She made a showy entrance—an impressive retinue of attendants and camels loaded with perfume and much gold and precious stones. She emptied her heart to Solo-

NEW INTERNATIONAL VERSION

on her mind. ²Solomon answered all her questions; nothing was too hard for him to explain to her. ³When the queen of Sheba saw the wisdom of Solomon, as well as the palace he had built, ⁴the food on his table, the seating of his officials, the attending servants in their robes, the cup-bearers in their robes and the burnt offerings he made at *a* the temple of the LORD, she was overwhelmed.

⁵She said to the king, "The report I heard in my own country about your achievements and your wisdom is true. ⁶But I did not believe what they said until I came and saw with my own eyes. Indeed, not even half the greatness of your wisdom was told me; you have far exceeded the report I heard. ⁷How happy your men must be! How happy your officials, who continually stand before you and hear your wisdom! ⁸Praise be to the LORD your God, who has delighted in you and placed you on his throne as king to rule for the LORD your God. Because of the love of your God for Israel and his desire to uphold them forever, he has made you king over them, to maintain justice and righteousness."

⁹Then she gave the king 120 talents *b* of gold, large quantities of spices, and precious stones. There had never been such spices as those the queen of Sheba gave to King Solomon.

¹⁰(The men of Hiram and the men of Solomon brought gold from Ophir; they also brought algumwood *c* and precious stones. ¹¹The king used the algumwood to make steps for the temple of the LORD and for the royal palace, and to make harps and lyres for the musicians. Nothing like them had ever been seen in Judah.)

¹²King Solomon gave the queen of Sheba all she desired and asked for; he gave her more than she had brought to him. Then she left and returned with her retinue to her own country.

SOLOMON'S SPLENDOR

¹³The weight of the gold that Solomon received yearly was 666 talents, *d* ¹⁴not including the revenues brought in by merchants and traders. Also all the kings of Arabia and the governors of the land brought gold and silver to Solomon.

¹⁵King Solomon made two hundred large shields of hammered gold; six hundred bekas *e* of hammered gold went into each shield. ¹⁶He also made three hundred small shields of hammered gold, with three hundred bekas *f* of gold in each

THE MESSAGE

mon, talking over everything she cared about. And Solomon answered everything she put to him—nothing stumped him. When the queen of Sheba experienced for herself Solomon's wisdom and saw with her own eyes the palace he had built, the meals that were served, the impressive array of court officials, the sharply dressed waiters, the cupbearers, and then the elaborate worship extravagant with Whole-Burnt-Offerings at The Temple of GOD, it all took her breath away.

9.5-8   She said to the king, "It's all true! Your reputation for accomplishment and wisdom that reached all the way to my country is confirmed. I wouldn't have believed it if I hadn't seen it for myself; they didn't exaggerate! Such wisdom and elegance—far more than I could ever have imagined. Lucky the men and women who work for you, getting to be around you every day and hear your wise words firsthand! And blessed be your GOD who has taken such a liking to you, making you king. Clearly, GOD's love for Israel is behind this, making you king to keep a just order and nurture a God-pleasing people."

9.9-11   She then gave the king four and a half tons of gold and sack after sack of spices and precious stones. There hasn't been a cargo of spices like the shipload the queen of Sheba brought to King Solomon. The ships of Hiram also imported gold from Ophir along with fragrant sandalwood and expensive gems. The king used the sandalwood for fine cabinetry in The Temple of GOD and the royal palace, and for making harps and dulcimers for the musicians. Nothing like that shipment of sandalwood has been seen since.

9.12   King Solomon, for his part, gave the queen of Sheba all her heart's desire—everything she asked for. She took away more than she brought. Satisfied, she returned home with her train of servants.

☩

9.13-14   Solomon received twenty-five tons of gold annually. This was above and beyond the taxes and profit on trade with merchants and traders. All kings of Arabia and various and assorted governors also brought silver and gold to Solomon.

9.15-16   King Solomon crafted 200 body-length shields of hammered gold—about fifteen pounds of gold to each shield—and about 300

---

a 4 Or *the ascent by which he went up to*   *b 9* That is, about 4 1/2 tons (about 4 metric tons)   *c 10* Probably a variant of *almugwood*   *d 13* That is, about 25 tons (about 23 metric tons)   *e 15* That is, about 7 1/2 pounds (about 3.5 kilograms)   *f 16* That is, about 3 3/4 pounds (about 1.7 kilograms)

NEW INTERNATIONAL VERSION

shield. The king put them in the Palace of the Forest of Lebanon.

17Then the king made a great throne inlaid with ivory and overlaid with pure gold. 18The throne had six steps, and a footstool of gold was attached to it. On both sides of the seat were armrests, with a lion standing beside each of them. 19Twelve lions stood on the six steps, one at either end of each step. Nothing like it had ever been made for any other kingdom. 20All King Solomon's goblets were gold, and all the household articles in the Palace of the Forest of Lebanon were pure gold. Nothing was made of silver, because silver was considered of little value in Solomon's day. 21The king had a fleet of trading ships*a* manned by Hiram's*b* men. Once every three years it returned, carrying gold, silver and ivory, and apes and baboons.

22King Solomon was greater in riches and wisdom than all the other kings of the earth. 23All the kings of the earth sought audience with Solomon to hear the wisdom God had put in his heart. 24Year after year, everyone who came brought a gift—articles of silver and gold, and robes, weapons and spices, and horses and mules.

25Solomon had four thousand stalls for horses and chariots, and twelve thousand horses,*c* which he kept in the chariot cities and also with him in Jerusalem. 26He ruled over all the kings from the River*d* to the land of the Philistines, as far as the border of Egypt. 27The king made silver as common in Jerusalem as stones, and cedar as plentiful as sycamore-fig trees in the foothills. 28Solomon's horses were imported from Egypt*e* and from all other countries.

SOLOMON'S DEATH

29As for the other events of Solomon's reign, from beginning to end, are they not written in the records of Nathan the prophet, in the prophecy of Ahijah the Shilonite and in the visions of Iddo the seer concerning Jeroboam son of Nebat? 30Solomon reigned in Jerusalem over all Israel forty years. 31Then he rested with his fathers and was buried in the city of David his father. And Rehoboam his son succeeded him as king.

ISRAEL REBELS AGAINST REHOBOAM

10 Rehoboam went to Shechem, for all the Israelites had gone there to make him

THE MESSAGE

small shields about half that size. He stored the shields in the House of the Forest of Lebanon.

9.17-19 The king made a massive throne of ivory with a veneer of gold. The throne had six steps leading up to it with an attached footstool of gold. The armrests on each side were flanked by lions. Lions, twelve of them, were placed at either end of the six steps. There was no throne like it in any other kingdom.

9.20 King Solomon's chalices and tankards were made of gold, and all the dinnerware and serving utensils in the House of the Forest of Lebanon were pure gold. Nothing was made of silver; silver was considered common and cheap in the time of Solomon.

9.21 The king's ships, manned by Hiram's sailors, made a round trip to Tarshish every three years, returning with a cargo of gold, silver, and ivory, apes and peacocks.

9.22-24 King Solomon was richer and wiser than all the kings of the earth—he surpassed them all. Kings came from all over the world to be with Solomon and get in on the wisdom God had given him. Everyone who came brought gifts—artifacts of gold and silver, fashionable robes and gowns, the latest in weapons, exotic spices, horses, and mules—parades of visitors, year after year.

9.25-28 Solomon collected horses and chariots. He had 4,000 stalls for horses and chariots, and 12,000 horsemen in barracks in the chariot-cities and in Jerusalem. He ruled over all the kings from the River Euphrates in the east, throughout the Philistine country, and as far west as the border of Egypt. The king made silver as common as rocks and cedar as common as the fig trees in the lowland hills. He carried on a brisk horse-trading business with Egypt and other places.

✝

9.29-31 The rest of Solomon's life and rule, from start to finish, one can read in the records of Nathan the prophet, the prophecy of Ahijah of Shiloh, and in the visions of Iddo the seer concerning Jeroboam son of Nebat. Solomon ruled in Jerusalem over all Israel for forty years. Solomon died and was buried in the City of David his father. His son Rehoboam was the next king.

KING REHOBOAM

10.1-2 **10** Rehoboam traveled to Shechem where all Israel had gathered to inaugurate

---

a 21 Hebrew of ships that could go to Tarshish
b 21 Hebrew Huram, a variant of Hiram
c 25 Or charioteers   d 26 That is, the Euphrates
e 28 Or possibly Muzur, a region in Cilicia

NEW INTERNATIONAL VERSION

king. ²When Jeroboam son of Nebat heard this (he was in Egypt, where he had fled from King Solomon), he returned from Egypt. ³So they sent for Jeroboam, and he and all Israel went to Rehoboam and said to him: ⁴"Your father put a heavy yoke on us, but now lighten the harsh labor and the heavy yoke he put on us, and we will serve you."

⁵Rehoboam answered, "Come back to me in three days." So the people went away.

⁶Then King Rehoboam consulted the elders who had served his father Solomon during his lifetime. "How would you advise me to answer these people?" he asked.

⁷They replied, "If you will be kind to these people and please them and give them a favorable answer, they will always be your servants."

⁸But Rehoboam rejected the advice the elders gave him and consulted the young men who had grown up with him and were serving him. ⁹He asked them, "What is your advice? How should we answer these people who say to me, 'Lighten the yoke your father put on us'?"

¹⁰The young men who had grown up with him replied, "Tell the people who have said to you, 'Your father put a heavy yoke on us, but make our yoke lighter'—tell them, 'My little finger is thicker than my father's waist. ¹¹My father laid on you a heavy yoke; I will make it even heavier. My father scourged you with whips; I will scourge you with scorpions.'"

¹²Three days later Jeroboam and all the people returned to Rehoboam, as the king had said, "Come back to me in three days." ¹³The king answered them harshly. Rejecting the advice of the elders, ¹⁴he followed the advice of the young men and said, "My father made your yoke heavy; I will make it even heavier. My father scourged you with whips; I will scourge you with scorpions." ¹⁵So the king did not listen to the people, for this turn of events was from God, to fulfill the word the LORD had spoken to Jeroboam son of Nebat through Ahijah the Shilonite.

¹⁶When all Israel saw that the king refused to listen to them, they answered the king:

"What share do we have in David,
    what part in Jesse's son?
To your tents, O Israel!
    Look after your own house, O David!"

THE MESSAGE

him as king. Jeroboam was then in Egypt, where he had taken asylum from King Solomon; when he got the report of Solomon's death, he came back.

10.3-4   Summoned by Israel, Jeroboam and all Israel went to Rehoboam and said, "Your father made life hard for us—worked our fingers to the bone. Give us a break; lighten up on us and we'll willingly serve you."

10.5   "Give me," said Rehoboam, "three days to think it over; then come back." So the people left.

10.6   King Rehoboam talked it over with the elders who had advised his father when he was alive: "What's your counsel? How do you suggest that I answer the people?"

10.7   They said, "If you will be a servant to this people, be considerate of their needs and respond with compassion, work things out with them, they'll end up doing anything for you."

10.8-9   But he rejected the counsel of the elders and asked the young men he'd grown up with who were now currying his favor, "What do you think? What should I say to these people who are saying, 'Give us a break from your father's harsh ways—lighten up on us'?"

10.10-11   The young turks he'd grown up with said, "These people who complain, 'Your father was too hard on us; lighten up'—well, tell them this: 'My little finger is thicker than my father's waist. If you think life under my father was hard, you haven't seen the half of it. My father thrashed you with whips; I'll beat you bloody with chains!'"

10.12-14   Three days later Jeroboam and the people showed up, just as Rehoboam had directed when he said, "Give me three days to think it over; then come back." The king's answer was harsh and rude. He spurned the counsel of the elders and went with the advice of the younger set: "If you think life under my father was hard, you haven't seen the half of it: my father thrashed you with whips; I'll beat you bloody with chains!"

10.15   Rehoboam turned a deaf ear to the people. God was behind all this, confirming the message that he had given to Jeroboam son of Nebat through Ahijah of Shiloh.

10.16-17   When all Israel realized that the king hadn't listened to a word they'd said, they stood up to him and said,

Get lost, David!
We've had it with you, son of Jesse!
Let's get out of here, Israel, and fast!
From now on, David, mind your own
    business.

NEW INTERNATIONAL VERSION

So all the Israelites went home. [17]But as for the Israelites who were living in the towns of Judah, Rehoboam still ruled over them.

[18]King Rehoboam sent out Adoniram,[a] who was in charge of forced labor, but the Israelites stoned him to death. King Rehoboam, however, managed to get into his chariot and escape to Jerusalem. [19]So Israel has been in rebellion against the house of David to this day.

11 When Rehoboam arrived in Jerusalem, he mustered the house of Judah and Benjamin—a hundred and eighty thousand fighting men—to make war against Israel and to regain the kingdom for Rehoboam.

[2]But this word of the LORD came to Shemaiah the man of God: [3]"Say to Rehoboam son of Solomon king of Judah and to all the Israelites in Judah and Benjamin, [4]'This is what the LORD says: Do not go up to fight against your brothers. Go home, every one of you, for this is my doing.' " So they obeyed the words of the LORD and turned back from marching against Jeroboam.

REHOBOAM FORTIFIES JUDAH

[5]Rehoboam lived in Jerusalem and built up towns for defense in Judah: [6]Bethlehem, Etam, Tekoa, [7]Beth Zur, Soco, Adullam, [8]Gath, Mareshah, Ziph, [9]Adoraim, Lachish, Azekah, [10]Zorah, Aijalon and Hebron. These were fortified cities in Judah and Benjamin. [11]He strengthened their defenses and put commanders in them, with supplies of food, olive oil and wine. [12]He put shields and spears in all the cities, and made them very strong. So Judah and Benjamin were his.

[13]The priests and Levites from all their districts throughout Israel sided with him. [14]The Levites even abandoned their pasturelands and property, and came to Judah and Jerusalem because Jeroboam and his sons had rejected them as priests of the LORD. [15]And he appointed his own priests for the high places and for the goat and calf idols he had made. [16]Those from every tribe of Israel who set their hearts on seeking the LORD, the God of Israel, followed the Levites to Jerusalem to offer sacrifices to the LORD, the God of their fathers. [17]They strengthened the kingdom of Judah and supported Rehoboam son of Solomon three years, walking in the ways of David and Solomon during this time.

REHOBOAM'S FAMILY

[18]Rehoboam married Mahalath, who was the

THE MESSAGE

And with that they left. Rehoboam continued to rule only those who lived in the towns of Judah.

10.18-19   When King Rehoboam next sent out Adoniram, head of the workforce, the Israelites ganged up on him, pelted him with stones, and killed him. King Rehoboam jumped in his chariot and escaped to Jerusalem as fast as he could. Israel has been in rebellion against the Davidic dynasty ever since.

11.1   11 When Rehoboam got back to Jerusalem he called up the men of the tribes of Judah and Benjamin, 180,000 of their best soldiers, to go to war against Israel and recover the kingdom.

11.2-4   At the same time the word of GOD came to Shemaiah, a holy man, "Tell this to Rehoboam son of Solomon, king of Judah, along with all the Israelites in Judah and Benjamin, This is GOD's word: Don't march out; don't fight against your brothers the Israelites. Go back home, every last one of you; *I'm* in charge here." And they did it; they did what GOD said and went home.

11.5-12   Rehoboam continued to live in Jerusalem but built up a defense system for Judah all around: in Bethlehem, Etam, Tekoa, Beth Zur, Soco, Adullam, Gath, Mareshah, Ziph, Adoraim, Lachish, Azekah, Zorah, Aijalon, and Hebron—a line of defense protecting Judah and Benjamin. He beefed up the fortifications, appointed commanders, and put in supplies of food, olive oil, and wine. He installed arms—large shields and spears—in all the forts, making them very strong. So Judah and Benjamin were secure for the time.

11.13-17   The priests and Levites from all over Israel came and made themselves available to Rehoboam. The Levites left their pastures and properties and moved to Judah and Jerusalem because Jeroboam and his sons had dismissed them from the priesthood of GOD and replaced them with his own priests to preside over the worship centers at which he had installed goat and calf demon-idols. Everyone from all the tribes of Israel who determined to seek the GOD of Israel migrated with the priests and Levites to Jerusalem to worship there, sacrificing to the GOD of their ancestors. That gave a tremendous boost to the kingdom of Judah. They stuck with Rehoboam son of Solomon for three years, loyal to the ways of David and Solomon for this period.

11.18-21   Rehoboam married Mahalath daughter of

---

a 18 Hebrew *Hadoram,* a variant of *Adoniram*

NEW INTERNATIONAL VERSION

daughter of David's son Jerimoth and of Abihail, the daughter of Jesse's son Eliab. [19]She bore him sons: Jeush, Shemariah and Zaham. [20]Then he married Maacah daughter of Absalom, who bore him Abijah, Attai, Ziza and Shelomith. [21]Rehoboam loved Maacah daughter of Absalom more than any of his other wives and concubines. In all, he had eighteen wives and sixty concubines, twenty-eight sons and sixty daughters.

[22]Rehoboam appointed Abijah son of Maacah to be the chief prince among his brothers, in order to make him king. [23]He acted wisely, dispersing some of his sons throughout the districts of Judah and Benjamin, and to all the fortified cities. He gave them abundant provisions and took many wives for them.

SHISHAK ATTACKS JERUSALEM

12 After Rehoboam's position as king was established and he had become strong, he and all Israel[a] with him abandoned the law of the LORD. [2]Because they had been unfaithful to the LORD, Shishak king of Egypt attacked Jerusalem in the fifth year of King Rehoboam. [3]With twelve hundred chariots and sixty thousand horsemen and the innumerable troops of Libyans, Sukkites and Cushites[b] that came with him from Egypt, [4]he captured the fortified cities of Judah and came as far as Jerusalem.

[5]Then the prophet Shemaiah came to Rehoboam and to the leaders of Judah who had assembled in Jerusalem for fear of Shishak, and he said to them, "This is what the LORD says, 'You have abandoned me; therefore, I now abandon you to Shishak.'"

[6]The leaders of Israel and the king humbled themselves and said, "The LORD is just."

[7]When the LORD saw that they humbled themselves, this word of the LORD came to Shemaiah: "Since they have humbled themselves, I will not destroy them but will soon give them deliverance. My wrath will not be poured out on Jerusalem through Shishak. [8]They will, however, become subject to him, so that they may learn the difference between serving me and serving the kings of other lands."

[9]When Shishak king of Egypt attacked Jerusalem, he carried off the treasures of the temple of the LORD and the treasures of the royal palace. He took everything, including the gold shields Solomon had made. [10]So King Rehoboam made bronze shields to replace them and assigned these to the commanders of the guard on duty at the entrance to the royal palace. [11]Whenever the

a 1 That is, Judah, as frequently in 2 Chronicles *b 3* That is, people from the upper Nile region

THE MESSAGE

Jerimoth, David's son, and Abihail daughter of Eliab, Jesse's son. Mahalath bore him Jeush, Shemariah, and Zaham. Then he married Maacah, Absalom's daughter, and she bore him Abijah, Attai, Ziza, and Shelomith. Maacah was Rehoboam's favorite wife; he loved her more than all his other wives and concubines put together (and he had a lot—eighteen wives and sixty concubines who produced twenty-eight sons and sixty daughters!).

11.22-23 Rehoboam designated Abijah son of Maacah as the "first son" and leader of the brothers— he intended to make him the next king. He was shrewd in deploying his sons in all the fortress cities that made up his defense system in Judah and Benjamin; he kept them happy with much food and many wives.

12.1 **12** By the time Rehoboam had secured his kingdom and was strong again, he, and all Israel with him, had virtually abandoned GOD and his ways.

✝

12.2-4 In Rehoboam's fifth year, because he and the people were unfaithful to GOD, Shishak king of Egypt invaded as far as Jerusalem. He came with 1,200 chariots and 60,000 cavalry, and soldiers from all over—the Egyptian army included Libyans, Sukkites, and Ethiopians. They took the fortress cities of Judah and advanced as far as Jerusalem itself.

12.5 Then the prophet Shemaiah, accompanied by the leaders of Judah who had retreated to Jerusalem before Shishak, came to Rehoboam and said, "GOD's word: You abandoned me; now I abandon you to Shishak."

12.6 The leaders of Israel and the king were repentant and said, "GOD is right."

12.7-8 When GOD saw that they were humbly repentant, the word of GOD came to Shemaiah: "Because they are humble, I'll not destroy them—I'll give them a break; I won't use Shishak to express my wrath against Jerusalem. What I will do, though, is make them Shishak's subjects—they'll learn the difference between serving me and serving human kings."

12.9 Then Shishak king of Egypt attacked Jerusalem. He plundered the treasury of The Temple of GOD and the treasury of the royal palace—he took everything he could lay his hands on. He even took the gold shields that Solomon had made.

12.10-11 King Rehoboam replaced the gold shields with bronze shields and gave them to the guards who were posted at the entrance to the

NEW INTERNATIONAL VERSION

king went to the LORD's temple, the guards went with him, bearing the shields, and afterward they returned them to the guardroom. [12]Because Rehoboam humbled himself, the LORD's anger turned from him, and he was not totally destroyed. Indeed, there was some good in Judah.

[13]King Rehoboam established himself firmly in Jerusalem and continued as king. He was forty-one years old when he became king, and he reigned seventeen years in Jerusalem, the city the LORD had chosen out of all the tribes of Israel in which to put his Name. His mother's name was Naamah; she was an Ammonite. [14]He did evil because he had not set his heart on seeking the LORD.

[15]As for the events of Rehoboam's reign, from beginning to end, are they not written in the records of Shemaiah the prophet and of Iddo the seer that deal with genealogies? There was continual warfare between Rehoboam and Jeroboam. [16]Rehoboam rested with his fathers and was buried in the City of David. And Abijah his son succeeded him as king.

ABIJAH KING OF JUDAH

13 In the eighteenth year of the reign of Jeroboam, Abijah became king of Judah, [2]and he reigned in Jerusalem three years. His mother's name was Maacah,[a] a daughter[b] of Uriel of Gibeah.

There was war between Abijah and Jeroboam. [3]Abijah went into battle with a force of four hundred thousand able fighting men, and Jeroboam drew up a battle line against him with eight hundred thousand able troops.

[4]Abijah stood on Mount Zemaraim, in the hill country of Ephraim, and said, "Jeroboam and all Israel, listen to me! [5]Don't you know that the LORD, the God of Israel, has given the kingship of Israel to David and his descendants forever by a covenant of salt? [6]Yet Jeroboam son of Nebat, an official of Solomon son of David, rebelled against his master. [7]Some worthless scoundrels gathered around him and opposed Rehoboam son of Solomon when he was young and indecisive and not strong enough to resist them.

[8]"And now you plan to resist the kingdom of the LORD, which is in the hands of David's descendants. You are indeed a vast army and have with you the golden calves that Jeroboam made to be your gods. [9]But didn't you drive out the

[a] 2 Most Septuagint manuscripts and Syriac (see also 2 Chron. 11:20 and 1 Kings 15:2); Hebrew *Micaiah*
[b] 2 Or *granddaughter*

THE MESSAGE

royal palace. Whenever the king went to GOD's Temple, the guards went with him carrying the shields, but they always returned them to the guardroom.

12.12   Because Rehoboam was repentant, GOD's anger was blunted, so he wasn't totally destroyed. The picture wasn't entirely bleak—there were some good things going on in Judah.

12.13-14   King Rehoboam regrouped and reestablished his rule in Jerusalem. He was forty-one years old when he became king and continued as king for seventeen years in Jerusalem, the city GOD chose out of all the tribes of Israel as the special presence of his Name. His mother was Naamah from Ammon. But the final verdict on Rehoboam was that he was a bad king—GOD was not important to him; his heart neither cared for nor sought after GOD.

12.15-16   The history of Rehoboam, from start to finish, is written in the memoirs of Shemaiah the prophet and Iddo the seer that contain the family trees. There was war between Rehoboam and Jeroboam the whole time. Rehoboam died and was buried with his ancestors in the City of David. His son Abijah ruled after him.

KING ABIJAH

13 In the eighteenth year of the rule of King Jeroboam, Abijah took over the throne of Judah. He ruled in Jerusalem three years. His mother was Maacah daughter of Uriel of Gibeah.

13.2-3   War broke out between Abijah and Jeroboam. Abijah started out with 400,000 of his best soldiers; Jeroboam countered with 800,000 of his best.

13.4-7   Abijah took a prominent position on Mount Zemaraim in the hill country of Ephraim and gave this speech: "Listen, Jeroboam and all Israel! Don't you realize that GOD, the one and only God of Israel, established David and his sons as the permanent rulers of Israel, ratified by a 'covenant of salt'—GOD's kingdom ruled by GOD's king? And what happened? Jeroboam, the son of Solomon's slave Nebat, rebelled against his master. All the riff-raff joined his cause and were too much for Rehoboam, Solomon's true heir. Rehoboam didn't know his way around—besides he was a real wimp; he couldn't stand up against them.

13.8-9   "Taking advantage of that weakness, you are asserting yourself against the very rule of GOD that is delegated to David's descendants—you think you are so big with your huge army backed up by the golden-calf idols that Jeroboam made for you as gods! But just look at what

NEW INTERNATIONAL VERSION

priests of the LORD, the sons of Aaron, and the Levites, and make priests of your own as the peoples of other lands do? Whoever comes to consecrate himself with a young bull and seven rams may become a priest of what are not gods.

10 "As for us, the LORD is our God, and we have not forsaken him. The priests who serve the LORD are sons of Aaron, and the Levites assist them. 11 Every morning and evening they present burnt offerings and fragrant incense to the LORD. They set out the bread on the ceremonially clean table and light the lamps on the gold lampstand every evening. We are observing the requirements of the LORD our God. But you have forsaken him. 12 God is with us; he is our leader. His priests with their trumpets will sound the battle cry against you. Men of Israel, do not fight against the LORD, the God of your fathers, for you will not succeed."

13 Now Jeroboam had sent troops around to the rear, so that while he was in front of Judah the ambush was behind them. 14 Judah turned and saw that they were being attacked at both front and rear. Then they cried out to the LORD. The priests blew their trumpets 15 and the men of Judah raised the battle cry. At the sound of their battle cry, God routed Jeroboam and all Israel before Abijah and Judah. 16 The Israelites fled before Judah, and God delivered them into their hands. 17 Abijah and his men inflicted heavy losses on them, so that there were five hundred thousand casualties among Israel's able men. 18 The men of Israel were subdued on that occasion, and the men of Judah were victorious because they relied on the LORD, the God of their fathers.

19 Abijah pursued Jeroboam and took from him the towns of Bethel, Jeshanah and Ephron, with their surrounding villages. 20 Jeroboam did not regain power during the time of Abijah. And the LORD struck him down and he died.

21 But Abijah grew in strength. He married fourteen wives and had twenty-two sons and sixteen daughters.

22 The other events of Abijah's reign, what he did and what he said, are written in the annotations of the prophet Iddo.

14 And Abijah rested with his fathers and was buried in the City of David. Asa his son succeeded him as king, and in his days the country was at peace for ten years.

THE MESSAGE

you've done—you threw out the priests of GOD, the sons of Aaron, and the Levites, and made priests to suit yourselves, priests just like the pagans have. Anyone who shows up with enough money to pay for it can be a priest! A priest of No-God!

13.10-11 "But for the rest of us in Judah, we're sticking with GOD. We have not traded him in for the latest model—we're keeping the tried and true priests of Aaron to lead us to GOD and the Levites to lead us in worship by sacrificing Whole-Burnt-Offerings and aromatic incense to GOD at the daily morning and evening prayers, setting out fresh holy bread on a clean table, and lighting the lamps on the golden Lampstand every night. We continue doing what GOD told us to in the way he told us to do it; but you have rid yourselves of him.

13.12 "Can't you see the obvious? God is on our side; he's our leader. And his priests with trumpets are all ready to blow the signal to battle. O Israel—don't fight against GOD, the God of your ancestors. You will not win this battle."

13.13-18 While Abijah was speaking, Jeroboam had sent men around to take them by surprise from the rear: Jeroboam in front of Judah and the ambush behind. When Judah looked back, they saw they were attacked front and back. They prayed desperately to GOD, the priests blew their trumpets, and the soldiers of Judah shouted their battle cry. At the battle cry, God routed Jeroboam and all Israel before Abijah and Judah. The army of Israel scattered before Judah; God gave them the victory. Abijah and his troops slaughtered them—500,000 of Israel's best fighters were killed that day. The army of Israel fell flat on its face—a humiliating defeat. The army of Judah won hands down because they trusted GOD, the God of their ancestors.

13.19-21 Abijah followed up his victory by pursuing Jeroboam, taking the towns of Bethel, Jeshanah, and Ephron with their surrounding villages. Jeroboam never did recover from his defeat while Abijah lived. Later on GOD struck him down and he died. Meanwhile Abijah flourished; he married fourteen wives and ended up with a family of twenty-two sons and sixteen daughters.

13.22 The rest of the history of Abijah, what he did and said, is written in the study written by Iddo the prophet.

KING ASA

14.1 **14** Abijah died and was buried with his ancestors in the City of David. His son Asa became the next king.

For ten years into Asa's reign the country was at peace.

NEW INTERNATIONAL VERSION

Asa King of Judah

²Asa did what was good and right in the eyes of the LORD his God. ³He removed the foreign altars and the high places, smashed the sacred stones and cut down the Asherah poles.ᵃ ⁴He commanded Judah to seek the LORD, the God of their fathers, and to obey his laws and commands. ⁵He removed the high places and incense altars in every town in Judah, and the kingdom was at peace under him. ⁶He built up the fortified cities of Judah, since the land was at peace. No one was at war with him during those years, for the LORD gave him rest.

⁷"Let us build up these towns," he said to Judah, "and put walls around them, with towers, gates and bars. The land is still ours, because we have sought the LORD our God; we sought him and he has given us rest on every side." So they built and prospered.

⁸Asa had an army of three hundred thousand men from Judah, equipped with large shields and with spears, and two hundred and eighty thousand from Benjamin, armed with small shields and with bows. All these were brave fighting men.

⁹Zerah the Cushite marched out against them with a vast armyᵇ and three hundred chariots, and came as far as Mareshah. ¹⁰Asa went out to meet him, and they took up battle positions in the Valley of Zephathah near Mareshah.

¹¹Then Asa called to the LORD his God and said, "LORD, there is no one like you to help the powerless against the mighty. Help us, O LORD our God, for we rely on you, and in your name we have come against this vast army. O LORD, you are our God; do not let man prevail against you."

¹²The LORD struck down the Cushites before Asa and Judah. The Cushites fled, ¹³and Asa and his army pursued them as far as Gerar. Such a great number of Cushites fell that they could not recover; they were crushed before the LORD and his forces. The men of Judah carried off a large amount of plunder. ¹⁴They destroyed all the villages around Gerar, for the terror of the LORD had fallen upon them. They plundered all these villages, since there was much booty there. ¹⁵They also attacked the camps of the herdsmen and carried off droves of sheep and goats and camels. Then they returned to Jerusalem.

THE MESSAGE

14.2-6 Asa was a good king. He did things right in GOD's eyes. He cleaned house: got rid of the pagan altars and shrines, smashed the sacred stone pillars, and chopped down the sex-and-religion groves (Asherim). He told Judah to center their lives in GOD, the God of their fathers, to do what the law said, and to follow the commandments. Because he got rid of all the pagan shrines and altars in the cities of Judah, his kingdom was at peace. Because the land was quiet and there was no war, he was able to build up a good defense system in Judah. GOD kept the peace.

14.7 Asa said to his people, "While we have the chance and the land is quiet, let's build a solid defense system, fortifying our cities with walls, towers, gates, and bars. We have this peaceful land because we sought GOD; he has given us rest from all troubles." So they built and enjoyed prosperity.

14.8 Asa had an army of 300,000 Judeans, equipped with shields and spears, and another 280,000 Benjaminites who were shield bearers and archers. They were all courageous warriors.

14.9-11 Zerah the Ethiopian went to war against Asa with an army of a million plus 300 chariots and got as far as Mareshah. Asa met him there and prepared to fight from the Valley of Zephathah near Mareshah. Then Asa prayed to GOD, " O GOD, you aren't impressed by numbers or intimidated by a show of force once you decide to help: Help us, O GOD; we have come out to meet this huge army because we trust in you and who you are. Don't let mere mortals stand against you!"

14.12-15 GOD defeated the Ethiopians before Asa and Judah; the Ethiopians ran for their lives. Asa and his men chased them as far as Gerar; so many of the Ethiopians were killed that there was no fight left in them—a massacre before GOD and his troops; Judah carted off loads of plunder. They devastated all the towns around Gerar whose people were helpless, paralyzed by the fear of GOD, and looted the country. They also attacked herdsmen and brought back a lot of sheep and camels to Jerusalem.

ᵃ 3 That is, symbols of the goddess Asherah; here and elsewhere in 2 Chronicles   ᵇ 9 Hebrew *with an army of a thousand thousands* or *with an army of thousands upon thousands*

NEW INTERNATIONAL VERSION

ASA'S REFORM

15 The Spirit of God came upon Azariah son of Oded. ²He went out to meet Asa and said to him, "Listen to me, Asa and all Judah and Benjamin. The LORD is with you when you are with him. If you seek him, he will be found by you, but if you forsake him, he will forsake you. ³For a long time Israel was without the true God, without a priest to teach and without the law. ⁴But in their distress they turned to the LORD, the God of Israel, and sought him, and he was found by them. ⁵In those days it was not safe to travel about, for all the inhabitants of the lands were in great turmoil. ⁶One nation was being crushed by another and one city by another, because God was troubling them with every kind of distress. ⁷But as for you, be strong and do not give up, for your work will be rewarded."

⁸When Asa heard these words and the prophecy of Azariah son of*ᵃ* Oded the prophet, he took courage. He removed the detestable idols from the whole land of Judah and Benjamin and from the towns he had captured in the hills of Ephraim. He repaired the altar of the LORD that was in front of the portico of the LORD's temple.

⁹Then he assembled all Judah and Benjamin and the people from Ephraim, Manasseh and Simeon who had settled among them, for large numbers had come over to him from Israel when they saw that the LORD his God was with him.

¹⁰They assembled at Jerusalem in the third month of the fifteenth year of Asa's reign. ¹¹At that time they sacrificed to the LORD seven hundred head of cattle and seven thousand sheep and goats from the plunder they had brought back. ¹²They entered into a covenant to seek the LORD, the God of their fathers, with all their heart and soul. ¹³All who would not seek the LORD, the God of Israel, were to be put to death, whether small or great, man or woman. ¹⁴They took an oath to the LORD with loud acclamation, with shouting and with trumpets and horns. ¹⁵All Judah rejoiced about the oath because they had sworn it wholeheartedly. They sought God eagerly, and he was found by them. So the LORD gave them rest on every side.

¹⁶King Asa also deposed his grandmother Maacah from her position as queen mother, because she had made a repulsive Asherah pole. Asa cut

THE MESSAGE

15 Then Azariah son of Obed, moved by the Spirit of God, went out to meet Asa. He said, "Listen carefully, Asa, and listen Judah and Benjamin: GOD will stick with you as long as you stick with him. If you look for him he will let himself be found; but if you leave him he'll leave you. For a long time Israel didn't have the real God, nor did they have the help of priest or teacher or book. But when they were in trouble and got serious, and decided to seek GOD, the God of Israel, GOD let himself be found. At that time it was a dog-eat-dog world; life was constantly up for grabs—no one, regardless of country, knew what the next day might bring. Nation battered nation, city pummeled city. God let loose every kind of trouble among them.

¹⁵.⁷ "But it's different with you: Be strong. Take heart. Payday is coming!"

¹⁵.⁸⁻⁹ Asa heard the prophecy of Azariah son of Obed, took a deep breath, then rolled up his sleeves, and went to work: He cleaned out the obscene and polluting sacred shrines from the whole country of Judah and Benjamin and from the towns he had taken in the hill country of Ephraim. He spruced up the Altar of GOD that was in front of The Temple porch. Then he called an assembly for all Judah and Benjamin, including those from Ephraim, Manasseh, and Simeon who were living there at the time (for many from Israel had left their homes and joined forces with Asa when they saw that GOD was on his side).

¹⁵.¹⁰⁻¹⁵ They all arrived in Jerusalem in the third month of the fifteenth year of Asa's reign for a great assembly of worship. From their earlier plunder they offered sacrifices of 700 oxen and 7,000 sheep for the worship. Then they bound themselves in a covenant to seek GOD, the God of their fathers, wholeheartedly, holding nothing back. And they agreed that anyone who refused to seek GOD, the God of Israel, should be killed, no matter who it was, young or old, man or woman. They shouted out their promise to GOD, a joyful sound accompanied with blasts from trumpets and rams' horns. The whole country felt good about the covenant promise—they had given their promise joyfully from the heart. Anticipating the best, they had sought God—and he showed up, ready to be found. GOD gave them peace within and without—a most peaceable kingdom!

¹⁵.¹⁶⁻¹⁹ In his clean-up of the country, Asa went so far as to remove his mother, Queen Maacah, from her throne because she had built a shockingly obscene image of the sex goddess Ashe-

---

ᵃ 8 Vulgate and Syriac (see also Septuagint and verse 1); Hebrew does not have *Azariah son of.*

NEW INTERNATIONAL VERSION

the pole down, broke it up and burned it in the Kidron Valley. ¹⁷Although he did not remove the high places from Israel, Asa's heart was fully committed ᴌto the Lᴏʀᴅᴊ all his life. ¹⁸He brought into the temple of God the silver and gold and the articles that he and his father had dedicated.

¹⁹There was no more war until the thirty-fifth year of Asa's reign.

ASA'S LAST YEARS

16 In the thirty-sixth year of Asa's reign Baasha king of Israel went up against Judah and fortified Ramah to prevent anyone from leaving or entering the territory of Asa king of Judah.

²Asa then took the silver and gold out of the treasuries of the Lᴏʀᴅ's temple and of his own palace and sent it to Ben-Hadad king of Aram, who was ruling in Damascus. ³"Let there be a treaty between me and you," he said, "as there was between my father and your father. See, I am sending you silver and gold. Now break your treaty with Baasha king of Israel so he will withdraw from me."

⁴Ben-Hadad agreed with King Asa and sent the commanders of his forces against the towns of Israel. They conquered Ijon, Dan, Abel Maim*ᵃ* and all the store cities of Naphtali. ⁵When Baasha heard this, he stopped building Ramah and abandoned his work. ⁶Then King Asa brought all the men of Judah, and they carried away from Ramah the stones and timber Baasha had been using. With them he built up Geba and Mizpah.

⁷At that time Hanani the seer came to Asa king of Judah and said to him: "Because you relied on the king of Aram and not on the Lᴏʀᴅ your God, the army of the king of Aram has escaped from your hand. ⁸Were not the Cushites*ᵇ* and Libyans a mighty army with great numbers of chariots and horsemen*ᶜ*? Yet when you relied on the Lᴏʀᴅ, he delivered them into your hand. ⁹For the eyes of the Lᴏʀᴅ range throughout the earth to strengthen those whose hearts are fully committed to him. You have done a foolish thing, and from now on you will be at war."

¹⁰Asa was angry with the seer because of this; he was so enraged that he put him in prison. At the same time Asa brutally oppressed some of the people.

¹¹The events of Asa's reign, from beginning to end, are written in the book of the kings of Judah and Israel. ¹²In the thirty-ninth year of his reign Asa was afflicted with a disease in his feet. Though his disease was severe, even in his illness he did

THE MESSAGE

rah. Asa tore it down, smashed it, and burned it up in the Kidron Valley. Unfortunately he didn't get rid of the local sex-and-religion shrines. But he was well-intentioned—his heart was in the right place, loyal to Gᴏᴅ. All the gold and silver vessels and artifacts that he and his father had consecrated for holy use he installed in The Temple of God. There wasn't a trace of war up to the thirty-fifth year of Asa's reign.

16.1 **16** But in the thirty-sixth year of Asa's reign, Baasha king of Israel attacked. He started it by building a fort at Ramah and closing the border between Israel and Judah to keep Asa king of Judah from leaving or entering.

16.2-3   Asa took silver and gold from the treasuries of The Temple of Gᴏᴅ and the royal palace and sent it to Ben-Hadad, king of Aram who lived in Damascus, with this message: "Let's make a treaty like the one between our fathers. I'm showing my good faith with this gift of silver and gold. Break your deal with Baasha king of Israel so he'll quit fighting against me."

16.4-5   Ben-Hadad went along with King Asa and sent his troops against the towns of Israel. They sacked Ijon, Dan, Abel Maim, and all the store-cities of Naphtali. When Baasha got the report, he quit fortifying Ramah.

16.6   Then King Asa issued orders to his people in Judah to haul away the logs and stones Baasha had used in the fortification of Ramah and used them himself to fortify Geba and Mizpah.

16.7-9   Just after that, Hanani the seer came to Asa king of Judah and said, "Because you went for help to the king of Aram and didn't ask Gᴏᴅ for help, you've lost a victory over the army of the king of Aram. Didn't the Ethiopians and Libyans come against you with superior forces, completely outclassing you with their chariots and cavalry? But you asked Gᴏᴅ for help and he gave you the victory. Gᴏᴅ is always on the alert, constantly on the lookout for people who are totally committed to him. You were foolish to go for human help when you could have had God's help. Now you're in trouble—one round of war after another."

16.10   At that, Asa lost his temper. Angry, he put Hanani in the stocks. At the same time Asa started abusing some of the people.

16.11-14   A full account of Asa is written in *The Chronicles of the Kings of Judah.* In the thirty-ninth year of his reign Asa came down with a severe case of foot infection. He didn't ask Gᴏᴅ

ᵃ 4 Also known as *Abel Beth Maacah*   *ᵇ 8* That is, people from the upper Nile region   *ᶜ 8* Or *charioteers*

not seek help from the LORD, but only from the physicians. ¹³Then in the forty-first year of his reign Asa died and rested with his fathers. ¹⁴They buried him in the tomb that he had cut out for himself in the City of David. They laid him on a bier covered with spices and various blended perfumes, and they made a huge fire in his honor.

JEHOSHAPHAT KING OF JUDAH

17 Jehoshaphat his son succeeded him as king and strengthened himself against Israel. ²He stationed troops in all the fortified cities of Judah and put garrisons in Judah and in the towns of Ephraim that his father Asa had captured.

³The LORD was with Jehoshaphat because in his early years he walked in the ways his father David had followed. He did not consult the Baals ⁴but sought the God of his father and followed his commands rather than the practices of Israel. ⁵The LORD established the kingdom under his control; and all Judah brought gifts to Jehoshaphat, so that he had great wealth and honor. ⁶His heart was devoted to the ways of the LORD; furthermore, he removed the high places and the Asherah poles from Judah.

⁷In the third year of his reign he sent his officials Ben-Hail, Obadiah, Zechariah, Nethanel and Micaiah to teach in the towns of Judah. ⁸With them were certain Levites—Shemaiah, Nethaniah, Zebadiah, Asahel, Shemiramoth, Jehonathan, Adonijah, Tobijah and Tob-Adonijah—and the priests Elishama and Jehoram. ⁹They taught throughout Judah, taking with them the Book of the Law of the LORD; they went around to all the towns of Judah and taught the people.

¹⁰The fear of the LORD fell on all the kingdoms of the lands surrounding Judah, so that they did not make war with Jehoshaphat. ¹¹Some Philistines brought Jehoshaphat gifts and silver as tribute, and the Arabs brought him flocks: seven thousand seven hundred rams and seven thousand seven hundred goats.

¹²Jehoshaphat became more and more powerful; he built forts and store cities in Judah ¹³and had large supplies in the towns of Judah. He also kept experienced fighting men in Jerusalem. ¹⁴Their enrollment by families was as follows:

From Judah, commanders of units of 1,000:
Adnah the commander, with 300,000 fighting men;
¹⁵next, Jehohanan the commander, with 280,000;
¹⁶next, Amasiah son of Zicri, who volun-

for help, but went instead to the doctors. Then Asa died; he died in the forty-first year of his reign. They buried him in a mausoleum that he had built for himself in the City of David. They laid him in a crypt full of aromatic oils and spices. Then they had a huge bonfire in his memory.

JEHOSHAPHAT OF JUDAH

17.1-6 **17** Asa's son Jehoshaphat was the next king; he started out by working on his defense system against Israel. He put troops in all the fortress cities of Judah and deployed garrisons throughout Judah and in the towns of Ephraim that his father Asa had captured. GOD was on Jehoshaphat's side because he stuck to the ways of his father Asa's early years. He didn't fool around with the popular Baal religion—he was a seeker and follower of the God of his father and was obedient to him; he wasn't like Israel. And GOD secured the kingdom under his rule, gave him a firm grip on it. And everyone in Judah showed their appreciation by bringing gifts. Jehoshaphat ended up very rich and much honored. He was single-minded in following GOD; and he got rid of the local sex-and-religion shrines.

17.7-9 In the third year of his reign he sent his officials—excellent men, every one of them—Ben-Hail, Obadiah, Zechariah, Nethanel, and Micaiah on a teaching mission to the cities of Judah. They were accompanied by Levites—Shemaiah, Nethaniah, Zebadiah, Asahel, Shemiramoth, Jehonathan, Adonijah, Tobijah, and Tob-Adonijah; the priests Elishama and Jehoram were also in the company. They made a circuit of the towns of Judah, teaching the people and using the Book of The Revelation of GOD as their text.

17.10-12 There was a strong sense of the fear of GOD in all the kingdoms around Judah—they didn't dare go to war against Jehoshaphat. Some Philistines even brought gifts and a load of silver to Jehoshaphat, and the desert bedouin brought flocks—7,700 rams and 7,700 goats. So Jehoshaphat became stronger by the day, and constructed more and more forts and store-cities—an age of prosperity for Judah!

17.13-19 He also had excellent fighting men stationed in Jerusalem. The captains of the military units of Judah, classified according to families, were: Captain Adnah with 300,000 soldiers; his associate Captain Jehohanan with 280,000; his associate Amasiah son of Zicri, a volunteer for

NEW INTERNATIONAL VERSION

teered himself for the service of the LORD, with 200,000.

¹⁷From Benjamin:

Eliada, a valiant soldier, with 200,000 men armed with bows and shields;

¹⁸next, Jehozabad, with 180,000 men armed for battle.

¹⁹These were the men who served the king, besides those he stationed in the fortified cities throughout Judah.

MICAIAH PROPHESIES AGAINST AHAB

18 Now Jehoshaphat had great wealth and honor, and he allied himself with Ahab by marriage. ²Some years later he went down to visit Ahab in Samaria. Ahab slaughtered many sheep and cattle for him and the people with him and urged him to attack Ramoth Gilead. ³Ahab king of Israel asked Jehoshaphat king of Judah, "Will you go with me against Ramoth Gilead?"

Jehoshaphat replied, "I am as you are, and my people as your people; we will join you in the war." ⁴But Jehoshaphat also said to the king of Israel, "First seek the counsel of the LORD."

⁵So the king of Israel brought together the prophets—four hundred men—and asked them, "Shall we go to war against Ramoth Gilead, or shall I refrain?"

"Go," they answered, "for God will give it into the king's hand."

⁶But Jehoshaphat asked, "Is there not a prophet of the LORD here whom we can inquire of?"

⁷The king of Israel answered Jehoshaphat, "There is still one man through whom we can inquire of the LORD, but I hate him because he never prophesies anything good about me, but always bad. He is Micaiah son of Imlah."

"The king should not say that," Jehoshaphat replied.

⁸So the king of Israel called one of his officials and said, "Bring Micaiah son of Imlah at once."

⁹Dressed in their royal robes, the king of Israel and Jehoshaphat king of Judah were sitting on their thrones at the threshing floor by the entrance to the gate of Samaria, with all the prophets prophesying before them. ¹⁰Now Zedekiah son of Kenaanah had made iron horns, and he declared, "This is what the LORD says: 'With these you will gore the Arameans until they are destroyed.' "

¹¹All the other prophets were prophesying the same thing. "Attack Ramoth Gilead and be victorious," they said, "for the LORD will give it into the king's hand."

¹²The messenger who had gone to summon

THE MESSAGE

GOD, with 200,000. Officer Eliada represented Benjamin with 200,000 fully equipped with bow and shield; and his associate was Jehozabad with 180,000 armed and ready for battle. These were under the direct command of the king; in addition there were the troops assigned to the fortress cities spread all over Judah.

18 But even though Jehoshaphat was very rich and much honored, he made a marriage alliance with Ahab of Israel. Some time later he paid a visit to Ahab at Samaria. Ahab celebrated his visit with a feast—a huge barbecue with all the lamb and beef you could eat. But Ahab had a hidden agenda; he wanted Jehoshaphat's support in attacking Ramoth Gilead. Then Ahab brought it into the open: "Will you join me in attacking Ramoth Gilead?" Jehoshaphat said, "You bet. I'm with you all the way; you can count on me and my troops."

18.4 Then Jehoshaphat said, "But before you do anything, ask GOD for guidance."

18.5 The king of Israel got the prophets together—all 400 of them—and put the question to them: "Should I attack Ramoth Gilead or should I hold back?"

"Go for it," they said. "God will hand it over to the king."

18.6 But Jehoshaphat dragged his feet, "Is there another prophet of GOD around here we can consult? Let's get a second opinion."

18.7 The king of Israel told Jehoshaphat, "As a matter of fact, there is another. But I hate him. He never preaches anything good to me, only doom, doom, doom—Micaiah son of Imlah."

"The king shouldn't talk about a prophet like that!" said Jehoshaphat.

18.8 So the king of Israel ordered one of his men, "Quickly, get Micaiah son of Imlah."

18.9-11 Meanwhile, the king of Israel and Jehoshaphat were seated on their thrones, dressed in their royal robes, resplendent in front of the Samaria city gates. All the prophets were staging a prophecy-performance for their benefit. Zedekiah son of Kenaanah had even made a set of iron horns, and brandishing them, called out, "GOD's word! With these horns you'll gore Aram until there's nothing left of them!" All the prophets chimed in, "Yes! Go for Ramoth Gilead! An easy victory! GOD's gift to the king!"

18.12 The messenger who went to get Micaiah told

NEW INTERNATIONAL VERSION

Micaiah said to him, "Look, as one man the other prophets are predicting success for the king. Let your word agree with theirs, and speak favorably."

¹³But Micaiah said, "As surely as the LORD lives, I can tell him only what my God says."

¹⁴When he arrived, the king asked him, "Micaiah, shall we go to war against Ramoth Gilead, or shall I refrain?"

"Attack and be victorious," he answered, "for they will be given into your hand."

¹⁵The king said to him, "How many times must I make you swear to tell me nothing but the truth in the name of the LORD?"

¹⁶Then Micaiah answered, "I saw all Israel scattered on the hills like sheep without a shepherd, and the LORD said, 'These people have no master. Let each one go home in peace.' "

¹⁷The king of Israel said to Jehoshaphat, "Didn't I tell you that he never prophesies anything good about me, but only bad?"

¹⁸Micaiah continued, "Therefore hear the word of the LORD: I saw the LORD sitting on his throne with all the host of heaven standing on his right and on his left. ¹⁹And the LORD said, 'Who will entice Ahab king of Israel into attacking Ramoth Gilead and going to his death there?'

"One suggested this, and another that. ²⁰Finally, a spirit came forward, stood before the LORD and said, 'I will entice him.'

" 'By what means?' the LORD asked.

²¹" 'I will go and be a lying spirit in the mouths of all his prophets,' he said.

" 'You will succeed in enticing him,' said the LORD. 'Go and do it.'

²²"So now the LORD has put a lying spirit in the mouths of these prophets of yours. The LORD has decreed disaster for you."

²³Then Zedekiah son of Kenaanah went up and slapped Micaiah in the face. "Which way did the spirit from*ᵃ* the LORD go when he went from me to speak to you?" he asked.

²⁴Micaiah replied, "You will find out on the day you go to hide in an inner room."

²⁵The king of Israel then ordered, "Take Micaiah and send him back to Amon the ruler of the city and to Joash the king's son, ²⁶and say, 'This is what the king says: Put this fellow in prison

THE MESSAGE

him, "The prophets have all said Yes to the king. Make it unanimous—vote Yes!"

18.13 But Micaiah said, "As sure as GOD lives, what God says, I'll say."

18.14 With Micaiah before him, the king asked him, "So, Micaiah—do we attack Ramoth Gilead? Or do we hold back?"

"Go ahead," he said, "an easy victory! God's gift to the king."

18.15 "Not so fast," said the king. "How many times have I made you promise under oath to tell me the truth and nothing but the truth?"

18.16 "All right," said Micaiah, "since you insist . . .

I saw all of Israel scattered over the hills,
 sheep with no shepherd.
Then GOD spoke, 'These poor people
 have no one to tell them what to do.
Let them go home and do
 the best they can for themselves.' "

18.17 The king of Israel turned to Jehoshaphat, "See! What did I tell you? He never has a good word for me from GOD, only doom."

18.18-21 Micaiah kept on, "I'm not done yet; listen to GOD's word:

I saw GOD enthroned,
 and all the Angel Armies of heaven
standing at attention,
 ranged on his right and his left.
And GOD said, "How can we seduce Ahab
 into attacking Ramoth Gilead?"
Some said this,
 and some said that.
Then a bold angel stepped out,
 stood before GOD, and said,
"I'll seduce him."
 "And how will you do it?" said GOD.
"Easy," said the angel,
 "I'll get all the prophets to lie."
"That should do it," said GOD;
 "On your way—seduce him!"

18.22 "And that's what has happened. GOD filled the mouths of your puppet prophets with seductive lies. GOD has pronounced your doom."

18.23 Just then Zedekiah son of Kenaanah came up and slapped Micaiah in the face, saying, "Since when did the Spirit of GOD leave me and take up with you?"

18.24 Micaiah said, "You'll know soon enough; you'll know it when you're frantically and futilely looking for a place to hide."

18.25-26 The king of Israel had heard enough: "Get Micaiah out of here! Turn him over to Amon the city magistrate and to Joash the king's son with this message: 'King's orders! Lock him up

ᵃ 23 Or Spirit of

NEW INTERNATIONAL VERSION

and give him nothing but bread and water until I return safely.' "

²⁷Micaiah declared, "If you ever return safely, the LORD has not spoken through me." Then he added, "Mark my words, all you people!"

AHAB KILLED AT RAMOTH GILEAD

²⁸So the king of Israel and Jehoshaphat king of Judah went up to Ramoth Gilead. ²⁹The king of Israel said to Jehoshaphat, "I will enter the battle in disguise, but you wear your royal robes." So the king of Israel disguised himself and went into battle.

³⁰Now the king of Aram had ordered his chariot commanders, "Do not fight with anyone, small or great, except the king of Israel." ³¹When the chariot commanders saw Jehoshaphat, they thought, "This is the king of Israel." So they turned to attack him, but Jehoshaphat cried out, and the LORD helped him. God drew them away from him, ³²for when the chariot commanders saw that he was not the king of Israel, they stopped pursuing him.

³³But someone drew his bow at random and hit the king of Israel between the sections of his armor. The king told the chariot driver, "Wheel around and get me out of the fighting. I've been wounded." ³⁴All day long the battle raged, and the king of Israel propped himself up in his chariot facing the Arameans until evening. Then at sunset he died.

19 When Jehoshaphat king of Judah returned safely to his palace in Jerusalem, ²Jehu the seer, the son of Hanani, went out to meet him and said to the king, "Should you help the wicked and love*ᵃ* those who hate the LORD? Because of this, the wrath of the LORD is upon you. ³There is, however, some good in you, for you have rid the land of the Asherah poles and have set your heart on seeking God."

JEHOSHAPHAT APPOINTS JUDGES

⁴Jehoshaphat lived in Jerusalem, and he went out again among the people from Beersheba to the hill country of Ephraim and turned them back to the LORD, the God of their fathers. ⁵He appointed judges in the land, in each of the fortified cities of Judah. ⁶He told them, "Consider carefully what you do, because you are not judging for man but

THE MESSAGE

in jail; keep him on bread and water until I'm back in one piece.' "

18.27 Micaiah said,

If you ever get back in one piece,
I'm no prophet of GOD.

He added,

When it happens, O people,
remember where you heard it!

18.28-29 So the king of Israel and Jehoshaphat king of Judah went ahead and attacked Ramoth Gilead. The king of Israel said to Jehoshaphat, "Wear my kingly robe; I'm going into battle disguised." So the king of Israel entered the battle in disguise.

18.30 Meanwhile, the king of Aram had ordered his chariot commanders (there were thirty-two of them), "Don't bother with anyone whether small or great; go after the king of Israel and him only."

18.31-32 When the chariot commanders saw Jehoshaphat, they said, "There he is! The king of Israel!" and took after him. Jehoshaphat yelled out, and the chariot commanders realized they had the wrong man—it wasn't the king of Israel after all. God intervened and they let him go.

18.33 Just then someone, without aiming, shot an arrow into the crowd and hit the king of Israel in the chink of his armor. The king told his charioteer, "Turn back! Get me out of here—I'm wounded."

18.34 All day the fighting continued, hot and heavy. Propped up in his chariot, the king watched from the sidelines. He died that evening.

19.1-3 **19** But Jehoshaphat king of Judah got home safe and sound. Jehu, son of Hanani the seer, confronted King Jehoshaphat: "You have no business helping evil, cozying up to GOD-haters. Because you did this, GOD is good and angry with you. But you're not all bad—you made a clean sweep of the polluting sex-and-religion shrines; and you were single-minded in seeking God."

19.4 Jehoshaphat kept his residence in Jerusalem but made a regular round of visits among the people, from Beersheba in the south to Mount Ephraim in the north, urging them to return to GOD, the God of their ancestors.

19.5-7 And he was diligent in appointing judges in the land—each of the fortress cities had its judge. He charged the judges: "This is serious work; do it carefully. You are not merely judg-

---

ᵃ 2 Or and make alliances with

NEW INTERNATIONAL VERSION

for the LORD, who is with you whenever you give a verdict. [7]Now let the fear of the LORD be upon you. Judge carefully, for with the LORD our God there is no injustice or partiality or bribery."

[8]In Jerusalem also, Jehoshaphat appointed some of the Levites, priests and heads of Israelite families to administer the law of the LORD and to settle disputes. And they lived in Jerusalem. [9]He gave them these orders: "You must serve faithfully and wholeheartedly in the fear of the LORD. [10]In every case that comes before you from your fellow countrymen who live in the cities—whether bloodshed or other concerns of the law, commands, decrees or ordinances—you are to warn them not to sin against the LORD; otherwise his wrath will come on you and your brothers. Do this, and you will not sin.

[11]"Amariah the chief priest will be over you in any matter concerning the LORD, and Zebadiah son of Ishmael, the leader of the tribe of Judah, will be over you in any matter concerning the king, and the Levites will serve as officials before you. Act with courage, and may the LORD be with those who do well."

JEHOSHAPHAT DEFEATS MOAB AND AMMON

20 After this, the Moabites and Ammonites with some of the Meunites[a] came to make war on Jehoshaphat.

[2]Some men came and told Jehoshaphat, "A vast army is coming against you from Edom,[b] from the other side of the Sea.[c] It is already in Hazazon Tamar" (that is, En Gedi). [3]Alarmed, Jehoshaphat resolved to inquire of the LORD, and he proclaimed a fast for all Judah. [4]The people of Judah came together to seek help from the LORD; indeed, they came from every town in Judah to seek him.

[5]Then Jehoshaphat stood up in the assembly of Judah and Jerusalem at the temple of the LORD in the front of the new courtyard [6]and said:

"O LORD, God of our fathers, are you not the God who is in heaven? You rule over all the kingdoms of the nations. Power and might are in your hand, and no one can withstand you. [7]O our God, did you not drive out the inhabitants of this land before your people Israel and give it forever to the descendants of Abraham your friend? [8]They have lived in it and have built in it a sanctuary for your Name, saying, [9]'If calamity comes upon us, whether the sword of judgment, or plague or famine, we will stand in your presence before this temple

---

a 1 Some Septuagint manuscripts; Hebrew *Ammonites*
b 2 One Hebrew manuscript; most Hebrew manuscripts,
Septuagint and Vulgate *Aram*   c 2 That is, the Dead Sea

THE MESSAGE

ing between men and women; these are GOD's judgments that you are passing on. Live in the fear of GOD—be most careful, for GOD hates dishonesty, partiality, and bribery."

19.8-10 In Jerusalem Jehoshaphat also appointed Levites, priests, and family heads to decide on matters that had to do with worship and mediating local differences. He charged them: "Do your work in the fear of GOD; be dependable and honest in your duties. When a case comes before you involving any of your fellow citizens, whether it seems large (like murder) or small (like matters of interpretation of the law), you are responsible for warning them that they are dealing with GOD. Make that explicit, otherwise both you and they are going to be dealing with GOD's wrath. Do your work well or you'll end up being as guilty as they are.

19.11 "Amariah the chief priest is in charge of all cases regarding the worship of GOD; Zebadiah son of Ishmael, the leader of the tribe of Judah, is in charge of all civil cases; the Levites will keep order in the courts. Be bold and diligent. And GOD be with you as you do your best."

✠

20.1-2 **20** Some time later the Moabites and Ammonites, accompanied by Meunites, joined forces to make war on Jehoshaphat. Jehoshaphat received this intelligence report: "A huge force is on its way from beyond the Dead Sea to fight you. There's no time to waste—they're already at Hazazon Tamar, the oasis of En Gedi."

20.3-4 Shaken, Jehoshaphat prayed. He went to GOD for help and ordered a nationwide fast. The country of Judah united in seeking GOD's help—they came from all the cities of Judah to pray to GOD.

20.5-9 Then Jehoshaphat took a position before the assembled people of Judah and Jerusalem at The Temple of GOD in front of the new courtyard and said, "O GOD, God of our ancestors, are you not God in heaven above and ruler of all kingdoms below? You hold all power and might in your fist—no one stands a chance against you! And didn't you make the natives of this land leave as you brought your people Israel in, turning it over permanently to your people Israel, the descendants of Abraham your friend? They have lived here and built a holy house of worship to honor you, saying, 'When the worst happens—whether war or flood or disease or famine—and we take our place before this Temple (we know you are personally

NEW INTERNATIONAL VERSION

that bears your Name and will cry out to you in our distress, and you will hear us and save us.'

¹⁰"But now here are men from Ammon, Moab and Mount Seir, whose territory you would not allow Israel to invade when they came from Egypt; so they turned away from them and did not destroy them. ¹¹See how they are repaying us by coming to drive us out of the possession you gave us as an inheritance. ¹²O our God, will you not judge them? For we have no power to face this vast army that is attacking us. We do not know what to do, but our eyes are upon you."

¹³All the men of Judah, with their wives and children and little ones, stood there before the LORD.

¹⁴Then the Spirit of the LORD came upon Jahaziel son of Zechariah, the son of Benaiah, the son of Jeiel, the son of Mattaniah, a Levite and descendant of Asaph, as he stood in the assembly.

¹⁵He said: "Listen, King Jehoshaphat and all who live in Judah and Jerusalem! This is what the LORD says to you: 'Do not be afraid or discouraged because of this vast army. For the battle is not yours, but God's. ¹⁶Tomorrow march down against them. They will be climbing up by the Pass of Ziz, and you will find them at the end of the gorge in the Desert of Jeruel. ¹⁷You will not have to fight this battle. Take up your positions; stand firm and see the deliverance the LORD will give you, O Judah and Jerusalem. Do not be afraid; do not be discouraged. Go out to face them tomorrow, and the LORD will be with you.'"

¹⁸Jehoshaphat bowed with his face to the ground, and all the people of Judah and Jerusalem fell down in worship before the LORD. ¹⁹Then some Levites from the Kohathites and Korahites stood up and praised the LORD, the God of Israel, with a very loud voice.

²⁰Early in the morning they left for the Desert of Tekoa. As they set out, Jehoshaphat stood and said, "Listen to me, Judah and people of Jerusalem! Have faith in the LORD your God and you will be upheld; have faith in his prophets and you will be successful." ²¹After consulting the people, Jehoshaphat appointed men to sing to the LORD and to praise him for the splendor of his[a] holiness as they went out at the head of the army, saying:

"Give thanks to the LORD,
  for his love endures forever."

[a] 21 Or *him with the splendor of*

THE MESSAGE

present in this place!) and pray out our pain and trouble, we know that you will listen and give victory.'

20.10-12 "And now it's happened: men from Ammon, Moab, and Mount Seir have shown up. You didn't let Israel touch them when we got here at first—we detoured around them and didn't lay a hand on them. And now they've come to kick us out of the country you gave us. O dear God, won't you take care of them? We're helpless before this vandal horde ready to attack us. We don't know what to do; we're looking to you."

20.13 Everyone in Judah was there—little children, wives, sons—all present and attentive to GOD.

20.14-17 Then Jahaziel was moved by the Spirit of GOD to speak from the midst of the congregation. (Jahaziel was the son of Zechariah, the son of Benaiah, the son of Jeiel, the son of Mattaniah the Levite of the Asaph clan.) He said, "Attention everyone—all of you from out of town, all you from Jerusalem, and you King Jehoshaphat—GOD's word: Don't be afraid; don't pay any mind to this vandal horde. This is God's war, not yours. Tomorrow you'll go after them; see, they're already on their way up the slopes of Ziz; you'll meet them at the end of the ravine near the wilderness of Jeruel. You won't have to lift a hand in this battle; just stand firm, Judah and Jerusalem, and watch GOD's saving work for you take shape. Don't be afraid, don't waver. March out boldly tomorrow—GOD is with you."

20.18-19 Then Jehoshaphat knelt down, bowing with his face to the ground. All Judah and Jerusalem did the same, worshiping GOD. The Levites (both Kohathites and Korahites) stood to their feet to praise GOD, the God of Israel; they praised at the top of their lungs!

20.20 They were up early in the morning, ready to march into the wilderness of Tekoa. As they were leaving, Jehoshaphat stood up and said, "Listen Judah and Jerusalem! Listen to what I have to say! Believe firmly in GOD, your God, and your lives will be firm! Believe in your prophets and you'll come out on top!"

20.21 After talking it over with the people, Jehoshaphat appointed a choir for GOD; dressed in holy robes, they were to march ahead of the troops, singing,

Give thanks to GOD,
His love never quits.

NEW INTERNATIONAL VERSION

²²As they began to sing and praise, the LORD set ambushes against the men of Ammon and Moab and Mount Seir who were invading Judah, and they were defeated. ²³The men of Ammon and Moab rose up against the men from Mount Seir to destroy and annihilate them. After they finished slaughtering the men from Seir, they helped to destroy one another.

²⁴When the men of Judah came to the place that overlooks the desert and looked toward the vast army, they saw only dead bodies lying on the ground; no one had escaped. ²⁵So Jehoshaphat and his men went to carry off their plunder, and they found among them a great amount of equipment and clothing*a* and also articles of value—more than they could take away. There was so much plunder that it took three days to collect it. ²⁶On the fourth day they assembled in the Valley of Beracah, where they praised the LORD. This is why it is called the Valley of Beracah*b* to this day.

²⁷Then, led by Jehoshaphat, all the men of Judah and Jerusalem returned joyfully to Jerusalem, for the LORD had given them cause to rejoice over their enemies. ²⁸They entered Jerusalem and went to the temple of the LORD with harps and lutes and trumpets.

²⁹The fear of God came upon all the kingdoms of the countries when they heard how the LORD had fought against the enemies of Israel. ³⁰And the kingdom of Jehoshaphat was at peace, for his God had given him rest on every side.

THE END OF JEHOSHAPHAT'S REIGN

³¹So Jehoshaphat reigned over Judah. He was thirty-five years old when he became king of Judah, and he reigned in Jerusalem twenty-five years. His mother's name was Azubah daughter of Shilhi. ³²He walked in the ways of his father Asa and did not stray from them; he did what was right in the eyes of the LORD. ³³The high places, however, were not removed, and the people still had not set their hearts on the God of their fathers.

³⁴The other events of Jehoshaphat's reign, from beginning to end, are written in the annals of Jehu son of Hanani, which are recorded in the book of the kings of Israel.

³⁵Later, Jehoshaphat king of Judah made an alliance with Ahaziah king of Israel, who was guilty of wickedness. ³⁶He agreed with him to construct a fleet of trading ships.*c* After these were built at Ezion Geber, ³⁷Eliezer son of Dodavahu of Mareshah prophesied against Jehosha-

THE MESSAGE

20.22-23 As soon as they started shouting and praising, GOD set ambushes against the men of Ammon, Moab, and Mount Seir as they were attacking Judah, and they all ended up dead. The Ammonites and Moabites mistakenly attacked those from Mount Seir and massacred them. Then, further confused, they went at each other, and all ended up killed.

20.24 As Judah came up over the rise, looking into the wilderness for the horde of barbarians, they looked on a killing field of dead bodies—not a living soul among them.

20.25-26 When Jehoshaphat and his people came to carry off the plunder they found more loot than they could carry off—equipment, clothing, valuables. It took three days to cart it away! On the fourth day they came together at the Valley of Blessing (Beracah) and blessed GOD (that's how it got the name, Valley of Blessing).

20.27-28 Jehoshaphat then led all the men of Judah and Jerusalem back to Jerusalem—an exuberant parade. GOD had given them joyful relief from their enemies! They entered Jerusalem and came to The Temple of GOD with all the instruments of the band playing.

20.29-30 When the surrounding kingdoms got word that GOD had fought Israel's enemies, the fear of God descended on them. Jehoshaphat heard no more from them; as long as Jehoshaphat reigned, peace reigned.

20.31-33 That about sums up Jehoshaphat's reign over Judah. He was thirty-five years old when he became king and ruled as king in Jerusalem for twenty-five years. His mother was Azubah daughter of Shilhi. He continued the kind of life characteristic of his father Asa—no detours, no dead-ends—pleasing GOD with his life. But he failed to get rid of the neighborhood sex-and-religion shrines—people continued to pray and worship at these idolatrous god shops.

20.34 The rest of Jehoshaphat's life, from start to finish, is written in the memoirs of Jehu son of Hanani, which are included in the *Royal Annals of Israel's Kings.*

20.35-37 Late in life Jehoshaphat formed a trading syndicate with Ahaziah king of Israel—which was very wrong of him to do. He went in as partner with him to build ocean-going ships at Ezion Geber to trade with Tarshish. Eliezer son of Dodavahu of Mareshah preached against Je-

---

a 25 Some Hebrew manuscripts and Vulgate; most Hebrew manuscripts *corpses*   *b 26 Beracah* means *praise.*
c 36 Hebrew *of ships that could go to Tarshish*

NEW INTERNATIONAL VERSION

phat, saying, "Because you have made an alliance with Ahaziah, the LORD will destroy what you have made." The ships were wrecked and were not able to set sail to trade. *a*

21 Then Jehoshaphat rested with his fathers and was buried with them in the City of David. And Jehoram his son succeeded him as king. ²Jehoram's brothers, the sons of Jehoshaphat, were Azariah, Jehiel, Zechariah, Azariahu, Michael and Shephatiah. All these were sons of Jehoshaphat king of Israel. *b* ³Their father had given them many gifts of silver and gold and articles of value, as well as fortified cities in Judah, but he had given the kingdom to Jehoram because he was his firstborn son.

JEHORAM KING OF JUDAH

⁴When Jehoram established himself firmly over his father's kingdom, he put all his brothers to the sword along with some of the princes of Israel. ⁵Jehoram was thirty-two years old when he became king, and he reigned in Jerusalem eight years. ⁶He walked in the ways of the kings of Israel, as the house of Ahab had done, for he married a daughter of Ahab. He did evil in the eyes of the LORD. ⁷Nevertheless, because of the covenant the LORD had made with David, the LORD was not willing to destroy the house of David. He had promised to maintain a lamp for him and his descendants forever.

⁸In the time of Jehoram, Edom rebelled against Judah and set up its own king. ⁹So Jehoram went there with his officers and all his chariots. The Edomites surrounded him and his chariot commanders, but he rose up and broke through by night. ¹⁰To this day Edom has been in rebellion against Judah.

Libnah revolted at the same time, because Jehoram had forsaken the LORD, the God of his fathers. ¹¹He had also built high places on the hills of Judah and had caused the people of Jerusalem to prostitute themselves and had led Judah astray.

¹²Jehoram received a letter from Elijah the prophet, which said:

"This is what the LORD, the God of your father David, says: 'You have not walked in the ways of your father Jehoshaphat or of Asa king of Judah. ¹³But you have walked in the ways of the kings of Israel, and you have led Judah and the people of Jerusalem to prostitute themselves, just as the house of Ahab did. You have also murdered your

THE MESSAGE

hoshaphat's venture: "Because you joined forces with Ahaziah, GOD has shipwrecked your work." The ships were smashed and nothing ever came of the trade partnership.

21 21.1 Jehoshaphat died and was buried in the family cemetery in the City of David. Jehoram his son was the next king.

KING JEHORAM

21.2-4 Jehoram's brothers were Azariah, Jehiel, Zechariah, Azariahu, Michael, and Shephatiah—the sons of Jehoshaphat king of Judah. Their father had lavished them with gifts—silver, gold, and other valuables, plus the fortress cities in Judah. But Jehoram was his firstborn son and he gave him the kingdom of Judah. But when Jehoram had taken over his father's kingdom and had secured his position, he killed all his brothers along with some of the government officials.

21.5-7 Jehoram was thirty-two years old when he became king and ruled in Jerusalem for eight years. He imitated Israel's kings and married into the Ahab dynasty. GOD considered him an evil man. But despite that, because of his covenant with David, GOD was not yet ready to destroy the descendants of David; he had, after all, promised to keep a light burning for David and his sons.

21.8-9 During Jehoram's reign, Edom revolted from Judah's rule and set up their own king. Jehoram responded by setting out with his officers and chariots. Edom surrounded him, but in the middle of the night he and his charioteers broke through the lines and hit Edom hard.

21.10-11 Edom continues in revolt against Judah right up to the present. Even little Libnah revolted at that time. The evidence accumulated: Since Jehoram had abandoned GOD, the God of his ancestors, God was abandoning him. He even went so far as to build pagan sacred shrines in the mountains of Judah. He brazenly led Jerusalem away from God, seducing the whole country.

21.12-15 One day he got a letter from Elijah the prophet. It read, "From GOD, the God of your ancestor David—a message: Because you have not kept to the ways of Jehoshaphat your father and Asa your grandfather, kings of Judah, but have taken up with the ways of the kings of Israel in the north, leading Judah and Jerusalem away from God, going step by step down the apostate path of Ahab and his crew—why, you

NEW INTERNATIONAL VERSION

own brothers, members of your father's house, men who were better than you. [14]So now the LORD is about to strike your people, your sons, your wives and everything that is yours, with a heavy blow. [15]You yourself will be very ill with a lingering disease of the bowels, until the disease causes your bowels to come out.' "

[16]The LORD aroused against Jehoram the hostility of the Philistines and of the Arabs who lived near the Cushites. [17]They attacked Judah, invaded it and carried off all the goods found in the king's palace, together with his sons and wives. Not a son was left to him except Ahaziah,[a] the youngest.

[18]After all this, the LORD afflicted Jehoram with an incurable disease of the bowels. [19]In the course of time, at the end of the second year, his bowels came out because of the disease, and he died in great pain. His people made no fire in his honor, as they had for his fathers.

[20]Jehoram was thirty-two years old when he became king, and he reigned in Jerusalem eight years. He passed away, to no one's regret, and was buried in the City of David, but not in the tombs of the kings.

AHAZIAH KING OF JUDAH

22 The people of Jerusalem made Ahaziah, Jehoram's youngest son, king in his place, since the raiders, who came with the Arabs into the camp, had killed all the older sons. So Ahaziah son of Jehoram king of Judah began to reign.

[2]Ahaziah was twenty-two[b] years old when he became king, and he reigned in Jerusalem one year. His mother's name was Athaliah, a granddaughter of Omri.

[3]He too walked in the ways of the house of Ahab, for his mother encouraged him in doing wrong. [4]He did evil in the eyes of the LORD, as the house of Ahab had done, for after his father's death they became his advisers, to his undoing. [5]He also followed their counsel when he went with Joram[c] son of Ahab king of Israel to war against Hazael king of Aram at Ramoth Gilead. The Arameans wounded Joram; [6]so he returned to Jezreel to recover from the wounds they had inflicted on him at Ramoth[d] in his battle with Hazael king of Aram.

Then Ahaziah[e] son of Jehoram king of Judah

THE MESSAGE

even killed your own brothers, all of them better men than you!—GOD is going to afflict your people, your wives, your sons, and everything you have with a terrible plague. And you are going to come down with a terrible disease of the colon, painful and humiliating."

21.16-20   The trouble started with an invasion. GOD incited the Philistines and the Arabs who lived near the Ethiopians to attack Jehoram. They came to the borders of Judah, forced their way in, and plundered the place—robbing the royal palace of everything in it including his wives and sons. One son, his youngest, Ahaziah, was left behind. The terrible and fatal disease in his colon followed. After about two years he was totally incontinent and died writhing in pain. His people didn't honor him by lighting a great bonfire, as was customary with his ancestors. He was thirty-two years old when he became king and reigned for eight years in Jerusalem. There were no tears shed when he died—it was good riddance!—and they buried him in the City of David, but not in the royal cemetery.

KING AHAZIAH

22.1-6   **22** The people of Jerusalem made Ahaziah, Jehoram's youngest son, king. Raiders from the desert, who had come with the Arabs against the settlement, had killed all the older sons. That's how Ahaziah son of Jehoram king of Judah became king. Ahaziah was twenty-two years old when he became king, but reigned only one year in Jerusalem. His mother was Athaliah, granddaughter of Omri. He lived and ruled just like the Ahab family had done, his mother training him in evil ways. GOD also considered him evil, related by both marriage and sin to the Ahab clan. After the death of his father, he attended the sin school of Ahab, and graduated with a degree in doom. He did what they taught him, went with Joram son of Ahab king of Israel in the war against Hazael king of Aram at Ramoth Gilead. Joram, wounded by the Arameans, retreated to Jezreel to recover from the wounds he received in Ramah in his war with Hazael king of Aram. Ahaziah son of

---

a 17 Hebrew *Jehoahaz,* a variant of *Ahaziah*   *b 2* Some Septuagint manuscripts and Syriac (see also 2 Kings 8:26); Hebrew *forty-two*   *c 5* Hebrew *Jehoram,* a variant of *Joram;* also in verses 6 and 7   *d 6* Hebrew *Ramah,* a variant of *Ramoth*   *e 6* Some Hebrew manuscripts, Septuagint, Vulgate and Syriac (see also 2 Kings 8:29); most Hebrew manuscripts *Azariah*

NEW INTERNATIONAL VERSION	THE MESSAGE

NEW INTERNATIONAL VERSION

went down to Jezreel to see Joram son of Ahab because he had been wounded.

⁷Through Ahaziah's visit to Joram, God brought about Ahaziah's downfall. When Ahaziah arrived, he went out with Joram to meet Jehu son of Nimshi, whom the LORD had anointed to destroy the house of Ahab. ⁸While Jehu was executing judgment on the house of Ahab, he found the princes of Judah and the sons of Ahaziah's relatives, who had been attending Ahaziah, and he killed them. ⁹He then went in search of Ahaziah, and his men captured him while he was hiding in Samaria. He was brought to Jehu and put to death. They buried him, for they said, "He was a son of Jehoshaphat, who sought the LORD with all his heart." So there was no one in the house of Ahaziah powerful enough to retain the kingdom.

ATHALIAH AND JOASH

¹⁰When Athaliah the mother of Ahaziah saw that her son was dead, she proceeded to destroy the whole royal family of the house of Judah. ¹¹But Jehosheba,ᵃ the daughter of King Jehoram, took Joash son of Ahaziah and stole him away from among the royal princes who were about to be murdered and put him and his nurse in a bedroom. Because Jehosheba,ᵃ the daughter of King Jehoram and wife of the priest Jehoiada, was Ahaziah's sister, she hid the child from Athaliah so she could not kill him. ¹²He remained hidden with them at the temple of God for six years while Athaliah ruled the land.

23 In the seventh year Jehoiada showed his strength. He made a covenant with the commanders of units of a hundred: Azariah son of Jeroham, Ishmael son of Jehohanan, Azariah son of Obed, Maaseiah son of Adaiah, and Elishaphat son of Zicri. ²They went throughout Judah and gathered the Levites and the heads of Israelite families from all the towns. When they came to Jerusalem, ³the whole assembly made a covenant with the king at the temple of God.

Jehoiada said to them, "The king's son shall reign, as the LORD promised concerning the descendants of David. ⁴Now this is what you are to do: A third of you priests and Levites who are going on duty on the Sabbath are to keep watch

THE MESSAGE

Jehoram king of Judah paid a visit to Joram son of Ahab on his sickbed at Jezreel.

²²·⁷⁻⁹ The fate of Ahaziah when he went to visit was God's judgment on him. When Ahaziah arrived at Jezreel, he and Joram met with Jehu son of Nimshi, whom GOD had already authorized to destroy the dynasty of Ahab. Jehu, already at work, executing doom on the dynasty of Ahab, came upon the captains of Judah and Ahaziah's nephews, part of the Ahaziah delegation, and killed them outright. Then he sent out a search party looking for Ahaziah himself. They found him hiding out in Samaria and hauled him back to Jehu. And Jehu killed him.

They didn't, though, just leave his body there. Out of respect for his grandfather Jehoshaphat, famous as a sincere seeker after GOD, they gave him a decent burial. But there was no one left in Ahaziah's family capable of ruling the kingdom.

QUEEN ATHALIAH

²²·¹⁰⁻¹² When Ahaziah's mother Athaliah saw that her son was dead, she took over. She began by massacring the entire royal family. Jehosheba, daughter of King Jehoram, took Ahaziah's son Joash, and kidnapped him from among the king's sons slated for slaughter. She hid him and his nurse in a private room away from Athaliah. So Jehosheba, daughter of King Jehoram and Ahaziah's sister—she was also the wife of Jehoiada the priest—saved Joash from the murderous Queen Athaliah. He was there with her, hidden away for six years in The Temple of God. Athaliah, oblivious to his existence, ruled the country.

²³·¹⁻³ **23** In the seventh year the priest Jehoiada decided to make his move and worked out a strategy with certain influential officers in the army. He picked Azariah son of Jeroham, Ishmael son of Jehohanan, Azariah son of Obed, Maaseiah son of Adaiah, and Elishaphat son of Zicri as his associates. They dispersed throughout Judah and called in the Levites from all the towns in Judah along with the heads of families. They met in Jerusalem. The gathering met in The Temple of God. They made a covenant there in The Temple.

²³·³⁻⁷ The priest Jehoiada showed them the young prince and addressed them: "Here he is—the son of the king. He is going to rule just as GOD promised regarding the sons of David. Now this is what you must do: A third of you priests and Levites who come on duty on the Sabbath are to be posted as security guards at the gates;

ᵃ 11 Hebrew *Jehoshabeath*, a variant of *Jehosheba*

NEW INTERNATIONAL VERSION

at the doors, ⁵a third of you at the royal palace and a third at the Foundation Gate, and all the other men are to be in the courtyards of the temple of the LORD. ⁶No one is to enter the temple of the LORD except the priests and Levites on duty; they may enter because they are consecrated, but all the other men are to guard what the LORD has assigned to them.ᵃ ⁷The Levites are to station themselves around the king, each man with his weapons in his hand. Anyone who enters the temple must be put to death. Stay close to the king wherever he goes."

⁸The Levites and all the men of Judah did just as Jehoiada the priest ordered. Each one took his men—those who were going on duty on the Sabbath and those who were going off duty—for Jehoiada the priest had not released any of the divisions. ⁹Then he gave the commanders of units of a hundred the spears and the large and small shields that had belonged to King David and that were in the temple of God. ¹⁰He stationed all the men, each with his weapon in his hand, around the king—near the altar and the temple, from the south side to the north side of the temple.

¹¹Jehoiada and his sons brought out the king's son and put the crown on him; they presented him with a copy of the covenant and proclaimed him king. They anointed him and shouted, "Long live the king!"

¹²When Athaliah heard the noise of the people running and cheering the king, she went to them at the temple of the LORD. ¹³She looked, and there was the king, standing by his pillar at the entrance. The officers and the trumpeters were beside the king, and all the people of the land were rejoicing and blowing trumpets, and singers with musical instruments were leading the praises. Then Athaliah tore her robes and shouted, "Treason! Treason!"

¹⁴Jehoiada the priest sent out the commanders of units of a hundred, who were in charge of the troops, and said to them: "Bring her out between the ranksᵇ and put to the sword anyone who follows her." For the priest had said, "Do not put her to death at the temple of the LORD." ¹⁵So they seized her as she reached the entrance of the Horse Gate on the palace grounds, and there they put her to death.

¹⁶Jehoiada then made a covenant that he and the people and the kingᶜ would be the LORD's people. ¹⁷All the people went to the temple of Baal and tore it down. They smashed the altars and idols and killed Mattan the priest of Baal in front of the altars.

THE MESSAGE

another third will guard the palace; and the other third will guard the foundation gate. All the people will gather in the courtyards of The Temple of GOD. No one may enter The Temple of GOD except the priests and designated Levites—they are permitted in because they've been consecrated, but all the people must do the work assigned them. The Levites are to form a ring around the young king, weapons at the ready. Kill anyone who tries to break through your ranks. Your job is to stay with the king at all times and places, coming and going."

23.8-10 All the Levites and officers obeyed the orders of Jehoiada the priest. Each took charge of his men, both those who came on duty on the Sabbath and those who went off duty on the Sabbath, for Jehoiada the priest hadn't exempted any of them from duty. Then the priest armed the officers with spears and the large and small shields originally belonging to King David that were stored in The Temple of God. Well-armed, the guards took up their assigned positions for protecting the king, from one end of The Temple to the other, surrounding both Altar and Temple.

23.11 Then the priest brought the prince into view, crowned him, handed him the scroll of God's covenant, and made him king. As Jehoiada and his sons anointed him they shouted, "Long live the king!"

23.12-13 Athaliah, hearing all the commotion, the people running around and praising the king, came to The Temple to see what was going on. Astonished, she saw the young king standing at the entrance flanked by the captains and heralds, with everybody beside themselves with joy, trumpets blaring, the choir and orchestra leading the praise. Athaliah ripped her robes in dismay and shouted, "Treason! Treason!"

23.14-15 Jehoiada the priest ordered the military officers, "Drag her outside—and kill anyone who tries to follow her!" (The priest had said, "Don't kill her inside The Temple of GOD.") So they dragged her out to the palace's horse corral and there they killed her.

23.16 Jehoiada now made a covenant between himself and the king and the people: they were to be GOD's special people.

23.17 The people poured into the temple of Baal and tore it down, smashing altar and images to smithereens. They killed Mattan the priest of Baal in front of the altar.

ᵃ 6 Or to observe the LORD's command ⌊not to enter⌋   ᵇ 14 Or out from the precincts   ᶜ 16 Or covenant between ⌊the LORD⌋ and the people and the king that they (see 2 Kings 11:17)

NEW INTERNATIONAL VERSION

¹⁸Then Jehoiada placed the oversight of the temple of the LORD in the hands of the priests, who were Levites, to whom David had made assignments in the temple, to present the burnt offerings of the LORD as written in the Law of Moses, with rejoicing and singing, as David had ordered. ¹⁹He also stationed doorkeepers at the gates of the LORD's temple so that no one who was in any way unclean might enter.

²⁰He took with him the commanders of hundreds, the nobles, the rulers of the people and all the people of the land and brought the king down from the temple of the LORD. They went into the palace through the Upper Gate and seated the king on the royal throne, ²¹and all the people of the land rejoiced. And the city was quiet, because Athaliah had been slain with the sword.

JOASH REPAIRS THE TEMPLE

24 Joash was seven years old when he became king, and he reigned in Jerusalem forty years. His mother's name was Zibiah; she was from Beersheba. ²Joash did what was right in the eyes of the LORD all the years of Jehoiada the priest. ³Jehoiada chose two wives for him, and he had sons and daughters.

⁴Some time later Joash decided to restore the temple of the LORD. ⁵He called together the priests and Levites and said to them, "Go to the towns of Judah and collect the money due annually from all Israel, to repair the temple of your God. Do it now." But the Levites did not act at once.

⁶Therefore the king summoned Jehoiada the chief priest and said to him, "Why haven't you required the Levites to bring in from Judah and Jerusalem the tax imposed by Moses the servant of the LORD and by the assembly of Israel for the Tent of the Testimony?"

⁷Now the sons of that wicked woman Athaliah had broken into the temple of God and had used even its sacred objects for the Baals.

⁸At the king's command, a chest was made and placed outside, at the gate of the temple of the LORD. ⁹A proclamation was then issued in Judah and Jerusalem that they should bring to the LORD the tax that Moses the servant of God had required of Israel in the desert. ¹⁰All the officials and all the people brought their contributions gladly, dropping them into the chest until it was full. ¹¹Whenever the chest was brought in by the Levites to the king's officials and they saw

THE MESSAGE

23.18-21   Jehoiada turned the care of GOD's Temple over to the priests and Levites, the way David had directed originally. They were to offer the Whole-Burnt-Offerings of GOD as set out in The Revelation of Moses, and with praise and song as directed by David. He also assigned security guards at the gates of GOD's Temple so that no one who was unprepared could enter. Then he got everyone together—officers, nobles, governors, and the people themselves—and escorted the king down from The Temple of GOD, through the Upper Gate, and placed him on the royal throne. Everybody celebrated the event. And the city was safe and undisturbed—Athaliah had been killed; no more Athaliah terror.

KING JOASH

24.1   **24** Joash was seven years old when he became king; he was king for forty years in Jerusalem. His mother's name was Gazelle (Zibiah). She was from Beersheba.

24.2-3   Taught and trained by Jehoiada the priest, Joash did what pleased GOD throughout Jehoiada's lifetime. Jehoiada picked out two wives for him; he had a family of both sons and daughters.

24.4-6   The time came when Joash determined to renovate The Temple of GOD. He got the priests and Levites together and said, "Circulate through the towns of Judah every year and collect money from the people to repair The Temple of your God. You are in charge of carrying this out." But the Levites dragged their feet and didn't do anything.

24.7   Then the king called in Jehoiada the chief priest and said, "Why haven't you made the Levites bring in from Judah and Jerusalem the tax Moses, servant of GOD and the congregation, set for the upkeep of the place of worship? You can see how bad things are—wicked Queen Athaliah and her sons let The Temple of God go to ruin and took all its sacred artifacts for use in Baal worship."

24.8-9   Following the king's orders, they made a chest and placed it at the entrance to The Temple of GOD. Then they sent out a tax notice throughout Judah and Jerusalem: "Pay the tax that Moses the servant of GOD set when Israel was in the wilderness."

24.10   The people and their leaders were glad to do it and cheerfully brought their money until the chest was full.

24.11-14   Whenever the Levites brought the chest in for a royal audit and found it to be full, the

NEW INTERNATIONAL VERSION

that there was a large amount of money, the royal secretary and the officer of the chief priest would come and empty the chest and carry it back to its place. They did this regularly and collected a great amount of money. ¹²The king and Jehoiada gave it to the men who carried out the work required for the temple of the LORD. They hired masons and carpenters to restore the LORD's temple, and also workers in iron and bronze to repair the temple.

¹³The men in charge of the work were diligent, and the repairs progressed under them. They rebuilt the temple of God according to its original design and reinforced it. ¹⁴When they had finished, they brought the rest of the money to the king and Jehoiada, and with it were made articles for the LORD's temple: articles for the service and for the burnt offerings, and also dishes and other objects of gold and silver. As long as Jehoiada lived, burnt offerings were presented continually in the temple of the LORD.

¹⁵Now Jehoiada was old and full of years, and he died at the age of a hundred and thirty. ¹⁶He was buried with the kings in the City of David, because of the good he had done in Israel for God and his temple.

THE WICKEDNESS OF JOASH

¹⁷After the death of Jehoiada, the officials of Judah came and paid homage to the king, and he listened to them. ¹⁸They abandoned the temple of the LORD, the God of their fathers, and worshiped Asherah poles and idols. Because of their guilt, God's anger came upon Judah and Jerusalem. ¹⁹Although the LORD sent prophets to the people to bring them back to him, and though they testified against them, they would not listen.

²⁰Then the Spirit of God came upon Zechariah son of Jehoiada the priest. He stood before the people and said, "This is what God says: 'Why do you disobey the LORD's commands? You will not prosper. Because you have forsaken the LORD, he has forsaken you.'"

²¹But they plotted against him, and by order of the king they stoned him to death in the courtyard of the LORD's temple. ²²King Joash did not remember the kindness Zechariah's father Jehoiada had shown him but killed his son, who said as he lay dying, "May the LORD see this and call you to account."

²³At the turn of the year,[a] the army of Aram marched against Joash; it invaded Judah and Jerusalem and killed all the leaders of the people. They sent all the plunder to their king in Damascus. ²⁴Although the Aramean army had

[a] 23 Probably in the spring

THE MESSAGE

king's secretary and the official of the chief priest would empty the chest and put it back in its place. Day after day they did this and collected a lot of money. The king and Jehoiada gave the money to the managers of The Temple project; they in turn paid the masons and carpenters for the repair work on The Temple of GOD. The construction workers kept at their jobs steadily until the restoration was complete—the house of GOD as good as new! When they had finished the work, they returned the surplus money to the king and Jehoiada, who used the money for making sacred vessels for Temple worship, vessels for the daily worship, for the Whole-Burnt-Offerings, bowls, and other gold and silver liturgical artifacts.

²⁴.¹⁴-¹⁶ Whole-Burnt-Offerings were made regularly in The Temple of GOD throughout Jehoiada's lifetime. He died at a ripe old age—130 years old! They buried him in the royal cemetery because he had such a distinguished life of service to Israel and God and God's Temple.

²⁴.¹⁷-¹⁹ But after the death of Jehoiada things fell apart. The leaders of Judah made a formal presentation to the king and he went along with them. Things went from bad to worse; they deserted The Temple of GOD and took up with the cult of sex goddesses. An angry cloud hovered over Judah and Jerusalem because of this sin. GOD sent prophets to straighten them out, warning of judgment. But nobody paid attention.

²⁴.²⁰ Then the Spirit of God moved Zechariah son of Jehoiada the priest to speak up: "God's word: Why have you deliberately walked away from GOD's commandments? You can't live this way! If you walk out on GOD, he'll walk out on you."

²⁴.²¹-²² But they worked out a plot against Zechariah, and with the complicity of the king—he actually gave the order!—they murdered him, pelting him with rocks, right in the court of The Temple of GOD. That's the thanks King Joash showed the loyal Jehoiada, the priest who had made him king. He murdered Jehoiada's son. Zechariah's last words were, "Look, GOD! Make them pay for this!"

²⁴.²³-²⁴ A year or so later Aramean troops attacked Joash. They invaded Judah and Jerusalem, massacred the leaders, and shipped all their plunder back to the king in Damascus. The Arame-

NEW INTERNATIONAL VERSION

come with only a few men, the LORD delivered into their hands a much larger army. Because Judah had forsaken the LORD, the God of their fathers, judgment was executed on Joash. ²⁵When the Arameans withdrew, they left Joash severely wounded. His officials conspired against him for murdering the son of Jehoiada the priest, and they killed him in his bed. So he died and was buried in the City of David, but not in the tombs of the kings.

²⁶Those who conspired against him were Zabad,ᵃ son of Shimeath an Ammonite woman, and Jehozabad, son of Shimrithᵇ a Moabite woman. ²⁷The account of his sons, the many prophecies about him, and the record of the restoration of the temple of God are written in the annotations on the book of the kings. And Amaziah his son succeeded him as king.

AMAZIAH KING OF JUDAH

25 Amaziah was twenty-five years old when he became king, and he reigned in Jerusalem twenty-nine years. His mother's name was Jehoaddinᶜ; she was from Jerusalem. ²He did what was right in the eyes of the LORD, but not wholeheartedly. ³After the kingdom was firmly in his control, he executed the officials who had murdered his father the king. ⁴Yet he did not put their sons to death, but acted in accordance with what is written in the Law, in the Book of Moses, where the LORD commanded: "Fathers shall not be put to death for their children, nor children put to death for their fathers; each is to die for his own sins."ᵈ

⁵Amaziah called the people of Judah together and assigned them according to their families to commanders of thousands and commanders of hundreds for all Judah and Benjamin. He then mustered those twenty years old or more and found that there were three hundred thousand men ready for military service, able to handle the spear and shield. ⁶He also hired a hundred thousand fighting men from Israel for a hundred talentsᵉ of silver.

⁷But a man of God came to him and said, "O king, these troops from Israel must not march with you, for the LORD is not with Israel—not with any of the people of Ephraim. ⁸Even if you go and fight courageously in battle, God will overthrow you before the enemy, for God has the power to help or to overthrow."

THE MESSAGE

an army was quite small, but GOD used them to wipe out Joash's large army—their punishment for deserting GOD, the God of their ancestors. Arameans implemented God's judgment against Joash.

²⁴·²⁵⁻²⁷   They left Joash badly wounded and his own servants finished him off—it was a palace conspiracy, avenging the murder of the son of Jehoiada the priest. They killed him in his bed. Afterward they buried him in the City of David, but he was not honored with a grave in the royal cemetery. The temple conspirators were Zabad, whose mother was Shimeath from Ammon, and Jehozabad, whose mother was Shimrith from Moab. The story of his sons, the many sermons preached to Joash, and the account of his repairs on The Temple of God can be found contained in the commentary on the royal history.

Amaziah, Joash's son, was the next king.

KING AMAZIAH

²⁵·¹⁻⁴ **25** Amaziah was twenty-five years old when he became king and reigned twenty-nine years in Jerusalem. His mother was Jehoaddin from Jerusalem. He lived well before GOD, doing the right thing for the most part. But he wasn't wholeheartedly devoted to God. When he had the affairs of the kingdom well in hand, he executed the palace guard who had assassinated his father the king. But he didn't kill the sons of the assassins—he was mindful of what GOD commanded in The Revelation of Moses, that parents shouldn't be executed for their childrens' sins, nor children for their parents'. We each pay personally for our sins.

²⁵·⁵⁻⁶   Amaziah organized Judah and sorted out Judah and Benjamin by families and by military units. Men twenty years and older had to register—they ended up with 300,000 judged capable of military service. In addition he hired 100,000 soldiers from Israel in the north at a cost of about four and a half tons of silver.

²⁵·⁷⁻⁸   A holy man showed up and said, "No, O King—don't let those northern Israelite soldiers into your army; GOD is not on their side, nor with any of the Ephraimites. Instead, you go by yourself and be strong. God and God only has the power to help or hurt your cause."

ᵃ 26 A variant of *Jozabad*   ᵇ 26 A variant of *Shomer*
ᶜ 1 Hebrew *Jehoaddan*, a variant of *Jehoaddin*
ᵈ 4 Deut. 24:16   ᵉ 6 That is, about 3 3/4 tons (about 3.4 metric tons); also in verse 9

NEW INTERNATIONAL VERSION

⁹Amaziah asked the man of God, "But what about the hundred talents I paid for these Israelite troops?"

The man of God replied, "The LORD can give you much more than that."

¹⁰So Amaziah dismissed the troops who had come to him from Ephraim and sent them home. They were furious with Judah and left for home in a great rage.

¹¹Amaziah then marshaled his strength and led his army to the Valley of Salt, where he killed ten thousand men of Seir. ¹²The army of Judah also captured ten thousand men alive, took them to the top of a cliff and threw them down so that all were dashed to pieces.

¹³Meanwhile the troops that Amaziah had sent back and had not allowed to take part in the war raided Judean towns from Samaria to Beth Horon. They killed three thousand people and carried off great quantities of plunder.

¹⁴When Amaziah returned from slaughtering the Edomites, he brought back the gods of the people of Seir. He set them up as his own gods, bowed down to them and burned sacrifices to them. ¹⁵The anger of the LORD burned against Amaziah, and he sent a prophet to him, who said, "Why do you consult this people's gods, which could not save their own people from your hand?"

¹⁶While he was still speaking, the king said to him, "Have we appointed you an adviser to the king? Stop! Why be struck down?"

So the prophet stopped but said, "I know that God has determined to destroy you, because you have done this and have not listened to my counsel."

¹⁷After Amaziah king of Judah consulted his advisers, he sent this challenge to Jehoash[a] son of Jehoahaz, the son of Jehu, king of Israel: "Come, meet me face to face."

¹⁸But Jehoash king of Israel replied to Amaziah king of Judah: "A thistle in Lebanon sent a message to a cedar in Lebanon, 'Give your daughter to my son in marriage.' Then a wild beast in Lebanon came along and trampled the thistle underfoot. ¹⁹You say to yourself that you have defeated Edom, and now you are arrogant and proud. But stay at home! Why ask for trouble and cause your own downfall and that of Judah also?"

²⁰Amaziah, however, would not listen, for God so worked that he might hand them over to ⌞Jehoash⌟, because they sought the gods of

[a] 17 Hebrew *Joash*, a variant of *Jehoash*; also in verses 18, 21, 23 and 25

THE MESSAGE

²⁵·⁹ But Amaziah said to the holy man, "But what about all this money—these tons of silver I have already paid out to hire these men?"

"GOD's help is worth far more to you than that," said the holy man.

²⁵·¹⁰ So Amaziah fired the soldiers he had hired from the north and sent them home. They were very angry at losing their jobs and went home seething.

²⁵·¹¹⁻¹² But Amaziah was optimistic. He led his troops into the Valley of Salt and killed 10,000 men of Seir. They took another 10,000 as prisoners, led them to the top of the Rock, and pushed them off a cliff. They all died in the fall, smashed on the rocks.

²⁵·¹³ But the troops Amaziah had dismissed from his army, angry over their lost opportunity for plunder, rampaged through the towns of Judah all the way from Samaria to Beth Horon, killing 3,000 people and taking much plunder.

²⁵·¹⁴⁻¹⁵ On his return from the destruction of the Edomites, Amaziah brought back the gods of the men of Seir and installed them as his own gods, worshiping them and burning incense to them. *That* ignited GOD's anger; a fiery blast of GOD's wrath put into words by a God-sent prophet: "What is this? Why on earth would you pray to inferior gods who couldn't so much as help their own people from you—gods weaker than Amaziah?"

²⁵·¹⁶ Amaziah interrupted him, "Did I ask for your opinion? Shut up or get thrown out!"

The prophet quit speaking, but not before he got in one last word: "I have it on good authority: God has made up his mind to throw *you* out because of what you've done, and because you wouldn't listen to me."

✝

²⁵·¹⁷ One day Amaziah sent envoys to Jehoash son of Jehoahaz, the son of Jehu, king of Israel, challenging him to a fight: "Come and meet with me, I dare you. Let's have it out face to face!"

²⁵·¹⁸⁻¹⁹ Jehoash king of Israel replied to Amaziah king of Judah, "One day a thistle in Lebanon sent word to a cedar in Lebanon, 'Give your daughter to my son in marriage.' But then a wild animal of Lebanon passed by and stepped on the thistle, crushing it. Just because you've defeated Edom in battle, you now think you're a big shot. Go ahead and be proud, but stay home. Why press your luck? Why bring defeat on yourself and Judah?"

²⁵·²⁰⁻²² Amaziah wouldn't take no for an answer— God had already decided to let Jehoash defeat him because he had defected to the gods of

NEW INTERNATIONAL VERSION

Edom. ²¹So Jehoash king of Israel attacked. He and Amaziah king of Judah faced each other at Beth Shemesh in Judah. ²²Judah was routed by Israel, and every man fled to his home. ²³Jehoash king of Israel captured Amaziah king of Judah, the son of Joash, the son of Ahaziah,^a at Beth Shemesh. Then Jehoash brought him to Jerusalem and broke down the wall of Jerusalem from the Ephraim Gate to the Corner Gate—a section about six hundred feet^b long. ²⁴He took all the gold and silver and all the articles found in the temple of God that had been in the care of Obed-Edom, together with the palace treasures and the hostages, and returned to Samaria.

²⁵Amaziah son of Joash king of Judah lived for fifteen years after the death of Jehoash son of Jehoahaz king of Israel. ²⁶As for the other events of Amaziah's reign, from beginning to end, are they not written in the book of the kings of Judah and Israel? ²⁷From the time that Amaziah turned away from following the LORD, they conspired against him in Jerusalem and he fled to Lachish, but they sent men after him to Lachish and killed him there. ²⁸He was brought back by horse and was buried with his fathers in the City of Judah.

UZZIAH KING OF JUDAH

26 Then all the people of Judah took Uzziah,^c who was sixteen years old, and made him king in place of his father Amaziah. ²He was the one who rebuilt Elath and restored it to Judah after Amaziah rested with his fathers.

³Uzziah was sixteen years old when he became king, and he reigned in Jerusalem fifty-two years. His mother's name was Jecoliah; she was from Jerusalem. ⁴He did what was right in the eyes of the LORD, just as his father Amaziah had done. ⁵He sought God during the days of Zechariah, who instructed him in the fear^d of God. As long as he sought the LORD, God gave him success.

⁶He went to war against the Philistines and broke down the walls of Gath, Jabneh and Ashdod. He then rebuilt towns near Ashdod and elsewhere among the Philistines. ⁷God helped him against the Philistines and against the Arabs who lived in Gur Baal and against the Meunites. ⁸The Ammonites brought tribute to Uzziah, and

THE MESSAGE

Edom. So Jehoash king of Israel came on ahead and confronted Amaziah king of Judah. They met at Beth Shemesh, a town of Judah. Judah was thoroughly beaten by Israel—all the soldiers straggled home in defeat.

25.23-24 Jehoash king of Israel captured Amaziah king of Judah, the son of Joash, the son of Ahaziah, at Beth Shemesh. But Jehoash didn't stop at that; he went on to attack Jerusalem. He demolished the Wall of Jerusalem all the way from the Ephraim Gate to the Corner Gate—a stretch of about six hundred feet. He looted the gold, silver, and furnishings—anything he found that was worth taking—from both the palace and The Temple of God—and, for good measure, he took hostages. Then he returned to Samaria.

25.25-26 Amaziah son of Joash king of Judah continued as king fifteen years after the death of Jehoash son of Jehoahaz king of Israel. The rest of the life and times of Amaziah from start to finish is written in the *Royal Annals of the Kings of Judah and Israel.*

25.27-28 During those last days, after Amaziah had defected from GOD, they cooked up a plot against Amaziah in Jerusalem, and he had to flee to Lachish. But they tracked him down in Lachish and killed him there. They brought him back on horseback and buried him in Jerusalem with his ancestors in the City of David.

KING UZZIAH

26.1-2 **26** The people of Judah then took Uzziah, who was only sixteen years old, and made him king in place of his father Amaziah. The first thing he did after his father was dead and buried was to recover Elath for Judah and rebuild it.

26.3-5 Uzziah was sixteen years old when he became king and reigned for fifty-two years in Jerusalem. His mother was Jecoliah from Jerusalem. He behaved well in the eyes of GOD, following in the footsteps of his father Amaziah. He was a loyal seeker of God. He was well trained by his pastor and teacher Zechariah to live in reverent obedience before God, and for as long as Zechariah lived, Uzziah lived a godly life. And God prospered him.

26.6-8 He ventured out and fought the Philistines, breaking into the fortress cities of Gath, Jabneh, and Ashdod. He also built settlements around Ashdod and other Philistine areas. God helped him in his wars with the Philistines, the Arabs in Gur Baal, and the Meunites. The Ammonites also paid tribute. Uzziah became fa-

---

^a 23 Hebrew *Jehoahaz*, a variant of *Ahaziah*   ^b 23 Hebrew *four hundred cubits* (about 180 meters)   ^c 1 Also called *Azariah*   ^d 5 Many Hebrew manuscripts, Septuagint and Syriac; other Hebrew manuscripts *vision*

NEW INTERNATIONAL VERSION

his fame spread as far as the border of Egypt, because he had become very powerful.

⁹Uzziah built towers in Jerusalem at the Corner Gate, at the Valley Gate and at the angle of the wall, and he fortified them. ¹⁰He also built towers in the desert and dug many cisterns, because he had much livestock in the foothills and in the plain. He had people working his fields and vineyards in the hills and in the fertile lands, for he loved the soil.

¹¹Uzziah had a well-trained army, ready to go out by divisions according to their numbers as mustered by Jeiel the secretary and Maaseiah the officer under the direction of Hananiah, one of the royal officials. ¹²The total number of family leaders over the fighting men was 2,600. ¹³Under their command was an army of 307,500 men trained for war, a powerful force to support the king against his enemies. ¹⁴Uzziah provided shields, spears, helmets, coats of armor, bows and slingstones for the entire army. ¹⁵In Jerusalem he made machines designed by skillful men for use on the towers and on the corner defenses to shoot arrows and hurl large stones. His fame spread far and wide, for he was greatly helped until he became powerful.

¹⁶But after Uzziah became powerful, his pride led to his downfall. He was unfaithful to the Lord his God, and entered the temple of the Lord to burn incense on the altar of incense. ¹⁷Azariah the priest with eighty other courageous priests of the Lord followed him in. ¹⁸They confronted him and said, "It is not right for you, Uzziah, to burn incense to the Lord. That is for the priests, the descendants of Aaron, who have been consecrated to burn incense. Leave the sanctuary, for you have been unfaithful; and you will not be honored by the Lord God."

¹⁹Uzziah, who had a censer in his hand ready to burn incense, became angry. While he was raging at the priests in their presence before the incense altar in the Lord's temple, leprosy*ᵃ* broke out on his forehead. ²⁰When Azariah the chief priest and all the other priests looked at him, they saw that he had leprosy on his forehead, so they hurried him out. Indeed, he himself was eager to leave, because the Lord had afflicted him.

²¹King Uzziah had leprosy until the day he died. He lived in a separate house*ᵇ*—leprous, and excluded from the temple of the Lord. Jotham his son had charge of the palace and governed the people of the land.

ᵃ 19 The Hebrew word was used for various diseases affecting the skin—not necessarily leprosy; also in verses 20, 21 and 23.   ᵇ 21 Or in a house where he was relieved of responsibilities

THE MESSAGE

mous, his reputation extending all the way to Egypt. He became quite powerful.

26:9-10   Uzziah constructed defense towers in Jerusalem at the Corner Gate, the Valley Gate, and at the corner of the wall. He also built towers and dug cisterns out in the country. He had herds of cattle down in the foothills and out on the plains, had farmers and vinedressers at work in the hills and fields—he loved growing things.

26:11-15   On the military side, Uzziah had a well-prepared army ready to fight. They were organized by companies under the direction of Jeiel the secretary, Maaseiah the field captain, and Hananiah of the general staff. The roster of family leaders over the fighting men accounted for 2,600. Under them were reinforcement troops numbering 307,000, with 500 of them on constant alert—a strong royal defense against any attack. Uzziah had them well-armed with shields, spears, helmets, armor, bows, and slingshots. He also installed the latest in military technology on the towers and corners of Jerusalem for shooting arrows and hurling stones. He became well known for all this—a famous king. Everything seemed to go his way.

26:16-18   But then the strength and success went to his head. Arrogant and proud, he fell. One day, contemptuous of God, he walked into The Temple of God like he owned it and took over, burning incense on the Incense Altar. The priest Azariah, backed up by eighty brave priests of God, tried to prevent him. They confronted Uzziah: "You must not, you *cannot* do this, Uzziah—only the Aaronite priests, especially consecrated for the work, are permitted to burn incense. Get out of God's Temple; you are unfaithful and a disgrace!"

26:19-21   But Uzziah, censer in hand, was already in the middle of doing it and angrily rebuffed the priests. He lost his temper; angry words were exchanged—and then, even as they quarreled, a skin disease appeared on his forehead. As soon as they saw it, the chief priest Azariah and the other priests got him out of there as fast as they could. He hurried out—he knew that God then and there had given him the disease. Uzziah had his skin disease for the rest of his life and had to live in quarantine; he was not permitted to set foot in The Temple of God. His son Jotham, who managed the royal palace, took over the government of the country.

NEW INTERNATIONAL VERSION

²²The other events of Uzziah's reign, from beginning to end, are recorded by the prophet Isaiah son of Amoz. ²³Uzziah rested with his fathers and was buried near them in a field for burial that belonged to the kings, for people said, "He had leprosy." And Jotham his son succeeded him as king.

JOTHAM KING OF JUDAH

27 Jotham was twenty-five years old when he became king, and he reigned in Jerusalem sixteen years. His mother's name was Jerusha daughter of Zadok. ²He did what was right in the eyes of the LORD, just as his father Uzziah had done, but unlike him he did not enter the temple of the LORD. The people, however, continued their corrupt practices. ³Jotham rebuilt the Upper Gate of the temple of the LORD and did extensive work on the wall at the hill of Ophel. ⁴He built towns in the Judean hills and forts and towers in the wooded areas.

⁵Jotham made war on the king of the Ammonites and conquered them. That year the Ammonites paid him a hundred talents[a] of silver, ten thousand cors[b] of wheat and ten thousand cors of barley. The Ammonites brought him the same amount also in the second and third years. ⁶Jotham grew powerful because he walked steadfastly before the LORD his God.

⁷The other events in Jotham's reign, including all his wars and the other things he did, are written in the book of the kings of Israel and Judah. ⁸He was twenty-five years old when he became king, and he reigned in Jerusalem sixteen years. ⁹Jotham rested with his fathers and was buried in the City of David. And Ahaz his son succeeded him as king.

AHAZ KING OF JUDAH

28 Ahaz was twenty years old when he became king, and he reigned in Jerusalem sixteen years. Unlike David his father, he did not do what was right in the eyes of the LORD. ²He walked in the ways of the kings of Israel and also made cast idols for worshiping the Baals. ³He burned sacrifices in the Valley of Ben Hinnom and sacrificed his sons in the fire, following the detestable ways of the nations the LORD had driven out before the Israelites. ⁴He offered sacrifices and burned incense at the high places, on the hilltops and under every spreading tree.

⁵Therefore the LORD his God handed him over to the king of Aram. The Arameans defeated him

---

[a] 5 That is, about 3 3/4 tons (about 3.4 metric tons)
[b] 5 That is, probably about 62,000 bushels (about 2,200 kiloliters)

THE MESSAGE

26.22-23 The rest of the history of Uzziah, from start to finish, was written by the prophet Isaiah son of Amoz. When Uzziah died, they buried him with his ancestors in a field next to the royal cemetery. His skin disease disqualified him from burial in the royal cemetery. His son Jotham became the next king.

KING JOTHAM

27.1-2 **27** Jotham was twenty-five years old when he became king; he reigned sixteen years at Jerusalem. His mother was Jerusha the daughter of Zadok. In GOD's eyes he lived a good life, following the path marked out by his father Uzziah. Unlike his father, though, he didn't desecrate The Temple of GOD. But the people pushed right on in their lives of corruption.

27.3-6 Jotham constructed the Upper Gate of The Temple of GOD, considerably extended the Wall of the Ophel, and built cities in the high country of Judah and forts and towers down in the forests. He fought and beat the king of the Ammonites—that year the Ammonites turned over three and a quarter tons of silver and about sixty-five thousand bushels of wheat, and another sixty-five thousand bushels of barley. They repeated this for the next two years. Jotham's strength was rooted in his steady and determined life of obedience to GOD.

27.7-9 The rest of the history of Jotham, including his wars and achievements, are all written in the *Royal Annals of the Kings of Israel and Judah*. He was twenty-five years old when he became king; he reigned for sixteen years at Jerusalem. Jotham died and was buried in the City of David. His son Ahaz became the next king.

KING AHAZ

28.1-4 **28** Ahaz was twenty years old when he became king and reigned sixteen years in Jerusalem. He didn't live right in the eyes of GOD; he wasn't at all like his ancestor David. Instead he followed in the track of Israel in the north, even casting metal figurines for worshiping the pagan Baal gods. He participated in the outlawed burning of incense in the Valley of Ben Hinnom and—incredibly!—indulged in the outrageous practice of "passing his sons through the fire," a truly abominable thing he picked up from the pagans GOD had earlier thrown out of the country. He also joined in the activities of the neighborhood sex-and-religion shrines that flourished all over the place.

28.5-8 GOD, fed up, handed him over to the king of Aram, who beat him badly and took many pris-

NEW INTERNATIONAL VERSION

and took many of his people as prisoners and brought them to Damascus.

He was also given into the hands of the king of Israel, who inflicted heavy casualties on him. 6In one day Pekah son of Remaliah killed a hundred and twenty thousand soldiers in Judah—because Judah had forsaken the LORD, the God of their fathers. 7Zicri, an Ephraimite warrior, killed Maaseiah the king's son, Azrikam the officer in charge of the palace, and Elkanah, second to the king. 8The Israelites took captive from their kinsmen two hundred thousand wives, sons and daughters. They also took a great deal of plunder, which they carried back to Samaria.

9But a prophet of the LORD named Oded was there, and he went out to meet the army when it returned to Samaria. He said to them, "Because the LORD, the God of your fathers, was angry with Judah, he gave them into your hand. But you have slaughtered them in a rage that reaches to heaven. 10And now you intend to make the men and women of Judah and Jerusalem your slaves. But aren't you also guilty of sins against the LORD your God? 11Now listen to me! Send back your fellow countrymen you have taken as prisoners, for the LORD's fierce anger rests on you."

12Then some of the leaders in Ephraim—Azariah son of Jehohanan, Berekiah son of Meshillemoth, Jehizkiah son of Shallum, and Amasa son of Hadlai—confronted those who were arriving from the war. 13"You must not bring those prisoners here," they said, "or we will be guilty before the LORD. Do you intend to add to our sin and guilt? For our guilt is already great, and his fierce anger rests on Israel."

14So the soldiers gave up the prisoners and plunder in the presence of the officials and all the assembly. 15The men designated by name took the prisoners, and from the plunder they clothed all who were naked. They provided them with clothes and sandals, food and drink, and healing balm. All those who were weak they put on donkeys. So they took them back to their fellow countrymen at Jericho, the City of Palms, and returned to Samaria.

16At that time King Ahaz sent to the king*a* of Assyria for help. 17The Edomites had again come and attacked Judah and carried away prisoners, 18while the Philistines had raided towns in the foothills and in the Negev of Judah. They captured and occupied Beth Shemesh, Aijalon and Gederoth, as well as Soco, Timnah and Gimzo, with their surrounding villages. 19The LORD had

---

a 16 One Hebrew manuscript, Septuagint and Vulgate (see also 2 Kings 16:7); most Hebrew manuscripts *kings*

THE MESSAGE

oners to Damascus. God also let the king of Israel loose on him and that resulted in a terrible slaughter: Pekah son of Remaliah killed 120,000 in one day, all of them first-class soldiers, and all because they had deserted GOD, the God of their ancestors. Furthermore, Zicri, an Ephraimite hero, killed the king's son Maaseiah, Azrikam the palace steward, and Elkanah, second in command to the king. And that wasn't the end of it—the Israelites captured 200,000 men, women, and children, besides huge cartloads of plunder that they took to Samaria.

28.9-11   GOD's prophet Oded was in the neighborhood. He met the army when it entered Samaria and said, "Stop right where you are and listen! GOD, the God of your ancestors, was angry with Judah and used you to punish them; but you took things into your own hands and used *your* anger, uncalled for and irrational, to turn your brothers and sisters from Judah and Jerusalem into slaves. Don't you see that this is a terrible sin against your GOD? Careful now; do exactly what I say—return these captives, every last one of them. If you don't, you'll find out how real anger, GOD's anger, works."

28.12-13   Some of their Ephraimite leaders—Azariah son of Jehohanan, Berekiah son of Meshillemoth, Jehizkiah son of Shallum, and Amasa son of Hadlai—stood up against the returning army and said, "Don't bring the captives here! We've already sinned against GOD; and now you are about to compound our sin and guilt. We're guilty enough as it is, enough to set off an explosion of divine anger."

28.14-15   So the soldiers turned over both the captives and the plunder to the leaders and the people. Personally designated men gathered the captives together, dressed the ones who were naked using clothing from the stores of plunder, put shoes on their feet, gave them all a square meal, provided first aid to the injured, put the weak ones on donkeys, and then escorted them to Jericho, the City of Palms, restoring them to their families. Then they went back to Samaria.

28.16-21   At about that time King Ahaz sent to the king of Assyria asking for personal help. The Edomites had come back and given Judah a bad beating, taking off a bunch of captives. Adding insult to injury the Philistines raided the cities in the foothills to the west and the southern desert and captured Beth Shemesh, Aijalon, and Gederoth, along with Soco, Timnah, and Gimzo, with their surrounding villages, and moved in, making themselves at

NEW INTERNATIONAL VERSION

humbled Judah because of Ahaz king of Israel,[a] for he had promoted wickedness in Judah and had been most unfaithful to the LORD. [20]Tiglath-Pileser[b] king of Assyria came to him, but he gave him trouble instead of help. [21]Ahaz took some of the things from the temple of the LORD and from the royal palace and from the princes and presented them to the king of Assyria, but that did not help him.

[22]In his time of trouble King Ahaz became even more unfaithful to the LORD. [23]He offered sacrifices to the gods of Damascus, who had defeated him; for he thought, "Since the gods of the kings of Aram have helped them, I will sacrifice to them so they will help me." But they were his downfall and the downfall of all Israel.

[24]Ahaz gathered together the furnishings from the temple of God and took them away.[c] He shut the doors of the LORD's temple and set up altars at every street corner in Jerusalem. [25]In every town in Judah he built high places to burn sacrifices to other gods and provoked the LORD, the God of his fathers, to anger.

[26]The other events of his reign and all his ways, from beginning to end, are written in the book of the kings of Judah and Israel. [27]Ahaz rested with his fathers and was buried in the city of Jerusalem, but he was not placed in the tombs of the kings of Israel. And Hezekiah his son succeeded him as king.

HEZEKIAH PURIFIES THE TEMPLE

29 Hezekiah was twenty-five years old when he became king, and he reigned in Jerusalem twenty-nine years. His mother's name was Abijah daughter of Zechariah. [2]He did what was right in the eyes of the LORD, just as his father David had done.

[3]In the first month of the first year of his reign, he opened the doors of the temple of the LORD and repaired them. [4]He brought in the priests and the Levites, assembled them in the square on the east side [5]and said: "Listen to me, Levites! Consecrate yourselves now and consecrate the temple of the LORD, the God of your fathers. Remove all defilement from the sanctuary. [6]Our fathers were unfaithful; they did evil in the eyes of the LORD our God and forsook him. They

THE MESSAGE

home. Arrogant King Ahaz, acting as if he could do without God's help, had unleashed an epidemic of depravity. Judah, brought to its knees by GOD, was now reduced to begging for a handout. But the king of Assyria, Tiglath-Pileser, wouldn't help—he came instead and humiliated Ahaz even more by attacking and bullying him. Desperate, Ahaz ransacked The Temple of GOD, the royal palace, and every other place he could think of, scraping together everything he could, and gave it to the king of Assyria—and got nothing in return, not a bit of help.

28.22-25 But King Ahaz didn't learn his lesson—at the very time that everyone was turning against him, he continued to be against GOD! He offered sacrifices to the gods of Damascus. He had just been defeated by Damascus; he thought, "If I worship the gods who helped Damascus, those gods just might help me too." But things only went from bad to worse: first Ahaz in ruins and then the country. He cleaned out The Temple of God of everything useful and valuable, boarded up the doors of The Temple, and then went out and set up pagan shrines for his own use all over Jerusalem. And not only in Jerusalem, but all over Judah—neighborhood shrines for worshiping any and every god on sale. And was GOD ever angry!

28.26-27 The rest of Ahaz's infamous life, all that he did from start to finish, is written in the *Royal Annals of the Kings of Judah and Israel*. When Ahaz died, they buried him in Jerusalem, but he was not honored with a burial in the cemetery of the kings. His son Hezekiah was the next king.

KING HEZEKIAH

29.1-2 **29** Hezekiah became king when he was twenty-five years old and was king in Jerusalem for twenty-nine years. His mother was Abijah daughter of Zechariah. In GOD's opinion he was a good king; he kept to the standards of his ancestor David.

29.3-9 In the first month of the first year of his reign, Hezekiah, having first repaired the doors of The Temple of GOD, threw them open to the public. He assembled the priests and Levites in the court on the east side and said, "Levites, listen! Consecrate yourselves and consecrate The Temple of GOD—give this much-defiled place a good housecleaning. Our ancestors went wrong and lived badly before GOD—they

---

[a] 19 That is, Judah, as frequently in 2 Chronicles
[b] 20 Hebrew *Tilgath-Pilneser*, a variant of *Tiglath-Pileser*
[c] 24 Or *and cut them up*

NEW INTERNATIONAL VERSION

turned their faces away from the LORD's dwelling place and turned their backs on him. [7]They also shut the doors of the portico and put out the lamps. They did not burn incense or present any burnt offerings at the sanctuary to the God of Israel. [8]Therefore, the anger of the LORD has fallen on Judah and Jerusalem; he has made them an object of dread and horror and scorn, as you can see with your own eyes. [9]This is why our fathers have fallen by the sword and why our sons and daughters and our wives are in captivity. [10]Now I intend to make a covenant with the LORD, the God of Israel, so that his fierce anger will turn away from us. [11]My sons, do not be negligent now, for the LORD has chosen you to stand before him and serve him, to minister before him and to burn incense."

[12]Then these Levites set to work:
from the Kohathites,
  Mahath son of Amasai and Joel son of Azariah;
from the Merarites,
  Kish son of Abdi and Azariah son of Jehallelel;
from the Gershonites,
  Joah son of Zimmah and Eden son of Joah;
[13]from the descendants of Elizaphan,
  Shimri and Jeiel;
from the descendants of Asaph,
  Zechariah and Mattaniah;
[14]from the descendants of Heman,
  Jehiel and Shimei;
from the descendants of Jeduthun,
  Shemaiah and Uzziel.

[15]When they had assembled their brothers and consecrated themselves, they went in to purify the temple of the LORD, as the king had ordered, following the word of the LORD. [16]The priests went into the sanctuary of the LORD to purify it. They brought out to the courtyard of the LORD's temple everything unclean that they found in the temple of the LORD. The Levites took it and carried it out to the Kidron Valley. [17]They began the consecration on the first day of the first month, and by the eighth day of the month they reached the portico of the LORD. For eight more days they consecrated the temple of the LORD itself, finishing on the sixteenth day of the first month.

[18]Then they went in to King Hezekiah and reported: "We have purified the entire temple of the LORD, the altar of burnt offering with all its utensils, and the table for setting out the consecrated bread, with all its articles. [19]We have prepared and consecrated all the articles that King Ahaz removed in his unfaithfulness while he was king. They are now in front of the LORD's altar."

THE MESSAGE

discarded him, turned away from this house where we meet with GOD, and walked off. They boarded up the doors, turned out the lights, and canceled all the acts of worship of the GOD of Israel in the holy Temple. And because of that, GOD's anger flared up and he turned those people into a public exhibit of disaster, a moral history lesson—look and read! This is why our ancestors were killed, and this is why our wives and sons and daughters were taken prisoner and made slaves.

29.10-11 "I have decided to make a covenant with the GOD of Israel and turn history around so that GOD will no longer be angry with us. Children, don't drag your feet in this! GOD has chosen you to take your place before him to serve in conducting and leading worship—*this* is your life work; make sure you do it and do it well."

29.12-17 The Levites stood at attention: Mahath son of Amasai and Joel son of Azariah from the Kohathites; Kish son of Abdi and Azariah son of Jehallelel from the Merarites; Joah son of Zimmah and Eden son of Joah from the Gershonites; Shimri and Jeiel sons of Elizaphan; Zechariah and Mattaniah sons of Asaph; Jehiel and Shimei of the family of Heman; Shemaiah and Uzziel of the family of Jeduthun. They presented themselves and their brothers, consecrated themselves, and set to work cleaning up The Temple of GOD as the king had directed—as GOD directed! The priests started from the inside and worked out; they emptied the place of the accumulation of defiling junk—pagan rubbish that had no business in that holy place—and the Levites hauled it off to the Kidron Valley. They began the Temple cleaning on the first day of the first month and by the eighth day they had worked their way out to the porch—eight days it took them to clean and consecrate The Temple itself, and in eight more days they had finished with the entire Temple complex.

29.18-19 Then they reported to Hezekiah the king, "We have cleaned up the entire Temple of GOD, including the Altar of Whole-Burnt-Offering and the Table of the Bread of the Presence with their furnishings. We have also cleaned up and consecrated all the vessels which King Ahaz had gotten rid of during his misrule. Take a look; we have repaired them. They're all there in front of the Altar of GOD."

NEW INTERNATIONAL VERSION

²⁰Early the next morning King Hezekiah gathered the city officials together and went up to the temple of the LORD. ²¹They brought seven bulls, seven rams, seven male lambs and seven male goats as a sin offering for the kingdom, for the sanctuary and for Judah. The king commanded the priests, the descendants of Aaron, to offer these on the altar of the LORD. ²²So they slaughtered the bulls, and the priests took the blood and sprinkled it on the altar; next they slaughtered the rams and sprinkled their blood on the altar; then they slaughtered the lambs and sprinkled their blood on the altar. ²³The goats for the sin offering were brought before the king and the assembly, and they laid their hands on them. ²⁴The priests then slaughtered the goats and presented their blood on the altar for a sin offering to atone for all Israel, because the king had ordered the burnt offering and the sin offering for all Israel.

²⁵He stationed the Levites in the temple of the LORD with cymbals, harps and lyres in the way prescribed by David and Gad the king's seer and Nathan the prophet; this was commanded by the LORD through his prophets. ²⁶So the Levites stood ready with David's instruments, and the priests with their trumpets.

²⁷Hezekiah gave the order to sacrifice the burnt offering on the altar. As the offering began, singing to the LORD began also, accompanied by trumpets and the instruments of David king of Israel. ²⁸The whole assembly bowed in worship, while the singers sang and the trumpeters played. All this continued until the sacrifice of the burnt offering was completed.

²⁹When the offerings were finished, the king and everyone present with him knelt down and worshiped. ³⁰King Hezekiah and his officials ordered the Levites to praise the LORD with the words of David and of Asaph the seer. So they sang praises with gladness and bowed their heads and worshiped.

³¹Then Hezekiah said, "You have now dedicated yourselves to the LORD. Come and bring sacrifices and thank offerings to the temple of the LORD." So the assembly brought sacrifices and thank offerings, and all whose hearts were willing brought burnt offerings.

³²The number of burnt offerings the assembly brought was seventy bulls, a hundred rams and two hundred male lambs—all of them for burnt offerings to the LORD. ³³The animals consecrated as sacrifices amounted to six hundred bulls and three thousand sheep and goats. ³⁴The priests, however, were too few to skin all the burnt offerings; so their kinsmen the Levites helped them

THE MESSAGE

29.20-24 Then Hezekiah the king went to work: He got all the leaders of the city together and marched to The Temple of GOD. They brought with them seven bulls, seven rams, seven lambs, and seven he-goats to sacrifice as an Absolution-Offering for the royal family, for the Sanctuary, and for Judah as a whole; he directed the Aaronite priests to sacrifice them on the Altar of GOD. The priests butchered the bulls and then took the blood and sprinkled it on the Altar, and then the same with the rams and lambs. Finally they brought the goats up; the king and congregation laid their hands upon them. The priests butchered them and made an Absolution-Offering with their blood at the Altar to atone for the sin of all Israel—the king had ordered that the Whole-Burnt-Offering and the Absolution-Offering be for all Israel.

29.25-26 The king ordered the Levites to take their places in The Temple of GOD with their musical instruments—cymbals, harps, zithers—following the original instructions of David, Gad the king's seer, and Nathan the prophet; this was GOD's command conveyed by his prophets. The Levites formed the orchestra of David, while the priests took up the trumpets.

29.27-30 Then Hezekiah gave the signal to begin: The Whole-Burnt-Offering was offered on the Altar; at the same time the sacred choir began singing, backed up by the trumpets and the David orchestra while the entire congregation worshiped. The singers sang and the trumpeters played all during the sacrifice of the Whole-Burnt-Offering. When the offering of the sacrifice was completed, the king and everyone there knelt to the ground and worshiped. Then Hezekiah the king and the leaders told the Levites to finish things off with anthems of praise to GOD using lyrics by David and Asaph the seer. They sang their praises with joy and reverence, kneeling in worship.

29.31-35 Hezekiah then made this response: "The dedication is complete—you're consecrated to GOD. Now you're ready: Come forward and bring your sacrifices and Thank-Offerings to The Temple of GOD."

And come they did. Everyone in the congregation brought sacrifices and Thank-Offerings and some, overflowing with generosity, even brought Whole-Burnt-Offerings, a generosity expressed in seventy bulls, a hundred rams, and two hundred lambs—all for Whole-Burnt-Offerings for GOD! The total number of animals consecrated for sacrifice that day amounted to 600 bulls and 3,000 sheep. They ran out of priests qualified to slaughter all the Whole-Burnt-Offerings so their brother Levites

NEW INTERNATIONAL VERSION

until the task was finished and until other priests had been consecrated, for the Levites had been more conscientious in consecrating themselves than the priests had been. ³⁵There were burnt offerings in abundance, together with the fat of the fellowship offerings ᵃ and the drink offerings that accompanied the burnt offerings.

So the service of the temple of the LORD was reestablished. ³⁶Hezekiah and all the people rejoiced at what God had brought about for his people, because it was done so quickly.

HEZEKIAH CELEBRATES THE PASSOVER

30 Hezekiah sent word to all Israel and Judah and also wrote letters to Ephraim and Manasseh, inviting them to come to the temple of the LORD in Jerusalem and celebrate the Passover to the LORD, the God of Israel. ²The king and his officials and the whole assembly in Jerusalem decided to celebrate the Passover in the second month. ³They had not been able to celebrate it at the regular time because not enough priests had consecrated themselves and the people had not assembled in Jerusalem. ⁴The plan seemed right both to the king and to the whole assembly. ⁵They decided to send a proclamation throughout Israel, from Beersheba to Dan, calling the people to come to Jerusalem and celebrate the Passover to the LORD, the God of Israel. It had not been celebrated in large numbers according to what was written.

⁶At the king's command, couriers went throughout Israel and Judah with letters from the king and from his officials, which read:

"People of Israel, return to the LORD, the God of Abraham, Isaac and Israel, that he may return to you who are left, who have escaped from the hand of the kings of Assyria. ⁷Do not be like your fathers and brothers, who were unfaithful to the LORD, the God of their fathers, so that he made them an object of horror, as you see. ⁸Do not be stiff-necked, as your fathers were; submit to the LORD. Come to the sanctuary, which he has consecrated forever. Serve the LORD your God, so that his fierce anger will turn away from you. ⁹If you return to the LORD, then your brothers and your children will be shown compassion by their captors and will come back to this land, for the LORD your God is gracious and compassionate. He will not turn his face from you if you return to him."

THE MESSAGE

stepped in and helped out while other priests consecrated themselves for the work. It turned out that the Levites had been more responsible in making sure they were properly consecrated than the priests had been. Besides the overflow of Whole-Burnt-Offerings there were also choice pieces for the Peace-Offerings and lavish libations that went with the Whole-Burnt-Offerings. The worship in The Temple of GOD was on a firm footing again!

29.36   Hezekiah and the congregation celebrated: God had established a firm foundation for the lives of the people—and so quickly!

✝

30.1-5 **30** Then Hezekiah invited all of Israel and Judah, with personal letters to Ephraim and Manasseh, to come to The Temple of GOD in Jerusalem to celebrate the Passover to Israel's God. The king and his officials and the congregation in Jerusalem had decided to celebrate Passover in the second month. They hadn't been able to celebrate it at the regular time because not enough of the priests were yet personally prepared and the people hadn't had time to gather in Jerusalem. Under these circumstances, the revised date was approved by both king and people and they sent out the invitation from one end of the country to the other, from Beersheba in the south to Dan in the north: "Come and celebrate the Passover to Israel's God in Jerusalem." No one living had ever celebrated it properly.

30.6-9   The king gave the orders, and the couriers delivered the invitations from the king and his leaders throughout Israel and Judah. The invitation read: "O Israelites! Come back to GOD, the God of Abraham, Isaac, and Israel, so that he can return to you who have survived the predations of the kings of Assyria. Don't repeat the sins of your ancestors who turned their backs on GOD, the God of their ancestors who then brought them to ruin—you can see the ruins all around you. Don't be pigheaded as your ancestors were. Clasp GOD's outstretched hand. Come to his Temple of holy worship, consecrated for all time. Serve GOD, *your* God. You'll no longer be in danger of his hot anger. If you come back to GOD, your captive relatives and children will be treated compassionately and allowed to come home. Your GOD is gracious and kind and won't snub you—come back and he'll welcome you with open arms."

ᵃ 35 Traditionally *peace offerings*

NEW INTERNATIONAL VERSION

¹⁰The couriers went from town to town in Ephraim and Manasseh, as far as Zebulun, but the people scorned and ridiculed them. ¹¹Nevertheless, some men of Asher, Manasseh and Zebulun humbled themselves and went to Jerusalem. ¹²Also in Judah the hand of God was on the people to give them unity of mind to carry out what the king and his officials had ordered, following the word of the LORD.

¹³A very large crowd of people assembled in Jerusalem to celebrate the Feast of Unleavened Bread in the second month. ¹⁴They removed the altars in Jerusalem and cleared away the incense altars and threw them into the Kidron Valley.

¹⁵They slaughtered the Passover lamb on the fourteenth day of the second month. The priests and the Levites were ashamed and consecrated themselves and brought burnt offerings to the temple of the LORD. ¹⁶Then they took up their regular positions as prescribed in the Law of Moses the man of God. The priests sprinkled the blood handed to them by the Levites. ¹⁷Since many in the crowd had not consecrated themselves, the Levites had to kill the Passover lambs for all those who were not ceremonially clean and could not consecrate ˌtheir lambsˌ to the LORD. ¹⁸Although most of the many people who came from Ephraim, Manasseh, Issachar and Zebulun had not purified themselves, yet they ate the Passover, contrary to what was written. But Hezekiah prayed for them, saying, "May the LORD, who is good, pardon everyone ¹⁹who sets his heart on seeking God—the LORD, the God of his fathers—even if he is not clean according to the rules of the sanctuary." ²⁰And the LORD heard Hezekiah and healed the people.

²¹The Israelites who were present in Jerusalem celebrated the Feast of Unleavened Bread for seven days with great rejoicing, while the Levites and priests sang to the LORD every day, accompanied by the LORD's instruments of praise.ᵃ

²²Hezekiah spoke encouragingly to all the Levites, who showed good understanding of the service of the LORD. For the seven days they ate their assigned portion and offered fellowship offeringsᵇ and praised the LORD, the God of their fathers.

ᵃ 21 Or priests praised the LORD every day with resounding instruments belonging to the LORD   ᵇ 22 Traditionally peace offerings

THE MESSAGE

30.10-12   So the couriers set out, going from city to city through the country of Ephraim and Manasseh, as far north as Zebulun. But the people poked fun at them, treated them as a joke. But not all; some from Asher, Manasseh, and Zebulun weren't too proud to accept the invitation and come to Jerusalem. It was better in Judah—God worked powerfully among them to make it unanimous, responding to the orders sent out by the king and his officials, orders backed up by the word of GOD.

30.13-17   It turned out that there was a tremendous crowd of people when the time came in the second month to celebrate the Passover (sometimes called the Feast of Unraised Bread). First they went to work and got rid of all the pagan altars that were in Jerusalem—hauled them off and dumped them in the Kidron Valley. Then, on the fourteenth day of the second month, they slaughtered the Passover lambs. The priests and Levites weren't ready; but now, embarrassed in their laziness, they consecrated themselves and brought Whole-Burnt-Offerings to The Temple of GOD. Ready now, they stood at their posts as designated by The Revelation of Moses the holy man; the priests sprinkled the blood the Levites handed to them. Because so many in the congregation had not properly prepared themselves by consecration and so were not qualified, the Levites took charge of the slaughter of the Passover lambs so that they would be properly consecrated to GOD.

30.18-19   There were a lot of people, especially those from Ephraim, Manasseh, Issachar, and Zebulun, who did not eat the Passover meal because they had not prepared themselves adequately. Hezekiah prayed for these as follows: "May GOD who is all good, pardon and forgive everyone who sincerely desires GOD, the God of our ancestors. Even—especially!—these who do not meet the literal conditions stated for access to The Temple."

30.20   GOD responded to Hezekiah's prayer and healed the people.

30.21-22   All the Israelites present in Jerusalem celebrated the Passover (Feast of Unraised Bread) for seven days, celebrated exuberantly. The Levites and priests praised GOD day after day, filling the air with praise sounds of percussion and brass. Hezekiah commended the Levites for the superb way in which they had led the people in the worship of GOD.

30.22-23   When the feast and festival—that glorious seven days of worship, the making of offerings, and the praising of GOD, the God of their ancestors—were over, the tables cleared and the

NEW INTERNATIONAL VERSION

²³The whole assembly then agreed to celebrate the festival seven more days; so for another seven days they celebrated joyfully. ²⁴Hezekiah king of Judah provided a thousand bulls and seven thousand sheep and goats for the assembly, and the officials provided them with a thousand bulls and ten thousand sheep and goats. A great number of priests consecrated themselves. ²⁵The entire assembly of Judah rejoiced, along with the priests and Levites and all who had assembled from Israel, including the aliens who had come from Israel and those who lived in Judah. ²⁶There was great joy in Jerusalem, for since the days of Solomon son of David king of Israel there had been nothing like this in Jerusalem. ²⁷The priests and the Levites stood to bless the people, and God heard them, for their prayer reached heaven, his holy dwelling place.

31 When all this had ended, the Israelites who were there went out to the towns of Judah, smashed the sacred stones and cut down the Asherah poles. They destroyed the high places and the altars throughout Judah and Benjamin and in Ephraim and Manasseh. After they had destroyed all of them, the Israelites returned to their own towns and to their own property.

CONTRIBUTIONS FOR WORSHIP

²Hezekiah assigned the priests and Levites to divisions—each of them according to their duties as priests or Levites—to offer burnt offerings and fellowship offerings,ᵃ to minister, to give thanks and to sing praises at the gates of the LORD's dwelling. ³The king contributed from his own possessions for the morning and evening burnt offerings and for the burnt offerings on the Sabbaths, New Moons and appointed feasts as written in the Law of the LORD. ⁴He ordered the people living in Jerusalem to give the portion due the priests and Levites so they could devote themselves to the Law of the LORD. ⁵As soon as the order went out, the Israelites generously gave the firstfruits of their grain, new wine, oil and honey and all that the fields produced. They brought a great amount, a tithe of everything. ⁶The men of Israel and Judah who lived in the towns of Judah also brought a tithe of their herds and flocks and a tithe of the holy things dedicated to the LORD their God, and they piled them in heaps. ⁷They began doing this in

ᵃ 2 Traditionally *peace offerings*

THE MESSAGE

floors swept, they all decided to keep going for another seven days! So they just kept on celebrating, and as joyfully as they began.

30:24-26 Hezekiah king of Judah gave 1,000 bulls and 7,000 sheep for the congregation's worship; the officials gave an additional 1,000 bulls and 10,000 sheep. And there turned out to be plenty of consecrated priests—qualified and well-prepared. The whole congregation of Judah, the priests and Levites, the congregation that came in from Israel, and the resident aliens from both Israel and Judah, were all in on the joyous celebration. Jerusalem was bursting with joy—nothing like this had taken place in Jerusalem since Solomon son of David king of Israel had built and dedicated The Temple.

30:27 The priests and Levites had the last word: they stood and blessed the people. And God listened, listened as the ascending sound of their prayers entered his holy heaven.

✝

31:1 **31** After the Passover celebration, they all took off for the cities of Judah and smashed the phallic stone monuments, chopped down the sacred Asherah groves, and demolished the neighborhood sex-and-religion shrines and local god shops. They didn't stop until they had been all through Judah, Benjamin, Ephraim, and Manasseh. Then they all went back home and resumed their everyday lives.

31:2 Hezekiah organized the groups of priests and Levites for their respective tasks, handing out job descriptions for conducting the services of worship: making the various offerings, and making sure that thanks and praise took place wherever and whenever GOD was worshiped.

31:3 He also designated his personal contribution for the Whole-Burnt-Offerings for the morning and evening worship, for Sabbaths, for New Moon festivals, and for the special worship days set down in The Revelation of GOD.

31:4 In addition, he asked the people who lived in Jerusalem to be responsible for providing for the priests and Levites so they, without distraction or concern, could give themselves totally to The Revelation of GOD.

31:5-7 As soon as Hezekiah's orders had gone out, the Israelites responded generously: firstfruits of the grain harvest, new wine, oil, honey—everything they grew. They didn't hold back, turning over a tithe of everything. They also brought in a tithe of their cattle, sheep, and anything else they owned that had been dedicated to GOD. Everything was sorted and piled in mounds. They started doing this in the third

NEW INTERNATIONAL VERSION

the third month and finished in the seventh month. ⁸When Hezekiah and his officials came and saw the heaps, they praised the LORD and blessed his people Israel.

⁹Hezekiah asked the priests and Levites about the heaps; ¹⁰and Azariah the chief priest, from the family of Zadok, answered, "Since the people began to bring their contributions to the temple of the LORD, we have had enough to eat and plenty to spare, because the LORD has blessed his people, and this great amount is left over."

¹¹Hezekiah gave orders to prepare storerooms in the temple of the LORD, and this was done. ¹²Then they faithfully brought in the contributions, tithes and dedicated gifts. Conaniah, a Levite, was in charge of these things, and his brother Shimei was next in rank. ¹³Jehiel, Azaziah, Nahath, Asahel, Jerimoth, Jozabad, Eliel, Ismakiah, Mahath and Benaiah were supervisors under Conaniah and Shimei his brother, by appointment of King Hezekiah and Azariah the official in charge of the temple of God.

¹⁴Kore son of Imnah the Levite, keeper of the East Gate, was in charge of the freewill offerings given to God, distributing the contributions made to the LORD and also the consecrated gifts. ¹⁵Eden, Miniamin, Jeshua, Shemaiah, Amariah and Shecaniah assisted him faithfully in the towns of the priests, distributing to their fellow priests according to their divisions, old and young alike.

¹⁶In addition, they distributed to the males three years old or more whose names were in the genealogical records—all who would enter the temple of the LORD to perform the daily duties of their various tasks, according to their responsibilities and their divisions. ¹⁷And they distributed to the priests enrolled by their families in the genealogical records and likewise to the Levites twenty years old or more, according to their responsibilities and their divisions. ¹⁸They included all the little ones, the wives, and the sons and daughters of the whole community listed in these genealogical records. For they were faithful in consecrating themselves.

¹⁹As for the priests, the descendants of Aaron, who lived on the farm lands around their towns or in any other towns, men were designated by name to distribute portions to every male among them and to all who were recorded in the genealogies of the Levites.

²⁰This is what Hezekiah did throughout Judah, doing what was good and right and faithful before the LORD his God. ²¹In everything that he undertook in the service of God's temple and in obedience to the law and the commands, he sought his God and worked wholeheartedly. And so he prospered.

THE MESSAGE

month and didn't finish until the seventh month.

31.8-9   When Hezekiah and his leaders came and saw the extent of the mounds of gifts, they praised GOD and commended God's people Israel. Hezekiah then consulted the priests and Levites on how to handle the abundance of offerings.

31.10   Azariah, chief priest of the family of Zadok, answered, "From the moment of this huge outpouring of gifts to The Temple of GOD, there has been plenty to eat for everyone with food left over. GOD has blessed his people—just look at the evidence!"

31.11-18   Hezekiah then ordered storerooms to be prepared in The Temple of GOD. When they were ready, they brought in all the offerings of tithes and sacred gifts. They put Conaniah the Levite in charge with his brother Shimei as assistant. Jehiel, Azaziah, Nahath, Asahel, Jerimoth, Jozabad, Eliel, Ismakiah, Mahath, and Benaiah were project managers under the direction of Conaniah and Shimei, carrying out the orders of King Hezekiah and Azariah the chief priest of The Temple of God. Kore son of Imnah the Levite, security guard of the East Gate, was in charge of the Freewill-Offerings of God and responsible for distributing the offerings and sacred gifts. Faithful support out in the priestly cities was provided by Eden, Miniamin, Jeshua, Shemaiah, Amariah, and Shecaniah. They were even-handed in their distributions to their coworkers (all males thirty years and older) in each of their respective divisions as they entered The Temple of GOD each day to do their assigned work (their work was all organized by divisions). The divisions comprised officially registered priests by family and Levites twenty years and older by job description. The official family tree included everyone in the entire congregation—their small children, wives, sons, and daughters. The ardent dedication they showed in bringing themselves and their gifts to worship was total—no one was left out.

31.19   The Aaronites, the priests who lived out on the pastures that belonged to the priest-cities, had reputable men on hand to distribute regular rations to every priest—everyone listed in the official family tree of the Levites.

31.20-21   Hezekiah carried out this work and kept it up everywhere in Judah. He was the very best—good, right, and true before his GOD. Everything he took up, whether it had to do with worship in God's Temple or the carrying out of God's Law and Commandments, he did well in a spirit of prayerful worship. He was a great success.

☩

NEW INTERNATIONAL VERSION

SENNACHERIB THREATENS JERUSALEM

32 After all that Hezekiah had so faithfully done, Sennacherib king of Assyria came and invaded Judah. He laid siege to the fortified cities, thinking to conquer them for himself. ²When Hezekiah saw that Sennacherib had come and that he intended to make war on Jerusalem, ³he consulted with his officials and military staff about blocking off the water from the springs outside the city, and they helped him. ⁴A large force of men assembled, and they blocked all the springs and the stream that flowed through the land. "Why should the kings*a* of Assyria come and find plenty of water?" they said. ⁵Then he worked hard repairing all the broken sections of the wall and building towers on it. He built another wall outside that one and reinforced the supporting terraces*b* of the City of David. He also made large numbers of weapons and shields.

⁶He appointed military officers over the people and assembled them before him in the square at the city gate and encouraged them with these words: ⁷"Be strong and courageous. Do not be afraid or discouraged because of the king of Assyria and the vast army with him, for there is a greater power with us than with him. ⁸With him is only the arm of flesh, but with us is the LORD our God to help us and to fight our battles." And the people gained confidence from what Hezekiah the king of Judah said.

⁹Later, when Sennacherib king of Assyria and all his forces were laying siege to Lachish, he sent his officers to Jerusalem with this message for Hezekiah king of Judah and for all the people of Judah who were there:

¹⁰"This is what Sennacherib king of Assyria says: On what are you basing your confidence, that you remain in Jerusalem under siege? ¹¹When Hezekiah says, 'The LORD our God will save us from the hand of the king of Assyria,' he is misleading you, to let you die of hunger and thirst. ¹²Did not Hezekiah himself remove this god's high places and altars, saying to Judah and Jerusalem, 'You must worship before one altar and burn sacrifices on it'?

¹³"Do you not know what I and my fathers have done to all the peoples of the other lands? Were the gods of those nations ever able to deliver their land from my hand? ¹⁴Who of all the gods of these nations that my fathers destroyed has been able to save his people from me? How then can your god deliver you from my hand?

a 4 Hebrew; Septuagint and Syriac king *b 5 Or the Millo*

THE MESSAGE

32 ³²·¹ And then, after this exemplary track record, this: Sennacherib king of Assyria came and attacked Judah. He put the fortified cities under siege, determined to take them.

³²·²⁻⁴ When Hezekiah realized that Sennacherib's strategy was to take Jerusalem, he talked to his advisors and military leaders about eliminating all the water supplies outside the city; they thought it was a good idea. There was a great turnout of people to plug the springs and tear down the aqueduct. They said, "Why should the kings of Assyria march in and be furnished with running water?"

³²·⁵⁻⁶ Hezekiah also went to work repairing every part of the city wall that was damaged, built defensive towers on it, built another wall of defense further out, and reinforced the defensive rampart (the Millo) of the old City of David. He also built up a large store of armaments—spears and shields. He then appointed military officers to be responsible for the people and got them all together at the public square in front of the city gate.

³²·⁶⁻⁸ Hezekiah rallied the people, saying, "Be strong! Take courage! Don't be intimidated by the king of Assyria and his troops—there are more on our side than on their side. He only has a bunch of mere men; we have our GOD to help us and fight for us!"

Morale surged. Hezekiah's words put steel in their spines.

³²·⁹⁻¹⁵ Later on, Sennacherib, who had set up camp a few miles away at Lachish, sent messengers to Jerusalem, addressing Judah through Hezekiah: "A proclamation of Sennacherib king of Assyria: You poor people—do you think you're safe in that so-called fortress of Jerusalem? You're sitting ducks. Do you think Hezekiah will save you? Don't be stupid—Hezekiah has fed you a pack of lies. When he says, 'GOD will save us from the power of the king of Assyria,' he's lying—you're all going to end up dead. Wasn't it Hezekiah who cleared out all the neighborhood worship shrines and told you, 'There is only one legitimate place to worship'? Do you have any idea what I and my ancestors have done to all the countries around here? Has there been a single god anywhere strong enough to stand up against me? Can you name one god among all the nations that either I or my ancestors have ravaged that so much as lifted a finger against me? So what makes you think you'll make out any better with your

NEW INTERNATIONAL VERSION

¹⁵Now do not let Hezekiah deceive you and mislead you like this. Do not believe him, for no god of any nation or kingdom has been able to deliver his people from my hand or the hand of my fathers. How much less will your god deliver you from my hand!"

¹⁶Sennacherib's officers spoke further against the LORD God and against his servant Hezekiah. ¹⁷The king also wrote letters insulting the LORD, the God of Israel, and saying this against him: "Just as the gods of the peoples of the other lands did not rescue their people from my hand, so the god of Hezekiah will not rescue his people from my hand." ¹⁸Then they called out in Hebrew to the people of Jerusalem who were on the wall, to terrify them and make them afraid in order to capture the city. ¹⁹They spoke about the God of Jerusalem as they did about the gods of the other peoples of the world—the work of men's hands.

²⁰King Hezekiah and the prophet Isaiah son of Amoz cried out in prayer to heaven about this. ²¹And the LORD sent an angel, who annihilated all the fighting men and the leaders and officers in the camp of the Assyrian king. So he withdrew to his own land in disgrace. And when he went into the temple of his god, some of his sons cut him down with the sword.

²²So the LORD saved Hezekiah and the people of Jerusalem from the hand of Sennacherib king of Assyria and from the hand of all others. He took care of them*ᵃ* on every side. ²³Many brought offerings to Jerusalem for the LORD and valuable gifts for Hezekiah king of Judah. From then on he was highly regarded by all the nations.

HEZEKIAH'S PRIDE, SUCCESS AND DEATH

²⁴In those days Hezekiah became ill and was at the point of death. He prayed to the LORD, who answered him and gave him a miraculous sign. ²⁵But Hezekiah's heart was proud and he did not respond to the kindness shown him; therefore the LORD's wrath was on him and on Judah and Jerusalem. ²⁶Then Hezekiah repented of the pride of his heart, as did the people of Jerusalem; therefore the LORD's wrath did not come upon them during the days of Hezekiah.

²⁷Hezekiah had very great riches and honor, and he made treasuries for his silver and gold and for his precious stones, spices, shields and all kinds of valuables. ²⁸He also made buildings to store the harvest of grain, new wine and oil; and he made stalls for various kinds of cattle,

THE MESSAGE

god? Don't let Hezekiah fool you; don't let him get by with his barefaced lies; don't trust him. No god of any country or kingdom ever has been one bit of help against me or my ancestors—what kind of odds does that give your god?"

32.16 The messengers felt free to throw in their personal comments, putting down both GOD and God's servant Hezekiah.

32.17 Sennacherib continued to send letters insulting the GOD of Israel: "The gods of the nations were powerless to help their people; the god of Hezekiah is no better, probably worse."

32.18-19 The messengers would come up to the wall of Jerusalem and shout up to the people standing on the wall, shouting their propaganda in Hebrew, trying to scare them into demoralized submission. They contemptuously lumped the God of Jerusalem in with the handmade gods of other peoples.

32.20-21 King Hezekiah, joined by the prophet Isaiah son of Amoz, responded by praying, calling up to heaven. GOD answered by sending an angel who wiped out everyone in the Assyrian camp, both warriors and officers. Sennacherib was forced to return home in disgrace, tail between his legs. When he went into the temple of his god, his own sons killed him.

32.22-23 GOD saved Hezekiah and the citizens of Jerusalem from Sennacherib king of Assyria and everyone else. And he continued to take good care of them. People streamed into Jerusalem bringing offerings for the worship of GOD and expensive presents to Hezekiah king of Judah. All the surrounding nations were impressed—Hezekiah's stock soared.

✝

32.24 Some time later Hezekiah became deathly sick. He prayed to GOD and was given a reassuring sign.

32.25-26 But the sign, instead of making Hezekiah grateful, made him arrogant. This made GOD angry, and his anger spilled over on Judah and Jerusalem. But then Hezekiah, and Jerusalem with him, repented of his arrogance, and GOD withdrew his anger while Hezekiah lived.

32.27-31 Hezekiah ended up very wealthy and much honored. He built treasuries for all his silver, gold, precious stones, spices, shields, and valuables, barns for the grain, new wine, and olive oil, stalls for his various breeds of cattle, and

---

ᵃ 22 Hebrew; Septuagint and Vulgate He gave them rest

NEW INTERNATIONAL VERSION

and pens for the flocks. [29]He built villages and acquired great numbers of flocks and herds, for God had given him very great riches.

[30]It was Hezekiah who blocked the upper outlet of the Gihon spring and channeled the water down to the west side of the City of David. He succeeded in everything he undertook. [31]But when envoys were sent by the rulers of Babylon to ask him about the miraculous sign that had occurred in the land, God left him to test him and to know everything that was in his heart.

[32]The other events of Hezekiah's reign and his acts of devotion are written in the vision of the prophet Isaiah son of Amoz in the book of the kings of Judah and Israel. [33]Hezekiah rested with his fathers and was buried on the hill where the tombs of David's descendants are. All Judah and the people of Jerusalem honored him when he died. And Manasseh his son succeeded him as king.

MANASSEH KING OF JUDAH

33 Manasseh was twelve years old when he became king, and he reigned in Jerusalem fifty-five years. [2]He did evil in the eyes of the LORD, following the detestable practices of the nations the LORD had driven out before the Israelites. [3]He rebuilt the high places his father Hezekiah had demolished; he also erected altars to the Baals and made Asherah poles. He bowed down to all the starry hosts and worshiped them. [4]He built altars in the temple of the LORD, of which the LORD had said, "My Name will remain in Jerusalem forever." [5]In both courts of the temple of the LORD, he built altars to all the starry hosts. [6]He sacrificed his sons in[a] the fire in the Valley of Ben Hinnom, practiced sorcery, divination and witchcraft, and consulted mediums and spiritists. He did much evil in the eyes of the LORD, provoking him to anger.

[7]He took the carved image he had made and put it in God's temple, of which God had said to David and to his son Solomon, "In this temple and in Jerusalem, which I have chosen out of all the tribes of Israel, I will put my Name forever. [8]I

THE MESSAGE

pens for his flocks. He founded royal cities for himself and built up huge stocks of sheep and cattle. God saw to it that he was extravagantly rich. Hezekiah was also responsible for diverting the upper outlet of the Gihon spring and rerouting the water to the west side of the City of David. Hezekiah succeeded in everything he did. But when the rulers of Babylon sent emissaries to find out about the sign from God that had taken place earlier, God left him on his own to see what he would do; he wanted to test his heart.

⸸

32:32-33 The rest of the history of Hezekiah and his life of loyal service, you can read for yourself—it's written in the vision of the prophet Isaiah son of Amoz in the *Royal Annals of the Kings of Judah and Israel*. When Hezekiah died, they buried him in the upper part of the King David cemetery. Everyone in Judah and Jerusalem came to the funeral. He was buried in great honor.

Manasseh his son was the next king.

KING MANASSEH

33:1-6 **33** Manasseh was twelve years old when he became king. He ruled for fifty-five years in Jerusalem. In GOD's opinion he was a bad king—an evil king. He reintroduced all the moral rot and spiritual corruption that had been scoured from the country when GOD dispossessed the pagan nations in favor of the children of Israel. He rebuilt the sex-and-religion shrines that his father Hezekiah had torn down, he built altars and phallic images for the sex god Baal and the sex goddess Asherah and worshiped the cosmic powers, taking orders from the constellations. He built shrines to the cosmic powers and placed them in both courtyards of The Temple of GOD, the very Jerusalem Temple dedicated exclusively by GOD's decree to GOD's Name ("in Jerusalem I place my Name"). He burned his own sons in a sacrificial rite in the Valley of Ben Hinnom. He practiced witchcraft and fortunetelling. He held séances and consulted spirits from the underworld. Much evil—in GOD's view a career in evil. And GOD was angry.

33:7-8 As a last straw he placed a carved image of the sex goddess Asherah that he had commissioned in The Temple of God, a flagrant and provocative violation of God's well-known command to both David and Solomon, "In this Temple and in this city Jerusalem, my choice out of all the tribes of Israel, I place my Name—exclusively and forever." He had prom-

---

[a] 6 Or *He made his sons pass through*

NEW INTERNATIONAL VERSION

will not again make the feet of the Israelites leave the land I assigned to your forefathers, if only they will be careful to do everything I commanded them concerning all the laws, decrees and ordinances given through Moses." ⁹But Manasseh led Judah and the people of Jerusalem astray, so that they did more evil than the nations the LORD had destroyed before the Israelites.

¹⁰The LORD spoke to Manasseh and his people, but they paid no attention. ¹¹So the LORD brought against them the army commanders of the king of Assyria, who took Manasseh prisoner, put a hook in his nose, bound him with bronze shackles and took him to Babylon. ¹²In his distress he sought the favor of the LORD his God and humbled himself greatly before the God of his fathers. ¹³And when he prayed to him, the LORD was moved by his entreaty and listened to his plea; so he brought him back to Jerusalem and to his kingdom. Then Manasseh knew that the LORD is God.

¹⁴Afterward he rebuilt the outer wall of the City of David, west of the Gihon spring in the valley, as far as the entrance of the Fish Gate and encircling the hill of Ophel; he also made it much higher. He stationed military commanders in all the fortified cities in Judah.

¹⁵He got rid of the foreign gods and removed the image from the temple of the LORD, as well as all the altars he had built on the temple hill and in Jerusalem; and he threw them out of the city. ¹⁶Then he restored the altar of the LORD and sacrificed fellowship offerings ᵃ and thank offerings on it, and told Judah to serve the LORD, the God of Israel. ¹⁷The people, however, continued to sacrifice at the high places, but only to the LORD their God.

¹⁸The other events of Manasseh's reign, including his prayer to his God and the words the seers spoke to him in the name of the LORD, the God of Israel, are written in the annals of the kings of Israel. ᵇ ¹⁹His prayer and how God was moved by his entreaty, as well as all his sins and unfaithfulness, and the sites where he built high places and set up Asherah poles and idols before he humbled himself—all are written in the records of the seers. ᶜ ²⁰Manasseh rested with his fathers and was buried in his palace. And Amon his son succeeded him as king.

THE MESSAGE

ised, "Never again will I let my people Israel wander off from this land I've given to their ancestors. But on this condition, that they keep everything I've commanded in the instructions my servant Moses passed on to them."

33.9-10   But Manasseh led Judah and the citizens of Jerusalem off the beaten path into practices of evil exceeding even the evil of the pagan nations that GOD had earlier destroyed. When GOD spoke to Manasseh and his people about this, they ignored him.

33.11-13   Then GOD directed the leaders of the troops of the king of Assyria to come after Manasseh. They put a hook in his nose, shackles on his feet, and took him off to Babylon. Now that he was in trouble, he went to his knees in prayer asking for help—total repentance before the God of his ancestors. As he prayed, GOD was touched; GOD listened and brought him back to Jerusalem as king. That convinced Manasseh that GOD was in control.

33.14-17   After that Manasseh rebuilt the outside defensive wall of the City of David to the west of the Gihon spring in the valley. It went from the Fish Gate and around the hill of Ophel. He also increased its height. He tightened up the defense system by posting army captains in all the fortress cities of Judah. He also did a good spring cleaning on The Temple, carting out the pagan idols and the goddess statue. He took all the altars he had set up on The Temple hill and throughout Jerusalem and dumped them outside the city. He put the Altar of GOD back in working order and restored worship, sacrificing Peace-Offerings and Thank-Offerings. He issued orders to the people: "You shall serve and worship GOD, the God of Israel." But the people didn't take him seriously—they used the name "GOD" but kept on going to the old pagan neighborhood shrines and doing the same old things.

33.18-19   The rest of the history of Manasseh—his prayer to his God, and the sermons the prophets personally delivered by authority of GOD, the God of Israel—this is all written in *The Chronicles of the Kings of Israel*. His prayer and how God was touched by his prayer, a list of all his sins and the things he did wrong, the actual places where he built the pagan shrines, the installation of the sex-goddess Asherah sites, and the idolatrous images that he worshiped previous to his conversion—this is all described in the records of the prophets.

33.20   When Manasseh died, they buried him in the palace garden. His son Amon was the next king.

ᵃ 16 Traditionally *peace offerings*   ᵇ 18 That is, Judah, as frequently in 2 Chronicles   ᶜ 19 One Hebrew manuscript and Septuagint; most Hebrew manuscripts *of Hozai*

NEW INTERNATIONAL VERSION

AMON KING OF JUDAH

21Amon was twenty-two years old when he became king, and he reigned in Jerusalem two years. 22He did evil in the eyes of the LORD, as his father Manasseh had done. Amon worshiped and offered sacrifices to all the idols Manasseh had made. 23But unlike his father Manasseh, he did not humble himself before the LORD; Amon increased his guilt.

24Amon's officials conspired against him and assassinated him in his palace. 25Then the people of the land killed all who had plotted against King Amon, and they made Josiah his son king in his place.

JOSIAH'S REFORMS

34 Josiah was eight years old when he became king, and he reigned in Jerusalem thirty-one years. 2He did what was right in the eyes of the LORD and walked in the ways of his father David, not turning aside to the right or to the left.

3In the eighth year of his reign, while he was still young, he began to seek the God of his father David. In his twelfth year he began to purge Judah and Jerusalem of high places, Asherah poles, carved idols and cast images. 4Under his direction the altars of the Baals were torn down; he cut to pieces the incense altars that were above them, and smashed the Asherah poles, the idols and the images. These he broke to pieces and scattered over the graves of those who had sacrificed to them. 5He burned the bones of the priests on their altars, and so he purged Judah and Jerusalem. 6In the towns of Manasseh, Ephraim and Simeon, as far as Naphtali, and in the ruins around them, 7he tore down the altars and the Asherah poles and crushed the idols to powder and cut to pieces all the incense altars throughout Israel. Then he went back to Jerusalem.

8In the eighteenth year of Josiah's reign, to purify the land and the temple, he sent Shaphan son of Azaliah and Maaseiah the ruler of the city, with Joah son of Joahaz, the recorder, to repair the temple of the LORD his God.

9They went to Hilkiah the high priest and gave him the money that had been brought into the temple of God, which the Levites who were the doorkeepers had collected from the people of Manasseh, Ephraim and the entire remnant of Israel and from all the people of Judah and Benjamin and the inhabitants of Jerusalem. 10Then they entrusted it to the men appointed to supervise the work on the LORD's temple. These men paid the workers who repaired and restored the

THE MESSAGE

KING AMON

33.21-23 Amon was twenty-two years old when he became king. He was king for two years in Jerusalem. In GOD's opinion he lived an evil life, just like his father Manasseh, but he never did repent to GOD as Manasseh repented. He just kept at it, going from one thing to another.

33.24-25 In the end Amon's servants revolted and assassinated him—killed the king right in his own palace. The citizens in their turn then killed the king's assassins. The citizens then crowned Josiah, Amon's son, as king.

KING JOSIAH

34.1-2 **34** Josiah was eight years old when he became king. He ruled for thirty-one years in Jerusalem. He behaved well before GOD. He kept straight on the path blazed by his ancestor David, not one step to the left or right.

34.3-7 When he had been king for eight years—he was still only a teenager—he began to seek the God of David his ancestor. Four years later, the twelfth year of his reign, he set out to cleanse the neighborhood of sex-and-religion shrines, and get rid of the sacred Asherah groves and the god and goddess figurines, whether carved or cast, from Judah. He wrecked the Baal shrines, tore down the altars connected with them, and scattered the debris and ashes over the graves of those who had worshiped at them. He burned the bones of the priests on the same altars they had used when alive. He scrubbed the place clean, Judah and Jerusalem, clean inside and out. The clean-up campaign ranged outward to the cities of Manasseh, Ephraim, Simeon, and the surrounding neighborhoods—as far north as Naphtali. Throughout Israel he demolished the altars and Asherah groves, pulverized the god and goddess figures, chopped up the neighborhood shrines into firewood. With Israel once more intact, he returned to Jerusalem.

34.8-13 One day in the eighteenth year of his kingship, with the cleanup of country and Temple complete, King Josiah sent Shaphan son of Azaliah, Maaseiah the mayor of the city, and Joah son of Joahaz the historian to renovate The Temple of GOD. First they turned over to Hilkiah the high priest all the money collected by the Levitical security guards from Manasseh and Ephraim and the rest of Israel, and from Judah and Benjamin and the citizens of Jerusalem. It was then put into the hands of the foremen managing the work on The Temple of GOD who then passed it on to the workers repairing

NEW INTERNATIONAL VERSION

temple. ¹¹They also gave money to the carpenters and builders to purchase dressed stone, and timber for joists and beams for the buildings that the kings of Judah had allowed to fall into ruin.

¹²The men did the work faithfully. Over them to direct them were Jahath and Obadiah, Levites descended from Merari, and Zechariah and Meshullam, descended from Kohath. The Levites—all who were skilled in playing musical instruments— ¹³had charge of the laborers and supervised all the workers from job to job. Some of the Levites were secretaries, scribes and doorkeepers.

THE BOOK OF THE LAW FOUND

¹⁴While they were bringing out the money that had been taken into the temple of the LORD, Hilkiah the priest found the Book of the Law of the LORD that had been given through Moses. ¹⁵Hilkiah said to Shaphan the secretary, "I have found the Book of the Law in the temple of the LORD." He gave it to Shaphan.

¹⁶Then Shaphan took the book to the king and reported to him: "Your officials are doing everything that has been committed to them. ¹⁷They have paid out the money that was in the temple of the LORD and have entrusted it to the supervisors and workers." ¹⁸Then Shaphan the secretary informed the king, "Hilkiah the priest has given me a book." And Shaphan read from it in the presence of the king.

¹⁹When the king heard the words of the Law, he tore his robes. ²⁰He gave these orders to Hilkiah, Ahikam son of Shaphan, Abdon son of Micah,ᵃ Shaphan the secretary and Asaiah the king's attendant: ²¹"Go and inquire of the LORD for me and for the remnant in Israel and Judah about what is written in this book that has been found. Great is the LORD's anger that is poured out on us because our fathers have not kept the word of the LORD; they have not acted in accordance with all that is written in this book."

²²Hilkiah and those the king had sent with himᵇ went to speak to the prophetess Huldah, who was the wife of Shallum son of Tokhath,ᶜ the son of Hasrah,ᵈ keeper of the wardrobe. She lived in Jerusalem, in the Second District.

²³She said to them, "This is what the LORD, the God of Israel, says: Tell the man who sent you to me, ²⁴'This is what the LORD says: I am going to bring disaster on this place and its people—all the curses written in the book that has been read in the presence of the king of Judah.

THE MESSAGE

GOD's Temple—the carpenters, construction workers, and masons—so they could buy the lumber and dressed stone for rebuilding the foundations the kings of Judah had allowed to fall to pieces. The workmen were honest and diligent. Their foremen were Jahath and Obadiah, the Merarite Levites, and Zechariah and Meshullam from the Kohathites—these managed the project. The Levites—they were all skilled musicians—were in charge of the common laborers and supervised the workers as they went from job to job. The Levites also served as accountants, managers, and security guards.

34.14-17   While the money that had been given for The Temple of GOD was being received and dispersed, Hilkiah the high priest found a copy of The Revelation of Moses. He reported to Shaphan the royal secretary, "I've just found the Book of GOD's Revelation, instructing us in GOD's way—found it in The Temple!" He gave it to Shaphan, who then gave it to the king. And along with the book, he gave this report: "The job is complete—everything you ordered done is done. They took all the money that was collected in The Temple of GOD and handed it over to the managers and workers."

34.18   And then Shaphan told the king, "Hilkiah the priest gave me a book." Shaphan proceeded to read it out to the king.

34.19-21   When the king heard what was written in the book, GOD's Revelation, he ripped his robes in dismay. And then he called for Hilkiah, Ahikam son of Shaphan, Abdon son of Micah, Shaphan the royal secretary, and Asaiah the king's personal aide. He ordered them all: "Go and pray to GOD for me and what's left of Israel and Judah. Find out what we must do in response to what is written in this book that has just been found! GOD's anger must be burning furiously against us—our ancestors haven't obeyed a thing written in this book of GOD, followed none of the instructions directed to us."

34.22-25   Hilkiah and those picked by the king went straight to Huldah the prophetess. She was the wife of Shallum son of Tokhath, the son of Hasrah, who was in charge of the palace wardrobe. She lived in Jerusalem in the Second Quarter. The men consulted with her. In response to them she said, "GOD's word, the God of Israel: Tell the man who sent you here, 'GOD has spoken, I'm on my way to bring the doom of judgment on this place and this people. Every word written in the book read by the king of Judah

---

ᵃ 20 Also called *Acbor son of Micaiah*   ᵇ 22 One Hebrew manuscript, Vulgate and Syriac; most Hebrew manuscripts do not have *had sent with him.*   ᶜ 22 Also called *Tikvah*
ᵈ 22 Also called *Harhas*

NEW INTERNATIONAL VERSION

25Because they have forsaken me and burned incense to other gods and provoked me to anger by all that their hands have made,ᵃ my anger will be poured out on this place and will not be quenched.' 26Tell the king of Judah, who sent you to inquire of the LORD, 'This is what the LORD, the God of Israel, says concerning the words you heard: 27Because your heart was responsive and you humbled yourself before God when you heard what he spoke against this place and its people, and because you humbled yourself before me and tore your robes and wept in my presence, I have heard you, declares the LORD. 28Now I will gather you to your fathers, and you will be buried in peace. Your eyes will not see all the disaster I am going to bring on this place and on those who live here.' "

So they took her answer back to the king.

29Then the king called together all the elders of Judah and Jerusalem. 30He went up to the temple of the LORD with the men of Judah, the people of Jerusalem, the priests and the Levites—all the people from the least to the greatest. He read in their hearing all the words of the Book of the Covenant, which had been found in the temple of the LORD. 31The king stood by his pillar and renewed the covenant in the presence of the LORD—to follow the LORD and keep his commands, regulations and decrees with all his heart and all his soul, and to obey the words of the covenant written in this book.

32Then he had everyone in Jerusalem and Benjamin pledge themselves to it; the people of Jerusalem did this in accordance with the covenant of God, the God of their fathers.

33Josiah removed all the detestable idols from all the territory belonging to the Israelites, and he had all who were present in Israel serve the LORD their God. As long as he lived, they did not fail to follow the LORD, the God of their fathers.

JOSIAH CELEBRATES THE PASSOVER

35 Josiah celebrated the Passover to the LORD in Jerusalem, and the Passover lamb was slaughtered on the fourteenth day of the first month. 2He appointed the priests to their duties and encouraged them in the service of the LORD's temple. 3He said to the Levites, who instructed all Israel and who had been consecrated to the LORD: "Put the sacred ark in the temple that Solomon son of David king of Israel built. It is not to

ᵃ 25 Or *by everything they have done*

THE MESSAGE

will happen. And why? Because they've deserted me and taken up with other gods; they've made me thoroughly angry by setting up their god-making businesses. My anger is raging white-hot against this place and nobody is going to put it out.'

34.26-28 "And also tell the king of Judah, since he sent you to ask GOD for direction, GOD's comment on what he read in the book: 'Because you took seriously the doom of judgment I spoke against this place and people, and because you responded in humble repentance, tearing your robe in dismay and weeping before me, I'm taking you seriously. GOD's word. I'll take care of you; you'll have a quiet death and be buried in peace. You won't be around to see the doom that I'm going to bring upon this place and people.' "

The men took her message back to the king.

34.29-31 The king acted immediately, assembling all the elders of Judah and Jerusalem, and then proceeding to The Temple of GOD bringing everyone in his train—priests and prophets and people ranging from the least to the greatest. Then he read out publicly everything written in the Book of the Covenant that was found in The Temple of GOD. The king stood by his pillar and before GOD solemnly committed himself to the covenant: to follow GOD believingly and obediently; to follow his instructions, heart and soul, on what to believe and do; to confirm with his life the entire covenant, all that was written in the book.

34.32 Then he made everyone in Jerusalem and Benjamin commit themselves. And they did it. They committed themselves to the covenant of God, the God of their ancestors.

34.33 Josiah did a thorough job of cleaning up the pollution that had spread throughout Israelite territory and got everyone started fresh again, serving and worshiping their GOD. All through Josiah's life the people kept to the straight and narrow, obediently following GOD, the God of their ancestors.

✝

35.1-4 **35** Josiah celebrated the Passover to GOD in Jerusalem. They killed the Passover lambs on the fourteenth day of the first month. He gave the priests detailed instructions and encouraged them in the work of leading worship in The Temple of GOD. He also told the Levites who were in charge of teaching and guiding Israel in all matters of worship (they were especially consecrated for this), "Place the sacred Chest in The Temple that Solomon son of David, the king of Israel, built. You don't have

NEW INTERNATIONAL VERSION

be carried about on your shoulders. Now serve the LORD your God and his people Israel. ⁴Prepare yourselves by families in your divisions, according to the directions written by David king of Israel and by his son Solomon.

⁵"Stand in the holy place with a group of Levites for each subdivision of the families of your fellow countrymen, the lay people. ⁶Slaughter the Passover lambs, consecrate yourselves and prepare ⌐the lambs⌐ for your fellow countrymen, doing what the LORD commanded through Moses."

⁷Josiah provided for all the lay people who were there a total of thirty thousand sheep and goats for the Passover offerings, and also three thousand cattle—all from the king's own possessions.

⁸His officials also contributed voluntarily to the people and the priests and Levites. Hilkiah, Zechariah and Jehiel, the administrators of God's temple, gave the priests twenty-six hundred Passover offerings and three hundred cattle. ⁹Also Conaniah along with Shemaiah and Nethanel, his brothers, and Hashabiah, Jeiel and Jozabad, the leaders of the Levites, provided five thousand Passover offerings and five hundred head of cattle for the Levites.

¹⁰The service was arranged and the priests stood in their places with the Levites in their divisions as the king had ordered. ¹¹The Passover lambs were slaughtered, and the priests sprinkled the blood handed to them, while the Levites skinned the animals. ¹²They set aside the burnt offerings to give them to the subdivisions of the families of the people to offer to the LORD, as is written in the Book of Moses. They did the same with the cattle. ¹³They roasted the Passover animals over the fire as prescribed, and boiled the holy offerings in pots, caldrons and pans and served them quickly to all the people. ¹⁴After this, they made preparations for themselves and for the priests, because the priests, the descendants of Aaron, were sacrificing the burnt offerings and the fat portions until nightfall. So the Levites made preparations for themselves and for the Aaronic priests.

¹⁵The musicians, the descendants of Asaph, were in the places prescribed by David, Asaph, Heman and Jeduthun the king's seer. The gatekeepers at each gate did not need to leave their posts, because their fellow Levites made the preparations for them.

¹⁶So at that time the entire service of the LORD was carried out for the celebration of the Passover and the offering of burnt offerings on the altar of the LORD, as King Josiah had ordered.

THE MESSAGE

to carry it around on your shoulders any longer! Serve GOD and God's people Israel. Organize yourselves by families for your respective responsibilities, following the instructions left by David king of Israel and Solomon his son.

35.5-6 "Take your place in the sanctuary—a team of Levites for every grouping of your fellow citizens, the laity. Your job is to kill the Passover lambs, then consecrate yourselves and prepare the lambs so that everyone will be able to keep the Passover exactly as GOD commanded through Moses."

35.7-9 Josiah personally donated 30,000 sheep, lambs, and goats and 3,000 bulls—everything needed for the Passover celebration was there. His officials also pitched in on behalf of the people, including the priests and the Levites. Hilkiah, Zechariah, and Jehiel, leaders in The Temple of God, gave 2,600 lambs and 300 bulls to the priests for the Passover offerings. Conaniah, his brothers Shemaiah and Nethanel, along with the Levitical chiefs Hashabiah, Jeiel, and Jozabad, donated 5,000 lambs and 500 bulls to the Levites for the Passover offerings.

35.10-13 Preparations were complete for the service of worship; the priests took up their positions and the Levites were at their posts as instructed by the king. They killed the Passover lambs, and while the priests sprinkled the blood from the lambs, the Levites skinned them out. Then they set aside the Whole-Burnt-Offering for presentation to the family groupings of the people so that each group could offer it to GOD following the instructions in the Book of Moses. They did the same with the cattle. They roasted the Passover lamb according to the instructions and boiled the consecrated offerings in pots and kettles and pans and promptly served the people.

35.14 After the people had eaten the holy meal, the Levites served themselves and the Aaronite priests—the priests were busy late into the night making the offerings at the Altar.

35.15 The Asaph singers were all in their places following the instructions of David, Asaph, Heman, and Jeduthun the king's seer. The security guards were on duty at each gate—the Levites also served them because they couldn't leave their posts.

35.16-19 Everything went without a hitch in the worship of GOD that day as they celebrated the Passover and the offering of the Whole-Burnt-Offering on the Altar of GOD. It went just as Josiah had ordered. The Israelites celebrated the

NEW INTERNATIONAL VERSION

[17]The Israelites who were present celebrated the Passover at that time and observed the Feast of Unleavened Bread for seven days. [18]The Passover had not been observed like this in Israel since the days of the prophet Samuel; and none of the kings of Israel had ever celebrated such a Passover as did Josiah, with the priests, the Levites and all Judah and Israel who were there with the people of Jerusalem. [19]This Passover was celebrated in the eighteenth year of Josiah's reign.

THE DEATH OF JOSIAH

[20]After all this, when Josiah had set the temple in order, Neco king of Egypt went up to fight at Carchemish on the Euphrates, and Josiah marched out to meet him in battle. [21]But Neco sent messengers to him, saying, "What quarrel is there between you and me, O king of Judah? It is not you I am attacking at this time, but the house with which I am at war. God has told me to hurry; so stop opposing God, who is with me, or he will destroy you."

[22]Josiah, however, would not turn away from him, but disguised himself to engage him in battle. He would not listen to what Neco had said at God's command but went to fight him on the plain of Megiddo.

[23]Archers shot King Josiah, and he told his officers, "Take me away; I am badly wounded." [24]So they took him out of his chariot, put him in the other chariot he had and brought him to Jerusalem, where he died. He was buried in the tombs of his fathers, and all Judah and Jerusalem mourned for him.

[25]Jeremiah composed laments for Josiah, and to this day all the men and women singers commemorate Josiah in the laments. These became a tradition in Israel and are written in the Laments.

[26]The other events of Josiah's reign and his acts of devotion, according to what is written in the Law of the LORD— [27]all the events, from beginning to end, are written in the book of the kings of Israel and Judah.

36

[1]And the people of the land took Jehoahaz son of Josiah and made him king in Jerusalem in place of his father.

JEHOAHAZ KING OF JUDAH

[2]Jehoahaz[a] was twenty-three years old when he became king, and he reigned in Jerusalem three months. [3]The king of Egypt dethroned him in Jerusalem and imposed on Judah a levy of a

---

a 2 Hebrew Joahaz, *a variant of* Jehoahaz; *also in verse 4*

THE MESSAGE

Passover, also known as the Feast of Unraised Bread, for seven days. The Passover hadn't been celebrated like this since the days of Samuel the prophet. None of the kings had done it. But Josiah, the priests, the Levites, all Judah and Israel who were there that week, plus the citizens of Jerusalem—*they* did it. In the eighteenth year of the rule of King Josiah, this Passover was celebrated.

35.20 Some time later, after Josiah's reformation of The Temple, Neco king of Egypt marched out toward Carchemish on the Euphrates River on his way to war. Josiah went out to fight him.

35.21 Neco sent messengers to Josiah saying, "What do we have against each other, O king of Judah? I haven't come to fight against you but against the country with whom I'm at war. God commanded me to hurry, so don't get in my way; you'll only interfere with God, who is on my side in this, and he'll destroy you."

35.22-23 But Josiah was spoiling for a fight and wouldn't listen to a thing Neco said (in actuality it was God who said it). Though King Josiah disguised himself when they met on the plain of Megiddo, archers shot him anyway.

The king said to his servants, "Get me out of here—I'm badly wounded."

35.24-25 So his servants took him out of his chariot and laid him down in an ambulance chariot and drove him back to Jerusalem. He died there and was buried in the family cemetery. Everybody in Judah and Jerusalem attended the funeral. Jeremiah composed an anthem of lament for Josiah. The anthem is still sung by the choirs of Israel to this day. The anthem is written in the Laments.

35.26-36.1 The rest of the history of Josiah, his exemplary and devout life, conformed to The Revelation of GOD. The whole story, from start to finish, is written in the *Royal Annals of the Kings of Israel and Judah*. By popular choice, Jehoahaz son of Josiah was made king at Jerusalem, succeeding his father.

KING JEHOAHAZ

36.2-3 **36** Jehoahaz was twenty-three years old when he began to rule. He was king in Jerusalem for a mere three months. The king of Egypt dethroned him and forced the country

NEW INTERNATIONAL VERSION

hundred talents[a] of silver and a talent[b] of gold. [4]The king of Egypt made Eliakim, a brother of Jehoahaz, king over Judah and Jerusalem and changed Eliakim's name to Jehoiakim. But Neco took Eliakim's brother Jehoahaz and carried him off to Egypt.

JEHOIAKIM KING OF JUDAH

[5]Jehoiakim was twenty-five years old when he became king, and he reigned in Jerusalem eleven years. He did evil in the eyes of the LORD his God. [6]Nebuchadnezzar king of Babylon attacked him and bound him with bronze shackles to take him to Babylon. [7]Nebuchadnezzar also took to Babylon articles from the temple of the LORD and put them in his temple[c] there.

[8]The other events of Jehoiakim's reign, the detestable things he did and all that was found against him, are written in the book of the kings of Israel and Judah. And Jehoiachin his son succeeded him as king.

JEHOIACHIN KING OF JUDAH

[9]Jehoiachin was eighteen[d] years old when he became king, and he reigned in Jerusalem three months and ten days. He did evil in the eyes of the LORD. [10]In the spring, King Nebuchadnezzar sent for him and brought him to Babylon, together with articles of value from the temple of the LORD, and he made Jehoiachin's uncle,[e] Zedekiah, king over Judah and Jerusalem.

ZEDEKIAH KING OF JUDAH

[11]Zedekiah was twenty-one years old when he became king, and he reigned in Jerusalem eleven years. [12]He did evil in the eyes of the LORD his God and did not humble himself before Jeremiah the prophet, who spoke the word of the LORD. [13]He also rebelled against King Nebuchadnezzar, who had made him take an oath in God's name. He became stiff-necked and hardened his heart and would not turn to the LORD, the God of Israel. [14]Furthermore, all the leaders of the priests and the people became more and more unfaithful, following all the detestable practices of the nations and defiling the temple of the LORD, which he had consecrated in Jerusalem.

THE FALL OF JERUSALEM

[15]The LORD, the God of their fathers, sent word to them through his messengers again and again, because he had pity on his people and on

---

[a] 3 That is, about 3 3/4 tons (about 3.4 metric tons)
[b] 3 That is, about 75 pounds (about 34 kilograms)
[c] 7 Or palace   [d] 9 One Hebrew manuscript, some Septuagint manuscripts and Syriac (see also 2 Kings 24:8); most Hebrew manuscripts eight   [e] 10 Hebrew brother, that is, relative (see 2 Kings 24:17)

THE MESSAGE

to pay him nearly four tons of silver and seventy-five pounds of gold.

KING JEHOIAKIM

36.4 Neco king of Egypt then made Eliakim, Jehoahaz's brother, king of Judah and Jerusalem, but changed his name to Jehoiakim; then he took Jehoahaz back with him to Egypt.

36.5 Jehoiakim was twenty-five years old when he began to rule; he was king for eleven years in Jerusalem. In GOD's opinion he was an evil king.

36.6-7 Nebuchadnezzar king of Babylon made war against him, and bound him in bronze chains, intending to take him prisoner to Babylon. Nebuchadnezzar also took things from The Temple of GOD to Babylon and put them in his royal palace.

36.8 The rest of the history of Jehoiakim, the outrageous sacrilege he committed and what happened to him as a consequence, is all written in the *Royal Annals of the Kings of Israel and Judah*. Jehoiachin his son became the next king.

KING JEHOIACHIN

36.9-10 Jehoiachin was eighteen years old when he became king. But he ruled for only three months and ten days in Jerusalem. In GOD's opinion he was an evil king. In the spring King Nebuchadnezzar ordered him brought to Babylon along with the valuables remaining in The Temple of GOD. Then he made his uncle Zedekiah a puppet king over Judah and Jerusalem.

KING ZEDEKIAH

36.11-13 Zedekiah was twenty-one years old when he started out as king. He was king in Jerusalem for eleven years. As far as GOD was concerned, he was just one more evil king; there wasn't a trace of contrition in him when the prophet Jeremiah preached GOD's word to him. Then he compounded his troubles by rebelling against King Nebuchadnezzar, who earlier had made him swear in God's name that he would be loyal. He became set in his own stubborn ways— he never gave GOD a thought; repentance never entered his mind.

36.14 The evil mindset spread to the leaders and priests and filtered down to the people—it kicked off an epidemic of evil, repeating the abominations of the pagans and polluting The Temple of GOD so recently consecrated in Jerusalem.

36.15-17 GOD, the God of their ancestors, repeatedly sent warning messages to them. Out of compassion for both his people and his Temple he

NEW INTERNATIONAL VERSION

his dwelling place. ¹⁶But they mocked God's messengers, despised his words and scoffed at his prophets until the wrath of the LORD was aroused against his people and there was no remedy. ¹⁷He brought up against them the king of the Babylonians,ᵃ who killed their young men with the sword in the sanctuary, and spared neither young man nor young woman, old man or aged. God handed all of them over to Nebuchadnezzar. ¹⁸He carried to Babylon all the articles from the temple of God, both large and small, and the treasures of the LORD's temple and the treasures of the king and his officials. ¹⁹They set fire to God's temple and broke down the wall of Jerusalem; they burned all the palaces and destroyed everything of value there.

²⁰He carried into exile to Babylon the remnant, who escaped from the sword, and they became servants to him and his sons until the kingdom of Persia came to power. ²¹The land enjoyed its sabbath rests; all the time of its desolation it rested, until the seventy years were completed in fulfillment of the word of the LORD spoken by Jeremiah.

²²In the first year of Cyrus king of Persia, in order to fulfill the word of the LORD spoken by Jeremiah, the LORD moved the heart of Cyrus king of Persia to make a proclamation throughout his realm and to put it in writing:

²³"This is what Cyrus king of Persia says:

" 'The LORD, the God of heaven, has given me all the kingdoms of the earth and he has appointed me to build a temple for him at Jerusalem in Judah. Anyone of his people among you—may the LORD his God be with him, and let him go up.' "

THE MESSAGE

wanted to give them every chance possible. But they wouldn't listen; they poked fun at God's messengers, despised the message itself, and in general treated the prophets like idiots. GOD became more and more angry until there was no turning back—GOD called in Nebuchadnezzar king of Babylon, who came and killed indiscriminately—and right in The Temple itself; it was a ruthless massacre: young men and virgins, the elderly and weak—they were all the same to him.

36.18-20 And then he plundered The Temple of everything valuable, cleaned it out completely; he emptied the treasuries of The Temple of God, the treasuries of the king and his officials, and hauled it all, people and possessions, off to Babylon. He burned The Temple of God to the ground, knocked down the wall of Jerusalem, and set fire to all the buildings—everything valuable was burned up. Any survivor was taken prisoner into exile in Babylon and made a slave to Nebuchadnezzar and his family. The exile and slavery lasted until the kingdom of Persia took over.

36.21 This is exactly the message of GOD that Jeremiah had preached: the desolate land put to an extended sabbath rest, a seventy-year Sabbath rest making up for all the unkept Sabbaths.

KING CYRUS

36.22-23 In the first year of Cyrus king of Persia—this fulfilled the message of GOD preached by Jeremiah—GOD moved Cyrus king of Persia to make an official announcement throughout his kingdom; he wrote it out as follows: "From Cyrus king of Persia a proclamation: GOD, the God of the heavens, has given me all the kingdoms of the earth. He has also assigned me to build him a Temple of worship at Jerusalem in Judah. All who belong to GOD's people are urged to return—and may your GOD be with you! Move forward!"

ᵃ 17 Or *Chaldeans*

EZRA

EZRA

CYRUS HELPS THE EXILES TO RETURN

1 In the first year of Cyrus king of Persia, in order to fulfill the word of the LORD spoken by Jeremiah, the LORD moved the heart of Cyrus king of Persia to make a proclamation throughout his realm and to put it in writing:

2"This is what Cyrus king of Persia says:

" 'The LORD, the God of heaven, has given me all the kingdoms of the earth and he has appointed me to build a temple for him at Jerusalem in Judah. 3Anyone of his people among you—may his God be with him, and let him go up to Jerusalem in Judah and build the temple of the LORD, the God of Israel, the God who is in Jerusalem. 4And the people of any place where survivors may now be living are to provide him with silver and gold, with goods and livestock, and with freewill offerings for the temple of God in Jerusalem.' "

5Then the family heads of Judah and Benjamin, and the priests and Levites—everyone whose heart God had moved—prepared to go up and build the house of the LORD in Jerusalem. 6All their neighbors assisted them with articles of silver and gold, with goods and livestock, and with valuable gifts, in addition to all the freewill offerings. 7Moreover, King Cyrus brought out the articles belonging to the temple of the LORD, which Nebuchadnezzar had carried away from Jerusalem and had placed in the temple of his god.[a] 8Cyrus king of Persia had them brought by Mithredath the treasurer, who counted them out to Sheshbazzar the prince of Judah.

9This was the inventory:

gold dishes	30
silver dishes	1,000
silver pans[b]	29
10 gold bowls	30
matching silver bowls	410
other articles	1,000

CYRUS KING OF PERSIA: "BUILD THE TEMPLE OF GOD!"

1.1-4 **1** In the first year of Cyrus king of Persia— this fulfilled the Message of GOD preached by Jeremiah—GOD prodded Cyrus king of Persia to make an official announcement throughout his kingdom. He wrote it out as follows:

From Cyrus king of Persia, a Proclamation: GOD, the God of the heavens, has given me all the kingdoms of the earth. He has also assigned me to build him a Temple of worship in Jerusalem, Judah. Who among you belongs to his people? God be with you! Go to Jerusalem which is in Judah and build The Temple of GOD, the God of Israel, Jerusalem's God. Those who stay behind, wherever they happen to live, will support them with silver, gold, tools, and pack animals, along with Freewill-Offerings for The Temple of God in Jerusalem.

1.5-6 The heads of the families of Judah and Benjamin, along with the priests and Levites— everyone, in fact, God prodded—set out to build The Temple of GOD in Jerusalem. Their neighbors rallied behind them enthusiastically with silver, gold, tools, pack animals, expensive gifts, and, over and above these, Freewill-Offerings.

1.7-10 Also, King Cyrus turned over to them all the vessels and utensils from The Temple of GOD that Nebuchadnezzar had hauled from Jerusalem and put in the temple of his gods. Cyrus king of Persia put Mithredath the treasurer in charge of the transfer; he provided a full inventory for Sheshbazzar the prince of Judah, including the following:

30 gold dishes
1,000 silver dishes
29 silver pans
30 gold bowls
410 duplicate silver bowls
1,000 miscellaneous items.

---

[a] 7 Or *gods*   [b] 9 The meaning of the Hebrew for this word is uncertain.

NEW INTERNATIONAL VERSION

¹¹In all, there were 5,400 articles of gold and of silver. Sheshbazzar brought all these along when the exiles came up from Babylon to Jerusalem.

THE LIST OF THE EXILES WHO RETURNED

2 Now these are the people of the province who came up from the captivity of the exiles, whom Nebuchadnezzar king of Babylon had taken captive to Babylon (they returned to Jerusalem and Judah, each to his own town, ²in company with Zerubbabel, Jeshua, Nehemiah, Seraiah, Reelaiah, Mordecai, Bilshan, Mispar, Bigvai, Rehum and Baanah):

The list of the men of the people of Israel:

³the descendants of Parosh	2,172
⁴of Shephatiah	372
⁵of Arah	775
⁶of Pahath-Moab (through the line of Jeshua and Joab)	2,812
⁷of Elam	1,254
⁸of Zattu	945
⁹of Zaccai	760
¹⁰of Bani	642
¹¹of Bebai	623
¹²of Azgad	1,222
¹³of Adonikam	666
¹⁴of Bigvai	2,056
¹⁵of Adin	454
¹⁶of Ater (through Hezekiah)	98
¹⁷of Bezai	323
¹⁸of Jorah	112
¹⁹of Hashum	223
²⁰of Gibbar	95
²¹the men of Bethlehem	123
²²of Netophah	56
²³of Anathoth	128
²⁴of Azmaveth	42
²⁵of Kiriath Jearim,ᵃ Kephirah and Beeroth	743
²⁶of Ramah and Geba	621
²⁷of Micmash	122
²⁸of Bethel and Ai	223
²⁹of Nebo	52
³⁰of Magbish	156
³¹of the other Elam	1,254
³²of Harim	320
³³of Lod, Hadid and Ono	725
³⁴of Jericho	345
³⁵of Senaah	3,630

³⁶The priests:

the descendants of Jedaiah (through the family of Jeshua)	973

ᵃ 25 See Septuagint (see also Neh. 7:29); Hebrew *Kiriath Arim*.

THE MESSAGE

1.11   All told, there were 5,400 gold and silver articles that Sheshbazzar took with him when he brought the exiles back from Babylon to Jerusalem.

2.1-58 2 These are the people from the province who now returned from the captivity, exiles whom Nebuchadnezzar king of Babylon had carried off captive. They returned to Jerusalem and Judah, each to his hometown. They came in company with Zerubbabel, Jeshua, Nehemiah, Seraiah, Reelaiah, Mordecai, Bilshan, Mispar, Bigvai, Rehum, and Baanah.

The numbers of the returning Israelites by families of origin were as follows:

Parosh, 2,172
Shephatiah, 372
Arah, 775
Pahath-Moab (sons of Jeshua and Joab), 2,812
Elam, 1,254
Zattu, 945
Zaccai, 760
Bani, 642
Bebai, 623
Azgad, 1,222
Adonikam, 666
Bigvai, 2,056
Adin, 454
Ater (sons of Hezekiah), 98
Bezai, 323
Jorah, 112
Hashum, 223
Gibbar, 95.

Israelites identified by place of origin were as follows:
Bethlehem, 123
Netophah, 56
Anathoth, 128
Azmaveth, 42
Kiriath Jearim, Kephirah, and Beeroth, 743
Ramah and Geba, 621
Micmash, 122
Bethel and Ai, 223
Nebo, 52
Magbish, 156
Elam (the other one), 1,254
Harim, 320
Lod, Hadid, and Ono, 725
Jericho, 345
Senaah, 3,630.

Priestly families:
Jedaiah (sons of Jeshua), 973

NEW INTERNATIONAL VERSION

³⁷of Immer   1,052
³⁸of Pashhur   1,247
³⁹of Harim   1,017

⁴⁰The Levites:

the descendants of Jeshua and Kadmiel
(through the line of Hodaviah)   74

⁴¹The singers:

the descendants of Asaph   128

⁴²The gatekeepers of the temple:

the descendants of
Shallum, Ater, Talmon,
Akkub, Hatita and Shobai   139

⁴³The temple servants:

the descendants of
Ziha, Hasupha, Tabbaoth,
⁴⁴Keros, Siaha, Padon,
⁴⁵Lebanah, Hagabah, Akkub,
⁴⁶Hagab, Shalmai, Hanan,
⁴⁷Giddel, Gahar, Reaiah,
⁴⁸Rezin, Nekoda, Gazzam,
⁴⁹Uzza, Paseah, Besai,
⁵⁰Asnah, Meunim, Nephusim,
⁵¹Bakbuk, Hakupha, Harhur,
⁵²Bazluth, Mehida, Harsha,
⁵³Barkos, Sisera, Temah,
⁵⁴Neziah and Hatipha.

⁵⁵The descendants of the servants of Solomon:

the descendants of
Sotai, Hassophereth, Peruda,
⁵⁶Jaala, Darkon, Giddel,
⁵⁷Shephatiah, Hattil,
Pokereth-Hazzebaim and Ami

⁵⁸The temple servants and the
descendants of the servants of
Solomon   392

⁵⁹The following came up from the towns
of Tel Melah, Tel Harsha, Kerub, Addon
and Immer, but they could not show that
their families were descended from Israel:

⁶⁰The descendants of
Delaiah, Tobiah and Nekoda   652

⁶¹And from among the priests:

The descendants of
Hobaiah, Hakkoz and Barzillai (a
man who had married a daughter of
Barzillai the Gileadite and was called
by that name).

⁶²These searched for their family records, but they could not find them and so

THE MESSAGE

Immer, 1,052
Pashhur, 1,247
Harim, 1,017.
Levitical families:
Jeshua and Kadmiel (sons of Hodaviah),
74.
Singers:
Asaph's family line, 128.
Security guard families:
Shallum, Ater, Talmon, Akkub, Hatita,
and Shobai, 139.
Families of temple support staff:
Ziha, Hasupha, Tabbaoth,
Keros, Siaha, Padon,
Lebanah, Hagabah, Akkub,
Hagab, Shalmai, Hanan,
Giddel, Gahar, Reaiah,
Rezin, Nekoda, Gazzam,
Uzza, Paseah, Besai,
Asnah, Meunim, Nephussim,
Bakbuk, Hakupha, Harhur,
Bazluth, Mehida, Harsha,
Barkos, Sisera, Temah,
Neziah, and Hatipha.
Families of Solomon's servants:
Sotai, Hassophereth, Peruda,
Jaala, Darkon, Giddel,
Shephatiah, Hattil, Pokereth-Hazzebaim,
and Ami.
Temple support staff and Solomon's servants
added up to 392.

^{2.59-60}   These are those who came from Tel Melah,
Tel Harsha, Kerub, Addon, and Immer. They
weren't able to prove their ancestry, whether
they were true Israelites or not:

^{2.61}   Delaiah, Tobiah, and Nekoda, 652 in all.
Likewise with these priestly families:
Hobaiah, Hakkoz, and Barzillai, who had
married a daughter of Barzillai the
Gileadite and took that name.

^{2.62-63} They had thoroughly searched for their family records but couldn't find them. And so they

NEW INTERNATIONAL VERSION

were excluded from the priesthood as unclean. ⁶³The governor ordered them not to eat any of the most sacred food until there was a priest ministering with the Urim and Thummim.

⁶⁴The whole company numbered 42,360, ⁶⁵besides their 7,337 menservants and maidservants; and they also had 200 men and women singers. ⁶⁶They had 736 horses, 245 mules, ⁶⁷435 camels and 6,720 donkeys.

⁶⁸When they arrived at the house of the LORD in Jerusalem, some of the heads of the families gave freewill offerings toward the rebuilding of the house of God on its site. ⁶⁹According to their ability they gave to the treasury for this work 61,000 drachmas^a of gold, 5,000 minas^b of silver and 100 priestly garments.

⁷⁰The priests, the Levites, the singers, the gatekeepers and the temple servants settled in their own towns, along with some of the other people, and the rest of the Israelites settled in their towns.

REBUILDING THE ALTAR

3 When the seventh month came and the Israelites had settled in their towns, the people assembled as one man in Jerusalem. ²Then Jeshua son of Jozadak and his fellow priests and Zerubbabel son of Shealtiel and his associates began to build the altar of the God of Israel to sacrifice burnt offerings on it, in accordance with what is written in the Law of Moses the man of God. ³Despite their fear of the peoples around them, they built the altar on its foundation and sacrificed burnt offerings on it to the LORD, both the morning and evening sacrifices. ⁴Then in accordance with what is written, they celebrated the Feast of Tabernacles with the required number of burnt offerings prescribed for each day. ⁵After that, they presented the regular burnt offerings, the New Moon sacrifices and the sacrifices for all the appointed sacred feasts of the LORD, as well as those brought as freewill offerings to the LORD. ⁶On the first day of the seventh month they began to offer burnt offerings to the LORD, though the foundation of the LORD's temple had not yet been laid.

REBUILDING THE TEMPLE

⁷Then they gave money to the masons and carpenters, and gave food and drink and oil to

^a 69 That is, about 1,100 pounds (about 500 kilograms)
^b 69 That is, about 3 tons (about 2.9 metric tons)

THE MESSAGE

were barred from priestly work as ritually unclean. The governor ruled that they could not eat from the holy food until a priest could determine their status with the Urim and Thummim.

2.64-67 The total count for the congregation was 42,360. That did not include the male and female slaves, which numbered 7,337. There were also 200 male and female singers, and they had 736 horses, 245 mules, 435 camels, and 6,720 donkeys.

✠

2.68-69 Some of the heads of families, on arriving at The Temple of GOD in Jerusalem, made Freewill-Offerings toward the rebuilding of The Temple of God on its site. They gave to the building fund as they were able, about 1,100 pounds of gold, about three tons of silver, and 100 priestly robes.

2.70 The priests, Levites, and some of the people lived in Jerusalem. The singers, security guards, and temple support staff found places in their hometowns. All the Israelites found a place to live.

THE BUILDING BEGUN: "THE FOUNDATION OF THE TEMPLE WAS LAID"

3.1-2 **3** When the seventh month came and the Israelites had settled into their towns, the people assembled together in Jerusalem. Jeshua son of Jozadak and his brother priests, along with Zerubbabel, the son of Shealtiel, and his relatives, went to work and built the Altar of the God of Israel to offer Whole-Burnt-Offerings on it as written in The Revelation of Moses the man of God.

3.3-5 Even though they were afraid of what their non-Israelite neighbors might do, they went ahead anyway and set up the Altar on its foundations and offered Whole-Burnt-Offerings on it morning and evening. They also celebrated the Festival of Booths as prescribed and the daily Whole-Burnt-Offerings set for each day. And they presented the regular Whole-Burnt-Offerings for Sabbaths, New Moons, and GOD's Holy Festivals, as well as Freewill-Offerings for GOD.

3.6 They began offering Whole-Burnt-Offerings to GOD from the very first day of the seventh month, even though The Temple of GOD's foundation had not yet been laid.

3.7 They gave money to hire masons and carpenters. They gave food, drink, and oil to the

NEW INTERNATIONAL VERSION

the people of Sidon and Tyre, so that they would bring cedar logs by sea from Lebanon to Joppa, as authorized by Cyrus king of Persia.

⁸In the second month of the second year after their arrival at the house of God in Jerusalem, Zerubbabel son of Shealtiel, Jeshua son of Jozadak and the rest of their brothers (the priests and the Levites and all who had returned from the captivity to Jerusalem) began the work, appointing Levites twenty years of age and older to supervise the building of the house of the LORD. ⁹Jeshua and his sons and brothers and Kadmiel and his sons (descendants of Hodaviah*) and the sons of Henadad and their sons and brothers—all Levites—joined together in supervising those working on the house of God.

¹⁰When the builders laid the foundation of the temple of the LORD, the priests in their vestments and with trumpets, and the Levites (the sons of Asaph) with cymbals, took their places to praise the LORD, as prescribed by David king of Israel. ¹¹With praise and thanksgiving they sang to the LORD:

"He is good;
    his love to Israel endures forever."

And all the people gave a great shout of praise to the LORD, because the foundation of the house of the LORD was laid. ¹²But many of the older priests and Levites and family heads, who had seen the former temple, wept aloud when they saw the foundation of this temple being laid, while many others shouted for joy. ¹³No one could distinguish the sound of the shouts of joy from the sound of weeping, because the people made so much noise. And the sound was heard far away.

OPPOSITION TO THE REBUILDING

4 When the enemies of Judah and Benjamin heard that the exiles were building a temple for the LORD, the God of Israel, ²they came to Zerubbabel and to the heads of the families and said, "Let us help you build because, like you, we seek your God and have been sacrificing to him since the time of Esarhaddon king of Assyria, who brought us here."

³But Zerubbabel, Jeshua and the rest of the heads of the families of Israel answered, "You have no part with us in building a temple to our God. We alone will build it for the LORD, the God of Israel, as King Cyrus, the king of Persia, commanded us."

⁴Then the peoples around them set out to discourage the people of Judah and make them

a 9 Hebrew *Yehudah*, probably a variant of *Hodaviah*

THE MESSAGE

Sidonians and Tyrians in exchange for the cedar lumber they had brought by sea from Lebanon to Joppa, a shipment authorized by Cyrus the king of Persia.

3.8-9 In the second month of the second year after their arrival at The Temple of God in Jerusalem, Zerubbabel son of Shealtiel, and Jeshua son of Jozadak, in company with their brother priests and Levites and everyone else who had come back to Jerusalem from captivity, got started. They appointed the Levites twenty years of age and older to direct the rebuilding of The Temple of GOD. Jeshua and his family joined Kadmiel, Binnui, and Hodaviah, along with the extended family of Henadad—all Levites—to direct the work crew on The Temple of God.

3.10-11 When the workers laid the foundation of The Temple of GOD, the priests in their robes stood up with trumpets, and the Levites, sons of Asaph, with cymbals, to praise GOD in the tradition of David king of Israel. They sang antiphonally praise and thanksgiving to GOD:

Yes! GOD is good!
    Oh yes—he'll never quit loving Israel!

3.11-13 All the people boomed out hurrahs, praising GOD as the foundation of The Temple of GOD was laid. As many were noisily shouting with joy, many of the older priests, Levites, and family heads who had seen the first Temple, when they saw the foundations of this Temple laid, wept loudly for joy. People couldn't distinguish the shouting from the weeping. The sound of their voices reverberated for miles around.

THE BUILDING STOPPED: CEASE REBUILDING IN THAT CITY

4.1-2 4 Old enemies of Judah and Benjamin heard that the exiles were building The Temple of the GOD of Israel. They came to Zerubbabel and the family heads and said, "We'll help you build. We worship your God the same as you. We've been offering sacrifices to him since Esarhaddon king of Assyria brought us here."

4.3 Zerubbabel, Jeshua, and the rest of the family heads of Israel said to them, "Nothing doing. Building The Temple of our God is not the same thing to you as to us. We alone will build for the GOD of Israel. We're the ones King Cyrus of Persia commanded to do it."

4.4-5 So these people started beating down the morale of the people of Judah, harassing them

NEW INTERNATIONAL VERSION

afraid to go on building.*ᵃ* ⁵They hired counselors to work against them and frustrate their plans during the entire reign of Cyrus king of Persia and down to the reign of Darius king of Persia.

LATER OPPOSITION UNDER XERXES AND ARTAXERXES

⁶At the beginning of the reign of Xerxes,*ᵇ* they lodged an accusation against the people of Judah and Jerusalem.

⁷And in the days of Artaxerxes king of Persia, Bishlam, Mithredath, Tabeel and the rest of his associates wrote a letter to Artaxerxes. The letter was written in Aramaic script and in the Aramaic language.*ᶜ,ᵈ*

⁸Rehum the commanding officer and Shimshai the secretary wrote a letter against Jerusalem to Artaxerxes the king as follows:

⁹Rehum the commanding officer and Shimshai the secretary, together with the rest of their associates—the judges and officials over the men from Tripolis, Persia,*ᵉ* Erech and Babylon, the Elamites of Susa, ¹⁰and the other people whom the great and honorable Ashurbanipal*ᶠ* deported and settled in the city of Samaria and elsewhere in Trans-Euphrates.

¹¹(This is a copy of the letter they sent him.)

To King Artaxerxes,

From your servants, the men of Trans-Euphrates:

¹²The king should know that the Jews who came up to us from you have gone to Jerusalem and are rebuilding that rebellious and wicked city. They are restoring the walls and repairing the foundations.

¹³Furthermore, the king should know that if this city is built and its walls are restored, no more taxes, tribute or duty will be paid, and the royal revenues will suffer. ¹⁴Now since we are under obligation to the palace and it is not proper for us to see the king dishonored, we are sending this message to inform the king, ¹⁵so that a search may be made in the archives of your predecessors. In these records you will find that this city is a rebellious city, troublesome to kings and provinces, a place of rebellion from ancient times. That is why this city

---

ᵃ 4 Or and troubled them as they built   ᵇ 6 Hebrew Ahasuerus, a variant of Xerxes' Persian name   ᶜ 7 Or written in Aramaic and translated   ᵈ 7 The text of Ezra 4:8–6:18 is in Aramaic.   ᵉ 9 Or officials, magistrates and governors over the men from   ᶠ 10 Aramaic Osnappar, a variant of Ashurbanipal

THE MESSAGE

as they built. They even hired propagandists to sap their resolve. They kept this up for about fifteen years, throughout the lifetime of Cyrus king of Persia and on into the reign of Darius king of Persia.

⁴.⁶ In fact, in the reign of Xerxes, at the beginning of his reign, they wrote an accusation against those living in Judah and Jerusalem.

⁴.⁷ Again later, in the time of Artaxerxes, Bishlam, Mithredath, Tabeel, and their associates wrote regarding the Jerusalem business to Artaxerxes king of Persia. The letter was written in Aramaic and translated. (What follows is written in Aramaic.)

⁴.⁸⁻¹⁶ Rehum the commanding officer and Shimshai the secretary wrote a letter against Jerusalem to Artaxerxes the king as follows:

From: Rehum the commanding officer and Shimshai the secretary, backed by the rest of their associates, the judges and officials over the people from Tripolis, Persia, Erech, and Babylon, Elamites of Susa, and all the others whom the great and honorable Ashurbanipal deported and settled in the city of Samaria and other places in the land across the Euphrates.

(This is the copy of the letter they sent to him.)

To: King Artaxerxes from your servants from the land across the Euphrates.

We are here to inform the king that the Jews who came from you to us have arrived in Jerusalem and have set about rebuilding that rebellious and evil city. They are busy at work finishing the walls and rebuilding the foundations. The king needs to know that once that city is rebuilt and the wall completed they will no longer pay a penny of tribute, tax, or duty. The royal treasury will feel the loss. We're loyal to the king and cannot sit idly by while our king is being insulted—that's why we are passing this information on. We suggest that you look into the court records of your ancestors; you'll learn from those books that that city is a rebellious city, a thorn in the side to kings and provinces, an historic center of unrest and revolt. That's why the city was wiped out.

NEW INTERNATIONAL VERSION

was destroyed. [16]We inform the king that if this city is built and its walls are restored, you will be left with nothing in Trans-Euphrates.

[17]The king sent this reply:

To Rehum the commanding officer, Shimshai the secretary and the rest of their associates living in Samaria and elsewhere in Trans-Euphrates:

Greetings.

[18]The letter you sent us has been read and translated in my presence. [19]I issued an order and a search was made, and it was found that this city has a long history of revolt against kings and has been a place of rebellion and sedition. [20]Jerusalem has had powerful kings ruling over the whole of Trans-Euphrates, and taxes, tribute and duty were paid to them. [21]Now issue an order to these men to stop work, so that this city will not be rebuilt until I so order. [22]Be careful not to neglect this matter. Why let this threat grow, to the detriment of the royal interests?

[23]As soon as the copy of the letter of King Artaxerxes was read to Rehum and Shimshai the secretary and their associates, they went immediately to the Jews in Jerusalem and compelled them by force to stop.

[24]Thus the work on the house of God in Jerusalem came to a standstill until the second year of the reign of Darius king of Persia.

TATTENAI'S LETTER TO DARIUS

5 Now Haggai the prophet and Zechariah the prophet, a descendant of Iddo, prophesied to the Jews in Judah and Jerusalem in the name of the God of Israel, who was over them. [2]Then Zerubbabel son of Shealtiel and Jeshua son of Jozadak set to work to rebuild the house of God in Jerusalem. And the prophets of God were with them, helping them.

[3]At that time Tattenai, governor of Trans-Euphrates, and Shethar-Bozenai and their associates went to them and asked, "Who authorized you to rebuild this temple and restore this structure?" [4]They also asked, "What are the names of the men constructing this building?" [a] [5]But the eye of their God was watching over the elders of the Jews, and they were not stopped until

[a] 4 See Septuagint; Aramaic [4]We told them the names of the men constructing this building.

THE MESSAGE

We are letting the king know that if that city gets rebuilt and its walls restored, you'll end up with nothing in your province beyond the Euphrates.

4.17-22 The king sent his reply to Rehum the commanding officer, Shimshai the secretary, and the rest of their associates who lived in Samaria and other places beyond the Euphrates.

Peace be with you. The letter that you sent has been translated and read to me. I gave orders to search the records, and sure enough it turns out that this city has revolted against kings time and again—rebellion is an old story there. I find that they've had their share of strong kings who have taken over beyond the Euphrates and exacted taxes, tribute, and duty. So do this: Order these men to stop work immediately—not a lick of rebuilding in that city unless I order it. Act quickly and firmly; they've done enough damage to kings!

4.23 The letter of King Artaxerxes was read to Rehum and Shimshai the secretary and their associates. They lost no time. They went to the Jews in Jerusalem and made them quit work.

4.24 That put a stop to the work on The Temple of God in Jerusalem. Nothing more was done until the second year of the reign of Darius king of Persia.

THE BUILDING RESUMED: "HELP THE LEADERS IN THE REBUILDING"

5.1-2 5 Meanwhile the prophets Haggai and Zechariah son of Iddo were preaching to the Jews in Judah and Jerusalem in the authority of the God of Israel who ruled them. And so Zerubbabel son of Shealtiel and Jeshua son of Jozadak started again, rebuilding The Temple of God in Jerusalem. The prophets of God were right there helping them.

5.3-4 Tattenai was governor of the land beyond the Euphrates at this time. Tattenai, Shethar-Bozenai, and their associates came to the Israelites and asked, "Who issued you a permit to rebuild this Temple and restore it to use?" Then we told them the names of the men responsible for this construction work.

5.5 But God had his eye on the leaders of the Jews, and the work wasn't stopped until a re-

NEW INTERNATIONAL VERSION

a report could go to Darius and his written reply be received.

⁶This is a copy of the letter that Tattenai, governor of Trans-Euphrates, and Shethar-Bozenai and their associates, the officials of Trans-Euphrates, sent to King Darius. ⁷The report they sent him read as follows:

To King Darius:

Cordial greetings.

⁸The king should know that we went to the district of Judah, to the temple of the great God. The people are building it with large stones and placing the timbers in the walls. The work is being carried on with diligence and is making rapid progress under their direction.

⁹We questioned the elders and asked them, "Who authorized you to rebuild this temple and restore this structure?" ¹⁰We also asked them their names, so that we could write down the names of their leaders for your information.

¹¹This is the answer they gave us:

"We are the servants of the God of heaven and earth, and we are rebuilding the temple that was built many years ago, one that a great king of Israel built and finished. ¹²But because our fathers angered the God of heaven, he handed them over to Nebuchadnezzar the Chaldean, king of Babylon, who destroyed this temple and deported the people to Babylon.

¹³"However, in the first year of Cyrus king of Babylon, King Cyrus issued a decree to rebuild this house of God. ¹⁴He even removed from the temple ᵃ of Babylon the gold and silver articles of the house of God, which Nebuchadnezzar had taken from the temple in Jerusalem and brought to the temple ᵃ in Babylon.

"Then King Cyrus gave them to a man named Sheshbazzar, whom he had appointed governor, ¹⁵and he told him, 'Take these articles and go and deposit them in the temple in Jerusalem. And rebuild the house of God on its site.' ¹⁶So this Sheshbazzar came and laid the foundations of the house of God in Jerusalem. From that day to the present it has been under construction but is not yet finished."

¹⁷Now if it pleases the king, let a search be made in the royal archives of Babylon to see if King Cyrus did in fact issue a decree

THE MESSAGE

port could reach Darius and an official reply be returned.

5.6-7 Tattenai, governor of the land beyond the Euphrates, and Shethar-Bozenai and his associates—the officials of that land—sent a letter to Darius the king. This is what they wrote to him:

To Darius the king. Peace and blessing!

5.8 We want to report to the king that we went to the province of Judah, to The Temple of the great God that is being rebuilt with large stones. Timbers are being fitted into the walls; the work is going on with great energy and in good time.

5.9-10 We asked the leaders, "Who issued you the permit to rebuild this Temple and restore it to use?" We also asked for their names so we could pass them on to you and have a record of the men at the head of the construction work.

5.11-12 This is what they told us: "We are servants of the God of the heavens and the earth. We are rebuilding The Temple that was built a long time ago. A great king of Israel built it, the entire structure. But our ancestors made the God of the heavens really angry and he turned them over to Nebuchadnezzar, king of Babylon, the Chaldean, who knocked this Temple down and took the people to Babylon in exile.

5.13-16 "But when Cyrus became king of Babylon, in his first year he issued a building permit to rebuild this Temple of God. He also gave back the gold and silver vessels of The Temple of God that Nebuchadnezzar had carted off and put in the Babylon temple. Cyrus the king removed them from the temple of Babylon and turned them over to Sheshbazzar, the man he had appointed governor. He told him, 'Take these vessels and place them in The Temple of Jerusalem and rebuild The Temple of God on its original site.' And Sheshbazzar did it. He laid the foundation of The Temple of God in Jerusalem. It has been under construction ever since but it is not yet finished."

5.17 So now, if it please the king, look up the records in the royal archives in Babylon and see if it is indeed a fact that Cyrus the king issued an official building

---

ᵃ 14 Or *palace*

NEW INTERNATIONAL VERSION

to rebuild this house of God in Jerusalem. Then let the king send us his decision in this matter.

THE DECREE OF DARIUS

6 King Darius then issued an order, and they searched in the archives stored in the treasury at Babylon. ²A scroll was found in the citadel of Ecbatana in the province of Media, and this was written on it:

Memorandum:

³In the first year of King Cyrus, the king issued a decree concerning the temple of God in Jerusalem:

Let the temple be rebuilt as a place to present sacrifices, and let its foundations be laid. It is to be ninety feet*a* high and ninety feet wide, ⁴with three courses of large stones and one of timbers. The costs are to be paid by the royal treasury. ⁵Also, the gold and silver articles of the house of God, which Nebuchadnezzar took from the temple in Jerusalem and brought to Babylon, are to be returned to their places in the temple in Jerusalem; they are to be deposited in the house of God.

⁶Now then, Tattenai, governor of Trans-Euphrates, and Shethar-Bozenai and you, their fellow officials of that province, stay away from there. ⁷Do not interfere with the work on this temple of God. Let the governor of the Jews and the Jewish elders rebuild this house of God on its site.

⁸Moreover, I hereby decree what you are to do for these elders of the Jews in the construction of this house of God:

The expenses of these men are to be fully paid out of the royal treasury, from the revenues of Trans-Euphrates, so that the work will not stop. ⁹Whatever is needed—young bulls, rams, male lambs for burnt offerings to the God of heaven, and wheat, salt, wine and oil, as requested by the priests in Jerusalem—must be given them daily without fail, ¹⁰so that they may offer sacrifices pleasing to the God of heaven and pray for the well-being of the king and his sons.

¹¹Furthermore, I decree that if anyone changes this edict, a beam is to be pulled from his house and he is to be lifted up and impaled on it. And for this crime his house is to be made a pile of rubble. ¹²May

THE MESSAGE

permit authorizing the rebuilding of The Temple of God in Jerusalem. And then send the king's ruling on this matter to us.

6.1-3 **6** So King Darius ordered a search through the records in the archives in Babylon. Eventually a scroll was turned up in the fortress of Ecbatana over in the province of Media, with this writing on it:

Memorandum

In his first year as king, Cyrus issued an official decree regarding The Temple of God in Jerusalem, as follows:

6.3-5   The Temple where sacrifices are offered is to be rebuilt on new foundations. It is to be ninety feet high and ninety feet wide with three courses of large stones topped with one course of timber. The cost is to be paid from the royal bank. The gold and silver vessels from The Temple of God that Nebuchadnezzar carried to Babylon are to be returned to The Temple at Jerusalem, each to its proper place; place them in The Temple of God.

6.6-7   Now listen, Tattenai governor of the land beyond the Euphrates, Shethar-Bozenai, associates, and all officials of that land: Stay out of their way. Leave the governor and leaders of the Jews alone so they can work on that Temple of God as they rebuild it.

6.8-10   I hereby give official orders on how you are to help the leaders of the Jews in the rebuilding of that Temple of God:

1. All construction costs are to be paid to these men from the royal bank out of the taxes coming in from the land beyond the Euphrates. And pay them on time, without delays.

2. Whatever is required for their worship—young bulls, rams, and lambs for Whole-Burnt-Offerings to the God-of-Heaven; and whatever wheat, salt, wine, and anointing oil the priests of Jerusalem request—is to be given to them daily without delay so that they may make sacrifices to the God-of-Heaven and pray for the life of the king and his sons.

6.11-12   I've issued an official decree that anyone who violates this order is to be impaled on a timber torn out of his own house, and the house itself made a ma-

---

a 3 Aramaic *sixty cubits* (about 27 meters)

NEW INTERNATIONAL VERSION

God, who has caused his Name to dwell there, overthrow any king or people who lifts a hand to change this decree or to destroy this temple in Jerusalem.

I Darius have decreed it. Let it be carried out with diligence.

COMPLETION AND DEDICATION OF THE TEMPLE

¹³Then, because of the decree King Darius had sent, Tattenai, governor of Trans-Euphrates, and Shethar-Bozenai and their associates carried it out with diligence. ¹⁴So the elders of the Jews continued to build and prosper under the preaching of Haggai the prophet and Zechariah, a descendant of Iddo. They finished building the temple according to the command of the God of Israel and the decrees of Cyrus, Darius and Artaxerxes, kings of Persia. ¹⁵The temple was completed on the third day of the month Adar, in the sixth year of the reign of King Darius.

¹⁶Then the people of Israel—the priests, the Levites and the rest of the exiles—celebrated the dedication of the house of God with joy. ¹⁷For the dedication of this house of God they offered a hundred bulls, two hundred rams, four hundred male lambs and, as a sin offering for all Israel, twelve male goats, one for each of the tribes of Israel. ¹⁸And they installed the priests in their divisions and the Levites in their groups for the service of God at Jerusalem, according to what is written in the Book of Moses.

THE PASSOVER

¹⁹On the fourteenth day of the first month, the exiles celebrated the Passover. ²⁰The priests and Levites had purified themselves and were all ceremonially clean. The Levites slaughtered the Passover lamb for all the exiles, for their brothers the priests and for themselves. ²¹So the Israelites who had returned from the exile ate it, together with all who had separated themselves from the unclean practices of their Gentile neighbors in order to seek the LORD, the God of Israel. ²²For seven days they celebrated with joy the Feast of Unleavened Bread, because the LORD had filled them with joy by changing the attitude of the king of Assyria, so that he assisted them in the work on the house of God, the God of Israel.

EZRA COMES TO JERUSALEM

7 After these things, during the reign of Artaxerxes king of Persia, Ezra son of Seraiah,

THE MESSAGE

nure pit. And may the God who put his Name on that place wipe out any king or people who dares to defy this decree and destroy The Temple of God at Jerusalem.

I, Darius, have issued an official decree. Carry it out precisely and promptly.

6.13 Tattenai governor of the land across the Euphrates, Shethar-Bozenai, and their associates did it: They carried out the decree of Darius precisely and promptly.

THE BUILDING COMPLETED: "EXUBERANTLY CELEBRATED THE DEDICATION"

6.14-15 So the leaders of the Jews continued to build; the work went well under the preaching of the prophets Haggai and Zechariah son of Iddo. They completed the rebuilding under orders of the God of Israel and authorization by Cyrus, Darius, and Artaxerxes, kings of Persia. The Temple was completed on the third day of the month Adar in the sixth year of the reign of King Darius.

6.16-18 And then the Israelites celebrated—priests, Levites, every last exile, exuberantly celebrated the dedication of The Temple of God. At the dedication of this Temple of God they sacrificed a hundred bulls, two hundred rams, and four hundred lambs—and, as an Absolution-Offering for all Israel, twelve he-goats, one for each of the twelve tribes of Israel. They placed the priests in their divisions and the Levites in their places for the service of God at Jerusalem—all as written out in the Book of Moses.

⸸

6.19 On the fourteenth day of the first month, the exiles celebrated the Passover.

6.20 All the priests and Levites had purified themselves—all, no exceptions. They were all ritually clean. The Levites slaughtered the Passover lamb for the exiles, their brother priests, and themselves.

6.21-22 Then the Israelites who had returned from exile, along with everyone who had removed themselves from the defilements of the nations to join them and seek GOD, the God of Israel, ate the Passover. With great joy they celebrated the Feast of Unraised Bread for seven days. GOD had plunged them into a sea of joy; he had changed the mind of the king of Assyria to back them in rebuilding The Temple of God, the God of Israel.

EZRA ARRIVES

7.1-5 **7** After all this, Ezra. It was during the reign of Artaxerxes king of Persia. Ezra was the

NEW INTERNATIONAL VERSION

the son of Azariah, the son of Hilkiah, ²the son of Shallum, the son of Zadok, the son of Ahitub, ³the son of Amariah, the son of Azariah, the son of Meraioth, ⁴the son of Zerahiah, the son of Uzzi, the son of Bukki, ⁵the son of Abishua, the son of Phinehas, the son of Eleazar, the son of Aaron the chief priest— ⁶this Ezra came up from Babylon. He was a teacher well versed in the Law of Moses, which the LORD, the God of Israel, had given. The king had granted him everything he asked, for the hand of the LORD his God was on him. ⁷Some of the Israelites, including priests, Levites, singers, gatekeepers and temple servants, also came up to Jerusalem in the seventh year of King Artaxerxes.

⁸Ezra arrived in Jerusalem in the fifth month of the seventh year of the king. ⁹He had begun his journey from Babylon on the first day of the first month, and he arrived in Jerusalem on the first day of the fifth month, for the gracious hand of his God was on him. ¹⁰For Ezra had devoted himself to the study and observance of the Law of the LORD, and to teaching its decrees and laws in Israel.

KING ARTAXERXES' LETTER TO EZRA

¹¹This is a copy of the letter King Artaxerxes had given to Ezra the priest and teacher, a man learned in matters concerning the commands and decrees of the LORD for Israel:

¹² *ᵃ* Artaxerxes, king of kings,

To Ezra the priest, a teacher of the Law of the God of heaven:

Greetings.

¹³Now I decree that any of the Israelites in my kingdom, including priests and Levites, who wish to go to Jerusalem with you, may go. ¹⁴You are sent by the king and his seven advisers to inquire about Judah and Jerusalem with regard to the Law of your God, which is in your hand. ¹⁵Moreover, you are to take with you the silver and gold that the king and his advisers have freely given to the God of Israel, whose dwelling is in Jerusalem, ¹⁶together with all the silver and gold you may obtain from the province of Babylon, as well as the freewill offerings of the people and priests for the temple of their God in Jerusalem. ¹⁷With this money be sure to buy bulls, rams and male lambs, together with their grain offerings and drink offerings, and sacrifice them on the altar of the temple of your God in Jerusalem.

ᵃ 12 The text of Ezra 7:12-26 is in Aramaic.

THE MESSAGE

son of Seraiah, son of Azariah, son of Hilkiah, son of Shallum, son of Zadok, son of Ahitub, son of Amariah, son of Azariah, son of Meraioth, son of Zerahiah, son of Uzzi, son of Bukki, son of Abishua, son of Phinehas, son of Eleazar, son of Aaron the high priest.

7.6-7   That's Ezra. He arrived from Babylon, a scholar well-practiced in the Revelation of Moses that the GOD of Israel had given. Because GOD's hand was on Ezra, the king gave him everything he asked for. Some of the Israelites—priests, Levites, singers, temple security guards, and temple slaves—went with him to Jerusalem. It was in the seventh year of Artaxerxes the king.

7.8-10   They arrived at Jerusalem in the fifth month of the seventh year of the king's reign. Ezra had scheduled their departure from Babylon on the first day of the first month; they arrived in Jerusalem on the first day of the fifth month under the generous guidance of his God. Ezra had committed himself to studying the Revelation of GOD, to living it, and to teaching Israel to live its truths and ways.

⸏

7.11   What follows is the letter that King Artaxerxes gave Ezra, priest and scholar, expert in matters involving the truths and ways of GOD concerning Israel:

7.12-20   Artaxerxes, King of Kings, to Ezra the priest, a scholar of the Teaching of the God-of-Heaven.
Peace. I hereby decree that any of the people of Israel living in my kingdom who want to go to Jerusalem, including their priests and Levites, may go with you. You are being sent by the king and his seven advisors to carry out an investigation of Judah and Jerusalem in relation to the Teaching of your God that you are carrying with you. You are also authorized to take the silver and gold that the king and his advisors are giving for the God of Israel, whose residence is in Jerusalem, along with all the silver and gold that has been collected from the generously donated offerings all over Babylon, including that from the people and the priests, for The Temple of their God in Jerusalem. Use this money carefully to buy bulls, rams, lambs, and the ingredients for Grain-Offerings and Drink-Offerings and then offer them on the Altar of The Temple of your God in Jerusalem.

NEW INTERNATIONAL VERSION

¹⁸You and your brother Jews may then do whatever seems best with the rest of the silver and gold, in accordance with the will of your God. ¹⁹Deliver to the God of Jerusalem all the articles entrusted to you for worship in the temple of your God. ²⁰And anything else needed for the temple of your God that you may have occasion to supply, you may provide from the royal treasury.

²¹Now I, King Artaxerxes, order all the treasurers of Trans-Euphrates to provide with diligence whatever Ezra the priest, a teacher of the Law of the God of heaven, may ask of you— ²²up to a hundred talents*ᵃ* of silver, a hundred cors*ᵇ* of wheat, a hundred baths*ᶜ* of wine, a hundred baths*ᶜ* of olive oil, and salt without limit. ²³Whatever the God of heaven has prescribed, let it be done with diligence for the temple of the God of heaven. Why should there be wrath against the realm of the king and of his sons? ²⁴You are also to know that you have no authority to impose taxes, tribute or duty on any of the priests, Levites, singers, gatekeepers, temple servants or other workers at this house of God.

²⁵And you, Ezra, in accordance with the wisdom of your God, which you possess, appoint magistrates and judges to administer justice to all the people of Trans-Euphrates—all who know the laws of your God. And you are to teach any who do not know them. ²⁶Whoever does not obey the law of your God and the law of the king must surely be punished by death, banishment, confiscation of property, or imprisonment.

²⁷Praise be to the Lᴏʀᴅ, the God of our fathers, who has put it into the king's heart to bring honor to the house of the Lᴏʀᴅ in Jerusalem in this way ²⁸and who has extended his good favor to me before the king and his advisers and all the king's powerful officials. Because the hand of the Lᴏʀᴅ my God was on me, I took courage and gathered leading men from Israel to go up with me.

THE MESSAGE

You are free to use whatever is left over from the silver and gold for what you and your brothers decide is in keeping with the will of your God. Deliver to the God of Jerusalem the vessels given to you for the services of worship in The Temple of your God. Whatever else you need for The Temple of your God you may pay for out of the royal bank.

7.21-23 I, Artaxerxes the king, have formally authorized and ordered all the treasurers of the land across the Euphrates to give Ezra the priest, scholar of the Teaching of the God-of-Heaven, the full amount of whatever he asks for up to a hundred talents of silver, six hundred and fifty bushels of wheat, and six hundred and seven gallons each of wine and olive oil. There is no limit on the salt. Everything the God-of-Heaven requires for The Temple of God must be given without hesitation. Why would the king and his sons risk stirring up his wrath?

7.24 Also, let it be clear that no one is permitted to impose tribute, tax, or duty on any priest, Levite, singer, temple security guard, temple servant, or any other worker connected with The Temple of God.

7.25 I authorize you, Ezra, exercising the wisdom of God that you have in your hands, to appoint magistrates and judges so they can administer justice among all the people of the land across the Euphrates who live by the Teaching of your God. Anyone who does not know the Teaching, you teach them.

7.26 Anyone who does not obey the Teaching of your God and the king must be tried and sentenced at once—death, banishment, a fine, prison, whatever.

Eᴢʀᴀ: "I Wᴀs Rᴇᴀᴅʏ ᴛᴏ Gᴏ"

7.27-28 Blessed be Gᴏᴅ, the God-of-Our-Fathers, who put it in the mind of the king to beautify The Temple of Gᴏᴅ in Jerusalem! Not only that, he caused the king and all his advisors and influential officials actually to like me and back me. My God was on my side and I was ready to go. And I organized all the leaders of Israel to go with me.

ᵃ 22 That is, about 3 3/4 tons (about 3.4 metric tons)
ᵇ 22 That is, probably about 600 bushels (about 22 kiloliters)   ᶜ 22 That is, probably about 600 gallons (about 2.2 kiloliters)

NEW INTERNATIONAL VERSION

LIST OF THE FAMILY HEADS RETURNING WITH EZRA

8 These are the family heads and those registered with them who came up with me from Babylon during the reign of King Artaxerxes:

2 of the descendants of Phinehas, Gershom;
of the descendants of Ithamar, Daniel;
of the descendants of David, Hattush 3 of the descendants of Shecaniah;

of the descendants of Parosh, Zechariah, and with him were registered 150 men;
4 of the descendants of Pahath-Moab, Eliehoenai son of Zerahiah, and with him 200 men;
5 of the descendants of Zattu,^a Shecaniah son of Jahaziel, and with him 300 men;
6 of the descendants of Adin, Ebed son of Jonathan, and with him 50 men;
7 of the descendants of Elam, Jeshaiah son of Athaliah, and with him 70 men;
8 of the descendants of Shephatiah, Zebadiah son of Michael, and with him 80 men;
9 of the descendants of Joab, Obadiah son of Jehiel, and with him 218 men;
10 of the descendants of Bani,^b Shelomith son of Josiphiah, and with him 160 men;
11 of the descendants of Bebai, Zechariah son of Bebai, and with him 28 men;
12 of the descendants of Azgad, Johanan son of Hakkatan, and with him 110 men;
13 of the descendants of Adonikam, the last ones, whose names were Eliphelet, Jeuel and Shemaiah, and with them 60 men;
14 of the descendants of Bigvai, Uthai and Zaccur, and with them 70 men.

THE RETURN TO JERUSALEM

15 I assembled them at the canal that flows toward Ahava, and we camped there three days. When I checked among the people and the priests, I found no Levites there. 16 So I summoned Eliezer, Ariel, Shemaiah, Elnathan, Jarib, Elnathan, Nathan, Zechariah and Meshullam, who were leaders, and Joiarib and Elnathan, who were men of learning, 17 and I sent them to Iddo, the leader in Casiphia. I told them what to say to Iddo and his kinsmen, the temple servants in Casiphia, so that they might bring attendants to us for the house of our God. 18 Because the gracious hand of our God was on us, they brought us Sherebiah, a capable man, from the descendants of Mahli son of Levi, the son of Israel, and Sherebiah's sons and brothers, 18 men; 19 and

---

^a 5 Some Septuagint manuscripts (also 1 Esdras 8:32); Hebrew does not have *Zattu*. ^b 10 Some Septuagint manuscripts (also 1 Esdras 8:36); Hebrew does not have *Bani*.

THE MESSAGE

8.1-14 **8** These are the family heads and those who signed up to go up with me from Babylon in the reign of Artaxerxes the king:

From the family of Phinehas: Gershom
Family of Ithamar: Daniel
Family of David: Hattush
Family of Shecaniah
Family of Parosh: Zechariah, and with him 150 men signed up
Family of Pahath-Moab: Eliehoenai son of Zerahiah, and 200 men
Family of Zattu: Shecaniah son of Jahaziel, and 300 men
Family of Adin: Ebed son of Jonathan, and 50 men
Family of Elam: Jeshaiah son of Athaliah, and 70 men
Family of Shephatiah: Zebadiah son of Michael, and 80 men
Family of Joab: Obadiah son of Jehiel, and 218 men
Family of Bani: Shelomith son of Josiphiah, and 160 men
Family of Bebai: Zechariah son of Bebai, and 28 men
Family of Azgad: Johanan son of Hakkatan, and 110 men
Family of Adonikam (bringing up the rear): their names were
Eliphelet, Jeuel, Shemaiah, and 60 men
Family of Bigvai: Uthai and Zaccur, and 70 men.

8.15-17 I gathered them together at the canal that runs to Ahava. We camped there three days. I looked them over and found that they were all laymen and priests but no Levites. So I sent for the leaders Eliezer, Ariel, Shemaiah, Elnathan, Jarib, Elnathan, Nathan, Zechariah, and Meshullam, and for the teachers Joiarib and Elnathan. I then sent them to Iddo, who is head of the town of Casiphia, and told them what to say to Iddo and his relatives who lived there in Casiphia: "Send us ministers for The Temple of God."

8.18-20 Well, the generous hand of our God was on us, and they brought back to us a wise man from the family of Mahli son of Levi, the son of Israel. His name was Sherebiah. With sons and brothers they numbered eighteen. They also

NEW INTERNATIONAL VERSION

Hashabiah, together with Jeshaiah from the descendants of Merari, and his brothers and nephews, 20 men. ²⁰They also brought 220 of the temple servants—a body that David and the officials had established to assist the Levites. All were registered by name.

²¹There, by the Ahava Canal, I proclaimed a fast, so that we might humble ourselves before our God and ask him for a safe journey for us and our children, with all our possessions. ²²I was ashamed to ask the king for soldiers and horsemen to protect us from enemies on the road, because we had told the king, "The gracious hand of our God is on everyone who looks to him, but his great anger is against all who forsake him." ²³So we fasted and petitioned our God about this, and he answered our prayer.

²⁴Then I set apart twelve of the leading priests, together with Sherebiah, Hashabiah and ten of their brothers, ²⁵and I weighed out to them the offering of silver and gold and the articles that the king, his advisers, his officials and all Israel present there had donated for the house of our God. ²⁶I weighed out to them 650 talents*ᵃ* of silver, silver articles weighing 100 talents,*ᵇ* 100 talents*ᵇ* of gold, ²⁷20 bowls of gold valued at 1,000 darics,*ᶜ* and two fine articles of polished bronze, as precious as gold.

²⁸I said to them, "You as well as these articles are consecrated to the LORD. The silver and gold are a freewill offering to the LORD, the God of your fathers. ²⁹Guard them carefully until you weigh them out in the chambers of the house of the LORD in Jerusalem before the leading priests and the Levites and the family heads of Israel." ³⁰Then the priests and Levites received the silver and gold and sacred articles that had been weighed out to be taken to the house of our God in Jerusalem.

³¹On the twelfth day of the first month we set out from the Ahava Canal to go to Jerusalem. The hand of our God was on us, and he protected us from enemies and bandits along the way. ³²So we arrived in Jerusalem, where we rested three days.

³³On the fourth day, in the house of our God, we weighed out the silver and gold and the sacred articles into the hands of Meremoth son of Uriah, the priest. Eleazar son of Phinehas was with him, and so were the Levites Jozabad son of Jeshua and Noadiah son of Binnui. ³⁴Everything was accounted for by number and weight, and the entire weight was recorded at that time.

ᵃ 26 That is, about 25 tons (about 22 metric tons)
ᵇ 26 That is, about 3 3/4 tons (about 3.4 metric tons)
ᶜ 27 That is, about 19 pounds (about 8.5 kilograms)

THE MESSAGE

brought Hashabiah and Jeshaiah of the family of Merari, with brothers and their sons, another twenty. And then there were 220 temple servants, descendants of the temple servants that David and the princes had assigned to help the Levites in their work. They were all signed up by name.

8.21-22   I proclaimed a fast there beside the Ahava Canal, a fast to humble ourselves before our God and pray for wise guidance for our journey—all our people and possessions. I was embarrassed to ask the king for a cavalry bodyguard to protect us from bandits on the road. We had just told the king, "Our God lovingly looks after all those who seek him, but turns away in disgust from those who leave him."

8.23   So we fasted and prayed about these concerns. And he listened.

8.24-27   Then I picked twelve of the leading priests—Sherebiah and Hashabiah with ten of their brothers. I weighed out for them the silver, the gold, the vessels, and the offerings for The Temple of our God that the king, his advisors, and all the Israelites had given:

   25 tons of silver
   100 vessels of silver valued at three and three-quarter tons of gold
   20 gold bowls weighing eighteen and a half pounds
   2 vessels of bright red copper, as valuable as gold.

8.28-29   I said to them, "You are holy to GOD and these vessels are holy. The silver and gold are Freewill-Offerings to the GOD of your ancestors. Guard them with your lives until you're able to weigh them out in a secure place in The Temple of our God for the priests and Levites and family heads who are in charge in Jerusalem."

8.30   The priests and Levites took charge of all that had been weighed out to them, and prepared to deliver it to Jerusalem to The Temple of our God.

8.31   We left the Ahava Canal on the twelfth day of the first month to travel to Jerusalem. God was with us all the way and kept us safe from bandits and highwaymen.

8.32-34   We arrived in Jerusalem and waited there three days. On the fourth day the silver and gold and vessels were weighed out in The Temple of our God into the hands of Meremoth son of Uriah, the priest. Eleazar son of Phinehas was there with him, also the Levites Jozabad son of Jeshua and Noadiah son of Binnui. Everything was counted and weighed and the totals recorded.

NEW INTERNATIONAL VERSION

³⁵Then the exiles who had returned from captivity sacrificed burnt offerings to the God of Israel: twelve bulls for all Israel, ninety-six rams, seventy-seven male lambs and, as a sin offering, twelve male goats. All this was a burnt offering to the LORD. ³⁶They also delivered the king's orders to the royal satraps and to the governors of Trans-Euphrates, who then gave assistance to the people and to the house of God.

EZRA'S PRAYER ABOUT INTERMARRIAGE

9 After these things had been done, the leaders came to me and said, "The people of Israel, including the priests and the Levites, have not kept themselves separate from the neighboring peoples with their detestable practices, like those of the Canaanites, Hittites, Perizzites, Jebusites, Ammonites, Moabites, Egyptians and Amorites. ²They have taken some of their daughters as wives for themselves and their sons, and have mingled the holy race with the peoples around them. And the leaders and officials have led the way in this unfaithfulness."

³When I heard this, I tore my tunic and cloak, pulled hair from my head and beard and sat down appalled. ⁴Then everyone who trembled at the words of the God of Israel gathered around me because of this unfaithfulness of the exiles. And I sat there appalled until the evening sacrifice.

⁵Then, at the evening sacrifice, I rose from my self-abasement, with my tunic and cloak torn, and fell on my knees with my hands spread out to the LORD my God ⁶and prayed:

"O my God, I am too ashamed and disgraced to lift up my face to you, my God, because our sins are higher than our heads and our guilt has reached to the heavens. ⁷From the days of our forefathers until now, our guilt has been great. Because of our sins, we and our kings and our priests have been subjected to the sword and captivity, to pillage and humiliation at the hand of foreign kings, as it is today. ⁸"But now, for a brief moment, the LORD our God has been gracious in leaving us a remnant and giving us a firm place in his sanctuary, and so our God gives light to our eyes and a little relief in our bondage. ⁹Though we are slaves, our God has not

THE MESSAGE

8.35 When they arrived, the exiles, now returned from captivity, offered Whole-Burnt-Offerings to the God of Israel:

12 bulls, representing all Israel
96 rams
77 lambs
12 he-goats as an Absolution-Offering.

All of this was sacrificed as a Whole-Burnt-Offering to GOD.

8.36 They also delivered the king's orders to the king's provincial administration assigned to the land beyond the Euphrates. They, in turn, gave their support to the people and The Temple of God.

EZRA PRAYS: "LOOK AT US . . . GUILTY BEFORE YOU"

9.1-2 **9** After all this was done, the leaders came to me and said, "The People of Israel, priests and Levites included, have not kept themselves separate from the neighboring people around here with all their vulgar obscenities—Canaanites, Hittites, Perizzites, Jebusites, Ammonites, Moabites, Egyptians, Amorites. They have given some of their daughters in marriage to them and have taken some of their daughters for marriage to their sons. The holy seed is now all mixed in with these other peoples. And our leaders have led the way in this betrayal."

9.3 When I heard all this, I ripped my clothes and my cape; I pulled hair from my head and out of my beard; I slumped to the ground, appalled.

9.4-6 Many were in fear and trembling because of what God was saying about the betrayal by the exiles. They gathered around me as I sat there in despair, waiting for the evening sacrifice. At the evening sacrifice I picked myself up from my utter devastation, and in my ripped clothes and cape fell to my knees and stretched out my hands to GOD, my God. And I prayed:

9.6-7 "My dear God, I'm so totally ashamed, I can't bear to face you. O my God—our iniquities are piled up so high that we can't see out; our guilt touches the skies. We've been stuck in a muck of guilt since the time of our ancestors until right now; we and our kings and priests, because of our sins, have been turned over to foreign kings, to killing, to captivity, to looting, and to public shame—just as you see us now.

9.8-9 "Now for a brief time GOD, our God, has allowed us, this battered band, to get a firm foothold in his holy place so that our God may brighten our eyes and lighten our burdens as we serve out this hard sentence. We were slaves; yet even as slaves, our God didn't aban-

NEW INTERNATIONAL VERSION

deserted us in our bondage. He has shown us kindness in the sight of the kings of Persia: He has granted us new life to rebuild the house of our God and repair its ruins, and he has given us a wall of protection in Judah and Jerusalem.

¹⁰"But now, O our God, what can we say after this? For we have disregarded the commands ¹¹you gave through your servants the prophets when you said: 'The land you are entering to possess is a land polluted by the corruption of its peoples. By their detestable practices they have filled it with their impurity from one end to the other. ¹²Therefore, do not give your daughters in marriage to their sons or take their daughters for your sons. Do not seek a treaty of friendship with them at any time, that you may be strong and eat the good things of the land and leave it to your children as an everlasting inheritance.'

¹³"What has happened to us is a result of our evil deeds and our great guilt, and yet, our God, you have punished us less than our sins have deserved and have given us a remnant like this. ¹⁴Shall we again break your commands and intermarry with the peoples who commit such detestable practices? Would you not be angry enough with us to destroy us, leaving us no remnant or survivor? ¹⁵O LORD, God of Israel, you are righteous! We are left this day as a remnant. Here we are before you in our guilt, though because of it not one of us can stand in your presence."

THE PEOPLE'S CONFESSION OF SIN

10 While Ezra was praying and confessing, weeping and throwing himself down before the house of God, a large crowd of Israelites—men, women and children—gathered around him. They too wept bitterly. ²Then Shecaniah son of Jehiel, one of the descendants of Elam, said to Ezra, "We have been unfaithful to our God by marrying foreign women from the peoples around us. But in spite of this, there is still hope for Israel. ³Now let us make a covenant before our God to send away all these women and their children, in accordance with the counsel of my lord and of those who fear the commands of our God. Let it be done according to the Law. ⁴Rise up; this matter is in your hands. We will support you, so take courage and do it."

⁵So Ezra rose up and put the leading priests and Levites and all Israel under oath to do what

THE MESSAGE

don us. He has put us in the good graces of the kings of Persia and given us the heart to build The Temple of our God, restore its ruins, and construct a defensive wall in Judah and Jerusalem.

9.10-12 "And now, our God, after all this what can we say for ourselves? For we have thrown your commands to the wind, the commands you gave us through your servants the prophets. They told us, 'The land you're taking over is a polluted land, polluted with the obscene vulgarities of the people who live there; they've filled it with their moral rot from one end to the other. Whatever you do, don't give your daughters in marriage to their sons nor marry your sons to their daughters. Don't cultivate their good opinion; don't make over them and get them to like you so you can make a lot of money and build up a tidy estate to hand down to your children.'

9.13-15 "And now this, on top of all we've already suffered because of our evil ways and accumulated guilt, even though you, dear God, punished us far less than we deserved and even went ahead and gave us this present escape. Yet here we are, at it again, breaking your commandments by intermarrying with the people who practice all these obscenities! Are you angry to the point of wiping us out completely, without even a few stragglers, with no way out at all? You are the righteous GOD of Israel. We are, right now, a small band of escapees. Look at us, openly standing here, guilty before you. No one can last long like this."

EZRA TAKES CHARGE

10.1 **10** Ezra wept, prostrate in front of The Temple of God. As he prayed and confessed, a huge number of the men, women, and children of Israel gathered around him. All the people were now weeping as if their hearts would break.

10.2-3 Shecaniah son of Jehiel of the family of Elam, acting as spokesman, said to Ezra: "We betrayed our God by marrying foreign wives from the people around here. But all is not lost; there is still hope for Israel. Let's make a covenant right now with our God, agreeing to get rid of all these wives and their children, just as my master and those who honor God's commandment are saying. It's what The Revelation says, so let's do it.

10.4 "Now get up, Ezra. Take charge—we're behind you. Don't back down."

10.5 So Ezra stood up and had the leaders of the priests, the Levites, and all Israel solemnly

NEW INTERNATIONAL VERSION

had been suggested. And they took the oath. ⁶Then Ezra withdrew from before the house of God and went to the room of Jehohanan son of Eliashib. While he was there, he ate no food and drank no water, because he continued to mourn over the unfaithfulness of the exiles.

⁷A proclamation was then issued throughout Judah and Jerusalem for all the exiles to assemble in Jerusalem. ⁸Anyone who failed to appear within three days would forfeit all his property, in accordance with the decision of the officials and elders, and would himself be expelled from the assembly of the exiles.

⁹Within the three days, all the men of Judah and Benjamin had gathered in Jerusalem. And on the twentieth day of the ninth month, all the people were sitting in the square before the house of God, greatly distressed by the occasion and because of the rain. ¹⁰Then Ezra the priest stood up and said to them, "You have been unfaithful; you have married foreign women, adding to Israel's guilt. ¹¹Now make confession to the LORD, the God of your fathers, and do his will. Separate yourselves from the peoples around you and from your foreign wives."

¹²The whole assembly responded with a loud voice: "You are right! We must do as you say. ¹³But there are many people here and it is the rainy season; so we cannot stand outside. Besides, this matter cannot be taken care of in a day or two, because we have sinned greatly in this thing. ¹⁴Let our officials act for the whole assembly. Then let everyone in our towns who has married a foreign woman come at a set time, along with the elders and judges of each town, until the fierce anger of our God in this matter is turned away from us." ¹⁵Only Jonathan son of Asahel and Jahzeiah son of Tikvah, supported by Meshullam and Shabbethai the Levite, opposed this.

¹⁶So the exiles did as was proposed. Ezra the priest selected men who were family heads, one from each family division, and all of them designated by name. On the first day of the tenth month they sat down to investigate the cases, ¹⁷and by the first day of the first month they finished dealing with all the men who had married foreign women.

THE MESSAGE

swear to do what Shecaniah proposed. And they did it.

10.6   Then Ezra left the plaza in front of The Temple of God and went to the home of Jehohanan son of Eliashib where he stayed, still fasting from food and drink, continuing his mourning over the betrayal by the exiles.

✛

10.7-8 A notice was then sent throughout Judah and Jerusalem ordering all the exiles to meet in Jerusalem. Anyone who failed to show up in three days, in compliance with the ruling of the leaders and elders, would have all his possessions confiscated and be thrown out of the congregation of the returned exiles.

10.9   All the men of Judah and Benjamin met in Jerusalem within the three days. It was the twentieth day of the ninth month. They all sat down in the plaza in front of The Temple of God. Because of the business before them, and aggravated by the buckets of rain coming down on them, they were restless, uneasy, and anxious.

10.10-11 Ezra the priest stood up and spoke: "You've broken trust. You've married foreign wives. You've piled guilt on Israel. Now make your confession to GOD, the God of your ancestors, and do what he wants you to do: Separate yourselves from the people of the land and from your foreign wives."

10.12   The whole congregation responded with a shout, "Yes, we'll do it—just the way you said it!"

10.13-14 They also said, "But look, do you see how many people there are out here? And it's the rainy season; you can't expect us to stand out here soaking wet until this is done—why, it will take days! A lot of us are deeply involved in this transgression. Let our leaders act on behalf of the whole congregation. Have everybody who lives in cities and who has married a foreign wife come at an appointed time, accompanied by the elders and judges of each city. We'll keep at this until the hot anger of our God over this thing is turned away."

10.15-17 Only Jonathan son of Asahel and Jahzeiah son of Tikvah, supported by Meshullam and Shabbethai the Levite, opposed this. So the exiles went ahead with the plan. Ezra the priest picked men who were family heads, each one by name. They sat down together on the first day of the tenth month to pursue the matter. By the first day of the first month they had finished dealing with every man who had married a foreign wife.

✛

NEW INTERNATIONAL VERSION	THE MESSAGE

NEW INTERNATIONAL VERSION

THOSE GUILTY OF INTERMARRIAGE

18Among the descendants of the priests, the following had married foreign women:

From the descendants of Jeshua son of Jozadak, and his brothers: Maaseiah, Eliezer, Jarib and Gedaliah. **19**(They all gave their hands in pledge to put away their wives, and for their guilt they each presented a ram from the flock as a guilt offering.)

20From the descendants of Immer:
Hanani and Zebadiah.

21From the descendants of Harim:
Maaseiah, Elijah, Shemaiah, Jehiel and Uzziah.

22From the descendants of Pashhur:
Elioenai, Maaseiah, Ishmael, Nethanel, Jozabad and Elasah.

23Among the Levites:

Jozabad, Shimei, Kelaiah (that is, Kelita), Pethahiah, Judah and Eliezer.

24From the singers:
Eliashib.

From the gatekeepers:
Shallum, Telem and Uri.

25And among the other Israelites:

From the descendants of Parosh:
Ramiah, Izziah, Malkijah, Mijamin, Eleazar, Malkijah and Benaiah.

26From the descendants of Elam:
Mattaniah, Zechariah, Jehiel, Abdi, Jeremoth and Elijah.

27From the descendants of Zattu:
Elioenai, Eliashib, Mattaniah, Jeremoth, Zabad and Aziza.

28From the descendants of Bebai:
Jehohanan, Hananiah, Zabbai and Athlai.

29From the descendants of Bani:
Meshullam, Malluch, Adaiah, Jashub, Sheal and Jeremoth.

30From the descendants of Pahath-Moab:
Adna, Kelal, Benaiah, Maaseiah, Mattaniah, Bezalel, Binnui and Manasseh.

31From the descendants of Harim:
Eliezer, Ishijah, Malkijah, Shemaiah, Shimeon, **32**Benjamin, Malluch and Shemariah.

33From the descendants of Hashum:
Mattenai, Mattattah, Zabad, Eliphelet, Jeremai, Manasseh and Shimei.

34From the descendants of Bani:
Maadai, Amram, Uel, **35**Benaiah, Bedeiah, Keluhi, **36**Vaniah, Meremoth, Eliashib, **37**Mattaniah, Mattenai and Jaasu.

THE MESSAGE

10.18-19 Among the families of priests, the following were found to have married foreign wives:

The family of Jeshua son of Jozadak and his brothers: Maaseiah, Eliezer, Jarib, and Gedaliah. They all promised to divorce their wives and sealed it with a handshake. For their guilt they brought a ram from the flock as a Compensation-Offering.

10.20 The family of Immer: Hanani and Zebadiah.

10.21 The family of Harim: Maaseiah, Elijah, Shemaiah, Jehiel, and Uzziah.

10.22 The family of Pashhur: Elioenai, Maaseiah, Ishmael, Nethanel, Jozabad, and Elasah.

10.23 From the Levites: Jozabad, Shimei, Kelaiah—that is, Kelita—Pethahiah, Judah, and Eliezer.

10.24 From the singers: Eliashib.
From the temple security guards: Shallum, Telem, and Uri.

10.25 And from the other Israelites:
The family of Parosh: Ramiah, Izziah, Malkijah, Mijamin, Eleazar, Malkijah, and Benaiah.

10.26 The family of Elam: Mattaniah, Zechariah, Jehiel, Abdi, Jeremoth, and Elijah.

10.27 The family of Zattu: Elioenai, Eliashib, Mattaniah, Jeremoth, Zabad, and Aziza.

10.28 The family of Bebai: Jehohanan, Hananiah, Zabbai, and Athlai.

10.29 The family of Bani: Meshullam, Malluch, Adaiah, Jashub, Sheal, and Jeremoth.

10.30 The family of Pahath-Moab: Adna, Kelal, Benaiah, Maaseiah, Mattaniah, Bezalel, Binnui, and Manasseh.

10.31-32 The family of Harim: Eliezer, Ishijah, Malkijah, Shemaiah, Shimeon, Benjamin, Malluch, and Shemariah.

10.33 The family of Hashum: Mattenai, Mattattah, Zabad, Eliphelet, Jeremai, Manasseh, and Shimei.

10.34-37 The family of Bani: Maadai, Amram, Uel, Benaiah, Bedeiah, Keluhi, Vaniah, Meremoth, Eliashib, Mattaniah, Mattenai, and Jaasu.

NEW INTERNATIONAL VERSION

³⁸From the descendants of Binnui:^a
 Shimei, ³⁹Shelemiah, Nathan, Adaiah,
 ⁴⁰Macnadebai, Shashai, Sharai, ⁴¹Azarel,
 Shelemiah, Shemariah, ⁴²Shallum, Ama-
 riah and Joseph.
⁴³From the descendants of Nebo:
 Jeiel, Mattithiah, Zabad, Zebina, Jaddai,
 Joel and Benaiah.

⁴⁴All these had married foreign women, and
some of them had children by these wives.^b

THE MESSAGE

10.38-42 The family of Binnui: Shimei, Shelemiah,
 Nathan, Adaiah, Macnadebai, Shashai, Sharai,
 Azarel, Shelemiah, Shemariah, Shallum, Amari-
 ah, and Joseph.

10.43 The family of Nebo: Jeiel, Mattithiah, Zabad,
 Zebina, Jaddai, Joel, and Benaiah.

10.44 All these had married foreign wives and
 some had also had children by them.

---

^a 37,38 See Septuagint (also 1 Esdras 9:34); Hebrew *Jaasu*
³⁸*and Bani and Binnui,*   ^b 44 Or *and they sent them away
with their children*

NEHEMIAH

NEHEMIAH

NEHEMIAH'S PRAYER

1 The words of Nehemiah son of Hacaliah:

In the month of Kislev in the twentieth year, while I was in the citadel of Susa, ²Hanani, one of my brothers, came from Judah with some other men, and I questioned them about the Jewish remnant that survived the exile, and also about Jerusalem.

³They said to me, "Those who survived the exile and are back in the province are in great trouble and disgrace. The wall of Jerusalem is broken down, and its gates have been burned with fire."

⁴When I heard these things, I sat down and wept. For some days I mourned and fasted and prayed before the God of heaven. ⁵Then I said:

"O LORD, God of heaven, the great and awesome God, who keeps his covenant of love with those who love him and obey his commands, ⁶let your ear be attentive and your eyes open to hear the prayer your servant is praying before you day and night for your servants, the people of Israel. I confess the sins we Israelites, including myself and my father's house, have committed against you. ⁷We have acted very wickedly toward you. We have not obeyed the commands, decrees and laws you gave your servant Moses.

⁸"Remember the instruction you gave your servant Moses, saying, 'If you are unfaithful, I will scatter you among the nations, ⁹but if you return to me and obey my commands, then even if your exiled people are at the farthest horizon, I will gather them from there and bring them to the place I have chosen as a dwelling for my Name.'

¹⁰"They are your servants and your people, whom you redeemed by your great strength and your mighty hand. ¹¹O Lord, let your ear be attentive to the prayer of this your servant and to the prayer of your servants who delight in revering your name. Give your servant success today by granting him favor in the presence of this man."

I was cupbearer to the king.

1 1.1-2 The memoirs of Nehemiah son of Hacaliah.

It was the month of Kislev in the twentieth year. At the time I was in the palace complex at Susa. Hanani, one of my brothers, had just arrived from Judah with some fellow Jews. I asked them about the conditions among the Jews there who had survived the exile, and about Jerusalem.

1.3 They told me, "The exile survivors who are left there in the province are in bad shape. Conditions are appalling. The wall of Jerusalem is still rubble; the city gates are still cinders."

1.4 When I heard this, I sat down and wept. I mourned for days, fasting and praying before the God-of-Heaven.

1.5-6 I said, "GOD, God-of-Heaven, the great and awesome God, loyal to his covenant and faithful to those who love him and obey his commands: Look at me, listen to me. Pay attention to this prayer of your servant that I'm praying day and night in intercession for your servants, the People of Israel, confessing the sins of the People of Israel. And I'm including myself, I and my ancestors, among those who have sinned against you.

1.7-9 "We've treated you like dirt: We haven't done what you told us, haven't followed your commands, and haven't respected the decisions you gave to Moses your servant. All the same, remember the warning you posted to your servant Moses: 'If you betray me, I'll scatter you to the four winds, but if you come back to me and do what I tell you, I'll gather up all these scattered peoples from wherever they ended up and put them back in the place I chose to mark with my Name.'

1.10-11 "Well, there they are—your servants, your people whom you so powerfully and impressively redeemed. O Master, listen to me, listen to your servant's prayer—and yes, to all your servants who delight in honoring you—and make me successful today so that I get what I want from the king."

I was cupbearer to the king.

NEW INTERNATIONAL VERSION

Artaxerxes Sends Nehemiah to Jerusalem

2 In the month of Nisan in the twentieth year of King Artaxerxes, when wine was brought for him, I took the wine and gave it to the king. I had not been sad in his presence before; ²so the king asked me, "Why does your face look so sad when you are not ill? This can be nothing but sadness of heart."

I was very much afraid, ³but I said to the king, "May the king live forever! Why should my face not look sad when the city where my fathers are buried lies in ruins, and its gates have been destroyed by fire?"

⁴The king said to me, "What is it you want?"

Then I prayed to the God of heaven, ⁵and I answered the king, "If it pleases the king and if your servant has found favor in his sight, let him send me to the city in Judah where my fathers are buried so that I can rebuild it."

⁶Then the king, with the queen sitting beside him, asked me, "How long will your journey take, and when will you get back?" It pleased the king to send me; so I set a time.

⁷I also said to him, "If it pleases the king, may I have letters to the governors of Trans-Euphrates, so that they will provide me safe-conduct until I arrive in Judah? ⁸And may I have a letter to Asaph, keeper of the king's forest, so he will give me timber to make beams for the gates of the citadel by the temple and for the city wall and for the residence I will occupy?" And because the gracious hand of my God was upon me, the king granted my requests. ⁹So I went to the governors of Trans-Euphrates and gave them the king's letters. The king had also sent army officers and cavalry with me.

¹⁰When Sanballat the Horonite and Tobiah the Ammonite official heard about this, they were very much disturbed that someone had come to promote the welfare of the Israelites.

Nehemiah Inspects Jerusalem's Walls

¹¹I went to Jerusalem, and after staying there three days ¹²I set out during the night with a few men. I had not told anyone what my God had put in my heart to do for Jerusalem. There were no mounts with me except the one I was riding on.

¹³By night I went out through the Valley Gate toward the Jackal*ª* Well and the Dung Gate, examining the walls of Jerusalem, which had been broken down, and its gates, which had been destroyed by fire. ¹⁴Then I moved on toward the Fountain Gate and the King's Pool, but there was not enough room for my mount to get through;

THE MESSAGE

2 It was the month of Nisan in the twentieth year of Artaxerxes the king. At the hour for serving wine I brought it in and gave it to the king. I had never been hangdog in his presence before, so he asked me, "Why the long face? You're not sick are you? Or are you depressed?"

2.1-2

That made me all the more agitated. I said, "Long live the king! And why shouldn't I be depressed when the city, the city where all my family is buried, is in ruins and the city gates have been reduced to cinders?"

2.2-3

The king then asked me, "So what do you want?"

Praying under my breath to the God-of-Heaven, I said, "If it please the king, and if the king thinks well of me, send me to Judah, to the city where my family is buried, so that I can rebuild it."

2.4-5

The king, with the queen sitting alongside him, said, "How long will your work take and when would you expect to return?"

2.6

I gave him a time, and the king gave his approval to send me.

Then I said, "If it please the king, provide me with letters to the governors across the Euphrates that authorize my travel through to Judah; and also an order to Asaph, keeper of the king's forest, to supply me with timber for the beams of The Temple fortress, the wall of the city, and the house where I'll be living."

2.7-8

The generous hand of my God was with me in this and the king gave them to me. When I met the governors across The River (the Euphrates) I showed them the king's letters. The king even sent along a cavalry escort.

2.8-9

When Sanballat the Horonite and Tobiah the Ammonite official heard about this, they were very upset, angry that anyone would come to look after the interests of the People of Israel.

2.10

"Come—Let's Build the Wall of Jerusalem"

And so I arrived in Jerusalem. After I had been there three days, I got up in the middle of the night, I and a few men who were with me. I hadn't told anyone what my God had put in my heart to do for Jerusalem. The only animal with us was the one I was riding.

2.11-12

Under cover of night I went past the Valley Gate toward the Dragon's Fountain to the Dung Gate looking over the walls of Jerusalem, which had been broken through and whose gates had been burned up. I then crossed to the Fountain Gate and headed for the King's Pool but there wasn't enough room for the donkey I was riding to get through. So I went up

2.13-16

ª 13 Or Serpent or Fig

NEW INTERNATIONAL VERSION

¹⁵so I went up the valley by night, examining the wall. Finally, I turned back and reentered through the Valley Gate. ¹⁶The officials did not know where I had gone or what I was doing, because as yet I had said nothing to the Jews or the priests or nobles or officials or any others who would be doing the work.

¹⁷Then I said to them, "You see the trouble we are in: Jerusalem lies in ruins, and its gates have been burned with fire. Come, let us rebuild the wall of Jerusalem, and we will no longer be in disgrace." ¹⁸I also told them about the gracious hand of my God upon me and what the king had said to me.

They replied, "Let us start rebuilding." So they began this good work.

¹⁹But when Sanballat the Horonite, Tobiah the Ammonite official and Geshem the Arab heard about it, they mocked and ridiculed us. "What is this you are doing?" they asked. "Are you rebelling against the king?"

²⁰I answered them by saying, "The God of heaven will give us success. We his servants will start rebuilding, but as for you, you have no share in Jerusalem or any claim or historic right to it."

BUILDERS OF THE WALL

3 Eliashib the high priest and his fellow priests went to work and rebuilt the Sheep Gate. They dedicated it and set its doors in place, building as far as the Tower of the Hundred, which they dedicated, and as far as the Tower of Hananel. ²The men of Jericho built the adjoining section, and Zaccur son of Imri built next to them.

³The Fish Gate was rebuilt by the sons of Hassenaah. They laid its beams and put its doors and bolts and bars in place. ⁴Meremoth son of Uriah, the son of Hakkoz, repaired the next section. Next to him Meshullam son of Berekiah, the son of Meshezabel, made repairs, and next to him Zadok son of Baana also made repairs. ⁵The next section was repaired by the men of Tekoa, but their nobles would not put their shoulders to the work under their supervisors. ᵃ

⁶The Jeshanah ᵇ Gate was repaired by Joiada son of Paseah and Meshullam son of Besodeiah. They laid its beams and put its doors and bolts and bars in place. ⁷Next to them, repairs were made by men from Gibeon and Mizpah—Melatiah of Gibeon and Jadon of Meronoth—places under the authority of the governor of Trans-Euphrates. ⁸Uzziel son of Harhaiah, one of the goldsmiths, repaired the next section; and Hana-

ᵃ *5 Or their Lord or the governor*   ᵇ *6 Or Old*

THE MESSAGE

the valley in the dark continuing my inspection of the wall. I came back in through the Valley Gate. The local officials had no idea where I'd gone or what I was doing—I hadn't breathed a word to the Jews, priests, nobles, local officials, or anyone else who would be working on the job.

2.17-18 Then I gave them my report: "Face it: we're in a bad way here. Jerusalem is a wreck; its gates are burned up. Come—let's build the wall of Jerusalem and not live with this disgrace any longer." I told them how God was supporting me and how the king was backing me up.

They said, "We're with you. Let's get started." They rolled up their sleeves, ready for the good work.

2.19 When Sanballat the Horonite, Tobiah the Ammonite official, and Geshem the Arab heard about it, they laughed at us, mocking, "Ha! What do you think you're doing? Do you think you can cross the king?"

2.20 I shot back, "The God-of-Heaven will make sure we succeed. We're his servants and we're going to work, rebuilding. You can keep your nose out of it. You get no say in this—Jerusalem's none of your business!"

✝

3.1-2 **3** The high priest Eliashib and his fellow priests were up and at it: They went to work on the Sheep Gate; they repaired it and hung its doors, continuing on as far as the Tower of the Hundred and the Tower of Hananel. The men of Jericho worked alongside them; and next to them, Zaccur son of Imri.

3.3-5 The Fish Gate was built by the Hassenaah brothers; they repaired it, hung its doors, and installed its bolts and bars. Meremoth son of Uriah, the son of Hakkoz, worked; next to him Meshullam son of Berekiah, the son of Meshezabel; next to him Zadok son of Baana; and next to him the Tekoites (except for their nobles, who wouldn't work with their master and refused to get their hands dirty with such work).

3.6-8 The Jeshanah Gate was rebuilt by Joiada son of Paseah and Meshullam son of Besodeiah; they repaired it, hung its doors, and installed its bolts and bars. Melatiah the Gibeonite, Jadon the Meronothite, and the men of Gibeon and Mizpah, which was under the rule of the governor from across the Euphrates, worked alongside them. Uzziel son of Harhaiah of the goldsmiths' guild worked next to him, and next

NEW INTERNATIONAL VERSION

niah, one of the perfume-makers, made repairs next to that. They restored[a] Jerusalem as far as the Broad Wall. [9]Rephaiah son of Hur, ruler of a half-district of Jerusalem, repaired the next section. [10]Adjoining this, Jedaiah son of Harumaph made repairs opposite his house, and Hattush son of Hashabneiah made repairs next to him. [11]Malkijah son of Harim and Hasshub son of Pahath-Moab repaired another section and the Tower of the Ovens. [12]Shallum son of Hallohesh, ruler of a half-district of Jerusalem, repaired the next section with the help of his daughters.

[13]The Valley Gate was repaired by Hanun and the residents of Zanoah. They rebuilt it and put its doors and bolts and bars in place. They also repaired five hundred yards[b] of the wall as far as the Dung Gate.

[14]The Dung Gate was repaired by Malkijah son of Recab, ruler of the district of Beth Hakkerem. He rebuilt it and put its doors and bolts and bars in place.

[15]The Fountain Gate was repaired by Shallun son of Col-Hozeh, ruler of the district of Mizpah. He rebuilt it, roofing it over and putting its doors and bolts and bars in place. He also repaired the wall of the Pool of Siloam,[c] by the King's Garden, as far as the steps going down from the City of David. [16]Beyond him, Nehemiah son of Azbuk, ruler of a half-district of Beth Zur, made repairs up to a point opposite the tombs[d] of David, as far as the artificial pool and the House of the Heroes.

[17]Next to him, the repairs were made by the Levites under Rehum son of Bani. Beside him, Hashabiah, ruler of half the district of Keilah, carried out repairs for his district. [18]Next to him, the repairs were made by their countrymen under Binnui[e] son of Henadad, ruler of the other half-district of Keilah. [19]Next to him, Ezer son of Jeshua, ruler of Mizpah, repaired another section, from a point facing the ascent to the armory as far as the angle. [20]Next to him, Baruch son of Zabbai zealously repaired another section, from the angle to the entrance of the house of Eliashib the high priest. [21]Next to him, Meremoth son of Uriah, the son of Hakkoz, repaired another section, from the entrance of Eliashib's house to the end of it.

[22]The repairs next to him were made by the priests from the surrounding region. [23]Beyond

THE MESSAGE

to him Hananiah, one of the perfumers. They rebuilt the wall of Jerusalem as far as the Broad Wall.

[3.9-10] The next section was worked on by Rephaiah son of Hur, mayor of a half-district of Jerusalem. Next to him Jedaiah son of Harumaph rebuilt the front of his house; Hattush son of Hashabneiah worked next to him.

[3.11-12] Malkijah son of Harim and Hasshub son of Pahath-Moab rebuilt another section that included the Tower of Furnaces. Working next to him was Shallum son of Hallohesh, mayor of the other half-district of Jerusalem, along with his daughters.

[3.13] The Valley Gate was rebuilt by Hanun and villagers of Zanoah; they repaired it, hung its doors, and installed its bolts and bars. They went on to repair 1,500 feet of the wall, as far as the Dung Gate.

[3.14] The Dung Gate itself was rebuilt by Malkijah son of Recab, the mayor of the district of Beth Hakkerem; he repaired it, hung its doors, and installed its bolts and bars.

[3.15] The Fountain Gate was rebuilt by Shallun son of Col-Hozeh, mayor of the Mizpah district; he repaired it, roofed it, hung its doors, and installed its bolts and bars. He also rebuilt the wall of the Pool of Siloam at the King's Garden as far as the steps that go down from the City of David.

[3.16] After him came Nehemiah son of Azbuk, mayor of half the district of Beth Zur. He worked from just in front of the Tomb of David as far as the Pool and the House of Heroes.

[3.17-18] Levites under Rehum son of Bani were next in line. Alongside them, Hashabiah, mayor of half the district of Keilah, represented his district in the rebuilding. Next to him their brothers continued the rebuilding under Binnui son of Henadad, mayor of the other half-district of Keilah.

[3.19-23] The section from in front of the Ascent to the Armory as far as the Angle was rebuilt by Ezer son of Jeshua, the mayor of Mizpah. From the Angle to the door of the house of Eliashib the high priest was done by Baruch son of Zabbai. Meremoth son of Uriah, the son of Hakkoz, took it from the door of Eliashib's house to the end of Eliashib's house. Priests from the neighborhood went on from there. Benjamin

---

[a] 8 Or *They left out part of*   [b] 13 Hebrew *a thousand cubits* (about 450 meters)   [c] 15 Hebrew *Shelah,* a variant of *Shiloah,* that is, Siloam   [d] 16 Hebrew; Septuagint, some Vulgate manuscripts and Syriac *tomb*   [e] 18 Two Hebrew manuscripts and Syriac (see also Septuagint and verse 24); most Hebrew manuscripts *Bavvai*

NEW INTERNATIONAL VERSION

them, Benjamin and Hasshub made repairs in front of their house; and next to them, Azariah son of Maaseiah, the son of Ananiah, made repairs beside his house. 24Next to him, Binnui son of Henadad repaired another section, from Azariah's house to the angle and the corner, 25and Palal son of Uzai worked opposite the angle and the tower projecting from the upper palace near the court of the guard. Next to him, Pedaiah son of Parosh 26and the temple servants living on the hill of Ophel made repairs up to a point opposite the Water Gate toward the east and the projecting tower. 27Next to them, the men of Tekoa repaired another section, from the great projecting tower to the wall of Ophel.

28Above the Horse Gate, the priests made repairs, each in front of his own house. 29Next to them, Zadok son of Immer made repairs opposite his house. Next to him, Shemaiah son of Shecaniah, the guard at the East Gate, made repairs. 30Next to him, Hananiah son of Shelemiah, and Hanun, the sixth son of Zalaph, repaired another section. Next to them, Meshullam son of Berekiah made repairs opposite his living quarters. 31Next to him, Malkijah, one of the goldsmiths, made repairs as far as the house of the temple servants and the merchants, opposite the Inspection Gate, and as far as the room above the corner; 32and between the room above the corner and the Sheep Gate the goldsmiths and merchants made repairs.

OPPOSITION TO THE REBUILDING

4 When Sanballat heard that we were rebuilding the wall, he became angry and was greatly incensed. He ridiculed the Jews, 2and in the presence of his associates and the army of Samaria, he said, "What are those feeble Jews doing? Will they restore their wall? Will they offer sacrifices? Will they finish in a day? Can they bring the stones back to life from those heaps of rubble—burned as they are?"

3Tobiah the Ammonite, who was at his side, said, "What they are building—if even a fox climbed up on it, he would break down their wall of stones!"

4Hear us, O our God, for we are despised. Turn their insults back on their own heads. Give them over as plunder in a land of captivity. 5Do not cover up their guilt or blot out their sins from your sight, for they have thrown insults in the face ofᵃ the builders.

6So we rebuilt the wall till all of it reached

ᵃ 5 Or have provoked you to anger before

THE MESSAGE

and Hasshub worked on the wall in front of their house, and Azariah son of Maaseiah, the son of Ananiah, did the work alongside his house.

3.24-27 The section from the house of Azariah to the Angle at the Corner was rebuilt by Binnui son of Henadad. Palal son of Uzai worked opposite the Angle and the tower that projects from the Upper Palace of the king near the Court of the Guard. Next to him Pedaiah son of Parosh and The Temple support staff who lived on the hill of Ophel worked up to the point opposite the Water Gate eastward and the projecting tower. The men of Tekoa did the section from the great projecting tower as far as the wall of Ophel.

3.28-30 Above the Horse Gate the priests worked, each priest repairing the wall in front of his own house. After them Zadok son of Immer rebuilt in front of his house and after him Shemaiah son of Shecaniah, the keeper of the East Gate; then Hananiah son of Shelemiah and Hanun, the sixth son of Zalaph; then Meshullam son of Berekiah rebuilt the wall in front of his storage shed.

3.31-32 Malkijah the goldsmith repaired the wall as far as the house of The Temple support staff and merchants, up to the Inspection Gate, and the Upper Room at the Corner. The goldsmiths and the merchants made the repairs between the Upper Room at the Corner and the Sheep Gate.

"I STATIONED ARMED GUARDS"

4.1-2 4 When Sanballat heard that we were rebuilding the wall he exploded in anger, vilifying the Jews. In the company of his Samaritan cronies and military he let loose: "What are these miserable Jews doing? Do they think they can get everything back to normal overnight? Make building stones out of make-believe?"

4.3 At his side, Tobiah the Ammonite jumped in and said, "That's right! What do they think they're building? Why, if a fox climbed that wall, it would fall to pieces under his weight."

4.4-5 Nehemiah prayed, "Oh listen to us, dear God. We're so despised: Boomerang their ridicule on their heads; have their enemies cart them off as war trophies to a land of no return; don't forgive their iniquity, don't wipe away their sin—they've insulted the builders!"

4.6 We kept at it, repairing and rebuilding the wall. The whole wall was soon joined together

NEW INTERNATIONAL VERSION

half its height, for the people worked with all their heart.

7But when Sanballat, Tobiah, the Arabs, the Ammonites and the men of Ashdod heard that the repairs to Jerusalem's walls had gone ahead and that the gaps were being closed, they were very angry. 8They all plotted together to come and fight against Jerusalem and stir up trouble against it. 9But we prayed to our God and posted a guard day and night to meet this threat.

10Meanwhile, the people in Judah said, "The strength of the laborers is giving out, and there is so much rubble that we cannot rebuild the wall."

11Also our enemies said, "Before they know it or see us, we will be right there among them and will kill them and put an end to the work."

12Then the Jews who lived near them came and told us ten times over, "Wherever you turn, they will attack us."

13Therefore I stationed some of the people behind the lowest points of the wall at the exposed places, posting them by families, with their swords, spears and bows. 14After I looked things over, I stood up and said to the nobles, the officials and the rest of the people, "Don't be afraid of them. Remember the Lord, who is great and awesome, and fight for your brothers, your sons and your daughters, your wives and your homes."

15When our enemies heard that we were aware of their plot and that God had frustrated it, we all returned to the wall, each to his own work.

16From that day on, half of my men did the work, while the other half were equipped with spears, shields, bows and armor. The officers posted themselves behind all the people of Judah 17who were building the wall. Those who carried materials did their work with one hand and held a weapon in the other, 18and each of the builders wore his sword at his side as he worked. But the man who sounded the trumpet stayed with me.

19Then I said to the nobles, the officials and the rest of the people, "The work is extensive and spread out, and we are widely separated from each other along the wall. 20Wherever you hear the sound of the trumpet, join us there. Our God will fight for us!"

21So we continued the work with half the men holding spears, from the first light of dawn till the stars came out. 22At that time I also said to the people, "Have every man and his helper stay inside Jerusalem at night, so they can serve us as guards by night and workmen by day."

THE MESSAGE

and halfway to its intended height because the people had a heart for the work.

4:7-9 When Sanballat, Tobiah, the Arabs, the Ammonites, and the Ashdodites heard that the repairs of the walls of Jerusalem were going so well—that the breaks in the wall were being fixed—they were absolutely furious. They put their heads together and decided to fight against Jerusalem and create as much trouble as they could. We countered with prayer to our God and set a round-the-clock guard against them.

4:10 But soon word was going around in Judah,

The builders are pooped,
   the rubbish piles up;
We're in over our heads,
   we can't build this wall.

4:11-12 And all this time our enemies were saying, "They won't know what hit them. Before they know it we'll be at their throats, killing them right and left. *That* will put a stop to the work!" The Jews who were their neighbors kept reporting, "They have us surrounded; they're going to attack!" If we heard it once, we heard it ten times.

4:13-14 So I stationed armed guards at the most vulnerable places of the wall and assigned people by families with their swords, lances, and bows. After looking things over I stood up and spoke to the nobles, officials, and everyone else: "Don't be afraid of them. Put your minds on the Master, great and awesome, and then fight for your brothers, your sons, your daughters, your wives, and your homes."

4:15-18 Our enemies learned that we knew all about their plan and that God had frustrated it. And we went back to the wall and went to work. From then on half of my young men worked while the other half stood guard with lances, shields, bows, and mail armor. Military officers served as backup for everyone in Judah who was at work rebuilding the wall. The common laborers held a tool in one hand and a spear in the other. Each of the builders had a sword strapped to his side as he worked. I kept the trumpeter at my side to sound the alert.

4:19-20 Then I spoke to the nobles and officials and everyone else: "There's a lot of work going on and we are spread out all along the wall, separated from each other. When you hear the trumpet call, join us there; our God will fight for us."

4:21 And so we kept working, from first light until the stars came out, half of us holding lances.

4:22 I also instructed the people, "Each person and his helper is to stay inside Jerusalem— guards by night and workmen by day."

NEW INTERNATIONAL VERSION

²³Neither I nor my brothers nor my men nor the guards with me took off our clothes; each had his weapon, even when he went for water. *a*

Nehemiah Helps the Poor

5 Now the men and their wives raised a great outcry against their Jewish brothers. ²Some were saying, "We and our sons and daughters are numerous; in order for us to eat and stay alive, we must get grain."

³Others were saying, "We are mortgaging our fields, our vineyards and our homes to get grain during the famine."

⁴Still others were saying, "We have had to borrow money to pay the king's tax on our fields and vineyards. ⁵Although we are of the same flesh and blood as our countrymen and though our sons are as good as theirs, yet we have to subject our sons and daughters to slavery. Some of our daughters have already been enslaved, but we are powerless, because our fields and our vineyards belong to others."

⁶When I heard their outcry and these charges, I was very angry. ⁷I pondered them in my mind and then accused the nobles and officials. I told them, "You are exacting usury from your own countrymen!" So I called together a large meeting to deal with them ⁸and said: "As far as possible, we have bought back our Jewish brothers who were sold to the Gentiles. Now you are selling your brothers, only for them to be sold back to us!" They kept quiet, because they could find nothing to say.

⁹So I continued, "What you are doing is not right. Shouldn't you walk in the fear of our God to avoid the reproach of our Gentile enemies? ¹⁰I and my brothers and my men are also lending the people money and grain. But let the exacting of usury stop! ¹¹Give back to them immediately their fields, vineyards, olive groves and houses, and also the usury you are charging them—the hundredth part of the money, grain, new wine and oil."

¹²"We will give it back," they said. "And we will not demand anything more from them. We will do as you say."

Then I summoned the priests and made the nobles and officials take an oath to do what they had promised. ¹³I also shook out the folds of my robe and said, "In this way may God shake out of his house and possessions every man who does not keep this promise. So may such a man be shaken out and emptied!"

At this the whole assembly said, "Amen," and

THE MESSAGE

4.23 We all slept in our clothes—I, my brothers, my workmen, and the guards backing me up. And each one kept his spear in his hand, even when getting water.

The "Great Protest"

5.1-2 5 A great protest was mounted by the people, including the wives, against their fellow Jews. Some said, "We have big families, and we need food just to survive."

5.3 Others said, "We're having to mortgage our fields and vineyards and homes to get enough grain to keep from starving."

5.4-5 And others said, "We're having to borrow money to pay the royal tax on our fields and vineyards. Look: We're the same flesh and blood as our brothers here; our children are just as good as theirs. Yet here we are having to sell our children off as slaves—some of our daughters have already been sold—and we can't do anything about it because our fields and vineyards are owned by somebody else."

5.6-7 I got really angry when I heard their protest and complaints. After thinking it over, I called the nobles and officials on the carpet. I said, "Each one of you is gouging his brother."

5.7-8 Then I called a big meeting to deal with them. I told them, "We did everything we could to buy back our Jewish brothers who had to sell themselves as slaves to foreigners. And now you're selling these same brothers back into debt slavery! Does that mean that we have to buy them back again?"

They said nothing. What could they say?

5.9 "What you're doing is wrong. Is there no fear of God left in you? Don't you care what the nations around here, our enemies, think of you?

5.10-11 "I and my brothers and the people working for me have also loaned them money. But this gouging them with interest has to stop. Give them back their foreclosed fields, vineyards, olive groves, and homes right now. And forgive your claims on their money, grain, new wine, and olive oil."

5.12-13 They said, "We'll give it all back. We won't make any more demands on them. We'll do everything you say."

Then I called the priests together and made them promise to keep their word. Then I emptied my pockets, turning them inside out, and said, "So may God empty the pockets and house of everyone who doesn't keep this promise—turned inside out and emptied."

Everyone gave a wholehearted "Yes, we'll do

---

a 23 The meaning of the Hebrew for this clause is uncertain.

NEW INTERNATIONAL VERSION

praised the LORD. And the people did as they had promised.

[14]Moreover, from the twentieth year of King Artaxerxes, when I was appointed to be their governor in the land of Judah, until his thirty-second year—twelve years—neither I nor my brothers ate the food allotted to the governor. [15]But the earlier governors—those preceding me—placed a heavy burden on the people and took forty shekels[a] of silver from them in addition to food and wine. Their assistants also lorded it over the people. But out of reverence for God I did not act like that. [16]Instead, I devoted myself to the work on this wall. All my men were assembled there for the work; we[b] did not acquire any land.

[17]Furthermore, a hundred and fifty Jews and officials ate at my table, as well as those who came to us from the surrounding nations. [18]Each day one ox, six choice sheep and some poultry were prepared for me, and every ten days an abundant supply of wine of all kinds. In spite of all this, I never demanded the food allotted to the governor, because the demands were heavy on these people.

[19]Remember me with favor, O my God, for all I have done for these people.

FURTHER OPPOSITION TO THE REBUILDING

6 When word came to Sanballat, Tobiah, Geshem the Arab and the rest of our enemies that I had rebuilt the wall and not a gap was left in it—though up to that time I had not set the doors in the gates— [2]Sanballat and Geshem sent me this message: "Come, let us meet together in one of the villages[c] on the plain of Ono."

But they were scheming to harm me; [3]so I sent messengers to them with this reply: "I am carrying on a great project and cannot go down. Why should the work stop while I leave it and go down to you?" [4]Four times they sent me the same message, and each time I gave them the same answer.

[5]Then, the fifth time, Sanballat sent his aide to me with the same message, and in his hand was an unsealed letter [6]in which was written:

"It is reported among the nations—and Geshem[d] says it is true—that you and the Jews are plotting to revolt, and therefore you are building the wall. Moreover, ac-

THE MESSAGE

it!" and praised GOD. And the people did what they promised.

"REMEMBER IN MY FAVOR, O MY GOD"

[5.14-16] From the time King Artaxerxes appointed me as their governor in the land of Judah—from the twentieth to the thirty-second year of his reign, twelve years—neither I nor my brothers used the governor's food allowance. Governors who had preceded me had oppressed the people by taxing them forty shekels of silver (about a pound) a day for food and wine while their underlings bullied the people unmercifully. But out of fear of God I did none of that. I had work to do; I worked on this wall. All my men were on the job to do the work. We didn't have time to line our own pockets.

[5.17-18] I fed one hundred and fifty Jews and officials at my table in addition to those who showed up from the surrounding nations. One ox, six choice sheep, and some chickens were prepared for me daily, and every ten days a large supply of wine was delivered. Even so, I didn't use the food allowance provided for the governor—the people had it hard enough as it was.

[5.19] Remember in my favor, O my God,
Everything I've done for these people.

"I'M DOING A GREAT WORK; I CAN'T COME DOWN"

[6.1-2] **6** When Sanballat, Tobiah, Geshem the Arab, and the rest of our enemies heard that I had rebuilt the wall and that there were no more breaks in it—even though I hadn't yet installed the gates—Sanballat and Geshem sent this message: "Come and meet with us at Kephirim in the valley of Ono."

[6.2-3] I knew they were scheming to hurt me so I sent messengers back with this: "I'm doing a great work; I can't come down. Why should the work come to a standstill just so I can come down to see you?"

[6.4] Four times they sent this message and four times I gave them my answer.

[6.5-6] The fifth time—same messenger, same message—Sanballat sent an unsealed letter with this message:

[6.6-7] "The word is out among the nations—and Geshem says it's true—that you and the Jews are planning to rebel. That's why you are rebuilding the wall. The word is that you want to

---

[a] 15 That is, about 1 pound (about 0.5 kilogram)
[b] 16 Most Hebrew manuscripts; some Hebrew manuscripts, Septuagint, Vulgate and Syriac I   [c] 2 Or in Kephirim
[d] 6 Hebrew Gashmu, a variant of Geshem

NEW INTERNATIONAL VERSION

cording to these reports you are about to become their king [7]and have even appointed prophets to make this proclamation about you in Jerusalem: 'There is a king in Judah!' Now this report will get back to the king; so come, let us confer together."

[8]I sent him this reply: "Nothing like what you are saying is happening; you are just making it up out of your head."

[9]They were all trying to frighten us, thinking, "Their hands will get too weak for the work, and it will not be completed."

ʟBut I prayed,ʜ "Now strengthen my hands."

[10]One day I went to the house of Shemaiah son of Delaiah, the son of Mehetabel, who was shut in at his home. He said, "Let us meet in the house of God, inside the temple, and let us close the temple doors, because men are coming to kill you—by night they are coming to kill you."

[11]But I said, "Should a man like me run away? Or should one like me go into the temple to save his life? I will not go!" [12]I realized that God had not sent him, but that he had prophesied against me because Tobiah and Sanballat had hired him. [13]He had been hired to intimidate me so that I would commit a sin by doing this, and then they would give me a bad name to discredit me.

[14]Remember Tobiah and Sanballat, O my God, because of what they have done; remember also the prophetess Noadiah and the rest of the prophets who have been trying to intimidate me.

THE COMPLETION OF THE WALL

[15]So the wall was completed on the twenty-fifth of Elul, in fifty-two days. [16]When all our enemies heard about this, all the surrounding nations were afraid and lost their self-confidence, because they realized that this work had been done with the help of our God.

[17]Also, in those days the nobles of Judah were sending many letters to Tobiah, and replies from Tobiah kept coming to them. [18]For many in Judah were under oath to him, since he was son-in-law to Shecaniah son of Arah, and his son Jehohanan had married the daughter of Meshullam son of Berekiah. [19]Moreover, they kept reporting to me his good deeds and then telling him what I said. And Tobiah sent letters to intimidate me.

THE MESSAGE

be king and that you have appointed prophets to announce in Jerusalem, 'There's a king in Judah!' The king is going to be told all this—don't you think we should sit down and have a talk?"

6.8   I sent him back this: "There's nothing to what you're saying. You've made it all up."

6.9   They were trying to intimidate us into quitting. They thought, "They'll give up; they'll never finish it."

I prayed, "Give me strength."

⸕

6.10   Then I met secretly with Shemaiah son of Delaiah, the son of Mehetabel, at his house. He said:

Let's meet at the house of God,
    inside The Temple;
Let's find safety behind locked doors
    because they're coming to kill you,
Yes, coming by night to kill you.

6.11   I said, "Why would a man like me run for cover? And why would a man like me use The Temple as a hideout? I won't do it."

6.12-13   I sensed that God hadn't sent this man. The so-called prophecy he spoke to me was the work of Tobiah and Sanballat; they had hired him. He had been hired to scare me off—trick me—a layman, into desecrating The Temple and ruining my good reputation so they could accuse me.

6.14   "O my God, don't let Tobiah and Sanballat get by with all the mischief they've done. And the same goes for the prophetess Noadiah and the other prophets who have been trying to undermine my confidence."

⸕

6.15-16   The wall was finished on the twenty-fifth day of Elul. It had taken fifty-two days. When all our enemies heard the news and all the surrounding nations saw it, our enemies totally lost their nerve. They knew that God was behind this work.

6.17-19   All during this time letters were going back and forth constantly between the nobles of Judah and Tobiah. Many of the nobles had ties to him because he was son-in-law to Shecaniah son of Arah and his son Jehohanan had married the daughter of Meshullam son of Berekiah. They kept telling me all the good things he did and then would report back to him anything I would say. And then Tobiah would send letters to intimidate me.

NEW INTERNATIONAL VERSION

7 After the wall had been rebuilt and I had set the doors in place, the gatekeepers and the singers and the Levites were appointed. ²I put in charge of Jerusalem my brother Hanani, along with*ᵃ* Hananiah the commander of the citadel, because he was a man of integrity and feared God more than most men do. ³I said to them, "The gates of Jerusalem are not to be opened until the sun is hot. While the gatekeepers are still on duty, have them shut the doors and bar them. Also appoint residents of Jerusalem as guards, some at their posts and some near their own houses."

THE LIST OF THE EXILES WHO RETURNED

⁴Now the city was large and spacious, but there were few people in it, and the houses had not yet been rebuilt. ⁵So my God put it into my heart to assemble the nobles, the officials and the common people for registration by families. I found the genealogical record of those who had been the first to return. This is what I found written there:

⁶These are the people of the province who came up from the captivity of the exiles whom Nebuchadnezzar king of Babylon had taken captive (they returned to Jerusalem and Judah, each to his own town, ⁷in company with Zerubbabel, Jeshua, Nehemiah, Azariah, Raamiah, Nahamani, Mordecai, Bilshan, Mispereth, Bigvai, Nehum and Baanah):

The list of the men of Israel:

⁸the descendants of Parosh	2,172
⁹of Shephatiah	372
¹⁰of Arah	652
¹¹of Pahath-Moab (through the line of Jeshua and Joab)	2,818
¹²of Elam	1,254
¹³of Zattu	845
¹⁴of Zaccai	760
¹⁵of Binnui	648
¹⁶of Bebai	628
¹⁷of Azgad	2,322
¹⁸of Adonikam	667
¹⁹of Bigvai	2,067
²⁰of Adin	655
²¹of Ater (through Hezekiah)	98
²²of Hashum	328
²³of Bezai	324
²⁴of Hariph	112
²⁵of Gibeon	95

THE MESSAGE

THE WALL REBUILT: NAMES AND NUMBERS

7.1-2 7 After the wall was rebuilt and I had installed the doors, and the security guards, the singers, and the Levites were appointed, I put my brother Hanani, along with Hananiah the captain of the citadel, in charge of Jerusalem because he was an honest man and feared God more than most men.

7.3 I gave them this order: "Don't open the gates of Jerusalem until the sun is up. And shut and bar the gates while the guards are still on duty. Appoint the guards from the citizens of Jerusalem and assign them to posts in front of their own homes."

7.4 The city was large and spacious with only a few people in it and the houses not yet rebuilt.

7.5 God put it in my heart to gather the nobles, the officials, and the people in general to be registered. I found the genealogical record of those who were in the first return from exile. This is the record I found:

7.6-60 These are the people of the province who returned from the captivity of the Exile, the ones Nebuchadnezzar king of Babylon had carried off captive; they came back to Jerusalem and Judah, each going to his own town. They came back in the company of Zerubbabel, Jeshua, Nehemiah, Azariah, Raamiah, Nahamani, Mordecai, Bilshan, Mispereth, Bigvai, Nehum, and Baanah.

The numbers of the men of the People of Israel by families of origin:
Parosh, 2,172
Shephatiah, 372
Arah, 652
Pahath-Moab (sons of Jeshua and Joab), 2,818
Elam, 1,254
Zattu, 845
Zaccai, 760
Binnui, 648
Bebai, 628
Azgad, 2,322
Adonikam, 667
Bigvai, 2,067
Adin, 655
Ater (sons of Hezekiah), 98
Hashum, 328
Bezai, 324
Hariph, 112
Gibeon, 95.
Israelites identified by place of origin:

ᵃ 2 Or Hanani, that is,

NEW INTERNATIONAL VERSION	THE MESSAGE

NEW INTERNATIONAL VERSION

26 the men of Bethlehem and
Netophah 188
27 of Anathoth 128
28 of Beth Azmaveth 42
29 of Kiriath Jearim, Kephirah and
Beeroth 743
30 of Ramah and Geba 621
31 of Micmash 122
32 of Bethel and Ai 123
33 of the other Nebo 52
34 of the other Elam 1,254
35 of Harim 320
36 of Jericho 345
37 of Lod, Hadid and Ono 721
38 of Senaah 3,930

39 The priests:

the descendants of Jedaiah
(through the family of Jeshua) 973
40 of Immer 1,052
41 of Pashhur 1,247
42 of Harim 1,017

43 The Levites:

the descendants of Jeshua (through
Kadmiel through the line of
Hodaviah) 74

44 The singers:

the descendants of Asaph 148

45 The gatekeepers:

the descendants of
Shallum, Ater, Talmon, Akkub,
Hatita and Shobai 138

46 The temple servants:

the descendants of
Ziha, Hasupha, Tabbaoth,
47 Keros, Sia, Padon,
48 Lebana, Hagaba, Shalmai,
49 Hanan, Giddel, Gahar,
50 Reaiah, Rezin, Nekoda,
51 Gazzam, Uzza, Paseah,
52 Besai, Meunim, Nephusim,
53 Bakbuk, Hakupha, Harhur,
54 Bazluth, Mehida, Harsha,
55 Barkos, Sisera, Temah,
56 Neziah and Hatipha

57 The descendants of the servants of Solomon:

the descendants of
Sotai, Sophereth, Perida,
58 Jaala, Darkon, Giddel,
59 Shephatiah, Hattil,
Pokereth-Hazzebaim and Amon

THE MESSAGE

Bethlehem and Netophah, 188
Anathoth, 128
Beth Azmaveth, 42
Kiriath Jearim, Kephirah, and Beeroth,
743
Ramah and Geba, 621
Micmash, 122
Bethel and Ai, 123
Nebo (the other one), 52
Elam (the other one), 1,254
Harim, 320
Jericho, 345
Lod, Hadid, and Ono, 721
Senaah, 3,930.
Priestly families:
Jedaiah (sons of Jeshua), 973
Immer, 1,052
Pashhur, 1,247
Harim, 1,017.
Levitical families:
Jeshua (sons of Kadmiel and of
Hodaviah), 74.
Singers:
Asaph's family line, 148.
Security guard families:
Shallum, Ater, Talmon, Akkub, Hatita,
and Shobai, 138.
Families of support staff:
Ziha, Hasupha, Tabbaoth,
Keros, Sia, Padon,
Lebana, Hagaba, Shalmai,
Hanan, Giddel, Gahar,
Reaiah, Rezin, Nekoda,
Gazzam, Uzza, Paseah,
Besai, Meunim, Nephussim,
Bakbuk, Hakupha, Harhur,
Bazluth, Mehida, Harsha,
Barkos, Sisera, Temah,
Neziah, and Hatipha.
Families of Solomon's servants:
Sotai, Sophereth, Perida,
Jaala, Darkon, Giddel,
Shephatiah, Hattil, Pokereth-Hazzebaim,
and Amon.

NEW INTERNATIONAL VERSION

⁶⁰The temple servants and the descendants of the servants of Solomon   392

⁶¹The following came up from the towns of Tel Melah, Tel Harsha, Kerub, Addon and Immer, but they could not show that their families were descended from Israel:

⁶²the descendants of
Delaiah, Tobiah and Nekoda   642

⁶³And from among the priests:

the descendants of
Hobaiah, Hakkoz and Barzillai (a man who had married a daughter of Barzillai the Gileadite and was called by that name).
⁶⁴These searched for their family records, but they could not find them and so were excluded from the priesthood as unclean. ⁶⁵The governor, therefore, ordered them not to eat any of the most sacred food until there should be a priest ministering with the Urim and Thummim.

⁶⁶The whole company numbered 42,360, ⁶⁷besides their 7,337 menservants and maidservants; and they also had 245 men and women singers. ⁶⁸There were 736 horses, 245 mules,ᵃ ⁶⁹435 camels and 6,720 donkeys.

⁷⁰Some of the heads of the families contributed to the work. The governor gave to the treasury 1,000 drachmasᵇ of gold, 50 bowls and 530 garments for priests. ⁷¹Some of the heads of the families gave to the treasury for the work 20,000 drachmasᶜ of gold and 2,200 minasᵈ of silver. ⁷²The total given by the rest of the people was 20,000 drachmas of gold, 2,000 minasᵉ of silver and 67 garments for priests.

⁷³The priests, the Levites, the gatekeepers, the singers and the temple servants, along with certain of the people and the rest of the Israelites, settled in their own towns.

Ezra Reads the Law

When the seventh month came and the Israelites had settled in their towns,

8 ¹all the people assembled as one man in the square before the Water Gate. They told Ezra

---

ᵃ 68 Some Hebrew manuscripts (see also Ezra 2:66); most Hebrew manuscripts do not have this verse.   ᵇ 70 That is, about 19 pounds (about 8.5 kilograms)   ᶜ 71 That is, about 375 pounds (about 170 kilograms); also in verse 72
ᵈ 71 That is, about 1 1/3 tons (about 1.2 metric tons)
ᵉ 72 That is, about 1 1/4 tons (about 1.1 metric tons)

THE MESSAGE

The Temple support staff and Solomon's servants added up to 392.

7.61-63   These are those who came from Tel Melah, Tel Harsha, Kerub, Addon, and Immer. They weren't able to prove their ancestry, whether they were true Israelites or not:

The sons of Delaiah, Tobiah, and Nekoda, 642.
Likewise with these priestly families:
The sons of Hobaiah, Hakkoz, and Barzillai, who had married a daughter of Barzillai the Gileadite and took that name.

7.64-65   They looked high and low for their family records but couldn't find them. And so they were barred from priestly work as ritually unclean. The governor ruled that they could not eat from the holy food until a priest could determine their status by using the Urim and Thummim.

7.66-69   The total count for the congregation was 42,360. That did not include the male and female slaves who numbered 7,337. There were also 245 male and female singers. And there were 736 horses, 245 mules, 435 camels, and 6,720 donkeys.

7.70-72   Some of the heads of families made voluntary offerings for the work. The governor made a gift to the treasury of 1,000 drachmas of gold (about nineteen pounds), 50 bowls, and 530 garments for the priests. Some of the heads of the families made gifts to the treasury for the work; it came to 20,000 drachmas of gold and 2,200 minas of silver (about one and a third tons). Gifts from the rest of the people totaled 20,000 drachmas of gold (about 375 pounds), 2,000 minas of silver, and 67 garments for the priests.

7.73   The priests, Levites, security guards, singers, and Temple support staff, along with some others, and the rest of the People of Israel, all found a place to live in their own towns.

Ezra and the Revelation

8.1   **8** By the time the seventh month arrived, the People of Israel were settled in their towns. Then all the people gathered as one person in the town square in front of the Water Gate and

NEW INTERNATIONAL VERSION

the scribe to bring out the Book of the Law of Moses, which the LORD had commanded for Israel.

²So on the first day of the seventh month Ezra the priest brought the Law before the assembly, which was made up of men and women and all who were able to understand. ³He read it aloud from daybreak till noon as he faced the square before the Water Gate in the presence of the men, women and others who could understand. And all the people listened attentively to the Book of the Law.

⁴Ezra the scribe stood on a high wooden platform built for the occasion. Beside him on his right stood Mattithiah, Shema, Anaiah, Uriah, Hilkiah and Maaseiah; and on his left were Pedaiah, Mishael, Malkijah, Hashum, Hashbaddanah, Zechariah and Meshullam.

⁵Ezra opened the book. All the people could see him because he was standing above them; and as he opened it, the people all stood up. ⁶Ezra praised the LORD, the great God; and all the people lifted their hands and responded, "Amen! Amen!" Then they bowed down and worshiped the LORD with their faces to the ground.

⁷The Levites—Jeshua, Bani, Sherebiah, Jamin, Akkub, Shabbethai, Hodiah, Maaseiah, Kelita, Azariah, Jozabad, Hanan and Pelaiah—instructed the people in the Law while the people were standing there. ⁸They read from the Book of the Law of God, making it clear*ᵃ* and giving the meaning so that the people could understand what was being read.

⁹Then Nehemiah the governor, Ezra the priest and scribe, and the Levites who were instructing the people said to them all, "This day is sacred to the LORD your God. Do not mourn or weep." For all the people had been weeping as they listened to the words of the Law.

¹⁰Nehemiah said, "Go and enjoy choice food and sweet drinks, and send some to those who have nothing prepared. This day is sacred to our Lord. Do not grieve, for the joy of the LORD is your strength."

¹¹The Levites calmed all the people, saying, "Be still, for this is a sacred day. Do not grieve."

¹²Then all the people went away to eat and drink, to send portions of food and to celebrate with great joy, because they now understood the words that had been made known to them.

¹³On the second day of the month, the heads of all the families, along with the priests and the

THE MESSAGE

asked the scholar Ezra to bring the Book of The Revelation of Moses that GOD had commanded for Israel.

8.2-3   So Ezra the priest brought The Revelation to the congregation, which was made up of both men and women—everyone capable of understanding. It was the first day of the seventh month. He read it facing the town square at the Water Gate from early dawn until noon in the hearing of the men and women, all who could understand it. And all the people listened—they were all ears—to the Book of The Revelation.

8.4   The scholar Ezra stood on a wooden platform constructed for the occasion. He was flanked on the right by Mattithiah, Shema, Anaiah, Uriah, Hilkiah, and Maaseiah, and on the left by Pedaiah, Mishael, Malkijah, Hashum, Hashbaddanah, Zechariah, and Meshullam.

8.5-6   Ezra opened the book. Every eye was on him (he was standing on the raised platform) and as he opened the book everyone stood. Then Ezra praised GOD, the great God, and all the people responded, "Oh Yes! Yes!" with hands raised high. And then they fell to their knees in worship of GOD, their faces to the ground.

8.7-8   Jeshua, Bani, Sherebiah, Jamin, Akkub, Shabbethai, Hodiah, Maaseiah, Kelita, Azariah, Jozabad, Hanan, and Pelaiah, all Levites, explained The Revelation while people stood, listening respectfully. They translated the Book of The Revelation of God so the people could understand it and then explained the reading.

8.9   Nehemiah the governor, along with Ezra the priest and scholar and the Levites who were teaching the people, said to all the people, "This day is holy to GOD, your God. Don't weep and carry on." They said this because all the people were weeping as they heard the words of The Revelation.

8.10   He continued, "Go home and prepare a feast, holiday food and drink; and share it with those who don't have anything: This day is holy to God. Don't feel bad. The joy of GOD is your strength!"

8.11   The Levites calmed the people, "Quiet now. This is a holy day. Don't be upset."

8.12   So the people went off to feast, eating and drinking and including the poor in a great celebration. Now they got it; they understood the reading that had been given to them.

✠

8.13-15   On the second day of the month the family heads of all the people, the priests, and the Le-

---

ᵃ8 Or *God, translating it*

NEW INTERNATIONAL VERSION

Levites, gathered around Ezra the scribe to give attention to the words of the Law. [14]They found written in the Law, which the LORD had commanded through Moses, that the Israelites were to live in booths during the feast of the seventh month [15]and that they should proclaim this word and spread it throughout their towns and in Jerusalem: "Go out into the hill country and bring back branches from olive and wild olive trees, and from myrtles, palms and shade trees, to make booths"—as it is written.[a]

[16]So the people went out and brought back branches and built themselves booths on their own roofs, in their courtyards, in the courts of the house of God and in the square by the Water Gate and the one by the Gate of Ephraim. [17]The whole company that had returned from exile built booths and lived in them. From the days of Joshua son of Nun until that day, the Israelites had not celebrated it like this. And their joy was very great.

[18]Day after day, from the first day to the last, Ezra read from the Book of the Law of God. They celebrated the feast for seven days, and on the eighth day, in accordance with the regulation, there was an assembly.

THE ISRAELITES CONFESS THEIR SINS

9 On the twenty-fourth day of the same month, the Israelites gathered together, fasting and wearing sackcloth and having dust on their heads. [2]Those of Israelite descent had separated themselves from all foreigners. They stood in their places and confessed their sins and the wickedness of their fathers. [3]They stood where they were and read from the Book of the Law of the LORD their God for a quarter of the day, and spent another quarter in confession and in worshiping the LORD their God. [4]Standing on the stairs were the Levites—Jeshua, Bani, Kadmiel, Shebaniah, Bunni, Sherebiah, Bani and Kenani—who called with loud voices to the LORD their God. [5]And the Levites—Jeshua, Kadmiel, Bani, Hashabneiah, Sherebiah, Hodiah, Shebaniah and Pethahiah—said: "Stand up and praise the LORD your God, who is from everlasting to everlasting.[b]"

"Blessed be your glorious name, and may it be exalted above all blessing and praise. [6]You alone are the LORD. You made the heavens, even the highest heavens, and all their starry host, the earth and all that is on it, the seas and all that is in them. You

THE MESSAGE

vites gathered around Ezra the scholar to get a deeper understanding of the words of The Revelation. They found written in The Revelation that GOD commanded through Moses that the People of Israel are to live in booths during the festival of the seventh month. So they published this decree and had it posted in all their cities and in Jerusalem: "Go into the hills and collect olive branches, pine branches, myrtle branches, palm branches, and any other leafy branches to make booths, as it is written."

☩

8.16-17 So the people went out, brought in branches, and made themselves booths on their roofs, courtyards, the courtyards of The Temple of God, the Water Gate plaza, and the Ephraim Gate plaza. The entire congregation that had come back from exile made booths and lived in them. The People of Israel hadn't done this from the time of Joshua son of Nun until that very day—a terrific day! Great joy!

8.18 Ezra read from the Book of The Revelation of God each day, from the first to the last day—they celebrated the feast for seven days. On the eighth day they held a solemn assembly in accordance with the decree.

9.1-3 **9** Then on the twenty-fourth day of this month, the People of Israel gathered for a fast, wearing burlap and faces smudged with dirt as signs of repentance. The Israelites broke off all relations with foreigners, stood up, and confessed their sins and the iniquities of their parents. While they stood there in their places, they read from the Book of The Revelation of GOD, their God, for a quarter of the day. For another quarter of the day they confessed and worshiped their GOD.

9.4-5 A group of Levites—Jeshua, Bani, Kadmiel, Shebaniah, Bunni, Sherebiah, Bani, and Kenani—stood on the platform and cried out to GOD, their God, in a loud voice. The Levites Jeshua, Kadmiel, Bani, Hashabneiah, Sherebiah, Hodiah, Shebaniah, and Pethahiah said, "On your feet! Bless GOD, your God, for ever and ever!"

9.5-6 Blessed be your glorious name,
    exalted above all blessing and praise!
You're the one,
    GOD, you alone;
You made the heavens,
    the heavens of heavens, and all angels;
The earth and everything on it,
    the seas and everything in them;

---

[a] 15 See Lev. 23:37-40.   [b] 5 Or God for ever and ever

NEW INTERNATIONAL VERSION

give life to everything, and the multitudes of heaven worship you.

⁷"You are the LORD God, who chose Abram and brought him out of Ur of the Chaldeans and named him Abraham. ⁸You found his heart faithful to you, and you made a covenant with him to give to his descendants the land of the Canaanites, Hittites, Amorites, Perizzites, Jebusites and Girgashites. You have kept your promise because you are righteous.

⁹"You saw the suffering of our forefathers in Egypt; you heard their cry at the Red Sea.ᵃ ¹⁰You sent miraculous signs and wonders against Pharaoh, against all his officials and all the people of his land, for you knew how arrogantly the Egyptians treated them. You made a name for yourself, which remains to this day. ¹¹You divided the sea before them, so that they passed through it on dry ground, but you hurled their pursuers into the depths, like a stone into mighty waters. ¹²By day you led them with a pillar of cloud, and by night with a pillar of fire to give them light on the way they were to take.

¹³"You came down on Mount Sinai; you spoke to them from heaven. You gave them regulations and laws that are just and right, and decrees and commands that are good. ¹⁴You made known to them your holy Sabbath and gave them commands, decrees and laws through your servant Moses. ¹⁵In their hunger you gave them bread from heaven and in their thirst you brought them water from the rock; you told them to go in and take possession of the land you had sworn with uplifted hand to give them.

¹⁶"But they, our forefathers, became arrogant and stiff-necked, and did not obey your commands. ¹⁷They refused to listen and failed to remember the miracles you performed among them. They became stiff-necked and in their rebellion appointed a

ᵃ 9 Hebrew *Yam Suph*; that is, Sea of Reeds

THE MESSAGE

You keep them all alive;
   heaven's angels worship you!

9.7-8 You're the one, GOD, *the* God
   who chose Abram
And brought him from Ur of the Chaldees
   and changed his name to Abraham.
You found his heart to be steady and true to
   you
   and signed a covenant with him,
A covenant to give him the land of the
   Canaanites,
   the Hittites, and the Amorites,
The Perizzites, Jebusites, and Girgashites,
   —to give it to his descendants.
And you kept your word
   because you are righteous.

9.9-15 You saw the anguish of our parents in Egypt.
   You heard their cries at the Red Sea;
You amazed Pharaoh, his servants, and the
   people of his land
   with wonders and miracle-signs.
You knew their bullying arrogance against
   your people;
   you made a name for yourself that lasts to
     this day.
You split the sea before them;
   they crossed through and never got their
     feet wet;
You pitched their pursuers into the deep;
   they sank like a rock in the storm-tossed
     sea.
By day you led them with a Pillar of Cloud,
   and by night with a Pillar of Fire
To show them the way
   they were to travel.
You came down onto Mount Sinai,
   you spoke to them out of heaven;
You gave them instructions on how to live
   well,
   true teaching, sound rules and commands;
You introduced them
   to your Holy Sabbath;
Through your servant Moses you decreed
   commands, rules, and instruction.
You gave bread from heaven for their hunger,
   you sent water from the rock for their
     thirst.

9.16-19 You told them to enter and take the land,
   which you promised to give them.

But they, our ancestors, were arrogant;
   bullheaded, they wouldn't obey your
     commands.
They turned a deaf ear, they refused
   to remember the miracles you had done for
     them;
They turned stubborn, got it into their heads

NEW INTERNATIONAL VERSION

leader in order to return to their slavery. But you are a forgiving God, gracious and compassionate, slow to anger and abounding in love. Therefore you did not desert them, [18]even when they cast for themselves an image of a calf and said, 'This is your god, who brought you up out of Egypt,' or when they committed awful blasphemies.

[19]"Because of your great compassion you did not abandon them in the desert. By day the pillar of cloud did not cease to guide them on their path, nor the pillar of fire by night to shine on the way they were to take. [20]You gave your good Spirit to instruct them. You did not withhold your manna from their mouths, and you gave them water for their thirst. [21]For forty years you sustained them in the desert; they lacked nothing, their clothes did not wear out nor did their feet become swollen.

[22]"You gave them kingdoms and nations, allotting to them even the remotest frontiers. They took over the country of Sihon[a] king of Heshbon and the country of Og king of Bashan. [23]You made their sons as numerous as the stars in the sky, and you brought them into the land that you told their fathers to enter and possess. [24]Their sons went in and took possession of the land. You subdued before them the Canaanites, who lived in the land; you handed the Canaanites over to them, along with their kings and the peoples of the land, to deal with them as they pleased. [25]They captured fortified cities and fertile land; they took possession of houses filled with all kinds of good things, wells already dug, vineyards, olive groves and fruit trees in abundance. They ate to the full and were well-nourished; they reveled in your great goodness.

[26]"But they were disobedient and rebelled against you; they put your law behind their backs. They killed your prophets, who had admonished them in order to turn them back to you; they committed awful blasphemies. [27]So you handed them over to their enemies, who oppressed them. But when they were oppressed they cried out to you. From heaven you heard

THE MESSAGE

to return to their Egyptian slavery.
And you, a forgiving God,
    gracious and compassionate,
Incredibly patient, with tons of love—
    you didn't dump them.
Yes, even when they cast a sculpted calf
    and said, "This is your god
Who brought you out of Egypt,"
    and continued from bad to worse,
You in your amazing compassion
    didn't walk off and leave them in the desert.
The Pillar of Cloud didn't leave them;
    daily it continued to show them their route;
The Pillar of Fire did the same by night,
    showed them the right way to go.

9.20-23 You gave them your good Spirit
    to teach them to live wisely.
You never stinted with your manna,
    gave them plenty of water to drink.
You supported them forty years in that desert;
    they had everything they needed;
Their clothes didn't wear out
    and their feet never blistered.
You gave them kingdoms and peoples,
    establishing generous boundaries.
They took over the country of Sihon king of
        Heshbon
    and the country of Og king of Bashan.
You multiplied children for them,
    rivaling the stars in the night skies,
And you brought them into the land
    that you promised their ancestors
    they would get and own.

9.24-25 Well, they entered all right,
    they took it and settled in.
The Canaanites who lived there
    you brought to their knees before them.
You turned over their land, kings, and peoples
    to do with as they pleased.
They took strong cities and fertile fields,
    they took over well-furnished houses,
Cisterns, vineyards, olive groves,
    and lush, extensive orchards.
And they ate, grew fat on the fat of the land;
    they reveled in your bountiful goodness.

9.26-31 But then they mutinied, rebelled against you,
    threw out your laws and killed your
        prophets,
The very prophets who tried to get them back
        on your side—
    and then things went from bad to worse.
You turned them over to their enemies,
    who made life rough for them.
But when they called out for help in their
        troubles
    you listened from heaven;

NEW INTERNATIONAL VERSION

them, and in your great compassion you gave them deliverers, who rescued them from the hand of their enemies.

28"But as soon as they were at rest, they again did what was evil in your sight. Then you abandoned them to the hand of their enemies so that they ruled over them. And when they cried out to you again, you heard from heaven, and in your compassion you delivered them time after time.

29"You warned them to return to your law, but they became arrogant and disobeyed your commands. They sinned against your ordinances, by which a man will live if he obeys them. Stubbornly they turned their backs on you, became stiffnecked and refused to listen. 30For many years you were patient with them. By your Spirit you admonished them through your prophets. Yet they paid no attention, so you handed them over to the neighboring peoples. 31But in your great mercy you did not put an end to them or abandon them, for you are a gracious and merciful God.

32"Now therefore, O our God, the great, mighty and awesome God, who keeps his covenant of love, do not let all this hardship seem trifling in your eyes—the hardship that has come upon us, upon our kings and leaders, upon our priests and prophets, upon our fathers and all your people, from the days of the kings of Assyria until today. 33In all that has happened to us, you have been just; you have acted faithfully, while we did wrong. 34Our kings, our leaders, our priests and our fathers did not follow your law; they did not pay attention to your commands or the warnings you gave them. 35Even while they were in their kingdom, enjoying your great goodness to them in the spacious and fertile

THE MESSAGE

And in keeping with your bottomless compassion
    you gave them saviors:
Saviors who saved them
    from the cruel abuse of their enemies.
But as soon as they had it easy again
    they were right back at it—more evil.
So you turned away and left them again to
    their fate,
    to the enemies who came right back.
They cried out to you again; in your great
    compassion
    you heard and helped them again.
This went on over and over and over.
You warned them to return to your
    Revelation,
    they responded with haughty arrogance:
They flouted your commands, spurned your
    rules
    —the very words by which men and
      women live!
They set their jaws in defiance,
    they turned their backs on you and didn't
      listen.
You put up with them year after year
    and warned them by your spirit through
      your prophets;
But when they refused to listen
    you abandoned them to foreigners.
Still, because of your great compassion,
    you didn't make a total end to them.
You didn't walk out and leave them for good;
    yes, you *are* a God of grace and
      compassion.

9.32-37 And now, our God, the great God,
    God majestic and terrible, loyal in covenant
      and love,
Don't treat lightly the trouble that has come
    to us,
    to our kings and princes, our priests and
      prophets,
Our ancestors, and all your people from the
    time
    of the Assyrian kings right down to today.
You are not to blame
    for all that has come down on us;
You did everything right,
    we did everything wrong.
None of our kings, princes, priests, or
    ancestors
    followed your Revelation;
They ignored your commands,
    dismissed the warnings you gave them.
Even when they had their own kingdom
    and were enjoying your generous goodness,
Living in that spacious and fertile land
    that you spread out before them,

<table>
<tr><th>NEW INTERNATIONAL VERSION</th><th>THE MESSAGE</th></tr>
</table>

NEW INTERNATIONAL VERSION

land you gave them, they did not serve you or turn from their evil ways.

³⁶"But see, we are slaves today, slaves in the land you gave our forefathers so they could eat its fruit and the other good things it produces. ³⁷Because of our sins, its abundant harvest goes to the kings you have placed over us. They rule over our bodies and our cattle as they please. We are in great distress.

THE AGREEMENT OF THE PEOPLE

³⁸"In view of all this, we are making a binding agreement, putting it in writing, and our leaders, our Levites and our priests are affixing their seals to it."

10 Those who sealed it were:

Nehemiah the governor, the son of Hacaliah.

Zedekiah, ²Seraiah, Azariah, Jeremiah, ³Pashhur, Amariah, Malkijah, ⁴Hattush, Shebaniah, Malluch, ⁵Harim, Meremoth, Obadiah, ⁶Daniel, Ginnethon, Baruch, ⁷Meshullam, Abijah, Mijamin, ⁸Maaziah, Bilgai and Shemaiah. These were the priests.

⁹The Levites:

Jeshua son of Azaniah, Binnui of the sons of Henadad, Kadmiel, ¹⁰and their associates: Shebaniah, Hodiah, Kelita, Pelaiah, Hanan, ¹¹Mica, Rehob, Hashabiah, ¹²Zaccur, Sherebiah, Shebaniah, ¹³Hodiah, Bani and Beninu.

¹⁴The leaders of the people:

Parosh, Pahath-Moab, Elam, Zattu, Bani, ¹⁵Bunni, Azgad, Bebai, ¹⁶Adonijah, Bigvai, Adin, ¹⁷Ater, Hezekiah, Azzur, ¹⁸Hodiah, Hashum, Bezai, ¹⁹Hariph, Anathoth, Nebai, ²⁰Magpiash, Meshullam, Hezir, ²¹Meshezabel, Zadok, Jaddua, ²²Pelatiah, Hanan, Anaiah, ²³Hoshea, Hananiah, Hasshub, ²⁴Hallohesh, Pilha, Shobek, ²⁵Rehum, Hashabnah, Maaseiah, ²⁶Ahiah, Hanan, Anan, ²⁷Malluch, Harim and Baanah.

THE MESSAGE

They didn't serve you
    or turn their backs on the practice of evil.
And here we are, slaves again today;
    and here's the land you gave our ancestors
So they could eat well and enjoy a good life,
    and now look at us—no better than slaves
        on this land.
Its wonderful crops go to the kings
    you put over us because of our sins;
They act like they own our bodies
    and do whatever they like with our cattle.
    We're in deep trouble.

9.38   "Because of all this we are drawing up a binding pledge, a sealed document signed by our princes, our Levites, and our priests."

✞

10.1-8 **10** The sealed document bore these signatures:

Nehemiah the governor, son of Hacaliah,
Zedekiah, Seraiah, Azariah, Jeremiah,
Pashhur, Amariah, Malkijah,
Hattush, Shebaniah, Malluch,
Harim, Meremoth, Obadiah,
Daniel, Ginnethon, Baruch,
Meshullam, Abijah, Mijamin,
Maaziah, Bilgai, and Shemaiah.
These were the priests.

10.9-13 The Levites:

Jeshua son of Azaniah, Binnui of the sons of Henadad, Kadmiel,
and their kinsmen: Shebaniah, Hodiah, Kelita, Pelaiah, Hanan,
Mica, Rehob, Hashabiah,
Zaccur, Sherebiah, Shebaniah,
Hodiah, Bani, and Beninu.

10.14-27 The heads of the people:

Parosh, Pahath-Moab, Elam, Zattu, Bani,
Bunni, Azgad, Bebai,
Adonijah, Bigvai, Adin,
Ater, Hezekiah, Azzur,
Hodiah, Hashum, Bezai,
Hariph, Anathoth, Nebai,
Magpiash, Meshullam, Hezir,
Meshezabel, Zadok, Jaddua,
Pelatiah, Hanan, Anaiah,
Hoshea, Hananiah, Hasshub,
Hallohesh, Pilha, Shobek,
Rehum, Hashabnah, Maaseiah,
Ahiah, Hanan, Anan,
Malluch, Harim, and Baanah.

NEW INTERNATIONAL VERSION

28 "The rest of the people—priests, Levites, gatekeepers, singers, temple servants and all who separated themselves from the neighboring peoples for the sake of the Law of God, together with their wives and all their sons and daughters who are able to understand— 29 all these now join their brothers the nobles, and bind themselves with a curse and an oath to follow the Law of God given through Moses the servant of God and to obey carefully all the commands, regulations and decrees of the LORD our Lord.

30 "We promise not to give our daughters in marriage to the peoples around us or take their daughters for our sons.

31 "When the neighboring peoples bring merchandise or grain to sell on the Sabbath, we will not buy from them on the Sabbath or on any holy day. Every seventh year we will forgo working the land and will cancel all debts.

32 "We assume the responsibility for carrying out the commands to give a third of a shekel*a* each year for the service of the house of our God: 33 for the bread set out on the table; for the regular grain offerings and burnt offerings; for the offerings on the Sabbaths, New Moon festivals and appointed feasts; for the holy offerings; for sin offerings to make atonement for Israel; and for all the duties of the house of our God.

34 "We—the priests, the Levites and the people—have cast lots to determine when each of our families is to bring to the house of our God at set times each year a contribution of wood to burn on the altar of the LORD our God, as it is written in the Law.

35 "We also assume responsibility for bringing to the house of the LORD each year the firstfruits of our crops and of every fruit tree.

36 "As it is also written in the Law, we will bring the firstborn of our sons and of our cattle, of our herds and of our flocks to the house of our God, to the priests ministering there.

37 "Moreover, we will bring to the storerooms of the house of our God, to the priests, the first of our ground meal, of our ⌊grain⌋ offerings, of the fruit of all our trees and of our new wine and oil. And we will bring a tithe of our crops to the Levites, for it is the Levites who collect the tithes in all the towns where we work. 38 A priest descended from Aaron is to accompany the

THE MESSAGE

10.28-30 The rest of the people, priests, Levites, security guards, singers, Temple staff, and all who separated themselves from the foreign neighbors to keep The Revelation of God, together with their wives, sons, daughters—everyone old enough to understand—all joined their noble kinsmen in a binding oath to follow The Revelation of God given through Moses the servant of God, to keep and carry out all the commandments of GOD our Master, all his decisions and standards. Thus:

10.30 We will not marry our daughters to our foreign neighbors nor let our sons marry their daughters.

10.31 When the foreign neighbors bring goods or grain to sell on the Sabbath we won't trade with them—not on the Sabbath or any other holy day.

10.31 Every seventh year we will leave the land fallow and cancel all debts.

10.32-33 We accept the responsibility for paying an annual tax of one-third of a shekel (about an eighth ounce) for providing The Temple of our God with
bread for the Table
regular Grain-Offerings
regular Whole-Burnt-Offerings
offerings for the Sabbaths, New Moons, and appointed feasts
Dedication-Offerings
Absolution-Offerings to atone for Israel
maintenance of The Temple of our God.

10.34 We—priests, Levites, and the people—have cast lots to see when each of our families will bring wood for burning on the Altar of our GOD, following the yearly schedule set down in The Revelation.

10.35-36 We take responsibility for delivering annually to The Temple of GOD the first-fruits of our crops and our orchards, our firstborn sons and cattle, and the first-born from our herds and flocks for the priests who serve in The Temple of our God—just as it is set down in The Revelation.

10.37-39 We will bring the best of our grain, of our contributions, of the fruit of every tree, of wine, and of oil to the priests in the storerooms of The Temple of our God.

We will bring the tithes from our fields to the Levites, since the Levites are appointed to collect the tithes in the towns where we work. We'll see to it that a priest descended from Aaron will super-

a 32 That is, about 1/8 ounce (about 4 grams)

NEW INTERNATIONAL VERSION

Levites when they receive the tithes, and the Levites are to bring a tenth of the tithes up to the house of our God, to the storerooms of the treasury. ³⁹The people of Israel, including the Levites, are to bring their contributions of grain, new wine and oil to the storerooms where the articles for the sanctuary are kept and where the ministering priests, the gatekeepers and the singers stay.

"We will not neglect the house of our God."

THE NEW RESIDENTS OF JERUSALEM

11 Now the leaders of the people settled in Jerusalem, and the rest of the people cast lots to bring one out of every ten to live in Jerusalem, the holy city, while the remaining nine were to stay in their own towns. ²The people commended all the men who volunteered to live in Jerusalem.

³These are the provincial leaders who settled in Jerusalem (now some Israelites, priests, Levites, temple servants and descendants of Solomon's servants lived in the towns of Judah, each on his own property in the various towns, ⁴while other people from both Judah and Benjamin lived in Jerusalem):

From the descendants of Judah:

Athaiah son of Uzziah, the son of Zechariah, the son of Amariah, the son of Shephatiah, the son of Mahalalel, a descendant of Perez; ⁵and Maaseiah son of Baruch, the son of Col-Hozeh, the son of Hazaiah, the son of Adaiah, the son of Joiarib, the son of Zechariah, a descendant of Shelah. ⁶The descendants of Perez who lived in Jerusalem totaled 468 able men.

⁷From the descendants of Benjamin:

Sallu son of Meshullam, the son of Joed, the son of Pedaiah, the son of Kolaiah, the son of Maaseiah, the son of Ithiel, the son of Jeshaiah, ⁸and his followers, Gabbai and Sallai—928 men. ⁹Joel son of Zicri was their chief officer, and Judah son of Hassenuah was over the Second District of the city.

¹⁰From the priests:

Jedaiah; the son of Joiarib; Jakin; ¹¹Seraiah son of Hilkiah, the son of Meshullam, the son of Zadok, the son of Meraioth, the son of Ahitub, supervisor in the house of God, ¹²and their associates, who carried on work for the temple—822 men; Adaiah son of

THE MESSAGE

vise the Levites as they collect the tithes and make sure that they take a tenth of the tithes to the treasury in The Temple of our God. We'll see to it that the People of Israel and Levites bring the grain, wine, and oil to the storage rooms where the vessels of the Sanctuary are kept and where the priests who serve, the security guards, and the choir meet.

We will not neglect The Temple of our God.

^{11.1-2} **11** The leaders of the people were already living in Jerusalem, so the rest of the people drew lots to get one out of ten to move to Jerusalem, the holy city, while the other nine remained in their towns. The people applauded those who voluntarily offered to live in Jerusalem.

^{11.3-4} These are the leaders in the province who resided in Jerusalem (some Israelites, priests, Levites, Temple staff, and descendants of Solomon's slaves lived in the towns of Judah on their own property in various towns; others from both Judah and Benjamin lived in Jerusalem):

^{11.4-6} From the family of Judah:

Athaiah son of Uzziah, the son of Zechariah, the son of Amariah, the son of Shephatiah, the son of Mahalalel, from the family line of Perez; Maaseiah son of Baruch, the son of Col-Hozeh, the son of Hazaiah, the son of Adaiah, the son of Joiarib, the son of Zechariah, the son of the Shilonite. The descendants of Perez who lived in Jerusalem numbered 468 valiant men.

^{11.7-9} From the family of Benjamin:

Sallu son of Meshullam, the son of Joed, the son of Pedaiah, the son of Kolaiah, the son of Maaseiah, the son of Ithiel, the son of Jeshaiah, and his brothers Gabbai and Sallai: 928 men. Joel son of Zicri was their chief and Judah son of Hassenuah was second in command over the city.

^{11.10-14} From the priests:

Jedaiah son of Joiarib; Jakin; Seraiah son of Hilkiah, the son of Meshullam, the son of Zadok, the son of Meraioth, the son of Ahitub, supervisor of The Temple of God, along with their associates responsible for work in The Temple: 822 men. Also Adaiah son of Jeroham,

NEW INTERNATIONAL VERSION

Jeroham, the son of Pelaliah, the son of Amzi, the son of Zechariah, the son of Pashhur, the son of Malkijah, [13]and his associates, who were heads of families—242 men; Amashsai son of Azarel, the son of Ahzai, the son of Meshillemoth, the son of Immer, [14]and his[a] associates, who were able men—128. Their chief officer was Zabdiel son of Haggedolim.

[15]From the Levites:

Shemaiah son of Hasshub, the son of Azrikam, the son of Hashabiah, the son of Bunni; [16]Shabbethai and Jozabad, two of the heads of the Levites, who had charge of the outside work of the house of God; [17]Mattaniah son of Mica, the son of Zabdi, the son of Asaph, the director who led in thanksgiving and prayer; Bakbukiah, second among his associates; and Abda son of Shammua, the son of Galal, the son of Jeduthun. [18]The Levites in the holy city totaled 284.

[19]The gatekeepers:

Akkub, Talmon and their associates, who kept watch at the gates—172 men.

[20]The rest of the Israelites, with the priests and Levites, were in all the towns of Judah, each on his ancestral property.

[21]The temple servants lived on the hill of Ophel, and Ziha and Gishpa were in charge of them.

[22]The chief officer of the Levites in Jerusalem was Uzzi son of Bani, the son of Hashabiah, the son of Mattaniah, the son of Mica. Uzzi was one of Asaph's descendants, who were the singers responsible for the service of the house of God. [23]The singers were under the king's orders, which regulated their daily activity.

[24]Pethahiah son of Meshezabel, one of the descendants of Zerah son of Judah, was the king's agent in all affairs relating to the people.

[25]As for the villages with their fields, some of the people of Judah lived in Kiriath Arba and its surrounding settlements, in Dibon and its settlements, in Jekabzeel and its villages, [26]in Jeshua, in Moladah, in Beth Pelet, [27]in Hazar Shual, in Beersheba and its settlements, [28]in Ziklag, in Meconah and its settlements, [29]in En Rimmon, in Zorah, in Jarmuth, [30]Zanoah, Adullam and their villages, in Lachish and its fields, and in

THE MESSAGE

the son of Pelaliah, the son of Amzi, the son of Zechariah, the son of Pashhur, the son of Malkijah, and his associates who were heads of families: 242 men; Amashsai son of Azarel, the son of Ahzai, the son of Meshillemoth, the son of Immer, and his associates, all valiant men: 128 men. Their commander was Zabdiel son of Haggedolim.

11.15-18 From the Levites:

Shemaiah son of Hasshub, the son of Azrikam, the son of Hashabiah, the son of Bunni; Shabbethai and Jozabad, two of the leaders of the Levites who were in charge of the outside work of The Temple of God; Mattaniah son of Mica, the son of Zabdi, the son of Asaph, the director who led in thanksgiving and prayer; Bakbukiah, second among his associates; and Abda son of Shammua, the son of Galal, the son of Jeduthun. The Levites in the holy city totaled 284.

11.19 From the security guards:

Akkub, Talmon, and their associates who kept watch over the gates: 172 men.

11.20 The rest of the Israelites, priests, and Levites were in all the towns of Judah, each on his own family property.

11.21 The Temple staff lived on the hill Ophel. Ziha and Gishpa were responsible for them.

11.22-23 The chief officer over the Levites in Jerusalem was Uzzi son of Bani, the son of Hashabiah, the son of Mattaniah, the son of Mica. Uzzi was one of Asaph's descendants, singers who led worship in The Temple of God. The singers got their orders from the king, who drew up their daily schedule.

11.24 Pethahiah son of Meshezabel, a descendant of Zerah son of Judah, represented the people's concerns at the royal court.

11.25-30 Some of the Judeans lived in the villages near their farms:

Kiriath Arba (Hebron) and suburbs
Dibon and suburbs
Jekabzeel and suburbs
Jeshua
Moladah
Beth Pelet
Hazar Shual
Beersheba and suburbs
Ziklag
Meconah and suburbs
En Rimmon
Zorah
Jarmuth
Zanoah
Adullam and their towns
Lachish and its fields

NEW INTERNATIONAL VERSION

Azekah and its settlements. So they were living all the way from Beersheba to the Valley of Hinnom.

³¹The descendants of the Benjamites from Geba lived in Micmash, Aija, Bethel and its settlements, ³²in Anathoth, Nob and Ananiah, ³³in Hazor, Ramah and Gittaim, ³⁴in Hadid, Zeboim and Neballat, ³⁵in Lod and Ono, and in the Valley of the Craftsmen.

³⁶Some of the divisions of the Levites of Judah settled in Benjamin.

PRIESTS AND LEVITES

12 These were the priests and Levites who returned with Zerubbabel son of Shealtiel and with Jeshua:

Seraiah, Jeremiah, Ezra,
²Amariah, Malluch, Hattush,
³Shecaniah, Rehum, Meremoth,
⁴Iddo, Ginnethon,ᵃ Abijah,
⁵Mijamin,ᵇ Moadiah, Bilgah,
⁶Shemaiah, Joiarib, Jedaiah,
⁷Sallu, Amok, Hilkiah and Jedaiah.

These were the leaders of the priests and their associates in the days of Jeshua.

⁸The Levites were Jeshua, Binnui, Kadmiel, Sherebiah, Judah, and also Mattaniah, who, together with his associates, was in charge of the songs of thanksgiving. ⁹Bakbukiah and Unni, their associates, stood opposite them in the services.

¹⁰Jeshua was the father of Joiakim, Joiakim the father of Eliashib, Eliashib the father of Joiada, ¹¹Joiada the father of Jonathan, and Jonathan the father of Jaddua.

¹²In the days of Joiakim, these were the heads of the priestly families:

of Seraiah's family, Meraiah;
of Jeremiah's, Hananiah;
¹³of Ezra's, Meshullam;
of Amariah's, Jehohanan;
¹⁴of Malluch's, Jonathan;
of Shecaniah's,ᶜ Joseph;
¹⁵of Harim's, Adna;
of Meremoth's,ᵈ Helkai;
¹⁶of Iddo's, Zechariah;

ᵃ 4 Many Hebrew manuscripts and Vulgate (see also Neh. 12:16); most Hebrew manuscripts *Ginnethoi*
ᵇ 5 A variant of *Miniamin*   ᶜ 14 Very many Hebrew manuscripts, some Septuagint manuscripts and Syriac (see also Neh. 12:3); most Hebrew manuscripts *Shebaniah's*
ᵈ 15 Some Septuagint manuscripts (see also Neh. 12:3); Hebrew *Meraioth's*

THE MESSAGE

Azekah and suburbs.
They were living all the way from Beersheba to the Valley of Hinnom.

11.31-36   The Benjaminites from Geba lived in:
Micmash
Aijah
Bethel and its suburbs
Anathoth
Nob and Ananiah
Hazor
Ramah and Gittaim
Hadid, Zeboim, and Neballat
Lod and Ono and the Valley of the
    Craftsmen.

Also some of the Levitical groups of Judah were assigned to Benjamin.

12.1-7   **12** These are the priests and Levites who came up with Zerubbabel son of Shealtiel and with Jeshua:

Seraiah, Jeremiah, Ezra,
Amariah, Malluch, Hattush,
Shecaniah, Rehum, Meremoth,
Iddo, Ginnethon, Abijah,
Mijamin, Moadiah, Bilgah,
Shemaiah, Joiarib, Jedaiah,
Sallu, Amok, Hilkiah, and Jedaiah.

These were the leaders of the priests during the time of Jeshua.

12.8-9   And the Levites:
Jeshua, Binnui, Kadmiel, Sherebiah,
Judah; Mattaniah, with his brothers, was
in charge of songs of praise, and their
brothers Bakbukiah and Unni stood
opposite them in the services of
worship.

12.10-11   Jeshua fathered Joiakim,
Joiakim fathered Eliashib,
Eliashib fathered Joiada,
Joiada fathered Jonathan,
and Jonathan fathered Jaddua.

12.12-21   During the time of Joiakim, these were the heads of the priestly families:
of the family of Seraiah, Meraiah;
of Jeremiah, Hananiah;
of Ezra, Meshullam;
of Amariah, Jehohanan;
of Malluch, Jonathan;
of Shecaniah, Joseph;
of Harim, Adna;
of Meremoth, Helkai;
of Iddo, Zechariah;

NEW INTERNATIONAL VERSION

of Ginnethon's, Meshullam;
¹⁷ of Abijah's, Zicri;
of Miniamin's and of Moadiah's, Piltai;
¹⁸ of Bilgah's, Shammua;
of Shemaiah's, Jehonathan;
¹⁹ of Joiarib's, Mattenai;
of Jedaiah's, Uzzi;
²⁰ of Sallu's, Kallai;
of Amok's, Eber;
²¹ of Hilkiah's, Hashabiah;
of Jedaiah's, Nethanel.

²²The family heads of the Levites in the days of Eliashib, Joiada, Johanan and Jaddua, as well as those of the priests, were recorded in the reign of Darius the Persian. ²³The family heads among the descendants of Levi up to the time of Johanan son of Eliashib were recorded in the book of the annals. ²⁴And the leaders of the Levites were Hashabiah, Sherebiah, Jeshua son of Kadmiel, and their associates, who stood opposite them to give praise and thanksgiving, one section responding to the other, as prescribed by David the man of God.

²⁵Mattaniah, Bakbukiah, Obadiah, Meshullam, Talmon and Akkub were gatekeepers who guarded the storerooms at the gates. ²⁶They served in the days of Joiakim son of Jeshua, the son of Jozadak, and in the days of Nehemiah the governor and of Ezra the priest and scribe.

DEDICATION OF THE WALL OF JERUSALEM

²⁷At the dedication of the wall of Jerusalem, the Levites were sought out from where they lived and were brought to Jerusalem to celebrate joyfully the dedication with songs of thanksgiving and with the music of cymbals, harps and lyres. ²⁸The singers also were brought together from the region around Jerusalem—from the villages of the Netophathites, ²⁹from Beth Gilgal, and from the area of Geba and Azmaveth, for the singers had built villages for themselves around Jerusalem. ³⁰When the priests and Levites had purified themselves ceremonially, they purified the people, the gates and the wall.

³¹I had the leaders of Judah go up on top*a* of the wall. I also assigned two large choirs to give thanks. One was to proceed on top*b* of the wall to the right, toward the Dung Gate. ³²Hoshaiah and half the leaders of Judah followed them, ³³along with Azariah, Ezra, Meshullam, ³⁴Judah,

a 31 Or go alongside   b 31 Or proceed alongside

THE MESSAGE

of Ginnethon, Meshullam;
of Abijah, Zicri;
of Miniamin and Moadiah, Piltai;
of Bilgah, Shammua;
of Shemaiah, Jehonathan;
of Joiarib, Mattenai;
of Jedaiah, Uzzi;
of Sallu, Kallai;
of Amok, Eber;
of Hilkiah, Hashabiah;
and of Jedaiah, Nethanel.

12.22   During the time of Eliashib, Joiada, Johanan, and Jaddua, the Levites were registered as heads of families. During the reign of Darius the Persian, the priests were registered.

12.23-24   The Levites who were heads of families were registered in the Book of the Chronicles until the time of Johanan son of Eliashib. These were:

Hashabiah,
Sherebiah,
and Jeshua son of Kadmiel.

Their brothers stood opposite them to give praise and thanksgiving, one side responding to the other, as had been directed by David the man of God.

12.25-26   The security guards included:

Mattaniah,
Bakbukiah,
Obadiah,
Meshullam,
Talmon,
and Akkub.

They guarded the storerooms at the gates. They lived during the time of Joiakim son of Jeshua, the son of Jozadak, the time of Nehemiah the governor and of Ezra the priest and scholar.

DEDICATION OF THE WALL

12.27-29 When it came time for the dedication of the wall, they tracked down and brought in the Levites from all their homes in Jerusalem to carry out the dedication exuberantly: thanksgiving hymns, songs, cymbals, harps, and lutes. The singers assembled from all around Jerusalem, from the villages of the Netophathites, from Beth Gilgal, from the farms at Geba and Azmaveth—the singers had built villages for themselves all around Jerusalem.

12.30   The priests and Levites ceremonially purified themselves; then they did the same for the people, the gates, and the wall.

12.31-36   I had the leaders of Judah come up on the wall, and I appointed two large choirs. One proceeded on the wall to the right toward the Dung Gate. Hashaiah and half the leaders of Judah followed them, including Azariah, Ezra,

NEW INTERNATIONAL VERSION

Benjamin, Shemaiah, Jeremiah, [35]as well as some priests with trumpets, and also Zechariah son of Jonathan, the son of Shemaiah, the son of Mattaniah, the son of Micaiah, the son of Zaccur, the son of Asaph, [36]and his associates—Shemaiah, Azarel, Milalai, Gilalai, Maai, Nethanel, Judah and Hanani—with musical instruments ⌊prescribed by⌋ David the man of God. Ezra the scribe led the procession. [37]At the Fountain Gate they continued directly up the steps of the City of David on the ascent to the wall and passed above the house of David to the Water Gate on the east.

[38]The second choir proceeded in the opposite direction. I followed them on top[a] of the wall, together with half the people—past the Tower of the Ovens to the Broad Wall, [39]over the Gate of Ephraim, the Jeshanah[b] Gate, the Fish Gate, the Tower of Hananel and the Tower of the Hundred, as far as the Sheep Gate. At the Gate of the Guard they stopped.

[40]The two choirs that gave thanks then took their places in the house of God; so did I, together with half the officials, [41]as well as the priests—Eliakim, Maaseiah, Miniamin, Micaiah, Elioenai, Zechariah and Hananiah with their trumpets— [42]and also Maaseiah, Shemaiah, Eleazar, Uzzi, Jehohanan, Malkijah, Elam and Ezer. The choirs sang under the direction of Jezrahiah. [43]And on that day they offered great sacrifices, rejoicing because God had given them great joy. The women and children also rejoiced. The sound of rejoicing in Jerusalem could be heard far away.

[44]At that time men were appointed to be in charge of the storerooms for the contributions, firstfruits and tithes. From the fields around the towns they were to bring into the storerooms the portions required by the Law for the priests and the Levites, for Judah was pleased with the ministering priests and Levites. [45]They performed the service of their God and the service of purification, as did also the singers and gatekeepers, according to the commands of David and his son Solomon. [46]For long ago, in the days of David and Asaph, there had been directors for the singers and for the songs of praise and thanksgiving to God. [47]So in the days of Zerubbabel and of Nehemiah, all Israel contributed the daily portions for the singers and gatekeepers. They also set aside the portion for the other Levites, and the Levites set aside the portion for the descendants of Aaron.

THE MESSAGE

Meshullam, Judah, Benjamin, Shemaiah, and Jeremiah. Some of the young priests had trumpets. Next, playing the musical instruments of David the man of God, came Zechariah son of Jonathan, the son of Shemaiah, the son of Mattaniah, the son of Micaiah, the son of Zaccur, the son of Asaph, and his brothers Shemaiah, Azarel, Milalai, Gilalai, Maai, Nethanel, Judah, and Hanani. Ezra the scholar led them.

12.37 At the Fountain Gate they went straight ahead, up the steps of the City of David using the wall stairway above the house of David to the Water Gate on the east.

12.38-39 The other choir proceeded to the left. I and half of the people followed them on the wall from the Tower of Furnaces to the Broad Wall, over the Ephraim Gate, the Jeshanah Gate, the Fish Gate, the Tower of Hananel, and the Tower of the Hundred as far as the Sheep Gate, stopping at the Prison Gate.

12.40-42 The two choirs then took their places in The Temple of God. I was there with half of the officials, along with the priests Eliakim, Maaseiah, Miniamin, Micaiah, Elioenai, Zechariah, and Hananiah with their trumpets. Also Maaseiah, Shemaiah, Eleazar, Uzzi, Jehohanan, Malkijah, Elam, and Ezer. The singers, directed by Jezrahiah, made the rafters ring.

12.43 That day they offered great sacrifices, an exuberant celebration because God had filled them with great joy. The women and children raised their happy voices with all the rest. Jerusalem's jubilation was heard far and wide.

✠

12.44-46 That same day men were appointed to be responsible for the storerooms for the offerings, the firstfruits, and the tithes. They saw to it that the portion directed by The Revelation for the priests and Levites was brought in from the farms connected to the towns. Judah was so appreciative of the priests and Levites and their service; they, along with the singers and security guards, had done everything so well, conducted the worship of their God and the ritual of ceremonial cleansing in a way that would have made David and his son Solomon proud. That's the way it was done in the olden days, the days of David and Asaph, when they had choir directors for singing songs of praise and thanksgiving to God.

12.47 During the time of Zerubbabel and Nehemiah, all Israel contributed the daily allowances for the singers and security guards. They also set aside what was dedicated to the Levites, and the Levites did the same for the Aaronites.

✠

---

[a] 38 Or *them alongside*   [b] 39 Or *Old*

NEW INTERNATIONAL VERSION

NEHEMIAH'S FINAL REFORMS

13 On that day the Book of Moses was read aloud in the hearing of the people and there it was found written that no Ammonite or Moabite should ever be admitted into the assembly of God, ²because they had not met the Israelites with food and water but had hired Balaam to call a curse down on them. (Our God, however, turned the curse into a blessing.) ³When the people heard this law, they excluded from Israel all who were of foreign descent.

⁴Before this, Eliashib the priest had been put in charge of the storerooms of the house of our God. He was closely associated with Tobiah, ⁵and he had provided him with a large room formerly used to store the grain offerings and incense and temple articles, and also the tithes of grain, new wine and oil prescribed for the Levites, singers and gatekeepers, as well as the contributions for the priests.

⁶But while all this was going on, I was not in Jerusalem, for in the thirty-second year of Artaxerxes king of Babylon I had returned to the king. Some time later I asked his permission ⁷and came back to Jerusalem. Here I learned about the evil thing Eliashib had done in providing Tobiah a room in the courts of the house of God. ⁸I was greatly displeased and threw all Tobiah's household goods out of the room. ⁹I gave orders to purify the rooms, and then I put back into them the equipment of the house of God, with the grain offerings and the incense.

¹⁰I also learned that the portions assigned to the Levites had not been given to them, and that all the Levites and singers responsible for the service had gone back to their own fields. ¹¹So I rebuked the officials and asked them, "Why is the house of God neglected?" Then I called them together and stationed them at their posts.

¹²All Judah brought the tithes of grain, new wine and oil into the storerooms. ¹³I put Shelemiah the priest, Zadok the scribe, and a Levite named Pedaiah in charge of the storerooms and made Hanan son of Zaccur, the son of Mattaniah, their assistant, because these men were considered trustworthy. They were made responsible for distributing the supplies to their brothers.

¹⁴Remember me for this, O my God, and do not blot out what I have so faithfully done for the house of my God and its services.

¹⁵In those days I saw men in Judah treading

THE MESSAGE

13.1-3 **13** Also on that same day there was a reading from the Book of Moses in the hearing of the people. It was found written there that no Ammonite or Moabite was permitted to enter the congregation of God, because they hadn't welcomed the People of Israel with food and drink; they even hired Balaam to work against them by cursing them, but our God turned the curse into a blessing. When they heard the reading of The Revelation, they excluded all foreigners from Israel.

⁜

13.4-5 Some time before this, Eliashib the priest had been put in charge of the storerooms of The Temple of God. He was close to Tobiah and had made available to him a large storeroom that had been used to store Grain-Offerings, incense, worship vessels, and the tithes of grain, wine, and oil for the Levites, singers, and security guards, and the offerings for the priests.

13.6-9 When this was going on I wasn't there in Jerusalem; in the thirty-second year of Artaxerxes king of Babylon, I had traveled back to the king. But later I asked for his permission to leave again. I arrived in Jerusalem and learned of the wrong that Eliashib had done in turning over to him a room in the courts of The Temple of God. I was angry, really angry, and threw everything in the room out into the street, all of Tobiah's stuff. Then I ordered that they ceremonially cleanse the room. Only then did I put back the worship vessels of The Temple of God, along with the Grain-Offerings and the incense.

13.10-13 And then I learned that the Levites hadn't been given their regular food allotments. So the Levites and singers who led the services of worship had all left and gone back to their farms. I called the officials on the carpet, "Why has The Temple of God been abandoned?" I got everyone back again and put them back on their jobs so that all Judah was again bringing in the tithe of grain, wine, and oil to the storerooms. I put Shelemiah the priest, Zadok the scribe, and a Levite named Pedaiah in charge of the storerooms. I made Hanan son of Zaccur, the son of Mattaniah, their right-hand man. These men had a reputation for honesty and hard work. They were responsible for distributing the rations to their brothers.

13.14 Remember me, O my God, for this. Don't ever forget the devoted work I have done for The Temple of God and its worship.

13.15-16 During those days, while back in Judah, I

NEW INTERNATIONAL VERSION

winepresses on the Sabbath and bringing in grain and loading it on donkeys, together with wine, grapes, figs and all other kinds of loads. And they were bringing all this into Jerusalem on the Sabbath. Therefore I warned them against selling food on that day. ¹⁶Men from Tyre who lived in Jerusalem were bringing in fish and all kinds of merchandise and selling them in Jerusalem on the Sabbath to the people of Judah. ¹⁷I rebuked the nobles of Judah and said to them, "What is this wicked thing you are doing—desecrating the Sabbath day? ¹⁸Didn't your forefathers do the same things, so that our God brought all this calamity upon us and upon this city? Now you are stirring up more wrath against Israel by desecrating the Sabbath."

¹⁹When evening shadows fell on the gates of Jerusalem before the Sabbath, I ordered the doors to be shut and not opened until the Sabbath was over. I stationed some of my own men at the gates so that no load could be brought in on the Sabbath day. ²⁰Once or twice the merchants and sellers of all kinds of goods spent the night outside Jerusalem. ²¹But I warned them and said, "Why do you spend the night by the wall? If you do this again, I will lay hands on you." From that time on they no longer came on the Sabbath. ²²Then I commanded the Levites to purify themselves and go and guard the gates in order to keep the Sabbath day holy.

Remember me for this also, O my God, and show mercy to me according to your great love.

²³Moreover, in those days I saw men of Judah who had married women from Ashdod, Ammon and Moab. ²⁴Half of their children spoke the language of Ashdod or the language of one of the other peoples, and did not know how to speak the language of Judah. ²⁵I rebuked them and called curses down on them. I beat some of the men and pulled out their hair. I made them take an oath in God's name and said: "You are not to give your daughters in marriage to their sons, nor are you to take their daughters in marriage for your sons or for yourselves. ²⁶Was it not because of marriages like these that Solomon king of Israel sinned? Among the many nations there was no king like him. He was loved by his God, and God made him king over all Israel, but even he was led into sin by foreign women. ²⁷Must we hear now that you too are doing all this terrible wickedness and are being unfaithful to our God by marrying foreign women?"

THE MESSAGE

also noticed that people treaded wine presses, brought in sacks of grain, and loaded up their donkeys on the Sabbath. They brought wine, grapes, figs, and all kinds of stuff to sell on the Sabbath. So I spoke up and warned them about selling food on that day. Tyrians living there brought in fish and whatever else, selling it to Judeans—*in Jerusalem*, mind you!—on the Sabbath.

13.17-18   I confronted the leaders of Judah: "What's going on here? This evil! Profaning the Sabbath! Isn't this exactly what your ancestors did? And because of it didn't God bring down on us and this city all this misery? And here you are adding to it—accumulating more wrath on Jerusalem by profaning the Sabbath."

13.19   As the gates of Jerusalem were darkened by the shadows of the approaching Sabbath, I ordered the doors shut and not to be opened until the Sabbath was over. I placed some of my servants at the gates to make sure that nothing to be sold would get in on the Sabbath day.

13.20-21   Traders and dealers in various goods camped outside the gates once or twice. But I took them to task. I said, "You have no business camping out here by the wall. If I find you here again, I'll use force to drive you off."

And that did it; they didn't come back on the Sabbath.

13.22   Then I directed the Levites to ceremonially cleanse themselves and take over as guards at the gates to keep the sanctity of the Sabbath day.

Remember me also for this, my God. Treat me with mercy according to your great and steadfast love.

✛

13.23-27   Also in those days I saw Jews who had married women from Ashdod, Ammon, and Moab. Half the children couldn't even speak the language of Judah; all they knew was the language of Ashdod or some other tongue. So I took those men to task, gave them a piece of my mind, even slapped some of them and jerked them by the hair. I made them swear to God: "Don't marry your daughters to their sons; and don't let their daughters marry your sons—and don't you yourselves marry them! Didn't Solomon the king of Israel sin because of women just like these? Even though there was no king quite like him, and God loved him and made him king over all Israel, foreign women were his downfall. Do you call this obedience—engaging in this extensive evil, showing yourselves faithless to God by marrying foreign wives?"

NEW INTERNATIONAL VERSION

²⁸One of the sons of Joiada son of Eliashib the high priest was son-in-law to Sanballat the Horonite. And I drove him away from me.

²⁹Remember them, O my God, because they defiled the priestly office and the covenant of the priesthood and of the Levites.

³⁰So I purified the priests and the Levites of everything foreign, and assigned them duties, each to his own task. ³¹I also made provision for contributions of wood at designated times, and for the firstfruits.

Remember me with favor, O my God.

THE MESSAGE

13.28   One of the sons of Joiada, the son of Eliashib the high priest, was a son-in-law of Sanballat the Horonite; I drove him out of my presence.

13.29   Remember them, O my God, how they defiled the priesthood and the covenant of the priests and Levites.

13.30-31 All in all I cleansed them from everything foreign. I organized the orders of service for the priests and Levites so that each man knew his job. I arranged for a regular supply of altar wood at the appointed times and for the firstfruits.

Remember me, O my God, for good.

ESTHER

ESTHER

QUEEN VASHTI DEPOSED

1 This is what happened during the time of Xerxes,[a] the Xerxes who ruled over 127 provinces stretching from India to Cush[b]: ²At that time King Xerxes reigned from his royal throne in the citadel of Susa, ³and in the third year of his reign he gave a banquet for all his nobles and officials. The military leaders of Persia and Media, the princes, and the nobles of the provinces were present.

⁴For a full 180 days he displayed the vast wealth of his kingdom and the splendor and glory of his majesty. ⁵When these days were over, the king gave a banquet, lasting seven days, in the enclosed garden of the king's palace, for all the people from the least to the greatest, who were in the citadel of Susa. ⁶The garden had hangings of white and blue linen, fastened with cords of white linen and purple material to silver rings on marble pillars. There were couches of gold and silver on a mosaic pavement of porphyry, marble, mother-of-pearl and other costly stones. ⁷Wine was served in goblets of gold, each one different from the other, and the royal wine was abundant, in keeping with the king's liberality. ⁸By the king's command each guest was allowed to drink in his own way, for the king instructed all the wine stewards to serve each man what he wished.

⁹Queen Vashti also gave a banquet for the women in the royal palace of King Xerxes.

¹⁰On the seventh day, when King Xerxes was in high spirits from wine, he commanded the seven eunuchs who served him—Mehuman, Biztha, Harbona, Bigtha, Abagtha, Zethar and Carcas— ¹¹to bring before him Queen Vashti, wearing her royal crown, in order to display her beauty to the people and nobles, for she was lovely to look at. ¹²But when the attendants delivered the king's command, Queen Vashti refused to come. Then the king became furious and burned with anger.

¹³Since it was customary for the king to con-

1.1-3 **1** This is the story of something that happened in the time of Xerxes, the Xerxes who ruled from India to Ethiopia—127 provinces in all. King Xerxes ruled from his royal throne in the palace complex of Susa. In the third year of his reign he gave a banquet for all his officials and ministers. The military brass of Persia and Media were also there, along with the princes and governors of the provinces.

1.4-7 For six months he put on exhibit the huge wealth of his empire and its stunningly beautiful royal splendors. At the conclusion of the exhibit, the king threw a weeklong party for everyone living in Susa, the capital—important and unimportant alike. The party was in the garden courtyard of the king's summer house. The courtyard was elaborately decorated with white and blue cotton curtains tied with linen and purple cords to silver rings on marble columns. Silver and gold couches were arranged on a mosaic pavement of porphyry, marble, mother-of-pearl, and colored stones. Drinks were served in gold chalices, each chalice one-of-a-kind. The royal wine flowed freely—a generous king!

1.8-9 The guests could drink as much as they liked—king's orders!—with waiters at their elbows to refill the drinks. Meanwhile, Queen Vashti was throwing a separate party for women inside King Xerxes' royal palace.

1.10-11 On the seventh day of the party, the king, high on the wine, ordered the seven eunuchs who were his personal servants (Mehuman, Biztha, Harbona, Bigtha, Abagtha, Zethar, and Carcas) to bring him Queen Vashti resplendent in her royal crown. He wanted to show off her beauty to the guests and officials. She was extremely good-looking.

1.12-15 But Queen Vashti refused to come, refused the summons delivered by the eunuchs. The king lost his temper. Seething with anger over her insolence, the king called in his counselors, all experts in legal matters. It was the king's

---

a 1 Hebrew *Ahasuerus*, a variant of Xerxes' Persian name; here and throughout Esther   *b 1* That is, the upper Nile region

sult experts in matters of law and justice, he spoke with the wise men who understood the times [14]and were closest to the king—Carshena, Shethar, Admatha, Tarshish, Meres, Marsena and Memucan, the seven nobles of Persia and Media who had special access to the king and were highest in the kingdom.

[15]"According to law, what must be done to Queen Vashti?" he asked. "She has not obeyed the command of King Xerxes that the eunuchs have taken to her."

[16]Then Memucan replied in the presence of the king and the nobles, "Queen Vashti has done wrong, not only against the king but also against all the nobles and the peoples of all the provinces of King Xerxes. [17]For the queen's conduct will become known to all the women, and so they will despise their husbands and say, 'King Xerxes commanded Queen Vashti to be brought before him, but she would not come.' [18]This very day the Persian and Median women of the nobility who have heard about the queen's conduct will respond to all the king's nobles in the same way. There will be no end of disrespect and discord.

[19]"Therefore, if it pleases the king, let him issue a royal decree and let it be written in the laws of Persia and Media, which cannot be repealed, that Vashti is never again to enter the presence of King Xerxes. Also let the king give her royal position to someone else who is better than she. [20]Then when the king's edict is proclaimed throughout all his vast realm, all the women will respect their husbands, from the least to the greatest."

[21]The king and his nobles were pleased with this advice, so the king did as Memucan proposed. [22]He sent dispatches to all parts of the kingdom, to each province in its own script and to each people in its own language, proclaiming in each people's tongue that every man should be ruler over his own household.

ESTHER MADE QUEEN

2 Later when the anger of King Xerxes had subsided, he remembered Vashti and what she had done and what he had decreed about her. [2]Then the king's personal attendants proposed, "Let a search be made for beautiful young virgins for the king. [3]Let the king appoint commissioners in every province of his realm to bring all these beautiful girls into the harem at the citadel of Susa. Let them be placed under the care of Hegai, the king's eunuch, who is in charge of the women; and let beauty treatments be given to them. [4]Then let the girl who pleases the king be queen instead of Vashti." This advice appealed to the king, and he followed it.

practice to consult his expert advisors. Those closest to him were Carshena, Shethar, Admatha, Tarshish, Meres, Marsena, and Memucan, the seven highest-ranking princes of Persia and Media, the inner circle with access to the king's ear. He asked them what legal recourse they had against Queen Vashti for not obeying King Xerxes' summons delivered by the eunuchs.

1.16-18   Memucan spoke up in the council of the king and princes: "It's not only the king Queen Vashti has insulted, it's all of us, leaders and people alike in every last one of King Xerxes' provinces. The word's going to get out: 'Did you hear the latest about Queen Vashti? King Xerxes ordered her to be brought before him and she wouldn't do it!' When the women hear it, they'll start treating their husbands with contempt. The day the wives of the Persian and Mede officials get wind of the queen's insolence, they'll be out of control. Is that what we want, a country of angry women who don't know their place?

1.19-20   "So, if the king agrees, let him pronounce a royal ruling and have it recorded in the laws of the Persians and Medes so that it cannot be revoked, that Vashti is permanently banned from King Xerxes' presence. And then let the king give her royal position to a woman who knows her place. When the king's ruling becomes public knowledge throughout the kingdom, extensive as it is, every woman, regardless of her social position, will show proper respect to her husband."

1.21-22   The king and the princes liked this. The king did what Memucan proposed. He sent bulletins to every part of the kingdom, to each province in its own script, to each people in their own language: "Every man is master of his own house; whatever he says, goes."

2.1-4   **2** Later, when King Xerxes' anger had cooled and he was having second thoughts about what Vashti had done and what he had ordered against her, the king's young attendants stepped in and got the ball rolling: "Let's begin a search for beautiful young virgins for the king. Let the king appoint officials in every province of his kingdom to bring every beautiful young virgin to the palace complex of Susa and to the harem run by Hegai, the king's eunuch who oversees the women; he will put them through their beauty treatments. Then let the girl who best pleases the king be made queen in place of Vashti."

The king liked this advice and took it.

⊹

NEW INTERNATIONAL VERSION

⁵Now there was in the citadel of Susa a Jew of the tribe of Benjamin, named Mordecai son of Jair, the son of Shimei, the son of Kish, ⁶who had been carried into exile from Jerusalem by Nebuchadnezzar king of Babylon, among those taken captive with Jehoiachin*ª* king of Judah. ⁷Mordecai had a cousin named Hadassah, whom he had brought up because she had neither father nor mother. This girl, who was also known as Esther, was lovely in form and features, and Mordecai had taken her as his own daughter when her father and mother died.

⁸When the king's order and edict had been proclaimed, many girls were brought to the citadel of Susa and put under the care of Hegai. Esther also was taken to the king's palace and entrusted to Hegai, who had charge of the harem. ⁹The girl pleased him and won his favor. Immediately he provided her with her beauty treatments and special food. He assigned to her seven maids selected from the king's palace and moved her and her maids into the best place in the harem.

¹⁰Esther had not revealed her nationality and family background, because Mordecai had forbidden her to do so. ¹¹Every day he walked back and forth near the courtyard of the harem to find out how Esther was and what was happening to her.

¹²Before a girl's turn came to go in to King Xerxes, she had to complete twelve months of beauty treatments prescribed for the women, six months with oil of myrrh and six with perfumes and cosmetics. ¹³And this is how she would go to the king: Anything she wanted was given her to take with her from the harem to the king's palace. ¹⁴In the evening she would go there and in the morning return to another part of the harem to the care of Shaashgaz, the king's eunuch who was in charge of the concubines. She would not return to the king unless he was pleased with her and summoned her by name.

¹⁵When the turn came for Esther (the girl Mordecai had adopted, the daughter of his uncle Abihail) to go to the king, she asked for nothing other than what Hegai, the king's eunuch who was in charge of the harem, suggested. And Esther won the favor of everyone who saw her. ¹⁶She was taken to King Xerxes in the royal residence in the tenth month, the month of Tebeth, in the seventh year of his reign.

¹⁷Now the king was attracted to Esther more than to any of the other women, and she won his favor and approval more than any of the other virgins. So he set a royal crown on her head and made her queen instead of Vashti. ¹⁸And the

---

THE MESSAGE

2.5-7 Now there was a Jew who lived in the palace complex in Susa. His name was Mordecai the son of Jair, the son of Shimei, the son of Kish—a Benjaminite. His ancestors had been taken from Jerusalem with the exiles and carried off with King Jehoiachin of Judah by King Nebuchadnezzar of Babylon into exile. Mordecai had reared his cousin Hadassah, otherwise known as Esther, since she had no father or mother. The girl had a good figure and a beautiful face. After her parents died, Mordecai had adopted her.

2.8 When the king's order had been publicly posted, many young girls were brought to the palace complex of Susa and given over to Hegai who was overseer of the women. Esther was among them.

2.9-10 Hegai liked Esther and took a special interest in her. Right off he started her beauty treatments, ordered special food, assigned her seven personal maids from the palace, and put her and her maids in the best rooms in the harem. Esther didn't say anything about her family and racial background because Mordecai had told her not to.

2.11 Every day Mordecai strolled beside the court of the harem to find out how Esther was and get news of what she was doing.

2.12-14 Each girl's turn came to go in to King Xerxes after she had completed the twelve months of prescribed beauty treatments—six months' treatment with oil of myrrh followed by six months with perfumes and various cosmetics. When it was time for the girl to go to the king, she was given whatever she wanted to take with her when she left the harem for the king's quarters. She would go there in the evening; in the morning she would return to a second harem overseen by Shaashgaz, the king's eunuch in charge of the concubines. She never again went back to the king unless the king took a special liking to her and asked for her by name.

2.15 When it was Esther's turn to go to the king (Esther the daughter of Abihail the uncle of Mordecai, who had adopted her as his daughter), she asked for nothing other than what Hegai, the king's eunuch in charge of the harem, had recommended. Esther, just as she was, won the admiration of everyone who saw her.

2.16 She was taken to King Xerxes in the royal palace in the tenth month, the month of Tebeth, in the seventh year of the king's reign.

2.17-18 The king fell in love with Esther far more than with any of his other women or any of the other virgins—he was totally smitten by her. He placed a royal crown on her head and made her queen in place of Vashti. Then the

---

ª 6 Hebrew Jeconiah, a variant of Jehoiachin

NEW INTERNATIONAL VERSION

king gave a great banquet, Esther's banquet, for all his nobles and officials. He proclaimed a holiday throughout the provinces and distributed gifts with royal liberality.

MORDECAI UNCOVERS A CONSPIRACY

[19]When the virgins were assembled a second time, Mordecai was sitting at the king's gate. [20]But Esther had kept secret her family background and nationality just as Mordecai had told her to do, for she continued to follow Mordecai's instructions as she had done when he was bringing her up.

[21]During the time Mordecai was sitting at the king's gate, Bigthana[a] and Teresh, two of the king's officers who guarded the doorway, became angry and conspired to assassinate King Xerxes. [22]But Mordecai found out about the plot and told Queen Esther, who in turn reported it to the king, giving credit to Mordecai. [23]And when the report was investigated and found to be true, the two officials were hanged on a gallows.[b] All this was recorded in the book of the annals in the presence of the king.

HAMAN'S PLOT TO DESTROY THE JEWS

3 After these events, King Xerxes honored Haman son of Hammedatha, the Agagite, elevating him and giving him a seat of honor higher than that of all the other nobles. [2]All the royal officials at the king's gate knelt down and paid honor to Haman, for the king had commanded this concerning him. But Mordecai would not kneel down or pay him honor.

[3]Then the royal officials at the king's gate asked Mordecai, "Why do you disobey the king's command?" [4]Day after day they spoke to him but he refused to comply. Therefore they told Haman about it to see whether Mordecai's behavior would be tolerated, for he had told them he was a Jew.

[5]When Haman saw that Mordecai would not kneel down or pay him honor, he was enraged. [6]Yet having learned who Mordecai's people were, he scorned the idea of killing only Mordecai. Instead Haman looked for a way to destroy all Mordecai's people, the Jews, throughout the whole kingdom of Xerxes.

[7]In the twelfth year of King Xerxes, in the first month, the month of Nisan, they cast the *pur* (that is, the lot) in the presence of Haman to select a day and month. And the lot fell on[c] the twelfth month, the month of Adar.

[8]Then Haman said to King Xerxes, "There is a

---

a 21 Hebrew *Bigthan,* a variant of *Bigthana*   *b 23* Or *were hung* (or *impaled*) *on poles*; similarly elsewhere in Esther   *c 7* Septuagint; Hebrew does not have *And the lot fell on.*

THE MESSAGE

king gave a great banquet for all his nobles and officials—"Esther's Banquet." He proclaimed a holiday for all the provinces and handed out gifts with royal generosity.

2.19-20 On one of the occasions when the virgins were being gathered together, Mordecai was sitting at the King's Gate. All this time, Esther had kept her family background and race a secret as Mordecai had ordered; Esther still did what Mordecai told her, just as when she was being raised by him.

2.21-22 On this day, with Mordecai sitting at the King's Gate, Bigthana and Teresh, two of the king's eunuchs who guarded the entrance, had it in for the king and were making plans to kill King Xerxes. But Mordecai learned of the plot and told Queen Esther, who then told King Xerxes, giving credit to Mordecai. When the thing was investigated and confirmed as true, the two men were hanged on a gallows. This was all written down in a logbook kept for the king's use.

3.1-2 **3** Some time later, King Xerxes promoted Haman son of Hammedatha the Agagite, making him the highest-ranking official in the government. All the king's servants at the King's Gate used to honor him by bowing down and kneeling before Haman—that's what the king had commanded.

3.2-4 Except Mordecai. Mordecai wouldn't do it, wouldn't bow down and kneel. The king's servants at the King's Gate asked Mordecai about it: "Why do you cross the king's command?" Day after day they spoke to him about this but he wouldn't listen, so they went to Haman to see whether something shouldn't be done about it. Mordecai had told them that he was a Jew.

3.5-6 When Haman saw for himself that Mordecai didn't bow down and kneel before him, he was outraged. Meanwhile, having learned that Mordecai was a Jew, Haman hated to waste his fury on just one Jew; he looked for a way to eliminate not just Mordecai but all Jews throughout the whole kingdom of Xerxes.

3.7 In the first month, the month of Nisan, of the twelfth year of Xerxes, the *pur*—that is, the lot—was cast under Haman's charge to determine the propitious day and month. The lot turned up the thirteenth day of the twelfth month, which is the month of Adar.

3.8-9 Haman then spoke with King Xerxes: "There

NEW INTERNATIONAL VERSION

certain people dispersed and scattered among the peoples in all the provinces of your kingdom whose customs are different from those of all other people and who do not obey the king's laws; it is not in the king's best interest to tolerate them. ⁹If it pleases the king, let a decree be issued to destroy them, and I will put ten thousand talents[a] of silver into the royal treasury for the men who carry out this business."

¹⁰So the king took his signet ring from his finger and gave it to Haman son of Hammedatha, the Agagite, the enemy of the Jews. ¹¹"Keep the money," the king said to Haman, "and do with the people as you please."

¹²Then on the thirteenth day of the first month the royal secretaries were summoned. They wrote out in the script of each province and in the language of each people all Haman's orders to the king's satraps, the governors of the various provinces and the nobles of the various peoples. These were written in the name of King Xerxes himself and sealed with his own ring. ¹³Dispatches were sent by couriers to all the king's provinces with the order to destroy, kill and annihilate all the Jews—young and old, women and little children—on a single day, the thirteenth day of the twelfth month, the month of Adar, and to plunder their goods. ¹⁴A copy of the text of the edict was to be issued as law in every province and made known to the people of every nationality so they would be ready for that day.

¹⁵Spurred on by the king's command, the couriers went out, and the edict was issued in the citadel of Susa. The king and Haman sat down to drink, but the city of Susa was bewildered.

Mordecai Persuades Esther to Help

4 When Mordecai learned of all that had been done, he tore his clothes, put on sackcloth and ashes, and went out into the city, wailing loudly and bitterly. ²But he went only as far as the king's gate, because no one clothed in sackcloth was allowed to enter it. ³In every province to which the edict and order of the king came, there was great mourning among the Jews, with fasting, weeping and wailing. Many lay in sackcloth and ashes.

⁴When Esther's maids and eunuchs came and told her about Mordecai, she was in great distress. She sent clothes for him to put on instead of his sackcloth, but he would not accept them. ⁵Then Esther summoned Hathach, one of the king's eunuchs assigned to attend her, and or-

THE MESSAGE

is an odd set of people scattered through the provinces of your kingdom who don't fit in. Their customs and ways are different from those of everybody else. Worse, they disregard the king's laws. They're an affront; the king shouldn't put up with them. If it please the king, let orders be given that they be destroyed. I'll pay for it myself. I'll deposit 375 tons of silver in the royal bank to finance the operation."

3.10   The king slipped his signet ring from his hand and gave it to Haman son of Hammedatha the Agagite, archenemy of the Jews.

3.11   "Go ahead," the king said to Haman. "It's your money—do whatever you want with those people."

3.12   The king's secretaries were brought in on the thirteenth day of the first month. The orders were written out word for word as Haman had addressed them to the king's satraps, the governors of every province, and the officials of every people. They were written in the script of each province and the language of each people in the name of King Xerxes and sealed with the royal signet ring.

3.13-14   Bulletins were sent out by couriers to all the king's provinces with orders to massacre, kill, and eliminate all the Jews—youngsters and old men, women and babies—on a single day, the thirteenth day of the twelfth month, the month Adar, and to plunder their goods. Copies of the bulletin were to be posted in each province, publicly available to all peoples, to get them ready for that day.

3.15   At the king's command, the couriers took off; the order was also posted in the palace complex of Susa. The king and Haman sat back and had a drink while the city of Susa reeled from the news.

4.1-3   4 When Mordecai learned what had been done, he ripped his clothes to shreds and put on sackcloth and ashes. Then he went out in the streets of the city crying out in loud and bitter cries. He came only as far as the King's Gate, for no one dressed in sackcloth was allowed to enter the King's Gate. As the king's order was posted in every province, there was loud lament among the Jews—fasting, weeping, wailing. And most of them stretched out on sackcloth and ashes.

4.4-8   Esther's maids and eunuchs came and told her. The queen was stunned. She sent fresh clothes to Mordecai so he could take off his sackcloth but he wouldn't accept them. Esther called for Hathach, one of the royal eunuchs whom the king had assigned to wait on her,

NEW INTERNATIONAL VERSION

dered him to find out what was troubling Mordecai and why.

⁶So Hathach went out to Mordecai in the open square of the city in front of the king's gate. ⁷Mordecai told him everything that had happened to him, including the exact amount of money Haman had promised to pay into the royal treasury for the destruction of the Jews. ⁸He also gave him a copy of the text of the edict for their annihilation, which had been published in Susa, to show to Esther and explain it to her, and he told him to urge her to go into the king's presence to beg for mercy and plead with him for her people.

⁹Hathach went back and reported to Esther what Mordecai had said. ¹⁰Then she instructed him to say to Mordecai, ¹¹"All the king's officials and the people of the royal provinces know that for any man or woman who approaches the king in the inner court without being summoned the king has but one law: that he be put to death. The only exception to this is for the king to extend the gold scepter to him and spare his life. But thirty days have passed since I was called to go to the king."

¹²When Esther's words were reported to Mordecai, ¹³he sent back this answer: "Do not think that because you are in the king's house you alone of all the Jews will escape. ¹⁴For if you remain silent at this time, relief and deliverance for the Jews will arise from another place, but you and your father's family will perish. And who knows but that you have come to royal position for such a time as this?"

¹⁵Then Esther sent this reply to Mordecai: ¹⁶"Go, gather together all the Jews who are in Susa, and fast for me. Do not eat or drink for three days, night or day. I and my maids will fast as you do. When this is done, I will go to the king, even though it is against the law. And if I perish, I perish."

¹⁷So Mordecai went away and carried out all of Esther's instructions.

ESTHER'S REQUEST TO THE KING

5 On the third day Esther put on her royal robes and stood in the inner court of the palace, in front of the king's hall. The king was sitting on his royal throne in the hall, facing the entrance. ²When he saw Queen Esther standing in the court, he was pleased with her and held out to her the gold scepter that was in his hand. So Esther approached and touched the tip of the scepter.

³Then the king asked, "What is it, Queen Esther? What is your request? Even up to half the kingdom, it will be given you."

THE MESSAGE

and told him to go to Mordecai and get the full story of what was happening. So Hathach went to Mordecai in the town square in front of the King's Gate. Mordecai told him everything that had happened to him. He also told him the exact amount of money that Haman had promised to deposit in the royal bank to finance the massacre of the Jews. Mordecai also gave him a copy of the bulletin that had been posted in Susa ordering the massacre so he could show it to Esther when he reported back with instructions to go to the king and intercede and plead with him for her people.

4.9-11 Hathach came back and told Esther everything Mordecai had said. Esther talked it over with Hathach and then sent him back to Mordecai with this message: "Everyone who works for the king here, and even the people out in the provinces, knows that there is a single fate for every man or woman who approaches the king without being invited: death. The one exception is if the king extends his gold scepter; then he or she may live. And it's been thirty days now since I've been invited to come to the king."

4.12-14 When Hathach told Mordecai what Esther had said, Mordecai sent her this message: "Don't think that just because you live in the king's house you're the one Jew who will get out of this alive. If you persist in staying silent at a time like this, help and deliverance will arrive for the Jews from someplace else; but you and your family will be wiped out. Who knows? Maybe you were made queen for just such a time as this."

4.15-16 Esther sent back her answer to Mordecai: "Go and get all the Jews living in Susa together. Fast for me. Don't eat or drink for three days, either day or night. I and my maids will fast with you. If you will do this, I'll go to the king, even though it's forbidden. If I die, I die."

4.17 Mordecai left and carried out Esther's instructions.

✝

5.1-3 **5** Three days later Esther dressed in her royal robes and took up a position in the inner court of the palace in front of the king's throne room. The king was on his throne facing the entrance. When he noticed Queen Esther standing in the court, he was pleased to see her; the king extended the gold scepter in his hand. Esther approached and touched the tip of the scepter. The king asked, "And what's your desire, Queen Esther? What do you want? Ask and it's yours—even if it's half my kingdom!"

NEW INTERNATIONAL VERSION

⁴"If it pleases the king," replied Esther, "let the king, together with Haman, come today to a banquet I have prepared for him."

⁵"Bring Haman at once," the king said, "so that we may do what Esther asks."

So the king and Haman went to the banquet Esther had prepared. ⁶As they were drinking wine, the king again asked Esther, "Now what is your petition? It will be given you. And what is your request? Even up to half the kingdom, it will be granted."

⁷Esther replied, "My petition and my request is this: ⁸If the king regards me with favor and if it pleases the king to grant my petition and fulfill my request, let the king and Haman come tomorrow to the banquet I will prepare for them. Then I will answer the king's question."

HAMAN'S RAGE AGAINST MORDECAI

⁹Haman went out that day happy and in high spirits. But when he saw Mordecai at the king's gate and observed that he neither rose nor showed fear in his presence, he was filled with rage against Mordecai. ¹⁰Nevertheless, Haman restrained himself and went home.

Calling together his friends and Zeresh, his wife, ¹¹Haman boasted to them about his vast wealth, his many sons, and all the ways the king had honored him and how he had elevated him above the other nobles and officials. ¹²"And that's not all," Haman added. "I'm the only person Queen Esther invited to accompany the king to the banquet she gave. And she has invited me along with the king tomorrow. ¹³But all this gives me no satisfaction as long as I see that Jew Mordecai sitting at the king's gate."

¹⁴His wife Zeresh and all his friends said to him, "Have a gallows built, seventy-five feet*ᵃ* high, and ask the king in the morning to have Mordecai hanged on it. Then go with the king to the dinner and be happy." This suggestion delighted Haman, and he had the gallows built.

MORDECAI HONORED

6 That night the king could not sleep; so he ordered the book of the chronicles, the record of his reign, to be brought in and read to him. ²It was found recorded there that Mordecai had exposed Bigthana and Teresh, two of the king's officers who guarded the doorway, who had conspired to assassinate King Xerxes.

³"What honor and recognition has Mordecai received for this?" the king asked.

"Nothing has been done for him," his attendants answered.

THE MESSAGE

5.4 "If it please the king," said Esther, "let the king come with Haman to a dinner I've prepared for him."

5.5-6 "Get Haman at once," said the king, "so we can go to dinner with Esther."

So the king and Haman joined Esther at the dinner she had arranged. As they were drinking the wine, the king said, "Now, what is it you want? Half of my kingdom isn't too much to ask! Just ask."

5.7-8 Esther answered, "Here's what I want. If the king favors me and is pleased to do what I desire and ask, let the king and Haman come again tomorrow to the dinner that I will fix for them. Then I'll give a straight answer to the king's question."

✛

5.9-13 Haman left the palace that day happy, beaming. And then he saw Mordecai sitting at the King's Gate ignoring him, oblivious to him. Haman was furious with Mordecai. But he held himself in and went on home. He got his friends together with his wife Zeresh and started bragging about how much money he had, his many sons, all the times the king had honored him, and his promotion to the highest position in the government. "On top of all that," Haman continued, "Queen Esther invited me to a private dinner she gave for the king, just the three of us. And she's invited me to another one tomorrow. But I can't enjoy any of it when I see Mordecai the Jew sitting at the King's Gate."

5.14 His wife Zeresh and all his friends said, "Build a gallows seventy-five feet high. First thing in the morning speak with the king; get him to order Mordecai hanged on it. Then happily go with the king to dinner."

Haman liked that. He had the gallows built.

✛

6.1-2 **6** That night the king couldn't sleep. He ordered the record book, the day-by-day journal of events, to be brought and read to him. They came across the story there about the time that Mordecai had exposed the plot of Bigthana and Teresh—the two royal eunuchs who guarded the entrance and who had conspired to assassinate King Xerxes.

6.3 The king asked, "What great honor was given to Mordecai for this?"

"Nothing," replied the king's servants who were in attendance. "Nothing has been done for him."

ᵃ 14 Hebrew *fifty cubits* (about 23 meters)

NEW INTERNATIONAL VERSION

⁴The king said, "Who is in the court?" Now Haman had just entered the outer court of the palace to speak to the king about hanging Mordecai on the gallows he had erected for him.

⁵His attendants answered, "Haman is standing in the court."

"Bring him in," the king ordered.

⁶When Haman entered, the king asked him, "What should be done for the man the king delights to honor?"

Now Haman thought to himself, "Who is there that the king would rather honor than me?" ⁷So he answered the king, "For the man the king delights to honor, ⁸have them bring a royal robe the king has worn and a horse the king has ridden, one with a royal crest placed on its head. ⁹Then let the robe and horse be entrusted to one of the king's most noble princes. Let them robe the man the king delights to honor, and lead him on the horse through the city streets, proclaiming before him, 'This is what is done for the man the king delights to honor!' "

¹⁰"Go at once," the king commanded Haman. "Get the robe and the horse and do just as you have suggested for Mordecai the Jew, who sits at the king's gate. Do not neglect anything you have recommended."

¹¹So Haman got the robe and the horse. He robed Mordecai, and led him on horseback through the city streets, proclaiming before him, "This is what is done for the man the king delights to honor!"

¹²Afterward Mordecai returned to the king's gate. But Haman rushed home, with his head covered in grief, ¹³and told Zeresh his wife and all his friends everything that had happened to him.

His advisers and his wife Zeresh said to him, "Since Mordecai, before whom your downfall has started, is of Jewish origin, you cannot stand against him—you will surely come to ruin!" ¹⁴While they were still talking with him, the king's eunuchs arrived and hurried Haman away to the banquet Esther had prepared.

HAMAN HANGED

7 So the king and Haman went to dine with Queen Esther, ²and as they were drinking wine on that second day, the king again asked, "Queen Esther, what is your petition? It will be given you. What is your request? Even up to half the kingdom, it will be granted."

³Then Queen Esther answered, "If I have

THE MESSAGE

6.4 The king said, "Is there anybody out in the court?"

Now Haman had just come into the outer court of the king's palace to talk to the king about hanging Mordecai on the gallows he had built for him.

6.5 The king's servants said, "Haman is out there, waiting in the court."

"Bring him in," said the king.

6.6-9 When Haman entered, the king said, "What would be appropriate for the man the king especially wants to honor?"

Haman thought to himself, "He must be talking about honoring me—who else?" So he answered the king, "For the man the king delights to honor, do this: Bring a royal robe that the king has worn and a horse the king has ridden, one with a royal crown on its head. Then give the robe and the horse to one of the king's most noble princes. Have him robe the man whom the king especially wants to honor; have the prince lead him on horseback through the city square, proclaiming before him, 'This is what is done for the man whom the king especially wants to honor!' "

6.10 "Go and do it," the king said to Haman. "Don't waste another minute. Take the robe and horse and do what you have proposed to Mordecai the Jew who sits at the King's Gate. Don't leave out a single detail of your plan."

6.11 So Haman took the robe and horse; he robed Mordecai and led him through the city square, proclaiming before him, "This is what is done for the man whom the king especially wants to honor!"

6.12-13 Then Mordecai returned to the King's Gate, but Haman fled to his house, thoroughly mortified, hiding his face. When Haman had finished telling his wife Zeresh and all his friends everything that had happened to him, his knowledgeable friends who were there and his wife Zeresh said, "If this Mordecai is in fact a Jew, your bad luck has only begun. You don't stand a chance against him—you're as good as ruined."

6.14 While they were still talking, the king's eunuchs arrived and hurried Haman off to the dinner that Esther had prepared.

✝

7.1-2 **7** So the king and Haman went to dinner with Queen Esther. At this second dinner, while they were drinking wine the king again asked, "Queen Esther, what would you like? Half of my kingdom! Just ask and it's yours."

7.3 Queen Esther answered, "If I have found fa-

NEW INTERNATIONAL VERSION

found favor with you, O king, and if it pleases your majesty, grant me my life—this is my petition. And spare my people—this is my request. [4]For I and my people have been sold for destruction and slaughter and annihilation. If we had merely been sold as male and female slaves, I would have kept quiet, because no such distress would justify disturbing the king. [a]"

[5]King Xerxes asked Queen Esther, "Who is he? Where is the man who has dared to do such a thing?"

[6]Esther said, "The adversary and enemy is this vile Haman."

Then Haman was terrified before the king and queen. [7]The king got up in a rage, left his wine and went out into the palace garden. But Haman, realizing that the king had already decided his fate, stayed behind to beg Queen Esther for his life.

[8]Just as the king returned from the palace garden to the banquet hall, Haman was falling on the couch where Esther was reclining.

The king exclaimed, "Will he even molest the queen while she is with me in the house?"

As soon as the word left the king's mouth, they covered Haman's face. [9]Then Harbona, one of the eunuchs attending the king, said, "A gallows seventy-five feet [b] high stands by Haman's house. He had it made for Mordecai, who spoke up to help the king."

The king said, "Hang him on it!" [10]So they hanged Haman on the gallows he had prepared for Mordecai. Then the king's fury subsided.

THE KING'S EDICT IN BEHALF OF THE JEWS

8 That same day King Xerxes gave Queen Esther the estate of Haman, the enemy of the Jews. And Mordecai came into the presence of the king, for Esther had told how he was related to her. [2]The king took off his signet ring, which he had reclaimed from Haman, and presented it to Mordecai. And Esther appointed him over Haman's estate.

[3]Esther again pleaded with the king, falling at his feet and weeping. She begged him to put an end to the evil plan of Haman the Agagite, which he had devised against the Jews. [4]Then the king extended the gold scepter to Esther and she arose and stood before him.

[5]"If it pleases the king," she said, "and if he regards me with favor and thinks it the right

THE MESSAGE

vor in your eyes, O King, and if it please the king, give me my life, and give my people their lives.

[7.4] "We've been sold, I and my people, to be destroyed—sold to be massacred, eliminated. If we had just been sold off into slavery, I wouldn't even have brought it up; our troubles wouldn't have been worth bothering the king over."

[7.5] King Xerxes exploded, "Who? Where is he? This is monstrous!"

[7.6] "An enemy. An adversary. This evil Haman," said Esther.

Haman was terror-stricken before the king and queen.

[7.7-8] The king, raging, left his wine and stalked out into the palace garden.

Haman stood there pleading with Queen Esther for his life—he could see that the king was finished with him and that he was doomed. As the king came back from the palace garden into the banquet hall, Haman was groveling at the couch on which Esther reclined. The king roared out, "Will he even molest the queen while I'm just around the corner?"

When that word left the king's mouth, all the blood drained from Haman's face.

[7.9] Harbona, one of the eunuchs attending the king, spoke up: "Look over there! There's the gallows that Haman had built for Mordecai, who saved the king's life. It's right next to Haman's house—seventy-five feet high!"

The king said, "Hang him on it!"

[7.10] So Haman was hanged on the very gallows that he had built for Mordecai. And the king's hot anger cooled.

⊹

[8.1-2] **8** That same day King Xerxes gave Queen Esther the estate of Haman, archenemy of the Jews. And Mordecai came before the king because Esther had explained their relationship. The king took off his signet ring, which he had taken back from Haman, and gave it to Mordecai. Esther appointed Mordecai over Haman's estate.

[8.3-6] Then Esther again spoke to the king, falling at his feet, begging with tears to counter the evil of Haman the Agagite and revoke the plan that he had plotted against the Jews. The king extended his gold scepter to Esther. She got to her feet and stood before the king. She said, "If it please the king and he regards me with favor and thinks this is right, and if he has any affec-

---

[a] 4 Or quiet, but the compensation our adversary offers cannot be compared with the loss the king would suffer   [b] 9 Hebrew fifty cubits (about 23 meters)

NEW INTERNATIONAL VERSION

thing to do, and if he is pleased with me, let an order be written overruling the dispatches that Haman son of Hammedatha, the Agagite, devised and wrote to destroy the Jews in all the king's provinces. [6]For how can I bear to see disaster fall on my people? How can I bear to see the destruction of my family?"

[7]King Xerxes replied to Queen Esther and to Mordecai the Jew, "Because Haman attacked the Jews, I have given his estate to Esther, and they have hanged him on the gallows. [8]Now write another decree in the king's name in behalf of the Jews as seems best to you, and seal it with the king's signet ring—for no document written in the king's name and sealed with his ring can be revoked."

[9]At once the royal secretaries were summoned—on the twenty-third day of the third month, the month of Sivan. They wrote out all Mordecai's orders to the Jews, and to the satraps, governors and nobles of the 127 provinces stretching from India to Cush.[a] These orders were written in the script of each province and the language of each people and also to the Jews in their own script and language. [10]Mordecai wrote in the name of King Xerxes, sealed the dispatches with the king's signet ring, and sent them by mounted couriers, who rode fast horses especially bred for the king.

[11]The king's edict granted the Jews in every city the right to assemble and protect themselves; to destroy, kill and annihilate any armed force of any nationality or province that might attack them and their women and children; and to plunder the property of their enemies. [12]The day appointed for the Jews to do this in all the provinces of King Xerxes was the thirteenth day of the twelfth month, the month of Adar. [13]A copy of the text of the edict was to be issued as law in every province and made known to the people of every nationality so that the Jews would be ready on that day to avenge themselves on their enemies.

[14]The couriers, riding the royal horses, raced out, spurred on by the king's command. And the edict was also issued in the citadel of Susa.

[15]Mordecai left the king's presence wearing royal garments of blue and white, a large crown of gold and a purple robe of fine linen. And the city of Susa held a joyous celebration. [16]For the Jews it was a time of happiness and joy, gladness and honor. [17]In every province and in every city, wherever the edict of the king went, there was joy and gladness among the Jews, with feasting and celebrating. And many people of other nationalities became Jews because fear of the Jews had seized them.

[a] 9 That is, the upper Nile region

THE MESSAGE

tion for me at all, let an order be written that cancels the bulletins authorizing the plan of Haman son of Hammedatha the Agagite to annihilate the Jews in all the king's provinces. How can I stand to see this catastrophe wipe out my people? How can I bear to stand by and watch the massacre of my own relatives?"

8.7-8 King Xerxes said to Queen Esther and Mordecai the Jew: "I've given Haman's estate to Esther and he's been hanged on the gallows because he attacked the Jews. So go ahead now and write whatever you decide on behalf of the Jews; then seal it with the signet ring." (An order written in the king's name and sealed with his signet ring is irrevocable.)

8.9 So the king's secretaries were brought in on the twenty-third day of the third month, the month of Sivan, and the order regarding the Jews was written word for word as Mordecai dictated and was addressed to the satraps, governors, and officials of the provinces from India to Ethiopia, 127 provinces in all, to each province in its own script and each people in their own language, including the Jews in their script and language.

8.10 He wrote under the name of King Xerxes and sealed the order with the royal signet ring; he sent out the bulletins by couriers on horseback, riding the fastest royal steeds bred from the royal stud.

8.11-13 The king's order authorized the Jews in every city to arm and defend themselves to the death, killing anyone who threatened them or their women and children, and confiscating for themselves anything owned by their enemies. The day set for this in all King Xerxes' provinces was the thirteenth day of the twelfth month, the month of Adar. The order was posted in public places in each province so everyone could read it, authorizing the Jews to be prepared on that day to avenge themselves on their enemies.

8.14 The couriers, fired up by the king's order, raced off on their royal horses. At the same time, the order was posted in the palace complex of Susa.

8.15-17 Mordecai walked out of the king's presence wearing a royal robe of violet and white, a huge gold crown, and a purple cape of fine linen. The city of Susa exploded with joy. For Jews it was all sunshine and laughter: they celebrated, they were honored. It was that way all over the country, in every province, every city when the king's bulletin was posted: the Jews took to the streets in celebration, cheering, and feasting. Not only that, but many non-Jews became Jews—now it was dangerous *not* to be a Jew!

☩

NEW INTERNATIONAL VERSION

TRIUMPH OF THE JEWS

9 On the thirteenth day of the twelfth month, the month of Adar, the edict commanded by the king was to be carried out. On this day the enemies of the Jews had hoped to overpower them, but now the tables were turned and the Jews got the upper hand over those who hated them. ²The Jews assembled in their cities in all the provinces of King Xerxes to attack those seeking their destruction. No one could stand against them, because the people of all the other nationalities were afraid of them. ³And all the nobles of the provinces, the satraps, the governors and the king's administrators helped the Jews, because fear of Mordecai had seized them. ⁴Mordecai was prominent in the palace; his reputation spread throughout the provinces, and he became more and more powerful.

⁵The Jews struck down all their enemies with the sword, killing and destroying them, and they did what they pleased to those who hated them. ⁶In the citadel of Susa, the Jews killed and destroyed five hundred men. ⁷They also killed Parshandatha, Dalphon, Aspatha, ⁸Poratha, Adalia, Aridatha, ⁹Parmashta, Arisai, Aridai and Vaizatha, ¹⁰the ten sons of Haman son of Hammedatha, the enemy of the Jews. But they did not lay their hands on the plunder.

¹¹The number of those slain in the citadel of Susa was reported to the king that same day. ¹²The king said to Queen Esther, "The Jews have killed and destroyed five hundred men and the ten sons of Haman in the citadel of Susa. What have they done in the rest of the king's provinces? Now what is your petition? It will be given you. What is your request? It will also be granted."

¹³"If it pleases the king," Esther answered, "give the Jews in Susa permission to carry out this day's edict tomorrow also, and let Haman's ten sons be hanged on gallows."

¹⁴So the king commanded that this be done. An edict was issued in Susa, and they hanged the ten sons of Haman. ¹⁵The Jews in Susa came together on the fourteenth day of the month of Adar, and they put to death in Susa three hundred men, but they did not lay their hands on the plunder.

¹⁶Meanwhile, the remainder of the Jews who were in the king's provinces also assembled to protect themselves and get relief from their enemies. They killed seventy-five thousand of them but did not lay their hands on the plunder. ¹⁷This happened on the thirteenth day of the

THE MESSAGE

9 On the thirteenth day of the twelfth month, the month of Adar, the king's order came into effect. This was the very day that the enemies of the Jews had planned to overpower them, but the tables were now turned: the Jews overpowered those who hated them! The Jews had gathered in the cities throughout King Xerxes' provinces to lay hands on those who were seeking their ruin. Not one man was able to stand up against them—fear made cowards of them all. What's more, all the government officials, satraps, governors—everyone who worked for the king—actually helped the Jews because of Mordecai; they were afraid of him. Mordecai by now was a power in the palace. As Mordecai became more and more powerful, his reputation had grown in all the provinces.

9.5-9 So the Jews finished off all their enemies with the sword, slaughtering them right and left, and did as they pleased to those who hated them. In the palace complex of Susa the Jews massacred five hundred men. They also killed the ten sons of Haman son of Hammedatha, the archenemy of the Jews:

Parshandatha	Dalphon
Aspatha	Poratha
Adalia	Aridatha
Parmashta	Arisai
Aridai	Vaizatha

9.10-12 But they took no plunder. That day, when it was all over, the number of those killed in the palace complex was given to the king. The king told Queen Esther, "In the palace complex alone here in Susa the Jews have killed five hundred men, plus Haman's ten sons. Think of the killing that must have been done in the rest of the provinces! What else do you want? Name it and it's yours. Your wish is my command."

9.13 "If it please the king," Queen Esther responded, "give the Jews of Susa permission to extend the terms of the order another day. And have the bodies of Haman's ten sons hanged in public display on the gallows."

9.14 The king commanded it: The order was extended; the bodies of Haman's ten sons were publicly hanged.

9.15 The Jews in Susa went at it again. On the fourteenth day of Adar they killed another three hundred men in Susa. But again they took no plunder.

9.16-19 Meanwhile in the rest of the king's provinces, the Jews had organized and defended themselves, freeing themselves from oppression. On the thirteenth day of the month of

NEW INTERNATIONAL VERSION

month of Adar, and on the fourteenth they rested and made it a day of feasting and joy.

PURIM CELEBRATED

[18]The Jews in Susa, however, had assembled on the thirteenth and fourteenth, and then on the fifteenth they rested and made it a day of feasting and joy.

[19]That is why rural Jews—those living in villages—observe the fourteenth of the month of Adar as a day of joy and feasting, a day for giving presents to each other.

[20]Mordecai recorded these events, and he sent letters to all the Jews throughout the provinces of King Xerxes, near and far, [21]to have them celebrate annually the fourteenth and fifteenth days of the month of Adar [22]as the time when the Jews got relief from their enemies, and as the month when their sorrow was turned into joy and their mourning into a day of celebration. He wrote them to observe the days as days of feasting and joy and giving presents of food to one another and gifts to the poor.

[23]So the Jews agreed to continue the celebration they had begun, doing what Mordecai had written to them. [24]For Haman son of Hammedatha, the Agagite, the enemy of all the Jews, had plotted against the Jews to destroy them and had cast the *pur* (that is, the lot) for their ruin and destruction. [25]But when the plot came to the king's attention,[a] he issued written orders that the evil scheme Haman had devised against the Jews should come back onto his own head, and that he and his sons should be hanged on the gallows. [26](Therefore these days were called Purim, from the word *pur*.) Because of everything written in this letter and because of what they had seen and what had happened to them, [27]the Jews took it upon themselves to establish the custom that they and their descendants and all who join them should without fail observe these two days every year, in the way prescribed and at the time appointed. [28]These days should be remembered and observed in every generation by every family, and in every province and in every city. And these days of Purim should never cease to be celebrated by the Jews, nor should the memory of them die out among their descendants.

[29]So Queen Esther, daughter of Abihail, along with Mordecai the Jew, wrote with full authority to confirm this second letter concerning Purim. [30]And Mordecai sent letters to all the Jews in the 127 provinces of the kingdom of Xerxes—words

[a] 25 Or *when Esther came before the king*

THE MESSAGE

Adar, they killed 75,000 of those who hated them but did not take any plunder. The next day, the fourteenth, they took it easy and celebrated with much food and laughter. But in Susa, since the Jews had banded together on both the thirteenth and fourteenth days, they made the fifteenth their holiday for laughing and feasting. (This accounts for why Jews living out in the country in the rural villages remember the fourteenth day of Adar for celebration, their day for parties and the exchange of gifts.)

⊹

9.20-22 Mordecai wrote all this down and sent copies to all the Jews in all King Xerxes' provinces, regardless of distance, calling for an annual celebration on the fourteenth and fifteenth days of Adar as the occasion when Jews got relief from their enemies, the month in which their sorrow turned to joy, mourning somersaulted into a holiday for parties and fun and laughter, the sending and receiving of presents and of giving gifts to the poor.

9.23 And they did it. What started then became a tradition, continuing the practice of what Mordecai had written to them.

⊹

9.24-26 Haman son of Hammedatha, the Agagite, the archenemy of all Jews, had schemed to destroy all Jews. He had cast the *pur* (the lot) to throw them into a panic and destroy them. But when Queen Esther intervened with the king, he gave written orders that the evil scheme that Haman had worked out should boomerang back on his own head. He and his sons were hanged on the gallows. That's why these days are called "Purim," from the word *pur* or "lot."

9.26-28 Therefore, because of everything written in this letter and because of all that they had been through, the Jews agreed to continue. It became a tradition for them, their children, and all future converts to remember these two days every year on the specified dates set down in the letter. These days are to be remembered and kept by every single generation, every last family, every province and city. These days of Purim must never be neglected among the Jews; the memory of them must never die out among their descendants.

9.29-32 Queen Esther, the daughter of Abihail, backed Mordecai the Jew, using her full queenly authority in this second Purim letter to endorse and ratify what he wrote. Calming and reassuring letters went out to all the Jews throughout the 127 provinces of Xerxes' king-

NEW INTERNATIONAL VERSION

of goodwill and assurance— [31] to establish these days of Purim at their designated times, as Mordecai the Jew and Queen Esther had decreed for them, and as they had established for themselves and their descendants in regard to their times of fasting and lamentation. [32] Esther's decree confirmed these regulations about Purim, and it was written down in the records.

THE GREATNESS OF MORDECAI

10 King Xerxes imposed tribute throughout the empire, to its distant shores. [2] And all his acts of power and might, together with a full account of the greatness of Mordecai to which the king had raised him, are they not written in the book of the annals of the kings of Media and Persia? [3] Mordecai the Jew was second in rank to King Xerxes, preeminent among the Jews, and held in high esteem by his many fellow Jews, because he worked for the good of his people and spoke up for the welfare of all the Jews.

THE MESSAGE

dom to fix these days of Purim their assigned place on the calendar, dates set by Mordecai the Jew—what they had agreed to for themselves and their descendants regarding their fasting and mourning. Esther's word confirmed the tradition of Purim and was written in the book.

✣

10.1-2 **10** King Xerxes imposed taxes from one end of his empire to the other. For the rest of it, King Xerxes' extensive accomplishments, along with a detailed account of the brilliance of Mordecai, whom the king had promoted, that's all written in *The Chronicles of the Kings of Media and Persia.*

10.3   Mordecai the Jew ranked second in command to King Xerxes. He was popular among the Jews and greatly respected by them. He worked hard for the good of his people; he cared for the peace and prosperity of his race.

JOB

JOB

PROLOGUE

1 In the land of Uz there lived a man whose name was Job. This man was blameless and upright; he feared God and shunned evil. ²He had seven sons and three daughters, ³and he owned seven thousand sheep, three thousand camels, five hundred yoke of oxen and five hundred donkeys, and had a large number of servants. He was the greatest man among all the people of the East.

⁴His sons used to take turns holding feasts in their homes, and they would invite their three sisters to eat and drink with them. ⁵When a period of feasting had run its course, Job would send and have them purified. Early in the morning he would sacrifice a burnt offering for each of them, thinking, "Perhaps my children have sinned and cursed God in their hearts." This was Job's regular custom.

JOB'S FIRST TEST

⁶One day the angels*a* came to present themselves before the LORD, and Satan*b* also came with them. ⁷The LORD said to Satan, "Where have you come from?"

Satan answered the LORD, "From roaming through the earth and going back and forth in it."

⁸Then the LORD said to Satan, "Have you considered my servant Job? There is no one on earth like him; he is blameless and upright, a man who fears God and shuns evil."

⁹"Does Job fear God for nothing?" Satan replied. ¹⁰"Have you not put a hedge around him and his household and everything he has? You have blessed the work of his hands, so that his flocks and herds are spread throughout the land. ¹¹But stretch out your hand and strike everything he has, and he will surely curse you to your face."

¹²The LORD said to Satan, "Very well, then, everything he has is in your hands, but on the man himself do not lay a finger."

Then Satan went out from the presence of the LORD.

A MAN DEVOTED TO GOD

1.1-3 **1** Job was a man who lived in Uz. He was honest inside and out, a man of his word, who was totally devoted to God and hated evil with a passion. He had seven sons and three daughters. He was also very wealthy—seven thousand head of sheep, three thousand camels, five hundred teams of oxen, five hundred donkeys, and a huge staff of servants—the most influential man in all the East!

1.4-5 His sons used to take turns hosting parties in their homes, always inviting their three sisters to join them in their merrymaking. When the parties were over, Job would get up early in the morning and sacrifice a burnt offering for each of his children, thinking, "Maybe one of them sinned by defying God inwardly." Job made a habit of this sacrificial atonement, just in case they'd sinned.

THE FIRST TEST: FAMILY AND FORTUNE

1.6-7 One day when the angels came to report to GOD, Satan, who was the Designated Accuser, came along with them. GOD singled out Satan and said, "What have you been up to?"

Satan answered GOD, "Going here and there, checking things out on earth."

1.8 GOD said to Satan, "Have you noticed my friend Job? There's no one quite like him—honest and true to his word, totally devoted to God and hating evil."

1.9-10 Satan retorted, "So do you think Job does all that out of the sheer goodness of his heart? Why, no one ever had it so good! You pamper him like a pet, make sure nothing bad ever happens to him or his family or his possessions, bless everything he does—he can't lose!

1.11 "But what do you think would happen if you reached down and took away everything that is his? He'd curse you right to your face, that's what."

1.12 GOD replied, "We'll see. Go ahead—do what you want with all that is his. Just don't hurt *him*." Then Satan left the presence of GOD.

---

a 6 Hebrew the sons of God   *b 6 Satan means accuser.*

NEW INTERNATIONAL VERSION

¹³One day when Job's sons and daughters were feasting and drinking wine at the oldest brother's house, ¹⁴a messenger came to Job and said, "The oxen were plowing and the donkeys were grazing nearby, ¹⁵and the Sabeans attacked and carried them off. They put the servants to the sword, and I am the only one who has escaped to tell you!"

¹⁶While he was still speaking, another messenger came and said, "The fire of God fell from the sky and burned up the sheep and the servants, and I am the only one who has escaped to tell you!"

¹⁷While he was still speaking, another messenger came and said, "The Chaldeans formed three raiding parties and swept down on your camels and carried them off. They put the servants to the sword, and I am the only one who has escaped to tell you!"

¹⁸While he was still speaking, yet another messenger came and said, "Your sons and daughters were feasting and drinking wine at the oldest brother's house, ¹⁹when suddenly a mighty wind swept in from the desert and struck the four corners of the house. It collapsed on them and they are dead, and I am the only one who has escaped to tell you!"

²⁰At this, Job got up and tore his robe and shaved his head. Then he fell to the ground in worship ²¹and said:

"Naked I came from my mother's womb,
   and naked I will depart.ᵃ
The Lord gave and the Lord has taken away;
   may the name of the Lord be praised."

²²In all this, Job did not sin by charging God with wrongdoing.

Job's Second Test

2 On another day the angelsᵇ came to present themselves before the Lord, and Satan also came with them to present himself before him. ²And the Lord said to Satan, "Where have you come from?"

Satan answered the Lord, "From roaming through the earth and going back and forth in it."

³Then the Lord said to Satan, "Have you considered my servant Job? There is no one on earth like him; he is blameless and upright, a man who fears God and shuns evil. And he still maintains his integrity, though you incited me against him to ruin him without any reason."

⁴"Skin for skin!" Satan replied. "A man will give all he has for his own life. ⁵But stretch out your hand and strike his flesh and bones, and he will surely curse you to your face."

THE MESSAGE

1.13-15 Sometime later, while Job's children were having one of their parties at the home of the oldest son, a messenger came to Job and said, "The oxen were plowing and the donkeys grazing in the field next to us when Sabeans attacked. They stole the animals and killed the field hands. I'm the only one to get out alive and tell you what happened."

1.16 While he was still talking, another messenger arrived and said, "Bolts of lightning struck the sheep and the shepherds and fried them—burned them to a crisp. I'm the only one to get out alive and tell you what happened."

1.17 While he was still talking, another messenger arrived and said, "Chaldeans coming from three directions raided the camels and massacred the camel drivers. I'm the only one to get out alive and tell you what happened."

1.18-19 While he was still talking, another messenger arrived and said, "Your children were having a party at the home of the oldest brother when a tornado swept in off the desert and struck the house. It collapsed on the young people and they died. I'm the only one to get out alive and tell you what happened."

1.20 Job got to his feet, ripped his robe, shaved his head, then fell to the ground and worshiped:

1.21 Naked I came from my mother's womb,
   naked I'll return to the womb of the earth.
God gives, God takes.
   God's name be ever blessed.

1.22 Not once through all this did Job sin; not once did he blame God.

The Second Test: Health

2 2.1-3 One day when the angels came to report to God, Satan also showed up. God singled out Satan, saying, "And what have you been up to?" Satan answered God, "Oh, going here and there, checking things out." Then God said to Satan, "Have you noticed my friend Job? There's no one quite like him, is there—honest and true to his word, totally devoted to God and hating evil? He still has a firm grip on his integrity! You tried to trick me into destroying him, but it didn't work."

2.4-5 Satan answered, "A human would do anything to save his life. But what do you think would happen if you reached down and took away his health? He'd curse you to your face, that's what."

ᵃ 21 Or will return there   ᵇ 1 Hebrew the sons of God

NEW INTERNATIONAL VERSION

⁶The LORD said to Satan, "Very well, then, he is in your hands; but you must spare his life."

⁷So Satan went out from the presence of the LORD and afflicted Job with painful sores from the soles of his feet to the top of his head. ⁸Then Job took a piece of broken pottery and scraped himself with it as he sat among the ashes.

⁹His wife said to him, "Are you still holding on to your integrity? Curse God and die!"

¹⁰He replied, "You are talking like a foolish*ᵃ* woman. Shall we accept good from God, and not trouble?"

In all this, Job did not sin in what he said.

JOB'S THREE FRIENDS

¹¹When Job's three friends, Eliphaz the Temanite, Bildad the Shuhite and Zophar the Naamathite, heard about all the troubles that had come upon him, they set out from their homes and met together by agreement to go and sympathize with him and comfort him. ¹²When they saw him from a distance, they could hardly recognize him; they began to weep aloud, and they tore their robes and sprinkled dust on their heads. ¹³Then they sat on the ground with him for seven days and seven nights. No one said a word to him, because they saw how great his suffering was.

JOB SPEAKS

3 After this, Job opened his mouth and cursed the day of his birth. ²He said:

³ "May the day of my birth perish,
  and the night it was said, 'A boy is born!'
⁴That day—may it turn to darkness;
  may God above not care about it;
  may no light shine upon it.
⁵May darkness and deep shadow*ᵇ* claim it
      once more;
  may a cloud settle over it;
  may blackness overwhelm its light.
⁶That night—may thick darkness seize it;
  may it not be included among the days of
      the year
  nor be entered in any of the months.
⁷May that night be barren;
  may no shout of joy be heard in it.

THE MESSAGE

2.6   GOD said, "All right. Go ahead—you can do what you like with him. But mind you, don't kill him."

2.7-8   Satan left GOD and struck Job with terrible sores. Job was ulcers and scabs from head to foot. They itched and oozed so badly that he took a piece of broken pottery to scrape himself, then went and sat on a trash heap, among the ashes.

2.9   His wife said, "Still holding on to your precious integrity, are you? Curse God and be done with it!"

2.10   He told her, "You're talking like an empty-headed fool. We take the good days from God—why not also the bad days?"

Not once through all this did Job sin. He said nothing against God.

JOB'S THREE FRIENDS

2.11-13   Three of Job's friends heard of all the trouble that had fallen on him. Each traveled from his own country—Eliphaz from Teman, Bildad from Shuhah, Zophar from Naamath—and went together to Job to keep him company and comfort him. When they first caught sight of him, they couldn't believe what they saw—they hardly recognized him! They cried out in lament, ripped their robes, and dumped dirt on their heads as a sign of their grief. Then they sat with him on the ground. Seven days and nights they sat there without saying a word. They could see how rotten he felt, how deeply he was suffering.

JOB CRIES OUT

WHAT'S THE POINT OF LIFE?

3.1-2   **3** Then Job broke the silence. He spoke up and cursed his fate:

3.3-10   "Obliterate the day I was born.
      Blank out the night I was conceived!
Let it be a black hole in space.
      May God above forget it ever happened.
      Erase it from the books!
May the day of my birth be buried in deep
          darkness,
      shrouded by the fog,
      swallowed by the night.
And the night of my conception—the devil
          take it!
      Rip the date off the calendar,
      delete it from the almanac.
Oh, turn that night into pure nothingness—
      no sounds of pleasure from that night, ever!

ᵃ *10* The Hebrew word rendered *foolish* denotes moral deficiency.   ᵇ *5* Or *and the shadow of death*

NEW INTERNATIONAL VERSION

⁸ May those who curse days*ᵃ* curse that day,
    those who are ready to rouse Leviathan.
⁹ May its morning stars become dark;
    may it wait for daylight in vain
    and not see the first rays of dawn,
¹⁰ for it did not shut the doors of the womb
      on me
    to hide trouble from my eyes.

¹¹ "Why did I not perish at birth,
    and die as I came from the womb?
¹² Why were there knees to receive me
    and breasts that I might be nursed?
¹³ For now I would be lying down in peace;
    I would be asleep and at rest
¹⁴ with kings and counselors of the earth,
    who built for themselves places now lying
      in ruins,
¹⁵ with rulers who had gold,
    who filled their houses with silver.
¹⁶ Or why was I not hidden in the ground like
      a stillborn child,
    like an infant who never saw the light of
      day?
¹⁷ There the wicked cease from turmoil,
    and there the weary are at rest.
¹⁸ Captives also enjoy their ease;
    they no longer hear the slave driver's
      shout.
¹⁹ The small and the great are there,
    and the slave is freed from his master.

²⁰ "Why is light given to those in misery,
    and life to the bitter of soul,
²¹ to those who long for death that does not
      come,
    who search for it more than for hidden
      treasure,
²² who are filled with gladness
    and rejoice when they reach the grave?
²³ Why is life given to a man
    whose way is hidden,
    whom God has hedged in?
²⁴ For sighing comes to me instead of food;
    my groans pour out like water.
²⁵ What I feared has come upon me;
    what I dreaded has happened to me.
²⁶ I have no peace, no quietness;
    I have no rest, but only turmoil."

ELIPHAZ

4 Then Eliphaz the Temanite replied:

² "If someone ventures a word with you, will
      you be impatient?

ᵃ 8 Or the sea

THE MESSAGE

May those who are good at cursing curse that
      day.
    Unleash the sea beast, Leviathan, on it.
May its morning stars turn to black cinders,
    waiting for a daylight that never comes,
    never once seeing the first light of dawn.
And why? Because it released me from my
      mother's womb
    into a life with so much trouble.

3:11-19 "Why didn't I die at birth,
    my first breath out of the womb my last?
Why were there arms to rock me,
    and breasts for me to drink from?
I could be resting in peace right now,
    asleep forever, feeling no pain,
In the company of kings and statesmen
    in their royal ruins,
Or with princes resplendent
    in their gold and silver tombs.
Why wasn't I stillborn and buried
    with all the babies who never saw light,
Where the wicked no longer trouble anyone
    and bone-weary people get a long-deserved
      rest?
Prisoners sleep undisturbed,
    never again to wake up to the bark of the
      guards.
The small and the great are equals in that place,
    and slaves are free from their masters.

3:20-23 "Why does God bother giving light to the
      miserable,
    why bother keeping bitter people alive,
Those who want in the worst way to die, and
      can't,
    who can't imagine anything better than death,
Who count the day of their death and burial
    the happiest day of their life?
What's the point of life when it doesn't make
      sense,
    when God blocks all the roads to meaning?

3:24-26 "Instead of bread I get groans for my supper,
    then leave the table and vomit my anguish.
The worst of my fears has come true,
    what I've dreaded most has happened.
My repose is shattered, my peace destroyed.
    No rest for me, ever—death has invaded life."

ELIPHAZ SPEAKS OUT

NOW *YOU'RE* THE ONE IN TROUBLE

4:1-6 **4** Then Eliphaz from Teman spoke up:

"Would you mind if I said something to you?

NEW INTERNATIONAL VERSION

But who can keep from speaking?
3 Think how you have instructed many,
  how you have strengthened feeble hands.
4 Your words have supported those who
    stumbled;
  you have strengthened faltering knees.
5 But now trouble comes to you, and you are
    discouraged;
  it strikes you, and you are dismayed.
6 Should not your piety be your confidence
  and your blameless ways your hope?

7 "Consider now: Who, being innocent, has
    ever perished?
  Where were the upright ever destroyed?
8 As I have observed, those who plow evil
  and those who sow trouble reap it.
9 At the breath of God they are destroyed;
  at the blast of his anger they perish.
10 The lions may roar and growl,
  yet the teeth of the great lions are broken.
11 The lion perishes for lack of prey,
  and the cubs of the lioness are scattered.

12 "A word was secretly brought to me,
  my ears caught a whisper of it.
13 Amid disquieting dreams in the night,
  when deep sleep falls on men,
14 fear and trembling seized me
  and made all my bones shake.
15 A spirit glided past my face,
  and the hair on my body stood on end.
16 It stopped,
  but I could not tell what it was.
  A form stood before my eyes,
  and I heard a hushed voice:
17 'Can a mortal be more righteous than God?
  Can a man be more pure than his Maker?
18 If God places no trust in his servants,
  if he charges his angels with error,
19 how much more those who live in houses of
    clay,
  whose foundations are in the dust,
  who are crushed more readily than a
    moth!
20 Between dawn and dusk they are broken to
    pieces;
  unnoticed, they perish forever.

THE MESSAGE

Under the circumstances it's hard to keep
    quiet.
You yourself have done this plenty of times,
    spoken words
  that clarify, encouraged those who were
    about to quit.
Your words have put stumbling people on
    their feet,
  put fresh hope in people about to collapse.
But now *you're* the one in trouble—you're
    hurting!
  You've been hit hard and you're reeling
    from the blow.
But shouldn't your devout life give you
    confidence now?
  Shouldn't your exemplary life give you hope?

4.7-11 "Think! Has a truly innocent person ever
    ended up on the scrap heap?
  Do genuinely upright people ever lose out
    in the end?
It's my observation that those who plow evil
  and sow trouble reap evil and trouble.
One breath from God and they fall apart,
  one blast of his anger and there's nothing
    left of them.
The mighty lion, king of the beasts, roars
    mightily,
  but when he's toothless he's useless—
No teeth, no prey—and the cubs
  wander off to fend for themselves.

4.12-16 "A word came to me in secret—
  a mere whisper of a word, but I heard it
    clearly.
It came in a scary dream one night,
  after I had fallen into a deep, deep sleep.
Dread stared me in the face, and Terror.
  I was scared to death—I shook from head
    to foot.
A spirit glided right in front of me—
  the hair on my head stood on end.
I couldn't tell what it was that appeared there—
  a blur . . . and then I heard a muffled voice:

4.17-21 " 'How can mere mortals be more righteous
    than God?
  How can humans be purer than their
    Creator?
Why, God doesn't even trust his own servants,
  doesn't even cheer his angels,
So how much less these bodies composed of
    mud,
  fragile as moths?
These bodies of ours are here today and gone
    tomorrow,
  and no one even notices—gone without a
    trace.

NEW INTERNATIONAL VERSION

²¹Are not the cords of their tent pulled up,
    so that they die without wisdom?'ᵃ

5 "Call if you will, but who will answer you?
    To which of the holy ones will you turn?
²Resentment kills a fool,
    and envy slays the simple.
³I myself have seen a fool taking root,
    but suddenly his house was cursed.
⁴His children are far from safety,
    crushed in court without a defender.
⁵The hungry consume his harvest,
    taking it even from among thorns,
    and the thirsty pant after his wealth.
⁶For hardship does not spring from the soil,
    nor does trouble sprout from the ground.
⁷Yet man is born to trouble
    as surely as sparks fly upward.

⁸"But if it were I, I would appeal to God;
    I would lay my cause before him.
⁹He performs wonders that cannot be
        fathomed,
    miracles that cannot be counted.
¹⁰He bestows rain on the earth;
    he sends water upon the countryside.
¹¹The lowly he sets on high,
    and those who mourn are lifted to safety.
¹²He thwarts the plans of the crafty,
    so that their hands achieve no success.
¹³He catches the wise in their craftiness,
    and the schemes of the wily are swept
        away.
¹⁴Darkness comes upon them in the daytime;
    at noon they grope as in the night.
¹⁵He saves the needy from the sword in their
        mouth;
    he saves them from the clutches of the
        powerful.
¹⁶So the poor have hope,
    and injustice shuts its mouth.

¹⁷"Blessed is the man whom God corrects;
    so do not despise the discipline of the
        Almighty.ᵇ

THE MESSAGE

When the tent stakes are ripped up, the tent
        collapses—
    we die and are never the wiser for having
        lived.'

DON'T BLAME FATE WHEN THINGS GO WRONG

5.1-7 5 "Call for help, Job, if you think anyone
        will answer!
    To which of the holy angels will you turn?
The hot temper of a fool eventually kills him,
    the jealous anger of a simpleton does her in.
I've seen it myself—seen fools putting down
        roots,
    and then, suddenly, their houses are cursed.
Their children out in the cold, abused and
        exploited,
    with no one to stick up for them.
Hungry people off the street plunder their
        harvests,
    cleaning them out completely, taking
        thorns and all,
    insatiable for everything they have.
Don't blame fate when things go wrong—
    trouble doesn't come from nowhere.
It's human! Mortals are born and bred for
        trouble,
    as certainly as sparks fly upward.

WHAT A BLESSING WHEN GOD CORRECTS YOU!

5.8-16 "If I were in your shoes, I'd go straight to God,
    I'd throw myself on the mercy of God.
After all, he's famous for great and unexpected
        acts;
    there's no end to his surprises.
He gives rain, for instance, across the wide earth,
    sends water to irrigate the fields.
He raises up the down-and-out,
    gives firm footing to those sinking in grief.
He aborts the schemes of conniving crooks,
    so that none of their plots come to term.
He catches the know-it-alls in their
        conspiracies—
    all that intricate intrigue swept out with the
        trash!
Suddenly they're disoriented, plunged into
        darkness;
    they can't see to put one foot in front of the
        other.
But the downtrodden are saved by God,
    saved from the murderous plots, saved
        from the iron fist.
And so the poor continue to hope,
    while injustice is bound and gagged.

5.17-19 "So, what a blessing when God steps in and
        corrects you!
    Mind you, don't despise the discipline of
        Almighty God!

ᵃ 21 Some interpreters end the quotation after verse 17.
ᵇ 17 Hebrew Shaddai; here and throughout Job

NEW INTERNATIONAL VERSION

¹⁸ For he wounds, but he also binds up;
 he injures, but his hands also heal.
¹⁹ From six calamities he will rescue you;
 in seven no harm will befall you.
²⁰ In famine he will ransom you from death,
 and in battle from the stroke of the sword.
²¹ You will be protected from the lash of the
 tongue,
 and need not fear when destruction
 comes.
²² You will laugh at destruction and famine,
 and need not fear the beasts of the earth.
²³ For you will have a covenant with the stones
 of the field,
 and the wild animals will be at peace with
 you.
²⁴ You will know that your tent is secure;
 you will take stock of your property and
 find nothing missing.
²⁵ You will know that your children will be
 many,
 and your descendants like the grass of the
 earth.
²⁶ You will come to the grave in full vigor,
 like sheaves gathered in season.

²⁷ "We have examined this, and it is true.
 So hear it and apply it to yourself."

JOB

6 Then Job replied:

² "If only my anguish could be weighed
 and all my misery be placed on the scales!
³ It would surely outweigh the sand of the
 seas—
 no wonder my words have been
 impetuous.
⁴ The arrows of the Almighty are in me,
 my spirit drinks in their poison;
 God's terrors are marshaled against me.
⁵ Does a wild donkey bray when it has grass,
 or an ox bellow when it has fodder?
⁶ Is tasteless food eaten without salt,
 or is there flavor in the white of an egg*a*?
⁷ I refuse to touch it;
 such food makes me ill.

⁸ "Oh, that I might have my request,
 that God would grant what I hope for,
⁹ that God would be willing to crush me,
 to let loose his hand and cut me off!

a 6 The meaning of the Hebrew for this phrase is uncertain.

THE MESSAGE

True, he wounds, but he also dresses the
 wound;
 the same hand that hurts you, heals you.
From one disaster after another he delivers you;
 no matter what the calamity, the evil can't
 touch you—

5.20-26 "In famine, he'll keep you from starving,
 in war, from being gutted by the sword.
You'll be protected from vicious gossip
 and live fearless through any catastrophe.
You'll shrug off disaster and famine,
 and stroll fearlessly among wild animals.
You'll be on good terms with rocks and
 mountains;
 wild animals will become your good friends.
You'll know that your place on earth is safe,
 you'll look over your goods and find
 nothing amiss.
You'll see your children grow up,
 your family lovely and lissome as orchard
 grass.
You'll arrive at your grave ripe with many
 good years,
 like sheaves of golden grain at harvest.

5.27 "Yes, this is the way things are—my word of
 honor!
 Take it to heart and you won't go wrong."

JOB REPLIES TO ELIPHAZ

GOD HAS DUMPED THE WORKS ON ME

6.1-7 **6** Job answered:

"If my misery could be weighed,
 if you could pile the whole bitter load on
 the scales,
It would be heavier than all the sand of the sea!
 Is it any wonder that I'm screaming like a
 caged cat?
The arrows of God Almighty are in me,
 poison arrows—and I'm poisoned all
 through!
God has dumped the whole works on me.
Donkeys bray and cows moo when they run
 out of pasture—
 so don't expect me to keep quiet in this.
Do you see what God has dished out for me?
 It's enough to turn anyone's stomach!
Everything in me is repulsed by it—
 it makes me sick.

PRESSED PAST THE LIMITS

6.8-13 "All I want is an answer to one prayer,
 a last request to be honored:
Let God step on me—squash me like a bug,
 and be done with me for good.

NEW INTERNATIONAL VERSION

¹⁰Then I would still have this consolation—
    my joy in unrelenting pain—
  that I had not denied the words of the
    Holy One.

¹¹ "What strength do I have, that I should still
    hope?
  What prospects, that I should be patient?
¹²Do I have the strength of stone?
    Is my flesh bronze?
¹³Do I have any power to help myself,
    now that success has been driven
      from me?

¹⁴ "A despairing man should have the devotion
    of his friends,
  even though he forsakes the fear of the
    Almighty.
¹⁵But my brothers are as undependable as
    intermittent streams,
  as the streams that overflow
¹⁶when darkened by thawing ice
    and swollen with melting snow,
¹⁷but that cease to flow in the dry season,
    and in the heat vanish from their channels.
¹⁸Caravans turn aside from their routes;
    they go up into the wasteland and perish.
¹⁹The caravans of Tema look for water,
    the traveling merchants of Sheba look in
      hope.
²⁰They are distressed, because they had been
    confident;
  they arrive there, only to be disappointed.
²¹Now you too have proved to be of no help;
    you see something dreadful and are afraid.
²²Have I ever said, 'Give something on my
    behalf,
  pay a ransom for me from your wealth,
²³deliver me from the hand of the enemy,
    ransom me from the clutches of the
      ruthless'?

²⁴ "Teach me, and I will be quiet;
    show me where I have been wrong.
²⁵How painful are honest words!
    But what do your arguments prove?
²⁶Do you mean to correct what I say,
    and treat the words of a despairing man as
      wind?
²⁷You would even cast lots for the fatherless
    and barter away your friend.

²⁸ "But now be so kind as to look at me.
    Would I lie to your face?
²⁹Relent, do not be unjust;
    reconsider, for my integrity is at stake.ᵃ
³⁰Is there any wickedness on my lips?
    Can my mouth not discern malice?

ᵃ 29 Or my righteousness still stands

THE MESSAGE

I'd at least have the satisfaction
    of not having blasphemed the Holy God,
    before being pressed past the limits.
Where's the strength to keep my hopes up?
    What future do I have to keep me going?
Do you think I have nerves of steel?
    Do you think I'm made of iron?
Do you think I can pull myself up by my
      bootstraps?
    Why, I don't even have any boots!

MY SO-CALLED FRIENDS

6.14-23 "When desperate people give up on God
      Almighty,
    their friends, at least, should stick with them.
But my brothers are fickle as a gulch in the
      desert—
    one day they're gushing with water
From melting ice and snow
    cascading out of the mountains,
But by midsummer they're dry,
    gullies baked dry in the sun.
Travelers who spot them and go out of their
      way for a drink,
    end up in a waterless gulch and die of thirst.
Merchant caravans from Tema see them and
      expect water,
    tourists from Sheba hope for a cool drink.
They arrive so confident—but what a
      disappointment!
    They get there, and their faces fall!
And you, my so-called friends, are no better—
      there's nothing to you!
    One look at a hard scene and you shrink in
      fear.
It's not as though I asked you for anything—
    I didn't ask you for one red cent—
Nor did I beg you to go out on a limb for me.
    So why all this dodging and shuffling?

6.24-27 "Confront me with the truth and I'll shut up,
    show me where I've gone off the track.
Honest words never hurt anyone,
    but what's the point of all this pious bluster?
You pretend to tell me what's wrong with my
      life,
    but treat my words of anguish as so much
      hot air.
Are people mere things to you?
    Are friends just items of profit and loss?

6.28-30 "Look me in the eyes!
    Do you think I'd lie to your face?
Think it over—no double-talk!
    Think carefully—my integrity is on the line!
Can you detect anything false in what I say?
    Don't you trust me to discern good from
      evil?

NEW INTERNATIONAL VERSION

7 "Does not man have hard service on earth?
Are not his days like those of a hired
man?
2 Like a slave longing for the evening
shadows,
or a hired man waiting eagerly for his
wages,
3 so I have been allotted months of futility,
and nights of misery have been assigned
to me.
4 When I lie down I think, 'How long before I
get up?'
The night drags on, and I toss till dawn.
5 My body is clothed with worms and scabs,
my skin is broken and festering.

6 "My days are swifter than a weaver's shuttle,
and they come to an end without hope.
7 Remember, O God, that my life is but a
breath;
my eyes will never see happiness again.
8 The eye that now sees me will see me no
longer;
you will look for me, but I will be no
more.
9 As a cloud vanishes and is gone,
so he who goes down to the grave*a* does
not return.
10 He will never come to his house again;
his place will know him no more.

11 "Therefore I will not keep silent;
I will speak out in the anguish of my
spirit,
I will complain in the bitterness of my
soul.
12 Am I the sea, or the monster of the deep,
that you put me under guard?
13 When I think my bed will comfort me
and my couch will ease my complaint,
14 even then you frighten me with dreams
and terrify me with visions,
15 so that I prefer strangling and death,
rather than this body of mine.
16 I despise my life; I would not live forever.
Let me alone; my days have no meaning.

17 "What is man that you make so much of
him,
that you give him so much attention,
18 that you examine him every morning
and test him every moment?
19 Will you never look away from me,
or let me alone even for an instant?
20 If I have sinned, what have I done to you,
O watcher of men?

THE MESSAGE

THERE'S NOTHING TO MY LIFE

7 7.1-6 "Human life is a struggle, isn't it?
It's a life sentence to hard labor.
Like field hands longing for quitting time
and working stiffs with nothing to hope for
but payday,
I'm given a life that meanders and goes
nowhere—
months of aimlessness, nights of misery!
I go to bed and think, 'How long till I can
get up?'
I toss and turn as the night drags on—and
I'm fed up!
I'm covered with maggots and scabs.
My skin gets scaly and hard, then oozes
with pus.
My days come and go swifter than the click of
knitting needles,
and then the yarn runs out—an unfinished
life!

7.7-10 "God, don't forget that I'm only a puff of air!
These eyes have had their last look at
goodness.
And your eyes have seen the last of me;
even while you're looking, there'll be
nothing left to look at.
When a cloud evaporates, it's gone for good;
those who go to the grave never come back.
They don't return to visit their families;
never again will friends drop in for coffee.

7.11-16 "And so I'm not keeping one bit of this quiet,
I'm laying it all out on the table;
my complaining to high heaven is bitter,
but honest.
Are you going to put a muzzle on me,
the way you quiet the sea and still the storm?
If I say, 'I'm going to bed, then I'll feel better.
A little nap will lift my spirits,'
You come and so scare me with nightmares
and frighten me with ghosts
That I'd rather strangle in the bedclothes
than face this kind of life any longer.
I hate this life! Who needs any more of this?
Let me alone! There's nothing to my life—
it's nothing but smoke.

7.17-21 "What are mortals anyway, that you bother
with them,
that you even give them the time of day?
That you check up on them every morning,
looking in on them to see how they're doing?
Let up on me, will you?
Can't you even let me spit in peace?
Even suppose I'd sinned—how would that
hurt you?
You're responsible for every human being.

NEW INTERNATIONAL VERSION

Why have you made me your target?
Have I become a burden to you?[a]
²¹ Why do you not pardon my offenses
and forgive my sins?
For I will soon lie down in the dust;
you will search for me, but I will be no
more."

BILDAD

8 Then Bildad the Shuhite replied:

² "How long will you say such things?
Your words are a blustering wind.
³ Does God pervert justice?
Does the Almighty pervert what is right?
⁴ When your children sinned against him,
he gave them over to the penalty of their
sin.
⁵ But if you will look to God
and plead with the Almighty,
⁶ if you are pure and upright,
even now he will rouse himself on your
behalf
and restore you to your rightful place.
⁷ Your beginnings will seem humble,
so prosperous will your future be.

⁸ "Ask the former generations
and find out what their fathers learned,
⁹ for we were born only yesterday and know
nothing,
and our days on earth are but a shadow.
¹⁰ Will they not instruct you and tell you?
Will they not bring forth words from their
understanding?
¹¹ Can papyrus grow tall where there is no
marsh?
Can reeds thrive without water?
¹² While still growing and uncut,
they wither more quickly than grass.
¹³ Such is the destiny of all who forget God;
so perishes the hope of the godless.
¹⁴ What he trusts in is fragile[b];
what he relies on is a spider's web.
¹⁵ He leans on his web, but it gives way;
he clings to it, but it does not hold.

ᵃ 20 A few manuscripts of the Masoretic Text, an ancient
Hebrew scribal tradition and Septuagint; most manuscripts
of the Masoretic Text *I have become a burden to myself.*
ᵇ 14 The meaning of the Hebrew for this word is uncertain.

THE MESSAGE

Don't you have better things to do than pick
on me?
Why make a federal case out of me?
Why don't you just forgive my sins
and start me off with a clean slate?
The way things are going, I'll soon be dead.
You'll look high and low, but I won't be
around."

BILDAD'S RESPONSE

DOES GOD MESS UP?

8.1-7 **8** Bildad from Shuhah was next to speak:

"How can you keep on talking like this?
You're talking nonsense, and noisy
nonsense at that.
Does God mess up?
Does God Almighty ever get things
backwards?
It's plain that your children sinned against
him—
otherwise, why would God have punished
them?
Here's what you must do—and don't put it off
any longer:
Get down on your knees before God
Almighty.
If you're as innocent and upright as you say,
it's not too late—he'll come running;
he'll set everything right again, reestablish
your fortunes.
Even though you're not much right now,
you'll end up better than ever.

TO HANG YOUR LIFE FROM ONE THIN THREAD

8.8-19 "Put the question to our ancestors,
study what they learned from their ancestors.
For we're newcomers at this, with a lot to learn,
and not too long to learn it.
So why not let the ancients teach you, tell you
what's what,
instruct you in what they knew from
experience?
Can mighty pine trees grow tall without soil?
Can luscious tomatoes flourish without
water?
Blossoming flowers look great before they're
cut or picked,
but without soil or water they wither more
quickly than grass.
That's what happens to all who forget God—
all their hopes come to nothing.
They hang their life from one thin thread,
they hitch their fate to a spider web.
One jiggle and the thread breaks,
one jab and the web collapses.

NEW INTERNATIONAL VERSION

16 He is like a well-watered plant in the
      sunshine,
    spreading its shoots over the garden;
17 it entwines its roots around a pile of rocks
      and looks for a place among the stones.
18 But when it is torn from its spot,
      that place disowns it and says, 'I never
        saw you.'
19 Surely its life withers away,
      and[a] from the soil other plants grow.

20 "Surely God does not reject a blameless man
      or strengthen the hands of evildoers.
21 He will yet fill your mouth with laughter
      and your lips with shouts of joy.
22 Your enemies will be clothed in shame,
      and the tents of the wicked will be no
        more."

JOB

9 Then Job replied:

2 "Indeed, I know that this is true.
      But how can a mortal be righteous before
        God?
3 Though one wished to dispute with him,
      he could not answer him one time out of
        a thousand.
4 His wisdom is profound, his power is vast.
      Who has resisted him and come out
        unscathed?
5 He moves mountains without their
      knowing it
    and overturns them in his anger.
6 He shakes the earth from its place
      and makes its pillars tremble.
7 He speaks to the sun and it does not shine;
      he seals off the light of the stars.
8 He alone stretches out the heavens
      and treads on the waves of the sea.
9 He is the Maker of the Bear and Orion,
      the Pleiades and the constellations of the
        south.
10 He performs wonders that cannot be
      fathomed,
    miracles that cannot be counted.
11 When he passes me, I cannot see him;
      when he goes by, I cannot perceive him.
12 If he snatches away, who can stop him?
      Who can say to him, 'What are you doing?'
13 God does not restrain his anger;
      even the cohorts of Rahab cowered at his
        feet.

a 19 Or Surely all the joy it has / is that

THE MESSAGE

Or they're like weeds springing up in the
      sunshine,
    invading the garden,
Spreading everywhere, overtaking the flowers,
      getting a foothold even in the rocks.
But when the gardener rips them out by the
      roots,
    the garden doesn't miss them one bit.
The sooner the godless are gone, the better;
      then good plants can grow in their place.

8.20-22 "There's no way that God will reject a good
        person,
      and there is no way he'll help a bad one.
God will let you laugh again;
      you'll raise the roof with shouts of joy,
With your enemies thoroughly discredited,
      their house of cards collapsed."

JOB CONTINUES

HOW CAN MERE MORTALS GET RIGHT
WITH GOD?

9.1-13 9 Job continued by saying:

"So what's new? I know all this.
      The question is, 'How can mere mortals get
        right with God?'
If we wanted to bring our case before him,
      what chance would we have? Not one in a
        thousand!
God's wisdom is so deep, God's power so
      immense,
    who could take him on and come out in
      one piece?
He moves mountains before they know what's
      happened,
    flips them on their heads on a whim.
He gives the earth a good shaking up,
      rocks it down to its very foundations.
He tells the sun, 'Don't shine,' and it doesn't;
      he pulls the blinds on the stars.
All by himself he stretches out the heavens
      and strides on the waves of the sea.
He designed the Big Dipper and Orion,
      the Pleiades and Alpha Centauri.
We'll never comprehend all the great things he
      does;
    his miracle-surprises can't be counted.
Somehow, though he moves right in front of
      me, I don't see him;
    quietly but surely he's active, and I miss it.
If he steals you blind, who can stop him?
      Who's going to say, 'Hey, what are you
        doing?'
God doesn't hold back on his anger;
      even dragon-bred monsters cringe before
        him.

NEW INTERNATIONAL VERSION

¹⁴ "How then can I dispute with him?
　　How can I find words to argue with him?
¹⁵ Though I were innocent, I could not answer
　　　him;
　　I could only plead with my Judge for
　　　mercy.
¹⁶ Even if I summoned him and he responded,
　　I do not believe he would give me a
　　　hearing.
¹⁷ He would crush me with a storm
　　and multiply my wounds for no reason.
¹⁸ He would not let me regain my breath
　　but would overwhelm me with misery.
¹⁹ If it is a matter of strength, he is mighty!
　　And if it is a matter of justice, who will
　　　summon him^a?
²⁰ Even if I were innocent, my mouth would
　　　condemn me;
　　if I were blameless, it would pronounce
　　　me guilty.

²¹ "Although I am blameless,
　　I have no concern for myself;
　　I despise my own life.
²² It is all the same; that is why I say,
　　'He destroys both the blameless and the
　　　wicked.'
²³ When a scourge brings sudden death,
　　he mocks the despair of the innocent.
²⁴ When a land falls into the hands of the
　　　wicked,
　　he blindfolds its judges.
　　If it is not he, then who is it?

²⁵ "My days are swifter than a runner;
　　they fly away without a glimpse of joy.
²⁶ They skim past like boats of papyrus,
　　like eagles swooping down on their prey.
²⁷ If I say, 'I will forget my complaint,
　　I will change my expression, and smile,'
²⁸ I still dread all my sufferings,
　　for I know you will not hold me innocent.
²⁹ Since I am already found guilty,
　　why should I struggle in vain?
³⁰ Even if I washed myself with soap^b
　　and my hands with washing soda,

THE MESSAGE

9.14-20 "So how could I ever argue with him,
　　construct a defense that would influence
　　　God?
Even though I'm innocent I could never
　　　prove it;
　　I can only throw myself on the Judge's
　　　mercy.
If I called on God and he himself
　　　answered me,
　　then, and only then, would I believe that
　　　he'd heard me.
As it is, he knocks me about from pillar to
　　　post,
　　beating me up, black and blue, for no good
　　　reason.
He won't even let me catch my breath,
　　piles bitterness upon bitterness.
If it's a question of who's stronger, he wins,
　　　hands down!
　　If it's a question of justice, who'll serve him
　　　the subpoena?
Even though innocent, anything I say
　　　incriminates me;
　　blameless as I am, my defense just makes
　　　me sound worse.

IF GOD'S NOT RESPONSIBLE, WHO IS?

9.21-24 "Believe me, I'm blameless.
　　I don't understand what's going on.
　　I hate my life!
Since either way it ends up the same, I can
　　　only conclude
　　that God destroys the good right along with
　　　the bad.
When calamity hits and brings sudden death,
　　he folds his arms, aloof from the despair of
　　　the innocent.
He lets the wicked take over running the world,
　　he installs judges who can't tell right from
　　　wrong.
　　If he's not responsible, who is?

9.25-31 "My time is short—what's left of my life races
　　　off
　　too fast for me to even glimpse the good.
My life is going fast, like a ship under full sail,
　　like an eagle plummeting to its prey.
Even if I say, 'I'll put all this behind me,
　　I'll look on the bright side and force a smile,'
All these troubles would still be like grit in my
　　　gut
　　since it's clear you're not going to let up.
The verdict has already been handed down—
　　　'Guilty!'—
　　so what's the use of protests or appeals?
Even if I scrub myself all over
　　and wash myself with the strongest soap I
　　　can find,

^{a} 19 See Septuagint; Hebrew me.　　^{b} 30 Or snow

NEW INTERNATIONAL VERSION

³¹ you would plunge me into a slime pit
    so that even my clothes would detest me.

³² "He is not a man like me that I might answer
    him,
    that we might confront each other in court.
³³ If only there were someone to arbitrate
    between us,
    to lay his hand upon us both,
³⁴ someone to remove God's rod from me,
    so that his terror would frighten me no
    more.
³⁵ Then I would speak up without fear of him,
    but as it now stands with me, I cannot.

10 ¹ "I loathe my very life;
    therefore I will give free rein to my
    complaint
    and speak out in the bitterness of my
    soul.
² I will say to God: Do not condemn me,
    but tell me what charges you have
    against me.
³ Does it please you to oppress me,
    to spurn the work of your hands,
    while you smile on the schemes of the
    wicked?
⁴ Do you have eyes of flesh?
    Do you see as a mortal sees?
⁵ Are your days like those of a mortal
    or your years like those of a man,
⁶ that you must search out my faults
    and probe after my sin—
⁷ though you know that I am not guilty
    and that no one can rescue me from your
    hand?

⁸ "Your hands shaped me and made me.
    Will you now turn and destroy me?
⁹ Remember that you molded me like clay.
    Will you now turn me to dust again?
¹⁰ Did you not pour me out like milk
    and curdle me like cheese,
¹¹ clothe me with skin and flesh
    and knit me together with bones and
    sinews?
¹² You gave me life and showed me kindness,
    and in your providence watched over my
    spirit.

THE MESSAGE

It wouldn't last—you'd push me into a pigpen,
    or worse,
    so nobody could stand me for the stink.

^{9.32-35} "God and I are not equals; I can't bring a case
    against him.
    We'll never enter a courtroom as peers.
How I wish we had an arbitrator
    to step in and let me get on with life—
To break God's death grip on me,
    to free me from this terror so I could
    breathe again.
Then I'd speak up and state my case boldly.
    As things stand, there is no way I can do it.

To Find Some Skeleton in My Closet

^{10.1} **10** "I can't stand my life—I hate it!
    I'm putting it all out on the table,
    all the bitterness of my life—I'm holding
    back nothing."

^{10.2-7} Job prayed:

"Here's what I want to say:
Don't, God, bring in a verdict of guilty
    without letting me know the charges you're
    bringing.
How does this fit into what you once called
    'good'—
    giving me a hard time, spurning me,
    a life you shaped by your very own hands,
    and then blessing the plots of the wicked?
You don't look at things the way we mortals do.
    You're not taken in by appearances, are you?
Unlike us, you're not working against a
    deadline.
    You have all eternity to work things out.
So what's this all about, anyway—this
    compulsion
    to dig up some dirt, to find some skeleton
    in my closet?
You know good and well I'm not guilty.
    You also know no one can help me.

^{10.8-12} "You made me like a handcrafted piece of
    pottery—
    and now are you going to smash me to
    pieces?
Don't you remember how beautifully you
    worked my clay?
    Will you reduce me now to a mud pie?
Oh, that marvel of conception as you stirred
    together
    semen and ovum—
What a miracle of skin and bone,
    muscle and brain!
You gave me life itself, and incredible love.
    You watched and guarded every breath I
    took.

NEW INTERNATIONAL VERSION

13 "But this is what you concealed in your heart,
and I know that this was in your mind:
14 If I sinned, you would be watching me
and would not let my offense go
unpunished.
15 If I am guilty—woe to me!
Even if I am innocent, I cannot lift my head,
for I am full of shame
and drowned in a my affliction.
16 If I hold my head high, you stalk me like a
lion
and again display your awesome power
against me.
17 You bring new witnesses against me
and increase your anger toward me;
your forces come against me wave upon
wave.

18 "Why then did you bring me out of the womb?
I wish I had died before any eye saw me.
19 If only I had never come into being,
or had been carried straight from the
womb to the grave!
20 Are not my few days almost over?
Turn away from me so I can have a
moment's joy
21 before I go to the place of no return,
to the land of gloom and deep shadow, b
22 to the land of deepest night,
of deep shadow and disorder,
where even the light is like darkness."

ZOPHAR

11

Then Zophar the Naamathite replied:

2 "Are all these words to go unanswered?
Is this talker to be vindicated?
3 Will your idle talk reduce men to silence?
Will no one rebuke you when you mock?
4 You say to God, 'My beliefs are flawless
and I am pure in your sight.'
5 Oh, how I wish that God would speak,
that he would open his lips against you
6 and disclose to you the secrets of wisdom,
for true wisdom has two sides.
Know this: God has even forgotten some
of your sin.

7 "Can you fathom the mysteries of God?

---

a 15 Or and aware of   b 21 Or and the shadow of death;
also in verse 22

THE MESSAGE

10.13-17 "But you never told me about this part.
I should have known that there was more
to it—
That if I so much as missed a step, you'd
notice and pounce,
wouldn't let me get by with a thing.
If I'm truly guilty, I'm doomed.
But if I'm innocent, it's no better—I'm still
doomed.
My belly is full of bitterness.
I'm up to my ears in a swamp of affliction.
I try to make the best of it, try to brave it out,
but you're too much for me,
relentless, like a lion on the prowl.
You line up fresh witnesses against me.
You compound your anger
and pile on the grief and pain!

10.18-22 "So why did you have me born?
I wish no one had ever laid eyes on me!
I wish I'd never lived—a stillborn,
buried without ever having breathed.
Isn't it time to call it quits on my life?
Can't you let up, and let me smile just once
Before I die and am buried,
before I'm nailed into my coffin, sealed in
the ground,
And banished for good to the land of the
dead,
blind in the final dark?"

ZOPHAR'S COUNSEL

HOW WISDOM LOOKS FROM THE INSIDE

11.1-6 # 11

Now it was the turn of Zophar from
Naamath:

"What a flood of words! Shouldn't we put a
stop to it?
Should this kind of loose talk be permitted?
Job, do you think you can carry on like this
and we'll say nothing?
That we'll let you rail and mock and not
step in?
You claim, 'My doctrine is sound
and my conduct impeccable.'
How I wish God would give you a piece of his
mind,
tell you what's what!
I wish he'd show you how wisdom looks from
the inside,
for true wisdom is mostly 'inside.'
But you can be sure of this,
you haven't gotten half of what you
deserve.

11.7-12 "Do you think you can explain the mystery of
God?

NEW INTERNATIONAL VERSION

Can you probe the limits of the Almighty?
8 They are higher than the heavens—what can
    you do?
  They are deeper than the depths of the
    grave^a—what can you know?
9 Their measure is longer than the earth
    and wider than the sea.

10 "If he comes along and confines you in prison
    and convenes a court, who can oppose
    him?
11 Surely he recognizes deceitful men;
    and when he sees evil, does he not take
    note?
12 But a witless man can no more become wise
    than a wild donkey's colt can be born a
    man.^b

13 "Yet if you devote your heart to him
    and stretch out your hands to him,
14 if you put away the sin that is in your hand
    and allow no evil to dwell in your tent,
15 then you will lift up your face without
    shame;
    you will stand firm and without fear.
16 You will surely forget your trouble,
    recalling it only as waters gone by.
17 Life will be brighter than noonday,
    and darkness will become like morning.
18 You will be secure, because there is hope;
    you will look about you and take your
    rest in safety.
19 You will lie down, with no one to make you
    afraid,
    and many will court your favor.
20 But the eyes of the wicked will fail,
    and escape will elude them;
    their hope will become a dying gasp."

JOB

12

Then Job replied:

2 "Doubtless you are the people,
    and wisdom will die with you!
3 But I have a mind as well as you;
    I am not inferior to you.
    Who does not know all these things?

4 "I have become a laughingstock to my
    friends,
    though I called upon God and he
    answered—
    a mere laughingstock, though righteous
    and blameless!

THE MESSAGE

Do you think you can diagram God
    Almighty?
God is far higher than you can imagine,
    far deeper than you can comprehend,
Stretching farther than earth's horizons,
    far wider than the endless ocean.
If he happens along, throws you in jail
    then hauls you into court, can you do
    anything about it?
He sees through vain pretensions,
    spots evil a long way off—
    no one pulls the wool over *his* eyes!
Hollow men, hollow women, will wise up
    about the same time mules learn to talk.

REACH OUT TO GOD

11.13-20 "Still, if you set your heart on God
    and reach out to him,
If you scrub your hands of sin
    and refuse to entertain evil in your home,
You'll be able to face the world unashamed
    and keep a firm grip on life, guiltless and
    fearless.
You'll forget your troubles;
    they'll be like old, faded photographs.
Your world will be washed in sunshine,
    every shadow dispersed by dayspring.
Full of hope, you'll relax, confident again;
    you'll look around, sit back, and take it
    easy.
Expansive, without a care in the world,
    you'll be hunted out by many for your
    blessing.
But the wicked will see none of this.
    They're headed down a dead-end road
    with nothing to look forward to—nothing."

JOB ANSWERS ZOPHAR

PUT YOUR EAR TO THE EARTH

12.1-3 # 12

Job answered:

"I'm sure you speak for all the experts,
    and when you die there'll be no one left to
    tell us how to live.
But don't forget that I also have a brain—
    I don't intend to play second fiddle to you.
    It doesn't take an expert to know these
    things.

12.4-6 "I'm ridiculed by my friends:
    'So that's the man who had conversations
    with God!'
Ridiculed without mercy:
    'Look at the man who never did wrong!'

---

^a 8 Hebrew *than Sheol*   ^b 12 Or *wild donkey can be born tame*

NEW INTERNATIONAL VERSION

⁵Men at ease have contempt for misfortune
    as the fate of those whose feet are
      slipping.
⁶The tents of marauders are undisturbed,
    and those who provoke God are secure—
    those who carry their god in their hands. ᵃ

⁷ "But ask the animals, and they will teach
      you,
    or the birds of the air, and they will tell
      you;
⁸or speak to the earth, and it will teach you,
    or let the fish of the sea inform you.
⁹Which of all these does not know
    that the hand of the LORD has done this?
¹⁰In his hand is the life of every creature
    and the breath of all mankind.
¹¹Does not the ear test words
    as the tongue tastes food?
¹²Is not wisdom found among the aged?
    Does not long life bring understanding?

¹³ "To God belong wisdom and power;
    counsel and understanding are his.
¹⁴What he tears down cannot be rebuilt;
    the man he imprisons cannot be released.
¹⁵If he holds back the waters, there is drought;
    if he lets them loose, they devastate the
      land.
¹⁶To him belong strength and victory;
    both deceived and deceiver are his.
¹⁷He leads counselors away stripped
    and makes fools of judges.
¹⁸He takes off the shackles put on by kings
    and ties a loincloth ᵇ around their waist.
¹⁹He leads priests away stripped
    and overthrows men long established.
²⁰He silences the lips of trusted advisers
    and takes away the discernment of elders.
²¹He pours contempt on nobles
    and disarms the mighty.
²²He reveals the deep things of darkness
    and brings deep shadows into the light.
²³He makes nations great, and destroys them;
    he enlarges nations, and disperses them.
²⁴He deprives the leaders of the earth of their
      reason;
    he sends them wandering through a
      trackless waste.
²⁵They grope in darkness with no light;
    he makes them stagger like drunkards.

ᵃ 6 Or secure / in what God's hand brings them
ᵇ 18 Or shackles of kings / and ties a belt

THE MESSAGE

It's easy for the well-to-do to point their
    fingers in blame,
    for the well-fixed to pour scorn on the
      strugglers.
Crooks reside safely in high-security houses,
    insolent blasphemers live in luxury;
    they've bought and paid for a god who'll
      protect them.

¹²·⁷⁻¹² "But ask the animals what they think—let
    them teach you;
    let the birds tell you what's going on.
Put your ear to the earth—learn the basics.
    Listen—the fish in the ocean will tell you
      their stories.
Isn't it clear that they all know and agree
    that GOD is sovereign, that he holds all
      things in his hand—
Every living soul, yes,
    every breathing creature?
Isn't this all just common sense,
    as common as the sense of taste?
Do you think the elderly have a corner on
      wisdom,
    that you have to grow old before you
      understand life?

FROM GOD WE LEARN HOW TO LIVE

¹²·¹³⁻²⁵ "True wisdom and real power belong to God;
    from him we learn how to live,
    and also what to live for.
If he tears something down, it's down for good;
    if he locks people up, they're locked up for
      good.
If he holds back the rain, there's a drought;
    if he lets it loose, there's a flood.
Strength and success belong to God;
    both deceived and deceiver must answer to
      him.
He strips experts of their vaunted credentials,
    exposes judges as witless fools.
He divests kings of their royal garments,
    then ties a rag around their waists.
He strips priests of their robes,
    and fires high officials from their jobs.
He forces trusted sages to keep silence,
    deprives elders of their good sense and
      wisdom.
He dumps contempt on famous people,
    disarms the strong and mighty.
He shines a spotlight into caves of darkness,
    hauls deepest darkness into the noonday sun.
He makes nations rise and then fall,
    builds up some and abandons others.
He robs world leaders of their reason,
    and sends them off into no man's land.
They grope in the dark without a clue,
    lurching and staggering like drunks.

NEW INTERNATIONAL VERSION

13 "My eyes have seen all this,
  my ears have heard and understood it.
2 What you know, I also know;
  I am not inferior to you.
3 But I desire to speak to the Almighty
  and to argue my case with God.
4 You, however, smear me with lies;
  you are worthless physicians, all of you!
5 If only you would be altogether silent!
  For you, that would be wisdom.
6 Hear now my argument;
  listen to the plea of my lips.
7 Will you speak wickedly on God's behalf?
  Will you speak deceitfully for him?
8 Will you show him partiality?
  Will you argue the case for God?
9 Would it turn out well if he examined you?
  Could you deceive him as you might
    deceive men?
10 He would surely rebuke you
  if you secretly showed partiality.
11 Would not his splendor terrify you?
  Would not the dread of him fall on you?
12 Your maxims are proverbs of ashes;
  your defenses are defenses of clay.

13 "Keep silent and let me speak;
  then let come to me what may.
14 Why do I put myself in jeopardy
  and take my life in my hands?
15 Though he slay me, yet will I hope in him;
  I will surely[a] defend my ways to his face.
16 Indeed, this will turn out for my deliverance,
  for no godless man would dare come
    before him!
17 Listen carefully to my words;
  let your ears take in what I say.
18 Now that I have prepared my case,
  I know I will be vindicated.
19 Can anyone bring charges against me?
  If so, I will be silent and die.

20 "Only grant me these two things, O God,
  and then I will not hide from you:

---

[a] 15 Or *He will surely slay me; I have no hope — / yet I will*

THE MESSAGE

I'm Taking My Case to God

13.1-5 **13** "Yes, I've seen all this with my own
      eyes,
  heard and understood it with my very own
    ears.
Everything you know, I know,
  so I'm not taking a back seat to any of you.
I'm taking my case straight to God Almighty;
  I've had it with you—I'm going directly to
    God.
You graffiti my life with lies.
  You're a bunch of pompous quacks!
I wish you'd shut your mouths—
  silence is your only claim to wisdom.

13.6-12 "Listen now while I make my case,
  consider my side of things for a change.
Or are you going to keep on lying 'to do God a
    service'?
  to make up stories 'to get him off the
    hook'?
Why do you always take his side?
  Do you think he needs a lawyer to defend
    himself?
How would you fare if you were in the dock?
  Your lies might convince a jury—but would
    they convince *God*?
He'd reprimand you on the spot
  if he detected a bias in your witness.
Doesn't his splendor put you in awe?
  Aren't you afraid to speak cheap lies before
    him?
Your wise sayings are knickknack wisdom,
  good for nothing but gathering dust.

13.13-19 "So hold your tongue while I have my say,
  then I'll take whatever I have coming to me.
Why do I go out on a limb like this
  and take my life in my hands?
Because even if he killed me, I'd keep on
    hoping.
  I'd defend my innocence to the very end.
Just wait, this is going to work out for the
    best—my salvation!
  If I were guilt-stricken do you think I'd be
    doing this—
  laying myself on the line before God?
You'd better pay attention to what I'm telling
    you,
  listen carefully with both ears.
Now that I've laid out my defense,
  I'm sure that I'll be acquitted.
Can anyone prove charges against me?
  I've said my piece. I rest my case.

Why Does God Stay Hidden and Silent?

13.20-27 "Please, God, I have two requests;
  grant them so I'll know I count with you:

NEW INTERNATIONAL VERSION

²¹Withdraw your hand far from me,
and stop frightening me with your terrors.
²²Then summon me and I will answer,
or let me speak, and you reply.
²³How many wrongs and sins have I
committed?
Show me my offense and my sin.
²⁴Why do you hide your face
and consider me your enemy?
²⁵Will you torment a windblown leaf?
Will you chase after dry chaff?
²⁶For you write down bitter things against me
and make me inherit the sins of my
youth.
²⁷You fasten my feet in shackles;
you keep close watch on all my paths
by putting marks on the soles of my feet.

²⁸"So man wastes away like something rotten,
like a garment eaten by moths.

14 "Man born of woman
is of few days and full of trouble.
²He springs up like a flower and withers
away;
like a fleeting shadow, he does not endure.
³Do you fix your eye on such a one?
Will you bring him*a* before you for
judgment?
⁴Who can bring what is pure from the
impure?
No one!
⁵Man's days are determined;
you have decreed the number of his
months
and have set limits he cannot exceed.
⁶So look away from him and let him alone,
till he has put in his time like a hired
man.

⁷"At least there is hope for a tree:
If it is cut down, it will sprout again,
and its new shoots will not fail.
⁸Its roots may grow old in the ground
and its stump die in the soil,
⁹yet at the scent of water it will bud
and put forth shoots like a plant.
¹⁰But man dies and is laid low;
he breathes his last and is no more.
¹¹As water disappears from the sea
or a riverbed becomes parched and dry,

THE MESSAGE

First, lay off the afflictions;
the terror is too much for me.
Second, address me directly so I can answer
you,
or let me speak and then you answer me.
How many sins have been charged
against me?
Show me the list—how bad is it?
Why do you stay hidden and silent?
Why treat me like I'm your enemy?
Why kick me around like an old tin can?
Why beat a dead horse?
You compile a long list of mean things
about me,
even hold me accountable for the sins of
my youth.
You hobble me so I can't move about.
You watch every move I make,
and brand me as a dangerous character.

13.28 "Like something rotten, human life fast
decomposes,
like a moth-eaten shirt or a mildewed
blouse.

IF WE DIE, WILL WE LIVE AGAIN?

14.1-17 **14** "We're all adrift in the same boat:
too few days, too many troubles.
We spring up like wildflowers in the desert
and then wilt,
transient as the shadow of a cloud.
Do you occupy your time with such fragile
wisps?
Why even bother hauling me into court?
There's nothing much to us to start with;
how do you expect us to amount to
anything?
Mortals have a limited life span.
You've already decided how long we'll
live—
you set the boundary and no one can
cross it.
So why not give us a break? Ease up!
Even ditchdiggers get occasional days off.
For a tree there is always hope.
Chop it down and it still has a chance—
its roots can put out fresh sprouts.
Even if its roots are old and gnarled,
its stump long dormant,
At the first whiff of water it comes to life,
buds and grows like a sapling.
But men and women? They die and stay dead.
They breathe their last, and that's it.
Like lakes and rivers that have dried up,
parched reminders of what once was,

---

a 3 Septuagint, Vulgate and Syriac; Hebrew *me*

NEW INTERNATIONAL VERSION

¹²so man lies down and does not rise;
 till the heavens are no more, men will not
  awake
 or be roused from their sleep.

¹³"If only you would hide me in the grave^a
 and conceal me till your anger has passed!
If only you would set me a time
 and then remember me!
¹⁴If a man dies, will he live again?
 All the days of my hard service
 I will wait for my renewal^b to come.
¹⁵You will call and I will answer you;
 you will long for the creature your hands
  have made.
¹⁶Surely then you will count my steps
 but not keep track of my sin.
¹⁷My offenses will be sealed up in a bag;
 you will cover over my sin.

¹⁸"But as a mountain erodes and crumbles
 and as a rock is moved from its place,
¹⁹as water wears away stones
 and torrents wash away the soil,
 so you destroy man's hope.
²⁰You overpower him once for all, and he is
  gone;
 you change his countenance and send
  him away.
²¹If his sons are honored, he does not know it;
 if they are brought low, he does not see it.
²²He feels but the pain of his own body
 and mourns only for himself."

ELIPHAZ

15 Then Eliphaz the Temanite replied:

²"Would a wise man answer with empty
  notions
 or fill his belly with the hot east wind?
³Would he argue with useless words,
 with speeches that have no value?
⁴But you even undermine piety
 and hinder devotion to God.
⁵Your sin prompts your mouth;
 you adopt the tongue of the crafty.
⁶Your own mouth condemns you, not mine;
 your own lips testify against you.

⁷"Are you the first man ever born?

^a 13 Hebrew *Sheol*   ^b 14 Or *release*

THE MESSAGE

So mortals lie down and never get up,
 never wake up again—never.
Why don't you just bury me alive,
 get me out of the way until your anger
  cools?
But don't leave me there!
 Set a date when you'll see me again.
If we humans die, will we live again? That's
  my question.
 All through these difficult days I keep
  hoping,
 waiting for the final change—for
  resurrection!
Homesick with longing for the creature you
  made,
 you'll call—and I'll answer!
You'll watch over every step I take,
 but you won't keep track of my missteps.
My sins will be stuffed in a sack
 and thrown into the sea—sunk in deep
  ocean.

^{14.18-22} "Meanwhile, mountains wear down
 and boulders break up,
Stones wear smooth
 and soil erodes,
 as you relentlessly grind down our hope.
You're too much for us.
 As always, you get the last word.
We don't like it and our faces show it,
 but you send us off anyway.
If our children do well for themselves, we
  never know it;
 if they do badly, we're spared the hurt.
Body and soul, that's it for us—
 a lifetime of pain, a lifetime of sorrow."

ELIPHAZ ATTACKS AGAIN

YOU TRIVIALIZE RELIGION

^{15.1-16} # 15 Eliphaz of Teman spoke a second time:

"If you were truly wise, would you sound so
  much like a
 windbag, belching hot air?
Would you talk nonsense in the middle of a
  serious argument,
 babbling baloney?
Look at you! You trivialize religion,
 turn spiritual conversation into empty
  gossip.
It's your sin that taught you to talk this way.
 You chose an education in fraud.
Your own words have exposed your guilt.
 It's nothing I've said—you've incriminated
  yourself!
Do you think you're the first person to have to
  deal with these things?

NEW INTERNATIONAL VERSION

Were you brought forth before the hills?
8 Do you listen in on God's council?
   Do you limit wisdom to yourself?
9 What do you know that we do not know?
   What insights do you have that we do not
      have?
10 The gray-haired and the aged are on our
      side,
   men even older than your father.
11 Are God's consolations not enough for you,
   words spoken gently to you?
12 Why has your heart carried you away,
   and why do your eyes flash,
13 so that you vent your rage against God
   and pour out such words from your
      mouth?

14 "What is man, that he could be pure,
   or one born of woman, that he could be
      righteous?
15 If God places no trust in his holy ones,
   if even the heavens are not pure in his
      eyes,
16 how much less man, who is vile and corrupt,
   who drinks up evil like water!

17 "Listen to me and I will explain to you;
   let me tell you what I have seen,
18 what wise men have declared,
   hiding nothing received from their fathers
19 (to whom alone the land was given
   when no alien passed among them):
20 All his days the wicked man suffers torment,
   the ruthless through all the years stored
      up for him.
21 Terrifying sounds fill his ears;
   when all seems well, marauders attack
      him.
22 He despairs of escaping the darkness;
   he is marked for the sword.
23 He wanders about—food for vultures[a];
   he knows the day of darkness is at hand.
24 Distress and anguish fill him with terror;
   they overwhelm him, like a king poised to
      attack,
25 because he shakes his fist at God
   and vaunts himself against the Almighty,

THE MESSAGE

Have you been around as long as the hills?
Were you listening in when God planned all
      this?
   Do you think you're the only one who
      knows anything?
What do you know that we don't know?
   What insights do you have that we've
      missed?
Gray beards and white hair back us up—
   old folks who've been around a lot longer
      than you.
Are God's promises not enough for you,
   spoken so gently and tenderly?
Why do you let your emotions take over,
   lashing out and spitting fire,
Pitting your whole being against God
   by letting words like this come out of your
      mouth?
Do you think it's possible for any mere mortal
      to be sinless in God's sight,
   for anyone born of a human mother to get
      it all together?
Why, God can't even trust his holy angels.
   He sees the flaws in the very heavens
      themselves,
So how much less we humans, smelly and
      foul,
   who lap up evil like water?

ALWAYS AT ODDS WITH GOD

15.17-26 "I've a thing or two to tell you, so listen up!
   I'm letting you in on my views;
It's what wise men and women have always
      taught,
   holding nothing back from what *they* were
      taught
By their parents, back in the days
   when they had this land all to themselves:
Those who live by their own rules, not God's,
   can expect nothing but trouble,
   and the longer they live, the worse it gets.
Every little sound terrifies them.
   Just when they think they have it made,
      disaster strikes.
They despair of things ever getting better—
   they're on the list of people for whom
      things always turn out for the
      worst.
They wander here and there,
   never knowing where the next meal is
      coming from—
   every day is doomsday!
They live in constant terror,
   always with their backs up against the wall
Because they insist on shaking their fists at
      God,
   defying God Almighty to his face,

---

[a] 23 Or *about, looking for food*

NEW INTERNATIONAL VERSION

26 defiantly charging against him
 with a thick, strong shield.

27 "Though his face is covered with fat
 and his waist bulges with flesh,
28 he will inhabit ruined towns
 and houses where no one lives,
 houses crumbling to rubble.
29 He will no longer be rich and his wealth will
 not endure,
 nor will his possessions spread over the
 land.
30 He will not escape the darkness;
 a flame will wither his shoots,
 and the breath of God's mouth will carry
 him away.
31 Let him not deceive himself by trusting what
 is worthless,
 for he will get nothing in return.
32 Before his time he will be paid in full,
 and his branches will not flourish.
33 He will be like a vine stripped of its unripe
 grapes,
 like an olive tree shedding its blossoms.
34 For the company of the godless will be barren,
 and fire will consume the tents of those
 who love bribes.
35 They conceive trouble and give birth to evil;
 their womb fashions deceit."

JOB

16 Then Job replied:

2 "I have heard many things like these;
 miserable comforters are you all!
3 Will your long-winded speeches never end?
 What ails you that you keep on arguing?
4 I also could speak like you,
 if you were in my place;
 I could make fine speeches against you
 and shake my head at you.
5 But my mouth would encourage you;
 comfort from my lips would bring you
 relief.

6 "Yet if I speak, my pain is not relieved;
 and if I refrain, it does not go away.
7 Surely, O God, you have worn me out;
 you have devastated my entire household.
8 You have bound me—and it has become a
 witness;
 my gauntness rises up and testifies
 against me.
9 God assails me and tears me in his anger

THE MESSAGE

Always and ever at odds with God,
 always on the defensive.

15.27-35 "Even if they're the picture of health,
 trim and fit and youthful,
They'll end up living in a ghost town
 sleeping in a hovel not fit for a dog,
 a ramshackle shack.
They'll never get ahead,
 never amount to a hill of beans.
And then death—don't think they'll escape
 that!
 They'll end up shriveled weeds,
 brought down by a puff of God's breath.
There's a lesson here: Whoever invests in lies,
 gets lies for interest,
 Paid in full before the due date.
 Some investment!
They'll be like fruit frost-killed before it
 ripens,
 like buds sheared off before they bloom.
The godless are fruitless—a barren crew;
 a life built on bribes goes up in smoke.
They have sex with sin and give birth to evil.
 Their lives are wombs for breeding deceit."

JOB DEFENDS HIMSELF

IF YOU WERE IN MY SHOES

16.1-5 # 16 Then Job defended himself:

"I've had all I can take of your talk.
 What a bunch of miserable comforters!
Is there no end to your windbag speeches?
 What's your problem that you go on and on
 like this?
If you were in my shoes,
 I could talk just like you.
I could put together a terrific harangue
 and really let you have it.
But I'd never do that. I'd console and comfort,
 make things better, not worse!

16.6-14 "When I speak up, I feel no better;
 if I say nothing, that doesn't help either.
I feel worn down.
 God, you have wasted me totally—me and
 my family!
You've shriveled me like a dried prune,
 showing the world that you're against me.
My gaunt face stares back at me from the
 mirror,
 a mute witness to your treatment of me.
Your anger tears at me,

NEW INTERNATIONAL VERSION

and gnashes his teeth at me;
my opponent fastens on me his piercing
eyes.
¹⁰Men open their mouths to jeer at me;
they strike my cheek in scorn
and unite together against me.
¹¹God has turned me over to evil men
and thrown me into the clutches of the
wicked.
¹²All was well with me, but he shattered me;
he seized me by the neck and crushed me.
He has made me his target;
¹³   his archers surround me.
Without pity, he pierces my kidneys
and spills my gall on the ground.
¹⁴Again and again he bursts upon me;
he rushes at me like a warrior.

¹⁵"I have sewed sackcloth over my skin
and buried my brow in the dust.
¹⁶My face is red with weeping,
deep shadows ring my eyes;
¹⁷yet my hands have been free of violence
and my prayer is pure.

¹⁸"O earth, do not cover my blood;
may my cry never be laid to rest!
¹⁹Even now my witness is in heaven;
my advocate is on high.
²⁰My intercessor is my friend ᵃ
as my eyes pour out tears to God;
²¹on behalf of a man he pleads with God
as a man pleads for his friend.

²²"Only a few years will pass
before I go on the journey of no return.

17

¹My spirit is broken,
my days are cut short,
the grave awaits me.
²Surely mockers surround me;
my eyes must dwell on their hostility.

³"Give me, O God, the pledge you demand.
Who else will put up security for me?

ᵃ 20 Or My friends treat me with scorn

THE MESSAGE

your teeth rip me to shreds,
your eyes burn holes in me—God, my
enemy!
People take one look at me and gasp.
Contemptuous, they slap me around
and gang up against me.
And God just stands there and lets them do it,
lets wicked people do what they want
with me.
I was contentedly minding my business when
God beat me up.
He grabbed me by the neck and threw me
around.
He set me up as his target,
then rounded up archers to shoot at me.
Merciless, they shot me full of arrows;
bitter bile poured from my gut to the
ground.
He burst in on me, onslaught after onslaught,
charging me like a mad bull.

16.15-17 "I sewed myself a shroud and wore it like a
shirt;
I lay face down in the dirt.
Now my face is blotched red from weeping;
look at the dark shadows under my eyes,
Even though I've never hurt a soul
and my prayers are sincere!

THE ONE WHO REPRESENTS MORTALS
BEFORE GOD

16.18-22 "O Earth, don't cover up the wrong done
to me!
Don't muffle my cry!
There must be Someone in heaven who knows
the truth about me,
in highest heaven, some Attorney who can
clear my name—
My Champion, my Friend,
while I'm weeping my eyes out before God.
I appeal to the One who represents mortals
before God
as a neighbor stands up for a neighbor.

"Only a few years are left
before I set out on the road of no return.

17.1-2 # 17

"My spirit is broken,
my days used up,
my grave dug and waiting.
See how these mockers close in on me?
How long do I have to put up with their
insolence?

17.3-5 "O God, pledge your support for me.
Give it to me in writing, with your
signature.
You're the only one who can do it!

NEW INTERNATIONAL VERSION

⁴You have closed their minds to
    understanding;
    therefore you will not let them triumph.
⁵If a man denounces his friends for reward,
    the eyes of his children will fail.

⁶"God has made me a byword to everyone,
    a man in whose face people spit.
⁷My eyes have grown dim with grief;
    my whole frame is but a shadow.
⁸Upright men are appalled at this;
    the innocent are aroused against the
        ungodly.
⁹Nevertheless, the righteous will hold to their
    ways,
    and those with clean hands will grow
        stronger.

¹⁰"But come on, all of you, try again!
    I will not find a wise man among you.
¹¹My days have passed, my plans are shattered,
    and so are the desires of my heart.
¹²These men turn night into day;
    in the face of darkness they say, 'Light is
        near.'
¹³If the only home I hope for is the grave,ᵃ
    if I spread out my bed in darkness,
¹⁴if I say to corruption, 'You are my father,'
    and to the worm, 'My mother' or 'My
        sister,'
¹⁵where then is my hope?
    Who can see any hope for me?
¹⁶Will it go down to the gates of deathᵃ?
    Will we descend together into the dust?"

BILDAD

18 Then Bildad the Shuhite replied:

²"When will you end these speeches?
    Be sensible, and then we can talk.
³Why are we regarded as cattle
    and considered stupid in your sight?
⁴You who tear yourself to pieces in your
    anger,

ᵃ 13,16 Hebrew *Sheol*

THE MESSAGE

These people are so useless!
    You know firsthand how stupid they
        can be.
    You wouldn't let them have the last word,
        would you?
Those who betray their own friends
    leave a legacy of abuse to their children.

17.6-8 "God, you've made me the talk of the town—
    people spit in my face;
I can hardly see from crying so much;
    I'm nothing but skin and bones.
Decent people can't believe what they're
        seeing;
    the good-hearted wake up and insist I've
        given up on God.

17.9 "But principled people hold tight, keep a firm
        grip on life,
    sure that their clean, pure hands will get
        stronger and stronger!

17.10-16 "Maybe you'd all like to start over,
    to try it again, the bunch of you.
So far I haven't come across one scrap
    of wisdom in anything you've said.
My life's about over. All my plans are
        smashed,
    all my hopes are snuffed out—
My hope that night would turn into day,
    my hope that dawn was about to break.
If all I have to look forward to is a home in
        the graveyard,
    if my only hope for comfort is a well-built
        coffin,
If a family reunion means going six feet under,
    and the only family that shows up is
        worms,
Do you call that hope?
    Who on earth could find any hope in that?
No. If hope and I are to be buried together,
    I suppose you'll all come to the double
        funeral!"

BILDAD'S SECOND ATTACK

PLUNGED FROM LIGHT INTO DARKNESS

18.1-4 **18** Bildad from Shuhah chimed in:

"How monotonous these word games are
        getting!
    Get serious! We need to get down to
        business.
Why do you treat your friends like slow-
        witted animals?
    You look down on us as if we don't know
        anything.
Why are you working yourself up like this?

NEW INTERNATIONAL VERSION

is the earth to be abandoned for your
sake?
Or must the rocks be moved from their
place?

5 "The lamp of the wicked is snuffed out;
the flame of his fire stops burning.
6 The light in his tent becomes dark;
the lamp beside him goes out.
7 The vigor of his step is weakened;
his own schemes throw him down.
8 His feet thrust him into a net
and he wanders into its mesh.
9 A trap seizes him by the heel;
a snare holds him fast.
10 A noose is hidden for him on the ground;
a trap lies in his path.
11 Terrors startle him on every side
and dog his every step.
12 Calamity is hungry for him;
disaster is ready for him when he falls.
13 It eats away parts of his skin;
death's firstborn devours his limbs.
14 He is torn from the security of his tent
and marched off to the king of terrors.
15 Fire resides[a] in his tent;
burning sulfur is scattered over his
dwelling.
16 His roots dry up below
and his branches wither above.
17 The memory of him perishes from the earth;
he has no name in the land.
18 He is driven from light into darkness
and is banished from the world.
19 He has no offspring or descendants among
his people,
no survivor where once he lived.
20 Men of the west are appalled at his fate;
men of the east are seized with horror.
21 Surely such is the dwelling of an evil man;
such is the place of one who knows not
God."

JOB

19 Then Job replied:

2 "How long will you torment me
and crush me with words?
3 Ten times now you have reproached me;
shamelessly you attack me.
4 If it is true that I have gone astray,

a 15 Or Nothing he had remains

THE MESSAGE

Do you want the world redesigned to suit
you?
Should reality be suspended to
accommodate you?

18.5-21 "Here's the rule: The light of the wicked is put
out.
Their flame dies down and is extinguished.
Their house goes dark—
every lamp in the place goes out.
Their strong strides weaken, falter;
they stumble into their own traps.
They get all tangled up
in their own red tape,
Their feet are grabbed and caught,
their necks in a noose.
They trip on ropes they've hidden,
and fall into pits they've dug themselves.
Terrors come at them from all sides.
They run helter-skelter.
The hungry grave is ready
to gobble them up for supper,
To lay them out for a gourmet meal,
a treat for ravenous Death.
They are snatched from their home sweet
home
and marched straight to the death house.
Their lives go up in smoke;
acid rain soaks their ruins.
Their roots rot
and their branches wither.
They'll never again be remembered—
nameless in unmarked graves.
They are plunged from light into darkness,
banished from the world.
And they leave empty-handed—not one single
child—
nothing to show for their life on this earth.
Westerners are aghast at their fate,
easterners are horrified:
'Oh no! So this is what happens to perverse
people.
This is how the God-ignorant end up!' "

JOB ANSWERS BILDAD

I CALL FOR HELP AND NO ONE BOTHERS

19.1-6 **19** Job answered:

"How long are you going to keep battering
away at me,
pounding me with these harangues?
Time after time after time you jump all over
me.
Do you have no conscience, abusing me
like this?
Even if I have, somehow or other, gotten off
the track,

NEW INTERNATIONAL VERSION

my error remains my concern alone.
⁵ If indeed you would exalt yourselves
above me
and use my humiliation against me,
⁶ then know that God has wronged me
and drawn his net around me.

⁷ "Though I cry, 'I've been wronged!' I get no
response;
though I call for help, there is no justice.
⁸ He has blocked my way so I cannot pass;
he has shrouded my paths in darkness.
⁹ He has stripped me of my honor
and removed the crown from my head.
¹⁰ He tears me down on every side till I am
gone;
he uproots my hope like a tree.
¹¹ His anger burns against me;
he counts me among his enemies.
¹² His troops advance in force;
they build a siege ramp against me
and encamp around my tent.

¹³ "He has alienated my brothers from me;
my acquaintances are completely
estranged from me.
¹⁴ My kinsmen have gone away;
my friends have forgotten me.
¹⁵ My guests and my maidservants count me a
stranger;
they look upon me as an alien.
¹⁶ I summon my servant, but he does not
answer,
though I beg him with my own mouth.
¹⁷ My breath is offensive to my wife;
I am loathsome to my own brothers.
¹⁸ Even the little boys scorn me;
when I appear, they ridicule me.
¹⁹ All my intimate friends detest me;
those I love have turned against me.
²⁰ I am nothing but skin and bones;
I have escaped with only the skin of my
teeth. ᵃ

²¹ "Have pity on me, my friends, have pity,
for the hand of God has struck me.
²² Why do you pursue me as God does?
Will you never get enough of my flesh?

²³ "Oh, that my words were recorded,
that they were written on a scroll,
²⁴ that they were inscribed with an iron tool
on ᵇ lead,
or engraved in rock forever!
²⁵ I know that my Redeemer ᶜ lives,
and that in the end he will stand upon the
earth. ᵈ

THE MESSAGE

what business is that of yours?
Why do you insist on putting me down,
using my troubles as a stick to beat me?
Tell it to God—he's the one behind all this,
he's the one who dragged me into this
mess.

19.7-12 "Look at me—I shout 'Murder!' and I'm
ignored;
I call for help and no one bothers to stop.
God threw a barricade across my path—I'm
stymied;
he turned out all the lights—I'm stuck in
the dark.
He destroyed my reputation,
robbed me of all self-respect.
He tore me apart piece by piece—I'm ruined!
Then he yanked out hope by the roots.
He's angry with me—oh, how he's angry!
He treats me like his worst enemy.
He has launched a major campaign
against me,
using every weapon he can think of,
coming at me from all sides at once.

I Know That God Lives

19.13-20 "God alienated my family from me;
everyone who knows me avoids me.
My relatives and friends have all left;
houseguests forget I ever existed.
The servant girls treat me like a bum off the
street,
look at me like they've never seen me
before.
I call my attendant and he ignores me,
ignores me even though I plead with him.
My wife can't stand to be around me anymore.
I'm repulsive to my family.
Even street urchins despise me;
when I come out, they taunt and jeer.
Everyone I've ever been close to abhors me;
my dearest loved ones reject me.
I'm nothing but a bag of bones;
my life hangs by a thread.

19.21-22 "Oh, friends, dear friends, take pity on me.
God has come down hard on me!
Do you have to be hard on me too?
Don't you ever tire of abusing me?

19.23-27 "If only my words were written in a book—
better yet, chiseled in stone!
Still, I know that God lives—the One who
gives me back my life—
and eventually he'll take his stand on earth.

ᵃ 20 Or *only my gums*   ᵇ 24 Or *and*   ᶜ 25 Or *defender*
ᵈ 25 Or *upon my grave*

NEW INTERNATIONAL VERSION

²⁶And after my skin has been destroyed,
yet ᵃ in ᵇ my flesh I will see God;
²⁷I myself will see him
with my own eyes—I, and not another.
How my heart yearns within me!

²⁸"If you say, 'How we will hound him,
since the root of the trouble lies in him,' ᶜ
²⁹you should fear the sword yourselves;
for wrath will bring punishment by the
sword,
and then you will know that there is
judgment. ᵈ"

ZOPHAR

20 Then Zophar the Naamathite replied:

²"My troubled thoughts prompt me to answer
because I am greatly disturbed.
³I hear a rebuke that dishonors me,
and my understanding inspires me to
reply.

⁴"Surely you know how it has been from of
old,
ever since man ᵉ was placed on the earth,
⁵that the mirth of the wicked is brief,
the joy of the godless lasts but a moment.
⁶Though his pride reaches to the heavens
and his head touches the clouds,
⁷he will perish forever, like his own dung;
those who have seen him will say, 'Where
is he?'
⁸Like a dream he flies away, no more to be
found,
banished like a vision of the night.
⁹The eye that saw him will not see him again;
his place will look on him no more.
¹⁰His children must make amends to the poor;
his own hands must give back his wealth.
¹¹The youthful vigor that fills his bones
will lie with him in the dust.

¹²"Though evil is sweet in his mouth
and he hides it under his tongue,
¹³though he cannot bear to let it go
and keeps it in his mouth,
¹⁴yet his food will turn sour in his stomach;
it will become the venom of serpents
within him.
¹⁵He will spit out the riches he swallowed;

ᵃ 26 Or And after I awake, / though this ⸤body⸥ has been
destroyed, / then   ᵇ 26 Or / apart from   ᶜ 28 Many
Hebrew manuscripts, Septuagint and Vulgate; most Hebrew
manuscripts me   ᵈ 29 Or / that you may come to know the
Almighty   ᵉ 4 Or Adam

THE MESSAGE

And I'll see him—even though I get skinned
alive!—
see God myself, with my very own eyes.
Oh, how I long for that day!

¹⁹.²⁸⁻²⁹ "If you're thinking, 'How can we get through
to him,
get him to see that his trouble is all his own
fault?'
Forget it. Start worrying about *yourselves*.
Worry about your own sins and God's
coming judgment,
for judgment is most certainly on the way."

ZOPHAR ATTACKS JOB—
THE SECOND ROUND

SAVORING EVIL AS A DELICACY

²⁰.¹⁻³ **20** Zophar from Naamath again took his
turn:

"I can't believe what I'm hearing!
You've put my teeth on edge, my stomach
in a knot.
How dare you insult my intelligence like this!
Well, here's a piece of my mind!

²⁰.⁴⁻¹¹ "Don't you even know the basics,
how things have been since the earliest
days,
when Adam and Eve were first placed on
earth?
The good times of the wicked are short-lived;
godless joy is only momentary.
The evil might become world famous,
strutting at the head of the celebrity parade,
But still end up in a pile of dung.
Acquaintances look at them with disgust
and say, 'What's that?'
They fly off like a dream that can't be
remembered,
like a shadowy illusion that vanishes in the
light.
Though once notorious public figures, now
they're nobodies,
unnoticed, whether they come or go.
Their children will go begging on skid row,
and they'll have to give back their ill-gotten
gain.
Right in the prime of life,
and youthful and vigorous, they'll die.

²⁰.¹²⁻¹⁹ "They savor evil as a delicacy,
roll it around on their tongues,
Prolong the flavor, a dalliance in decadence—
real gourmets of evil!
But then they get stomach cramps,
a bad case of food poisoning.
They gag on all that rich food;

NEW INTERNATIONAL VERSION

God will make his stomach vomit
them up.
16 He will suck the poison of serpents;
the fangs of an adder will kill him.
17 He will not enjoy the streams,
the rivers flowing with honey and cream.
18 What he toiled for he must give back
uneaten;
he will not enjoy the profit from his
trading.
19 For he has oppressed the poor and left them
destitute;
he has seized houses he did not build.

20 "Surely he will have no respite from his
craving;
he cannot save himself by his treasure.
21 Nothing is left for him to devour;
his prosperity will not endure.
22 In the midst of his plenty, distress will
overtake him;
the full force of misery will come upon
him.
23 When he has filled his belly,
God will vent his burning anger against
him
and rain down his blows upon him.
24 Though he flees from an iron weapon,
a bronze-tipped arrow pierces him.
25 He pulls it out of his back,
the gleaming point out of his liver.
Terrors will come over him;
26 total darkness lies in wait for his
treasures.
A fire unfanned will consume him
and devour what is left in his tent.
27 The heavens will expose his guilt;
the earth will rise up against him.
28 A flood will carry off his house,
rushing waters[a] on the day of God's
wrath.
29 Such is the fate God allots the wicked,
the heritage appointed for them by God."

JOB

21

Then Job replied:

2 "Listen carefully to my words;
let this be the consolation you give me.
3 Bear with me while I speak,
and after I have spoken, mock on.

4 "Is my complaint directed to man?
Why should I not be impatient?

---

[a] 28 Or *The possessions in his house will be carried off, /
washed away*

THE MESSAGE

God makes them vomit it up.
They gorge on evil, make a diet of that
poison—
a deadly diet—and it kills them.
No quiet picnics for them beside gentle
streams
with fresh-baked bread and cheese, and
tall, cool drinks.
They spit out their food half-chewed,
unable to relax and enjoy anything they've
worked for.
And why? Because they exploited the poor,
took what never belonged to them.

20.20-29 "Such God-denying people are never content
with what they have or who they
are;
their greed drives them relentlessly.
They plunder everything
but they can't hold on to any of it.
Just when they think they have it all, disaster
strikes;
they're served up a plate full of misery.
When they've filled their bellies with that,
God gives them a taste of his anger,
and they get to chew on that for a while.
As they run for their lives from one disaster,
they run smack into another.
They're knocked around from pillar to post,
beaten to within an inch of their lives.
They're trapped in a house of horrors,
and see their loot disappear down a black
hole.
Their lives are a total loss—
not a penny to their name, not so much as
a bean.
God will strip them of their sin-soaked clothes
and hang their dirty laundry out for all
to see.
Life is a complete wipeout for them,
nothing surviving God's wrath.
There! That's God's blueprint for the wicked—
what they have to look forward to."

JOB'S RESPONSE

WHY DO THE WICKED HAVE IT SO GOOD?

21.1-3 # 21

Job replied:

"Now listen to me carefully, please listen,
at least do me the favor of listening.
Put up with me while I have my say—
then you can mock me later to your heart's
content.

21.4-16 "It's not *you* I'm complaining to—it's *God*.
Is it any wonder I'm getting fed up with his
silence?

NEW INTERNATIONAL VERSION

⁵Look at me and be astonished;
  clap your hand over your mouth.
⁶When I think about this, I am terrified;
  trembling seizes my body.
⁷Why do the wicked live on,
  growing old and increasing in power?
⁸They see their children established around
    them,
  their offspring before their eyes.
⁹Their homes are safe and free from fear;
  the rod of God is not upon them.
¹⁰Their bulls never fail to breed;
  their cows calve and do not miscarry.
¹¹They send forth their children as a flock;
  their little ones dance about.
¹²They sing to the music of tambourine and
    harp;
  they make merry to the sound of the flute.
¹³They spend their years in prosperity
  and go down to the grave ᵃ in peace. ᵇ
¹⁴Yet they say to God, 'Leave us alone!
  We have no desire to know your ways.
¹⁵Who is the Almighty, that we should serve
    him?
  What would we gain by praying to him?'
¹⁶But their prosperity is not in their own
    hands,
  so I stand aloof from the counsel of the
    wicked.

¹⁷"Yet how often is the lamp of the wicked
    snuffed out?
  How often does calamity come upon
    them,
  the fate God allots in his anger?
¹⁸How often are they like straw before the
    wind,
  like chaff swept away by a gale?
¹⁹⌊It is said,⌋ 'God stores up a man's
    punishment for his sons.'
  Let him repay the man himself, so that he
    will know it!
²⁰Let his own eyes see his destruction;
  let him drink of the wrath of the
    Almighty. ᶜ
²¹For what does he care about the family he
    leaves behind
  when his allotted months come to an end?

²²"Can anyone teach knowledge to God,
  since he judges even the highest?
²³One man dies in full vigor,
  completely secure and at ease,
²⁴his body ᵈ well nourished,

ᵃ 13 Hebrew Sheol   ᵇ 13 Or in an instant
ᶜ 17-20 Verses 17 and 18 may be taken as exclamations and
19 and 20 as declarations.   ᵈ 24 The meaning of the
Hebrew for this word is uncertain.

THE MESSAGE

Take a good look at me. Aren't you appalled
    by what's happened?
  No! Don't say anything. I can do without
    your comments.
When I look back, I go into shock,
  my body is racked with spasms.
Why do the wicked have it so good,
  live to a ripe old age and get rich?
They get to see their children succeed,
  get to watch and enjoy their grandchildren.
Their homes are peaceful and free from fear;
  they never experience God's disciplining
    rod.
Their bulls breed with great vigor
  and their cows calve without fail.
They send their children out to play
  and watch them frolic like spring lambs.
They make music with fiddles and flutes,
  have good times singing and dancing.
They have a long life on easy street,
  and die painlessly in their sleep.
They say to God, 'Get lost!
  We've no interest in you or your ways.
Why should we have dealings with God
    Almighty?
  What's there in it for us?'
But they're wrong, dead wrong—they're not
    gods.
  It's beyond me how they can carry on like
    this!

21.17-21 "Still, how often does it happen that the
    wicked fail,
  or disaster strikes,
  or they get their just deserts?
How often are they blown away by bad luck?
  Not very often.
You might say, 'God is saving up the
    punishment for their children.'
  I say, 'Give it to them right now so they'll
    know what they've done!'
They deserve to experience the effects of their
    evil,
  feel the full force of God's wrath firsthand.
What do they care what happens to their
    families
  after they're safely tucked away in the
    grave?

FANCY FUNERALS WITH ALL THE TRIMMINGS
21.22-26 "But who are we to tell God how to run his
    affairs?
  He's dealing with matters that are way over
    our heads.
Some people die in the prime of life,
  with everything going for them—

NEW INTERNATIONAL VERSION

his bones rich with marrow.
²⁵ Another man dies in bitterness of soul,
  never having enjoyed anything good.
²⁶ Side by side they lie in the dust,
  and worms cover them both.

²⁷ "I know full well what you are thinking,
  the schemes by which you would
    wrong me.
²⁸ You say, 'Where now is the great man's
    house,
  the tents where wicked men lived?'
²⁹ Have you never questioned those who travel?
  Have you paid no regard to their
    accounts—
³⁰ that the evil man is spared from the day of
    calamity,
  that he is delivered from ᵃ the day of
    wrath?
³¹ Who denounces his conduct to his face?
  Who repays him for what he has done?
³² He is carried to the grave,
  and watch is kept over his tomb.
³³ The soil in the valley is sweet to him;
  all men follow after him,
  and a countless throng goes ᵇ before him.

³⁴ "So how can you console me with your
    nonsense?
  Nothing is left of your answers but
    falsehood!"

ELIPHAZ

22 Then Eliphaz the Temanite replied:

² "Can a man be of benefit to God?
  Can even a wise man benefit him?
³ What pleasure would it give the Almighty if
    you were righteous?
  What would he gain if your ways were
    blameless?

⁴ "Is it for your piety that he rebukes you
  and brings charges against you?
⁵ Is not your wickedness great?
  Are not your sins endless?
⁶ You demanded security from your brothers
    for no reason;
  you stripped men of their clothing,
    leaving them naked.
⁷ You gave no water to the weary

THE MESSAGE

fat and sassy.
Others die bitter and bereft,
  never getting a taste of happiness.
They're laid out side by side in the cemetery,
  where the worms can't tell one from the
    other.

²¹·²⁷⁻³³ "I'm not deceived. I know what you're up to,
  the plans you're cooking up to bring me
    down.
Naively you claim that the castles of tyrants
    fall to pieces,
  that the achievements of the wicked
    collapse.
Have you ever asked world travelers how they
    see it?
  Have you not listened to their stories
Of evil men and women who got off scot-free,
  who never had to pay for their wickedness?
Did anyone ever confront them with their
    crimes?
  Did they ever have to face the music?
Not likely—they're given fancy funerals
  with all the trimmings,
Gently lowered into expensive graves,
  with everyone telling lies about how
    wonderful they were.

²¹·³⁴ "So how do you expect me to get any comfort
    from your nonsense?
  Your so-called comfort is a tissue of lies."

ELIPHAZ ATTACKS JOB—
THE THIRD ROUND

COME TO TERMS WITH GOD

²²·¹⁻¹¹ **22** Once again Eliphaz the Temanite took
    up his theme:

"Are any of us strong enough to give God a
    hand,
  or smart enough to give him advice?
So what if you were righteous—would God
    Almighty even notice?
  Even if you gave a perfect performance, do
    you think
  he'd applaud?
Do you think it's because he cares about your
    purity
  that he's disciplining you, putting you on
    the spot?
Hardly! It's because you're a first-class moral
    failure,
  because there's no end to your sins.
When people came to you for help,
  you took the shirts off their backs,
    exploited their helplessness.
You wouldn't so much as give a drink to the
    thirsty,

ᵃ 30 Or *man is reserved for the day of calamity, / that he is brought forth to* ᵇ 33 Or / *as a countless throng went*

and you withheld food from the hungry,
⁸ though you were a powerful man, owning
land—
an honored man, living on it.
⁹ And you sent widows away empty-handed
and broke the strength of the fatherless.
¹⁰ That is why snares are all around you,
why sudden peril terrifies you,
¹¹ why it is so dark you cannot see,
and why a flood of water covers you.

¹² "Is not God in the heights of heaven?
And see how lofty are the highest stars!
¹³ Yet you say, 'What does God know?
Does he judge through such darkness?
¹⁴ Thick clouds veil him, so he does not see us
as he goes about in the vaulted heavens.'
¹⁵ Will you keep to the old path
that evil men have trod?
¹⁶ They were carried off before their time,
their foundations washed away by a flood.
¹⁷ They said to God, 'Leave us alone!
What can the Almighty do to us?'
¹⁸ Yet it was he who filled their houses with
good things,
so I stand aloof from the counsel of the
wicked.

¹⁹ "The righteous see their ruin and rejoice;
the innocent mock them, saying,
²⁰ 'Surely our foes are destroyed,
and fire devours their wealth.'

²¹ "Submit to God and be at peace with him;
in this way prosperity will come to you.
²² Accept instruction from his mouth
and lay up his words in your heart.
²³ If you return to the Almighty, you will be
restored:
If you remove wickedness far from your
tent
²⁴ and assign your nuggets to the dust,
your gold of Ophir to the rocks in the
ravines,
²⁵ then the Almighty will be your gold,
the choicest silver for you.
²⁶ Surely then you will find delight in the
Almighty
and will lift up your face to God.
²⁷ You will pray to him, and he will hear you,
and you will fulfill your vows.

or food, not even a scrap, to the hungry.
And there you sat, strong and honored by
everyone,
surrounded by immense wealth!
You turned poor widows away from your
door;
heartless, you crushed orphans.
Now you're the one trapped in terror,
paralyzed by fear.
Suddenly the tables have turned!
How do you like living in the dark, sightless,
up to your neck in flood waters?

22.12-14 "You agree, don't you, that God is in charge?
He runs the universe—just look at the
stars!
Yet you dare raise questions: 'What does God
know?
From that distance and darkness, how can
he judge?
He roams the heavens wrapped in clouds,
so how can he see us?'

22.15-18 "Are you going to persist in that tired old line
that wicked men and women have always
used?
Where did it get them? They died young,
flash floods sweeping them off to their
doom.
They told God, 'Get lost!
What good is God Almighty to us?'
And yet it was God who gave them everything
they had.
It's beyond me how they can carry on like
this!

22.19-20 "Good people see bad people crash, and call
for a celebration.
Relieved, they crow,
'At last! Our enemies—wiped out.
Everything they had and stood for is up in
smoke!'

22.21-25 "Give in to God, come to terms with him
and everything will turn out just fine.
Let him tell you what to do;
take his words to heart.
Come back to God Almighty
and he'll rebuild your life.
Clean house of everything evil.
Relax your grip on your money
and abandon your gold-plated luxury.
God Almighty will be your treasure,
more wealth than you can imagine.

22.26-30 "You'll take delight in God, the Mighty One,
and look to him joyfully, boldly.
You'll pray to him and he'll listen;
he'll help you do what you've promised.

NEW INTERNATIONAL VERSION

28 What you decide on will be done,
  and light will shine on your ways.
29 When men are brought low and you say, 'Lift
    them up!'
  then he will save the downcast.
30 He will deliver even one who is not innocent,
  who will be delivered through the
    cleanness of your hands."

JOB

23

Then Job replied:

2 "Even today my complaint is bitter;
  his hand*a* is heavy in spite of*b* my
    groaning.
3 If only I knew where to find him;
  if only I could go to his dwelling!
4 I would state my case before him
  and fill my mouth with arguments.
5 I would find out what he would answer me,
  and consider what he would say.
6 Would he oppose me with great power?
  No, he would not press charges against me.
7 There an upright man could present his case
    before him,
  and I would be delivered forever from my
    judge.

8 "But if I go to the east, he is not there;
  if I go to the west, I do not find him.
9 When he is at work in the north, I do not see
    him;
  when he turns to the south, I catch no
    glimpse of him.
10 But he knows the way that I take;
  when he has tested me, I will come forth
    as gold.
11 My feet have closely followed his steps;
  I have kept to his way without turning
    aside.
12 I have not departed from the commands of
    his lips;
  I have treasured the words of his mouth
    more than my daily bread.

13 "But he stands alone, and who can oppose
    him?
  He does whatever he pleases.
14 He carries out his decree against me,
  and many such plans he still has in store.
15 That is why I am terrified before him;
  when I think of all this, I fear him.
16 God has made my heart faint;
  the Almighty has terrified me.

---

a 2 Septuagint and Syriac; Hebrew / *the hand on me*
b 2 Or *heavy on me in*

THE MESSAGE

You'll decide what you want and it will
    happen;
  your life will be bathed in light.
To those who feel low you'll say, 'Chin up! Be
    brave!'
  and God will save them.
Yes, even the guilty will escape,
  escape through God's grace in your life."

JOB'S DEFENSE

I'M COMPLETELY IN THE DARK

23.1-7

23

Job replied:

"I'm not letting up—I'm standing my ground.
  My complaint is legitimate.
God has no right to treat me like this—
  it isn't fair!
If I knew where on earth to find him,
  I'd go straight to him.
I'd lay my case before him face-to-face,
  give him all my arguments firsthand.
I'd find out exactly what he's thinking,
  discover what's going on in his head.
Do you think he'd dismiss me or bully me?
  No, he'd take me seriously.
He'd see a straight-living man standing before
    him;
  my Judge would acquit me for good of all
    charges.

23.8-9 "I travel East looking for him—I find no one;
  then West, but not a trace;
I go North, but he's hidden his tracks;
  then South, but not even a glimpse.

23.10-12 "But he knows where I am and what I've
    done.
  He can cross-examine me all he wants, and
    I'll pass the test with honors.
I've followed him closely, my feet in his
    footprints,
  not once swerving from his way.
I've obeyed every word he's spoken,
  and not just obeyed his advice—I've
    treasured it.

23.13-17 "But he is singular and sovereign. Who can
    argue with him?
  He does what he wants, when he wants to.
He'll complete in detail what he's decided
    about me,
  and whatever else he determines to do.
Is it any wonder that I dread meeting him?
  Whenever I think about it, I get scared all
    over again.
God makes my heart sink!
  God Almighty gives me the shudders!

NEW INTERNATIONAL VERSION

¹⁷Yet I am not silenced by the darkness,
by the thick darkness that covers my face.

24 "Why does the Almighty not set times
for judgment?
Why must those who know him look in
vain for such days?
²Men move boundary stones;
they pasture flocks they have stolen.
³They drive away the orphan's donkey
and take the widow's ox in pledge.
⁴They thrust the needy from the path
and force all the poor of the land into
hiding.
⁵Like wild donkeys in the desert,
the poor go about their labor of foraging
food;
the wasteland provides food for their
children.
⁶They gather fodder in the fields
and glean in the vineyards of the wicked.
⁷Lacking clothes, they spend the night naked;
they have nothing to cover themselves in
the cold.
⁸They are drenched by mountain rains
and hug the rocks for lack of shelter.
⁹The fatherless child is snatched from the
breast;
the infant of the poor is seized for a debt.
¹⁰Lacking clothes, they go about naked;
they carry the sheaves, but still go hungry.
¹¹They crush olives among the terraces^a;
they tread the winepresses, yet suffer
thirst.
¹²The groans of the dying rise from the city,
and the souls of the wounded cry out for
help.
But God charges no one with wrongdoing.

¹³"There are those who rebel against the light,
who do not know its ways
or stay in its paths.
¹⁴When daylight is gone, the murderer
rises up
and kills the poor and needy;
in the night he steals forth like a thief.
¹⁵The eye of the adulterer watches for dusk;
he thinks, 'No eye will see me,'
and he keeps his face concealed.
¹⁶In the dark, men break into houses,
but by day they shut themselves in;
they want nothing to do with the light.
¹⁷For all of them, deep darkness is their
morning^b;

---

^a 11 Or olives between the millstones; the meaning of the
Hebrew for this word is uncertain.   ^b 17 Or them, their
morning is like the shadow of death

THE MESSAGE

I'm completely in the dark,
I can't see my hand in front of my face.

AN ILLUSION OF SECURITY

24.1-12 # 24 "But if Judgment Day isn't hidden from
the Almighty,
why are we kept in the dark?
There are people out there getting by with
murder—
stealing and lying and cheating.
They rip off the poor
and exploit the unfortunate,
Push the helpless into the ditch,
bully the weak so that they fear for their
lives.
The poor, like stray dogs and cats,
scavenge for food in back alleys.
They sort through the garbage of the rich,
eke out survival on handouts.
Homeless, they shiver through cold nights on
the street;
they've no place to lay their heads.
Exposed to the weather, wet and frozen,
they huddle in makeshift shelters.
Nursing mothers have their babies snatched
from them;
the infants of the poor are kidnapped and
sold.
They go about patched and threadbare;
even the hard workers go hungry.
No matter how back-breaking their labor,
they can never make ends meet.
People are dying right and left, groaning in
torment.
The wretched cry out for help
and God does nothing, acts like nothing's
wrong!

24.13-17 "Then there are those who avoid light at all
costs,
who scorn the light-filled path.
When the sun goes down, the murderer
gets up—
kills the poor and robs the defenseless.
Sexual predators can't wait for nightfall,
thinking, 'No one can see us now.'
Burglars do their work at night,
but keep well out of sight through the day.
They want nothing to do with light.
Deep darkness is morning for that bunch;

NEW INTERNATIONAL VERSION

they make friends with the terrors of
darkness. [a]

18 "Yet they are foam on the surface of the water;
their portion of the land is cursed,
so that no one goes to the vineyards.
19 As heat and drought snatch away the melted
snow,
so the grave [b] snatches away those who
have sinned.
20 The womb forgets them,
the worm feasts on them;
evil men are no longer remembered
but are broken like a tree.
21 They prey on the barren and childless woman,
and to the widow show no kindness.
22 But God drags away the mighty by his power;
though they become established, they
have no assurance of life.
23 He may let them rest in a feeling of security,
but his eyes are on their ways.
24 For a little while they are exalted, and then
they are gone;
they are brought low and gathered up like
all others;
they are cut off like heads of grain.

25 "If this is not so, who can prove me false
and reduce my words to nothing?"

BILDAD

25 Then Bildad the Shuhite replied:

2 "Dominion and awe belong to God;
he establishes order in the heights of
heaven.
3 Can his forces be numbered?
Upon whom does his light not rise?
4 How then can a man be righteous before
God?
How can one born of woman be pure?
5 If even the moon is not bright
and the stars are not pure in his eyes,
6 how much less man, who is but a maggot—
a son of man, who is only a worm!"

JOB

26 Then Job replied:

2 "How you have helped the powerless!

THE MESSAGE

they make the terrors of darkness their
companions in crime.

24.18-25 "They are scraps of wood floating on the
water—
useless, cursed junk, good for nothing.
As surely as snow melts under the hot,
summer sun,
sinners disappear in the grave.
The womb has forgotten them, worms have
relished them—
nothing that is evil lasts.
Unscrupulous,
they prey on those less fortunate.
However much they strut and flex their
muscles,
there's nothing to them. They're hollow.
They may have an illusion of security,
but God has his eye on them.
They may get their brief successes,
but then it's over, nothing to show for it.
Like yesterday's newspaper,
they're used to wrap up the garbage.
You're free to try to prove me a liar,
but you won't be able to do it."

BILDAD'S THIRD ATTACK

25.1-6 EVEN THE STARS AREN'T PERFECT IN GOD'S EYES

25 Bildad the Shuhite again attacked Job:

"God is sovereign, God is fearsome—
everything in the cosmos fits and works in
his plan.
Can anyone count his angel armies?
Is there any place where his light doesn't
shine?
How can a mere mortal presume to stand up
to God?
How can an ordinary person pretend to be
guiltless?
Why, even the moon has its flaws,
even the stars aren't perfect in God's eyes,
So how much less, plain men and women—
slugs and maggots by comparison!"

JOB'S DEFENSE

GOD SETS A BOUNDARY BETWEEN LIGHT AND
DARKNESS

26 Job answered:

26.1-4 "Well, you've certainly been a great help to a
helpless man!

---

a 17 Or of the shadow of death   *b 19 Hebrew Sheol*

NEW INTERNATIONAL VERSION

How you have saved the arm that is feeble!
³What advice you have offered to one without
wisdom!
And what great insight you have displayed!
⁴Who has helped you utter these words?
And whose spirit spoke from your mouth?

⁵ "The dead are in deep anguish,
those beneath the waters and all that live
in them.
⁶Death*a* is naked before God;
Destruction*b* lies uncovered.
⁷He spreads out the northern ⌊skies⌋ over
empty space;
he suspends the earth over nothing.
⁸He wraps up the waters in his clouds,
yet the clouds do not burst under their
weight.
⁹He covers the face of the full moon,
spreading his clouds over it.
¹⁰He marks out the horizon on the face of the
waters
for a boundary between light and darkness.
¹¹The pillars of the heavens quake,
aghast at his rebuke.
¹²By his power he churned up the sea;
by his wisdom he cut Rahab to pieces.
¹³By his breath the skies became fair;
his hand pierced the gliding serpent.
¹⁴And these are but the outer fringe of his works;
how faint the whisper we hear of him!
Who then can understand the thunder of
his power?"

27 And Job continued his discourse:

² "As surely as God lives, who has denied me
justice,
the Almighty, who has made me taste
bitterness of soul,
³as long as I have life within me,
the breath of God in my nostrils,
⁴my lips will not speak wickedness,
and my tongue will utter no deceit.
⁵I will never admit you are in the right;
till I die, I will not deny my integrity.
⁶I will maintain my righteousness and never
let go of it;
my conscience will not reproach me as
long as I live.

⁷ "May my enemies be like the wicked,
my adversaries like the unjust!
⁸For what hope has the godless when he is
cut off,
when God takes away his life?

a 6 Hebrew Sheol   b 6 Hebrew Abaddon

THE MESSAGE

You came to the rescue just in the nick of
time!
What wonderful advice you've given to a
mixed-up man!
What amazing insights you've provided!
Where in the world did you learn all this?
How did you become so inspired?

26.5-14 "All the buried dead are in torment,
and all who've been drowned in the deep,
deep sea.
Hell is ripped open before God,
graveyards dug up and exposed.
He spreads the skies over unformed space,
hangs the earth out in empty space.
He pours water into cumulus cloud-bags
and the bags don't burst.
He makes the moon wax and wane,
putting it through its phases.
He draws the horizon out over the ocean,
sets a boundary between light and
darkness.
Thunder crashes and rumbles in the skies.
Listen! It's God raising his voice!
By his power he stills sea storms,
by his wisdom he tames sea monsters.
With one breath he clears the sky,
with one finger he crushes the sea serpent.
And this is only the beginning,
a mere whisper of his rule.
Whatever would we do if he *really* raised
his voice!"

No Place to Hide

27.1-6 **27** Having waited for Zophar, Job now resumed his defense:

"God-Alive! He's denied me justice!
God Almighty! He's ruined my life!
But for as long as I draw breath,
and for as long as God breathes life
into me,
I refuse to say one word that isn't true.
I refuse to confess to any charge that's false.
There is no way I'll ever agree to your
accusations.
I'll not deny my integrity even if it costs me
my life.
I'm holding fast to my integrity and not
loosening my grip—
and, believe me, I'll never regret it.

27.7-10 "Let my enemy be exposed as wicked!
Let my adversary be proven guilty!
What hope do people without God have when
life is cut short?
when God puts an end to life?

NEW INTERNATIONAL VERSION

⁹Does God listen to his cry
  when distress comes upon him?
¹⁰Will he find delight in the Almighty?
  Will he call upon God at all times?

¹¹ "I will teach you about the power of God;
  the ways of the Almighty I will not
    conceal.
¹²You have all seen this yourselves.
  Why then this meaningless talk?

¹³ "Here is the fate God allots to the wicked,
  the heritage a ruthless man receives from
    the Almighty:
¹⁴However many his children, their fate is the
    sword;
  his offspring will never have enough to
    eat.
¹⁵The plague will bury those who survive him,
  and their widows will not weep for them.
¹⁶Though he heaps up silver like dust
  and clothes like piles of clay,
¹⁷what he lays up the righteous will wear,
  and the innocent will divide his silver.
¹⁸The house he builds is like a moth's cocoon,
  like a hut made by a watchman.
¹⁹He lies down wealthy, but will do so no
    more;
  when he opens his eyes, all is gone.
²⁰Terrors overtake him like a flood;
  a tempest snatches him away in the night.
²¹The east wind carries him off, and he is
    gone;
  it sweeps him out of his place.
²²It hurls itself against him without mercy
  as he flees headlong from its power.
²³It claps its hands in derision
  and hisses him out of his place.

28 "There is a mine for silver
  and a place where gold is refined.
²Iron is taken from the earth,
  and copper is smelted from ore.
³Man puts an end to the darkness;
  he searches the farthest recesses
  for ore in the blackest darkness.
⁴Far from where people dwell he cuts a shaft,
  in places forgotten by the foot of man;
  far from men he dangles and sways.

THE MESSAGE

Do you think God will listen to their cry for
    help
  when disaster hits?
What interest have they ever shown in the
    Almighty?
  Have they ever been known to pray before?

27.11-12 "I've given you a clear account of God in action,
  suppressed nothing regarding God Almighty.
The evidence is right before you. You can all
    see it for yourselves,
  so why do you keep talking nonsense?

27.13-23 "I'll quote your own words back to you:

" 'This is how God treats the wicked,
  this is what evil people can expect from
    God Almighty:
Their children—all of them—will die violent
    deaths;
  they'll never have enough bread to put on
    the table.
They'll be wiped out by the plague,
  and none of the widows will shed a tear
    when they're gone.
Even if they make a lot of money
  and are resplendent in the latest fashions,
It's the good who will end up wearing the
    clothes
  and the decent who will divide up the money.
They build elaborate houses
  that won't survive a single winter.
They go to bed wealthy
  and wake up poor.
Terrors pour in on them like flash floods—
  a tornado snatches them away in the
    middle of the night,
A cyclone sweeps them up—gone!
  Not a trace of them left, not even a footprint.
Catastrophes relentlessly pursue them;
  they run this way and that, but there's no
    place to hide—
Pummeled by the weather,
  blown to kingdom come by the storm.'

WHERE DOES WISDOM COME FROM?

28.1-11 **28** "We all know how silver seams the
    rocks,
  we've seen the stuff from which gold is
    refined,
We're aware of how iron is dug out of the
    ground
  and copper is smelted from rock.
Miners penetrate the earth's darkness,
  searching the roots of the mountains for ore,
  digging away in the suffocating darkness.
Far from civilization, far from the traffic,
  they cut a shaft,
  and are lowered into it by ropes.

NEW INTERNATIONAL VERSION

⁵The earth, from which food comes,
    is transformed below as by fire;
⁶sapphires^a come from its rocks,
    and its dust contains nuggets of gold.
⁷No bird of prey knows that hidden path,
    no falcon's eye has seen it.
⁸Proud beasts do not set foot on it,
    and no lion prowls there.
⁹Man's hand assaults the flinty rock
    and lays bare the roots of the mountains.
¹⁰He tunnels through the rock;
    his eyes see all its treasures.
¹¹He searches^b the sources of the rivers
    and brings hidden things to light.

¹²"But where can wisdom be found?
    Where does understanding dwell?
¹³Man does not comprehend its worth;
    it cannot be found in the land of the
        living.
¹⁴The deep says, 'It is not in me';
    the sea says, 'It is not with me.'
¹⁵It cannot be bought with the finest gold,
    nor can its price be weighed in silver.
¹⁶It cannot be bought with the gold of Ophir,
    with precious onyx or sapphires.
¹⁷Neither gold nor crystal can compare with it,
    nor can it be had for jewels of gold.
¹⁸Coral and jasper are not worthy of mention;
    the price of wisdom is beyond rubies.
¹⁹The topaz of Cush cannot compare with it;
    it cannot be bought with pure gold.

²⁰"Where then does wisdom come from?
    Where does understanding dwell?
²¹It is hidden from the eyes of every living
        thing,
    concealed even from the birds of the air.
²²Destruction^c and Death say,
    'Only a rumor of it has reached our ears.'
²³God understands the way to it
    and he alone knows where it dwells,
²⁴for he views the ends of the earth
    and sees everything under the heavens.
²⁵When he established the force of the wind
    and measured out the waters,
²⁶when he made a decree for the rain
    and a path for the thunderstorm,
²⁷then he looked at wisdom and appraised it;
    he confirmed it and tested it.
²⁸And he said to man,
    'The fear of the Lord—that is wisdom,
    and to shun evil is understanding.' "

^a 6 Or lapis lazuli; also in verse 16   ^b 11 Septuagint,
Aquila and Vulgate; Hebrew He dams up   ^c 22 Hebrew
Abaddon

THE MESSAGE

Earth's surface is a field for grain,
    but its depths are a forge
Firing sapphires from stones
    and chiseling gold from rocks.
Vultures are blind to its riches,
    hawks never lay eyes on it.
Wild animals are oblivious to it,
    lions don't know it's there.
Miners hammer away at the rock,
    they uproot the mountains.
They tunnel through the rock
    and find all kinds of beautiful gems.
They discover the origins of rivers,
    and bring earth's secrets to light.

28.12-19 "But where, oh where, will they find Wisdom?
    Where does Insight hide?
Mortals don't have a clue,
    haven't the slightest idea where to look.
Earth's depths say, 'It's not here';
    ocean deeps echo, 'Never heard of it.'
It can't be bought with the finest gold;
    no amount of silver can get it.
Even famous Ophir gold can't buy it,
    not even diamonds and sapphires.
Neither gold nor emeralds are comparable;
    extravagant jewelry can't touch it.
Pearl necklaces and ruby bracelets—why
        bother?
    None of this is even a down payment on
        Wisdom!
Pile gold and African diamonds as high as you
        will,
    they can't hold a candle to Wisdom.

28.20-22 "So where does Wisdom come from?
    And where does Insight live?
It can't be found by looking, no matter
    how deep you dig, no matter how high you
        fly.
If you search through the graveyard and
        question the dead,
    they say, 'We've only heard rumors of it.'

28.23-28 "God alone knows the way to Wisdom,
    he knows the exact place to find it.
He knows where everything is on earth,
    he sees everything under heaven.
After he commanded the winds to blow
    and measured out the waters,
Arranged for the rain
    and set off explosions of thunder and
        lightning,
He focused on Wisdom,
    made sure it was all set and tested and
        ready.
Then he addressed the human race: 'Here it is!
    Fear-of-the-Lord—that's Wisdom,
    and Insight means shunning evil.' "

NEW INTERNATIONAL VERSION

29 Job continued his discourse:

2 "How I long for the months gone by,
  for the days when God watched over me,
3 when his lamp shone upon my head
  and by his light I walked through
    darkness!
4 Oh, for the days when I was in my prime,
  when God's intimate friendship blessed
    my house,
5 when the Almighty was still with me
  and my children were around me,
6 when my path was drenched with cream
  and the rock poured out for me streams of
    olive oil.

7 "When I went to the gate of the city
  and took my seat in the public square,
8 the young men saw me and stepped aside
  and the old men rose to their feet;
9 the chief men refrained from speaking
  and covered their mouths with their hands;
10 the voices of the nobles were hushed,
  and their tongues stuck to the roof of
    their mouths.
11 Whoever heard me spoke well of me,
  and those who saw me commended me,
12 because I rescued the poor who cried for
    help,
  and the fatherless who had none to assist
    him.
13 The man who was dying blessed me;
  I made the widow's heart sing.
14 I put on righteousness as my clothing;
  justice was my robe and my turban.
15 I was eyes to the blind
  and feet to the lame.
16 I was a father to the needy;
  I took up the case of the stranger.
17 I broke the fangs of the wicked
  and snatched the victims from their teeth.

18 "I thought, 'I will die in my own house,
  my days as numerous as the grains of sand.
19 My roots will reach to the water,
  and the dew will lie all night on my
    branches.
20 My glory will remain fresh in me,
  the bow ever new in my hand.'

21 "Men listened to me expectantly,
  waiting in silence for my counsel.
22 After I had spoken, they spoke no more;
  my words fell gently on their ears.
23 They waited for me as for showers
  and drank in my words as the spring rain.
24 When I smiled at them, they scarcely
    believed it;

THE MESSAGE

WHEN GOD WAS STILL BY MY SIDE

29.1-6 **29** Job now resumed his response:

"Oh, how I long for the good old days,
  when God took such very good care of me.
He always held a lamp before me
  and I walked through the dark by its light.
Oh, how I miss those golden years
  when God's friendship graced my home,
When the Mighty One was still by my side
  and my children were all around me,
When everything was going my way,
  and nothing seemed too difficult.

29.7-20 "When I walked downtown
  and sat with my friends in the public
    square,
Young and old greeted me with respect;
  I was honored by everyone in town.
When I spoke, everyone listened;
  they hung on my every word.
People who knew me spoke well of me;
  my reputation went ahead of me.
I was known for helping people in trouble
  and standing up for those who were down
    on their luck.
The dying blessed me,
  and the bereaved were cheered by my
    visits.
All my dealings with people were good.
  I was known for being fair to everyone I
    met.
I was eyes to the blind
  and feet to the lame,
Father to the needy,
  and champion of abused aliens.
I grabbed street thieves by the scruff of the
    neck
  and made them give back what they'd
    stolen.
I thought, 'I'll die peacefully in my own bed,
  grateful for a long and full life,
A life deep-rooted and well-watered,
  a life limber and dew-fresh,
My soul suffused with glory
  and my body robust until the day I die.'

29.21-25 "Men and women listened when I spoke,
  hung expectantly on my every word.
After I spoke, they'd be quiet,
  taking it all in.
They welcomed my counsel like spring rain,
  drinking it all in.
When I smiled at them, they could hardly
    believe it;

NEW INTERNATIONAL VERSION

the light of my face was precious to them. *a*
²⁵ I chose the way for them and sat as their chief;
    I dwelt as a king among his troops;
    I was like one who comforts mourners.

30 "But now they mock me,
    men younger than I,
whose fathers I would have disdained
    to put with my sheep dogs.
² Of what use was the strength of their hands
        to me,
    since their vigor had gone from them?
³ Haggard from want and hunger,
    they roamed *b* the parched land
    in desolate wastelands at night.
⁴ In the brush they gathered salt herbs,
    and their food *c* was the root of the broom
        tree.
⁵ They were banished from their fellow men,
    shouted at as if they were thieves.
⁶ They were forced to live in the dry stream beds,
    among the rocks and in holes in the ground.
⁷ They brayed among the bushes
    and huddled in the undergrowth.
⁸ A base and nameless brood,
    they were driven out of the land.

⁹ "And now their sons mock me in song;
    I have become a byword among them.
¹⁰ They detest me and keep their distance;
    they do not hesitate to spit in my face.
¹¹ Now that God has unstrung my bow and
        afflicted me,
    they throw off restraint in my presence.
¹² On my right the tribe *d* attacks;
    they lay snares for my feet,
    they build their siege ramps against me.
¹³ They break up my road;
    they succeed in destroying me—
    without anyone's helping them. *e*
¹⁴ They advance as through a gaping breach;
    amid the ruins they come rolling in.
¹⁵ Terrors overwhelm me;
    my dignity is driven away as by the wind,
    my safety vanishes like a cloud.

¹⁶ "And now my life ebbs away;
    days of suffering grip me.
¹⁷ Night pierces my bones;
    my gnawing pains never rest.
¹⁸ In his great power ⌊God⌋ becomes like
        clothing to me *f*;
    he binds me like the neck of my garment.

---

a 24 The meaning of the Hebrew for this clause is
uncertain.   *b* 3 Or *gnawed*   *c* 4 Or *fuel*
d 12 The meaning of the Hebrew for this word is uncertain.
e 13 Or *me. / 'No one can help him,' ⌊they say⌋.*
f 18 Hebrew; Septuagint ⌊*God*⌋ *grasps my clothing*

THE MESSAGE

their faces lit up, their troubles took wing!
I was their leader, establishing the mood
    and setting the pace by which they lived.
    Where I led, they followed.

THE PAIN NEVER LETS UP

 30.1-8 **30** "But no longer. Now I'm the butt of
    their jokes—
    young ruffians! whippersnappers!
Why, I considered their fathers
    mere inexperienced pups.
But they are worse than dogs—good for
        nothing,
    stray, mangy animals,
Half-starved, scavenging the back alleys,
    howling at the moon;
Homeless guttersnipes
    chewing on old bones and licking old tin
        cans;
Outcasts from the community,
    cursed as dangerous delinquents.
Nobody would put up with them;
    they were driven from the neighborhood.
You could hear them out there at the edge of
        town,
    yelping and barking, huddled in junkyards,
A gang of beggars and no-names,
    thrown out on their ears.

30.9-15 "But now I'm the one they're after,
    mistreating me, taunting and mocking.
They abhor me, they abuse me.
    How dare those scoundrels—they spit in
        my face!
Now that God has undone me and left me in a
        heap,
    they hold nothing back. Anything goes.
They come at me from my blind side,
    trip me up, then jump on me while I'm
        down.
They throw every kind of obstacle in my path,
    determined to ruin me—
    and no one lifts a finger to help me!
They violate my broken body,
    trample through the rubble of my ruined
        life.
Terrors assault me—
    my dignity in shreds,
    salvation up in smoke.

30.16-19 "And now my life drains out,
    as suffering seizes and grips me hard.
Night gnaws at my bones;
    the pain never lets up.
I am tied hand and foot, my neck in a noose.
    I twist and turn.

NEW INTERNATIONAL VERSION

¹⁹He throws me into the mud,
and I am reduced to dust and ashes.

²⁰ "I cry out to you, O God, but you do not
answer;
I stand up, but you merely look at me.
²¹You turn on me ruthlessly;
with the might of your hand you attack
me.
²²You snatch me up and drive me before the
wind;
you toss me about in the storm.
²³I know you will bring me down to death,
to the place appointed for all the living.

²⁴ "Surely no one lays a hand on a broken man
when he cries for help in his distress.
²⁵Have I not wept for those in trouble?
Has not my soul grieved for the poor?
²⁶Yet when I hoped for good, evil came;
when I looked for light, then came
darkness.
²⁷The churning inside me never stops;
days of suffering confront me.
²⁸I go about blackened, but not by the sun;
I stand up in the assembly and cry for
help.
²⁹I have become a brother of jackals,
a companion of owls.
³⁰My skin grows black and peels;
my body burns with fever.
³¹My harp is tuned to mourning,
and my flute to the sound of wailing.

31 "I made a covenant with my eyes
not to look lustfully at a girl.
²For what is man's lot from God above,
his heritage from the Almighty on high?
³Is it not ruin for the wicked,
disaster for those who do wrong?
⁴Does he not see my ways
and count my every step?

⁵ "If I have walked in falsehood
or my foot has hurried after deceit—
⁶let God weigh me in honest scales
and he will know that I am blameless—
⁷if my steps have turned from the path,
if my heart has been led by my eyes,
or if my hands have been defiled,
⁸then may others eat what I have sown,
and may my crops be uprooted.

⁹ "If my heart has been enticed by a woman,
or if I have lurked at my neighbor's door,

THE MESSAGE

Thrown facedown in the muck,
I'm a muddy mess, inside and out.

WHAT DID I DO TO DESERVE THIS?

30.20-23 "I shout for help, God, and get nothing, no
answer!
I stand to face you in protest, and you give
me a blank stare!
You've turned into my tormenter—
you slap me around, knock me about.
You raised me up so I was riding high
and then dropped me, and I crashed.
I know you're determined to kill me,
to put me six feet under.

30.24-31 "What did I do to deserve this?
Did I ever hit anyone who was calling for
help?
Haven't I wept for those who live a hard life,
been heartsick over the lot of the poor?
But where did it get me?
I expected good but evil showed up.
I looked for light but darkness fell.
My stomach's in a constant churning, never
settles down.
Each day confronts me with more suffering.
I walk under a black cloud. The sun is gone.
I stand in the congregation and protest.
I howl with the jackals,
I hoot with the owls.
I'm black and blue all over,
burning up with fever.
My fiddle plays nothing but the blues;
my mouth harp wails laments.

WHAT CAN I EXPECT FROM GOD?

31.1-4 **31** "I made a solemn pact with myself
never to undress a girl with my eyes.
So what can I expect from God?
What do I deserve from God Almighty
above?
Isn't calamity reserved for the wicked?
Isn't disaster supposed to strike those who
do wrong?
Isn't God looking, observing how I live?
Doesn't he mark every step I take?

31.5-8 "Have I walked hand in hand with falsehood,
or hung out in the company of deceit?
Weigh me on a set of honest scales
so God has proof of my integrity.
If I've strayed off the straight and narrow,
wanted things I had no right to,
messed around with sin,
Go ahead, then—
give my portion to someone who deserves it.

31.9-12 "If I've let myself be seduced by a woman
and conspired to go to bed with her,

NEW INTERNATIONAL VERSION

¹⁰ then may my wife grind another man's grain,
and may other men sleep with her.
¹¹ For that would have been shameful,
a sin to be judged.
¹² It is a fire that burns to Destruction*;
it would have uprooted my harvest.

¹³ "If I have denied justice to my menservants
and maidservants
when they had a grievance against me,
¹⁴ what will I do when God confronts me?
What will I answer when called to account?
¹⁵ Did not he who made me in the womb make
them?
Did not the same one form us both within
our mothers?

¹⁶ "If I have denied the desires of the poor
or let the eyes of the widow grow weary,
¹⁷ if I have kept my bread to myself,
not sharing it with the fatherless—
¹⁸ but from my youth I reared him as would a
father,
and from my birth I guided the widow—
¹⁹ if I have seen anyone perishing for lack of
clothing,
or a needy man without a garment,
²⁰ and his heart did not bless me
for warming him with the fleece from my
sheep,
²¹ if I have raised my hand against the
fatherless,
knowing that I had influence in court,
²² then let my arm fall from the shoulder,
let it be broken off at the joint.
²³ For I dreaded destruction from God,
and for fear of his splendor I could not do
such things.

²⁴ "If I have put my trust in gold
or said to pure gold, 'You are my security,'
²⁵ if I have rejoiced over my great wealth,
the fortune my hands had gained,
²⁶ if I have regarded the sun in its radiance
or the moon moving in splendor,
²⁷ so that my heart was secretly enticed
and my hand offered them a kiss of
homage,
²⁸ then these also would be sins to be judged,
for I would have been unfaithful to God
on high.

²⁹ "If I have rejoiced at my enemy's misfortune
or gloated over the trouble that came to
him—
³⁰ I have not allowed my mouth to sin
by invoking a curse against his life—
³¹ if the men of my household have never said,

a 12 Hebrew Abaddon

THE MESSAGE

Fine, my wife has every right to go ahead
and sleep with anyone she wants to.
For disgusting behavior like that,
I'd deserve the worst punishment you
could hand out.
Adultery is a fire that burns the house down;
I wouldn't expect anything I count dear to
survive it.

31:13-15 "Have I ever been unfair to my employees
when they brought a complaint to me?
What, then, will I do when God confronts me?
When God examines my books, what can I
say?
Didn't the same God who made me, make them?
Aren't we all made of the same stuff, equals
before God?

31:16-18 "Have I ignored the needs of the poor,
turned my back on the indigent,
Taken care of my own needs and fed my own
face
while they languished?
Wasn't my home always open to them?
Weren't they always welcome at my table?

31:19-20 "Have I ever left a poor family shivering in the
cold
when they had no warm clothes?
Didn't the poor bless me when they saw me
coming,
knowing I'd brought coats from my closet?

31:21-23 "If I've ever used my strength and influence
to take advantage of the unfortunate,
Go ahead, break both my arms,
cut off all my fingers!
The fear of God has kept me from these
things—
how else could I ever face him?

IF ONLY SOMEONE WOULD GIVE ME A HEARING!

31:24-28 "Did I set my heart on making big money
or worship at the bank?
Did I boast about my wealth,
show off because I was well-off?
Was I ever so awed by the sun's brilliance
and moved by the moon's beauty
That I let myself become seduced by them
and worshiped them on the sly?
If so, I would deserve the worst of
punishments,
for I would be betraying God himself.

31:29-30 "Did I ever crow over my enemy's ruin?
Or gloat over my rival's bad luck?
No, I never said a word of detraction,
never cursed them, even under my breath.

31:31-34 "Didn't those who worked for me say,

NEW INTERNATIONAL VERSION

'Who has not had his fill of Job's meat?'—
³² but no stranger had to spend the night in the
street,
for my door was always open to the
traveler—
³³ if I have concealed my sin as men do,^a
by hiding my guilt in my heart
³⁴ because I so feared the crowd
and so dreaded the contempt of the clans
that I kept silent and would not go
outside—

³⁵ ("Oh, that I had someone to hear me!
I sign now my defense—let the Almighty
answer me;
let my accuser put his indictment in
writing.
³⁶ Surely I would wear it on my shoulder,
I would put it on like a crown.
³⁷ I would give him an account of my every
step;
like a prince I would approach him.)—

³⁸ "if my land cries out against me
and all its furrows are wet with tears,
³⁹ if I have devoured its yield without payment
or broken the spirit of its tenants,
⁴⁰ then let briers come up instead of wheat
and weeds instead of barley."

The words of Job are ended.

ELIHU

32 So these three men stopped answering
Job, because he was righteous in his own
eyes. ² But Elihu son of Barakel the Buzite, of the
family of Ram, became very angry with Job for
justifying himself rather than God. ³ He was also
angry with the three friends, because they had
found no way to refute Job, and yet had con-
demned him.^b ⁴ Now Elihu had waited before
speaking to Job because they were older than he.
⁵ But when he saw that the three men had noth-
ing more to say, his anger was aroused.

⁶ So Elihu son of Barakel the Buzite said:

"I am young in years,
and you are old;
that is why I was fearful,
not daring to tell you what I know.
⁷ I thought, 'Age should speak;

THE MESSAGE

'He fed us well. There were always second
helpings'?
And no stranger ever had to spend a night in
the street;
my doors were always open to travelers.
Did I hide my sin the way Adam did,
or conceal my guilt behind closed doors
Because I was afraid what people would say,
fearing the gossip of the neighbors so much
That I turned myself into a recluse?
You know good and well that I didn't.

^{31.35-37} "Oh, if only someone would give me a hearing!
I've signed my name to my defense—let the
Almighty One answer!
I want to see my indictment in writing.
Anyone's welcome to read my defense;
I'll write it on a poster and carry it around
town.
I'm prepared to account for every move I've
ever made—
to anyone and everyone, prince or pauper.

^{31.38-39} "If the very ground that I farm accuses me,
if even the furrows fill with tears from my
abuse,
If I've ever raped the earth for my own profit
or dispossessed its rightful owners,
Then curse it with thistles instead of wheat,
curse it with weeds instead of barley."

The words of Job to his three friends were
finished.

ELIHU SPEAKS

GOD'S SPIRIT MAKES WISDOM POSSIBLE

^{32.1-5} **32** Job's three friends now fell silent. They
were talked out, stymied because Job
wouldn't budge an inch—wouldn't admit to an
ounce of guilt. Then Elihu lost his temper.
(Elihu was the son of Barakel the Buzite from
the clan of Ram.) He blazed out in anger
against Job for pitting his righteousness against
God's. He was also angry with the three friends
because they had neither come up with an answer nor proved Job wrong. Elihu had waited
with Job while they spoke because they were
all older than he. But when he saw that the
three other men had exhausted their arguments, he exploded with pent-up anger.

^{32.6-10} This is what Elihu, son of Barakel the Buzite,
said:

"I'm a young man,
and you are all old and experienced.
That's why I kept quiet
and held back from joining the discussion.
I kept thinking, 'Experience will tell.

---

^a 33 Or *as Adam did* ^b 3 Masoretic Text; an ancient
Hebrew scribal tradition *Job, and so had condemned God*

NEW INTERNATIONAL VERSION

advanced years should teach wisdom.'
⁸But it is the spirit*a* in a man,
    the breath of the Almighty, that gives him
      understanding.
⁹It is not only the old*b* who are wise,
    not only the aged who understand what is
      right.

¹⁰"Therefore I say: Listen to me;
    I too will tell you what I know.
¹¹I waited while you spoke,
    I listened to your reasoning;
while you were searching for words,
¹²   I gave you my full attention.
But not one of you has proved Job wrong;
    none of you has answered his arguments.
¹³Do not say, 'We have found wisdom;
    let God refute him, not man.'
¹⁴But Job has not marshaled his words
    against me,
    and I will not answer him with your
      arguments.

¹⁵"They are dismayed and have no more to
    say;
    words have failed them.
¹⁶Must I wait, now that they are silent,
    now that they stand there with no reply?
¹⁷I too will have my say;
    I too will tell what I know.
¹⁸For I am full of words,
    and the spirit within me compels me;
¹⁹inside I am like bottled-up wine,
    like new wineskins ready to burst.
²⁰I must speak and find relief;
    I must open my lips and reply.
²¹I will show partiality to no one,
    nor will I flatter any man;
²²for if I were skilled in flattery,
    my Maker would soon take me away.

33 "But now, Job, listen to my words;
    pay attention to everything I say.
²I am about to open my mouth;
    my words are on the tip of my tongue.
³My words come from an upright heart;
    my lips sincerely speak what I know.
⁴The Spirit of God has made me;
    the breath of the Almighty gives me life.
⁵Answer me then, if you can;
    prepare yourself and confront me.

THE MESSAGE

The longer you live, the wiser you become.'
But I see I was wrong—it's God's Spirit in a
    person,
    the breath of the Almighty One, that makes
      wise human insight possible.
The experts have no corner on wisdom;
    getting old doesn't guarantee good sense.
So I've decided to speak up. Listen well!
    I'm going to tell you exactly what I think.

32.11-14 "I hung on your words while you spoke,
    listened carefully to your arguments.
While you searched for the right words,
    I was all ears.
And now what have you proved? Nothing.
    Nothing you say has even touched Job.
And don't excuse yourselves by saying, 'We've
    done our best.
    Now it's up to God to talk sense into him.'
Job has yet to contend with me.
    And rest assured, I won't be using *your*
      arguments!

32.15-22 "Do you three have nothing else to say?
    Of *course* you don't! You're total frauds!
Why should I wait any longer,
    now that you're stopped dead in your tracks?
I'm ready to speak my piece. That's right!
    It's my turn—and it's about time!
I've got a lot to say,
    and I'm bursting to say it.
The pressure has built up, like lava beneath
    the earth.
    I'm a volcano ready to blow.
I *have* to speak—I have no choice.
    I have to say what's on my heart,
And I'm going to say it straight—
    the truth, the whole truth, and nothing but
    the truth.
I was never any good at bootlicking;
    my Maker would make short work of me if
      I started in now!

33 "So please, Job, hear me out,
    honor me by listening to me.
What I'm about to say
    has been carefully thought out.
I have no ulterior motives in this;
    I'm speaking honestly from my heart.
The Spirit of God made me what I am,
    the breath of God Almighty gave me life!

GOD ALWAYS ANSWERS, ONE WAY OR ANOTHER

33.5-7 "And if you think you can prove me wrong,
    do it.
    Lay out your arguments. Stand up for
      yourself!

a 8 Or *Spirit;* also in verse 18   *b 9* Or *many;* or *great*

NEW INTERNATIONAL VERSION

⁶I am just like you before God;
 I too have been taken from clay.
⁷No fear of me should alarm you,
 nor should my hand be heavy upon you.

⁸"But you have said in my hearing—
 I heard the very words—
⁹'I am pure and without sin;
 I am clean and free from guilt.
¹⁰Yet God has found fault with me;
 he considers me his enemy.
¹¹He fastens my feet in shackles;
 he keeps close watch on all my paths.'

¹²"But I tell you, in this you are not right,
 for God is greater than man.
¹³Why do you complain to him
 that he answers none of man's words*a*?
¹⁴For God does speak—now one way, now
  another—
 though man may not perceive it.
¹⁵In a dream, in a vision of the night,
 when deep sleep falls on men
 as they slumber in their beds,
¹⁶he may speak in their ears
 and terrify them with warnings,
¹⁷to turn man from wrongdoing
 and keep him from pride,
¹⁸to preserve his soul from the pit,*b*
 his life from perishing by the sword.*c*
¹⁹Or a man may be chastened on a bed of pain
 with constant distress in his bones,
²⁰so that his very being finds food repulsive
 and his soul loathes the choicest meal.
²¹His flesh wastes away to nothing,
 and his bones, once hidden, now stick
  out.
²²His soul draws near to the pit,*d*
 and his life to the messengers of death.*e*

²³"Yet if there is an angel on his side
 as a mediator, one out of a thousand,
 to tell a man what is right for him,
²⁴to be gracious to him and say,
 'Spare him from going down to the pit*f*;
 I have found a ransom for him'—
²⁵then his flesh is renewed like a child's;
 it is restored as in the days of his youth.
²⁶He prays to God and finds favor with him,
 he sees God's face and shouts for joy;
 he is restored by God to his righteous
  state.

a 13 Or that he does not answer for any of his actions
b 18 Or preserve him from the grave   *c 18 Or from crossing*
the River   *d 22 Or He draws near to the grave*   *e 22 Or to*
the dead   *f 24 Or grave*

THE MESSAGE

Look, I'm human—no better than you;
 we're both made of the same kind of mud.
So let's work this through together;
 don't let my aggressiveness overwhelm you.

33.8-11 "Here's what you said.
 I heard you say it with my own ears.
You said, 'I'm pure—I've done nothing wrong.
 Believe me, I'm clean—my conscience is
  clear.
But God keeps picking on me;
 he treats me like I'm his enemy.
He's thrown me in jail;
 he keeps me under constant surveillance.'

33.12-14 "But let me tell you, Job, you're wrong, dead
  wrong!
 God is far greater than any human.
So how dare you haul him into court,
 and then complain that he won't answer
  your charges?
God always answers, one way or another,
 even when people don't recognize his
  presence.

33.15-18 "In a dream, for instance, a vision at night,
 when men and women are deep in sleep,
 fast asleep in their beds—
God opens their ears
 and impresses them with warnings
To turn them back from something bad they're
  planning,
 from some reckless choice,
And keep them from an early grave,
 from the river of no return.

33.19-22 "Or, God might get their attention through
  pain,
 by throwing them on a bed of suffering,
So they can't stand the sight of food,
 have no appetite for their favorite treats.
They lose weight, wasting away to nothing,
 reduced to a bag of bones.
They hang on the cliff-edge of death,
 knowing the next breath may be their last.

33.23-25 "But even then an angel could come,
 a champion—there are thousands of them!—
 to take up your cause,
A messenger who would mercifully intervene,
 canceling the death sentence with the
  words:
 'I've come up with the ransom!'
Before you know it, you're healed,
 the very picture of health!

33.26-28 "Or, you may fall on your knees and pray—to
  God's delight!
 You'll see God's smile and celebrate,
 finding yourself set right with God.

NEW INTERNATIONAL VERSION

²⁷Then he comes to men and says,
    'I sinned, and perverted what was right,
    but I did not get what I deserved.
²⁸He redeemed my soul from going down to
        the pit,ᵃ
    and I will live to enjoy the light.'

²⁹"God does all these things to a man—
    twice, even three times—
³⁰to turn back his soul from the pit,ᵇ
    that the light of life may shine on him.

³¹"Pay attention, Job, and listen to me;
    be silent, and I will speak.
³²If you have anything to say, answer me;
    speak up, for I want you to be cleared.
³³But if not, then listen to me;
    be silent, and I will teach you wisdom."

34

Then Elihu said:

²"Hear my words, you wise men;
    listen to me, you men of learning.
³For the ear tests words
    as the tongue tastes food.
⁴Let us discern for ourselves what is right;
    let us learn together what is good.

⁵"Job says, 'I am innocent,
    but God denies me justice.
⁶Although I am right,
    I am considered a liar;
although I am guiltless,
    his arrow inflicts an incurable wound.'
⁷What man is like Job,
    who drinks scorn like water?
⁸He keeps company with evildoers;
    he associates with wicked men.
⁹For he says, 'It profits a man nothing
    when he tries to please God.'

¹⁰"So listen to me, you men of understanding.
    Far be it from God to do evil,
    from the Almighty to do wrong.
¹¹He repays a man for what he has done;
    he brings upon him what his conduct
        deserves.
¹²It is unthinkable that God would do wrong,
    that the Almighty would pervert justice.
¹³Who appointed him over the earth?

ᵃ 28 Or redeemed me from going down to the grave
ᵇ 30 Or turn him back from the grave

THE MESSAGE

You'll sing God's praises to everyone you meet,
    testifying, 'I messed up my life—
    and let me tell you, it wasn't worth it.
But God stepped in and saved me from certain
        death.
    I'm alive again! Once more I see the light!'

33.29-30 "This is the way God works.
    Over and over again
He pulls our souls back from certain
        destruction
    so we'll see the light—and *live* in the light!

33.31-33 "Keep listening, Job.
    Don't interrupt—I'm not finished yet.
But if you think of anything I should know,
        tell me.
There's nothing I'd like better than to see
        your name cleared.
Meanwhile, keep listening. Don't distract me
        with interruptions.
I'm going to teach you the basics of wisdom."

ELIHU'S SECOND SPEECH

IT'S IMPOSSIBLE FOR GOD TO DO EVIL

34.1-4 # 34 Elihu continued:

"So, my fine friends—listen to me,
    and see what you think of this.
Isn't it just common sense—
    as common as the sense of taste—
To put our heads together
    and figure out what's going on here?

34.5-9 "We've all heard Job say, 'I'm in the right,
    but God won't give me a fair trial.
When I defend myself, I'm called a liar to my
        face.
I've done nothing wrong, and I get
        punished anyway.'
Have you ever heard anything to beat this?
    Does nothing faze this man Job?
Do you think he's spent too much time in bad
        company,
    hanging out with the wrong crowd,
So that now he's parroting their line:
    'It doesn't pay to try to please God'?

34.10-15 "You're veterans in dealing with these matters;
    certainly we're of one mind on this.
It's impossible for God to do anything evil;
    no way can the Mighty One do wrong.
He makes us pay for exactly what we've
        done—no more, no less.
Our chickens always come home to roost.
It's impossible for God to do anything wicked,
    for the Mighty One to subvert justice.
He's the one who runs the earth!

NEW INTERNATIONAL VERSION

Who put him in charge of the whole
world?
¹⁴ If it were his intention
and he withdrew his spirit *a* and breath,
¹⁵ all mankind would perish together
and man would return to the dust.

¹⁶ "If you have understanding, hear this;
listen to what I say.
¹⁷ Can he who hates justice govern?
Will you condemn the just and mighty
One?
¹⁸ Is he not the One who says to kings, 'You are
worthless,'
and to nobles, 'You are wicked,'
¹⁹ who shows no partiality to princes
and does not favor the rich over the poor,
for they are all the work of his hands?
²⁰ They die in an instant, in the middle of the
night;
the people are shaken and they pass away;
the mighty are removed without human
hand.

²¹ "His eyes are on the ways of men;
he sees their every step.
²² There is no dark place, no deep shadow,
where evildoers can hide.
²³ God has no need to examine men further,
that they should come before him for
judgment.
²⁴ Without inquiry he shatters the mighty
and sets up others in their place.
²⁵ Because he takes note of their deeds,
he overthrows them in the night and they
are crushed.
²⁶ He punishes them for their wickedness
where everyone can see them,
²⁷ because they turned from following him
and had no regard for any of his ways.
²⁸ They caused the cry of the poor to come
before him,
so that he heard the cry of the needy.
²⁹ But if he remains silent, who can condemn
him?
If he hides his face, who can see him?
Yet he is over man and nation alike,
³⁰   to keep a godless man from ruling,
from laying snares for the people.

³¹ "Suppose a man says to God,
'I am guilty but will offend no more.
³² Teach me what I cannot see;
if I have done wrong, I will not do so
again.'

a 14 Or Spirit

THE MESSAGE

He cradles the whole world in his hand!
If he decided to hold his breath,
every man, woman, and child would die for
lack of air.

GOD IS WORKING BEHIND THE SCENES

34:16-20 "So, Job, use your head;
this is all pretty obvious.
Can someone who hates order, keep order?
Do you dare condemn the righteous,
mighty God?
Doesn't God always tell it like it is,
exposing corrupt rulers as scoundrels and
criminals?
Does he play favorites with the rich and
famous and slight the poor?
Isn't he equally responsible to everybody?
Don't people who deserve it die without
notice?
Don't wicked rulers tumble to their doom?
When the so-called great ones are wiped out,
we know God is working behind the scenes.

34:21-28 "He has his eyes on every man and woman.
He doesn't miss a trick.
There is no night dark enough, no shadow
deep enough,
to hide those who do evil.
God doesn't need to gather any more
evidence;
their sin is an open-and-shut case.
He deposes the so-called high and mighty
without asking questions,
and replaces them at once with others.
Nobody gets by with anything; overnight,
judgment is signed, sealed, and delivered.
He punishes the wicked for their wickedness
out in the open where everyone can see it,
Because they quit following him,
no longer even thought about him or his
ways.
Their apostasy was announced by the cry of
the poor;
the cry of the afflicted got God's attention.

BECAUSE YOU REFUSE TO LIVE ON GOD'S TERMS

34:29-30 "If God is silent, what's that to you?
If he turns his face away, what can you do
about it?
But whether silent or hidden, he's there,
ruling,
so that those who hate God won't take over
and ruin people's lives.

34:31-33 "So why don't you simply confess to God?
Say, 'I sinned, but I'll sin no more.
Teach me to see what I still don't see.
Whatever evil I've done, I'll do it no more.'

NEW INTERNATIONAL VERSION

³³Should God then reward you on your terms,
  when you refuse to repent?
You must decide, not I;
  so tell me what you know.

³⁴"Men of understanding declare,
  wise men who hear me say to me,
³⁵'Job speaks without knowledge;
  his words lack insight.'
³⁶Oh, that Job might be tested to the utmost
  for answering like a wicked man!
³⁷To his sin he adds rebellion;
  scornfully he claps his hands among us
  and multiplies his words against God."

35 Then Elihu said:

²"Do you think this is just?
  You say, 'I will be cleared by God.'^a
³Yet you ask him, 'What profit is it to me,^b
  and what do I gain by not sinning?'

⁴"I would like to reply to you
  and to your friends with you.
⁵Look up at the heavens and see;
  gaze at the clouds so high above you.
⁶If you sin, how does that affect him?
  If your sins are many, what does that do to
    him?
⁷If you are righteous, what do you give to
    him,
  or what does he receive from your hand?
⁸Your wickedness affects only a man like
    yourself,
  and your righteousness only the sons of
    men.

⁹"Men cry out under a load of oppression;
  they plead for relief from the arm of the
    powerful.
¹⁰But no one says, 'Where is God my Maker,
  who gives songs in the night,
¹¹who teaches more to us than to^c the beasts
    of the earth

THE MESSAGE

Just because you refuse to live on God's terms,
  do you think he should start living on yours?
You choose. I can't do it for you.
  Tell me what you decide.

^{34.34-37}"All right-thinking people say—
  and the wise who have listened to me
    concur—
'Job is an ignoramus.
  He talks utter nonsense.'
Job, you need to be pushed to the wall and
    called to account
  for wickedly talking back to God the way
    you have.
You've compounded your original sin
  by rebelling against God's discipline,
Defiantly shaking your fist at God,
  piling up indictments against the Almighty
    One."

ELIHU'S THIRD SPEECH

WHEN GOD MAKES CREATION A CLASSROOM

^{35.1-3}**35** Elihu lit into Job again:

"Does this kind of thing make any sense?
  First you say, 'I'm perfectly innocent before
    God.'
And then you say, 'It doesn't make a bit of
    difference
  whether I've sinned or not.'

^{35.4-8}"Well, I'm going to show you
  that you don't know what you're talking
    about,
  neither you nor your friends.
Look up at the sky. Take a long hard look.
  See those clouds towering above you?
If you sin, what difference could that make to
    God?
  No matter how much you sin, will it matter
    to him?
Even if you're good, what would God get out
    of that?
  Do you think he's dependent on your
    accomplishments?
The only ones who care whether you're good
    or bad
  are your family and friends and neighbors.
  God's not dependent on your behavior.

^{35.9-15}"When times get bad, people cry out for help.
  They cry for relief from being kicked around,
But never give God a thought when things go
    well,
  when God puts spontaneous songs in their
    hearts,
When God sets out the entire creation as a
    science classroom,

---

^a 2 Or My righteousness is more than God's   ^b 3 Or you
^c 11 Or teaches us by

NEW INTERNATIONAL VERSION

and makes us wiser than *a* the birds of the
air?'
¹²He does not answer when men cry out
because of the arrogance of the wicked.
¹³Indeed, God does not listen to their empty
plea;
the Almighty pays no attention to it.
¹⁴How much less, then, will he listen
when you say that you do not see him,
that your case is before him
and you must wait for him,
¹⁵and further, that his anger never punishes
and he does not take the least notice of
wickedness. *b*
¹⁶So Job opens his mouth with empty talk;
without knowledge he multiplies words.'

36 Elihu continued:

² "Bear with me a little longer and I will show
you
that there is more to be said in God's
behalf.
³I get my knowledge from afar;
I will ascribe justice to my Maker.
⁴Be assured that my words are not false;
one perfect in knowledge is with you.

⁵ "God is mighty, but does not despise men;
he is mighty, and firm in his purpose.
⁶He does not keep the wicked alive
but gives the afflicted their rights.
⁷He does not take his eyes off the righteous;
he enthrones them with kings
and exalts them forever.
⁸But if men are bound in chains,
held fast by cords of affliction,
⁹he tells them what they have done—
that they have sinned arrogantly.
¹⁰He makes them listen to correction
and commands them to repent of their evil.
¹¹If they obey and serve him,
they will spend the rest of their days in
prosperity
and their years in contentment.
¹²But if they do not listen,
they will perish by the sword*c*
and die without knowledge.

¹³ "The godless in heart harbor resentment;
even when he fetters them, they do not
cry for help.
¹⁴They die in their youth,
among male prostitutes of the shrines.

THE MESSAGE

using birds and beasts to teach wisdom.
People are arrogantly indifferent to God—
until, of course, they're in trouble,
and then God is indifferent to them.
There's nothing behind such prayers except
panic;
the Almighty pays them no mind.
So why would he notice you
just because you say you're tired of waiting
to be heard,
Or waiting for him to get good and angry
and do something about the world's
problems?

35.16 "Job, you talk sheer nonsense—
nonstop nonsense!"

THOSE WHO LEARN FROM THEIR SUFFERING

36.1-4 **36** Here Elihu took a deep breath, but kept
going:

"Stay with me a little longer. I'll convince you.
There's still more to be said on God's side.
I learned all this firsthand from the Source;
everything I know about justice I owe to
my Maker himself.
Trust me, I'm giving you undiluted truth;
believe me, I know these things inside and
out.

36.5-15 "It's true that God is all-powerful,
but he doesn't bully innocent people.
For the wicked, though, it's a different story—
he doesn't give them the time of day,
but champions the rights of their victims.
He never takes his eyes off the righteous;
he honors them lavishly, promotes them
endlessly.
When things go badly,
when affliction and suffering descend,
God tells them where they've gone wrong,
shows them how their pride has caused
their trouble.
He forces them to heed his warning,
tells them they must repent of their bad
life.
If they obey and serve him,
they'll have a good, long life on easy street.
But if they disobey, they'll be cut down in
their prime
and never know the first thing about life.
Angry people without God pile grievance
upon grievance,
always blaming others for their troubles.
Living it up in sexual excesses,
virility wasted, they die young.

---

a 11 Or us wise by *b 15 Symmachus, Theodotion and
Vulgate; the meaning of the Hebrew for this word is
uncertain. c 12 Or will cross the River*

NEW INTERNATIONAL VERSION

¹⁵ But those who suffer he delivers in their
suffering;
he speaks to them in their affliction.

¹⁶ "He is wooing you from the jaws of distress
to a spacious place free from restriction,
to the comfort of your table laden with
choice food.
¹⁷ But now you are laden with the judgment
due the wicked;
judgment and justice have taken hold of
you.
¹⁸ Be careful that no one entices you by riches;
do not let a large bribe turn you aside.
¹⁹ Would your wealth
or even all your mighty efforts
sustain you so you would not be in
distress?
²⁰ Do not long for the night,
to drag people away from their homes. ᵃ
²¹ Beware of turning to evil,
which you seem to prefer to affliction.

²² "God is exalted in his power.
Who is a teacher like him?
²³ Who has prescribed his ways for him,
or said to him, 'You have done wrong'?
²⁴ Remember to extol his work,
which men have praised in song.
²⁵ All mankind has seen it;
men gaze on it from afar.
²⁶ How great is God—beyond our
understanding!
The number of his years is past finding
out.

²⁷ "He draws up the drops of water,
which distill as rain to the streams ᵇ;
²⁸ the clouds pour down their moisture
and abundant showers fall on mankind.
²⁹ Who can understand how he spreads out the
clouds,
how he thunders from his pavilion?
³⁰ See how he scatters his lightning about him,
bathing the depths of the sea.
³¹ This is the way he governs ᶜ the nations
and provides food in abundance.
³² He fills his hands with lightning
and commands it to strike its mark.
³³ His thunder announces the coming storm;
even the cattle make known its
approach. ᵈ

ᵃ 20 The meaning of the Hebrew for verses 18-20 is
uncertain.   ᵇ 27 Or distill from the mist as rain
ᶜ 31 Or nourishes   ᵈ 33 Or announces his coming— / the
One zealous against evil

THE MESSAGE

But those who learn from their suffering,
God delivers from their suffering.

OBSESSED WITH PUTTING THE BLAME ON GOD

36.16-21 "Oh, Job, don't you see how God's wooing you
from the jaws of danger?
How he's drawing you into wide-open places—
inviting you to feast at a table laden with
blessings?
And here you are laden with the guilt of the
wicked,
obsessed with putting the blame on God!
Don't let your great riches mislead you;
don't think you can bribe your way out of
this.
Did you plan to buy your way out of this?
Not on your life!
And don't think that night,
when people sleep off their troubles,
will bring you any relief.
Above all, don't make things worse with more
evil—
that's what's behind your suffering as it is!

36.22-25 "Do you have any idea how powerful God is?
Have you ever heard of a teacher like him?
Has anyone ever had to tell him what to do,
or correct him, saying, 'You did that all
wrong!'?
Remember, then, to praise his workmanship,
which is so often celebrated in song.
Everybody sees it;
nobody is too far away to see it.

NO ONE CAN ESCAPE FROM GOD

36.26 "Take a long, hard look. See how great he is—
infinite,
greater than anything you could ever
imagine or figure out!

36.27-33 "He pulls water up out of the sea,
distills it, and fills up his rain-cloud cisterns.
Then the skies open up
and pour out soaking showers on everyone.
Does anyone have the slightest idea how this
happens?
How he arranges the clouds, how he speaks
in thunder?
Just look at that lightning, his sky-filling light
show
illumining the dark depths of the sea!
These are the symbols of his sovereignty,
his generosity, his loving care.
He hurls arrows of light,
taking sure and accurate aim.
The High God roars in the thunder,
angry against evil.

NEW INTERNATIONAL VERSION	THE MESSAGE

37 "At this my heart pounds
and leaps from its place.
² Listen! Listen to the roar of his voice,
to the rumbling that comes from his
mouth.
³ He unleashes his lightning beneath the
whole heaven
and sends it to the ends of the earth.
⁴ After that comes the sound of his roar;
he thunders with his majestic voice.
When his voice resounds,
he holds nothing back.
⁵ God's voice thunders in marvelous ways;
he does great things beyond our
understanding.
⁶ He says to the snow, 'Fall on the earth,'
and to the rain shower, 'Be a mighty
downpour.'
⁷ So that all men he has made may know his
work,
he stops every man from his labor. *ᵃ*
⁸ The animals take cover;
they remain in their dens.
⁹ The tempest comes out from its chamber,
the cold from the driving winds.
¹⁰ The breath of God produces ice,
and the broad waters become frozen.
¹¹ He loads the clouds with moisture;
he scatters his lightning through them.
¹² At his direction they swirl around
over the face of the whole earth
to do whatever he commands them.
¹³ He brings the clouds to punish men,
or to water his earth *ᵇ* and show his love.

¹⁴ "Listen to this, Job;
stop and consider God's wonders.
¹⁵ Do you know how God controls the clouds
and makes his lightning flash?
¹⁶ Do you know how the clouds hang poised,
those wonders of him who is perfect in
knowledge?
¹⁷ You who swelter in your clothes
when the land lies hushed under the
south wind,
¹⁸ can you join him in spreading out the skies,
hard as a mirror of cast bronze?

¹⁹ "Tell us what we should say to him;
we cannot draw up our case because of
our darkness.

---

37 ³⁷·¹⁻¹³ "Whenever this happens, my heart
stops—
I'm stunned, I can't catch my breath.
Listen to it! Listen to his thunder,
the rolling, rumbling thunder of his voice.
He lets loose his lightnings from horizon to
horizon,
lighting up the earth from pole to pole.
In their wake, the thunder echoes his voice,
powerful and majestic.
He lets out all the stops, he holds nothing
back.
No one can mistake that voice—
His word thundering so wondrously,
his mighty acts staggering our
understanding.
He orders the snow, 'Blanket the earth!'
and the rain, 'Soak the whole countryside!'
No one can escape the weather—it's *there*.
And no one can escape from God.
Wild animals take shelter,
crawling into their dens,
When blizzards roar out of the north
and freezing rain crusts the land.
It's God's breath that forms the ice,
it's God's breath that turns lakes and rivers
solid.
And yes, it's God who fills clouds with
rainwater
and hurls lightning from them every which
way.
He puts them through their paces—first this
way, then that—
commands them to do what he says all over
the world.
Whether for discipline or grace or extravagant
love,
he makes sure they make their mark.

A TERRIBLE BEAUTY STREAMS FROM GOD
³⁷·¹⁴⁻¹⁸ "Job, are you listening? Have you noticed all
this?
Stop in your tracks! Take in God's miracle-
wonders!
Do you have any idea how God does it all,
how he makes bright lightning from dark
storms,
How he piles up the cumulus clouds—
all these miracle-wonders of a perfect
Mind?
Why, you don't even know how to keep cool
on a sweltering hot day,
So how could you even dream
of making a dent in that hot-tin-roof sky?

³⁷·¹⁹⁻²² "If you're so smart, give us a lesson in how to
address God.
We're in the dark and can't figure it out.

---

*ᵃ 7 Or / he fills all men with fear by his power   ᵇ 13 Or to
favor them*

NEW INTERNATIONAL VERSION

²⁰Should he be told that I want to speak?
  Would any man ask to be swallowed up?
²¹Now no one can look at the sun,
  bright as it is in the skies
  after the wind has swept them clean.
²²Out of the north he comes in golden
    splendor;
  God comes in awesome majesty.
²³The Almighty is beyond our reach and
    exalted in power;
  in his justice and great righteousness, he
    does not oppress.
²⁴Therefore, men revere him,
  for does he not have regard for all the
    wise in heart?^a"

THE LORD SPEAKS

38 Then the LORD answered Job out of the
    storm. He said:

²"Who is this that darkens my counsel
  with words without knowledge?
³Brace yourself like a man;
  I will question you,
  and you shall answer me.

⁴"Where were you when I laid the earth's
    foundation?
  Tell me, if you understand.
⁵Who marked off its dimensions? Surely you
    know!
  Who stretched a measuring line across it?
⁶On what were its footings set,
  or who laid its cornerstone—
⁷while the morning stars sang together
  and all the angels^b shouted for joy?

⁸"Who shut up the sea behind doors
  when it burst forth from the womb,
⁹when I made the clouds its garment
  and wrapped it in thick darkness,
¹⁰when I fixed limits for it
  and set its doors and bars in place,
¹¹when I said, 'This far you may come and no
    farther;
  here is where your proud waves halt'?

¹²"Have you ever given orders to the morning,
  or shown the dawn its place,
¹³that it might take the earth by the edges
  and shake the wicked out of it?
¹⁴The earth takes shape like clay under a seal;

---

^a 24 Or for he does not have regard for any who think they are
wise.   ^b 7 Hebrew the sons of God

THE MESSAGE

Do you think I'm dumb enough to challenge
    God?
  Wouldn't that just be asking for trouble?
No one in his right mind stares straight at the
    sun
  on a clear and cloudless day.
As gold comes from the northern mountains,
  so a terrible beauty streams from God.

^{37.23-24} "Mighty God! Far beyond our reach!
  Unsurpassable in power and justice!
  It's unthinkable that he'd treat anyone
    unfairly.
So bow to him in deep reverence, one and all!
  If you're wise, you'll most certainly worship
    him."

GOD CONFRONTS JOB

HAVE YOU GOTTEN TO THE BOTTOM
OF THINGS?

^{38.1} **38** And now, finally, GOD answered Job
    from the eye of a violent storm. He said:

^{38.2-11} "Why do you confuse the issue?
  Why do you talk without knowing what
    you're talking about?
Pull yourself together, Job!
  Up on your feet! Stand tall!
I have some questions for you,
  and I want some straight answers.
Where were you when I created the earth?
  Tell me, since you know so much!
Who decided on its size? Certainly you'll
    know that!
  Who came up with the blueprints and
    measurements?
How was its foundation poured,
  and who set the cornerstone,
While the morning stars sang in chorus
  and all the angels shouted praise?
And who took charge of the ocean
  when it gushed forth like a baby from the
    womb?
That was me! I wrapped it in soft clouds,
  and tucked it in safely at night.
Then I made a playpen for it,
  a strong playpen so it couldn't run loose,
And said, 'Stay here, this is your place.
  Your wild tantrums are confined to this
    place.'

^{38.12-15} "And have you ever ordered Morning,
    'Get up!'
  told Dawn, 'Get to work!'
So you could seize Earth like a blanket
  and shake out the wicked like
    cockroaches?
As the sun brings everything to light,

NEW INTERNATIONAL VERSION

its features stand out like those of a
garment.
¹⁵ The wicked are denied their light,
and their upraised arm is broken.

¹⁶ "Have you journeyed to the springs of the
sea
or walked in the recesses of the deep?
¹⁷ Have the gates of death been shown to you?
Have you seen the gates of the shadow of
death*ᵃ*?
¹⁸ Have you comprehended the vast expanses
of the earth?
Tell me, if you know all this.

¹⁹ "What is the way to the abode of light?
And where does darkness reside?
²⁰ Can you take them to their places?
Do you know the paths to their
dwellings?
²¹ Surely you know, for you were already born!
You have lived so many years!

²² "Have you entered the storehouses of the
snow
or seen the storehouses of the hail,
²³ which I reserve for times of trouble,
for days of war and battle?
²⁴ What is the way to the place where the
lightning is dispersed,
or the place where the east winds are
scattered over the earth?
²⁵ Who cuts a channel for the torrents of rain,
and a path for the thunderstorm,
²⁶ to water a land where no man lives,
a desert with no one in it,
²⁷ to satisfy a desolate wasteland
and make it sprout with grass?
²⁸ Does the rain have a father?
Who fathers the drops of dew?
²⁹ From whose womb comes the ice?
Who gives birth to the frost from the
heavens
³⁰ when the waters become hard as stone,
when the surface of the deep is frozen?

³¹ "Can you bind the beautiful*ᵇ* Pleiades?
Can you loose the cords of Orion?
³² Can you bring forth the constellations in
their seasons*ᶜ*
or lead out the Bear*ᵈ* with its cubs?
³³ Do you know the laws of the heavens?
Can you set up ⌊God's*ᵉ*⌋ dominion over
the earth?

ᵃ 17 Or gates of deep shadows   *ᵇ 31 Or the twinkling; or*
the chains of the   *ᶜ 32 Or the morning star in its season*
ᵈ 32 Or out Leo   *ᵉ 33 Or his; or their*

THE MESSAGE

brings out all the colors and shapes,
The cover of darkness is snatched from the
wicked—
they're caught in the very act!

38.16-18 "Have you ever gotten to the true bottom of
things,
explored the labyrinthine caves of deep
ocean?
Do you know the first thing about death?
Do you have one clue regarding death's
dark mysteries?
And do you have any idea how large this
earth is?
Speak up if you have even the beginning of
an answer.

38.19-21 "Do you know where Light comes from
and where Darkness lives
So you can take them by the hand
and lead them home when they get lost?
Why, of *course* you know that.
You've known them all your life,
grown up in the same neighborhood with
them!

38.22-30 "Have you ever traveled to where snow is
made,
seen the vault where hail is stockpiled,
The arsenals of hail and snow that I keep in
readiness
for times of trouble and battle and war?
Can you find your way to where lightning is
launched,
or to the place from which the wind blows?
Who do you suppose carves canyons
for the downpours of rain, and charts
the route of thunderstorms
That bring water to unvisited fields,
deserts no one ever lays eyes on,
Drenching the useless wastelands
so they're carpeted with wildflowers and
grass?
And who do you think is the father of rain
and dew,
the mother of ice and frost?
You don't for a minute imagine
these marvels of weather just happen, do
you?

38.31-33 "Can you catch the eye of the beautiful
Pleiades sisters,
or distract Orion from his hunt?
Can you get Venus to look your way,
or get the Great Bear and her cubs to come
out and play?
Do you know the first thing about the sky's
constellations
and how they affect things on Earth?

34 "Can you raise your voice to the clouds
    and cover yourself with a flood of water?
35 Do you send the lightning bolts on their
    way?
    Do they report to you, 'Here we are'?
36 Who endowed the heart *a* with wisdom
    or gave understanding to the mind *a*?
37 Who has the wisdom to count the clouds?
    Who can tip over the water jars of the
      heavens
38 when the dust becomes hard
    and the clods of earth stick together?

39 "Do you hunt the prey for the lioness
    and satisfy the hunger of the lions
40 when they crouch in their dens
    or lie in wait in a thicket?
41 Who provides food for the raven
    when its young cry out to God
    and wander about for lack of food?

39

"Do you know when the mountain
    goats give birth?
    Do you watch when the doe bears her
      fawn?
2 Do you count the months till they bear?
    Do you know the time they give birth?
3 They crouch down and bring forth their
    young;
    their labor pains are ended.
4 Their young thrive and grow strong in the
    wilds;
    they leave and do not return.

5 "Who let the wild donkey go free?
    Who untied his ropes?
6 I gave him the wasteland as his home,
    the salt flats as his habitat.
7 He laughs at the commotion in the town;
    he does not hear a driver's shout.
8 He ranges the hills for his pasture
    and searches for any green thing.

9 "Will the wild ox consent to serve you?
    Will he stay by your manger at night?
10 Can you hold him to the furrow with a
    harness?
    Will he till the valleys behind you?
11 Will you rely on him for his great strength?
    Will you leave your heavy work to him?
12 Can you trust him to bring in your grain
    and gather it to your threshing floor?

38.34-35 "Can you get the attention of the clouds,
    and commission a shower of rain?
Can you take charge of the lightning bolts
    and have them report to you for orders?

WHAT DO YOU HAVE TO SAY FOR YOURSELF?

38.36-38 "Who do you think gave weather-wisdom to
    the ibis,
    and storm-savvy to the rooster?
Does anyone know enough to number all the
    clouds
    or tip over the rain barrels of heaven
When the earth is cracked and dry,
    the ground baked hard as a brick?

38.39-41 "Can you teach the lioness to stalk her prey
    and satisfy the appetite of her cubs
As they crouch in their den,
    waiting hungrily in their cave?
And who sets out food for the ravens
    when their young cry to God,
    fluttering about because they have no food?

39

39.1-4 "Do you know the month when
    mountain goats give birth?
    Have you ever watched a doe bear her
      fawn?
Do you know how many months she is
    pregnant?
    Do you know the season of her delivery,
    when she crouches down and drops her
      offspring?
Her young ones flourish and are soon on their
    own;
    they leave and don't come back.

39.5-8 "Who do you think set the wild donkey free,
    opened the corral gates and let him go?
I gave him the whole wilderness to roam in,
    the rolling plains and wide-open places.
He laughs at his city cousins, who are
    harnessed and harried.
    He's oblivious to the cries of teamsters.
He grazes freely through the hills,
    nibbling anything that's green.

39.9-12 "Will the wild buffalo condescend to serve
    you,
    volunteer to spend the night in your barn?
Can you imagine hitching your plow to a
    buffalo
    and getting him to till your fields?
He's hugely strong, yes, but could you trust
    him,
    would you dare turn the job over to him?
You wouldn't for a minute depend on him,
    would you,
    to do what you said when you said it?

---

a 36 The meaning of the Hebrew for this word is uncertain.

NEW INTERNATIONAL VERSION	THE MESSAGE

NEW INTERNATIONAL VERSION

13 "The wings of the ostrich flap joyfully,
    but they cannot compare with the pinions
      and feathers of the stork.
14 She lays her eggs on the ground
    and lets them warm in the sand,
15 unmindful that a foot may crush them,
    that some wild animal may trample them.
16 She treats her young harshly, as if they were
      not hers;
    she cares not that her labor was in vain,
17 for God did not endow her with wisdom
    or give her a share of good sense.
18 Yet when she spreads her feathers to run,
    she laughs at horse and rider.

19 "Do you give the horse his strength
    or clothe his neck with a flowing mane?
20 Do you make him leap like a locust,
    striking terror with his proud snorting?
21 He paws fiercely, rejoicing in his strength,
    and charges into the fray.
22 He laughs at fear, afraid of nothing;
    he does not shy away from the sword.
23 The quiver rattles against his side,
    along with the flashing spear and lance.
24 In frenzied excitement he eats up the
      ground;
    he cannot stand still when the trumpet
      sounds.
25 At the blast of the trumpet he snorts, 'Aha!'
    He catches the scent of battle from afar,
    the shout of commanders and the battle
      cry.

26 "Does the hawk take flight by your wisdom
    and spread his wings toward the south?
27 Does the eagle soar at your command
    and build his nest on high?
28 He dwells on a cliff and stays there at night;
    a rocky crag is his stronghold.
29 From there he seeks out his food;
    his eyes detect it from afar.
30 His young ones feast on blood,
    and where the slain are, there is he."

40 The LORD said to Job:

2 "Will the one who contends with the
      Almighty correct him?
    Let him who accuses God answer him!"

THE MESSAGE

39.13-18 "The ostrich flaps her wings futilely—
    all those beautiful feathers, but useless!
She lays her eggs on the hard ground,
    leaves them there in the dirt, exposed to
      the weather,
Not caring that they might get stepped on and
      cracked
    or trampled by some wild animal.
She's negligent with her young, as if they
      weren't even hers.
    She cares nothing about anything.
She wasn't created very smart, that's for sure,
    wasn't given her share of good sense.
But when she runs, oh, how she runs,
    laughing, leaving horse and rider in the
      dust.

39.19-25 "Are you the one who gave the horse his
      prowess
    and adorned him with a shimmering mane?
Did you create him to prance proudly
    and strike terror with his royal snorts?
He paws the ground fiercely, eager and
      spirited,
    then charges into the fray.
He laughs at danger, fearless,
    doesn't shy away from the sword.
The banging and clanging
    of quiver and lance don't faze him.
He quivers with excitement, and at the
      trumpet blast
    races off at a gallop.
At the sound of the trumpet he neighs
      mightily,
    smelling the excitement of battle from a
      long way off,
    catching the rolling thunder of the war cries.

39.26-30 "Was it through your know how that the
      hawk learned to fly,
    soaring effortlessly on thermal updrafts?
Did you command the eagle's flight,
    and teach her to build her nest in the
      heights,
Perfectly at home on the high cliff-face,
    invulnerable on pinnacle and crag?
From her perch she searches for prey,
    spies it at a great distance.
Her young gorge themselves on carrion;
    wherever there's a roadkill, you'll see her
      circling."

40.1-2 **40** GOD then confronted Job directly:

"Now what do you have to say for yourself?
    Are you going to haul me, the Mighty One,
      into court and press charges?"

NEW INTERNATIONAL VERSION

³Then Job answered the LORD:

⁴"I am unworthy—how can I reply to you?
  I put my hand over my mouth.
⁵I spoke once, but I have no answer—
  twice, but I will say no more."

⁶Then the LORD spoke to Job out of the storm:

⁷"Brace yourself like a man;
  I will question you,
  and you shall answer me.

⁸"Would you discredit my justice?
  Would you condemn me to justify
    yourself?
⁹Do you have an arm like God's,
  and can your voice thunder like his?
¹⁰Then adorn yourself with glory and
    splendor,
  and clothe yourself in honor and majesty.
¹¹Unleash the fury of your wrath,
  look at every proud man and bring him
    low,
¹²look at every proud man and humble him,
  crush the wicked where they stand.
¹³Bury them all in the dust together;
  shroud their faces in the grave.
¹⁴Then I myself will admit to you
  that your own right hand can save you.

¹⁵"Look at the behemoth,^a
  which I made along with you
  and which feeds on grass like an ox.
¹⁶What strength he has in his loins,
  what power in the muscles of his belly!
¹⁷His tail^b sways like a cedar;
  the sinews of his thighs are close-knit.
¹⁸His bones are tubes of bronze,
  his limbs like rods of iron.
¹⁹He ranks first among the works of God,
  yet his Maker can approach him with his
    sword.
²⁰The hills bring him their produce,
  and all the wild animals play nearby.
²¹Under the lotus plants he lies,
  hidden among the reeds in the marsh.
²²The lotuses conceal him in their shadow;
  the poplars by the stream surround him.
²³When the river rages, he is not alarmed;

THE MESSAGE

JOB ANSWERS GOD

I'M READY TO SHUT UP AND LISTEN

40.3-5 Job answered:

"I'm speechless, in awe—words fail me.
  I should never have opened my mouth!
I've talked too much, way too much.
  I'm ready to shut up and listen."

GOD'S SECOND SET OF QUESTIONS

I WANT STRAIGHT ANSWERS

40.6-7 GOD addressed Job next from the eye of the storm, and this is what he said:

"I have some more questions for you,
  and I want straight answers.

40.8-14 "Do you presume to tell me what I'm doing
    wrong?
  Are you calling me a sinner so you can be a
    saint?
Do you have an arm like my arm?
  Can you shout in thunder the way I can?
Go ahead, show your stuff.
  Let's see what you're made of, what you
    can do.
Unleash your outrage.
  Target the arrogant and lay them flat.
Target the arrogant and bring them to their
    knees.
  Stop the wicked in their tracks—make
    mincemeat of them!
Dig a mass grave and dump them in it—
  faceless corpses in an unmarked grave.
I'll gladly step aside and hand things over to
    you—
  you can surely save yourself with no help
    from me!

40.15-24 "Look at the land beast, Behemoth. I created
    him as well as you.
  Grazing on grass, docile as a cow—
Just look at the strength of his back,
  the powerful muscles of his belly.
His tail sways like a cedar in the wind;
  his huge legs are like beech trees.
His skeleton is made of steel,
  every bone in his body hard as steel.
Most magnificent of all my creatures,
  but I still lead him around like a lamb!
The grass-covered hills serve him meals,
  while field mice frolic in his shadow.
He takes afternoon naps under shade trees,
  cools himself in the reedy swamps,
Lazily cool in the leafy shadows
  as the breeze moves through the willows.
And when the river rages he doesn't budge,

^a 15 Possibly the hippopotamus or the elephant
^b 17 Possibly trunk

NEW INTERNATIONAL VERSION

he is secure, though the Jordan should
surge against his mouth.
24 Can anyone capture him by the eyes,ᵃ
or trap him and pierce his nose?

41 "Can you pull in the leviathanᵇ with a
fishhook
or tie down his tongue with a rope?
2 Can you put a cord through his nose
or pierce his jaw with a hook?
3 Will he keep begging you for mercy?
Will he speak to you with gentle words?
4 Will he make an agreement with you
for you to take him as your slave for life?
5 Can you make a pet of him like a bird
or put him on a leash for your girls?
6 Will traders barter for him?
Will they divide him up among the
merchants?
7 Can you fill his hide with harpoons
or his head with fishing spears?
8 If you lay a hand on him,
you will remember the struggle and never
do it again!
9 Any hope of subduing him is false;
the mere sight of him is overpowering.
10 No one is fierce enough to rouse him.
Who then is able to stand against me?
11 Who has a claim against me that I must pay?
Everything under heaven belongs to me.

12 "I will not fail to speak of his limbs,
his strength and his graceful form.
13 Who can strip off his outer coat?
Who would approach him with a bridle?
14 Who dares open the doors of his mouth,
ringed about with his fearsome teeth?
15 His back hasᶜ rows of shields
tightly sealed together;
16 each is so close to the next
that no air can pass between.
17 They are joined fast to one another;
they cling together and cannot be parted.
18 His snorting throws out flashes of light;
his eyes are like the rays of dawn.
19 Firebrands stream from his mouth;
sparks of fire shoot out.

ᵃ 24 Or *by a water hole*   ᵇ 1 Possibly the crocodile
ᶜ 15 Or *His pride is his*

THE MESSAGE

stolid and unperturbed even when the
Jordan goes wild.
But you'd never want him for a pet—
you'd never be able to housebreak him!

I RUN THIS UNIVERSE

41.1-11 **41** "Or can you pull in the sea beast,
Leviathan, with a fly rod
and stuff him in your creel?
Can you lasso him with a rope,
or snag him with an anchor?
Will he beg you over and over for mercy,
or flatter you with flowery speech?
Will he apply for a job with you
to run errands and serve you the rest of
your life?
Will you play with him as if he were a pet
goldfish?
Will you make him the mascot of the
neighborhood children?
Will you put him on display in the market
and have shoppers haggle over the price?
Could you shoot him full of arrows like a pin
cushion,
or drive harpoons into his huge head?
If you so much as lay a hand on him,
you won't live to tell the story.
What hope would you have with such a
creature?
Why, one look at him would do you in!
If you can't hold your own against his
glowering visage,
how, then, do you expect to stand up
to *me*?
Who could confront me and get by with it?
I'm in *charge* of all this—I *run* this
universe!

41.12-17 "But I've more to say about Leviathan, the sea
beast,
his enormous bulk, his beautiful shape.
Who would even dream of piercing that tough
skin
or putting those jaws into bit and bridle?
And who would dare knock at the door of his
mouth
filled with row upon row of fierce teeth?
His pride is invincible;
nothing can make a dent in that pride.
Nothing can get through that proud skin—
impervious to weapons and weather,
The thickest and toughest of hides,
impenetrable!

41.18-34 "He snorts and the world lights up with fire,
he blinks and the dawn breaks.
Comets pour out of his mouth,
fireworks arc and branch.

NEW INTERNATIONAL VERSION

²⁰Smoke pours from his nostrils
    as from a boiling pot over a fire of reeds.
²¹His breath sets coals ablaze,
    and flames dart from his mouth.
²²Strength resides in his neck;
    dismay goes before him.
²³The folds of his flesh are tightly joined;
    they are firm and immovable.
²⁴His chest is hard as rock,
    hard as a lower millstone.
²⁵When he rises up, the mighty are terrified;
    they retreat before his thrashing.
²⁶The sword that reaches him has no effect,
    nor does the spear or the dart or the
        javelin.
²⁷Iron he treats like straw
    and bronze like rotten wood.
²⁸Arrows do not make him flee;
    slingstones are like chaff to him.
²⁹A club seems to him but a piece of straw;
    he laughs at the rattling of the lance.
³⁰His undersides are jagged potsherds,
    leaving a trail in the mud like a threshing
        sledge.
³¹He makes the depths churn like a boiling
        caldron
    and stirs up the sea like a pot of ointment.
³²Behind him he leaves a glistening wake;
    one would think the deep had white hair.
³³Nothing on earth is his equal—
    a creature without fear.
³⁴He looks down on all that are haughty;
    he is king over all that are proud."

JOB

42

    Then Job replied to the LORD:

²"I know that you can do all things;
    no plan of yours can be thwarted.
³You asked, 'Who is this that obscures my
        counsel without knowledge?'
    Surely I spoke of things I did not
        understand,
    things too wonderful for me to know.

⁴"You said, 'Listen now, and I will speak;
    I will question you,
    and you shall answer me.'
⁵My ears had heard of you
    but now my eyes have seen you.

THE MESSAGE

Smoke erupts from his nostrils
    like steam from a boiling pot.
He blows and fires blaze;
    flames of fire stream from his mouth.
All muscle he is—sheer and seamless muscle.
    To meet him is to dance with death.
Sinewy and lithe,
    there's not a soft spot in his entire body—
As tough inside as out,
    rock-hard, invulnerable.
Even angels run for cover when he surfaces,
    cowering before his tail-thrashing turbulence.
Javelins bounce harmlessly off his hide,
    harpoons ricochet wildly.
Iron bars are so much straw to him,
    bronze weapons beneath notice.
Arrows don't even make him blink;
    bullets make no more impression than
        raindrops.
A battle ax is nothing but a splinter of kindling;
    he treats a brandished harpoon as a joke.
His belly is armor-plated, inexorable—
    unstoppable as a barge.
He roils deep ocean the way you'd boil water,
    he whips the sea like you'd whip an egg
        into batter.
With a luminous trail stretching out behind
        him,
    you might think Ocean had grown a gray
        beard!
There's nothing on this earth quite like him,
    not an ounce of fear in *that* creature!
He surveys all the high and mighty—
    king of the ocean, king of the deep!"

JOB WORSHIPS GOD

I BABBLED ON ABOUT THINGS FAR BEYOND ME

^{42.1-6} **42** Job answered GOD:

"I'm convinced: You can do anything and
        everything.
    Nothing and no one can upset your plans.
You asked, 'Who is this muddying the water,
    ignorantly confusing the issue, second-
        guessing my purposes?'
I admit it. I was the one. I babbled on about
        things far beyond me,
    made small talk about wonders way over
        my head.
You told me, 'Listen, and let me do the talking.
    Let me ask the questions. *You* give the
        answers.'
I admit I once lived by rumors of you;
    now I have it all firsthand—from my own
        eyes and ears!

NEW INTERNATIONAL VERSION

⁶Therefore I despise myself
and repent in dust and ashes.”

EPILOGUE

⁷After the LORD had said these things to Job, he said to Eliphaz the Temanite, “I am angry with you and your two friends, because you have not spoken of me what is right, as my servant Job has. ⁸So now take seven bulls and seven rams and go to my servant Job and sacrifice a burnt offering for yourselves. My servant Job will pray for you, and I will accept his prayer and not deal with you according to your folly. You have not spoken of me what is right, as my servant Job has.” ⁹So Eliphaz the Temanite, Bildad the Shuhite and Zophar the Naamathite did what the LORD told them; and the LORD accepted Job’s prayer.

¹⁰After Job had prayed for his friends, the LORD made him prosperous again and gave him twice as much as he had before. ¹¹All his brothers and sisters and everyone who had known him before came and ate with him in his house. They comforted and consoled him over all the trouble the LORD had brought upon him, and each one gave him a piece of silver*a* and a gold ring.

¹²The LORD blessed the latter part of Job’s life more than the first. He had fourteen thousand sheep, six thousand camels, a thousand yoke of oxen and a thousand donkeys. ¹³And he also had seven sons and three daughters. ¹⁴The first daughter he named Jemimah, the second Keziah and the third Keren-Happuch. ¹⁵Nowhere in all the land were there found women as beautiful as Job’s daughters, and their father granted them an inheritance along with their brothers.

¹⁶After this, Job lived a hundred and forty years; he saw his children and their children to the fourth generation. ¹⁷And so he died, old and full of years.

THE MESSAGE

I’m sorry—forgive me. I’ll never do that again,
I promise!
I’ll never again live on crusts of hearsay,
crumbs of rumor.”

GOD RESTORES JOB

I WILL ACCEPT HIS PRAYER

42.7-8 After GOD had finished addressing Job, he turned to Eliphaz the Temanite and said, “I’ve had it with you and your two friends. I’m fed up! You haven’t been honest either with me or about me—not the way my friend Job has. So here’s what you must do. Take seven bulls and seven rams, and go to my friend Job. Sacrifice a burnt offering on your own behalf. My friend Job will pray for you, and I will accept his prayer. He will ask me not to treat you as you deserve for talking nonsense about me, and for not being honest with me, as he has.”

42.9 They did it. Eliphaz the Temanite, Bildad the Shuhite, and Zophar the Naamathite did what GOD commanded. And GOD accepted Job’s prayer.

42.10-11 After Job had interceded for his friends, GOD restored his fortune—and then doubled it! All his brothers and sisters and friends came to his house and celebrated. They told him how sorry they were, and consoled him for all the trouble GOD had brought him. Each of them brought generous housewarming gifts.

42.12-15 GOD blessed Job’s later life even more than his earlier life. He ended up with fourteen thousand sheep, six thousand camels, one thousand teams of oxen, and one thousand donkeys. He also had seven sons and three daughters. He named the first daughter Dove, the second, Cinnamon, and the third, Dark-eyes. There was not a woman in that country as beautiful as Job’s daughters. Their father treated them as equals with their brothers, providing the same inheritance.

42.16-17 Job lived on another hundred and forty years, living to see his children and grandchildren—four generations of them! Then he died—an old man, a full life.

---

a 11 Hebrew *him a kesitah*; a kesitah was a unit of money of unknown weight and value.

PSALMS

PSALMS

BOOK I

Psalms 1–41

PSALM 1

¹Blessed is the man
    who does not walk in the counsel of the
      wicked
  or stand in the way of sinners
    or sit in the seat of mockers.
²But his delight is in the law of the LORD,
    and on his law he meditates day and
      night.
³He is like a tree planted by streams of water,
    which yields its fruit in season
  and whose leaf does not wither.
    Whatever he does prospers.

⁴Not so the wicked!
    They are like chaff
    that the wind blows away.
⁵Therefore the wicked will not stand in the
      judgment,
    nor sinners in the assembly of the
      righteous.
⁶For the LORD watches over the way of the
      righteous,
    but the way of the wicked will perish.

PSALM 2

¹Why do the nations conspire[a]
    and the peoples plot in vain?
²The kings of the earth take their stand
    and the rulers gather together
  against the LORD
    and against his Anointed One.[b]
³"Let us break their chains," they say,
    "and throw off their fetters."

⁴The One enthroned in heaven laughs;
    the Lord scoffs at them.
⁵Then he rebukes them in his anger
    and terrifies them in his wrath, saying,

1.1 **1** How well God must like you—
    you don't hang out at Sin Saloon,
    you don't slink along Dead-End Road,
    you don't go to Smart-Mouth College.

1.2-3 Instead you thrill to GOD's Word,
    you chew on Scripture day and night.
You're a tree replanted in Eden,
    bearing fresh fruit every month,
Never dropping a leaf,
    always in blossom.

1.4-5 You're not at all like the wicked,
    who are mere windblown dust—
Without defense in court,
    unfit company for innocent people.

1.6 GOD charts the road you take.
    The road *they* take is Skid Row.

2.1-6 **2** Why the big noise, nations?
    Why the mean plots, peoples?
Earth-leaders push for position,
Demagogues and delegates meet for summit
      talks,
The God-deniers, the Messiah-defiers:
"Let's get free of God!
Cast loose from Messiah!"
Heaven-throned God breaks out laughing.
At first he's amused at their presumption;
Then he gets good and angry.
Furiously, he shuts them up:

---

[a] 1 Hebrew; Septuagint *rage*   [b] 2 Or *anointed one*

NEW INTERNATIONAL VERSION

6 "I have installed my King[a]
  on Zion, my holy hill."

7 I will proclaim the decree of the LORD:

He said to me, "You are my Son[b];
  today I have become your Father.[c]
8 Ask of me,
  and I will make the nations your
    inheritance,
  the ends of the earth your possession.
9 You will rule them with an iron scepter[d];
  you will dash them to pieces like pottery."

10 Therefore, you kings, be wise;
  be warned, you rulers of the earth.
11 Serve the LORD with fear
  and rejoice with trembling.
12 Kiss the Son, lest he be angry
  and you be destroyed in your way,
for his wrath can flare up in a moment.
  Blessed are all who take refuge in him.

PSALM 3

A psalm of David. When he fled from his son
Absalom.

1 O LORD, how many are my foes!
  How many rise up against me!
2 Many are saying of me,
  "God will not deliver him."   *Selah*[e]

3 But you are a shield around me, O LORD;
  you bestow glory on me and lift[f] up my
    head.
4 To the LORD I cry aloud,
  and he answers me from his holy hill.
                                        Selah

5 I lie down and sleep;
  I wake again, because the LORD
    sustains me.
6 I will not fear the tens of thousands
  drawn up against me on every side.

7 Arise, O LORD!
  Deliver me, O my God!
Strike all my enemies on the jaw;
  break the teeth of the wicked.

8 From the LORD comes deliverance.
  May your blessing be on your people.
                                        Selah

THE MESSAGE

"Don't you know there's a King in Zion? A
    coronation banquet
  Is spread for him on the holy summit."

2.7-9 Let me tell you what GOD said next.
  He said, "You're my son,
  And today is your birthday.
  What do you want? Name it:
  Nations as a present? continents as a prize?
  You can command them all to dance for you,
  Or throw them out with tomorrow's trash."

2.10-12 So, rebel-kings, use your heads;
  Upstart-judges, learn your lesson:
  Worship GOD in adoring embrace,
  Celebrate in trembling awe. Kiss Messiah!
  Your very lives are in danger, you know;
  His anger is about to explode,
  But if you make a run for God—you won't
    regret it!

A David psalm, when he escaped for his life
from Absalom, his son.

3.1-2 **3** GOD! Look! Enemies past counting!
        Enemies sprouting like mushrooms,
  Mobs of them all around me, roaring their
    mockery:
  "Hah! No help for *him* from God!"

3.3-4 But you, GOD, shield me on all sides;
  You ground my feet, you lift my head high;
  With all my might I shout up to GOD,
  His answers thunder from the holy mountain.

3.5-6 I stretch myself out. I sleep.
  Then I'm up again—rested, tall and steady,
  Fearless before the enemy mobs
  Coming at me from all sides.

3.7 Up, GOD! My God, help me!
  Slap their faces,
  First this cheek, then the other,
  Your fist hard in their teeth!

3.8 Real help comes from GOD.
  Your blessing clothes your people!

---

[a] 6 Or *king*   [b] 7 Or *son*; also in verse 12   [c] 7 Or *have*
begotten you   [d] 9 Or *will break them with a rod of iron*
[e] 2 A word of uncertain meaning, occurring frequently in
the Psalms; possibly a musical term   [f] 3 Or LORD, / *my*
Glorious One, who lifts

NEW INTERNATIONAL VERSION

PSALM 4

For the director of music. With stringed
instruments. A psalm of David.

¹Answer me when I call to you,
   O my righteous God.
 Give me relief from my distress;
   be merciful to me and hear my prayer.

²How long, O men, will you turn my glory
      into shame *a*?
   How long will you love delusions and
      seek false gods *b*?   *Selah*
³Know that the LORD has set apart the godly
      for himself;
   the LORD will hear when I call to him.

⁴In your anger do not sin;
   when you are on your beds,
   search your hearts and be silent.   *Selah*
⁵Offer right sacrifices
   and trust in the LORD.

⁶Many are asking, "Who can show us any
      good?"
   Let the light of your face shine upon us,
      O LORD.
⁷You have filled my heart with greater joy
   than when their grain and new wine
      abound.
⁸I will lie down and sleep in peace,
   for you alone, O LORD,
   make me dwell in safety.

PSALM 5

For the director of music. For flutes. A psalm
of David.

¹Give ear to my words, O LORD,
   consider my sighing.
²Listen to my cry for help,
   my King and my God,
   for to you I pray.
³In the morning, O LORD, you hear my voice;
   in the morning I lay my requests before
      you
   and wait in expectation.

⁴You are not a God who takes pleasure in evil;
   with you the wicked cannot dwell.
⁵The arrogant cannot stand in your presence;
   you hate all who do wrong.
⁶You destroy those who tell lies;
   bloodthirsty and deceitful men
   the LORD abhors.

⁷But I, by your great mercy,
   will come into your house;

THE MESSAGE

A David psalm

4.1 **4** When I call, give me answers. God, take
         my side!
    Once, in a tight place, you gave me room;
    Now I'm in trouble again: grace me! hear me!

4.2 You rabble—how long do I put up with your
         scorn?
    How long will you lust after lies?
    How long will you live crazed by illusion?

4.3 Look at this: look
    Who got picked by GOD!
    He listens the split second I call to him.

4.4-5 Complain if you must, but don't lash out.
    Keep your mouth shut, and let your heart do
         the talking.
    Build your case before God and wait for his
         verdict.

4.6-7 Why is everyone hungry for *more?* "More,
         more," they say.
    "More, more."
    I have God's more-than-enough,
    More joy in one ordinary day

4.7-8 Than they get in all their shopping sprees.
    At day's end I'm ready for sound sleep,
    For you, GOD, have put my life back together.

A David psalm

5.1-3 **5** Listen, GOD! Please, pay attention!
         Can you make sense of these ramblings,
            my groans and cries?
               King-God, I need your help.
    Every morning
       you'll hear me at it again.
    Every morning
       I lay out the pieces of my life
       on your altar
       and watch for fire to descend.

5.4-6 You don't socialize with Wicked,
       or invite Evil over as your houseguest.
    Hot-Air-Boaster collapses in front of you;
       you shake your head over Mischief-Maker.
    GOD destroys Lie-Speaker;
       Blood-Thirsty and Truth-Bender disgust
         you.

5.7-8 And here I am, your invited guest—
       it's incredible!
    I enter your house; here I am,

---

a 2 Or you dishonor my Glorious One   *b 2 Or seek lies*

NEW INTERNATIONAL VERSION

in reverence will I bow down
 toward your holy temple.
[8] Lead me, O LORD, in your righteousness
 because of my enemies—
 make straight your way before me.

[9] Not a word from their mouth can be trusted;
 their heart is filled with destruction.
Their throat is an open grave;
 with their tongue they speak deceit.
[10] Declare them guilty, O God!
 Let their intrigues be their downfall.
Banish them for their many sins,
 for they have rebelled against you.

[11] But let all who take refuge in you be glad;
 let them ever sing for joy.
Spread your protection over them,
 that those who love your name may
 rejoice in you.
[12] For surely, O LORD, you bless the righteous;
 you surround them with your favor as
 with a shield.

PSALM 6

For the director of music. With stringed
instruments. According to *sheminith.* [a] A psalm
of David.

[1] O LORD, do not rebuke me in your anger
 or discipline me in your wrath.
[2] Be merciful to me, LORD, for I am faint;
 O LORD, heal me, for my bones are in
 agony.
[3] My soul is in anguish.
 How long, O LORD, how long?

[4] Turn, O LORD, and deliver me;
 save me because of your unfailing love.
[5] No one remembers you when he is dead.
 Who praises you from the grave [b]?

[6] I am worn out from groaning;
 all night long I flood my bed with
 weeping
 and drench my couch with tears.
[7] My eyes grow weak with sorrow;
 they fail because of all my foes.

[8] Away from me, all you who do evil,
 for the LORD has heard my weeping.
[9] The LORD has heard my cry for mercy;
 the LORD accepts my prayer.
[10] All my enemies will be ashamed and
 dismayed;
 they will turn back in sudden disgrace.

THE MESSAGE

prostrate in your inner sanctum,
Waiting for directions
 to get me safely through enemy lines.

5.9-10 Every word they speak is a land mine;
 their lungs breathe out poison gas.
Their throats are gaping graves,
 their tongues slick as mudslides.
Pile on the guilt, God!
 Let their so-called wisdom wreck them.
Kick them out! They've had their chance.

5.11-12 But you'll welcome us with open arms
 when we run for cover to you.
Let the party last all night!
 Stand guard over our celebration.
You are famous, GOD, for welcoming God-
 seekers,
 for decking us out in delight.

A David psalm

6.1-2 **6** Please, GOD, no more yelling,
 no more trips to the woodshed.
Treat me nice for a change;
 I'm so starved for affection.

6.2-3 Can't you see I'm black and blue,
 beat up badly in bones and soul?
GOD, how long will it take
 for you to let up?

6.4-5 Break in, GOD, and break up this fight;
 if you love me at all, get me out of here.
I'm no good to you dead, am I?
 I can't sing in your choir if I'm buried in
 some tomb!

6.6-7 I'm tired of all this—so tired. My bed
 has been floating forty days and nights
On the flood of my tears.
 My mattress is soaked, soggy with tears.
The sockets of my eyes are black holes;
 nearly blind, I squint and grope.

6.8-9 Get out of here, you Devil's crew:
 at last GOD has heard my sobs.
My requests have all been granted,
 my prayers are answered.

6.10 Cowards, my enemies disappear.
 Disgraced, they turn tail and run.

---

[a] Title: Probably a musical term [b] 5 Hebrew *Sheol*

NEW INTERNATIONAL VERSION

PSALM 7

A *shiggaion*[a] of David, which he sang to the LORD
concerning Cush, a Benjamite.

[1] O LORD my God, I take refuge in you;
    save and deliver me from all who
        pursue me,
[2] or they will tear me like a lion
    and rip me to pieces with no one to
        rescue me.

[3] O LORD my God, if I have done this
    and there is guilt on my hands—
[4] if I have done evil to him who is at peace
        with me
    or without cause have robbed my foe—
[5] then let my enemy pursue and overtake me;
    let him trample my life to the ground
    and make me sleep in the dust.   *Selah*

[6] Arise, O LORD, in your anger;
    rise up against the rage of my enemies.
    Awake, my God; decree justice.
[7] Let the assembled peoples gather around
        you.
    Rule over them from on high;
[8]   let the LORD judge the peoples.
    Judge me, O LORD, according to my
        righteousness,
    according to my integrity, O Most High.
[9] O righteous God,
    who searches minds and hearts,
    bring to an end the violence of the wicked
    and make the righteous secure.

[10] My shield[b] is God Most High,
    who saves the upright in heart.
[11] God is a righteous judge,
    a God who expresses his wrath every day.
[12] If he does not relent,
    he[c] will sharpen his sword;
    he will bend and string his bow.
[13] He has prepared his deadly weapons;
    he makes ready his flaming arrows.

[14] He who is pregnant with evil
    and conceives trouble gives birth to
        disillusionment.
[15] He who digs a hole and scoops it out
    falls into the pit he has made.
[16] The trouble he causes recoils on himself;
    his violence comes down on his own
        head.

---

[a] Title: Probably a literary or musical term
[b] 10 Or *sovereign*   [c] 12 Or *If a man does not repent, / God*

THE MESSAGE

A David psalm

7.1-2 **7** GOD! God! I am running to you for dear life;
        the chase is wild.
    If they catch me, I'm finished:
        ripped to shreds by foes fierce as lions,
        dragged into the forest and left
        unlooked for, unremembered.

7.3-5 GOD, if I've done what they say—
        betrayed my friends,
        ripped off my enemies—
    If my hands are really that dirty,
        let them get me, walk all over me,
        leave me flat on my face in the dirt.

7.6-8 Stand up, GOD; pit your holy fury
        against my furious enemies.
    Wake up, God. My accusers have packed
        the courtroom; it's judgment time.
    Take your place on the bench, reach for your
        gavel,
        throw out the false charges against me.
    I'm ready, confident in your verdict:
        "Innocent."

7.9-11 Close the book on Evil, GOD,
        but publish your mandate for us.
    You get us ready for life:
        you probe for our soft spots,
        you knock off our rough edges.
    And I'm feeling so fit, so safe:
        made right, kept right.
    God in solemn honor does things right,
        but his nerves are sandpapered raw.

7.11-13 Nobody gets by with anything.
        God is already in action—
    Sword honed on his whetstone,
        bow strung, arrow on the string,
    Lethal weapons in hand,
        each arrow a flaming missile.

7.14 Look at that guy!
        He had sex with sin,
        he's pregnant with evil.
    Oh, look! He's having
        the baby—a Lie-Baby!

7.15-16 See that man shoveling day after day,
        digging, then concealing, his man-trap
        down that lonely stretch of road?
    Go back and look again—you'll see him in it
        headfirst,
        legs waving in the breeze.
    That's what happens:
        mischief backfires;
        violence boomerangs.

NEW INTERNATIONAL VERSION

¹⁷ I will give thanks to the LORD because of his
righteousness
and will sing praise to the name of the
LORD Most High.

PSALM 8

For the director of music. According to *gittith*. ^{*a*}
A psalm of David.

¹ O LORD, our Lord,
how majestic is your name in all the
earth!

You have set your glory
above the heavens.
² From the lips of children and infants
you have ordained praise^{*b*}
because of your enemies,
to silence the foe and the avenger.

³ When I consider your heavens,
the work of your fingers,
the moon and the stars,
which you have set in place,
⁴ what is man that you are mindful of him,
the son of man that you care for him?
⁵ You made him a little lower than the
heavenly beings^{*c*}
and crowned him with glory and honor.

⁶ You made him ruler over the works of your
hands;
you put everything under his feet:
⁷ all flocks and herds,
and the beasts of the field,
⁸ the birds of the air,
and the fish of the sea,
all that swim the paths of the seas.

⁹ O LORD, our Lord,
how majestic is your name in all the
earth!

PSALM 9 ^{*d*}

For the director of music. To the tune of, "The
Death of the Son." A psalm of David.

¹ I will praise you, O LORD, with all my heart;
I will tell of all your wonders.
² I will be glad and rejoice in you;
I will sing praise to your name, O Most
High.

³ My enemies turn back;
they stumble and perish before you.

THE MESSAGE

^{7.17} I'm thanking God, who makes things right.
I'm singing the fame of heaven-high GOD.

A David psalm

^{8.1} **8** GOD, brilliant Lord,
yours is a household name.

^{8.2} Nursing infants gurgle choruses about you;
toddlers shout the songs
That drown out enemy talk,
and silence atheist babble.

^{8.3-4} I look up at your macro-skies, dark and
enormous,
your handmade sky-jewelry,
Moon and stars mounted in their settings.
Then I look at my micro-self and wonder,
Why do you bother with us?
Why take a second look our way?

^{8.5-8} Yet we've so narrowly missed being gods,
bright with Eden's dawn light.
You put us in charge of your handcrafted
world,
repeated to us your Genesis-charge,
Made us lords of sheep and cattle,
even animals out in the wild,
Birds flying and fish swimming,
whales singing in the ocean deeps.

^{8.9} GOD, brilliant Lord,
your name echoes around the world.

A David psalm

^{9.1-2} **9** I'm thanking you, GOD, from a full heart,
I'm writing the book on your wonders.
I'm whistling, laughing, and jumping for joy;
I'm singing your song, High God.

^{9.3-4} The day my enemies turned tail and ran,
they stumbled on you and fell on their
faces.

---

^{*a*} Title: Probably a musical term   ^{*b*} 2 Or *strength*
^{*c*} 5 Or *than God*   ^{*d*} Psalms 9 and 10 may have been
originally a single acrostic poem, the stanzas of which begin
with the successive letters of the Hebrew alphabet. In the
Septuagint they constitute one psalm.

NEW INTERNATIONAL VERSION

⁴For you have upheld my right and my cause;
  you have sat on your throne, judging
    righteously.
⁵You have rebuked the nations and destroyed
    the wicked;
  you have blotted out their name for ever
    and ever.
⁶Endless ruin has overtaken the enemy,
  you have uprooted their cities;
  even the memory of them has perished.

⁷The LORD reigns forever;
  he has established his throne for
    judgment.
⁸He will judge the world in righteousness;
  he will govern the peoples with justice.
⁹The LORD is a refuge for the oppressed,
  a stronghold in times of trouble.
¹⁰Those who know your name will trust in
    you,
  for you, LORD, have never forsaken those
    who seek you.

¹¹Sing praises to the LORD, enthroned in Zion;
  proclaim among the nations what he has
    done.
¹²For he who avenges blood remembers;
  he does not ignore the cry of the afflicted.

¹³O LORD, see how my enemies persecute me!
  Have mercy and lift me up from the gates
    of death,
¹⁴that I may declare your praises
  in the gates of the Daughter of Zion
  and there rejoice in your salvation.

¹⁵The nations have fallen into the pit they
    have dug;
  their feet are caught in the net they have
    hidden.
¹⁶The LORD is known by his justice;
  the wicked are ensnared by the work of
    their hands.   *Higgaion.* ᵃ *Selah*
¹⁷The wicked return to the grave,ᵇ
  all the nations that forget God.
¹⁸But the needy will not always be forgotten,
  nor the hope of the afflicted ever perish.

¹⁹Arise, O LORD, let not man triumph;
  let the nations be judged in your
    presence.
²⁰Strike them with terror, O LORD;
  let the nations know they are but men.
    Selah

THE MESSAGE

You took over and set everything right;
  when I needed you, you were there, taking
    charge.

9.5-6 You blow the whistle on godless nations;
  you throw dirty players out of the game,
  wipe their names right off the roster.
Enemies disappear from the sidelines,
  their reputation trashed,
  their names erased from the halls of fame.

9.7-8 GOD holds the high center,
  he sees and sets the world's mess right.
He decides what is right for us earthlings,
  gives people their just deserts.

9.9-10 GOD's a safe-house for the battered,
  a sanctuary during bad times.
The moment you arrive, you relax;
  you're never sorry you knocked.

9.11-12 Sing your songs to Zion-dwelling GOD,
  tell his stories to everyone you meet:
How he tracks down killers
  yet keeps his eye on us,
  registers every whimper and moan.

9.13-14 Be kind to me, GOD;
  I've been kicked around long enough.
Once you've pulled me back
  from the gates of death,
I'll write the book on Hallelujahs;
  on the corner of Main and First
  I'll hold a street meeting;
I'll be the song leader; we'll fill the air
  with salvation songs.

9.15-16 They're trapped, those godless countries,
  in the very snares they set,
Their feet all tangled
  in the net they spread.
They have no excuse;
  the way God works is well-known.
The cunning machinery made by the wicked
  has maimed their own hands.

9.17-20 The wicked bought a one-way
  ticket to hell.
No longer will the poor be nameless—
  no more humiliation for the humble.
Up, GOD! Aren't you fed up with their empty
    strutting?
  Expose these grand pretensions!
Shake them up, GOD!
  Show them how silly they look.

ᵃ 16 Or *Meditation*; possibly a musical notation
ᵇ 17 Hebrew *Sheol*

NEW INTERNATIONAL VERSION

PSALM 10[a]

[1] Why, O Lord, do you stand far off?
Why do you hide yourself in times of
trouble?

[2] In his arrogance the wicked man hunts
down the weak,
who are caught in the schemes he devises.
[3] He boasts of the cravings of his heart;
he blesses the greedy and reviles the Lord.
[4] In his pride the wicked does not seek him;
in all his thoughts there is no room for
God.
[5] His ways are always prosperous;
he is haughty and your laws are far from
him;
he sneers at all his enemies.
[6] He says to himself, "Nothing will shake me;
I'll always be happy and never have
trouble."
[7] His mouth is full of curses and lies and
threats;
trouble and evil are under his tongue.
[8] He lies in wait near the villages;
from ambush he murders the innocent,
watching in secret for his victims.
[9] He lies in wait like a lion in cover;
he lies in wait to catch the helpless;
he catches the helpless and drags them off
in his net.
[10] His victims are crushed, they collapse;
they fall under his strength.
[11] He says to himself, "God has forgotten;
he covers his face and never sees."

[12] Arise, Lord! Lift up your hand, O God.
Do not forget the helpless.
[13] Why does the wicked man revile God?
Why does he say to himself,
"He won't call me to account"?
[14] But you, O God, do see trouble and grief;
you consider it to take it in hand.
The victim commits himself to you;
you are the helper of the fatherless.
[15] Break the arm of the wicked and evil man;
call him to account for his wickedness
that would not be found out.

[16] The Lord is King for ever and ever;
the nations will perish from his land.
[17] You hear, O Lord, the desire of the afflicted;
you encourage them, and you listen to
their cry,

---

[a] Psalms 9 and 10 may have been originally a single acrostic
poem, the stanzas of which begin with the successive letters
of the Hebrew alphabet. In the Septuagint they constitute
one psalm.

THE MESSAGE

10 10.1-2 God, are you avoiding me?
Where are you when I need you?
Full of hot air, the wicked
are hot on the trail of the poor.
Trip them up, tangle them up
in their fine-tuned plots.

10.3-4 The wicked are windbags,
the swindlers have foul breath.
The wicked snub God,
their noses stuck high in the air.
Their graffiti are scrawled on the walls:
"Catch us if you can!" "God is dead."

10.5-6 They care nothing for what you think;
if you get in their way, they blow you off.
They live (they think) a charmed life:
"We can't go wrong. This is our lucky
year!"

10.7-8 They carry a mouthful of hexes,
their tongues spit venom like adders.
They hide behind ordinary people,
then pounce on their victims.

10.9 They mark the luckless,
then wait like a hunter in a blind;
When the poor wretch wanders too close,
they stab him in the back.

10.10-11 The hapless fool is kicked to the ground,
the unlucky victim is brutally axed.
He thinks God has dumped him,
he's sure that God is indifferent to his
plight.

10.12-13 Time to get up, God—get moving.
The luckless think they're Godforsaken.
They wonder why the wicked scorn God
and get away with it,
Why the wicked are so cocksure
they'll never come up for audit.

10.14 But you know all about it—
the contempt, the abuse.
I dare to believe that the luckless
will get lucky someday in you.
You won't let them down:
orphans won't be orphans forever.

10.15-16 Break the wicked right arms,
break all the evil left arms.
Search and destroy
every sign of crime.
God's grace and order wins;
godlessness loses.

10.17-18 The victim's faint pulse picks up;
the hearts of the hopeless pump red blood
as you put your ear to their lips.

NEW INTERNATIONAL VERSION

¹⁸defending the fatherless and the oppressed,
in order that man, who is of the earth,
may terrify no more.

PSALM 11

For the director of music. Of David.

¹In the LORD I take refuge.
How then can you say to me:
"Flee like a bird to your mountain.
²For look, the wicked bend their bows;
they set their arrows against the strings
to shoot from the shadows
at the upright in heart.
³When the foundations are being destroyed,
what can the righteous do^a?"

⁴The LORD is in his holy temple;
the LORD is on his heavenly throne.
He observes the sons of men;
his eyes examine them.
⁵The LORD examines the righteous,
but the wicked^b and those who love
violence
his soul hates.
⁶On the wicked he will rain
fiery coals and burning sulfur;
a scorching wind will be their lot.

⁷For the LORD is righteous,
he loves justice;
upright men will see his face.

PSALM 12

*For the director of music. According
to sheminith.^c A psalm of David.*

¹Help, LORD, for the godly are no more;
the faithful have vanished from among
men.
²Everyone lies to his neighbor;
their flattering lips speak with deception.

³May the LORD cut off all flattering lips
and every boastful tongue
⁴that says, "We will triumph with our
tongues;
we own our lips^d—who is our master?"

⁵"Because of the oppression of the weak
and the groaning of the needy,
I will now arise," says the LORD.

---

[a] 3 Or *what is the Righteous One doing*   [b] 5 Or *The LORD, the Righteous One, examines the wicked, /*   [c] Title: Probably a musical term   [d] 4 Or */ our lips are our plowshares*

THE MESSAGE

Orphans get parents,
the homeless get homes.
The reign of terror is over,
the rule of the gang lords is ended.

A David psalm

11 ^{11.1-3} I've already run for dear life
straight to the arms of GOD.
So why would I run away now
when you say,

"Run to the mountains; the evil
bows are bent, the wicked arrows
Aimed to shoot under cover of darkness
at every heart open to God.
The bottom's dropped out of the country;
good people don't have a chance"?

^{11.4-6}But GOD hasn't moved to the mountains;
his holy address hasn't changed.
He's in charge, as always, his eyes
taking everything in, his eyelids
Unblinking, examining Adam's unruly brood
inside and out, not missing a thing.
He tests the good and the bad alike;
if anyone cheats, God's outraged.
Fail the test and you're out,
out in a hail of firestones,
Drinking from a canteen
filled with hot desert wind.

^{11.7}GOD's business is putting things right;
he loves getting the lines straight,
Setting us straight. Once we're standing tall,
we can look him straight in the eye.

A David psalm

12 ^{12.1-2} Quick, GOD, I need your helping hand!
The last decent person just went down,
All the friends I depended on gone.
Everyone talks in lie language;
Lies slide off their oily lips.
They doubletalk with forked tongues.

^{12.3-4}Slice their lips off their faces! Pull
The braggart tongues from their mouths!
I'm tired of hearing, "We can talk anyone into
anything!
Our lips manage the world."

^{12.5}Into the hovels of the poor,
Into the dark streets where the homeless
groan, God speaks:
"I've had enough; I'm on my way

NEW INTERNATIONAL VERSION

"I will protect them from those who
malign them."
6 And the words of the LORD are flawless,
like silver refined in a furnace of clay,
purified seven times.

7 O LORD, you will keep us safe
and protect us from such people forever.
8 The wicked freely strut about
when what is vile is honored among men.

PSALM 13

For the director of music. A psalm of David.

1 How long, O LORD? Will you forget me
forever?
How long will you hide your face from
me?
2 How long must I wrestle with my thoughts
and every day have sorrow in my heart?
How long will my enemy triumph over
me?

3 Look on me and answer, O LORD my God.
Give light to my eyes, or I will sleep in
death;
4 my enemy will say, "I have overcome him,"
and my foes will rejoice when I fall.

5 But I trust in your unfailing love;
my heart rejoices in your salvation.
6 I will sing to the LORD,
for he has been good to me.

PSALM 14

For the director of music. Of David.

1 The fool[a] says in his heart,
"There is no God."
They are corrupt, their deeds are vile;
there is no one who does good.

2 The LORD looks down from heaven
on the sons of men
to see if there are any who understand,
any who seek God.
3 All have turned aside,
they have together become corrupt;
there is no one who does good,
not even one.

4 Will evildoers never learn—

---

a 1 The Hebrew words rendered *fool* in Psalms denote one
who is morally deficient.

THE MESSAGE

To heal the ache in the heart of the wretched."
12.6-8 God's words are pure words,
Pure silver words refined seven times
In the fires of his word-kiln,
Pure on earth as well as in heaven.
GOD, keep us safe from their lies,
From the wicked who stalk us with lies,
From the wicked who collect honors
For their wonderful lies.

A David psalm

13.1-2 **13** Long enough, GOD—
you've ignored me long enough.
I've looked at the back of your head
long enough. Long enough
I've carried this ton of trouble,
lived with a stomach full of pain.
Long enough my arrogant enemies
have looked down their noses at me.

13.3-4 Take a good look at me, GOD, my God;
I want to look life in the eye,
So no enemy can get the best of me
or laugh when I fall on my face.

13.5-6 I've thrown myself headlong into your arms—
I'm celebrating your rescue.
I'm singing at the top of my lungs,
I'm so full of answered prayers.

A David psalm

14.1 **14** Bilious and bloated, they gas,
"God is gone."
Their words are poison gas,
fouling the air; they poison
Rivers and skies;
thistles are their cash crop.

14.2 GOD sticks his head out of heaven.
He looks around.
He's looking for someone not stupid—
one man, even, God-expectant,
just one God-ready woman.

14.3 He comes up empty. A string
of zeros. Useless, unshepherded
Sheep, taking turns pretending
to be Shepherd.
The ninety and nine
follow their fellow.

14.4 Don't they know anything,
all these impostors?
Don't they know

NEW INTERNATIONAL VERSION	THE MESSAGE

those who devour my people as men eat
    bread
  and who do not call on the LORD?
⁵ There they are, overwhelmed with dread,
  for God is present in the company of the
    righteous.
⁶ You evildoers frustrate the plans of the poor,
  but the LORD is their refuge.

⁷ Oh, that salvation for Israel would come out
    of Zion!
  When the LORD restores the fortunes of
    his people,
  let Jacob rejoice and Israel be glad!

PSALM 15

A psalm of David.

¹ LORD, who may dwell in your sanctuary?
  Who may live on your holy hill?

² He whose walk is blameless
  and who does what is righteous,
who speaks the truth from his heart
³ and has no slander on his tongue,
  who does his neighbor no wrong
  and casts no slur on his fellowman,
⁴ who despises a vile man
  but honors those who fear the LORD,
  who keeps his oath
    even when it hurts,
⁵ who lends his money without usury
  and does not accept a bribe against the
    innocent.

He who does these things
  will never be shaken.

PSALM 16

A *miktam*^a of David.

¹ Keep me safe, O God,
  for in you I take refuge.

² I said to the LORD, "You are my Lord;
  apart from you I have no good thing."
³ As for the saints who are in the land,
  they are the glorious ones in whom is all
    my delight.^b
⁴ The sorrows of those will increase
  who run after other gods.
  I will not pour out their libations of blood
  or take up their names on my lips.

⁵ LORD, you have assigned me my portion and
    my cup;

---

they can't get away with this—
  Treating people like a fast-food meal
    over which they're too busy to pray?

14.5-6 Night is coming for them, and nightmares,
    for God takes the side of victims.
  Do you think you can mess
    with the dreams of the poor?
  You can't, for God
    makes their dreams come true.

14.7 Is there anyone around to save Israel?
    Yes. God is around; GOD turns life around.
  Turned-around Jacob skips rope,
    turned-around Israel sings laughter.

A David psalm

15.1 **15** GOD, who gets invited
         to dinner at your place?
  How do we get on your guest list?

15.2 "Walk straight,
    act right,
      tell the truth.

15.3-4 "Don't hurt your friend,
    don't blame your neighbor;
      despise the despicable.

15.5 "Keep your word even when it costs you,
    make an honest living,
      never take a bribe.

  "You'll never get
  blacklisted
  if you live like this."

A David song

16.1-2 **16** Keep me safe, O God,
         I've run for dear life to you.
  I say to GOD, "Be my Lord!"
    Without you, nothing makes sense.

16.3 And these God-chosen lives all around—
    what splendid friends they make!

16.4 Don't just go shopping for a god.
    Gods are not for sale.
  I swear I'll never treat god-names
    like brand-names.

16.5-6 My choice is you, GOD, first and only.

---

^a Title: Probably a literary or musical term   ^b 3 Or *As for
the pagan priests who are in the land / and the nobles in whom
all delight, I said:*

NEW INTERNATIONAL VERSION

you have made my lot secure.
⁶ The boundary lines have fallen for me in
pleasant places;
surely I have a delightful inheritance.

⁷ I will praise the LORD, who counsels me;
even at night my heart instructs me.
⁸ I have set the LORD always before me.
Because he is at my right hand,
I will not be shaken.

⁹ Therefore my heart is glad and my tongue
rejoices;
my body also will rest secure,
¹⁰ because you will not abandon me to the
grave,ᵃ
nor will you let your Holy Oneᵇ see decay.
¹¹ You have madeᶜ known to me the path of
life;
you will fill me with joy in your presence,
with eternal pleasures at your right hand.

PSALM 17

A prayer of David.

¹ Hear, O LORD, my righteous plea;
listen to my cry.
Give ear to my prayer—
it does not rise from deceitful lips.
² May my vindication come from you;
may your eyes see what is right.

³ Though you probe my heart and examine me
at night,
though you test me, you will find
nothing;
I have resolved that my mouth will not
sin.
⁴ As for the deeds of men—
by the word of your lips
I have kept myself
from the ways of the violent.
⁵ My steps have held to your paths;
my feet have not slipped.

⁶ I call on you, O God, for you will answer
me;
give ear to me and hear my prayer.
⁷ Show the wonder of your great love,
you who save by your right hand
those who take refuge in you from their
foes.
⁸ Keep me as the apple of your eye;
hide me in the shadow of your wings
⁹ from the wicked who assail me,
from my mortal enemies who surround
me.

ᵃ 10 Hebrew *Sheol*   ᵇ 10 Or *your faithful one*
ᶜ 11 Or *You will make*

THE MESSAGE

And now I find I'm *your* choice!
You set me up with a house and yard.
And then you made me your heir!

16.7-8 The wise counsel GOD gives when I'm awake
is confirmed by my sleeping heart.
Day and night I'll stick with GOD;
I've got a good thing going and I'm not
letting go.

16.9-10 I'm happy from the inside out,
and from the outside in, I'm firmly formed.
You canceled my ticket to hell—
that's not my destination!

16.11 Now you've got my feet on the life path,
all radiant from the shining of your face.
Ever since you took my hand,
I'm on the right way.

A David prayer

17.1-2 **17** Listen while I build my case, GOD,
the most honest prayer you'll ever
hear.
Show the world I'm innocent—
in your heart you know I am.

17.3 Go ahead, examine me from inside out,
surprise me in the middle of the night—
You'll find I'm just what I say I am.
My words don't run loose.

17.4-5 I'm not trying to get my way
in the world's way.
I'm trying to get *your* way,
your Word's way.
I'm staying on your trail;
I'm putting one foot
In front of the other.
I'm not giving up.

17.6-7 I call to you, God, because I'm sure of an
answer.
So—answer! bend your ear! listen sharp!
Paint grace-graffiti on the fences;
take in your frightened children who
Are running from the neighborhood bullies
straight to you.

17.8-9 Keep your eye on me;
hide me under your cool wing feathers
From the wicked who are out to get me,
from mortal enemies closing in.

NEW INTERNATIONAL VERSION

¹⁰ They close up their callous hearts,
  and their mouths speak with arrogance.
¹¹ They have tracked me down, they now
    surround me,
  with eyes alert, to throw me to the
    ground.
¹² They are like a lion hungry for prey,
  like a great lion crouching in cover.

¹³ Rise up, O LORD, confront them, bring them
    down;
  rescue me from the wicked by your
    sword.
¹⁴ O LORD, by your hand save me from such
    men,
  from men of this world whose reward is
    in this life.

You still the hunger of those you cherish;
  their sons have plenty,
  and they store up wealth for their
    children.
¹⁵ And I—in righteousness I will see your face;
  when I awake, I will be satisfied with
    seeing your likeness.

PSALM 18

For the director of music. Of David the servant of
  the LORD. He sang to the LORD the words of this
  song when the LORD delivered him from the hand
  of all his enemies and from the hand of Saul.
  He said:

¹ I love you, O LORD, my strength.

² The LORD is my rock, my fortress and my
    deliverer;
  my God is my rock, in whom I take
    refuge.
  He is my shield and the horn^a of my
    salvation, my stronghold.
³ I call to the LORD, who is worthy of praise,
  and I am saved from my enemies.

⁴ The cords of death entangled me;
  the torrents of destruction
    overwhelmed me.
⁵ The cords of the grave^b coiled around me;
  the snares of death confronted me.
⁶ In my distress I called to the LORD;
  I cried to my God for help.
From his temple he heard my voice;
  my cry came before him, into his ears.

⁷ The earth trembled and quaked,
  and the foundations of the mountains
    shook;
  they trembled because he was angry.

^a 2 *Horn* here symbolizes strength.   ^b 5 Hebrew *Sheol*

THE MESSAGE

^{17.10-14} Their hearts are hard as nails,
  their mouths blast hot air.
They are after me, nipping my heels,
  determined to bring me down,
Lions ready to rip me apart,
  young lions poised to pounce.
Up, GOD: beard them! break them!
  By your sword, free me from their clutches;
Barehanded, GOD, break these mortals,
  these flat-earth people who can't think
    beyond today.

I'd like to see their bellies
  swollen with famine food,
The weeds they've sown
  harvested and baked into famine bread,
With second helpings for their children
  and crusts for their babies to chew on.

^{17.15} And me? I plan on looking
  you full in the face. When I get up,
I'll see your full stature
  and live heaven on earth.

A David song, which he sang to God after being
  saved from all his enemies and from Saul.

^{18.1-2} **18** I love you, GOD—
  you make me strong.
GOD is bedrock under my feet,
  the castle in which I live,
  my rescuing knight.
My God—the high crag
  where I run for dear life,
  hiding behind the boulders,
  safe in the granite hideout.

^{18.3} I sing to GOD, the Praise-Lofty,
  and find myself safe and saved.

^{18.4-5} The hangman's noose was tight at my throat;
  devil waters rushed over me.
Hell's ropes cinched me tight;
  death traps barred every exit.

^{18.6} A hostile world! I call to GOD,
  I cry to God to help me.
From his palace he hears my call;
  my cry brings me right into his presence—
    a private audience!

^{18.7-15} Earth wobbles and lurches;
  huge mountains shake like leaves,
Quake like aspen leaves
  because of his rage.

NEW INTERNATIONAL VERSION

8 Smoke rose from his nostrils;
    consuming fire came from his mouth,
    burning coals blazed out of it.
9 He parted the heavens and came down;
    dark clouds were under his feet.
10 He mounted the cherubim and flew;
    he soared on the wings of the wind.
11 He made darkness his covering, his canopy
        around him—
    the dark rain clouds of the sky.
12 Out of the brightness of his presence clouds
        advanced,
    with hailstones and bolts of lightning.
13 The LORD thundered from heaven;
    the voice of the Most High resounded. *a*
14 He shot his arrows and scattered ⌊the
        enemies⌋,
    great bolts of lightning and routed them.
15 The valleys of the sea were exposed
    and the foundations of the earth laid bare
    at your rebuke, O LORD,
    at the blast of breath from your nostrils.

16 He reached down from on high and took
        hold of me;
    he drew me out of deep waters.
17 He rescued me from my powerful enemy,
    from my foes, who were too strong for
        me.
18 They confronted me in the day of my
        disaster,
    but the LORD was my support.
19 He brought me out into a spacious place;
    he rescued me because he delighted in
        me.

20 The LORD has dealt with me according to my
        righteousness;
    according to the cleanness of my hands he
        has rewarded me.
21 For I have kept the ways of the LORD;
    I have not done evil by turning from my
        God.
22 All his laws are before me;
    I have not turned away from his decrees.
23 I have been blameless before him
    and have kept myself from sin.
24 The LORD has rewarded me according to my
        righteousness,
    according to the cleanness of my hands in
        his sight.

25 To the faithful you show yourself faithful,
    to the blameless you show yourself
        blameless,
26 to the pure you show yourself pure,

*a 13 Some Hebrew manuscripts and Septuagint (see also
2 Samuel 22:14); most Hebrew manuscripts resounded, /
amid hailstones and bolts of lightning*

THE MESSAGE

His nostrils flare, bellowing smoke;
    his mouth spits fire.
Tongues of fire dart in and out;
    he lowers the sky.
He steps down;
    under his feet an abyss opens up.
He's riding a winged creature,
    swift on wind-wings.
Now he's wrapped himself
    in a trenchcoat of black-cloud darkness.
But his cloud-brightness bursts through,
    spraying hailstones and fireballs.
Then GOD thundered out of heaven;
    the High God gave a great shout,
    spraying hailstones and fireballs.
God shoots his arrows—pandemonium!
    He hurls his lightnings—a rout!
The secret sources of ocean are exposed,
    the hidden depths of earth lie uncovered
The moment you roar in protest,
    let loose your hurricane anger.

18.16-19 But me he caught—reached all the way
        from sky to sea; he pulled me out
    Of that ocean of hate, that enemy chaos,
        the void in which I was drowning.
    They hit me when I was down,
        but GOD stuck by me.
    He stood me up on a wide-open field;
        I stood there saved—surprised to be loved!

18.20-24 GOD made my life complete
        when I placed all the pieces before him.
    When I got my act together,
        he gave me a fresh start.
    Now I'm alert to GOD's ways;
        I don't take God for granted.
    Every day I review the ways he works;
        I try not to miss a trick.
    I feel put back together,
        and I'm watching my step.
    GOD rewrote the text of my life
        when I opened the book of my heart to his
            eyes.

18.25-27 The good people taste your goodness,
    The whole people taste your health,
    The true people taste your truth,

NEW INTERNATIONAL VERSION

but to the crooked you show yourself
  shrewd.
27 You save the humble
  but bring low those whose eyes are
    haughty.
28 You, O LORD, keep my lamp burning;
  my God turns my darkness into light.
29 With your help I can advance against a
    troop*a*;
  with my God I can scale a wall.

30 As for God, his way is perfect;
  the word of the LORD is flawless.
He is a shield
  for all who take refuge in him.
31 For who is God besides the LORD?
  And who is the Rock except our God?
32 It is God who arms me with strength
  and makes my way perfect.
33 He makes my feet like the feet of a deer;
  he enables me to stand on the heights.
34 He trains my hands for battle;
  my arms can bend a bow of bronze.
35 You give me your shield of victory,
  and your right hand sustains me;
  you stoop down to make me great.
36 You broaden the path beneath me,
  so that my ankles do not turn.

37 I pursued my enemies and overtook them;
  I did not turn back till they were
    destroyed.
38 I crushed them so that they could not rise;
  they fell beneath my feet.
39 You armed me with strength for battle;
  you made my adversaries bow at my feet.
40 You made my enemies turn their backs in
    flight,
  and I destroyed my foes.
41 They cried for help, but there was no one to
    save them—
  to the LORD, but he did not answer.
42 I beat them as fine as dust borne on the
    wind;
  I poured them out like mud in the streets.

43 You have delivered me from the attacks of
    the people;
  you have made me the head of nations;
  people I did not know are subject to me.
44 As soon as they hear me, they obey me;
  foreigners cringe before me.
45 They all lose heart;
  they come trembling from their
    strongholds.

46 The LORD lives! Praise be to my Rock!
  Exalted be God my Savior!

a 29 Or can run through a barricade

THE MESSAGE

The bad ones can't figure you out.
You take the side of the down-and-out,
But the stuck-up you take down a peg.

18.28-29 Suddenly, GOD, you floodlight my life;
  I'm blazing with glory, God's glory!
I smash the bands of marauders,
  I vault the highest fences.

18.30 What a God! His road
  stretches straight and smooth.
Every GOD-direction is road-tested.
  Everyone who runs toward him
Makes it.

18.31-42 Is there any god like GOD?
  Are we not at bedrock?
Is not this the God who armed me,
  then aimed me in the right direction?
Now I run like a deer;
  I'm king of the mountain.
He shows me how to fight;
  I can bend a bronze bow!
You protect me with salvation-armor;
  you hold me up with a firm hand,
  caress me with your gentle ways.
You cleared the ground under me
  so my footing was firm.
When I chased my enemies I caught them;
  I didn't let go till they were dead men.
I nailed them; they were down for good;
  then I walked all over them.
You armed me well for this fight,
  you smashed the upstarts.
You made my enemies turn tail,
  and I wiped out the haters.
They cried "uncle"
  but Uncle didn't come;
They yelled for GOD
  and got no for an answer.
I ground them to dust; they gusted in the
    wind.
  I threw them out, like garbage in the gutter.

18.43-45 You rescued me from a squabbling people;
  you made me a leader of nations.
People I'd never heard of served me;
  the moment they got wind of me they
    listened.
The foreign devils gave up; they came
  on their bellies, crawling from their
    hideouts.

18.46-48 Live, GOD! Blessings from my Rock,
  my free and freeing God, towering!

NEW INTERNATIONAL VERSION

⁴⁷He is the God who avenges me,
    who subdues nations under me,
⁴⁸   who saves me from my enemies.
You exalted me above my foes;
    from violent men you rescued me.
⁴⁹Therefore I will praise you among the
        nations, O LORD;
    I will sing praises to your name.

⁵⁰He gives his king great victories;
    he shows unfailing kindness to his
        anointed,
    to David and his descendants forever.

PSALM 19

For the director of music. A psalm of David.

¹ The heavens declare the glory of God;
    the skies proclaim the work of his hands.
² Day after day they pour forth speech;
    night after night they display knowledge.
³ There is no speech or language
    where their voice is not heard.ᵃ
⁴ Their voiceᵇ goes out into all the earth,
    their words to the ends of the world.

    In the heavens he has pitched a tent for the
        sun,
⁵   which is like a bridegroom coming forth
        from his pavilion,
    like a champion rejoicing to run his
        course.
⁶ It rises at one end of the heavens
    and makes its circuit to the other;
    nothing is hidden from its heat.

⁷ The law of the LORD is perfect,
    reviving the soul.
    The statutes of the LORD are trustworthy,
        making wise the simple.
⁸ The precepts of the LORD are right,
    giving joy to the heart.
    The commands of the LORD are radiant,
        giving light to the eyes.
⁹ The fear of the LORD is pure,
    enduring forever.
    The ordinances of the LORD are sure
        and altogether righteous.
¹⁰ They are more precious than gold,
    than much pure gold;
    they are sweeter than honey,
        than honey from the comb.

THE MESSAGE

This God set things right for me
    and shut up the people who talked back.
He rescued me from enemy anger,
    he pulled me from the grip of upstarts,
He saved me from the bullies.

18.49-50 That's why I'm thanking you, GOD,
    all over the world.
That's why I'm singing songs
    that rhyme your name.
God's king takes the trophy;
    God's chosen is beloved.
I mean David and all his children—
    always.

A David psalm

19.1-2 **19** God's glory is on tour in the skies,
    God-craft on exhibit across the
        horizon.
Madame Day holds classes every morning,
    Professor Night lectures each evening.

19.3-4 Their words aren't heard,
    their voices aren't recorded,
But their silence fills the earth:
    unspoken truth is spoken everywhere.

19.4-5 God makes a huge dome
    for the sun—a superdome!
The morning sun's a new husband
    leaping from his honeymoon bed,
The daybreaking sun an athlete
    racing to the tape.

19.6 That's how God's Word vaults across the skies
    from sunrise to sunset,
Melting ice, scorching deserts,
    warming hearts to faith.

19.7-9 The revelation of GOD is whole
    and pulls our lives together.
The signposts of GOD are clear
    and point out the right road.
The life-maps of GOD are right,
    showing the way to joy.
The directions of GOD are plain
    and easy on the eyes.
GOD's reputation is twenty-four-carat gold,
    with a lifetime guarantee.
The decisions of GOD are accurate
    down to the nth degree.

19.10 God's Word is better than a diamond,
    better than a diamond set between
        emeralds.
You'll like it better than strawberries in spring,
    better than red, ripe strawberries.

ᵃ 3 Or *They have no speech, there are no words; / no sound is heard from them*   ᵇ 4 Septuagint, Jerome and Syriac; Hebrew *line*

NEW INTERNATIONAL VERSION

¹¹By them is your servant warned;
  in keeping them there is great reward.

¹²Who can discern his errors?
  Forgive my hidden faults.
¹³Keep your servant also from willful sins;
  may they not rule over me.
Then will I be blameless,
  innocent of great transgression.

¹⁴May the words of my mouth and the
    meditation of my heart
  be pleasing in your sight,
  O LORD, my Rock and my Redeemer.

PSALM 20

For the director of music. A psalm of David.

¹May the LORD answer you when you are in
    distress;
  may the name of the God of Jacob protect
    you.
²May he send you help from the sanctuary
  and grant you support from Zion.
³May he remember all your sacrifices
  and accept your burnt offerings.   *Selah*
⁴May he give you the desire of your heart
  and make all your plans succeed.
⁵We will shout for joy when you are
    victorious
  and will lift up our banners in the name
    of our God.
  May the LORD grant all your requests.

⁶Now I know that the LORD saves his
    anointed;
  he answers him from his holy heaven
  with the saving power of his right hand.
⁷Some trust in chariots and some in horses,
  but we trust in the name of the LORD our
    God.
⁸They are brought to their knees and fall,
  but we rise up and stand firm.

⁹O LORD, save the king!
  Answer^a us when we call!

PSALM 21

For the director of music. A psalm of David.

¹O LORD, the king rejoices in your strength.
  How great is his joy in the victories you
    give!
²You have granted him the desire of his heart

THE MESSAGE

^{19.11-14} There's more: God's Word warns us of danger
  and directs us to hidden treasure.
Otherwise how will we find our way?
  Or know when we play the fool?
Clean the slate, God, so we can start the day
    fresh!
  Keep me from stupid sins,
  from thinking I can take over your work;
Then I can start this day sun-washed,
  scrubbed clean of the grime of sin.
These are the words in my mouth;
  these are what I chew on and pray.
Accept them when I place them
  on the morning altar,
O God, my Altar-Rock,
  God, Priest-of-My-Altar.

A David psalm

^{20.1-4} **20** GOD answer you on the day you crash,
    The name God-of-Jacob put you out of
      harm's reach,
  Send reinforcements from Holy Hill,
  Dispatch from Zion fresh supplies,
  Exclaim over your offerings,
  Celebrate your sacrifices,
  Give you what your heart desires,
  Accomplish your plans.

^{20.5} When you win, we plan to raise the roof
    and lead the parade with our banners.
  May all your wishes come true!

^{20.6} That clinches it—help's coming,
    an answer's on the way,
    everything's going to work out.

^{20.7-8} See those people polishing their chariots,
    and those others grooming their horses?
  But we're making garlands for GOD our
      God.
  The chariots will rust,
    those horses pull up lame—
    and we'll be on our feet, standing tall.

^{20.9} Make the king a winner, GOD;
    the day we call, give us your answer.

A David psalm

^{21.1-7} **21** Your strength, GOD, is the king's
    strength.
  Helped, he's hollering Hosannas.
  You gave him exactly what he wanted;

NEW INTERNATIONAL VERSION	THE MESSAGE

NEW INTERNATIONAL VERSION

and have not withheld the request of his
lips.   *Selah*
³ You welcomed him with rich blessings
and placed a crown of pure gold on his
head.
⁴ He asked you for life, and you gave it to
him—
length of days, for ever and ever.
⁵ Through the victories you gave, his glory is
great;
you have bestowed on him splendor and
majesty.
⁶ Surely you have granted him eternal
blessings
and made him glad with the joy of your
presence.
⁷ For the king trusts in the LORD;
through the unfailing love of the Most
High
he will not be shaken.

⁸ Your hand will lay hold on all your enemies;
your right hand will seize your foes.
⁹ At the time of your appearing
you will make them like a fiery furnace.
In his wrath the LORD will swallow them up,
and his fire will consume them.
¹⁰ You will destroy their descendants from the
earth,
their posterity from mankind.
¹¹ Though they plot evil against you
and devise wicked schemes, they cannot
succeed;
¹² for you will make them turn their backs
when you aim at them with drawn bow.

¹³ Be exalted, O LORD, in your strength;
we will sing and praise your might.

PSALM 22

*For the director of music. To the tune of, "The
Doe of the Morning." A psalm of David.*

¹ My God, my God, why have you forsaken me?
Why are you so far from saving me,
so far from the words of my groaning?
² O my God, I cry out by day, but you do not
answer,
by night, and am not silent.

³ Yet you are enthroned as the Holy One;
you are the praise of Israel. ᵃ
⁴ In you our fathers put their trust;
they trusted and you delivered them.
⁵ They cried to you and were saved;
in you they trusted and were not
disappointed.

THE MESSAGE

you didn't hold back.
You filled his arms with gifts;
you gave him a right royal welcome.
He wanted a good life; you gave it to him,
and then made it a *long* life as a bonus.
You lifted him high and bright as a cumulus
cloud,
then dressed him in rainbow colors.
You pile blessings on him;
you make him glad when you smile.
Is it any wonder the king loves GOD?
that he's sticking with the Best?

21.8-12 With a fistful of enemies in one hand
and a fistful of haters in the other,
You radiate with such brilliance
that they cringe as before a furnace.
Now the furnace swallows them whole,
the fire eats them alive!
You purge the earth of their progeny,
you wipe the slate clean.
All their evil schemes, the plots they cook up,
have fizzled—every one.
You sent them packing;
they couldn't face you.

21.13 Show your strength, GOD, so no one can miss
it.
We are out singing the good news!

A David psalm

22.1-2 **22** God, God . . . my God!
Why did you dump me
miles from nowhere?
Doubled up with pain, I call to God
all the day long. No answer. Nothing.
I keep at it all night, tossing and turning.

22.3-5 And you! Are you indifferent, above it all,
leaning back on the cushions of Israel's
praise?
We know you were there for our parents:
they cried for your help and you gave it;
they trusted and lived a good life.

ᵃ 3 Or *Yet you are holy, / enthroned on the praises of Israel*

NEW INTERNATIONAL VERSION

⁶But I am a worm and not a man,
  scorned by men and despised by the
    people.
⁷All who see me mock me;
  they hurl insults, shaking their heads:
⁸"He trusts in the LORD;
  let the LORD rescue him.
 Let him deliver him,
  since he delights in him."

⁹Yet you brought me out of the womb;
  you made me trust in you
    even at my mother's breast.
¹⁰From birth I was cast upon you;
  from my mother's womb you have been
    my God.
¹¹Do not be far from me,
  for trouble is near
    and there is no one to help.

¹²Many bulls surround me;
  strong bulls of Bashan encircle me.
¹³Roaring lions tearing their prey
  open their mouths wide against me.
¹⁴I am poured out like water,
  and all my bones are out of joint.
 My heart has turned to wax;
  it has melted away within me.
¹⁵My strength is dried up like a potsherd,
  and my tongue sticks to the roof of my
    mouth;
 you lay me ᵃ in the dust of death.
¹⁶Dogs have surrounded me;
  a band of evil men has encircled me,
 they have pierced ᵇ my hands and my feet.
¹⁷I can count all my bones;
  people stare and gloat over me.
¹⁸They divide my garments among them
  and cast lots for my clothing.

¹⁹But you, O LORD, be not far off;
  O my Strength, come quickly to help me.
²⁰Deliver my life from the sword,
  my precious life from the power of the
    dogs.
²¹Rescue me from the mouth of the lions;
  save ᶜ me from the horns of the wild oxen.

²²I will declare your name to my brothers;
  in the congregation I will praise you.
²³You who fear the LORD, praise him!
  All you descendants of Jacob, honor him!
  Revere him, all you descendants of Israel!
²⁴For he has not despised or disdained
  the suffering of the afflicted one;

ᵃ 15 Or / I am laid   ᵇ 16 Some Hebrew manuscripts,
Septuagint and Syriac; most Hebrew manuscripts / like the
lion,   ᶜ 21 Or / you have heard

THE MESSAGE

22.6-8 And here I am, a nothing—an earthworm,
    something to step on, to squash.
 Everyone pokes fun at me;
    they make faces at me, they shake their
      heads:
 "Let's see how GOD handles this one;
    since God likes him so much, let *him* help
      him!"

22.9-11 And to think you were midwife at my birth,
    setting me at my mother's breasts!
 When I left the womb you cradled me;
    since the moment of birth you've been my
      God.
 Then you moved far away
    and trouble moved in next-door.
 I need a neighbor.

22.12-13 Herds of bulls come at me,
    the raging bulls stampede,
 Horns lowered, nostrils flaring,
    like a herd of buffalo on the move.

22.14-15 I'm a bucket kicked over and spilled,
    every joint in my body has been pulled
      apart.
 My heart is a blob
    of melted wax in my gut.
 I'm dry as a bone,
    my tongue black and swollen.
 They have laid me out for burial
    in the dirt.

22.16-18 Now packs of wild dogs come at me;
    thugs gang up on me.
 They pin me down hand and foot,
    and lock me in a cage—a bag
 Of bones in a cage, stared at
    by every passerby.
 They take my wallet and the shirt off my back,
    and then throw dice for my clothes.

22.19-21 You, GOD—don't put off my rescue!
    Hurry and help me!
 Don't let them cut my throat;
    don't let those mongrels devour me.
 If you don't show up soon,
    I'm done for—gored by the bulls,
      meat for the lions.

22.22-24 Here's the story I'll tell my friends when they
    come to worship,
    and punctuate it with Hallelujahs:
 Shout Hallelujah, you God-worshipers;
    give glory, you sons of Jacob;
    adore him, you daughters of Israel.
 He has never let you down,
    never looked the other way
    when you were being kicked around.

NEW INTERNATIONAL VERSION	THE MESSAGE

NEW INTERNATIONAL VERSION

he has not hidden his face from him
   but has listened to his cry for help.

25 From you comes the theme of my praise in
      the great assembly;
   before those who fear you[a] will I fulfill
     my vows.
26 The poor will eat and be satisfied;
   they who seek the LORD will praise him—
   may your hearts live forever!
27 All the ends of the earth
   will remember and turn to the LORD,
and all the families of the nations
   will bow down before him,
28 for dominion belongs to the LORD
   and he rules over the nations.

29 All the rich of the earth will feast and
     worship;
   all who go down to the dust will kneel
     before him—
   those who cannot keep themselves alive.
30 Posterity will serve him;
   future generations will be told about the
     Lord.
31 They will proclaim his righteousness
   to a people yet unborn—
   for he has done it.

PSALM 23

A psalm of David.

1 The LORD is my shepherd, I shall not be in
   want.
2   He makes me lie down in green pastures,
he leads me beside quiet waters,
3   he restores my soul.
He guides me in paths of righteousness
   for his name's sake.
4 Even though I walk
   through the valley of the shadow of
     death,[b]
I will fear no evil,
   for you are with me;
your rod and your staff,
   they comfort me.

5 You prepare a table before me
   in the presence of my enemies.

THE MESSAGE

He has never wandered off to do his own
     thing;
   he has been right there, listening.

22.25-26 Here in this great gathering for worship
   I have discovered this praise-life.
And I'll do what I promised right here
   in front of the God-worshipers.
Down-and-outers sit at GOD's table
   and eat their fill.
Everyone on the hunt for God
   is here, praising him.
"Live it up, from head to toe.
   Don't ever quit!"

22.27-28 From the four corners of the earth
   people are coming to their senses,
   are running back to GOD.
Long-lost families
   are falling on their faces before him.
GOD has taken charge;
   from now on he has the last word.

22.29 All the power-mongers are before him
     —worshiping!
All the poor and powerless, too
     —worshiping!
Along with those who never got it together
     —worshiping!

22.30-31 Our children and their children
   will get in on this
As the word is passed along
   from parent to child.
Babies not yet conceived
   will hear the good news—
   that God does what he says.

A David psalm

23.1-3 **23** GOD, my shepherd!
     I don't need a thing.
You have bedded me down in lush meadows,
   you find me quiet pools to drink from.
True to your word,
   you let me catch my breath
   and send me in the right direction.

23.4 Even when the way goes through
     Death Valley,
I'm not afraid
   when you walk at my side.
Your trusty shepherd's crook
   makes me feel secure.

23.5 You serve me a six-course dinner
   right in front of my enemies.

---

a 25 Hebrew *him*   *b 4* Or *through the darkest valley*

NEW INTERNATIONAL VERSION

You anoint my head with oil;
my cup overflows.
⁶ Surely goodness and love will follow me
all the days of my life,
and I will dwell in the house of the LORD
forever.

PSALM 24

Of David. A psalm.

¹ The earth is the LORD's, and everything in it,
the world, and all who live in it;
² for he founded it upon the seas
and established it upon the waters.

³ Who may ascend the hill of the LORD?
Who may stand in his holy place?
⁴ He who has clean hands and a pure heart,
who does not lift up his soul to an idol
or swear by what is false. ᵃ
⁵ He will receive blessing from the LORD
and vindication from God his Savior.
⁶ Such is the generation of those who seek
him,
who seek your face, O God of Jacob. ᵇ
Selah

⁷ Lift up your heads, O you gates;
be lifted up, you ancient doors,
that the King of glory may come in.
⁸ Who is this King of glory?
The LORD strong and mighty,
the LORD mighty in battle.
⁹ Lift up your heads, O you gates;
lift them up, you ancient doors,
that the King of glory may come in.
¹⁰ Who is he, this King of glory?
The LORD Almighty—
he is the King of glory. *Selah*

PSALM 25 ᶜ

Of David.

¹ To you, O LORD, I lift up my soul;
² in you I trust, O my God.
Do not let me be put to shame,
nor let my enemies triumph over me.
³ No one whose hope is in you
will ever be put to shame,
but they will be put to shame
who are treacherous without excuse.

ᵃ 4 Or *swear falsely*   ᵇ 6 Two Hebrew manuscripts and
Syriac (see also Septuagint); most Hebrew manuscripts *face,
Jacob*   ᶜ This psalm is an acrostic poem, the verses of
which begin with the successive letters of the Hebrew
alphabet.

THE MESSAGE

You revive my drooping head;
my cup brims with blessing.
23.6 Your beauty and love chase after me
every day of my life.
I'm back home in the house of GOD
for the rest of my life.

A David psalm

24.1-2 **24** GOD claims Earth and everything in it,
GOD claims World and all who live
on it.
He built it on Ocean foundations,
laid it out on River girders.

24.3-4 Who can climb Mount GOD?
Who can scale the holy north-face?
Only the clean-handed,
only the pure-hearted;
Men who won't cheat,
women who won't seduce.

24.5-6 GOD is at their side;
with GOD's help they make it.
This, Jacob, is what happens
to God-seekers, God-questers.

24.7 Wake up, you sleepyhead city!
Wake up, you sleepyhead people!
King-Glory is ready to enter.

24.8 Who is this King-Glory?
GOD, armed
and battle-ready.

24.9 Wake up, you sleepyhead city!
Wake up, you sleepyhead people!
King-Glory is ready to enter.

24.10 Who is this King-Glory?
GOD of the Angel Armies:
he is King-Glory.

A David psalm

25.1-2 **25** My head is high, GOD, held high;
I'm looking to you, GOD;
No hangdog skulking for me.

25.3 I've thrown in my lot with you;
You won't embarrass me, will you?
Or let my enemies get the best of me?

Don't embarrass any of us
Who went out on a limb for you.
It's the traitors who should be humiliated.

NEW INTERNATIONAL VERSION

⁴Show me your ways, O LORD,
   teach me your paths;
⁵guide me in your truth and teach me,
   for you are God my Savior,
   and my hope is in you all day long.
⁶Remember, O LORD, your great mercy and
      love,
   for they are from of old.
⁷Remember not the sins of my youth
   and my rebellious ways;
according to your love remember me,
   for you are good, O LORD.

⁸Good and upright is the LORD;
   therefore he instructs sinners in his ways.
⁹He guides the humble in what is right
   and teaches them his way.
¹⁰All the ways of the LORD are loving and
      faithful
   for those who keep the demands of his
      covenant.
¹¹For the sake of your name, O LORD,
   forgive my iniquity, though it is great.
¹²Who, then, is the man that fears the LORD?
   He will instruct him in the way chosen for
      him.
¹³He will spend his days in prosperity,
   and his descendants will inherit the land.
¹⁴The LORD confides in those who fear him;
   he makes his covenant known to them.
¹⁵My eyes are ever on the LORD,
   for only he will release my feet from the
      snare.

¹⁶Turn to me and be gracious to me,
   for I am lonely and afflicted.
¹⁷The troubles of my heart have multiplied;
   free me from my anguish.
¹⁸Look upon my affliction and my distress
   and take away all my sins.
¹⁹See how my enemies have increased
   and how fiercely they hate me!
²⁰Guard my life and rescue me;
   let me not be put to shame,
   for I take refuge in you.
²¹May integrity and uprightness protect me,
   because my hope is in you.

²²Redeem Israel, O God,
   from all their troubles!

THE MESSAGE

25.4 Show me how you work, GOD;
   School me in your ways.

25.5 Take me by the hand;
   Lead me down the path of truth.
   You are my Savior, aren't you?

25.6 Mark the milestones of your mercy and love,
      GOD;
   Rebuild the ancient landmarks!

25.7 Forget that I sowed wild oats;
   Mark me with your sign of love.
   Plan only the best for me, GOD!

25.8 GOD is fair and just;
   He corrects the misdirected,
   Sends them in the right direction.

25.9 He gives the rejects his hand,
   And leads them step-by-step.

25.10 From now on every road you travel
   Will take you to GOD.
   Follow the Covenant signs;
   Read the charted directions.

25.11 Keep up your reputation, GOD;
   Forgive my bad life;
   It's been a very bad life.

25.12 My question: What are God-worshipers like?
   Your answer: Arrows aimed at God's bull's-eye.

25.13 They settle down in a promising place;
   Their kids inherit a prosperous farm.

25.14 God-friendship is for God-worshipers;
   They are the ones he confides in.

25.15 If I keep my eyes on GOD,
   I won't trip over my own feet.

25.16 Look at me and help me!
   I'm all alone and in big trouble.

25.17 My heart and kidneys are fighting each other;
   Call a truce to this civil war.

25.18 Take a hard look at my life of hard labor,
   Then lift this ton of sin.

25.19 Do you see how many people
   Have it in for me?
   How viciously they hate me?

25.20 Keep watch over me and keep me out of
      trouble;
   Don't let me down when I run to you.

25.21 Use all your skill to put me together;
   I wait to see your finished product.

25.22 GOD, give your people a break
   From this run of bad luck.

NEW INTERNATIONAL VERSION

PSALM 26

Of David.

1 Vindicate me, O LORD,
  for I have led a blameless life;
 I have trusted in the LORD
  without wavering.
2 Test me, O LORD, and try me,
  examine my heart and my mind;
3 for your love is ever before me,
  and I walk continually in your truth.
4 I do not sit with deceitful men,
  nor do I consort with hypocrites;
5 I abhor the assembly of evildoers
  and refuse to sit with the wicked.
6 I wash my hands in innocence,
  and go about your altar, O LORD,
7 proclaiming aloud your praise
  and telling of all your wonderful deeds.
8 I love the house where you live, O LORD,
  the place where your glory dwells.

9 Do not take away my soul along with
   sinners,
  my life with bloodthirsty men,
10 in whose hands are wicked schemes,
  whose right hands are full of bribes.
11 But I lead a blameless life;
  redeem me and be merciful to me.

12 My feet stand on level ground;
  in the great assembly I will praise the
  LORD.

PSALM 27

Of David.

1 The LORD is my light and my salvation—
  whom shall I fear?
 The LORD is the stronghold of my life—
  of whom shall I be afraid?
2 When evil men advance against me
  to devour my flesh,[a]
 when my enemies and my foes attack me,
  they will stumble and fall.
3 Though an army besiege me,
  my heart will not fear;
 though war break out against me,
  even then will I be confident.

a 2 Or to slander me

THE MESSAGE

A David psalm

26.1 **26** Clear my name, GOD;
   I've kept an honest shop.
 I've thrown in my lot with you, GOD, and
  I'm not budging.

26.2 Examine me, GOD, from head to foot,
  order your battery of tests.
 Make sure I'm fit
  inside and out

26.3 So I never lose
  sight of your love,
 But keep in step with you,
  never missing a beat.

26.4-5 I don't hang out with tricksters,
  I don't pal around with thugs;
 I hate that pack of gangsters,
  I don't deal with double-dealers.

26.6-7 I scrub my hands with purest soap,
  then join hands with the others in the great
   circle,
  dancing around your altar, GOD,
 Singing God-songs at the top of my lungs,
  telling God-stories.

26.8-10 GOD, I love living with you;
  your house glows with your glory.
 When it's time for spring cleaning,
  don't sweep me out with the quacks and
   crooks,
 Men with bags of dirty tricks,
  women with purses stuffed with bribe-
   money.

26.11-12 You know I've been aboveboard with you;
  now be aboveboard with me.
 I'm on the level with you, GOD;
  I bless you every chance I get.

A David psalm

27.1 **27** Light, space, zest—
   that's GOD!
 So, with him on my side I'm fearless,
  afraid of no one and nothing.

27.2 When vandal hordes ride down
  ready to eat me alive,
 Those bullies and toughs
  fall flat on their faces.

27.3 When besieged,
  I'm calm as a baby.
 When all hell breaks loose,
  I'm collected and cool.

NEW INTERNATIONAL VERSION

⁴ One thing I ask of the LORD,
   this is what I seek:
that I may dwell in the house of the LORD
   all the days of my life,
to gaze upon the beauty of the LORD
   and to seek him in his temple.
⁵ For in the day of trouble
   he will keep me safe in his dwelling;
he will hide me in the shelter of his
      tabernacle
   and set me high upon a rock.
⁶ Then my head will be exalted
   above the enemies who surround me;
at his tabernacle will I sacrifice with shouts
      of joy;
   I will sing and make music to the LORD.

⁷ Hear my voice when I call, O LORD;
   be merciful to me and answer me.
⁸ My heart says of you, "Seek his ᵃ face!"
   Your face, LORD, I will seek.
⁹ Do not hide your face from me,
   do not turn your servant away in anger;
   you have been my helper.
Do not reject me or forsake me,
   O God my Savior.
¹⁰ Though my father and mother forsake me,
   the LORD will receive me.
¹¹ Teach me your way, O LORD;
   lead me in a straight path
   because of my oppressors.
¹² Do not turn me over to the desire of my foes,
   for false witnesses rise up against me,
   breathing out violence.

¹³ I am still confident of this:
   I will see the goodness of the LORD
   in the land of the living.
¹⁴ Wait for the LORD;
   be strong and take heart
   and wait for the LORD.

PSALM 28

Of David.

¹ To you I call, O LORD my Rock;
   do not turn a deaf ear to me.
For if you remain silent,
   I will be like those who have gone down
      to the pit.
² Hear my cry for mercy
   as I call to you for help,

ᵃ 8 Or *To you, O my heart, he has said, "Seek my*

THE MESSAGE

27.4 I'm asking GOD for one thing,
   only one thing:
To live with him in his house
   my whole life long.
I'll contemplate his beauty;
   I'll study at his feet.

27.5 That's the only quiet, secure place
   in a noisy world,
The perfect getaway,
   far from the buzz of traffic.

27.6 God holds me head and shoulders
   above all who try to pull me down.
I'm headed for his place to offer anthems
   that will raise the roof!
Already I'm singing God-songs;
   I'm making music to GOD.

27.7-9 Listen, GOD, I'm calling at the top of my
      lungs:
   "Be good to me! Answer me!"
When my heart whispered, "Seek God,"
   my whole being replied,
   "I'm seeking him!"
Don't hide from me now!

27.9-10 You've always been right there for me;
   don't turn your back on me now.
Don't throw me out, don't abandon me;
   you've always kept the door open.
My father and mother walked out and left me,
   but GOD took me in.

27.11-12 Point me down your highway, GOD;
   direct me along a well-lighted street;
   show my enemies whose side you're on.
Don't throw me to the dogs,
   those liars who are out to get me,
   filling the air with their threats.

27.13-14 I'm sure now I'll see God's goodness
   in the exuberant earth.
Stay with GOD!
   Take heart. Don't quit.
I'll say it again:
   Stay with GOD.

A David psalm

28.1 **28** Don't turn a deaf ear
         when I call you, GOD.
If all I get from you is
   deafening silence,
I'd be better off
   in the Black Hole.

28.2 I'm letting you know what I need,
   calling out for help

NEW INTERNATIONAL VERSION

as I lift up my hands
   toward your Most Holy Place.

3 Do not drag me away with the wicked,
   with those who do evil,
who speak cordially with their neighbors
   but harbor malice in their hearts.
4 Repay them for their deeds
   and for their evil work;
repay them for what their hands have done
   and bring back upon them what they
     deserve.
5 Since they show no regard for the works of
     the LORD
   and what his hands have done,
he will tear them down
   and never build them up again.

6 Praise be to the LORD,
   for he has heard my cry for mercy.
7 The LORD is my strength and my shield;
   my heart trusts in him, and I am helped.
My heart leaps for joy
   and I will give thanks to him in song.

8 The LORD is the strength of his people,
   a fortress of salvation for his anointed
     one.
9 Save your people and bless your inheritance;
   be their shepherd and carry them forever.

PSALM 29

A psalm of David.

1 Ascribe to the LORD, O mighty ones,
   ascribe to the LORD glory and strength.
2 Ascribe to the LORD the glory due his name;
   worship the LORD in the splendor of his[a]
     holiness.

3 The voice of the LORD is over the waters;
   the God of glory thunders,
   the LORD thunders over the mighty
     waters.
4 The voice of the LORD is powerful;
   the voice of the LORD is majestic.
5 The voice of the LORD breaks the cedars;
   the LORD breaks in pieces the cedars of
     Lebanon.
6 He makes Lebanon skip like a calf,
   Sirion[b] like a young wild ox.

THE MESSAGE

And lifting my arms
   toward your inner sanctum.

28.3-4 Don't shove me into
   the same jail cell with those crooks,
With those who are
   full-time employees of evil.
They talk a good line of "peace,"
   then moonlight for the Devil.

Pay them back for what they've done,
   for how bad they've been.
Pay them back for their long hours
   in the Devil's workshop;
Then cap it with a huge bonus.

28.5 Because they have no idea how God works
   or what he is up to,
God will smash them to smithereens
   and walk away from the ruins.

28.6-7 Blessed be GOD—
   he heard me praying.
He proved he's on my side;
   I've thrown my lot in with him.

Now I'm jumping for joy,
   and shouting and singing my thanks to
     him.

28.8-9 GOD is all strength for his people,
   ample refuge for his chosen leader;
Save your people
   and bless your heritage.
Care for them;
   carry them like a good shepherd.

A David psalm

29.1-2 **29** Bravo, GOD, bravo!
   Gods and all angels shout, "Encore!"
In awe before the glory,
   in awe before God's visible power.
Stand at attention!
   Dress your best to honor him!

29.3 GOD thunders across the waters,
Brilliant, his voice and his face, streaming
     brightness—
   GOD, across the flood waters.

29.4 GOD's thunder tympanic,
   GOD's thunder symphonic.

29.5 GOD's thunder smashes cedars,
   GOD topples the northern cedars.

29.6 The mountain ranges skip like spring colts,
   The high ridges jump like wild kid goats.

---

a 2 Or LORD with the splendor of   b 6 That is, Mount
Hermon

NEW INTERNATIONAL VERSION

⁷The voice of the LORD strikes
   with flashes of lightning.
⁸The voice of the LORD shakes the desert;
   the LORD shakes the Desert of Kadesh.
⁹The voice of the LORD twists the oaks*ᵃ*
   and strips the forests bare.
   And in his temple all cry, "Glory!"

¹⁰The LORD sits*ᵇ* enthroned over the flood;
   the LORD is enthroned as King forever.
¹¹The LORD gives strength to his people;
   the LORD blesses his people with peace.

PSALM 30

*A psalm. A song. For the dedication of the
   temple.ᶜ Of David.*

¹I will exalt you, O LORD,
   for you lifted me out of the depths
   and did not let my enemies gloat over me.
²O LORD my God, I called to you for help
   and you healed me.
³O LORD, you brought me up from the grave*ᵈ*;
   you spared me from going down into the
      pit.

⁴Sing to the LORD, you saints of his;
   praise his holy name.
⁵For his anger lasts only a moment,
   but his favor lasts a lifetime;
weeping may remain for a night,
   but rejoicing comes in the morning.

⁶When I felt secure, I said,
   "I will never be shaken."
⁷O LORD, when you favored me,
   you made my mountain*ᵉ* stand firm;
but when you hid your face,
   I was dismayed.

⁸To you, O LORD, I called;
   to the Lord I cried for mercy:
⁹"What gain is there in my destruction,*ᶠ*
   in my going down into the pit?
Will the dust praise you?
   Will it proclaim your faithfulness?
¹⁰Hear, O LORD, and be merciful to me;
   O LORD, be my help."

¹¹You turned my wailing into dancing;
   you removed my sackcloth and clothed
      me with joy,
¹²that my heart may sing to you and not be silent.
   O LORD my God, I will give you thanks
      forever.

*ᵃ 9 Or LORD makes the deer give birth   ᵇ 10 Or sat
ᶜ Title: Or palace   ᵈ 3 Hebrew Sheol   ᵉ 7 Or hill country
ᶠ 9 Or there if I am silenced*

THE MESSAGE

29.7-8 GOD's thunder spits fire.
   GOD thunders, the wilderness quakes;
   He makes the desert of Kadesh shake.

29.9 GOD's thunder sets the oak trees dancing
   A wild dance, whirling; the pelting rain strips
      their branches.
   We fall to our knees—we call out, "Glory!"

29.10 Above the floodwaters is GOD's throne
   from which his power flows,
   from which he rules the world.

29.11 GOD makes his people strong.
   GOD gives his people peace.

A David psalm

30.1 **30** I give you all the credit, GOD—
   you got me out of that mess,
   you didn't let my foes gloat.

30.2-3 GOD, my God, I yelled for help
   and you put me together.
   GOD, you pulled me out of the grave,
   gave me another chance at life
   when I was down-and-out.

30.4-5 All you saints! Sing your hearts out to GOD!
   Thank him to his face!
   He gets angry once in a while, but across
   a lifetime there is only love.
   The nights of crying your eyes out
   give way to days of laughter.

30.6-7 When things were going great
   I crowed, "I've got it made.
   I'm GOD's favorite.
   He made me king of the mountain."
   Then you looked the other way
   and I fell to pieces.

30.8-10 I called out to you, GOD;
   I laid my case before you:
   "Can you sell me for a profit when I'm dead?
   auction me off at a cemetery yard sale?
   When I'm 'dust to dust' my songs
   and stories of you won't sell.
   So listen! and be kind!
   Help me out of this!"

30.11-12 You did it: you changed wild lament
   into whirling dance;
   You ripped off my black mourning band
   and decked me with wildflowers.
   I'm about to burst with song;
   I can't keep quiet about you.
   GOD, my God,
   I can't thank you enough.

NEW INTERNATIONAL VERSION

PSALM 31

For the director of music. A psalm of David.

[1] In you, O LORD, I have taken refuge;
    let me never be put to shame;
    deliver me in your righteousness.
[2] Turn your ear to me,
    come quickly to my rescue;
  be my rock of refuge,
    a strong fortress to save me.
[3] Since you are my rock and my fortress,
    for the sake of your name lead and
        guide me.
[4] Free me from the trap that is set for me,
    for you are my refuge.
[5] Into your hands I commit my spirit;
    redeem me, O LORD, the God of truth.

[6] I hate those who cling to worthless idols;
    I trust in the LORD.
[7] I will be glad and rejoice in your love,
    for you saw my affliction
    and knew the anguish of my soul.
[8] You have not handed me over to the enemy
    but have set my feet in a spacious place.

[9] Be merciful to me, O LORD, for I am in
        distress;
    my eyes grow weak with sorrow,
    my soul and my body with grief.
[10] My life is consumed by anguish
    and my years by groaning;
  my strength fails because of my affliction,[a]
    and my bones grow weak.
[11] Because of all my enemies,
    I am the utter contempt of my neighbors;
  I am a dread to my friends—
    those who see me on the street flee
        from me.
[12] I am forgotten by them as though I were
        dead;
    I have become like broken pottery.
[13] For I hear the slander of many;
    there is terror on every side;
  they conspire against me
    and plot to take my life.

[14] But I trust in you, O LORD;
    I say, "You are my God."
[15] My times are in your hands;
    deliver me from my enemies
    and from those who pursue me.
[16] Let your face shine on your servant;
    save me in your unfailing love.
[17] Let me not be put to shame, O LORD,
    for I have cried out to you;
  but let the wicked be put to shame

---

a 10 Or guilt

THE MESSAGE

A David psalm

31.1-2 **31** I run to you, GOD; I run for dear life.
        Don't let me down!
    Take me seriously this time!
Get down on my level and listen,
    and please—no procrastination!
Your granite cave a hiding place,
    your high cliff aerie a place of safety.

31.3-5 You're my cave to hide in,
    my cliff to climb.
Be my safe leader,
    be my true mountain guide.
Free me from hidden traps;
    I want to hide in you.
I've put my life in your hands.
    You won't drop me,
    you'll never let me down.

31.6-13 I hate all this silly religion,
    but you, GOD, I trust.
I'm leaping and singing in the circle of your
        love;
    you saw my pain,
    you disarmed my tormentors,
You didn't leave me in their clutches
    but gave me room to breathe.
Be kind to me, GOD—
    I'm in deep, deep trouble again.
I've cried my eyes out;
    I feel hollow inside.
My life leaks away, groan by groan;
    my years fade out in sighs.
My troubles have worn me out,
    turned my bones to powder.
To my enemies I'm a monster;
    I'm ridiculed by the neighbors.
My friends are horrified;
    they cross the street to avoid me.
They want to blot me from memory,
    forget me like a corpse in a grave,
    discard me like a broken dish in the trash.
The street-talk gossip has me
    "criminally insane"!
Behind locked doors they plot
    how to ruin me for good.

31.14-18 Desperate, I throw myself on you:
    you are my God!
Hour by hour I place my days in your hand,
    safe from the hands out to get me.
Warm me, your servant, with a smile;
    save me because you love me.
Don't embarrass me by not showing up;
    I've given you plenty of notice.
Embarrass the wicked, stand them up,
    leave them stupidly shaking their heads

NEW INTERNATIONAL VERSION

and lie silent in the grave.*ᵃ*
¹⁸ Let their lying lips be silenced,
    for with pride and contempt
    they speak arrogantly against the
        righteous.

¹⁹ How great is your goodness,
    which you have stored up for those who
        fear you,
  which you bestow in the sight of men
    on those who take refuge in you.
²⁰ In the shelter of your presence you hide
        them
    from the intrigues of men;
  in your dwelling you keep them safe
    from accusing tongues.

²¹ Praise be to the LORD,
    for he showed his wonderful love to me
    when I was in a besieged city.
²² In my alarm I said,
    "I am cut off from your sight!"
  Yet you heard my cry for mercy
    when I called to you for help.

²³ Love the LORD, all his saints!
    The LORD preserves the faithful,
    but the proud he pays back in full.
²⁴ Be strong and take heart,
    all you who hope in the LORD.

PSALM 32

Of David. A *maskil.*ᵇ

¹ Blessed is he
    whose transgressions are forgiven,
    whose sins are covered.
² Blessed is the man
    whose sin the LORD does not count
        against him
    and in whose spirit is no deceit.

³ When I kept silent,
    my bones wasted away
    through my groaning all day long.
⁴ For day and night
    your hand was heavy upon me;
  my strength was sapped
    as in the heat of summer.   *Selah*
⁵ Then I acknowledged my sin to you
    and did not cover up my iniquity.
  I said, "I will confess
    my transgressions to the LORD"—
  and you forgave
    the guilt of my sin.   *Selah*

THE MESSAGE

as they drift down to hell.
Gag those loudmouthed liars
    who heckle me, your follower,
    with jeers and catcalls.

31.19-22 What a stack of blessing you have piled up
    for those who worship you,
Ready and waiting for all who run to you
    to escape an unkind world.
You hide them safely away
    from the opposition.
As you slam the door on those oily, mocking
        faces,
    you silence the poisonous gossip.
Blessed GOD!
    His love is the wonder of the world.
Trapped by a siege, I panicked.
    "Out of sight, out of mind," I said.
But you heard me say it,
    you heard and listened.

31.23 Love GOD, all you saints;
    GOD takes care of all who stay close to him,
But he pays back in full
    those arrogant enough to go it alone.

31.24 Be brave. Be strong. Don't give up.
    Expect GOD to get here soon.

A David psalm

32.1 **32** Count yourself lucky, how happy you
        must be—
you get a fresh start,
    your slate's wiped clean.

32.2 Count yourself lucky—
    GOD holds nothing against you
    and you're holding nothing back from him.

32.3 When I kept it all inside,
    my bones turned to powder,
    my words became daylong groans.

32.4 The pressure never let up;
    all the juices of my life dried up.

32.5 Then I let it all out;
    I said, "I'll make a clean breast of my
        failures to GOD."

Suddenly the pressure was gone—
    my guilt dissolved,
    my sin disappeared.

ᵃ 17 Hebrew *Sheol*   *ᵇ* Title: Probably a literary or musical term

NEW INTERNATIONAL VERSION

⁶Therefore let everyone who is godly pray to
    you
    while you may be found;
surely when the mighty waters rise,
    they will not reach him.
⁷You are my hiding place;
    you will protect me from trouble
    and surround me with songs of
        deliverance.   *Selah*

⁸I will instruct you and teach you in the way
    you should go;
    I will counsel you and watch over you.
⁹Do not be like the horse or the mule,
    which have no understanding
but must be controlled by bit and bridle
    or they will not come to you.
¹⁰Many are the woes of the wicked,
    but the LORD's unfailing love
    surrounds the man who trusts in him.

¹¹Rejoice in the LORD and be glad, you
    righteous;
    sing, all you who are upright in heart!

PSALM 33

¹Sing joyfully to the LORD, you righteous;
    it is fitting for the upright to praise him.
²Praise the LORD with the harp;
    make music to him on the ten-stringed
        lyre.
³Sing to him a new song;
    play skillfully, and shout for joy.

⁴For the word of the LORD is right and true;
    he is faithful in all he does.
⁵The LORD loves righteousness and justice;
    the earth is full of his unfailing love.

⁶By the word of the LORD were the heavens
    made,
    their starry host by the breath of his
        mouth.
⁷He gathers the waters of the sea into jars^{*a*};
    he puts the deep into storehouses.
⁸Let all the earth fear the LORD;
    let all the people of the world revere him.
⁹For he spoke, and it came to be;
    he commanded, and it stood firm.
¹⁰The LORD foils the plans of the nations;
    he thwarts the purposes of the peoples.
¹¹But the plans of the LORD stand firm forever,
    the purposes of his heart through all
        generations.

¹²Blessed is the nation whose God is the LORD,
    the people he chose for his inheritance.

a 7 Or sea as into a heap

THE MESSAGE

32.6 These things add up. Every one of us needs to
    pray;
    when all hell breaks loose and the dam
        bursts
    we'll be on high ground, untouched.

32.7 GOD's my island hideaway,
    keeps danger far from the shore,
    throws garlands of hosannas around my
        neck.

32.8 Let me give you some good advice;
    I'm looking you in the eye
    and giving it to you straight:

32.9 "Don't be ornery like a horse or mule
    that needs bit and bridle
    to stay on track."

32.10 God-defiers are always in trouble;
    GOD-affirmers find themselves loved
    every time they turn around.

32.11 Celebrate GOD.
    Sing together—everyone!
    All you honest hearts, raise the roof!

33.1-3 **33** Good people, cheer GOD!
    Right-living people sound best when
        praising.
Use guitars to reinforce your Hallelujahs!
    Play his praise on a grand piano!
Invent your own new song to him;
    give him a trumpet fanfare.

33.4-5 For GOD's Word is solid to the core;
    everything he makes is sound inside and
        out.
He loves it when everything fits,
    when his world is in plumb-line true.
Earth is drenched
    in GOD's affectionate satisfaction.

33.6-7 The skies were made by GOD's command;
    he breathed the word and the stars popped
        out.
He scooped Sea into his jug,
    put Ocean in his keg.

33.8-9 Earth-creatures, bow before GOD;
    world-dwellers—down on your knees!
Here's why: he spoke and there it was,
    in place the moment he said so.

33.10-12 GOD takes the wind out of Babel pretense,
    he shoots down the world's power-schemes.
GOD's plan for the world stands up,
    all his designs are made to last.
Blessed is the country with GOD for God;
    blessed are the people he's put in his will.

NEW INTERNATIONAL VERSION

13 From heaven the LORD looks down
   and sees all mankind;
14 from his dwelling place he watches
   all who live on earth—
15 he who forms the hearts of all,
   who considers everything they do.
16 No king is saved by the size of his army;
   no warrior escapes by his great strength.
17 A horse is a vain hope for deliverance;
   despite all its great strength it cannot
   save.
18 But the eyes of the LORD are on those who
   fear him,
   on those whose hope is in his unfailing
   love,
19 to deliver them from death
   and keep them alive in famine.

20 We wait in hope for the LORD;
   he is our help and our shield.
21 In him our hearts rejoice,
   for we trust in his holy name.
22 May your unfailing love rest upon us,
   O LORD,
   even as we put our hope in you.

PSALM 34 [a]

Of David. When he pretended to be insane before
Abimelech, who drove him away, and he left.

1 I will extol the LORD at all times;
   his praise will always be on my lips.
2 My soul will boast in the LORD;
   let the afflicted hear and rejoice.
3 Glorify the LORD with me;
   let us exalt his name together.

4 I sought the LORD, and he answered me;
   he delivered me from all my fears.
5 Those who look to him are radiant;
   their faces are never covered with shame.
6 This poor man called, and the LORD heard
   him;
   he saved him out of all his troubles.
7 The angel of the LORD encamps around those
   who fear him,
   and he delivers them.

8 Taste and see that the LORD is good;
   blessed is the man who takes refuge in
   him.
9 Fear the LORD, you his saints,
   for those who fear him lack nothing.

[a] This psalm is an acrostic poem, the verses of which begin
with the successive letters of the Hebrew alphabet.

THE MESSAGE

33.13-15 From high in the skies GOD looks around,
   he sees all Adam's brood.
   From where he sits
   he overlooks all us earth-dwellers.
   He has shaped each person in turn;
   now he watches everything we do.

33.16-17 No king succeeds with a big army alone,
   no warrior wins by brute strength.
   Horsepower is not the answer;
   no one gets by on muscle alone.

33.18-19 Watch this: God's eye is on those who respect
   him,
   the ones who are looking for his love.
   He's ready to come to their rescue in bad
   times;
   in lean times he keeps body and soul
   together.

33.20-22 We're depending on GOD;
   he's everything we need.
   What's more, our hearts brim with joy
   since we've taken for our own his holy
   name.
   Love us, GOD, with all you've got—
   that's what we're depending on.

A David psalm, when he outwitted Abimelech
and got away.

34.1 **34** I bless GOD every chance I get;
   my lungs expand with his praise.

34.2 I live and breathe GOD;
   if things aren't going well, hear this and be
   happy:

34.3 Join me in spreading the news;
   together let's get the word out.

34.4 GOD met me more than halfway,
   he freed me from my anxious fears.

34.5 Look at him; give him your warmest smile.
   Never hide your feelings from him.

34.6 When I was desperate, I called out,
   and GOD got me out of a tight spot.

34.7 GOD's angel sets up a circle
   of protection around us while we pray.

34.8 Open your mouth and taste, open your eyes
   and see—
   how good GOD is.
   Blessed are you who run to him.

34.9 Worship GOD if you want the best;
   worship opens doors to all his goodness.

NEW INTERNATIONAL VERSION

[10] The lions may grow weak and hungry,
 but those who seek the LORD lack no good
  thing.

[11] Come, my children, listen to me;
 I will teach you the fear of the LORD.
[12] Whoever of you loves life
 and desires to see many good days,
[13] keep your tongue from evil
 and your lips from speaking lies.
[14] Turn from evil and do good;
 seek peace and pursue it.

[15] The eyes of the LORD are on the righteous
 and his ears are attentive to their cry;
[16] the face of the LORD is against those who do
  evil,
  to cut off the memory of them from the
   earth.

[17] The righteous cry out, and the LORD hears
  them;
  he delivers them from all their troubles.
[18] The LORD is close to the brokenhearted
 and saves those who are crushed in spirit.

[19] A righteous man may have many troubles,
 but the LORD delivers him from them all;
[20] he protects all his bones,
 not one of them will be broken.

[21] Evil will slay the wicked;
 the foes of the righteous will be
  condemned.
[22] The LORD redeems his servants;
 no one will be condemned who takes
  refuge in him.

PSALM 35

Of David.

[1] Contend, O LORD, with those who contend
  with me;
  fight against those who fight against me.
[2] Take up shield and buckler;
 arise and come to my aid.
[3] Brandish spear and javelin[a]
 against those who pursue me.
 Say to my soul,
  "I am your salvation."

[4] May those who seek my life
 be disgraced and put to shame;
 may those who plot my ruin
 be turned back in dismay.
[5] May they be like chaff before the wind,
 with the angel of the LORD driving them
  away;

THE MESSAGE

34.10 Young lions on the prowl get hungry,
 but GOD-seekers are full of God.

34.11 Come, children, listen closely;
 I'll give you a lesson in GOD worship.

34.12 Who out there has a lust for life?
 Can't wait each day to come upon beauty?

34.13 Guard your tongue from profanity,
 and no more lying through your teeth.

34.14 Turn your back on sin; do something good.
 Embrace peace—don't let it get away!

34.15 GOD keeps an eye on his friends,
 his ears pick up every moan and groan.

34.16 GOD won't put up with rebels;
 he'll cull them from the pack.

34.17 Is anyone crying for help? GOD is listening,
 ready to rescue you.

34.18 If your heart is broken, you'll find GOD right
  there;
  if you're kicked in the gut, he'll help you catch
   your breath.

34.19 Disciples so often get into trouble;
 still, GOD is there every time.

34.20 He's your bodyguard, shielding every bone;
 not even a finger gets broken.

34.21 The wicked commit slow suicide;
 they waste their lives hating the good.

34.22 GOD pays for each slave's freedom;
 no one who runs to him loses out.

A David psalm

35.1-3 **35** Harass these hecklers, GOD,
  punch these bullies in the nose.
 Grab a weapon, anything at hand;
  stand up for me!
 Get ready to throw the spear, aim the javelin,
  at the people who are out to get me.
 Reassure me; let me hear you say,
  "I'll save you."

35.4-8 When those thugs try to knife me in the back,
 make them look foolish.
 Frustrate all those
 who are plotting my downfall.
 Make them like cinders in a high wind,
  with GOD's angel working the bellows.

---

a 3 Or and block the way

NEW INTERNATIONAL VERSION	THE MESSAGE

NEW INTERNATIONAL VERSION

⁶may their path be dark and slippery,
  with the angel of the LORD pursuing them.
⁷Since they hid their net for me without cause
  and without cause dug a pit for me,
⁸may ruin overtake them by surprise—
  may the net they hid entangle them,
  may they fall into the pit, to their ruin.
⁹Then my soul will rejoice in the LORD
  and delight in his salvation.
¹⁰My whole being will exclaim,
  "Who is like you, O LORD?
You rescue the poor from those too strong
    for them,
  the poor and needy from those who rob
    them."

¹¹Ruthless witnesses come forward;
  they question me on things I know
    nothing about.
¹²They repay me evil for good
  and leave my soul forlorn.
¹³Yet when they were ill, I put on sackcloth
  and humbled myself with fasting.
When my prayers returned to me
    unanswered,
¹⁴ I went about mourning
    as though for my friend or brother.
  I bowed my head in grief
    as though weeping for my mother.
¹⁵But when I stumbled, they gathered in glee;
  attackers gathered against me when I was
    unaware.
  They slandered me without ceasing.
¹⁶Like the ungodly they maliciously mocked[a];
  they gnashed their teeth at me.
¹⁷O Lord, how long will you look on?
  Rescue my life from their ravages,
  my precious life from these lions.
¹⁸I will give you thanks in the great assembly;
  among throngs of people I will praise you.

¹⁹Let not those gloat over me
  who are my enemies without cause;
let not those who hate me without reason
  maliciously wink the eye.
²⁰They do not speak peaceably,
  but devise false accusations
  against those who live quietly in the land.
²¹They gape at me and say, "Aha! Aha!
  With our own eyes we have seen it."

THE MESSAGE

Make their road lightless and mud-slick,
  with GOD's angel on their tails.
Out of sheer cussedness they set a trap to
    catch me;
  for no good reason they dug a ditch to
    stop me.
Surprise them with your ambush—
  catch them in the very trap they set,
  the disaster they planned for me.

35:9-10 But let me run loose and free,
  celebrating GOD's great work,
Every bone in my body laughing, singing,
  "GOD,
    there's no one like you.
You put the down-and-out on their feet
  and protect the unprotected from bullies!"

35:11-12 Hostile accusers appear out of nowhere,
  they stand up and badger me.
They pay me back misery for mercy,
  leaving my soul empty.

35:13-14 When they were sick, I dressed in black;
  instead of eating, I prayed.
My prayers were like lead in my gut,
  like I'd lost my best friend, my brother.
I paced, distraught as a motherless child,
  hunched and heavyhearted.

35:15-16 But when I was down
  they threw a party!
All the nameless riffraff of the town came
  chanting insults about me.
Like barbarians desecrating a shrine,
  they destroyed my reputation.

35:17-18 GOD, how long are you going
  to stand there doing nothing?
Save me from their brutalities;
  everything I've got is being thrown to the
    lions.
I will give you full credit
  when everyone gathers for worship;
When the people turn out in force
  I will say my Hallelujahs.

35:19-21 Don't let these liars, my enemies,
  have a party at my expense,
Those who hate me for no reason,
  winking and rolling their eyes.
No good is going to come
  from that crowd;
They spend all their time cooking up gossip
  against those who mind their own business.
They open their mouths
  in ugly grins,
Mocking, "Ha-ha, ha-ha, thought you'd get
    away with it?
  We've caught you hands down!"

---

a 16 Septuagint; Hebrew may mean *ungodly circle of
mockers.*

NEW INTERNATIONAL VERSION

²² O Lord, you have seen this; be not silent.
  Do not be far from me, O Lord.
²³ Awake, and rise to my defense!
  Contend for me, my God and Lord.
²⁴ Vindicate me in your righteousness, O Lord
    my God;
  do not let them gloat over me.
²⁵ Do not let them think, "Aha, just what we
    wanted!"
  or say, "We have swallowed him up."

²⁶ May all who gloat over my distress
  be put to shame and confusion;
  may all who exalt themselves over me
  be clothed with shame and disgrace.
²⁷ May those who delight in my vindication
  shout for joy and gladness;
  may they always say, "The Lord be exalted,
  who delights in the well-being of his
    servant."
²⁸ My tongue will speak of your righteousness
  and of your praises all day long.

PSALM 36

For the director of music. Of David the servant
of the Lord.

¹ An oracle is within my heart
  concerning the sinfulness of the wicked: ᵃ
There is no fear of God
  before his eyes.
² For in his own eyes he flatters himself
  too much to detect or hate his sin.
³ The words of his mouth are wicked and
    deceitful;
  he has ceased to be wise and to do good.
⁴ Even on his bed he plots evil;
  he commits himself to a sinful course
  and does not reject what is wrong.

⁵ Your love, O Lord, reaches to the heavens,
  your faithfulness to the skies.
⁶ Your righteousness is like the mighty
    mountains,
  your justice like the great deep.

THE MESSAGE

35.22 Don't you see what they're doing, God?
  You're not going to let them
  Get by with it, are you? Not going to walk off
  without *doing* something, are you?

35.23-26 Please get up—wake up! Tend to my case.
  My God, my Lord—my life is on the line.
  Do what you think is right, God, my God,
  but don't make me pay for their good time.
  Don't let them say to themselves,
    "Ha-ha, we got what we wanted."
  Don't let them say,
    "We've chewed him up and spit him out."
  Let those who are being hilarious
  at my expense
  Be made to look ridiculous.
  Make them wear donkey's ears;
  Pin them with the donkey's tail,
  who made themselves so high and mighty!

35.27-28 But those who want
  the best for me,
  Let them have the last word—a glad shout!—
  and say, over and over and over,
    "God is great—everything works
  together for good for his servant."
  I'll tell the world how great and good you are,
  I'll shout Hallelujah all day, every day.

A David psalm

36.1-4 **36** The God-rebel tunes in to sedition—
    all ears, eager to sin.
  He has no regard for God,
  he stands insolent before him.
  He has smooth-talked himself
  into believing
  That his evil
  will never be noticed.
  Words gutter from his mouth,
  dishwater dirty.
  Can't remember when he
  did anything decent.
  Every time he goes to bed,
  he fathers another evil plot.
  When he's loose on the streets,
  nobody's safe.
  He plays with fire
  and doesn't care who gets burned.

36.5-6 God's love is meteoric,
  his loyalty astronomic,
  His purpose titanic,
  his verdicts oceanic.
  Yet in his largeness
  nothing gets lost;

ᵃ 1 Or *heart: / Sin proceeds from the wicked.*

NEW INTERNATIONAL VERSION

O LORD, you preserve both man and beast.
7 How priceless is your unfailing love!
Both high and low among men
  find*ª* refuge in the shadow of your wings.
8 They feast on the abundance of your house;
  you give them drink from your river of
    delights.
9 For with you is the fountain of life;
  in your light we see light.

10 Continue your love to those who know you,
  your righteousness to the upright in
    heart.
11 May the foot of the proud not come against
    me,
  nor the hand of the wicked drive me away.
12 See how the evildoers lie fallen—
  thrown down, not able to rise!

PSALM 37*ᵇ*

Of David.

1 Do not fret because of evil men
  or be envious of those who do wrong;
2 for like the grass they will soon wither,
  like green plants they will soon die away.

3 Trust in the LORD and do good;
  dwell in the land and enjoy safe pasture.
4 Delight yourself in the LORD
  and he will give you the desires of your
    heart.

5 Commit your way to the LORD;
  trust in him and he will do this:
6 He will make your righteousness shine like
    the dawn,
  the justice of your cause like the noonday
    sun.

7 Be still before the LORD and wait patiently for
    him;
  do not fret when men succeed in their
    ways,
  when they carry out their wicked schemes.

8 Refrain from anger and turn from wrath;
  do not fret—it leads only to evil.
9 For evil men will be cut off,
  but those who hope in the LORD will
    inherit the land.

10 A little while, and the wicked will be no
    more;
  though you look for them, they will not
    be found.

THE MESSAGE

Not a man, not a mouse,
  slips through the cracks.

36.7-9 How exquisite your love, O God!
  How eager we are to run under your wings,
To eat our fill at the banquet you spread
  as you fill our tankards with Eden spring
    water.
You're a fountain of cascading light,
  and you open our eyes to light.

36.10-12 Keep on loving your friends;
  do your work in welcoming hearts.
Don't let the bullies kick me around,
  the moral midgets slap me down.
Send the upstarts sprawling
  flat on their faces in the mud.

A David psalm

37.1-2 **37** Don't bother your head with braggarts
  or wish you could succeed like the
    wicked.
In no time they'll shrivel like grass clippings
  and wilt like cut flowers in the sun.

37.3-4 Get insurance with GOD and do a good deed,
  settle down and stick to your last.
Keep company with GOD,
  get in on the best.

37.5-6 Open up before GOD, keep nothing back;
  he'll do whatever needs to be done:
He'll validate your life in the clear light of day
  and stamp you with approval at high noon.

37.7 Quiet down before GOD,
  be prayerful before him.
Don't bother with those who climb the ladder,
  who elbow their way to the top.

37.8-9 Bridle your anger, trash your wrath,
  cool your pipes—it only makes things
    worse.
Before long the crooks will be bankrupt;
  GOD-investors will soon own the store.

37.10-11 Before you know it, the wicked will have
    had it;
  you'll stare at his once famous place and—
    nothing!

---

*ª 7 Or love, O God! / Men find; or love! / Both heavenly beings
and men / find   ᵇ This psalm is an acrostic poem, the
stanzas of which begin with the successive letters of the
Hebrew alphabet.*

NEW INTERNATIONAL VERSION

¹¹ But the meek will inherit the land
    and enjoy great peace.

¹² The wicked plot against the righteous
    and gnash their teeth at them;
¹³ but the Lord laughs at the wicked,
    for he knows their day is coming.

¹⁴ The wicked draw the sword
    and bend the bow
  to bring down the poor and needy,
    to slay those whose ways are upright.
¹⁵ But their swords will pierce their own hearts,
    and their bows will be broken.

¹⁶ Better the little that the righteous have
    than the wealth of many wicked;
¹⁷ for the power of the wicked will be broken,
    but the Lord upholds the righteous.

¹⁸ The days of the blameless are known to the
    Lord,
    and their inheritance will endure forever.
¹⁹ In times of disaster they will not wither;
    in days of famine they will enjoy plenty.

²⁰ But the wicked will perish:
    The Lord's enemies will be like the beauty
      of the fields,
    they will vanish—vanish like smoke.

²¹ The wicked borrow and do not repay,
    but the righteous give generously;
²² those the Lord blesses will inherit the land,
    but those he curses will be cut off.

²³ If the Lord delights in a man's way,
    he makes his steps firm;
²⁴ though he stumble, he will not fall,
    for the Lord upholds him with his hand.

²⁵ I was young and now I am old,
    yet I have never seen the righteous forsaken
    or their children begging bread.
²⁶ They are always generous and lend freely;
    their children will be blessed.

²⁷ Turn from evil and do good;
    then you will dwell in the land forever.
²⁸ For the Lord loves the just
    and will not forsake his faithful ones.

They will be protected forever,
    but the offspring of the wicked will be cut
      off;
²⁹ the righteous will inherit the land
    and dwell in it forever.

³⁰ The mouth of the righteous man utters
    wisdom,
    and his tongue speaks what is just.
³¹ The law of his God is in his heart;
    his feet do not slip.

THE MESSAGE

Down-to-earth people will move in and take
    over,
    relishing a huge bonanza.

37.12-13 Bad guys have it in for the good guys,
    obsessed with doing them in.
But God isn't losing any sleep; to him
    they're a joke with no punch line.

37.14-15 Bullies brandish their swords,
    pull back on their bows with a flourish.
They're out to beat up on the harmless,
    or mug that nice man out walking his dog.
A banana peel lands them flat on their faces—
    slapstick figures in a moral circus.

37.16-17 Less is more and more is less.
    One righteous will outclass fifty wicked,
For the wicked are moral weaklings
    but the righteous are God-strong.

37.18-19 God keeps track of the decent folk;
    what they do won't soon be forgotten.
In hard times, they'll hold their heads high;
    when the shelves are bare, they'll be full.

37.20 God-despisers have had it;
    God's enemies are finished—
Stripped bare like vineyards at harvest time,
    vanished like smoke in thin air.

37.21-22 Wicked borrows and never returns;
    Righteous gives and gives.
Generous gets it all in the end;
    Stingy is cut off at the pass.

37.23-24 Stalwart walks in step with God;
    his path blazed by God, he's happy.
If he stumbles, he's not down for long;
    God has a grip on his hand.

37.25-26 I once was young, now I'm a graybeard—
    not once have I seen an abandoned believer,
    or his kids out roaming the streets.
Every day he's out giving and lending,
    his children making him proud.

37.27-28 Turn your back on evil,
    work for the good and don't quit.
God loves this kind of thing,
    never turns away from his friends.

37.28-29 Live this way and you've got it made,
    but bad eggs will be tossed out.
The good get planted on good land
    and put down healthy roots.

37.30-31 Righteous chews on wisdom like a dog on a
    bone,
    rolls virtue around on his tongue.
His heart pumps God's Word like blood
    through his veins;
    his feet are as sure as a cat's.

NEW INTERNATIONAL VERSION

³² The wicked lie in wait for the righteous,
  seeking their very lives;
³³ but the LORD will not leave them in their
    power
  or let them be condemned when brought
    to trial.

³⁴ Wait for the LORD
  and keep his way.
He will exalt you to inherit the land;
  when the wicked are cut off, you will
    see it.

³⁵ I have seen a wicked and ruthless man
  flourishing like a green tree in its native
    soil,
³⁶ but he soon passed away and was no more;
  though I looked for him, he could not be
    found.

³⁷ Consider the blameless, observe the upright;
  there is a future *a* for the man of peace.
³⁸ But all sinners will be destroyed;
  the future *b* of the wicked will be cut off.

³⁹ The salvation of the righteous comes from
    the LORD;
  he is their stronghold in time of trouble.
⁴⁰ The LORD helps them and delivers them;
  he delivers them from the wicked and
    saves them,
  because they take refuge in him.

PSALM 38

A psalm of David. A petition.

¹ O LORD, do not rebuke me in your anger
  or discipline me in your wrath.
² For your arrows have pierced me,
  and your hand has come down upon me.
³ Because of your wrath there is no health in
    my body;
  my bones have no soundness because of
    my sin.
⁴ My guilt has overwhelmed me
  like a burden too heavy to bear.

⁵ My wounds fester and are loathsome
  because of my sinful folly.
⁶ I am bowed down and brought very low;
  all day long I go about mourning.
⁷ My back is filled with searing pain;
  there is no health in my body.
⁸ I am feeble and utterly crushed;
  I groan in anguish of heart.

⁹ All my longings lie open before you, O Lord;
  my sighing is not hidden from you.

a 37 Or there will be posterity   *b 38 Or posterity*

THE MESSAGE

^{37.32-33} Wicked sets a watch for Righteous,
  he's out for the kill.
GOD, alert, is also on watch—
  Wicked won't hurt a hair of his head.

^{37.34} Wait passionately for GOD,
  don't leave the path.
He'll give you your place in the sun
  while you watch the wicked lose it.

^{37.35-36} I saw Wicked bloated like a toad,
  croaking pretentious nonsense.
The next time I looked there was nothing—
  a punctured bladder, vapid and limp.

^{37.37-38} Keep your eye on the healthy soul,
  scrutinize the straight life;
There's a future
  in strenuous wholeness.
But the willful will soon be discarded;
  insolent souls are on a dead-end street.

^{37.39-40} The spacious, free life is from GOD,
  it's also protected and safe.
GOD-strengthened, we're delivered from evil—
  when we run to him, he saves us.

A David psalm

^{38.1-2} **38** Take a deep breath, GOD; calm down—
  don't be so hasty with your punishing
    rod.
Your sharp-pointed arrows of rebuke draw
    blood;
  my backside smarts from your caning.

^{38.3-4} I've lost twenty pounds in two months
  because of your accusation.
My bones are brittle as dry sticks
  because of my sin.
I'm swamped by my bad behavior,
  collapsed under gunnysacks of guilt.

^{38.5-8} The cuts in my flesh stink and grow maggots
  because I've lived so badly.
And now I'm flat on my face
  feeling sorry for myself morning to night.
All my insides are on fire,
  my body is a wreck.
I'm on my last legs; I've had it—
  my life is a vomit of groans.

^{38.9-16} Lord, my longings are sitting in plain sight,
  my groans an old story to you.

NEW INTERNATIONAL VERSION

¹⁰ My heart pounds, my strength fails me;
  even the light has gone from my eyes.
¹¹ My friends and companions avoid me
    because of my wounds;
  my neighbors stay far away.
¹² Those who seek my life set their traps,
  those who would harm me talk of my
    ruin;
  all day long they plot deception.

¹³ I am like a deaf man, who cannot hear,
  like a mute, who cannot open his mouth;
¹⁴ I have become like a man who does not hear,
  whose mouth can offer no reply.
¹⁵ I wait for you, O LORD;
  you will answer, O Lord my God.
¹⁶ For I said, "Do not let them gloat
  or exalt themselves over me when my foot
    slips."

¹⁷ For I am about to fall,
  and my pain is ever with me.
¹⁸ I confess my iniquity;
  I am troubled by my sin.
¹⁹ Many are those who are my vigorous
    enemies;
  those who hate me without reason are
    numerous.
²⁰ Those who repay my good with evil
  slander me when I pursue what is good.

²¹ O LORD, do not forsake me;
  be not far from me, O my God.
²² Come quickly to help me,
  O Lord my Savior.

PSALM 39

For the director of music. For Jeduthun. A psalm
of David.

¹ I said, "I will watch my ways
  and keep my tongue from sin;
  I will put a muzzle on my mouth
  as long as the wicked are in my presence."
² But when I was silent and still,
  not even saying anything good,
  my anguish increased.
³ My heart grew hot within me,
  and as I meditated, the fire burned;
  then I spoke with my tongue:

⁴ "Show me, O LORD, my life's end
  and the number of my days;
  let me know how fleeting is my life.
⁵ You have made my days a mere handbreadth;
  the span of my years is as nothing before
    you.
  Each man's life is but a breath.   *Selah*

THE MESSAGE

My heart's about to break;
  I'm a burned-out case.
Cataracts blind me to God and good;
  old friends avoid me like the plague.
My cousins never visit,
  my neighbors stab me in the back.
My competitors blacken my name,
  devoutly they pray for my ruin.
But I'm deaf and mute to it all,
  ears shut, mouth shut.
I don't hear a word they say,
  don't speak a word in response.
What I do, GOD, is wait for you,
  wait for my Lord, my God—you *will*
    answer!
I wait and pray so they won't laugh me off,
  won't smugly strut off when I stumble.

38:17-20 I'm on the edge of losing it—
  the pain in my gut keeps burning.
I'm ready to tell my story of failure,
  I'm no longer smug in my sin.
My enemies are alive and in action,
  a lynch mob after my neck.
I give out good and get back evil
  from God-haters who can't stand a God-
    lover.

38:21-22 Don't dump me, GOD;
  my God, don't stand me up.
Hurry and help me;
  I want some wide-open space in my life!

A David psalm

39:1-3 **39** I'm determined to watch steps and
    tongue
  so they won't land me in trouble.
I decided to hold my tongue
  as long as Wicked is in the room.
"Mum's the word," I said, and kept quiet.
  But the longer I kept silence
The worse it got—
  my insides got hotter and hotter.
My thoughts boiled over;
  I spilled my guts.

39:4-6 "Tell me, what's going on, GOD?
  How long do I have to live?
  Give me the bad news!
You've kept me on pretty short rations;
  my life is string too short to be saved.

NEW INTERNATIONAL VERSION

⁶Man is a mere phantom as he goes to and
      fro:
    He bustles about, but only in vain;
    he heaps up wealth, not knowing who
        will get it.

⁷"But now, Lord, what do I look for?
    My hope is in you.
⁸Save me from all my transgressions;
    do not make me the scorn of fools.
⁹I was silent; I would not open my mouth,
    for you are the one who has done this.
¹⁰Remove your scourge from me;
    I am overcome by the blow of your hand.
¹¹You rebuke and discipline men for their sin;
    you consume their wealth like a moth—
    each man is but a breath.   *Selah*

¹²"Hear my prayer, O LORD,
    listen to my cry for help;
    be not deaf to my weeping.
  For I dwell with you as an alien,
    a stranger, as all my fathers were.
¹³Look away from me, that I may rejoice again
    before I depart and am no more."

PSALM 40

For the director of music. Of David. A psalm.

¹I waited patiently for the LORD;
    he turned to me and heard my cry.
²He lifted me out of the slimy pit,
    out of the mud and mire;
  he set my feet on a rock
    and gave me a firm place to stand.
³He put a new song in my mouth,
    a hymn of praise to our God.
  Many will see and fear
    and put their trust in the LORD.

⁴Blessed is the man
    who makes the LORD his trust,
  who does not look to the proud,
    to those who turn aside to false gods.*ᵃ*
⁵Many, O LORD my God,
    are the wonders you have done.
  The things you planned for us
    no one can recount to you;
  were I to speak and tell of them,
    they would be too many to declare.

⁶Sacrifice and offering you did not desire,
    but my ears you have pierced*ᵇ, ᶜ*;

THE MESSAGE

  Oh! we're all puffs of air.
    Oh! we're all shadows in a campfire.
  Oh! we're just spit in the wind.
    We make our pile, and then we leave it.

39.7-11 "What am I doing in the meantime, Lord?
    Hoping, that's what I'm doing—hoping
  You'll save me from a rebel life,
    save me from the contempt of dunces.
  I'll say no more, I'll shut my mouth,
    since you, Lord, are behind all this.
    But I can't take it much longer.
  When you put us through the fire
    to purge us from our sin,
    our dearest idols go up in smoke.
  Are we also nothing but smoke?

39.12-13 "Ah, GOD, listen to my prayer, my
      cry—open your ears.
  Don't be callous;
    just look at these tears of mine.
  I'm a stranger here. I don't know my way—
    a migrant like my whole family.
  Give me a break, cut me some slack
    before it's too late and I'm out of here."

A David psalm

40.1-3 **40** I waited and waited and waited for GOD.
        At last he looked; finally he listened.
  He lifted me out of the ditch,
    pulled me from deep mud.
  He stood me up on a solid rock
    to make sure I wouldn't slip.
  He taught me how to sing the latest God-song,
    a praise-song to our God.
  More and more people are seeing this:
    they enter the mystery,
    abandoning themselves to GOD.

40.4-5 Blessed are you who give yourselves over to
        GOD,
    turn your backs on the world's "sure
        thing,"
  ignore what the world worships;
  The world's a huge stockpile
    of GOD-wonders and God-thoughts.
  Nothing and no one
    comes close to you!
  I start talking about you, telling what I know,
    and quickly run out of words.
  Neither numbers nor words
    account for you.

40.6 Doing something for you, bringing something
        to you—
    that's not what you're after.
  Being religious, acting pious—

ᵃ 4 Or *to falsehood*   *ᵇ 6* Hebrew; Septuagint *but a body you
have prepared for me* (see also Symmachus and Theodotion)
ᶜ 6 Or *opened*

NEW INTERNATIONAL VERSION

burnt offerings and sin offerings
    you did not require.
⁷Then I said, "Here I am, I have come—
    it is written about me in the scroll. *ᵃ*
⁸I desire to do your will, O my God;
    your law is within my heart."

⁹I proclaim righteousness in the great
        assembly;
    I do not seal my lips,
        as you know, O LORD.
¹⁰I do not hide your righteousness in my
        heart;
    I speak of your faithfulness and salvation.
    I do not conceal your love and your truth
        from the great assembly.

¹¹Do not withhold your mercy from me,
        O LORD;
    may your love and your truth always
        protect me.
¹²For troubles without number surround me;
    my sins have overtaken me, and I cannot
        see.
    They are more than the hairs of my head,
        and my heart fails within me.

¹³Be pleased, O LORD, to save me;
    O LORD, come quickly to help me.
¹⁴May all who seek to take my life
        be put to shame and confusion;
    may all who desire my ruin
        be turned back in disgrace.
¹⁵May those who say to me, "Aha! Aha!"
        be appalled at their own shame.
¹⁶But may all who seek you
        rejoice and be glad in you;
    may those who love your salvation always
        say,
        "The LORD be exalted!"

¹⁷Yet I am poor and needy;
    may the Lord think of me.
    You are my help and my deliverer;
        O my God, do not delay.

THE MESSAGE

that's not what you're asking for.
You've opened my ears
    so I can listen.

40.7-8 So I answered, "I'm coming.
    I read in your letter what you wrote
        about me,
And I'm coming to the party
    you're throwing for me."
That's when God's Word entered my life,
    became part of my very being.

40.9-10 I've preached you to the whole congregation,
    I've kept back nothing, GOD—you know
        that.
I didn't keep the news of your ways
    a secret, didn't keep it to myself.
I told it all, how dependable you are, how
        thorough.
    I didn't hold back pieces of love and truth
For myself alone. I told it all,
    let the congregation know the whole story.

40.11-12 Now GOD, don't hold out on me,
    don't hold back your passion.
Your love and truth
    are all that keeps me together.
When troubles ganged up on me,
    a mob of sins past counting,
I was so swamped by guilt
    I couldn't see my way clear.
More guilt in my heart than hair on my head,
    so heavy the guilt that my heart gave out.

40.13-15 Soften up, GOD, and intervene;
    hurry and get me some help,
So those who are trying to kidnap my soul
    will be embarrassed and lose face,
So anyone who gets a kick out of making me
        miserable
    will be heckled and disgraced,
So those who pray for my ruin
    will be booed and jeered without mercy.

40.16-17 But all who are hunting for you—
    oh, let them sing and be happy.
Let those who know what you're all about
    tell the world you're great and not quitting.
And me? I'm a mess. I'm nothing and have
        nothing:
    make something of me.
You can do it; you've got what it takes—
    but God, don't put it off.

ᵃ 7 Or come / with the scroll written for me

NEW INTERNATIONAL VERSION

PSALM 41

For the director of music. A psalm of David.

¹Blessed is he who has regard for the weak;
  the LORD delivers him in times of trouble.
²The LORD will protect him and preserve his
    life;
  he will bless him in the land
  and not surrender him to the desire of his
    foes.
³The LORD will sustain him on his sickbed
  and restore him from his bed of illness.

⁴I said, "O LORD, have mercy on me;
  heal me, for I have sinned against you."
⁵My enemies say of me in malice,
  "When will he die and his name perish?"
⁶Whenever one comes to see me,
  he speaks falsely, while his heart gathers
    slander;
  then he goes out and spreads it abroad.

⁷All my enemies whisper together against me;
  they imagine the worst for me, saying,
⁸"A vile disease has beset him;
  he will never get up from the place where
    he lies."
⁹Even my close friend, whom I trusted,
  he who shared my bread,
  has lifted up his heel against me.

¹⁰But you, O LORD, have mercy on me;
  raise me up, that I may repay them.
¹¹I know that you are pleased with me,
  for my enemy does not triumph over me.
¹²In my integrity you uphold me
  and set me in your presence forever.

¹³Praise be to the LORD, the God of Israel,
  from everlasting to everlasting.
    Amen and Amen.

THE MESSAGE

A David psalm

41 ⁴¹·¹⁻³ Dignify those who are down on their
    luck;
  you'll feel good—*that's* what GOD does.
GOD looks after us all,
  makes us robust with life—
Lucky to be in the land,
  we're free from enemy worries.
Whenever we're sick and in bed,
  GOD becomes our nurse,
  nurses us back to health.

⁴¹·⁴⁻⁷ I said, "GOD, be gracious!
  Put me together again—
  my sins have torn me to pieces."
My enemies are wishing the worst for me;
  they make bets on what day I will die.
If someone comes to see me,
  he mouths empty platitudes,
All the while gathering gossip about me
  to entertain the street-corner crowd.
These "friends" who hate me
  whisper slanders all over town.
They form committees
  to plan misery for me.

⁴¹·⁸⁻⁹ The rumor goes out, "He's got some dirty,
    deadly disease. The doctors
  have given up on him."
Even my best friend, the one I always told
    everything
  —he ate meals at my house all the time!—
  has bitten my hand.

⁴¹·¹⁰ GOD, give grace, get me up on my feet.
  I'll show them a thing or two.

⁴¹·¹¹⁻¹² Meanwhile, I'm sure you're on my side—
  no victory shouts yet from the enemy
    camp!
You know me inside and out, you hold me
    together,
  you never fail to stand me tall in your
    presence
  so I can look you in the eye.

⁴¹·¹³ Blessed is GOD, Israel's God,
  always, always, always.
  Yes. Yes. Yes.

NEW INTERNATIONAL VERSION

BOOK II

Psalms 42–72

PSALM 42 [a]

For the director of music. A *maskil* [b] of the Sons
of Korah.

[1] As the deer pants for streams of water,
so my soul pants for you, O God.
[2] My soul thirsts for God, for the living God.
When can I go and meet with God?
[3] My tears have been my food
day and night,
while men say to me all day long,
"Where is your God?"
[4] These things I remember
as I pour out my soul:
how I used to go with the multitude,
leading the procession to the house of
God,
with shouts of joy and thanksgiving
among the festive throng.

[5] Why are you downcast, O my soul?
Why so disturbed within me?
Put your hope in God,
for I will yet praise him,
my Savior and [6] my God.

My [c] soul is downcast within me;
therefore I will remember you
from the land of the Jordan,
the heights of Hermon—from Mount
Mizar.
[7] Deep calls to deep
in the roar of your waterfalls;
all your waves and breakers
have swept over me.

[8] By day the LORD directs his love,
at night his song is with me—
a prayer to the God of my life.

[9] I say to God my Rock,
"Why have you forgotten me?
Why must I go about mourning,
oppressed by the enemy?"
[10] My bones suffer mortal agony
as my foes taunt me,
saying to me all day long,
"Where is your God?"

THE MESSAGE

A psalm of the sons of Korah

42.1-3 **42** A white-tailed deer drinks
from the creek;
I want to drink God,
deep draughts of God.
I'm thirsty for God-alive.
I wonder, "Will I ever make it—
arrive and drink in God's presence?"
I'm on a diet of tears—
tears for breakfast, tears for supper.
All day long
people knock at my door,
Pestering,
"Where is this God of yours?"

42.4 These are the things I go over and over,
emptying out the pockets of my life.
I was always at the head of the worshiping
crowd,
right out in front,
Leading them all,
eager to arrive and worship,
Shouting praises, singing thanksgiving—
celebrating, all of us, God's feast!

42.5 Why are you down in the dumps, dear soul?
Why are you crying the blues?
Fix my eyes on God—
soon I'll be praising again.
He puts a smile on my face.
He's my God.

42.6-8 When my soul is in the dumps, I rehearse
everything I know of you,
From Jordan depths to Hermon heights,
including Mount Mizar.
Chaos calls to chaos,
to the tune of whitewater rapids.
Your breaking surf, your thundering breakers
crash and crush me.
Then GOD promises to love me all day,
sing songs all through the night!
My life is God's prayer.

42.9-10 Sometimes I ask God, my rock-solid God,
"Why did you let me down?
Why am I walking around in tears,
harassed by enemies?"
They're out for the kill, these
tormentors with their obscenities,
Taunting day after day,
"Where is this God of yours?"

---

[a] In many Hebrew manuscripts Psalms 42 and 43 constitute
one psalm.   [b] Title: Probably a literary or musical term
[c] 5,6 A few Hebrew manuscripts, Septuagint and Syriac;
most Hebrew manuscripts *praise him for his saving help.* /
[6]*O my God, my*

NEW INTERNATIONAL VERSION

[11] Why are you downcast, O my soul?
  Why so disturbed within me?
Put your hope in God,
  for I will yet praise him,
  my Savior and my God.

PSALM 43 [a]

[1] Vindicate me, O God,
  and plead my cause against an ungodly
    nation;
  rescue me from deceitful and wicked men.
[2] You are God my stronghold.
  Why have you rejected me?
Why must I go about mourning,
  oppressed by the enemy?
[3] Send forth your light and your truth,
  let them guide me;
let them bring me to your holy mountain,
  to the place where you dwell.
[4] Then will I go to the altar of God,
  to God, my joy and my delight.
I will praise you with the harp,
  O God, my God.

[5] Why are you downcast, O my soul?
  Why so disturbed within me?
Put your hope in God,
  for I will yet praise him,
  my Savior and my God.

PSALM 44

For the director of music. Of the Sons of Korah.
A *maskil.* [b]

[1] We have heard with our ears, O God;
  our fathers have told us
what you did in their days,
  in days long ago.
[2] With your hand you drove out the nations
  and planted our fathers;
you crushed the peoples
  and made our fathers flourish.
[3] It was not by their sword that they won the
    land,
  nor did their arm bring them victory;
it was your right hand, your arm,
  and the light of your face, for you loved
    them.

[4] You are my King and my God,
  who decrees [c] victories for Jacob.

[a] In many Hebrew manuscripts Psalms 42 and 43 constitute
one psalm.   [b] Title: Probably a literary or musical term
[c] 4 Septuagint, Aquila and Syriac; Hebrew *King, O God; /
command*

THE MESSAGE

42.11 Why are you down in the dumps, dear soul?
  Why are you crying the blues?
Fix my eyes on God—
  soon I'll be praising again.
He puts a smile on my face.
  He's my God.

43.1-2 **43** Clear my name, God; stick up for me
    against these loveless, immoral people.
Get me out of here, away
  from these lying degenerates.
I counted on you, God.
  Why did you walk out on me?
Why am I pacing the floor, wringing my
    hands
  over these outrageous people?

43.3-4 Give me your lantern and compass,
  give me a map,
So I can find my way to the sacred mountain,
  to the place of your presence,
To enter the place of worship,
  meet my exuberant God,
Sing my thanks with a harp,
  magnificent God, my God.

43.5 Why are you down in the dumps, dear soul?
  Why are you crying the blues?
Fix my eyes on God—
  soon I'll be praising again.
He puts a smile on my face.
  He's my God.

A psalm of the sons of Korah

44.1-3 **44** We've been hearing about this, God,
    all our lives.
Our fathers told us the stories
  their fathers told them,
How single-handedly you weeded out the
    godless
  from the fields and planted us,
How you sent those people packing
  but gave us a fresh start.
We didn't fight for this land;
  we didn't work for it—it was a gift!
You gave it, smiling as you gave it,
  delighting as you gave it.

44.4-8 You're my King, O God—
  command victories for Jacob!

NEW INTERNATIONAL VERSION

⁵ Through you we push back our enemies;
    through your name we trample our foes.
⁶ I do not trust in my bow,
    my sword does not bring me victory;
⁷ but you give us victory over our enemies,
    you put our adversaries to shame.
⁸ In God we make our boast all day long,
    and we will praise your name forever.
                    Selah

⁹ But now you have rejected and humbled us;
    you no longer go out with our armies.
¹⁰ You made us retreat before the enemy,
    and our adversaries have plundered us.
¹¹ You gave us up to be devoured like sheep
    and have scattered us among the nations.
¹² You sold your people for a pittance,
    gaining nothing from their sale.

¹³ You have made us a reproach to our
      neighbors,
    the scorn and derision of those around us.
¹⁴ You have made us a byword among the
      nations;
    the peoples shake their heads at us.
¹⁵ My disgrace is before me all day long,
    and my face is covered with shame
¹⁶ at the taunts of those who reproach and
      revile me,
    because of the enemy, who is bent on
      revenge.

¹⁷ All this happened to us,
    though we had not forgotten you
    or been false to your covenant.
¹⁸ Our hearts had not turned back;
    our feet had not strayed from your path.
¹⁹ But you crushed us and made us a haunt for
      jackals
    and covered us over with deep darkness.

²⁰ If we had forgotten the name of our God
    or spread out our hands to a foreign god,
²¹ would not God have discovered it,
    since he knows the secrets of the heart?
²² Yet for your sake we face death all day long;
    we are considered as sheep to be
      slaughtered.

²³ Awake, O Lord! Why do you sleep?
    Rouse yourself! Do not reject us forever.
²⁴ Why do you hide your face
    and forget our misery and oppression?

²⁵ We are brought down to the dust;
    our bodies cling to the ground.
²⁶ Rise up and help us;
    redeem us because of your unfailing love.

THE MESSAGE

With your help we'll wipe out our enemies,
    in your name we'll stomp them to dust.
I don't trust in weapons;
    my sword won't save me—
But it's you, you who saved us from the
      enemy;
    you made those who hate us lose face.
All day we parade God's praise—
    we thank you by name over and over.

44.9-12 But now you've walked off and left us,
    you've disgraced us and won't fight for us.
You made us turn tail and run;
    those who hate us have cleaned us out.
You delivered us as sheep to the butcher,
    you scattered us to the four winds.
You sold your people at a discount—
    you made nothing on the sale.

44.13-16 You made people on the street,
    urchins, poke fun and call us names.
You made us a joke among the godless,
    a cheap joke among the rabble.
Every day I'm up against it,
    my nose rubbed in my shame—
Gossip and ridicule fill the air,
    people out to get me crowd the street.

44.17-19 All this came down on us,
    and we've done nothing to deserve it.
We never betrayed your Covenant: our hearts
    were never false, our feet never left your
      path.
Do we deserve torture in a den of jackals?
    or lockup in a black hole?

44.20-22 If we had forgotten to pray to our God
    or made fools of ourselves with store-
      bought gods,
Wouldn't God have figured this out?
    We can't hide things from him.
No, you decided to make us martyrs,
    lambs assigned for sacrifice each day.

44.23-26 Get up, GOD! Are you going to sleep all day?
    Wake up! Don't you care what happens
      to us?
Why do you bury your face in the pillow?
    Why pretend things are just fine with us?
And here we are—flat on our faces in the dirt,
    held down with a boot on our necks.
Get up and come to our rescue.
    If you love us so much, *Help us!*

NEW INTERNATIONAL VERSION

PSALM 45

For the director of music. To the tune of
"Lilies." Of the Sons of Korah. A *maskil.* [a]
A wedding song.

¹ My heart is stirred by a noble theme
    as I recite my verses for the king;
    my tongue is the pen of a skillful writer.

² You are the most excellent of men
    and your lips have been anointed with
        grace,
    since God has blessed you forever.
³ Gird your sword upon your side, O mighty
        one;
    clothe yourself with splendor and majesty.
⁴ In your majesty ride forth victoriously
    in behalf of truth, humility and
        righteousness;
    let your right hand display awesome
        deeds.
⁵ Let your sharp arrows pierce the hearts of
        the king's enemies;
    let the nations fall beneath your feet.
⁶ Your throne, O God, will last for ever and
        ever;
    a scepter of justice will be the scepter of
        your kingdom.
⁷ You love righteousness and hate wickedness;
    therefore God, your God, has set you
        above your companions
    by anointing you with the oil of joy.
⁸ All your robes are fragrant with myrrh and
        aloes and cassia;
    from palaces adorned with ivory
    the music of the strings makes you glad.
⁹ Daughters of kings are among your honored
        women;
    at your right hand is the royal bride in
        gold of Ophir.

¹⁰ Listen, O daughter, consider and give ear:
    Forget your people and your father's
        house.
¹¹ The king is enthralled by your beauty;
    honor him, for he is your lord.
¹² The Daughter of Tyre will come with a gift, [b]
    men of wealth will seek your favor.

¹³ All glorious is the princess within her
        chamber;
    her gown is interwoven with gold.
¹⁴ In embroidered garments she is led to the
        king;
    her virgin companions follow her
    and are brought to you.

---

a Title: Probably a literary or musical term   *b* 12 Or *A
Tyrian robe is among the gifts*

THE MESSAGE

A wedding song of the sons of Korah

45.1 **45** My heart bursts its banks,
        spilling beauty and goodness.
I pour it out in a poem to the king,
    shaping the river into words:

✝

45.2-4 "You're the handsomest of men;
    every word from your lips is sheer grace,
    and God has blessed you, blessed you so
        much.
Strap your sword to your side, warrior!
    Accept praise! Accept due honor!
    Ride majestically! Ride triumphantly!
Ride on the side of truth!
    Ride for the righteous meek!

45.4-5 "Your instructions are glow-in-the-dark;
    you shoot sharp arrows
Into enemy hearts; the king's
    foes lie down in the dust, beaten.

45.6-7 "Your throne is God's throne,
    ever and always;
The scepter of your royal rule
    measures right living.
You love the right
    and hate the wrong.
And that is why God, your very own God,
    poured fragrant oil on your head,
Marking you out as king
    from among your dear companions.

45.8-9 "Your ozone-drenched garments
    are fragrant with mountain breeze.
Chamber music—from the throne room—
    makes you want to dance.
Kings' daughters are maids in your court,
    the Bride glittering with golden jewelry.

✝

45.10-12 "Now listen, daughter, don't miss a word:
    forget your country, put your home behind
        you.
Be *here*—the king is wild for you.
    Since he's your lord, adore him.
Wedding gifts pour in from Tyre;
    rich guests shower you with presents."

45.13-15 (Her wedding dress is dazzling,
    lined with gold by the weavers;
All her dresses and robes
    are woven with gold.
She is led to the king,
    followed by her virgin companions.

NEW INTERNATIONAL VERSION

15 They are led in with joy and gladness;
  they enter the palace of the king.

16 Your sons will take the place of your fathers;
  you will make them princes throughout
    the land.

17 I will perpetuate your memory through all
    generations;
  therefore the nations will praise you for
    ever and ever.

PSALM 46

For the director of music. Of the Sons of Korah.
According to *alamoth.* *a* A song.

1 God is our refuge and strength,
  an ever-present help in trouble.

2 Therefore we will not fear, though the earth
    give way
  and the mountains fall into the heart of
    the sea,

3 though its waters roar and foam
  and the mountains quake with their
    surging.   *Selah*

4 There is a river whose streams make glad the
    city of God,
  the holy place where the Most High
    dwells.

5 God is within her, she will not fall;
  God will help her at break of day.

6 Nations are in uproar, kingdoms fall;
  he lifts his voice, the earth melts.

7 The LORD Almighty is with us;
  the God of Jacob is our fortress.   *Selah*

8 Come and see the works of the LORD,
  the desolations he has brought on the
    earth.

9 He makes wars cease to the ends of the
    earth;
  he breaks the bow and shatters the spear,
  he burns the shields*b* with fire.

10 "Be still, and know that I am God;
  I will be exalted among the nations,
  I will be exalted in the earth."

11 The LORD Almighty is with us;
  the God of Jacob is our fortress.   *Selah*

PSALM 47

For the director of music. Of the Sons of Korah.
A psalm.

1 Clap your hands, all you nations;
  shout to God with cries of joy.

2 How awesome is the LORD Most High,
  the great King over all the earth!

a Title: Probably a musical term   *b* 9 Or *chariots*

THE MESSAGE

A procession of joy and laughter!
  a grand entrance to the king's palace!)

45.16-17 "Set your mind now on sons—
  don't dote on father and grandfather.
You'll set your sons up as princes
  all over the earth.
I'll make you famous for generations;
  you'll be the talk of the town
  for a long, long time."

A song of the sons of Korah

46.1-3 **46** God is a safe place to hide,
  ready to help when we need him.
We stand fearless at the cliff-edge of doom,
  courageous in seastorm and earthquake,
Before the rush and roar of oceans,
  the tremors that shift mountains.

  Jacob-wrestling God fights for us,
  GOD of the Angel Armies protects us.

46.4-6 River fountains splash joy, cooling God's city,
  this sacred haunt of the Most High.
God lives here, the streets are safe,
  God at your service from crack of dawn.
Godless nations rant and rave, kings and
    kingdoms threaten,
  but Earth does anything he says.

46.7 Jacob-wrestling God fights for us,
  GOD of the Angel Armies protects us.

46.8-10 Attention, all! See the marvels of GOD!
  He plants flowers and trees all over the
    earth,
Bans war from pole to pole,
  breaks all the weapons across his knee.
"Step out of the traffic! Take a long,
  loving look at me, your High God,
  above politics, above everything."

46.11 Jacob-wrestling God fights for us,
  GOD of the Angel Armies protects us.

A psalm of the sons of Korah

47.1-9 **47** Applause, everyone. Bravo,
    bravissimo!
  Shout God-songs at the top of your lungs!
GOD Most High is stunning,
  astride land and ocean.

NEW INTERNATIONAL VERSION

³He subdued nations under us,
 peoples under our feet.
⁴He chose our inheritance for us,
 the pride of Jacob, whom he loved. *Selah*

⁵God has ascended amid shouts of joy,
 the LORD amid the sounding of trumpets.
⁶Sing praises to God, sing praises;
 sing praises to our King, sing praises.

⁷For God is the King of all the earth;
 sing to him a psalm*ᵃ* of praise.
⁸God reigns over the nations;
 God is seated on his holy throne.
⁹The nobles of the nations assemble
 as the people of the God of Abraham,
for the kings*ᵇ* of the earth belong to God;
 he is greatly exalted.

PSALM 48

A song. A psalm of the Sons of Korah.

¹Great is the LORD, and most worthy of praise,
 in the city of our God, his holy mountain.
²It is beautiful in its loftiness,
 the joy of the whole earth.
Like the utmost heights of Zaphon*ᶜ* is Mount
  Zion,
 the*ᵈ* city of the Great King.
³God is in her citadels;
 he has shown himself to be her fortress.

⁴When the kings joined forces,
 when they advanced together,
⁵they saw ₍her₎ and were astounded;
 they fled in terror.
⁶Trembling seized them there,
 pain like that of a woman in labor.
⁷You destroyed them like ships of Tarshish
 shattered by an east wind.

⁸As we have heard,
 so have we seen
in the city of the LORD Almighty,
 in the city of our God:
God makes her secure forever. *Selah*

⁹Within your temple, O God,
 we meditate on your unfailing love.
¹⁰Like your name, O God,
 your praise reaches to the ends of the
  earth;
 your right hand is filled with righteousness.
¹¹Mount Zion rejoices,
 the villages of Judah are glad
 because of your judgments.

ᵃ 7 Or *a maskil* (probably a literary or musical term)
ᵇ 9 Or *shields*   *ᶜ 2 Zaphon* can refer to a sacred mountain
or the direction north.   *ᵈ 2* Or *earth, / Mount Zion, on the
northern side / of the*

THE MESSAGE

He crushes hostile people,
 puts nations at our feet.
He set us at the head of the line,
 prize-winning Jacob, his favorite.
Loud cheers as God climbs the mountain,
 a ram's horn blast at the summit.
Sing songs to God, sing out!
 Sing to our King, sing praise!
He's Lord over earth,
 so sing your best songs to God.
God is Lord of godless nations—
 sovereign, he's King of the mountain.
Princes from all over are gathered,
 people of Abraham's God.
The powers of earth are God's—
 he soars over all.

A psalm of the sons of Korah

48.1-3 **48** GOD majestic,
 praise abounds in our God-city!
His sacred mountain,
 breathtaking in its heights—earth's joy.
Zion Mountain looms in the North,
 city of the world-King.
God in his citadel peaks
 impregnable.

48.4-6 The kings got together,
 they united and came.
They took one look and shook their heads,
 they scattered and ran away.
They doubled up in pain
 like a woman having a baby.

48.7-8 You smashed the ships of Tarshish
 with a storm out of the East.
We heard about it, then we saw it
 with our eyes—
In GOD's city of angel armies,
 in the city our God
Set on firm foundations,
 firm forever.

48.9-10 We pondered your love-in-action, God,
 waiting in your temple:
Your name, God, evokes a train
 of Hallelujahs wherever
It is spoken, near and far;
 your arms are heaped with goodness-in-
  action.

48.11 Be glad, Zion Mountain;
 Dance, Judah's daughters!
 He does what he said he'd do!

NEW INTERNATIONAL VERSION

¹²Walk about Zion, go around her,
 count her towers,
¹³consider well her ramparts,
 view her citadels,
 that you may tell of them to the next
 generation.
¹⁴For this God is our God for ever and ever;
 he will be our guide even to the end.

PSALM 49

For the director of music. Of the Sons of Korah.
A psalm.

¹Hear this, all you peoples;
 listen, all who live in this world,
²both low and high,
 rich and poor alike:
³My mouth will speak words of wisdom;
 the utterance from my heart will give
 understanding.
⁴I will turn my ear to a proverb;
 with the harp I will expound my riddle:

⁵Why should I fear when evil days come,
 when wicked deceivers surround me—
⁶those who trust in their wealth
 and boast of their great riches?
⁷No man can redeem the life of another
 or give to God a ransom for him—
⁸the ransom for a life is costly,
 no payment is ever enough—
⁹that he should live on forever
 and not see decay.

¹⁰For all can see that wise men die;
 the foolish and the senseless alike perish
 and leave their wealth to others.
¹¹Their tombs will remain their houses[a]
 forever,
 their dwellings for endless generations,
 though they had[b] named lands after
 themselves.

¹²But man, despite his riches, does not endure;
 he is[c] like the beasts that perish.

¹³This is the fate of those who trust in
 themselves,
 and of their followers, who approve their
 sayings.   *Selah*
¹⁴Like sheep they are destined for the grave,[d]
 and death will feed on them.
 The upright will rule over them in the
 morning;
 their forms will decay in the grave,[d]

---

a 11 Septuagint and Syriac; Hebrew *In their thoughts their houses will remain*   *b 11* Or */ for they have*   *c 12* Hebrew; Septuagint and Syriac read verse 12 the same as verse 20.
d 14 Hebrew *Sheol*; also in verse 15

THE MESSAGE

48.12-14 Circle Zion, take her measure,
 count her fortress peaks,
 Gaze long at her sloping bulwark,
 climb her citadel heights—
 Then you can tell the next generation
 detail by detail the story of God,
 Our God forever,
 who guides us till the end of time.

A psalm of the sons of Korah

49.1-2 **49** Listen, everyone, listen—
 earth-dwellers, don't miss this.
 All you haves
 and have-nots,
 All together now: listen.

49.3-4 I set plainspoken wisdom before you,
 my heart-seasoned understandings of life.
 I fine-tuned my ear to the sayings of the wise,
 I solve life's riddle with the help of a harp.

49.5-6 So why should I fear in bad times,
 hemmed in by enemy malice,
 Shoved around by bullies,
 demeaned by the arrogant rich?

49.7-9 Really! There's no such thing as self-rescue,
 pulling yourself up by your bootstraps.
 The cost of rescue is beyond our means,
 and even then it doesn't guarantee
 Life forever, or insurance
 against the Black Hole.

49.10-11 Anyone can see that the brightest and best
 die,
 wiped out right along with fools and
 dunces.
 They leave all their prowess behind,
 move into their new home, The Coffin,
 The cemetery their permanent address.
 And to think they named counties after
 themselves!

49.12 We aren't immortal. We don't last long.
 Like our dogs, we age and weaken. And
 die.

49.13-15 This is what happens to those who live for the
 moment,
 who only look out for themselves:
 Death herds them like sheep straight to hell;
 they disappear down the gullet of the
 grave;
 They waste away to nothing—

NEW INTERNATIONAL VERSION

far from their princely mansions.
¹⁵But God will redeem my life *ᵃ* from the grave;
he will surely take me to himself.   *Selah*

¹⁶Do not be overawed when a man grows rich,
when the splendor of his house increases;
¹⁷for he will take nothing with him when he
dies,
his splendor will not descend with him.
¹⁸Though while he lived he counted himself
blessed—
and men praise you when you prosper—
¹⁹he will join the generation of his fathers,
who will never see the light ⌊of life⌋.

²⁰A man who has riches without
understanding
is like the beasts that perish.

PSALM 50

A psalm of Asaph.

¹The Mighty One, God, the Lord,
speaks and summons the earth
from the rising of the sun to the place
where it sets.
²From Zion, perfect in beauty,
God shines forth.
³Our God comes and will not be silent;
a fire devours before him,
and around him a tempest rages.
⁴He summons the heavens above,
and the earth, that he may judge his
people:
⁵"Gather to me my consecrated ones,
who made a covenant with me by
sacrifice."
⁶And the heavens proclaim his righteousness,
for God himself is judge.   *Selah*

⁷"Hear, O my people, and I will speak,
O Israel, and I will testify against you:
I am God, your God.
⁸I do not rebuke you for your sacrifices
or your burnt offerings, which are ever
before me.
⁹I have no need of a bull from your stall
or of goats from your pens,
¹⁰for every animal of the forest is mine,
and the cattle on a thousand hills.
¹¹I know every bird in the mountains,
and the creatures of the field are mine.
¹²If I were hungry I would not tell you,
for the world is mine, and all that is in it.
¹³Do I eat the flesh of bulls
or drink the blood of goats?

THE MESSAGE

nothing left but a marker in a cemetery.
But me? God snatches me from the clutch of
death,
he reaches down and grabs me.

⁴⁹·¹⁶⁻¹⁹ So don't be impressed with those who get rich
and pile up fame and fortune.
They can't take it with them;
fame and fortune all get left behind.
Just when they think they've arrived
and folks praise them because they've made
good,
They enter the family burial plot
where they'll never see sunshine again.

⁴⁹·²⁰   We aren't immortal. We don't last long.
Like our dogs, we age and weaken. And
die.

An Asaph psalm

⁵⁰·¹⁻³ **50** The God of gods—it's God!—speaks
out, shouts, "Earth!"
welcomes the sun in the east,
farewells the disappearing sun in the west.
From the dazzle of Zion,
God blazes into view.
Our God makes his entrance,
he's not shy in his coming.
Starbursts of fireworks precede him.

⁵⁰·⁴⁻⁵ He summons heaven and earth as a jury,
he's taking his people to court:
"Round up my saints who swore
on the Bible their loyalty to me."

⁵⁰·⁶ The whole cosmos attests to the fairness of
this court,
that here *God* is judge.

⁵⁰·⁷⁻¹⁵ "Are you listening, dear people? I'm getting
ready to speak;
Israel, I'm about ready to bring you to trial.
This is God, your God,
speaking to you.
I don't find fault with your acts of worship,
the frequent burnt sacrifices you offer.
But why should I want your blue-ribbon bull,
or more and more goats from your herds?
Every creature in the forest is mine,
the wild animals on all the mountains.
I know every mountain bird by name;
the scampering field mice are my friends.
If I get hungry, do you think I'd tell you?
All creation and its bounty are mine.
Do you think I feast on venison?
or drink draughts of goats' blood?

ᵃ 15 Or soul

NEW INTERNATIONAL VERSION

14 Sacrifice thank offerings to God,
  fulfill your vows to the Most High,
15 and call upon me in the day of trouble;
  I will deliver you, and you will
      honor me."

16 But to the wicked, God says:

"What right have you to recite my laws
  or take my covenant on your lips?
17 You hate my instruction
  and cast my words behind you.
18 When you see a thief, you join with him;
  you throw in your lot with adulterers.
19 You use your mouth for evil
  and harness your tongue to deceit.
20 You speak continually against your brother
  and slander your own mother's son.
21 These things you have done and I kept
      silent;
  you thought I was altogether *a* like you.
But I will rebuke you
  and accuse you to your face.

22 "Consider this, you who forget God,
  or I will tear you to pieces, with none to
      rescue:
23 He who sacrifices thank offerings honors me,
  and he prepares the way
  so that I may show him *b* the salvation of
      God."

PSALM 51

For the director of music. A psalm of David.
When the prophet Nathan came to him after
David had committed adultery with Bathsheba.

1 Have mercy on me, O God,
  according to your unfailing love;
according to your great compassion
  blot out my transgressions.
2 Wash away all my iniquity
  and cleanse me from my sin.

3 For I know my transgressions,
  and my sin is always before me.
4 Against you, you only, have I sinned
  and done what is evil in your sight,
so that you are proved right when you speak
  and justified when you judge.
5 Surely I was sinful at birth,
  sinful from the time my mother
      conceived me.
6 Surely you desire truth in the inner parts *c*;
  you teach *d* me wisdom in the inmost
      place.

THE MESSAGE

Spread for me a banquet of praise,
  serve High God a feast of kept promises,
And call for help when you're in trouble—
  I'll help you, and you'll honor me."

50.16-21 Next, God calls up the wicked:

"What are you up to, quoting my laws,
  talking like we are good friends?
You never answer the door when I call;
  you treat my words like garbage.
If you find a thief, you make him your buddy;
  adulterers are your friends of choice.
Your mouth drools filth;
  lying is a serious art form with you.
You stab your own brother in the back,
  rip off your little sister.
I kept a quiet patience while you did these
      things;
  you thought I went along with your game.
I'm calling you on the carpet, *now*,
  laying your wickedness out in plain sight.

50.22-23 "Time's up for playing fast and
      loose with me.
I'm ready to pass sentence,
  and there's no help in sight!
It's the praising life that honors me.
  As soon as you set your foot on the Way,
I'll show you my salvation."

A David psalm, after he was confronted by
Nathan about the affair with Bathsheba.

51.1-3 **51** Generous in love—God, give grace!
      Huge in mercy—wipe out my bad
          record.
Scrub away my guilt,
  soak out my sins in your laundry.
I know how bad I've been;
  my sins are staring me down.

51.4-6 You're the One I've violated, and you've seen
  it all, seen the full extent of my evil.
You have all the facts before you;
  whatever you decide about me is fair.
I've been out of step with you for a long time,
  in the wrong since before I was born.
What you're after is truth from the inside out.
  Enter me, then; conceive a new, true life.

---

*a 21 Or thought the 'I AM' was   b 23 Or and to him who
considers his way / I will show   c 6 The meaning of the
Hebrew for this phrase is uncertain.   d 6 Or you
desired . . . ; / you taught*

NEW INTERNATIONAL VERSION

7 Cleanse me with hyssop, and I will be clean;
  wash me, and I will be whiter than snow.
8 Let me hear joy and gladness;
  let the bones you have crushed rejoice.
9 Hide your face from my sins
  and blot out all my iniquity.

10 Create in me a pure heart, O God,
  and renew a steadfast spirit within me.
11 Do not cast me from your presence
  or take your Holy Spirit from me.
12 Restore to me the joy of your salvation
  and grant me a willing spirit, to
    sustain me.

13 Then I will teach transgressors your ways,
  and sinners will turn back to you.
14 Save me from bloodguilt, O God,
  the God who saves me,
  and my tongue will sing of your
    righteousness.
15 O Lord, open my lips,
  and my mouth will declare your praise.
16 You do not delight in sacrifice, or I would
    bring it;
  you do not take pleasure in burnt
    offerings.
17 The sacrifices of God are*a* a broken spirit;
  a broken and contrite heart,
  O God, you will not despise.

18 In your good pleasure make Zion prosper;
  build up the walls of Jerusalem.
19 Then there will be righteous sacrifices,
  whole burnt offerings to delight you;
  then bulls will be offered on your altar.

PSALM 52

For the director of music. A *maskil*[b] of David.
When Doeg the Edomite had gone to Saul and
  told him: "David has gone to the house
  of Ahimelech."

1 Why do you boast of evil, you mighty man?
  Why do you boast all day long,
  you who are a disgrace in the eyes of
    God?
2 Your tongue plots destruction;
  it is like a sharpened razor,
  you who practice deceit.
3 You love evil rather than good,
  falsehood rather than speaking the truth.
                                         Selah

4 You love every harmful word,
  O you deceitful tongue!

a 17 Or My sacrifice, O God, is   *b Title: Probably a literary
or musical term*

THE MESSAGE

51.7-15 Soak me in your laundry and I'll come out
    clean,
  scrub me and I'll have a snow-white life.
Tune me in to foot-tapping songs,
  set these once-broken bones to dancing.
Don't look too close for blemishes,
  give me a clean bill of health.
God, make a fresh start in me,
  shape a Genesis week from the chaos of my
    life.
Don't throw me out with the trash,
  or fail to breathe holiness in me.
Bring me back from gray exile,
  put a fresh wind in my sails!
Give me a job teaching rebels your ways
  so the lost can find their way home.
Commute my death sentence, God, my
    salvation God,
  and I'll sing anthems to your life-giving
    ways.
Unbutton my lips, dear God;
  I'll let loose with your praise.

51.16-17 Going through the motions doesn't please
    you,
  a flawless performance is nothing to you.
I learned God-worship
  when my pride was shattered.
Heart-shattered lives ready for love
  don't for a moment escape God's notice.

51.18-19 Make Zion the place you delight in,
  repair Jerusalem's broken-down walls.
Then you'll get real worship from us,
  acts of worship small and large,
Including all the bulls
  they can heave onto your altar!

A David psalm, when Doeg the Edomite
reported to Saul, "David's at Ahimelech's house."

52.1-4 **52** Why do you brag of evil, "Big Man"?
    God's mercy carries the day.
You scheme catastrophe;
  your tongue cuts razor-sharp,
  artisan in lies.
You love evil more than good,
  you call black white.
You love malicious gossip,
  you foul-mouth.

NEW INTERNATIONAL VERSION

5 Surely God will bring you down to
    everlasting ruin:
He will snatch you up and tear you from
    your tent;
he will uproot you from the land of the
    living.   *Selah*
6 The righteous will see and fear;
    they will laugh at him, saying,
7 "Here now is the man
    who did not make God his stronghold
but trusted in his great wealth
    and grew strong by destroying others!"

8 But I am like an olive tree
    flourishing in the house of God;
I trust in God's unfailing love
    for ever and ever.
9 I will praise you forever for what you have
    done;
in your name I will hope, for your name is
    good.
I will praise you in the presence of your
    saints.

PSALM 53

For the director of music. According
to *mahalath.* [a] A *maskil* [b] of David.

1 The fool says in his heart,
    "There is no God."
They are corrupt, and their ways are vile;
    there is no one who does good.

2 God looks down from heaven
    on the sons of men
to see if there are any who understand,
    any who seek God.
3 Everyone has turned away,
    they have together become corrupt;
there is no one who does good,
    not even one.

4 Will the evildoers never learn—
    those who devour my people as men eat
    bread
    and who do not call on God?
5 There they were, overwhelmed with dread,
    where there was nothing to dread.
God scattered the bones of those who
    attacked you;
    you put them to shame, for God despised
    them.

THE MESSAGE

52.5 God will tear you limb from limb,
    sweep you up and throw you out,
Pull you up by the roots
    from the land of life.

52.6-7 Good people will watch and
    worship. They'll laugh in relief:
"Big Man bet on the wrong horse,
    trusted in big money,
    made his living from catastrophe."

52.8 And I'm an olive tree,
    growing green in God's house.
I trusted in the generous mercy
    of God then and now.

52.9 I thank you always
    that you went into action.
And I'll stay right here,
    your good name my hope,
    in company with your faithful friends.

A David psalm

53.1-2 **53** Bilious and bloated, they gas,
    "God is gone."
It's poison gas—
    they foul themselves, they poison
Rivers and skies;
    thistles are their cash crop.
God sticks his head out of heaven.
    He looks around.
He's looking for someone not stupid—
    one man, even, God-expectant,
    just one God-ready woman.

53.3 He comes up empty. A string
    of zeros. Useless, unshepherded
Sheep, taking turns pretending
    to be Shepherd.
The ninety and nine
    follow the one.

53.4 Don't they know anything,
    all these impostors?
Don't they know
    they can't get away with this,
Treating people like a fast-food meal
    over which they're too busy to pray?

53.5 Night is coming for them, and nightmare—
    a nightmare they'll never wake up from.
God will make hash of these squatters,
    send them packing for good.

---

[a] Title: Probably a musical term   [b] Title: Probably a
literary or musical term

NEW INTERNATIONAL VERSION

⁶Oh, that salvation for Israel would come out
of Zion!
When God restores the fortunes of his
people,
let Jacob rejoice and Israel be glad!

PSALM 54

For the director of music. With stringed
instruments. A *maskil*[a] of David. When the
Ziphites had gone to Saul and said, "Is not David
hiding among us?"

¹Save me, O God, by your name;
vindicate me by your might.
²Hear my prayer, O God;
listen to the words of my mouth.

³Strangers are attacking me;
ruthless men seek my life—
men without regard for God.   *Selah*

⁴Surely God is my help;
the Lord is the one who sustains me.

⁵Let evil recoil on those who slander me;
in your faithfulness destroy them.

⁶I will sacrifice a freewill offering to you;
I will praise your name, O LORD,
for it is good.
⁷For he has delivered me from all my troubles,
and my eyes have looked in triumph on
my foes.

PSALM 55

For the director of music. With stringed
instruments. A *maskil*[a] of David.

¹Listen to my prayer, O God,
do not ignore my plea;
²   hear me and answer me.
My thoughts trouble me and I am distraught
³   at the voice of the enemy,
at the stares of the wicked;
for they bring down suffering upon me
and revile me in their anger.

⁴My heart is in anguish within me;
the terrors of death assail me.
⁵Fear and trembling have beset me;
horror has overwhelmed me.
⁶I said, "Oh, that I had the wings of a dove!
I would fly away and be at rest—
⁷I would flee far away
and stay in the desert;   *Selah*
⁸I would hurry to my place of shelter,
far from the tempest and storm."

---

[a] Title: Probably a literary or musical term

THE MESSAGE

53.6 Is there anyone around to save Israel?
God turns life around.
Turned-around Jacob skips rope,
turned-around Israel sings laughter.

A David psalm, when the Ziphites reported
to Saul, "David is hiding out with us."

54.1-2 **54** God, for your sake, help me!
Use your influence to clear me.
Listen, God—I'm desperate.
Don't be too busy to hear me.

54.3 Outlaws are out to get me,
hit men are trying to kill me.
Nothing will stop them;
God means nothing to them.

54.4-5 Oh, look! God's right here helping!
GOD's on my side,
Evil is looping back on my enemies.
Don't let up! Finish them off!

54.6-7 I'm ready now to worship, so ready.
I thank you, GOD—you're so good.
You got me out of every scrape,
and I saw my enemies get it.

A David psalm

55.1-3 **55** Open your ears, God, to my prayer;
don't pretend you don't hear me
knocking.
Come close and whisper your answer.
I really need you.
I shudder at the mean voice,
quail before the evil eye,
As they pile on the guilt,
stockpile angry slander.

55.4-8 My insides are turned inside out;
specters of death have me down.
I shake with fear,
I shudder from head to foot.
"Who will give me wings," I ask—
"wings like a dove?"
Get me out of here on dove wings;
I want some peace and quiet.
I want a walk in the country,
I want a cabin in the woods.
I'm desperate for a change
from rage and stormy weather.

NEW INTERNATIONAL VERSION

⁹ Confuse the wicked, O Lord, confound their
       speech,
   for I see violence and strife in the city.
¹⁰ Day and night they prowl about on its walls;
   malice and abuse are within it.
¹¹ Destructive forces are at work in the city;
   threats and lies never leave its streets.

¹² If an enemy were insulting me,
   I could endure it;
 if a foe were raising himself against me,
   I could hide from him.
¹³ But it is you, a man like myself,
   my companion, my close friend,
¹⁴ with whom I once enjoyed sweet fellowship
   as we walked with the throng at the house
       of God.

¹⁵ Let death take my enemies by surprise;
   let them go down alive to the grave,ᵃ
   for evil finds lodging among them.

¹⁶ But I call to God,
   and the LORD saves me.
¹⁷ Evening, morning and noon
   I cry out in distress,
   and he hears my voice.
¹⁸ He ransoms me unharmed
   from the battle waged against me,
   even though many oppose me.
¹⁹ God, who is enthroned forever,
   will hear them and afflict them—   *Selah*
 men who never change their ways
   and have no fear of God.

²⁰ My companion attacks his friends;
   he violates his covenant.
²¹ His speech is smooth as butter,
   yet war is in his heart;
 his words are more soothing than oil,
   yet they are drawn swords.

²² Cast your cares on the LORD
   and he will sustain you;
   he will never let the righteous fall.
²³ But you, O God, will bring down the wicked
   into the pit of corruption;
 bloodthirsty and deceitful men
   will not live out half their days.

 But as for me, I trust in you.

ᵃ 15 Hebrew *Sheol*

THE MESSAGE

55.9-11 Come down hard, Lord—slit their tongues.
       I'm appalled how they've split the city
 Into rival gangs
       prowling the alleys
 Day and night spoiling for a fight,
       trash piled in the streets,
 Even shopkeepers gouging and cheating
       in broad daylight.

55.12-14 This isn't the neighborhood bully
       mocking me—I could take that.
 This isn't a foreign devil spitting
       invective—I could tune that out.
 It's *you!* We grew up together!
       You! My best friend!
 Those long hours of leisure as we walked
       arm in arm, God a third party to our
           conversation.

55.15 Haul my betrayers off alive to hell—let them
       experience the horror, let them
       feel every desolate detail of a damned life.

55.16-19 I call to God;
       GOD will help me.
 At dusk, dawn, and noon I sigh
       deep sighs—he hears, he rescues.
 My life is well and whole, secure
       in the middle of danger
 Even while thousands
       are lined up against me.
 God hears it all, and from his judge's bench
       puts them in their place.
 But, set in their ways, they won't change;
       they pay him no mind.

55.20-21 And this, my best friend, betrayed his best
           friends;
       his life betrayed his word.
 All my life I've been charmed by his speech,
       never dreaming he'd turn on me.
 His words, which were music to my ears,
       turned to daggers in my heart.

55.22-23 Pile your troubles on GOD's shoulders—
       he'll carry your load, he'll help you out.
 He'll never let good people
       topple into ruin.
 But you, God, will throw the others
       into a muddy bog,
 Cut the lifespan of assassins
       and traitors in half.

 And I trust in you.

NEW INTERNATIONAL VERSION

PSALM 56

For the director of music. To the tune of "A
Dove on Distant Oaks." Of David. A *miktam.* [a]
When the Philistines had seized him in Gath.

[1] Be merciful to me, O God, for men hotly
    pursue me;
  all day long they press their attack.
[2] My slanderers pursue me all day long;
  many are attacking me in their pride.

[3] When I am afraid,
  I will trust in you.
[4] In God, whose word I praise,
  in God I trust; I will not be afraid.
  What can mortal man do to me?

[5] All day long they twist my words;
  they are always plotting to harm me.
[6] They conspire, they lurk,
  they watch my steps,
  eager to take my life.

[7] On no account let them escape;
  in your anger, O God, bring down the
    nations.
[8] Record my lament;
  list my tears on your scroll[b]—
  are they not in your record?

[9] Then my enemies will turn back
  when I call for help.
  By this I will know that God is for me.
[10] In God, whose word I praise,
  in the LORD, whose word I praise—
[11] in God I trust; I will not be afraid.
  What can man do to me?

[12] I am under vows to you, O God;
  I will present my thank offerings to you.
[13] For you have delivered me[c] from death
  and my feet from stumbling,
  that I may walk before God
  in the light of life.[d]

THE MESSAGE

A David psalm, when he was captured by the
Philistines in Gath.

56.1-4 **56** Take my side, God—I'm getting kicked
    around,
  stomped on every day.
Not a day goes by
  but somebody beats me up;
They make it their duty
  to beat me up.
When I get really afraid
  I come to you in trust.
I'm proud to praise God;
  fearless now, I trust in God.
  What can mere mortals do?

56.5-6 They don't let up—
  they smear my reputation
  and huddle to plot my collapse.
They gang up,
  sneak together through the alleys
To take me by surprise,
  wait their chance to get me.

56.7 Pay them back in evil!
  Get angry, God!
  Down with these people!

56.8 You've kept track of my every toss and turn
  through the sleepless nights,
Each tear entered in your ledger,
  each ache written in your book.

56.9 If my enemies run away,
  turn tail when I yell at them,
Then I'll know
  that God is on my side.

56.10-11 I'm proud to praise God,
  proud to praise GOD.
Fearless now, I trust in God;
  what can mere mortals do to me?

56.12-13 God, you did everything you promised,
  and I'm thanking you with all my heart.
You pulled me from the brink of death,
  my feet from the cliff-edge of doom.
Now I stroll at leisure with God
  in the sunlit fields of life.

---

[a] Title: Probably a literary or musical term   [b] 8 Or / put
my tears in your wineskin   [c] 13 Or my soul   [d] 13 Or the
land of the living

NEW INTERNATIONAL VERSION

PSALM 57

For the director of music. ⌐To the tune of⌐ "Do
Not Destroy." Of David. A *miktam.* *ª* When he had
fled from Saul into the cave.

¹ Have mercy on me, O God, have mercy
on me,
for in you my soul takes refuge.
I will take refuge in the shadow of your
wings
until the disaster has passed.

² I cry out to God Most High,
to God, who fulfills ⌐his purpose⌐ for me.
³ He sends from heaven and saves me,
rebuking those who hotly pursue me;
Selah
God sends his love and his faithfulness.

⁴ I am in the midst of lions;
I lie among ravenous beasts—
men whose teeth are spears and arrows,
whose tongues are sharp swords.

⁵ Be exalted, O God, above the heavens;
let your glory be over all the earth.

⁶ They spread a net for my feet—
I was bowed down in distress.
They dug a pit in my path—
but they have fallen into it themselves.
Selah

⁷ My heart is steadfast, O God,
my heart is steadfast;
I will sing and make music.
⁸ Awake, my soul!
Awake, harp and lyre!
I will awaken the dawn.

⁹ I will praise you, O Lord, among the nations;
I will sing of you among the peoples.
¹⁰ For great is your love, reaching to the
heavens;
your faithfulness reaches to the skies.

¹¹ Be exalted, O God, above the heavens;
let your glory be over all the earth.

PSALM 58

For the director of music. ⌐To the tune of⌐ "Do
Not Destroy." Of David. A *miktam.* *ª*

¹ Do you rulers indeed speak justly?
Do you judge uprightly among men?
² No, in your heart you devise injustice,
and your hands mete out violence on the
earth.

THE MESSAGE

A David psalm, when he hid in a cave
from Saul.

57.1-3 **57** Be good to me, God—and now!
I've run to you for dear life.
I'm hiding out under your wings
until the hurricane blows over.
I call out to High God,
the God who holds me together.
He sends orders from heaven and saves me,
he humiliates those who kick me around.
God delivers generous love,
he makes good on his word.

57.4 I find myself in a pride of lions
who are wild for a taste of human flesh;
Their teeth are lances and arrows,
their tongues are sharp daggers.

57.5 Soar high in the skies, O God!
Cover the whole earth with your glory!

57.6 They booby-trapped my path;
I thought I was dead and done for.
They dug a mantrap to catch me,
and fell in headlong themselves.

57.7-8 I'm ready, God, so ready,
ready from head to toe,
Ready to sing, ready to raise a tune:
"Wake up, soul!
Wake up, harp! wake up, lute!
Wake up, you sleepyhead sun!"

57.9-10 I'm thanking you, GOD, out loud in the
streets,
singing your praises in town and country.
The deeper your love, the higher it goes;
every cloud is a flag to your faithfulness.

57.11 Soar high in the skies, O God!
Cover the whole earth with your glory!

A David psalm

58.1-2 **58** Is this any way to run a country?
Is there an honest politician in the
house?
Behind the scenes you brew cauldrons of evil,
behind closed doors you make deals with
demons.

ª Title: Probably a literary or musical term

NEW INTERNATIONAL VERSION

³ Even from birth the wicked go astray;
  from the womb they are wayward and
    speak lies.
⁴ Their venom is like the venom of a snake,
  like that of a cobra that has stopped its
    ears,
⁵ that will not heed the tune of the charmer,
  however skillful the enchanter may be.

⁶ Break the teeth in their mouths, O God;
  tear out, O LORD, the fangs of the lions!
⁷ Let them vanish like water that flows away;
  when they draw the bow, let their arrows
    be blunted.
⁸ Like a slug melting away as it moves along,
  like a stillborn child, may they not see the
    sun.
⁹ Before your pots can feel ⌐the heat of⌐ the
    thorns—
  whether they be green or dry—the wicked
    will be swept away.ᵃ
¹⁰ The righteous will be glad when they are
    avenged,
  when they bathe their feet in the blood of
    the wicked.
¹¹ Then men will say,
  "Surely the righteous still are rewarded;
    surely there is a God who judges the
      earth."

PSALM 59

For the director of music. ⌐To the tune of⌐ "Do
Not Destroy." Of David. A *miktam.ᵇ* When Saul
had sent men to watch David's house in order
to kill him.

¹ Deliver me from my enemies, O God;
  protect me from those who rise up
    against me.
² Deliver me from evildoers
  and save me from bloodthirsty men.

³ See how they lie in wait for me!
  Fierce men conspire against me
  for no offense or sin of mine, O LORD.
⁴ I have done no wrong, yet they are ready to
    attack me.
  Arise to help me; look on my plight!
⁵ O LORD God Almighty, the God of Israel,
  rouse yourself to punish all the nations;
  show no mercy to wicked traitors.   *Selah*

⁶ They return at evening,
  snarling like dogs,
  and prowl about the city.

THE MESSAGE

58.3-5 The wicked crawl from the wrong side of the
    cradle;
  their first words out of the womb are lies.
Poison, lethal rattlesnake poison,
  drips from their forked tongues—
Deaf to threats, deaf to charm,
  decades of wax built up in their ears.

58.6-9 God, smash their teeth to bits,
  leave them toothless tigers.
Let their lives be buckets of water spilled,
  all that's left, a damp stain in the sand.
Let them be trampled grass
  worn smooth by the traffic.
Let them dissolve into snail slime,
  be a miscarried fetus that never sees
    sunlight.
Before what they cook up is half-done, God,
  throw it out with the garbage!

58.10-11 The righteous will call up their friends
  when they see the wicked get their reward,
Serve up their blood in goblets
  as they toast one another,
Everyone cheering, "It's worth it to play by the
    rules!
  God's handing out trophies and tending the
    earth!"

A David psalm, when Saul set a watch
on David's house in order to kill him.

59.1-2 **59** My God! Rescue me from my enemies,
        defend me from these mutineers.
Rescue me from their dirty tricks,
  save me from their hit men.

59.3-4 Desperadoes have ganged up on me,
  they're hiding in ambush for me.
I did nothing to deserve this, GOD,
  crossed no one, wronged no one.
All the same, they're after me,
  determined to get me.

59.4-5 Wake up and see for yourself! You're GOD,
  God of the Angel Armies, Israel's God!
Get on the job and take care of these pagans,
  don't be soft on these hard cases.

59.6-7 They return when the sun goes down,
  They howl like coyotes, ringing the city.

ᵃ 9 The meaning of the Hebrew for this verse is uncertain.
ᵇ Title: Probably a literary or musical term

NEW INTERNATIONAL VERSION

⁷ See what they spew from their mouths—
they spew out swords from their lips,
and they say, "Who can hear us?"
⁸ But you, O Lord, laugh at them;
you scoff at all those nations.

⁹ O my Strength, I watch for you;
you, O God, are my fortress, ¹⁰ my loving
God.

God will go before me
and will let me gloat over those who
slander me.
¹¹ But do not kill them, O Lord our shield,ᵃ
or my people will forget.
In your might make them wander about,
and bring them down.
¹² For the sins of their mouths,
for the words of their lips,
let them be caught in their pride.
For the curses and lies they utter,
¹³ consume them in wrath,
consume them till they are no more.
Then it will be known to the ends of the
earth
that God rules over Jacob. *Selah*

¹⁴ They return at evening,
snarling like dogs,
and prowl about the city.
¹⁵ They wander about for food
and howl if not satisfied.
¹⁶ But I will sing of your strength,
in the morning I will sing of your love;
for you are my fortress,
my refuge in times of trouble.

¹⁷ O my Strength, I sing praise to you;
you, O God, are my fortress, my loving
God.

PSALM 60

For the director of music. To the tune of, "The
Lily of the Covenant." A *miktam*ᵇ of David. For
teaching. When he fought Aram Naharaimᶜ and
Aram Zobah,ᵈ and when Joab returned and
struck down twelve thousand Edomites in
the Valley of Salt.

¹ You have rejected us, O God, and burst forth
upon us;
you have been angry—now restore us!
² You have shaken the land and torn it open;
mend its fractures, for it is quaking.

THE MESSAGE

Then suddenly they're all at the gate,
Snarling invective, drawn daggers in their
teeth.
They think they'll never get caught.

59.8-10 But you, God, break out laughing;
you treat the godless nations like jokes.
Strong God, I'm watching you do it,
I can always count on you.
God in dependable love shows up on time,
shows me my enemies in ruin.

59.11-13 Don't make quick work of them, God,
lest my people forget.
Bring them down in slow motion,
take them apart piece by piece.
Let all their mean-mouthed arrogance
catch up with them,
Catch them out and bring them down
—every muttered curse
—every barefaced lie.
Finish them off in fine style!
Finish them off for good!
Then all the world will see
that God rules well in Jacob,
everywhere that God's in charge.

59.14-15 They return when the sun goes down,
They howl like coyotes, ringing the city.
They scavenge for bones,
And bite the hand that feeds them.

59.16-17 And me? I'm singing your prowess,
shouting at cockcrow your largesse,
For you've been a safe place for me,
a good place to hide.
Strong God, I'm watching you do it,
I can always count on you—
God, my dependable love.

A David psalm, when he fought against Aram-
naharaim and Aram-zobah and Joab killed
twelve thousand Edomites at the Valley of Salt.

60.1-2 **60** God! you walked off and left us,
kicked our defenses to bits
And stalked off angry.
Come back. Oh please, come back!

You shook earth to the foundations,
ripped open huge crevasses.
Heal the breaks! Everything's
coming apart at the seams.

ᵃ 11 Or *sovereign*   ᵇ Title: Probably a literary or musical
term   ᶜ Title: That is, Arameans of Northwest
Mesopotamia   ᵈ Title: That is, Arameans of central Syria

NEW INTERNATIONAL VERSION

3 You have shown your people desperate
  times;
 you have given us wine that makes us
  stagger.
4 But for those who fear you, you have raised a
  banner
 to be unfurled against the bow.   *Selah*

5 Save us and help us with your right hand,
 that those you love may be delivered.
6 God has spoken from his sanctuary:
 "In triumph I will parcel out Shechem
 and measure off the Valley of Succoth.
7 Gilead is mine, and Manasseh is mine;
 Ephraim is my helmet,
 Judah my scepter.
8 Moab is my washbasin,
 upon Edom I toss my sandal;
 over Philistia I shout in triumph."

9 Who will bring me to the fortified city?
 Who will lead me to Edom?
10 Is it not you, O God, you who have rejected
  us
 and no longer go out with our armies?
11 Give us aid against the enemy,
 for the help of man is worthless.
12 With God we will gain the victory,
 and he will trample down our enemies.

PSALM 61

For the director of music. With stringed
instruments. Of David.

1 Hear my cry, O God;
 listen to my prayer.

2 From the ends of the earth I call to you,
 I call as my heart grows faint;
 lead me to the rock that is higher than I.
3 For you have been my refuge,
 a strong tower against the foe.

4 I long to dwell in your tent forever
 and take refuge in the shelter of your
  wings.   *Selah*
5 For you have heard my vows, O God;
 you have given me the heritage of those
  who fear your name.

6 Increase the days of the king's life,
 his years for many generations.
7 May he be enthroned in God's presence
  forever;
 appoint your love and faithfulness to
  protect him.

8 Then will I ever sing praise to your name
 and fulfill my vows day after day.

THE MESSAGE

60.3-5 You made your people look doom in the face,
 then gave us cheap wine to drown our
  troubles.
Then you planted a flag to rally your people,
 an unfurled flag to look to for courage.
Now do something quickly, answer right now,
 so the one you love best is saved.

60.6-8 That's when God spoke in holy splendor,
 "Bursting with joy,
I make a present of Shechem,
 I hand out Succoth Valley as a gift.
Gilead's in my pocket,
 to say nothing of Manasseh.
Ephraim's my hard hat,
 Judah my hammer;
Moab's a scrub bucket,
 I mop the floor with Moab,
Spit on Edom,
 rain fireworks all over Philistia."

60.9-10 Who will take me to the thick of the fight?
 Who'll show me the road to Edom?
You aren't giving up on us, are you, God?
 refusing to go out with our troops?

60.11-12 Give us help for the hard task;
 human help is worthless.
In God we'll do our very best;
 he'll flatten the opposition for good.

A David psalm

61.1-2 **61** God, listen to me shout,
 bend an ear to my prayer.
When I'm far from anywhere,
 down to my last gasp,
I call out, "Guide me
 up High Rock Mountain!"

61.3-5 You've always given me breathing room,
 a place to get away from it all,
A lifetime pass to your safe-house,
 an open invitation as your guest.
You've always taken me seriously, God,
 made me welcome among those who know
  and love you.

61.6-8 Let the days of the king add up
 to years and years of good rule.
Set his throne in the full light of God;
 post Steady Love and Good Faith as
  lookouts,
And I'll be the poet who sings your glory—
 and live what I sing every day.

NEW INTERNATIONAL VERSION

PSALM 62

For the director of music. For Jeduthun. A psalm
of David.

1 My soul finds rest in God alone;
    my salvation comes from him.
2 He alone is my rock and my salvation;
    he is my fortress, I will never be shaken.

3 How long will you assault a man?
    Would all of you throw him down—
    this leaning wall, this tottering fence?
4 They fully intend to topple him
    from his lofty place;
    they take delight in lies.
  With their mouths they bless,
    but in their hearts they curse.   *Selah*

5 Find rest, O my soul, in God alone;
    my hope comes from him.
6 He alone is my rock and my salvation;
    he is my fortress, I will not be shaken.
7 My salvation and my honor depend on
        God *a*;
    he is my mighty rock, my refuge.
8 Trust in him at all times, O people;
    pour out your hearts to him,
    for God is our refuge.   *Selah*

9 Lowborn men are but a breath,
    the highborn are but a lie;
  if weighed on a balance, they are nothing;
    together they are only a breath.
10 Do not trust in extortion
    or take pride in stolen goods;
  though your riches increase,
    do not set your heart on them.

11 One thing God has spoken,
    two things have I heard:
  that you, O God, are strong,
12   and that you, O Lord, are loving.
  Surely you will reward each person
    according to what he has done.

THE MESSAGE

A David psalm

62.1-2 **62** God, the one and only—
    I'll wait as long as he says.
Everything I need comes from him,
    so why not?
He's solid rock under my feet,
    breathing room for my soul,
An impregnable castle:
    I'm set for life.

62.3-4 How long will you gang up on me?
    How long will you run with the bullies?
There's nothing to you, any of you—
    rotten floorboards, worm-eaten rafters,
Anthills plotting to bring down mountains,
    far gone in make-believe.
You talk a good line,
    but every "blessing" breathes a curse.

62.5-6 God, the one and only—
    I'll wait as long as he says.
Everything I hope for comes from him,
    so why not?
He's solid rock under my feet,
    breathing room for my soul,
An impregnable castle:
    I'm set for life.

62.7-8 My help and glory are in God
    —granite-strength and safe-harbor-God—
So trust him absolutely, people;
    lay your lives on the line for him.
    God is a safe place to be.

62.9 Man as such is smoke,
    woman as such, a mirage.
Put them together, they're nothing;
    two times nothing is nothing.

62.10 And a windfall, if it comes—
    don't make too much of it.

62.11 God said this once and for all;
    how many times
Have I heard it repeated?
    "Strength comes
Straight from God."

62.12 Love to you, Lord God!
    You pay a fair wage for a good day's work!

---

a 7 Or / God Most High is my salvation and my honor

NEW INTERNATIONAL VERSION

PSALM 63

A psalm of David. When he was in the Desert of Judah.

¹ O God, you are my God,
    earnestly I seek you;
my soul thirsts for you,
    my body longs for you,
in a dry and weary land
    where there is no water.

² I have seen you in the sanctuary
    and beheld your power and your glory.
³ Because your love is better than life,
    my lips will glorify you.
⁴ I will praise you as long as I live,
    and in your name I will lift up my hands.
⁵ My soul will be satisfied as with the richest
    of foods;
    with singing lips my mouth will praise
    you.

⁶ On my bed I remember you;
    I think of you through the watches of the
    night.
⁷ Because you are my help,
    I sing in the shadow of your wings.
⁸ My soul clings to you;
    your right hand upholds me.

⁹ They who seek my life will be destroyed;
    they will go down to the depths of the
    earth.
¹⁰ They will be given over to the sword
    and become food for jackals.

¹¹ But the king will rejoice in God;
    all who swear by God's name will praise
    him,
    while the mouths of liars will be silenced.

PSALM 64

For the director of music. A psalm of David.

¹ Hear me, O God, as I voice my complaint;
    protect my life from the threat of the
    enemy.
² Hide me from the conspiracy of the wicked,
    from that noisy crowd of evildoers.

³ They sharpen their tongues like swords
    and aim their words like deadly arrows.
⁴ They shoot from ambush at the innocent
    man;
    they shoot at him suddenly, without fear.

⁵ They encourage each other in evil plans,
    they talk about hiding their snares;

THE MESSAGE

A David psalm, when he was out in the Judean wilderness.

63.1 **63** God—you're my God!
    I can't get enough of you!
I've worked up such hunger and thirst for
    God,
    traveling across dry and weary deserts.

63.2-4 So here I am in the place of worship, eyes
    open,
    drinking in your strength and glory.
In your generous love I am really living at
    last!
    My lips brim praises like fountains.
I bless you every time I take a breath;
    My arms wave like banners of praise to
    you.

63.5-8 I eat my fill of prime rib and gravy;
    I smack my lips. It's time to shout praises!
If I'm sleepless at midnight,
    I spend the hours in grateful reflection.
Because you've always stood up for me,
    I'm free to run and play.
I hold on to you for dear life,
    and you hold me steady as a post.

63.9-11 Those who are out to get me are marked for
    doom,
    marked for death, bound for hell.
They'll die violent deaths;
    jackals will tear them limb from limb.
But the king is glad in God;
    his true friends spread the joy,
While small-minded gossips
    are gagged for good.

A David psalm

64.1 **64** Listen and help, O God.
    I'm reduced to a whine
And a whimper, obsessed
    with feelings of doomsday.

64.2-6 Don't let them find me—
    the conspirators out to get me,
Using their tongues as weapons,
    flinging poison words,
    poison-tipped arrow-words.
They shoot from ambush,
    shoot without warning,
    not caring who they hit.
They keep fit doing calisthenics
    of evil purpose,
They keep lists of the traps

NEW INTERNATIONAL VERSION

they say, "Who will see them *a*?"
6 They plot injustice and say,
    "We have devised a perfect plan!"
    Surely the mind and heart of man are
        cunning.

7 But God will shoot them with arrows;
    suddenly they will be struck down.
8 He will turn their own tongues against them
    and bring them to ruin;
    all who see them will shake their heads in
        scorn.

9 All mankind will fear;
    they will proclaim the works of God
    and ponder what he has done.
10 Let the righteous rejoice in the LORD
    and take refuge in him;
    let all the upright in heart praise him!

PSALM 65

For the director of music. A psalm of David.
A song.

1 Praise awaits *b* you, O God, in Zion;
    to you our vows will be fulfilled.
2 O you who hear prayer,
    to you all men will come.
3 When we were overwhelmed by sins,
    you forgave *c* our transgressions.
4 Blessed are those you choose
    and bring near to live in your courts!
  We are filled with the good things of your
        house,
    of your holy temple.

5 You answer us with awesome deeds of
        righteousness,
    O God our Savior,
  the hope of all the ends of the earth
    and of the farthest seas,
6 who formed the mountains by your power,
    having armed yourself with strength,
7 who stilled the roaring of the seas,
    the roaring of their waves,
    and the turmoil of the nations.
8 Those living far away fear your wonders;
    where morning dawns and evening fades
    you call forth songs of joy.

9 You care for the land and water it;
    you enrich it abundantly.
  The streams of God are filled with water
    to provide the people with grain,
    for so you have ordained it. *d*
10 You drench its furrows

THE MESSAGE

they've secretly set.
They say to each other,
    "No one can catch us,
    no one can detect our perfect crime."
The Detective detects the mystery
    in the dark of the cellar heart.

64:7-8 The God of the Arrow shoots!
    They double up in pain,
Fall flat on their faces
    in full view of the grinning crowd.

64:9-10 Everyone sees it. God's
    work is the talk of the town.
Be glad, good people! Fly to GOD!
    Good-hearted people, make praise your
        habit.

A David psalm

65:1-2 **65** Silence is praise to you,
        Zion-dwelling God,
And also obedience.
    You hear the prayer in it all.

65:2-8 We all arrive at your doorstep sooner
    or later, loaded with guilt,
Our sins too much for us—
    but you get rid of them once and for all.
Blessed are the chosen! Blessed the guest
    at home in your place!
We expect our fill of good things
    in your house, your heavenly manse.
All your salvation wonders
    are on display in your trophy room.
Earth-Tamer, Ocean-Pourer,
    Mountain-Maker, Hill-Dresser,
Muzzler of sea storm and wave crash,
    of mobs in noisy riot—
Far and wide they'll come to a stop,
    they'll stare in awe, in wonder.
Dawn and dusk take turns
    calling, "Come and worship."

65:9-13 Oh, visit the earth,
    ask her to join the dance!
Deck her out in spring showers,
    fill the God-River with living water.
Paint the wheat fields golden.
    Creation was made for this!
Drench the plowed fields,

---

a 5 Or *us*   *b* 1 Or *befits*; the meaning of the Hebrew for
this word is uncertain.   *c* 3 Or *made atonement for*
d 9 Or *for that is how you prepare the land*

NEW INTERNATIONAL VERSION

and level its ridges;
you soften it with showers
and bless its crops.
¹¹ You crown the year with your bounty,
and your carts overflow with abundance.
¹² The grasslands of the desert overflow;
the hills are clothed with gladness.
¹³ The meadows are covered with flocks
and the valleys are mantled with grain;
they shout for joy and sing.

PSALM 66

For the director of music. A song. A psalm.

¹ Shout with joy to God, all the earth!
²   Sing the glory of his name;
make his praise glorious!
³ Say to God, "How awesome are your deeds!
So great is your power
that your enemies cringe before you.
⁴ All the earth bows down to you;
they sing praise to you,
they sing praise to your name."   *Selah*

⁵ Come and see what God has done,
how awesome his works in man's behalf!
⁶ He turned the sea into dry land,
they passed through the waters on foot—
come, let us rejoice in him.
⁷ He rules forever by his power,
his eyes watch the nations—
let not the rebellious rise up against him.   *Selah*

⁸ Praise our God, O peoples,
let the sound of his praise be heard;
⁹ he has preserved our lives
and kept our feet from slipping.
¹⁰ For you, O God, tested us;
you refined us like silver.
¹¹ You brought us into prison
and laid burdens on our backs.
¹² You let men ride over our heads;
we went through fire and water,
but you brought us to a place of
abundance.

¹³ I will come to your temple with burnt
offerings
and fulfill my vows to you—
¹⁴ vows my lips promised and my mouth spoke
when I was in trouble.
¹⁵ I will sacrifice fat animals to you

THE MESSAGE

soak the dirt clods
With rainfall as harrow and rake
bring her to blossom and fruit.
Snow-crown the peaks with splendor,
scatter rose petals down your paths,
All through the wild meadows, rose petals.
Set the hills to dancing,
Dress the canyon walls with live sheep,
a drape of flax across the valleys.
Let them shout, and shout, and shout!
Oh, oh, let them sing!

66.1-4 **66** All together now—applause for God!
Sing songs to the tune of his glory,
set glory to the rhythms of his praise.
Say of God, "We've never seen anything like
him!"
When your enemies see you in action,
they slink off like scolded dogs.
The whole earth falls to its knees—
it worships you, sings to you,
can't stop enjoying your name and fame.

66.5-6 Take a good look at God's wonders—
they'll take your breath away.
He converted sea to dry land;
travelers crossed the river on foot.
Now isn't that cause for a song?

66.7 Ever sovereign in his high tower, he keeps
his eye on the godless nations.
Rebels don't dare
raise a finger against him.

66.8-12 Bless our God, O peoples!
Give him a thunderous welcome!
Didn't he set us on the road to life?
Didn't he keep us out of the ditch?
He trained us first,
passed us like silver through refining fires,
Brought us into hardscrabble country,
pushed us to our very limit,
Road-tested us inside and out,
took us to hell and back;
Finally he brought us
to this well-watered place.

66.13-15 I'm bringing my prizes and presents to your
house.
I'm doing what I said I'd do,
What I solemnly swore I'd do
that day when I was in so much trouble:
The choicest cuts of meat
for the sacrificial meal;
Even the fragrance
of roasted lamb is like a meal!

NEW INTERNATIONAL VERSION

and an offering of rams;
I will offer bulls and goats.   *Selah*

[16] Come and listen, all you who fear God;
let me tell you what he has done for me.
[17] I cried out to him with my mouth;
his praise was on my tongue.
[18] If I had cherished sin in my heart,
the Lord would not have listened;
[19] but God has surely listened
and heard my voice in prayer.
[20] Praise be to God,
who has not rejected my prayer
or withheld his love from me!

PSALM 67

*For the director of music. With stringed
instruments. A psalm. A song.*

[1] May God be gracious to us and bless us
and make his face shine upon us,   *Selah*
[2] that your ways may be known on earth,
your salvation among all nations.

[3] May the peoples praise you, O God;
may all the peoples praise you.
[4] May the nations be glad and sing for joy,
for you rule the peoples justly
and guide the nations of the earth.   *Selah*
[5] May the peoples praise you, O God;
may all the peoples praise you.

[6] Then the land will yield its harvest,
and God, our God, will bless us.
[7] God will bless us,
and all the ends of the earth will fear him.

PSALM 68

*For the director of music. Of David. A psalm.
A song.*

[1] May God arise, may his enemies be
scattered;
may his foes flee before him.
[2] As smoke is blown away by the wind,
may you blow them away;
as wax melts before the fire,
may the wicked perish before God.
[3] But may the righteous be glad
and rejoice before God;
may they be happy and joyful.

[4] Sing to God, sing praise to his name,
extol him who rides on the clouds[a]—
his name is the LORD—
and rejoice before him.

a 4 Or / prepare the way for him who rides through the deserts

THE MESSAGE

Or make it an ox
garnished with goat meat!

[66.16-20] All believers, come here and listen,
let me tell you what God did for me.
I called out to him with my mouth,
my tongue shaped the sounds of music.
If I had been cozy with evil,
the Lord would never have listened.
But he most surely *did* listen,
he came on the double when he heard my
prayer.
Blessed be God: he didn't turn a deaf ear,
he stayed with me, loyal in his love.

[67.1-7] **67** God, mark us with grace
and blessing! Smile!
The whole country will see how you work,
all the godless nations see how you save.
God! Let people thank and enjoy you.
Let all people thank and enjoy you.
Let all far-flung people become happy
and shout their happiness because
You judge them fair and square,
you tend the far-flung peoples.
God! Let people thank and enjoy you.
Let all people thank and enjoy you.
Earth, display your exuberance!
You mark us with blessing, O God, our
God.
You mark us with blessing, O God.
Earth's four corners—honor him!

A David psalm

[68.1-4] **68** Up with God!
Down with his enemies!
Adversaries, run for the hills!
Gone like a puff of smoke,
like a blob of wax in the fire—
one look at God and the wicked vanish.
When the righteous see God in action
they'll laugh, they'll sing,
they'll laugh and sing for joy.
Sing hymns to God;
all heaven, sing out;
clear the way for the coming of Cloud-
Rider.
Enjoy GOD,
cheer when you see him!

NEW INTERNATIONAL VERSION

⁵A father to the fatherless, a defender of
    widows,
    is God in his holy dwelling.
⁶God sets the lonely in families,ᵃ
    he leads forth the prisoners with singing;
    but the rebellious live in a sun-scorched
       land.

⁷When you went out before your people, O
       God,
    when you marched through the
       wasteland,   *Selah*
⁸the earth shook,
    the heavens poured down rain,
  before God, the One of Sinai,
    before God, the God of Israel.
⁹You gave abundant showers, O God;
    you refreshed your weary inheritance.
¹⁰Your people settled in it,
    and from your bounty, O God, you
       provided for the poor.

¹¹The Lord announced the word,
    and great was the company of those who
       proclaimed it:
¹²"Kings and armies flee in haste;
    in the camps men divide the plunder.
¹³Even while you sleep among the campfires,ᵇ
    the wings of ⌐myᒋ dove are sheathed with
       silver,
    its feathers with shining gold."
¹⁴When the Almightyᶜ scattered the kings in
       the land,
    it was like snow fallen on Zalmon.

¹⁵The mountains of Bashan are majestic
       mountains;
    rugged are the mountains of Bashan.
¹⁶Why gaze in envy, O rugged mountains,
    at the mountain where God chooses to
       reign,
    where the LORD himself will dwell
       forever?
¹⁷The chariots of God are tens of thousands
    and thousands of thousands;
    the Lord ⌐has comeᒋ from Sinai into his
       sanctuary.
¹⁸When you ascended on high,
    you led captives in your train;
    you received gifts from men,
  even fromᵈ the rebellious—
    that you,ᵉ O LORD God, might dwell there.

¹⁹Praise be to the Lord, to God our Savior,
    who daily bears our burdens.   *Selah*

THE MESSAGE

68.5-6 Father of orphans,
    champion of widows,
    is God in his holy house.
God makes homes for the homeless,
    leads prisoners to freedom,
    but leaves rebels to rot in hell.

68.7-10 God, when you took the lead with your
       people,
    when you marched out into the wild,
Earth shook, sky broke out in a sweat;
    God was on the march.
Even Sinai trembled at the sight of God on the
       move,
    at the sight of Israel's God.
You pour out rain in buckets, O God;
    thorn and cactus become an oasis
For your people to camp in and enjoy.
    You set them up in business;
    they went from rags to riches.

68.11-14 The Lord gave the word;
    thousands called out the good news:
"Kings of the armies
    are on the run, on the run!"
While housewives, safe and sound back home,
    divide up the plunder,
    the plunder of Canaanite silver and gold.
On that day that Shaddai scattered the kings,
    snow fell on Black Mountain.

68.15-16 You huge mountains, Bashan mountains,
    mighty mountains, dragon mountains.
All you mountains not chosen,
    sulk now, and feel sorry for yourselves,
For this is the mountain God has chosen to
       live on;
    he'll rule from this mountain forever.

68.17-18 The chariots of God, twice ten thousand,
    and thousands more besides,
The Lord in the lead, riding down Sinai—
    straight to the Holy Place!
You climbed to the High Place, captives in
       tow,
    your arms full of booty from rebels,
And now you sit there in state,
    GOD, sovereign GOD!

68.19-23 Blessed be the Lord—
    day after day he carries us along.

ᵃ 6 Or *the desolate in a homeland*   ᵇ 13 Or *saddlebags*
ᶜ 14 Hebrew *Shaddai*   ᵈ 18 Or *gifts for men, / even*
ᵉ 18 Or *they*

NEW INTERNATIONAL VERSION

20 Our God is a God who saves;
  from the Sovereign LORD comes escape
    from death.
21 Surely God will crush the heads of his
    enemies,
  the hairy crowns of those who go on in
    their sins.
22 The Lord says, "I will bring them from
    Bashan;
  I will bring them from the depths of the
    sea,
23 that you may plunge your feet in the blood
    of your foes,
  while the tongues of your dogs have their
    share."

24 Your procession has come into view, O God,
  the procession of my God and King into
    the sanctuary.
25 In front are the singers, after them the
    musicians;
  with them are the maidens playing
    tambourines.
26 Praise God in the great congregation;
  praise the LORD in the assembly of Israel.
27 There is the little tribe of Benjamin, leading
    them,
  there the great throng of Judah's princes,
  and there the princes of Zebulun and of
    Naphtali.

28 Summon your power, O God*a*;
  show us your strength, O God, as you
    have done before.
29 Because of your temple at Jerusalem
  kings will bring you gifts.
30 Rebuke the beast among the reeds,
  the herd of bulls among the calves of the
    nations.
  Humbled, may it bring bars of silver.
  Scatter the nations who delight in war.
31 Envoys will come from Egypt;
  Cush*b* will submit herself to God.

32 Sing to God, O kingdoms of the earth,
  sing praise to the Lord, *Selah*
33 to him who rides the ancient skies above,
  who thunders with mighty voice.
34 Proclaim the power of God,
  whose majesty is over Israel,
  whose power is in the skies.
35 You are awesome, O God, in your sanctuary;
  the God of Israel gives power and strength
    to his people.

  Praise be to God!

*a 28 Many Hebrew manuscripts, Septuagint and Syriac;
most Hebrew manuscripts Your God has summoned power for
you   b 31 That is, the upper Nile region*

THE MESSAGE

He's our Savior, our God, oh yes!
  He's God-for-us, he's God-who-saves-us.
Lord GOD knows all
  death's ins and outs.
What's more, he made heads roll,
  split the skulls of the enemy
As he marched out of heaven,
  saying, "I tied up the Dragon in knots,
  put a muzzle on the Deep Blue Sea."
You can wade through your enemies' blood,
  and your dogs taste of your enemies from
    your boots.

68.24-31 See God on parade
  to the sanctuary, my God,
  my King on the march!
Singers out front, the band behind,
  maidens in the middle with castanets.
The whole choir blesses God.
  Like a fountain of praise, Israel blesses
    GOD.
Look—little Benjamin's out
  front and leading
Princes of Judah in their royal robes,
  princes of Zebulon, princes of Naphtali.
Parade your power, O God,
  the power, O God, that made us what we
    are.
Your temple, High God, is Jerusalem;
  kings bring gifts to you.
Rebuke that old crocodile, Egypt,
  with her herd of wild bulls and calves,
Rapacious in her lust for silver,
  crushing peoples, spoiling for a fight.
Let Egyptian traders bring blue cloth
  and Cush come running to God, her hands
    outstretched.

68.32-34 Sing, O kings of the earth!
  Sing praises to the Lord!
There he is: Sky-Rider,
  striding the ancient skies.
Listen—he's calling in thunder,
  rumbling, rolling thunder.
Call out "Bravo!" to God,
  the High God of Israel.
His splendor and strength
  rise huge as thunderheads.

68.35 A terrible beauty, O God,
  streams from your sanctuary.
It's Israel's strong God! He gives
  power and might to his people!
O you, his people—bless God!

NEW INTERNATIONAL VERSION

PSALM 69

For the director of music. To the tune of "Lilies." Of David.

[1] Save me, O God,
for the waters have come up to my neck.
[2] I sink in the miry depths,
where there is no foothold.
I have come into the deep waters;
the floods engulf me.
[3] I am worn out calling for help;
my throat is parched.
My eyes fail,
looking for my God.
[4] Those who hate me without reason
outnumber the hairs of my head;
many are my enemies without cause,
those who seek to destroy me.
I am forced to restore
what I did not steal.

[5] You know my folly, O God;
my guilt is not hidden from you.

[6] May those who hope in you
not be disgraced because of me,
O Lord, the LORD Almighty;
may those who seek you
not be put to shame because of me,
O God of Israel.
[7] For I endure scorn for your sake,
and shame covers my face.
[8] I am a stranger to my brothers,
an alien to my own mother's sons;
[9] for zeal for your house consumes me,
and the insults of those who insult you
fall on me.
[10] When I weep and fast,
I must endure scorn;
[11] when I put on sackcloth,
people make sport of me.
[12] Those who sit at the gate mock me,
and I am the song of the drunkards.

[13] But I pray to you, O LORD,
in the time of your favor;
in your great love, O God,
answer me with your sure salvation.
[14] Rescue me from the mire,
do not let me sink;
deliver me from those who hate me,
from the deep waters.
[15] Do not let the floodwaters engulf me
or the depths swallow me up
or the pit close its mouth over me.

THE MESSAGE

A David psalm

69.1 **69** God, God, save me!
I'm in over my head,

69.2 Quicksand under me, swamp water over me;
I'm going down for the third time.

69.3 I'm hoarse from calling for help,
Bleary-eyed from searching the sky for God.

69.4 I've got more enemies than hairs on my head;
Sneaks and liars are out to knife me in the
back.

What I never stole
Must I now give back?

69.5 God, you know every sin I've committed;
My life's a wide-open book before you.

69.6 Don't let those who look to you in hope
Be discouraged by what happens to me,
Dear Lord! GOD of the armies!

Don't let those out looking for you
Come to a dead end by following me—
Please, dear God of Israel!

69.7 Because of you I look like an idiot,
I walk around ashamed to show my face.

69.8 My brothers shun me like a bum off the street;
My family treats me like an unwanted guest.

69.9 I love you more than I can say.
Because I'm madly in love with you,
They blame me for everything they dislike
about you.

69.10 When I poured myself out in prayer and fasting,
All it got me was more contempt.

69.11 When I put on a sad face,
They treated me like a clown.

69.12 Now drunks and gluttons
Make up drinking songs about me.

69.13 And me? I pray.
GOD, it's time for a break!

God, answer in love!
Answer with your sure salvation!

69.14 Rescue me from the swamp,
Don't let me go under for good,

Pull me out of the clutch of the enemy;
This whirlpool is sucking me down.

69.15 Don't let the swamp be my grave, the Black
Hole
Swallow me, its jaws clenched around me.

NEW INTERNATIONAL VERSION

¹⁶Answer me, O LORD, out of the goodness of
    your love;
    in your great mercy turn to me.
¹⁷Do not hide your face from your servant;
    answer me quickly, for I am in trouble.
¹⁸Come near and rescue me;
    redeem me because of my foes.

¹⁹You know how I am scorned, disgraced and
    shamed;
    all my enemies are before you.
²⁰Scorn has broken my heart
    and has left me helpless;
  I looked for sympathy, but there was none,
    for comforters, but I found none.
²¹They put gall in my food
    and gave me vinegar for my thirst.

²²May the table set before them become a
    snare;
    may it become retribution and ^{a} a trap.
²³May their eyes be darkened so they cannot
    see,
    and their backs be bent forever.
²⁴Pour out your wrath on them;
    let your fierce anger overtake them.
²⁵May their place be deserted;
    let there be no one to dwell in their tents.
²⁶For they persecute those you wound
    and talk about the pain of those you hurt.
²⁷Charge them with crime upon crime;
    do not let them share in your salvation.
²⁸May they be blotted out of the book of life
    and not be listed with the righteous.

²⁹I am in pain and distress;
    may your salvation, O God, protect me.

³⁰I will praise God's name in song
    and glorify him with thanksgiving.
³¹This will please the LORD more than an ox,
    more than a bull with its horns and hoofs.
³²The poor will see and be glad—
    you who seek God, may your hearts live!
³³The LORD hears the needy
    and does not despise his captive people.

³⁴Let heaven and earth praise him,
    the seas and all that move in them,
³⁵for God will save Zion
    and rebuild the cities of Judah.

^{a} 22 Or snare / and their fellowship become

THE MESSAGE

69.16 Now answer me, GOD, because you love me;
    Let me see your great mercy full-face.

69.17 Don't look the other way; your servant can't
    take it.
    I'm in trouble. Answer right now!

69.18 Come close, God; get me out of here.
    Rescue me from this deathtrap.

69.19 You know how they kick me around—
    Pin on me the donkey's ears, the dunce's cap.

69.20 I'm broken by their taunts,
    Flat on my face, reduced to a nothing.

I looked in vain for one friendly face. Not one.
    I couldn't find one shoulder to cry on.

69.21 They put poison in my soup,
    Vinegar in my drink.

69.22 Let their supper be bait in a trap that snaps
    shut;
    May their best friends be trappers who'll skin
    them alive.

69.23 Make them become blind as bats,
    Give them the shakes from morning to night.

69.24 Let them know what you think of them,
    Blast them with your red-hot anger.

69.25 Burn down their houses,
    Leave them desolate with nobody at home.

69.26 They gossiped about the one you disciplined,
    Made up stories about anyone wounded by
        God.

69.27 Pile on the guilt,
    Don't let them off the hook.

69.28 Strike their names from the list of the living;
    No rock-carved honor for them among the
        righteous.

69.29 I'm hurt and in pain;
    Give me space for healing, and mountain air.

69.30 Let me shout God's name with a praising song,
    Let me tell his greatness in a prayer of thanks.

69.31 For GOD, this is better than oxen on the altar,
    Far better than blue-ribbon bulls.

69.32 The poor in spirit see and are glad—
    Oh, you God-seekers, take heart!

69.33 For GOD listens to the poor,
    He doesn't walk out on the wretched.

69.34 You heavens, praise him; praise him, earth;
    Also ocean and all things that swim in it.

69.35 For God is out to help Zion,
    Rebuilding the wrecked towns of Judah.

NEW INTERNATIONAL VERSION

Then people will settle there and possess it;
36 the children of his servants will inherit it,
and those who love his name will dwell
there.

PSALM 70

For the director of music. Of David. A petition.

¹ Hasten, O God, to save me;
O LORD, come quickly to help me.
² May those who seek my life
be put to shame and confusion;
may all who desire my ruin
be turned back in disgrace.
³ May those who say to me, "Aha! Aha!"
turn back because of their shame.
⁴ But may all who seek you
rejoice and be glad in you;
may those who love your salvation always
say,
"Let God be exalted!"

⁵ Yet I am poor and needy;
come quickly to me, O God.
You are my help and my deliverer;
O LORD, do not delay.

PSALM 71

¹ In you, O LORD, I have taken refuge;
let me never be put to shame.
² Rescue me and deliver me in your
righteousness;
turn your ear to me and save me.
³ Be my rock of refuge,
to which I can always go;
give the command to save me,
for you are my rock and my fortress.
⁴ Deliver me, O my God, from the hand of the
wicked,
from the grasp of evil and cruel men.

⁵ For you have been my hope, O Sovereign
LORD,
my confidence since my youth.
⁶ From birth I have relied on you;
you brought me forth from my mother's
womb.
I will ever praise you.
⁷ I have become like a portent to many,
but you are my strong refuge.
⁸ My mouth is filled with your praise,
declaring your splendor all day long.

⁹ Do not cast me away when I am old;
do not forsake me when my strength is
gone.
¹⁰ For my enemies speak against me;
those who wait to kill me conspire together.

THE MESSAGE

Guess who will live there—
The proud owners of the land?

69.36 No, the children of his servants will get it,
The lovers of his name will live in it.

A David prayer

70.1-3 **70** God! Please hurry to my rescue!
GOD, come quickly to my side!
Those who are out to get me—
let them fall all over themselves.
Those who relish my downfall—
send them down a blind alley.
Give them a taste of their own medicine,
those gossips off clucking their tongues.

70.4 Let those on the hunt for you
sing and celebrate.
Let all who love your saving way
say over and over, "God is mighty!"

70.5 But I've lost it. I'm wasted.
God—quickly, quickly!
Quick to my side, quick to my rescue!
GOD, don't lose a minute.

71.1-3 **71** I run for dear life to GOD,
I'll never live to regret it.
Do what you do so well:
get me out of this mess and up on my feet.
Put your ear to the ground and listen,
give me space for salvation.
Be a guest room where I can retreat;
you said your door was always open!
You're my salvation—my vast, granite fortress.

71.4-7 My God, free me from the grip of Wicked,
from the clutch of Bad and Bully.
You keep me going when times are tough—
my bedrock, GOD, since my childhood.
I've hung on you from the day of my birth,
the day you took me from the cradle;
I'll never run out of praise.
Many gasp in alarm when they see me,
but you take me in stride.

71.8-11 Just as each day brims with your beauty,
my mouth brims with praise.
But don't turn me out to pasture when I'm old
or put me on the shelf when I can't pull my
weight.
My enemies are talking behind my back,
watching for their chance to knife me.

NEW INTERNATIONAL VERSION

11 They say, "God has forsaken him;
   pursue him and seize him,
   for no one will rescue him."
12 Be not far from me, O God;
   come quickly, O my God, to help me.
13 May my accusers perish in shame;
   may those who want to harm me
   be covered with scorn and disgrace.

14 But as for me, I will always have hope;
   I will praise you more and more.
15 My mouth will tell of your righteousness,
   of your salvation all day long,
   though I know not its measure.
16 I will come and proclaim your mighty acts,
      O Sovereign LORD;
   I will proclaim your righteousness, yours
      alone.
17 Since my youth, O God, you have taught me,
   and to this day I declare your marvelous
      deeds.
18 Even when I am old and gray,
   do not forsake me, O God,
   till I declare your power to the next
      generation,
   your might to all who are to come.

19 Your righteousness reaches to the skies,
      O God,
   you who have done great things.
   Who, O God, is like you?
20 Though you have made me see troubles,
      many and bitter,
   you will restore my life again;
   from the depths of the earth
   you will again bring me up.
21 You will increase my honor
   and comfort me once again.

22 I will praise you with the harp
   for your faithfulness, O my God;
   I will sing praise to you with the lyre,
      O Holy One of Israel.
23 My lips will shout for joy
   when I sing praise to you—
   I, whom you have redeemed.
24 My tongue will tell of your righteous acts
   all day long,
   for those who wanted to harm me
   have been put to shame and confusion.

PSALM 72

Of Solomon.

1 Endow the king with your justice, O God,
   the royal son with your righteousness.
2 He will*a* judge your people in righteousness,
   your afflicted ones with justice.

a 2 Or May he; similarly in verses 3-11 and 17

THE MESSAGE

The gossip is: "God has abandoned him.
   Pounce on him now; no one will help
      him."
71.12-16 God, don't just watch from the sidelines.
   Come on! Run to my side!
My accusers—make them lose face.
   Those out to get me—make them look
Like idiots, while I stretch out, reaching for
      you,
   and daily add praise to praise.
I'll write the book on your righteousness,
   talk up your salvation the livelong day,
   never run out of good things to write or
      say.
I come in the power of the Lord GOD,
   I post signs marking his right-of-way.

71.17-24 You got me when I was an unformed youth,
   God, and taught me everything I know.
Now I'm telling the world your wonders;
   I'll keep at it until I'm old and gray.
God, don't walk off and leave me
   until I get out the news
Of your strong right arm to this world,
   news of your power to the world yet to
      come,
Your famous and righteous
   ways, O God.
God, you've done it all!
   Who is quite like you?
You, who made me stare trouble in the face,
   Turn me around;
Now let me look life in the face.
   I've been to the bottom;
Bring me up, streaming with honors;
   turn to me, be tender to me,
And I'll take up the lute and thank you
   to the tune of your faithfulness, God.
I'll make music for you on a harp,
   Holy One of Israel.
When I open up in song to you,
   I let out lungsful of praise,
   my rescued life a song.
All day long I'm chanting
   about you and your righteous ways,
While those who tried to do me in
   slink off looking ashamed.

A Solomon psalm

72.1-8 **72** Give the gift of wise rule to the king,
      O God,
   the gift of just rule to the crown prince.
May he judge your people rightly,
   be honorable to your meek and lowly.

NEW INTERNATIONAL VERSION

³ The mountains will bring prosperity to the
people,
the hills the fruit of righteousness.
⁴ He will defend the afflicted among the people
and save the children of the needy;
he will crush the oppressor.

⁵ He will endure[a] as long as the sun,
as long as the moon, through all
generations.
⁶ He will be like rain falling on a mown field,
like showers watering the earth.
⁷ In his days the righteous will flourish;
prosperity will abound till the moon is no
more.

⁸ He will rule from sea to sea
and from the River[b] to the ends of the
earth.[c]
⁹ The desert tribes will bow before him
and his enemies will lick the dust.
¹⁰ The kings of Tarshish and of distant shores
will bring tribute to him;
the kings of Sheba and Seba
will present him gifts.
¹¹ All kings will bow down to him
and all nations will serve him.

¹² For he will deliver the needy who cry out,
the afflicted who have no one to help.
¹³ He will take pity on the weak and the needy
and save the needy from death.
¹⁴ He will rescue them from oppression and
violence,
for precious is their blood in his sight.

¹⁵ Long may he live!
May gold from Sheba be given him.
May people ever pray for him
and bless him all day long.
¹⁶ Let grain abound throughout the land;
on the tops of the hills may it sway.
Let its fruit flourish like Lebanon;
let it thrive like the grass of the field.
¹⁷ May his name endure forever;
may it continue as long as the sun.

All nations will be blessed through him,
and they will call him blessed.

¹⁸ Praise be to the LORD God, the God of Israel,
who alone does marvelous deeds.
¹⁹ Praise be to his glorious name forever;
may the whole earth be filled with his glory.
Amen and Amen.

²⁰ This concludes the prayers of David son of
Jesse.

---

a 5 Septuagint; Hebrew *You will be feared*   *b 8* That is, the
Euphrates   *c 8* Or *the end of the land*

THE MESSAGE

Let the mountains give exuberant witness;
shape the hills with the contours of right
living.
Please stand up for the poor,
help the children of the needy,
come down hard on the cruel tyrants.
Outlast the sun, outlive the moon—
age after age after age.
Be rainfall on cut grass,
earth-refreshing rain showers.
Let righteousness burst into blossom
and peace abound until the moon fades to
nothing.
Rule from sea to sea,
from the River to the Rim.

72.9-14 Foes will fall on their knees before God,
his enemies lick the dust.
Kings remote and legendary will pay homage,
kings rich and resplendent will turn over
their wealth.
All kings will fall down and worship,
and godless nations sign up to serve him,
Because he rescues the poor at the first sign of
need,
the destitute who have run out of luck.
He opens a place in his heart for the down-
and-out,
he restores the wretched of the earth.
He frees them from tyranny and torture—
when they bleed, he bleeds;
when they die, he dies.

72.15-17 And live! Oh, let him live!
Deck him out in Sheba gold.
Offer prayers unceasing to him,
bless him from morning to night.
Fields of golden grain in the land,
cresting the mountains in wild exuberance,
Cornucopias of praise, praises
springing from the city like grass from the
earth.
May he never be forgotten,
his fame shine on like sunshine.
May all godless people enter his circle of
blessing
and bless the One who blessed them.

72.18-20 Blessed GOD, Israel's God,
the one and only wonder-working God!
Blessed always his blazing glory!
All earth brims with his glory.
Yes and Yes and Yes.

NEW INTERNATIONAL VERSION

BOOK III

Psalms 73–89

PSALM 73

A psalm of Asaph.

¹ Surely God is good to Israel,
   to those who are pure in heart.

² But as for me, my feet had almost slipped;
   I had nearly lost my foothold.
³ For I envied the arrogant
   when I saw the prosperity of the wicked.

⁴ They have no struggles;
   their bodies are healthy and strong.ᵃ
⁵ They are free from the burdens common to
      man;
   they are not plagued by human ills.
⁶ Therefore pride is their necklace;
   they clothe themselves with violence.
⁷ From their callous hearts comes iniquityᵇ;
   the evil conceits of their minds know no
      limits.
⁸ They scoff, and speak with malice;
   in their arrogance they threaten
      oppression.
⁹ Their mouths lay claim to heaven,
   and their tongues take possession of the
      earth.
¹⁰ Therefore their people turn to them
   and drink up waters in abundance.ᶜ
¹¹ They say, "How can God know?
   Does the Most High have knowledge?"

¹² This is what the wicked are like—
   always carefree, they increase in wealth.

¹³ Surely in vain have I kept my heart pure;
   in vain have I washed my hands in
      innocence.
¹⁴ All day long I have been plagued;
   I have been punished every morning.

¹⁵ If I had said, "I will speak thus,"
   I would have betrayed your children.
¹⁶ When I tried to understand all this,
   it was oppressive to me
¹⁷ till I entered the sanctuary of God;
   then I understood their final destiny.

¹⁸ Surely you place them on slippery ground;
   you cast them down to ruin.
¹⁹ How suddenly are they destroyed,
   completely swept away by terrors!

ᵃ 4 With a different word division of the Hebrew; Masoretic
Text *struggles at their death; / their bodies are healthy*
ᵇ 7 Syriac (see also Septuagint); Hebrew *Their eyes bulge
with fat*   ᶜ 10 The meaning of the Hebrew for this verse is
uncertain.

THE MESSAGE

An Asaph psalm

73.1-5 **73** No doubt about it! God is good—
   good to good people, good to the
      good-hearted.
But I nearly missed it,
   missed seeing his goodness.
I was looking the other way,
   looking up to the people
At the top,
   envying the wicked who have it made,
Who have nothing to worry about,
   not a care in the whole wide world.

73.6-10 Pretentious with arrogance,
   they wear the latest fashions in violence,
Pampered and overfed,
   decked out in silk bows of silliness.
They jeer, using words to kill;
   they bully their way with words.
They're full of hot air,
   loudmouths disturbing the peace.
People actually listen to them—can you
      believe it?
   Like thirsty puppies, they lap up their
      words.

73.11-14 What's going on here? Is God out to lunch?
   Nobody's tending the store.
The wicked get by with everything;
   they have it made, piling up riches.
I've been stupid to play by the rules;
   what has it gotten me?
A long run of bad luck, that's what—
   a slap in the face every time I walk out the
      door.

73.15-20 If I'd have given in and talked like this,
   I would have betrayed your dear children.
Still, when I tried to figure it out,
   all I got was a splitting headache . . .
Until I entered the sanctuary of God.
   Then I saw the whole picture:
The slippery road you've put them on,
   with a final crash in a ditch of delusions.
In the blink of an eye, disaster!
   A blind curve in the dark, and—nightmare!

NEW INTERNATIONAL VERSION

²⁰ As a dream when one awakes,
so when you arise, O Lord,
you will despise them as fantasies.

²¹ When my heart was grieved
and my spirit embittered,
²² I was senseless and ignorant;
I was a brute beast before you.

²³ Yet I am always with you;
you hold me by my right hand.
²⁴ You guide me with your counsel,
and afterward you will take me into glory.
²⁵ Whom have I in heaven but you?
And earth has nothing I desire besides
you.
²⁶ My flesh and my heart may fail,
but God is the strength of my heart
and my portion forever.

²⁷ Those who are far from you will perish;
you destroy all who are unfaithful to you.
²⁸ But as for me, it is good to be near God.
I have made the Sovereign LORD my
refuge;
I will tell of all your deeds.

PSALM 74

A maskil^a of Asaph.

¹ Why have you rejected us forever, O God?
Why does your anger smolder against the
sheep of your pasture?
² Remember the people you purchased of old,
the tribe of your inheritance, whom you
redeemed—
Mount Zion, where you dwelt.
³ Turn your steps toward these everlasting
ruins,
all this destruction the enemy has brought
on the sanctuary.

⁴ Your foes roared in the place where you met
with us;
they set up their standards as signs.
⁵ They behaved like men wielding axes
to cut through a thicket of trees.
⁶ They smashed all the carved paneling
with their axes and hatchets.
⁷ They burned your sanctuary to the ground;
they defiled the dwelling place of your
Name.
⁸ They said in their hearts, "We will crush
them completely!"
They burned every place where God was
worshiped in the land.

^a Title: Probably a literary or musical term

THE MESSAGE

We wake up and rub our eyes. . . . Nothing.
There's nothing to them. And there never
was.

^{73.21-24} When I was beleaguered and bitter,
totally consumed by envy,
I was totally ignorant, a dumb ox
in your very presence.
I'm still in your presence,
but you've taken my hand.
You wisely and tenderly lead me,
and then you bless me.

^{73.25-28} You're all I want in heaven!
You're all I want on earth!
When my skin sags and my bones get brittle,
GOD is rock-firm and faithful.
Look! Those who left you are falling apart!
Deserters, they'll never be heard from
again.
But I'm in the very presence of God—
oh, how refreshing it is!
I've made Lord GOD my home.
God, I'm telling the world what you do!

An Asaph psalm

^{74.1} **74** You walked off and left us, and never
looked back.
God, how could you do that?
We're your very own sheep;
how can you stomp off in anger?

^{74.2-3} Refresh your memory of us—you bought us a
long time ago.
Your most precious tribe—you paid a good
price for us!
Your very own Mount Zion—you actually
lived here once!
Come and visit the site of disaster,
see how they've wrecked the sanctuary.

^{74.4-8} While your people were at worship, your
enemies barged in,
brawling and scrawling graffiti.
They set fire to the porch;
axes swinging, they chopped up the
woodwork,
Beat down the doors with sledgehammers,
then split them into kindling.
They burned your holy place to the ground,
violated the place of worship.
They said to themselves, "We'll wipe them all
out,"
and burned down all the places of worship.

NEW INTERNATIONAL VERSION

⁹ We are given no miraculous signs;
  no prophets are left,
  and none of us knows how long this will be.

¹⁰ How long will the enemy mock you, O God?
  Will the foe revile your name forever?
¹¹ Why do you hold back your hand, your right
    hand?
  Take it from the folds of your garment
    and destroy them!

¹² But you, O God, are my king from of old;
  you bring salvation upon the earth.
¹³ It was you who split open the sea by your
    power;
  you broke the heads of the monster in the
    waters.
¹⁴ It was you who crushed the heads of
    Leviathan
  and gave him as food to the creatures of
    the desert.
¹⁵ It was you who opened up springs and
    streams;
  you dried up the ever flowing rivers.
¹⁶ The day is yours, and yours also the night;
  you established the sun and moon.
¹⁷ It was you who set all the boundaries of the
    earth;
  you made both summer and winter.

¹⁸ Remember how the enemy has mocked you,
    O Lord,
  how foolish people have reviled your
    name.
¹⁹ Do not hand over the life of your dove to
    wild beasts;
  do not forget the lives of your afflicted
    people forever.
²⁰ Have regard for your covenant,
  because haunts of violence fill the dark
    places of the land.
²¹ Do not let the oppressed retreat in disgrace;
  may the poor and needy praise your
    name.

²² Rise up, O God, and defend your cause;
  remember how fools mock you all day long.
²³ Do not ignore the clamor of your
    adversaries,
  the uproar of your enemies, which rises
    continually.

PSALM 75

For the director of music. To the tune of, "Do
Not Destroy." A psalm of Asaph. A song.

¹ We give thanks to you, O God,
  we give thanks, for your Name is near;
  men tell of your wonderful deeds.

THE MESSAGE

74.9-17 There's not a sign or symbol of God in sight,
  nor anyone to speak in his name,
  no one who knows what's going on.
How long, God, will barbarians blaspheme,
  enemies curse and get by with it?
Why don't you do something? How long are
    you going
  to sit there with your hands folded in your
    lap?
God is my King from the very start;
  he works salvation in the womb of the
    earth.
With one blow you split the sea in two,
  you made mincemeat of the dragon Tannin.
You lopped off the heads of Leviathan,
  then served them up in a stew for the
    animals.
With your finger you opened up springs and
    creeks,
  and dried up the wild floodwaters.
You own the day, you own the night;
  you put stars and sun in place.
You laid out the four corners of earth,
  shaped the seasons of summer and winter.

74.18-21 Mark and remember, God, all the enemy
    taunts, each idiot desecration.
Don't throw your lambs to the wolves;
  after all we've been through, don't forget us.
Remember your promises;
  the city is in darkness, the countryside
    violent.
Don't leave the victims to rot in the street;
  make them a choir that sings your praises.

74.22-23 On your feet, O God—
  stand up for yourself!
Do you hear what they're saying about you,
  all the vile obscenities?
Don't tune out their malicious filth,
  the brawling invective that never lets up.

An Asaph psalm

75.1 **75** We thank you, God, we thank you—
  your Name is our favorite word;
  your mighty works are all we talk about.

NEW INTERNATIONAL VERSION

2 You say, "I choose the appointed time;
　　it is I who judge uprightly.
3 When the earth and all its people quake,
　　it is I who hold its pillars firm.　　*Selah*
4 To the arrogant I say, 'Boast no more,'
　　and to the wicked, 'Do not lift up your
　　　horns.
5 Do not lift your horns against heaven;
　　do not speak with outstretched neck.' "

6 No one from the east or the west
　　or from the desert can exalt a man.
7 But it is God who judges:
　　He brings one down, he exalts another.
8 In the hand of the LORD is a cup
　　full of foaming wine mixed with spices;
　he pours it out, and all the wicked of the
　　earth
　　drink it down to its very dregs.

9 As for me, I will declare this forever;
　　I will sing praise to the God of Jacob.
10 I will cut off the horns of all the wicked,
　　but the horns of the righteous will be
　　　lifted up.

PSALM 76

For the director of music. With stringed
instruments. A psalm of Asaph. A song.

1 In Judah God is known;
　　his name is great in Israel.
2 His tent is in Salem,
　　his dwelling place in Zion.
3 There he broke the flashing arrows,
　　the shields and the swords, the weapons
　　　of war.　　*Selah*

4 You are resplendent with light,
　　more majestic than mountains rich with
　　　game.
5 Valiant men lie plundered,
　　they sleep their last sleep;
　not one of the warriors
　　can lift his hands.
6 At your rebuke, O God of Jacob,
　　both horse and chariot lie still.
7 You alone are to be feared.
　　Who can stand before you when you are
　　　angry?
8 From heaven you pronounced judgment,
　　and the land feared and was quiet—
9 when you, O God, rose up to judge,
　　to save all the afflicted of the land.　　*Selah*

THE MESSAGE

75.2-4 You say, "I'm calling this meeting to order,
　　I'm ready to set things right.
When the earth goes topsy-turvy
　　And nobody knows which end is up,
I nail it all down,
　　I put everything in place again.
I say to the smart alecks, 'That's enough,'
　　to the bullies, 'Not so fast.' "

75.5-6 Don't raise your fist against High God.
　　Don't raise your voice against Rock of Ages.
He's the One from east to west;
　　from desert to mountains, he's the One.

75.7-8 God rules: he brings this one down to his
　　　knees,
　　pulls that one up on her feet.
GOD has a cup in his hand,
　　a bowl of wine, full to the brim.
He draws from it and pours;
　　it's drained to the dregs.
Earth's wicked ones drink it all,
　　drink it down to the last bitter drop!

75.9-10 And I'm telling the story of God Eternal,
　　singing the praises of Jacob's God.
The fists of the wicked
　　are bloody stumps,
The arms of the righteous
　　are lofty green branches.

An Asaph psalm

76.1-3 **76** God is well-known in Judah;
　　in Israel, he's a household name.
He keeps a house in Salem,
　　his own suite of rooms in Zion.
That's where, using arrows for kindling,
　　he made a bonfire of weapons of war.

76.4-6 Oh, how bright you shine!
　　Outshining their huge piles of loot!
The warriors were plundered
　　and left there impotent.
And now there's nothing to them,
　　nothing to show for their swagger and
　　　threats.
Your sudden roar, God of Jacob,
　　knocked the wind out of horse and rider.

76.7-10 Fierce you are, and fearsome!
　　Who can stand up to your rising anger?
From heaven you thunder judgment;
　　earth falls to her knees and holds her
　　　breath.
God stands tall and makes things right,
　　he saves all the wretched on earth.

NEW INTERNATIONAL VERSION

¹⁰Surely your wrath against men brings you
    praise,
  and the survivors of your wrath are
    restrained. ᵃ

¹¹Make vows to the LORD your God and fulfill
    them;
  let all the neighboring lands
    bring gifts to the One to be feared.
¹²He breaks the spirit of rulers;
  he is feared by the kings of the earth.

PSALM 77

For the director of music. For Jeduthun.
Of Asaph. A psalm.

¹I cried out to God for help;
  I cried out to God to hear me.
²When I was in distress, I sought the Lord;
  at night I stretched out untiring hands
  and my soul refused to be comforted.

³I remembered you, O God, and I groaned;
  I mused, and my spirit grew faint.   *Selah*
⁴You kept my eyes from closing;
  I was too troubled to speak.
⁵I thought about the former days,
  the years of long ago;
⁶I remembered my songs in the night.
  My heart mused and my spirit inquired:

⁷"Will the Lord reject forever?
  Will he never show his favor again?
⁸Has his unfailing love vanished forever?
  Has his promise failed for all time?
⁹Has God forgotten to be merciful?
  Has he in anger withheld his
    compassion?"   *Selah*

¹⁰Then I thought, "To this I will appeal:
  the years of the right hand of the Most
    High."
¹¹I will remember the deeds of the LORD;
  yes, I will remember your miracles of long
    ago.
¹²I will meditate on all your works
  and consider all your mighty deeds.

¹³Your ways, O God, are holy.
  What god is so great as our God?
¹⁴You are the God who performs miracles;
  you display your power among the
    peoples.
¹⁵With your mighty arm you redeemed your
    people,
  the descendants of Jacob and Joseph.
                    Selah

ᵃ *10 Or Surely the wrath of men brings you praise, / and with the remainder of wrath you arm yourself*

THE MESSAGE

Instead of smoldering rage—God-praise!
  All that sputtering rage—now a garland for
    God!
⁷⁶·¹¹⁻¹²Do for GOD what you said you'd do—
  he is, after all, your God.
Let everyone in town bring offerings
  to the One Who Watches our every move.
Nobody gets by with anything,
  no one plays fast and loose with him.

An Asaph psalm

⁷⁷·¹ **77** I yell out to my God, I yell with all my
    might,
  I yell at the top of my lungs. He listens.

⁷⁷·²⁻⁶I found myself in trouble and went looking for
    my Lord;
  my life was an open wound that wouldn't
    heal.
When friends said, "Everything will turn out
    all right,"
  I didn't believe a word they said.
I remember God—and shake my head.
  I bow my head—then wring my hands.
I'm awake all night—not a wink of sleep;
  I can't even say what's bothering me.
I go over the days one by one,
  I ponder the years gone by.
I strum my lute all through the night,
  wondering how to get my life together.

⁷⁷·⁷⁻¹⁰Will the Lord walk off and leave us for good?
  Will he never smile again?
Is his love worn threadbare?
  Has his salvation promise burned out?
Has God forgotten his manners?
  Has he angrily stalked off and left us?
"Just my luck," I said. "The High God goes
    out of business
  just the moment I need him."

⁷⁷·¹¹⁻¹²Once again I'll go over what GOD has done,
  lay out on the table the ancient wonders;
I'll ponder all the things you've accomplished,
  and give a long, loving look at your acts.

⁷⁷·¹³⁻¹⁵O God! Your way is holy!
  No god is great like God!
You're the God who makes things happen;
  you showed everyone what you can do—
You pulled your people out of the worst kind
    of trouble,
  rescued the children of Jacob and Joseph.

NEW INTERNATIONAL VERSION

16 The waters saw you, O God,
    the waters saw you and writhed;
    the very depths were convulsed.
17 The clouds poured down water,
    the skies resounded with thunder;
    your arrows flashed back and forth.
18 Your thunder was heard in the whirlwind,
    your lightning lit up the world;
    the earth trembled and quaked.
19 Your path led through the sea,
    your way through the mighty waters,
    though your footprints were not seen.

20 You led your people like a flock
    by the hand of Moses and Aaron.

PSALM 78

A maskil [a] *of Asaph.*

1 O my people, hear my teaching;
    listen to the words of my mouth.
2 I will open my mouth in parables,
    I will utter hidden things, things from of
    old—
3 what we have heard and known,
    what our fathers have told us.
4 We will not hide them from their children;
    we will tell the next generation
    the praiseworthy deeds of the LORD,
    his power, and the wonders he has done.
5 He decreed statutes for Jacob
    and established the law in Israel,
    which he commanded our forefathers
    to teach their children,
6 so the next generation would know them,
    even the children yet to be born,
    and they in turn would tell their children.
7 Then they would put their trust in God
    and would not forget his deeds
    but would keep his commands.
8 They would not be like their forefathers—
    a stubborn and rebellious generation,
    whose hearts were not loyal to God,
    whose spirits were not faithful to him.

9 The men of Ephraim, though armed with
    bows,
    turned back on the day of battle;
10 they did not keep God's covenant
    and refused to live by his law.
11 They forgot what he had done,
    the wonders he had shown them.
12 He did miracles in the sight of their fathers
    in the land of Egypt, in the region of
    Zoan.
13 He divided the sea and led them through;
    he made the water stand firm like a wall.

[a] Title: Probably a literary or musical term

THE MESSAGE

77.16-19 Ocean saw you in action, God,
    saw you and trembled with fear;
    Deep Ocean was scared to death.
Clouds belched buckets of rain,
    Sky exploded with thunder,
    your arrows flashing this way and that.
From Whirlwind came your thundering voice,
    Lightning exposed the world,
    Earth reeled and rocked.
You strode right through Ocean,
    walked straight through roaring Ocean,
    but nobody saw you come or go.

77.20 Hidden in the hands of Moses and Aaron,
You led your people like a flock of sheep.

An Asaph psalm

78.1-4 **78** Listen, dear friends, to God's truth,
    bend your ears to what I tell you.
I'm chewing on the morsel of a proverb;
    I'll let you in on the sweet old truths,
Stories we heard from our fathers,
    counsel we learned at our mother's knee.
We're not keeping this to ourselves,
    we're passing it along to the next
        generation—
GOD's fame and fortune,
    the marvelous things he has done.

78.5-8 He planted a witness in Jacob,
    set his Word firmly in Israel,
Then commanded our parents
    to teach it to their children
So the next generation would know,
    and all the generations to come—
Know the truth and tell the stories
    so their children can trust in God,
Never forget the works of God
    but keep his commands to the letter.
Heaven forbid they should be like their
        parents,
    bullheaded and bad,
A fickle and faithless bunch
    who never stayed true to God.

78.9-16 The Ephraimites, armed to the teeth,
    ran off when the battle began.
They were cowards to God's Covenant,
    refused to walk by his Word.
They forgot what he had done—
    marvels he'd done right before their eyes.
He performed miracles in plain sight of their
        parents
    in Egypt, out on the fields of Zoan.
He split the Sea and they walked right
        through it;
    he piled the waters to the right and the left.

NEW INTERNATIONAL VERSION

¹⁴He guided them with the cloud by day
    and with light from the fire all night.
¹⁵He split the rocks in the desert
    and gave them water as abundant as the
        seas;
¹⁶he brought streams out of a rocky crag
    and made water flow down like rivers.

¹⁷But they continued to sin against him,
    rebelling in the desert against the Most
        High.
¹⁸They willfully put God to the test
    by demanding the food they craved.
¹⁹They spoke against God, saying,
    "Can God spread a table in the desert?
²⁰When he struck the rock, water gushed out,
    and streams flowed abundantly.
  But can he also give us food?
    Can he supply meat for his people?"
²¹When the LORD heard them, he was very
        angry;
    his fire broke out against Jacob,
    and his wrath rose against Israel,
²²for they did not believe in God
    or trust in his deliverance.
²³Yet he gave a command to the skies above
    and opened the doors of the heavens;
²⁴he rained down manna for the people to eat,
    he gave them the grain of heaven.
²⁵Men ate the bread of angels;
    he sent them all the food they could eat.
²⁶He let loose the east wind from the heavens
    and led forth the south wind by his
        power.
²⁷He rained meat down on them like dust,
    flying birds like sand on the seashore.
²⁸He made them come down inside their
        camp,
    all around their tents.
²⁹They ate till they had more than enough,
    for he had given them what they craved.
³⁰But before they turned from the food they
        craved,
    even while it was still in their mouths,
³¹God's anger rose against them;
    he put to death the sturdiest among them,
    cutting down the young men of Israel.

³²In spite of all this, they kept on sinning;
    in spite of his wonders, they did not
        believe.
³³So he ended their days in futility
    and their years in terror.

THE MESSAGE

He led them by day with a cloud,
    led them all the night long with a fiery
        torch.
He split rocks in the wilderness,
    gave them all they could drink from
        underground springs;
He made creeks flow out from sheer rock,
    and water pour out like a river.

78:17-20 All they did was sin even more,
    rebel in the desert against the High God.
They tried to get their own way with God,
    clamored for favors, for special attention.
They whined like spoiled children,
    "Why can't God give us a decent meal in
        this desert?
Sure, he struck the rock and the water flowed,
    creeks cascaded from the rock.
But how about some fresh-baked bread?
    How about a nice cut of meat?"

78:21-31 When GOD heard that, he was furious—
    his anger flared against Jacob,
    he lost his temper with Israel.
It was clear they didn't believe God,
    had no intention of trusting in his help.
But God helped them anyway, commanded
        the clouds
    and gave orders that opened the gates of
        heaven.
He rained down showers of manna to eat,
    he gave them the Bread of Heaven.
They ate the bread of the mighty angels;
    he sent them all the food they could eat.
He let East Wind break loose from the skies,
    gave a strong push to South Wind.
This time it was birds that rained down—
    succulent birds, an abundance of birds.
He aimed them right for the center of their
        camp;
    all round their tents there were birds.
They ate and had their fill;
    he handed them everything they craved on
        a platter.
But their greed knew no bounds;
    they stuffed their mouths with more and
        more.
Finally, God was fed up, his anger erupted—
    he cut down their brightest and best,
    he laid low Israel's finest young men.

78:32-37 And—can you believe it?—they kept right on
        sinning;
    all those wonders and they still wouldn't
        believe!
So their lives dribbled off to nothing—
    nothing to show for their lives but a ghost
        town.

NEW INTERNATIONAL VERSION

34 Whenever God slew them, they would seek
       him;
    they eagerly turned to him again.
35 They remembered that God was their Rock,
    that God Most High was their Redeemer.
36 But then they would flatter him with their
       mouths,
    lying to him with their tongues;
37 their hearts were not loyal to him,
    they were not faithful to his covenant.
38 Yet he was merciful;
    he forgave their iniquities
    and did not destroy them.
 Time after time he restrained his anger
    and did not stir up his full wrath.
39 He remembered that they were but flesh,
    a passing breeze that does not return.

40 How often they rebelled against him in the
       desert
    and grieved him in the wasteland!
41 Again and again they put God to the test;
    they vexed the Holy One of Israel.
42 They did not remember his power—
    the day he redeemed them from the
       oppressor,
43 the day he displayed his miraculous signs in
       Egypt,
    his wonders in the region of Zoan.
44 He turned their rivers to blood;
    they could not drink from their streams.
45 He sent swarms of flies that devoured them,
    and frogs that devastated them.
46 He gave their crops to the grasshopper,
    their produce to the locust.
47 He destroyed their vines with hail
    and their sycamore-figs with sleet.
48 He gave over their cattle to the hail,
    their livestock to bolts of lightning.
49 He unleashed against them his hot anger,
    his wrath, indignation and hostility—
    a band of destroying angels.
50 He prepared a path for his anger;
    he did not spare them from death
    but gave them over to the plague.
51 He struck down all the firstborn of Egypt,
    the firstfruits of manhood in the tents of
       Ham.
52 But he brought his people out like a flock;
    he led them like sheep through the desert.
53 He guided them safely, so they were
       unafraid;
    but the sea engulfed their enemies.
54 Thus he brought them to the border of his
       holy land,
    to the hill country his right hand had
       taken.

THE MESSAGE

When he cut them down, they came running
       for help;
    they turned and pled for mercy.
They gave witness that God was their rock,
    that High God was their redeemer,
But they didn't mean a word of it;
    they lied through their teeth the whole
       time.
They could not have cared less about him,
    wanted nothing to do with his Covenant.

78.38-55 And God? Compassionate!
    Forgave the sin! Didn't destroy!
Over and over he reined in his anger,
    restrained his considerable wrath.
He knew what they were made of;
    he knew there wasn't much to them,
How often in the desert they had spurned
       him,
    tried his patience in those wilderness years.
Time and again they pushed him to the limit,
    provoked Israel's Holy God.
How quickly they forgot what he'd done,
    forgot their day of rescue from the enemy,
When he did miracles in Egypt,
    wonders on the plain of Zoan.
He turned the River and its streams to
       blood—
    not a drop of water fit to drink.
He sent flies, which ate them alive,
    and frogs, which bedeviled them.
He turned their harvest over to caterpillars,
    everything they had worked for to the
       locusts.
He flattened their grapevines with hail;
    a killing frost ruined their orchards.
He pounded their cattle with hail,
    let thunderbolts loose on their herds.
His anger flared,
    a wild firestorm of havoc,
An advance guard of disease-carrying angels
    to clear the ground, preparing the way
       before him.
He didn't spare those people,
    he let the plague rage through their lives.
He killed all the Egyptian firstborns,
    lusty infants, offspring of Ham's virility.
Then he led his people out like sheep,
    took his flock safely through the
       wilderness.
He took good care of them; they had nothing
       to fear.
    The Sea took care of their enemies for
       good.
He brought them into his holy land,
    this mountain he claimed for his own.

NEW INTERNATIONAL VERSION

⁵⁵He drove out nations before them
    and allotted their lands to them as an
      inheritance;
    he settled the tribes of Israel in their
      homes.
⁵⁶But they put God to the test
    and rebelled against the Most High;
    they did not keep his statutes.
⁵⁷Like their fathers they were disloyal and
      faithless,
    as unreliable as a faulty bow.
⁵⁸They angered him with their high places;
    they aroused his jealousy with their idols.
⁵⁹When God heard them, he was very angry;
    he rejected Israel completely.
⁶⁰He abandoned the tabernacle of Shiloh,
    the tent he had set up among men.
⁶¹He sent the ark of his might into captivity,
    his splendor into the hands of the enemy.
⁶²He gave his people over to the sword;
    he was very angry with his inheritance.
⁶³Fire consumed their young men,
    and their maidens had no wedding songs;
⁶⁴their priests were put to the sword,
    and their widows could not weep.
⁶⁵Then the Lord awoke as from sleep,
    as a man wakes from the stupor of wine.
⁶⁶He beat back his enemies;
    he put them to everlasting shame.
⁶⁷Then he rejected the tents of Joseph,
    he did not choose the tribe of Ephraim;
⁶⁸but he chose the tribe of Judah,
    Mount Zion, which he loved.
⁶⁹He built his sanctuary like the heights,
    like the earth that he established forever.
⁷⁰He chose David his servant
    and took him from the sheep pens;
⁷¹from tending the sheep he brought him
    to be the shepherd of his people Jacob,
    of Israel his inheritance.
⁷²And David shepherded them with integrity
      of heart;
    with skillful hands he led them.

PSALM 79

A psalm of Asaph.

¹O God, the nations have invaded your
      inheritance;
    they have defiled your holy temple,
    they have reduced Jerusalem to rubble.

THE MESSAGE

He scattered everyone who got in their way;
    he staked out an inheritance for them—
    the tribes of Israel all had their own places.

78.56-64 But they kept on giving him a hard time,
    rebelled against God, the High God,
    refused to do anything he told them.
They were worse, if that's possible, than their
      parents:
    traitors—crooked as a corkscrew.
Their pagan orgies provoked God's anger,
    their obscene idolatries broke his heart.
When God heard their carryings-on, he was
      furious;
    he posted a huge No over Israel.
He walked off and left Shiloh empty,
    abandoned the shrine where he had met
      with Israel.
He let his pride and joy go to the dogs,
    turned his back on the pride of his life.
He turned them loose on fields of battle;
    angry, he let them fend for themselves.
Their young men went to war and never came
      back;
    their young women waited in vain.
Their priests were massacred,
    and their widows never shed a tear.

78.65-72 Suddenly the Lord was up on his feet
    like someone roused from deep sleep,
    shouting like a drunken warrior.
He hit his enemies hard, sent them running,
    yelping, not daring to look back.
He disqualified Joseph as leader,
    told Ephraim he didn't have what it takes,
And chose the Tribe of Judah instead,
    Mount Zion, which he loves so much.
He built his sanctuary there, resplendent,
    solid and lasting as the earth itself.
Then he chose David, his servant,
    handpicked him from his work in the
      sheep pens.
One day he was caring for the ewes and their
      lambs,
    the next day God had him shepherding
      Jacob,
    his people Israel, his prize possession.
His good heart made him a good shepherd;
    he guided the people wisely and well.

An Asaph psalm

79.1-4 **79** God! Barbarians have broken into your
      home,
    violated your holy temple,
    left Jerusalem a pile of rubble!

NEW INTERNATIONAL VERSION

2 They have given the dead bodies of your
   servants
   as food to the birds of the air,
   the flesh of your saints to the beasts of the
      earth.
3 They have poured out blood like water
   all around Jerusalem,
   and there is no one to bury the dead.
4 We are objects of reproach to our neighbors,
   of scorn and derision to those around us.

5 How long, O LORD? Will you be angry
      forever?
   How long will your jealousy burn like
      fire?
6 Pour out your wrath on the nations
   that do not acknowledge you,
   on the kingdoms
   that do not call on your name;
7 for they have devoured Jacob
   and destroyed his homeland.
8 Do not hold against us the sins of the
      fathers;
   may your mercy come quickly to meet us,
   for we are in desperate need.

9 Help us, O God our Savior,
   for the glory of your name;
   deliver us and forgive our sins
   for your name's sake.
10 Why should the nations say,
   "Where is their God?"
   Before our eyes, make known among the
      nations
   that you avenge the outpoured blood of
      your servants.
11 May the groans of the prisoners come before
      you;
   by the strength of your arm
   preserve those condemned to die.

12 Pay back into the laps of our neighbors
      seven times
   the reproach they have hurled at you,
   O Lord.
13 Then we your people, the sheep of your
      pasture,
   will praise you forever;
   from generation to generation
   we will recount your praise.

PSALM 80

For the director of music. To the tune of, "The
Lilies of the Covenant." Of Asaph. A psalm.

1 Hear us, O Shepherd of Israel,
   you who lead Joseph like a flock;
you who sit enthroned between the
      cherubim, shine forth

THE MESSAGE

They've served up the corpses of your
      servants
   as carrion food for birds of prey,
Threw the bones of your holy people
   out to the wild animals to gnaw on.
They dumped out their blood
   like buckets of water.
All around Jerusalem, their bodies
   were left to rot, unburied.
We're nothing but a joke to our neighbors,
   graffiti scrawled on the city walls.

79.5-7 How long do we have to put up with this,
      GOD?
   Do you have it in for us for good?
   Will your smoldering rage never cool down?
If you're going to be angry, be angry
   with the pagans who care nothing about
      you,
   or your rival kingdoms who ignore you.
They're the ones who ruined Jacob,
   who wrecked and looted the place where
      he lived.

79.8-10 Don't blame us for the sins of our parents.
   Hurry up and help us; we're at the end of
      our rope.
You're famous for helping; God, give *us* a break.
   Your reputation is on the line.
Pull us out of this mess, forgive us our sins—
   do what you're famous for doing!
Don't let the heathen get by with their sneers:
   "Where's your God? Is he out to lunch?"
Go public and show the godless world
   that they can't kill your servants and get by
      with it.

79.11-13 Give groaning prisoners a hearing;
   pardon those on death row from their
      doom—you can do it!
Give our jeering neighbors what they've got
      coming to them;
   let their God-taunts boomerang and knock
      them flat.
Then we, your people, the ones you love and
      care for,
   will thank you over and over and over.
We'll tell everyone we meet
   how wonderful you are, how praiseworthy
      you are!

An Asaph psalm

80.1-2 **80** Listen, Shepherd, Israel's Shepherd—
         get all your Joseph sheep together.
Throw beams of light
   from your dazzling throne

NEW INTERNATIONAL VERSION

² before Ephraim, Benjamin and Manasseh.
Awaken your might;
  come and save us.

³ Restore us, O God;
  make your face shine upon us,
  that we may be saved.

⁴ O Lord God Almighty,
  how long will your anger smolder
  against the prayers of your people?
⁵ You have fed them with the bread of tears;
  you have made them drink tears by the
    bowlful.
⁶ You have made us a source of contention to
    our neighbors,
  and our enemies mock us.

⁷ Restore us, O God Almighty;
  make your face shine upon us,
  that we may be saved.

⁸ You brought a vine out of Egypt;
  you drove out the nations and planted it.
⁹ You cleared the ground for it,
  and it took root and filled the land.
¹⁰ The mountains were covered with its shade,
  the mighty cedars with its branches.
¹¹ It sent out its boughs to the Sea,ᵃ
  its shoots as far as the River.ᵇ

¹² Why have you broken down its walls
  so that all who pass by pick its grapes?
¹³ Boars from the forest ravage it
  and the creatures of the field feed on it.
¹⁴ Return to us, O God Almighty!
  Look down from heaven and see!
  Watch over this vine,
¹⁵   the root your right hand has planted,
  the sonᶜ you have raised up for yourself.

¹⁶ Your vine is cut down, it is burned with fire;
  at your rebuke your people perish.
¹⁷ Let your hand rest on the man at your right
    hand,
  the son of man you have raised up for
    yourself.
¹⁸ Then we will not turn away from you;
  revive us, and we will call on your name.

¹⁹ Restore us, O Lord God Almighty;
  make your face shine upon us,
  that we may be saved.

THE MESSAGE

So Ephraim, Benjamin, and Manasseh
  can see where they're going.
Get out of bed—you've slept long enough!
  Come on the run before it's too late.

80.3   God, come back!
  Smile your blessing smile:
  That will be our salvation.

80.4-6 God, God of the Angel Armies,
    how long will you smolder like a sleeping
      volcano
    while your people call for fire and
      brimstone?
  You put us on a diet of tears,
    bucket after bucket of salty tears to drink.
  You make us look ridiculous to our friends;
    our enemies poke fun day after day.

80.7   God of the Angel Armies, come back!
  Smile your blessing smile:
  That will be our salvation.

80.8-18 Remember how you brought a young vine
      from Egypt,
    cleared out the brambles and briers
    and planted your very own vineyard?
  You prepared the good earth,
    you planted her roots deep;
    the vineyard filled the land.
  Your vine soared high and shaded the
      mountains,
    even dwarfing the giant cedars.
  Your vine ranged west to the Sea,
    east to the River.
  So why do you no longer protect your vine?
    Trespassers pick its grapes at will;
  Wild pigs crash through and crush it,
    and the mice nibble away at what's left.
  God of the Angel Armies, turn our way!
    Take a good look at what's happened
    and attend to this vine.
  Care for what you once tenderly planted—
    the vine you raised from a shoot.
  And those who dared to set it on fire—
    give them a look that will kill!
  Then take the hand of your once-favorite
      child,
    the child you raised to adulthood.
  We will never turn our back on you;
    breathe life into our lungs so we can shout
      your name!

80.19   God, God of the Angel Armies, come back!
  Smile your blessing smile:
  That will be our salvation.

ᵃ 11 Probably the Mediterranean   ᵇ 11 That is, the
Euphrates   ᶜ 15 Or *branch*

NEW INTERNATIONAL VERSION

PSALM 81

For the director of music. According to *gittith.* ª
Of Asaph.

¹ Sing for joy to God our strength;
   shout aloud to the God of Jacob!
² Begin the music, strike the tambourine,
   play the melodious harp and lyre.

³ Sound the ram's horn at the New Moon,
   and when the moon is full, on the day of
      our Feast;
⁴ this is a decree for Israel,
   an ordinance of the God of Jacob.
⁵ He established it as a statute for Joseph
   when he went out against Egypt,
   where we heard a language we did not
      understand. ᵇ

⁶ He says, "I removed the burden from their
      shoulders;
   their hands were set free from the basket.
⁷ In your distress you called and I rescued
      you,
   I answered you out of a thundercloud;
   I tested you at the waters of Meribah.
                                    Selah

⁸ "Hear, O my people, and I will warn you—
   if you would but listen to me, O Israel!
⁹ You shall have no foreign god among you;
   you shall not bow down to an alien god.
¹⁰ I am the LORD your God,
   who brought you up out of Egypt.
   Open wide your mouth and I will fill it.

¹¹ "But my people would not listen to me;
   Israel would not submit to me.
¹² So I gave them over to their stubborn hearts
   to follow their own devices.

¹³ "If my people would but listen to me,
   if Israel would follow my ways,
¹⁴ how quickly would I subdue their enemies
   and turn my hand against their foes!
¹⁵ Those who hate the LORD would cringe
      before him,
   and their punishment would last forever.
¹⁶ But you would be fed with the finest of
      wheat;
   with honey from the rock I would satisfy
      you."

PSALM 82

A psalm of Asaph.

¹ God presides in the great assembly;
   he gives judgment among the "gods":

ª Title: Probably a musical term   ᵇ 5 Or / *and we heard a
voice we had not known*

THE MESSAGE

An Asaph psalm

81 A song to our strong God!
   a shout to the God of Jacob!

81.1-5 Anthems from the choir, music from the band,
   sweet sounds from lute and harp,
Trumpets and trombones and horns:
   it's festival day, a feast to God!
A day decreed by God,
   solemnly ordered by the God of Jacob.
He commanded Joseph to keep this day
   so we'd never forget what he did in Egypt.

I hear this most gentle whisper from One
I never guessed would speak to me:

81.6-7 "I took the world off your shoulders,
   freed you from a life of hard labor.
You called to me in your pain;
   I got you out of a bad place.
I answered you from where the thunder hides,
   I proved you at Meribah Fountain.

81.8-10 "Listen, dear ones—get this straight;
   O Israel, don't take this lightly.
Don't take up with strange gods,
   don't worship the latest in gods.
I'm GOD, your God, the very God
   who rescued you from doom in Egypt,
Then fed you all you could eat,
   filled your hungry stomachs.

81.11-12 "But my people didn't listen,
   Israel paid no attention;
So I let go of the reins and told them, 'Run!
   Do it your own way!'

81.13-16 "Oh, dear people, will you listen to me now?
   Israel, will you follow my map?
I'll make short work of your enemies,
   give your foes the back of my hand.
I'll send the GOD-haters cringing like dogs,
   never to be heard from again.
You'll feast on my fresh-baked bread
   spread with butter and rock-pure honey."

An Asaph psalm

82 God calls the judges into his
         courtroom,
82.1 he puts all the judges in the dock.

NEW INTERNATIONAL VERSION

² "How long will you[a] defend the unjust
    and show partiality to the wicked? *Selah*
³ Defend the cause of the weak and fatherless;
    maintain the rights of the poor and
      oppressed.
⁴ Rescue the weak and needy;
    deliver them from the hand of the wicked.

⁵ "They know nothing, they understand
      nothing.
They walk about in darkness;
    all the foundations of the earth are
      shaken.

⁶ "I said, 'You are "gods";
    you are all sons of the Most High.'
⁷ But you will die like mere men;
    you will fall like every other ruler."

⁸ Rise up, O God, judge the earth,
    for all the nations are your inheritance.

PSALM 83

A song. A psalm of Asaph.

¹ O God, do not keep silent;
    be not quiet, O God, be not still.
² See how your enemies are astir,
    how your foes rear their heads.
³ With cunning they conspire against your
      people;
    they plot against those you cherish.
⁴ "Come," they say, "let us destroy them as a
      nation,
    that the name of Israel be remembered no
      more."

⁵ With one mind they plot together;
    they form an alliance against you—
⁶ the tents of Edom and the Ishmaelites,
    of Moab and the Hagrites,
⁷ Gebal,[b] Ammon and Amalek,
    Philistia, with the people of Tyre.
⁸ Even Assyria has joined them
    to lend strength to the descendants of Lot.
        Selah

⁹ Do to them as you did to Midian,
    as you did to Sisera and Jabin at the river
      Kishon,
¹⁰ who perished at Endor
    and became like refuse on the ground.
¹¹ Make their nobles like Oreb and Zeeb,
    all their princes like Zebah and
      Zalmunna,

THE MESSAGE

82.2-4 "Enough! You've corrupted justice long
      enough,
    you've let the wicked get away with
      murder.
You're here to defend the defenseless,
    to make sure that underdogs get a fair
      break;
Your job is to stand up for the powerless,
    and prosecute all those who exploit them."

82.5 Ignorant judges! Head-in-the-sand judges!
    They haven't a clue to what's going on.
And now everything's falling apart,
    the world's coming unglued.

82.6-7 "I commissioned you judges, each one of you,
    deputies of the High God,
But you've betrayed your commission
    and now you're stripped of your rank,
      busted."

82.8 O God, give them their just deserts!
    You've got the whole world in your hands!

An Asaph psalm

83.1-5 **83** GOD, don't shut me out;
    don't give me the silent treatment,
      O God.
Your enemies are out there whooping it up,
    the God-haters are living it up;
They're plotting to do your people in,
    conspiring to rob you of your precious
      ones.
"Let's wipe this nation from the face of the
      earth,"
    they say; "scratch Israel's name off the
      books."
And now they're putting their heads together,
    making plans to get rid of you.

83.6-8 Edom and the Ishmaelites,
    Moab and the Hagrites,
Gebal and Ammon and Amalek,
    Philistia and the Tyrians,
And now Assyria has joined up,
    Giving muscle to the gang of Lot.

83.9-12 Do to them what you did to Midian,
    to Sisera and Jabin at Kishon Brook;
They came to a bad end at Endor,
    nothing but dung for the garden.
Cut down their leaders as you did Oreb and
      Zeeb,
    their princes to nothings like Zebah and
      Zalmunna,

---

a 2 The Hebrew is plural.   *b* 7 That is, Byblos

NEW INTERNATIONAL VERSION

¹²who said, "Let us take possession
  of the pasturelands of God."

¹³Make them like tumbleweed, O my God,
  like chaff before the wind.
¹⁴As fire consumes the forest
  or a flame sets the mountains ablaze,
¹⁵so pursue them with your tempest
  and terrify them with your storm.
¹⁶Cover their faces with shame
  so that men will seek your name, O LORD.

¹⁷May they ever be ashamed and dismayed;
  may they perish in disgrace.
¹⁸Let them know that you, whose name is the
  LORD—
  that you alone are the Most High over all
  the earth.

PSALM 84

For the director of music. According to gittith. *ᵃ
Of the Sons of Korah. A psalm.*

¹How lovely is your dwelling place,
  O LORD Almighty!
²My soul yearns, even faints,
  for the courts of the LORD;
my heart and my flesh cry out
  for the living God.

³Even the sparrow has found a home,
  and the swallow a nest for herself,
  where she may have her young—
a place near your altar,
  O LORD Almighty, my King and my God.
⁴Blessed are those who dwell in your house;
  they are ever praising you.   *Selah*

⁵Blessed are those whose strength is in you,
  who have set their hearts on pilgrimage.
⁶As they pass through the Valley of Baca,
  they make it a place of springs;
  the autumn rains also cover it with
  pools.ᵇ
⁷They go from strength to strength,
  till each appears before God in Zion.

⁸Hear my prayer, O LORD God Almighty;
  listen to me, O God of Jacob.   *Selah*
⁹Look upon our shield,ᶜ O God;
  look with favor on your anointed one.

¹⁰Better is one day in your courts
  than a thousand elsewhere;
I would rather be a doorkeeper in the house
  of my God

THE MESSAGE

With their empty brags, "We're grabbing it all,
  grabbing God's gardens for ourselves."

83.13-18 My God! I've had it with them!
  Blow them away!
Tumbleweeds in the desert waste,
  charred sticks in the burned-over ground.
Knock the breath right out of them, so they're
  gasping
  for breath, gasping, "GOD."
Bring them to the end of their rope,
  and leave them there dangling, helpless.
Then they'll learn your name: "GOD,"
  the one and only High God on earth.

A Korah psalm

84.1-2 **84** What a beautiful home, GOD of the
  Angel Armies!
I've always longed to live in a place like
  this,
Always dreamed of a room in your house,
  where I could sing for joy to God-alive!

84.3-4 Birds find nooks and crannies in your house,
  sparrows and swallows make nests there.
They lay their eggs and raise their young,
  singing their songs in the place where we
  worship.
GOD of the Angel Armies! King! God!
  How blessed they are to live and sing there!

84.5-7 And how blessed all those in whom you live,
  whose lives become roads you travel;
They wind through lonesome valleys, come
  upon brooks,
  discover cool springs and pools brimming
  with rain!
God-traveled, these roads curve up the
  mountain, and
  at the last turn—Zion! God in full view!

84.8-9 God of the Angel Armies, listen:
  O God of Jacob, open your ears—I'm
  praying!
Look at our shields, glistening in the sun,
  our faces, shining with your gracious
  anointing.

84.10-12 One day spent in your house, this beautiful
  place of worship,
  beats thousands spent on Greek island
  beaches.
I'd rather scrub floors in the house of my God

ᵃ *Title: Probably a musical term*   ᵇ *6 Or* blessings
ᶜ *9 Or* sovereign

NEW INTERNATIONAL VERSION

than dwell in the tents of the wicked.
[11] For the LORD God is a sun and shield;
the LORD bestows favor and honor;
no good thing does he withhold
from those whose walk is blameless.

[12] O LORD Almighty,
blessed is the man who trusts in you.

PSALM 85

For the director of music. Of the Sons of Korah.
A psalm.

[1] You showed favor to your land, O LORD;
you restored the fortunes of Jacob.
[2] You forgave the iniquity of your people
and covered all their sins.   *Selah*
[3] You set aside all your wrath
and turned from your fierce anger.

[4] Restore us again, O God our Savior,
and put away your displeasure toward us.
[5] Will you be angry with us forever?
Will you prolong your anger through all
generations?
[6] Will you not revive us again,
that your people may rejoice in you?
[7] Show us your unfailing love, O LORD,
and grant us your salvation.

[8] I will listen to what God the LORD will say;
he promises peace to his people, his
saints—
but let them not return to folly.
[9] Surely his salvation is near those who fear
him,
that his glory may dwell in our land.

[10] Love and faithfulness meet together;
righteousness and peace kiss each other.
[11] Faithfulness springs forth from the earth,
and righteousness looks down from
heaven.
[12] The LORD will indeed give what is good,
and our land will yield its harvest.
[13] Righteousness goes before him
and prepares the way for his steps.

PSALM 86

A prayer of David.

[1] Hear, O LORD, and answer me,
for I am poor and needy.
[2] Guard my life, for I am devoted to you.
You are my God; save your servant
who trusts in you.
[3] Have mercy on me, O Lord,
for I call to you all day long.
[4] Bring joy to your servant,

THE MESSAGE

than be honored as a guest in the palace of
sin.
All sunshine and sovereign is GOD,
generous in gifts and glory.
He doesn't scrimp with his traveling
companions.
It's smooth sailing all the way with GOD of
the Angel Armies.

A Korah psalm

85.1-3 **85** GOD, you smiled on your good earth!
You brought good times back to Jacob!
You lifted the cloud of guilt from your people,
you put their sins far out of sight.
You took back your sin-provoked threats,
you cooled your hot, righteous anger.

85.4-7 Help us again, God of our help;
don't hold a grudge against us forever.
You aren't going to keep this up, are you?
scowling and angry, year after year?
Why not help us make a fresh start—a
resurrection life?
Then your people will laugh and sing!
Show us how much you love us, GOD!
Give us the salvation we need!

85.8-9 I can't wait to hear what he'll say.
GOD's about to pronounce his people well,
The holy people he loves so much,
so they'll never again live like fools.
See how close his salvation is to those who
fear him?
Our country is home base for Glory!

85.10-13 Love and Truth meet in the street,
Right Living and Whole Living embrace
and kiss!
Truth sprouts green from the ground,
Right Living pours down from the skies!
Oh yes! GOD gives Goodness and Beauty;
our land responds with Bounty and
Blessing.
Right Living strides out before him,
and clears a path for his passage.

A David psalm

86.1-7 **86** Bend an ear, GOD; answer me.
I'm one miserable wretch!
Keep me safe—haven't I lived a good life?
Help your servant—I'm depending on you!
You're my God; have mercy on me.
I count on you from morning to night.
Give your servant a happy life;

NEW INTERNATIONAL VERSION

for to you, O Lord,
I lift up my soul.

⁵You are forgiving and good, O Lord,
abounding in love to all who call to you.
⁶Hear my prayer, O LORD;
listen to my cry for mercy.
⁷In the day of my trouble I will call to you,
for you will answer me.

⁸Among the gods there is none like you,
O Lord;
no deeds can compare with yours.
⁹All the nations you have made
will come and worship before you,
O Lord;
they will bring glory to your name.
¹⁰For you are great and do marvelous deeds;
you alone are God.

¹¹Teach me your way, O LORD,
and I will walk in your truth;
give me an undivided heart,
that I may fear your name.
¹²I will praise you, O Lord my God, with all
my heart;
I will glorify your name forever.
¹³For great is your love toward me;
you have delivered me from the depths of
the grave.ᵃ

¹⁴The arrogant are attacking me, O God;
a band of ruthless men seeks my life—
men without regard for you.
¹⁵But you, O Lord, are a compassionate and
gracious God,
slow to anger, abounding in love and
faithfulness.
¹⁶Turn to me and have mercy on me;
grant your strength to your servant
and save the son of your maidservant.ᵇ
¹⁷Give me a sign of your goodness,
that my enemies may see it and be put to
shame,
for you, O LORD, have helped me and
comforted me.

PSALM 87

Of the Sons of Korah. A psalm. A song.

¹He has set his foundation on the holy
mountain;
²   the LORD loves the gates of Zion
more than all the dwellings of Jacob.
³Glorious things are said of you,
O city of God: *Selah*

THE MESSAGE

I put myself in your hands!
You're well-known as good and forgiving,
bighearted to all who ask for help.
Pay attention, GOD, to my prayer;
bend down and listen to my cry for help.
Every time I'm in trouble I call on you,
confident that you'll answer.

86.8-10 There's no one quite like you among the gods,
O Lord,
and nothing to compare with your works.
All the nations you made are on their way,
ready to give honor to you, O Lord,
Ready to put your beauty on display,
parading your greatness,
And the great things you do—
God, you're the one, there's no one but
you!

86.11-17 Train me, GOD, to walk straight;
then I'll follow your true path.
Put me together, one heart and mind;
then, undivided, I'll worship in joyful fear.
From the bottom of my heart I thank you,
dear Lord;
I've never kept secret what you're up to.
You've always been great toward me—what
love!
You snatched me from the brink of
disaster!
God, these bullies have reared their heads!
A gang of thugs is after me—
and they don't care a thing about you.
But you, O God, are both tender and kind,
not easily angered, immense in love,
and you never, never quit.
So look me in the eye and show kindness,
give your servant the strength to go on,
save your dear, dear child!
Make a show of how much you love me
so the bullies who hate me will stand there
slack-jawed,
As you, GOD, gently and powerfully
put me back on my feet.

A Korah psalm

87.1-3 **87** He founded Zion on the Holy
Mountain—
and oh, how GOD loves his home!
Loves it far better than all
the homes of Jacob put together!
God's hometown—oh!
everyone there is talking about you!

ᵃ 13 Hebrew *Sheol*   ᵇ 16 Or *save your faithful son*

NEW INTERNATIONAL VERSION

4 "I will record Rahab[a] and Babylon
    among those who acknowledge me—
Philistia too, and Tyre, along with Cush[b]—
    and will say, 'This[c] one was born in
        Zion.' "

5 Indeed, of Zion it will be said,
    "This one and that one were born in her,
    and the Most High himself will establish
        her."
6 The LORD will write in the register of the
        peoples:
    "This one was born in Zion."   *Selah*
7 As they make music they will sing,
    "All my fountains are in you."

PSALM 88

A song. A psalm of the Sons of Korah. For the
    director of music. According to *mahalath
    leannoth.*[d] A *maskil*[e] of Heman the Ezrahite.

1 O LORD, the God who saves me,
    day and night I cry out before you.
2 May my prayer come before you;
    turn your ear to my cry.

3 For my soul is full of trouble
    and my life draws near the grave.[f]
4 I am counted among those who go down to
        the pit;
    I am like a man without strength.
5 I am set apart with the dead,
    like the slain who lie in the grave,
whom you remember no more,
    who are cut off from your care.

6 You have put me in the lowest pit,
    in the darkest depths.
7 Your wrath lies heavily upon me;
    you have overwhelmed me with all your
        waves.   *Selah*
8 You have taken from me my closest friends
    and have made me repulsive to them.
I am confined and cannot escape;
9   my eyes are dim with grief.

I call to you, O LORD, every day;
    I spread out my hands to you.
10 Do you show your wonders to the dead?
    Do those who are dead rise up and praise
        you?   *Selah*
11 Is your love declared in the grave,
    your faithfulness in Destruction[g]?

---

a 4 A poetic name for Egypt   b 4 That is, the upper Nile
region   c 4 Or *"O Rahab and Babylon, / Philistia, Tyre and
Cush, / I will record concerning those who acknowledge me: /
'This*   d Title: Possibly a tune, "The Suffering of Affliction"
e Title: Probably a literary or musical term   f 3 Hebrew
Sheol   g 11 Hebrew *Abaddon*

THE MESSAGE

87.4 I name them off, those among whom I'm famous:
    Egypt and Babylon,
        also Philistia,
    even Tyre, along with Cush.
Word's getting around; they point them out:
    "This one was born again here!"

87.5 The word's getting out on Zion:
    "Men and women, right and left,
        get born again in her!"

87.6 GOD registers their names in his book:
    "This one, this one, and this one—
        born again, right here."

87.7 Singers and dancers give credit to Zion:
    "All my springs are in you!"

A Korah prayer of Heman

88.1-9 **88** GOD, you're my last chance of the day.
    I spend the night on my knees before
        you.
Put me on your salvation agenda;
    take notes on the trouble I'm in.
I've had my fill of trouble;
    I'm camped on the edge of hell.
I'm written off as a lost cause,
    one more statistic, a hopeless case.
Abandoned as already dead,
    one more body in a stack of corpses,
And not so much as a gravestone—
    I'm a black hole in oblivion.
You've dropped me into a bottomless pit,
    sunk me in a pitch-black abyss.
I'm battered senseless by your rage,
    relentlessly pounded by your waves of
        anger.
You turned my friends against me,
    made me horrible to them.
I'm caught in a maze and can't find my way
        out,
    blinded by tears of pain and frustration.

88.9-12 I call to you, GOD; all day I call.
    I wring my hands, I plead for help.
Are the dead a live audience for your
        miracles?
    Do ghosts ever join the choirs that praise
        you?
Does your love make any difference in a
        graveyard?
    Is your faithful presence noticed in the
        corridors of hell?

NEW INTERNATIONAL VERSION

¹²Are your wonders known in the place of
darkness,
or your righteous deeds in the land of
oblivion?

¹³But I cry to you for help, O LORD;
in the morning my prayer comes before
you.
¹⁴Why, O LORD, do you reject me
and hide your face from me?

¹⁵From my youth I have been afflicted and
close to death;
I have suffered your terrors and am in
despair.
¹⁶Your wrath has swept over me;
your terrors have destroyed me.
¹⁷All day long they surround me like a flood;
they have completely engulfed me.
¹⁸You have taken my companions and loved
ones from me;
the darkness is my closest friend.

PSALM 89

A maskil[a] *of Ethan the Ezrahite.*

¹I will sing of the LORD's great love forever;
with my mouth I will make your
faithfulness known through all
generations.
²I will declare that your love stands firm
forever,
that you established your faithfulness in
heaven itself.

³You said, "I have made a covenant with my
chosen one,
I have sworn to David my servant,
⁴'I will establish your line forever
and make your throne firm through all
generations.' "   *Selah*

⁵The heavens praise your wonders, O LORD,
your faithfulness too, in the assembly of
the holy ones.
⁶For who in the skies above can compare
with the LORD?
Who is like the LORD among the heavenly
beings?
⁷In the council of the holy ones God is greatly
feared;
he is more awesome than all who
surround him.
⁸O LORD God Almighty, who is like you?
You are mighty, O LORD, and your
faithfulness surrounds you.

THE MESSAGE

Are your marvelous wonders ever seen in the
dark,
your righteous ways noticed in the Land of
No Memory?

88.13-18 I'm standing my ground, GOD, shouting for
help,
at my prayers every morning, on my knees
each daybreak.
Why, GOD, do you turn a deaf ear?
Why do you make yourself scarce?
For as long as I remember I've been hurting;
I've taken the worst you can hand out, and
I've had it.
Your wildfire anger has blazed through my
life;
I'm bleeding, black and blue.
You've attacked me fiercely from every side,
raining down blows till I'm nearly dead.
You made lover and neighbor alike dump me;
the only friend I have left is Darkness.

An Ethan prayer

89.1-4 **89** Your love, GOD, is my song, and I'll
sing it!
I'm forever telling everyone how faithful
you are.
I'll never quit telling the story of your love—
how you built the cosmos
and guaranteed everything in it.
Your love has always been our lives'
foundation,
your fidelity has been the roof over our
world.
You once said, "I joined forces with my
chosen leader,
I pledged my word to my servant, David,
saying,
'Everyone descending from you is guaranteed
life;
I'll make your rule as solid and lasting as
rock.' "

89.5-18 GOD! Let the cosmos praise your wonderful
ways,
the choir of holy angels sing anthems to
your faithful ways!
Search high and low, scan skies and land,
you'll find nothing and no one quite like
GOD.
The holy angels are in awe before him;
he looms immense and august over
everyone around him.
GOD of the Angel Armies, who is like you,
powerful and faithful from every angle?

---

[a] Title: Probably a literary or musical term

NEW INTERNATIONAL VERSION

⁹You rule over the surging sea;
  when its waves mount up, you still them.
¹⁰You crushed Rahab like one of the slain;
  with your strong arm you scattered your
    enemies.
¹¹The heavens are yours, and yours also the
    earth;
  you founded the world and all that is in it.
¹²You created the north and the south;
  Tabor and Hermon sing for joy at your name.
¹³Your arm is endued with power;
  your hand is strong, your right hand
    exalted.

¹⁴Righteousness and justice are the foundation
    of your throne;
  love and faithfulness go before you.
¹⁵Blessed are those who have learned to
    acclaim you,
  who walk in the light of your presence,
    O Lord.
¹⁶They rejoice in your name all day long;
  they exult in your righteousness.
¹⁷For you are their glory and strength,
  and by your favor you exalt our horn.ᵃ
¹⁸Indeed, our shieldᵇ belongs to the Lord,
  our king to the Holy One of Israel.

¹⁹Once you spoke in a vision,
  to your faithful people you said:
  "I have bestowed strength on a warrior;
  I have exalted a young man from among
    the people.
²⁰I have found David my servant;
  with my sacred oil I have anointed him.
²¹My hand will sustain him;
  surely my arm will strengthen him.
²²No enemy will subject him to tribute;
  no wicked man will oppress him.
²³I will crush his foes before him
  and strike down his adversaries.
²⁴My faithful love will be with him,
  and through my name his hornᶜ will be
    exalted.
²⁵I will set his hand over the sea,
  his right hand over the rivers.
²⁶He will call out to me, 'You are my Father,
  my God, the Rock my Savior.'
²⁷I will also appoint him my firstborn,
  the most exalted of the kings of the earth.
²⁸I will maintain my love to him forever,
  and my covenant with him will never fail.
²⁹I will establish his line forever,
  his throne as long as the heavens endure.

³⁰"If his sons forsake my law
  and do not follow my statutes,

ᵃ *17 Horn* here symbolizes strong one.   ᵇ *18* Or *sovereign*
ᶜ *24 Horn* here symbolizes strength.

THE MESSAGE

You put the arrogant ocean in its place
  and calm its waves when they turn unruly.
You gave that old hag Egypt the back of your
    hand,
  you brushed off your enemies with a flick
    of your wrist.
You own the cosmos—you made everything
    in it,
  everything from atom to archangel.
You positioned the North and South Poles;
  the mountains Tabor and Hermon sing
    duets to you.
With your well-muscled arm and your grip of
    steel—
  nobody trifles with you!
The Right and Justice are the roots of your
    rule;
  Love and Truth are its fruits.
Blessed are the people who know the
    passwords of praise,
  who shout on parade in the bright presence
    of God.
Delighted, they dance all day long; they know
  who you are, what you do—they can't keep
    it quiet!
Your vibrant beauty has gotten inside us—
  you've been so good to us! We're walking
    on air!
All we are and have we owe to God,
  Holy God of Israel, our King!

89:19-37 A long time ago you spoke in a vision,
  you spoke to your faithful beloved:
  "I've crowned a hero,
  I chose the best I could find;
I found David, my servant,
  poured holy oil on his head,
And I'll keep my hand steadily on him,
  yes, I'll stick with him through thick and thin.
No enemy will get the best of him,
  no scoundrel will do him in.
I'll weed out all who oppose him,
  I'll clean out all who hate him.
I'm with him for good and I'll love him forever;
  I've set him on high—he's riding high!
I've put Ocean in his one hand, River in the
    other;
  he'll call out, 'Oh, my Father—my God, my
    Rock of Salvation!'
Yes, I'm setting him apart as the First of the
    royal line,
  High King over all of earth's kings.
I'll preserve him eternally in my love,
  I'll faithfully do all I so solemnly promised.
I'll guarantee his family tree
  and underwrite his rule.
If his children refuse to do what I tell them,
  if they refuse to walk in the way I show them,

NEW INTERNATIONAL VERSION

³¹ if they violate my decrees
    and fail to keep my commands,
³² I will punish their sin with the rod,
    their iniquity with flogging;
³³ but I will not take my love from him,
    nor will I ever betray my faithfulness.
³⁴ I will not violate my covenant
    or alter what my lips have uttered.
³⁵ Once for all, I have sworn by my holiness—
    and I will not lie to David—
³⁶ that his line will continue forever
    and his throne endure before me like the sun;
³⁷ it will be established forever like the moon,
    the faithful witness in the sky."   *Selah*

³⁸ But you have rejected, you have spurned,
    you have been very angry with your
        anointed one.
³⁹ You have renounced the covenant with your
        servant
    and have defiled his crown in the dust.
⁴⁰ You have broken through all his walls
    and reduced his strongholds to ruins.
⁴¹ All who pass by have plundered him;
    he has become the scorn of his neighbors.
⁴² You have exalted the right hand of his foes;
    you have made all his enemies rejoice.
⁴³ You have turned back the edge of his sword
    and have not supported him in battle.
⁴⁴ You have put an end to his splendor
    and cast his throne to the ground.
⁴⁵ You have cut short the days of his youth;
    you have covered him with a mantle of
        shame.   *Selah*

⁴⁶ How long, O L<small>ORD</small>? Will you hide yourself
        forever?
    How long will your wrath burn like fire?
⁴⁷ Remember how fleeting is my life.
    For what futility you have created all men!
⁴⁸ What man can live and not see death,
    or save himself from the power of the
        grave ^{*a*}?   *Selah*
⁴⁹ O Lord, where is your former great love,
    which in your faithfulness you swore to
        David?
⁵⁰ Remember, Lord, how your servant has ^{*b*}
        been mocked,
    how I bear in my heart the taunts of all
        the nations,
⁵¹ the taunts with which your enemies have
        mocked, O L<small>ORD</small>,
    with which they have mocked every step
        of your anointed one.

⁵² Praise be to the L<small>ORD</small> forever!
    Amen and Amen.

^{*a*} 48 Hebrew *Sheol*   ^{*b*} 50 Or *your servants have*

THE MESSAGE

If they spit on the directions I give them
    and tear up the rules I post for them—
I'll rub their faces in the dirt of their rebellion
    and make them face the music.
But I'll never throw them out,
    never abandon or disown them.
Do you think I'd withdraw my holy promise?
    or take back words I'd already spoken?
I've given my word, my whole and holy word;
    do you think I would lie to David?
His family tree is here for good,
    his sovereignty as sure as the sun,
Dependable as the phases of the moon,
    inescapable as weather."

^{89.38-51} But G<small>OD</small>, you did walk off and leave us,
    you lost your temper with the one you
        anointed.
You tore up the promise you made to your
        servant,
    you stomped his crown in the mud.
You blasted his home to kingdom come,
    reduced his city to a pile of rubble
Picked clean by wayfaring strangers,
    a joke to all the neighbors.
You declared a holiday for all his enemies,
    and they're celebrating for all they're worth.
Angry, you opposed him in battle,
    refused to fight on his side;
You robbed him of his splendor, humiliated
        this warrior,
    ground his kingly honor in the dirt.
You took the best years of his life
    and left him an impotent, ruined husk.
How long do we put up with this, G<small>OD</small>?
    Are you gone for good? Will you hold this
        grudge forever?
Remember my sorrow and how short life is.
    Did you create men and women for nothing
        but this?
We'll see death soon enough. Everyone does.
    And there's no back door out of hell.
So where is the love you're so famous for,
        Lord?
    What happened to your promise to David?
Take a good look at your servant, dear Lord;
    I'm the butt of the jokes of all nations,
The taunting jokes of your enemies, G<small>OD</small>,
    as they dog the steps of your dear anointed.

    Blessed be G<small>OD</small> forever and always!
        Yes. Oh, yes.

NEW INTERNATIONAL VERSION

BOOK IV

Psalms 90–106

PSALM 90

A prayer of Moses the man of God.

1 Lord, you have been our dwelling place
  throughout all generations.
2 Before the mountains were born
  or you brought forth the earth and the
    world,
  from everlasting to everlasting you are
    God.

3 You turn men back to dust,
  saying, "Return to dust, O sons of men."
4 For a thousand years in your sight
  are like a day that has just gone by,
  or like a watch in the night.
5 You sweep men away in the sleep of death;
  they are like the new grass of the
    morning—
6 though in the morning it springs up new,
  by evening it is dry and withered.

7 We are consumed by your anger
  and terrified by your indignation.
8 You have set our iniquities before you,
  our secret sins in the light of your presence.
9 All our days pass away under your wrath;
  we finish our years with a moan.
10 The length of our days is seventy years—
  or eighty, if we have the strength;
  yet their span*a* is but trouble and sorrow,
  for they quickly pass, and we fly away.

11 Who knows the power of your anger?
  For your wrath is as great as the fear that
    is due you.
12 Teach us to number our days aright,
  that we may gain a heart of wisdom.

13 Relent, O LORD! How long will it be?
  Have compassion on your servants.
14 Satisfy us in the morning with your unfailing
    love,
  that we may sing for joy and be glad all
    our days.
15 Make us glad for as many days as you have
    afflicted us,
  for as many years as we have seen trouble.
16 May your deeds be shown to your servants,
  your splendor to their children.

17 May the favor*b* of the Lord our God rest
    upon us;
  establish the work of our hands for us—
  yes, establish the work of our hands.

THE MESSAGE

A prayer of Moses, man of God

90.1-2 **90** God, it seems you've been our home
      forever;
  long before the mountains were born,
  Long before you brought earth itself to birth,
  from "once upon a time" to "kingdom
    come"—you are God.

90.3-11 So don't return us to mud, saying,
  "Back to where you came from!"
  Patience! You've got all the time in the
    world—whether
  a thousand years or a day, it's all the same
    to you.
  Are we no more to you than a wispy dream,
  no more than a blade of grass
  That springs up gloriously with the rising sun
  and is cut down without a second thought?
  Your anger is far and away too much for us;
  we're at the end of our rope.
  You keep track of all our sins; every misdeed
  since we were children is entered in your
    books.
  All we can remember is that frown on your
    face.
  Is that all we're ever going to get?
  We live for seventy years or so
  (with luck we might make it to eighty),
  And what do we have to show for it? Trouble.
  Toil and trouble and a marker in the
    graveyard.
  Who can make sense of such rage,
  such anger against the very ones who fear
    you?

90.12-17 Oh! Teach us to live well!
  Teach us to live wisely and well!
  Come back, GOD—how long do we have to
    wait?—
  and treat your servants with kindness for a
    change.
  Surprise us with love at daybreak;
  then we'll skip and dance all the day long.
  Make up for the bad times with some good
    times;
  we've seen enough evil to last a lifetime.
  Let your servants see what you're best at—
  the ways you rule and bless your children.
  And let the loveliness of our Lord, our God,
    rest on us,
  confirming the work that we do.
  Oh, yes. Affirm the work that we do!

---

a 10 Or yet the best of them   b 17 Or beauty

NEW INTERNATIONAL VERSION

PSALM 91

¹ He who dwells in the shelter of the Most
      High
   will rest in the shadow of the Almighty. *a*
² I will say *b* of the LORD, "He is my refuge and
      my fortress,
   my God, in whom I trust."

³ Surely he will save you from the fowler's
      snare
   and from the deadly pestilence.
⁴ He will cover you with his feathers,
   and under his wings you will find refuge;
   his faithfulness will be your shield and
      rampart.
⁵ You will not fear the terror of night,
   nor the arrow that flies by day,
⁶ nor the pestilence that stalks in the
      darkness,
   nor the plague that destroys at midday.
⁷ A thousand may fall at your side,
   ten thousand at your right hand,
   but it will not come near you.
⁸ You will only observe with your eyes
   and see the punishment of the wicked.

⁹ If you make the Most High your dwelling—
   even the LORD, who is my refuge—
¹⁰ then no harm will befall you,
   no disaster will come near your tent.
¹¹ For he will command his angels concerning
      you
   to guard you in all your ways;
¹² they will lift you up in their hands,
   so that you will not strike your foot
      against a stone.
¹³ You will tread upon the lion and the cobra;
   you will trample the great lion and the
      serpent.

¹⁴ "Because he loves me," says the LORD, "I will
      rescue him;
   I will protect him, for he acknowledges
      my name.
¹⁵ He will call upon me, and I will answer him;
   I will be with him in trouble,
   I will deliver him and honor him.
¹⁶ With long life will I satisfy him
   and show him my salvation."

PSALM 92

A psalm. A song. For the Sabbath day.

¹ It is good to praise the LORD
   and make music to your name, O Most
      High,
² to proclaim your love in the morning

THE MESSAGE

91 You who sit down in the High God's
         presence,
   spend the night in Shaddai's shadow,
Say this: "GOD, you're my refuge.
   I trust in you and I'm safe!"
That's right—he rescues you from hidden
      traps,
   shields you from deadly hazards.
His huge outstretched arms protect you—
   under them you're perfectly safe;
   his arms fend off all harm.
Fear nothing—not wild wolves in the night,
   not flying arrows in the day,
Not disease that prowls through the darkness,
   not disaster that erupts at high noon.
Even though others succumb all around,
   drop like flies right and left,
   no harm will even graze you.
You'll stand untouched, watch it all from a
         distance,
   watch the wicked turn into corpses.
Yes, because GOD's your refuge,
   the High God your very own home,
Evil can't get close to you,
   harm can't get through the door.
He ordered his angels
   to guard you wherever you go.
If you stumble, they'll catch you;
   their job is to keep you from falling.
You'll walk unharmed among lions and
         snakes,
   and kick young lions and serpents from the
         path.

91.14-16 "If you'll hold on to me for dear life," says
         GOD,
   "I'll get you out of any trouble.
I'll give you the best of care
   if you'll only get to know and trust me.
Call me and I'll answer, be at your side in bad
         times;
   I'll rescue you, then throw you a party.
I'll give you a long life,
   give you a long drink of salvation!"

A Sabbath song

92.1-3 **92** What a beautiful thing, GOD, to give
         thanks,
   to sing an anthem to you, the High God!
To announce your love each daybreak,

91.1-13

---

a 1 Hebrew Shaddai   *b 2 Or He says*

NEW INTERNATIONAL VERSION

and your faithfulness at night,
³ to the music of the ten-stringed lyre
and the melody of the harp.

⁴ For you make me glad by your deeds,
O Lord;
I sing for joy at the works of your hands.
⁵ How great are your works, O Lord,
how profound your thoughts!
⁶ The senseless man does not know,
fools do not understand,
⁷ that though the wicked spring up like grass
and all evildoers flourish,
they will be forever destroyed.

⁸ But you, O Lord, are exalted forever.

⁹ For surely your enemies, O Lord,
surely your enemies will perish;
all evildoers will be scattered.
¹⁰ You have exalted my horn*ª* like that of a wild
ox;
fine oils have been poured upon me.
¹¹ My eyes have seen the defeat of my
adversaries;
my ears have heard the rout of my wicked
foes.

¹² The righteous will flourish like a palm tree,
they will grow like a cedar of Lebanon;
¹³ planted in the house of the Lord,
they will flourish in the courts of our God.
¹⁴ They will still bear fruit in old age,
they will stay fresh and green,
¹⁵ proclaiming, "The Lord is upright;
he is my Rock, and there is no wickedness
in him."

PSALM 93

¹ The Lord reigns, he is robed in majesty;
the Lord is robed in majesty
and is armed with strength.
The world is firmly established;
it cannot be moved.
² Your throne was established long ago;
you are from all eternity.

³ The seas have lifted up, O Lord,
the seas have lifted up their voice;
the seas have lifted up their pounding
waves.
⁴ Mightier than the thunder of the great waters,
mightier than the breakers of the sea—
the Lord on high is mighty.

⁵ Your statutes stand firm;
holiness adorns your house
for endless days, O Lord.

THE MESSAGE

sing your faithful presence all through the
night,
Accompanied by dulcimer and harp,
the full-bodied music of strings.

92.4-9 You made me so happy, God.
I saw your work and I shouted for joy.
How magnificent your work, God!
How profound your thoughts!
Dullards never notice what you do;
fools never do get it.
When the wicked popped up like weeds
and all the evil men and women took over,
You mowed them down,
finished them off once and for all.
You, God, are High and Eternal.
Look at your enemies, God!
Look at your enemies—ruined!
Scattered to the winds, all those hirelings of
evil!

92.10-14 But you've made me strong as a charging
bison,
you've honored me with a festive parade.
The sight of my critics going down is still
fresh,
the rout of my malicious detractors.
My ears are filled with the sounds of promise:
"Good people will prosper like palm trees,
Grow tall like Lebanon cedars;
transplanted to God's courtyard,
They'll grow tall in the presence of God,
lithe and green, virile still in old age."

92.15 Such witnesses to upright God!
My Mountain, my huge, holy Mountain!

93.1-2 **93** God is King, robed and ruling,
God is robed and surging with
strength.

And yes, the world is firm, immovable,
Your throne ever firm—you're Eternal!

93.3-4 Sea storms are up, God,
Sea storms wild and roaring,
Sea storms with thunderous breakers.

Stronger than wild sea storms,
Mightier than sea-storm breakers,
Mighty God rules from High Heaven.

93.5 What you say goes—it always has.
"Beauty" and "Holy" mark your palace rule,
God, to the very end of time.

ª 10 Horn here symbolizes strength.

NEW INTERNATIONAL VERSION

PSALM 94

1 O LORD, the God who avenges,
  O God who avenges, shine forth.
2 Rise up, O Judge of the earth;
  pay back to the proud what they deserve.
3 How long will the wicked, O LORD,
  how long will the wicked be jubilant?

4 They pour out arrogant words;
  all the evildoers are full of boasting.
5 They crush your people, O LORD;
  they oppress your inheritance.
6 They slay the widow and the alien;
  they murder the fatherless.
7 They say, "The LORD does not see;
  the God of Jacob pays no heed."

8 Take heed, you senseless ones among the
      people;
  you fools, when will you become wise?
9 Does he who implanted the ear not hear?
  Does he who formed the eye not see?
10 Does he who disciplines nations not punish?
  Does he who teaches man lack
      knowledge?
11 The LORD knows the thoughts of man;
  he knows that they are futile.

12 Blessed is the man you discipline, O LORD,
  the man you teach from your law;
13 you grant him relief from days of trouble,
  till a pit is dug for the wicked.
14 For the LORD will not reject his people;
  he will never forsake his inheritance.
15 Judgment will again be founded on
      righteousness,
  and all the upright in heart will follow it.

16 Who will rise up for me against the wicked?
  Who will take a stand for me against
      evildoers?
17 Unless the LORD had given me help,
  I would soon have dwelt in the silence of
      death.
18 When I said, "My foot is slipping,"
  your love, O LORD, supported me.
19 When anxiety was great within me,
  your consolation brought joy to my soul.

20 Can a corrupt throne be allied with you—
  one that brings on misery by its decrees?
21 They band together against the righteous
  and condemn the innocent to death.
22 But the LORD has become my fortress,
  and my God the rock in whom I take
      refuge.
23 He will repay them for their sins
  and destroy them for their wickedness;
  the LORD our God will destroy them.

THE MESSAGE

94.1-2 **94** GOD, put an end to evil;
      avenging God, show your colors!
  Judge of the earth, take your stand;
    throw the book at the arrogant.

94.3-4 GOD, the wicked get away with murder—
      how long will you let this go on?
  They brag and boast
    and crow about their crimes!

94.5-7 They walk all over your people, GOD,
      exploit and abuse your precious people.
  They take out anyone who gets in their way;
    if they can't use them, they kill them.
  They think, "GOD isn't looking,
    Jacob's God is out to lunch."

94.8-11 Well, think again, you idiots,
      fools—how long before you get smart?
  Do you think Ear-Maker doesn't hear,
      Eye-Shaper doesn't see?
  Do you think the trainer of nations doesn't
      correct,
    the teacher of Adam doesn't know?
  GOD knows, all right—
    knows your stupidity,
    sees your shallowness.

94.12-15 How blessed the man you train, GOD,
      the woman you instruct in your Word,
  Providing a circle of quiet within the clamor
      of evil,
    while a jail is being built for the wicked.
  GOD will never walk away from his people,
    never desert his precious people.
  Rest assured that justice is on its way
    and every good heart put right.

94.16-19 Who stood up for me against the wicked?
      Who took my side against evil workers?
  If GOD hadn't been there for me,
    I never would have made it.
  The minute I said, "I'm slipping, I'm falling,"
    your love, GOD, took hold and held me fast.
  When I was upset and beside myself,
    you calmed me down and cheered me up.

94.20-23 Can Misrule have anything in common with
      you?
    Can Troublemaker pretend to be on your
      side?
  They ganged up on good people,
    plotted behind the backs of the innocent.
  But GOD became my hideout,
    God was my high mountain retreat,
  Then boomeranged their evil back on them:
    for their evil ways he wiped them out,
    our GOD cleaned them out for good.

NEW INTERNATIONAL VERSION

PSALM 95

1 Come, let us sing for joy to the LORD;
  let us shout aloud to the Rock of our
    salvation.
2 Let us come before him with thanksgiving
  and extol him with music and song.

3 For the LORD is the great God,
  the great King above all gods.
4 In his hand are the depths of the earth,
  and the mountain peaks belong to him.
5 The sea is his, for he made it,
  and his hands formed the dry land.

6 Come, let us bow down in worship,
  let us kneel before the LORD our Maker;
7 for he is our God
  and we are the people of his pasture,
    the flock under his care.

  Today, if you hear his voice,
8   do not harden your hearts as you did at
      Meribah,*a*
  as you did that day at Massah*b* in the
      desert,
9 where your fathers tested and tried me,
  though they had seen what I did.
10 For forty years I was angry with that
      generation;
  I said, "They are a people whose hearts go
      astray,
  and they have not known my ways."
11 So I declared on oath in my anger,
  "They shall never enter my rest."

PSALM 96

1 Sing to the LORD a new song;
  sing to the LORD, all the earth.
2 Sing to the LORD, praise his name;
  proclaim his salvation day after day.
3 Declare his glory among the nations,
  his marvelous deeds among all peoples.

4 For great is the LORD and most worthy of
      praise;
  he is to be feared above all gods.
5 For all the gods of the nations are idols,
  but the LORD made the heavens.
6 Splendor and majesty are before him;
  strength and glory are in his sanctuary.

---

a 8 Meribah means quarreling. *b 8 Massah means testing.*

THE MESSAGE

95 95.1-2 Come, let's shout praises to GOD,
  raise the roof for the Rock who
    saved us!
Let's march into his presence singing praises,
  lifting the rafters with our hymns!

95.3-5 And why? Because GOD is the best,
  High King over all the gods.
In one hand he holds deep caves and caverns,
  in the other hand grasps the high
    mountains.
He made Ocean—he owns it!
  His hands sculpted Earth!

95.6-7 So come, let us worship: bow before him,
  on your knees before GOD, who made us!
Oh yes, he's our God,
  and we're the people he pastures, the flock
    he feeds.

95.7-11 Drop everything and listen, listen as he
      speaks:
  "Don't turn a deaf ear as in the Bitter
      Uprising,
As on the day of the Wilderness Test,
  when your ancestors turned and put *me* to
    the test.
For forty years they watched me at work
      among them,
  as over and over they tried my patience.
And I was provoked—oh, was I provoked!
  'Can't they keep their minds on God for
    five minutes?
Do they simply refuse to walk down my
    road?'
Exasperated, I exploded,
  'They'll never get where they're headed,
  never be able to sit down and rest.'"

96 96.1-2 Sing GOD a brand-new song!
  Earth and everyone in it, sing!
Sing to GOD—*worship* GOD!

96.2-3 Shout the news of his victory from sea to sea,
Take the news of his glory to the lost,
News of his wonders to one and all!

96.4-5 For GOD is great, and worth a thousand
      Hallelujahs.
His terrible beauty makes the gods look
      cheap;
Pagan gods are mere tatters and rags.

96.5-6 GOD made the heavens—
Royal splendor radiates from him,
A powerful beauty sets him apart.

NEW INTERNATIONAL VERSION

⁷Ascribe to the LORD, O families of nations,
    ascribe to the LORD glory and strength.
⁸Ascribe to the LORD the glory due his name;
    bring an offering and come into his
        courts.
⁹Worship the LORD in the splendor of his*ᵃ*
        holiness;
    tremble before him, all the earth.

¹⁰Say among the nations, "The LORD reigns."
    The world is firmly established, it cannot
        be moved;
    he will judge the peoples with equity.
¹¹Let the heavens rejoice, let the earth be glad;
    let the sea resound, and all that is in it;
¹²   let the fields be jubilant, and everything in
        them.
    Then all the trees of the forest will sing for
        joy;
¹³   they will sing before the LORD, for he
        comes,
    he comes to judge the earth.
    He will judge the world in righteousness
    and the peoples in his truth.

PSALM 97

¹The LORD reigns, let the earth be glad;
    let the distant shores rejoice.

²Clouds and thick darkness surround him;
    righteousness and justice are the
        foundation of his throne.
³Fire goes before him
    and consumes his foes on every side.
⁴His lightning lights up the world;
    the earth sees and trembles.
⁵The mountains melt like wax before the
        LORD,
    before the Lord of all the earth.
⁶The heavens proclaim his righteousness,
    and all the peoples see his glory.

⁷All who worship images are put to shame,
    those who boast in idols—
    worship him, all you gods!

⁸Zion hears and rejoices
    and the villages of Judah are glad
    because of your judgments, O LORD.
⁹For you, O LORD, are the Most High over all
        the earth;
    you are exalted far above all gods.

ᵃ 9 Or LORD *with the splendor of*

THE MESSAGE

96.7 Bravo, GOD, Bravo!
    Everyone join in the great shout: Encore!
    In awe before the beauty, in awe before the
        might.

96.8-9 Bring gifts and celebrate,
    Bow before the beauty of GOD,
    Then to your knees—everyone worship!

96.10 Get out the message—GOD Rules!
    He put the world on a firm foundation;
    He treats everyone fair and square.

96.11 Let's hear it from Sky,
    With Earth joining in,
    And a huge round of applause from Sea.

96.12 Let Wilderness turn cartwheels,
    Animals, come dance,
    Put every tree of the forest in the choir—

96.13 An extravaganza before GOD as he comes,
    As he comes to set everything right on earth,
    Set everything right, treat everyone fair.

97.1 **97** GOD rules: *there's* something to shout
        over!
    On the double, mainlands and islands—
        celebrate!

97.2 Bright clouds and storm clouds circle 'round
        him;
    Right and justice anchor his rule.

97.3 Fire blazes out before him,
    Flaming high up the craggy mountains.

97.4 His lightnings light up the world;
    Earth, wide-eyed, trembles in fear.

97.5 The mountains take one look at GOD
    And melt, melt like wax before earth's Lord.

97.6 The heavens announce that he'll set
        everything right,
    And everyone will see it happen—glorious!

97.7-8 All who serve handcrafted gods will be
        sorry—
    And they were so proud of their ragamuffin
        gods!

    On your knees, all you gods—worship him!
    And Zion, you listen and take heart!

    Daughters of Zion, sing your hearts out:
    GOD has done it all, has set everything right.

97.9 You, GOD, are High God of the cosmos,
    Far, far higher than any of the gods.

¹⁰Let those who love the LORD hate evil,
 for he guards the lives of his faithful ones
 and delivers them from the hand of the
  wicked.
¹¹Light is shed upon the righteous
 and joy on the upright in heart.
¹²Rejoice in the LORD, you who are righteous,
 and praise his holy name.

PSALM 98

A psalm.

¹Sing to the LORD a new song,
 for he has done marvelous things;
his right hand and his holy arm
 have worked salvation for him.
²The LORD has made his salvation known
 and revealed his righteousness to the
  nations.
³He has remembered his love
 and his faithfulness to the house of Israel;
all the ends of the earth have seen
 the salvation of our God.

⁴Shout for joy to the LORD, all the earth,
 burst into jubilant song with music;
⁵make music to the LORD with the harp,
 with the harp and the sound of singing,
⁶with trumpets and the blast of the ram's
  horn—
 shout for joy before the LORD, the King.

⁷Let the sea resound, and everything in it,
 the world, and all who live in it.
⁸Let the rivers clap their hands,
 let the mountains sing together for joy;
⁹let them sing before the LORD,
 for he comes to judge the earth.
He will judge the world in righteousness
 and the peoples with equity.

PSALM 99

¹The LORD reigns,
 let the nations tremble;
he sits enthroned between the cherubim,
 let the earth shake.
²Great is the LORD in Zion;
 he is exalted over all the nations.
³Let them praise your great and awesome
  name—
 he is holy.

⁴The King is mighty, he loves justice—
 you have established equity;

97.10 GOD loves all who hate evil,
 And those who love him he keeps safe,
 Snatches them from the grip of the wicked.

97.11 Light-seeds are planted in the souls of God's
  people,
 Joy-seeds are planted in good heart-soil.

97.12 So, God's people, shout praise to GOD,
 Give thanks to our Holy God!

98.1 **98** Sing to GOD a brand-new song.
   He's made a world of wonders!

He rolled up his sleeves,
He set things right.

98.2 GOD made history with salvation,
 He showed the world what he could do.

98.3 He remembered to love us, a bonus
 To his dear family, Israel—indefatigable love.

The whole earth comes to attention.
Look—God's work of salvation!

98.4 Shout your praises to GOD, everybody!
 Let loose and sing! Strike up the band!

98.5 Round up an orchestra to play for GOD,
 Add on a hundred-voice choir.

98.6 Feature trumpets and big trombones,
 Fill the air with praises to King GOD.

98.7 Let the sea and its fish give a round of
  applause,
 With everything living on earth joining in.

98.8 Let ocean breakers call out, "Encore!"
 And mountains harmonize the finale—

98.9 A tribute to GOD when he comes,
 When he comes to set the earth right.

He'll straighten out the whole world,
He'll put the world right, and everyone in it.

99.1-3 **99** GOD rules. On your toes, everybody!
   He rules from his angel throne—take
   notice!
GOD looms majestic in Zion,
He towers in splendor over all the big names.
Great and terrible your beauty: let everyone
  praise you!
 Holy. Yes, holy.

99.4-5 Strong King, lover of justice,
 You laid things out fair and square;

NEW INTERNATIONAL VERSION

in Jacob you have done
what is just and right.
[5] Exalt the LORD our God
and worship at his footstool;
he is holy.

[6] Moses and Aaron were among his priests,
Samuel was among those who called on
his name;
they called on the LORD
and he answered them.
[7] He spoke to them from the pillar of cloud;
they kept his statutes and the decrees he
gave them.

[8] O LORD our God,
you answered them;
you were to Israel[a] a forgiving God,
though you punished their misdeeds.[b]
[9] Exalt the LORD our God
and worship at his holy mountain,
for the LORD our God is holy.

PSALM 100

A psalm. For giving thanks.

[1] Shout for joy to the LORD, all the earth.
[2]   Worship the LORD with gladness;
come before him with joyful songs.
[3] Know that the LORD is God.
It is he who made us, and we are his[c];
we are his people, the sheep of his
pasture.

[4] Enter his gates with thanksgiving
and his courts with praise;
give thanks to him and praise his name.
[5] For the LORD is good and his love endures
forever;
his faithfulness continues through all
generations.

PSALM 101

Of David. A psalm.

[1] I will sing of your love and justice;
to you, O LORD, I will sing praise.
[2] I will be careful to lead a blameless life—
when will you come to me?

I will walk in my house
with blameless heart.
[3] I will set before my eyes
no vile thing.

The deeds of faithless men I hate;
they will not cling to me.

THE MESSAGE

You set down the foundations in Jacob,
Foundation stones of just and right ways.
Honor GOD, our God; worship his rule!
Holy. Yes, holy.

99.6-9 Moses and Aaron were his priests,
Samuel among those who prayed to him.
They prayed to GOD and he answered them;
He spoke from the pillar of cloud.
And they did what he said; they kept the law
he gave them.
And then GOD, our God, answered them
(But you were never soft on their sins).
Lift high GOD, our God; worship at his holy
mountain.
Holy. Yes, holy is GOD our God.

A thanksgiving psalm

100.1-2 **100** On your feet now—applaud GOD!
Bring a gift of laughter,
sing yourselves into his presence.

100.3 Know this: GOD is God, and God, GOD.
He made us; we didn't make him.
We're his people, his well-tended sheep.

100.4 Enter with the password: "Thank you!"
Make yourselves at home, talking praise.
Thank him. Worship him.

100.5 For GOD is sheer beauty,
all-generous in love,
loyal always and ever.

A David psalm

101.1-8 **101** My theme song is God's love and
justice,
and I'm singing it right to you, GOD.
I'm finding my way down the road of right
living,
but how long before you show up?
I'm doing the very best I can,
and I'm doing it at home, where it counts.
I refuse to take a second look
at corrupting people and degrading things.
I reject made-in-Canaan gods,
stay clear of contamination.

---

a 8 Hebrew *them*   *b 8* Or / *an avenger of the wrongs done to
them*   *c 3* Or *and not we ourselves*

NEW INTERNATIONAL VERSION

⁴Men of perverse heart shall be far from me;
    I will have nothing to do with evil.

⁵Whoever slanders his neighbor in secret,
    him will I put to silence;
whoever has haughty eyes and a proud heart,
    him will I not endure.

⁶My eyes will be on the faithful in the land,
    that they may dwell with me;
he whose walk is blameless
    will minister to me.

⁷No one who practices deceit
    will dwell in my house;
no one who speaks falsely
    will stand in my presence.

⁸Every morning I will put to silence
    all the wicked in the land;
I will cut off every evildoer
    from the city of the LORD.

PSALM 102

A prayer of an afflicted man. When he is faint
and pours out his lament before the LORD.

¹Hear my prayer, O LORD;
    let my cry for help come to you.
²Do not hide your face from me
    when I am in distress.
Turn your ear to me;
    when I call, answer me quickly.

³For my days vanish like smoke;
    my bones burn like glowing embers.
⁴My heart is blighted and withered like grass;
    I forget to eat my food.
⁵Because of my loud groaning
    I am reduced to skin and bones.
⁶I am like a desert owl,
    like an owl among the ruins.
⁷I lie awake; I have become
    like a bird alone on a roof.
⁸All day long my enemies taunt me;
    those who rail against me use my name as
    a curse.
⁹For I eat ashes as my food
    and mingle my drink with tears
¹⁰because of your great wrath,
    for you have taken me up and thrown me
    aside.
¹¹My days are like the evening shadow;
    I wither away like grass.

¹²But you, O LORD, sit enthroned forever;
    your renown endures through all
    generations.
¹³You will arise and have compassion on Zion,
    for it is time to show favor to her;

THE MESSAGE

The crooked in heart keep their distance;
    I refuse to shake hands with those who
      plan evil.
I put a gag on the gossip
    who bad-mouths his neighbor;
I can't stand
    arrogance.
But I have my eye on salt-of-the-earth
    people—
    they're the ones I want working with me;
Men and women on the straight and narrow—
    these are the ones I want at my side.
But no one who traffics in lies
    gets a job with me; I have no patience with
      liars.
I've rounded up all the wicked like cattle
    and herded them right out of the country.
I purged GOD's city
    of all who make a business of evil.

A prayer of one whose life is falling to pieces,
and who lets God know just how bad it is.

102.1-2 **102** GOD, listen! Listen to my prayer,
    listen to the pain in my cries.
Don't turn your back on me
    just when I need you so desperately.
Pay attention! This is a cry for *help!*
    And hurry—this can't wait!

102.3-11 I'm wasting away to nothing,
    I'm burning up with fever.
I'm a ghost of my former self,
    half-consumed already by terminal illness.
My jaws ache from gritting my teeth;
    I'm nothing but skin and bones.
I'm like a buzzard in the desert,
    a crow perched on the rubble.
Insomniac, I twitter away,
    mournful as a sparrow in the gutter.
All day long my enemies taunt me,
    while others just curse.
They bring in meals—casseroles of ashes!
    I draw drink from a barrel of my tears.
And all because of your furious anger;
    you swept me up and threw me out.
There's nothing left of me—
    a withered weed, swept clean from the
      path.

102.12-17 Yet you, GOD, are sovereign still,
    always and ever sovereign.
You'll get up from your throne and help
    Zion—

NEW INTERNATIONAL VERSION

the appointed time has come.
¹⁴ For her stones are dear to your servants;
  her very dust moves them to pity.
¹⁵ The nations will fear the name of the LORD,
  all the kings of the earth will revere your
    glory.
¹⁶ For the LORD will rebuild Zion
  and appear in his glory.
¹⁷ He will respond to the prayer of the
    destitute;
  he will not despise their plea.

¹⁸ Let this be written for a future generation,
  that a people not yet created may praise
    the LORD:
¹⁹ "The LORD looked down from his sanctuary
    on high,
  from heaven he viewed the earth,
²⁰ to hear the groans of the prisoners
  and release those condemned to death."
²¹ So the name of the LORD will be declared in
    Zion
  and his praise in Jerusalem
²² when the peoples and the kingdoms
  assemble to worship the LORD.

²³ In the course of my life ᵃ he broke my
    strength;
  he cut short my days.
²⁴ So I said:
  "Do not take me away, O my God, in the
    midst of my days;
  your years go on through all generations.
²⁵ In the beginning you laid the foundations of
    the earth,
  and the heavens are the work of your
    hands.
²⁶ They will perish, but you remain;
  they will all wear out like a garment.
  Like clothing you will change them
  and they will be discarded.
²⁷ But you remain the same,
  and your years will never end.
²⁸ The children of your servants will live in
      your presence;
  their descendants will be established
    before you."

PSALM 103

Of David.

¹ Praise the LORD, O my soul;
  all my inmost being, praise his holy name.
² Praise the LORD, O my soul,
  and forget not all his benefits—
³ who forgives all your sins
  and heals all your diseases,

ᵃ 23 Or *By his power*

THE MESSAGE

it's time for compassionate help.
Oh, how your servants love this city's rubble
  and weep with compassion over its dust!
The godless nations will sit up and take notice
  —see your glory, worship your name—
When GOD rebuilds Zion,
  when he shows up in all his glory,
When he attends to the prayer of the
    wretched,
  He won't dismiss their prayer.

102.18-22 Write this down for the next generation
  so people not yet born will praise GOD:
"GOD looked out from his high holy place;
  from heaven he surveyed the earth.
He listened to the groans of the doomed,
  he opened the doors of their death cells."
Write it so the story can be told in Zion,
  so GOD's praise will be sung in Jerusalem's
    streets
And wherever people gather together
  along with their rulers to worship him.

102.23-28 GOD sovereignly brought me to my knees,
  he cut me down in my prime.
"Oh, don't," I prayed, "please don't let me die.
  You have more years than you know what
    to do with!
You laid earth's foundations a long time ago,
  and handcrafted the very heavens;
You'll still be around when they're long gone,
  threadbare and discarded like an old suit of
    clothes.
You'll throw them away like a worn-out coat,
  but year after year you're as good as new.
Your servants' children will have a good place
    to live
  and their children will be at home with
    you."

A David psalm

103.1-2 **103** O my soul, bless GOD.
  From head to toe, I'll bless his holy
    name!
O my soul, bless GOD,
  don't forget a single blessing!

103.3-5 He forgives your sins—every one.
  He heals your diseases—every one.

NEW INTERNATIONAL VERSION

⁴who redeems your life from the pit
  and crowns you with love and
    compassion,
⁵who satisfies your desires with good things
  so that your youth is renewed like the
    eagle's.

⁶The LORD works righteousness
  and justice for all the oppressed.

⁷He made known his ways to Moses,
  his deeds to the people of Israel:
⁸The LORD is compassionate and gracious,
  slow to anger, abounding in love.
⁹He will not always accuse,
  nor will he harbor his anger forever;
¹⁰he does not treat us as our sins deserve
  or repay us according to our iniquities.
¹¹For as high as the heavens are above the
    earth,
  so great is his love for those who fear him;
¹²as far as the east is from the west,
  so far has he removed our transgressions
    from us.
¹³As a father has compassion on his children,
  so the LORD has compassion on those who
    fear him;
¹⁴for he knows how we are formed,
  he remembers that we are dust.
¹⁵As for man, his days are like grass,
  he flourishes like a flower of the field;
¹⁶the wind blows over it and it is gone,
  and its place remembers it no more.
¹⁷But from everlasting to everlasting
  the LORD's love is with those who fear him,
  and his righteousness with their children's
    children—
¹⁸with those who keep his covenant
  and remember to obey his precepts.

¹⁹The LORD has established his throne in
    heaven,
  and his kingdom rules over all.

²⁰Praise the LORD, you his angels,
  you mighty ones who do his bidding,
  who obey his word.
²¹Praise the LORD, all his heavenly hosts,
  you his servants who do his will.
²²Praise the LORD, all his works
  everywhere in his dominion.

  Praise the LORD, O my soul.

PSALM 104

¹Praise the LORD, O my soul.

O LORD my God, you are very great;
  you are clothed with splendor and
    majesty.

THE MESSAGE

He redeems you from hell—saves your life!
He crowns you with love and mercy—a
    paradise crown.
He wraps you in goodness—beauty eternal.
He renews your youth—you're always
    young in his presence.

103.6-18 GOD makes everything come out right;
  he puts victims back on their feet.
He showed Moses how he went about his
    work,
  opened up his plans to all Israel.
GOD is sheer mercy and grace;
  not easily angered, he's rich in love.
He doesn't endlessly nag and scold,
  nor hold grudges forever.
He doesn't treat us as our sins deserve,
  nor pay us back in full for our wrongs.
As high as heaven is over the earth,
  so strong is his love to those who fear him.
And as far as sunrise is from sunset,
  he has separated us from our sins.
As parents feel for their children,
  GOD feels for those who fear him.
He knows us inside and out,
  keeps in mind that we're made of mud.
Men and women don't live very long;
  like wildflowers they spring up and
    blossom,
But a storm snuffs them out just as quickly,
  leaving nothing to show they were here.
GOD's love, though, is ever and always,
  eternally present to all who fear him,
Making everything right for them and their
    children
  as they follow his Covenant ways
  and remember to do whatever he said.

103.19-22 GOD has set his throne in heaven;
  he rules over us all. He's the King!
So bless GOD, you angels,
  ready and able to fly at his bidding,
  quick to hear and do what he says.
Bless GOD, all you armies of angels,
  alert to respond to whatever he wills.
Bless GOD, all creatures, wherever you are—
  everything and everyone made by GOD.

And you, O my soul, bless GOD!

104.1-14 **104** O my soul, bless GOD!

GOD, my God, how great you are!
  beautifully, gloriously robed,

NEW INTERNATIONAL VERSION

²He wraps himself in light as with a garment;
  he stretches out the heavens like a tent
³   and lays the beams of his upper chambers
    on their waters.
 He makes the clouds his chariot
  and rides on the wings of the wind.
⁴He makes winds his messengers,^a
  flames of fire his servants.

⁵He set the earth on its foundations;
  it can never be moved.
⁶You covered it with the deep as with a
    garment;
  the waters stood above the mountains.
⁷But at your rebuke the waters fled,
  at the sound of your thunder they took to
    flight;
⁸they flowed over the mountains,
  they went down into the valleys,
  to the place you assigned for them.
⁹You set a boundary they cannot cross;
  never again will they cover the earth.

¹⁰He makes springs pour water into the
    ravines;
  it flows between the mountains.
¹¹They give water to all the beasts of the field;
  the wild donkeys quench their thirst.
¹²The birds of the air nest by the waters;
  they sing among the branches.
¹³He waters the mountains from his upper
    chambers;
  the earth is satisfied by the fruit of his
    work.
¹⁴He makes grass grow for the cattle,
  and plants for man to cultivate—
  bringing forth food from the earth:
¹⁵wine that gladdens the heart of man,
  oil to make his face shine,
  and bread that sustains his heart.
¹⁶The trees of the LORD are well watered,
  the cedars of Lebanon that he planted.
¹⁷There the birds make their nests;
  the stork has its home in the pine trees.
¹⁸The high mountains belong to the wild goats;
  the crags are a refuge for the coneys.^b

¹⁹The moon marks off the seasons,
  and the sun knows when to go down.
²⁰You bring darkness, it becomes night,
  and all the beasts of the forest prowl.
²¹The lions roar for their prey
  and seek their food from God.
²²The sun rises, and they steal away;
  they return and lie down in their dens.
²³Then man goes out to his work,
  to his labor until evening.

THE MESSAGE

Dressed up in sunshine,
  and all heaven stretched out for your tent.
You built your palace on the ocean deeps,
  made a chariot out of clouds and took off
    on wind-wings.
You commandeered winds as messengers,
  appointed fire and flame as ambassadors.
You set earth on a firm foundation
  so that nothing can shake it, ever.
You blanketed earth with ocean,
  covered the mountains with deep waters;
Then you roared and the water ran away—
  your thunder crash put it to flight.
Mountains pushed up, valleys spread out
  in the places you assigned them.
You set boundaries between earth and sea;
  never again will earth be flooded.
You started the springs and rivers,
  sent them flowing among the hills.
All the wild animals now drink their fill,
  wild donkeys quench their thirst.
Along the riverbanks the birds build nests,
  ravens make their voices heard.
You water the mountains from your heavenly
    cisterns;
  earth is supplied with plenty of water.
You make grass grow for the livestock,
  hay for the animals that plow the ground.

104.14-23 Oh yes, God brings grain from the land,
  wine to make people happy,
Their faces glowing with health,
  a people well-fed and hearty.
GOD's trees are well-watered—
  the Lebanon cedars he planted.
Birds build their nests in those trees;
  look—the stork at home in the treetop.
Mountain goats climb about the cliffs;
  badgers burrow among the rocks.
The moon keeps track of the seasons,
  the sun is in charge of each day.
When it's dark and night takes over,
  all the forest creatures come out.
The young lions roar for their prey,
  clamoring to God for their supper.
When the sun comes up, they vanish,
  lazily stretched out in their dens.
Meanwhile, men and women go out to work,
  busy at their jobs until evening.

---

^a 4 Or *angels*   ^b 18 That is, the hyrax or rock badger

NEW INTERNATIONAL VERSION

²⁴How many are your works, O Lord!
In wisdom you made them all;
the earth is full of your creatures.
²⁵There is the sea, vast and spacious,
teeming with creatures beyond number—
living things both large and small.
²⁶There the ships go to and fro,
and the leviathan, which you formed to
frolic there.

²⁷These all look to you
to give them their food at the proper time.
²⁸When you give it to them,
they gather it up;
when you open your hand,
they are satisfied with good things.
²⁹When you hide your face,
they are terrified;
when you take away their breath,
they die and return to the dust.
³⁰When you send your Spirit,
they are created,
and you renew the face of the earth.

³¹May the glory of the Lord endure forever;
may the Lord rejoice in his works—
³²he who looks at the earth, and it trembles,
who touches the mountains, and they
smoke.

³³I will sing to the Lord all my life;
I will sing praise to my God as long as I
live.
³⁴May my meditation be pleasing to him,
as I rejoice in the Lord.
³⁵But may sinners vanish from the earth
and the wicked be no more.

Praise the Lord, O my soul.

Praise the Lord. ᵃ

PSALM 105

¹Give thanks to the Lord, call on his name;
make known among the nations what he
has done.
²Sing to him, sing praise to him;
tell of all his wonderful acts.
³Glory in his holy name;
let the hearts of those who seek the Lord
rejoice.
⁴Look to the Lord and his strength;
seek his face always.

⁵Remember the wonders he has done,
his miracles, and the judgments he
pronounced,

ᵃ 35 Hebrew Hallelu Yah; in the Septuagint this line stands
at the beginning of Psalm 105.

THE MESSAGE

104.24-30 What a wildly wonderful world, God!
You made it all, with Wisdom at your side,
made earth overflow with your wonderful
creations.
Oh, look—the deep, wide sea,
brimming with fish past counting,
sardines and sharks and salmon.
Ships plow those waters,
and Leviathan, your pet dragon, romps in
them.
All the creatures look expectantly to you
to give them their meals on time.
You come, and they gather around;
you open your hand and they eat from it.
If you turned your back,
they'd die in a minute—
Take back your Spirit and they die,
revert to original mud;
Send out your Spirit and they spring to life—
the whole countryside in bloom and
blossom.

104.31-32 The glory of God—let it last forever!
Let God enjoy his creation!
He takes one look at earth and triggers an
earthquake,
points a finger at the mountains, and
volcanoes erupt.

104.33-35 Oh, let me sing to God all my life long,
sing hymns to my God as long as I live!
Oh, let my song please him;
I'm so pleased to be singing to God.
But clear the ground of sinners—
no more godless men and women!

O my soul, bless God!

105.1-6 # 105 Hallelujah!

Thank God! Pray to him by name!
Tell everyone you meet what he has done!
Sing him songs, belt out hymns,
translate his wonders into music!
Honor his holy name with Hallelujahs,
you who seek God. Live a happy life!
Keep your eyes open for God, watch for his
works;
be alert for signs of his presence.
Remember the world of wonders he has made,
his miracles, and the verdicts he's
rendered—

NEW INTERNATIONAL VERSION

⁶ O descendants of Abraham his servant,
O sons of Jacob, his chosen ones.
⁷ He is the LORD our God;
his judgments are in all the earth.

⁸ He remembers his covenant forever,
the word he commanded, for a thousand
generations,
⁹ the covenant he made with Abraham,
the oath he swore to Isaac.
¹⁰ He confirmed it to Jacob as a decree,
to Israel as an everlasting covenant:
¹¹ "To you I will give the land of Canaan
as the portion you will inherit."

¹² When they were but few in number,
few indeed, and strangers in it,
¹³ they wandered from nation to nation,
from one kingdom to another.
¹⁴ He allowed no one to oppress them;
for their sake he rebuked kings:
¹⁵ "Do not touch my anointed ones;
do my prophets no harm."

¹⁶ He called down famine on the land
and destroyed all their supplies of food;
¹⁷ and he sent a man before them—
Joseph, sold as a slave.
¹⁸ They bruised his feet with shackles,
his neck was put in irons,
¹⁹ till what he foretold came to pass,
till the word of the LORD proved him true.
²⁰ The king sent and released him,
the ruler of peoples set him free.
²¹ He made him master of his household,
ruler over all he possessed,
²² to instruct his princes as he pleased
and teach his elders wisdom.

²³ Then Israel entered Egypt;
Jacob lived as an alien in the land of Ham.
²⁴ The LORD made his people very fruitful;
he made them too numerous for their
foes,
²⁵ whose hearts he turned to hate his people,
to conspire against his servants.
²⁶ He sent Moses his servant,
and Aaron, whom he had chosen.
²⁷ They performed his miraculous signs among
them,
his wonders in the land of Ham.
²⁸ He sent darkness and made the land dark—
for had they not rebelled against his
words?
²⁹ He turned their waters into blood,
causing their fish to die.
³⁰ Their land teemed with frogs,
which went up into the bedrooms of their
rulers.

THE MESSAGE

O seed of Abraham, his servant,
O child of Jacob, his chosen.

105.7-15 He's GOD, our God,
in charge of the whole earth.
And he remembers, remembers his
Covenant—
for a thousand generations he's been as
good as his word.
It's the Covenant he made with Abraham,
the same oath he swore to Isaac,
The very statute he established with Jacob,
the eternal Covenant with Israel,
Namely, "I give you the land.
Canaan is your hill-country inheritance."
When they didn't count for much,
a mere handful, and strangers at that,
Wandering from country to country,
drifting from pillar to post,
He permitted no one to abuse them.
He told kings to keep their hands off:
"Don't you dare lay a hand on my anointed,
don't hurt a hair on the heads of my
prophets."

105.16-22 Then he called down a famine on the country,
he broke every last blade of wheat.
But he sent a man on ahead:
Joseph, sold as a slave.
They put cruel chains on his ankles,
an iron collar around his neck,
Until God's word came to the Pharaoh,
and GOD confirmed his promise.
God sent the king to release him.
The Pharaoh set Joseph free;
He appointed him master of his palace,
put him in charge of all his business
To personally instruct his princes
and train his advisors in wisdom.

105.23-42 Then Israel entered Egypt,
Jacob immigrated to the Land of Ham.
God gave his people lots of babies;
soon their numbers alarmed their foes.
He turned the Egyptians against his people;
they abused and cheated God's servants.
Then he sent his servant Moses,
and Aaron, whom he also chose.
They worked marvels in that spiritual
wasteland,
miracles in the Land of Ham.
He spoke, "Darkness!" and it turned dark—
they couldn't see what they were doing.
He turned all their water to blood
so that all their fish died;
He made frogs swarm through the land,
even into the king's bedroom;

NEW INTERNATIONAL VERSION

³¹He spoke, and there came swarms of flies,
  and gnats throughout their country.
³²He turned their rain into hail,
  with lightning throughout their land;
³³he struck down their vines and fig trees
  and shattered the trees of their country.
³⁴He spoke, and the locusts came,
  grasshoppers without number;
³⁵they ate up every green thing in their land,
  ate up the produce of their soil.
³⁶Then he struck down all the firstborn in
    their land,
  the firstfruits of all their manhood.

³⁷He brought out Israel, laden with silver and
    gold,
  and from among their tribes no one
    faltered.
³⁸Egypt was glad when they left,
  because dread of Israel had fallen on
    them.
³⁹He spread out a cloud as a covering,
  and a fire to give light at night.
⁴⁰They asked, and he brought them quail
  and satisfied them with the bread of
    heaven.
⁴¹He opened the rock, and water gushed out;
  like a river it flowed in the desert.

⁴²For he remembered his holy promise
  given to his servant Abraham.
⁴³He brought out his people with rejoicing,
  his chosen ones with shouts of joy;
⁴⁴he gave them the lands of the nations,
  and they fell heir to what others had
    toiled for—
⁴⁵that they might keep his precepts
  and observe his laws.

  Praise the LORD.ᵃ

PSALM 106

¹Praise the LORD.ᵇ

Give thanks to the LORD, for he is good;
  his love endures forever.
²Who can proclaim the mighty acts of the
    LORD
  or fully declare his praise?
³Blessed are they who maintain justice,
  who constantly do what is right.
⁴Remember me, O LORD, when you show
    favor to your people,
  come to my aid when you save them,
⁵that I may enjoy the prosperity of your
    chosen ones,

THE MESSAGE

He gave the word and flies swarmed,
  gnats filled the air.
He substituted hail for rain,
  he stabbed their land with lightning;
He wasted their vines and fig trees,
  smashed their groves of trees to splinters;
With a word he brought in locusts,
  millions of locusts, armies of locusts;
They consumed every blade of grass in the
    country
  and picked the ground clean of produce;
He struck down every firstborn in the land,
  the first fruits of their virile powers.
He led Israel out, their arms filled with loot,
  and not one among his tribes even
    stumbled.
Egypt was glad to have them go—
  they were scared to death of them.
God spread a cloud to keep them cool
    through the day
  and a fire to light their way through the
    night;
They prayed and he brought quail,
  filled them with the bread of heaven;
He opened the rock and water poured out;
  it flowed like a river through that desert—
All because he remembered his Covenant,
  his promise to Abraham, his servant.

105.43-45 Remember this! He led his people out singing
    for joy;
  his chosen people marched, singing their
    hearts out!
He made them a gift of the country they
    entered,
  helped them seize the wealth of the nations
So they could do everything he told them—
  could follow his instructions to the letter.

Hallelujah!

106.1-3 **106** Hallelujah!
  Thank GOD! And why?
  Because he's good, because his love lasts.
But who on earth can do it—
  declaim GOD's mighty acts, broadcast all his
    praises?
You're one happy man when you do what's
    right,
  one happy woman when you form the
    habit of justice.

106.4-5 Remember me, GOD, when you enjoy your
    people;
  include me when you save them;
I want to see your chosen succeed,

ᵃ 45 Hebrew *Hallelu Yah*   ᵇ 1 Hebrew *Hallelu Yah*; also in
verse 48

NEW INTERNATIONAL VERSION	THE MESSAGE

NEW INTERNATIONAL VERSION

that I may share in the joy of your nation
and join your inheritance in giving praise.

⁶We have sinned, even as our fathers did;
we have done wrong and acted wickedly.
⁷When our fathers were in Egypt,
they gave no thought to your miracles;
they did not remember your many
kindnesses,
and they rebelled by the sea, the Red Sea.*ᵃ*
⁸Yet he saved them for his name's sake,
to make his mighty power known.
⁹He rebuked the Red Sea, and it dried up;
he led them through the depths as
through a desert.
¹⁰He saved them from the hand of the foe;
from the hand of the enemy he redeemed
them.
¹¹The waters covered their adversaries;
not one of them survived.
¹²Then they believed his promises
and sang his praise.

¹³But they soon forgot what he had done
and did not wait for his counsel.
¹⁴In the desert they gave in to their craving;
in the wasteland they put God to the test.
¹⁵So he gave them what they asked for,
but sent a wasting disease upon them.
¹⁶In the camp they grew envious of Moses
and of Aaron, who was consecrated to the
LORD.
¹⁷The earth opened up and swallowed Dathan;
it buried the company of Abiram.
¹⁸Fire blazed among their followers;
a flame consumed the wicked.

¹⁹At Horeb they made a calf
and worshiped an idol cast from metal.
²⁰They exchanged their Glory
for an image of a bull, which eats grass.
²¹They forgot the God who saved them,
who had done great things in Egypt,
²²miracles in the land of Ham
and awesome deeds by the Red Sea.
²³So he said he would destroy them—
had not Moses, his chosen one,
stood in the breach before him
to keep his wrath from destroying them.

ᵃ 7 Hebrew *Yam Suph*; that is, Sea of Reeds; also in verses 9 and 22

THE MESSAGE

celebrate with your celebrating nation,
join the Hallelujahs of your pride and joy!

¹⁰⁶·⁶⁻¹² We've sinned a lot, both we and our parents;
We've fallen short, hurt a lot of people.
After our parents left Egypt,
they took your wonders for granted,
forgot your great and wonderful love.
They were barely beyond the Red Sea
when they defied the High God
—the very place he saved them!
—the place he revealed his amazing power!
He rebuked the Red Sea so that it dried up on
the spot
—he paraded them right through!
—no one so much as got wet feet!
He saved them from a life of oppression,
pried them loose from the grip of the
enemy.
Then the waters flowed back on their
oppressors;
there wasn't a single survivor.
Then they believed his words were true
and broke out in songs of praise.

¹⁰⁶·¹³⁻¹⁸ But it wasn't long before they forgot the whole
thing,
wouldn't wait to be told what to do.
They only cared about pleasing themselves in
that desert,
provoked God with their insistent
demands.
He gave them exactly what they asked for—
but along with it they got an empty heart.
One day in camp some grew jealous of Moses,
also of Aaron, holy priest of GOD.
The ground opened and swallowed Dathan,
then buried Abiram's gang.
Fire flared against that rebel crew
and torched them to a cinder.

¹⁰⁶·¹⁹⁻²² They cast in metal a bull calf at Horeb
and worshiped the statue they'd made.
They traded the Glory
for a cheap piece of sculpture—a grass-
chewing bull!
They forgot God, their very own Savior,
who turned things around in Egypt,
Who created a world of wonders in the Land
of Ham,
who gave that stunning performance at the
Red Sea.

¹⁰⁶·²³⁻²⁷ Fed up, God decided to get rid of them—
and except for Moses, his chosen, he would
have.
But Moses stood in the gap and deflected
God's anger,
prevented it from destroying them utterly.

NEW INTERNATIONAL VERSION	THE MESSAGE

NEW INTERNATIONAL VERSION

²⁴ Then they despised the pleasant land;
    they did not believe his promise.
²⁵ They grumbled in their tents
    and did not obey the LORD.
²⁶ So he swore to them with uplifted hand
    that he would make them fall in the
    desert,
²⁷ make their descendants fall among the
    nations
    and scatter them throughout the lands.

²⁸ They yoked themselves to the Baal of Peor
    and ate sacrifices offered to lifeless gods;
²⁹ they provoked the LORD to anger by their
    wicked deeds,
    and a plague broke out among them.
³⁰ But Phinehas stood up and intervened,
    and the plague was checked.
³¹ This was credited to him as righteousness
    for endless generations to come.

³² By the waters of Meribah they angered the
    LORD,
    and trouble came to Moses because of
    them;
³³ for they rebelled against the Spirit of God,
    and rash words came from Moses' lips. *ᵃ*

³⁴ They did not destroy the peoples
    as the LORD had commanded them,
³⁵ but they mingled with the nations
    and adopted their customs.
³⁶ They worshiped their idols,
    which became a snare to them.
³⁷ They sacrificed their sons
    and their daughters to demons.
³⁸ They shed innocent blood,
    the blood of their sons and daughters,
    whom they sacrificed to the idols of Canaan,
    and the land was desecrated by their
    blood.
³⁹ They defiled themselves by what they did;
    by their deeds they prostituted
    themselves.

⁴⁰ Therefore the LORD was angry with his
    people
    and abhorred his inheritance.
⁴¹ He handed them over to the nations,
    and their foes ruled over them.
⁴² Their enemies oppressed them
    and subjected them to their power.
⁴³ Many times he delivered them,
    but they were bent on rebellion
    and they wasted away in their sin.

⁴⁴ But he took note of their distress
    when he heard their cry;

THE MESSAGE

They went on to reject the Blessed Land,
    didn't believe a word of what God
    promised.
They found fault with the life they had
    and turned a deaf ear to GOD's voice.
Exasperated, God swore
    that he'd lay them low in the desert,
Scattering their children hither and yon,
    strewing them all over the earth.

106.28-31 Then they linked up with Baal Peor,
    attending funeral banquets and eating idol
    food.
That made God so angry
    that a plague spread through their ranks;
Phinehas stood up and pled their case
    and the plague was stopped.
This was counted to his credit;
    his descendants will never forget it.

106.32-33 They angered God again at Meribah Springs;
    this time Moses got mixed up in their evil;
Because they defied GOD yet again,
    Moses exploded and lost his temper.

106.34-39 They didn't wipe out those godless cultures
    as ordered by GOD;
Instead they intermarried with the heathen,
    and in time became just like them.
They worshiped their idols,
    were caught in the trap of idols.
They sacrificed their sons and daughters
    at the altars of demon gods.
They slit the throats of their babies,
    murdered their infant girls and boys.
They offered their babies to Canaan's gods;
    the blood of their babies stained the land.
Their way of life stank to high heaven;
    they lived like whores.

106.40-43 And GOD was furious—a wildfire anger;
    he couldn't stand even to look at his
    people.
He turned them over to the heathen
    so that the people who hated them ruled
    them.
Their enemies made life hard for them;
    they were tyrannized under that rule.
Over and over God rescued them, but they
    never learned—
    until finally their sins destroyed them.

106.44-46 Still, when God saw the trouble they were in
    and heard their cries for help,

ᵃ 33 Or against his spirit, / and rash words came from his lips

NEW INTERNATIONAL VERSION

⁴⁵ for their sake he remembered his covenant
and out of his great love he relented.
⁴⁶ He caused them to be pitied
by all who held them captive.

⁴⁷ Save us, O LORD our God,
and gather us from the nations,
that we may give thanks to your holy name
and glory in your praise.

⁴⁸ Praise be to the LORD, the God of Israel,
from everlasting to everlasting.
Let all the people say, "Amen!"

Praise the LORD.

BOOK V

Psalms 107–150

PSALM 107

¹ Give thanks to the LORD, for he is good;
his love endures forever.
² Let the redeemed of the LORD say this—
those he redeemed from the hand of the
foe,
³ those he gathered from the lands,
from east and west, from north and
south. *ᵃ*

⁴ Some wandered in desert wastelands,
finding no way to a city where they could
settle.
⁵ They were hungry and thirsty,
and their lives ebbed away.
⁶ Then they cried out to the LORD in their
trouble,
and he delivered them from their distress.
⁷ He led them by a straight way
to a city where they could settle.
⁸ Let them give thanks to the LORD for his
unfailing love
and his wonderful deeds for men,
⁹ for he satisfies the thirsty
and fills the hungry with good things.

¹⁰ Some sat in darkness and the deepest gloom,
prisoners suffering in iron chains,
¹¹ for they had rebelled against the words of
God
and despised the counsel of the Most
High.
¹² So he subjected them to bitter labor;
they stumbled, and there was no one to
help.
¹³ Then they cried to the LORD in their trouble,
and he saved them from their distress.

THE MESSAGE

He remembered his Covenant with them,
and, immense with love, took them by the
hand.
He poured out his mercy on them
while their captors looked on, amazed.

106.47 Save us, GOD, our God!
Gather us back out of exile
So we can give thanks to your holy name
and join in the glory when you are praised!

106.48 Blessed be GOD, Israel's God!
Bless now, bless always!
Oh! Let everyone say Amen!
Hallelujah!

107.1-3 **107** Oh, thank GOD—he's so good!
His love never runs out.
All of you set free by GOD, tell the world!
Tell how he freed you from oppression,
Then rounded you up from all over the place,
from the four winds, from the seven seas.

107.4-9 Some of you wandered for years in the desert,
looking but not finding a good place to
live,
Half-starved and parched with thirst,
staggering and stumbling, on the brink of
exhaustion.
Then, in your desperate condition, you called
out to GOD.
He got you out in the nick of time;
He put your feet on a wonderful road
that took you straight to a good place to
live.
So thank GOD for his marvelous love,
for his miracle mercy to the children he
loves.
He poured great draughts of water down
parched throats;
the starved and hungry got plenty to eat.

107.10-16 Some of you were locked in a dark cell,
cruelly confined behind bars,
Punished for defying God's Word,
for turning your back on the High God's
counsel—
A hard sentence, and your hearts so heavy,
and not a soul in sight to help.
Then you called out to GOD in your desperate
condition;
he got you out in the nick of time.

ᵃ 3 Hebrew *north and the sea*

NEW INTERNATIONAL VERSION

¹⁴He brought them out of darkness and the
  deepest gloom
  and broke away their chains.
¹⁵Let them give thanks to the LORD for his
  unfailing love
  and his wonderful deeds for men,
¹⁶for he breaks down gates of bronze
  and cuts through bars of iron.

¹⁷Some became fools through their rebellious
  ways
  and suffered affliction because of their
  iniquities.
¹⁸They loathed all food
  and drew near the gates of death.
¹⁹Then they cried to the LORD in their trouble,
  and he saved them from their distress.
²⁰He sent forth his word and healed them;
  he rescued them from the grave.
²¹Let them give thanks to the LORD for his
  unfailing love
  and his wonderful deeds for men.
²²Let them sacrifice thank offerings
  and tell of his works with songs of joy.

²³Others went out on the sea in ships;
  they were merchants on the mighty
  waters.
²⁴They saw the works of the LORD,
  his wonderful deeds in the deep.
²⁵For he spoke and stirred up a tempest
  that lifted high the waves.
²⁶They mounted up to the heavens and went
  down to the depths;
  in their peril their courage melted away.
²⁷They reeled and staggered like drunken men;
  they were at their wits' end.
²⁸Then they cried out to the LORD in their
  trouble,
  and he brought them out of their distress.
²⁹He stilled the storm to a whisper;
  the waves of the sea were hushed.
³⁰They were glad when it grew calm,
  and he guided them to their desired
  haven.
³¹Let them give thanks to the LORD for his
  unfailing love
  and his wonderful deeds for men.
³²Let them exalt him in the assembly of the
  people
  and praise him in the council of the
  elders.

³³He turned rivers into a desert,
  flowing springs into thirsty ground,
³⁴and fruitful land into a salt waste,
  because of the wickedness of those who
  lived there.

THE MESSAGE

He led you out of your dark, dark cell,
  broke open the jail and led you out.
So thank GOD for his marvelous love,
  for his miracle mercy to the children he
  loves;
He shattered the heavy jailhouse doors,
  he snapped the prison bars like
  matchsticks!

107.17-22 Some of you were sick because you'd lived a
  bad life,
  your bodies feeling the effects of your sin;
You couldn't stand the sight of food,
  so miserable you thought you'd be better
  off dead.
Then you called out to GOD in your desperate
  condition;
  he got you out in the nick of time.
He spoke the word that healed you,
  that pulled you back from the brink of death.
So thank GOD for his marvelous love,
  for his miracle mercy to the children he
  loves;
Offer thanksgiving sacrifices,
  tell the world what he's done—sing it out!

107.23-32 Some of you set sail in big ships;
  you put to sea to do business in faraway
  ports.
Out at sea you saw GOD in action,
  saw his breathtaking ways with the ocean:
With a word he called up the wind—
  an ocean storm, towering waves!
You shot high in the sky, then the bottom
  dropped out;
  your hearts were stuck in your throats.
You were spun like a top, you reeled like a
  drunk,
  you didn't know which end was up.
Then you called out to GOD in your desperate
  condition;
  he got you out in the nick of time.
He quieted the wind down to a whisper,
  put a muzzle on all the big waves.
And you were so glad when the storm died
  down,
  and he led you safely back to harbor.
So thank GOD for his marvelous love,
  for his miracle mercy to the children he
  loves.
Lift high your praises when the people
  assemble,
  shout Hallelujah when the elders meet!

107.33-41 GOD turned rivers into wasteland,
  springs of water into sunbaked mud;
Luscious orchards became alkali flats
  because of the evil of the people who lived
  there.

NEW INTERNATIONAL VERSION

35 He turned the desert into pools of water
and the parched ground into flowing
springs;
36 there he brought the hungry to live,
and they founded a city where they could
settle.
37 They sowed fields and planted vineyards
that yielded a fruitful harvest;
38 he blessed them, and their numbers greatly
increased,
and he did not let their herds diminish.

39 Then their numbers decreased, and they
were humbled
by oppression, calamity and sorrow;
40 he who pours contempt on nobles
made them wander in a trackless waste.
41 But he lifted the needy out of their affliction
and increased their families like flocks.
42 The upright see and rejoice,
but all the wicked shut their mouths.

43 Whoever is wise, let him heed these things
and consider the great love of the LORD.

PSALM 108

A song. A psalm of David.

1 My heart is steadfast, O God;
I will sing and make music with all my
soul.
2 Awake, harp and lyre!
I will awaken the dawn.
3 I will praise you, O LORD, among the
nations;
I will sing of you among the peoples.
4 For great is your love, higher than the
heavens;
your faithfulness reaches to the skies.
5 Be exalted, O God, above the heavens,
and let your glory be over all the earth.

6 Save us and help us with your right hand,
that those you love may be delivered.
7 God has spoken from his sanctuary:
"In triumph I will parcel out Shechem
and measure off the Valley of Succoth.
8 Gilead is mine, Manasseh is mine;
Ephraim is my helmet,
Judah my scepter.
9 Moab is my washbasin,
upon Edom I toss my sandal;
over Philistia I shout in triumph."

10 Who will bring me to the fortified city?
Who will lead me to Edom?

THE MESSAGE

Then he changed wasteland into fresh pools
of water,
arid earth into springs of water,
Brought in the hungry and settled them there;
they moved in—what a great place to live!
They sowed the fields, they planted vineyards,
they reaped a bountiful harvest.
He blessed them and they prospered greatly;
their herds of cattle never decreased.
But abuse and evil and trouble declined
as he heaped scorn on princes and sent
them away.
He gave the poor a safe place to live,
treated their clans like well-cared-for sheep.

107.42-43 Good people see this and are glad;
bad people are speechless, stopped in their
tracks.
If you are really wise, you'll think this over—
it's time you appreciated GOD's deep love.

A David prayer

108.1-2 **108** I'm ready, God, so ready,
ready from head to toe.
Ready to sing,
ready to raise a God-song:
"Wake, soul! Wake, lute!
Wake up, you sleepyhead sun!"

108.3-6 I'm thanking you, GOD, out in the streets,
singing your praises in town and country.
The deeper your love, the higher it goes;
every cloud's a flag to your faithfulness.
Soar high in the skies, O God!
Cover the whole earth with your glory!
And for the sake of the one you love so much,
reach down and help me—answer me!

108.7-9 That's when God spoke in holy splendor:
"Brimming over with joy,
I make a present of Shechem,
I hand out Succoth Valley as a gift.
Gilead's in my pocket,
to say nothing of Manasseh.
Ephraim's my hard hat,
Judah my hammer.
Moab's a scrub bucket—
I mop the floor with Moab,
Spit on Edom,
rain fireworks all over Philistia."

108.10-11 Who will take me to the thick of the fight?
Who'll show me the road to Edom?

NEW INTERNATIONAL VERSION

¹¹Is it not you, O God, you who have
    rejected us
  and no longer go out with our armies?
¹²Give us aid against the enemy,
    for the help of man is worthless.
¹³With God we will gain the victory,
    and he will trample down our enemies.

PSALM 109

For the director of music. Of David. A psalm.

¹O God, whom I praise,
    do not remain silent,
²for wicked and deceitful men
    have opened their mouths against me;
  they have spoken against me with lying
    tongues.
³With words of hatred they surround me;
    they attack me without cause.
⁴In return for my friendship they accuse me,
    but I am a man of prayer.
⁵They repay me evil for good,
    and hatred for my friendship.

⁶Appoint^{*a*} an evil man^{*b*} to oppose him;
    let an accuser^{*c*} stand at his right hand.
⁷When he is tried, let him be found guilty,
    and may his prayers condemn him.
⁸May his days be few;
    may another take his place of leadership.
⁹May his children be fatherless
    and his wife a widow.
¹⁰May his children be wandering beggars;
    may they be driven^{*d*} from their ruined
    homes.
¹¹May a creditor seize all he has;
    may strangers plunder the fruits of his
    labor.
¹²May no one extend kindness to him
    or take pity on his fatherless children.
¹³May his descendants be cut off,
    their names blotted out from the next
    generation.
¹⁴May the iniquity of his fathers be
    remembered before the LORD;
  may the sin of his mother never be blotted
    out.
¹⁵May their sins always remain before the
    LORD,
  that he may cut off the memory of them
    from the earth.

¹⁶For he never thought of doing a kindness,
    but hounded to death the poor
  and the needy and the brokenhearted.

*a 6 Or They say:, "Appoint (with quotation marks at the
end of verse 19)*   *b 6 Or the Evil One*   *c 6 Or let Satan*
d 10 Septuagint; Hebrew sought

THE MESSAGE

You aren't giving up on us, are you, God?
  refusing to go out with our troops?
^{108.12-13} Give us help for the hard task;
    human help is worthless.
In God we'll do our very best;
    he'll flatten the opposition for good.

A David prayer

^{109.1-5} **109** My God, don't turn a deaf ear to my
    hallelujah prayer.
Liars are pouring out invective on me;
Their lying tongues are like a pack of dogs out
    to get me,
  barking their hate, nipping my heels—and
    for no reason!
I loved them and now they slander me—
    yes, me!—
  and treat my prayer like a crime;
They return my good with evil,
    they return my love with hate.

^{109.6-20} Send the Evil One to accuse my accusing
    judge;
  dispatch Satan to prosecute him.
When he's judged, let the verdict be, "Guilty,"
  and when he prays, let his prayer turn to
    sin.
Give him a short life,
    and give his job to somebody else.
Make orphans of his children,
    dress his wife in widow's weeds;
Turn his children into begging street urchins,
    evicted from their homes—homeless.
May the bank foreclose and wipe him out,
    and strangers, like vultures, pick him clean.
May there be no one around to help him out,
    no one willing to give his orphans a break.
Chop down his family tree
    so that nobody even remembers his name.
But erect a memorial to the sin of his father,
    and make sure his mother's name is there,
    too—
Their sins recorded forever before GOD,
    but they themselves sunk in oblivion.
That's all he deserves since he was never once
    kind,
  hounded the afflicted and heartbroken to
    their graves.

NEW INTERNATIONAL VERSION	THE MESSAGE

NEW INTERNATIONAL VERSION

17 He loved to pronounce a curse—
　may it[a] come on him;
he found no pleasure in blessing—
　may it be[b] far from him.
18 He wore cursing as his garment;
　it entered into his body like water,
　into his bones like oil.
19 May it be like a cloak wrapped about him,
　like a belt tied forever around him.
20 May this be the LORD's payment to my
　　accusers,
　to those who speak evil of me.

21 But you, O Sovereign LORD,
　deal well with me for your name's sake;
　out of the goodness of your love,
　　deliver me.
22 For I am poor and needy,
　and my heart is wounded within me.
23 I fade away like an evening shadow;
　I am shaken off like a locust.
24 My knees give way from fasting;
　my body is thin and gaunt.
25 I am an object of scorn to my accusers;
　when they see me, they shake their heads.

26 Help me, O LORD my God;
　save me in accordance with your love.
27 Let them know that it is your hand,
　that you, O LORD, have done it.
28 They may curse, but you will bless;
　when they attack they will be put to
　　shame,
　but your servant will rejoice.
29 My accusers will be clothed with disgrace
　and wrapped in shame as in a cloak.

30 With my mouth I will greatly extol the LORD;
　in the great throng I will praise him.
31 For he stands at the right hand of the needy
　　one,
　to save his life from those who condemn
　　him.

PSALM 110

Of David. A psalm.

1 The LORD says to my Lord:
　"Sit at my right hand
until I make your enemies
　a footstool for your feet."

2 The LORD will extend your mighty scepter
　　from Zion;
　you will rule in the midst of your
　　enemies.

THE MESSAGE

Since he loved cursing so much,
　let curses rain down;
Since he had no taste for blessing,
　let blessings flee far from him.
He dressed up in curses like a fine suit of
　　clothes;
　he drank curses, took his baths in curses.
So give him a gift—a costume of curses;
　he can wear curses every day of the week!
That's what they'll get, those out to get me—
　an avalanche of just deserts from GOD.

109.21-25 Oh, GOD, my Lord, step in;
　work a miracle for me—you can do it!
Get me out of here—your love is so great!—
　I'm at the end of my rope, my life in ruins.
I'm fading away to nothing, passing away,
　my youth gone, old before my time.
I'm weak from hunger and can hardly
　　stand up,
　my body a rack of skin and bones.
I'm a joke in poor taste to those who see me;
　they take one look and shake their heads.

109.26-29 Help me, oh help me, GOD, my God,
　save me through your wonderful love;
Then they'll know that your hand is in this,
　that you, GOD, have been at work.
Let them curse all they want;
　you do the blessing.
Let them be jeered by the crowd when they
　　stand up,
　followed by cheers for me, your servant.
Dress my accusers in clothes dirty with
　　shame,
　discarded and humiliating old ragbag
　　clothes.

109.30-31 My mouth's full of great praise for GOD,
　I'm singing his hallelujahs surrounded by
　　crowds,
For he's always at hand to take the side of the
　　needy,
　to rescue a life from the unjust judge.

A David prayer

110.1-3 **110** The word of GOD to my Lord:
　"Sit alongside me here on my
　　throne
until I make your enemies a stool for your
　　feet."
You were forged a strong scepter by GOD of
　　Zion;
　now rule, though surrounded by enemies!

---

a 17 Or *curse, / and it has*　　b 17 Or *blessing, / and it is*

NEW INTERNATIONAL VERSION

³ Your troops will be willing
    on your day of battle.
Arrayed in holy majesty,
    from the womb of the dawn
    you will receive the dew of your youth. ᵃ

⁴ The LORD has sworn
    and will not change his mind:
"You are a priest forever,
    in the order of Melchizedek."

⁵ The Lord is at your right hand;
    he will crush kings on the day of his
        wrath.
⁶ He will judge the nations, heaping up the
        dead
    and crushing the rulers of the whole
        earth.
⁷ He will drink from a brook beside the way ᵇ;
    therefore he will lift up his head.

PSALM 111 ᶜ

¹ Praise the LORD. ᵈ

I will extol the LORD with all my heart
    in the council of the upright and in the
        assembly.
² Great are the works of the LORD;
    they are pondered by all who delight in
        them.
³ Glorious and majestic are his deeds,
    and his righteousness endures forever.
⁴ He has caused his wonders to be
        remembered;
    the LORD is gracious and compassionate.
⁵ He provides food for those who fear him;
    he remembers his covenant forever.
⁶ He has shown his people the power of his
        works,
    giving them the lands of other nations.
⁷ The works of his hands are faithful and just;
    all his precepts are trustworthy.
⁸ They are steadfast for ever and ever,
    done in faithfulness and uprightness.
⁹ He provided redemption for his people;
    he ordained his covenant forever—
    holy and awesome is his name.

¹⁰ The fear of the LORD is the beginning of
        wisdom;
    all who follow his precepts have good
        understanding.
    To him belongs eternal praise.

THE MESSAGE

Your people will freely join you, resplendent
        in holy armor
    on the great day of your conquest,
Join you at the fresh break of day,
    join you with all the vigor of youth.

110.4-7 GOD gave his word and he won't take it back:
    you're the permanent priest, the
        Melchizedek priest.
The Lord stands true at your side,
    crushing kings in his terrible wrath,
Bringing judgment on the nations,
    handing out convictions wholesale,
    crushing opposition across the wide earth.
The King-Maker put his King on the throne;
    the True King rules with head held high!

111.1-10 **111** Hallelujah!
    I give thanks to GOD with
        everything I've got—
Wherever good people gather, and in the
        congregation.
GOD's works are so great, worth
A lifetime of study—endless enjoyment!
Splendor and beauty mark his craft;
    His generosity never gives out.
His miracles are his memorial—
This GOD of Grace, this GOD of Love.
He gave food to those who fear him,
He remembered to keep his ancient promise.
He proved to his people that he could do what
        he said:
Hand them the nations on a platter—a gift!
He manufactures truth and justice;
All his products are guaranteed to last—
Never out-of-date, never obsolete, rust-proof.
All that he makes and does is honest and true:
He paid the ransom for his people,
He ordered his Covenant kept forever.
He's so personal and holy, worthy of our
        respect.
The good life begins in the fear of GOD—
Do that and you'll know the blessing of GOD.
His Hallelujah lasts forever!

ᵃ 3 Or / your young men will come to you like the dew
ᵇ 7 Or / The One who grants succession will set him in
authority   ᶜ This psalm is an acrostic poem, the lines of
which begin with the successive letters of the Hebrew
alphabet.   ᵈ 1 Hebrew Hallelu Yah

NEW INTERNATIONAL VERSION	THE MESSAGE

NEW INTERNATIONAL VERSION

PSALM 112 *ᵃ*

¹ Praise the LORD. *ᵇ*

Blessed is the man who fears the LORD,
    who finds great delight in his commands.

² His children will be mighty in the land;
    the generation of the upright will be
      blessed.
³ Wealth and riches are in his house,
    and his righteousness endures forever.
⁴ Even in darkness light dawns for the
    upright,
    for the gracious and compassionate and
      righteous man. *ᶜ*
⁵ Good will come to him who is generous and
    lends freely,
    who conducts his affairs with justice.
⁶ Surely he will never be shaken;
    a righteous man will be remembered
      forever.
⁷ He will have no fear of bad news;
    his heart is steadfast, trusting in the LORD.
⁸ His heart is secure, he will have no fear;
    in the end he will look in triumph on his
      foes.
⁹ He has scattered abroad his gifts to the poor,
    his righteousness endures forever;
    his horn *ᵈ* will be lifted high in honor.

¹⁰ The wicked man will see and be vexed,
    he will gnash his teeth and waste away;
    the longings of the wicked will come to
      nothing.

PSALM 113

¹ Praise the LORD. *ᵉ*

Praise, O servants of the LORD,
    praise the name of the LORD.
² Let the name of the LORD be praised,
    both now and forevermore.
³ From the rising of the sun to the place where
    it sets,
    the name of the LORD is to be praised.

⁴ The LORD is exalted over all the nations,
    his glory above the heavens.
⁵ Who is like the LORD our God,
    the One who sits enthroned on high,
⁶ who stoops down to look
    on the heavens and the earth?

THE MESSAGE

112 ¹²⁻¹⁰ Hallelujah!
Blessed man, blessed woman, who
    fear GOD,
Who cherish and relish his commandments,
Their children robust on the earth,
And the homes of the upright—how blessed!
Their houses brim with wealth
And a generosity that never runs dry.
Sunrise breaks through the darkness for good
    people—
God's grace and mercy and justice!
The good person is generous and lends
    lavishly;
No shuffling or stumbling around for this one,
But a sterling and solid and lasting reputation.
Unfazed by rumor and gossip,
Heart ready, trusting in GOD,
Spirit firm, unperturbed,
Ever blessed, relaxed among enemies,
They lavish gifts on the poor—
A generosity that goes on, and on, and on.
An honored life! A beautiful life!
Someone wicked takes one look and rages,
Blusters away but ends up speechless.
There's nothing to the dreams of the wicked.
    Nothing.

113 ¹¹³⁻³ Hallelujah!
You who serve GOD, praise GOD!
    Just to speak his name is praise!
Just to remember GOD is a blessing—
    now and tomorrow and always.
From east to west, from dawn to dusk,
    keep lifting all your praises to GOD!

¹¹³⁴⁻⁹ GOD is higher than anything and anyone,
    outshining everything you can see in the
      skies.
Who can compare with GOD, our God,
    so majestically enthroned,
Surveying his magnificent
    heavens and earth?

ᵃ This psalm is an acrostic poem, the lines of which begin
with the successive letters of the Hebrew alphabet.
ᵇ 1 Hebrew *Hallelu Yah*   *ᶜ* 4 Or *for [the LORD] is gracious
and compassionate and righteous*   *ᵈ* 9 *Horn* here
symbolizes dignity.   *ᵉ* 1 Hebrew *Hallelu Yah*; also in
verse 9

NEW INTERNATIONAL VERSION

⁷He raises the poor from the dust
  and lifts the needy from the ash heap;
⁸he seats them with princes,
  with the princes of their people.
⁹He settles the barren woman in her home
  as a happy mother of children.

  Praise the LORD.

PSALM 114

¹When Israel came out of Egypt,
  the house of Jacob from a people of
    foreign tongue,
²Judah became God's sanctuary,
  Israel his dominion.

³The sea looked and fled,
  the Jordan turned back;
⁴the mountains skipped like rams,
  the hills like lambs.

⁵Why was it, O sea, that you fled,
  O Jordan, that you turned back,
⁶you mountains, that you skipped like rams,
  you hills, like lambs?

⁷Tremble, O earth, at the presence of the
    Lord,
  at the presence of the God of Jacob,
⁸who turned the rock into a pool,
  the hard rock into springs of water.

PSALM 115

¹Not to us, O LORD, not to us
  but to your name be the glory,
  because of your love and faithfulness.

²Why do the nations say,
  "Where is their God?"
³Our God is in heaven;
  he does whatever pleases him.
⁴But their idols are silver and gold,
  made by the hands of men.
⁵They have mouths, but cannot speak,
  eyes, but they cannot see;
⁶they have ears, but cannot hear,
  noses, but they cannot smell;
⁷they have hands, but cannot feel,
  feet, but they cannot walk;
  nor can they utter a sound with their
    throats.
⁸Those who make them will be like them,
  and so will all who trust in them.

THE MESSAGE

He picks up the poor from out of the dirt,
  rescues the wretched who've been thrown
    out with the trash,
Seats them among the honored guests,
  a place of honor among the brightest and
    best.
He gives childless couples a family,
  gives them joy as the parents of children.
Hallelujah!

114.1-8 **114** After Israel left Egypt,
  the clan of Jacob left those
    barbarians behind;
Judah became holy land for him,
  Israel the place of holy rule.
Sea took one look and ran the other way;
  River Jordan turned around and ran off.
The mountains turned playful and skipped
    like rams,
  the hills frolicked like spring lambs.
What's wrong with you, Sea, that you ran
    away?
  and you, River Jordan, that you turned and
    ran off?
And mountains, why did you skip like rams?
  and you, hills, frolic like spring lambs?
Tremble, Earth! You're in the Lord's presence!
  in the presence of Jacob's God.
He turned the rock into a pool of cool water,
  turned flint into fresh spring water.

115.1-2 **115** Not for our sake, GOD, no, not for
  our sake,
  but for your name's sake, show your glory.
Do it on account of your merciful love,
  do it on account of your faithful ways.
Do it so none of the nations can say,
  "Where now, oh where is their God?"

115.3-8 Our God is in heaven
  doing whatever he wants to do.
Their gods are metal and wood,
  handmade in a basement shop:
Carved mouths that can't talk,
  painted eyes that can't see,
Tin ears that can't hear,
  molded noses that can't smell,
Hands that can't grasp, feet that can't walk or
    run,
  throats that never utter a sound.
Those who make them have become just like
    them,
  have become just like the gods they trust.

NEW INTERNATIONAL VERSION	THE MESSAGE

NEW INTERNATIONAL VERSION

⁹O house of Israel, trust in the LORD—
he is their help and shield.
¹⁰O house of Aaron, trust in the LORD—
he is their help and shield.
¹¹You who fear him, trust in the LORD—
he is their help and shield.

¹²The LORD remembers us and will bless us:
He will bless the house of Israel,
he will bless the house of Aaron,
¹³he will bless those who fear the LORD—
small and great alike.

¹⁴May the LORD make you increase,
both you and your children.
¹⁵May you be blessed by the LORD,
the Maker of heaven and earth.

¹⁶The highest heavens belong to the LORD,
but the earth he has given to man.
¹⁷It is not the dead who praise the LORD,
those who go down to silence;
¹⁸it is we who extol the LORD,
both now and forevermore.

Praise the LORD.ᵃ

PSALM 116

¹I love the LORD, for he heard my voice;
he heard my cry for mercy.
²Because he turned his ear to me,
I will call on him as long as I live.

³The cords of death entangled me,
the anguish of the graveᵇ came upon me;
I was overcome by trouble and sorrow.
⁴Then I called on the name of the LORD:
"O LORD, save me!"

⁵The LORD is gracious and righteous;
our God is full of compassion.
⁶The LORD protects the simplehearted;
when I was in great need, he saved me.

⁷Be at rest once more, O my soul,
for the LORD has been good to you.

⁸For you, O LORD, have delivered my soul
from death,
my eyes from tears,
my feet from stumbling,
⁹that I may walk before the LORD
in the land of the living.
¹⁰I believed; thereforeᶜ I said,
"I am greatly afflicted."
¹¹And in my dismay I said,
"All men are liars."

THE MESSAGE

115.9-11 But you, Israel: put your trust in GOD!
—trust your Helper! trust your Ruler!
Clan of Aaron, trust in GOD!
—trust your Helper! trust your Ruler!
You who fear GOD, trust in GOD!
—trust your Helper! trust your Ruler!

115.12-16 O GOD, remember us and bless us,
bless the families of Israel and Aaron.
And let GOD bless all who fear GOD—
bless the small, bless the great.
Oh, let GOD enlarge your families—
giving growth to you, growth to your
children.
May you be blessed by GOD,
by GOD, who made heaven and earth.
The heaven of heavens is for GOD,
but he put us in charge of the earth.

115.17-18 Dead people can't praise GOD—
not a word to be heard from those buried in
the ground.
But we bless GOD, oh yes—
we bless him now, we bless him always!
Hallelujah!

116.1-6 **116** I love GOD because he listened
to me,
listened as I begged for mercy.
He listened so intently
as I laid out my case before him.
Death stared me in the face,
hell was hard on my heels.
Up against it, I didn't know which way to
turn;
then I called out to GOD for help:
"Please, GOD!" I cried out.
"Save my life!"
GOD is gracious—it is he who makes things
right,
our most compassionate God.
GOD takes the side of the helpless;
when I was at the end of my rope, he
saved me.

116.7-8 I said to myself, "Relax and rest.
GOD has showered you with blessings.
Soul, you've been rescued from death;
Eye, you've been rescued from tears;
And you, Foot, were kept from stumbling."

116.9-11 I'm striding in the presence of GOD,
alive in the land of the living!
I stayed faithful, though bedeviled,
and despite a ton of bad luck,
Despite giving up on the human race,
saying, "They're all liars and cheats."

ᵃ 18 Hebrew *Hallelu Yah*   ᵇ 3 Hebrew *Sheol*
ᶜ 10 Or *believed even when*

NEW INTERNATIONAL VERSION

¹²How can I repay the LORD
  for all his goodness to me?
¹³I will lift up the cup of salvation
  and call on the name of the LORD.
¹⁴I will fulfill my vows to the LORD
  in the presence of all his people.

¹⁵Precious in the sight of the LORD
  is the death of his saints.
¹⁶O LORD, truly I am your servant;
  I am your servant, the son of your
    maidservant[a];
  you have freed me from my chains.

¹⁷I will sacrifice a thank offering to you
  and call on the name of the LORD.
¹⁸I will fulfill my vows to the LORD
  in the presence of all his people,
¹⁹in the courts of the house of the LORD—
  in your midst, O Jerusalem.

  Praise the LORD.[b]

PSALM 117

¹Praise the LORD, all you nations;
  extol him, all you peoples.
²For great is his love toward us,
  and the faithfulness of the LORD endures
    forever.

  Praise the LORD.[b]

PSALM 118

¹Give thanks to the LORD, for he is good;
  his love endures forever.

²Let Israel say:
  "His love endures forever."
³Let the house of Aaron say:
  "His love endures forever."
⁴Let those who fear the LORD say:
  "His love endures forever."

⁵In my anguish I cried to the LORD,
  and he answered by setting me free.
⁶The LORD is with me; I will not be afraid.
  What can man do to me?
⁷The LORD is with me; he is my helper.
  I will look in triumph on my enemies.

⁸It is better to take refuge in the LORD
  than to trust in man.
⁹It is better to take refuge in the LORD
  than to trust in princes.

¹⁰All the nations surrounded me,
  but in the name of the LORD I cut them
    off.

THE MESSAGE

¹¹⁶·¹²⁻¹⁹ What can I give back to GOD
  for the blessings he's poured out on me?
I'll lift high the cup of salvation—a toast to
    GOD!
  I'll pray in the name of GOD;
I'll complete what I promised GOD I'd do,
  and I'll do it together with his people.
When they arrive at the gates of death,
  GOD welcomes those who love him.
Oh, GOD, here I am, your servant,
  your faithful servant: set me free for your
    service!
I'm ready to offer the thanksgiving sacrifice
  and pray in the name of GOD.
I'll complete what I promised GOD I'd do,
  and I'll do it in company with his people,
In the place of worship, in GOD's house,
  in Jerusalem, GOD's city.
Hallelujah!

¹¹⁷·¹⁻² **117** Praise GOD, everybody!
  Applaud GOD, all people!
His love has taken over our lives;
  GOD's faithful ways are eternal.
  Hallelujah!

¹¹⁸·¹⁻⁴ **118** Thank GOD because he's good,
  because his love never quits.
Tell the world, Israel,
  "His love never quits."
And you, clan of Aaron, tell the world,
  "His love never quits."
And you who fear GOD, join in,
  "His love never quits."

¹¹⁸·⁵⁻¹⁶ Pushed to the wall, I called to GOD;
  from the wide open spaces, he answered.
GOD's now at my side and I'm not afraid;
  who would dare lay a hand on me?
GOD's my strong champion;
  I flick off my enemies like flies.
Far better to take refuge in GOD
  than trust in people;
Far better to take refuge in GOD
  than trust in celebrities.
Hemmed in by barbarians,
  in GOD's name I rubbed their faces in the
    dirt;

---

[a] 16 Or *servant, your faithful son*   [b] 19,2 Hebrew *Hallelu
Yah*

NEW INTERNATIONAL VERSION

11 They surrounded me on every side,
    but in the name of the LORD I cut them
        off.
12 They swarmed around me like bees,
    but they died out as quickly as burning
        thorns;
    in the name of the LORD I cut them off.

13 I was pushed back and about to fall,
    but the LORD helped me.
14 The LORD is my strength and my song;
    he has become my salvation.

15 Shouts of joy and victory
    resound in the tents of the righteous:
    "The LORD's right hand has done mighty
        things!
16   The LORD's right hand is lifted high;
    the LORD's right hand has done mighty
        things!"

17 I will not die but live,
    and will proclaim what the LORD has
        done.
18 The LORD has chastened me severely,
    but he has not given me over to death.

19 Open for me the gates of righteousness;
    I will enter and give thanks to the LORD.
20 This is the gate of the LORD
    through which the righteous may enter.
21 I will give you thanks, for you answered me;
    you have become my salvation.

22 The stone the builders rejected
    has become the capstone;
23 the LORD has done this,
    and it is marvelous in our eyes.
24 This is the day the LORD has made;
    let us rejoice and be glad in it.

25 O LORD, save us;
    O LORD, grant us success.
26 Blessed is he who comes in the name of the
        LORD.
    From the house of the LORD we bless
        you. *a*
27 The LORD is God,
    and he has made his light shine upon us.
    With boughs in hand, join in the festal
        procession
    up *b* to the horns of the altar.

28 You are my God, and I will give you thanks;
    you are my God, and I will exalt you.

29 Give thanks to the LORD, for he is good;
    his love endures forever.

THE MESSAGE

Hemmed in and with no way out,
    in GOD's name I rubbed their faces in the
        dirt;
Like swarming bees, like wild prairie fire, they
        hemmed me in;
    in GOD's name I rubbed their faces in the
        dirt.
I was right on the cliff-edge, ready to fall,
    when GOD grabbed and held me.
GOD's my strength, he's also my song,
    and now he's my salvation.
Hear the shouts, hear the triumph songs
    in the camp of the saved?
        "The hand of GOD has turned the tide!
        The hand of GOD is raised in victory!
        The hand of GOD has turned the tide!"

118.17-20 I didn't die. I *lived!*
    And now I'm telling the world what GOD
        did.
GOD tested me, he pushed me hard,
    but he didn't hand me over to Death.
Swing wide the city gates—the *righteous*
        gates!
    I'll walk right through and thank GOD!
This Temple Gate belongs to GOD,
    so the victors can enter and praise.

118.21-25 Thank you for responding to me;
    you've truly become my salvation!
The stone the masons discarded as flawed
    is now the capstone!
This is GOD's work.
    We rub our eyes—we can hardly believe it!
This is the very day GOD acted—
    let's celebrate and be festive!
Salvation now, GOD. Salvation now!
    Oh yes, GOD—a free and full life!

118.26-29 Blessed are you who enter in GOD's name—
    from GOD's house we bless you!
GOD is God,
    he has bathed us in light.
Festoon the shrine with garlands,
    hang colored banners above the altar!
You're my God, and I thank you.
    O my God, I lift high your praise.
Thank GOD—he's so good.
    His love never quits!

---

a 26 The Hebrew is plural.   *b* 27 Or *Bind the festal
sacrifice with ropes / and take it*

NEW INTERNATIONAL VERSION

PSALM 119[a]

א ALEPH

1 Blessed are they whose ways are blameless,
  who walk according to the law of the
   LORD.
2 Blessed are they who keep his statutes
  and seek him with all their heart.
3 They do nothing wrong;
  they walk in his ways.
4 You have laid down precepts
  that are to be fully obeyed.
5 Oh, that my ways were steadfast
  in obeying your decrees!
6 Then I would not be put to shame
  when I consider all your commands.
7 I will praise you with an upright heart
  as I learn your righteous laws.
8 I will obey your decrees;
  do not utterly forsake me.

ב BETH

9 How can a young man keep his way pure?
  By living according to your word.
10 I seek you with all my heart;
  do not let me stray from your commands.
11 I have hidden your word in my heart
  that I might not sin against you.
12 Praise be to you, O LORD;
  teach me your decrees.
13 With my lips I recount
  all the laws that come from your mouth.
14 I rejoice in following your statutes
  as one rejoices in great riches.
15 I meditate on your precepts
  and consider your ways.
16 I delight in your decrees;
  I will not neglect your word.

ג GIMEL

17 Do good to your servant, and I will live;
  I will obey your word.
18 Open my eyes that I may see
  wonderful things in your law.
19 I am a stranger on earth;
  do not hide your commands from me.
20 My soul is consumed with longing
  for your laws at all times.
21 You rebuke the arrogant, who are cursed

---

a This psalm is an acrostic poem; the verses of each stanza
begin with the same letter of the Hebrew alphabet.

THE MESSAGE

119.1-8 **119** You're blessed when you stay on
  course,
  walking steadily on the road revealed by
   GOD.
You're blessed when you follow his directions,
  doing your best to find him.
That's right—you don't go off on your own;
  you walk straight along the road he set.
You, GOD, prescribed the right way to live;
  now you expect us to live it.
Oh, that my steps might be steady,
  keeping to the course you set;
Then I'd never have any regrets
  in comparing my life with your counsel.
I thank you for speaking straight from your
    heart;
  I learn the pattern of your righteous ways.
I'm going to do what you tell me to do;
  don't ever walk off and leave me.

⁜

119.9-16 How can a young person live a clean life?
  By carefully reading the map of your Word.
I'm single-minded in pursuit of you;
  don't let me miss the road signs you've
    posted.
I've banked your promises in the vault of my
    heart
  so I won't sin myself bankrupt.
Be blessed, GOD;
  train me in your ways of wise living.
I'll transfer to my lips
  all the counsel that comes from your
    mouth;
I delight far more in what you tell me about
    living
  than in gathering a pile of riches.
I ponder every morsel of wisdom from you,
  I attentively watch how you've done it.
I relish everything you've told me of life,
  I won't forget a word of it.

⁜

119.17-24 Be generous with me and I'll live a full life;
  not for a minute will I take my eyes off
    your road.
Open my eyes so I can see
  what you show me of your miracle-
    wonders.
I'm a stranger in these parts;
  give me clear directions.
My soul is starved and hungry, ravenous!—
  insatiable for your nourishing commands.
And those who think they know so much,

NEW INTERNATIONAL VERSION

and who stray from your commands.
²² Remove from me scorn and contempt,
 for I keep your statutes.
²³ Though rulers sit together and slander me,
 your servant will meditate on your
  decrees.
²⁴ Your statutes are my delight;
 they are my counselors.

ד DALETH

²⁵ I am laid low in the dust;
 preserve my life according to your word.
²⁶ I recounted my ways and you answered me;
 teach me your decrees.
²⁷ Let me understand the teaching of your
  precepts;
 then I will meditate on your wonders.
²⁸ My soul is weary with sorrow;
 strengthen me according to your word.
²⁹ Keep me from deceitful ways;
 be gracious to me through your law.
³⁰ I have chosen the way of truth;
 I have set my heart on your laws.
³¹ I hold fast to your statutes, O LORD;
 do not let me be put to shame.
³² I run in the path of your commands,
 for you have set my heart free.

ה HE

³³ Teach me, O LORD, to follow your decrees;
 then I will keep them to the end.
³⁴ Give me understanding, and I will keep your
  law
 and obey it with all my heart.
³⁵ Direct me in the path of your commands,
 for there I find delight.
³⁶ Turn my heart toward your statutes
 and not toward selfish gain.
³⁷ Turn my eyes away from worthless things;
 preserve my life according to your word. ᵃ
³⁸ Fulfill your promise to your servant,
 so that you may be feared.
³⁹ Take away the disgrace I dread,
 for your laws are good.
⁴⁰ How I long for your precepts!
 Preserve my life in your righteousness.

ו WAW

⁴¹ May your unfailing love come to me,
  O LORD,
 your salvation according to your promise;

ᵃ *37* Two manuscripts of the Masoretic Text and Dead Sea
Scrolls; most manuscripts of the Masoretic Text *life in your
way*

THE MESSAGE

ignoring everything you tell them—let
  them have it!
Don't let them mock and humiliate me;
 I've been careful to do just what you said.
While bad neighbors maliciously gossip
  about me,
 I'm absorbed in pondering your wise
  counsel.
Yes, your sayings on life are what give me
  delight;
 I listen to them as to good neighbors!

119.25-32 I'm feeling terrible—I couldn't feel worse!
 Get me on my feet again. You promised,
  remember?
When I told my story, you responded;
 train me well in your deep wisdom.
Help me understand these things inside and
  out
 so I can ponder your miracle-wonders.
My sad life's dilapidated, a falling-down barn;
 build me up again by your Word.
Barricade the road that goes Nowhere;
 grace me with your clear revelation.
I choose the true road to Somewhere,
 I post your road signs at every curve and
  corner.
I grasp and cling to whatever you tell me;
 GOD, don't let me down!
I'll run the course you lay out for me
 if you'll just show me how.

119.33-40 GOD, teach me lessons for living
 so I can stay the course.
Give me insight so I can do what you tell
  me—
 my whole life one long, obedient response.
Guide me down the road of your
  commandments;
 I love traveling this freeway!
Give me a bent for your words of wisdom,
 and not for piling up loot.
Divert my eyes from toys and trinkets,
 invigorate me on the pilgrim way.
Affirm your promises to me—
 promises made to all who fear you.
Deflect the harsh words of my critics—
 but what you say is always so good.
See how hungry I am for your counsel;
 preserve my life through your righteous
  ways!

119.41-48 Let your love, GOD, shape my life
 with salvation, exactly as you promised;

NEW INTERNATIONAL VERSION

⁴²then I will answer the one who taunts me,
  for I trust in your word.
⁴³Do not snatch the word of truth from my
      mouth,
  for I have put my hope in your laws.
⁴⁴I will always obey your law,
  for ever and ever.
⁴⁵I will walk about in freedom,
  for I have sought out your precepts.
⁴⁶I will speak of your statutes before kings
  and will not be put to shame,
⁴⁷for I delight in your commands
  because I love them.
⁴⁸I lift up my hands to*ᵃ* your commands,
      which I love,
  and I meditate on your decrees.

ז Zayin

⁴⁹Remember your word to your servant,
  for you have given me hope.
⁵⁰My comfort in my suffering is this:
  Your promise preserves my life.
⁵¹The arrogant mock me without restraint,
  but I do not turn from your law.
⁵²I remember your ancient laws, O Lord,
  and I find comfort in them.
⁵³Indignation grips me because of the wicked,
  who have forsaken your law.
⁵⁴Your decrees are the theme of my song
  wherever I lodge.
⁵⁵In the night I remember your name, O Lord,
  and I will keep your law.
⁵⁶This has been my practice:
  I obey your precepts.

ח Heth

⁵⁷You are my portion, O Lord;
  I have promised to obey your words.
⁵⁸I have sought your face with all my heart;
  be gracious to me according to your
      promise.
⁵⁹I have considered my ways
  and have turned my steps to your statutes.
⁶⁰I will hasten and not delay
  to obey your commands.
⁶¹Though the wicked bind me with ropes,
  I will not forget your law.
⁶²At midnight I rise to give you thanks
  for your righteous laws.
⁶³I am a friend to all who fear you,
  to all who follow your precepts.
⁶⁴The earth is filled with your love, O Lord;
  teach me your decrees.

ᵃ 48 Or *for*

THE MESSAGE

Then I'll be able to stand up to mockery
  because I trusted your Word.
Don't ever deprive me of truth, not ever—
  your commandments are what I depend on.
Oh, I'll guard with my life what you've
      revealed to me,
  guard it now, guard it ever;
And I'll stride freely through wide open spaces
  as I look for your truth and your wisdom;
Then I'll tell the world what I find,
  speak out boldly in public, unembarrassed.
I cherish your commandments—oh, how I
      love them!—
  relishing every fragment of your counsel.

119.49-56 Remember what you said to me, your
      servant—
  I hang on to these words for dear life!
These words hold me up in bad times;
  yes, your promises rejuvenate me.
The insolent ridicule me without mercy,
  but I don't budge from your revelation.
I watch for your ancient landmark words,
  and know I'm on the right track.
But when I see the wicked ignore your
      directions,
  I'm beside myself with anger.
I set your instructions to music
  and sing them as I walk this pilgrim way.
I meditate on your name all night, God,
  treasuring your revelation, O God.
Still, I walk through a rain of derision
  because I live by your Word and counsel.

119.57-64 Because you have satisfied me, God, I promise
  to do everything you say.
I beg you from the bottom of my heart: smile,
  be gracious to me just as you promised.
When I took a long, careful look at your ways,
  I got my feet back on the trail you blazed.
I was up at once, didn't drag my feet,
  was quick to follow your orders.
The wicked hemmed me in—there was no
      way out—
  but not for a minute did I forget your plan
      for me.
I get up in the middle of the night to thank
      you;
  your decisions are so right, so true—I can't
      wait till morning!
I'm a friend and companion of all who fear you,
  of those committed to living by your rules.
Your love, God, fills the earth!
  Train me to live by your counsel.

✝

NEW INTERNATIONAL VERSION	THE MESSAGE

ט TETH

⁶⁵ Do good to your servant
according to your word, O LORD.
⁶⁶ Teach me knowledge and good judgment,
for I believe in your commands.
⁶⁷ Before I was afflicted I went astray,
but now I obey your word.
⁶⁸ You are good, and what you do is good;
teach me your decrees.
⁶⁹ Though the arrogant have smeared me with
lies,
I keep your precepts with all my heart.
⁷⁰ Their hearts are callous and unfeeling,
but I delight in your law.
⁷¹ It was good for me to be afflicted
so that I might learn your decrees.
⁷² The law from your mouth is more precious
to me
than thousands of pieces of silver and
gold.

119.65-72 Be good to your servant, GOD;
be as good as your Word.
Train me in good common sense;
I'm thoroughly committed to living your
way.
Before I learned to answer you, I wandered all
over the place,
but now I'm in step with your Word.
You are good, and the source of good;
train me in your goodness.
The godless spread lies about me,
but I focus my attention on what you are
saying;
They're bland as a bucket of lard,
while I dance to the tune of your
revelation.
My troubles turned out all for the best—
they forced me to learn from your
textbook.
Truth from your mouth means more to me
than striking it rich in a gold mine.

י YODH

⁷³ Your hands made me and formed me;
give me understanding to learn your
commands.
⁷⁴ May those who fear you rejoice when they
see me,
for I have put my hope in your word.
⁷⁵ I know, O LORD, that your laws are righteous,
and in faithfulness you have afflicted me.
⁷⁶ May your unfailing love be my comfort,
according to your promise to your
servant.
⁷⁷ Let your compassion come to me that I may
live,
for your law is my delight.
⁷⁸ May the arrogant be put to shame for
wronging me without cause;
but I will meditate on your precepts.
⁷⁹ May those who fear you turn to me,
those who understand your statutes.
⁸⁰ May my heart be blameless toward your
decrees,
that I may not be put to shame.

119.73-80 With your very own hands you formed me;
now breathe your wisdom over me so I can
understand you.
When they see me waiting, expecting your
Word,
those who fear you will take heart and be
glad.
I can see now, GOD, that your decisions are
right;
your testing has taught me what's true and
right.
Oh, love me—and right now!—hold me tight!
just the way you promised.
Now comfort me so I can live, really live;
your revelation is the tune I dance to.
Let the fast-talking tricksters be exposed as
frauds;
they tried to sell me a bill of goods,
but I kept my mind fixed on your counsel.
Let those who fear you turn to me
for evidence of your wise guidance.
And let me live whole and holy, soul and body,
so I can always walk with my head held
high.

כ KAPH

⁸¹ My soul faints with longing for your
salvation,
but I have put my hope in your word.
⁸² My eyes fail, looking for your promise;
I say, "When will you comfort me?"
⁸³ Though I am like a wineskin in the smoke,

119.81-88 I'm homesick—longing for your salvation;
I'm waiting for your word of hope.
My eyes grow heavy watching for some sign of
your promise;
how long must I wait for your comfort?
There's smoke in my eyes—they burn and
water,

NEW INTERNATIONAL VERSION

I do not forget your decrees.
84 How long must your servant wait?
When will you punish my persecutors?
85 The arrogant dig pitfalls for me,
contrary to your law.
86 All your commands are trustworthy;
help me, for men persecute me without
cause.
87 They almost wiped me from the earth,
but I have not forsaken your precepts.
88 Preserve my life according to your love,
and I will obey the statutes of your
mouth.

ל LAMEDH

89 Your word, O LORD, is eternal;
it stands firm in the heavens.
90 Your faithfulness continues through all
generations;
you established the earth, and it endures.
91 Your laws endure to this day,
for all things serve you.
92 If your law had not been my delight,
I would have perished in my affliction.
93 I will never forget your precepts,
for by them you have preserved my life.
94 Save me, for I am yours;
I have sought out your precepts.
95 The wicked are waiting to destroy me,
but I will ponder your statutes.
96 To all perfection I see a limit;
but your commands are boundless.

מ MEM

97 Oh, how I love your law!
I meditate on it all day long.
98 Your commands make me wiser than my
enemies,
for they are ever with me.
99 I have more insight than all my teachers,
for I meditate on your statutes.
100 I have more understanding than the elders,
for I obey your precepts.
101 I have kept my feet from every evil path
so that I might obey your word.

THE MESSAGE

but I keep a steady gaze on the instructions
you post.
How long do I have to put up with all this?
How long till you haul my tormentors into
court?
The arrogant godless try to throw me off
track,
ignorant as they are of God and his ways.
Everything you command is a sure thing,
but they harass me with lies. Help!
They've pushed and pushed—they never let
up—
but I haven't relaxed my grip on your
counsel.
In your great love revive me
so I can alertly obey your every word.

✠

119.89-96 What you say goes, GOD,
and *stays*, as permanent as the heavens.
Your truth never goes out of fashion;
it's as up-to-date as the earth when the sun
comes up.
Your Word and truth are dependable as ever;
that's what you ordered—you set the earth
going.
If your revelation hadn't delighted me so,
I would have given up when the hard times
came.
But I'll never forget the advice you gave me;
you saved my life with those wise words.
Save me! I'm all yours.
I look high and low for your words of
wisdom.
The wicked lie in ambush to destroy me,
but I'm only concerned with your plans
for me.
I see the limits to everything human,
but the horizons can't contain your
commands!

✠

119.97- Oh, how I love all you've revealed;
104 I reverently ponder it all the day long.
Your commands give me an edge on my
enemies;
they never become obsolete.
I've even become smarter than my teachers
since I've pondered and absorbed your
counsel.
I've become wiser than the wise old sages
simply by doing what you tell me.
I watch my step, avoiding the ditches and ruts
of evil
so I can spend all my time keeping your
Word.

NEW INTERNATIONAL VERSION

102 I have not departed from your laws,
    for you yourself have taught me.
103 How sweet are your words to my taste,
    sweeter than honey to my mouth!
104 I gain understanding from your precepts;
    therefore I hate every wrong path.

ב Nun

105 Your word is a lamp to my feet
    and a light for my path.
106 I have taken an oath and confirmed it,
    that I will follow your righteous laws.
107 I have suffered much;
    preserve my life, O Lord, according to
      your word.
108 Accept, O Lord, the willing praise of my
      mouth,
    and teach me your laws.
109 Though I constantly take my life in my
      hands,
    I will not forget your law.
110 The wicked have set a snare for me,
    but I have not strayed from your precepts.
111 Your statutes are my heritage forever;
    they are the joy of my heart.
112 My heart is set on keeping your decrees
    to the very end.

ס Samekh

113 I hate double-minded men,
    but I love your law.
114 You are my refuge and my shield;
    I have put my hope in your word.
115 Away from me, you evildoers,
    that I may keep the commands of my
      God!
116 Sustain me according to your promise, and I
      will live;
    do not let my hopes be dashed.
117 Uphold me, and I will be delivered;
    I will always have regard for your decrees.
118 You reject all who stray from your decrees,
    for their deceitfulness is in vain.
119 All the wicked of the earth you discard like
      dross;
    therefore I love your statutes.
120 My flesh trembles in fear of you;
    I stand in awe of your laws.

ע Ayin

121 I have done what is righteous and just;
    do not leave me to my oppressors.
122 Ensure your servant's well-being;

THE MESSAGE

I never make detours from the route you laid
    out;
    you gave me such good directions.
Your words are so choice, so tasty;
    I prefer them to the best home cooking.
With your instruction, I understand life;
    that's why I hate false propaganda.

119.105- By your words I can see where I'm going;
   112   they throw a beam of light on my dark
      path.
I've committed myself and I'll never turn back
    from living by your righteous order.
Everything's falling apart on me, God;
    put me together again with your Word.
Festoon me with your finest sayings, God;
    teach me your holy rules.
My life is as close as my own hands,
    but I don't forget what you have revealed.
The wicked do their best to throw me off
      track,
    but I don't swerve an inch from your
      course.
I inherited your book on living; it's mine
      forever—
    what a gift! And how happy it makes me!
I concentrate on doing exactly what you say—
    I always have and always will.

119.113- I hate the two-faced,
   120   but I love your clear-cut revelation.
You're my place of quiet retreat;
    I wait for your Word to renew me.
Get out of my life, evildoers,
    so I can keep my God's commands.
Take my side as you promised; I'll live then
      for sure.
    Don't disappoint all my grand hopes.
Stick with me and I'll be all right;
    I'll give total allegiance to your definitions
      of life.
Expose all who drift away from your sayings;
    their casual idolatry is lethal.
You reject earth's wicked as so much rubbish;
    therefore I lovingly embrace everything you
      say.
I shiver in awe before you;
    your decisions leave me speechless with
      reverence.

119.121- I stood up for justice and the right;
   128   don't leave me to the mercy of my
      oppressors.
Take the side of your servant, good God;

NEW INTERNATIONAL VERSION

let not the arrogant oppress me.
123 My eyes fail, looking for your salvation,
looking for your righteous promise.
124 Deal with your servant according to your
love
and teach me your decrees.
125 I am your servant; give me discernment
that I may understand your statutes.
126 It is time for you to act, O LORD;
your law is being broken.
127 Because I love your commands
more than gold, more than pure gold,
128 and because I consider all your precepts
right,
I hate every wrong path.

פ PE

129 Your statutes are wonderful;
therefore I obey them.
130 The unfolding of your words gives light;
it gives understanding to the simple.
131 I open my mouth and pant,
longing for your commands.
132 Turn to me and have mercy on me,
as you always do to those who love your
name.
133 Direct my footsteps according to your word;
let no sin rule over me.
134 Redeem me from the oppression of men,
that I may obey your precepts.
135 Make your face shine upon your servant
and teach me your decrees.
136 Streams of tears flow from my eyes,
for your law is not obeyed.

צ TSADHE

137 Righteous are you, O LORD,
and your laws are right.
138 The statutes you have laid down are
righteous;
they are fully trustworthy.
139 My zeal wears me out,
for my enemies ignore your words.
140 Your promises have been thoroughly tested,
and your servant loves them.
141 Though I am lowly and despised,
I do not forget your precepts.
142 Your righteousness is everlasting
and your law is true.
143 Trouble and distress have come upon me,
but your commands are my delight.

THE MESSAGE

don't let the godless take advantage of me.
I can't keep my eyes open any longer, waiting
for you
to keep your promise to set everything
right.
Let your love dictate how you deal with me;
teach me from your textbook on life.
I'm your servant—help me understand what
that means,
the inner meaning of your instructions.
It's time to act, GOD;
they've made a shambles of your revelation!
Yea-Saying God, I love what you command,
I love it better than gold and gemstones;
Yea-Saying God, I honor everything you tell
me,
I despise every deceitful detour.

✠

119.129- Every word you give me is a miracle word—
136   how could I help but obey?
Break open your words, let the light shine out,
let ordinary people see the meaning.
Mouth open and panting,
I wanted your commands more than
anything.
Turn my way, look kindly on me,
as you always do to those who personally
love you.
Steady my steps with your Word of promise
so nothing malign gets the better of me.
Rescue me from the grip of bad men and
women
so I can live life your way.
Smile on me, your servant;
teach me the right way to live.
I cry rivers of tears
because nobody's living by your book!

✠

119.137- You *are* right and you *do* right, GOD;
144   your decisions are right on target.
You rightly instruct us in how to live
ever faithful to you.
My rivals nearly did me in,
they persistently ignored your
commandments.
Your promise has been tested through and
through,
and I, your servant, love it dearly.
I'm too young to be important,
but I don't forget what you tell me.
Your righteousness is eternally right,
your revelation is the only truth.
Even though troubles came down on me hard,
your commands always gave me delight.

NEW INTERNATIONAL VERSION

¹⁴⁴Your statutes are forever right;
  give me understanding that I may live.

ק QOPH

¹⁴⁵I call with all my heart; answer me, O LORD,
  and I will obey your decrees.
¹⁴⁶I call out to you; save me
  and I will keep your statutes.
¹⁴⁷I rise before dawn and cry for help;
  I have put my hope in your word.
¹⁴⁸My eyes stay open through the watches of
    the night,
  that I may meditate on your promises.
¹⁴⁹Hear my voice in accordance with your love;
  preserve my life, O LORD, according to
    your laws.
¹⁵⁰Those who devise wicked schemes are near,
  but they are far from your law.
¹⁵¹Yet you are near, O LORD,
  and all your commands are true.
¹⁵²Long ago I learned from your statutes
  that you established them to last forever.

ר RESH

¹⁵³Look upon my suffering and deliver me,
  for I have not forgotten your law.
¹⁵⁴Defend my cause and redeem me;
  preserve my life according to your
    promise.
¹⁵⁵Salvation is far from the wicked,
  for they do not seek out your decrees.
¹⁵⁶Your compassion is great, O LORD;
  preserve my life according to your laws.
¹⁵⁷Many are the foes who persecute me,
  but I have not turned from your statutes.
¹⁵⁸I look on the faithless with loathing,
  for they do not obey your word.
¹⁵⁹See how I love your precepts;
  preserve my life, O LORD, according to
    your love.
¹⁶⁰All your words are true;
  all your righteous laws are eternal.

ש SIN AND SHIN

¹⁶¹Rulers persecute me without cause,
  but my heart trembles at your word.
¹⁶²I rejoice in your promise
  like one who finds great spoil.
¹⁶³I hate and abhor falsehood
  but I love your law.
¹⁶⁴Seven times a day I praise you
  for your righteous laws.

THE MESSAGE

The way you tell me to live is always right;
  help me understand it so I can live to the
    fullest.

☩

119.145- I call out at the top of my lungs,
  152   "GOD! Answer! I'll do whatever you say."
      I called to you, "Save me
        so I can carry out all your instructions."
      I was up before sunrise,
        crying for help, hoping for a word from you.
      I stayed awake all night,
        prayerfully pondering your promise.
      In your love, listen to me;
        in your justice, GOD, keep me alive.
      As those out to get me come closer and closer,
        they go farther and farther from the truth
          you reveal;
      But you're the closest of all to me, GOD,
        and all your judgments true.
      I've known all along from the evidence of
          your words
        that you meant them to last forever.

☩

119.153- Take a good look at my trouble, and help me—
  160   I haven't forgotten your revelation.
      Take my side and get me out of this;
        give me back my life, just as you promised.
      "Salvation" is only gibberish to the wicked
        because they've never looked it up in your
          dictionary.
      Your mercies, GOD, run into the billions;
        following your guidelines, revive me.
      My antagonists are too many to count,
        but I don't swerve from the directions you
          gave.
      I took one look at the quitters and was filled
          with loathing;
        they walked away from your promises so
          casually!
      Take note of how I love what you tell me;
        out of your life of love, prolong my life.
      Your words all add up to the sum total: Truth.
        Your righteous decisions are eternal.

☩

119.161- I've been slandered unmercifully by the
  168   politicians,
        but my awe at your words keeps me stable.
      I'm ecstatic over what you say,
        like one who strikes it rich.
      I hate lies—can't stand them!—
        but I love what you have revealed.
      Seven times each day I stop and shout praises
        for the way you keep everything running
          right.

NEW INTERNATIONAL VERSION

¹⁶⁵Great peace have they who love your law,
and nothing can make them stumble.
¹⁶⁶I wait for your salvation, O LORD,
and I follow your commands.
¹⁶⁷I obey your statutes,
for I love them greatly.
¹⁶⁸I obey your precepts and your statutes,
for all my ways are known to you.

ת TAW

¹⁶⁹May my cry come before you, O LORD;
give me understanding according to your
word.
¹⁷⁰May my supplication come before you;
deliver me according to your promise.
¹⁷¹May my lips overflow with praise,
for you teach me your decrees.
¹⁷²May my tongue sing of your word,
for all your commands are righteous.
¹⁷³May your hand be ready to help me,
for I have chosen your precepts.
¹⁷⁴I long for your salvation, O LORD,
and your law is my delight.
¹⁷⁵Let me live that I may praise you,
and may your laws sustain me.
¹⁷⁶I have strayed like a lost sheep.
Seek your servant,
for I have not forgotten your commands.

PSALM 120

A song of ascents.

¹I call on the LORD in my distress,
and he answers me.
²Save me, O LORD, from lying lips
and from deceitful tongues.

³What will he do to you,
and what more besides, O deceitful
tongue?
⁴He will punish you with a warrior's sharp
arrows,
with burning coals of the broom tree.

⁵Woe to me that I dwell in Meshech,
that I live among the tents of Kedar!
⁶Too long have I lived
among those who hate peace.
⁷I am a man of peace;
but when I speak, they are for war.

THE MESSAGE

For those who love what you reveal,
everything fits—
no stumbling around in the dark for them.
I wait expectantly for your salvation;
GOD, I do what you tell me.
My soul guards and keeps all your
instructions—
oh, how much I love them!
I follow your directions, abide by your
counsel;
my life's an open book before you.

✠

119.169- Let my cry come right into your presence,
176   GOD;
provide me with the insight that comes
only from your Word.
Give my request your personal attention,
rescue me on the terms of your promise.
Let praise cascade off my lips;
after all, you've taught me the truth about
life!
And let your promises ring from my tongue;
every order you've given is right.
Put your hand out and steady me
since I've chosen to live by your counsel.
I'm homesick, GOD, for your salvation;
I love it when you show yourself!
Invigorate my soul so I can praise you well,
use your decrees to put iron in my soul.
And should I wander off like a lost sheep—
seek me!
I'll recognize the sound of your voice.

A pilgrim song

120.1-2 **120** I'm in trouble. I cry to GOD,
desperate for an answer:
"Deliver me from the liars, GOD!
They smile so sweetly but lie through their
teeth."

120.3-4 Do you know what's next, can you see what's
coming,
all you barefaced liars?
Pointed arrows and burning coals
will be your reward.

120.5-7 I'm doomed to live in Meshech,
cursed with a home in Kedar,
My whole life lived camping
among quarreling neighbors.
I'm all for peace, but the minute
I tell them so, they go to war!

NEW INTERNATIONAL VERSION

PSALM 121

A song of ascents.

[1] I lift up my eyes to the hills—
where does my help come from?
[2] My help comes from the LORD,
the Maker of heaven and earth.

[3] He will not let your foot slip—
he who watches over you will not
slumber;
[4] indeed, he who watches over Israel
will neither slumber nor sleep.

[5] The LORD watches over you—
the LORD is your shade at your right hand;
[6] the sun will not harm you by day,
nor the moon by night.

[7] The LORD will keep you from all harm—
he will watch over your life;
[8] the LORD will watch over your coming and
going
both now and forevermore.

PSALM 122

A song of ascents. Of David.

[1] I rejoiced with those who said to me,
"Let us go to the house of the LORD."
[2] Our feet are standing
in your gates, O Jerusalem.

[3] Jerusalem is built like a city
that is closely compacted together.
[4] That is where the tribes go up,
the tribes of the LORD,
to praise the name of the LORD
according to the statute given to Israel.
[5] There the thrones for judgment stand,
the thrones of the house of David.

[6] Pray for the peace of Jerusalem:
"May those who love you be secure.
[7] May there be peace within your walls
and security within your citadels."
[8] For the sake of my brothers and friends,
I will say, "Peace be within you."
[9] For the sake of the house of the LORD our
God,
I will seek your prosperity.

PSALM 123

A song of ascents.

[1] I lift up my eyes to you,
to you whose throne is in heaven.

THE MESSAGE

A pilgrim song

121 121.1-2 I look up to the mountains;
does my strength come from
mountains?
No, my strength comes from GOD,
who made heaven, and earth, and
mountains.

121.3-4 He won't let you stumble,
your Guardian God won't fall asleep.
Not on your life! Israel's
Guardian will never doze or sleep.

121.5-6 GOD's your Guardian,
right at your side to protect you—
Shielding you from sunstroke,
sheltering you from moonstroke.

121.7-8 GOD guards you from every evil,
he guards your very life.
He guards you when you leave and when you
return,
he guards you now, he guards you always.

A pilgrim song of David

122 122.1-2 When they said, "Let's go to the
house of GOD,"
my heart leaped for joy.
And now we're here, O Jerusalem,
inside Jerusalem's walls!

122.3-5 Jerusalem, well-built city,
built as a place for worship!
The city to which the tribes ascend,
all GOD's tribes go up to worship,
To give thanks to the name of GOD—
this is what it means to be Israel.
Thrones for righteous judgment
are set there, famous David-thrones.

122.6-9 Pray for Jerusalem's peace!
Prosperity to all you Jerusalem-lovers!
Friendly insiders, get along!
Hostile outsiders, keep your distance!
For the sake of my family and friends,
I say it again: live in peace!
For the sake of the house of our God, GOD,
I'll do my very best for you.

A pilgrim song

123 123.1-4 I look to you, heaven-dwelling
God,
look up to you for help.

NEW INTERNATIONAL VERSION

²As the eyes of slaves look to the hand of
their master,
as the eyes of a maid look to the hand of
her mistress,
so our eyes look to the LORD our God,
till he shows us his mercy.

³Have mercy on us, O LORD, have mercy on
us,
for we have endured much contempt.
⁴We have endured much ridicule from the
proud,
much contempt from the arrogant.

PSALM 124

A song of ascents. Of David.

¹If the LORD had not been on our side—
let Israel say—
²if the LORD had not been on our side
when men attacked us,
³when their anger flared against us,
they would have swallowed us alive;
⁴the flood would have engulfed us,
the torrent would have swept over us,
⁵the raging waters
would have swept us away.

⁶Praise be to the LORD,
who has not let us be torn by their teeth.
⁷We have escaped like a bird
out of the fowler's snare;
the snare has been broken,
and we have escaped.
⁸Our help is in the name of the LORD,
the Maker of heaven and earth.

PSALM 125

A song of ascents.

¹Those who trust in the LORD are like Mount
Zion,
which cannot be shaken but endures
forever.
²As the mountains surround Jerusalem,
so the LORD surrounds his people
both now and forevermore.

³The scepter of the wicked will not remain
over the land allotted to the righteous,
for then the righteous might use
their hands to do evil.

⁴Do good, O LORD, to those who are good,
to those who are upright in heart.

THE MESSAGE

Like servants, alert to their master's
commands,
like a maiden attending her lady,
We're watching and waiting, holding our
breath,
awaiting your word of mercy.
Mercy, GOD, mercy!
We've been kicked around long enough,
Kicked in the teeth by complacent rich men,
kicked when we're down by arrogant
brutes.

A pilgrim song of David

124.1-5 **124** If GOD hadn't been for us
—all together now, Israel, sing
out!—
If GOD hadn't been for us
when everyone went against us,
We would have been swallowed alive
by their violent anger,
Swept away by the flood of rage,
drowned in the torrent;
We would have lost our lives
in the wild, raging water.

124.6 Oh, blessed be GOD!
He didn't go off and leave us.
He didn't abandon us defenseless,
helpless as a rabbit in a pack of snarling
dogs.

124.7 We've flown free from their fangs,
free of their traps, free as a bird.
Their grip is broken;
we're free as a bird in flight.

124.8 GOD's strong name is our help,
the same GOD who made heaven and earth.

A pilgrim song

125.1-5 **125** Those who trust in GOD
are like Zion Mountain:
Nothing can move it, a rock-solid mountain
you can always depend on.
Mountains encircle Jerusalem,
and GOD encircles his people—
always has and always will.
The fist of the wicked
will never violate
What is due the righteous,
provoking wrongful violence.
Be good to your good people, GOD,
to those whose hearts are right!

NEW INTERNATIONAL VERSION

⁵But those who turn to crooked ways
    the LORD will banish with the evildoers.

Peace be upon Israel.

PSALM 126

A song of ascents.

¹When the LORD brought back the captives
    to*ᵃ* Zion,
  we were like men who dreamed.*ᵇ*
²Our mouths were filled with laughter,
    our tongues with songs of joy.
Then it was said among the nations,
  "The LORD has done great things for
    them."
³The LORD has done great things for us,
    and we are filled with joy.

⁴Restore our fortunes,*ᶜ* O LORD,
    like streams in the Negev.
⁵Those who sow in tears
    will reap with songs of joy.
⁶He who goes out weeping,
    carrying seed to sow,
will return with songs of joy,
    carrying sheaves with him.

PSALM 127

A song of ascents. Of Solomon.

¹Unless the LORD builds the house,
    its builders labor in vain.
Unless the LORD watches over the city,
    the watchmen stand guard in vain.
²In vain you rise early
    and stay up late,
toiling for food to eat—
  for he grants sleep to*ᵈ* those he loves.

³Sons are a heritage from the LORD,
    children a reward from him.
⁴Like arrows in the hands of a warrior
    are sons born in one's youth.
⁵Blessed is the man
    whose quiver is full of them.
They will not be put to shame
  when they contend with their enemies in
    the gate.

PSALM 128

A song of ascents.

¹Blessed are all who fear the LORD,
    who walk in his ways.

ᵃ 1 Or LORD restored the fortunes of   *ᵇ 1 Or men restored to
health*   *ᶜ 4 Or Bring back our captives*   *ᵈ 2 Or eat— / for
while they sleep he provides for*

THE MESSAGE

GOD will round up the backsliders,
    corral them with the incorrigibles.
Peace over Israel!

A pilgrim song

126 126.1-3 It seemed like a dream, too good to
    be true,
  when GOD returned Zion's exiles.
We laughed, we sang,
  we couldn't believe our good fortune.
We were the talk of the nations—
  "GOD was wonderful to them!"
GOD *was* wonderful to us;
  we are one happy people.

126.4-6 And now, GOD, do it again—
  bring rains to our drought-stricken lives
So those who planted their crops in despair
  will shout hurrahs at the harvest,
So those who went off with heavy hearts
  will come home laughing, with armloads of
    blessing.

A pilgrim song of Solomon

127 127.1-2 If GOD doesn't build the house,
    the builders only build shacks.
If GOD doesn't guard the city,
  the night watchman might as well nap.
It's useless to rise early and go to bed late,
  and work your worried fingers to the bone.
Don't you know he enjoys
  giving rest to those he loves?

127.3-5 Don't you see that children are GOD's best gift?
  the fruit of the womb his generous legacy?
Like a warrior's fistful of arrows
  are the children of a vigorous youth.
Oh, how blessed are you parents,
  with your quivers full of children!
Your enemies don't stand a chance against
    you;
  you'll sweep them right off your doorstep.

A pilgrim song

128 128.1-2 All you who fear GOD, how blessed
    you are!
  how happily you walk on his smooth
    straight road!

NEW INTERNATIONAL VERSION

² You will eat the fruit of your labor;
blessings and prosperity will be yours.
³ Your wife will be like a fruitful vine
within your house;
your sons will be like olive shoots
around your table.
⁴ Thus is the man blessed
who fears the LORD.

⁵ May the LORD bless you from Zion
all the days of your life;
may you see the prosperity of Jerusalem,
⁶ and may you live to see your children's
children.

Peace be upon Israel.

PSALM 129

A song of ascents.

¹ They have greatly oppressed me from my
youth—
let Israel say—
² they have greatly oppressed me from my
youth,
but they have not gained the victory
over me.
³ Plowmen have plowed my back
and made their furrows long.
⁴ But the LORD is righteous;
he has cut me free from the cords of the
wicked.

⁵ May all who hate Zion
be turned back in shame.
⁶ May they be like grass on the roof,
which withers before it can grow;
⁷ with it the reaper cannot fill his hands,
nor the one who gathers fill his arms.
⁸ May those who pass by not say,
"The blessing of the LORD be upon you;
we bless you in the name of the LORD."

PSALM 130

A song of ascents.

¹ Out of the depths I cry to you, O LORD;
² O Lord, hear my voice.
Let your ears be attentive
to my cry for mercy.

³ If you, O LORD, kept a record of sins,
O Lord, who could stand?
⁴ But with you there is forgiveness;
therefore you are feared.

⁵ I wait for the LORD, my soul waits,
and in his word I put my hope.

THE MESSAGE

You worked hard and deserve all you've got
coming.
Enjoy the blessing! Revel in the goodness!

128.3-4 Your wife will bear children as a vine bears
grapes,
your household lush as a vineyard,
The children around your table
as fresh and promising as young olive
shoots.
Stand in awe of God's Yes.
Oh, how he blesses the one who fears GOD!

128.5-6 Enjoy the good life in Jerusalem
every day of your life.
And enjoy your grandchildren.
Peace to Israel!

A pilgrim song

129.1-4 **129** "They've kicked me around ever
since I was young"
—this is how Israel tells it—
"They've kicked me around ever since I was
young,
but they never could keep me down.
Their plowmen plowed long furrows
up and down my back;
Then GOD ripped the harnesses
of the evil plowmen to shreds."

129.5-8 Oh, let all those who hate Zion
grovel in humiliation;
Let them be like grass in shallow ground
that withers before the harvest,
Before the farmhands can gather it in,
the harvesters get in the crop,
Before the neighbors have a chance to call out,
"Congratulations on your wonderful crop!
We bless you in GOD's name!"

A pilgrim song

130.1-2 **130** Help, GOD—the bottom has fallen
out of my life!
Master, hear my cry for help!
Listen hard! Open your ears!
Listen to my cries for mercy.

130.3-4 If you, GOD, kept records on wrongdoings,
who would stand a chance?
As it turns out, forgiveness is your habit,
and that's why you're worshiped.

130.5-6 I pray to GOD—my life a prayer—
and wait for what he'll say and do.

NEW INTERNATIONAL VERSION

6 My soul waits for the Lord
    more than watchmen wait for the
       morning,
    more than watchmen wait for the
       morning.

7 O Israel, put your hope in the LORD,
    for with the LORD is unfailing love
    and with him is full redemption.
8 He himself will redeem Israel
    from all their sins.

PSALM 131

A song of ascents. Of David.

1 My heart is not proud, O LORD,
    my eyes are not haughty;
I do not concern myself with great matters
    or things too wonderful for me.
2 But I have stilled and quieted my soul;
    like a weaned child with its mother,
    like a weaned child is my soul within me.

3 O Israel, put your hope in the LORD
    both now and forevermore.

PSALM 132

A song of ascents.

1 O LORD, remember David
    and all the hardships he endured.

2 He swore an oath to the LORD
    and made a vow to the Mighty One of
       Jacob:
3 "I will not enter my house
    or go to my bed—
4 I will allow no sleep to my eyes,
    no slumber to my eyelids,
5 till I find a place for the LORD,
    a dwelling for the Mighty One of Jacob."

6 We heard it in Ephrathah,
    we came upon it in the fields of Jaar*a; b*
7 "Let us go to his dwelling place;
    let us worship at his footstool—
8 arise, O LORD, and come to your resting
       place,
    you and the ark of your might.
9 May your priests be clothed with
       righteousness;
    may your saints sing for joy."

THE MESSAGE

My life's on the line before God, my Lord,
    waiting and watching till morning,
    waiting and watching till morning.

130.7-8 O Israel, wait and watch for GOD—
    with GOD's arrival comes love,
    with GOD's arrival comes generous
       redemption.
No doubt about it—he'll redeem Israel,
    buy back Israel from captivity to sin.

A pilgrim song

131.1 **131** GOD, I'm not trying to rule the
    roost,
    I don't want to be king of the mountain.
I haven't meddled where I have no business
    or fantasized grandiose plans.

131.2 I've kept my feet on the ground,
    I've cultivated a quiet heart.
Like a baby content in its mother's arms,
    my soul is a baby content.

131.3 Wait, Israel, for GOD. Wait with hope.
    Hope now; hope always!

A pilgrim song

132.1-5 **132** O GOD, remember David,
    remember all his troubles!
And remember how he promised GOD,
    made a vow to the Strong God of Jacob,
"I'm not going home,
    and I'm not going to bed,
I'm not going to sleep,
    not even take time to rest,
Until I find a home for GOD,
    a house for the Strong God of Jacob."

132.6-7 Remember how we got the news in
       Ephrathah,
    learned all about it at Jaar Meadows?
We shouted, "Let's go to the shrine
       dedication!
    Let's worship at God's own footstool!"

132.8-10 Up, GOD, enjoy your new place of quiet
       repose,
    you and your mighty covenant ark;
Get your priests all dressed up in justice;
    prompt your worshipers to sing this prayer:

---

a 6 That is, Kiriath Jearim   *b* 6 Or *heard of it in Ephrathah,
/ we found it in the fields of Jaar.* (And no quotes around
verses 7-9)

NEW INTERNATIONAL VERSION	THE MESSAGE

NEW INTERNATIONAL VERSION

¹⁰ For the sake of David your servant,
    do not reject your anointed one.

¹¹ The LORD swore an oath to David,
    a sure oath that he will not revoke:
"One of your own descendants
    I will place on your throne—
¹² if your sons keep my covenant
    and the statutes I teach them,
then their sons will sit
    on your throne for ever and ever."

¹³ For the LORD has chosen Zion,
    he has desired it for his dwelling:
¹⁴ "This is my resting place for ever and ever;
    here I will sit enthroned, for I have
      desired it—
¹⁵ I will bless her with abundant provisions;
    her poor will I satisfy with food.
¹⁶ I will clothe her priests with salvation,
    and her saints will ever sing for joy.

¹⁷ "Here I will make a horn ^a grow for David
    and set up a lamp for my anointed one.
¹⁸ I will clothe his enemies with shame,
    but the crown on his head will be
      resplendent."

PSALM 133

A song of ascents. Of David.

¹ How good and pleasant it is
    when brothers live together in unity!
² It is like precious oil poured on the head,
    running down on the beard,
running down on Aaron's beard,
    down upon the collar of his robes.
³ It is as if the dew of Hermon
    were falling on Mount Zion.
For there the LORD bestows his blessing,
    even life forevermore.

PSALM 134

A song of ascents.

¹ Praise the LORD, all you servants of the LORD
    who minister by night in the house of the
      LORD.
² Lift up your hands in the sanctuary
    and praise the LORD.

³ May the LORD, the Maker of heaven and
      earth,
    bless you from Zion.

THE MESSAGE

"Honor your servant David;
    don't disdain your anointed one."

132.11-18 GOD gave David his word,
    he won't back out on this promise:
"One of your sons
    I will set on your throne;
If your sons stay true to my Covenant
    and learn to live the way I teach them,
Their sons will continue the line—
    always a son to sit on your throne.
Yes—I, GOD, chose Zion,
    the place I wanted for my shrine;
This will always be my home;
    this is what I want, and I'm here for good.
I'll shower blessings on the pilgrims who
      come here,
    and give supper to those who arrive
      hungry;
I'll dress my priests in salvation clothes;
    the holy people will sing their hearts out!
Oh, I'll make the place radiant for David!
    I'll fill it with light for my anointed!
I'll dress his enemies in dirty rags,
    but I'll make his crown sparkle with
      splendor."

A pilgrim song of David

133.1-3 **133** How wonderful, how beautiful,
    when brothers and sisters get
      along!
It's like costly anointing oil
    flowing down head and beard,
Flowing down Aaron's beard,
    flowing down the collar of his priestly
      robes.
It's like the dew on Mount Hermon
    flowing down the slopes of Zion.
Yes, that's where GOD commands the blessing,
    ordains eternal life.

A pilgrim song

134.1-3 **134** Come, bless GOD,
    all you servants of GOD!
You priests of GOD, posted to the nightwatch
    in GOD's shrine,
Lift your praising hands to the Holy Place,
    and bless GOD.
In turn, may GOD of Zion bless you—
    GOD who made heaven and earth!

---

^a 17 *Horn* here symbolizes strong one, that is, king.

NEW INTERNATIONAL VERSION

PSALM 135

[1] Praise the LORD. [a]

Praise the name of the LORD;
  praise him, you servants of the LORD,
[2] you who minister in the house of the LORD,
  in the courts of the house of our God.

[3] Praise the LORD, for the LORD is good;
  sing praise to his name, for that is pleasant.
[4] For the LORD has chosen Jacob to be his own,
  Israel to be his treasured possession.

[5] I know that the LORD is great,
  that our Lord is greater than all gods.
[6] The LORD does whatever pleases him,
  in the heavens and on the earth,
  in the seas and all their depths.
[7] He makes clouds rise from the ends of the
    earth;
  he sends lightning with the rain
  and brings out the wind from his storehouses.

[8] He struck down the firstborn of Egypt,
  the firstborn of men and animals.
[9] He sent his signs and wonders into your
    midst, O Egypt,
  against Pharaoh and all his servants.
[10] He struck down many nations
  and killed mighty kings—
[11] Sihon king of the Amorites,
  Og king of Bashan
  and all the kings of Canaan—
[12] and he gave their land as an inheritance,
  an inheritance to his people Israel.

[13] Your name, O LORD, endures forever,
  your renown, O LORD, through all
    generations.
[14] For the LORD will vindicate his people
  and have compassion on his servants.

[15] The idols of the nations are silver and gold,
  made by the hands of men.
[16] They have mouths, but cannot speak,
  eyes, but they cannot see;
[17] they have ears, but cannot hear,
  nor is there breath in their mouths.
[18] Those who make them will be like them,
  and so will all who trust in them.

[19] O house of Israel, praise the LORD;
  O house of Aaron, praise the LORD;
[20] O house of Levi, praise the LORD;
  you who fear him, praise the LORD.
[21] Praise be to the LORD from Zion,
  to him who dwells in Jerusalem.

Praise the LORD.

[a] *1* Hebrew *Hallelu Yah*; also in verses 3 and 21

THE MESSAGE

135.1-4 **135** Hallelujah!
  Praise the name of GOD,
  praise the works of GOD.
All you priests on duty in GOD's temple,
  serving in the sacred halls of our God,
Shout "Hallelujah!" because GOD's so good,
  sing anthems to his beautiful name.
And why? Because GOD chose Jacob,
  embraced Israel as a prize possession.

135.5-12 I too give witness to the greatness of GOD,
  our Lord, high above all other gods.
He does just as he pleases—
  however, wherever, whenever.
He makes the weather—clouds and thunder,
  lightning and rain, wind pouring out of the
    north.
He struck down the Egyptian firstborn,
  both human and animal firstborn.
He made Egypt sit up and take notice,
  confronted Pharaoh and his servants with
    miracles.
Yes, he struck down great nations,
  he slew mighty kings—
Sihon king of the Amorites, also Og of
    Bashan—
  every last one of the Canaanite kings!
Then he turned their land over to Israel,
  a gift of good land to his people.

135.13-18 GOD, your name is eternal,
  GOD, you'll never be out-of-date.
GOD stands up for his people,
  GOD holds the hands of his people.
The gods of the godless nations are mere
    trinkets,
  made for quick sale in the markets:
Chiseled mouths that can't talk,
  painted eyes that can't see,
Carved ears that can't hear—
  dead wood! cold metal!
Those who make and trust them
  become like them.

135.19-21 Family of Israel, bless GOD!
  Family of Aaron, bless GOD!
Family of Levi, bless GOD!
  You who fear GOD, bless GOD!
Oh, blessed be GOD of Zion,
  First Citizen of Jerusalem!
Hallelujah!

NEW INTERNATIONAL VERSION

PSALM 136

¹Give thanks to the LORD, for he is good.
His love endures forever.
²Give thanks to the God of gods.
His love endures forever.
³Give thanks to the Lord of lords:
His love endures forever.

⁴to him who alone does great wonders,
His love endures forever.
⁵who by his understanding made the heavens,
His love endures forever.
⁶who spread out the earth upon the waters,
His love endures forever.
⁷who made the great lights—
His love endures forever.
⁸the sun to govern the day,
His love endures forever.
⁹the moon and stars to govern the night;
His love endures forever.

¹⁰to him who struck down the firstborn of
Egypt
His love endures forever.
¹¹and brought Israel out from among them
His love endures forever.
¹²with a mighty hand and outstretched arm;
His love endures forever.

¹³to him who divided the Red Sea*ᵃ* asunder
His love endures forever.
¹⁴and brought Israel through the midst of it,
His love endures forever.
¹⁵but swept Pharaoh and his army into the
Red Sea;
His love endures forever.

¹⁶to him who led his people through the
desert,
His love endures forever.
¹⁷who struck down great kings,
His love endures forever.
¹⁸and killed mighty kings—
His love endures forever.
¹⁹Sihon king of the Amorites
His love endures forever.
²⁰and Og king of Bashan—
His love endures forever.
²¹and gave their land as an inheritance,
His love endures forever.
²²an inheritance to his servant Israel;
His love endures forever.

²³to the One who remembered us in our low
estate
His love endures forever.

ᵃ 13 Hebrew *Yam Suph*; that is, Sea of Reeds; also in
verse 15

THE MESSAGE

136 Thank GOD! He deserves your
thanks.
His love never quits.
Thank the God of all gods,
His love never quits.
Thank the Lord of all lords.
His love never quits.

136.1-3

136.4-22 Thank the miracle-working God,
His love never quits.
The God whose skill formed the cosmos,
His love never quits.
The God who laid out earth on ocean
foundations,
His love never quits.
The God who filled the skies with light,
His love never quits.
The sun to watch over the day,
His love never quits.
Moon and stars as guardians of the night,
His love never quits.
The God who struck down the Egyptian
firstborn,
His love never quits.
And rescued Israel from Egypt's oppression,
His love never quits.
Took Israel in hand with his powerful hand,
His love never quits.
Split the Red Sea right in half,
His love never quits.
Led Israel right through the middle,
His love never quits.
Dumped Pharaoh and his army in the sea,
His love never quits.
The God who marched his people through the
desert,
His love never quits.
Smashed huge kingdoms right and left,
His love never quits.
Struck down the famous kings,
His love never quits.
Struck Sihon the Amorite king,
His love never quits.
Struck Og the Bashanite king,
His love never quits.
Then distributed their land as booty,
His love never quits.
Handed the land over to Israel.
His love never quits.

136.23-26 God remembered us when we were down,
His love never quits.

NEW INTERNATIONAL VERSION

²⁴ and freed us from our enemies,
> *His love endures forever.*
²⁵ and who gives food to every creature.
> *His love endures forever.*

²⁶ Give thanks to the God of heaven.
> *His love endures forever.*

PSALM 137

¹ By the rivers of Babylon we sat and wept
> when we remembered Zion.
² There on the poplars
> we hung our harps,
³ for there our captors asked us for songs,
> our tormentors demanded songs of joy;
> they said, "Sing us one of the songs of
> Zion!"

⁴ How can we sing the songs of the LORD
> while in a foreign land?
⁵ If I forget you, O Jerusalem,
> may my right hand forget ʟits skilʟ.
⁶ May my tongue cling to the roof of my
> mouth
> if I do not remember you,
> if I do not consider Jerusalem
> my highest joy.

⁷ Remember, O LORD, what the Edomites did
> on the day Jerusalem fell.
> "Tear it down," they cried,
> "tear it down to its foundations!"

⁸ O Daughter of Babylon, doomed to
> destruction,
> happy is he who repays you
> for what you have done to us—
⁹ he who seizes your infants
> and dashes them against the rocks.

PSALM 138

Of David.

¹ I will praise you, O LORD, with all my heart;
> before the "gods" I will sing your praise.
² I will bow down toward your holy temple
> and will praise your name
> for your love and your faithfulness,
> for you have exalted above all things
> your name and your word.
³ When I called, you answered me;
> you made me bold and stouthearted.

⁴ May all the kings of the earth praise you,
> O LORD,
> when they hear the words of your mouth.
⁵ May they sing of the ways of the LORD,
> for the glory of the LORD is great.

THE MESSAGE

Rescued us from the trampling boot,
> *His love never quits.*
Takes care of everyone in time of need.
> *His love never quits.*
Thank God, who did it all!
> *His love never quits!*

137.1-3 **137** Alongside Babylon's rivers
> we sat on the banks; we cried and
> cried,
> remembering the good old days in Zion.
Alongside the quaking aspens
> we stacked our unplayed harps;
That's where our captors demanded songs,
> sarcastic and mocking:
> "Sing us a happy Zion song!"

137.4-6 Oh, how could we ever sing GOD's song
> in this wasteland?
If I ever forget you, Jerusalem,
> let my fingers wither and fall off like leaves.
Let my tongue swell and turn black
> if I fail to remember you,
If I fail, O dear Jerusalem,
> to honor you as my greatest.

137.7-9 GOD, remember those Edomites,
> and remember the ruin of Jerusalem,
That day they yelled out,
> "Wreck it, smash it to bits!"
And you, Babylonians—ravagers!
> A reward to whoever gets back at you
> for all you've done to us;
Yes, a reward to the one who grabs your
> babies
> and smashes their heads on the rocks!

A David psalm

138.1-3 **138** Thank you! Everything in me says
> "Thank you!"
> Angels listen as I sing my thanks.
I kneel in worship facing your holy temple
> and say it again: "Thank you!"
Thank you for your love,
> thank you for your faithfulness;
Most holy is your name,
> most holy is your Word.
The moment I called out, you stepped in;
> you made my life large with strength.

138.4-6 When they hear what you have to say, GOD,
> all earth's kings will say "Thank you."
They'll sing of what you've done:
> "How great the glory of GOD!"

NEW INTERNATIONAL VERSION

⁶Though the LORD is on high, he looks upon
  the lowly,
   but the proud he knows from afar.
⁷Though I walk in the midst of trouble,
   you preserve my life;
  you stretch out your hand against the anger
   of my foes,
   with your right hand you save me.
⁸The LORD will fulfill ⌊his purpose⌋ for me;
   your love, O LORD, endures forever—
   do not abandon the works of your hands.

PSALM 139

For the director of music. Of David. A psalm.

¹O LORD, you have searched me
   and you know me.
²You know when I sit and when I rise;
   you perceive my thoughts from afar.
³You discern my going out and my lying
   down;
   you are familiar with all my ways.
⁴Before a word is on my tongue
   you know it completely, O LORD.

⁵You hem me in—behind and before;
   you have laid your hand upon me.
⁶Such knowledge is too wonderful for me,
   too lofty for me to attain.

⁷Where can I go from your Spirit?
   Where can I flee from your presence?
⁸If I go up to the heavens, you are there;
   if I make my bed in the depths,ᵃ you are
    there.
⁹If I rise on the wings of the dawn,
   if I settle on the far side of the sea,
¹⁰even there your hand will guide me,
   your right hand will hold me fast.

¹¹If I say, "Surely the darkness will hide me
   and the light become night around me,"
¹²even the darkness will not be dark to you;
   the night will shine like the day,
   for darkness is as light to you.

¹³For you created my inmost being;
   you knit me together in my mother's
    womb.
¹⁴I praise you because I am fearfully and
    wonderfully made;
   your works are wonderful,
   I know that full well.
¹⁵My frame was not hidden from you
   when I was made in the secret place.

THE MESSAGE

And here's why: GOD, high above, sees far
   below;
   no matter the distance, he knows
    everything about us.

138.7-8 When I walk into the thick of trouble,
    keep me alive in the angry turmoil.
With one hand
   strike my foes,
With your other hand
   save me.
Finish what you started in me, GOD.
   Your love is eternal—don't quit on me now.

A David psalm

139.1-6 **139** GOD, investigate my life;
       get all the facts firsthand.
I'm an open book to you;
   even from a distance, you know what I'm
    thinking.
You know when I leave and when I get back;
   I'm never out of your sight.
You know everything I'm going to say
   before I start the first sentence.
I look behind me and you're there,
   then up ahead and you're there, too—
   your reassuring presence, coming and
    going.
This is too much, too wonderful—
   I can't take it all in!

139.7-12 Is there anyplace I can go to avoid your Spirit?
    to be out of your sight?
If I climb to the sky, you're there!
   If I go underground, you're there!
If I flew on morning's wings
   to the far western horizon,
You'd find me in a minute—
   you're already there waiting!
Then I said to myself, "Oh, he even sees me in
    the dark!
   At night I'm immersed in the light!"
It's a fact: darkness isn't dark to you;
   night and day, darkness and light, they're
    all the same to you.

139.13-16 Oh yes, you shaped me first inside, then out;
    you formed me in my mother's womb.
I thank you, High God—you're breathtaking!
   Body and soul, I am marvelously made!
   I worship in adoration—what a creation!
You know me inside and out,
   you know every bone in my body;
You know exactly how I was made, bit by bit,

ᵃ 8 Hebrew *Sheol*

NEW INTERNATIONAL VERSION

When I was woven together in the depths of
the earth,
16 your eyes saw my unformed body.
All the days ordained for me
were written in your book
before one of them came to be.

17 How precious to*a* me are your thoughts,
O God!
How vast is the sum of them!
18 Were I to count them,
they would outnumber the grains of sand.
When I awake,
I am still with you.

19 If only you would slay the wicked, O God!
Away from me, you bloodthirsty men!
20 They speak of you with evil intent;
your adversaries misuse your name.
21 Do I not hate those who hate you, O LORD,
and abhor those who rise up against you?
22 I have nothing but hatred for them;
I count them my enemies.

23 Search me, O God, and know my heart;
test me and know my anxious thoughts.
24 See if there is any offensive way in me,
and lead me in the way everlasting.

PSALM 140

For the director of music. A psalm of David.

1 Rescue me, O LORD, from evil men;
protect me from men of violence,
2 who devise evil plans in their hearts
and stir up war every day.
3 They make their tongues as sharp as a
serpent's;
the poison of vipers is on their lips. *Selah*

4 Keep me, O LORD, from the hands of the
wicked;
protect me from men of violence
who plan to trip my feet.
5 Proud men have hidden a snare for me;
they have spread out the cords of their net
and have set traps for me along my path.
Selah

6 O LORD, I say to you, "You are my God."
Hear, O LORD, my cry for mercy.

THE MESSAGE

how I was sculpted from nothing into
something.
Like an open book, you watched me grow
from conception to birth;
all the stages of my life were spread out
before you,
The days of my life all prepared
before I'd even lived one day.

139.17-22 Your thoughts—how rare, how beautiful!
God, I'll never comprehend them!
I couldn't even begin to count them—
any more than I could count the sand of
the sea.
Oh, let me rise in the morning and live always
with you!
And please, God, do away with wickedness
for good!
And you murderers—out of here!—
all the men and women who belittle you,
God,
infatuated with cheap god-imitations.
See how I hate those who hate you, GOD,
see how I loathe all this godless arrogance;
I hate it with pure, unadulterated hatred.
Your enemies are my enemies!

139.23-24 Investigate my life, O God,
find out everything about me;
Cross-examine and test me,
get a clear picture of what I'm about;
See for yourself whether I've done anything
wrong—
then guide me on the road to eternal life.

A David psalm

140.1-5 **140** GOD, get me out of here, away from
this evil;
protect me from these vicious people.
All they do is think up new ways to be bad;
they spend their days plotting war games.
They practice the sharp rhetoric of hate and
hurt,
speak venomous words that maim and kill.
GOD, keep me out of the clutch of these
wicked ones,
protect me from these vicious people;
Stuffed with self-importance, they plot ways
to trip me up,
determined to bring me down.
These crooks invent traps to catch me
and do their best to incriminate me.

140.6-8 I prayed, "GOD, you're my God!
Listen, GOD! Mercy!

---

a 17 Or concerning

NEW INTERNATIONAL VERSION

⁷ O Sovereign Lᴏʀᴅ, my strong deliverer,
  who shields my head in the day of
      battle—
⁸ do not grant the wicked their desires,
      O Lᴏʀᴅ;
  do not let their plans succeed,
  or they will become proud.   *Selah*

⁹ Let the heads of those who surround me
  be covered with the trouble their lips have
      caused.
¹⁰ Let burning coals fall upon them;
  may they be thrown into the fire,
  into miry pits, never to rise.
¹¹ Let slanderers not be established in the land;
  may disaster hunt down men of violence.

¹² I know that the Lᴏʀᴅ secures justice for the
      poor
  and upholds the cause of the needy.
¹³ Surely the righteous will praise your name
  and the upright will live before you.

PSALM 141

A psalm of David.

¹ O Lᴏʀᴅ, I call to you; come quickly to me.
  Hear my voice when I call to you.
² May my prayer be set before you like incense;
  may the lifting up of my hands be like the
      evening sacrifice.

³ Set a guard over my mouth, O Lᴏʀᴅ;
  keep watch over the door of my lips.
⁴ Let not my heart be drawn to what is evil,
  to take part in wicked deeds
with men who are evildoers;
  let me not eat of their delicacies.

⁵ Let a righteous man*ᵃ* strike me—it is a
      kindness;
  let him rebuke me—it is oil on my head.
  My head will not refuse it.

Yet my prayer is ever against the deeds of
      evildoers;
⁶ their rulers will be thrown down from the
      cliffs,
  and the wicked will learn that my words
      were well spoken.
⁷ ᵼThey will say,ᶜ "As one plows and breaks up
      the earth,
  so our bones have been scattered at the
      mouth of the grave.ᵇ"

⁸ But my eyes are fixed on you, O Sovereign
      Lᴏʀᴅ;
  in you I take refuge—do not give me over
      to death.

THE MESSAGE

Gᴏᴅ, my Lord, Strong Savior,
  protect me when the fighting breaks out!
Don't let the wicked have their way, Gᴏᴅ,
  don't give them an inch!"

140.9-11 These troublemakers all around me—
  let them drown in their own verbal poison.
Let God pile hellfire on them,
  let him bury them alive in crevasses!
These loudmouths—
  don't let them be taken seriously;
These savages—
  let the Devil hunt them down!

140.12-13 I know that you, Gᴏᴅ, are on the side of
      victims,
  that you care for the rights of the poor.
And I know that the righteous personally
      thank you,
  that good people are secure in your
      presence.

A David psalm

141.1-2 **141** Gᴏᴅ, come close. Come quickly!
          Open your ears—it's my voice
          you're hearing!
Treat my prayer as sweet incense rising;
  my raised hands are my evening prayers.

141.3-7 Post a guard at my mouth, Gᴏᴅ,
  set a watch at the door of my lips.
Don't let me so much as dream of evil
  or thoughtlessly fall into bad company.
And these people who only do wrong—
  don't let them lure me with their sweet
      talk!
May the Just One set me straight,
  may the Kind One correct me,
Don't let sin anoint my head.
  I'm praying hard against their evil ways!
Oh, let their leaders be pushed off a high rock
      cliff;
  make them face the music.
Like a rock pulverized by a maul,
  let their bones be scattered at the gates of
      hell.

141.8-10 But Gᴏᴅ, dear Lord,
  I only have eyes for you.
Since I've run for dear life to you,
  take good care of me.

ᵃ 5 Or *Let the Righteous One*   ᵇ 7 Hebrew *Sheol*

NEW INTERNATIONAL VERSION

⁹Keep me from the snares they have laid
    for me,
  from the traps set by evildoers.
¹⁰Let the wicked fall into their own nets,
  while I pass by in safety.

PSALM 142

A maskil ᵃ of David. When he was in the cave.
A prayer.

¹I cry aloud to the LORD;
  I lift up my voice to the LORD for mercy.
²I pour out my complaint before him;
  before him I tell my trouble.

³When my spirit grows faint within me,
  it is you who know my way.
In the path where I walk
  men have hidden a snare for me.
⁴Look to my right and see;
  no one is concerned for me.
I have no refuge;
  no one cares for my life.

⁵I cry to you, O LORD;
  I say, "You are my refuge,
  my portion in the land of the living."
⁶Listen to my cry,
  for I am in desperate need;
rescue me from those who pursue me,
  for they are too strong for me.
⁷Set me free from my prison,
  that I may praise your name.

Then the righteous will gather about me
  because of your goodness to me.

PSALM 143

A psalm of David.

¹O LORD, hear my prayer,
  listen to my cry for mercy;
in your faithfulness and righteousness
  come to my relief.
²Do not bring your servant into judgment,
  for no one living is righteous before you.

³The enemy pursues me,
  he crushes me to the ground;
he makes me dwell in darkness
  like those long dead.
⁴So my spirit grows faint within me;
  my heart within me is dismayed.

⁵I remember the days of long ago;
  I meditate on all your works
  and consider what your hands have done.

ᵃ Title: Probably a literary or musical term

THE MESSAGE

Protect me from their evil scheming,
  from all their demonic subterfuge.
Let the wicked fall flat on their faces,
  while I walk off without a scratch.

A David prayer—when he was in the cave.

142 ¹⁴²·¹⁻² I cry out loudly to GOD,
  loudly I plead with GOD for mercy.
I spill out all my complaints before him,
  and spell out my troubles in detail:

¹⁴²·³⁻⁷ "As I sink in despair, my spirit ebbing away,
  you know how I'm feeling,
Know the danger I'm in,
  the traps hidden in my path.
Look right, look left—
  there's not a soul who cares what happens!
I'm up against it, with no exit—
  bereft, left alone.
I cry out, GOD, call out:
  'You're my last chance, my only hope for
    life!'
Oh listen, please listen;
  I've never been this low.
Rescue me from those who are hunting me
    down;
  I'm no match for them.
Get me out of this dungeon
  so I can thank you in public.
Your people will form a circle around me
  and you'll bring me showers of blessing!"

A David psalm

143 ¹⁴³·¹⁻² Listen to this prayer of mine, GOD;
  pay attention to what I'm asking.
Answer me—you're famous for your answers!
  Do what's right for me.
But don't, please don't, haul me into court;
  not a person alive would be acquitted there.

¹⁴³·³⁻⁶ The enemy hunted me down;
  he kicked me and stomped me within an
    inch of my life.
He put me in a black hole,
  buried me like a corpse in that dungeon.
I sat there in despair, my spirit draining away,
  my heart heavy, like lead.
I remembered the old days,
  went over all you've done, pondered the
    ways you've worked,

NEW INTERNATIONAL VERSION

⁶I spread out my hands to you;
  my soul thirsts for you like a parched
      land. *Selah*

⁷Answer me quickly, O LORD;
  my spirit fails.
  Do not hide your face from me
    or I will be like those who go down to the
      pit.
⁸Let the morning bring me word of your
      unfailing love,
    for I have put my trust in you.
  Show me the way I should go,
    for to you I lift up my soul.
⁹Rescue me from my enemies, O LORD,
    for I hide myself in you.
¹⁰Teach me to do your will,
    for you are my God;
  may your good Spirit
    lead me on level ground.

¹¹For your name's sake, O LORD, preserve my
      life;
    in your righteousness, bring me out of
      trouble.
¹²In your unfailing love, silence my enemies;
    destroy all my foes,
    for I am your servant.

PSALM 144

Of David.

¹Praise be to the LORD my Rock,
  who trains my hands for war,
  my fingers for battle.
²He is my loving God and my fortress,
  my stronghold and my deliverer,
  my shield, in whom I take refuge,
  who subdues peoples*a* under me.

³O LORD, what is man that you care for him,
  the son of man that you think of him?
⁴Man is like a breath;
  his days are like a fleeting shadow.

⁵Part your heavens, O LORD, and come down;
  touch the mountains, so that they smoke.
⁶Send forth lightning and scatter ⌊the
      enemies⌋;
  shoot your arrows and rout them.
⁷Reach down your hand from on high;
  deliver me and rescue me
  from the mighty waters,
  from the hands of foreigners
⁸whose mouths are full of lies,
  whose right hands are deceitful.

THE MESSAGE

Stretched out my hands to you,
  as thirsty for you as a desert thirsty for rain.
143.7-10 Hurry with your answer, GOD!
  I'm nearly at the end of my rope.
Don't turn away; don't ignore me!
  That would be certain death.
If you wake me each morning with the sound
      of your loving voice,
  I'll go to sleep each night trusting in you.
Point out the road I must travel;
  I'm all ears, all eyes before you.
Save me from my enemies, GOD—
  you're my only hope!
Teach me how to live to please you,
  because you're my God.
Lead me by your blessed Spirit
  into cleared and level pastureland.

143.11-12 Keep up your reputation, God—give me life!
  In your justice, get me out of this trouble!
In your great love, vanquish my enemies;
  make a clean sweep of those who harass
      me.
And why? Because I'm your servant.

A David psalm

144.1-2 **144** Blessed be GOD, my mountain,
  who trains me to fight fair and well.
He's the bedrock on which I stand,
  the castle in which I live,
  my rescuing knight,
The high crag where I run for dear life,
  while he lays my enemies low.

144.3-4 I wonder why you care, GOD—
  why do you bother with us at all?
All we are is a puff of air;
  we're like shadows in a campfire.

144.5-8 Step down out of heaven, GOD;
  ignite volcanoes in the hearts of the
      mountains.
Hurl your lightnings in every direction;
  shoot your arrows this way and that.
Reach all the way from sky to sea:
  pull me out of the ocean of hate,
  out of the grip of those barbarians
Who lie through their teeth,
  who shake your hand
  then knife you in the back.

a 2 Many manuscripts of the Masoretic Text, Dead Sea
Scrolls, Aquila, Jerome and Syriac; most manuscripts of the
Masoretic Text *subdues my people*

NEW INTERNATIONAL VERSION

⁹I will sing a new song to you, O God;
  on the ten-stringed lyre I will make music
    to you,
¹⁰to the One who gives victory to kings,
  who delivers his servant David from the
    deadly sword.

¹¹Deliver me and rescue me
  from the hands of foreigners
whose mouths are full of lies,
  whose right hands are deceitful.

¹²Then our sons in their youth
  will be like well-nurtured plants,
and our daughters will be like pillars
  carved to adorn a palace.
¹³Our barns will be filled
  with every kind of provision.
Our sheep will increase by thousands,
  by tens of thousands in our fields;
¹⁴ our oxen will draw heavy loads. ᵃ
There will be no breaching of walls,
  no going into captivity,
  no cry of distress in our streets.

¹⁵Blessed are the people of whom this is true;
  blessed are the people whose God is the
    LORD.

PSALM 145 ᵇ

A psalm of praise. Of David.

¹I will exalt you, my God the King;
  I will praise your name for ever and ever.
²Every day I will praise you
  and extol your name for ever and ever.

³Great is the LORD and most worthy of praise;
  his greatness no one can fathom.
⁴One generation will commend your works to
    another;
  they will tell of your mighty acts.
⁵They will speak of the glorious splendor of
    your majesty,
  and I will meditate on your wonderful
    works. ᶜ
⁶They will tell of the power of your awesome
    works,
  and I will proclaim your great deeds.
⁷They will celebrate your abundant goodness
  and joyfully sing of your righteousness.

⁸The LORD is gracious and compassionate,
  slow to anger and rich in love.

ᵃ 14 Or *our chieftains will be firmly established*   ᵇ This
psalm is an acrostic poem, the verses of which (including
verse 13b) begin with the successive letters of the Hebrew
alphabet.   ᶜ 5 Dead Sea Scrolls and Syriac (see also
Septuagint); Masoretic Text *On the glorious splendor of your
majesty / and on your wonderful works I will meditate*

THE MESSAGE

144.9-10 O God, let me sing a new song to you,
  let me play it on a twelve-string guitar—
A song to the God who saved the king,
  the God who rescued David, his servant.

144.11 Rescue me from the enemy sword,
  release me from the grip of those
    barbarians
Who lie through their teeth,
  who shake your hand
    then knife you in the back.

144.12-14 Make our sons in their prime
  like sturdy oak trees,
Our daughters as shapely and bright
  as fields of wildflowers.
Fill our barns with great harvest,
  fill our fields with huge flocks;
Protect us from invasion and exile—
  eliminate the crime in our streets.

144.15 How blessed the people who have all this!
How blessed the people who have GOD for
  God!

David's praise

145.1 **145** I lift you high in praise, my God,
  O my King!
  and I'll bless your name into eternity.

145.2 I'll bless you every day,
  and keep it up from now to eternity.

145.3 GOD is magnificent; he can never be praised
    enough.
  There are no boundaries to his greatness.

145.4 Generation after generation stands in awe of
    your work;
  each one tells stories of your mighty acts.

145.5 Your beauty and splendor have everyone
    talking;
  I compose songs on your wonders.

145.6 Your marvelous doings are headline news;
  I could write a book full of the details of
    your greatness.

145.7 The fame of your goodness spreads across the
    country;
  your righteousness is on everyone's lips.

145.8 GOD is all mercy and grace—
  not quick to anger, is rich in love.

NEW INTERNATIONAL VERSION	THE MESSAGE

NEW INTERNATIONAL VERSION

⁹ The LORD is good to all;
    he has compassion on all he has made.
¹⁰ All you have made will praise you, O LORD;
    your saints will extol you.
¹¹ They will tell of the glory of your kingdom
    and speak of your might,
¹² so that all men may know of your mighty
       acts
    and the glorious splendor of your
       kingdom.
¹³ Your kingdom is an everlasting kingdom,
    and your dominion endures through all
       generations.

The LORD is faithful to all his promises
    and loving toward all he has made. *ᵃ*
¹⁴ The LORD upholds all those who fall
    and lifts up all who are bowed down.
¹⁵ The eyes of all look to you,
    and you give them their food at the
       proper time.
¹⁶ You open your hand
    and satisfy the desires of every living
       thing.

¹⁷ The LORD is righteous in all his ways
    and loving toward all he has made.
¹⁸ The LORD is near to all who call on him,
    to all who call on him in truth.
¹⁹ He fulfills the desires of those who fear him;
    he hears their cry and saves them.
²⁰ The LORD watches over all who love him,
    but all the wicked he will destroy.

²¹ My mouth will speak in praise of the LORD.
    Let every creature praise his holy name
      for ever and ever.

PSALM 146

¹ Praise the LORD. *ᵇ*

Praise the LORD, O my soul.
²   I will praise the LORD all my life;
    I will sing praise to my God as long as I
      live.

³ Do not put your trust in princes,
    in mortal men, who cannot save.
⁴ When their spirit departs, they return to the
      ground;
    on that very day their plans come to
      nothing.

⁵ Blessed is he whose help is the God of Jacob,
    whose hope is in the LORD his God,

THE MESSAGE

145.9 GOD is good to one and all;
    everything he does is suffused with grace.

145.10-11 Creation and creatures applaud you, GOD;
    your holy people bless you.

They talk about the glories of your rule,
    they exclaim over your splendor,

145.12 Letting the world know of your power for
      good,
    the lavish splendor of your kingdom.

145.13 Your kingdom is a kingdom eternal;
    you never get voted out of office.

GOD always does what he says,
    and is gracious in everything he does.

145.14 GOD gives a hand to those down on their luck,
    gives a fresh start to those ready to quit.

145.15 All eyes are on you, expectant;
    you give them their meals on time.

145.16 Generous to a fault,
    you lavish your favor on all creatures.

145.17 Everything GOD does is right—
    the trademark on all his works is love.

145.18 GOD's there, listening for all who pray,
    for all who pray and mean it.

145.19 He does what's best for those who fear him—
    hears them call out, and saves them.

145.20 GOD sticks by all who love him,
    but it's all over for those who don't.

145.21 My mouth is filled with GOD's praise.
    Let everything living bless him,
    bless his holy name from now to eternity!

146.1-2 **146** Hallelujah!
    O my soul, praise GOD!
All my life long I'll praise GOD,
    singing songs to my God as long as I live.

146.3-9 Don't put your life in the hands of experts
    who know nothing of life, of *salvation* life.
Mere humans don't have what it takes;
    when they die, their projects die with them.
Instead, get help from the God of Jacob,
    put your hope in GOD and know real
      blessing!

ᵃ 13 One manuscript of the Masoretic Text, Dead Sea
Scrolls and Syriac (see also Septuagint); most manuscripts
of the Masoretic Text do not have the last two lines of
verse 13. *ᵇ 1* Hebrew *Hallelu Yah*; also in verse 10

NEW INTERNATIONAL VERSION

⁶the Maker of heaven and earth,
    the sea, and everything in them—
    the LORD, who remains faithful forever.
⁷He upholds the cause of the oppressed
    and gives food to the hungry.
The LORD sets prisoners free,
⁸   the LORD gives sight to the blind,
the LORD lifts up those who are bowed down,
    the LORD loves the righteous.
⁹The LORD watches over the alien
    and sustains the fatherless and the widow,
    but he frustrates the ways of the wicked.

¹⁰The LORD reigns forever,
    your God, O Zion, for all generations.

Praise the LORD.

PSALM 147

¹Praise the LORD. *ª*

How good it is to sing praises to our God,
    how pleasant and fitting to praise him!

²The LORD builds up Jerusalem;
    he gathers the exiles of Israel.
³He heals the brokenhearted
    and binds up their wounds.
⁴He determines the number of the stars
    and calls them each by name.
⁵Great is our Lord and mighty in power;
    his understanding has no limit.
⁶The LORD sustains the humble
    but casts the wicked to the ground.

⁷Sing to the LORD with thanksgiving;
    make music to our God on the harp.
⁸He covers the sky with clouds;
    he supplies the earth with rain
    and makes grass grow on the hills.
⁹He provides food for the cattle
    and for the young ravens when they call.

¹⁰His pleasure is not in the strength of the
        horse,
    nor his delight in the legs of a man;
¹¹the LORD delights in those who fear him,
    who put their hope in his unfailing love.

¹²Extol the LORD, O Jerusalem;
    praise your God, O Zion,
¹³for he strengthens the bars of your gates
    and blesses your people within you.
¹⁴He grants peace to your borders
    and satisfies you with the finest of wheat.

¹⁵He sends his command to the earth;
    his word runs swiftly.

THE MESSAGE

GOD made sky and soil,
    sea and all the fish in it.
He always does what he says—
    he defends the wronged,
    he feeds the hungry.
GOD frees prisoners—
    he gives sight to the blind,
    he lifts up the fallen.
GOD loves good people, protects strangers,
    takes the side of orphans and widows,
    but makes short work of the wicked.

146.10 GOD's in charge—*always*.
    Zion's God is God for good!
    Hallelujah!

147.1 **147** Hallelujah!
    It's a good thing to sing praise to
        our God;
    praise is beautiful, praise is fitting.

147.2-6 GOD's the one who rebuilds Jerusalem,
    who regathers Israel's scattered exiles.
He heals the heartbroken
    and bandages their wounds.
He counts the stars
    and assigns each a name.
Our Lord is great, with limitless strength;
    we'll never comprehend what he knows
        and does.
GOD puts the fallen on their feet again
    and pushes the wicked into the ditch.

147.7-11 Sing to GOD a thanksgiving hymn,
    play music on your instruments to God,
Who fills the sky with clouds,
    preparing rain for the earth,
Then turning the mountains green with grass,
    feeding both cattle and crows.
He's not impressed with horsepower;
    the size of our muscles means little to him.
Those who fear GOD get GOD's attention;
    they can depend on his strength.

147.12-18 Jerusalem, worship GOD!
    Zion, praise your God!
He made your city secure,
    he blessed your children among you.
He keeps the peace at your borders,
    he puts the best bread on your tables.
He launches his promises earthward—
    how swift and sure they come!

ª 1 Hebrew *Hallelu Yah*; also in verse 20

NEW INTERNATIONAL VERSION

¹⁶He spreads the snow like wool
  and scatters the frost like ashes.
¹⁷He hurls down his hail like pebbles.
  Who can withstand his icy blast?
¹⁸He sends his word and melts them;
  he stirs up his breezes, and the waters
    flow.

¹⁹He has revealed his word to Jacob,
  his laws and decrees to Israel.
²⁰He has done this for no other nation;
  they do not know his laws.

  Praise the LORD.

PSALM 148

¹Praise the LORD. *ᵃ*

Praise the LORD from the heavens,
  praise him in the heights above.
²Praise him, all his angels,
  praise him, all his heavenly hosts.
³Praise him, sun and moon,
  praise him, all you shining stars.
⁴Praise him, you highest heavens
  and you waters above the skies.
⁵Let them praise the name of the LORD,
  for he commanded and they were created.
⁶He set them in place for ever and ever;
  he gave a decree that will never pass away.

⁷Praise the LORD from the earth,
  you great sea creatures and all ocean
    depths,
⁸lightning and hail, snow and clouds,
  stormy winds that do his bidding,
⁹you mountains and all hills,
  fruit trees and all cedars,
¹⁰wild animals and all cattle,
  small creatures and flying birds,
¹¹kings of the earth and all nations,
  you princes and all rulers on earth,
¹²young men and maidens,
  old men and children.

¹³Let them praise the name of the LORD,
  for his name alone is exalted;
  his splendor is above the earth and the
    heavens.
¹⁴He has raised up for his people a horn, *ᵇ*
  the praise of all his saints,
  of Israel, the people close to his heart.

  Praise the LORD.

THE MESSAGE

He spreads snow like a white fleece,
  he scatters frost like ashes,
He broadcasts hail like birdseed—
  who can survive his winter?
Then he gives the command and it all melts;
  he breathes on winter—suddenly it's
    spring!

147.19-20 He speaks the same way to Jacob,
  speaks words that work to Israel.
He never did this to the other nations;
  they never heard such commands.
Hallelujah!

148.1-5 # 148 Hallelujah!
  Praise GOD from heaven,
    praise him from the mountaintops;
Praise him, all you his angels,
  praise him, all you his warriors,
Praise him, sun and moon,
  praise him, you morning stars;
Praise him, high heaven,
  praise him, heavenly rain clouds;
Praise, oh let them praise the name of GOD—
  he spoke the word, and there they were!

148.6 He set them in place
  from all time to eternity;
He gave his orders,
  and that's it!

148.7-12 Praise GOD from earth,
  you sea dragons, you fathomless ocean
    deeps;
Fire and hail, snow and ice,
  hurricanes obeying his orders;
Mountains and all hills,
  apple orchards and cedar forests;
Wild beasts and herds of cattle,
  snakes, and birds in flight;
Earth's kings and all races,
  leaders and important people,
Robust men and women in their prime,
  and yes, graybeards and little children.

148.13-14 Let them praise the name of GOD—
  it's the only Name worth praising.
His radiance exceeds anything in earth and
    sky;
  he's built a monument—his very own
    people!

Praise from all who love GOD!
  Israel's children, intimate friends of GOD.
Hallelujah!

ᵃ 1 Hebrew *Hallelu Yah*; also in verse 14   *ᵇ 14 Horn* here
symbolizes strong one, that is, king.

NEW INTERNATIONAL VERSION

PSALM 149

¹ Praise the LORD. *a*

Sing to the LORD a new song,
  his praise in the assembly of the saints.

² Let Israel rejoice in their Maker;
  let the people of Zion be glad in their
    King.
³ Let them praise his name with dancing
  and make music to him with tambourine
    and harp.
⁴ For the LORD takes delight in his people;
  he crowns the humble with salvation.
⁵ Let the saints rejoice in this honor
  and sing for joy on their beds.

⁶ May the praise of God be in their mouths
  and a double-edged sword in their hands,
⁷ to inflict vengeance on the nations
  and punishment on the peoples,
⁸ to bind their kings with fetters,
  their nobles with shackles of iron,
⁹ to carry out the sentence written against
    them.
  This is the glory of all his saints.

Praise the LORD.

PSALM 150

¹ Praise the LORD. *b*

Praise God in his sanctuary;
  praise him in his mighty heavens.
² Praise him for his acts of power;
  praise him for his surpassing greatness.
³ Praise him with the sounding of the trumpet,
  praise him with the harp and lyre,
⁴ praise him with tambourine and dancing,
  praise him with the strings and flute,
⁵ praise him with the clash of cymbals,
  praise him with resounding cymbals.

⁶ Let everything that has breath praise the
    LORD.

Praise the LORD.

THE MESSAGE

149 149.1-4 Hallelujah!
  Sing to GOD a brand-new song,
praise him in the company of all who love
    him.
Let all Israel celebrate their Sovereign Creator,
  Zion's children exult in their King.
Let them praise his name in dance;
  strike up the band and make great music!
And why? Because GOD delights in his people,
  festoons plain folk with salvation garlands!

149.5-9 Let true lovers break out in praise,
  sing out from wherever they're sitting,
Shout the high praises of God,
  brandish their swords in the wild sword-
    dance—
A portent of vengeance on the God-defying
    nations,
  a signal that punishment's coming,
Their kings chained and hauled off to jail,
  their leaders behind bars for good,
The judgment on them carried out to the
    letter
  —and all who love God in the seat of
    honor!
Hallelujah!

150 150.1-6 Hallelujah!
  Praise God in his holy house of
    worship,
praise him under the open skies;
Praise him for his acts of power,
  praise him for his magnificent greatness;
Praise with a blast on the trumpet,
  praise by strumming soft strings;
Praise him with castanets and dance,
  praise him with banjo and flute;
Praise him with cymbals and a big bass drum,
  praise him with fiddles and mandolin.
Let every living, breathing creature praise
    GOD!
  Hallelujah!

PROVERBS

PROLOGUE: PURPOSE AND THEME

1 The proverbs of Solomon son of David, king of Israel:

2 for attaining wisdom and discipline;
for understanding words of insight;
3 for acquiring a disciplined and prudent life,
doing what is right and just and fair;
4 for giving prudence to the simple,
knowledge and discretion to the young—
5 let the wise listen and add to their learning,
and let the discerning get guidance—
6 for understanding proverbs and parables,
the sayings and riddles of the wise.

7 The fear of the LORD is the beginning of knowledge,
but fools[a] despise wisdom and discipline.

EXHORTATIONS TO EMBRACE WISDOM

WARNING AGAINST ENTICEMENT

8 Listen, my son, to your father's instruction
and do not forsake your mother's teaching.
9 They will be a garland to grace your head
and a chain to adorn your neck.

10 My son, if sinners entice you,
do not give in to them.
11 If they say, "Come along with us;
let's lie in wait for someone's blood,
let's waylay some harmless soul;
12 let's swallow them alive, like the grave,[b]
and whole, like those who go down to the pit;
13 we will get all sorts of valuable things
and fill our houses with plunder;
14 throw in your lot with us,
and we will share a common purse"—
15 my son, do not go along with them,
do not set foot on their paths;

---

a 7 The Hebrew words rendered *fool* in Proverbs, and often elsewhere in the Old Testament, denote one who is morally deficient.   b 12 Hebrew *Sheol*

PROVERBS

WISE SAYINGS OF SOLOMON

A MANUAL FOR LIVING

1.1-6 **1** These are the wise sayings of Solomon,
David's son, Israel's king—
Written down so we'll know how to live well and right,
to understand what life means and where it's going;
A manual for living,
for learning what's right and just and fair;
To teach the inexperienced the ropes
and give our young people a grasp on reality.
There's something here also for seasoned men and women,
still a thing or two for the experienced to learn—
Fresh wisdom to probe and penetrate,
the rhymes and reasons of wise men and women.

START WITH GOD

1.7 Start with GOD—the first step in learning is bowing down to GOD;
only fools thumb their noses at such wisdom and learning.

1.8-19 Pay close attention, friend, to what your father tells you;
never forget what you learned at your mother's knee.
Wear their counsel like flowers in your hair,
like rings on your fingers.
Dear friend, if bad companions tempt you,
don't go along with them.
If they say—"Let's go out and raise some hell.
Let's beat up some old man, mug some old woman.
Let's pick them clean
and get them ready for their funerals.
We'll load up on top-quality loot.
We'll haul it home by the truckload.
Join us for the time of your life!
With us, it's share and share alike!"—
Oh, friend, don't give them a second look;
don't listen to them for a minute.

NEW INTERNATIONAL VERSION

¹⁶ for their feet rush into sin,
    they are swift to shed blood.
¹⁷ How useless to spread a net
    in full view of all the birds!
¹⁸ These men lie in wait for their own blood;
    they waylay only themselves!
¹⁹ Such is the end of all who go after ill-gotten
        gain;
    it takes away the lives of those who get it.

WARNING AGAINST REJECTING WISDOM
²⁰ Wisdom calls aloud in the street,
    she raises her voice in the public squares;
²¹ at the head of the noisy streets*a* she cries out,
    in the gateways of the city she makes her
        speech:

²² "How long will you simple ones*b* love your
        simple ways?
    How long will mockers delight in mockery
    and fools hate knowledge?
²³ If you had responded to my rebuke,
    I would have poured out my heart to you
    and made my thoughts known to you.
²⁴ But since you rejected me when I called
    and no one gave heed when I stretched
        out my hand,
²⁵ since you ignored all my advice
    and would not accept my rebuke,
²⁶ I in turn will laugh at your disaster;
    I will mock when calamity overtakes
        you—
²⁷ when calamity overtakes you like a storm,
    when disaster sweeps over you like a
        whirlwind,
    when distress and trouble overwhelm
        you.

²⁸ "Then they will call to me but I will not
        answer;
    they will look for me but will not find me.
²⁹ Since they hated knowledge
    and did not choose to fear the LORD,
³⁰ since they would not accept my advice
    and spurned my rebuke,
³¹ they will eat the fruit of their ways
    and be filled with the fruit of their
        schemes.
³² For the waywardness of the simple will kill
        them,
    and the complacency of fools will destroy
        them;
³³ but whoever listens to me will live in safety
    and be at ease, without fear of harm."

a 21 Hebrew; Septuagint / *on the tops of the walls*
b 22 The Hebrew word rendered *simple* in Proverbs
generally denotes one without moral direction and inclined
to evil.

THE MESSAGE

They're racing to a very bad end,
    hurrying to ruin everything they lay
        hands on.
Nobody robs a bank
    with everyone watching,
Yet that's what these people are doing—
    they're doing themselves in.
When you grab all you can get, that's what
        happens:
    the more you get, the less you are.

LADY WISDOM
1.20-21 Lady Wisdom goes out in the street and
        shouts.
    At the town center she makes her speech.
In the middle of the traffic she takes her stand.
    At the busiest corner she calls out:

1.22-24 "Simpletons! How long will you wallow in
        ignorance?
    Cynics! How long will you feed your
        cynicism?
Idiots! How long will you refuse to learn?
    About face! I can revise your life.
Look, I'm ready to pour out my spirit on you;
    I'm ready to tell you all I know.
As it is, I've called, but you've turned a deaf ear;
    I've reached out to you, but you've
        ignored me.

1.25-28 "Since you laugh at my counsel
    and make a joke of my advice,
How can I take you seriously?
    I'll turn the tables and joke about *your*
        troubles!
What if the roof falls in,
    and your whole life goes to pieces?
What if catastrophe strikes and there's nothing
    to show for your life but rubble and ashes?
You'll need me then. You'll call for me, but
        don't expect an answer.
    No matter how hard you look, you won't
        find me.

1.29-33 "Because you hated Knowledge
    and had nothing to do with the Fear-of-
        GOD,
Because you wouldn't take my advice
    and brushed aside all my offers to train
        you,
Well, you've made your bed—now lie in it;
    you wanted your own way—now, how do
        you like it?
Don't you see what happens, you simpletons,
        you idiots?
    Carelessness kills; complacency is murder.
First pay attention to me, and then relax.
    Now you can take it easy—you're in good
        hands."

NEW INTERNATIONAL VERSION

Moral Benefits of Wisdom

2 My son, if you accept my words
  and store up my commands within you,
[2] turning your ear to wisdom
  and applying your heart to understanding,
[3] and if you call out for insight
  and cry aloud for understanding,
[4] and if you look for it as for silver
  and search for it as for hidden treasure,
[5] then you will understand the fear of the
    Lord
  and find the knowledge of God.
[6] For the Lord gives wisdom,
  and from his mouth come knowledge and
    understanding.
[7] He holds victory in store for the upright,
  he is a shield to those whose walk is
    blameless,
[8] for he guards the course of the just
  and protects the way of his faithful ones.

[9] Then you will understand what is right and
    just
  and fair—every good path.
[10] For wisdom will enter your heart,
  and knowledge will be pleasant to your
    soul.
[11] Discretion will protect you,
  and understanding will guard you.

[12] Wisdom will save you from the ways of
    wicked men,
  from men whose words are perverse,
[13] who leave the straight paths
  to walk in dark ways,
[14] who delight in doing wrong
  and rejoice in the perverseness of evil,
[15] whose paths are crooked
  and who are devious in their ways.

[16] It will save you also from the adulteress,
  from the wayward wife with her seductive
    words,
[17] who has left the partner of her youth
  and ignored the covenant she made before
    God.[a]
[18] For her house leads down to death
  and her paths to the spirits of the dead.
[19] None who go to her return
  or attain the paths of life.

THE MESSAGE

Make Insight Your Priority

2.1-5 **2** Good friend, take to heart what I'm telling
    you;
  collect my counsels and guard them with
    your life.
Tune your ears to the world of Wisdom;
  set your heart on a life of Understanding.
That's right—if you make Insight your
    priority,
  and won't take no for an answer,
Searching for it like a prospector panning for
    gold,
  like an adventurer on a treasure hunt,
Believe me, before you know it Fear-of-God
    will be yours;
  you'll have come upon the Knowledge of
    God.

2.6-8 And here's why: God gives out Wisdom free,
  is plainspoken in Knowledge and
    Understanding.
He's a rich mine of Common Sense for those
    who live well,
  a personal bodyguard to the candid and
    sincere.
He keeps his eye on all who live honestly,
  and pays special attention to his loyally
    committed ones.

2.9-15 So now you can pick out what's true and fair,
  find all the good trails!
Lady Wisdom will be your close friend,
  and Brother Knowledge your pleasant
    companion.
Good Sense will scout ahead for danger,
  Insight will keep an eye out for you.
They'll keep you from making wrong turns,
  or following the bad directions
Of those who are lost themselves
  and can't tell a trail from a tumbleweed,
These losers who make a game of evil
  and throw parties to celebrate perversity,
Traveling paths that go nowhere,
  wandering in a maze of detours and dead
    ends.

2.16-19 Wise friends will rescue you from the
    Temptress—
  that smooth-talking Seductress
Who's faithless to the husband she married
    years ago,
  never gave a second thought to her
    promises before God.
Her whole way of life is doomed;
  every step she takes brings her closer to
    hell.
No one who joins her company ever comes
    back,
  ever sets foot on the path to real living.

---

[a] 17 Or covenant of her God

NEW INTERNATIONAL VERSION

20 Thus you will walk in the ways of good men
and keep to the paths of the righteous.
21 For the upright will live in the land,
and the blameless will remain in it;
22 but the wicked will be cut off from the land,
and the unfaithful will be torn from it.

FURTHER BENEFITS OF WISDOM

3 My son, do not forget my teaching,
but keep my commands in your heart,
2 for they will prolong your life many years
and bring you prosperity.

3 Let love and faithfulness never leave you;
bind them around your neck,
write them on the tablet of your heart.
4 Then you will win favor and a good name
in the sight of God and man.

5 Trust in the LORD with all your heart
and lean not on your own understanding;
6 in all your ways acknowledge him,
and he will make your paths straight. *a*

7 Do not be wise in your own eyes;
fear the LORD and shun evil.
8 This will bring health to your body
and nourishment to your bones.

9 Honor the LORD with your wealth,
with the firstfruits of all your crops;
10 then your barns will be filled to overflowing,
and your vats will brim over with new
wine.

11 My son, do not despise the LORD's discipline
and do not resent his rebuke,
12 because the LORD disciplines those he loves,
as a father *b* the son he delights in.

13 Blessed is the man who finds wisdom,
the man who gains understanding,
14 for she is more profitable than silver
and yields better returns than gold.
15 She is more precious than rubies;
nothing you desire can compare with her.
16 Long life is in her right hand;
in her left hand are riches and honor.
17 Her ways are pleasant ways,
and all her paths are peace.
18 She is a tree of life to those who embrace
her;
those who lay hold of her will be blessed.

THE MESSAGE

2.20-22 So—join the company of good men and
women,
keep your feet on the tried and true paths.
It's the men who walk straight who will settle
this land,
the women with integrity who will last
here.
The corrupt will lose their lives;
the dishonest will be gone for good.

DON'T ASSUME YOU KNOW IT ALL

3.1-2 3 Good friend, don't forget all I've taught
you;
take to heart my commands.
They'll help you live a long, long time,
a long life lived full and well.

3.3-4 Don't lose your grip on Love and Loyalty.
Tie them around your neck; carve their
initials on your heart.
Earn a reputation for living well
in God's eyes and the eyes of the people.

3.5-12 Trust GOD from the bottom of your heart;
don't try to figure out everything on your
own.
Listen for GOD's voice in everything you do,
everywhere you go;
he's the one who will keep you on track.
Don't assume that you know it all.
Run to GOD! Run from evil!
Your body will glow with health,
your very bones will vibrate with life!
Honor GOD with everything you own;
give him the first and the best.
Your barns will burst,
your wine vats will brim over.
But don't, dear friend, resent GOD's discipline;
don't sulk under his loving correction.
It's the child he loves that GOD corrects;
a father's delight is behind all this.

THE VERY TREE OF LIFE

3.13-18 You're blessed when you meet Lady Wisdom,
when you make friends with Madame
Insight.
She's worth far more than money in the bank;
her friendship is better than a big salary.
Her value exceeds all the trappings of wealth;
nothing you could wish for holds a candle
to her.
With one hand she gives long life,
with the other she confers recognition.
Her manner is beautiful,
her life wonderfully complete.
She's the very Tree of Life to those who
embrace her.
Hold her tight—and be blessed!

*a 6 Or will direct your paths   b 12 Hebrew; Septuagint /
and he punishes*

NEW INTERNATIONAL VERSION

¹⁹ By wisdom the LORD laid the earth's
        foundations,
    by understanding he set the heavens in
        place;
²⁰ by his knowledge the deeps were divided,
    and the clouds let drop the dew.

²¹ My son, preserve sound judgment and
        discernment,
    do not let them out of your sight;
²² they will be life for you,
    an ornament to grace your neck.
²³ Then you will go on your way in safety,
    and your foot will not stumble;
²⁴ when you lie down, you will not be afraid;
    when you lie down, your sleep will be
        sweet.
²⁵ Have no fear of sudden disaster
    or of the ruin that overtakes the wicked,
²⁶ for the LORD will be your confidence
    and will keep your foot from being
        snared.

²⁷ Do not withhold good from those who
        deserve it,
    when it is in your power to act.
²⁸ Do not say to your neighbor,
    "Come back later; I'll give it tomorrow"—
    when you now have it with you.

²⁹ Do not plot harm against your neighbor,
    who lives trustfully near you.
³⁰ Do not accuse a man for no reason—
    when he has done you no harm.

³¹ Do not envy a violent man
    or choose any of his ways,
³² for the LORD detests a perverse man
    but takes the upright into his confidence.

³³ The LORD's curse is on the house of the
        wicked,
    but he blesses the home of the righteous.
³⁴ He mocks proud mockers
    but gives grace to the humble.
³⁵ The wise inherit honor,
    but fools he holds up to shame.

WISDOM IS SUPREME

4 Listen, my sons, to a father's instruction;
    pay attention and gain understanding.
² I give you sound learning,
    so do not forsake my teaching.

THE MESSAGE

3.19-20 With Lady Wisdom, GOD formed Earth;
    with Madame Insight, he raised Heaven.
They knew when to signal rivers and springs
        to the surface,
    and dew to descend from the night skies.

NEVER WALK AWAY

3.21-26 Dear friend, guard Clear Thinking and
            Common Sense with your life;
    don't for a minute lose sight of them.
They'll keep your soul alive and well,
    they'll keep you fit and attractive.
You'll travel safely,
    you'll neither tire nor trip.
You'll take afternoon naps without a worry,
    you'll enjoy a good night's sleep.
No need to panic over alarms or surprises,
    or predictions that doomsday's just around
        the corner,
Because GOD will be right there with you;
    he'll keep you safe and sound.

3.27-29 Never walk away from someone who deserves
            help;
    your hand is *God's* hand for that person.
Don't tell your neighbor, "Maybe some other
            time,"
    or, "Try me tomorrow,"
    when the money's right there in your
        pocket.
Don't figure ways of taking advantage of your
            neighbor
    when he's sitting there trusting and
        unsuspecting.

3.30-32 Don't walk around with a chip on your
            shoulder,
    always spoiling for a fight.
Don't try to be like those who shoulder their
            way through life.
    Why be a bully?
"Why not?" you say. Because GOD can't stand
            twisted souls.
    It's the straightforward who get his respect.

3.33-35 GOD's curse blights the house of the wicked,
    but he blesses the home of the righteous.
He gives proud skeptics a cold shoulder,
    but if you're down on your luck, he's right
        there to help.
Wise living gets rewarded with honor;
    stupid living gets the booby prize.

YOUR LIFE IS AT STAKE

4.1-2 **4** Listen, friends, to some fatherly advice;
    sit up and take notice so you'll know
        how to live.
I'm giving you good counsel;
    don't let it go in one ear and out the other.

NEW INTERNATIONAL VERSION

³When I was a boy in my father's house,
  still tender, and an only child of my
    mother,
⁴he taught me and said,
  "Lay hold of my words with all your
    heart;
  keep my commands and you will live.
⁵Get wisdom, get understanding;
  do not forget my words or swerve from
    them.
⁶Do not forsake wisdom, and she will protect
    you;
  love her, and she will watch over you.
⁷Wisdom is supreme; therefore get wisdom.
  Though it cost all you have,ᵃ get
    understanding.
⁸Esteem her, and she will exalt you;
  embrace her, and she will honor you.
⁹She will set a garland of grace on your head
  and present you with a crown of
    splendor."

¹⁰Listen, my son, accept what I say,
  and the years of your life will be many.
¹¹I guide you in the way of wisdom
  and lead you along straight paths.
¹²When you walk, your steps will not be
    hampered;
  when you run, you will not stumble.
¹³Hold on to instruction, do not let it go;
  guard it well, for it is your life.
¹⁴Do not set foot on the path of the wicked
  or walk in the way of evil men.
¹⁵Avoid it, do not travel on it;
  turn from it and go on your way.
¹⁶For they cannot sleep till they do evil;
  they are robbed of slumber till they make
    someone fall.
¹⁷They eat the bread of wickedness
  and drink the wine of violence.

¹⁸The path of the righteous is like the first
    gleam of dawn,
  shining ever brighter till the full light of
    day.
¹⁹But the way of the wicked is like deep
    darkness;
  they do not know what makes them
    stumble.

²⁰My son, pay attention to what I say;
  listen closely to my words.
²¹Do not let them out of your sight,
  keep them within your heart;

ᵃ 7 Or *Whatever else you get*

THE MESSAGE

4.3-9 When I was a boy at my father's knee,
  the pride and joy of my mother,
He would sit me down and drill me:
  "Take this to heart. Do what I tell you—
    live!
Sell everything and buy Wisdom! Forage for
    Understanding!
  Don't forget one word! Don't deviate an
    inch!
Never walk away from Wisdom—she guards
    your life;
  love her—she keeps her eye on you.
Above all and before all, do this: Get Wisdom!
  Write this at the top of your list: Get
    Understanding!
Throw your arms around her—believe me,
    you won't regret it;
  never let her go—she'll make your life
    glorious.
She'll garland your life with grace,
  she'll festoon your days with beauty."

4.10-15 Dear friend, take my advice;
  it will add years to your life.
I'm writing out clear directions to Wisdom
    Way,
  I'm drawing a map to Righteous Road.
I don't want you ending up in blind alleys,
  or wasting time making wrong turns.
Hold tight to good advice; don't relax your
    grip.
  Guard it well—your life is at stake!
Don't take Wicked Bypass;
  don't so much as set foot on that road.
Stay clear of it; give it a wide berth.
  Make a detour and be on your way.

4.16-17 Evil people are restless
  unless they're making trouble;
They can't get a good night's sleep
  unless they've made life miserable for
    somebody.
Perversity is their food and drink,
  violence their drug of choice.

4.18-19 The ways of right-living people glow with
    light;
  the longer they live, the brighter they
    shine.
But the road of wrongdoing gets darker and
    darker—
  travelers can't see a thing; they fall flat on
    their faces.

LEARN IT BY HEART
4.20-22 Dear friend, listen well to my words;
  tune your ears to my voice.
Keep my message in plain view at all times.
  Concentrate! Learn it by heart!

NEW INTERNATIONAL VERSION

²² for they are life to those who find them
    and health to a man's whole body.
²³ Above all else, guard your heart,
    for it is the wellspring of life.
²⁴ Put away perversity from your mouth;
    keep corrupt talk far from your lips.
²⁵ Let your eyes look straight ahead,
    fix your gaze directly before you.
²⁶ Make level^a paths for your feet
    and take only ways that are firm.
²⁷ Do not swerve to the right or the left;
    keep your foot from evil.

WARNING AGAINST ADULTERY

5 My son, pay attention to my wisdom,
    listen well to my words of insight,
² that you may maintain discretion
    and your lips may preserve knowledge.
³ For the lips of an adulteress drip honey,
    and her speech is smoother than oil;
⁴ but in the end she is bitter as gall,
    sharp as a double-edged sword.
⁵ Her feet go down to death;
    her steps lead straight to the grave.^b
⁶ She gives no thought to the way of life;
    her paths are crooked, but she knows it
    not.

⁷ Now then, my sons, listen to me;
    do not turn aside from what I say.
⁸ Keep to a path far from her,
    do not go near the door of her house,
⁹ lest you give your best strength to others
    and your years to one who is cruel,
¹⁰ lest strangers feast on your wealth
    and your toil enrich another man's house.
¹¹ At the end of your life you will groan,
    when your flesh and body are spent.
¹² You will say, "How I hated discipline!
    How my heart spurned correction!
¹³ I would not obey my teachers
    or listen to my instructors.
¹⁴ I have come to the brink of utter ruin
    in the midst of the whole assembly."

THE MESSAGE

Those who discover these words live, really
    live;
    body and soul, they're bursting with health.

4.23-27 Keep vigilant watch over your heart;
    that's where life starts.
Don't talk out of both sides of your mouth;
    avoid careless banter, white lies, and gossip.
Keep your eyes straight ahead;
    ignore all sideshow distractions.
Watch your step,
    and the road will stretch out smooth before
      you.
Look neither right nor left;
    leave evil in the dust.

NOTHING BUT SIN AND BONES

5.1-2 **5** Dear friend, pay close attention to this, my
      wisdom;
    listen very closely to the way I see it.
Then you'll acquire a taste for good sense;
    what I tell you will keep you out of trouble.

5.3-6 The lips of a seductive woman are oh so
      sweet,
    her soft words are oh so smooth.
But it won't be long before she's gravel in your
      mouth,
    a pain in your gut, a wound in your heart.
She's dancing down the primrose path to
      Death;
    she's headed straight for Hell and taking
      you with her.
She hasn't a clue about Real Life,
    about who she is or where she's going.

5.7-14 So, my friend, listen closely;
    don't treat my words casually.
Keep your distance from such a woman;
    absolutely stay out of her neighborhood.
You don't want to squander your wonderful
      life,
    to waste your precious life among the
      hardhearted.
Why should you allow strangers to take
      advantage of you?
    Why be exploited by those who care
      nothing for you?
You don't want to end your life full of regrets,
    nothing but sin and bones,
Saying, "Oh, why didn't I do what they told
      me?
    Why did I reject a disciplined life?
Why didn't I listen to my mentors,
    or take my teachers seriously?
My life is ruined!
    I haven't one blessed thing to show for my
      life!"

^a 26 Or *Consider the*   ^b 5 Hebrew *Sheol*

NEW INTERNATIONAL VERSION

¹⁵ Drink water from your own cistern,
 running water from your own well.
¹⁶ Should your springs overflow in the streets,
 your streams of water in the public
 squares?
¹⁷ Let them be yours alone,
 never to be shared with strangers.
¹⁸ May your fountain be blessed,
 and may you rejoice in the wife of your
 youth.
¹⁹ A loving doe, a graceful deer—
 may her breasts satisfy you always,
 may you ever be captivated by her love.
²⁰ Why be captivated, my son, by an
 adulteress?
 Why embrace the bosom of another man's
 wife?

²¹ For a man's ways are in full view of the LORD,
 and he examines all his paths.
²² The evil deeds of a wicked man ensnare him;
 the cords of his sin hold him fast.
²³ He will die for lack of discipline,
 led astray by his own great folly.

WARNINGS AGAINST FOLLY

6 My son, if you have put up security for
 your neighbor,
 if you have struck hands in pledge for
 another,
² if you have been trapped by what you said,
 ensnared by the words of your mouth,
³ then do this, my son, to free yourself,
 since you have fallen into your neighbor's
 hands:
 Go and humble yourself;
 press your plea with your neighbor!
⁴ Allow no sleep to your eyes,
 no slumber to your eyelids.
⁵ Free yourself, like a gazelle from the hand of
 the hunter,
 like a bird from the snare of the fowler.

⁶ Go to the ant, you sluggard;
 consider its ways and be wise!
⁷ It has no commander,
 no overseer or ruler,
⁸ yet it stores its provisions in summer
 and gathers its food at harvest.

THE MESSAGE

NEVER TAKE LOVE FOR GRANTED

5.15-16 Do you know the saying, "Drink from your
 own rain barrel,
 draw water from your own spring-fed
 well"?
 It's true. Otherwise, you may one day come
 home
 and find your barrel empty and your well
 polluted.

5.17-20 Your spring water is for you and you only,
 not to be passed around among strangers.
 Bless your fresh-flowing fountain!
 Enjoy the wife you married as a young
 man!
 Lovely as an angel, beautiful as a rose—
 don't ever quit taking delight in her body.
 Never take her love for granted!
 Why would you trade enduring intimacies for
 cheap thrills with a whore?
 for dalliance with a promiscuous stranger?

5.21-23 Mark well that GOD doesn't miss a move you
 make;
 he's aware of every step you take.
 The shadow of your sin will overtake you;
 you'll find yourself stumbling all over
 yourself in the dark.
 Death is the reward of an undisciplined life;
 your foolish decisions trap you in a dead
 end.

LIKE A DEER FROM THE HUNTER

6.1-5 **6** Dear friend, if you've gone into hock with
 your neighbor
 or locked yourself into a deal with a
 stranger,
 If you've impulsively promised the shirt off
 your back
 and now find yourself shivering out in the
 cold,
 Friend, don't waste a minute, get yourself out
 of that mess.
 You're in that man's clutches!
 Go, put on a long face; act desperate.
 Don't procrastinate—
 there's no time to lose.
 Run like a deer from the hunter,
 fly like a bird from the trapper!

A LESSON FROM THE ANT

6.6-11 You lazy fool, look at an ant.
 Watch it closely; let it teach you a thing or
 two.
 Nobody has to tell it what to do.
 All summer it stores up food;
 at harvest it stockpiles provisions.

NEW INTERNATIONAL VERSION

⁹How long will you lie there, you sluggard?
  When will you get up from your sleep?
¹⁰A little sleep, a little slumber,
  a little folding of the hands to rest—
¹¹and poverty will come on you like a bandit
  and scarcity like an armed man. ᵃ

¹²A scoundrel and villain,
  who goes about with a corrupt mouth,
¹³ who winks with his eye,
  signals with his feet
  and motions with his fingers,
¹⁴ who plots evil with deceit in his heart—
  he always stirs up dissension.
¹⁵Therefore disaster will overtake him in an
    instant;
  he will suddenly be destroyed—without
    remedy.

¹⁶There are six things the LORD hates,
  seven that are detestable to him:
¹⁷ haughty eyes,
  a lying tongue,
  hands that shed innocent blood,
¹⁸ a heart that devises wicked schemes,
  feet that are quick to rush into evil,
¹⁹ a false witness who pours out lies
  and a man who stirs up dissension
    among brothers.

Warning Against Adultery

²⁰My son, keep your father's commands
  and do not forsake your mother's
    teaching.
²¹Bind them upon your heart forever;
  fasten them around your neck.
²²When you walk, they will guide you;
  when you sleep, they will watch over you;
  when you awake, they will speak to you.
²³For these commands are a lamp,
  this teaching is a light,
  and the corrections of discipline
  are the way to life,
²⁴keeping you from the immoral woman,
  from the smooth tongue of the wayward
    wife.
²⁵Do not lust in your heart after her beauty
  or let her captivate you with her eyes,
²⁶for the prostitute reduces you to a loaf of
    bread,

ᵃ 11 Or like a vagrant / and scarcity like a beggar

THE MESSAGE

So how long are you going to laze around
    doing nothing?
  How long before you get out of bed?
A nap here, a nap there, a day off here, a day
    off there,
  sit back, take it easy—do you know what
    comes next?
Just this: You can look forward to a dirt-poor
    life,
  poverty your permanent houseguest!

Always Cooking Up Something Nasty

6.12-15 Riffraff and rascals
  talk out of both sides of their mouths.
They wink at each other, they shuffle their
    feet,
  they cross their fingers behind their backs.
Their perverse minds are always cooking up
    something nasty,
  always stirring up trouble.
Catastrophe is just around the corner for
    them,
  a total smash-up, their lives ruined beyond
    repair.

Seven Things God Hates

6.16-19 Here are six things GOD hates,
  and one more that he loathes with a
    passion:

    eyes that are arrogant,
    a tongue that lies,
    hands that murder the innocent,
    a heart that hatches evil plots,
    feet that race down a wicked track,
    a mouth that lies under oath,
    a troublemaker in the family.

Warning on Adultery

6.20-23 Good friend, follow your father's good advice;
  don't wander off from your mother's
    teachings.
Wrap yourself in them from head to foot;
  wear them like a scarf around your neck.
Wherever you walk, they'll guide you;
  whenever you rest, they'll guard you;
  when you wake up, they'll tell you what's
    next.
For sound advice is a beacon,
  good teaching is a light,
  moral discipline is a life path.

6.24-35 They'll protect you from wanton women,
  from the seductive talk of some temptress.
Don't lustfully fantasize on her beauty,
  nor be taken in by her bedroom eyes.
You can buy an hour with a whore for a loaf of
    bread,

NEW INTERNATIONAL VERSION

and the adulteress preys upon your very
  life.
27 Can a man scoop fire into his lap
  without his clothes being burned?
28 Can a man walk on hot coals
  without his feet being scorched?
29 So is he who sleeps with another man's wife;
  no one who touches her will go
  unpunished.

30 Men do not despise a thief if he steals
  to satisfy his hunger when he is starving.
31 Yet if he is caught, he must pay sevenfold,
  though it costs him all the wealth of his
  house.
32 But a man who commits adultery lacks
  judgment;
  whoever does so destroys himself.
33 Blows and disgrace are his lot,
  and his shame will never be wiped away;
34 for jealousy arouses a husband's fury,
  and he will show no mercy when he takes
  revenge.
35 He will not accept any compensation;
  he will refuse the bribe, however great it
  is.

Warning Against the Adulteress

7 My son, keep my words
  and store up my commands within you.
2 Keep my commands and you will live;
  guard my teachings as the apple of your
  eye.
3 Bind them on your fingers;
  write them on the tablet of your heart.
4 Say to wisdom, "You are my sister,"
  and call understanding your kinsman;
5 they will keep you from the adulteress,
  from the wayward wife with her seductive
  words.

6 At the window of my house
  I looked out through the lattice.
7 I saw among the simple,
  I noticed among the young men,
  a youth who lacked judgment.
8 He was going down the street near her
  corner,
  walking along in the direction of her house
9 at twilight, as the day was fading,
  as the dark of night set in.

10 Then out came a woman to meet him,
  dressed like a prostitute and with crafty
  intent.
11 (She is loud and defiant,
  her feet never stay at home;
12 now in the street, now in the squares,
  at every corner she lurks.)

THE MESSAGE

but a wanton woman may well eat *you*
  alive.
Can you build a fire in your lap
  and not burn your pants?
Can you walk barefoot on hot coals
  and not get blisters?
It's the same when you have sex with your
  neighbor's wife:
  Touch her and you'll pay for it. No excuses.
Hunger is no excuse
  for a thief to steal;
When he's caught he has to pay it back,
  even if he has to put his whole house in
  hock.
Adultery is a brainless act,
  soul-destroying, self-destructive;
Expect a bloody nose, a black eye,
  and a reputation ruined for good.
For jealousy detonates rage in a cheated
  husband;
  wild for revenge, he won't make
  allowances.
Nothing you say or pay will make it all right;
  neither bribes nor reason will satisfy him.

Dressed to Seduce

7.1-5 7 Dear friend, do what I tell you;
  treasure my careful instructions.
Do what I say and you'll live well.
  My teaching is as precious as your
  eyesight—guard it!
Write it out on the back of your hands;
  etch it on the chambers of your heart.
Talk to Wisdom as to a sister.
  Treat Insight as your companion.
They'll be with you to fend off the
  Temptress—
  that smooth-talking, honey-tongued
  Seductress.

7.6-12 As I stood at the window of my house
  looking out through the shutters,
Watching the mindless crowd stroll by,
  I spotted a young man without any sense
Arriving at the corner of the street where she
  lived,
  then turning up the path to her house.
It was dusk, the evening coming on,
  the darkness thickening into night.
Just then, a woman met him—
  she'd been lying in wait for him, dressed to
  seduce him.
Brazen and brash she was,
  restless and roaming, never at home,
Walking the streets, loitering in the mall,
  hanging out at every corner in town.

NEW INTERNATIONAL VERSION

¹³ She took hold of him and kissed him
  and with a brazen face she said:

¹⁴ "I have fellowship offerings*ᵃ* at home;
  today I fulfilled my vows.
¹⁵ So I came out to meet you;
  I looked for you and have found you!
¹⁶ I have covered my bed
  with colored linens from Egypt.
¹⁷ I have perfumed my bed
  with myrrh, aloes and cinnamon.
¹⁸ Come, let's drink deep of love till morning;
  let's enjoy ourselves with love!
¹⁹ My husband is not at home;
  he has gone on a long journey.
²⁰ He took his purse filled with money
  and will not be home till full moon."

²¹ With persuasive words she led him astray;
  she seduced him with her smooth talk.
²² All at once he followed her
  like an ox going to the slaughter,
  like a deer*ᵇ* stepping into a noose*ᶜ*
²³   till an arrow pierces his liver,
  like a bird darting into a snare,
  little knowing it will cost him his life.

²⁴ Now then, my sons, listen to me;
  pay attention to what I say.
²⁵ Do not let your heart turn to her ways
  or stray into her paths.
²⁶ Many are the victims she has brought down;
  her slain are a mighty throng.
²⁷ Her house is a highway to the grave,*ᵈ*
  leading down to the chambers of death.

WISDOM'S CALL

8 Does not wisdom call out?
  Does not understanding raise her voice?
² On the heights along the way,
  where the paths meet, she takes her stand;
³ beside the gates leading into the city,
  at the entrances, she cries aloud:
⁴ "To you, O men, I call out;
  I raise my voice to all mankind.
⁵ You who are simple, gain prudence;
  you who are foolish, gain understanding.
⁶ Listen, for I have worthy things to say;
  I open my lips to speak what is right.
⁷ My mouth speaks what is true,
  for my lips detest wickedness.
⁸ All the words of my mouth are just;

THE MESSAGE

7.13-20 She threw her arms around him and kissed
  him,
  boldly took his arm and said,
"I've got all the makings for a feast—
  today I made my offerings, my vows are all
  paid,
So now I've come to find you,
  hoping to catch sight of your face—and
  here you are!
I've spread fresh, clean sheets on my bed,
  colorful imported linens.
My bed is aromatic with spices
  and exotic fragrances.
Come, let's make love all night,
  spend the night in ecstatic lovemaking!
My husband's not home; he's away on
  business,
  and he won't be back for a month."

7.21-23 Soon she has him eating out of her hand,
  bewitched by her honeyed speech.
Before you know it, he's trotting behind her,
  like a calf led to the butcher shop,
Like a stag lured into ambush
  and then shot with an arrow,
Like a bird flying into a net
  not knowing that its flying life is over.

7.24-27 So, friends, listen to me,
  take these words of mine most seriously.
Don't fool around with a woman like that;
  don't even stroll through her
  neighborhood.
Countless victims come under her spell;
  she's the death of many a poor man.
She runs a halfway house to hell,
  fits you out with a shroud and a coffin.

LADY WISDOM CALLS OUT

8.1-11 **8** Do you hear Lady Wisdom calling?
  Can you hear Madame Insight raising
  her voice?
She's taken her stand at First and Main,
  at the busiest intersection.
Right in the city square
  where the traffic is thickest, she shouts,
"You—I'm talking to all of you,
  everyone out here on the streets!
Listen, you idiots—learn good sense!
  You blockheads—shape up!
Don't miss a word of this—I'm telling you
  how to live well,
  I'm telling you how to live at your best.
My mouth chews and savors and relishes
  truth—
  I can't stand the taste of evil!
You'll only hear true and right words from my
  mouth;

ᵃ 14 Traditionally *peace offerings*   *ᵇ 22* Syriac (see also
Septuagint); Hebrew *fool*   *ᶜ 22* The meaning of the
Hebrew for this line is uncertain.   *ᵈ 27* Hebrew *Sheol*

NEW INTERNATIONAL VERSION

none of them is crooked or perverse.
9 To the discerning all of them are right;
  they are faultless to those who have
    knowledge.
10 Choose my instruction instead of silver,
  knowledge rather than choice gold,
11 for wisdom is more precious than rubies,
  and nothing you desire can compare with
    her.

12 "I, wisdom, dwell together with prudence;
  I possess knowledge and discretion.
13 To fear the LORD is to hate evil;
  I hate pride and arrogance,
  evil behavior and perverse speech.
14 Counsel and sound judgment are mine;
  I have understanding and power.
15 By me kings reign
  and rulers make laws that are just;
16 by me princes govern,
  and all nobles who rule on earth. *a*
17 I love those who love me,
  and those who seek me find me.
18 With me are riches and honor,
  enduring wealth and prosperity.
19 My fruit is better than fine gold;
  what I yield surpasses choice silver.
20 I walk in the way of righteousness,
  along the paths of justice,
21 bestowing wealth on those who love me
  and making their treasuries full.

22 "The LORD brought me forth as the first of
    his works, *b, c*
  before his deeds of old;
23 I was appointed *d* from eternity,
  from the beginning, before the world
    began.
24 When there were no oceans, I was given
    birth,
  when there were no springs abounding
    with water;
25 before the mountains were settled in place,
  before the hills, I was given birth,
26 before he made the earth or its fields
  or any of the dust of the world.
27 I was there when he set the heavens in place,

THE MESSAGE

not one syllable will be twisted or skewed.
You'll recognize this as true—you with open
    minds;
  truth-ready minds will see it at once.
Prefer my life-disciplines over chasing after
    money,
  and God-knowledge over a lucrative career.
For Wisdom is better than all the trappings of
    wealth;
  nothing you could wish for holds a candle
    to her.

8.12-21 "I am Lady Wisdom, and I live next to Sanity;
  Knowledge and Discretion live just down
    the street.
The Fear-of-GOD means hating Evil,
  whose ways I hate with a passion—
  pride and arrogance and crooked talk.
Good counsel and common sense are my
    characteristics;
  I am both Insight and the Virtue to live it
    out.
With my help, leaders rule,
  and lawmakers legislate fairly;
With my help, governors govern,
  along with all in legitimate authority.
I love those who love me;
  those who look for me find me.
Wealth and Glory accompany me—
  also substantial Honor and a Good Name.
My benefits are worth more than a big salary,
    even a *very* big salary;
  the returns on me exceed any imaginable
    bonus.
You can find me on Righteous Road—that's
    where I walk—
  at the intersection of Justice Avenue,
Handing out life to those who love me,
  filling their arms with life—armloads of
    life!

8.22-31 "GOD sovereignly made me—the first, the
    basic—
  before he did anything else.
I was brought into being a long time ago,
  well before Earth got its start.
I arrived on the scene before Ocean,
  yes, even before Springs and Rivers and
    Lakes.
Before Mountains were sculpted and Hills
    took shape,
  I was already there, newborn;
Long before GOD stretched out Earth's
    Horizons,
  and tended to the minute details of Soil and
    Weather,
And set Sky firmly in place,
  I was there.

---

a 16 Many Hebrew manuscripts and Septuagint; most
Hebrew manuscripts *and nobles—all righteous rulers*
b 22 Or *way*; or *dominion*   *c* 22 Or *The* LORD *possessed me
at the beginning of his work*; or *The* LORD *brought me forth at
the beginning of his work*   *d* 23 Or *fashioned*

NEW INTERNATIONAL VERSION

when he marked out the horizon on the
face of the deep,
28 when he established the clouds above
and fixed securely the fountains of the
deep,
29 when he gave the sea its boundary
so the waters would not overstep his
command,
and when he marked out the foundations of
the earth.
30 Then I was the craftsman at his side.
I was filled with delight day after day,
rejoicing always in his presence,
31 rejoicing in his whole world
and delighting in mankind.

32 "Now then, my sons, listen to me;
blessed are those who keep my ways.
33 Listen to my instruction and be wise;
do not ignore it.
34 Blessed is the man who listens to me,
watching daily at my doors,
waiting at my doorway.
35 For whoever finds me finds life
and receives favor from the LORD.
36 But whoever fails to find me harms himself;
all who hate me love death."

INVITATIONS OF WISDOM AND OF FOLLY

9 Wisdom has built her house;
she has hewn out its seven pillars.
2 She has prepared her meat and mixed her
wine;
she has also set her table.
3 She has sent out her maids, and she calls
from the highest point of the city.
4 "Let all who are simple come in here!"
she says to those who lack judgment.
5 "Come, eat my food
and drink the wine I have mixed.
6 Leave your simple ways and you will live;
walk in the way of understanding.

THE MESSAGE

When he mapped and gave borders to wild
Ocean,
built the vast vault of Heaven,
and installed the fountains that fed Ocean,
When he drew a boundary for Sea,
posted a sign that said, NO TRESPASSING,
And then staked out Earth's foundations,
I was right there with him, making sure
everything fit.
Day after day I was there, with my joyful
applause,
always enjoying his company,
Delighted with the world of things and
creatures,
happily celebrating the human family.

8.32-36 "So, my dear friends, listen carefully;
those who embrace these my ways are most
blessed.
Mark a life of discipline and live wisely;
don't squander your precious life.
Blessed the man, blessed the woman, who
listens to me,
awake and ready for me each morning,
alert and responsive as I start my day's
work.
When you find me, you find life, real life,
to say nothing of GOD's good pleasure.
But if you wrong me, you damage your very
soul;
when you reject me, you're flirting with
death."

LADY WISDOM GIVES A DINNER PARTY

9.1-6 9 Lady Wisdom has built and furnished her
home;
it's supported by seven hewn timbers.
The banquet meal is ready to be served: lamb
roasted,
wine poured out, table set with silver and
flowers.
Having dismissed her serving maids,
Lady Wisdom goes to town, stands in a
prominent place,
and invites everyone within sound of her
voice:
"Are you confused about life, don't know
what's going on?
Come with me, oh come, have dinner
with me!
I've prepared a wonderful spread—fresh-
baked bread,
roast lamb, carefully selected wines.
Leave your impoverished confusion and *live!*
Walk up the street to a life with meaning."

✛

NEW INTERNATIONAL VERSION

7 "Whoever corrects a mocker invites insult;
  whoever rebukes a wicked man incurs
    abuse.
8 Do not rebuke a mocker or he will hate you;
  rebuke a wise man and he will love you.
9 Instruct a wise man and he will be wiser
    still;
  teach a righteous man and he will add to
    his learning.

10 "The fear of the LORD is the beginning of
    wisdom,
  and knowledge of the Holy One is
    understanding.
11 For through me your days will be many,
  and years will be added to your life.
12 If you are wise, your wisdom will reward
    you;
  if you are a mocker, you alone will suffer."

13 The woman Folly is loud;
  she is undisciplined and without
    knowledge.
14 She sits at the door of her house,
  on a seat at the highest point of the city,
15 calling out to those who pass by,
  who go straight on their way.
16 "Let all who are simple come in here!"
  she says to those who lack judgment.
17 "Stolen water is sweet;
  food eaten in secret is delicious!"
18 But little do they know that the dead are
    there,
  that her guests are in the depths of the
    grave. *a*

PROVERBS OF SOLOMON

10 The proverbs of Solomon:

A wise son brings joy to his father,
  but a foolish son grief to his mother.
2 Ill-gotten treasures are of no value,
  but righteousness delivers from death.
3 The LORD does not let the righteous go
    hungry
  but he thwarts the craving of the wicked.
4 Lazy hands make a man poor,
  but diligent hands bring wealth.

THE MESSAGE

9.7-12 If you reason with an arrogant cynic, you'll get
    slapped in the face;
  confront bad behavior and get a kick in the
    shins.
So don't waste your time on a scoffer;
  all you'll get for your pains is abuse.
But if you correct those who care about life,
  that's different—they'll love you for it!
Save your breath for the wise—they'll be wiser
    for it;
  tell good people what you know—they'll
    profit from it.
Skilled living gets its start in the Fear-of-GOD,
  insight into life from knowing a Holy God.
It's through me, Lady Wisdom, that your life
    deepens,
  and the years of your life ripen.
Live wisely and wisdom will permeate your
    life;
  mock life and life will mock you.

MADAME WHORE CALLS OUT, TOO

9.13-18 Then there's this other woman, Madame
    Whore—
  brazen, empty-headed, frivolous.
She sits on the front porch
  of her house on Main Street,
And as people walk by minding
  their own business, calls out,
"Are you confused about life, don't know
    what's going on?
  Steal off with me, I'll show you a good
    time!
No one will ever know—I'll give you the
    time of your life."
But they don't know about all the skeletons in
    her closet,
  that all her guests end up in hell.

THE WISE SAYINGS OF SOLOMON

AN HONEST LIFE IS IMMORTAL

10.1 **10** Wise son, glad father;
    stupid son, sad mother.

10.2 Ill-gotten gain gets you nowhere;
  an honest life is immortal.

10.3 GOD won't starve an honest soul,
  but he frustrates the appetites of the wicked.

10.4 Sloth makes you poor;
  diligence brings wealth.

a 18 Hebrew *Sheol*

NEW INTERNATIONAL VERSION

⁵He who gathers crops in summer is a wise son,
  but he who sleeps during harvest is a
    disgraceful son.

⁶Blessings crown the head of the righteous,
  but violence overwhelms the mouth of
    the wicked.ᵃ

⁷The memory of the righteous will be a
    blessing,
  but the name of the wicked will rot.

⁸The wise in heart accept commands,
  but a chattering fool comes to ruin.

⁹The man of integrity walks securely,
  but he who takes crooked paths will be
    found out.

¹⁰He who winks maliciously causes grief,
  and a chattering fool comes to ruin.

¹¹The mouth of the righteous is a fountain of
    life,
  but violence overwhelms the mouth of
    the wicked.

¹²Hatred stirs up dissension,
  but love covers over all wrongs.

¹³Wisdom is found on the lips of the
    discerning,
  but a rod is for the back of him who lacks
    judgment.

¹⁴Wise men store up knowledge,
  but the mouth of a fool invites ruin.

¹⁵The wealth of the rich is their fortified city,
  but poverty is the ruin of the poor.

¹⁶The wages of the righteous bring them life,
  but the income of the wicked brings them
    punishment.

¹⁷He who heeds discipline shows the way to
    life,
  but whoever ignores correction leads
    others astray.

¹⁸He who conceals his hatred has lying lips,
  and whoever spreads slander is a fool.

¹⁹When words are many, sin is not absent,
  but he who holds his tongue is wise.

²⁰The tongue of the righteous is choice silver,
  but the heart of the wicked is of little
    value.

²¹The lips of the righteous nourish many,
  but fools die for lack of judgment.

THE MESSAGE

10.5 Make hay while the sun shines—that's smart;
    go fishing during harvest—that's stupid.

10.6 Blessings accrue on a good and honest life,
    but the mouth of the wicked is a dark cave
      of abuse.

10.7 A good and honest life is a blessed memorial;
    a wicked life leaves a rotten stench.

10.8 A wise heart takes orders;
    an empty head will come unglued.

10.9 Honesty lives confident and carefree,
    but Shifty is sure to be exposed.

10.10 An evasive eye is a sign of trouble ahead,
    but an open, face-to-face meeting results in
      peace.

10.11 The mouth of a good person is a deep, life-
      giving well,
    but the mouth of the wicked is a dark cave
      of abuse.

10.12 Hatred starts fights,
    but love pulls a quilt over the bickering.

10.13 You'll find wisdom on the lips of a person of
      insight,
    but the shortsighted needs a slap in the
      face.

10.14 The wise accumulate knowledge—a true
      treasure;
    know-it-alls talk too much—a sheer waste.

THE ROAD TO LIFE IS A DISCIPLINED LIFE

10.15 The wealth of the rich is their bastion;
    the poverty of the indigent is their ruin.

10.16 The wage of a good person is exuberant life;
    an evil person ends up with nothing but
      sin.

10.17 The road to life is a disciplined life;
    ignore correction and you're lost for good.

10.18 Liars secretly hoard hatred;
    fools openly spread slander.

10.19 The more talk, the less truth;
    the wise measure their words.

10.20 The speech of a good person is worth waiting
      for;
    the blabber of the wicked is worthless.

10.21 The talk of a good person is rich fare for
      many,
    but chatterboxes die of an empty heart.

ᵃ 6 Or *but the mouth of the wicked conceals violence*; also in
verse 11

NEW INTERNATIONAL VERSION

22 The blessing of the LORD brings wealth,
and he adds no trouble to it.

23 A fool finds pleasure in evil conduct,
but a man of understanding delights in
wisdom.

24 What the wicked dreads will overtake him;
what the righteous desire will be granted.

25 When the storm has swept by, the wicked are
gone,
but the righteous stand firm forever.

26 As vinegar to the teeth and smoke to the eyes,
so is a sluggard to those who send him.

27 The fear of the LORD adds length to life,
but the years of the wicked are cut short.

28 The prospect of the righteous is joy,
but the hopes of the wicked come to
nothing.

29 The way of the LORD is a refuge for the
righteous,
but it is the ruin of those who do evil.

30 The righteous will never be uprooted,
but the wicked will not remain in the land.

31 The mouth of the righteous brings forth
wisdom,
but a perverse tongue will be cut out.

32 The lips of the righteous know what is
fitting,
but the mouth of the wicked only what is
perverse.

11 The LORD abhors dishonest scales,
but accurate weights are his delight.

2 When pride comes, then comes disgrace,
but with humility comes wisdom.

3 The integrity of the upright guides them,
but the unfaithful are destroyed by their
duplicity.

4 Wealth is worthless in the day of wrath,
but righteousness delivers from death.

5 The righteousness of the blameless makes a
straight way for them,
but the wicked are brought down by their
own wickedness.

6 The righteousness of the upright delivers
them,
but the unfaithful are trapped by evil
desires.

THE MESSAGE

FEAR-OF-GOD EXPANDS YOUR LIFE

10.22 GOD's blessing makes life rich;
nothing we do can improve on God.

10.23 An empty-head thinks mischief is fun,
but a mindful person relishes wisdom.

10.24 The nightmares of the wicked come true;
what the good people desire, they get.

10.25 When the storm is over, there's nothing left of
the wicked;
good people, firm on their rock foundation,
aren't even fazed.

10.26 A lazy employee will give you nothing but
trouble;
it's vinegar in the mouth, smoke in the
eyes.

10.27 The Fear-of-GOD expands your life;
a wicked life is a puny life.

10.28 The aspirations of good people end in
celebration;
the ambitions of bad people crash.

10.29 GOD is solid backing to a well-lived life,
but he calls into question a shabby
performance.

10.30 Good people *last*—they can't be moved;
the wicked are here today, gone tomorrow.

10.31 A good person's mouth is a clear fountain of
wisdom;
a foul mouth is a stagnant swamp.

10.32 The speech of a good person clears the air;
the words of the wicked pollute it.

WITHOUT GOOD DIRECTION, PEOPLE LOSE THEIR WAY

11.1 GOD hates cheating in the marketplace;
he loves it when business is aboveboard.

11.2 The stuck-up fall flat on their faces,
but down-to-earth people stand firm.

11.3 The integrity of the honest keeps them on
track;
the deviousness of crooks brings them to
ruin.

11.4 A thick bankroll is no help when life falls
apart,
but a principled life can stand up to the
worst.

11.5 Moral character makes for smooth traveling;
an evil life is a hard life.

11.6 Good character is the best insurance;
crooks get trapped in their sinful lust.

NEW INTERNATIONAL VERSION

⁷ When a wicked man dies, his hope perishes;
    all he expected from his power comes to
      nothing.

⁸ The righteous man is rescued from trouble,
    and it comes on the wicked instead.

⁹ With his mouth the godless destroys his
      neighbor,
    but through knowledge the righteous
      escape.

¹⁰ When the righteous prosper, the city
      rejoices;
    when the wicked perish, there are shouts
      of joy.

¹¹ Through the blessing of the upright a city is
      exalted,
    but by the mouth of the wicked it is
      destroyed.

¹² A man who lacks judgment derides his
      neighbor,
    but a man of understanding holds his
      tongue.

¹³ A gossip betrays a confidence,
    but a trustworthy man keeps a secret.

¹⁴ For lack of guidance a nation falls,
    but many advisers make victory sure.

¹⁵ He who puts up security for another will
      surely suffer,
    but whoever refuses to strike hands in
      pledge is safe.

¹⁶ A kindhearted woman gains respect,
    but ruthless men gain only wealth.

¹⁷ A kind man benefits himself,
    but a cruel man brings trouble on himself.

¹⁸ The wicked man earns deceptive wages,
    but he who sows righteousness reaps a
      sure reward.

¹⁹ The truly righteous man attains life,
    but he who pursues evil goes to his death.

²⁰ The LORD detests men of perverse heart
    but he delights in those whose ways are
      blameless.

²¹ Be sure of this: The wicked will not go
      unpunished,
    but those who are righteous will go free.

²² Like a gold ring in a pig's snout
    is a beautiful woman who shows no
      discretion.

THE MESSAGE

11.7 When the wicked die, that's it—
    the story's over, end of hope.

11.8 A good person is saved from much trouble;
    a bad person runs straight into it.

11.9 The loose tongue of the godless spreads
      destruction;
    the common sense of the godly preserves
      them.

11.10 When it goes well for good people, the whole
      town cheers;
    when it goes badly for bad people, the town
      celebrates.

11.11 When right-living people bless the city, it
      flourishes;
    evil talk turns it into a ghost town in no
      time.

11.12 Mean-spirited slander is heartless;
    quiet discretion accompanies good sense.

11.13 A gadabout gossip can't be trusted with a
      secret,
    but someone of integrity won't violate a
      confidence.

11.14 Without good direction, people lose their way;
    the more wise counsel you follow, the
      better your chances.

11.15 Whoever makes deals with strangers is sure to
      get burned;
    if you keep a cool head, you'll avoid rash
      bargains.

11.16 A woman of gentle grace gets respect,
    but men of rough violence grab for loot.

A GOD-SHAPED LIFE

11.17 When you're kind to others, you help
      yourself;
    when you're cruel to others, you hurt
      yourself.

11.18 Bad work gets paid with a bad check;
    good work gets solid pay.

11.19 Take your stand with God's loyal community
      and live,
    or chase after phantoms of evil and die.

11.20 GOD can't stand deceivers,
    but oh how he relishes integrity.

11.21 Count on this: The wicked won't get off scot-
      free,
    and God's loyal people will triumph.

11.22 Like a gold ring in a pig's snout
    is a beautiful face on an empty head.

NEW INTERNATIONAL VERSION

23 The desire of the righteous ends only in
      good,
    but the hope of the wicked only in wrath.

24 One man gives freely, yet gains even more;
    another withholds unduly, but comes to
      poverty.

25 A generous man will prosper;
    he who refreshes others will himself be
      refreshed.

26 People curse the man who hoards grain,
    but blessing crowns him who is willing to
      sell.

27 He who seeks good finds goodwill,
    but evil comes to him who searches for it.

28 Whoever trusts in his riches will fall,
    but the righteous will thrive like a green
      leaf.

29 He who brings trouble on his family will
      inherit only wind,
    and the fool will be servant to the wise.

30 The fruit of the righteous is a tree of life,
    and he who wins souls is wise.

31 If the righteous receive their due on earth,
    how much more the ungodly and the
      sinner!

12 Whoever loves discipline loves
      knowledge,
    but he who hates correction is stupid.

2 A good man obtains favor from the Lord,
    but the Lord condemns a crafty man.

3 A man cannot be established through
      wickedness,
    but the righteous cannot be uprooted.

4 A wife of noble character is her husband's
      crown,
    but a disgraceful wife is like decay in his
      bones.

5 The plans of the righteous are just,
    but the advice of the wicked is deceitful.

6 The words of the wicked lie in wait for
      blood,
    but the speech of the upright rescues
      them.

7 Wicked men are overthrown and are no
      more,
    but the house of the righteous stands
      firm.

THE MESSAGE

11.23 The desires of good people lead straight to the
      best,
    but wicked ambition ends in angry
      frustration.

11.24 The world of the generous gets larger and
      larger;
    the world of the stingy gets smaller and
      smaller.

11.25 The one who blesses others is abundantly
      blessed;
    those who help others are helped.

11.26 Curses on those who drive a hard bargain!
    Blessings on all who play fair and square!

11.27 The one who seeks good finds delight;
    the student of evil becomes evil.

11.28 A life devoted to things is a dead life, a stump;
    a God-shaped life is a flourishing tree.

11.29 Exploit or abuse your family, and end up with
      a fistful of air;
    common sense tells you it's a stupid way to
      live.

11.30 A good life is a fruit-bearing tree;
    a violent life destroys souls.

11.31 If good people barely make it,
    what's in store for the bad!

IF YOU LOVE LEARNING

12.1 **12** If you love learning, you love the
      discipline that goes with it—
    how shortsighted to refuse correction!

12.2 A good person basks in the delight of God,
    and he wants nothing to do with devious
      schemers.

12.3 You can't find firm footing in a swamp,
    but life rooted in God stands firm.

12.4 A hearty wife invigorates her husband,
    but a frigid woman is cancer in the bones.

12.5 The thinking of principled people makes for
      justice;
    the plots of degenerates corrupt.

12.6 The words of the wicked kill;
    the speech of the upright saves.

12.7 Wicked people fall to pieces—there's nothing
      to them;
    the homes of good people hold together.

NEW INTERNATIONAL VERSION

⁸A man is praised according to his wisdom,
but men with warped minds are despised.

⁹Better to be a nobody and yet have a servant
than pretend to be somebody and have no
food.

¹⁰A righteous man cares for the needs of his
animal,
but the kindest acts of the wicked are
cruel.

¹¹He who works his land will have abundant
food,
but he who chases fantasies lacks
judgment.

¹²The wicked desire the plunder of evil men,
but the root of the righteous flourishes.

¹³An evil man is trapped by his sinful talk,
but a righteous man escapes trouble.

¹⁴From the fruit of his lips a man is filled with
good things
as surely as the work of his hands rewards
him.

¹⁵The way of a fool seems right to him,
but a wise man listens to advice.

¹⁶A fool shows his annoyance at once,
but a prudent man overlooks an insult.

¹⁷A truthful witness gives honest testimony,
but a false witness tells lies.

¹⁸Reckless words pierce like a sword,
but the tongue of the wise brings healing.

¹⁹Truthful lips endure forever,
but a lying tongue lasts only a moment.

²⁰There is deceit in the hearts of those who
plot evil,
but joy for those who promote peace.

²¹No harm befalls the righteous,
but the wicked have their fill of trouble.

²²The LORD detests lying lips,
but he delights in men who are truthful.

²³A prudent man keeps his knowledge to
himself,
but the heart of fools blurts out folly.

²⁴Diligent hands will rule,
but laziness ends in slave labor.

²⁵An anxious heart weighs a man down,
but a kind word cheers him up.

²⁶A righteous man is cautious in friendship,ᵃ

ᵃ 26 Or *man is a guide to his neighbor*

THE MESSAGE

12.8 A person who talks sense is honored;
airheads are held in contempt.

12.9 Better to be ordinary and work for a living
than act important and starve in the
process.

12.10 Good people are good to their animals;
the "good-hearted" bad people kick and
abuse them.

12.11 The one who stays on the job has food on the
table;
the witless chase whims and fancies.

12.12 What the wicked construct finally falls into
ruin,
while the roots of the righteous give life,
and more life.

WISE PEOPLE TAKE ADVICE

12.13 The gossip of bad people gets them in trouble;
the conversation of good people keeps
them out of it.

12.14 Well-spoken words bring satisfaction;
well-done work has its own reward.

12.15 Fools are headstrong and do what they like;
wise people take advice.

12.16 Fools have short fuses and explode all too
quickly;
the prudent quietly shrug off insults.

12.17 Truthful witness by a good person clears the
air,
but liars lay down a smoke screen of deceit.

12.18 Rash language cuts and maims,
but there is healing in the words of the
wise.

12.19 Truth lasts;
lies are here today, gone tomorrow.

12.20 Evil scheming distorts the schemer;
peace-planning brings joy to the planner.

12.21 No evil can overwhelm a good person,
but the wicked have their hands full of it.

12.22 God can't stomach liars;
he loves the company of those who keep
their word.

12.23 Prudent people don't flaunt their knowledge;
talkative fools broadcast their silliness.

12.24 The diligent find freedom in their work;
the lazy are oppressed by work.

12.25 Worry weighs us down;
a cheerful word picks us up.

12.26 A good person survives misfortune,

NEW INTERNATIONAL VERSION

but the way of the wicked leads them
astray.

²⁷ The lazy man does not roast ᵃ his game,
but the diligent man prizes his possessions.

²⁸ In the way of righteousness there is life;
along that path is immortality.

13 A wise son heeds his father's instruction,
but a mocker does not listen to rebuke.

² From the fruit of his lips a man enjoys good
things,
but the unfaithful have a craving for
violence.

³ He who guards his lips guards his life,
but he who speaks rashly will come to
ruin.

⁴ The sluggard craves and gets nothing,
but the desires of the diligent are fully
satisfied.

⁵ The righteous hate what is false,
but the wicked bring shame and disgrace.

⁶ Righteousness guards the man of integrity,
but wickedness overthrows the sinner.

⁷ One man pretends to be rich, yet has
nothing;
another pretends to be poor, yet has great
wealth.

⁸ A man's riches may ransom his life,
but a poor man hears no threat.

⁹ The light of the righteous shines brightly,
but the lamp of the wicked is snuffed out.

¹⁰ Pride only breeds quarrels,
but wisdom is found in those who take
advice.

¹¹ Dishonest money dwindles away,
but he who gathers money little by little
makes it grow.

¹² Hope deferred makes the heart sick,
but a longing fulfilled is a tree of life.

¹³ He who scorns instruction will pay for it,
but he who respects a command is
rewarded.

¹⁴ The teaching of the wise is a fountain of life,
turning a man from the snares of death.

¹⁵ Good understanding wins favor,
but the way of the unfaithful is hard. ᵇ

ᵃ 27 The meaning of the Hebrew for this word is uncertain.
ᵇ 15 Or *unfaithful does not endure*

THE MESSAGE

but a wicked life invites disaster.

12.27 A lazy life is an empty life,
but "early to rise" gets the job done.

12.28 Good men and women travel right into life;
sin's detours take you straight to hell.

WALK WITH THE WISE

13.1 **13** Intelligent children listen to their
parents;
foolish children do their own thing.

13.2 The good acquire a taste for helpful
conversation;
bullies push and shove their way through
life.

13.3 Careful words make for a careful life;
careless talk may ruin everything.

13.4 Indolence wants it all and gets nothing;
the energetic have something to show for
their lives.

13.5 A good person hates false talk;
a bad person wallows in gibberish.

13.6 A God-loyal life keeps you on track;
sin dumps the wicked in the ditch.

13.7 A pretentious, showy life is an empty life;
a plain and simple life is a full life.

13.8 The rich can be sued for everything they have,
but the poor are free of such threats.

13.9 The lives of good people are brightly lit
streets;
the lives of the wicked are dark alleys.

13.10 Arrogant know-it-alls stir up discord,
but wise men and women listen to each
other's counsel.

13.11 Easy come, easy go,
but steady diligence pays off.

13.12 Unrelenting disappointment leaves you
heartsick,
but a sudden good break can turn life
around.

13.13 Ignore the Word and suffer;
honor God's commands and grow rich.

13.14 The teaching of the wise is a fountain of life,
so, no more drinking from death-tainted
wells!

13.15 Sound thinking makes for gracious living,
but liars walk a rough road.

NEW INTERNATIONAL VERSION

¹⁶Every prudent man acts out of knowledge,
　　but a fool exposes his folly.

¹⁷A wicked messenger falls into trouble,
　　but a trustworthy envoy brings healing.

¹⁸He who ignores discipline comes to poverty
　　and shame,
　　but whoever heeds correction is honored.

¹⁹A longing fulfilled is sweet to the soul,
　　but fools detest turning from evil.

²⁰He who walks with the wise grows wise,
　　but a companion of fools suffers harm.

²¹Misfortune pursues the sinner,
　　but prosperity is the reward of the
　　righteous.

²²A good man leaves an inheritance for his
　　children's children,
　　but a sinner's wealth is stored up for the
　　righteous.

²³A poor man's field may produce abundant
　　food,
　　but injustice sweeps it away.

²⁴He who spares the rod hates his son,
　　but he who loves him is careful to
　　discipline him.

²⁵The righteous eat to their hearts' content,
　　but the stomach of the wicked goes
　　hungry.

14 The wise woman builds her house,
　　but with her own hands the foolish one
　　tears hers down.

²He whose walk is upright fears the LORD,
　　but he whose ways are devious despises
　　him.

³A fool's talk brings a rod to his back,
　　but the lips of the wise protect them.

⁴Where there are no oxen, the manger is
　　empty,
　　but from the strength of an ox comes an
　　abundant harvest.

⁵A truthful witness does not deceive,
　　but a false witness pours out lies.

⁶The mocker seeks wisdom and finds none,
　　but knowledge comes easily to the
　　discerning.

⁷Stay away from a foolish man,
　　for you will not find knowledge on his
　　lips.

THE MESSAGE

13.16 A commonsense person *lives* good sense;
　　fools litter the country with silliness.

13.17 Irresponsible talk makes a real mess of things,
　　but a reliable reporter is a healing presence.

13.18 Refuse discipline and end up homeless;
　　embrace correction and live an honored
　　life.

13.19 Souls who follow their hearts thrive;
　　fools bent on evil despise matters of soul.

13.20 Become wise by walking with the wise;
　　hang out with fools and watch your life fall
　　to pieces.

13.21 Disaster entraps sinners,
　　but God-loyal people get a good life.

13.22 A good life gets passed on to the
　　grandchildren;
　　ill-gotten wealth ends up with good people.

13.23 Banks foreclose on the farms of the poor,
　　or else the poor lose their shirts to crooked
　　lawyers.

13.24 A refusal to correct is a refusal to love;
　　love your children by disciplining them.

13.25 An appetite for good brings much satisfaction,
　　but the belly of the wicked always wants
　　more.

A WAY THAT LEADS TO HELL

14.1 **14** Lady Wisdom builds a lovely home;
　　Sir Fool comes along and tears it down
　　brick by brick.

14.2 An honest life shows respect for GOD;
　　a degenerate life is a slap in his face.

14.3 Frivolous talk provokes a derisive smile;
　　wise speech evokes nothing but respect.

14.4 No cattle, no crops;
　　a good harvest requires a strong ox for the
　　plow.

14.5 A true witness never lies;
　　a false witness makes a business of it.

14.6 Cynics look high and low for wisdom—and
　　never find it;
　　the open-minded find it right on their
　　doorstep!

14.7 Escape quickly from the company of fools;
　　they're a waste of your time, a waste of
　　your words.

NEW INTERNATIONAL VERSION

8 The wisdom of the prudent is to give
thought to their ways,
but the folly of fools is deception.

9 Fools mock at making amends for sin,
but goodwill is found among the upright.

10 Each heart knows its own bitterness,
and no one else can share its joy.

11 The house of the wicked will be destroyed,
but the tent of the upright will flourish.

12 There is a way that seems right to a man,
but in the end it leads to death.

13 Even in laughter the heart may ache,
and joy may end in grief.

14 The faithless will be fully repaid for their
ways,
and the good man rewarded for his.

15 A simple man believes anything,
but a prudent man gives thought to his
steps.

16 A wise man fears the LORD and shuns evil,
but a fool is hotheaded and reckless.

17 A quick-tempered man does foolish things,
and a crafty man is hated.

18 The simple inherit folly,
but the prudent are crowned with
knowledge.

19 Evil men will bow down in the presence of
the good,
and the wicked at the gates of the
righteous.

20 The poor are shunned even by their
neighbors,
but the rich have many friends.

21 He who despises his neighbor sins,
but blessed is he who is kind to the needy.

22 Do not those who plot evil go astray?
But those who plan what is good find*a*
love and faithfulness.

23 All hard work brings a profit,
but mere talk leads only to poverty.

24 The wealth of the wise is their crown,
but the folly of fools yields folly.

25 A truthful witness saves lives,
but a false witness is deceitful.

26 He who fears the LORD has a secure fortress,
and for his children it will be a refuge.

a 22 Or show

THE MESSAGE

14.8 The wisdom of the wise keeps life on track;
the foolishness of fools lands them in the
ditch.

14.9 The stupid ridicule right and wrong,
but a moral life is a favored life.

14.10 The person who shuns the bitter moments of
friends
will be an outsider at their celebrations.

14.11 Lives of careless wrongdoing are tumbledown
shacks;
holy living builds soaring cathedrals.

14.12-13 There's a way of life that looks harmless
enough;
look again—it leads straight to hell.
Sure, those people appear to be having a good
time,
but all that laughter will end in heartbreak.

SIFT AND WEIGH EVERY WORD

14.14 A mean person gets paid back in meanness,
a gracious person in grace.

14.15 The gullible believe anything they're told;
the prudent sift and weigh every word.

14.16 The wise watch their steps and avoid evil;
fools are headstrong and reckless.

14.17 The hotheaded do things they'll later regret;
the coldhearted get the cold shoulder.

14.18 Foolish dreamers live in a world of illusion;
wise realists plant their feet on the ground.

14.19 Eventually, evil will pay tribute to good;
the wicked will respect God-loyal people.

14.20 An unlucky loser is shunned by all,
but everyone loves a winner.

14.21 It's criminal to ignore a neighbor in need,
but compassion for the poor—what a
blessing!

14.22 Isn't it obvious that conspirators lose out,
while the thoughtful win love and trust?

14.23 Hard work always pays off;
mere talk puts no bread on the table.

14.24 The wise accumulate wisdom;
fools get stupider by the day.

14.25 Souls are saved by truthful witness
and betrayed by the spread of lies.

14.26 The Fear-of-GOD builds up confidence,
and makes a world safe for your children.

NEW INTERNATIONAL VERSION

²⁷The fear of the LORD is a fountain of life,
   turning a man from the snares of death.

²⁸A large population is a king's glory,
   but without subjects a prince is ruined.

²⁹A patient man has great understanding,
   but a quick-tempered man displays folly.

³⁰A heart at peace gives life to the body,
   but envy rots the bones.

³¹He who oppresses the poor shows contempt
   for their Maker,
   but whoever is kind to the needy honors
   God.

³²When calamity comes, the wicked are
   brought down,
   but even in death the righteous have a
   refuge.

³³Wisdom reposes in the heart of the
   discerning
   and even among fools she lets herself be
   known. *a*

³⁴Righteousness exalts a nation,
   but sin is a disgrace to any people.

³⁵A king delights in a wise servant,
   but a shameful servant incurs his wrath.

15 A gentle answer turns away wrath,
   but a harsh word stirs up anger.

²The tongue of the wise commends
   knowledge,
   but the mouth of the fool gushes folly.

³The eyes of the LORD are everywhere,
   keeping watch on the wicked and the
   good.

⁴The tongue that brings healing is a tree of
   life,
   but a deceitful tongue crushes the spirit.

⁵A fool spurns his father's discipline,
   but whoever heeds correction shows
   prudence.

⁶The house of the righteous contains great
   treasure,
   but the income of the wicked brings them
   trouble.

⁷The lips of the wise spread knowledge;
   not so the hearts of fools.

*a 33 Hebrew; Septuagint and Syriac / but in the heart of fools
she is not known*

THE MESSAGE

14.27 The Fear-of-God is a spring of living water
   so you won't go off drinking from poisoned
   wells.

14.28 The mark of a good leader is loyal followers;
   leadership is nothing without a following.

14.29 Slowness to anger makes for deep
   understanding;
   a quick-tempered person stockpiles
   stupidity.

14.30 A sound mind makes for a robust body,
   but runaway emotions corrode the bones.

14.31 You insult your Maker when you exploit the
   powerless;
   when you're kind to the poor, you honor
   God.

14.32 The evil of bad people leaves them out in the
   cold;
   the integrity of good people creates a safe
   place for living.

14.33 Lady Wisdom is at home in an understanding
   heart—
   fools never even get to say hello.

14.34 God-devotion makes a country strong;
   God-avoidance leaves people weak.

14.35 Diligent work gets a warm commendation;
   shiftless work earns an angry rebuke.

GOD DOESN'T MISS A THING

15.1 **15** A gentle response defuses anger,
   but a sharp tongue kindles a
   temper-fire.

15.2 Knowledge flows like spring water from the
   wise;
   fools are leaky faucets, dripping nonsense.

15.3 GOD doesn't miss a thing—
   he's alert to good and evil alike.

15.4 Kind words heal and help;
   cutting words wound and maim.

15.5 Moral dropouts won't listen to their elders;
   welcoming correction is a mark of good
   sense.

15.6 The lives of God-loyal people flourish;
   a misspent life is soon bankrupt.

15.7 Perceptive words spread knowledge;
   fools are hollow—there's nothing to them.

NEW INTERNATIONAL VERSION

⁸ The LORD detests the sacrifice of the wicked,
   but the prayer of the upright pleases him.

⁹ The LORD detests the way of the wicked
   but he loves those who pursue
      righteousness.

¹⁰ Stern discipline awaits him who leaves the
      path;
   he who hates correction will die.

¹¹ Death and Destruction *ᵃ* lie open before the
      LORD—
   how much more the hearts of men!

¹² A mocker resents correction;
   he will not consult the wise.

¹³ A happy heart makes the face cheerful,
   but heartache crushes the spirit.

¹⁴ The discerning heart seeks knowledge,
   but the mouth of a fool feeds on folly.

¹⁵ All the days of the oppressed are wretched,
   but the cheerful heart has a continual
      feast.

¹⁶ Better a little with the fear of the LORD
   than great wealth with turmoil.

¹⁷ Better a meal of vegetables where there is
      love
   than a fattened calf with hatred.

¹⁸ A hot-tempered man stirs up dissension,
   but a patient man calms a quarrel.

¹⁹ The way of the sluggard is blocked with
      thorns,
   but the path of the upright is a highway.

²⁰ A wise son brings joy to his father,
   but a foolish man despises his mother.

²¹ Folly delights a man who lacks judgment,
   but a man of understanding keeps a
      straight course.

²² Plans fail for lack of counsel,
   but with many advisers they succeed.

²³ A man finds joy in giving an apt reply—
   and how good is a timely word!

²⁴ The path of life leads upward for the wise
   to keep him from going down to the
      grave. *ᵇ*

THE MESSAGE

15.8 GOD can't stand pious poses,
   but he delights in genuine prayers.

15.9 A life frittered away disgusts GOD;
   he loves those who run straight for the
      finish line.

15.10 It's a school of hard knocks for those who
      leave God's path,
   a dead-end street for those who hate God's
      rules.

15.11 Even hell holds no secrets from GOD—
   do you think he can't read human hearts?

LIFE ASCENDS TO THE HEIGHTS

15.12 Know-it-alls don't like being told what to do;
   they avoid the company of wise men and
      women.

15.13 A cheerful heart brings a smile to your face;
   a sad heart makes it hard to get through the
      day.

15.14 An intelligent person is always eager to take
      in more truth;
   fools feed on fast-food fads and fancies.

15.15 A miserable heart means a miserable life;
   a cheerful heart fills the day with song.

15.16 A simple life in the Fear-of-GOD
   is better than a rich life with a ton of
      headaches.

15.17 Better a bread crust shared in love
   than a slab of prime rib served in hate.

15.18 Hot tempers start fights;
   a calm, cool spirit keeps the peace.

15.19 The path of lazy people is overgrown with
      briers;
   the diligent walk down a smooth road.

15.20 Intelligent children make their parents proud;
   lazy students embarrass their parents.

15.21 The empty-headed treat life as a plaything;
   the perceptive grasp its meaning and make
      a go of it.

15.22 Refuse good advice and watch your plans fail;
   take good counsel and watch them
      succeed.

15.23 Congenial conversation—what a pleasure!
   The right word at the right time—
      beautiful!

15.24 Life ascends to the heights for the
      thoughtful—
   it's a clean about-face from descent into
      hell.

ᵃ 11 Hebrew *Sheol* and *Abaddon*   *ᵇ 24* Hebrew *Sheol*

NEW INTERNATIONAL VERSION	THE MESSAGE

NEW INTERNATIONAL VERSION

[25] The Lord tears down the proud man's house
  but he keeps the widow's boundaries
    intact.

[26] The Lord detests the thoughts of the wicked,
  but those of the pure are pleasing to him.

[27] A greedy man brings trouble to his family,
  but he who hates bribes will live.

[28] The heart of the righteous weighs its
    answers,
  but the mouth of the wicked gushes evil.

[29] The Lord is far from the wicked
  but he hears the prayer of the righteous.

[30] A cheerful look brings joy to the heart,
  and good news gives health to the bones.

[31] He who listens to a life-giving rebuke
  will be at home among the wise.

[32] He who ignores discipline despises himself,
  but whoever heeds correction gains
    understanding.

[33] The fear of the Lord teaches a man wisdom,[a]
  and humility comes before honor.

16 To man belong the plans of the heart,
  but from the Lord comes the reply of
    the tongue.

[2] All a man's ways seem innocent to him,
  but motives are weighed by the Lord.

[3] Commit to the Lord whatever you do,
  and your plans will succeed.

[4] The Lord works out everything for his own
    ends—
  even the wicked for a day of disaster.

[5] The Lord detests all the proud of heart.
  Be sure of this: They will not go
    unpunished.

[6] Through love and faithfulness sin is atoned
    for;
  through the fear of the Lord a man avoids
    evil.

[7] When a man's ways are pleasing to the Lord,
  he makes even his enemies live at peace
    with him.

THE MESSAGE

15.25 God smashes the pretensions of the arrogant;
  he stands with those who have no standing.

15.26 God can't stand evil scheming,
  but he puts words of grace and beauty on
    display.

15.27 A greedy and grasping person destroys
    community;
  those who refuse to exploit live and let live.

15.28 Prayerful answers come from God-loyal
    people;
  the wicked are sewers of abuse.

15.29 God keeps his distance from the wicked;
  he closely attends to the prayers of God-
    loyal people.

15.30 A twinkle in the eye means joy in the heart,
  and good news makes you feel fit as a
    fiddle.

15.31 Listen to good advice if you want to live well,
  an honored guest among wise men and
    women.

15.32 An undisciplined, self-willed life is puny;
  an obedient, God-willed life is spacious.

15.33 Fear-of-God is a school in skilled living—
  first you learn humility, then you
    experience glory.

EVERYTHING WITH A PLACE AND A PURPOSE

16.1 **16** Mortals make elaborate plans,
  but God has the last word.

16.2 Humans are satisfied with whatever looks
    good;
  God probes for what *is* good.

16.3 Put God in charge of your work,
  then what you've planned will take place.

16.4 God made everything with a place and
    purpose;
  even the wicked are included—but for
    judgment.

16.5 God can't stomach arrogance or pretense;
  believe me, he'll put those upstarts in their
    place.

16.6 Guilt is banished through love and truth;
  Fear-of-God deflects evil.

16.7 When God approves of your life,
  even your enemies will end up shaking
    your hand.

---

[a] 33 Or *Wisdom teaches the fear of the Lord*

NEW INTERNATIONAL VERSION	THE MESSAGE

NEW INTERNATIONAL VERSION

8 Better a little with righteousness
  than much gain with injustice.

9 In his heart a man plans his course,
  but the LORD determines his steps.

10 The lips of a king speak as an oracle,
  and his mouth should not betray justice.

11 Honest scales and balances are from the
  LORD;
  all the weights in the bag are of his
  making.

12 Kings detest wrongdoing,
  for a throne is established through
  righteousness.

13 Kings take pleasure in honest lips;
  they value a man who speaks the truth.

14 A king's wrath is a messenger of death,
  but a wise man will appease it.

15 When a king's face brightens, it means life;
  his favor is like a rain cloud in spring.

16 How much better to get wisdom than gold,
  to choose understanding rather than
  silver!

17 The highway of the upright avoids evil;
  he who guards his way guards his life.

18 Pride goes before destruction,
  a haughty spirit before a fall.

19 Better to be lowly in spirit and among the
  oppressed
  than to share plunder with the proud.

20 Whoever gives heed to instruction prospers,
  and blessed is he who trusts in the LORD.

21 The wise in heart are called discerning,
  and pleasant words promote instruction. *a*

22 Understanding is a fountain of life to those
  who have it,
  but folly brings punishment to fools.

23 A wise man's heart guides his mouth,
  and his lips promote instruction. *b*

24 Pleasant words are a honeycomb,
  sweet to the soul and healing to the
  bones.

25 There is a way that seems right to a man,
  but in the end it leads to death.

26 The laborer's appetite works for him;
  his hunger drives him on.

THE MESSAGE

16.8 Far better to be right and poor
  than to be wrong and rich.

16.9 We plan the way we want to live,
  but only GOD makes us able to live it.

IT PAYS TO TAKE LIFE SERIOUSLY

16.10 A good leader motivates,
  doesn't mislead, doesn't exploit.

16.11 GOD cares about honesty in the workplace;
  your business is his business.

16.12 Good leaders abhor wrongdoing of all kinds;
  sound leadership has a moral foundation.

16.13 Good leaders cultivate honest speech;
  they love advisors who tell them the truth.

16.14 An intemperate leader wreaks havoc in lives;
  you're smart to stay clear of someone like
  that.

16.15 Good-tempered leaders invigorate lives;
  they're like spring rain and sunshine.

16.16 Get wisdom—it's worth more than money;
  choose insight over income every time.

16.17 The road of right living bypasses evil;
  watch your step and save your life.

16.18 First pride, then the crash—
  the bigger the ego, the harder the fall.

16.19 It's better to live humbly among the poor
  than to live it up among the rich and
  famous.

16.20 It pays to take life seriously;
  things work out when you trust in GOD.

16.21 A wise person gets known for insight;
  gracious words add to one's reputation.

16.22 True intelligence is a spring of fresh water,
  while fools sweat it out the hard way.

16.23 They make a lot of sense, these wise folks;
  whenever they speak, their reputation
  increases.

16.24 Gracious speech is like clover honey—
  good taste to the soul, quick energy for the
  body.

16.25 There's a way that looks harmless enough;
  look again—it leads straight to hell.

16.26 Appetite is an incentive to work;
  hunger makes you work all the harder.

---

a 21 Or words make a man persuasive   *b 23 Or mouth / and
makes his lips persuasive*

NEW INTERNATIONAL VERSION

27 A scoundrel plots evil,
  and his speech is like a scorching fire.

28 A perverse man stirs up dissension,
  and a gossip separates close friends.

29 A violent man entices his neighbor
  and leads him down a path that is not
  good.

30 He who winks with his eye is plotting
  perversity;
  he who purses his lips is bent on evil.

31 Gray hair is a crown of splendor;
  it is attained by a righteous life.

32 Better a patient man than a warrior,
  a man who controls his temper than one
  who takes a city.

33 The lot is cast into the lap,
  but its every decision is from the LORD.

17 Better a dry crust with peace and quiet
  than a house full of feasting,*a* with strife.

2 A wise servant will rule over a disgraceful
  son,
  and will share the inheritance as one of
  the brothers.

3 The crucible for silver and the furnace for
  gold,
  but the LORD tests the heart.

4 A wicked man listens to evil lips;
  a liar pays attention to a malicious
  tongue.

5 He who mocks the poor shows contempt for
  their Maker;
  whoever gloats over disaster will not go
  unpunished.

6 Children's children are a crown to the aged,
  and parents are the pride of their children.

7 Arrogant*b* lips are unsuited to a fool—
  how much worse lying lips to a ruler!

8 A bribe is a charm to the one who gives it;
  wherever he turns, he succeeds.

9 He who covers over an offense promotes
  love,
  but whoever repeats the matter separates
  close friends.

10 A rebuke impresses a man of discernment
  more than a hundred lashes a fool.

THE MESSAGE

16.27 Mean people spread mean gossip;
  their words smart and burn.

16.28 Troublemakers start fights;
  gossips break up friendships.

16.29 Calloused climbers betray their very own
  friends;
  they'd stab their own grandmothers in the
  back.

16.30 A shifty eye betrays an evil intention;
  a clenched jaw signals trouble ahead.

16.31 Gray hair is a mark of distinction,
  the award for a God-loyal life.

16.32 Moderation is better than muscle,
  self-control better than political power.

16.33 Make your motions and cast your votes,
  but GOD has the final say.

A WHACK ON THE HEAD OF A FOOL

17.1 **17** A meal of bread and water in contented
  peace
  is better than a banquet spiced with
  quarrels.

17.2 A wise servant takes charge of an unruly child
  and is honored as one of the family.

17.3 As silver in a crucible and gold in a pan,
  so our lives are assayed by GOD.

17.4 Evil people relish malicious conversation;
  the ears of liars itch for dirty gossip.

17.5 Whoever mocks poor people, insults their
  Creator;
  gloating over misfortune is a punishable
  crime.

17.6 Old people are distinguished by
  grandchildren;
  children take pride in their parents.

17.7 We don't expect eloquence from fools,
  nor do we expect lies from our leaders.

17.8 Receiving a gift is like getting a rare gemstone;
  any way you look at it, you see beauty
  refracted.

17.9 Overlook an offense and bond a friendship;
  fasten on to a slight and—good-bye, friend!

17.10 A quiet rebuke to a person of good sense
  does more than a whack on the head of a
  fool.

a 1 Hebrew *sacrifices*   *b* 7 Or *Eloquent*

NEW INTERNATIONAL VERSION

11 An evil man is bent only on rebellion;
  a merciless official will be sent against
    him.

12 Better to meet a bear robbed of her cubs
  than a fool in his folly.

13 If a man pays back evil for good,
  evil will never leave his house.

14 Starting a quarrel is like breaching a dam;
  so drop the matter before a dispute breaks
    out.

15 Acquitting the guilty and condemning the
    innocent—
  the LORD detests them both.

16 Of what use is money in the hand of a fool,
  since he has no desire to get wisdom?

17 A friend loves at all times,
  and a brother is born for adversity.

18 A man lacking in judgment strikes hands in
    pledge
  and puts up security for his neighbor.

19 He who loves a quarrel loves sin;
  he who builds a high gate invites
    destruction.

20 A man of perverse heart does not prosper;
  he whose tongue is deceitful falls into
    trouble.

21 To have a fool for a son brings grief;
  there is no joy for the father of a fool.

22 A cheerful heart is good medicine,
  but a crushed spirit dries up the bones.

23 A wicked man accepts a bribe in secret
  to pervert the course of justice.

24 A discerning man keeps wisdom in view,
  but a fool's eyes wander to the ends of the
    earth.

25 A foolish son brings grief to his father
  and bitterness to the one who bore him.

26 It is not good to punish an innocent man,
  or to flog officials for their integrity.

27 A man of knowledge uses words with
    restraint,
  and a man of understanding is even-
    tempered.

28 Even a fool is thought wise if he keeps silent,
  and discerning if he holds his tongue.

THE MESSAGE

17.11 Criminals out looking for nothing but trouble
  won't have to wait long—they'll meet it
    coming and going!

17.12 Better to meet a grizzly robbed of her cubs
  than a fool hellbent on folly.

17.13 Those who return evil for good
  will meet their own evil returning.

17.14 The start of a quarrel is like a leak in a dam,
  so stop it before it bursts.

17.15 Whitewashing bad people and throwing mud
      on good people
  are equally abhorrent to GOD.

17.16 What's this? Fools out shopping for wisdom!
  They wouldn't recognize it if they saw it!

ONE WHO KNOWS MUCH SAYS LITTLE

17.17 Friends love through all kinds of weather,
  and families stick together in all kinds of
    trouble.

17.18 It's stupid to try to get something for nothing,
  or run up huge bills you can never pay.

17.19 The person who courts sin, marries trouble;
  build a wall, invite a burglar.

17.20 A bad motive can't achieve a good end;
  double-talk brings you double trouble.

17.21 Having a fool for a child is misery;
  it's no fun being the parent of a dolt.

17.22 A cheerful disposition is good for your health;
  gloom and doom leave you bone-tired.

17.23 The wicked take bribes under the table;
  they show nothing but contempt for
    justice.

17.24 The perceptive find wisdom in their own front
      yard;
  fools look for it everywhere but right here.

17.25 A surly, stupid child is sheer pain to a father,
  a bitter pill for a mother to swallow.

17.26 It's wrong to penalize good behavior,
  or make good citizens pay for the crimes of
    others.

17.27 The one who knows much says little;
  an understanding person remains calm.

17.28 Even dunces who keep quiet are thought to be
      wise;
  as long as they keep their mouths shut,
    they're smart.

NEW INTERNATIONAL VERSION

18 An unfriendly man pursues selfish ends;
he defies all sound judgment.

² A fool finds no pleasure in understanding
but delights in airing his own opinions.

³ When wickedness comes, so does contempt,
and with shame comes disgrace.

⁴ The words of a man's mouth are deep waters,
but the fountain of wisdom is a bubbling
brook.

⁵ It is not good to be partial to the wicked
or to deprive the innocent of justice.

⁶ A fool's lips bring him strife,
and his mouth invites a beating.

⁷ A fool's mouth is his undoing,
and his lips are a snare to his soul.

⁸ The words of a gossip are like choice morsels;
they go down to a man's inmost parts.

⁹ One who is slack in his work
is brother to one who destroys.

¹⁰ The name of the LORD is a strong tower;
the righteous run to it and are safe.

¹¹ The wealth of the rich is their fortified city;
they imagine it an unscalable wall.

¹² Before his downfall a man's heart is proud,
but humility comes before honor.

¹³ He who answers before listening—
that is his folly and his shame.

¹⁴ A man's spirit sustains him in sickness,
but a crushed spirit who can bear?

¹⁵ The heart of the discerning acquires
knowledge;
the ears of the wise seek it out.

¹⁶ A gift opens the way for the giver
and ushers him into the presence of the
great.

¹⁷ The first to present his case seems right,
till another comes forward and questions
him.

¹⁸ Casting the lot settles disputes
and keeps strong opponents apart.

¹⁹ An offended brother is more unyielding than
a fortified city,
and disputes are like the barred gates of a
citadel.

²⁰ From the fruit of his mouth a man's stomach
is filled;
with the harvest from his lips he is satisfied.

THE MESSAGE

WORDS KILL, WORDS GIVE LIFE

18.1 **18** Loners who care only for themselves
spit on the common good.

18.2 Fools care nothing for thoughtful discourse;
all they do is run off at the mouth.

18.3 When wickedness arrives, shame's not far
behind;
contempt for life is contemptible.

18.4 Many words rush along like rivers in flood,
but deep wisdom flows up from artesian
springs.

18.5 It's not right to go easy on the guilty,
or come down hard on the innocent.

18.6 The words of a fool start fights;
do him a favor and gag him.

18.7 Fools are undone by their big mouths;
their souls are crushed by their words.

18.8 Listening to gossip is like eating cheap candy;
do you really want junk like that in your
belly?

18.9 Slack habits and sloppy work
are as bad as vandalism.

18.10 GOD's name is a place of protection—
good people can run there and be safe.

18.11 The rich think their wealth protects them;
they imagine themselves safe behind it.

18.12 Pride first, then the crash,
but humility is precursor to honor.

18.13 Answering before listening
is both stupid and rude.

18.14 A healthy spirit conquers adversity,
but what can you do when the spirit is
crushed?

18.15 Wise men and women are always learning,
always listening for fresh insights.

18.16 A gift gets attention;
it buys the attention of eminent people.

18.17 The first speech in a court case is always
convincing—
until the cross-examination starts!

18.18 You may have to draw straws
when faced with a tough decision.

18.19 Do a favor and win a friend forever;
nothing can untie that bond.

18.20 Words satisfy the mind as much as fruit does
the stomach;
good talk is as gratifying as a good harvest.

NEW INTERNATIONAL VERSION

21 The tongue has the power of life and death,
and those who love it will eat its fruit.

22 He who finds a wife finds what is good
and receives favor from the LORD.

23 A poor man pleads for mercy,
but a rich man answers harshly.

24 A man of many companions may come to ruin,
but there is a friend who sticks closer
than a brother.

19 Better a poor man whose walk is
blameless
than a fool whose lips are perverse.

2 It is not good to have zeal without
knowledge,
nor to be hasty and miss the way.

3 A man's own folly ruins his life,
yet his heart rages against the LORD.

4 Wealth brings many friends,
but a poor man's friend deserts him.

5 A false witness will not go unpunished,
and he who pours out lies will not go free.

6 Many curry favor with a ruler,
and everyone is the friend of a man who
gives gifts.

7 A poor man is shunned by all his relatives—
how much more do his friends avoid him!
Though he pursues them with pleading,
they are nowhere to be found. *a*

8 He who gets wisdom loves his own soul;
he who cherishes understanding prospers.

9 A false witness will not go unpunished,
and he who pours out lies will perish.

10 It is not fitting for a fool to live in luxury—
how much worse for a slave to rule over
princes!

11 A man's wisdom gives him patience;
it is to his glory to overlook an offense.

12 A king's rage is like the roar of a lion,
but his favor is like dew on the grass.

13 A foolish son is his father's ruin,
and a quarrelsome wife is like a constant
dripping.

14 Houses and wealth are inherited from
parents,
but a prudent wife is from the LORD.

*a 7 The meaning of the Hebrew for this sentence is
uncertain.*

THE MESSAGE

18.21 Words kill, words give life;
they're either poison or fruit—you choose.

18.22 Find a good spouse, you find a good life—
and even more: the favor of GOD!

18.23 The poor speak in soft supplications;
the rich bark out answers.

18.24 Friends come and friends go,
but a true friend sticks by you like family.

IF YOU QUIT LISTENING

19.1 **19** Better to be poor and honest
than a rich person no one can trust.

19.2 Ignorant zeal is worthless;
haste makes waste.

19.3 People ruin their lives by their own stupidity,
so why does GOD always get blamed?

19.4 Wealth attracts friends as honey draws flies,
but poor people are avoided like a plague.

19.5 Perjury won't go unpunished.
Would you let a liar go free?

19.6 Lots of people flock around a generous
person;
everyone's a friend to the philanthropist.

19.7 When you're down on your luck, even your
family avoids you—
yes, even your best friends wish you'd get
lost.
If they see you coming, they look the other
way—
out of sight, out of mind.

19.8 Grow a wise heart—you'll do yourself a favor;
keep a clear head—you'll find a good life.

19.9 The person who tells lies gets caught;
the person who spreads rumors is ruined.

19.10 Blockheads shouldn't live on easy street
any more than workers should give orders
to their boss.

19.11 Smart people know how to hold their tongue;
their grandeur is to forgive and forget.

19.12 Mean-tempered leaders are like mad dogs;
the good-natured are like fresh morning
dew.

9.13 A parent is worn to a frazzle by a stupid child;
a nagging spouse is a leaky faucet.

19.14 House and land are handed down from
parents,
but a congenial spouse comes straight from
GOD.

NEW INTERNATIONAL VERSION

¹⁵ Laziness brings on deep sleep,
and the shiftless man goes hungry.

¹⁶ He who obeys instructions guards his life,
but he who is contemptuous of his ways
will die.

¹⁷ He who is kind to the poor lends to the Lord,
and he will reward him for what he has
done.

¹⁸ Discipline your son, for in that there is hope;
do not be a willing party to his death.

¹⁹ A hot-tempered man must pay the penalty;
if you rescue him, you will have to do it
again.

²⁰ Listen to advice and accept instruction,
and in the end you will be wise.

²¹ Many are the plans in a man's heart,
but it is the Lord's purpose that prevails.

²² What a man desires is unfailing love ᵃ;
better to be poor than a liar.

²³ The fear of the Lord leads to life:
Then one rests content, untouched by
trouble.

²⁴ The sluggard buries his hand in the dish;
he will not even bring it back to his mouth!

²⁵ Flog a mocker, and the simple will learn
prudence;
rebuke a discerning man, and he will gain
knowledge.

²⁶ He who robs his father and drives out his
mother
is a son who brings shame and disgrace.

²⁷ Stop listening to instruction, my son,
and you will stray from the words of
knowledge.

²⁸ A corrupt witness mocks at justice,
and the mouth of the wicked gulps down
evil.

²⁹ Penalties are prepared for mockers,
and beatings for the backs of fools.

20 Wine is a mocker and beer a brawler;
whoever is led astray by them is not
wise.

² A king's wrath is like the roar of a lion;
he who angers him forfeits his life.

³ It is to a man's honor to avoid strife,
but every fool is quick to quarrel.

ᵃ 22 Or *A man's greed is his shame*

THE MESSAGE

19.15 Life collapses on loafers;
lazybones go hungry.

19.16 Keep the rules and keep your life;
careless living kills.

19.17 Mercy to the needy is a loan to God,
and God pays back those loans in full.

19.18 Discipline your children while you still have
the chance;
indulging them destroys them.

19.19 Let angry people endure the backlash of their
own anger;
if you try to make it better, you'll only
make it worse.

19.20 Take good counsel and accept correction—
that's the way to live wisely and well.

19.21 We humans keep brainstorming options and
plans,
but God's purpose prevails.

19.22 It's only human to want to make a buck,
but it's better to be poor than a liar.

19.23 Fear-of-God is life itself,
a full life, and serene—no nasty surprises.

19.24 Some people dig a fork into the pie
but are too lazy to raise it to their mouth.

19.25 Punish the insolent—make an example of
them.
Who knows? Somebody might learn a good
lesson.

19.26 Kids who lash out against their parents
are an embarrassment and disgrace.

19.27 If you quit listening, dear child, and strike off
on your own,
you'll soon be out of your depth.

19.28 An unprincipled witness desecrates justice;
the mouths of the wicked spew malice.

19.29 The irreverent have to learn reverence the
hard way;
only a slap in the face brings fools to
attention.

DEEP WATER IN THE HEART

20.1 **20** Wine makes you mean, beer makes
you quarrelsome—
a staggering drunk is not much fun.

20.2 Quick-tempered leaders are like mad dogs—
cross them and they bite your head off.

20.3 It's a mark of good character to avert quarrels,
but fools love to pick fights.

NEW INTERNATIONAL VERSION

⁴ A sluggard does not plow in season;
    so at harvest time he looks but finds
        nothing.

⁵ The purposes of a man's heart are deep
        waters,
    but a man of understanding draws them
        out.

⁶ Many a man claims to have unfailing love,
    but a faithful man who can find?

⁷ The righteous man leads a blameless life;
    blessed are his children after him.

⁸ When a king sits on his throne to judge,
    he winnows out all evil with his eyes.

⁹ Who can say, "I have kept my heart pure;
    I am clean and without sin"?

¹⁰ Differing weights and differing measures—
    the LORD detests them both.

¹¹ Even a child is known by his actions,
    by whether his conduct is pure and right.

¹² Ears that hear and eyes that see—
    the LORD has made them both.

¹³ Do not love sleep or you will grow poor;
    stay awake and you will have food to
        spare.

¹⁴ "It's no good, it's no good!" says the buyer;
    then off he goes and boasts about his
        purchase.

¹⁵ Gold there is, and rubies in abundance,
    but lips that speak knowledge are a rare
        jewel.

¹⁶ Take the garment of one who puts up
        security for a stranger;
    hold it in pledge if he does it for a
        wayward woman.

¹⁷ Food gained by fraud tastes sweet to a man,
    but he ends up with a mouth full of
        gravel.

¹⁸ Make plans by seeking advice;
    if you wage war, obtain guidance.

¹⁹ A gossip betrays a confidence;
    so avoid a man who talks too much.

²⁰ If a man curses his father or mother,
    his lamp will be snuffed out in pitch
        darkness.

²¹ An inheritance quickly gained at the
        beginning
    will not be blessed at the end.

THE MESSAGE

20.4 A farmer too lazy to plant in the spring
    has nothing to harvest in the fall.

20.5 Knowing what is right is like deep water in
        the heart;
    a wise person draws from the well within.

20.6 Lots of people claim to be loyal and loving,
    but where on earth can you find one?

20.7 God-loyal people, living honest lives,
    make it much easier for their children.

20.8-9 Leaders who know their business and care
    keep a sharp eye out for the shoddy and
        cheap,
    For who among us can be trusted
    to be always diligent and honest?

20.10 Switching price tags and padding the expense
        account
    are two things GOD hates.

20.11 Young people eventually reveal by their actions
    if their motives are on the up and up.

DRINKING FROM THE CHALICE OF KNOWLEDGE

20.12 Ears that hear and eyes that see—
    we get our basic equipment from GOD!

20.13 Don't be too fond of sleep; you'll end up in the
        poorhouse.
    Wake up and get up; then there'll be food
        on the table.

20.14 The shopper says, "That's junk—I'll take it off
        your hands,"
    then goes off boasting of the bargain.

20.15 Drinking from the beautiful chalice of
        knowledge
    is better than adorning oneself with gold
        and rare gems.

20.16 Hold tight to collateral on any loan to a stranger;
    beware of accepting what a transient has
        pawned.

20.17 Stolen bread tastes sweet,
    but soon your mouth is full of gravel.

20.18 Form your purpose by asking for counsel,
    then carry it out using all the help you can
        get.

20.19 Gossips can't keep secrets,
    so never confide in blabbermouths.

20.20 Anyone who curses father and mother
    extinguishes light and exists benighted.

THE VERY STEPS WE TAKE

20.21 A bonanza at the beginning
    is no guarantee of blessing at the end.

NEW INTERNATIONAL VERSION

²² Do not say, "I'll pay you back for this wrong!"
   Wait for the LORD, and he will deliver you.

²³ The LORD detests differing weights,
   and dishonest scales do not please him.

²⁴ A man's steps are directed by the LORD.
   How then can anyone understand his own
   way?

²⁵ It is a trap for a man to dedicate something
   rashly
   and only later to consider his vows.

²⁶ A wise king winnows out the wicked;
   he drives the threshing wheel over them.

²⁷ The lamp of the LORD searches the spirit of a
   man *a*;
   it searches out his inmost being.

²⁸ Love and faithfulness keep a king safe;
   through love his throne is made secure.

²⁹ The glory of young men is their strength,
   gray hair the splendor of the old.

³⁰ Blows and wounds cleanse away evil,
   and beatings purge the inmost being.

21

The king's heart is in the hand of the
LORD;
   he directs it like a watercourse wherever
   he pleases.

² All a man's ways seem right to him,
   but the LORD weighs the heart.

³ To do what is right and just
   is more acceptable to the LORD than
   sacrifice.

⁴ Haughty eyes and a proud heart,
   the lamp of the wicked, are sin!

⁵ The plans of the diligent lead to profit
   as surely as haste leads to poverty.

⁶ A fortune made by a lying tongue
   is a fleeting vapor and a deadly snare. *b*

⁷ The violence of the wicked will drag them
   away,
   for they refuse to do what is right.

⁸ The way of the guilty is devious,
   but the conduct of the innocent is upright.

⁹ Better to live on a corner of the roof
   than share a house with a quarrelsome
   wife.

*a 27 Or The spirit of man is the LORD's lamp   b 6 Some
Hebrew manuscripts, Septuagint and Vulgate; most Hebrew
manuscripts vapor for those who seek death*

THE MESSAGE

20.22 Don't ever say, "I'll get you for that!"
   Wait for GOD; he'll settle the score.

20.23 GOD hates cheating in the marketplace;
   rigged scales are an outrage.

20.24 The very steps we take come from GOD;
   otherwise how would we know where we're
   going?

20.25 An impulsive vow is a trap;
   later you'll wish you could get out of it.

20.26 After careful scrutiny, a wise leader
   makes a clean sweep of rebels and dolts.

20.27 GOD is in charge of human life,
   watching and examining us inside and out.

20.28 Love and truth form a good leader;
   sound leadership is founded on loving
   integrity.

20.29 Youth may be admired for vigor,
   but gray hair gives prestige to old age.

20.30 A good thrashing purges evil;
   punishment goes deep within us.

GOD EXAMINES OUR MOTIVES

21.1 Good leadership is a channel of water
   controlled by God;
   he directs it to whatever ends he chooses.

21.2 We justify our actions by appearances;
   GOD examines our motives.

21.3 Clean living before God and justice with our
   neighbors
   mean far more to GOD than religious
   performance.

21.4 Arrogance and pride—distinguishing marks in
   the wicked—
   are just plain sin.

21.5 Careful planning puts you ahead in the long run;
   hurry and scurry puts you further behind.

21.6 Make it to the top by lying and cheating;
   get paid with smoke and a promotion—to
   death!

21.7 The wicked get buried alive by their loot
   because they refuse to use it to help others.

21.8 Mixed motives twist life into tangles;
   pure motives take you straight down the
   road.

DO YOUR BEST, PREPARE FOR THE WORST

21.9 Better to live alone in a tumbledown shack
   than share a mansion with a nagging
   spouse.

NEW INTERNATIONAL VERSION

¹⁰ The wicked man craves evil;
  his neighbor gets no mercy from him.

¹¹ When a mocker is punished, the simple gain
    wisdom;
  when a wise man is instructed, he gets
    knowledge.

¹² The Righteous One*ᵃ* takes note of the house
    of the wicked
  and brings the wicked to ruin.

¹³ If a man shuts his ears to the cry of the poor,
  he too will cry out and not be answered.

¹⁴ A gift given in secret soothes anger,
  and a bribe concealed in the cloak pacifies
    great wrath.

¹⁵ When justice is done, it brings joy to the
    righteous
  but terror to evildoers.

¹⁶ A man who strays from the path of
    understanding
  comes to rest in the company of the dead.

¹⁷ He who loves pleasure will become poor;
  whoever loves wine and oil will never be
    rich.

¹⁸ The wicked become a ransom for the righteous,
  and the unfaithful for the upright.

¹⁹ Better to live in a desert
  than with a quarrelsome and ill-tempered
    wife.

²⁰ In the house of the wise are stores of choice
    food and oil,
  but a foolish man devours all he has.

²¹ He who pursues righteousness and love
  finds life, prosperity*ᵇ* and honor.

²² A wise man attacks the city of the mighty
  and pulls down the stronghold in which
    they trust.

²³ He who guards his mouth and his tongue
  keeps himself from calamity.

²⁴ The proud and arrogant man—"Mocker" is
    his name;
  he behaves with overweening pride.

²⁵ The sluggard's craving will be the death of him,
  because his hands refuse to work.
²⁶ All day long he craves for more,
  but the righteous give without sparing.

²⁷ The sacrifice of the wicked is detestable—
  how much more so when brought with
    evil intent!

THE MESSAGE

²¹·¹⁰ Wicked souls love to make trouble;
  they feel nothing for friends and neighbors.

²¹·¹¹ Simpletons only learn the hard way,
  but the wise learn by listening.

²¹·¹² A God-loyal person will see right through the
    wicked
  and undo the evil they've planned.

²¹·¹³ If you stop your ears to the cries of the poor,
  your cries will go unheard, unanswered.

²¹·¹⁴ A quietly given gift soothes an irritable
    person;
  a heartfelt present cools a hot temper.

²¹·¹⁵ Good people celebrate when justice triumphs,
  but for the workers of evil it's a bad day.

²¹·¹⁶ Whoever wanders off the straight and narrow
  ends up in a congregation of ghosts.

²¹·¹⁷ You're addicted to thrills? What an empty life!
  The pursuit of pleasure is never satisfied.

²¹·¹⁸ What a bad person plots against the good,
    boomerangs;
  the plotter gets it in the end.

²¹·¹⁹ Better to live in a tent in the wild
  than with a cross and petulant spouse.

²¹·²⁰ Valuables are safe in a wise person's home;
  fools put it all out for yard sales.

²¹·²¹ Whoever goes hunting for what is right and
    kind
  finds life itself—*glorious* life!

²¹·²² One sage entered a whole city of armed
    soldiers—
  their trusted defenses fell to pieces!

²¹·²³ Watch your words and hold your tongue;
  you'll save yourself a lot of grief.

²¹·²⁴ You know their names—Brash, Impudent,
    Blasphemer—
  intemperate hotheads, every one.

²¹·²⁵ Lazy people finally die of hunger
  because they won't get up and go to work.

²¹·²⁶ Sinners are always wanting what they don't
    have;
  the God-loyal are always giving what they
    do have.

²¹·²⁷ Religious performance by the wicked stinks;
  it's even worse when they use it to get
    ahead.

ᵃ 12 Or *The righteous man*   ᵇ 21 Or *righteousness*

NEW INTERNATIONAL VERSION

28 A false witness will perish,
  and whoever listens to him will be
    destroyed forever.[a]

29 A wicked man puts up a bold front,
  but an upright man gives thought to his
    ways.

30 There is no wisdom, no insight, no plan
  that can succeed against the LORD.

31 The horse is made ready for the day of battle,
  but victory rests with the LORD.

22 A good name is more desirable than
    great riches;
  to be esteemed is better than silver or
    gold.

2 Rich and poor have this in common:
  The LORD is the Maker of them all.

3 A prudent man sees danger and takes refuge,
  but the simple keep going and suffer for
    it.

4 Humility and the fear of the LORD
  bring wealth and honor and life.

5 In the paths of the wicked lie thorns and
    snares,
  but he who guards his soul stays far from
    them.

6 Train[b] a child in the way he should go,
  and when he is old he will not turn from
    it.

7 The rich rule over the poor,
  and the borrower is servant to the lender.

8 He who sows wickedness reaps trouble,
  and the rod of his fury will be destroyed.

9 A generous man will himself be blessed,
  for he shares his food with the poor.

10 Drive out the mocker, and out goes strife;
  quarrels and insults are ended.

11 He who loves a pure heart and whose speech
    is gracious
  will have the king for his friend.

12 The eyes of the LORD keep watch over
    knowledge,
  but he frustrates the words of the
    unfaithful.

13 The sluggard says, "There is a lion outside!"
  or, "I will be murdered in the streets!"

THE MESSAGE

21.28 A lying witness is unconvincing;
  a person who speaks truth is respected.

21.29 Unscrupulous people fake it a lot;
  honest people are sure of their steps.

21.30 Nothing clever, nothing conceived, nothing
    contrived,
  can get the better of GOD.

21.31 Do your best, prepare for the worst—
  then trust GOD to bring victory.

THE CURE COMES THROUGH DISCIPLINE

22.1 **22** A sterling reputation is better than
    striking it rich;
  a gracious spirit is better than money in the
    bank.

22.2 The rich and the poor shake hands as
    equals—
  GOD made them both!

22.3 A prudent person sees trouble coming and
    ducks;
  a simpleton walks in blindly and is
    clobbered.

22.4 The payoff for meekness and Fear-of-GOD
  is plenty and honor and a satisfying life.

22.5 The perverse travel a dangerous road,
    potholed and mud-slick;
  if you know what's good for you, stay clear
    of it.

22.6 Point your kids in the right direction—
  when they're old they won't be lost.

22.7 The poor are always ruled over by the rich,
  so don't borrow and put yourself under
    their power.

22.8 Whoever sows sin reaps weeds,
  and bullying anger sputters into nothing.

22.9 Generous hands are blessed hands
  because they give bread to the poor.

22.10 Kick out the troublemakers and things will
    quiet down;
  you need a break from bickering and
    griping!

22.11 GOD loves the pure-hearted and well-spoken;
  good leaders also delight in their
    friendship.

22.12 GOD guards knowledge with a passion,
  but he'll have nothing to do with
    deception.

22.13 The loafer says, "There's a lion on the loose!
  If I go out I'll be eaten alive!"

NEW INTERNATIONAL VERSION

[14] The mouth of an adulteress is a deep pit;
  he who is under the Lord's wrath will fall
    into it.

[15] Folly is bound up in the heart of a child,
  but the rod of discipline will drive it far
    from him.

[16] He who oppresses the poor to increase his
    wealth
  and he who gives gifts to the rich—both
    come to poverty.

SAYINGS OF THE WISE

[17] Pay attention and listen to the sayings of the
    wise;
  apply your heart to what I teach,
[18] for it is pleasing when you keep them in
    your heart
  and have all of them ready on your lips.
[19] So that your trust may be in the Lord,
  I teach you today, even you.
[20] Have I not written thirty[a] sayings for you,
  sayings of counsel and knowledge,
[21] teaching you true and reliable words,
  so that you can give sound answers
    to him who sent you?

[22] Do not exploit the poor because they are
    poor
  and do not crush the needy in court,
[23] for the Lord will take up their case
  and will plunder those who plunder them.

[24] Do not make friends with a hot-tempered
    man,
  do not associate with one easily angered,
[25] or you may learn his ways
  and get yourself ensnared.

[26] Do not be a man who strikes hands in pledge
  or puts up security for debts;
[27] if you lack the means to pay,
  your very bed will be snatched from
    under you.

[28] Do not move an ancient boundary stone
  set up by your forefathers.

[29] Do you see a man skilled in his work?
  He will serve before kings;
  he will not serve before obscure men.

THE MESSAGE

[22.14] The mouth of a whore is a bottomless pit;
  you'll fall in that pit if you're on the outs
    with God.

[22.15] Young people are prone to foolishness and fads;
  the cure comes through tough-minded
    discipline.

[22.16] Exploit the poor or glad-hand the rich—
    whichever,
  you'll end up the poorer for it.

THE THIRTY PRECEPTS OF THE SAGES

DON'T MOVE BACK THE BOUNDARY LINES

[22.17-21] Listen carefully to my wisdom;
  take to heart what I can teach you.
You'll treasure its sweetness deep within;
  you'll give it bold expression in your speech.
To make sure your foundation is trust in God,
  I'm laying it all out right now just for you.
I'm giving you thirty sterling principles—
  tested guidelines to live by.
Believe me—these are truths that work,
  and will keep you accountable
    to those who sent you.

1

[22.22-23] Don't walk on the poor just because they're
    poor,
  and don't use your position to crush the weak,
Because God will come to their defense;
  the life you took, he'll take from you and
    give back to them.

2

[22.24-25] Don't hang out with angry people;
  don't keep company with hotheads.
Bad temper is contagious—
  don't get infected.

3

[22.26-27] Don't gamble on the pot of gold at the end of
    the rainbow,
  hocking your house against a lucky chance.
The time will come when you have to pay up;
  you'll be left with nothing but the shirt on
    your back.

4

[22.28] Don't stealthily move back the boundary lines
  staked out long ago by your ancestors.

5

[22.29] Observe people who are good at their work—
  skilled workers are always in demand and
    admired;
  they don't take a back seat to anyone.

---

a 20 Or not formerly written; or not written excellent

NEW INTERNATIONAL VERSION	THE MESSAGE

NEW INTERNATIONAL VERSION

23 When you sit to dine with a ruler,
note well what[a] is before you,
² and put a knife to your throat
if you are given to gluttony.
³ Do not crave his delicacies,
for that food is deceptive.

⁴ Do not wear yourself out to get rich;
have the wisdom to show restraint.
⁵ Cast but a glance at riches, and they are
gone,
for they will surely sprout wings
and fly off to the sky like an eagle.

⁶ Do not eat the food of a stingy man,
do not crave his delicacies;
⁷ for he is the kind of man
who is always thinking about the cost.[b]
"Eat and drink," he says to you,
but his heart is not with you.
⁸ You will vomit up the little you have eaten
and will have wasted your compliments.

⁹ Do not speak to a fool,
for he will scorn the wisdom of your
words.

¹⁰ Do not move an ancient boundary stone
or encroach on the fields of the fatherless,
¹¹ for their Defender is strong;
he will take up their case against you.

¹² Apply your heart to instruction
and your ears to words of knowledge.

¹³ Do not withhold discipline from a child;
if you punish him with the rod, he will
not die.
¹⁴ Punish him with the rod
and save his soul from death.[c]

¹⁵ My son, if your heart is wise,
then my heart will be glad;
¹⁶ my inmost being will rejoice
when your lips speak what is right.

¹⁷ Do not let your heart envy sinners,
but always be zealous for the fear of the
LORD.
¹⁸ There is surely a future hope for you,

THE MESSAGE

RESTRAIN YOURSELF

6

23.1-3 **23** When you go out to dinner with an
influential person,
mind your manners:
Don't gobble your food,
don't talk with your mouth full.
And don't stuff yourself;
bridle your appetite.

7

23.4-5 Don't wear yourself out trying to get rich;
restrain yourself!
Riches disappear in the blink of an eye;
wealth sprouts wings
and flies off into the wild blue yonder.

8

23.6-8 Don't accept a meal from a tightwad;
don't expect anything special.
He'll be as stingy with you as he is with
himself;
he'll say, "Eat! Drink!" but won't mean a
word of it.
His miserly serving will turn your stomach
when you realize the meal's a sham.

9

23.9 Don't bother talking sense to fools;
they'll only poke fun at your words.

10

23.10-11 Don't stealthily move back the boundary lines
or cheat orphans out of their property,
For they have a powerful Advocate
who will go to bat for them.

11

23.12 Give yourselves to disciplined instruction;
open your ears to tested knowledge.

12

23.13-14 Don't be afraid to correct your young ones;
a spanking won't kill them.
A good spanking, in fact, might save them
from something worse than death.

13

23.15-16 Dear child, if you become wise,
I'll be one happy parent.
My heart will dance and sing
to the tuneful truth you'll speak.

14

23.17-18 Don't for a minute envy careless rebels;
soak yourself in the Fear-of-GOD—
That's where your future lies.

ª 1 Or who *ᵇ 7 Or for as he thinks within himself, / so he
is; or for as he puts on a feast, / so he is* *ᶜ 14 Hebrew Sheol*

NEW INTERNATIONAL VERSION

and your hope will not be cut off.

¹⁹ Listen, my son, and be wise,
and keep your heart on the right path.
²⁰ Do not join those who drink too much wine
or gorge themselves on meat,
²¹ for drunkards and gluttons become poor,
and drowsiness clothes them in rags.

²² Listen to your father, who gave you life,
and do not despise your mother when she
is old.
²³ Buy the truth and do not sell it;
get wisdom, discipline and
understanding.
²⁴ The father of a righteous man has great joy;
he who has a wise son delights in him.
²⁵ May your father and mother be glad;
may she who gave you birth rejoice!

²⁶ My son, give me your heart
and let your eyes keep to my ways,
²⁷ for a prostitute is a deep pit
and a wayward wife is a narrow well.
²⁸ Like a bandit she lies in wait,
and multiplies the unfaithful among men.

²⁹ Who has woe? Who has sorrow?
Who has strife? Who has complaints?
Who has needless bruises? Who has
bloodshot eyes?
³⁰ Those who linger over wine,
who go to sample bowls of mixed wine.
³¹ Do not gaze at wine when it is red,
when it sparkles in the cup,
when it goes down smoothly!
³² In the end it bites like a snake
and poisons like a viper.
³³ Your eyes will see strange sights
and your mind imagine confusing things.
³⁴ You will be like one sleeping on the high
seas,
lying on top of the rigging.
³⁵ "They hit me," you will say, "but I'm not
hurt!
They beat me, but I don't feel it!
When will I wake up
so I can find another drink?"

THE MESSAGE

Then you won't be left with an armload of
nothing.

15

23.19-21 Oh listen, dear child—become wise;
point your life in the right direction.
Don't drink too much wine and get drunk;
don't eat too much food and get fat.
Drunks and gluttons will end up on skid row,
in a stupor and dressed in rags.

BUY WISDOM, EDUCATION, INSIGHT

16

23.22-25 Listen with respect to the father who raised
you,
and when your mother grows old, don't
neglect her.
Buy truth—don't sell it for love or money;
buy wisdom, buy education, buy insight.
Parents rejoice when their children turn out
well;
wise children become proud parents.
So make your father happy!
Make your mother proud!

17

23.26 Dear child, I want your full attention;
please do what I show you.

23.27-28 A whore is a bottomless pit;
a loose woman can get you in deep trouble
fast.
She'll take you for all you've got;
she's worse than a pack of thieves.

18

23.29-35 Who are the people who are always crying the
blues?
Who do you know who reeks of self-pity?
Who keeps getting beat up for no reason at
all?
Whose eyes are bleary and bloodshot?
It's those who spend the night with a bottle,
for whom drinking is serious business.
Don't judge wine by its label,
or its bouquet, or its full-bodied flavor.
Judge it rather by the hangover it leaves you
with—
the splitting headache, the queasy stomach.
Do you really prefer seeing double,
with your speech all slurred,
Reeling and seasick,
drunk as a sailor?
"They hit me," you'll say, "but it didn't hurt;
they beat on me, but I didn't feel a thing.
When I'm sober enough to manage it,
bring me another drink!"

NEW INTERNATIONAL VERSION

24 Do not envy wicked men,
do not desire their company;
² for their hearts plot violence,
and their lips talk about making trouble.

³ By wisdom a house is built,
and through understanding it is
established;
⁴ through knowledge its rooms are filled
with rare and beautiful treasures.

⁵ A wise man has great power,
and a man of knowledge increases
strength;
⁶ for waging war you need guidance,
and for victory many advisers.

⁷ Wisdom is too high for a fool;
in the assembly at the gate he has nothing
to say.

⁸ He who plots evil
will be known as a schemer.
⁹ The schemes of folly are sin,
and men detest a mocker.

¹⁰ If you falter in times of trouble,
how small is your strength!

¹¹ Rescue those being led away to death;
hold back those staggering toward
slaughter.
¹² If you say, "But we knew nothing about
this,"
does not he who weighs the heart perceive
it?
Does not he who guards your life know it?
Will he not repay each person according
to what he has done?

¹³ Eat honey, my son, for it is good;
honey from the comb is sweet to your
taste.
¹⁴ Know also that wisdom is sweet to your
soul;
if you find it, there is a future hope for
you,
and your hope will not be cut off.

¹⁵ Do not lie in wait like an outlaw against a
righteous man's house,
do not raid his dwelling place;
¹⁶ for though a righteous man falls seven times,
he rises again,

THE MESSAGE

INTELLIGENCE OUTRANKS MUSCLE

19

24.1-2 **24** Don't envy bad people;
don't even want to be around them.
All they think about is causing a disturbance;
all they talk about is making trouble.

20

24.3-4 It takes wisdom to build a house,
and understanding to set it on a firm
foundation;
It takes knowledge to furnish its rooms
with fine furniture and beautiful draperies.

21

24.5-6 It's better to be wise than strong;
intelligence outranks muscle any day.
Strategic planning is the key to warfare;
to win, you need a lot of good counsel.

22

24.7 Wise conversation is way over the head of fools;
in a serious discussion they haven't a clue.

23

24.8-9 The person who's always cooking up some evil
soon gets a reputation as prince of rogues.
Fools incubate sin;
cynics desecrate beauty.

RESCUE THE PERISHING

24

24.10 If you fall to pieces in a crisis,
there wasn't much to you in the first place.

25

24.11-12 Rescue the perishing;
don't hesitate to step in and help.
If you say, "Hey, that's none of my business,"
will that get you off the hook?
Someone is watching you closely, you know—
Someone not impressed with weak excuses.

26

24.13-14 Eat honey, dear child—it's good for you—
and delicacies that melt in your mouth.
Likewise knowledge,
and wisdom for your soul—
Get that and your future's secured,
your hope is on solid rock.

27

24.15-16 Don't interfere with good people's lives;
don't try to get the best of them.
No matter how many times you trip them up,
God-loyal people don't stay down long;
Soon they're up on their feet,

NEW INTERNATIONAL VERSION

but the wicked are brought down by
calamity.

17 Do not gloat when your enemy falls;
when he stumbles, do not let your heart
rejoice,
18 or the LORD will see and disapprove
and turn his wrath away from him.

19 Do not fret because of evil men
or be envious of the wicked,
20 for the evil man has no future hope,
and the lamp of the wicked will be
snuffed out.

21 Fear the LORD and the king, my son,
and do not join with the rebellious,
22 for those two will send sudden destruction
upon them,
and who knows what calamities they can
bring?

FURTHER SAYINGS OF THE WISE

23 These also are sayings of the wise:

To show partiality in judging is not good:
24 Whoever says to the guilty, "You are
innocent"—
peoples will curse him and nations
denounce him.
25 But it will go well with those who convict
the guilty,
and rich blessing will come upon them.

26 An honest answer
is like a kiss on the lips.

27 Finish your outdoor work
and get your fields ready;
after that, build your house.

28 Do not testify against your neighbor without
cause,
or use your lips to deceive.
29 Do not say, "I'll do to him as he has done to
me;
I'll pay that man back for what he did."

30 I went past the field of the sluggard,
past the vineyard of the man who lacks
judgment;
31 thorns had come up everywhere,
the ground was covered with weeds,
and the stone wall was in ruins.
32 I applied my heart to what I observed
and learned a lesson from what I saw:
33 A little sleep, a little slumber,
a little folding of the hands to rest—

THE MESSAGE

while the wicked end up flat on their faces.

28

24.17-18 Don't laugh when your enemy falls;
don't crow over his collapse.
GOD might see, and become very provoked,
and then take pity on his plight.

29

24.19-20 Don't bother your head with braggarts
or wish you could succeed like the wicked.
Those people have no future at all;
they're headed down a dead-end street.

30

24.21-22 Fear GOD, dear child—respect your leaders;
don't be defiant or mutinous.
Without warning your life can turn upside-
down,
and who knows how or when it might
happen?

MORE SAYINGS OF THE WISE

AN HONEST ANSWER

24.23 It's wrong, very wrong,
to go along with injustice.

24.24-25 Whoever whitewashes the wicked
gets a black mark in the history books,
But whoever exposes the wicked
will be thanked and rewarded.

24.26 An honest answer
is like a warm hug.

24.27 First plant your fields;
then build your barn.

24.28-29 Don't talk about your neighbors behind their
backs—
no slander or gossip, please.
Don't say to anyone, "I'll get back at you for
what you did to me.
I'll make you pay for what you did!"

24.30-34 One day I walked by the field of an old
lazybones,
and then passed the vineyard of a lout;
They were overgrown with weeds,
thick with thistles, all the fences broken down.
I took a long look and pondered what I saw;
the fields preached me a sermon and I
listened:
"A nap here, a nap there, a day off here, a day
off there,
sit back, take it easy—do you know what
comes next?
Just this: You can look forward to a dirt-poor
life,

NEW INTERNATIONAL VERSION

³⁴ and poverty will come on you like a bandit
and scarcity like an armed man. ᵃ

MORE PROVERBS OF SOLOMON

25 These are more proverbs of Solomon,
copied by the men of Hezekiah king of
Judah:

² It is the glory of God to conceal a matter;
to search out a matter is the glory of
kings.

³ As the heavens are high and the earth is deep,
so the hearts of kings are unsearchable.

⁴ Remove the dross from the silver,
and out comes material for ᵇ the
silversmith;

⁵ remove the wicked from the king's presence,
and his throne will be established through
righteousness.

⁶ Do not exalt yourself in the king's presence,
and do not claim a place among great men;

⁷ it is better for him to say to you, "Come up
here,"
than for him to humiliate you before a
nobleman.

What you have seen with your eyes
⁸   do not bring ᶜ hastily to court,
for what will you do in the end
if your neighbor puts you to shame?

⁹ If you argue your case with a neighbor,
do not betray another man's confidence,

¹⁰ or he who hears it may shame you
and you will never lose your bad
reputation.

¹¹ A word aptly spoken
is like apples of gold in settings of silver.

¹² Like an earring of gold or an ornament of
fine gold
is a wise man's rebuke to a listening ear.

¹³ Like the coolness of snow at harvest time
is a trustworthy messenger to those who
send him;
he refreshes the spirit of his masters.

¹⁴ Like clouds and wind without rain
is a man who boasts of gifts he does not
give.

¹⁵ Through patience a ruler can be persuaded,
and a gentle tongue can break a bone.

ᵃ 34 Or *like a vagrant / and scarcity like a beggar*
ᵇ 4 Or *comes a vessel from*   ᶜ 7,8 Or *nobleman / on whom
you had set your eyes. / ⁸Do not go*

THE MESSAGE

with poverty as your permanent
houseguest!"

FURTHER WISE SAYINGS OF SOLOMON

THE RIGHT WORD AT THE RIGHT TIME

25.1 **25** There are also these proverbs of
Solomon,
collected by scribes of Hezekiah, king of
Judah.

25.2 God delights in concealing things;
scientists delight in discovering things.

25.3 Like the horizons for breadth and the ocean
for depth,
the understanding of a good leader is broad
and deep.

25.4-5 Remove impurities from the silver
and the silversmith can craft a fine chalice;
Remove the wicked from leadership
and authority will be credible and God-
honoring.

25.6-7 Don't work yourself into the spotlight;
don't push your way into the place of
prominence.
It's better to be promoted to a place of honor
than face humiliation by being demoted.

25.8 Don't jump to conclusions—there may be
a perfectly good explanation for what you
just saw.

25.9-10 In the heat of an argument,
don't betray confidences;
Word is sure to get around,
and no one will trust you.

25.11-12 The right word at the right time
is like a custom-made piece of jewelry,
And a wise friend's timely reprimand
is like a gold ring slipped on your finger.

25.13 Reliable friends who do what they say
are like cool drinks in sweltering heat—
refreshing!

25.14 Like billowing clouds that bring no rain
is the person who talks big but never
produces.

25.15 Patient persistence pierces through
indifference;
gentle speech breaks down rigid defenses.

NEW INTERNATIONAL VERSION

¹⁶ If you find honey, eat just enough—
    too much of it, and you will vomit.
¹⁷ Seldom set foot in your neighbor's house—
    too much of you, and he will hate you.

¹⁸ Like a club or a sword or a sharp arrow
    is the man who gives false testimony
    against his neighbor.

¹⁹ Like a bad tooth or a lame foot
    is reliance on the unfaithful in times of
    trouble.

²⁰ Like one who takes away a garment on a
    cold day,
    or like vinegar poured on soda,
    is one who sings songs to a heavy heart.

²¹ If your enemy is hungry, give him food to
    eat;
    if he is thirsty, give him water to drink.
²² In doing this, you will heap burning coals on
    his head,
    and the LORD will reward you.

²³ As a north wind brings rain,
    so a sly tongue brings angry looks.

²⁴ Better to live on a corner of the roof
    than share a house with a quarrelsome
    wife.

²⁵ Like cold water to a weary soul
    is good news from a distant land.

²⁶ Like a muddied spring or a polluted well
    is a righteous man who gives way to the
    wicked.

²⁷ It is not good to eat too much honey,
    nor is it honorable to seek one's own
    honor.

²⁸ Like a city whose walls are broken down
    is a man who lacks self-control.

26 Like snow in summer or rain in harvest,
    honor is not fitting for a fool.

² Like a fluttering sparrow or a darting
    swallow,
    an undeserved curse does not come to
    rest.

³ A whip for the horse, a halter for the donkey,
    and a rod for the backs of fools!

⁴ Do not answer a fool according to his folly,
    or you will be like him yourself.

THE MESSAGE

A PERSON WITHOUT SELF-CONTROL

25.16-17 When you're given a box of candy, don't gulp
    it all down;
    eat too much chocolate and you'll make
    yourself sick;
    And when you find a friend, don't outwear
    your welcome;
    show up at all hours and he'll soon get
    fed up.

25.18 Anyone who tells lies against the neighbors
    in court or on the street is a loose cannon.

25.19 Trusting a double-crosser when you're in
    trouble
    is like biting down on an abscessed tooth.

25.20 Singing light songs to the heavyhearted
    is like pouring salt in their wounds.

25.21-22 If you see your enemy hungry, go buy him
    lunch;
    if he's thirsty, bring him a drink.
    Your generosity will surprise him with
    goodness,
    and GOD will look after you.

25.23 A north wind brings stormy weather,
    and a gossipy tongue stormy looks.

25.24 Better to live alone in a tumbledown shack
    than share a mansion with a nagging spouse.

25.25 Like a cool drink of water when you're worn
    out and weary
    is a letter from a long-lost friend.

25.26 A good person who gives in to a bad person
    is a muddied spring, a polluted well.

25.27 It's not smart to stuff yourself with sweets,
    nor is glory piled on glory good for you.

25.28 A person without self-control
    is like a house with its doors and windows
    knocked out.

FOOLS RECYCLE SILLINESS

26.1 **26** We no more give honors to fools
    than pray for snow in summer or rain
    during harvest.

26.2 You have as little to fear from an undeserved
    curse
    as from the dart of a wren or the swoop of a
    swallow.

26.3 A whip for the racehorse, a tiller for the
    sailboat—
    and a stick for the back of fools!

26.4 Don't respond to the stupidity of a fool;
    you'll only look foolish yourself.

NEW INTERNATIONAL VERSION

⁵Answer a fool according to his folly,
   or he will be wise in his own eyes.

⁶Like cutting off one's feet or drinking
      violence
   is the sending of a message by the hand of
      a fool.

⁷Like a lame man's legs that hang limp
   is a proverb in the mouth of a fool.

⁸Like tying a stone in a sling
   is the giving of honor to a fool.

⁹Like a thornbush in a drunkard's hand
   is a proverb in the mouth of a fool.

¹⁰Like an archer who wounds at random
   is he who hires a fool or any passer-by.

¹¹As a dog returns to its vomit,
   so a fool repeats his folly.

¹²Do you see a man wise in his own eyes?
   There is more hope for a fool than for
      him.

¹³The sluggard says, "There is a lion in the
      road,
   a fierce lion roaming the streets!"

¹⁴As a door turns on its hinges,
   so a sluggard turns on his bed.

¹⁵The sluggard buries his hand in the dish;
   he is too lazy to bring it back to his
      mouth.

¹⁶The sluggard is wiser in his own eyes
   than seven men who answer discreetly.

¹⁷Like one who seizes a dog by the ears
   is a passer-by who meddles in a quarrel
      not his own.

¹⁸Like a madman shooting
   firebrands or deadly arrows
¹⁹is a man who deceives his neighbor
   and says, "I was only joking!"

²⁰Without wood a fire goes out;
   without gossip a quarrel dies down.

²¹As charcoal to embers and as wood to fire,
   so is a quarrelsome man for kindling
      strife.

²²The words of a gossip are like choice
      morsels;
   they go down to a man's inmost parts.

²³Like a coating of glaze*ᵃ* over earthenware
   are fervent lips with an evil heart.

ᵃ 23 With a different word division of the Hebrew;
Masoretic Text *of silver dross*

THE MESSAGE

26.5 Answer a fool in simple terms
   so he doesn't get a swelled head.

26.6 You're only asking for trouble
   when you send a message by a fool.

26.7 A proverb quoted by fools
   is limp as a wet noodle.

26.8 Putting a fool in a place of honor
   is like setting a mud brick on a marble
      column.

26.9 To ask a moron to quote a proverb
   is like putting a scalpel in the hands of a
      drunk.

26.10 Hire a fool or a drunk
   and you shoot yourself in the foot.

26.11 As a dog eats its own vomit,
   so fools recycle silliness.

26.12 See that man who thinks he's so smart?
   You can expect far more from a fool than
      from him.

26.13 Loafers say, "It's dangerous out there!
   Tigers are prowling the streets!"
   and then pull the covers back over their
      heads.

26.14 Just as a door turns on its hinges,
   so a lazybones turns back over in bed.

26.15 A shiftless sluggard puts his fork in the pie,
   but is too lazy to lift it to his mouth.

LIKE GLAZE ON CRACKED POTTERY
26.16 Dreamers fantasize their self-importance;
   they think they are smarter
   than a whole college faculty.

26.17 You grab a mad dog by the ears
   when you butt into a quarrel that's none of
      your business.

26.18-19 People who shrug off deliberate deceptions,
   saying, "I didn't mean it, I was only
      joking,"
   Are worse than careless campers
   who walk away from smoldering campfires.

26.20 When you run out of wood, the fire goes out;
   when the gossip ends, the quarrel dies
      down.

26.21 A quarrelsome person in a dispute
   is like kerosene thrown on a fire.

26.22 Listening to gossip is like eating cheap candy;
   do you want junk like that in your belly?

26.23 Smooth talk from an evil heart
   is like glaze on cracked pottery.

NEW INTERNATIONAL VERSION

24 A malicious man disguises himself with his
  lips,
  but in his heart he harbors deceit.
25 Though his speech is charming, do not
  believe him,
  for seven abominations fill his heart.
26 His malice may be concealed by deception,
  but his wickedness will be exposed in the
  assembly.

27 If a man digs a pit, he will fall into it;
  if a man rolls a stone, it will roll back on
  him.

28 A lying tongue hates those it hurts,
  and a flattering mouth works ruin.

27 Do not boast about tomorrow,
  for you do not know what a day may
  bring forth.

2 Let another praise you, and not your own
  mouth;
  someone else, and not your own lips.

3 Stone is heavy and sand a burden,
  but provocation by a fool is heavier than
  both.

4 Anger is cruel and fury overwhelming,
  but who can stand before jealousy?

5 Better is open rebuke
  than hidden love.

6 Wounds from a friend can be trusted,
  but an enemy multiplies kisses.

7 He who is full loathes honey,
  but to the hungry even what is bitter
  tastes sweet.

8 Like a bird that strays from its nest
  is a man who strays from his home.

9 Perfume and incense bring joy to the heart,
  and the pleasantness of one's friend
  springs from his earnest counsel.

10 Do not forsake your friend and the friend of
  your father,
  and do not go to your brother's house
  when disaster strikes you—
  better a neighbor nearby than a brother
  far away.

11 Be wise, my son, and bring joy to my heart;
  then I can answer anyone who treats me
  with contempt.

THE MESSAGE

26.24-26 Your enemy shakes hands and greets you like
  an old friend,
  all the while conniving against you.
When he speaks warmly to you, don't believe
  him for a minute;
  he's just waiting for the chance to rip you
  off.
No matter how cunningly he conceals his
  malice,
  eventually his evil will be exposed in
  public.

26.27 Malice backfires;
  spite boomerangs.

26.28 Liars hate their victims;
  flatterers sabotage trust.

You Don't Know Tomorrow

27.1 27 Don't brashly announce what you're
  going to do tomorrow;
  you don't know the first thing about
  tomorrow.

27.2 Don't call attention to yourself;
  let others do that for you.

27.3 Carrying a log across your shoulders
  while you're hefting a boulder with your
  arms
  Is nothing compared to the burden
  of putting up with a fool.

27.4 We're blasted by anger and swamped by rage,
  but who can survive jealousy?

27.5 A spoken reprimand is better
  than approval that's never expressed.

27.6 The wounds from a lover are worth it;
  kisses from an enemy do you in.

27.7 When you've stuffed yourself, you refuse
  dessert;
  when you're starved, you could eat a horse.

27.8 People who won't settle down, wandering
  hither and yon,
  are like restless birds, flitting to and fro.

27.9 Just as lotions and fragrance give sensual
  delight,
  a sweet friendship refreshes the soul.

27.10 Don't leave your friends or your parents' friends
  and run home to your family when things
  get rough;
  Better a nearby friend
  than a distant family.

27.11 Become wise, dear child, and make me happy;
  then nothing the world throws my way will
  upset me.

NEW INTERNATIONAL VERSION

¹² The prudent see danger and take refuge,
　　but the simple keep going and suffer for it.

¹³ Take the garment of one who puts up
　　security for a stranger;
　　hold it in pledge if he does it for a
　　wayward woman.

¹⁴ If a man loudly blesses his neighbor early in
　　the morning,
　　it will be taken as a curse.

¹⁵ A quarrelsome wife is like
　　a constant dripping on a rainy day;
¹⁶ restraining her is like restraining the wind
　　or grasping oil with the hand.

¹⁷ As iron sharpens iron,
　　so one man sharpens another.

¹⁸ He who tends a fig tree will eat its fruit,
　　and he who looks after his master will be
　　honored.

¹⁹ As water reflects a face,
　　so a man's heart reflects the man.

²⁰ Death and Destruction*a* are never satisfied,
　　and neither are the eyes of man.

²¹ The crucible for silver and the furnace for
　　gold,
　　but man is tested by the praise he receives.

²² Though you grind a fool in a mortar,
　　grinding him like grain with a pestle,
　　you will not remove his folly from him.

²³ Be sure you know the condition of your
　　flocks,
　　give careful attention to your herds;
²⁴ for riches do not endure forever,
　　and a crown is not secure for all
　　generations.
²⁵ When the hay is removed and new growth
　　appears
　　and the grass from the hills is gathered in,
²⁶ the lambs will provide you with clothing,
　　and the goats with the price of a field.
²⁷ You will have plenty of goats' milk
　　to feed you and your family
　　and to nourish your servant girls.

28 The wicked man flees though no one
　　　　pursues,
　　but the righteous are as bold as a lion.

² When a country is rebellious, it has many
　　rulers,

THE MESSAGE

27.12 A prudent person sees trouble coming and
　　　ducks;
　　　a simpleton walks in blindly and is
　　　clobbered.

27.13 Hold tight to collateral on any loan to a
　　　stranger;
　　　be wary of accepting what a transient has
　　　pawned.

27.14 If you wake your friend in the early morning
　　　by shouting "Rise and shine!"
　　　It will sound to him
　　　more like a curse than a blessing.

27.15-16 A nagging spouse is like
　　　the drip, drip, drip of a leaky faucet;
　　　You can't turn it off,
　　　and you can't get away from it.

Your Face Mirrors Your Heart
27.17 You use steel to sharpen steel,
　　　and one friend sharpens another.

27.18 If you care for your orchard, you'll enjoy its
　　　fruit;
　　　if you honor your boss, you'll be honored.

27.19 Just as water mirrors your face,
　　　so your face mirrors your heart.

27.20 Hell has a voracious appetite,
　　　and lust just never quits.

27.21 The purity of silver and gold is tested
　　　by putting them in the fire;
　　　The purity of human hearts is tested
　　　by giving them a little fame.

27.22 Pound on a fool all you like—
　　　you can't pound out foolishness.

27.23-27 Know your sheep by name;
　　　carefully attend to your flocks;
　　　(Don't take them for granted;
　　　possessions don't last forever, you know.)
　　　And then, when the crops are in
　　　and the harvest is stored in the barns,
　　　You can knit sweaters from lambs' wool,
　　　and sell your goats for a profit;
　　　There will be plenty of milk and meat
　　　to last your family through the winter.

If You Desert God's Law
28.1 **28** The wicked are edgy with guilt, ready
　　　　　to run off
　　　even when no one's after them;
　　　Honest people are relaxed and confident,
　　　bold as lions.

28.2 When the country is in chaos,
　　　everybody has a plan to fix it—

a 20 Hebrew *Sheol and Abaddon*

NEW INTERNATIONAL VERSION

but a man of understanding and
knowledge maintains order.

³ A ruler*ᵃ* who oppresses the poor
is like a driving rain that leaves no crops.

⁴ Those who forsake the law praise the wicked,
but those who keep the law resist them.

⁵ Evil men do not understand justice,
but those who seek the LORD understand
it fully.

⁶ Better a poor man whose walk is blameless
than a rich man whose ways are perverse.

⁷ He who keeps the law is a discerning son,
but a companion of gluttons disgraces his
father.

⁸ He who increases his wealth by exorbitant
interest
amasses it for another, who will be kind to
the poor.

⁹ If anyone turns a deaf ear to the law,
even his prayers are detestable.

¹⁰ He who leads the upright along an evil path
will fall into his own trap,
but the blameless will receive a good
inheritance.

¹¹ A rich man may be wise in his own eyes,
but a poor man who has discernment sees
through him.

¹² When the righteous triumph, there is great
elation;
but when the wicked rise to power, men
go into hiding.

¹³ He who conceals his sins does not prosper,
but whoever confesses and renounces
them finds mercy.

¹⁴ Blessed is the man who always fears the LORD,
but he who hardens his heart falls into
trouble.

¹⁵ Like a roaring lion or a charging bear
is a wicked man ruling over a helpless people.

¹⁶ A tyrannical ruler lacks judgment,
but he who hates ill-gotten gain will enjoy
a long life.

¹⁷ A man tormented by the guilt of murder
will be a fugitive till death;
let no one support him.

¹⁸ He whose walk is blameless is kept safe,
but he whose ways are perverse will
suddenly fall.

ᵃ 3 Or A poor man

THE MESSAGE

But it takes a leader of real understanding
to straighten things out.

28.3 The wicked who oppress the poor
are like a hailstorm that beats down the
harvest.

28.4 If you desert God's law, you're free to embrace
depravity;
if you love God's law, you fight for it tooth
and nail.

28.5 Justice makes no sense to the evilminded;
those who seek GOD know it inside and
out.

28.6 It's better to be poor and direct
than rich and crooked.

28.7 Practice God's law—get a reputation for
wisdom;
hang out with a loose crowd—embarrass
your family.

28.8 Get as rich as you want
through cheating and extortion,
But eventually some friend of the poor
is going to give it all back to them.

28.9 God has no use for the prayers
of the people who won't listen to him.

28.10 Lead good people down a wrong path
and you'll come to a bad end;
do good and you'll be rewarded for it.

28.11 The rich think they know it all,
but the poor can see right through them.

28.12 When good people are promoted, everything
is great,
but when the bad are in charge, watch out!

28.13 You can't whitewash your sins and get by
with it;
you find mercy by admitting and leaving
them.

28.14 A tenderhearted person lives a blessed life;
a hardhearted person lives a hard life.

28.15 Lions roar and bears charge—
and the wicked lord it over the poor.

28.16 Among leaders who lack insight, abuse
abounds,
but for one who hates corruption, the
future is bright.

28.17 A murderer haunted by guilt
is doomed—there's no helping him.

28.18 Walk straight—live well and be saved;
a devious life is a doomed life.

NEW INTERNATIONAL VERSION

¹⁹He who works his land will have abundant
food,
but the one who chases fantasies will have
his fill of poverty.

²⁰A faithful man will be richly blessed,
but one eager to get rich will not go
unpunished.

²¹To show partiality is not good—
yet a man will do wrong for a piece of
bread.

²²A stingy man is eager to get rich
and is unaware that poverty awaits him.

²³He who rebukes a man will in the end gain
more favor
than he who has a flattering tongue.

²⁴He who robs his father or mother
and says, "It's not wrong"—
he is partner to him who destroys.

²⁵A greedy man stirs up dissension,
but he who trusts in the Lord will prosper.

²⁶He who trusts in himself is a fool,
but he who walks in wisdom is kept safe.

²⁷He who gives to the poor will lack nothing,
but he who closes his eyes to them
receives many curses.

²⁸When the wicked rise to power, people go
into hiding;
but when the wicked perish, the righteous
thrive.

29 A man who remains stiff-necked after
many rebukes
will suddenly be destroyed—without
remedy.

²When the righteous thrive, the people
rejoice;
when the wicked rule, the people groan.

³A man who loves wisdom brings joy to his
father,
but a companion of prostitutes squanders
his wealth.

⁴By justice a king gives a country stability,
but one who is greedy for bribes tears it
down.

⁵Whoever flatters his neighbor
is spreading a net for his feet.

⁶An evil man is snared by his own sin,

THE MESSAGE

DOING GREAT HARM IN SEEMINGLY
HARMLESS WAYS

28.19 Work your garden—you'll end up with plenty
of food;
play and party—you'll end up with an
empty plate.

28.20 Committed and persistent work pays off;
get-rich-quick schemes are ripoffs.

28.21 Playing favorites is always a bad thing;
you can do great harm in seemingly
harmless ways.

28.22 A miser in a hurry to get rich
doesn't know that he'll end up broke.

28.23 In the end, serious reprimand is appreciated
far more than bootlicking flattery.

28.24 Anyone who robs father and mother
and says, "So, what's wrong with that?"
is worse than a pirate.

28.25 A grasping person stirs up trouble,
but trust in GOD brings a sense of well-being.

28.26 If you think you know it all, you're a fool for
sure;
real survivors learn wisdom from others.

28.27 Be generous to the poor—you'll never go
hungry;
shut your eyes to their needs, and run a
gauntlet of curses.

28.28 When corruption takes over, good people go
underground,
but when the crooks are thrown out, it's
safe to come out.

IF PEOPLE CAN'T SEE WHAT GOD IS DOING

29.1 **29** For people who hate discipline
and only get more stubborn,
There'll come a day when life tumbles in and
they break,
but by then it'll be too late to help them.

29.2 When good people run things, everyone is
glad,
but when the ruler is bad, everyone groans.

29.3 If you love wisdom, you'll delight your parents,
but you'll destroy their trust if you run with
whores.

29.4 A leader of good judgment gives stability;
an exploiting leader leaves a trail of waste.

29.5 A flattering neighbor is up to no good;
he's probably planning to take advantage of
you.

29.6 Evil people fall into their own traps;

NEW INTERNATIONAL VERSION

but a righteous one can sing and be glad.

7 The righteous care about justice for the poor,
but the wicked have no such concern.

8 Mockers stir up a city,
but wise men turn away anger.

9 If a wise man goes to court with a fool,
the fool rages and scoffs, and there is no
peace.

10 Bloodthirsty men hate a man of integrity
and seek to kill the upright.

11 A fool gives full vent to his anger,
but a wise man keeps himself under
control.

12 If a ruler listens to lies,
all his officials become wicked.

13 The poor man and the oppressor have this in
common:
The LORD gives sight to the eyes of both.

14 If a king judges the poor with fairness,
his throne will always be secure.

15 The rod of correction imparts wisdom,
but a child left to himself disgraces his
mother.

16 When the wicked thrive, so does sin,
but the righteous will see their downfall.

17 Discipline your son, and he will give you
peace;
he will bring delight to your soul.

18 Where there is no revelation, the people cast
off restraint;
but blessed is he who keeps the law.

19 A servant cannot be corrected by mere
words;
though he understands, he will not
respond.

20 Do you see a man who speaks in haste?
There is more hope for a fool than for
him.

21 If a man pampers his servant from youth,
he will bring grief *a* in the end.

22 An angry man stirs up dissension,
and a hot-tempered one commits many
sins.

23 A man's pride brings him low,
but a man of lowly spirit gains honor.

24 The accomplice of a thief is his own enemy;
he is put under oath and dare not testify.

a 21 The meaning of the Hebrew for this word is uncertain.

THE MESSAGE

good people run the other way, glad to
escape.

29.7 The good-hearted understand what it's like to
be poor;
the hardhearted haven't the faintest idea.

29.8 A gang of cynics can upset a whole city;
a group of sages can calm everyone down.

29.9 A sage trying to work things out with a fool
gets only scorn and sarcasm for his trouble.

29.10 Murderers hate honest people;
moral folks encourage them.

29.11 A fool lets it all hang out;
a sage quietly mulls it over.

29.12 When a leader listens to malicious gossip,
all the workers get infected with evil.

29.13 The poor and their abusers have at least
something in common:
they can both *see*—their sight, GOD's gift!

29.14 Leadership gains authority and respect
when the voiceless poor are treated fairly.

29.15 Wise discipline imparts wisdom;
spoiled adolescents embarrass their parents.

29.16 When degenerates take charge, crime runs wild,
but the righteous will eventually observe
their collapse.

29.17 Discipline your children; you'll be glad you
did—
they'll turn out delightful to live with.

29.18 If people can't see what God is doing,
they stumble all over themselves;
But when they attend to what he reveals,
they are most blessed.

29.19 It takes more than talk to keep workers in line;
mere words go in one ear and out the other.

29.20 Observe the people who always talk before
they think—
even simpletons are better off than they are.

29.21 If you let people treat you like a doormat,
you'll be quite forgotten in the end.

29.22 Angry people stir up a lot of discord;
the intemperate stir up trouble.

29.23 Pride lands you flat on your face;
humility prepares you for honors.

29.24 Befriend an outlaw
and become an enemy to yourself.
When the victims cry out,
you'll be included in their curses
if you're a coward to their cause in court.

NEW INTERNATIONAL VERSION

²⁵ Fear of man will prove to be a snare,
   but whoever trusts in the Lord is kept
      safe.

²⁶ Many seek an audience with a ruler,
   but it is from the Lord that man gets
      justice.

²⁷ The righteous detest the dishonest;
   the wicked detest the upright.

SAYINGS OF AGUR

30 The sayings of Agur son of Jakeh—an oracle ª:

This man declared to Ithiel,
   to Ithiel and to Ucal: ᵇ

² "I am the most ignorant of men;
   I do not have a man's understanding.
³ I have not learned wisdom,
   nor have I knowledge of the Holy One.
⁴ Who has gone up to heaven and come down?
   Who has gathered up the wind in the
      hollow of his hands?
   Who has wrapped up the waters in his cloak?
   Who has established all the ends of the
      earth?
   What is his name, and the name of his son?
      Tell me if you know!

⁵ "Every word of God is flawless;
   he is a shield to those who take refuge in
      him.
⁶ Do not add to his words,
   or he will rebuke you and prove you a liar.

⁷ "Two things I ask of you, O Lord;
   do not refuse me before I die:
⁸ Keep falsehood and lies far from me;
   give me neither poverty nor riches,
   but give me only my daily bread.
⁹ Otherwise, I may have too much and disown
      you
   and say, 'Who is the Lord?'
   Or I may become poor and steal,
   and so dishonor the name of my God.

¹⁰ "Do not slander a servant to his master,
   or he will curse you, and you will pay
      for it.

¹¹ "There are those who curse their fathers
   and do not bless their mothers;
¹² those who are pure in their own eyes
   and yet are not cleansed of their filth;

ª 1 Or *Jakeh of Massa*   ᵇ 1 Masoretic Text; with a different
word division of the Hebrew *declared,* "I am weary, O God; /
I am weary, O God, and faint.

THE MESSAGE

29.25 The fear of human opinion disables;
   trusting in God protects you from that.

29.26 Everyone tries to get help from the leader,
   but only God will give us justice.

29.27 Good people can't stand the sight of deliberate
      evil;
   the wicked can't stand the sight of well-
      chosen goodness.

THE WORDS OF AGUR BEN YAKEH

GOD? WHO NEEDS HIM?

30.1-2 **30** The skeptic swore, "There is no God!
   No God!—I can do anything I want!
I'm more animal than human;
   so-called human intelligence escapes me.

30.3-4 "I flunked 'wisdom.'
   I see no evidence of a holy God.
Has anyone ever seen Anyone
   climb into Heaven and take charge?
   grab the winds and control them?
   gather the rains in his bucket?
   stake out the ends of the earth?
Just tell me his name, tell me the names of his
      sons.
   Come on now—tell me!"

30.5-6 The believer replied, "Every promise of God
      proves true;
   he protects everyone who runs to him for
      help.
So don't second-guess him;
   he might take you to task and show up
      your lies."

30.7-9 And then he prayed, "God, I'm asking for two
      things
   before I die; don't refuse me—
Banish lies from my lips
   and liars from my presence.
Give me enough food to live on,
   neither too much nor too little.
If I'm too full, I might get independent,
   saying, 'God? Who needs him?'
If I'm poor, I might steal
   and dishonor the name of my God."

✝

30.10 Don't blow the whistle on your fellow workers
      behind their backs;
   They'll accuse you of being underhanded,
   and then *you'll* be the guilty one!

30.11 Don't curse your father
   or fail to bless your mother.

30.12 Don't imagine yourself to be quite presentable
   when you haven't had a bath in weeks.

NEW INTERNATIONAL VERSION

¹³ those whose eyes are ever so haughty,
   whose glances are so disdainful;
¹⁴ those whose teeth are swords
   and whose jaws are set with knives
to devour the poor from the earth,
   the needy from among mankind.

¹⁵ "The leech has two daughters.
   'Give! Give!' they cry.

"There are three things that are never
   satisfied,
   four that never say, 'Enough!':
¹⁶ the grave,ᵃ the barren womb,
   land, which is never satisfied with water,
   and fire, which never says, 'Enough!'

¹⁷ "The eye that mocks a father,
   that scorns obedience to a mother,
will be pecked out by the ravens of the
   valley,
   will be eaten by the vultures.

¹⁸ "There are three things that are too amazing
   for me,
   four that I do not understand:
¹⁹ the way of an eagle in the sky,
   the way of a snake on a rock,
the way of a ship on the high seas,
   and the way of a man with a maiden.

²⁰ "This is the way of an adulteress:
   She eats and wipes her mouth
   and says, 'I've done nothing wrong.'

²¹ "Under three things the earth trembles,
   under four it cannot bear up:
²² a servant who becomes king,
   a fool who is full of food,
²³ an unloved woman who is married,
   and a maidservant who displaces her
      mistress.

²⁴ "Four things on earth are small,
   yet they are extremely wise:
²⁵ Ants are creatures of little strength,

THE MESSAGE

30.13 Don't be stuck-up
   and think you're better than everyone else.

30.14 Don't be greedy,
   merciless and cruel as wolves,
Tearing into the poor and feasting on them,
   shredding the needy to pieces only to
      discard them.

30.15-16 A leech has twin daughters
   named "Gimme" and "Gimme more."

FOUR INSATIABLES
Three things are never satisfied,
   no, there are four that never say, "That's
      enough, thank you!"—

   hell,
   a barren womb,
   a parched land,
   a forest fire.

                            ✝

30.17 An eye that disdains a father
   and despises a mother—
that eye will be plucked out by wild vultures
   and consumed by young eagles.

FOUR MYSTERIES
30.18-19 Three things amaze me,
   no, four things I'll never understand—

   how an eagle flies so high in the sky,
   how a snake glides over a rock,
   how a ship navigates the ocean,
   why adolescents act the way they do.

                            ✝

30.20 Here's how a prostitute operates:
   she has sex with her client,
Takes a bath,
   then asks, "Who's next?"

FOUR INTOLERABLES
30.21-23 Three things are too much for even the earth
      to bear,
   yes, four things shake its foundations—

   when the janitor becomes the boss,
   when a fool gets rich,
   when a whore is voted "woman of the
      year,"
   when a "girlfriend" replaces a faithful
      wife.

FOUR SMALL WONDERS
30.24-28 There are four small creatures,
   wisest of the wise they are—

   ants—frail as they are,

ᵃ 16 Hebrew *Sheol*

NEW INTERNATIONAL VERSION

yet they store up their food in the
summer;
²⁶ coneys^a are creatures of little power,
yet they make their home in the crags;
²⁷ locusts have no king,
yet they advance together in ranks;
²⁸ a lizard can be caught with the hand,
yet it is found in kings' palaces.

²⁹ "There are three things that are stately in
their stride,
four that move with stately bearing:
³⁰ a lion, mighty among beasts,
who retreats before nothing;
³¹ a strutting rooster, a he-goat,
and a king with his army around him.^b

³² "If you have played the fool and exalted
yourself,
or if you have planned evil,
clap your hand over your mouth!
³³ For as churning the milk produces butter,
and as twisting the nose produces blood,
so stirring up anger produces strife."

Sayings of King Lemuel

31 The sayings of King Lemuel—an oracle^c
his mother taught him:

² "O my son, O son of my womb,
O son of my vows,^d
³ do not spend your strength on women,
your vigor on those who ruin kings.

⁴ "It is not for kings, O Lemuel—
not for kings to drink wine,
not for rulers to crave beer,
⁵ lest they drink and forget what the law
decrees,
and deprive all the oppressed of their rights.
⁶ Give beer to those who are perishing,
wine to those who are in anguish;
⁷ let them drink and forget their poverty
and remember their misery no more.

⁸ "Speak up for those who cannot speak for
themselves,
for the rights of all who are destitute.
⁹ Speak up and judge fairly;
defend the rights of the poor and needy."

THE MESSAGE

get plenty of food in for the winter;
marmots—vulnerable as they are,
manage to arrange for rock-solid
homes;
locusts—leaderless insects,
yet they strip the field like an army
regiment;
lizards—easy enough to catch,
but they sneak past vigilant palace
guards.

Four Dignitaries

^{30.29-31} There are three solemn dignitaries,
four that are impressive in their bearing—

a lion, king of the beasts, deferring to
none;
a rooster, proud and strutting;
a billy goat;
a head of state in stately procession.

^{30.32-33} If you're dumb enough to call attention to
yourself
by offending people and making rude
gestures,
Don't be surprised if someone bloodies your
nose.
Churned milk turns into butter;
riled emotions turn into fist fights.

Speak Out for Justice

^{31.1} **31** The words of King Lemuel,
the strong advice his mother gave him:

^{31.2-3} "Oh, son of mine, what can you be
thinking of!
Child whom I bore! The son I dedicated to
God!
Don't dissipate your virility on fortune-
hunting women,
promiscuous women who shipwreck leaders.

^{31.4-7} "Leaders can't afford to make fools of
themselves,
gulping wine and swilling beer,
Lest, hung over, they don't know right from
wrong,
and the people who depend on them are
hurt.
Use wine and beer only as sedatives,
to kill the pain and dull the ache
Of the terminally ill,
for whom life is a living death.

^{31.8-9} "Speak up for the people who have no voice,
for the rights of all the down-and-outers.
Speak out for justice!
Stand up for the poor and destitute!"

---

^a 26 That is, the hyrax or rock badger   ^b 31 Or king
secure against revolt   ^c 1 Or of Lemuel king of Massa, which
^d 2 Or / the answer to my prayers

NEW INTERNATIONAL VERSION	THE MESSAGE

NEW INTERNATIONAL VERSION

EPILOGUE: THE WIFE OF NOBLE CHARACTER

10 [a] A wife of noble character who can find?
　　She is worth far more than rubies.
11 Her husband has full confidence in her
　　and lacks nothing of value.
12 She brings him good, not harm,
　　all the days of her life.
13 She selects wool and flax
　　and works with eager hands.
14 She is like the merchant ships,
　　bringing her food from afar.
15 She gets up while it is still dark;
　　she provides food for her family
　　and portions for her servant girls.
16 She considers a field and buys it;
　　out of her earnings she plants a vineyard.
17 She sets about her work vigorously;
　　her arms are strong for her tasks.
18 She sees that her trading is profitable,
　　and her lamp does not go out at night.
19 In her hand she holds the distaff
　　and grasps the spindle with her fingers.
20 She opens her arms to the poor
　　and extends her hands to the needy.
21 When it snows, she has no fear for her
　　　household;
　　for all of them are clothed in scarlet.
22 She makes coverings for her bed;
　　she is clothed in fine linen and purple.
23 Her husband is respected at the city gate,
　　where he takes his seat among the elders
　　　of the land.
24 She makes linen garments and sells them,
　　and supplies the merchants with sashes.
25 She is clothed with strength and dignity;
　　she can laugh at the days to come.
26 She speaks with wisdom,
　　and faithful instruction is on her tongue.
27 She watches over the affairs of her
　　　household
　　and does not eat the bread of idleness.
28 Her children arise and call her blessed;
　　her husband also, and he praises her:
29 "Many women do noble things,
　　but you surpass them all."
30 Charm is deceptive, and beauty is fleeting;
　　but a woman who fears the LORD is to be
　　　praised.
31 Give her the reward she has earned,
　　and let her works bring her praise at the
　　　city gate.

[a] 10 Verses 10-31 are an acrostic, each verse beginning with
a successive letter of the Hebrew alphabet.

THE MESSAGE

HYMN TO A GOOD WIFE

31.10-31 A good woman is hard to find,
　　and worth far more than diamonds.
Her husband trusts her without reserve,
　　and never has reason to regret it.
Never spiteful, she treats him generously
　　all her life long.
She shops around for the best yarns and
　　　cottons,
　　and enjoys knitting and sewing.
She's like a trading ship that sails to faraway
　　　places
　　and brings back exotic surprises.
She's up before dawn, preparing breakfast
　　for her family and organizing her day.
She looks over a field and buys it,
　　then, with money she's put aside, plants a
　　　garden.
First thing in the morning, she dresses for
　　　work,
　　rolls up her sleeves, eager to get started.
She senses the worth of her work,
　　is in no hurry to call it quits for the day.
She's skilled in the crafts of home and hearth,
　　diligent in homemaking.
She's quick to assist anyone in need,
　　reaches out to help the poor.
She doesn't worry about her family when it
　　　snows;
　　their winter clothes are all mended and
　　　ready to wear.
She makes her own clothing,
　　and dresses in colorful linens and silks.
Her husband is greatly respected
　　when he deliberates with the city fathers.
She designs gowns and sells them,
　　brings the sweaters she knits to the dress
　　　shops.
Her clothes are well-made and elegant,
　　and she always faces tomorrow with a
　　　smile.
When she speaks she has something
　　　worthwhile to say,
　　and she always says it kindly.
She keeps an eye on everyone in her
　　　household,
　　and keeps them all busy and productive.
Her children respect and bless her;
　　her husband joins in with words of praise:
"Many women have done wonderful things,
　　but you've outclassed them all!"
Charm can mislead and beauty soon fades.
　　The woman to be admired and praised
　　is the woman who lives in the Fear-of-GOD.
Give her everything she deserves!
　　Festoon her life with praises!

ECCLESIASTES

ECCLESIASTES

EVERYTHING IS MEANINGLESS

1 The words of the Teacher,[a] son of David,
king in Jerusalem:

2 "Meaningless! Meaningless!"
   says the Teacher.
  "Utterly meaningless!
   Everything is meaningless."

3 What does man gain from all his labor
   at which he toils under the sun?
4 Generations come and generations go,
   but the earth remains forever.
5 The sun rises and the sun sets,
   and hurries back to where it rises.
6 The wind blows to the south
   and turns to the north;
  round and round it goes,
   ever returning on its course.
7 All streams flow into the sea,
   yet the sea is never full.
  To the place the streams come from,
   there they return again.
8 All things are wearisome,
   more than one can say.
  The eye never has enough of seeing,
   nor the ear its fill of hearing.
9 What has been will be again,
   what has been done will be done again;
   there is nothing new under the sun.
10 Is there anything of which one can say,
   "Look! This is something new"?
  It was here already, long ago;
   it was here before our time.
11 There is no remembrance of men of old,
   and even those who are yet to come
  will not be remembered
   by those who follow.

WISDOM IS MEANINGLESS

12 I, the Teacher, was king over Israel in Jerusa-

THE QUESTER

1.1 **1** These are the words of the Quester, David's
son and king in Jerusalem:

1.2-11   Smoke, nothing but smoke. [That's what
         the Quester says.]
      There's nothing to anything—it's all
         smoke.
   What's there to show for a lifetime of work,
      a lifetime of working your fingers to the
         bone?
   One generation goes its way, the next one
      arrives,
      but nothing changes—it's business as
         usual for old planet earth.
   The sun comes up and the sun goes down,
      then does it again, and again—the same
         old round.
   The wind blows south, the wind blows
      north.
      Around and around and around it blows,
         blowing this way, then that—the
            whirling, erratic wind.
   All the rivers flow into the sea,
      but the sea never fills up.
   The rivers keep flowing to the same old
      place,
      and then start all over and do it again.
   Everything's boring, utterly boring—
      no one can find any meaning in it.
   Boring to the eye,
      boring to the ear.
   What was will be again,
      what happened will happen again.
   There's nothing new on this earth.
      Year after year it's the same old thing.
   Does someone call out, "Hey, *this* is new"?
      Don't get excited—it's the same old story.
   Nobody remembers what happened
      yesterday.
      And the things that will happen
         tomorrow?
   Nobody'll remember them either.
      Don't count on being remembered.

I'VE SEEN IT ALL

1.12-14 Call me "the Quester." I've been king over Isra-

---

a 1 Or *leader of the assembly*; also in verses 2 and 12

NEW INTERNATIONAL VERSION

lem. ¹³I devoted myself to study and to explore by wisdom all that is done under heaven. What a heavy burden God has laid on men! ¹⁴I have seen all the things that are done under the sun; all of them are meaningless, a chasing after the wind.

¹⁵What is twisted cannot be straightened;
   what is lacking cannot be counted.

¹⁶I thought to myself, "Look, I have grown and increased in wisdom more than anyone who has ruled over Jerusalem before me; I have experienced much of wisdom and knowledge." ¹⁷Then I applied myself to the understanding of wisdom, and also of madness and folly, but I learned that this, too, is a chasing after the wind.

¹⁸For with much wisdom comes much sorrow;
   the more knowledge, the more grief.

PLEASURES ARE MEANINGLESS

2 I thought in my heart, "Come now, I will test you with pleasure to find out what is good." But that also proved to be meaningless. ²"Laughter," I said, "is foolish. And what does pleasure accomplish?" ³I tried cheering myself with wine, and embracing folly—my mind still guiding me with wisdom. I wanted to see what was worthwhile for men to do under heaven during the few days of their lives.

⁴I undertook great projects: I built houses for myself and planted vineyards. ⁵I made gardens and parks and planted all kinds of fruit trees in them. ⁶I made reservoirs to water groves of flourishing trees. ⁷I bought male and female slaves and had other slaves who were born in my house. I also owned more herds and flocks than anyone in Jerusalem before me. ⁸I amassed silver and gold for myself, and the treasure of kings and provinces. I acquired men and women singers, and a harem*ᵃ* as well—the delights of the heart of man. ⁹I became greater by far than

THE MESSAGE

el in Jerusalem. I looked most carefully into everything, searched out all that is done on this earth. And let me tell you, there's not much to write home about. God hasn't made it easy for us. I've seen it all and it's nothing but smoke—smoke, and spitting into the wind.

1.15 Life's a corkscrew that can't be straightened,
   A minus that won't add up.

1.16-17 I said to myself, "I know more and I'm wiser than anyone before me in Jerusalem. I've stock-piled wisdom and knowledge." What I've finally concluded is that so-called wisdom and knowledge are mindless and witless—nothing but spitting into the wind.

1.18 Much learning earns you much trouble.
   The more you know, the more you hurt.

2.1-3 2 I said to myself, "Let's go for it—experiment with pleasure, have a good time!" But there was nothing to it, nothing but smoke.

What do I think of the fun-filled life?
   Insane! Inane!
   My verdict on the pursuit of happiness?
   Who needs it?
With the help of a bottle of wine
   and all the wisdom I could muster,
I tried my level best
   to penetrate the absurdity of life.
I wanted to get a handle on anything useful
   we mortals might do
   during the years we spend on this earth.

I NEVER SAID NO TO MYSELF

2.4-8 Oh, I did great things:
   built houses,
   planted vineyards,
   designed gardens and parks
      and planted a variety of fruit trees in
         them,
   made pools of water
      to irrigate the groves of trees.
I bought slaves, male and female,
   who had children, giving me even
      more slaves;
   then I acquired large herds and flocks,
      larger than any before me in
         Jerusalem.
I piled up silver and gold,
   loot from kings and kingdoms.
I gathered a chorus of singers to entertain
      me with song,
   and—most exquisite of all pleasures—
      voluptuous maidens for my bed.

2.9-10 Oh, how I prospered! I left all my predeces-

ᵃ 8 The meaning of the Hebrew for this phrase is uncertain.

NEW INTERNATIONAL VERSION

anyone in Jerusalem before me. In all this my wisdom stayed with me.

¹⁰I denied myself nothing my eyes desired;
  I refused my heart no pleasure.
My heart took delight in all my work,
  and this was the reward for all my labor.
¹¹Yet when I surveyed all that my hands had done
  and what I had toiled to achieve,
everything was meaningless, a chasing after the wind;
  nothing was gained under the sun.

WISDOM AND FOLLY ARE MEANINGLESS

¹²Then I turned my thoughts to consider wisdom,
  and also madness and folly.
What more can the king's successor do
  than what has already been done?
¹³I saw that wisdom is better than folly,
  just as light is better than darkness.
¹⁴The wise man has eyes in his head,
  while the fool walks in the darkness;
but I came to realize
  that the same fate overtakes them both.

¹⁵Then I thought in my heart,

"The fate of the fool will overtake me also.
  What then do I gain by being wise?"
I said in my heart,
  "This too is meaningless."
¹⁶For the wise man, like the fool, will not be long remembered;
  in days to come both will be forgotten.
Like the fool, the wise man too must die!

TOIL IS MEANINGLESS

¹⁷So I hated life, because the work that is done under the sun was grievous to me. All of it is meaningless, a chasing after the wind. ¹⁸I hated all the things I had toiled for under the sun, because I must leave them to the one who comes after me. ¹⁹And who knows whether he will be a wise man or a fool? Yet he will have control over all the work into which I have poured my effort and skill under the sun. This too is meaningless. ²⁰So my heart began to despair over all my toilsome labor under the sun. ²¹For a man may do his work with wisdom, knowledge and skill, and then he must leave all he owns to someone who has not worked for it. This too is meaningless and a great misfortune. ²²What does a man get for all the toil and anxious striving with which he labors under the sun? ²³All his days his work is pain and grief; even at night his mind does not rest. This too is meaningless.

THE MESSAGE

sors in Jerusalem far behind, left them behind in the dust. What's more, I kept a clear head through it all. Everything I wanted I took—I never said no to myself. I gave in to every impulse, held back nothing. I sucked the marrow of pleasure out of every task—my reward to myself for a hard day's work!

I HATE LIFE

2.11 Then I took a good look at everything I'd done, looked at all the sweat and hard work. But when I looked, I saw nothing but smoke. Smoke and spitting into the wind. There was nothing to any of it. Nothing.

2.12-14 And then I took a hard look at what's smart and what's stupid. What's left to do after you've been king? That's a hard act to follow. You just do what you can, and that's it. But I did see that it's better to be smart than stupid, just as light is better than darkness. Even so, though the smart ones see where they're going and the stupid ones grope in the dark, they're all the same in the end. One fate for all—and that's it.

2.15-16 When I realized that my fate's the same as the fool's, I had to ask myself, "So why bother being wise?" It's all smoke, nothing but smoke. The smart and the stupid both disappear out of sight. In a day or two they're both forgotten. Yes, both the smart and the stupid die, and that's it.

2.17 I hate life. As far as I can see, what happens on earth is a bad business. It's smoke—and spitting into the wind.

2.18-19 And I hated everything I'd accomplished and accumulated on this earth. I can't take it with me—no, I have to leave it to whoever comes after me. Whether they're worthy or worthless—and who's to tell?—they'll take over the earthly results of my intense thinking and hard work. Smoke.

2.20-23 That's when I called it quits, gave up on anything that could be hoped for on this earth. What's the point of working your fingers to the bone if you hand over what you worked for to someone who never lifted a finger for it? Smoke, that's what it is. A bad business from start to finish. So what do you get from a life of hard labor? Pain and grief from dawn to dusk. Never a decent night's rest. Nothing but smoke.

NEW INTERNATIONAL VERSION

²⁴A man can do nothing better than to eat and drink and find satisfaction in his work. This too, I see, is from the hand of God, ²⁵for without him, who can eat or find enjoyment? ²⁶To the man who pleases him, God gives wisdom, knowledge and happiness, but to the sinner he gives the task of gathering and storing up wealth to hand it over to the one who pleases God. This too is meaningless, a chasing after the wind.

A TIME FOR EVERYTHING

3 There is a time for everything,
      and a season for every activity under
        heaven:

2   a time to be born and a time to die,
      a time to plant and a time to uproot,
3   a time to kill and a time to heal,
      a time to tear down and a time to build,
4   a time to weep and a time to laugh,
      a time to mourn and a time to dance,
5   a time to scatter stones and a time to
        gather them,
      a time to embrace and a time to refrain,
6   a time to search and a time to give up,
      a time to keep and a time to throw away,
7   a time to tear and a time to mend,
      a time to be silent and a time to speak,
8   a time to love and a time to hate,
      a time for war and a time for peace.

⁹What does the worker gain from his toil? ¹⁰I have seen the burden God has laid on men. ¹¹He has made everything beautiful in its time. He has also set eternity in the hearts of men; yet they cannot fathom what God has done from beginning to end. ¹²I know that there is nothing better for men than to be happy and do good while they live. ¹³That everyone may eat and drink, and find satisfaction in all his toil—this is the gift of God. ¹⁴I know that everything God does will endure forever; nothing can be added to it and nothing taken from it. God does it so that men will revere him.

¹⁵Whatever is has already been,
      and what will be has been before;
      and God will call the past to account.^a

^a 15 Or God calls back the past

THE MESSAGE

2.24-26   The best you can do with your life is have a good time and get by the best you can. The way I see it, that's it—divine fate. Whether we feast or fast, it's up to God. God may give wisdom and knowledge and joy to his favorites, but sinners are assigned a life of hard labor, and end up turning their wages over to God's favorites. Nothing but smoke—and spitting into the wind.

THERE'S A RIGHT TIME FOR EVERYTHING

3.1   **3** There's an opportune time to do things, a
         right time for everything on the earth:

3.2-8   A right time for birth and another for
           death,
         A right time to plant and another to reap,
         A right time to kill and another to heal,
         A right time to destroy and another to
           construct,
         A right time to cry and another to laugh,
         A right time to lament and another to
           cheer,
         A right time to make love and another to
           abstain,
         A right time to embrace and another to
           part,
         A right time to search and another to count
           your losses,
         A right time to hold on and another to
           let go,
         A right time to rip out and another to
           mend,
         A right time to shut up and another to
           speak up,
         A right time to love and another to hate,
         A right time to wage war and another to
           make peace.

3.9-13   But in the end, does it really make a difference what anyone does? I've had a good look at what God has given us to do—busywork, mostly. True, God made everything beautiful in itself and in its time—but he's left us in the dark, so we can never know what God is up to, whether he's coming or going. I've decided that there's nothing better to do than go ahead and have a good time and get the most we can out of life. That's it—eat, drink, and make the most of your job. It's God's gift.

3.14   I've also concluded that whatever God does, that's the way it's going to be, always. No addition, no subtraction. God's done it and that's it. That's so we'll quit asking questions and simply worship in holy fear.

3.15   Whatever was, is.
         Whatever will be, is.
         That's how it always is with God.

NEW INTERNATIONAL VERSION

¹⁶And I saw something else under the sun:

In the place of judgment—wickedness was
there,
in the place of justice—wickedness was
there.

¹⁷I thought in my heart,

"God will bring to judgment
both the righteous and the wicked,
for there will be a time for every activity,
a time for every deed."

¹⁸I also thought, "As for men, God tests them
so that they may see that they are like the animals. ¹⁹Man's fate is like that of the animals; the
same fate awaits them both: As one dies, so dies
the other. All have the same breath^a; man has
no advantage over the animal. Everything is
meaningless. ²⁰All go to the same place; all come
from dust, and to dust all return. ²¹Who knows
if the spirit of man rises upward and if the spirit
of the animal^b goes down into the earth?"

²²So I saw that there is nothing better for a
man than to enjoy his work, because that is his
lot. For who can bring him to see what will happen after him?

OPPRESSION, TOIL, FRIENDLESSNESS

4 Again I looked and saw all the oppression
that was taking place under the sun:

I saw the tears of the oppressed—
and they have no comforter;
power was on the side of their oppressors—
and they have no comforter.
²And I declared that the dead,
who had already died,
are happier than the living,
who are still alive.
³But better than both
is he who has not yet been,
who has not seen the evil
that is done under the sun.

⁴And I saw that all labor and all achievement
spring from man's envy of his neighbor. This too
is meaningless, a chasing after the wind.

⁵The fool folds his hands
and ruins himself.
⁶Better one handful with tranquillity
than two handfuls with toil
and chasing after the wind.

⁷Again I saw something meaningless under
the sun:

^a 19 Or spirit   ^b 21 Or Who knows the spirit of man, which
rises upward, or the spirit of the animal, which

THE MESSAGE

GOD'S TESTING US

3.16-18 I took another good look at what's going on:
The very place of judgment—corrupt! The
place of righteousness—corrupt! I said to myself, "God will judge righteous and wicked."
There's a right time for every thing, every
deed—and there's no getting around it. I said to
myself regarding the human race, "God's testing the lot of us, showing us up as nothing but
animals."

3.19-22   Humans and animals come to the same
end—humans die, animals die. We all breathe
the same air. So there's really no advantage in
being human. None. Everything's smoke. We
all end up in the same place—we all came from
dust, we all end up as dust. Nobody knows for
sure that the human spirit rises to heaven or
that the animal spirit sinks into the earth. So I
made up my mind that there's nothing better
for us men and women than to have a good
time in whatever we do—that's our lot. Who
knows if there's anything else to life?

SLOW SUICIDE

4.1-3 **4** Next I turned my attention to all the outrageous violence that takes place on this
planet—the tears of the victims, no one to
comfort them; the iron grip of oppressors, no
one to rescue the victims from them. So I congratulated the dead who are already dead instead of the living who are still alive. But luck-
ier than the dead or the living is the person
who has never even been, who has never seen
the bad business that takes place on this earth.

4.4   Then I observed all the work and ambition
motivated by envy. What a waste! Smoke. And
spitting into the wind.

4.5   The fool sits back and takes it easy,
His sloth is slow suicide.

4.6   One handful of peaceful repose
Is better than two fistfuls of worried
work—
More spitting into the wind.

WHY AM I WORKING LIKE A DOG?

4.7-8 I turned my head and saw yet another wisp of
smoke on its way to nothingness: a solitary

NEW INTERNATIONAL VERSION

8 There was a man all alone;
    he had neither son nor brother.
There was no end to his toil,
    yet his eyes were not content with his
        wealth.
"For whom am I toiling," he asked,
    "and why am I depriving myself of
        enjoyment?"
This too is meaningless—
    a miserable business!

9 Two are better than one,
    because they have a good return for their
        work:
10 If one falls down,
    his friend can help him up.
But pity the man who falls
    and has no one to help him up!
11 Also, if two lie down together, they will keep
        warm.
    But how can one keep warm alone?
12 Though one may be overpowered,
    two can defend themselves.
A cord of three strands is not quickly
    broken.

ADVANCEMENT IS MEANINGLESS

13 Better a poor but wise youth than an old but
foolish king who no longer knows how to take
warning. 14 The youth may have come from prison to the kingship, or he may have been born in
poverty within his kingdom. 15 I saw that all who
lived and walked under the sun followed the
youth, the king's successor. 16 There was no end
to all the people who were before them. But those
who came later were not pleased with the successor. This too is meaningless, a chasing after the
wind.

STAND IN AWE OF GOD

5 Guard your steps when you go to the house
of God. Go near to listen rather than to offer
the sacrifice of fools, who do not know that they
do wrong.

2 Do not be quick with your mouth,
    do not be hasty in your heart
        to utter anything before God.
God is in heaven
    and you are on earth,
        so let your words be few.
3 As a dream comes when there are many
        cares,
    so the speech of a fool when there are
        many words.

4 When you make a vow to God, do not delay

THE MESSAGE

person, completely alone—no children, no
family, no friends—yet working obsessively late
into the night, compulsively greedy for more
and more, never bothering to ask, "Why am I
working like a dog, never having any fun? And
who cares?" More smoke. A bad business.

4.9-10 It's better to have a partner than go it alone.
        Share the work, share the wealth.
        And if one falls down, the other helps,
        But if there's no one to help, tough!

4.11 Two in a bed warm each other.
        Alone, you shiver all night.

4.12 By yourself you're unprotected.
        With a friend you can face the worst.
        Can you round up a third?
        A three-stranded rope isn't easily snapped.

⊹

4.13-16 A poor youngster with some wisdom is better
        off than an old but foolish king who doesn't
        know which end is up. I saw a youth just like
        this start with nothing and go from rags to
        riches, and I saw everyone rally to the rule
        of this young successor to the king. Even so,
        the excitement died quickly, the throngs of
        people soon lost interest. Can't you see it's only
        smoke? And spitting into the wind?

GOD'S IN CHARGE, NOT YOU

5.1 **5** Watch your step when you enter God's
        house.
        Enter to learn. That's far better than
            mindlessly offering a sacrifice,
        Doing more harm than good.

5.2 Don't shoot off your mouth, or speak
            before you think.
        Don't be too quick to tell God what you
            think he wants to hear.
        God's in charge, not you—the less you
            speak, the better.

5.3 Over-work makes for restless sleep.
        Over-talk shows you up as a fool.

5.4-5 When you tell God you'll do something, do
        it—now.

NEW INTERNATIONAL VERSION

in fulfilling it. He has no pleasure in fools; fulfill your vow. [5]It is better not to vow than to make a vow and not fulfill it. [6]Do not let your mouth lead you into sin. And do not protest to the ⌐temple⌐ messenger, "My vow was a mistake." Why should God be angry at what you say and destroy the work of your hands? [7]Much dreaming and many words are meaningless. Therefore stand in awe of God.

RICHES ARE MEANINGLESS

[8]If you see the poor oppressed in a district, and justice and rights denied, do not be surprised at such things; for one official is eyed by a higher one, and over them both are others higher still. [9]The increase from the land is taken by all; the king himself profits from the fields.

[10]Whoever loves money never has money
    enough;
  whoever loves wealth is never satisfied
    with his income.
  This too is meaningless.

[11]As goods increase,
  so do those who consume them.
And what benefit are they to the owner
  except to feast his eyes on them?

[12]The sleep of a laborer is sweet,
  whether he eats little or much,
but the abundance of a rich man
  permits him no sleep.

[13]I have seen a grievous evil under the sun:

wealth hoarded to the harm of its owner,
[14] or wealth lost through some misfortune,
so that when he has a son
  there is nothing left for him.
[15]Naked a man comes from his mother's
    womb,
  and as he comes, so he departs.
He takes nothing from his labor
  that he can carry in his hand.

[16]This too is a grievous evil:

As a man comes, so he departs,
  and what does he gain,
  since he toils for the wind?
[17]All his days he eats in darkness,
  with great frustration, affliction and anger.

[18]Then I realized that it is good and proper for a man to eat and drink, and to find satisfaction

THE MESSAGE

God takes no pleasure in foolish gabble.
  Vow it, then do it.
Far better not to vow in the first place than
  to vow and not pay up.

5.6 Don't let your mouth make a total sinner of
    you.
When called to account, you won't get by
    with "Sorry, I didn't mean it."
Why risk provoking God to angry
    retaliation?

5.7 But against all illusion and fantasy and
    empty talk
There's always this rock foundation: Fear
    God!

A SALARY OF SMOKE

5.8-9 Don't be too upset when you see the poor kicked around, and justice and right violated all over the place. Exploitation filters down from one petty official to another. There's no end to it, and nothing can be done about it. But the good earth doesn't cheat anyone—even a bad king is honestly served by a field.

5.10 The one who loves money is never satisfied
    with money,
Nor the one who loves wealth with big
    profits. More smoke.

5.11 The more loot you get, the more looters
    show up.
And what fun is that—to be robbed in
    broad daylight?

5.12 Hard and honest work earns a good night's
    sleep,
Whether supper is beans or steak.
But a rich man's belly gives him insomnia.

5.13-17 Here's a piece of bad luck I've seen happen:
A man hoards far more wealth than is good
    for him
And then loses it all in a bad business deal.
He fathered a child but hasn't a cent left to
    give him.
He arrived naked from the womb of his
    mother;
He'll leave in the same condition—with
    nothing.
This is bad luck, for sure—naked he came,
    naked he went.
So what was the point of working for a
    salary of smoke?
All for a miserable life spent in the dark?

MAKE THE MOST OF WHAT GOD GIVES

5.18-20 After looking at the way things are on this earth, here's what I've decided is the best way to live:

NEW INTERNATIONAL VERSION

in his toilsome labor under the sun during the few days of life God has given him—for this is his lot. ¹⁹Moreover, when God gives any man wealth and possessions, and enables him to enjoy them, to accept his lot and be happy in his work—this is a gift of God. ²⁰He seldom reflects on the days of his life, because God keeps him occupied with gladness of heart.

6 I have seen another evil under the sun, and it weighs heavily on men: ²God gives a man wealth, possessions and honor, so that he lacks nothing his heart desires, but God does not enable him to enjoy them, and a stranger enjoys them instead. This is meaningless, a grievous evil.

³A man may have a hundred children and live many years; yet no matter how long he lives, if he cannot enjoy his prosperity and does not receive proper burial, I say that a stillborn child is better off than he. ⁴It comes without meaning, it departs in darkness, and in darkness its name is shrouded. ⁵Though it never saw the sun or knew anything, it has more rest than does that man— ⁶even if he lives a thousand years twice over but fails to enjoy his prosperity. Do not all go to the same place?

⁷ All man's efforts are for his mouth,
  yet his appetite is never satisfied.
⁸What advantage has a wise man
  over a fool?
What does a poor man gain
  by knowing how to conduct himself
    before others?
⁹Better what the eye sees
  than the roving of the appetite.
This too is meaningless,
  a chasing after the wind.

¹⁰Whatever exists has already been named,
  and what man is has been known;
no man can contend
  with one who is stronger than he.
¹¹The more the words,
  the less the meaning,
  and how does that profit anyone?

¹²For who knows what is good for a man in life, during the few and meaningless days he passes through like a shadow? Who can tell him what will happen under the sun after he is gone?

WISDOM

7 A good name is better than fine perfume,
  and the day of death better than the day
    of birth.

THE MESSAGE

Take care of yourself, have a good time, and make the most of whatever job you have for as long as God gives you life. And that's about it. That's the human lot. Yes, we should make the most of what God gives, both the bounty and the capacity to enjoy it, accepting what's given and delighting in the work. It's God's gift! God deals out joy in the present, the *now*. It's useless to brood over how long we might live.

THINGS ARE BAD

6.1-2 **6** I looked long and hard at what goes on around here, and let me tell you, things are bad. And people feel it. There are people, for instance, on whom God showers everything— money, property, reputation—all they ever wanted or dreamed of. And then God doesn't let them enjoy it. Some stranger comes along and has all the fun. It's more of what I'm calling *smoke*. A bad business.

6.3-5 Say a couple have scores of children and live a long, long life but never enjoy themselves— even though they end up with a big funeral! I'd say that a stillborn baby gets the better deal. It gets its start in a mist and ends up in the dark—unnamed. It sees nothing and knows nothing, but is better off by far than anyone living.

6.6 Even if someone lived a thousand years— make it two thousand!—but didn't enjoy anything, what's the point? Doesn't everyone end up in the same place?

6.7 We work to feed our appetites;
  Meanwhile our souls go hungry.

6.8-9 So what advantage has a sage over a fool, or over some poor wretch who barely gets by? Just grab whatever you can while you can; don't assume something better might turn up by and by. All it amounts to anyway is smoke. And spitting into the wind.

6.10 Whatever happens, happens. Its destiny is
  fixed.
You can't argue with fate.

6.11-12 The more words that are spoken, the more smoke there is in the air. And who is any better off? And who knows what's best for us as we live out our meager smoke-and-shadow lives? And who can tell any of us the next chapter of our lives?

DON'T TAKE ANYTHING FOR GRANTED

7.1 **7** A good reputation is better than a fat bank
    account.
  Your death date tells more than your birth
    date.

NEW INTERNATIONAL VERSION

²It is better to go to a house of mourning
    than to go to a house of feasting,
for death is the destiny of every man;
    the living should take this to heart.
³Sorrow is better than laughter,
    because a sad face is good for the heart.
⁴The heart of the wise is in the house of
        mourning,
    but the heart of fools is in the house of
        pleasure.
⁵It is better to heed a wise man's rebuke
    than to listen to the song of fools.
⁶Like the crackling of thorns under the pot,
    so is the laughter of fools.
    This too is meaningless.

⁷Extortion turns a wise man into a fool,
    and a bribe corrupts the heart.

⁸The end of a matter is better than its
        beginning,
    and patience is better than pride.
⁹Do not be quickly provoked in your spirit,
    for anger resides in the lap of fools.

¹⁰Do not say, "Why were the old days better
        than these?"
    For it is not wise to ask such questions.

¹¹Wisdom, like an inheritance, is a good thing
    and benefits those who see the sun.
¹²Wisdom is a shelter
    as money is a shelter,
but the advantage of knowledge is this:
    that wisdom preserves the life of its
        possessor.

¹³Consider what God has done:

Who can straighten
    what he has made crooked?
¹⁴When times are good, be happy;
    but when times are bad, consider:
God has made the one
    as well as the other.
Therefore, a man cannot discover
    anything about his future.

¹⁵In this meaningless life of mine I have seen
both of these:

a righteous man perishing in his
        righteousness,
    and a wicked man living long in his
        wickedness.
¹⁶Do not be overrighteous,
    neither be overwise—
    why destroy yourself?
¹⁷Do not be overwicked,
    and do not be a fool—
    why die before your time?

THE MESSAGE

7.2   You learn more at a funeral than at a
            feast—
        After all, that's where we'll end up. We
            might discover something from it.

7.3   Crying is better than laughing.
        It blotches the face but it scours the heart.

7.4   Sages invest themselves in hurt and
            grieving.
        Fools waste their lives in fun and games.

7.5   You'll get more from the rebuke of a sage
        Than from the song and dance of fools.

7.6   The giggles of fools are like the crackling of
            twigs
        Under the cooking pot. And like smoke.

7.7   Brutality stupefies even the wise
        And destroys the strongest heart.

7.8   Endings are better than beginnings.
        Sticking to it is better than standing out.

7.9   Don't be quick to fly off the handle.
        Anger boomerangs. You can spot a fool by
            the lumps on his head.

7.10   Don't always be asking, "Where are the
            good old days?"
        Wise folks don't ask questions like that.

7.11-12 Wisdom is better when it's paired with
            money,
        Especially if you get both while you're still
            living.
        Double protection: wisdom and wealth!
        Plus this bonus: Wisdom energizes its
            owner.

7.13   Take a good look at God's work.
        Who could simplify and reduce Creation's
            curves and angles
        To a plain straight line?

7.14   On a good day, enjoy yourself;
        On a bad day, examine your conscience.
        God arranges for both kinds of days
        So that we won't take anything for granted.

STAY IN TOUCH WITH BOTH SIDES

7.15-17 I've seen it all in my brief and pointless life—
        here a good person cut down in the middle of
        doing good, there a bad person living a long
        life of sheer evil. So don't knock yourself out
        being good, and don't go overboard being wise.
        Believe me, you won't get anything out of it.
        But don't press your luck by being bad, either.
        And don't be reckless. Why die needlessly?

NEW INTERNATIONAL VERSION

¹⁸ It is good to grasp the one
  and not let go of the other.
 The man who fears God will avoid all
  ⌊extremes⌋. *ᵃ*

¹⁹ Wisdom makes one wise man more powerful
  than ten rulers in a city.

²⁰ There is not a righteous man on earth
  who does what is right and never sins.

²¹ Do not pay attention to every word people
  say,
  or you may hear your servant cursing
   you—
²² for you know in your heart
  that many times you yourself have cursed
   others.

²³ All this I tested by wisdom and I said,

 "I am determined to be wise"—
  but this was beyond me.
²⁴ Whatever wisdom may be,
  it is far off and most profound—
  who can discover it?
²⁵ So I turned my mind to understand,
   to investigate and to search out wisdom
    and the scheme of things
 and to understand the stupidity of
    wickedness
  and the madness of folly.

²⁶ I find more bitter than death
  the woman who is a snare,
 whose heart is a trap
  and whose hands are chains.
 The man who pleases God will escape her,
  but the sinner she will ensnare.

²⁷ "Look," says the Teacher, *ᵇ* "this is what I
have discovered:

 "Adding one thing to another to discover the
   scheme of things—
²⁸ while I was still searching
  but not finding—
 I found one ⌊upright⌋ man among a
    thousand,
  but not one ⌊upright⌋ woman among them
   all.
²⁹ This only have I found:
  God made mankind upright,
  but men have gone in search of many
   schemes."

8 Who is like the wise man?
 Who knows the explanation of things?

THE MESSAGE

7.18 It's best to stay in touch with both sides of
an issue. A person who fears God deals responsibly with all of reality, not just a piece of it.

7.19 Wisdom puts more strength in one wise
    person
 Than ten strong men give to a city.

7.20 There's not one totally good person on
    earth,
 Not one who is truly pure and sinless.

7.21-22 Don't eavesdrop on the conversation of
    others.
 What if the gossip's about you and you'd
    rather not hear it?
 You've done that a few times, haven't you—
    said things
 Behind someone's back you wouldn't say to
    his face?

HOW TO INTERPRET THE MEANING OF LIFE

7.23-25 I tested everything in my search for wisdom. I
set out to be wise, but it was beyond me, far beyond me, and deep—oh so deep! Does anyone
ever find it? I concentrated with all my might,
studying and exploring and seeking wisdom—
the meaning of life. I also wanted to identify
evil and stupidity, foolishness and craziness.

7.26-29 One discovery: A woman can be a bitter pill
to swallow, full of seductive scheming and
grasping. The lucky escape her; the undiscern-
ing get caught. At least this is my experience—
what I, the Quester, have pieced together as
I've tried to make sense of life. But the wisdom
I've looked for I haven't found. I didn't find one
man or woman in a thousand worth my while.
Yet I did spot one ray of light in this murk: God
made men and women true and upright; *we're*
the ones who've made a mess of things.

8.1 **8** There's nothing better than being wise,
 Knowing how to interpret the meaning of
    life.

NEW INTERNATIONAL VERSION

Wisdom brightens a man's face
and changes its hard appearance.

OBEY THE KING

²Obey the king's command, I say, because you took an oath before God. ³Do not be in a hurry to leave the king's presence. Do not stand up for a bad cause, for he will do whatever he pleases. ⁴Since a king's word is supreme, who can say to him, "What are you doing?"

⁵Whoever obeys his command will come to
no harm,
and the wise heart will know the proper
time and procedure.
⁶For there is a proper time and procedure for
every matter,
though a man's misery weighs heavily
upon him.

⁷Since no man knows the future,
who can tell him what is to come?
⁸No man has power over the wind to
contain it ᵃ;
so no one has power over the day of his
death.
As no one is discharged in time of war,
so wickedness will not release those who
practice it.

⁹All this I saw, as I applied my mind to everything done under the sun. There is a time when a man lords it over others to his own ᵇ hurt. ¹⁰Then too, I saw the wicked buried—those who used to come and go from the holy place and receive praise ᶜ in the city where they did this. This too is meaningless. ¹¹When the sentence for a crime is not quickly carried out, the hearts of the people are filled with schemes to do wrong. ¹²Although a wicked man commits a hundred crimes and still lives a long time, I know that it will go better with God-fearing men, who are reverent before God. ¹³Yet because the wicked do not fear God, it will not go well with them, and their days will not lengthen like a shadow.

¹⁴There is something else meaningless that occurs on earth: righteous men who get what the wicked deserve, and wicked men who get what the righteous deserve. This too, I say, is meaningless. ¹⁵So I commend the enjoyment of life, because nothing is better for a man under the sun than to eat and drink and be glad. Then

---

ᵃ 8 Or over his spirit to retain it   ᵇ 9 Or to their
ᶜ 10 Some Hebrew manuscripts and Septuagint (Aquila);
most Hebrew manuscripts and are forgotten

THE MESSAGE

Wisdom puts light in the eyes,
And gives gentleness to words and
manners.

NO ONE CAN CONTROL THE WIND

8.2-7 Do what your king commands; you gave a sacred oath of obedience. Don't worryingly second-guess your orders or try to back out when the task is unpleasant. You're serving his pleasure, not yours. The king has the last word. Who dares say to him, "What are you doing?" Carrying out orders won't hurt you a bit; the wise person obeys promptly and accurately. Yes, there's a right time and way for everything, even though, unfortunately, we miss it for the most part. It's true that no one knows what's going to happen, or when. Who's around to tell us?

8.8   No one can control the wind or lock it in a
box.
No one has any say-so regarding the day of
death.
No one can stop a battle in its tracks.
No one who does evil can be saved by evil.

8.9   All this I observed as I tried my best to understand all that's going on in this world. As long as men and women have the power to hurt each other, this is the way it is.

ONE FATE FOR EVERYBODY

8.10 One time I saw wicked men given a solemn burial in holy ground. When the people returned to the city, they delivered flowery eulogies—and in the very place where wicked acts were done by those very men! More smoke. Indeed.

8.11   Because the sentence against evil deeds is so long in coming, people in general think they can get by with murder.

8.12-13   Even though a person sins and gets by with it hundreds of times throughout a long life, I'm still convinced that the good life is reserved for the person who fears God, who lives reverently in his presence, and that the evil person will not experience a "good" life. No matter how many days he lives, they'll all be as flat and colorless as a shadow—because he doesn't fear God.

8.14 Here's something that happens all the time and makes no sense at all: Good people get what's coming to the wicked, and bad people get what's coming to the good. I tell you, this makes no sense. It's smoke.

8.15   So, I'm all for just going ahead and having a good time—the best possible. The only earthly good men and women can look forward to is to eat and drink well and have a good time—com-

NEW INTERNATIONAL VERSION

joy will accompany him in his work all the days of the life God has given him under the sun.

¹⁶When I applied my mind to know wisdom and to observe man's labor on earth—his eyes not seeing sleep day or night— ¹⁷then I saw all that God has done. No one can comprehend what goes on under the sun. Despite all his efforts to search it out, man cannot discover its meaning. Even if a wise man claims he knows, he cannot really comprehend it.

A Common Destiny for All

9 So I reflected on all this and concluded that the righteous and the wise and what they do are in God's hands, but no man knows whether love or hate awaits him. ²All share a common destiny—the righteous and the wicked, the good and the bad,ᵃ the clean and the unclean, those who offer sacrifices and those who do not.

As it is with the good man,
so with the sinner;
as it is with those who take oaths,
so with those who are afraid to take them.

³This is the evil in everything that happens under the sun: The same destiny overtakes all. The hearts of men, moreover, are full of evil and there is madness in their hearts while they live, and afterward they join the dead. ⁴Anyone who is among the living has hopeᵇ—even a live dog is better off than a dead lion!

⁵For the living know that they will die,
but the dead know nothing;
they have no further reward,
and even the memory of them is
forgotten.
⁶Their love, their hate
and their jealousy have long since vanished;
never again will they have a part
in anything that happens under the sun.

⁷Go, eat your food with gladness, and drink your wine with a joyful heart, for it is now that God favors what you do. ⁸Always be clothed in white, and always anoint your head with oil. ⁹Enjoy life with your wife, whom you love, all the days of this meaningless life that God has given you under the sun—all your meaningless days. For this is your lot in life and in your toilsome labor under the sun. ¹⁰Whatever your hand finds to do, do it with all your might, for in the grave,ᶜ where you are going, there is neither working nor planning nor knowledge nor wisdom.

ᵃ *2 Septuagint (Aquila), Vulgate and Syriac; Hebrew does not have* and the bad. *ᵇ 4 Or* What then is to be chosen? With all who live, there is hope *ᶜ 10 Hebrew* Sheol

THE MESSAGE

pensation for the struggle for survival these few years God gives us on earth.

8.16-17 When I determined to load up on wisdom and examine everything taking place on earth, I realized that if you keep your eyes open day and night without even blinking, you'll still never figure out the meaning of what God is doing on this earth. Search as hard as you like, you're not going to make sense of it. No matter how smart you are, you won't get to the bottom of it.

9.1-3 **9** Well, I took all this in and thought it through, inside and out. Here's what I understood: The good, the wise, and all that they do are in God's hands—but, day by day, whether it's love or hate they're dealing with, they don't know.

Anything's possible. It's one fate for everybody—righteous and wicked, good people, bad people, the nice and the nasty, worshipers and non-worshipers, committed and uncommitted. I find this outrageous—the worst thing about living on this earth—that everyone's lumped together in one fate. Is it any wonder that so many people are obsessed with evil? Is it any wonder that people go crazy right and left? Life leads to death. That's it.

Seize Life!

9.4-6 Still, anyone selected out for life has hope, for, as they say, "A living dog is better than a dead lion." The living at least know *something*, even if it's only that they're going to die. But the dead know nothing and get nothing. They're a minus that no one remembers. Their loves, their hates, yes, even their dreams, are long gone. There's not a trace of them left in the affairs of this earth.

9.7-10 Seize life! Eat bread with gusto,
Drink wine with a robust heart.
Oh yes—God takes pleasure in *your* pleasure!
Dress festively every morning.
Don't skimp on colors and scarves.
Relish life with the spouse you love
Each and every day of your precarious life.
Each day is God's gift. It's all you get in
exchange
For the hard work of staying alive.
Make the most of each one!
Whatever turns up, grab it and do it. And
heartily!
This is your last and only chance at it,
For there's neither work to do nor thoughts
to think
In the company of the dead, where you're
most certainly headed.

⊹

NEW INTERNATIONAL VERSION

¹¹I have seen something else under the sun:

The race is not to the swift
  or the battle to the strong,
nor does food come to the wise
  or wealth to the brilliant
  or favor to the learned;
but time and chance happen to them all.

¹²Moreover, no man knows when his hour will come:

As fish are caught in a cruel net,
  or birds are taken in a snare,
so men are trapped by evil times
  that fall unexpectedly upon them.

WISDOM BETTER THAN FOLLY

¹³I also saw under the sun this example of wisdom that greatly impressed me: ¹⁴There was once a small city with only a few people in it. And a powerful king came against it, surrounded it and built huge siegeworks against it. ¹⁵Now there lived in that city a man poor but wise, and he saved the city by his wisdom. But nobody remembered that poor man. ¹⁶So I said, "Wisdom is better than strength." But the poor man's wisdom is despised, and his words are no longer heeded.

¹⁷The quiet words of the wise are more to be heeded
  than the shouts of a ruler of fools.
¹⁸Wisdom is better than weapons of war,
  but one sinner destroys much good.

10 As dead flies give perfume a bad smell,
  so a little folly outweighs wisdom and honor.
²The heart of the wise inclines to the right,
  but the heart of the fool to the left.
³Even as he walks along the road,
  the fool lacks sense
  and shows everyone how stupid he is.
⁴If a ruler's anger rises against you,
  do not leave your post;
  calmness can lay great errors to rest.

⁵There is an evil I have seen under the sun,
  the sort of error that arises from a ruler:
⁶Fools are put in many high positions,
  while the rich occupy the low ones.

THE MESSAGE

9.11 I took another walk around the neighborhood and realized that on this earth as it is—

The race is not always to the swift,
Nor the battle to the strong,
Nor satisfaction to the wise,
Nor riches to the smart,
Nor grace to the learned.
Sooner or later bad luck hits us all.

9.12 No one can predict misfortune.
Like fish caught in a cruel net or birds in a trap,
So men and women are caught
By accidents evil and sudden.

WISDOM IS BETTER THAN MUSCLE

9.13-15 One day as I was observing how wisdom fares on this earth, I saw something that made me sit up and take notice. There was a small town with only a few people in it. A strong king came and mounted an attack, building trenches and attack posts around it. There was a poor but wise man in that town whose wisdom saved the town, but he was promptly forgotten. (He was only a poor man, after all.)

9.16 All the same, I still say that wisdom is better than muscle, even though the wise poor man was treated with contempt and soon forgotten.

9.17 The quiet words of the wise are more effective
Than the ranting of a king of fools.

9.18 Wisdom is better than warheads,
But one hothead can ruin the good earth.

10 10.1 Dead flies in perfume make it stink,
And a little foolishness decomposes much wisdom.

10.2 Wise thinking leads to right living;
Stupid thinking leads to wrong living.

10.3 Fools on the road have no sense of direction.
The way they walk tells the story: "There goes the fool again!"

10.4 If a ruler loses his temper against you, don't panic;
A calm disposition quiets intemperate rage.

✠

10.5-7 Here's a piece of bad business I've seen on this earth,
An error that can be blamed on whoever is in charge:
Immaturity is given a place of prominence,
While maturity is made to take a back seat.

NEW INTERNATIONAL VERSION

⁷ I have seen slaves on horseback,
  while princes go on foot like slaves.

⁸ Whoever digs a pit may fall into it;
  whoever breaks through a wall may be
      bitten by a snake.
⁹ Whoever quarries stones may be injured by
      them;
  whoever splits logs may be endangered by
      them.

¹⁰ If the ax is dull
  and its edge unsharpened,
  more strength is needed
  but skill will bring success.

¹¹ If a snake bites before it is charmed,
  there is no profit for the charmer.

¹² Words from a wise man's mouth are
      gracious,
  but a fool is consumed by his own lips.
¹³ At the beginning his words are folly;
  at the end they are wicked madness—
¹⁴   and the fool multiplies words.

No one knows what is coming—
  who can tell him what will happen after
      him?

¹⁵ A fool's work wearies him;
  he does not know the way to town.

¹⁶ Woe to you, O land whose king was a
      servant ᵃ
  and whose princes feast in the morning.
¹⁷ Blessed are you, O land whose king is of
      noble birth
  and whose princes eat at a proper time—
  for strength and not for drunkenness.

¹⁸ If a man is lazy, the rafters sag;
  if his hands are idle, the house leaks.

¹⁹ A feast is made for laughter,
  and wine makes life merry,
  but money is the answer for everything.

²⁰ Do not revile the king even in your
      thoughts,
  or curse the rich in your bedroom,
  because a bird of the air may carry your
      words,
  and a bird on the wing may report what
      you say.

THE MESSAGE

I've seen unproven upstarts riding in style,
While experienced veterans are put out to
      pasture.

✛

10.8   Caution: The trap you set might catch you.
       Warning: Your accomplice in crime might
           double-cross you.

10.9   Safety first: Quarrying stones is dangerous.
       Be alert: Felling trees is hazardous.

10.10 Remember: The duller the ax the harder
           the work;
       Use your head: The more brains, the less
           muscle.

10.11 If the snake bites before it's been charmed,
       What's the point in then sending for the
           charmer?

✛

10.12-13 The words of a wise person are gracious.
          The talk of a fool self-destructs—
          He starts out talking nonsense
          And ends up spouting insanity and evil.

10.14 Fools talk way too much,
       Chattering stuff they know nothing about.

10.15 A decent day's work so fatigues fools
       That they can't find their way back to town.

✛

10.16-17 Unlucky the land whose king is a young
              pup,
          And whose princes party all night.
          Lucky the land whose king is mature,
          Where the princes behave themselves
          And don't drink themselves silly.

✛

10.18 A shiftless man lives in a tumbledown
           shack;
       A lazy woman ends up with a leaky roof.

10.19 Laughter and bread go together,
       And wine gives sparkle to life—
       But it's money that makes the world go
           around.

10.20 Don't bad-mouth your leaders, not even
           under your breath,
       And don't abuse your betters, even in the
           privacy of your home.
       Loose talk has a way of getting picked up
           and spread around.
       Little birds drop the crumbs of your gossip
           far and wide.

ᵃ 16 Or *king is a child*

NEW INTERNATIONAL VERSION

BREAD UPON THE WATERS

11 Cast your bread upon the waters,
for after many days you will find it
again.
² Give portions to seven, yes to eight,
for you do not know what disaster may
come upon the land.

³ If clouds are full of water,
they pour rain upon the earth.
Whether a tree falls to the south or to the
north,
in the place where it falls, there will it lie.
⁴ Whoever watches the wind will not plant;
whoever looks at the clouds will not reap.

⁵ As you do not know the path of the wind,
or how the body is formed *a* in a mother's
womb,
so you cannot understand the work of God,
the Maker of all things.

⁶ Sow your seed in the morning,
and at evening let not your hands be idle,
for you do not know which will succeed,
whether this or that,
or whether both will do equally well.

REMEMBER YOUR CREATOR WHILE YOUNG

⁷ Light is sweet,
and it pleases the eyes to see the sun.
⁸ However many years a man may live,
let him enjoy them all.
But let him remember the days of darkness,
for they will be many.
Everything to come is meaningless.

⁹ Be happy, young man, while you are young,
and let your heart give you joy in the days
of your youth.
Follow the ways of your heart
and whatever your eyes see,
but know that for all these things
God will bring you to judgment.
¹⁰ So then, banish anxiety from your heart
and cast off the troubles of your body,
for youth and vigor are meaningless.

12 Remember your Creator
in the days of your youth,
before the days of trouble come
and the years approach when you will say,

*a 5 Or know how life (or the spirit) / enters the body being
formed*

THE MESSAGE

11 11.1 Be generous: Invest in acts of charity.
Charity yields high returns.

11.2 Don't hoard your goods; spread them
around.
Be a blessing to others. This could be your
last night.

11.3-4 When the clouds are full of water, it rains.
When the wind blows down a tree, it lies
where it falls.
Don't sit there watching the wind. Do your
own work.
Don't stare at the clouds. Get on with your
life.

11.5 Just as you'll never understand
the mystery of life forming in a pregnant
woman,
So you'll never understand
the mystery at work in all that God does.

11.6 Go to work in the morning
and stick to it until evening without
watching the clock.
You never know from moment to moment
how your work will turn out in the end.

BEFORE THE YEARS TAKE THEIR TOLL

11.7-8 Oh, how sweet the light of day,
And how wonderful to live in the sunshine!
Even if you live a long time, don't take a
single day for granted.
Take delight in each light-filled hour,
Remembering that there will also be many
dark days
And that most of what comes your way is
smoke.

11.9 You who are young, make the most of your
youth.
Relish your youthful vigor.
Follow the impulses of your heart.
If something looks good to you, pursue it.
But know also that not just anything goes;
You have to answer to God for every last bit
of it.

11.10 Live footloose and fancy free—
You won't be young forever.
Youth lasts about as long as smoke.

12 12.1-2 Honor and enjoy your Creator while
you're still young,
Before the years take their toll and your
vigor wanes,

NEW INTERNATIONAL VERSION

"I find no pleasure in them"—
² before the sun and the light
and the moon and the stars grow dark,
and the clouds return after the rain;
³ when the keepers of the house tremble,
and the strong men stoop,
when the grinders cease because they are
few,
and those looking through the windows
grow dim;
⁴ when the doors to the street are closed
and the sound of grinding fades;
when men rise up at the sound of birds,
but all their songs grow faint;
⁵ when men are afraid of heights
and of dangers in the streets;
when the almond tree blossoms
and the grasshopper drags himself along
and desire no longer is stirred.
Then man goes to his eternal home
and mourners go about the streets.

⁶ Remember him—before the silver cord is
severed,
or the golden bowl is broken;
before the pitcher is shattered at the spring,
or the wheel broken at the well,
⁷ and the dust returns to the ground it came
from,
and the spirit returns to God who gave it.

⁸ "Meaningless! Meaningless!" says the
Teacher.*a*
"Everything is meaningless!"

THE CONCLUSION OF THE MATTER

⁹ Not only was the Teacher wise, but also he
imparted knowledge to the people. He pondered
and searched out and set in order many proverbs. ¹⁰ The Teacher searched to find just the
right words, and what he wrote was upright and
true.

¹¹ The words of the wise are like goads, their
collected sayings like firmly embedded nails—
given by one Shepherd. ¹² Be warned, my son, of
anything in addition to them.
Of making many books there is no end, and
much study wearies the body.

¹³ Now all has been heard;
here is the conclusion of the matter:
Fear God and keep his commandments,
for this is the whole ⌊duty⌋ of man.
¹⁴ For God will bring every deed into
judgment,
including every hidden thing,
whether it is good or evil.

THE MESSAGE

Before your vision dims and the world
blurs
And the winter years keep you close to the
fire.

12.3-5 In old age, your body no longer serves you
so well.
Muscles slacken, grip weakens, joints
stiffen.
The shades are pulled down on the world.
You can't come and go at will. Things grind
to a halt.
The hum of the household fades away.
You are wakened now by bird-song.
Hikes to the mountains are a thing of the
past.
Even a stroll down the road has its terrors.
Your hair turns apple-blossom white,
Adorning a fragile and impotent matchstick
body.
Yes, you're well on your way to eternal rest,
While your friends make plans for your
funeral.

12.6-7 Life, lovely while it lasts, is soon over.
Life as we know it, precious and beautiful,
ends.
The body is put back in the same ground it
came from.
The spirit returns to God, who first
breathed it.

12.8 It's all smoke, nothing but smoke.
The Quester says that everything's smoke.

THE FINAL WORD

12.9-10 Besides being wise himself, the Quester also
taught others knowledge. He weighed, examined, and arranged many proverbs. The Quester
did his best to find the right words and write
the plain truth.

12.11 The words of the wise prod us to live well.
They're like nails hammered home, holding
life together.
They are given by God, the one Shepherd.

12.12-13 But regarding anything beyond this, dear
friend, go easy. There's no end to the publishing
of books, and constant study wears you out so
you're no good for anything else. The last and
final word is this:

Fear God.
Do what he tells you.

12.14 And that's it. Eventually God will bring
everything that we do out into the open and
judge it according to its hidden intent, whether
it's good or evil.

a 8 Or the leader of the assembly; also in verses 9 and 10

SONG OF SONGS

SONG OF SONGS

1 Solomon's Song of Songs.

BELOVED [a]

2 Let him kiss me with the kisses of his mouth—
   for your love is more delightful than wine.
3 Pleasing is the fragrance of your perfumes;
   your name is like perfume poured out.
   No wonder the maidens love you!
4 Take me away with you—let us hurry!
   Let the king bring me into his chambers.

FRIENDS

   We rejoice and delight in you [b];
   we will praise your love more than wine.

BELOVED

   How right they are to adore you!

5 Dark am I, yet lovely,
   O daughters of Jerusalem,
   dark like the tents of Kedar,
   like the tent curtains of Solomon. [c]
6 Do not stare at me because I am dark,
   because I am darkened by the sun.
   My mother's sons were angry with me
   and made me take care of the vineyards;
   my own vineyard I have neglected.
7 Tell me, you whom I love, where you graze
      your flock
   and where you rest your sheep at midday.
   Why should I be like a veiled woman
   beside the flocks of your friends?

FRIENDS

8 If you do not know, most beautiful of
      women,
   follow the tracks of the sheep
   and graze your young goats
   by the tents of the shepherds.

---

[a] Primarily on the basis of the gender of the Hebrew
pronouns used, male and female speakers are indicated in
the margins by the captions *Lover* and *Beloved* respectively.
The words of others are marked *Friends*. In some instances
the divisions and their captions are debatable.
[b] 4 The Hebrew is masculine singular.   [c] 5 Or *Salma*

1.1 **1** The Song—best of all songs—Solomon's
      song!

THE WOMAN

1.2-3 Kiss me—full on the mouth!
      Yes! For your love is better than wine,
      headier than your aromatic oils.
   The syllables of your name murmur like a
      meadow brook.
   No wonder everyone loves to say your
      name!

1.4 Take me away with you! Let's run off
      together!
   An elopement with my King-Lover!
   We'll celebrate, we'll sing,
      we'll make great music.
   Yes! For your love is better than vintage wine.
   Everyone loves you—of course! And why
      not?

1.5-6 I am weathered but still elegant,
      oh, dear sisters in Jerusalem,
   Weather-darkened like Kedar desert tents,
      time-softened like Solomon's Temple
         hangings.
   Don't look down on me because I'm dark,
      darkened by the sun's harsh rays.
   My brothers ridiculed me and sent me to
         work in the fields.
   They made me care for the face of the
         earth,
      but I had no time to care for my own face.

1.7 Tell me where you're working
      —I love you so much—
   Tell me where you're tending your flocks,
      where you let them rest at noontime.
   Why should I be the one left out,
      outside the orbit of your tender care?

THE MAN

1.8 If you can't find me, loveliest of all women,
      it's all right. Stay with your flocks.
   Lead your lambs to good pasture.
      Stay with your shepherd neighbors.

NEW INTERNATIONAL VERSION

LOVER

⁹ I liken you, my darling, to a mare
    harnessed to one of the chariots of
        Pharaoh.
¹⁰ Your cheeks are beautiful with earrings,
    your neck with strings of jewels.
¹¹ We will make you earrings of gold,
    studded with silver.

BELOVED

¹² While the king was at his table,
    my perfume spread its fragrance.
¹³ My lover is to me a sachet of myrrh
    resting between my breasts.
¹⁴ My lover is to me a cluster of henna
        blossoms
    from the vineyards of En Gedi.

LOVER

¹⁵ How beautiful you are, my darling!
    Oh, how beautiful!
    Your eyes are doves.

BELOVED

¹⁶ How handsome you are, my lover!
    Oh, how charming!
    And our bed is verdant.

LOVER

¹⁷ The beams of our house are cedars;
    our rafters are firs.

BELOVED *ᵃ*

2 I am a rose *ᵇ* of Sharon,
    a lily of the valleys.

LOVER

² Like a lily among thorns
    is my darling among the maidens.

BELOVED

³ Like an apple tree among the trees of the
        forest
    is my lover among the young men.
 I delight to sit in his shade,
    and his fruit is sweet to my taste.
⁴ He has taken me to the banquet hall,
    and his banner over me is love.
⁵ Strengthen me with raisins,
    refresh me with apples,
    for I am faint with love.
⁶ His left arm is under my head,
    and his right arm embraces me.

ᵃ Or Lover   *ᵇ 1 Possibly a member of the crocus family*

THE MESSAGE

THE WOMAN

1.9-11 You remind me of Pharaoh's
    well-groomed and satiny mares.
Pendant earrings line the elegance of your
    cheeks;
    strands of jewels illumine the curve of your
        throat.
I'm making jewelry for you, gold and silver
    jewelry
    that will mark and accent your beauty.

THE WOMAN

1.12-14 When my King-Lover lay down beside me,
    my fragrance filled the room.
His head resting between my breasts—
    the head of my lover was a sachet of sweet
        myrrh.
My beloved is a bouquet of wildflowers
    picked just for me from the fields of
        Engedi.

THE MAN

1.15 Oh, my dear friend! You're so beautiful!
    And your eyes so beautiful—like doves!

THE WOMAN

1.16-17 And you, my dear lover—you're so
        handsome!
    And the bed we share is like a forest glen.
We enjoy a canopy of cedars
    enclosed by cypresses, fragrant and green.

2.1 **2** I'm just a wildflower picked from the
        plains of Sharon,
    a lotus blossom from the valley pools.

THE MAN

2.2 A lotus blossoming in a swamp of weeds—
    that's my dear friend among the girls in the
        village.

THE WOMAN

2.3-4 As an apricot tree stands out in the forest,
    my lover stands above the young men in
        town.
All I want is to sit in his shade,
    to taste and savor his delicious love.
He took me home with him for a festive meal,
    but his eyes feasted on *me*!

2.5-6 Oh! Give me something refreshing to eat—
    and quickly!
    Apricots, raisins—anything. I'm about to
        faint with love!
His left hand cradles my head,
    and his right arm encircles my waist!

NEW INTERNATIONAL VERSION

⁷Daughters of Jerusalem, I charge you
  by the gazelles and by the does of the
    field:
Do not arouse or awaken love
  until it so desires.

⁸Listen! My lover!
  Look! Here he comes,
leaping across the mountains,
  bounding over the hills.
⁹My lover is like a gazelle or a young stag.
  Look! There he stands behind our wall,
gazing through the windows,
  peering through the lattice.
¹⁰My lover spoke and said to me,
  "Arise, my darling,
  my beautiful one, and come with me.
¹¹See! The winter is past;
  the rains are over and gone.
¹²Flowers appear on the earth;
  the season of singing has come,
the cooing of doves
  is heard in our land.
¹³The fig tree forms its early fruit;
  the blossoming vines spread their
    fragrance.
Arise, come, my darling;
  my beautiful one, come with me."

LOVER

¹⁴My dove in the clefts of the rock,
  in the hiding places on the mountainside,
show me your face,
  let me hear your voice;
for your voice is sweet,
  and your face is lovely.
¹⁵Catch for us the foxes,
  the little foxes
that ruin the vineyards,
  our vineyards that are in bloom.

BELOVED

¹⁶My lover is mine and I am his;
  he browses among the lilies.
¹⁷Until the day breaks
  and the shadows flee,
turn, my lover,
  and be like a gazelle
or like a young stag
  on the rugged hills. ᵃ

3 All night long on my bed
  I looked for the one my heart loves;
I looked for him but did not find him.

ᵃ 17 Or the hills of Bether

THE MESSAGE

2.7 Oh, let me warn you, sisters in Jerusalem,
  by the gazelles, yes, by all the wild deer:
Don't excite love, don't stir it up,
  until the time is ripe—and you're ready.

2.8-10 Look! Listen! There's my lover!
  Do you see him coming?
Vaulting the mountains,
  leaping the hills.
My lover is like a gazelle, graceful;
  like a young stag, virile.
Look at him there, on tiptoe at the gate,
  all ears, all eyes—ready!
My lover has arrived
  and he's speaking to me!

THE MAN

2.10-14 Get up, my dear friend,
  fair and beautiful lover—come to me!
Look around you: Winter is over;
  the winter rains are over, gone!
Spring flowers are in blossom all over.
  The whole world's a choir—and singing!
Spring warblers are filling the forest
  with sweet arpeggios.
Lilacs are exuberantly purple and perfumed,
  and cherry trees fragrant with blossoms.
Oh, get up, dear friend,
  my fair and beautiful lover—come to me!
Come, my shy and modest dove—
  leave your seclusion, come out in the open.
Let me see your face,
  let me hear your voice.
For your voice is soothing
  and your face is ravishing.

THE WOMAN

2.15 Then you must protect me from the foxes,
  foxes on the prowl,
Foxes who would like nothing better
  than to get into our flowering garden.

2.16-17 My lover is mine, and I am his.
  Nightly he strolls in our garden,
Delighting in the flowers
  until dawn breathes its light and night slips
    away.

Turn to me, dear lover.
  Come like a gazelle.
Leap like a wild stag
  on delectable mountains!

3.1-4 **3** Restless in bed and sleepless through the
    night,
  I longed for my lover.
I wanted him desperately. His absence was
    painful.

NEW INTERNATIONAL VERSION

² I will get up now and go about the city,
   through its streets and squares;
I will search for the one my heart loves.
   So I looked for him but did not find him.
³ The watchmen found me
   as they made their rounds in the city.
   "Have you seen the one my heart loves?"
⁴ Scarcely had I passed them
   when I found the one my heart loves.
I held him and would not let him go
   till I had brought him to my mother's
      house,
   to the room of the one who conceived me.
⁵ Daughters of Jerusalem, I charge you
   by the gazelles and by the does of the field:
Do not arouse or awaken love
   until it so desires.

⁶ Who is this coming up from the desert
   like a column of smoke,
perfumed with myrrh and incense
   made from all the spices of the merchant?
⁷ Look! It is Solomon's carriage,
   escorted by sixty warriors,
   the noblest of Israel,
⁸ all of them wearing the sword,
   all experienced in battle,
each with his sword at his side,
   prepared for the terrors of the night.
⁹ King Solomon made for himself the carriage;
   he made it of wood from Lebanon.
¹⁰ Its posts he made of silver,
   its base of gold.
Its seat was upholstered with purple,
   its interior lovingly inlaid
   by*ᵃ* the daughters of Jerusalem.
¹¹ Come out, you daughters of Zion,
   and look at King Solomon wearing the
      crown,
   the crown with which his mother
      crowned him
on the day of his wedding,
   the day his heart rejoiced.

LOVER

4 How beautiful you are, my darling!
   Oh, how beautiful!
   Your eyes behind your veil are doves.
Your hair is like a flock of goats
   descending from Mount Gilead.
² Your teeth are like a flock of sheep just shorn,
   coming up from the washing.
Each has its twin;
   not one of them is alone.
³ Your lips are like a scarlet ribbon;
   your mouth is lovely.

THE MESSAGE

So I got up, went out and roved the city,
   hunting through streets and down alleys.
I wanted my lover in the worst way!
   I looked high and low, and didn't find him.
And then the night watchmen found me
   as they patrolled the darkened city.
   "Have you seen my dear lost love?" I asked.
No sooner had I left them than I found him,
   found my dear lost love.
I threw my arms around him and held him
      tight,
   wouldn't let him go until I had him home
      again,
   safe at home beside the fire.

3.5   Oh, let me warn you, sisters in Jerusalem,
   by the gazelles, yes, by all the wild deer:
Don't excite love, don't stir it up,
   until the time is ripe—and you're ready.

3.6-10   What's this I see, approaching from the desert,
   raising clouds of dust,
Filling the air with sweet smells
   and pungent aromatics?
Look! It's Solomon's carriage,
   carried and guarded by sixty soldiers,
   sixty of Israel's finest,
All of them armed to the teeth,
   trained for battle,
   ready for anything, anytime.
King Solomon once had a carriage built
   from fine-grained Lebanon cedar.
He had it framed with silver and roofed with
      gold.
   The cushions were covered with a purple
      fabric,
   the interior lined with tooled leather.

3.11   Come and look, sisters in Jerusalem.
   Oh, sisters of Zion, don't miss this!
My King-Lover,
   dressed and garlanded for his wedding,
   his heart full, bursting with joy!

THE MAN

4.1-5   **4** You're so beautiful, my darling,
   so beautiful, and your dove eyes are
      veiled
By your hair as it flows and shimmers,
   like a flock of goats in the distance
   streaming down a hillside in the sunshine.
Your smile is generous and full—
   expressive and strong and clean.
Your lips are jewel red,
   your mouth elegant and inviting,

ᵃ 10 Or its inlaid interior a gift of love / from

NEW INTERNATIONAL VERSION

Your temples behind your veil
    are like the halves of a pomegranate.
[4] Your neck is like the tower of David,
    built with elegance[a];
on it hang a thousand shields,
    all of them shields of warriors.
[5] Your two breasts are like two fawns,
    like twin fawns of a gazelle
    that browse among the lilies.
[6] Until the day breaks
    and the shadows flee,
I will go to the mountain of myrrh
    and to the hill of incense.
[7] All beautiful you are, my darling;
    there is no flaw in you.

[8] Come with me from Lebanon, my bride,
    come with me from Lebanon.
Descend from the crest of Amana,
    from the top of Senir, the summit of Hermon,
from the lions' dens
    and the mountain haunts of the leopards.
[9] You have stolen my heart, my sister, my bride;
    you have stolen my heart
with one glance of your eyes,
    with one jewel of your necklace.
[10] How delightful is your love, my sister, my
    bride!
    How much more pleasing is your love
      than wine,
    and the fragrance of your perfume than
      any spice!
[11] Your lips drop sweetness as the honeycomb,
    my bride;
    milk and honey are under your tongue.
    The fragrance of your garments is like
      that of Lebanon.
[12] You are a garden locked up, my sister, my bride;
    you are a spring enclosed, a sealed fountain.
[13] Your plants are an orchard of pomegranates
    with choice fruits,
    with henna and nard,
[14]   nard and saffron,
    calamus and cinnamon,
    with every kind of incense tree,
    with myrrh and aloes
    and all the finest spices.
[15] You are[b] a garden fountain,
    a well of flowing water
    streaming down from Lebanon.

BELOVED

[16] Awake, north wind,
    and come, south wind!
Blow on my garden,
    that its fragrance may spread abroad.

[a] 4 The meaning of the Hebrew for this word is uncertain.
[b] 15 Or I am (spoken by the Beloved)

THE MESSAGE

your veiled cheeks soft and radiant.
The smooth, lithe lines of your neck
    command notice—all heads turn in awe
      and admiration!
Your breasts are like fawns,
    twins of a gazelle, grazing among the first
      spring flowers.

4.6-7 The sweet, fragrant curves of your body,
    the soft, spiced contours of your flesh
Invite me, and I come. I stay
    until dawn breathes its light and night slips
      away.
You're beautiful from head to toe, my dear love,
    beautiful beyond compare, absolutely
      flawless.

4.8-15 Come with me from Lebanon, my bride.
    Leave Lebanon behind, and come.
Leave your high mountain hideaway.
    Abandon your wilderness seclusion,
Where you keep company with lions
    and panthers guard your safety.
You've captured my heart, dear friend.
    You looked at me, and I fell in love.
    One look my way and I was hopelessly in
      love!
How beautiful your love, dear, dear friend—
    far more pleasing than a fine, rare wine,
    your fragrance more exotic than select
      spices.
The kisses of your lips are honey, my love,
    every syllable you speak a delicacy to savor.
Your clothes smell like the wild outdoors,
    the ozone scent of high mountains.
Dear lover and friend, you're a secret garden,
    a private and pure fountain.
Body and soul, you are paradise,
    a whole orchard of succulent fruits—
Ripe apricots and peaches,
    oranges and pears;
Nut trees and cinnamon,
    and all scented woods;
Mint and lavender,
    and all herbs aromatic;
A garden fountain, sparkling and splashing,
    fed by spring waters from the Lebanon
      mountains.

THE WOMAN

4.16 Wake up, North Wind,
    get moving, South Wind!
Breathe on my garden,
    fill the air with spice fragrance.

NEW INTERNATIONAL VERSION

Let my lover come into his garden
  and taste its choice fruits.

LOVER

5 I have come into my garden, my sister, my
      bride;
  I have gathered my myrrh with my spice.
I have eaten my honeycomb and my honey;
  I have drunk my wine and my milk.

FRIENDS

  Eat, O friends, and drink;
    drink your fill, O lovers.

BELOVED

²I slept but my heart was awake.
    Listen! My lover is knocking:
  "Open to me, my sister, my darling,
    my dove, my flawless one.
  My head is drenched with dew,
    my hair with the dampness of the night."
³I have taken off my robe—
    must I put it on again?
  I have washed my feet—
    must I soil them again?
⁴My lover thrust his hand through the
      latch-opening;
    my heart began to pound for him.
⁵I arose to open for my lover,
    and my hands dripped with myrrh,
  my fingers with flowing myrrh,
    on the handles of the lock.
⁶I opened for my lover,
    but my lover had left; he was gone.
  My heart sank at his departure.ᵃ
  I looked for him but did not find him.
    I called him but he did not answer.
⁷The watchmen found me
    as they made their rounds in the city.
  They beat me, they bruised me;
    they took away my cloak,
    those watchmen of the walls!
⁸O daughters of Jerusalem, I charge you—
    if you find my lover,
  what will you tell him?
    Tell him I am faint with love.

FRIENDS

⁹How is your beloved better than others,
    most beautiful of women?

THE MESSAGE

Oh, let my lover enter his garden!
  Yes, let him eat the fine, ripe fruits.

THE MAN

5.1 **5** I went to my garden, dear friend, best
          lover!
    breathed the sweet fragrance.
  I ate the fruit and honey,
    I drank the nectar and wine.

Celebrate with me, friends!
  Raise your glasses—"To life! To love!"

THE WOMAN

5.2 I was sound asleep, but in my dreams I was
          wide awake.
    Oh, listen! It's the sound of my lover
          knocking, calling!

THE MAN

"Let me in, dear companion, dearest friend,
    my dove, consummate lover!
  I'm soaked with the dampness of the night,
    drenched with dew, shivering and cold."

THE WOMAN

5.3 "But I'm in my nightgown—do you expect me
          to get dressed?
    I'm bathed and in bed—do you want me to
          get dirty?"

5.4-7 But my lover wouldn't take no for an answer,
    and the longer he knocked, the more
          excited I became.
  I got up to open the door to my lover,
    sweetly ready to receive him,
  Desiring and expectant
    as I turned the door handle.
  But when I opened the door he was gone.
    My loved one had tired of waiting and left.
  And I died inside—oh, I felt so bad!
    I ran out looking for him
  But he was nowhere to be found.
    I called into the darkness—but no answer.
  The night watchmen found me
    as they patrolled the streets of the city.
  They slapped and beat and bruised me,
    ripping off my clothes,
  These watchmen,
    who were supposed to be guarding the city.

5.8 I beg you, sisters in Jerusalem—
    if you find my lover,
  Please tell him I want him,
    that I'm heartsick with love for him.

THE CHORUS

5.9 What's so great about your lover, fair lady?

ᵃ 6 Or *heart had gone out to him when he spoke*

NEW INTERNATIONAL VERSION

How is your beloved better than others,
that you charge us so?

BELOVED

¹⁰ My lover is radiant and ruddy,
outstanding among ten thousand.
¹¹ His head is purest gold;
his hair is wavy
and black as a raven.
¹² His eyes are like doves
by the water streams,
washed in milk,
mounted like jewels.
¹³ His cheeks are like beds of spice
yielding perfume.
His lips are like lilies
dripping with myrrh.
¹⁴ His arms are rods of gold
set with chrysolite.
His body is like polished ivory
decorated with sapphires.ᵃ
¹⁵ His legs are pillars of marble
set on bases of pure gold.
His appearance is like Lebanon,
choice as its cedars.
¹⁶ His mouth is sweetness itself;
he is altogether lovely.
This is my lover, this my friend,
O daughters of Jerusalem.

FRIENDS

6 Where has your lover gone,
most beautiful of women?
Which way did your lover turn,
that we may look for him with you?

BELOVED

² My lover has gone down to his garden,
to the beds of spices,
to browse in the gardens
and to gather lilies.
³ I am my lover's and my lover is mine;
he browses among the lilies.

LOVER

⁴ You are beautiful, my darling, as Tirzah,
lovely as Jerusalem,
majestic as troops with banners.
⁵ Turn your eyes from me;
they overwhelm me.
Your hair is like a flock of goats
descending from Gilead.
⁶ Your teeth are like a flock of sheep

ᵃ 14 Or lapis lazuli

THE MESSAGE

What's so special about him that you beg for
our help?

THE WOMAN

5.10-16 My dear lover glows with health—
red-blooded, radiant!
He's one in a million.
There's no one quite like him!
My golden one, pure and untarnished,
with raven black curls tumbling across his
shoulders.
His eyes are like doves, soft and bright,
but deep-set, brimming with meaning, like
wells of water.
His face is rugged, his beard smells like sage,
His voice, his words, warm and reassuring.
Fine muscles ripple beneath his skin,
quiet and beautiful.
His torso is the work of a sculptor,
hard and smooth as ivory.
He stands tall, like a cedar,
strong and deep-rooted,
A rugged mountain of a man,
aromatic with wood and stone.
His words are kisses, his kisses words.
Everything about him delights me, thrills
me through and through!

That's my lover, that's my man,
dear Jerusalem sisters.

THE CHORUS

6.1 **6** So where has this love of yours gone,
fair one?
Where on earth can he be?
Can we help you look for him?

THE WOMAN

6.2-3 Never mind. My lover is already on his way to
his garden,
to browse among the flowers, touching the
colors and forms.
I am my lover's and my lover is mine.
He caresses the sweet-smelling flowers.

THE MAN

6.4-7 Dear, dear friend and lover,
you're as beautiful as Tirzah, city of delights,
Lovely as Jerusalem, city of dreams,
the ravishing visions of my ecstasy.
Your beauty is too much for me—I'm in over
my head.
I'm not used to this! I can't take it in.
Your hair flows and shimmers
like a flock of goats in the distance
streaming down a hillside in the sunshine.
Your smile is generous and full—

coming up from the washing.
Each has its twin,
    not one of them is alone.
7 Your temples behind your veil
    are like the halves of a pomegranate.
8 Sixty queens there may be,
    and eighty concubines,
    and virgins beyond number;
9 but my dove, my perfect one, is unique,
    the only daughter of her mother,
    the favorite of the one who bore her.
The maidens saw her and called her blessed;
    the queens and concubines praised her.

FRIENDS

10 Who is this that appears like the dawn,
    fair as the moon, bright as the sun,
    majestic as the stars in procession?

LOVER

11 I went down to the grove of nut trees
    to look at the new growth in the valley,
to see if the vines had budded
    or the pomegranates were in bloom.
12 Before I realized it,
    my desire set me among the royal chariots
        of my people. *a*

FRIENDS

13 Come back, come back, O Shulammite;
    come back, come back, that we may gaze
        on you!

LOVER

Why would you gaze on the Shulammite
    as on the dance of Mahanaim?

7 How beautiful your sandaled feet,
    O prince's daughter!
Your graceful legs are like jewels,
    the work of a craftsman's hands.
2 Your navel is a rounded goblet
    that never lacks blended wine.
Your waist is a mound of wheat
    encircled by lilies.
3 Your breasts are like two fawns,
    twins of a gazelle.
4 Your neck is like an ivory tower.
Your eyes are the pools of Heshbon
    by the gate of Bath Rabbim.
Your nose is like the tower of Lebanon
    looking toward Damascus.
5 Your head crowns you like Mount Carmel.
    Your hair is like royal tapestry;

*a 12 Or among the chariots of Amminadab; or among the
chariots of the people of the prince*

expressive and strong and clean.
Your veiled cheeks
    are soft and radiant.

6.8-9 There's no one like her on earth,
    never has been, never will be.
She's a woman beyond compare.
    My dove is perfection,
Pure and innocent as the day she was born,
    and cradled in joy by her mother.
Everyone who came by to see her
    exclaimed and admired her—
All the fathers and mothers, the neighbors and
        friends,
    blessed and praised her:

6.10 "Has anyone ever seen anything like this—
    dawn-fresh, moon-lovely, sun-radiant,
    ravishing as the night sky with its galaxies
        of stars?"

6.11-12 One day I went strolling through the orchard,
    looking for signs of spring,
Looking for buds about to burst into flower,
    anticipating readiness, ripeness.
Before I knew it my heart was raptured,
    carried away by lofty thoughts!

6.13 Dance, dance, dear Shulammite, Angel-
        Princess!
    Dance, and we'll feast our eyes on your
        grace!
Everyone wants to see the Shulammite dance
    her victory dances of love and peace.

7.1-9 **7** Shapely and graceful your sandaled feet,
    and queenly your movement—
Your limbs are lithe and elegant,
    the work of a master artist.
Your body is a chalice,
    wine-filled.
Your skin is silken and tawny
    like a field of wheat touched by the breeze.
Your breasts are like fawns,
    twins of a gazelle.
Your neck is carved ivory, curved and slender.
Your eyes are wells of light, deep with mystery.
    Quintessentially feminine!
Your profile turns all heads,
    commanding attention.
The feelings I get when I see the high
        mountain ranges
    —stirrings of desire, longings for the
        heights—

NEW INTERNATIONAL VERSION

the king is held captive by its tresses.
⁶ How beautiful you are and how pleasing,
O love, with your delights!
⁷ Your stature is like that of the palm,
and your breasts like clusters of fruit.
⁸ I said, "I will climb the palm tree;
I will take hold of its fruit."
May your breasts be like the clusters of the
vine,
the fragrance of your breath like apples,
⁹ and your mouth like the best wine.

BELOVED

May the wine go straight to my lover,
flowing gently over lips and teeth. *a*
¹⁰ I belong to my lover,
and his desire is for me.
¹¹ Come, my lover, let us go to the countryside,
let us spend the night in the villages. *b*
¹² Let us go early to the vineyards
to see if the vines have budded,
if their blossoms have opened,
and if the pomegranates are in bloom—
there I will give you my love.
¹³ The mandrakes send out their fragrance,
and at our door is every delicacy,
both new and old,
that I have stored up for you, my lover.

8 If only you were to me like a brother,
who was nursed at my mother's breasts!
Then, if I found you outside,
I would kiss you,
and no one would despise me.
² I would lead you
and bring you to my mother's house—
she who has taught me.
I would give you spiced wine to drink,
the nectar of my pomegranates.
³ His left arm is under my head
and his right arm embraces me.
⁴ Daughters of Jerusalem, I charge you:
Do not arouse or awaken love
until it so desires.

FRIENDS

⁵ Who is this coming up from the desert
leaning on her lover?

*a 9 Septuagint, Aquila, Vulgate and Syriac; Hebrew lips of
sleepers   b 11 Or henna bushes*

THE MESSAGE

Remind me of you,
and I'm spoiled for anyone else!
Your beauty, within and without, is absolute,
dear lover, close companion.
You are tall and supple, like the palm tree,
and your full breasts are like sweet clusters
of dates.
I say, "I'm going to climb that palm tree!
I'm going to caress its fruit!"
Oh yes! Your breasts
will be clusters of sweet fruit to me,
Your breath clean and cool like fresh mint,
your tongue and lips like the best wine.

THE WOMAN

7.9-12 Yes, and yours are, too—my love's kisses
flow from his lips to mine.
I am my lover's.
I'm all he wants. I'm all the world to him!
Come, dear lover—
let's tramp through the countryside.
Let's sleep at some wayside inn,
then rise early and listen to bird-song.
Let's look for wildflowers in bloom,
blackberry bushes blossoming white,
Fruit trees festooned
with cascading flowers.
And there I'll give myself to you,
my love to your love!

7.13 Love-apples drench us with fragrance,
fertility surrounds, suffuses us,
Fruits fresh and preserved
that I've kept and saved just for you, my love.

8 I wish you'd been my twin brother,
sharing with me the breasts of my mother,
Playing outside in the street,
kissing in plain view of everyone,
and no one thinking anything of it.
I'd take you by the hand and bring you home
where I was raised by my mother.
You'd drink my wine
and kiss my cheeks.

8.3-4 Imagine! His left hand cradling my head,
his right arm around my waist!
Oh, let me warn you, sisters in Jerusalem:
Don't excite love, don't stir it up,
until the time is ripe—and you're ready.

THE CHORUS

8.5 Who is this I see coming up from the country,
arm in arm with her lover?

NEW INTERNATIONAL VERSION

BELOVED

Under the apple tree I roused you;
   there your mother conceived you,
   there she who was in labor gave you birth.
⁶Place me like a seal over your heart,
   like a seal on your arm;
for love is as strong as death,
   its jealousy*a* unyielding as the grave.*b*
It burns like blazing fire,
   like a mighty flame.*c*
⁷Many waters cannot quench love;
   rivers cannot wash it away.
If one were to give
   all the wealth of his house for love,
   it*d* would be utterly scorned.

FRIENDS

⁸We have a young sister,
   and her breasts are not yet grown.
What shall we do for our sister
   for the day she is spoken for?
⁹If she is a wall,
   we will build towers of silver on her.
If she is a door,
   we will enclose her with panels of cedar.

BELOVED

¹⁰I am a wall,
   and my breasts are like towers.
Thus I have become in his eyes
   like one bringing contentment.
¹¹Solomon had a vineyard in Baal Hamon;
   he let out his vineyard to tenants.
Each was to bring for its fruit
   a thousand shekels*e* of silver.
¹²But my own vineyard is mine to give;
   the thousand shekels are for you,
      O Solomon,
   and two hundred*f* are for those who tend
      its fruit.

LOVER

¹³You who dwell in the gardens
   with friends in attendance,
   let me hear your voice!

BELOVED

¹⁴Come away, my lover,
   and be like a gazelle
or like a young stag
   on the spice-laden mountains.

THE MESSAGE

THE MAN

I found you under the apricot tree,
   and woke you up to love.
Your mother went into labor under that tree,
   and under that very tree she bore you.

THE WOMAN

8.6-8 Hang my locket around your neck,
   wear my ring on your finger.
Love is invincible facing danger and death.
   Passion laughs at the terrors of hell.
The fire of love stops at nothing—
   it sweeps everything before it.
Flood waters can't drown love,
   torrents of rain can't put it out.
Love can't be bought, love can't be sold—
   it's not to be found in the marketplace.
My brothers used to worry about me:

8.8-9 "Our little sister has no breasts.
   What shall we do with our little sister
      when men come asking for her?
She's a virgin and vulnerable,
   and we'll protect her.
If they think she's a wall, we'll top it with
      barbed wire.
   If they think she's a door, we'll
      barricade it."

8.10 Dear brothers, I'm a walled-in virgin still,
   but my breasts are full—
And when my lover sees me,
   he knows he'll soon be satisfied.

THE MAN

8.11-12 King Solomon may have vast vineyards
   in lush, fertile country,
Where he hires others to work the ground.
   People pay anything to get in on that
      bounty.
But *my* vineyard is all mine,
   and I'm keeping it to myself.
You can have your vast vineyards, Solomon,
   you and your greedy guests!

8.13 Oh, lady of the gardens,
   my friends are with me listening.
   Let me hear your voice!

THE WOMAN

8.14 Run to me, dear lover.
   Come like a gazelle.
Leap like a wild stag
   on the spice mountains.

---

a 6 Or *ardor*   *b* 6 Hebrew *Sheol*   *c* 6 Or / *like the very
flame of the* LORD   *d* 7 Or *he*   *e* 11 That is, about 25
pounds (about 11.5 kilograms); also in verse 12
f 12 That is, about 5 pounds (about 2.3 kilograms)

ISAIAH

ISAIAH

MESSAGES OF JUDGMENT

QUIT YOUR WORSHIP CHARADES

1 The vision concerning Judah and Jerusalem that Isaiah son of Amoz saw during the reigns of Uzziah, Jotham, Ahaz and Hezekiah, kings of Judah.

1.1 **1** The vision that Isaiah son of Amoz saw regarding Judah and Jerusalem during the times of the kings of Judah: Uzziah, Jotham, Ahaz, and Hezekiah.

A REBELLIOUS NATION

2 Hear, O heavens! Listen, O earth!
    For the LORD has spoken:
"I reared children and brought them up,
    but they have rebelled against me.
3 The ox knows his master,
    the donkey his owner's manger,
but Israel does not know,
    my people do not understand."

4 Ah, sinful nation,
    a people loaded with guilt,
a brood of evildoers,
    children given to corruption!
They have forsaken the LORD;
    they have spurned the Holy One of Israel
    and turned their backs on him.

5 Why should you be beaten anymore?
    Why do you persist in rebellion?
Your whole head is injured,
    your whole heart afflicted.
6 From the sole of your foot to the top of your
        head
    there is no soundness—
only wounds and welts
    and open sores,
not cleansed or bandaged
    or soothed with oil.

7 Your country is desolate,
    your cities burned with fire;
your fields are being stripped by foreigners
    right before you,
    laid waste as when overthrown by
        strangers.
8 The Daughter of Zion is left
    like a shelter in a vineyard,
like a hut in a field of melons,
    like a city under siege.

1.2-4 Heaven and earth, you're the jury.
        Listen to GOD's case:
"I had children and raised them well,
    and they turned on me.
The ox knows who's boss,
    the mule knows the hand that feeds him,
But not Israel.
    My people don't know up from down.
Shame! Misguided GOD-dropouts,
    staggering under their guilt-baggage,
Gang of miscreants,
    band of vandals—
My people have walked out on me, their GOD,
    turned their backs on The Holy of Israel,
    walked off and never looked back.

1.5-9 "Why bother even trying to do anything with
            you
        when you just keep to your bullheaded
            ways?
You keep beating your heads against brick
            walls.
    Everything within you protests against you.
From the bottom of your feet to the top of
            your head,
    nothing's working right.
Wounds and bruises and running sores—
    untended, unwashed, unbandaged.
Your country is laid waste,
    your cities burned down.
Your land is destroyed by outsiders while you
            watch,
    reduced to rubble by barbarians.
Daughter Zion is deserted—
    like a tumbledown shack on a dead-end
            street,
Like a tarpaper shanty on the wrong side of
            the tracks,
    like a sinking ship abandoned by the rats.

NEW INTERNATIONAL VERSION

⁹Unless the LORD Almighty
    had left us some survivors,
we would have become like Sodom,
    we would have been like Gomorrah.

¹⁰Hear the word of the LORD,
    you rulers of Sodom;
listen to the law of our God,
    you people of Gomorrah!
¹¹"The multitude of your sacrifices—
    what are they to me?" says the LORD.
"I have more than enough of burnt offerings,
    of rams and the fat of fattened animals;
I have no pleasure
    in the blood of bulls and lambs and goats.
¹²When you come to appear before me,
    who has asked this of you,
this trampling of my courts?
¹³Stop bringing meaningless offerings!
    Your incense is detestable to me.
New Moons, Sabbaths and convocations—
    I cannot bear your evil assemblies.
¹⁴Your New Moon festivals and your
        appointed feasts
    my soul hates.
They have become a burden to me;
    I am weary of bearing them.
¹⁵When you spread out your hands in prayer,
    I will hide my eyes from you;
even if you offer many prayers,
    I will not listen.
Your hands are full of blood;
¹⁶   wash and make yourselves clean.
Take your evil deeds
    out of my sight!
Stop doing wrong,
¹⁷   learn to do right!
Seek justice,
    encourage the oppressed. ^a
Defend the cause of the fatherless,
    plead the case of the widow.

¹⁸"Come now, let us reason together,"
    says the LORD.
"Though your sins are like scarlet,

a 17 Or / rebuke the oppressor

THE MESSAGE

If GOD-of-the-Angel-Armies hadn't left us a
    few survivors,
    we'd be as desolate as Sodom, doomed just
        like Gomorrah.

^{1.10} "Listen to my Message,
    you Sodom-schooled leaders.
Receive God's revelation,
    you Gomorrah-schooled people.

^{1.11-12} "Why this frenzy of sacrifices?"
    GOD's asking.
"Don't you think I've had my fill of burnt
        sacrifices,
    rams and plump grain-fed calves?
Don't you think I've had my fill
    of blood from bulls, lambs, and goats?
When you come before me,
    who ever gave you the idea of acting like
        this,
Running here and there, doing this and that—
    all this sheer *commotion* in the place
        provided for worship?

^{1.13-17} "Quit your worship charades.
    I can't stand your trivial religious games:
Monthly conferences, weekly Sabbaths,
        special meetings—
    meetings, meetings, meetings—I can't
        stand one more!
Meetings for this, meetings for that. I hate
    them!
    You've worn me out!
I'm sick of your religion, religion, religion,
    while you go right on sinning.
When you put on your next prayer-
        performance,
    I'll be looking the other way.
No matter how long or loud or often you pray,
    I'll not be listening.
And do you know why? Because you've been
        tearing
    people to pieces, and your hands are
        bloody.
Go home and wash up.
    Clean up your act.
Sweep your lives clean of your evildoings
    so I don't have to look at them any longer.
Say no to wrong.
    Learn to do good.
Work for justice.
    Help the down-and-out.
Stand up for the homeless.
    Go to bat for the defenseless.

LET'S ARGUE THIS OUT

^{1.18-20} "Come. Sit down. Let's argue this out."
    This is GOD's Message:
"If your sins are blood-red,

NEW INTERNATIONAL VERSION

they shall be as white as snow;
though they are red as crimson,
they shall be like wool.
¹⁹ If you are willing and obedient,
you will eat the best from the land;
²⁰ but if you resist and rebel,
you will be devoured by the sword."
For the mouth of the LORD
has spoken.

²¹ See how the faithful city
has become a harlot!
She once was full of justice;
righteousness used to dwell in her—
but now murderers!
²² Your silver has become dross,
your choice wine is diluted with water.
²³ Your rulers are rebels,
companions of thieves;
they all love bribes
and chase after gifts.
They do not defend the cause of the
fatherless;
the widow's case does not come before
them.
²⁴ Therefore the Lord, the LORD Almighty,
the Mighty One of Israel, declares:
"Ah, I will get relief from my foes
and avenge myself on my enemies.
²⁵ I will turn my hand against you;
I will thoroughly purge away your dross
and remove all your impurities.
²⁶ I will restore your judges as in days of old,
your counselors as at the beginning.
Afterward you will be called
the City of Righteousness,
the Faithful City."

²⁷ Zion will be redeemed with justice,
her penitent ones with righteousness.
²⁸ But rebels and sinners will both be broken,
and those who forsake the LORD will
perish.

²⁹ "You will be ashamed because of the sacred
oaks
in which you have delighted;
you will be disgraced because of the gardens
that you have chosen.
³⁰ You will be like an oak with fading leaves,
like a garden without water.
³¹ The mighty man will become tinder
and his work a spark;
both will burn together,
with no one to quench the fire."

THE MESSAGE

they'll be snow-white.
If they're red like crimson,
they'll be like wool.
If you'll willingly obey,
you'll feast like kings.
But if you're willful and stubborn,
you'll die like dogs."
That's right. GOD says so.

THOSE WHO WALK OUT ON GOD

1.21-23 Oh! Can you believe it? The chaste city
has become a whore!
She was once all justice,
everyone living as good neighbors,
And now they're all
at one another's throats.
Your coins are all counterfeits.
Your wine is watered down.
Your leaders are turncoats
who keep company with crooks.
They sell themselves to the highest bidder
and grab anything not nailed down.
They never stand up for the homeless,
never stick up for the defenseless.

1.24-31 This Decree, therefore, of the Master, GOD-of-
the-Angel-Armies,
the Strong One of Israel:
"This is it! I'll get my oppressors off my back.
I'll get back at my enemies.
I'll give you the back of my hand,
purge the junk from your life, clean you
up.
I'll set honest judges and wise counselors
among you
just like it was back in the beginning.
Then you'll be renamed
City-That-Treats-People-Right, the True-
Blue City."
GOD's right ways will put Zion right again.
GOD's right actions will restore her
penitents.
But it's curtains for rebels and GOD-traitors,
a dead end for those who walk out on GOD.
"Your dalliances in those oak grove shrines
will leave you looking mighty foolish,
All that fooling around in god and goddess
gardens
that you thought was the latest thing.
You'll end up like an oak tree
with all its leaves falling off,
Like an unwatered garden,
withered and brown.
'The Big Man' will turn out to be dead bark
and twigs,
and his 'work,' the spark that starts the fire
That exposes man and work both
as nothing but cinders and smoke."

NEW INTERNATIONAL VERSION

THE MOUNTAIN OF THE LORD

2 This is what Isaiah son of Amoz saw concerning Judah and Jerusalem:

[2] In the last days

the mountain of the LORD's temple will be
established
as chief among the mountains;
it will be raised above the hills,
and all nations will stream to it.

[3] Many peoples will come and say,

"Come, let us go up to the mountain of the
LORD,
to the house of the God of Jacob.
He will teach us his ways,
so that we may walk in his paths."
The law will go out from Zion,
the word of the LORD from Jerusalem.
[4] He will judge between the nations
and will settle disputes for many peoples.
They will beat their swords into plowshares
and their spears into pruning hooks.
Nation will not take up sword against
nation,
nor will they train for war anymore.

[5] Come, O house of Jacob,
let us walk in the light of the LORD.

THE DAY OF THE LORD

[6] You have abandoned your people,
the house of Jacob.
They are full of superstitions from the East;
they practice divination like the
Philistines
and clasp hands with pagans.
[7] Their land is full of silver and gold;
there is no end to their treasures.
Their land is full of horses;
there is no end to their chariots.
[8] Their land is full of idols;
they bow down to the work of their
hands,
to what their fingers have made.
[9] So man will be brought low
and mankind humbled—
do not forgive them. [a]

[10] Go into the rocks,
hide in the ground
from dread of the LORD
and the splendor of his majesty!
[11] The eyes of the arrogant man will be
humbled
and the pride of men brought low;
the LORD alone will be exalted in that day.

---

[a] 9 Or *not raise them up*

THE MESSAGE

CLIMB GOD'S MOUNTAIN

2.1-5 **2** The Message Isaiah got regarding Judah
and Jerusalem:

There's a day coming
when the mountain of GOD's House
Will be The Mountain—
solid, towering over all mountains.
All nations will river toward it,
people from all over set out for it.
They'll say, "Come,
let's climb GOD's Mountain,
go to the House of the God of Jacob.
He'll show us the way he works
so we can live the way we're made."
Zion's the source of the revelation.
GOD's Message comes from Jerusalem.
He'll settle things fairly between nations.
He'll make things right between many
peoples.
They'll turn their swords into shovels,
their spears into hoes.
No more will nation fight nation;
they won't play war anymore.
Come, family of Jacob,
let's live in the light of GOD.

2.6-9 GOD, you've walked out on your family Jacob
because their world is full of hokey
religion,
Philistine witchcraft, and pagan hocus-pocus,
a world rolling in wealth,
Stuffed with things,
no end to its machines and gadgets,
And gods—gods of all sorts and sizes.
These people make their own gods and
worship what they make.
A degenerate race, facedown in the gutter.
Don't bother with them! They're not worth
forgiving!

PRETENTIOUS EGOS BROUGHT DOWN TO EARTH

2.10 Head for the hills,
hide in the caves
From the terror of GOD,
from his dazzling presence.

2.11-17 People with a big head are headed for a fall,
pretentious egos brought down a peg.
It's GOD alone at front-and-center
on the Day we're talking about,

NEW INTERNATIONAL VERSION	THE MESSAGE

NEW INTERNATIONAL VERSION

¹²The Lord Almighty has a day in store
  for all the proud and lofty,
  for all that is exalted
  (and they will be humbled),
¹³for all the cedars of Lebanon, tall and lofty,
  and all the oaks of Bashan,
¹⁴for all the towering mountains
  and all the high hills,
¹⁵for every lofty tower
  and every fortified wall,
¹⁶for every trading ship*a*
  and every stately vessel.
¹⁷The arrogance of man will be brought low
  and the pride of men humbled;
  the Lord alone will be exalted in that day,
¹⁸ and the idols will totally disappear.

¹⁹Men will flee to caves in the rocks
  and to holes in the ground
  from dread of the Lord
  and the splendor of his majesty,
  when he rises to shake the earth.
²⁰In that day men will throw away
  to the rodents and bats
  their idols of silver and idols of gold,
  which they made to worship.
²¹They will flee to caverns in the rocks
  and to the overhanging crags
  from dread of the Lord
  and the splendor of his majesty,
  when he rises to shake the earth.

²²Stop trusting in man,
  who has but a breath in his nostrils.
  Of what account is he?

JUDGMENT ON JERUSALEM AND JUDAH

3 See now, the Lord,
  the Lord Almighty,
  is about to take from Jerusalem and Judah
  both supply and support:
  all supplies of food and all supplies of water,
² the hero and warrior,
  the judge and prophet,
  the soothsayer and elder,
³the captain of fifty and man of rank,
  the counselor, skilled craftsman and
  clever enchanter.

THE MESSAGE

The Day that God-of-the-Angel-Armies
  is matched against all big-talking rivals,
  against all swaggering big names;
Against all giant sequoias
  hugely towering,
  and against the expansive chestnut;
Against Kilimanjaro and Annapurna,
  against the ranges of Alps and Andes;
Against every soaring skyscraper,
  against all proud obelisks and statues;
Against ocean-going luxury liners,
  against elegant three-masted schooners.
The swelled big heads will be punctured
    bladders,
  the pretentious egos brought down to earth,
Leaving God alone at front-and-center
  on the Day we're talking about.

2.18 And all those sticks and stones
  dressed up to look like gods
  will be gone for good.

2.19 Clamber into caves in the cliffs,
  duck into any hole you can find.
Hide from the terror of God,
  from his dazzling presence,
When he assumes his full stature on earth,
  towering and terrifying.

2.20-21 On that Day men and women will take
  the sticks and stones
They've decked out in gold and silver
  to look like gods and then worshiped,
And they will dump them
  in any ditch or gully,
Then run for rock caves
  and cliff hideouts
To hide from the terror of God,
  from his dazzling presence,
When he assumes his full stature on earth,
  towering and terrifying.

2.22 Quit scraping and fawning over mere humans,
  so full of themselves, so full of hot air!
  Can't you see there's nothing to them?

JERUSALEM ON ITS LAST LEGS

3.1-7 **3** The Master, God-of-the-Angel-Armies,
  is emptying Jerusalem and Judah
Of all the basic necessities,
  plain bread and water to begin with.
He's withdrawing police and protection,
  judges and courts,
  pastors and teachers,
  captains and generals,
  doctors and nurses,
  and, yes, even the repairmen and
    jacks-of-all-trades.

---

a 16 Hebrew *every ship of Tarshish*

NEW INTERNATIONAL VERSION	THE MESSAGE

NEW INTERNATIONAL VERSION

⁴I will make boys their officials;
   mere children will govern them.
⁵People will oppress each other—
   man against man, neighbor against
      neighbor.
The young will rise up against the old,
   the base against the honorable.

⁶A man will seize one of his brothers
   at his father's home, and say,
"You have a cloak, you be our leader;
   take charge of this heap of ruins!"
⁷But in that day he will cry out,
   "I have no remedy.
I have no food or clothing in my house;
   do not make me the leader of the people."

⁸Jerusalem staggers,
   Judah is falling;
their words and deeds are against the LORD,
   defying his glorious presence.
⁹The look on their faces testifies against
      them;
   they parade their sin like Sodom;
   they do not hide it.
Woe to them!
   They have brought disaster upon
      themselves.

¹⁰Tell the righteous it will be well with them,
   for they will enjoy the fruit of their deeds.
¹¹Woe to the wicked! Disaster is upon them!
   They will be paid back for what their hands
      have done.

¹²Youths oppress my people,
   women rule over them.
O my people, your guides lead you astray;
   they turn you from the path.

¹³The LORD takes his place in court;
   he rises to judge the people.
¹⁴The LORD enters into judgment
   against the elders and leaders of his
      people:
"It is you who have ruined my vineyard;
   the plunder from the poor is in your
      houses.
¹⁵What do you mean by crushing my people
   and grinding the faces of the poor?"
                  declares the Lord,
               the LORD Almighty.

¹⁶The LORD says,
   "The women of Zion are haughty,
walking along with outstretched necks,
   flirting with their eyes,
tripping along with mincing steps,
   with ornaments jingling on their ankles.

THE MESSAGE

He says, "I'll put little kids in charge of the
      city.
   Schoolboys and schoolgirls will order
      everyone around.
People will be at each other's throats,
   stabbing one another in the back:
Neighbor against neighbor, young against old,
   the no-account against the well-respected.
One brother will grab another and say,
   'You look like you've got a head on your
      shoulders.
Do something!
   Get us out of this mess.'
And he'll say, 'Me? Not me! I don't have a clue.
   Don't put me in charge of anything.'

3.8-9 "Jerusalem's on its last legs.
   Judah is soon down for the count.
Everything people say and do
   is at cross-purposes with GOD,
   a slap in my face.
Brazen in their depravity,
   they flout their sins like degenerate Sodom.
Doom to their eternal souls! They've made
      their bed;
   now they'll sleep in it.

3.10-11 "Reassure the righteous
   that their good living will pay off.
But doom to the wicked! Disaster!
   Everything they did will be done to them.

3.12 "Skinny kids terrorize my people.
   Silly girls bully them around.
My dear people! Your leaders are taking you
      down a blind alley.
   They're sending you off on a wild goose
      chase."

A CITY BROUGHT TO HER KNEES BY HER SORROWS

3.13-15 GOD enters the courtroom.
   He takes his place at the bench to judge his
      people.
GOD calls for order in the court,
   hauls the leaders of his people into the dock:
"You've played havoc with this country.
   Your houses are stuffed with what you've
      stolen from the poor.
What is this anyway? Stomping on my people,
   grinding the faces of the poor into the dirt?"
That's what the Master,
   GOD-of-the-Angel-Armies, says.

3.16-17 GOD says, "Zion women are stuck-up,
   prancing around in their high heels,
Making eyes at all the men in the street,
   swinging their hips,
Tossing their hair,
   gaudy and garish in cheap jewelry."

NEW INTERNATIONAL VERSION

¹⁷ Therefore the Lord will bring sores on the
heads of the women of Zion;
the LORD will make their scalps bald."

¹⁸In that day the Lord will snatch away their
finery: the bangles and headbands and crescent
necklaces, ¹⁹the earrings and bracelets and veils,
²⁰the headdresses and ankle chains and sashes,
the perfume bottles and charms, ²¹the signet
rings and nose rings, ²²the fine robes and the
capes and cloaks, the purses ²³and mirrors, and
the linen garments and tiaras and shawls.

²⁴ Instead of fragrance there will be a stench;
instead of a sash, a rope;
instead of well-dressed hair, baldness;
instead of fine clothing, sackcloth;
instead of beauty, branding.
²⁵ Your men will fall by the sword,
your warriors in battle.
²⁶ The gates of Zion will lament and mourn;
destitute, she will sit on the ground.

4 ¹In that day seven women
will take hold of one man
and say, "We will eat our own food
and provide our own clothes;
only let us be called by your name.
Take away our disgrace!"

THE BRANCH OF THE LORD

²In that day the Branch of the LORD will be
beautiful and glorious, and the fruit of the land
will be the pride and glory of the survivors in Israel. ³Those who are left in Zion, who remain in
Jerusalem, will be called holy, all who are recorded among the living in Jerusalem. ⁴The Lord will
wash away the filth of the women of Zion; he
will cleanse the bloodstains from Jerusalem by a
spirit*a* of judgment and a spirit*a* of fire. ⁵Then
the LORD will create over all of Mount Zion and
over those who assemble there a cloud of smoke
by day and a glow of flaming fire by night; over
all the glory will be a canopy. ⁶It will be a shelter
and shade from the heat of the day, and a refuge
and hiding place from the storm and rain.

a 4 Or the Spirit

THE MESSAGE

The Master will fix it so those Zion women
will all turn bald—
Scabby, bald-headed women.
The Master will do it.

3.18-23 The time is coming when the Master will
strip them of their fancy baubles—the dangling
earrings, anklets and bracelets, combs and mirrors and silk scarves, diamond brooches and
pearl necklaces, the rings on their fingers and
the rings on their toes, the latest fashions in
hats, exotic perfumes and aphrodisiacs, gowns
and capes, all the world's finest in fabrics and
design.

3.24 Instead of wearing seductive scents,
these women are going to smell like rotting
cabbages;
Instead of modeling flowing gowns,
they'll be sporting rags;
Instead of their stylish hairdos,
scruffy heads;
Instead of beauty marks,
scabs and scars.

3.25-26 Your finest fighting men will be killed,
your soldiers left dead on the battlefield.
The entrance gate to Zion will be clotted
with people mourning their dead—
A city stooped under the weight of her loss,
brought to her knees by her sorrows.

✠

4.1 **4** That will be the day when seven women
will gang up on one man, saying,
"We'll take care of ourselves,
get our own food and clothes.
Just give us a child. Make us pregnant
so we'll have something to live for!"

GOD'S BRANCH

4.2-4 And that's when GOD's Branch will sprout green
and lush. The produce of the country will give
Israel's survivors something to be proud of
again. Oh, they'll hold their heads high! Everyone left behind in Zion, all the discards and rejects in Jerusalem, will be reclassified as
"holy"—alive and therefore precious. GOD will
give Zion's women a good bath. He'll scrub the
bloodstained city of its violence and brutality,
purge the place with a firestorm of judgment.

4.5-6 Then GOD will bring back the ancient pillar
of cloud by day and the pillar of fire by night
and mark Mount Zion and everyone in it with
his glorious presence, his immense, protective
presence, shade from the burning sun and shelter from the driving rain.

NEW INTERNATIONAL VERSION

THE SONG OF THE VINEYARD

5 I will sing for the one I love
  a song about his vineyard:
My loved one had a vineyard
  on a fertile hillside.
² He dug it up and cleared it of stones
  and planted it with the choicest vines.
He built a watchtower in it
  and cut out a winepress as well.
Then he looked for a crop of good grapes,
  but it yielded only bad fruit.

³ "Now you dwellers in Jerusalem and men of
    Judah,
  judge between me and my vineyard.
⁴ What more could have been done for my
    vineyard
  than I have done for it?
When I looked for good grapes,
  why did it yield only bad?
⁵ Now I will tell you
  what I am going to do to my vineyard:
I will take away its hedge,
  and it will be destroyed;
I will break down its wall,
  and it will be trampled.
⁶ I will make it a wasteland,
  neither pruned nor cultivated,
  and briers and thorns will grow there.
I will command the clouds
  not to rain on it."

⁷ The vineyard of the LORD Almighty
  is the house of Israel,
and the men of Judah
  are the garden of his delight.
And he looked for justice, but saw bloodshed;
  for righteousness, but heard cries of distress.

WOES AND JUDGMENTS

⁸ Woe to you who add house to house
  and join field to field
till no space is left
  and you live alone in the land.

⁹ The LORD Almighty has declared in my hearing:

  "Surely the great houses will become desolate,
    the fine mansions left without occupants.
¹⁰ A ten-acre*ᵃ* vineyard will produce only a
      bath*ᵇ* of wine,
  a homer*ᶜ* of seed only an ephah*ᵈ* of
      grain."

ᵃ *10* Hebrew *ten-yoke,* that is, the land plowed by 10 yoke
of oxen in one day ᵇ *10* That is, probably about 6 gallons
(about 22 liters) ᶜ *10* That is, probably about 6 bushels
(about 220 liters) ᵈ *10* That is, probably about 3/5
bushel (about 22 liters)

THE MESSAGE

LOOKING FOR A CROP OF JUSTICE

5 5.1-2 I'll sing a ballad to the one I love,
  a love ballad about his vineyard:
The one I love had a vineyard,
  a fine, well-placed vineyard.
He hoed the soil and pulled the weeds,
  and planted the very best vines.
He built a lookout, built a winepress,
  a vineyard to be proud of.
He looked for a vintage yield of grapes,
  but for all his pains he got junk grapes.

5.3-4 "Now listen to what I'm telling you,
  you who live in Jerusalem and Judah.
What do you think is going on
  between me and my vineyard?
Can you think of anything I could have done
  to my vineyard that I didn't do?
When I expected good grapes,
  why did I get bitter grapes?

5.5-6 "Well now, let me tell you
  what I'll do to my vineyard:
I'll tear down its fence
  and let it go to ruin.
I'll knock down the gate
  and let it be trampled.
I'll turn it into a patch of weeds, untended,
      uncared for—
  thistles and thorns will take over.
I'll give orders to the clouds:
  'Don't rain on that vineyard, ever!' "

5.7 Do you get it? The vineyard of GOD-of-the-
      Angel-Armies
  is the country of Israel.
All the men and women of Judah
  are the garden he was so proud of.
He looked for a crop of justice
  and saw them murdering each other.
He looked for a harvest of righteousness
  and heard only the moans of victims.

YOU WHO CALL EVIL GOOD AND GOOD EVIL

5.8-10 Doom to you who buy up all the houses
  and grab all the land for yourselves—
Evicting the old owners,
  posting NO TRESPASSING signs,
Taking over the country,
  leaving everyone homeless and landless.
I overheard GOD-of-the-Angel-Armies say:
"Those mighty houses will end up empty.
  Those extravagant estates will be deserted.
A ten-acre vineyard will produce a pint of
      wine,
  a fifty-pound sack of seed, a quart of grain."

NEW INTERNATIONAL VERSION	THE MESSAGE

NEW INTERNATIONAL VERSION

[11] Woe to those who rise early in the morning
  to run after their drinks,
who stay up late at night
  till they are inflamed with wine.
[12] They have harps and lyres at their banquets,
  tambourines and flutes and wine,
but they have no regard for the deeds of the
  LORD,
  no respect for the work of his hands.
[13] Therefore my people will go into exile
  for lack of understanding;
their men of rank will die of hunger
  and their masses will be parched with
    thirst.
[14] Therefore the grave[a] enlarges its appetite
  and opens its mouth without limit;
into it will descend their nobles and masses
  with all their brawlers and revelers.
[15] So man will be brought low
  and mankind humbled,
  the eyes of the arrogant humbled.
[16] But the LORD Almighty will be exalted by his
    justice,
  and the holy God will show himself holy
    by his righteousness.
[17] Then sheep will graze as in their own
      pasture;
  lambs will feed[b] among the ruins of the
    rich.

[18] Woe to those who draw sin along with cords
    of deceit,
  and wickedness as with cart ropes,
[19] to those who say, "Let God hurry,
  let him hasten his work
    so we may see it.
Let it approach,
  let the plan of the Holy One of Israel
    come,
    so we may know it."

[20] Woe to those who call evil good
    and good evil,
who put darkness for light
  and light for darkness,
who put bitter for sweet
  and sweet for bitter.

[21] Woe to those who are wise in their own eyes
  and clever in their own sight.

[22] Woe to those who are heroes at drinking wine
  and champions at mixing drinks,
[23] who acquit the guilty for a bribe,
  but deny justice to the innocent.
[24] Therefore, as tongues of fire lick up straw
  and as dry grass sinks down in the flames,

THE MESSAGE

5.11-17 Doom to those who get up early
  and start drinking booze before breakfast,
Who stay up all hours of the night
  drinking themselves into a stupor
They make sure their banquets are
      well-furnished
  with harps and flutes and plenty of wine,
But they'll have nothing to do with the work
    of GOD,
  pay no mind to what he is doing.
Therefore my people will end up in exile
  because they don't know the score.
Their "big men" will starve to death
  and the common people die of thirst.
Sheol developed a huge appetite,
  swallowing people nonstop!
Big people and little people alike
  down that gullet, to say nothing of all the
    drunks.
The down-and-out on a par
  with the high-and-mighty,
Windbag boasters crumpled,
  flaccid as a punctured bladder.
But by working justice,
  GOD-of-the-Angel-Armies will be a mountain.
By working righteousness,
  Holy God will show what "holy" is.
And lambs will graze
  as if they owned the place,
Kids and calves
  right at home in the ruins.

5.18-19 Doom to you who use lies to sell evil,
  who haul sin to market by the truckload,
Who say, "What's God waiting for?
  Let him get a move on so we can see it.
Whatever The Holy of Israel has cooked up,
  we'd like to check it out."

5.20 Doom to you who call evil good
  and good evil,
Who put darkness in place of light
  and light in place of darkness,
Who substitute bitter for sweet
  and sweet for bitter!

5.21-23 Doom to you who think you're so smart,
  who hold such a high opinion of
    yourselves!
All you're good at is drinking—champion
    boozers
  who collect trophies from drinking bouts
And then line your pockets with bribes from
    the guilty
  while you violate the rights of the innocent.

5.24 But they won't get by with it. As fire eats
    stubble
  and dry grass goes up in smoke,

---

[a] 14 Hebrew *Sheol*   [b] 17 Septuagint; Hebrew / *strangers will eat*

NEW INTERNATIONAL VERSION

so their roots will decay
    and their flowers blow away like dust;
for they have rejected the law of the LORD
        Almighty
    and spurned the word of the Holy One of
        Israel.
25 Therefore the LORD's anger burns against his
        people;
    his hand is raised and he strikes them
        down.
The mountains shake,
    and the dead bodies are like refuse in the
        streets.

Yet for all this, his anger is not turned away,
    his hand is still upraised.

26 He lifts up a banner for the distant nations,
    he whistles for those at the ends of the
        earth.
Here they come,
    swiftly and speedily!
27 Not one of them grows tired or stumbles,
    not one slumbers or sleeps;
not a belt is loosened at the waist,
    not a sandal thong is broken.
28 Their arrows are sharp,
    all their bows are strung;
their horses' hoofs seem like flint,
    their chariot wheels like a whirlwind.
29 Their roar is like that of the lion,
    they roar like young lions;
they growl as they seize their prey
    and carry it off with no one to rescue.
30 In that day they will roar over it
    like the roaring of the sea.
And if one looks at the land,
    he will see darkness and distress;
    even the light will be darkened by the
        clouds.

ISAIAH'S COMMISSION

6 In the year that King Uzziah died, I saw the
Lord seated on a throne, high and exalted,
and the train of his robe filled the temple.
²Above him were seraphs, each with six wings:
With two wings they covered their faces, with
two they covered their feet, and with two they
were flying. ³And they were calling to one another:

"Holy, holy, holy is the LORD Almighty;
    the whole earth is full of his glory."

⁴At the sound of their voices the doorposts and
thresholds shook and the temple was filled with
smoke.

THE MESSAGE

Their souls will atrophy,
    their achievements crumble into dust,
Because they said no to the revelation
    of GOD-of-the-Angel-Armies,
Would have nothing to do
    with The Holy of Israel.

5.25-30 That's why GOD flamed out in anger against
            his people,
    reached out and knocked them down.
The mountains trembled
    as their dead bodies piled up in the streets.
But even after that, he was still angry,
    his fist still raised, ready to hit them again.
He raises a flag, signaling a distant nation,
    whistles for people at the ends of the earth.
And here they come—
    on the run!
None drag their feet, no one stumbles,
    no one sleeps or dawdles.
Shirts are on and pants buckled,
    every boot is spit-polished and tied.
Their arrows are sharp,
    bows strung,
The hooves of their horses shod,
    chariot wheels greased.
Roaring like a pride of lions,
    the full-throated roars of young lions,
They growl and seize their prey,
    dragging it off—no rescue for that one!
They'll roar and roar and roar on that Day,
    like the roar of ocean billows.
Look as long and hard as you like at that land,
    you'll see nothing but darkness and
        trouble.
Every light in the sky
    will be blacked out by the clouds.

HOLY, HOLY, HOLY!

6.1-8 6 In the year that King Uzziah died, I saw the
Master sitting on a throne—high, exalt-
ed!—and the train of his robes filled the Temple. Angel-seraphs hovered above him, each
with six wings. With two wings they covered
their faces, with two their feet, and with two
they flew. And they called back and forth one
to the other,

Holy, Holy, Holy is GOD-of-the-Angel-
    Armies.
His bright glory fills the whole earth."

The foundations trembled at the sound of the
angel voices, and then the whole house filled
with smoke. I said,

NEW INTERNATIONAL VERSION

⁵"Woe to me!" I cried. "I am ruined! For I am a man of unclean lips, and I live among a people of unclean lips, and my eyes have seen the King, the LORD Almighty."

⁶Then one of the seraphs flew to me with a live coal in his hand, which he had taken with tongs from the altar. ⁷With it he touched my mouth and said, "See, this has touched your lips; your guilt is taken away and your sin atoned for."

⁸Then I heard the voice of the Lord saying, "Whom shall I send? And who will go for us?"

And I said, "Here am I. Send me!"

⁹He said, "Go and tell this people:

" 'Be ever hearing, but never understanding;
    be ever seeing, but never perceiving.'
¹⁰Make the heart of this people calloused;
    make their ears dull
    and close their eyes.*
Otherwise they might see with their eyes,
    hear with their ears,
    understand with their hearts,
and turn and be healed."

¹¹Then I said, "For how long, O Lord?"

And he answered:

"Until the cities lie ruined
    and without inhabitant,
until the houses are left deserted
    and the fields ruined and ravaged,
¹²until the LORD has sent everyone far away
    and the land is utterly forsaken.
¹³And though a tenth remains in the land,
    it will again be laid waste.
But as the terebinth and oak
    leave stumps when they are cut down,
    so the holy seed will be the stump in the
        land."

THE MESSAGE

"Doom! It's Doomsday!
    I'm as good as dead!
Every word I've ever spoken is tainted—
    blasphemous even!
And the people I live with talk the same way,
    using words that corrupt and desecrate.
And here I've looked God in the face!
    The King! GOD-of-the-Angel-Armies!"

Then one of the angel-seraphs flew to me. He held a live coal that he had taken with tongs from the altar. He touched my mouth with the coal and said,

"Look. This coal has touched your lips.
    Gone your guilt,
    your sins wiped out."

And then I heard the voice of the Master:
    "Whom shall I send?
    Who will go for us?"
I spoke up,
    "I'll go.
    Send me!"

⊹

6.9-10 He said, "Go and tell this people:

" 'Listen hard, but you aren't going to get it;
    look hard, but you won't catch on.'
Make these people blockheads,
    with fingers in their ears and blindfolds on
        their eyes,
So they won't see a thing,
    won't hear a word,
So they won't have a clue about what's going
        on
and, yes, so they won't turn around and be
        made whole."

6.11-13 Astonished, I said,
    "And Master, how long is this to go on?"
He said, "Until the cities are emptied out,
    not a soul left in the cities—
Houses empty of people,
    countryside empty of people.
Until I, GOD, get rid of everyone, sending
        them off,
    the land totally empty.
And even if some should survive, say a tenth,
    the devastation will start up again.
The country will look like pine and oak forest
    with every tree cut down—
Every tree a stump, a huge field of stumps.
    But there's a holy seed in those stumps."

ᵃ 9,10 Hebrew; Septuagint *'You will be ever hearing, but never understanding; / you will be ever seeing, but never perceiving.' / ¹⁰This people's heart has become calloused; / they hardly hear with their ears, / and they have closed their eyes*

NEW INTERNATIONAL VERSION

THE SIGN OF IMMANUEL

7 When Ahaz son of Jotham, the son of Uzziah, was king of Judah, King Rezin of Aram and Pekah son of Remaliah king of Israel marched up to fight against Jerusalem, but they could not overpower it.

²Now the house of David was told, "Aram has allied itself with[a] Ephraim"; so the hearts of Ahaz and his people were shaken, as the trees of the forest are shaken by the wind.

³Then the LORD said to Isaiah, "Go out, you and your son Shear-Jashub,[b] to meet Ahaz at the end of the aqueduct of the Upper Pool, on the road to the Washerman's Field. ⁴Say to him, 'Be careful, keep calm and don't be afraid. Do not lose heart because of these two smoldering stubs of firewood—because of the fierce anger of Rezin and Aram and of the son of Remaliah. ⁵Aram, Ephraim and Remaliah's son have plotted your ruin, saying, ⁶"Let us invade Judah; let us tear it apart and divide it among ourselves, and make the son of Tabeel king over it." ⁷Yet this is what the Sovereign LORD says:

" 'It will not take place,
    it will not happen,
⁸for the head of Aram is Damascus,
    and the head of Damascus is only Rezin.
Within sixty-five years
    Ephraim will be too shattered to be a
        people.
⁹The head of Ephraim is Samaria,
    and the head of Samaria is only Remaliah's
        son.
If you do not stand firm in your faith,
    you will not stand at all.' "

¹⁰Again the LORD spoke to Ahaz, ¹¹"Ask the LORD your God for a sign, whether in the deepest depths or in the highest heights."

¹²But Ahaz said, "I will not ask; I will not put the LORD to the test."

¹³Then Isaiah said, "Hear now, you house of David! Is it not enough to try the patience of men? Will you try the patience of my God also? ¹⁴Therefore the Lord himself will give you[c] a sign: The virgin will be with child and will give birth to a son, and[d] will call him Immanuel.[e] ¹⁵He will eat curds and honey when he knows enough to reject the wrong and choose the right. ¹⁶But before the boy knows enough to reject the wrong and choose the right, the land of the two kings you dread will be laid waste. ¹⁷The LORD

---

a 2 Or *has set up camp in*   *b 3 Shear-Jashub* means *a remnant will return.*   *c 14* The Hebrew is plural.
d 14 Masoretic Text; Dead Sea Scrolls *and he* or *and they*
e 14 Immanuel means *God with us.*

THE MESSAGE

A VIRGIN WILL BEAR A SON

7.1-2 **7** During the time that Ahaz son of Jotham, son of Uzziah, was king of Judah, King Rezin of Aram and King Pekah son of Remaliah of Israel attacked Jerusalem, but the attack sputtered out. When the Davidic government learned that Aram had joined forces with Ephraim (that is, Israel), Ahaz and his people were badly shaken. They shook like trees in the wind.

7.3-6   Then GOD told Isaiah, "Go and meet Ahaz. Take your son Shear-jashub (A-Remnant-Will-Return) with you. Meet him south of the city at the end of the aqueduct where it empties into the upper pool on the road to the public laundry. Tell him, Listen, calm down. Don't be afraid. And don't panic over these two burnt-out cases, Rezin of Aram and the son of Remaliah. They talk big but there's nothing to them. Aram, along with Ephraim's son of Remaliah, have plotted to do you harm. They've conspired against you, saying, 'Let's go to war against Judah, dismember it, take it for ourselves, and set the son of Tabeel up as a puppet king over it.'

7.7-9   But GOD, the Master, says,

"It won't happen.
    Nothing will come of it
Because the capital of Aram is Damascus
    and the king of Damascus is a mere man,
        Rezin.
As for Ephraim, in sixty-five years
    it will be rubble, nothing left of it.
The capital of Ephraim is Samaria,
    and the king of Samaria is the mere son of
        Remaliah.
If you don't take your stand in faith,
    you won't have a leg to stand on."

7.10-11 GOD spoke again to Ahaz. This time he said, "Ask for a sign from your GOD. Ask anything. Be extravagant. Ask for the moon!"

7.12   But Ahaz said, "I'd never do that. I'd never make demands like that on GOD!"

7.13-17   So Isaiah told him, "Then listen to this, government of David! It's bad enough that you make people tired with your pious, timid hypocrisies, but now you're making God tired. So the Master is going to give you a sign anyway. Watch for this: A girl who is presently a virgin will get pregnant. She'll bear a son and name him Immanuel (God-With-Us). By the time the child is twelve years old, able to make moral decisions, the threat of war will be over. Relax, those two kings that have you so worried will be out of the picture. But also be

NEW INTERNATIONAL VERSION	THE MESSAGE

will bring on you and on your people and on the house of your father a time unlike any since Ephraim broke away from Judah—he will bring the king of Assyria."

¹⁸In that day the LORD will whistle for flies from the distant streams of Egypt and for bees from the land of Assyria. ¹⁹They will all come and settle in the steep ravines and in the crevices in the rocks, on all the thornbushes and at all the water holes. ²⁰In that day the Lord will use a razor hired from beyond the River ᵃ—the king of Assyria—to shave your head and the hair of your legs, and to take off your beards also. ²¹In that day, a man will keep alive a young cow and two goats. ²²And because of the abundance of the milk they give, he will have curds to eat. All who remain in the land will eat curds and honey. ²³In that day, in every place where there were a thousand vines worth a thousand silver shekels, ᵇ there will be only briers and thorns. ²⁴Men will go there with bow and arrow, for the land will be covered with briers and thorns. ²⁵As for all the hills once cultivated by the hoe, you will no longer go there for fear of the briers and thorns; they will become places where cattle are turned loose and where sheep run.

ASSYRIA, THE LORD'S INSTRUMENT

8 The LORD said to me, "Take a large scroll and write on it with an ordinary pen: Maher-Shalal-Hash-Baz. ᶜ ²And I will call in Uriah the priest and Zechariah son of Jeberekiah as reliable witnesses for me."

³Then I went to the prophetess, and she conceived and gave birth to a son. And the LORD said to me, "Name him Maher-Shalal-Hash-Baz. ⁴Before the boy knows how to say 'My father' or 'My mother,' the wealth of Damascus and the plunder of Samaria will be carried off by the king of Assyria."

⁵The LORD spoke to me again:

⁶ "Because this people has rejected
   the gently flowing waters of Shiloah
and rejoices over Rezin
   and the son of Remaliah,
⁷ therefore the Lord is about to bring against
   them
   the mighty floodwaters of the River ᵃ—

---

warned: GOD will bring on you and your people and your government a judgment worse than anything since the time the kingdom split, when Ephraim left Judah. The king of Assyria is coming!"

7.18-19 That's when GOD will whistle for the flies at the headwaters of Egypt's Nile, and whistle for the bees in the land of Assyria. They'll come and infest every nook and cranny of this country. There'll be no getting away from them.

7.20 And that's when the Master will take the razor rented from across the Euphrates—the king of Assyria no less!—and shave the hair off your heads and genitals, leaving you shamed, exposed, and denuded. He'll shave off your beards while he's at it.

7.21-22 It will be a time when survivors will count themselves lucky to have a cow and a couple of sheep. At least they'll have plenty of milk! Whoever's left in the land will learn to make do with the simplest foods—curds, whey, and honey.

7.23-25 But that's not the end of it. This country that used to be covered with fine vineyards—thousands of them, worth millions!—will revert to a weed patch. Weeds and thorn bushes everywhere! Good for nothing except, perhaps, hunting rabbits. Cattle and sheep will forage as best they can in the fields of weeds—but there won't be a trace of all those fertile and well-tended gardens and fields.

✛

8.1 **8** Then GOD told me, "Get a big sheet of paper and write in indelible ink, 'This belongs to Maher-shalal-hash-baz (Spoil-Speeds-Plunder-Hurries).'"

8.2-3 I got two honest men, Uriah the priest and Zechariah son of Jeberekiah, to witness the document. Then I went home to my wife, the prophetess. She conceived and gave birth to a son.

8.3-4 GOD told me, "Name him Maher-shalal-hash-baz. Before that baby says 'Daddy' or 'Mamma' the king of Assyria will have plundered the wealth of Damascus and the riches of Samaria."

✛

8.5-8 GOD spoke to me again, saying:

"Because this people has turned its back
   on the gently flowing stream of Shiloah
And gotten all excited over Rezin
   and the son of Remaliah,
I'm stepping in and facing them with
   the wild floodwaters of the Euphrates,

ᵃ 20,7 That is, the Euphrates   ᵇ 23 That is, about 25 pounds (about 11.5 kilograms)   ᶜ 1 Maher-Shalal-Hash-Baz means quick to the plunder, swift to the spoil; also in verse 3.

NEW INTERNATIONAL VERSION

the king of Assyria with all his pomp.
It will overflow all its channels,
    run over all its banks
[8] and sweep on into Judah, swirling over it,
    passing through it and reaching up to the
        neck.
Its outspread wings will cover the breadth of
    your land,
    O Immanuel[a]!"

[9] Raise the war cry,[b] you nations, and be
    shattered!
    Listen, all you distant lands.
Prepare for battle, and be shattered!
Prepare for battle, and be shattered!
[10] Devise your strategy, but it will be thwarted;
    propose your plan, but it will not stand,
for God is with us.[c]

FEAR GOD

[11] The LORD spoke to me with his strong hand
upon me, warning me not to follow the way of
this people. He said:

[12] "Do not call conspiracy
    everything that these people call
        conspiracy[d];
do not fear what they fear,
    and do not dread it.
[13] The LORD Almighty is the one you are to
        regard as holy,
he is the one you are to fear,
he is the one you are to dread,
[14] and he will be a sanctuary;
    but for both houses of Israel he will be
a stone that causes men to stumble
    and a rock that makes them fall.
And for the people of Jerusalem he will be
    a trap and a snare.
[15] Many of them will stumble;
    they will fall and be broken,
    they will be snared and captured."

[16] Bind up the testimony
    and seal up the law among my disciples.
[17] I will wait for the LORD,
    who is hiding his face from the house of
        Jacob.
I will put my trust in him.

[18] Here am I, and the children the LORD has
given me. We are signs and symbols in Israel
from the LORD Almighty, who dwells on Mount
Zion.

---

[a] 8 *Immanuel* means *God with us.*   [b] 9 Or *Do your worst*
[c] 10 Hebrew *Immanuel*   [d] 12 Or *Do not call for a treaty /
every time these people call for a treaty*

THE MESSAGE

The king of Assyria and all his fanfare,
    a river in flood, bursting its banks,
Pouring into Judah, sweeping everything
    before it,
    water up to your necks,
A huge wingspan of a raging river,
    O Immanuel, spreading across your land."

        ✝

8.9-10 But face the facts, all you oppressors, and then
    wring your hands.
    Listen, all of you, far and near.
Prepare for the worst and wring your hands.
    Yes, prepare for the worst and wring your
        hands!
Plan and plot all you want—nothing will
    come of it.
    All your talk is mere talk, empty words,
Because when all is said and done,
    the last word is Immanuel—God-With-Us.

A BOULDER BLOCKING YOUR WAY

8.11-15 GOD spoke strongly to me, grabbed me with
both hands and warned me not to go along
with this people. He said:

"Don't be like this people,
    always afraid somebody is plotting against
        them.
Don't fear what they fear.
    Don't take on their worries.
If you're going to worry,
    worry about The Holy. Fear GOD-of-the-
        Angel-Armies.
The Holy can be either a Hiding Place
    or a Boulder blocking your way,
The Rock standing in the willful way
    of both houses of Israel,
A barbed-wire Fence preventing trespass
    to the citizens of Jerusalem.
Many of them are going to run into that Rock
    and get their bones broken,
Get tangled up in that barbed wire
    and not get free of it."

        ✝

8.16-18 Gather up the testimony,
    preserve the teaching for my followers,
While I wait for GOD as long as he remains in
        hiding,
    while I wait and hope for him.
I stand my ground and hope,
    I and the children GOD gave me as signs to
        Israel,
Warning signs and hope signs from GOD-of-
    the-Angel-Armies,
    who makes his home in Mount Zion.

NEW INTERNATIONAL VERSION

[19]When men tell you to consult mediums and spiritists, who whisper and mutter, should not a people inquire of their God? Why consult the dead on behalf of the living? [20]To the law and to the testimony! If they do not speak according to this word, they have no light of dawn. [21]Distressed and hungry, they will roam through the land; when they are famished, they will become enraged and, looking upward, will curse their king and their God. [22]Then they will look toward the earth and see only distress and darkness and fearful gloom, and they will be thrust into utter darkness.

TO US A CHILD IS BORN

9 Nevertheless, there will be no more gloom for those who were in distress. In the past he humbled the land of Zebulun and the land of Naphtali, but in the future he will honor Galilee of the Gentiles, by the way of the sea, along the Jordan—

[2] The people walking in darkness
  have seen a great light;
on those living in the land of the shadow of
    death[a]
  a light has dawned.
[3] You have enlarged the nation
  and increased their joy;
they rejoice before you
  as people rejoice at the harvest,
as men rejoice
  when dividing the plunder.
[4] For as in the day of Midian's defeat,
  you have shattered
the yoke that burdens them,
  the bar across their shoulders,
  the rod of their oppressor.
[5] Every warrior's boot used in battle
  and every garment rolled in blood
will be destined for burning,
  will be fuel for the fire.
[6] For to us a child is born,
  to us a son is given,
  and the government will be on his
    shoulders.
And he will be called
  Wonderful Counselor,[b] Mighty God,
  Everlasting Father, Prince of Peace.

THE MESSAGE

8.19-22 When people tell you, "Try out the
    fortunetellers.
  Consult the spiritualists.
Why not tap into the spirit-world,
  get in touch with the dead?"
Tell them, "No, we're going to study the
    Scriptures."
  People who try the other ways get
    nowhere—a dead end!
Frustrated and famished,
  they try one thing after another.
When nothing works out they get angry,
  cursing first this god and then that one,
Looking this way and that,
  up, down, and sideways—and seeing
    nothing,
A blank wall, an empty hole.
  They end up in the dark with nothing.

A CHILD HAS BEEN BORN—FOR US!

9.1 **9** But there'll be no darkness for those who
    were in trouble. Earlier he did bring the
lands of Zebulun and Naphtali into disrepute,
but the time is coming when he'll make that
whole area glorious—the road along the Sea,
the country past the Jordan, international Galilee.

9.2-7 The people who walked in darkness
  have seen a great light.
For those who lived in a land of deep
    shadows—
  light! sunbursts of light!
You repopulated the nation,
  you expanded its joy.
Oh, they're so glad in your presence!
  Festival joy!
The joy of a great celebration,
  sharing rich gifts and warm greetings.
The abuse of oppressors and cruelty of
    tyrants—
  all their whips and cudgels and curses—
Is gone, done away with, a deliverance
  as surprising and sudden as Gideon's old
    victory over Midian.
The boots of all those invading troops,
  along with their shirts soaked with
    innocent blood,
Will be piled in a heap and burned,
  a fire that will burn for days!
For a child has been born—for us!
  the gift of a son—for us!
He'll take over
  the running of the world.
His names will be: Amazing Counselor,
  Strong God,
Eternal Father,
  Prince of Wholeness.

---

[a] 2 Or land of darkness   [b] 6 Or Wonderful, Counselor

NEW INTERNATIONAL VERSION

⁷ Of the increase of his government and peace
there will be no end.
He will reign on David's throne
and over his kingdom,
establishing and upholding it
with justice and righteousness
from that time on and forever.
The zeal of the LORD Almighty
will accomplish this.

THE LORD'S ANGER AGAINST ISRAEL

⁸ The Lord has sent a message against Jacob;
it will fall on Israel.
⁹ All the people will know it—
Ephraim and the inhabitants of Samaria—
who say with pride
and arrogance of heart,
¹⁰ "The bricks have fallen down,
but we will rebuild with dressed stone;
the fig trees have been felled,
but we will replace them with cedars."
¹¹ But the LORD has strengthened Rezin's foes
against them
and has spurred their enemies on.
¹² Arameans from the east and Philistines from
the west
have devoured Israel with open mouth.

Yet for all this, his anger is not turned away,
his hand is still upraised.

¹³ But the people have not returned to him who
struck them,
nor have they sought the LORD Almighty.
¹⁴ So the LORD will cut off from Israel both
head and tail,
both palm branch and reed in a single
day;
¹⁵ the elders and prominent men are the head,
the prophets who teach lies are the tail.
¹⁶ Those who guide this people mislead them,
and those who are guided are led astray.
¹⁷ Therefore the Lord will take no pleasure in
the young men,
nor will he pity the fatherless and
widows,
for everyone is ungodly and wicked,
every mouth speaks vileness.

Yet for all this, his anger is not turned away,
his hand is still upraised.

¹⁸ Surely wickedness burns like a fire;
it consumes briers and thorns,
it sets the forest thickets ablaze,

THE MESSAGE

His ruling authority will grow,
and there'll be no limits to the wholeness
he brings.
He'll rule from the historic David throne
over that promised kingdom.
He'll put that kingdom on a firm footing
and keep it going
With fair dealing and right living,
beginning now and lasting always.
The zeal of GOD-of-the-Angel-Armies
will do all this.

GOD ANSWERED FIRE WITH FIRE

9.8-10 The Master sent a message against Jacob.
It landed right on Israel's doorstep.
All the people soon heard the message,
Ephraim and the citizens of Samaria.
But they were a proud and arrogant bunch.
They dismissed the message, saying,
"Things aren't that bad.
We can handle anything that comes.
If our buildings are knocked down,
we'll rebuild them bigger and finer.
If our forests are cut down,
we'll replant them with finer trees."

9.11-12 So GOD incited their adversaries against them,
stirred up their enemies to attack:
From the east, Arameans; from the west,
Philistines.
They made hash of Israel.
But even after that, he was still angry,
his fist still raised, ready to hit them again.

9.13-17 But the people paid no mind to him who hit
them,
didn't seek GOD-of-the-Angel-Armies.
So GOD hacked off Israel's head and tail,
palm branch and reed, both on the same
day.
The big-head elders were the head,
the lying prophets were the tail.
Those who were supposed to lead this people
led them down blind alleys,
And those who followed the leaders
ended up lost and confused.
That's why the Master lost interest in the
young men,
had no feeling for their orphans and
widows.
All of them were godless and evil,
talking filth and folly.
And even after that, he was still angry,
his fist still raised, ready to hit them again.

9.18-21 Their wicked lives raged like an out-of-control
fire,
the kind that burns everything in its path—
Trees and bushes, weeds and grasses—

NEW INTERNATIONAL VERSION

so that it rolls upward in a column of
smoke.
¹⁹ By the wrath of the LORD Almighty
the land will be scorched
and the people will be fuel for the fire;
no one will spare his brother.
²⁰ On the right they will devour,
but still be hungry;
on the left they will eat,
but not be satisfied.
Each will feed on the flesh of his own
offspring*:
²¹ Manasseh will feed on Ephraim, and
Ephraim on Manasseh;
together they will turn against Judah.

Yet for all this, his anger is not turned away,
his hand is still upraised.

10 Woe to those who make unjust laws,
to those who issue oppressive decrees,
² to deprive the poor of their rights
and withhold justice from the oppressed
of my people,
making widows their prey
and robbing the fatherless.
³ What will you do on the day of reckoning,
when disaster comes from afar?
To whom will you run for help?
Where will you leave your riches?
⁴ Nothing will remain but to cringe among the
captives
or fall among the slain.

Yet for all this, his anger is not turned away,
his hand is still upraised.

GOD'S JUDGMENT ON ASSYRIA

⁵ "Woe to the Assyrian, the rod of my anger,
in whose hand is the club of my wrath!
⁶ I send him against a godless nation,
I dispatch him against a people who
anger me,
to seize loot and snatch plunder,
and to trample them down like mud in
the streets.
⁷ But this is not what he intends,
this is not what he has in mind;
his purpose is to destroy,
to put an end to many nations.
⁸ 'Are not my commanders all kings?' he says.
⁹ 'Has not Calno fared like Carchemish?
Is not Hamath like Arpad,
and Samaria like Damascus?
¹⁰ As my hand seized the kingdoms of the idols,

THE MESSAGE

filling the skies with smoke.
GOD-of-the-Angel-Armies answered fire with
fire,
set the whole country on fire,
Turned the people into consuming fires,
consuming one another in their lusts—
Appetites insatiable, stuffing and gorging
themselves left and right with people and
things.
But still they starved. Not even their children
were safe from their rapacious hunger.
Manasseh ate Ephraim, and Ephraim
Manasseh,
and then the two ganged up against Judah.
And after that, he was still angry,
his fist still raised, ready to hit them again.

✛

YOU WHO LEGISLATE EVIL

10.1-4 **10** Doom to you who legislate evil,
who make laws that make victims—
Laws that make misery for the poor,
that rob my destitute people of dignity,
Exploiting defenseless widows,
taking advantage of homeless children.
What will you have to say on Judgment Day,
when Doomsday arrives out of the blue?
Who will you get to help you?
What good will your money do you?
A sorry sight you'll be then, huddled with the
prisoners,
or just some corpses stacked in the street.

Even after all this, God is still angry,
his fist still raised, ready to hit them again.

DOOM TO ASSYRIA!

10.5-11 "Doom to Assyria, weapon of my anger.
My wrath is a cudgel in his hands!
I send him against a godless nation,
against the people I'm angry with.
I command him to strip them clean, rob them
blind,
and then push their faces in the mud and
leave them.
But Assyria has another agenda;
he has something else in mind.
He's out to destroy utterly,
to stamp out as many nations as he can.
Assyria says, 'Aren't my commanders all
kings?
Can't they do whatever they like?
Didn't I destroy Calno as well as Carchemish?
Hamath as well as Arpad? Level Samaria as
I did Damascus?
I've eliminated kingdoms full of gods

---

a 20 Or arm

NEW INTERNATIONAL VERSION

kingdoms whose images excelled those of
Jerusalem and Samaria—
¹¹ shall I not deal with Jerusalem and her
images
as I dealt with Samaria and her idols?' "

¹²When the Lord has finished all his work
against Mount Zion and Jerusalem, he will say, "I
will punish the king of Assyria for the willful
pride of his heart and the haughty look in his
eyes. ¹³For he says:

" 'By the strength of my hand I have done
this,
and by my wisdom, because I have
understanding.
I removed the boundaries of nations,
I plundered their treasures;
like a mighty one I subdued*a* their kings.
¹⁴ As one reaches into a nest,
so my hand reached for the wealth of the
nations;
as men gather abandoned eggs,
so I gathered all the countries;
not one flapped a wing,
or opened its mouth to chirp.' "

¹⁵ Does the ax raise itself above him who
swings it,
or the saw boast against him who uses it?
As if a rod were to wield him who lifts it up,
or a club brandish him who is not wood!
¹⁶ Therefore, the Lord, the Lord Almighty,
will send a wasting disease upon his
sturdy warriors;
under his pomp a fire will be kindled
like a blazing flame.
¹⁷ The Light of Israel will become a fire,
their Holy One a flame;
in a single day it will burn and consume
his thorns and his briers.
¹⁸ The splendor of his forests and fertile fields
it will completely destroy,
as when a sick man wastes away.
¹⁹ And the remaining trees of his forests will be
so few
that a child could write them down.

THE REMNANT OF ISRAEL
²⁰ In that day the remnant of Israel,

THE MESSAGE

far more impressive than anything in
Jerusalem and Samaria.
So what's to keep me from destroying
Jerusalem
in the same way I destroyed Samaria and all
her god-idols?' "

10.12-13   When the Master has finished dealing with
Mount Zion and Jerusalem, he'll say, "Now it's
Assyria's turn. I'll punish the bragging arrogance of the king of Assyria, his high and
mighty posturing, the way he goes around saying,

10.13-14   " 'I've done all this by myself.
I know more than anyone.
I've wiped out the boundaries of whole
countries.
I've walked in and taken anything I wanted.
I charged in like a bull
and toppled their kings from their thrones.
I reached out my hand and took all that they
treasured
as easily as a boy taking a bird's eggs from a
nest.
Like a farmer gathering eggs from the
henhouse,
I gathered the world in my basket,
And no one so much as fluttered a wing
or squawked or even chirped.' "

10.15-19   Does an ax take over from the one who
swings it?
Does a saw act more important than the
sawyer?
As if a shovel did its shoveling by using a
ditch digger!
As if a hammer used the carpenter to
pound nails!
Therefore the Master, GOD-of-the-Angel-
Armies,
will send a debilitating disease on his
robust Assyrian fighters.
Under the canopy of God's bright glory
a fierce fire will break out.
Israel's Light will burst into a conflagration.
The Holy will explode into a firestorm,
And in one day burn to cinders
every last Assyrian thornbush.
GOD will destroy the splendid trees and lush
gardens.
The Assyrian body and soul will waste
away to nothing
like a disease-ridden invalid.
A child could count what's left of the trees
on the fingers of his two hands.

☩

10.20-23   And on that Day also, what's left of Israel, the

---

a 13 Or *I subdued the mighty,*

NEW INTERNATIONAL VERSION

the survivors of the house of Jacob,
will no longer rely on him
who struck them down
but will truly rely on the LORD,
the Holy One of Israel.
²¹ A remnant will return,ᵃ a remnant of Jacob
will return to the Mighty God.
²² Though your people, O Israel, be like the
sand by the sea,
only a remnant will return.
Destruction has been decreed,
overwhelming and righteous.
²³ The Lord, the LORD Almighty, will carry out
the destruction decreed upon the whole
land.

²⁴ Therefore, this is what the Lord, the LORD
Almighty, says:

"O my people who live in Zion,
do not be afraid of the Assyrians,
who beat you with a rod
and lift up a club against you, as Egypt
did.
²⁵ Very soon my anger against you will end
and my wrath will be directed to their
destruction."

²⁶ The LORD Almighty will lash them with a
whip,
as when he struck down Midian at the
rock of Oreb;
and he will raise his staff over the waters,
as he did in Egypt.
²⁷ In that day their burden will be lifted from
your shoulders,
their yoke from your neck;
the yoke will be broken
because you have grown so fat.ᵇ

²⁸ They enter Aiath;
they pass through Migron;
they store supplies at Micmash.
²⁹ They go over the pass, and say,
"We will camp overnight at Geba."
Ramah trembles;
Gibeah of Saul flees.
³⁰ Cry out, O Daughter of Gallim!
Listen, O Laishah!
Poor Anathoth!
³¹ Madmenah is in flight;
the people of Gebim take cover.
³² This day they will halt at Nob;
they will shake their fist
at the mount of the Daughter of Zion,
at the hill of Jerusalem.

THE MESSAGE

ragtag survivors of Jacob, will no longer be fascinated by abusive, battering Assyria. They'll
lean on GOD, The Holy—yes, truly. The ragtag
remnant—what's left of Jacob—will come back
to the Strong God. Your people Israel were
once like the sand on the seashore, but only a
scattered few will return. Destruction is ordered, brimming over with righteousness. For
the Master, GOD-of-the-Angel-Armies, will finish here what he started all over the globe.

¹⁰·²⁴⁻²⁷ Therefore the Master, GOD-of-the-Angel-Armies, says: "My dear, dear people who live in
Zion, don't be terrorized by the Assyrians when
they beat you with clubs and threaten you with
rods like the Egyptians once did. In just a short
time my anger against you will be spent and
I'll turn my destroying anger on them. I, GOD-
of-the-Angel-Armies, will go after them with a
cat-o'-nine-tails and finish them off decisively—as Gideon downed Midian at the rock
Oreb, as Moses turned the tables on Egypt. On
that day, Assyria will be pulled off your back,
and the yoke of slavery lifted from your neck."

✝

¹⁰·²⁷⁻³² Assyria's on the move: up from Rimmon,
on to Aiath,
through Migron,
with a bivouac at Micmash.
They've crossed the pass,
set camp at Geba for the night.
Ramah trembles with fright.
Gibeah of Saul has run off.
Cry for help, daughter of Gallim!
Listen to her, Laishah!
Do something, Anathoth!
Madmenah takes to the hills.
The people of Gebim flee in panic.
The enemy's soon at Nob—nearly there!
In sight of the city he shakes his fist
At the mount of dear daughter Zion,
the hill of Jerusalem.

ᵃ *21* Hebrew *shear-jashub*; also in verse 22   ᵇ *27* Hebrew;
Septuagint *broken / from your shoulders*

NEW INTERNATIONAL VERSION

33 See, the Lord, the LORD Almighty,
    will lop off the boughs with great power.
The lofty trees will be felled,
    the tall ones will be brought low.
34 He will cut down the forest thickets with
        an ax;
    Lebanon will fall before the Mighty One.

THE BRANCH FROM JESSE

11 A shoot will come up from the stump of
        Jesse;
    from his roots a Branch will bear fruit.
2 The Spirit of the LORD will rest on him—
    the Spirit of wisdom and of
        understanding,
    the Spirit of counsel and of power,
    the Spirit of knowledge and of the fear of
        the LORD—
3 and he will delight in the fear of the LORD.

He will not judge by what he sees with his
        eyes,
    or decide by what he hears with his ears;
4 but with righteousness he will judge the
        needy,
    with justice he will give decisions for the
        poor of the earth.
He will strike the earth with the rod of his
        mouth;
    with the breath of his lips he will slay the
        wicked.
5 Righteousness will be his belt
    and faithfulness the sash around his waist.

6 The wolf will live with the lamb,
    the leopard will lie down with the goat,
the calf and the lion and the yearling*a*
        together;
    and a little child will lead them.
7 The cow will feed with the bear,
    their young will lie down together,
    and the lion will eat straw like the ox.
8 The infant will play near the hole of the
        cobra,
    and the young child put his hand into the
        viper's nest.
9 They will neither harm nor destroy
    on all my holy mountain,
for the earth will be full of the knowledge of
        the LORD
    as the waters cover the sea.

THE MESSAGE

10.33-34 But now watch this: The Master, GOD-of-the-
        Angel-Armies,
    swings his ax and lops the branches,
Chops down the giant trees,
    lays flat the towering forest-on-the-march.
His ax will make toothpicks of that forest,
    that Lebanon-like army reduced to
        kindling.

A GREEN SHOOT FROM JESSE'S STUMP

11.1-5 11 A green Shoot will sprout from Jesse's
        stump,
    from his roots a budding Branch.
The life-giving Spirit of GOD will hover over
        him,
    the Spirit that brings wisdom and
        understanding,
The Spirit that gives direction and builds
        strength,
    the Spirit that instills knowledge and
        Fear-of-GOD.
Fear-of-GOD
    will be all his joy and delight.
He won't judge by appearances,
    won't decide on the basis of hearsay.
He'll judge the needy by what is right,
    render decisions on earth's poor with
        justice.
His words will bring everyone to awed
        attention.
    A mere breath from his lips will topple the
        wicked.
Each morning he'll pull on sturdy work
        clothes and boots,
    and build righteousness and faithfulness in
        the land.

A LIVING KNOWLEDGE OF GOD

11.6-9 The wolf will romp with the lamb,
    the leopard sleep with the kid.
Calf and lion will eat from the same trough,
    and a little child will tend them.
Cow and bear will graze the same pasture,
    their calves and cubs grow up together,
    and the lion eat straw like the ox.
The nursing child will crawl over rattlesnake
        dens,
    the toddler stick his hand down the hole of
        a serpent.
Neither animal nor human will hurt or kill
    on my holy mountain.
The whole earth will be brimming with
        knowing God-Alive,
    a living knowledge of God ocean-deep,
        ocean-wide.

✣

---

a 6 Hebrew; Septuagint *lion will feed*

NEW INTERNATIONAL VERSION

¹⁰In that day the Root of Jesse will stand as a banner for the peoples; the nations will rally to him, and his place of rest will be glorious. ¹¹In that day the Lord will reach out his hand a second time to reclaim the remnant that is left of his people from Assyria, from Lower Egypt, from Upper Egypt,ᵃ from Cush,ᵇ from Elam, from Babylonia,ᶜ from Hamath and from the islands of the sea.

¹²He will raise a banner for the nations
    and gather the exiles of Israel;
he will assemble the scattered people of
        Judah
    from the four quarters of the earth.
¹³Ephraim's jealousy will vanish,
    and Judah's enemiesᵈ will be cut off;
Ephraim will not be jealous of Judah,
    nor Judah hostile toward Ephraim.
¹⁴They will swoop down on the slopes of
        Philistia to the west;
    together they will plunder the people to
        the east.
They will lay hands on Edom and Moab,
    and the Ammonites will be subject to
        them.
¹⁵The Lord will dry up
    the gulf of the Egyptian sea;
with a scorching wind he will sweep his
        hand
    over the Euphrates River.ᵉ
He will break it up into seven streams
    so that men can cross over in sandals.
¹⁶There will be a highway for the remnant of
        his people
    that is left from Assyria,
as there was for Israel
    when they came up from Egypt.

SONGS OF PRAISE

12 In that day you will say:

"I will praise you, O Lord.
    Although you were angry with me,
your anger has turned away
    and you have comforted me.
²Surely God is my salvation;
    I will trust and not be afraid.
The Lord, the Lord, is my strength and my
        song;
    he has become my salvation."
³With joy you will draw water
    from the wells of salvation.

⁴In that day you will say:

THE MESSAGE

11.10 On that day, Jesse's Root will be raised high, posted as a rallying banner for the peoples. The nations will all come to him. His headquarters will be glorious.

11.11   Also on that day, the Master for the second time will reach out to bring back what's left of his scattered people. He'll bring them back from Assyria, Egypt, Pathros, Ethiopia, Elam, Sinar, Hamath, and the ocean islands.

11.12-16 And he'll raise that rallying banner high,
        visible to all nations,
    gather in all the scattered exiles of Israel,
Pull in all the dispersed refugees of Judah
    from the four winds and the seven seas.
The jealousy of Ephraim will dissolve,
    the hostility of Judah will vanish—
Ephraim no longer the jealous rival of Judah,
    Judah no longer the hostile rival of
        Ephraim!
Blood brothers united, they'll pounce on the
        Philistines in the west,
    join forces to plunder the people in the
        east.
They'll attack Edom and Moab.
    The Ammonites will fall into line.
God will once again dry up Egypt's Red Sea,
    making for an easy crossing.
He'll send a blistering wind
    down on the great River Euphrates,
Reduce it to seven mere trickles.
    None even need get their feet wet!
In the end there'll be a highway all the way
        from Assyria,
    easy traveling for what's left of God's
        people—
A highway just like the one Israel had
    when he marched up out of Egypt.

MY STRENGTH AND SONG

12.1 **12** And you will say in that day,
    "I thank you, God.
You were angry
    but your anger wasn't forever.
You withdrew your anger
    and moved in and comforted me.

12.2 "Yes, indeed—God is my salvation.
    I trust, I won't be afraid.
God—yes God!—is my strength and song,
    best of all, my salvation!"

12.3-4 Joyfully you'll pull up buckets of water
    from the wells of salvation.
And as you do it, you'll say,

ᵃ 11 Hebrew *from Pathros*   ᵇ 11 That is, the upper Nile region   ᶜ 11 Hebrew *Shinar*   ᵈ 13 Or *hostility*   ᵉ 15 Hebrew *the River*

NEW INTERNATIONAL VERSION

"Give thanks to the LORD, call on his name;
  make known among the nations what he
    has done,
  and proclaim that his name is exalted.
⁵Sing to the LORD, for he has done glorious
    things;
  let this be known to all the world.
⁶Shout aloud and sing for joy, people of Zion,
  for great is the Holy One of Israel among
    you."

A PROPHECY AGAINST BABYLON

13 An oracle concerning Babylon that Isaiah
  son of Amoz saw:

²Raise a banner on a bare hilltop,
  shout to them;
beckon to them
  to enter the gates of the nobles.
³I have commanded my holy ones;
  I have summoned my warriors to carry
    out my wrath—
  those who rejoice in my triumph.

⁴Listen, a noise on the mountains,
  like that of a great multitude!
Listen, an uproar among the kingdoms,
  like nations massing together!
The LORD Almighty is mustering
  an army for war.
⁵They come from faraway lands,
  from the ends of the heavens—
the LORD and the weapons of his wrath—
  to destroy the whole country.

⁶Wail, for the day of the LORD is near;
  it will come like destruction from the
    Almighty. *ᵃ*
⁷Because of this, all hands will go limp,
  every man's heart will melt.
⁸Terror will seize them,
  pain and anguish will grip them;
  they will writhe like a woman in labor.
They will look aghast at each other,
  their faces aflame.

⁹See, the day of the LORD is coming
  —a cruel day, with wrath and fierce
    anger—
to make the land desolate
  and destroy the sinners within it.
¹⁰The stars of heaven and their constellations
  will not show their light.
The rising sun will be darkened
  and the moon will not give its light.
¹¹I will punish the world for its evil,
  the wicked for their sins.

ᵃ 6 Hebrew *Shaddai*

THE MESSAGE

"Give thanks to GOD.
Call out his name.
  Ask him anything!
Shout to the nations, tell them what he's done,
  spread the news of his great reputation!

¹²·⁵⁻⁶ "Sing praise-songs to GOD. He's done it all!
  Let the whole earth know what he's done!
Raise the roof! Sing your hearts out, O Zion!
  The Greatest lives among you: The Holy of
    Israel."

BABYLON IS DOOMED!

¹³·¹ **13** The Message on Babylon. Isaiah son of
  Amoz saw it:

¹³·²⁻³ "Run up a flag on an open hill.
  Yell loud. Get their attention.
Wave them into formation.
  Direct them to the nerve center of power.
I've taken charge of my special forces,
  called up my crack troops.
They're bursting with pride and passion
  to carry out my angry judgment."

¹³·⁴⁻⁵ Thunder rolls off the mountains
  like a mob huge and noisy—
Thunder of kingdoms in an uproar,
  nations assembling for war.
GOD-of-the-Angel-Armies is calling
  his army into battle formation.
They come from far-off countries,
  they pour in across the horizon.
It's GOD on the move with the weapons of his
    wrath,
  ready to destroy the whole country.

¹³·⁶⁻⁸ Wail! GOD's Day of Judgment is near—
  an avalanche crashing down from the
    Strong God!
Everyone paralyzed in the panic,
  hysterical and unstrung,
Doubled up in pain
  like a woman giving birth to a baby.
Horrified—everyone they see
  is like a face out of a nightmare.

⸸

¹³·⁹⁻¹⁶ "Watch now. GOD's Judgment Day comes.
  Cruel it is, a day of wrath and anger,
A day to waste the earth
  and clean out all the sinners.
The stars in the sky, the great parade of
    constellations,
  will be nothing but black holes.
The sun will come up as a black disk,
  and the moon a blank nothing.
I'll put a full stop to the evil on earth,
  terminate the dark acts of the wicked.

NEW INTERNATIONAL VERSION

I will put an end to the arrogance of the
  haughty
  and will humble the pride of the ruthless.
¹²I will make man scarcer than pure gold,
  more rare than the gold of Ophir.
¹³Therefore I will make the heavens tremble;
  and the earth will shake from its place
  at the wrath of the LORD Almighty,
  in the day of his burning anger.

¹⁴Like a hunted gazelle,
  like sheep without a shepherd,
  each will return to his own people,
  each will flee to his native land.
¹⁵Whoever is captured will be thrust through;
  all who are caught will fall by the sword.
¹⁶Their infants will be dashed to pieces before
  their eyes;
  their houses will be looted and their wives
  ravished.

¹⁷See, I will stir up against them the Medes,
  who do not care for silver
  and have no delight in gold.
¹⁸Their bows will strike down the young men;
  they will have no mercy on infants
  nor will they look with compassion on
  children.
¹⁹Babylon, the jewel of kingdoms,
  the glory of the Babylonians'ᵃ pride,
  will be overthrown by God
  like Sodom and Gomorrah.
²⁰She will never be inhabited
  or lived in through all generations;
  no Arab will pitch his tent there,
  no shepherd will rest his flocks there.
²¹But desert creatures will lie there,
  jackals will fill her houses;
  there the owls will dwell,
  and there the wild goats will leap about.
²²Hyenas will howl in her strongholds,
  jackals in her luxurious palaces.
  Her time is at hand,
  and her days will not be prolonged.

14 The LORD will have compassion on
    Jacob;
  once again he will choose Israel
  and will settle them in their own land.

ᵃ 19 Or Chaldeans'

THE MESSAGE

I'll gag all braggarts and boasters—not a peep
    anymore from them—
  and trip strutting tyrants, leave them flat on
    their faces.
Proud humanity will disappear from the earth.
  I'll make mortals rarer than hens' teeth.
And yes, I'll even make the sky shake,
  and the earth quake to its roots
Under the wrath of GOD-of-the-Angel-Armies,
  the Judgment Day of his raging anger.
Like a hunted white-tailed deer,
  like lost sheep with no shepherd,
People will huddle with a few of their own
    kind,
  run off to some makeshift shelter.
But tough luck to stragglers—they'll be killed
    on the spot,
  throats cut, bellies ripped open,
Babies smashed on the rocks
  while mothers and fathers watch,
Houses looted,
  wives raped.

¹³·¹⁷⁻²² "And now watch this:
  Against Babylon, I'm inciting the Medes,
A ruthless bunch indifferent to bribes,
  the kind of brutality that no one can blunt.
They massacre the young,
  wantonly kick and kill even babies.
And Babylon, most glorious of all kingdoms,
  the pride and joy of Chaldeans,
Will end up smoking and stinking like Sodom,
  and, yes, like Gomorrah, when God had
    finished with them.
No one will live there anymore,
  generation after generation a ghost town.
Not even Bedouins will pitch tents there.
  Shepherds will give it a wide berth.
But strange and wild animals will like it just
    fine,
  filling the vacant houses with eerie night
    sounds.
Skunks will make it their home,
  and unspeakable night hags will haunt it.
Hyenas will curdle your blood with their
    laughing,
  and the howling of coyotes will give you
    the shivers.

"Babylon is doomed.
  It won't be long now."

NOW YOU ARE NOTHING

¹⁴·¹⁻² **14** But not so with Jacob. GOD will have
    compassion on Jacob. Once again he'll
choose Israel. He'll establish them in their own

NEW INTERNATIONAL VERSION	THE MESSAGE

NEW INTERNATIONAL VERSION

Aliens will join them
  and unite with the house of Jacob.
² Nations will take them
  and bring them to their own place.
And the house of Israel will possess the
    nations
  as menservants and maidservants in the
    LORD's land.
They will make captives of their captors
  and rule over their oppressors.

³ On the day the LORD gives you relief from suffering and turmoil and cruel bondage, ⁴you will take up this taunt against the king of Babylon:

How the oppressor has come to an end!
  How his fury*a* has ended!
⁵ The LORD has broken the rod of the wicked,
  the scepter of the rulers,
⁶ which in anger struck down peoples
  with unceasing blows,
and in fury subdued nations
  with relentless aggression.
⁷ All the lands are at rest and at peace;
  they break into singing.
⁸ Even the pine trees and the cedars of
    Lebanon
  exult over you and say,
"Now that you have been laid low,
  no woodsman comes to cut us down."

⁹ The grave*b* below is all astir
  to meet you at your coming;
it rouses the spirits of the departed to greet
    you—
  all those who were leaders in the world;
it makes them rise from their thrones—
  all those who were kings over the nations.
¹⁰ They will all respond,
  they will say to you,
"You also have become weak, as we are;
  you have become like us."
¹¹ All your pomp has been brought down to the
    grave,
  along with the noise of your harps;
maggots are spread out beneath you
  and worms cover you.

¹² How you have fallen from heaven,
  O morning star, son of the dawn!
You have been cast down to the earth,
  you who once laid low the nations!
¹³ You said in your heart,
  "I will ascend to heaven;
I will raise my throne

THE MESSAGE

country. Outsiders will be attracted and throw their lot in with Jacob. The nations among whom they lived will actually escort them back home, and then Israel will pay them back by making slaves of them, men and women alike, possessing them as slaves in GOD's country, capturing those who had captured them, ruling over those who had abused them.

14.3-4 When GOD has given you time to recover from the abuse and trouble and harsh servitude that you had to endure, you can amuse yourselves by taking up this satire, a taunt against the king of Babylon:

14.4-6 Can you believe it? The tyrant is gone!
    The tyranny is over!
GOD has broken the rule of the wicked,
    the power of the bully-rulers
That crushed many people.
    A relentless rain of cruel outrage
Established a violent rule of anger
    rife with torture and persecution.

14.7-10 And now it's over, the whole earth quietly at
      rest.
    Burst into song! Make the rafters ring!
Ponderosa pine trees are happy,
    giant Lebanon cedars are relieved, saying,
"Since you've been cut down,
    there's no one around to cut us down."
And the underworld dead are all excited,
    preparing to welcome you when you come.
Getting ready to greet you are the ghostly
      dead,
    all the famous names of earth.
All the buried kings of the nations
    will stand up on their thrones
With well-prepared speeches,
    royal invitations to death:
"Now you are as nothing as we are!
    Make yourselves at home with us dead
      folks!"

14.11 This is where your pomp and fine music led
      you, Babylon,
    to your underworld private chambers,
A king-size mattress of maggots for repose
    and a quilt of crawling worms for warmth.

14.12 What a comedown this, O Babylon!
    Daystar! Son of Dawn!
Flat on your face in the underworld mud,
    you, famous for flattening nations!

14.13-14 You said to yourself,
    "I'll climb to heaven.
I'll set my throne

---

a 4 Dead Sea Scrolls, Septuagint and Syriac; the meaning of the word in the Masoretic Text is uncertain.   *b 9* Hebrew *Sheol*; also in verses 11 and 15

NEW INTERNATIONAL VERSION

above the stars of God;
I will sit enthroned on the mount of
assembly,
on the utmost heights of the sacred
mountain. [a]
14 I will ascend above the tops of the clouds;
I will make myself like the Most High."
15 But you are brought down to the grave,
to the depths of the pit.

16 Those who see you stare at you,
they ponder your fate:
"Is this the man who shook the earth
and made kingdoms tremble,
17 the man who made the world a desert,
who overthrew its cities
and would not let his captives go home?"

18 All the kings of the nations lie in state,
each in his own tomb.
19 But you are cast out of your tomb
like a rejected branch;
you are covered with the slain,
with those pierced by the sword,
those who descend to the stones of the
pit.
Like a corpse trampled underfoot,
20   you will not join them in burial,
for you have destroyed your land
and killed your people.

The offspring of the wicked
will never be mentioned again.
21 Prepare a place to slaughter his sons
for the sins of their forefathers;
they are not to rise to inherit the land
and cover the earth with their cities.

22 "I will rise up against them,"
declares the LORD Almighty.
"I will cut off from Babylon her name and
survivors,
her offspring and descendants,"
declares the LORD.
23 "I will turn her into a place for owls
and into swampland;
I will sweep her with the broom of
destruction,"
declares the LORD Almighty.

A PROPHECY AGAINST ASSYRIA

24 The LORD Almighty has sworn,

"Surely, as I have planned, so it will be,
and as I have purposed, so it will stand.
25 I will crush the Assyrian in my land;
on my mountains I will trample him
down.

THE MESSAGE

over the stars of God.
I'll run the assembly of angels
that meets on sacred Mount Zaphon.
I'll climb to the top of the clouds.
I'll take over as King of the Universe!"

14.15-17 But you didn't make it, did you?
Instead of climbing up, you came down—
Down with the underground dead,
down to the abyss of the Pit.
People will stare and muse:
"Can this be the one
Who terrorized earth and its kingdoms,
turned earth to a moonscape,
Wasted its cities,
shut up his prisoners to a living death?"

14.18-20 Other kings get a decent burial,
honored with eulogies and placed in a
tomb.
But you're dumped in a ditch unburied,
like a stray dog or cat,
Covered with rotting bodies,
murdered and indigent corpses.
Your dead body desecrated, mutilated—
no state funeral for you!
You've left your land in ruins,
left a legacy of massacre.
The progeny of your evil life
will never be named. Oblivion!

14.21 Get a place ready to slaughter the sons of the
wicked
and wipe out their father's line.
Unthinkable that they should own a square
foot of land
or desecrate the face of the world with their
cities!

14.22-23   "I will confront them"—Decree of GOD-of-
the-Angel-Armies—"and strip Babylon of name
and survivors, children and grandchildren."
GOD's Decree. "I'll make it a worthless swamp
and give it as a prize to the hedgehog. And then
I'll bulldoze it out of existence." Decree of GOD-
of-the-Angel-Armies.

WHO COULD EVER CANCEL SUCH PLANS?
14.24-27 GOD-of-the-Angel-Armies speaks:

"Exactly as I planned,
it will happen.
Following my blueprints,
it will take shape.
I will shatter the Assyrian who trespasses my
land
and stomp him into the dirt on my
mountains.

---

[a] 13 Or *the north; Hebrew Zaphon*

NEW INTERNATIONAL VERSION

His yoke will be taken from my people,
    and his burden removed from their
        shoulders."

26 This is the plan determined for the whole
        world;
    this is the hand stretched out over all
        nations.
27 For the LORD Almighty has purposed, and
        who can thwart him?
    His hand is stretched out, and who can
        turn it back?

A PROPHECY AGAINST THE PHILISTINES

28 This oracle came in the year King Ahaz
died:

29 Do not rejoice, all you Philistines,
    that the rod that struck you is broken;
from the root of that snake will spring up a
        viper,
    its fruit will be a darting, venomous
        serpent.
30 The poorest of the poor will find pasture,
    and the needy will lie down in safety.
But your root I will destroy by famine;
    it will slay your survivors.

31 Wail, O gate! Howl, O city!
    Melt away, all you Philistines!
A cloud of smoke comes from the north,
    and there is not a straggler in its ranks.
32 What answer shall be given
    to the envoys of that nation?
"The LORD has established Zion,
    and in her his afflicted people will find
        refuge."

A PROPHECY AGAINST MOAB

15 An oracle concerning Moab:

Ar in Moab is ruined,
    destroyed in a night!
Kir in Moab is ruined,
    destroyed in a night!
2 Dibon goes up to its temple,
    to its high places to weep;
Moab wails over Nebo and Medeba.
Every head is shaved
    and every beard cut off.
3 In the streets they wear sackcloth;
    on the roofs and in the public squares
they all wail,
    prostrate with weeping.
4 Heshbon and Elealeh cry out,
    their voices are heard all the way to Jahaz.
Therefore the armed men of Moab cry out,
    and their hearts are faint.

THE MESSAGE

I will ban his taking and making of slaves
    and lift the weight of oppression from all
        shoulders."
This is the plan,
    planned for the whole earth,
And this is the hand that will do it,
    reaching into every nation.
GOD-of-the-Angel-Armies has planned it.
    Who could ever cancel such plans?
His is the hand that's reached out.
    Who could brush it aside?

14.28-31   In the year King Ahaz died, this Message
        came:

Hold it, Philistines! It's too soon to celebrate
    the defeat of your cruel oppressor.
From the death throes of that snake a worse
        snake will come,
    and from that, one even worse.
The poor won't have to worry.
    The needy will escape the terror.
But you Philistines will be plunged into
        famine,
    and those who don't starve, God will kill.
Wail and howl, proud city!
    Fall prostrate in fear, Philistia!
On the northern horizon, smoke from burned
        cities,
    the wake of a brutal, disciplined destroyer.

14.32   What does one say to
        outsiders who ask questions?
Tell them, "GOD has established Zion.
    Those in need and in trouble find refuge in
        her."

POIGNANT CRIES REVERBERATE THROUGH MOAB

15.1-4 **15** A Message concerning Moab:

Village Ar of Moab is in ruins,
    destroyed in a night raid.
Village Kir of Moab is in ruins,
    destroyed in a night raid.
Village Dibon climbs to its chapel in the hills,
    goes up to lament.
Moab weeps and wails
    over Nebo and Medba.
Every head is shaved bald,
    every beard shaved clean.
They pour into the streets wearing black,
    go up on the roofs, take to the town square,
Everyone in tears,
    everyone in grief.
Towns Heshbon and Elealeh cry long and loud.
    The sound carries as far as Jahaz.
Moab sobs, shaking in grief.
    The soul of Moab trembles.

NEW INTERNATIONAL VERSION

5 My heart cries out over Moab;
  her fugitives flee as far as Zoar,
  as far as Eglath Shelishiyah.
They go up the way to Luhith,
  weeping as they go;
  on the road to Horonaim
  they lament their destruction.
6 The waters of Nimrim are dried up
  and the grass is withered;
  the vegetation is gone
  and nothing green is left.
7 So the wealth they have acquired and
    stored up
  they carry away over the Ravine of the
    Poplars.
8 Their outcry echoes along the border of
    Moab;
  their wailing reaches as far as Eglaim,
  their lamentation as far as Beer Elim.
9 Dimon's *a* waters are full of blood,
  but I will bring still more upon Dimon *a*—
  a lion upon the fugitives of Moab
  and upon those who remain in the land.

16 Send lambs as tribute
    to the ruler of the land,
  from Sela, across the desert,
    to the mount of the Daughter of Zion.
2 Like fluttering birds
    pushed from the nest,
  so are the women of Moab
    at the fords of the Arnon.

3 "Give us counsel,
    render a decision.
  Make your shadow like night—
    at high noon.
  Hide the fugitives,
    do not betray the refugees.
4 Let the Moabite fugitives stay with you;
    be their shelter from the destroyer."

  The oppressor will come to an end,
    and destruction will cease;
    the aggressor will vanish from the land.
5 In love a throne will be established;
    in faithfulness a man will sit on it—
    one from the house *b* of David—
  one who in judging seeks justice
    and speeds the cause of righteousness.

6 We have heard of Moab's pride—

THE MESSAGE

15.5-9 Oh, how I grieve for Moab!
  Refugees stream to Zoar
  and then on to Eglath-shelishiyah.
Up the slopes of Luhith they weep;
  on the road to Horonaim they cry their
    loss.
The springs of Nimrim are dried up—
  grass brown, buds stunted, nothing grows.
They leave, carrying all their possessions
  on their backs, everything they own,
Making their way as best they can
  across Willow Creek to safety.
Poignant cries reverberate
  all through Moab,
Gut-wrenching sobs as far as Eglaim,
  heart-racking sobs all the way to Beer-elim.
The banks of the Dibon crest with blood,
  but God has worse in store for Dibon:
A lion—a lion to finish off the fugitives,
  to clean up whoever's left in the land.

A NEW GOVERNMENT IN THE DAVID TRADITION

16.1-4 **16** "Dispatch a gift of lambs," says Moab,
    "to the leaders in Jerusalem—
  Lambs from Sela sent across the desert
    to buy the goodwill of Jerusalem.
The towns and people of Moab
  are at a loss,
New-hatched birds knocked from the nest,
  fluttering helplessly
At the banks of the Arnon River,
  unable to cross:
'Tell us what to do,
  help us out!
Protect us,
  hide us!
Give the refugees from Moab
  sanctuary with you.
Be a safe place for those on the run
  from the killing fields.' "

16.4-5 "When this is all over," Judah answers,
    "the tyrant toppled,
The killing at an end,
  all signs of these cruelties long gone,
A new government of love will be established
  in the venerable David tradition.
A Ruler you can depend upon
  will head this government,
A Ruler passionate for justice,
  a Ruler quick to set things right."

⚜

16.6-12 We've heard—everyone's heard!—of Moab's
    pride,

NEW INTERNATIONAL VERSION

her overweening pride and conceit,
her pride and her insolence—
but her boasts are empty.
⁷ Therefore the Moabites wail,
they wail together for Moab.
Lament and grieve
for the men*ᵃ* of Kir Hareseth.
⁸ The fields of Heshbon wither,
the vines of Sibmah also.
The rulers of the nations
have trampled down the choicest vines,
which once reached Jazer
and spread toward the desert.
Their shoots spread out
and went as far as the sea.
⁹ So I weep, as Jazer weeps,
for the vines of Sibmah.
O Heshbon, O Elealeh,
I drench you with tears!
The shouts of joy over your ripened fruit
and over your harvests have been stilled.
¹⁰ Joy and gladness are taken away from the
orchards;
no one sings or shouts in the vineyards;
no one treads out wine at the presses,
for I have put an end to the shouting.
¹¹ My heart laments for Moab like a harp,
my inmost being for Kir Hareseth.
¹² When Moab appears at her high place,
she only wears herself out;
when she goes to her shrine to pray,
it is to no avail.

¹³ This is the word the Lord has already spoken concerning Moab. ¹⁴ But now the Lord says: "Within three years, as a servant bound by contract would count them, Moab's splendor and all her many people will be despised, and her survivors will be very few and feeble."

AN ORACLE AGAINST DAMASCUS

17 An oracle concerning Damascus:

"See, Damascus will no longer be a city
but will become a heap of ruins.
² The cities of Aroer will be deserted
and left to flocks, which will lie down,
with no one to make them afraid.

ᵃ 7 Or "raisin cakes," a wordplay

THE MESSAGE

world-famous for pride—
Arrogant, self-important, insufferable,
full of hot air.
So now let Moab lament for a change,
with antiphonal mock-laments from the
neighbors!
What a shame! How terrible!
No more fine fruitcakes and Kir-hareseth
candies!
All those lush Heshbon fields dried up,
the rich Sibmah vineyards withered!
Foreign thugs have crushed and torn out
the famous grapevines
That once reached all the way to Jazer,
right to the edge of the desert,
Ripped out the crops in every direction
as far as the eye can see.
I'll join the weeping. I'll weep right along with
Jazer,
weep for the Sibmah vineyards.
And yes, Heshbon and Elealeh,
I'll mingle my tears with your tears!
The joyful shouting at harvest is gone.
Instead of song and celebration, dead
silence.
No more boisterous laughter in the orchards,
no more hearty work songs in the
vineyards.
Instead of the bustle and sound of good work
in the fields,
silence—deathly and deadening silence.
My heartstrings throb like harp strings for
Moab,
my soul in sympathy for sad Kir-heres.
When Moab trudges to the shrine to pray,
he wastes both time and energy.
Going to the sanctuary and praying for relief
is useless. Nothing ever happens.

16.13-14   This is God's earlier Message on Moab. God's updated Message is, "In three years, no longer than the term of an enlisted soldier, Moab's impressive presence will be gone, that splendid hot-air balloon will be punctured, and instead of a vigorous population, just a few shuffling bums cadging handouts."

DAMASCUS: A PILE OF DUST AND RUBBLE

17.1-3   **17** A Message concerning Damascus:

"Watch this: Damascus undone as a city,
a pile of dust and rubble!
Her towns emptied of people.
The sheep and goats will move in
And take over the towns
as if they owned them—which they will!

NEW INTERNATIONAL VERSION

³The fortified city will disappear from
Ephraim,
and royal power from Damascus;
the remnant of Aram will be
like the glory of the Israelites,"
declares the LORD Almighty.

⁴"In that day the glory of Jacob will fade;
the fat of his body will waste away.
⁵It will be as when a reaper gathers the
standing grain
and harvests the grain with his arm—
as when a man gleans heads of grain
in the Valley of Rephaim.
⁶Yet some gleanings will remain,
as when an olive tree is beaten,
leaving two or three olives on the topmost
branches,
four or five on the fruitful boughs,"
declares the LORD, the God
of Israel.

⁷In that day men will look to their Maker
and turn their eyes to the Holy One of
Israel.
⁸They will not look to the altars,
the work of their hands,
and they will have no regard for the Asherah
poles ᵃ
and the incense altars their fingers have
made.

⁹In that day their strong cities, which they left
because of the Israelites, will be like places abandoned to thickets and undergrowth. And all will
be desolation.

¹⁰You have forgotten God your Savior;
you have not remembered the Rock, your
fortress.
Therefore, though you set out the finest
plants
and plant imported vines,
¹¹though on the day you set them out, you
make them grow,
and on the morning when you plant
them, you bring them to bud,
yet the harvest will be as nothing
in the day of disease and incurable pain.

¹²Oh, the raging of many nations—
they rage like the raging sea!
Oh, the uproar of the peoples—
they roar like the roaring of great waters!
¹³Although the peoples roar like the roar of
surging waters,
when he rebukes them they flee far away,

ᵃ 8 That is, symbols of the goddess Asherah

THE MESSAGE

Not a sign of a fort is left in Ephraim,
not a trace of government left in Damascus.
What's left of Aram?
The same as what's left of Israel—not
much."
Decree of GOD-of-the-Angel-Armies.

THE DAY IS COMING

17:4-6 "The Day is coming when Jacob's robust
splendor goes pale
and his well-fed body turns skinny.
The country will be left empty, picked clean
as a field harvested by field hands.
She'll be like a few stalks of barley left
standing
in the lush Valley of Rephaim after harvest,
Or like the couple of ripe olives overlooked
in the top of the olive tree,
Or the four or five apples
that the pickers couldn't reach in the
orchard."
Decree of the GOD of Israel.

17:7-8 Yes, the Day is coming when people will notice The One Who Made Them, take a long
hard look at The Holy of Israel. They'll lose interest in all the stuff they've made—altars and
monuments and rituals, their homemade, handmade religion—however impressive it is.

17:9 And yes, the Day is coming when their
fortress cities will be abandoned—the very
same cities that the Hivites and Amorites abandoned when Israel invaded! And the country
will be empty, desolate.

YOU HAVE FORGOTTEN GOD

17:10-11 And why? Because you have forgotten God-
Your-Salvation,
not remembered your Rock-of-Refuge.
And so, even though you are very religious,
planting all sorts of bushes and herbs and
trees
to honor and influence your fertility gods,
And even though you make them grow so
well,
bursting with buds and sprouts and
blossoms,
Nothing will come of them. Instead of a
harvest
you'll get nothing but grief and pain, pain,
pain.

17:12-13 Oh my! Thunder! A thundering herd of people!
Thunder like the crashing of ocean waves!
Nations roaring, roaring,
like the roar of a massive waterfall,
Roaring like a deafening Niagara!
But God will silence them with a word,

NEW INTERNATIONAL VERSION

driven before the wind like chaff on the hills,
    like tumbleweed before a gale.
[14] In the evening, sudden terror!
    Before the morning, they are gone!
This is the portion of those who loot us,
    the lot of those who plunder us.

A Prophecy Against Cush

18 Woe to the land of whirring wings[a]
    along the rivers of Cush,[b]
[2] which sends envoys by sea
    in papyrus boats over the water.

Go, swift messengers,
to a people tall and smooth-skinned,
    to a people feared far and wide,
an aggressive nation of strange speech,
    whose land is divided by rivers.

[3] All you people of the world,
    you who live on the earth,
when a banner is raised on the mountains,
    you will see it,
and when a trumpet sounds,
    you will hear it.
[4] This is what the Lord says to me:
    "I will remain quiet and will look on from
      my dwelling place,
like shimmering heat in the sunshine,
    like a cloud of dew in the heat of harvest."
[5] For, before the harvest, when the blossom is
      gone
    and the flower becomes a ripening grape,
he will cut off the shoots with pruning
      knives,
    and cut down and take away the
      spreading branches.
[6] They will all be left to the mountain birds of
      prey
    and to the wild animals;
the birds will feed on them all summer,
    the wild animals all winter.

[7] At that time gifts will be brought to the Lord
Almighty

from a people tall and smooth-skinned,
    from a people feared far and wide,
an aggressive nation of strange speech,
    whose land is divided by rivers—

the gifts will be brought to Mount Zion, the
place of the Name of the Lord Almighty.

THE MESSAGE

And then he'll blow them away like dead
    leaves off a tree,
    like down from a thistle.
17.14 At bedtime, terror fills the air.
    By morning it's gone—not a sign of it
      anywhere!
This is what happens to those who would
      ruin us,
    this is the fate of those out to get us.

People Mighty and Merciless

18.1-2 **18** Doom to the land of flies and mosquitoes
    beyond the Ethiopian rivers,
Shipping emissaries all over the world,
    down rivers and across seas.

Go, swift messengers,
    go to this people tall and handsome,
This people held in respect everywhere,
    this people mighty and merciless,
    from the land crisscrossed with rivers.

18.3 Everybody everywhere,
    all earth-dwellers:
When you see a flag flying on the mountain,
    look!
    When you hear the trumpet blown, listen!

18.4-6 For here's what God told me:

"I'm not going to say anything,
    but simply look on from where I live,
Quiet as warmth that comes from the sun,
    silent as dew during harvest."
And then, just before harvest, after the
      blossom
    has turned into a maturing grape,
He'll step in and prune back the new shoots,
    ruthlessly hack off all the growing
      branches.
He'll leave them piled on the ground
    for birds and animals to feed on—
Fodder for the summering birds,
    fodder for the wintering animals.

18.7 Then tribute will be brought to God-of-the-
      Angel-Armies,
    brought from this people tall and
      handsome,
This people once held in respect everywhere,
    this people once mighty and merciless,
From the land crisscrossed with rivers,
    to Mount Zion, God's place.

---

a 1 Or *of locusts*   *b 1* That is, the upper Nile region

NEW INTERNATIONAL VERSION

A PROPHECY ABOUT EGYPT

19 An oracle concerning Egypt:

See, the LORD rides on a swift cloud
  and is coming to Egypt.
The idols of Egypt tremble before him,
  and the hearts of the Egyptians melt
    within them.

2 "I will stir up Egyptian against Egyptian—
  brother will fight against brother,
  neighbor against neighbor,
  city against city,
  kingdom against kingdom.
3 The Egyptians will lose heart,
  and I will bring their plans to nothing;
they will consult the idols and the spirits of
    the dead,
  the mediums and the spiritists.
4 I will hand the Egyptians over
  to the power of a cruel master,
and a fierce king will rule over them,"
  declares the Lord, the LORD Almighty.

5 The waters of the river will dry up,
  and the riverbed will be parched and dry.
6 The canals will stink;
  the streams of Egypt will dwindle and
    dry up.
The reeds and rushes will wither,
7   also the plants along the Nile,
  at the mouth of the river.
Every sown field along the Nile
  will become parched, will blow away and
    be no more.
8 The fishermen will groan and lament,
  all who cast hooks into the Nile;
those who throw nets on the water
  will pine away.
9 Those who work with combed flax will despair,
  the weavers of fine linen will lose hope.
10 The workers in cloth will be dejected,
  and all the wage earners will be sick at
    heart.

11 The officials of Zoan are nothing but fools;
  the wise counselors of Pharaoh give
    senseless advice.
How can you say to Pharaoh,
  "I am one of the wise men,
  a disciple of the ancient kings"?

12 Where are your wise men now?
  Let them show you and make known
what the LORD Almighty
  has planned against Egypt.
13 The officials of Zoan have become fools,
  the leaders of Memphis*a* are deceived;

THE MESSAGE

ANARCHY AND CHAOS AND KILLING!

19.1 **19** A Message concerning Egypt:

Watch this! GOD riding on a fast-moving
    cloud,
  moving in on Egypt!
The god-idols of Egypt shudder and shake,
  Egyptians paralyzed by panic.

19.2-4 God says, "I'll make Egyptian fight Egyptian,
  brother fight brother, neighbor fight
    neighbor,
City fight city, kingdom fight kingdom—
  anarchy and chaos and killing!
I'll knock the wind out of the Egyptians.
  They won't know coming from going.
They'll go to their god-idols for answers;
  they'll conjure ghosts and hold séances,
    desperate for answers.
But I'll turn the Egyptians
  over to a tyrant most cruel.
I'll put them under the rule of a mean,
    merciless king."
  Decree of the Master, GOD-of-the-Angel-
    Armies.

19.5-10 The River Nile will dry up,
  the riverbed baked dry in the sun.
The canals will become stagnant and stink,
  every stream touching the Nile dry up.
River vegetation will rot away
  the banks of the Nile-baked clay,
The riverbed hard and smooth,
  river grasses dried up and gone with the
    wind.
Fishermen will complain
  that the fishing's been ruined.
Textile workers will be out of work, all
    weavers
  and workers in linen and cotton and wool
Dispirited, depressed in their forced
    idleness—
  everyone who works for a living, jobless.

19.11-15 The princes of Zoan are fools,
  the advisors of Pharaoh stupid.
How could any of you dare tell Pharaoh,
  "Trust me: I'm wise. I know what's going
    on.
  Why, I'm descended from the old wisdom
    of Egypt"?
There's not a wise man or woman left in the
    country.
  If there were, one of them would tell you
  what GOD-of-the-Angel-Armies has in mind
    for Egypt.
As it is, the princes of Zoan are all fools
  and the princes of Memphis, dunces.

NEW INTERNATIONAL VERSION

the cornerstones of her peoples
have led Egypt astray.
¹⁴ The LORD has poured into them
a spirit of dizziness;
they make Egypt stagger in all that she does,
as a drunkard staggers around in his
vomit.
¹⁵ There is nothing Egypt can do—
head or tail, palm branch or reed.

¹⁶ In that day the Egyptians will be like women. They will shudder with fear at the uplifted hand that the LORD Almighty raises against them. ¹⁷ And the land of Judah will bring terror to the Egyptians; everyone to whom Judah is mentioned will be terrified, because of what the LORD Almighty is planning against them.

¹⁸ In that day five cities in Egypt will speak the language of Canaan and swear allegiance to the LORD Almighty. One of them will be called the City of Destruction.ᵃ

¹⁹ In that day there will be an altar to the LORD in the heart of Egypt, and a monument to the LORD at its border. ²⁰ It will be a sign and witness to the LORD Almighty in the land of Egypt. When they cry out to the LORD because of their oppressors, he will send them a savior and defender, and he will rescue them. ²¹ So the LORD will make himself known to the Egyptians, and in that day they will acknowledge the LORD. They will worship with sacrifices and grain offerings; they will make vows to the LORD and keep them. ²² The LORD will strike Egypt with a plague; he will strike them and heal them. They will turn to the LORD, and he will respond to their pleas and heal them.

²³ In that day there will be a highway from Egypt to Assyria. The Assyrians will go to Egypt and the Egyptians to Assyria. The Egyptians and Assyrians will worship together. ²⁴ In that day Israel will be the third, along with Egypt and Assyria, a blessing on the earth. ²⁵ The LORD Almighty will bless them, saying, "Blessed be Egypt my people, Assyria my handiwork, and Israel my inheritance."

A PROPHECY AGAINST EGYPT AND CUSH

20 In the year that the supreme commander, sent by Sargon king of Assyria, came to Ashdod and attacked and captured it— ²at that time the LORD spoke through Isaiah son of

---

ᵃ *18* Most manuscripts of the Masoretic Text; some manuscripts of the Masoretic Text, Dead Sea Scrolls and Vulgate *City of the Sun* (that is, Heliopolis)

THE MESSAGE

The honored pillars of your society
have led Egypt into detours and dead ends.
GOD has scrambled their brains,
Egypt's become a falling-down-in-his-own-
vomit drunk.
Egypt's hopeless, past helping,
a senile, doddering old fool.

✝

19.16-17 On that Day, Egyptians will be like hysterical schoolgirls, screaming at the first hint of action from GOD-of-the-Angel-Armies. Little Judah will strike terror in Egyptians! Say "Judah" to an Egyptian and see panic. The word triggers fear of the GOD-of-the-Angel-Armies' plan against Egypt.

19.18 On that Day, more than one city in Egypt will learn to speak the language of faith and promise to follow GOD-of-the-Angel-Armies. One of these cities will be honored with the title "City of the Sun."

19.19-22 On that Day, there will be a place of worship to GOD in the center of Egypt and a monument to GOD at its border. It will show how the GOD-of-the-Angel-Armies has helped the Egyptians. When they cry out in prayer to GOD because of oppressors, he'll send them help, a savior who will keep them safe and take care of them. GOD will openly show himself to the Egyptians and they'll get to know him on that Day. They'll worship him seriously with sacrifices and burnt offerings. They'll make vows and keep them. GOD will wound Egypt, first hit and then heal. Egypt will come back to GOD, and GOD will listen to their prayers and heal them, heal them from head to toe.

19.23 On that Day, there will be a highway all the way from Egypt to Assyria: Assyrians will have free range in Egypt and Egyptians in Assyria. No longer rivals, they'll worship together, Egyptians and Assyrians!

19.24-25 On that Day, Israel will take its place alongside Egypt and Assyria, sharing the blessing from the center. GOD-of-the-Angel-Armies, who blessed Israel, will generously bless them all: "Blessed be Egypt, my people! . . . Blessed be Assyria, work of my hands! . . . Blessed be Israel, my heritage!"

EXPOSED TO MOCKERY AND JEERS

20.1-2 **20** In the year the field commander, sent by King Sargon of Assyria, came to Ashdod and fought and took it, GOD told Isaiah

NEW INTERNATIONAL VERSION

Amoz. He said to him, "Take off the sackcloth from your body and the sandals from your feet." And he did so, going around stripped and barefoot.

³Then the LORD said, "Just as my servant Isaiah has gone stripped and barefoot for three years, as a sign and portent against Egypt and Cush,ᵃ ⁴so the king of Assyria will lead away stripped and barefoot the Egyptian captives and Cushite exiles, young and old, with buttocks bared—to Egypt's shame. ⁵Those who trusted in Cush and boasted in Egypt will be afraid and put to shame. ⁶In that day the people who live on this coast will say, 'See what has happened to those we relied on, those we fled to for help and deliverance from the king of Assyria! How then can we escape?' "

A PROPHECY AGAINST BABYLON

21 An oracle concerning the Desert by the Sea:

Like whirlwinds sweeping through the
    southland,
an invader comes from the desert,
    from a land of terror.

²A dire vision has been shown to me:
    The traitor betrays, the looter takes loot.
Elam, attack! Media, lay siege!
    I will bring to an end all the groaning she
    caused.

³At this my body is racked with pain,
    pangs seize me, like those of a woman in
    labor;
I am staggered by what I hear,
    I am bewildered by what I see.
⁴My heart falters,
    fear makes me tremble;
the twilight I longed for
    has become a horror to me.

⁵They set the tables,
    they spread the rugs,
    they eat, they drink!
Get up, you officers,
    oil the shields!

⁶This is what the Lord says to me:

"Go, post a lookout
    and have him report what he sees.
⁷When he sees chariots
    with teams of horses,

ᵃ 3 That is, the upper Nile region; also in verse 5

THE MESSAGE

son of Amoz, "Go, take off your clothes and sandals," and Isaiah did it, going about naked and barefooted.

20.3-6 Then GOD said, "Just as my servant Isaiah has walked around town naked and barefooted for three years as a warning sign to Egypt and Ethiopia, so the king of Assyria is going to come and take the Egyptians as captives and the Ethiopians as exiles. He'll take young and old alike and march them out of there naked and barefooted, exposed to mockery and jeers—the bared buttocks of Egypt on parade! Everyone who has put hope in Ethiopia and expected help from Egypt will be thrown into confusion. Everyone who lives along this coast will say, 'Look at them! Naked and barefooted, shuffling off to exile! And we thought they were our best hope, that they'd rescue us from the king of Assyria. *Now* what's going to happen to us? How are we going to get out of this?' "

THE BETRAYER BETRAYED

21 A Message concerning the desert at the sea:

As tempests drive through the Negev Desert,
    coming out of the desert, that terror-filled
        place,
A hard vision is given me:
    The betrayer betrayed, the plunderer
        plundered.
Attack, Elam!
    Lay siege, Media!
Persians, attack!
    Attack, Babylon!
I'll put an end to
    all the moaning and groaning.
Because of this news I'm doubled up in pain,
    writhing in pain like a woman having a
        baby,
Baffled by what I hear,
    undone by what I see.
Absolutely stunned,
    horror-stricken,
I had hoped for a relaxed evening,
    but it has turned into a nightmare.

21.5 The banquet is spread,
    the guests reclining in luxurious ease,
Eating and drinking, having a good time,
    and then, "To arms, princes! The fight
        is on!"

21.6-9 The Master told me, "Go, post a lookout.
    Have him report whatever he spots.
When he sees horses and wagons in battle
    formation,

NEW INTERNATIONAL VERSION

riders on donkeys
  or riders on camels,
let him be alert,
  fully alert.' "

8And the lookout[a] shouted,

"Day after day, my lord, I stand on the
    watchtower;
  every night I stay at my post.
9Look, here comes a man in a chariot
  with a team of horses.
And he gives back the answer:
  'Babylon has fallen, has fallen!
All the images of its gods
  lie shattered on the ground!' "

10O my people, crushed on the threshing floor,
  I tell you what I have heard
from the LORD Almighty,
  from the God of Israel.

A PROPHECY AGAINST EDOM

11An oracle concerning Dumah[b]:

Someone calls to me from Seir,
  "Watchman, what is left of the night?
  Watchman, what is left of the night?"
12The watchman replies,
  "Morning is coming, but also the night.
If you would ask, then ask;
  and come back yet again."

A PROPHECY AGAINST ARABIA

13An oracle concerning Arabia:

You caravans of Dedanites,
  who camp in the thickets of Arabia,
14 bring water for the thirsty;
you who live in Tema,
  bring food for the fugitives.
15They flee from the sword,
  from the drawn sword,
from the bent bow
  and from the heat of battle.

16This is what the Lord says to me: "Within
one year, as a servant bound by contract would
count it, all the pomp of Kedar will come to an
end. 17The survivors of the bowmen, the warriors of Kedar, will be few." The LORD, the God of
Israel, has spoken.

A PROPHECY ABOUT JERUSALEM

22 An oracle concerning the Valley of Vision:

What troubles you now,

THE MESSAGE

lines of donkeys and columns of camels,
Tell him to keep his ear to the ground,
  note every whisper, every rumor."
Just then, the lookout shouted,
  "I'm at my post, Master,
Sticking to my post day after day
  and all through the night!
I watched them come,
  the horses and wagons in battle formation.
I heard them call out the war news in headlines:
  'Babylon fallen! Fallen!
And all its precious god-idols
  smashed to pieces on the ground.' "

21.10 Dear Israel, you've been through a lot,
  you've been put through the mill.
The good news I get from GOD-of-the-Angel-
    Armies,
  the God of Israel, I now pass on to you.

✝

21.11-12 A Message concerning Edom:

A voice calls to me
  from the Seir mountains in Edom,
"Night watchman! How long till daybreak?
  How long will this night last?"
The night watchman calls back,
  "Morning's coming,
But for now it's still night.
  If you ask me again, I'll give the same
    answer."

✝

21.13-15 A Message concerning Arabia:

You'll have to camp out in the desert
    badlands,
  you caravans of Dedanites.
Haul water to the thirsty,
  greet fugitives with bread.
Show your desert hospitality,
  you who live in Tema.
The desert's swarming with refugees
  escaping the horrors of war.

21.16-17   The Master told me, "Hang on. Within one
year—I'll sign a contract on it!—the arrogant
brutality of Kedar, those hooligans of the
desert, will be over, nothing much left of the
Kedar toughs." The GOD of Israel says so.

A COUNTRY OF COWARDS

21.1-3 **22** A Message concerning the Valley of Vision:

What's going on here anyway?

---

[a] 8 Dead Sea Scrolls and Syriac; Masoretic Text *A lion*
[b] 11 *Dumah* means *silence* or *stillness,* a wordplay on *Edom.*

NEW INTERNATIONAL VERSION

that you have all gone up on the roofs,
² O town full of commotion,
    O city of tumult and revelry?
Your slain were not killed by the sword,
    nor did they die in battle.
³ All your leaders have fled together;
    they have been captured without using
        the bow.
All you who were caught were taken
        prisoner together,
    having fled while the enemy was still far
        away.
⁴ Therefore I said, "Turn away from me;
    let me weep bitterly.
Do not try to console me
    over the destruction of my people."

⁵ The Lord, the LORD Almighty, has a day
    of tumult and trampling and terror
        in the Valley of Vision,
    a day of battering down walls
        and of crying out to the mountains.
⁶ Elam takes up the quiver,
    with her charioteers and horses;
    Kir uncovers the shield.
⁷ Your choicest valleys are full of chariots,
    and horsemen are posted at the city gates;
⁸   the defenses of Judah are stripped away.

And you looked in that day
    to the weapons in the Palace of the Forest;
⁹ you saw that the City of David
    had many breaches in its defenses;
you stored up water
    in the Lower Pool.
¹⁰ You counted the buildings in Jerusalem
    and tore down houses to strengthen the
        wall.
¹¹ You built a reservoir between the two walls
    for the water of the Old Pool,
but you did not look to the One who
        made it,
    or have regard for the One who planned it
        long ago.

¹² The Lord, the LORD Almighty,
    called you on that day
to weep and to wail,
    to tear out your hair and put on
        sackcloth.
¹³ But see, there is joy and revelry,
    slaughtering of cattle and killing of sheep,
    eating of meat and drinking of wine!
"Let us eat and drink," you say,
    "for tomorrow we die!"

THE MESSAGE

All this partying and noisemaking,
    Shouting and cheering in the streets,
        the city noisy with celebrations!
You have no brave soldiers to honor,
    no combat heroes to be proud of.
Your leaders were all cowards,
    captured without even lifting a sword,
A country of cowards
    captured escaping the battle.

YOU LOOKED, BUT YOU NEVER LOOKED TO HIM

22.4-8 In the midst of the shouting, I said, "Let me
        alone.
    Let me grieve by myself.
Don't tell me it's going to be all right.
    These people are doomed. It's *not* all right."
For the Master, GOD-of-the-Angel-Armies,
    is bringing a day noisy with mobs of
        people,
Jostling and stampeding in the Valley of Vision,
    knocking down walls
    and hollering to the mountains, "Attack!
        Attack!"
Old enemies Elam and Kir arrive armed to the
        teeth—
    weapons and chariots and cavalry.
Your fine valleys are noisy with war,
    chariots and cavalry charging this way and
        that.
God has left Judah exposed and
        defenseless.

22.8-11   You assessed your defenses that Day, in-
spected your arsenal of weapons in the Forest
Armory. You found the weak places in the city
walls that needed repair. You secured the water
supply at the Lower Pool. You took an inventory of the houses in Jerusalem and tore down
some to get bricks to fortify the city wall. You
built a large cistern to ensure plenty of water.
    You looked and looked and looked, but you
never looked to him who gave you this city,
never once consulted the One who has long
had plans for this city.

22.12-13 The Master, GOD-of-the-Angel-Armies,
    called out on that Day,
Called for a day of repentant tears,
    called you to dress in somber clothes of
        mourning.
But what do *you* do? You throw a party!
    Eating and drinking and dancing in the
        streets!
You barbecue bulls and sheep, and throw a
        huge feast—
    slabs of meat, kegs of beer.
"Seize the day! Eat and drink!
    Tomorrow we die!"

NEW INTERNATIONAL VERSION

¹⁴The LORD Almighty has revealed this in my hearing: "Till your dying day this sin will not be atoned for," says the Lord, the LORD Almighty.

¹⁵This is what the Lord, the LORD Almighty, says:

"Go, say to this steward,
  to Shebna, who is in charge of the palace:
¹⁶What are you doing here and who gave you
      permission
  to cut out a grave for yourself here,
hewing your grave on the height
  and chiseling your resting place in the
      rock?

¹⁷"Beware, the LORD is about to take firm hold
      of you
  and hurl you away, O you mighty man.
¹⁸He will roll you up tightly like a ball
  and throw you into a large country.
There you will die
  and there your splendid chariots will
      remain—
  you disgrace to your master's house!
¹⁹I will depose you from your office,
  and you will be ousted from your
      position.

²⁰"In that day I will summon my servant, Eliakim son of Hilkiah. ²¹I will clothe him with your robe and fasten your sash around him and hand your authority over to him. He will be a father to those who live in Jerusalem and to the house of Judah. ²²I will place on his shoulder the key to the house of David; what he opens no one can shut, and what he shuts no one can open. ²³I will drive him like a peg into a firm place; he will be a seat*ᵃ* of honor for the house of his father. ²⁴All the glory of his family will hang on him: its offspring and offshoots—all its lesser vessels, from the bowls to all the jars.

²⁵"In that day," declares the LORD Almighty, "the peg driven into the firm place will give way; it will be sheared off and will fall, and the load hanging on it will be cut down." The LORD has spoken.

A PROPHECY ABOUT TYRE

23 An oracle concerning Tyre:

Wail, O ships of Tarshish!
  For Tyre is destroyed
    and left without house or harbor.
From the land of Cyprus*ᵇ*
    word has come to them.

THE MESSAGE

22.14   GOD-of-the-Angel-Armies whispered to me his verdict on this frivolity: "You'll pay for this outrage until the day you die." The Master, GOD-of-the-Angel-Armies, says so.

THE KEY OF THE DAVIDIC HERITAGE

22.15-19   The Master, GOD-of-the-Angel-Armies, spoke: "Come. Go to this steward, Shebna, who is in charge of all the king's affairs, and tell him: What's going on here? You're an outsider here and yet you act like you own the place, make a big, fancy tomb for yourself where everyone can see it, making sure everyone will think you're important. GOD is about to sack you, to throw you to the dogs. He'll grab you by the hair, swing you round and round dizzyingly, and then let you go, sailing through the air like a ball, until you're out of sight. Where you'll land, nobody knows. And there you'll die, and all the stuff you've collected heaped on your grave. You've disgraced your master's house! You're fired—and good riddance!

22.20-24   "On that Day I'll replace Shebna. I will call my servant Eliakim son of Hilkiah. I'll dress him in your robe. I'll put your belt on him. I'll give him your authority. He'll be a father-leader to Jerusalem and the government of Judah. I'll give him the key of the Davidic heritage. He'll have the run of the place—open any door and keep it open, lock any door and keep it locked. I'll pound him like a nail into a solid wall. He'll secure the Davidic tradition. Everything will hang on him—not only the fate of Davidic descendants but also the detailed daily operations of the house, including cups and cutlery.

22.25   "And then the Day will come," says GOD-of-the-Angel-Armies, "when that nail will come loose and fall out, break loose from that solid wall—and everything hanging on it will go with it." That's what will happen. GOD says so.

IT WAS ALL NUMBERS, DEAD NUMBERS, PROFIT AND LOSS

23.1-4   # 23 Wail, ships of Tarshish,
      your strong seaports all in ruins!
When the ships returned from Cyprus,
      they saw the destruction.

ᵃ 23 Or throne   *ᵇ 1 Hebrew Kittim*

NEW INTERNATIONAL VERSION

² Be silent, you people of the island
    and you merchants of Sidon,
      whom the seafarers have enriched.
³ On the great waters
    came the grain of the Shihor;
    the harvest of the Nile*a* was the revenue of Tyre,
    and she became the marketplace of the
      nations.

⁴ Be ashamed, O Sidon, and you, O fortress of
    the sea,
    for the sea has spoken:
"I have neither been in labor nor given birth;
    I have neither reared sons nor brought up
      daughters."
⁵ When word comes to Egypt,
    they will be in anguish at the report from
      Tyre.

⁶ Cross over to Tarshish;
    wail, you people of the island.
⁷ Is this your city of revelry,
    the old, old city,
whose feet have taken her
    to settle in far-off lands?
⁸ Who planned this against Tyre,
    the bestower of crowns,
whose merchants are princes,
    whose traders are renowned in the earth?
⁹ The LORD Almighty planned it,
    to bring low the pride of all glory
    and to humble all who are renowned on
      the earth.

¹⁰ Till*b* your land as along the Nile,
    O Daughter of Tarshish,
    for you no longer have a harbor.
¹¹ The LORD has stretched out his hand over
    the sea
    and made its kingdoms tremble.
He has given an order concerning Phoenicia*c*
    that her fortresses be destroyed.
¹² He said, "No more of your reveling,
    O Virgin Daughter of Sidon, now crushed!

"Up, cross over to Cyprus*d*;
    even there you will find no rest."
¹³ Look at the land of the Babylonians,*e*
    this people that is now of no account!
The Assyrians have made it
    a place for desert creatures;
they raised up their siege towers,
    they stripped its fortresses bare
    and turned it into a ruin.

*a 2,3 Masoretic Text; one Dead Sea Scroll Sidon, / who cross
over the sea; / your envoys ³are on the great waters. / The grain
of the Shihor, / the harvest of the Nile,*   *b 10 Dead Sea
Scrolls and some Septuagint manuscripts; Masoretic Text Go
through*   *c 11 Hebrew Canaan*   *d 12 Hebrew Kittim*
e 13 Or Chaldeans

THE MESSAGE

Hold your tongue, you who live on the
    seacoast,
    merchants of Sidon.
Your people sailed the deep seas,
    buying and selling,
Making money on wheat from Shihor,
    grown along the Nile—
    multinational broker in grains!
Hang your head in shame, Sidon. The Sea
    speaks up,
    the powerhouse of the ocean says,
"I've never had labor pains, never had a baby,
    never reared children to adulthood,
Never gave life, never worked with life.
    It was all numbers, dead numbers, profit
      and loss."

23.5 When Egypt gets the report on Tyre,
    what wailing! what wringing of hands!

NOTHING LEFT HERE TO BE PROUD OF

23.6-12 Visit Tarshish, you who live on the seacoast.
    Take a good, long look and wail—yes, cry
      buckets of tears!
Is this the city you remember as energetic and
    alive,
    bustling with activity, this historic old city,
Expanding throughout the globe,
    buying and selling all over the world?
And who is behind the collapse of Tyre,
    the Tyre that controlled the world markets?
Tyre's merchants were the business tycoons.
    Tyre's traders called all the shots.
GOD-of-the-Angel-Armies ordered the crash
    to show the sordid backside of pride
    and puncture the inflated reputations.
Sail for home, O ships of Tarshish.
    There are no docks left in this harbor.
GOD reached out to the sea and sea traders,
    threw the sea kingdoms into turmoil.
GOD ordered the destruction
    of the seacoast cities, the centers of
      commerce.
GOD said, "There's nothing left here to be
    proud of,
    bankrupt and bereft Sidon.
Do you want to make a new start in Cyprus?
    Don't count on it. Nothing there will work
      out for you either."

23.13   Look at what happened to Babylon: There's
nothing left of it. Assyria turned it into a desert,
into a refuge for wild dogs and stray cats. They
brought in their big siege engines, tore down
the buildings, and left nothing behind but rubble.

NEW INTERNATIONAL VERSION

¹⁴Wail, you ships of Tarshish;
  your fortress is destroyed!

¹⁵At that time Tyre will be forgotten for seventy years, the span of a king's life. But at the end of these seventy years, it will happen to Tyre as in the song of the prostitute:

¹⁶"Take up a harp, walk through the city,
  O prostitute forgotten;
play the harp well, sing many a song,
  so that you will be remembered."

¹⁷At the end of seventy years, the LORD will deal with Tyre. She will return to her hire as a prostitute and will ply her trade with all the kingdoms on the face of the earth. ¹⁸Yet her profit and her earnings will be set apart for the LORD; they will not be stored up or hoarded. Her profits will go to those who live before the LORD, for abundant food and fine clothes.

THE LORD'S DEVASTATION OF THE EARTH

24 See, the LORD is going to lay waste the
  earth
  and devastate it;
he will ruin its face
  and scatter its inhabitants—
²it will be the same
  for priest as for people,
  for master as for servant,
  for mistress as for maid,
  for seller as for buyer,
  for borrower as for lender,
  for debtor as for creditor.
³The earth will be completely laid waste
  and totally plundered.
            The LORD has spoken
                this word.

⁴The earth dries up and withers,
  the world languishes and withers,
  the exalted of the earth languish.
⁵The earth is defiled by its people;
  they have disobeyed the laws,
violated the statutes
  and broken the everlasting covenant.
⁶Therefore a curse consumes the earth;
  its people must bear their guilt.
Therefore earth's inhabitants are burned up,
  and very few are left.
⁷The new wine dries up and the vine withers;
  all the merrymakers groan.
⁸The gaiety of the tambourines is stilled,

THE MESSAGE

23.14 Wail, ships of Tarshish,
  your strong seaports all in ruins!

✝

23.15-16 For the next seventy years, a king's lifetime, Tyre will be forgotten. At the end of the seventy years, Tyre will stage a comeback, but it will be the comeback of a worn-out whore, as in the song:

"Take a harp, circle the city,
  unremembered whore.
Sing your old songs, your many old songs.
  Maybe someone will remember."

23.17-18 At the end of the seventy years, GOD will look in on Tyre. She'll go back to her old whoring trade, selling herself to the highest bidder, doing anything with anyone—promiscuous with all the kingdoms of earth—for a fee. But everything she gets, all the money she takes in, will be turned over to GOD. It will not be put in banks. Her profits will be put to the use of GOD-Aware, GOD-Serving-People, providing plenty of food and the best of clothing.

THE LANDSCAPE WILL BE A MOONSCAPE

24.1-3 **24** Danger ahead! GOD's about to ravish
  the earth
  and leave it in ruins,
Rip everything out by the roots
  and send everyone scurrying:
    priests and laypeople alike,
    owners and workers alike,
    celebrities and nobodies alike,
    buyers and sellers alike,
    bankers and beggars alike,
    the haves and have-nots alike.
The landscape will be a moonscape,
  totally wasted.
And why? Because GOD says so.
  He's issued the orders.

24.4 The earth turns gaunt and gray,
  the world silent and sad,
  sky and land lifeless, colorless.

EARTH POLLUTED BY ITS VERY OWN PEOPLE

24.5-13 Earth is polluted by its very own people,
  who have broken its laws,
Disrupted its order,
  violated the sacred and eternal covenant.
Therefore a curse, like a cancer,
  ravages the earth.
Its people pay the price of their sacrilege.
  They dwindle away, dying out one by one.
No more wine, no more vineyards,
  no more songs or singers.
The laughter of castanets is gone,

NEW INTERNATIONAL VERSION

the noise of the revelers has stopped,
the joyful harp is silent.
⁹No longer do they drink wine with a song;
the beer is bitter to its drinkers.
¹⁰The ruined city lies desolate;
the entrance to every house is barred.
¹¹In the streets they cry out for wine;
all joy turns to gloom,
all gaiety is banished from the earth.
¹²The city is left in ruins,
its gate is battered to pieces.
¹³So will it be on the earth
and among the nations,
as when an olive tree is beaten,
or as when gleanings are left after the
grape harvest.

¹⁴They raise their voices, they shout for joy;
from the west they acclaim the LORD's
majesty.
¹⁵Therefore in the east give glory to the LORD;
exalt the name of the LORD, the God of
Israel,
in the islands of the sea.
¹⁶From the ends of the earth we hear singing:
"Glory to the Righteous One."

But I said, "I waste away, I waste away!
Woe to me!
The treacherous betray!
With treachery the treacherous betray!"
¹⁷Terror and pit and snare await you,
O people of the earth.
¹⁸Whoever flees at the sound of terror
will fall into a pit;
whoever climbs out of the pit
will be caught in a snare.

The floodgates of the heavens are opened,
the foundations of the earth shake.
¹⁹The earth is broken up,
the earth is split asunder,
the earth is thoroughly shaken.
²⁰The earth reels like a drunkard,
it sways like a hut in the wind;
so heavy upon it is the guilt of its rebellion
that it falls—never to rise again.

²¹In that day the LORD will punish
the powers in the heavens above
and the kings on the earth below.
²²They will be herded together
like prisoners bound in a dungeon;
they will be shut up in prison
and be punished[a] after many days.

ᵃ 22 Or released

THE MESSAGE

the shouts of celebrants, gone,
the laughter of fiddles, gone.
No more parties with toasts of champagne.
Serious drinkers gag on their drinks.
The chaotic cities are unlivable. Anarchy
reigns.
Every house is boarded up, condemned.
People riot in the streets for wine,
but the good times are gone forever—
no more joy for this old world.
The city is dead and deserted,
bulldozed into piles of rubble.
That's the way it will be on this earth.
This is the fate of all nations:
An olive tree shaken clean of its olives,
a grapevine picked clean of its grapes.

24.14-16 But there are some who will break into glad
song.
Out of the west they'll shout of GOD's
majesty.
Yes, from the east GOD's glory will ascend.
Every island of the sea
Will broadcast GOD's fame,
the fame of the God of Israel.
From the four winds and the seven seas we
hear the singing:
"All praise to the Righteous One!"

24.16-20 But I said, "That's all well and good for
somebody,
but all I can see is doom, doom, and more
doom."
All of them at one another's throats,
yes, all of them at one another's throats.
Terror and pits and booby traps
are everywhere, whoever you are.
If you run from the terror,
you'll fall into the pit.
If you climb out of the pit,
you'll get caught in the trap.
Chaos pours out of the skies.
The foundations of earth are crumbling.
Earth is smashed to pieces,
earth is ripped to shreds,
earth is wobbling out of control,
Earth staggers like a drunk,
sways like a shack in a high wind.
Its piled-up sins are too much for it.
It collapses and won't get up again.

24.21-23 That's when GOD will call on the carpet
rebel powers in the skies and
Rebel kings on earth.
They'll be rounded up like prisoners in a
jail,
Corralled and locked up in a jail,
and then sentenced and put to hard labor.

NEW INTERNATIONAL VERSION

²³The moon will be abashed, the sun ashamed;
  for the LORD Almighty will reign
on Mount Zion and in Jerusalem,
  and before its elders, gloriously.

PRAISE TO THE LORD

25 O LORD, you are my God;
  I will exalt you and praise your name,
for in perfect faithfulness
  you have done marvelous things,
  things planned long ago.
²You have made the city a heap of rubble,
  the fortified town a ruin,
the foreigners' stronghold a city no more;
  it will never be rebuilt.
³Therefore strong peoples will honor you;
  cities of ruthless nations will revere you.
⁴You have been a refuge for the poor,
  a refuge for the needy in his distress,
a shelter from the storm
  and a shade from the heat.
For the breath of the ruthless
  is like a storm driving against a wall
⁵ and like the heat of the desert.
You silence the uproar of foreigners;
  as heat is reduced by the shadow of a
    cloud,
  so the song of the ruthless is stilled.

⁶On this mountain the LORD Almighty will
    prepare
  a feast of rich food for all peoples,
a banquet of aged wine—
  the best of meats and the finest of wines.
⁷On this mountain he will destroy
  the shroud that enfolds all peoples,
the sheet that covers all nations;
⁸ he will swallow up death forever.
The Sovereign LORD will wipe away the tears
  from all faces;
he will remove the disgrace of his people
  from all the earth.
              The LORD has spoken.

⁹In that day they will say,

"Surely this is our God;
  we trusted in him, and he saved us.
This is the LORD, we trusted in him;
  let us rejoice and be glad in his salvation."

¹⁰The hand of the LORD will rest on this
    mountain;

THE MESSAGE

Shamefaced moon will cower, humiliated,
  red-faced sun will skulk, disgraced,
Because GOD-of-the-Angel-Armies will take
    over,
  ruling from Mount Zion and Jerusalem,
Splendid and glorious
  before all his leaders.

GOD'S HAND RESTS ON THIS MOUNTAIN

25.1-5 **25** GOD, you are *my* God.
  I celebrate you. I praise you.
You've done your share of miracle-wonders,
  well-thought-out plans, solid and sure.
Here you've reduced the city to rubble,
  the strong city to a pile of stones.
The enemy Big City is a non-city,
  never to be a city again.
Superpowers will see it and honor you,
  brutal oppressors bow in worshipful
    reverence.
They'll see that you take care of the poor,
  that you take care of poor people in
    trouble,
Provide a warm, dry place in bad weather,
  provide a cool place when it's hot.
Brutal oppressors are like a winter blizzard
  and vicious foreigners like high noon in the
    desert.
But you, shelter from the storm and shade
    from the sun,
  shut the mouths of the big-mouthed
    bullies.

25.6-8 But here on this mountain, GOD-of-the-Angel-
    Armies
  will throw a feast for all the people of the
    world,
A feast of the finest foods, a feast with vintage
    wines,
  a feast of seven courses, a feast lavish with
    gourmet desserts.
And here on this mountain, GOD will banish
  the pall of doom hanging over all peoples,
The shadow of doom darkening all nations.
  Yes, he'll banish death forever.
And GOD will wipe the tears from every face.
  He'll remove every sign of disgrace
From his people, wherever they are.
  Yes! GOD says so!

25.9-10 Also at that time, people will say,
  "Look at what's happened! This is our God!
We waited for him and he showed up and
    saved us!
  This GOD, the one we waited for!
Let's celebrate, sing the joys of his salvation.
  GOD's hand rests on this mountain!"

NEW INTERNATIONAL VERSION

but Moab will be trampled under him
  as straw is trampled down in the manure.
[11] They will spread out their hands in it,
  as a swimmer spreads out his hands to
    swim.
God will bring down their pride
  despite the cleverness[a] of their hands.
[12] He will bring down your high fortified walls
  and lay them low;
he will bring them down to the ground,
  to the very dust.

A Song of Praise

26 In that day this song will be sung in the
  land of Judah:

We have a strong city;
  God makes salvation
  its walls and ramparts.
[2] Open the gates
  that the righteous nation may enter,
  the nation that keeps faith.
[3] You will keep in perfect peace
  him whose mind is steadfast,
  because he trusts in you.
[4] Trust in the LORD forever,
  for the LORD, the LORD, is the Rock
    eternal.
[5] He humbles those who dwell on high,
  he lays the lofty city low;
he levels it to the ground
  and casts it down to the dust.
[6] Feet trample it down—
  the feet of the oppressed,
  the footsteps of the poor.

[7] The path of the righteous is level;
  O upright One, you make the way of the
    righteous smooth.
[8] Yes, LORD, walking in the way of your laws,[b]
  we wait for you;
your name and renown
  are the desire of our hearts.
[9] My soul yearns for you in the night;
  in the morning my spirit longs for you.
When your judgments come upon the earth,
  the people of the world learn
    righteousness.
[10] Though grace is shown to the wicked,
  they do not learn righteousness;
even in a land of uprightness they go on
    doing evil
  and regard not the majesty of the LORD.
[11] O LORD, your hand is lifted high,
  but they do not see it.

THE MESSAGE

25.10-12 As for the Moabites, they'll be treated like
    refuse,
  waste shoveled into a cesspool.
Thrash away as they will,
  like swimmers trying to stay afloat,
They'll sink in the sewage.
  Their pride will pull them under.
Their famous fortifications will crumble to
    nothing,
  those mighty walls reduced to dust.

STRETCH THE BORDERS OF LIFE

26.1-6 **26** At that time, this song
  will be sung in the country of Judah:
We have a strong city, Salvation City,
  built and fortified with salvation.
Throw wide the gates
  so good and true people can enter.
People with their minds set on you,
  you keep completely whole,
Steady on their feet,
  because they keep at it and don't quit.
Depend on GOD and keep at it
  because in the LORD GOD you have a sure
    thing.
Those who lived high and mighty
  he knocked off their high horse.
He used the city built on the hill
  as fill for the marshes.
All the exploited and outcast peoples
  build their lives on the reclaimed land.

26.7-10 The path of right-living people is level.
  The Leveler evens the road for the
    right-living.
We're in no hurry, GOD. We're content to
    linger
  in the path sign-posted with your
    decisions.
Who you are and what you've done
  are all we'll ever want.
Through the night my soul longs for you.
  Deep from within me my spirit reaches out
    to you.
When your decisions are on public display,
  everyone learns how to live right.
If the wicked are shown grace,
  they don't seem to get it.
In the land of right living, they persist in
    wrong living,
  blind to the splendor of GOD.

26.11-15 You hold your hand up high, GOD,
  but they don't see it.

---

a 11 The meaning of the Hebrew for this word is uncertain.
b 8 Or *judgments*

NEW INTERNATIONAL VERSION

Let them see your zeal for your people and
    be put to shame;
  let the fire reserved for your enemies
    consume them.

12 LORD, you establish peace for us;
  all that we have accomplished you have
    done for us.
13 O LORD, our God, other lords besides you
    have ruled over us,
  but your name alone do we honor.
14 They are now dead, they live no more;
    those departed spirits do not rise.
  You punished them and brought them to
    ruin;
  you wiped out all memory of them.
15 You have enlarged the nation, O LORD;
  you have enlarged the nation.
  You have gained glory for yourself;
    you have extended all the borders of the
    land.

16 LORD, they came to you in their distress;
  when you disciplined them,
  they could barely whisper a prayer. *a*
17 As a woman with child and about to give
    birth
  writhes and cries out in her pain,
  so were we in your presence, O LORD.
18 We were with child, we writhed in pain,
  but we gave birth to wind.
  We have not brought salvation to the earth;
  we have not given birth to people of the
    world.

19 But your dead will live;
  their bodies will rise.
  You who dwell in the dust,
  wake up and shout for joy.
  Your dew is like the dew of the morning;
  the earth will give birth to her dead.

20 Go, my people, enter your rooms
  and shut the doors behind you;
  hide yourselves for a little while
  until his wrath has passed by.
21 See, the LORD is coming out of his dwelling
  to punish the people of the earth for their
    sins.
  The earth will disclose the blood shed upon
    her;
  she will conceal her slain no longer.

---

*a 16 The meaning of the Hebrew for this clause is
uncertain.*

THE MESSAGE

Open their eyes to what you do,
  to see your zealous love for your people.
Shame them. Light a fire under them.
  Get the attention of these enemies of yours.
GOD, order a peaceful and whole life for us
  because everything we've done, you've
    done for us.
O GOD, our God, we've had other masters
    rule us,
  but you're the only Master we've ever
    known.
The dead don't talk,
  ghosts don't walk,
Because you've said, "Enough—that's all for
    you,"
  and wiped them off the books.
But the living you make larger than life.
  The more life you give, the more glory you
    display,
  and stretch the borders to accommodate
    more living!

26.16-18 O GOD, they begged you for help when they
    were in trouble,
  when your discipline was so heavy
  they could barely whisper a prayer.
Like a woman having a baby,
  writhing in distress, screaming her pain
  as the baby is being born,
That's how we were because of you, O GOD.
  We were pregnant full-term.
We writhed in labor but bore no baby.
  We gave birth to wind.
Nothing came of our labor.
  We produced nothing living.
  We couldn't save the world.

26.19 But friends, your dead will live,
  your corpses will get to their feet.
All you dead and buried,
  wake up! Sing!
Your dew is morning dew
  catching the first rays of sun,
The earth bursting with life,
  giving birth to the dead.

26.20-21 Come, my people, go home
  and shut yourselves in.
Go into seclusion for a while
  until the punishing wrath is past,
Because GOD is sure to come from his place
  to punish the wrong of the people on earth.
Earth itself will point out the bloodstains;
  it will show where the murdered have been
    hidden away.

NEW INTERNATIONAL VERSION

DELIVERANCE OF ISRAEL

27 In that day,

the LORD will punish with his sword,
his fierce, great and powerful sword,
Leviathan the gliding serpent,
Leviathan the coiling serpent;
he will slay the monster of the sea.

2 In that day—

"Sing about a fruitful vineyard:
3 I, the LORD, watch over it;
I water it continually.
I guard it day and night
so that no one may harm it.
4 I am not angry.
If only there were briers and thorns
confronting me!
I would march against them in battle;
I would set them all on fire.
5 Or else let them come to me for refuge;
let them make peace with me,
yes, let them make peace with me."

6 In days to come Jacob will take root,
Israel will bud and blossom
and fill all the world with fruit.

7 Has ⌊the LORD⌋ struck her
as he struck down those who struck her?
Has she been killed
as those were killed who killed her?
8 By warfare*a* and exile you contend with
her—
with his fierce blast he drives her out,
as on a day the east wind blows.
9 By this, then, will Jacob's guilt be atoned for,
and this will be the full fruitage of the
removal of his sin:
When he makes all the altar stones
to be like chalk stones crushed to pieces,
no Asherah poles*b* or incense altars
will be left standing.
10 The fortified city stands desolate,
an abandoned settlement, forsaken like
the desert;
there the calves graze,
there they lie down;
they strip its branches bare.
11 When its twigs are dry, they are broken off
and women come and make fires with
them.
For this is a people without understanding;

THE MESSAGE

SELECTED GRAIN BY GRAIN

27 At that time GOD will unsheathe his
sword,
his merciless, massive, mighty sword.
He'll punish the serpent Leviathan as it flees,
the serpent Leviathan thrashing in flight.
He'll kill that old dragon
that lives in the sea.

27.2-5 "At that same time, a fine vineyard will
appear.
There's something to sing about!
I, GOD, tend it.
I keep it well-watered.
I keep careful watch over it
so that no one can damage it.
I'm not angry. I care.
Even if it gives me thistles and
thornbushes,
I'll just pull them out
and burn them up.
Let that vine cling to me for safety,
let it find a good and whole life with me,
let it hold on for a good and whole life."

27.6 The days are coming when Jacob
shall put down roots,
Israel blossom and grow fresh branches,
and fill the world with its fruit.

27.7-11 Has GOD knocked them to the ground
as he knocked down those who hit them?
Oh, no.
Were they killed
as their killers were killed? Again, no.
He was hard on them all right. The exile was a
harsh sentence.
He blew them away on a fierce blast of
wind.
But the good news is that through this
experience
Jacob's guilt was taken away.
The evidence that his sin is removed will be
this:
He will tear down the alien altars,
take them apart stone by stone,
And then crush the stones into gravel
and clean out all the sex-and-religion
shrines.
For there's nothing left of that pretentious
grandeur.
Nobody lives there anymore. It's unlivable.
But animals do just fine,
browsing and bedding down.
And it's not a bad place to get firewood.
Dry twigs and dead branches are plentiful.
It's the leavings of a people with no sense of
God.

---

a 8 See Septuagint; the meaning of the Hebrew for this word
is uncertain.   *b 9* That is, symbols of the goddess Asherah

NEW INTERNATIONAL VERSION

so their Maker has no compassion on
them,
and their Creator shows them no favor.

¹²In that day the LORD will thresh from the flowing Euphrates[a] to the Wadi of Egypt, and you, O Israelites, will be gathered up one by one. ¹³And in that day a great trumpet will sound. Those who were perishing in Assyria and those who were exiled in Egypt will come and worship the LORD on the holy mountain in Jerusalem.

WOE TO EPHRAIM

28 Woe to that wreath, the pride of
Ephraim's drunkards,
to the fading flower, his glorious beauty,
set on the head of a fertile valley—
to that city, the pride of those laid low by
wine!
² See, the Lord has one who is powerful and
strong.
Like a hailstorm and a destructive wind,
like a driving rain and a flooding downpour,
he will throw it forcefully to the ground.
³ That wreath, the pride of Ephraim's
drunkards,
will be trampled underfoot.
⁴ That fading flower, his glorious beauty,
set on the head of a fertile valley,
will be like a fig ripe before harvest—
as soon as someone sees it and takes it in
his hand,
he swallows it.

⁵ In that day the LORD Almighty
will be a glorious crown,
a beautiful wreath
for the remnant of his people.
⁶ He will be a spirit of justice
to him who sits in judgment,
a source of strength
to those who turn back the battle at the
gate.

⁷ And these also stagger from wine
and reel from beer:
Priests and prophets stagger from beer
and are befuddled with wine;
they reel from beer,
they stagger when seeing visions,
they stumble when rendering decisions.
⁸ All the tables are covered with vomit
and there is not a spot without filth.

a 12 Hebrew *River*

THE MESSAGE

So, the God who made them
Will have nothing to do with them.
He who formed them will turn his back on
them.

27.12-13 At that time GOD will thresh
from the River Euphrates to the Brook of
Egypt,
And you, people of Israel,
will be selected grain by grain.
At that same time a great trumpet will be
blown,
calling home the exiles from Assyria,
Welcoming home the refugees from Egypt
to come and worship GOD on the holy
mountain, Jerusalem.

GOD WILL SPEAK IN BABY TALK

28.1-4 **28** Doom to the pretentious drunks of
Ephraim,
shabby and washed out and seedy—
Tipsy, sloppy-fat, beer-bellied parodies
of a proud and handsome past.
Watch closely: GOD has someone picked out,
someone tough and strong to flatten them.
Like a hailstorm, like a hurricane, like a flash
flood,
one-handed he'll throw them to the
ground.
Samaria, the party hat on Israel's head,
will be knocked off with one blow.
It will disappear quicker than
a piece of meat tossed to a dog.

28.5-6 At that time, GOD-of-the-Angel-Armies will be
the beautiful crown on the head of what's
left of his people:
Energy and insights of justice to those who
guide and decide,
strength and prowess to those who guard
and protect.

28.7-8 These also, the priest and prophet, stagger
from drink,
weaving, falling-down drunks,
Besotted with wine and whiskey,
can't see straight, can't talk sense.
Every table is covered with vomit.
They *live* in vomit.

NEW INTERNATIONAL VERSION

⁹ "Who is it he is trying to teach?
    To whom is he explaining his message?
To children weaned from their milk,
    to those just taken from the breast?
¹⁰ For it is:
    Do and do, do and do,
    rule on rule, rule on rule*ᵃ*;
    a little here, a little there."

¹¹ Very well then, with foreign lips and strange
        tongues
    God will speak to this people,
¹² to whom he said,
    "This is the resting place, let the weary
        rest";
and, "This is the place of repose"—
    but they would not listen.
¹³ So then, the word of the LORD to them will
        become:
    Do and do, do and do,
    rule on rule, rule on rule;
    a little here, a little there—
so that they will go and fall backward,
    be injured and snared and captured.

¹⁴ Therefore hear the word of the LORD, you
        scoffers
    who rule this people in Jerusalem.
¹⁵ You boast, "We have entered into a covenant
        with death,
    with the grave*ᵇ* we have made an
        agreement.
When an overwhelming scourge sweeps by,
    it cannot touch us,
for we have made a lie our refuge
    and falsehood*ᶜ* our hiding place."

¹⁶ So this is what the Sovereign LORD says:

"See, I lay a stone in Zion,
    a tested stone,
a precious cornerstone for a sure foundation;
    the one who trusts will never be
        dismayed.
¹⁷ I will make justice the measuring line
    and righteousness the plumb line;
hail will sweep away your refuge, the lie,
    and water will overflow your hiding place.
¹⁸ Your covenant with death will be annulled;
    your agreement with the grave will not
        stand.

ᵃ 10 Hebrew */sav lasav sav lasav / kav lakav kav lakav*
(possibly meaningless sounds; perhaps a mimicking of the
prophet's words); also in verse 13   *ᵇ 15* Hebrew *Sheol*;
also in verse 18   *ᶜ 15* Or *false gods*

THE MESSAGE

28.9-10 "Is that so? And who do you think you are to
        teach us?
    Who are you to lord it over us?
We're not babies in diapers
    to be talked down to by such as you—
'Da, da, da, da,
    blah, blah, blah, blah.
That's a good little girl,
    that's a good little boy.' "

28.11-12 But that's exactly how you will be addressed.
    God will speak to this people
In baby talk, one syllable at a time—
    and he'll do it through foreign oppressors.
He said before, "This is the time and place to
        rest,
    to give rest to the weary.
This is the place to lay down your burden."
    But they won't listen.

28.13 So GOD will start over with the simple basics
    and address them in baby talk, one syllable
        at a time—
"Da, da, da, da,
    blah, blah, blah, blah.
That's a good little girl,
    that's a good little boy."
And like toddlers, they will get up and fall
        down,
    get bruised and confused and lost.

28.14-15 Now listen to GOD's Message, you scoffers,
    you who rule this people in Jerusalem.
You say, "We've taken out good life insurance.
    We've hedged all our bets, covered all our
        bases.
No disaster can touch us. We've thought of
        everything.
    We're advised by the experts. We're set."

THE MEANING OF THE STONE

28.16-17 But the Master, GOD, has something to say to
        this:

"Watch closely. I'm laying a foundation in
        Zion,
    a solid granite foundation, squared and
        true.
And this is the meaning of the stone:
    A TRUSTING LIFE WON'T TOPPLE.
I'll make justice the measuring stick
    and righteousness the plumb line for the
        building.
A hailstorm will knock down the shantytown
        of lies,
    and a flash flood will wash out the rubble.

28.18-22 "Then you'll see that your precious life
        insurance policy
    wasn't worth the paper it was written on.

NEW INTERNATIONAL VERSION

When the overwhelming scourge sweeps by,
  you will be beaten down by it.
19 As often as it comes it will carry you away;
  morning after morning, by day and by
    night,
  it will sweep through."

The understanding of this message
  will bring sheer terror.
20 The bed is too short to stretch out on,
  the blanket too narrow to wrap around
    you.
21 The LORD will rise up as he did at Mount
    Perazim,
  he will rouse himself as in the Valley of
    Gibeon—
to do his work, his strange work,
  and perform his task, his alien task.
22 Now stop your mocking,
  or your chains will become heavier;
the Lord, the LORD Almighty, has told me
  of the destruction decreed against the
    whole land.

23 Listen and hear my voice;
  pay attention and hear what I say.
24 When a farmer plows for planting, does he
    plow continually?
  Does he keep on breaking up and
    harrowing the soil?
25 When he has leveled the surface,
  does he not sow caraway and scatter
    cummin?
  Does he not plant wheat in its place, *a*
  barley in its plot, *a*
  and spelt in its field?
26 His God instructs him
  and teaches him the right way.

27 Caraway is not threshed with a sledge,
  nor is a cartwheel rolled over cummin;
caraway is beaten out with a rod,
  and cummin with a stick.
28 Grain must be ground to make bread;
  so one does not go on threshing it forever.
Though he drives the wheels of his threshing
    cart over it,
  his horses do not grind it.
29 All this also comes from the LORD Almighty,
  wonderful in counsel and magnificent in
    wisdom.

WOE TO DAVID'S CITY

29 Woe to you, Ariel, Ariel,
  the city where David settled!
  Add year to year

THE MESSAGE

Your careful precautions against death
  were a pack of illusions and lies.
When the disaster happens,
  you'll be crushed by it.
Every time disaster comes, you'll be in on it—
  disaster in the morning, disaster at night."
Every report of disaster
  will send you cowering in terror.
There will be no place where you can rest,
  nothing to hide under.
GOD will rise to full stature,
  raging as he did long ago on Mount Perazim
And in the valley of Gibeon against the
    Philistines.
  But this time it's against *you.*
Hard to believe, but true.
  Not what you'd expect, but it's coming.
Sober up, friends, and don't scoff.
  Scoffing will just make it worse.
I've heard the orders issued for destruction,
    orders from
GOD-of-the-Angel-Armies—ending up in an
    international disaster.

☩

28.23-26 Listen to me now.
  Give me your closest attention.
Do farmers plow and plow and do nothing but
    plow?
  Or harrow and harrow and do nothing but
    harrow?
After they've prepared the ground, don't they
    plant?
  Don't they scatter dill and spread cumin,
Plant wheat and barley in the fields
  and raspberries along the borders?
They know exactly what to do and when to do
    it.
  Their God is their teacher.

28.27-29 And at the harvest, the delicate herbs and
    spices,
  the dill and cumin, are treated delicately.
On the other hand, wheat is threshed and
    milled, but still not endlessly.
  The farmer knows how to treat each kind
    of grain.
He's learned it all from GOD-of-the-Angel-
    Armies,
  who knows everything about when and
    how and where.

BLIND YOURSELVES SO THAT YOU SEE NOTHING

29.1-4 **29** Doom, Ariel, Ariel,
  the city where David set camp!
Let the years add up,

---

a 25 The meaning of the Hebrew for this word is uncertain.

NEW INTERNATIONAL VERSION

and let your cycle of festivals go on.
² Yet I will besiege Ariel;
　　she will mourn and lament,
　　she will be to me like an altar hearth. *ᵃ*
³ I will encamp against you all around;
　　I will encircle you with towers
　　and set up my siege works against you.
⁴ Brought low, you will speak from the
　　　　ground;
　　your speech will mumble out of the dust.
Your voice will come ghostlike from the
　　　　earth;
　　out of the dust your speech will whisper.

⁵ But your many enemies will become like fine
　　　　dust,
　　the ruthless hordes like blown chaff.
Suddenly, in an instant,
⁶　　the LORD Almighty will come
with thunder and earthquake and great
　　　　noise,
　　with windstorm and tempest and flames
　　　　of a devouring fire.
⁷ Then the hordes of all the nations that fight
　　　　against Ariel,
　　that attack her and her fortress and
　　　　besiege her,
will be as it is with a dream,
　　with a vision in the night—
⁸ as when a hungry man dreams that he is
　　　　eating,
　　but he awakens, and his hunger remains;
as when a thirsty man dreams that he is
　　　　drinking,
　　but he awakens faint, with his thirst
　　　　unquenched.
So will it be with the hordes of all the
　　　　nations
　　that fight against Mount Zion.

⁹ Be stunned and amazed,
　　blind yourselves and be sightless;
be drunk, but not from wine,
　　stagger, but not from beer.
¹⁰ The LORD has brought over you a deep sleep:
　　He has sealed your eyes (the prophets);
　　he has covered your heads (the seers).

¹¹ For you this whole vision is nothing but
words sealed in a scroll. And if you give the
scroll to someone who can read, and say to him,
"Read this, please," he will answer, "I can't; it is
sealed." ¹²Or if you give the scroll to someone
who cannot read, and say, "Read this, please,"
he will answer, "I don't know how to read."

THE MESSAGE

　　let the festivals run their cycles,
But I'm not letting up on Jerusalem.
　　The moaning and groaning will continue.
　　Jerusalem to me is an Ariel.
Like David, I'll set up camp against you.
　　I'll set siege, build towers,
　　bring in siege engines, build siege ramps.
Driven into the ground, you'll speak,
　　you'll mumble words from the dirt—
Your voice from the ground, like the
　　　　muttering of a ghost.
　　Your speech will whisper from the dust.

29.5-8 But it will be your enemies who are beaten to
　　　　dust,
　　the mob of tyrants who will be blown away
　　　　like chaff.
Because, surprise, as if out of nowhere,
　　a visit from GOD-of-the-Angel-Armies,
With thunderclaps, earthquakes, and
　　　　earsplitting noise,
　　backed up by hurricanes, tornadoes, and
　　　　lightning strikes,
And the mob of enemies at war with Ariel,
　　all who trouble and hassle and torment her,
　　will turn out to be a bad dream, a
　　　　nightmare.
Like a hungry man dreaming he's eating steak
　　and wakes up hungry as ever,
Like a thirsty woman dreaming she's drinking
　　　　iced tea
　　and wakes up thirsty as ever,
So that mob of nations at war against Mount
　　　　Zion
　　will wake up and find they haven't shot an
　　　　arrow,
　　haven't killed a single soul.

29.9-10 Drug yourselves so you feel nothing.
　　Blind yourselves so you see nothing.
Get drunk, but not on wine.
　　Black out, but not from whiskey.
For GOD has rocked you into a deep, deep
　　　　sleep,
　　put the discerning prophets to sleep,
　　put the farsighted seers to sleep.

YOU HAVE EVERYTHING BACKWARD

29.11-12 What you've been shown here is somewhat like
a letter in a sealed envelope. If you give it to
someone who can read and tell her, "Read this,"
she'll say, "I can't. The envelope is sealed." And
if you give it to someone who can't read and
tell him, "Read this," he'll say, "I can't read."

✝

ᵃ 2 The Hebrew for *altar hearth* sounds like the Hebrew for
Ariel.

NEW INTERNATIONAL VERSION

13 The Lord says:

"These people come near to me with their
　　mouth
　　and honor me with their lips,
　　but their hearts are far from me.
Their worship of me
　　is made up only of rules taught by men. *a*
14 Therefore once more I will astound these
　　people
　　with wonder upon wonder;
the wisdom of the wise will perish,
　　the intelligence of the intelligent will
　　vanish."
15 Woe to those who go to great depths
　　to hide their plans from the LORD,
who do their work in darkness and think,
　　"Who sees us? Who will know?"
16 You turn things upside down,
　　as if the potter were thought to be like the
　　clay!
Shall what is formed say to him who
　　formed it,
　　"He did not make me"?
Can the pot say of the potter,
　　"He knows nothing"?

17 In a very short time, will not Lebanon be
　　turned into a fertile field
　　and the fertile field seem like a forest?
18 In that day the deaf will hear the words of
　　the scroll,
　　and out of gloom and darkness
　　the eyes of the blind will see.
19 Once more the humble will rejoice in the
　　LORD;
　　the needy will rejoice in the Holy One of
　　Israel.
20 The ruthless will vanish,
　　the mockers will disappear,
　　and all who have an eye for evil will be
　　cut down—
21 those who with a word make a man out to be
　　guilty,
　　who ensnare the defender in court
　　and with false testimony deprive the
　　innocent of justice.

22 Therefore this is what the LORD, who redeemed Abraham, says to the house of Jacob:

"No longer will Jacob be ashamed;
　　no longer will their faces grow pale.

THE MESSAGE

29.13-14 The Master said:

"These people make a big show of saying the
　　right thing,
　　but their hearts aren't in it.
Because they act like they're worshiping me
　　but don't mean it,
I'm going to step in and shock them awake,
　　astonish them, stand them on their ears.
The wise ones who had it all figured out
　　will be exposed as fools.
The smart people who thought they knew
　　everything
　　will turn out to know nothing."

29.15-16 Doom to you! You pretend to have the inside
　　track.
　　You shut GOD out and work behind the
　　scenes,
Plotting the future as if you knew everything,
　　acting mysterious, never showing your
　　hand.
You have everything backward!
　　You treat the potter as a lump of clay.
Does a book say to its author,
　　"He didn't write a word of me"?
Does a meal say to the woman who cooked it,
　　"She had nothing to do with this"?

29.17-21 And then before you know it,
　　and without you having anything to do
　　with it,
Wasted Lebanon will be transformed into lush
　　gardens,
　　and Mount Carmel reforested.
At that time the deaf will hear
　　word-for-word what's been written.
After a lifetime in the dark,
　　the blind will see.
The castoffs of society will be laughing and
　　dancing in GOD,
　　the down-and-outs shouting praise to The
　　Holy of Israel.
For there'll be no more gangs on the street.
　　Cynical scoffers will be an extinct species.
Those who never missed a chance to hurt or
　　demean
　　will never be heard of again:
Gone the people who corrupted the courts,
　　gone the people who cheated the poor,
　　gone the people who victimized the
　　innocent.

29.22-24 And finally this, GOD's Message for the family
　　of Jacob,
　　the same GOD who redeemed Abraham:
"No longer will Jacob hang his head in shame,
　　no longer grow gaunt and pale with
　　waiting.

---

a 13 Hebrew; Septuagint *They worship me in vain; / their
teachings are but rules taught by men*

NEW INTERNATIONAL VERSION	THE MESSAGE

NEW INTERNATIONAL VERSION

23 When they see among them their children,
the work of my hands,
they will keep my name holy;
they will acknowledge the holiness of the
Holy One of Jacob,
and will stand in awe of the God of Israel.
24 Those who are wayward in spirit will gain
understanding;
those who complain will accept
instruction."

WOE TO THE OBSTINATE NATION

30 "Woe to the obstinate children,"
declares the LORD,
"to those who carry out plans that are not
mine,
forming an alliance, but not by my Spirit,
heaping sin upon sin;
2 who go down to Egypt
without consulting me;
who look for help to Pharaoh's protection,
to Egypt's shade for refuge.
3 But Pharaoh's protection will be to your
shame,
Egypt's shade will bring you disgrace.
4 Though they have officials in Zoan
and their envoys have arrived in Hanes,
5 everyone will be put to shame
because of a people useless to them,
who bring neither help nor advantage,
but only shame and disgrace."

6 An oracle concerning the animals of the Negev:

Through a land of hardship and distress,
of lions and lionesses,
of adders and darting snakes,
the envoys carry their riches on donkeys'
backs,
their treasures on the humps of camels,
to that unprofitable nation,
7   to Egypt, whose help is utterly useless.
Therefore I call her
Rahab the Do-Nothing.

8 Go now, write it on a tablet for them,
inscribe it on a scroll,
that for the days to come
it may be an everlasting witness.
9 These are rebellious people, deceitful
children,
children unwilling to listen to the LORD's
instruction.
10 They say to the seers,
"See no more visions!"

THE MESSAGE

For he's going to see his children,
my personal gift to him—lots of children.
And these children will honor me
by living holy lives.
In holy worship they'll honor the Holy One of
Jacob
and stand in holy awe of the God of Israel.
Those who got off-track will get back
on-track,
and complainers and whiners learn
gratitude."

ALL SHOW, NO SUBSTANCE

30.1-5 **30** "Doom, rebel children!"
GOD's Decree.
"You make plans, but not mine.
You make deals, but not in my Spirit.
You pile sin on sin,
one sin on top of another,
Going off to Egypt
without so much as asking me,
Running off to Pharaoh for protection,
expecting to hide out in Egypt.
Well, some protection Pharaoh will be!
Some hideout, Egypt!
They look big and important, true,
with officials strategically established in
Zoan in the north and Hanes in the south,
but there's nothing to them.
Anyone stupid enough to trust them
will end up looking stupid—
All show, no substance,
an embarrassing farce."

30.6-7 And this note on the animals of the Negev
encountered on the road to Egypt:
A most dangerous, treacherous route,
menaced by lions and deadly snakes.
And you're going to lug all your stuff down
there,
your donkeys and camels loaded down
with bribes,
Thinking you can buy protection
from that hollow farce of a nation?
Egypt is all show, no substance.
My name for her is Toothless Dragon.

THIS IS A REBEL GENERATION

30.8-11 So, go now and write all this down.
Put it in a book
So that the record will be there
to instruct the coming generations,
Because this is a rebel generation,
a people who lie,
A people unwilling to listen
to anything GOD tells them.
They tell their spiritual leaders,
"Don't bother us with irrelevancies."

NEW INTERNATIONAL VERSION

and to the prophets,
　"Give us no more visions of what is right!
Tell us pleasant things,
　prophesy illusions.
11 Leave this way,
　get off this path,
and stop confronting us
　with the Holy One of Israel!"

12 Therefore, this is what the Holy One of Israel says:

"Because you have rejected this message,
　relied on oppression
　and depended on deceit,
13 this sin will become for you
　like a high wall, cracked and bulging,
　that collapses suddenly, in an instant.
14 It will break in pieces like pottery,
　shattered so mercilessly
that among its pieces not a fragment will be
　　found
for taking coals from a hearth
　or scooping water out of a cistern."

15 This is what the Sovereign LORD, the Holy One of Israel, says:

"In repentance and rest is your salvation,
　in quietness and trust is your strength,
　but you would have none of it.
16 You said, 'No, we will flee on horses.'
　Therefore you will flee!
You said, 'We will ride off on swift horses.'
　Therefore your pursuers will be swift!
17 A thousand will flee
　at the threat of one;
at the threat of five
　you will all flee away,
till you are left
　like a flagstaff on a mountaintop,
　like a banner on a hill."

18 Yet the LORD longs to be gracious to you;
　he rises to show you compassion.
For the LORD is a God of justice.
　Blessed are all who wait for him!

19 O people of Zion, who live in Jerusalem, you will weep no more. How gracious he will be when you cry for help! As soon as he hears, he

THE MESSAGE

They tell their preachers,
　"Don't waste our time on impracticalities.
Tell us what makes us feel better.
　Don't bore us with obsolete religion.
That stuff means nothing to us.
　Quit hounding us with The Holy of Israel."

30.12-14 Therefore, The Holy of Israel says this:
　"Because you scorn this Message,
Preferring to live by injustice
　and shape your lives on lies,
This perverse way of life
　will be like a towering, badly built wall
That slowly, slowly tilts and shifts,
　and then one day, without warning,
　　collapses—
Smashed to bits like a piece of pottery,
　smashed beyond recognition or repair,
Useless, a pile of debris
　to be swept up and thrown in the trash."

GOD TAKES THE TIME TO DO EVERYTHING RIGHT

30.15-17 GOD, the Master, The Holy of Israel,
　has this solemn counsel:
"Your salvation requires you to turn back
　　to me
and stop your silly efforts to save
　　yourselves.
Your strength will come from settling down
　in complete dependence on me—
The very thing
　you've been unwilling to do.
You've said, 'Nothing doing! We'll rush off on
　　horseback!'
You'll rush off, all right! Just not far
　　enough!
You've said, 'We'll ride off on fast horses!'
　Do you think your pursuers ride old nags?
Think again: A thousand of you will scatter
　　before one attacker.
Before a mere five you'll all run off.
There'll be nothing left of you—
　a flagpole on a hill with no flag,
　a signpost on a roadside with the sign torn
　　off."

30.18 But GOD's not finished. He's waiting around to
　be gracious to you.
He's gathering strength to show mercy to
　you.
GOD takes the time to do everything right—
　everything.
Those who wait around for him are the
　lucky ones.

30.19-22 Oh yes, people of Zion, citizens of Jerusalem, your time of tears is over. Cry for help and you'll find it's grace and more grace. The mo-

NEW INTERNATIONAL VERSION

will answer you. ²⁰Although the Lord gives you the bread of adversity and the water of affliction, your teachers will be hidden no more; with your own eyes you will see them. ²¹Whether you turn to the right or to the left, your ears will hear a voice behind you, saying, "This is the way; walk in it." ²²Then you will defile your idols overlaid with silver and your images covered with gold; you will throw them away like a menstrual cloth and say to them, "Away with you!"

²³He will also send you rain for the seed you sow in the ground, and the food that comes from the land will be rich and plentiful. In that day your cattle will graze in broad meadows. ²⁴The oxen and donkeys that work the soil will eat fodder and mash, spread out with fork and shovel. ²⁵In the day of great slaughter, when the towers fall, streams of water will flow on every high mountain and every lofty hill. ²⁶The moon will shine like the sun, and the sunlight will be seven times brighter, like the light of seven full days, when the LORD binds up the bruises of his people and heals the wounds he inflicted.

²⁷See, the Name of the LORD comes from afar,
  with burning anger and dense clouds of
    smoke;
  his lips are full of wrath,
    and his tongue is a consuming fire.
²⁸His breath is like a rushing torrent,
    rising up to the neck.
  He shakes the nations in the sieve of
    destruction;
  he places in the jaws of the peoples
    a bit that leads them astray.
²⁹And you will sing
    as on the night you celebrate a holy
      festival;
  your hearts will rejoice
    as when people go up with flutes
  to the mountain of the LORD,
    to the Rock of Israel.
³⁰The LORD will cause men to hear his majestic
    voice
  and will make them see his arm coming
    down
  with raging anger and consuming fire,
    with cloudburst, thunderstorm and hail.
³¹The voice of the LORD will shatter Assyria;
    with his scepter he will strike them down.
³²Every stroke the LORD lays on them
    with his punishing rod
  will be to the music of tambourines and
    harps,
    as he fights them in battle with the blows
      of his arm.

THE MESSAGE

ment he hears, he'll answer. Just as the Master kept you alive during the hard times, he'll keep your teacher alive and present among you. Your teacher will be right there, local and on the job, urging you on whenever you wander left or right: "This is the right road. Walk down this road." You'll scrap your expensive and fashionable god-images. You'll throw them in the trash as so much garbage, saying, "Good riddance!"

30.23-26   God will provide rain for the seeds you sow. The grain that grows will be abundant. Your cattle will range far and wide. Oblivious to war and earthquake, the oxen and donkeys you use for hauling and plowing will be fed well near running brooks that flow freely from mountains and hills. Better yet, on the Day GOD heals his people of the wounds and bruises from the time of punishment, moonlight will flare into sunlight, and sunlight, like a whole week of sunshine at once, will flood the land.

✠

30.27-28 Look, GOD's on his way,
    and from a long way off!
  Smoking with anger,
    immense as he comes into view,
  Words steaming from his mouth,
    searing, indicting words!
  A torrent of words, a flash flood of words
    sweeping everyone into the vortex of his
      words.
  He'll shake down the nations in a sieve of
    destruction,
    herd them into a dead end.

30.29-33 But *you* will sing,
    sing through an all-night holy feast!
  Your hearts will burst with song,
    make music like the sound of flutes on
      parade,
  En route to the mountain of GOD,
    on the way to the Rock of Israel.
  GOD will sound out in grandiose thunder,
    display his hammering arm,
  Furiously angry, showering sparks—
    cloudburst, storm, hail!
  Oh yes, at GOD's thunder
    Assyria will cower under the clubbing.
  Every blow GOD lands on them with his club
    is in time to the music of drums and pipes,
  GOD in all-out, two-fisted battle,
    fighting against them.

NEW INTERNATIONAL VERSION

33 Topheth has long been prepared;
  it has been made ready for the king.
Its fire pit has been made deep and wide,
  with an abundance of fire and wood;
the breath of the LORD,
  like a stream of burning sulfur,
  sets it ablaze.

WOE TO THOSE WHO RELY ON EGYPT

31 Woe to those who go down to Egypt for
      help,
  who rely on horses,
who trust in the multitude of their chariots
  and in the great strength of their
      horsemen,
but do not look to the Holy One of Israel,
  or seek help from the LORD.
2 Yet he too is wise and can bring disaster;
  he does not take back his words.
He will rise up against the house of the
      wicked,
  against those who help evildoers.
3 But the Egyptians are men and not God;
  their horses are flesh and not spirit.
When the LORD stretches out his hand,
  he who helps will stumble,
  he who is helped will fall;
  both will perish together.

4 This is what the LORD says to me:

"As a lion growls,
  a great lion over his prey—
and though a whole band of shepherds
  is called together against him,
he is not frightened by their shouts
  or disturbed by their clamor—
so the LORD Almighty will come down
  to do battle on Mount Zion and on its
      heights.
5 Like birds hovering overhead,
  the LORD Almighty will shield Jerusalem;
he will shield it and deliver it,
  he will 'pass over' it and will rescue it."

6 Return to him you have so greatly revolted
against, O Israelites. 7 For in that day every one
of you will reject the idols of silver and gold
your sinful hands have made.

8 "Assyria will fall by a sword that is not of
      man;
  a sword, not of mortals, will devour them.
They will flee before the sword
  and their young men will be put to forced
      labor.

THE MESSAGE

Topheth's fierce fires are well prepared,
  ready for the Assyrian king.
The Topheth furnace is deep and wide,
  well stoked with hot-burning wood.
GOD's breath, like a river of burning pitch,
  starts the fire.

IMPRESSED BY MILITARY MATHEMATICS

31.1-3 **31** Doom to those who go off to Egypt
        thinking that horses can help them,
Impressed by military mathematics,
  awed by sheer numbers of chariots and
      riders—
And to The Holy of Israel, not even a glance,
  not so much as a prayer to GOD.
Still, he must be reckoned with,
  a most wise God who knows what he's
      doing.
He can call down catastrophe.
  He's a God who does what he says.
He intervenes in the work of those who do
      wrong,
  stands up against interfering evildoers.
Egyptians are mortal, not God,
  and their horses are flesh, not Spirit.
When GOD gives the signal, helpers and
      helped alike
  will fall in a heap and share the same dirt
      grave.

☩

31.4-5 This is what GOD told me:

"Like a lion, king of the beasts,
  that gnaws and chews and worries its prey,
Not fazed in the least by a bunch of shepherds
  who arrive to chase it off,
So GOD-of-the-Angel-Armies comes down
  to fight on Mount Zion, to make war from
      its heights.
And like a huge eagle hovering in the sky,
  GOD-of-the-Angel-Armies protects Jerusa-
      lem.
I'll protect and rescue it.
  Yes, I'll hover and deliver."

31.6-7 Repent, return, dear Israel, to the One you
so cruelly abandoned. On the day you return,
you'll throw away—every last one of you—the
no-gods your sinful hands made from metal
and wood.

31.8-9 "Assyrians will fall dead,
  killed by a sword-thrust but not by a soldier,
  laid low by a sword not swung by a mortal.
Assyrians will run from that sword, run for
      their lives,
  and their prize young men made slaves.

NEW INTERNATIONAL VERSION

⁹ Their stronghold will fall because of terror;
  at sight of the battle standard their
    commanders will panic,"
declares the LORD,
  whose fire is in Zion,
  whose furnace is in Jerusalem.

THE KINGDOM OF RIGHTEOUSNESS

32 See, a king will reign in righteousness
    and rulers will rule with justice.
² Each man will be like a shelter from the
      wind
  and a refuge from the storm,
  like streams of water in the desert
    and the shadow of a great rock in a thirsty
      land.

³ Then the eyes of those who see will no
      longer be closed,
  and the ears of those who hear will listen.
⁴ The mind of the rash will know and
      understand,
  and the stammering tongue will be fluent
    and clear.
⁵ No longer will the fool be called noble
  nor the scoundrel be highly respected.
⁶ For the fool speaks folly,
  his mind is busy with evil:
He practices ungodliness
  and spreads error concerning the LORD;
the hungry he leaves empty
  and from the thirsty he withholds water.
⁷ The scoundrel's methods are wicked,
  he makes up evil schemes
to destroy the poor with lies,
  even when the plea of the needy is just.
⁸ But the noble man makes noble plans,
  and by noble deeds he stands.

THE WOMEN OF JERUSALEM

⁹ You women who are so complacent,
  rise up and listen to me;
you daughters who feel secure,
  hear what I have to say!
¹⁰ In little more than a year
  you who feel secure will tremble;
the grape harvest will fail,
  and the harvest of fruit will not come.
¹¹ Tremble, you complacent women;
  shudder, you daughters who feel secure!
Strip off your clothes,
  put sackcloth around your waists.
¹² Beat your breasts for the pleasant fields,
  for the fruitful vines
¹³ and for the land of my people,
  a land overgrown with thorns and
    briers—

THE MESSAGE

Terrorized, that rock-solid people will fall to
    pieces,
  their leaders scatter hysterically."
GOD's Decree on Assyria.
  His fire blazes in Zion,
  his furnace burns hot in Jerusalem.

SAFE HOUSES, QUIET GARDENS

32:1-8 **32** But look! A king will rule in the right
        way,
  and his leaders will carry out justice.
Each one will stand as a shelter from high
      winds,
  provide safe cover in stormy weather.
Each will be cool running water in parched
      land,
  a huge granite outcrop giving shade in the
    desert.
Anyone who looks will see,
  anyone who listens will hear.
The impulsive will make sound decisions,
  the tongue-tied will speak with eloquence.
No more will fools become celebrities,
  nor crooks be rewarded with fame.
For fools are fools and that's that,
  thinking up new ways to do mischief.
They leave a wake of wrecked lives
  and lies about GOD,
Turning their backs on the homeless hungry,
  ignoring those dying of thirst in the streets.
And the crooks? Underhanded sneaks they
      are,
  inventive in sin and scandal,
Exploiting the poor with scams and lies,
  unmoved by the victimized poor.
But those who are noble make noble plans,
  and stand for what is noble.

☩

32:9-14 Take your stand, indolent women!
    Listen to me!
Indulgent, indolent women,
  listen closely to what I have to say.
In just a little over a year from now,
  you'll be shaken out of your lazy lives.
The grape harvest will fail,
  and there'll be no fruit on the trees.
Oh tremble, you indolent women.
  Get serious, you pampered dolls!
Strip down and discard your silk fineries.
  Put on funeral clothes.
Shed honest tears for the lost harvest,
  the failed vintage.
Weep for my people's gardens and farms
  that grow nothing but thistles and
    thornbushes.

NEW INTERNATIONAL VERSION	THE MESSAGE

yes, mourn for all houses of merriment
 and for this city of revelry.
[14] The fortress will be abandoned,
 the noisy city deserted;
 citadel and watchtower will become a
 wasteland forever,
 the delight of donkeys, a pasture for
 flocks,
[15] till the Spirit is poured upon us from on
 high,
 and the desert becomes a fertile field,
 and the fertile field seems like a forest.
[16] Justice will dwell in the desert
 and righteousness live in the fertile field.
[17] The fruit of righteousness will be peace;
 the effect of righteousness will be
 quietness and confidence forever.
[18] My people will live in peaceful dwelling
 places,
 in secure homes,
 in undisturbed places of rest.
[19] Though hail flattens the forest
 and the city is leveled completely,
[20] how blessed you will be,
 sowing your seed by every stream,
 and letting your cattle and donkeys range
 free.

DISTRESS AND HELP

33 Woe to you, O destroyer,
 you who have not been destroyed!
 Woe to you, O traitor,
 you who have not been betrayed!
 When you stop destroying,
 you will be destroyed;
 when you stop betraying,
 you will be betrayed.

[2] O LORD, be gracious to us;
 we long for you.
 Be our strength every morning,
 our salvation in time of distress.
[3] At the thunder of your voice, the peoples flee;
 when you rise up, the nations scatter.
[4] Your plunder, O nations, is harvested as by
 young locusts;
 like a swarm of locusts men pounce on it.

[5] The LORD is exalted, for he dwells on high;
 he will fill Zion with justice and
 righteousness.
[6] He will be the sure foundation for your
 times,
 a rich store of salvation and wisdom and
 knowledge;
 the fear of the LORD is the key to this
 treasure. [a]

Cry tears, real tears, for the happy homes no
 longer happy,
 the merry city no longer merry.
The royal palace is deserted,
 the bustling city quiet as a morgue,
The emptied parks and playgrounds
 taken over by wild animals,
 delighted with their new home.

32.15-20 Yes, weep and grieve until the Spirit is poured
 down on us from above
And the badlands desert grows crops
 and the fertile fields become forests.
Justice will move into the badlands desert.
 Right will build a home in the fertile field.
And where there's Right, there'll be Peace
 and the progeny of Right: quiet lives and
 endless trust.
My people will live in a peaceful
 neighborhood—
 in safe houses, in quiet gardens.
The forest of your pride will be clear-cut,
 the city showing off your power leveled.
But you will enjoy a blessed life,
 planting well-watered fields and gardens,
 with your farm animals grazing freely.

THE GROUND UNDER OUR FEET MOURNS

33.1 **33** Doom to you, Destroyer,
 not yet destroyed;
And doom to you, Betrayer,
 not yet betrayed.
When you finish destroying,
 your turn will come—destroyed!
When you quit betraying,
 your turn will come—betrayed!

33.2-4 GOD, treat us kindly. You're our only hope.
 First thing in the morning, be there for us!
 When things go bad, help us out!
You spoke in thunder and everyone ran.
 You showed up and nations scattered.
Your people, for a change, got in on the loot,
 picking the field clean of the enemy spoils.

33.5-6 GOD is supremely esteemed. His center holds.
 Zion brims over with all that is just and
 right.
GOD keeps your days stable and secure—
 salvation, wisdom, and knowledge in
 surplus,
 and best of all, Zion's treasure, Fear-of-GOD.

---

a 6 Or *is a treasure from him*

NEW INTERNATIONAL VERSION

[7] Look, their brave men cry aloud in the
            streets;
      the envoys of peace weep bitterly.
[8] The highways are deserted,
      no travelers are on the roads.
   The treaty is broken,
      its witnesses[a] are despised,
      no one is respected.
[9] The land mourns[b] and wastes away,
      Lebanon is ashamed and withers;
   Sharon is like the Arabah,
      and Bashan and Carmel drop their leaves.

[10] "Now will I arise," says the LORD.
      "Now will I be exalted;
      now will I be lifted up.
[11] You conceive chaff,
      you give birth to straw;
      your breath is a fire that consumes you.
[12] The peoples will be burned as if to lime;
      like cut thornbushes they will be set
            ablaze."

[13] You who are far away, hear what I have done;
      you who are near, acknowledge my
            power!
[14] The sinners in Zion are terrified;
      trembling grips the godless:
   "Who of us can dwell with the consuming
            fire?
   Who of us can dwell with everlasting
            burning?"
[15] He who walks righteously
      and speaks what is right,
   who rejects gain from extortion
      and keeps his hand from accepting bribes,
   who stops his ears against plots of murder
      and shuts his eyes against contemplating
            evil—
[16] this is the man who will dwell on the heights,
      whose refuge will be the mountain fortress.
   His bread will be supplied,
      and water will not fail him.

[17] Your eyes will see the king in his beauty
      and view a land that stretches afar.
[18] In your thoughts you will ponder the former
            terror:
   "Where is that chief officer?
   Where is the one who took the revenue?
   Where is the officer in charge of the
            towers?"
[19] You will see those arrogant people no more,
      those people of an obscure speech,
      with their strange, incomprehensible
            tongue.

---

[a] 8 Dead Sea Scrolls; Masoretic Text / *the cities*
[b] 9 Or *dries up*

THE MESSAGE

33:7-9 But look! Listen!
      Tough men weep openly.
      Peacemaking diplomats are in bitter tears.
   The roads are empty—
      not a soul out on the streets.
   The peace treaty is broken,
      its conditions violated,
      its signers reviled.
   The very ground under our feet mourns,
      the Lebanon mountains hang their heads,
   Flowering Sharon is a weed-choked gully,
      and the forests of Bashan and Carmel? Bare
            branches.

33:10-12 "Now I'm stepping in," GOD says.
      "From now on, I'm taking over.
      The gloves come off. Now see how mighty
            I am.
   There's nothing to you.
      Pregnant with chaff, you produce straw
            babies;
      full of hot air, you self-destruct.
   You're good for nothing but fertilizer and fuel.
      Earth to earth—and the sooner the better.

33:13-14 "If you're far away,
      get the reports on what I've done,
   And if you're in the neighborhood,
      pay attention to my record.
   The sinners in Zion are rightly terrified;
      the godless are at their wit's end:
   'Who among us can survive this firestorm?
      Who of us can get out of this purge with
            our lives?'"

33:15-16 The answer's simple:
      Live right,
      speak the truth,
      despise exploitation,
      refuse bribes,
      reject violence,
      avoid evil amusements.
   This is how you raise your standard of living!
      A safe and stable way to live.
      A nourishing, satisfying way to live.

GOD MAKES ALL THE DECISIONS HERE

33:17-19 Oh, you'll see the king—a beautiful sight!
      And you'll take in the wide vistas of land.
   In your mind you'll go over the old terrors:
      "What happened to that Assyrian inspector
            who condemned and confiscated?
   And the one who gouged us of taxes?
      And that cheating moneychanger?"
   Gone! Out of sight forever! Their insolence
      nothing now but a fading stain on the carpet!
   No more putting up with a language you can't
            understand,
      no more sounds of gibberish in your ears.

NEW INTERNATIONAL VERSION

²⁰Look upon Zion, the city of our festivals;
   your eyes will see Jerusalem,
   a peaceful abode, a tent that will not be
      moved;
   its stakes will never be pulled up,
      nor any of its ropes broken.
²¹There the LORD will be our Mighty One.
   It will be like a place of broad rivers and
      streams.
   No galley with oars will ride them,
      no mighty ship will sail them.
²²For the LORD is our judge,
   the LORD is our lawgiver,
   the LORD is our king;
      it is he who will save us.

²³Your rigging hangs loose:
   The mast is not held secure,
      the sail is not spread.
   Then an abundance of spoils will be divided
      and even the lame will carry off plunder.
²⁴No one living in Zion will say, "I am ill";
   and the sins of those who dwell there will
      be forgiven.

JUDGMENT AGAINST THE NATIONS

34 Come near, you nations, and listen;
   pay attention, you peoples!
   Let the earth hear, and all that is in it,
      the world, and all that comes out of it!
²The LORD is angry with all nations;
   his wrath is upon all their armies.
   He will totally destroy^a them,
      he will give them over to slaughter.
³Their slain will be thrown out,
   their dead bodies will send up a stench;
   the mountains will be soaked with their
      blood.
⁴All the stars of the heavens will be dissolved
   and the sky rolled up like a scroll;
   all the starry host will fall
      like withered leaves from the vine,
      like shriveled figs from the fig tree.

⁵My sword has drunk its fill in the heavens;
   see, it descends in judgment on Edom,
   the people I have totally destroyed.
⁶The sword of the LORD is bathed in blood,
   it is covered with fat—
   the blood of lambs and goats,
      fat from the kidneys of rams.

THE MESSAGE

^{33.20-22} Just take a look at Zion, will you?
   Centering our worship in festival feasts!
Feast your eyes on Jerusalem,
   a quiet and permanent place to live.
No more pulling up stakes and moving on,
   no more patched-together lean-tos.
Instead, GOD! GOD majestic, God himself the
      place
   in a country of broad rivers and streams,
But rivers blocked to invading ships,
   off-limits to predatory pirates.
For GOD makes all the decisions here. GOD is
      our king.
   GOD runs this place and he'll keep us safe.

^{33.23} Ha! Your sails are in shreds,
   your mast wobbling,
   your hold leaking.
The plunder is free for the taking, free for
      all—
   for weak and strong, insiders and outsiders.

^{33.24} No one in Zion will say, "I'm sick."
   Best of all, they'll all live guilt-free.

THE FIRES BURNING DAY AND NIGHT

^{34.1} **34** Draw in close now, nations. Listen
      carefully,
   you people. Pay attention!
Earth, you too, and everything in you.
   World, and all that comes from you.

^{34.2-4} And here's why: GOD is angry,
   good and angry with all the nations,
So blazingly angry at their arms and armies
   that he's going to rid earth of them, wipe
      them out.
The corpses, thrown in a heap,
   will stink like the town dump in midsummer,
Their blood flowing off the mountains
   like creeks in spring runoff.
Stars will fall out of the sky
   like overripe, rotting fruit in the orchard,
And the sky itself will be folded up like a
      blanket
   and put away in a closet.
All that army of stars, shriveled to nothing,
   like leaves and fruit in autumn, dropping
      and rotting!

^{34.5-7} "Once I've finished with earth and sky,
   I'll start in on Edom.
I'll come down hard on Edom,
   a people I've slated for total termination."
GOD has a sword, thirsty for blood and more
      blood,
   a sword hungry for well-fed flesh,
Lamb and goat blood,
   the suet-rich kidneys of rams.

---

^a 2 The Hebrew term refers to the irrevocable giving over of
things or persons to the LORD, often by totally destroying
them; also in verse 5.

NEW INTERNATIONAL VERSION

For the LORD has a sacrifice in Bozrah
    and a great slaughter in Edom.
⁷ And the wild oxen will fall with them,
    the bull calves and the great bulls.
Their land will be drenched with blood,
    and the dust will be soaked with fat.

⁸ For the LORD has a day of vengeance,
    a year of retribution, to uphold Zion's
    cause.
⁹ Edom's streams will be turned into pitch,
    her dust into burning sulfur;
    her land will become blazing pitch!
¹⁰ It will not be quenched night and day;
    its smoke will rise forever.
From generation to generation it will lie
    desolate;
    no one will ever pass through it again.
¹¹ The desert owl ᵃ and screech owl ᵃ will
    possess it;
    the great owl ᵃ and the raven will nest
    there.
God will stretch out over Edom
    the measuring line of chaos
    and the plumb line of desolation.
¹² Her nobles will have nothing there to be
    called a kingdom,
    all her princes will vanish away.
¹³ Thorns will overrun her citadels,
    nettles and brambles her strongholds.
She will become a haunt for jackals,
    a home for owls.
¹⁴ Desert creatures will meet with hyenas,
    and wild goats will bleat to each other;
there the night creatures will also repose
    and find for themselves places of rest.
¹⁵ The owl will nest there and lay eggs,
    she will hatch them, and care for her
      young under the shadow of her
      wings;
there also the falcons will gather,
    each with its mate.

¹⁶ Look in the scroll of the LORD and read:

None of these will be missing,
    not one will lack her mate.
For it is his mouth that has given the order,
    and his Spirit will gather them together.
¹⁷ He allots their portions;
    his hand distributes them by measure.
They will possess it forever
    and dwell there from generation to
      generation.

THE MESSAGE

Yes, GOD has scheduled a sacrifice in Bozrah,
    the capital,
    the whole country of Edom a
      slaughterhouse.
A wholesale slaughter, wild animals
    and farm animals alike slaughtered.
The whole country soaked with blood,
    all the ground greasy with fat.

³⁴·⁸⁻¹⁵ It's GOD's scheduled time for vengeance,
    the year all Zion's accounts are settled.
Edom's streams will flow sluggish, thick with
    pollution,
    the soil sterile, poisoned with waste,
The whole country
    a smoking, stinking garbage dump—
The fires burning day and night,
    the skies black with endless smoke.
Generation after generation of wasteland—
    no more travelers through this country!
Vultures and skunks will police the streets;
    owls and crows will feel at home there.
God will reverse creation. Chaos!
    He will cancel fertility. Emptiness!
Leaders will have no one to lead.
    They'll name it No Kingdom There,
A country where all kings
    and princes are unemployed.
Thistles will take over, covering the castles,
    fortresses conquered by weeds and
      thornbushes.
Wild dogs will prowl the ruins,
    ostriches have the run of the place.
Wildcats and hyenas will hunt together,
    demons and devils dance through the
      night.
The night-demon Lilith, evil and rapacious,
    will establish permanent quarters.
Scavenging carrion birds will breed and
      brood,
    infestations of ominous evil.

³⁴·¹⁶⁻¹⁷ Get and read GOD's book:
    None of this is going away,
    this breeding, brooding evil.
GOD has personally commanded it all.
    His Spirit set it in motion.
GOD has assigned them their place,
    decreed their fate in detail.
This is permanent—
    generation after generation, the same old
      thing.

ᵃ 11 The precise identification of these birds is uncertain.

NEW INTERNATIONAL VERSION

JOY OF THE REDEEMED

35 The desert and the parched land will be glad;
    the wilderness will rejoice and blossom.
Like the crocus, ²it will burst into bloom;
    it will rejoice greatly and shout for joy.
The glory of Lebanon will be given to it,
    the splendor of Carmel and Sharon;
they will see the glory of the LORD,
    the splendor of our God.

³Strengthen the feeble hands,
    steady the knees that give way;
⁴say to those with fearful hearts,
    "Be strong, do not fear;
your God will come,
    he will come with vengeance;
with divine retribution
    he will come to save you."

⁵Then will the eyes of the blind be opened
    and the ears of the deaf unstopped.
⁶Then will the lame leap like a deer,
    and the mute tongue shout for joy.
Water will gush forth in the wilderness
    and streams in the desert.
⁷The burning sand will become a pool,
    the thirsty ground bubbling springs.
In the haunts where jackals once lay,
    grass and reeds and papyrus will grow.

⁸And a highway will be there;
    it will be called the Way of Holiness.
The unclean will not journey on it;
    it will be for those who walk in that Way;
    wicked fools will not go about on it. ᵃ
⁹No lion will be there,
    nor will any ferocious beast get up on it;
    they will not be found there.
But only the redeemed will walk there,
10   and the ransomed of the LORD will return.
They will enter Zion with singing;
    everlasting joy will crown their heads.
Gladness and joy will overtake them,
    and sorrow and sighing will flee away.

SENNACHERIB THREATENS JERUSALEM

36 In the fourteenth year of King Hezekiah's reign, Sennacherib king of Assyria attacked all the fortified cities of Judah and cap-

THE MESSAGE

THE VOICELESS BREAK INTO SONG

35.1-2 **35** Wilderness and desert will sing joyously,
    the badlands will celebrate and flower—
Like the crocus in spring, bursting into blossom,
    a symphony of song and color.
Mountain glories of Lebanon—a gift.
    Awesome Carmel, stunning Sharon—gifts.
GOD's resplendent glory, fully on display.
    GOD awesome, GOD majestic.

35.3-4 Energize the limp hands,
    strengthen the rubbery knees.
Tell fearful souls,
    "Courage! Take heart!
GOD is here, right here,
    on his way to put things right
And redress all wrongs.
    He's on his way! He'll save you!"

35.5-7 Blind eyes will be opened,
    deaf ears unstopped,
Lame men and women will leap like deer,
    the voiceless break into song.
Springs of water will burst out in the wilderness,
    streams flow in the desert.
Hot sands will become a cool oasis,
    thirsty ground a splashing fountain.
Even lowly jackals will have water to drink,
    and barren grasslands flourish richly.

35.8-10 There will be a highway
    called the Holy Road.
No one rude or rebellious
    is permitted on this road.
It's for GOD's people exclusively—
    impossible to get lost on this road.
    Not even fools can get lost on it.
No lions on this road,
    no dangerous wild animals—
Nothing and no one dangerous or threatening.
    Only the redeemed will walk on it.
The people GOD has ransomed
    will come back on this road.
They'll sing as they make their way home to Zion,
    unfading halos of joy encircling their heads,
Welcomed home with gifts of joy and gladness
    as all sorrows and sighs scurry into the night.

IT'S THEIR FATE THAT'S AT STAKE

36.1-3 **36** In the fourteenth year of King Hezekiah, Sennacherib king of Assyria made war on all the fortress cities of Judah and took

---

ᵃ 8 Or / the simple will not stray from it

NEW INTERNATIONAL VERSION

tured them. ²Then the king of Assyria sent his field commander with a large army from Lachish to King Hezekiah at Jerusalem. When the commander stopped at the aqueduct of the Upper Pool, on the road to the Washerman's Field, ³Eliakim son of Hilkiah the palace administrator, Shebna the secretary, and Joah son of Asaph the recorder went out to him.

⁴The field commander said to them, "Tell Hezekiah,

" 'This is what the great king, the king of Assyria, says: On what are you basing this confidence of yours? ⁵You say you have strategy and military strength—but you speak only empty words. On whom are you depending, that you rebel against me? ⁶Look now, you are depending on Egypt, that splintered reed of a staff, which pierces a man's hand and wounds him if he leans on it! Such is Pharaoh king of Egypt to all who depend on him. ⁷And if you say to me, "We are depending on the LORD our God"—isn't he the one whose high places and altars Hezekiah removed, saying to Judah and Jerusalem, "You must worship before this altar"?

⁸" 'Come now, make a bargain with my master, the king of Assyria: I will give you two thousand horses—if you can put riders on them! ⁹How then can you repulse one officer of the least of my master's officials, even though you are depending on Egypt for chariots and horsemen? ¹⁰Furthermore, have I come to attack and destroy this land without the LORD? The LORD himself told me to march against this country and destroy it.' "

¹¹Then Eliakim, Shebna and Joah said to the field commander, "Please speak to your servants in Aramaic, since we understand it. Don't speak to us in Hebrew in the hearing of the people on the wall."

¹²But the commander replied, "Was it only to your master and you that my master sent me to say these things, and not to the men sitting on the wall—who, like you, will have to eat their own filth and drink their own urine?"

¹³Then the commander stood and called out in Hebrew, "Hear the words of the great king, the king of Assyria! ¹⁴This is what the king says: Do not let Hezekiah deceive you. He cannot deliver you! ¹⁵Do not let Hezekiah persuade you to trust in the LORD when he says, 'The LORD will surely deliver us; this city will not be given into the hand of the king of Assyria.'

THE MESSAGE

them. Then the king of Assyria sent his general, the "Rabshekah," accompanied by a huge army, from Lachish to Jerusalem to King Hezekiah. The general stopped at the aqueduct where it empties into the upper pool on the road to the public laundry. Three men went out to meet him: Eliakim son of Hilkiah, in charge of the palace; Shebna the secretary; and Joah son of Asaph, the official historian.

36.4-7   The Rabshekah said to them, "Tell Hezekiah that the Great King, the king of Assyria, says this: 'What kind of backing do you think you have against me? You're bluffing and I'm calling your bluff. Your words are no match for my weapons. What kind of backup do you have now that you've rebelled against me? Egypt? Don't make me laugh. Egypt is a rubber crutch. Lean on Egypt and you'll end up flat on your face. That's all Pharaoh king of Egypt is to anyone who leans on him. And if you try to tell me, "We're leaning on our GOD," isn't it a bit late? Hasn't Hezekiah just gotten rid of all the places of worship, telling you, "You've got to worship at *this* altar"?

36.8-9   " 'Be reasonable. Face the facts: My master the king of Assyria will give you two thousand horses if you can put riders on them. You can't do it, can you? So how do you think, depending on flimsy Egypt's chariots and riders, you can stand up against even the lowest-ranking captain in my master's army?

36.10   " 'And besides, do you think I came all this way to destroy this land without first getting GOD's blessing? It was your GOD who told me, Make war on this land. Destroy it.' "

36.11   Eliakim, Shebna, and Joah answered the Rabshekah, "Please talk to us in Aramaic. We understand Aramaic. Don't talk to us in Hebrew within earshot of all the people gathered around."

36.12   But the Rabshekah replied, "Do you think my master has sent me to give this message to your master and you but not also to the people clustered here? It's their fate that's at stake. They're the ones who are going to end up eating their own excrement and drinking their own urine."

36.13-15   Then the Rabshekah stood up and called out loudly in Hebrew, the common language, "Listen to the message of the great king, the king of Assyria! Don't listen to Hezekiah's lies. He can't save you. And don't pay any attention to Hezekiah's pious sermons telling you to lean on GOD, telling you 'GOD will save us, depend on it. GOD won't let this city fall to the king of Assyria.'

NEW INTERNATIONAL VERSION

¹⁶"Do not listen to Hezekiah. This is what the king of Assyria says: Make peace with me and come out to me. Then every one of you will eat from his own vine and fig tree and drink water from his own cistern, ¹⁷until I come and take you to a land like your own—a land of grain and new wine, a land of bread and vineyards.

¹⁸"Do not let Hezekiah mislead you when he says, 'The LORD will deliver us.' Has the god of any nation ever delivered his land from the hand of the king of Assyria? ¹⁹Where are the gods of Hamath and Arpad? Where are the gods of Sepharvaim? Have they rescued Samaria from my hand? ²⁰Who of all the gods of these countries has been able to save his land from me? How then can the LORD deliver Jerusalem from my hand?"

²¹But the people remained silent and said nothing in reply, because the king had commanded, "Do not answer him."

²²Then Eliakim son of Hilkiah the palace administrator, Shebna the secretary, and Joah son of Asaph the recorder went to Hezekiah, with their clothes torn, and told him what the field commander had said.

JERUSALEM'S DELIVERANCE FORETOLD

37 When King Hezekiah heard this, he tore his clothes and put on sackcloth and went into the temple of the LORD. ²He sent Eliakim the palace administrator, Shebna the secretary, and the leading priests, all wearing sackcloth, to the prophet Isaiah son of Amoz. ³They told him, "This is what Hezekiah says: This day is a day of distress and rebuke and disgrace, as when children come to the point of birth and there is no strength to deliver them. ⁴It may be that the LORD your God will hear the words of the field commander, whom his master, the king of Assyria, has sent to ridicule the living God, and that he will rebuke him for the words the LORD your God has heard. Therefore pray for the remnant that still survives."

⁵When King Hezekiah's officials came to Isaiah, ⁶Isaiah said to them, "Tell your master, 'This is what the LORD says: Do not be afraid of what you have heard—those words with which the underlings of the king of Assyria have blasphemed me. ⁷Listen! I am going to put a spirit in him so that when he hears a certain report, he will return to his own country, and there I will have him cut down with the sword.'"

⁸When the field commander heard that the king of Assyria had left Lachish, he withdrew and found the king fighting against Libnah.

THE MESSAGE

36.16-20   "Don't listen to Hezekiah. Listen to the king of Assyria's offer: 'Make peace with me. Come and join me. Everyone will end up with a good life, with plenty of land and water, and eventually something far better. I'll turn you loose in wide open spaces, with more than enough fertile and productive land for everyone.' Don't let Hezekiah mislead you with his lies, 'GOD will save us.' Has that ever happened? Has any god in history ever gotten the best of the king of Assyria? Look around you. Where are the gods of Hamath and Arpad? The gods of Sepharvaim? Did the gods do anything for Samaria? Name one god that has ever saved its countries from me. So what makes you think that GOD could save Jerusalem from me?'"

36.21   The three men were silent. They said nothing, for the king had already commanded, "Don't answer him."

36.22   Then Eliakim son of Hilkiah, the palace administrator, Shebna the secretary, and Joah son of Asaph, the court historian, tearing their clothes in defeat and despair, went back and reported what the Rabshekah had said to Hezekiah.

THE ONLY GOD THERE IS

37.1-2   **37** When King Hezekiah heard the report, he also tore his clothes and dressed in rough, penitential burlap gunnysacks, and went into the sanctuary of GOD. He sent Eliakim the palace administrator, Shebna the secretary, and the senior priests, all of them also dressed in penitential burlap, to the prophet Isaiah son of Amoz.

37.3-4   They said to him, "Hezekiah says, 'This is a black day. We're in crisis. We're like pregnant women without even the strength to have a baby! Do you think your GOD heard what the Rabshekah said, sent by his master the king of Assyria to mock the living God? And do you think your GOD will do anything about it? Pray for us, Isaiah. Pray for those of us left here holding the fort!'"

37.5-7   Then King Hezekiah's servants came to Isaiah. Isaiah said, "Tell your master this: 'GOD's Message: Don't be upset by what you've heard, all those words the servants of the Assyrian king have used to mock me. I personally will take care of him. I'll arrange it so that he'll get a rumor of bad news back home and rush home to take care of it. And he'll die there. Killed—a violent death.'"

37.8   The Rabshekah left and found the king of Assyria fighting against Libnah. (He had gotten word that the king had left Lachish.)

NEW INTERNATIONAL VERSION

⁹Now Sennacherib received a report that Tirhakah, the Cushite*a* king ⌊of Egypt⌋, was marching out to fight against him. When he heard it, he sent messengers to Hezekiah with this word: ¹⁰"Say to Hezekiah king of Judah: Do not let the god you depend on deceive you when he says, 'Jerusalem will not be handed over to the king of Assyria.' ¹¹Surely you have heard what the kings of Assyria have done to all the countries, destroying them completely. And will you be delivered? ¹²Did the gods of the nations that were destroyed by my forefathers deliver them—the gods of Gozan, Haran, Rezeph and the people of Eden who were in Tel Assar? ¹³Where is the king of Hamath, the king of Arpad, the king of the city of Sepharvaim, or of Hena or Ivvah?"

HEZEKIAH'S PRAYER

¹⁴Hezekiah received the letter from the messengers and read it. Then he went up to the temple of the LORD and spread it out before the LORD. ¹⁵And Hezekiah prayed to the LORD: ¹⁶"O LORD Almighty, God of Israel, enthroned between the cherubim, you alone are God over all the kingdoms of the earth. You have made heaven and earth. ¹⁷Give ear, O LORD, and hear; open your eyes, O LORD, and see; listen to all the words Sennacherib has sent to insult the living God.

¹⁸"It is true, O LORD, that the Assyrian kings have laid waste all these peoples and their lands. ¹⁹They have thrown their gods into the fire and destroyed them, for they were not gods but only wood and stone, fashioned by human hands. ²⁰Now, O LORD our God, deliver us from his hand, so that all kingdoms on earth may know that you alone, O LORD, are God.*b*"

SENNACHERIB'S FALL

²¹Then Isaiah son of Amoz sent a message to Hezekiah: "This is what the LORD, the God of Israel, says: Because you have prayed to me concerning Sennacherib king of Assyria, ²²this is the word the LORD has spoken against him:

"The Virgin Daughter of Zion
    despises and mocks you.
The Daughter of Jerusalem
    tosses her head as you flee.
²³Who is it you have insulted and
    blasphemed?

THE MESSAGE

37.9-13 Just then the Assyrian king received an intelligence report on King Tirhakah of Ethiopia: "He is on his way to make war on you."

On hearing that, he sent messengers to Hezekiah with instructions to deliver this message: "Don't let your GOD, on whom you so naively lean, deceive you, promising that Jerusalem won't fall to the king of Assyria. Use your head! Look around at what the kings of Assyria have done all over the world—one country after another devastated! And do you think you're going to get off? Have any of the gods of any of these countries ever stepped in and saved them, even one of these nations my predecessors destroyed—Gozan, Haran, Rezeph, and the people of Eden who lived in Telassar? Look around. Do you see anything left of the king of Hamath, the king of Arpad, the king of the city of Sepharvaim, the king of Hena, the king of Ivvah?"

37.14 Hezekiah took the letter from the hands of the messengers and read it. Then he went into the sanctuary of GOD and spread the letter out before GOD.

37.15-20 Then Hezekiah prayed to GOD: "GOD-of-the-Angel-Armies, enthroned over the cherubim-angels, you are God, the only God there is, God of all kingdoms on earth. You *made* heaven and earth. Listen, O GOD, and hear. Look, O GOD, and see. Mark all these words of Sennacherib that he sent to mock the living God. It's quite true, O GOD, that the kings of Assyria have devastated all the nations and their lands. They've thrown their gods into the trash and burned them—no great achievement since they were no-gods anyway, gods made in workshops, carved from wood and chiseled from rock. An end to the no-gods! But now step in, O GOD, our God. Save us from him. Let all the kingdoms of earth know that you and you alone are GOD."

⊹

37.21-25 Then Isaiah son of Amoz sent this word to Hezekiah: "GOD's Message, the God of Israel: Because you brought King Sennacherib of Assyria to me in prayer, here is my answer, GOD's answer:

" 'She has no use for you, Sennacherib,
        nothing but contempt,
    this virgin daughter Zion.
She spits at you and turns on her heel,
    this daughter Jerusalem.

" 'Who do you think you've been mocking
        and reviling
    all these years?

---

a 9 That is, from the upper Nile region   *b 20* Dead Sea Scrolls (see also 2 Kings 19:19); Masoretic Text *alone are the* LORD

NEW INTERNATIONAL VERSION

Against whom have you raised your voice
and lifted your eyes in pride?
Against the Holy One of Israel!
24 By your messengers
you have heaped insults on the Lord.
And you have said,
'With my many chariots
I have ascended the heights of the mountains,
the utmost heights of Lebanon.
I have cut down its tallest cedars,
the choicest of its pines.
I have reached its remotest heights,
the finest of its forests.
25 I have dug wells in foreign lands[a]
and drunk the water there.
With the soles of my feet
I have dried up all the streams of Egypt.'

26 "Have you not heard?
Long ago I ordained it.
In days of old I planned it;
now I have brought it to pass,
that you have turned fortified cities
into piles of stone.
27 Their people, drained of power,
are dismayed and put to shame.
They are like plants in the field,
like tender green shoots,
like grass sprouting on the roof,
scorched[b] before it grows up.

28 "But I know where you stay
and when you come and go
and how you rage against me.
29 Because you rage against me
and because your insolence has reached
my ears,
I will put my hook in your nose
and my bit in your mouth,
and I will make you return
by the way you came.

30 "This will be the sign for you, O Hezekiah:

"This year you will eat what grows by itself,
and the second year what springs from that.
But in the third year sow and reap,
plant vineyards and eat their fruit.
31 Once more a remnant of the house of Judah
will take root below and bear fruit above.
32 For out of Jerusalem will come a remnant,
and out of Mount Zion a band of
survivors.
The zeal of the Lord Almighty
will accomplish this.

*a 25 Dead Sea Scrolls (see also 2 Kings 19:24); Masoretic
Text does not have in foreign lands.   b 27 Some
manuscripts of the Masoretic Text, Dead Sea Scrolls and
some Septuagint manuscripts (see also 2 Kings 19:26); most
manuscripts of the Masoretic Text roof / and terraced fields*

THE MESSAGE

Who do you think you've been jeering
and treating with such utter contempt
All these years?
The Holy of Israel!
You've used your servants to mock the Master.
You've bragged, "With my fleet of chariots
I've gone to the highest mountain ranges,
penetrated the far reaches of Lebanon,
Chopped down its giant cedars,
its finest cypresses.
I conquered its highest peak,
explored its deepest forest.
I dug wells
and drank my fill.
I emptied the famous rivers of Egypt
with one kick of my foot.

37.26-27 " 'Haven't you gotten the news
that I've been behind this all along?
This is a longstanding plan of mine
and I'm just now making it happen,
using you to devastate strong cities,
turning them into piles of rubble
and leaving their citizens helpless,
bewildered, and confused,
drooping like unwatered plants,
stunted like withered seedlings.

37.28-29 " 'I know all about your pretentious poses,
your officious comings and goings,
and, yes, the tantrums you throw against
me.
Because of all your wild raging against me,
your unbridled arrogance that I keep
hearing of,
I'll put my hook in your nose
and my bit in your mouth.
I'll show you who's boss. I'll turn you around
and take you back to where you came from.

37.30-32 " 'And this, Hezekiah, will be your confirming sign: This year's crops will be slim pickings,
and next year it won't be much better. But in
three years, farming will be back to normal,
with regular sowing and reaping, planting and
harvesting. What's left of the people of Judah
will put down roots and make a new start. The
people left in Jerusalem will get moving again.
Mount Zion survivors will take hold again. The
zeal of God-of-the-Angel-Armies will do all
this.'

✛

NEW INTERNATIONAL VERSION

³³"Therefore this is what the LORD says concerning the king of Assyria:

"He will not enter this city
  or shoot an arrow here.
He will not come before it with shield
  or build a siege ramp against it.
³⁴By the way that he came he will return;
  he will not enter this city,"
                    declares the LORD.
³⁵"I will defend this city and save it,
    for my sake and for the sake of David my
      servant!"

³⁶Then the angel of the LORD went out and put to death a hundred and eighty-five thousand men in the Assyrian camp. When the people got up the next morning—there were all the dead bodies! ³⁷So Sennacherib king of Assyria broke camp and withdrew. He returned to Nineveh and stayed there.

³⁸One day, while he was worshiping in the temple of his god Nisroch, his sons Adrammelech and Sharezer cut him down with the sword, and they escaped to the land of Ararat. And Esarhaddon his son succeeded him as king.

HEZEKIAH'S ILLNESS

38 In those days Hezekiah became ill and was at the point of death. The prophet Isaiah son of Amoz went to him and said, "This is what the LORD says: Put your house in order, because you are going to die; you will not recover."

²Hezekiah turned his face to the wall and prayed to the LORD, ³"Remember, O LORD, how I have walked before you faithfully and with wholehearted devotion and have done what is good in your eyes." And Hezekiah wept bitterly.

⁴Then the word of the LORD came to Isaiah: ⁵"Go and tell Hezekiah, 'This is what the LORD, the God of your father David, says: I have heard your prayer and seen your tears; I will add fifteen years to your life. ⁶And I will deliver you and this city from the hand of the king of Assyria. I will defend this city.

⁷"'This is the LORD's sign to you that the LORD will do what he has promised: ⁸I will make the shadow cast by the sun go back the ten steps it has gone down on the stairway of Ahaz.'" So the sunlight went back the ten steps it had gone down.

THE MESSAGE

37.33-35 "Finally, this is GOD's verdict on the king of Assyria:

" 'Don't worry, he won't enter this city,
    won't let loose a single arrow,
Won't brandish so much as one shield,
    let alone build a siege ramp against it.
He'll go back the same way he came.
    He won't set a foot in this city.
    GOD's Decree.
I've got my hand on this city
    to save it,
Save it for my very own sake,
    but also for the sake of my David dynasty.' "

37.36-38   Then the Angel of GOD arrived and struck the Assyrian camp—185,000 Assyrians died. By the time the sun came up, they were all dead—an army of corpses! Sennacherib, king of Assyria, got out of there fast, back home to Nineveh. As he was worshiping in the sanctuary of his god Nisroch, he was murdered by his sons Adrammelech and Sharezer. They escaped to the land of Ararat. His son Esar-haddon became the next king.

TIME SPENT IN DEATH'S WAITING ROOM

38.1 **38** At that time, Hezekiah got sick. He was about to die. The prophet Isaiah son of Amoz visited him and said, "GOD says, 'Prepare your affairs and your family. This is it: You're going to die. You're not going to get well.' "

38.2-3   Hezekiah turned away from Isaiah and, facing the wall, prayed to GOD: "GOD, please, I beg you: Remember how I've lived my life. I've lived faithfully in your presence, lived out of a heart that was totally yours. You've seen how I've lived, the good that I have done." And Hezekiah wept as he prayed—painful tears.

38.4-6   Then GOD told Isaiah, "Go and speak with Hezekiah. Give him this Message from me, GOD, the God of your ancestor David: 'I've heard your prayer. I have seen your tears. Here's what I'll do: I'll add fifteen years to your life. And I'll save both you and this city from the king of Assyria. I have my hand on this city.

38.7-8   " 'And this is your confirming sign, confirming that I, GOD, will do exactly what I have promised. Watch for this: As the sun goes down and the shadow lengthens on the sundial of Ahaz, I'm going to reverse the shadow ten notches on the dial.' " And that's what happened: The declining sun's shadow reversed ten notches on the dial.

✠

NEW INTERNATIONAL VERSION

⁹A writing of Hezekiah king of Judah after his illness and recovery:

¹⁰I said, "In the prime of my life
    must I go through the gates of death *a*
    and be robbed of the rest of my years?"
¹¹I said, "I will not again see the LORD,
    the LORD, in the land of the living;
no longer will I look on mankind,
    or be with those who now dwell in this
      world. *b*
¹²Like a shepherd's tent my house
    has been pulled down and taken from me.
Like a weaver I have rolled up my life,
    and he has cut me off from the loom;
    day and night you made an end of me.
¹³I waited patiently till dawn,
    but like a lion he broke all my bones;
    day and night you made an end of me.
¹⁴I cried like a swift or thrush,
    I moaned like a mourning dove.
My eyes grew weak as I looked to the
      heavens.
    I am troubled; O Lord, come to my aid!"

¹⁵But what can I say?
    He has spoken to me, and he himself has
      done this.
I will walk humbly all my years
    because of this anguish of my soul.
¹⁶Lord, by such things men live;
    and my spirit finds life in them too.
You restored me to health
    and let me live.
¹⁷Surely it was for my benefit
    that I suffered such anguish.
In your love you kept me
    from the pit of destruction;
you have put all my sins
    behind your back.
¹⁸For the grave *a* cannot praise you,
    death cannot sing your praise;
those who go down to the pit
    cannot hope for your faithfulness.
¹⁹The living, the living—they praise you,
    as I am doing today;
fathers tell their children
    about your faithfulness.

---

a 10,18 Hebrew *Sheol*   *b 11* A few Hebrew manuscripts;
most Hebrew manuscripts *in the place of cessation*

THE MESSAGE

38.9-15 This is what Hezekiah king of Judah wrote after he'd been sick and then recovered from his sickness:

In the very prime of life
    I have to leave.
Whatever time I have left
    is spent in death's waiting room.
No more glimpses of GOD
    in the land of the living,
No more meetings with my neighbors,
    no more rubbing shoulders with friends.
This body I inhabit is taken down
    and packed away like a camper's tent.
Like a weaver, I've rolled up the carpet of my
      life
    as God cuts me free of the loom
And at day's end sweeps up the scraps and
      pieces.
    I cry for help until morning.
Like a lion, God pummels and pounds me,
    relentlessly finishing me off.
I squawk like a doomed hen,
    moan like a dove.
My eyes ache from looking up for help:
    "Master, I'm in trouble! Get me out of
      this!"
But what's the use? God himself gave me the
      word.
    He's done it to me.
I can't sleep—
    I'm that upset, that troubled.

38.16-19 O Master, these are the conditions in which
      people live,
    and yes, in these very conditions my spirit
      is still alive—
    fully recovered with a fresh infusion of life!
It seems it was good for me
    to go through all those troubles.
Throughout them all you held tight to my
      lifeline.
    You never let me tumble over the edge into
      nothing.
But my sins you let go of,
    threw them over your shoulder—good
      riddance!
The dead don't thank you,
    and choirs don't sing praises from the
      morgue.
Those buried six feet under
    don't witness to your faithful ways.
It's the living—live men, live women—who
      thank you,
    just as I'm doing right now.
Parents give their children
    full reports on your faithful ways.

⊹

NEW INTERNATIONAL VERSION

20 The LORD will save me,
  and we will sing with stringed
    instruments
  all the days of our lives
    in the temple of the LORD.

21 Isaiah had said, "Prepare a poultice of figs and apply it to the boil, and he will recover." 22 Hezekiah had asked, "What will be the sign that I will go up to the temple of the LORD?"

ENVOYS FROM BABYLON

39 At that time Merodach-Baladan son of Baladan king of Babylon sent Hezekiah letters and a gift, because he had heard of his illness and recovery. 2 Hezekiah received the envoys gladly and showed them what was in his storehouses—the silver, the gold, the spices, the fine oil, his entire armory and everything found among his treasures. There was nothing in his palace or in all his kingdom that Hezekiah did not show them.

3 Then Isaiah the prophet went to King Hezekiah and asked, "What did those men say, and where did they come from?"

"From a distant land," Hezekiah replied. "They came to me from Babylon."

4 The prophet asked, "What did they see in your palace?"

"They saw everything in my palace," Hezekiah said. "There is nothing among my treasures that I did not show them."

5 Then Isaiah said to Hezekiah, "Hear the word of the LORD Almighty: 6 The time will surely come when everything in your palace, and all that your fathers have stored up until this day, will be carried off to Babylon. Nothing will be left, says the LORD. 7 And some of your descendants, your own flesh and blood who will be born to you, will be taken away, and they will become eunuchs in the palace of the king of Babylon."

8 "The word of the LORD you have spoken is good," Hezekiah replied. For he thought, "There will be peace and security in my lifetime."

COMFORT FOR GOD'S PEOPLE

40 Comfort, comfort my people,
  says your God.
2 Speak tenderly to Jerusalem,
  and proclaim to her

THE MESSAGE

38.20 GOD saves and will save me.
  As fiddles and mandolins strike up the
    tunes,
  We'll sing, oh we'll sing, sing,
    for the rest of our lives in the Sanctuary of
      GOD.

38.21-22 Isaiah had said, "Prepare a poultice of figs and put it on the boil so he may recover." Hezekiah had said, "What is my cue that it's all right to enter again the Sanctuary of GOD?"

THERE WILL BE NOTHING LEFT

39.1 **39** Sometime later, King Merodach-baladan son of Baladan of Babylon sent messengers with greetings and a gift to Hezekiah. He had heard that Hezekiah had been sick and was now well.

39.2 Hezekiah received the messengers warmly. He took them on a tour of his royal precincts, proudly showing them all his treasures: silver, gold, spices, expensive oils, all his weapons—everything out on display. There was nothing in his house or kingdom that Hezekiah didn't show them.

39.3 Later the prophet Isaiah showed up. He asked Hezekiah, "What were these men up to? What did they say? And where did they come from?"

Hezekiah said, "They came from a long way off, from Babylon."

39.4 "And what did they see in your palace?"

"Everything," said Hezekiah. "I showed them the works, opened all the doors and impressed them with it all."

39.5-7 Then Isaiah said to Hezekiah, "Now listen to this Message from GOD-of-the-Angel-Armies: I have to warn you, the time is coming when everything in this palace, along with everything your ancestors accumulated before you, will be hauled off to Babylon. GOD says that there will be nothing left. Nothing. And not only your things but your *sons*. Some of your sons will be taken into exile, ending up as eunuchs in the palace of the king of Babylon."

39.8 Hezekiah replied to Isaiah, "Good. If GOD says so, it's good." Within himself he was thinking, "But surely nothing bad will happen in my lifetime. I'll enjoy peace and stability as long as I live."

MESSAGES OF COMFORT

PREPARE FOR GOD'S ARRIVAL

40.1-2 **40** "Comfort, oh comfort my people,"
  says your God.
  "Speak softly and tenderly to Jerusalem,
    but also make it very clear

NEW INTERNATIONAL VERSION

that her hard service has been completed,
  that her sin has been paid for,
that she has received from the LORD's hand
  double for all her sins.

[3] A voice of one calling:
"In the desert prepare
  the way for the LORD[a];
make straight in the wilderness
  a highway for our God.[b]
[4] Every valley shall be raised up,
  every mountain and hill made low;
the rough ground shall become level,
  the rugged places a plain.
[5] And the glory of the LORD will be revealed,
  and all mankind together will see it.
            For the mouth of the LORD
                    has spoken."

[6] A voice says, "Cry out."
  And I said, "What shall I cry?"

"All men are like grass,
  and all their glory is like the flowers of
    the field.
[7] The grass withers and the flowers fall,
  because the breath of the LORD blows on
    them.
  Surely the people are grass.
[8] The grass withers and the flowers fall,
  but the word of our God stands forever."

[9] You who bring good tidings to Zion,
  go up on a high mountain.
You who bring good tidings to Jerusalem,[c]
  lift up your voice with a shout,
lift it up, do not be afraid;
  say to the towns of Judah,
  "Here is your God!"
[10] See, the Sovereign LORD comes with power,
  and his arm rules for him.
See, his reward is with him,
  and his recompense accompanies him.
[11] He tends his flock like a shepherd:
  He gathers the lambs in his arms
and carries them close to his heart;
  he gently leads those that have young.

[12] Who has measured the waters in the hollow
    of his hand,
  or with the breadth of his hand marked
    off the heavens?
Who has held the dust of the earth in a
    basket,
  or weighed the mountains on the scales
  and the hills in a balance?

THE MESSAGE

That she has served her sentence,
  that her sin is taken care of—forgiven!
She's been punished enough and more than
    enough,
  and now it's over and done with."

40.3-5 Thunder in the desert!
  "Prepare for GOD's arrival!
Make the road straight and smooth,
  a highway fit for our God.
Fill in the valleys,
  level off the hills,
Smooth out the ruts,
  clear out the rocks.
Then GOD's bright glory will shine
  and everyone will see it.
Yes. Just as GOD has said."

40.6 A voice says, "Shout!"
  I said, "What shall I shout?"

40.6-8 "These people are nothing but grass,
  their love fragile as wildflowers.
The grass withers, the wildflowers fade,
  if GOD so much as puffs on them.
Aren't these people just so much grass?
True, the grass withers and the wildflowers
    fade,
  but our God's Word stands firm and
    forever."

40.9-11 Climb a high mountain, Zion.
  You're the preacher of good news.
Raise your voice. Make it good and loud, Jeru-
    salem.
  You're the preacher of good news.
  Speak loud and clear. Don't be timid!
Tell the cities of Judah,
  "Look! Your God!"
Look at him! GOD, the Master, comes in
    power,
  ready to go into action.
He is going to pay back his enemies
  and reward those who have loved him.
Like a shepherd, he will care for his flock,
  gathering the lambs in his arms,
Hugging them as he carries them,
  leading the nursing ewes to good pasture.

THE CREATOR OF ALL YOU CAN SEE OR IMAGINE

40.12-17 Who has scooped up the ocean
  in his two hands,
    or measured the sky between his thumb
      and little finger,
Who has put all the earth's dirt in one of his
    baskets,
  weighed each mountain and hill?

---

[a] 3 Or A voice of one calling in the desert: / "Prepare the way
for the LORD   [b] 3 Hebrew; Septuagint make straight the
paths of our God   [c] 9 Or O Zion, bringer of good tidings, / go
up on a high mountain. / O Jerusalem, bringer of good tidings

NEW INTERNATIONAL VERSION

¹³ Who has understood the mind^a of the LORD,
  or instructed him as his counselor?
¹⁴ Whom did the LORD consult to enlighten
    him,
  and who taught him the right way?
Who was it that taught him knowledge
  or showed him the path of
    understanding?

¹⁵ Surely the nations are like a drop in a
    bucket;
  they are regarded as dust on the scales;
he weighs the islands as though they were
  fine dust.
¹⁶ Lebanon is not sufficient for altar fires,
  nor its animals enough for burnt
    offerings.
¹⁷ Before him all the nations are as nothing;
  they are regarded by him as worthless
    and less than nothing.

¹⁸ To whom, then, will you compare God?
  What image will you compare him to?
¹⁹ As for an idol, a craftsman casts it,
  and a goldsmith overlays it with gold
  and fashions silver chains for it.
²⁰ A man too poor to present such an offering
  selects wood that will not rot.
He looks for a skilled craftsman
  to set up an idol that will not topple.

²¹ Do you not know?
  Have you not heard?
Has it not been told you from the beginning?
  Have you not understood since the earth
    was founded?
²² He sits enthroned above the circle of the
    earth,
  and its people are like grasshoppers.
He stretches out the heavens like a canopy,
  and spreads them out like a tent to live in.
²³ He brings princes to naught
  and reduces the rulers of this world to
    nothing.
²⁴ No sooner are they planted,
  no sooner are they sown,
  no sooner do they take root in the
    ground,
than he blows on them and they wither,
  and a whirlwind sweeps them away like
    chaff.

²⁵ "To whom will you compare me?
  Or who is my equal?" says the Holy One.
²⁶ Lift your eyes and look to the heavens:
  Who created all these?
He who brings out the starry host one by
  one,

THE MESSAGE

Who could ever have told GOD what to do
  or taught him his business?
What expert would he have gone to for
    advice,
  what school would he attend to learn
    justice?
What god do you suppose might have taught
    him what he knows,
  showed him how things work?
Why, the nations are but a drop in a bucket,
  a mere smudge on a window.
Watch him sweep up the islands
  like so much dust off the floor!
There aren't enough trees in Lebanon
  nor enough animals in those vast forests
  to furnish adequate fuel and offerings for
    his worship.
All the nations add up to simply nothing
    before him—
  less than nothing is more like it. A minus.

^{40.18-20} So who even comes close to being like God?
  To whom or what can you compare him?
Some no-god idol? Ridiculous!
  It's made in a workshop, cast in bronze,
Given a thin veneer of gold,
  and draped with silver filigree.
Or, perhaps someone will select a fine wood—
  olive wood, say—that won't rot,
Then hire a woodcarver to make a no-god,
  giving special care to its base so it won't tip
    over!

^{40.21-24} Have you not been paying attention?
  Have you not been listening?
Haven't you heard these stories all your life?
  Don't you understand the foundation of all
    things?
God sits high above the round ball of earth.
  The people look like mere ants.
He stretches out the skies like a canvas—
  yes, like a tent canvas to live under.
He ignores what all the princes say and do.
  The rulers of the earth count for nothing.
Princes and rulers don't amount to much.
  Like seeds barely rooted, just sprouted,
They shrivel when God blows on them.
  Like flecks of chaff, they're gone with the
    wind.

^{40.25-26} "So—who is like me?
  Who holds a candle to me?" says The Holy.
Look at the night skies:
  Who do you think made all this?
Who marches this army of stars out each
    night,

^a 13 Or *Spirit*; or *spirit*

NEW INTERNATIONAL VERSION	THE MESSAGE

NEW INTERNATIONAL VERSION

and calls them each by name.
Because of his great power and mighty
strength,
not one of them is missing.

27 Why do you say, O Jacob,
and complain, O Israel,
"My way is hidden from the LORD;
my cause is disregarded by my God"?
28 Do you not know?
Have you not heard?
The LORD is the everlasting God,
the Creator of the ends of the earth.
He will not grow tired or weary,
and his understanding no one can fathom.
29 He gives strength to the weary
and increases the power of the weak.
30 Even youths grow tired and weary,
and young men stumble and fall;
31 but those who hope in the LORD
will renew their strength.
They will soar on wings like eagles;
they will run and not grow weary,
they will walk and not be faint.

THE HELPER OF ISRAEL

41 "Be silent before me, you islands!
Let the nations renew their strength!
Let them come forward and speak;
let us meet together at the place of
judgment.

2 "Who has stirred up one from the east,
calling him in righteousness to his
service *a* ?
He hands nations over to him
and subdues kings before him.
He turns them to dust with his sword,
to windblown chaff with his bow.
3 He pursues them and moves on unscathed,
by a path his feet have not traveled before.
4 Who has done this and carried it through,
calling forth the generations from the
beginning?
I, the LORD—with the first of them
and with the last—I am he."

5 The islands have seen it and fear;
the ends of the earth tremble.
They approach and come forward;
6 each helps the other
and says to his brother, "Be strong!"
7 The craftsman encourages the goldsmith,
and he who smooths with the hammer
spurs on him who strikes the anvil.

THE MESSAGE

counts them off, calls each by name
—so magnificent! so powerful!—
and never overlooks a single one?

40.27-31 Why would you ever complain, O Jacob,
or, whine, Israel, saying,
"GOD has lost track of me.
He doesn't care what happens to me"?
Don't you know anything? Haven't you been
listening?
GOD doesn't come and go. God *lasts.*
He's Creator of all you can see or imagine.
He doesn't get tired out, doesn't pause to catch
his breath.
And he knows *everything,* inside and out.
He energizes those who get tired,
gives fresh strength to dropouts.
For even young people tire and drop out,
young folk in their prime stumble and fall.
But those who wait upon GOD get fresh
strength.
They spread their wings and soar like
eagles,
They run and don't get tired,
they walk and don't lag behind.

DO YOU FEEL LIKE A LOWLY WORM?

41.1 **41** "Quiet down, far-flung ocean islands.
Listen!
Sit down and rest, everyone. Recover your
strength.
Gather around me. Say what's on your heart.
Together let's decide what's right.

41.2-3 "Who got things rolling here,
got this champion from the east on the
move?
Who recruited him for this job,
then rounded up and corralled the nations
so he could run roughshod over kings?
He's off and running,
pulverizing nations into dust,
leaving only stubble and chaff in his wake.
He chases them and comes through unscathed,
his feet scarcely touching the path.

41.4 "Who did this? Who made it happen?
Who always gets things started?
I did. GOD. I'm first on the scene.
I'm also the last to leave.

41.5-7 "Far-flung ocean islands see it and panic.
The ends of the earth are shaken.
Fearfully they huddle together.
They try to help each other out,
making up stories in the dark.
The godmakers in the workshops
go into overtime production, crafting new
models of no-gods,

---

a 2 Or / *whom victory meets at every step*

NEW INTERNATIONAL VERSION	THE MESSAGE

He says of the welding, "It is good."
He nails down the idol so it will not
    topple.

8 "But you, O Israel, my servant,
    Jacob, whom I have chosen,
    you descendants of Abraham my friend,
9 I took you from the ends of the earth,
    from its farthest corners I called you.
I said, 'You are my servant';
    I have chosen you and have not rejected
    you.
10 So do not fear, for I am with you;
    do not be dismayed, for I am your God.
I will strengthen you and help you;
    I will uphold you with my righteous right
    hand.

11 "All who rage against you
    will surely be ashamed and disgraced;
those who oppose you
    will be as nothing and perish.
12 Though you search for your enemies,
    you will not find them.
Those who wage war against you
    will be as nothing at all.
13 For I am the LORD, your God,
    who takes hold of your right hand
and says to you, Do not fear;
    I will help you.
14 Do not be afraid, O worm Jacob,
    O little Israel,
for I myself will help you," declares the
    LORD,
    your Redeemer, the Holy One of Israel.
15 "See, I will make you into a threshing sledge,
    new and sharp, with many teeth.
You will thresh the mountains and crush
    them,
    and reduce the hills to chaff.
16 You will winnow them, the wind will pick
    them up,
    and a gale will blow them away.
But you will rejoice in the LORD
    and glory in the Holy One of Israel.

17 "The poor and needy search for water,
    but there is none;
    their tongues are parched with thirst.
But I the LORD will answer them;
    I, the God of Israel, will not forsake them.

Urging one another on—'Good job!' 'Great
    design!'—
    pounding in nails at the base
    so that the things won't tip over.

41.8-10 "But you, Israel, are my servant.
    You're Jacob, my first choice,
    descendants of my good friend Abraham.
I pulled you in from all over the world,
    called you in from every dark corner of the
    earth,
Telling you, 'You're my servant, serving on my
    side.
    I've picked you. I haven't dropped you.'
Don't panic. I'm with you.
    There's no need to fear for I'm your God.
I'll give you strength. I'll help you.
    I'll hold you steady, keep a firm grip on you.

41.11-13 "Count on it: Everyone who had it in for you
    will end up out in the cold—
    real losers.
Those who worked against you
    will end up empty-handed—
    nothing to show for their lives.
When you go out looking for your old
    adversaries
    you won't find them—
Not a trace of your old enemies,
    not even a memory.
That's right. Because I, your GOD,
    have a firm grip on you and I'm not letting
    go.
I'm telling you, 'Don't panic.
    I'm right here to help you.'

41.14-16 "Do you feel like a lowly worm, Jacob?
    Don't be afraid.
Feel like a fragile insect, Israel?
    I'll help you.
I, GOD, want to reassure you.
    The God who buys you back, The Holy of
    Israel.
I'm transforming you from worm to harrow,
    from insect to iron.
As a sharp-toothed harrow you'll smooth out
    the mountains,
    turn those tough old hills into loamy soil.
You'll open the rough ground to the weather,
    to the blasts of sun and wind and rain.
But you'll be confident and exuberant,
    expansive in The Holy of Israel!

41.17-20 "The poor and homeless are desperate for water,
    their tongues parched and no water to be
    found.
But I'm there to be found, I'm there for them,
    and I, God of Israel, will not leave them
    thirsty.

NEW INTERNATIONAL VERSION

¹⁸ I will make rivers flow on barren heights,
　　and springs within the valleys.
I will turn the desert into pools of water,
　　and the parched ground into springs.
¹⁹ I will put in the desert
　　the cedar and the acacia, the myrtle and
　　　　the olive.
I will set pines in the wasteland,
　　the fir and the cypress together,
²⁰ so that people may see and know,
　　may consider and understand,
that the hand of the LORD has done this,
　　that the Holy One of Israel has created it.

²¹ "Present your case," says the LORD.
　　"Set forth your arguments," says Jacob's
　　　　King.
²² "Bring in your idols to tell us
　　what is going to happen.
Tell us what the former things were,
　　so that we may consider them
　　and know their final outcome.
Or declare to us the things to come,
²³ 　tell us what the future holds,
　　so we may know that you are gods.
Do something, whether good or bad,
　　so that we will be dismayed and filled
　　　　with fear.
²⁴ But you are less than nothing
　　and your works are utterly worthless;
　　he who chooses you is detestable.

²⁵ "I have stirred up one from the north, and he
　　　　comes—
　　one from the rising sun who calls on my
　　　　name.
He treads on rulers as if they were mortar,
　　as if he were a potter treading the clay.
²⁶ Who told of this from the beginning, so we
　　　　could know,
　　or beforehand, so we could say, 'He was
　　　　right'?
No one told of this,
　　no one foretold it,
　　no one heard any words from you.
²⁷ I was the first to tell Zion, 'Look, here they
　　　　are!'
　　I gave to Jerusalem a messenger of good
　　　　tidings.
²⁸ I look but there is no one—
　　no one among them to give counsel,
　　no one to give answer when I ask them.
²⁹ See, they are all false!
　　Their deeds amount to nothing;
　　their images are but wind and confusion.

THE MESSAGE

I'll open up rivers for them on the barren hills,
　　spout fountains in the valleys.
I'll turn the baked-clay badlands into a cool
　　　　pond,
　　the waterless waste into splashing creeks.
I'll plant the red cedar in that treeless
　　　　wasteland,
　　also acacia, myrtle, and olive.
I'll place the cypress in the desert,
　　with plenty of oaks and pines.
Everyone will see this. No one can miss it—
　　unavoidable, indisputable evidence
That I, GOD, personally did this.
　　It's created and signed by The Holy of
　　　　Israel.

^{41.21-24} "Set out your case for your gods," says GOD.
　　"Bring your evidence," says the King of
　　　　Jacob.
"Take the stand on behalf of your idols, offer
　　　　arguments,
　　assemble reasons.
Spread out the facts before us
　　so that we can assess them ourselves.
Ask them, 'If you are gods, explain what the
　　　　past means—
　　or, failing that, tell us what will happen in
　　　　the future.
Can't do that?
　　How about doing something—anything!
Good or bad—whatever.
　　Can you hurt us or help us? Do we need to
　　　　be afraid?'
They say nothing, because they are nothing—
　　sham gods, no-gods, fool-making gods.

^{41.25-29} "I, God, started someone out from the north
　　　　and he's come.
　　He was called out of the east by name.
He'll stomp the rulers into the mud
　　the way a potter works the clay.
Let me ask you, Did anyone guess that this
　　　　might happen?
　　Did anyone tell us earlier so we might
　　　　confirm it
　　with 'Yes, he's right!'?
No one mentioned it, no one announced it,
　　no one heard a peep out of you.
But I told Zion all about this beforehand.
　　I gave Jerusalem a preacher of good news.
But around here there's no one—
　　no one who knows what's going on.
　　I ask, but no one can tell me the score.
Nothing here. It's all smoke and hot air—
　　sham gods, hollow gods, no-gods.

NEW INTERNATIONAL VERSION

THE SERVANT OF THE LORD

42 "Here is my servant, whom I uphold,
my chosen one in whom I delight;
I will put my Spirit on him
and he will bring justice to the nations.
² He will not shout or cry out,
or raise his voice in the streets.
³ A bruised reed he will not break,
and a smoldering wick he will not snuff
out.
In faithfulness he will bring forth justice;
⁴   he will not falter or be discouraged
till he establishes justice on earth.
In his law the islands will put their hope."

⁵ This is what God the LORD says—
he who created the heavens and stretched
them out,
who spread out the earth and all that
comes out of it,
who gives breath to its people,
and life to those who walk on it:
⁶ "I, the LORD, have called you in
righteousness;
I will take hold of your hand.
I will keep you and will make you
to be a covenant for the people
and a light for the Gentiles,
⁷ to open eyes that are blind,
to free captives from prison
and to release from the dungeon those
who sit in darkness.

⁸ "I am the LORD; that is my name!
I will not give my glory to another
or my praise to idols.
⁹ See, the former things have taken place,
and new things I declare;
before they spring into being
I announce them to you."

SONG OF PRAISE TO THE LORD

¹⁰ Sing to the LORD a new song,
his praise from the ends of the earth,
you who go down to the sea, and all that is
in it,
you islands, and all who live in them.
¹¹ Let the desert and its towns raise their
voices;
let the settlements where Kedar lives
rejoice.

THE MESSAGE

GOD'S SERVANT WILL SET EVERYTHING RIGHT

42.1-4 **42** "Take a good look at my servant.
I'm backing him to the hilt.
He's the one I chose,
and I couldn't be more pleased with him.
I've bathed him with my Spirit, my *life.*
He'll set everything right among the
nations.
He won't call attention to what he does
with loud speeches or gaudy parades.
He won't brush aside the bruised and the hurt
and he won't disregard the small and
insignificant,
but he'll steadily and firmly set things right.
He won't tire out and quit. He won't be
stopped
until he's finished his work—to set things
right on earth.
Far-flung ocean islands
wait expectantly for his teaching."

THE GOD WHO MAKES US ALIVE WITH HIS OWN LIFE

42.5-9 GOD'S Message,
the God who created the cosmos, stretched
out the skies,
laid out the earth and all that grows from it,
Who breathes life into earth's people,
makes them alive with his own life:
"I am GOD. I have called you to live right and
well.
I have taken responsibility for you, kept
you safe.
I have set you among my people to bind them
to me,
and provided you as a lighthouse to the
nations,
To make a start at bringing people into the
open, into light:
opening blind eyes,
releasing prisoners from dungeons,
emptying the dark prisons.
I am GOD. That's my name.
I don't franchise my glory,
don't endorse the no-god idols.
Take note: The earlier predictions of judgment
have been fulfilled.
I'm announcing the new salvation work.
Before it bursts on the scene,
I'm telling you all about it."

42.10-16 Sing to GOD a brand-new song,
sing his praises all over the world!
Let the sea and its fish give a round of
applause,
with all the far-flung islands joining in.
Let the desert and its camps raise a tune,
calling the Kedar nomads to join in.

NEW INTERNATIONAL VERSION

Let the people of Sela sing for joy;
    let them shout from the mountaintops.
[12] Let them give glory to the LORD
    and proclaim his praise in the islands.
[13] The LORD will march out like a mighty man,
    like a warrior he will stir up his zeal;
with a shout he will raise the battle cry
    and will triumph over his enemies.

[14] "For a long time I have kept silent,
    I have been quiet and held myself back.
But now, like a woman in childbirth,
    I cry out, I gasp and pant.
[15] I will lay waste the mountains and hills
    and dry up all their vegetation;
I will turn rivers into islands
    and dry up the pools.
[16] I will lead the blind by ways they have not
        known,
    along unfamiliar paths I will guide them;
I will turn the darkness into light before
        them
    and make the rough places smooth.
These are the things I will do;
    I will not forsake them.
[17] But those who trust in idols,
    who say to images, 'You are our gods,'
    will be turned back in utter shame.

ISRAEL BLIND AND DEAF

[18] "Hear, you deaf;
    look, you blind, and see!
[19] Who is blind but my servant,
    and deaf like the messenger I send?
Who is blind like the one committed to me,
    blind like the servant of the LORD?
[20] You have seen many things, but have paid no
        attention;
    your ears are open, but you hear
        nothing."
[21] It pleased the LORD
    for the sake of his righteousness
    to make his law great and glorious.
[22] But this is a people plundered and looted,
    all of them trapped in pits
    or hidden away in prisons.
They have become plunder,
    with no one to rescue them;
they have been made loot,
    with no one to say, "Send them back."

[23] Which of you will listen to this
    or pay close attention in time to come?
[24] Who handed Jacob over to become loot,
    and Israel to the plunderers?

THE MESSAGE

Let the villagers in Sela round up a choir
    and perform from the tops of the
        mountains.
Make GOD's glory resound;
    echo his praises from coast to coast.
GOD steps out like he means business.
    You can see he's primed for action.
He shouts, announcing his arrival;
    he takes charge and his enemies fall into
        line:

42.14-16 "I've been quiet long enough.
    I've held back, biting my tongue.
But now I'm letting loose, letting go,
    like a woman who's having a baby—
Stripping the hills bare,
    withering the wildflowers,
Drying up the rivers,
    turning lakes into mudflats.
But I'll take the hand of those who don't know
        the way,
    who can't see where they're going.
I'll be a personal guide to them,
    directing them through unknown country.
I'll be right there to show them what roads to
        take,
    make sure they don't fall into the ditch.
These are the things I'll be doing for them—
    sticking with them, not leaving them for a
        minute."

42.17 But those who invested in the no-gods
    are bankrupt—dead broke.

YOU'VE SEEN A LOT, BUT LOOKED AT NOTHING

42.18-25 Pay attention! Are you deaf?
    Open your eyes! Are you blind?
You're my servant, and you're not looking!
    You're my messenger, and you're not
        listening!
The very people I depended upon, servants of
        GOD,
    blind as a bat—willfully blind!
You've seen a lot, but looked at nothing.
    You've heard everything, but listened to
        nothing.
GOD intended, out of the goodness of his
        heart,
    to be lavish in his revelation.
But this is a people battered and cowed,
    shut up in attics and closets,
Victims licking their wounds,
    feeling ignored, abandoned.
But is anyone out there listening?
    Is anyone paying attention to what's
        coming?
Who do you think turned Jacob over to the
        thugs,
    let loose the robbers on Israel?

NEW INTERNATIONAL VERSION

Was it not the LORD,
  against whom we have sinned?
For they would not follow his ways;
  they did not obey his law.
²⁵ So he poured out on them his burning anger,
  the violence of war.
It enveloped them in flames, yet they did not
    understand;
  it consumed them, but they did not take it
    to heart.

ISRAEL'S ONLY SAVIOR

43 But now, this is what the LORD says—
  he who created you, O Jacob,
  he who formed you, O Israel:
"Fear not, for I have redeemed you;
  I have summoned you by name; you are
    mine.
² When you pass through the waters,
  I will be with you;
and when you pass through the rivers,
  they will not sweep over you.
When you walk through the fire,
  you will not be burned;
  the flames will not set you ablaze.
³ For I am the LORD, your God,
  the Holy One of Israel, your Savior;
I give Egypt for your ransom,
  Cush^a and Seba in your stead.
⁴ Since you are precious and honored in my
    sight,
  and because I love you,
I will give men in exchange for you,
  and people in exchange for your life.
⁵ Do not be afraid, for I am with you;
  I will bring your children from the east
  and gather you from the west.
⁶ I will say to the north, 'Give them up!'
  and to the south, 'Do not hold them back.'
Bring my sons from afar
  and my daughters from the ends of the
    earth—
⁷ everyone who is called by my name,
  whom I created for my glory,
  whom I formed and made."

⁸ Lead out those who have eyes but are blind,
  who have ears but are deaf.
⁹ All the nations gather together
  and the peoples assemble.
Which of them foretold this
  and proclaimed to us the former things?

^a 3 That is, the upper Nile region

THE MESSAGE

Wasn't it GOD himself, this God against whom
    we've sinned—
  not doing what he commanded,
  not listening to what he said?
Isn't it God's anger that's behind all this,
  God's punishing power?
Their whole world collapsed but they still
    didn't get it;
  their life is in ruins but they don't take it to
    heart.

WHEN YOU'RE BETWEEN A ROCK AND A HARD PLACE

43.1-4 **43** But now, GOD's Message,
  the God who made you in the first
    place, Jacob,
  the One who got you started, Israel:
"Don't be afraid, I've redeemed you.
  I've called your name. You're mine.
When you're in over your head, I'll be there
    with you.
  When you're in rough waters, you will not
    go down.
When you're between a rock and a hard place,
  it won't be a dead end—
Because I am GOD, your personal God,
  The Holy of Israel, your Savior.
I paid a huge price for you:
  all of Egypt, with rich Cush and Seba
    thrown in!
That's how much you mean to me!
  That's how much I love you!
I'd sell off the whole world to get you back,
  trade the creation just for you.

43.5-7 "So don't be afraid: I'm with you.
  I'll round up all your scattered children,
  pull them in from east and west.
I'll send orders north and south:
  'Send them back.
Return my sons from distant lands,
  my daughters from faraway places.
I want them back, every last one who bears
    my name,
  every man, woman, and child
Whom I created for my glory,
  yes, personally formed and made each
    one.' "

✠

43.8-13 Get the blind and deaf out here and ready—
  the blind (though there's nothing wrong
    with their eyes)
  and the deaf (though there's nothing wrong
    with their ears).
Then get the other nations out here and ready.
  Let's see what they have to say about this,
  how they account for what's happened.

NEW INTERNATIONAL VERSION

Let them bring in their witnesses to prove
    they were right,
  so that others may hear and say, "It is
    true."
¹⁰ "You are my witnesses," declares the LORD,
    "and my servant whom I have chosen,
  so that you may know and believe me
    and understand that I am he.
Before me no god was formed,
    nor will there be one after me.
¹¹ I, even I, am the LORD,
    and apart from me there is no savior.
¹² I have revealed and saved and proclaimed—
    I, and not some foreign god among you.
You are my witnesses," declares the LORD,
    "that I am God.
¹³   Yes, and from ancient days I am he.
No one can deliver out of my hand.
    When I act, who can reverse it?"

GOD'S MERCY AND ISRAEL'S UNFAITHFULNESS
¹⁴ This is what the LORD says—
    your Redeemer, the Holy One of Israel:
"For your sake I will send to Babylon
    and bring down as fugitives all the
    Babylonians,ᵃ
  in the ships in which they took pride.
¹⁵ I am the LORD, your Holy One,
    Israel's Creator, your King."

¹⁶ This is what the LORD says—
    he who made a way through the sea,
    a path through the mighty waters,
¹⁷ who drew out the chariots and horses,
    the army and reinforcements together,
and they lay there, never to rise again,
    extinguished, snuffed out like a wick:
¹⁸ "Forget the former things;
    do not dwell on the past.
¹⁹ See, I am doing a new thing!
    Now it springs up; do you not perceive it?
I am making a way in the desert
    and streams in the wasteland.
²⁰ The wild animals honor me,
    the jackals and the owls,
because I provide water in the desert
    and streams in the wasteland,
to give drink to my people, my chosen,
²¹   the people I formed for myself
    that they may proclaim my praise.

ᵃ 14 Or Chaldeans

THE MESSAGE

Let them present their expert witnesses
    and make their case;
  let them try to convince us what they say is
    true.
"But *you* are my witnesses." GOD's Decree.
    "You're my handpicked servant
So that you'll come to know and trust me,
    understand both *that* I am and *who* I am.
Previous to me there was no such thing as a
    god,
    nor will there be after me.
I, yes I, am GOD.
    I'm the only Savior there is.
I spoke, I saved, I told you what existed
    long before these upstart gods appeared on
    the scene.
And you know it, you're my witnesses,
    you're the evidence." GOD's Decree.
"Yes, I am God.
    I've always been God
    and I always will be God.
No one can take anything from me.
    I make; who can unmake it?"

YOU DIDN'T EVEN DO THE MINIMUM
43.14-15 GOD, your Redeemer,
    The Holy of Israel, says:
"Just for you, I will march on Babylon.
    I'll turn the tables on the Babylonians.
Instead of whooping it up,
    they'll be wailing.
I am GOD, your Holy One,
    Creator of Israel, your King."

43.16-21 This is what GOD says,
    the God who builds a road right through
    the ocean,
  who carves a path through pounding
    waves,
The God who summons horses and chariots
    and armies—
  they lie down and then can't get up;
  they're snuffed out like so many candles:
"Forget about what's happened;
    don't keep going over old history.
Be alert, be present. I'm about to do
    something brand-new.
    It's bursting out! Don't you see it?
There it is! I'm making a road through the
    desert,
    rivers in the badlands.
Wild animals will say 'Thank you!'
    —the coyotes and the buzzards—
Because I provided water in the desert,
    rivers through the sun-baked earth,
Drinking water for the people I chose,
    the people I made especially for myself,
    a people custom-made to praise me.

NEW INTERNATIONAL VERSION

22 "Yet you have not called upon me, O Jacob,
	you have not wearied yourselves for me,
		O Israel.
23 You have not brought me sheep for burnt
		offerings,
	nor honored me with your sacrifices.
I have not burdened you with grain offerings
	nor wearied you with demands for
		incense.
24 You have not bought any fragrant calamus
		for me,
	or lavished on me the fat of your
		sacrifices.
But you have burdened me with your sins
	and wearied me with your offenses.

25 "I, even I, am he who blots out
	your transgressions, for my own sake,
	and remembers your sins no more.
26 Review the past for me,
	let us argue the matter together;
	state the case for your innocence.
27 Your first father sinned;
	your spokesmen rebelled against me.
28 So I will disgrace the dignitaries of your
		temple,
	and I will consign Jacob to destruction[a]
	and Israel to scorn.

ISRAEL THE CHOSEN

44 "But now listen, O Jacob, my servant,
	Israel, whom I have chosen.
2 This is what the LORD says—
	he who made you, who formed you in the
		womb,
	and who will help you:
	Do not be afraid, O Jacob, my servant,
	Jeshurun, whom I have chosen.
3 For I will pour water on the thirsty land,
	and streams on the dry ground;
I will pour out my Spirit on your offspring,
	and my blessing on your descendants.
4 They will spring up like grass in a meadow,
	like poplar trees by flowing streams.
5 One will say, 'I belong to the LORD';
	another will call himself by the name of
		Jacob;
still another will write on his hand, 'The
		LORD's,'
	and will take the name Israel.

THE LORD, NOT IDOLS

6 "This is what the LORD says—
	Israel's King and Redeemer, the LORD
		Almighty:

---

[a] 28 The Hebrew term refers to the irrevocable giving over
of things or persons to the LORD, often by totally destroying
them.

THE MESSAGE

43.22-24 "But you didn't pay a bit of attention to me,
		Jacob.
	You so quickly tired of me, Israel.
You wouldn't even bring sheep for offerings in
		worship.
	You couldn't be bothered with sacrifices.
It wasn't that I asked that much from you.
	I didn't expect expensive presents.
But you didn't even do the minimum—
	so stingy with me, so closefisted.
Yet you haven't been stingy with your sins.
	You've been plenty generous with them—
		and I'm fed up.

43.25 "But I, yes I, am the one
	who takes care of your sins—that's what I
		do.
	I don't keep a list of your sins.

43.26-28 "So, make your case against me. Let's have
		this out.
	Make your arguments. Prove you're in the
		right.
Your original ancestor started the sinning,
	and everyone since has joined in.
That's why I had to disqualify the Temple
		leaders,
	repudiate Jacob and discredit Israel.

PROUD TO BE CALLED ISRAEL

44.1-5 "But for now, dear servant Jacob, listen—
	yes, you, Israel, my personal choice.
GOD who made you has something to say to
		you;
	the God who formed you in the womb
		wants to help you.
Don't be afraid, dear servant Jacob,
	Jeshurun, the one I chose.
For I will pour water on the thirsty ground
	and send streams coursing through the
		parched earth.
I will pour my Spirit into your descendants
	and my blessing on your children.
They shall sprout like grass on the prairie,
	like willows alongside creeks.
This one will say, 'I am GOD's,'
	and another will go by the name Jacob;
That one will write on his hand 'GOD's
		property'—
	and be proud to be called Israel."

44.6-8 GOD, King of Israel,
	your Redeemer, GOD-of-the-Angel-Armies,
		says:

NEW INTERNATIONAL VERSION

I am the first and I am the last;
    apart from me there is no God.
7 Who then is like me? Let him proclaim it.
    Let him declare and lay out before me
what has happened since I established my
        ancient people,
    and what is yet to come—
    yes, let him foretell what will come.
8 Do not tremble, do not be afraid.
    Did I not proclaim this and foretell it long
        ago?
You are my witnesses. Is there any God
        besides me?
    No, there is no other Rock; I know not
        one."

9 All who make idols are nothing,
    and the things they treasure are worthless.
Those who would speak up for them are
        blind;
    they are ignorant, to their own shame.
10 Who shapes a god and casts an idol,
    which can profit him nothing?
11 He and his kind will be put to shame;
    craftsmen are nothing but men.
Let them all come together and take their
        stand;
    they will be brought down to terror and
        infamy.

12 The blacksmith takes a tool
    and works with it in the coals;
he shapes an idol with hammers,
    he forges it with the might of his arm.
He gets hungry and loses his strength;
    he drinks no water and grows faint.
13 The carpenter measures with a line
    and makes an outline with a marker;
he roughs it out with chisels
    and marks it with compasses.
He shapes it in the form of man,
    of man in all his glory,
    that it may dwell in a shrine.
14 He cut down cedars,
    or perhaps took a cypress or oak.
He let it grow among the trees of the forest,
    or planted a pine, and the rain made it
        grow.
15 It is man's fuel for burning;
    some of it he takes and warms himself,
    he kindles a fire and bakes bread.
But he also fashions a god and worships it;
    he makes an idol and bows down to it.
16 Half of the wood he burns in the fire;
    over it he prepares his meal,
    he roasts his meat and eats his fill.
He also warms himself and says,
    "Ah! I am warm; I see the fire."

THE MESSAGE

"I'm first, I'm last, and everything in between.
    I'm the only God there is.
Who compares with me?
    Speak up. See if you measure up.
From the beginning, who else has always
        announced what's coming?
    So what is coming next? Anybody want to
        venture a try?
Don't be afraid, and don't worry:
    Haven't I always kept you informed, told
        you what was going on?
You're my eyewitnesses:
    Have you ever come across a God, a real
        God, other than me?
    There's no Rock like me that I know of."

LOVER OF EMPTINESS

44.9-11 All those who make no-god idols don't amount
to a thing, and what they work so hard at making is nothing. Their little puppet-gods see
nothing and know nothing—they're total em-
barrassments! Who would bother making gods
that can't do anything, that can't "*god*"? Watch
all the no-god worshipers hide their faces in
shame. Watch the no-god makers slink off humiliated when their idols fail them. Get them
out here in the open. Make them face God-reality.

44.12   The blacksmith makes his no-god, works it
over in his forge, hammering it on his anvil—
such hard work! He works away, fatigued with
hunger and thirst.

44.13-17   The woodworker draws up plans for his no-
god, traces it on a block of wood. He shapes it
with chisels and planes into human shape—a
beautiful woman, a handsome man, ready to
be placed in a chapel. He first cuts down a
cedar, or maybe picks out a pine or oak, and
lets it grow strong in the forest, nourished by
the rain. Then it can serve a double purpose:
Part he uses as firewood for keeping warm and
baking bread; from the other part he makes a
god that he worships—carves it into a god
shape and prays before it. With half he makes a
fire to warm himself and barbecue his supper.
He eats his fill and sits back satisfied with his
stomach full and his feet warmed by the fire:
"Ah, this is the life." And he still has half left

NEW INTERNATIONAL VERSION	THE MESSAGE

NEW INTERNATIONAL VERSION

¹⁷ From the rest he makes a god, his idol;
    he bows down to it and worships.
He prays to it and says,
    "Save me; you are my god."
¹⁸ They know nothing, they understand
        nothing;
    their eyes are plastered over so they
        cannot see,
    and their minds closed so they cannot
        understand.
¹⁹ No one stops to think,
    no one has the knowledge or
        understanding to say,
"Half of it I used for fuel;
    I even baked bread over its coals,
    I roasted meat and I ate.
Shall I make a detestable thing from what is
        left?
    Shall I bow down to a block of wood?"
²⁰ He feeds on ashes, a deluded heart misleads
        him;
    he cannot save himself, or say,
    "Is not this thing in my right hand a lie?"

²¹ "Remember these things, O Jacob,
    for you are my servant, O Israel.
I have made you, you are my servant;
    O Israel, I will not forget you.
²² I have swept away your offenses like a cloud,
    your sins like the morning mist.
Return to me,
    for I have redeemed you."

²³ Sing for joy, O heavens, for the LORD has
        done this;
    shout aloud, O earth beneath.
Burst into song, you mountains,
    you forests and all your trees,
for the LORD has redeemed Jacob,
    he displays his glory in Israel.

JERUSALEM TO BE INHABITED
²⁴ "This is what the LORD says—
    your Redeemer, who formed you in the
        womb:

I am the LORD,
    who has made all things,
    who alone stretched out the heavens,
    who spread out the earth by myself,

²⁵ who foils the signs of false prophets
    and makes fools of diviners,
who overthrows the learning of the wise
    and turns it into nonsense,
²⁶ who carries out the words of his servants
    and fulfills the predictions of his
        messengers,

THE MESSAGE

for a god, made to his personal design—a
handy, convenient no-god to worship whenever so inclined. Whenever the need strikes him
he prays to it, "Save me. You're my god."

^{44.18-19}   Pretty stupid, wouldn't you say? Don't they
have eyes in their heads? Are their brains working at all? Doesn't it occur to them to say, "Half
of this tree I used for firewood: I baked bread,
roasted meat, and enjoyed a good meal. And
now I've used the rest to make an abominable
no-god. Here I am praying to a stick of wood!"

^{44.20}   This lover of emptiness, of nothing, is so out
of touch with reality, so far gone, that he can't
even look at what he's doing, can't even look at
the no-god stick of wood in his hand and say,
"This is crazy."

✝

^{44.21-22} "Remember these things, O Jacob.
    Take it seriously, Israel, that you're my
        servant.
I made you, *shaped* you: You're my servant.
    O Israel, I'll never forget you.
I've wiped the slate of all your wrongdoings.
    There's nothing left of your sins.
Come back to me, come back.
    I've redeemed you."

^{44.23} High heavens, sing!
    GOD has done it.
Deep earth, shout!
    And you mountains, sing!
    A forest choir of oaks and pines and cedars!
GOD has redeemed Jacob.
    GOD's glory is on display in Israel.

^{44.24} GOD, your Redeemer,
    who shaped your life in your mother's
        womb, says:
"I am GOD. I made all that is.
    With no help from you I spread out the
        skies
    and laid out the earth."

^{44.25-28} He makes the magicians look ridiculous
    and turns fortunetellers into jokes.
He makes the experts look trivial
    and their latest knowledge look silly.
But he backs the word of his servant
    and confirms the counsel of his
        messengers.

NEW INTERNATIONAL VERSION	THE MESSAGE

NEW INTERNATIONAL VERSION

who says of Jerusalem, 'It shall be inhabited,'
   of the towns of Judah, 'They shall be
      built,'
  and of their ruins, 'I will restore them,'
27 who says to the watery deep, 'Be dry,
  and I will dry up your streams,'
28 who says of Cyrus, 'He is my shepherd
  and will accomplish all that I please;
  he will say of Jerusalem, "Let it be
     rebuilt,"
  and of the temple, "Let its foundations be
     laid." '

45 "This is what the LORD says to his
     anointed,
  to Cyrus, whose right hand I take hold of
to subdue nations before him
  and to strip kings of their armor,
to open doors before him
  so that gates will not be shut:
2 I will go before you
  and will level the mountains*a*;
I will break down gates of bronze
  and cut through bars of iron.
3 I will give you the treasures of darkness,
  riches stored in secret places,
so that you may know that I am the LORD,
  the God of Israel, who summons you by
    name.
4 For the sake of Jacob my servant,
  of Israel my chosen,
I summon you by name
  and bestow on you a title of honor,
  though you do not acknowledge me.
5 I am the LORD, and there is no other;
  apart from me there is no God.
I will strengthen you,
  though you have not acknowledged me,
6 so that from the rising of the sun
  to the place of its setting
men may know there is none besides me.
  I am the LORD, and there is no other.
7 I form the light and create darkness,
  I bring prosperity and create disaster;
  I, the LORD, do all these things.

8 "You heavens above, rain down
     righteousness;
  let the clouds shower it down.
Let the earth open wide,
  let salvation spring up,
let righteousness grow with it;
  I, the LORD, have created it.

9 "Woe to him who quarrels with his Maker,

THE MESSAGE

He says to Jerusalem, "Be inhabited,"
  and to the cities of Judah, "Be rebuilt,"
  and to the ruins, "I raise you up."
He says to Ocean, "Dry up.
  I'm drying up your rivers."
He says to Cyrus, "My shepherd—
  everything I want, you'll do it."
He says to Jerusalem, "Be built,"
  and to the Temple, "Be established."

THE GOD WHO FORMS LIGHT AND DARKNESS

45.1-7 45 GOD's Message to his anointed,
  to Cyrus, whom he took by the hand
To give the task of taming the nations,
  of terrifying their kings—
He gave him free rein,
  no restrictions:
"I'll go ahead of you,
  clearing and paving the road.
I'll break down bronze city gates,
  smash padlocks, kick down barred
    entrances.
I'll lead you to buried treasures,
  secret caches of valuables—
Confirmations that it is, in fact, I, GOD,
  the God of Israel, who calls you by your
    name.
It's because of my dear servant Jacob,
  Israel my chosen,
That I've singled you out, called you by name,
  and given you this privileged work.
  And you don't even know me!
I am GOD, the only God there is.
  Besides me there are no real gods.
I'm the one who armed you for this work,
  though you don't even know me,
So that everyone, from east to west, will know
  that I have no god-rivals.
  I am GOD, the only God there is.
I form light and create darkness,
  I make harmonies and create discords.
  I, GOD, do all these things.

45.8-10 "Open up, heavens, and rain.
  Clouds, pour out buckets of my goodness!
Loosen up, earth, and bloom salvation;
  sprout right living.
  I, GOD, generate all this.
But doom to you who fight your Maker—

---

a 2 Dead Sea Scrolls and Septuagint; the meaning of the
word in the Masoretic Text is uncertain.

NEW INTERNATIONAL VERSION

to him who is but a potsherd among the
potsherds on the ground.
Does the clay say to the potter,
'What are you making?'
Does your work say,
'He has no hands'?
¹⁰Woe to him who says to his father,
'What have you begotten?'
or to his mother,
'What have you brought to birth?'

¹¹"This is what the LORD says—
the Holy One of Israel, and its Maker:
Concerning things to come,
do you question me about my children,
or give me orders about the work of my
hands?
¹²It is I who made the earth
and created mankind upon it.
My own hands stretched out the heavens;
I marshaled their starry hosts.
¹³I will raise up Cyrus ᵃ in my righteousness:
I will make all his ways straight.
He will rebuild my city
and set my exiles free,
but not for a price or reward,
says the LORD Almighty."

¹⁴This is what the LORD says:

"The products of Egypt and the merchandise
of Cush, ᵇ
and those tall Sabeans—
they will come over to you
and will be yours;
they will trudge behind you,
coming over to you in chains.
They will bow down before you
and plead with you, saying,
'Surely God is with you, and there is no
other;
there is no other god.' "

¹⁵Truly you are a God who hides himself,
O God and Savior of Israel.
¹⁶All the makers of idols will be put to shame
and disgraced;
they will go off into disgrace together.
¹⁷But Israel will be saved by the LORD
with an everlasting salvation;
you will never be put to shame or disgraced,
to ages everlasting.

¹⁸For this is what the LORD says—
he who created the heavens,

THE MESSAGE

you're a pot at odds with the potter!
Does clay talk back to the potter:
'What are you doing? What clumsy
fingers!'
Would a sperm say to a father,
'Who gave you permission to use me to
make a baby?'
Or a fetus to a mother,
'Why have you cooped me up in this
belly?' "

45.11-13 Thus GOD, The Holy of Israel, Israel's Maker,
says:
"Do you question who or what I'm
making?
Are you telling me what I can or cannot
do?
I made earth,
and I created man and woman to live on it.
I handcrafted the skies
and direct all the constellations in their
turnings.
And now I've got Cyrus on the move.
I've rolled out the red carpet before him.
He will build my city.
He will bring home my exiles.
I didn't hire him to do this. I *told* him.
I, GOD-of-the-Angel-Armies."

✜

45.14 GOD says:

"The workers of Egypt, the merchants of
Ethiopia,
and those statuesque Sabeans
Will all come over to you—all yours.
Docile in chains, they'll follow you,
Hands folded in reverence, praying before
you:
'Amazing! God is with you!
There is no other God—none.' "

LOOK AT THE EVIDENCE
45.15-17 Clearly, you are a God who works behind the
scenes,
God of Israel, Savior God.
Humiliated, all those others
will be ashamed to show their faces in
public.
Out of work and at loose ends, the makers of
no-god idols
won't know what to do with themselves.
The people of Israel, though, are saved by
you, GOD,
saved with an eternal salvation.
They won't be ashamed,
they won't be at loose ends, ever.

GOD, Creator of the heavens—

ᵃ 13 Hebrew *him* ᵇ 14 That is, the upper Nile region

NEW INTERNATIONAL VERSION	THE MESSAGE

NEW INTERNATIONAL VERSION

he is God;
he who fashioned and made the earth,
    he founded it;
he did not create it to be empty,
    but formed it to be inhabited—
he says:
"I am the LORD,
    and there is no other.
¹⁹ I have not spoken in secret,
    from somewhere in a land of darkness;
I have not said to Jacob's descendants,
    'Seek me in vain.'
I, the LORD, speak the truth;
    I declare what is right.

²⁰ "Gather together and come;
    assemble, you fugitives from the nations.
Ignorant are those who carry about idols of
      wood,
who pray to gods that cannot save.
²¹ Declare what is to be, present it—
    let them take counsel together.
Who foretold this long ago,
    who declared it from the distant past?
Was it not I, the LORD?
    And there is no God apart from me,
a righteous God and a Savior;
    there is none but me.

²² "Turn to me and be saved,
    all you ends of the earth;
for I am God, and there is no other.
²³ By myself I have sworn,
    my mouth has uttered in all integrity
    a word that will not be revoked:
Before me every knee will bow;
    by me every tongue will swear.
²⁴ They will say of me, 'In the LORD alone
    are righteousness and strength.' "
All who have raged against him
    will come to him and be put to shame.
²⁵ But in the LORD all the descendants of Israel
    will be found righteous and will exult.

THE MESSAGE

he is, remember, *God*.
Maker of earth—
    he put it on its foundations, built it from
      scratch.
He didn't go to all that trouble
    to just leave it empty, nothing in it.
He made it to be lived in.

45.18-24   This GOD says:

"I am GOD,
    the one and only.
I don't just talk to myself
    or mumble under my breath.
I never told Jacob,
    'Seek me in emptiness, in dark
      nothingness.'
I am GOD. I work out in the open,
    saying what's right, setting things right.
So gather around, come on in,
    all you refugees and castoffs.
They don't seem to know much, do they—
    those who carry around their no-god
      blocks of wood,
    praying for help to a dead stick?
So tell me what you think. Look at the
      evidence.
Put your heads together. Make your case.
Who told you, and a long time ago, what's
      going on here?
    Who made sense of things for you?
Wasn't I the one? GOD?
    It had to be me. I'm the only God there is—
The only God who does things right
    and knows how to help.
So turn to me and be helped—saved!—
    everyone, whoever and wherever you are.
I am GOD,
    the only God there is, the one and only.
I promise in my own name:
    Every word out of my mouth does what it
      says.
    I never take back what I say.
Everyone is going to end up kneeling before
      me.
    Everyone is going to end up saying of me,
'Yes! Salvation and strength are in GOD!' "

45.24-25   All who have raged against him
    will be brought before him,
    disgraced by their unbelief.
And all who are connected with Israel
    will have a robust, praising, good life in
      GOD!

NEW INTERNATIONAL VERSION	THE MESSAGE

NEW INTERNATIONAL VERSION

GODS OF BABYLON

46 Bel bows down, Nebo stoops low;
their idols are borne by beasts of
burden. *a*
The images that are carried about are
burdensome,
a burden for the weary.
² They stoop and bow down together;
unable to rescue the burden,
they themselves go off into captivity.

³ "Listen to me, O house of Jacob,
all you who remain of the house of Israel,
you whom I have upheld since you were
conceived,
and have carried since your birth.
⁴ Even to your old age and gray hairs
I am he, I am he who will sustain you.
I have made you and I will carry you;
I will sustain you and I will rescue you.

⁵ "To whom will you compare me or count me
equal?
To whom will you liken me that we may
be compared?
⁶ Some pour out gold from their bags
and weigh out silver on the scales;
they hire a goldsmith to make it into a god,
and they bow down and worship it.
⁷ They lift it to their shoulders and carry it;
they set it up in its place, and there it
stands.
From that spot it cannot move.
Though one cries out to it, it does not
answer;
it cannot save him from his troubles.

⁸ "Remember this, fix it in mind,
take it to heart, you rebels.
⁹ Remember the former things, those of long
ago;
I am God, and there is no other;
I am God, and there is none like me.
¹⁰ I make known the end from the beginning,
from ancient times, what is still to come.
I say: My purpose will stand,
and I will do all that I please.
¹¹ From the east I summon a bird of prey;
from a far-off land, a man to fulfill my
purpose.
What I have said, that will I bring about;
what I have planned, that will I do.
¹² Listen to me, you stubborn-hearted,
you who are far from righteousness.

THE MESSAGE

THIS IS SERIOUS BUSINESS, REBELS

46.1-2 **46** The god Bel falls down, god Nebo
slumps.
The no-god hunks of wood are loaded on
mules
And have to be hauled off,
wearing out the poor mules—
Dead weight, burdens who can't bear burdens,
hauled off to captivity.

46.3-4 "Listen to me, family of Jacob,
everyone that's left of the family of Israel.
I've been carrying you on my back
from the day you were born,
And I'll keep on carrying you when you're old.
I'll be there, bearing you when you're old
and gray.
I've done it and will keep on doing it,
carrying you on my back, saving you.

46.5-7 "So to whom will you compare me, the
Incomparable?
Can you picture me without reducing me?
People with a lot of money
hire craftsmen to make them gods.
The artisan delivers the god,
and they kneel and worship it!
They carry it around in holy parades,
then take it home and put it on a shelf.
And there it sits, day in and day out,
a dependable god, always right where you
put it.
Say anything you want to it, it never talks
back.
Of course, it never *does* anything either!

46.8-11 "Think about this. Wrap your minds around it.
This is serious business, rebels. Take it to
heart.
Remember your history,
your long and rich history.
I am GOD, the only God you've had or ever
will have—
incomparable, irreplaceable—
From the very beginning
telling you what the ending will be,
All along letting you in
on what is going to happen,
Assuring you, 'I'm in this for the long haul,
I'll do exactly what I set out to do,'
Calling that eagle, Cyrus, out of the east,
from a far country the man I chose to help
me.
I've said it, and I'll most certainly do it.
I've planned it, so it's as good as done.

46.12-13 "Now listen to me:
You're a hardheaded bunch and hard to
help.

NEW INTERNATIONAL VERSION

13 I am bringing my righteousness near,
 it is not far away;
 and my salvation will not be delayed.
I will grant salvation to Zion,
 my splendor to Israel.

THE FALL OF BABYLON

47 "Go down, sit in the dust,
 Virgin Daughter of Babylon;
sit on the ground without a throne,
 Daughter of the Babylonians. *a*
No more will you be called
 tender or delicate.
2 Take millstones and grind flour;
 take off your veil.
Lift up your skirts, bare your legs,
 and wade through the streams.
3 Your nakedness will be exposed
 and your shame uncovered.
I will take vengeance;
 I will spare no one."

4 Our Redeemer—the LORD Almighty is his
 name—
 is the Holy One of Israel.

5 "Sit in silence, go into darkness,
 Daughter of the Babylonians;
no more will you be called
 queen of kingdoms.
6 I was angry with my people
 and desecrated my inheritance;
I gave them into your hand,
 and you showed them no mercy.
Even on the aged
 you laid a very heavy yoke.
7 You said, 'I will continue forever—
 the eternal queen!'
But you did not consider these things
 or reflect on what might happen.

8 "Now then, listen, you wanton creature,
 lounging in your security
and saying to yourself,
 'I am, and there is none besides me.
I will never be a widow
 or suffer the loss of children.'
9 Both of these will overtake you
 in a moment, on a single day:
 loss of children and widowhood.
They will come upon you in full measure,
 in spite of your many sorceries
 and all your potent spells.

a 1 Or *Chaldeans*; also in verse 5

THE MESSAGE

I'm ready to help you right now.
 Deliverance is not a long-range plan.
 Salvation isn't on hold.
I'm putting salvation to work in Zion now,
 and glory in Israel.

THE PARTY'S OVER

47.1-3 **47** "Get off your high horse and sit in the
 dirt,
 virgin daughter of Babylon.
No more throne for you—sit on the ground,
 daughter of the Chaldeans.
Nobody will be calling you 'charming'
 and 'alluring' anymore. Get used to it.
Get a job, any old job:
 Clean gutters, scrub toilets.
Hock your gowns and scarves,
 put on overalls—the party's over.
Your nude body will be on public display,
 exposed to vulgar taunts.
It's vengeance time, and I'm taking vengeance.
 No one gets let off the hook."

YOU'RE ACTING LIKE THE CENTER OF THE UNIVERSE

47.4-13 Our Redeemer speaks,
 named GOD-of-the-Angel-Armies, The Holy
 of Israel:
"Shut up and get out of the way,
 daughter of Chaldeans.
You'll no longer be called
 'First Lady of the Kingdoms.'
I was fed up with my people,
 thoroughly disgusted with my progeny.
I turned them over to you,
 but you had no compassion.
You put old men and women
 to cruel, hard labor.
You said, 'I'm the First Lady.
 I'll always be the pampered darling.'
You took nothing seriously, took nothing to
 heart,
 never gave tomorrow a thought.
Well, start thinking, playgirl.
 You're acting like the center of the
 universe,
Smugly saying to yourself, 'I'm Number One.
 There's nobody but me.
I'll never be a widow, I'll never lose my
 children.'
Those two things are going to hit you both at
 once,
 suddenly, on the same day:
Spouse and children gone, a total loss,
 despite your many enchantments and
 charms.

NEW INTERNATIONAL VERSION

¹⁰ You have trusted in your wickedness
    and have said, 'No one sees me.'
Your wisdom and knowledge mislead you
    when you say to yourself,
    'I am, and there is none besides me.'
¹¹ Disaster will come upon you,
    and you will not know how to conjure it
        away.
A calamity will fall upon you
    that you cannot ward off with a ransom;
a catastrophe you cannot foresee
    will suddenly come upon you.

¹² "Keep on, then, with your magic spells
    and with your many sorceries,
    which you have labored at since
        childhood.
Perhaps you will succeed,
    perhaps you will cause terror.
¹³ All the counsel you have received has only
        worn you out!
Let your astrologers come forward,
    those stargazers who make predictions
        month by month,
let them save you from what is coming
        upon you.
¹⁴ Surely they are like stubble;
    the fire will burn them up.
They cannot even save themselves
    from the power of the flame.
Here are no coals to warm anyone;
    here is no fire to sit by.
¹⁵ That is all they can do for you—
    these you have labored with
    and trafficked with since childhood.
Each of them goes on in his error;
    there is not one that can save you.

STUBBORN ISRAEL

48 "Listen to this, O house of Jacob,
    you who are called by the name of Israel
    and come from the line of Judah,
you who take oaths in the name of the LORD
    and invoke the God of Israel—
    but not in truth or righteousness—
² you who call yourselves citizens of the holy
        city
    and rely on the God of Israel—
    the LORD Almighty is his name:
³ I foretold the former things long ago,
    my mouth announced them and I made
        them known;
    then suddenly I acted, and they came to
        pass.
⁴ For I knew how stubborn you were;
    the sinews of your neck were iron,

THE MESSAGE

You were so confident and comfortable in
        your evil life,
    saying, 'No one sees me.'
You thought you knew so much, had
        everything figured out.
    What delusion!
    Smugly telling yourself, 'I'm Number One.
        There's nobody but me.'
Ruin descends—
    you can't charm it away.
Disaster strikes—
    you can't cast it off with spells.
Catastrophe, sudden and total—
    and you're totally at sea, totally bewildered!
But don't give up. From your great repertoire
    of enchantments there must be one you
        haven't yet tried.
You've been at this a long time.
    Surely *something* will work.
I know you're exhausted trying out remedies,
    but don't give up.
Call in the astrologers and stargazers.
    They're good at this. Surely they can work
        up something!

47.14-15 "Fat chance. You'd be grasping at straws
    that are already in the fire,
A fire that is even now raging.
    Your 'experts' are in it and won't get out.
It's not a fire for cooking venison stew,
    not a fire to warm you on a winter night!
That's the fate of your friends in sorcery, your
        magician buddies
    you've been in cahoots with all your life.
They reel, confused, bumping into one
        another.
    None of them bother to help you.

TESTED IN THE FURNACE OF AFFLICTION

48.1-11 **48** "And now listen to this, family of Jacob,
    you who are called by the name Israel:
Who got you started in the loins of Judah,
    you who use GOD's name to back up your
        promises
    and pray to the God of Israel?
But do you mean it?
    Do you live like it?
You claim to be citizens of the Holy City;
    you act as though you lean on the God of
        Israel,
    named GOD-of-the-Angel-Armies.
For a long time now, I've let you in on the way
        I work:
    I told you what I was going to do
        beforehand,
    then I did it and it was done, and that's
        that.
I know you're a bunch of hardheads,

NEW INTERNATIONAL VERSION

your forehead was bronze.
5 Therefore I told you these things long ago;
    before they happened I announced them
        to you
so that you could not say,
    'My idols did them;
    my wooden image and metal god
        ordained them.'
6 You have heard these things; look at them
        all.
    Will you not admit them?

"From now on I will tell you of new things,
    of hidden things unknown to you.
7 They are created now, and not long ago;
    you have not heard of them before today.
So you cannot say,
    'Yes, I knew of them.'
8 You have neither heard nor understood;
    from of old your ear has not been open.
Well do I know how treacherous you are;
    you were called a rebel from birth.
9 For my own name's sake I delay my wrath;
    for the sake of my praise I hold it back
        from you,
    so as not to cut you off.
10 See, I have refined you, though not as silver;
    I have tested you in the furnace of
        affliction.
11 For my own sake, for my own sake, I do this.
    How can I let myself be defamed?
    I will not yield my glory to another.

ISRAEL FREED

12 "Listen to me, O Jacob,
    Israel, whom I have called:
I am he;
    I am the first and I am the last.
13 My own hand laid the foundations of the
        earth,
    and my right hand spread out the
        heavens;
when I summon them,
    they all stand up together.

14 "Come together, all of you, and listen:
    Which of ⌊the idols⌋ has foretold these
        things?
The LORD's chosen ally
    will carry out his purpose against
        Babylon;
    his arm will be against the Babylonians. ᵃ
15 I, even I, have spoken;
    yes, I have called him.
I will bring him,
    and he will succeed in his mission.

THE MESSAGE

obstinate and flint-faced,
So I got a running start and began telling you
    what was going on before it even
        happened.
That is why you can't say,
    'My god-idol did this.'
    'My favorite god-carving commanded this.'
You have all this evidence
    confirmed by your own eyes and ears.
    Shouldn't you be talking about it?
And that was just the beginning.
    I have a lot more to tell you,
    things you never knew existed.
This isn't a variation on the same old thing.
    This is new, brand-new,
    something you'd never guess or dream up.
When you hear this you won't be able to say,
    'I knew that all along.'
You've never been good listeners to me.
    You have a history of ignoring me,
A sorry track record of fickle attachments—
    rebels from the womb.
But out of the sheer goodness of my heart,
    because of who I am,
I keep a tight rein on my anger and hold my
        temper.
    I don't wash my hands of you.
Do you see what I've done?
    I've refined you, but not without fire.
    I've tested you like silver in the furnace of
        affliction.
Out of myself, simply because of who I am, I
        do what I do.
    I have my reputation to keep up.
    I'm not playing second fiddle to either gods
        or people.

48.12-13 "Listen, Jacob. Listen, Israel—
    I'm the One who named you!
I'm the One.
    I got things started and, yes, I'll wrap them
        up.
Earth is my work, handmade.
    And the skies—I made them too, horizon
        to horizon.
When I speak, they're on their feet, at
        attention.

48.14-16 "Come everybody, gather around, listen:
    Who among the gods has delivered the
        news?
I, GOD, love this man Cyrus, and I'm using
        him
    to do what I want with Babylon.
I, yes I, have spoken. I've called him.
    I've brought him here. He'll be successful.

ᵃ 14 Or Chaldeans; also in verse 20

NEW INTERNATIONAL VERSION

¹⁶"Come near me and listen to this:

"From the first announcement I have not
    spoken in secret;
  at the time it happens, I am there."

And now the Sovereign LORD has sent me,
    with his Spirit.

¹⁷This is what the LORD says—
    your Redeemer, the Holy One of Israel:
"I am the LORD your God,
    who teaches you what is best for you,
    who directs you in the way you
      should go.
¹⁸If only you had paid attention to my
      commands,
    your peace would have been like a river,
    your righteousness like the waves of the
      sea.
¹⁹Your descendants would have been like the
      sand,
    your children like its numberless grains;
  their name would never be cut off
    nor destroyed from before me."

²⁰Leave Babylon,
    flee from the Babylonians!
  Announce this with shouts of joy
    and proclaim it.
  Send it out to the ends of the earth;
    say, "The LORD has redeemed his servant
      Jacob."
²¹They did not thirst when he led them
      through the deserts;
    he made water flow for them from the rock;
  he split the rock
    and water gushed out.

²²"There is no peace," says the LORD, "for the
    wicked."

THE SERVANT OF THE LORD

49 Listen to me, you islands;
    hear this, you distant nations:
  Before I was born the LORD called me;
    from my birth he has made mention of my
      name.
²He made my mouth like a sharpened sword,
    in the shadow of his hand he hid me;
  he made me into a polished arrow
    and concealed me in his quiver.
³He said to me, "You are my servant,
    Israel, in whom I will display my
      splendor."
⁴But I said, "I have labored to no purpose;
    I have spent my strength in vain and for
      nothing.
  Yet what is due me is in the LORD's hand,
    and my reward is with my God."

THE MESSAGE

Come close, listen carefully:
    I've never kept secrets from you.
    I've always been present with you."

YOUR PROGENY, LIKE GRAINS OF SAND

^{48.16-19} And now, the Master, GOD, sends me and his
      Spirit
    with this Message from GOD,
    your Redeemer, The Holy of Israel:
"I am GOD, your God,
    who teaches you how to live right and well.
    I show you what to do, where to go.
  If you had listened all along to what I told
      you,
    your life would have flowed full like a river,
    blessings rolling in like waves from the sea.
  Children and grandchildren are like sand,
    your progeny like grains of sand.
  There would be no end of them,
    no danger of losing touch with me."

^{48.20} Get out of Babylon! Run from the
      Babylonians!
    Shout the news. Broadcast it.
  Let the world know, the whole world.
    Tell them, "GOD redeemed his dear servant
      Jacob!"

^{48.21} They weren't thirsty when he led them
      through the deserts.
    He made water pour out of the rock;
    he split the rock and the water gushed.

^{48.22} "There is no peace," says GOD, "for the
      wicked."

A LIGHT FOR THE NATIONS

^{49.1-3} **49** Listen, far-flung islands,
    pay attention, faraway people:
  GOD put me to work from the day I was born.
    The moment I entered the world he
      named me.
  He gave me speech that would cut and
      penetrate.
    He kept his hand on me to protect me.
  He made me his straight arrow
    and hid me in his quiver.
  He said to me, "You're my dear servant,
    Israel, through whom I'll shine."

^{49.4} But I said, "I've worked for nothing.
    I've nothing to show for a life of hard work.
  Nevertheless, I'll let GOD have the last word.
    I'll let him pronounce his verdict."

NEW INTERNATIONAL VERSION

⁵And now the LORD says—
 he who formed me in the womb to be his
 servant
to bring Jacob back to him
 and gather Israel to himself,
for I am honored in the eyes of the LORD
 and my God has been my strength—
⁶he says:
"It is too small a thing for you to be my
 servant
 to restore the tribes of Jacob
 and bring back those of Israel I have kept.
I will also make you a light for the Gentiles,
 that you may bring my salvation to the
 ends of the earth."

⁷This is what the LORD says—
 the Redeemer and Holy One of Israel—
to him who was despised and abhorred by
 the nation,
 to the servant of rulers:
"Kings will see you and rise up,
 princes will see and bow down,
because of the LORD, who is faithful,
 the Holy One of Israel, who has chosen you."

RESTORATION OF ISRAEL
 ⁸This is what the LORD says:

"In the time of my favor I will answer you,
 and in the day of salvation I will help you;
I will keep you and will make you
 to be a covenant for the people,
to restore the land
 and to reassign its desolate inheritances,
⁹to say to the captives, 'Come out,'
 and to those in darkness, 'Be free!'

"They will feed beside the roads
 and find pasture on every barren hill.
¹⁰They will neither hunger nor thirst,
 nor will the desert heat or the sun beat
 upon them.
He who has compassion on them will guide
 them
 and lead them beside springs of water.
¹¹I will turn all my mountains into roads,
 and my highways will be raised up.
¹²See, they will come from afar—
 some from the north, some from the west,
 some from the region of Aswan. ^a"

¹³Shout for joy, O heavens;
 rejoice, O earth;
 burst into song, O mountains!
For the LORD comforts his people
 and will have compassion on his afflicted
 ones.

^a 12 Dead Sea Scrolls; Masoretic Text *Sinim*

THE MESSAGE

49.5-6 "And now," GOD says,
 this God who took me in hand
 from the moment of birth to be his servant,
To bring Jacob back home to him,
 to set a reunion for Israel—
What an honor for me in GOD's eyes!
 That God should be my strength!
He says, "But that's not a big enough job for
 my servant—
 just to recover the tribes of Jacob,
 merely to round up the strays of Israel.
I'm setting you up as a light for the *nations*
 so that my salvation becomes *global!*"

49.7 GOD, Redeemer of Israel, The Holy of Israel,
 says to the despised one, kicked around by
 the nations,
 slave labor to the ruling class:
"Kings will see, get to their feet—the princes,
 too—
 and then fall on their faces in homage
Because of GOD, who has faithfully kept his
 word,
 The Holy of Israel, who has chosen you."

49.8-12 GOD also says:

"When the time's ripe, I answer you.
 When victory's due, I help you.
I form you and use you
 to reconnect the people with me,
To put the land in order,
 to resettle families on the ruined properties.
I tell prisoners, 'Come on out. You're free!'
 and those huddled in fear, 'It's all right. It's
 safe now.'
There'll be foodstands along all the roads,
 picnics on all the hills—
Nobody hungry, nobody thirsty,
 shade from the sun, shelter from the wind,
For the Compassionate One guides them,
 takes them to the best springs.
I'll make all my mountains into roads,
 turn them into a superhighway.
Look: These coming from far countries,
 and those, out of the north,
These streaming in from the west,
 and those from all the way down the Nile!"

49.13 Heavens, raise the roof! Earth, wake the dead!
 Mountains, send up cheers!
GOD has comforted his people.
 He has tenderly nursed his beaten-up,
 beaten-down people.

NEW INTERNATIONAL VERSION

¹⁴ But Zion said, "The LORD has forsaken me,
  the Lord has forgotten me."

¹⁵ "Can a mother forget the baby at her breast
    and have no compassion on the child she
      has borne?
  Though she may forget,
    I will not forget you!
¹⁶ See, I have engraved you on the palms of my
      hands;
    your walls are ever before me.
¹⁷ Your sons hasten back,
    and those who laid you waste depart from
      you.
¹⁸ Lift up your eyes and look around;
    all your sons gather and come to you.
  As surely as I live," declares the LORD,
    "you will wear them all as ornaments;
    you will put them on, like a bride.

¹⁹ "Though you were ruined and made desolate
    and your land laid waste,
  now you will be too small for your people,
    and those who devoured you will be far
      away.
²⁰ The children born during your bereavement
    will yet say in your hearing,
  'This place is too small for us;
    give us more space to live in.'
²¹ Then you will say in your heart,
    'Who bore me these?
  I was bereaved and barren;
    I was exiled and rejected.
  Who brought these up?
  I was left all alone,
    but these—where have they come from?' "

²² This is what the Sovereign LORD says:

"See, I will beckon to the Gentiles,
    I will lift up my banner to the peoples;
  they will bring your sons in their arms
    and carry your daughters on their
      shoulders.
²³ Kings will be your foster fathers,
    and their queens your nursing mothers.
  They will bow down before you with their
      faces to the ground;
    they will lick the dust at your feet.
  Then you will know that I am the LORD;
    those who hope in me will not be
      disappointed."

²⁴ Can plunder be taken from warriors,
    or captives rescued from the fierce^a?

THE MESSAGE

^{49.14} But Zion said, "I don't get it. GOD has left me.
    My Master has forgotten I even exist."

^{49.15-18} "Can a mother forget the infant at her breast,
    walk away from the baby she bore?
  But even if mothers forget,
    I'd never forget you—never.
  Look, I've written your names on the backs of
      my hands.
    The walls you're rebuilding are never out of
      my sight.
  Your builders are faster than your wreckers.
    The demolition crews are gone for good.
  Look up, look around, look well!
    See them all gathering, coming to you?
  As sure as I am the living God"—GOD's
      Decree—
    "you're going to put them on like so much
      jewelry,
    you're going to use them to dress up like a
      bride.

^{49.19-21} "And your ruined land?
    Your devastated, decimated land?
  Filled with more people than you know what
      to do with!
    And your barbarian enemies, a fading
      memory.
  The children born in your exile will be saying,
    'It's getting too crowded here. I need more
      room.'
  And you'll say to yourself,
    'Where on earth did these children come
      from?
  I lost everything, had nothing, was exiled and
      penniless.
    So who reared these children?
    How did these children get here?' "

^{49.22-23} The Master, GOD, says:

"Look! I signal to the nations,
    I raise my flag to summon the people.
  Here they'll come: women carrying your little
      boys in their arms,
    men carrying your little girls on their
      shoulders.
  Kings will be your babysitters,
    princesses will be your nursemaids.
  They'll offer to do all your drudge work—
    scrub your floors, do your laundry.
  You'll know then that I am GOD.
    No one who hopes in me ever regrets it."

^{49.24-26} Can plunder be retrieved from a giant,
    prisoners of war gotten back from a tyrant?

---

^a 24 Dead Sea Scrolls, Vulgate and Syriac (see also
Septuagint and verse 25); Masoretic Text *righteous*

NEW INTERNATIONAL VERSION

²⁵But this is what the LORD says:

"Yes, captives will be taken from warriors,
  and plunder retrieved from the fierce;
I will contend with those who contend with
    you,
  and your children I will save.
²⁶I will make your oppressors eat their own
    flesh;
  they will be drunk on their own blood, as
    with wine.
Then all mankind will know
  that I, the LORD, am your Savior,
  your Redeemer, the Mighty One of Jacob."

ISRAEL'S SIN AND THE SERVANT'S OBEDIENCE

50 This is what the LORD says:

"Where is your mother's certificate of divorce
  with which I sent her away?
Or to which of my creditors
  did I sell you?
Because of your sins you were sold;
  because of your transgressions your
    mother was sent away.
²When I came, why was there no one?
  When I called, why was there no one to
    answer?
Was my arm too short to ransom you?
  Do I lack the strength to rescue you?
By a mere rebuke I dry up the sea,
  I turn rivers into a desert;
their fish rot for lack of water
  and die of thirst.
³I clothe the sky with darkness
  and make sackcloth its covering."

⁴The Sovereign LORD has given me an
    instructed tongue,
  to know the word that sustains the weary.
He wakens me morning by morning,
  wakens my ear to listen like one being
    taught.
⁵The Sovereign LORD has opened my ears,
  and I have not been rebellious;
  I have not drawn back.
⁶I offered my back to those who beat me,
  my cheeks to those who pulled out my
    beard;
I did not hide my face
  from mocking and spitting.
⁷Because the Sovereign LORD helps me,
  I will not be disgraced.
Therefore have I set my face like flint,

THE MESSAGE

But GOD says, "Even if a giant grips the
    plunder
  and a tyrant holds my people prisoner,
I'm the one who's on your side,
  defending your cause, rescuing your
    children.
And your enemies, crazed and desperate, will
    turn on themselves,
  killing each other in a frenzy of
    self-destruction.
Then everyone will know that I, GOD,
  have saved you—I, the Mighty One of
    Jacob."

WHO OUT THERE FEARS GOD?

50.1-3 **50** GOD says:

"Can you produce your mother's divorce
    papers
  proving I got rid of her?
Can you produce a receipt
  proving I sold you?
Of course you can't.
  It's your sins that put you here,
  your wrongs that got you shipped out.
So why didn't anyone come when I knocked?
  Why didn't anyone answer when I called?
Do you think I've forgotten how to help?
  Am I so decrepit that I can't deliver?
I'm as powerful as ever,
  and can reverse what I once did:
I can dry up the sea with a word,
  turn river water into desert sand,
And leave the fish stinking in the sun,
  stranded on dry land . . .
Turn all the lights out in the sky
  and pull down the curtain."

✛

50.4-9 The Master, GOD, has given me
  a well-taught tongue,
So I know how to encourage tired people.
  He wakes me up in the morning,
Wakes me up, opens my ears
  to listen as one ready to take orders.
The Master, GOD, opened my ears,
  and I didn't go back to sleep,
  didn't pull the covers back over my head.
I followed orders,
  stood there and took it while they beat me,
  held steady while they pulled out my beard,
Didn't dodge their insults,
  faced them as they spit in my face.
And the Master, GOD, stays right there and
    helps me,
  so I'm not disgraced.
Therefore I set my face like flint,

NEW INTERNATIONAL VERSION	THE MESSAGE

NEW INTERNATIONAL VERSION

and I know I will not be put to shame.
⁸He who vindicates me is near.
  Who then will bring charges against me?
  Let us face each other!
Who is my accuser?
  Let him confront me!
⁹It is the Sovereign LORD who helps me.
  Who is he that will condemn me?
They will all wear out like a garment;
  the moths will eat them up.

¹⁰Who among you fears the LORD
  and obeys the word of his servant?
Let him who walks in the dark,
  who has no light,
trust in the name of the LORD
  and rely on his God.
¹¹But now, all you who light fires
  and provide yourselves with flaming
    torches,
go, walk in the light of your fires
  and of the torches you have set ablaze.
This is what you shall receive from my hand:
  You will lie down in torment.

EVERLASTING SALVATION FOR ZION

51 "Listen to me, you who pursue
      righteousness
  and who seek the LORD:
Look to the rock from which you were cut
  and to the quarry from which you were
    hewn;
  ²look to Abraham, your father,
    and to Sarah, who gave you birth.
  When I called him he was but one,
    and I blessed him and made him many.
  ³The LORD will surely comfort Zion
    and will look with compassion on all her
      ruins;
  he will make her deserts like Eden,
    her wastelands like the garden of the
      LORD.
  Joy and gladness will be found in her,
    thanksgiving and the sound of singing.

  ⁴"Listen to me, my people;
    hear me, my nation:
  The law will go out from me;
    my justice will become a light to the
      nations.
  ⁵My righteousness draws near speedily,
    my salvation is on the way,
    and my arm will bring justice to the
      nations.
  The islands will look to me

THE MESSAGE

confident that I'll never regret this.
My champion is right here.
  Let's take our stand together!
Who dares bring suit against me?
  Let him try!
Look! the Master, GOD, is right here.
  Who would dare call me guilty?
Look! My accusers are a clothes bin of
    threadbare
  socks and shirts, fodder for moths!

✠

50.10-11 Who out there fears GOD,
      actually listens to the voice of his servant?
  For anyone out there who doesn't know where
        you're going,
    anyone groping in the dark,
  Here's what: Trust in GOD.
    Lean on your God!
  But if all you're after is making trouble,
    playing with fire,
  Go ahead and see where it gets you.
    Set your fires, stir people up, blow on the
        flames,
  But don't expect me to just stand there and
      watch.
    I'll hold your feet to those flames.

COMMITTED TO SEEKING GOD

51.1-3 **51** "Listen to me, all you who are serious
        about right living
    and committed to seeking GOD.
  Ponder the rock from which you were cut,
    the quarry from which you were dug.
  Yes, ponder Abraham, your father,
    and Sarah, who bore you.
  Think of it! One solitary man when I called
        him,
    but once I blessed him, he multiplied.
  Likewise I, GOD, will comfort Zion,
    comfort all her mounds of ruins.
  I'll transform her dead ground into Eden,
    her moonscape into the garden of GOD,
  A place filled with exuberance and laughter,
    thankful voices and melodic songs.

51.4-6 "Pay attention, my people.
    Listen to me, nations.
  Revelation flows from me.
    My decisions light up the world.
  My deliverance arrives on the run,
    my salvation right on time.
    I'll bring justice to the peoples.
  Even faraway islands will look to me

NEW INTERNATIONAL VERSION

and wait in hope for my arm.
⁶Lift up your eyes to the heavens,
    look at the earth beneath;
the heavens will vanish like smoke,
    the earth will wear out like a garment
    and its inhabitants die like flies.
But my salvation will last forever,
    my righteousness will never fail.

⁷"Hear me, you who know what is right,
    you people who have my law in your
        hearts:
Do not fear the reproach of men
    or be terrified by their insults.
⁸For the moth will eat them up like a
        garment;
    the worm will devour them like wool.
But my righteousness will last forever,
    my salvation through all generations."

⁹Awake, awake! Clothe yourself with
        strength,
    O arm of the LORD;
awake, as in days gone by,
    as in generations of old.
Was it not you who cut Rahab to pieces,
    who pierced that monster through?
¹⁰Was it not you who dried up the sea,
    the waters of the great deep,
who made a road in the depths of the sea
    so that the redeemed might cross over?
¹¹The ransomed of the LORD will return.
    They will enter Zion with singing;
    everlasting joy will crown their heads.
Gladness and joy will overtake them,
    and sorrow and sighing will flee away.

¹²"I, even I, am he who comforts you.
    Who are you that you fear mortal men,
    the sons of men, who are but grass,
¹³that you forget the LORD your Maker,
    who stretched out the heavens
    and laid the foundations of the earth,
that you live in constant terror every day
    because of the wrath of the oppressor,
    who is bent on destruction?
For where is the wrath of the oppressor?
¹⁴   The cowering prisoners will soon be set
        free;
they will not die in their dungeon,
    nor will they lack bread.
¹⁵For I am the LORD your God,
    who churns up the sea so that its waves
        roar—
    the LORD Almighty is his name.
¹⁶I have put my words in your mouth
    and covered you with the shadow of my
        hand—
    I who set the heavens in place,

THE MESSAGE

and take hope in my saving power.
Look up at the skies,
    ponder the earth under your feet.
The skies will fade out like smoke,
    the earth will wear out like work pants,
    and the people will die off like flies.
But my salvation will last forever,
    my setting-things-right will never be
        obsolete.

51.7-8 "Listen now, you who know right from wrong,
    you who hold my teaching inside you:
Pay no attention to insults, and when mocked
    don't let it get you down.
Those insults and mockeries are moth-eaten,
    from brains that are termite-ridden,
But my setting-things-right lasts,
    my salvation goes on and on and on."

51.9-11 Wake up, wake up, flex your muscles, GOD!
    Wake up as in the old days, in the long ago.
Didn't you once make mincemeat of Rahab,
    dispatch the old chaos-dragon?
And didn't you once dry up the sea,
    the powerful waters of the deep,
And then made the bottom of the ocean a
        road
    for the redeemed to walk across?
In the same way GOD's ransomed will come
        back,
    come back to Zion cheering, shouting,
Joy eternal wreathing their heads,
    exuberant ecstasies transporting them—
    and not a sign of moans or groans.

WHAT ARE YOU AFRAID OF—OR WHO?

51.12-16 "I, I'm the One comforting you.
    What are you afraid of—or who?
Some man or woman who'll soon be dead?
    Some poor wretch destined for dust?
You've forgotten me, GOD, who made you,
    who unfurled the skies, who founded the
        earth.
And here you are, quaking like an aspen
    before the tantrums of a tyrant
    who thinks he can kick down the world.
But what will come of the tantrums?
    The victims will be released before you
        know it.
They're not going to die.
    They're not even going to go hungry.
For I am GOD, your very own God,
    who stirs up the sea and whips up the
        waves,
    named GOD-of-the-Angel-Armies.
I teach you how to talk, word by word,
    and personally watch over you,
Even while I'm unfurling the skies,

NEW INTERNATIONAL VERSION	THE MESSAGE

NEW INTERNATIONAL VERSION

who laid the foundations of the earth,
and who say to Zion, 'You are my people.' "

THE CUP OF THE LORD'S WRATH

¹⁷ Awake, awake!
   Rise up, O Jerusalem,
you who have drunk from the hand of the
   LORD
   the cup of his wrath,
you who have drained to its dregs
   the goblet that makes men stagger.
¹⁸ Of all the sons she bore
   there was none to guide her;
of all the sons she reared
   there was none to take her by the hand.
¹⁹ These double calamities have come upon you—
   who can comfort you?—
ruin and destruction, famine and sword—
   who can*ᵃ* console you?
²⁰ Your sons have fainted;
   they lie at the head of every street,
   like antelope caught in a net.
They are filled with the wrath of the LORD
   and the rebuke of your God.

²¹ Therefore hear this, you afflicted one,
   made drunk, but not with wine.
²² This is what your Sovereign LORD says,
   your God, who defends his people:
"See, I have taken out of your hand
   the cup that made you stagger;
from that cup, the goblet of my wrath,
   you will never drink again.
²³ I will put it into the hands of your tormentors,
   who said to you,
   'Fall prostrate that we may walk over you.'
And you made your back like the ground,
   like a street to be walked over."

52 Awake, awake, O Zion,
   clothe yourself with strength.
Put on your garments of splendor,
   O Jerusalem, the holy city.
The uncircumcised and defiled
   will not enter you again.
² Shake off your dust;
   rise up, sit enthroned, O Jerusalem.
Free yourself from the chains on your neck,
   O captive Daughter of Zion.

³ For this is what the LORD says:

"You were sold for nothing,
   and without money you will be
     redeemed."

ᵃ 19 Dead Sea Scrolls, Septuagint, Vulgate and Syriac;
Masoretic Text / *how can I*

THE MESSAGE

setting earth on solid foundations,
and greeting Zion: 'Welcome, my people!' "

51.17-20 So wake up! Rub the sleep from your eyes!
   Up on your feet, Jerusalem!
You've drunk the cup GOD handed you,
   the strong drink of his anger.
You drank it down to the last drop,
   staggered and collapsed, dead-drunk.
And nobody to help you home,
   no one among your friends or children
   to take you by the hand and put you in
     bed.
You've been hit with a double dose of trouble
   —does anyone care?
Assault and battery, hunger and death
   —will anyone comfort?
Your sons and daughters have passed out,
   strewn in the streets like stunned rabbits,
Sleeping off the strong drink of GOD's anger,
   the rage of your God.

51.21-23 Therefore listen, please,
   you with your splitting headaches,
You who are nursing the hangovers
   that didn't come from drinking wine.
Your Master, your GOD, has something to say,
   your God has taken up his people's case:
"Look, I've taken back the drink that sent you
     reeling.
   No more drinking from that jug of my
     anger!
I've passed it over to your abusers to drink,
     those who ordered you,
   'Down on the ground so we can walk all
     over you!'
And you had to do it. Flat on the ground,
   you were the dirt under their feet."

GOD IS LEADING YOU OUT OF HERE

52.1-2 **52** Wake up, wake up! Pull on your
     boots, Zion!
Dress up in your Sunday best, Jerusalem,
     holy city!
Those who want no part of God have been
     culled out.
   They won't be coming along.
Brush off the dust and get to your feet, captive
     Jerusalem!
Throw off your chains, captive daughter of
     Zion!

52.3   GOD says, "You were sold for nothing. You're
being bought back for nothing."

NEW INTERNATIONAL VERSION

⁴For this is what the Sovereign LORD says:

"At first my people went down to Egypt to
    live;
    lately, Assyria has oppressed them.

⁵"And now what do I have here?" declares the
LORD.

"For my people have been taken away for
        nothing,
    and those who rule them mock,ᵃ"
                        declares the LORD.
"And all day long
    my name is constantly blasphemed.
⁶Therefore my people will know my name;
    therefore in that day they will know
that it is I who foretold it.
    Yes, it is I."

⁷How beautiful on the mountains
    are the feet of those who bring good news,
who proclaim peace,
    who bring good tidings,
    who proclaim salvation,
who say to Zion,
    "Your God reigns!"
⁸Listen! Your watchmen lift up their voices;
    together they shout for joy.
When the LORD returns to Zion,
    they will see it with their own eyes.
⁹Burst into songs of joy together,
    you ruins of Jerusalem,
for the LORD has comforted his people,
    he has redeemed Jerusalem.
¹⁰The LORD will lay bare his holy arm
    in the sight of all the nations,
and all the ends of the earth will see
    the salvation of our God.

¹¹Depart, depart, go out from there!
    Touch no unclean thing!
Come out from it and be pure,
    you who carry the vessels of the LORD.
¹²But you will not leave in haste
    or go in flight;
for the LORD will go before you,
    the God of Israel will be your rear guard.

THE SUFFERING AND GLORY OF THE SERVANT
¹³See, my servant will act wiselyᵇ;
    he will be raised and lifted up and highly
        exalted.
¹⁴Just as there were many who were appalled
        at himᶜ—
    his appearance was so disfigured beyond
        that of any man

THE MESSAGE

52.4-6   Again, the Master, GOD, says, "Early on, my
people went to Egypt and lived, strangers in
the land. At the other end, Assyria oppressed
them. And now, what have I here?" GOD's Decree. "My people are hauled off again for no
reason at all. Tyrants on the warpath, whooping
it up, and day after day, incessantly, my reputation blackened. Now it's time that my people
know who I am, what I'm made of—yes, that I
have something to say. Here I am!"

52.7-10   How beautiful on the mountains
        are the feet of the messenger bringing good
            news,
    Breaking the news that all's well,
        proclaiming good times, announcing
            salvation,
        telling Zion, "Your God reigns!"
    Voices! Listen! Your scouts are shouting,
            thunderclap shouts,
        shouting in joyful unison.
    They see with their own eyes
        GOD coming back to Zion.
    Break into song! Boom it out, ruins of
            Jerusalem:
        "GOD has comforted his people!
        He's redeemed Jerusalem!"
    GOD has rolled up his sleeves.
        All the nations can see his holy, muscled
            arm.
    Everyone, from one end of the earth to the
            other,
        sees him at work, doing his salvation work.

52.11-12 Out of here! Out of here! Leave this place!
        Don't look back. Don't contaminate
            yourselves with plunder.
    Just leave, but leave clean. Purify yourselves
        in the process of worship, carrying the holy
            vessels of GOD.
    But you don't have to be in a hurry.
        You're not running from anybody!
    GOD is leading you out of here,
        and the God of Israel is also your rear
            guard.

IT WAS OUR PAINS HE CARRIED
52.13-15 "Just watch my servant blossom!
        Exalted, tall, head and shoulders above the
            crowd!
    But he didn't begin that way.
        At first everyone was appalled.
    He didn't even look human—

ᵃ 5 Dead Sea Scrolls and Vulgate; Masoretic Text *wail*
ᵇ 13 Or *will prosper*   ᶜ 14 Hebrew *you*

NEW INTERNATIONAL VERSION

and his form marred beyond human
likeness—
[15] so will he sprinkle many nations,[a]
and kings will shut their mouths because
of him.
For what they were not told, they will see,
and what they have not heard, they will
understand.

53 Who has believed our message
and to whom has the arm of the LORD
been revealed?
[2] He grew up before him like a tender shoot,
and like a root out of dry ground.
He had no beauty or majesty to attract us to
him,
nothing in his appearance that we should
desire him.
[3] He was despised and rejected by men,
a man of sorrows, and familiar with
suffering.
Like one from whom men hide their faces
he was despised, and we esteemed him
not.

[4] Surely he took up our infirmities
and carried our sorrows,
yet we considered him stricken by God,
smitten by him, and afflicted.
[5] But he was pierced for our transgressions,
he was crushed for our iniquities;
the punishment that brought us peace was
upon him,
and by his wounds we are healed.
[6] We all, like sheep, have gone astray,
each of us has turned to his own way;
and the LORD has laid on him
the iniquity of us all.

[7] He was oppressed and afflicted,
yet he did not open his mouth;
he was led like a lamb to the slaughter,
and as a sheep before her shearers is
silent,
so he did not open his mouth.
[8] By oppression[b] and judgment he was taken
away.
And who can speak of his descendants?
For he was cut off from the land of the
living;
for the transgression of my people he was
stricken.[c]

a 15 Hebrew; Septuagint *so will many nations marvel at him*
b 8 Or *From arrest*   *c 8* Or *away. / Yet who of his generation
considered / that he was cut off from the land of the living / for
the transgression of my people, / to whom the blow was due?*

THE MESSAGE

a ruined face, disfigured past recognition.
Nations all over the world will be in awe,
taken aback,
kings shocked into silence when they see
him.
For what was unheard of they'll see with their
own eyes,
what was unthinkable they'll have right
before them."

53 53.1 Who believes what we've heard and
seen?
Who would have thought GOD's saving
power would look like this?

53.2-6 The servant grew up before God—a scrawny
seedling,
a scrubby plant in a parched field.
There was nothing attractive about him,
nothing to cause us to take a second look.
He was looked down on and passed over,
a man who suffered, who knew pain
firsthand.
One look at him and people turned away.
We looked down on him, thought he was
scum.
But the fact is, it was *our* pains he carried—
our disfigurements, all the things wrong
with *us*.
We thought he brought it on himself,
that God was punishing him for his own
failures.
But it was our sins that did that to him,
that ripped and tore and crushed him—*our*
sins!
He took the punishment, and that made us
whole.
Through his bruises we get healed.
We're all like sheep who've wandered off and
gotten lost.
We've all done our own thing, gone our
own way.
And GOD has piled all our sins, everything
we've done wrong,
on him, on him.

53.7-9 He was beaten, he was tortured,
but he didn't say a word.
Like a lamb taken to be slaughtered
and like a sheep being sheared,
he took it all in silence.
Justice miscarried, and he was led off—
and did anyone really know what was
happening?
He died without a thought for his own
welfare,
beaten bloody for the sins of my people.

NEW INTERNATIONAL VERSION

⁹ He was assigned a grave with the wicked,
  and with the rich in his death,
though he had done no violence,
  nor was any deceit in his mouth.

¹⁰ Yet it was the LORD's will to crush him and
    cause him to suffer,
  and though the LORD makes ᵃ his life a
    guilt offering,
  he will see his offspring and prolong his
    days,
  and the will of the LORD will prosper in
    his hand.
¹¹ After the suffering of his soul,
  he will see the light ⌊of life⌋ ᵇ and be
    satisfied ᶜ;
by his knowledge ᵈ my righteous servant will
    justify many,
  and he will bear their iniquities.
¹² Therefore I will give him a portion among
    the great, ᵉ
  and he will divide the spoils with the
    strong, ᶠ
because he poured out his life unto death,
  and was numbered with the transgressors.
For he bore the sin of many,
  and made intercession for the
    transgressors.

THE FUTURE GLORY OF ZION

54 "Sing, O barren woman,
  you who never bore a child;
burst into song, shout for joy,
  you who were never in labor;
because more are the children of the desolate
    woman
  than of her who has a husband,"
                          says the LORD.
² "Enlarge the place of your tent,
  stretch your tent curtains wide,
    do not hold back;
  lengthen your cords,
    strengthen your stakes.
³ For you will spread out to the right and to
    the left;
  your descendants will dispossess nations
    and settle in their desolate cities.

⁴ "Do not be afraid; you will not suffer shame.
  Do not fear disgrace; you will not be
    humiliated.

ᵃ *10 Hebrew though you make*   ᵇ *11 Dead Sea Scrolls (see
also Septuagint); Masoretic Text does not have the light ⌊of
life⌋.*   ᶜ *11 Or (with Masoretic Text) ¹¹He will see the result
of the suffering of his soul / and be satisfied*   ᵈ *11 Or by
knowledge of him*   ᵉ *12 Or many*   ᶠ *12 Or numerous*

THE MESSAGE

They buried him with the wicked,
  threw him in a grave with a rich man,
Even though he'd never hurt a soul
  or said one word that wasn't true.

53.10 Still, it's what GOD had in mind all along,
    to crush him with pain.
The plan was that he give himself as an
    offering for sin
  so that he'd see life come from it—life, life,
    and more life.
And GOD's plan will deeply prosper through
    him.

53.11-12 Out of that terrible travail of soul,
    he'll see that it's worth it and be glad he did
    it.
Through what he experienced, my righteous
    one, my servant,
  will make many "righteous ones,"
  as he himself carries the burden of their sins.
Therefore I'll reward him extravagantly—
  the best of everything, the highest
    honors—
Because he looked death in the face and didn't
    flinch,
  because he embraced the company of the
    lowest.
He took on his own shoulders the sin of the
    many,
  he took up the cause of all the black sheep.

SPREAD OUT! THINK BIG!

54.1-6 **54** "Sing, barren woman, who has never
    had a baby.
  Fill the air with song, you who've never
    experienced childbirth,
You're ending up with far more children
  than all those childbearing women." GOD
    says so!
"Clear lots of ground for your tents!
  Make your tents large. Spread out! Think
    big!
Use plenty of rope,
  drive the tent pegs deep.
You're going to need lots of elbow room
  for your growing family.
You're going to take over whole nations;
  you're going to resettle abandoned cities.
Don't be afraid—you're not going to be
    embarrassed.
  Don't hold back—you're not going to come
    up short.

NEW INTERNATIONAL VERSION

You will forget the shame of your youth
  and remember no more the reproach of
    your widowhood.
⁵ For your Maker is your husband—
  the Lord Almighty is his name—
  the Holy One of Israel is your Redeemer;
  he is called the God of all the earth.
⁶ The Lord will call you back
  as if you were a wife deserted and
    distressed in spirit—
  a wife who married young,
    only to be rejected," says your God.
⁷ "For a brief moment I abandoned you,
  but with deep compassion I will bring you
    back.
⁸ In a surge of anger
  I hid my face from you for a moment,
  but with everlasting kindness
  I will have compassion on you,"
  says the Lord your Redeemer.

⁹ "To me this is like the days of Noah,
  when I swore that the waters of Noah
    would never again cover the earth.
  So now I have sworn not to be angry with
    you,
  never to rebuke you again.
¹⁰ Though the mountains be shaken
  and the hills be removed,
  yet my unfailing love for you will not be
    shaken
  nor my covenant of peace be removed,"
  says the Lord, who has compassion on
    you.

¹¹ "O afflicted city, lashed by storms and not
    comforted,
  I will build you with stones of turquoise,ᵃ
  your foundations with sapphires.ᵇ
¹² I will make your battlements of rubies,
  your gates of sparkling jewels,
  and all your walls of precious stones.
¹³ All your sons will be taught by the Lord,
  and great will be your children's peace.
¹⁴ In righteousness you will be established:
  Tyranny will be far from you;
  you will have nothing to fear.
  Terror will be far removed;
  it will not come near you.
¹⁵ If anyone does attack you, it will not be my
    doing;
  whoever attacks you will surrender to
    you.
¹⁶ "See, it is I who created the blacksmith

ᵃ 11 The meaning of the Hebrew for this word is uncertain.
ᵇ 11 Or *lapis lazuli*

THE MESSAGE

You'll forget all about the humiliations of your
    youth,
  and the indignities of being a widow will
    fade from memory.
For your Maker is your bridegroom,
  his name, God-of-the-Angel-Armies!
Your Redeemer is The Holy of Israel,
  known as God of the whole earth.
You were like an abandoned wife, devastated
    with grief,
  and God welcomed you back,
Like a woman married young
  and then left," says your God.

54:7-8   Your Redeemer God says:

"I left you, but only for a moment.
  Now, with enormous compassion, I'm
    bringing you back.
In an outburst of anger I turned my back on
    you—
  but only for a moment.
It's with lasting love
  that I'm tenderly caring for you.

54:9-10 "This exile is just like the days of Noah
    for me:
  I promised then that the waters of Noah
    would never again flood the earth.
I'm promising now no more anger,
  no more dressing you down.
For even if the mountains walk away
  and the hills fall to pieces,
My love won't walk away from you,
  my covenant commitment of peace won't
    fall apart."
  The God who has compassion on you
    says so.

54:11-17 "Afflicted city, storm-battered, unpitied:
  I'm about to rebuild you with stones of
    turquoise,
Lay your foundations with sapphires,
  construct your towers with rubies,
Your gates with jewels,
  and all your walls with precious stones.
All your children will have God for their
    teacher—
  what a mentor for your children!
You'll be built solid, grounded in
    righteousness,
  far from any trouble—nothing to fear!
  far from terror—it won't even come close!
If anyone attacks you,
  don't for a moment suppose that I sent
    them,
And if any should attack,
  nothing will come of it.
I create the blacksmith

NEW INTERNATIONAL VERSION

who fans the coals into flame
and forges a weapon fit for its work.
And it is I who have created the destroyer to
work havoc;
17 no weapon forged against you will prevail,
and you will refute every tongue that
accuses you.
This is the heritage of the servants of the
LORD,
and this is their vindication from me,"
declares the LORD.

INVITATION TO THE THIRSTY

55 "Come, all you who are thirsty,
come to the waters;
and you who have no money,
come, buy and eat!
Come, buy wine and milk
without money and without cost.
2 Why spend money on what is not bread,
and your labor on what does not satisfy?
Listen, listen to me, and eat what is good,
and your soul will delight in the richest of
fare.
3 Give ear and come to me;
hear me, that your soul may live.
I will make an everlasting covenant with
you,
my faithful love promised to David.
4 See, I have made him a witness to the
peoples,
a leader and commander of the peoples.
5 Surely you will summon nations you know
not,
and nations that do not know you will
hasten to you,
because of the LORD your God,
the Holy One of Israel,
for he has endowed you with splendor."

6 Seek the LORD while he may be found;
call on him while he is near.
7 Let the wicked forsake his way
and the evil man his thoughts.
Let him turn to the LORD, and he will have
mercy on him,
and to our God, for he will freely pardon.

8 "For my thoughts are not your thoughts,
neither are your ways my ways,"
declares the LORD.
9 "As the heavens are higher than the earth,
so are my ways higher than your ways
and my thoughts than your thoughts.

THE MESSAGE

who fires up his forge
and makes a weapon designed to kill.
I also create the destroyer—
but no weapon that can hurt you has ever
been forged.
Any accuser who takes you to court
will be dismissed as a liar.
This is what GOD's servants can expect.
I'll see to it that everything works out for
the best."
GOD's Decree.

BUY WITHOUT MONEY

55.1-5 **55** "Hey there! All who are thirsty,
come to the water!
Are you penniless?
Come anyway—buy and eat!
Come, buy your drinks, buy wine and milk.
Buy without money—everything's free!
Why do you spend your money on junk food,
your hard-earned cash on cotton candy?
Listen to me, listen well: Eat only the best,
fill yourself with only the finest.
Pay attention, come close now,
listen carefully to my life-giving, life-
nourishing words.
I'm making a lasting covenant commitment
with you,
the same that I made with David: sure,
solid, enduring love.
I set him up as a witness to the nations,
made him a prince and leader of the
nations,
And now I'm doing it to you:
You'll summon nations you've never
heard of,
and nations who've never heard of you
will come running to you
Because of me, your GOD,
because The Holy of Israel has honored
you."

55.6-7 Seek GOD while he's here to be found,
pray to him while he's close at hand.
Let the wicked abandon their way of life
and the evil their way of thinking.
Let them come back to GOD, who is merciful,
come back to our God, who is lavish with
forgiveness.

55.8-11 "I don't think the way you think.
The way you work isn't the way I work."
GOD's Decree.
"For as the sky soars high above earth,
so the way I work surpasses the way you
work,
and the way I think is beyond the way you
think.

NEW INTERNATIONAL VERSION

¹⁰As the rain and the snow
    come down from heaven,
and do not return to it
    without watering the earth
and making it bud and flourish,
    so that it yields seed for the sower and
        bread for the eater,
¹¹so is my word that goes out from my mouth:
    It will not return to me empty,
but will accomplish what I desire
    and achieve the purpose for which I
        sent it.
¹²You will go out in joy
    and be led forth in peace;
the mountains and hills
    will burst into song before you,
and all the trees of the field
    will clap their hands.
¹³Instead of the thornbush will grow the pine
        tree,
    and instead of briers the myrtle will grow.
This will be for the LORD's renown,
    for an everlasting sign,
    which will not be destroyed."

SALVATION FOR OTHERS

56 This is what the LORD says:

"Maintain justice
    and do what is right,
for my salvation is close at hand
    and my righteousness will soon be
        revealed.
²Blessed is the man who does this,
    the man who holds it fast,
who keeps the Sabbath without
        desecrating it,
    and keeps his hand from doing any evil."

³Let no foreigner who has bound himself to
        the LORD say,
    "The LORD will surely exclude me from
        his people."
And let not any eunuch complain,
    "I am only a dry tree."

⁴For this is what the LORD says:

"To the eunuchs who keep my Sabbaths,
    who choose what pleases me
    and hold fast to my covenant—
⁵to them I will give within my temple and its
        walls
    a memorial and a name
    better than sons and daughters;

THE MESSAGE

Just as rain and snow descend from the skies
    and don't go back until they've watered the
        earth,
Doing their work of making things grow and
        blossom,
    producing seed for farmers and food for the
        hungry,
So will the words that come out of my mouth
    not come back empty-handed.
They'll do the work I sent them to do,
    they'll complete the assignment I gave
        them.

^{55.12-13} "So you'll go out in joy,
    you'll be led into a whole and complete life.
The mountains and hills will lead the parade,
    bursting with song.
All the trees of the forest will join the
        procession,
    exuberant with applause.
No more thistles, but giant sequoias,
    no more thornbushes, but stately pines—
Monuments to me, to GOD,
    living and lasting evidence of GOD."

MESSAGES OF HOPE

SALVATION IS JUST AROUND THE CORNER

^{56.1-3} **56** GOD's Message:

"Guard my common good:
    Do what's right and do it in the right way,
For salvation is just around the corner,
    my setting-things-right is about to go into
        action.
How blessed are you who enter into these
        things,
    you men and women who embrace them,
Who keep Sabbath and don't defile it,
    who watch your step and don't do anything
        evil!
Make sure no outsider who now follows GOD
    ever has occasion to say, 'GOD put me in
        second-class.
    I don't really belong.'
And make sure no physically mutilated person
    is ever made to think, 'I'm damaged goods.
    I don't really belong.'"

^{56.4-5} For GOD says:

"To the mutilated who keep my Sabbaths
    and choose what delights me
    and keep a firm grip on my covenant,
I'll provide them an honored place
    in my family and within my city,
    even more honored than that of sons and
        daughters.

NEW INTERNATIONAL VERSION

I will give them an everlasting name
    that will not be cut off.
⁶ And foreigners who bind themselves to the
    LORD
    to serve him,
to love the name of the LORD,
    and to worship him,
all who keep the Sabbath without
        desecrating it
    and who hold fast to my covenant—
⁷ these I will bring to my holy mountain
    and give them joy in my house of prayer.
Their burnt offerings and sacrifices
    will be accepted on my altar;
for my house will be called
    a house of prayer for all nations."
⁸ The Sovereign LORD declares—
    he who gathers the exiles of Israel:
"I will gather still others to them
    besides those already gathered."

GOD'S ACCUSATION AGAINST THE WICKED

⁹ Come, all you beasts of the field,
    come and devour, all you beasts of the
        forest!
¹⁰ Israel's watchmen are blind,
    they all lack knowledge;
they are all mute dogs,
    they cannot bark;
they lie around and dream,
    they love to sleep.
¹¹ They are dogs with mighty appetites;
    they never have enough.
They are shepherds who lack understanding;
    they all turn to their own way,
    each seeks his own gain.
¹² "Come," each one cries, "let me get wine!
    Let us drink our fill of beer!
And tomorrow will be like today,
    or even far better."

57 The righteous perish,
    and no one ponders it in his heart;
devout men are taken away,
    and no one understands
that the righteous are taken away
    to be spared from evil.
² Those who walk uprightly
    enter into peace;
    they find rest as they lie in death.

³ "But you—come here, you sons of a
        sorceress,
    you offspring of adulterers and
        prostitutes!

THE MESSAGE

I'll confer permanent honors on them
    that will never be revoked.
56.6-8 "And as for the outsiders who now follow me,
    working for me, loving my name,
    and wanting to be my servants—
All who keep Sabbath and don't defile it,
    holding fast to my covenant—
I'll bring them to my holy mountain
    and give them joy in my house of prayer.
They'll be welcome to worship the same as the
        'insiders,'
    to bring burnt offerings and sacrifices to
        my altar.
Oh yes, my house of worship
    will be known as a house of prayer for all
        people."
The Decree of the Master, GOD himself,
    who gathers in the exiles of Israel:
"I will gather others also,
    gather them in with those already
        gathered."

⊹

56.9-12 A call to the savage beasts: Come on the run.
    Come, devour, beast barbarians!
For Israel's watchmen are blind, the whole lot
        of them.
    They have no idea what's going on.
They're dogs without sense enough to bark,
    lazy dogs, dreaming in the sun—
But hungry dogs, they do know how to eat,
    voracious dogs, with never enough.
And these are Israel's shepherds!
    They know nothing, understand nothing.
They all look after themselves,
    grabbing whatever's not nailed down.
"Come," they say, "let's have a party.
    Let's go out and get drunk!"
And tomorrow, more of the same:
    "Let's live it up!"

NEVER TIRED OF TRYING NEW RELIGIONS

57.1-2 **57** Meanwhile, right-living people die
    and no one gives them a thought.
God-fearing people are carted off
    and no one even notices.
The right-living people are out of their misery,
    they're finally at rest.
They lived well and with dignity
    and now they're finally at peace.

⊹

57.3-10 "But you, children of a witch, come here!
    Sons of a slut, daughters of a whore.

NEW INTERNATIONAL VERSION

⁴Whom are you mocking?
 At whom do you sneer
 and stick out your tongue?
Are you not a brood of rebels,
 the offspring of liars?
⁵You burn with lust among the oaks
 and under every spreading tree;
you sacrifice your children in the ravines
 and under the overhanging crags.
⁶ₗThe idolsₗ among the smooth stones of the
 ravines are your portion;
 they, they are your lot.
Yes, to them you have poured out drink
 offerings
 and offered grain offerings.
 In the light of these things, should I
 relent?
⁷You have made your bed on a high and lofty
 hill;
 there you went up to offer your sacrifices.
⁸Behind your doors and your doorposts
 you have put your pagan symbols.
Forsaking me, you uncovered your bed,
 you climbed into it and opened it wide;
you made a pact with those whose beds you
 love,
 and you looked on their nakedness.
⁹You went to Molech ᵃ with olive oil
 and increased your perfumes.
You sent your ambassadors ᵇ far away;
 you descended to the grave ᶜ itself!
¹⁰You were wearied by all your ways,
 but you would not say, 'It is hopeless.'
You found renewal of your strength,
 and so you did not faint.

¹¹ "Whom have you so dreaded and feared
 that you have been false to me,
and have neither remembered me
 nor pondered this in your hearts?
Is it not because I have long been silent
 that you do not fear me?
¹²I will expose your righteousness and your
 works,
 and they will not benefit you.
¹³When you cry out for help,
 let your collection ₗof idolsₗ save you!
The wind will carry all of them off,
 a mere breath will blow them away.
But the man who makes me his refuge
 will inherit the land
 and possess my holy mountain."

THE MESSAGE

What business do you have taunting,
 sneering, and sticking out your tongue?
Do you have any idea what wretches you've
 turned out to be?
 A race of rebels, a generation of liars.
You satisfy your lust any place you find some
 shade
 and fornicate at whim.
You kill your children at any convenient
 spot—
 any cave or crevasse will do.
You take stones from the creek
 and set up your sex-and-religion shrines.
You've chosen your fate.
 Your worship will be your doom.
You've climbed a high mountain
 to practice your foul sex-and-death
 religion.
Behind closed doors
 you assemble your precious gods and
 goddesses.
Deserting me, you've gone all out, stripped
 down
 and made your bed your place of worship.
You've climbed into bed with the 'sacred'
 whores
 and loved every minute of it,
 adoring every curve of their naked bodies.
You anoint your king-god with ointments
 and lavish perfumes on yourselves.
You send scouts to search out the latest in
 religion,
 send them all the way to hell and back.
You wear yourselves out trying the new and
 the different,
 and never see what a waste it all is.
You've always found strength for the latest fad,
 never got tired of trying new religions.

⁵⁷·¹¹⁻¹³ "Who talked you into the pursuit of this
 nonsense,
 leaving me high and dry,
 forgetting you ever knew me?
Because I don't yell and make a scene
 do you think I don't exist?
I'll go over, detail by detail, all your 'righteous'
 attempts at religion,
 and expose the absurdity of it all.
Go ahead, cry for help to your collection of
 no-gods:
 A good wind will blow them away.
 They're smoke, nothing but smoke.

"But anyone who runs to me for help
 will inherit the land,
 will end up owning my holy mountain!"

☩

NEW INTERNATIONAL VERSION

COMFORT FOR THE CONTRITE

14And it will be said:

"Build up, build up, prepare the road!
    Remove the obstacles out of the way of
        my people."
15For this is what the high and lofty One
        says—
    he who lives forever, whose name is holy:
"I live in a high and holy place,
    but also with him who is contrite and
        lowly in spirit,
to revive the spirit of the lowly
    and to revive the heart of the contrite.
16I will not accuse forever,
    nor will I always be angry,
for then the spirit of man would grow faint
        before me—
    the breath of man that I have created.
17I was enraged by his sinful greed;
    I punished him, and hid my face in anger,
    yet he kept on in his willful ways.
18I have seen his ways, but I will heal him;
    I will guide him and restore comfort to
        him,
19   creating praise on the lips of the mourners
        in Israel.
Peace, peace, to those far and near,"
    says the LORD. "And I will heal them."
20But the wicked are like the tossing sea,
    which cannot rest,
    whose waves cast up mire and mud.
21"There is no peace," says my God, "for the
        wicked."

TRUE FASTING

58 "Shout it aloud, do not hold back.
    Raise your voice like a trumpet.
Declare to my people their rebellion
    and to the house of Jacob their sins.
2For day after day they seek me out;
    they seem eager to know my ways,
as if they were a nation that does what is
        right
    and has not forsaken the commands of its
        God.
They ask me for just decisions
    and seem eager for God to come near
        them.
3'Why have we fasted,' they say,
    'and you have not seen it?
Why have we humbled ourselves,
    and you have not noticed?'

THE MESSAGE

57.14 Someone says: "Build, build! Make a road!
    Clear the way, remove the rocks
    from the road my people will travel."

57.15-21 A Message from the high and towering God,
    who lives in Eternity,
    whose name is Holy:
"I live in the high and holy places,
    but also with the low-spirited, the spirit-
        crushed,
And what I do is put new spirit in them,
    get them up and on their feet again.
For I'm not going to haul people into court
        endlessly,
    I'm not going to be angry forever.
Otherwise, people would lose heart.
    These souls I created would tire out and
        give up.
I was angry, good and angry, because of Israel's
        sins.
    I struck him hard and turned away in
        anger,
    while he kept at his stubborn, willful ways.
When I looked again and saw what he was
        doing,
    I decided to heal him, lead him, and
        comfort him,
    creating a new language of praise for the
        mourners.
Peace to the far-off, peace to the near-at-
        hand," says GOD—
    "and yes, I will heal them.
But the wicked are storm-battered seas
    that can't quiet down.
    The waves stir up garbage and mud.
There's no peace," God says, "for the wicked.

YOUR PRAYERS WON'T GET OFF THE GROUND

58.1-3 58 "Shout! A full-throated shout!
    Hold nothing back—a trumpet-blast
        shout!
Tell my people what's wrong with their lives,
    face my family Jacob with their sins!
They're busy, busy, busy at worship,
    and love studying all about me.
To all appearances they're a nation of right-
        living people—
    law-abiding, God-honoring.
They ask me, 'What's the right thing to do?'
    and love having me on their side.
But they also complain,
    'Why do we fast and you don't look our
        way?
    Why do we humble ourselves and you
        don't even notice?'

NEW INTERNATIONAL VERSION

"Yet on the day of your fasting, you do as
you please
and exploit all your workers.
[4] Your fasting ends in quarreling and strife,
and in striking each other with wicked
fists.
You cannot fast as you do today
and expect your voice to be heard on
high.
[5] Is this the kind of fast I have chosen,
only a day for a man to humble himself?
Is it only for bowing one's head like a reed
and for lying on sackcloth and ashes?
Is that what you call a fast,
a day acceptable to the LORD?

[6] "Is not this the kind of fasting I have chosen:
to loose the chains of injustice
and untie the cords of the yoke,
to set the oppressed free
and break every yoke?
[7] Is it not to share your food with the hungry
and to provide the poor wanderer with
shelter—
when you see the naked, to clothe him,
and not to turn away from your own flesh
and blood?
[8] Then your light will break forth like the
dawn,
and your healing will quickly appear;
then your righteousness[a] will go before you,
and the glory of the LORD will be your rear
guard.
[9] Then you will call, and the LORD will answer;
you will cry for help, and he will say:
Here am I.

"If you do away with the yoke of oppression,
with the pointing finger and malicious
talk,
[10] and if you spend yourselves in behalf of the
hungry
and satisfy the needs of the oppressed,
then your light will rise in the darkness,
and your night will become like the
noonday.
[11] The LORD will guide you always;
he will satisfy your needs in a sun-
scorched land
and will strengthen your frame.
You will be like a well-watered garden,
like a spring whose waters never fail.
[12] Your people will rebuild the ancient ruins
and will raise up the age-old foundations;

THE MESSAGE

58.3-5 "Well, here's why:

"The bottom line on your 'fast days' is profit.
You drive your employees much too hard.
You fast, but at the same time you bicker and
fight.
You fast, but you swing a mean fist.
The kind of fasting you do
won't get your prayers off the ground.
Do you think this is the kind of fast day I'm
after:
a day to show off humility?
To put on a pious long face
and parade around solemnly in black?
Do you call *that* fasting,
a fast day that I, GOD, would like?

58.6-9 "This is the kind of fast day I'm after:
to break the chains of injustice,
get rid of exploitation in the workplace,
free the oppressed,
cancel debts.
What I'm interested in seeing you do is:
sharing your food with the hungry,
inviting the homeless poor into your
homes,
putting clothes on the shivering ill-clad,
being available to your own families.
Do this and the lights will turn on,
and your lives will turn around at once.
Your righteousness will pave your way.
The GOD of glory will secure your passage.
Then when you pray, GOD will answer.
You'll call out for help and I'll say, 'Here
I am.'

A FULL LIFE IN THE EMPTIEST OF PLACES
58.9-12 "If you get rid of unfair practices,
quit blaming victims,
quit gossiping about other people's sins,
If you are generous with the hungry
and start giving yourselves to the down-
and-out,
Your lives will begin to glow in the darkness,
your shadowed lives will be bathed in
sunlight.
I will always show you where to go.
I'll give you a full life in the emptiest of
places—
firm muscles, strong bones.
You'll be like a well-watered garden,
a gurgling spring that never runs dry.
You'll use the old rubble of past lives to build
anew,
rebuild the foundations from out of your
past.
You'll be known as those who can fix
anything,

[a] 8 Or your righteous One

NEW INTERNATIONAL VERSION

you will be called Repairer of Broken Walls,
Restorer of Streets with Dwellings.

13 "If you keep your feet from breaking the
Sabbath
and from doing as you please on my holy
day,
if you call the Sabbath a delight
and the LORD's holy day honorable,
and if you honor it by not going your own
way
and not doing as you please or speaking
idle words,
14 then you will find your joy in the LORD,
and I will cause you to ride on the heights
of the land
and to feast on the inheritance of your
father Jacob."
The mouth of the LORD
has spoken.

SIN, CONFESSION AND REDEMPTION

59 Surely the arm of the LORD is not too
short to save,
nor his ear too dull to hear.
2 But your iniquities have separated
you from your God;
your sins have hidden his face from you,
so that he will not hear.
3 For your hands are stained with blood,
your fingers with guilt.
Your lips have spoken lies,
and your tongue mutters wicked things.
4 No one calls for justice;
no one pleads his case with integrity.
They rely on empty arguments and speak
lies;
they conceive trouble and give birth to
evil.
5 They hatch the eggs of vipers
and spin a spider's web.
Whoever eats their eggs will die,
and when one is broken, an adder is
hatched.
6 Their cobwebs are useless for clothing;
they cannot cover themselves with what
they make.
Their deeds are evil deeds,
and acts of violence are in their hands.
7 Their feet rush into sin;
they are swift to shed innocent blood.
Their thoughts are evil thoughts;
ruin and destruction mark their ways.

THE MESSAGE

restore old ruins, rebuild and renovate,
make the community livable again.

58.13-14 "If you watch your step on the Sabbath
and don't use my holy day for personal
advantage,
If you treat the Sabbath as a day of joy,
GOD's holy day as a celebration,
If you honor it by refusing 'business as usual,'
making money, running here and there—
Then you'll be free to enjoy GOD!
Oh, I'll make you ride high and soar above
it all.
I'll make you feast on the inheritance of your
ancestor Jacob."
Yes! GOD says so!

WE LONG FOR LIGHT BUT SINK INTO DARKNESS

59.1-8 **59** Look! Listen!
GOD's arm is not amputated—he can
still save.
GOD's ears are not stopped up—he can still
hear.
There's nothing wrong with God; the wrong is
in *you.*
Your wrongheaded lives caused the split
between you and God.
Your sins got between you so that he
doesn't hear.
Your hands are drenched in blood,
your fingers dripping with guilt,
Your lips smeared with lies,
your tongue swollen from muttering
obscenities.
No one speaks up for the right,
no one deals fairly.
They trust in illusion, they tell lies,
they get pregnant with mischief and have
sin-babies.
They hatch snake eggs and weave spider
webs.
Eat an egg and die; break an egg and get a
snake!
The spider webs are no good for shirts or
shawls.
No one can wear these weavings!
They weave wickedness,
they hatch violence.
They compete in the race to do evil
and run to be the first to murder.
They plan and plot evil, think and breathe
evil,
and leave a trail of wrecked lives behind
them.

NEW INTERNATIONAL VERSION

⁸ The way of peace they do not know;
    there is no justice in their paths.
They have turned them into crooked roads;
    no one who walks in them will know
        peace.

⁹ So justice is far from us,
    and righteousness does not reach us.
We look for light, but all is darkness;
    for brightness, but we walk in deep
        shadows.
¹⁰ Like the blind we grope along the wall,
    feeling our way like men without eyes.
At midday we stumble as if it were twilight;
    among the strong, we are like the dead.
¹¹ We all growl like bears;
    we moan mournfully like doves.
We look for justice, but find none;
    for deliverance, but it is far away.

¹² For our offenses are many in your sight,
    and our sins testify against us.
Our offenses are ever with us,
    and we acknowledge our iniquities:
¹³ rebellion and treachery against the LORD,
    turning our backs on our God,
fomenting oppression and revolt,
    uttering lies our hearts have conceived.
¹⁴ So justice is driven back,
    and righteousness stands at a distance;
truth has stumbled in the streets,
    honesty cannot enter.
¹⁵ Truth is nowhere to be found,
    and whoever shuns evil becomes a prey.

The LORD looked and was displeased
    that there was no justice.
¹⁶ He saw that there was no one,
    he was appalled that there was no one to
        intervene;
so his own arm worked salvation for him,
    and his own righteousness sustained him.
¹⁷ He put on righteousness as his breastplate,
    and the helmet of salvation on his head;
he put on the garments of vengeance
    and wrapped himself in zeal as in a cloak.
¹⁸ According to what they have done,
    so will he repay
wrath to his enemies
    and retribution to his foes;
    he will repay the islands their due.
¹⁹ From the west, men will fear the name of the
    LORD,

THE MESSAGE

They know nothing about peace
    and less than nothing about justice.
They make tortuously twisted roads.
    No peace for the wretch who walks down
        those roads!

59.9-11 Which means that we're a far cry from fair
        dealing,
    and we're not even close to right living.
We long for light but sink into darkness,
    long for brightness but stumble through
        the night.
Like the blind, we inch along a wall,
    groping eyeless in the dark.
We shuffle our way in broad daylight,
    like the dead, but somehow walking.
We're no better off than bears, groaning,
    and no worse off than doves, moaning.
We look for justice—not a sign of it;
    for salvation—not so much as a hint.

59.12-15 Our wrongdoings pile up before you, God,
    our sins stand up and accuse us.
Our wrongdoings stare us down;
    we know in detail what we've done:
Mocking and denying GOD,
    not following our God,
Spreading false rumors, inciting sedition,
    pregnant with lies, muttering malice.
Justice is beaten back,
    Righteousness is banished to the sidelines,
Truth staggers down the street,
    Honesty is nowhere to be found,
Good is missing in action.
    Anyone renouncing evil is beaten and
        robbed.

59.15-19 GOD looked and saw evil looming on the
        horizon—
    so much evil and no sign of Justice.
He couldn't believe what he saw:
    not a soul around to correct this awful
        situation.
So he did it himself, took on the work of
        Salvation,
    fueled by his own Righteousness.
He dressed in Righteousness, put it on like a
        suit of armor,
    with Salvation on his head like a helmet,
Put on Judgment like an overcoat,
    and threw a cloak of Passion across his
        shoulders.
He'll make everyone pay for what they've
        done:
    fury for his foes, just deserts for his
        enemies.
    Even the far-off islands will get paid off in
        full.
In the west they'll fear the name of GOD,

NEW INTERNATIONAL VERSION

and from the rising of the sun, they will
revere his glory.
For he will come like a pent-up flood
that the breath of the LORD drives along. *a*

20 "The Redeemer will come to Zion,
to those in Jacob who repent of their
sins,"
declares the LORD.

21 "As for me, this is my covenant with them,"
says the LORD. "My Spirit, who is on you, and
my words that I have put in your mouth will not
depart from your mouth, or from the mouths of
your children, or from the mouths of their descendants from this time on and forever," says
the LORD.

THE GLORY OF ZION

60 "Arise, shine, for your light has come,
and the glory of the LORD rises upon
you.
2 See, darkness covers the earth
and thick darkness is over the peoples,
but the LORD rises upon you
and his glory appears over you.
3 Nations will come to your light,
and kings to the brightness of your dawn.

4 "Lift up your eyes and look about you:
All assemble and come to you;
your sons come from afar,
and your daughters are carried on the
arm.
5 Then you will look and be radiant,
your heart will throb and swell with joy;
the wealth on the seas will be brought to
you,
to you the riches of the nations will come.
6 Herds of camels will cover your land,
young camels of Midian and Ephah.
And all from Sheba will come,
bearing gold and incense
and proclaiming the praise of the LORD.
7 All Kedar's flocks will be gathered to you,
the rams of Nebaioth will serve you;
they will be accepted as offerings on my
altar,
and I will adorn my glorious temple.

8 "Who are these that fly along like clouds,
like doves to their nests?
9 Surely the islands look to me;

*a 19 Or When the enemy comes in like a flood, / the Spirit of
the LORD will put him to flight*

THE MESSAGE

in the east they'll fear the glory of GOD,
For he'll arrive like a river in flood stage,
whipped to a torrent by the wind of GOD.

59.20 "I'll arrive in Zion as Redeemer,
to those in Jacob who leave their sins."
GOD's Decree.

59.21 "As for me," GOD says, "this is my covenant
with them: My Spirit that I've placed upon you
and the words that I've given you to speak,
they're not going to leave your mouths nor the
mouths of your children nor the mouths of
your grandchildren. You will keep repeating
these words and won't ever stop." GOD's orders.

PEOPLE RETURNING FOR THE REUNION

60.1-7 **60** "Get out of bed, Jerusalem!
Wake up. Put your face in the sunlight.
GOD's bright glory has risen for you.
The whole earth is wrapped in darkness,
all people sunk in deep darkness,
But GOD rises on you,
his sunrise glory breaks over you.
Nations will come to your light,
kings to your sunburst brightness.
Look up! Look around!
Watch as they gather, watch as they
approach you:
Your sons coming from great distances,
your daughters carried by their nannies.
When you see them coming you'll smile—big
smiles!
Your heart will swell and, yes, burst!
All those people returning by sea for the
reunion,
a rich harvest of exiles gathered in from the
nations!
And then streams of camel caravans as far as
the eye can see,
young camels of nomads in Midian and
Ephah,
Pouring in from the south from Sheba,
loaded with gold and frankincense,
preaching the praises of GOD.
And yes, a great roundup
of flocks from the nomads in Kedar and
Nebaioth,
Welcome gifts for worship at my altar
as I bathe my glorious Temple in splendor.

WHAT'S THAT WE SEE IN THE DISTANCE?

60.8-22 "What's that we see in the distance,
a cloud on the horizon, like doves
darkening the sky?
It's ships from the distant islands,

NEW INTERNATIONAL VERSION

in the lead are the ships of Tarshish,[a]
bringing your sons from afar,
   with their silver and gold,
to the honor of the LORD your God,
   the Holy One of Israel,
   for he has endowed you with splendor.

10 "Foreigners will rebuild your walls,
   and their kings will serve you.
Though in anger I struck you,
   in favor I will show you compassion.
11 Your gates will always stand open,
   they will never be shut, day or night,
so that men may bring you the wealth of the
      nations—
   their kings led in triumphal procession.
12 For the nation or kingdom that will not
      serve you will perish;
   it will be utterly ruined.

13 "The glory of Lebanon will come to you,
   the pine, the fir and the cypress together,
to adorn the place of my sanctuary;
   and I will glorify the place of my feet.
14 The sons of your oppressors will come
      bowing before you;
   all who despise you will bow down at
      your feet
and will call you the City of the LORD,
   Zion of the Holy One of Israel.

15 "Although you have been forsaken and
      hated,
   with no one traveling through,
I will make you the everlasting pride
   and the joy of all generations.
16 You will drink the milk of nations
   and be nursed at royal breasts.
Then you will know that I, the LORD, am
      your Savior,
   your Redeemer, the Mighty One of Jacob.
17 Instead of bronze I will bring you gold,
   and silver in place of iron.
Instead of wood I will bring you bronze,
   and iron in place of stones.
I will make peace your governor
   and righteousness your ruler.
18 No longer will violence be heard in your
      land,
   nor ruin or destruction within your
      borders,
but you will call your walls Salvation
   and your gates Praise.
19 The sun will no more be your light by day,
   nor will the brightness of the moon shine
      on you,
for the LORD will be your everlasting light,

THE MESSAGE

the famous Tarshish ships
Returning your children from faraway places,
   loaded with riches, with silver and gold,
And backed by the name of your GOD, The
      Holy of Israel,
   showering you with splendor.
Foreigners will rebuild your walls,
   and their kings assist you in the conduct of
      worship.
When I was angry I hit you hard.
   It's my desire now to be tender.
Your Jerusalem gates will always be open
   —open house day and night!—
Receiving deliveries of wealth from all
      nations,
   and their kings, the delivery boys!
Any nation or kingdom that doesn't deliver
      will perish;
   those nations will be totally wasted.
The rich woods of Lebanon will be delivered
   —all that cypress and oak and pine—
To give a splendid elegance to my Sanctuary,
   as I make my footstool glorious.
The descendants of your oppressor
   will come bowing and scraping to you.
All who looked down at you in contempt
   will lick your boots.
They'll confer a title on you: City of GOD,
   Zion of The Holy of Israel.
Not long ago you were despised refuse—
   out-of-the-way, unvisited, ignored.
But now I've put you on your feet,
   towering and grand forever, a joy to
      look at!
When you suck the milk of nations
   and the breasts of royalty,
You'll know that I, GOD, am your Savior,
   your Redeemer, Champion of Jacob.
I'll give you only the best—no more hand-me-
      downs!
   Gold instead of bronze, silver instead of
      iron,
   bronze instead of wood, iron instead of
      stones.
I'll install Peace to run your country,
   make Righteousness your boss.
There'll be no more stories of crime in your
      land,
   no more robberies, no more vandalism.
You'll name your main street Salvation Way,
   and install Praise Park at the center of
      town.
You'll have no more need of the sun by day
   nor the brightness of the moon at night.
GOD will be your eternal light,

NEW INTERNATIONAL VERSION

and your God will be your glory.
20 Your sun will never set again,
  and your moon will wane no more;
the LORD will be your everlasting light,
  and your days of sorrow will end.
21 Then will all your people be righteous
  and they will possess the land forever.
They are the shoot I have planted,
  the work of my hands,
  for the display of my splendor.
22 The least of you will become a thousand,
  the smallest a mighty nation.
I am the LORD;
  in its time I will do this swiftly."

THE YEAR OF THE LORD'S FAVOR

61 The Spirit of the Sovereign LORD is
  on me,
  because the LORD has anointed me
  to preach good news to the poor.
He has sent me to bind up the
  brokenhearted,
  to proclaim freedom for the captives
  and release from darkness for the
  prisoners,[a]
2 to proclaim the year of the LORD's favor
  and the day of vengeance of our God,
to comfort all who mourn,
3   and provide for those who grieve in
  Zion—
to bestow on them a crown of beauty
  instead of ashes,
the oil of gladness
  instead of mourning,
and a garment of praise
  instead of a spirit of despair.
They will be called oaks of righteousness,
  a planting of the LORD
  for the display of his splendor.

4 They will rebuild the ancient ruins
  and restore the places long devastated;
they will renew the ruined cities
  that have been devastated for generations.
5 Aliens will shepherd your flocks;
  foreigners will work your fields and
  vineyards.
6 And you will be called priests of the LORD,
  you will be named ministers of our God.
You will feed on the wealth of nations,
  and in their riches you will boast.

7 Instead of their shame
  my people will receive a double portion,
and instead of disgrace
  they will rejoice in their inheritance;

THE MESSAGE

your God will bathe you in splendor.
Your sun will never go down,
  your moon will never fade.
I will be your eternal light.
  Your days of grieving are over.
All your people will live right and well,
  in permanent possession of the land.
They're the green shoot that I planted,
  planted with my own hands to display my
  glory.
The runt will become a great tribe,
  the weakling become a strong nation.
I am GOD.
  At the right time I'll make it happen."

ANNOUNCE FREEDOM TO ALL CAPTIVES

61.1-7 **61** The Spirit of GOD, the Master, is on me
  because GOD anointed me.
He sent me to preach good news to the poor,
  heal the heartbroken,
Announce freedom to all captives,
  pardon all prisoners.
GOD sent me to announce the year of his
  grace—
  a celebration of God's destruction of our
  enemies—
  and to comfort all who mourn,
To care for the needs of all who mourn in
  Zion,
  give them bouquets of roses instead of
  ashes,
Messages of joy instead of news of doom,
  a praising heart instead of a languid spirit.
Rename them "Oaks of Righteousness"
  planted by GOD to display his glory.
They'll rebuild the old ruins,
  raise a new city out of the wreckage.
They'll start over on the ruined cities,
  take the rubble left behind and make it
  new.
You'll hire outsiders to herd your flocks
  and foreigners to work your fields,
But you'll have the title "Priests of GOD,"
  honored as ministers of our God.
You'll feast on the bounty of nations,
  you'll bask in their glory.
Because you got a double dose of trouble
  and more than your share of contempt,

---

a 1 Hebrew; Septuagint the blind

NEW INTERNATIONAL VERSION

and so they will inherit a double portion in
their land,
and everlasting joy will be theirs.

⁸ "For I, the LORD, love justice;
I hate robbery and iniquity.
In my faithfulness I will reward them
and make an everlasting covenant with
them.
⁹ Their descendants will be known among the
nations
and their offspring among the peoples.
All who see them will acknowledge
that they are a people the LORD has
blessed."

¹⁰ I delight greatly in the LORD;
my soul rejoices in my God.
For he has clothed me with garments of
salvation
and arrayed me in a robe of righteousness,
as a bridegroom adorns his head like a
priest,
and as a bride adorns herself with her
jewels.
¹¹ For as the soil makes the sprout come up
and a garden causes seeds to grow,
so the Sovereign LORD will make
righteousness and praise
spring up before all nations.

ZION'S NEW NAME

62 For Zion's sake I will not keep silent,
for Jerusalem's sake I will not remain
quiet,
till her righteousness shines out like the
dawn,
her salvation like a blazing torch.
² The nations will see your righteousness,
and all kings your glory;
you will be called by a new name
that the mouth of the LORD will bestow.
³ You will be a crown of splendor in the LORD's
hand,
a royal diadem in the hand of your God.
⁴ No longer will they call you Deserted,
or name your land Desolate.
But you will be called Hephzibah,ᵃ
and your land Beulahᵇ;
for the LORD will take delight in you,
and your land will be married.
⁵ As a young man marries a maiden,
so will your sonsᶜ marry you;
as a bridegroom rejoices over his bride,
so will your God rejoice over you.

THE MESSAGE

Your inheritance in the land will be doubled
and your joy go on forever.

⁶¹·⁸⁻⁹ "Because I, GOD, love fair dealing
and hate thievery and crime,
I'll pay your wages on time and in full,
and establish my eternal covenant with
you.
Your descendants will become well-known all
over.
Your children in foreign countries
Will be recognized at once
as the people I have blessed."

⁶¹·¹⁰⁻¹¹ I will sing for joy in GOD,
explode in praise from deep in my soul!
He dressed me up in a suit of salvation,
he outfitted me in a robe of righteousness,
As a bridegroom who puts on a tuxedo
and a bride a jeweled tiara.
For as the earth bursts with spring
wildflowers,
and as a garden cascades with blossoms,
So the Master, GOD, brings righteousness into
full bloom
and puts praise on display before the
nations.

LOOK, YOUR SAVIOR COMES!

⁶²·¹⁻⁵ **62** Regarding Zion, I can't keep my mouth
shut,
regarding Jerusalem, I can't hold my tongue,
Until her righteousness blazes down like the
sun
and her salvation flames up like a torch.
Foreign countries will see your righteousness,
and world leaders your glory.
You'll get a brand-new name
straight from the mouth of GOD.
You'll be a stunning crown in the palm of
GOD's hand,
a jeweled gold cup held high in the hand of
your God.
No more will anyone call you Rejected,
and your country will no more be called
Ruined.
You'll be called Hephzibah (My Delight),
and your land Beulah (Married),
Because GOD delights in you
and your land will be like a wedding
celebration.
For as a young man marries his virgin bride,
so your builder marries you,
And as a bridegroom is happy in his bride,
so your God is happy with you.

ᵃ 4 *Hephzibah* means *my delight is in her.*   ᵇ 4 *Beulah*
means *married.*   ᶜ 5 Or *Builder*

NEW INTERNATIONAL VERSION

⁶ I have posted watchmen on your walls,
  O Jerusalem;
  they will never be silent day or night.
You who call on the LORD,
  give yourselves no rest,
⁷ and give him no rest till he establishes
  Jerusalem
  and makes her the praise of the earth.

⁸ The LORD has sworn by his right hand
  and by his mighty arm:
"Never again will I give your grain
  as food for your enemies,
and never again will foreigners drink the
  new wine
  for which you have toiled;
⁹ but those who harvest it will eat it
  and praise the LORD,
and those who gather the grapes will drink it
  in the courts of my sanctuary."

¹⁰ Pass through, pass through the gates!
  Prepare the way for the people.
Build up, build up the highway!
  Remove the stones.
Raise a banner for the nations.

¹¹ The LORD has made proclamation
  to the ends of the earth:
"Say to the Daughter of Zion,
  'See, your Savior comes!
See, his reward is with him,
  and his recompense accompanies him.' "
¹² They will be called the Holy People,
  the Redeemed of the LORD;
and you will be called Sought After,
  the City No Longer Deserted.

GOD'S DAY OF VENGEANCE AND REDEMPTION

63 Who is this coming from Edom,
  from Bozrah, with his garments stained
  crimson?
Who is this, robed in splendor,
  striding forward in the greatness of his
  strength?

"It is I, speaking in righteousness,
  mighty to save."

² Why are your garments red,
  like those of one treading the winepress?

³ "I have trodden the winepress alone;
  from the nations no one was with me.
I trampled them in my anger
  and trod them down in my wrath;
their blood spattered my garments,
  and I stained all my clothing.
⁴ For the day of vengeance was in my heart,

THE MESSAGE

62.6-7 I've posted watchmen on your walls,
  Jerusalem.
Day and night they keep at it, praying,
  calling out,
  reminding GOD to remember.
They are to give him no peace until he does
  what he said,
  until he makes Jerusalem famous as the
  City of Praise.

62.8-9 GOD has taken a solemn oath,
  an oath he means to keep:
"Never again will I open your grain-filled
  barns
  to your enemies to loot and eat.
Never again will foreigners drink the wine
  that you worked so hard to produce.
No. The farmers who grow the food will eat
  the food
  and praise GOD for it.
And those who make the wine will drink the
  wine
  in my holy courtyards."

62.10-12 Walk out of the gates. Get going!
  Get the road ready for the people.
Build the highway. Get at it!
  Clear the debris,
  hoist high a flag, a signal to all peoples!
Yes! GOD has broadcast to all the world:
  "Tell daughter Zion, 'Look! Your Savior
  comes,
Ready to do what he said he'd do,
  prepared to complete what he promised.' "
Zion will be called new names: Holy People,
  GOD-Redeemed,
  Sought-Out, City-Not-Forsaken.

WHO GOES THERE?

63.1 **63** The watchmen call out,
  "Who goes there, marching out of
  Edom,
  out of Bozrah in clothes dyed red?
Name yourself, so splendidly dressed,
  advancing, bristling with power!"

"It is I: I speak what is right,
  I, mighty to save!"

63.2 "And why are your robes so red,
  your clothes dyed red like those who tread
  grapes?"

63.3-6 "I've been treading the winepress alone.
  No one was there to help me.
Angrily, I stomped the grapes;
  raging, I trampled the people.
Their blood spurted all over me—
  all my clothes were soaked with blood.
I was set on vengeance.

NEW INTERNATIONAL VERSION

and the year of my redemption has come.
⁵I looked, but there was no one to help,
  I was appalled that no one gave support;
so my own arm worked salvation for me,
  and my own wrath sustained me.
⁶I trampled the nations in my anger;
  in my wrath I made them drunk
  and poured their blood on the ground."

PRAISE AND PRAYER

⁷I will tell of the kindnesses of the LORD,
  the deeds for which he is to be praised,
  according to all the LORD has done
    for us—
yes, the many good things he has done
  for the house of Israel,
  according to his compassion and many
    kindnesses.
⁸He said, "Surely they are my people,
  sons who will not be false to me";
  and so he became their Savior.
⁹In all their distress he too was distressed,
  and the angel of his presence saved them.
In his love and mercy he redeemed them;
  he lifted them up and carried them
  all the days of old.
¹⁰Yet they rebelled
  and grieved his Holy Spirit.
So he turned and became their enemy
  and he himself fought against them.

¹¹Then his people recalled ᵃ the days of old,
  the days of Moses and his people—
where is he who brought them through the
    sea,
  with the shepherd of his flock?
Where is he who set
  his Holy Spirit among them,
¹²who sent his glorious arm of power
  to be at Moses' right hand,
who divided the waters before them,
  to gain for himself everlasting renown,
¹³who led them through the depths?
Like a horse in open country,
  they did not stumble;
¹⁴like cattle that go down to the plain,
  they were given rest by the Spirit of the
    LORD.
This is how you guided your people
  to make for yourself a glorious name.

¹⁵Look down from heaven and see
  from your lofty throne, holy and glorious.

ᵃ 11 Or But may he recall

THE MESSAGE

The time for redemption had arrived.
I looked around for someone to help
  —no one.
I couldn't believe it
  —not one volunteer.
So I went ahead and did it myself,
  fed and fueled by my rage.
I trampled the people in my anger,
  crushed them under foot in my wrath,
  soaked the earth with their lifeblood."

ALL THE THINGS GOD HAS DONE THAT NEED
PRAISING

63.7-9 I'll make a list of GOD's gracious dealings,
  all the things GOD has done that need
    praising,
All the generous bounties of GOD,
  his great goodness to the family of Israel—
Compassion lavished,
  love extravagant.
He said, "Without question these are my
    people,
  children who would never betray me."
So he became their Savior.
  In all their troubles,
  he was troubled, too.
He didn't send someone else to help them.
  He did it himself, in person.
Out of his own love and pity
  he redeemed them.
He rescued them and carried them along
  for a long, long time.

63.10 But they turned on him;
  they grieved his Holy Spirit.
So he turned on them,
  became their enemy and fought them.

63.11-14 Then they remembered the old days,
  the days of Moses, God's servant:
"Where is he who brought the shepherds of
    his flock
  up and out of the sea?
And what happened to the One who set
  his Holy Spirit within them?
Who linked his arm with Moses' right arm,
  divided the waters before them,
Making him famous ever after,
  and led them through the muddy abyss
  as surefooted as horses on hard, level
    ground?
Like a herd of cattle led to pasture,
  the Spirit of GOD gave them rest."

63.14-19 That's how you led your people!
  That's how you became so famous!
Look down from heaven, look at us!
  Look out the window of your holy and
    magnificent house!

NEW INTERNATIONAL VERSION

Where are your zeal and your might?
  Your tenderness and compassion are
    withheld from us.
16 But you are our Father,
  though Abraham does not know us
    or Israel acknowledge us;
  you, O LORD, are our Father,
    our Redeemer from of old is your name.
17 Why, O LORD, do you make us wander from
      your ways
  and harden our hearts so we do not revere
    you?
  Return for the sake of your servants,
    the tribes that are your inheritance.
18 For a little while your people possessed your
      holy place,
  but now our enemies have trampled down
    your sanctuary.
19 We are yours from of old;
  but you have not ruled over them,
    they have not been called by your name. *a*

64 Oh, that you would rend the heavens
      and come down,
  that the mountains would tremble before
    you!
2 As when fire sets twigs ablaze
    and causes water to boil,
  come down to make your name known to
      your enemies
  and cause the nations to quake before
    you!
3 For when you did awesome things that we
      did not expect,
  you came down, and the mountains
    trembled before you.
4 Since ancient times no one has heard,
    no ear has perceived,
  no eye has seen any God besides you,
    who acts on behalf of those who wait for
      him.
5 You come to the help of those who gladly do
      right,
    who remember your ways.
  But when we continued to sin against them,
    you were angry.
  How then can we be saved?
6 All of us have become like one who is
      unclean,
  and all our righteous acts are like filthy
    rags;
  we all shrivel up like a leaf,
    and like the wind our sins sweep us away.

*a 19 Or We are like those you have never ruled, / like those
never called by your name*

THE MESSAGE

Whatever happened to your passion,
  your famous mighty acts,
Your heartfelt pity, your compassion?
  Why are you holding back?
You are our Father.
  Abraham and Israel are long dead.
  They wouldn't know us from Adam.
But you're our *living* Father,
  our Redeemer, famous from eternity!
Why, GOD, did you make us wander from your
      ways?
  Why did you make us cold and stubborn
    so that we no longer worshiped you in
      awe?
Turn back for the sake of your servants.
  You own us! We belong to you!
For a while your holy people had it good,
  but now our enemies have wrecked your
    holy place.
For a long time now, you've paid no attention
    to us.
  It's like you never knew us.

CAN WE BE SAVED?

64.1-7 **64** Oh, that you would rip open the
      heavens and descend,
  make the mountains shudder at your
    presence—
As when a forest catches fire,
  as when fire makes a pot to boil—
To shock your enemies into facing you,
  make the nations shake in their boots!
You did terrible things we never expected,
  descended and made the mountains
    shudder at your presence.
Since before time began
  no one has ever imagined,
No ear heard, no eye seen, a God like you
  who works for those who wait for him.
You meet those who happily do what is right,
  who keep a good memory of the way you
    work.
But how angry you've been with us!
  We've sinned and kept at it so long!
  Is there any hope for us? Can we be saved?
We're all sin-infected, sin-contaminated.
  Our best efforts are grease-stained rags.
We dry up like autumn leaves—
  sin-dried, we're blown off by the wind.

NEW INTERNATIONAL VERSION

7 No one calls on your name
  or strives to lay hold of you;
for you have hidden your face from us
  and made us waste away because of our
    sins.

8 Yet, O LORD, you are our Father.
  We are the clay, you are the potter;
  we are all the work of your hand.
9 Do not be angry beyond measure, O LORD;
  do not remember our sins forever.
Oh, look upon us, we pray,
  for we are all your people.
10 Your sacred cities have become a desert;
  even Zion is a desert, Jerusalem a
    desolation.
11 Our holy and glorious temple, where our
    fathers praised you,
  has been burned with fire,
  and all that we treasured lies in ruins.
12 After all this, O LORD, will you hold yourself
    back?
  Will you keep silent and punish us
    beyond measure?

JUDGMENT AND SALVATION

65 "I revealed myself to those who did not
    ask for me;
  I was found by those who did not
    seek me.
To a nation that did not call on my name,
  I said, 'Here am I, here am I.'
2 All day long I have held out my hands
  to an obstinate people,
who walk in ways not good,
  pursuing their own imaginations—
3 a people who continually provoke me
  to my very face,
offering sacrifices in gardens
  and burning incense on altars of brick;
4 who sit among the graves
  and spend their nights keeping secret
    vigil;
who eat the flesh of pigs,
  and whose pots hold broth of unclean
    meat;
5 who say, 'Keep away; don't come near me,
  for I am too sacred for you!'
Such people are smoke in my nostrils,
  a fire that keeps burning all day.

6 "See, it stands written before me:
  I will not keep silent but will pay back in
    full;
  I will pay it back into their laps—

THE MESSAGE

No one prays to you
  or makes the effort to reach out to you
Because you've turned away from us,
  left us to stew in our sins.

64.8-12 Still, GOD, you are our Father.
  We're the clay and you're our potter:
  All of us are what you made us.
Don't be too angry with us, O GOD.
  Don't keep a permanent account of
    wrongdoing.
  Keep in mind, please, we are your people—
    all of us.
Your holy cities are all ghost towns:
  Zion's a ghost town,
  Jerusalem's a field of weeds.
Our holy and beautiful Temple,
  which our ancestors filled with your
    praises,
Was burned down by fire,
  all our lovely parks and gardens in ruins.
In the face of all this,
  are you going to sit there unmoved, GOD?
Aren't you going to say something?
  Haven't you made us miserable long
    enough?

THE PEOPLE WHO BOTHERED TO REACH OUT
TO GOD

65.1-7 65 "I've made myself available
    to those who haven't bothered to ask.
I'm here, ready to be found
  by those who haven't bothered to look.
I kept saying 'I'm here, I'm right here'
  to a nation that ignored me.
I reached out day after day
  to a people who turned their backs on me,
People who make wrong turns,
  who insist on doing things their own way.
They get on my nerves,
  are rude to my face day after day,
Make up their own kitchen religion,
  a potluck religious stew.
They spend the night in tombs
  to get messages from the dead,
Eat forbidden foods
  and drink a witch's brew of potions and
    charms.
They say, 'Keep your distance.
  Don't touch me. I'm holier than thou.'
These people gag me.
  I can't stand their stench.
Look at this! Their sins are all written out—
  I have the list before me.
I'm not putting up with this any longer.
  I'll pay them the wages

NEW INTERNATIONAL VERSION

⁷both your sins and the sins of your fathers,"
  says the LORD.
"Because they burned sacrifices on the
    mountains
  and defied me on the hills,
I will measure into their laps
  the full payment for their former deeds."

⁸This is what the LORD says:

"As when juice is still found in a cluster of
    grapes
  and men say, 'Don't destroy it,
  there is yet some good in it,'
so will I do in behalf of my servants;
  I will not destroy them all.
⁹I will bring forth descendants from Jacob,
  and from Judah those who will possess
    my mountains;
my chosen people will inherit them,
  and there will my servants live.
¹⁰Sharon will become a pasture for flocks,
  and the Valley of Achor a resting place for
    herds,
  for my people who seek me.

¹¹"But as for you who forsake the LORD
  and forget my holy mountain,
who spread a table for Fortune
  and fill bowls of mixed wine for Destiny,
¹²I will destine you for the sword,
  and you will all bend down for the
    slaughter;
for I called but you did not answer,
  I spoke but you did not listen.
You did evil in my sight
  and chose what displeases me."

¹³Therefore this is what the Sovereign LORD
says:

"My servants will eat,
  but you will go hungry;
my servants will drink,
  but you will go thirsty;
my servants will rejoice,
  but you will be put to shame.
¹⁴My servants will sing
  out of the joy of their hearts,
but you will cry out
  from anguish of heart
  and wail in brokenness of spirit.
¹⁵You will leave your name
  to my chosen ones as a curse;
the Sovereign LORD will put you to death,
  but to his servants he will give another
    name.
¹⁶Whoever invokes a blessing in the land

THE MESSAGE

They have coming for their sins.
  And for the sins of their parents lumped in,
  a bonus." GOD says so.
"Because they've practiced their blasphemous
    worship,
  mocking me at their hillside shrines,
I'll let loose the consequences
  and pay them in full for their actions."

65.8-10 GOD's Message:

"But just as one bad apple doesn't ruin the
    whole bushel,
  there are still plenty of good apples left.
So I'll preserve those in Israel who obey me.
  I won't destroy the whole nation.
I'll bring out my true children from Jacob
  and the heirs of my mountains from Judah.
My chosen will inherit the land,
  my servants will move in.
The lush valley of Sharon in the west
  will be a pasture for flocks,
And in the east, the valley of Achor,
  a place for herds to graze.
These will be for the people
  who bothered to reach out to me, who
    wanted me in their lives,
  who actually bothered to look for me.

✝

65.11-12 "But you who abandon me, your GOD,
  who forget the holy mountains,
Who hold dinners for Lady Luck
  and throw cocktail parties for Sir Fate,
Well, you asked for it. Fate it will be:
  your destiny, Death.
For when I invited you, you ignored me;
  when I spoke to you, you brushed me off.
You did the very things I exposed as evil;
  you chose what I hate."

65.13-16   Therefore, this is the Message from the Master, GOD:

"My servants will eat,
  and you'll go hungry;
My servants will drink,
  and you'll go thirsty;
My servants will rejoice,
  and you'll hang your heads.
My servants will laugh from full hearts,
  and you'll cry out heartbroken,
yes, wail from crushed spirits.
Your legacy to my chosen
  will be your name reduced to a cussword.
I, GOD, will put you to death
  and give a new name to my servants.
Then whoever prays a blessing in the land

NEW INTERNATIONAL VERSION

will do so by the God of truth;
he who takes an oath in the land
will swear by the God of truth.
For the past troubles will be forgotten
and hidden from my eyes.

NEW HEAVENS AND A NEW EARTH

¹⁷ "Behold, I will create
new heavens and a new earth.
The former things will not be remembered,
nor will they come to mind.
¹⁸ But be glad and rejoice forever
in what I will create,
for I will create Jerusalem to be a delight
and its people a joy.
¹⁹ I will rejoice over Jerusalem
and take delight in my people;
the sound of weeping and of crying
will be heard in it no more.

²⁰ "Never again will there be in it
an infant who lives but a few days,
or an old man who does not live out his
years;
he who dies at a hundred
will be thought a mere youth;
he who fails to reach ᵃ a hundred
will be considered accursed.
²¹ They will build houses and dwell in them;
they will plant vineyards and eat their
fruit.
²² No longer will they build houses and others
live in them,
or plant and others eat.
For as the days of a tree,
so will be the days of my people;
my chosen ones will long enjoy
the works of their hands.
²³ They will not toil in vain
or bear children doomed to misfortune;
for they will be a people blessed by the LORD,
they and their descendants with them.
²⁴ Before they call I will answer;
while they are still speaking I will hear.
²⁵ The wolf and the lamb will feed together,
and the lion will eat straw like the ox,
but dust will be the serpent's food.
They will neither harm nor destroy
on all my holy mountain,"
says the LORD.

THE MESSAGE

will use my faithful name for the blessing,
And whoever takes an oath in the land
will use my faithful name for the oath,
Because the earlier troubles are gone and
forgotten,
banished far from my sight.

NEW HEAVENS AND A NEW EARTH

65.17-25 "Pay close attention now:
I'm creating new heavens and a new earth.
All the earlier troubles, chaos, and pain
are things of the past, to be forgotten.
Look ahead with joy.
Anticipate what I'm creating:
I'll create Jerusalem as sheer joy,
create my people as pure delight.
I'll take joy in Jerusalem,
take delight in my people:
No more sounds of weeping in the city,
no cries of anguish;
No more babies dying in the cradle,
or old people who don't enjoy a full
lifetime;
One-hundredth birthdays will be considered
normal—
anything less will seem like a cheat.
They'll build houses
and move in.
They'll plant fields
and eat what they grow.
No more building a house
that some outsider takes over,
No more planting fields
that some enemy confiscates,
For my people will be as long-lived as trees,
my chosen ones will have satisfaction in
their work.
They won't work and have nothing come of it,
they won't have children snatched out from
under them.
For they themselves are plantings blessed by
GOD,
with their children and grandchildren
likewise GOD-blessed.
Before they call out, I'll answer.
Before they've finished speaking, I'll have
heard.
Wolf and lamb will graze the same meadow,
lion and ox eat straw from the same trough,
but snakes—they'll get a diet of dirt!
Neither animal nor human will hurt or kill
anywhere on my Holy Mountain," says
GOD.

ᵃ 20 Or / the sinner who reaches

NEW INTERNATIONAL VERSION

JUDGMENT AND HOPE

66

This is what the LORD says:

"Heaven is my throne,
  and the earth is my footstool.
Where is the house you will build for me?
  Where will my resting place be?
2 Has not my hand made all these things,
  and so they came into being?"
                        declares the LORD.

"This is the one I esteem:
  he who is humble and contrite in spirit,
  and trembles at my word.
3 But whoever sacrifices a bull
  is like one who kills a man,
and whoever offers a lamb,
  like one who breaks a dog's neck;
whoever makes a grain offering
  is like one who presents pig's blood,
and whoever burns memorial incense,
  like one who worships an idol.
They have chosen their own ways,
  and their souls delight in their
    abominations;
4 so I also will choose harsh treatment for
    them
  and will bring upon them what they
    dread.
For when I called, no one answered,
  when I spoke, no one listened.
They did evil in my sight
  and chose what displeases me."

5 Hear the word of the LORD,
  you who tremble at his word:
"Your brothers who hate you,
  and exclude you because of my name,
    have said,
'Let the LORD be glorified,
  that we may see your joy!'
  Yet they will be put to shame.
6 Hear that uproar from the city,
  hear that noise from the temple!
It is the sound of the LORD
  repaying his enemies all they deserve.

7 "Before she goes into labor,
  she gives birth;
before the pains come upon her,
  she delivers a son.
8 Who has ever heard of such a thing?
  Who has ever seen such things?
Can a country be born in a day
  or a nation be brought forth in a moment?
Yet no sooner is Zion in labor
  than she gives birth to her children.
9 Do I bring to the moment of birth

THE MESSAGE

LIVING WORSHIP TO GOD

66

66.1-2 GOD'S Message:

"Heaven's my throne,
  earth is my footstool.
What sort of house could you build for me?
  What holiday spot reserve for me?
I made all this! I own all this!"
    GOD'S Decree.
"But there is something I'm looking for:
  a person simple and plain,
  reverently responsive to what I say.

66.3-4 "Your acts of worship
  are acts of sin:
Your sacrificial slaughter of the ox
  is no different from murdering the
    neighbor;
Your offerings for worship,
  no different from dumping pig's blood on
    the altar;
Your presentation of memorial gifts,
  no different from honoring a no-god idol.
You choose self-serving worship,
  you delight in self-centered worship—
    disgusting!
Well, I choose to expose your nonsense
  and let you realize your worst fears,
Because when I invited you, you ignored me;
  when I spoke to you, you brushed me off.
You did the very things I exposed as evil,
  you chose what I hate."

66.5 But listen to what GOD has to say
  to you who reverently respond to his Word:
"Your own families hate you
  and turn you out because of me.
They taunt you, 'Let us see GOD's glory!
  If God's so great, why aren't you happy?'
But they're the ones
  who are going to end up shamed."

✝

66.6 Rumbles of thunder from the city!
  A voice out of the Temple!
GOD's voice,
  handing out judgment to his enemies:

66.7-9 "Before she went into labor,
  she had the baby.
Before the birth pangs hit,
  she delivered a son.
Has anyone ever heard of such a thing?
  Has anyone seen anything like this?
A country born in a day?
  A nation born in a flash?
But Zion was barely in labor
  when she had her babies!
Do I open the womb

NEW INTERNATIONAL VERSION

and not give delivery?" says the LORD.
  "Do I close up the womb
    when I bring to delivery?" says your God.
¹⁰ "Rejoice with Jerusalem and be glad for her,
    all you who love her;
  rejoice greatly with her,
    all you who mourn over her.
¹¹ For you will nurse and be satisfied
    at her comforting breasts;
  you will drink deeply
    and delight in her overflowing
      abundance."

¹² For this is what the LORD says:

  "I will extend peace to her like a river,
    and the wealth of nations like a flooding
      stream;
  you will nurse and be carried on her arm
    and dandled on her knees.
¹³ As a mother comforts her child,
    so will I comfort you;
  and you will be comforted over
    Jerusalem."

¹⁴ When you see this, your heart will rejoice
    and you will flourish like grass;
  the hand of the LORD will be made known to
    his servants,
    but his fury will be shown to his foes.
¹⁵ See, the LORD is coming with fire,
    and his chariots are like a whirlwind;
  he will bring down his anger with fury,
    and his rebuke with flames of fire.
¹⁶ For with fire and with his sword
    the LORD will execute judgment upon all
      men,
  and many will be those slain by the LORD.

¹⁷ "Those who consecrate and purify themselves to go into the gardens, following the one
in the midst of*a* those who eat the flesh of pigs
and rats and other abominable things—they will
meet their end together," declares the LORD.

¹⁸ "And I, because of their actions and their
imaginations, am about to come*b* and gather all
nations and tongues, and they will come and see
my glory.

¹⁹ "I will set a sign among them, and I will
send some of those who survive to the nations—
to Tarshish, to the Libyans*c* and Lydians (famous
as archers), to Tubal and Greece, and to the distant islands that have not heard of my fame
or seen my glory. They will proclaim my glory
among the nations. ²⁰ And they will bring all

THE MESSAGE

and not deliver the baby?
Do I, the One who delivers babies,
  shut the womb?

66.10-11 "Rejoice, Jerusalem,
  and all who love her, celebrate!
And all you who have shed tears over her,
  join in the happy singing.
You newborns can satisfy yourselves
  at her nurturing breasts.
Yes, delight yourselves and drink your fill
  at her ample bosom."

66.12-13   GOD's Message:

"I'll pour robust well-being into her like a
    river,
  the glory of nations like a river in flood.
You'll nurse at her breasts,
  nestle in her bosom,
  and be bounced on her knees.
As a mother comforts her child,
  so I'll comfort you.
You will be comforted in Jerusalem."

66.14-16 You'll see all this and burst with joy
  —you'll feel ten feet tall—
As it becomes apparent that GOD is on your
    side
  and against his enemies.
For GOD arrives like wildfire
  and his chariots like a tornado,
A furious outburst of anger,
  a rebuke fierce and fiery.
For it's by fire that GOD brings judgment,
  a death sentence on the human race.
Many, oh so many,
  are under GOD's sentence of death:

66.17 "All who enter the sacred groves for initiation
in those unholy rituals that climaxed in that
foul and obscene meal of pigs and mice will eat
together and then die together." GOD's Decree.

66.18-21   "I know everything they've ever done or
thought. I'm going to come and then gather
everyone—all nations, all languages. They'll
come and see my glory. I'll set up a station at
the center. I'll send the survivors of judgment
all over the world: Spain and Africa, Turkey
and Greece, and the far-off islands that have
never heard of me, who know nothing of what
I've done nor who I am. I'll send them out as
missionaries to preach my glory among the nations. They'll return with all your long-lost

---

a 17 Or *gardens behind one of your temples, and*
b 18 The meaning of the Hebrew for this clause is
uncertain.   *c* 19 Some Septuagint manuscripts *Put*
(Libyans); Hebrew *Pul*

NEW INTERNATIONAL VERSION

your brothers, from all the nations, to my holy mountain in Jerusalem as an offering to the LORD—on horses, in chariots and wagons, and on mules and camels," says the LORD. "They will bring them, as the Israelites bring their grain offerings, to the temple of the LORD in ceremonially clean vessels. ²¹And I will select some of them also to be priests and Levites," says the LORD.

²²"As the new heavens and the new earth that I make will endure before me," declares the LORD, "so will your name and descendants endure. ²³From one New Moon to another and from one Sabbath to another, all mankind will come and bow down before me," says the LORD. ²⁴"And they will go out and look upon the dead bodies of those who rebelled against me; their worm will not die, nor will their fire be quenched, and they will be loathsome to all mankind."

THE MESSAGE

brothers and sisters from all over the world. They'll bring them back and offer them in living worship to GOD. They'll bring them on horses and wagons and carts, on mules and camels, straight to my holy mountain Jerusalem," says GOD. "They'll present them just as Israelites present their offerings in a ceremonial vessel in the Temple of GOD. I'll even take some of them and make them priests and Levites," says GOD.

66.22-23 "For just as the new heavens and new earth
    that I am making will stand firm
        before me"
    —GOD's Decree—
"So will your children
    and your reputation stand firm.
Month after month and week by week,
    everyone will come to worship me," GOD
        says.

66.24 "And then they'll go out and look at what
        happened
    to those who rebelled against me. Corpses!
Maggots endlessly eating away on them,
    an endless supply of fuel for fires.
Everyone who sees what's happened
    and smells the stench retches."

JEREMIAH

JEREMIAH

DEMOLISH, AND THEN START OVER

1.1-4 **1** The words of Jeremiah son of Hilkiah, one of the priests at Anathoth in the territory of Benjamin. ²The word of the LORD came to him in the thirteenth year of the reign of Josiah son of Amon king of Judah, ³and through the reign of Jehoiakim son of Josiah king of Judah, down to the fifth month of the eleventh year of Zedekiah son of Josiah king of Judah, when the people of Jerusalem went into exile.

1 The Message of Jeremiah son of Hilkiah of the family of priests who lived in Anathoth in the country of Benjamin. GOD's Message began to come to him during the thirteenth year that Josiah son of Amos reigned over Judah. It continued to come to him during the time Jehoiakim son of Josiah reigned over Judah. And it continued to come to him clear down to the fifth month of the eleventh year of the reign of Zedekiah son of Josiah over Judah, the year that Jerusalem was taken into exile. This is what GOD said:

THE CALL OF JEREMIAH

⁴The word of the LORD came to me, saying,

⁵"Before I formed you in the womb I knew*ᵃ* you,
  before you were born I set you apart;
  I appointed you as a prophet to the
    nations."

1.5 "Before I shaped you in the womb,
  I knew all about you.
Before you saw the light of day,
  I had holy plans for you:
A prophet to the nations—
  that's what I had in mind for you."

⁶"Ah, Sovereign LORD," I said, "I do not know how to speak; I am only a child."
⁷But the LORD said to me, "Do not say, 'I am only a child.' You must go to everyone I send you to and say whatever I command you. ⁸Do not be afraid of them, for I am with you and will rescue you," declares the LORD.
⁹Then the LORD reached out his hand and touched my mouth and said to me, "Now, I have put my words in your mouth. ¹⁰See, today I appoint you over nations and kingdoms to uproot and tear down, to destroy and overthrow, to build and to plant."
¹¹The word of the LORD came to me: "What do you see, Jeremiah?"
"I see the branch of an almond tree," I replied.

1.6 But I said, "Hold it, Master GOD! Look at me. I don't know anything. I'm only a boy!"

1.7-8 GOD told me, "Don't say, 'I'm only a boy.'
  I'll tell you where to go and you'll go there.
I'll tell you what to say and you'll say it.
  Don't be afraid of a soul.
I'll be right there, looking after you."
  GOD's Decree.

1.9-10 GOD reached out, touched my mouth, and said,
  "Look! I've just put my words in your
    mouth—hand-delivered!
See what I've done? I've given you a job to do
  among nations and governments—a
    red-letter day!
Your job is to pull up and tear down,
  take apart and demolish,
And then start over,
  building and planting."

STAND UP AND SAY YOUR PIECE

1.11-12 GOD's Message came to me: "What do you see, Jeremiah?"
  I said, "A walking stick—that's all."

NEW INTERNATIONAL VERSION

¹²The LORD said to me, "You have seen correctly, for I am watching[a] to see that my word is fulfilled."

¹³The word of the LORD came to me again: "What do you see?"

"I see a boiling pot, tilting away from the north," I answered.

¹⁴The LORD said to me, "From the north disaster will be poured out on all who live in the land. ¹⁵I am about to summon all the peoples of the northern kingdoms," declares the LORD.

"Their kings will come and set up their
thrones
in the entrance of the gates of Jerusalem;
they will come against all her surrounding
walls
and against all the towns of Judah.
¹⁶I will pronounce my judgments on my
people
because of their wickedness in
forsaking me,
in burning incense to other gods
and in worshiping what their hands have
made.

¹⁷"Get yourself ready! Stand up and say to them whatever I command you. Do not be terrified by them, or I will terrify you before them. ¹⁸Today I have made you a fortified city, an iron pillar and a bronze wall to stand against the whole land—against the kings of Judah, its officials, its priests and the people of the land. ¹⁹They will fight against you but will not overcome you, for I am with you and will rescue you," declares the LORD.

ISRAEL FORSAKES GOD

2 The word of the LORD came to me: ²"Go and proclaim in the hearing of Jerusalem:

" 'I remember the devotion of your youth,
how as a bride you loved me
and followed me through the desert,
through a land not sown.
³Israel was holy to the LORD,

[a] 12 The Hebrew for *watching* sounds like the Hebrew for *almond tree*.

THE MESSAGE

And GOD said, "Good eyes! I'm sticking with
you.
I'll make every word I give you come true."

1.13-15 GOD'S Message came again: "So what do you
see now?"
I said, "I see a boiling pot, tipped down
toward us."
Then GOD told me, "Disaster will pour out of
the north
on everyone living in this land.
Watch for this: I'm calling all the kings out of
the north."
GOD'S Decree.

1.15-16 "They'll come and set up headquarters
facing Jerusalem's gates,
Facing all the city walls,
facing all the villages of Judah.
I'll pronounce my judgment on the people of
Judah
for walking out on me—what a terrible
thing to do!—
And courting other gods with their offerings,
worshiping as gods sticks they'd carved,
stones they'd painted.

1.17 "But you—up on your feet and get dressed for
work!
Stand up and say your piece. Say exactly
what I tell you to say.
Don't pull your punches
or I'll pull you out of the lineup.

1.18-19 "Stand at attention while I prepare you for
your work.
I'm making you as impregnable as a castle,
Immovable as a steel post,
solid as a concrete block wall.
You're a one-man defense system
against this culture,
Against Judah's kings and princes,
against the priests and local leaders.
They'll fight you, but they won't
even scratch you.
I'll back you up every inch of the way."
GOD'S Decree.

ISRAEL WAS GOD'S HOLY CHOICE

2.1-3 **2** GOD'S Message came to me. It went like
this:
"Get out in the streets and call to Jerusalem,
'GOD'S Message!
I remember your youthful loyalty,
our love as newlyweds.
You stayed with me through the wilderness
years,
stuck with me through all the hard places.
Israel was GOD'S holy choice,

NEW INTERNATIONAL VERSION

the firstfruits of his harvest;
all who devoured her were held guilty,
and disaster overtook them,' "
declares the LORD.

⁴Hear the word of the LORD, O house of
Jacob,
all you clans of the house of Israel.

⁵This is what the LORD says:

"What fault did your fathers find in me,
that they strayed so far from me?
They followed worthless idols
and became worthless themselves.
⁶They did not ask, 'Where is the LORD,
who brought us up out of Egypt
and led us through the barren wilderness,
through a land of deserts and rifts,
a land of drought and darkness,ᵃ
a land where no one travels and no one
lives?'
⁷I brought you into a fertile land
to eat its fruit and rich produce.
But you came and defiled my land
and made my inheritance detestable.
⁸The priests did not ask,
'Where is the LORD?'
Those who deal with the law did not
know me;
the leaders rebelled against me.
The prophets prophesied by Baal,
following worthless idols.

⁹"Therefore I bring charges against you
again,"
declares the LORD.
"And I will bring charges against your
children's children.
¹⁰Cross over to the coasts of Kittimᵇ and look,
send to Kedarᶜ and observe closely;
see if there has ever been anything like
this:
¹¹Has a nation ever changed its gods?
(Yet they are not gods at all.)
But my people have exchanged theirᵈ Glory
for worthless idols.
¹²Be appalled at this, O heavens,
and shudder with great horror,"
declares the LORD.
¹³"My people have committed two sins:
They have forsaken me,

ᵃ 6 Or *and the shadow of death*   ᵇ 10 That is, Cyprus and
western coastlands   ᶜ 10 The home of Bedouin tribes in
the Syro-Arabian desert   ᵈ 11 Masoretic Text; an ancient
Hebrew scribal tradition *my*

THE MESSAGE

the pick of the crop.
Anyone who laid a hand on her
would soon wish he hadn't!' "
GOD's Decree.

☩

2.4-6 Hear GOD's Message, House of Jacob!
Yes, you—House of Israel!
GOD's Message: "What did your ancestors find
fault with in me
that they drifted so far from me,
Took up with Sir Windbag
and turned into windbags themselves?
It never occurred to them to say, 'Where's
GOD,
the God who got us out of Egypt,
Who took care of us through thick and thin,
those rough-and-tumble
wilderness years of parched deserts and
death valleys,
A land that no one who enters comes out of,
a cruel, inhospitable land?'

2.7-8 "I brought you to a garden land
where you could eat lush fruit.
But you barged in and polluted my land,
trashed and defiled my dear land.
The priests never thought to ask, 'Where's
GOD?'
The religion experts knew nothing of me.
The rulers defied me.
The prophets preached god Baal
And chased empty god-dreams and silly god-
schemes.

2.9-11 "Because of all this, I'm bringing charges
against you"
—GOD's Decree—
"charging you and your children and your
grandchildren.
Look around. Have you ever seen anything
quite like this?
Sail to the western islands and look.
Travel to the Kedar wilderness and look.
Look closely. Has this ever happened
before,
That a nation has traded in its gods
for gods that aren't even close to gods?
But my people have traded my Glory
for empty god-dreams and silly god-
schemes.

2.12-13 "Stand in shock, heavens, at what you see!
Throw up your hands in disbelief—this
can't be!"
GOD's Decree.
"My people have committed a compound sin:
they've walked out on me, the fountain

NEW INTERNATIONAL VERSION

the spring of living water,
and have dug their own cisterns,
broken cisterns that cannot hold water.
¹⁴ Is Israel a servant, a slave by birth?
Why then has he become plunder?
¹⁵ Lions have roared;
they have growled at him.
They have laid waste his land;
his towns are burned and deserted.
¹⁶ Also, the men of Memphis *ᵃ* and Tahpanhes
have shaved the crown of your head. *ᵇ*
¹⁷ Have you not brought this on yourselves
by forsaking the Lord your God
when he led you in the way?
¹⁸ Now why go to Egypt
to drink water from the Shihor *ᶜ*?
And why go to Assyria
to drink water from the River *ᵈ*?
¹⁹ Your wickedness will punish you;
your backsliding will rebuke you.
Consider then and realize
how evil and bitter it is for you
when you forsake the Lord your God
and have no awe of me,"
declares the Lord,
the Lord Almighty.

²⁰ "Long ago you broke off your yoke
and tore off your bonds;
you said, 'I will not serve you!'
Indeed, on every high hill
and under every spreading tree
you lay down as a prostitute.
²¹ I had planted you like a choice vine
of sound and reliable stock.
How then did you turn against me
into a corrupt, wild vine?
²² Although you wash yourself with soda
and use an abundance of soap,
the stain of your guilt is still before me,"
declares the Sovereign
Lord.
²³ "How can you say, 'I am not defiled;
I have not run after the Baals'?

ᵃ 16 Hebrew *Noph*   *ᵇ 16* Or *have cracked your skull*
ᶜ 18 That is, a branch of the Nile   *ᵈ 18* That is, the
Euphrates

THE MESSAGE

Of fresh flowing waters, and then dug
cisterns—
cisterns that leak, cisterns that are no better
than sieves.

²·¹⁴⁻¹⁷ "Isn't Israel a valued servant,
born into a family with place and position?
So how did she end up a piece of meat
fought over by snarling and roaring lions?
There's nothing left of her but a few old bones,
her towns trashed and deserted.
Egyptians from the cities of Memphis and
Tahpanhes
have broken your skulls.
And why do you think all this has happened?
Isn't it because you walked out on your
God
just as he was beginning to lead you in the
right way?

²·¹⁸⁻¹⁹ "And now, what do you think you'll get by
going off to Egypt?
Maybe a cool drink of Nile River water?
Or what do you think you'll get by going off
to Assyria?
Maybe a long drink of Euphrates River
water?
Your evil ways will get you a sound thrashing,
that's what you'll get.
You'll pay dearly for your disloyal ways.
Take a long, hard look at what you've done
and its bitter results.
Was it worth it to have walked out on your
God?"
God's Decree, Master God-of-the-Angel-
Armies.

Addicted to Alien Gods

²·²⁰⁻²² "A long time ago you broke out of the
harness.
You shook off all restraints.
You said, 'I will not serve!'
and off you went,
Visiting every sex-and-religion shrine on the
way,
like a common whore.
You were a select vine when I planted you
from completely reliable stock.
And look how you've turned out—
a tangle of rancid growth, a poor excuse for
a vine.
Scrub, using the strongest soaps.
Scour your skin raw.
The sin-grease won't come out. I can't stand to
even look at you!"
God's Decree, the Master's Decree.

²·²³⁻²⁴ "How dare you tell me, 'I'm not stained by sin.
I've never chased after the Baal sex gods'!

NEW INTERNATIONAL VERSION

See how you behaved in the valley;
  consider what you have done.
You are a swift she-camel
  running here and there,
24 a wild donkey accustomed to the desert,
  sniffing the wind in her craving—
  in her heat who can restrain her?
Any males that pursue her need not tire
    themselves;
  at mating time they will find her.
25 Do not run until your feet are bare
  and your throat is dry.
But you said, 'It's no use!
  I love foreign gods,
  and I must go after them.'

26 "As a thief is disgraced when he is caught,
  so the house of Israel is disgraced—
they, their kings and their officials,
  their priests and their prophets.
27 They say to wood, 'You are my father,'
  and to stone, 'You gave me birth.'
They have turned their backs to me
  and not their faces;
yet when they are in trouble, they say,
  'Come and save us!'
28 Where then are the gods you made for
    yourselves?
  Let them come if they can save you
  when you are in trouble!
For you have as many gods
  as you have towns, O Judah.

29 "Why do you bring charges against me?
  You have all rebelled against me,"
            declares the LORD.
30 "In vain I punished your people;
  they did not respond to correction.
Your sword has devoured your prophets
  like a ravening lion.

31 "You of this generation, consider the word
of the LORD:

"Have I been a desert to Israel
  or a land of great darkness?
Why do my people say, 'We are free to roam;
  we will come to you no more'?

THE MESSAGE

Well, look at the tracks you've left behind in
    the valley.
  How do you account for what is written in
    the desert dust—
Tracks of a camel in heat, running this way
    and that,
  tracks of a wild donkey in rut,
Sniffing the wind for the slightest scent of sex.
  Who could possibly corral her!
On the hunt for sex, sex, and more sex—
  insatiable, indiscriminate, promiscuous.

2.25 "Slow down. Take a deep breath. What's the
    hurry?
  Why wear yourself out? Just what are you
    after anyway?
But you say, 'I can't help it.
  I'm addicted to alien gods. I can't quit.'

✝

2.26-28 "Just as a thief is chagrined, but only when
    caught,
  so the people of Israel are chagrined,
Caught along with their kings and princes,
  their priests and prophets.
They walk up to a tree and say, 'My father!'
  They pick up a stone and say, 'My mother!
    You bore me!'
All I ever see of them is their backsides.
  They never look me in the face.
But when things go badly, they don't hesitate
    to come running,
  calling out, 'Get a move on! Save us!'
Why not go to your handcrafted gods you're
    so fond of?
  Rouse them. Let them save you from your
    bad times.
You've got more gods, Judah,
  than you know what to do with.

TRYING OUT ANOTHER SIN-PROJECT

2.29-30 "What do you have against me,
  running off to assert your 'independence'?"
    GOD's Decree.
"I've wasted my time trying to train your
    children.
  They've paid no attention to me, ignored
    my discipline.
And you've gotten rid of your God-messengers,
  treating them like dirt and sweeping them
    away.

2.31-32 "What a generation you turned out to be!
  Didn't I tell you? Didn't I warn you?
Have I let you down, Israel?
  Am I nothing but a dead-end street?
Why do my people say, 'Good riddance!
  From now on we're on our own'?

NEW INTERNATIONAL VERSION

32 Does a maiden forget her jewelry,
    a bride her wedding ornaments?
Yet my people have forgotten me,
    days without number.
33 How skilled you are at pursuing love!
    Even the worst of women can learn from
        your ways.
34 On your clothes men find
    the lifeblood of the innocent poor,
    though you did not catch them
        breaking in.
    Yet in spite of all this
35   you say, 'I am innocent;
    he is not angry with me.'
But I will pass judgment on you
    because you say, 'I have not sinned.'
36 Why do you go about so much,
    changing your ways?
You will be disappointed by Egypt
    as you were by Assyria.
37 You will also leave that place
    with your hands on your head,
for the LORD has rejected those you trust;
    you will not be helped by them.

3 "If a man divorces his wife
    and she leaves him and marries another
        man,
should he return to her again?
    Would not the land be completely
        defiled?
But you have lived as a prostitute with many
        lovers—
    would you now return to me?"
                        declares the LORD.
2 "Look up to the barren heights and see.
    Is there any place where you have not
        been ravished?
By the roadside you sat waiting for lovers,
    sat like a nomad*a* in the desert.

a 2 Or an Arab

THE MESSAGE

Young women don't forget their jewelry, do
        they?
    Brides don't show up without their veils, do
        they?
But my people forget me.
    Day after day after day they never give me a
        thought.

                    ✝

2.33-35 "What an impressive start you made
    to get the most out of life.
You founded schools of sin,
    taught graduate courses in evil!
And now you're sending out graduates,
        resplendent in cap and gown—
    except the gowns are stained with the
        blood of your victims!
All that blood convicts you.
    You cut and hurt a lot of people to get
        where you are.
And yet you have the gall to say, 'I've done
        nothing wrong.
    God doesn't mind. He hasn't punished me,
        has he?'
Don't look now, but judgment's on the way,
    aimed at you who say, 'I've done nothing
        wrong.'

2.36-37 "You think it's just a small thing, don't you,
    to try out another sin-project when the first
        one fails?
But Egypt will leave you in the lurch
    the same way that Assyria did.
You're going to walk away from there
    wringing your hands.
I, GOD, have blacklisted those you trusted.
    You'll get not a lick of help from them."

YOUR SEX-AND-RELIGION OBSESSIONS

3.1 **3** GOD'S Message came to me as follows:

"If a man's wife
    walks out on him
And marries another man,
    can he take her back as if nothing had
        happened?
Wouldn't that raise a huge stink
    in the land?
And isn't that what you've done—
    'whored' your way with god after god?
And now you want to come back as if nothing
        had happened."
    GOD'S Decree.

3.2-5 "Look around at the hills.
    Where have you *not* had sex?
You've camped out like hunters stalking deer.
    You've solicited many lover-gods,

NEW INTERNATIONAL VERSION

You have defiled the land
  with your prostitution and wickedness.
³ Therefore the showers have been withheld,
  and no spring rains have fallen.
Yet you have the brazen look of a prostitute;
  you refuse to blush with shame.
⁴ Have you not just called to me:
  'My Father, my friend from my youth,
⁵ will you always be angry?
  Will your wrath continue forever?'
This is how you talk,
  but you do all the evil you can."

UNFAITHFUL ISRAEL

⁶During the reign of King Josiah, the LORD said to me, "Have you seen what faithless Israel has done? She has gone up on every high hill and under every spreading tree and has committed adultery there. ⁷I thought that after she had done all this she would return to me but she did not, and her unfaithful sister Judah saw it. ⁸I gave faithless Israel her certificate of divorce and sent her away because of all her adulteries. Yet I saw that her unfaithful sister Judah had no fear; she also went out and committed adultery. ⁹Because Israel's immorality mattered so little to her, she defiled the land and committed adultery with stone and wood. ¹⁰In spite of all this, her unfaithful sister Judah did not return to me with all her heart, but only in pretense," declares the LORD.

¹¹The LORD said to me, "Faithless Israel is more righteous than unfaithful Judah. ¹²Go, proclaim this message toward the north:

" 'Return, faithless Israel,' declares the LORD,
  'I will frown on you no longer,
for I am merciful,' declares the LORD,
  'I will not be angry forever.
¹³ Only acknowledge your guilt—
  you have rebelled against the LORD your
    God,
you have scattered your favors to foreign
    gods
  under every spreading tree,
  and have not obeyed me,' "
                    declares the LORD.

¹⁴"Return, faithless people," declares the LORD, "for I am your husband. I will choose you—one from a town and two from a clan—and bring you to Zion. ¹⁵Then I will give you

THE MESSAGE

Like a streetwalking whore
  chasing after other gods.
And so the rain has stopped.
  No more rain from the skies!
But it doesn't even faze you. Brazen as whores,
  you carry on as if you've done nothing
    wrong.
Then you have the nerve to call out, 'My
    father!
You took care of me when I was a child.
  Why not now?
Are you going to keep up your anger
    nonstop?'
  That's your line. Meanwhile you keep
    sinning nonstop."

ADMIT YOUR GOD-DEFIANCE

3.6-10 GOD spoke to me during the reign of King Josiah: "You have noticed, haven't you, how fickle Israel has visited every hill and grove of trees as a whore at large? I assumed that after she had gotten it out of her system, she'd come back, but she didn't. Her flighty sister, Judah, saw what she did. She also saw that because of fickle Israel's loose morals I threw her out, gave her her walking papers. But that didn't faze flighty sister Judah. She went out, big as you please, and took up a whore's life also. She took up cheap sex-and-religion as a sideline diversion, an indulgent recreation, and used anything and anyone, flouting sanity and sanctity alike, stinking up the country. And not once in all this did flighty sister Judah even give me a nod, although she made a show of it from time to time." GOD's Decree.

3.11-12 Then GOD told me, "Fickle Israel was a good sight better than flighty Judah. Go and preach this message. Face north toward Israel and say:

3.12-15 " 'Turn back, fickle Israel.
  I'm not just hanging back to punish you.
I'm committed in love to you.
  My anger doesn't seethe nonstop.
Just admit your guilt.
  Admit your God-defiance.
Admit to your promiscuous life with casual
    partners,
  pulling strangers into the sex-and-religion
    groves
While turning a deaf ear to me.' "
    GOD's Decree.
"Come back, wandering children!"
    GOD's Decree.
"I, yes I, am your true husband.
  I'll pick you out one by one—
This one from the city, these two from the
    country—
  and bring you to Zion.

NEW INTERNATIONAL VERSION

shepherds after my own heart, who will lead you with knowledge and understanding. ¹⁶In those days, when your numbers have increased greatly in the land," declares the LORD, "men will no longer say, 'The ark of the covenant of the LORD.' It will never enter their minds or be remembered; it will not be missed, nor will another one be made. ¹⁷At that time they will call Jerusalem The Throne of the LORD, and all nations will gather in Jerusalem to honor the name of the LORD. No longer will they follow the stubbornness of their evil hearts. ¹⁸In those days the house of Judah will join the house of Israel, and together they will come from a northern land to the land I gave your forefathers as an inheritance.

¹⁹"I myself said,

" 'How gladly would I treat you like sons
    and give you a desirable land,
    the most beautiful inheritance of any
        nation.'
I thought you would call me 'Father'
    and not turn away from following me.
²⁰But like a woman unfaithful to her husband,
    so you have been unfaithful to me,
        O house of Israel,"
                    declares the LORD.

²¹A cry is heard on the barren heights,
    the weeping and pleading of the people of
        Israel,
because they have perverted their ways
    and have forgotten the LORD their God.

²²"Return, faithless people;
    I will cure you of backsliding."

"Yes, we will come to you,
    for you are the LORD our God.
²³Surely the ⌊idolatrous⌋ commotion on the
        hills
    and mountains is a deception;
surely in the LORD our God
    is the salvation of Israel.
²⁴From our youth shameful gods have
        consumed
    the fruits of our fathers' labor—
their flocks and herds,
    their sons and daughters.
²⁵Let us lie down in our shame,

THE MESSAGE

I'll give you good shepherd-rulers who rule
        my way,
    who rule you with intelligence and
        wisdom.

3.16   "And this is what will happen: You will increase and prosper in the land. The time will come"—GOD's Decree!—"when no one will say any longer, 'Oh, for the good old days! Remember the Ark of the Covenant?' It won't even occur to anyone to say it—'the good old days.' The so-called good old days of the Ark are gone for good.

3.17   "Jerusalem will be the new Ark—'GOD's Throne.' All the godless nations, no longer stuck in the ruts of their evil ways, will gather there to honor GOD.

3.18   "At that time, the House of Judah will join up with the House of Israel. Holding hands, they'll leave the north country and come to the land I willed to your ancestors.

✣

3.19-20 "I planned what I'd say if you returned to me:
        'Good! I'll bring you back into the family.
I'll give you choice land,
        land that the godless nations would die for.'
And I imagined that you would say, 'Dear
        father!'
    and would never again go off and leave me.
But no luck. Like a false-hearted woman
        walking out on her husband,
    you, the whole family of Israel, have
            proven false to me."
        GOD's Decree.

3.21-22 The sound of voices comes drifting out of the
            hills,
        the unhappy sound of Israel's crying,
Israel lamenting the wasted years,
        never once giving her God a thought.
"Come back, wandering children!
        I can heal your wanderlust!"

✣

3.22-25 "We're here! We've come back to you.
        You're our own true GOD!
All that popular religion was a cheap lie,
        duped crowds buying up the latest in gods.
We're back! Back to our true GOD,
        the salvation of Israel.
The Fraud picked us clean, swindled us
        of what our ancestors bequeathed us,
Gypped us out of our inheritance—
        God-blessed flocks and God-given
            children.
We made our bed and now lie in it,

NEW INTERNATIONAL VERSION

and let our disgrace cover us.
We have sinned against the LORD our God,
both we and our fathers;
from our youth till this day
we have not obeyed the LORD our God."

4 "If you will return, O Israel,
    return to me,"
                    declares the LORD.
"If you put your detestable idols out of my
        sight
    and no longer go astray,
2 and if in a truthful, just and righteous way
    you swear, 'As surely as the LORD lives,'
then the nations will be blessed by him
    and in him they will glory."

3 This is what the LORD says to the men of Judah and to Jerusalem:

"Break up your unplowed ground
    and do not sow among thorns.
4 Circumcise yourselves to the LORD,
    circumcise your hearts,
    you men of Judah and people of
        Jerusalem,
or my wrath will break out and burn like fire
    because of the evil you have done—
    burn with no one to quench it.

DISASTER FROM THE NORTH

5 "Announce in Judah and proclaim in
        Jerusalem and say:
    'Sound the trumpet throughout the land!'
Cry aloud and say:
    'Gather together!
    Let us flee to the fortified cities!'
6 Raise the signal to go to Zion!
    Flee for safety without delay!
For I am bringing disaster from the north,
    even terrible destruction."

7 A lion has come out of his lair;
    a destroyer of nations has set out.
He has left his place
    to lay waste your land.
Your towns will lie in ruins
    without inhabitant.

THE MESSAGE

all tangled up in the dirty sheets of
        dishonor.
All because we sinned against our GOD,
    we and our fathers and mothers.
From the time we took our first steps, said
        our first words,
    we've been rebels, disobeying the voice of
        our GOD."

☩

4.1-2 **4** "If you want to come back, O Israel,
        you must really come back to me.
You must get rid of your stinking sin
        paraphernalia
    and not wander away from me anymore.
Then you can say words like, 'As GOD
        lives . . .'
    and have them mean something true and
        just and right.
And the godless nations will get caught up in
        the blessing
    and find something in Israel to write home
        about."

☩

4.3-4 Here's another Message from GOD
        to the people of Judah and Jerusalem:
"Plow your unplowed fields,
    but then don't plant weeds in the soil!
Yes, circumcise your *lives* for God's sake.
    Plow your unplowed hearts,
    all you people of Judah and Jerusalem.
Prevent fire—the fire of my anger—
    for once it starts it can't be put out.
Your wicked ways
    are fuel for the fire.

GOD'S SLEDGEHAMMER ANGER

4.5-8 "Sound the alarm in Judah,
        broadcast the news in Jerusalem.
Say, 'Blow the ram's horn trumpet through the
        land!'
    Shout out—a bullhorn bellow!—
'Close ranks!
    Run for your lives to the shelters!'
Send up a flare warning Zion:
    'Not a minute to lose! Don't sit on your
        hands!'
Disaster's descending from the north. I set it
        off!
    When it lands, it will shake the
        foundations.
Invaders have pounced like a lion from its
        cover,
    ready to rip nations to shreds,
Leaving your land in wrack and ruin,
    your cities in rubble, abandoned.

NEW INTERNATIONAL VERSION

⁸So put on sackcloth,
　　lament and wail,
　for the fierce anger of the LORD
　　has not turned away from us.

⁹"In that day," declares the LORD,
　　"the king and the officials will lose heart,
　the priests will be horrified,
　　and the prophets will be appalled."

¹⁰Then I said, "Ah, Sovereign LORD, how completely you have deceived this people and Jerusalem by saying, 'You will have peace,' when the sword is at our throats."

¹¹At that time this people and Jerusalem will be told, "A scorching wind from the barren heights in the desert blows toward my people, but not to winnow or cleanse; ¹²a wind too strong for that comes from me.ᵃ Now I pronounce my judgments against them."

¹³Look! He advances like the clouds,
　　his chariots come like a whirlwind,
　his horses are swifter than eagles.
　　Woe to us! We are ruined!
¹⁴O Jerusalem, wash the evil from your heart
　　and be saved.
　How long will you harbor wicked
　　thoughts?
¹⁵A voice is announcing from Dan,
　　proclaiming disaster from the hills of
　　　Ephraim.
¹⁶"Tell this to the nations,
　　proclaim it to Jerusalem:
　'A besieging army is coming from a distant
　　　land,
　　raising a war cry against the cities of
　　　Judah.
¹⁷They surround her like men guarding a field,
　　because she has rebelled against me,' "
　　　　　　　　　　　　　　declares the LORD.
¹⁸"Your own conduct and actions
　　have brought this upon you.
　This is your punishment.
　　How bitter it is!
　　How it pierces to the heart!"

¹⁹Oh, my anguish, my anguish!
　　I writhe in pain.
　Oh, the agony of my heart!
　　My heart pounds within me,

ᵃ *12 Or comes at my command*

THE MESSAGE

Dress in funereal black.
　　Weep and wail,
For GOD's sledgehammer anger
　　has slammed into us head-on.

4.9 "When this happens"
　　—GOD's Decree—
"King and princes will lose heart;
　　priests will be baffled and prophets stand
　　　dumbfounded."

4.10 Then I said, "Alas, Master GOD!
　　You've fed lies to this people, this
　　　Jerusalem.
You assured them, 'All is well, don't worry,'
　　at the very moment when the sword was at
　　　their throats."

　　　　　　　　　☩

4.11-12 At that time, this people, yes, this very
　　　Jerusalem,
　　will be told in plain words:
"The northern hordes are sweeping in
　　from the desert steppes—
A wind that's up to no good, a gale-force wind.
　　I ordered this wind.
I'm pronouncing
　　my hurricane judgment on my people."

YOUR EVIL LIFE IS PIERCING YOUR HEART

4.13-14 Look at them! Like banks of storm clouds,
　　racing, tumbling, their chariots a tornado,
Their horses faster than eagles!
　　Woe to us! We're done for!
Jerusalem! Scrub the evil from your lives
　　so you'll be fit for salvation.
How much longer will you harbor
　　devious and malignant designs within you?

4.15-17 What's this? A messenger from Dan?
　　Bad news from Ephraim's hills!
Make the report public.
　　Broadcast the news to Jerusalem:
"Invaders from far off are
　　raising war cries against Judah's towns.
They're all over her, like a dog on a bone.
　　And why? Because she rebelled
　　　against me."
　　　GOD's Decree.

4.18 "It's the way you've lived
　　that's brought all this on you.
The bitter taste is from your evil life.
　　That's what's piercing your heart."

　　　　　　　　　☩

4.19-21 I'm doubled up with cramps in my belly—
　　a poker burns in my gut.
My insides are tearing me up,

NEW INTERNATIONAL VERSION

I cannot keep silent.
For I have heard the sound of the trumpet;
I have heard the battle cry.
20 Disaster follows disaster;
the whole land lies in ruins.
In an instant my tents are destroyed,
my shelter in a moment.
21 How long must I see the battle standard
and hear the sound of the trumpet?

22 "My people are fools;
they do not know me.
They are senseless children;
they have no understanding.
They are skilled in doing evil;
they know not how to do good."

23 I looked at the earth,
and it was formless and empty;
and at the heavens,
and their light was gone.
24 I looked at the mountains,
and they were quaking;
all the hills were swaying.
25 I looked, and there were no people;
every bird in the sky had flown away.
26 I looked, and the fruitful land was a desert;
all its towns lay in ruins
before the LORD, before his fierce anger.

27 This is what the LORD says:

"The whole land will be ruined,
though I will not destroy it completely.
28 Therefore the earth will mourn
and the heavens above grow dark,
because I have spoken and will not relent,
I have decided and will not turn back."

29 At the sound of horsemen and archers
every town takes to flight.
Some go into the thickets;
some climb up among the rocks.
All the towns are deserted;
no one lives in them.

30 What are you doing, O devastated one?
Why dress yourself in scarlet
and put on jewels of gold?
Why shade your eyes with paint?

THE MESSAGE

never a moment's peace.
The ram's horn trumpet blast rings in my ears,
the signal for all-out war.
Disaster hard on the heels of disaster,
the whole country in ruins!
In one stroke my home is destroyed,
the walls flattened in the blink of an eye.
How long do I have to look at the warning
flares,
listen to the siren of danger?

EXPERTS AT EVIL

4.22 "What fools my people are!
They have no idea who I am.
A company of half-wits,
dopes and donkeys all!
Experts at evil
but klutzes at good."

4.23-26 I looked at the earth—
it was back to pre-Genesis chaos and
emptiness.
I looked at the skies,
and not a star to be seen.
I looked at the mountains—
they were trembling like aspen leaves,
And all the hills
rocking back and forth in the wind.
I looked—what's this! Not a man or woman in
sight,
and not a bird to be seen in the skies.
I looked—this can't be! Every garden and
orchard shriveled up.
All the towns were ghost towns.
And all this because of GOD,
because of the blazing anger of GOD.

4.27-28 Yes, this is GOD's Word on the matter:

"The whole country will be laid waste—
still it won't be the end of the world.
The earth will mourn
and the skies lament
Because I've given my word and won't take it
back.
I've decided and won't change my mind."

YOU'RE NOT GOING TO SEDUCE ANYONE

4.29 Someone shouts, "Horsemen and archers!"
and everybody runs for cover.
They hide in ditches,
they climb into caves.
The cities are emptied,
not a person left anywhere.

4.30-31 And you, what do you think you're up to?
Dressing up in party clothes,
Decking yourselves out in jewelry,
putting on lipstick and rouge and mascara!

NEW INTERNATIONAL VERSION

You adorn yourself in vain.
Your lovers despise you;
they seek your life.

31 I hear a cry as of a woman in labor,
a groan as of one bearing her first child—
the cry of the Daughter of Zion gasping for
breath,
stretching out her hands and saying,
"Alas! I am fainting;
my life is given over to murderers."

NOT ONE IS UPRIGHT

5 "Go up and down the streets of Jerusalem,
look around and consider,
search through her squares.
If you can find but one person
who deals honestly and seeks the truth,
I will forgive this city.
2 Although they say, 'As surely as the LORD
lives,'
still they are swearing falsely."

3 O LORD, do not your eyes look for truth?
You struck them, but they felt no pain;
you crushed them, but they refused
correction.
They made their faces harder than stone
and refused to repent.
4 I thought, "These are only the poor;
they are foolish,
for they do not know the way of the LORD,
the requirements of their God.
5 So I will go to the leaders
and speak to them;
surely they know the way of the LORD,
the requirements of their God."
But with one accord they too had broken off
the yoke
and torn off the bonds.
6 Therefore a lion from the forest will attack
them,
a wolf from the desert will ravage them,
a leopard will lie in wait near their towns
to tear to pieces any who venture out,
for their rebellion is great
and their backslidings many.

7 "Why should I forgive you?
Your children have forsaken me
and sworn by gods that are not gods.

THE MESSAGE

Your primping goes for nothing.
You're not going to seduce anyone. They're
out to *kill* you!
And what's that I hear? The cry of a woman in
labor,
the screams of a mother giving birth to her
firstborn.
It's the cry of Daughter Zion, gasping for
breath,
reaching out for help:
"Help, oh help me! I'm dying!
The killers are on me!"

SINS ARE PILED SKY-HIGH

5.1-2 5 "Patrol Jerusalem's streets.
Look around. Take note.
Search the market squares.
See if you can find one man, one woman,
A single soul who does what is right
and tries to live a true life.
I want to forgive that person."
GOD's Decree.
"But if all they do is say, 'As sure as GOD
lives . . .'
they're nothing but a bunch of liars."

5.3-6 But you, GOD,
you have an eye for truth, don't you?
You hit them hard, but it didn't faze them.
You disciplined them, but they refused
correction.
Hardheaded, harder than rock,
they wouldn't change.
Then I said to myself, "Well, these are just
poor people.
They don't know any better.
They were never taught anything about GOD.
They never went to prayer meetings.
I'll find some people from the best families.
I'll talk to them.
They'll know what's going on, the way GOD
works.
They'll know the score."
But they were no better! Rebels all!
Off doing their own thing.
The invaders are ready to pounce and kill,
like a mountain lion, a wilderness wolf,
Panthers on the prowl.
The streets aren't safe anymore.
And why? Because the people's sins are piled
sky-high;
their betrayals are past counting.

5.7-9 "Why should I even bother with you any
longer?
Your children wander off, leaving me,
Taking up with gods
that aren't even gods.

NEW INTERNATIONAL VERSION

I supplied all their needs,
yet they committed adultery
and thronged to the houses of prostitutes.
8 They are well-fed, lusty stallions,
each neighing for another man's wife.
9 Should I not punish them for this?"
declares the LORD.
"Should I not avenge myself
on such a nation as this?

10 "Go through her vineyards and ravage them,
but do not destroy them completely.
Strip off her branches,
for these people do not belong to the
LORD.
11 The house of Israel and the house of Judah
have been utterly unfaithful to me,"
declares the LORD.

12 They have lied about the LORD;
they said, "He will do nothing!
No harm will come to us;
we will never see sword or famine.
13 The prophets are but wind
and the word is not in them;
so let what they say be done to them."

14 Therefore this is what the LORD God Almighty says:

"Because the people have spoken these
words,
I will make my words in your mouth a fire
and these people the wood it consumes.
15 O house of Israel," declares the LORD,
"I am bringing a distant nation against
you—
an ancient and enduring nation,
a people whose language you do not
know,
whose speech you do not understand.
16 Their quivers are like an open grave;
all of them are mighty warriors.
17 They will devour your harvests and food,
devour your sons and daughters;
they will devour your flocks and herds,
devour your vines and fig trees.
With the sword they will destroy
the fortified cities in which you trust.

18 "Yet even in those days," declares the LORD,
"I will not destroy you completely. 19 And when

THE MESSAGE

I satisfied their deepest needs, and then they
went off with the 'sacred' whores,
left me for orgies in sex shrines!
A bunch of well-groomed, lusty stallions,
each one pawing and snorting for his
neighbor's wife.
Do you think I'm going to stand around and
do nothing?"
GOD's Decree.
"Don't you think I'll take serious measures
against a people like this?

EYES THAT DON'T REALLY LOOK, EARS THAT
DON'T REALLY LISTEN

5.10-11 "Go down the rows of vineyards and rip out
the vines,
but not all of them. Leave a few.
Prune back those vines!
That growth didn't come from GOD!
They've betrayed me over and over again,
Judah and Israel both."
GOD's Decree.

5.12-13 "They've spread lies about GOD.
They've said, 'There's nothing to him.
Nothing bad will happen to us,
neither famine nor war will come our way.
The prophets are all windbags.
They speak nothing but nonsense.' "

5.14 Therefore, this is what GOD said to me, GOD-
of-the-Angel-Armies:

"Because they have talked this way,
they are going to eat those words.
Watch now! I'm putting my words
as fire in your mouth.
And the people are a pile of kindling
ready to go up in flames.

5.15-17 "Attention! I'm bringing a far-off nation
against you, O house of Israel."
GOD's Decree.
"A solid nation,
an ancient nation,
A nation that speaks another language.
You won't understand a word they say.
When they aim their arrows, you're as good as
dead.
They're a nation of real fighters!
They'll clean you out of house and home,
rob you of crops and children alike.
They'll feast on your sheep and cattle,
strip your vines and fig trees.
And the fortresses that made you feel so
safe—
leveled with a stroke of the sword!

5.18-19 "Even then, as bad as it will be"—GOD's Decree!—"it will not be the end of the world for

NEW INTERNATIONAL VERSION

the people ask, 'Why has the LORD our God done all this to us?' you will tell them, 'As you have forsaken me and served foreign gods in your own land, so now you will serve foreigners in a land not your own.'

20 "Announce this to the house of Jacob
    and proclaim it in Judah:
21 Hear this, you foolish and senseless people,
    who have eyes but do not see,
    who have ears but do not hear:
22 Should you not fear me?" declares the LORD.
    "Should you not tremble in my presence?
  I made the sand a boundary for the sea,
    an everlasting barrier it cannot cross.
  The waves may roll, but they cannot prevail;
    they may roar, but they cannot cross it.
23 But these people have stubborn and
        rebellious hearts;
    they have turned aside and gone away.
24 They do not say to themselves,
    'Let us fear the LORD our God,
  who gives autumn and spring rains in
        season,
    who assures us of the regular weeks of
        harvest.'
25 Your wrongdoings have kept these away;
    your sins have deprived you of good.

26 "Among my people are wicked men
    who lie in wait like men who snare birds
    and like those who set traps to catch men.
27 Like cages full of birds,
    their houses are full of deceit;
  they have become rich and powerful
28   and have grown fat and sleek.
  Their evil deeds have no limit;
    they do not plead the case of the
        fatherless to win it,
    they do not defend the rights of the poor.
29 Should I not punish them for this?"
    declares the LORD.
  "Should I not avenge myself
    on such a nation as this?

THE MESSAGE

you. And when people ask, 'Why did our GOD do all this to us?' you must say to them, 'It's tit for tat. Just as you left me and served foreign gods in your own country, so now you must serve foreigners in their own country.'

5.20-25 "Tell the house of Jacob this,
    put out this bulletin in Judah:
  Listen to this,
    you scatterbrains, airheads,
  With eyes that see but don't really look,
    and ears that hear but don't really listen.
  Why don't you honor me?
    Why aren't you in awe before me?
  Yes, *me*, who made the shorelines
    to contain the ocean waters.
  I drew a line in the sand
    that cannot be crossed.
  Waves roll in but cannot get through;
    breakers crash but that's the end of them.
  But this people—what a people!
    Uncontrollable, untameable runaways.
  It never occurs to them to say,
    'How can we honor our GOD with our lives,
  The God who gives rain in both spring and
        autumn
    and maintains the rhythm of the seasons,
  Who sets aside time each year for harvest
    and keeps everything running smoothly
        for us?'
  Of course you don't! Your bad behavior blinds
        you to all this.
    Your sins keep my blessings at a distance.

TO STAND FOR NOTHING AND STAND UP
FOR NO ONE

5.26-29 "My people are infiltrated by wicked men,
    unscrupulous men on the hunt.
  They set traps for the unsuspecting.
    Their victims are innocent men and
        women.
  Their houses are stuffed with ill-gotten gain,
    like a hunter's bag full of birds.
  Pretentious and powerful and rich,
    hugely obese, oily with rolls of fat.
  Worse, they have no conscience.
    Right and wrong mean nothing to them.
  They stand for nothing, stand up for no one,
    throw orphans to the wolves, exploit the
        poor.
  Do you think I'll stand by and do nothing
        about this?"
    GOD's Decree.
  "Don't you think I'll take serious measures
    against a people like this?

☩

NEW INTERNATIONAL VERSION

30 "A horrible and shocking thing
   has happened in the land:
31 The prophets prophesy lies,
   the priests rule by their own authority,
and my people love it this way.
   But what will you do in the end?

Jerusalem Under Siege

6 "Flee for safety, people of Benjamin!
   Flee from Jerusalem!
Sound the trumpet in Tekoa!
   Raise the signal over Beth Hakkerem!
For disaster looms out of the north,
   even terrible destruction.
2 I will destroy the Daughter of Zion,
   so beautiful and delicate.
3 Shepherds with their flocks will come
         against her;
   they will pitch their tents around her,
   each tending his own portion."

4 "Prepare for battle against her!
   Arise, let us attack at noon!
But, alas, the daylight is fading,
   and the shadows of evening grow long.
5 So arise, let us attack at night
   and destroy her fortresses!"

6 This is what the LORD Almighty says:

"Cut down the trees
   and build siege ramps against Jerusalem.
This city must be punished;
   it is filled with oppression.
7 As a well pours out its water,
   so she pours out her wickedness.
Violence and destruction resound in her;
   her sickness and wounds are ever
         before me.
8 Take warning, O Jerusalem,
   or I will turn away from you
and make your land desolate
   so no one can live in it."

9 This is what the LORD Almighty says:

"Let them glean the remnant of Israel
   as thoroughly as a vine;
pass your hand over the branches again,
   like one gathering grapes."

10 To whom can I speak and give warning?
   Who will listen to me?

THE MESSAGE

5.30-31 "Unspeakable! Sickening!
   What's happened in this country?
Prophets preach lies
   and priests hire on as their assistants.
And my people love it. They eat it up!
   But what will you do when it's time to pick
         up the pieces?

A City Full of Lies

6.1-5 6 "Run for your lives, children of Benjamin!
   Get out of Jerusalem, and now!
Give a blast on the ram's horn in Blastville.
   Send up smoke signals from Smoketown.
Doom pours out of the north—
   massive terror!
I have likened my dear daughter Zion
   to a lovely meadow.
Well, now 'shepherds' from the north have
         discovered her
   and brought in their flocks of soldiers.
They've pitched camp all around her,
   and plan where they'll 'graze.'
And then, 'Prepare to attack! The fight is on!
   To arms! We'll strike at noon!
Oh, it's too late? Day is dying?
   Evening shadows are upon us?
Well, up anyway! We'll attack by night
   and tear apart her defenses stone by
         stone.' "

6.6-8   GOD-of-the-Angel-Armies gave the orders:

"Chop down her trees.
   Build a siege ramp against Jerusalem,
A city full of brutality,
   bursting with violence.
Just as a well holds a good supply of water,
   she supplies wickedness nonstop.
The streets echo the cries: 'Violence! Rape!'
   Victims, bleeding and moaning, lie all over
         the place.
You're in deep trouble, Jerusalem.
   You've pushed me to the limit.
You're on the brink of being wiped out,
   being turned into a ghost town."

6.9   More orders from GOD-of-the-Angel-
         Armies:

"Time's up! Harvest the grapes for judgment.
   Salvage what's left of Israel.
Go back over the vines.
   Pick them clean, every last grape.

Is Anybody Listening?

6.10-11 "I've got something to say. Is anybody
         listening?
   I've a warning to post. Will anyone notice?

NEW INTERNATIONAL VERSION

Their ears are closed[a]
    so they cannot hear.
The word of the LORD is offensive to them;
    they find no pleasure in it.
11 But I am full of the wrath of the LORD,
    and I cannot hold it in.

"Pour it out on the children in the street
    and on the young men gathered together;
both husband and wife will be caught in it,
    and the old, those weighed down with
        years.
12 Their houses will be turned over to others,
    together with their fields and their wives,
when I stretch out my hand
    against those who live in the land,"
                    declares the LORD.
13 "From the least to the greatest,
    all are greedy for gain;
prophets and priests alike,
    all practice deceit.
14 They dress the wound of my people
    as though it were not serious.
'Peace, peace,' they say,
    when there is no peace.
15 Are they ashamed of their loathsome
        conduct?
    No, they have no shame at all;
    they do not even know how to blush.
So they will fall among the fallen;
    they will be brought down when I punish
        them,"
                    says the LORD.

16 This is what the LORD says:

"Stand at the crossroads and look;
    ask for the ancient paths,
ask where the good way is, and walk in it,
    and you will find rest for your souls.
    But you said, 'We will not walk in it.'
17 I appointed watchmen over you and said,
    'Listen to the sound of the trumpet!'
    But you said, 'We will not listen.'
18 Therefore hear, O nations;
    observe, O witnesses,
    what will happen to them.
19 Hear, O earth:
I am bringing disaster on this people,
    the fruit of their schemes,
because they have not listened to my words
    and have rejected my law.

---

a 10 Hebrew *uncircumcised*

THE MESSAGE

It's hopeless! Their ears are stuffed with
    wax—
    deaf as a post, blind as a bat.
It's hopeless! They've tuned out GOD.
    They don't want to hear from me.
But I'm bursting with the wrath of GOD.
    I can't hold it in much longer.

6.11-12 "So dump it on the children in the streets.
    Let it loose on the gangs of youth.
For no one's exempt: Husbands and wives will
        be taken,
    the old and those ready to die;
Their homes will be given away—
    all they own, even their loved ones—
When I give the signal
    against all who live in this country."
        GOD's Decree.

6.13-15 "Everyone's after the dishonest dollar,
    little people and big people alike.
Prophets and priests and everyone in between
    twist words and doctor truth.
My people are broken—shattered!—
    and they put on band-aids,
Saying, 'It's not so bad. You'll be just fine.'
    But things are not 'just fine'!
Do you suppose they are embarrassed
    over this outrage?
No, they have no shame.
    They don't even know how to blush.
There's no hope for them. They've hit bottom
    and there's no getting up.
As far as I'm concerned,
    they're finished."
        GOD has spoken.

DEATH IS ON THE PROWL

6.16-20 GOD's Message yet again:

"Go stand at the crossroads and look around.
    Ask for directions to the old road,
The tried and true road. Then take it.
    Discover the right route for your souls.
But they said, 'Nothing doing.
    We aren't going that way.'
I even provided watchmen for them
    to warn them, to set off the alarm.
But the people said, 'It's a false alarm.
    It doesn't concern us.'
And so I'm calling in the nations as witnesses:
    'Watch, witnesses, what happens to them!'
And, 'Pay attention, earth!
    Don't miss these bulletins.'
I'm visiting catastrophe on this people, the
        end result
    of the games they've been playing with me.
They've ignored everything I've said,
    had nothing but contempt for my teaching.

NEW INTERNATIONAL VERSION

²⁰What do I care about incense from Sheba
    or sweet calamus from a distant land?
Your burnt offerings are not acceptable;
    your sacrifices do not please me."

²¹Therefore this is what the LORD says:

"I will put obstacles before this people.
    Fathers and sons alike will stumble over
        them;
    neighbors and friends will perish."

²²This is what the LORD says:

"Look, an army is coming
    from the land of the north;
a great nation is being stirred up
    from the ends of the earth.
²³They are armed with bow and spear;
    they are cruel and show no mercy.
They sound like the roaring sea
    as they ride on their horses;
they come like men in battle formation
    to attack you, O Daughter of Zion."

²⁴We have heard reports about them,
    and our hands hang limp.
Anguish has gripped us,
    pain like that of a woman in labor.
²⁵Do not go out to the fields
    or walk on the roads,
for the enemy has a sword,
    and there is terror on every side.
²⁶O my people, put on sackcloth
    and roll in ashes;
mourn with bitter wailing
    as for an only son,
for suddenly the destroyer
    will come upon us.

²⁷"I have made you a tester of metals
    and my people the ore,
that you may observe
    and test their ways.
²⁸They are all hardened rebels,
    going about to slander.
They are bronze and iron;
    they all act corruptly.
²⁹The bellows blow fiercely
    to burn away the lead with fire,
but the refining goes on in vain;
    the wicked are not purged out.
³⁰They are called rejected silver,
    because the LORD has rejected them."

THE MESSAGE

What would I want with incense brought in
        from Sheba,
    rare spices from exotic places?
Your burnt sacrifices in worship give me no
        pleasure.
    Your religious rituals mean nothing to me."

6.21   So listen to this. Here's GOD's verdict on your
way of life:

"Watch out! I'm putting roadblocks and
        barriers
    on the road you're taking.
They'll send you sprawling,
    parents and children, neighbors and
        friends—
    and that will be the end of the lot of you."

6.22-23   And listen to this verdict from GOD:

"Look out! An invasion from the north,
    a mighty power on the move from a
        faraway place:
Armed to the teeth,
    vicious and pitiless,
Booming like sea storm and thunder—tramp,
        tramp, tramp—
    riding hard on war horses,
In battle formation
    against you, dear Daughter Zion!"

6.24-25   We've heard the news,
    and we're as limp as wet dishrags.
We're paralyzed with fear.
    Terror has a death grip on our throats.
Don't dare go outdoors!
    Don't leave the house!
Death is on the prowl.
    Danger everywhere!

6.26   "Dear Daughter Zion: Dress in black.
    Blacken your face with ashes.
Weep most bitterly,
    as for an only child.
The countdown has begun . . .
    six, five, four, three . . .
    The Terror is on us!"

✠

6.27-30   GOD gave me this task:

"I have made you the examiner of my people,
    to examine and weigh their lives.
They're a thickheaded, hard-nosed bunch,
    rotten to the core, the lot of them.
Refining fires are cranked up to white heat,
    but the ore stays a lump, unchanged.
It's useless to keep trying any longer.
    Nothing can refine evil out of them.
Men will give up and call them 'slag,'
    thrown on the slag heap by me, their GOD."

NEW INTERNATIONAL VERSION

FALSE RELIGION WORTHLESS

7 This is the word that came to Jeremiah from the LORD: ²"Stand at the gate of the LORD's house and there proclaim this message:

" 'Hear the word of the LORD, all you people of Judah who come through these gates to worship the LORD. ³This is what the LORD Almighty, the God of Israel, says: Reform your ways and your actions, and I will let you live in this place. ⁴Do not trust in deceptive words and say, "This is the temple of the LORD, the temple of the LORD, the temple of the LORD!" ⁵If you really change your ways and your actions and deal with each other justly, ⁶if you do not oppress the alien, the fatherless or the widow and do not shed innocent blood in this place, and if you do not follow other gods to your own harm, ⁷then I will let you live in this place, in the land I gave your forefathers for ever and ever. ⁸But look, you are trusting in deceptive words that are worthless.

⁹" 'Will you steal and murder, commit adultery and perjury,*a* burn incense to Baal and follow other gods you have not known, ¹⁰and then come and stand before me in this house, which bears my Name, and say, "We are safe"—safe to do all these detestable things? ¹¹Has this house, which bears my Name, become a den of robbers to you? But I have been watching! declares the LORD.

¹²" 'Go now to the place in Shiloh where I first made a dwelling for my Name, and see what I did to it because of the wickedness of my people Israel. ¹³While you were doing all these things, declares the LORD, I spoke to you again and again, but you did not listen; I called you, but you did not answer. ¹⁴Therefore, what I did to Shiloh I will now do to the house that bears my Name, the temple you trust in, the place I gave to you and your fathers. ¹⁵I will thrust you from my presence, just as I did all your brothers, the people of Ephraim.'

a 9 Or and swear by false gods

THE MESSAGE

THE NATION THAT WOULDN'T OBEY GOD

7 The Message from GOD to Jeremiah: "Stand in the gate of GOD's Temple and preach this Message.

7.1-2

7.2-3 "Say, 'Listen, all you people of Judah who come through these gates to worship GOD. GOD-of-the-Angel-Armies, Israel's God, has this to say to you:

7.3-7 " 'Clean up your act—the way you live, the things you do—so I can make my home with you in this place. Don't for a minute believe the lies being spoken here—"This is GOD's Temple, GOD's Temple, GOD's Temple!" Total nonsense! Only if you clean up your act (the way you live, the things you do), only if you do a total spring cleaning on the way you live and treat your neighbors, only if you quit exploiting the street people and orphans and widows, no longer taking advantage of innocent people on this very site and no longer destroying your souls by using this Temple as a front for other gods—only *then* will I move into your neighborhood. Only then will this country I gave your ancestors be my permanent home, my Temple.

7.8-11 " 'Get smart! Your leaders are handing you a pack of lies, and you're swallowing them! Use your heads! Do you think you can rob and murder, have sex with the neighborhood wives, tell lies nonstop, worship the local gods, and buy every novel religious commodity on the market—and then march into this Temple, set apart for my worship, and say, "We're safe!" thinking that the place itself gives you a license to go on with all this outrageous sacrilege? A cave full of criminals! Do you think you can turn this Temple, set apart for my worship, into something like that? Well, think again. I've got eyes in my head. I can see what's going on.' " GOD's Decree!

7.12 " 'Take a trip down to the place that was once in Shiloh, where I met my people in the early days. Take a look at those ruins, what I did to it because of the evil ways of my people Israel.

7.13-15 " 'So now, because of the way you have lived and failed to listen, even though time and again I took you aside and talked seriously with you, and because you refused to change when I called you to repent, I'm going to do to this Temple, set aside for my worship, this place you think is going to keep you safe no matter what, this place I gave as a gift to your ancestors and you, the same as I did to Shiloh. And as for you, I'm going to get rid of you, the same as I got rid of those old relatives of yours around Shiloh, your fellow Israelites in that former kingdom to the north.'

NEW INTERNATIONAL VERSION

16"So do not pray for this people nor offer any plea or petition for them; do not plead with me, for I will not listen to you. 17Do you not see what they are doing in the towns of Judah and in the streets of Jerusalem? 18The children gather wood, the fathers light the fire, and the women knead the dough and make cakes of bread for the Queen of Heaven. They pour out drink offerings to other gods to provoke me to anger. 19But am I the one they are provoking? declares the LORD. Are they not rather harming themselves, to their own shame?

20" 'Therefore this is what the Sovereign LORD says: My anger and my wrath will be poured out on this place, on man and beast, on the trees of the field and on the fruit of the ground, and it will burn and not be quenched.

21" 'This is what the LORD Almighty, the God of Israel, says: Go ahead, add your burnt offerings to your other sacrifices and eat the meat yourselves! 22For when I brought your forefathers out of Egypt and spoke to them, I did not just give them commands about burnt offerings and sacrifices, 23but I gave them this command: Obey me, and I will be your God and you will be my people. Walk in all the ways I command you, that it may go well with you. 24But they did not listen or pay attention; instead, they followed the stubborn inclinations of their evil hearts. They went backward and not forward. 25From the time your forefathers left Egypt until now, day after day, again and again I sent you my servants the prophets. 26But they did not listen to me or pay attention. They were stiff-necked and did more evil than their forefathers.'

27"When you tell them all this, they will not listen to you; when you call to them, they will not answer. 28Therefore say to them, 'This is the nation that has not obeyed the LORD its God or responded to correction. Truth has perished; it has vanished from their lips. 29Cut off your hair and throw it away; take up a lament on the barren heights, for the LORD has rejected and abandoned this generation that is under his wrath.

THE VALLEY OF SLAUGHTER

30" 'The people of Judah have done evil in my eyes, declares the LORD. They have set up their

THE MESSAGE

7.16-18   "And you, Jeremiah, don't waste your time praying for this people. Don't offer to make petitions or intercessions. Don't bother me with them. I'm not listening. Can't you see what they're doing in all the villages of Judah and in the Jerusalem streets? Why, they've got the children gathering wood while the fathers build fires and the mothers make bread to be offered to 'the Queen of Heaven'! And as if that weren't bad enough, they go around pouring out libations to any other gods they come across, just to hurt me.

7.19   "But is it me they're hurting?" GOD's Decree! "Aren't they just hurting themselves? Exposing themselves shamefully? Making themselves ridiculous?

7.20   "Here's what the Master GOD has to say: 'My white-hot anger is about to descend on this country and everything in it—people and animals, trees in the field and vegetables in the garden—a raging wildfire that no one can put out.'

7.21-23   "The Message from GOD-of-the-Angel-Armies, Israel's God: 'Go ahead! Put your burnt offerings with all your other sacrificial offerings and make a good meal for yourselves. I sure don't want them! When I delivered your ancestors out of Egypt, I never said anything to them about wanting burnt offerings and sacrifices as such. But I did say this, commanded this: "Obey me. Do what I say and I will be your God and you will be my people. Live the way I tell you. Do what I command so that your lives will go well."

7.24-26   " 'But do you think they listened? Not a word of it. They did just what they wanted to do, indulged any and every evil whim and got worse day by day. From the time your ancestors left the land of Egypt until now, I've supplied a steady stream of my servants the prophets, but do you think the people listened? Not once. Stubborn as mules and worse than their ancestors!'

7.27-28   "Tell them all this, but don't expect them to listen. Call out to them, but don't expect an answer. Tell them, 'You are the nation that wouldn't obey GOD, that refused all discipline. Truth has disappeared. There's not a trace of it left in your mouths.

7.29   " 'So shave your heads.
       Go bald to the hills and lament,
    For GOD has rejected and left
       this generation that has made him so
          angry.'

7.30-31   "The people of Judah have lived evil lives while I've stood by and watched." GOD's Decree.

NEW INTERNATIONAL VERSION

detestable idols in the house that bears my Name and have defiled it. 31They have built the high places of Topheth in the Valley of Ben Hinnom to burn their sons and daughters in the fire—something I did not command, nor did it enter my mind. 32So beware, the days are coming, declares the LORD, when people will no longer call it Topheth or the Valley of Ben Hinnom, but the Valley of Slaughter, for they will bury the dead in Topheth until there is no more room. 33Then the carcasses of this people will become food for the birds of the air and the beasts of the earth, and there will be no one to frighten them away. 34I will bring an end to the sounds of joy and gladness and to the voices of bride and bridegroom in the towns of Judah and the streets of Jerusalem, for the land will become desolate.

8 " 'At that time, declares the LORD, the bones of the kings and officials of Judah, the bones of the priests and prophets, and the bones of the people of Jerusalem will be removed from their graves. 2They will be exposed to the sun and the moon and all the stars of the heavens, which they have loved and served and which they have followed and consulted and worshiped. They will not be gathered up or buried, but will be like refuse lying on the ground. 3Wherever I banish them, all the survivors of this evil nation will prefer death to life, declares the LORD Almighty.'

SIN AND PUNISHMENT

4"Say to them, 'This is what the LORD says:

" 'When men fall down, do they not get up?
    When a man turns away, does he not
        return?
5Why then have these people turned away?
    Why does Jerusalem always turn away?
They cling to deceit;
    they refuse to return.
6I have listened attentively,
    but they do not say what is right.
No one repents of his wickedness,
    saying, "What have I done?"
Each pursues his own course
    like a horse charging into battle.
7Even the stork in the sky
    knows her appointed seasons,
and the dove, the swift and the thrush

THE MESSAGE

"In deliberate insult to me, they've set up their obscene god-images in the very Temple that was built to honor me. They've constructed Topheth altars for burning babies in prominent places all through the valley of Ben-hinnom, altars for burning their sons and daughters alive in the fire—a shocking perversion of all that I am and all I command.

7.32-34   "But soon, very soon"—GOD's Decree!—"the names Topheth and Ben-hinnom will no longer be used. They'll call the place what it is: Murder Meadow. Corpses will be stacked up in Topheth because there's no room left to bury them! Corpses abandoned in the open air, fed on by crows and coyotes, who have the run of the place. And I'll empty both smiles and laughter from the villages of Judah and the streets of Jerusalem. No wedding songs, no holiday sounds. *Dead* silence.

✝

8.1-2   **8** "And when the time comes"—GOD's Decree!—"I'll see to it that they dig up the bones of the kings of Judah, the bones of the princes and priests and prophets, and yes, even the bones of the common people. They'll dig them up and spread them out like a congregation at worship before sun, moon, and stars, all those sky gods they've been so infatuated with all these years, following their 'lucky stars' in doglike devotion. The bones will be left scattered and exposed, to reenter the soil as fertilizer, like manure.

8.3   "Everyone left—all from this evil generation unlucky enough to still be alive in whatever godforsaken place I will have driven them to— will wish they were dead." Decree of GOD-of-the-Angel-Armies.

TO KNOW EVERYTHING BUT GOD'S WORD

8.4-7   "Tell them this, GOD's Message:

" 'Do people fall down and not get up?
    Or take the wrong road and then just keep
        going?
So why does this people go backward,
    and just keep on going—*backward!*
They stubbornly hold on to their illusions,
    refuse to change direction.
I listened carefully
    but heard not so much as a whisper.
No one expressed one word of regret.
    Not a single "I'm sorry" did I hear.
They just kept at it, blindly and stupidly
    banging their heads against a brick wall.
Cranes know when it's time
    to move south for winter.
And robins, warblers, and bluebirds

NEW INTERNATIONAL VERSION

observe the time of their migration.
But my people do not know
  the requirements of the LORD.

8 " 'How can you say, "We are wise,
  for we have the law of the LORD,"
when actually the lying pen of the scribes
  has handled it falsely?
9 The wise will be put to shame;
  they will be dismayed and trapped.
Since they have rejected the word of the
  LORD,
  what kind of wisdom do they have?
10 Therefore I will give their wives to other
    men
  and their fields to new owners.
From the least to the greatest,
  all are greedy for gain;
prophets and priests alike,
  all practice deceit.
11 They dress the wound of my people
  as though it were not serious.
"Peace, peace," they say,
  when there is no peace.
12 Are they ashamed of their loathsome
    conduct?
  No, they have no shame at all;
  they do not even know how to blush.
So they will fall among the fallen;
  they will be brought down when they are
    punished,
               says the LORD.

13 " 'I will take away their harvest,
            declares the LORD.
There will be no grapes on the vine.
There will be no figs on the tree,
  and their leaves will wither.
What I have given them
  will be taken from them. *a* ' "

14 "Why are we sitting here?
  Gather together!
Let us flee to the fortified cities
  and perish there!
For the LORD our God has doomed us to
    perish
  and given us poisoned water to drink,
  because we have sinned against him.
15 We hoped for peace
  but no good has come,
for a time of healing
  but there was only terror.

THE MESSAGE

know when it's time to come back again.
But my people? My people know nothing,
  not the first thing of GOD and his rule.

8.8-9 " 'How can you say, "We know the score.
  We're the proud owners of GOD's
    revelation"?
Look where it's gotten you—stuck in illusion.
  Your religion experts have taken you for a
    ride!
Your know-it-alls will be unmasked,
  caught and shown up for what they are.
Look at them! They know everything but
    GOD's Word.
  Do you call that "knowing"?

8.10-12 " 'So here's what will happen to the know-it-
    alls:
  I'll make them wifeless and homeless.
Everyone's after the dishonest dollar,
  little people and big people alike.
Prophets and priests and everyone in-between
  twist words and doctor truth.
My dear Daughter—my people—broken,
    shattered,
  and yet they put on band-aids,
Saying, "It's not so bad. You'll be just fine."
  But things are not "just fine"!
Do you suppose they are embarrassed
  over this outrage?
Not really. They have no shame.
  They don't even know how to blush.
There's no hope for them. They've hit bottom
  and there's no getting up.
As far as I'm concerned,
  they're finished.' " GOD has spoken.

✠

8.13 " 'I went out to see if I could salvage
    anything' "
  —GOD's Decree—
" 'but found nothing:
Not a grape, not a fig,
  just a few withered leaves.
I'm taking back
  everything I gave them.' "

8.14-16 So why are we sitting here, doing nothing?
  Let's get organized.
Let's go to the big city
  and at least die fighting.
We've gotten GOD's ultimatum:
  We're damned if we do and damned if we
    don't—
  damned because of our sin against him.
We hoped things would turn out for the best,
  but it didn't happen that way.
We were waiting around for healing—
  and terror showed up!

---

a 13 The meaning of the Hebrew for this sentence is
uncertain.

NEW INTERNATIONAL VERSION

¹⁶ The snorting of the enemy's horses
  is heard from Dan;
at the neighing of their stallions
  the whole land trembles.
They have come to devour
  the land and everything in it,
  the city and all who live there."

¹⁷ "See, I will send venomous snakes among
    you,
  vipers that cannot be charmed,
  and they will bite you,"
                    declares the LORD.

¹⁸ O my Comforter^a in sorrow,
  my heart is faint within me.
¹⁹ Listen to the cry of my people
  from a land far away:
"Is the LORD not in Zion?
  Is her King no longer there?"

"Why have they provoked me to anger with
    their images,
  with their worthless foreign idols?"

²⁰ "The harvest is past,
  the summer has ended,
  and we are not saved."

²¹ Since my people are crushed, I am crushed;
  I mourn, and horror grips me.
²² Is there no balm in Gilead?
  Is there no physician there?
Why then is there no healing
  for the wound of my people?

9 ¹ Oh, that my head were a spring of water
    and my eyes a fountain of tears!
I would weep day and night
  for the slain of my people.
² Oh, that I had in the desert
  a lodging place for travelers,
so that I might leave my people
  and go away from them;
for they are all adulterers,
  a crowd of unfaithful people.

³ "They make ready their tongue
  like a bow, to shoot lies;
it is not by truth
  that they triumph^b in the land.
They go from one sin to another;
  they do not acknowledge me,"
                    declares the LORD.
⁴ "Beware of your friends;
  do not trust your brothers.

---

^a 18 The meaning of the Hebrew for this word is uncertain.
^b 3 Or *lies; / they are not valiant for truth*

THE MESSAGE

From Dan at the northern borders
  we hear the hooves of horses,
Horses galloping, horses neighing.
  The ground shudders and quakes.
They're going to swallow up the whole
    country.
  Towns and people alike—fodder for war.

^{8.17} " 'What's more, I'm dispatching
  poisonous snakes among you,
Snakes that can't be charmed,
  snakes that will bite you and kill you.' "
    GOD's Decree!

ADVANCING FROM ONE EVIL TO THE NEXT

^{8.18-22} I drown in grief.
  I'm heartsick.
Oh, listen! Please listen! It's the cry of my dear
    people
  reverberating through the country.
Is GOD no longer in Zion?
  Has the King gone away?
Can you tell me why they flaunt their
    plaything-gods,
  their silly, imported no-gods before me?
The crops are in, the summer is over,
  but for us nothing's changed.
  We're still waiting to be rescued.
For my dear broken people, I'm heartbroken.
  I weep, seized by grief.
Are there no healing ointments in Gilead?
  Isn't there a doctor in the house?
So why can't something be done
  to heal and save my dear, dear people?

          ✝

^{9.1-2} **9** I wish my head were a well of water
    and my eyes fountains of tears
So I could weep day and night
  for casualties among my dear, dear people.
At times I wish I had a wilderness hut,
  a backwoods cabin,
Where I could get away from my people
  and never see them again.
They're a faithless, feckless bunch,
  a congregation of degenerates.

          ✝

^{9.3-6} "Their tongues shoot out lies
  like a bow shoots arrows—
A mighty army of liars,
  the sworn enemies of truth.
They advance from one evil to the next,
  ignorant of me."
    GOD's Decree.
"Be wary of even longtime neighbors.
  Don't even trust your grandmother!

NEW INTERNATIONAL VERSION

For every brother is a deceiver,[a]
   and every friend a slanderer.
[5] Friend deceives friend,
   and no one speaks the truth.
They have taught their tongues to lie;
   they weary themselves with sinning.
[6] You[b] live in the midst of deception;
   in their deceit they refuse to
      acknowledge me,"
                    declares the LORD.

[7] Therefore this is what the LORD Almighty
says:

"See, I will refine and test them,
   for what else can I do
   because of the sin of my people?
[8] Their tongue is a deadly arrow;
   it speaks with deceit.
With his mouth each speaks cordially to his
      neighbor,
   but in his heart he sets a trap for him.
[9] Should I not punish them for this?"
   declares the LORD.
"Should I not avenge myself
   on such a nation as this?"

[10] I will weep and wail for the mountains
   and take up a lament concerning the
      desert pastures.
They are desolate and untraveled,
   and the lowing of cattle is not heard.
The birds of the air have fled
   and the animals are gone.

[11] "I will make Jerusalem a heap of ruins,
   a haunt of jackals;
and I will lay waste the towns of Judah
   so no one can live there."

[12] What man is wise enough to understand
this? Who has been instructed by the LORD and
can explain it? Why has the land been ruined
and laid waste like a desert that no one can
cross?

[13] The LORD said, "It is because they have forsaken my law, which I set before them; they have
not obeyed me or followed my law. [14] Instead,
they have followed the stubbornness of their
hearts; they have followed the Baals, as their fa-

*a 4 Or a deceiving Jacob   b 6 That is, Jeremiah (the
Hebrew is singular)*

THE MESSAGE

Brother schemes against brother,
   like old cheating Jacob.
Friend against friend
   spreads malicious gossip.
Neighbors gyp neighbors,
   never telling the truth.
They've trained their tongues to tell lies,
   and now they can't tell the truth.
They pile wrong upon wrong, stack lie upon
      lie,
   and refuse to know me."
      GOD'S Decree.

9.7-9   Therefore, GOD-of-the-Angel-Armies says:

"Watch this! I'll melt them down
   and see what they're made of.
What else can I do
   with a people this wicked?
Their tongues are poison arrows!
   Deadly lies stream from their mouths.
Neighbor greets neighbor with a smile,
   'Good morning! How're things?'
   while scheming to do away with him.
Do you think I'm going to stand around and
      do nothing?"
      GOD'S Decree.
"Don't you think I'll take serious measures
   against a people like this?

9.10-11   "I'm lamenting the loss of the mountain
      pastures.
   I'm chanting dirges for the old grazing
      grounds.
They've become deserted wastelands too
      dangerous for travelers.
   No sounds of sheep bleating or cattle
      mooing.
Birds and wild animals, all gone.
   Nothing stirring, no sounds of life.
I'm going to make Jerusalem a pile of rubble,
   fit for nothing but stray cats and dogs.
I'm going to reduce Judah's towns to piles of
      ruins
   where no one lives!"

✝

9.12   I asked, "Is there anyone around bright enough
to tell us what's going on here? Anyone who
has the inside story from GOD and can let us in
on it?
   "Why is the country wasted?
   "Why no travelers in this desert?"

9.13-15   GOD'S answer: "Because they abandoned my
plain teaching. They wouldn't listen to anything
I said, refused to live the way I told them to. Instead they lived any way they wanted and took
up with the Baal gods, who they thought would
give them what they wanted—following the ex-

NEW INTERNATIONAL VERSION

thers taught them." ¹⁵Therefore, this is what the Lord Almighty, the God of Israel, says: "See, I will make this people eat bitter food and drink poisoned water. ¹⁶I will scatter them among nations that neither they nor their fathers have known, and I will pursue them with the sword until I have destroyed them."

¹⁷This is what the Lord Almighty says:

"Consider now! Call for the wailing women
        to come;
    send for the most skillful of them.
¹⁸Let them come quickly
    and wail over us
till our eyes overflow with tears
    and water streams from our eyelids.
¹⁹The sound of wailing is heard from Zion:
    'How ruined we are!
    How great is our shame!
We must leave our land
    because our houses are in ruins.' "

²⁰Now, O women, hear the word of the Lord;
    open your ears to the words of his mouth.
Teach your daughters how to wail;
    teach one another a lament.
²¹Death has climbed in through our windows
    and has entered our fortresses;
it has cut off the children from the streets
    and the young men from the public
        squares.

²²Say, "This is what the Lord declares:

" 'The dead bodies of men will lie
    like refuse on the open field,
like cut grain behind the reaper,
    with no one to gather them.' "

²³This is what the Lord says:

"Let not the wise man boast of his wisdom
    or the strong man boast of his strength
    or the rich man boast of his riches,
²⁴but let him who boasts boast about this:
    that he understands and knows me,
that I am the Lord, who exercises kindness,
    justice and righteousness on earth,
    for in these I delight,"
                        declares the Lord.

THE MESSAGE

ample of their parents." And this is the consequence. God-of-the-Angel-Armies says so:

    "I'll feed them with pig slop.
    "I'll give them poison to drink.
9.16   "Then I'll scatter them far and wide among
godless peoples that neither they nor their parents have ever heard of, and I'll send Death in pursuit until there's nothing left of them."

A Life That Is All Outside but No Inside
9.17-19 A Message from God-of-the-Angel-Armies:

"Look over the trouble we're in and call for
        help.
    Send for some singers who can help us
        mourn our loss.
Tell them to hurry—
    to help us express our loss and lament,
Help us get our tears flowing,
    make tearful music of our crying.
Listen to it!
    Listen to that torrent of tears out of Zion:
'We're a ruined people,
    we're a shamed people!
We've been driven from our homes
    and must leave our land!' "

                    ✜

9.20-21 Mourning women! Oh, listen to God's Message!
    Open your ears. Take in what he says.
Teach your daughters songs for the dead
    and your friends the songs of heartbreak.
Death has climbed in through the window,
    broken into our bedrooms.
Children on the playgrounds drop dead,
    and young men and women collapse at
        their games.

9.22   Speak up! "God's Message:

" 'Dead bodies everywhere, scattered at random
    like sheep and goat dung in the fields,
Like wheat cut down by reapers
    and left to rot where it falls.' "

9.23-24   God's Message:

"Don't let the wise brag of their wisdom.
    Don't let heroes brag of their exploits.
Don't let the rich brag of their riches.
    If you brag, brag of this and this only:
That you understand and know me.
    I'm God, and I act in loyal love.
I do what's right and set things right and fair,
    and delight in those who do the same
        things.
These are my trademarks."
    God's Decree.

                    ✜

NEW INTERNATIONAL VERSION

²⁵"The days are coming," declares the LORD, "when I will punish all who are circumcised only in the flesh— ²⁶Egypt, Judah, Edom, Ammon, Moab and all who live in the desert in distant places. ^a For all these nations are really uncircumcised, and even the whole house of Israel is uncircumcised in heart."

GOD AND IDOLS

10 Hear what the LORD says to you, O house of Israel. ²This is what the LORD says:

"Do not learn the ways of the nations
  or be terrified by signs in the sky,
  though the nations are terrified by them.
³For the customs of the peoples are
    worthless;
  they cut a tree out of the forest,
  and a craftsman shapes it with his chisel.
⁴They adorn it with silver and gold;
  they fasten it with hammer and nails
  so it will not totter.
⁵Like a scarecrow in a melon patch,
  their idols cannot speak;
they must be carried
  because they cannot walk.
Do not fear them;
  they can do no harm
  nor can they do any good."

⁶No one is like you, O LORD;
  you are great,
  and your name is mighty in power.
⁷Who should not revere you,
  O King of the nations?
  This is your due.
Among all the wise men of the nations
  and in all their kingdoms,
  there is no one like you.
⁸They are all senseless and foolish;
  they are taught by worthless wooden
    idols.
⁹Hammered silver is brought from Tarshish
  and gold from Uphaz.
What the craftsman and goldsmith have
    made
  is then dressed in blue and purple—
  all made by skilled workers.
¹⁰But the LORD is the true God;
  he is the living God, the eternal King.
When he is angry, the earth trembles;
  the nations cannot endure his wrath.

¹¹"Tell them this: 'These gods, who did not make the heavens and the earth, will perish from the earth and from under the heavens.' " ^b

THE MESSAGE

^{9.25-26} "Stay alert! It won't be long now"—GOD's Decree!—"when I will personally deal with everyone whose life is all outside but no inside: Egypt, Judah, Edom, Ammon, Moab. All these nations are big on performance religion—including Israel, who is no better."

THE STICK GODS

10 Listen to the Message that GOD is sending your way, House of Israel. Listen most carefully:

"Don't take the godless nations as your
    models.
  Don't be impressed by their glamour and
    glitz,
  no matter how much they're impressed.
The religion of these peoples
  is nothing but smoke.
An idol is nothing but a tree chopped down,
  then shaped by a woodsman's ax.
They trim it with tinsel and balls,
  use hammer and nails to keep it upright.
It's like a scarecrow in a cabbage patch—can't
    talk!
  Dead wood that has to be carried—can't
    walk!
Don't be impressed by such stuff.
  It's useless for either good or evil."

^{10.6-9} All this is nothing compared to you, O GOD.
  You're wondrously great, famously great.
Who can fail to be impressed by you, King of
    the nations?
  It's your very nature to be worshiped!
Look far and wide among the elite of the
    nations.
  The best they can come up with is nothing
    compared to you.
Stupidly, they line them up—a lineup of
    sticks,
  good for nothing but making smoke.
Gilded with silver foil from Tarshish,
  covered with gold from Uphaz,
Hung with violet and purple fabrics—
  no matter how fancy the sticks, they're still
    sticks.

^{10.10} But GOD is the real thing—
  the living God, the eternal King.
When he's angry, Earth shakes.
  Yes, and the godless nations quake.

^{10.11-15} "Tell them this: 'The stick gods
  who made nothing, neither sky nor earth,
Will come to nothing
  on the earth and under the sky.' "

---

^a 26 Or *desert and who clip the hair by their foreheads*
^b 11 The text of this verse is in Aramaic.

NEW INTERNATIONAL VERSION

¹²But God made the earth by his power;
  he founded the world by his wisdom
  and stretched out the heavens by his
    understanding.
¹³When he thunders, the waters in the
    heavens roar;
  he makes clouds rise from the ends of the
    earth.
  He sends lightning with the rain
    and brings out the wind from his
    storehouses.

¹⁴Everyone is senseless and without
    knowledge;
  every goldsmith is shamed by his idols.
  His images are a fraud;
    they have no breath in them.
¹⁵They are worthless, the objects of mockery;
    when their judgment comes, they will
    perish.
¹⁶He who is the Portion of Jacob is not like
    these,
  for he is the Maker of all things,
  including Israel, the tribe of his
    inheritance—
  the LORD Almighty is his name.

COMING DESTRUCTION

¹⁷Gather up your belongings to leave the land,
  you who live under siege.
¹⁸For this is what the LORD says:
  "At this time I will hurl out
    those who live in this land;
  I will bring distress on them
    so that they may be captured."

¹⁹Woe to me because of my injury!
  My wound is incurable!
  Yet I said to myself,
  "This is my sickness, and I must
    endure it."
²⁰My tent is destroyed;
  all its ropes are snapped.
  My sons are gone from me and are no more;
  no one is left now to pitch my tent
    or to set up my shelter.
²¹The shepherds are senseless
  and do not inquire of the LORD;
  so they do not prosper
  and all their flock is scattered.
²²Listen! The report is coming—
  a great commotion from the land of the
    north!
  It will make the towns of Judah desolate,
    a haunt of jackals.

THE MESSAGE

But it is God whose power made the earth,
  whose wisdom gave shape to the world,
  who crafted the cosmos.
He thunders, and rain pours down.
  He sends the clouds soaring.
He embellishes the storm with lightnings,
  launches wind from his warehouse.
Stick-god worshipers looking mighty foolish,
  god-makers embarrassed by their
    handmade gods!
Their gods are frauds—dead sticks,
  deadwood gods, tasteless jokes.
  When the fires of judgment come, they'll be
    ashes.

¹⁰·¹⁶ But the Portion-of-Jacob is the real thing.
  He put the whole universe together
And pays special attention to Israel.
  His name? GOD-of-the-Angel-Armies!

✠

¹⁰·¹⁷⁻¹⁸ Grab your bags,
  all you who are under attack.
GOD has given notice:
  "Attention! I'm evicting
Everyone who lives here,
  And right now—yes, right now!
I'm going to press them to the limit,
  squeeze the life right out of them."

✠

¹⁰·¹⁹⁻²⁰ But it's a black day for me!
  Hopelessly wounded,
I said, "Why, oh why
  did I think I could bear it?"
My house is ruined—
  the roof caved in.
Our children are gone—
  we'll never see them again.
No one left to help in rebuilding,
  no one to make a new start!

¹⁰·²¹ It's because our leaders are stupid.
  They never asked GOD for counsel,
And so nothing worked right.
  The people are scattered all over.

¹⁰·²² But listen! Something's coming!
  A big commotion from the northern
    borders!
Judah's towns about to be smashed,
  left to all the stray dogs and cats!

NEW INTERNATIONAL VERSION

JEREMIAH'S PRAYER

²³ I know, O LORD, that a man's life is not his
own;
it is not for man to direct his steps.
²⁴ Correct me, LORD, but only with justice—
not in your anger,
lest you reduce me to nothing.
²⁵ Pour out your wrath on the nations
that do not acknowledge you,
on the peoples who do not call on your
name.
For they have devoured Jacob;
they have devoured him completely
and destroyed his homeland.

THE COVENANT IS BROKEN

11 This is the word that came to Jeremiah
from the LORD: ²"Listen to the terms of
this covenant and tell them to the people of Judah and to those who live in Jerusalem. ³Tell
them that this is what the LORD, the God of Israel, says: 'Cursed is the man who does not obey
the terms of this covenant— ⁴the terms I commanded your forefathers when I brought them
out of Egypt, out of the iron-smelting furnace.' I
said, 'Obey me and do everything I command
you, and you will be my people, and I will be
your God. ⁵Then I will fulfill the oath I swore to
your forefathers, to give them a land flowing
with milk and honey'—the land you possess today."

I answered, "Amen, LORD."

⁶The LORD said to me, "Proclaim all these
words in the towns of Judah and in the streets of
Jerusalem: 'Listen to the terms of this covenant
and follow them. ⁷From the time I brought your
forefathers up from Egypt until today, I warned
them again and again, saying, "Obey me." ⁸But
they did not listen or pay attention; instead, they
followed the stubbornness of their evil hearts.
So I brought on them all the curses of the covenant I had commanded them to follow but that
they did not keep.' "

⁹Then the LORD said to me, "There is a con-
spiracy among the people of Judah and those
who live in Jerusalem. ¹⁰They have returned to
the sins of their forefathers, who refused to listen
to my words. They have followed other gods to
serve them. Both the house of Israel and the

THE MESSAGE

^{10:23-25} I know, GOD, that mere mortals
can't run their own lives,
That men and women
don't have what it takes to take charge of
life.
So correct us, GOD, as you see best.
Don't lose your temper. That would be the
end of us.
Vent your anger on the godless nations,
who refuse to acknowledge you,
And on the people
who won't pray to you—
The very ones who've made hash out of Jacob,
yes, made hash
And devoured him whole,
people and pastures alike.

THE TERMS OF THIS COVENANT

^{11:1} **11** The Message that came to Jeremiah
from GOD:

^{11:2-4} "Preach to the people of Judah and citizens
of Jerusalem. Tell them this: 'This is GOD's Message, the Message of Israel's God to you. Anyone who does not keep the terms of this covenant is cursed. The terms are clear. I made
them plain to your ancestors when I delivered
them from Egypt, out of the iron furnace of
suffering.

^{11:4-5} "'Obey what I tell you. Do exactly what I
command you. Your obedience will close the
deal. You'll be mine and I'll be yours. This will
provide the conditions in which I will be able
to do what I promised your ancestors: to give
them a fertile and lush land. And, as you know,
that's what I did.' "

"Yes, GOD," I replied. "That's true."

^{11:6-8} GOD continued: "Preach all this in the towns
of Judah and the streets of Jerusalem. Say, 'Listen to the terms of this covenant and carry
them out! I warned your ancestors when I
delivered them from Egypt and I've kept up the
warnings. I haven't quit warning them for a
moment. I warned them from morning to
night: "Obey me or else!" But they didn't obey.
They paid no attention to me. They did whatever they wanted to do, whenever they wanted
to do it, until finally I stepped in and ordered
the punishments set out in the covenant,
which, despite all my warnings, they had ignored.' "

^{11:9-10} Then GOD said, "There's a conspiracy among
the people of Judah and the citizens of Jerusalem. They've plotted to reenact the sins of
their ancestors—the ones who disobeyed me
and decided to go after other gods and worship
them. Israel and Judah are in this together,

NEW INTERNATIONAL VERSION	THE MESSAGE

house of Judah have broken the covenant I made with their forefathers. [11]Therefore this is what the LORD says: 'I will bring on them a disaster they cannot escape. Although they cry out to me, I will not listen to them. [12]The towns of Judah and the people of Jerusalem will go and cry out to the gods to whom they burn incense, but they will not help them at all when disaster strikes. [13]You have as many gods as you have towns, O Judah; and the altars you have set up to burn incense to that shameful god Baal are as many as the streets of Jerusalem.'

[14]"Do not pray for this people nor offer any plea or petition for them, because I will not listen when they call to me in the time of their distress.

[15]"What is my beloved doing in my temple
    as she works out her evil schemes with
        many?
Can consecrated meat avert ⌊your
        punishment⌋?
When you engage in your wickedness,
    then you rejoice.*a*"

[16]The LORD called you a thriving olive tree
    with fruit beautiful in form.
But with the roar of a mighty storm
    he will set it on fire,
    and its branches will be broken.

[17]The LORD Almighty, who planted you, has decreed disaster for you, because the house of Israel and the house of Judah have done evil and provoked me to anger by burning incense to Baal.

PLOT AGAINST JEREMIAH
[18]Because the LORD revealed their plot to me, I knew it, for at that time he showed me what they were doing. [19]I had been like a gentle lamb led to the slaughter; I did not realize that they had plotted against me, saying,

"Let us destroy the tree and its fruit;
    let us cut him off from the land of the
        living,
    that his name be remembered no more."
[20]But, O LORD Almighty, you who judge
    righteously

---

mindlessly breaking the covenant I made with their ancestors."

11.11-13 "Well, your God has something to say about this: Watch out! I'm about to visit doom on you, and no one will get out of it. You're going to cry for help but I won't listen. Then all the people in Judah and Jerusalem will start praying to the gods you've been sacrificing to all these years, but it won't do a bit of good. You've got as many gods as you have villages, Judah! And you've got enough altars for sacrifices to that impotent sex god Baal to put one on every street corner in Jerusalem!"

11.14 "And as for you, Jeremiah, I don't want you praying for this people. Nothing! Not a word of petition. Indeed, I'm not going to listen to a single syllable of their crisis-prayers."

PROMISES AND PIOUS PROGRAMS
11.15-16 "What business do the ones I love have
        figuring out
    how to get off the hook? And right in the
        house of worship!
Do you think making promises and devising
        pious programs
    will save you from doom?
Do you think you can get out of this
    by becoming more religious?
A mighty oak tree, majestic and glorious—
    that's how I once described you.
But it will only take a clap of thunder and a
        bolt of lightning
    to leave you a shattered wreck.

11.17 "I, GOD-of-the-Angel-Armies, who planted you—yes, I have pronounced doom on you. Why? Because of the disastrous life you've lived, Israel and Judah alike, goading me to anger with your continuous worship and offerings to that sorry god Baal."

☩

11.18-19 GOD told me what was going on. That's how I
        knew.
    You, GOD, opened my eyes to their evil
        scheming.
I had no idea what was going on—naive as a
        lamb
    being led to slaughter!
I didn't know they had it in for me,
    didn't know of their behind-the-scenes plots:
"Let's get rid of the preacher.
    That will stop the sermons!
Let's get rid of him for good.
    He won't be remembered for long."

11.20 Then I said, "GOD-of-the-Angel-Armies,
    you're a fair judge.

---

a 15 Or Could consecrated meat avert your punishment? /
Then you would rejoice

NEW INTERNATIONAL VERSION

and test the heart and mind,
let me see your vengeance upon them,
for to you I have committed my cause.

21 "Therefore this is what the LORD says about the men of Anathoth who are seeking your life and saying, 'Do not prophesy in the name of the LORD or you will die by our hands'— 22 therefore this is what the LORD Almighty says: 'I will punish them. Their young men will die by the sword, their sons and daughters by famine. 23 Not even a remnant will be left to them, because I will bring disaster on the men of Anathoth in the year of their punishment.' "

JEREMIAH'S COMPLAINT

12 You are always righteous, O LORD,
when I bring a case before you.
Yet I would speak with you about your
justice:
Why does the way of the wicked prosper?
Why do all the faithless live at ease?
2 You have planted them, and they have taken
root;
they grow and bear fruit.
You are always on their lips
but far from their hearts.
3 Yet you know me, O LORD;
you see me and test my thoughts about
you.
Drag them off like sheep to be butchered!
Set them apart for the day of slaughter!
4 How long will the land lie parched [a]
and the grass in every field be withered?
Because those who live in it are wicked,
the animals and birds have perished.
Moreover, the people are saying,
"He will not see what happens to us."

GOD'S ANSWER

5 "If you have raced with men on foot
and they have worn you out,
how can you compete with horses?
If you stumble in safe country, [b]
how will you manage in the thickets by [c]
the Jordan?
6 Your brothers, your own family—
even they have betrayed you;
they have raised a loud cry against you.

THE MESSAGE

You examine and cross-examine
human actions and motives.
I want to see these people shown up and put
down!
I'm an open book before you. Clear my
name."

11.21-23 That sent a signal to GOD, who spoke up: "Here's what I'll do to the men of Anathoth who are trying to murder you, the men who say, 'Don't preach to us in GOD's name or we'll kill you.' Yes, it's GOD-of-the-Angel-Armies speaking. Indeed! I'll call them to account: Their young people will die in battle, their children will die of starvation, and there will be no one left at all, none. I'm visiting the men of Anathoth with doom. Doomsday!"

WHAT MAKES YOU THINK YOU CAN RACE
AGAINST HORSES?

12.1-4 **12** You are right, O GOD, and you set
things right.
I can't argue with that. But I do have some
questions:
Why do bad people have it so good?
Why do con artists make it big?
You planted them and they put down roots.
They flourished and produced fruit.
They talk as if they're old friends with you,
but they couldn't care less about you.
Meanwhile, you know *me* inside and out.
You don't let me get by with a thing!
Make them pay for the way they live,
pay with their lives, like sheep marked for
slaughter.
How long do we have to put up with this—
the country depressed, the farms in ruin—
And all because of wickedness, these wicked
lives?
Even animals and birds are dying off
Because they'll have nothing to do with God
and think God has nothing to do with
them.

✝

12.5-6 "So, Jeremiah, if you're worn out in this
footrace with men,
what makes you think you can race against
horses?
And if you can't keep your wits during times
of calm,
what's going to happen when troubles
break loose
like the Jordan in flood?
Those closest to you, your own brothers and
cousins,
are working against you.

---

[a] 4 Or *land mourn*   [b] 5 Or *If you put your trust in a land of safety*   [c] 5 Or *the flooding of*

NEW INTERNATIONAL VERSION

Do not trust them,
though they speak well of you.

7 "I will forsake my house,
abandon my inheritance;
I will give the one I love
into the hands of her enemies.
8 My inheritance has become to me
like a lion in the forest.
She roars at me;
therefore I hate her.
9 Has not my inheritance become to me
like a speckled bird of prey
that other birds of prey surround and
attack?
Go and gather all the wild beasts;
bring them to devour.
10 Many shepherds will ruin my vineyard
and trample down my field;
they will turn my pleasant field
into a desolate wasteland.
11 It will be made a wasteland,
parched and desolate before me;
the whole land will be laid waste
because there is no one who cares.
12 Over all the barren heights in the desert
destroyers will swarm,
for the sword of the LORD will devour
from one end of the land to the other;
no one will be safe.
13 They will sow wheat but reap thorns;
they will wear themselves out but gain
nothing.
So bear the shame of your harvest
because of the LORD's fierce anger."

14 This is what the LORD says: "As for all my wicked neighbors who seize the inheritance I gave my people Israel, I will uproot them from their lands and I will uproot the house of Judah from among them. 15 But after I uproot them, I will again have compassion and will bring each of them back to his own inheritance and his own country. 16 And if they learn well the ways of my people and swear by my name, saying, 'As surely as the LORD lives'—even as they once taught my people to swear by Baal—then they will be established among my people. 17 But if any nation does not listen, I will completely uproot and destroy it," declares the LORD.

THE MESSAGE

They're out to get you. They'll stop at nothing.
Don't trust them, especially when they're
smiling.

✝

12.7-11 "I will abandon the House of Israel,
walk away from my beloved people.
I will turn over those I most love
to those who are her enemies.
She's been, this one I held dear,
like a snarling lion in the jungle,
Growling and baring her teeth at me—
and I can't take it anymore.
Has this one I hold dear become a preening
peacock?
But isn't she under attack by vultures?
Then invite all the hungry animals at large,
invite them in for a free meal!
Foreign, scavenging shepherds
will loot and trample my fields,
Turn my beautiful, well-cared-for fields
into vacant lots of tin cans and thistles.
They leave them littered with junk—
a ruined land, a land in lament.
The whole countryside is a wasteland,
and no one will really care.

✝

12.12-13 "The barbarians will invade,
swarm over hills and plains.
The judgment sword of GOD will take its toll
from one end of the land to the other.
Nothing living will be safe.
They will plant wheat and reap weeds.
Nothing they do will work out.
They will look at their meager crops and
wring their hands.
All this the result of GOD's fierce anger!"

✝

12.14-17 GOD's Message: "Regarding all the bad neighbors who abused the land I gave to Israel as their inheritance: I'm going to pluck them out of their lands, and then pluck Judah out from among them. Once I've pulled the bad neighbors out, I will relent and take them tenderly to my heart and put them back where they belong, put each of them back in their home country, on their family farms. Then if they will get serious about living my way and pray to me as well as they taught my people to pray to that god Baal, everything will go well for them. But if they won't listen, then I'll pull them out of their land by the roots and cart them off to the dump. Total destruction!" GOD's Decree.

NEW INTERNATIONAL VERSION

A LINEN BELT

13 This is what the LORD said to me: "Go and buy a linen belt and put it around your waist, but do not let it touch water." ²So I bought a belt, as the LORD directed, and put it around my waist.

³Then the word of the LORD came to me a second time: ⁴"Take the belt you bought and are wearing around your waist, and go now to Perath[a] and hide it there in a crevice in the rocks." ⁵So I went and hid it at Perath, as the LORD told me.

⁶Many days later the LORD said to me, "Go now to Perath and get the belt I told you to hide there." ⁷So I went to Perath and dug up the belt and took it from the place where I had hidden it, but now it was ruined and completely useless.

⁸Then the word of the LORD came to me: ⁹"This is what the LORD says: 'In the same way I will ruin the pride of Judah and the great pride of Jerusalem. ¹⁰These wicked people, who refuse to listen to my words, who follow the stubbornness of their hearts and go after other gods to serve and worship them, will be like this belt—completely useless! ¹¹For as a belt is bound around a man's waist, so I bound the whole house of Israel and the whole house of Judah to me,' declares the LORD, 'to be my people for my renown and praise and honor. But they have not listened.'

WINESKINS

¹²"Say to them: 'This is what the LORD, the God of Israel, says: Every wineskin should be filled with wine.' And if they say to you, 'Don't we know that every wineskin should be filled with wine?' ¹³then tell them, 'This is what the LORD says: I am going to fill with drunkenness all who live in this land, including the kings who sit on David's throne, the priests, the prophets and all those living in Jerusalem. ¹⁴I will smash them one against the other, fathers and sons alike, declares the LORD. I will allow no pity or mercy or compassion to keep me from destroying them.' "

THREAT OF CAPTIVITY

¹⁵ Hear and pay attention,
  do not be arrogant,
  for the LORD has spoken.
¹⁶ Give glory to the LORD your God
  before he brings the darkness,
 before your feet stumble
  on the darkening hills.

THE MESSAGE

PEOPLE WHO DO ONLY WHAT THEY WANT TO DO

13.1-2 **13** GOD told me, "Go and buy yourself some linen shorts. Put them on and keep them on. Don't even take them off to wash them." So I bought the shorts as GOD directed and put them on.

13.3-5 Then GOD told me, "Take the shorts that you bought and go straight to Perath and hide them there in a crack in the rock." So I did what GOD told me and hid them at Perath.

13.6-7 Next, after quite a long time, GOD told me, "Go back to Perath and get the linen shorts I told you to hide there." So I went back to Perath and dug them out of the place where I had hidden them. The shorts by then had rotted and were worthless.

13.8-11 GOD explained, "This is the way I am going to ruin the pride of Judah and the great pride of Jerusalem—a wicked bunch of people who won't obey me, who do only what they want to do, who chase after all kinds of no-gods and worship them. They're going to turn out as rotten as these old shorts. Just as shorts clothe and protect, so I kept the whole family of Israel under my care"—GOD's Decree—"so that everyone could see they were my people, a people I could show off to the world and be proud of. But they refused to do a thing I said.

13.12 "And then tell them this: 'GOD's Message, personal from the God of Israel: Every wine jug should be full of wine.'

"And they'll say, 'Of course. We know that. Every wine jug should be full of wine!'

13.13-14 "Then you'll say, 'This is what GOD says: Watch closely. I'm going to fill every person who lives in this country—the kings who rule from David's throne, the priests, the prophets, the citizens of Jerusalem—with wine that will make them drunk. And then I'll smash them, smash the wine-filled jugs—old and young alike. Nothing will stop me. Not an ounce of pity or mercy or compassion will slow me down. Every last drunken jug of them will be smashed!' "

THE LIGHT YOU ALWAYS TOOK FOR GRANTED

13.15-17 Then I said, Listen. Listen carefully: Don't stay
  stuck in your ways!
 It's GOD's Message we're dealing with here.
 Let your lives glow bright before GOD
  before he turns out the lights,
 Before you trip and fall
  on the dark mountain paths.

---

[a] 4 Or possibly *the Euphrates*; also in verses 5-7

NEW INTERNATIONAL VERSION	THE MESSAGE

NEW INTERNATIONAL VERSION

You hope for light,
  but he will turn it to thick darkness
  and change it to deep gloom.
¹⁷But if you do not listen,
  I will weep in secret
  because of your pride;
my eyes will weep bitterly,
  overflowing with tears,
  because the LORD's flock will be taken
    captive.

¹⁸Say to the king and to the queen mother,
  "Come down from your thrones,
for your glorious crowns
  will fall from your heads."
¹⁹The cities in the Negev will be shut up,
  and there will be no one to open them.
All Judah will be carried into exile,
  carried completely away.

²⁰Lift up your eyes and see
  those who are coming from the north.
Where is the flock that was entrusted to you,
  the sheep of which you boasted?
²¹What will you say when ˻the LORD˼ sets over
    you
  those you cultivated as your special allies?
Will not pain grip you
  like that of a woman in labor?
²²And if you ask yourself,
  "Why has this happened to me?"—
it is because of your many sins
  that your skirts have been torn off
  and your body mistreated.
²³Can the Ethiopian^a change his skin
  or the leopard its spots?
Neither can you do good
  who are accustomed to doing evil.

²⁴"I will scatter you like chaff
  driven by the desert wind.
²⁵This is your lot,
  the portion I have decreed for you,"
                declares the LORD,
  "because you have forgotten me
  and trusted in false gods.
²⁶I will pull up your skirts over your face
  that your shame may be seen—
²⁷your adulteries and lustful neighings,
  your shameless prostitution!

THE MESSAGE

The light you always took for granted will go
    out
  and the world will turn black.
If you people won't listen,
  I'll go off by myself and weep over you,
Weep because of your stubborn arrogance,
  bitter, bitter tears,
Rivers of tears from my eyes,
  because GOD's sheep will end up in exile.

^{13.18-19} Tell the king and the queen-mother,
  "Come down off your high horses.
Your dazzling crowns
  will tumble off your heads."
The villages in the Negev will be surrounded,
  everyone trapped,
And Judah dragged off to exile,
  the whole country dragged to oblivion.

^{13.20-22} Look, look, Jerusalem!
  Look at the enemies coming out of the
    north!
What will become of your flocks of people,
  the beautiful flocks in your care?
How are you going to feel when the people
  you've played up to, looked up to all these
    years
Now look down on you? You didn't expect
    this?
  Surprise! The pain of a woman having a
    baby!
Do I hear you saying,
  "What's going on here? Why me?"
The answer's simple: You're guilty,
  hugely guilty.
Your guilt has your life endangered,
  your guilt has you writhing in pain.

^{13.23} Can an African change skin?
  Can a leopard get rid of its spots?
So what are the odds on you doing good,
  you who are so long-practiced in evil?

^{13.24-27} "I'll blow these people away—
  like wind-blown leaves.
You have it coming to you.
  I've measured it out precisely."
    GOD's Decree.
"It's because you forgot me
  and embraced the Big Lie,
  that so-called god Baal.
I'm the one who will rip off your clothes,
  expose and shame you before the watching
    world.
Your obsessions with gods, gods, and more gods,
  your goddess affairs, your god-adulteries.

---

^a 23 Hebrew *Cushite* (probably a person from the upper
Nile region)

NEW INTERNATIONAL VERSION

I have seen your detestable acts
    on the hills and in the fields.
Woe to you, O Jerusalem!
    How long will you be unclean?"

DROUGHT, FAMINE, SWORD

14 This is the word of the LORD to Jeremiah
    concerning the drought:

² "Judah mourns,
    her cities languish;
they wail for the land,
    and a cry goes up from Jerusalem.
³ The nobles send their servants for water;
    they go to the cisterns
    but find no water.
They return with their jars unfilled;
    dismayed and despairing,
    they cover their heads.
⁴ The ground is cracked
    because there is no rain in the land;
the farmers are dismayed
    and cover their heads.
⁵ Even the doe in the field
    deserts her newborn fawn
    because there is no grass.
⁶ Wild donkeys stand on the barren heights
    and pant like jackals;
their eyesight fails
    for lack of pasture."

⁷ Although our sins testify against us,
    O LORD, do something for the sake of
        your name.
For our backsliding is great;
    we have sinned against you.
⁸ O Hope of Israel,
    its Savior in times of distress,
why are you like a stranger in the land,
    like a traveler who stays only a night?
⁹ Why are you like a man taken by surprise,
    like a warrior powerless to save?
You are among us, O LORD,
    and we bear your name;
    do not forsake us!

¹⁰ This is what the LORD says about this people:

"They greatly love to wander;
    they do not restrain their feet.
So the LORD does not accept them;
    he will now remember their wickedness
    and punish them for their sins."

THE MESSAGE

Gods on the hills, gods in the fields—
    every time I look you're off with another
        god.
O Jerusalem, what a sordid life!
    Is there any hope for you!"

TIME AND AGAIN WE'VE BETRAYED GOD

14.1-6 **14** GOD's Message that came to Jeremiah re-
    garding the drought:

"Judah weeps,
    her cities mourn.
The people fall to the ground, moaning,
    while sounds of Jerusalem's sobs rise
        up, up.
The rich people sent their servants for water.
    They went to the cisterns, but the cisterns
        were dry.
They came back with empty buckets,
    wringing their hands, shaking their heads.
All the farm work has stopped.
    Not a drop of rain has fallen.
The farmers don't know what to do.
    They wring their hands, they shake their
        heads.
Even the doe abandons her fawn in the field
    because there is no grass—
Eyes glazed over, on her last legs,
    nothing but skin and bones."

14.7-9 We know we're guilty. We've lived bad lives—
    but do something, GOD. Do it for *your*
        sake!
Time and time again we've betrayed you.
    No doubt about it—we've sinned against
        you.
Hope of Israel! Our only hope!
    Israel's last chance in this trouble!
Why are you acting like a tourist,
    taking in the sights, here today and gone
        tomorrow?
Why do you just stand there and stare,
    like someone who doesn't know what to do
        in a crisis?
But GOD, you are, in fact, *here*, here *with us!*
    You know who we are—you named us!
    Don't leave us in the lurch.

14.10 Then GOD said of these people:

"Since they loved to wander this way and that,
    never giving a thought to where they were
        going,
I will now have nothing more to do with
    them—
    except to note their guilt and punish their
        sins."

NEW INTERNATIONAL VERSION

¹¹Then the LORD said to me, "Do not pray for the well-being of this people. ¹²Although they fast, I will not listen to their cry; though they offer burnt offerings and grain offerings, I will not accept them. Instead, I will destroy them with the sword, famine and plague."

¹³But I said, "Ah, Sovereign LORD, the prophets keep telling them, 'You will not see the sword or suffer famine. Indeed, I will give you lasting peace in this place.' "

¹⁴Then the LORD said to me, "The prophets are prophesying lies in my name. I have not sent them or appointed them or spoken to them. They are prophesying to you false visions, divinations, idolatries*a* and the delusions of their own minds. ¹⁵Therefore, this is what the LORD says about the prophets who are prophesying in my name: I did not send them, yet they are saying, 'No sword or famine will touch this land.' Those same prophets will perish by sword and famine. ¹⁶And the people they are prophesying to will be thrown out into the streets of Jerusalem because of the famine and sword. There will be no one to bury them or their wives, their sons or their daughters. I will pour out on them the calamity they deserve.

¹⁷"Speak this word to them:

" 'Let my eyes overflow with tears
    night and day without ceasing;
for my virgin daughter—my people—
    has suffered a grievous wound,
    a crushing blow.
¹⁸If I go into the country,
    I see those slain by the sword;
if I go into the city,
    I see the ravages of famine.
Both prophet and priest
    have gone to a land they know not.' "

¹⁹Have you rejected Judah completely?
    Do you despise Zion?
Why have you afflicted us
    so that we cannot be healed?
We hoped for peace
    but no good has come,
for a time of healing
    but there is only terror.
²⁰O LORD, we acknowledge our wickedness
    and the guilt of our fathers;
    we have indeed sinned against you.

a 14 Or *visions, worthless divinations*

THE MESSAGE

THE KILLING FIELDS

14:11-12 GOD said to me, "Don't pray that everything will turn out all right for this people. When they skip their meals in order to pray, I won't listen to a thing they say. When they redouble their prayers, bringing all kinds of offerings from their herds and crops, I'll not accept them. I'm finishing them off with war and famine and disease."

14:13 I said, "But Master, GOD! Their preachers have been telling them that everything is going to be all right—no war and no famine—that there's nothing to worry about."

14:14 Then GOD said, "These preachers are liars, and they use my name to cover their lies. I never sent them, I never commanded them, and I don't talk with them. The sermons they've been handing out are sheer illusion, tissues of lies, whistlings in the dark.

14:15-16 "So this is my verdict on them: All the preachers who preach using my name as their text, preachers I never sent in the first place, preachers who say, 'War and famine will never come here'—these preachers will die in war and by starvation. And the people to whom they've been preaching will end up as corpses, victims of war and starvation, thrown out in the streets of Jerusalem unburied—no funerals for them or their wives or their children! I'll make sure they get the full brunt of all their evil.

14:17-18 "And you, Jeremiah, will say this to them:

" 'My eyes pour out tears.
    Day and night, the tears never quit.
My dear, dear people are battered and bruised,
    hopelessly and cruelly wounded.
I walk out into the fields,
    shocked by the killing fields strewn with
        corpses.
I walk into the city,
    shocked by the sight of starving bodies.
And I watch the preachers and priests
    going about their business as if nothing's
        happened!' "

14:19-22 God, have you said your final No to Judah?
    Can you simply not stand Zion any longer?
If not, why have you treated us like this,
    beaten us nearly to death?
We hoped for peace—
    nothing good came from it;
We looked for healing—
    and got kicked in the stomach.
We admit, O GOD, how bad we've lived,
    and our ancestors, how bad they were.
We've sinned, they've sinned,
    we've all sinned against you!

NEW INTERNATIONAL VERSION

²¹ For the sake of your name do not despise us;
  do not dishonor your glorious throne.
Remember your covenant with us
  and do not break it.
²² Do any of the worthless idols of the nations
    bring rain?
  Do the skies themselves send down
    showers?
No, it is you, O LORD our God.
  Therefore our hope is in you,
  for you are the one who does all this.

15 Then the LORD said to me: "Even if Moses and Samuel were to stand before me, my heart would not go out to this people. Send them away from my presence! Let them go! ² And if they ask you, 'Where shall we go?' tell them, 'This is what the LORD says:

" 'Those destined for death, to death;
  those for the sword, to the sword;
  those for starvation, to starvation;
  those for captivity, to captivity.'

³ "I will send four kinds of destroyers against them," declares the LORD, "the sword to kill and the dogs to drag away and the birds of the air and the beasts of the earth to devour and destroy. ⁴ I will make them abhorrent to all the kingdoms of the earth because of what Manasseh son of Hezekiah king of Judah did in Jerusalem.

⁵ "Who will have pity on you, O Jerusalem?
  Who will mourn for you?
  Who will stop to ask how you are?
⁶ You have rejected me," declares the LORD.
  "You keep on backsliding.
So I will lay hands on you and destroy you;
  I can no longer show compassion.
⁷ I will winnow them with a winnowing fork
  at the city gates of the land.
I will bring bereavement and destruction on
    my people,
  for they have not changed their ways.
⁸ I will make their widows more numerous
  than the sand of the sea.
At midday I will bring a destroyer
  against the mothers of their young men;
suddenly I will bring down on them
  anguish and terror.
⁹ The mother of seven will grow faint
  and breathe her last.
Her sun will set while it is still day;
  she will be disgraced and humiliated.

THE MESSAGE

Your reputation is at stake! Don't quit on us!
  Don't walk out and abandon your glorious
    Temple!
Remember your covenant.
  Don't break faith with us!
Can the no-gods of the godless nations cause
    rain?
  Can the sky water the earth by itself?
You're the one, O GOD, who does this.
  So you're the one for whom we wait.
You made it all,
  you do it all.

15.1-2 **15** Then GOD said to me: "Jeremiah, even if Moses and Samuel stood here and made their case, I wouldn't feel a thing for this people. Get them out of here. Tell them to get lost! And if they ask you, 'So where do we go?' tell them GOD says,

" 'If you're assigned to die, go and die;
  if assigned to war, go and get killed;
If assigned to starve, go starve;
  if assigned to exile, off to exile you go!'

15.3-4 "I've arranged for four kinds of punishment: death in battle, the corpses dropped off by killer dogs, the rest picked clean by vultures, the bones gnawed by hyenas. They'll be a sight to see, a sight to shock the whole world—and all because of Manasseh son of Hezekiah and all he did in Jerusalem.

15.5 "Who do you think will feel sorry for you,
    Jerusalem?
  Who do you think will waste tears on you?
Who will bother to take the time to ask,
  'So, how are things going?'

15.6-9 "*You* left *me*, remember?" GOD's Decree.
  "You turned your back and walked out.
So I will grab you and hit you hard.
  I'm tired of letting you off the hook.
I threw you to the four winds
  and let the winds scatter you like leaves.
I made sure you'll lose everything,
  since nothing makes you change.
I created more widows among you
  than grains of sand on the ocean beaches.
At noon mothers will get the news
  of their sons killed in action.
Sudden anguish for the mothers—
  all those terrible deaths.
A mother of seven falls to the ground,
    gasping for breath,
Robbed of her children in their prime.
  Her sun sets at high noon!

NEW INTERNATIONAL VERSION

I will put the survivors to the sword
before their enemies,"
                    declares the LORD.

¹⁰Alas, my mother, that you gave me birth,
a man with whom the whole land strives
and contends!
I have neither lent nor borrowed,
yet everyone curses me.

¹¹The LORD said,

"Surely I will deliver you for a good purpose;
surely I will make your enemies plead
with you
in times of disaster and times of distress.

¹²"Can a man break iron—
iron from the north—or bronze?
¹³Your wealth and your treasures
I will give as plunder, without charge,
because of all your sins
throughout your country.
¹⁴I will enslave you to your enemies
in ᵃ a land you do not know,
for my anger will kindle a fire
that will burn against you."

¹⁵You understand, O LORD;
remember me and care for me.
Avenge me on my persecutors.
You are long-suffering—do not take me
away;
think of how I suffer reproach for your
sake.
¹⁶When your words came, I ate them;
they were my joy and my heart's delight,
for I bear your name,
O LORD God Almighty.
¹⁷I never sat in the company of revelers,
never made merry with them;
I sat alone because your hand was on me
and you had filled me with indignation.
¹⁸Why is my pain unending
and my wound grievous and incurable?
Will you be to me like a deceptive brook,
like a spring that fails?

¹⁹Therefore this is what the LORD says:

"If you repent, I will restore you
that you may serve me;

ᵃ *14 Some Hebrew manuscripts, Septuagint and Syriac (see
also Jer. 17:4); most Hebrew manuscripts* I will cause your
enemies to bring you / into

THE MESSAGE

Then I'll round up any of you that are left
alive
and see that you're killed by your enemies."
GOD's Decree.

GIVING EVERYTHING AWAY FOR NOTHING

15.10-11 Unlucky mother—that you had me as a son,
given the unhappy job of indicting the
whole country!
I've never hurt or harmed a soul,
and yet everyone is out to get me.
But, GOD knows, I've done everything I could
to help them,
prayed for them and against their enemies.
I've always been on their side, trying to stave
off disaster.
God knows how I've tried!

15.12-14 "O Israel, O Judah, what are your chances
against the iron juggernaut from the north?
In punishment for your sins, I'm giving away
everything you've got, giving it away for
nothing.
I'll make you slaves to your enemies
in a strange and far-off land.
My anger is blazing and fierce,
burning in hot judgment against you."

15.15-18 You know where I am, GOD! Remember what
I'm doing here!
Take my side against my detractors.
Don't stand back while they ruin me.
Just look at the abuse I'm taking!
When your words showed up, I ate them—
swallowed them whole. What a feast!
What delight I took in being yours,
O GOD, GOD-of-the-Angel-Armies!
I never joined the party crowd
in their laughter and their fun.
Led by you, I went off by myself.
You'd filled me with indignation. Their sin
had me seething.
But why, why this chronic pain,
this ever worsening wound and no healing
in sight?
You're nothing, GOD, but a mirage,
a lovely oasis in the distance—and then
nothing!

15.19-21 This is how GOD answered me:

"Take back those words, and I'll take you
back.
Then you'll stand tall before me.

NEW INTERNATIONAL VERSION

if you utter worthy, not worthless, words,
you will be my spokesman.
Let this people turn to you,
but you must not turn to them.
²⁰ I will make you a wall to this people,
a fortified wall of bronze;
they will fight against you
but will not overcome you,
for I am with you
to rescue and save you,"
declares the LORD.
²¹ "I will save you from the hands of the
wicked
and redeem you from the grasp of the
cruel."

DAY OF DISASTER

16 Then the word of the LORD came to me: ²"You must not marry and have sons or daughters in this place." ³For this is what the LORD says about the sons and daughters born in this land and about the women who are their mothers and the men who are their fathers: ⁴"They will die of deadly diseases. They will not be mourned or buried but will be like refuse lying on the ground. They will perish by sword and famine, and their dead bodies will become food for the birds of the air and the beasts of the earth."

⁵For this is what the LORD says: "Do not enter a house where there is a funeral meal; do not go to mourn or show sympathy, because I have withdrawn my blessing, my love and my pity from this people," declares the LORD. ⁶"Both high and low will die in this land. They will not be buried or mourned, and no one will cut himself or shave his head for them. ⁷No one will offer food to comfort those who mourn for the dead—not even for a father or a mother—nor will anyone give them a drink to console them.

⁸"And do not enter a house where there is feasting and sit down to eat and drink. ⁹For this is what the LORD Almighty, the God of Israel, says: Before your eyes and in your days I will bring an end to the sounds of joy and gladness and to the voices of bride and bridegroom in this place.

¹⁰"When you tell these people all this and they ask you, 'Why has the LORD decreed such a great disaster against us? What wrong have we done? What sin have we committed against the LORD our God?' ¹¹then say to them, 'It is because your fathers forsook me,' declares the LORD, 'and followed other gods and served and worshiped them. They forsook me and did not keep my law. ¹²But you have behaved more wickedly than your fathers. See how each of you is following

THE MESSAGE

Use words truly and well. Don't stoop to
cheap whining.
Then, but only then, you'll speak for me.
Let your words change *them.*
Don't change your words to suit them.
I'll turn you into a steel wall,
a thick steel wall, impregnable.
They'll attack you but won't put a dent in you
because I'm at your side, defending and
delivering."
GOD's Decree.
"I'll deliver you from the grip of the wicked.
I'll get you out of the clutch of the
ruthless."

CAN MORTALS MANUFACTURE GODS?

16.1 **16** GOD's Message to me:
16.2-4 "Jeremiah, don't get married. Don't raise a family here. I have signed the death warrant on all the children born in this country, the mothers who bear them and the fathers who beget them—an epidemic of death. Death unlamented, the dead unburied, dead bodies decomposing and stinking like dung, all the killed and starved corpses served up as meals for carrion crows and mongrel dogs!"

16.5-7 GOD continued: "Don't enter a house where there's mourning. Don't go to the funeral. Don't sympathize. I've quit caring about what happens to this people." GOD's Decree. "No more loyal love on my part, no more compassion. The famous and obscure will die alike here, unlamented and unburied. No funerals will be conducted, no one will give them a second thought, no one will care, no one will say, 'I'm sorry,' no one will so much as offer a cup of tea, not even for the mother or father.

16.8 "And if there happens to be a feast celebrated, don't go there either to enjoy the festivities."

16.9 GOD-of-the-Angel-Armies, the God of Israel, says, "Watch this! I'm about to banish smiles and laughter from this place. No more brides and bridegrooms celebrating. And I'm doing it in your lifetime, before your very eyes.

16.10-13 "When you tell this to the people and they ask, 'Why is GOD talking this way, threatening us with all these calamities? We're not criminals, after all. What have we done to our GOD to be treated like this?' tell them this: 'It's because your ancestors left me, walked off and never looked back. They took up with the no-gods, worshiped and doted on them, and ignored me and wouldn't do a thing I told them. And *you're* even *worse!* Take a good look in the mirror—each of you doing whatever you want,

NEW INTERNATIONAL VERSION

the stubbornness of his evil heart instead of obeying me. ¹³So I will throw you out of this land into a land neither you nor your fathers have known, and there you will serve other gods day and night, for I will show you no favor.'

¹⁴"However, the days are coming," declares the LORD, "when men will no longer say, 'As surely as the LORD lives, who brought the Israelites up out of Egypt,' ¹⁵but they will say, 'As surely as the LORD lives, who brought the Israelites up out of the land of the north and out of all the countries where he had banished them.' For I will restore them to the land I gave their forefathers.

¹⁶"But now I will send for many fishermen," declares the LORD, "and they will catch them. After that I will send for many hunters, and they will hunt them down on every mountain and hill and from the crevices of the rocks. ¹⁷My eyes are on all their ways; they are not hidden from me, nor is their sin concealed from my eyes. ¹⁸I will repay them double for their wickedness and their sin, because they have defiled my land with the lifeless forms of their vile images and have filled my inheritance with their detestable idols."

¹⁹O LORD, my strength and my fortress,
　my refuge in time of distress,
to you the nations will come
　from the ends of the earth and say,
"Our fathers possessed nothing but false
　　gods,
　worthless idols that did them no good.
²⁰Do men make their own gods?
　Yes, but they are not gods!"

²¹"Therefore I will teach them—
　this time I will teach them
　my power and might.
Then they will know
　that my name is the LORD.

17 "Judah's sin is engraved with an iron
　　tool,
　inscribed with a flint point,
on the tablets of their hearts
　and on the horns of their altars.
²Even their children remember

THE MESSAGE

whenever you want, refusing to pay attention to me. And for this I'm getting rid of you, throwing you out in the cold, into a far and strange country. You can worship your precious no-gods there to your heart's content. Rest assured, I won't bother you anymore.'

✝

^{16.14-15} "On the other hand, don't miss this: The time is coming when no one will say any longer, 'As sure as GOD lives, the God who delivered Israel from Egypt.' What they'll say is, 'As sure as GOD lives, the God who brought Israel back from the land of the north, brought them back from all the places where he'd scattered them.' That's right, I'm going to bring them back to the land I first gave to their ancestors.

✝

^{16.16-17} "Now, watch for what comes next: I'm going to assemble a bunch of fishermen." GOD's Decree! "They'll go fishing for my people and pull them in for judgment. Then I'll send out a party of hunters, and they'll hunt them out in all the mountains, hills, and caves. I'm watching their every move. I haven't lost track of a single one of them, neither them nor their sins.

^{16.18} "They won't get by with a thing. They'll pay double for everything they did wrong. They've made a complete mess of things, littering their lives with their obscene no-gods, leaving piles of stinking god-junk all over the place."

^{16.19-20} GOD, my strength, my stronghold,
　my safe retreat when trouble descends:
The godless nations will come
　from earth's four corners, saying,
"Our ancestors lived on lies,
　useless illusions, all smoke."
Can mortals manufacture gods?
　Their factories turn out no-gods!

^{16.21} "Watch closely now. I'm going to teach these
　　wrongheaded people.
　Starting right now, I'm going to teach them
Who I am and what I do,
　teach them the meaning of my name,
　　GOD—'I AM.'

THE HEART IS HOPELESSLY DARK AND DECEITFUL

^{17.1-2} **17** "Judah's sin is engraved
　　with a steel chisel,
A steel chisel with a diamond point—
　engraved on their granite hearts,
　engraved on the stone corners of their
　　altars.
The evidence against them is plain to see:

NEW INTERNATIONAL VERSION

their altars and Asherah poles[a]
beside the spreading trees
and on the high hills.
³My mountain in the land
and your[b] wealth and all your treasures
I will give away as plunder,
together with your high places,
because of sin throughout your country.
⁴Through your own fault you will lose
the inheritance I gave you.
I will enslave you to your enemies
in a land you do not know,
for you have kindled my anger,
and it will burn forever."

⁵This is what the LORD says:

"Cursed is the one who trusts in man,
who depends on flesh for his strength
and whose heart turns away from the
LORD.
⁶He will be like a bush in the wastelands;
he will not see prosperity when it comes.
He will dwell in the parched places of the
desert,
in a salt land where no one lives.

⁷ "But blessed is the man who trusts in the
LORD,
whose confidence is in him.
⁸He will be like a tree planted by the water
that sends out its roots by the stream.
It does not fear when heat comes;
its leaves are always green.
It has no worries in a year of drought
and never fails to bear fruit."

⁹The heart is deceitful above all things
and beyond cure.
Who can understand it?

¹⁰ "I the LORD search the heart
and examine the mind,
to reward a man according to his conduct,
according to what his deeds deserve."

¹¹Like a partridge that hatches eggs it did not
lay
is the man who gains riches by unjust
means.
When his life is half gone, they will desert
him,
and in the end he will prove to be a fool.

¹²A glorious throne, exalted from the
beginning,
is the place of our sanctuary.
¹³O LORD, the hope of Israel,

---

a 2 That is, symbols of the goddess Asherah
b 2,3 Or *hills / ³and the mountains of the land. / Your*

THE MESSAGE

sex-and-religion altars and sacred sex
shrines
Anywhere there's a grove of trees,
anywhere there's an available hill.

17.3-4 "I'll use your mountains as roadside stands
for giving away everything you have.
All your 'things' will serve as reparations
for your sins all over the country.
You'll lose your gift of land,
The inheritance I gave you.
I'll make you slaves of your enemies
in a far-off and strange land.
My anger is hot and blazing and fierce,
and no one will put it out."

✝

GOD's Message:

17.5-6 "Cursed is the strong one
who depends on mere humans,
Who thinks he can make it on muscle alone
and sets GOD aside as dead weight.
He's like a tumbleweed on the prairie,
out of touch with the good earth.
He lives rootless and aimless
in a land where nothing grows.

17.7-8 "But blessed is the man who trusts me, GOD,
the woman who sticks with GOD.
They're like trees replanted in Eden,
putting down roots near the rivers—
Never a worry through the hottest of
summers,
never dropping a leaf,
Serene and calm through droughts,
bearing fresh fruit every season.

✝

17.9-10 "The heart is hopelessly dark and deceitful,
a puzzle that no one can figure out.
But I, GOD, search the heart
and examine the mind.
I get to the heart of the human.
I get to the root of things.
I treat them as they really are,
not as they pretend to be."

✝

17.11 Like a cowbird that cheats by laying its eggs
in another bird's nest
Is the person who gets rich by cheating.
When the eggs hatch, the deceit is exposed.
What a fool he'll look like then!

✝

17.12-13 From early on your Sanctuary was set high,
a throne of glory, exalted!
O GOD, you're the hope of Israel.

NEW INTERNATIONAL VERSION

all who forsake you will be put to shame.
Those who turn away from you will be
    written in the dust
because they have forsaken the LORD,
    the spring of living water.

14 Heal me, O LORD, and I will be healed;
    save me and I will be saved,
    for you are the one I praise.
15 They keep saying to me,
    "Where is the word of the LORD?
    Let it now be fulfilled!"
16 I have not run away from being your
        shepherd;
    you know I have not desired the day of
        despair.
    What passes my lips is open before you.
17 Do not be a terror to me;
    you are my refuge in the day of disaster.
18 Let my persecutors be put to shame,
    but keep me from shame;
let them be terrified,
    but keep me from terror.
Bring on them the day of disaster;
    destroy them with double destruction.

KEEPING THE SABBATH HOLY

19 This is what the LORD said to me: "Go and
stand at the gate of the people, through which
the kings of Judah go in and out; stand also at all
the other gates of Jerusalem. 20 Say to them, 'Hear
the word of the LORD, O kings of Judah and all
people of Judah and everyone living in Jerusalem
who come through these gates. 21 This is what
the LORD says: Be careful not to carry a load on
the Sabbath day or bring it through the gates
of Jerusalem. 22 Do not bring a load out of your
houses or do any work on the Sabbath, but keep
the Sabbath day holy, as I commanded your forefathers. 23 Yet they did not listen or pay attention; they were stiff-necked and would not listen
or respond to discipline. 24 But if you are careful
to obey me, declares the LORD, and bring no load
through the gates of this city on the Sabbath,
but keep the Sabbath day holy by not doing any
work on it, 25 then kings who sit on David's
throne will come through the gates of this city
with their officials. They and their officials will
come riding in chariots and on horses, accompanied by the men of Judah and those living in Jerusalem, and this city will be inhabited forever.
26 People will come from the towns of Judah and
the villages around Jerusalem, from the territory
of Benjamin and the western foothills, from the
hill country and the Negev, bringing burnt offerings and sacrifices, grain offerings, incense and
thank offerings to the house of the LORD. 27 But if

THE MESSAGE

All who leave you end up as fools,
Deserters with nothing to show for their lives,
    who walk off from GOD, fountain of living
        waters—
    and wind up dead!

☩

17.14-18 GOD, pick up the pieces.
    Put me back together again.
    You are my praise!
Listen to how they talk about me:
    "So where's this 'Word of GOD'?
    We'd like to see something happen!"
But it wasn't my idea to call for Doomsday.
    I never wanted trouble.
You know what I've said.
    It's all out in the open before you.
Don't add to my troubles.
    Give me some relief!
Let those who harass me be harassed, not me.
    Let *them* be disgraced, not me.
Bring down upon them the day of doom.
    Lower the boom. *Boom!*

KEEP THE SABBATH DAY HOLY

17.19-20 GOD's Message to me: "Go stand in the People's
Gate, the one used by Judah's kings as they
come and go, and then proceed in turn to all
the gates of Jerusalem. Tell them: 'Listen, you
kings of Judah, listen to GOD's Message—and
all you people who go in and out of these gates,
you listen!

17.21-23 " 'This is GOD's Message. Be careful, if you care
about your lives, not to desecrate the Sabbath
by turning it into just another workday, lug-
ging stuff here and there. Don't use the Sabbath
to do business as usual. Keep the Sabbath day
holy, as I commanded your ancestors. They never did it, as you know. They paid no attention to
what I said and went about their own business,
refusing to be guided or instructed by me.

17.24-26 " 'But now, take seriously what I tell you.
Quit desecrating the Sabbath by busily going
about your own work, and keep the Sabbath
day holy by not doing business as usual. Then
kings from the time of David and their officials will continue to ride through these gates
on horses or in chariots. The people of Judah
and citizens of Jerusalem will continue to pass
through them, too. Jerusalem will always be
filled with people. People will stream in from
all over Judah, from the province of Benjamin,
from the Jerusalem suburbs, from foothills and
mountains and deserts. They'll come to worship, bringing all kinds of offerings—animals,
grains, incense, expressions of thanks—into
the Sanctuary of GOD.

NEW INTERNATIONAL VERSION

you do not obey me to keep the Sabbath day holy by not carrying any load as you come through the gates of Jerusalem on the Sabbath day, then I will kindle an unquenchable fire in the gates of Jerusalem that will consume her fortresses.' "

AT THE POTTER'S HOUSE

18 This is the word that came to Jeremiah from the LORD: ²"Go down to the potter's house, and there I will give you my message." ³So I went down to the potter's house, and I saw him working at the wheel. ⁴But the pot he was shaping from the clay was marred in his hands; so the potter formed it into another pot, shaping it as seemed best to him.

⁵Then the word of the LORD came to me: ⁶"O house of Israel, can I not do with you as this potter does?" declares the LORD. "Like clay in the hand of the potter, so are you in my hand, O house of Israel. ⁷If at any time I announce that a nation or kingdom is to be uprooted, torn down and destroyed, ⁸and if that nation I warned repents of its evil, then I will relent and not inflict on it the disaster I had planned. ⁹And if at another time I announce that a nation or kingdom is to be built up and planted, ¹⁰and if it does evil in my sight and does not obey me, then I will reconsider the good I had intended to do for it.

¹¹"Now therefore say to the people of Judah and those living in Jerusalem, 'This is what the LORD says: Look! I am preparing a disaster for you and devising a plan against you. So turn from your evil ways, each one of you, and reform your ways and your actions.' ¹²But they will reply, 'It's no use. We will continue with our own plans; each of us will follow the stubbornness of his evil heart.' "

¹³Therefore this is what the LORD says:

"Inquire among the nations:
    Who has ever heard anything like this?
A most horrible thing has been done
    by Virgin Israel.
¹⁴Does the snow of Lebanon
    ever vanish from its rocky slopes?
Do its cool waters from distant sources
    ever cease to flow?ᵃ
¹⁵Yet my people have forgotten me;
    they burn incense to worthless idols,
which made them stumble in their ways
    and in the ancient paths.
They made them walk in bypaths
    and on roads not built up.

ᵃ *14* The meaning of the Hebrew for this sentence is uncertain.

THE MESSAGE

17.27 " 'But if you won't listen to me, won't keep the Sabbath holy, won't quit using the Sabbath for doing your own work, busily going in and out of the city gates on your self-important business, then I'll burn the gates down. In fact, I'll burn the whole city down, palaces and all, with a fire nobody will be able to put out!' "

TO WORSHIP THE BIG LIE

18.1-2 **18** GOD told Jeremiah, "Up on your feet! Go to the potter's house. When you get there, I'll tell you what I have to say."

18.3-4 So I went to the potter's house, and sure enough, the potter was there, working away at his wheel. Whenever the pot the potter was working on turned out badly, as sometimes happens when you are working with clay, the potter would simply start over and use the same clay to make another pot.

18.5-10 Then GOD's Message came to me: "Can't I do just as this potter does, people of Israel?" GOD's Decree! "Watch this potter. In the same way that this potter works his clay, I work on you, people of Israel. At any moment I may decide to pull up a people or a country by the roots and get rid of them. But if they repent of their wicked lives, I will think twice and start over with them. At another time I might decide to plant a people or country, but if they don't cooperate and won't listen to me, I will think again and give up on the plans I had for them.

18.11 "So, tell the people of Judah and citizens of Jerusalem my Message: 'Danger! I'm shaping doom against you, laying plans against you. Turn back from your doomed way of life. Straighten out your lives.'

18.12 "But they'll just say, 'Why should we? What's the point? We'll live just the way we've always lived, doom or no doom.' "

⊹

18.13-17 GOD's Message:

"Ask around.
    Survey the godless nations.
Has anyone heard the likes of this?
    Virgin Israel has become a slut!
Does snow disappear from the Lebanon
        peaks?
    Do alpine streams run dry?
But my people have left me
    to worship the Big Lie.
They've gotten off the track,
    the old, well-worn trail,
And now bushwhack through underbrush
    in a tangle of roots and vines.

NEW INTERNATIONAL VERSION

¹⁶Their land will be laid waste,
an object of lasting scorn;
all who pass by will be appalled
and will shake their heads.
¹⁷Like a wind from the east,
I will scatter them before their enemies;
I will show them my back and not my face
in the day of their disaster."

¹⁸They said, "Come, let's make plans against Jeremiah; for the teaching of the law by the priest will not be lost, nor will counsel from the wise, nor the word from the prophets. So come, let's attack him with our tongues and pay no attention to anything he says."

¹⁹Listen to me, O LORD;
hear what my accusers are saying!
²⁰Should good be repaid with evil?
Yet they have dug a pit for me.
Remember that I stood before you
and spoke in their behalf
to turn your wrath away from them.
²¹So give their children over to famine;
hand them over to the power of the
sword.
Let their wives be made childless and
widows;
let their men be put to death,
their young men slain by the sword in
battle.
²²Let a cry be heard from their houses
when you suddenly bring invaders against
them,
for they have dug a pit to capture me
and have hidden snares for my feet.
²³But you know, O LORD,
all their plots to kill me.
Do not forgive their crimes
or blot out their sins from your sight.
Let them be overthrown before you;
deal with them in the time of your anger.

19 This is what the LORD says: "Go and buy a clay jar from a potter. Take along some of the elders of the people and of the priests ²and go out to the Valley of Ben Hinnom, near the entrance of the Potsherd Gate. There proclaim the words I tell you, ³and say, 'Hear the word of the LORD, O kings of Judah and people of Jerusalem. This is what the LORD Almighty, the God of Israel, says: Listen! I am going to bring a disaster on this place that will make the ears of everyone who hears of it tingle. ⁴For they have forsaken

THE MESSAGE

Their land's going to end up a mess—
a fool's memorial to be spit on.
Travelers passing through
will shake their heads in disbelief.
I'll scatter my people before their enemies,
like autumn leaves in a high wind.
On their day of doom, they'll stare at my back
as I walk away,
catching not so much as a glimpse of my
face."

☩

18.18 Some of the people said, "Come on, let's cook up a plot against Jeremiah. We'll still have the priests to teach us the law, wise counselors to give us advice, and prophets to tell us what God has to say. Come on, let's discredit him so we don't have to put up with him any longer."

18.19-23 And I said to GOD:

"GOD, listen to me!
Just listen to what my enemies are saying.
Should I get paid evil for good?
That's what they're doing. They've made
plans to kill me!
Remember all the times I stood up for them
before you,
speaking up for them,
trying to soften your anger?
But enough! Let their children starve!
Let them be massacred in battle!
Let their wives be childless and widowed,
their friends die and their proud young
men be killed.
Let cries of panic sound from their homes
as you surprise them with war parties!
They're all set to lynch me.
The noose is practically around my neck!
But you know all this, GOD.
You know they're determined to kill me.
Don't whitewash their crimes,
don't overlook a single sin!
Round the bunch of them up before you.
Strike while the iron of your anger is hot!"

SMASHING THE CLAY POT

19.1-2 **19** GOD said to me, "Go, buy a clay pot. Then get a few leaders from the people and a few of the leading priests and go out to the Valley of Ben-hinnom, just outside the Potsherd Gate, and preach there what I tell you.

19.3-5 "Say, 'Listen to GOD's Word, you kings of Judah and people of Jerusalem! This is the Message from GOD-of-the-Angel-Armies, the God of Israel. I'm about to bring doom crashing down on this place. Oh, and will ears ever ring! Doom—because they've walked off and left me,

NEW INTERNATIONAL VERSION	THE MESSAGE

me and made this a place of foreign gods; they have burned sacrifices in it to gods that neither they nor their fathers nor the kings of Judah ever knew, and they have filled this place with the blood of the innocent. ⁵They have built the high places of Baal to burn their sons in the fire as offerings to Baal—something I did not command or mention, nor did it enter my mind. ⁶So beware, the days are coming, declares the LORD, when people will no longer call this place Topheth or the Valley of Ben Hinnom, but the Valley of Slaughter.

⁷"'In this place I will ruin*a* the plans of Judah and Jerusalem. I will make them fall by the sword before their enemies, at the hands of those who seek their lives, and I will give their carcasses as food to the birds of the air and the beasts of the earth. ⁸I will devastate this city and make it an object of scorn; all who pass by will be appalled and will scoff because of all its wounds. ⁹I will make them eat the flesh of their sons and daughters, and they will eat one another's flesh during the stress of the siege imposed on them by the enemies who seek their lives.'

¹⁰"Then break the jar while those who go with you are watching, ¹¹and say to them, 'This is what the LORD Almighty says: I will smash this nation and this city just as this potter's jar is smashed and cannot be repaired. They will bury the dead in Topheth until there is no more room. ¹²This is what I will do to this place and to those who live here, declares the LORD. I will make this city like Topheth. ¹³The houses in Jerusalem and those of the kings of Judah will be defiled like this place, Topheth—all the houses where they burned incense on the roofs to all the starry hosts and poured out drink offerings to other gods.'"

¹⁴Jeremiah then returned from Topheth, where the LORD had sent him to prophesy, and stood in the court of the LORD's temple and said to all the people, ¹⁵"This is what the LORD Almighty, the God of Israel, says: 'Listen! I am going to bring on this city and the villages around it every disaster I pronounced against them, because they were stiff-necked and would not listen to my words.'"

JEREMIAH AND PASHHUR

20 When the priest Pashhur son of Immer, the chief officer in the temple of the LORD, heard Jeremiah prophesying these things, ²he had Jeremiah the prophet beaten and put in the stocks at the Upper Gate of Benjamin at the LORD's temple. ³The next day, when Pashhur released him from the stocks, Jeremiah said to

and made this place strange by worshiping strange gods, gods never heard of by them, their parents, or the old kings of Judah. Doom—because they have massacred innocent people. Doom—because they've built altars to that no-god Baal, and burned their own children alive in the fire as offerings to Baal, an atrocity I never ordered, never so much as hinted at!

19.6-9 "'And so it's pay day, and soon'—GOD's Decree!—'this place will no longer be known as Topheth or Valley of Ben-hinnom, but Massacre Meadows. I'm canceling all the plans Judah and Jerusalem had for this place, and I'll have them killed by their enemies. I'll stack their dead bodies to be eaten by carrion crows and wild dogs. I'll turn this city into such a museum of atrocities that anyone coming near will be shocked speechless by the savage brutality. The people will turn into cannibals. Dehumanized by the pressure of the enemy siege, they'll eat their own children! Yes, they'll eat one another, family and friends alike.'

19.10-13 "Say all this, and then smash the pot in front of the men who have come with you. Then say, 'This is what GOD-of-the-Angel-Armies says: I'll smash this people and this city like a man who smashes a clay pot into so many pieces it can never be put together again. They'll bury bodies here in Topheth until there's no more room. And the whole city will become a Topheth. The city will be turned by people and kings alike into a center for worshiping the star gods and goddesses, turned into an open grave, the whole city an open grave, stinking like a sewer, like Topheth.'"

19.14-15 Then Jeremiah left Topheth, where GOD had sent him to preach the sermon, and took his stand in the court of GOD's Temple and said to the people, "This is the Message from GOD-of-the-Angel-Armies to you: 'Warning! Danger! I'm bringing down on this city and all the surrounding towns the doom that I have pronounced. They're set in their ways and won't budge. They refuse to do a thing I say.'"

LIFE'S BEEN NOTHING BUT TROUBLE AND TEARS

20.1-5 **20** The priest Pashur son of Immer was the senior priest in GOD's Temple. He heard Jeremiah preach this sermon. He whipped Jeremiah the prophet and put him in the stocks at the Upper Benjamin Gate of GOD's Temple. The next day Pashur came and let him go. Jeremiah

---

a 7 The Hebrew for *ruin* sounds like the Hebrew for *jar* (see verses 1 and 10).

NEW INTERNATIONAL VERSION

him, "The LORD's name for you is not Pashhur, but Magor-Missabib. *a* ⁴For this is what the LORD says: 'I will make you a terror to yourself and to all your friends; with your own eyes you will see them fall by the sword of their enemies. I will hand all Judah over to the king of Babylon, who will carry them away to Babylon or put them to the sword. ⁵I will hand over to their enemies all the wealth of this city—all its products, all its valuables and all the treasures of the kings of Judah. They will take it away as plunder and carry it off to Babylon. ⁶And you, Pashhur, and all who live in your house will go into exile to Babylon. There you will die and be buried, you and all your friends to whom you have prophesied lies.'"

JEREMIAH'S COMPLAINT

⁷O LORD, you deceived*b* me, and I was
        deceived*b*;
    you overpowered me and prevailed.
I am ridiculed all day long;
    everyone mocks me.
⁸Whenever I speak, I cry out
    proclaiming violence and destruction.
So the word of the LORD has brought me
    insult and reproach all day long.
⁹But if I say, "I will not mention him
    or speak any more in his name,"
his word is in my heart like a fire,
    a fire shut up in my bones.
I am weary of holding it in;
    indeed, I cannot.
¹⁰I hear many whispering,
    "Terror on every side!
    Report him! Let's report him!"
All my friends
    are waiting for me to slip, saying,
"Perhaps he will be deceived;
    then we will prevail over him
    and take our revenge on him."

¹¹But the LORD is with me like a mighty
        warrior;
    so my persecutors will stumble and not
        prevail.
They will fail and be thoroughly disgraced;
    their dishonor will never be forgotten.
¹²O LORD Almighty, you who examine the
        righteous
    and probe the heart and mind,
let me see your vengeance upon them,
    for to you I have committed my cause.

THE MESSAGE

told him, "GOD has a new name for you: not Pashur but Danger-Everywhere, because GOD says, 'You're a danger to yourself and everyone around you. All your friends are going to get killed in battle while you stand there and watch. What's more, I'm turning all of Judah over to the king of Babylon to do whatever he likes with them—haul them off into exile, kill them at whim. Everything worth anything in this city, property and possessions along with everything in the royal treasury—I'm handing it all over to the enemy. They'll rummage through it and take what they want back to Babylon.

20.6   "'And you, Pashur, you and everyone in your family will be taken prisoner into exile—that's right, exile in Babylon. You'll die and be buried there, you and all your cronies to whom you preached your lies.'"

20.7-10 You pushed me into this, GOD, and I let you
        do it.
    You were too much for me.
And now I'm a public joke.
    They all poke fun at me.
Every time I open my mouth
    I'm shouting, "Murder!" or "Rape!"
And all I get for my GOD-warnings
    are insults and contempt.
But if I say, "Forget it!
    No more GOD-Messages from me!"
The words are fire in my belly,
    a burning in my bones.
I'm worn out trying to hold it in.
    I can't do it any longer!
Then I hear whispering behind my back:
    "There goes old 'Danger-Everywhere.' Shut
        him up! Report him!"
Old friends watch, hoping I'll fall flat on my
        face:
    "One misstep and we'll have him. We'll get
        rid of him for good!"

20.11 But GOD, a most fierce warrior, is at my side.
    Those who are after me will be sent
        sprawling—
Slapstick buffoons falling all over themselves,
    a spectacle of humiliation no one will ever
        forget.

20.12 Oh, GOD-of-the-Angel-Armies, no one fools
        you.
    You see through everyone, everything.
I want to see you pay them back for what
        they've done.
    I rest my case with you.

NEW INTERNATIONAL VERSION	THE MESSAGE

NEW INTERNATIONAL VERSION

13 Sing to the LORD!
  Give praise to the LORD!
He rescues the life of the needy
  from the hands of the wicked.

14 Cursed be the day I was born!
  May the day my mother bore me not be
    blessed!
15 Cursed be the man who brought my father
    the news,
  who made him very glad, saying,
    "A child is born to you—a son!"
16 May that man be like the towns
    the LORD overthrew without pity.
  May he hear wailing in the morning,
    a battle cry at noon.
17 For he did not kill me in the womb,
    with my mother as my grave,
  her womb enlarged forever.
18 Why did I ever come out of the womb
  to see trouble and sorrow
  and to end my days in shame?

GOD REJECTS ZEDEKIAH'S REQUEST

21 The word came to Jeremiah from the
LORD when King Zedekiah sent to him
Pashhur son of Malkijah and the priest Zephaniah son of Maaseiah. They said: 2 "Inquire now of
the LORD for us because Nebuchadnezzar[a] king
of Babylon is attacking us. Perhaps the LORD will
perform wonders for us as in times past so that
he will withdraw from us."

3 But Jeremiah answered them, "Tell Zedekiah,
4 'This is what the LORD, the God of Israel, says: I
am about to turn against you the weapons of war
that are in your hands, which you are using to
fight the king of Babylon and the Babylonians[b]
who are outside the wall besieging you. And I
will gather them inside this city. 5 I myself will
fight against you with an outstretched hand and
a mighty arm in anger and fury and great wrath.
6 I will strike down those who live in this city—
both men and animals—and they will die of a
terrible plague. 7 After that, declares the LORD, I
will hand over Zedekiah king of Judah, his officials and the people in this city who survive the
plague, sword and famine, to Nebuchadnezzar
king of Babylon and to their enemies who seek
their lives. He will put them to the sword; he
will show them no mercy or pity or compassion.'

8 "Furthermore, tell the people, 'This is what

THE MESSAGE

20.13 Sing to GOD! All praise to GOD!
  He saves the weak from the grip of the
    wicked.

✠

20.14-18 Curse the day
  I was born!
The day my mother bore me—
  a curse on it, I say!
And curse the man who delivered
  the news to my father:
"You've got a new baby—a boy baby!"
  (How happy it made him.)
Let that birth notice be blacked out,
  deleted from the records,
And the man who brought it haunted to his
    death
  with the bad news he brought.
He should have killed me before I was born,
  with that womb as my tomb,
My mother pregnant for the rest of her life
  with a baby dead in her womb.
Why, oh why, did I ever leave that womb?
  Life's been nothing but trouble and tears,
  and what's coming is more of the same.

START EACH DAY WITH A SENSE OF JUSTICE

21.1-2 **21** GOD's Message to Jeremiah when King
Zedekiah sent Pashur son of Malkijah
and the priest Zephaniah son of Maaseiah to
him with this request: "Nebuchadnezzar, king
of Babylon, has waged war against us. Pray to
GOD for us. Ask him for help. Maybe GOD will
intervene with one of his famous miracles and
make him leave."

21.3-7   But Jeremiah said, "Tell Zedekiah: 'This
is the GOD of Israel's Message to you: You can
say goodbye to your army, watch morale and
weapons flushed down the drain. I'm going to
personally lead the king of Babylon and the
Chaldeans, against whom you're fighting so
hard, right into the city itself. I'm joining *their*
side and fighting against *you*, fighting all-out,
holding nothing back. And in fierce anger. I'm
prepared to wipe out the population of this
city, people and animals alike, in a raging epidemic. And then I will personally deliver Zedekiah king of Judah, his princes, and any survivors left in the city who haven't died from
disease, been killed, or starved. I'll deliver them
to Nebuchadnezzar, king of Babylon—yes,
hand them over to their enemies, who have
come to kill them. He'll kill them ruthlessly,
showing no mercy.'

21.8-10   "And then tell the people at large, 'GOD's

---

*a 2 Hebrew Nebuchadrezzar, of which Nebuchadnezzar is a
variant; here and often in Jeremiah and Ezekiel*
b 4 Or Chaldeans; also in verse 9

NEW INTERNATIONAL VERSION

the LORD says: See, I am setting before you the way of life and the way of death. ⁹Whoever stays in this city will die by the sword, famine or plague. But whoever goes out and surrenders to the Babylonians who are besieging you will live; he will escape with his life. ¹⁰I have determined to do this city harm and not good, declares the LORD. It will be given into the hands of the king of Babylon, and he will destroy it with fire.'

¹¹"Moreover, say to the royal house of Judah, 'Hear the word of the LORD; ¹²O house of David, this is what the LORD says:

" 'Administer justice every morning;
    rescue from the hand of his oppressor
    the one who has been robbed,
or my wrath will break out and burn like fire
    because of the evil you have done—
    burn with no one to quench it.
¹³I am against you, ⌊Jerusalem,⌋
    you who live above this valley
    on the rocky plateau,
                        declares the LORD—
you who say, "Who can come against us?
    Who can enter our refuge?"
¹⁴I will punish you as your deeds deserve,
                        declares the LORD.
I will kindle a fire in your forests
    that will consume everything around
    you.' "

JUDGMENT AGAINST EVIL KINGS

22 This is what the LORD says: "Go down to the palace of the king of Judah and proclaim this message there: ²'Hear the word of the LORD, O king of Judah, you who sit on David's throne—you, your officials and your people who come through these gates. ³This is what the LORD says: Do what is just and right. Rescue from the hand of his oppressor the one who has been robbed. Do no wrong or violence to the alien, the fatherless or the widow, and do not shed innocent blood in this place. ⁴For if you are careful to carry out these commands, then kings who sit on David's throne will come through the gates of this palace, riding in chariots and on horses, accompanied by their officials and their people. ⁵But if you do not obey these commands, declares the LORD, I swear by myself that this palace will become a ruin.' "

⁶For this is what the LORD says about the palace of the king of Judah:

THE MESSAGE

Message to you is this: Listen carefully. I'm giving you a choice: life or death. Whoever stays in this city will die—either in battle or by starvation or disease. But whoever goes out and surrenders to the Chaldeans who have surrounded the city will live. You'll lose everything—but not your life. I'm determined to see this city destroyed. I'm that angry with this place! GOD's Decree. I'm going to give it to the king of Babylon, and he's going to burn it to the ground.'

21.11-14 "To the royal house of Judah, listen to GOD's
        Message!
    House of David, listen—GOD's Message to
        you:
'Start each day by dealing with justice.
    Rescue victims from their exploiters.
Prevent fire—the fire of my anger—
    for once it starts, it can't be put out.
Your evil regime
    is fuel for my anger.
Don't you realize that I'm against you,
    yes, *against* you.
You think you've got it made,
    all snug and secure.
You say, "Who can possibly get to us?
    Who can crash our party?"
Well, I can—and will!
    I'll punish your evil regime.
I'll start a fire that will rage unchecked,
    burn everything in sight to cinders.' "

WALKING OUT ON THE COVENANT OF GOD

22.1-3 **22** GOD's orders: "Go to the royal palace and deliver this Message. Say, 'Listen to what GOD says, O King of Judah, you who sit on David's throne—you and your officials and all the people who go in and out of these palace gates. This is GOD's Message: Attend to matters of justice. Set things right between people. Rescue victims from their exploiters. Don't take advantage of the homeless, the orphans, the widows. Stop the murdering!

22.4-5 " 'If you obey these commands, then kings who follow in the line of David will continue to go in and out of these palace gates mounted on horses and riding in chariots—they and their officials and the citizens of Judah. But if you don't obey these commands, then I swear—GOD's Decree!—this palace will end up a heap of rubble.' "

22.6-7 This is GOD's verdict on Judah's royal palace:

NEW INTERNATIONAL VERSION

"Though you are like Gilead to me,
   like the summit of Lebanon,
I will surely make you like a desert,
   like towns not inhabited.
⁷I will send destroyers against you,
   each man with his weapons,
and they will cut up your fine cedar beams
   and throw them into the fire.

⁸"People from many nations will pass by this city and will ask one another, 'Why has the LORD done such a thing to this great city?' ⁹And the answer will be: 'Because they have forsaken the covenant of the LORD their God and have worshiped and served other gods.' "

¹⁰Do not weep for the dead ⌊king⌋ or mourn
     his loss;
rather, weep bitterly for him who is
     exiled,
because he will never return
   nor see his native land again.

¹¹For this is what the LORD says about Shallum[a] son of Josiah, who succeeded his father as king of Judah but has gone from this place: "He will never return. ¹²He will die in the place where they have led him captive; he will not see this land again."

¹³"Woe to him who builds his palace by
     unrighteousness,
   his upper rooms by injustice,
making his countrymen work for nothing,
   not paying them for their labor.
¹⁴He says, 'I will build myself a great palace
   with spacious upper rooms.'
So he makes large windows in it,
   panels it with cedar
   and decorates it in red.

¹⁵"Does it make you a king
   to have more and more cedar?
Did not your father have food and drink?
   He did what was right and just,
   so all went well with him.
¹⁶He defended the cause of the poor and
     needy,
   and so all went well.
Is that not what it means to know me?"
   declares the LORD.
¹⁷"But your eyes and your heart
   are set only on dishonest gain,
on shedding innocent blood
   and on oppression and extortion."

¹⁸Therefore this is what the LORD says about Jehoiakim son of Josiah king of Judah:

THE MESSAGE

"I number you among my favorite places—
   like the lovely hills of Gilead,
   like the soaring peaks of Lebanon.
Yet I swear I'll turn you into a wasteland,
   as empty as a ghost town.
I'll hire a demolition crew,
   well-equipped with sledgehammers and
     wrecking bars,
Pound the country to a pulp
   and burn it all up.

22:8-9   "Travelers from all over will come through here and say to one another, 'Why would GOD do such a thing to this wonderful city?' They'll be told, 'Because they walked out on the covenant of their GOD, took up with other gods and worshiped them.' ".

BUILDING A FINE HOUSE BUT DESTROYING LIVES

22:10 Don't weep over dead King Josiah.
   Don't waste your tears.
Weep for his exiled son:
   He's gone for good.
   He'll never see home again.

22:11-12   For this is GOD's Word on Shallum son of Josiah, who succeeded his father as king of Judah: "He's gone from here, gone for good. He'll die in the place they've taken him to. He'll never see home again."

☩

22:13-17 "Doom to him who builds palaces but bullies
     people,
   who makes a fine house but destroys lives,
Who cheats his workers
   and won't pay them for their work,
Who says, 'I'll build me an elaborate mansion
   with spacious rooms and fancy windows.
I'll bring in rare and expensive woods
   and the latest in interior decor.'
So, that makes you a king—
   living in a fancy palace?
Your father got along just fine, didn't he?
   He did what was right and treated people
     fairly,
And things went well with him.
   He stuck up for the down-and-out,
And things went well for Judah.
   Isn't this what it means to know me?"
     GOD's Decree!
"But you're blind and brainless.
   All you think about is yourself,
Taking advantage of the weak,
   bulldozing your way, bullying victims."

22:18-19 This is God's epitaph on Jehoiakim son of
     Josiah king of Judah:

---

a 11 Also called *Jehoahaz*

NEW INTERNATIONAL VERSION

"They will not mourn for him:
    'Alas, my brother! Alas, my sister!'
They will not mourn for him:
    'Alas, my master! Alas, his splendor!'
¹⁹He will have the burial of a donkey—
    dragged away and thrown
        outside the gates of Jerusalem."

²⁰"Go up to Lebanon and cry out,
    let your voice be heard in Bashan,
cry out from Abarim,
    for all your allies are crushed.
²¹I warned you when you felt secure,
    but you said, 'I will not listen!'
This has been your way from your youth;
    you have not obeyed me.
²²The wind will drive all your shepherds away,
    and your allies will go into exile.
Then you will be ashamed and disgraced
    because of all your wickedness.
²³You who live in 'Lebanon,'*ᵃ*
    who are nestled in cedar buildings,
how you will groan when pangs come upon
        you,
    pain like that of a woman in labor!

²⁴"As surely as I live," declares the Lᴏʀᴅ, "even if you, Jehoiachin*ᵇ* son of Jehoiakim king of Judah, were a signet ring on my right hand, I would still pull you off. ²⁵I will hand you over to those who seek your life, those you fear—to Nebuchadnezzar king of Babylon and to the Babylonians.*ᶜ* ²⁶I will hurl you and the mother who gave you birth into another country, where neither of you was born, and there you both will die. ²⁷You will never come back to the land you long to return to."

²⁸Is this man Jehoiachin a despised, broken
        pot,
    an object no one wants?
Why will he and his children be hurled out,
    cast into a land they do not know?
²⁹O land, land, land,
    hear the word of the Lᴏʀᴅ!
³⁰This is what the Lᴏʀᴅ says:
"Record this man as if childless,
    a man who will not prosper in his
        lifetime,
for none of his offspring will prosper,
    none will sit on the throne of David
    or rule anymore in Judah."

ᵃ 23 That is, the palace in Jerusalem (see 1 Kings 7:2)
ᵇ 24 Hebrew Coniah, a variant of Jehoiachin; also in verse 28
ᶜ 25 Or Chaldeans

THE MESSAGE

"Doom to this man!
Nobody will shed tears over him,
    'Poor, poor brother!'
Nobody will shed tears over him,
    'Poor, poor master!'
They'll give him a donkey's funeral,
    drag him out of the city and dump him.

Yᴏᴜ'ᴠᴇ Mᴀᴅᴇ ᴀ Tᴏᴛᴀʟ Mᴇss ᴏꜰ Yᴏᴜʀ Lɪꜰᴇ

^{22.20-23}"People of Jerusalem, climb a Lebanon peak
        and weep,
    climb a Bashan mountain and wail,
Climb the Abarim ridge and cry—
    you've made a total mess of your life.
I spoke to you when everything was going
        your way.
    You said, 'I'm not interested.'
You've been that way as long as I've known
        you,
    never listened to a thing I said.
All your leaders will be blown away,
    all your friends end up in exile,
And you'll find yourself in the gutter,
    disgraced by your evil life.
You big-city people thought you were so
        important,
    thought you were 'king of the mountain'!
You're soon going to be doubled up in pain,
    pain worse than the pangs of childbirth.

✝

^{22.24-26}"As sure as I am the living God"—Gᴏᴅ's Decree—"even if you, Jehoiachin son of Jehoiakim king of Judah, were the signet ring on my right hand, I'd pull you off and give you to those who are out to kill you, to Nebuchadnezzar king of Babylon and the Chaldeans, and then throw you, both you and your mother, into a foreign country, far from your place of birth. There you'll both die.

^{22.27}   "You'll be homesick, desperately homesick, but you'll never get home again."

^{22.28-30}Is Jehoiachin a leaky bucket,
    a rusted-out pail good for nothing?
Why else would he be thrown away, he and
        his children,
    thrown away to a foreign place?
O land, land, land,
    listen to Gᴏᴅ's Message!
This is Gᴏᴅ's verdict:
"Write this man off as if he were childless,
    a man who will never amount to anything.
Nothing will ever come of his life.
    He's the end of the line, the last of the
        kings.

NEW INTERNATIONAL VERSION

THE RIGHTEOUS BRANCH

23 "Woe to the shepherds who are destroying and scattering the sheep of my pasture!" declares the LORD. ²Therefore this is what the LORD, the God of Israel, says to the shepherds who tend my people: "Because you have scattered my flock and driven them away and have not bestowed care on them, I will bestow punishment on you for the evil you have done," declares the LORD. ³"I myself will gather the remnant of my flock out of all the countries where I have driven them and will bring them back to their pasture, where they will be fruitful and increase in number. ⁴I will place shepherds over them who will tend them, and they will no longer be afraid or terrified, nor will any be missing," declares the LORD.

⁵"The days are coming," declares the LORD,
    "when I will raise up to David*ᵃ* a
        righteous Branch,
    a King who will reign wisely
        and do what is just and right in the land.
⁶In his days Judah will be saved
        and Israel will live in safety.
    This is the name by which he will be called:
        The LORD Our Righteousness.

⁷"So then, the days are coming," declares the LORD, "when people will no longer say, 'As surely as the LORD lives, who brought the Israelites up out of Egypt,' ⁸but they will say, 'As surely as the LORD lives, who brought the descendants of Israel up out of the land of the north and out of all the countries where he had banished them.' Then they will live in their own land."

LYING PROPHETS

⁹Concerning the prophets:

My heart is broken within me;
    all my bones tremble.
I am like a drunken man,
    like a man overcome by wine,
because of the LORD
    and his holy words.
¹⁰The land is full of adulterers;
    because of the curse*ᵇ* the land lies
        parched*ᶜ*
    and the pastures in the desert are
        withered.
The ˌprophetsˌ follow an evil course
    and use their power unjustly.

THE MESSAGE

AN AUTHENTIC DAVID-BRANCH

23 23.1-4 "Doom to the shepherd-leaders who butcher and scatter my sheep!" GOD'S Decree. "So here is what I, GOD, Israel's God, say to the shepherd-leaders who misled my people: 'You've scattered my sheep. You've driven them off. You haven't kept your eye on them. Well, let me tell you, I'm keeping my eye on *you*, keeping track of your criminal behavior. I'll take over and gather what's left of my sheep, gather them in from all the lands where I've driven them. I'll bring them back where they belong, and they'll recover and flourish. I'll set shepherd-leaders over them who will take good care of them. They won't live in fear or panic anymore. All the lost sheep rounded up!' GOD'S Decree."

23.5-6 "Time's coming"—GOD's Decree—
    "when I'll establish a truly righteous
        David-Branch,
    A ruler who knows how to rule justly.
        He'll make sure of justice and keep people
            united.
    In his time Judah will be secure again
        and Israel will live in safety.
    This is the name they'll give him:
        'GOD-Who-Puts-Everything-Right.'

23.7-8 "So watch for this. The time's coming"—GOD's Decree—"when no one will say, 'As sure as GOD lives, the God who brought the Israelites out of Egypt,' but, 'As sure as GOD lives, the God who brought the descendants of Israel back from the north country and from the other countries where he'd driven them, so that they can live on their own good earth.' "

THE "EVERYTHING WILL TURN OUT FINE" SERMON

23.9 My head is reeling,
    my limbs are limp,
I'm staggering like a drunk,
    seeing double from too much wine—
And all because of GOD,
    because of his holy words.

23.10-12 Now for what GOD says regarding the lying prophets:

"Can you believe it? A country teeming with
        adulterers!
    faithless, promiscuous idolater-adulterers!
They're a curse on the land.
    The land's a wasteland.
Their unfaithfulness
    is turning the country into a cesspool,

ᵃ 5 Or *up from David's line*   *ᵇ 10* Or *because of these things*
ᶜ 10 Or *land mourns*

NEW INTERNATIONAL VERSION

¹¹ "Both prophet and priest are godless;
   even in my temple I find their
      wickedness,"
         declares the LORD.
¹² "Therefore their path will become slippery;
   they will be banished to darkness
   and there they will fall.
I will bring disaster on them
   in the year they are punished,"
         declares the LORD.

¹³ "Among the prophets of Samaria
   I saw this repulsive thing:
They prophesied by Baal
   and led my people Israel astray.
¹⁴ And among the prophets of Jerusalem
   I have seen something horrible:
They commit adultery and live a lie.
They strengthen the hands of evildoers,
   so that no one turns from his wickedness.
They are all like Sodom to me;
   the people of Jerusalem are like
      Gomorrah."

¹⁵ Therefore, this is what the LORD Almighty
says concerning the prophets:

"I will make them eat bitter food
   and drink poisoned water,
because from the prophets of Jerusalem
   ungodliness has spread throughout the
      land."

¹⁶ This is what the LORD Almighty says:

"Do not listen to what the prophets are
      prophesying to you;
   they fill you with false hopes.
They speak visions from their own minds,
   not from the mouth of the LORD.
¹⁷ They keep saying to those who despise me,
   'The LORD says: You will have peace.'
And to all who follow the stubbornness of
      their hearts
   they say, 'No harm will come to you.'
¹⁸ But which of them has stood in the council
      of the LORD
   to see or to hear his word?
   Who has listened and heard his word?
¹⁹ See, the storm of the LORD
   will burst out in wrath,
a whirlwind swirling down
   on the heads of the wicked.

THE MESSAGE

Prophets and priests devoted to desecration.
   They have nothing to do with me as their
      God.
My very own Temple, mind you—
   mud-spattered with their crimes." GOD's
      Decree.
"But they won't get by with it.
   They'll find themselves on a slippery slope,
Careening into the darkness,
   somersaulting into the pitch-black dark.
I'll make them pay for their crimes.
   It will be the Year of Doom." GOD's Decree.

23.13-14 "Over in Samaria I saw prophets
   acting like silly fools—shocking!
They preached using that no-god Baal for a
      text,
   messing with the minds of my people.
And the Jerusalem prophets are even worse—
      horrible!—
   sex-driven, living a lie,
Subsidizing a culture of wickedness,
   and never giving it a second thought.
They're as bad as those wretches in old
      Sodom,
   the degenerates of old Gomorrah."

23.15   So here's the Message to the prophets from
GOD-of-the-Angel-Armies:

"I'll cook them a supper of maggoty meat
   with after-dinner drinks of strychnine.
The Jerusalem prophets are behind all this.
   They're the cause of the godlessness
      polluting this country."

23.16-17 A Message from GOD-of-the-Angel-Armies:

"Don't listen to the sermons of the prophets.
   It's all hot air. Lies, lies, and more lies.
They make it all up.
   Not a word they speak comes from me.
They preach their 'Everything Will Turn Out
      Fine' sermon
   to congregations with no taste for God,
Their 'Nothing Bad Will Ever Happen to You'
      sermon
   to people who are set in their own ways.

23.18-20 "Have any of these prophets bothered to meet
      with me,
   the true GOD?
      bothered to take in what *I* have to say?
      listened to and then *lived out* my Word?
Look out! GOD's hurricane will be let loose—
   my hurricane blast,
Spinning the heads of the wicked like tops!

NEW INTERNATIONAL VERSION

²⁰ The anger of the LORD will not turn back
until he fully accomplishes
the purposes of his heart.
In days to come
you will understand it clearly.
²¹ I did not send these prophets,
yet they have run with their message;
I did not speak to them,
yet they have prophesied.
²² But if they had stood in my council,
they would have proclaimed my words to
my people
and would have turned them from their evil
ways
and from their evil deeds.

²³ "Am I only a God nearby,"
declares the LORD,
"and not a God far away?
²⁴ Can anyone hide in secret places
so that I cannot see him?"
declares the LORD.
"Do not I fill heaven and earth?"
declares the LORD.

²⁵ "I have heard what the prophets say who prophesy lies in my name. They say, 'I had a dream! I had a dream!' ²⁶ How long will this continue in the hearts of these lying prophets, who prophesy the delusions of their own minds? ²⁷ They think the dreams they tell one another will make my people forget my name, just as their fathers forgot my name through Baal worship. ²⁸ Let the prophet who has a dream tell his dream, but let the one who has my word speak it faithfully. For what has straw to do with grain?" declares the LORD. ²⁹ "Is not my word like fire," declares the LORD, "and like a hammer that breaks a rock in pieces?

³⁰ "Therefore," declares the LORD, "I am against the prophets who steal from one another words supposedly from me. ³¹ Yes," declares the LORD, "I am against the prophets who wag their own tongues and yet declare, 'The LORD de-

THE MESSAGE

God's raging anger won't let up
Until I've made a clean sweep,
completing the job I began.
When the job's done,
you'll see that it's been well done.

QUIT THE "GOD TOLD ME THIS" KIND OF TALK

23.21-22 "I never sent these prophets,
but they ran anyway.
I never spoke to them,
but they preached away.
If they'd have bothered to sit down and meet
with me,
they'd have preached my Message to my
people.
They'd have gotten them back on the right
track,
gotten them out of their evil ruts.

✝

23.23-24 "Am I not a God near at hand"—GOD's
Decree—
"and not a God far off?
Can anyone hide out in a corner
where I can't see him?"
GOD's Decree.
"Am I not present everywhere,
whether seen or unseen?"
GOD's Decree.

✝

23.25-27 "I know what they're saying, all these prophets who preach lies using me as their text, saying 'I had this dream! I had this dream!' How long do I have to put up with this? Do these prophets give two cents about me as they preach their lies and spew out their grandiose delusions? They swap dreams with one another, feed on each other's delusive dreams, trying to distract my people from me just as their ancestors were distracted by the no-god Baal.

23.28-29 "You prophets who do nothing but dream—
go ahead and tell your silly dreams.
But you prophets who have a message
from me—
tell it truly and faithfully.
What does straw have in common with
wheat?
Nothing else is like GOD's Decree.
Isn't my Message like fire?" GOD's Decree.
"Isn't it like a sledgehammer busting a
rock?

23.30-31 "I've had it with the 'prophets' who get all their sermons secondhand from each other. Yes, I've had it with them. They make up stuff and then pretend it's a real sermon.

NEW INTERNATIONAL VERSION

clares.' ³²Indeed, I am against those who prophesy false dreams," declares the LORD. "They tell them and lead my people astray with their reckless lies, yet I did not send or appoint them. They do not benefit these people in the least," declares the LORD.

FALSE ORACLES AND FALSE PROPHETS

³³"When these people, or a prophet or a priest, ask you, 'What is the oracle^a of the LORD?' say to them, 'What oracle?^b I will forsake you, declares the LORD.' ³⁴If a prophet or a priest or anyone else claims, 'This is the oracle of the LORD,' I will punish that man and his household. ³⁵This is what each of you keeps on saying to his friend or relative: 'What is the LORD's answer?' or 'What has the LORD spoken?' ³⁶But you must not mention 'the oracle of the LORD' again, because every man's own word becomes his oracle and so you distort the words of the living God, the LORD Almighty, our God. ³⁷This is what you keep saying to a prophet: 'What is the LORD's answer to you?' or 'What has the LORD spoken?' ³⁸Although you claim, 'This is the oracle of the LORD,' this is what the LORD says: You used the words, 'This is the oracle of the LORD,' even though I told you that you must not claim, 'This is the oracle of the LORD.' ³⁹Therefore, I will surely forget you and cast you out of my presence along with the city I gave to you and your fathers. ⁴⁰I will bring upon you everlasting disgrace—everlasting shame that will not be forgotten."

TWO BASKETS OF FIGS

24 After Jehoiachin^c son of Jehoiakim king of Judah and the officials, the craftsmen and the artisans of Judah were carried into exile from Jerusalem to Babylon by Nebuchadnezzar king of Babylon, the LORD showed me two baskets of figs placed in front of the temple of the LORD. ²One basket had very good figs, like those that ripen early; the other basket had very poor figs, so bad they could not be eaten.

³Then the LORD asked me, "What do you see, Jeremiah?"

"Figs," I answered. "The good ones are very good, but the poor ones are so bad they cannot be eaten."

^a 33 Or *burden* (see Septuagint and Vulgate)
^b 33 Hebrew; Septuagint and Vulgate *'You are the burden.*
(The Hebrew for *oracle* and *burden* is the same.)
^c 1 Hebrew *Jeconiah,* a variant of *Jehoiachin*

THE MESSAGE

23.32   "Oh yes, I've had it with the prophets who preach the lies they dream up, spreading them all over the country, ruining the lives of my people with their cheap and reckless lies.

   "I never sent these prophets, never authorized a single one of them. They do nothing for this people—*nothing!*" GOD's Decree.

23.33   "And anyone, including prophets and priests, who asks, 'What's GOD got to say about all this, what's troubling him?' tell him, 'You, you're the trouble, and I'm getting rid of you.' " GOD's Decree.

23.34   "And if anyone, including prophets and priests, goes around saying glibly 'GOD's Message! GOD's Message!' I'll punish him and his family.

23.35-36   "Instead of claiming to know what GOD says, ask questions of one another, such as 'How do we understand GOD in this?' But don't go around pretending to know it all, saying 'God told me this . . . God told me that. . . .' I don't want to hear it anymore. Only the person I authorize speaks for me. Otherwise, my Message gets twisted, the Message of the living GOD-of-the-Angel-Armies.

23.37-38   "You can ask the prophets, 'How did GOD answer you? What did he tell you?' But don't pretend that you know all the answers yourselves and talk like you know it all. I'm telling you: Quit the 'God told me this . . . God told me that . . .' kind of talk.

23.39-40   "Are you paying attention? You'd better, because I'm about to take you in hand and throw you to the ground, you and this entire city that I gave to your ancestors. I've had it with the lot of you. You're never going to live this down. You're going down in history as a disgrace."

TWO BASKETS OF FIGS

24.1-2 **24** GOD showed me two baskets of figs placed in front of the Temple of GOD. This was after Nebuchadnezzar king of Babylon had taken Jehoiachin son of Jehoiakim king of Judah from Jerusalem into exile in Babylon, along with the leaders of Judah, the craftsmen, and the skilled laborers. In one basket the figs were of the finest quality, ripe and ready to eat. In the other basket the figs were rotten, so rotten they couldn't be eaten.

24.3   GOD said to me, "Jeremiah, what do you see?"

   "Figs," I said. "Excellent figs of the finest quality, and also rotten figs, so rotten they can't be eaten."

NEW INTERNATIONAL VERSION

⁴Then the word of the LORD came to me: ⁵"This is what the LORD, the God of Israel, says: 'Like these good figs, I regard as good the exiles from Judah, whom I sent away from this place to the land of the Babylonians.ᵃ ⁶My eyes will watch over them for their good, and I will bring them back to this land. I will build them up and not tear them down; I will plant them and not uproot them. ⁷I will give them a heart to know me, that I am the LORD. They will be my people, and I will be their God, for they will return to me with all their heart.

⁸" 'But like the poor figs, which are so bad they cannot be eaten,' says the LORD, 'so will I deal with Zedekiah king of Judah, his officials and the survivors from Jerusalem, whether they remain in this land or live in Egypt. ⁹I will make them abhorrent and an offense to all the kingdoms of the earth, a reproach and a byword, an object of ridicule and cursing, wherever I banish them. ¹⁰I will send the sword, famine and plague against them until they are destroyed from the land I gave to them and their fathers.' "

SEVENTY YEARS OF CAPTIVITY

25 The word came to Jeremiah concerning all the people of Judah in the fourth year of Jehoiakim son of Josiah king of Judah, which was the first year of Nebuchadnezzar king of Babylon. ²So Jeremiah the prophet said to all the people of Judah and to all those living in Jerusalem: ³For twenty-three years—from the thirteenth year of Josiah son of Amon king of Judah until this very day—the word of the LORD has come to me and I have spoken to you again and again, but you have not listened.

⁴And though the LORD has sent all his servants the prophets to you again and again, you have not listened or paid any attention. ⁵They said, "Turn now, each of you, from your evil ways and your evil practices, and you can stay in the land the LORD gave to you and your fathers for ever and ever. ⁶Do not follow other gods to serve and worship them; do not provoke me to anger with what your hands have made. Then I will not harm you."

⁷"But you did not listen to me," declares the LORD, "and you have provoked me with what your hands have made, and you have brought harm to yourselves."

⁸Therefore the LORD Almighty says this: "Because you have not listened to my words, ⁹I will

ᵃ 5 Or Chaldeans

THE MESSAGE

24.4-6 Then GOD told me, "This is the Message from the GOD of Israel: The exiles from here that I've sent off to the land of the Babylonians are like the good figs, and I'll make sure they get good treatment. I'll keep my eye on them so that their lives are good, and I'll bring them back to this land. I'll build them up, not tear them down; I'll plant them, not uproot them.

24.7 "And I'll give them a heart to know me, GOD. They'll be my people and I'll be their God, for they'll have returned to me with all their hearts.

24.8-10 "But like the rotten figs, so rotten they can't be eaten, is Zedekiah king of Judah. Rotten figs—that's how I'll treat him and his leaders, along with the survivors here and those down in Egypt. I'll make them something that the whole world will look on as disgusting—repugnant outcasts, their names used as curse words wherever in the world I drive them. And I'll make sure they die like flies—from war, starvation, disease, whatever—until the land I once gave to them and their ancestors is completely rid of them."

DON'T FOLLOW THE GOD-FADS OF THE DAY

25.1 **25** This is the Message given to Jeremiah for all the people of Judah. It came in the fourth year of Jehoiakim son of Josiah king of Judah. It was the first year of Nebuchadnezzar king of Babylon.

25.2 Jeremiah the prophet delivered the Message to all the people of Judah and citizens of Jerusalem:

25.3 From the thirteenth year of Josiah son of Amon king of Judah right up to the present day—twenty-three years it's been!—GOD's Word has come to me, and from early each morning to late every night I've passed it on to you. And you haven't listened to a word of it!

25.4-6 Not only that, but GOD also sent a steady stream of prophets to you who were just as persistent as me, and you never listened. They told you, "Turn back—right now, each one of you!—from your evil way of life and bad behavior, and live in the land GOD gave you and your ancestors, the land he intended to give you forever. Don't follow the god-fads of the day, taking up and worshiping these no-gods. Don't make me angry with your god-business-es, making and selling gods—a dangerous business!

25.7 "You refused to listen to any of this, and now I am really angry. These god-making businesses of yours are your doom."

25.8-11 The verdict of GOD-of-the-Angel-Armies on all this: "Because you have refused to listen to

NEW INTERNATIONAL VERSION

summon all the peoples of the north and my servant Nebuchadnezzar king of Babylon," declares the LORD, "and I will bring them against this land and its inhabitants and against all the surrounding nations. I will completely destroy[a] them and make them an object of horror and scorn, and an everlasting ruin. [10]I will banish from them the sounds of joy and gladness, the voices of bride and bridegroom, the sound of millstones and the light of the lamp. [11]This whole country will become a desolate wasteland, and these nations will serve the king of Babylon seventy years.

[12]"But when the seventy years are fulfilled, I will punish the king of Babylon and his nation, the land of the Babylonians,[b] for their guilt," declares the LORD, "and will make it desolate forever. [13]I will bring upon that land all the things I have spoken against it, all that are written in this book and prophesied by Jeremiah against all the nations. [14]They themselves will be enslaved by many nations and great kings; I will repay them according to their deeds and the work of their hands."

THE CUP OF GOD'S WRATH

[15]This is what the LORD, the God of Israel, said to me: "Take from my hand this cup filled with the wine of my wrath and make all the nations to whom I send you drink it. [16]When they drink it, they will stagger and go mad because of the sword I will send among them."

[17]So I took the cup from the LORD's hand and made all the nations to whom he sent me drink it: [18]Jerusalem and the towns of Judah, its kings and officials, to make them a ruin and an object of horror and scorn and cursing, as they are today; [19]Pharaoh king of Egypt, his attendants, his officials and all his people, [20]and all the foreign people there; all the kings of Uz; all the kings of the Philistines (those of Ashkelon, Gaza, Ekron, and the people left at Ashdod); [21]Edom, Moab and Ammon; [22]all the kings of Tyre and Sidon; the kings of the coastlands across the sea; [23]Dedan, Tema, Buz and all who are in distant places[c]; [24]all the kings of Arabia and all the kings of the foreign people who live in the desert; [25]all the kings of Zimri, Elam and Media; [26]and all the kings of the north, near and far, one after the other—all the kingdoms on the face of the

THE MESSAGE

what I've said, I'm stepping in. I'm sending for the armies out of the north headed by Nebuchadnezzar king of Babylon, my servant in this, and I'm setting them on this land and people and even the surrounding countries. I'm devoting the whole works to total destruction—a horror to top all the horrors in history. And I'll banish every sound of joy—singing, laughter, marriage festivities, genial workmen, candlelit suppers. The whole landscape will be one vast wasteland. These countries will be in subjection to the king of Babylon for seventy years.

25.12-14 "Once the seventy years is up, I'll punish the king of Babylon and the whole nation of Babylon for their sin. Then *they'll* be the wasteland. Everything that I said I'd do to that country, I'll do—everything that's written in this book, everything Jeremiah preached against all the godless nations. Many nations and great kings will make slaves of the Babylonians, paying them back for everything they've done to others. They won't get by with anything." GOD's Decree.

GOD PUTS THE HUMAN RACE ON TRIAL

25.15-16 This is a Message that the GOD of Israel gave me: "Take this cup filled with the wine of my wrath that I'm handing to you. Make all the nations where I send you drink it down. They'll drink it and get drunk, staggering in delirium because of the killing that I'm going to unleash among them."

25.17-26 I took the cup from GOD's hand and made them drink it, all the nations to which he sent me:

Jerusalem and the towns of Judah, along with their kings and leaders, turning them into a vast wasteland, a horror to look at, a cussword—which, in fact, they now are;

Pharaoh king of Egypt with his attendants and leaders, plus all his people and the melting pot of foreigners collected there;

All the kings of Uz;

All the kings of the Philistines from Ashkelon, Gaza, Ekron, and what's left of Ashdod;

Edom, Moab, and the Ammonites;

All the kings of Tyre, Sidon, and the coastlands across the sea;

Dedan, Tema, Buz, and the nomads on the fringe of the desert;

All the kings of Arabia and the various Bedouin sheiks and chieftains wandering about in the desert;

All the kings of Zimri, Elam, and the Medes;

All the kings from the north countries near and far, one by one;

All the kingdoms on planet Earth . . .

---

[a] 9 The Hebrew term refers to the irrevocable giving over of things or persons to the LORD, often by totally destroying them.   [b] 12 Or *Chaldeans*   [c] 23 Or *who clip the hair by their foreheads*

NEW INTERNATIONAL VERSION

earth. And after all of them, the king of She-shach[a] will drink it too.

27 "Then tell them, 'This is what the LORD Almighty, the God of Israel, says: Drink, get drunk and vomit, and fall to rise no more because of the sword I will send among you.' 28 But if they refuse to take the cup from your hand and drink, tell them, 'This is what the LORD Almighty says: You must drink it! 29 See, I am beginning to bring disaster on the city that bears my Name, and will you indeed go unpunished? You will not go unpunished, for I am calling down a sword upon all who live on the earth, declares the LORD Almighty.'

30 "Now prophesy all these words against them and say to them:

" 'The LORD will roar from on high;
    he will thunder from his holy dwelling
    and roar mightily against his land.
He will shout like those who tread the
        grapes,
    shout against all who live on the earth.
31 The tumult will resound to the ends of the
        earth,
    for the LORD will bring charges against the
        nations;
he will bring judgment on all mankind
    and put the wicked to the sword,' "
                        declares the LORD.

32 This is what the LORD Almighty says:

"Look! Disaster is spreading
    from nation to nation;
a mighty storm is rising
    from the ends of the earth."

33 At that time those slain by the LORD will be everywhere—from one end of the earth to the other. They will not be mourned or gathered up or buried, but will be like refuse lying on the ground.

34 Weep and wail, you shepherds;
    roll in the dust, you leaders of the flock.
For your time to be slaughtered has come;
    you will fall and be shattered like fine
        pottery.
35 The shepherds will have nowhere to flee,
    the leaders of the flock no place to escape.
36 Hear the cry of the shepherds,
    the wailing of the leaders of the flock,

THE MESSAGE

And the king of Sheshak (that is, Babylon) will be the last to drink.

25.27 "Tell them, 'These are orders from GOD-of-the-Angel-Armies, the God of Israel: Drink and get drunk and vomit. Fall on your faces and don't get up again. You're slated for a massacre.'

25.28 "If any of them refuse to take the cup from you and drink it, say to them, 'GOD-of-the-Angel-Armies has ordered you to drink. So drink!

25.29 " 'Prepare for the worst! I'm starting off the catastrophe in the city that I claim as my own, so don't think you are going to get out of it. No, you're not getting out of anything. It's the sword and nothing but the sword against everyone everywhere!' " The GOD-of-the-Angel-Armies' Decree.

"Preach it all, Jeremiah. Preach the entire Message to them. Say:

25.30-31 " 'GOD roars like a lion from high heaven;
    thunder rolls out from his holy dwelling—
Ear-splitting bellows against his people,
    shouting hurrahs like workers in harvest.
The noise reverberates all over the earth;
    everyone everywhere hears it.
GOD makes his case against the godless
        nations.
He's about to put the human race on trial.
For the wicked the verdict is clear-cut:
    death by the sword.' " GOD's Decree.

                        ✠

25.32 A Message from GOD-of-the-Angel-Armies:

"Prepare for the worst! Doomsday!
    Disaster is spreading from nation to nation.
A huge storm is about to rage
    all across planet Earth."

                        ✠

25.33 Laid end to end, those killed in GOD's judgment that day will stretch from one end of the earth to the other. No tears will be shed and no burials conducted. The bodies will be left where they fall, like so much horse dung fertilizing the fields.

                        ✠

25.34-38 Wail, shepherds! Cry out for help!
    Grovel in the dirt, you masters of flocks!
Time's up—you're slated for the
        slaughterhouse,
    like a choice ram with its throat cut.
There's no way out for the rulers,
    no escape for those shepherds.
Hear that? Rulers crying for help,
    shepherds of the flock wailing!

---

a 26 Sheshach is a cryptogram for Babylon.

NEW INTERNATIONAL VERSION

for the LORD is destroying their pasture.
[37] The peaceful meadows will be laid waste
because of the fierce anger of the LORD.
[38] Like a lion he will leave his lair,
and their land will become desolate
because of the sword[a] of the oppressor
and because of the LORD's fierce anger.

JEREMIAH THREATENED WITH DEATH

26 Early in the reign of Jehoiakim son of Josiah king of Judah, this word came from the LORD: [2]"This is what the LORD says: Stand in the courtyard of the LORD's house and speak to all the people of the towns of Judah who come to worship in the house of the LORD. Tell them everything I command you; do not omit a word. [3]Perhaps they will listen and each will turn from his evil way. Then I will relent and not bring on them the disaster I was planning because of the evil they have done. [4]Say to them, 'This is what the LORD says: If you do not listen to me and follow my law, which I have set before you, [5]and if you do not listen to the words of my servants the prophets, whom I have sent to you again and again (though you have not listened), [6]then I will make this house like Shiloh and this city an object of cursing among all the nations of the earth.'"

[7]The priests, the prophets and all the people heard Jeremiah speak these words in the house of the LORD. [8]But as soon as Jeremiah finished telling all the people everything the LORD had commanded him to say, the priests, the prophets and all the people seized him and said, "You must die! [9]Why do you prophesy in the LORD's name that this house will be like Shiloh and this city will be desolate and deserted?" And all the people crowded around Jeremiah in the house of the LORD.

[10]When the officials of Judah heard about these things, they went up from the royal palace to the house of the LORD and took their places at the entrance of the New Gate of the LORD's house. [11]Then the priests and the prophets said to the officials and all the people, "This man should be sentenced to death because he has prophesied against this city. You have heard it with your own ears!"

[12]Then Jeremiah said to all the officials and all the people: "The LORD sent me to prophesy

THE MESSAGE

GOD is about to ravage their fine pastures.
The peaceful sheepfolds will be silent with
death,
silenced by GOD's deadly anger.
God will come out into the open
like a lion leaping from its cover,
And the country will be torn to pieces,
ripped and ravaged by his anger.

CHANGE THE WAY YOU'RE LIVING

26.1 **26** At the beginning of the reign of Jehoiakim son of Josiah king of Judah, this Message came from GOD to Jeremiah:

26.2-3 "GOD's Message: Stand in the court of GOD's Temple and preach to the people who come from all over Judah to worship in GOD's Temple. Say everything I tell you to say to them. Don't hold anything back. Just maybe they'll listen and turn back from their bad lives. Then I'll reconsider the disaster that I'm planning to bring on them because of their evil behavior.

26.4-6 "Say to them, 'This is GOD's Message: If you refuse to listen to me and live by my teaching that I've revealed so plainly to you, and if you continue to refuse to listen to my servants the prophets that I tirelessly keep on sending to you—but you've never listened! Why would you start now?—then I'll make this Temple a pile of ruins like Shiloh, and I'll make this city nothing but a bad joke worldwide.'"

26.7-9 Everybody there—priests, prophets, and people—heard Jeremiah preaching this Message in the Temple of GOD. When Jeremiah had finished his sermon, saying everything God had commanded him to say, the priests and prophets and people all grabbed him, yelling, "Death! You're going to die for this! How dare you preach—and using GOD's name!—saying that this Temple will become a heap of rubble like Shiloh and this city be wiped out without a soul left in it!"

All the people mobbed Jeremiah right in the Temple itself.

✝

26.10 Officials from the royal court of Judah were told of this. They left the palace immediately and came to GOD's Temple to investigate. They held court on the spot, at the New Gate entrance to GOD's Temple.

26.11 The prophets and priests spoke first, addressing the officials, but also the people: "Death to this man! He deserves nothing less than death! He has preached against this city—you've heard the evidence with your own ears."

26.12-13 Jeremiah spoke next, publicly addressing the officials before the crowd: "GOD sent me to

---

[a] 38 Some Hebrew manuscripts and Septuagint (see also Jer. 46:16 and 50:16); most Hebrew manuscripts *anger*

NEW INTERNATIONAL VERSION

against this house and this city all the things you have heard. ¹³Now reform your ways and your actions and obey the LORD your God. Then the LORD will relent and not bring the disaster he has pronounced against you. ¹⁴As for me, I am in your hands; do with me whatever you think is good and right. ¹⁵Be assured, however, that if you put me to death, you will bring the guilt of innocent blood on yourselves and on this city and on those who live in it, for in truth the LORD has sent me to you to speak all these words in your hearing."

¹⁶Then the officials and all the people said to the priests and the prophets, "This man should not be sentenced to death! He has spoken to us in the name of the LORD our God."

¹⁷Some of the elders of the land stepped forward and said to the entire assembly of people, ¹⁸"Micah of Moresheth prophesied in the days of Hezekiah king of Judah. He told all the people of Judah, 'This is what the LORD Almighty says:

" 'Zion will be plowed like a field,
    Jerusalem will become a heap of rubble,
      the temple hill a mound overgrown with
        thickets.'ᵃ

¹⁹"Did Hezekiah king of Judah or anyone else in Judah put him to death? Did not Hezekiah fear the LORD and seek his favor? And did not the LORD relent, so that he did not bring the disaster he pronounced against them? We are about to bring a terrible disaster on ourselves!"

²⁰(Now Uriah son of Shemaiah from Kiriath Jearim was another man who prophesied in the name of the LORD; he prophesied the same things against this city and this land as Jeremiah did. ²¹When King Jehoiakim and all his officers and officials heard his words, the king sought to put him to death. But Uriah heard of it and fled in fear to Egypt. ²²King Jehoiakim, however, sent Elnathan son of Acbor to Egypt, along with some other men. ²³They brought Uriah out of Egypt and took him to King Jehoiakim, who had him struck down with a sword and his body thrown into the burial place of the common people.)

²⁴Furthermore, Ahikam son of Shaphan supported Jeremiah, and so he was not handed over to the people to be put to death.

ᵃ *18* Micah 3:12

THE MESSAGE

preach against both this Temple and city everything that's been reported to you. So do something about it! Change the way you're living, change your behavior. Listen obediently to the Message of your GOD. Maybe GOD will reconsider the disaster he has threatened.

26.14-15   "As for me, I'm at your mercy—do whatever you think is best. But take warning: If you kill me, you're killing an innocent man, and you and the city and the people in it will be liable. I didn't say any of this on my own. GOD sent me and told me what to say. You've been listening to GOD speak, not Jeremiah."

26.16   The court officials, backed by the people, then handed down their ruling to the priests and prophets: "Acquittal. No death sentence for this man. He has spoken to us with the authority of our GOD."

26.17-18   Then some of the respected leaders stood up and addressed the crowd: "In the reign of Hezekiah king of Judah, Micah of Moresheth preached to the people of Judah this sermon: This is GOD-of-the-Angel-Armies' Message for you:

" 'Because of people like you,
    Zion will be turned back into farmland,
Jerusalem end up as a pile of rubble,
    and instead of the Temple on the mountain,
    a few scraggly scrub pines.'

26.19   "Did King Hezekiah or anyone else in Judah kill Micah of Moresheth because of that sermon? Didn't Hezekiah honor him and pray for mercy from GOD? And then didn't GOD call off the disaster he had threatened?

"Friends, we're at the brink of bringing a terrible calamity upon ourselves."

☩

26.20-23   (At another time there had been a man, Uriah son of Shemaiah from Kiriath-jearim, who had preached similarly in the name of GOD. He preached against this same city and country just as Jeremiah did. When King Jehoiakim and his royal court heard his sermon, they determined to kill him. Uriah, afraid for his life, went into hiding in Egypt. King Jehoiakim sent Elnathan son of Achbor with a posse of men after him. They brought him back from Egypt and presented him to the king. And the king had him killed. They dumped his body unceremoniously outside the city.

26.24   But in Jeremiah's case, Ahikam son of Shaphan stepped forward and took his side, preventing the mob from lynching him.)

NEW INTERNATIONAL VERSION

JUDAH TO SERVE NEBUCHADNEZZAR

27 Early in the reign of Zedekiah[a] son of Josiah king of Judah, this word came to Jeremiah from the LORD: [2]This is what the LORD said to me: "Make a yoke out of straps and crossbars and put it on your neck. [3]Then send word to the kings of Edom, Moab, Ammon, Tyre and Sidon through the envoys who have come to Jerusalem to Zedekiah king of Judah. [4]Give them a message for their masters and say, 'This is what the LORD Almighty, the God of Israel, says: "Tell this to your masters: [5]With my great power and outstretched arm I made the earth and its people and the animals that are on it, and I give it to anyone I please. [6]Now I will hand all your countries over to my servant Nebuchadnezzar king of Babylon; I will make even the wild animals subject to him. [7]All nations will serve him and his son and his grandson until the time for his land comes; then many nations and great kings will subjugate him.

[8]" ' "If, however, any nation or kingdom will not serve Nebuchadnezzar king of Babylon or bow its neck under his yoke, I will punish that nation with the sword, famine and plague, declares the LORD, until I destroy it by his hand. [9]So do not listen to your prophets, your diviners, your interpreters of dreams, your mediums or your sorcerers who tell you, 'You will not serve the king of Babylon.' [10]They prophesy lies to you that will only serve to remove you far from your lands; I will banish you and you will perish. [11]But if any nation will bow its neck under the yoke of the king of Babylon and serve him, I will let that nation remain in its own land to till it and to live there, declares the LORD." ' "

[12]I gave the same message to Zedekiah king of Judah. I said, "Bow your neck under the yoke of the king of Babylon; serve him and his people, and you will live. [13]Why will you and your people die by the sword, famine and plague with which the LORD has threatened any nation that will not serve the king of Babylon? [14]Do not listen to the words of the prophets who say to you, 'You will not serve the king of Babylon,' for they are prophesying lies to you. [15]I have not sent them,' declares the LORD. 'They are prophesying lies in my name. Therefore, I will banish you and you will perish, both you and the prophets who prophesy to you.' "

[16]Then I said to the priests and all these people, "This is what the LORD says: Do not listen to

THE MESSAGE

HARNESS YOURSELVES UP TO THE YOKE

27.1-4 **27** Early in the reign of Zedekiah son of Josiah king of Judah, Jeremiah received this Message from GOD: "Make a harness and a yoke and then harness yourself up. Send a message to the kings of Edom, Moab, Ammon, Tyre, and Sidon. Send it through their ambassadors who have come to Jerusalem to see Zedekiah king of Judah. Give them this charge to take back to their masters: 'This is a Message from GOD-of-the-Angel-Armies, the God of Israel. Tell your masters:

27.5-8 " 'I'm the one who made the earth, man and woman, and all the animals in the world. I did it on my own without asking anyone's help and I hand it out to whomever I will. Here and now I give all these lands over to my servant Nebuchadnezzar king of Babylon. I have made even the wild animals subject to him. All nations will be under him, then his son, and then his grandson. Then his country's time will be up and the tables will be turned: *Babylon* will be the underdog servant. But until then, any nation or kingdom that won't submit to Nebuchadnezzar king of Babylon must take the yoke of the king of Babylon and harness up. I'll punish that nation with war and starvation and disease until I've got them where I want them.

27.9-11 " 'So don't for a minute listen to all your prophets and spiritualists and fortunetellers, who claim to know the future and who tell you not to give in to the king of Babylon. They're handing you a line of lies, barefaced lies, that will end up putting you in exile far from home. I myself will drive you out of your lands, and that'll be the end of you. But the nation that accepts the yoke of the king of Babylon and does what he says, I'll let that nation stay right where it is, minding its own business.' "

27.12-15 Then I gave this same message to Zedekiah king of Judah: "Harness yourself up to the yoke of the king of Babylon. Serve him and his people. Live a long life! Why choose to get killed or starve to death or get sick and die, which is what GOD has threatened to any nation that won't throw its lot in with Babylon? Don't listen to the prophets who are telling you not to submit to the king of Babylon. They're telling you lies, *preaching* lies. GOD's Word on this is, 'I didn't send those prophets, but they keep preaching lies, claiming I sent them. If you listen to them, I'll end up driving you out of here and that will be the end of you, both you and the lying prophets.' "

27.16-22 And finally I spoke to the priests and the people at large: "This is GOD's Message: Don't listen to the preaching of the prophets who

NEW INTERNATIONAL VERSION

the prophets who say, 'Very soon now the articles from the LORD's house will be brought back from Babylon.' They are prophesying lies to you. ¹⁷Do not listen to them. Serve the king of Babylon, and you will live. Why should this city become a ruin? ¹⁸If they are prophets and have the word of the LORD, let them plead with the LORD Almighty that the furnishings remaining in the house of the LORD and in the palace of the king of Judah and in Jerusalem not be taken to Babylon. ¹⁹For this is what the LORD Almighty says about the pillars, the Sea, the movable stands and the other furnishings that are left in this city, ²⁰which Nebuchadnezzar king of Babylon did not take away when he carried Jehoiachin*a* son of Jehoiakim king of Judah into exile from Jerusalem to Babylon, along with all the nobles of Judah and Jerusalem— ²¹yes, this is what the LORD Almighty, the God of Israel, says about the things that are left in the house of the LORD and in the palace of the king of Judah and in Jerusalem: ²²'They will be taken to Babylon and there they will remain until the day I come for them,' declares the LORD. 'Then I will bring them back and restore them to this place.' "

THE FALSE PROPHET HANANIAH

28 In the fifth month of that same year, the fourth year, early in the reign of Zedekiah king of Judah, the prophet Hananiah son of Azzur, who was from Gibeon, said to me in the house of the LORD in the presence of the priests and all the people: ²"This is what the LORD Almighty, the God of Israel, says: 'I will break the yoke of the king of Babylon. ³Within two years I will bring back to this place all the articles of the LORD's house that Nebuchadnezzar king of Babylon removed from here and took to Babylon. ⁴I will also bring back to this place Jehoiachin*a* son of Jehoiakim king of Judah and all the other exiles from Judah who went to Babylon,' declares the LORD, 'for I will break the yoke of the king of Babylon.' "

⁵Then the prophet Jeremiah replied to the prophet Hananiah before the priests and all the people who were standing in the house of the LORD. ⁶He said, "Amen! May the LORD do so! May the LORD fulfill the words you have prophesied by bringing the articles of the LORD's house and all the exiles back to this place from Babylon. ⁷Nevertheless, listen to what I have to say in your hearing and in the hearing of all the people: ⁸From early times the prophets who preceded you and me have prophesied war, disaster and plague against many countries and great king-

THE MESSAGE

keep telling you, 'Trust us: The furnishings, plundered from GOD's Temple, are going to be returned from Babylon any day now.' That's a lie. Don't listen to them. Submit to the king of Babylon and live a long life. Why do something that will destroy this city and leave it a heap of rubble? If they are real prophets and have a Message from GOD, let them come to GOD-of-the-Angel-Armies in prayer so that the furnishings that are still left in GOD's Temple, the king's palace, and Jerusalem aren't also lost to Babylon. That's because GOD-of-the-Angel-Armies has already spoken about the Temple furnishings that remain—the pillars, the great bronze basin, the stands, and all the other bowls and chalices that Nebuchadnezzar king of Babylon didn't take when he took Jehoiachin son of Jehoiakim off to Babylonian exile along with all the leaders of Judah and Jerusalem. He said that the furnishings left behind in the Temple of GOD and in the royal palace and in Jerusalem will be taken off to Babylon and stay there until, in GOD's words, 'I take the matter up again and bring them back where they belong.' "

FROM A WOODEN TO AN IRON YOKE

28 Later that same year (it was in the fifth month of King Zedekiah's fourth year) Hananiah son of Azzur, a prophet from Gibeon, confronted Jeremiah in the Temple of GOD in front of the priests and all the people who were there. Hananiah said:

"This Message is straight from GOD-of-the-Angel-Armies, the God of Israel: 'I will most certainly break the yoke of the king of Babylon. Before two years are out I'll have all the furnishings of GOD's Temple back here, all the things that Nebuchadnezzar king of Babylon plundered and hauled off to Babylon. I'll also bring back Jehoiachin son of Jehoiakim king of Judah and all the exiles who were taken off to Babylon.' GOD's Decree. 'Yes, I will break the king of Babylon's yoke. You'll no longer be in harness to him.' "

Prophet Jeremiah stood up to Prophet Hananiah in front of the priests and all the people who were in GOD's Temple that day. Prophet Jeremiah said, "Wonderful! Would that it were true—that GOD would validate your preaching by bringing the Temple furnishings and all the exiles back from Babylon. But listen to me, listen closely. Listen to what I tell both you and all the people here today: The old prophets, the ones before our time, preached judgment against many countries and kingdoms, warning of war and disaster and plague. So any prophet

a 20,4 Hebrew *Jeconiah,* a variant of *Jehoiachin*

NEW INTERNATIONAL VERSION

doms. ⁹But the prophet who prophesies peace will be recognized as one truly sent by the LORD only if his prediction comes true."

¹⁰Then the prophet Hananiah took the yoke off the neck of the prophet Jeremiah and broke it, ¹¹and he said before all the people, "This is what the LORD says: 'In the same way will I break the yoke of Nebuchadnezzar king of Babylon off the neck of all the nations within two years.' " At this, the prophet Jeremiah went on his way.

¹²Shortly after the prophet Hananiah had broken the yoke off the neck of the prophet Jeremiah, the word of the LORD came to Jeremiah: ¹³"Go and tell Hananiah, 'This is what the LORD says: You have broken a wooden yoke, but in its place you will get a yoke of iron. ¹⁴This is what the LORD Almighty, the God of Israel, says: I will put an iron yoke on the necks of all these nations to make them serve Nebuchadnezzar king of Babylon, and they will serve him. I will even give him control over the wild animals.' "

¹⁵Then the prophet Jeremiah said to Hananiah the prophet, "Listen, Hananiah! The LORD has not sent you, yet you have persuaded this nation to trust in lies. ¹⁶Therefore, this is what the LORD says: 'I am about to remove you from the face of the earth. This very year you are going to die, because you have preached rebellion against the LORD.' "

¹⁷In the seventh month of that same year, Hananiah the prophet died.

A LETTER TO THE EXILES

29 This is the text of the letter that the prophet Jeremiah sent from Jerusalem to the surviving elders among the exiles and to the priests, the prophets and all the other people Nebuchadnezzar had carried into exile from Jerusalem to Babylon. ²(This was after King Jehoiachin*ᵃ* and the queen mother, the court officials and the leaders of Judah and Jerusalem, the craftsmen and the artisans had gone into exile from Jerusalem.) ³He entrusted the letter to Elasah son of Shaphan and to Gemariah son of Hilkiah, whom Zedekiah king of Judah sent to King Nebuchadnezzar in Babylon. It said:

⁴This is what the LORD Almighty, the God of Israel, says to all those I carried into exile from Jerusalem to Babylon: ⁵"Build houses and settle down; plant gardens and eat what they produce. ⁶Marry and have sons and daughters; find wives for your

---

THE MESSAGE

who preaches that everything is just fine and there's nothing to worry about stands out like a sore thumb. We'll wait and see. If it happens, it happens—and then we'll know that GOD sent him."

28.10-11 At that, Hananiah grabbed the yoke from Jeremiah's shoulders and smashed it. And then he addressed the people: "This is GOD's Message: In just this way I will smash the yoke of the king of Babylon and get him off the neck of all the nations—and within two years."

Jeremiah walked out.

28.12-14 Later, sometime after Hananiah had smashed the yoke from off his shoulders, Jeremiah received this Message from GOD: "Go back to Hananiah and tell him, 'This is GOD's Message: You smashed the wooden yoke-bars; now you've got iron yoke-bars. This is a Message from GOD-of-the-Angel-Armies, Israel's own God: I've put an iron yoke on all these nations. They're harnessed to Nebuchadnezzar king of Babylon. They'll do just what he tells them. Why, I'm even putting him in charge of the wild animals.' "

28.15-16 So prophet Jeremiah told prophet Hananiah, "Hold it, Hananiah! GOD never sent you. You've talked the whole country into believing a pack of lies! And so GOD says, 'You claim to be sent? I'll send you all right—right off the face of the earth! Before the year is out, you'll be dead because you fomented sedition against GOD.' "

28.17 Prophet Hananiah died that very year, in the seventh month.

PLANS TO GIVE YOU THE FUTURE YOU HOPE FOR

29.1-2 **29** This is the letter that the prophet Jeremiah sent from Jerusalem to what was left of the elders among the exiles, to the priests and prophets and all the exiles whom Nebuchadnezzar had taken to Babylon from Jerusalem, including King Jehoiachin, the queen mother, the government leaders, and all the skilled laborers and craftsmen.

29.3 The letter was carried by Elasah son of Shaphan and Gemariah son of Hilkiah, whom Zedekiah king of Judah had sent to Nebuchadnezzar king of Babylon. The letter said:

29.4 This is the Message from GOD-of-the-Angel-Armies, Israel's God, to all the exiles I've taken from Jerusalem to Babylon:

29.5 "Build houses and make yourselves at home.

"Put in gardens and eat what grows in that country.

29.6 "Marry and have children. Encourage your children to marry and have children so

NEW INTERNATIONAL VERSION

sons and give your daughters in marriage, so that they too may have sons and daughters. Increase in number there; do not decrease. ⁷Also, seek the peace and prosperity of the city to which I have carried you into exile. Pray to the LORD for it, because if it prospers, you too will prosper." ⁸Yes, this is what the LORD Almighty, the God of Israel, says: "Do not let the prophets and diviners among you deceive you. Do not listen to the dreams you encourage them to have. ⁹They are prophesying lies to you in my name. I have not sent them," declares the LORD.

¹⁰This is what the LORD says: "When seventy years are completed for Babylon, I will come to you and fulfill my gracious promise to bring you back to this place. ¹¹For I know the plans I have for you," declares the LORD, "plans to prosper you and not to harm you, plans to give you hope and a future. ¹²Then you will call upon me and come and pray to me, and I will listen to you. ¹³You will seek me and find me when you seek me with all your heart. ¹⁴I will be found by you," declares the LORD, "and will bring you back from captivity.ᵃ I will gather you from all the nations and places where I have banished you," declares the LORD, "and will bring you back to the place from which I carried you into exile."

¹⁵You may say, "The LORD has raised up prophets for us in Babylon," ¹⁶but this is what the LORD says about the king who sits on David's throne and all the people who remain in this city, your countrymen who did not go with you into exile— ¹⁷yes, this is what the LORD Almighty says: "I will send the sword, famine and plague against them and I will make them like poor figs that are so bad they cannot be eaten. ¹⁸I will pursue them with the sword, famine and plague and will make them abhorrent to all the kingdoms of the earth and an object of cursing and horror, of scorn and reproach, among all the nations where I drive them. ¹⁹For they have not listened to my words," declares the LORD, "words that I sent to them again and again by my servants the prophets. And you exiles have not listened either," declares the LORD.

THE MESSAGE

that you'll thrive in that country and not waste away.

29.7   "Make yourselves at home there and work for the country's welfare.

"Pray for Babylon's well-being. If things go well for Babylon, things will go well for you."

29.8-9   Yes. Believe it or not, this is the Message from GOD-of-the-Angel-Armies, Israel's God: "Don't let all those so-called preachers and know-it-alls who are all over the place there take you in with their lies. Don't pay any attention to the fantasies they keep coming up with to please you. They're a bunch of liars preaching lies—and claiming I sent them! I never sent them, believe me." GOD's Decree!

29.10-11   This is GOD's Word on the subject: "As soon as Babylon's seventy years are up and not a day before, I'll show up and take care of you as I promised and bring you back home. I know what I'm doing. I have it all planned out—plans to take care of you, not abandon you, plans to give you the future you hope for.

29.12   "When you call on me, when you come and pray to me, I'll listen.

29.13-14   "When you come looking for me, you'll find me.

"Yes, when you get serious about finding me and want it more than anything else, I'll make sure you won't be disappointed." GOD's Decree.

29.14   "I'll turn things around for you. I'll bring you back from all the countries into which I drove you"—GOD's Decree—"bring you home to the place from which I sent you off into exile. You can count on it.

29.15-19   "But for right now, because you've taken up with these newfangled prophets who set themselves up as 'Babylonian specialists,' spreading the word 'GOD sent them just for us!' GOD is setting the record straight: As for the king still sitting on David's throne and all the people left in Jerusalem who didn't go into exile with you, they're facing bad times. GOD-of-the-Angel-Armies says, 'Watch this! Catastrophe is on the way: war, hunger, disease! They're a barrel of rotten apples. I'll rid the country of them through war and hunger and disease. The whole world is going to hold its nose at the smell, shut its eyes at the horrible sight. They'll end up in slum ghettos because they wouldn't listen to a thing I said when I sent my servant-prophets preaching tirelessly and urgently. No, they wouldn't listen to a word I said.' " GOD's Decree.

ᵃ 14 Or will restore your fortunes

NEW INTERNATIONAL VERSION

²⁰Therefore, hear the word of the LORD, all you exiles whom I have sent away from Jerusalem to Babylon. ²¹This is what the LORD Almighty, the God of Israel, says about Ahab son of Kolaiah and Zedekiah son of Maaseiah, who are prophesying lies to you in my name: "I will hand them over to Nebuchadnezzar king of Babylon, and he will put them to death before your very eyes. ²²Because of them, all the exiles from Judah who are in Babylon will use this curse: 'The LORD treat you like Zedekiah and Ahab, whom the king of Babylon burned in the fire.' ²³For they have done outrageous things in Israel; they have committed adultery with their neighbors' wives and in my name have spoken lies, which I did not tell them to do. I know it and am a witness to it," declares the LORD.

MESSAGE TO SHEMAIAH

²⁴Tell Shemaiah the Nehelamite, ²⁵"This is what the LORD Almighty, the God of Israel, says: You sent letters in your own name to all the people in Jerusalem, to Zephaniah son of Maaseiah the priest, and to all the other priests. You said to Zephaniah, ²⁶'The LORD has appointed you priest in place of Jehoiada to be in charge of the house of the LORD; you should put any madman who acts like a prophet into the stocks and neck-irons. ²⁷So why have you not reprimanded Jeremiah from Anathoth, who poses as a prophet among you? ²⁸He has sent this message to us in Babylon: It will be a long time. Therefore build houses and settle down; plant gardens and eat what they produce.' "

²⁹Zephaniah the priest, however, read the letter to Jeremiah the prophet. ³⁰Then the word of the LORD came to Jeremiah: ³¹"Send this message to all the exiles: 'This is what the LORD says about Shemaiah the Nehelamite: Because Shemaiah has prophesied to you, even though I did not send him, and has led you to believe a lie, ³²this is what the LORD says: I will surely punish Shemaiah the Nehelamite and his descendants. He will have no one left among this people, nor will he see the good things I will do for my people, declares the LORD, because he has preached rebellion against me.' "

THE MESSAGE

29.20-23   "And you—you exiles whom I sent out of Jerusalem to Babylon—listen to GOD's Message to you. As far as Ahab son of Kolaiah and Zedekiah son of Maaseiah are concerned, the 'Babylonian specialists' who are preaching lies in my name, I will turn them over to Nebuchadnezzar king of Babylon, who will kill them while you watch. The exiles from Judah will take what they see at the execution and use it as a curse: 'GOD fry you to a crisp like the king of Babylon fried Zedekiah and Ahab in the fire!' Those two men, sex predators and prophet-impostors, got what they deserved. They pulled every woman they got their hands on into bed—their neighbors' wives, no less—and preached lies claiming it was my Message. I never sent those men. I've never had anything to do with them." GOD's Decree.

"They won't get away with a thing. I've witnessed it all."

29.24-26   And this is the Message for Shemaiah the Nehelamite: "GOD-of-the-Angel-Armies, the God of Israel, says: You took it on yourself to send letters to all the people in Jerusalem and to the priest Zephaniah son of Maaseiah and the company of priests. In your letter you told Zephaniah that GOD set you up as priest replacing priest Jehoiadah. He's put you in charge of GOD's Temple and made you responsible for locking up any crazy fellow off the street who takes it into his head to be a prophet.

29.27-28   "So why haven't you done anything about muzzling Jeremiah of Anathoth, who's going around posing as a prophet? He's gone so far as to write to us in Babylon, 'It's going to be a long exile, so build houses and make yourselves at home. Plant gardens and prepare Babylonian recipes.' "

29.29   The priest Zephaniah read that letter to the prophet Jeremiah.

✝

29.30-32   Then GOD told Jeremiah, "Send this Message to the exiles. Tell them what GOD says about Shemaiah the Nehelamite: Shemaiah is preaching lies to you. I didn't send him. He is seducing you into believing lies. So this is GOD's verdict: I will punish Shemaiah the Nehelamite and his whole family. He's going to end up with nothing and no one. No one from his family will be around to see any of the good that I am going to do for my people because he has preached rebellion against me." GOD's Decree.

NEW INTERNATIONAL VERSION

RESTORATION OF ISRAEL

30 This is the word that came to Jeremiah from the LORD: ²"This is what the LORD, the God of Israel, says: 'Write in a book all the words I have spoken to you. ³The days are coming,' declares the LORD, 'when I will bring my people Israel and Judah back from captivity ᵃ and restore them to the land I gave their forefathers to possess,' says the LORD."

⁴These are the words the LORD spoke concerning Israel and Judah: ⁵"This is what the LORD says:

" 'Cries of fear are heard—
    terror, not peace.
⁶Ask and see:
    Can a man bear children?
Then why do I see every strong man
    with his hands on his stomach like a
        woman in labor,
    every face turned deathly pale?
⁷How awful that day will be!
    None will be like it.
It will be a time of trouble for Jacob,
    but he will be saved out of it.

⁸" 'In that day,' declares the LORD Almighty,
    'I will break the yoke off their necks
and will tear off their bonds;
    no longer will foreigners enslave them.
⁹Instead, they will serve the LORD their God
    and David their king,
    whom I will raise up for them.

¹⁰" 'So do not fear, O Jacob my servant;
    do not be dismayed, O Israel,'
                    declares the LORD.
'I will surely save you out of a distant place,
    your descendants from the land of their
        exile.
Jacob will again have peace and security,
    and no one will make him afraid.
¹¹I am with you and will save you,'
    declares the LORD.
'Though I completely destroy all the nations
    among which I scatter you,
    I will not completely destroy you.
I will discipline you but only with justice;
    I will not let you go entirely unpunished.'

¹²"This is what the LORD says:

" 'Your wound is incurable,
    your injury beyond healing.
¹³There is no one to plead your cause,
    no remedy for your sore,
    no healing for you.
¹⁴All your allies have forgotten you;

ᵃ 3 Or will restore the fortunes of my people Israel and Judah

THE MESSAGE

DON'T DESPAIR, ISRAEL

30.1-2 **30** This is the Message Jeremiah received from GOD: "GOD's Message, the God of Israel: 'Write everything I tell you in a book.

30.3 " 'Look. The time is coming when I will turn everything around for my people, both Israel and Judah. I, GOD, say so. I'll bring them back to the land I gave their ancestors, and they'll take up ownership again.' "

30.4 This is the way GOD put it to Israel and Judah:

30.5-7 "GOD's Message:

" 'Cries of panic are being heard.
    The peace has been shattered.
Ask around! Look around!
    Can men bear babies?
So why do I see all these he-men
    holding their bellies like women in labor,
Faces contorted,
    pale as death?
The blackest of days,
    no day like it ever!
A time of deep trouble for Jacob—
    but he'll come out of it alive.

30.8-9 " 'And then I'll enter the darkness.
    I'll break the yoke from their necks,
Cut them loose from the harness.
    No more slave labor to foreigners!
They'll serve their GOD
    and the David-King I'll establish for them.

30.10-11 " 'So fear no more, Jacob, dear servant.
    Don't despair, Israel.
Look up! I'll save you out of faraway places,
    I'll bring your children back from exile.
Jacob will come back and find life good,
    safe and secure.
I'll be with you. I'll save you.
    I'll finish off all the godless nations
Among which I've scattered you,
    but I won't finish you off.
I'll punish you, but fairly.
    I won't send you off with just a slap on the
        wrist.'

30.12-15 "This is GOD's Message:

" 'You're a burned-out case,
    as good as dead.
Everyone has given up on you.
    You're hopeless.
All your fair-weather friends have skipped
        town

NEW INTERNATIONAL VERSION

they care nothing for you.
I have struck you as an enemy would
and punished you as would the cruel,
because your guilt is so great
and your sins so many.
¹⁵ Why do you cry out over your wound,
your pain that has no cure?
Because of your great guilt and many sins
I have done these things to you.

¹⁶ " 'But all who devour you will be devoured;
all your enemies will go into exile.
Those who plunder you will be plundered;
all who make spoil of you I will despoil.
¹⁷ But I will restore you to health
and heal your wounds,'
declares the LORD,
'because you are called an outcast,
Zion for whom no one cares.'

¹⁸ "This is what the LORD says:

" 'I will restore the fortunes of Jacob's tents
and have compassion on his dwellings;
the city will be rebuilt on her ruins,
and the palace will stand in its proper
place.
¹⁹ From them will come songs of thanksgiving
and the sound of rejoicing.
I will add to their numbers,
and they will not be decreased;
I will bring them honor,
and they will not be disdained.
²⁰ Their children will be as in days of old,
and their community will be established
before me;
I will punish all who oppress them.
²¹ Their leader will be one of their own;
their ruler will arise from among them.
I will bring him near and he will come close
to me,
for who is he who will devote himself
to be close to me?'
declares the LORD.
²² " 'So you will be my people,
and I will be your God.' "

²³ See, the storm of the LORD
will burst out in wrath,
a driving wind swirling down
on the heads of the wicked.
²⁴ The fierce anger of the LORD will not turn
back
until he fully accomplishes
the purposes of his heart.
In days to come
you will understand this.

THE MESSAGE

without giving you a second thought.
But I delivered the knockout blow,
a punishment you will never forget,
Because of the enormity of your guilt,
the endless list of your sins.
So why all this self-pity, licking your wounds?
You deserve all this, and more.
Because of the enormity of your guilt,
the endless list of your sins,
I've done all this to you.

30.16-17 " 'Everyone who hurt you will be hurt;
your enemies will end up as slaves.
Your plunderers will be plundered;
your looters will become loot.
As for you, I'll come with healing,
curing the incurable,
Because they all gave up on you
and dismissed you as hopeless—
that good-for-nothing Zion.'

30.18-21 "Again, GOD's Message:

" 'I'll turn things around for Jacob.
I'll compassionately come in and rebuild
homes.
The town will be rebuilt on its old foundations;
the mansions will be splendid again.
Thanksgivings will pour out of the windows;
laughter will spill through the doors.
Things will get better and better.
Depression days are over.
They'll thrive, they'll flourish.
The days of contempt will be over.
They'll look forward to having children again,
to being a community in which I take pride.
I'll punish anyone who hurts them,
and their prince will come from their own
ranks.
One of their own people shall be their leader.
Their ruler will come from their own ranks.
I'll grant him free and easy access to me.
Would anyone dare to do that on his own,
to enter my presence uninvited?' GOD's
Decree.

30.22 " 'And that's it: You'll be my very own people,
I'll be your very own God.' "

30.23-24 Look out! GOD's hurricane is let loose,
his hurricane blast,
Spinning the heads of the wicked like dust
devils!
God's raging anger won't let up
Until he's made a clean sweep
completing the job he began.
When the job's done
you'll see it's been well done.

⊹

NEW INTERNATIONAL VERSION

31 "At that time," declares the LORD, "I will be the God of all the clans of Israel, and they will be my people."

² This is what the LORD says:

"The people who survive the sword
    will find favor in the desert;
    I will come to give rest to Israel."

³ The LORD appeared to us in the past,[a] saying:

"I have loved you with an everlasting love;
    I have drawn you with loving-kindness.
⁴ I will build you up again
    and you will be rebuilt, O Virgin Israel.
Again you will take up your tambourines
    and go out to dance with the joyful.
⁵ Again you will plant vineyards
    on the hills of Samaria;
the farmers will plant them
    and enjoy their fruit.
⁶ There will be a day when watchmen cry out
    on the hills of Ephraim,
'Come, let us go up to Zion,
    to the LORD our God.' "

⁷ This is what the LORD says:

"Sing with joy for Jacob;
    shout for the foremost of the nations.
Make your praises heard, and say,
    'O LORD, save your people,
    the remnant of Israel.'
⁸ See, I will bring them from the land of the
        north
    and gather them from the ends of the
        earth.
Among them will be the blind and the lame,
    expectant mothers and women in labor;
    a great throng will return.

THE MESSAGE

31 "And when that happens"—GOD's
    Decree—
"it will be plain as the sun at high noon:
I'll be the God of every man, woman, and
        child in Israel
    and they shall be my very own people."

✝

³¹·²⁻⁶ This is the way GOD put it:

"They found grace out in the desert,
    these people who survived the killing.
Israel, out looking for a place to rest,
    met God out looking for them!"
GOD told them, "I've never quit loving you
        and never will.
    Expect love, love, and more love!
And so now I'll start over with you and build
        you up again,
    dear virgin Israel.
You'll resume your singing,
    grabbing tambourines and joining the
        dance.
You'll go back to your old work of planting
        vineyards
    on the Samaritan hillsides,
And sit back and enjoy the fruit—
    oh, how you'll enjoy those harvests!
The time's coming when watchmen will call
        out
    from the hilltops of Ephraim:
'On your feet! Let's go to Zion,
    go to meet our GOD!' "

✝

³¹·⁷ Oh yes, GOD says so:

"Shout for joy at the top of your lungs for
        Jacob!
    Announce the good news to the number-
        one nation!
Raise cheers! Sing praises. Say,
    'GOD has saved his people,
    saved the core of Israel.'

"Watch what comes next:

³¹·⁸ "I'll bring my people back
    from the north country
And gather them up from the ends of the
        earth,
    gather those who've gone blind
And those who are lame and limping,
    gather pregnant women,
Even the mothers whose birth pangs have
        started,
    bring them all back, a huge crowd!

---

[a] 3 Or LORD *has appeared to us from afar*

NEW INTERNATIONAL VERSION

⁹They will come with weeping;
  they will pray as I bring them back.
I will lead them beside streams of water
  on a level path where they will not
    stumble,
because I am Israel's father,
  and Ephraim is my firstborn son.

¹⁰"Hear the word of the LORD, O nations;
  proclaim it in distant coastlands:
'He who scattered Israel will gather them
  and will watch over his flock like a
    shepherd.'
¹¹For the LORD will ransom Jacob
  and redeem them from the hand of those
    stronger than they.
¹²They will come and shout for joy on the
    heights of Zion;
  they will rejoice in the bounty of the
    LORD—
the grain, the new wine and the oil,
  the young of the flocks and herds.
They will be like a well-watered garden,
  and they will sorrow no more.
¹³Then maidens will dance and be glad,
  young men and old as well.
I will turn their mourning into gladness;
  I will give them comfort and joy instead
    of sorrow.
¹⁴I will satisfy the priests with abundance,
  and my people will be filled with my
    bounty,"
                              declares the LORD.

¹⁵This is what the LORD says:

"A voice is heard in Ramah,
  mourning and great weeping,
Rachel weeping for her children
  and refusing to be comforted,
  because her children are no more."

¹⁶This is what the LORD says:

"Restrain your voice from weeping
  and your eyes from tears,
for your work will be rewarded,"
                              declares the LORD.
"They will return from the land of the
    enemy.
¹⁷So there is hope for your future,"
                              declares the LORD.
"Your children will return to their own
    land.

¹⁸"I have surely heard Ephraim's moaning:
'You disciplined me like an unruly calf,
  and I have been disciplined.
Restore me, and I will return,
  because you are the LORD my God.

THE MESSAGE

31.9 "Watch them come! They'll come weeping for
      joy
  as I take their hands and lead them,
Lead them to fresh flowing brooks,
  lead them along smooth, uncluttered paths.
Yes, it's because I'm Israel's Father
  and Ephraim's my firstborn son!

31.10-14 "Hear this, nations! GOD's Message!
  Broadcast this all over the world!
Tell them, 'The One who scattered Israel
  will gather them together again.
From now on he'll keep a careful eye on them,
  like a shepherd with his flock.'
I, GOD, will pay a stiff ransom price for Jacob;
  I'll free him from the grip of the Babylonian
    bully.
The people will climb up Zion's slopes
    shouting with joy,
  their faces beaming because of GOD's
    bounty—
Grain and wine and oil,
  flocks of sheep, herds of cattle.
Their lives will be like a well-watered garden,
  never again left to dry up.
Young women will dance and be happy,
  young men and old men will join in.
I'll convert their weeping into laughter,
  lavishing comfort, invading their grief with
    joy.
I'll make sure that their priests get three
    square meals a day
  and that my people have more than
    enough.'" GOD's Decree.

✠

31.15-17 Again, GOD's Message:

"Listen to this! Laments coming out of
    Ramah,
  wild and bitter weeping.
It's Rachel weeping for her children,
  Rachel refusing all solace.
Her children are gone,
  gone—long gone into exile."
But GOD says, "Stop your incessant weeping,
  hold back your tears.
Collect wages from your grief work." GOD's
    Decree.
  "They'll be coming back home!
There's hope for your children." GOD's Decree.

31.18-19 "I've heard the contrition of Ephraim.
  Yes, I've heard it clearly, saying,
'You trained me well.
  You broke me, a wild yearling horse, to the
    saddle.
Now put me, trained and obedient, to use.
  You are my GOD.

NEW INTERNATIONAL VERSION

¹⁹After I strayed,
  I repented;
after I came to understand,
  I beat my breast.
I was ashamed and humiliated
  because I bore the disgrace of my youth.'
²⁰Is not Ephraim my dear son,
  the child in whom I delight?
Though I often speak against him,
  I still remember him.
Therefore my heart yearns for him;
  I have great compassion for him,"
                    declares the LORD.

²¹"Set up road signs;
  put up guideposts.
Take note of the highway,
  the road that you take.
Return, O Virgin Israel,
  return to your towns.
²²How long will you wander,
  O unfaithful daughter?
The LORD will create a new thing on earth—
  a woman will surround^a a man."

²³This is what the LORD Almighty, the God of Israel, says: "When I bring them back from captivity,^b the people in the land of Judah and in its towns will once again use these words: 'The LORD bless you, O righteous dwelling, O sacred mountain.' ²⁴People will live together in Judah and all its towns—farmers and those who move about with their flocks. ²⁵I will refresh the weary and satisfy the faint."

²⁶At this I awoke and looked around. My sleep had been pleasant to me.

²⁷"The days are coming," declares the LORD, "when I will plant the house of Israel and the house of Judah with the offspring of men and of animals. ²⁸Just as I watched over them to uproot and tear down, and to overthrow, destroy and bring disaster, so I will watch over them to build and to plant," declares the LORD. ²⁹"In those days people will no longer say,

'The fathers have eaten sour grapes,
  and the children's teeth are set on edge.'

³⁰Instead, everyone will die for his own sin; whoever eats sour grapes—his own teeth will be set on edge.

THE MESSAGE

After those years of running loose, I repented.
  After you trained me to obedience,
I was ashamed of my past, my wild, unruly past.
  Humiliated, I beat on my chest.
Will I ever live this down?'

31.20 "Oh! Ephraim is my dear, dear son,
  my child in whom I take pleasure!
Every time I mention his name,
  my heart bursts with longing for him!
Everything in me cries out for him.
  Softly and tenderly I wait for him." GOD'S
    Decree.

31.21-22 "Set up signposts to mark your trip home.
  Get a good map.
Study the road conditions.
  The road out is the road back.
Come back, dear virgin Israel,
  come back to your hometowns.
How long will you flit here and there,
    indecisive?
  How long before you make up your fickle
    mind?
GOD will create a new thing in this land:
  A transformed woman will embrace the
    transforming GOD!"

✝

31.23-24 A Message from Israel's GOD-of-the-Angel-Armies: "When I've turned everything around and brought my people back, the old expressions will be heard on the streets: 'GOD bless you!' . . . 'O True Home!' . . . 'O Holy Mountain!' All Judah's people, whether in town or country, will get along just fine with each other.

31.25 I'll refresh tired bodies;
  I'll restore tired souls.

31.26   Just then I woke up and looked around—what a pleasant and satisfying sleep!

✝

31.27-28 "Be ready. The time's coming"—GOD'S Decree—"when I will plant people and animals in Israel and Judah, just as a farmer plants seed. And in the same way that earlier I relentlessly pulled up and tore down, took apart and demolished, so now I am sticking with them as they start over, building and planting.

31.29   "When that time comes you won't hear the old proverb anymore,

Parents ate the green apples,
  their children got the stomachache.

31.30 "No, each person will pay for his own sin. You eat green apples, you're the one who gets sick.

✝

---

^a 22 Or *will go about seeking*; or *will protect*   ^b 23 Or I *restore their fortunes*

NEW INTERNATIONAL VERSION

³¹ "The time is coming," declares the LORD,
  "when I will make a new covenant
with the house of Israel
  and with the house of Judah.
³² It will not be like the covenant
  I made with their forefathers
when I took them by the hand
  to lead them out of Egypt,
because they broke my covenant,
  though I was a husband to*ᵃ* them,*ᵇ*
            declares the LORD.
³³ "This is the covenant I will make with the
      house of Israel
  after that time," declares the LORD.
"I will put my law in their minds
  and write it on their hearts.
I will be their God,
  and they will be my people.
³⁴ No longer will a man teach his neighbor,
  or a man his brother, saying, 'Know the
      LORD,'
because they will all know me,
  from the least of them to the greatest,"
            declares the LORD.
"For I will forgive their wickedness
  and will remember their sins no more."

³⁵ This is what the LORD says,

he who appoints the sun
  to shine by day,
who decrees the moon and stars
  to shine by night,
who stirs up the sea
  so that its waves roar—
  the LORD Almighty is his name:
³⁶ "Only if these decrees vanish from my sight,"
  declares the LORD,
"will the descendants of Israel ever cease
  to be a nation before me."

³⁷ This is what the LORD says:

"Only if the heavens above can be measured
  and the foundations of the earth below be
      searched out
will I reject all the descendants of Israel
  because of all they have done,"
            declares the LORD.

³⁸ "The days are coming," declares the LORD,
"when this city will be rebuilt for me from the
Tower of Hananel to the Corner Gate. ³⁹ The
measuring line will stretch from there straight
to the hill of Gareb and then turn to Goah. ⁴⁰ The
whole valley where dead bodies and ashes are
thrown, and all the terraces out to the Kidron

THE MESSAGE

31.31-32 "That's right. The time is coming when I will
make a brand-new covenant with Israel and Judah. It won't be a repeat of the covenant I made
with their ancestors when I took their hand to
lead them out of the land of Egypt. They broke
that covenant even though I did my part as
their Master." GOD's Decree.

31.33-34   "This is the brand-new covenant that I will
make with Israel when the time comes. I will
put my law within them—write it on their
hearts!—and be their God. And they will be
my people. They will no longer go around setting up schools to teach each other about GOD.
They'll know me firsthand, the dull and the
bright, the smart and the slow. I'll wipe the
slate clean for each of them. I'll forget they ever
sinned!" GOD's Decree.

IF THIS ORDERED COSMOS EVER FELL
TO PIECES

31.35 GOD's Message, from the God who lights up
            the day with sun and
  brightens the night with moon and stars,
Who whips the ocean into a billowy froth,
  whose name is GOD-of-the-Angel-Armies:

31.36 "If this ordered cosmos ever fell to pieces,
  fell into chaos before me"—GOD's Decree—
"Then and only then might Israel fall apart
  and disappear as a nation before me."

31.37 GOD's Message:

"If the skies could be measured with a
      yardstick
  and the earth explored to its core,
Then and only then would I turn my back on
      Israel,
  disgusted with all they've done." GOD's
            Decree.

31.38-40 "The time is coming"—it's GOD's Decree—"when
GOD's city will be rebuilt, rebuilt all the way from
the Citadel of Hanamel to the Corner Gate. The
master plan will extend west to Gareb Hill and
then around to Goath. The whole valley to the
south where incinerated corpses are dumped—a
death valley if there ever was one!—and all the
terraced fields out to the Brook Kidron on the

NEW INTERNATIONAL VERSION

Valley on the east as far as the corner of the Horse Gate, will be holy to the LORD. The city will never again be uprooted or demolished."

JEREMIAH BUYS A FIELD

32 This is the word that came to Jeremiah from the LORD in the tenth year of Zedekiah king of Judah, which was the eighteenth year of Nebuchadnezzar. ²The army of the king of Babylon was then besieging Jerusalem, and Jeremiah the prophet was confined in the courtyard of the guard in the royal palace of Judah.

³Now Zedekiah king of Judah had imprisoned him there, saying, "Why do you prophesy as you do? You say, 'This is what the LORD says: I am about to hand this city over to the king of Babylon, and he will capture it. ⁴Zedekiah king of Judah will not escape out of the hands of the Babylonians[a] but will certainly be handed over to the king of Babylon, and will speak with him face to face and see him with his own eyes. ⁵He will take Zedekiah to Babylon, where he will remain until I deal with him, declares the LORD. If you fight against the Babylonians, you will not succeed.' "

⁶Jeremiah said, "The word of the LORD came to me: ⁷Hanamel son of Shallum your uncle is going to come to you and say, 'Buy my field at Anathoth, because as nearest relative it is your right and duty to buy it.'

⁸"Then, just as the LORD had said, my cousin Hanamel came to me in the courtyard of the guard and said, 'Buy my field at Anathoth in the territory of Benjamin. Since it is your right to redeem it and possess it, buy it for yourself.'

"I knew that this was the word of the LORD; ⁹so I bought the field at Anathoth from my cousin Hanamel and weighed out for him seventeen shekels[b] of silver. ¹⁰I signed and sealed the deed, had it witnessed, and weighed out the silver on the scales. ¹¹I took the deed of purchase—the sealed copy containing the terms and conditions, as well as the unsealed copy— ¹²and I gave this deed to Baruch son of Neriah, the son of Mahseiah, in the presence of my cousin Hanamel and of the witnesses who had signed the deed and of all the Jews sitting in the courtyard of the guard.

¹³"In their presence I gave Baruch these instructions: ¹⁴'This is what the LORD Almighty, the God of Israel, says: Take these documents, both the sealed and unsealed copies of the deed of purchase, and put them in a clay jar so they will last a long time. ¹⁵For this is what the LORD Almighty, the God of Israel, says: Houses, fields and vineyards will again be bought in this land.'

---

[a] 4 Or *Chaldeans*; also in verses 5, 24, 25, 28, 29 and 43
[b] 9 That is, about 7 ounces (about 200 grams)

THE MESSAGE

east as far north as the Horse Gate will be consecrated to me as a holy place.

"This city will never again be torn down or destroyed."

KILLING AND DISEASE ARE ON OUR DOORSTEP

32.1-5 **32** The Message Jeremiah received from GOD in the tenth year of Zedekiah king of Judah. It was the eighteenth year of Nebuchadnezzar. At that time the army of the king of Babylon was holding Jerusalem under siege. Jeremiah was shut up in jail in the royal palace. Zedekiah, king of Judah, had locked him up, complaining, "How dare you preach, saying, 'GOD says, I'm warning you: I will hand this city over to the king of Babylon and he will take it over. Zedekiah king of Judah will be handed over to the Chaldeans along with the city. He will be handed over to the king of Babylon and forced to face the music. He'll be hauled off to Babylon where he'll stay until I deal with him. GOD's Decree. Fight against the Babylonians all you want—it won't get you anywhere.' "

32.6-7 Jeremiah said, "GOD's Message came to me like this: Prepare yourself! Hanamel, your uncle Shallum's son, is on his way to see you. He is going to say, 'Buy my field in Anathoth. You have the legal right to buy it.'

32.8 "And sure enough, just as GOD had said, my cousin Hanamel came to me while I was in jail and said, 'Buy my field in Anathoth in the territory of Benjamin, for you have the legal right to keep it in the family. Buy it. Take it over.'

"That did it. I knew it was GOD's Message.

32.9-12 "So I bought the field at Anathoth from my cousin Hanamel. I paid him seventeen silver shekels. I followed all the proper procedures: In the presence of witnesses I wrote out the bill of sale, sealed it, and weighed out the money on the scales. Then I took the deed of purchase—the sealed copy that contained the contract and its conditions and also the open copy—and gave them to Baruch son of Neriah, the son of Mahseiah. All this took place in the presence of my cousin Hanamel and the witnesses who had signed the deed, as the Jews who were at the jail that day looked on.

32.13-15 "Then, in front of all of them, I told Baruch, 'These are orders from GOD-of-the-Angel-Armies, the God of Israel: Take these documents—both the sealed and the open deeds—and put them for safekeeping in a pottery jar. For GOD-of-the-Angel-Armies, the God of Israel, says, "Life is going to return to normal. Homes and fields and vineyards are again going to be bought in this country." '

NEW INTERNATIONAL VERSION

¹⁶"After I had given the deed of purchase to Baruch son of Neriah, I prayed to the LORD:

¹⁷"Ah, Sovereign LORD, you have made the heavens and the earth by your great power and outstretched arm. Nothing is too hard for you. ¹⁸You show love to thousands but bring the punishment for the fathers' sins into the laps of their children after them. O great and powerful God, whose name is the LORD Almighty, ¹⁹great are your purposes and mighty are your deeds. Your eyes are open to all the ways of men; you reward everyone according to his conduct and as his deeds deserve. ²⁰You performed miraculous signs and wonders in Egypt and have continued them to this day, both in Israel and among all mankind, and have gained the renown that is still yours. ²¹You brought your people Israel out of Egypt with signs and wonders, by a mighty hand and an outstretched arm and with great terror. ²²You gave them this land you had sworn to give their forefathers, a land flowing with milk and honey. ²³They came in and took possession of it, but they did not obey you or follow your law; they did not do what you commanded them to do. So you brought all this disaster upon them.

²⁴"See how the siege ramps are built up to take the city. Because of the sword, famine and plague, the city will be handed over to the Babylonians who are attacking it. What you said has happened, as you now see. ²⁵And though the city will be handed over to the Babylonians, you, O Sovereign LORD, say to me, 'Buy the field with silver and have the transaction witnessed.' "

²⁶Then the word of the LORD came to Jeremiah: ²⁷"I am the LORD, the God of all mankind. Is anything too hard for me? ²⁸Therefore, this is what the LORD says: I am about to hand this city over to the Babylonians and to Nebuchadnezzar king of Babylon, who will capture it. ²⁹The Babylonians who are attacking this city will come in and set it on fire; they will burn it down, along with the houses where the people provoked me to anger by burning incense on the roofs to Baal and by pouring out drink offerings to other gods.

³⁰"The people of Israel and Judah have done nothing but evil in my sight from their youth; indeed, the people of Israel have done nothing but provoke me with what their hands have made, declares the LORD. ³¹From the day it was built until now, this city has so aroused my anger and

THE MESSAGE

32.16-19 "And then, having handed over the legal documents to Baruch son of Neriah, I prayed to GOD, 'Dear GOD, my Master, you created earth and sky by your great power—by merely stretching out your arm! There is nothing you can't do. You're loyal in your steadfast love to thousands upon thousands—but you also make children live with the fallout from their parents' sins. Great and powerful God, named GOD-of-the-Angel-Armies, determined in purpose and relentless in following through, you see everything that men and women do and respond appropriately to the way they live, to the things they do.

32.20-23 " 'You performed signs and wonders in the country of Egypt and continue to do so right into the present, right here in Israel and everywhere else, too. You've made a reputation for yourself that doesn't diminish. You brought your people Israel out of Egypt with signs and wonders—a powerful deliverance!—by merely stretching out your arm. You gave them this land and solemnly promised to their ancestors a bountiful and fertile land. But when they entered the land and took it over, they didn't listen to you. They didn't do what you commanded. They wouldn't listen to a thing you told them. And so you brought this disaster on them.

32.24-25 " 'Oh, look at the siege ramps already set in place to take the city. Killing and starvation and disease are on our doorstep. The Babylonians are attacking! The Word you spoke is coming to pass—it's daily news! And yet you, GOD, the Master, even though it is certain that the city will be turned over to the Babylonians, also told me, Buy the field. Pay for it in cash. And make sure there are witnesses.' "

✝

32.26-30 Then GOD's Message came again to Jeremiah: "Stay alert! I am GOD, the God of everything living. Is there anything I can't do? So listen to GOD's Message: No doubt about it, I'm handing this city over to the Babylonians and Nebuchadnezzar king of Babylon. He'll take it. The attacking Chaldeans will break through and burn the city down: All those houses whose roofs were used as altars for offerings to Baal and the worship of who knows how many other gods provoked me. It isn't as if this were the first time they had provoked me. The people of Israel and Judah have been doing this for a long time—doing what I hate, making me angry by the way they live." GOD's Decree.

32.31-35 "This city has made me angry from the day they built it, and now I've had my fill. I'm de-

NEW INTERNATIONAL VERSION

wrath that I must remove it from my sight. ³²The people of Israel and Judah have provoked me by all the evil they have done—they, their kings and officials, their priests and prophets, the men of Judah and the people of Jerusalem. ³³They turned their backs to me and not their faces; though I taught them again and again, they would not listen or respond to discipline. ³⁴They set up their abominable idols in the house that bears my Name and defiled it. ³⁵They built high places for Baal in the Valley of Ben Hinnom to sacrifice their sons and daughters*ᵃ* to Molech, though I never commanded, nor did it enter my mind, that they should do such a detestable thing and so make Judah sin.

³⁶"You are saying about this city, 'By the sword, famine and plague it will be handed over to the king of Babylon'; but this is what the LORD, the God of Israel, says: ³⁷I will surely gather them from all the lands where I banish them in my furious anger and great wrath; I will bring them back to this place and let them live in safety. ³⁸They will be my people, and I will be their God. ³⁹I will give them singleness of heart and action, so that they will always fear me for their own good and the good of their children after them. ⁴⁰I will make an everlasting covenant with them: I will never stop doing good to them, and I will inspire them to fear me, so that they will never turn away from me. ⁴¹I will rejoice in doing them good and will assuredly plant them in this land with all my heart and soul.

⁴²"This is what the LORD says: As I have brought all this great calamity on this people, so I will give them all the prosperity I have promised them. ⁴³Once more fields will be bought in this land of which you say, 'It is a desolate waste, without men or animals, for it has been handed over to the Babylonians.' ⁴⁴Fields will be bought for silver, and deeds will be signed, sealed and witnessed in the territory of Benjamin, in the villages around Jerusalem, in the towns of Judah and in the towns of the hill country, of the western foothills and of the Negev, because I will restore their fortunes,*ᵇ* declares the LORD."

THE MESSAGE

stroying it. I can't stand to look any longer at the wicked lives of the people of Israel and Judah, deliberately making me angry, the whole lot of them—kings and leaders and priests and preachers, in the country and in the city. They've turned their backs on me—won't even look me in the face!—even though I took great pains to teach them how to live. They refused to listen, refused to be taught. Why, they even set up obscene god and goddess statues in the Temple built in my honor—an outrageous desecration! And then they went out and built shrines to the god Baal in the valley of Hinnom, where they burned their children in sacrifice to the god Molech—I can hardly conceive of such evil!—turning the whole country into one huge act of sin.

✝

32.36 "But there is also this Message from me, the GOD of Israel, to this city of which you have said, 'In killing and starvation and disease this city will be delivered up to the king of Babylon':

32.37-40 " 'Watch for this! I will collect them from all the countries to which I will have driven them in my anger and rage and indignation. Yes, I'll bring them all back to this place and let them live here in peace. They will be my people, I will be their God. I'll make them of one mind and heart, always honoring me, so that they can live good and whole lives, they and their children after them. What's more, I'll make a covenant with them that will last forever, a covenant to stick with them no matter what, and work for their good. I'll fill their hearts with a deep respect for me so they'll not even *think* of turning away from me.

32.41 " 'Oh how I'll rejoice in them! Oh how I'll delight in doing good things for them! Heart and soul, I'll plant them in this country and keep them here!'

32.42-44 "Yes, this is GOD's Message: 'I will certainly bring this huge catastrophe on this people, but I will also usher in a wonderful life of prosperity. I promise. Fields are going to be bought here again, yes, in this very country that you assume is going to end up desolate—gone to the dogs, unlivable, wrecked by the Babylonians. Yes, people will buy farms again, and legally, with deeds of purchase, sealed documents, proper witnesses—and right here in the territory of Benjamin, and in the area around Jerusalem, around the villages of Judah and the hill country, the Shephelah and the Negev. I will restore everything that was lost.' GOD's Decree."

ᵃ 35 Or *to make their sons and daughters pass through* the *fire* ; *ᵇ 44* Or *will bring them back from captivity*

NEW INTERNATIONAL VERSION

PROMISE OF RESTORATION

33 While Jeremiah was still confined in the courtyard of the guard, the word of the LORD came to him a second time: ²This is what the LORD says, he who made the earth, the LORD who formed it and established it—the LORD is his name: ³'Call to me and I will answer you and tell you great and unsearchable things you do not know.' ⁴For this is what the LORD, the God of Israel, says about the houses in this city and the royal palaces of Judah that have been torn down to be used against the siege ramps and the sword ⁵in the fight with the Babylonians[a]: 'They will be filled with the dead bodies of the men I will slay in my anger and wrath. I will hide my face from this city because of all its wickedness.

⁶"'Nevertheless, I will bring health and healing to it; I will heal my people and will let them enjoy abundant peace and security. ⁷I will bring Judah and Israel back from captivity[b] and will rebuild them as they were before. ⁸I will cleanse them from all the sin they have committed against me and will forgive all their sins of rebellion against me. ⁹Then this city will bring me renown, joy, praise and honor before all nations on earth that hear of all the good things I do for it; and they will be in awe and will tremble at the abundant prosperity and peace I provide for it.'

¹⁰"This is what the LORD says: 'You say about this place, "It is a desolate waste, without men or animals." Yet in the towns of Judah and the streets of Jerusalem that are deserted, inhabited by neither men nor animals, there will be heard once more ¹¹the sounds of joy and gladness, the voices of bride and bridegroom, and the voices of those who bring thank offerings to the house of the LORD, saying,

"Give thanks to the LORD Almighty,
    for the LORD is good;
    his love endures forever."

For I will restore the fortunes of the land as they were before,' says the LORD.

¹²"This is what the LORD Almighty says: 'In this place, desolate and without men or animals—in all its towns there will again be pastures for shepherds to rest their flocks. ¹³In the towns of the hill country, of the western foothills and of the Negev, in the territory of Benjamin, in the villages around Jerusalem and in the towns of Judah, flocks will again pass under the hand of the one who counts them,' says the LORD.

---

a 5 Or Chaldeans   b 7 Or will restore the fortunes of Judah and Israel

THE MESSAGE

THINGS YOU COULD NEVER FIGURE OUT ON YOUR OWN

33.1 **33** While Jeremiah was still locked up in jail, a second Message from GOD was given to him:

33.2-3 "This is GOD's Message, the God who made earth, made it livable and lasting, known everywhere as GOD: 'Call to me and I will answer you. I'll tell you marvelous and wondrous things that you could never figure out on your own.'

33.4-5 "This is what GOD, the God of Israel, has to say about what's going on in this city, about the homes of both people and kings that have been demolished, about all the ravages of war and the killing by the Chaldeans, and about the streets littered with the dead bodies of those killed because of my raging anger—about all that's happened because the evil actions in this city have turned my stomach in disgust.

33.6-9 "But now take another look. I'm going to give this city a thorough renovation, working a true healing inside and out. I'm going to show them life whole, life brimming with blessings. I'll restore everything that was lost to Judah and Jerusalem. I'll build everything back as good as new. I'll scrub them clean from the dirt they've done against me. I'll forgive everything they've done wrong, forgive all their rebellions. And Jerusalem will be a center of joy and praise and glory for all the countries on earth. They'll get reports on all the good I'm doing for her. They'll be in awe of the blessings I am pouring on her.

33.10-11 "Yes, GOD's Message: 'You're going to look at this place, these empty and desolate towns of Judah and streets of Jerusalem, and say, "A wasteland. Unlivable. Not even a dog could live here." But the time is coming when you're going to hear laughter and celebration, marriage festivities, people exclaiming, "Thank GOD-of-the-Angel-Armies. He's so good! His love never quits," as they bring thank offerings into GOD's Temple. I'll restore everything that was lost in this land. I'll make everything as good as new.' I, GOD, say so.

33.12-13 "GOD-of-the-Angel-Armies says: 'This coming desolation, unfit for even a stray dog, is once again going to become a pasture for shepherds who care for their flocks. You'll see flocks everywhere—in the mountains around the towns of the Shephelah and Negev, all over the territory of Benjamin, around Jerusalem and the towns of Judah—flocks under the care of shepherds who keep track of each sheep.' GOD says so.

NEW INTERNATIONAL VERSION

14 " 'The days are coming,' declares the LORD, 'when I will fulfill the gracious promise I made to the house of Israel and to the house of Judah.

15 " 'In those days and at that time
    I will make a righteous Branch sprout
        from David's line;
    he will do what is just and right in the
        land.
16 In those days Judah will be saved
    and Jerusalem will live in safety.
    This is the name by which it *a* will be called:
    The LORD Our Righteousness.'

17 For this is what the LORD says: 'David will never fail to have a man to sit on the throne of the house of Israel, 18 nor will the priests, who are Levites, ever fail to have a man to stand before me continually to offer burnt offerings, to burn grain offerings and to present sacrifices.' "

19 The word of the LORD came to Jeremiah: 20 "This is what the LORD says: 'If you can break my covenant with the day and my covenant with the night, so that day and night no longer come at their appointed time, 21 then my covenant with David my servant—and my covenant with the Levites who are priests ministering before me—can be broken and David will no longer have a descendant to reign on his throne. 22 I will make the descendants of David my servant and the Levites who minister before me as countless as the stars of the sky and as measureless as the sand on the seashore.' "

23 The word of the LORD came to Jeremiah: 24 "Have you not noticed that these people are saying, 'The LORD has rejected the two kingdoms *b* he chose'? So they despise my people and no longer regard them as a nation. 25 This is what the LORD says: 'If I have not established my covenant with day and night and the fixed laws of heaven and earth, 26 then I will reject the descendants of Jacob and David my servant and will not choose one of his sons to rule over the descendants of Abraham, Isaac and Jacob. For I will restore their fortunes *c* and have compassion on them.' "

WARNING TO ZEDEKIAH

34 While Nebuchadnezzar king of Babylon and all his army and all the kingdoms and peoples in the empire he ruled were fighting

a 16 Or he   *b* 24 Or families   *c* 26 Or will bring them back from captivity

THE MESSAGE

A FRESH AND TRUE SHOOT FROM THE DAVID-TREE

33.14-18 " 'Watch for this: The time is coming'—GOD's Decree—'when I will keep the promise I made to the families of Israel and Judah. When that time comes, I will make a fresh and true shoot sprout from the David-Tree. He will run this country honestly and fairly. He will set things right. That's when Judah will be secure and Jerusalem live in safety. The motto for the city will be, "GOD Has Set Things Right for Us." GOD has made it clear that there will always be a descendant of David ruling the people of Israel and that there will always be Levitical priests on hand to offer burnt offerings, present grain offerings, and carry on the sacrificial worship in my honor.' "

✝

33.19-22 GOD's Message to Jeremiah: "GOD says, 'If my covenant with day and my covenant with night ever fell apart so that day and night became haphazard and you never knew which was coming and when, then and only then would my covenant with my servant David fall apart and his descendants no longer rule. The same goes for the Levitical priests who serve me. Just as you can't number the stars in the sky nor measure the sand on the seashore, neither will you be able to account for the descendants of David my servant and the Levites who serve me.' "

✝

33.23-24 GOD's Message to Jeremiah: "Have you heard the saying that's making the rounds: 'The two families GOD chose, Israel and Judah, he disowned'? And have you noticed that my people are treated with contempt, with rumors afoot that there's nothing to them anymore?

33.25-26 "Well, here's GOD's response: 'If my covenant with day and night wasn't in working order, if sky and earth weren't functioning the way I set them going, then, but only then, you might think I had disowned the descendants of Jacob and of my servant David, and that I wouldn't set up any of David's descendants over the descendants of Abraham, Isaac, and Jacob. But as it is, I will give them back everything they've lost. The last word is, I will have mercy on them.' "

FREEDOM TO THE SLAVES

34.1 **34** GOD's Message to Jeremiah at the time King Nebuchadnezzar of Babylon mounted an all-out attack on Jerusalem and all

NEW INTERNATIONAL VERSION	THE MESSAGE

NEW INTERNATIONAL VERSION

against Jerusalem and all its surrounding towns, this word came to Jeremiah from the LORD: ²"This is what the LORD, the God of Israel, says: Go to Zedekiah king of Judah and tell him, 'This is what the LORD says: I am about to hand this city over to the king of Babylon, and he will burn it down. ³You will not escape from his grasp but will surely be captured and handed over to him. You will see the king of Babylon with your own eyes, and he will speak with you face to face. And you will go to Babylon.

⁴" 'Yet hear the promise of the LORD, O Zedekiah king of Judah. This is what the LORD says concerning you: You will not die by the sword; ⁵you will die peacefully. As people made a funeral fire in honor of your fathers, the former kings who preceded you, so they will make a fire in your honor and lament, "Alas, O master!" I myself make this promise, declares the LORD.' "

⁶Then Jeremiah the prophet told all this to Zedekiah king of Judah, in Jerusalem, ⁷while the army of the king of Babylon was fighting against Jerusalem and the other cities of Judah that were still holding out—Lachish and Azekah. These were the only fortified cities left in Judah.

FREEDOM FOR SLAVES

⁸The word came to Jeremiah from the LORD after King Zedekiah had made a covenant with all the people in Jerusalem to proclaim freedom for the slaves. ⁹Everyone was to free his Hebrew slaves, both male and female; no one was to hold a fellow Jew in bondage. ¹⁰So all the officials and people who entered into this covenant agreed that they would free their male and female slaves and no longer hold them in bondage. They agreed, and set them free. ¹¹But afterward they changed their minds and took back the slaves they had freed and enslaved them again.

¹²Then the word of the LORD came to Jeremiah: ¹³"This is what the LORD, the God of Israel, says: I made a covenant with your forefathers when I brought them out of Egypt, out of the land of slavery. I said, ¹⁴'Every seventh year each of you must free any fellow Hebrew who has sold himself to you. After he has served you six years, you must let him go free.'ᵃ Your fathers, however, did not listen to me or pay attention to me. ¹⁵Recently you repented and did what is right in my sight: Each of you proclaimed freedom to his countrymen. You even made a covenant before me in the house that bears my Name. ¹⁶But now you have turned around and profaned my name; each of you has taken back the male and female slaves you had set free to go

ᵃ *14* Deut. 15:12

THE MESSAGE

the towns around it with his armies and allies and everyone he could muster:

34.2-3 "I, GOD, the God of Israel, direct you to go and tell Zedekiah king of Judah: 'This is GOD's Message. Listen to me. I am going to hand this city over to the king of Babylon, and he is going to burn it to the ground. And don't think you'll get away. You'll be captured and be his prisoner. You will have a personal confrontation with the king of Babylon and be taken off with him, captive, to Babylon.

34.4-5 " 'But listen, O Zedekiah king of Judah, to the rest of the Message of GOD. You won't be killed. You'll die a peaceful death. They will honor you with funeral rites as they honored your ancestors, the kings who preceded you. They will properly mourn your death, weeping, "Master, master!" This is a solemn promise. GOD's Decree.' "

34.6-7 The prophet Jeremiah gave this Message to Zedekiah king of Judah in Jerusalem, gave it to him word for word. It was at the very time that the king of Babylon was mounting his all-out attack on Jerusalem and whatever cities in Judah that were still standing—only Lachish and Azekah, as it turned out (they were the only fortified cities left in Judah).

✝

34.8-10 GOD delivered a Message to Jeremiah after King Zedekiah made a covenant with the people of Jerusalem to decree freedom to the slaves who were Hebrews, both men and women. The covenant stipulated that no one in Judah would own a fellow Jew as a slave. All the leaders and people who had signed the covenant set free the slaves, men and women alike.

34.11 But a little while later, they reneged on the covenant, broke their promise and forced their former slaves to become slaves again.

34.12-14 Then Jeremiah received this Message from GOD: "GOD, the God of Israel, says, 'I made a covenant with your ancestors when I delivered them out of their slavery in Egypt. At the time I made it clear: "At the end of seven years, each of you must free any fellow Hebrew who has had to sell himself to you. After he has served six years, set him free." But your ancestors totally ignored me.

34.15-16 " 'And now, *you*—what have you done? First you turned back to the right way and did the right thing, decreeing freedom for your brothers and sisters—and you made it official in a solemn covenant in my Temple. And then you turned right around and broke your word, making a mockery of both me and the covenant, and made them all slaves again, these

NEW INTERNATIONAL VERSION

where they wished. You have forced them to become your slaves again.

17"Therefore, this is what the LORD says: You have not obeyed me; you have not proclaimed freedom for your fellow countrymen. So I now proclaim 'freedom' for you, declares the LORD— 'freedom' to fall by the sword, plague and famine. I will make you abhorrent to all the kingdoms of the earth. 18The men who have violated my covenant and have not fulfilled the terms of the covenant they made before me, I will treat like the calf they cut in two and then walked between its pieces. 19The leaders of Judah and Jerusalem, the court officials, the priests and all the people of the land who walked between the pieces of the calf, 20I will hand over to their enemies who seek their lives. Their dead bodies will become food for the birds of the air and the beasts of the earth.

21"I will hand Zedekiah king of Judah and his officials over to their enemies who seek their lives, to the army of the king of Babylon, which has withdrawn from you. 22I am going to give the order, declares the LORD, and I will bring them back to this city. They will fight against it, take it and burn it down. And I will lay waste the towns of Judah so no one can live there."

THE RECABITES

35 This is the word that came to Jeremiah from the LORD during the reign of Jehoiakim son of Josiah king of Judah: 2"Go to the Recabite family and invite them to come to one of the side rooms of the house of the LORD and give them wine to drink."

3So I went to get Jaazaniah son of Jeremiah, the son of Habazziniah, and his brothers and all his sons—the whole family of the Recabites. 4I brought them into the house of the LORD, into the room of the sons of Hanan son of Igdaliah the man of God. It was next to the room of the officials, which was over that of Maaseiah son of Shallum the doorkeeper. 5Then I set bowls full of wine and some cups before the men of the Recabite family and said to them, "Drink some wine."

6But they replied, "We do not drink wine, because our forefather Jonadab son of Recab gave us this command: 'Neither you nor your descendants must ever drink wine. 7Also you must never build houses, sow seed or plant vineyards; you must never have any of these things, but must always live in tents. Then you will live a long time in the land where you are nomads.'

THE MESSAGE

men and women you'd just set free. You forced them back into slavery.

34.17-20 " 'So here is what I, GOD, have to say: You have not obeyed me and set your brothers and sisters free. Here is what I'm going to do: I'm going to set *you* free—GOD's Decree—free to get killed in war or by disease or by starvation. I'll make you a spectacle of horror. People all over the world will take one look at you and shudder. Everyone who violated my covenant, who didn't do what was solemnly promised in the covenant ceremony when they split the young bull into two halves and walked between them, all those people that day who walked between the two halves of the bull— leaders of Judah and Jerusalem, palace officials, priests, and all the rest of the people—I'm handing the lot of them over to their enemies who are out to kill them. Their dead bodies will be carrion food for vultures and stray dogs.

34.21-22 " 'As for Zedekiah king of Judah and his palace staff, I'll also hand them over to their enemies, who are out to kill them. The army of the king of Babylon has pulled back for a time, but not for long, for I'm going to issue orders that will bring them back to this city. They'll attack and take it and burn it to the ground. The surrounding cities of Judah will fare no better. I'll turn them into ghost towns, unlivable and unlived in.' " GOD's Decree.

MEETING IN GOD's TEMPLE

35.1 **35** The Message that Jeremiah received from GOD ten years earlier, during the time of Jehoiakim son of Josiah king of Israel:

35.2 "Go visit the Recabite community. Invite them to meet with you in one of the rooms in GOD's Temple. And serve them wine."

35.3-4 So I went and got Jaazaniah son of Jeremiah, son of Habazziniah, along with all his brothers and sons—the whole community of the Recabites as it turned out—and brought them to GOD's Temple and to the meeting room of Hanan son of Igdaliah, a man of God. It was next to the meeting room of the Temple officials and just over the apartment of Maaseiah son of Shallum, who was in charge of Temple affairs.

35.5 Then I set out chalices and pitchers of wine for the Recabites and said, "A toast! Drink up!"

35.6-7 But they wouldn't do it. "We don't drink wine," they said. "Our ancestor Jonadab son of Recab commanded us, 'You are not to drink wine, you or your children, ever. Neither shall you build houses or settle down, planting fields and gardens and vineyards. Don't own property. Live in tents as nomads so that you will live well and prosper in a wandering life.'

NEW INTERNATIONAL VERSION

⁸We have obeyed everything our forefather Jonadab son of Recab commanded us. Neither we nor our wives nor our sons and daughters have ever drunk wine ⁹or built houses to live in or had vineyards, fields or crops. ¹⁰We have lived in tents and have fully obeyed everything our forefather Jonadab commanded us. ¹¹But when Nebuchadnezzar king of Babylon invaded this land, we said, 'Come, we must go to Jerusalem to escape the Babylonian*ᵃ* and Aramean armies.' So we have remained in Jerusalem."

¹²Then the word of the LORD came to Jeremiah, saying: ¹³"This is what the LORD Almighty, the God of Israel, says: Go and tell the men of Judah and the people of Jerusalem, 'Will you not learn a lesson and obey my words?' declares the LORD. ¹⁴'Jonadab son of Recab ordered his sons not to drink wine and this command has been kept. To this day they do not drink wine, because they obey their forefather's command. But I have spoken to you again and again, yet you have not obeyed me. ¹⁵Again and again I sent all my servants the prophets to you. They said, "Each of you must turn from your wicked ways and reform your actions; do not follow other gods to serve them. Then you will live in the land I have given to you and your fathers." But you have not paid attention or listened to me. ¹⁶The descendants of Jonadab son of Recab have carried out the command their forefather gave them, but these people have not obeyed me.'

¹⁷"Therefore, this is what the LORD God Almighty, the God of Israel, says: 'Listen! I am going to bring on Judah and on everyone living in Jerusalem every disaster I pronounced against them. I spoke to them, but they did not listen; I called to them, but they did not answer.' "

¹⁸Then Jeremiah said to the family of the Recabites, "This is what the LORD Almighty, the God of Israel, says: 'You have obeyed the command of your forefather Jonadab and have followed all his instructions and have done everything he ordered.' ¹⁹Therefore, this is what the LORD Almighty, the God of Israel, says: 'Jonadab son of Recab will never fail to have a man to serve me.' "

THE MESSAGE

35.8-10 "And we've done it, done everything Jonadab son of Recab commanded. We and our wives, our sons and daughters, drink no wine at all. We don't build houses. We don't have vineyards or fields or gardens. We live in tents as nomads. We've listened to our ancestor Jonadab and we've done everything he commanded us.

35.11 "But when Nebuchadnezzar king of Babylon invaded our land, we said, 'Let's go to Jerusalem and get out of the path of the Chaldean and Aramean armies, find ourselves a safe place.' That's why we're living in Jerusalem right now."

WHY WON'T YOU LEARN YOUR LESSON?

35.12-15 Then Jeremiah received this Message from GOD: "GOD-of-the-Angel-Armies, the God of Israel, wants you to go tell the people of Judah and the citizens of Jerusalem that I say, 'Why won't you learn your lesson and do what I tell you?' GOD's Decree. 'The commands of Jonadab son of Recab to his sons have been carried out to the letter. He told them not to drink wine, and they haven't touched a drop to this very day. They honored and obeyed their ancestor's command. But look at you! I have gone to a lot of trouble to get your attention, and you've ignored me. I sent prophet after prophet to you, all of them my servants, to tell you from early morning to late at night to change your life, make a clean break with your evil past and do what is right, to not take up with every Tom, Dick, and Harry of a god that comes down the pike, but settle down and be faithful in this country I gave your ancestors.

35.15-16 " 'And what do I get from you? Deaf ears. The descendants of Jonadab son of Recab carried out to the letter what their ancestor commanded them, but this people ignores me.'

35.17 "So here's what is going to happen. GOD-of-the-Angel-Armies, the God of Israel, says, 'I will bring calamity down on the heads of the people of Judah and Jerusalem—the very calamity I warned you was coming—because you turned a deaf ear when I spoke, turned your backs when I called.' "

35.18-19 Then, turning to the Recabite community, Jeremiah said, "And this is what GOD-of-the-Angel-Armies, the God of Israel, says to you: Because you have done what Jonadab your ancestor told you, obeyed his commands and followed through on his instructions, receive this Message from GOD-of-the-Angel-Armies, the God of Israel: There will always be a descendant of Jonadab son of Recab at my service! Always!' "

NEW INTERNATIONAL VERSION

JEHOIAKIM BURNS JEREMIAH'S SCROLL

36 In the fourth year of Jehoiakim son of Josiah king of Judah, this word came to Jeremiah from the LORD: ²"Take a scroll and write on it all the words I have spoken to you concerning Israel, Judah and all the other nations from the time I began speaking to you in the reign of Josiah till now. ³Perhaps when the people of Judah hear about every disaster I plan to inflict on them, each of them will turn from his wicked way; then I will forgive their wickedness and their sin."

⁴So Jeremiah called Baruch son of Neriah, and while Jeremiah dictated all the words the LORD had spoken to him, Baruch wrote them on the scroll. ⁵Then Jeremiah told Baruch, "I am restricted; I cannot go to the LORD's temple. ⁶So you go to the house of the LORD on a day of fasting and read to the people from the scroll the words of the LORD that you wrote as I dictated. Read them to all the people of Judah who come in from their towns. ⁷Perhaps they will bring their petition before the LORD, and each will turn from his wicked ways, for the anger and wrath pronounced against this people by the LORD are great."

⁸Baruch son of Neriah did everything Jeremiah the prophet told him to do; at the LORD's temple he read the words of the LORD from the scroll. ⁹In the ninth month of the fifth year of Jehoiakim son of Josiah king of Judah, a time of fasting before the LORD was proclaimed for all the people in Jerusalem and those who had come from the towns of Judah. ¹⁰From the room of Gemariah son of Shaphan the secretary, which was in the upper courtyard at the entrance of the New Gate of the temple, Baruch read to all the people at the LORD's temple the words of Jeremiah from the scroll.

¹¹When Micaiah son of Gemariah, the son of Shaphan, heard all the words of the LORD from the scroll, ¹²he went down to the secretary's room in the royal palace, where all the officials were sitting: Elishama the secretary, Delaiah son of Shemaiah, Elnathan son of Acbor, Gemariah son of Shaphan, Zedekiah son of Hananiah, and all the other officials. ¹³After Micaiah told them everything he had heard Baruch read to the people from the scroll, ¹⁴all the officials sent Jehudi

THE MESSAGE

READING GOD'S MESSAGE

36.1 **36** In the fourth year of Jehoiakim son of Josiah king of Judah, Jeremiah received this Message from GOD:

36.2 "Get a scroll and write down everything I've told you regarding Israel and Judah and all the other nations from the time I first started speaking to you in Josiah's reign right up to the present day.

36.3 "Maybe the community of Judah will finally get it, finally understand the catastrophe that I'm planning for them, turn back from their bad lives, and let me forgive their perversity and sin."

36.4 So Jeremiah called in Baruch son of Neriah. Jeremiah dictated and Baruch wrote down on a scroll everything that GOD had said to him.

36.5-6 Then Jeremiah told Baruch, "I'm blacklisted. I can't go into GOD's Temple, so you'll have to go in my place. Go into the Temple and read everything you've written at my dictation. Wait for a day of fasting when everyone is there to hear you. And make sure that all the people who come from the Judean villages hear you.

36.7 "Maybe, just maybe, they'll start praying and GOD will hear their prayers. Maybe they'll turn back from their bad lives. This is no light matter. GOD has certainly let them know how angry he is!"

36.8 Baruch son of Neriah did everything Jeremiah the prophet told him to do. In the Temple of GOD he read the Message of GOD from the scroll.

36.9 It came about in December of the fifth year of Jehoiakim son of Josiah king of Judah that all the people of Jerusalem, along with all the people from the Judean villages, were there in Jerusalem to observe a fast to GOD.

36.10 Baruch took the scroll to the Temple and read out publicly the words of Jeremiah. He read from the meeting room of Gemariah son of Shaphan the secretary of state, which was in the upper court right next to the New Gate of GOD's Temple. Everyone could hear him.

36.11-12 The moment Micaiah the son of Gemariah heard what was being read from the scroll—GOD's Message!—he went straight to the palace and to the chambers of the secretary of state where all the government officials were holding a meeting: Elishama the secretary, Delaiah son of Shemaiah, Elnathan son of Achbor, Gemariah son of Shaphan, Zedekiah son of Hananiah, and all the other government officials.

36.13 Micaiah reported everything he had heard Baruch read from the scroll as the officials listened.

36.14 Immediately they dispatched Jehudi son of

NEW INTERNATIONAL VERSION

son of Nethaniah, the son of Shelemiah, the son of Cushi, to say to Baruch, "Bring the scroll from which you have read to the people and come." So Baruch son of Neriah went to them with the scroll in his hand. ¹⁵They said to him, "Sit down, please, and read it to us."

So Baruch read it to them. ¹⁶When they heard all these words, they looked at each other in fear and said to Baruch, "We must report all these words to the king." ¹⁷Then they asked Baruch, "Tell us, how did you come to write all this? Did Jeremiah dictate it?"

¹⁸"Yes," Baruch replied, "he dictated all these words to me, and I wrote them in ink on the scroll."

¹⁹Then the officials said to Baruch, "You and Jeremiah, go and hide. Don't let anyone know where you are."

²⁰After they put the scroll in the room of Elishama the secretary, they went to the king in the courtyard and reported everything to him. ²¹The king sent Jehudi to get the scroll, and Jehudi brought it from the room of Elishama the secretary and read it to the king and all the officials standing beside him. ²²It was the ninth month and the king was sitting in the winter apartment, with a fire burning in the firepot in front of him. ²³Whenever Jehudi had read three or four columns of the scroll, the king cut them off with a scribe's knife and threw them into the firepot, until the entire scroll was burned in the fire. ²⁴The king and all his attendants who heard all these words showed no fear, nor did they tear their clothes. ²⁵Even though Elnathan, Delaiah and Gemariah urged the king not to burn the scroll, he would not listen to them. ²⁶Instead, the king commanded Jerahmeel, a son of the king, Seraiah son of Azriel and Shelemiah son of Abdeel to arrest Baruch the scribe and Jeremiah the prophet. But the LORD had hidden them.

²⁷After the king burned the scroll containing the words that Baruch had written at Jeremiah's dictation, the word of the LORD came to Jeremiah: ²⁸"Take another scroll and write on it all the words that were on the first scroll, which Jehoiakim king of Judah burned up. ²⁹Also tell Jehoiakim king of Judah, 'This is what the LORD says: You burned that scroll and said, "Why did you write on it that the king of Babylon would certainly come and destroy this land and cut off both men and animals from it?" ³⁰Therefore, this

THE MESSAGE

Nethaniah, son of Semaiah, son of Cushi, to Baruch, ordering him, "Take the scroll that you have read to the people and bring it here." So Baruch went and retrieved the scroll.

36.15 The officials told him, "Sit down. Read it to us, please." Baruch read it.

36.16 When they had heard it all, they were upset. They talked it over. "We've got to tell the king all this."

36.17 They asked Baruch, "Tell us, how did you come to write all this? Was it at Jeremiah's dictation?"

36.18 Baruch said, "That's right. Every word right from his own mouth. And I wrote it down, word for word, with pen and ink."

36.19 The government officials told Baruch, "You need to get out of here. Go into hiding, you and Jeremiah. Don't let anyone know where you are!"

36.20-21 The officials went to the court of the palace to report to the king, having put the scroll for safekeeping in the office of Elishama the secretary of state. The king sent Jehudi to get the scroll. He brought it from the office of Elishama the secretary. Jehudi then read it to the king and the officials who were in the king's service.

36.22-23 It was December. The king was sitting in his winter quarters in front of a charcoal fire. After Jehudi would read three or four columns, the king would cut them off the scroll with his pocketknife and throw them in the fire. He continued in this way until the entire scroll had been burned up in the fire.

36.24-26 Neither the king nor any of his officials showed the slightest twinge of conscience as they listened to the messages read. Elnathan, Delaiah, and Gemariah tried to convince the king not to burn the scroll, but he brushed them off. He just plowed ahead and ordered Prince Jerahameel, Seraiah son of Azriel, and Shelemiah son of Abdeel to arrest Jeremiah the prophet and his secretary Baruch. But GOD had hidden them away.

✛

36.27-28 After the king had burned the scroll that Baruch had written at Jeremiah's dictation, Jeremiah received this Message from GOD: "Get another blank scroll and do it all over again. Write out everything that was in that first scroll that Jehoiakim king of Judah burned up.

36.29 "And send this personal message to Jehoiakim king of Judah: 'GOD says, You had the gall to burn this scroll and then the nerve to say, "What kind of nonsense is this written here—that the king of Babylon will come and destroy this land and kill everything in it?"

NEW INTERNATIONAL VERSION

is what the LORD says about Jehoiakim king of Judah: He will have no one to sit on the throne of David; his body will be thrown out and exposed to the heat by day and the frost by night. ³¹I will punish him and his children and his attendants for their wickedness; I will bring on them and those living in Jerusalem and the people of Judah every disaster I pronounced against them, because they have not listened.' "

³²So Jeremiah took another scroll and gave it to the scribe Baruch son of Neriah, and as Jeremiah dictated, Baruch wrote on it all the words of the scroll that Jehoiakim king of Judah had burned in the fire. And many similar words were added to them.

JEREMIAH IN PRISON

37 Zedekiah son of Josiah was made king of Judah by Nebuchadnezzar king of Babylon; he reigned in place of Jehoiachin*ᵃ* son of Jehoiakim. ²Neither he nor his attendants nor the people of the land paid any attention to the words the LORD had spoken through Jeremiah the prophet.

³King Zedekiah, however, sent Jehucal son of Shelemiah with the priest Zephaniah son of Maaseiah to Jeremiah the prophet with this message: "Please pray to the LORD our God for us."

⁴Now Jeremiah was free to come and go among the people, for he had not yet been put in prison. ⁵Pharaoh's army had marched out of Egypt, and when the Babylonians*ᵇ* who were besieging Jerusalem heard the report about them, they withdrew from Jerusalem.

⁶Then the word of the LORD came to Jeremiah the prophet: ⁷"This is what the LORD, the God of Israel, says: Tell the king of Judah, who sent you to inquire of me, 'Pharaoh's army, which has marched out to support you, will go back to its own land, to Egypt. ⁸Then the Babylonians will return and attack this city; they will capture it and burn it down.'

⁹"This is what the LORD says: Do not deceive yourselves, thinking, 'The Babylonians will surely leave us.' They will not! ¹⁰Even if you were to defeat the entire Babylonian*ᶜ* army that is attacking you and only wounded men were left in their tents, they would come out and burn this city down."

¹¹After the Babylonian army had withdrawn

ᵃ 1 Hebrew Coniah, *a variant of* Jehoiachin
ᵇ 5 Or Chaldeans; *also in verses 8, 9, 13 and 14*
ᶜ 10 Or Chaldean; *also in verse 11*

THE MESSAGE

³⁶·³⁰⁻³¹ " 'Well, do you want to know what GOD says about Jehoiakim king of Judah? This: No descendant of his will ever rule from David's throne. His corpse will be thrown in the street and left unburied, exposed to the hot sun and the freezing night. I will punish him and his children and the officials in his government for their blatant sin. I'll let loose on them and everyone in Jerusalem the doomsday disaster of which I warned them but they spit at.' "

³⁶·³² So Jeremiah went and got another scroll and gave it to Baruch son of Neriah, his secretary. At Jeremiah's dictation he again wrote down everything that Jehoiakim king of Judah had burned in the fire. There were also generous additions, but of the same kind of thing.

IN AN UNDERGROUND DUNGEON

³⁷·¹⁻² **37** King Zedekiah son of Josiah, a puppet king set on the throne by Nebuchadnezzar king of Babylon in the land of Judah, was now king in place of Jehoiachin son of Jehoiakim. But neither he nor his officials nor the people themselves paid a bit of attention to the Message GOD gave by Jeremiah the prophet.

³⁷·³ However, King Zedekiah sent Jehucal son of Shelemiah, and Zephaniah the priest, son of Maaseiah, to Jeremiah the prophet, saying, "Pray for us—pray hard!—to the Master, our GOD."

³⁷·⁴⁻⁵ Jeremiah was still moving about freely among the people in those days. This was before he had been put in jail. Pharaoh's army was marching up from Egypt. The Chaldeans fighting against Jerusalem heard that the Egyptians were coming and pulled back.

³⁷·⁶⁻¹⁰ Then Jeremiah the prophet received this Message from GOD: "I, the GOD of Israel, want you to give this Message to the king of Judah, who has just sent you to me to find out what he should do. Tell him, 'Get this: Pharaoh's army, which is on its way to help you, isn't going to stick it out. No sooner will they get here than they'll leave and go home to Egypt. And then the Babylonians will come back and resume their attack, capture this city and burn it to the ground. I, GOD, am telling you: Don't kid yourselves, reassuring one another, "The Babylonians will leave in a few days." I tell you, they aren't leaving. Why, even if you defeated the entire attacking Chaldean army and all that was left were a few wounded soldiers in their tents, the wounded would still do the job and burn this city to the ground.' "

✛

³⁷·¹¹⁻¹³ When the Chaldean army pulled back from

NEW INTERNATIONAL VERSION

from Jerusalem because of Pharaoh's army, ¹²Jeremiah started to leave the city to go to the territory of Benjamin to get his share of the property among the people there. ¹³But when he reached the Benjamin Gate, the captain of the guard, whose name was Irijah son of Shelemiah, the son of Hananiah, arrested him and said, "You are deserting to the Babylonians!"

¹⁴"That's not true!" Jeremiah said. "I am not deserting to the Babylonians." But Irijah would not listen to him; instead, he arrested Jeremiah and brought him to the officials. ¹⁵They were angry with Jeremiah and had him beaten and imprisoned in the house of Jonathan the secretary, which they had made into a prison.

¹⁶Jeremiah was put into a vaulted cell in a dungeon, where he remained a long time. ¹⁷Then King Zedekiah sent for him and had him brought to the palace, where he asked him privately, "Is there any word from the LORD?"

"Yes," Jeremiah replied, "you will be handed over to the king of Babylon."

¹⁸Then Jeremiah said to King Zedekiah, "What crime have I committed against you or your officials or this people, that you have put me in prison? ¹⁹Where are your prophets who prophesied to you, 'The king of Babylon will not attack you or this land'? ²⁰But now, my lord the king, please listen. Let me bring my petition before you: Do not send me back to the house of Jonathan the secretary, or I will die there."

²¹King Zedekiah then gave orders for Jeremiah to be placed in the courtyard of the guard and given bread from the street of the bakers each day until all the bread in the city was gone. So Jeremiah remained in the courtyard of the guard.

JEREMIAH THROWN INTO A CISTERN

38 Shephatiah son of Mattan, Gedaliah son of Pashhur, Jehucal*ᵃ* son of Shelemiah, and Pashhur son of Malkijah heard what Jeremiah was telling all the people when he said, ²"This is what the LORD says: 'Whoever stays in this city will die by the sword, famine or plague, but whoever goes over to the Babylonians*ᵇ* will live. He will escape with his life; he will live.' ³And this is what the LORD says: 'This city will certainly be handed over to the army of the king of Babylon, who will capture it.' "

⁴Then the officials said to the king, "This man should be put to death. He is discouraging the

THE MESSAGE

Jerusalem, Jeremiah left Jerusalem to go over to the territory of Benjamin to take care of some personal business. When he got to the Benjamin Gate, the officer on guard there, Irijah son of Shelemiah, son of Hananiah, grabbed Jeremiah the prophet, accusing him, "You're deserting to the Chaldeans!"

"That's a lie," protested Jeremiah. "I wouldn't think of deserting to the Chaldeans."

37.14-16 But Irijah wouldn't listen to him. He arrested him and took him to the police. The police were furious with Jeremiah. They beat him up and threw him into jail in the house of Jonathan the secretary of state. (They were using the house for a prison cell.) So Jeremiah entered an underground cell in a cistern turned into a dungeon. He stayed there a long time.

37.17 Later King Zedekiah had Jeremiah brought to him. The king questioned him privately, "Is there a Message from GOD?"

"There certainly is," said Jeremiah. "You're going to be turned over to the king of Babylon."

37.18-20 Jeremiah continued speaking to King Zedekiah: "Can you tell me why you threw me into prison? What crime did I commit against you or your officials or this people? And tell me, whatever has become of your prophets who preached all those sermons saying that the king of Babylon would never attack you or this land? Listen to me, please, my master—my king! Please don't send me back to that dungeon in the house of Jonathan the secretary. I'll die there!"

37.21 So King Zedekiah ordered that Jeremiah be assigned to the courtyard of the palace guards. He was given a loaf of bread from Bakers' Alley every day until all the bread in the city was gone. And that's where Jeremiah remained—in the courtyard of the palace guards.

FROM THE DUNGEON TO THE PALACE

38.1 **38** Shaphatiah son of Mattan, Gedaliah son of Pashur, Jehucal son of Shelemiah, and Pashur son of Malkijah heard what Jeremiah was telling the people, namely:

38.2 "This is GOD's Message: 'Whoever stays in this town will die—will be killed or starve to death or get sick and die. But those who go over to the Babylonians will save their necks and live.'

38.3 "And, GOD's sure Word: 'This city is destined to fall to the army of the king of Babylon. He's going to take it over.' "

38.4 These officials told the king, "Please, kill this man. He's got to go! He's ruining the re-

---

ᵃ 1 Hebrew *Jucal,* a variant of *Jehucal*   *ᵇ* 2 Or *Chaldeans*; also in verses 18, 19 and 23

NEW INTERNATIONAL VERSION	THE MESSAGE

soldiers who are left in this city, as well as all the people, by the things he is saying to them. This man is not seeking the good of these people but their ruin."

⁵"He is in your hands," King Zedekiah answered. "The king can do nothing to oppose you."

⁶So they took Jeremiah and put him into the cistern of Malkijah, the king's son, which was in the courtyard of the guard. They lowered Jeremiah by ropes into the cistern; it had no water in it, only mud, and Jeremiah sank down into the mud.

⁷But Ebed-Melech, a Cushite,ᵃ an officialᵇ in the royal palace, heard that they had put Jeremiah into the cistern. While the king was sitting in the Benjamin Gate, ⁸Ebed-Melech went out of the palace and said to him, ⁹"My lord the king, these men have acted wickedly in all they have done to Jeremiah the prophet. They have thrown him into a cistern, where he will starve to death when there is no longer any bread in the city."

¹⁰Then the king commanded Ebed-Melech the Cushite, "Take thirty men from here with you and lift Jeremiah the prophet out of the cistern before he dies."

¹¹So Ebed-Melech took the men with him and went to a room under the treasury in the palace. He took some old rags and worn-out clothes from there and let them down with ropes to Jeremiah in the cistern. ¹²Ebed-Melech the Cushite said to Jeremiah, "Put these old rags and worn-out clothes under your arms to pad the ropes." Jeremiah did so, ¹³and they pulled him up with the ropes and lifted him out of the cistern. And Jeremiah remained in the courtyard of the guard.

ZEDEKIAH QUESTIONS JEREMIAH AGAIN

¹⁴Then King Zedekiah sent for Jeremiah the prophet and had him brought to the third entrance to the temple of the LORD. "I am going to ask you something," the king said to Jeremiah. "Do not hide anything from me."

¹⁵Jeremiah said to Zedekiah, "If I give you an answer, will you not kill me? Even if I did give you counsel, you would not listen to me."

¹⁶But King Zedekiah swore this oath secretly to Jeremiah: "As surely as the LORD lives, who has given us breath, I will neither kill you nor hand you over to those who are seeking your life."

¹⁷Then Jeremiah said to Zedekiah, "This is what the LORD God Almighty, the God of Israel, says: 'If you surrender to the officers of the king of Babylon, your life will be spared and this city will not be burned down; you and your family

solve of the soldiers who are still left in the city, as well as the people themselves, by spreading these words. This man isn't looking after the good of this people. He's trying to ruin us!"

38.5 King Zedekiah caved in: "If you say so. Go ahead, handle it your way. You're too much for me."

38.6 So they took Jeremiah and threw him into the cistern of Malkijah the king's son that was in the courtyard of the palace guard. They lowered him down with ropes. There wasn't any water in the cistern, only mud. Jeremiah sank into the mud.

38.7-9 Ebed-melech the Ethiopian, a court official assigned to the royal palace, heard that they had thrown Jeremiah into the cistern. While the king was holding court in the Benjamin Gate, Ebed-melek went immediately from the palace to the king and said, "My master, O king—these men are committing a great crime in what they're doing, throwing Jeremiah the prophet into the cistern and leaving him there to starve. He's as good as dead. There isn't a scrap of bread left in the city."

38.10 So the king ordered Ebed-melek the Ethiopian, "Get three men and pull Jeremiah the prophet out of the cistern before he dies."

38.11-12 Ebed-melek got three men and went to the palace wardrobe and got some scraps of old clothing, which they tied together and lowered down with ropes to Jeremiah in the cistern. Ebed-melek the Ethiopian called down to Jeremiah, "Put these scraps of old clothing under your armpits and around the ropes."

Jeremiah did what he said.

38.13 And so they pulled Jeremiah up out of the cistern by the ropes. But he was still confined in the courtyard of the palace guard.

38.14 Later, King Zedekiah sent for Jeremiah the prophet and had him brought to the third entrance of the Temple of GOD. The king said to Jeremiah, "I'm going to ask you something. Don't hold anything back from me."

38.15 Jeremiah said, "If I told you the whole truth, you'd kill me. And no matter what I said, you wouldn't pay any attention anyway."

38.16 Zedekiah swore to Jeremiah right there, but in secret, "As sure as GOD lives, who gives *us* life, I won't kill you, nor will I turn you over to the men who are trying to kill you."

38.17-18 So Jeremiah told Zedekiah, "This is the Message from GOD, GOD-of-the-Angel-Armies, the God of Israel: 'If you will turn yourself over to the generals of the king of Babylon, you will live, this city won't be burned down, and your

---

ᵃ 7 Probably from the upper Nile region   ᵇ 7 Or *a eunuch*

NEW INTERNATIONAL VERSION

will live. ¹⁸But if you will not surrender to the officers of the king of Babylon, this city will be handed over to the Babylonians and they will burn it down; you yourself will not escape from their hands.' "

¹⁹King Zedekiah said to Jeremiah, "I am afraid of the Jews who have gone over to the Babylonians, for the Babylonians may hand me over to them and they will mistreat me."

²⁰"They will not hand you over," Jeremiah replied. "Obey the Lord by doing what I tell you. Then it will go well with you, and your life will be spared. ²¹But if you refuse to surrender, this is what the Lord has revealed to me: ²²All the women left in the palace of the king of Judah will be brought out to the officials of the king of Babylon. Those women will say to you:

" 'They misled you and overcame you—
    those trusted friends of yours.
Your feet are sunk in the mud;
    your friends have deserted you.'

²³"All your wives and children will be brought out to the Babylonians. You yourself will not escape from their hands but will be captured by the king of Babylon; and this city will*a* be burned down."

²⁴Then Zedekiah said to Jeremiah, "Do not let anyone know about this conversation, or you may die. ²⁵If the officials hear that I talked with you, and they come to you and say, 'Tell us what you said to the king and what the king said to you; do not hide it from us or we will kill you,' ²⁶then tell them, 'I was pleading with the king not to send me back to Jonathan's house to die there.' "

²⁷All the officials did come to Jeremiah and question him, and he told them everything the king had ordered him to say. So they said no more to him, for no one had heard his conversation with the king.

²⁸And Jeremiah remained in the courtyard of the guard until the day Jerusalem was captured.

THE FALL OF JERUSALEM

39 This is how Jerusalem was taken: ¹In the ninth year of Zedekiah king of Judah, in the tenth month, Nebuchadnezzar king of Babylon marched against Jerusalem with his whole army and laid siege to it. ²And on the ninth day of the fourth month of Zedekiah's eleventh year, the city wall was broken through. ³Then all the

---

THE MESSAGE

family will live. But if you don't turn yourself over to the generals of the king of Babylon, this city will go into the hands of the Chaldeans and they'll burn it down. And don't for a minute think there's any escape for you.' "

38.19 King Zedekiah said to Jeremiah, "But I'm afraid of the Judeans who have already deserted to the Chaldeans. If they get hold of me, they'll rough me up good."

38.20-22 Jeremiah assured him, "They won't get hold of you. Listen, please. Listen to God's voice. I'm telling you this for your own good so that you'll live. But if you refuse to turn yourself over, this is what God has shown me will happen: Picture this in your mind—all the women still left in the palace of the king of Judah, led out to the officers of the king of Babylon, and as they're led out they are saying:

" 'They lied to you and did you in,
    those so-called friends of yours;
And now you're stuck, about knee-deep in
    mud,
    and your "friends," where are they now?'

38.23 "They'll take all your wives and children and give them to the Chaldeans. And you, don't think you'll get out of this—the king of Babylon will seize you and then burn this city to the ground."

38.24-26 Zedekiah said to Jeremiah, "Don't let anyone know of this conversation, if you know what's good for you. If the government officials get wind that I've been talking with you, they may come and say, 'Tell us what went on between you and the king, what you said and what he said. Hold nothing back and we won't kill you.' If this happens, tell them, 'I presented my case to the king so that he wouldn't send me back to the dungeon of Jonathan to die there.' "

38.27 And sure enough, all the officials came to Jeremiah and asked him. He responded as the king had instructed. So they quit asking. No one had overheard the conversation.

38.28 Jeremiah lived in the courtyard of the palace guards until the day that Jerusalem was captured.

BAD NEWS, NOT GOOD NEWS

39.1-2 **39** In the ninth year and tenth month of Zedekiah king of Judah, Nebuchadnezzar king of Babylon came with his entire army and laid siege to Jerusalem. In the eleventh year and fourth month, on the ninth day of Zedekiah's reign, they broke through into the city.

---

a 23 Or and you will cause this city to

NEW INTERNATIONAL VERSION

officials of the king of Babylon came and took seats in the Middle Gate: Nergal-Sharezer of Samgar, Nebo-Sarsekim*a* a chief officer, Nergal-Sharezer a high official and all the other officials of the king of Babylon. *4*When Zedekiah king of Judah and all the soldiers saw them, they fled; they left the city at night by way of the king's garden, through the gate between the two walls, and headed toward the Arabah.*b*

*5*But the Babylonian*c* army pursued them and overtook Zedekiah in the plains of Jericho. They captured him and took him to Nebuchadnezzar king of Babylon at Riblah in the land of Hamath, where he pronounced sentence on him. *6*There at Riblah the king of Babylon slaughtered the sons of Zedekiah before his eyes and also killed all the nobles of Judah. *7*Then he put out Zedekiah's eyes and bound him with bronze shackles to take him to Babylon.

*8*The Babylonians*d* set fire to the royal palace and the houses of the people and broke down the walls of Jerusalem. *9*Nebuzaradan commander of the imperial guard carried into exile to Babylon the people who remained in the city, along with those who had gone over to him, and the rest of the people. *10*But Nebuzaradan the commander of the guard left behind in the land of Judah some of the poor people, who owned nothing; and at that time he gave them vineyards and fields.

*11*Now Nebuchadnezzar king of Babylon had given these orders about Jeremiah through Nebuzaradan commander of the imperial guard: *12*"Take him and look after him; don't harm him but do for him whatever he asks." *13*So Nebuzaradan the commander of the guard, Nebushazban a chief officer, Nergal-Sharezer a high official and all the other officers of the king of Babylon *14*sent and had Jeremiah taken out of the courtyard of the guard. They turned him over to Gedaliah son of Ahikam, the son of Shaphan, to take him back to his home. So he remained among his own people.

*15*While Jeremiah had been confined in the courtyard of the guard, the word of the LORD came to him: *16*"Go and tell Ebed-Melech the Cushite, 'This is what the LORD Almighty, the God of Israel, says: I am about to fulfill my

THE MESSAGE

39.3 All the officers of the king of Babylon came and set themselves up as a ruling council from the Middle Gate: Nergal-sharezer of Simmagar, Nebushazban the Rabsaris, Nergal-sharezer the Rabmag, along with all the other officials of the king of Babylon.

39.4-7 When Zedekiah king of Judah and his remaining soldiers saw this, they ran for their lives. They slipped out at night on a path in the king's garden through the gate between two walls and headed for the wilderness, toward the Jordan Valley. The Babylonian army chased them and caught Zedekiah in the wilderness of Jericho. They seized him and took him to Nebuchadnezzar king of Babylon at Riblah in the country of Hamath. Nebuchadnezzar decided his fate. The king of Babylon killed all the sons of Zedekiah in Riblah right before his eyes and then killed all the nobles of Judah. After Zedekiah had seen the slaughter, Nebuchadnezzar blinded him, chained him up, and then took him off to Babylon.

39.8-10 Meanwhile, the Babylonians burned down the royal palace, the Temple, and all the homes of the people. They leveled the walls of Jerusalem. Nebuzaradan, commander of the king's bodyguard, rounded up everyone left in the city, along with those who had surrendered to him, and herded them off to exile in Babylon. He didn't bother taking the few poor people who had nothing. He left them in the land of Judah to eke out a living as best they could in the vineyards and fields.

✟

39.11-12 Nebuchadnezzar king of Babylon gave Nebuzaradan captain of the king's bodyguard special orders regarding Jeremiah: "Look out for him. Make sure nothing bad happens to him. Give him anything he wants."

39.13-14 So Nebuzaradan, chief of the king's bodyguard, along with Nebushazban the Rabsaris, Nergal-sharezer the Rabmag, and all the chief officers of the king of Babylon, sent for Jeremiah, taking him from the courtyard of the royal guards and putting him under the care of Gedaliah son of Ahikam, the son of Shaphan, to be taken home. And so he was able to live with the people.

✟

39.15-18 Earlier, while Jeremiah was still in custody in the courtyard of the royal guards, GOD's Message came to him: "Go and speak with Ebed-melek the Ethiopian. Tell him, GOD-of-the-Angel-Armies, the God of Israel, says, Listen carefully: I will do exactly what I said I would

---

a 3 Or Nergal-Sharezer, Samgar-Nebo, Sarsekim   b 4 Or the Jordan Valley   c 5 Or Chaldean   d 8 Or Chaldeans

NEW INTERNATIONAL VERSION

words against this city through disaster, not prosperity. At that time they will be fulfilled before your eyes. ¹⁷But I will rescue you on that day, declares the LORD; you will not be handed over to those you fear. ¹⁸I will save you; you will not fall by the sword but will escape with your life, because you trust in me, declares the LORD.' "

JEREMIAH FREED

40 The word came to Jeremiah from the LORD after Nebuzaradan commander of the imperial guard had released him at Ramah. He had found Jeremiah bound in chains among all the captives from Jerusalem and Judah who were being carried into exile to Babylon. ²When the commander of the guard found Jeremiah, he said to him, "The LORD your God decreed this disaster for this place. ³And now the LORD has brought it about; he has done just as he said he would. All this happened because you people sinned against the LORD and did not obey him. ⁴But today I am freeing you from the chains on your wrists. Come with me to Babylon, if you like, and I will look after you; but if you do not want to, then don't come. Look, the whole country lies before you; go wherever you please." ⁵However, before Jeremiah turned to go,ᵃ Nebuzaradan added, "Go back to Gedaliah son of Ahikam, the son of Shaphan, whom the king of Babylon has appointed over the towns of Judah, and live with him among the people, or go anywhere else you please."

Then the commander gave him provisions and a present and let him go. ⁶So Jeremiah went to Gedaliah son of Ahikam at Mizpah and stayed with him among the people who were left behind in the land.

GEDALIAH ASSASSINATED

⁷When all the army officers and their men who were still in the open country heard that the king of Babylon had appointed Gedaliah son of Ahikam as governor over the land and had put him in charge of the men, women and children who were the poorest in the land and who had not been carried into exile to Babylon, ⁸they came to Gedaliah at Mizpah—Ishmael son of Nethaniah, Johanan and Jonathan the sons of Kareah, Seraiah son of Tanhumeth, the sons of Ephai the Netophathite, and Jaazaniahᵇ the son of the Maacathite, and their men. ⁹Gedaliah son of Ahikam, the son of Shaphan, took an oath to reassure them and their men. "Do not be afraid

---

ᵃ 5 Or *Jeremiah answered*   ᵇ 8 Hebrew *Jezaniah*, a variant of *Jaazaniah*

THE MESSAGE

do to this city—bad news, not good news. When it happens, you will be there to see it. But I'll deliver you on that doomsday. You won't be handed over to those men whom you have good reason to fear. Yes, I'll most certainly save you. You won't be killed. You'll walk out of there safe and sound because you trusted me.' " GOD's Decree.

GO AND LIVE WHEREVER YOU WISH

40.1 **40** GOD's Message to Jeremiah after Nebuzaradan captain of the bodyguard set him free at Ramah. When Nebuzaradan came upon him, he was in chains, along with all the other captives from Jerusalem and Judah who were being herded off to exile in Babylon.

40.2-3 The captain of the bodyguard singled out Jeremiah and said to him, "Your GOD pronounced doom on this place. GOD came and did what he had warned he'd do because you all sinned against GOD and wouldn't do what he told you. So now you're all suffering the consequences.

40.4-5 "But today, Jeremiah, I'm setting you free, taking the chains off your hands. If you'd like to come to Babylon with me, come along. I'll take good care of you. But if you don't want to come to Babylon with me, that's just fine, too. Look, the whole land stretches out before you. Do what you like. Go and live wherever you wish. If you want to stay home, go back to Gedaliah son of Ahikam, son of Shaphan. The king of Babylon made him governor of the cities of Judah. Stay with him and your people. Or go wherever you'd like. It's up to you."

The captain of the bodyguard gave him food for the journey and a parting gift, and sent him off.

40.6 Jeremiah went to Gedaliah son of Ahikam at Mizpah and made his home with him and the people who were left behind in the land.

TAKE CARE OF THE LAND

40.7-8 When the army leaders and their men, who had been hiding out in the fields, heard that the king of Babylon had appointed Gedaliah son of Ahikam as governor of the land, putting him in charge of the men, women, and children of the poorest of the poor who hadn't been taken off to exile in Babylon, they came to Gedaliah at Mizpah: Ishmael son of Nethaniah, Johanan and Jonathan the sons of Kareah, Seraiah son of Tanhumeth, the sons of Ephai the Netophathite, and Jaazaniah son of the Maacathite, accompanied by their men.

40.9 Gedaliah son of Ahikam, the son of Shaphan, promised them and their men, "You have

NEW INTERNATIONAL VERSION

to serve the Babylonians,*a*" he said. "Settle down in the land and serve the king of Babylon, and it will go well with you. ¹⁰I myself will stay at Mizpah to represent you before the Babylonians who come to us, but you are to harvest the wine, summer fruit and oil, and put them in your storage jars, and live in the towns you have taken over."

¹¹When all the Jews in Moab, Ammon, Edom and all the other countries heard that the king of Babylon had left a remnant in Judah and had appointed Gedaliah son of Ahikam, the son of Shaphan, as governor over them, ¹²they all came back to the land of Judah, to Gedaliah at Mizpah, from all the countries where they had been scattered. And they harvested an abundance of wine and summer fruit.

¹³Johanan son of Kareah and all the army officers still in the open country came to Gedaliah at Mizpah ¹⁴and said to him, "Don't you know that Baalis king of the Ammonites has sent Ishmael son of Nethaniah to take your life?" But Gedaliah son of Ahikam did not believe them.

¹⁵Then Johanan son of Kareah said privately to Gedaliah in Mizpah, "Let me go and kill Ishmael son of Nethaniah, and no one will know it. Why should he take your life and cause all the Jews who are gathered around you to be scattered and the remnant of Judah to perish?"

¹⁶But Gedaliah son of Ahikam said to Johanan son of Kareah, "Don't do such a thing! What you are saying about Ishmael is not true."

41 In the seventh month Ishmael son of Nethaniah, the son of Elishama, who was of royal blood and had been one of the king's officers, came with ten men to Gedaliah son of Ahikam at Mizpah. While they were eating together there, ²Ishmael son of Nethaniah and the ten men who were with him got up and struck down Gedaliah son of Ahikam, the son of Shaphan, with the sword, killing the one whom the king of Babylon had appointed as governor over the land. ³Ishmael also killed all the Jews who were with Gedaliah at Mizpah, as well as the Babylonian*b* soldiers who were there.

⁴The day after Gedaliah's assassination, before anyone knew about it, ⁵eighty men who had shaved off their beards, torn their clothes and

THE MESSAGE

nothing to fear from the Chaldean officials. Stay here on the land. Be subject to the king of Babylon. You'll get along just fine.

40.10 "My job is to stay here in Mizpah and be your advocate before the Chaldeans when they show up. Your job is to take care of the land: Make wine, harvest the summer fruits, press olive oil. Store it all in pottery jugs and settle into the towns that you have taken over."

40.11-12 The Judeans who had escaped to Moab, Ammon, Edom, and other countries heard that the king of Babylon had left a few survivors in Judah and made Gedaliah son of Ahikam, son of Shaphan, governor over them. They all started coming back to Judah from all the places where they'd been scattered. They came to Judah and to Gedaliah at Mizpah and went to work gathering in a huge supply of wine and summer fruits.

✠

40.13-14 One day Johanan son of Kareah and all the officers of the army who had been hiding out in the backcountry came to Gedaliah at Mizpah and told him, "You know, don't you, that Baaliss king of Ammon has sent Ishmael son of Nethaniah to kill you?" But Gedaliah son of Ahikam didn't believe them.

40.15 Then Johanan son of Kareah took Gedaliah aside privately in Mizpah: "Let me go and kill Ishmael son of Nethaniah. No one needs to know about it. Why should we let him kill you and plunge the land into anarchy? Why let everyone you've taken care of be scattered and what's left of Judah destroyed?"

40.16 But Gedaliah son of Ahikam told Johanan son of Kareah, "Don't do it. I forbid it. You're spreading a false rumor about Ishmael."

MURDER

41.1-3 **41** But in the seventh month, Ishmael son of Nethaniah, son of Elishama, came. He had royal blood in his veins and had been one of the king's high-ranking officers. He paid a visit to Gedaliah son of Ahikam at Mizpah with ten of his men. As they were eating together, Ishmael and his ten men jumped to their feet and knocked Gedaliah down and killed him, killed the man the king of Babylon had appointed governor of the land. Ishmael also killed all the Judeans who were with Gedaliah in Mizpah, as well as the Chaldean soldiers who were stationed there.

41.4-5 On the second day after the murder of Gedaliah—no one yet knew of it—men arrived from Shechem, Shiloh, and Samaria, eighty of them, with their beards shaved, their clothing ripped,

cut themselves came from Shechem, Shiloh and Samaria, bringing grain offerings and incense with them to the house of the LORD. ⁶Ishmael son of Nethaniah went out from Mizpah to meet them, weeping as he went. When he met them, he said, "Come to Gedaliah son of Ahikam." ⁷When they went into the city, Ishmael son of Nethaniah and the men who were with him slaughtered them and threw them into a cistern. ⁸But ten of them said to Ishmael, "Don't kill us! We have wheat and barley, oil and honey, hidden in a field." So he let them alone and did not kill them with the others. ⁹Now the cistern where he threw all the bodies of the men he had killed along with Gedaliah was the one King Asa had made as part of his defense against Baasha king of Israel. Ishmael son of Nethaniah filled it with the dead.

¹⁰Ishmael made captives of all the rest of the people who were in Mizpah—the king's daughters along with all the others who were left there, over whom Nebuzaradan commander of the imperial guard had appointed Gedaliah son of Ahikam. Ishmael son of Nethaniah took them captive and set out to cross over to the Ammonites.

¹¹When Johanan son of Kareah and all the army officers who were with him heard about all the crimes Ishmael son of Nethaniah had committed, ¹²they took all their men and went to fight Ishmael son of Nethaniah. They caught up with him near the great pool in Gibeon. ¹³When all the people Ishmael had with him saw Johanan son of Kareah and the army officers who were with him, they were glad. ¹⁴All the people Ishmael had taken captive at Mizpah turned and went over to Johanan son of Kareah. ¹⁵But Ishmael son of Nethaniah and eight of his men escaped from Johanan and fled to the Ammonites.

FLIGHT TO EGYPT

¹⁶Then Johanan son of Kareah and all the army officers who were with him led away all the survivors from Mizpah whom he had recovered from Ishmael son of Nethaniah after he had assassinated Gedaliah son of Ahikam: the soldiers, women, children and court officials he had brought from Gibeon. ¹⁷And they went on, stopping at Geruth Kimham near Bethlehem on their way to Egypt ¹⁸to escape the Babylonians.ᵃ They were afraid of them because Ishmael son of Nethaniah had killed Gedaliah son of Ahikam, whom the king of Babylon had appointed as governor over the land.

ᵃ *18 Or Chaldeans*

and gashes on their bodies. They were pilgrims carrying grain offerings and incense on their way to worship at the Temple in Jerusalem.

41.6 Ishmael son of Nethaniah went out from Mizpah to welcome them, weeping ostentatiously. When he greeted them he invited them in: "Come and meet Gedaliah son of Ahikam."

41.7-8 But as soon as they were inside the city, Ishmael son of Nethaniah and his henchmen slaughtered the pilgrims and dumped the bodies in a cistern. Ten of the men talked their way out of the massacre. They bargained with Ishmael, "Don't kill us. We have a hidden store of wheat, barley, olive oil, and honey out in the fields." So he held back and didn't kill them with their fellow pilgrims.

41.9 Ishmael's reason for dumping the bodies into a cistern was to cover up the earlier murder of Gedaliah. The cistern had been built by king Asa as a defense against Baasha king of Israel. This was the cistern that Ishmael son of Nethaniah filled with the slaughtered men.

41.10 Ishmael then took everyone else in Mizpah, including the king's daughters entrusted to the care of Gedaliah son of Ahikam by Nebuzaradan the captain of the bodyguard, as prisoners. Rounding up the prisoners, Ishmael son of Nethaniah proceeded to take them over into the country of Ammon.

41.11-12 Johanan son of Kareah and all the army officers with him heard about the atrocities committed by Ishmael son of Nethaniah. They set off at once after Ishmael son of Nethaniah. They found him at the large pool at Gibeon.

41.13-15 When all the prisoners from Mizpah who had been taken by Ishmael saw Johanan son of Kareah and the army officers with him, they couldn't believe their eyes. They were so happy! They all rallied around Johanan son of Kareah and headed back home. But Ishmael son of Nethaniah got away, escaping from Johanan with eight men into the land of Ammon.

41.16 Then Johanan son of Kareah and the army officers with him gathered together what was left of the people whom Ishmael son of Nethaniah had taken prisoner from Mizpah after the murder of Gedaliah son of Ahikam—men, women, children, eunuchs—and brought them back from Gibeon.

41.17-18 They set out at once for Egypt to get away from the Chaldeans, stopping on the way at Geruth-kimham near Bethlehem. They were afraid of what the Chaldeans might do in retaliation of Ishmael son of Nethaniah's murder of Gedaliah son of Ahikam, whom the king of Babylon had appointed as governor of the country.

NEW INTERNATIONAL VERSION

42 Then all the army officers, including Johanan son of Kareah and Jezaniah[a] son of Hoshaiah, and all the people from the least to the greatest approached ²Jeremiah the prophet and said to him, "Please hear our petition and pray to the LORD your God for this entire remnant. For as you now see, though we were once many, now only a few are left. ³Pray that the LORD your God will tell us where we should go and what we should do."

⁴"I have heard you," replied Jeremiah the prophet. "I will certainly pray to the LORD your God as you have requested; I will tell you everything the LORD says and will keep nothing back from you."

⁵Then they said to Jeremiah, "May the LORD be a true and faithful witness against us if we do not act in accordance with everything the LORD your God sends you to tell us. ⁶Whether it is favorable or unfavorable, we will obey the LORD our God, to whom we are sending you, so that it will go well with us, for we will obey the LORD our God."

⁷Ten days later the word of the LORD came to Jeremiah. ⁸So he called together Johanan son of Kareah and all the army officers who were with him and all the people from the least to the greatest. ⁹He said to them, "This is what the LORD, the God of Israel, to whom you sent me to present your petition, says: ¹⁰'If you stay in this land, I will build you up and not tear you down; I will plant you and not uproot you, for I am grieved over the disaster I have inflicted on you. ¹¹Do not be afraid of the king of Babylon, whom you now fear. Do not be afraid of him, declares the LORD, for I am with you and will save you and deliver you from his hands. ¹²I will show you compassion so that he will have compassion on you and restore you to your land.'

¹³"However, if you say, 'We will not stay in this land,' and so disobey the LORD your God, ¹⁴and if you say, 'No, we will go and live in Egypt, where we will not see war or hear the trumpet or be hungry for bread,' ¹⁵then hear the word of the LORD, O remnant of Judah. This is what the LORD Almighty, the God of Israel, says: 'If you are determined to go to Egypt and you do go to settle there, ¹⁶then the sword you fear will overtake you there, and the famine you dread will follow you into Egypt, and there you will die. ¹⁷Indeed, all who are determined to go to Egypt to settle there will die by the sword, famine and plague; not one of them will survive or escape the disaster I will bring on them.' ¹⁸This is what the LORD Almighty, the God of Israel,

---

THE MESSAGE

WHAT YOU FEAR WILL CATCH UP WITH YOU

42 42.1-3 All the army officers, led by Johanan son of Kareah and Jezaniah son of Hoshaiah, accompanied by all the people, small and great, came to Jeremiah the prophet and said, "We have a request. Please listen. Pray to your GOD for us, what's left of us. You can see for yourself how few we are! Pray that your GOD will tell us the way we should go and what we should do."

42.4 Jeremiah the prophet said, "I hear your request. And I will pray to your GOD as you have asked. Whatever GOD says, I'll pass on to you. I'll tell you everything, holding nothing back."

42.5-6 They said to Jeremiah, "Let GOD be our witness, a true and faithful witness against us, if we don't do everything that your GOD directs you to tell us. Whether we like it or not, we'll do it. We'll obey whatever our GOD tells us. Yes, count on us. We'll do it."

42.7-8 Ten days later GOD's Message came to Jeremiah. He called together Johanan son of Kareah and all the army officers with him, including all the people, regardless of how much clout they had.

42.9-12 He then spoke: "This is the Message from GOD, the God of Israel, to whom you sent me to present your prayer. He says, 'If you are ready to stick it out in this land, I will build you up and not drag you down, I will plant you and not pull you up like a weed. I feel deep compassion on account of the doom I have visited on you. You don't have to fear the king of Babylon. Your fears are for nothing. I'm on your side, ready to save and deliver you from anything he might do. I'll pour mercy on you. What's more, *he* will show you mercy! He'll let you come back to your very own land.'

42.13-17 "But do not say, 'We're not staying around this place,' refusing to obey the command of your GOD and saying instead, 'No! We're off to Egypt, where things are peaceful—no wars, no attacking armies, plenty of food. We're going to live there.' If what's left of Judah is headed down that road, then listen to GOD's Message. This is what GOD-of-the-Angel-Armies says: 'If you have determined to go to Egypt and make that your home, then the very wars you fear will catch up with you in Egypt and the starvation you dread will track you down in Egypt. You'll die there! Every last one of you who is determined to go to Egypt and make it your home will either be killed, starve, or get sick and die. No survivors, not one! No one will escape the doom that I'll bring upon you.'

42.18 "This is the Message from GOD-of-the-Angel-Armies, the God of Israel: 'In the same way

NEW INTERNATIONAL VERSION

says: 'As my anger and wrath have been poured out on those who lived in Jerusalem, so will my wrath be poured out on you when you go to Egypt. You will be an object of cursing and horror, of condemnation and reproach; you will never see this place again.'

¹⁹"O remnant of Judah, the LORD has told you, 'Do not go to Egypt.' Be sure of this: I warn you today ²⁰that you made a fatal mistake *ᵃ* when you sent me to the LORD your God and said, 'Pray to the LORD our God for us; tell us everything he says and we will do it.' ²¹I have told you today, but you still have not obeyed the LORD your God in all he sent me to tell you. ²²So now, be sure of this: You will die by the sword, famine and plague in the place where you want to go to settle."

43 When Jeremiah finished telling the people all the words of the LORD their God—everything the LORD had sent him to tell them—²Azariah son of Hoshaiah and Johanan son of Kareah and all the arrogant men said to Jeremiah, "You are lying! The LORD our God has not sent you to say, 'You must not go to Egypt to settle there.' ³But Baruch son of Neriah is inciting you against us to hand us over to the Babylonians, *ᵇ* so they may kill us or carry us into exile to Babylon."

⁴So Johanan son of Kareah and all the army officers and all the people disobeyed the LORD's command to stay in the land of Judah. ⁵Instead, Johanan son of Kareah and all the army officers led away all the remnant of Judah who had come back to live in the land of Judah from all the nations where they had been scattered. ⁶They also led away all the men, women and children and the king's daughters whom Nebuzaradan commander of the imperial guard had left with Gedaliah son of Ahikam, the son of Shaphan, and Jeremiah the prophet and Baruch son of Neriah. ⁷So they entered Egypt in disobedience to the LORD and went as far as Tahpanhes.

⁸In Tahpanhes the word of the LORD came to Jeremiah: ⁹"While the Jews are watching, take some large stones with you and bury them in clay in the brick pavement at the entrance to Pharaoh's palace in Tahpanhes. ¹⁰Then say to

THE MESSAGE

that I swept the citizens of Jerusalem away with my anger and wrath, I'll do the same thing all over again in Egypt. You'll end up being cursed, reviled, ridiculed, and mocked. And you'll never see your homeland again.'

42.19-20 "GOD has plainly told you, you leftovers from Judah, 'Don't go to Egypt.' Could anything be plainer? I warn you this day that you are living out a fantasy. You're making a fatal mistake.

"Didn't you just now send me to your GOD, saying, 'Pray for us to our GOD. Tell us everything that GOD says and we'll do it all'?

42.21-22 "Well, now I've told you, told you everything he said, and you haven't obeyed a word of it, not a single word of what your GOD sent me to tell you. So now let me tell you what will happen next: You'll be killed, you'll starve to death, you'll get sick and die in the wonderful country where you've determined to go and live."

DEATH! EXILE! SLAUGHTER!

43.1-3 **43** When Jeremiah finished telling all the people the whole Message that their GOD had sent him to give them—all these words—Azariah son of Hoshaiah and Johanan son of Kareah, backed by all the self-important men, said to Jeremiah, "Liar! Our GOD never sent you with this message telling us not to go to Egypt and live there. Baruch son of Neriah is behind this. He has turned you against us. He's playing into the hands of the Babylonians so we'll either end up being killed or taken off to exile in Babylon."

43.4 Johanan son of Kareah and the army officers, and the people along with them, wouldn't listen to GOD's Message that they stay in the land of Judah and live there.

43.5-7 Johanan son of Kareah and the army officers gathered up everyone who was left from Judah, who had come back after being scattered all over the place—the men, women, and children, the king's daughters, all the people that Nebuzaradan captain of the bodyguard had left in the care of Gedaliah son of Ahikam, the son of Shaphan, and last but not least, Jeremiah the prophet and Baruch son of Neriah. They entered the land of Egypt in total disobedience of GOD's Message and arrived at the city of Tahpanhes.

43.8-9 While in Tahpanhes, GOD's Word came to Jeremiah: "Pick up some large stones and cover them with mortar in the vicinity of the pavement that leads up to the building set aside for Pharaoh's use in Tahpanhes. Make sure some of the men of Judah are watching.

ᵃ 20 Or you erred in your hearts   *ᵇ 3 Or Chaldeans*

NEW INTERNATIONAL VERSION

them, 'This is what the LORD Almighty, the God of Israel, says: I will send for my servant Nebuchadnezzar king of Babylon, and I will set his throne over these stones I have buried here; he will spread his royal canopy above them. [11]He will come and attack Egypt, bringing death to those destined for death, captivity to those destined for captivity, and the sword to those destined for the sword. [12]He[a] will set fire to the temples of the gods of Egypt; he will burn their temples and take their gods captive. As a shepherd wraps his garment around him, so will he wrap Egypt around himself and depart from there unscathed. [13]There in the temple of the sun[b] in Egypt he will demolish the sacred pillars and will burn down the temples of the gods of Egypt.'"

DISASTER BECAUSE OF IDOLATRY

44 This word came to Jeremiah concerning all the Jews living in Lower Egypt—in Migdol, Tahpanhes and Memphis[c]—and in Upper Egypt[d]: [2]"This is what the LORD Almighty, the God of Israel, says: You saw the great disaster I brought on Jerusalem and on all the towns of Judah. Today they lie deserted and in ruins [3]because of the evil they have done. They provoked me to anger by burning incense and by worshiping other gods that neither they nor you nor your fathers ever knew. [4]Again and again I sent my servants the prophets, who said, 'Do not do this detestable thing that I hate!' [5]But they did not listen or pay attention; they did not turn from their wickedness or stop burning incense to other gods. [6]Therefore, my fierce anger was poured out; it raged against the towns of Judah and the streets of Jerusalem and made them the desolate ruins they are today.

[7]"Now this is what the LORD God Almighty, the God of Israel, says: Why bring such great disaster on yourselves by cutting off from Judah the men and women, the children and infants, and so leave yourselves without a remnant? [8]Why provoke me to anger with what your hands have made, burning incense to other gods in Egypt, where you have come to live? You will destroy yourselves and make yourselves an object of cursing and reproach among all the na-

THE MESSAGE

43.10-13 "Then address them: 'This is what GOD-of-the-Angel-Armies says: Be on the lookout! I'm sending for and bringing Nebuchadnezzar the king of Babylon—my servant, mind you!—and he'll set up his throne on these very stones that I've had buried here and he'll spread out his canopy over them. He'll come and absolutely smash Egypt, sending each to his assigned fate: death, exile, slaughter. He'll burn down the temples of Egypt's gods. He'll either burn up the gods or haul them off as booty. Like a shepherd who picks lice from his robes, he'll pick Egypt clean. And then he'll walk away without a hand being laid on him. He'll shatter the sacred obelisks at Egypt's House of the Sun and make a huge bonfire of the temples of Egypt's gods.'"

THE SAME FATE WILL FALL UPON ALL

44.1-6 **44** The Message that Jeremiah received for all the Judeans who lived in the land of Egypt, who had their homes in Migdol, Tahpanhes, Noph, and the land of Pathros: "This is what GOD-of-the-Angel-Armies, the God of Israel, says: 'You saw with your own eyes the terrible doom that I brought down on Jerusalem and the Judean cities. Look at what's left: ghost towns of rubble and smoking ruins, and all because they took up with evil ways, making me angry by going off to offer sacrifices and worship the latest in gods—no-gods that neither they nor you nor your ancestors knew the first thing about. Morning after morning and long into the night I kept after you, sending you all those prophets, my servants, begging you, "Please, please—don't do this, don't fool around in this loathsome gutter of gods that I hate with a passion." But do you think anyone paid the least bit of attention or repented of evil or quit offering sacrifices to the no-gods? Not one. So I let loose with my anger, a firestorm of wrath in the cities of Judah and the streets of Jerusalem, and left them in ruins and wasted. And they're *still* in ruins and wasted.'

44.7-8 "This is the Message of GOD, GOD-of-the-Angel-Armies, the God of Israel: 'So why are you ruining your lives by amputating yourselves—man, woman, child, and baby—from the life of Judah, leaving yourselves isolated, unconnected? And why do you deliberately make me angry by what you do, offering sacrifices to these no-gods in the land of Egypt where you've come to live? You'll only destroy yourselves and make yourselves an example used in curses and an object of ridicule among all the nations of the earth.

---

[a] 12 Or I   [b] 13 Or in Heliopolis   [c] 1 Hebrew Noph
[d] 1 Hebrew in Pathros

NEW INTERNATIONAL VERSION

tions on earth. ⁹Have you forgotten the wickedness committed by your fathers and by the kings and queens of Judah and the wickedness committed by you and your wives in the land of Judah and the streets of Jerusalem? ¹⁰To this day they have not humbled themselves or shown reverence, nor have they followed my law and the decrees I set before you and your fathers.

¹¹"Therefore, this is what the LORD Almighty, the God of Israel, says: I am determined to bring disaster on you and to destroy all Judah. ¹²I will take away the remnant of Judah who were determined to go to Egypt to settle there. They will all perish in Egypt; they will fall by the sword or die from famine. From the least to the greatest, they will die by sword or famine. They will become an object of cursing and horror, of condemnation and reproach. ¹³I will punish those who live in Egypt with the sword, famine and plague, as I punished Jerusalem. ¹⁴None of the remnant of Judah who have gone to live in Egypt will escape or survive to return to the land of Judah, to which they long to return and live; none will return except a few fugitives."

¹⁵Then all the men who knew that their wives were burning incense to other gods, along with all the women who were present—a large assembly—and all the people living in Lower and Upper Egypt,ᵃ said to Jeremiah, ¹⁶"We will not listen to the message you have spoken to us in the name of the LORD! ¹⁷We will certainly do everything we said we would: We will burn incense to the Queen of Heaven and will pour out drink offerings to her just as we and our fathers, our kings and our officials did in the towns of Judah and in the streets of Jerusalem. At that time we had plenty of food and were well off and suffered no harm. ¹⁸But ever since we stopped burning incense to the Queen of Heaven and pouring out drink offerings to her, we have had nothing and have been perishing by sword and famine."

¹⁹The women added, "When we burned incense to the Queen of Heaven and poured out drink offerings to her, did not our husbands know that we were making cakes like her image and pouring out drink offerings to her?"

²⁰Then Jeremiah said to all the people, both

THE MESSAGE

44:9-11   "'Have you so soon forgotten the evil lives of your ancestors, the evil lives of the kings of Judah and their wives, to say nothing of your own evil lives, you and your wives, the evil you flaunted in the land of Judah and the streets of Jerusalem? And to this day, there's not a trace of remorse, not a sign of reverence, nobody caring about living by what I tell them or following my instructions that I've set out so plainly before you and your parents! So this is what GOD-of-the-Angel-Armies decrees:

44:11-14   "'Watch out! I've decided to bring doom on you and get rid of everyone connected with Judah. I'm going to take what's left of Judah, those who have decided to go to Egypt and live there, and finish them off. In Egypt they will either be killed or starve to death. The same fate will fall upon both the obscure and the important. Regardless of their status, they will either be killed or starve. You'll end up cursed, reviled, ridiculed, and mocked. I'll give those who are in Egypt the same medicine I gave those in Jerusalem: massacre, starvation, and disease. None of those who managed to get out of Judah alive and get away to Egypt are going to make it back to the Judah for which they're so homesick. None will make it back, except maybe a few fugitives.'"

MAKING GODDESS COOKIES

44:15-18   The men who knew that their wives had been burning sacrifices to the no-gods, joined by a large crowd of women, along with virtually everyone living in Pathros of Egypt, answered Jeremiah: "We're having nothing to do with what you tell us is GOD's Message. We're going to go right on offering sacrifices to the Queen of Heaven and pouring out drink offerings to her, keeping up the traditions set by our ancestors, our kings and government leaders in the cities of Judah and the streets of Jerusalem in the good old days. We had a good life then—lots of food, rising standard of living, and no bad luck. But the moment we quit sacrificing to the Queen of Heaven and pouring out offerings to her, everything fell apart. We've had nothing but massacres and starvation ever since."

44:19   And then the women chimed in: "Yes! Absolutely! We're going to keep at it, offering sacrifices to the Queen of Heaven and pouring out offerings to her. Aren't our husbands behind us? They like it that we make goddess cookies and pour out our offerings to her."

✝

44:20-23   Then Jeremiah spoke up, confronting the men

NEW INTERNATIONAL VERSION

men and women, who were answering him, 21"Did not the LORD remember and think about the incense burned in the towns of Judah and the streets of Jerusalem by you and your fathers, your kings and your officials and the people of the land? 22When the LORD could no longer endure your wicked actions and the detestable things you did, your land became an object of cursing and a desolate waste without inhabitants, as it is today. 23Because you have burned incense and have sinned against the LORD and have not obeyed him or followed his law or his decrees or his stipulations, this disaster has come upon you, as you now see."

24Then Jeremiah said to all the people, including the women, "Hear the word of the LORD, all you people of Judah in Egypt. 25This is what the LORD Almighty, the God of Israel, says: You and your wives have shown by your actions what you promised when you said, 'We will certainly carry out the vows we made to burn incense and pour out drink offerings to the Queen of Heaven.'

"Go ahead then, do what you promised! Keep your vows! 26But hear the word of the LORD, all Jews living in Egypt: 'I swear by my great name,' says the LORD, 'that no one from Judah living anywhere in Egypt will ever again invoke my name or swear, "As surely as the Sovereign LORD lives." 27For I am watching over them for harm, not for good; the Jews in Egypt will perish by sword and famine until they are all destroyed. 28Those who escape the sword and return to the land of Judah from Egypt will be very few. Then the whole remnant of Judah who came to live in Egypt will know whose word will stand—mine or theirs.

29" 'This will be the sign to you that I will punish you in this place,' declares the LORD, 'so that you will know that my threats of harm against you will surely stand.' 30This is what the LORD says: 'I am going to hand Pharaoh Hophra king of Egypt over to his enemies who seek his life, just as I handed Zedekiah king of Judah over to Nebuchadnezzar king of Babylon, the enemy who was seeking his life.' "

A MESSAGE TO BARUCH

45 This is what Jeremiah the prophet told Baruch son of Neriah in the fourth year of Jehoiakim son of Josiah king of Judah, after Baruch had written on a scroll the words Jeremiah was then dictating: 2"This is what the LORD, the God of Israel, says to you, Baruch: 3You said,

THE MESSAGE

and the women, all the people who had answered so insolently. He said, "The sacrifices that you and your parents, your kings, your government officials, and the common people of the land offered up in the cities of Judah and the streets of Jerusalem—don't you think GOD noticed? He noticed, all right. And he got fed up. Finally, he couldn't take your evil behavior and your disgusting acts any longer. Your land became a wasteland, a death valley, a horror story, a ghost town. And it continues to be just that. This doom has come upon you because you kept offering all those sacrifices, and you sinned against GOD! You refused to listen to him, wouldn't live the way he directed, ignored the covenant conditions."

44.24-25 Jeremiah kept going, but now zeroed in on the women: "Listen, all you who are from Judah and living in Egypt—please, listen to GOD's Word. GOD-of-the-Angel-Armies, the God of Israel, says: 'You women! You said it and then you did it. You said, "We're going to keep the vows we made to sacrifice to the Queen of Heaven and pour out offerings to her, and nobody's going to stop us!" '

44.25-27 "Well, go ahead. Keep your vows. Do it up big. But also listen to what GOD has to say about it, all you who are from Judah but live in Egypt: 'I swear by my great name, backed by everything I am—this is GOD speaking!—that never again shall my name be used in vows, such as "As sure as the Master, GOD, lives!" by anyone in the whole country of Egypt. I've targeted each one of you for doom. The good is gone for good.

44.27-28 " 'All the Judeans in Egypt will die off by massacre or starvation until they're wiped out. The few who get out of Egypt alive and back to Judah will be very few, hardly worth counting. Then that ragtag bunch that left Judah to live in Egypt will know who had the last word.

44.29-30 " 'And this will be the evidence: I will bring punishment right here, and by this you'll know that the decrees of doom against you are the real thing. Watch for this sign of doom: I will give Pharaoh Hophra king of Egypt over to his enemies, those who are out to kill him, exactly as I gave Zedekiah king of Judah to his enemy Nebuchadnezzar, who was after him.' "

GOD'S PILING ON THE PAIN

45.1 **45** This is what Jeremiah told Baruch one day in the fourth year of Jehoiakim's reign as he was taking dictation from the prophet:

45.2-3 "These are the words of GOD, the God of Israel, to you, Baruch. You say, 'These are bad

NEW INTERNATIONAL VERSION

'Woe to me! The LORD has added sorrow to my pain; I am worn out with groaning and find no rest.'"

⁴The LORD said, "Say this to him: 'This is what the LORD says: I will overthrow what I have built and uproot what I have planted, throughout the land. ⁵Should you then seek great things for yourself? Seek them not. For I will bring disaster on all people, declares the LORD, but wherever you go I will let you escape with your life.'"

A MESSAGE ABOUT EGYPT

46 This is the word of the LORD that came to Jeremiah the prophet concerning the nations:

²Concerning Egypt:

This is the message against the army of Pharaoh Neco king of Egypt, which was defeated at Carchemish on the Euphrates River by Nebuchadnezzar king of Babylon in the fourth year of Jehoiakim son of Josiah king of Judah:

³"Prepare your shields, both large and small,
    and march out for battle!
⁴Harness the horses,
    mount the steeds!
Take your positions
    with helmets on!
Polish your spears,
    put on your armor!
⁵What do I see?
    They are terrified,
they are retreating,
    their warriors are defeated.
They flee in haste
    without looking back,
    and there is terror on every side,"
                    declares the LORD.
⁶"The swift cannot flee
    nor the strong escape.
In the north by the River Euphrates
    they stumble and fall.

⁷"Who is this that rises like the Nile,
    like rivers of surging waters?
⁸Egypt rises like the Nile,
    like rivers of surging waters.
She says, 'I will rise and cover the earth;
    I will destroy cities and their people.'
⁹Charge, O horses!
    Drive furiously, O charioteers!
March on, O warriors—
    men of Cush*a* and Put who carry shields,
    men of Lydia who draw the bow.

a 9 That is, the upper Nile region

THE MESSAGE

times for me! It's one thing after another. GOD is piling on the pain. I'm worn out and there's no end in sight.'

45.4-5   "But GOD says, 'Look around. What I've built I'm about to wreck, and what I've planted I'm about to rip up. And I'm doing it everywhere—all over the whole earth! So forget about making any big plans for yourself. Things are going to get worse before they get better. But don't worry. I'll keep you alive through the whole business.'"

YOU VAINLY COLLECT MEDICINES

46.1   **46** GOD's Messages through the prophet Jeremiah regarding the godless nations.

46.2-5   The Message to Egypt and the army of Pharaoh Neco king of Egypt at the time it was defeated by Nebuchadnezzar king of Babylon while camped at Carchemish on the Euphrates River in the fourth year of the reign of Jehoiakim king of Judah:

" 'Present arms!
    March to the front!
Harness the horses!
    Up in the saddles!
Battle formation! Helmets on,
    spears sharpened, armor in place!'
But what's this I see?
    They're scared out of their wits!
They break ranks and run for cover.
    Their soldiers panic.
They run this way and that,
    stampeding blindly.
It's total chaos, total confusion, danger
                    everywhere!"
    GOD's Decree.

46.6   "The swiftest runners won't get away,
    the strongest soldiers won't escape.
In the north country, along the River
                    Euphrates,
    they'll stagger, stumble, and fall.

46.7-9   "Who is this like the Nile in flood?
    like its streams torrential?
Why, it's Egypt like the Nile in flood,
    like its streams torrential,
Saying, 'I'll take over the world.
    I'll wipe out cities and peoples.'
Run, horses!
    Roll, chariots!
Advance, soldiers
    from Cush and Put with your shields,
Soldiers from Lud,
    experts with bow and arrow.

NEW INTERNATIONAL VERSION

¹⁰ But that day belongs to the Lord, the LORD
Almighty—
    a day of vengeance, for vengeance on his
      foes.
The sword will devour till it is satisfied,
    till it has quenched its thirst with blood.
For the Lord, the LORD Almighty, will offer
    sacrifice
    in the land of the north by the River
      Euphrates.

¹¹ "Go up to Gilead and get balm,
    O Virgin Daughter of Egypt.
But you multiply remedies in vain;
    there is no healing for you.
¹² The nations will hear of your shame;
    your cries will fill the earth.
One warrior will stumble over another;
    both will fall down together."

¹³ This is the message the LORD spoke to Jeremiah the prophet about the coming of Nebuchadnezzar king of Babylon to attack Egypt:

¹⁴ "Announce this in Egypt, and proclaim it in
    Migdol;
    proclaim it also in Memphis*a* and
      Tahpanhes:
'Take your positions and get ready,
    for the sword devours those around you.'
¹⁵ Why will your warriors be laid low?
    They cannot stand, for the LORD will push
      them down.
¹⁶ They will stumble repeatedly;
    they will fall over each other.
They will say, 'Get up, let us go back
    to our own people and our native lands,
    away from the sword of the oppressor.'
¹⁷ There they will exclaim,
    'Pharaoh king of Egypt is only a loud
      noise;
    he has missed his opportunity.'

¹⁸ "As surely as I live," declares the King,
    whose name is the LORD Almighty,
"one will come who is like Tabor among the
    mountains,
    like Carmel by the sea.
¹⁹ Pack your belongings for exile,
    you who live in Egypt,
for Memphis will be laid waste
    and lie in ruins without inhabitant.

²⁰ "Egypt is a beautiful heifer,
    but a gadfly is coming
    against her from the north.
²¹ The mercenaries in her ranks

a 14 Hebrew Noph; also in verse 19

THE MESSAGE

46.10 "But it's not your day. It's the Master's, me,
    GOD-of-the-Angel-Armies—
    the day when I have it out with my
      enemies,
The day when Sword puts an end to my
    enemies,
    when Sword exacts vengeance.
I, the Master, GOD-of-the-Angel-Armies,
    will pile them on an altar—a huge
      sacrifice!—
In the great north country,
    along the mighty Euphrates.

46.11-12 "Oh, virgin Daughter Egypt,
    climb into the mountains of Gilead, get
      healing balm.
You will vainly collect medicines,
    for nothing will be able to cure what ails
      you.
The whole world will hear your anguished
    cries.
    Your wails fill the earth,
As soldier falls against soldier
    and they all go down in a heap."

EGYPT'S ARMY SLITHERS LIKE A SNAKE

46.13 The Message that GOD gave to the prophet Jeremiah when Nebuchadnezzar king of Babylon was on his way to attack Egypt:

46.14 "Tell Egypt, alert Migdol,
    post warnings in Noph and Tahpanhes:
'Wake up! Be prepared!
    War's coming!'

46.15-19 "Why will your bull-god Apis run off?
    Because GOD will drive him off.
Your ragtag army will fall to pieces.
    The word is passing through the ranks,
'Let's get out of here while we still can.
    Let's head for home and save our skins.'
When they get home they'll nickname
    Pharaoh
    'Big-Talk-Bad-Luck.'
As sure as I am the living God"
    —the King's Decree, GOD-of-the-Angel-
      Armies is his name—
"A conqueror is coming: like Tabor, singular
    among mountains;
    like Carmel, jutting up from the sea!
So pack your bags for exile,
    you coddled daughters of Egypt,
For Memphis will soon be nothing,
    a vacant lot grown over with weeds.

46.20-21 "Too bad, Egypt, a beautiful sleek heifer
    attacked by a horsefly from the north!
All her hired soldiers are stationed to defend
    her—

NEW INTERNATIONAL VERSION

are like fattened calves.
They too will turn and flee together,
    they will not stand their ground,
for the day of disaster is coming upon them,
    the time for them to be punished.
22 Egypt will hiss like a fleeing serpent
    as the enemy advances in force;
they will come against her with axes,
    like men who cut down trees.
23 They will chop down her forest,"
                    declares the LORD,
    "dense though it be.
They are more numerous than locusts,
    they cannot be counted.
24 The Daughter of Egypt will be put to shame,
    handed over to the people of the north."

25 The LORD Almighty, the God of Israel, says: "I am about to bring punishment on Amon god of Thebes,[a] on Pharaoh, on Egypt and her gods and her kings, and on those who rely on Pharaoh. 26 I will hand them over to those who seek their lives, to Nebuchadnezzar king of Babylon and his officers. Later, however, Egypt will be inhabited as in times past," declares the LORD.

27 "Do not fear, O Jacob my servant;
    do not be dismayed, O Israel.
I will surely save you out of a distant place,
    your descendants from the land of their
        exile.
Jacob will again have peace and security,
    and no one will make him afraid.
28 Do not fear, O Jacob my servant,
    for I am with you," declares the LORD.
"Though I completely destroy all the nations
    among which I scatter you,
    I will not completely destroy you.
I will discipline you but only with justice;
    I will not let you go entirely unpunished."

A MESSAGE ABOUT THE PHILISTINES

47 This is the word of the LORD that came to Jeremiah the prophet concerning the Philistines before Pharaoh attacked Gaza:

2 This is what the LORD says:

"See how the waters are rising in the north;
    they will become an overflowing torrent.

THE MESSAGE

like well-fed calves they are.
But when their lives are on the line, they'll run
        off,
    cowards every one.
When the going gets tough,
    they'll take the easy way out.

46.22-24 "Egypt will slither and hiss like a snake
    as the enemy army comes in force.
They will rush in, swinging axes
    like lumberjacks cutting down trees.
They'll level the country"—GOD's Decree—
        "nothing
    and no one standing for as far as you can
        see.
The invaders will be a swarm of locusts,
    innumerable, past counting.
Daughter Egypt will be ravished,
    raped by vandals from the north."

46.25-26 GOD-of-the-Angel-Armies, the God of Israel, says, "Watch out when I visit doom on the god Amon of Thebes, Egypt and its gods and kings, Pharaoh and those who trust in him. I'll turn them over to those who are out to kill them, to Nebuchadnezzar and his military. Egypt will be set back a thousand years. Eventually people will live there again." GOD's Decree.

✝

46.27-28 "But you, dear Jacob my servant, you have
        nothing to fear.
    Israel, there's no need to worry.
Look up! I'll save you from that far country,
    I'll get your children out of the land of
        exile.
Things are going to be normal again for Jacob,
    safe and secure, smooth sailing.
Yes, dear Jacob my servant, you have nothing
        to fear.
    Depend on it, I'm on your side.
I'll finish off all the godless nations
    among which I've scattered you,
But I won't finish you off.
    I have more work left to do on you.
I'll punish you, but fairly.
    No, I'm not finished with you yet."

IT'S DOOMSDAY FOR PHILISTINES

47 47.1-5 GOD's Message to the prophet Jeremiah regarding the Philistines just before Pharaoh attacked Gaza. This is what GOD says:

"Look out! Water will rise in the north
        country,
    swelling like a river in flood.

NEW INTERNATIONAL VERSION	THE MESSAGE

NEW INTERNATIONAL VERSION

They will overflow the land and everything
in it,
the towns and those who live in them.
The people will cry out;
all who dwell in the land will wail
3 at the sound of the hoofs of galloping steeds,
at the noise of enemy chariots
and the rumble of their wheels.
Fathers will not turn to help their children;
their hands will hang limp.
4 For the day has come
to destroy all the Philistines
and to cut off all survivors
who could help Tyre and Sidon.
The LORD is about to destroy the Philistines,
the remnant from the coasts of Caphtor. *a*
5 Gaza will shave her head in mourning;
Ashkelon will be silenced.
O remnant on the plain,
how long will you cut yourselves?

6 " 'Ah, sword of the LORD,' ⌊you cry,⌋
'how long till you rest?
Return to your scabbard;
cease and be still.'
7 But how can it rest
when the LORD has commanded it,
when he has ordered it
to attack Ashkelon and the coast?"

A MESSAGE ABOUT MOAB

48 Concerning Moab:

This is what the LORD Almighty, the God of Israel, says:

"Woe to Nebo, for it will be ruined.
Kiriathaim will be disgraced and captured;
the stronghold *b* will be disgraced and
shattered.
2 Moab will be praised no more;
in Heshbon *c* men will plot her downfall:
'Come, let us put an end to that nation.'
You too, O Madmen, *d* will be silenced;
the sword will pursue you.
3 Listen to the cries from Horonaim,
cries of great havoc and destruction.
4 Moab will be broken;
her little ones will cry out. *e*
5 They go up the way to Luhith,
weeping bitterly as they go;
on the road down to Horonaim
anguished cries over the destruction are
heard.

THE MESSAGE

The torrent will flood the land,
washing away city and citizen.
Men and women will scream in terror,
wails from every door and window,
As the thunder from the hooves of the horses
will be heard,
the clatter of chariots, the banging of
wheels.
Fathers, paralyzed by fear,
won't even grab up their babies
Because it will be doomsday for Philistines,
one and all,
no hope of help for Tyre and Sidon.
GOD will finish off the Philistines,
what's left of those from the island of Crete.
Gaza will be shaved bald as an egg,
Ashkelon struck dumb as a post.
You're on your last legs.
How long will you keep flailing?

47.6 "Oh, Sword of GOD,
how long will you keep this up?
Return to your scabbard.
Haven't you had enough? Can't you call it
quits?

47.7 "But how can it quit
when I, GOD, command the action?
I've ordered it to cut down
Ashkelon and the seacoast."

GET OUT WHILE YOU CAN!

48.1-10 **48** The Message on Moab from GOD-of-
the-Angel-Armies, the God of Israel:

"Doom to Nebo! Leveled to the ground!
Kiriathaim demeaned and defeated,
The mighty fortress reduced to a molehill,
Moab's glory—dust and ashes.
Conspirators plot Heshbon's doom:
'Come, let's wipe Moab off the map.'
Dungface Dimon will loudly lament,
as killing follows killing.
Listen! A cry out of Horonaim:
'Disaster—doom and more doom!'
Moab will be shattered.
Her cries will be heard clear down in Zoar.
Up the ascent of Luhith
climbers weep,
And down the descent from Horonaim,
cries of loss and devastation.

---

a 4 That is, Crete   *b 1* Or / *Misgab*   *c 2* The Hebrew for
Heshbon sounds like the Hebrew for *plot*.   *d 2* The name
of the Moabite town Madmen sounds like the Hebrew for *be
silenced*.   *e 4* Hebrew; Septuagint / *proclaim it to Zoar*

NEW INTERNATIONAL VERSION

⁶ Flee! Run for your lives;
    become like a bush*ᵃ* in the desert.
⁷ Since you trust in your deeds and riches,
    you too will be taken captive,
and Chemosh will go into exile,
    together with his priests and officials.
⁸ The destroyer will come against every town,
    and not a town will escape.
The valley will be ruined
    and the plateau destroyed,
    because the LORD has spoken.
⁹ Put salt on Moab,
    for she will be laid waste*ᵇ*;
her towns will become desolate,
    with no one to live in them.

¹⁰ "A curse on him who is lax in doing the
        LORD's work!
A curse on him who keeps his sword from
        bloodshed!

¹¹ "Moab has been at rest from youth,
    like wine left on its dregs,
not poured from one jar to another—
    she has not gone into exile.
So she tastes as she did,
    and her aroma is unchanged.
¹² But days are coming,"
    declares the LORD,
"when I will send men who pour from jars,
    and they will pour her out;
they will empty her jars
    and smash her jugs.
¹³ Then Moab will be ashamed of Chemosh,
    as the house of Israel was ashamed
when they trusted in Bethel.

¹⁴ "How can you say, 'We are warriors,
    men valiant in battle'?
¹⁵ Moab will be destroyed and her towns
        invaded;
her finest young men will go down in the
        slaughter,"
declares the King, whose name is the
        LORD Almighty.
¹⁶ "The fall of Moab is at hand;
    her calamity will come quickly.
¹⁷ Mourn for her, all who live around her,
    all who know her fame;
say, 'How broken is the mighty scepter,
    how broken the glorious staff!'

¹⁸ "Come down from your glory
    and sit on the parched ground,
O inhabitants of the Daughter of Dibon,
for he who destroys Moab
    will come up against you

ᵃ 6 Or *like Aroer*   *ᵇ 9* Or *Give wings to Moab, / for she will fly away*

THE MESSAGE

Oh, run for your lives! Get out while you can!
    Survive by your wits in the wild!
You trusted in thick walls and big money, yes?
    But it won't help you now.
Your big god Chemosh will be hauled off,
    his priests and managers with him.
A wrecker will wreck every city.
    Not a city will survive.
The valley fields will be ruined,
    the plateau pastures destroyed, just as I
        told you.
Cover the land of Moab with salt.
    Make sure nothing ever grows here again.
Her towns will all be ghost towns.
    Nobody will ever live here again.
Sloppy work in GOD's name is cursed,
    and cursed all halfhearted use of the sword.

48.11-17 "Moab has always taken it easy—
    lazy as a dog in the sun,
Never had to work for a living,
    never faced any trouble,
Never had to grow up,
    never once worked up a sweat.
But those days are a thing of the past.
    I'll put him to work at hard labor.
That will wake him up to the world of hard
        knocks.
    That will smash his illusions.
Moab will be as ashamed of god Chemosh
    as Israel was ashamed of her Bethel calf-
        gods,
    the calf-gods she thought were so great.
For how long do you think you'll be saying,
    'We're tough.
    We can beat anyone anywhere'?
The destruction of Moab has already begun.
    Her choice young soldiers are lying dead
        right now."
The King's Decree—
    his full name, GOD-of-the-Angel-Armies.
"Yes. Moab's doom is on countdown,
    disaster targeted and launched.
Weep for Moab, friends and neighbors,
    all who know how famous he's been.
Lament, 'His mighty scepter snapped in two
        like a toothpick,
    that magnificent royal staff!'

48.18-20 "Come down from your high horse, pampered
        beauty of Dibon.
    Sit in dog dung.
The destroyer of Moab will come against you.

<table>
<tr><td>

NEW INTERNATIONAL VERSION

and ruin your fortified cities.
¹⁹ Stand by the road and watch,
  you who live in Aroer.
Ask the man fleeing and the woman
    escaping,
  ask them, 'What has happened?'
²⁰ Moab is disgraced, for she is shattered.
  Wail and cry out!
Announce by the Arnon
  that Moab is destroyed.
²¹ Judgment has come to the plateau—
  to Holon, Jahzah and Mephaath,
²² to Dibon, Nebo and Beth Diblathaim,
²³ to Kiriathaim, Beth Gamul and Beth Meon,
²⁴ to Kerioth and Bozrah—
  to all the towns of Moab, far and near.
²⁵ Moab's horn ᵃ is cut off;
  her arm is broken,"
                declares the Lord.

²⁶ "Make her drunk,
  for she has defied the Lord.
Let Moab wallow in her vomit;
  let her be an object of ridicule.
²⁷ Was not Israel the object of your ridicule?
  Was she caught among thieves,
that you shake your head in scorn
  whenever you speak of her?
²⁸ Abandon your towns and dwell among the
    rocks,
  you who live in Moab.
Be like a dove that makes its nest
  at the mouth of a cave.

²⁹ "We have heard of Moab's pride—
  her overweening pride and conceit,
her pride and arrogance
  and the haughtiness of her heart.
³⁰ I know her insolence but it is futile,"
                declares the Lord,
  "and her boasts accomplish nothing.
³¹ Therefore I wail over Moab,
  for all Moab I cry out,
  I moan for the men of Kir Hareseth.
³² I weep for you, as Jazer weeps,
  O vines of Sibmah.
Your branches spread as far as the sea;
  they reached as far as the sea of Jazer.
The destroyer has fallen
  on your ripened fruit and grapes.
³³ Joy and gladness are gone
  from the orchards and fields of Moab.
I have stopped the flow of wine from the
    presses;
  no one treads them with shouts of joy.
Although there are shouts,
  they are not shouts of joy.

</td><td>

THE MESSAGE

He'll wreck your safe, secure houses.
Stand on the roadside,
  pampered women of Aroer.
Interview the refugees who are running away.
  Ask them, 'What's happened? And why?'
Moab will be an embarrassing memory,
    nothing left of the place.
  Wail and weep your eyes out!
Tell the bad news along the Arnon river.
  Tell the world that Moab is no more.

48.21-24 "My judgment will come to the plateau cit-
ies: on Holon, Jahzah, and Mephaath; on Di-
bon, Nebo, and Beth-diblathaim; on Kiriatha-
im, Beth-gamul, and Beth-meon; on Kerioth,
Bozrah, and all the cities of Moab, far and near.

48.25 "Moab's link to power is severed.
  Moab's arm is broken." God's Decree.

THE SHEER NOTHINGNESS OF MOAB

48.26-27 "Turn Moab into a drunken sot, drunk on the
wine of my wrath, a dung-faced drunk, filling
the country with vomit—Moab a falling-down
drunk, a joke in bad taste. Wasn't it you, Moab,
who made crude jokes over Israel? And when
they were caught in bad company, didn't you
cluck and gossip and snicker?

48.28 "Leave town! Leave! Look for a home in the
      cliffs,
  you who grew up in Moab.
Try living like a dove
  who nests high in the river gorge.

48.29-33 "We've all heard of Moab's pride,
    that legendary pride,
The strutting, bullying, puffed-up pride,
    the insufferable arrogance.
I know"—God's Decree—"his rooster-crowing
      pride,
  the inflated claims, the sheer nothingness
      of Moab.
But I will weep for Moab,
  yes, I will mourn for the people of Moab.
  I will even mourn for the people of Kir-
      heres.
I'll weep for the grapevines of Sibmah
  and join Jazer in her weeping—
Grapevines that once reached the Dead Sea
  with tendrils as far as Jazer.
Your summer fruit and your bursting grapes
  will be looted by brutal plunderers,
Lush Moab stripped
  of song and laughter.
And yes, I'll shut down the winepresses,
  stop all the shouts and hurrahs of harvest.

</td></tr>
</table>

ᵃ 25 Horn here symbolizes strength.

NEW INTERNATIONAL VERSION

34 "The sound of their cry rises
  from Heshbon to Elealeh and Jahaz,
from Zoar as far as Horonaim and Eglath
    Shelishiyah,
  for even the waters of Nimrim are
    dried up.
35 In Moab I will put an end
  to those who make offerings on the high
    places
  and burn incense to their gods,"
                declares the LORD.
36 "So my heart laments for Moab like a flute;
  it laments like a flute for the men of Kir
    Hareseth.
  The wealth they acquired is gone.
37 Every head is shaved
  and every beard cut off;
every hand is slashed
  and every waist is covered with sackcloth.
38 On all the roofs in Moab
  and in the public squares
there is nothing but mourning,
  for I have broken Moab
  like a jar that no one wants,"
                declares the LORD.
39 "How shattered she is! How they wail!
  How Moab turns her back in shame!
Moab has become an object of ridicule,
  an object of horror to all those around
    her."

40 This is what the LORD says:

"Look! An eagle is swooping down,
  spreading its wings over Moab.
41 Kerioth* will be captured
  and the strongholds taken.
In that day the hearts of Moab's warriors
  will be like the heart of a woman in labor.
42 Moab will be destroyed as a nation
  because she defied the LORD.
43 Terror and pit and snare await you,
  O people of Moab,"
                declares the LORD.
44 "Whoever flees from the terror
  will fall into a pit,
whoever climbs out of the pit
  will be caught in a snare;
for I will bring upon Moab
  the year of her punishment,"
                declares the LORD.

45 "In the shadow of Heshbon
  the fugitives stand helpless,
for a fire has gone out from Heshbon,
  a blaze from the midst of Sihon;
it burns the foreheads of Moab,

a 41 Or The cities

THE MESSAGE

48.34   "Heshbon and Elealeh will cry out, and the people in Jahaz will hear the cries. They will hear them all the way from Zoar to Horonaim and Eglath-shelishiyah. Even the waters of Nimrim will be dried up.

48.35   "I will put a stop in Moab"—GOD's Decree—"to all hiking to the high places to offer burnt sacrifices to the gods.

48.36   "My heart moans for Moab, for the men of Kir-heres, like soft flute sounds carried by the wind. They've lost it all. They've got nothing.

48.37   "Everywhere you look are signs of mourning:
  heads shaved, beards cut,
Hands scratched and bleeding,
  clothes ripped and torn.

48.38   "In every house in Moab there'll be loud lamentation, on every street in Moab, loud lamentation. As with a pottery jug that no one wants, I'll smash Moab to bits." GOD's Decree.

48.39   "Moab ruined!
  Moab shamed and ashamed to be seen!
Moab a cruel joke!
  The stark horror of Moab!"

                ✝

48.40-42 GOD's verdict on Moab. Indeed!

"Look! An eagle is about to swoop down
  and spread its wings over Moab.
The towns will be captured,
  the fortresses taken.
Brave warriors will double up in pain, helpless
    to fight,
  like a woman giving birth to a baby.
There'll be nothing left of Moab, nothing at
    all,
  because of his defiant arrogance against me.

48.43-44 "Terror and pit and trap
  are what you have facing you, Moab."
                GOD's Decree.
"A man running in terror
  will fall into a trap.
A man climbing out of a pit
  will be caught in a trap.
This is my agenda for Moab
  on doomsday." GOD's Decree.

48.45-47 "On the outskirts of Heshbon,
  refugees will pull up short, worn out.
Fire will flame high from Heshbon,
  a firestorm raging from the capital of
    Sihon's kingdom.
It will burn off Moab's eyebrows,

NEW INTERNATIONAL VERSION

the skulls of the noisy boasters.
⁴⁶Woe to you, O Moab!
    The people of Chemosh are destroyed;
your sons are taken into exile
    and your daughters into captivity.

⁴⁷"Yet I will restore the fortunes of Moab
    in days to come,"
                        declares the LORD.

Here ends the judgment on Moab.

A MESSAGE ABOUT AMMON

49 Concerning the Ammonites:

This is what the LORD says:

"Has Israel no sons?
    Has she no heirs?
Why then has Molech*ᵃ* taken possession of
        Gad?
    Why do his people live in its towns?
²But the days are coming,"
    declares the LORD,
"when I will sound the battle cry
    against Rabbah of the Ammonites;
it will become a mound of ruins,
    and its surrounding villages will be set on
        fire.
Then Israel will drive out
    those who drove her out,"
                        says the LORD.
³"Wail, O Heshbon, for Ai is destroyed!
    Cry out, O inhabitants of Rabbah!
Put on sackcloth and mourn;
    rush here and there inside the walls,
for Molech will go into exile,
    together with his priests and officials.
⁴Why do you boast of your valleys,
    boast of your valleys so fruitful?
O unfaithful daughter,
    you trust in your riches and say,
    'Who will attack me?'
⁵I will bring terror on you
    from all those around you,"
                        declares the Lord,
                        the LORD Almighty.
"Every one of you will be driven away,
    and no one will gather the fugitives.

⁶"Yet afterward, I will restore the fortunes of
        the Ammonites,"
                        declares the LORD.

A MESSAGE ABOUT EDOM

⁷Concerning Edom:

This is what the LORD Almighty says:

ᵃ 1 Or their king; Hebrew malcam; also in verse 3

THE MESSAGE

will scorch the skull of the braggarts.
That's all for you, Moab!
    You worshipers of Chemosh will be
        finished off!
Your sons will be trucked off to prison camps;
    your daughters will be herded into exile.
But yet there's a day that's coming
    when I'll put things right in Moab.

    "For now, that's the judgment on Moab."

YOU'RE A BROKEN-DOWN HAS-BEEN

49.1-6 **49** GOD's Message on the Ammonites:

"Doesn't Israel have any children,
    no one to step into her inheritance?
So why is the god Milcom taking over Gad's
        land,
    his followers moving into its towns?
But not for long! The time's coming"
    —GOD's Decree—
"When I'll fill the ears of Rabbah, Ammon's
        big city,
    with battle cries.
She'll end up a pile of rubble,
    all her towns burned to the ground.
Then Israel will kick out the invaders.
    I, GOD, say so, and it will *be* so.
Wail Heshbon, Ai is in ruins.
    Villages of Rabbah, wring your hands!
Dress in mourning, weep buckets of tears.
    Go into hysterics, run around in circles!
Your god Milcom will be hauled off to exile,
    and all his priests and managers right with
        him.
Why do you brag of your once-famous
        strength?
    You're a broken-down has-been, a castoff
Who fondles his trophies and dreams of glory
        days
    and vainly thinks, 'No one can lay a hand
        on me.'
Well, think again. I'll face you with terror
        from all sides."
    Word of the Master, GOD-of-the-Angel-
        Armies.
"You'll be stampeded headlong,
    with no one to round up the runaways.
Still, the time will come
    when I will make things right with
        Ammon." GOD's Decree.

STRUTTING ACROSS THE STAGE OF HISTORY

49.7-11 The Message of GOD-of-the-Angel-Armies on
Edom:

NEW INTERNATIONAL VERSION	THE MESSAGE

NEW INTERNATIONAL VERSION

"Is there no longer wisdom in Teman?
  Has counsel perished from the prudent?
  Has their wisdom decayed?
⁸Turn and flee, hide in deep caves,
  you who live in Dedan,
for I will bring disaster on Esau
  at the time I punish him.
⁹If grape pickers came to you,
  would they not leave a few grapes?
If thieves came during the night,
  would they not steal only as much as they
    wanted?
¹⁰But I will strip Esau bare;
  I will uncover his hiding places,
  so that he cannot conceal himself.
His children, relatives and neighbors will
    perish,
  and he will be no more.
¹¹Leave your orphans; I will protect their lives.
  Your widows too can trust in me."

¹²This is what the LORD says: "If those who do
not deserve to drink the cup must drink it, why
should you go unpunished? You will not go unpunished, but must drink it. ¹³I swear by myself," declares the LORD, "that Bozrah will become a ruin and an object of horror, of reproach
and of cursing; and all its towns will be in ruins
forever."

¹⁴I have heard a message from the LORD:
  An envoy was sent to the nations to say,
"Assemble yourselves to attack it!
  Rise up for battle!"

¹⁵"Now I will make you small among the
    nations,
  despised among men.
¹⁶The terror you inspire
  and the pride of your heart have deceived
    you,
you who live in the clefts of the rocks,
  who occupy the heights of the hill.
Though you build your nest as high as the
    eagle's,
  from there I will bring you down,"
                        declares the LORD.
¹⁷"Edom will become an object of horror;
  all who pass by will be appalled and will
    scoff
  because of all its wounds.
¹⁸As Sodom and Gomorrah were overthrown,
  along with their neighboring towns,"
                        says the LORD,
"so no one will live there;
  no man will dwell in it.

¹⁹"Like a lion coming up from Jordan's
    thickets

THE MESSAGE

"Is there nobody wise left in famous Teman?
  no one with a sense of reality?
Has their wisdom gone wormy and rotten?
  Run for your lives! Get out while you can!
Find a good place to hide,
  you who live in Dedan!
I'm bringing doom to Esau.
  It's time to settle accounts.
When harvesters work your fields,
  don't they leave gleanings?
When burglars break into your house,
  don't they take only what they want?
But I'll strip Esau clean.
  I'll search out every nook and cranny.
I'll destroy everything connected with him,
  children and relatives and neighbors.
There'll be no one left who will be able to say,
  'I'll take care of your orphans.
  Your widows can depend on me.' "

49.12-13   Indeed. GOD says, "I tell you, if there are people who have to drink the cup of God's wrath
even though they don't deserve it, why would
you think you'd get off? You won't get off. You'll
drink it. Oh yes, you'll drink every drop. And as
for Bozrah, your capital, I swear by all that I
am"—GOD's Decree—"that that city will end up
a pile of charred ruins, a stinking garbage
dump, an obscenity—and all her daughter-cities
with her."

49.14 I've just heard the latest from GOD.
  He's sent an envoy to the nations:
"Muster your troops and attack Edom.
  Present arms! Go to war!"

49.15-16 "Ah, Edom, I'm dropping you to last place
    among nations,
  the bottom of the heap, kicked around.
You think you're so great—
  strutting across the stage of history,
Living high in the impregnable rocks,
  acting like king of the mountain.
You think you're above it all, don't you,
  like an eagle in its aerie?
Well, you're headed for a fall.
  I'll bring you crashing to the ground."
        GOD's Decree.

49.17-18   "Edom will end up trash. Stinking, despicable trash. A wonder of the world in reverse.
She'll join Sodom and Gomorrah and their
neighbors in the sewers of history." GOD says
so.

"No one will live there,
  no mortal soul move in there.

49.19 "Watch this: Like a lion coming up
  from the thick jungle of the Jordan

NEW INTERNATIONAL VERSION

to a rich pastureland,
I will chase Edom from its land in an instant.
Who is the chosen one I will appoint for this?
Who is like me and who can challenge me?
And what shepherd can stand against me?"

20 Therefore, hear what the LORD has planned against Edom,
what he has purposed against those who live in Teman:
The young of the flock will be dragged away;
he will completely destroy their pasture because of them.
21 At the sound of their fall the earth will tremble;
their cry will resound to the Red Sea. *a*
22 Look! An eagle will soar and swoop down,
spreading its wings over Bozrah.
In that day the hearts of Edom's warriors
will be like the heart of a woman in labor.

A MESSAGE ABOUT DAMASCUS
23 Concerning Damascus:

"Hamath and Arpad are dismayed,
for they have heard bad news.
They are disheartened,
troubled like *b* the restless sea.
24 Damascus has become feeble,
she has turned to flee
and panic has gripped her;
anguish and pain have seized her,
pain like that of a woman in labor.
25 Why has the city of renown not been abandoned,
the town in which I delight?
26 Surely, her young men will fall in the streets;
all her soldiers will be silenced in that day,"
declares the LORD Almighty.
27 "I will set fire to the walls of Damascus;
it will consume the fortresses of Ben-Hadad."

A MESSAGE ABOUT KEDAR AND HAZOR
28 Concerning Kedar and the kingdoms of Hazor, which Nebuchadnezzar king of Babylon attacked:

This is what the LORD says:

"Arise, and attack Kedar
and destroy the people of the East.
29 Their tents and their flocks will be taken;
their shelters will be carried off

THE MESSAGE

Looking for prey in the mountain pastures,
I will come upon Edom and pounce.
I'll take my pick of the flock—and who's to stop me?
The shepherds of Edom are helpless before me."

49:20-22 So, listen to this plan that GOD has worked out against Edom, the blueprint of what he's prepared for those who live in Teman:

"Believe it or not, the young, the vulnerable—
mere lambs and kids—will be dragged off.
Believe it or not, the flock
in shock, helpless to help, will watch it happen.
The very earth will shudder because of their cries,
cries of anguish heard at the distant Red Sea.
Look! An eagle soars, swoops down,
spreads its wings over Bozrah.
Brave warriors will double up in pain, helpless to fight,
like a woman giving birth to a baby."

THE BLOOD WILL DRAIN FROM THE FACE OF DAMASCUS
49:23-27 The Message on Damascus:

"Hamath and Arpad will be in shock
when they hear the bad news.
Their hearts will melt in fear
as they pace back and forth in worry.
The blood will drain from the face of Damascus
as she turns to flee.
Hysterical, she'll fall to pieces,
disabled, like a woman in childbirth.
And now how lonely—bereft, abandoned!
The once famous city, the once happy city.
Her bright young men dead in the streets,
her brave warriors silent as death.
On that day"—Decree of GOD-of-the-Angel-Armies—
"I'll start a fire at the wall of Damascus
that will burn down all of Ben-hadad's forts."

FIND A SAFE PLACE TO HIDE
49:28-33 The Message on Kedar and the sheikdoms of Hazor who were attacked by Nebuchadnezzar king of Babylon. This is GOD's Message:

"On your feet! Attack Kedar!
Plunder the Bedouin nomads from the east.
Grab their blankets and pots and pans.

---

a 21 Hebrew *Yam Suph*; that is, Sea of Reeds   *b 23* Hebrew *on* or *by*

NEW INTERNATIONAL VERSION

with all their goods and camels.
Men will shout to them,
'Terror on every side!'

30 "Flee quickly away!
Stay in deep caves, you who live in
Hazor,"
declares the LORD.
"Nebuchadnezzar king of Babylon has
plotted against you;
he has devised a plan against you.

31 "Arise and attack a nation at ease,
which lives in confidence,"
declares the LORD,
"a nation that has neither gates nor bars;
its people live alone.
32 Their camels will become plunder,
and their large herds will be booty.
I will scatter to the winds those who are in
distant places*a*
and will bring disaster on them from
every side,"
declares the LORD.
33 "Hazor will become a haunt of jackals,
a desolate place forever.
No one will live there;
no man will dwell in it."

A Message About Elam

34 This is the word of the LORD that came to
Jeremiah the prophet concerning Elam, early in
the reign of Zedekiah king of Judah:

35 This is what the LORD Almighty says:

"See, I will break the bow of Elam,
the mainstay of their might.
36 I will bring against Elam the four winds
from the four quarters of the heavens;
I will scatter them to the four winds,
and there will not be a nation
where Elam's exiles do not go.
37 I will shatter Elam before their foes,
before those who seek their lives;
I will bring disaster upon them,
even my fierce anger,"
declares the LORD.
"I will pursue them with the sword
until I have made an end of them.
38 I will set my throne in Elam
and destroy her king and officials,"
declares the LORD.

39 "Yet I will restore the fortunes of Elam
in days to come,"
declares the LORD.

THE MESSAGE

Steal their camels.
Traumatize them, shouting, 'Terror! Death!
Doom!
Danger everywhere!'
Oh, run for your lives,
You nomads from Hazor." GOD's Decree.
"Find a safe place to hide.
Nebuchadnezzar king of Babylon
has plans to wipe you out,
to go after you with a vengeance:
'After them,' he says. 'Go after these relaxed
nomads
who live free and easy in the desert,
Who live in the open with no doors to lock,
who live off by themselves.'
Their camels are there for the taking,
their herds and flocks, easy picking.
I'll scatter them to the four winds,
these defenseless nomads on the fringes of
the desert.
I'll bring terror from every direction.
They won't know what hit them." GOD's
Decree.
"Jackals will take over the camps of Hazor,
camps abandoned to wind and sand.
No one will live there,
no mortal soul move in there."

The Winds Will Blow Away Elam

49.34-39 GOD's Message to the prophet Jeremiah on Elam
at the outset of the reign of Zedekiah king of Judah. This is what GOD-of-the-Angel-Armies
says:

"Watch this! I'll break Elam's bow,
her weapon of choice, across my knee.
Then I'll let four winds loose on Elam,
winds from the four corners of earth.
I'll blow them away in all directions,
landing homeless Elamites in every country
on earth.
They'll live in constant fear and terror
among enemies who want to kill them.
I'll bring doom on them,
my anger-fueled doom.
I'll set murderous hounds on their heels
until there's nothing left of them.
And then I'll set up my throne in Elam,
having thrown out the king and his
henchmen.
But the time will come when I make
everything right for Elam again." GOD's
Decree.

a 32 Or who clip the hair by their foreheads

NEW INTERNATIONAL VERSION

A MESSAGE ABOUT BABYLON

50 This is the word the LORD spoke through Jeremiah the prophet concerning Babylon and the land of the Babylonians[a]:

2 "Announce and proclaim among the nations,
    lift up a banner and proclaim it;
    keep nothing back, but say,
'Babylon will be captured;
    Bel will be put to shame,
    Marduk filled with terror.
Her images will be put to shame
    and her idols filled with terror.'
3 A nation from the north will attack her
    and lay waste her land.
No one will live in it;
    both men and animals will flee away.

4 "In those days, at that time,"
    declares the LORD,
"the people of Israel and the people of Judah
        together
    will go in tears to seek the LORD their
        God.
5 They will ask the way to Zion
    and turn their faces toward it.
They will come and bind themselves to the
        LORD
    in an everlasting covenant
    that will not be forgotten.

6 "My people have been lost sheep;
    their shepherds have led them astray
    and caused them to roam on the
        mountains.
They wandered over mountain and hill
    and forgot their own resting place.
7 Whoever found them devoured them;
    their enemies said, 'We are not guilty,
for they sinned against the LORD, their true
        pasture,
    the LORD, the hope of their fathers.'

8 "Flee out of Babylon;
    leave the land of the Babylonians,
    and be like the goats that lead the flock.
9 For I will stir up and bring against Babylon
    an alliance of great nations from the land
        of the north.
They will take up their positions against her,
    and from the north she will be captured.
Their arrows will be like skilled warriors
    who do not return empty-handed.
10 So Babylonia[b] will be plundered;
    all who plunder her will have their fill,"
                declares the LORD.

THE MESSAGE

GET OUT OF BABYLON AS FAST AS YOU CAN

50:1-3 **50** The Message of GOD through the prophet Jeremiah on Babylon, land of the Chaldeans:

"Get the word out to the nations! Preach it!
    Go public with this, broadcast it far and
        wide:
Babylon taken, god-Bel hanging his head in
        shame,
    god-Marduk exposed as a fraud.
All her god-idols shuffling in shame,
    all her play-gods exposed as cheap frauds.
For a nation will come out of the north to
        attack her,
    reduce her cities to rubble.
Empty of life—no animals, no people—
    not a sound, not a movement, not a breath.

50:4-5 "In those days, at that time"—GOD's Decree—
    "the people of Israel will come,
And the people of Judah with them.
    Walking and weeping, they'll seek me, their
        GOD.
They'll ask directions to Zion
    and set their faces toward Zion.
They'll come and hold tight to GOD,
    bound in a covenant eternal they'll never
        forget.

50:6-7 "My people were lost sheep.
    Their shepherds led them astray.
They abandoned them in the mountains
    where they wandered aimless through the
        hills.
They lost track of home,
    couldn't remember where they came from.
Everyone who met them took advantage of
        them.
    Their enemies had no qualms:
'Fair game' they said. 'They walked out on GOD.
    They abandoned the True Pasture, the hope
        of their parents.'

50:8-10 "But now, get out of Babylon as fast as you can.
    Be rid of that Babylonian country.
On your way. Good sheepdogs lead, but don't
        you be led.
    Lead the way home!
Do you see what I'm doing?
    I'm rallying a host of nations against
        Babylon.
They'll come out of the north,
    attack and take her.
Oh, they know how to fight, these armies.
    They never come home empty-handed.
Babylon is ripe for picking!
    All her plunderers will fill their bellies!"
                GOD's Decree.

---

[a] 1 Or *Chaldeans*; also in verses 8, 25, 35 and 45
[b] 10 Or *Chaldea*

NEW INTERNATIONAL VERSION

¹¹ "Because you rejoice and are glad,
      you who pillage my inheritance,
   because you frolic like a heifer threshing
         grain
      and neigh like stallions,
¹² your mother will be greatly ashamed;
      she who gave you birth will be disgraced.
   She will be the least of the nations—
      a wilderness, a dry land, a desert.
¹³ Because of the LORD's anger she will not be
         inhabited
      but will be completely desolate.
   All who pass Babylon will be horrified and
         scoff
      because of all her wounds.

¹⁴ "Take up your positions around Babylon,
      all you who draw the bow.
   Shoot at her! Spare no arrows,
      for she has sinned against the LORD.
¹⁵ Shout against her on every side!
      She surrenders, her towers fall,
      her walls are torn down.
   Since this is the vengeance of the LORD,
      take vengeance on her;
      do to her as she has done to others.
¹⁶ Cut off from Babylon the sower,
      and the reaper with his sickle at harvest.
   Because of the sword of the oppressor
      let everyone return to his own people,
      let everyone flee to his own land.

¹⁷ "Israel is a scattered flock
      that lions have chased away.
   The first to devour him
      was the king of Assyria;
   the last to crush his bones
      was Nebuchadnezzar king of Babylon."

¹⁸ Therefore this is what the LORD Almighty,
the God of Israel, says:

   "I will punish the king of Babylon and his
         land
      as I punished the king of Assyria.
¹⁹ But I will bring Israel back to his own
         pasture
      and he will graze on Carmel and Bashan;
   his appetite will be satisfied
      on the hills of Ephraim and Gilead.

THE MESSAGE

^{50:11-16} "You Babylonians had a good time while it
         lasted, didn't you?
   You lived it up, exploiting and using my
         people,
   Frisky calves romping in lush pastures,
      wild stallions out having a good time!
   Well, your mother would hardly be proud of
         you.
      The woman who bore you wouldn't be
         pleased.
   Look at what's come of you! A nothing
         nation!
      Rubble and garbage and weeds!
   Emptied of life by my holy anger,
      a desert of death and emptiness.
   Travelers who pass by Babylon will gasp,
         appalled,
      shaking their heads at such a comedown.
   Gang up on Babylon! Pin her down!
      Throw everything you have against her.
   Hold nothing back. Knock her flat.
      She's sinned—oh, how she's sinned,
         against me!
   Shout battle cries from every direction.
      All the fight has gone out of her.
   Her defenses have been flattened,
      her walls smashed.
   'Operation GOD's Vengeance.'
      Pile on the vengeance!
   Do to her as she has done.
      Give her a good dose of her own medicine!
   Destroy her farms and farmers,
      ravage her fields, empty her barns.
   And you captives, while the destruction rages,
      get out while the getting's good,
      get out fast and run for home.

                    ☩

^{50:17} "Israel is a scattered flock,
      hunted down by lions.
   The king of Assyria started the carnage.
      The king of Babylon, Nebuchadnezzar,
   Has completed the job,
      gnawing the bones clean."

^{50:18-20} And now this is what GOD-of-the-Angel-
         Armies,
      the God of Israel, has to say:
   "Just watch! I'm bringing doom on the king of
         Babylon and his land,
      the same doom I brought on the king of
         Assyria.
   But Israel I'll bring home to good pastures.
      He'll graze on the hills of Carmel and
         Bashan,
   On the slopes of Ephraim and Gilead.
      He will eat to his heart's content.

NEW INTERNATIONAL VERSION	THE MESSAGE

NEW INTERNATIONAL VERSION

²⁰In those days, at that time,"
  declares the LORD,
"search will be made for Israel's guilt,
  but there will be none,
and for the sins of Judah,
  but none will be found,
  for I will forgive the remnant I spare.

²¹ "Attack the land of Merathaim
  and those who live in Pekod.
Pursue, kill and completely destroy *ᵃ* them,"
  declares the LORD.
"Do everything I have commanded you.
²² The noise of battle is in the land,
  the noise of great destruction!
²³ How broken and shattered
  is the hammer of the whole earth!
How desolate is Babylon
  among the nations!
²⁴ I set a trap for you, O Babylon,
  and you were caught before you knew it;
you were found and captured
  because you opposed the LORD.
²⁵ The LORD has opened his arsenal
  and brought out the weapons of his wrath,
for the Sovereign LORD Almighty has work
    to do
  in the land of the Babylonians.
²⁶ Come against her from afar.
  Break open her granaries;
  pile her up like heaps of grain.
Completely destroy her
  and leave her no remnant.
²⁷ Kill all her young bulls;
  let them go down to the slaughter!
Woe to them! For their day has come,
  the time for them to be punished.
²⁸ Listen to the fugitives and refugees from
    Babylon
  declaring in Zion
how the LORD our God has taken vengeance,
  vengeance for his temple.

²⁹ "Summon archers against Babylon,
  all those who draw the bow.
Encamp all around her;
  let no one escape.
Repay her for her deeds;
  do to her as she has done.
For she has defied the LORD,
  the Holy One of Israel.
³⁰ Therefore, her young men will fall in the
    streets;
  all her soldiers will be silenced in that day,"
    declares the LORD.

THE MESSAGE

In those days and at that time"—GOD's
    Decree—
"they'll look high and low for a sign of
    Israel's guilt—nothing;
Search nook and cranny for a trace of Judah's
    sin—nothing.
These people that I've saved will start out
  with a clean slate.

✠

⁵⁰·²¹ "Attack Merathaim, land of rebels!
  Go after Pekod, country of doom!
Hunt them down. Make a clean sweep." GOD's
    Decree.
"These are my orders. Do what I tell you.

⁵⁰·²²⁻²⁴ "The thunderclap of battle
  shakes the foundations!
The Hammer has been hammered,
  smashed and splintered,
Babylon pummeled
  beyond recognition.
I set out a trap and you were caught in it.
  O Babylon, you never knew what hit you,
Caught and held in the steel grip of that trap!
  That's what you get for taking on GOD.

⁵⁰·²⁵⁻²⁸ "I, GOD, opened my arsenal.
  I brought out my weapons of wrath.
The Master, GOD-of-the-Angel-Armies,
  has a job to do in Babylon.
Come at her from all sides!
  Break into her granaries!
Shovel her into piles and burn her up.
  Leave nothing! Leave no one!
Kill all her young turks.
  Send them to their doom!
Doom to them! Yes, Doomsday!
  The clock has finally run out on them.
And here's a surprise:
  Runaways and escapees from Babylon
Show up in Zion reporting the news of GOD's
    vengeance,
  taking vengeance for my own Temple.

⁵⁰·²⁹⁻³⁰ "Call in the troops against Babylon,
  anyone who can shoot straight!
Tighten the noose!
  Leave no loopholes!
Give her back as good as she gave,
  a dose of her own medicine!
Her brazen insolence is an outrage
  against GOD, The Holy of Israel.
And now she pays: her young strewn dead in
    the streets,
  her soldiers dead, silent forever." GOD's
    Decree.

ᵃ 21 The Hebrew term refers to the irrevocable giving over
of things or persons to the LORD, often by totally destroying
them; also in verse 26.

NEW INTERNATIONAL VERSION

31 "See, I am against you, O arrogant one,"
    declares the Lord, the LORD Almighty,
"for your day has come,
    the time for you to be punished.
32 The arrogant one will stumble and fall
    and no one will help her up;
I will kindle a fire in her towns
    that will consume all who are around
        her."

33 This is what the LORD Almighty says:

"The people of Israel are oppressed,
    and the people of Judah as well.
All their captors hold them fast,
    refusing to let them go.
34 Yet their Redeemer is strong;
    the LORD Almighty is his name.
He will vigorously defend their cause
    so that he may bring rest to their land,
    but unrest to those who live in Babylon.

35 "A sword against the Babylonians!"
    declares the LORD—
"against those who live in Babylon
    and against her officials and wise men!
36 A sword against her false prophets!
    They will become fools.
A sword against her warriors!
    They will be filled with terror.
37 A sword against her horses and chariots
    and all the foreigners in her ranks!
    They will become women.
A sword against her treasures!
    They will be plundered.
38 A drought on*a* her waters!
    They will dry up.
For it is a land of idols,
    idols that will go mad with terror.

39 "So desert creatures and hyenas will live
        there,
    and there the owl will dwell.
It will never again be inhabited
    or lived in from generation to generation.
40 As God overthrew Sodom and Gomorrah
    along with their neighboring towns,"
                declares the LORD,
"so no one will live there;
    no man will dwell in it.

41 "Look! An army is coming from the north;
    a great nation and many kings
    are being stirred up from the ends of the
        earth.

a 38 Or A sword against

THE MESSAGE

50:31-32 "Do you get it, Mister Pride? I'm your
        enemy!"
    Decree of the Master, GOD-of-the-Angel-
        Armies.
"Time's run out on you:
    That's right: It's Doomsday.
Mister Pride will fall flat on his face.
    No one will offer him a hand.
I'll set his towns on fire.
    The fire will spread wild through the
        country."

✝

50:33-34 And here's more from GOD-of-the-Angel-Armies:

"The people of Israel are beaten down,
    the people of Judah along with them.
Their oppressors have them in a grip of steel.
    They won't let go.
But the Rescuer is strong:
    GOD-of-the-Angel-Armies.
Yes, I will take their side,
    I'll come to their rescue.
I'll soothe their land,
    but rough up the people of Babylon.

50:35-40 "It's all-out war in Babylon"—GOD's Decree—
    "total war against people, leaders, and the
        wise!
War to the death on her boasting pretenders,
    fools one and all!
    War to the death on her soldiers, cowards
        to a man!
War to the death on her hired killers, gutless
        wonders!
    War to the death on her banks—looted!
War to the death on her water supply—
        drained dry!
    A land of make-believe gods gone crazy—
        hobgoblins!
The place will be haunted with jackals and
        scorpions,
    night-owls and vampire bats.
No one will ever live there again.
    The land will reek with the stench of death.
It will join Sodom and Gomorrah and their
        neighbors,
    the cities I did away with." GOD's Decree.
"No one will live there again.
    No one will again draw breath in that land,
        ever.

50:41-43 "And now, watch this! People pouring
    out of the north, hordes of people,
A mob of kings stirred up
    from far-off places.

NEW INTERNATIONAL VERSION

⁴²They are armed with bows and spears;
    they are cruel and without mercy.
They sound like the roaring sea
    as they ride on their horses;
they come like men in battle formation
    to attack you, O Daughter of Babylon.
⁴³The king of Babylon has heard reports about
    them,
    and his hands hang limp.
Anguish has gripped him,
    pain like that of a woman in labor.
⁴⁴Like a lion coming up from Jordan's thickets
    to a rich pastureland,
I will chase Babylon from its land in an
    instant.
    Who is the chosen one I will appoint for
        this?
Who is like me and who can challenge me?
    And what shepherd can stand
        against me?"
⁴⁵Therefore, hear what the LORD has planned
    against Babylon,
    what he has purposed against the land of
        the Babylonians:
The young of the flock will be dragged away;
    he will completely destroy their pasture
        because of them.
⁴⁶At the sound of Babylon's capture the earth
    will tremble;
    its cry will resound among the nations.

51

This is what the LORD says:

"See, I will stir up the spirit of a destroyer
    against Babylon and the people of Leb
        Kamai.ᵃ
²I will send foreigners to Babylon
    to winnow her and to devastate her land;
they will oppose her on every side
    in the day of her disaster.
³Let not the archer string his bow,
    nor let him put on his armor.
Do not spare her young men;
    completely destroyᵇ her army.
⁴They will fall down slain in Babylon,ᶜ
    fatally wounded in her streets.
⁵For Israel and Judah have not been forsaken

ᵃ 1 Leb Kamai is a cryptogram for Chaldea, that is,
Babylonia.   ᵇ 3 The Hebrew term refers to the irrevocable
giving over of things or persons to the LORD, often by totally
destroying them.   ᶜ 4 Or Chaldea

THE MESSAGE

Flourishing deadly weapons,
    barbarians they are, cruel and pitiless.
Roaring and relentless, like ocean breakers,
    they come riding fierce stallions,
In battle formation, ready to fight
    you, Daughter Babylon!
Babylon's king hears them coming.
    He goes white as a ghost, limp as a dishrag.
Terror-stricken, he doubles up in pain,
        helpless to fight,
    like a woman giving birth to a baby.

50.44   "And now watch this: Like a lion coming up
    from the thick jungle of the Jordan,
Looking for prey in the mountain pastures,
    I'll take over and pounce.
I'll take my pick of the flock—and who's to
        stop me?
    All the so-called shepherds are helpless
        before me."

50.45-46   So, listen to this plan that GOD has worked
out against Babylon, the blueprint of what he's
prepared for dealing with Chaldea:

Believe it or not, the young,
    the vulnerable—mere lambs and kids—will
        be dragged off.
Believe it or not, the flock
    in shock, helpless to help, watches it
        happen.
When the shout goes up, "Babylon's down!"
    the very earth will shudder at the sound.
    The news will be heard all over the world.

HURRICANE PERSIA

51.1-5 # 51

There's more. GOD says more:

"Watch this:
    I'm whipping up
A death-dealing hurricane against Babylon—
        'Hurricane Persia'—
    against all who live in that perverse land.
I'm sending a cleanup crew into Babylon.
    They'll clean the place out from top to
        bottom.
When they get through there'll be nothing left
        of her
    worth taking or talking about.
They won't miss a thing.
    A total and final Doomsday!
Fighters will fight with everything they've got.
    It's no holds barred.
They will spare nothing and no one.
    It's final and wholesale destruction—the end!
Babylon littered with the wounded,
    streets piled with corpses.
It turns out that Israel and Judah
    are not widowed after all.

NEW INTERNATIONAL VERSION

by their God, the LORD Almighty,
though their land *a* is full of guilt
   before the Holy One of Israel.

6 "Flee from Babylon!
   Run for your lives!
   Do not be destroyed because of her sins.
It is time for the LORD's vengeance;
   he will pay her what she deserves.
7 Babylon was a gold cup in the LORD's hand;
   she made the whole earth drunk.
The nations drank her wine;
   therefore they have now gone mad.
8 Babylon will suddenly fall and be broken.
   Wail over her!
Get balm for her pain;
   perhaps she can be healed.

9 " 'We would have healed Babylon,
   but she cannot be healed;
let us leave her and each go to his own land,
   for her judgment reaches to the skies,
   it rises as high as the clouds.'

10 " 'The LORD has vindicated us;
   come, let us tell in Zion
   what the LORD our God has done.'

11 "Sharpen the arrows,
   take up the shields!
The LORD has stirred up the kings of the
   Medes,
   because his purpose is to destroy Babylon.
The LORD will take vengeance,
   vengeance for his temple.
12 Lift up a banner against the walls of
   Babylon!
   Reinforce the guard,
station the watchmen,
   prepare an ambush!
The LORD will carry out his purpose,
   his decree against the people of Babylon.
13 You who live by many waters
   and are rich in treasures,
your end has come,
   the time for you to be cut off.

THE MESSAGE

As their God, GOD-of-the-Angel-Armies, I am
   still alive and well,
   committed to them even though
They filled their land with sin
   against Israel's most Holy God.

51.6-8 "Get out of Babylon as fast as you can.
   Run for your lives! Save your necks!
Don't linger and lose your lives to my
   vengeance on her
   as I pay her back for her sins.
Babylon was a fancy gold chalice
   held in my hand,
Filled with the wine of my anger
   to make the whole world drunk.
The nations drank the wine
   and they've all gone crazy.
Babylon herself will stagger and crash,
   senseless in a drunken stupor—tragic!
Get anointing balm for her wound.
   Maybe she can be cured."

✠

51.9 "We did our best, but she can't be helped.
   Babylon is past fixing.
Give her up to her fate.
   Go home.
The judgment on her will be vast,
   a skyscraper-memorial of vengeance.

YOUR LIFELINE IS CUT

51.10 "GOD has set everything right for us.
   Come! Let's tell the good news
Back home in Zion.
   Let's tell what our GOD did to set things
   right.

51.11-13 "Sharpen the arrows!
   Fill the quivers!
GOD has stirred up the kings of the Medes,
   infecting them with war fever: 'Destroy
   Babylon!'
GOD's on the warpath.
   He's out to avenge his Temple.
Give the signal to attack Babylon's walls.
   Station guards around the clock.
Bring in reinforcements.
   Set men in ambush.
GOD will do what he planned,
   what he said he'd do to the people of
   Babylon.
You have more water than you need,
   you have more money than you need—
But your life is over,
   your lifeline cut."

✠

a 5 Or / *and the land of the Babylonians*

NEW INTERNATIONAL VERSION

¹⁴ The Lord Almighty has sworn by himself:
  I will surely fill you with men, as with a
    swarm of locusts,
  and they will shout in triumph over you.

¹⁵ "He made the earth by his power;
  he founded the world by his wisdom
  and stretched out the heavens by his
    understanding.
¹⁶ When he thunders, the waters in the
    heavens roar;
  he makes clouds rise from the ends of the
    earth.
  He sends lightning with the rain
  and brings out the wind from his
    storehouses.

¹⁷ "Every man is senseless and without
    knowledge;
  every goldsmith is shamed by his idols.
  His images are a fraud;
  they have no breath in them.
¹⁸ They are worthless, the objects of mockery;
  when their judgment comes, they will
    perish.
¹⁹ He who is the Portion of Jacob is not like these,
  for he is the Maker of all things,
  including the tribe of his inheritance—
  the Lord Almighty is his name.

²⁰ "You are my war club,
  my weapon for battle—
  with you I shatter nations,
  with you I destroy kingdoms,
²¹ with you I shatter horse and rider,
  with you I shatter chariot and driver,
²² with you I shatter man and woman,
  with you I shatter old man and youth,
  with you I shatter young man and maiden,
²³ with you I shatter shepherd and flock,
  with you I shatter farmer and oxen,
  with you I shatter governors and officials.

²⁴ "Before your eyes I will repay Babylon and
all who live in Babylonia*a* for all the wrong they
have done in Zion," declares the Lord.

²⁵ "I am against you, O destroying mountain,
  you who destroy the whole earth,"
                    declares the Lord.
  "I will stretch out my hand against you,
  roll you off the cliffs,
  and make you a burned-out mountain.
²⁶ No rock will be taken from you for a
    cornerstone,
  nor any stone for a foundation,
  for you will be desolate forever,"
                    declares the Lord.

a 24 Or Chaldea; also in verse 35

THE MESSAGE

51.14 God-of-the-Angel-Armies has solemnly
    sworn:
  "I'll fill this place with soldiers.
  They'll swarm through here like locusts
  chanting victory songs over you."

☩

51.15-19 By his power he made earth.
  His wisdom gave shape to the world.
  He crafted the cosmos.
  He thunders and rain pours down.
  He sends the clouds soaring.
  He embellishes the storm with lightnings,
  launches the wind from his warehouse.
  Stick-god worshipers look mighty foolish!
  god-makers embarrassed by their
    handmade gods!
  Their gods are frauds, dead sticks—
  deadwood gods, tasteless jokes.
  They're nothing but stale smoke.
  When the smoke clears, they're gone.
  But the Portion-of-Jacob is the real thing;
  he put the whole universe together,
  With special attention to Israel.
  His name? God-of-the-Angel-Armies!

They'll Sleep and Never Wake Up

51.20-23 God says, "You, Babylon, are my hammer,
  my weapon of war.
  I'll use you to smash godless nations,
  use you to knock kingdoms to bits.
  I'll use you to smash horse and rider,
  use you to smash chariot and driver.
  I'll use you to smash man and woman,
  use you to smash the old man and the boy.
  I'll use you to smash the young man and
    young woman,
  use you to smash shepherd and sheep.
  I'll use you to smash farmer and yoked oxen,
  use you to smash governors and senators.

51.24 "Judeans, you'll see it with your own eyes.
  I'll pay Babylon and all the Chaldeans back for
  all the evil they did in Zion." God's Decree.

51.25-26 "I'm your enemy, Babylon, Mount Destroyer,
  you ravager of the whole earth.
  I'll reach out, I'll take you in my hand,
  and I'll crush you till there's no mountain
    left.
  I'll turn you into a gravel pit—
  no more cornerstones cut from you,
  No more foundation stones quarried from
    you!
  Nothing left of you but gravel." God's
    Decree.

☩

NEW INTERNATIONAL VERSION

27 "Lift up a banner in the land!
  Blow the trumpet among the nations!
Prepare the nations for battle against her;
  summon against her these kingdoms:
  Ararat, Minni and Ashkenaz.
Appoint a commander against her;
  send up horses like a swarm of locusts.
28 Prepare the nations for battle against her—
  the kings of the Medes,
their governors and all their officials,
  and all the countries they rule.
29 The land trembles and writhes,
  for the LORD's purposes against Babylon
    stand—
to lay waste the land of Babylon
  so that no one will live there.
30 Babylon's warriors have stopped fighting;
  they remain in their strongholds.
Their strength is exhausted;
  they have become like women.
Her dwellings are set on fire;
  the bars of her gates are broken.
31 One courier follows another
  and messenger follows messenger
to announce to the king of Babylon
  that his entire city is captured,
32 the river crossings seized,
  the marshes set on fire,
  and the soldiers terrified."

33 This is what the LORD Almighty, the God of
Israel, says:

"The Daughter of Babylon is like a threshing
    floor
  at the time it is trampled;
  the time to harvest her will soon come."

34 "Nebuchadnezzar king of Babylon has
    devoured us,
  he has thrown us into confusion,
  he has made us an empty jar.
Like a serpent he has swallowed us
  and filled his stomach with our delicacies,
  and then has spewed us out.
35 May the violence done to our flesh[a] be upon
    Babylon,"
  say the inhabitants of Zion.
"May our blood be on those who live in
    Babylonia,"
  says Jerusalem.

36 Therefore, this is what the LORD says:

"See, I will defend your cause
  and avenge you;
I will dry up her sea
  and make her springs dry.

---

[a] 35 Or *done to us and to our children*

THE MESSAGE

51.27-28 "Raise the signal in the land,
  blow the shofar-trumpet for the nations.
Consecrate the nations for holy work against
    her.
  Call kingdoms into service against her.
  Enlist Ararat, Minni, and Ashkenaz.
Appoint a field marshal against her,
  and round up horses, locust hordes of
    horses!
Consecrate the nations for holy work against
    her—
  the king of the Medes, his leaders and
    people.

51.29-33 "The very land trembles in terror, writhes in
    pain,
  terrorized by my plans against Babylon,
Plans to turn the country of Babylon
  into a lifeless moonscape—a wasteland.
Babylon's soldiers have quit fighting.
  They hide out in ruins and caves—
Cowards who've given up without a fight,
  exposed as cowering milksops.
Babylon's houses are going up in flames,
  the city gates torn off their hinges.
Runner after runner comes racing in,
  each on the heels of the last,
Bringing reports to the king of Babylon
  that his city is a lost cause.
The fords of the rivers are all taken.
  Wildfire rages through the swamp grass.
Soldiers desert left and right.
  I, GOD-of-the-Angel-Armies, said it would
    happen:
'Daughter Babylon is a threshing floor
  at threshing time.
Soon, oh very soon, her harvest will come
  and then the chaff will fly!'

51.34-37 "Nebuchadnezzar king of Babylon
  chewed up my people and spit out the
    bones.
He wiped his dish clean, pushed back his
    chair,
  and belched—a huge gluttonous belch.
Lady Zion says,
  'The brutality done to me be done to
    Babylon!'
And Jerusalem says,
  'The blood spilled from me be charged to
    the Chaldeans!'
Then I, GOD, step in and say,
  'I'm on your side, taking up your cause.
I'm your Avenger. You'll get your revenge.
  I'll dry up her rivers, plug up her springs.

NEW INTERNATIONAL VERSION

³⁷Babylon will be a heap of ruins,
    a haunt of jackals,
an object of horror and scorn,
    a place where no one lives.
³⁸Her people all roar like young lions,
    they growl like lion cubs.
³⁹But while they are aroused,
    I will set out a feast for them
    and make them drunk,
so that they shout with laughter—
    then sleep forever and not awake,"
                    declares the LORD.
⁴⁰"I will bring them down
    like lambs to the slaughter,
    like rams and goats.

⁴¹"How Sheshach^a will be captured,
    the boast of the whole earth seized!
What a horror Babylon will be
    among the nations!
⁴²The sea will rise over Babylon;
    its roaring waves will cover her.
⁴³Her towns will be desolate,
    a dry and desert land,
a land where no one lives,
    through which no man travels.
⁴⁴I will punish Bel in Babylon
    and make him spew out what he has
        swallowed.
The nations will no longer stream to him.
    And the wall of Babylon will fall.

⁴⁵"Come out of her, my people!
    Run for your lives!
    Run from the fierce anger of the LORD.
⁴⁶Do not lose heart or be afraid
    when rumors are heard in the land;
one rumor comes this year, another the next,
    rumors of violence in the land
    and of ruler against ruler.
⁴⁷For the time will surely come
    when I will punish the idols of Babylon;
her whole land will be disgraced
    and her slain will all lie fallen within her.
⁴⁸Then heaven and earth and all that is in
        them
    will shout for joy over Babylon,
for out of the north
    destroyers will attack her,"
                    declares the LORD.

THE MESSAGE

Babylon will be a pile of rubble,
    scavenged by stray dogs and cats,
A dumping ground for garbage,
    a godforsaken ghost town.'

⁵¹·³⁸⁻⁴⁰ "The Babylonians will be like lions and their
        cubs,
    ravenous, roaring for food.
I'll fix them a meal, all right—a banquet, in
        fact.
    They'll drink themselves falling-down
        drunk.
Dead drunk, they'll sleep—and sleep, and
        sleep . . .
    and they'll never wake up." GOD's Decree.
"I'll haul these 'lions' off to the slaughterhouse
    like the lambs, rams, and goats,
    never to be heard of again.

⁵¹·⁴¹⁻⁴⁸ "Babylon is finished—
    the pride of the whole earth is flat on her
        face.
What a comedown for Babylon,
    to end up inglorious in the sewer!
Babylon drowned in chaos,
    battered by waves of enemy soldiers.
Her towns stink with decay and rot,
    the land empty and bare and sterile.
No one lives in these towns anymore.
    Travelers give them a wide berth.
I'll bring doom on the glutton god-Bel in
        Babylon.
    I'll make him vomit up all he gulped down.
No more visitors stream into this place,
    admiring and gawking at the wonders of
        Babylon.
    The wonders of Babylon are no more.
Run for your lives, my dear people!
    Run, and don't look back!
Get out of this place while you can,
    this place torched by GOD's raging anger.
Don't lose hope. Don't ever give up
    when the rumors pour in hot and heavy.
One year it's this, the next year it's that—
    rumors of violence, rumors of war.
Trust me, the time is coming
    when I'll put the no-gods of Babylon in
        their place.
I'll show up the whole country as a sickening
        fraud,
    with dead bodies strewn all over the place.
Heaven and earth, angels and people,
    will throw a victory party over Babylon
When the avenging armies from the north
    descend on her." GOD's Decree!

---

^a 41 *Sheshach* is a cryptogram for Babylon.

NEW INTERNATIONAL VERSION

⁴⁹ "Babylon must fall because of Israel's slain,
    just as the slain in all the earth
    have fallen because of Babylon.
⁵⁰ You who have escaped the sword,
    leave and do not linger!
  Remember the LORD in a distant land,
    and think on Jerusalem."

⁵¹ "We are disgraced,
    for we have been insulted
    and shame covers our faces,
  because foreigners have entered
    the holy places of the LORD's house."

⁵² "But days are coming," declares the LORD,
    "when I will punish her idols,
  and throughout her land
    the wounded will groan.
⁵³ Even if Babylon reaches the sky
    and fortifies her lofty stronghold,
  I will send destroyers against her,"
                    declares the LORD.

⁵⁴ "The sound of a cry comes from Babylon,
    the sound of great destruction
    from the land of the Babylonians.ᵃ
⁵⁵ The LORD will destroy Babylon;
    he will silence her noisy din.
  Waves ∟of enemies⌐ will rage like great
      waters;
    the roar of their voices will resound.
⁵⁶ A destroyer will come against Babylon;
    her warriors will be captured,
    and their bows will be broken.
  For the LORD is a God of retribution;
    he will repay in full.
⁵⁷ I will make her officials and wise men
      drunk,
    her governors, officers and warriors as
      well;
  they will sleep forever and not awake,"
    declares the King, whose name is the
      LORD Almighty.

⁵⁸ This is what the LORD Almighty says:

"Babylon's thick wall will be leveled

THE MESSAGE

REMEMBER GOD IN YOUR LONG AND DISTANT EXILE

51.49-50 "Babylon must fall—
    compensation for the war dead in Israel.
  Babylonians will be killed
    because of all that Babylonian killing.
  But you exiles who have escaped a Babylonian
      death,
    get out! And fast!
  Remember GOD in your long and distant exile.
    Keep Jerusalem alive in your memory."

51.51 How we've been humiliated, taunted and
      abused,
    kicked around for so long that we hardly
      know who we are!
  And we hardly know what to think—
    our old Sanctuary, GOD's house, desecrated
      by strangers.

51.52-53 "I know, but trust me: The time is coming"
    —GOD's Decree.
  "When I will bring doom on her no-god idols,
    and all over this land her wounded will
      groan.
  Even if Babylon climbed a ladder to the moon
    and pulled up the ladder so that no one
      could get to her,
  That wouldn't stop me.
    I'd make sure my avengers would reach
      her."
        GOD's Decree.

51.54-56 "But now listen! Do you hear it? A cry out of
      Babylon!
    An unearthly wail out of Chaldea!
  GOD is taking his wrecking bar to Babylon.
    We'll be hearing the last of her noise—
  Death throes like the crashing of waves,
    death rattles like the roar of cataracts.
  The avenging destroyer is about to enter
      Babylon:
    Her soldiers are taken, her weapons are
      trashed.
  Indeed, GOD is a God who evens things out.
    All end up with their just deserts.

51.57 "I'll get them drunk, the whole lot of them—
    princes, sages, governors, soldiers.
  Dead drunk, they'll sleep—and sleep and
      sleep . . .
    and never wake up." The King's Decree.
  His name? GOD-OF-THE-ANGEL-ARMIES!

51.58   GOD-OF-THE-ANGEL-ARMIES speaks:

"The city walls of Babylon—those massive
      walls!—
    will be flattened.
  And those city gates—huge gates!—

NEW INTERNATIONAL VERSION

and her high gates set on fire;
    the peoples exhaust themselves for nothing,
      the nations' labor is only fuel for the
        flames."

⁵⁹This is the message Jeremiah gave to the staff officer Seraiah son of Neriah, the son of Mahseiah, when he went to Babylon with Zedekiah king of Judah in the fourth year of his reign. ⁶⁰Jeremiah had written on a scroll about all the disasters that would come upon Babylon—all that had been recorded concerning Babylon. ⁶¹He said to Seraiah, "When you get to Babylon, see that you read all these words aloud. ⁶²Then say, 'O LORD, you have said you will destroy this place, so that neither man nor animal will live in it; it will be desolate forever.' ⁶³When you finish reading this scroll, tie a stone to it and throw it into the Euphrates. ⁶⁴Then say, 'So will Babylon sink to rise no more because of the disaster I will bring upon her. And her people will fall.' "

The words of Jeremiah end here.

THE FALL OF JERUSALEM

52 Zedekiah was twenty-one years old when he became king, and he reigned in Jerusalem eleven years. His mother's name was Hamutal daughter of Jeremiah; she was from Libnah. ²He did evil in the eyes of the LORD, just as Jehoiakim had done. ³It was because of the LORD's anger that all this happened to Jerusalem and Judah, and in the end he thrust them from his presence.

Now Zedekiah rebelled against the king of Babylon.

⁴So in the ninth year of Zedekiah's reign, on the tenth day of the tenth month, Nebuchadnezzar king of Babylon marched against Jerusalem with his whole army. They camped outside the city and built siege works all around it. ⁵The city was kept under siege until the eleventh year of King Zedekiah.

⁶By the ninth day of the fourth month the famine in the city had become so severe that there was no food for the people to eat. ⁷Then the city wall was broken through, and the whole army fled. They left the city at night through the gate between the two walls near the king's garden, though the Babylonians*ᵃ* were surrounding

ᵃ 7 Or *Chaldeans*; also in verse 17

THE MESSAGE

will be set on fire.
The harder you work at this empty life,
    the less you are.
Nothing comes of ambition like this
    but ashes."

✠

51.59 Jeremiah the prophet gave a job to Seraiah son of Neriah, son of Mahseiah, when Seraiah went with Zedekiah king of Judah to Babylon. It was in the fourth year of Zedekiah's reign. Seraiah was in charge of travel arrangements.

51.60-62 Jeremiah had written down in a little booklet all the bad things that would come down on Babylon. He told Seraiah, "When you get to Babylon, read this out in public. Read, 'You, O GOD, said that you would destroy this place so that nothing could live here, neither human nor animal—a wasteland to top all wastelands, an eternal nothing.'

51.63-64 "When you've finished reading the page, tie a stone to it, throw it into the River Euphrates, and watch it sink. Then say, 'That's how Babylon will sink to the bottom and stay there after the disaster I'm going to bring upon her.' "

THE DESTRUCTION OF JERUSALEM AND EXILE OF JUDAH

52 Zedekiah was twenty-one years old when he started out as king. He was king in Jerusalem for eleven years. His mother's name was Hamutal, the daughter of Jeremiah. Her hometown was Libnah.

52.2 As far as GOD was concerned, Zedekiah was just one more evil king, a carbon copy of Jehoiakim.

52.3-5 The source of all this doom to Jerusalem and Judah was GOD's anger. GOD turned his back on them as an act of judgment.

Zedekiah revolted against the king of Babylon. Nebuchadnezzar set out for Jerusalem with a full army. He set up camp and sealed off the city by building siege mounds around it. He arrived on the ninth year and tenth month of Zedekiah's reign. The city was under siege for nineteen months (until the eleventh year of Zedekiah).

52.6-8 By the fourth month of Zedekiah's eleventh year, on the ninth day of the month, the famine was so bad that there wasn't so much as a crumb of bread for anyone. Then the Babylonians broke through the city walls. Under cover of the night darkness, the entire Judean army fled through an opening in the wall (it was the gate between the two walls above the King's Garden). They slipped through the lines of the Babylonians who surrounded the city and

NEW INTERNATIONAL VERSION

the city. They fled toward the Arabah,[a] [8]but the Babylonian[b] army pursued King Zedekiah and overtook him in the plains of Jericho. All his soldiers were separated from him and scattered, [9]and he was captured.

He was taken to the king of Babylon at Riblah in the land of Hamath, where he pronounced sentence on him. [10]There at Riblah the king of Babylon slaughtered the sons of Zedekiah before his eyes; he also killed all the officials of Judah. [11]Then he put out Zedekiah's eyes, bound him with bronze shackles and took him to Babylon, where he put him in prison till the day of his death.

[12]On the tenth day of the fifth month, in the nineteenth year of Nebuchadnezzar king of Babylon, Nebuzaradan commander of the imperial guard, who served the king of Babylon, came to Jerusalem. [13]He set fire to the temple of the LORD, the royal palace and all the houses of Jerusalem. Every important building he burned down. [14]The whole Babylonian army under the commander of the imperial guard broke down all the walls around Jerusalem. [15]Nebuzaradan the commander of the guard carried into exile some of the poorest people and those who remained in the city, along with the rest of the craftsmen[c] and those who had gone over to the king of Babylon. [16]But Nebuzaradan left behind the rest of the poorest people of the land to work the vineyards and fields.

[17]The Babylonians broke up the bronze pillars, the movable stands and the bronze Sea that were at the temple of the LORD and they carried all the bronze to Babylon. [18]They also took away the pots, shovels, wick trimmers, sprinkling bowls, dishes and all the bronze articles used in the temple service. [19]The commander of the imperial guard took away the basins, censers, sprinkling bowls, pots, lampstands, dishes and bowls used for drink offerings—all that were made of pure gold or silver.

[20]The bronze from the two pillars, the Sea and the twelve bronze bulls under it, and the movable stands, which King Solomon had made for the temple of the LORD, was more than could be weighed. [21]Each of the pillars was eighteen cubits high and twelve cubits in circumference[d]; each was four fingers thick, and hollow. [22]The bronze capital on top of the one pillar was five cubits[e] high and was decorated with a network and pomegranates of bronze all around. The oth-

THE MESSAGE

headed for the Jordan into the Arabah Valley, but the Babylonians were in full pursuit. They caught up with them in the Plains of Jericho. But by then Zedekiah's army had deserted and was scattered.

52:9-11 The Babylonians captured Zedekiah and marched him off to the king of Babylon at Riblah in Hamath, who tried and sentenced him on the spot. The king of Babylon then killed Zedekiah's sons right before his eyes. The summary murder of his sons was the last thing Zedekiah saw, for they then blinded him. The king of Babylon followed that up by killing all the officials of Judah. Securely handcuffed, Zedekiah was hauled off to Babylon. The king of Babylon threw him in prison, where he stayed until the day he died.

52:12-16 In the nineteenth year of Nebuchadnezzar king of Babylon on the seventh day of the fifth month, Nebuzaradan, the king of Babylon's chief deputy, arrived in Jerusalem. He burned the Temple of GOD to the ground, went on to the royal palace, and then finished off the city. He burned the whole place down. He put the Babylonian troops he had with him to work knocking down the city walls. Finally, he rounded up everyone left in the city, including those who had earlier deserted to the king of Babylon, and took them off into exile. He left a few poor dirt farmers behind to tend the vineyards and what was left of the fields.

52:17-19 The Babylonians broke up the bronze pillars, the bronze washstands, and the huge bronze basin (the Sea) that were in the Temple of GOD, and hauled the bronze off to Babylon. They also took the various bronze-crafted liturgical accessories, as well as the gold and silver censers and sprinkling bowls, used in the services of Temple worship. The king's deputy didn't miss a thing. He took every scrap of precious metal he could find.

52:20-23 The amount of bronze they got from the two pillars, the Sea, the twelve bronze bulls that supported the Sea, and the ten washstands that Solomon had made for the Temple of GOD was enormous. They couldn't weigh it all! Each pillar stood twenty-seven feet high with a circumference of eighteen feet. The pillars were hollow, the bronze a little less than an inch thick. Each pillar was topped with an ornate capital of bronze pomegranates and filigree, which added

---

[a] 7 Or *the Jordan Valley*   [b] 8 Or *Chaldean*; also in verse 14
[c] 15 Or *populace*   [d] 21 That is, about 27 feet (about 8.1 meters) high and 18 feet (about 5.4 meters) in circumference   [e] 22 That is, about 7 1/2 feet (about 2.3 meters)

NEW INTERNATIONAL VERSION

er pillar, with its pomegranates, was similar. ²³There were ninety-six pomegranates on the sides; the total number of pomegranates above the surrounding network was a hundred.

²⁴The commander of the guard took as prisoners Seraiah the chief priest, Zephaniah the priest next in rank and the three doorkeepers. ²⁵Of those still in the city, he took the officer in charge of the fighting men, and seven royal advisers. He also took the secretary who was chief officer in charge of conscripting the people of the land and sixty of his men who were found in the city. ²⁶Nebuzaradan the commander took them all and brought them to the king of Babylon at Riblah. ²⁷There at Riblah, in the land of Hamath, the king had them executed.

So Judah went into captivity, away from her land. ²⁸This is the number of the people Nebuchadnezzar carried into exile:

in the seventh year, 3,023 Jews;
²⁹in Nebuchadnezzar's eighteenth year,
832 people from Jerusalem;
³⁰in his twenty-third year,
745 Jews taken into exile by Nebuzaradan the commander of the imperial guard.
There were 4,600 people in all.

JEHOIACHIN RELEASED

³¹In the thirty-seventh year of the exile of Jehoiachin king of Judah, in the year Evil-Merodach^a became king of Babylon, he released Jehoiachin king of Judah and freed him from prison on the twenty-fifth day of the twelfth month. ³²He spoke kindly to him and gave him a seat of honor higher than those of the other kings who were with him in Babylon. ³³So Jehoiachin put aside his prison clothes and for the rest of his life ate regularly at the king's table. ³⁴Day by day the king of Babylon gave Jehoiachin a regular allowance as long as he lived, till the day of his death.

THE MESSAGE

another seven and a half feet to its height. There were ninety-six pomegranates evenly spaced—in all, a hundred pomegranates worked into the filigree.

52.24-27 The king's deputy took a number of special prisoners: Seraiah the chief priest, Zephaniah the associate priest, three wardens, the chief remaining army officer, seven of the king's counselors who happened to be in the city, the chief recruiting officer for the army, and sixty men of standing from among the people who were still there. Nebuzaradan the king's deputy marched them all off to the king of Babylon at Riblah. And there at Riblah, in the land of Hamath, the king of Babylon killed the lot of them in cold blood.

Judah went into exile, orphaned from her land.

✝

52.28 3,023 men of Judah were taken into exile by Nebuchadnezzar in the seventh year of his reign.

52.29 832 from Jerusalem were taken in the eighteenth year of his reign.

52.30 745 men from Judah were taken off by Nebuzaradan, the king's chief deputy, in Nebuchadnezzar's twenty-third year.

The total number of exiles was 4,600.

✝

52.31-34 When Jehoiachin king of Judah had been in exile for thirty-seven years, Evil-Merodach became king in Babylon and let Jehoiachin out of prison. This release took place on the twenty-fifth day of the twelfth month. The king treated him most courteously and gave him preferential treatment beyond anything experienced by the political prisoners held in Babylon. Jehoiachin took off his prison garb and from then on ate his meals in company with the king. The king provided everything he needed to live comfortably for the rest of his life.

---

^a 31 Also called *Amel-Marduk*.

LAMENTATIONS

LAMENTATIONS

1 ^a How deserted lies the city,
    once so full of people!
How like a widow is she,
    who once was great among the nations!
She who was queen among the provinces
    has now become a slave.

² Bitterly she weeps at night,
    tears are upon her cheeks.
Among all her lovers
    there is none to comfort her.
All her friends have betrayed her;
    they have become her enemies.

³ After affliction and harsh labor,
    Judah has gone into exile.
She dwells among the nations;
    she finds no resting place.
All who pursue her have overtaken her
    in the midst of her distress.

⁴ The roads to Zion mourn,
    for no one comes to her appointed feasts.
All her gateways are desolate,
    her priests groan,
her maidens grieve,
    and she is in bitter anguish.

⁵ Her foes have become her masters;
    her enemies are at ease.
The LORD has brought her grief
    because of her many sins.
Her children have gone into exile,
    captive before the foe.

⁶ All the splendor has departed
    from the Daughter of Zion.
Her princes are like deer
    that find no pasture;
in weakness they have fled
    before the pursuer.

⁷ In the days of her affliction and wandering
    Jerusalem remembers all the treasures
    that were hers in days of old.

---

^a This chapter is an acrostic poem, the verses of which
begin with the successive letters of the Hebrew alphabet.

WORTHLESS, CHEAP, ABJECT!

1.1 **1** Oh, oh, oh . . .
    How empty the city, once teeming with
        people.
A widow, this city, once in the front rank of
        nations,
    once queen of the ball, she's now a drudge
        in the kitchen.

1.2 She cries herself to sleep each night, tears
        soaking her pillow.
No one's left among her lovers to sit and
        hold her hand.
    Her friends have all dumped her.

1.3 After years of pain and hard labor, Judah has
        gone into exile.
    She camps out among the nations, never
        feels at home.
    Hunted by all, she's stuck between a rock
        and a hard place.

1.4 Zion's roads weep, empty of pilgrims headed
        to the feasts.
    All her city gates are deserted, her priests in
        despair.
    Her virgins are sad. How bitter her fate.

1.5 Her enemies have become her masters. Her
        foes are living it up
    because GOD laid her low, punishing her
        repeated rebellions.
    Her children, prisoners of the enemy,
        trudge into exile.

1.6 All beauty has drained from Daughter Zion's
        face.
    Her princes are like deer famished for food,
        chased to exhaustion by hunters.

1.7 Jerusalem remembers the day she lost
        everything,

NEW INTERNATIONAL VERSION

When her people fell into enemy hands,
　　there was no one to help her.
Her enemies looked at her
　　and laughed at her destruction.

8 Jerusalem has sinned greatly
　　and so has become unclean.
All who honored her despise her,
　　for they have seen her nakedness;
she herself groans
　　and turns away.

9 Her filthiness clung to her skirts;
　　she did not consider her future.
Her fall was astounding;
　　there was none to comfort her.
"Look, O Lord, on my affliction,
　　for the enemy has triumphed."

10 The enemy laid hands
　　on all her treasures;
she saw pagan nations
　　enter her sanctuary—
those you had forbidden
　　to enter your assembly.

11 All her people groan
　　as they search for bread;
they barter their treasures for food
　　to keep themselves alive.
"Look, O Lord, and consider,
　　for I am despised."

12 "Is it nothing to you, all you who pass by?
　　Look around and see.
Is any suffering like my suffering
　　that was inflicted on me,
that the Lord brought on me
　　in the day of his fierce anger?

13 "From on high he sent fire,
　　sent it down into my bones.
He spread a net for my feet
　　and turned me back.
He made me desolate,
　　faint all the day long.

14 "My sins have been bound into a yoke *a*;
　　by his hands they were woven together.
They have come upon my neck
　　and the Lord has sapped my strength.
He has handed me over
　　to those I cannot withstand.

15 "The Lord has rejected
　　all the warriors in my midst;
he has summoned an army against me
　　to *b* crush my young men.
In his winepress the Lord has trampled
　　the Virgin Daughter of Judah.

*a 14 Most Hebrew manuscripts; Septuagint He kept watch
over my sins   b 15 Or has set a time for me / when he will*

THE MESSAGE

when her people fell into enemy hands,
　　and not a soul there to help.
Enemies looked on and laughed, laughed at
　　her helpless silence.

1.8 Jerusalem, who outsinned the whole world, is
　　an outcast.
All who admired her despise her now that
　　they see beneath the surface.
Miserable, she groans and turns away in
　　shame.

1.9 She played fast and loose with life, she never
　　considered tomorrow,
and now she's crashed royally, with no one
　　to hold her hand:
"Look at my pain, O God! And how the
　　enemy cruelly struts."

1.10 The enemy reached out to take all her favorite
　　things. She watched
as pagans barged into her Sanctuary, those
　　very people for whom
you posted orders: KEEP OUT: THIS ASSEMBLY
　　OFF-LIMITS.

1.11 All the people groaned, so desperate for food,
　　so desperate to stay alive
that they bartered their favorite things for a
　　bit of breakfast:
"O God, look at me! Worthless, cheap,
　　abject!

1.12 "And you passersby, look at me! Have you
　　ever seen anything like this?
Ever seen pain like my pain, seen what he
　　did to me,
what *God* did to me in his rage?

1.13 "He struck me with lightning, skewered me
　　from head to foot,
then he set traps all around so I could
　　hardly move.
He left me with nothing—left me sick, and
　　sick of living.

1.14 "He wove my sins into a rope
　　and harnessed me to captivity's yoke.
I'm goaded by cruel taskmasters.

1.15 "The Master piled up my best soldiers in a
　　heap,
then called in thugs to break their fine
　　young necks.
The Master crushed the life out of fair
　　virgin Judah.

NEW INTERNATIONAL VERSION

¹⁶ "This is why I weep
and my eyes overflow with tears.
No one is near to comfort me,
no one to restore my spirit.
My children are destitute
because the enemy has prevailed."

¹⁷ Zion stretches out her hands,
but there is no one to comfort her.
The Lord has decreed for Jacob
that his neighbors become his foes;
Jerusalem has become
an unclean thing among them.

¹⁸ "The Lord is righteous,
yet I rebelled against his command.
Listen, all you peoples;
look upon my suffering.
My young men and maidens
have gone into exile.

¹⁹ "I called to my allies
but they betrayed me.
My priests and my elders
perished in the city
while they searched for food
to keep themselves alive.

²⁰ "See, O Lord, how distressed I am!
I am in torment within,
and in my heart I am disturbed,
for I have been most rebellious.
Outside, the sword bereaves;
inside, there is only death.

²¹ "People have heard my groaning,
but there is no one to comfort me.
All my enemies have heard of my distress;
they rejoice at what you have done.
May you bring the day you have announced
so they may become like me.

²² "Let all their wickedness come before you;
deal with them
as you have dealt with me
because of all my sins.
My groans are many
and my heart is faint."

2 ^a How the Lord has covered the Daughter of
Zion
with the cloud of his anger^b!
He has hurled down the splendor of Israel
from heaven to earth;

^a This chapter is an acrostic poem, the verses of which
begin with the successive letters of the Hebrew alphabet.
^b 1 Or *How the Lord in his anger / has treated the Daughter of
Zion with contempt*

THE MESSAGE

1.16 "For all this I weep, weep buckets of tears,
and not a soul within miles around cares
for my soul.
My children are wasted, my enemy got his
way."

1.17 Zion reached out for help, but no one helped.
God ordered Jacob's enemies to surround
him,
and now no one wants anything to do with
Jerusalem.

1.18 "God has right on his side. I'm the one who
did wrong.
Listen everybody! Look at what I'm going
through!
My fair young women, my fine young men,
all herded into exile!

1.19 "I called to my friends; they betrayed me.
My priests and my leaders only looked after
themselves,
trying but failing to save their own skins.

1.20 "O God, look at the trouble I'm in! My
stomach in knots,
my heart wrecked by a life of rebellion.
Massacres in the streets, starvation in the
houses.

1.21 "Oh, listen to my groans. No one listens, no
one cares.
When my enemies heard of the trouble you
gave me, they cheered.
Bring on Judgment Day! Let them get what
I got!

1.22 "Take a good look at their evil ways and give
it to them!
Give them what you gave me for my sins.
Groaning in pain, body and soul, I've had
all I can take."

God Walked Away from His Holy Temple

2.1 **2** Oh, oh, oh . . .
How the Master has cut down Daughter
Zion
from the skies, dashed Israel's glorious city
to earth,

NEW INTERNATIONAL VERSION

he has not remembered his footstool
  in the day of his anger.

²Without pity the Lord has swallowed up
  all the dwellings of Jacob;
in his wrath he has torn down
  the strongholds of the Daughter of Judah.
He has brought her kingdom and its princes
  down to the ground in dishonor.

³In fierce anger he has cut off
  every horn^a of Israel.
He has withdrawn his right hand
  at the approach of the enemy.
He has burned in Jacob like a flaming fire
  that consumes everything around it.

⁴Like an enemy he has strung his bow;
  his right hand is ready.
Like a foe he has slain
  all who were pleasing to the eye;
he has poured out his wrath like fire
  on the tent of the Daughter of Zion.

⁵The Lord is like an enemy;
  he has swallowed up Israel.
He has swallowed up all her palaces
  and destroyed her strongholds.
He has multiplied mourning and lamentation
  for the Daughter of Judah.

⁶He has laid waste his dwelling like a garden;
  he has destroyed his place of meeting.
The LORD has made Zion forget
  her appointed feasts and her Sabbaths;
in his fierce anger he has spurned
  both king and priest.

⁷The Lord has rejected his altar
  and abandoned his sanctuary.
He has handed over to the enemy
  the walls of her palaces;
they have raised a shout in the house of the
  LORD
  as on the day of an appointed feast.

⁸The LORD determined to tear down
  the wall around the Daughter of Zion.
He stretched out a measuring line
  and did not withhold his hand from
    destroying.
He made ramparts and walls lament;
  together they wasted away.

⁹Her gates have sunk into the ground;
  their bars he has broken and destroyed.
Her king and her princes are exiled among
    the nations,
  the law is no more,

^a 3 Or / all the strength; or every king; horn here symbolizes
strength.

THE MESSAGE

in his anger treated his favorite as
  throwaway junk.

2.2 The Master, without a second thought, took
  Israel in one gulp.
Raging, he smashed Judah's defenses,
  made hash of her king and princes.

2.3 His anger blazing, he knocked Israel flat,
  broke Israel's arm and turned his back just
    as the enemy approached,
came on Jacob like a wildfire from every
  direction.

2.4 Like an enemy, he aimed his bow, bared his
  sword,
and killed our young men, our pride and
  joy.
His anger, like fire, burned down the
  homes in Zion.

2.5 The Master became the enemy. He had Israel
  for supper.
He chewed up and spit out all the defenses.
He left Daughter Judah moaning and
  groaning.

2.6 He plowed up his old trysting place, trashed
  his favorite rendezvous.
GOD wiped out Zion's memories of feast
  days and Sabbaths,
angrily sacked king and priest alike.

2.7 GOD abandoned his altar, walked away from
  his holy Temple
and turned the fortifications over to the
  enemy.
As they cheered in GOD's Temple, you'd
  have thought it was a feast day!

2.8 GOD drew up plans to tear down the walls of
  Daughter Zion.
He assembled his crew, set to work and
  went at it.
Total demolition! The stones wept!

2.9 Her city gates, iron bars and all, disappeared
  in the rubble:
her kings and princes off to exile—no one
  left to instruct or lead;

NEW INTERNATIONAL VERSION	THE MESSAGE

NEW INTERNATIONAL VERSION

and her prophets no longer find
    visions from the LORD.

10 The elders of the Daughter of Zion
    sit on the ground in silence;
they have sprinkled dust on their heads
    and put on sackcloth.
The young women of Jerusalem
    have bowed their heads to the ground.

11 My eyes fail from weeping,
    I am in torment within,
my heart is poured out on the ground
    because my people are destroyed,
because children and infants faint
    in the streets of the city.

12 They say to their mothers,
    "Where is bread and wine?"
as they faint like wounded men
    in the streets of the city,
as their lives ebb away
    in their mothers' arms.

13 What can I say for you?
    With what can I compare you,
    O Daughter of Jerusalem?
To what can I liken you,
    that I may comfort you,
    O Virgin Daughter of Zion?
Your wound is as deep as the sea.
    Who can heal you?

14 The visions of your prophets
    were false and worthless;
they did not expose your sin
    to ward off your captivity.
The oracles they gave you
    were false and misleading.

15 All who pass your way
    clap their hands at you;
they scoff and shake their heads
    at the Daughter of Jerusalem:
"Is this the city that was called
    the perfection of beauty,
    the joy of the whole earth?"

16 All your enemies open their mouths
    wide against you;
they scoff and gnash their teeth
    and say, "We have swallowed her up.
This is the day we have waited for;
    we have lived to see it."

17 The LORD has done what he planned;
    he has fulfilled his word,
    which he decreed long ago.
He has overthrown you without pity,

THE MESSAGE

    her prophets useless—they neither saw nor
        heard anything from GOD.

2.10 The elders of Daughter Zion sit silent on the
        ground.
    They throw dust on their heads, dress in
        rough penitential burlap—
    the young virgins of Jerusalem, their faces
        creased with the dirt.

2.11 My eyes are blind with tears, my stomach in a
        knot.
    My insides have turned to jelly over my
        people's fate.
    Babies and children are fainting all over the
        place,

2.12 Calling to their mothers, "I'm hungry! I'm
        thirsty!"
    then fainting like dying soldiers in the
        streets,
    breathing their last in their mothers' laps.

2.13 How can I understand your plight, dear
        Jerusalem?
    What can I say to give you comfort, dear
        Zion?
    Who can put you together again? This
        bust-up is past understanding.

2.14 Your prophets courted you with sweet talk.
    They didn't face you with your sin so that
        you could repent.
    Their sermons were all wishful thinking,
        deceptive illusions.

2.15 Astonished, passersby can't believe what they
        see.
    They rub their eyes, they shake their heads
        over Jerusalem.
    Is this the city voted "Most Beautiful" and
        "Best Place to Live"?

2.16 But now your enemies gape, slack-jawed.
    Then they rub their hands in glee: "We've
        got them!
    We've been waiting for this! Here it is!"

2.17 GOD did carry out, item by item, exactly what
        he said he'd do.
    He always said he'd do this. Now he's done
        it—torn the place down.

NEW INTERNATIONAL VERSION	THE MESSAGE

NEW INTERNATIONAL VERSION

he has let the enemy gloat over you,
    he has exalted the horn[a] of your foes.

18 The hearts of the people
    cry out to the Lord.
O wall of the Daughter of Zion,
    let your tears flow like a river
    day and night;
give yourself no relief,
    your eyes no rest.

19 Arise, cry out in the night,
    as the watches of the night begin;
pour out your heart like water
    in the presence of the Lord.
Lift up your hands to him
    for the lives of your children,
who faint from hunger
    at the head of every street.

20 "Look, O LORD, and consider:
    Whom have you ever treated like this?
Should women eat their offspring,
    the children they have cared for?
Should priest and prophet be killed
    in the sanctuary of the Lord?

21 "Young and old lie together
    in the dust of the streets;
my young men and maidens
    have fallen by the sword.
You have slain them in the day of your anger;
    you have slaughtered them without pity.

22 "As you summon to a feast day,
    so you summoned against me terrors on
        every side.
In the day of the LORD's anger
    no one escaped or survived;
those I cared for and reared,
    my enemy has destroyed."

3 [b] I am the man who has seen affliction
    by the rod of his wrath.
2 He has driven me away and made me walk
    in darkness rather than light;
3 indeed, he has turned his hand against me
    again and again, all day long.

4 He has made my skin and my flesh grow old
    and has broken my bones.
5 He has besieged me and surrounded me
    with bitterness and hardship.
6 He has made me dwell in darkness
    like those long dead.

THE MESSAGE

He's let your enemies walk all over you,
    declared them world champions!

2.18 Give out heart-cries to the Master, dear
    repentant Zion.
Let the tears roll like a river, day and night,
    and keep at it—no time-outs. Keep those
    tears flowing!

2.19 As each night watch begins, get up and cry
    out in prayer.
Pour your heart out face to face with the
    Master.
Lift high your hands. Beg for the lives of
    your children
who are starving to death out on the
    streets.

2.20 "Look at us, GOD. Think it over. Have you
    ever treated *anyone* like this?
Should women eat their own babies, the
    very children they raised?
Should priests and prophets be murdered
    in the Master's own Sanctuary?

2.21 "Boys and old men lie in the gutters of the
    streets,
my young men and women killed in their
    prime.
Angry, you killed them in cold blood, cut
    them down without mercy.

2.22 "You invited, like friends to a party, men to
    swoop down in attack
so that on the big day of GOD's wrath no
    one would get away.
The children I loved and reared—gone,
    gone, gone."

GOD LOCKED ME UP IN DEEP DARKNESS

3.1-3 3 I'm the man who has seen trouble,
    trouble coming from the lash of GOD's
    anger.
He took me by the hand and walked me
    into pitch-black darkness.
Yes, he's given me the back of his hand
    over and over and over again.

3.4-6 He turned me into a scarecrow
    of skin and bones, then broke the bones.
He hemmed me in, ganged up on me,
    poured on the trouble and hard times.
He locked me up in deep darkness,
    like a corpse nailed inside a coffin.

---

a 17 Horn here symbolizes strength.   *b* This chapter is an acrostic poem; the verses of each stanza begin with the successive letters of the Hebrew alphabet, and the verses within each stanza begin with the same letter.

NEW INTERNATIONAL VERSION

7 He has walled me in so I cannot escape;
  he has weighed me down with chains.
8 Even when I call out or cry for help,
  he shuts out my prayer.
9 He has barred my way with blocks of stone;
  he has made my paths crooked.

10 Like a bear lying in wait,
  like a lion in hiding,
11 he dragged me from the path and
      mangled me
  and left me without help.
12 He drew his bow
  and made me the target for his arrows.

13 He pierced my heart
  with arrows from his quiver.
14 I became the laughingstock of all my people;
  they mock me in song all day long.
15 He has filled me with bitter herbs
  and sated me with gall.

16 He has broken my teeth with gravel;
  he has trampled me in the dust.
17 I have been deprived of peace;
  I have forgotten what prosperity is.
18 So I say, "My splendor is gone
  and all that I had hoped from the LORD."

19 I remember my affliction and my wandering,
  the bitterness and the gall.
20 I well remember them,
  and my soul is downcast within me.
21 Yet this I call to mind
  and therefore I have hope:

22 Because of the LORD's great love we are not
      consumed,
  for his compassions never fail.
23 They are new every morning;
  great is your faithfulness.
24 I say to myself, "The LORD is my portion;
  therefore I will wait for him."

25 The LORD is good to those whose hope is in
      him,
  to the one who seeks him;
26 it is good to wait quietly
  for the salvation of the LORD.
27 It is good for a man to bear the yoke
  while he is young.

28 Let him sit alone in silence,
  for the LORD has laid it on him.

THE MESSAGE

3.7-9 He shuts me in so I'll never get out,
  manacles my hands, shackles my feet.
  Even when I cry out and plead for help,
    he locks up my prayers and throws away
      the key.
  He sets up blockades with quarried limestone.
    He's got me cornered.

3.10-12 He's a prowling bear tracking me down,
  a lion in hiding ready to pounce.
  He knocked me from the path and ripped me
      to pieces.
    When he finished, there was nothing left
      of me.
  He took out his bow and arrows
    and used me for target practice.

3.13-15 He shot me in the stomach
  with arrows from his quiver.
  Everyone took me for a joke,
    made me the butt of their mocking ballads.
  He forced rotten, stinking food down my
      throat,
    bloated me with vile drinks.

3.16-18 He ground my face into the gravel.
  He pounded me into the mud.
  I gave up on life altogether.
    I've forgotten what the good life is like.
  I said to myself, "This is it. I'm finished.
    GOD is a lost cause."

IT'S A GOOD THING TO HOPE FOR HELP
FROM GOD

3.19-21 I'll never forget the trouble, the utter lostness,
  the taste of ashes, the poison I've
      swallowed.
  I remember it all—oh, how well I
      remember—
    the feeling of hitting the bottom.
  But there's one other thing I remember,
    and remembering, I keep a grip on hope:

3.22-24 GOD's loyal love couldn't have run out,
  his merciful love couldn't have dried up.
  They're created new every morning.
    How great your faithfulness!
  I'm sticking with GOD (I say it over and over).
    He's all I've got left.

3.25-27 GOD proves to be good to the man who
      passionately waits,
  to the woman who diligently seeks.
  It's a good thing to quietly hope,
    quietly hope for help from GOD.
  It's a good thing when you're young
    to stick it out through the hard times.

3.28-30 When life is heavy and hard to take,
  go off by yourself. Enter the silence.

NEW INTERNATIONAL VERSION

²⁹ Let him bury his face in the dust—
     there may yet be hope.
³⁰ Let him offer his cheek to one who would
          strike him,
     and let him be filled with disgrace.

³¹ For men are not cast off
     by the Lord forever.
³² Though he brings grief, he will show
          compassion,
     so great is his unfailing love.
³³ For he does not willingly bring affliction
     or grief to the children of men.

³⁴ To crush underfoot
     all prisoners in the land,
³⁵ to deny a man his rights
     before the Most High,
³⁶ to deprive a man of justice—
     would not the Lord see such things?

³⁷ Who can speak and have it happen
     if the Lord has not decreed it?
³⁸ Is it not from the mouth of the Most High
     that both calamities and good things
          come?
³⁹ Why should any living man complain
     when punished for his sins?

⁴⁰ Let us examine our ways and test them,
     and let us return to the LORD.
⁴¹ Let us lift up our hearts and our hands
     to God in heaven, and say:
⁴² "We have sinned and rebelled
     and you have not forgiven.

⁴³ "You have covered yourself with anger and
          pursued us;
     you have slain without pity.
⁴⁴ You have covered yourself with a cloud
     so that no prayer can get through.
⁴⁵ You have made us scum and refuse
     among the nations.

⁴⁶ "All our enemies have opened their mouths
     wide against us.
⁴⁷ We have suffered terror and pitfalls,
     ruin and destruction."
⁴⁸ Streams of tears flow from my eyes
     because my people are destroyed.

⁴⁹ My eyes will flow unceasingly,
     without relief,
⁵⁰ until the LORD looks down
     from heaven and sees.

THE MESSAGE

Bow in prayer. Don't ask questions:
     Wait for hope to appear.
Don't run from trouble. Take it full-face.
     The "worst" is never the worst.

3.31-33 Why? Because the Master won't ever
     walk out and fail to return.
If he works severely, he also works tenderly.
     His stockpiles of loyal love are immense.
He takes no pleasure in making life hard,
     in throwing roadblocks in the way:

3.34-36 Stomping down hard
     on luckless prisoners,
Refusing justice to victims
     in the court of High God,
Tampering with evidence—
     the Master does not approve of such things.

GOD SPEAKS BOTH GOOD THINGS AND HARD
THINGS INTO BEING

3.37-39 Who do you think "spoke and it happened"?
     It's the Master who gives such orders.
Doesn't the High God speak everything,
     good things and hard things alike, into
          being?
And why would anyone gifted with life
     complain when punished for sin?

3.40-42 Let's take a good look at the way we're living
     and reorder our lives under GOD.
Let's lift our hearts and hands at one and the
          same time,
     praying to God in heaven:
"We've been contrary and willful,
     and you haven't forgiven.

3.43-45 "You lost your temper with us, holding
          nothing back.
     You chased us and cut us down without
          mercy.
You wrapped yourself in thick blankets of
          clouds
     so no prayers could get through.
You treated us like dirty dishwater,
     threw us out in the backyard of the nations.

3.46-48 "Our enemies shout abuse,
     their mouths full of derision, spitting
          invective.
We've been to hell and back.
     We've nowhere to turn, nowhere to go.
Rivers of tears pour from my eyes
     at the smashup of my dear people.

3.49-51 "The tears stream from my eyes,
     an artesian well of tears,
Until you, GOD, look down from on high,
     look and see my tears.

NEW INTERNATIONAL VERSION

⁵¹ What I see brings grief to my soul
  because of all the women of my city.

⁵² Those who were my enemies without cause
  hunted me like a bird.
⁵³ They tried to end my life in a pit
  and threw stones at me;
⁵⁴ the waters closed over my head,
  and I thought I was about to be cut off.

⁵⁵ I called on your name, O LORD,
  from the depths of the pit.
⁵⁶ You heard my plea: "Do not close your ears
  to my cry for relief."
⁵⁷ You came near when I called you,
  and you said, "Do not fear."

⁵⁸ O Lord, you took up my case;
  you redeemed my life.
⁵⁹ You have seen, O LORD, the wrong done
    to me.
  Uphold my cause!
⁶⁰ You have seen the depth of their vengeance,
  all their plots against me.

⁶¹ O LORD, you have heard their insults,
  all their plots against me—
⁶² what my enemies whisper and mutter
  against me all day long.
⁶³ Look at them! Sitting or standing,
  they mock me in their songs.

⁶⁴ Pay them back what they deserve, O LORD,
  for what their hands have done.
⁶⁵ Put a veil over their hearts,
  and may your curse be on them!
⁶⁶ Pursue them in anger and destroy them
  from under the heavens of the LORD.

4 ᵃ How the gold has lost its luster,
  the fine gold become dull!
The sacred gems are scattered
  at the head of every street.

² How the precious sons of Zion,
  once worth their weight in gold,
are now considered as pots of clay,
  the work of a potter's hands!

³ Even jackals offer their breasts
  to nurse their young,

ᵃ This chapter is an acrostic poem, the verses of which
begin with the successive letters of the Hebrew alphabet.

THE MESSAGE

When I see what's happened to the young
    women in the city,
  the pain breaks my heart.

3.52-54 "Enemies with no reason to be enemies
    hunted me down like a bird.
They threw me into a pit,
    then pelted me with stones.
Then the rains came and filled the pit.
    The water rose over my head. I said, 'It's all
      over.'

3.55-57 "I called out your name, O GOD,
    called from the bottom of the pit.
You listened when I called out, 'Don't shut
      your ears!
    Get me out of here! Save me!'
You came close when I called out.
    You said, 'It's going to be all right.'

3.58-60 "You took my side, Master;
    you brought me back alive!
GOD, you saw the wrongs heaped on me.
    Give me my day in court!
Yes, you saw their mean-minded schemes,
    their plots to destroy me.

3.61-63 "You heard, GOD, their vicious gossip,
    their behind-my-back plots to ruin me.
They never quit, these enemies of mine,
      dreaming up mischief,
    hatching out malice, day after day after day.
Sitting down or standing up—just look at
      them!—
    they mock me with vulgar doggerel.

3.64-66 "Make them pay for what they've done, GOD.
    Give them their just deserts.
Break their miserable hearts!
    Damn their eyes!
Get good and angry. Hunt them down.
    Make a total demolition here under your
      heaven!"

WAKING UP WITH NOTHING

4.1 **4** Oh, oh, oh . . .
    How gold is treated like dirt,
  the finest gold thrown out with the
      garbage,
Priceless jewels scattered all over,
    jewels loose in the gutters.

4.2 And the people of Zion, once prized,
    far surpassing their weight in gold,
Are now treated like cheap pottery,
    like everyday pots and bowls mass-
      produced by a potter.

4.3 Even wild jackals nurture their babies,
    give them their breasts to suckle.

NEW INTERNATIONAL VERSION

but my people have become heartless
  like ostriches in the desert.

⁴Because of thirst the infant's tongue
  sticks to the roof of its mouth;
the children beg for bread,
  but no one gives it to them.

⁵Those who once ate delicacies
  are destitute in the streets.
Those nurtured in purple
  now lie on ash heaps.

⁶The punishment of my people
  is greater than that of Sodom,
which was overthrown in a moment
  without a hand turned to help her.

⁷Their princes were brighter than snow
  and whiter than milk,
their bodies more ruddy than rubies,
  their appearance like sapphires. ᵃ

⁸But now they are blacker than soot;
  they are not recognized in the streets.
Their skin has shriveled on their bones;
  it has become as dry as a stick.

⁹Those killed by the sword are better off
  than those who die of famine;
racked with hunger, they waste away
  for lack of food from the field.

¹⁰With their own hands compassionate
    women
  have cooked their own children,
who became their food
  when my people were destroyed.

¹¹The Lᴏʀᴅ has given full vent to his wrath;
  he has poured out his fierce anger.
He kindled a fire in Zion
  that consumed her foundations.

¹²The kings of the earth did not believe,
  nor did any of the world's people,
that enemies and foes could enter
  the gates of Jerusalem.

¹³But it happened because of the sins of her
    prophets
  and the iniquities of her priests,
who shed within her
  the blood of the righteous.

¹⁴Now they grope through the streets
  like men who are blind.
They are so defiled with blood
  that no one dares to touch their garments.

THE MESSAGE

But my people have turned cruel to their
    babies,
  like an ostrich in the wilderness.

4.4 Babies have nothing to drink.
  Their tongues stick to the roofs of their
    mouths.
Little children ask for bread
  but no one gives them so much as a crust.

4.5 People used to the finest cuisine
  forage for food in the streets.
People used to the latest in fashions
  pick through the trash for something to
    wear.

4.6 The evil guilt of my dear people
  was worse than the sin of Sodom—
The city was destroyed in a flash,
  and no one around to help.

4.7 The splendid and sacred nobles
  once glowed with health.
Their bodies were robust and ruddy,
  their beards like carved stone.

4.8 But now they are smeared with soot,
  unrecognizable in the street,
Their bones sticking out,
  their skin dried out like old leather.

4.9 Better to have been killed in battle
  than killed by starvation.
Better to have died of battle wounds
  than to slowly starve to death.

4.10 Nice and kindly women
  boiled their own children for supper.
This was the only food in town
  when my dear people were broken.

4.11 Gᴏᴅ let all his anger loose, held nothing back.
  He poured out his raging wrath.
He set a fire in Zion
  that burned it to the ground.

4.12 The kings of the earth couldn't believe it.
  World rulers were in shock,
Watching old enemies march in big as you
    please,
  right through Jerusalem's gates.

4.13 Because of the sins of her prophets
  and the evil of her priests,
Who exploited good and trusting people,
  robbing them of their lives,

4.14 These prophets and priests blindly grope their
    way through the streets,
  grimy and stained from their dirty lives,
Wasted by their wasted lives,
  shuffling from fatigue, dressed in rags.

ᵃ 7 Or lapis lazuli

NEW INTERNATIONAL VERSION	THE MESSAGE

NEW INTERNATIONAL VERSION

15 "Go away! You are unclean!" men cry to
them.
"Away! Away! Don't touch us!"
When they flee and wander about,
people among the nations say,
"They can stay here no longer."

16 The LORD himself has scattered them;
he no longer watches over them.
The priests are shown no honor,
the elders no favor.

17 Moreover, our eyes failed,
looking in vain for help;
from our towers we watched
for a nation that could not save us.

18 Men stalked us at every step,
so we could not walk in our streets.
Our end was near, our days were numbered,
for our end had come.

19 Our pursuers were swifter
than eagles in the sky;
they chased us over the mountains
and lay in wait for us in the desert.

20 The LORD's anointed, our very life breath,
was caught in their traps.
We thought that under his shadow
we would live among the nations.

21 Rejoice and be glad, O Daughter of Edom,
you who live in the land of Uz.
But to you also the cup will be passed;
you will be drunk and stripped naked.

22 O Daughter of Zion, your punishment will
end;
he will not prolong your exile.
But, O Daughter of Edom, he will punish
your sin
and expose your wickedness.

5 Remember, O LORD, what has happened
to us;
look, and see our disgrace.
2 Our inheritance has been turned over to
aliens,
our homes to foreigners.
3 We have become orphans and fatherless,
our mothers like widows.

THE MESSAGE

4.15 People yell at them, "Get out of here, dirty old
men!
Get lost, don't touch us, don't infect us!"
They have to leave town. They wander off.
Nobody wants them to stay here.
Everyone knows, wherever they wander,
that they've been kicked out of their own
hometown.

4.16 GOD himself scattered them.
No longer does he look out for them.
He has nothing to do with the priests;
he cares nothing for the elders.

4.17 We watched and watched,
wore our eyes out looking for help. And
nothing.
We mounted our lookouts and looked
for the help that never showed up.

4.18 They tracked us down, those hunters.
It wasn't safe to go out in the street.
Our end was near, our days numbered.
We were doomed.

4.19 They came after us faster than eagles in flight,
pressed us hard in the mountains,
ambushed us in the desert.

4.20 Our king, our life's breath, the anointed of
GOD,
was caught in their traps—
Our king under whose protection
we always said we'd live.

4.21 Celebrate while you can, O Edom!
Live it up in Uz!
For it won't be long before you drink this cup,
too.
You'll find out what it's like to drink God's
wrath,
Get drunk on God's wrath
and wake up with nothing, stripped naked.

4.22 And that's it for you, Zion. The punishment's
complete.
You won't have to go through this exile
again.
But Edom, your time is coming:
He'll punish your evil life, put all your sins
on display.

GIVE US A FRESH START

5.1-22 **5** "Remember, GOD, all we've been through.
Study our plight, the black mark we've
made in history.
Our precious land has been given to outsiders,
our homes to strangers.
Orphans we are, not a father in sight,
and our mothers no better than widows.

NEW INTERNATIONAL VERSION

⁴We must buy the water we drink;
   our wood can be had only at a price.
⁵Those who pursue us are at our heels;
   we are weary and find no rest.
⁶We submitted to Egypt and Assyria
   to get enough bread.
⁷Our fathers sinned and are no more,
   and we bear their punishment.
⁸Slaves rule over us,
   and there is none to free us from their
      hands.
⁹We get our bread at the risk of our lives
   because of the sword in the desert.
¹⁰Our skin is hot as an oven,
   feverish from hunger.
¹¹Women have been ravished in Zion,
   and virgins in the towns of Judah.
¹²Princes have been hung up by their hands;
   elders are shown no respect.
¹³Young men toil at the millstones;
   boys stagger under loads of wood.
¹⁴The elders are gone from the city gate;
   the young men have stopped their music.
¹⁵Joy is gone from our hearts;
   our dancing has turned to mourning.
¹⁶The crown has fallen from our head.
   Woe to us, for we have sinned!
¹⁷Because of this our hearts are faint,
   because of these things our eyes grow dim
¹⁸for Mount Zion, which lies desolate,
   with jackals prowling over it.

¹⁹You, O Lord, reign forever;
   your throne endures from generation to
      generation.
²⁰Why do you always forget us?
   Why do you forsake us so long?
²¹Restore us to yourself, O Lord, that we may
      return;
   renew our days as of old
²²unless you have utterly rejected us
   and are angry with us beyond measure.

THE MESSAGE

We have to pay to drink our own water.
   Even our firewood comes at a price.
We're nothing but slaves, bullied and bowed,
   worn out and without any rest.
We sold ourselves to Assyria and Egypt
   just to get something to eat.
Our parents sinned and are no more,
   and now we're paying for the wrongs they
      did.
Slaves rule over us;
   there's no escape from their grip.
We risk our lives to gather food
   in the bandit-infested desert.
Our skin has turned black as an oven,
   dried out like old leather from the famine.
Our wives were raped in the streets in Zion,
   and our virgins in the cities of Judah.
They hanged our princes by their hands,
   dishonored our elders.
Strapping young men were put to women's
      work,
   mere boys forced to do men's work.
The city gate is empty of wise elders.
   Music from the young is heard no more.
All the joy is gone from our hearts.
   Our dances have turned into dirges.
The crown of glory has toppled from our
      head.
   Woe! Woe! Would that we'd never sinned!
Because of all this we're heartsick;
   we can't see through the tears.
On Mount Zion, wrecked and ruined,
   jackals pace and prowl.
And yet, God, you're sovereign still,
   your throne intact and eternal.
So why do you keep forgetting us?
   Why dump us and leave us like this?
Bring us back to you, God—we're ready to
      come back.
   Give us a fresh start.
As it is, you've cruelly disowned us.
   You've been so very angry with us."

EZEKIEL

EZEKIEL

THE LIVING CREATURES AND THE GLORY OF THE LORD

1 In the[a] thirtieth year, in the fourth month on the fifth day, while I was among the exiles by the Kebar River, the heavens were opened and I saw visions of God.

²On the fifth of the month—it was the fifth year of the exile of King Jehoiachin— ³the word of the LORD came to Ezekiel the priest, the son of Buzi,[b] by the Kebar River in the land of the Babylonians.[c] There the hand of the LORD was upon him.

⁴I looked, and I saw a windstorm coming out of the north—an immense cloud with flashing lightning and surrounded by brilliant light. The center of the fire looked like glowing metal, ⁵and in the fire was what looked like four living creatures. In appearance their form was that of a man, ⁶but each of them had four faces and four wings. ⁷Their legs were straight; their feet were like those of a calf and gleamed like burnished bronze. ⁸Under their wings on their four sides they had the hands of a man. All four of them had faces and wings, ⁹and their wings touched one another. Each one went straight ahead; they did not turn as they moved.

¹⁰Their faces looked like this: Each of the four had the face of a man, and on the right side each had the face of a lion, and on the left the face of an ox; each also had the face of an eagle. ¹¹Such were their faces. Their wings were spread out upward; each had two wings, one touching the wing of another creature on either side, and two wings covering its body. ¹²Each one went straight ahead. Wherever the spirit would go, they would go, without turning as they went. ¹³The appearance of the living creatures was like burning coals of fire or like torches. Fire moved back and forth among the creatures; it was bright, and lightning flashed out of it. ¹⁴The creatures sped back and forth like flashes of lightning.

¹⁵As I looked at the living creatures, I saw a wheel on the ground beside each creature with

WHEELS WITHIN WHEELS, LIKE A GYROSCOPE

1.1 1 When I was thirty years of age, I was living with the exiles on the Kebar River. On the fifth day of the fourth month, the sky opened up and I saw visions of God.

1.2-3 (It was the fifth day of the month in the fifth year of the exile of King Jehoiachin that GOD's Word came to Ezekiel the priest, the son of Buzi, on the banks of the Kebar River in the country of Babylon. GOD's hand came upon him that day.)

1.4-9 I looked: I saw an immense dust storm come from the north, an immense cloud with lightning flashing from it, a huge ball of fire glowing like bronze. Within the fire were what looked like four creatures vibrant with life. Each had the form of a human being, but each also had four faces and four wings. Their legs were as sturdy and straight as columns, but their feet were hoofed like those of a calf and sparkled from the fire like burnished bronze. On all four sides under their wings they had human hands. All four had both faces and wings, with the wings touching one another. They turned neither one way nor the other; they went straight forward.

1.10-12 Their faces looked like this: In front a human face, on the right side the face of a lion, on the left the face of an ox, and in back the face of an eagle. So much for the faces. The wings were spread out with the tips of one pair touching the creature on either side; the other pair of wings covered its body. Each creature went straight ahead. Wherever the spirit went, they went. They didn't turn as they went.

1.13-14 The four creatures looked like a blazing fire, or like fiery torches. Tongues of fire shot back and forth between the creatures, and out of the fire, bolts of lightning. The creatures flashed back and forth like strikes of lightning.

1.15-16 As I watched the four creatures, I saw something that looked like a wheel on the ground beside each of the four-faced creatures. This is

---

[a] 1 Or _my_   [b] 3 Or _Ezekiel son of Buzi the priest_
[c] 3 Or _Chaldeans_

NEW INTERNATIONAL VERSION

its four faces. ¹⁶This was the appearance and structure of the wheels: They sparkled like chrysolite, and all four looked alike. Each appeared to be made like a wheel intersecting a wheel. ¹⁷As they moved, they would go in any one of the four directions the creatures faced; the wheels did not turn about*ᵃ* as the creatures went. ¹⁸Their rims were high and awesome, and all four rims were full of eyes all around.

¹⁹When the living creatures moved, the wheels beside them moved; and when the living creatures rose from the ground, the wheels also rose. ²⁰Wherever the spirit would go, they would go, and the wheels would rise along with them, because the spirit of the living creatures was in the wheels. ²¹When the creatures moved, they also moved; when the creatures stood still, they also stood still; and when the creatures rose from the ground, the wheels rose along with them, because the spirit of the living creatures was in the wheels.

²²Spread out above the heads of the living creatures was what looked like an expanse, sparkling like ice, and awesome. ²³Under the expanse their wings were stretched out one toward the other, and each had two wings covering its body. ²⁴When the creatures moved, I heard the sound of their wings, like the roar of rushing waters, like the voice of the Almighty,*ᵇ* like the tumult of an army. When they stood still, they lowered their wings.

²⁵Then there came a voice from above the expanse over their heads as they stood with lowered wings. ²⁶Above the expanse over their heads was what looked like a throne of sapphire,*ᶜ* and high above on the throne was a figure like that of a man. ²⁷I saw that from what appeared to be his waist up he looked like glowing metal, as if full of fire, and that from there down he looked like fire; and brilliant light surrounded him. ²⁸Like the appearance of a rainbow in the clouds on a rainy day, so was the radiance around him.

This was the appearance of the likeness of the glory of the LORD. When I saw it, I fell facedown, and I heard the voice of one speaking.

EZEKIEL'S CALL

2 He said to me, "Son of man, stand up on your feet and I will speak to you." ²As he spoke, the Spirit came into me and raised me to my feet, and I heard him speaking to me.

³He said: "Son of man, I am sending you to the Israelites, to a rebellious nation that has rebelled against me; they and their fathers have been in revolt against me to this very day. ⁴The

THE MESSAGE

what the wheels looked like: They were identical wheels, sparkling like diamonds in the sun. It looked like they were wheels within wheels, like a gyroscope.

1.17-21 They went in any one of the four directions they faced, but straight, not veering off. The rims were immense, circled with eyes. When the living creatures went, the wheels went; when the living creatures lifted off, the wheels lifted off. Wherever the spirit went, they went, the wheels sticking right with them, for the spirit of the living creatures was in the wheels. When the creatures went, the wheels went; when the creatures stopped, the wheels stopped; when the creatures lifted off, the wheels lifted off, because the spirit of the living creatures was in the wheels.

1.22-24 Over the heads of the living creatures was something like a dome, shimmering like a sky full of cut glass, vaulted over their heads. Under the dome one set of wings was extended toward the others, with another set of wings covering their bodies. When they moved I heard their wings—it was like the roar of a great waterfall, like the voice of The Strong God, like the noise of a battlefield. When they stopped, they folded their wings.

1.25-28 And then, as they stood with folded wings, there was a voice from above the dome over their heads. Above the dome there was something that looked like a throne, sky-blue like a sapphire, with a humanlike figure towering above the throne. From what I could see, from the waist up he looked like burnished bronze and from the waist down like a blazing fire. Brightness everywhere! The way a rainbow springs out of the sky on a rainy day—that's what it was like. It turned out to be the Glory of GOD!

When I saw all this, I fell to my knees, my face to the ground. Then I heard a voice.

✝

2.1 **2** It said, "Son of man, stand up. I have something to say to you."

2.2 The moment I heard the voice, the Spirit entered me and put me on my feet. As he spoke to me, I listened.

2.3-7 He said, "Son of man, I'm sending you to the family of Israel, a rebellious nation if there ever was one. They and their ancestors have fomented rebellion right up to the present.

ᵃ 17 Or aside   *ᵇ 24 Hebrew Shaddai*   *ᶜ 26 Or lapis lazuli*

NEW INTERNATIONAL VERSION

people to whom I am sending you are obstinate and stubborn. Say to them, 'This is what the Sovereign LORD says.' 5And whether they listen or fail to listen—for they are a rebellious house—they will know that a prophet has been among them. 6And you, son of man, do not be afraid of them or their words. Do not be afraid, though briers and thorns are all around you and you live among scorpions. Do not be afraid of what they say or terrified by them, though they are a rebellious house. 7You must speak my words to them, whether they listen or fail to listen, for they are rebellious. 8But you, son of man, listen to what I say to you. Do not rebel like that rebellious house; open your mouth and eat what I give you."

9Then I looked, and I saw a hand stretched out to me. In it was a scroll, 10which he unrolled before me. On both sides of it were written words of lament and mourning and woe.

3 And he said to me, "Son of man, eat what is before you, eat this scroll; then go and speak to the house of Israel." 2So I opened my mouth, and he gave me the scroll to eat.

3Then he said to me, "Son of man, eat this scroll I am giving you and fill your stomach with it." So I ate it, and it tasted as sweet as honey in my mouth.

4He then said to me: "Son of man, go now to the house of Israel and speak my words to them. 5You are not being sent to a people of obscure speech and difficult language, but to the house of Israel— 6not to many peoples of obscure speech and difficult language, whose words you cannot understand. Surely if I had sent you to them, they would have listened to you. 7But the house of Israel is not willing to listen to you because they are not willing to listen to me, for the whole house of Israel is hardened and obstinate. 8But I will make you as unyielding and hardened as they are. 9I will make your forehead like the hardest stone, harder than flint. Do not be afraid of them or terrified by them, though they are a rebellious house."

10And he said to me, "Son of man, listen carefully and take to heart all the words I speak to you. 11Go now to your countrymen in exile and speak to them. Say to them, 'This is what the Sovereign LORD says,' whether they listen or fail to listen."

12Then the Spirit lifted me up, and I heard behind me a loud rumbling sound—May the glory of the LORD be praised in his dwelling place!—13the sound of the wings of the living creatures

THE MESSAGE

They're a hard case, these people to whom I'm sending you—hardened in their sin. Tell them, 'This is the Message of GOD, the Master.' They are a defiant bunch. Whether or not they listen, at least they'll know that a prophet's been here. But don't be afraid of them, son of man, and don't be afraid of anything they say. Don't be afraid when living among them is like stepping on thorns or finding scorpions in your bed. Don't be afraid of their mean words or their hard looks. They're a bunch of rebels. Your job is to speak to them. Whether they listen is not your concern. They're hardened rebels.

2.8 "Only take care, son of man, that you don't rebel like these rebels. Open your mouth and eat what I give you."

2.9-10 When I looked he had his hand stretched out to me, and in the hand a book, a scroll. He unrolled the scroll. On both sides, front and back, were written lamentations and mourning and doom.

WARN THESE PEOPLE

3.1 3 He told me, "Son of man, eat what you see. Eat this book. Then go and speak to the family of Israel."

3.2-3 As I opened my mouth, he gave me the scroll to eat, saying, "Son of man, eat this book that I am giving you. Make a full meal of it!"

So I ate it. It tasted so good—just like honey.

3.4-6 Then he told me, "Son of man, go to the family of Israel and speak my Message. Look, I'm not sending you to a people who speak a hard-to-learn language with words you can hardly pronounce. If I had sent you to such people, their ears would have perked up and they would have listened immediately.

3.7-9 "But it won't work that way with the family of Israel. They won't listen to you because they won't listen to me. They are, as I said, a hard case, hardened in their sin. But I'll make you as hard in your way as they are in theirs. I'll make your face as hard as rock, harder than granite. Don't let them intimidate you. Don't be afraid of them, even though they're a bunch of rebels."

3.10-11 Then he said, "Son of man, get all these words that I'm giving you inside you. Listen to them obediently. Make them your own. And now go. Go to the exiles, your people, and speak. Tell them, 'This is the Message of GOD, the Master.' Speak your piece, whether they listen or not."

3.12-13 Then the Spirit picked me up. Behind me I heard a great commotion—"Blessed be the Glory of GOD in his Sanctuary!"—the wings of the living creatures beating against each other, the

NEW INTERNATIONAL VERSION

brushing against each other and the sound of the wheels beside them, a loud rumbling sound. ¹⁴The Spirit then lifted me up and took me away, and I went in bitterness and in the anger of my spirit, with the strong hand of the LORD upon me. ¹⁵I came to the exiles who lived at Tel Abib near the Kebar River. And there, where they were living, I sat among them for seven days—overwhelmed.

WARNING TO ISRAEL

¹⁶At the end of seven days the word of the LORD came to me: ¹⁷"Son of man, I have made you a watchman for the house of Israel; so hear the word I speak and give them warning from me. ¹⁸When I say to a wicked man, 'You will surely die,' and you do not warn him or speak out to dissuade him from his evil ways in order to save his life, that wicked man will die forᵃ his sin, and I will hold you accountable for his blood. ¹⁹But if you do warn the wicked man and he does not turn from his wickedness or from his evil ways, he will die for his sin; but you will have saved yourself.

²⁰"Again, when a righteous man turns from his righteousness and does evil, and I put a stumbling block before him, he will die. Since you did not warn him, he will die for his sin. The righteous things he did will not be remembered, and I will hold you accountable for his blood. ²¹But if you do warn the righteous man not to sin and he does not sin, he will surely live because he took warning, and you will have saved yourself."

²²The hand of the LORD was upon me there, and he said to me, "Get up and go out to the plain, and there I will speak to you." ²³So I got up and went out to the plain. And the glory of the LORD was standing there, like the glory I had seen by the Kebar River, and I fell facedown.

²⁴Then the Spirit came into me and raised me to my feet. He spoke to me and said: "Go, shut yourself inside your house. ²⁵And you, son of man, they will tie with ropes; you will be bound so that you cannot go out among the people. ²⁶I will make your tongue stick to the roof of your mouth so that you will be silent and unable to rebuke them, though they are a rebellious house. ²⁷But when I speak to you, I will open your mouth and you shall say to them, 'This is what the Sovereign LORD says.' Whoever will listen let him listen, and whoever will refuse let him refuse; for they are a rebellious house.

ᵃ 18 Or in; also in verses 19 and 20

THE MESSAGE

whirling wheels, the rumble of a great earthquake.

3.14-15 The Spirit lifted me and took me away. I went bitterly and angrily. I didn't want to go. But GOD had me in his grip. I arrived among the exiles who lived near the Kebar River at Tel Aviv. I came to where they were living and sat there for seven days, appalled.

3.16 At the end of the seven days, I received this Message from GOD:

3.17-19 "Son of man, I've made you a watchman for the family of Israel. Whenever you hear me say something, warn them for me. If I say to the wicked, 'You are going to die,' and you don't sound the alarm warning them that it's a matter of life or death, they will die and it will be your fault. I'll hold you responsible. But if you warn the wicked and they keep right on sinning anyway, they'll most certainly die for their sin, but *you* won't die. You'll have saved your life.

3.20-21 "And if the righteous turn back from living righteously and take up with evil when I step in and put them in a hard place, they'll die. If you haven't warned them, they'll die because of their sins, and none of the right things they've done will count for anything—and I'll hold you responsible. But if you warn these righteous people not to sin and they listen to you, they'll live because they took the warning—and again, you'll have saved your life."

3.22 GOD grabbed me by the shoulder and said, "Get up. Go out on the plain. I want to talk with you."

3.23 So I got up and went out on the plain. I couldn't believe my eyes: the Glory of GOD! Right there! It was like the Glory I had seen at the Kebar River. I fell to the ground, prostrate.

3.24-26 Then the Spirit entered me and put me on my feet. He said, "Go home and shut the door behind you." And then something odd: "Son of man: They'll tie you hand and foot with ropes so you can't leave the house. I'll make your tongue stick to the roof of your mouth so you won't be able to talk and tell the people what they're doing wrong, even though they are a bunch of rebels.

3.27 "But then when the time is ripe, I'll free your tongue and you'll say, 'This is what GOD, the Master, says: . . .' From then on it's up to them. They can listen or not listen, whichever they like. They *are* a bunch of rebels!

NEW INTERNATIONAL VERSION

SIEGE OF JERUSALEM SYMBOLIZED

4 "Now, son of man, take a clay tablet, put it in front of you and draw the city of Jerusalem on it. ²Then lay siege to it: Erect siege works against it, build a ramp up to it, set up camps against it and put battering rams around it. ³Then take an iron pan, place it as an iron wall between you and the city and turn your face toward it. It will be under siege, and you shall besiege it. This will be a sign to the house of Israel.

⁴"Then lie on your left side and put the sin of the house of Israel upon yourself.ª You are to bear their sin for the number of days you lie on your side. ⁵I have assigned you the same number of days as the years of their sin. So for 390 days you will bear the sin of the house of Israel.

⁶"After you have finished this, lie down again, this time on your right side, and bear the sin of the house of Judah. I have assigned you 40 days, a day for each year. ⁷Turn your face toward the siege of Jerusalem and with bared arm prophesy against her. ⁸I will tie you up with ropes so that you cannot turn from one side to the other until you have finished the days of your siege.

⁹"Take wheat and barley, beans and lentils, millet and spelt; put them in a storage jar and use them to make bread for yourself. You are to eat it during the 390 days you lie on your side. ¹⁰Weigh out twenty shekelsᵇ of food to eat each day and eat it at set times. ¹¹Also measure out a sixth of a hinᶜ of water and drink it at set times. ¹²Eat the food as you would a barley cake; bake it in the sight of the people, using human excrement for fuel." ¹³The LORD said, "In this way the people of Israel will eat defiled food among the nations where I will drive them."

¹⁴Then I said, "Not so, Sovereign LORD! I have never defiled myself. From my youth until now I have never eaten anything found dead or torn by wild animals. No unclean meat has ever entered my mouth."

¹⁵"Very well," he said, "I will let you bake your bread over cow manure instead of human excrement."

¹⁶He then said to me: "Son of man, I will cut off the supply of food in Jerusalem. The people will eat rationed food in anxiety and drink rationed water in despair, ¹⁷for food and water will be scarce. They will be appalled at the sight of each other and will waste away because ofᵈ their sin.

ª *4 Or your side*   ᵇ *10 That is, about 8 ounces (about 0.2 kilogram)*   ᶜ *11 That is, about 2/3 quart (about 0.6 liter)*   ᵈ *17 Or away in*

THE MESSAGE

THIS IS WHAT SIN DOES

4.1-3 **4** "Now, son of man, take a brick and place it before you. Draw a picture of the city Jerusalem on it. Then make a model of a military siege against the brick: Build siege walls, construct a ramp, set up army camps, lay in battering rams around it. Then get an iron skillet and place it upright between you and the city—an iron wall. Face the model: The city shall be under siege and you shall be the besieger. This is a sign to the family of Israel.

4.4-5 "Next lie on your left side and place the sin of the family of Israel on yourself. You will bear their sin for as many days as you lie on your side. The number of days you bear their sin will match the number of years of their sin, namely, 390. For 390 days you will bear the sin of the family of Israel.

4.6-7 "Then, after you have done this, turn over and lie down on your right side and bear the sin of the family of Judah. Your assignment this time is to lie there for forty days, a day for each year of their sin. Look straight at the siege of Jerusalem. Roll up your sleeve, shake your bare arm, and preach against her.

4.8 "I will tie you up with ropes, tie you so you can't move or turn over until you have finished the days of the siege.

4.9-12 "Next I want you to take wheat and barley, beans and lentils, dried millet and spelt, and mix them in a bowl to make a flat bread. This is your food ration for the 390 days you lie on your side. Measure out about half a pound for each day and eat it on schedule. Also measure out your daily ration of about a pint of water and drink it on schedule. Eat the bread as you would a muffin. Bake the muffins out in the open where everyone can see you, using dried human dung for fuel."

4.13 GOD said, "This is what the people of Israel are going to do: Among the pagan nations where I will drive them, they will eat foods that are strictly taboo to a holy people."

4.14 I said, "GOD, my Master! Never! I've never contaminated myself with food like that. Since my youth I've never eaten anything forbidden by law, nothing found dead or violated by wild animals. I've never taken a single bite of forbidden food."

4.15 "All right," he said. "I'll let you bake your bread over cow dung instead of human dung."

4.16-17 Then he said to me, "Son of man, I'm going to cut off all food from Jerusalem. The people will live on starvation rations, worrying where the next meal's coming from, scrounging for the next drink of water. Famine conditions. People will look at one another, see nothing but skin and bones, and shake their heads. This is what sin does."

NEW INTERNATIONAL VERSION

5 "Now, son of man, take a sharp sword and use it as a barber's razor to shave your head and your beard. Then take a set of scales and divide up the hair. ²When the days of your siege come to an end, burn a third of the hair with fire inside the city. Take a third and strike it with the sword all around the city. And scatter a third to the wind. For I will pursue them with drawn sword. ³But take a few strands of hair and tuck them away in the folds of your garment. ⁴Again, take a few of these and throw them into the fire and burn them up. A fire will spread from there to the whole house of Israel.

⁵"This is what the Sovereign LORD says: This is Jerusalem, which I have set in the center of the nations, with countries all around her. ⁶Yet in her wickedness she has rebelled against my laws and decrees more than the nations and countries around her. She has rejected my laws and has not followed my decrees.

⁷"Therefore this is what the Sovereign LORD says: You have been more unruly than the nations around you and have not followed my decrees or kept my laws. You have not even*ᵃ* conformed to the standards of the nations around you.

⁸"Therefore this is what the Sovereign LORD says: I myself am against you, Jerusalem, and I will inflict punishment on you in the sight of the nations. ⁹Because of all your detestable idols, I will do to you what I have never done before and will never do again. ¹⁰Therefore in your midst fathers will eat their children, and children will eat their fathers. I will inflict punishment on you and will scatter all your survivors to the winds. ¹¹Therefore as surely as I live, declares the Sovereign LORD, because you have defiled my sanctuary with all your vile images and detestable practices, I myself will withdraw my favor; I will not look on you with pity or spare you. ¹²A third of your people will die of the plague or perish by famine inside you; a third will fall by the sword outside your walls; and a third I will scatter to the winds and pursue with drawn sword.

¹³"Then my anger will cease and my wrath against them will subside, and I will be avenged. And when I have spent my wrath upon them, they will know that I the LORD have spoken in my zeal.

¹⁴"I will make you a ruin and a reproach among the nations around you, in the sight of all who pass by. ¹⁵You will be a reproach and a taunt, a warning and an object of horror to the

ᵃ 7 Most Hebrew manuscripts; some Hebrew manuscripts and Syriac You have

THE MESSAGE

A JEALOUS GOD, NOT TO BE TRIFLED WITH

5 "Now, son of man, take a sharp sword and use it as a straight razor, shaving your head and your beard. Then, using a set of balancing scales, divide the hair into thirds. When the days of the siege are over, take one-third of the hair and burn it inside the city. Take another third, chop it into bits with the sword and sprinkle it around the city. The final third you'll throw to the wind. Then I'll go after them with a sword.

⁵·³·⁴ "Retrieve a few of the hairs and slip them into your pocket. Take some of them and throw them into the fire—burn them up. From them, fire will spread to the whole family of Israel.

⁵·⁵·⁶ "This is what GOD, the Master, says: This means *Jerusalem.* I set her at the center of the world, all the nations ranged around her. But she rebelled against my laws and ordinances, rebelled far worse than the nations ranged around her—sheer wickedness!—refused my guidance, ignored my directions.

⁵·⁷ "Therefore this is what GOD, the Master, says: You've been more headstrong and willful than any of the nations around you, refusing my guidance, ignoring my directions. You've sunk to the gutter level of those around you.

⁵·⁸·¹⁰ "Therefore this is what GOD, the Master, says: I'm setting myself against you—yes, against you, Jerusalem. I'm going to punish you in full sight of the nations. Because of your disgusting no-god idols, I'm going to do something to you that I've never done before and will never do again: turn families into cannibals—parents eating children, children eating parents! Punishment indeed. And whoever's left over I'll throw to the winds.

⁵·¹¹·¹² "Therefore, as sure as I am the living God—Decree of GOD, the Master—because you've polluted my Sanctuary with your obscenities and disgusting no-god idols, I'm pulling out. Not an ounce of pity will I show you. A third of your people will die of either disease or hunger inside the city, a third will be killed outside the city, and a third will be thrown to the winds and chased by killers.

⁵·¹³ "Only then will I calm down and let my anger cool. Then you'll know that I was serious about this all along, that I'm a jealous God and not to be trifled with.

⁵·¹⁴·¹⁵ "When I get done with you, you'll be a pile of rubble. Nations who walk by will make coarse jokes. When I finish my angry punishment and searing rebukes, you'll be reduced to an object of ridicule and mockery, turned into a horror story circulating among the surrounding

NEW INTERNATIONAL VERSION

nations around you when I inflict punishment on you in anger and in wrath and with stinging rebuke. I the LORD have spoken. ¹⁶When I shoot at you with my deadly and destructive arrows of famine, I will shoot to destroy you. I will bring more and more famine upon you and cut off your supply of food. ¹⁷I will send famine and wild beasts against you, and they will leave you childless. Plague and bloodshed will sweep through you, and I will bring the sword against you. I the LORD have spoken."

A PROPHECY AGAINST THE MOUNTAINS OF ISRAEL

6 The word of the LORD came to me: ²"Son of man, set your face against the mountains of Israel; prophesy against them ³and say: 'O mountains of Israel, hear the word of the Sovereign LORD. This is what the Sovereign LORD says to the mountains and hills, to the ravines and valleys: I am about to bring a sword against you, and I will destroy your high places. ⁴Your altars will be demolished and your incense altars will be smashed; and I will slay your people in front of your idols. ⁵I will lay the dead bodies of the Israelites in front of their idols, and I will scatter your bones around your altars. ⁶Wherever you live, the towns will be laid waste and the high places demolished, so that your altars will be laid waste and devastated, your idols smashed and ruined, your incense altars broken down, and what you have made wiped out. ⁷Your people will fall slain among you, and you will know that I am the LORD.

⁸"'But I will spare some, for some of you will escape the sword when you are scattered among the lands and nations. ⁹Then in the nations where they have been carried captive, those who escape will remember me—how I have been grieved by their adulterous hearts, which have turned away from me, and by their eyes, which have lusted after their idols. They will loathe themselves for the evil they have done and for all their detestable practices. ¹⁰And they will know that I am the LORD; I did not threaten in vain to bring this calamity on them.

¹¹"'This is what the Sovereign LORD says: Strike your hands together and stamp your feet and cry out "Alas!" because of all the wicked and detestable practices of the house of Israel, for they will fall by the sword, famine and plague. ¹²He that is far away will die of the plague, and he that is near will fall by the sword, and he that survives and is spared will die of famine. So will I spend my wrath upon them. ¹³And they will know that I am the LORD, when their people lie slain among their idols around their altars, on every high hill and on all the

THE MESSAGE

nations. I, GOD, have spoken.

5.16-17 "When I shoot my lethal famine arrows at you, I'll shoot to kill. Then I'll step up the famine and cut off food supplies. Famine and more famine—and then I'll send in the wild animals to finish off your children. Epidemic disease, unrestrained murder, death—and I will have sent it! I, GOD, have spoken."

TURN ISRAEL INTO WASTELAND

6.1-7 6 Then the Word of GOD came to me: "Son of man, now turn and face the mountains of Israel and preach against them: 'O Mountains of Israel, listen to the Message of GOD, the Master. GOD, the Master, speaks to the mountains and hills, to the ravines and the valleys: I'm about to destroy your sacred god and goddess shrines. I'll level your altars, bust up your sun-god pillars, and kill your people as they bow down to your no-god idols. I'll stack the dead bodies of Israelites in front of your idols and then scatter your bones around your shrines. Every place where you've lived, the towns will be torn down and the pagan shrines demolished—altars busted up, idols smashed, all your custom-made sun-god pillars in ruins. Corpses everywhere you look! Then you'll know that I am GOD.

6.8-10 "'But I'll let a few escape the killing as you are scattered through other lands and nations. In the foreign countries where they're taken as prisoners of war, they'll remember me. They'll realize how devastated I was by their betrayals, by their voracious lust for gratifying themselves in their idolatries. They'll be disgusted with their evil ways, disgusting to God in the way they've lived. They'll know that I am GOD. They'll know that my judgment against them was no empty threat.

6.11-14 "'This is what GOD, the Master, says: Clap your hands, stamp your feet, yell out, "No, no, no!" because of all the evil obscenities rife in Israel. They're going to be killed, dying of hunger, dying of disease—death everywhere you look, people dropping like flies, people far away dying, people nearby dying, and whoever's left in the city starving to death. Why? Because I'm angry, furiously angry. They'll realize that I am GOD when they see their people's corpses strewn over and around all their ruined sex-and-religion shrines on the bare hills

NEW INTERNATIONAL VERSION	THE MESSAGE

mountaintops, under every spreading tree and every leafy oak—places where they offered fragrant incense to all their idols. ¹⁴And I will stretch out my hand against them and make the land a desolate waste from the desert to Diblah*ᵃ*—wherever they live. Then they will know that I am the LORD.' "

THE END HAS COME

7 The word of the LORD came to me: ²"Son of man, this is what the Sovereign LORD says to the land of Israel: The end! The end has come upon the four corners of the land. ³The end is now upon you and I will unleash my anger against you. I will judge you according to your conduct and repay you for all your detestable practices. ⁴I will not look on you with pity or spare you; I will surely repay you for your conduct and the detestable practices among you. Then you will know that I am the LORD.

⁵"This is what the Sovereign LORD says: Disaster! An unheard-of*ᵇ* disaster is coming. ⁶The end has come! The end has come! It has roused itself against you. It has come! ⁷Doom has come upon you—you who dwell in the land. The time has come, the day is near; there is panic, not joy, upon the mountains. ⁸I am about to pour out my wrath on you and spend my anger against you; I will judge you according to your conduct and repay you for all your detestable practices. ⁹I will not look on you with pity or spare you; I will repay you in accordance with your conduct and the detestable practices among you. Then you will know that it is I the LORD who strikes the blow.

¹⁰"The day is here! It has come! Doom has burst forth, the rod has budded, arrogance has blossomed! ¹¹Violence has grown into*ᶜ* a rod to punish wickedness; none of the people will be left, none of that crowd—no wealth, nothing of value. ¹²The time has come, the day has arrived.

---

and in the lush fertility groves, in all the places where they indulged their sensual rites. I'll bring my hand down hard on them, demolish the country wherever they live, turn it into wasteland from one end to the other, from the wilderness to Riblah. Then they'll know that I am GOD!' "

FATE HAS CAUGHT UP WITH YOU

7 ⁷·¹⁻⁴ GOD's Word came to me, saying, "You, son of man—GOD, the Master, has this Message for the land of Israel:

" 'Endtime.
> The end of business as usual for everyone.
It's all over. The end is upon you.
> I've launched my anger against you.
I've issued my verdict on the way you live.
> I'll make you pay for your disgusting
>> obscenities.
I won't look the other way,
> I won't feel sorry for you.
I'll make you pay for the way you've lived:
> Your disgusting obscenities will boomerang
>> on you,
> and you'll realize that I am GOD.'

⁷·⁵⁻⁹ "I, GOD, the Master, say:
> 'Disaster after disaster! Look, it comes!
Endtime—
> the end comes.
The end is ripe. Watch out, it's coming!
> This is your fate, you who live in this land.
Time's up.
> It's zero hour.
No dragging of feet now,
> no bargaining for more time.
Soon now I'll pour my wrath on you,
> pay out my anger against you,
Render my verdict on the way you've lived,
> make you pay for your disgusting obscenities.
I won't look the other way,
> I won't feel sorry for you.
I'll make you pay for the way you've lived.
> Your disgusting obscenities will boomerang
>> on you.
Then you'll realize
> that it is I, GOD, who has hit you.

⁷·¹⁰⁻¹³ " 'Judgment Day!
> Fate has caught up with you.
The scepter outsized and pretentious,
> pride bursting all bounds,
Violence strutting,
> brandishing the evil scepter.
But there's nothing to them,
> and nothing will be left of them.
Time's up.
> Countdown: five, four, three, two . . .

ᵃ 14 Most Hebrew manuscripts; a few Hebrew manuscripts *Riblah*   *ᵇ 5* Most Hebrew manuscripts; some Hebrew manuscripts and Syriac *Disaster after*   *ᶜ 11* Or *The violent one has become*

NEW INTERNATIONAL VERSION

Let not the buyer rejoice nor the seller grieve, for wrath is upon the whole crowd. ¹³The seller will not recover the land he has sold as long as both of them live, for the vision concerning the whole crowd will not be reversed. Because of their sins, not one of them will preserve his life. ¹⁴Though they blow the trumpet and get everything ready, no one will go into battle, for my wrath is upon the whole crowd.

¹⁵"Outside is the sword, inside are plague and famine; those in the country will die by the sword, and those in the city will be devoured by famine and plague. ¹⁶All who survive and escape will be in the mountains, moaning like doves of the valleys, each because of his sins. ¹⁷Every hand will go limp, and every knee will become as weak as water. ¹⁸They will put on sackcloth and be clothed with terror. Their faces will be covered with shame and their heads will be shaved. ¹⁹They will throw their silver into the streets, and their gold will be an unclean thing. Their silver and gold will not be able to save them in the day of the LORD's wrath. They will not satisfy their hunger or fill their stomachs with it, for it has made them stumble into sin. ²⁰They were proud of their beautiful jewelry and used it to make their detestable idols and vile images. Therefore I will turn these into an unclean thing for them. ²¹I will hand it all over as plunder to foreigners and as loot to the wicked of the earth, and they will defile it. ²²I will turn my face away from them, and they will desecrate my treasured place; robbers will enter it and desecrate it.

²³"Prepare chains, because the land is full of bloodshed and the city is full of violence. ²⁴I will bring the most wicked of the nations to take possession of their houses; I will put an end to the pride of the mighty, and their sanctuaries will be desecrated. ²⁵When terror comes, they will seek

THE MESSAGE

Buyer, don't crow; seller, don't worry:
    Judgment wrath has turned the world
        topsy-turvy.
The bottom has dropped out of buying and
      selling.
    It will never be the same again.
But don't fantasize an upturn in the market.
    The country is bankrupt because of its sins,
    and it's not going to get any better.

7.14-16 " 'The trumpet signals the call to battle:
    "Present arms!"
But no one marches into battle.
    My wrath has them paralyzed!
On the open roads you're killed,
    or else you go home and die of hunger and
        disease.
Either get murdered out in the country
    or die of sickness or hunger in town.
Survivors run for the hills.
    They moan like doves in the valleys,
Each one moaning
    for his own sins.

7.17-18 " 'Every hand hangs limp,
    every knee turns to rubber.
They dress in rough burlap—
    sorry scarecrows,
Shifty and shamefaced,
    with their heads shaved bald.

7.19-27 " 'They throw their money into the gutters.
    Their hard-earned cash stinks like garbage.
They find that it won't buy a thing
    they either want or need on Judgment Day.
They tripped on money
    and fell into sin.
Proud and pretentious with their jewels,
    they deck out their vile and vulgar no-gods
      in finery.
    I'll make those god-obscenities a stench in
      their nostrils.
I'll give away their religious junk—
    strangers will pick it up for free,
    the godless spit on it and make jokes.
I'll turn my face so I won't have to look
    as my treasured place and people are
      violated,
As violent strangers walk in
    and desecrate place and people—
A bloody massacre,
    as crime and violence fill the city.
I'll bring in the dregs of humanity
    to move into their houses.
I'll put a stop to the boasting and strutting
    of the high-and-mighty,
And see to it that there'll be nothing holy
    left in their holy places.
Catastrophe descends. They look for peace,

NEW INTERNATIONAL VERSION

peace, but there will be none. ²⁶Calamity upon calamity will come, and rumor upon rumor. They will try to get a vision from the prophet; the teaching of the law by the priest will be lost, as will the counsel of the elders. ²⁷The king will mourn, the prince will be clothed with despair, and the hands of the people of the land will tremble. I will deal with them according to their conduct, and by their own standards I will judge them. Then they will know that I am the LORD."

IDOLATRY IN THE TEMPLE

8 In the sixth year, in the sixth month on the fifth day, while I was sitting in my house and the elders of Judah were sitting before me, the hand of the Sovereign LORD came upon me there. ²I looked, and I saw a figure like that of a man.ᵃ From what appeared to be his waist down he was like fire, and from there up his appearance was as bright as glowing metal. ³He stretched out what looked like a hand and took me by the hair of my head. The Spirit lifted me up between earth and heaven and in visions of God he took me to Jerusalem, to the entrance to the north gate of the inner court, where the idol that provokes to jealousy stood. ⁴And there before me was the glory of the God of Israel, as in the vision I had seen in the plain.

⁵Then he said to me, "Son of man, look toward the north." So I looked, and in the entrance north of the gate of the altar I saw this idol of jealousy.

⁶And he said to me, "Son of man, do you see what they are doing—the utterly detestable things the house of Israel is doing here, things that will drive me far from my sanctuary? But you will see things that are even more detestable."

⁷Then he brought me to the entrance to the court. I looked, and I saw a hole in the wall. ⁸He said to me, "Son of man, now dig into the wall." So I dug into the wall and saw a doorway there.

⁹And he said to me, "Go in and see the wicked and detestable things they are doing here." ¹⁰So I went in and looked, and I saw portrayed all over the walls all kinds of crawling things and detestable animals and all the idols of the house of Israel. ¹¹In front of them stood seventy

---

THE MESSAGE

but there's no peace to be found—
Disaster on the heels of disaster,
 one rumor after another.
They clamor for the prophet to tell them
 what's up,
 but nobody knows anything.
Priests don't have a clue;
 the elders don't know what to say.
The king holds his head in despair;
 the prince is devastated.
The common people are paralyzed.
 Gripped by fear, they can't move.
I'll deal with them where they are,
 judge them on their terms.
 They'll know that I am GOD.' "

THE SPIRIT CARRIED ME IN VISIONS

8.1-4 **8** In the sixth year, in the sixth month and the fifth day, while I was sitting at home meeting with the leaders of Judah, it happened that the hand of my Master, GOD, gripped me. When I looked, I was astonished. What I saw looked like a man—from the waist down like fire and from the waist up like highly burnished bronze. He reached out what looked like a hand and grabbed me by the hair. The Spirit swept me high in the air and carried me in visions of God to Jerusalem, to the entrance of the north gate of the Temple's inside court where the image of the sex goddess that makes God so angry had been set up. Right before me was the Glory of the God of Israel, exactly like the vision I had seen out on the plain.

8.5 He said to me, "Son of man, look north." I looked north and saw it: Just north of the entrance loomed the altar of the sex goddess, Asherah, that makes God so angry.

8.6 Then he said, "Son of man, do you see what they're doing? Outrageous obscenities! And doing them right here! It's enough to drive me right out of my own Temple. But you're going to see worse yet."

⊹

8.7 He brought me to the door of the Temple court. I looked and saw a gaping hole in the wall.

8.8 He said, "Son of man, dig through the wall." I dug through the wall and came upon a door.

8.9 He said, "Now walk through the door and take a look at the obscenities they're engaging in."

8.10-11 I entered and looked. I couldn't believe my eyes: Painted all over the walls were pictures of reptiles and animals and monsters—the whole pantheon of Egyptian gods and goddesses—being worshiped by Israel. In the middle of the

---

ᵃ *2 Or saw a fiery figure*

NEW INTERNATIONAL VERSION

elders of the house of Israel, and Jaazaniah son of Shaphan was standing among them. Each had a censer in his hand, and a fragrant cloud of incense was rising.

¹²He said to me, "Son of man, have you seen what the elders of the house of Israel are doing in the darkness, each at the shrine of his own idol? They say, 'The LORD does not see us; the LORD has forsaken the land.'" ¹³Again, he said, "You will see them doing things that are even more detestable."

¹⁴Then he brought me to the entrance to the north gate of the house of the LORD, and I saw women sitting there, mourning for Tammuz. ¹⁵He said to me, "Do you see this, son of man? You will see things that are even more detestable than this."

¹⁶He then brought me into the inner court of the house of the LORD, and there at the entrance to the temple, between the portico and the altar, were about twenty-five men. With their backs toward the temple of the LORD and their faces toward the east, they were bowing down to the sun in the east.

¹⁷He said to me, "Have you seen this, son of man? Is it a trivial matter for the house of Judah to do the detestable things they are doing here? Must they also fill the land with violence and continually provoke me to anger? Look at them putting the branch to their nose! ¹⁸Therefore I will deal with them in anger; I will not look on them with pity or spare them. Although they shout in my ears, I will not listen to them."

IDOLATERS KILLED

9 Then I heard him call out in a loud voice, "Bring the guards of the city here, each with a weapon in his hand." ²And I saw six men coming from the direction of the upper gate, which faces north, each with a deadly weapon in his hand. With them was a man clothed in linen who had a writing kit at his side. They came in and stood beside the bronze altar.

³Now the glory of the God of Israel went up from above the cherubim, where it had been, and moved to the threshold of the temple. Then the LORD called to the man clothed in linen who had the writing kit at his side ⁴and said to him, "Go throughout the city of Jerusalem and put a mark on the foreheads of those who grieve and lament over all the detestable things that are done in it."

⁵As I listened, he said to the others, "Follow him through the city and kill, without showing pity or compassion. ⁶Slaughter old men, young men and maidens, women and children, but do not touch anyone who has the mark. Begin at

THE MESSAGE

room were seventy of the leaders of Israel, with Jaazaniah son of Shaphan standing in the middle. Each held his censer with the incense rising in a fragrant cloud.

8.12   He said, "Son of man, do you see what the elders are doing here in the dark, each one before his favorite god-picture? They tell themselves, 'GOD doesn't see us. GOD has forsaken the country.'"

8.13   Then he said, "You're going to see worse yet."

✝

8.14-15 He took me to the entrance at the north gate of the Temple of GOD. I saw women sitting there, weeping for Tammuz, the Babylonian fertility god. He said, "Have you gotten an eyeful, son of man? You're going to see worse yet."

✝

8.16   Finally, he took me to the inside court of the Temple of GOD. There between the porch and the altar were about twenty-five men. Their backs were to GOD's Temple. They were facing east, bowing in worship to the sun.

8.17-18 He said, "Have you seen enough, son of man? Isn't it bad enough that Judah engages in these outrageous obscenities? They fill the country with violence and now provoke me even further with their obscene gestures. That's it. They have an angry God on their hands! From now on, no mercy. They can shout all they want, but I'm not listening."

A MARK ON THE FOREHEAD

9.1   **9** Then I heard him call out loudly, "Executioners, come! And bring your deadly weapons with you."

9.2   Six men came down the road from the upper gate that faces north, each carrying his lethal weapon. With them was a man dressed in linen with a writing case slung from his shoulder. They entered and stood by the bronze altar.

9.3-4   The Glory of the God of Israel ascended from his usual place above the cherubim-angels, moved to the threshold of the Temple, and called to the man with the writing case who was dressed in linen: "Go through the streets of Jerusalem and put a mark on the forehead of everyone who is in anguish over the outrageous obscenities being done in the city."

9.5-6   I listened as he went on to address the executioners: "Follow him through the city and kill. Feel sorry for no one. Show no compassion. Kill old men and women, young men and women, mothers and children. But don't lay a hand on anyone with the mark. Start at my Temple."

NEW INTERNATIONAL VERSION

my sanctuary." So they began with the elders who were in front of the temple.

⁷Then he said to them, "Defile the temple and fill the courts with the slain. Go!" So they went out and began killing throughout the city. ⁸While they were killing and I was left alone, I fell facedown, crying out, "Ah, Sovereign LORD! Are you going to destroy the entire remnant of Israel in this outpouring of your wrath on Jerusalem?"

⁹He answered me, "The sin of the house of Israel and Judah is exceedingly great; the land is full of bloodshed and the city is full of injustice. They say, 'The LORD has forsaken the land; the LORD does not see.' ¹⁰So I will not look on them with pity or spare them, but I will bring down on their own heads what they have done."

¹¹Then the man in linen with the writing kit at his side brought back word, saying, "I have done as you commanded."

THE GLORY DEPARTS FROM THE TEMPLE

10 I looked, and I saw the likeness of a throne of sapphire*ᵃ* above the expanse that was over the heads of the cherubim. ²The LORD said to the man clothed in linen, "Go in among the wheels beneath the cherubim. Fill your hands with burning coals from among the cherubim and scatter them over the city." And as I watched, he went in.

³Now the cherubim were standing on the south side of the temple when the man went in, and a cloud filled the inner court. ⁴Then the glory of the LORD rose from above the cherubim and moved to the threshold of the temple. The cloud filled the temple, and the court was full of the radiance of the glory of the LORD. ⁵The sound of the wings of the cherubim could be heard as far away as the outer court, like the voice of God Almighty*ᵇ* when he speaks.

⁶When the LORD commanded the man in linen, "Take fire from among the wheels, from among the cherubim," the man went in and stood beside a wheel. ⁷Then one of the cherubim reached out his hand to the fire that was among them. He took up some of it and put it into the hands of the man in linen, who took it and went out. ⁸(Under the wings of the cherubim could be seen what looked like the hands of a man.)

⁹I looked, and I saw beside the cherubim four wheels, one beside each of the cherubim; the wheels sparkled like chrysolite. ¹⁰As for their appearance, the four of them looked alike; each

THE MESSAGE

They started with the leaders in front of the Temple.

9.7-8 He told the executioners, "Desecrate the Temple. Fill it with corpses. Then go out and continue the killing." So they went out and struck the city.

While the massacre went forward, I was left alone. I fell on my face in prayer: "Oh, oh, GOD, my Master! Are you going to kill everyone left in Israel in this pouring out of your anger on Jerusalem?"

9.9-10 He said, "The guilt of Israel and Judah is enormous. The land is swollen with murder. The city is bloated with injustice. They all say, 'GOD has forsaken the country. He doesn't see anything we do.' Well, I do see, and I'm not feeling sorry for any of them. They're going to pay for what they've done."

9.11 Just then, the man dressed in linen and carrying the writing case came back and reported, "I've done what you told me."

THE TEMPLE, FILLED WITH THE PRESENCE OF GOD

10.1 **10** When I next looked, oh! Above the dome over the heads of the cherubim-angels was what looked like a throne, sky-blue, like a sapphire!

10.2 GOD said to the man dressed in linen, "Enter the place of the wheels under the cherubim-angels. Fill your hands with burning coals from beneath the cherubim and scatter them over the city."

10.2-5 I watched as he entered. The cherubim were standing on the south side of the Temple when the man entered. A cloud filled the inside courtyard. Then the Glory of GOD ascended from the cherubim and moved to the threshold of the Temple. The cloud filled the Temple. Court and Temple were both filled with the blazing presence of the Glory of GOD. And the sound! The wings of the cherubim were audible all the way to the outer court—the sound of the voice was like The Strong God in thunder.

10.6-8 When GOD commanded the man dressed in linen, "Take fire from among the wheels, from between the cherubim," he went in and stood beside a wheel. One of the cherubim reached into the fire, took some coals, and put them in the hands of the man dressed in linen. He took them and went out. Something that looked like a human hand could be seen under the wings of the cherubim.

10.9-13 And then I saw four wheels beside the cherubim, one beside each cherub. The wheels radiating were sparkling like diamonds in the sun. All four wheels looked alike, each like a

---

ᵃ 1 Or *lapis lazuli*   *ᵇ* 5 Hebrew *El-Shaddai*

NEW INTERNATIONAL VERSION

was like a wheel intersecting a wheel. ¹¹As they moved, they would go in any one of the four directions the cherubim faced; the wheels did not turn about*ª* as the cherubim went. The cherubim went in whatever direction the head faced, without turning as they went. ¹²Their entire bodies, including their backs, their hands and their wings, were completely full of eyes, as were their four wheels. ¹³I heard the wheels being called "the whirling wheels." ¹⁴Each of the cherubim had four faces: One face was that of a cherub, the second the face of a man, the third the face of a lion, and the fourth the face of an eagle.

¹⁵Then the cherubim rose upward. These were the living creatures I had seen by the Kebar River. ¹⁶When the cherubim moved, the wheels beside them moved; and when the cherubim spread their wings to rise from the ground, the wheels did not leave their side. ¹⁷When the cherubim stood still, they also stood still; and when the cherubim rose, they rose with them, because the spirit of the living creatures was in them.

¹⁸Then the glory of the LORD departed from over the threshold of the temple and stopped above the cherubim. ¹⁹While I watched, the cherubim spread their wings and rose from the ground, and as they went, the wheels went with them. They stopped at the entrance to the east gate of the LORD's house, and the glory of the God of Israel was above them. ²⁰These were the living creatures I had seen beneath the God of Israel by the Kebar River, and I realized that they were cherubim. ²¹Each had four faces and four wings, and under their wings was what looked like the hands of a man. ²²Their faces had the same appearance as those I had seen by the Kebar River. Each one went straight ahead.

JUDGMENT ON ISRAEL'S LEADERS

11 Then the Spirit lifted me up and brought me to the gate of the house of the LORD that faces east. There at the entrance to the gate were twenty-five men, and I saw among them Jaazaniah son of Azzur and Pelatiah son of Benaiah, leaders of the people. ²The LORD said to me, "Son of man, these are the men who are plotting evil and giving wicked advice in this city. ³They say, 'Will it not soon be time to build houses?*ᵇ* This city is a cooking pot, and we are the meat.' ⁴Therefore prophesy against them; prophesy, son of man."

⁵Then the Spirit of the LORD came upon me, and he told me to say: "This is what the LORD says: That is what you are saying, O house of Israel, but I know what is going through your

ª 11 Or aside   ᵇ 3 Or This is not the time to build houses.

THE MESSAGE

wheel within a wheel. When they moved, they went in any of the four directions but in a perfectly straight line. Where the cherubim went, the wheels went straight ahead. The cherubim were full of eyes in their backs, hands, and wings. The wheels likewise were full of eyes. I heard the wheels called "wheels within wheels."

10.14   Each of the cherubim had four faces: the first, of an angel; the second, a human; the third, a lion; the fourth, an eagle.

10.15-17   Then the cherubim ascended. They were the same living creatures I had seen at the Kebar River. When the cherubim moved, the wheels beside them moved. When the cherubim spread their wings to take off from the ground, the wheels stayed right with them. When the cherubim stopped, the wheels stopped. When the cherubim rose, the wheels rose, because the spirit of the living creatures was also in the wheels.

10.18-19   Then the Glory of GOD left the Temple entrance and hovered over the cherubim. I watched as the cherubim spread their wings and left the ground, the wheels right with them. They stopped at the entrance of the east gate of the Temple. The Glory of the God of Israel was above them.

10.20-22   These were the same living creatures I had seen previously beneath the God of Israel at the Kebar River. I recognized them as cherubim. Each had four faces and four wings. Under their wings was what looked like human hands. Their faces looked exactly like those I had seen at the Kebar River. Each went straight ahead.

A NEW HEART AND A NEW SPIRIT

11.1 **11** Then the Spirit picked me up and took me to the gate of the Temple that faces east. There were twenty-five men standing at the gate. I recognized the leaders, Jaazaniah son of Azzur and Pelatiah son of Benaiah.

11.2-3   GOD said, "Son of man, these are the men who draw up blueprints for sin, who think up new programs for evil in this city. They say, 'We can make anything happen here. We're the best. We're the choice pieces of meat in the soup pot.'

11.4   "Oppose them, son of man. Preach against them."

11.5-6   Then the Spirit of GOD came upon me and told me what to say: "This is what GOD says: 'That's a fine public speech, Israel, but I know what you are thinking. You've murdered a lot of

NEW INTERNATIONAL VERSION

mind. ⁶You have killed many people in this city and filled its streets with the dead.

⁷"Therefore this is what the Sovereign LORD says: The bodies you have thrown there are the meat and this city is the pot, but I will drive you out of it. ⁸You fear the sword, and the sword is what I will bring against you, declares the Sovereign LORD. ⁹I will drive you out of the city and hand you over to foreigners and inflict punishment on you. ¹⁰You will fall by the sword, and I will execute judgment on you at the borders of Israel. Then you will know that I am the LORD. ¹¹This city will not be a pot for you, nor will you be the meat in it; I will execute judgment on you at the borders of Israel. ¹²And you will know that I am the LORD, for you have not followed my decrees or kept my laws but have conformed to the standards of the nations around you."

¹³Now as I was prophesying, Pelatiah son of Benaiah died. Then I fell facedown and cried out in a loud voice, "Ah, Sovereign LORD! Will you completely destroy the remnant of Israel?"

¹⁴The word of the LORD came to me: ¹⁵"Son of man, your brothers—your brothers who are your blood relatives*a* and the whole house of Israel—are those of whom the people of Jerusalem have said, 'They are*b* far away from the LORD; this land was given to us as our possession.'

PROMISED RETURN OF ISRAEL

¹⁶"Therefore say: 'This is what the Sovereign LORD says: Although I sent them far away among the nations and scattered them among the countries, yet for a little while I have been a sanctuary for them in the countries where they have gone.'

¹⁷"Therefore say: 'This is what the Sovereign LORD says: I will gather you from the nations and bring you back from the countries where you have been scattered, and I will give you back the land of Israel again.'

¹⁸"They will return to it and remove all its vile images and detestable idols. ¹⁹I will give them an undivided heart and put a new spirit in them; I will remove from them their heart of stone and give them a heart of flesh. ²⁰Then they will follow my decrees and be careful to keep my laws. They will be my people, and I will be their God. ²¹But as for those whose hearts are devoted to their vile images and detestable idols, I will bring down on their own heads what they have done, declares the Sovereign LORD."

²²Then the cherubim, with the wheels beside them, spread their wings, and the glory of the God of Israel was above them. ²³The glory of the LORD went up from within the city and stopped

---

THE MESSAGE

people in this city. The streets are piled high with corpses.'

11.7-12   "Therefore this is what GOD, the Master, says: 'The corpses that you've piled in the streets are the meat and this city is the soup pot, and *you're* not even in the pot! I'm throwing you out! You fear war, but war is what you're going to get. I'm bringing war against you. I'm throwing you out of this city, giving you over to foreigners, and punishing you good. You'll be killed in battle. I'll carry out judgment on you at the borders of Israel. Then you'll realize that I am GOD. This city will not be your soup pot and you won't be the choice pieces of meat in it either. Hardly. I will carry out judgment on you at the borders of Israel and you'll realize that I am GOD, for you haven't followed my statutes and ordinances. Instead of following my ways, you've sunk to the level of the laws of the nations around you.' "

11.13   Even while I was preaching, Pelatiah son of Benaiah died. I fell down, face to the ground, and prayed loudly, "O Master, GOD! Will you completely wipe out what's left of Israel?"

11.14-15   The answer from GOD came back: "Son of man, your brothers—I mean the whole people of Israel who are in exile with you—are the people of whom the citizens of Jerusalem are saying, 'They're in the far country, far from GOD. This land has been given to us to own.'

11.16-20   "Well, tell them this: 'This is your Message from GOD, the Master. True, I sent you to the far country and scattered you through other lands. All the same, I've provided you a temporary sanctuary in the countries where you've gone. I will gather you back from those countries and lands where you've been scattered and give you back the land of Israel. You'll come back and clean house, throw out all the rotten images and obscene idols. I'll give you a new heart. I'll put a new spirit in you. I'll cut out your stone heart and replace it with a red-blooded, firm-muscled heart. Then you'll obey my statutes and be careful to obey my commands. You'll be my people! I'll be your God!

11.21   " 'But not those who are self-willed and addicted to their rotten images and obscene idols! I'll see that they're paid in full for what they've done.' Decree of GOD, the Master."

11.22-23   Then the cherubim spread their wings, with the wheels beside them and the Glory of the God of Israel hovering over them. The Glory of GOD ascended from within the city and rested on the mountain to the east of the city.

✛

---

a 15 Or are in exile with you (see Septuagint and Syriac)
b 15 Or those to whom the people of Jerusalem have said, 'Stay

NEW INTERNATIONAL VERSION

above the mountain east of it. [24]The Spirit lifted me up and brought me to the exiles in Babylonia[a] in the vision given by the Spirit of God.

Then the vision I had seen went up from me, [25]and I told the exiles everything the LORD had shown me.

THE EXILE SYMBOLIZED

12 The word of the LORD came to me: [2]"Son of man, you are living among a rebellious people. They have eyes to see but do not see and ears to hear but do not hear, for they are a rebellious people.

[3]"Therefore, son of man, pack your belongings for exile and in the daytime, as they watch, set out and go from where you are to another place. Perhaps they will understand, though they are a rebellious house. [4]During the daytime, while they watch, bring out your belongings packed for exile. Then in the evening, while they are watching, go out like those who go into exile. [5]While they watch, dig through the wall and take your belongings out through it. [6]Put them on your shoulder as they are watching and carry them out at dusk. Cover your face so that you cannot see the land, for I have made you a sign to the house of Israel."

[7]So I did as I was commanded. During the day I brought out my things packed for exile. Then in the evening I dug through the wall with my hands. I took my belongings out at dusk, carrying them on my shoulders while they watched.

[8]In the morning the word of the LORD came to me: [9]"Son of man, did not that rebellious house of Israel ask you, 'What are you doing?'

[10]"Say to them, 'This is what the Sovereign LORD says: This oracle concerns the prince in Jerusalem and the whole house of Israel who are there.' [11]Say to them, 'I am a sign to you.'

"As I have done, so it will be done to them. They will go into exile as captives.

[12]"The prince among them will put his things on his shoulder at dusk and leave, and a hole will be dug in the wall for him to go through. He will cover his face so that he cannot see the land. [13]I will spread my net for him, and he will be caught in my snare; I will bring him to Babylonia, the land of the Chaldeans, but he will not see it, and there he will die. [14]I will scatter to the winds all those around him—his staff and all his troops—and I will pursue them with drawn sword.

[15]"They will know that I am the LORD, when I disperse them among the nations and scatter

[a] 24 Or *Chaldea*

THE MESSAGE

Then, still in the vision given me by the Spirit of God, the Spirit took me and carried me back to the exiles in Babylon. And then the vision left me. I told the exiles everything that GOD had shown me.

PUT THE BUNDLE ON YOUR SHOULDER AND WALK INTO THE NIGHT

12 GOD's Message came to me: "Son of man, you're living with a bunch of rebellious people. They have eyes but don't see a thing, they have ears but don't hear a thing. They're rebels all. So, son of man, pack up your exile duffel bags. Leave in broad daylight with everyone watching and go off, as if into exile. Maybe then they'll understand what's going on, rebels though they are. You'll take up your baggage while they watch, a bundle of the bare necessities of someone going into exile, and toward evening leave, just like a person going off into exile. As they watch, dig through the wall of the house and carry your bundle through it. In full sight of the people, put the bundle on your shoulder and walk out into the night. Cover your face so you won't have to look at what you'll never see again. I'm using you as a sign for the family of Israel."

I did exactly as he commanded me. I got my stuff together and brought it out in the street where everyone could see me, bundled it up the way someone being taken off into exile would, and then, as the sun went down, made a hole in the wall of the house with my hands. As it grew dark and as they watched, I left, throwing my bundle across my shoulders.

The next morning GOD spoke to me: "Son of man, when anyone in Israel, that bunch of rebels, asks you, 'What are you doing?' Tell them, 'GOD, the Master, says that this Message especially concerns the prince in Jerusalem—Zedekiah—but includes all the people of Israel.'

"Also tell them, 'I am drawing a picture for you. As I am now doing, it will be done to all the people of Israel. They will go into exile as captives.'

"The prince will put his bundle on his shoulders in the dark and leave. He'll dig through the wall of the house, covering his face so he won't have to look at the land he'll never see again. But I'll make sure he gets caught and is taken to Babylon. Blinded, he'll never see that land in which he'll die. I'll scatter to the four winds those who helped him escape, along with his troops, and many will die in battle. They'll realize that I am GOD when I scatter them among foreign countries.

NEW INTERNATIONAL VERSION

them through the countries. ¹⁶But I will spare a few of them from the sword, famine and plague, so that in the nations where they go they may acknowledge all their detestable practices. Then they will know that I am the LORD."

¹⁷The word of the LORD came to me: ¹⁸"Son of man, tremble as you eat your food, and shudder in fear as you drink your water. ¹⁹Say to the people of the land: 'This is what the Sovereign LORD says about those living in Jerusalem and in the land of Israel: They will eat their food in anxiety and drink their water in despair, for their land will be stripped of everything in it because of the violence of all who live there. ²⁰The inhabited towns will be laid waste and the land will be desolate. Then you will know that I am the LORD.' "

²¹The word of the LORD came to me: ²²"Son of man, what is this proverb you have in the land of Israel: 'The days go by and every vision comes to nothing'? ²³Say to them, 'This is what the Sovereign LORD says: I am going to put an end to this proverb, and they will no longer quote it in Israel.' Say to them, 'The days are near when every vision will be fulfilled. ²⁴For there will be no more false visions or flattering divinations among the people of Israel. ²⁵But I the LORD will speak what I will, and it shall be fulfilled without delay. For in your days, you rebellious house, I will fulfill whatever I say, declares the Sovereign LORD.' "

²⁶The word of the LORD came to me: ²⁷"Son of man, the house of Israel is saying, 'The vision he sees is for many years from now, and he prophesies about the distant future.'

²⁸"Therefore say to them, 'This is what the Sovereign LORD says: None of my words will be delayed any longer; whatever I say will be fulfilled, declares the Sovereign LORD.' "

FALSE PROPHETS CONDEMNED

13 The word of the LORD came to me: ²"Son of man, prophesy against the prophets of Israel who are now prophesying. Say to those who prophesy out of their own imagination: 'Hear the word of the LORD! ³This is what the Sovereign LORD says: Woe to the foolish*a* prophets who follow their own spirit and have seen nothing! ⁴Your prophets, O Israel, are like jackals among ruins. ⁵You have not gone up to the breaks in the wall to repair it for the house of Is-

a 3 Or *wicked*

THE MESSAGE

12.16   "I'll permit a few of them to escape the killing, starvation, and deadly sickness so that they can confess among the foreign countries all the disgusting obscenities they've been involved in. They will realize that I am GOD."

✝

12.17-20 GOD's Message came to me: "Son of man, eat your meals shaking in your boots, drink your water trembling with fear. Tell the people of this land, everyone living in Jerusalem and Israel, GOD's Message: 'You'll eat your meals shaking in your boots and drink your water in terror because your land is going to be stripped bare as punishment for the brutality rampant in it. All the cities and villages will be emptied out and the fields destroyed. Then you'll realize that I am GOD.' "

✝

12.21-22 GOD's Message came to me: "Son of man, what's this proverb making the rounds in the land of Israel that says, 'Everything goes on the same as ever; all the prophetic warnings are false alarms'?

12.23-25   "Tell them, 'GOD, the Master, says, This proverb's going to have a short life!'

"Tell them, 'Time's about up. Every warning is about to come true. False alarms and easygoing preaching are a thing of the past in the life of Israel. I, GOD, am doing the speaking. What I say happens. None of what I say is on hold. What I say, I'll do—and soon, you rebels!' Decree of God the Master."

✝

12.26-28 GOD's Message came to me: "Son of man, do you hear what Israel is saying: that the alarm the prophet raises is for a long time off, that he's preaching about the far-off future? Well, tell them, 'GOD, the Master, says, "Nothing of what I say is on hold. What I say happens." ' Decree of GOD, the Master."

✝

PEOPLE WHO LOVE LISTENING TO LIES

13.1-2   **13** GOD's Message came to me: "Son of man, preach against the prophets of Israel who are making things up out of their own heads and calling it 'prophesying.'

13.2-6   "Preach to them the real thing. Tell them, 'Listen to GOD's Message!' GOD, the Master, pronounces doom on the empty-headed prophets who do their own thing and know nothing of what's going on! Your prophets, Israel, are like jackals scavenging through the ruins. They haven't lifted a finger to repair the defenses of the city and have risked nothing to help Israel

NEW INTERNATIONAL VERSION

rael so that it will stand firm in the battle on the day of the LORD. [6]Their visions are false and their divinations a lie. They say, "The LORD declares," when the LORD has not sent them; yet they expect their words to be fulfilled. [7]Have you not seen false visions and uttered lying divinations when you say, "The LORD declares," though I have not spoken?

[8]" 'Therefore this is what the Sovereign LORD says: Because of your false words and lying visions, I am against you, declares the Sovereign LORD. [9]My hand will be against the prophets who see false visions and utter lying divinations. They will not belong to the council of my people or be listed in the records of the house of Israel, nor will they enter the land of Israel. Then you will know that I am the Sovereign LORD.

[10]" 'Because they lead my people astray, saying, "Peace," when there is no peace, and because, when a flimsy wall is built, they cover it with whitewash, [11]therefore tell those who cover it with whitewash that it is going to fall. Rain will come in torrents, and I will send hailstones hurtling down, and violent winds will burst forth. [12]When the wall collapses, will people not ask you, "Where is the whitewash you covered it with?"

[13]" 'Therefore this is what the Sovereign LORD says: In my wrath I will unleash a violent wind, and in my anger hailstones and torrents of rain will fall with destructive fury. [14]I will tear down the wall you have covered with whitewash and will level it to the ground so that its foundation will be laid bare. When it[a] falls, you will be destroyed in it; and you will know that I am the LORD. [15]So I will spend my wrath against the wall and against those who covered it with whitewash. I will say to you, "The wall is gone and so are those who whitewashed it, [16]those prophets of Israel who prophesied to Jerusalem and saw visions of peace for her when there was no peace, declares the Sovereign LORD." '

[17]"Now, son of man, set your face against the daughters of your people who prophesy out of their own imagination. Prophesy against them [18]and say, 'This is what the Sovereign LORD says: Woe to the women who sew magic charms on all their wrists and make veils of various lengths for their heads in order to ensnare people. Will you ensnare the lives of my people but preserve your own? [19]You have profaned me among my people for a few handfuls of barley and scraps of bread. By lying to my people, who listen to lies, you have killed those who should not have died and have spared those who should not live.

[a] 14 Or *the city*

THE MESSAGE

stand on GOD's Day of Judgment. All they do is fantasize comforting illusions and preach lying sermons. They say 'GOD says . . .' when GOD hasn't so much as breathed in their direction. And yet they stand around thinking that something they said is going to happen.

13:7-9 "Haven't you fantasized sheer nonsense? Aren't your sermons tissues of lies, saying 'GOD says . . .' when I've done nothing of the kind? Therefore—and this is the Message of GOD, the Master, remember—I'm dead set against prophets who substitute illusions for visions and use sermons to tell lies. I'm going to ban them from the council of my people, remove them from membership in Israel, and outlaw them from the land of Israel. Then you'll realize that I am GOD, the Master.

13:10-12 "The fact is that they've lied to my people. They've said, 'No problem; everything's just fine,' when things are not at all fine. When people build a wall, they're right behind them slapping on whitewash. Tell those who are slapping on the whitewash, 'When a torrent of rain comes and the hailstones crash down and the hurricane sweeps in and the wall collapses, what's the good of the whitewash that you slapped on so liberally, making it look so good?'

13:13-14 "And that's exactly what will happen. I, GOD, the Master, say so: 'I'll let the hurricane of my wrath loose, a torrent of my hailstone-anger. I'll make that wall you've slapped with whitewash collapse. I'll level it to the ground so that only the foundation stones will be left. And in the ruin you'll all die. You'll realize then that I am GOD.

13:15-16 " 'I'll dump my wrath on that wall, all of it, and on those who plastered it with whitewash. I will say to them, There is no wall, and those who did such a good job of whitewashing it wasted their time, those prophets of Israel who preached to Jerusalem and announced all their visions telling us things were just fine when they weren't at all fine. Decree of GOD, the Master.'

13:17-19 "And the women prophets—son of man, take your stand against the women prophets who make up stuff out of their own minds. Oppose them. Say 'Doom' to the women who sew magic bracelets and head scarves to suit every taste, devices to trap souls. Say, 'Will you kill the souls of my people, use living souls to make yourselves rich and popular? You have profaned me among my people just to get ahead yourselves, used me to make yourselves look good—killing souls who should never have died and coddling souls who shouldn't live. You've lied to people who love listening to lies.'

NEW INTERNATIONAL VERSION

²⁰" 'Therefore this is what the Sovereign LORD says: I am against your magic charms with which you ensnare people like birds and I will tear them from your arms; I will set free the people that you ensnare like birds. ²¹I will tear off your veils and save my people from your hands, and they will no longer fall prey to your power. Then you will know that I am the LORD. ²²Because you disheartened the righteous with your lies, when I had brought them no grief, and because you encouraged the wicked not to turn from their evil ways and so save their lives, ²³therefore you will no longer see false visions or practice divination. I will save my people from your hands. And then you will know that I am the LORD.' "

IDOLATERS CONDEMNED

14 Some of the elders of Israel came to me and sat down in front of me. ²Then the word of the LORD came to me: ³"Son of man, these men have set up idols in their hearts and put wicked stumbling blocks before their faces. Should I let them inquire of me at all? ⁴Therefore speak to them and tell them, 'This is what the Sovereign LORD says: When any Israelite sets up idols in his heart and puts a wicked stumbling block before his face and then goes to a prophet, I the LORD will answer him myself in keeping with his great idolatry. ⁵I will do this to recapture the hearts of the people of Israel, who have all deserted me for their idols.'

⁶"Therefore say to the house of Israel, 'This is what the Sovereign LORD says: Repent! Turn from your idols and renounce all your detestable practices!

⁷" 'When any Israelite or any alien living in Israel separates himself from me and sets up idols in his heart and puts a wicked stumbling block before his face and then goes to a prophet to inquire of me, I the LORD will answer him myself. ⁸I will set my face against that man and make him an example and a byword. I will cut him off from my people. Then you will know that I am the LORD.

⁹" 'And if the prophet is enticed to utter a prophecy, I the LORD have enticed that prophet, and I will stretch out my hand against him and destroy him from among my people Israel. ¹⁰They will bear their guilt—the prophet will be as guilty as the one who consults him. ¹¹Then the people of Israel will no longer stray from me, nor will they defile themselves anymore with all

THE MESSAGE

13.20-21   "Therefore GOD says, 'I am against all the devices and techniques you use to hunt down souls. I'll rip them out of your hands. I'll free the souls you're trying to catch. I'll rip your magic bracelets and scarves to shreds and deliver my people from your influence so they'll no longer be victimized by you. That's how you'll come to realize that I am GOD.

13.22-23   " 'Because you've confounded and confused good people, unsuspecting and innocent people, with your lies, and because you've made it easy for others to persist in evil so that it wouldn't even dawn on them to turn to me so I could save them, as of now you're finished. No more delusion-mongering from you, no more sermonic lies. I'm going to rescue my people from your clutches. And you'll realize that I am GOD.' "

IDOLS IN THEIR HEARTS

14.1-5   **14** Some of the leaders of Israel approached me and sat down with me. GOD's Message came to me: "Son of Man, these people have installed idols in their hearts. They have embraced the wickedness that will ruin them. Why should I even bother with their prayers? Therefore tell them, 'The Message of GOD, the Master: All in Israel who install idols in their hearts and embrace the wickedness that will ruin them and still have the gall to come to a prophet, be on notice: I, GOD, will step in and personally answer them as they come dragging along their mob of idols. I am ready to go to work on the hearts of the house of Israel, all of whom have left me for their idols.'

14.6-8   "Therefore, say to the house of Israel: 'GOD, the Master, says, Repent! Turn your backs on your no-god idols. Turn your backs on all your outrageous obscenities. To every last person from the house of Israel, including any of the resident aliens who live in Israel—all who turn their backs on me and embrace idols, who install the wickedness that will ruin them at the center of their lives and then have the gall to go to the prophet to ask me questions—I, GOD, will step in and give the answer myself. I'll oppose those people to their faces, make an example of them—a warning lesson—and get rid of them so you will realize that I am GOD.

14.9-11   " 'If a prophet is deceived and tells these idolaters the lies they want to hear, I, GOD, get blamed for those lies. He won't get by with it. I'll grab him by the scruff of the neck and get him out of there. They'll be equally guilty, the prophet and the one who goes to the prophet, so that the house of Israel will never again wander off my paths and make themselves filthy in their re-

NEW INTERNATIONAL VERSION

their sins. They will be my people, and I will be their God, declares the Sovereign LORD.' "

JUDGMENT INESCAPABLE

¹²The word of the LORD came to me: ¹³"Son of man, if a country sins against me by being unfaithful and I stretch out my hand against it to cut off its food supply and send famine upon it and kill its men and their animals, ¹⁴even if these three men—Noah, Daniel[a] and Job—were in it, they could save only themselves by their righteousness, declares the Sovereign LORD.

¹⁵"Or if I send wild beasts through that country and they leave it childless and it becomes desolate so that no one can pass through it because of the beasts, ¹⁶as surely as I live, declares the Sovereign LORD, even if these three men were in it, they could not save their own sons or daughters. They alone would be saved, but the land would be desolate.

¹⁷"Or if I bring a sword against that country and say, 'Let the sword pass throughout the land,' and I kill its men and their animals, ¹⁸as surely as I live, declares the Sovereign LORD, even if these three men were in it, they could not save their own sons or daughters. They alone would be saved.

¹⁹"Or if I send a plague into that land and pour out my wrath upon it through bloodshed, killing its men and their animals, ²⁰as surely as I live, declares the Sovereign LORD, even if Noah, Daniel and Job were in it, they could save neither son nor daughter. They would save only themselves by their righteousness.

²¹"For this is what the Sovereign LORD says: How much worse will it be when I send against Jerusalem my four dreadful judgments—sword and famine and wild beasts and plague—to kill its men and their animals! ²²Yet there will be some survivors—sons and daughters who will be brought out of it. They will come to you, and when you see their conduct and their actions, you will be consoled regarding the disaster I have brought upon Jerusalem—every disaster I have brought upon it. ²³You will be consoled when you see their conduct and their actions, for you will know that I have done nothing in it without cause, declares the Sovereign LORD."

JERUSALEM, A USELESS VINE

15 The word of the LORD came to me: ²"Son of man, how is the wood of a vine better than that of a branch on any of the trees in the

---

[a] *14 Or Danel*; the Hebrew spelling may suggest a person other than the prophet Daniel; also in verse 20.

THE MESSAGE

bellions, but will rather be my people, just as I am their God. Decree of GOD, the Master.' "

✝

14.12-14 GOD's Message came to me: "Son of man, when a country sins against me by living faithlessly and I reach out and destroy its food supply by bringing on a famine, wiping out humans and animals alike, even if Noah, Daniel, and Job—the Big Three—were alive at the time, it wouldn't do the population any good. Their righteousness would only save their own lives." Decree of GOD, the Master.

14.15-16 "Or, if I make wild animals go through the country so that everyone has to leave and the country becomes wilderness and no one dares enter it anymore because of the wild animals, even if these three men were living there, as sure as I am the living God, neither their sons nor daughters would be rescued, but only those three, and the country would revert to wilderness.

14.17-18 "Or, if I bring war on that country and give the order, 'Let the killing begin!' leaving both people and animals dead, even if those three men were alive at the time, as sure as I am the living God, neither sons nor daughters would be rescued, but only these three.

14.19-20 "Or, if I visit a deadly disease on that country, pouring out my lethal anger, killing both people and animals, and Noah, Daniel, and Job happened to be alive at the time, as sure as I am the living God, not a son, not a daughter, would be rescued. Only these three would be delivered because of their righteousness.

14.21-23 "Now then, that's the picture," says GOD, the Master, "once I've sent my four catastrophic judgments on Jerusalem—war, famine, wild animals, disease—to kill off people and animals alike. But look! Believe it or not, there'll be survivors. Some of their sons and daughters will be brought out. When they come out to you and their salvation is right in your face, you'll see for yourself the life they've been saved from. You'll know that this severe judgment I brought on Jerusalem was worth it, that it had to be. Yes, when you see in detail the kind of lives they've been living, you'll feel much better. You'll see the reason behind all that I've done in Jerusalem." Decree of GOD, the Master.

USED AS FUEL FOR THE FIRE

15.1-3 **15** GOD's Message came to me: "Son of man, how would you compare the wood of a vine with the branches of any tree

NEW INTERNATIONAL VERSION

forest? ³Is wood ever taken from it to make anything useful? Do they make pegs from it to hang things on? ⁴And after it is thrown on the fire as fuel and the fire burns both ends and chars the middle, is it then useful for anything? ⁵If it was not useful for anything when it was whole, how much less can it be made into something useful when the fire has burned it and it is charred?

⁶"Therefore this is what the Sovereign LORD says: As I have given the wood of the vine among the trees of the forest as fuel for the fire, so will I treat the people living in Jerusalem. ⁷I will set my face against them. Although they have come out of the fire, the fire will yet consume them. And when I set my face against them, you will know that I am the LORD. ⁸I will make the land desolate because they have been unfaithful, declares the Sovereign LORD."

AN ALLEGORY OF UNFAITHFUL JERUSALEM

16 The word of the LORD came to me: ²"Son of man, confront Jerusalem with her detestable practices ³and say, 'This is what the Sovereign LORD says to Jerusalem: Your ancestry and birth were in the land of the Canaanites; your father was an Amorite and your mother a Hittite. ⁴On the day you were born your cord was not cut, nor were you washed with water to make you clean, nor were you rubbed with salt or wrapped in cloths. ⁵No one looked on you with pity or had compassion enough to do any of these things for you. Rather, you were thrown out into the open field, for on the day you were born you were despised.

⁶" 'Then I passed by and saw you kicking about in your blood, and as you lay there in your blood I said to you, "Live!"ᵃ ⁷I made you grow like a plant of the field. You grew up and developed and became the most beautiful of jewels.ᵇ Your breasts were formed and your hair grew, you who were naked and bare.

⁸" 'Later I passed by, and when I looked at you and saw that you were old enough for love, I spread the corner of my garment over you and covered your nakedness. I gave you my solemn oath and entered into a covenant with you, declares the Sovereign LORD, and you became mine.

⁹" 'I bathedᶜ you with water and washed the blood from you and put ointments on you. ¹⁰I

THE MESSAGE

you'd find in the forest? Is vine wood ever used to make anything? Is it used to make pegs to hang things from?

15.4 "I don't think so. At best it's good for fuel. Look at it: a flimsy piece of vine, thrown in the fire and then rescued—the ends burned off and the middle charred. Now is it good for anything?

15.5 "Hardly. When it was whole it wasn't good for anything. Half-burned is no improvement. What's it good for?

15.6-8 "So here's the Message of GOD, the Master: Like the wood of the vine I selected from among the trees of the forest and used as fuel for the fire, just so I'll treat those who live in Jerusalem. I am dead set against them. Even though at one time they got out of the fire charred, the fire's going to burn them up. When I take my stand against them, you'll realize that I am GOD. I'll turn this country into a wilderness because they've been faithless." Decree of GOD, the Master.

YOUR BEAUTY WENT TO YOUR HEAD

16 GOD's Message came to me: "Son of man, confront Jerusalem with her outrageous violations. Say this: 'The Message of GOD, the Master, to Jerusalem: You were born and bred among Canaanites. Your father was an Amorite and your mother a Hittite.

16.4-5 " 'On the day you were born your umbilical cord was not cut, you weren't bathed and cleaned up, you weren't rubbed with salt, you weren't wrapped in a baby blanket. No one cared a fig for you. No one did one thing to care for you tenderly in these ways. You were thrown out into a vacant lot and left there, dirty and unwashed—a newborn nobody wanted.

16.6-7 " 'And then I came by. I saw you all miserable and bloody. Yes, I said to you, lying there helpless and filthy, "Live! Grow up like a plant in the field!" And you did. You grew up. You grew tall and matured as a woman, full-breasted, with flowing hair. But you were naked and vulnerable, fragile and exposed.

16.8-14 " 'I came by again and saw you, saw that you were ready for love and a lover. I took care of you, dressed you and protected you. I promised you my love and entered the covenant of marriage with you. I, GOD, the Master, gave my word. You became mine. I gave you a good bath, washing off all that old blood, and anointed you with aromatic oils. I dressed you in a colorful

---

ᵃ 6 A few Hebrew manuscripts, Septuagint and Syriac; most Hebrew manuscripts *"Live!" And as you lay there in your blood I said to you, "Live!"*   ᵇ 7 Or *became mature*
ᶜ 9 Or *I had bathed*

NEW INTERNATIONAL VERSION

clothed you with an embroidered dress and put leather sandals on you. I dressed you in fine linen and covered you with costly garments. ¹¹I adorned you with jewelry: I put bracelets on your arms and a necklace around your neck, ¹²and I put a ring on your nose, earrings on your ears and a beautiful crown on your head. ¹³So you were adorned with gold and silver; your clothes were of fine linen and costly fabric and embroidered cloth. Your food was fine flour, honey and olive oil. You became very beautiful and rose to be a queen. ¹⁴And your fame spread among the nations on account of your beauty, because the splendor I had given you made your beauty perfect, declares the Sovereign LORD.

¹⁵ 'But you trusted in your beauty and used your fame to become a prostitute. You lavished your favors on anyone who passed by and your beauty became his.ª ¹⁶You took some of your garments to make gaudy high places, where you carried on your prostitution. Such things should not happen, nor should they ever occur. ¹⁷You also took the fine jewelry I gave you, the jewelry made of my gold and silver, and you made for yourself male idols and engaged in prostitution with them. ¹⁸And you took your embroidered clothes to put on them, and you offered my oil and incense before them. ¹⁹Also the food I provided for you—the fine flour, olive oil and honey I gave you to eat—you offered as fragrant incense before them. That is what happened, declares the Sovereign LORD.

²⁰ 'And you took your sons and daughters whom you bore to me and sacrificed them as food to the idols. Was your prostitution not enough? ²¹You slaughtered my children and sacrificed themᵇ to the idols. ²²In all your detestable practices and your prostitution you did not remember the days of your youth, when you were naked and bare, kicking about in your blood.

²³ 'Woe! Woe to you, declares the Sovereign LORD. In addition to all your other wickedness, ²⁴you built a mound for yourself and made a lofty shrine in every public square. ²⁵At the head of every street you built your lofty shrines and degraded your beauty, offering your body with increasing promiscuity to anyone who passed by. ²⁶You engaged in prostitution with the Egyptians, your lustful neighbors, and provoked me to anger with your increasing promiscuity. ²⁷So I stretched out my hand against you and reduced your territory; I gave you over to the greed of your enemies, the daughters of the Philistines, who were shocked by your lewd conduct. ²⁸You

ª 15 Most Hebrew manuscripts; one Hebrew manuscript (see some Septuagint manuscripts) *by. Such a thing should not happen*   ᵇ 21 Or *and made them pass through ⸤the fire⸥*

THE MESSAGE

gown and put leather sandals on your feet. I gave you linen blouses and a fashionable wardrobe of expensive clothing. I adorned you with jewelry: I placed bracelets on your wrists, fitted you out with a necklace, emerald rings, sapphire earrings, and a diamond tiara. You were provided with everything precious and beautiful: with exquisite clothes and elegant food, garnished with honey and oil. You were absolutely stunning. You were a queen! You became world-famous, a legendary beauty brought to perfection by my adornments. Decree of GOD, the Master.

16.15-16   " 'But your beauty went to your head and you became a common whore, grabbing anyone coming down the street and taking him into your bed. You took your fine dresses and made "tents" of them, using them as brothels in which you practiced your trade. This kind of thing should never happen, never.

WHAT A SICK SOUL!

16.17-19   " 'And then you took all that fine jewelry I gave you, my gold and my silver, and made pornographic images of them for your brothels. You decorated your beds with fashionable silks and cottons, and perfumed them with my aromatic oils and incense. And then you set out the wonderful foods I provided—the fresh breads and fruits, with fine herbs and spices, which were my gifts to you—and you served them as delicacies in your whorehouses. That's what happened, says GOD, the Master.

16.20-21   " 'And then you took your sons and your daughters, whom you had given birth to as my children, and you killed them, sacrificing them to idols. Wasn't it bad enough that you had become a whore? And now you're a murderer, killing my children and sacrificing them to idols.

16.22   " 'Not once during these years of outrageous obscenities and whorings did you remember your infancy, when you were naked and exposed, a blood-smeared newborn.

16.23-24   " 'And then to top off all your evil acts, you built your bold brothels in every town square. Doom! Doom to you, says GOD, the Master! At every major intersection you built your bold brothels and exposed your sluttish sex, spreading your legs for everyone who passed by.

16.25-27   " 'And then you went international with your whoring. You fornicated with the Egyptians, seeking them out in their sex orgies. The more promiscuous you became, the angrier I got. Finally, I intervened, reduced your borders and turned you over to the rapacity of your enemies. Even the Philistine women—can you believe it?—were shocked at your sluttish life.

NEW INTERNATIONAL VERSION

engaged in prostitution with the Assyrians too, because you were insatiable; and even after that, you still were not satisfied. ²⁹Then you increased your promiscuity to include Babylonia,^{*a*} a land of merchants, but even with this you were not satisfied.

³⁰" 'How weak-willed you are, declares the Sovereign LORD, when you do all these things, acting like a brazen prostitute! ³¹When you built your mounds at the head of every street and made your lofty shrines in every public square, you were unlike a prostitute, because you scorned payment.

³²" 'You adulterous wife! You prefer strangers to your own husband! ³³Every prostitute receives a fee, but you give gifts to all your lovers, bribing them to come to you from everywhere for your illicit favors. ³⁴So in your prostitution you are the opposite of others; no one runs after you for your favors. You are the very opposite, for you give payment and none is given to you.

³⁵" 'Therefore, you prostitute, hear the word of the LORD! ³⁶This is what the Sovereign LORD says: Because you poured out your wealth^{*b*} and exposed your nakedness in your promiscuity with your lovers, and because of all your detestable idols, and because you gave them your children's blood, ³⁷therefore I am going to gather all your lovers, with whom you found pleasure, those you loved as well as those you hated. I will gather them against you from all around and will strip you in front of them, and they will see all your nakedness. ³⁸I will sentence you to the punishment of women who commit adultery and who shed blood; I will bring upon you the blood vengeance of my wrath and jealous anger. ³⁹Then I will hand you over to your lovers, and they will tear down your mounds and destroy your lofty shrines. They will strip you of your clothes and take your fine jewelry and leave you naked and bare. ⁴⁰They will bring a mob against you, who will stone you and hack you to pieces with their swords. ⁴¹They will burn down your houses and inflict punishment on you in the sight of many women. I will put a stop to your prostitution, and you will no longer pay your lovers. ⁴²Then my wrath against you will subside and my jealous anger will turn away from you; I will be calm and no longer angry.

⁴³" 'Because you did not remember the days of your youth but enraged me with all these things, I will surely bring down on your head what you have done, declares the Sovereign LORD. Did you not add lewdness to all your other detestable practices?

⁴⁴" 'Everyone who quotes proverbs will quote

^{*a*} 29 Or *Chaldea*   ^{*b*} 36 Or *lust*

THE MESSAGE

16.28-29   " 'You went on to fornicate with the Assyrians. Your appetite was insatiable. But still you weren't satisfied. You took on the Babylonians, a country of businessmen, and *still* you weren't satisfied.

16.30-31   " 'What a sick soul! Doing all this stuff—the champion whore! You built your bold brothels at every major intersection, opened up your whorehouses in every neighborhood, but you were different from regular whores in that you wouldn't accept a fee.

16.32-34   " 'Wives who are unfaithful to their husbands accept gifts from their lovers. And men commonly pay their whores. But you pay your lovers! You bribe men from all over to come to bed with you! You're just the opposite of the regular whores who get paid for sex. Instead, you pay men for *their* favors! You even pervert whoredom!

16.35-38   " 'Therefore, whore, listen to GOD's Message: I, GOD, the Master, say, Because you've been unrestrained in your promiscuity, stripped down for every lover, flaunting your sex, and because of your pornographic idols and all the slaughtered children you offered to them, therefore, because of all this, I'm going to get all your lovers together, all those you've used for your own pleasure, the ones you loved and the ones you loathed. I'll assemble them as a courtroom of spectators around you. In broad daylight I'll strip you naked before them— they'll see what you *really* look like. Then I'll sentence you to the punishment for an adulterous woman and a murderous woman. I'll give you a taste of my wrath!

16.39-41   " 'I'll gather all your lovers around you and turn you over to them. They'll tear down your bold brothels and sex shrines. They'll rip off your clothes, take your jewels, and leave you naked and exposed. Then they'll call for a mass meeting. The mob will stone you and hack you to pieces with their swords. They'll burn down your houses. A massive judgment—with all the women watching!

16.41-42   " 'I'll have put a full stop to your whoring life—no more paying lovers to come to your bed! By then my anger will be played out. My jealousy will subside.

16.43   " 'Because you didn't remember what happened when you were young but made me angry with all this behavior, I'll make you pay for your waywardness. Didn't you just exponentially compound your outrageous obscenities with all your sluttish ways?

16.44-45   " 'Everyone who likes to use proverbs will

NEW INTERNATIONAL VERSION

this proverb about you: "Like mother, like daughter." [45]You are a true daughter of your mother, who despised her husband and her children; and you are a true sister of your sisters, who despised their husbands and their children. Your mother was a Hittite and your father an Amorite. [46]Your older sister was Samaria, who lived to the north of you with her daughters; and your younger sister, who lived to the south of you with her daughters, was Sodom. [47]You not only walked in their ways and copied their detestable practices, but in all your ways you soon became more depraved than they. [48]As surely as I live, declares the Sovereign LORD, your sister Sodom and her daughters never did what you and your daughters have done.

[49]" 'Now this was the sin of your sister Sodom: She and her daughters were arrogant, overfed and unconcerned; they did not help the poor and needy. [50]They were haughty and did detestable things before me. Therefore I did away with them as you have seen. [51]Samaria did not commit half the sins you did. You have done more detestable things than they, and have made your sisters seem righteous by all these things you have done. [52]Bear your disgrace, for you have furnished some justification for your sisters. Because your sins were more vile than theirs, they appear more righteous than you. So then, be ashamed and bear your disgrace, for you have made your sisters appear righteous.

[53]" 'However, I will restore the fortunes of Sodom and her daughters and of Samaria and her daughters, and your fortunes along with them, [54]so that you may bear your disgrace and be ashamed of all you have done in giving them comfort. [55]And your sisters, Sodom with her daughters and Samaria with her daughters, will return to what they were before; and you and your daughters will return to what you were before. [56]You would not even mention your sister Sodom in the day of your pride, [57]before your wickedness was uncovered. Even so, you are now scorned by the daughters of Edom[a] and all her neighbors and the daughters of the Philistines—all those around you who despise you. [58]You will bear the consequences of your lewdness and your detestable practices, declares the LORD.

[59]" 'This is what the Sovereign LORD says: I will deal with you as you deserve, because you have despised my oath by breaking the covenant. [60]Yet I will remember the covenant I made with

---

[a] 57 Many Hebrew manuscripts and Syriac; most Hebrew manuscripts, Septuagint and Vulgate *Aram*

THE MESSAGE

use this one: "Like mother, like daughter." You're the daughter of your mother, who couldn't stand her husband and children. And you're a true sister of your sisters, who couldn't stand their husbands and children. Your mother was a Hittite and your father an Amorite.

16.46-48 " 'Your older sister is Samaria. She lived to the north of you with her daughters. Your younger sister is Sodom, who lived to the south of you with her daughters. Haven't you lived just like they did? Haven't you engaged in outrageous obscenities just like they did? In fact, it didn't take you long to catch up and pass them! As sure as I am the living God!—Decree of GOD, the Master—your sister Sodom and her daughters never even came close to what you and your daughters have done.

16.49-50 " 'The sin of your sister Sodom was this: She lived with her daughters in the lap of luxury—proud, gluttonous, and lazy. They ignored the oppressed and the poor. They put on airs and lived obscene lives. And you know what happened: I did away with them.

16.51-52 " 'And Samaria. Samaria didn't sin half as much as you. You've committed far more obscenities than she ever did. Why, you make your two sisters look good in comparison with what you've done! Face it, your sisters look mighty good compared with you. Because you've outsinned them so completely, you've actually made them look righteous. Aren't you ashamed? But you're going to have to live with it. What a reputation to carry into history: outsinning your two sisters!

16.53-58 " 'But I'm going to reverse their fortunes, the fortunes of Sodom and her daughters and the fortunes of Samaria and her daughters. And—get this—*your* fortunes right along with them! Still, you're going to have to live with your shame. And by facing and accepting your shame, you're going to provide some comfort to your two sisters. Your sisters, Sodom with her daughters and Samaria with her daughters, will become what they were before, and you will become what you were before. Remember the days when you were putting on airs, acting so high and mighty, looking down on sister Sodom? That was before your evil ways were exposed. And now *you're* the butt of contempt, despised by the Edomite women, the Philistine women, and everybody else around. But you have to face it, to accept the shame of your obscene and vile life. Decree of GOD, the Master.

16.59-63 " 'GOD, the Master, says, I'll do to you just as you have already done, you who have treated my oath with contempt and broken the covenant. All the same, I'll remember the covenant

NEW INTERNATIONAL VERSION

you in the days of your youth, and I will establish an everlasting covenant with you. 61Then you will remember your ways and be ashamed when you receive your sisters, both those who are older than you and those who are younger. I will give them to you as daughters, but not on the basis of my covenant with you. 62So I will establish my covenant with you, and you will know that I am the LORD. 63Then, when I make atonement for you for all you have done, you will remember and be ashamed and never again open your mouth because of your humiliation, declares the Sovereign LORD.' "

TWO EAGLES AND A VINE

17 The word of the LORD came to me: 2"Son of man, set forth an allegory and tell the house of Israel a parable. 3Say to them, 'This is what the Sovereign LORD says: A great eagle with powerful wings, long feathers and full plumage of varied colors came to Lebanon. Taking hold of the top of a cedar, 4he broke off its topmost shoot and carried it away to a land of merchants, where he planted it in a city of traders.

5" 'He took some of the seed of your land and put it in fertile soil. He planted it like a willow by abundant water, 6and it sprouted and became a low, spreading vine. Its branches turned toward him, but its roots remained under it. So it became a vine and produced branches and put out leafy boughs.

7" 'But there was another great eagle with powerful wings and full plumage. The vine now sent out its roots toward him from the plot where it was planted and stretched out its branches to him for water. 8It had been planted in good soil by abundant water so that it would produce branches, bear fruit and become a splendid vine.'

9"Say to them, 'This is what the Sovereign LORD says: Will it thrive? Will it not be uprooted and stripped of its fruit so that it withers? All its new growth will wither. It will not take a strong

THE MESSAGE

I made with you when you were young and I'll make a new covenant with you that will last forever. You'll remember your sorry past and be properly contrite when you receive back your sisters, both the older and the younger. I'll give them to you as daughters, but not as participants in your covenant. I'll firmly establish my covenant with you and you'll know that I am GOD. You'll remember your past life and face the shame of it, but when I make atonement for you, make everything right after all you've done, it will leave you speechless.' "
Decree of GOD, the Master.

THE GREAT TREE IS MADE SMALL AND THE SMALL TREE GREAT

17.1-6 **17** GOD's Message came to me: "Son of man, make a riddle for the house of Israel. Tell them a story. Say, 'GOD, the Master, says:

" 'A great eagle
  with a huge wingspan and long feathers,
In full plumage and bright colors,
  came to Lebanon
And took the top off a cedar,
  broke off the top branch,
Took it to a land of traders,
  and set it down in a city of shopkeepers.
Then he took a cutting from the land
  and planted it in good, well-watered soil,
  like a willow on a riverbank.
It sprouted into a flourishing vine,
  low to the ground.
Its branches grew toward the eagle
  and the roots became established—
A vine putting out shoots,
  developing branches.

17.7-8 " 'There was another great eagle
  with a huge wingspan and thickly
    feathered.
This vine sent out its roots toward him
  from the place where it was planted.
Its branches reached out to him
  so he could water it
  from a long distance.
It had been planted
  in good, well-watered soil,
And it put out branches and bore fruit,
  and became a noble vine.

17.9-10 " 'GOD, the Master, says,
  Will it thrive?
Won't he just pull it up by the roots
  and leave the grapes to rot
And the branches to shrivel up,
  a withered, dead vine?
It won't take much strength

NEW INTERNATIONAL VERSION

arm or many people to pull it up by the roots. ¹⁰Even if it is transplanted, will it thrive? Will it not wither completely when the east wind strikes it—wither away in the plot where it grew?' "

¹¹Then the word of the LORD came to me: ¹²"Say to this rebellious house, 'Do you not know what these things mean?' Say to them: 'The king of Babylon went to Jerusalem and carried off her king and her nobles, bringing them back with him to Babylon. ¹³Then he took a member of the royal family and made a treaty with him, putting him under oath. He also carried away the leading men of the land, ¹⁴so that the kingdom would be brought low, unable to rise again, surviving only by keeping his treaty. ¹⁵But the king rebelled against him by sending his envoys to Egypt to get horses and a large army. Will he succeed? Will he who does such things escape? Will he break the treaty and yet escape?

¹⁶" 'As surely as I live, declares the Sovereign LORD, he shall die in Babylon, in the land of the king who put him on the throne, whose oath he despised and whose treaty he broke. ¹⁷Pharaoh with his mighty army and great horde will be of no help to him in war, when ramps are built and siege works erected to destroy many lives. ¹⁸He despised the oath by breaking the covenant. Because he had given his hand in pledge and yet did all these things, he shall not escape.

¹⁹" 'Therefore this is what the Sovereign LORD says: As surely as I live, I will bring down on his head my oath that he despised and my covenant that he broke. ²⁰I will spread my net for him, and he will be caught in my snare. I will bring him to Babylon and execute judgment upon him there because he was unfaithful to me. ²¹All his fleeing troops will fall by the sword, and the survivors will be scattered to the winds. Then you will know that I the LORD have spoken.

²²"'This is what the Sovereign LORD says: I myself will take a shoot from the very top of a cedar and plant it; I will break off a tender sprig from its topmost shoots and plant it on a high and lofty mountain. ²³On the mountain heights of Israel I will plant it; it will produce branches and bear fruit and become a splendid cedar. Birds of every kind will nest in it; they will find shelter in the shade of its branches. ²⁴All the trees of the field will know that I the LORD bring down the tall tree and make the low tree grow

THE MESSAGE

or many hands to pull it up.
Even if it's transplanted,
  will it thrive?
When the hot east wind strikes it,
  won't it shrivel up?
Won't it dry up and blow away
  from the place where it was planted?' "

✝

17.11-12 GOD's Message came to me: "Tell this house of rebels, 'Do you get it? Do you know what this means?'

17.12-14 "Tell them, 'The king of Babylon came to Jerusalem and took its king and its leaders back to Babylon. He took one of the royal family and made a covenant with him, making him swear his loyalty. The king of Babylon took all the top leaders into exile to make sure that this kingdom stayed weak—didn't get any big ideas of itself—and kept the covenant with him so that it would have a future.

17.15 " 'But he rebelled and sent emissaries to Egypt to recruit horses and a big army. Do you think that's going to work? Are they going to get by with this? Does anyone break a covenant and get off scot-free?

17.16-18 " 'As sure as I am the living God, this king who broke his pledge of loyalty and his covenant will die in that country, in Babylon. Pharaoh with his big army—all those soldiers!—won't lift a finger to fight for him when Babylon sets siege to the city and kills everyone inside. Because he broke his word and broke the covenant, even though he gave his solemn promise, because he went ahead and did all these things anyway, he won't escape.

17.19-21 " 'Therefore, GOD, the Master, says, As sure as I am the living God, because the king despised my oath and broke my covenant, I'll bring the consequences crashing down on his head. I'll send out a search party and catch him. I'll take him to Babylon and have him brought to trial because of his total disregard for me. All his elite soldiers, along with the rest of the army, will be killed in battle, and whoever is left will be scattered to the four winds. Then you'll realize that I, GOD, have spoken.

17.22-24 " 'GOD, the Master, says, I personally will take a shoot from the top of the towering cedar, a cutting from the crown of the tree, and plant it on a high and towering mountain, on the high mountain of Israel. It will grow, putting out branches and fruit—a majestic cedar. Birds of every sort and kind will live under it. They'll build nests in the shade of its branches. All the trees of the field will recognize that I, GOD, made the great tree small and the small tree

NEW INTERNATIONAL VERSION

tall. I dry up the green tree and make the dry tree flourish.

" 'I the LORD have spoken, and I will do it.' "

THE SOUL WHO SINS WILL DIE

18 The word of the LORD came to me: 2 "What do you people mean by quoting this proverb about the land of Israel:

" 'The fathers eat sour grapes,
  and the children's teeth are set on edge'?

3 "As surely as I live, declares the Sovereign LORD, you will no longer quote this proverb in Israel. 4 For every living soul belongs to me, the father as well as the son—both alike belong to me. The soul who sins is the one who will die.

5 "Suppose there is a righteous man
  who does what is just and right.
6 He does not eat at the mountain shrines
  or look to the idols of the house of Israel.
He does not defile his neighbor's wife
  or lie with a woman during her period.
7 He does not oppress anyone,
  but returns what he took in pledge for a
    loan.
He does not commit robbery
  but gives his food to the hungry
  and provides clothing for the naked.
8 He does not lend at usury
  or take excessive interest. *a*
He withholds his hand from doing wrong
  and judges fairly between man and man.
9 He follows my decrees
  and faithfully keeps my laws.
That man is righteous;
  he will surely live,
              declares the Sovereign
                        LORD.

10 "Suppose he has a violent son, who sheds blood or does any of these other things *b* 11 (though the father has done none of them):

"He eats at the mountain shrines.
He defiles his neighbor's wife.
12 He oppresses the poor and needy.
He commits robbery.
He does not return what he took in pledge.
He looks to the idols.
He does detestable things.
13 He lends at usury and takes excessive interest.

Will such a man live? He will not! Because he has done all these detestable things, he will surely be put to death and his blood will be on his own head.

THE MESSAGE

great, made the green tree turn dry and the dry tree sprout green branches. I, GOD, said it— and I did it.' "

JUDGED ACCORDING TO THE WAY YOU LIVE

18.1-2 **18** GOD's Message to me: "What do you people mean by going around the country repeating the saying,

The parents ate green apples,
The children got stomachache?

18.3-4 "As sure as I'm the living God, you're not going to repeat this saying in Israel any longer. Every soul—man, woman, child—belongs to me, parent and child alike. You die for your own sin, not another's.

18.5-9 "Imagine a person who lives well, treating others fairly, keeping good relationships—

doesn't eat at the pagan shrines,
doesn't worship the idols so popular in
  Israel,
doesn't seduce a neighbor's spouse,
doesn't indulge in casual sex,
doesn't bully anyone,
doesn't pile up bad debts,
doesn't steal,
doesn't refuse food to the hungry,
doesn't refuse clothing to the ill-clad,
doesn't exploit the poor,
doesn't live by impulse and greed,
doesn't treat one person better than
  another,
But lives by my statutes and faithfully
  honors and obeys my laws.
This person who lives upright and well
  shall live a full and true life.
      Decree of GOD, the Master.

18.10-13 "But if this person has a child who turns violent and murders and goes off and does any of these things, even though the parent has done none of them—

eats at the pagan shrines,
seduces his neighbor's spouse,
bullies the weak,
steals,
piles up bad debts,
admires idols,
commits outrageous obscenities,
exploits the poor

"—do you think this person, the child, will live? Not a chance! Because he's done all these vile things, he'll die. And his death will be his own fault.

---

a 8 Or *take interest;* similarly in verses 13 and 17
b 10 Or *things to a brother*

NEW INTERNATIONAL VERSION

¹⁴"But suppose this son has a son who sees all the sins his father commits, and though he sees them, he does not do such things:

¹⁵"He does not eat at the mountain shrines
　　or look to the idols of the house of Israel.
　He does not defile his neighbor's wife.
¹⁶He does not oppress anyone
　　or require a pledge for a loan.
　He does not commit robbery
　　but gives his food to the hungry
　　and provides clothing for the naked.
¹⁷He withholds his hand from sin[a]
　　and takes no usury or excessive interest.
　He keeps my laws and follows my decrees.

He will not die for his father's sin; he will surely live. ¹⁸But his father will die for his own sin, because he practiced extortion, robbed his brother and did what was wrong among his people.

¹⁹"Yet you ask, 'Why does the son not share the guilt of his father?' Since the son has done what is just and right and has been careful to keep all my decrees, he will surely live. ²⁰The soul who sins is the one who will die. The son will not share the guilt of the father, nor will the father share the guilt of the son. The righteousness of the righteous man will be credited to him, and the wickedness of the wicked will be charged against him.

²¹"But if a wicked man turns away from all the sins he has committed and keeps all my decrees and does what is just and right, he will surely live; he will not die. ²²None of the offenses he has committed will be remembered against him. Because of the righteous things he has done, he will live. ²³Do I take any pleasure in the death of the wicked? declares the Sovereign LORD. Rather, am I not pleased when they turn from their ways and live?

²⁴"But if a righteous man turns from his righteousness and commits sin and does the same detestable things the wicked man does, will he live? None of the righteous things he has done will be remembered. Because of the unfaithfulness he is guilty of and because of the sins he has committed, he will die.

THE MESSAGE

18.14-17　"Now look: Suppose that this child has a child who sees all the sins done by his parent. The child sees them, but doesn't follow in the parent's footsteps—

　　doesn't eat at the pagan shrines,
　　doesn't worship the popular idols of
　　　Israel,
　　doesn't seduce his neighbor's spouse,
　　doesn't bully anyone,
　　doesn't refuse to loan money,
　　doesn't steal,
　　doesn't refuse food to the hungry,
　　doesn't refuse to give clothes to the ill-
　　　clad,
　　doesn't live by impulse and greed,
　　doesn't exploit the poor.
　He does what I say;
　　he performs my laws and lives by my
　　　statutes.

18.17-18　"This person will not die for the sins of the parent; he will live truly and well. But the parent will die for what the parent did, for the sins of—

　　oppressing the weak,
　　robbing brothers and sisters,
　　doing what is dead wrong in the
　　　community.

18.19-20　"Do you need to ask, 'So why does the child not share the guilt of the parent?'

　"Isn't it plain? It's because the child did what is fair and right. Since the child was careful to do what is lawful and right, the child will live truly and well. The soul that sins is the soul that dies. The child does not share the guilt of the parent, nor the parent the guilt of the child. If you live upright and well, you get the credit; if you live a wicked life, you're guilty as charged.

18.21-23　"But a wicked person who turns his back on that life of sin and keeps all my statutes, living a just and righteous life, he'll live, really live. He won't die. I won't keep a list of all the things he did wrong. He will live. Do you think I take any pleasure in the death of wicked men and women? Isn't it my pleasure that they turn around, no longer living wrong but living right—really living?

18.24　"The same thing goes for a good person who turns his back on an upright life and starts sinning, plunging into the same vile obscenities that the wicked person practices. Will this person live? I don't keep a list of all the things this person did right, like money in the bank he can draw on. Because of his defection, because he accumulates sin, he'll die.

[a] 17 Septuagint (see also verse 8); Hebrew *from the poor*

NEW INTERNATIONAL VERSION

25 "Yet you say, 'The way of the Lord is not just.' Hear, O house of Israel: Is my way unjust? Is it not your ways that are unjust? 26 If a righteous man turns from his righteousness and commits sin, he will die for it; because of the sin he has committed he will die. 27 But if a wicked man turns away from the wickedness he has committed and does what is just and right, he will save his life. 28 Because he considers all the offenses he has committed and turns away from them, he will surely live; he will not die. 29 Yet the house of Israel says, 'The way of the Lord is not just.' Are my ways unjust, O house of Israel? Is it not your ways that are unjust?

30 "Therefore, O house of Israel, I will judge you, each one according to his ways, declares the Sovereign Lord. Repent! Turn away from all your offenses; then sin will not be your downfall. 31 Rid yourselves of all the offenses you have committed, and get a new heart and a new spirit. Why will you die, O house of Israel? 32 For I take no pleasure in the death of anyone, declares the Sovereign Lord. Repent and live!

A Lament for Israel's Princes

19 "Take up a lament concerning the princes of Israel 2 and say:

" 'What a lioness was your mother
    among the lions!
She lay down among the young lions
    and reared her cubs.
3 She brought up one of her cubs,
    and he became a strong lion.
He learned to tear the prey
    and he devoured men.
4 The nations heard about him,
    and he was trapped in their pit.
They led him with hooks
    to the land of Egypt.

5 " 'When she saw her hope unfulfilled,
    her expectation gone,
she took another of her cubs
    and made him a strong lion.
6 He prowled among the lions,
    for he was now a strong lion.
He learned to tear the prey
    and he devoured men.
7 He broke down[a] their strongholds
    and devastated their towns.
The land and all who were in it
    were terrified by his roaring.
8 Then the nations came against him,
    those from regions round about.
They spread their net for him,

[a] 7 Targum (see Septuagint); Hebrew He knew

THE MESSAGE

18.25-28 "Do I hear you saying, 'That's not fair! God's not fair!'?

"Listen, Israel. I'm not fair? You're the ones who aren't fair! If a good person turns away from his good life and takes up sinning, he'll die for it. He'll die for his own sin. Likewise, if a bad person turns away from his bad life and starts living a good life, a fair life, he will save his life. Because he faces up to all the wrongs he's committed and puts them behind him, he will live, really live. He won't die.

18.29 "And yet Israel keeps on whining, 'That's not fair! God's not fair.'

"I'm not fair, Israel? You're the ones who aren't fair.

18.30-32 "The upshot is this, Israel: I'll judge each of you according to the way you live. So turn around! Turn your backs on your rebellious living so that sin won't drag you down. Clean house. No more rebellions, please. Get a new heart! Get a new spirit! Why would you choose to die, Israel? I take no pleasure in anyone's death. Decree of God, the Master.

"Make a clean break! Live!"

A Story of Two Lions

19.1-4 **19** Sing the blues over the princes of Israel. Say:

What a lioness was your mother
    among lions!
She crouched in a pride of young lions.
    Her cubs grew large.
She reared one of her cubs to maturity,
    a robust young lion.
He learned to hunt.
    He ate men.
Nations sounded the alarm.
    He was caught in a trap.
They took him with hooks
    and dragged him to Egypt.

19.5-9 When the lioness saw she was luckless,
    that her hope for that cub was gone,
She took her other cub
    and made him a strong young lion.
He prowled with the lions,
    a robust young lion.
He learned to hunt.
    He ate men.
He rampaged through their defenses,
    left their cities in ruins.
The country and everyone in it
    was terrorized by the roars of the lion.
The nations got together to hunt him.
    Everyone joined the hunt.
They set out their traps

NEW INTERNATIONAL VERSION

and he was trapped in their pit.
⁹ With hooks they pulled him into a cage
    and brought him to the king of Babylon.
They put him in prison,
    so his roar was heard no longer
    on the mountains of Israel.

¹⁰ " 'Your mother was like a vine in your
    vineyard*ᵃ*
    planted by the water;
it was fruitful and full of branches
    because of abundant water.
¹¹ Its branches were strong,
    fit for a ruler's scepter.
It towered high
    above the thick foliage,
conspicuous for its height
    and for its many branches.
¹² But it was uprooted in fury
    and thrown to the ground.
The east wind made it shrivel,
    it was stripped of its fruit;
its strong branches withered
    and fire consumed them.
¹³ Now it is planted in the desert,
    in a dry and thirsty land.
¹⁴ Fire spread from one of its main*ᵇ* branches
    and consumed its fruit.
No strong branch is left on it
    fit for a ruler's scepter.'

This is a lament and is to be used as a lament."

Rebellious Israel

20 In the seventh year, in the fifth month on the tenth day, some of the elders of Israel came to inquire of the LORD, and they sat down in front of me.

² Then the word of the LORD came to me: ³ "Son of man, speak to the elders of Israel and say to them, 'This is what the Sovereign LORD says: Have you come to inquire of me? As surely as I live, I will not let you inquire of me, declares the Sovereign LORD.'

⁴ "Will you judge them? Will you judge them, son of man? Then confront them with the detestable practices of their fathers ⁵ and say to them: 'This is what the Sovereign LORD says: On the day I chose Israel, I swore with uplifted hand to the descendants of the house of Jacob and revealed myself to them in Egypt. With uplifted hand I said to them, "I am the LORD your God." ⁶ On that day I swore to them that I would bring them out of Egypt into a land I had searched out

THE MESSAGE

and caught him.
They put a wooden collar on him
    and took him to the king of Babylon.
No more would that voice be heard
    disturbing the peace in the mountains of
        Israel!

¹⁹·¹⁰⁻¹⁴ Here's another way to put it:
    Your mother was like a vine in a vineyard,
        transplanted alongside streams of water,
    Luxurious in branches and grapes
        because of the ample water.
    It grew sturdy branches
        fit to be carved into a royal scepter.
    It grew high, reaching into the clouds.
        Its branches filled the horizon,
        and everyone could see it.
    Then it was ripped up in a rage
        and thrown to the ground.
    The hot east wind shriveled it up
        and stripped its fruit.
    The sturdy branches dried out,
        fit for nothing but kindling.
    Now it's a stick stuck out in the desert,
        a bare stick in a desert of death,
    Good for nothing but making fires,
        campfires in the desert.
    Not a hint now of those sturdy branches
        fit for use as a royal scepter!

(This is a sad song, a text for singing the blues.)

GET RID OF ALL THE THINGS YOU'VE BECOME ADDICTED TO

²⁰·¹ **20** In the seventh year, the fifth month, on the tenth day of the month, some of the leaders of Israel came to ask for guidance from GOD. They sat down before me.

²⁰·²⁻³ Then GOD's Message came to me: "Son of man, talk with the leaders of Israel. Tell them, 'GOD, the Master, says, "Have you come to ask me questions? As sure as I am the living God, I'll not put up with questions from you. Decree of GOD, the Master." '

²⁰·⁴⁻⁵ "Son of man, why don't *you* do it? Yes, go ahead. Hold them accountable. Confront them with the outrageous obscenities of their parents. Tell them that GOD, the Master, says:

²⁰·⁵⁻⁶ " 'On the day I chose Israel, I revealed myself to them in the country of Egypt, raising my hand in a solemn oath to the people of Jacob, in which I said, "I am GOD, your personal God." On the same day that I raised my hand in the solemn oath, I promised them that I would take them out of the country of Egypt and bring them into a country that I had

---

ᵃ 10 Two Hebrew manuscripts; most Hebrew manuscripts
your blood   *ᵇ 14* Or *from under its*

NEW INTERNATIONAL VERSION

for them, a land flowing with milk and honey, the most beautiful of all lands. [7]And I said to them, "Each of you, get rid of the vile images you have set your eyes on, and do not defile yourselves with the idols of Egypt. I am the Lord your God."

[8]" 'But they rebelled against me and would not listen to me; they did not get rid of the vile images they had set their eyes on, nor did they forsake the idols of Egypt. So I said I would pour out my wrath on them and spend my anger against them in Egypt. [9]But for the sake of my name I did what would keep it from being profaned in the eyes of the nations they lived among and in whose sight I had revealed myself to the Israelites by bringing them out of Egypt. [10]Therefore I led them out of Egypt and brought them into the desert. [11]I gave them my decrees and made known to them my laws, for the man who obeys them will live by them. [12]Also I gave them my Sabbaths as a sign between us, so they would know that I the Lord made them holy.

[13]" 'Yet the people of Israel rebelled against me in the desert. They did not follow my decrees but rejected my laws—although the man who obeys them will live by them—and they utterly desecrated my Sabbaths. So I said I would pour out my wrath on them and destroy them in the desert. [14]But for the sake of my name I did what would keep it from being profaned in the eyes of the nations in whose sight I had brought them out. [15]Also with uplifted hand I swore to them in the desert that I would not bring them into the land I had given them—a land flowing with milk and honey, most beautiful of all lands— [16]because they rejected my laws and did not follow my decrees and desecrated my Sabbaths. For their hearts were devoted to their idols. [17]Yet I looked on them with pity and did not destroy them or put an end to them in the desert. [18]I said to their children in the desert, "Do not follow the statutes of your fathers or keep their laws or defile yourselves with their idols. [19]I am the Lord your God; follow my decrees and be careful to keep my laws. [20]Keep my Sabbaths holy, that they may be a sign between us. Then you will know that I am the Lord your God."

[21]" 'But the children rebelled against me: They did not follow my decrees, they were not careful to keep my laws—although the man who obeys them will live by them—and they desecrated my

THE MESSAGE

searched out just for them, a country flowing with milk and honey, a jewel of a country.

20.7   " 'At that time I told them, "Get rid of all the vile things that you've become addicted to. Don't make yourselves filthy with the Egyptian no-god idols. *I alone* am God, your God."

20.8-10   " 'But they rebelled against me, wouldn't listen to a word I said. None got rid of the vile things they were addicted to. They held on to the no-gods of Egypt as if for dear life. I seriously considered inflicting my anger on them in force right there in Egypt. Then I thought better of it. I acted out of who I was, not by how I felt. And I acted in a way that would evoke honor, not blasphemy, from the nations around them, nations who had seen me reveal myself by promising to lead my people out of Egypt. And then I did it: I led them out of Egypt into the desert.

20.11-12   " 'I gave them laws for living, showed them how to live well and obediently before me. I also gave them my weekly holy rest days, my "Sabbaths," a kind of signpost erected between me and them to show them that I, God, am in the business of making them holy.

20.13-17   " 'But Israel rebelled against me in the desert. They didn't follow my statutes. They despised my laws for living well and obediently in the ways I had set out. And they totally desecrated my holy Sabbaths. I seriously considered unleashing my anger on them right there in the desert. But I thought better of it and acted out of who I was, not by what I felt, so that I might be honored and not blasphemed by the nations who had seen me bring them out. But I did lift my hand in a solemn oath there in the desert and promise them that I would not bring them into the country flowing with milk and honey that I had chosen for them, that jewel among all lands. I canceled my promise because they despised my laws for living obediently, wouldn't follow my statutes, and went ahead and desecrated my holy Sabbaths. They preferred living by their no-god idols. But I didn't go all the way: I didn't wipe them out, didn't finish them off in the desert.

20.18-20   " 'Then I addressed myself to their children in the desert: "Don't do what your parents did. Don't take up their practices. Don't make yourselves filthy with their no-god idols. I myself am God, your God: Keep my statutes and live by my laws. Keep my Sabbaths as holy rest days, signposts between me and you, signaling that I am God, *your* God."

20.21-22   " 'But the children also rebelled against me. They neither followed my statutes nor kept my laws for living upright and well. And they des-

NEW INTERNATIONAL VERSION

Sabbaths. So I said I would pour out my wrath on them and spend my anger against them in the desert. ²²But I withheld my hand, and for the sake of my name I did what would keep it from being profaned in the eyes of the nations in whose sight I had brought them out. ²³Also with uplifted hand I swore to them in the desert that I would disperse them among the nations and scatter them through the countries, ²⁴because they had not obeyed my laws but had rejected my decrees and desecrated my Sabbaths, and their eyes ⌐lusted⌐ after their fathers' idols. ²⁵I also gave them over to statutes that were not good and laws they could not live by; ²⁶I let them become defiled through their gifts—the sacrifice of every firstborn*ᵃ*—that I might fill them with horror so they would know that I am the LORD.'

²⁷"Therefore, son of man, speak to the people of Israel and say to them, 'This is what the Sovereign LORD says: In this also your fathers blasphemed me by forsaking me: ²⁸When I brought them into the land I had sworn to give them and they saw any high hill or any leafy tree, there they offered their sacrifices, made offerings that provoked me to anger, presented their fragrant incense and poured out their drink offerings. ²⁹Then I said to them: What is this high place you go to?'" (It is called Bamah*ᵇ* to this day.)

JUDGMENT AND RESTORATION

³⁰"Therefore say to the house of Israel: 'This is what the Sovereign LORD says: Will you defile yourselves the way your fathers did and lust after their vile images? ³¹When you offer your gifts—the sacrifice of your sons in*ᶜ* the fire—you continue to defile yourselves with all your idols to this day. Am I to let you inquire of me, O house of Israel? As surely as I live, declares the Sovereign LORD, I will not let you inquire of me.

³²"'You say, "We want to be like the nations, like the peoples of the world, who serve wood and stone." But what you have in mind will never happen. ³³As surely as I live, declares the Sovereign LORD, I will rule over you with a mighty hand and an outstretched arm and with outpoured wrath. ³⁴I will bring you from the nations and gather you from the countries where you have been scattered—with a mighty hand and an outstretched arm and with outpoured wrath. ³⁵I will bring you into the desert of the nations and there, face to face, I will execute

---

ᵃ 26 Or —making every firstborn pass through ⌐the fire⌐
ᵇ 29 Bamah means high place.   ᶜ 31 Or —making your sons pass through

THE MESSAGE

ecrated my Sabbaths. I seriously considered dumping my anger on them, right there in the desert. But I thought better of it and acted out of who I was, not by what I felt, so that I might be honored and not blasphemed by the nations who had seen me bring them out.

20.23-26   "'But I did lift my hand in solemn oath there in the desert, and swore that I would scatter them all over the world, disperse them every which way because they didn't keep my laws nor live by my statutes. They desecrated my Sabbaths and remained addicted to the no-god idols of their parents. Since they were determined to live bad lives, I myself gave them statutes that could not produce goodness and laws that did not produce life. I abandoned them. Filthy in the gutter, they perversely sacrificed their firstborn children in the fire. The very horror should have shocked them into recognizing that I am GOD.'

20.27-29   "Therefore, speak to Israel, son of man. Tell them that GOD says, 'As if that wasn't enough, your parents further insulted me by betraying me. When I brought them into that land that I had solemnly promised with my upraised hand to give them, every time they saw a hill with a sex-and-religion shrine on it or a grove of trees where the sacred whores practiced, they were there, buying into the whole pagan system. I said to them, "What hill do you go to?"' (It's still called "Whore Hills.")

20.30-31   "Therefore, say to Israel, 'The Message of GOD, the Master: You're making your lives filthy by copying the ways of your parents. In repeating their vile practices, you've become whores yourselves. In burning your children as sacrifices, you've become as filthy as your no-god idols—as recently as today!

"'Am I going to put up with questions from people like you, Israel? As sure as I am the living God, I, GOD, the Master, refuse to be called into question by you!

20.32   "'What you're secretly thinking is never going to happen. You're thinking, "We're going to be like everybody else, just like the other nations. We're going to worship gods we can make and control."

20.33-35   "'As sure as I am the living God, says GOD, the Master, think again! With a mighty show of strength and a terrifying rush of anger, I will be King over you! I'll bring you back from the nations, collect you out of the countries to which you've been scattered, with a mighty show of strength and a terrifying rush of anger. I'll bring you to the desert of nations and haul you into court, where you'll be face to face with judgment.

NEW INTERNATIONAL VERSION

judgment upon you. ³⁶As I judged your fathers in the desert of the land of Egypt, so I will judge you, declares the Sovereign LORD. ³⁷I will take note of you as you pass under my rod, and I will bring you into the bond of the covenant. ³⁸I will purge you of those who revolt and rebel against me. Although I will bring them out of the land where they are living, yet they will not enter the land of Israel. Then you will know that I am the LORD.

³⁹" 'As for you, O house of Israel, this is what the Sovereign LORD says: Go and serve your idols, every one of you! But afterward you will surely listen to me and no longer profane my holy name with your gifts and idols. ⁴⁰For on my holy mountain, the high mountain of Israel, declares the Sovereign LORD, there in the land the entire house of Israel will serve me, and there I will accept them. There I will require your offerings and your choice gifts,*a* along with all your holy sacrifices. ⁴¹I will accept you as fragrant incense when I bring you out from the nations and gather you from the countries where you have been scattered, and I will show myself holy among you in the sight of the nations. ⁴²Then you will know that I am the LORD, when I bring you into the land of Israel, the land I had sworn with uplifted hand to give to your fathers. ⁴³There you will remember your conduct and all the actions by which you have defiled yourselves, and you will loathe yourselves for all the evil you have done. ⁴⁴You will know that I am the LORD, when I deal with you for my name's sake and not according to your evil ways and your corrupt practices, O house of Israel, declares the Sovereign LORD.' "

PROPHECY AGAINST THE SOUTH

⁴⁵The word of the LORD came to me: ⁴⁶"Son of man, set your face toward the south; preach against the south and prophesy against the forest of the southland. ⁴⁷Say to the southern forest: 'Hear the word of the LORD. This is what the Sovereign LORD says: I am about to set fire to you, and it will consume all your trees, both green and dry. The blazing flame will not be quenched, and every face from south to north will be scorched by it. ⁴⁸Everyone will see that I the LORD have kindled it; it will not be quenched.' "

⁴⁹Then I said, "Ah, Sovereign LORD! They are saying of me, 'Isn't he just telling parables?' "

BABYLON, GOD'S SWORD OF JUDGMENT

21 The word of the LORD came to me: ²"Son of man, set your face against Jerusalem and preach against the sanctuary. Prophesy

a 40 Or and the gifts of your firstfruits

THE MESSAGE

20.36-38 " 'As I faced your parents with judgment in the desert of Egypt, so I'll face you with judgment. I'll scrutinize and search every person as you arrive, and I'll bring you under the bond of the covenant. I'll cull out the rebels and traitors. I'll lead them out of their exile, but I won't bring them back to Israel.

" 'Then you'll realize that I am GOD.

20.39-43 " 'But you, people of Israel, this is the Message of GOD, the Master, to you: Go ahead, serve your no-god idols! But later, you'll think better of it and quit throwing filth and mud on me with your pagan offerings and no-god idols. For on my holy mountain, the high mountain of Israel, I, GOD, the Master, tell you that the entire people of Israel will worship me. I'll receive them there with open arms. I'll demand your best gifts and offerings, all your holy sacrifices. What's more, I'll receive you as the best kind of offerings when I bring you back from all the lands and countries in which you've been scattered. I'll demonstrate in the eyes of the world that I am The Holy. When I return you to the land of Israel, the land that I solemnly promised with upraised arm to give to your parents, you'll realize that I am GOD. Then and there you'll remember all that you've done, the way you've lived that has made you so filthy—and you'll loathe yourselves.

20.44 " 'But, dear Israel, you'll also realize that I am GOD when I respond to you out of who I am, not by what I feel about the evil lives you've lived, the corrupt history you've compiled. Decree of GOD, the Master.' "

NOBODY WILL PUT OUT THE FIRE

20.45-46 GOD's Message came to me: "Son of man, face south. Let the Message roll out against the south. Prophesy against the wilderness forest of the south.

20.47-48 "Tell the forest of the south, 'Listen to the Message of GOD! GOD, the Master, says, I'll set a fire in you that will burn up every tree, dead trees and live trees alike. Nobody will put out the fire. The whole country from south to north will be blackened by it. Everyone is going to see that I, GOD, started the fire and that it's not going to be put out.' "

20.49 And I said, "O GOD, everyone is saying of me, 'He just makes up stories.' "

A SWORD! A SWORD!

21.1-5 **21** GOD's Message came to me: "Son of man, now face Jerusalem and let the Message roll out against the Sanctuary. Prophe-

NEW INTERNATIONAL VERSION

against the land of Israel ³and say to her: 'This is what the LORD says: I am against you. I will draw my sword from its scabbard and cut off from you both the righteous and the wicked. ⁴Because I am going to cut off the righteous and the wicked, my sword will be unsheathed against everyone from south to north. ⁵Then all people will know that I the LORD have drawn my sword from its scabbard; it will not return again.'

⁶"Therefore groan, son of man! Groan before them with broken heart and bitter grief. ⁷And when they ask you, 'Why are you groaning?' you shall say, 'Because of the news that is coming. Every heart will melt and every hand go limp; every spirit will become faint and every knee become as weak as water.' It is coming! It will surely take place, declares the Sovereign LORD."

⁸The word of the LORD came to me: ⁹"Son of man, prophesy and say, 'This is what the Lord says:

" 'A sword, a sword,
    sharpened and polished—
¹⁰sharpened for the slaughter,
    polished to flash like lightning!

" 'Shall we rejoice in the scepter of my son ⌊Judah⌋? The sword despises every such stick.

¹¹ " 'The sword is appointed to be polished,
    to be grasped with the hand;
it is sharpened and polished,
    made ready for the hand of the slayer.
¹²Cry out and wail, son of man,
    for it is against my people;
    it is against all the princes of Israel.
They are thrown to the sword
    along with my people.
Therefore beat your breast.

¹³ " 'Testing will surely come. And what if the scepter ⌊of Judah⌋, which the sword despises, does not continue? declares the Sovereign LORD.'

¹⁴"So then, son of man, prophesy
    and strike your hands together.
Let the sword strike twice,
    even three times.
It is a sword for slaughter—
    a sword for great slaughter,
    closing in on them from every side.
¹⁵So that hearts may melt
    and the fallen be many,
I have stationed the sword for slaughter*ᵃ*
    at all their gates.
Oh! It is made to flash like lightning,
    it is grasped for slaughter.

ᵃ 15 Septuagint; the meaning of the Hebrew for this word is uncertain.

THE MESSAGE

sy against the land of Israel. Say, 'GOD's Message: I'm against you. I'm pulling my sword from its sheath and killing both the wicked and the righteous. Because I'm treating everyone the same, good and bad, everyone from south to north is going to feel my sword! Everyone will know that I mean business.'

21.6 "So, son of man, groan! Double up in pain. Make a scene!

21.7 "When they ask you, 'Why all this groaning, this carrying on?' say, 'Because of the news that's coming. It'll knock the breath out of everyone. Hearts will stop cold, knees turn to rubber. Yes, it's coming. No stopping it. Decree of GOD, the Master.' "

✝

21.8-10 GOD's Message to me: "Son of man, prophesy. Tell them, 'The Master says:

" 'A sword! A sword!
    razor-sharp and polished,
Sharpened to kill,
    polished to flash like lightning!

" 'My child, you've despised the scepter of
        Judah
    by worshiping every tree-idol.

21.11 " 'The sword is made to glisten,
    to be held and brandished.
It's sharpened and polished,
    ready to be brandished by the killer.'

21.12 "Yell out and wail, son of man.
    The sword is against my people!
The princes of Israel
    and my people—abandoned to the sword!
Wring your hands!
    Tear out your hair!

21.13 " 'Testing comes.
    Why have you despised discipline?
You can't get around it.
    Decree of GOD, the Master.'

21.14-17 "So, prophesy, son of man!
    Clap your hands. Get their attention.
Tell them that the sword's coming down
    once, twice, three times.
It's a sword to kill,
    a sword for a massacre,
A sword relentless,
    a sword inescapable—
People collapsing right and left,
    going down like dominoes.
I've stationed a murderous sword
    at every gate in the city,
Flashing like lightning,
    brandished murderously.

NEW INTERNATIONAL VERSION

¹⁶O sword, slash to the right,
  then to the left,
    wherever your blade is turned.
¹⁷I too will strike my hands together,
  and my wrath will subside.
  I the LORD have spoken."

¹⁸The word of the LORD came to me: ¹⁹"Son of man, mark out two roads for the sword of the king of Babylon to take, both starting from the same country. Make a signpost where the road branches off to the city. ²⁰Mark out one road for the sword to come against Rabbah of the Ammonites and another against Judah and fortified Jerusalem. ²¹For the king of Babylon will stop at the fork in the road, at the junction of the two roads, to seek an omen: He will cast lots with arrows, he will consult his idols, he will examine the liver. ²²Into his right hand will come the lot for Jerusalem, where he is to set up battering rams, to give the command to slaughter, to sound the battle cry, to set battering rams against the gates, to build a ramp and to erect siege works. ²³It will seem like a false omen to those who have sworn allegiance to him, but he will remind them of their guilt and take them captive.

²⁴"Therefore this is what the Sovereign LORD says: 'Because you people have brought to mind your guilt by your open rebellion, revealing your sins in all that you do—because you have done this, you will be taken captive.

²⁵" 'O profane and wicked prince of Israel, whose day has come, whose time of punishment has reached its climax, ²⁶this is what the Sovereign LORD says: Take off the turban, remove the crown. It will not be as it was: The lowly will be exalted and the exalted will be brought low. ²⁷A ruin! A ruin! I will make it a ruin! It will not be restored until he comes to whom it rightfully belongs; to him I will give it.'

²⁸"And you, son of man, prophesy and say, 'This is what the Sovereign LORD says about the Ammonites and their insults:

" 'A sword, a sword,
    drawn for the slaughter,
  polished to consume
    and to flash like lightning!
²⁹Despite false visions concerning you
    and lying divinations about you,
  it will be laid on the necks
    of the wicked who are to be slain,
  whose day has come,
    whose time of punishment has reached its
      climax.
³⁰Return the sword to its scabbard.
  In the place where you were created,

THE MESSAGE

Cut to the right, thrust to the left,
  murderous, sharp-edged sword!
Then I'll clap my hands,
  a signal that my anger is spent.
  I, GOD, have spoken."

✛

^{21.18-22} GOD's Message came to me: "Son of man, lay out two roads for the sword of the king of Babylon to take. Start them from the same place. Place a signpost at the beginning of each road. Post one sign to mark the road of the sword to Rabbah of the Ammonites. Post the other to mark the road to Judah and Fort Jerusalem. The king of Babylon stands at the fork in the road and he decides by divination which of the two roads to take. He draws straws, he throws god-dice, he examines a goat liver. He opens his right hand: The omen says, 'Head for Jerusalem!' So he's on his way with battering rams, roused to kill, sounding the battle cry, pounding down city gates, building siege works.

^{21.23} "To the Judah leaders, who themselves have sworn oaths, it will seem like a false divination, but he will remind them of their guilt, and so they'll be captured.

^{21.24} "So this is what GOD, the Master, says: 'Because your sin is now out in the open so everyone can see what you've been doing, you'll be taken captive.

^{21.25-27} " 'O Zedekiah, blasphemous and evil prince of Israel: Time's up. It's "punishment payday." GOD says, Take your royal crown off your head. No more "business as usual." The underdog will be promoted and the top dog will be demoted. Ruins, ruins, ruins! I'll turn the whole place into ruins. And ruins it will remain until the one comes who has a right to it. Then I'll give it to him.'

^{21.28-32} "But, son of man, your job is to prophesy. Tell them, 'This is the Message from GOD, the Master, against the Ammonites and against their cruel taunts:

" 'A sword! A sword!
    Bared to kill,
  Sharp as a razor,
    flashing like lightning.
  Despite false sword propaganda
    circulated in Ammon,
  The sword will sever Ammonite necks,
    for whom it's punishment payday.
  Return the sword to the sheath! I'll judge you
    in your home country,

NEW INTERNATIONAL VERSION	THE MESSAGE

NEW INTERNATIONAL VERSION

in the land of your ancestry,
    I will judge you.
³¹ I will pour out my wrath upon you
    and breathe out my fiery anger against
        you;
I will hand you over to brutal men,
    men skilled in destruction.
³² You will be fuel for the fire,
    your blood will be shed in your land,
you will be remembered no more;
    for I the LORD have spoken.' "

JERUSALEM'S SINS

22 The word of the LORD came to me: ² "Son of man, will you judge her? Will you judge this city of bloodshed? Then confront her with all her detestable practices ³ and say: 'This is what the Sovereign LORD says: O city that brings on herself doom by shedding blood in her midst and defiles herself by making idols, ⁴ you have become guilty because of the blood you have shed and have become defiled by the idols you have made. You have brought your days to a close, and the end of your years has come. Therefore I will make you an object of scorn to the nations and a laughingstock to all the countries. ⁵ Those who are near and those who are far away will mock you, O infamous city, full of turmoil.

⁶ " 'See how each of the princes of Israel who are in you uses his power to shed blood. ⁷ In you they have treated father and mother with contempt; in you they have oppressed the alien and mistreated the fatherless and the widow. ⁸ You have despised my holy things and desecrated my Sabbaths. ⁹ In you are slanderous men bent on shedding blood; in you are those who eat at the mountain shrines and commit lewd acts. ¹⁰ In you are those who dishonor their fathers' bed; in you are those who violate women during their period, when they are ceremonially unclean. ¹¹ In you one man commits a detestable offense with his neighbor's wife, another shamefully defiles his daughter-in-law, and another violates his sister, his own father's daughter. ¹² In you men accept bribes to shed blood; you take usury and excessive interest^a and make unjust gain from your neighbors by extortion. And you have forgotten me, declares the Sovereign LORD.

¹³ " 'I will surely strike my hands together at the unjust gain you have made and at the blood you have shed in your midst. ¹⁴ Will your courage endure or your hands be strong in the day I deal with you? I the LORD have spoken, and I will do it. ¹⁵ I will disperse you among the na-

THE MESSAGE

in the land where you grew up.
I'll empty out my wrath on you,
    breathe hot anger down your neck.
I'll give you to vicious men
    skilled in torture.
You'll end up as stove-wood.
    Corpses will litter your land.
Not so much as a memory will be left of you.
    I, GOD, have said so.' "

THE SCARECROW OF THE NATIONS

22.1-5 **22** GOD's Message came to me: "Son of man, are you going to judge this bloody city or not? Come now, are you going to judge her? Do it! Face her with all her outrageous obscenities. Tell her, 'This is what GOD, the Master, says: You're a city murderous at the core, just asking for punishment. You're a city obsessed with no-god idols, making yourself filthy. In all your killing, you've piled up guilt. In all your idol-making, you've become filthy. You've forced a premature end to your existence. I'll put you on exhibit as the scarecrow of the nations, the world's worst joke. From far and near they'll deride you as infamous in filth, notorious for chaos.

22.6-12 " 'Your leaders, the princes of Israel among you, compete in crime. You're a community that's insolent to parents, abusive to outsiders, oppressive against orphans and widows. You treat my holy things with contempt and desecrate my Sabbaths. You have people spreading lies and spilling blood, flocking to the hills to the sex shrines and fornicating unrestrained. Incest is common. Men force themselves on women regardless of whether they're ready or willing. Sex is now anarchy. Anyone is fair game: neighbor, daughter-in-law, sister. Murder is for hire, usury is rampant, extortion is commonplace.

" 'And you've forgotten *me*. Decree of GOD, the Master.

22.13-14 " 'Now look! I've clapped my hands, calling everyone's attention to your rapacious greed and your bloody brutalities. Can you stick with it? Will you be able to keep at this once I start dealing with you?

22.14-16 " 'I, GOD, have spoken. I'll put an end to this. I'll throw you to the four winds. I'll scatter you

---

^a 12 Or *usury and interest*

NEW INTERNATIONAL VERSION

tions and scatter you through the countries; and I will put an end to your uncleanness. 16When you have been defiled*a* in the eyes of the nations, you will know that I am the Lord.' "

17Then the word of the Lord came to me: 18"Son of man, the house of Israel has become dross to me; all of them are the copper, tin, iron and lead left inside a furnace. They are but the dross of silver. 19Therefore this is what the Sovereign Lord says: 'Because you have all become dross, I will gather you into Jerusalem. 20As men gather silver, copper, iron, lead and tin into a furnace to melt it with a fiery blast, so will I gather you in my anger and my wrath and put you inside the city and melt you. 21I will gather you and I will blow on you with my fiery wrath, and you will be melted inside her. 22As silver is melted in a furnace, so you will be melted inside her, and you will know that I the Lord have poured out my wrath upon you.' "

23Again the word of the Lord came to me: 24"Son of man, say to the land, 'You are a land that has had no rain or showers*b* in the day of wrath.' 25There is a conspiracy of her princes*c* within her like a roaring lion tearing its prey; they devour people, take treasures and precious things and make many widows within her. 26Her priests do violence to my law and profane my holy things; they do not distinguish between the holy and the common; they teach that there is no difference between the unclean and the clean; and they shut their eyes to the keeping of my Sabbaths, so that I am profaned among them. 27Her officials within her are like wolves tearing their prey; they shed blood and kill people to make unjust gain. 28Her prophets whitewash these deeds for them by false visions and lying divinations. They say, 'This is what the Sovereign Lord says'—when the Lord has not spoken. 29The people of the land practice extortion and commit robbery; they oppress the poor and needy and mistreat the alien, denying them justice.

30"I looked for a man among them who would build up the wall and stand before me in the gap on behalf of the land so I would not have to destroy it, but I found none. 31So I will pour out my wrath on them and consume them with my fiery anger, bringing down on their own heads all they have done, declares the Sovereign Lord."

THE MESSAGE

all over the world. I'll put a full stop to your filthy living. You will be defiled, spattered with your own mud in the eyes of the nations. And you'll recognize that I am God.' "

22.17-22   God's Message came to me: "Son of man, the people of Israel are slag to me, the useless by-product of refined copper, tin, iron, and lead left at the smelter—a worthless slag heap. So tell them, 'God, the Master, has spoken: Because you've all become worthless slag, you're on notice: I'll assemble you in Jerusalem. As men gather silver, copper, iron, lead, and tin into a furnace and blow fire on it to melt it down, so in my wrath I'll gather you and melt you down. I'll blow on you with the fire of my wrath to melt you down in the furnace. As silver is melted down, you'll be melted down. That should get through to you. Then you'll recognize that I, God, have let my wrath loose on you.' "

22.23-25   God's Message came to me: "Son of man, tell her, 'You're a land that during the time I was angry with you got no rain, not so much as a spring shower. The leaders among you became desperate, like roaring, ravaging lions killing indiscriminately. They grabbed and looted, leaving widows in their wake.

22.26-29   " 'Your priests violated my law and desecrated my holy things. They can't tell the difference between sacred and secular. They tell people there's no difference between right and wrong. They're contemptuous of my holy Sabbaths, profaning me by trying to pull me down to their level. Your politicians are like wolves prowling and killing and rapaciously taking whatever they want. Your preachers cover up for the politicians by pretending to have received visions and special revelations. They say, "This is what God, the Master, says . . ." when God hasn't said so much as one word. Extortion is rife, robbery is epidemic, the poor and needy are abused, outsiders are kicked around at will, with no access to justice.'

22.30-31   "I looked for someone to stand up for me against all this, to repair the defenses of the city, to take a stand for me and stand in the gap to protect this land so I wouldn't have to destroy it. I couldn't find anyone. Not one. So I'll empty out my wrath on them, burn them to a crisp with my hot anger, serve them with the consequences of all they've done. Decree of God, the Master."

---

a 16 Or *When I have allotted you your inheritance*
b 24 Septuagint; Hebrew *has not been cleansed or rained on*
c 25 Septuagint; Hebrew *prophets*

NEW INTERNATIONAL VERSION

Two Adulterous Sisters

23 The word of the Lord came to me: [2]"Son of man, there were two women, daughters of the same mother. [3]They became prostitutes in Egypt, engaging in prostitution from their youth. In that land their breasts were fondled and their virgin bosoms caressed. [4]The older was named Oholah, and her sister was Oholibah. They were mine and gave birth to sons and daughters. Oholah is Samaria, and Oholibah is Jerusalem.

[5]"Oholah engaged in prostitution while she was still mine; and she lusted after her lovers, the Assyrians—warriors [6]clothed in blue, governors and commanders, all of them handsome young men, and mounted horsemen. [7]She gave herself as a prostitute to all the elite of the Assyrians and defiled herself with all the idols of everyone she lusted after. [8]She did not give up the prostitution she began in Egypt, when during her youth men slept with her, caressed her virgin bosom and poured out their lust upon her.

[9]"Therefore I handed her over to her lovers, the Assyrians, for whom she lusted. [10]They stripped her naked, took away her sons and daughters and killed her with the sword. She became a byword among women, and punishment was inflicted on her.

[11]"Her sister Oholibah saw this, yet in her lust and prostitution she was more depraved than her sister. [12]She too lusted after the Assyrians—governors and commanders, warriors in full dress, mounted horsemen, all handsome young men. [13]I saw that she too defiled herself; both of them went the same way.

[14]"But she carried her prostitution still further. She saw men portrayed on a wall, figures of Chaldeans[a] portrayed in red, [15]with belts around their waists and flowing turbans on their heads; all of them looked like Babylonian chariot officers, natives of Chaldea.[b] [16]As soon as she saw them, she lusted after them and sent messengers to them in Chaldea. [17]Then the Babylonians came to her, to the bed of love, and in their lust they defiled her. After she had been defiled by them, she turned away from them in disgust. [18]When she carried on her prostitution openly and exposed her nakedness, I turned away from her in disgust, just as I had turned away from her sister. [19]Yet she became more and more promiscuous as she recalled the days of her youth, when she was a prostitute in Egypt. [20]There she lusted after her lovers, whose genitals were like those of donkeys and whose emission was like

THE MESSAGE

Wild with Lust

23 God's Message came to me: "Son of man, there were two women, daughters of the same mother. They became whores in Egypt, whores from a young age. Their breasts were fondled, their young bosoms caressed. The older sister was named Oholah, the younger was Oholibah. They were my daughters, and they gave birth to sons and daughters.

"Oholah is Samaria and Oholibah is Jerusalem.

[23.5-8] "Oholah started whoring while she was still mine. She lusted after Assyrians as lovers: military men smartly uniformed in blue, ambassadors and governors, good-looking young men mounted on fine horses. Her lust was unrestrained. She was a whore to the Assyrian elite. She compounded her filth with the idols of those to whom she gave herself in lust. She never slowed down. The whoring she began while young in Egypt she continued, sleeping with men who played with her breasts and spent their lust on her.

[23.9-10] "So I left her to her Assyrian lovers, for whom she was so obsessed with lust. They ripped off her clothes, took away her children, and then, the final indignity, killed her. Among women her name became Shame—history's judgment on her.

[23.11-18] "Her sister Oholibah saw all this, but she became even worse than her sister in lust and whoring, if you can believe it. She also went crazy with lust for Assyrians: ambassadors and governors, military men smartly dressed and mounted on fine horses—the Assyrian elite. And I saw that she also had become incredibly filthy. Both women followed the same path. But Oholibah surpassed her sister. When she saw figures of Babylonians carved in relief on the walls and painted red, fancy belts around their waists, elaborate turbans on their heads, all of them looking important—famous Babylonians!—she went wild with lust and sent invitations to them in Babylon. The Babylonians came on the run, fornicated with her, made her dirty inside and out. When they had thoroughly debased her, she lost interest in them. Then she went public with her fornication. She exhibited her sex to the world.

[23.18-21] "I turned my back on her just as I had on her sister. But that didn't slow her down. She went at her whoring harder than ever. She remembered when she was young, just starting out as a whore in Egypt. That whetted her appetite for more virile, vulgar, and violent lovers—stallions obsessive in their lust. She

---

[a] 14 Or *Babylonians*   [b] 15 Or *Babylonia*; also in verse 16

NEW INTERNATIONAL VERSION

that of horses. ²¹So you longed for the lewdness of your youth, when in Egypt your bosom was caressed and your young breasts fondled.^a

²²"Therefore, Oholibah, this is what the Sovereign LORD says: I will stir up your lovers against you, those you turned away from in disgust, and I will bring them against you from every side— ²³the Babylonians and all the Chaldeans, the men of Pekod and Shoa and Koa, and all the Assyrians with them, handsome young men, all of them governors and commanders, chariot officers and men of high rank, all mounted on horses. ²⁴They will come against you with weapons,^b chariots and wagons and with a throng of people; they will take up positions against you on every side with large and small shields and with helmets. I will turn you over to them for punishment, and they will punish you according to their standards. ²⁵I will direct my jealous anger against you, and they will deal with you in fury. They will cut off your noses and your ears, and those of you who are left will fall by the sword. They will take away your sons and daughters, and those of you who are left will be consumed by fire. ²⁶They will also strip you of your clothes and take your fine jewelry. ²⁷So I will put a stop to the lewdness and prostitution you began in Egypt. You will not look on these things with longing or remember Egypt anymore.

²⁸"For this is what the Sovereign LORD says: I am about to hand you over to those you hate, to those you turned away from in disgust. ²⁹They will deal with you in hatred and take away everything you have worked for. They will leave you naked and bare, and the shame of your prostitution will be exposed. Your lewdness and promiscuity ³⁰have brought this upon you, because you lusted after the nations and defiled yourself with their idols. ³¹You have gone the way of your sister; so I will put her cup into your hand.

³²"This is what the Sovereign LORD says:

"You will drink your sister's cup,
   a cup large and deep;
it will bring scorn and derision,
   for it holds so much.
³³You will be filled with drunkenness and
      sorrow,
   the cup of ruin and desolation,
   the cup of your sister Samaria.
³⁴You will drink it and drain it dry;
   you will dash it to pieces
   and tear your breasts.

I have spoken, declares the Sovereign LORD.

---

^a 21 Syriac (see also verse 3); Hebrew caressed because of your young breasts   ^b 24 The meaning of the Hebrew for this word is uncertain.

THE MESSAGE

longed for the sexual prowess of her youth back in Egypt, where her firm young breasts were caressed and fondled.

23.22-27   " 'Therefore, Oholibah, this is the Message from GOD, the Master: I will incite your old lovers against you, lovers you got tired of and left in disgust. I'll bring them against you from every direction, Babylonians and all the Chaldeans, Pekod, Shoa, and Koa, and all Assyrians—good-looking young men, ambassadors and governors, elite officers and celebrities—all of them mounted on fine, spirited horses. They'll come down on you out of the north, armed to the teeth, bringing chariots and troops from all sides. I'll turn over the task of judgment to them. They'll punish you according to their rules. I'll stand totally and relentlessly against you as they rip into you furiously. They'll mutilate you, cutting off your ears and nose, killing at random. They'll enslave your children—and anybody left over will be burned. They'll rip off your clothes and steal your jewelry. I'll put a stop to your sluttish sex, the whoring life you began in Egypt. You won't look on whoring with fondness anymore. You won't think back on Egypt with stars in your eyes.

23.28-30   " 'A Message from GOD, the Master: I'm at the point of abandoning you to those you hate, to those by whom you're repulsed. They'll treat you hatefully, leave you publicly naked, your whore's body exposed in the cruel glare of the sun. Your sluttish lust will be exposed. Your lust has brought you to this condition because you whored with pagan nations and made yourself filthy with their no-god idols.

23.31-34   " 'You copied the life of your sister. Now I'll let you drink the cup she drank.

" 'This is the Message of GOD, the Master:

" 'You'll drink your sister's cup,
   a cup canyon-deep and ocean-wide.
You'll be shunned and taunted
   as you drink from that cup, full to the
      brim.
You'll be falling-down-drunk and the tears
      will flow
   as you drink from that cup titanic with
      terror:
   It's the cup of your sister Samaria.
You'll drink it dry,
   then smash it to bits and eat the pieces,
   and end up tearing at your breasts.
I've given the word—
   Decree of GOD, the Master.

NEW INTERNATIONAL VERSION

35 "Therefore this is what the Sovereign LORD says: Since you have forgotten me and thrust me behind your back, you must bear the consequences of your lewdness and prostitution."

36 The LORD said to me: "Son of man, will you judge Oholah and Oholibah? Then confront them with their detestable practices, 37 for they have committed adultery and blood is on their hands. They committed adultery with their idols; they even sacrificed their children, whom they bore to me,ᵃ as food for them. 38 They have also done this to me: At that same time they defiled my sanctuary and desecrated my Sabbaths. 39 On the very day they sacrificed their children to their idols, they entered my sanctuary and desecrated it. That is what they did in my house.

40 "They even sent messengers for men who came from far away, and when they arrived you bathed yourself for them, painted your eyes and put on your jewelry. 41 You sat on an elegant couch, with a table spread before it on which you had placed the incense and oil that belonged to me.

42 "The noise of a carefree crowd was around her; Sabeansᵇ were brought from the desert along with men from the rabble, and they put bracelets on the arms of the woman and her sister and beautiful crowns on their heads. 43 Then I said about the one worn out by adultery, 'Now let them use her as a prostitute, for that is all she is.' 44 And they slept with her. As men sleep with a prostitute, so they slept with those lewd women, Oholah and Oholibah. 45 But righteous men will sentence them to the punishment of women who commit adultery and shed blood, because they are adulterous and blood is on their hands.

46 "This is what the Sovereign LORD says: Bring a mob against them and give them over to terror and plunder. 47 The mob will stone them and cut them down with their swords; they will kill their sons and daughters and burn down their houses.

48 "So I will put an end to lewdness in the land, that all women may take warning and not imitate you. 49 You will suffer the penalty for your lewdness and bear the consequences of your sins of idolatry. Then you will know that I am the Sovereign LORD."

THE COOKING POT

24 In the ninth year, in the tenth month on the tenth day, the word of the LORD came to me: 2 "Son of man, record this date, this very date, because the king of Babylon has laid siege to Jerusalem this very day. 3 Tell this rebellious house a parable and say to them: 'This is what the Sovereign LORD says:

THE MESSAGE

23.35 " 'Therefore GOD, the Master, says, Because you've forgotten all about me, pushing me into the background, you now must pay for what you've done—pay for your sluttish sex and whoring life.' "

23.36-39 Then GOD said to me, "Son of man, will you confront Oholah and Oholibah with what they've done? Make them face their outrageous obscenities, obscenities ranging from adultery to murder. They committed adultery with their no-god idols, sacrificed the children they bore me in order to feed their idols! And there is also this: They've defiled my holy Sanctuary and desecrated my holy Sabbaths. The same day that they sacrificed their children to their idols, they walked into my Sanctuary and defiled it. That's what they did—in *my* house!

23.40-42 "Furthermore, they even sent out invitations by special messenger to men far away—and, sure enough, they came. They bathed themselves, put on makeup and provocative lingerie. They reclined on a sumptuous bed, aromatic with incense and oils—*my* incense and oils! The crowd gathered, jostling and pushing, a drunken rabble. They adorned the sisters with bracelets on their arms and tiaras on their heads.

23.43-44 "I said, 'She's burned out on sex!' but that didn't stop them. They kept banging on her doors night and day as men do when they're after a whore. That's how they used Oholah and Oholibah, the worn-out whores.

23.45 "Righteous men will pronounce judgment on them, giving out sentences for adultery and murder. That was their lifework: adultery and murder."

23.46-47 "GOD says, 'Let a mob loose on them: Terror! Plunder! Let the mob stone them and hack them to pieces—kill all their children, burn down their houses!

23.48-49 " 'I'll put an end to sluttish sex in this country so that all women will be well warned and not copy you. You'll pay the price for all your obsessive sex. You'll pay in full for your promiscuous affairs with idols. And you'll realize that I am GOD, the Master.' "

BRING THE POT TO A BOIL

24.1-5 **24** The Message of GOD came to me in the ninth year, the tenth month, and the tenth day of the month: "Son of man, write down this date. The king of Babylon has laid siege to Jerusalem this very day. Tell this company of rebels a story:

ᵃ 37 Or *even made the children they bore to me pass through the fire* ᵇ 42 Or *drunkards*

NEW INTERNATIONAL VERSION

" 'Put on the cooking pot; put it on
  and pour water into it.
⁴Put into it the pieces of meat,
  all the choice pieces—the leg and the
    shoulder.
Fill it with the best of these bones;
⁵ take the pick of the flock.
Pile wood beneath it for the bones;
  bring it to a boil
  and cook the bones in it.

⁶" 'For this is what the Sovereign LORD says:

" 'Woe to the city of bloodshed,
  to the pot now encrusted,
  whose deposit will not go away!
Empty it piece by piece
  without casting lots for them.

⁷" 'For the blood she shed is in her midst:
  She poured it on the bare rock;
she did not pour it on the ground,
  where the dust would cover it.
⁸To stir up wrath and take revenge
  I put her blood on the bare rock,
  so that it would not be covered.

⁹" 'Therefore this is what the Sovereign LORD says:

" 'Woe to the city of bloodshed!
  I, too, will pile the wood high.
¹⁰So heap on the wood
  and kindle the fire.
Cook the meat well,
  mixing in the spices;
  and let the bones be charred.
¹¹Then set the empty pot on the coals
  till it becomes hot and its copper glows
so its impurities may be melted
  and its deposit burned away.
¹²It has frustrated all efforts;
  its heavy deposit has not been removed,
  not even by fire.

¹³" 'Now your impurity is lewdness. Because I tried to cleanse you but you would not be cleansed from your impurity, you will not be clean again until my wrath against you has subsided.

¹⁴" 'I the LORD have spoken. The time has come for me to act. I will not hold back; I will not have pity, nor will I relent. You will be judged according to your conduct and your actions, declares the Sovereign LORD.' "

EZEKIEL'S WIFE DIES

¹⁵The word of the LORD came to me: ¹⁶"Son of man, with one blow I am about to take away from you the delight of your eyes. Yet do not la-

THE MESSAGE

" 'Put on the soup pot.
  Fill it with water.
Put chunks of meat into it,
  all the choice pieces—loin and brisket.
Pick out the best soup bones
  from the best of the sheep in the flock.
Pile wood beneath the pot.
  Bring it to a boil
  and cook the soup.

24.6 " 'GOD, the Master, says:

" 'Doom to the city of murder,
  to the pot thick with scum,
  thick with a filth that can't be scoured.
Empty the pot piece by piece;
  don't bother who gets what.

24.7-8 " 'The blood from murders
  has stained the whole city;
Blood runs bold on the street stones,
  with no one bothering to wash it off—
Blood out in the open to public view
  to provoke my wrath,
  to trigger my vengeance.

24.9-12 " 'Therefore, this is what GOD, the Master, says:

" 'Doom to the city of murder!
  I, too, will pile on the wood.
Stack the wood high,
  light the match,
Cook the meat, spice it well, pour out the
    broth,
  and then burn the bones.
Then I'll set the empty pot on the coals
  and heat it red-hot so the bronze glows,
So the germs are killed
  and the corruption is burned off.
But it's hopeless. It's too far gone.
  The filth is too thick.

24.13-14 " 'Your encrusted filth is your filthy sex. I wanted to clean you up, but you wouldn't let me. I'll make no more attempts at cleaning you up until my anger quiets down. I, GOD, have said it, and I'll do it. I'm not holding back. I've run out of compassion. I'm not changing my mind. You're getting exactly what's coming to you. Decree of GOD, the Master.' "

NO TEARS

24.15-17 GOD's Message came to me: "Son of man, I'm about to take from you the delight of your life—a real blow, I know. But, please, no tears.

NEW INTERNATIONAL VERSION

ment or weep or shed any tears. ¹⁷Groan quietly; do not mourn for the dead. Keep your turban fastened and your sandals on your feet; do not cover the lower part of your face or eat the customary food ⌐of mourners⌐.'"

¹⁸So I spoke to the people in the morning, and in the evening my wife died. The next morning I did as I had been commanded.

¹⁹Then the people asked me, "Won't you tell us what these things have to do with us?"

²⁰So I said to them, "The word of the LORD came to me: ²¹Say to the house of Israel, 'This is what the Sovereign LORD says: I am about to desecrate my sanctuary—the stronghold in which you take pride, the delight of your eyes, the object of your affection. The sons and daughters you left behind will fall by the sword. ²²And you will do as I have done. You will not cover the lower part of your face or eat the customary food ⌐of mourners⌐. ²³You will keep your turbans on your heads and your sandals on your feet. You will not mourn or weep but will waste away because of*ᵃ* your sins and groan among yourselves. ²⁴Ezekiel will be a sign to you; you will do just as he has done. When this happens, you will know that I am the Sovereign LORD.'

²⁵"And you, son of man, on the day I take away their stronghold, their joy and glory, the delight of their eyes, their heart's desire, and their sons and daughters as well— ²⁶on that day a fugitive will come to tell you the news. ²⁷At that time your mouth will be opened; you will speak with him and will no longer be silent. So you will be a sign to them, and they will know that I am the LORD."

A PROPHECY AGAINST AMMON

25 The word of the LORD came to me: ²"Son of man, set your face against the Ammonites and prophesy against them. ³Say to them, 'Hear the word of the Sovereign LORD. This is what the Sovereign LORD says: Because you said "Aha!" over my sanctuary when it was desecrated and over the land of Israel when it was laid waste and over the people of Judah when they went into exile, ⁴therefore I am going to give you to the people of the East as a possession. They will set up their camps and pitch their tents among you; they will eat your fruit and drink your milk. ⁵I will turn Rabbah into a pasture for camels and Ammon into a resting place for sheep. Then you will know that I am the LORD. ⁶For this is what the Sovereign LORD says: Because you have clapped your hands and stamped your feet, rejoicing with all the malice of your heart against the land of Israel, ⁷therefore

THE MESSAGE

Keep your grief to yourself. No public mourning. Get dressed as usual and go about your work—none of the usual funeral rituals.'"

24.18   I preached to the people in the morning. That evening my wife died. The next morning I did as I'd been told.

24.19   The people came to me, saying, "Tell us why you're acting like this. What does it mean, anyway?"

24.20-21   So I told them, "GOD's Word came to me, saying, 'Tell the family of Israel, This is what GOD, the Master, says: I will desecrate my Sanctuary, your proud impregnable fort, the delight of your life, your heart's desire. The children you left behind will be killed.

24.22-24   " 'Then you'll do exactly as I've done. You'll perform none of the usual funeral rituals. You'll get dressed as usual and go about your work. No tears. But your sins will eat away at you from within and you'll groan among yourselves. Ezekiel will be your example. The way he did it is the way you'll do it.

24.24   " 'When this happens you'll recognize that I am GOD, the Master.'"

24.25-27   "And you, son of man: The day I take away the people's refuge, their great joy, the delight of their life, what they've most longed for, along with all their children—on that very day a survivor will arrive and tell you what happened to the city. You'll break your silence and start talking again, talking to the survivor. Again, you'll be an example for them. And they'll recognize that I am GOD."

ACTS OF VENGEANCE

25 GOD's Message came to me:

25.1-5

"Son of man, face Ammon and preach against the people: Listen to the Message of GOD, the Master. This is what GOD has to say: Because you cheered when my Sanctuary was desecrated and the land of Judah was devastated and the people of Israel were taken into exile, I'm giving you over to the people of the east. They'll move in and make themselves at home, eating the food right off your tables and drinking your milk. I'll turn your capital, Rabbah, into pasture for camels and all your villages into corrals for flocks. Then you'll realize that I am GOD.

25.6-7   "GOD, the Master, says, Because you clapped and cheered, venting all your malicious contempt against the land of Israel, I'll step in and

---

ᵃ 23 Or away in

NEW INTERNATIONAL VERSION

I will stretch out my hand against you and give you as plunder to the nations. I will cut you off from the nations and exterminate you from the countries. I will destroy you, and you will know that I am the LORD.' "

A PROPHECY AGAINST MOAB

⁸"This is what the Sovereign LORD says: 'Because Moab and Seir said, "Look, the house of Judah has become like all the other nations," ⁹therefore I will expose the flank of Moab, beginning at its frontier towns—Beth Jeshimoth, Baal Meon and Kiriathaim—the glory of that land. ¹⁰I will give Moab along with the Ammonites to the people of the East as a possession, so that the Ammonites will not be remembered among the nations; ¹¹and I will inflict punishment on Moab. Then they will know that I am the LORD.' "

A PROPHECY AGAINST EDOM

¹²"This is what the Sovereign LORD says: 'Because Edom took revenge on the house of Judah and became very guilty by doing so, ¹³therefore this is what the Sovereign LORD says: I will stretch out my hand against Edom and kill its men and their animals. I will lay it waste, and from Teman to Dedan they will fall by the sword. ¹⁴I will take vengeance on Edom by the hand of my people Israel, and they will deal with Edom in accordance with my anger and my wrath; they will know my vengeance, declares the Sovereign LORD.' "

A PROPHECY AGAINST PHILISTIA

¹⁵"This is what the Sovereign LORD says: 'Because the Philistines acted in vengeance and took revenge with malice in their hearts, and with ancient hostility sought to destroy Judah, ¹⁶therefore this is what the Sovereign LORD says: I am about to stretch out my hand against the Philistines, and I will cut off the Kerethites and destroy those remaining along the coast. ¹⁷I will carry out great vengeance on them and punish them in my wrath. Then they will know that I am the LORD, when I take vengeance on them.' "

A PROPHECY AGAINST TYRE

26 In the eleventh year, on the first day of the month, the word of the LORD came to me: ²"Son of man, because Tyre has said of Jerusalem, 'Aha! The gate to the nations is broken, and its doors have swung open to me; now that she lies in ruins I will prosper,' ³therefore this is

THE MESSAGE

hand you out as loot—first come, first served. I'll cross you off the roster of nations. There'll be nothing left of you. And you'll realize that I am GOD."

25.8-11 "GOD, the Master, says: Because Moab said, 'Look, Judah's nothing special,' I'll lay wide open the flank of Moab by exposing its lovely frontier villages to attack: Beth-jeshimoth, Baal-meon, and Kiriathaim. I'll lump Moab in with Ammon and give them to the people of the east for the taking. Ammon won't be heard from again. I'll punish Moab severely. And they'll realize that I am GOD."

25.12-14 "GOD, the Master, says: Because Edom reacted against the people of Judah in spiteful revenge and was so criminally vengeful against them, therefore I, GOD, the Master, will oppose Edom and kill the lot of them, people and animals both. I'll waste it—corpses stretched from Teman to Dedan. I'll use my people Israel to bring my vengeance down on Edom. My wrath will fuel their action. And they'll realize it's *my* vengeance. Decree of GOD the Master."

25.15-17 "GOD, the Master, says: Because the Philistines were so spitefully vengeful—all those centuries of stored-up malice!—and did their best to destroy Judah, therefore I, GOD, the Master, will oppose the Philistines and cut down the Cretans and anybody else left along the seacoast. Huge acts of vengeance, massive punishments! When I bring vengeance, they'll realize that I am GOD."

AS THE WAVES OF THE SEA, SURGING AGAINST THE SHORE

26.1-2 **26** In the eleventh year, on the first day of the month, GOD's Message came to me: "Son of man, Tyre cheered when they got the news of Jerusalem, exclaiming,

" 'Good! The gateway city is smashed!
    Now all her business comes my way.
She's in ruins
    and I'm in clover.'

NEW INTERNATIONAL VERSION

what the Sovereign LORD says: I am against you, O Tyre, and I will bring many nations against you, like the sea casting up its waves. ⁴They will destroy the walls of Tyre and pull down her towers; I will scrape away her rubble and make her a bare rock. ⁵Out in the sea she will become a place to spread fishnets, for I have spoken, declares the Sovereign LORD. She will become plunder for the nations, ⁶and her settlements on the mainland will be ravaged by the sword. Then they will know that I am the LORD.

⁷For this is what the Sovereign LORD says: From the north I am going to bring against Tyre Nebuchadnezzar*ᵃ* king of Babylon, king of kings, with horses and chariots, with horsemen and a great army. ⁸He will ravage your settlements on the mainland with the sword; he will set up siege works against you, build a ramp up to your walls and raise his shields against you. ⁹He will direct the blows of his battering rams against your walls and demolish your towers with his weapons. ¹⁰His horses will be so many that they will cover you with dust. Your walls will tremble at the noise of the war horses, wagons and chariots when he enters your gates as men enter a city whose walls have been broken through. ¹¹The hoofs of his horses will trample all your streets; he will kill your people with the sword, and your strong pillars will fall to the ground. ¹²They will plunder your wealth and loot your merchandise; they will break down your walls and demolish your fine houses and throw your stones, timber and rubble into the sea. ¹³I will put an end to your noisy songs, and the music of your harps will be heard no more. ¹⁴I will make you a bare rock, and you will become a place to spread fishnets. You will never be rebuilt, for I the LORD have spoken, declares the Sovereign LORD.

¹⁵This is what the Sovereign LORD says to Tyre: Will not the coastlands tremble at the sound of your fall, when the wounded groan and the slaughter takes place in you? ¹⁶Then all the princes of the coast will step down from their thrones and lay aside their robes and take off their embroidered garments. Clothed with terror, they will sit on the ground, trembling every moment, appalled at you. ¹⁷Then they will take up a lament concerning you and say to you:

ᵃ 7 Hebrew *Nebuchadrezzar,* of which *Nebuchadnezzar* is a variant; here and often in Ezekiel and Jeremiah

THE MESSAGE

26.3-6 "Therefore, GOD, the Master, has this to say:

" 'I'm against you, Tyre,
   and I'll bring many nations surging against you,
   as the waves of the sea surging against the shore.
They'll smash the city walls of Tyre
   and break down her towers.
I'll wash away the soil
   and leave nothing but bare rock.
She'll be an island of bare rock in the ocean,
   good for nothing but drying fishnets.
Yes, I've said so.' Decree of GOD, the Master.
   'She'll be loot, free pickings for the nations!
Her surrounding villages will be butchered.
   Then they'll realize that I am GOD.'

26.7-14 "GOD, the Master, says: Look! Out of the north I'm bringing Nebuchadnezzar king of Babylon, a king's king, down on Tyre. He'll come with chariots and horses and riders—a huge army. He'll massacre your surrounding villages and lay siege to you. He'll build siege ramps against your walls. A forest of shields will advance against you! He'll pummel your walls with his battering rams and shatter your towers with his iron weapons. You'll be covered with dust from his horde of horses—a thundering herd of war horses pouring through the breaches, pulling chariots. Oh, it will be an earthquake of an army and a city in shock! Horses will stampede through the streets. Your people will be slaughtered and your huge pillars strewn like matchsticks. The invaders will steal and loot—all that wealth, all that stuff! They'll knock down your fine houses and dump the stone and timber rubble into the sea. And your parties, your famous good-time parties, will be no more. No more songs, no more lutes. I'll reduce you to an island of bare rock, good for nothing but drying fishnets. You'll never be rebuilt. I, GOD, have said so. Decree of GOD, the Master.

INTRODUCED TO THE TERRORS OF DEATH

26.15 "This is the Message of GOD, the Master, to Tyre: Won't the ocean islands shake at the crash of your collapse, at the groans of your wounded, at your mayhem and massacre?

26.16-18 "All up and down the coast, the princes will come down from their thrones, take off their royal robes and fancy clothes, and wrap themselves in sheer terror. They'll sit on the ground, shaken to the core, horrified at you. Then they'll begin chanting a funeral song over you:

NEW INTERNATIONAL VERSION

" 'How you are destroyed, O city of renown,
  peopled by men of the sea!
You were a power on the seas,
  you and your citizens;
you put your terror
  on all who lived there.
¹⁸ Now the coastlands tremble
  on the day of your fall;
the islands in the sea
  are terrified at your collapse.'

¹⁹ "This is what the Sovereign LORD says:
When I make you a desolate city, like cities no
longer inhabited, and when I bring the ocean
depths over you and its vast waters cover you,
²⁰ then I will bring you down with those who
go down to the pit, to the people of long ago. I
will make you dwell in the earth below, as in ancient ruins, with those who go down to the pit,
and you will not return or take your place*ᵃ* in
the land of the living. ²¹ I will bring you to a horrible end and you will be no more. You will be
sought, but you will never again be found, declares the Sovereign LORD."

A LAMENT FOR TYRE

27 The word of the LORD came to me: ² "Son
of man, take up a lament concerning
Tyre. ³ Say to Tyre, situated at the gateway to the
sea, merchant of peoples on many coasts, 'This is
what the Sovereign LORD says:

" 'You say, O Tyre,
  "I am perfect in beauty."
⁴ Your domain was on the high seas;
  your builders brought your beauty to
    perfection.
⁵ They made all your timbers
  of pine trees from Senir*ᵇ*;
they took a cedar from Lebanon
  to make a mast for you.
⁶ Of oaks from Bashan
  they made your oars;
of cypress wood*ᶜ* from the coasts of Cyprus*ᵈ*
  they made your deck, inlaid with ivory.
⁷ Fine embroidered linen from Egypt was your
    sail
  and served as your banner;
your awnings were of blue and purple
  from the coasts of Elishah.
⁸ Men of Sidon and Arvad were your oarsmen;
  your skilled men, O Tyre, were aboard as
    your seamen.
⁹ Veteran craftsmen of Gebal*ᵉ* were on board

THE MESSAGE

" 'Sunk! Sunk to the bottom of the sea,
  famous city on the sea!
Power of the seas,
  you and your people,
Intimidating everyone
  who lived in your shadows.
But now the islands are shaking
  at the sound of your crash,
Ocean islands in tremors
  from the impact of your fall.'

²⁶.¹⁹⁻²¹   "The Message of GOD, the Master: 'When I
turn you into a wasted city, a city empty of
people, a ghost town, and when I bring up the
great ocean deeps and cover you, then I'll push
you down among those who go to the grave,
the long, long dead. I'll make you live there, in
the grave in old ruins, with the buried dead.
You'll never see the land of the living again. I'll
introduce you to the terrors of death and that'll
be the end of you. They'll send out search parties for you, but you'll never be found. Decree
of GOD, the Master.' "

TYRE, GATEWAY TO THE SEA

²⁷.¹⁻⁹   **27** GOD's Message came to me: "You, son
of man, raise a funeral song over Tyre.
Tell Tyre, gateway to the sea, merchant to the
world, trader among the far-off islands, 'This is
what GOD, the Master, says:

" 'You boast, Tyre:
  "I'm the perfect ship—stately, handsome."
You ruled the high seas from
  a real beauty, crafted to perfection.
Your planking came from
  Mount Hermon junipers.
A Lebanon cedar
  supplied your mast.
They made your oars
  from sturdy Bashan oaks.
Cypress from Cyprus inlaid with ivory
  was used for the decks.
Your sail and flag were of colorful
  embroidered linen from Egypt.
Your purple deck awnings
  also came from Cyprus.
Men of Sidon and Arvad pulled the oars.
  Your seasoned seamen, O Tyre, were the
    crew.
Ship's carpenters

ᵃ 20 Septuagint; Hebrew *return, and I will give glory*
ᵇ 5 That is, Hermon   *ᶜ 6* Targum; the Masoretic Text has
a different division of the consonants.   *ᵈ 6* Hebrew *Kittim*
ᵉ 9 That is, Byblos

NEW INTERNATIONAL VERSION

as shipwrights to caulk your seams.
All the ships of the sea and their sailors
came alongside to trade for your wares.

10 " 'Men of Persia, Lydia and Put
served as soldiers in your army.
They hung their shields and helmets on your
walls,
bringing you splendor.
11 Men of Arvad and Helech
manned your walls on every side;
men of Gammad
were in your towers.
They hung their shields around your walls;
they brought your beauty to perfection.

12 " 'Tarshish did business with you because
of your great wealth of goods; they exchanged
silver, iron, tin and lead for your merchandise.
13 " 'Greece, Tubal and Meshech traded with
you; they exchanged slaves and articles of bronze
for your wares.
14 " 'Men of Beth Togarmah exchanged work
horses, war horses and mules for your merchandise.
15 " 'The men of Rhodes*a* traded with you, and
many coastlands were your customers; they paid
you with ivory tusks and ebony.
16 " 'Aram*b* did business with you because of
your many products; they exchanged turquoise,
purple fabric, embroidered work, fine linen, coral and rubies for your merchandise.
17 " 'Judah and Israel traded with you; they exchanged wheat from Minnith and confections,*c*
honey, oil and balm for your wares.
18 " 'Damascus, because of your many products and great wealth of goods, did business with
you in wine from Helbon and wool from Zahar.
19 " 'Danites and Greeks from Uzal bought
your merchandise; they exchanged wrought
iron, cassia and calamus for your wares.
20 " 'Dedan traded in saddle blankets with you.
21 " 'Arabia and all the princes of Kedar were
your customers; they did business with you in
lambs, rams and goats.
22 " 'The merchants of Sheba and Raamah traded with you; for your merchandise they exchanged the finest of all kinds of spices and precious stones, and gold.
23 " 'Haran, Canneh and Eden and merchants
of Sheba, Asshur and Kilmad traded with you.
24 In your marketplace they traded with you
beautiful garments, blue fabric, embroidered
work and multicolored rugs with cords twisted
and tightly knotted.

a 15 Septuagint; Hebrew *Dedan*   *b 16* Most Hebrew
manuscripts; some Hebrew manuscripts and Syriac *Edom*
c 17 The meaning of the Hebrew for this word is uncertain.

THE MESSAGE

were old salts from Byblos.
All the ships of the sea and their sailors
clustered around you to barter for your
goods.

27.10-11 " 'Your army was composed of soldiers
from Paras, Lud, and Put,
Elite troops in uniformed splendor.
They put you on the map!
Your city police were imported from
Arvad, Helech, and Gammad.
They hung their shields from the city walls,
a final, perfect touch to your beauty.

27.12 " 'Tarshish carried on business with you because of your great wealth. They worked for
you, trading in silver, iron, tin, and lead for
your products.
27.13 " 'Greece, Tubal, and Meshech did business
with you, trading slaves and bronze for your
products.
27.14 " 'Beth-togarmah traded work horses, war
horses, and mules for your products.
27.15 " 'The people of Rhodes did business with
you. Many far-off islands traded with you in
ivory and ebony.
27.16 " 'Edom did business with you because of
all your goods. They traded for your products
with agate, purple textiles, embroidered cloth,
fine linen, coral, and rubies.
27.17 " 'Judah and Israel did business with you.
They traded for your products with premium
wheat, millet, honey, oil, and balm.
27.18 " 'Damascus, attracted by your vast array of
products and well-stocked warehouses, carried
on business with you, trading in wine from
Helbon and wool from Zahar.
27.19 " 'Danites and Greeks from Uzal traded with
you, using wrought iron, cinnamon, and
spices.
27.20 " 'Dedan traded with you for saddle blankets.
27.21 " 'Arabia and all the Bedouin sheiks of Kedar
traded lambs, rams, and goats with you.
27.22 " 'Traders from Sheba and Raamah in South
Arabia carried on business with you in premium spices, precious stones, and gold.
27.23-24 " 'Haran, Canneh, and Eden from the east in
Assyria and Media traded with you, bringing
elegant clothes, dyed textiles, and elaborate
carpets to your bazaars.

NEW INTERNATIONAL VERSION

25 " 'The ships of Tarshish serve
    as carriers for your wares.
You are filled with heavy cargo
    in the heart of the sea.
26 Your oarsmen take you
    out to the high seas.
But the east wind will break you to pieces
    in the heart of the sea.
27 Your wealth, merchandise and wares,
    your mariners, seamen and shipwrights,
your merchants and all your soldiers,
    and everyone else on board
will sink into the heart of the sea
    on the day of your shipwreck.
28 The shorelands will quake
    when your seamen cry out.
29 All who handle the oars
    will abandon their ships;
the mariners and all the seamen
    will stand on the shore.
30 They will raise their voice
    and cry bitterly over you;
they will sprinkle dust on their heads
    and roll in ashes.
31 They will shave their heads because of you
    and will put on sackcloth.
They will weep over you with anguish of
        soul
    and with bitter mourning.
32 As they wail and mourn over you,
    they will take up a lament concerning
        you:
"Who was ever silenced like Tyre,
    surrounded by the sea?"
33 When your merchandise went out on the
        seas,
    you satisfied many nations;
with your great wealth and your wares
    you enriched the kings of the earth.
34 Now you are shattered by the sea
    in the depths of the waters;
your wares and all your company
    have gone down with you.
35 All who live in the coastlands
    are appalled at you;
their kings shudder with horror
    and their faces are distorted with fear.
36 The merchants among the nations hiss at
        you;
    you have come to a horrible end
    and will be no more.' "

A PROPHECY AGAINST THE KING OF TYRE

28 The word of the LORD came to me: 2 "Son of man, say to the ruler of Tyre, 'This is what the Sovereign LORD says:

" 'In the pride of your heart

THE MESSAGE

27.25   " 'The great Tarshish ships were your freighters, importing and exporting. Oh, it was big business for you, trafficking the seaways!

27.26-32 " 'Your sailors row mightily,
    taking you into the high seas.
Then a storm out of the east
    shatters your ship in the ocean deep.
Everything sinks—your rich goods and
        products,
    sailors and crew, ship's carpenters and
        soldiers,
Sink to the bottom of the sea.
    Total shipwreck.
The cries of your sailors
    reverberate on shore.
Sailors everywhere abandon ship.
    Veteran seamen swim for dry land.
They cry out in grief,
    a choir of bitter lament over you.
They smear their faces with ashes,
    shave their heads,
Wear rough burlap,
    wildly keening their loss.
They raise their funeral song:
    "Who on the high seas is like Tyre!"

27.33-36 " 'As you crisscrossed the seas with your
        products,
    you satisfied many peoples.
Your worldwide trade
    made earth's kings rich.
And now you're battered to bits by the waves,
    sunk to the bottom of the sea,
And everything you've bought and sold
    has sunk to the bottom with you.
Everyone on shore looks on in terror.
    The hair of kings stands on end,
    their faces drawn and haggard!
The buyers and sellers of the world
    throw up their hands:
This horror can't happen!
    Oh, this has happened!' "

THE MONEY HAS GONE TO YOUR HEAD

28.1-5 28 GOD's Message came to me, "Son of man, tell the prince of Tyre, 'This is what GOD, the Master, says:

" 'Your heart is proud,

NEW INTERNATIONAL VERSION

you say, "I am a god;
I sit on the throne of a god
  in the heart of the seas."
But you are a man and not a god,
  though you think you are as wise as a god.
[3] Are you wiser than Daniel[a]?
  Is no secret hidden from you?
[4] By your wisdom and understanding
  you have gained wealth for yourself
and amassed gold and silver
  in your treasuries.
[5] By your great skill in trading
  you have increased your wealth,
and because of your wealth
  your heart has grown proud.

[6] " 'Therefore this is what the Sovereign Lord says:

" 'Because you think you are wise,
  as wise as a god,
[7] I am going to bring foreigners against you,
  the most ruthless of nations;
they will draw their swords against your
      beauty and wisdom
  and pierce your shining splendor.
[8] They will bring you down to the pit,
  and you will die a violent death
  in the heart of the seas.
[9] Will you then say, "I am a god,"
  in the presence of those who kill you?
You will be but a man, not a god,
  in the hands of those who slay you.
[10] You will die the death of the uncircumcised
  at the hands of foreigners.

I have spoken, declares the Sovereign Lord.' "

[11] The word of the Lord came to me: [12] "Son of man, take up a lament concerning the king of Tyre and say to him: 'This is what the Sovereign Lord says:

" 'You were the model of perfection,
  full of wisdom and perfect in beauty.
[13] You were in Eden,
  the garden of God;
every precious stone adorned you:
  ruby, topaz and emerald,
  chrysolite, onyx and jasper,
  sapphire,[b] turquoise and beryl.[c]
Your settings and mountings[d] were made of
      gold;
  on the day you were created they were
      prepared.

---

[a] 3 Or *Danel*; the Hebrew spelling may suggest a person other than the prophet Daniel.   [b] 13 Or *lapis lazuli*
[c] 13 The precise identification of some of these precious stones is uncertain.   [d] 13 The meaning of the Hebrew for this phrase is uncertain.

THE MESSAGE

going around saying, "I'm a god.
I sit on God's divine throne,
  ruling the sea"—
You, a mere mortal,
  not even close to being a god,
A mere mortal
  trying to be a god.
Look, you think you're smarter than Daniel.
  No enigmas can stump you.
Your sharp intelligence
  made you world-wealthy.
You piled up gold and silver
  in your banks.
You used your head well,
  worked good deals, made a lot of money.
But the money has gone to your head,
  swelled your head—what a big head!

28:6-11   " 'Therefore, God, the Master, says:

" 'Because you're acting like a god,
  pretending to *be* a god,
I'm giving fair warning: I'm bringing strangers
      down on you,
  the most vicious of all nations.
They'll pull their swords and make hash
  of your reputation for knowing it all.
They'll puncture the balloon
  of your god-pretensions.
They'll bring you down from your self-made
      pedestal
  and bury you in the deep blue sea.
Will you protest to your assassins,
  "You can't do that! I'm a god"?
To them you're a mere mortal.
  They're killing a man, not a god.
You'll die like a stray dog,
  killed by strangers—
Because I said so.
  Decree of God, the Master.' "

28:11-19   God's Message came to me: "Son of man, raise a funeral song over the king of Tyre. Tell him, A Message from God, the Master:

"You had everything going for you.
  You were in Eden, God's garden.
You were dressed in splendor,
  your robe studded with jewels:
Carnelian, peridot, and moonstone,
  beryl, onyx, and jasper,
Sapphire, turquoise, and emerald,
  all in settings of engraved gold.
A robe was prepared for you
  the same day you were created.

NEW INTERNATIONAL VERSION

¹⁴You were anointed as a guardian cherub,
  for so I ordained you.
You were on the holy mount of God;
  you walked among the fiery stones.
¹⁵You were blameless in your ways
  from the day you were created
  till wickedness was found in you.
¹⁶Through your widespread trade
  you were filled with violence,
  and you sinned.
So I drove you in disgrace from the mount of
    God,
  and I expelled you, O guardian cherub,
  from among the fiery stones.
¹⁷Your heart became proud
  on account of your beauty,
and you corrupted your wisdom
  because of your splendor.
So I threw you to the earth;
  I made a spectacle of you before kings.
¹⁸By your many sins and dishonest trade
  you have desecrated your sanctuaries.
So I made a fire come out from you,
  and it consumed you,
and I reduced you to ashes on the ground
  in the sight of all who were watching.
¹⁹All the nations who knew you
  are appalled at you;
you have come to a horrible end
  and will be no more.' "

A PROPHECY AGAINST SIDON

²⁰The word of the LORD came to me: ²¹"Son of man, set your face against Sidon; prophesy against her ²²and say: 'This is what the Sovereign LORD says:

" 'I am against you, O Sidon,
  and I will gain glory within you.
They will know that I am the LORD,
  when I inflict punishment on her
  and show myself holy within her.
²³I will send a plague upon her
  and make blood flow in her streets.
The slain will fall within her,
  with the sword against her on every side.
Then they will know that I am the LORD.

²⁴" 'No longer will the people of Israel have malicious neighbors who are painful briers and sharp thorns. Then they will know that I am the Sovereign LORD.

THE MESSAGE

You were the anointed cherub.
  I placed you on the mountain of God.
You strolled in magnificence
  among the stones of fire.
From the day of your creation
  you were sheer perfection . . .
  and then imperfection—evil!—was
    detected in you.
In much buying and selling
  you turned violent, you sinned!
I threw you, disgraced, off the mountain of God.
  I threw you out—you, the anointed
    angel-cherub.
  No more strolling among the gems of fire
    for you!
Your beauty went to your head.
  You corrupted wisdom
  by using it to get worldly fame.
I threw you to the ground,
  sent you sprawling before an audience of
    kings
  and let them gloat over your demise.
By sin after sin after sin,
  by your corrupt ways of doing business,
  you defiled your holy places of worship.
So I set a fire around and within you.
  It burned you up. I reduced you to ashes.
All anyone sees now
  when they look for you is ashes,
  a pitiful mound of ashes.
All who once knew you
  now throw up their hands:
'This can't have happened!
  This *has* happened!' "

☩

^{28.20-23} GOD'S Message came to me: "Son of man, confront Sidon. Preach against it. Say, 'Message from GOD, the Master:

" 'Look! I'm against you, Sidon.
  I intend to be known for who I truly am
    among you.'
They'll know that I am GOD
  when I set things right
  and reveal my holy presence.
I'll order an epidemic of disease there,
  along with murder and mayhem in the
    streets.
People will drop dead right and left,
  as war presses in from every side.
Then they'll realize that I mean business,
  that I am GOD.

^{28.24} "No longer will Israel have to put up with
  their thistle-and-thorn neighbors
Who have treated them so contemptuously.
  And they also will realize that I am GOD."

NEW INTERNATIONAL VERSION

25 " 'This is what the Sovereign LORD says: When I gather the people of Israel from the nations where they have been scattered, I will show myself holy among them in the sight of the nations. Then they will live in their own land, which I gave to my servant Jacob. 26 They will live there in safety and will build houses and plant vineyards; they will live in safety when I inflict punishment on all their neighbors who maligned them. Then they will know that I am the LORD their God.' "

A PROPHECY AGAINST EGYPT

29 In the tenth year, in the tenth month on the twelfth day, the word of the LORD came to me: 2 "Son of man, set your face against Pharaoh king of Egypt and prophesy against him and against all Egypt. 3 Speak to him and say: 'This is what the Sovereign LORD says:

" 'I am against you, Pharaoh king of Egypt,
  you great monster lying among your
    streams.
You say, "The Nile is mine;
  I made it for myself."
4 But I will put hooks in your jaws
  and make the fish of your streams stick to
    your scales.
I will pull you out from among your streams,
  with all the fish sticking to your scales.
5 I will leave you in the desert,
  you and all the fish of your streams.
You will fall on the open field
  and not be gathered or picked up.
I will give you as food
  to the beasts of the earth and the birds of
    the air.

6 Then all who live in Egypt will know that I am the LORD.

" 'You have been a staff of reed for the house of Israel. 7 When they grasped you with their hands, you splintered and you tore open their shoulders; when they leaned on you, you broke and their backs were wrenched. [a]

8 " 'Therefore this is what the Sovereign LORD says: I will bring a sword against you and kill your men and their animals. 9 Egypt will become a desolate wasteland. Then they will know that I am the LORD.

" 'Because you said, "The Nile is mine; I made it," 10 therefore I am against you and against your streams, and I will make the land of Egypt a ruin and a desolate waste from Migdol to Aswan, as far as the border of Cush. [b] 11 No foot of man or

---

[a] 7 Syriac (see also Septuagint and Vulgate); Hebrew *and you caused their backs to stand*   [b] 10 That is, the upper Nile region

THE MESSAGE

28.25-26   GOD, the Master, says, "When I gather Israel from the peoples among whom they've been scattered and put my holiness on display among them with all the nations looking on, then they'll live in their own land that I gave to my servant Jacob. They'll live there in safety. They'll build houses. They'll plant vineyards, living in safety. Meanwhile, I'll bring judgment on all the neighbors who have treated them with such contempt. And they'll realize that I am GOD."

NEVER A WORLD POWER AGAIN

29.1-6   **29** In the tenth year, in the tenth month, on the twelfth day, GOD's Message came to me: "Son of man, confront Pharaoh king of Egypt. Preach against him and all the Egyptians. Tell him, 'GOD, the Master, says:

" 'Watch yourself, Pharaoh, king of Egypt.
  I'm dead set against you,
You lumbering old dragon,
  lolling and flaccid in the Nile,
Saying, "It's my Nile.
  I made it. It's mine."
I'll set hooks in your jaw;
  I'll make the fish of the Nile stick to your
    scales.
I'll pull you out of the Nile,
  with all the fish stuck to your scales.
Then I'll drag you out into the desert,
  you and all the Nile fish sticking to your
    scales.
You'll lie there in the open, rotting in the sun,
  meat to the wild animals and carrion birds.
Everybody living in Egypt
  will realize that I am GOD.

29.6-9   " 'Because you've been a flimsy reed crutch to Israel so that when they gripped you, you splintered and cut their hand, and when they leaned on you, you broke and sent them sprawling—Message of GOD, the Master—I'll bring war against you, do away with people and animals alike, and turn the country into an empty desert so they'll realize that I am GOD.

29.9-11   " 'Because you said, "It's my Nile. I made it. It's all mine," therefore I am against you and your rivers. I'll reduce Egypt to an empty, desolate wasteland all the way from Migdol in the north to Syene and the border of Ethiopia in the south. Not a human will be seen in it, nor

NEW INTERNATIONAL VERSION

animal will pass through it; no one will live there for forty years. ¹²I will make the land of Egypt desolate among devastated lands, and her cities will lie desolate forty years among ruined cities. And I will disperse the Egyptians among the nations and scatter them through the countries.

¹³" 'Yet this is what the Sovereign LORD says: At the end of forty years I will gather the Egyptians from the nations where they were scattered. ¹⁴I will bring them back from captivity and return them to Upper Egypt,ᵃ the land of their ancestry. There they will be a lowly kingdom. ¹⁵It will be the lowliest of kingdoms and will never again exalt itself above the other nations. I will make it so weak that it will never again rule over the nations. ¹⁶Egypt will no longer be a source of confidence for the people of Israel but will be a reminder of their sin in turning to her for help. Then they will know that I am the Sovereign LORD.' "

¹⁷In the twenty-seventh year, in the first month on the first day, the word of the LORD came to me: ¹⁸"Son of man, Nebuchadnezzar king of Babylon drove his army in a hard campaign against Tyre; every head was rubbed bare and every shoulder made raw. Yet he and his army got no reward from the campaign he led against Tyre. ¹⁹Therefore this is what the Sovereign LORD says: I am going to give Egypt to Nebuchadnezzar king of Babylon, and he will carry off its wealth. He will loot and plunder the land as pay for his army. ²⁰I have given him Egypt as a reward for his efforts because he and his army did it for me, declares the Sovereign LORD.

²¹"On that day I will make a hornᵇ grow for the house of Israel, and I will open your mouth among them. Then they will know that I am the LORD."

A LAMENT FOR EGYPT

30 The word of the LORD came to me: ²"Son of man, prophesy and say: 'This is what the Sovereign LORD says:

" 'Wail and say,
    "Alas for that day!"
³For the day is near,
    the day of the LORD is near—
a day of clouds,
    a time of doom for the nations.
⁴A sword will come against Egypt,
    and anguish will come upon Cush.ᶜ
When the slain fall in Egypt,
    her wealth will be carried away
    and her foundations torn down.

ᵃ 14 Hebrew to Pathros   ᵇ 21 Horn here symbolizes strength.   ᶜ 4 That is, the upper Nile region; also in verses 5 and 9

THE MESSAGE

will an animal move through it. It'll be just empty desert, empty for forty years.

29.12   " 'I'll make Egypt the most desolate of all desolations. For forty years I'll make her cities the most wasted of all wasted cities. I'll scatter Egyptians to the four winds, send them off every which way into exile.

29.13-16   " 'But,' says GOD, the Master, 'that's not the end of it. After the forty years, I'll gather up the Egyptians from all the places where they've been scattered. I'll put things back together again for Egypt. I'll bring her back to Pathros where she got her start long ago. There she'll start over again from scratch. She'll take her place at the bottom of the ladder and there she'll stay, never to climb that ladder again, never to be a world power again. Never again will Israel be tempted to rely on Egypt. All she'll be to Israel is a reminder of old sin. Then Egypt will realize that I am GOD, the Master.' "

✝

29.17-18   In the twenty-seventh year, in the first month, on the first day of the month, GOD's Message came to me: "Son of man, Nebuchadnezzar, king of Babylon, has worn out his army against Tyre. They've worked their fingers to the bone and have nothing to show for it.

29.19-20   "Therefore, GOD, the Master, says, 'I'm giving Egypt to Nebuchadnezzar king of Babylon. He'll haul away its wealth, pick the place clean. He'll pay his army with Egyptian plunder. He's been working for me all these years without pay. This is his pay: Egypt. Decree of GOD, the Master.

29.21   " 'And then I'll stir up fresh hope in Israel—the dawn of deliverance!—and I'll give you, Ezekiel, bold and confident words to speak. And they'll realize that I am GOD.' "

EGYPT ON FIRE

30.1-5   **30** GOD, the Master, spoke to me: "Son of man, preach. Give them the Message of GOD, the Master. Wail:

" 'Doomsday!'
    Time's up!
    GOD's big day of judgment is near.
Thick clouds are rolling in.
    It's doomsday for the nations.
Death will rain down on Egypt.
    Terror will paralyze Ethiopia
When they see the Egyptians killed,
    their wealth hauled off,
    their foundations demolished,

NEW INTERNATIONAL VERSION

[5]Cush and Put, Lydia and all Arabia, Libya[a] and the people of the covenant land will fall by the sword along with Egypt.

[6]" 'This is what the LORD says:

" 'The allies of Egypt will fall
and her proud strength will fail.
From Migdol to Aswan
they will fall by the sword within her,
    declares the Sovereign
        LORD.
[7]" 'They will be desolate
among desolate lands,
and their cities will lie
among ruined cities.
[8]Then they will know that I am the LORD,
when I set fire to Egypt
and all her helpers are crushed.

[9]" 'On that day messengers will go out from me in ships to frighten Cush out of her complacency. Anguish will take hold of them on the day of Egypt's doom, for it is sure to come.

[10]" 'This is what the Sovereign LORD says:

" 'I will put an end to the hordes of Egypt
by the hand of Nebuchadnezzar king of
        Babylon.
[11]He and his army—the most ruthless of
        nations—
will be brought in to destroy the land.
They will draw their swords against Egypt
and fill the land with the slain.
[12]I will dry up the streams of the Nile
and sell the land to evil men;
by the hand of foreigners
    I will lay waste the land and everything
        in it.

I the LORD have spoken.

[13]" 'This is what the Sovereign LORD says:

" 'I will destroy the idols
and put an end to the images in
        Memphis.[b]
No longer will there be a prince in Egypt,
and I will spread fear throughout the land.
[14]I will lay waste Upper Egypt,[c]
set fire to Zoan
and inflict punishment on Thebes.[d]
[15]I will pour out my wrath on Pelusium,[e]
the stronghold of Egypt,
and cut off the hordes of Thebes.
[16]I will set fire to Egypt;
Pelusium will writhe in agony.
Thebes will be taken by storm;

---

[a] 5 Hebrew *Cub*   [b] 13 Hebrew *Noph*; also in verse 16
[c] 14 Hebrew *waste Pathros*   [d] 14 Hebrew *No*; also in
verses 15 and 16   [e] 15 Hebrew *Sin*; also in verse 16

THE MESSAGE

And Ethiopia, Put, Lud, Arabia, Libya
—all of Egypt's old allies—
    killed right along with them.

30.6-8   " 'GOD says:

" 'Egypt's allies will fall
and her proud strength will collapse—
From Migdol in the north to Syene in the
        south,
a great slaughter in Egypt!
Decree of GOD, the Master.
Egypt, most desolate of the desolate,
her cities wasted beyond wasting,
Will realize that I am GOD
when I burn her down
and her helpers are knocked flat.

30.9   " 'When that happens, I'll send out messengers by ship to sound the alarm among the easygoing Ethiopians. They'll be terrorized. Egypt's doomed! Judgment's coming!

30.10-12   " 'GOD, the Master, says:

" 'I'll put a stop to Egypt's arrogance.
I'll use Nebuchadnezzar king of Babylon to
        do it.
He and his army, the most brutal of nations,
    shall be used to destroy the country.
They'll brandish their swords
    and fill Egypt with corpses.
I'll dry up the Nile
    and sell off the land to a bunch of crooks.
I'll hire outsiders to come in
    and waste the country, strip it clean.
I, GOD, have said so.

30.13-19   " 'And now this is what GOD, the Master,
        says:

" 'I'll smash all the no-god idols;
I'll topple all those huge statues in
        Memphis.
The prince of Egypt will be gone for good,
    and in his place I'll put *fear*—fear
        throughout Egypt!
I'll demolish Pathros,
    burn Zoan to the ground, and punish
        Thebes,
Pour my wrath on Pelusium, Egypt's fort,
    and knock Thebes off its proud pedestal.
I'll set Egypt on fire:
    Pelusium will writhe in pain,
Thebes blown away,

NEW INTERNATIONAL VERSION

Memphis will be in constant distress.
¹⁷ The young men of Heliopolis*a* and Bubastis*b*
will fall by the sword,
and the cities themselves will go into
captivity.
¹⁸ Dark will be the day at Tahpanhes
when I break the yoke of Egypt;
there her proud strength will come to an
end.
She will be covered with clouds,
and her villages will go into captivity.
¹⁹ So I will inflict punishment on Egypt,
and they will know that I am the LORD.' "

²⁰In the eleventh year, in the first month on
the seventh day, the word of the LORD came to
me: ²¹"Son of man, I have broken the arm of
Pharaoh king of Egypt. It has not been bound up
for healing or put in a splint so as to become
strong enough to hold a sword. ²²Therefore this is
what the Sovereign LORD says: I am against Pharaoh king of Egypt. I will break both his arms, the
good arm as well as the broken one, and make the
sword fall from his hand. ²³I will disperse the
Egyptians among the nations and scatter them
through the countries. ²⁴I will strengthen the
arms of the king of Babylon and put my sword in
his hand, but I will break the arms of Pharaoh,
and he will groan before him like a mortally
wounded man. ²⁵I will strengthen the arms of the
king of Babylon, but the arms of Pharaoh will fall
limp. Then they will know that I am the LORD,
when I put my sword into the hand of the king of
Babylon and he brandishes it against Egypt. ²⁶I
will disperse the Egyptians among the nations and
scatter them through the countries. Then they
will know that I am the LORD."

A CEDAR IN LEBANON

31 In the eleventh year, in the third month
on the first day, the word of the LORD
came to me: ²"Son of man, say to Pharaoh king
of Egypt and to his hordes:

" 'Who can be compared with you in
majesty?
³ Consider Assyria, once a cedar in Lebanon,
with beautiful branches overshadowing
the forest;
it towered on high,
its top above the thick foliage.
⁴ The waters nourished it,
deep springs made it grow tall;
their streams flowed
all around its base
and sent their channels
to all the trees of the field.

^a 17 Hebrew *Awen* (or *On*)   ^b 17 Hebrew *Pi Beseth*

THE MESSAGE

Memphis raped.
The young warriors of On and Pi-beseth
will be killed and the cities exiled.
A dark day for Tahpanhes
when I shatter Egypt,
When I break Egyptian power
and put an end to her arrogant oppression!
She'll disappear in a cloud of dust,
her cities hauled off as exiles.
That's how I'll punish Egypt,
and that's how she'll realize that I am
GOD.' "

✢

^{30.20} In the eleventh year, on the seventh day of the
first month, GOD's Message came to me:

^{30.21} "Son of man, I've broken the arm of Pharaoh
king of Egypt. And look! It hasn't been set. No
splint has been put on it so the bones can knit
and heal, so he can use a sword again.

^{30.22-26} "Therefore, GOD, the Master, says, I am dead
set against Pharaoh king of Egypt and will go
ahead and break his other arm—both arms broken! There's no way he'll ever swing a sword
again. I'll scatter Egyptians all over the world.
I'll make the arms of the king of Babylon strong
and put my sword in his hand, but I'll break
the arms of Pharaoh and he'll groan like one
who is mortally wounded. I'll make the arms of
the king of Babylon strong, but the arms of
Pharaoh shall go limp. The Egyptians will realize that I am GOD when I place my sword in the
hand of the king of Babylon. He'll wield it
against Egypt and I'll scatter Egyptians all over
the world. Then they'll realize that I am GOD."

THE FUNERAL OF THE BIG TREE

^{31.1-9} **31** In the eleventh year, on the first day of
the third month, GOD's Message came
to me: "Son of man, tell Pharaoh king of Egypt,
that pompous old goat:

" 'Who do you, astride the world,
think you really are?
Look! Assyria was a Big Tree, huge as a
Lebanon cedar,
beautiful limbs offering cool shade,
Skyscraper high,
piercing the clouds.
The waters gave it drink,
the primordial deep lifted it high,
Gushing out rivers around
the place where it was planted,
And then branching out in streams
to all the trees in the forest.

NEW INTERNATIONAL VERSION

⁵ So it towered higher
than all the trees of the field;
its boughs increased
and its branches grew long,
spreading because of abundant waters.
⁶ All the birds of the air
nested in its boughs,
all the beasts of the field
gave birth under its branches;
all the great nations
lived in its shade.
⁷ It was majestic in beauty,
with its spreading boughs,
for its roots went down
to abundant waters.
⁸ The cedars in the garden of God
could not rival it,
nor could the pine trees
equal its boughs,
nor could the plane trees
compare with its branches—
no tree in the garden of God
could match its beauty.
⁹ I made it beautiful
with abundant branches,
the envy of all the trees of Eden
in the garden of God.

10 " 'Therefore this is what the Sovereign LORD says: Because it towered on high, lifting its top above the thick foliage, and because it was proud of its height, 11 I handed it over to the ruler of the nations, for him to deal with according to its wickedness. I cast it aside, 12 and the most ruthless of foreign nations cut it down and left it. Its boughs fell on the mountains and in all the valleys; its branches lay broken in all the ravines of the land. All the nations of the earth came out from under its shade and left it. 13 All the birds of the air settled on the fallen tree, and all the beasts of the field were among its branches. 14 Therefore no other trees by the waters are ever to tower proudly on high, lifting their tops above the thick foliage. No other trees so well-watered are ever to reach such a height; they are all destined for death, for the earth below, among mortal men, with those who go down to the pit.

15 " 'This is what the Sovereign LORD says: On the day it was brought down to the grave*a* I covered the deep springs with mourning for it; I held back its streams, and its abundant waters were restrained. Because of it I clothed Lebanon with gloom, and all the trees of the field withered away. 16 I made the nations tremble at the sound of its fall when I brought it down to the grave with those who go down to the pit. Then

a 15 Hebrew Sheol; also in verses 16 and 17

THE MESSAGE

It was immense,
dwarfing all the trees in the forest—
Thick boughs, long limbs,
roots delving deep into earth's waters.
All the birds of the air
nested in its boughs.
All the wild animals
gave birth under its branches.
All the mighty nations
lived in its shade.
It was stunning in its majesty—
the reach of its branches!
the depth of its water-seeking roots!
Not a cedar in God's garden came close to it.
No pine tree was anything like it.
Mighty oaks looked like bushes
growing alongside it.
Not a tree in God's garden
was in the same class of beauty.
I made it beautiful,
a work of art in limbs and leaves,
The envy of every tree in Eden,
every last tree in God's garden.' "

31.10-13 Therefore, GOD, the Master, says, " 'Because it skyscrapered upwards, piercing the clouds, swaggering and proud of its stature, I turned it over to a world-famous leader to call its evil to account. I'd had enough. Outsiders, unbelievably brutal, felled it across the mountain ranges. Its branches were strewn through all the valleys, its leafy boughs clogging all the streams and rivers. Because its shade was gone, everybody walked off. No longer a tree—just a log. On that dead log birds perch. Wild animals burrow under it.

31.14 " 'That marks the end of the "big tree" nations. No more trees nourished from the great deep, no more cloud-piercing trees, no more earth-born trees taking over. They're all slated for death—back to earth, right along with men and women, for whom it's "dust to dust."

31.15-17 " 'The Message of GOD, the Master: On the day of the funeral of the Big Tree, I threw the great deep into mourning. I stopped the flow of its rivers, held back great seas, and wrapped the Lebanon mountains in black. All the trees of the forest fainted and fell. I made the whole world quake when it crashed, and threw it into the underworld to take its place with all else

NEW INTERNATIONAL VERSION	THE MESSAGE

all the trees of Eden, the choicest and best of Lebanon, all the trees that were well-watered, were consoled in the earth below. ¹⁷Those who lived in its shade, its allies among the nations, had also gone down to the grave with it, joining those killed by the sword.

¹⁸" 'Which of the trees of Eden can be compared with you in splendor and majesty? Yet you, too, will be brought down with the trees of Eden to the earth below; you will lie among the uncircumcised, with those killed by the sword.

" 'This is Pharaoh and all his hordes, declares the Sovereign LORD.' "

A LAMENT FOR PHARAOH

32 In the twelfth year, in the twelfth month on the first day, the word of the LORD came to me: ²"Son of man, take up a lament concerning Pharaoh king of Egypt and say to him:

" 'You are like a lion among the nations;
  you are like a monster in the seas
thrashing about in your streams,
  churning the water with your feet
  and muddying the streams.

³" 'This is what the Sovereign LORD says:

" 'With a great throng of people
  I will cast my net over you,
  and they will haul you up in my net.
⁴I will throw you on the land
  and hurl you on the open field.
I will let all the birds of the air settle on you
  and all the beasts of the earth gorge
    themselves on you.
⁵I will spread your flesh on the mountains
  and fill the valleys with your remains.
⁶I will drench the land with your flowing
    blood
  all the way to the mountains,
  and the ravines will be filled with your
    flesh.
⁷When I snuff you out, I will cover the
    heavens
  and darken their stars;
  I will cover the sun with a cloud,
  and the moon will not give its light.
⁸All the shining lights in the heavens
  I will darken over you;
  I will bring darkness over your land,
                declares the Sovereign
                              LORD.
⁹I will trouble the hearts of many peoples
  when I bring about your destruction
    among the nations,

that gets buried. All the trees of Eden and the finest and best trees of Lebanon, well-watered, were relieved—they had descended to the underworld with it—along with everyone who had lived in its shade and all who had been killed.

31.18   " 'Which of the trees of Eden came anywhere close to you in splendor and size? But you're slated to be cut down to take your place in the underworld with the trees of Eden, to be a dead log stacked with all the other dead logs, among the other uncircumcised who are dead and buried.

" 'This means Pharaoh, the pompous old goat.
   " 'Decree of GOD, the Master.' "

A CLOUD ACROSS THE SUN

32.1-2 **32** In the twelfth year, on the first day of the twelfth month, GOD's Message came to me: "Son of man, sing a funeral lament over Pharaoh king of Egypt. Tell him:

" 'You think you're a young lion
  prowling through the nations.
You're more like a dragon in the ocean,
  snorting and thrashing about.

32.3-10   " 'GOD, the Master, says:

" 'I'm going to throw my net over you
  —many nations will get in on this
              operation—
  and haul you out with my dragnet.
I'll dump you on the ground
  out in an open field
And bring in all the crows and vultures
  for a sumptuous carrion lunch.
I'll invite wild animals from all over the world
  to gorge on your guts.
I'll scatter hunks of your meat in the
              mountains
  and strew your bones in the valleys.
The country, right up to the mountains,
  will be drenched with your blood,
  your blood filling every ditch and channel.
When I blot you out,
  I'll pull the curtain on the skies
  and shut out the stars.
I'll throw a cloud across the sun
  and turn off the moonlight.
I'll turn out every light in the sky above you
  and put your land in the dark.
     Decree of GOD, the Master.
I'll shake up everyone worldwide
  when I take you off captive to strange and
    far-off countries.

NEW INTERNATIONAL VERSION

among[a] lands you have not known. ¹⁰I will cause many peoples to be appalled at you,

and their kings will shudder with horror because of you
when I brandish my sword before them.
On the day of your downfall
each of them will tremble
every moment for his life.

¹¹" 'For this is what the Sovereign LORD says:

" 'The sword of the king of Babylon
will come against you.
¹²I will cause your hordes to fall
by the swords of mighty men—
the most ruthless of all nations.
They will shatter the pride of Egypt,
and all her hordes will be overthrown.
¹³I will destroy all her cattle
from beside abundant waters
no longer to be stirred by the foot of man
or muddied by the hoofs of cattle.
¹⁴Then I will let her waters settle
and make her streams flow like oil,
declares the Sovereign
LORD.

¹⁵When I make Egypt desolate
and strip the land of everything in it,
when I strike down all who live there,
then they will know that I am the LORD.'

¹⁶"This is the lament they will chant for her. The daughters of the nations will chant it; for Egypt and all her hordes they will chant it, declares the Sovereign LORD."

¹⁷In the twelfth year, on the fifteenth day of the month, the word of the LORD came to me: ¹⁸"Son of man, wail for the hordes of Egypt and consign to the earth below both her and the daughters of mighty nations, with those who go down to the pit. ¹⁹Say to them, 'Are you more favored than others? Go down and be laid among the uncircumcised.' ²⁰They will fall among those killed by the sword. The sword is drawn; let her be dragged off with all her hordes. ²¹From within the grave[b] the mighty leaders will say of Egypt and her allies, 'They have come down and they lie with the uncircumcised, with those killed by the sword.'

²²"Assyria is there with her whole army; she is surrounded by the graves of all her slain, all who have fallen by the sword. ²³Their graves are in the depths of the pit and her army lies around

THE MESSAGE

I'll shock people with you.
Kings will take one look and shudder.
I'll shake my sword
and they'll shake in their boots.
On the day you crash, they'll tremble,
thinking, "That could be me!"

TO LAY YOUR PRIDE LOW

32:11-15 " 'GOD, the Master, says:

" 'The sword of the king of Babylon
is coming against you.
I'll use the swords of champions
to lay your pride low,
Use the most brutal of nations
to knock Egypt off her high horse,
to puncture that hot-air pomposity.
I'll destroy all their livestock
that graze along the river.
Neither human foot nor animal hoof
will muddy those waters anymore.
I'll clear their springs and streams,
make their rivers flow clean and smooth.
Decree of GOD, the Master.
When I turn Egypt back to the wild
and strip her clean of all her abundant
produce,
When I strike dead all who live there,
then they'll realize that I am GOD.'

32:16 "This is a funeral song. Chant it.
Daughters of the nations, chant it.
Chant it over Egypt for the death of its
pomp."
Decree of GOD, the Master.

32:17-19   In the twelfth year, on the fifteenth day of the first month, GOD's Message came to me:

"Son of man, lament over Egypt's pompous
ways.
Send her on her way.
Dispatch Egypt
and her proud daughter nations
To the underworld,
down to the country of the dead and
buried.
Say, 'You think you're so high and mighty?
Down! Take your place with the heathen in
that unhallowed grave!'

32:20-21   "She'll be dumped in with those killed in battle. The sword is bared. Drag her off in all her proud pomp! All the big men and their helpers down among the dead and buried will greet them: 'Welcome to the grave of the heathen! Join the ranks of the victims of war!'

32:22-23   "Assyria is there and its congregation, the whole nation a cemetery. Their graves are in the deepest part of the underworld, a congre-

---

a 9 Hebrew; Septuagint *bring you into captivity among the nations, / to*   *b 21* Hebrew *Sheol*; also in verse 27

NEW INTERNATIONAL VERSION

her grave. All who had spread terror in the land of the living are slain, fallen by the sword.

²⁴"Elam is there, with all her hordes around her grave. All of them are slain, fallen by the sword. All who had spread terror in the land of the living went down uncircumcised to the earth below. They bear their shame with those who go down to the pit. ²⁵A bed is made for her among the slain, with all her hordes around her grave. All of them are uncircumcised, killed by the sword. Because their terror had spread in the land of the living, they bear their shame with those who go down to the pit; they are laid among the slain.

²⁶"Meshech and Tubal are there, with all their hordes around their graves. All of them are uncircumcised, killed by the sword because they spread their terror in the land of the living. ²⁷Do they not lie with the other uncircumcised warriors who have fallen, who went down to the grave with their weapons of war, whose swords were placed under their heads? The punishment for their sins rested on their bones, though the terror of these warriors had stalked through the land of the living.

²⁸"You too, O Pharaoh, will be broken and will lie among the uncircumcised, with those killed by the sword.

²⁹"Edom is there, her kings and all her princes; despite their power, they are laid with those killed by the sword. They lie with the uncircumcised, with those who go down to the pit.

³⁰"All the princes of the north and all the Sidonians are there; they went down with the slain in disgrace despite the terror caused by their power. They lie uncircumcised with those killed by the sword and bear their shame with those who go down to the pit.

³¹"Pharaoh—he and all his army—will see them and he will be consoled for all his hordes that were killed by the sword, declares the Sovereign LORD. ³²Although I had him spread terror in the land of the living, Pharaoh and all his hordes will be laid among the uncircumcised, with those killed by the sword, declares the Sovereign LORD."

EZEKIEL A WATCHMAN

33 The word of the LORD came to me: ²"Son of man, speak to your countrymen and say to them: 'When I bring the sword against a land, and the people of the land choose one of their men and make him their watchman, ³and he sees the sword coming against the land and

THE MESSAGE

gation of graves, all killed in battle, these people who terrorized the land of the living.

32.24-25   "Elam is there in all her pride, a cemetery—all killed in battle, dumped in her heathen grave with the dead and buried, these people who terrorized the land of the living. They carry their shame with them, along with the others in the grave. They turned Elam into a resort for the pompous dead, landscaped with heathen graves, slaughtered in battle. They once terrorized the land of the living. Now they carry their shame down with the others in deep earth. They're in the section set aside for the slain in battle.

32.26-27   "Meshech-tubal is there in all her pride, a cemetery in uncircumcised ground, dumped in with those slaughtered in battle—just deserts for terrorizing the land of the living. Now they carry their shame down with the others in deep earth. They're in the section set aside for the slain. They're segregated from the heroes, the old-time giants who entered the grave in full battle dress, their swords placed under their heads and their shields covering their bones, those heroes who spread terror through the land of the living.

32.28   "And you, Egypt, will be dumped in a heathen grave, along with all the rest, in the section set aside for the slain.

32.29   "Edom is there, with her kings and princes. In spite of her vaunted greatness, she is dumped in a heathen grave with the others headed for the grave.

32.30   "The princes of the north are there, the whole lot of them, and all the Sidonians who carry their shame to their graves—all that terror they spread with their brute power!—dumped in unhallowed ground with those killed in battle, carrying their shame with the others headed for deep earth.

32.31   "Pharaoh will see them all and, pompous old goat that he is, take comfort in the company he'll keep—Pharaoh and his slaughtered army. Decree of GOD, the Master.

32.32   "I used him to spread terror in the land of the living and now I'm dumping him in heathen ground with those killed by the sword—Pharaoh and all his pomp. Decree of GOD, the Master."

YOU ARE THE WATCHMAN

33.1-5   **33** GOD's Message came to me: "Son of man, speak to your people. Tell them: 'If I bring war on this land and the people take one of their citizens and make him their watchman, and if the watchman sees war coming and

NEW INTERNATIONAL VERSION

blows the trumpet to warn the people, ⁴then if anyone hears the trumpet but does not take warning and the sword comes and takes his life, his blood will be on his own head. ⁵Since he heard the sound of the trumpet but did not take warning, his blood will be on his own head. If he had taken warning, he would have saved himself. ⁶But if the watchman sees the sword coming and does not blow the trumpet to warn the people and the sword comes and takes the life of one of them, that man will be taken away because of his sin, but I will hold the watchman accountable for his blood.'

⁷"Son of man, I have made you a watchman for the house of Israel; so hear the word I speak and give them warning from me. ⁸When I say to the wicked, 'O wicked man, you will surely die,' and you do not speak out to dissuade him from his ways, that wicked man will die for ᵃ his sin, and I will hold you accountable for his blood. ⁹But if you do warn the wicked man to turn from his ways and he does not do so, he will die for his sin, but you will have saved yourself.

¹⁰"Son of man, say to the house of Israel, 'This is what you are saying: "Our offenses and sins weigh us down, and we are wasting away because of ᵇ them. How then can we live?" ' ¹¹Say to them, 'As surely as I live, declares the Sovereign LORD, I take no pleasure in the death of the wicked, but rather that they turn from their ways and live. Turn! Turn from your evil ways! Why will you die, O house of Israel?'

¹²"Therefore, son of man, say to your countrymen, 'The righteousness of the righteous man will not save him when he disobeys, and the wickedness of the wicked man will not cause him to fall when he turns from it. The righteous man, if he sins, will not be allowed to live because of his former righteousness.' ¹³If I tell the righteous man that he will surely live, but then he trusts in his righteousness and does evil, none of the righteous things he has done will be remembered; he will die for the evil he has done. ¹⁴And if I say to the wicked man, 'You will surely die,' but he then turns away from his sin and does what is just and right— ¹⁵if he gives back what he took in pledge for a loan, returns what he has stolen, follows the decrees that give life, and does no evil, he will surely live; he will not die. ¹⁶None of the sins he has committed will be remembered against him. He has done what is just and right; he will surely live.

¹⁷"Yet your countrymen say, 'The way of the Lord is not just.' But it is their way that is not just. ¹⁸If a righteous man turns from his righteousness and does evil, he will die for it. ¹⁹And

THE MESSAGE

blows the trumpet, warning the people, then if anyone hears the sound of the trumpet and ignores it and war comes and takes him off, it's his own fault. He heard the alarm, he ignored it—it's his own fault. If he had listened, he would have saved his life.

33.6 " 'But if the watchman sees war coming and doesn't blow the trumpet, warning the people, and war comes and takes anyone off, I'll hold the watchman responsible for the bloodshed of any unwarned sinner.'

33.7-9 "You, son of man, are the watchman. I've made you a watchman for Israel. The minute you hear a message from me, warn them. If I say to the wicked, 'Wicked man, wicked woman, you're on the fast track to death!' and you don't speak up and warn the wicked to change their ways, the wicked will die unwarned in their sins and I'll hold you responsible for their bloodshed. But if you warn the wicked to change their ways and they don't do it, they'll die in their sins well-warned and at least you will have saved your own life.

33.10 "Son of man, speak to Israel. Tell them: 'You've said, "Our rebellions and sins are weighing us down. We're wasting away. How can we go on living?" '

33.11 "Tell them, 'As sure as I am the living God, I take no pleasure from the death of the wicked. I want the wicked to change their ways and live. Turn your life around! Reverse your evil ways! Why *die*, Israel?'

33.12-13 "There's more, son of man. Tell your people: 'A good person's good life won't save him when he decides to rebel, and a bad person's bad life won't prevent him from repenting of his rebellion. A good person who sins can't expect to live when he chooses to sin. It's true that I tell good people, "Live! Be alive!" But if they trust in their good deeds and turn to evil, that good life won't amount to a hill of beans. They'll die for their evil life.

33.14-16 " 'On the other hand, if I tell a wicked person, "You'll die for your wicked life," and he repents of his sin and starts living a righteous and just life—being generous to the down-and-out, restoring what he had stolen, cultivating life-nourishing ways that don't hurt others— he'll live. He won't die. None of his sins will be kept on the books. He's doing what's right, living a good life. He'll live.

33.17-19 " 'Your people say, "The Master's way isn't fair." But it's the way *they're* living that isn't fair. When good people turn back from living good lives and plunge into sin, they'll die for it. And

ᵃ 8 Or *in*; also in verse 9   ᵇ 10 Or *away in*

NEW INTERNATIONAL VERSION

if a wicked man turns away from his wickedness and does what is just and right, he will live by doing so. 20Yet, O house of Israel, you say, 'The way of the Lord is not just.' But I will judge each of you according to his own ways."

JERUSALEM'S FALL EXPLAINED

21In the twelfth year of our exile, in the tenth month on the fifth day, a man who had escaped from Jerusalem came to me and said, "The city has fallen!" 22Now the evening before the man arrived, the hand of the LORD was upon me, and he opened my mouth before the man came to me in the morning. So my mouth was opened and I was no longer silent.

23Then the word of the LORD came to me: 24"Son of man, the people living in those ruins in the land of Israel are saying, 'Abraham was only one man, yet he possessed the land. But we are many; surely the land has been given to us as our possession.' 25Therefore say to them, 'This is what the Sovereign LORD says: Since you eat meat with the blood still in it and look to your idols and shed blood, should you then possess the land? 26You rely on your sword, you do detestable things, and each of you defiles his neighbor's wife. Should you then possess the land?'

27"Say this to them: 'This is what the Sovereign LORD says: As surely as I live, those who are left in the ruins will fall by the sword, those out in the country I will give to the wild animals to be devoured, and those in strongholds and caves will die of a plague. 28I will make the land a desolate waste, and her proud strength will come to an end, and the mountains of Israel will become desolate so that no one will cross them. 29Then they will know that I am the LORD, when I have made the land a desolate waste because of all the detestable things they have done.'

30"As for you, son of man, your countrymen are talking together about you by the walls and at the doors of the houses, saying to each other, 'Come and hear the message that has come from the LORD.' 31My people come to you, as they usually do, and sit before you to listen to your words, but they do not put them into practice. With their mouths they express devotion, but their hearts are greedy for unjust gain. 32Indeed, to them you are nothing more than one who sings love songs with a beautiful voice and plays an instrument well, for they hear your words but do not put them into practice.

33"When all this comes true—and it surely will—then they will know that a prophet has been among them."

THE MESSAGE

when a wicked person turns away from his wicked life and starts living a just and righteous life, he'll come alive.

33.20 " 'Still, you keep on saying, "The Master's way isn't fair." We'll see, Israel. I'll decide on each of you exactly according to how you live.' "

✝

33.21 In the twelfth year of our exile, on the fifth day of the tenth month, a survivor from Jerusalem came to me and said, "The city's fallen."

33.22 The evening before the survivor arrived, the hand of GOD had been on me and restored my speech. By the time he arrived in the morning I was able to speak. I could talk again.

33.23-24 GOD's Message came to me: "Son of man, those who are living in the ruins back in Israel are saying, 'Abraham was only one man and he owned the whole country. But there are *lots* of us. Our ownership is even more certain.'

33.25-26 "So tell them, 'GOD the Master says, You eat flesh that contains blood, you worship no-god idols, you murder at will—and you expect to own this land? You rely on the sword, you engage in obscenities, you indulge in sex at random—anyone, anytime. And you still expect to own this land?'

33.27-28 "Tell them this, Ezekiel: 'The Message of GOD, the Master. As sure as I am the living God, those who are still alive in the ruins will be killed. Anyone out in the field I'll give to wild animals for food. Anyone hiding out in mountain forts and caves will die of disease. I'll make this country an empty wasteland—no more arrogant bullying! Israel's mountains will become dangerously desolate. No one will dare pass through them.'

33.29 "They'll realize that I am GOD when I devastate the country because of all the obscenities they've practiced.

33.30-32 "As for you, son of man, you've become quite the talk of the town. Your people meet on street corners and in front of their houses and say, 'Let's go hear the latest news from GOD.' They show up, as people tend to do, and sit in your company. They listen to you speak, but don't do a thing you say. They flatter you with compliments, but all they care about is making money and getting ahead. To them you're merely entertainment—a country singer of sad love songs, playing a guitar. They love to hear you talk, but nothing comes of it.

33.33 "But when all this happens—and it is going to happen!—they'll realize that a prophet was among them."

NEW INTERNATIONAL VERSION

SHEPHERDS AND SHEEP

34 The word of the LORD came to me: ²"Son of man, prophesy against the shepherds of Israel; prophesy and say to them: 'This is what the Sovereign LORD says: Woe to the shepherds of Israel who only take care of themselves! Should not shepherds take care of the flock? ³You eat the curds, clothe yourselves with the wool and slaughter the choice animals, but you do not take care of the flock. ⁴You have not strengthened the weak or healed the sick or bound up the injured. You have not brought back the strays or searched for the lost. You have ruled them harshly and brutally. ⁵So they were scattered because there was no shepherd, and when they were scattered they became food for all the wild animals. ⁶My sheep wandered over all the mountains and on every high hill. They were scattered over the whole earth, and no one searched or looked for them.

⁷" 'Therefore, you shepherds, hear the word of the LORD: ⁸As surely as I live, declares the Sovereign LORD, because my flock lacks a shepherd and so has been plundered and has become food for all the wild animals, and because my shepherds did not search for my flock but cared for themselves rather than for my flock, ⁹therefore, O shepherds, hear the word of the LORD: ¹⁰This is what the Sovereign LORD says: I am against the shepherds and will hold them accountable for my flock. I will remove them from tending the flock so that the shepherds can no longer feed themselves. I will rescue my flock from their mouths, and it will no longer be food for them.

¹¹" 'For this is what the Sovereign LORD says: I myself will search for my sheep and look after them. ¹²As a shepherd looks after his scattered flock when he is with them, so will I look after my sheep. I will rescue them from all the places where they were scattered on a day of clouds and darkness. ¹³I will bring them out from the nations and gather them from the countries, and I will bring them into their own land. I will pasture them on the mountains of Israel, in the ravines and in all the settlements in the land. ¹⁴I will tend them in a good pasture, and the mountain heights of Israel will be their grazing land. There they will lie down in good grazing land, and there they will feed in a rich pasture on the mountains of Israel. ¹⁵I myself will tend my sheep and have them lie down, declares the Sovereign LORD. ¹⁶I will search for the lost and bring back the strays. I will bind up the injured and strengthen the weak, but the sleek and the strong I will destroy. I will shepherd the flock with justice.

THE MESSAGE

WHEN THE SHEEP GET SCATTERED

34 34:1-6 GOD's Message came to me: "Son of man, prophesy against the shepherd-leaders of Israel. Yes, prophesy! Tell those shepherds, 'GOD, the Master, says: Doom to you shepherds of Israel, feeding your own mouths! Aren't shepherds supposed to feed sheep? You drink the milk, you make clothes from the wool, you roast the lambs, but you don't feed the sheep. You don't build up the weak ones, don't heal the sick, don't doctor the injured, don't go after the strays, don't look for the lost. You bully and badger them. And now they're scattered every which way because there was no shepherd—scattered and easy pickings for wolves and coyotes. Scattered—*my sheep!*—exposed and vulnerable across mountains and hills. My sheep scattered all over the world, and no one out looking for them!

34:7-9 " 'Therefore, shepherds, listen to the Message of GOD: As sure as I am the living God—Decree of GOD, the Master—because my sheep have been turned into mere prey, into easy meals for wolves because you shepherds ignored them and only fed yourselves, listen to what GOD has to say:

34:10 " 'Watch out! I'm coming down on the shepherds and taking my sheep back. They're fired as shepherds of my sheep. No more shepherds who just feed themselves! I'll rescue my sheep from their greed. They're not going to feed off my sheep any longer!

34:11-16 " 'GOD, the Master, says: From now on, *I myself* am the shepherd. I'm going looking for them. As shepherds go after their flocks when they get scattered, I'm going after my sheep. I'll rescue them from all the places they've been scattered to in the storms. I'll bring them back from foreign peoples, gather them from foreign countries, and bring them back to their home country. I'll feed them on the mountains of Israel, along the streams, among their own people. I'll lead them into lush pasture so they can roam the mountain pastures of Israel, graze at leisure, feed in the rich pastures on the mountains of Israel. And I myself will be the shepherd of my sheep. I myself will make sure they get plenty of rest. I'll go after the lost, I'll collect the strays, I'll doctor the injured, I'll build up the weak ones and oversee the strong ones so they're not exploited.

NEW INTERNATIONAL VERSION

17" 'As for you, my flock, this is what the Sovereign LORD says: I will judge between one sheep and another, and between rams and goats. 18Is it not enough for you to feed on the good pasture? Must you also trample the rest of your pasture with your feet? Is it not enough for you to drink clear water? Must you also muddy the rest with your feet? 19Must my flock feed on what you have trampled and drink what you have muddied with your feet?

20" 'Therefore this is what the Sovereign LORD says to them: See, I myself will judge between the fat sheep and the lean sheep. 21Because you shove with flank and shoulder, butting all the weak sheep with your horns until you have driven them away, 22I will save my flock, and they will no longer be plundered. I will judge between one sheep and another. 23I will place over them one shepherd, my servant David, and he will tend them; he will tend them and be their shepherd. 24I the LORD will be their God, and my servant David will be prince among them. I the LORD have spoken.

25" 'I will make a covenant of peace with them and rid the land of wild beasts so that they may live in the desert and sleep in the forests in safety. 26I will bless them and the places surrounding my hill.ᵃ I will send down showers in season; there will be showers of blessing. 27The trees of the field will yield their fruit and the ground will yield its crops; the people will be secure in their land. They will know that I am the LORD, when I break the bars of their yoke and rescue them from the hands of those who enslaved them. 28They will no longer be plundered by the nations, nor will wild animals devour them. They will live in safety, and no one will make them afraid. 29I will provide for them a land renowned for its crops, and they will no longer be victims of famine in the land or bear the scorn of the nations. 30Then they will know that I, the LORD their God, am with them and that they, the house of Israel, are my people, declares the Sovereign LORD. 31You my sheep, the sheep of my pasture, are people, and I am your God, declares the Sovereign LORD.' "

A PROPHECY AGAINST EDOM

35 The word of the LORD came to me: 2"Son of man, set your face against Mount Seir; prophesy against it 3and say: 'This is what the

THE MESSAGE

34.17-19 " 'And as for you, my dear flock, I'm stepping in and judging between one sheep and another, between rams and goats. Aren't you satisfied to feed in good pasture without taking over the whole place? Can't you be satisfied to drink from the clear stream without muddying the water with your feet? Why do the rest of my sheep have to make do with grass that's trampled down and water that's been muddied?

34.20-22 " 'Therefore, GOD, the Master, says: I myself am stepping in and making things right between the plump sheep and the skinny sheep. Because you forced your way with shoulder and rump and butted at all the weaker animals with your horns till you scattered them all over the hills, I'll come in and save my dear flock, no longer let them be pushed around. I'll step in and set things right between one sheep and another.

34.23-24 " 'I'll appoint one shepherd over them all: my servant David. He'll feed them. He'll be their shepherd. And I, GOD, will be their God. My servant David will be their prince. I, GOD, have spoken.

34.25-27 " 'I'll make a covenant of peace with them. I'll banish fierce animals from the country so the sheep can live safely in the wilderness and sleep in the forest. I'll make them and everything around my hill a blessing. I'll send down plenty of rain in season—showers of blessing! The trees in the orchards will bear fruit, the ground will produce, they'll feel content and safe on their land, and they'll realize that I am GOD when I break them out of their slavery and rescue them from their slave masters.

34.28-29 " 'No longer will they be exploited by outsiders and ravaged by fierce beasts. They'll live safe and sound, fearless and free. I'll give them rich gardens, lavish in vegetables—no more living half-starved, no longer taunted by outsiders.

34.30-31 " 'They'll know, beyond doubting, that I, GOD, am their God, that I'm with them and that they, the people Israel, are my people. Decree of GOD, the Master:

You are my dear flock,
    the flock of my pasture, my human
        flock,
And I am your God.
    Decree of GOD, the Master.' "

A PILE OF RUBBLE

35 GOD's Message came to me: "Son of man, confront Mount Seir. Prophesy against it! Tell them, 'GOD, the Master, says:

ᵃ 26 Or I will make them and the places surrounding my hill a blessing

Sovereign LORD says: I am against you, Mount Seir, and I will stretch out my hand against you and make you a desolate waste. ⁴I will turn your towns into ruins and you will be desolate. Then you will know that I am the LORD.

⁵" 'Because you harbored an ancient hostility and delivered the Israelites over to the sword at the time of their calamity, the time their punishment reached its climax, ⁶therefore as surely as I live, declares the Sovereign LORD, I will give you over to bloodshed and it will pursue you. Since you did not hate bloodshed, bloodshed will pursue you. ⁷I will make Mount Seir a desolate waste and cut off from it all who come and go. ⁸I will fill your mountains with the slain; those killed by the sword will fall on your hills and in your valleys and in all your ravines. ⁹I will make you desolate forever; your towns will not be inhabited. Then you will know that I am the LORD.

¹⁰" 'Because you have said, "These two nations and countries will be ours and we will take possession of them," even though I the LORD was there, ¹¹therefore as surely as I live, declares the Sovereign LORD, I will treat you in accordance with the anger and jealousy you showed in your hatred of them and I will make myself known among them when I judge you. ¹²Then you will know that I the LORD have heard all the contemptible things you have said against the mountains of Israel. You said, "They have been laid waste and have been given over to us to devour." ¹³You boasted against me and spoke against me without restraint, and I heard it. ¹⁴This is what the Sovereign LORD says: While the whole earth rejoices, I will make you desolate. ¹⁵Because you rejoiced when the inheritance of the house of Israel became desolate, that is how I will treat you. You will be desolate, O Mount Seir, you and all of Edom. Then they will know that I am the LORD.' "

A PROPHECY TO THE MOUNTAINS OF ISRAEL

36 "Son of man, prophesy to the mountains of Israel and say, 'O mountains of Israel, hear the word of the LORD. ²This is what the Sovereign LORD says: The enemy said of you, "Aha! The ancient heights have become our possession." ' ³Therefore prophesy and say, 'This is what the Sovereign LORD says: Because they ravaged and hounded you from every side so that you became the possession of the rest of the nations and the object of people's malicious talk and slander, ⁴therefore, O mountains of Israel, hear the word of the Sovereign LORD: This is what the Sovereign LORD says to the mountains and hills, to the ravines and valleys, to the desolate ruins and the

" 'I'm coming down hard on you, Mount Seir.
   I'm stepping in and turning you to a pile of rubble.
I'll reduce your towns to piles of rocks.
   There'll be nothing left of you.
   Then you'll realize that I am GOD.

35.5-9   " 'I'm doing this because you've kept this age-old grudge going against Israel: You viciously attacked them when they were already down, looking their final punishment in the face. Therefore, as sure as I am the living God, I'm lining you up for a real bloodbath. Since you loved blood so much, you'll be chased by rivers of blood. I'll reduce Mount Seir to a heap of rubble. No one will either come or go from that place! I'll blanket your mountains with corpses. Massacred bodies will cover your hills and fill up your valleys and ditches. I'll reduce you to ruins and all your towns will be ghost towns—population zero. Then you'll realize that I am GOD.

35.10-13   " 'Because you said, "These two nations, these two countries, are mine. I'm taking over" (even though GOD is right there watching, right there listening), I'll turn your hate-bloated anger and rage right back on you. You'll know I mean business when I bring judgment on you. You'll realize then that I, GOD, have overheard all the vile abuse you've poured out against the mountains of Israel, saying, "They're roadkill and we're going to eat them up." You've strutted around, talking so big, insolently pitting yourselves against me. And I've heard it all.

35.14-15   " 'This is the verdict of GOD, the Master: With the whole earth applauding, I'll demolish you. Since you danced in the streets, thinking it was so wonderful when Israel's inheritance was demolished, I'll give you the same treatment: demolition. Mount Seir demolished—yes, every square inch of Edom. Then they'll realize that I am GOD!'

BACK TO YOUR OWN LAND

36.1-5 **36** "And now, son of man, prophesy to the mountains of Israel. Say, 'Mountains of Israel, listen to GOD's Message. GOD, the Master, says, Because the enemy crowed over you, "Good! Those old hills are now ours!" now here is a prophecy in the name of GOD, the Master: Because nations came at you from all sides, ripping and plundering, hauling pieces of you off every which way, and you've become the butt of cheap gossip and jokes, therefore, Mountains of Israel, listen to the Message of GOD, the Master. My Message to mountains and hills, to ditches and valleys, to the heaps of rubble and the emp-

NEW INTERNATIONAL VERSION

deserted towns that have been plundered and ridiculed by the rest of the nations around you— [5]this is what the Sovereign LORD says: In my burning zeal I have spoken against the rest of the nations, and against all Edom, for with glee and with malice in their hearts they made my land their own possession so that they might plunder its pastureland.' [6]Therefore prophesy concerning the land of Israel and say to the mountains and hills, to the ravines and valleys: 'This is what the Sovereign LORD says: I speak in my jealous wrath because you have suffered the scorn of the nations. [7]Therefore this is what the Sovereign LORD says: I swear with uplifted hand that the nations around you will also suffer scorn.

[8]" 'But you, O mountains of Israel, will produce branches and fruit for my people Israel, for they will soon come home. [9]I am concerned for you and will look on you with favor; you will be plowed and sown, [10]and I will multiply the number of people upon you, even the whole house of Israel. The towns will be inhabited and the ruins rebuilt. [11]I will increase the number of men and animals upon you, and they will be fruitful and become numerous. I will settle people on you as in the past and will make you prosper more than before. Then you will know that I am the LORD. [12]I will cause people, my people Israel, to walk upon you. They will possess you, and you will be their inheritance; you will never again deprive them of their children.

[13]" 'This is what the Sovereign LORD says: Because people say to you, "You devour men and deprive your nation of its children," [14]therefore you will no longer devour men or make your nation childless, declares the Sovereign LORD. [15]No longer will I make you hear the taunts of the nations, and no longer will you suffer the scorn of the peoples or cause your nation to fall, declares the Sovereign LORD.' "

[16]Again the word of the LORD came to me: [17]"Son of man, when the people of Israel were living in their own land, they defiled it by their conduct and their actions. Their conduct was like a woman's monthly uncleanness in my sight. [18]So I poured out my wrath on them because they had shed blood in the land and because they had defiled it with their idols. [19]I dispersed them among the nations, and they were scattered through the countries; I judged them according to their conduct and their actions. [20]And wherever they went among the nations they profaned my holy name, for it was said of them, 'These are the LORD's people, and yet they had to leave his land.' [21]I had concern for my holy name, which the house of Israel profaned among the nations where they had gone.

THE MESSAGE

tied towns that are looted for plunder and turned into jokes by all the surrounding nations: Therefore, says GOD, the Master, now I'm speaking in a fiery rage against the rest of the nations, but especially against Edom, who in an orgy of violence and shameless insolence robbed me of my land, grabbed it for themselves.'

36.6-7 "Therefore prophesy over the land of Israel, preach to the mountains and hills, to every ditch and valley: 'The Message of GOD, the Master: Look! Listen! I'm angry—and I care. I'm speaking to you because you've been humiliated among the nations. Therefore I, GOD, the Master, am telling you that I've solemnly sworn that the nations around you are next. It's their turn to be humiliated.

36.8-12 " 'But you, Mountains of Israel, will burst with new growth, putting out branches and bearing fruit for my people Israel. My people are coming home! Do you see? I'm back again. I'm on your side. You'll be plowed and planted as before! I'll see to it that your population grows all over Israel, that the towns fill up with people, that the ruins are rebuilt. I'll make this place teem with life—human and animal. The country will burst into life, life, and more life, your towns and villages full of people just as in the old days. I'll treat you better than I ever have. And you'll realize that I am GOD. I'll put people over you—my own people Israel! They'll take care of you and you'll be their inheritance. Never again will you be a harsh and unforgiving land to them.

36.13-15 " 'GOD, the Master, says: Because you have a reputation of being a land that eats people alive and makes women barren, I'm now telling you that you'll never eat people alive again nor make women barren. Decree of GOD, the Master. And I'll never again let the taunts of outsiders be heard over you nor permit nations to look down on you. You'll no longer be a land that makes women barren. Decree of GOD, the Master.' "

36.16-21 GOD's Message came to me: "Son of man, when the people of Israel lived in their land, they polluted it by the way they lived. I poured out my anger on them because of the polluted blood they poured out on the ground. And so I got thoroughly angry with them polluting the country with their wanton murders and dirty gods. I kicked them out, exiled them to other countries. I sentenced them according to how they had lived. Wherever they went, they gave me a bad name. People said, 'These are GOD's people, but they got kicked off his land.' I suffered much pain over my holy reputation, which the people of Israel blackened in every country they entered.

NEW INTERNATIONAL VERSION

22"Therefore say to the house of Israel, 'This is what the Sovereign LORD says: It is not for your sake, O house of Israel, that I am going to do these things, but for the sake of my holy name, which you have profaned among the nations where you have gone. 23I will show the holiness of my great name, which has been profaned among the nations, the name you have profaned among them. Then the nations will know that I am the LORD, declares the Sovereign LORD, when I show myself holy through you before their eyes.

24" 'For I will take you out of the nations; I will gather you from all the countries and bring you back into your own land. 25I will sprinkle clean water on you, and you will be clean; I will cleanse you from all your impurities and from all your idols. 26I will give you a new heart and put a new spirit in you; I will remove from you your heart of stone and give you a heart of flesh. 27And I will put my Spirit in you and move you to follow my decrees and be careful to keep my laws. 28You will live in the land I gave your forefathers; you will be my people, and I will be your God. 29I will save you from all your uncleanness. I will call for the grain and make it plentiful and will not bring famine upon you. 30I will increase the fruit of the trees and the crops of the field, so that you will no longer suffer disgrace among the nations because of famine. 31Then you will remember your evil ways and wicked deeds, and you will loathe yourselves for your sins and detestable practices. 32I want you to know that I am not doing this for your sake, declares the Sovereign LORD. Be ashamed and disgraced for your conduct, O house of Israel!

33" 'This is what the Sovereign LORD says: On the day I cleanse you from all your sins, I will resettle your towns, and the ruins will be rebuilt. 34The desolate land will be cultivated instead of lying desolate in the sight of all who pass through it. 35They will say, "This land that was laid waste has become like the garden of Eden; the cities that were lying in ruins, desolate and destroyed, are now fortified and inhabited." 36Then the nations around you that remain will know that I the LORD have rebuilt what was destroyed and have replanted what was desolate. I the LORD have spoken, and I will do it.'

37"This is what the Sovereign LORD says: Once again I will yield to the plea of the house of Israel and do this for them: I will make their people as numerous as sheep, 38as numerous as the flocks for offerings at Jerusalem during her appointed feasts. So will the ruined cities be filled with flocks of people. Then they will know that I am the LORD."

THE MESSAGE

36.22-23 "Therefore, tell Israel, 'Message of GOD, the Master: I'm not doing this for you, Israel. I'm doing it for me, to save my character, my holy name, which you've blackened in every country where you've gone. I'm going to put my great and holy name on display, the name that has been ruined in so many countries, the name that you blackened wherever you went. Then the nations will realize who I really am, that I am GOD, when I show my holiness through you so that they can see it with their own eyes.

36.24-28 " 'For here's what I'm going to do: I'm going to take you out of these countries, gather you from all over, and bring you back to your own land. I'll pour pure water over you and scrub you clean. I'll give you a new heart, put a new spirit in you. I'll remove the stone heart from your body and replace it with a heart that's God-willed, not self-willed. I'll put my Spirit in you and make it possible for you to do what I tell you and live by my commands. You'll once again live in the land I gave your ancestors. You'll be my people! I'll be your God!

36.29-30 " 'I'll pull you out of that stinking pollution. I'll give personal orders to the wheat fields, telling them to grow bumper crops. I'll send no more famines. I'll make sure your fruit trees and field crops flourish. Other nations won't be able to hold you in contempt again because of famine.

36.31 " 'And then you'll think back over your terrible lives—the evil, the shame—and be thoroughly disgusted with yourselves, realizing how badly you've lived—all those obscenities you've carried out.

36.32 " 'I'm not doing this for you. Get this through your thick heads! Shame on you. What a mess you made of things, Israel!

36.33-36 " 'Message of GOD, the Master: On the day I scrub you clean from all your filthy living, I'll also make your cities livable. The ruins will be rebuilt. The neglected land will be worked again, no longer overgrown with weeds and thistles, worthless in the eyes of passersby. People will exclaim, "Why, this weed patch has been turned into a Garden of Eden! And the ruined cities, smashed into oblivion, are now thriving!" The nations around you that are still in existence will realize that I, GOD, rebuild ruins and replant empty waste places. I, GOD, said so, and I'll do it.

36.37-38 " 'Message of GOD, the Master: Yet again I'm going to do what Israel asks. I'll increase their population as with a flock of sheep. Like the milling flocks of sheep brought for sacrifices in Jerusalem during the appointed feasts, the ruined cities will be filled with flocks of people. And they'll realize that I am GOD.' "

NEW INTERNATIONAL VERSION

THE VALLEY OF DRY BONES

37 The hand of the LORD was upon me, and he brought me out by the Spirit of the LORD and set me in the middle of a valley; it was full of bones. ²He led me back and forth among them, and I saw a great many bones on the floor of the valley, bones that were very dry. ³He asked me, "Son of man, can these bones live?"

I said, "O Sovereign LORD, you alone know."

⁴Then he said to me, "Prophesy to these bones and say to them, 'Dry bones, hear the word of the LORD! ⁵This is what the Sovereign LORD says to these bones: I will make breath*ᵃ* enter you, and you will come to life. ⁶I will attach tendons to you and make flesh come upon you and cover you with skin; I will put breath in you, and you will come to life. Then you will know that I am the LORD.' "

⁷So I prophesied as I was commanded. And as I was prophesying, there was a noise, a rattling sound, and the bones came together, bone to bone. ⁸I looked, and tendons and flesh appeared on them and skin covered them, but there was no breath in them.

⁹Then he said to me, "Prophesy to the breath; prophesy, son of man, and say to it, 'This is what the Sovereign LORD says: Come from the four winds, O breath, and breathe into these slain, that they may live.' " ¹⁰So I prophesied as he commanded me, and breath entered them; they came to life and stood up on their feet—a vast army.

¹¹Then he said to me: "Son of man, these bones are the whole house of Israel. They say, 'Our bones are dried up and our hope is gone; we are cut off.' ¹²Therefore prophesy and say to them: 'This is what the Sovereign LORD says: O my people, I am going to open your graves and bring you up from them; I will bring you back to the land of Israel. ¹³Then you, my people, will know that I am the LORD, when I open your graves and bring you up from them. ¹⁴I will put my Spirit in you and you will live, and I will settle you in your own land. Then you will know that I the LORD have spoken, and I have done it, declares the LORD.' "

ONE NATION UNDER ONE KING

¹⁵The word of the LORD came to me: ¹⁶"Son of man, take a stick of wood and write on it, 'Belonging to Judah and the Israelites associated with him.' Then take another stick of wood, and write on it, 'Ephraim's stick, belonging to Joseph and all the house of Israel associated with him.' ¹⁷Join them together into one stick so that they will become one in your hand.

ᵃ 5 The Hebrew for this word can also mean *wind* or *spirit* (see verses 6-14).

THE MESSAGE

BREATH OF LIFE

37 GOD grabbed me. GOD's Spirit took me up and set me down in the middle of an open plain strewn with bones. He led me around and among them—a lot of bones! There were bones all over the plain—dry bones, bleached by the sun.

37.3   He said to me, "Son of man, can these bones live?"

I said, "Master GOD, only you know that."

37.4   He said to me, "Prophesy over these bones: 'Dry bones, listen to the Message of GOD!' "

37.5-6   GOD, the Master, told the dry bones, "Watch this: I'm bringing the breath of life to you and you'll come to life. I'll attach sinews to you, put meat on your bones, cover you with skin, and breathe life into you. You'll come alive and you'll realize that I am GOD!"

37.7-8   I prophesied just as I'd been commanded. As I prophesied, there was a sound and, oh, rustling! The bones moved and came together, bone to bone. I kept watching. Sinews formed, then muscles on the bones, then skin stretched over them. But they had no breath in them.

37.9   He said to me, "Prophesy to the breath. Prophesy, son of man. Tell the breath, 'GOD, the Master, says, Come from the four winds. Come, breath. Breathe on these slain bodies. Breathe life!' "

37.10   So I prophesied, just as he commanded me. The breath entered them and they came alive! They stood up on their feet, a huge army.

37.11   Then God said to me, "Son of man, these bones are the whole house of Israel. Listen to what they're saying: 'Our bones are dried up, our hope is gone, there's nothing left of us.'

37.12-14   "Therefore, prophesy. Tell them, 'GOD, the Master, says: I'll dig up your graves and bring you out alive—O my people! Then I'll take you straight to the land of Israel. When I dig up graves and bring you out as my people, you'll realize that I am GOD. I'll breathe my life into you and you'll live. Then I'll lead you straight back to your land and you'll realize that I am GOD. I've said it and I'll do it. GOD's Decree.' "

✝

37.15-17   GOD's Message came to me: "You, son of man: Take a stick and write on it, 'For Judah, with his Israelite companions.' Then take another stick and write on it, 'For Joseph—Ephraim's stick, together with all his Israelite companions.' Then tie the two sticks together so that you're holding one stick.

NEW INTERNATIONAL VERSION

18"When your countrymen ask you, 'Won't you tell us what you mean by this?' 19say to them, 'This is what the Sovereign LORD says: I am going to take the stick of Joseph—which is in Ephraim's hand—and of the Israelite tribes associated with him, and join it to Judah's stick, making them a single stick of wood, and they will become one in my hand.' 20Hold before their eyes the sticks you have written on 21and say to them, 'This is what the Sovereign LORD says: I will take the Israelites out of the nations where they have gone. I will gather them from all around and bring them back into their own land. 22I will make them one nation in the land, on the mountains of Israel. There will be one king over all of them and they will never again be two nations or be divided into two kingdoms. 23They will no longer defile themselves with their idols and vile images or with any of their offenses, for I will save them from all their sinful backsliding,*a* and I will cleanse them. They will be my people, and I will be their God.

24" 'My servant David will be king over them, and they will all have one shepherd. They will follow my laws and be careful to keep my decrees. 25They will live in the land I gave to my servant Jacob, the land where your fathers lived. They and their children and their children's children will live there forever, and David my servant will be their prince forever. 26I will make a covenant of peace with them; it will be an everlasting covenant. I will establish them and increase their numbers, and I will put my sanctuary among them forever. 27My dwelling place will be with them; I will be their God, and they will be my people. 28Then the nations will know that I the LORD make Israel holy, when my sanctuary is among them forever.' "

A PROPHECY AGAINST GOG

38 The word of the LORD came to me: 2"Son of man, set your face against Gog, of the land of Magog, the chief prince of*b* Meshech and Tubal; prophesy against him 3and say: 'This is what the Sovereign LORD says: I am against you, O Gog, chief prince of*c* Meshech and Tubal. 4I will turn you around, put hooks in your jaws and bring you out with your whole army—your horses, your horsemen fully armed, and a great horde with large and small shields, all of them brandishing their swords. 5Persia, Cush*d* and Put will be with them, all with shields and helmets, 6also Gomer with all its troops, and Beth Togar-

THE MESSAGE

37.18-19 "When your people ask you, 'Are you going to tell us what you're doing?' tell them, 'GOD, the Master, says, Watch me! I'll take the Joseph stick that is in Ephraim's hand, with the tribes of Israel connected with him, and lay the Judah stick on it. I'll make them into one stick. I'm holding one stick.'

37.20-24 "Then take the sticks you've inscribed and hold them up so the people can see them. Tell them, 'GOD, the Master, says, Watch me! I'm taking the Israelites out of the nations in which they've been exiled. I'll gather them in from all directions and bring them back home. I'll make them one nation in the land, on the mountains of Israel, and give them one king—one king over all of them. Never again will they be divided into two nations, two kingdoms. Never again will they pollute their lives with their no-god idols and all those vile obscenities and rebellions. I'll save them out of all their old sinful haunts. I'll clean them up. They'll be my people! I'll be their God! My servant David will be king over them. They'll all be under one shepherd.

37.24-27 " 'They'll follow my laws and keep my statutes. They'll live in the same land I gave my servant Jacob, the land where your ancestors lived. They and their children and their grandchildren will live there forever, and my servant David will be their prince forever. I'll make a covenant of peace with them that will hold everything together, an everlasting covenant. I'll make them secure and place my holy place of worship at the center of their lives forever. I'll live right there with them. I'll be their God! They'll be my people!

37.28 " 'The nations will realize that I, GOD, make Israel holy when my holy place of worship is established at the center of their lives forever.' "

GOD AGAINST GOG

38 GOD's Message came to me: "Son of man, confront Gog from the country of Magog, head of Meshech and Tubal. Prophesy against him. Say, 'GOD, the Master, says: Be warned, Gog. I am against you, head of Meshech and Tubal. I'm going to turn you around, put hooks in your jaws, and drag you off with your whole army, your horses and riders in full armor—all those shields and bucklers and swords—fighting men armed to the teeth! Persia and Cush and Put will be in the ranks, also well-armed, as will Gomer and its army and

---

a 23 Many Hebrew manuscripts (see also Septuagint); most Hebrew manuscripts *all their dwelling places where they sinned* *b 2* Or *the prince of Rosh,* *c 3* Or *Gog, prince of Rosh,* *d 5* That is, the upper Nile region

NEW INTERNATIONAL VERSION

mah from the far north with all its troops—the many nations with you.

⁷" 'Get ready; be prepared, you and all the hordes gathered about you, and take command of them. ⁸After many days you will be called to arms. In future years you will invade a land that has recovered from war, whose people were gathered from many nations to the mountains of Israel, which had long been desolate. They had been brought out from the nations, and now all of them live in safety. ⁹You and all your troops and the many nations with you will go up, advancing like a storm; you will be like a cloud covering the land.

¹⁰" 'This is what the Sovereign LORD says: On that day thoughts will come into your mind and you will devise an evil scheme. ¹¹You will say, "I will invade a land of unwalled villages; I will attack a peaceful and unsuspecting people—all of them living without walls and without gates and bars. ¹²I will plunder and loot and turn my hand against the resettled ruins and the people gathered from the nations, rich in livestock and goods, living at the center of the land." ¹³Sheba and Dedan and the merchants of Tarshish and all her villages*ᵃ* will say to you, "Have you come to plunder? Have you gathered your hordes to loot, to carry off silver and gold, to take away livestock and goods and to seize much plunder?" '

¹⁴"Therefore, son of man, prophesy and say to Gog: 'This is what the Sovereign LORD says: In that day, when my people Israel are living in safety, will you not take notice of it? ¹⁵You will come from your place in the far north, you and many nations with you, all of them riding on horses, a great horde, a mighty army. ¹⁶You will advance against my people Israel like a cloud that covers the land. In days to come, O Gog, I will bring you against my land, so that the nations may know me when I show myself holy through you before their eyes.

¹⁷" 'This is what the Sovereign LORD says: Are you not the one I spoke of in former days by my servants the prophets of Israel? At that time they prophesied for years that I would bring you against them. ¹⁸This is what will happen in that day: When Gog attacks the land of Israel, my hot anger will be aroused, declares the Sovereign LORD. ¹⁹In my zeal and fiery wrath I declare that at that time there shall be a great earthquake in the land of Israel. ²⁰The fish of the sea, the birds of the air, the beasts of the field, every creature that moves along the ground, and all the people on the face of the earth will tremble at my presence. The mountains will be overturned, the cliffs will crumble and every wall will fall to the

THE MESSAGE

Beth-togarmah out of the north with its army. Many nations will be with you!

⁣38.7-9 " 'Get ready to fight, you and the whole company that's been called out. Take charge and wait for orders. After a long time, you'll be given your orders. In the distant future you'll arrive at a country that has recovered from a devastating war. People from many nations will be gathered there on the mountains of Israel, for a long time now a wasteland. These people have been brought back from many countries and now live safe and secure. You'll rise like a thunderstorm and roll in like clouds and cover the land, you and the massed troops with you.

⁣38.10-12 " 'Message of GOD, the Master: At that time you'll start thinking things over and cook up an evil plot. You'll say, "I'm going to invade a country without defenses, attack an unsuspecting, carefree people going about their business—no gates to their cities, no locks on their doors. And I'm going to plunder the place, march right in and clean them out, this rebuilt country risen from the ashes, these returned exiles and their booming economy centered down at the navel of the earth."

⁣38.13 " 'Sheba and Dedan and Tarshish, traders all out to make a fast buck, will say, "So! You've opened a new market for plunder! You've brought in your troops to get rich quick!" '

⁣38.14-16 "Therefore, son of man, prophesy! Tell Gog, 'A Message from GOD, the Master: When my people Israel are established securely, will you make your move? Will you come down out of the far north, you and that mob of armies, charging out on your horses like a tidal wave across the land, and invade my people Israel, covering the country like a cloud? When the time's ripe, I'll unleash you against my land in such a way that the nations will recognize me, realize that through you, Gog, in full view of the nations, I am putting my holiness on display.

⁣38.17-22 " 'A Message of GOD, the Master: Years ago when I spoke through my servants, the prophets of Israel, wasn't it you I was talking about? Year after year they prophesied that I would bring you against them. And when the day comes, Gog, you will attack that land of Israel. Decree of GOD, the Master. My raging anger will erupt. Fueled by blazing jealousy, I tell you that then there will be an earthquake that rocks the land of Israel. Fish and birds and wild animals—even ants and beetles!—and every human being will tremble and shake before me. Mountains will disintegrate, terraces will crum-

---

ᵃ 13 Or her strong lions

NEW INTERNATIONAL VERSION

ground. ²¹I will summon a sword against Gog on all my mountains, declares the Sovereign LORD. Every man's sword will be against his brother. ²²I will execute judgment upon him with plague and bloodshed; I will pour down torrents of rain, hailstones and burning sulfur on him and on his troops and on the many nations with him. ²³And so I will show my greatness and my holiness, and I will make myself known in the sight of many nations. Then they will know that I am the LORD.'

39 "Son of man, prophesy against Gog and say: 'This is what the Sovereign LORD says: I am against you, O Gog, chief prince of*ᵃ* Meshech and Tubal. ²I will turn you around and drag you along. I will bring you from the far north and send you against the mountains of Israel. ³Then I will strike your bow from your left hand and make your arrows drop from your right hand. ⁴On the mountains of Israel you will fall, you and all your troops and the nations with you. I will give you as food to all kinds of carrion birds and to the wild animals. ⁵You will fall in the open field, for I have spoken, declares the Sovereign LORD. ⁶I will send fire on Magog and on those who live in safety in the coastlands, and they will know that I am the LORD.

⁷" 'I will make known my holy name among my people Israel. I will no longer let my holy name be profaned, and the nations will know that I the LORD am the Holy One in Israel. ⁸It is coming! It will surely take place, declares the Sovereign LORD. This is the day I have spoken of.

⁹" 'Then those who live in the towns of Israel will go out and use the weapons for fuel and burn them up—the small and large shields, the bows and arrows, the war clubs and spears. For seven years they will use them for fuel. ¹⁰They will not need to gather wood from the fields or cut it from the forests, because they will use the weapons for fuel. And they will plunder those who plundered them and loot those who looted them, declares the Sovereign LORD.

¹¹" 'On that day I will give Gog a burial place in Israel, in the valley of those who travel east toward*ᵇ* the Sea.*ᶜ* It will block the way of travelers, because Gog and all his hordes will be buried there. So it will be called the Valley of Hamon Gog.*ᵈ*

¹²" 'For seven months the house of Israel will be burying them in order to cleanse the land. ¹³All the people of the land will bury them, and the day I am glorified will be a memorable day for them, declares the Sovereign LORD.

THE MESSAGE

ble. I'll order all-out war against you, Gog—Decree of GOD, the Master—Gog killing Gog on all the mountains of Israel. I'll deluge Gog with judgment: disease and massacre, torrential rain and hail, volcanic lava pouring down on you and your mobs of troops and people.

38.23   " 'I'll show you how great I am, how holy I am. I'll make myself known all over the world. Then you'll realize that I am GOD.'

CALL THE WILD ANIMALS!

39.1-5   **39** "Son of man, prophesy against Gog. Say, 'A Message of GOD, the Master: I'm against you, Gog, head of Meshech and Tubal. I'm going to turn you around and drag you out, drag you out of the far north and down on the mountains of Israel. Then I'll knock your bow out of your left hand and your arrows from your right hand. On the mountains of Israel you'll be slaughtered, you and all your troops and the people with you. I'll serve you up as a meal to carrion birds and scavenging animals. You'll be killed in the open field. I've given my word. Decree of GOD, the Master.'

39.6   "I'll set fire to Magog and the far-off islands, where people are so seemingly secure. And they'll realize that I am GOD.

39.7   "I'll reveal my holy name among my people Israel. Never again will I let my holy name be dragged in the mud. Then the nations will realize that I, GOD, am The Holy in Israel.

39.8   "It's coming! Yes, it will happen! This is the day I've been telling you about.

39.9-10   "People will come out of the cities of Israel and make a huge bonfire of the weapons of war, piling on shields large and small, bows and arrows, clubs and spears, a fire they'll keep going for seven years. They won't need to go into the woods to get fuel for the fire. There'll be plenty of weapons to keep it going. They'll strip those who stripped them. They'll rob those who robbed them. Decree of GOD, the Master.

39.11   "At that time I'll set aside a burial ground for Gog in Israel at Traveler's Rest, just east of the sea. It will obstruct the route of travelers, blocking their way, the mass grave of Gog and his mob of an army. They'll call the place Gog's Mob.

39.12-16   "Israel will bury the corpses in order to clean up the land. It will take them seven months. All the people will turn out to help with the burials. It will be a big day for the people when it's all done and I'm given my due.

ᵃ 1 Or Gog, prince of Rosh,   *ᵇ 11 Or of*   *ᶜ 11 That is, the Dead Sea*   *ᵈ 11 Hamon Gog means hordes of Gog.*

NEW INTERNATIONAL VERSION

14 " 'Men will be regularly employed to cleanse the land. Some will go throughout the land and, in addition to them, others will bury those that remain on the ground. At the end of the seven months they will begin their search. 15As they go through the land and one of them sees a human bone, he will set up a marker beside it until the gravediggers have buried it in the Valley of Hamon Gog. 16(Also a town called Hamonah*a* will be there.) And so they will cleanse the land.'

17"Son of man, this is what the Sovereign LORD says: Call out to every kind of bird and all the wild animals: 'Assemble and come together from all around to the sacrifice I am preparing for you, the great sacrifice on the mountains of Israel. There you will eat flesh and drink blood. 18You will eat the flesh of mighty men and drink the blood of the princes of the earth as if they were rams and lambs, goats and bulls—all of them fattened animals from Bashan. 19At the sacrifice I am preparing for you, you will eat fat till you are glutted and drink blood till you are drunk. 20At my table you will eat your fill of horses and riders, mighty men and soldiers of every kind,' declares the Sovereign LORD.

21"I will display my glory among the nations, and all the nations will see the punishment I inflict and the hand I lay upon them. 22From that day forward the house of Israel will know that I am the LORD their God. 23And the nations will know that the people of Israel went into exile for their sin, because they were unfaithful to me. So I hid my face from them and handed them over to their enemies, and they all fell by the sword. 24I dealt with them according to their uncleanness and their offenses, and I hid my face from them.

25"Therefore this is what the Sovereign LORD says: I will now bring Jacob back from captivity*b* and will have compassion on all the people of Israel, and I will be zealous for my holy name. 26They will forget their shame and all the unfaithfulness they showed toward me when they lived in safety in their land with no one to make them afraid. 27When I have brought them back from the nations and have gathered them from the countries of their enemies, I will show myself holy through them in the sight of many nations. 28Then they will know that I am the LORD their God, for though I sent them into exile among the nations, I will gather them to their own land, not leaving any behind. 29I will no longer hide my face from them, for I will pour out my Spirit on the house of Israel, declares the Sovereign LORD."

THE MESSAGE

Men will be hired full-time for the cleanup burial operation and will go through the country looking for defiling, decomposing corpses. At the end of seven months, there'll be an all-out final search. Anyone who sees a bone will mark the place with a stick so the buriers can get it and bury it in the mass burial site, Gog's Mob. (A town nearby is called Mobville, or Hamonah.) That's how they'll clean up the land.

39.17-20 "Son of man, GOD, the Master, says: Call the birds! Call the wild animals! Call out, 'Gather and come, gather around my sacrificial meal that I'm preparing for you on the mountains of Israel. You'll eat meat and drink blood. You'll eat off the bodies of great heroes and drink the blood of famous princes as if they were so many rams and lambs, goats and bulls, the choicest grain-fed animals of Bashan. At the sacrificial meal I'm fixing for you, you'll eat fat till you're stuffed and drink blood till you're drunk. At the table I set for you, you'll stuff yourselves with horses and riders, heroes and fighters of every kind.' Decree of GOD, the Master.

39.21-24 "I'll put my glory on display among the nations and they'll all see the judgment I execute, see me at work handing out judgment. From that day on, Israel will realize that I am their GOD. And the nations will get the message that it was because of their sins that Israel went into exile. They were disloyal to me and I turned away from them. I turned them over to their enemies and they were all killed. I treated them as their polluted and sin-sated lives deserved. I turned away from them, refused to look at them.

39.25-29 "But now I will return Jacob back from exile, I'll be compassionate with all the people of Israel, and I'll be zealous for my holy name. Eventually the memory will fade, the memory of their shame over their betrayals of me when they lived securely in their own land, safe and unafraid. Once I've brought them back from foreign parts, gathered them in from enemy territories, I'll use them to demonstrate my holiness with all the nations watching. Then they'll realize for sure that I am their GOD, for even though I sent them off into exile, I will gather them back to their own land, leaving not one soul behind. After I've poured my Spirit on Israel, filled them with my life, I'll no longer turn away. I'll look them full in the face. Decree of GOD, the Master."

---

a 16 Hamonah means horde.   *b 25 Or now restore the fortunes of Jacob*

NEW INTERNATIONAL VERSION

THE NEW TEMPLE AREA

40 In the twenty-fifth year of our exile, at the beginning of the year, on the tenth of the month, in the fourteenth year after the fall of the city—on that very day the hand of the LORD was upon me and he took me there. ²In visions of God he took me to the land of Israel and set me on a very high mountain, on whose south side were some buildings that looked like a city. ³He took me there, and I saw a man whose appearance was like bronze; he was standing in the gateway with a linen cord and a measuring rod in his hand. ⁴The man said to me, "Son of man, look with your eyes and hear with your ears and pay attention to everything I am going to show you, for that is why you have been brought here. Tell the house of Israel everything you see."

THE EAST GATE TO THE OUTER COURT

⁵I saw a wall completely surrounding the temple area. The length of the measuring rod in the man's hand was six long cubits, each of which was a cubit*ᵃ* and a handbreadth.*ᵇ* He measured the wall; it was one measuring rod thick and one rod high.

⁶Then he went to the gate facing east. He climbed its steps and measured the threshold of the gate; it was one rod deep.*ᶜ* ⁷The alcoves for the guards were one rod long and one rod wide, and the projecting walls between the alcoves were five cubits thick. And the threshold of the gate next to the portico facing the temple was one rod deep.

⁸Then he measured the portico of the gateway; ⁹it*ᵈ* was eight cubits deep and its jambs were two cubits thick. The portico of the gateway faced the temple.

¹⁰Inside the east gate were three alcoves on each side; the three had the same measurements, and the faces of the projecting walls on each side had the same measurements. ¹¹Then he measured the width of the entrance to the gateway; it was ten cubits and its length was thirteen cubits. ¹²In front of each alcove was a wall one cubit high, and the alcoves were six cubits square. ¹³Then he measured the gateway from the top of the rear wall of one alcove to the top of the opposite one; the distance was twenty-five cubits from one parapet opening to the opposite one. ¹⁴He measured along the faces of the projecting walls all around the inside of the gateway—sixty

ᵃ 5 The common cubit was about 1 1/2 feet (about 0.5 meter). *ᵇ 5* That is, about 3 inches (about 8 centimeters) *ᶜ 6* Septuagint; Hebrew *deep, the first threshold, one rod deep* *ᵈ 8,9* Many Hebrew manuscripts, Septuagint, Vulgate and Syriac; most Hebrew manuscripts *gateway facing the temple; it was one rod deep. ⁹Then he measured the portico of the gateway; it*

THE MESSAGE

MEASURING THE TEMPLE COMPLEX

40.1-3 **40** In the twenty-fifth year of our exile, at the beginning of the year on the tenth of the month—it was the fourteenth year after the city fell—GOD touched me and brought me here. He brought me in divine vision to the land of Israel and set me down on a high mountain. To the south there were buildings that looked like a city. He took me there and I met a man deeply tanned, like bronze. He stood at the entrance holding a linen cord and a measuring stick.

40.4 The man said to me, "Son of man, look and listen carefully. Pay close attention to everything I'm going to show you. That's why you've been brought here. And then tell Israel everything you see."

✠

40.5 First I saw a wall around the outside of the Temple complex. The measuring stick in the man's hand was about ten feet long. He measured the thickness of the wall: about ten feet. The height was also about ten feet.

✠

40.6-7 He went into the gate complex that faced the east and went up the seven steps. He measured the depth of the outside threshold of the gate complex: ten feet. There were alcoves flanking the gate corridor, each ten feet square, each separated by a wall seven and a half feet thick. The inside threshold of the gate complex that led to the porch facing into the Temple courtyard was ten feet deep.

40.8-9 He measured the inside porch of the gate complex: twelve feet deep, flanked by pillars three feet thick. The porch opened onto the Temple courtyard.

40.10 Inside this east gate complex were three alcoves on each side. Each room was the same size and the separating walls were identical.

40.11 He measured the outside entrance to the gate complex: fifteen feet wide and nineteen and a half feet deep.

40.12 In front of each alcove was a low wall eighteen inches high. The alcoves were ten feet square.

40.13 He measured the width of the gate complex from the outside edge of the alcove roof on one side to the outside edge of the alcove roof on the other: thirty-seven and a half feet from one top edge to the other.

40.14 He measured the inside walls of the gate

NEW INTERNATIONAL VERSION

cubits. The measurement was up to the portico[a] facing the courtyard.[b] 15The distance from the entrance of the gateway to the far end of its portico was fifty cubits. 16The alcoves and the projecting walls inside the gateway were surmounted by narrow parapet openings all around, as was the portico; the openings all around faced inward. The faces of the projecting walls were decorated with palm trees.

The Outer Court

17Then he brought me into the outer court. There I saw some rooms and a pavement that had been constructed all around the court; there were thirty rooms along the pavement. 18It abutted the sides of the gateways and was as wide as they were long; this was the lower pavement. 19Then he measured the distance from the inside of the lower gateway to the outside of the inner court; it was a hundred cubits on the east side as well as on the north.

The North Gate

20Then he measured the length and width of the gate facing north, leading into the outer court. 21Its alcoves—three on each side—its projecting walls and its portico had the same measurements as those of the first gateway. It was fifty cubits long and twenty-five cubits wide. 22Its openings, its portico and its palm tree decorations had the same measurements as those of the gate facing east. Seven steps led up to it, with its portico opposite them. 23There was a gate to the inner court facing the north gate, just as there was on the east. He measured from one gate to the opposite one; it was a hundred cubits.

The South Gate

24Then he led me to the south side and I saw a gate facing south. He measured its jambs and its portico, and they had the same measurements as the others. 25The gateway and its portico had narrow openings all around, like the openings of the others. It was fifty cubits long and twenty-five cubits wide. 26Seven steps led up to it, with its portico opposite them; it had palm tree decorations on the faces of the projecting walls on each side. 27The inner court also had a gate facing south, and he measured from this gate to the outer gate on the south side; it was a hundred cubits.

Gates to the Inner Court

28Then he brought me into the inner court through the south gate, and he measured the

a 14 Septuagint; Hebrew *projecting wall*
b 14 The meaning of the Hebrew for this verse is uncertain.

THE MESSAGE

complex: ninety feet to the porch leading into the courtyard.

40.15 The distance from the entrance of the gate complex to the far end of the porch was seventy-five feet.

40.16 The alcoves and their connecting walls inside the gate complex were topped by narrow windows all the way around. The porch also. All the windows faced inward. The doorjambs between the alcoves were decorated with palm trees.

✠

40.17-19 The man then led me to the outside courtyard and all its rooms. A paved walkway had been built connecting the courtyard gates. Thirty rooms lined the courtyard. The walkway was the same length as the gateways. It flanked them and ran their entire length. This was the walkway for the outside courtyard. He measured the distance from the front of the entrance gateway across to the entrance of the inner court: one hundred fifty feet.

✠

40.19-23 Then he took me to the north side. Here was another gate complex facing north, exiting the outside courtyard. He measured its length and width. It had three alcoves on each side. Its gateposts and porch were the same as in the first gate: eighty-seven and a half feet by forty-three and three-quarters feet. The windows and palm trees were identical to the east gateway. Seven steps led up to it, and its porch faced inward. Opposite this gate complex was a gate complex to the inside courtyard, on the north as on the east. The distance between the two was one hundred seventy-five feet.

40.24-27 Then he took me to the south side, to the south gate complex. He measured its gateposts and its porch. It was the same size as the others. The porch with its windows was the same size as those previously mentioned. It also had seven steps up to it. Its porch opened onto the outside courtyard, with palm trees decorating its gateposts on both sides. Opposite to it, the gate complex for the inner court faced south. He measured the distance across the courtyard from gate to gate: one hundred seventy-five feet.

✠

40.28-31 He led me into the inside courtyard through the south gate complex. He measured it and

NEW INTERNATIONAL VERSION

south gate; it had the same measurements as the others. ²⁹Its alcoves, its projecting walls and its portico had the same measurements as the others. The gateway and its portico had openings all around. It was fifty cubits long and twenty-five cubits wide. ³⁰(The porticoes of the gateways around the inner court were twenty-five cubits wide and five cubits deep.) ³¹Its portico faced the outer court; palm trees decorated its jambs, and eight steps led up to it.

³²Then he brought me to the inner court on the east side, and he measured the gateway; it had the same measurements as the others. ³³Its alcoves, its projecting walls and its portico had the same measurements as the others. The gateway and its portico had openings all around. It was fifty cubits long and twenty-five cubits wide. ³⁴Its portico faced the outer court; palm trees decorated the jambs on either side, and eight steps led up to it.

³⁵Then he brought me to the north gate and measured it. It had the same measurements as the others, ³⁶as did its alcoves, its projecting walls and its portico, and it had openings all around. It was fifty cubits long and twenty-five cubits wide. ³⁷Its portico*ᵃ* faced the outer court; palm trees decorated the jambs on either side, and eight steps led up to it.

THE ROOMS FOR PREPARING SACRIFICES

³⁸A room with a doorway was by the portico in each of the inner gateways, where the burnt offerings were washed. ³⁹In the portico of the gateway were two tables on each side, on which the burnt offerings, sin offerings and guilt offerings were slaughtered. ⁴⁰By the outside wall of the portico of the gateway, near the steps at the entrance to the north gateway were two tables, and on the other side of the steps were two tables. ⁴¹So there were four tables on one side of the gateway and four on the other—eight tables in all—on which the sacrifices were slaughtered. ⁴²There were also four tables of dressed stone for the burnt offerings, each a cubit and a half long, a cubit and a half wide and a cubit high. On them were placed the utensils for slaughtering the burnt offerings and the other sacrifices. ⁴³And double-pronged hooks, each a handbreadth long, were attached to the wall all around. The tables were for the flesh of the offerings.

ROOMS FOR THE PRIESTS

⁴⁴Outside the inner gate, within the inner court, were two rooms, one*ᵇ* at the side of the

THE MESSAGE

found it the same as the outside ones. Its alcoves, connecting walls, and vestibule were the same. The gate complex and porch, windowed all around, measured eighty-seven and a half by forty-three and three-quarters feet. The vestibule of each of the gate complexes leading to the inside courtyard was forty-three and three-quarters by eight and three-quarters feet. Each vestibule faced the outside courtyard. Palm trees were carved on its doorposts. Eight steps led up to it.

40.32-34   He then took me to the inside courtyard on the east and measured the gate complex. It was identical to the others—alcoves, connecting walls, and vestibule all the same. The gate complex and vestibule had windows all around. It measured eighty-seven and a half by forty-three and three-quarters feet. Its porch faced the outside courtyard. There were palm trees on the doorposts on both sides. And it had eight steps.

40.35-37   He brought me to the gate complex to the north and measured it: same measurements. The alcoves, connecting walls, and vestibule with its windows: eighty-seven and a half by forty-three and three-quarters feet. Its porch faced the outside courtyard. There were palm trees on its doorposts on both sides. And it had eight steps.

⊹

40.38-43   There was a room with a door at the vestibule of the gate complex where the burnt offerings were cleaned. Two tables were placed within the vestibule, one on either side, on which the animals for burnt offerings, sin offerings, and guilt offerings were slaughtered. Two tables were also placed against both outside walls of the vestibule—four tables inside and four tables outside, eight tables in all for slaughtering the sacrificial animals. The four tables used for the burnt offerings were thirty-one and a half inches square and twenty-one inches high. The tools for slaughtering the sacrificial animals and other sacrifices were kept there. Meat hooks, three inches long, were fastened to the walls. The tables were for the sacrificial animals.

⊹

40.44-46   Right where the inside gate complex opened onto the inside courtyard there were two

---

ᵃ 37 Septuagint (see also verses 31 and 34); Hebrew *jambs*
ᵇ 44 Septuagint; Hebrew *were rooms for singers, which were*

NEW INTERNATIONAL VERSION

north gate and facing south, and another at the side of the south*a* gate and facing north. [45]He said to me, "The room facing south is for the priests who have charge of the temple, [46]and the room facing north is for the priests who have charge of the altar. These are the sons of Zadok, who are the only Levites who may draw near to the LORD to minister before him."

[47]Then he measured the court: It was square— a hundred cubits long and a hundred cubits wide. And the altar was in front of the temple.

THE TEMPLE

[48]He brought me to the portico of the temple and measured the jambs of the portico; they were five cubits wide on either side. The width of the entrance was fourteen cubits and its projecting walls were*b* three cubits wide on either side. [49]The portico was twenty cubits wide, and twelve*c* cubits from front to back. It was reached by a flight of stairs,*d* and there were pillars on each side of the jambs.

41 Then the man brought me to the outer sanctuary and measured the jambs; the width of the jambs was six cubits*e* on each side.*f* [2]The entrance was ten cubits wide, and the projecting walls on each side of it were five cubits wide. He also measured the outer sanctuary; it was forty cubits long and twenty cubits wide. [3]Then he went into the inner sanctuary and measured the jambs of the entrance; each was two cubits wide. The entrance was six cubits wide, and the projecting walls on each side of it were seven cubits wide. [4]And he measured the length of the inner sanctuary; it was twenty cubits, and its width was twenty cubits across the end of the outer sanctuary. He said to me, "This is the Most Holy Place."

[5]Then he measured the wall of the temple; it was six cubits thick, and each side room around the temple was four cubits wide. [6]The side rooms were on three levels, one above another, thirty on each level. There were ledges all around the wall of the temple to serve as supports for the side rooms, so that the supports were not inserted into the wall of the temple. [7]The side rooms all around the temple were wider at each successive level. The structure surrounding the temple was built in ascending stages, so that the rooms widened as one went

THE MESSAGE

rooms, one at the north gate facing south and the one at the south gate facing north. The man told me, "The room facing south is for the priests who are in charge of the Temple. And the room facing north is for the priests who are in charge of the altar. These priests are the sons of Zadok, the only sons of Levi permitted to come near to GOD to serve him."

40.47 He measured the inside courtyard: a hundred seventy-five feet square. The altar was in front of the Temple.

✛

40.48-49 He led me to the porch of the Temple and measured the gateposts of the porch: eight and three-quarters feet high on both sides. The entrance to the gate complex was twenty-one feet wide and its connecting walls were four and a half feet thick. The vestibule itself was thirty-five feet wide and twenty-one feet deep. Ten steps led up to the porch. Columns flanked the gateposts.

✛

41 He brought me into the Temple itself and measured the doorposts on each side. Each was ten and a half feet thick. The entrance was seventeen and a half feet wide. The walls on each side were eight and three-quarters feet thick.

He also measured the Temple Sanctuary: seventy feet by thirty-five feet.

41.3-4 He went further in and measured the doorposts at the entrance: Each was three and a half feet thick. The entrance itself was ten and a half feet wide, and the entrance walls were twelve and a quarter feet thick. He measured the inside Sanctuary, thirty-five feet square, set at the end of the main Sanctuary. He told me, "This is The Holy of Holies."

41.5-7 He measured the wall of the Temple. It was ten and a half feet thick. The side rooms around the Temple were seven feet wide. There were three floors of these side rooms, thirty rooms on each of the three floors. There were supporting beams around the Temple wall to hold up the side rooms, but they were free-standing, not attached to the wall itself. The side rooms around the Temple became wider from first floor to second floor to third floor. A

---

a 44 Septuagint; Hebrew *east*   *b* 48 Septuagint; Hebrew *entrance was*   *c* 49 Septuagint; Hebrew *eleven*
d 49 Hebrew; Septuagint *Ten steps led up to it*
e 1 The common cubit was about 1 1/2 feet (about 0.5 meter).   *f* 1 One Hebrew manuscript and Septuagint; most Hebrew manuscripts *side, the width of the tent*

NEW INTERNATIONAL VERSION

upward. A stairway went up from the lowest floor to the top floor through the middle floor.

⁸I saw that the temple had a raised base all around it, forming the foundation of the side rooms. It was the length of the rod, six long cubits. ⁹The outer wall of the side rooms was five cubits thick. The open area between the side rooms of the temple ¹⁰and the ⌊priests'⌋ rooms was twenty cubits wide all around the temple. ¹¹There were entrances to the side rooms from the open area, one on the north and another on the south; and the base adjoining the open area was five cubits wide all around.

¹²The building facing the temple courtyard on the west side was seventy cubits wide. The wall of the building was five cubits thick all around, and its length was ninety cubits.

¹³Then he measured the temple; it was a hundred cubits long, and the temple courtyard and the building with its walls were also a hundred cubits long. ¹⁴The width of the temple courtyard on the east, including the front of the temple, was a hundred cubits.

¹⁵Then he measured the length of the building facing the courtyard at the rear of the temple, including its galleries on each side; it was a hundred cubits.

The outer sanctuary, the inner sanctuary and the portico facing the court, ¹⁶as well as the thresholds and the narrow windows and galleries around the three of them—everything beyond and including the threshold was covered with wood. The floor, the wall up to the windows, and the windows were covered. ¹⁷In the space above the outside of the entrance to the inner sanctuary and on the walls at regular intervals all around the inner and outer sanctuary ¹⁸were carved cherubim and palm trees. Palm trees alternated with cherubim. Each cherub had two faces: ¹⁹the face of a man toward the palm tree on one side and the face of a lion toward the palm tree on the other. They were carved all around the whole temple. ²⁰From the floor to the area above the entrance, cherubim and palm trees were carved on the wall of the outer sanctuary.

²¹The outer sanctuary had a rectangular doorframe, and the one at the front of the Most Holy Place was similar. ²²There was a wooden altar three cubits high and two cubits square*ᵃ*; its corners, its base*ᵇ* and its sides were of wood. The man said to me, "This is the table that is before the LORD." ²³Both the outer sanctuary and the Most Holy Place had double doors. ²⁴Each door had two leaves—two hinged leaves for each

ᵃ 22 Septuagint; Hebrew *long*   ᵇ 22 Septuagint; Hebrew *length*

THE MESSAGE

staircase went from the bottom floor, through the middle, and then to the top floor.

41.8-11   I observed that the Temple had a ten-and-a-half-foot-thick raised base around it, which provided a foundation for the side rooms. The outside walls of the side rooms were eight and three-quarters feet thick. The open area between the side rooms of the Temple and the priests' rooms was a thirty-five-foot-wide strip all around the Temple. There were two entrances to the side rooms from the open area, one placed on the north side, the other on the south. There were eight and three-quarters feet of open space all around.

41.12   The house that faced the Temple courtyard to the west was one hundred twenty-two and a half feet wide, with eight-and-three-quarters-foot-thick walls. The length of the wall and building was one hundred fifty-seven and a half feet.

41.13-14   He measured the Temple: one hundred seventy-five feet long. The Temple courtyard and the house, including its walls, measured a hundred seventy-five feet. The breadth of the front of the Temple and the open area to the east was a hundred seventy-five feet.

41.15-18   He measured the length of the house facing the courtyard at the back of the Temple, including the shelters on each side: one hundred seventy-five feet. The main Sanctuary, the inner Sanctuary, and the vestibule facing the courtyard were paneled with wood, and had window frames and door frames in all three sections. From floor to windows the walls were paneled. Above the outside entrance to the inner Sanctuary and on the walls at regular intervals all around the inner Sanctuary and the main Sanctuary, angel-cherubim and palm trees were carved in alternating sequence.

41.18-20   Each angel-cherub had two faces: a human face toward the palm tree on the right and the face of a lion toward the palm tree on the left. They were carved around the entire Temple. The cherubim–palm tree motif was carved from floor to door height on the wall of the main Sanctuary.

41.21-22   The main Sanctuary had a rectangular doorframe. In front of the Holy Place was something that looked like an altar of wood, five and a quarter feet high and three and a half feet square. Its corners, base, and sides were of wood. The man said to me, "This is the table that stands before GOD."

41.23-26   Both the main Sanctuary and the Holy Place had double doors. Each door had two leaves: two hinged leaves for each door, one set swing-

NEW INTERNATIONAL VERSION

door. ²⁵And on the doors of the outer sanctuary were carved cherubim and palm trees like those carved on the walls, and there was a wooden overhang on the front of the portico. ²⁶On the sidewalls of the portico were narrow windows with palm trees carved on each side. The side rooms of the temple also had overhangs.

ROOMS FOR THE PRIESTS

42 Then the man led me northward into the outer court and brought me to the rooms opposite the temple courtyard and opposite the outer wall on the north side. ²The building whose door faced north was a hundred cubits*a* long and fifty cubits wide. ³Both in the section twenty cubits from the inner court and in the section opposite the pavement of the outer court, gallery faced gallery at the three levels. ⁴In front of the rooms was an inner passageway ten cubits wide and a hundred cubits*b* long. Their doors were on the north. ⁵Now the upper rooms were narrower, for the galleries took more space from them than from the rooms on the lower and middle floors of the building. ⁶The rooms on the third floor had no pillars, as the courts had; so they were smaller in floor space than those on the lower and middle floors. ⁷There was an outer wall parallel to the rooms and the outer court; it extended in front of the rooms for fifty cubits. ⁸While the row of rooms on the side next to the outer court was fifty cubits long, the row on the side nearest the sanctuary was a hundred cubits long. ⁹The lower rooms had an entrance on the east side as one enters them from the outer court.

¹⁰On the south side*c* along the length of the wall of the outer court, adjoining the temple courtyard and opposite the outer wall, were rooms ¹¹with a passageway in front of them. These were like the rooms on the north; they had the same length and width, with similar exits and dimensions. Similar to the doorways on the north ¹²were the doorways of the rooms on the south. There was a doorway at the beginning of the passageway that was parallel to the corresponding wall extending eastward, by which one enters the rooms.

¹³Then he said to me, "The north and south rooms facing the temple courtyard are the priests' rooms, where the priests who approach the LORD will eat the most holy offerings. There they will put the most holy offerings—the grain offerings, the sin offerings and the guilt offerings—for the place is holy. ¹⁴Once the priests

---

a 2 The common cubit was about 1 1/2 feet (about 0.5 meter).   b 4 Septuagint and Syriac; Hebrew and one cubit   c 10 Septuagint; Hebrew Eastward

THE MESSAGE

ing inward and the other set outward. The doors of the main Sanctuary were carved with angel-cherubim and palm trees. There was a canopy of wood in front of the vestibule outside. There were narrow windows alternating with carved palm trees on both sides of the porch.

✛

42 42.1-9 The man led me north into the outside courtyard and brought me to the rooms that are in front of the open space and the house facing north. The length of the house on the north was one hundred seventy-five feet, and its width eighty-seven and a half feet. Across the thirty-five feet that separated the inside courtyard from the paved walkway at the edge of the outside courtyard, the rooms rose level by level for three stories. In front of the rooms on the inside was a hallway seventeen and a half feet wide and one hundred seventy-five feet long. Its entrances were from the north. The upper rooms themselves were narrower, their galleries being wider than on the first and second floors of the building. The rooms on the third floor had no pillars like the pillars in the outside courtyard and were smaller than the rooms on the first and second floors. There was an outside wall parallel to the rooms and the outside courtyard. It fronted the rooms for eighty-seven and a half feet. The row of rooms facing the outside courtyard was eighty-seven and a half feet long. The row on the side nearest the Sanctuary was one hundred seventy-five feet long. The first-floor rooms had their entrance from the east, coming in from the outside courtyard.

42.10-12 On the south side along the length of the courtyard's outside wall and fronting on the Temple courtyard were rooms with a walkway in front of them. These were just like the rooms on the north—same exits and dimensions— with the main entrance from the east leading to the hallway and the doors to the rooms the same as those on the north side. The design on the south was a mirror image of that on the north.

42.13-14 Then he said to me, "The north and south rooms adjacent to the open area are holy rooms where the priests who come before GOD eat the holy offerings. There they place the holy offerings—grain offerings, sin offerings, and guilt offerings. These are set-apart rooms, holy space. After the priests have entered the Sanc-

NEW INTERNATIONAL VERSION

enter the holy precincts, they are not to go into the outer court until they leave behind the garments in which they minister, for these are holy. They are to put on other clothes before they go near the places that are for the people."

¹⁵When he had finished measuring what was inside the temple area, he led me out by the east gate and measured the area all around: ¹⁶He measured the east side with the measuring rod; it was five hundred cubits.ᵃ ¹⁷He measured the north side; it was five hundred cubitsᵇ by the measuring rod. ¹⁸He measured the south side; it was five hundred cubits by the measuring rod. ¹⁹Then he turned to the west side and measured; it was five hundred cubits by the measuring rod. ²⁰So he measured the area on all four sides. It had a wall around it, five hundred cubits long and five hundred cubits wide, to separate the holy from the common.

THE GLORY RETURNS TO THE TEMPLE

43 Then the man brought me to the gate facing east, ²and I saw the glory of the God of Israel coming from the east. His voice was like the roar of rushing waters, and the land was radiant with his glory. ³The vision I saw was like the vision I had seen when heᶜ came to destroy the city and like the visions I had seen by the Kebar River, and I fell facedown. ⁴The glory of the Lᴏʀᴅ entered the temple through the gate facing east. ⁵Then the Spirit lifted me up and brought me into the inner court, and the glory of the Lᴏʀᴅ filled the temple.

⁶While the man was standing beside me, I heard someone speaking to me from inside the temple. ⁷He said: "Son of man, this is the place of my throne and the place for the soles of my feet. This is where I will live among the Israelites forever. The house of Israel will never again defile my holy name—neither they nor their kings—by their prostitutionᵈ and the lifeless idolsᵉ of their kings at their high places. ⁸When they placed their threshold next to my threshold and their doorposts beside my doorposts, with only a wall between me and them, they defiled my holy name by their detestable practices. So I destroyed them in my anger. ⁹Now let them put away from me their prostitution and the lifeless idols of their kings, and I will live among them forever.

¹⁰"Son of man, describe the temple to the people of Israel, that they may be ashamed of their

ᵃ 16 See Septuagint of verse 17; Hebrew *rods*; also in verses 18 and 19.   ᵇ 17 Septuagint; Hebrew *rods*   ᶜ 3 Some Hebrew manuscripts and Vulgate; most Hebrew manuscripts *I*   ᵈ 7 Or *their spiritual adultery*; also in verse 9   ᵉ 7 Or *the corpses*; also in verse 9

THE MESSAGE

tuary, they must not return to the outside courtyard and mingle among the people until they change the sacred garments in which they minister and put on their regular clothes."

⁴²·¹⁵⁻¹⁶ After he had finished measuring what was inside the Temple area, he took me out the east gate and measured it from the outside. Using his measuring stick, he measured the east side: eight hundred seventy-five feet.

⁴²·¹⁷ He measured the north side: eight hundred seventy-five feet.

⁴²·¹⁸ He measured the south side: eight hundred seventy-five feet.

⁴²·¹⁹ Last of all he went to the west side and measured it: eight hundred seventy-five feet.

⁴²·²⁰ He measured the wall on all four sides. Each wall was eight hundred seventy-five feet. The walls separated the holy from the ordinary.

THE MEANING OF THE TEMPLE

⁴³·¹⁻³ **43** The man brought me to the east gate. Oh! The bright Glory of the God of Israel rivered out of the east sounding like the roar of floodwaters, and the earth itself glowed with the bright Glory. It looked just like what I had seen when he came to destroy the city, exactly like what I had seen earlier at the Kebar River. And again I fell, face to the ground.

⁴³·⁴⁻⁵ The bright Glory of Gᴏᴅ poured into the Temple through the east gate. The Spirit put me on my feet and led me to the inside courtyard and—oh! the bright Glory of Gᴏᴅ filled the Temple!

⁴³·⁶⁻⁹ I heard someone speaking to me from inside the Temple while the man stood beside me. He said, "Son of man, this is the place for my throne, the place I'll plant my feet. This is the place where I'll live with the Israelites forever. Neither the people of Israel nor their kings will ever again drag my holy name through the mud with their whoring and the no-god idols their kings set up at all the wayside shrines. When they set up their worship shrines right alongside mine with only a thin wall between them, they dragged my holy name through the mud with their obscene and vile worship. Is it any wonder that I destroyed them in anger? So let them get rid of their whoring ways and the stinking no-god idols introduced by their kings and I'll move in and live with them forever.

⁴³·¹⁰⁻¹¹ "Son of man, tell the people of Israel all about the Temple so they'll be dismayed by

NEW INTERNATIONAL VERSION

sins. Let them consider the plan, [11]and if they are ashamed of all they have done, make known to them the design of the temple—its arrangement, its exits and entrances—its whole design and all its regulations[a] and laws. Write these down before them so that they may be faithful to its design and follow all its regulations.

[12]"This is the law of the temple: All the surrounding area on top of the mountain will be most holy. Such is the law of the temple.

THE ALTAR

[13]"These are the measurements of the altar in long cubits, that cubit being a cubit[b] and a handbreadth[c]: Its gutter is a cubit deep and a cubit wide, with a rim of one span[d] around the edge. And this is the height of the altar: [14]From the gutter on the ground up to the lower ledge it is two cubits high and a cubit wide, and from the smaller ledge up to the larger ledge it is four cubits high and a cubit wide. [15]The altar hearth is four cubits high, and four horns project upward from the hearth. [16]The altar hearth is square, twelve cubits long and twelve cubits wide. [17]The upper ledge also is square, fourteen cubits long and fourteen cubits wide, with a rim of half a cubit and a gutter of a cubit all around. The steps of the altar face east."

[18]Then he said to me, "Son of man, this is what the Sovereign LORD says: These will be the regulations for sacrificing burnt offerings and sprinkling blood upon the altar when it is built: [19]You are to give a young bull as a sin offering to the priests, who are Levites, of the family of Zadok, who come near to minister before me, declares the Sovereign LORD. [20]You are to take some of its blood and put it on the four horns of the altar and on the four corners of the upper ledge and all around the rim, and so purify the altar and make atonement for it. [21]You are to take the bull for the sin offering and burn it in the designated part of the temple area outside the sanctuary.

[22]"On the second day you are to offer a male goat without defect for a sin offering, and the altar is to be purified as it was purified with the bull. [23]When you have finished purifying it, you are to offer a young bull and a ram from the flock, both without defect. [24]You are to offer them before the LORD, and the priests are to sprinkle salt on them and sacrifice them as a burnt offering to the LORD.

[a] 11 Some Hebrew manuscripts and Septuagint; most Hebrew manuscripts regulations and its whole design
[b] 13 The common cubit was about 1 1/2 feet (about 0.5 meter).   [c] 13 That is, about 3 inches (about 8 centimeters)   [d] 13 That is, about 9 inches (about 22 centimeters)

THE MESSAGE

their wayward lives. Get them to go over the layout. That will bring them up short. Show them the whole plan of the Temple, its ins and outs, the proportions, the regulations, and the laws. Draw a picture so they can see the design and meaning and live by its design and intent.

43.12   "This is the law of the Temple: As it radiates from the top of the mountain, everything around it becomes holy ground. Yes, this is law, the meaning, of the Temple.

✠

43.13-14 "These are the dimensions of the altar, using the long (twenty-one-inch) ruler. The gutter at its base is twenty-one inches deep and twenty-one inches wide, with a four-inch lip around its edge.

43.14-15 "The height of the altar is three and a half feet from the base to the first ledge and twenty inches wide. From the first ledge to the second ledge it is seven feet high and twenty-one inches wide. The altar hearth is another seven feet high. Four horns stick upward from the hearth twenty-one inches high.

43.16-17 "The top of the altar, the hearth, is square, twenty-one by twenty-one feet. The upper ledge is also square, twenty-four and a half feet on each side, with a ten-and-a-half-inch lip and a twenty-one-inch-wide gutter all the way around.

"The steps of the altar ascend from the east."

43.18   Then the man said to me, "Son of man, GOD, the Master, says: 'These are the ordinances for conduct at the altar when it is built, for sacrificing burnt offerings and sprinkling blood on it.

43.19-21   " 'For a sin offering, give a bull to the priests, the Levitical priests who are from the family of Zadok who come into my presence to serve me. Take some of its blood and smear it on the four horns of the altar that project from the four corners of the top ledge and all around the lip. That's to purify the altar and make it fit for the sacrifice. Then take the bull for the sin offerings and burn it in the place set aside for this in the courtyard outside the Sanctuary.

43.22-24   " 'On the second day, offer a male goat without blemish for a sin offering. Purify the altar the same as you purified it for the bull. Then, when you have purified it, offer a bull without blemish and a ram without blemish from the flock. Present them before GOD. Sprinkle salt on them and offer them as a burnt offering to GOD.

NEW INTERNATIONAL VERSION

²⁵"For seven days you are to provide a male goat daily for a sin offering; you are also to provide a young bull and a ram from the flock, both without defect. ²⁶For seven days they are to make atonement for the altar and cleanse it; thus they will dedicate it. ²⁷At the end of these days, from the eighth day on, the priests are to present your burnt offerings and fellowship offerings*a* on the altar. Then I will accept you, declares the Sovereign LORD."

THE PRINCE, THE LEVITES, THE PRIESTS

44 Then the man brought me back to the outer gate of the sanctuary, the one facing east, and it was shut. ²The LORD said to me, "This gate is to remain shut. It must not be opened; no one may enter through it. It is to remain shut because the LORD, the God of Israel, has entered through it. ³The prince himself is the only one who may sit inside the gateway to eat in the presence of the LORD. He is to enter by way of the portico of the gateway and go out the same way."

⁴Then the man brought me by way of the north gate to the front of the temple. I looked and saw the glory of the LORD filling the temple of the LORD, and I fell facedown.

⁵The LORD said to me, "Son of man, look carefully, listen closely and give attention to everything I tell you concerning all the regulations regarding the temple of the LORD. Give attention to the entrance of the temple and all the exits of the sanctuary. ⁶Say to the rebellious house of Israel, 'This is what the Sovereign LORD says: Enough of your detestable practices, O house of Israel! ⁷In addition to all your other detestable practices, you brought foreigners uncircumcised in heart and flesh into my sanctuary, desecrating my temple while you offered me food, fat and blood, and you broke my covenant. ⁸Instead of carrying out your duty in regard to my holy things, you put others in charge of my sanctuary. ⁹This is what the Sovereign LORD says: No foreigner uncircumcised in heart and flesh is to enter my sanctuary, not even the foreigners who live among the Israelites.

¹⁰"'The Levites who went far from me when Israel went astray and who wandered from me after their idols must bear the consequences of their sin. ¹¹They may serve in my sanctuary, having charge of the gates of the temple and serving in it; they may slaughter the burnt offerings and sacrifices for the people and stand before the people and serve them. ¹²But because they served them in the presence of their idols and made the house of Israel fall into sin, therefore I

THE MESSAGE

43.25-26 "'For seven days, prepare a goat for a sin offering daily, and also a bull and a ram from the flock, animals without blemish. For seven days the priests are to get the altar ready for its work, purifying it. This is how you dedicate it.

43.27 "'After these seven days of dedication, from the eighth day on, the priests will present your burnt offerings and your peace offerings. And I'll accept you with pleasure, with delight! Decree of GOD, the Master.'"

SANCTUARY RULES

44.1 44 Then the man brought me back to the outside gate complex of the Sanctuary that faces east. But it was shut.

44.2-3 GOD spoke to me: "This gate is shut and it's to stay shut. No one is to go through it because GOD, the God of Israel, has gone through it. It stays shut. Only the prince, because he's the prince, may sit there to eat in the presence of GOD. He is to enter the gate complex through the porch and leave by the same way."

44.4 The man led me through the north gate to the front of the Temple. I looked, and—oh!—the bright Glory of GOD filling the Temple of GOD! I fell on my face in worship.

44.5 GOD said to me, "Son of man, get a grip on yourself. Use your eyes, use your ears, pay careful attention to everything I tell you about the ordinances of this Temple of GOD, the way all the laws work, instructions regarding it and all the entrances and exits of the Sanctuary.

44.6-9 "Tell this bunch of rebels, this family Israel, 'Message of GOD, the Master: No more of these vile obscenities, Israel, dragging irreverent and unrepentant outsiders, uncircumcised in heart and flesh, into my Sanctuary, feeding them the sacrificial offerings as if it were the food for a neighborhood picnic. With all your vile obscenities, you've broken trust with me, the solemn covenant I made with you. You haven't taken care of my holy things. You've hired out the work to foreigners who care nothing for this place, my Sanctuary. No irreverent and unrepentant aliens, uncircumcised in heart or flesh, not even the ones who live among Israelites, are to enter my Sanctuary.'

44.10-14 "The Levites who walked off and left me, along with everyone else—all Israel—who took up with all the no-god idols, will pay for everything they did wrong. From now on they'll do only the menial work in the Sanctuary: guard the gates and help out with the Temple chores—and also kill the sacrificial animals for the people and serve them. Because they acted as priests to the no-god idols and made my people Israel stumble and fall, I've taken an

---

a 27 Traditionally peace offerings

NEW INTERNATIONAL VERSION

have sworn with uplifted hand that they must bear the consequences of their sin, declares the Sovereign LORD. ¹³They are not to come near to serve me as priests or come near any of my holy things or my most holy offerings; they must bear the shame of their detestable practices. ¹⁴Yet I will put them in charge of the duties of the temple and all the work that is to be done in it.

¹⁵" 'But the priests, who are Levites and descendants of Zadok and who faithfully carried out the duties of my sanctuary when the Israelites went astray from me, are to come near to minister before me; they are to stand before me to offer sacrifices of fat and blood, declares the Sovereign LORD. ¹⁶They alone are to enter my sanctuary; they alone are to come near my table to minister before me and perform my service.

¹⁷" 'When they enter the gates of the inner court, they are to wear linen clothes; they must not wear any woolen garment while ministering at the gates of the inner court or inside the temple. ¹⁸They are to wear linen turbans on their heads and linen undergarments around their waists. They must not wear anything that makes them perspire. ¹⁹When they go out into the outer court where the people are, they are to take off the clothes they have been ministering in and are to leave them in the sacred rooms, and put on other clothes, so that they do not consecrate the people by means of their garments.

²⁰" 'They must not shave their heads or let their hair grow long, but they are to keep the hair of their heads trimmed. ²¹No priest is to drink wine when he enters the inner court. ²²They must not marry widows or divorced women; they may marry only virgins of Israelite descent or widows of priests. ²³They are to teach my people the difference between the holy and the common and show them how to distinguish between the unclean and the clean.

²⁴" 'In any dispute, the priests are to serve as judges and decide it according to my ordinances. They are to keep my laws and my decrees for all my appointed feasts, and they are to keep my Sabbaths holy.

²⁵" 'A priest must not defile himself by going near a dead person; however, if the dead person was his father or mother, son or daughter, brother or unmarried sister, then he may defile himself. ²⁶After he is cleansed, he must wait seven days. ²⁷On the day he goes into the inner court

THE MESSAGE

oath to punish them. Decree of GOD, the Master. Yes, they'll pay for what they've done. They're fired from the priesthood. No longer will they come into my presence and take care of my holy things. No more access to The Holy Place! They'll have to live with what they've done, carry the shame of their vile and obscene lives. From now on, their job is to sweep up and run errands. That's it.

44.15-16 "But the Levitical priests who descend from Zadok, who faithfully took care of my Sanctuary when everyone else went off and left me, are going to come into my presence and serve me. They are going to carry out the priestly work of offering the solemn sacrifices of worship. Decree of GOD, the Master. They're the only ones permitted to enter my Sanctuary. They're the only ones to approach my table and serve me, accompanying me in my work.

44.17-19 "When they enter the gate complex of the inside courtyard, they are to dress in linen. No woolens are to be worn while serving at the gate complex of the inside courtyard or inside the Temple itself. They're to wear linen turbans on their heads and linen underclothes—nothing that makes them sweat. When they go out into the outside courtyard where the people gather, they must first change out of the clothes they have been serving in, leaving them in the sacred rooms where they change to their everyday clothes, so that they don't trivialize their holy work by the way they dress.

44.20 "They are to neither shave their heads nor let their hair become unkempt, but must keep their hair trimmed and neat.

44.21 "No priest is to drink on the job—no wine while in the inside courtyard.

44.22 "Priests are not to marry widows or divorcees, but only Israelite virgins or widows of priests.

44.23 "Their job is to teach my people the difference between the holy and the common, to show them how to discern between unclean and clean.

44.24 "When there's a difference of opinion, the priests will arbitrate. They'll decide on the basis of my judgments, laws, and statutes. They are in charge of making sure the appointed feasts are honored and my Sabbaths kept holy in the ways I've commanded.

44.25-27 "A priest must not contaminate himself by going near a corpse. But when the dead person is his father or mother, son or daughter, brother or unmarried sister, he can approach the dead. But after he has been purified, he must wait another seven days. Then, when he returns to the inside courtyard of the Sanctuary

NEW INTERNATIONAL VERSION

of the sanctuary to minister in the sanctuary, he is to offer a sin offering for himself, declares the Sovereign Lord.

28 " 'I am to be the only inheritance the priests have. You are to give them no possession in Israel; I will be their possession. 29 They will eat the grain offerings, the sin offerings and the guilt offerings; and everything in Israel devoted *a* to the Lord will belong to them. 30 The best of all the firstfruits and of all your special gifts will belong to the priests. You are to give them the first portion of your ground meal so that a blessing may rest on your household. 31 The priests must not eat anything, bird or animal, found dead or torn by wild animals.

Division of the Land

45 " 'When you allot the land as an inheritance, you are to present to the Lord a portion of the land as a sacred district, 25,000 cubits long and 20,000 *b* cubits wide; the entire area will be holy. 2 Of this, a section 500 cubits square is to be for the sanctuary, with 50 cubits around it for open land. 3 In the sacred district, measure off a section 25,000 cubits *c* long and 10,000 cubits *d* wide. In it will be the sanctuary, the Most Holy Place. 4 It will be the sacred portion of the land for the priests, who minister in the sanctuary and who draw near to minister before the Lord. It will be a place for their houses as well as a holy place for the sanctuary. 5 An area 25,000 cubits long and 10,000 cubits wide will belong to the Levites, who serve in the temple, as their possession for towns to live in. *e*

6 " 'You are to give the city as its property an area 5,000 cubits wide and 25,000 cubits long, adjoining the sacred portion; it will belong to the whole house of Israel.

7 " 'The prince will have the land bordering each side of the area formed by the sacred district and the property of the city. It will extend westward from the west side and eastward from the east side, running lengthwise from the western to the eastern border parallel to one of the tribal portions. 8 This land will be his possession in Israel. And my princes will no longer oppress my people but will allow the house of Israel to possess the land according to their tribes.

THE MESSAGE

to do his priestly work in the Sanctuary, he must first offer a sin offering for himself. Decree of God, the Master.

44.28-30 "As to priests owning land, I am their inheritance. Don't give any land in Israel to them. *I* am their 'land,' their inheritance. They'll take their meals from the grain offerings, the sin offerings, and the guilt offerings. Everything in Israel offered to God in worship is theirs. The best of everything grown, plus all special gifts, comes to the priests. All that is given in worship to God goes to them. Serve them first. Serve from your best and your home will be blessed.

44.31 "Priests are not to eat any meat from bird or animal unfit for ordinary human consumption, such as carcasses found dead on the road or in the field.

Sacred Space for God

45.1-4 "When you divide up the inheritance of the land, you must set aside part of the land as sacred space for God: approximately seven miles long by six miles wide, all of it holy ground. Within this rectangle, reserve a seven-hundred-fifty-foot square for the Sanctuary with a seventy-five-foot buffer zone surrounding it. Mark off within the sacred reserve a section seven miles long by three miles wide. The Sanctuary with its Holy of Holies will be placed there. This is where the priests will live, those who lead worship in the Sanctuary and serve God there. Their houses will be there along with The Holy Place.

45.5 "To the north of the sacred reserve, an area roughly seven miles long and two and a quarter miles wide will be set aside as land for the villages of the Levites who administer the affairs of worship in the Sanctuary.

45.6 "To the south of the sacred reserve, measure off a section seven miles long and about a mile and a half wide for the city itself, an area held in common by the whole family of Israel.

45.7-8 "The prince gets the land abutting the seven-mile east and west borders of the central sacred square, extending eastward toward the Jordan and westward toward the Mediterranean. This is the prince's possession in Israel. My princes will no longer bully my people, running roughshod over them. They'll respect the land as it has been allotted to the tribes.

---

a 29 The Hebrew term refers to the irrevocable giving over of things or persons to the Lord.   *b* 1 Septuagint (see also verses 3 and 5 and 48:9); Hebrew *10,000*   *c* 3 That is, about 7 miles (about 12 kilometers)   *d* 3 That is, about 3 miles (about 5 kilometers)   *e* 5 Septuagint; Hebrew *temple; they will have as their possession 20 rooms*

NEW INTERNATIONAL VERSION

9 " 'This is what the Sovereign LORD says: You have gone far enough, O princes of Israel! Give up your violence and oppression and do what is just and right. Stop dispossessing my people, declares the Sovereign LORD. 10You are to use accurate scales, an accurate ephah*a* and an accurate bath.*b* 11The ephah and the bath are to be the same size, the bath containing a tenth of a homer*c* and the ephah a tenth of a homer; the homer is to be the standard measure for both. 12The shekel*d* is to consist of twenty gerahs. Twenty shekels plus twenty-five shekels plus fifteen shekels equal one mina.*e*

OFFERINGS AND HOLY DAYS

13 " 'This is the special gift you are to offer: a sixth of an ephah from each homer of wheat and a sixth of an ephah from each homer of barley. 14The prescribed portion of oil, measured by the bath, is a tenth of a bath from each cor (which consists of ten baths or one homer, for ten baths are equivalent to a homer). 15Also one sheep is to be taken from every flock of two hundred from the well-watered pastures of Israel. These will be used for the grain offerings, burnt offerings and fellowship offerings*f* to make atonement for the people, declares the Sovereign LORD. 16All the people of the land will participate in this special gift for the use of the prince in Israel. 17It will be the duty of the prince to provide the burnt offerings, grain offerings and drink offerings at the festivals, the New Moons and the Sabbaths—at all the appointed feasts of the house of Israel. He will provide the sin offerings, grain offerings, burnt offerings and fellowship offerings to make atonement for the house of Israel.

18 " 'This is what the Sovereign LORD says: In the first month on the first day you are to take a young bull without defect and purify the sanctuary. 19The priest is to take some of the blood of the sin offering and put it on the doorposts of the temple, on the four corners of the upper ledge of the altar and on the gateposts of the inner court. 20You are to do the same on the seventh day of the month for anyone who sins unintentionally or through ignorance; so you are to make atonement for the temple.

21 " 'In the first month on the fourteenth day you are to observe the Passover, a feast lasting seven days, during which you shall eat bread made without yeast. 22On that day the prince is

---

a 10 An ephah was a dry measure.   *b 10* A bath was a liquid measure.   *c 11* A homer was a dry measure.
d 12 A shekel weighed about 2/5 ounce (about 11.5 grams).
e 12 That is, 60 shekels; the common mina was 50 shekels.
f 15 Traditionally *peace offerings*; also in verse 17

THE MESSAGE

45.9-12   "This is the Message of GOD, the Master: 'I've put up with you long enough, princes of Israel! Quit bullying and taking advantage of my people. Do what's just and right for a change. Use honest scales—honest weights and honest measures. Every pound must have sixteen ounces. Every gallon must measure four quarts. The ounce is the basic measure for both. And your coins must be honest—no wooden nickels!

EVERYONE IN THE LAND MUST CONTRIBUTE

45.13-15   " 'These are the prescribed offerings you are to supply: one-sixtieth part of your wheat, one-sixtieth part of your barley, one-hundredth part of your oil, one sheep out of every two hundred from the lush pastures of Israel. These will be used for the grain offerings, burnt offerings, and peace offerings for making the atonement sacrifices for the people. Decree of GOD, the Master.

45.16-17   " 'Everyone in the land must contribute to these special offerings that the prince in Israel will administer. It's the prince's job to provide the burnt offerings, grain offerings, and drink offerings at the Holy Festivals, the New Moons, and the Sabbaths—all the commanded feasts among the people of Israel. Sin offerings, grain offerings, burnt offerings, and peace offerings for making atonement for the people of Israel are his responsibility.

45.18-20   " 'This is the Message from GOD, the Master: On the first day of the first month, take an unblemished bull calf and purify the Sanctuary. The priest is to take blood from the sin offerings and rub it on the doorposts of the Temple, on the four corners of the ledge of the altar, and on the gate entrance to the inside courtyard. Repeat this ritual on the seventh day of the month for anyone who sins without knowing it. In this way you make atonement for the Temple.

45.21   " 'On the fourteenth day of the first month, you will observe the Passover, a feast of seven days. During the feast you will eat bread made without yeast.

45.22-23   " 'On Passover, the prince supplies a bull as

NEW INTERNATIONAL VERSION

to provide a bull as a sin offering for himself and for all the people of the land. ²³Every day during the seven days of the Feast he is to provide seven bulls and seven rams without defect as a burnt offering to the LORD, and a male goat for a sin of-fering. ²⁴He is to provide as a grain offering an ephah for each bull and an ephah for each ram, along with a hin*a* of oil for each ephah.

²⁵" 'During the seven days of the Feast, which begins in the seventh month on the fifteenth day, he is to make the same provision for sin offer-ings, burnt offerings, grain offerings and oil.

46 " 'This is what the Sovereign LORD says: The gate of the inner court facing east is to be shut on the six working days, but on the Sabbath day and on the day of the New Moon it is to be opened. ²The prince is to enter from the outside through the portico of the gateway and stand by the gatepost. The priests are to sacrifice his burnt offering and his fellowship offerings.*b* He is to worship at the threshold of the gateway and then go out, but the gate will not be shut until evening. ³On the Sabbaths and New Moons the people of the land are to worship in the pres-ence of the LORD at the entrance to that gateway. ⁴The burnt offering the prince brings to the LORD on the Sabbath day is to be six male lambs and a ram, all without defect. ⁵The grain offering given with the ram is to be an ephah,*c* and the grain offering with the lambs is to be as much as he pleases, along with a hin*a* of oil for each ephah. ⁶On the day of the New Moon he is to of-fer a young bull, six lambs and a ram, all without defect. ⁷He is to provide as a grain offering one ephah with the bull, one ephah with the ram, and with the lambs as much as he wants to give, along with a hin of oil with each ephah. ⁸When the prince enters, he is to go in through the por-tico of the gateway, and he is to come out the same way.

⁹" 'When the people of the land come before the LORD at the appointed feasts, whoever enters by the north gate to worship is to go out the south gate; and whoever enters by the south gate is to go out the north gate. No one is to return through the gate by which he entered, but each is to go out the opposite gate. ¹⁰The prince is to be among them, going in when they go in and going out when they go out.

¹¹" 'At the festivals and the appointed feasts, the grain offering is to be an ephah with a bull,

THE MESSAGE

a sin offering for himself and all the people of the country. Each day for each of the seven days of the feast, he will supply seven bulls and seven rams unblemished as a burnt offering to GOD, and also each day a male goat.

45.24 " 'He will supply about five and a half gal-lons of grain offering and a gallon of oil for each bull and each ram.

45.25 " 'On the fifteenth day of the seventh month, and on each of the seven days of the feast, he is to supply the same materials for sin offerings, burnt offerings, grain offerings, and oil.

☩

46.1-3 **46** " 'Message from GOD, the Master: The gate of the inside courtyard on the east is to be shut on the six working days, but open on the Sabbath. It is also to be open on the New Moon. The prince will enter through the entrance area of the gate complex and stand at the gateposts as the priests present his burnt offerings and peace offerings while he worships there on the porch. He will then leave, but the gate won't be shut until evening. On Sabbaths and New Moons, the people are to worship be-fore GOD at the outside entrance to that gate complex.

46.4-5 " 'The prince supplies for GOD the burnt of-fering for the Sabbath—six unblemished lambs and an unblemished ram. The grain offering to go with the ram is about five and a half gallons plus a gallon of oil, and a handful of grain for each lamb.

46.6-7 " 'At the New Moon he is to supply a bull calf, six lambs, and a ram, all without blemish. He will also supply five and a half gallons of grain offering and a gallon of oil for both ram and bull, and a handful of grain offering for each lamb.

46.8 " 'When the prince enters, he will go through the entrance vestibule of the gate com-plex and leave the same way.

46.9-10 " 'But when the people of the land come to worship GOD at the commanded feasts, those who enter through the north gate will exit from the south gate, and those who enter though the south gate will exit from the north gate. You don't exit the gate through which you enter, but through the opposite gate. The prince is to be there, mingling with them, going in and out with them.

46.11 " 'At the festivals and the commanded feasts, the appropriate grain offering is five and a half

---

^a 24,5 That is, probably about 4 quarts (about 4 liters)
^b 2 Traditionally *peace offerings*; also in verse 12   ^c 5 That is, probably about 3/5 bushel (about 22 liters)

NEW INTERNATIONAL VERSION

an ephah with a ram, and with the lambs as much as one pleases, along with a hin of oil for each ephah. [12]When the prince provides a freewill offering to the LORD—whether a burnt offering or fellowship offerings—the gate facing east is to be opened for him. He shall offer his burnt offering or his fellowship offerings as he does on the Sabbath day. Then he shall go out, and after he has gone out, the gate will be shut.

[13]"'Every day you are to provide a year-old lamb without defect for a burnt offering to the LORD; morning by morning you shall provide it. [14]You are also to provide with it morning by morning a grain offering, consisting of a sixth of an ephah with a third of a hin of oil to moisten the flour. The presenting of this grain offering to the LORD is a lasting ordinance. [15]So the lamb and the grain offering and the oil shall be provided morning by morning for a regular burnt offering.

[16]"'This is what the Sovereign LORD says: If the prince makes a gift from his inheritance to one of his sons, it will also belong to his descendants; it is to be their property by inheritance. [17]If, however, he makes a gift from his inheritance to one of his servants, the servant may keep it until the year of freedom; then it will revert to the prince. His inheritance belongs to his sons only; it is theirs. [18]The prince must not take any of the inheritance of the people, driving them off their property. He is to give his sons their inheritance out of his own property, so that none of my people will be separated from his property.'"

[19]Then the man brought me through the entrance at the side of the gate to the sacred rooms facing north, which belonged to the priests, and showed me a place at the western end. [20]He said to me, "This is the place where the priests will cook the guilt offering and the sin offering and bake the grain offering, to avoid bringing them into the outer court and consecrating the people."

[21]He then brought me to the outer court and led me around to its four corners, and I saw in each corner another court. [22]In the four corners of the outer court were enclosed[a] courts, forty cubits long and thirty cubits wide; each of the courts in the four corners was the same size. [23]Around the inside of each of the four courts was a ledge of stone, with places for fire built all around under the ledge. [24]He said to me, "These are the kitchens where those who minister at the temple will cook the sacrifices of the people."

THE MESSAGE

gallons, with a gallon of oil for the bull and ram and a handful of grain for each lamb.

46.12 "'When the prince brings a freewill offering to GOD, whether a burnt offering or a peace offering, the east gate is to be opened for him. He offers his burnt or peace offering the same as he does on the Sabbath. Then he leaves, and after he is out, the gate is shut.

46.13-15 "'Every morning you are to bring a yearling lamb unblemished for a burnt offering to GOD. Also, every morning bring a grain offering of about a gallon of grain with a quart or so of oil to moisten it. Presenting this grain offering to GOD is standard procedure. The lamb, the grain offering, and the oil for the burnt offering are a regular daily ritual.

46.16-18 "'A Message from GOD, the Master: If the prince deeds a gift from his inheritance to one of his sons, it stays in the family. But if he deeds a gift from his inheritance to a servant, the servant keeps it only until the year of liberation (the Jubilee year). After that, it comes back to the prince. His inheritance is only for his sons. It stays in the family. The prince must not take the inheritance from any of the people, dispossessing them of their land. He can give his sons only what he himself owns. None of my people are to be run off their land.'"

46.19-20 Then the man brought me through the north gate into the holy chambers assigned to the priests and showed me a back room to the west. He said, "This is the kitchen where the priests will cook the guilt offering and sin offering and bake the grain offering so that they won't have to do it in the outside courtyard and endanger the unprepared people out there with The Holy."

46.21-23 He proceeded to take me to the outside courtyard and around to each of its four corners. In each corner I observed another court. In each of the four corners of the outside courtyard were smaller courts sixty by forty-five feet, each the same size. On the inside walls of the courts was a stone shelf, and beneath the shelves, hearths for cooking.

46.24 He said, "These are the kitchens where those who serve in the Temple will cook the sacrifices of the people."

---

[a] 22 The meaning of the Hebrew for this word is uncertain.

NEW INTERNATIONAL VERSION	THE MESSAGE

THE RIVER FROM THE TEMPLE

47 The man brought me back to the entrance of the temple, and I saw water coming out from under the threshold of the temple toward the east (for the temple faced east). The water was coming down from under the south side of the temple, south of the altar. ²He then brought me out through the north gate and led me around the outside to the outer gate facing east, and the water was flowing from the south side.

³As the man went eastward with a measuring line in his hand, he measured off a thousand cubits*a* and then led me through water that was ankle-deep. ⁴He measured off another thousand cubits and led me through water that was knee-deep. He measured off another thousand and led me through water that was up to the waist. ⁵He measured off another thousand, but now it was a river that I could not cross, because the water had risen and was deep enough to swim in—a river that no one could cross. ⁶He asked me, "Son of man, do you see this?"

Then he led me back to the bank of the river. ⁷When I arrived there, I saw a great number of trees on each side of the river. ⁸He said to me, "This water flows toward the eastern region and goes down into the Arabah,*b* where it enters the Sea.*c* When it empties into the Sea,*c* the water there becomes fresh. ⁹Swarms of living creatures will live wherever the river flows. There will be large numbers of fish, because this water flows there and makes the salt water fresh; so where the river flows everything will live. ¹⁰Fishermen will stand along the shore; from En Gedi to En Eglaim there will be places for spreading nets. The fish will be of many kinds—like the fish of the Great Sea.*d* ¹¹But the swamps and marshes will not become fresh; they will be left for salt. ¹²Fruit trees of all kinds will grow on both banks of the river. Their leaves will not wither, nor will their fruit fail. Every month they will bear, because the water from the sanctuary flows to them. Their fruit will serve for food and their leaves for healing."

THE BOUNDARIES OF THE LAND

¹³This is what the Sovereign LORD says: "These are the boundaries by which you are to divide the land for an inheritance among the twelve tribes of Israel, with two portions for Joseph. ¹⁴You are to divide it equally among them. Because I swore with uplifted hand to give it to

---

TREES ON BOTH SIDES OF THE RIVER

47 Now he brought me back to the entrance to the Temple. I saw water pouring out from under the Temple porch to the east (the Temple faced east). The water poured from the south side of the Temple, south of the altar. He then took me out through the north gate and led me around the outside to the gate complex on the east. The water was gushing from under the south front of the Temple.

47.3-5 He walked to the east with a measuring tape and measured off fifteen hundred feet, leading me through water that was ankle-deep. He measured off another fifteen hundred feet, leading me through water that was knee-deep. He measured off another fifteen hundred feet, leading me through water waist-deep. He measured off another fifteen hundred feet. By now it was a river over my head, water to swim in, water no one could possibly walk through.

47.6-7 He said, "Son of man, have you had a good look?"

Then he took me back to the riverbank. While sitting on the bank, I noticed a lot of trees on both sides of the river.

47.8-10 He told me, "This water flows east, descends to the Arabah and then into the sea, the sea of stagnant waters. When it empties into those waters, the sea will become fresh. Wherever the river flows, life will flourish—great schools of fish—because the river is turning the salt sea into fresh water. Where the river flows, life abounds. Fishermen will stand shoulder to shoulder along the shore from En-gedi all the way north to En-eglaim, casting their nets. The sea will teem with fish of all kinds, like the fish of the Great Mediterranean.

47.11 "The swamps and marshes won't become fresh. They'll stay salty.

47.12 "But the river itself, on both banks, will grow fruit trees of all kinds. Their leaves won't wither, the fruit won't fail. Every month they'll bear fresh fruit because the river from the Sanctuary flows to them. Their fruit will be for food and their leaves for healing."

DIVIDE UP THIS LAND

47.13-14 A Message from GOD, the Master: "These are the boundaries by which you are to divide up the inheritance of the land for the twelve tribes of Israel, with Joseph getting two parcels. It is to be divided up equally. I swore in a solemn

---

a 3 That is, about 1,500 feet (about 450 meters)
b 8 Or *the Jordan Valley*   *c 8* That is, the Dead Sea
d 10 That is, the Mediterranean; also in verses 15, 19 and 20

your forefathers, this land will become your inheritance.

15"This is to be the boundary of the land:

"On the north side it will run from the Great Sea by the Hethlon road past Lebo*a* Hamath to Zedad, 16Berothah*b* and Sibraim (which lies on the border between Damascus and Hamath), as far as Hazer Hatticon, which is on the border of Hauran. 17The boundary will extend from the sea to Hazar Enan,*c* along the northern border of Damascus, with the border of Hamath to the north. This will be the north boundary.

18"On the east side the boundary will run between Hauran and Damascus, along the Jordan between Gilead and the land of Israel, to the eastern sea and as far as Tamar.*d* This will be the east boundary.

19"On the south side it will run from Tamar as far as the waters of Meribah Kadesh, then along the Wadi *of Egypt* to the Great Sea. This will be the south boundary.

20"On the west side, the Great Sea will be the boundary to a point opposite Lebo*e* Hamath. This will be the west boundary.

21"You are to distribute this land among yourselves according to the tribes of Israel. 22You are to allot it as an inheritance for yourselves and for the aliens who have settled among you and who have children. You are to consider them as native-born Israelites; along with you they are to be allotted an inheritance among the tribes of Israel. 23In whatever tribe the alien settles, there you are to give him his inheritance," declares the Sovereign LORD.

THE DIVISION OF THE LAND

48 "These are the tribes, listed by name: At the northern frontier, Dan will have one portion; it will follow the Hethlon road to Lebo*f* Hamath; Hazar Enan and the northern border of Damascus next to Hamath will be part of its border from the east side to the west side.

2"Asher will have one portion; it will border the territory of Dan from east to west.

3"Naphtali will have one portion; it will border the territory of Asher from east to west.

4"Manasseh will have one portion; it will border the territory of Naphtali from east to west.

oath to give it to your ancestors, swore that this land would be your inheritance.

47.15-17 "These are the boundaries of the land:

"The northern boundary runs from the Great Mediterranean Sea along the Hethlon road to where you turn off to the entrance of Hamath, Zedad, Berothah, and Sibraim, which lies between the territory of Damascus and the territory of Hamath, and on to Hazor-hatticon on the border of Hauran. The boundary runs from the Sea to Hazor-enon, with the territories of Damascus and Hamath to the north. That is the northern boundary.

47.18 "The eastern boundary runs between Damascus and Hauran, down along the Jordan between Gilead and the land of Israel to the Eastern Sea as far as Tamar. This is the eastern boundary.

47.19 "The southern boundary runs west from Tamar to the waters of Meribah-kadesh, along the Brook of Egypt, and out to the Great Mediterranean Sea. This is the southern boundary.

47.20 "The western boundary is formed by the Great Mediterranean Sea north to where the road turns east toward the entrance to Hamath. This is the western boundary.

47.21-23 "Divide up this land among the twelve tribes of Israel. Divide it up as your inheritance, and include in it the resident aliens who have made themselves at home among you and now have children. Treat them as if they were born there, just like yourselves. They also get an inheritance among the tribes of Israel. In whatever tribe the resident alien lives, there he gets his inheritance. Decree of GOD, the Master.

THE SANCTUARY OF GOD AT THE CENTER

48.1 48 "These are the tribes:

"Dan: one portion, along the northern boundary, following the Hethlon road that turns off to the entrance of Hamath as far as Hazor-enon so that the territory of Damascus lies to the north alongside Hamath, the northern border stretching from east to west.

48.2 "Asher: one portion, bordering Dan from east to west.

48.3 "Naphtali: one portion, bordering Asher from east to west.

48.4 "Manasseh: one portion, bordering Naphtali from east to west.

---

a 15 Or *past the entrance to*   *b* 15,16 See Septuagint and Ezekiel 48:1; Hebrew *road to go into Zedad,* 16Hamath, Berothah   *c* 17 Hebrew *Enon,* a variant of *Enan*
d 18 Septuagint and Syriac; Hebrew *Israel. You will measure to the eastern sea*   *e* 20 Or *opposite the entrance to*
f 1 Or *to the entrance to*

NEW INTERNATIONAL VERSION

5"Ephraim will have one portion; it will border the territory of Manasseh from east to west.

6"Reuben will have one portion; it will border the territory of Ephraim from east to west.

7"Judah will have one portion; it will border the territory of Reuben from east to west.

8"Bordering the territory of Judah from east to west will be the portion you are to present as a special gift. It will be 25,000 cubits*a* wide, and its length from east to west will equal one of the tribal portions; the sanctuary will be in the center of it.

9"The special portion you are to offer to the LORD will be 25,000 cubits long and 10,000 cubits*b* wide. 10This will be the sacred portion for the priests. It will be 25,000 cubits long on the north side, 10,000 cubits wide on the west side, 10,000 cubits wide on the east side and 25,000 cubits long on the south side. In the center of it will be the sanctuary of the LORD. 11This will be for the consecrated priests, the Zadokites, who were faithful in serving me and did not go astray as the Levites did when the Israelites went astray. 12It will be a special gift to them from the sacred portion of the land, a most holy portion, bordering the territory of the Levites.

13"Alongside the territory of the priests, the Levites will have an allotment 25,000 cubits long and 10,000 cubits wide. Its total length will be 25,000 cubits and its width 10,000 cubits. 14They must not sell or exchange any of it. This is the best of the land and must not pass into other hands, because it is holy to the LORD.

15"The remaining area, 5,000 cubits wide and 25,000 cubits long, will be for the common use of the city, for houses and for pastureland. The city will be in the center of it 16and will have these measurements: the north side 4,500 cubits, the south side 4,500 cubits, the east side 4,500 cubits, and the west side 4,500 cubits. 17The pastureland for the city will be 250 cubits on the north, 250 cubits on the south, 250 cubits on the east, and 250 cubits on the west. 18What remains of the area, bordering on the sacred portion and running the length of it, will be 10,000 cubits on the east side and 10,000 cubits on the west side. Its produce will supply food for the workers of the city. 19The workers from the city who farm it will come from all the tribes of Israel. 20The entire portion will be a square, 25,000 cubits on each side. As a special gift you will set aside the sacred portion, along with the property of the city.

21"What remains on both sides of the area formed by the sacred portion and the city prop-

THE MESSAGE

48.5 "Ephraim: one portion, bordering Manasseh from east to west.

48.6 "Reuben: one portion, bordering Ephraim from east to west.

48.7 "Judah: one portion, bordering Reuben from east to west.

48.8-9 "Bordering Judah from east to west is the consecrated area that you will set aside as holy: a square approximately seven by seven miles, with the Sanctuary set at the center. The consecrated area reserved for GOD is to be seven miles long and a little less than three miles wide.

48.10-12 "This is how it will be parceled out. The priest will get the area measuring seven miles on the north and south boundaries, with a width of a little more than three miles at the east and west boundaries. The Sanctuary of GOD will be at the center. This is for the consecrated priests, the Zadokites who stayed true in their service to me and didn't get off track as the Levites did when Israel wandered off the main road. This is their special gift, a gift from the land itself, most holy ground, bordering the section of the Levites.

48.13-14 "The Levites get a section equal in size to that of the priests, roughly seven by three miles. They are not permitted to sell or trade any of it. It's the choice part of the land, to say nothing of being holy to GOD.

48.15-19 "What's left of the 'sacred square'—each side measures out at seven miles by a mile and a half—is for ordinary use: the city and its buildings with open country around it, but the city at the center. The north, south, east, and west sides of the city are each about a mile and a half in length. A strip of pasture, one hundred twenty-five yards wide, will border the city on all sides. The remainder of this portion, three miles of countryside to the east and to the west of the sacred precinct, is for farming. It will supply food for the city. Workers from all the tribes of Israel will serve as field hands to farm the land.

48.20 "This dedicated area, set apart for holy purposes, will be a square, seven miles by seven miles, a 'holy square,' which includes the part set aside for the city.

48.21-22 "The rest of this land, the country stretching east to the Jordan and west to the Mediter-

---

a 8 That is, about 7 miles (about 12 kilometers)   *b* 9 That is, about 3 miles (about 5 kilometers)

NEW INTERNATIONAL VERSION

erty will belong to the prince. It will extend eastward from the 25,000 cubits of the sacred portion to the eastern border, and westward from the 25,000 cubits to the western border. Both these areas running the length of the tribal portions will belong to the prince, and the sacred portion with the temple sanctuary will be in the center of them. ²²So the property of the Levites and the property of the city will lie in the center of the area that belongs to the prince. The area belonging to the prince will lie between the border of Judah and the border of Benjamin.

²³"As for the rest of the tribes: Benjamin will have one portion; it will extend from the east side to the west side.

²⁴"Simeon will have one portion; it will border the territory of Benjamin from east to west.

²⁵"Issachar will have one portion; it will border the territory of Simeon from east to west.

²⁶"Zebulun will have one portion; it will border the territory of Issachar from east to west.

²⁷"Gad will have one portion; it will border the territory of Zebulun from east to west.

²⁸"The southern boundary of Gad will run south from Tamar to the waters of Meribah Kadesh, then along the Wadi ʟof Egyptʟ to the Great Sea.ᵃ

²⁹"This is the land you are to allot as an inheritance to the tribes of Israel, and these will be their portions," declares the Sovereign LORD.

THE GATES OF THE CITY

³⁰"These will be the exits of the city: Beginning on the north side, which is 4,500 cubits long, ³¹the gates of the city will be named after the tribes of Israel. The three gates on the north side will be the gate of Reuben, the gate of Judah and the gate of Levi.

³²"On the east side, which is 4,500 cubits long, will be three gates: the gate of Joseph, the gate of Benjamin and the gate of Dan.

³³"On the south side, which measures 4,500 cubits, will be three gates: the gate of Simeon, the gate of Issachar and the gate of Zebulun.

³⁴"On the west side, which is 4,500 cubits long, will be three gates: the gate of Gad, the gate of Asher and the gate of Naphtali.

³⁵"The distance all around will be 18,000 cubits.

"And the name of the city from that time on will be:

THE LORD IS THERE."

THE MESSAGE

ranean from the seven-mile sides of the 'holy square,' belongs to the prince. His land is sandwiched between the tribal portions north and south, and goes out both east and west from the 'sacred square' with its Temple at the center. The land set aside for the Levites on one side and the city on the other is in the middle of the territory assigned to the prince. The 'sacred square' is flanked east and west by the prince's land and bordered on the north and south by the territories of Judah and Benjamin respectively.

48.23 "And then the rest of the tribes:

"Benjamin: one portion, stretching from the eastern to the western boundary.

48.24 "Simeon: one portion, bordering Benjamin from east to west.

48.25 "Issachar: one portion, bordering Simeon from east to west.

48.26 "Zebulun: one portion, bordering Issachar from east to west.

48.27 "Gad: one portion, bordering Zebulun from east to west.

48.28 "The southern boundary of Gad will run south from Tamar to the waters of Meribah-ka-desh, along the Brook of Egypt and then out to the Great Mediterranean Sea.

48.29 "This is the land that you are to divide up among the tribes of Israel as their inheritance. These are their portions." Decree of GOD, the Master.

✝

48.30-31 "These are the gates of the city. On the north side, which is 2,250 yards long (the gates of the city are named after the tribes of Israel), three gates: the gate of Reuben, the gate of Judah, the gate of Levi.

48.32 "On the east side, measuring 2,250 yards, three gates: the gate of Joseph, the gate of Benjamin, the gate of Dan.

48.33 "On the south side, measuring 2,250 yards, three gates: the gate of Simeon, the gate of Issachar, the gate of Zebulun.

48.34 "On the west side, measuring 2,250 yards, three gates: the gate of Gad, the gate of Asher, the gate of Naphtali.

48.35 "The four sides of the city measure to a total of nearly six miles.

"From now on the name of the city will be YAHWEH-SHAMMAH:

"GOD-IS-THERE."

ᵃ 28 That is, the Mediterranean

DANIEL

DANIEL

DANIEL'S TRAINING IN BABYLON

1 In the third year of the reign of Jehoiakim king of Judah, Nebuchadnezzar king of Babylon came to Jerusalem and besieged it. ²And the Lord delivered Jehoiakim king of Judah into his hand, along with some of the articles from the temple of God. These he carried off to the temple of his god in Babylonia *a* and put in the treasure house of his god.

³Then the king ordered Ashpenaz, chief of his court officials, to bring in some of the Israelites from the royal family and the nobility— ⁴young men without any physical defect, handsome, showing aptitude for every kind of learning, well informed, quick to understand, and qualified to serve in the king's palace. He was to teach them the language and literature of the Babylonians. *b* ⁵The king assigned them a daily amount of food and wine from the king's table. They were to be trained for three years, and after that they were to enter the king's service.

⁶Among these were some from Judah: Daniel, Hananiah, Mishael and Azariah. ⁷The chief official gave them new names: to Daniel, the name Belteshazzar; to Hananiah, Shadrach; to Mishael, Meshach; and to Azariah, Abednego.

⁸But Daniel resolved not to defile himself with the royal food and wine, and he asked the chief official for permission not to defile himself this way. ⁹Now God had caused the official to show favor and sympathy to Daniel, ¹⁰but the official told Daniel, "I am afraid of my lord the king, who has assigned your *c* food and drink. Why should he see you looking worse than the other young men your age? The king would then have my head because of you."

¹¹Daniel then said to the guard whom the chief official had appointed over Daniel, Hananiah, Mishael and Azariah, ¹²"Please test your servants for ten days: Give us nothing but vegetables to eat and water to drink. ¹³Then compare our appearance with that of the young men who eat the royal food, and treat your servants in ac-

DANIEL WAS GIFTED BY GOD

1 1.1-2 It was the third year of King Jehoiakim's reign in Judah when King Nebuchadnezzar of Babylon declared war on Jerusalem and besieged the city. The Master handed King Jehoiakim of Judah over to him, along with some of the furnishings from the Temple of God. Nebuchadnezzar took king and furnishings to the country of Babylon, the ancient Shinar. He put the furnishings in the sacred treasury.

1.3-5 The king told Ashpenaz, head of the palace staff, to get some Israelites from the royal family and nobility—young men who were healthy and handsome, intelligent and well-educated, good prospects for leadership positions in the government, perfect specimens!—and indoctrinate them in the Babylonian language and the lore of magic and fortunetelling. The king then ordered that they be served from the same menu as the royal table—the best food, the finest wine. After three years of training they would be given positions in the king's court.

1.6-7 Four young men from Judah—Daniel, Hananiah, Mishael, and Azariah—were among those selected. The head of the palace staff gave them Babylonian names: Daniel was named Belteshazzar, Hananiah was named Shadrach, Mishael was named Meshach, Azariah was named Abednego.

1.8-10 But Daniel determined that he would not defile himself by eating the king's food or drinking his wine, so he asked the head of the palace staff to exempt him from the royal diet. The head of the palace staff, by God's grace, liked Daniel, but he warned him, "I'm afraid of what my master the king will do. He is the one who assigned this diet and if he sees that you are not as healthy as the rest, he'll have my head!"

1.11-13 But Daniel appealed to a steward who had been assigned by the head of the palace staff to be in charge of Daniel, Hananiah, Mishael, and Azariah: "Try us out for ten days on a simple diet of vegetables and water. Then compare us with the young men who eat from the royal menu. Make your decision on the basis of what you see."

NEW INTERNATIONAL VERSION

cordance with what you see." ¹⁴So he agreed to this and tested them for ten days.

¹⁵At the end of the ten days they looked healthier and better nourished than any of the young men who ate the royal food. ¹⁶So the guard took away their choice food and the wine they were to drink and gave them vegetables instead.

¹⁷To these four young men God gave knowledge and understanding of all kinds of literature and learning. And Daniel could understand visions and dreams of all kinds.

¹⁸At the end of the time set by the king to bring them in, the chief official presented them to Nebuchadnezzar. ¹⁹The king talked with them, and he found none equal to Daniel, Hananiah, Mishael and Azariah; so they entered the king's service. ²⁰In every matter of wisdom and understanding about which the king questioned them, he found them ten times better than all the magicians and enchanters in his whole kingdom.

²¹And Daniel remained there until the first year of King Cyrus.

NEBUCHADNEZZAR'S DREAM

2 In the second year of his reign, Nebuchadnezzar had dreams; his mind was troubled and he could not sleep. ²So the king summoned the magicians, enchanters, sorcerers and astrologersᵃ to tell him what he had dreamed. When they came in and stood before the king, ³he said to them, "I have had a dream that troubles me and I want to know what it means.ᵇ"

⁴Then the astrologers answered the king in Aramaic,ᶜ "O king, live forever! Tell your servants the dream, and we will interpret it."

⁵The king replied to the astrologers, "This is what I have firmly decided: If you do not tell me what my dream was and interpret it, I will have you cut into pieces and your houses turned into piles of rubble. ⁶But if you tell me the dream and explain it, you will receive from me gifts and rewards and great honor. So tell me the dream and interpret it for me."

⁷Once more they replied, "Let the king tell his servants the dream, and we will interpret it."

⁸Then the king answered, "I am certain that you are trying to gain time, because you realize that this is what I have firmly decided: ⁹If you do not tell me the dream, there is just one penalty for you. You have conspired to tell me misleading and wicked things, hoping the situation will

THE MESSAGE

¹·¹⁴⁻¹⁶ The steward agreed to do it and fed them vegetables and water for ten days. At the end of the ten days they looked better and more robust than all the others who had been eating from the royal menu. So the steward continued to exempt them from the royal menu of food and drink and served them only vegetables.

¹·¹⁷⁻¹⁹ God gave these four young men knowledge and skill in both books and life. In addition, Daniel was gifted in understanding all sorts of visions and dreams. At the end of the time set by the king for their training, the head of the royal staff brought them in to Nebuchadnezzar. When the king interviewed them, he found them far superior to all the other young men. None were a match for Daniel, Hananiah, Mishael, and Azariah.

¹·¹⁹⁻²⁰ And so they took their place in the king's service. Whenever the king consulted them on anything, on books or on life, he found them ten times better than all the magicians and enchanters in his kingdom put together.

¹·²¹ Daniel continued in the king's service until the first year in the reign of King Cyrus.

KING NEBUCHADNEZZAR'S DREAM

²·¹⁻³ 2 In the second year of his reign, King Nebuchadnezzar started having dreams that disturbed him deeply. He couldn't sleep. He called in all the Babylonian magicians, enchanters, sorcerers, and fortunetellers to interpret his dreams for him. When they came and lined up before the king, he said to them, "I had a dream that I can't get out of my mind. I can't sleep until I know what it means."

²·⁴ The fortunetellers, speaking in the Aramaic language, said, "Long live the king! Tell us the dream and we will interpret it."

²·⁵⁻⁶ The king answered the fortunetellers, "This is my decree: If you can't tell me both the dream itself and its interpretation, I'll have you ripped to pieces, limb from limb, and your homes torn down. But if you tell me both the dream and its interpretation, I'll lavish you with gifts and honors. So go to it: Tell me the dream and its interpretation."

²·⁷ They answered, "If it please your majesty, tell us the dream. We'll give the interpretation."

²·⁸⁻⁹ But the king said, "I know what you're up to—you're just playing for time. You know you're up a tree. You know that if you can't tell me my dream, you're doomed. I see right through you—you're going to cook up some fancy stories and confuse the issue until I change my mind. Nothing doing! First tell me

---

ᵃ 2 Or *Chaldeans*; also in verses 4, 5 and 10   ᵇ 3 Or *was*
ᶜ 4 The text from here through chapter 7 is in Aramaic.

NEW INTERNATIONAL VERSION

change. So then, tell me the dream, and I will know that you can interpret it for me."

¹⁰The astrologers answered the king, "There is not a man on earth who can do what the king asks! No king, however great and mighty, has ever asked such a thing of any magician or enchanter or astrologer. ¹¹What the king asks is too difficult. No one can reveal it to the king except the gods, and they do not live among men."

¹²This made the king so angry and furious that he ordered the execution of all the wise men of Babylon. ¹³So the decree was issued to put the wise men to death, and men were sent to look for Daniel and his friends to put them to death.

¹⁴When Arioch, the commander of the king's guard, had gone out to put to death the wise men of Babylon, Daniel spoke to him with wisdom and tact. ¹⁵He asked the king's officer, "Why did the king issue such a harsh decree?" Arioch then explained the matter to Daniel. ¹⁶At this, Daniel went in to the king and asked for time, so that he might interpret the dream for him.

¹⁷Then Daniel returned to his house and explained the matter to his friends Hananiah, Mishael and Azariah. ¹⁸He urged them to plead for mercy from the God of heaven concerning this mystery, so that he and his friends might not be executed with the rest of the wise men of Babylon. ¹⁹During the night the mystery was revealed to Daniel in a vision. Then Daniel praised the God of heaven ²⁰and said:

"Praise be to the name of God for ever and
    ever;
  wisdom and power are his.
²¹ He changes times and seasons;
  he sets up kings and deposes them.
He gives wisdom to the wise
  and knowledge to the discerning.
²² He reveals deep and hidden things;
  he knows what lies in darkness,
  and light dwells with him.
²³ I thank and praise you, O God of my fathers:
  You have given me wisdom and power,
you have made known to me what we asked
    of you,
  you have made known to us the dream of
    the king."

DANIEL INTERPRETS THE DREAM

²⁴Then Daniel went to Arioch, whom the king had appointed to execute the wise men of Babylon, and said to him, "Do not execute the wise men of Babylon. Take me to the king, and I will interpret his dream for him."

²⁵Arioch took Daniel to the king at once and said, "I have found a man among the exiles from

THE MESSAGE

the dream, then I'll know that you're on the up and up with the interpretation and not just blowing smoke in my eyes."

2.10-11   The fortunetellers said, "Nobody anywhere can do what you ask. And no king, great or small, has ever demanded anything like this from any magician, enchanter, or fortuneteller. What you're asking is impossible unless some god or goddess should reveal it—and they don't hang around with people like us."

2.12-13   That set the king off. He lost his temper and ordered the whole company of Babylonian wise men killed. When the death warrant was issued, Daniel and his companions were included. They also were marked for execution.

2.14-15   When Arioch, chief of the royal guards, was making arrangements for the execution, Daniel wisely took him aside and quietly asked what was going on: "Why this all of a sudden?"

2.15-16   After Arioch filled in the background, Daniel went to the king and asked for a little time so that he could interpret the dream.

2.17-18   Daniel then went home and told his companions Hananiah, Mishael, and Azariah what was going on. He asked them to pray to the God of heaven for mercy in solving this mystery so that the four of them wouldn't be killed along with the whole company of Babylonian wise men.

DREAM INTERPRETATION: A STORY OF FIVE KINGDOMS

2.19-23 That night the answer to the mystery was given to Daniel in a vision. Daniel blessed the God of heaven, saying,

"Blessed be the name of God,
  forever and ever.
He knows all, does all:
  He changes the seasons and guides history,
He raises up kings and also brings them
    down,
  he provides both intelligence and
    discernment,
He opens up the depths, tells secrets,
  sees in the dark—light spills out of him!
God of all my ancestors, all thanks! all praise!
  You made me wise and strong.
And now you've shown us what we asked for.
  You've solved the king's mystery."

2.24   So Daniel went back to Arioch, who had been put in charge of the execution. He said, "Call off the execution! Take me to the king and I'll interpret his dream."

2.25   Arioch didn't lose a minute. He ran to the king, bringing Daniel with him, and said, "I've

NEW INTERNATIONAL VERSION

Judah who can tell the king what his dream means."

²⁶The king asked Daniel (also called Belteshazzar), "Are you able to tell me what I saw in my dream and interpret it?"

²⁷Daniel replied, "No wise man, enchanter, magician or diviner can explain to the king the mystery he has asked about, ²⁸but there is a God in heaven who reveals mysteries. He has shown King Nebuchadnezzar what will happen in days to come. Your dream and the visions that passed through your mind as you lay on your bed are these:

²⁹"As you were lying there, O king, your mind turned to things to come, and the revealer of mysteries showed you what is going to happen. ³⁰As for me, this mystery has been revealed to me, not because I have greater wisdom than other living men, but so that you, O king, may know the interpretation and that you may understand what went through your mind.

³¹"You looked, O king, and there before you stood a large statue—an enormous, dazzling statue, awesome in appearance. ³²The head of the statue was made of pure gold, its chest and arms of silver, its belly and thighs of bronze, ³³its legs of iron, its feet partly of iron and partly of baked clay. ³⁴While you were watching, a rock was cut out, but not by human hands. It struck the statue on its feet of iron and clay and smashed them. ³⁵Then the iron, the clay, the bronze, the silver and the gold were broken to pieces at the same time and became like chaff on a threshing floor in the summer. The wind swept them away without leaving a trace. But the rock that struck the statue became a huge mountain and filled the whole earth.

³⁶"This was the dream, and now we will interpret it to the king. ³⁷You, O king, are the king of kings. The God of heaven has given you dominion and power and might and glory; ³⁸in your hands he has placed mankind and the beasts of the field and the birds of the air. Wherever they live, he has made you ruler over them all. You are that head of gold.

³⁹"After you, another kingdom will rise, inferior to yours. Next, a third kingdom, one of bronze, will rule over the whole earth. ⁴⁰Finally, there will be a fourth kingdom, strong as iron—for iron breaks and smashes everything—and as iron breaks things to pieces, so it will crush and break all the others. ⁴¹Just as you saw that the feet and toes were partly of baked clay and partly of iron, so this will be a divided kingdom; yet

THE MESSAGE

found a man from the exiles of Judah who can interpret the king's dream!"

2.26   The king asked Daniel (renamed in Babylonian, Belteshazzar), "Are you sure you can do this—tell me the dream I had and interpret it for me?"

2.27-28   Daniel answered the king, "No mere human can solve the king's mystery, I don't care who it is—no wise man, enchanter, magician, diviner. But there is a God in heaven who solves mysteries, and he has solved this one. He is letting King Nebuchadnezzar in on what is going to happen in the days ahead. This is the dream you had when you were lying on your bed, the vision that filled your mind:

2.29-30   "While you were stretched out on your bed, O king, thoughts came to you regarding what is coming in the days ahead. The Revealer of Mysteries showed you what will happen. But the interpretation is given through me, not because I'm any smarter than anyone else in the country, but so that you will know what it means, so that you will understand what you dreamed.

2.31-36   "What you saw, O king, was a huge statue standing before you, striking in appearance. And terrifying. The head of the statue was pure gold, the chest and arms were silver, the belly and hips were bronze, the legs were iron, and the feet were an iron-ceramic mixture. While you were looking at this statue, a stone cut out of a mountain by an invisible hand hit the statue, smashing its iron-ceramic feet. Then the whole thing fell to pieces—iron, tile, bronze, silver, and gold, smashed to bits. It was like scraps of old newspapers in a vacant lot in a hot dry summer, blown every which way by the wind, scattered to oblivion. But the stone that hit the statue became a huge mountain, dominating the horizon. This was your dream.

2.36-40   "And now we'll interpret it for the king. You, O king, are the most powerful king on earth. The God of heaven has given you the works: rule, power, strength, and glory. He has put you in charge of men and women, wild animals and birds, all over the world—you're the head ruler, you are the head of gold. But your rule will be taken over by another kingdom, inferior to yours, and that one by a third, a bronze kingdom, but still ruling the whole land, and after that by a fourth kingdom, iron-like in strength. Just as iron smashes things to bits, breaking and pulverizing, it will bust up the previous kingdoms.

2.41-43   "But then the feet and toes that ended up as a mixture of ceramic and iron will deteriorate into a mongrel kingdom with some remains of

NEW INTERNATIONAL VERSION

it will have some of the strength of iron in it, even as you saw iron mixed with clay. [42]As the toes were partly iron and partly clay, so this kingdom will be partly strong and partly brittle. [43]And just as you saw the iron mixed with baked clay, so the people will be a mixture and will not remain united, any more than iron mixes with clay.

[44]"In the time of those kings, the God of heaven will set up a kingdom that will never be destroyed, nor will it be left to another people. It will crush all those kingdoms and bring them to an end, but it will itself endure forever. [45]This is the meaning of the vision of the rock cut out of a mountain, but not by human hands—a rock that broke the iron, the bronze, the clay, the silver and the gold to pieces.

"The great God has shown the king what will take place in the future. The dream is true and the interpretation is trustworthy."

[46]Then King Nebuchadnezzar fell prostrate before Daniel and paid him honor and ordered that an offering and incense be presented to him. [47]The king said to Daniel, "Surely your God is the God of gods and the Lord of kings and a revealer of mysteries, for you were able to reveal this mystery."

[48]Then the king placed Daniel in a high position and lavished many gifts on him. He made him ruler over the entire province of Babylon and placed him in charge of all its wise men. [49]Moreover, at Daniel's request the king appointed Shadrach, Meshach and Abednego administrators over the province of Babylon, while Daniel himself remained at the royal court.

THE IMAGE OF GOLD AND THE FIERY FURNACE

3 King Nebuchadnezzar made an image of gold, ninety feet high and nine feet[a] wide, and set it up on the plain of Dura in the province of Babylon. [2]He then summoned the satraps, prefects, governors, advisers, treasurers, judges, magistrates and all the other provincial officials to come to the dedication of the image he had set up. [3]So the satraps, prefects, governors, advisers, treasurers, judges, magistrates and all the other provincial officials assembled for the dedication of the image that King Nebuchadnezzar had set up, and they stood before it.

[4]Then the herald loudly proclaimed, "This is what you are commanded to do, O peoples, nations and men of every language: [5]As soon as you hear the sound of the horn, flute, zither, lyre, harp, pipes and all kinds of music, you

[a] 1 Aramaic *sixty cubits high and six cubits wide* (about 27 meters high and 2.7 meters wide)

THE MESSAGE

iron in it. Just as the toes of the feet were part ceramic and part iron, it will end up a mixed bag of the breakable and unbreakable. That kingdom won't bond, won't hold together any more than iron and clay hold together.

2.44-45 "But throughout the history of these kingdoms, the God of heaven will be building a kingdom that will never be destroyed, nor will this kingdom ever fall under the domination of another. In the end it will crush the other kingdoms and finish them off and come through it all standing strong and eternal. It will be like the stone cut from the mountain by the invisible hand that crushed the iron, the bronze, the ceramic, the silver, and the gold.

"The great God has let the king know what will happen in the years to come. This is an accurate telling of the dream, and the interpretation is also accurate."

2.46-47 When Daniel finished, King Nebuchadnezzar fell on his face in awe before Daniel. He ordered the offering of sacrifices and burning of incense in Daniel's honor. He said to Daniel, "Your God is beyond question the God of all gods, the Master of all kings. And he solves all mysteries, I know, because you've solved this mystery."

2.48-49 Then the king promoted Daniel to a high position in the kingdom, lavished him with gifts, and made him governor over the entire province of the Babylon and the chief in charge of all the Babylonian wise men. At Daniel's request the king appointed Shadrach, Meshach, and Abednego to administrative posts throughout Babylon, while Daniel governed from the royal headquarters.

FOUR MEN IN THE FURNACE

3.1-3 **3** King Nebuchadnezzar built a gold statue, ninety feet high and nine feet thick. He set it up on the Dura plain in the province of Babylon. He then ordered all the important leaders in the province, everybody who was anybody, to the dedication ceremony of the statue. They all came for the dedication, all the important people, and took their places before the statue that Nebuchadnezzar had erected.

3.4-6 A herald then proclaimed in a loud voice: "Attention, everyone! Every race, color, and creed, listen! When you hear the band strike up—all the trumpets and trombones, the tubas and baritones, the drums and cymbals—fall to

NEW INTERNATIONAL VERSION

must fall down and worship the image of gold that King Nebuchadnezzar has set up. ⁶Whoever does not fall down and worship will immediately be thrown into a blazing furnace."

⁷Therefore, as soon as they heard the sound of the horn, flute, zither, lyre, harp and all kinds of music, all the peoples, nations and men of every language fell down and worshiped the image of gold that King Nebuchadnezzar had set up.

⁸At this time some astrologers *a* came forward and denounced the Jews. ⁹They said to King Nebuchadnezzar, "O king, live forever! ¹⁰You have issued a decree, O king, that everyone who hears the sound of the horn, flute, zither, lyre, harp, pipes and all kinds of music must fall down and worship the image of gold, ¹¹and that whoever does not fall down and worship will be thrown into a blazing furnace. ¹²But there are some Jews whom you have set over the affairs of the province of Babylon—Shadrach, Meshach and Abednego—who pay no attention to you, O king. They neither serve your gods nor worship the image of gold you have set up."

¹³Furious with rage, Nebuchadnezzar summoned Shadrach, Meshach and Abednego. So these men were brought before the king, ¹⁴and Nebuchadnezzar said to them, "Is it true, Shadrach, Meshach and Abednego, that you do not serve my gods or worship the image of gold I have set up? ¹⁵Now when you hear the sound of the horn, flute, zither, lyre, harp, pipes and all kinds of music, if you are ready to fall down and worship the image I made, very good. But if you do not worship it, you will be thrown immediately into a blazing furnace. Then what god will be able to rescue you from my hand?"

¹⁶Shadrach, Meshach and Abednego replied to the king, "O Nebuchadnezzar, we do not need to defend ourselves before you in this matter. ¹⁷If we are thrown into the blazing furnace, the God we serve is able to save us from it, and he will rescue us from your hand, O king. ¹⁸But even if he does not, we want you to know, O king, that we will not serve your gods or worship the image of gold you have set up."

¹⁹Then Nebuchadnezzar was furious with Shadrach, Meshach and Abednego, and his attitude toward them changed. He ordered the furnace heated seven times hotter than usual ²⁰and commanded some of the strongest soldiers in his army to tie up Shadrach, Meshach and Abednego and throw them into the blazing furnace. ²¹So these men, wearing their robes, trousers, turbans and other clothes, were bound and thrown into the blazing furnace. ²²The king's command was so urgent and the furnace so hot that the flames

a 8 Or Chaldeans

THE MESSAGE

your knees and worship the gold statue that King Nebuchadnezzar has set up. Anyone who does not kneel and worship shall be thrown immediately into a roaring furnace."

3.7 The band started to play, a huge band equipped with all the musical instruments of Babylon, and everyone—every race, color, and creed—fell to their knees and worshiped the gold statue that King Nebuchadnezzar had set up.

3.8-12 Just then, some Babylonian fortunetellers stepped up and accused the Jews. They said to King Nebuchadnezzar, "Long live the king! You gave strict orders, O king, that when the big band started playing, everyone had to fall to their knees and worship the gold statue, and whoever did not go to their knees and worship had it to be pitched into a roaring furnace. Well, there are some Jews here—Shadrach, Meshach, and Abednego—whom you have placed in high positions in the province of Babylon. These men are ignoring you, O king. They don't respect your gods and they won't worship the gold statue you set up."

3.13-15 Furious, King Nebuchadnezzar ordered Shadrach, Meshach, and Abednego to be brought in. When the men were brought in, Nebuchadnezzar asked, "Is it true, Shadrach, Meshach, and Abednego, that you don't respect my gods and refuse to worship the gold statue that I have set up? I'm giving you a second chance—but from now on, when the big band strikes up you must go to your knees and worship the statue I have made. If you don't worship it, you will be pitched into a roaring furnace, no questions asked. Who is the god who can rescue you from my power?"

3.16-18 Shadrach, Meshach, and Abednego answered King Nebuchadnezzar, "Your threat means nothing to us. If you throw us in the fire, the God we serve can rescue us from your roaring furnace and anything else you might cook up, O king. But even if he doesn't, it wouldn't make a bit of difference, O king. We still wouldn't serve your gods or worship the gold statue you set up."

3.19-23 Nebuchadnezzar, his face purple with anger, cut off Shadrach, Meshach, and Abednego. He ordered the furnace fired up seven times hotter than usual. He ordered some strong men from the army to tie them up, hands and feet, and throw them into the roaring furnace. Shadrach, Meshach, and Abednego, bound hand and foot, fully dressed from head to toe, were pitched into the roaring fire. Because the king was in such a hurry and the furnace was so hot, flames

NEW INTERNATIONAL VERSION

of the fire killed the soldiers who took up Shadrach, Meshach and Abednego, 23and these three men, firmly tied, fell into the blazing furnace.

24Then King Nebuchadnezzar leaped to his feet in amazement and asked his advisers, "Weren't there three men that we tied up and threw into the fire?"

They replied, "Certainly, O king."

25He said, "Look! I see four men walking around in the fire, unbound and unharmed, and the fourth looks like a son of the gods."

26Nebuchadnezzar then approached the opening of the blazing furnace and shouted, "Shadrach, Meshach and Abednego, servants of the Most High God, come out! Come here!"

So Shadrach, Meshach and Abednego came out of the fire, 27and the satraps, prefects, governors and royal advisers crowded around them. They saw that the fire had not harmed their bodies, nor was a hair of their heads singed; their robes were not scorched, and there was no smell of fire on them.

28Then Nebuchadnezzar said, "Praise be to the God of Shadrach, Meshach and Abednego, who has sent his angel and rescued his servants! They trusted in him and defied the king's command and were willing to give up their lives rather than serve or worship any god except their own God. 29Therefore I decree that the people of any nation or language who say anything against the God of Shadrach, Meshach and Abednego be cut into pieces and their houses be turned into piles of rubble, for no other god can save in this way."

30Then the king promoted Shadrach, Meshach and Abednego in the province of Babylon.

NEBUCHADNEZZAR'S DREAM OF A TREE

4 King Nebuchadnezzar,

To the peoples, nations and men of every language, who live in all the world:

May you prosper greatly!

2It is my pleasure to tell you about the miraculous signs and wonders that the Most High God has performed for me.

3How great are his signs,
how mighty his wonders!
His kingdom is an eternal kingdom;
his dominion endures from
generation to generation.

THE MESSAGE

from the furnace killed the men who carried Shadrach, Meshach, and Abednego to it, while the fire raged around Shadrach, Meshach, and Abednego.

3.24   Suddenly King Nebuchadnezzar jumped up in alarm and said, "Didn't we throw three men, bound hand and foot, into the fire?"

"That's right, O king," they said.

3.25   "But look!" he said. "I see four men, walking around freely in the fire, completely unharmed! And the fourth man looks like a son of the gods!"

3.26   Nebuchadnezzar went to the door of the roaring furnace and called in, "Shadrach, Meshach, and Abednego, servants of the High God, come out here!"

Shadrach, Meshach, and Abednego walked out of the fire.

3.27   All the important people, the government leaders and king's counselors, gathered around to examine them and discovered that the fire hadn't so much as touched the three men—not a hair singed, not a scorch mark on their clothes, not even the smell of fire on them!

3.28   Nebuchadnezzar said, "Blessed be the God of Shadrach, Meshach, and Abednego! He sent his angel and rescued his servants who trusted in him! They ignored the king's orders and laid their bodies on the line rather than serve or worship any god but their own.

3.29   "Therefore I issue this decree: Anyone anywhere, of any race, color, or creed, who says anything against the God of Shadrach, Meshach, and Abednego will be ripped to pieces, limb from limb, and their houses torn down. There has never been a god who can pull off a rescue like this."

3.30   Then the king promoted Shadrach, Meshach, and Abednego in the province of Babylon.

A DREAM OF A CHOPPED-DOWN TREE

4.1-2   4 King Nebuchadnezzar to everyone, everywhere—every race, color, and creed: "Peace and prosperity to all! It is my privilege to report to you the gracious miracles that the High God has done for me.

4.3   "His miracles are staggering,
his wonders are surprising.
His kingdom lasts and lasts,
his sovereign rule goes on forever.

NEW INTERNATIONAL VERSION

⁴I, Nebuchadnezzar, was at home in my palace, contented and prosperous. ⁵I had a dream that made me afraid. As I was lying in my bed, the images and visions that passed through my mind terrified me. ⁶So I commanded that all the wise men of Babylon be brought before me to interpret the dream for me. ⁷When the magicians, enchanters, astrologers ᵃ and diviners came, I told them the dream, but they could not interpret it for me. ⁸Finally, Daniel came into my presence and I told him the dream. (He is called Belteshazzar, after the name of my god, and the spirit of the holy gods is in him.)

⁹I said, "Belteshazzar, chief of the magicians, I know that the spirit of the holy gods is in you, and no mystery is too difficult for you. Here is my dream; interpret it for me. ¹⁰These are the visions I saw while lying in my bed: I looked, and there before me stood a tree in the middle of the land. Its height was enormous. ¹¹The tree grew large and strong and its top touched the sky; it was visible to the ends of the earth. ¹²Its leaves were beautiful, its fruit abundant, and on it was food for all. Under it the beasts of the field found shelter, and the birds of the air lived in its branches; from it every creature was fed.

¹³"In the visions I saw while lying in my bed, I looked, and there before me was a messenger,ᵇ a holy one, coming down from heaven. ¹⁴He called in a loud voice: 'Cut down the tree and trim off its branches; strip off its leaves and scatter its fruit. Let the animals flee from under it and the birds from its branches. ¹⁵But let the stump and its roots, bound with iron and bronze, remain in the ground, in the grass of the field.

" 'Let him be drenched with the dew of heaven, and let him live with the animals among the plants of the earth. ¹⁶Let his mind be changed from that of a man and let him be given the mind of an animal, till seven timesᶜ pass by for him.

¹⁷" 'The decision is announced by messengers, the holy ones declare the verdict, so that the living may know that the Most High is sovereign over the kingdoms of men and gives them to anyone he wishes and sets over them the lowliest of men.'

THE MESSAGE

4.4-7 "I, Nebuchadnezzar, was at home taking it easy in my palace, without a care in the world. But as I was stretched out on my bed I had a dream that scared me—a nightmare that shook me. I sent for all the wise men of Babylon so that they could interpret the dream for me. When they were all assembled—magicians, enchanters, fortunetellers, witches—I told them the dream. None could tell me what it meant.

4.8 "And then Daniel came in. His Babylonian name is Belteshazzar, named after my god, a man full of the divine Holy Spirit. I told him my dream.

4.9 " 'Belteshazzar,' I said, 'chief of the magicians, I know that you are a man full of the divine Holy Spirit and that there is no mystery that you can't solve. Listen to this dream that I had and interpret it for me.

4.10-12 " 'This is what I saw as I was stretched out on my bed. I saw a big towering tree at the center of the world. As I watched, the tree grew huge and strong. Its top reached the sky and it could be seen from the four corners of the earth. Its leaves were beautiful, its fruit abundant—enough food for everyone! Wild animals found shelter under it, birds nested in its branches, everything living was fed and sheltered by it.

4.13-15 " 'And this also is what I saw as I was stretched out on my bed. I saw a holy watchman descend from heaven, and call out:

Chop down the tree, lop off its branches,
    strip its leaves and scatter its fruit.
Chase the animals from beneath it
    and shoo the birds from its branches.
But leave the stump and roots in the
      ground,
    belted with a strap of iron and bronze in
      the grassy meadow.

4.15-16 Let him be soaked in heaven's dew
    and take his meals with the animals that
      graze.
Let him lose his mind
    and get an animal's mind in exchange,
And let this go on
    for seven seasons.

4.17 The angels announce this decree,
    the holy watchmen bring this sentence,
So that everyone living will know
    that the High God rules human
      kingdoms.
He arranges kingdom affairs however he
      wishes,
    and makes leaders out of losers.

✝

ᵃ 7 Or *Chaldeans* ᵇ 13 Or *watchman*; also in verses 17 and 23 ᶜ 16 Or *years*; also in verses 23, 25 and 32

NEW INTERNATIONAL VERSION	THE MESSAGE

NEW INTERNATIONAL VERSION

¹⁸"This is the dream that I, King Nebuchadnezzar, had. Now, Belteshazzar, tell me what it means, for none of the wise men in my kingdom can interpret it for me. But you can, because the spirit of the holy gods is in you."

DANIEL INTERPRETS THE DREAM

¹⁹Then Daniel (also called Belteshazzar) was greatly perplexed for a time, and his thoughts terrified him. So the king said, "Belteshazzar, do not let the dream or its meaning alarm you."

Belteshazzar answered, "My lord, if only the dream applied to your enemies and its meaning to your adversaries! ²⁰The tree you saw, which grew large and strong, with its top touching the sky, visible to the whole earth, ²¹with beautiful leaves and abundant fruit, providing food for all, giving shelter to the beasts of the field, and having nesting places in its branches for the birds of the air— ²²you, O king, are that tree! You have become great and strong; your greatness has grown until it reaches the sky, and your dominion extends to distant parts of the earth.

²³"You, O king, saw a messenger, a holy one, coming down from heaven and saying, 'Cut down the tree and destroy it, but leave the stump, bound with iron and bronze, in the grass of the field, while its roots remain in the ground. Let him be drenched with the dew of heaven; let him live like the wild animals, until seven times pass by for him.'

²⁴"This is the interpretation, O king, and this is the decree the Most High has issued against my lord the king: ²⁵You will be driven away from people and will live with the wild animals; you will eat grass like cattle and be drenched with the dew of heaven. Seven times will pass by for you until you acknowledge that the Most High is sovereign over the kingdoms of men and gives them to anyone he wishes. ²⁶The command to leave the stump of the tree with its roots means that your kingdom will be restored to you when you acknowledge that Heaven rules. ²⁷Therefore, O king, be pleased to accept my advice: Renounce your sins by doing what is right, and your wickedness by being kind to the oppressed. It may be that then your prosperity will continue."

THE MESSAGE

4.18 " 'This is what I, King Nebuchadnezzar, dreamed. It's your turn, Belteshazzar—interpret it for me. None of the wise men of Babylon could make heads or tails of it, but I'm sure you can do it. You're full of the divine Holy Spirit.' "

"YOU WILL GRAZE ON THE GRASS LIKE AN OX"

4.19 At first Daniel, who had been renamed Belteshazzar in Babylon, was upset. The thoughts that came swarming into his mind terrified him.

"Belteshazzar," the king said, "stay calm. Don't let the dream and its interpretation scare you."

"My master," said Belteshazzar, "I wish this dream were about your enemies and its interpretation for your foes.

4.20-22 "The tree you saw that grew so large and sturdy with its top touching the sky, visible from the four corners of the world; the tree with the luxuriant foliage and abundant fruit, enough for everyone; the tree under which animals took cover and in which birds built nests—you, O king, are that tree.

4.23-25 "You have grown great and strong. Your royal majesty reaches sky-high, and your sovereign rule stretches to the four corners of the world.

"But the part about the holy angel descending from heaven and proclaiming, 'Chop down the tree, destroy it, but leave stump and roots in the ground belted with a strap of iron and bronze in the grassy meadow; let him be soaked with heaven's dew and take his meals with the grazing animals for seven seasons'— this, O king, also refers to you. It means that the High God has sentenced my master the king: You will be driven away from human company and live with the wild animals. You will graze on grass like an ox. You will be soaked in heaven's dew. This will go on for seven seasons, and you will learn that the High God rules over human kingdoms and that he arranges all kingdom affairs.

4.26 "The part about the tree stump and roots being left means that your kingdom will still be there for you after you learn that it is heaven that runs things.

4.27 "So, king, take my advice: Make a clean break with your sins and start living for others. Quit your wicked life and look after the needs of the down-and-out. Then *you* will continue to have a good life."

NEW INTERNATIONAL VERSION	THE MESSAGE

THE LOSS AND REGAINING OF A MIND AND A KINGDOM

THE DREAM IS FULFILLED

28All this happened to King Nebuchadnezzar. **29**Twelve months later, as the king was walking on the roof of the royal palace of Babylon, **30**he said, "Is not this the great Babylon I have built as the royal residence, by my mighty power and for the glory of my majesty?"

31The words were still on his lips when a voice came from heaven, "This is what is decreed for you, King Nebuchadnezzar: Your royal authority has been taken from you. **32**You will be driven away from people and will live with the wild animals; you will eat grass like cattle. Seven times will pass by for you until you acknowledge that the Most High is sovereign over the kingdoms of men and gives them to anyone he wishes."

33Immediately what had been said about Nebuchadnezzar was fulfilled. He was driven away from people and ate grass like cattle. His body was drenched with the dew of heaven until his hair grew like the feathers of an eagle and his nails like the claws of a bird.

34At the end of that time, I, Nebuchadnezzar, raised my eyes toward heaven, and my sanity was restored. Then I praised the Most High; I honored and glorified him who lives forever.

His dominion is an eternal dominion;
　his kingdom endures from generation to
　　generation.
35All the peoples of the earth
　are regarded as nothing.
He does as he pleases
　with the powers of heaven
　and the peoples of the earth.
No one can hold back his hand
　or say to him: "What have you done?"

36At the same time that my sanity was restored, my honor and splendor were returned to me for the glory of my kingdom. My advisers and nobles sought me out, and I was restored to my throne and became even greater than before. **37**Now I, Nebuchadnezzar, praise and exalt and glorify the King of heaven, because everything he does is right and all his ways are just. And those who walk in pride he is able to humble.

4.28-30 All this happened to King Nebuchadnezzar. Just twelve months later, he was walking on the balcony of the royal palace in Babylon and boasted, "Look at this, Babylon the great! And I built it all by myself, a royal palace adequate to display my honor and glory!"

4.31-32 The words were no sooner out of his mouth than a voice out of heaven spoke, "This is the verdict on you, King Nebuchadnezzar: Your kingdom is taken from you. You will be driven out of human company and live with the wild animals. You will eat grass like an ox. The sentence is for seven seasons, enough time to learn that the High God rules human kingdoms and puts whomever he wishes in charge."

4.33 It happened at once. Nebuchadnezzar was driven out of human company, ate grass like an ox, and was soaked in heaven's dew. His hair grew like the feathers of an eagle and his nails like the claws of a hawk.

✝

4.34-35 "At the end of the seven years, I, Nebuchadnezzar, looked to heaven. I was given my mind back and I blessed the High God, thanking and glorifying God, who lives forever.

"His sovereign rule lasts and lasts,
　his kingdom never declines and falls.
Life on this earth doesn't add up to much,
　but God's heavenly army keeps everything
　　going.
No one can interrupt his work,
　no one can call his rule into question.

4.36-37 "At the same time that I was given back my mind, I was also given back my majesty and splendor, making my kingdom shine. All the leaders and important people came looking for me. I was reestablished as king in my kingdom and became greater than ever. And that's why I'm singing—I, Nebuchadnezzar—singing and praising the King of Heaven:

"Everything he does is right,
　and he does it the right way.
He knows how to turn a proud person
　into a humble man or woman."

NEW INTERNATIONAL VERSION

THE WRITING ON THE WALL

5 King Belshazzar gave a great banquet for a thousand of his nobles and drank wine with them. [2]While Belshazzar was drinking his wine, he gave orders to bring in the gold and silver goblets that Nebuchadnezzar his father[a] had taken from the temple in Jerusalem, so that the king and his nobles, his wives and his concubines might drink from them. [3]So they brought in the gold goblets that had been taken from the temple of God in Jerusalem, and the king and his nobles, his wives and his concubines drank from them. [4]As they drank the wine, they praised the gods of gold and silver, of bronze, iron, wood and stone.

[5]Suddenly the fingers of a human hand appeared and wrote on the plaster of the wall, near the lampstand in the royal palace. The king watched the hand as it wrote. [6]His face turned pale and he was so frightened that his knees knocked together and his legs gave way.

[7]The king called out for the enchanters, astrologers[b] and diviners to be brought and said to these wise men of Babylon, "Whoever reads this writing and tells me what it means will be clothed in purple and have a gold chain placed around his neck, and he will be made the third highest ruler in the kingdom."

[8]Then all the king's wise men came in, but they could not read the writing or tell the king what it meant. [9]So King Belshazzar became even more terrified and his face grew more pale. His nobles were baffled.

[10]The queen,[c] hearing the voices of the king and his nobles, came into the banquet hall. "O king, live forever!" she said. "Don't be alarmed! Don't look so pale! [11]There is a man in your kingdom who has the spirit of the holy gods in him. In the time of your father he was found to have insight and intelligence and wisdom like that of the gods. King Nebuchadnezzar your father—your father the king, I say—appointed him chief of the magicians, enchanters, astrologers and diviners. [12]This man Daniel, whom the king called Belteshazzar, was found to have a keen mind and knowledge and understanding, and also the ability to interpret dreams, explain riddles and solve difficult problems. Call for Daniel, and he will tell you what the writing means."

[13]So Daniel was brought before the king, and the king said to him, "Are you Daniel, one of the exiles my father the king brought from Judah? [14]I have heard that the spirit of the gods is in you and that you have insight, intelligence

THE MESSAGE

THE WRITING OF A DISEMBODIED HAND

5.1-4 5 King Belshazzar held a great feast for his one thousand nobles. The wine flowed freely. Belshazzar, heady with the wine, ordered that the gold and silver chalices his father Nebuchadnezzar had stolen from God's Temple of Jerusalem be brought in so that he and his nobles, his wives and concubines, could drink from them. When the gold and silver chalices were brought in, the king and his nobles, his wives and his concubines, drank wine from them. They drank the wine and drunkenly praised their gods made of gold and silver, bronze and iron, wood and stone.

5.5-7 At that very moment, the fingers of a human hand appeared and began writing on the lamp-illumined, whitewashed wall of the palace. When the king saw the disembodied hand writing away, he went white as a ghost, scared out of his wits. His legs went limp and his knees knocked. He yelled out for the enchanters, the fortunetellers, and the diviners to come. He told these Babylonian magi, "Anyone who can read this writing on the wall and tell me what it means will be famous and rich—purple robe, the great gold chain—and be third-in-command in the kingdom."

5.8-9 One after the other they tried, but could make no sense of it. They could neither read what was written nor interpret it to the king. So now the king was really frightened. All the blood drained from his face. The nobles were in a panic.

5.10-12 The queen heard of the hysteria among the king and his nobles and came to the banquet hall. She said, "Long live the king! Don't be upset. Don't sit around looking like ghosts. There is a man in your kingdom who is full of the divine Holy Spirit. During your father's time he was well known for his intellectual brilliance and spiritual wisdom. He was so good that your father, King Nebuchadnezzar, made him the head of all the magicians, enchanters, fortunetellers, and diviners. There was no one quite like him. He could do anything—interpret dreams, solve mysteries, explain puzzles. His name is Daniel, but he was renamed Belteshazzar by the king. Have Daniel called in. He'll tell you what is going on here."

5.13-16 So Daniel was called in. The king asked him, "Are you the Daniel who was one of the Jewish exiles my father brought here from Judah? I've heard about you—that you're full of the Holy Spirit, that you've got a brilliant mind, that you

---

[a] 2 Or *ancestor*; or *predecessor*; also in verses 11, 13 and 18
[b] 7 Or *Chaldeans*; also in verse 11   [c] 10 Or *queen mother*

NEW INTERNATIONAL VERSION

and outstanding wisdom. ¹⁵The wise men and enchanters were brought before me to read this writing and tell me what it means, but they could not explain it. ¹⁶Now I have heard that you are able to give interpretations and to solve difficult problems. If you can read this writing and tell me what it means, you will be clothed in purple and have a gold chain placed around your neck, and you will be made the third highest ruler in the kingdom."

¹⁷Then Daniel answered the king, "You may keep your gifts for yourself and give your rewards to someone else. Nevertheless, I will read the writing for the king and tell him what it means.

¹⁸"O king, the Most High God gave your father Nebuchadnezzar sovereignty and greatness and glory and splendor. ¹⁹Because of the high position he gave him, all the peoples and nations and men of every language dreaded and feared him. Those the king wanted to put to death, he put to death; those he wanted to spare, he spared; those he wanted to promote, he promoted; and those he wanted to humble, he humbled. ²⁰But when his heart became arrogant and hardened with pride, he was deposed from his royal throne and stripped of his glory. ²¹He was driven away from people and given the mind of an animal; he lived with the wild donkeys and ate grass like cattle; and his body was drenched with the dew of heaven, until he acknowledged that the Most High God is sovereign over the kingdoms of men and sets over them anyone he wishes.

²²"But you his son,ᵃ O Belshazzar, have not humbled yourself, though you knew all this. ²³Instead, you have set yourself up against the Lord of heaven. You had the goblets from his temple brought to you, and you and your nobles, your wives and your concubines drank wine from them. You praised the gods of silver and gold, of bronze, iron, wood and stone, which cannot see or hear or understand. But you did not honor the God who holds in his hand your life and all your ways. ²⁴Therefore he sent the hand that wrote the inscription.

²⁵"This is the inscription that was written:

MENE, MENE, TEKEL, PARSINᵇ

²⁶"This is what these words mean:

*Mene*ᶜ: God has numbered the days
of your reign and brought it to
an end.

ᵃ 22 Or descendant; or successor   ᵇ 25 Aramaic UPARSIN (that is, AND PARSIN)   ᶜ 26 Mene can mean numbered or mina (a unit of money).

THE MESSAGE

are incredibly wise. The wise men and enchanters were brought in here to read this writing on the wall and interpret it for me. They couldn't figure it out—not a word, not a syllable. But I've heard that you interpret dreams and solve mysteries. So—if you can read the writing and interpret it for me, you'll be rich and famous—a purple robe, the great gold chain around your neck—and third-in-command in the kingdom."

5.17 Daniel answered the king, "You can keep your gifts, or give them to someone else. But I will read the writing for the king and tell him what it means.

5.18-21 "Listen, O king! The High God gave your father Nebuchadnezzar a great kingdom and a glorious reputation. Because God made him so famous, people from everywhere, whatever their race, color, and creed, were totally intimidated by him. He killed or spared people on whim. He promoted or humiliated people capriciously. He developed a big head and a hard spirit. Then God knocked him off his high horse and stripped him of his fame. He was thrown out of human company, lost his mind, and lived like a wild animal. He ate grass like an ox and was soaked by heaven's dew until he learned his lesson: that the High God rules human kingdoms and puts anyone he wants in charge.

5.22-23 "You are his son and have known all this, yet you're as arrogant as he ever was. Look at you, setting yourself up in competition against the Master of heaven! You had the sacred chalices from his Temple brought into your drunken party so that you and your nobles, your wives and your concubines, could drink from them. You used the sacred chalices to toast your gods of silver and gold, bronze and iron, wood and stone—blind, deaf, and imbecile gods. But you treat with contempt the living God who holds your entire life from birth to death in his hand.

5.24-26 "God sent the hand that wrote on the wall, and this is what is written: MENE, TEQEL, and PERES. This is what the words mean:

"*Mene*: God has numbered the days of your rule and they don't add up.

NEW INTERNATIONAL VERSION

²⁷ *Tekel*^a: You have been weighed on the scales and found wanting.

²⁸ *Peres*^b: Your kingdom is divided and given to the Medes and Persians."

²⁹Then at Belshazzar's command, Daniel was clothed in purple, a gold chain was placed around his neck, and he was proclaimed the third highest ruler in the kingdom. ³⁰That very night Belshazzar, king of the Babylonians,^c was slain, ³¹and Darius the Mede took over the kingdom, at the age of sixty-two.

DANIEL IN THE DEN OF LIONS

6 It pleased Darius to appoint 120 satraps to rule throughout the kingdom, ²with three administrators over them, one of whom was Daniel. The satraps were made accountable to them so that the king might not suffer loss. ³Now Daniel so distinguished himself among the administrators and the satraps by his exceptional qualities that the king planned to set him over the whole kingdom. ⁴At this, the administrators and the satraps tried to find grounds for charges against Daniel in his conduct of government affairs, but they were unable to do so. They could find no corruption in him, because he was trustworthy and neither corrupt nor negligent. ⁵Finally these men said, "We will never find any basis for charges against this man Daniel unless it has something to do with the law of his God."

⁶So the administrators and the satraps went as a group to the king and said: "O King Darius, live forever! ⁷The royal administrators, prefects, satraps, advisers and governors have all agreed that the king should issue an edict and enforce the decree that anyone who prays to any god or man during the next thirty days, except to you, O king, shall be thrown into the lions' den. ⁸Now, O king, issue the decree and put it in writing so that it cannot be altered—in accordance with the laws of the Medes and Persians, which cannot be repealed." ⁹So King Darius put the decree in writing.

¹⁰Now when Daniel learned that the decree had been published, he went home to his upstairs room where the windows opened toward Jerusalem. Three times a day he got down on his knees and prayed, giving thanks to his God, just

THE MESSAGE

^{5.27} "*Teqel*: You have been weighed on the scales and you don't weigh much.

^{5.28} "*Peres*: Your kingdom has been divided up and handed over to the Medes and Persians."

✛

^{5.29} Belshazzar did what he had promised. He robed Daniel in purple, draped the great gold chain around his neck, and promoted him to third-in-charge in the kingdom.

^{5.30-31} That same night the Babylonian king Belshazzar was murdered. Darius the Mede was sixty-two years old when he succeeded him as king.

DANIEL IN THE LIONS' DEN

6 Darius reorganized his kingdom. He appointed one hundred twenty governors to administer all the parts of his realm. Over them were three vice-regents, one of whom was Daniel. The governors reported to the vice-regents, who made sure that everything was in order for the king. But Daniel, brimming with spirit and intelligence, so completely outclassed the other vice-regents and governors that the king decided to put him in charge of the whole kingdom.

^{6.4-5} The vice-regents and governors got together to find some old scandal or skeleton in Daniel's life that they could use against him, but they couldn't dig up anything. He was totally exemplary and trustworthy. They could find no evidence of negligence or misconduct. So they finally gave up and said, "We're never going to find anything against this Daniel unless we can cook up something religious."

^{6.6-7} The vice-regents and governors conspired together and then went to the king and said, "King Darius, live forever! We've convened your vice-regents, governors, and all your leading officials, and have agreed that the king should issue the following decree:

For the next thirty days no one is to pray to any god or mortal except you, O king. Anyone who disobeys will be thrown into the lions' den.

^{6.8} "Issue this decree, O king, and make it unconditional, as if written in stone like all the laws of the Medes and the Persians."

^{6.9} King Darius signed the decree.

^{6.10} When Daniel learned that the decree had been signed and posted, he continued to pray just as he had always done. His house had windows in the upstairs that opened toward Jerusalem. Three times a day he knelt there in prayer, thanking and praising his God.

---

^a 27 *Tekel* can mean *weighed* or *shekel*.   ^b 28 *Peres* (the singular of *Parsin*) can mean *divided* or *Persia* or *a half mina* or *a half shekel*.   ^c 30 Or *Chaldeans*

NEW INTERNATIONAL VERSION

as he had done before. ¹¹Then these men went as a group and found Daniel praying and asking God for help. ¹²So they went to the king and spoke to him about his royal decree: "Did you not publish a decree that during the next thirty days anyone who prays to any god or man except to you, O king, would be thrown into the lions' den?"

The king answered, "The decree stands—in accordance with the laws of the Medes and Persians, which cannot be repealed."

¹³Then they said to the king, "Daniel, who is one of the exiles from Judah, pays no attention to you, O king, or to the decree you put in writing. He still prays three times a day." ¹⁴When the king heard this, he was greatly distressed; he was determined to rescue Daniel and made every effort until sundown to save him.

¹⁵Then the men went as a group to the king and said to him, "Remember, O king, that according to the law of the Medes and Persians no decree or edict that the king issues can be changed."

¹⁶So the king gave the order, and they brought Daniel and threw him into the lions' den. The king said to Daniel, "May your God, whom you serve continually, rescue you!"

¹⁷A stone was brought and placed over the mouth of the den, and the king sealed it with his own signet ring and with the rings of his nobles, so that Daniel's situation might not be changed. ¹⁸Then the king returned to his palace and spent the night without eating and without any entertainment being brought to him. And he could not sleep.

¹⁹At the first light of dawn, the king got up and hurried to the lions' den. ²⁰When he came near the den, he called to Daniel in an anguished voice, "Daniel, servant of the living God, has your God, whom you serve continually, been able to rescue you from the lions?"

²¹Daniel answered, "O king, live forever! ²²My God sent his angel, and he shut the mouths of the lions. They have not hurt me, because I was found innocent in his sight. Nor have I ever done any wrong before you, O king."

²³The king was overjoyed and gave orders to lift Daniel out of the den. And when Daniel was lifted from the den, no wound was found on him, because he had trusted in his God.

²⁴At the king's command, the men who had falsely accused Daniel were brought in and thrown into the lions' den, along with their wives and children. And before they reached the floor of the den, the lions overpowered them and crushed all their bones.

THE MESSAGE

6.11-12 The conspirators came and found him praying, asking God for help. They went straight to the king and reminded him of the royal decree that he had signed. "Did you not," they said, "sign a decree forbidding anyone to pray to any god or man except you for the next thirty days? And anyone caught doing it would be thrown into the lions' den?"

"Absolutely," said the king. "Written in stone, like all the laws of the Medes and Persians."

6.13 Then they said, "Daniel, one of the Jewish exiles, ignores you, O king, and defies your decree. Three times a day he prays."

6.14 At this, the king was very upset and tried his best to get Daniel out of the fix he'd put him in. He worked at it the whole day long.

6.15 But then the conspirators were back: "Remember, O king, it's the law of the Medes and Persians that the king's decree can never be changed."

6.16 The king caved in and ordered Daniel brought and thrown into the lions' den. But he said to Daniel, "Your God, to whom you are so loyal, is going to get you out of this."

6.17 A stone slab was placed over the opening of the den. The king sealed the cover with his signet ring and the signet rings of all his nobles, fixing Daniel's fate.

6.18 The king then went back to his palace. He refused supper. He couldn't sleep. He spent the night fasting.

6.19-20 At daybreak the king got up and hurried to the lions' den. As he approached the den, he called out anxiously, "Daniel, servant of the living God, has your God, whom you serve so loyally, saved you from the lions?"

6.21-22 "O king, live forever!" said Daniel. "My God sent his angel, who closed the mouths of the lions so that they would not hurt me. I've been found innocent before God and also before you, O king. I've done nothing to harm you."

6.23 When the king heard these words, he was happy. He ordered Daniel taken up out of the den. When he was hauled up, there wasn't a scratch on him. He had trusted his God.

6.24 Then the king commanded that the conspirators who had informed on Daniel be thrown into the lions' den, along with their wives and children. Before they hit the floor, the lions had them in their jaws, tearing them to pieces.

NEW INTERNATIONAL VERSION

25 Then King Darius wrote to all the peoples, nations and men of every language throughout the land:

"May you prosper greatly!

26 "I issue a decree that in every part of my kingdom people must fear and reverence the God of Daniel.

"For he is the living God
and he endures forever;
his kingdom will not be destroyed,
his dominion will never end.
27 He rescues and he saves;
he performs signs and wonders
in the heavens and on the earth.
He has rescued Daniel
from the power of the lions."

28 So Daniel prospered during the reign of Darius and the reign of Cyrus*a* the Persian.

DANIEL'S DREAM OF FOUR BEASTS

7 In the first year of Belshazzar king of Babylon, Daniel had a dream, and visions passed through his mind as he was lying on his bed. He wrote down the substance of his dream.

2 Daniel said: "In my vision at night I looked, and there before me were the four winds of heaven churning up the great sea. 3 Four great beasts, each different from the others, came up out of the sea.

4 "The first was like a lion, and it had the wings of an eagle. I watched until its wings were torn off and it was lifted from the ground so that it stood on two feet like a man, and the heart of a man was given to it.

5 "And there before me was a second beast, which looked like a bear. It was raised up on one of its sides, and it had three ribs in its mouth between its teeth. It was told, 'Get up and eat your fill of flesh!'

6 "After that, I looked, and there before me was another beast, one that looked like a leopard. And on its back it had four wings like those of a bird. This beast had four heads, and it was given authority to rule.

7 "After that, in my vision at night I looked, and there before me was a fourth beast—terrifying and frightening and very powerful. It had large iron teeth; it crushed and devoured its victims and trampled underfoot whatever was left. It was different from all the former beasts, and it had ten horns.

8 "While I was thinking about the horns, there before me was another horn, a little one, which came up among them; and three of the first

---

a 28 Or Darius, that is, the reign of Cyrus

THE MESSAGE

6.25-27 King Darius published this proclamation to every race, color, and creed on earth:

Peace to you! Abundant peace!
I decree that Daniel's God shall be worshiped and feared in all parts of my kingdom.
He is the living God, world without end. His kingdom never falls.
His rule continues eternally.
He is a savior and rescuer.
He performs astonishing miracles in heaven and on earth.
He saved Daniel from the power of the lions.

6.28 From then on, Daniel was treated well during the reign of Darius, and also in the following reign of Cyrus the Persian.

A VISION OF FOUR ANIMALS

7.1 7 In the first year of the reign of King Belshazzar of Babylon, Daniel had a dream. What he saw as he slept in his bed terrified him—a real nightmare. Then he wrote out his dream:

7.2-3 "In my dream that night I saw the four winds of heaven whipping up a great storm on the sea. Four huge animals, each different from the others, ascended out of the sea.

7.4 "The first animal looked like a lion, but it had the wings of an eagle. While I watched, its wings were pulled off. It was then pulled erect so that it was standing on two feet like a man. Then a human heart was placed in it.

7.5 "Then I saw a second animal that looked like a bear. It lurched from side to side, holding three ribs in its jaws. It was told, 'Attack! Devour! Fill your belly!'

7.6 "Next I saw another animal. This one looked like a panther. It had four birdlike wings on its back. This animal had four heads and was made to rule.

7.7 "After that, a fourth animal appeared in my dream. This one was a grisly horror—hideous. It had huge iron teeth. It crunched and swallowed its victims. Anything left over, it trampled into the ground. It was different from the other animals—this one was a real monster. It had ten horns.

7.8 "As I was staring at the horns and trying to figure out what they meant, another horn sprouted up, a little horn. Three of the original horns were uprooted before it. This horn had eyes like the eyes of a man and a mouth that spoke boastfully.

⁹"As I looked,

"thrones were set in place,
    and the Ancient of Days took his seat.
His clothing was as white as snow;
    the hair of his head was white like wool.
His throne was flaming with fire,
    and its wheels were all ablaze.
¹⁰A river of fire was flowing,
    coming out from before him.
Thousands upon thousands attended him;
    ten thousand times ten thousand stood
        before him.
The court was seated,
    and the books were opened.

¹¹"Then I continued to watch because of the boastful words the horn was speaking. I kept looking until the beast was slain and its body destroyed and thrown into the blazing fire. ¹²(The other beasts had been stripped of their authority, but were allowed to live for a period of time.)

¹³"In my vision at night I looked, and there before me was one like a son of man, coming with the clouds of heaven. He approached the Ancient of Days and was led into his presence. ¹⁴He was given authority, glory and sovereign power; all peoples, nations and men of every language worshiped him. His dominion is an everlasting dominion that will not pass away, and his kingdom is one that will never be destroyed.

THE INTERPRETATION OF THE DREAM

¹⁵"I, Daniel, was troubled in spirit, and the visions that passed through my mind disturbed me. ¹⁶I approached one of those standing there and asked him the true meaning of all this.

"So he told me and gave me the interpretation of these things: ¹⁷'The four great beasts are four kingdoms that will rise from the earth. ¹⁸But the saints of the Most High will receive the kingdom and will possess it forever—yes, for ever and ever.'

¹⁹"Then I wanted to know the true meaning of the fourth beast, which was different from all the others and most terrifying, with its iron teeth and bronze claws—the beast that crushed and devoured its victims and trampled underfoot whatever was left. ²⁰I also wanted to know about the ten horns on its head and about the other horn that came up, before which three of them fell—the horn that looked more imposing than the others and that had eyes and a mouth that spoke boastfully. ²¹As I watched, this horn was waging war against the saints and defeating them, ²²until the Ancient of Days came and pro-

horns were pulled out to make room for it. There were human eyes in this little horn, and a big mouth speaking arrogantly.

7.9-10   "As I was watching all this,

"Thrones were set in place
    and The Old One sat down.
His robes were white as snow,
    his hair was white like wool.
His throne was flaming with fire,
    its wheels blazing.
A river of fire
    poured out of the throne.
Thousands upon thousands served him,
    tens of thousands attended him.
The courtroom was called to order,
    and the books were opened.

7.11-13   "I kept watching. The little horn was speaking arrogantly. Then, as I watched, the monster was killed and its body cremated in a roaring fire. The other animals lived on for a limited time, but they didn't really do anything, had no power to rule. My dream continued.

7.13-14   "I saw a human form, a son of man,
    arriving in a whirl of clouds.
He came to The Old One
    and was presented to him.
He was given power to rule—all the glory of
        royalty.
    Everyone—race, color, and creed—had to
        serve him.
His rule would be forever, never ending.
    His kingly rule would never be replaced.

7.15-16   "But as for me, Daniel, I was disturbed. All these dream-visions had me agitated. So I went up to one of those standing by and asked him the meaning of all this. And he told me, interpreting the dream for me:

7.17-18   " 'These four huge animals,' he said, 'mean that four kingdoms will appear on earth. But eventually the holy people of the High God will be given the kingdom and have it ever after—yes, forever and ever.'

7.19-22   "But I wanted to know more. I was curious about the fourth animal, the one so different from the others, the hideous monster with the iron teeth and the bronze claws, gulping down what it ripped to pieces and trampling the leftovers into the dirt. And I wanted to know about the ten horns on its head and the other horn that sprouted up while three of the original horns were removed. This new horn had eyes and a big mouth and spoke arrogantly, dominating the other horns. I watched as this horn was making war on God's holy people and getting the best of them. But then The Old One

NEW INTERNATIONAL VERSION

nounced judgment in favor of the saints of the Most High, and the time came when they possessed the kingdom.

²³"He gave me this explanation: 'The fourth beast is a fourth kingdom that will appear on earth. It will be different from all the other kingdoms and will devour the whole earth, trampling it down and crushing it. ²⁴The ten horns are ten kings who will come from this kingdom. After them another king will arise, different from the earlier ones; he will subdue three kings. ²⁵He will speak against the Most High and oppress his saints and try to change the set times and the laws. The saints will be handed over to him for a time, times and half a time. *ᵃ*

²⁶" 'But the court will sit, and his power will be taken away and completely destroyed forever. ²⁷Then the sovereignty, power and greatness of the kingdoms under the whole heaven will be handed over to the saints, the people of the Most High. His kingdom will be an everlasting kingdom, and all rulers will worship and obey him.'

²⁸"This is the end of the matter. I, Daniel, was deeply troubled by my thoughts, and my face turned pale, but I kept the matter to myself."

DANIEL'S VISION OF A RAM AND A GOAT

8 In the third year of King Belshazzar's reign, I, Daniel, had a vision, after the one that had already appeared to me. ²In my vision I saw myself in the citadel of Susa in the province of Elam; in the vision I was beside the Ulai Canal. ³I looked up, and there before me was a ram with two horns, standing beside the canal, and the horns were long. One of the horns was longer than the other but grew up later. ⁴I watched the ram as he charged toward the west and the north and the south. No animal could stand against him, and none could rescue from his power. He did as he pleased and became great.

⁵As I was thinking about this, suddenly a goat with a prominent horn between his eyes came from the west, crossing the whole earth without touching the ground. ⁶He came toward the two-horned ram I had seen standing beside the canal and charged at him in great rage. ⁷I saw him attack the ram furiously, striking the ram and shattering his two horns. The ram was powerless to stand against him; the goat knocked him to the ground and trampled on him, and none could rescue the ram from his power. ⁸The goat became very great, but at the height of his power

---

ᵃ *25 Or for a year, two years and half a year*

THE MESSAGE

intervened and decided things in favor of the people of the High God. In the end, God's holy people took over the kingdom.

7.23-25 "The bystander continued, telling me this: 'The fourth animal is a fourth kingdom that will appear on earth. It will be different from the first three kingdoms, a monster kingdom that will chew up everyone in sight and spit them out. The ten horns are ten kings, one after another, that will come from this kingdom. But then another king will arrive. He will be different from the earlier kings. He will begin by toppling three kings. Then he will blaspheme the High God, persecute the followers of the High God, and try to get rid of sacred worship and moral practice. God's holy people will be persecuted by him for a time, two times, half a time.

7.26-27 " 'But when the court comes to order, the horn will be stripped of its power and totally destroyed. Then the royal rule and the authority and the glory of all the kingdoms under heaven will be handed over to the people of the High God. Their royal rule will last forever. All other rulers will serve and obey them.'

7.28 "And there it ended. I, Daniel, was in shock. I was like a man who had seen a ghost. But I kept it all to myself.

A VISION OF A RAM AND A BILLY GOAT

8.1 **8** "In King Belshazzar's third year as king, another vision came to me, Daniel. This was now the second vision.

8.2-4 "In the vision, I saw myself in Susa, the capital city of the province Elam, standing at the Ulai Canal. Looking around, I was surprised to see a ram also standing at the gate. The ram had two huge horns, one bigger than the other, but the bigger horn was the last to appear. I watched as the ram charged: first west, then north, then south. No beast could stand up to him. He did just as he pleased, strutting as if he were king of the beasts.

8.5-7 "While I was watching this, wondering what it all meant, I saw a billy goat with an immense horn in the middle of its forehead come up out of the west and fly across the whole country, not once touching the ground. The billy goat approached the double-horned ram that I had earlier seen standing at the gate and, enraged, charged it viciously. I watched as, mad with rage, it charged the ram and hit it so hard that it broke off its two horns. The ram didn't stand a chance against it. The billy goat knocked the ram to the ground and stomped all over it. Nothing could have saved the ram from the goat.

8.8-12 "Then the billy goat swelled to an enormous size. At the height of its power its immense horn

NEW INTERNATIONAL VERSION

his large horn was broken off, and in its place four prominent horns grew up toward the four winds of heaven.

⁹Out of one of them came another horn, which started small but grew in power to the south and to the east and toward the Beautiful Land. ¹⁰It grew until it reached the host of the heavens, and it threw some of the starry host down to the earth and trampled on them. ¹¹It set itself up to be as great as the Prince of the host; it took away the daily sacrifice from him, and the place of his sanctuary was brought low. ¹²Because of rebellion, the host ⌊of the saints⌋ᵃ and the daily sacrifice were given over to it. It prospered in everything it did, and truth was thrown to the ground.

¹³Then I heard a holy one speaking, and another holy one said to him, "How long will it take for the vision to be fulfilled—the vision concerning the daily sacrifice, the rebellion that causes desolation, and the surrender of the sanctuary and of the host that will be trampled underfoot?"

¹⁴He said to me, "It will take 2,300 evenings and mornings; then the sanctuary will be reconsecrated."

THE INTERPRETATION OF THE VISION

¹⁵While I, Daniel, was watching the vision and trying to understand it, there before me stood one who looked like a man. ¹⁶And I heard a man's voice from the Ulai calling, "Gabriel, tell this man the meaning of the vision."

¹⁷As he came near the place where I was standing, I was terrified and fell prostrate. "Son of man," he said to me, "understand that the vision concerns the time of the end."

¹⁸While he was speaking to me, I was in a deep sleep, with my face to the ground. Then he touched me and raised me to my feet.

¹⁹He said: "I am going to tell you what will happen later in the time of wrath, because the vision concerns the appointed time of the end.ᵇ ²⁰The two-horned ram that you saw represents the kings of Media and Persia. ²¹The shaggy goat is the king of Greece, and the large horn between his eyes is the first king. ²²The four horns that replaced the one that was broken off represent four kingdoms that will emerge from his nation but will not have the same power.

²³"In the latter part of their reign, when rebels have become completely wicked, a stern-faced king, a master of intrigue, will arise. ²⁴He will become very strong, but not by his own power. He will cause astounding devastation and will

ᵃ 12 Or rebellion, the armies   ᵇ 19 Or because the end will be at the appointed time

THE MESSAGE

broke off and four other big horns sprouted in its place, pointing to the four points of the compass. And then from one of these big horns another horn sprouted. It started small, but then grew to an enormous size, facing south and east—toward lovely Palestine. The horn grew tall, reaching to the stars, the heavenly army, and threw some of the stars to the earth and stomped on them. It even dared to challenge the power of God, Prince of the Celestial Army! And then it threw out daily worship and desecrated the Sanctuary. As judgment against their sin, the holy people of God got the same treatment as the daily worship. The horn cast God's Truth aside. High-handed, it took over everything and everyone.

8.13 "Then I overheard two holy angels talking. One asked, 'How long is what we see here going to last—the abolishing of daily worship, this devastating judgment against sin, the kicking around of God's holy people and the Sanctuary?'

8.14 "The other answered, 'Over the course of 2,300 sacrifices, evening and morning. Then the Sanctuary will be set right again.'

✝

8.15 "While I, Daniel, was trying to make sense of what I was seeing, suddenly there was a humanlike figure standing before me.

8.16-17 "Then I heard a man's voice from over by the Ulai Canal calling out, 'Gabriel, tell this man what is going on. Explain the vision to him.' He came up to me, but when he got close I became terrified and fell facedown on the ground.

8.17-18 "He said, 'Understand that this vision has to do with the time of the end.' As soon as he spoke, I fainted, my face in the dirt. But he picked me up and put me on my feet.

8.19 "And then he continued, 'I want to tell you what is going to happen as the judgment days of wrath wind down, for there is going to be an end to all this.

8.20-22 " 'The double-horned ram you saw stands for the two kings of the Medes and Persians. The billy goat stands for the kingdom of the Greeks. The huge horn on its forehead is the first Greek king. The four horns that sprouted after it was broken off are the four kings that come after him, but without his power.

8.23-26 " 'As their kingdoms cool down
      and rebellions heat up,
A king will show up,
      hard-faced, a master trickster.
His power will swell enormously.
      He'll talk big, high-handedly,
Doing whatever he pleases,
      knocking off heroes and holy ones left and
            right.

NEW INTERNATIONAL VERSION

succeed in whatever he does. He will destroy the mighty men and the holy people. ²⁵He will cause deceit to prosper, and he will consider himself superior. When they feel secure, he will destroy many and take his stand against the Prince of princes. Yet he will be destroyed, but not by human power.

²⁶"The vision of the evenings and mornings that has been given you is true, but seal up the vision, for it concerns the distant future."

²⁷I, Daniel, was exhausted and lay ill for several days. Then I got up and went about the king's business. I was appalled by the vision; it was beyond understanding.

DANIEL'S PRAYER

9 In the first year of Darius son of Xerxes*ᵃ* (a Mede by descent), who was made ruler over the Babylonian*ᵇ* kingdom— ²in the first year of his reign, I, Daniel, understood from the Scriptures, according to the word of the LORD given to Jeremiah the prophet, that the desolation of Jerusalem would last seventy years. ³So I turned to the Lord God and pleaded with him in prayer and petition, in fasting, and in sackcloth and ashes.

⁴I prayed to the LORD my God and confessed:

"O Lord, the great and awesome God, who keeps his covenant of love with all who love him and obey his commands, ⁵we have sinned and done wrong. We have been wicked and have rebelled; we have turned away from your commands and laws. ⁶We have not listened to your servants the prophets, who spoke in your name to our kings, our princes and our fathers, and to all the people of the land.

⁷"Lord, you are righteous, but this day we are covered with shame—the men of Judah and people of Jerusalem and all Israel, both near and far, in all the countries where you have scattered us because of our unfaithfulness to you. ⁸O LORD, we and our kings, our princes and our fathers are covered with shame because we have sinned against you. ⁹The Lord our God is merciful and forgiving, even though we have rebelled against him; ¹⁰we have not obeyed the LORD our God or kept the laws he gave us through his servants the prophets. ¹¹All

THE MESSAGE

He'll plot and scheme to make crime flourish—
and oh, how it will flourish!
He'll think he's invincible
and get rid of anyone who gets in his way.
But when he takes on the Prince of all princes,
he'll be smashed to bits—
but not by human hands.
This vision of the 2,300 sacrifices, evening
and morning,
is accurate but confidential.
Keep it to yourself.
It refers to the far future.'

✛

8.27 "I, Daniel, walked around in a daze, unwell for days. Then I got a grip on myself and went back to work taking care of the king's affairs. But I continued to be upset by the vision. I couldn't make sense of it.

GOD'S COVENANT COMMITMENT

9.1-4 **9** "Darius, son of Ahasuerus, born a Mede, became king over the land of Babylon. In the first year of his reign, I, Daniel, was meditating on the Scriptures that gave, according to the Word of GOD to the prophet Jeremiah, the number of years that Jerusalem had to lie in ruins, namely, seventy. I turned to the Master God, asking for an answer—praying earnestly, fasting from meals, wearing rough penitential burlap, and kneeling in the ashes. I poured out my heart, baring my soul to GOD, my God:

9.4-8 " 'O Master, great and august God. You never waver in your covenant commitment, never give up on those who love you and do what you say. Yet we have sinned in every way imaginable. We've done evil things, rebelled, dodged and taken detours around your clearly marked paths. We've turned a deaf ear to your servants the prophets, who preached your Word to our kings and leaders, our parents, and all the people in the land. You have done everything right, Master, but all we have to show for our lives is guilt and shame, the whole lot of us—people of Judah, citizens of Jerusalem, Israel at home and Israel in exile in all the places we've been banished to because of our betrayal of you. Oh yes, GOD, we've been exposed in our shame, all of us—our kings, leaders, parents—before the whole world. And deservedly so, because of our sin.

9.9-12 " 'Compassion is our only hope, the compassion of you, the Master, our God, since in our rebellion we've forfeited our rights. We paid no attention to you when you told us how to live, the clear teaching that came through your servants the prophets. All of us in Israel

---

ᵃ 1 Hebrew *Ahasuerus*   *ᵇ* 1 Or *Chaldean*

NEW INTERNATIONAL VERSION

Israel has transgressed your law and turned away, refusing to obey you.

"Therefore the curses and sworn judgments written in the Law of Moses, the servant of God, have been poured out on us, because we have sinned against you. 12You have fulfilled the words spoken against us and against our rulers by bringing upon us great disaster. Under the whole heaven nothing has ever been done like what has been done to Jerusalem. 13Just as it is written in the Law of Moses, all this disaster has come upon us, yet we have not sought the favor of the LORD our God by turning from our sins and giving attention to your truth. 14The LORD did not hesitate to bring the disaster upon us, for the LORD our God is righteous in everything he does; yet we have not obeyed him.

15"Now, O Lord our God, who brought your people out of Egypt with a mighty hand and who made for yourself a name that endures to this day, we have sinned, we have done wrong. 16O Lord, in keeping with all your righteous acts, turn away your anger and your wrath from Jerusalem, your city, your holy hill. Our sins and the iniquities of our fathers have made Jerusalem and your people an object of scorn to all those around us.

17"Now, our God, hear the prayers and petitions of your servant. For your sake, O Lord, look with favor on your desolate sanctuary. 18Give ear, O God, and hear; open your eyes and see the desolation of the city that bears your Name. We do not make requests of you because we are righteous, but because of your great mercy. 19O Lord, listen! O Lord, forgive! O Lord, hear and act! For your sake, O my God, do not delay, because your city and your people bear your Name."

THE SEVENTY "SEVENS"

20While I was speaking and praying, confessing my sin and the sin of my people Israel and making my request to the LORD my God for his holy hill— 21while I was still in prayer, Gabriel, the man I had seen in the earlier vision, came to me in swift flight about the time of the evening sacrifice. 22He instructed me and said to me, "Daniel, I have now come to give you insight and understanding. 23As soon as you began to

THE MESSAGE

ignored what you said. We defied your instructions and did what we pleased. And now we're paying for it: The solemn curse written out plainly in the revelation to God's servant Moses is now doing its work among us, the wages of our sin against you. You did to us and our rulers what you said you would do: You brought this catastrophic disaster on us, the worst disaster on record—and in Jerusalem!

9.13-14 " 'Just as written in God's revelation to Moses, the catastrophe was total. Nothing was held back. We kept at our sinning, never giving you a second thought, oblivious to your clear warning, and so you had no choice but to let the disaster loose on us in full force. You, our GOD, had a perfect right to do this since we persistently and defiantly ignored you.

9.15-17 " 'Master, you are our God, for you delivered your people from the land of Egypt in a show of power—people are still talking about it! We confess that we have sinned, that we have lived bad lives. Following the lines of what you have always done in setting things right, setting *people* right, please stop being so angry with Jerusalem, your very own city, your holy mountain. We know it's our fault that this has happened, all because of our sins and our parents' sins, and now we're an embarrassment to everyone around us. We're a blot on the neighborhood. So listen, God, to this determined prayer of your servant. Have mercy on your ruined Sanctuary. Act out of who you are, not out of what we are.

9.18 " 'Turn your ears our way, God, and listen. Open your eyes and take a long look at our ruined city, this city named after you. We know that we don't deserve a hearing from you. Our appeal is to your compassion. This prayer is our last and only hope:

9.19 " 'Master, listen to us!
Master, forgive us!
Master, look at us and do something!
Master, don't put us off!
Your city and your people are named after
    you:
You have a stake in us!'

SEVENTY SEVENS

9.20-21 "While I was pouring out my heart, baring my sins and the sins of my people Israel, praying my life out before my GOD, interceding for the holy mountain of my God—while I was absorbed in this praying, the humanlike Gabriel, the one I had seen in an earlier vision, approached me, flying in like a bird about the time of evening worship.

9.22-23 "He stood before me and said, 'Daniel, I have come to make things plain to you. You had no

NEW INTERNATIONAL VERSION

pray, an answer was given, which I have come to tell you, for you are highly esteemed. Therefore, consider the message and understand the vision:

24"Seventy 'sevens'[a] are decreed for your people and your holy city to finish[b] transgression, to put an end to sin, to atone for wickedness, to bring in everlasting righteousness, to seal up vision and prophecy and to anoint the most holy.[c]

25"Know and understand this: From the issuing of the decree[d] to restore and rebuild Jerusalem until the Anointed One,[e] the ruler, comes, there will be seven 'sevens,' and sixty-two 'sevens.' It will be rebuilt with streets and a trench, but in times of trouble. 26After the sixty-two 'sevens,' the Anointed One will be cut off and will have nothing.[f] The people of the ruler who will come will destroy the city and the sanctuary. The end will come like a flood: War will continue until the end, and desolations have been decreed. 27He will confirm a covenant with many for one 'seven.'[g] In the middle of the 'seven'[g] he will put an end to sacrifice and offering. And on a wing ⌊of the temple⌋ he will set up an abomination that causes desolation, until the end that is decreed is poured out on him.[h]" [i]

DANIEL'S VISION OF A MAN

10 In the third year of Cyrus king of Persia, a revelation was given to Daniel (who was called Belteshazzar). Its message was true and it concerned a great war.[j] The understanding of the message came to him in a vision.

2At that time I, Daniel, mourned for three weeks. 3I ate no choice food; no meat or wine touched my lips; and I used no lotions at all until the three weeks were over.

4On the twenty-fourth day of the first month, as I was standing on the bank of the great river, the Tigris, 5I looked up and there before me was a man dressed in linen, with a belt of the finest gold around his waist. 6His body was like chrysolite, his face like lightning, his eyes like flaming torches, his arms and legs like the gleam of burnished bronze, and his voice like the sound of a multitude.

7I, Daniel, was the only one who saw the vision; the men with me did not see it, but such

---

a 24 Or 'weeks'; also in verses 25 and 26   h 24 Or restrain
c 24 Or Most Holy Place; or most holy One   d 25 Or word
e 25 Or an anointed one; also in verse 26   f 26 Or off and
will have no one; or off, but not for himself   g 27 Or 'week'
h 27 Or it   i 27 Or And one who causes desolation will
come upon the pinnacle of the abominable ⌊temple⌋, until the
end that is decreed is poured out on the desolated ⌊city⌋
j 1 Or true and burdensome

THE MESSAGE

sooner started your prayer when the answer was given. And now I'm here to deliver the answer to you. You are much loved! So listen carefully to the answer, the plain meaning of what is revealed:

9.24 " 'Seventy sevens are set for your people and for your holy city to throttle rebellion, stop sin, wipe out crime, set things right forever, confirm what the prophet saw, and anoint The Holy of Holies.

9.25-26 " 'Here is what you must understand: From the time the word goes out to rebuild Jerusalem until the coming of the Anointed Leader, there will be seven sevens. The rebuilding will take sixty-two sevens, including building streets and digging a moat. Those will be rough times. After the sixty-two sevens, the Anointed Leader will be killed—the end of him. The city and Sanctuary will be laid in ruins by the army of the newly arriving leader. The end will come in a rush, like a flood. War will rage right up to the end, desolation the order of the day.

9.27 " 'Then for one seven, he will forge many and strong alliances, but halfway through the seven he will banish worship and prayers. At the place of worship, a desecrating obscenity will be set up and remain until finally the desecrator himself is decisively destroyed.' "

A VISION OF A BIG WAR

10 In the third year of the reign of King Cyrus of Persia, a message was made plain to Daniel, whose Babylonian name was Belteshazzar. The message was true. It dealt with a big war. He understood the message, the understanding coming by revelation:

10.2-3 "During those days, I, Daniel, went into mourning over Jerusalem for three weeks. I ate only plain and simple food, no seasoning or meat or wine. I neither bathed nor shaved until the three weeks were up.

10.4-6 "On the twenty-fourth day of the first month I was standing on the bank of the great river, the Tigris. I looked up and to my surprise saw a man dressed in linen with a belt of pure gold around his waist. His body was hard and glistening, as if sculpted from a precious stone, his face radiant, his eyes bright and penetrating like torches, his arms and feet glistening like polished bronze, and his voice, deep and resonant, sounded like a huge choir of voices.

10.7-8 "I, Daniel, was the only one to see this. The men who were with me, although they didn't see

NEW INTERNATIONAL VERSION

terror overwhelmed them that they fled and hid themselves. [8]So I was left alone, gazing at this great vision; I had no strength left, my face turned deathly pale and I was helpless. [9]Then I heard him speaking, and as I listened to him, I fell into a deep sleep, my face to the ground.

[10]A hand touched me and set me trembling on my hands and knees. [11]He said, "Daniel, you who are highly esteemed, consider carefully the words I am about to speak to you, and stand up, for I have now been sent to you." And when he said this to me, I stood up trembling.

[12]Then he continued, "Do not be afraid, Daniel. Since the first day that you set your mind to gain understanding and to humble yourself before your God, your words were heard, and I have come in response to them. [13]But the prince of the Persian kingdom resisted me twenty-one days. Then Michael, one of the chief princes, came to help me, because I was detained there with the king of Persia. [14]Now I have come to explain to you what will happen to your people in the future, for the vision concerns a time yet to come."

[15]While he was saying this to me, I bowed with my face toward the ground and was speechless. [16]Then one who looked like a man[a] touched my lips, and I opened my mouth and began to speak. I said to the one standing before me, "I am overcome with anguish because of the vision, my lord, and I am helpless. [17]How can I, your servant, talk with you, my lord? My strength is gone and I can hardly breathe."

[18]Again the one who looked like a man touched me and gave me strength. [19]"Do not be afraid, O man highly esteemed," he said. "Peace! Be strong now; be strong."

When he spoke to me, I was strengthened and said, "Speak, my lord, since you have given me strength."

[20]So he said, "Do you know why I have come to you? Soon I will return to fight against the prince of Persia, and when I go, the prince of Greece will come; [21]but first I will tell you what is written in the Book of Truth. (No one supports me against them except Michael, your prince.

11 [1]And in the first year of Darius the Mede, I took my stand to support and protect him.)

THE MESSAGE

it, were overcome with fear and ran off and hid, fearing the worst. Left alone after the appearance, abandoned by my friends, I went weak in the knees, the blood drained from my face.

10.9-10 "I heard his voice. At the sound of it I fainted, fell flat on the ground, face in the dirt. A hand touched me and pulled me to my hands and knees.

10.11 " 'Daniel,' he said, 'man of quality, listen carefully to my message. And get up on your feet. Stand at attention. I've been sent to bring you news.'

"When he had said this, I stood up, but I was still shaking.

10.12-14 " 'Relax, Daniel,' he continued, 'don't be afraid. From the moment you decided to humble yourself to receive understanding, your prayer was heard, and I set out to come to you. But I was waylaid by the angel-prince of the kingdom of Persia and was delayed for a good three weeks. But then Michael, one of the chief angel-princes, intervened to help me. I left him there with the prince of the kingdom of Persia. And now I'm here to help you understand what will eventually happen to your people. The vision has to do with what's ahead.'

10.15-17 "While he was saying all this, I looked at the ground and said nothing. Then I was surprised by something like a human hand that touched my lips. I opened my mouth and started talking to the messenger: 'When I saw you, master, I was terror-stricken. My knees turned to water. I couldn't move. How can I, a lowly servant, speak to you, my master? I'm paralyzed. I can hardly breathe!'

10.18-19 "Then this humanlike figure touched me again and gave me strength. He said, 'Don't be afraid, friend. Peace. Everything is going to be all right. Take courage. Be strong.'

"Even as he spoke, courage surged up within me. I said, 'Go ahead, let my master speak. You've given me courage.'

10.20-21 "He said, 'Do you know why I've come here to you? I now have to go back to fight against the angel-prince of Persia, and when I get him out of the way, the angel-prince of Greece will arrive. But first let me tell you what's written in The True Book. No one helps me in my fight against these beings except Michael, your angel-prince.

✝

11 11.1 " 'And I, in my turn, have been helping him out as best I can ever since the first year in the reign of Darius the Mede.'

---

[a] 16 Most manuscripts of the Masoretic Text; one manuscript of the Masoretic Text, Dead Sea Scrolls and Septuagint *Then something that looked like a man's hand*

NEW INTERNATIONAL VERSION

THE KINGS OF THE SOUTH AND THE NORTH

2"Now then, I tell you the truth: Three more kings will appear in Persia, and then a fourth, who will be far richer than all the others. When he has gained power by his wealth, he will stir up everyone against the kingdom of Greece. 3Then a mighty king will appear, who will rule with great power and do as he pleases. 4After he has appeared, his empire will be broken up and parceled out toward the four winds of heaven. It will not go to his descendants, nor will it have the power he exercised, because his empire will be uprooted and given to others.

5"The king of the South will become strong, but one of his commanders will become even stronger than he and will rule his own kingdom with great power. 6After some years, they will become allies. The daughter of the king of the South will go to the king of the North to make an alliance, but she will not retain her power, and he and his power *a* will not last. In those days she will be handed over, together with her royal escort and her father *b* and the one who supported her.

7"One from her family line will arise to take her place. He will attack the forces of the king of the North and enter his fortress; he will fight against them and be victorious. 8He will also seize their gods, their metal images and their valuable articles of silver and gold and carry them off to Egypt. For some years he will leave the king of the North alone. 9Then the king of the North will invade the realm of the king of the South but will retreat to his own country. 10His sons will prepare for war and assemble a great army, which will sweep on like an irresistible flood and carry the battle as far as his fortress.

11"Then the king of the South will march out in a rage and fight against the king of the North, who will raise a large army, but it will be defeated. 12When the army is carried off, the king of the South will be filled with pride and will slaughter many thousands, yet he will not remain triumphant. 13For the king of the North will muster another army, larger than the first; and after several years, he will advance with a huge army fully equipped.

14"In those times many will rise against the king of the South. The violent men among your own people will rebel in fulfillment of the vision, but without success. 15Then the king of the North will come and build up siege ramps and will capture a fortified city. The forces of the South will be powerless to resist; even their best

a 6 Or *offspring*   *b* 6 Or *child* (see Vulgate and Syriac)

THE MESSAGE

THE KINGS OF THE SOUTH AND THE NORTH

11.2 " 'But now let me tell you the truth of how things stand: Three more kings of Persia will show up, and then a fourth will become richer than all of them. When he senses that he is powerful enough as a result of his wealth, he will go to war against the entire kingdom of Greece.

11.3-4 " 'Then a powerful king will show up and take over a huge territory and run things just as he pleases. But at the height of his power, with everything seemingly under control, his kingdom will split into four parts, like the four points of the compass. But his heirs won't get in on it. There will be no continuity with his kingship. Others will tear it to pieces and grab whatever they can get for themselves.

11.5-6 " 'Next the king of the south will grow strong, but one of his princes will grow stronger than he and rule an even larger territory. After a few years, the two of them will make a pact, and the daughter of the king of the south will marry the king of the north to cement the peace agreement. But her influence will weaken and her child will not survive. She and her servants, her child, and her husband will be betrayed.

11.6-9 " 'Sometime later a member of the royal family will show up and take over. He will take command of his army and invade the defenses of the king of the north and win a resounding victory. He will load up their tin gods and all the gold and silver trinkets that go with them and cart them off to Egypt. Eventually, the king of the north will recover and invade the country of the king of the south, but unsuccessfully. He will have to retreat.

11.10 " 'But then his sons will raise a huge army and rush down like a flood, a torrential attack, on the defenses of the south.

11.11-13 " 'Furious, the king of the south will come out and engage the king of the north and his huge army in battle and rout them. As the corpses are cleared from the field, the king, inflamed with bloodlust, will go on a bloodletting rampage, massacring tens of thousands. But his victory won't last long, for the king of the north will put together another army bigger than the last one, and after a few years he'll come back to do battle again with his immense army and endless supplies.

11.14 " 'In those times, many others will get into the act and go off to fight against the king of the south. Hotheads from your own people, drunk on dreams, will join them. But they'll sputter out.

11.15-17 " 'When the king of the north arrives, he'll build siege works and capture the outpost fortress city. The armies of the south will fall to pieces before him. Not even their famous com-

NEW INTERNATIONAL VERSION

troops will not have the strength to stand. [16]The invader will do as he pleases; no one will be able to stand against him. He will establish himself in the Beautiful Land and will have the power to destroy it. [17]He will determine to come with the might of his entire kingdom and will make an alliance with the king of the South. And he will give him a daughter in marriage in order to overthrow the kingdom, but his plans[a] will not succeed or help him. [18]Then he will turn his attention to the coastlands and will take many of them, but a commander will put an end to his insolence and will turn his insolence back upon him. [19]After this, he will turn back toward the fortresses of his own country but will stumble and fall, to be seen no more.

[20]"His successor will send out a tax collector to maintain the royal splendor. In a few years, however, he will be destroyed, yet not in anger or in battle.

[21]"He will be succeeded by a contemptible person who has not been given the honor of royalty. He will invade the kingdom when its people feel secure, and he will seize it through intrigue. [22]Then an overwhelming army will be swept away before him; both it and a prince of the covenant will be destroyed. [23]After coming to an agreement with him, he will act deceitfully, and with only a few people he will rise to power. [24]When the richest provinces feel secure, he will invade them and will achieve what neither his fathers nor his forefathers did. He will distribute plunder, loot and wealth among his followers. He will plot the overthrow of fortresses—but only for a time.

[25]"With a large army he will stir up his strength and courage against the king of the South. The king of the South will wage war with a large and very powerful army, but he will not be able to stand because of the plots devised against him. [26]Those who eat from the king's provisions will try to destroy him; his army will be swept away, and many will fall in battle. [27]The two kings, with their hearts bent on evil, will sit at the same table and lie to each other, but to no avail, because an end will still come at the appointed time. [28]The king of the North will return to his own country with great wealth, but his heart will be set against the holy covenant. He will take action against it and then return to his own country.

[29]"At the appointed time he will invade the South again, but this time the outcome will be different from what it was before. [30]Ships of the western coastlands[b] will oppose him, and he will lose heart. Then he will turn back and vent his

THE MESSAGE

mando shock troops will slow down the attacker. He'll march in big as you please, as if he owned the place. He'll take over that beautiful country, Palestine, and make himself at home in it. Then he'll proceed to get everything, lock, stock, and barrel, in his control. He'll cook up a peace treaty and even give his daughter in marriage to the king of the south in a plot to destroy him totally. But the plot will fizzle. It won't succeed.

11.18-19   " 'Later, he'll turn his attention to the coastal regions and capture a bunch of prisoners, but a general will step in and put a stop to his bullying ways. The bully will be bullied! He'll go back home and tend to his own military affairs. But by then he'll be washed up and soon will be heard of no more.

11.20   " 'He will be replaced shortly by a real loser, his rule, reputation, and authority already in shreds. And he won't last long. He'll slip out of history quietly, without even a fight.

11.21-24   " 'His place will be taken by a reject, a man spurned and passed over for advancement. He'll surprise everyone, seemingly coming out of nowhere, and will seize the kingdom. He'll come in like a steamroller, flattening the opposition. Even the Prince of the Covenant will be crushed. After negotiating a cease-fire, he'll betray its terms. With a few henchmen, he'll take total control. Arbitrarily and impulsively, he'll invade the richest provinces. He'll surpass all his ancestors, near and distant, in his rape of the country, grabbing and looting, living with his cronies in corrupt and lavish luxury.

11.24-26   " 'He will make plans against the fortress cities, but they'll turn out to be shortsighted. He'll get a great army together, all charged up to fight the king of the south. The king of the south in response will get his army—an even greater army—in place, ready to fight. But he won't be able to sustain that intensity for long because of the treacherous intrigue in his own ranks, his court having been honeycombed with vicious plots. His army will be smashed, the battlefield filled with corpses.

11.27   " 'The two kings, each with evil designs on the other, will sit at the conference table and trade lies. Nothing will come of the treaty, which is nothing but a tissue of lies anyway. But that's not the end of it. There's more to this story.

11.28   " 'The king of the north will go home loaded down with plunder, but his mind will be set on destroying the holy covenant as he passes through the country on his way home.

11.29-32   " 'One year later he will mount a fresh invasion of the south. But the second invasion won't compare to the first. When the Roman ships arrive, he will turn tail and go back

a 17 Or but she   b 30 Hebrew of Kittim

NEW INTERNATIONAL VERSION

fury against the holy covenant. He will return and show favor to those who forsake the holy covenant.

31 "His armed forces will rise up to desecrate the temple fortress and will abolish the daily sacrifice. Then they will set up the abomination that causes desolation. 32 With flattery he will corrupt those who have violated the covenant, but the people who know their God will firmly resist him.

33 "Those who are wise will instruct many, though for a time they will fall by the sword or be burned or captured or plundered. 34 When they fall, they will receive a little help, and many who are not sincere will join them. 35 Some of the wise will stumble, so that they may be refined, purified and made spotless until the time of the end, for it will still come at the appointed time.

THE KING WHO EXALTS HIMSELF

36 "The king will do as he pleases. He will exalt and magnify himself above every god and will say unheard-of things against the God of gods. He will be successful until the time of wrath is completed, for what has been determined must take place. 37 He will show no regard for the gods of his fathers or for the one desired by women, nor will he regard any god, but will exalt himself above them all. 38 Instead of them, he will honor a god of fortresses; a god unknown to his fathers he will honor with gold and silver, with precious stones and costly gifts. 39 He will attack the mightiest fortresses with the help of a foreign god and will greatly honor those who acknowledge him. He will make them rulers over many people and will distribute the land at a price. *a*

40 "At the time of the end the king of the South will engage him in battle, and the king of the North will storm out against him with chariots and cavalry and a great fleet of ships. He will invade many countries and sweep through them like a flood. 41 He will also invade the Beautiful Land. Many countries will fall, but Edom, Moab and the leaders of Ammon will be delivered from his hand. 42 He will extend his power over many countries; Egypt will not escape. 43 He will gain control of the treasures of gold and silver and all the riches of Egypt, with the Libyans and Nubians in submission. 44 But reports from the east and the north will alarm him, and he

a 39 Or land for a reward

THE MESSAGE

home. But as he passes through the country, he will be filled with anger at the holy covenant. He will take up with all those who betray the holy covenant, favoring them. The bodyguards surrounding him will march in and desecrate the Sanctuary and citadel. They'll throw out the daily worship and set up in its place the obscene sacrilege. The king of the north will play up to those who betray the holy covenant, corrupting them even further with his seductive talk, but those who stay courageously loyal to their God will take a strong stand.

11.33-35 " 'Those who keep their heads on straight will teach the crowds right from wrong by their example. They'll be put to severe testing for a season: some killed, some burned, some exiled, some robbed. When the testing is intense, they'll get some help, but not much. Many of the helpers will be halfhearted at best. The testing will refine, cleanse, and purify those who keep their heads on straight and stay true, for there is still more to come.

11.36-39 " 'Meanwhile, the king of the north will do whatever he pleases. He'll puff himself up and posture himself as greater than any god. He will even dare to brag and boast in defiance of the God of gods. And he'll get by with it for a while—until this time of wrathful judgment is completed, for what is decreed must be done. He will have no respect for the gods of his ancestors, not even that popular favorite among women, Adonis. Contemptuous of every god and goddess, the king of the north will puff himself up greater than all of them. He'll even stoop to despising the God of the holy ones, and in the place where God is worshiped he will put on exhibit, with a lavish show of silver and gold and jewels, a new god that no one has ever heard of. Marching under the banner of a strange god, he will attack the key fortresses. He will promote everyone who falls into line behind this god, putting them in positions of power and paying them off with grants of land.

11.40-45 " 'In the final wrap-up of this story, the king of the south will confront him. But the king of the north will come at him like a tornado. Unleashing chariots and horses and an armada of ships, he'll blow away anything in his path. As he enters the beautiful land, people will fall before him like dominoes. Only Edom, Moab, and a few Ammonites will escape. As he reaches out, grabbing country after country, not even Egypt will be exempt. He will confiscate the treasuries of Egyptian gold and silver and other valuables. The Libyans and Ethiopians will fall in with him. Then disturbing reports will come in from the north and east that will

NEW INTERNATIONAL VERSION

will set out in a great rage to destroy and annihilate many. ⁴⁵He will pitch his royal tents between the seas at ᵃ the beautiful holy mountain. Yet he will come to his end, and no one will help him.

THE END TIMES

12 "At that time Michael, the great prince who protects your people, will arise. There will be a time of distress such as has not happened from the beginning of nations until then. But at that time your people—everyone whose name is found written in the book—will be delivered. ²Multitudes who sleep in the dust of the earth will awake: some to everlasting life, others to shame and everlasting contempt. ³Those who are wise ᵇ will shine like the brightness of the heavens, and those who lead many to righteousness, like the stars for ever and ever. ⁴But you, Daniel, close up and seal the words of the scroll until the time of the end. Many will go here and there to increase knowledge."

⁵Then I, Daniel, looked, and there before me stood two others, one on this bank of the river and one on the opposite bank. ⁶One of them said to the man clothed in linen, who was above the waters of the river, "How long will it be before these astonishing things are fulfilled?"

⁷The man clothed in linen, who was above the waters of the river, lifted his right hand and his left hand toward heaven, and I heard him swear by him who lives forever, saying, "It will be for a time, times and half a time.ᶜ When the power of the holy people has been finally broken, all these things will be completed."

⁸I heard, but I did not understand. So I asked, "My lord, what will the outcome of all this be?"

⁹He replied, "Go your way, Daniel, because the words are closed up and sealed until the time of the end. ¹⁰Many will be purified, made spotless and refined, but the wicked will continue to be wicked. None of the wicked will understand, but those who are wise will understand.

THE MESSAGE

throw him into a panic. Towering in rage, he'll rush to stamp out the threat. But he'll no sooner have pitched camp between the Mediterranean Sea and the Holy Mountain—all those royal tents!—than he'll meet his end. And not a soul around who can help!

THE WORST TROUBLE THE WORLD HAS EVER SEEN

12.1-2 **12** " 'That's when Michael, the great angel-prince, champion of your people, will step in. It will be a time of trouble, the worst trouble the world has ever seen. But your people will be saved from the trouble, every last one found written in the Book. Many who have been long dead and buried will wake up, some to eternal life, others to eternal shame.

12.3   " 'Men and women who have lived wisely and well will shine brilliantly, like the cloudless, star-strewn night skies. And those who put others on the right path to life will glow like stars forever.

12.4   " 'This is a confidential report, Daniel, for your eyes and ears only. Keep it secret. Put the book under lock and key until the end. In the interim there is going to be a lot of frantic running around, trying to figure out what's going on.'

✠

12.5-6 "As I, Daniel, took all this in, two figures appeared, one standing on this bank of the river and one on the other bank. One of them asked a third man who was dressed in linen and who straddled the river, 'How long is this astonishing story to go on?'

12.7   "The man dressed in linen, who straddled the river, raised both hands to the skies. I heard him solemnly swear by the Eternal One that it would be a time, two times, and half a time, that when the oppressor of the holy people was brought down the story would be complete.

12.8   "I heard all this plainly enough, but I didn't understand it. So I asked, 'Master, can you explain this to me?'

12.9-10 " 'Go on about your business, Daniel,' he said. 'The message is confidential and under lock and key until the end, until things are about to be wrapped up. The populace will be washed clean and made like new. But the wicked will just keep on being wicked, without a clue about what is happening. Those who live wisely and well will understand what's going on.'

✠

ᵃ 45 Or the sea and   ᵇ 3 Or who impart wisdom   ᶜ 7 Or a year, two years and half a year

NEW INTERNATIONAL VERSION

11"From the time that the daily sacrifice is abolished and the abomination that causes desolation is set up, there will be 1,290 days. 12Blessed is the one who waits for and reaches the end of the 1,335 days.

13"As for you, go your way till the end. You will rest, and then at the end of the days you will rise to receive your allotted inheritance."

THE MESSAGE

12.11 "From the time that the daily worship is banished from the Temple and the obscene desecration is set up in its place, there will be 1,290 days.

12.12 "Blessed are those who patiently make it through the 1,335 days.

12.13 "And you? Go about your business without fretting or worrying. Relax. When it's all over, you will be on your feet to receive your reward."

HOSEA

HOSEA

1 The word of the LORD that came to Hosea son of Beeri during the reigns of Uzziah, Jotham, Ahaz and Hezekiah, kings of Judah, and during the reign of Jeroboam son of Jehoash[a] king of Israel:

HOSEA'S WIFE AND CHILDREN

²When the LORD began to speak through Hosea, the LORD said to him, "Go, take to yourself an adulterous wife and children of unfaithfulness, because the land is guilty of the vilest adultery in departing from the LORD." ³So he married Gomer daughter of Diblaim, and she conceived and bore him a son.

⁴Then the LORD said to Hosea, "Call him Jezreel, because I will soon punish the house of Jehu for the massacre at Jezreel, and I will put an end to the kingdom of Israel. ⁵In that day I will break Israel's bow in the Valley of Jezreel."

⁶Gomer conceived again and gave birth to a daughter. Then the LORD said to Hosea, "Call her Lo-Ruhamah,[b] for I will no longer show love to the house of Israel, that I should at all forgive them. ⁷Yet I will show love to the house of Judah; and I will save them—not by bow, sword or battle, or by horses and horsemen, but by the LORD their God."

1.1 **1** This is God's Message to Hosea son of Beeri. It came to him during the royal reigns of Judah's kings Uzziah, Jotham, Ahaz, and Hezekiah. This was also the time that Jeroboam son of Joash was king over Israel.

THIS WHOLE COUNTRY HAS BECOME A WHOREHOUSE

1.2 The first time GOD spoke to Hosea he said:

"Find a whore and marry her.
   Make this whore the mother of your
      children.
And here's why: This whole country
   has become a whorehouse, unfaithful to
      me, GOD."

1.3   Hosea did it. He picked Gomer daughter of Diblaim. She got pregnant and gave him a son.
1.4-5   Then GOD told him:

"Name him Jezreel. It won't be long now
      before
   I'll make the people of Israel pay for the
      massacre at Jezreel.
I'm calling it quits on the kingdom of
      Israel.
Payday is coming! I'm going to chop Israel's
      bows and arrows
   into kindling in the valley of Jezreel."

✠

1.6-7 Gomer got pregnant again. This time she had a daughter. GOD told Hosea:

"Name this one No-Mercy. I'm fed up with
      Israel.
I've run out of mercy. There's no more
      forgiveness.
Judah's another story. I'll continue having
      mercy on them.
I'll save them. It will be their GOD who
      saves them,
Not their armaments and armies,
   not their horsepower and manpower."

✠

---

a 1 Hebrew *Joash*, a variant of *Jehoash*   *b* 6 *Lo-Ruhamah* means *not loved.*

NEW INTERNATIONAL VERSION

8After she had weaned Lo-Ruhamah, Gomer had another son. 9Then the LORD said, "Call him Lo-Ammi,ª for you are not my people, and I am not your God.

10"Yet the Israelites will be like the sand on the seashore, which cannot be measured or counted. In the place where it was said to them, 'You are not my people,' they will be called 'sons of the living God.' 11The people of Judah and the people of Israel will be reunited, and they will appoint one leader and will come up out of the land, for great will be the day of Jezreel.

2 "Say of your brothers, 'My people,' and of your sisters, 'My loved one.'

ISRAEL PUNISHED AND RESTORED

2 "Rebuke your mother, rebuke her,
    for she is not my wife,
    and I am not her husband.
Let her remove the adulterous look from her face
    and the unfaithfulness from between her breasts.
3Otherwise I will strip her naked
    and make her as bare as on the day she was born;
I will make her like a desert,
    turn her into a parched land,
    and slay her with thirst.
4I will not show my love to her children,
    because they are the children of adultery.
5Their mother has been unfaithful
    and has conceived them in disgrace.
She said, 'I will go after my lovers,
    who give me my food and my water,
    my wool and my linen, my oil and my drink.'
6Therefore I will block her path with thornbushes;
    I will wall her in so that she cannot find her way.
7She will chase after her lovers but not catch them;
    she will look for them but not find them.
Then she will say,
    'I will go back to my husband as at first,
    for then I was better off than now.'
8She has not acknowledged that I was the one
    who gave her the grain, the new wine and oil,
who lavished on her the silver and gold—
    which they used for Baal.

ª 9 Lo-Ammi means not my people.

THE MESSAGE

1.8-9 After Gomer had weaned No-Mercy, she got pregnant yet again and had a son. GOD said:

"Name him Nobody. You've become nobodies to me,
    and I, GOD, am a nobody to you.

1.10-11 "But down the road the population of Israel is going to explode past counting, like sand on the ocean beaches. In the very place where they were once named Nobody, they will be named God's Somebody. Everybody in Judah and everybody in Israel will be assembled as one people. They'll choose a single leader. There'll be no stopping them—a great day in Jezreel!

☩

2.1 **2** "Rename your brothers 'God's Somebody.'
    Rename your sisters 'All Mercy.'

WILD WEEKENDS AND UNHOLY HOLIDAYS

2.2-13 "Haul your mother into court. Accuse her!
    She's no longer my wife.
    I'm no longer her husband.
Tell her to quit dressing like a whore,
    displaying her breasts for sale.
If she refuses, I'll rip off her clothes
    and expose her, naked as a newborn.
I'll turn her skin into dried-out leather,
    her body into a badlands landscape,
    a rack of bones in the desert.
I'll have nothing to do with her children,
    born one and all in a whorehouse.
Face it: Your mother's been a whore,
    bringing bastard children into the world.
She said, 'I'm off to see my lovers!
    They'll wine and dine me,
Dress and caress me,
    perfume and adorn me!'
But I'll fix her: I'll dump her in a field of thistles,
    then lose her in a dead-end alley.
She'll go on the hunt for her lovers
    but not bring down a single one.
She'll look high and low
    but won't find a one. Then she'll say,
'I'm going back to my husband, the one I started out with.
    That was a better life by far than this one.'
She didn't know that it was I all along
    who wined and dined and adorned her,
That I was the one who dressed her up
    in the big-city fashions and jewelry
    that she wasted on wild Baal-orgies.

NEW INTERNATIONAL VERSION

⁹"Therefore I will take away my grain when it
　　ripens,
　　and my new wine when it is ready.
　I will take back my wool and my linen,
　　intended to cover her nakedness.
¹⁰So now I will expose her lewdness
　　before the eyes of her lovers;
　　no one will take her out of my hands.
¹¹I will stop all her celebrations:
　　her yearly festivals, her New Moons,
　　her Sabbath days—all her appointed
　　　feasts.
¹²I will ruin her vines and her fig trees,
　　which she said were her pay from her
　　　lovers;
　I will make them a thicket,
　　and wild animals will devour them.
¹³I will punish her for the days
　　she burned incense to the Baals;
　she decked herself with rings and jewelry,
　　and went after her lovers,
　　but me she forgot,"
　　　　　　　　　　　declares the LORD.

¹⁴"Therefore I am now going to allure her;
　　I will lead her into the desert
　　and speak tenderly to her.
¹⁵There I will give her back her vineyards,
　　and will make the Valley of Achorᵃ a door
　　　of hope.
　There she will singᵇ as in the days of her
　　　youth,
　　as in the day she came up out of Egypt.

¹⁶"In that day," declares the LORD,
　　"you will call me 'my husband';
　　you will no longer call me 'my master.'ᶜ
¹⁷I will remove the names of the Baals from
　　　her lips;
　　no longer will their names be invoked.
¹⁸In that day I will make a covenant for them
　　with the beasts of the field and the birds
　　　of the air
　　and the creatures that move along the
　　　ground.
　Bow and sword and battle
　　I will abolish from the land,
　　so that all may lie down in safety.
¹⁹I will betroth you to me forever;
　　I will betroth you inᵈ righteousness and
　　　justice,
　　inᵉ love and compassion.
²⁰I will betroth you in faithfulness,
　　and you will acknowledge the LORD.

ᵃ 15 Achor means trouble.　ᵇ 15 Or respond
ᶜ 16 Hebrew baal　ᵈ 19 Or with; also in verse 20
ᵉ 19 Or with

THE MESSAGE

I'm about to bring her up short: No more
　　wining and dining!
　Silk lingerie and gowns are a thing of the
　　　past.
　I'll expose her genitals to the public.
　　All her fly-by-night lovers will be helpless
　　　to help her.
Party time is over. I'm calling a halt to the
　　whole business,
　　her wild weekends and unholy holidays.
I'll wreck her sumptuous gardens and
　　ornamental fountains,
　of which she bragged, 'Whoring paid for all
　　this!'
They will soon be dumping grounds for garbage,
　feeding grounds for stray dogs and cats.
I'll make her pay for her indulgence in
　　promiscuous religion—
　　all that sensuous Baal worship
And all the promiscuous sex that went with it,
　　stalking her lovers, dressed to kill,
And not a thought for me."
　　GOD's Message!

TO START ALL OVER AGAIN

2.14-15 "And now, here's what I'm going to do:
　　I'm going to start all over again.
I'm taking her back out into the wilderness
　　where we had our first date, and I'll court
　　　her.
I'll give her bouquets of roses.
　　I'll turn Heartbreak Valley into Acres of
　　　Hope.
She'll respond like she did as a young girl,
　　those days when she was fresh out of Egypt.

✝

2.16-20 "At that time"—this is GOD's Message still—
　　"you'll address me, 'Dear husband!'
Never again will you address me,
　　'My slave-master!'
I'll wash your mouth out with soap,
　　get rid of all the dirty false-god names,
　　not so much as a whisper of those names
　　　again.
At the same time I'll make a peace treaty
　　between you
　　and wild animals and birds and reptiles,
And get rid of all weapons of war.
　　Think of it! Safe from beasts and bullies!
And then I'll marry you for good—forever!
　　I'll marry you true and proper, in love and
　　　tenderness.
Yes, I'll marry you and neither leave you nor
　　　let you go.
　　You'll know me, GOD, for who I really am.

✝

NEW INTERNATIONAL VERSION

21 "In that day I will respond,"
    declares the LORD—
"I will respond to the skies,
    and they will respond to the earth;
22 and the earth will respond to the grain,
    the new wine and oil,
    and they will respond to Jezreel. *a*
23 I will plant her for myself in the land;
    I will show my love to the one I called
        'Not my loved one. *b*'
I will say to those called 'Not my people, *c*'
        'You are my people';
    and they will say, 'You are my God.' "

HOSEA'S RECONCILIATION WITH HIS WIFE

3 The LORD said to me, "Go, show your love to
    your wife again, though she is loved by an-
other and is an adulteress. Love her as the LORD
loves the Israelites, though they turn to other
gods and love the sacred raisin cakes."

2 So I bought her for fifteen shekels *d* of silver
and about a homer and a lethek *e* of barley. 3 Then
I told her, "You are to live with *f* me many days;
you must not be a prostitute or be intimate with
any man, and I will live with *f* you."

4 For the Israelites will live many days without king or prince, without sacrifice or sacred
stones, without ephod or idol. 5 Afterward the Israelites will return and seek the LORD their God
and David their king. They will come trembling
to the LORD and to his blessings in the last days.

THE CHARGE AGAINST ISRAEL

4 Hear the word of the LORD, you Israelites,
    because the LORD has a charge to bring
    against you who live in the land:
"There is no faithfulness, no love,
    no acknowledgment of God in the land.
2 There is only cursing, *g* lying and murder,
    stealing and adultery;

THE MESSAGE

2.21-23 "On the very same day, I'll answer"—this is
        GOD's Message—
"I'll answer the sky, sky will answer earth,
Earth will answer grain and wine and olive
        oil,
    and they'll all answer Jezreel.
I'll plant her in the good earth.
    I'll have mercy on No-Mercy.
I'll say to Nobody, 'You're my dear Somebody,'
    and he'll say 'You're my God!' "

IN TIME THEY'LL COME BACK

3.1 3 Then GOD ordered me, "Start all over:
        Love your wife again,
    your wife who's in bed with her latest
        boyfriend, your cheating wife.
Love her the way I, GOD, love the Israelite
        people,
    even as they flirt and party with every god
        that takes their fancy."

3.2-3 I did it. I paid good money to get her back.
        It cost me the price of a slave.
Then I told her, "From now on you're living
        with me.
    No more whoring, no more sleeping around.
    You're living with me and I'm living with
        you."

✞

3.4-5 The people of Israel are going to live a long
        time
    stripped of security and protection,
without religion and comfort,
    godless and prayerless.
But in time they'll come back, these Israelites,
    come back looking for their GOD and their
        David-King.
They'll come back chastened to reverence
    before GOD and his good gifts, ready for the
        End of the story of his love.

NO ONE IS FAITHFUL

4.1-3 4 Attention all Israelites! GOD's Message!
        GOD indicts the whole population:
"No one is faithful. No one loves.
    No one knows the first thing about God.
All this cussing and lying and killing, theft
        and loose sex,

---

a 22 *Jezreel* means *God plants.*   *b* 23 Hebrew *Lo-Ruhamah*
c 23 Hebrew *Lo-Ammi*   *d* 2 That is, about 6 ounces (about
170 grams)   *e* 2 That is, probably about 10 bushels
(about 330 liters)   *f* 3 Or *wait for*   *g* 2 That is, to
pronounce a curse upon

NEW INTERNATIONAL VERSION

they break all bounds,
 and bloodshed follows bloodshed.
3 Because of this the land mourns, *a*
 and all who live in it waste away;
the beasts of the field and the birds of the air
 and the fish of the sea are dying.

4 "But let no man bring a charge,
 let no man accuse another,
for your people are like those
 who bring charges against a priest.
5 You stumble day and night,
 and the prophets stumble with you.
So I will destroy your mother—
6 my people are destroyed from lack of
  knowledge.

"Because you have rejected knowledge,
 I also reject you as my priests;
because you have ignored the law of your
  God,
 I also will ignore your children.
7 The more the priests increased,
 the more they sinned against me;
they exchanged *b* their *c* Glory for
  something disgraceful.
8 They feed on the sins of my people
 and relish their wickedness.
9 And it will be: Like people, like priests.
 I will punish both of them for their ways
 and repay them for their deeds.

10 "They will eat but not have enough;
 they will engage in prostitution but not
  increase,
because they have deserted the Lord
 to give themselves 11 to prostitution,
to old wine and new,
 which take away the understanding 12 of
  my people.
They consult a wooden idol
 and are answered by a stick of wood.
A spirit of prostitution leads them astray;
 they are unfaithful to their God.
13 They sacrifice on the mountaintops
 and burn offerings on the hills,
under oak, poplar and terebinth,
 where the shade is pleasant.
Therefore your daughters turn to
  prostitution
 and your daughters-in-law to adultery.

14 "I will not punish your daughters
 when they turn to prostitution,

THE MESSAGE

sheer anarchy, one murder after another!
And because of all this, the very land itself
  weeps
 and everything in it is grief-stricken—
animals in the fields and birds on the wing,
 even the fish in the sea are listless, lifeless.

☩

4.4-10 "But don't look for someone to blame.
 No finger pointing!
You, priest, are the one in the dock.
 You stumble around in broad daylight,
And then the prophets take over and stumble
  all night.
 Your mother is as bad as you.
My people are ruined
 because they don't know what's right or
  true.
Because you've turned your back on
  knowledge,
 I've turned my back on you priests.
Because you refuse to recognize the revelation
  of God,
 I'm no longer recognizing your children.
The more priests, the more sin.
 They traded in their glory for shame.
They pig out on my people's sins.
 They can't wait for the latest in evil.
The result: You can't tell the people from the
  priests,
 the priests from the people.
I'm on my way to make them both pay
 and take the consequences of the bad lives
  they've lived.
They'll eat and be as hungry as ever,
 have sex and get no satisfaction.
They walked out on me, their God,
 for a life of rutting with whores.

They Make a Picnic Out of Religion

4.11-14 "Wine and whiskey
 leave my people in a stupor.
They ask questions of a dead tree,
 expect answers from a sturdy walking stick.
Drunk on sex, they can't find their way home.
 They've replaced their God with their
  genitals.
They worship on the tops of mountains,
 make a picnic out of religion.
Under the oaks and elms on the hills
 they stretch out and take it easy.
Before you know it, your daughters are
  whores
 and the wives of your sons are sleeping
  around.
But I'm not going after your whoring
  daughters

---

a 3 Or *dries up* *b* 7 Syriac and an ancient Hebrew scribal
tradition; Masoretic Text *I will exchange* *c* 7 Masoretic
Text; an ancient Hebrew scribal tradition *my*

NEW INTERNATIONAL VERSION

nor your daughters-in-law
    when they commit adultery,
because the men themselves consort with
    harlots
    and sacrifice with shrine prostitutes—
a people without understanding will come
    to ruin!

15 "Though you commit adultery, O Israel,
    let not Judah become guilty.

"Do not go to Gilgal;
    do not go up to Beth Aven. *a*
  And do not swear, 'As surely as the LORD
    lives!'
16 The Israelites are stubborn,
    like a stubborn heifer.
How then can the LORD pasture them
    like lambs in a meadow?
17 Ephraim is joined to idols;
    leave him alone!
18 Even when their drinks are gone,
    they continue their prostitution;
  their rulers dearly love shameful ways.
19 A whirlwind will sweep them away,
    and their sacrifices will bring them
    shame.

JUDGMENT AGAINST ISRAEL

5 "Hear this, you priests!
    Pay attention, you Israelites!
Listen, O royal house!
    This judgment is against you:
You have been a snare at Mizpah,
    a net spread out on Tabor.
2 The rebels are deep in slaughter.
    I will discipline all of them.
3 I know all about Ephraim;
    Israel is not hidden from me.
Ephraim, you have now turned to
    prostitution;
    Israel is corrupt.

4 "Their deeds do not permit them
    to return to their God.
A spirit of prostitution is in their heart;
    they do not acknowledge the LORD.
5 Israel's arrogance testifies against them;
  the Israelites, even Ephraim, stumble in
    their sin;
    Judah also stumbles with them.
6 When they go with their flocks and herds
    to seek the LORD,

*a 15 Beth Aven means house of wickedness (a name for
Bethel, which means house of God).*

THE MESSAGE

or the adulterous wives of your sons.
It's the men who pick up the whores that I'm
    after,
the men who worship at the holy
    whorehouses—
  a stupid people, ruined by whores!

✝

4.15-19 "You've ruined your own life, Israel—
    but don't drag Judah down with you!
Don't go to the sex shrine at Gilgal,
    don't go to that sin city Bethel,
Don't go around saying 'GOD bless you' and
    not mean it,
    taking God's name in vain.
Israel is stubborn as a mule.
  How can GOD lead him like a lamb to open
    pasture?
Ephraim is addicted to idols.
    Let him go.
When the beer runs out,
    it's sex, sex, and more sex.
Bold and sordid debauchery—
    how they love it!
The whirlwind has them in its clutches.
  Their sex-worship leaves them finally
    impotent.

THEY WOULDN'T RECOGNIZE GOD IF THEY SAW HIM

5.1-2 5 "Listen to this, priests!
    Attention, people of Israel!
Royal family—all ears!
    You're in charge of justice around here.
But what have you done? Exploited people at
    Mizpah,
    ripped them off on Tabor,
Victimized them at Shittim.
    I'm going to punish the lot of you.

5.3-4 "I know you, Ephraim, inside and out.
    Yes, Israel, I see right through you!
Ephraim, you've played your sex-and-religion
    games long enough.
    All Israel is thoroughly polluted.
They couldn't turn to God if they wanted to.
    Their evil life is a bad habit.
Every breath they take is a whore's breath.
  They wouldn't recognize GOD if they
    saw me.

5.5-7 "Bloated by arrogance, big as a house,
    they're a public disgrace,
The lot of them—Israel, Ephraim, Judah—
  lurching and weaving down their guilty
    streets.
When they decide to get their lives together
  and go off looking for GOD once again,

NEW INTERNATIONAL VERSION	THE MESSAGE

NEW INTERNATIONAL VERSION

they will not find him;
  he has withdrawn himself from them.
⁷ They are unfaithful to the LORD;
  they give birth to illegitimate children.
Now their New Moon festivals
  will devour them and their fields.

⁸ "Sound the trumpet in Gibeah,
  the horn in Ramah.
Raise the battle cry in Beth Aven ᵃ;
  lead on, O Benjamin.
⁹ Ephraim will be laid waste
  on the day of reckoning.
Among the tribes of Israel
  I proclaim what is certain.
¹⁰ Judah's leaders are like those
  who move boundary stones.
I will pour out my wrath on them
  like a flood of water.
¹¹ Ephraim is oppressed,
  trampled in judgment,
  intent on pursuing idols. ᵇ
¹² I am like a moth to Ephraim,
  like rot to the people of Judah.

¹³ "When Ephraim saw his sickness,
  and Judah his sores,
then Ephraim turned to Assyria,
  and sent to the great king for help.
But he is not able to cure you,
  not able to heal your sores.
¹⁴ For I will be like a lion to Ephraim,
  like a great lion to Judah.
I will tear them to pieces and go away;
  I will carry them off, with no one to
    rescue them.
¹⁵ Then I will go back to my place
  until they admit their guilt.
And they will seek my face;
  in their misery they will earnestly
    seek me."

ISRAEL UNREPENTANT

6 "Come, let us return to the LORD.
  He has torn us to pieces
  but he will heal us;
he has injured us
  but he will bind up our wounds.
² After two days he will revive us;
  on the third day he will restore us,

THE MESSAGE

They'll find it's too late.
  I, GOD, will be long gone.
They've played fast and loose with me for too
    long,
  filling the country with their bastard
    offspring.
A plague of locusts will
  devastate their violated land.

5.8-9 "Blow the ram's horn shofar in Gibeah,
  the bugle in Ramah!
Signal the invasion of Sin City!
  Scare the daylights out of Benjamin!
Ephraim will be left wasted,
  a lifeless moonscape.
I'm telling it straight, the unvarnished truth,
  to the tribes of Israel.

5.10 "Israel's rulers are crooks and thieves,
  cheating the people of their land,
And I'm angry, good and angry.
  Every inch of their bodies is going to feel
    my anger.

5.11-12 "Brutal Ephraim is himself brutalized—
  a taste of his own medicine!
He was so determined
  to do it his own worthless way.
Therefore I'm pus to Ephraim,
  dry rot in the house of Judah.

5.13 "When Ephraim saw he was sick
  and Judah saw his pus-filled sores,
Ephraim went running to Assyria,
  went for help to the big king.
But he can't heal you.
  He can't cure your oozing sores.

5.14-15 "I'm a grizzly charging Ephraim,
  a grizzly with cubs charging Judah.
I'll rip them to pieces—yes, I will!
  No one can stop me now.
I'll drag them off.
  No one can help them.
Then I'll go back to where I came from
  until they come to their senses.
When they finally hit rock bottom,
  maybe they'll come looking for me."

GANGS OF PRIESTS ASSAULTING WORSHIPERS

6.1-3 **6** "Come on, let's go back to GOD.
  He hurt us, but he'll heal us.
He hit us hard,
  but he'll put us right again.
In a couple of days we'll feel better.
  By the third day he'll have made us
    brand-new,

ᵃ 8 *Beth Aven* means *house of wickedness* (a name for Bethel,
which means *house of God*).   ᵇ 11 The meaning of the
Hebrew for this word is uncertain.

NEW INTERNATIONAL VERSION

that we may live in his presence.
³Let us acknowledge the LORD;
    let us press on to acknowledge him.
As surely as the sun rises,
    he will appear;
he will come to us like the winter rains,
    like the spring rains that water the earth."

⁴"What can I do with you, Ephraim?
    What can I do with you, Judah?
Your love is like the morning mist,
    like the early dew that disappears.
⁵Therefore I cut you in pieces with my
        prophets,
    I killed you with the words of my mouth;
    my judgments flashed like lightning upon
        you.
⁶For I desire mercy, not sacrifice,
    and acknowledgment of God rather than
        burnt offerings.
⁷Like Adam,ᵃ they have broken the
        covenant—
    they were unfaithful to me there.
⁸Gilead is a city of wicked men,
    stained with footprints of blood.
⁹As marauders lie in ambush for a man,
    so do bands of priests;
they murder on the road to Shechem,
    committing shameful crimes.
¹⁰I have seen a horrible thing
    in the house of Israel.
There Ephraim is given to prostitution
    and Israel is defiled.

¹¹"Also for you, Judah,
    a harvest is appointed.

"Whenever I would restore the fortunes of
    my people,

7¹ whenever I would heal Israel,
    the sins of Ephraim are exposed
    and the crimes of Samaria revealed.
They practice deceit,
    thieves break into houses,
    bandits rob in the streets;
²but they do not realize
    that I remember all their evil deeds.
Their sins engulf them;
    they are always before me.

ᵃ 7 Or *As at Adam;* or *Like men*

THE MESSAGE

Alive and on our feet,
    fit to face him.
We're ready to study GOD,
    eager for God-knowledge.
As sure as dawn breaks,
    so sure is his daily arrival.
He comes as rain comes,
    as spring rain refreshing the ground."

                    ☩

6.4-7 "What am I to do with you, Ephraim?
    What do I make of you, Judah?
Your declarations of love last no longer
    than morning mist and predawn dew.
That's why I use prophets to shake you to
        attention,
    why my words cut you to the quick:
To wake you up to my judgment
    blazing like light.
I'm after love that lasts, not more religion.
    I want you to know GOD, not go to more
        prayer meetings.
You broke the covenant—just like Adam!
    You broke faith with me—ungrateful
        wretches!

6.8-9 "Gilead has become Crime City—
    blood on the sidewalks, blood on the
        streets.
It used to be robbers who mugged
        pedestrians.
    Now it's gangs of priests
Assaulting worshipers on their way to
        Shechem.
    Nothing is sacred to them.

6.10 "I saw a shocking thing in the country of Israel:
    Ephraim worshiping in a religious
        whorehouse,
    and Israel in the mud right there with him.

6.11 "You're as bad as the worst of them, Judah.
    You've been sowing wild oats. Now it's
        harvest time.

DESPITE ALL THE SIGNS, ISRAEL IGNORES GOD

7.1-2 **7** "Every time I gave Israel a fresh start,
        wiped the slate clean and got them going
        again,
Ephraim soon filled the slate with new sins,
    the treachery of Samaria written out in bold
        print.
Two-faced and double-tongued,
    they steal you blind, pick you clean.
It never crosses their mind
    that I keep account of their every crime.
They're mud-spattered head to toe with the
        residue of sin.
    I see who they are and what they've done.

NEW INTERNATIONAL VERSION

³ "They delight the king with their
   wickedness,
   the princes with their lies.
⁴ They are all adulterers,
   burning like an oven
whose fire the baker need not stir
   from the kneading of the dough till it
   rises.
⁵ On the day of the festival of our king
   the princes become inflamed with wine,
   and he joins hands with the mockers.
⁶ Their hearts are like an oven;
   they approach him with intrigue.
Their passion smolders all night;
   in the morning it blazes like a flaming
   fire.
⁷ All of them are hot as an oven;
   they devour their rulers.
All their kings fall,
   and none of them calls on me.

⁸ "Ephraim mixes with the nations;
   Ephraim is a flat cake not turned over.
⁹ Foreigners sap his strength,
   but he does not realize it.
His hair is sprinkled with gray,
   but he does not notice.
¹⁰ Israel's arrogance testifies against him,
   but despite all this
he does not return to the LORD his God
   or search for him.

¹¹ "Ephraim is like a dove,
   easily deceived and senseless—
now calling to Egypt,
   now turning to Assyria.
¹² When they go, I will throw my net over
   them;
   I will pull them down like birds of the air.
When I hear them flocking together,
   I will catch them.
¹³ Woe to them,
   because they have strayed from me!
Destruction to them,
   because they have rebelled against me!
I long to redeem them
   but they speak lies against me.
¹⁴ They do not cry out to me from their hearts
   but wail upon their beds.
They gather together ª for grain and new
   wine
   but turn away from me.
¹⁵ I trained them and strengthened them,
   but they plot evil against me.
¹⁶ They do not turn to the Most High;
   they are like a faulty bow.

ª 14 Most Hebrew manuscripts; some Hebrew manuscripts
and Septuagint They slash themselves

THE MESSAGE

7.3-7 "They entertain the king with their evil circus,
   delight the princes with their acrobatic lies.
They're a bunch of overheated adulterers,
   like an oven that holds its heat
From the kneading of the dough
   to the rising of the bread.
On the royal holiday the princes get drunk
   on wine and the frenzy of the mocking
   mob.
They're like wood stoves,
   red-hot with lust.
Through the night their passion is banked;
   in the morning it blazes up, flames
   hungrily licking.
Murderous and volcanic,
   they incinerate their rulers.
Their kings fall one by one,
   and no one pays any attention to me.

7.8-10 "Ephraim mingles with the pagans,
   dissipating himself.
Ephraim is half-baked.
Strangers suck him dry
   but he doesn't even notice.
His hair has turned gray—
   he doesn't notice.
Bloated by arrogance, big as a house,
   Israel's a public disgrace.
Israel lumbers along oblivious to GOD,
   despite all the signs, ignoring GOD.

7.11-16 "Ephraim is bird-brained,
   mindless, clueless,
First chirping after Egypt,
   then fluttering after Assyria.
I'll throw my net over them. I'll clip their
   wings.
   I'll teach them to mind me!
Doom! They've run away from home.
   Now they're *really* in trouble! They've
   defied me.
And I'm supposed to help them
   while they feed me a line of lies?
Instead of crying out to me in heartfelt prayer,
   they whoop it up in bed with their whores,
Gash themselves bloody in their sex-and-
   religion orgies,
   but turn their backs on me.
I'm the one who gave them good minds and
   healthy bodies,
   and how am I repaid? With evil scheming!
They turn, but not to me—
   turn here, then there, like a weather vane.

NEW INTERNATIONAL VERSION

Their leaders will fall by the sword
  because of their insolent words.
For this they will be ridiculed
  in the land of Egypt.

ISRAEL TO REAP THE WHIRLWIND

8 "Put the trumpet to your lips!
  An eagle is over the house of the LORD
because the people have broken my
    covenant
  and rebelled against my law.
2 Israel cries out to me,
  'O our God, we acknowledge you!'
3 But Israel has rejected what is good;
  an enemy will pursue him.
4 They set up kings without my consent;
  they choose princes without my approval.
With their silver and gold
  they make idols for themselves
  to their own destruction.
5 Throw out your calf-idol, O Samaria!
  My anger burns against them.
How long will they be incapable of purity?
6   They are from Israel!
This calf—a craftsman has made it;
  it is not God.
It will be broken in pieces,
  that calf of Samaria.

7 "They sow the wind
  and reap the whirlwind.
The stalk has no head;
  it will produce no flour.
Were it to yield grain,
  foreigners would swallow it up.
8 Israel is swallowed up;
  now she is among the nations
  like a worthless thing.
9 For they have gone up to Assyria
  like a wild donkey wandering alone.
  Ephraim has sold herself to lovers.
10 Although they have sold themselves among
    the nations,
  I will now gather them together.
They will begin to waste away
  under the oppression of the mighty king.

11 "Though Ephraim built many altars for sin
    offerings,
  these have become altars for sinning.
12 I wrote for them the many things of my law,
  but they regarded them as something
    alien.

THE MESSAGE

Their rulers will be cut down, murdered—
  just deserts for their mocking blasphemies.
And the final sentence?
  Ridicule in the court of world opinion.

ALTARS FOR SINNING

8.1-3 **8** "Blow the trumpet! Sound the alarm!
  Vultures are circling over God's people
Who have broken my covenant
  and defied my revelation.
Predictably, Israel cries out, 'My God! We
    know you!'
  But they don't act like it.
Israel will have nothing to do with what's
    good,
  and now the enemy is after them.

8.4-10 "They crown kings, but without asking me.
  They set up princes but don't let me in
    on it.
Instead, they make idols, using silver and gold,
  idols that will be their ruin.
Throw that gold calf-god on the trash heap,
    Samaria!
  I'm seething with anger against that
    rubbish!
How long before they shape up?
  And they're Israelites!
A sculptor made that thing—
  it's not God.
That Samaritan calf
  will be broken to bits.
Look at them! Planting wind-seeds,
  they'll harvest tornadoes.
Wheat with no head
  produces no flour.
And even if it did,
  strangers would gulp it down.
Israel is swallowed up and spit out.
  Among the pagans they're a piece of junk.
They trotted off to Assyria:
  Why, even wild donkeys stick to their own
    kind,
  but donkey-Ephraim goes out and *pays* to
    get lovers.
Now, because of their whoring life among the
    pagans,
  I'm going to gather them together and
    confront them.
They're going to reap the consequences soon,
  feel what it's like to be oppressed by the big
    king.

8.11-14 "Ephraim has built a lot of altars,
  and then uses them for sinning.
  Can you believe it? Altars for sinning!
I write out my revelation for them in detail
  and they pretend they can't read it.

NEW INTERNATIONAL VERSION

¹³ They offer sacrifices given to me
  and they eat the meat,
    but the LORD is not pleased with them.
Now he will remember their wickedness
  and punish their sins:
    They will return to Egypt.
¹⁴ Israel has forgotten his Maker
  and built palaces;
  Judah has fortified many towns.
But I will send fire upon their cities
  that will consume their fortresses."

PUNISHMENT FOR ISRAEL

9 Do not rejoice, O Israel;
  do not be jubilant like the other nations.
For you have been unfaithful to your God;
  you love the wages of a prostitute
    at every threshing floor.
² Threshing floors and winepresses will not
      feed the people;
  the new wine will fail them.
³ They will not remain in the LORD's land;
  Ephraim will return to Egypt
  and eat unclean ᵃ food in Assyria.
⁴ They will not pour out wine offerings to the
      LORD,
  nor will their sacrifices please him.
Such sacrifices will be to them like the bread
      of mourners;
  all who eat them will be unclean.
This food will be for themselves;
  it will not come into the temple of the
    LORD.
⁵ What will you do on the day of your
      appointed feasts,
  on the festival days of the LORD?
⁶ Even if they escape from destruction,
  Egypt will gather them,
  and Memphis will bury them.
Their treasures of silver will be taken over by
      briers,
  and thorns will overrun their tents.
⁷ The days of punishment are coming,
  the days of reckoning are at hand.
  Let Israel know this.
Because your sins are so many
  and your hostility so great,
the prophet is considered a fool,
  the inspired man a maniac.
⁸ The prophet, along with my God,
  is the watchman over Ephraim, ᵇ
yet snares await him on all his paths,

THE MESSAGE

They offer sacrifices to me
  and then they feast on the meat.
GOD is not pleased!
I'm fed up—I'll keep remembering their guilt.
  I'll punish their sins
  and send them back to Egypt.
Israel has forgotten his Maker
  and gotten busy making palaces.
  Judah has gone in for a lot of fortress cities.
I'm sending fire on their cities
  to burn down their fortifications."

STARVED FOR GOD

9.1-6 **9** Don't waste your life in wild orgies, Israel.
  Don't party away your life with the
    heathen.
You walk away from your God at the drop of a
      hat
  and like a whore sell yourself
      promiscuously
  at every sex-and-religion party on the
      street.
All that party food won't fill you up.
  You'll end up hungrier than ever.
At this rate you'll not last long in GOD's land:
  Some of you are going to end up bankrupt
      in Egypt.
  Some of you will be disillusioned in
      Assyria.
As refugees in Egypt and Assyria,
  you won't have much chance to worship
      GOD—
Sentenced to rations of bread and water,
  and your souls polluted by the spirit-dirty
      air.
You'll be starved for GOD,
  exiled from GOD's own country.
Will you be homesick for the old Holy Days?
  Will you miss festival worship of GOD?
Be warned! When you escape from the frying
      pan of disaster,
  you'll fall into the fire of Egypt.
  Egypt will give you a fine funeral!
What use will all your god-inspired silver be
      then
  as you eke out a living in a field of weeds?

⊹

9.7-9 Time's up. Doom's at the doorstep.
  It's payday!
Did Israel bluster, "The prophet is crazy!
  The 'man of the Spirit' is nuts!"?
Think again. Because of your great guilt,
  you're in big trouble.
The prophet is looking out for Ephraim,
  working under God's orders.
But everyone is trying to trip him up.

ᵃ 3 That is, ceremonially unclean   ᵇ 8 Or The prophet is
the watchman over Ephraim, / the people of my God

NEW INTERNATIONAL VERSION

and hostility in the house of his God.
⁹They have sunk deep into corruption,
    as in the days of Gibeah.
God will remember their wickedness
    and punish them for their sins.

¹⁰"When I found Israel,
    it was like finding grapes in the desert;
when I saw your fathers,
    it was like seeing the early fruit on the fig
        tree.
But when they came to Baal Peor,
    they consecrated themselves to that
        shameful idol
    and became as vile as the thing they
        loved.
¹¹Ephraim's glory will fly away like a bird—
    no birth, no pregnancy, no conception.
¹²Even if they rear children,
    I will bereave them of every one.
Woe to them
    when I turn away from them!
¹³I have seen Ephraim, like Tyre,
    planted in a pleasant place.
But Ephraim will bring out
    their children to the slayer."

¹⁴Give them, O Lord—
    what will you give them?
Give them wombs that miscarry
    and breasts that are dry.

¹⁵"Because of all their wickedness in Gilgal,
    I hated them there.
Because of their sinful deeds,
    I will drive them out of my house.
I will no longer love them;
    all their leaders are rebellious.
¹⁶Ephraim is blighted,
    their root is withered,
    they yield no fruit.
Even if they bear children,
    I will slay their cherished offspring."

¹⁷My God will reject them
    because they have not obeyed him;
    they will be wanderers among the nations.

THE MESSAGE

He's hated right in God's house, of all
    places.
The people are going from bad to worse,
    rivaling that ancient and unspeakable crime
        at Gibeah.
God's keeping track of their guilt.
    He'll make them pay for their sins.

They Took to Sin Like a Pig to Filth

9.10-13 "Long ago when I came upon Israel,
    it was like finding grapes out in the desert.
When I found your ancestors, it was like
        finding
    a fig tree bearing fruit for the first time.
But when they arrived at Baal-peor, that pagan
        shrine,
    they took to sin like a pig to filth,
    wallowing in the mud with their newfound
        friends.
Ephraim is fickle and scattered, like a flock of
        blackbirds,
    their beauty dissipated in confusion and
        clamor,
Frenetic and noisy, frigid and barren,
    and nothing to show for it—neither
        conception nor childbirth.
Even if they did give birth, I'd declare them
    unfit parents and take away their children!
Yes indeed—a black day for them
    when I turn my back and walk off!
I see Ephraim letting his children run wild.
    He might just as well take them and kill
        them outright!"

9.14 Give it to them, God! But what?
    Give them a dried-up womb and shriveled
        breasts.

9.15-16 "All their evil came out into the open
    at the pagan shrine at Gilgal. Oh, how I
        hated them there!
Because of their evil practices,
    I'll kick them off my land.
I'm wasting no more love on them.
    Their leaders are a bunch of rebellious
        adolescents.
Ephraim is hit hard—
    roots withered, no more fruit.
Even if by some miracle they had children,
    the dear babies wouldn't live—I'd make
        sure of that!"

9.17 My God has washed his hands of them.
    They wouldn't listen.
They're doomed to be wanderers,
    vagabonds among the godless nations.

NEW INTERNATIONAL VERSION

10 Israel was a spreading vine;
he brought forth fruit for himself.
As his fruit increased,
he built more altars;
as his land prospered,
he adorned his sacred stones.
² Their heart is deceitful,
and now they must bear their guilt.
The LORD will demolish their altars
and destroy their sacred stones.

³ Then they will say, "We have no king
because we did not revere the LORD.
But even if we had a king,
what could he do for us?"
⁴ They make many promises,
take false oaths
and make agreements;
therefore lawsuits spring up
like poisonous weeds in a plowed field.
⁵ The people who live in Samaria fear
for the calf-idol of Beth Aven.ᵃ
Its people will mourn over it,
and so will its idolatrous priests,
those who had rejoiced over its splendor,
because it is taken from them into exile.
⁶ It will be carried to Assyria
as tribute for the great king.
Ephraim will be disgraced;
Israel will be ashamed of its wooden
idols.ᵇ
⁷ Samaria and its king will float away
like a twig on the surface of the waters.
⁸ The high places of wicknessᶜ will be
destroyed—
it is the sin of Israel.
Thorns and thistles will grow up
and cover their altars.
Then they will say to the mountains,
"Cover us!"
and to the hills, "Fall on us!"

⁹ "Since the days of Gibeah, you have sinned,
O Israel,
and there you have remained.ᵈ
Did not war overtake
the evildoers in Gibeah?
¹⁰ When I please, I will punish them;
nations will be gathered against them
to put them in bonds for their double sin.
¹¹ Ephraim is a trained heifer
that loves to thresh;

ᵃ 5 Beth Aven means house of wickedness (a name for Bethel,
which means house of God).   ᵇ 6 Or its counsel
ᶜ 8 Hebrew aven, a reference to Beth Aven (a derogatory
name for Bethel)   ᵈ 9 Or there a stand was taken

THE MESSAGE

YOU THOUGHT YOU COULD DO IT ALL ON YOUR OWN

10.1-2 **10** Israel was once a lush vine,
bountiful in grapes.
The more lavish the harvest,
the more promiscuous the worship.
The more money they got,
the more they squandered on gods-in-their-
own-image.
Their sweet smiles are sheer lies.
They're guilty as sin.
God will smash their worship shrines,
pulverize their god-images.

10.3-4 They go around saying,
"Who needs a king?
We couldn't care less about GOD,
so why bother with a king?
What difference would he make?"
They talk big,
lie through their teeth,
make deals.
But their high-sounding words
turn out to be empty words, litter in the
gutters.

10.5-6 The people of Samaria travel over to Crime
City
to worship the golden calf-god.
They go all out, prancing and hollering,
taken in by their showmen priests.
They act so important around the calf-god,
but are oblivious to the sham, the shame.
They have plans to take it to Assyria,
present it as a gift to the great king.
And so Ephraim makes a fool of himself,
disgraces Israel with his stupid idols.

10.7-8 Samaria is history. Its king
is a dead branch floating down the river.
Israel's favorite sin centers
will all be torn down.
Thistles and crabgrass
will decorate their ruined altars.
Then they'll say to the mountains, "Bury us!"
and to the hills, "Fall on us!"

10.9-10 You got your start in sin at Gibeah—
that ancient, unspeakable, shocking sin—
And you've been at it ever since.
And Gibeah will mark the end of it
in a war to end all the sinning.
I'll come to teach them a lesson.
Nations will gang up on them,
Making them learn the hard way
the sum of Gibeah plus Gibeah.

10.11-15 Ephraim was a trained heifer
that loved to thresh.

NEW INTERNATIONAL VERSION

so I will put a yoke
  on her fair neck.
I will drive Ephraim,
  Judah must plow,
  and Jacob must break up the ground.
¹²Sow for yourselves righteousness,
  reap the fruit of unfailing love,
and break up your unplowed ground;
  for it is time to seek the LORD,
until he comes
  and showers righteousness on you.
¹³But you have planted wickedness,
  you have reaped evil,
  you have eaten the fruit of deception.
Because you have depended on your own
      strength
  and on your many warriors,
¹⁴the roar of battle will rise against your people,
  so that all your fortresses will be
      devastated—
  as Shalman devastated Beth Arbel on the day
      of battle,
  when mothers were dashed to the ground
      with their children.
¹⁵Thus will it happen to you, O Bethel,
  because your wickedness is great.
When that day dawns,
  the king of Israel will be completely
      destroyed.

GOD'S LOVE FOR ISRAEL

11 "When Israel was a child, I loved him,
      and out of Egypt I called my son.
²But the more I ᵃ called Israel,
  the further they went from me. ᵇ
They sacrificed to the Baals
  and they burned incense to images.
³It was I who taught Ephraim to walk,
  taking them by the arms;
but they did not realize
  it was I who healed them.
⁴I led them with cords of human kindness,
  with ties of love;
I lifted the yoke from their neck
  and bent down to feed them.

⁵"Will they not return to Egypt
  and will not Assyria rule over them
  because they refuse to repent?
⁶Swords will flash in their cities,
  will destroy the bars of their gates
  and put an end to their plans.
⁷My people are determined to turn from me.
  Even if they call to the Most High,
  he will by no means exalt them.

THE MESSAGE

Passing by and seeing her strong, sleek neck,
  I wanted to harness Ephraim,
Put Ephraim to work in the fields—
  Judah plowing, Jacob harrowing:
Sow righteousness,
  reap love.
It's time to till the ready earth,
  it's time to dig in with GOD,
Until he arrives
  with righteousness ripe for harvest.
But instead you plowed wicked ways,
  reaped a crop of evil and ate a salad of lies.
You thought you could do it all on your own,
  flush with weapons and manpower.
But the volcano of war will erupt among your
      people.
  All your defense posts will be leveled
As viciously as king Shalman
  leveled the town of Beth-arba,
When mothers and their babies
  were smashed on the rocks.
That's what's ahead for you, you so-called
      people of God,
  because of your off-the-charts evil.
Some morning you're going to wake up
  and find Israel, king and kingdom, a
      blank—nothing.

ISRAEL PLAYED AT RELIGION WITH TOY GODS

11.1-9 **11** "When Israel was only a child, I loved
      him.
  I called out, 'My son!'—called him out of
      Egypt.
But when others called him,
  he ran off and left me.
He worshiped the popular sex gods,
  he played at religion with toy gods.
Still, I stuck with him. I led Ephraim.
  I rescued him from human bondage,
But he never acknowledged my help,
  never admitted that I was the one pulling
      his wagon,
That I lifted him, like a baby, to my cheek,
  that I bent down to feed him.
Now he wants to go *back* to Egypt or go over
      to Assyria—
  anything but return to me!
That's why his cities are unsafe—the murder
      rate skyrockets
  and every plan to improve things falls to
      pieces.
My people are hell-bent on leaving me.
  They pray to god Baal for help.
He doesn't lift a finger to help them.

ᵃ 2 Some Septuagint manuscripts; Hebrew *they*
ᵇ 2 Septuagint; Hebrew *them*

NEW INTERNATIONAL VERSION

8 "How can I give you up, Ephraim?
　How can I hand you over, Israel?
How can I treat you like Admah?
　How can I make you like Zeboiim?
My heart is changed within me;
　all my compassion is aroused.
9 I will not carry out my fierce anger,
　nor will I turn and devastate Ephraim.
For I am God, and not man—
　the Holy One among you.
I will not come in wrath. *a*
10 They will follow the LORD;
　he will roar like a lion.
When he roars,
　his children will come trembling from the
　　west.
11 They will come trembling
　like birds from Egypt,
　like doves from Assyria.
I will settle them in their homes,"
　declares the LORD.

ISRAEL'S SIN

12 Ephraim has surrounded me with lies,
　the house of Israel with deceit.
And Judah is unruly against God,
　even against the faithful Holy One.

12 1 Ephraim feeds on the wind;
　　he pursues the east wind all day
　and multiplies lies and violence.
He makes a treaty with Assyria
　and sends olive oil to Egypt.
2 The LORD has a charge to bring against
　　Judah;
　he will punish Jacob *b* according to his
　　ways
　and repay him according to his deeds.
3 In the womb he grasped his brother's heel;
　as a man he struggled with God.
4 He struggled with the angel and overcame
　　him;
　he wept and begged for his favor.
He found him at Bethel
　and talked with him there—
5 the LORD God Almighty,
　the LORD is his name of renown!
6 But you must return to your God;
　maintain love and justice,
　and wait for your God always.

THE MESSAGE

But how can I give up on you, Ephraim?
　How can I turn you loose, Israel?
How can I leave you to be ruined like Admah,
　devastated like luckless Zeboim?
I can't bear to even think such thoughts.
　My insides churn in protest.
And so I'm not going to act on my anger.
　I'm not going to destroy Ephraim.
And why? Because I am God and not a
　　human.
　I'm The Holy One and I'm here—in your
　　very midst.

11.10-12 "The people will end up following GOD.
　I will roar like a lion—
Oh, how I'll roar!
　My frightened children will come running
　　from the west.
Like frightened birds they'll come from Egypt,
　from Assyria like scared doves.
I'll move them back into their homes."
　GOD'S Word!

SOUL-DESTROYING LIES

Ephraim tells lies right and left.
　Not a word of Israel can be trusted.
Judah, meanwhile, is no better,
　addicted to cheap gods.

✛

12.1-5 **12** Ephraim, obsessed with god-fantasies,
　　chases ghosts and phantoms.
He tells lies nonstop,
　soul-destroying lies.
Both Ephraim and Judah made deals with
　　Assyria
　and tried to get an inside track with Egypt.
GOD is bringing charges against Israel.
　Jacob's children are hauled into court to be
　　punished.
In the womb, that heel, Jacob, got the best of
　　his brother.
　When he grew up, he tried to get the best
　　of GOD.
But GOD would not be bested.
　GOD bested him.
Brought to his knees,
　Jacob wept and prayed.
GOD found him at Bethel.
　That's where he spoke with him.
GOD is God-of-the-Angel-Armies,
　GOD-Revealed, GOD-Known.

✛

12.6 What are you waiting for? Return to your God!
　Commit yourself in love, in justice!
Wait for your God,
　and don't give up on him—ever!

---

a 9 Or come against any city　*b 2 Jacob means he grasps
the heel* (figuratively, *he deceives*).

NEW INTERNATIONAL VERSION

⁷The merchant uses dishonest scales;
  he loves to defraud.
⁸Ephraim boasts,
  "I am very rich; I have become wealthy.
With all my wealth they will not find in me
  any iniquity or sin."

⁹"I am the LORD your God,
  ⌊who brought you⌋ out of ᵃ Egypt;
I will make you live in tents again,
  as in the days of your appointed feasts.
¹⁰I spoke to the prophets,
  gave them many visions
  and told parables through them."

¹¹Is Gilead wicked?
  Its people are worthless!
Do they sacrifice bulls in Gilgal?
  Their altars will be like piles of stones
  on a plowed field.
¹²Jacob fled to the country of Aram ᵇ;
  Israel served to get a wife,
  and to pay for her he tended sheep.
¹³The LORD used a prophet to bring Israel up
  from Egypt,
  by a prophet he cared for him.
¹⁴But Ephraim has bitterly provoked him to
  anger;
  his Lord will leave upon him the guilt of
  his bloodshed
  and will repay him for his contempt.

THE LORD'S ANGER AGAINST ISRAEL

13 When Ephraim spoke, men trembled;
  he was exalted in Israel.
  But he became guilty of Baal worship and
  died.
²Now they sin more and more;
  they make idols for themselves from their
  silver,
cleverly fashioned images,
  all of them the work of craftsmen.
It is said of these people,
  "They offer human sacrifice
  and kiss ᶜ the calf-idols."
³Therefore they will be like the morning mist,
  like the early dew that disappears,
  like chaff swirling from a threshing floor,
  like smoke escaping through a window.

THE MESSAGE

12.7-8 The businessmen engage in wholesale fraud.
  They love to rip people off!
Ephraim boasted, "Look, I'm rich!
  I've made it big!
And look how well I've covered my tracks:
  not a hint of fraud, not a sign of sin!"

12.9-11 "But not so fast! I'm GOD, *your* God!
  Your God from the days in Egypt!
I'm going to put you back to living in tents,
  as in the old days when you worshiped in
  the wilderness.
I speak through the prophets
  to give clear pictures of the way things are.
  Using prophets, I tell revealing stories.
I show Gilead rampant with religious scandal
  and Gilgal teeming with empty-headed
  religion.
I expose their worship centers as
  stinking piles of garbage in their gardens."

12.12-14 Are you going to repeat the life of your
  ancestor Jacob?
  He ran off guilty to Aram,
Then sold his soul to get ahead,
  and made it big through treachery and
  deceit.
Your real identity is formed through God-sent
  prophets,
  who led you out of Egypt and served as
  faithful pastors.
As it is, Ephraim has continually
  and inexcusably insulted God.
Now he has to pay for his life-destroying
  ways.
  His Master will do to him what *he* has
  done.

RELIGION CUSTOMIZED TO TASTE

13.1-3 **13** God once let loose against Ephraim
  a terrifying sentence against Israel:
Caught and convicted
  in the lewd sex-worship of Baal—they
  died!
And now they're back in the sin business
  again,
  manufacturing god-images they can use,
Religion customized to taste. Professionals see
  to it:
  Anything you want in a god you can get.
Can you believe it? They sacrifice live babies
  to these dead gods—
  kill living babies and kiss golden calves!
And now there's nothing left to these people:
  hollow men, desiccated women,
Like scraps of paper blown down the street,
  like smoke in a gusty wind.

ᵃ 9 Or *God / ever since you were in*   ᵇ 12 That is,
Northwest Mesopotamia   ᶜ 2 Or *"Men who sacrifice / kiss*

NEW INTERNATIONAL VERSION

4 "But I am the LORD your God,
   ₗwho brought youₗ out of ᵃ Egypt.
You shall acknowledge no God but me,
   no Savior except me.
5 I cared for you in the desert,
   in the land of burning heat.
6 When I fed them, they were satisfied;
   when they were satisfied, they became
      proud;
   then they forgot me.
7 So I will come upon them like a lion,
   like a leopard I will lurk by the path.
8 Like a bear robbed of her cubs,
   I will attack them and rip them open.
Like a lion I will devour them;
   a wild animal will tear them apart.

9 "You are destroyed, O Israel,
   because you are against me, against your
      helper.
10 Where is your king, that he may save you?
   Where are your rulers in all your towns,
of whom you said,
   'Give me a king and princes'?
11 So in my anger I gave you a king,
   and in my wrath I took him away.
12 The guilt of Ephraim is stored up,
   his sins are kept on record.
13 Pains as of a woman in childbirth come to
      him,
   but he is a child without wisdom;
when the time arrives,
   he does not come to the opening of the
      womb.

14 "I will ransom them from the power of the
      grave ᵇ;
   I will redeem them from death.
Where, O death, are your plagues?
   Where, O grave, ᵇ is your destruction?

"I will have no compassion,
15   even though he thrives among his
      brothers.
An east wind from the LORD will come,
   blowing in from the desert;
his spring will fail
   and his well dry up.
His storehouse will be plundered
   of all its treasures.
16 The people of Samaria must bear their guilt,
   because they have rebelled against their
      God.

ᵃ 4 Or God / ever since you were in   ᵇ 14 Hebrew Sheol

THE MESSAGE

13.4-6 "I'm still your GOD,
   the God who saved you out of Egypt.
I'm the only real God you've ever known.
I'm the one and only God who delivers.
I took care of you during the wilderness hard
      times,
   those years when you had nothing.
I took care of you, took care of all your needs,
   gave you everything you needed.
You were spoiled. You thought you didn't
      need me.
   You forgot me.

13.7-12 "I'll charge them like a lion,
   like a leopard stalking in the brush.
I'll jump them like a sow grizzly robbed of her
      cubs.
   I'll rip out their guts.
Coyotes will make a meal of them.
   Crows will clean their bones.
I'm going to destroy you, Israel.
   Who is going to stop me?
Where is your trusty king you thought would
      save you?
   Where are all the local leaders you wanted
      so badly?
All these rulers you insisted on having,
   demanding, 'Give me a king! Give me
      leaders!'?
Well, long ago I gave you a king, but I wasn't
      happy about it.
   Now, fed up, I've gotten rid of him.
I have a detailed record of your infidelities—
   Ephraim's sin documented and stored in a
      safe-deposit box.

13.13-15 "When birth pangs signaled it was time to be
      born,
   Ephraim was too stupid to come out of the
      womb.
When the passage into life opened up,
   he didn't show.
Shall I intervene and pull them into life?
   Shall I snatch them from a certain death?
Who is afraid of you, Death?
   Who cares about your threats, Tomb?
In the end I'm abolishing regret,
   banishing sorrow,
Even though Ephraim ran wild,
   the black sheep of the family.

13.15-16 "GOD's tornado is on its way,
   roaring out of the desert.
It will devastate the country,
   leaving a trail of ruin and wreckage.
The cities will be gutted,
   dear possessions gone for good.
Now Samaria has to face the charges
   because she has rebelled against her God:

NEW INTERNATIONAL VERSION

They will fall by the sword;
>their little ones will be dashed to the
>>ground,
>their pregnant women ripped open."

REPENTANCE TO BRING BLESSING

14 Return, O Israel, to the LORD your God.
Your sins have been your downfall!
² Take words with you
>and return to the LORD.
Say to him:
>"Forgive all our sins
>and receive us graciously,
>>that we may offer the fruit of our lips. *ᵃ*
³ Assyria cannot save us;
>we will not mount war-horses.
We will never again say 'Our gods'
>to what our own hands have made,
>for in you the fatherless find compassion."

⁴ "I will heal their waywardness
>and love them freely,
>for my anger has turned away from them.
⁵ I will be like the dew to Israel;
>he will blossom like a lily.
Like a cedar of Lebanon
>he will send down his roots;
⁶   his young shoots will grow.
His splendor will be like an olive tree,
>his fragrance like a cedar of Lebanon.
⁷ Men will dwell again in his shade.
>He will flourish like the grain.
He will blossom like a vine,
>and his fame will be like the wine from
>>Lebanon.
⁸ O Ephraim, what more have I *ᵇ* to do with
>>idols?
>I will answer him and care for him.
I am like a green pine tree;
>your fruitfulness comes from me."

⁹ Who is wise? He will realize these things.
>Who is discerning? He will understand
>>them.
The ways of the LORD are right;
>the righteous walk in them,
>but the rebellious stumble in them.

THE MESSAGE

Her people will be killed, babies smashed on
>>the rocks,
>pregnant women ripped open."

COME BACK! RETURN TO YOUR GOD!

14.1-3 **14** O Israel, come back! Return to your
GOD!
You're down but you're not out.
Prepare your confession
>and come back to GOD.
Pray to him, "Take away our sin,
>accept our confession.
Receive as restitution
>our repentant prayers.
Assyria won't save us;
>horses won't get us where we want to go.
We'll never again say 'our god'
>to something we've made or made up.
You're our last hope. Is it not true
>that in you the orphan finds mercy?"

14.4-8 "I will heal their waywardness.
>I will love them lavishly. My anger is played
>>out.
I will make a fresh start with Israel.
>He'll burst into bloom like a crocus in the
>>spring.
He'll put down deep oak tree roots,
>he'll become a forest of oaks!
He'll become splendid—like a giant sequoia,
>his fragrance like a grove of cedars!
Those who live near him will be blessed by
>>him,
>be blessed and prosper like golden grain.
Everyone will be talking about them,
>spreading their fame as the vintage children
>>of God.
Ephraim is finished with gods that are
>>no-gods.
>From now on I'm the one who answers and
>>satisfies him.
I am like a luxuriant fruit tree.
>Everything you need is to be found in me."

14.9 If you want to live well,
>make sure you understand all of this.
If you know what's good for you,
>you'll learn this inside and out.
GOD's paths get you where you want to go.
>Right-living people walk them easily;
>wrong-living people are always tripping
>>and stumbling.

ᵃ 2 Or offer our lips as sacrifices of bulls   *ᵇ 8 Or What more has Ephraim*

JOEL

JOEL

GET IN TOUCH WITH REALITY—AND WEEP!

1 The word of the LORD that came to Joel son of Pethuel.

AN INVASION OF LOCUSTS

² Hear this, you elders;
   listen, all who live in the land.
Has anything like this ever happened in your
      days
   or in the days of your forefathers?
³ Tell it to your children,
   and let your children tell it to their
      children,
   and their children to the next generation.
⁴ What the locust swarm has left
   the great locusts have eaten;
what the great locusts have left
   the young locusts have eaten;
what the young locusts have left
   other locusts*a* have eaten.

⁵ Wake up, you drunkards, and weep!
   Wail, all you drinkers of wine;
wail because of the new wine,
   for it has been snatched from your lips.
⁶ A nation has invaded my land,
   powerful and without number;
it has the teeth of a lion,
   the fangs of a lioness.
⁷ It has laid waste my vines
   and ruined my fig trees.
It has stripped off their bark
   and thrown it away,
   leaving their branches white.

⁸ Mourn like a virgin*b* in sackcloth
   grieving for the husband*c* of her youth.
⁹ Grain offerings and drink offerings
   are cut off from the house of the LORD.
The priests are in mourning,
   those who minister before the LORD.
¹⁰ The fields are ruined,
   the ground is dried up*d*;

1.1-3 **1** GOD's Message to Joel son of Pethuel:

Attention, elder statesmen! Listen closely,
   everyone, whoever and wherever you are!
Have you ever heard of anything like this?
   Has anything like this ever happened
      before—ever?
Make sure you tell your children,
   and your children tell their children,
And their children *their* children.
   Don't let this message die out.

1.4 What the chewing locust left,
   the gobbling locust ate;
What the gobbling locust left,
   the munching locust ate;
What the munching locust left,
   the chomping locust ate.

1.5-7 Sober up, you drunks!
   Get in touch with reality—and weep!
Your supply of booze is cut off.
   You're on the wagon, like it or not.
My country's being invaded
   by an army invincible, past numbering,
Teeth like those of a lion,
   fangs like those of a tiger.
It has ruined my vineyards,
   stripped my orchards,
And clear-cut the country.
   The landscape's a moonscape.

1.8-10 Weep like a young virgin dressed in black,
   mourning the loss of her fiancé.
Without grain and grapes,
   worship has been brought to a standstill
   in the Sanctuary of GOD.
The priests are at a loss.
   GOD's ministers don't know what to do.
The fields are sterile.
   The very ground grieves.

---

a 4 The precise meaning of the four Hebrew words used
here for locusts is uncertain.   *b 8* Or *young woman*
c 8 Or *betrothed*   *d 10* Or *ground mourns*

NEW INTERNATIONAL VERSION

the grain is destroyed,
    the new wine is dried up,
    the oil fails.
11 Despair, you farmers,
    wail, you vine growers;
grieve for the wheat and the barley,
    because the harvest of the field is
        destroyed.
12 The vine is dried up
    and the fig tree is withered;
the pomegranate, the palm and the apple
        tree—
    all the trees of the field—are dried up.
Surely the joy of mankind
    is withered away.

A CALL TO REPENTANCE

13 Put on sackcloth, O priests, and mourn;
    wail, you who minister before the altar.
Come, spend the night in sackcloth,
    you who minister before my God;
for the grain offerings and drink offerings
    are withheld from the house of your God.
14 Declare a holy fast;
    call a sacred assembly.
Summon the elders
    and all who live in the land
to the house of the LORD your God,
    and cry out to the LORD.

15 Alas for that day!
    For the day of the LORD is near;
    it will come like destruction from the
        Almighty. *a*

16 Has not the food been cut off
    before our very eyes—
joy and gladness
    from the house of our God?
17 The seeds are shriveled
    beneath the clods. *b*
The storehouses are in ruins,
    the granaries have been broken down,
    for the grain has dried up.
18 How the cattle moan!
    The herds mill about
because they have no pasture;
    even the flocks of sheep are suffering.

19 To you, O LORD, I call,
    for fire has devoured the open pastures
    and flames have burned up all the trees of
        the field.
20 Even the wild animals pant for you;
    the streams of water have dried up
    and fire has devoured the open pastures.

THE MESSAGE

The wheat fields are lifeless,
    vineyards dried up, olive oil gone.
1.11-12 Dirt farmers, despair!
    Grape growers, wring your hands!
Lament the loss of wheat and barley.
    All crops have failed.
Vineyards dried up,
    fig trees withered,
Pomegranates, date palms, and apple trees—
    deadwood everywhere!
And joy is dried up and withered
    in the hearts of the people.

NOTHING'S GOING ON IN THE PLACE OF WORSHIP

1.13-14 And also you priests,
    put on your robes and join the outcry.
You who lead people in worship,
    lead them in lament.
Spend the night dressed in gunnysacks,
    you servants of my God.
Nothing's going on in the place of worship,
    no offerings, no prayers—nothing.
Declare a holy fast, call a special meeting,
    get the leaders together,
Round up everyone in the country.
    Get them into GOD's Sanctuary for serious
        prayer to GOD.

1.15-18 What a day! Doomsday!
    GOD's Judgment Day has come.
The Strong God has arrived.
    This is serious business!
Food is just a memory at our tables,
    as are joy and singing from God's Sanctuary.
The seeds in the field are dead,
    barns deserted,
Grain silos abandoned.
    Who needs them? The crops have failed!
The farm animals groan—oh, how they groan!
    The cattle mill around.
There's nothing for them to eat.
    Not even the sheep find anything.

1.19-20 GOD! I pray, I cry out to you!
    The fields are burning up,
The country is a dust bowl,
    forest and prairie fires rage unchecked.
Wild animals, dying of thirst,
    look to you for a drink.
Springs and streams are dried up.
    The whole country is burning up.

---

a 15 Hebrew *Shaddai*   *b* 17 The meaning of the Hebrew for this word is uncertain.

NEW INTERNATIONAL VERSION

AN ARMY OF LOCUSTS

2 Blow the trumpet in Zion;
sound the alarm on my holy hill.
Let all who live in the land tremble,
for the day of the LORD is coming.
It is close at hand—
2 a day of darkness and gloom,
a day of clouds and blackness.
Like dawn spreading across the mountains
a large and mighty army comes,
such as never was of old
nor ever will be in ages to come.

3 Before them fire devours,
behind them a flame blazes.
Before them the land is like the garden of
Eden,
behind them, a desert waste—
nothing escapes them.
4 They have the appearance of horses;
they gallop along like cavalry.
5 With a noise like that of chariots
they leap over the mountaintops,
like a crackling fire consuming stubble,
like a mighty army drawn up for battle.

6 At the sight of them, nations are in anguish;
every face turns pale.
7 They charge like warriors;
they scale walls like soldiers.
They all march in line,
not swerving from their course.
8 They do not jostle each other;
each marches straight ahead.
They plunge through defenses
without breaking ranks.
9 They rush upon the city;
they run along the wall.
They climb into the houses;
like thieves they enter through the
windows.

10 Before them the earth shakes,
the sky trembles,
the sun and moon are darkened,
and the stars no longer shine.
11 The LORD thunders
at the head of his army;
his forces are beyond number,
and mighty are those who obey his
command.
The day of the LORD is great;
it is dreadful.
Who can endure it?

REND YOUR HEART

12 "Even now," declares the LORD,
"return to me with all your heart,

THE MESSAGE

THE LOCUST ARMY

2 Blow the ram's horn trumpet in Zion!
Trumpet the alarm on my holy mountain!
Shake the country up!
GOD's Judgment's on its way—the Day's
almost here!
A black day! A Doomsday!
Clouds with no silver lining!
Like dawn light moving over the mountains,
a huge army is coming.
There's never been anything like it
and never will be again.
Wildfire burns everything before this army
and fire licks up everything in its wake.
Before it arrives, the country is like the
Garden of Eden.
When it leaves, it is Death Valley.
Nothing escapes unscathed.

2.4-6 The locust army seems all horses—
galloping horses, an army of horses.
It sounds like thunder
leaping on mountain ridges,
Or like the roar of wildfire
through grass and brush,
Or like an invincible army shouting for blood,
ready to fight, straining at the bit.
At the sight of this army,
the people panic, faces white with terror.

2.7-11 The invaders charge.
They climb barricades. Nothing stops
them.
Each soldier does what he's told,
so disciplined, so determined.
They don't get in each other's way.
Each one knows his job and does it.
Undaunted and fearless,
unswerving, unstoppable.
They storm the city,
swarm its defenses,
Loot the houses,
breaking down doors, smashing windows.
They arrive like an earthquake,
sweep through like a tornado.
Sun and moon turn out their lights,
stars black out.
GOD himself bellows in thunder
as he commands his forces.
Look at the size of that army!
And the strength of those who obey him!
GOD's Judgment Day—great and terrible.
Who can possibly survive this?

CHANGE YOUR LIFE

2.12 But there's also this, it's not too late—
GOD's personal Message!—
"Come back to me and really mean it!

NEW INTERNATIONAL VERSION

with fasting and weeping and mourning."

13 Rend your heart
    and not your garments.
Return to the LORD your God,
    for he is gracious and compassionate,
    slow to anger and abounding in love,
    and he relents from sending calamity.
14 Who knows? He may turn and have pity
    and leave behind a blessing—
grain offerings and drink offerings
    for the LORD your God.

15 Blow the trumpet in Zion,
    declare a holy fast,
    call a sacred assembly.
16 Gather the people,
    consecrate the assembly;
bring together the elders,
    gather the children,
    those nursing at the breast.
Let the bridegroom leave his room
    and the bride her chamber.
17 Let the priests, who minister before the
    LORD,
    weep between the temple porch and the
    altar.
Let them say, "Spare your people, O LORD.
    Do not make your inheritance an object of
    scorn,
    a byword among the nations.
Why should they say among the peoples,
    'Where is their God?' "

THE LORD'S ANSWER

18 Then the LORD will be jealous for his land
    and take pity on his people.
19 The LORD will reply[a] to them:

"I am sending you grain, new wine and oil,
    enough to satisfy you fully;
never again will I make you
    an object of scorn to the nations.

20 "I will drive the northern army far from you,
    pushing it into a parched and barren land,
with its front columns going into the eastern
    sea[b]
    and those in the rear into the western
    sea.[c]
And its stench will go up;
    its smell will rise."

Surely he has done great things.[d]
21   Be not afraid, O land;
    be glad and rejoice.

a 18,19 Or LORD was jealous . . . / and took pity . . . / 19 The LORD
replied   b 20 That is, the Dead Sea   c 20 That is, the
Mediterranean   d 20 Or rise. / Surely it has done great things."

THE MESSAGE

Come fasting and weeping, sorry for your
    sins!"

2.13-14 Change your life, not just your clothes.
    Come back to GOD, your God.
And here's why: God is kind and merciful.
    He takes a deep breath, puts up with a lot,
This most patient God, extravagant in love,
    always ready to cancel catastrophe.
Who knows? Maybe he'll do it now,
    maybe he'll turn around and show pity.
Maybe, when all's said and done,
    there'll be blessings full and robust for your
    GOD!

✝

2.15-17 Blow the ram's horn trumpet in Zion!
    Declare a day of repentance, a holy fast day.
Call a public meeting.
    Get everyone there. Consecrate the
    congregation.
Make sure the elders come,
    but bring in the children, too, even the
    nursing babies,
Even men and women on their honeymoon—
    interrupt them and get them there.
Between Sanctuary entrance and altar,
    let the priests, GOD's servants, weep tears of
    repentance.
Let them intercede: "Have mercy, GOD, on
    your people!
Don't abandon your heritage to contempt.
Don't let the pagans take over and rule them
    and sneer, 'And so where is this God of
    theirs?' "

✝

2.18-20 At that, GOD went into action to get his land
    back.
    He took pity on his people.
GOD answered and spoke to his people,
    "Look, listen—I'm sending a gift:
Grain and wine and olive oil.
    The fast is over—eat your fill!
I won't expose you any longer
    to contempt among the pagans.
I'll head off the final enemy coming out of the
    north
    and dump them in a wasteland.
Half of them will end up in the Dead Sea,
    the other half in the Mediterranean.
There they'll rot, a stench to high heaven.
    The bigger the enemy, the stronger the
    stench!"

THE TREES ARE BEARING FRUIT AGAIN

2.21-24 Fear not, earth! Be glad and celebrate!

NEW INTERNATIONAL VERSION

Surely the LORD has done great things.
22 Be not afraid, O wild animals,
for the open pastures are becoming green.
The trees are bearing their fruit;
the fig tree and the vine yield their riches.
23 Be glad, O people of Zion,
rejoice in the LORD your God,
for he has given you
the autumn rains in righteousness. *a*
He sends you abundant showers,
both autumn and spring rains, as before.
24 The threshing floors will be filled with grain;
the vats will overflow with new wine and
oil.

25 "I will repay you for the years the locusts
have eaten—
the great locust and the young locust,
the other locusts and the locust swarm *b*—
my great army that I sent among you.
26 You will have plenty to eat, until you are full,
and you will praise the name of the LORD
your God,
who has worked wonders for you;
never again will my people be shamed.
27 Then you will know that I am in Israel,
that I am the LORD your God,
and that there is no other;
never again will my people be shamed.

THE DAY OF THE LORD
28 "And afterward,
I will pour out my Spirit on all people.
Your sons and daughters will prophesy,
your old men will dream dreams,
your young men will see visions.
29 Even on my servants, both men and women,
I will pour out my Spirit in those days.
30 I will show wonders in the heavens
and on the earth,
blood and fire and billows of smoke.
31 The sun will be turned to darkness
and the moon to blood
before the coming of the great and
dreadful day of the LORD.
32 And everyone who calls
on the name of the LORD will be saved;
for on Mount Zion and in Jerusalem

THE MESSAGE

GOD has done great things.
Fear not, wild animals!
The fields and meadows are greening up.
The trees are bearing fruit again:
a bumper crop of fig trees and vines!
Children of Zion, celebrate!
Be glad in your GOD.
He's giving you a teacher
to train you how to live right—
Teaching, like rain out of heaven, showers of
words
to refresh and nourish your soul, just as he
used to do.
And plenty of food for your body—silos full
of grain,
casks of wine and barrels of olive oil.

✝

2.25-27 "I'll make up for the years of the locust,
the great locust devastation—
Locusts savage, locusts deadly,
fierce locusts, locusts of doom,
That great locust invasion
I sent your way.
You'll eat your fill of good food.
You'll be full of praises to your GOD,
The God who has set you back on your heels
in wonder.
Never again will my people be despised.
You'll know without question
that I'm in the thick of life with Israel,
That I'm your GOD, yes, *your* GOD,
the one and only real God.
Never again will my people be despised.

THE SUN TURNING BLACK AND THE MOON BLOOD-RED
2.28-32 "And that's just the beginning: After that—

"I will pour out my Spirit
on every kind of people:
Your sons will prophesy,
also your daughters.
Your old men will dream,
your young men will see visions.
I'll even pour out my Spirit on the servants,
men and women both.
I'll set wonders in the sky above
and signs on the earth below:
Blood and fire and billowing smoke,
the sun turning black and the moon blood-
red,
Before the Judgment Day of GOD,
the Day tremendous and awesome.
Whoever calls, 'Help, GOD!'
gets help.
On Mount Zion and in Jerusalem

---

a 23 Or / *the teacher for righteousness:* *b 25* The precise
meaning of the four Hebrew words used here for locusts is
uncertain.

NEW INTERNATIONAL VERSION

there will be deliverance,
as the LORD has said,
among the survivors
whom the LORD calls.

THE NATIONS JUDGED

3 "In those days and at that time,
when I restore the fortunes of Judah and
Jerusalem,
²I will gather all nations
and bring them down to the Valley of
Jehoshaphat.ᵃ
There I will enter into judgment against
them
concerning my inheritance, my people
Israel,
for they scattered my people among the
nations
and divided up my land.
³They cast lots for my people
and traded boys for prostitutes;
they sold girls for wine
that they might drink.

⁴"Now what have you against me, O Tyre and
Sidon and all you regions of Philistia? Are you
repaying me for something I have done? If you
are paying me back, I will swiftly and speedily
return on your own heads what you have done.
⁵For you took my silver and my gold and carried
off my finest treasures to your temples. ⁶You sold
the people of Judah and Jerusalem to the Greeks,
that you might send them far from their homeland.

⁷"See, I am going to rouse them out of the
places to which you sold them, and I will return
on your own heads what you have done. ⁸I will
sell your sons and daughters to the people of Judah, and they will sell them to the Sabeans, a
nation far away." The LORD has spoken.

⁹Proclaim this among the nations:
Prepare for war!
Rouse the warriors!
Let all the fighting men draw near and
attack.
¹⁰Beat your plowshares into swords
and your pruning hooks into spears.
Let the weakling say,
"I am strong!"

THE MESSAGE

there will be a great rescue—just as GOD
said.
Included in the survivors
are those that GOD calls.

GOD IS A SAFE HIDING PLACE

3.1-3 **3** "In those days, yes, at that very time
when I put life back together again for Judah and Jerusalem,
I'll assemble all the godless nations.
I'll lead them down into Judgment Valley
And put them all on trial, and judge them one
and all
because of their treatment of my own
people Israel.
They scattered my people all over the pagan
world
and grabbed my land for themselves.
They threw dice for my people
and used them for barter.
They would trade a boy for a whore,
sell a girl for a bottle of wine when they
wanted a drink.

✝

3.4-8 "As for you, Tyre and Sidon and Philistia,
why should I bother with you?
Are you trying to get back at me
for something I did to you?
If you are, forget it.
I'll see to it that it boomerangs on you.
You robbed me, cleaned me out of silver and
gold,
carted off everything valuable to furnish
your own temples.
You sold the people of Judah and Jerusalem
into slavery to the Greeks in faraway
places.
But I'm going to reverse your crime.
I'm going to free those slaves.
I'll have done to you what you did to them:
I'll sell your children as slaves to your
neighbors,
And they'll sell them to the far-off Sabeans."
GOD's Verdict.

✝

3.9-11 Announce this to the godless nations:
Prepare for battle!
Soldiers at attention!
Present arms! Advance!
Turn your shovels into swords,
turn your hoes into spears.
Let the weak one throw out his chest
and say, "I'm tough, I'm a fighter."

ᵃ 2 *Jehoshaphat* means *the* LORD *judges*; also in verse 12.

NEW INTERNATIONAL VERSION

¹¹Come quickly, all you nations from every
side,
and assemble there.

Bring down your warriors, O LORD!

¹²"Let the nations be roused;
let them advance into the Valley of
Jehoshaphat,
for there I will sit
to judge all the nations on every side.
¹³Swing the sickle,
for the harvest is ripe.
Come, trample the grapes,
for the winepress is full
and the vats overflow—
so great is their wickedness!"

¹⁴Multitudes, multitudes
in the valley of decision!
For the day of the LORD is near
in the valley of decision.
¹⁵The sun and moon will be darkened,
and the stars no longer shine.
¹⁶The LORD will roar from Zion
and thunder from Jerusalem;
the earth and the sky will tremble.
But the LORD will be a refuge for his people,
a stronghold for the people of Israel.

BLESSINGS FOR GOD'S PEOPLE

¹⁷"Then you will know that I, the LORD your
God,
dwell in Zion, my holy hill.
Jerusalem will be holy;
never again will foreigners invade her.

¹⁸"In that day the mountains will drip new
wine,
and the hills will flow with milk;
all the ravines of Judah will run with
water.
A fountain will flow out of the LORD's house
and will water the valley of acacias. ^a
¹⁹But Egypt will be desolate,
Edom a desert waste,
because of violence done to the people of
Judah,
in whose land they shed innocent blood.
²⁰Judah will be inhabited forever
and Jerusalem through all generations.
²¹Their bloodguilt, which I have not pardoned,
I will pardon."

The LORD dwells in Zion!

THE MESSAGE

Hurry up, pagans! Wherever you are, get a
move on!
Get your act together.
Prepare to be
shattered by GOD!

^{3.12} Let the pagan nations set out
for Judgment Valley.
There I'll take my place at the bench
and judge all the surrounding nations.

^{3.13} "Swing the sickle—
the harvest is ready.
Stomp on the grapes—
the winepress is full.
The wine vats are full,
overflowing with vintage evil.

^{3.14} "Mass confusion, mob uproar—
in Decision Valley!
GOD's Judgment Day has arrived
in Decision Valley.

^{3.15-17} "The sky turns black,
sun and moon go dark, stars burn out.
GOD roars from Zion, shouts from Jerusalem.
Earth and sky quake in terror.
But GOD is a safe hiding place,
a granite safe house for the children of
Israel.
Then you'll know for sure
that I'm *your* GOD,
Living in Zion,
my sacred mountain.
Jerusalem will be a sacred city,
posted: 'NO TRESPASSING.'

MILK RIVERING OUT OF THE HILLS

^{3.18-21} "What a day!
Wine streaming off the mountains,
Milk rivering out of the hills,
water flowing everywhere in Judah,
A fountain pouring out of GOD's Sanctuary,
watering all the parks and gardens!
But Egypt will be reduced to weeds in a vacant
lot,
Edom turned into barren badlands,
All because of brutalities to the Judean people,
the atrocities and murders of helpless
innocents.
Meanwhile, Judah will be filled with people,
Jerusalem inhabited forever.
The sins I haven't already forgiven, I'll
forgive."
GOD has moved into Zion for good.

^a 18 Or *Valley of Shittim*

AMOS

AMOS

1 The words of Amos, one of the shepherds of Tekoa—what he saw concerning Israel two years before the earthquake, when Uzziah was king of Judah and Jeroboam son of Jehoash[a] was king of Israel.

2He said:

"The LORD roars from Zion
   and thunders from Jerusalem;
the pastures of the shepherds dry up,[b]
   and the top of Carmel withers."

JUDGMENT ON ISRAEL'S NEIGHBORS

3This is what the LORD says:

"For three sins of Damascus,
   even for four, I will not turn back ⌞my
      wrath⌟.
Because she threshed Gilead
   with sledges having iron teeth,
4I will send fire upon the house of Hazael
   that will consume the fortresses of Ben-
      Hadad.
5I will break down the gate of Damascus;
   I will destroy the king who is in[c] the
      Valley of Aven[d]
and the one who holds the scepter in Beth
      Eden.
The people of Aram will go into exile to
      Kir,"
                      says the LORD.

6This is what the LORD says:

"For three sins of Gaza,
   even for four, I will not turn back ⌞my
      wrath⌟.
Because she took captive whole communities
   and sold them to Edom,
7I will send fire upon the walls of Gaza
   that will consume her fortresses.
8I will destroy the king[e] of Ashdod
   and the one who holds the scepter in
      Ashkelon.
I will turn my hand against Ekron,

1.1 1 The Message of Amos, one of the shepherds of Tekoa, that he received on behalf of Israel. It came to him in visions during the time that Uzziah was king of Judah and Jeroboam II son of Joash was king of Israel, two years before the big earthquake.

SWALLOWING THE SAME OLD LIES

1.2 The Message:

GOD roars from Zion,
   shouts from Jerusalem!
The thunderclap voice withers the pastures
      tended by shepherds,
   shrivels Mount Carmel's proud peak.

1.3-5 GOD'S Message:

"Because of the three great sins of Damascus
   —make that four—I'm not putting up with
      her any longer.
She pounded Gilead to a pulp, pounded her
      senseless
   with iron hammers and mauls.
For that, I'm setting the palace of Hazael on
      fire.
   I'm torching Ben-hadad's forts.
I'm going to smash the Damascus gates
   and banish the crime king who lives in Sin
      Valley,
   the vice boss who gives orders from
      Paradise Palace.
The people of the land will be sent back
   to where they came from—to Kir."
      GOD'S Decree.

1.6-8 GOD'S Message:

"Because of the three great sins of Gaza
   —make that four—I'm not putting up with
      her any longer.
She deported whole towns
   and then sold the people to Edom.
For that, I'm burning down the walls of Gaza,
   burning up all her forts.
I'll banish the crime king from Ashdod,
   the vice boss from Ashkelon.
I'll raise my fist against Ekron,

---

a 1 Hebrew *Joash*, a variant of *Jehoash*   b 2 Or *shepherds mourn*   c 5 Or *the inhabitants of*   d 5 *Aven* means *wickedness.*   e 8 Or *inhabitants*

NEW INTERNATIONAL VERSION

till the last of the Philistines is dead,"
　　　　says the Sovereign LORD.

⁹This is what the LORD says:

"For three sins of Tyre,
　　even for four, I will not turn back ⌐my
　　　　wrath⌐.
Because she sold whole communities of
　　captives to Edom,
　　disregarding a treaty of brotherhood,
¹⁰I will send fire upon the walls of Tyre
　　that will consume her fortresses."

¹¹This is what the LORD says:

"For three sins of Edom,
　　even for four, I will not turn back ⌐my
　　　　wrath⌐.
Because he pursued his brother with a
　　sword,
　　stifling all compassion,ᵃ
because his anger raged continually
　　and his fury flamed unchecked,
¹²I will send fire upon Teman
　　that will consume the fortresses of
　　　　Bozrah."

¹³This is what the LORD says:

"For three sins of Ammon,
　　even for four, I will not turn back ⌐my
　　　　wrath⌐.
Because he ripped open the pregnant women
　　of Gilead
　　in order to extend his borders,
¹⁴I will set fire to the walls of Rabbah
　　that will consume her fortresses
amid war cries on the day of battle,
　　amid violent winds on a stormy day.
¹⁵Her kingᵇ will go into exile,
　　he and his officials together,"
　　　　says the LORD.

2 This is what the LORD says:

"For three sins of Moab,
　　even for four, I will not turn back ⌐my
　　　　wrath⌐.
Because he burned, as if to lime,
　　the bones of Edom's king,
²I will send fire upon Moab
　　that will consume the fortresses of
　　　　Kerioth.ᶜ
Moab will go down in great tumult
　　amid war cries and the blast of the
　　　　trumpet.

ᵃ 11 Or sword / and destroyed his allies　　ᵇ 15 Or / Molech;
Hebrew malcam　　ᶜ 2 Or of her cities

THE MESSAGE

and what's left of the Philistines will die."
　　GOD's Decree.

1.9-10　　GOD's Message:

"Because of the three great sins of Tyre
　　—make that four—I'm not putting up with
　　　　her any longer.
She deported whole towns to Edom,
　　breaking the treaty she had with her kin.
For that, I'm burning down the walls of Tyre,
　　burning up all her forts."

1.11-12　　GOD's Message:

"Because of the three great sins of Edom
　　—make that four—I'm not putting up with
　　　　her any longer.
She hunts down her brother to murder him.
　　She has no pity, she has no heart.
Her anger rampages day and night.
　　Her meanness never takes a timeout.
For that, I'm burning down her capital,
　　　　Teman,
　　burning up the forts of Bozrah."

1.13-15　　GOD's Message:

"Because of the three great sins of Ammon
　　—make that four—I'm not putting up with
　　　　her any longer.
She ripped open pregnant women in Gilead
　　to get more land for herself.
For that, I'm burning down the walls of her
　　　　capital, Rabbah,
　　burning up her forts.
Battle shouts! War whoops!
　　with a tornado to finish things off!
The king has been carted off to exile,
　　the king and his princes with him."
　　　　GOD's Decree.

✠

2.1-3　　**2** GOD's Message:

"Because of the three great sins of Moab
　　—make that four—I'm not putting up with
　　　　her any longer.
She violated the corpse of Edom's king,
　　burning it to cinders.
For that, I'm burning down Moab,
　　burning down the forts of Kerioth.
Moab will die in the shouting,
　　go out in the blare of war trumpets.

NEW INTERNATIONAL VERSION

³ I will destroy her ruler
and kill all her officials with him,"
                        says the LORD.

⁴ This is what the LORD says:

"For three sins of Judah,
    even for four, I will not turn back ⌊my
        wrath⌋.
Because they have rejected the law of the
        LORD
    and have not kept his decrees,
because they have been led astray by false
        gods, ^a
    the gods ^b their ancestors followed,
⁵ I will send fire upon Judah
    that will consume the fortresses of
        Jerusalem."

JUDGMENT ON ISRAEL
⁶ This is what the LORD says:

"For three sins of Israel,
    even for four, I will not turn back ⌊my
        wrath⌋.
They sell the righteous for silver,
    and the needy for a pair of sandals.
⁷ They trample on the heads of the poor
    as upon the dust of the ground
    and deny justice to the oppressed.
Father and son use the same girl
    and so profane my holy name.
⁸ They lie down beside every altar
    on garments taken in pledge.
In the house of their god
    they drink wine taken as fines.

⁹ "I destroyed the Amorite before them,
    though he was tall as the cedars
    and strong as the oaks.
I destroyed his fruit above
    and his roots below.

¹⁰ "I brought you up out of Egypt,
    and I led you forty years in the desert
    to give you the land of the Amorites.
¹¹ I also raised up prophets from among your
        sons
    and Nazirites from among your young
        men.
Is this not true, people of Israel?"
                        declares the LORD.

^a 4 Or *by lies*   ^b 4 Or *lies*

THE MESSAGE

I'll remove the king from the center
    and kill all his princes with him."
        GOD'S Decree.

2.4-5   GOD'S Message:

"Because of the three great sins of Judah
    —make that four—I'm not putting up with
        them any longer.
They rejected GOD'S revelation,
    refused to keep my commands.
But they swallowed the same old lies
    that got their ancestors onto dead-end
        roads.
For that, I'm burning down Judah,
    burning down all the forts of Jerusalem."

DESTROYED FROM THE ROOTS UP
GOD'S Message:

2.6-8   "Because of the three great sins of Israel
    —make that four—I'm not putting up with
        them any longer.
They buy and sell upstanding people.
    People for them are only *things*—ways of
        making money.
They'd sell a poor man for a pair of shoes.
    They'd sell their own grandmother!
They grind the penniless into the dirt,
    shove the luckless into the ditch.
Everyone and his brother sleeps with the
        'sacred whore'—
    a sacrilege against my Holy Name.
Stuff they've extorted from the poor
    is piled up at the shrine of their god,
While they sit around drinking wine
    they've conned from their victims.

2.9-11   "In contrast, I was always on your side.
    I destroyed the Amorites who confronted
        you,
Amorites with the stature of great cedars,
    tough as thick oaks.
I destroyed them from the top branches down.
    I destroyed them from the roots up.
And yes, I'm the One who delivered you from
        Egypt,
    led you safely through the wilderness for
        forty years
And then handed you the country of the
        Amorites
    like a piece of cake on a platter.
I raised up some of your young men to be
        prophets,
    set aside your best youth for training in
        holiness.
Isn't this so, Israel?"
        GOD'S Decree.

NEW INTERNATIONAL VERSION

12 "But you made the Nazirites drink wine
   and commanded the prophets not to
     prophesy.

13 "Now then, I will crush you
   as a cart crushes when loaded with grain.
14 The swift will not escape,
   the strong will not muster their strength,
   and the warrior will not save his life.
15 The archer will not stand his ground,
   the fleet-footed soldier will not get away,
   and the horseman will not save his life.
16 Even the bravest warriors
   will flee naked on that day,"
                     declares the LORD.

WITNESSES SUMMONED AGAINST ISRAEL

3 Hear this word the LORD has spoken against
   you, O people of Israel—against the whole
family I brought up out of Egypt:

2 "You only have I chosen
   of all the families of the earth;
   therefore I will punish you
   for all your sins."

3 Do two walk together
   unless they have agreed to do so?
4 Does a lion roar in the thicket
   when he has no prey?
Does he growl in his den
   when he has caught nothing?
5 Does a bird fall into a trap on the ground
   where no snare has been set?
Does a trap spring up from the earth
   when there is nothing to catch?
6 When a trumpet sounds in a city,
   do not the people tremble?
When disaster comes to a city,
   has not the LORD caused it?

7 Surely the Sovereign LORD does nothing
   without revealing his plan
   to his servants the prophets.

8 The lion has roared—
   who will not fear?
The Sovereign LORD has spoken—
   who can but prophesy?

9 Proclaim to the fortresses of Ashdod
   and to the fortresses of Egypt:

THE MESSAGE

2.12-13 "But you made the youth-in-training break
     training,
   and you told the young prophets, 'Don't
     prophesy!'
You're too much for me.
   I'm hard-pressed—to the breaking point.
I'm like a wagon piled high and overloaded,
   creaking and groaning.

2.14-15 "When I go into action, what will you do?
   There's no place to run no matter how fast
     you run.
The strength of the strong won't count.
   Fighters won't make it.
Skilled archers won't make it.
   Fast runners won't make it.
Chariot drivers won't make it.
   Even the bravest of all your warriors
Won't make it.
   He'll run off for dear life, stripped naked."
     GOD's Decree.

THE LION HAS ROARED

3.1 3 Listen to this, Israel. GOD is calling you to
     account—and I mean all of you, everyone
connected with the family that he delivered out
of Egypt. Listen!

3.2 "Out of all the families on earth,
   I picked you.
Therefore, because of your special calling,
   I'm holding you responsible for all your sins."

3.3-7 Do two people walk hand in hand
   if they aren't going to the same place?
Does a lion roar in the forest
   if there's no carcass to devour?
Does a young lion growl with pleasure
   if he hasn't caught his supper?
Does a bird fall to the ground
   if it hasn't been hit with a stone?
Does a trap spring shut
   if nothing trips it?
When the alarm goes off in the city,
   aren't people alarmed?
And when disaster strikes the city,
   doesn't GOD stand behind it?
The fact is, GOD, the Master, does nothing
   without first telling his prophets the whole
     story.

3.8 The lion has roared—
   who isn't frightened?
GOD has spoken—
   what prophet can keep quiet?

✝

3.9-11 Announce to the forts of Assyria,
   announce to the forts of Egypt—

NEW INTERNATIONAL VERSION

"Assemble yourselves on the mountains of
    Samaria;
    see the great unrest within her
    and the oppression among her people."

10 "They do not know how to do right,"
    declares the LORD,
    "who hoard plunder and loot in their
        fortresses."

11 Therefore this is what the Sovereign LORD
says:

"An enemy will overrun the land;
    he will pull down your strongholds
    and plunder your fortresses."

12 This is what the LORD says:

"As a shepherd saves from the lion's mouth
    only two leg bones or a piece of an ear,
    so will the Israelites be saved,
those who sit in Samaria
    on the edge of their beds
    and in Damascus on their couches. *a*"

13 "Hear this and testify against the house of
Jacob," declares the Lord, the LORD God Almighty.

14 "On the day I punish Israel for her sins,
    I will destroy the altars of Bethel;
the horns of the altar will be cut off
    and fall to the ground.
15 I will tear down the winter house
    along with the summer house;
the houses adorned with ivory will be
        destroyed
    and the mansions will be demolished,"
        declares the LORD.

ISRAEL HAS NOT RETURNED TO GOD

4 Hear this word, you cows of Bashan on
    Mount Samaria,
    you women who oppress the poor and
        crush the needy
    and say to your husbands, "Bring us some
        drinks!"
2 The Sovereign LORD has sworn by his
        holiness:
"The time will surely come
when you will be taken away with hooks,
    the last of you with fishhooks.
3 You will each go straight out
    through breaks in the wall,
    and you will be cast out toward
        Harmon, *b*"
        declares the LORD.

a 12 The meaning of the Hebrew for this line is uncertain.
b 3 Masoretic Text; with a different word division of the
Hebrew (see Septuagint) out, O mountain of oppression

THE MESSAGE

Tell them, "Gather on the Samaritan
        mountains, take a good, hard look:
    what a snake pit of brutality and terror!
They can't—or won't—do one thing right."
    GOD said so.
"They stockpile violence and blight.
Therefore"—this is GOD's Word—"an enemy
        will surround the country.
He'll strip you of your power and plunder
        your forts."

3.12   GOD's Message:

"In the same way that a shepherd
    trying to save a lamb from a lion
Manages to recover
    just a pair of legs or the scrap of an ear,
So will little be saved of the Israelites
    who live in Samaria—
A couple of old chairs at most,
    the broken leg of a table.

3.13-15 "Listen and bring witness against Jacob's
        family"—
    this is God's Word, GOD-of-the-Angel-
        Armies!
"Note well! The day I make Israel pay for its
        sins,
    pay for the sin-altars of worship at Bethel,
The horned altars will all be dehorned
    and scattered around.
I'll tear down the winter palace,
    smash the summer palace—all your fancy
        buildings.
The luxury homes will be demolished,
    all those pretentious houses."
        GOD's Decree.

YOU NEVER GOT HUNGRY FOR GOD

4.1 4 "Listen to this, you cows of Bashan
    grazing on the slopes of Samaria.
You women! Mean to the poor,
    cruel to the down-and-out!
Indolent and pampered, you demand of your
        husbands,
    'Bring us a tall, cool drink!'

4.2-3 "This is serious—I, GOD, have sworn by my
        holiness!
    Be well warned: Judgment Day is coming!
They're going to rope you up and haul you
        off,
    keep the stragglers in line with cattle prods.
They'll drag you through the ruined city walls,
    forcing you out single file,
And kick you to kingdom come."
        GOD's Decree.

NEW INTERNATIONAL VERSION	THE MESSAGE

NEW INTERNATIONAL VERSION

4 "Go to Bethel and sin;
  go to Gilgal and sin yet more.
Bring your sacrifices every morning,
  your tithes every three years. *a*
5 Burn leavened bread as a thank offering
  and brag about your freewill offerings—
boast about them, you Israelites,
  for this is what you love to do,"
            declares the Sovereign
                          LORD.

6 "I gave you empty stomachs *b* in every city
  and lack of bread in every town,
  yet you have not returned to me,"
            declares the LORD.

7 "I also withheld rain from you
  when the harvest was still three months
    away.
I sent rain on one town,
  but withheld it from another.
One field had rain;
  another had none and dried up.
8 People staggered from town to town for
    water
  but did not get enough to drink,
  yet you have not returned to me,"
            declares the LORD.

9 "Many times I struck your gardens and
    vineyards,
  I struck them with blight and mildew.
Locusts devoured your fig and olive trees,
  yet you have not returned to me,"
            declares the LORD.

10 "I sent plagues among you
  as I did to Egypt.
I killed your young men with the sword,
  along with your captured horses.
I filled your nostrils with the stench of your
    camps,
  yet you have not returned to me,"
            declares the LORD.

11 "I overthrew some of you
  as I *c* overthrew Sodom and Gomorrah.
You were like a burning stick snatched from
    the fire,
  yet you have not returned to me,"
            declares the LORD.

12 "Therefore this is what I will do to you,
    Israel,

THE MESSAGE

4.4-5 "Come along to Bethel and sin!
  And then to Gilgal and sin some more!
Bring your sacrifices for morning worship.
  Every third day bring your tithe.
Burn pure sacrifices—thank offerings.
  Speak up—announce freewill offerings!
That's the sort of religious show
  you Israelites just love."
            GOD's Decree.

4.6 "You know, don't you, that I'm the One
  who emptied your pantries and cleaned out
      your cupboards,
Who left you hungry and standing in bread
      lines?
  But you never got hungry for me. You
      continued to ignore me."
            GOD's Decree.

4.7-8 "Yes, and I'm the One who stopped the rains
  three months short of harvest.
I'd make it rain on one village
  but not on another.
I'd make it rain on one field
  but not on another—and that one would
      dry up.
People would stagger from village to village
  crazed for water and never quenching their
      thirst.
But you never got thirsty for me.
  You ignored me."
            GOD's Decree.

4.9 "I hit your crops with disease
  and withered your orchards and gardens.
Locusts devoured your olive and fig trees,
  but you continued to ignore me."
            GOD's Decree.

4.10 "I revisited you with the old Egyptian plagues,
  killed your choice young men and prize
      horses.
The stink of rot in your camps was so strong
  that you held your noses—
But you didn't notice me.
  You continued to ignore me."
            GOD's Decree.

4.11 "I hit you with earthquake and fire,
  left you devastated like Sodom and
      Gomorrah.
You were like a burning stick
  snatched from the flames.
But you never looked my way.
  You continued to ignore me."
            GOD's Decree.

4.12 "All this I have done to you, Israel,
  and this is why I have done it.

---

*a 4 Or tithes on the third day   b 6 Hebrew you cleanness of
teeth   c 11 Hebrew God*

NEW INTERNATIONAL VERSION

and because I will do this to you,
prepare to meet your God, O Israel."

¹³He who forms the mountains,
creates the wind,
and reveals his thoughts to man,
he who turns dawn to darkness,
and treads the high places of the earth—
the LORD God Almighty is his name.

A LAMENT AND CALL TO REPENTANCE

5 Hear this word, O house of Israel, this lament I take up concerning you:

² "Fallen is Virgin Israel,
never to rise again,
deserted in her own land,
with no one to lift her up."

³This is what the Sovereign LORD says:

"The city that marches out a thousand strong
for Israel
will have only a hundred left;
the town that marches out a hundred strong
will have only ten left."

⁴This is what the LORD says to the house of Israel:

"Seek me and live;
⁵ do not seek Bethel,
do not go to Gilgal,
do not journey to Beersheba.
For Gilgal will surely go into exile,
and Bethel will be reduced to nothing. ᵃ"
⁶Seek the LORD and live,
or he will sweep through the house of
Joseph like a fire;
it will devour,
and Bethel will have no one to quench it.

⁷You who turn justice into bitterness
and cast righteousness to the ground
⁸(he who made the Pleiades and Orion,
who turns blackness into dawn
and darkens day into night,
who calls for the waters of the sea
and pours them out over the face of the
land—
the LORD is his name—
⁹he flashes destruction on the stronghold
and brings the fortified city to ruin),

THE MESSAGE

Time's up, O Israel!
Prepare to meet your God!"

4.13 Look who's here: Mountain-Shaper!
Wind-Maker!
He laid out the whole plot before Adam.
He brings everything out of nothing,
like dawn out of darkness.
He strides across the alpine ridges.
His name is GOD, God-of-the-Angel-
Armies.

ALL SHOW, NO SUBSTANCE

5.1 **5** Listen to this, family of Israel,
this Message I'm sending in bold print, this
tragic warning:

5.2 "Virgin Israel has fallen flat on her face.
She'll never stand up again.
She's been left where she's fallen.
No one offers to help her up."

5.3 This is the Message, GOD's Word:

"The city that marches out with a thousand
will end up with a hundred.
The city that marches out with a hundred
will end up with ten. Oh, family of Israel!"

5.4-5 GOD's Message to the family of Israel:

"Seek me and live.
Don't fool around at those shrines of
Bethel,
Don't waste time taking trips to Gilgal,
and don't bother going down to Beer-sheba.
Gilgal is here today and gone tomorrow
and Bethel is all show, no substance."

5.6 So seek GOD and live! You don't want to end
up
with nothing to show for your life
But a pile of ashes, a house burned to the
ground.
For God will send just such a fire,
and the firefighters will show up too late.

RAW TRUTH IS NEVER POPULAR

5.7-9 Woe to you who turn justice to vinegar
and stomp righteousness into the mud.
Do you realize where you are? You're in a
cosmos
star-flung with constellations by God,
A world God wakes up each morning
and puts to bed each night.
God dips water from the ocean
and gives the land a drink.
GOD, God-revealed, does all this.
And he can destroy it as easily as make it.
He can turn this vast wonder into total
waste.

ᵃ 5 Or *grief*; or *wickedness*; Hebrew *aven*, a reference to Beth
Aven (a derogatory name for Bethel)

NEW INTERNATIONAL VERSION

¹⁰you hate the one who reproves in court
   and despise him who tells the truth.

¹¹You trample on the poor
   and force him to give you grain.
Therefore, though you have built stone
      mansions,
   you will not live in them;
though you have planted lush vineyards,
   you will not drink their wine.
¹²For I know how many are your offenses
   and how great your sins.

You oppress the righteous and take bribes
   and you deprive the poor of justice in the
      courts.
¹³Therefore the prudent man keeps quiet in
      such times,
   for the times are evil.

¹⁴Seek good, not evil,
   that you may live.
Then the LORD God Almighty will be with
      you,
   just as you say he is.
¹⁵Hate evil, love good;
   maintain justice in the courts.
Perhaps the LORD God Almighty will have
      mercy
   on the remnant of Joseph.

¹⁶Therefore this is what the Lord, the LORD
God Almighty, says:

"There will be wailing in all the streets
   and cries of anguish in every public
      square.
The farmers will be summoned to weep
   and the mourners to wail.
¹⁷There will be wailing in all the vineyards,
   for I will pass through your midst,"
                              says the LORD.

THE DAY OF THE LORD
¹⁸Woe to you who long
   for the day of the LORD!
Why do you long for the day of the LORD?
   That day will be darkness, not light.
¹⁹It will be as though a man fled from a lion
   only to meet a bear,
as though he entered his house
   and rested his hand on the wall
   only to have a snake bite him.

THE MESSAGE

5.10-12 People hate this kind of talk.
   Raw truth is never popular.
But here it is, bluntly spoken:
   Because you run roughshod over the poor
      and take the bread right out of their
         mouths,
You're never going to move into
   the luxury homes you have built.
You're never going to drink wine
   from the expensive vineyards you've
      planted.
I know precisely the extent of your violations,
   the enormity of your sins. Appalling!
You bully right-living people,
   taking bribes right and left and kicking the
      poor when they're down.

5.13 Justice is a lost cause. Evil is epidemic.
   Decent people throw up their hands.
Protest and rebuke are useless,
   a waste of breath.

5.14 Seek good and not evil—
   and live!
You talk about GOD, the God-of-the-Angel-
      Armies,
   being your best friend.
Well, *live* like it,
   and maybe it will happen.

5.15 Hate evil and love good,
   then work it out in the public square.
Maybe GOD, the God-of-the-Angel-Armies,
   will notice your remnant and be gracious.

5.16-17   Now again, my Master's Message, GOD, God-
of-the-Angel-Armies:

"Go out into the streets and lament loudly!
   Fill the malls and shops with cries of
      doom!
Weep loudly, 'Not me! Not us, Not now!'
   Empty offices, stores, factories, workplaces.
Enlist everyone in the general lament.
   I want to hear it loud and clear when I
      make my visit."
      GOD's Decree.

TIME TO FACE HARD REALITY, NOT FANTASY
5.18-20 Woe to all of you who want GOD's Judgment
      Day!
   Why would you want to see GOD, want him
      to come?
When GOD comes, it will be bad news before
      it's good news,
   the worst of times, not the best of times.
Here's what it's like: A man runs from a lion
   right into the jaws of a bear.
A woman goes home after a hard day's work
   and is raped by a neighbor.

NEW INTERNATIONAL VERSION

²⁰Will not the day of the LORD be darkness,
    not light—
  pitch-dark, without a ray of brightness?

²¹"I hate, I despise your religious feasts;
    I cannot stand your assemblies.
²²Even though you bring me burnt offerings
      and grain offerings,
    I will not accept them.
  Though you bring choice fellowship
      offerings,*ᵃ*
    I will have no regard for them.
²³Away with the noise of your songs!
    I will not listen to the music of your
      harps.
²⁴But let justice roll on like a river,
    righteousness like a never-failing stream!

²⁵"Did you bring me sacrifices and offerings
    forty years in the desert, O house of
      Israel?
²⁶You have lifted up the shrine of your king,
    the pedestal of your idols,
  the star of your god*ᵇ*—
    which you made for yourselves.
²⁷Therefore I will send you into exile beyond
      Damascus,"
  says the LORD, whose name is God
      Almighty.

WOE TO THE COMPLACENT

6 Woe to you who are complacent in Zion,
    and to you who feel secure on Mount
      Samaria,
  you notable men of the foremost nation,
    to whom the people of Israel come!
²Go to Calneh and look at it;
    go from there to great Hamath,
    and then go down to Gath in Philistia.
  Are they better off than your two kingdoms?
    Is their land larger than yours?
³You put off the evil day
    and bring near a reign of terror.
⁴You lie on beds inlaid with ivory
    and lounge on your couches.
  You dine on choice lambs
    and fattened calves.
⁵You strum away on your harps like David
    and improvise on musical instruments.
⁶You drink wine by the bowlful
    and use the finest lotions,
  but you do not grieve over the ruin of
      Joseph.

*ᵃ 22 Traditionally peace offerings   ᵇ 26 Or lifted up
Sakkuth your king / and Kaiwan your idols, / your star-gods;
Septuagint lifted up the shrine of Molech / and the star of your
god Rephan, / their idols*

THE MESSAGE

At GOD'S coming we face hard reality, not
      fantasy—
  a black cloud with no silver lining.

5.21-24 "I can't stand your religious meetings.
    I'm fed up with your conferences and
      conventions.
  I want nothing to do with your religion
      projects,
    your pretentious slogans and goals.
  I'm sick of your fund-raising schemes,
    your public relations and image making.
  I've had all I can take of your noisy ego-music.
    When was the last time you sang to *me*?
  Do you know what I want?
    I want justice—oceans of it.
  I want fairness—rivers of it.
    That's what I want. That's *all* I want.

5.25-27   "Didn't you, dear family of Israel, worship
  me faithfully for forty years in the wilderness,
  bringing the sacrifices and offerings I commanded? How is it you've stooped to dragging
  gimcrack statues of your so-called rulers
  around, hauling the cheap images of all your
  star-gods here and there? Since you like them
  so much, you can take them with you when I
  drive you into exile beyond Damascus." GOD'S
  Message, God-of-the-Angel-Armies.

THOSE WHO LIVE ONLY FOR TODAY

6.1-2 **6** Woe to you who think you live on easy
        street in Zion,
    who think Mount Samaria is the good life.
  You assume you're at the top of the heap,
    voted the number-one best place to live.
  Well, wake up and look around. Get off your
      pedestal.
    Take a look at Calneh.
  Go and visit Great Hamath.
    Look in on Gath of the Philistines.
  Doesn't that take you off your high horse?
    Compared to them, you're not much, are you?

6.3-6 Woe to you who are rushing headlong to
        disaster!
    Catastrophe is just around the corner!
  Woe to those who live in luxury
    and expect everyone else to serve them!
  Woe to those who live only for today,
    indifferent to the fate of others!
  Woe to the playboys, the playgirls,
    who think life is a party held just for them!
  Woe to those addicted to feeling good—life
        without pain!
    those obsessed with looking good—life
        without wrinkles!
  They could not care less
    about their country going to ruin.

NEW INTERNATIONAL VERSION

⁷Therefore you will be among the first to go
into exile;
your feasting and lounging will end.

THE LORD ABHORS THE PRIDE OF ISRAEL

⁸The Sovereign LORD has sworn by himself—
the LORD God Almighty declares:

"I abhor the pride of Jacob
and detest his fortresses;
I will deliver up the city
and everything in it."

⁹If ten men are left in one house, they too will
die. ¹⁰And if a relative who is to burn the bodies
comes to carry them out of the house and asks
anyone still hiding there, "Is anyone with you?"
and he says, "No," then he will say, "Hush! We
must not mention the name of the LORD."

¹¹For the LORD has given the command,
and he will smash the great house into
pieces
and the small house into bits.

¹²Do horses run on the rocky crags?
Does one plow there with oxen?
But you have turned justice into poison
and the fruit of righteousness into
bitterness—
¹³you who rejoice in the conquest of Lo
Debarᵃ
and say, "Did we not take Karnaimᵇ by
our own strength?"

¹⁴For the LORD God Almighty declares,
"I will stir up a nation against you,
O house of Israel,
that will oppress you all the way
from Leboᶜ Hamath to the valley of the
Arabah."

LOCUSTS, FIRE AND A PLUMB LINE

7 This is what the Sovereign LORD showed me:
He was preparing swarms of locusts after the
king's share had been harvested and just as the
second crop was coming up. ²When they had
stripped the land clean, I cried out, "Sovereign
LORD, forgive! How can Jacob survive? He is so
small!"

³So the LORD relented.
"This will not happen," the LORD said.

⁴This is what the Sovereign LORD showed me:
The Sovereign LORD was calling for judgment by

THE MESSAGE

6.7 But here's what's *really* coming:
a forced march into exile.
They'll leave the country whining,
a rag-tag bunch of good-for-nothings.

YOU'VE MADE A SHAMBLES OF JUSTICE

6.8 GOD, the Master, has sworn, and solemnly
stands by his Word.
The God-of-the-Angel-Armies speaks:

"I hate the arrogance of Jacob.
I have nothing but contempt for his forts.
I'm about to hand over the city
and everyone in it."

6.9-10 Ten men are in a house, all dead. A relative
comes and gets the bodies to prepare them for a
decent burial. He discovers a survivor huddled
in a closet and asks, "Are there any more?" The
answer: "Not a soul. But hush! GOD must not
be mentioned in this desecrated place."

6.11 Note well: GOD issues the orders.
He'll knock large houses to smithereens.
He'll smash little houses to bits.

6.12-13 Do you hold a horse race in a field of rocks?
Do you plow the sea with oxen?
You'd cripple the horses
and drown the oxen.
And yet you've made a shambles of justice,
a bloated corpse of righteousness,
Bragging of your trivial pursuits,
beating up on the weak and crowing, "Look
what I've done!"

6.14 "Enjoy it while you can, you Israelites.
I've got a pagan army on the move against
you"
—this is your GOD speaking, God-of-the-
Angel-Armies—
"And they'll make hash of you,
from one end of the country to the other."

TO DIE HOMELESS AND FRIENDLESS

7.1-2 **7** GOD, my Master, showed me this vision: He
was preparing a locust swarm. The first cutting, which went to the king, was complete,
and the second crop was just sprouting. The
locusts ate everything green. Not even a blade
of grass was left.

I called out, "GOD, my Master! Excuse me,
but what's going to come of Jacob? He's so
small."

7.3 GOD gave in.
"It won't happen," he said.

✢

7.4 GOD showed me this vision: Oh! GOD, my Master GOD was calling up a firestorm. It burned

---

ᵃ 13 *Lo Debar* means *nothing*.   ᵇ 13 *Karnaim* means *horns*;
horn here symbolizes *strength*.   ᶜ 14 Or *from the entrance*
to

NEW INTERNATIONAL VERSION

fire; it dried up the great deep and devoured the land. ⁵Then I cried out, "Sovereign LORD, I beg you, stop! How can Jacob survive? He is so small!"

⁶So the LORD relented.

"This will not happen either," the Sovereign LORD said.

⁷This is what he showed me: The Lord was standing by a wall that had been built true to plumb, with a plumb line in his hand. ⁸And the LORD asked me, "What do you see, Amos?"

"A plumb line," I replied.

Then the Lord said, "Look, I am setting a plumb line among my people Israel; I will spare them no longer.

⁹ "The high places of Isaac will be destroyed
    and the sanctuaries of Israel will be ruined;
    with my sword I will rise against the
        house of Jeroboam."

AMOS AND AMAZIAH

¹⁰Then Amaziah the priest of Bethel sent a message to Jeroboam king of Israel: "Amos is raising a conspiracy against you in the very heart of Israel. The land cannot bear all his words. ¹¹For this is what Amos is saying:

" 'Jeroboam will die by the sword,
    and Israel will surely go into exile,
    away from their native land.' "

¹²Then Amaziah said to Amos, "Get out, you seer! Go back to the land of Judah. Earn your bread there and do your prophesying there. ¹³Don't prophesy anymore at Bethel, because this is the king's sanctuary and the temple of the kingdom."

¹⁴Amos answered Amaziah, "I was neither a prophet nor a prophet's son, but I was a shepherd, and I also took care of sycamore-fig trees. ¹⁵But the LORD took me from tending the flock and said to me, 'Go, prophesy to my people Israel.' ¹⁶Now then, hear the word of the LORD. You say,

" 'Do not prophesy against Israel,
    and stop preaching against the house of
        Isaac.'

¹⁷ "Therefore this is what the LORD says:

" 'Your wife will become a prostitute in the
        city,
    and your sons and daughters will fall by
        the sword.
Your land will be measured and divided up,
    and you yourself will die in a pagan ᵃ
        country.
And Israel will certainly go into exile,
    away from their native land.' "

ᵃ 17 Hebrew an unclean

THE MESSAGE

up the ocean. Then it burned up the Promised Land.

7.5   I said, "GOD, my Master! Hold it—please! What's going to come of Jacob? He's so small."

7.6   GOD gave in.

"All right, this won't happen either," GOD, my Master, said.

✝

7.7   GOD showed me this vision: My Master was standing beside a wall. In his hand he held a plumb line.

7.8-9   GOD said to me, "What do you see, Amos?"

I said, "A plumb line."

Then my Master said, "Look what I've done. I've hung a plumb line in the midst of my people Israel. I've spared them for the last time. This is it!

Isaac's sex-and-religion shrines will be
        smashed,
Israel's unholy shrines will be knocked to
        pieces.
I'm raising my sword against the royal
        family of Jeroboam."

7.10   Amaziah, priest at the shrine at Bethel, sent a message to Jeroboam, king of Israel:

"Amos is plotting to get rid of you; and he's doing it as an insider, working from within Israel. His talk will destroy the country. He's got to be silenced. Do you know what Amos is saying?

7.11   " 'Jeroboam will be killed.
        Israel is headed for exile.' "

7.12-13   Then Amaziah confronted Amos: "Seer, be on your way! Get out of here and go back to Judah where you came from! Hang out there. Do your preaching there. But no more preaching at Bethel! Don't show your face here again. This is the king's chapel. This is a royal shrine."

7.14-15   But Amos stood up to Amaziah: "I never set up to be a preacher, never had plans to be a preacher. I raised cattle and I pruned trees. Then GOD took me off the farm and said, 'Go preach to my people Israel.'

7.16-17   "So listen to GOD's Word. You tell me, 'Don't preach to Israel. Don't say anything against the family of Isaac.' But here's what GOD is telling you:

Your wife will become a whore in town.
Your children will get killed.
Your land will be auctioned off.
You will die homeless and friendless.
And Israel will be hauled off to exile, far
        from home."

NEW INTERNATIONAL VERSION

A BASKET OF RIPE FRUIT

8 This is what the Sovereign LORD showed me: a basket of ripe fruit. ²"What do you see, Amos?" he asked.

"A basket of ripe fruit," I answered.

Then the LORD said to me, "The time is ripe for my people Israel; I will spare them no longer.

³"In that day," declares the Sovereign LORD, "the songs in the temple will turn to wailing.ᵃ Many, many bodies—flung everywhere! Silence!"

⁴Hear this, you who trample the needy
   and do away with the poor of the land,

⁵saying,

"When will the New Moon be over
   that we may sell grain,
and the Sabbath be ended
   that we may market wheat?"—
skimping the measure,
   boosting the price
   and cheating with dishonest scales,
⁶buying the poor with silver
   and the needy for a pair of sandals,
   selling even the sweepings with the
      wheat.

⁷The LORD has sworn by the Pride of Jacob: "I will never forget anything they have done.

⁸"Will not the land tremble for this,
   and all who live in it mourn?
The whole land will rise like the Nile;
   it will be stirred up and then sink
   like the river of Egypt.

⁹"In that day," declares the Sovereign LORD,

"I will make the sun go down at noon
   and darken the earth in broad daylight.
¹⁰I will turn your religious feasts into
      mourning
   and all your singing into weeping.
I will make all of you wear sackcloth
   and shave your heads.
I will make that time like mourning for an
      only son
   and the end of it like a bitter day.

¹¹"The days are coming," declares the
      Sovereign LORD,
   "when I will send a famine through the
      land—
not a famine of food or a thirst for water,
   but a famine of hearing the words of the
      LORD.
¹²Men will stagger from sea to sea
   and wander from north to east,

ᵃ 3 Or "the temple singers will wail

THE MESSAGE

YOU WHO GIVE LITTLE AND TAKE MUCH

8.1 **8** My Master GOD showed me this vision: A bowl of fresh fruit.

8.2 He said, "What do you see, Amos?"
   I said, "A bowl of fresh, ripe fruit."
   GOD said, "Right. So, I'm calling it quits with my people Israel. I'm no longer acting as if everything is just fine."

8.3 "The royal singers will wail when it happens."
      My Master GOD said so.
   "Corpses will be strewn here, there, and
         everywhere.
      Hush!"

8.4-6 Listen to this, you who walk all over the
         weak,
      you who treat poor people as less than
         nothing,
   Who say, "When's my next paycheck coming
      so I can go out and live it up?
   How long till the weekend
      when I can go out and have a good time?"
   Who give little and take much,
      and never do an honest day's work.
   You exploit the poor, using them—
      and then, when they're used up, you
         discard them.

8.7-8 GOD swears against the arrogance of Jacob:
      "I'm keeping track of their every last sin."
   God's oath will shake earth's foundations,
      dissolve the whole world into tears.
   God's oath will sweep in like a river that rises,
      flooding houses and lands,
   And then recedes,
      leaving behind a sea of mud.

8.9-10 "On Judgment Day, watch out!"
      These are the words of GOD, my Master.
   "I'll turn off the sun at noon.
      In the middle of the day the earth will go
         black.
   I'll turn your parties into funerals
      and make every song you sing a dirge.
   Everyone will walk around in rags,
      with sunken eyes and bald heads.
   Think of the worst that could happen
      —your only son, say, murdered.
   That's a hint of Judgment Day
      —that and much more.

8.11-12 "Oh yes, Judgment Day is coming!"
      These are the words of my Master GOD.
   "I'll send a famine through the whole country.
      It won't be food or water that's lacking, but
         my Word.
   People will drift from one end of the country
         to the other,
      roam to the north, wander to the east.

NEW INTERNATIONAL VERSION

searching for the word of the LORD,
but they will not find it.

13 "In that day

"the lovely young women and strong young
men
will faint because of thirst.
14 They who swear by the shame *a* of Samaria,
or say, 'As surely as your god lives,
O Dan,'
or, 'As surely as the god *b* of Beersheba
lives'—
they will fall,
never to rise again."

ISRAEL TO BE DESTROYED

9 I saw the Lord standing by the altar, and he
said:

"Strike the tops of the pillars
so that the thresholds shake.
Bring them down on the heads of all the people;
those who are left I will kill with the sword.
Not one will get away,
none will escape.
2 Though they dig down to the depths of the
grave, *c*
from there my hand will take them.
Though they climb up to the heavens,
from there I will bring them down.
3 Though they hide themselves on the top of
Carmel,
there I will hunt them down and seize them.
Though they hide from me at the bottom of
the sea,
there I will command the serpent to bite
them.
4 Though they are driven into exile by their
enemies,
there I will command the sword to slay them.
I will fix my eyes upon them
for evil and not for good."

5 The Lord, the LORD Almighty,
he who touches the earth and it melts,
and all who live in it mourn—
the whole land rises like the Nile,
then sinks like the river of Egypt—
6 he who builds his lofty palace *d* in the heavens
and sets its foundation *e* on the earth,
who calls for the waters of the sea
and pours them out over the face of the
land—
the LORD is his name.

---

a 14 Or *by Ashima; or by the idol*   *b 14* Or *power*
c 2 Hebrew *to Sheol*   *d 6* The meaning of the Hebrew for
this phrase is uncertain.   *e 6* The meaning of the Hebrew
for this word is uncertain.

THE MESSAGE

They'll go anywhere, listen to anyone,
hoping to hear GOD's Word—but they won't
hear it.

8.13-14 "On Judgment Day,
lovely young girls will faint of Word-thirst,
robust young men will faint of God-thirst,
Along with those who take oaths at the
Samaria Sin-and-Sex Center,
saying, 'As the lord god of Dan is my witness!'
and 'The lady goddess of Beer-sheba bless
you!'
Their lives will fall to pieces.
They'll never put it together again."

ISRAEL THROWN INTO A SIEVE

9.1-4 **9** I saw my Master standing beside the altar at
the shrine. He said:

"Hit the tops of the shrine's pillars,
make the floor shake.
The roof's about to fall on the heads of the
people,
and whoever's still alive, I'll kill.
No one will get away,
no runaways will make it.
If they dig their way down into the
underworld,
I'll find them and bring them up.
If they climb to the stars,
I'll find them and bring them down.
If they hide out at the top of Mount Carmel,
I'll find them and bring them back.
If they dive to the bottom of the ocean,
I'll send Dragon to swallow them up.
If they're captured alive by their enemies,
I'll send Sword to kill them.
I've made up my mind
to hurt them, not help them."

9.5-6 My Master, GOD-of-the-Angel-Armies,
touches the earth, a mere touch, and it
trembles.
The whole world goes into mourning.
Earth swells like the Nile at flood stage;
then the water subsides, like the great Nile
of Egypt.
God builds his palace—towers soaring high in
the skies,
foundations set on the rock-firm earth.
He calls ocean waters and they come,
then he ladles them out on the earth.
GOD, your God, does all this.

✛

NEW INTERNATIONAL VERSION

7 "Are not you Israelites
the same to me as the Cushites[a]?"
declares the LORD.
"Did I not bring Israel up from Egypt,
the Philistines from Caphtor[b]
and the Arameans from Kir?

8 "Surely the eyes of the Sovereign LORD
are on the sinful kingdom.
I will destroy it
from the face of the earth—
yet I will not totally destroy
the house of Jacob,"
declares the LORD.
9 "For I will give the command,
and I will shake the house of Israel
among all the nations
as grain is shaken in a sieve,
and not a pebble will reach the ground.
10 All the sinners among my people
will die by the sword,
all those who say,
'Disaster will not overtake or meet us.'

ISRAEL'S RESTORATION

11 "In that day I will restore
David's fallen tent.
I will repair its broken places,
restore its ruins,
and build it as it used to be,
12 so that they may possess the remnant of
Edom
and all the nations that bear my name,[c]"
declares the LORD,
who will do these things.

13 "The days are coming," declares the LORD,

"when the reaper will be overtaken by the
plowman
and the planter by the one treading
grapes.
New wine will drip from the mountains
and flow from all the hills.
14 I will bring back my exiled[d] people Israel;
they will rebuild the ruined cities and live
in them.
They will plant vineyards and drink their
wine;
they will make gardens and eat their fruit.
15 I will plant Israel in their own land,
never again to be uprooted
from the land I have given them,"

says the LORD your God.

THE MESSAGE

9.7-8 "Do you Israelites think you're any better than
the far-off Cushites?" GOD's Decree.
"Am I not involved with all nations? Didn't I
bring Israel up from Egypt, the Philistines from
Caphtor, the Arameans from Qir? But you can
be sure that I, GOD, the Master, have my eye on
the Kingdom of Sin. I'm going to wipe it off
the face of the earth. Still, I won't totally destroy the family of Jacob." GOD's Decree.

9.9-10 "I'm still giving the orders around here. I'm
throwing Israel into a sieve among all the nations and shaking them good, shaking out all
the sin, all the sinners. No real grain will be
lost, but all the sinners will be sifted out and
thrown away, the people who say, 'Nothing bad
will ever happen in our lifetime. It won't even
come close.'

BLESSINGS LIKE WINE POURING
OFF THE MOUNTAINS

9.11-12 "But also on that Judgment Day I will restore
David's house that has fallen to pieces. I'll repair the holes in the roof, replace the broken
windows, fix it up like new. David's people will
be strong again and seize what's left of enemy
Edom, plus everyone else under my sovereign
judgment." GOD's Decree. He will do this.

9.13-15 "Yes indeed, it won't be long now." GOD's Decree.
"Things are going to happen so fast your
head will swim, one thing fast on the heels of
the other. You won't be able to keep up. Everything will be happening at once—and everywhere you look, blessings! Blessings like wine
pouring off the mountains and hills. I'll make
everything right again for my people Israel:

"They'll rebuild their ruined cities.
They'll plant vineyards and drink good
wine.
They'll work their gardens and eat fresh
vegetables.
And I'll plant *them*, plant them on their
own land.
They'll never again be uprooted from the
land I've given them."

GOD, your God, says so.

---

a 7 That is, people from the upper Nile region   b 7 That
is, Crete   c 12 Hebrew; Septuagint *so that the remnant of
men / and all the nations that bear my name may seek the
Lord*   d 14 Or *will restore the fortunes of my*

OBADIAH

OBADIAH

¹The vision of Obadiah.

This is what the Sovereign LORD says about Edom—

We have heard a message from the LORD:
    An envoy was sent to the nations to say,
"Rise, and let us go against her for battle"—

² "See, I will make you small among the
        nations;
    you will be utterly despised.
³ The pride of your heart has deceived you,
    you who live in the clefts of the rocks*a*
    and make your home on the heights,
    you who say to yourself,
    'Who can bring me down to the ground?'
⁴ Though you soar like the eagle
    and make your nest among the stars,
    from there I will bring you down,"
                        declares the LORD.
⁵ "If thieves came to you,
    if robbers in the night—
Oh, what a disaster awaits you—
    would they not steal only as much as they
        wanted?
If grape pickers came to you,
    would they not leave a few grapes?
⁶ But how Esau will be ransacked,
    his hidden treasures pillaged!
⁷ All your allies will force you to the border;
    your friends will deceive and overpower
        you;
those who eat your bread will set a trap for
    you,*b*
    but you will not detect it.

⁸ "In that day," declares the LORD,
    "will I not destroy the wise men of Edom,
    men of understanding in the mountains of
        Esau?
⁹ Your warriors, O Teman, will be terrified,
    and everyone in Esau's mountains
    will be cut down in the slaughter.

---

*a 3 Or of Sela   b 7 The meaning of the Hebrew for this
clause is uncertain.*

YOUR WORLD WILL COLLAPSE

1 Obadiah's Message to Edom
    from GOD, the Master.
We got the news straight from GOD
    by a special messenger sent out to the
        godless nations:

"On your feet, prepare for battle;
    get ready to make war on Edom!

✢

2-4 "Listen to this, Edom:
    I'm turning you to a no-account,
    the runt of the godless nations, despised.
You thought you were so great,
    perched high among the rocks, king of the
        mountain,
Thinking to yourself,
    'Nobody can get to me! Nobody can
        touch me!'
Think again. Even if, like an eagle,
    you hang out on a high cliff-face,
Even if you build your nest in the stars,
    I'll bring you down to earth."
        GOD's sure Word.

5-14 "If thieves crept up on you,
    they'd rob you blind—isn't that so?
If they mugged you on the streets at night,
    they'd pick you clean—isn't that so?
Oh, they'll take Esau apart, piece by piece,
    empty his purse and pockets.
All your old partners will drive you to the
        edge.
    Your old friends will lie to your face.
Your old drinking buddies will stab you in the
        back.
    Your world will collapse. You won't know
        what hit you.
So don't be surprised"—it's GOD's sure
        Word!—
    "when I wipe out all sages from Edom
    and rid the Esau mountains of its famous
        wise men.
Your great heroes will desert you, Teman.
    There'll be nobody left in Esau's mountains.

NEW INTERNATIONAL VERSION

¹⁰ Because of the violence against your brother
	Jacob,
	you will be covered with shame;
	you will be destroyed forever.
¹¹ On the day you stood aloof
	while strangers carried off his wealth
	and foreigners entered his gates
	and cast lots for Jerusalem,
	you were like one of them.
¹² You should not look down on your brother
	in the day of his misfortune,
	nor rejoice over the people of Judah
	in the day of their destruction,
	nor boast so much
	in the day of their trouble.
¹³ You should not march through the gates of
		my people
	in the day of their disaster,
	nor look down on them in their calamity
	in the day of their disaster,
	nor seize their wealth
	in the day of their disaster.
¹⁴ You should not wait at the crossroads
	to cut down their fugitives,
	nor hand over their survivors
	in the day of their trouble.

¹⁵ "The day of the LORD is near
	for all nations.
	As you have done, it will be done to you;
	your deeds will return upon your own
		head.
¹⁶ Just as you drank on my holy hill,
	so all the nations will drink continually;
	they will drink and drink
	and be as if they had never been.
¹⁷ But on Mount Zion will be deliverance;
	it will be holy,
	and the house of Jacob
	will possess its inheritance.
¹⁸ The house of Jacob will be a fire
	and the house of Joseph a flame;
	the house of Esau will be stubble,
	and they will set it on fire and consume it.
	There will be no survivors
	from the house of Esau."
				The LORD has spoken.

THE MESSAGE

Because of the murderous history compiled
	against your brother Jacob,
You will be looked down on by everyone.
	You'll lose your place in history.
On that day you stood there and didn't do
		anything.
	Strangers took your brother's army into
		exile.
Godless foreigners invaded and pillaged
		Jerusalem.
	You stood there and watched.
	You were as bad as they were.
You shouldn't have gloated over your brother
	when he was down-and-out.
You shouldn't have laughed and joked at
		Judah's sons
	when they were facedown in the mud.
You shouldn't have talked so big
	when everything was so bad.
You shouldn't have taken advantage of my
		people
	when their lives had fallen apart.
You of all people should not have been amused
	by their troubles, their wrecked nation.
You shouldn't have taken the shirt off their
		back
	when they were knocked flat, defenseless.
And you shouldn't have stood waiting at the
		outskirts
	and cut off refugees,
And traitorously turned in helpless survivors
	who had lost everything.

⊹

15-18 "GOD's Judgment Day is near
	for all the godless nations.
As you have done, it will be done to you.
	What you did will boomerang back
	and hit your own head.
Just as you partied on my holy mountain,
	all the godless nations will drink God's
		wrath.
They'll drink and drink and drink—
	they'll drink themselves to death.
But not so on Mount Zion—there's respite
		there!
	a safe and holy place!
The family of Jacob will take back their
		possessions
	from those who took them from them.
That's when the family of Jacob will catch fire,
	the family of Joseph become fierce flame,
	while the family of Esau will be straw.
Esau will go up in flames,
	nothing left of Esau but a pile of ashes."
		GOD said it, and it is so.

⊹

NEW INTERNATIONAL VERSION	THE MESSAGE

NEW INTERNATIONAL VERSION

¹⁹ People from the Negev will occupy
　　the mountains of Esau,
　and people from the foothills will possess
　　the land of the Philistines.
　They will occupy the fields of Ephraim and
　　Samaria,
　　and Benjamin will possess Gilead.
²⁰ This company of Israelite exiles who are in
　　Canaan
　　will possess ˪the land˩ as far as Zarephath;
　the exiles from Jerusalem who are in
　　Sepharad
　　will possess the towns of the Negev.
²¹ Deliverers will go up on ͣ Mount Zion
　　to govern the mountains of Esau.
　　And the kingdom will be the LORD's.

THE MESSAGE

19-21 People from the south will take over the Esau
　　mountains;
　people from the foothills will overrun the
　　Philistines.
　They'll take the farms of Ephraim and
　　Samaria,
　　and Benjamin will take Gilead.
　Earlier, Israelite exiles will come back
　　and take Canaanite land to the north at
　　Zarephath.
　Jerusalem exiles from the far northwest in
　　Sepharad
　　will come back and take the cities in the
　　south.
　The remnant of the saved in Mount Zion
　　will go into the mountains of Esau
　And rule justly and fairly,
　　a rule that honors GOD's kingdom.

ͣ 21 Or from

JONAH

JONAH

JONAH FLEES FROM THE LORD

1 The word of the LORD came to Jonah son of Amittai: ²"Go to the great city of Nineveh and preach against it, because its wickedness has come up before me."

³But Jonah ran away from the LORD and headed for Tarshish. He went down to Joppa, where he found a ship bound for that port. After paying the fare, he went aboard and sailed for Tarshish to flee from the LORD.

⁴Then the LORD sent a great wind on the sea, and such a violent storm arose that the ship threatened to break up. ⁵All the sailors were afraid and each cried out to his own god. And they threw the cargo into the sea to lighten the ship.

But Jonah had gone below deck, where he lay down and fell into a deep sleep. ⁶The captain went to him and said, "How can you sleep? Get up and call on your god! Maybe he will take notice of us, and we will not perish."

⁷Then the sailors said to each other, "Come, let us cast lots to find out who is responsible for this calamity." They cast lots and the lot fell on Jonah.

⁸So they asked him, "Tell us, who is responsible for making all this trouble for us? What do you do? Where do you come from? What is your country? From what people are you?"

⁹He answered, "I am a Hebrew and I worship the LORD, the God of heaven, who made the sea and the land."

¹⁰This terrified them and they asked, "What have you done?" (They knew he was running away from the LORD, because he had already told them so.)

¹¹The sea was getting rougher and rougher. So they asked him, "What should we do to you to make the sea calm down for us?"

¹²"Pick me up and throw me into the sea," he replied, "and it will become calm. I know that it is my fault that this great storm has come upon you."

RUNNING AWAY FROM GOD

1.1-2 **1** One day long ago, GOD's Word came to Jonah, Amittai's son: "Up on your feet and on your way to the big city of Nineveh! Preach to them. They're in a bad way and I can't ignore it any longer."

1.3 But Jonah got up and went the other direction to Tarshish, running away from GOD. He went down to the port of Joppa and found a ship headed for Tarshish. He paid the fare and went on board, joining those going to Tarshish—as far away from GOD as he could get.

1.4-6 But GOD sent a huge storm at sea, the waves towering.

The ship was about to break into pieces. The sailors were terrified. They called out in desperation to their gods. They threw everything they were carrying overboard to lighten the ship. Meanwhile, Jonah had gone down into the hold of the ship to take a nap. He was sound asleep. The captain came to him and said, "What's this? Sleeping! Get up! Pray to your god! Maybe your god will see we're in trouble and rescue us."

1.7 Then the sailors said to one another, "Let's get to the bottom of this. Let's draw straws to identify the culprit on this ship who's responsible for this disaster."

So they drew straws. Jonah got the short straw.

1.8 Then they grilled him: "Confess. Why this disaster? What is your work? Where do you come from? What country? What family?"

1.9 He told them, "I'm a Hebrew. I worship GOD, the God of heaven who made sea and land."

1.10 At that, the men were frightened, really frightened, and said, "What on earth have you done!" As Jonah talked, the sailors realized that he was running away from GOD.

1.11 They said to him, "What are we going to do with you—to get rid of this storm?" By this time the sea was wild, totally out of control.

1.12 Jonah said, "Throw me overboard, into the sea. Then the storm will stop. It's all my fault. I'm the cause of the storm. Get rid of me and you'll get rid of the storm."

NEW INTERNATIONAL VERSION

¹³Instead, the men did their best to row back to land. But they could not, for the sea grew even wilder than before. ¹⁴Then they cried to the LORD, "O LORD, please do not let us die for taking this man's life. Do not hold us accountable for killing an innocent man, for you, O LORD, have done as you pleased." ¹⁵Then they took Jonah and threw him overboard, and the raging sea grew calm. ¹⁶At this the men greatly feared the LORD, and they offered a sacrifice to the LORD and made vows to him.

¹⁷But the LORD provided a great fish to swallow Jonah, and Jonah was inside the fish three days and three nights.

JONAH'S PRAYER

2 From inside the fish Jonah prayed to the LORD his God. ²He said:

"In my distress I called to the LORD,
   and he answered me.
From the depths of the grave[a] I called for
   help,
   and you listened to my cry.
³You hurled me into the deep,
   into the very heart of the seas,
   and the currents swirled about me;
all your waves and breakers
   swept over me.
⁴I said, 'I have been banished
   from your sight;
yet I will look again
   toward your holy temple.'
⁵The engulfing waters threatened me,[b]
   the deep surrounded me;
   seaweed was wrapped around my head.
⁶To the roots of the mountains I sank down;
   the earth beneath barred me in forever.
But you brought my life up from the pit,
   O LORD my God.

⁷"When my life was ebbing away,
   I remembered you, LORD,
and my prayer rose to you,
   to your holy temple.

⁸"Those who cling to worthless idols
   forfeit the grace that could be theirs.
⁹But I, with a song of thanksgiving,
   will sacrifice to you.
What I have vowed I will make good.
   Salvation comes from the LORD."

¹⁰And the LORD commanded the fish, and it vomited Jonah onto dry land.

THE MESSAGE

₁.₁₃ But no. The men tried rowing back to shore. They made no headway. The storm only got worse and worse, wild and raging.

₁.₁₄ Then they prayed to GOD, "O GOD! Don't let us drown because of this man's life, and don't blame us for his death. You are GOD. Do what you think is best."

₁.₁₅ They took Jonah and threw him overboard. Immediately the sea was quieted down.

₁.₁₆ The sailors were impressed, no longer terrified by the sea, but in awe of GOD. They worshiped GOD, offered a sacrifice, and made vows.

₁.₁₇ Then GOD assigned a huge fish to swallow Jonah. Jonah was in the fish's belly three days and nights.

AT THE BOTTOM OF THE SEA

₂.₁₋₉ **2** Then Jonah prayed to his God from the belly of the fish.
   He prayed:

"In trouble, deep trouble, I prayed to GOD.
   He answered me.
From the belly of the grave I cried, 'Help!'
   You heard my cry.
You threw me into ocean's depths,
   into a watery grave,
With ocean waves, ocean breakers
   crashing over me.
I said, 'I've been thrown away,
   thrown out, out of your sight.
I'll never again lay eyes
   on your Holy Temple.'
Ocean gripped me by the throat.
   The ancient Abyss grabbed me and held
     tight.
My head was all tangled in seaweed
   at the bottom of the sea where the
     mountains take root.
I was as far down as a body can go,
   and the gates were slamming shut behind
     me forever—
Yet you pulled me up from that grave alive,
   O GOD, my God!
When my life was slipping away,
   I remembered GOD,
And my prayer got through to you,
   made it all the way to your Holy Temple.
Those who worship hollow gods, god-frauds,
   walk away from their only true love.
But I'm worshiping you, GOD,
   calling out in thanksgiving!
And I'll do what I promised I'd do!
   Salvation belongs to GOD!"

₂.₁₀ Then GOD spoke to the fish, and it vomited up Jonah on the seashore.

---

[a] 2 Hebrew *Sheol*   [b] 5 Or *waters were at my throat*

NEW INTERNATIONAL VERSION

Jonah Goes to Nineveh

3 Then the word of the LORD came to Jonah a second time: ²"Go to the great city of Nineveh and proclaim to it the message I give you."

³Jonah obeyed the word of the LORD and went to Nineveh. Now Nineveh was a very important city—a visit required three days. ⁴On the first day, Jonah started into the city. He proclaimed: "Forty more days and Nineveh will be overturned." ⁵The Ninevites believed God. They declared a fast, and all of them, from the greatest to the least, put on sackcloth.

⁶When the news reached the king of Nineveh, he rose from his throne, took off his royal robes, covered himself with sackcloth and sat down in the dust. ⁷Then he issued a proclamation in Nineveh:

"By the decree of the king and his nobles:

Do not let any man or beast, herd or flock, taste anything; do not let them eat or drink. ⁸But let man and beast be covered with sackcloth. Let everyone call urgently on God. Let them give up their evil ways and their violence. ⁹Who knows? God may yet relent and with compassion turn from his fierce anger so that we will not perish."

¹⁰When God saw what they did and how they turned from their evil ways, he had compassion and did not bring upon them the destruction he had threatened.

Jonah's Anger at the Lord's Compassion

4 But Jonah was greatly displeased and became angry. ²He prayed to the LORD, "O LORD, is this not what I said when I was still at home? That is why I was so quick to flee to Tarshish. I knew that you are a gracious and compassionate God, slow to anger and abounding in love, a God who relents from sending calamity. ³Now, O LORD, take away my life, for it is better for me to die than to live."

⁴But the LORD replied, "Have you any right to be angry?"

⁵Jonah went out and sat down at a place east of the city. There he made himself a shelter, sat in its shade and waited to see what would happen to the city. ⁶Then the LORD God provided a vine and made it grow up over Jonah to give

THE MESSAGE

Maybe God Will Change His Mind

3 3.1-2 Next, GOD spoke to Jonah a second time: "Up on your feet and on your way to the big city of Nineveh! Preach to them. They're in a bad way and I can't ignore it any longer."

3.3 This time Jonah started off straight for Nineveh, obeying GOD's orders to the letter.

3.3 Nineveh was a big city, very big—it took three days to walk across it.

3.4 Jonah entered the city, went one day's walk and preached, "In forty days Nineveh will be smashed."

3.5 The people of Nineveh listened, and trusted God. They proclaimed a citywide fast and dressed in burlap to show their repentance. Everyone did it—rich and poor, famous and obscure, leaders and followers.

3.6-9 When the message reached the king of Nineveh, he got up off his throne, threw down his royal robes, dressed in burlap, and sat down in the dirt. Then he issued a public proclamation throughout Nineveh, authorized by him and his leaders: "Not one drop of water, not one bite of food for man, woman, or animal, including your herds and flocks! Dress them all, both people and animals, in burlap, and send up a cry for help to God. Everyone must turn around, turn back from an evil life and the violent ways that stain their hands. Who knows? Maybe God will turn around and change his mind about us, quit being angry with us and let us live!"

3.10 God saw what they had done, that they had turned away from their evil lives. He *did* change his mind about them. What he said he would do to them he didn't do.

"I Knew This Was Going to Happen!"

4 4.1-2 Jonah was furious. He lost his temper. He yelled at GOD, "GOD! I knew it—when I was back home, I knew this was going to happen! That's why I ran off to Tarshish! I knew you were sheer grace and mercy, not easily angered, rich in love, and ready at the drop of a hat to turn your plans of punishment into a program of forgiveness!

4.3 "So, GOD, if you won't kill them, kill *me!* I'm better off dead!"

4.4 GOD said, "What do you have to be angry about?"

4.5 But Jonah just left. He went out of the city to the east and sat down in a sulk. He put together a makeshift shelter of leafy branches and sat there in the shade to see what would happen to the city.

4.6 GOD arranged for a broad-leafed tree to spring up. It grew over Jonah to cool him off

NEW INTERNATIONAL VERSION

shade for his head to ease his discomfort, and Jonah was very happy about the vine. 7But at dawn the next day God provided a worm, which chewed the vine so that it withered. 8When the sun rose, God provided a scorching east wind, and the sun blazed on Jonah's head so that he grew faint. He wanted to die, and said, "It would be better for me to die than to live."

9But God said to Jonah, "Do you have a right to be angry about the vine?"

"I do," he said. "I am angry enough to die."

10But the LORD said, "You have been concerned about this vine, though you did not tend it or make it grow. It sprang up overnight and died overnight. 11But Nineveh has more than a hundred and twenty thousand people who cannot tell their right hand from their left, and many cattle as well. Should I not be concerned about that great city?"

THE MESSAGE

and get him out of his angry sulk. Jonah was pleased and enjoyed the shade. Life was looking up.

4.7-8 But then God sent a worm. By dawn of the next day, the worm had bored into the shade tree and it withered away. The sun came up and God sent a hot, blistering wind from the east. The sun beat down on Jonah's head and he started to faint. He prayed to die: "I'm better off dead!"

4.9 Then God said to Jonah, "What right do you have to get angry about this shade tree?"

Jonah said, "Plenty of right. It's made me angry enough to die!"

4.10-11 GOD said, "What's this? How is it that you can change your feelings from pleasure to anger overnight about a mere shade tree that you did nothing to get? You neither planted nor watered it. It grew up one night and died the next night. So, why can't I likewise change what I feel about Nineveh from anger to pleasure, this big city of more than a hundred and twenty thousand childlike people who don't yet know right from wrong, to say nothing of all the innocent animals?"

MICAH

MICAH

1 The word of the LORD that came to Micah of Moresheth during the reigns of Jotham, Ahaz and Hezekiah, kings of Judah—the vision he saw concerning Samaria and Jerusalem.

2 Hear, O peoples, all of you,
    listen, O earth and all who are in it,
  that the Sovereign LORD may witness against
      you,
    the Lord from his holy temple.

JUDGMENT AGAINST SAMARIA AND JERUSALEM

3 Look! The LORD is coming from his dwelling
      place;
    he comes down and treads the high places
      of the earth.
4 The mountains melt beneath him
    and the valleys split apart,
  like wax before the fire,
    like water rushing down a slope.
5 All this is because of Jacob's transgression,
    because of the sins of the house of Israel.
  What is Jacob's transgression?
    Is it not Samaria?
  What is Judah's high place?
    Is it not Jerusalem?

6 "Therefore I will make Samaria a heap of
      rubble,
    a place for planting vineyards.
  I will pour her stones into the valley
    and lay bare her foundations.
7 All her idols will be broken to pieces;
    all her temple gifts will be burned with
      fire;
    I will destroy all her images.

1.1 1 GOD'S Message as it came to Micah of Moresheth. It came during the reigns of Jotham, Ahaz, and Hezekiah, kings of Judah. It had to do with what was going on in Samaria and Jerusalem.

GOD TAKES THE WITNESS STAND

1.2 Listen, people—all of you.
    Listen, earth, and everyone in it:
  The Master, GOD, takes the witness stand
      against you,
    the Master from his Holy Temple.

1.3-5 Look, here he comes! GOD, from his place!
    He comes down and strides across
      mountains and hills.
  Mountains sink under his feet,
    valleys split apart;
  The rock mountains crumble into gravel,
    the river valleys leak like sieves.
  All this because of Jacob's sin,
    because Israel's family did wrong.
  You ask, "So what is Jacob's sin?"
    Just look at Samaria—isn't it obvious?
  And all the sex-and-religion shrines in
      Judah—
    isn't Jerusalem responsible?

1.6-7 "I'm turning Samaria into a heap of rubble,
    a vacant lot littered with garbage.
  I'll dump the stones from her buildings in the
      valley
    and leave her abandoned foundations
      exposed.
  All her carved and cast gods and goddesses
    will be sold for stove wood and scrap
      metal,
  All her sacred fertility groves
    burned to the ground,
  All the sticks and stones she worshiped as
      gods,
    destroyed.

NEW INTERNATIONAL VERSION

Since she gathered her gifts from the wages
of prostitutes,
as the wages of prostitutes they will again
be used."

WEEPING AND MOURNING

[8] Because of this I will weep and wail;
I will go about barefoot and naked.
I will howl like a jackal
and moan like an owl.
[9] For her wound is incurable;
it has come to Judah.
It[a] has reached the very gate of my people,
even to Jerusalem itself.
[10] Tell it not in Gath[b];
weep not at all.[c]
In Beth Ophrah[d]
roll in the dust.
[11] Pass on in nakedness and shame,
you who live in Shaphir.[e]
Those who live in Zaanan[f]
will not come out.
Beth Ezel is in mourning;
its protection is taken from you.
[12] Those who live in Maroth[g] writhe in pain,
waiting for relief,
because disaster has come from the LORD,
even to the gate of Jerusalem.
[13] You who live in Lachish,[h]
harness the team to the chariot.
You were the beginning of sin
to the Daughter of Zion,
for the transgressions of Israel
were found in you.
[14] Therefore you will give parting gifts
to Moresheth Gath.
The town of Aczib[i] will prove deceptive
to the kings of Israel.
[15] I will bring a conqueror against you
who live in Mareshah.[j]
He who is the glory of Israel
will come to Adullam.
[16] Shave your heads in mourning
for the children in whom you delight;
make yourselves as bald as the vulture,
for they will go from you into exile.

---

[a] 9 Or *He*   [b] 10 *Gath* sounds like the Hebrew for *tell*.
[c] 10 Hebrew; Septuagint may suggest *not in Acco*. The
Hebrew for *in Acco* sounds like the Hebrew for *weep*.
[d] 10 *Beth Ophrah* means *house of dust*.   [e] 11 *Shaphir*
means *pleasant*.   [f] 11 *Zaanan* sounds like the Hebrew for
come out.   [g] 12 *Maroth* sounds like the Hebrew for *bitter*.
[h] 13 *Lachish* sounds like the Hebrew for *team*.   [i] 14 *Aczib*
means *deception*.   [j] 15 *Mareshah* sounds like the Hebrew
for *conqueror*.

THE MESSAGE

These were her earnings from her life as a
whore.
This is what happens to the fees of a
whore."

✛

1.8-9 This is why I lament and mourn.
This is why I go around in rags and
barefoot.
This is why I howl like a pack of coyotes,
and moan like a mournful owl in the night.
GOD has inflicted punishing wounds;
Judah has been wounded with no healing
in sight.
Judgment has marched through the city gates.
Jerusalem must face the charges.

✛

1.10-16 Don't gossip about this in Telltown.
Don't waste your tears.
In Dustville,
roll in the dust.
In Alarmtown,
the alarm is sounded.
The citizens of Exitburgh
will never get out alive.
Lament, Last-Stand City:
There's nothing in you left standing.
The villagers of Bittertown
wait in vain for sweet peace.
Harsh judgment has come from GOD
and entered Peace City.
All you who live in Chariotville,
get in your chariots for flight.
You led the daughter of Zion
into trusting not God but chariots.
Similar sins in Israel
also got their start in you.
Go ahead and give your goodbye gifts
to Goodbyeville.
Miragetown beckoned
but disappointed Israel's kings.
Inheritance City
has lost its inheritance.
Glorytown
has seen its last of glory.
Shave your heads in mourning
over the loss of your precious towns.
Go bald as a goose egg—they've gone
into exile and aren't coming back.

NEW INTERNATIONAL VERSION

Man's Plans and God's

2 Woe to those who plan iniquity,
to those who plot evil on their beds!
At morning's light they carry it out
because it is in their power to do it.
² They covet fields and seize them,
and houses, and take them.
They defraud a man of his home,
a fellowman of his inheritance.

³ Therefore, the LORD says:

"I am planning disaster against this people,
from which you cannot save yourselves.
You will no longer walk proudly,
for it will be a time of calamity.
⁴ In that day men will ridicule you;
they will taunt you with this mournful
song:
'We are utterly ruined;
my people's possession is divided up.
He takes it from me!
He assigns our fields to traitors.' "

⁵ Therefore you will have no one in the
assembly of the LORD
to divide the land by lot.

False Prophets

⁶ "Do not prophesy," their prophets say.
"Do not prophesy about these things;
disgrace will not overtake us."
⁷ Should it be said, O house of Jacob:
"Is the Spirit of the LORD angry?
Does he do such things?"

"Do not my words do good
to him whose ways are upright?
⁸ Lately my people have risen up
like an enemy.
You strip off the rich robe
from those who pass by without a care,
like men returning from battle.
⁹ You drive the women of my people
from their pleasant homes.
You take away my blessing
from their children forever.
¹⁰ Get up, go away!
For this is not your resting place,
because it is defiled,
it is ruined, beyond all remedy.
¹¹ If a liar and deceiver comes and says,

THE MESSAGE

God Has Had Enough

2.1-5 **2** Doom to those who plot evil,
who go to bed dreaming up crimes!
As soon as it's morning,
they're off, full of energy, doing what
they've planned.
They covet fields and grab them,
find homes and take them.
They bully the neighbor and his family,
see people only for what they can get out of
them.
GOD has had enough. He says,
"I have some plans of my own:
Disaster because of this interbreeding evil!
Your necks are on the line.
You're not walking away from this.
It's doomsday for you.
Mocking ballads will be sung of you,
and you yourselves will sing the blues:
'Our lives are ruined,
our homes and lands auctioned off.
They take everything, leave us nothing!
All is sold to the highest bidder.' "
And there'll be no one to stand up for you,
no one to speak for you before GOD and his
jury.

✛

2.6-7 "Don't preach," say the preachers.
"Don't preach such stuff.
Nothing bad will happen to us.
Talk like *this* to the family of Jacob?
Does GOD lose his temper?
Is this the way he acts?
Isn't he on the side of good people?
Doesn't he help those who help
themselves?"

✛

2.8-11 "What do you mean, 'good people'!
You're the enemy of my people!
You rob unsuspecting people
out for an evening stroll.
You take their coats off their backs
like soldiers who plunder the defenseless.
You drive the women of my people
out of their ample homes.
You make victims of the children
and leave them vulnerable to violence and
vice.
Get out of here, the lot of you.
You can't take it easy here!
You've polluted this place,
and now *you're* polluted—ruined!
If someone showed up with a good smile and
glib tongue
and told lies from morning to night—

NEW INTERNATIONAL VERSION

'I will prophesy for you plenty of wine
and beer,'
he would be just the prophet for this
people!

DELIVERANCE PROMISED

12 "I will surely gather all of you, O Jacob;
I will surely bring together the remnant of
Israel.
I will bring them together like sheep in a
pen,
like a flock in its pasture;
the place will throng with people.
13 One who breaks open the way will go up
before them;
they will break through the gate and go
out.
Their king will pass through before them,
the LORD at their head."

LEADERS AND PROPHETS REBUKED

3 Then I said,

"Listen, you leaders of Jacob,
you rulers of the house of Israel.
Should you not know justice,
2   you who hate good and love evil;
who tear the skin from my people
and the flesh from their bones;
3 who eat my people's flesh,
strip off their skin
and break their bones in pieces;
who chop them up like meat for the pan,
like flesh for the pot?"

4 Then they will cry out to the LORD,
but he will not answer them.
At that time he will hide his face from them
because of the evil they have done.

5 This is what the LORD says:

"As for the prophets
who lead my people astray,
if one feeds them,
they proclaim 'peace';
if he does not,
they prepare to wage war against him.
6 Therefore night will come over you, without
visions,
and darkness, without divination.
The sun will set for the prophets,
and the day will go dark for them.
7 The seers will be ashamed
and the diviners disgraced.

THE MESSAGE

'I'll preach sermons that will tell you
how you can get anything you want from
God:
More money, the best wines . . . you name
it'—
you'd hire him on the spot as your
preacher!

⚜

2.12-13 "I'm calling a meeting, Jacob.
I want everyone back—all the survivors of
Israel.
I'll get them together in one place—
like sheep in a fold, like cattle in a corral—
a milling throng of homebound people!
Then I, GOD, will burst all confinements
and lead them out into the open.
They'll follow their King.
I will be out in front leading them."

HATERS OF GOOD, LOVERS OF EVIL

3.1-3 **3** Then I said:

"Listen, leaders of Jacob, leaders of Israel:
Don't you know anything of justice?
Haters of good, lovers of evil:
Isn't justice in your job description?
But you skin my people alive.
You rip the meat off their bones.
You break up the bones, chop the meat,
and throw it in a pot for cannibal stew."

3.4 The time's coming, though, when these same
leaders
will cry out for help to GOD, but he won't
listen.
He'll turn his face the other way
because of their history of evil.

⚜

3.5-7 Here is GOD's Message to the prophets,
the preachers who lie to my people:
"For as long as they're well paid and well fed,
the prophets preach, 'Isn't life wonderful!
Peace to all!'
But if you don't pay up and jump on their
bandwagon,
their 'God bless you' turns into 'God damn
you.'
Therefore, you're going blind. You'll see
nothing.
You'll live in deep shadows and know
nothing.
The sun has set on the prophets.
They've had their day; from now on it's
night.
Visionaries will be confused,
experts will be all mixed up.

NEW INTERNATIONAL VERSION

They will all cover their faces
because there is no answer from God."

8 But as for me, I am filled with power,
with the Spirit of the LORD,
and with justice and might,
to declare to Jacob his transgression,
to Israel his sin.
9 Hear this, you leaders of the house of Jacob,
you rulers of the house of Israel,
who despise justice
and distort all that is right;
10 who build Zion with bloodshed,
and Jerusalem with wickedness.
11 Her leaders judge for a bribe,
her priests teach for a price,
and her prophets tell fortunes for money.
Yet they lean upon the LORD and say,
"Is not the LORD among us?
No disaster will come upon us."
12 Therefore because of you,
Zion will be plowed like a field,
Jerusalem will become a heap of rubble,
the temple hill a mound overgrown with
thickets.

THE MOUNTAIN OF THE LORD

4 In the last days

the mountain of the LORD's temple will be
established
as chief among the mountains;
it will be raised above the hills,
and peoples will stream to it.

2 Many nations will come and say,

"Come, let us go up to the mountain of the
LORD,
to the house of the God of Jacob.
He will teach us his ways,
so that we may walk in his paths."
The law will go out from Zion,
the word of the LORD from Jerusalem.
3 He will judge between many peoples
and will settle disputes for strong nations
far and wide.
They will beat their swords into plowshares
and their spears into pruning hooks.
Nation will not take up sword against
nation,
nor will they train for war anymore.
4 Every man will sit under his own vine
and under his own fig tree,

THE MESSAGE

They'll hide behind their reputations and
make lame excuses
to cover up their God-ignorance."

3.8 But me—I'm filled with GOD's power,
filled with GOD's Spirit of justice and
strength,
Ready to confront Jacob's crime
and Israel's sin.

3.9-12 The leaders of Jacob and
the leaders of Israel are
Leaders contemptuous of justice,
who twist and distort right living,
Leaders who build Zion by killing people,
who expand Jerusalem by committing
crimes.
Judges sell verdicts to the highest bidder,
priests mass-market their teaching,
prophets preach for high fees,
All the while posturing and pretending
dependence on GOD:
"We've got GOD on our side.
He'll protect us from disaster."
Because of people like you,
Zion will be turned back into farmland,
Jerusalem end up as a pile of rubble,
and instead of the Temple on the mountain,
a few scraggly scrub pines.

THE MAKING OF GOD'S PEOPLE

4.1-4 **4** But when all is said and done,
GOD's Temple on the mountain,
Firmly fixed, will dominate all mountains,
towering above surrounding hills.
People will stream to it
and many nations set out for it,
Saying, "Come, let's climb GOD's mountain.
Let's go to the Temple of Jacob's God.
He will teach us how to live.
We'll know how to live God's way."
True teaching will issue from Zion,
GOD's revelation from Jerusalem.
He'll establish justice in the rabble of nations
and settle disputes in faraway places.
They'll trade in their swords for shovels,
their spears for rakes and hoes.
Nations will quit fighting each other,
quit learning how to kill one another.
Each man will sit under his own shade tree,

NEW INTERNATIONAL VERSION

and no one will make them afraid,
for the LORD Almighty has spoken.
[5] All the nations may walk
in the name of their gods;
we will walk in the name of the LORD
our God for ever and ever.

THE LORD'S PLAN

[6] "In that day," declares the LORD,

"I will gather the lame;
I will assemble the exiles
and those I have brought to grief.
[7] I will make the lame a remnant,
those driven away a strong nation.
The LORD will rule over them in Mount Zion
from that day and forever.
[8] As for you, O watchtower of the flock,
O stronghold[a] of the Daughter of Zion,
the former dominion will be restored to you;
kingship will come to the Daughter of
Jerusalem."

[9] Why do you now cry aloud—
have you no king?
Has your counselor perished,
that pain seizes you like that of a woman
in labor?
[10] Writhe in agony, O Daughter of Zion,
like a woman in labor,
for now you must leave the city
to camp in the open field.
You will go to Babylon;
there you will be rescued.
There the LORD will redeem you
out of the hand of your enemies.

[11] But now many nations
are gathered against you.
They say, "Let her be defiled,
let our eyes gloat over Zion!"
[12] But they do not know
the thoughts of the LORD;
they do not understand his plan,
he who gathers them like sheaves to the
threshing floor.
[13] "Rise and thresh, O Daughter of Zion,
for I will give you horns of iron;

THE MESSAGE

each woman in safety will tend her own
garden.
GOD-of-the-Angel-Armies says so,
and he means what he says.

4.5 Meanwhile, all the other people live however
they wish,
picking and choosing their gods.
But we live honoring GOD,
and we're loyal to our God forever and ever.

4.6-7 "On that great day," GOD says,
"I will round up all the hurt and homeless,
everyone I have bruised or banished.
I will transform the battered into a company
of the elite.
I will make a strong nation out of the long
lost,
A showcase exhibit of GOD's rule in action,
as I rule from Mount Zion, from here to
eternity.

4.8 "And you stragglers around Jerusalem,
eking out a living in shantytowns:
The glory that once was will be again.
Jerusalem's daughter will be the kingdom
center."

☩

4.9-10 So why the doomsday hysterics?
You still have a king, don't you?
But maybe he's not doing his job
and you're panicked like a woman in labor.
Well, go ahead—twist and scream, Daughter
Jerusalem.
You *are* like a woman in childbirth.
You'll soon be out of the city, on your way
and camping in the open country.
And then you'll arrive in Babylon.
What you lost in Jerusalem will be found in
Babylon.
GOD will give you new life again.
He'll redeem you from your enemies.

4.11-12 But for right now, they're ganged up against you,
many godless peoples, saying,
"Kick her when she's down! Violate her!
We want to see Zion grovel in the dirt."
These blasphemers have no idea
what GOD is thinking and doing in this.
They don't know that this is the making of
GOD's people,
that they are wheat being threshed, gold
being refined.

4.13 On your feet, Daughter of Zion! Be threshed
of chaff,
be refined of dross.

---

[a] 8 Or *hill*

NEW INTERNATIONAL VERSION

I will give you hoofs of bronze
    and you will break to pieces many
        nations."

You will devote their ill-gotten gains to the
        LORD,
    their wealth to the Lord of all the earth.

A PROMISED RULER FROM BETHLEHEM

5 Marshal your troops, O city of troops,[a]
    for a siege is laid against us.
They will strike Israel's ruler
    on the cheek with a rod.

2 "But you, Bethlehem Ephrathah,
    though you are small among the clans[b] of
        Judah,
out of you will come for me
    one who will be ruler over Israel,
whose origins[c] are from of old,
    from ancient times.[d]"

3 Therefore Israel will be abandoned
    until the time when she who is in labor
        gives birth
and the rest of his brothers return
    to join the Israelites.

4 He will stand and shepherd his flock
    in the strength of the LORD,
    in the majesty of the name of the LORD his
        God.
And they will live securely, for then his
        greatness
    will reach to the ends of the earth.

5   And he will be their peace.

DELIVERANCE AND DESTRUCTION

When the Assyrian invades our land
    and marches through our fortresses,
we will raise against him seven shepherds,
    even eight leaders of men.

6 They will rule[e] the land of Assyria with the
        sword,
    the land of Nimrod with drawn sword.[f]
He will deliver us from the Assyrian
    when he invades our land
    and marches into our borders.

7 The remnant of Jacob will be
    in the midst of many peoples
like dew from the LORD,
    like showers on the grass,
which do not wait for man
    or linger for mankind.

8 The remnant of Jacob will be among the
        nations,

THE MESSAGE

I'm remaking you into a people invincible,
    into God's juggernaut to crush the godless
        peoples.
You'll bring their plunder as holy offerings to
        GOD,
    their wealth to the Master of the earth.

THE LEADER WHO WILL SHEPHERD-RULE ISRAEL

5.1 **5** But for now, prepare for the worst, victim
        daughter!
The siege is set against us.
They humiliate Israel's king,
    slapping him around like a rag doll.

5.2-4 But you, Bethlehem, David's country,
    the runt of the litter—
From you will come the leader
    who will shepherd-rule Israel.
He'll be no upstart, no pretender.
    His family tree is ancient and distinguished.
Meanwhile, Israel will be in foster homes
    until the birth pangs are over and the child
        is born,
And the scattered brothers come back
    home to the family of Israel.
He will stand tall in his shepherd-rule by
        GOD's strength,
    centered in the majesty of GOD-Revealed.
And the people will have a good and safe
        home,
    for the whole world will hold him in
        respect—
Peacemaker of the world!

5.5-6 And if some bullying Assyrian shows up,
    invades and violates our land, don't worry.
We'll put him in his place, send him packing,
    and watch his every move.
Shepherd-rule will extend as far as needed,
    to Assyria and all other Nimrod-bullies.
Our shepherd-ruler will save us from old or
        new enemies,
    from anyone who invades or violates our
        land.

5.7 The purged and select company of Jacob will
        be
    like an island in the sea of peoples.
They'll be like dew from GOD,
    like summer showers
Not mentioned in the weather forecast,
    not subject to calculation or control.

5.8-9 Yes, the purged and select company of Jacob
        will be

---

a 1 Or Strengthen your walls, O walled city   *b 2 Or rulers*
c 2 Hebrew goings out   *d 2 Or from days of eternity*
e 6 Or crush   *f 6 Or Nimrod in its gates*

NEW INTERNATIONAL VERSION	THE MESSAGE

NEW INTERNATIONAL VERSION

in the midst of many peoples,
like a lion among the beasts of the forest,
    like a young lion among flocks of sheep,
which mauls and mangles as it goes,
    and no one can rescue.
⁹Your hand will be lifted up in triumph over
        your enemies,
    and all your foes will be destroyed.

¹⁰"In that day," declares the LORD,

"I will destroy your horses from among you
    and demolish your chariots.
¹¹I will destroy the cities of your land
    and tear down all your strongholds.
¹²I will destroy your witchcraft
    and you will no longer cast spells.
¹³I will destroy your carved images
    and your sacred stones from among you;
you will no longer bow down
    to the work of your hands.
¹⁴I will uproot from among you your Asherah
        polesᵃ
    and demolish your cities.
¹⁵I will take vengeance in anger and wrath
    upon the nations that have not
        obeyed me."

THE LORD'S CASE AGAINST ISRAEL

6 Listen to what the LORD says:

"Stand up, plead your case before the
        mountains;
    let the hills hear what you have to say.
²Hear, O mountains, the LORD's accusation;
    listen, you everlasting foundations of the
        earth.
For the LORD has a case against his people;
    he is lodging a charge against Israel.

³"My people, what have I done to you?
    How have I burdened you? Answer me.
⁴I brought you up out of Egypt
    and redeemed you from the land of slavery.
I sent Moses to lead you,
    also Aaron and Miriam.
⁵My people, remember
    what Balak king of Moab counseled
    and what Balaam son of Beor answered.
Remember ⌊your journey⌋ from Shittim to
        Gilgal,
    that you may know the righteous acts of
        the LORD."

⁶With what shall I come before the LORD
    and bow down before the exalted God?
Shall I come before him with burnt offerings,

ᵃ 14 That is, symbols of the goddess Asherah

THE MESSAGE

like an island in the sea of peoples,
Like the king of beasts among wild beasts,
    like a young lion loose in a flock of sheep,
Killing and devouring the lambs
    and no one able to stop him.
With your arms raised in triumph over your
        foes,
    your enemies will be no more!

✛

5.10-15 "The day is coming"
    —GOD's Decree—
"When there will be no more war. None.
    I'll slaughter your war horses and demolish
        your chariots.
I'll dismantle military posts
    and level your fortifications.
I'll abolish your religious black markets,
    your underworld traffic in black magic.
I will smash your carved and cast gods
    and chop down your phallic posts.
No more taking control of the world,
    worshiping what you do or make.
I'll root out your sacred sex-and-power centers
    and destroy the God-defiant.
In raging anger, I'll make a clean sweep
    of godless nations who haven't listened."

WHAT GOD IS LOOKING FOR

6.1-2 **6** Listen now, listen to GOD:

"Take your stand in court.
    If you have a complaint, tell the mountains;
    make your case to the hills.
And now, Mountains, hear GOD's case;
    listen, Jury Earth—
For I am bringing charges against my people.
    I am building a case against Israel.

6.3-5 "Dear people, how have I done you wrong?
    Have I burdened you, worn you out?
        Answer!
I delivered you from a bad life in Egypt;
    I paid a good price to get you out of slavery.
I sent Moses to lead you—
    and Aaron and Miriam to boot!
Remember what Balak king of Moab tried to
        pull,
    and how Balaam son of Beor turned the
        tables on him.
Remember all those stories about Shittim and
        Gilgal.
    Keep all GOD's salvation stories fresh and
        present."

6.6-7 How can I stand up before GOD
    and show proper respect to the high God?
Should I bring an armload of offerings

NEW INTERNATIONAL VERSION

with calves a year old?
[7] Will the LORD be pleased with thousands of
rams,
with ten thousand rivers of oil?
Shall I offer my firstborn for my
transgression,
the fruit of my body for the sin of my
soul?
[8] He has showed you, O man, what is good.
And what does the LORD require of you?
To act justly and to love mercy
and to walk humbly with your God.

ISRAEL'S GUILT AND PUNISHMENT

[9] Listen! The LORD is calling to the city—
and to fear your name is wisdom—
"Heed the rod and the One who
appointed it.[a]
[10] Am I still to forget, O wicked house,
your ill-gotten treasures
and the short ephah,[b] which is accursed?
[11] Shall I acquit a man with dishonest scales,
with a bag of false weights?
[12] Her rich men are violent;
her people are liars
and their tongues speak deceitfully.
[13] Therefore, I have begun to destroy you,
to ruin you because of your sins.
[14] You will eat but not be satisfied;
your stomach will still be empty.[c]
You will store up but save nothing,
because what you save I will give to the
sword.
[15] You will plant but not harvest;
you will press olives but not use the oil on
yourselves,
you will crush grapes but not drink the
wine.
[16] You have observed the statutes of Omri
and all the practices of Ahab's house,
and you have followed their traditions.
Therefore I will give you over to ruin
and your people to derision;
you will bear the scorn of the nations.[d]"

---

[a] 9 The meaning of the Hebrew for this line is uncertain.
[b] 10 An ephah was a dry measure.   [c] 14 The meaning of
the Hebrew for this word is uncertain.   [d] 16 Septuagint;
Hebrew scorn due my people

THE MESSAGE

topped off with yearling calves?
Would GOD be impressed with thousands of
rams,
with buckets and barrels of olive oil?
Would he be moved if I sacrificed my
firstborn child,
my precious baby, to cancel my sin?

6.8 But he's already made it plain how to live,
what to do,
what GOD is looking for in men and
women.
It's quite simple: Do what is fair and just to
your neighbor,
be compassionate and loyal in your love,
And don't take yourself too seriously—
take God seriously.

6.9 Attention! GOD calls out to the city!
If you know what's good for you, you'll
listen.
So listen, all of you!
This is serious business.

6.10-16 "Do you expect me to overlook obscene
wealth
you've piled up by cheating and fraud?
Do you think I'll tolerate shady deals
and shifty scheming?
I'm tired of the violent rich
bullying their way with bluffs and lies.
I'm fed up. Beginning now, you're finished.
You'll pay for your sins down to your last
cent.
No matter how much you get, it will never be
enough—
hollow stomachs, empty hearts.
No matter how hard you work, you'll have
nothing to show for it—
bankrupt lives, wasted souls.
You'll plant grass
but never get a lawn.
You'll make jelly
but never spread it on your bread.
You'll press apples
but never drink the cider.
You have lived by the standards of your king,
Omri,
the decadent lifestyle of the family of Ahab.
Because you've slavishly followed their
fashions,
I'm forcing you into bankruptcy.
Your way of life will be laughed at, a tasteless
joke.
Your lives will be derided as futile and
fake."

NEW INTERNATIONAL VERSION

ISRAEL'S MISERY

7 What misery is mine!
I am like one who gathers summer fruit
at the gleaning of the vineyard;
there is no cluster of grapes to eat,
none of the early figs that I crave.
2 The godly have been swept from the land;
not one upright man remains.
All men lie in wait to shed blood;
each hunts his brother with a net.
3 Both hands are skilled in doing evil;
the ruler demands gifts,
the judge accepts bribes,
the powerful dictate what they desire—
they all conspire together.
4 The best of them is like a brier,
the most upright worse than a thorn
hedge.
The day of your watchmen has come,
the day God visits you.
Now is the time of their confusion.
5 Do not trust a neighbor;
put no confidence in a friend.
Even with her who lies in your embrace
be careful of your words.
6 For a son dishonors his father,
a daughter rises up against her mother,
a daughter-in-law against her mother-in-
law—
a man's enemies are the members of his
own household.

7 But as for me, I watch in hope for the LORD,
I wait for God my Savior;
my God will hear me.

ISRAEL WILL RISE

8 Do not gloat over me, my enemy!
Though I have fallen, I will rise.
Though I sit in darkness,
the LORD will be my light.
9 Because I have sinned against him,
I will bear the LORD's wrath,
until he pleads my case
and establishes my right.
He will bring me out into the light;
I will see his righteousness.
10 Then my enemy will see it
and will be covered with shame,
she who said to me,
"Where is the LORD your God?"
My eyes will see her downfall;
even now she will be trampled underfoot
like mire in the streets.

THE MESSAGE

STICK AROUND TO SEE WHAT GOD WILL DO

7.1-6 **7** I'm overwhelmed with sorrow!
sunk in a swamp of despair!
I'm like someone who goes to the garden
to pick cabbages and carrots and corn
And returns empty-handed,
finds nothing for soup or sandwich or
salad.
There's not a decent person in sight.
Right-living humans are extinct.
They're all out for one another's blood,
animals preying on each other.
They've all become experts in evil.
Corrupt leaders demand bribes.
The powerful rich
make sure they get what they want.
The best and brightest are thistles.
The top of the line is crabgrass.
But no longer: It's exam time.
Look at them slinking away in disgrace!
Don't trust your neighbor,
don't confide in your friend.
Watch your words,
even with your spouse.
Neighborhoods and families are falling to
pieces.
The closer they are—sons, daughters,
in-laws—
The worse they can be.
Your own family is the enemy.

✠

7.7 But me, I'm not giving up.
I'm sticking around to see what GOD will
do.
I'm waiting for God to make things right.
I'm counting on God to listen to me.

SPREADING YOUR WINGS

7.8-10 Don't, enemy, crow over me.
I'm down, but I'm not out.
I'm sitting in the dark right now,
but GOD is my light.
I can take GOD's punishing rage.
I deserve it—I sinned.
But it's not forever. He's on my side
and is going to get me out of this.
He'll turn on the lights and show me his ways.
I'll see the whole picture and how right
he is.
And my enemy will see it, too,
and be discredited—yes, disgraced!
This enemy who kept taunting,
"So where is this GOD of yours?"
I'm going to see it with these, my own eyes—
my enemy disgraced, trash in the gutter.

✠

NEW INTERNATIONAL VERSION

¹¹ The day for building your walls will come,
 the day for extending your boundaries.
¹² In that day people will come to you
 from Assyria and the cities of Egypt,
 even from Egypt to the Euphrates
 and from sea to sea
 and from mountain to mountain.
¹³ The earth will become desolate because of its
 inhabitants,
 as the result of their deeds.

PRAYER AND PRAISE

¹⁴ Shepherd your people with your staff,
 the flock of your inheritance,
 which lives by itself in a forest,
 in fertile pasturelands. ^a
 Let them feed in Bashan and Gilead
 as in days long ago.

¹⁵ "As in the days when you came out of Egypt,
 I will show them my wonders."

¹⁶ Nations will see and be ashamed,
 deprived of all their power.
 They will lay their hands on their mouths
 and their ears will become deaf.
¹⁷ They will lick dust like a snake,
 like creatures that crawl on the ground.
 They will come trembling out of their dens;
 they will turn in fear to the LORD our God
 and will be afraid of you.
¹⁸ Who is a God like you,
 who pardons sin and forgives the
 transgression
 of the remnant of his inheritance?
 You do not stay angry forever
 but delight to show mercy.
¹⁹ You will again have compassion on us;
 you will tread our sins underfoot
 and hurl all our iniquities into the depths
 of the sea.
²⁰ You will be true to Jacob,
 and show mercy to Abraham,
 as you pledged on oath to our fathers
 in days long ago.

THE MESSAGE

7.11-13 Oh, that will be a day! A day for rebuilding
 your city,
 a day for stretching your arms, spreading
 your wings!
 All your dispersed and scattered people will
 come back,
 old friends and family from faraway places,
 From Assyria in the east to Egypt in the west,
 from across the seas and out of the
 mountains.
 But there'll be a reversal for everyone else—
 massive depopulation—
 because of the way they lived, the things
 they did.

7.14-17 Shepherd, O GOD, your people with your staff,
 your dear and precious flock.
 Uniquely yours in a grove of trees,
 centered in lotus land.
 Let them graze in lush Bashan
 as in the old days in green Gilead.
 Reproduce the miracle-wonders
 of our exodus from Egypt.
 And the godless nations: Put them in their
 place—
 humiliated in their arrogance, speechless
 and clueless.
 Make them slink like snakes, crawl like
 cockroaches,
 come out of their holes from under their
 rocks
 And face our GOD.
 Fill them with holy fear and trembling.

✝

7.18-20 Where is the god who can compare with
 you—
 wiping the slate clean of guilt,
 Turning a blind eye, a deaf ear,
 to the past sins of your purged and
 precious people?
 You don't nurse your anger and don't stay
 angry long,
 for mercy is your specialty. That's what you
 love most.
 And compassion is on its way to us.
 You'll stamp out our wrongdoing.
 You'll sink our sins
 to the bottom of the ocean.
 You'll stay true to your word to Father Jacob
 and continue the compassion you showed
 Grandfather Abraham—
 Everything you promised our ancestors
 from a long time ago.

NAHUM

NAHUM

1 An oracle concerning Nineveh. The book of the vision of Nahum the Elkoshite.

THE LORD'S ANGER AGAINST NINEVEH

2 The LORD is a jealous and avenging God;
    the LORD takes vengeance and is filled
        with wrath.
The LORD takes vengeance on his foes
    and maintains his wrath against his
        enemies.
3 The LORD is slow to anger and great in
        power;
    the LORD will not leave the guilty
        unpunished.
His way is in the whirlwind and the storm,
    and clouds are the dust of his feet.
4 He rebukes the sea and dries it up;
    he makes all the rivers run dry.
Bashan and Carmel wither
    and the blossoms of Lebanon fade.
5 The mountains quake before him
    and the hills melt away.
The earth trembles at his presence,
    the world and all who live in it.
6 Who can withstand his indignation?
    Who can endure his fierce anger?
His wrath is poured out like fire;
    the rocks are shattered before him.

7 The LORD is good,
    a refuge in times of trouble.
He cares for those who trust in him,
8   but with an overwhelming flood
he will make an end of ⌊Nineveh⌋;
    he will pursue his foes into darkness.

9 Whatever they plot against the LORD
    he[a] will bring to an end;
    trouble will not come a second time.
10 They will be entangled among thorns
    and drunk from their wine;
    they will be consumed like dry stubble.[b]
11 From you, ⌊O Nineveh,⌋ has one come forth

GOD IS SERIOUS BUSINESS

1.1 1 A report on the problem of Nineveh, the way God gave Nahum of Elkosh to see it:

1.2-6 GOD is serious business.
    He won't be trifled with.
He avenges his foes.
    He stands up against his enemies, fierce
        and raging.
But GOD doesn't lose his temper.
    He's powerful, but it's a patient power.
Still, no one gets by with anything.
    Sooner or later, everyone pays.
Tornadoes and hurricanes
    are the wake of his passage,
Storm clouds are the dust
    he shakes off his feet.
He yells at the sea: It dries up.
    All the rivers run dry.
The Bashan and Carmel mountains shrivel,
    the Lebanon orchards shrivel.
Mountains quake in their roots,
    hills dissolve into mud flats.
Earth shakes in fear of GOD.
    The whole world's in a panic.
Who can face such towering anger?
    Who can stand up to this fierce rage?
His anger spills out like a river of lava,
    his fury shatters boulders.

1.7-10 GOD is good,
    a hiding place in tough times.
He recognizes and welcomes
    anyone looking for help,
No matter how desperate the trouble.
    But cozy islands of escape
He wipes right off the map.
    No one gets away from God.
Why waste time conniving against GOD?
    He's putting an end to all such scheming.
For troublemakers, no second chances.
    Like a pile of dry brush,
Soaked in oil,
    they'll go up in flames.

A THINK TANK FOR LIES

1.11 Nineveh's an anthill

_a 9 Or *What do you foes plot against the LORD? / He*
_b 10 The meaning of the Hebrew for this verse is uncertain.

NEW INTERNATIONAL VERSION	THE MESSAGE

NEW INTERNATIONAL VERSION

who plots evil against the LORD
and counsels wickedness.

12 This is what the LORD says:

"Although they have allies and are
    numerous,
they will be cut off and pass away.
Although I have afflicted you, ⌊O Judah,⌋
I will afflict you no more.
13 Now I will break their yoke from your neck
and tear your shackles away."

14 The LORD has given a command concerning
    you, ⌊Nineveh⌋:
"You will have no descendants to bear
    your name.
I will destroy the carved images and cast
    idols
that are in the temple of your gods.
I will prepare your grave,
    for you are vile."

15 Look, there on the mountains,
the feet of one who brings good news,
    who proclaims peace!
Celebrate your festivals, O Judah,
    and fulfill your vows.
No more will the wicked invade you;
they will be completely destroyed.

NINEVEH TO FALL

2 An attacker advances against you,
    ⌊Nineveh⌋.
Guard the fortress,
    watch the road,
brace yourselves,
    marshal all your strength!

2 The LORD will restore the splendor of Jacob
    like the splendor of Israel,
though destroyers have laid them waste
    and have ruined their vines.

3 The shields of his soldiers are red;
    the warriors are clad in scarlet.
The metal on the chariots flashes
    on the day they are made ready;
the spears of pine are brandished. a

4 The chariots storm through the streets,
rushing back and forth through the
    squares.

a 3 Hebrew; Septuagint and Syriac / the horsemen rush to and
fro

THE MESSAGE

of evil plots against GOD,
A think tank for lies
    that seduce and betray.

1.12-13 And GOD has something to say about all this:
"Even though you're on top of the world,
With all the applause and all the votes,
    you'll be mowed down flat.

"I've afflicted you, Judah, true,
    but I won't afflict you again.
From now on I'm taking the yoke from your
    neck
    and splitting it up for kindling.
I'm cutting you free
    from the ropes of your bondage."

☩

1.14 GOD's orders on Nineveh:

"You're the end of the line.
    It's all over with Nineveh.
I'm gutting your temple.
    Your gods and goddesses go in the trash.
I'm digging your grave. It's an unmarked
    grave.
You're nothing—no, you're *less* than
    nothing!"

1.15 Look! Striding across the mountains—
a messenger bringing the latest good news:
    peace!
A holiday, Judah! Celebrate!
    Worship and recommit to God!
No more worries about *this* enemy.
    This one is history. Close the books.

ISRAEL'S BEEN TO HELL AND BACK

2.1 2 The juggernaut's coming!
    Post guards, lay in supplies.
Get yourselves together,
    get ready for the big battle.

☩

2.2 GOD has restored the Pride of Jacob,
    the Pride of Israel.
Israel's lived through hard times.
    He's been to hell and back.

2.3-12 Weapons flash in the sun,
    the soldiers splendid in battle dress,
Chariots burnished and glistening,
    ready to charge,
A spiked forest of brandished spears,
    lethal on the horizon.
The chariots pour into the streets.
    They fill the public squares,

NEW INTERNATIONAL VERSION

They look like flaming torches;
　　they dart about like lightning.

⁵He summons his picked troops,
　　yet they stumble on their way.
They dash to the city wall;
　　the protective shield is put in place.
⁶The river gates are thrown open
　　and the palace collapses.
⁷It is decreed ᵃ that ⌊the city⌋
　　be exiled and carried away.
Its slave girls moan like doves
　　and beat upon their breasts.
⁸Nineveh is like a pool,
　　and its water is draining away.
"Stop! Stop!" they cry,
　　but no one turns back.
⁹Plunder the silver!
　　Plunder the gold!
The supply is endless,
　　the wealth from all its treasures!
¹⁰She is pillaged, plundered, stripped!
　　Hearts melt, knees give way,
　　bodies tremble, every face grows pale.

¹¹Where now is the lions' den,
　　the place where they fed their young,
where the lion and lioness went,
　　and the cubs, with nothing to fear?
¹²The lion killed enough for his cubs
　　and strangled the prey for his mate,
filling his lairs with the kill
　　and his dens with the prey.

¹³"I am against you,"
　　declares the LORD Almighty.
"I will burn up your chariots in smoke,
　　and the sword will devour your young
　　　lions.
I will leave you no prey on the earth.
　　The voices of your messengers
　　will no longer be heard."

WOE TO NINEVEH

3 Woe to the city of blood,
　　full of lies,
full of plunder,
　　never without victims!

THE MESSAGE

Flaming like torches in the sun,
　　like lightning darting and flashing.
The Assyrian king rallies his men,
　　but they stagger and stumble.
They run to the ramparts
　　to stem the tide, but it's too late.
Soldiers pour through the gates.
　　The palace is demolished.
Soon it's all over:
　　Nineveh stripped, Nineveh doomed,
Maids and slaves moaning like doves,
　　beating their breasts.
Nineveh is a tub
　　from which they've pulled the plug.
Cries go up, "Do something! Do something!"
　　but it's too late. Nineveh's soon empty—
　　　nothing.
Other cries come: "Plunder the silver!
　　Plunder the gold!
A bonanza of plunder!
　　Take everything you want!"
Doom! Damnation! Desolation!
　　Hearts sink,
　　knees fold,
　　stomachs retch,
　　faces blanch.
So, what happened to the famous
　　and fierce Assyrian lion
And all those cute Assyrian cubs?
　　To the lion and lioness
Cozy with their cubs,
　　fierce and fearless?
To the lion who always returned from the
　　　hunt
　　with fresh kills for lioness and cubs,
The lion lair heaped with bloody meat,
　　blood and bones for the royal lion feast?

✠

2.13 "Assyria, I'm your enemy,"
　　says GOD-of-the-Angel-Armies.
"I'll torch your chariots. They'll go up in
　　　smoke.
　'Lion Country' will be strewn with
　　　carcasses.
The war business is over—you're out of work:
　　You'll have no more wars to report,
No more victories to announce.
　　You're out of war work forever."

LET THE NATIONS GET THEIR FILL OF THE UGLY
TRUTH

3.1-4 **3** Doom to Murder City—
　　full of lies, bursting with loot, addicted
　　　to violence!

NEW INTERNATIONAL VERSION

²The crack of whips,
    the clatter of wheels,
galloping horses
    and jolting chariots!
³Charging cavalry,
    flashing swords
    and glittering spears!
Many casualties,
    piles of dead,
bodies without number,
    people stumbling over the corpses—
⁴all because of the wanton lust of a harlot,
    alluring, the mistress of sorceries,
who enslaved nations by her prostitution
    and peoples by her witchcraft.

⁵"I am against you," declares the Lord
      Almighty.
    "I will lift your skirts over your face.
I will show the nations your nakedness
    and the kingdoms your shame.
⁶I will pelt you with filth,
    I will treat you with contempt
    and make you a spectacle.
⁷All who see you will flee from you and say,
    'Nineveh is in ruins—who will mourn for
      her?'
    Where can I find anyone to comfort you?"

⁸Are you better than Thebes,ᵃ
    situated on the Nile,
    with water around her?
The river was her defense,
    the waters her wall.
⁹Cushᵇ and Egypt were her boundless
      strength;
    Put and Libya were among her allies.
¹⁰Yet she was taken captive
    and went into exile.
Her infants were dashed to pieces
    at the head of every street.
Lots were cast for her nobles,
    and all her great men were put in chains.
¹¹You too will become drunk;
    you will go into hiding
    and seek refuge from the enemy.

¹²All your fortresses are like fig trees
    with their first ripe fruit;
    when they are shaken,

THE MESSAGE

Horns blaring, wheels clattering,
    horses rearing, chariots lurching,
Horsemen galloping,
    brandishing swords and spears,
Dead bodies rotting in the street,
    corpses stacked like cordwood,
Bodies in every gutter and alley,
    clogging every intersection!
And whores! Whores without end!
    Whore City,
Fatally seductive, you're the Witch of
      Seduction,
    luring nations to their ruin with your evil
      spells.

        ✝

3.5-7 "I'm your enemy, Whore Nineveh—
    I, God-of-the-Angel-Armies!
I'll strip you of your seductive silk robes
    and expose you on the world stage.
I'll let the nations get their fill of the ugly
      truth
    of who you really are and have been all
      along.
I'll pelt you with dog dung
    and place you on a pedestal: 'Slut on
      Exhibit.'
Everyone who sees you will gag and say,
    'Nineveh's a pigsty:
What on earth did we ever see in her?
    Who would give her a second look? Ugh!' "

Past the Point of No Return

3.8-13 Do you think you're superior to Egyptian
      Thebes,
    proudly invincible on the River Nile,
Protected by the great River,
    walled in by the River, secure?
Ethiopia stood guard to the south,
    Egypt to the north.
Put and Libya, strong friends,
    were ready to step in and help.
But you know what happened to her:
    The whole city was marched off to a
      refugee camp,
Her babies smashed to death
    in public view on the streets,
Her prize leaders auctioned off,
    her celebrities put in chain gangs.
Expect the same treatment, Nineveh.
    You'll soon be staggering like a bunch of
      drunks,
Wondering what hit you,
    looking for a place to sleep it off.
All your forts are like peach trees,
    the lush peaches ripe, ready for the picking.
One shake of the tree and they fall

ᵃ 8 Hebrew *No Amon*   ᵇ 9 That is, the upper Nile region

NEW INTERNATIONAL VERSION

the figs fall into the mouth of the eater.
¹³Look at your troops—
    they are all women!
The gates of your land
    are wide open to your enemies;
    fire has consumed their bars.

¹⁴Draw water for the siege,
    strengthen your defenses!
Work the clay,
    tread the mortar,
    repair the brickwork!
¹⁵There the fire will devour you;
    the sword will cut you down
    and, like grasshoppers, consume you.
Multiply like grasshoppers,
    multiply like locusts!
¹⁶You have increased the number of your
        merchants
    till they are more than the stars of the sky,
but like locusts they strip the land
    and then fly away.
¹⁷Your guards are like locusts,
    your officials like swarms of locusts
    that settle in the walls on a cold day—
but when the sun appears they fly away,
    and no one knows where.

¹⁸O king of Assyria, your shepherds*ᵃ* slumber;
    your nobles lie down to rest.
Your people are scattered on the mountains
    with no one to gather them.
¹⁹Nothing can heal your wound;
    your injury is fatal.
Everyone who hears the news about you
    claps his hands at your fall,
for who has not felt
    your endless cruelty?

THE MESSAGE

straight into hungry mouths.
Face it: Your warriors are wimps.
    You're sitting ducks.
Your borders are gaping doors, inviting
    your enemies in. And who's to stop them?

3.14-15 Store up water for the siege.
    Shore up your defenses.
Get down to basics: Work the clay
    and make bricks.
Sorry. Too late.
    Enemy fire will burn you up.
Swords will cut you to pieces.
    You'll be chewed up as if by locusts.

3.15-17 Yes, as if by locusts—a fitting fate,
    for you yourselves are a locust plague.
You've multiplied shops and shopkeepers—
    more buyers and sellers than stars in the
        sky!
A plague of locusts, cleaning out the
        neighborhood
    and then flying off.
Your bureaucrats are locusts,
    your brokers and bankers are locusts.
Early on, they're all at your service,
    full of smiles and promises,
But later when you return with questions or
        complaints,
    you'll find they've flown off and are
        nowhere to be found.

3.18-19 King of Assyria! Your shepherd-leaders,
    in charge of caring for your people,
Are busy doing everything else but.
    They're not doing their job,
And your people are scattered and lost.
    There's no one to look after them.
You're past the point of no return.
    Your wound is fatal.
When the story of your fate gets out,
    the whole world will applaud and cry
        "Encore!"
Your cruel evil has seeped
    into every nook and cranny of the world.
    Everyone has felt it and suffered.

ᵃ 18 Or rulers

HABAKKUK

HABAKKUK

1 The oracle that Habakkuk the prophet received.

HABAKKUK'S COMPLAINT

² How long, O LORD, must I call for help,
    but you do not listen?
Or cry out to you, "Violence!"
    but you do not save?
³ Why do you make me look at injustice?
    Why do you tolerate wrong?
Destruction and violence are before me;
    there is strife, and conflict abounds.
⁴ Therefore the law is paralyzed,
    and justice never prevails.
The wicked hem in the righteous,
    so that justice is perverted.

THE LORD'S ANSWER

⁵ "Look at the nations and watch—
    and be utterly amazed.
For I am going to do something in your days
    that you would not believe,
    even if you were told.
⁶ I am raising up the Babylonians,ᵃ
    that ruthless and impetuous people,
who sweep across the whole earth
    to seize dwelling places not their own.
⁷ They are a feared and dreaded people;
    they are a law to themselves
    and promote their own honor.
⁸ Their horses are swifter than leopards,
    fiercer than wolves at dusk.
Their cavalry gallops headlong;
    their horsemen come from afar.
They fly like a vulture swooping to devour;
⁹   they all come bent on violence.
Their hordesᵇ advance like a desert wind
    and gather prisoners like sand.
¹⁰ They deride kings
    and scoff at rulers.
They laugh at all fortified cities;
    they build earthen ramps and capture
    them.

JUSTICE IS A JOKE

1.1-4 **1** The problem as God gave Habakkuk to
    see it:

GOD, how long do I have to cry out for help
    before you listen?
How many times do I have to yell, "Help!
        Murder! Police!"
    before you come to the rescue?
Why do you force me to look at evil,
    stare trouble in the face day after day?
Anarchy and violence break out,
    quarrels and fights all over the place.
Law and order fall to pieces.
    Justice is a joke.
The wicked have the righteous hamstrung
    and stand justice on its head.

GOD SAYS, "LOOK!"

1.5-11 "Look around at the godless nations.
    Look long and hard. Brace yourself for a
        shock.
Something's about to take place
    and you're going to find it hard to believe.
I'm about to raise up Babylonians to punish
        you,
    Babylonians, fierce and ferocious—
World-conquering Babylon,
    grabbing up nations right and left,
A dreadful and terrible people,
    making up its own rules as it goes.
Their horses run like the wind,
    attack like bloodthirsty wolves.
A stampede of galloping horses
    thunders out of nowhere.
They descend like vultures
    circling in on carrion.
They're out to kill. Death is on their minds.
    They collect victims like squirrels gathering
        nuts.
They mock kings,
    poke fun at generals,
Spit on forts,
    and leave them in the dust.

ᵃ 6 Or *Chaldeans*   ᵇ 9 The meaning of the Hebrew for this
word is uncertain.

NEW INTERNATIONAL VERSION

11 Then they sweep past like the wind and go
    on—
    guilty men, whose own strength is their
        god."

HABAKKUK'S SECOND COMPLAINT
12 O LORD, are you not from everlasting?
    My God, my Holy One, we will not die.
    O LORD, you have appointed them to execute
        judgment;
    O Rock, you have ordained them to
        punish.
13 Your eyes are too pure to look on evil;
    you cannot tolerate wrong.
    Why then do you tolerate the treacherous?
    Why are you silent while the wicked
    swallow up those more righteous than
        themselves?
14 You have made men like fish in the sea,
    like sea creatures that have no ruler.
15 The wicked foe pulls all of them up with
        hooks,
    he catches them in his net,
    he gathers them up in his dragnet;
    and so he rejoices and is glad.
16 Therefore he sacrifices to his net
    and burns incense to his dragnet,
    for by his net he lives in luxury
    and enjoys the choicest food.
17 Is he to keep on emptying his net,
    destroying nations without mercy?

2 I will stand at my watch
    and station myself on the ramparts;
I will look to see what he will say to me,
    and what answer I am to give to this
        complaint. a

THE LORD'S ANSWER
2 Then the LORD replied:

"Write down the revelation
    and make it plain on tablets
    so that a herald b may run with it.
3 For the revelation awaits an appointed time;
    it speaks of the end
    and will not prove false.

a 1 Or and what to answer when I am rebuked   b 2 Or so
that whoever reads it

THE MESSAGE

They'll all be blown away by the wind.
    Brazen in sin, they call strength their god."

WHY IS GOD SILENT NOW?
1.12-13 GOD, you're from eternity, aren't you?
    Holy God, we aren't going to die, are we?
GOD, you chose Babylonians for your
        judgment work?
    Rock-Solid God, you gave them the job of
        discipline?
But you can't be serious!
    You can't condone evil!
So why don't you do something about this?
    Why are you silent now?
This outrage! Evil men swallow up the
        righteous
    and you stand around and watch!

                    ✝

1.14-16 You're treating men and women
    as so many fish in the ocean,
Swimming without direction,
    swimming but not getting anywhere.
Then this evil Babylonian arrives and goes
        fishing.
    He pulls in a good catch.
He catches his limit and fills his creel—
    a good day of fishing! He's happy!
He praises his rod and reel,
    piles his fishing gear on an altar and
        worships it!
It's made his day,
    and he's going to eat well tonight!

                    ✝

1.17 Are you going to let this go on and on?
    Will you let this Babylonian fisherman
Fish like a weekend angler,
    killing people as if they're nothing but fish?

                    ✝

2.1 2 What's God going to say to my questions?
        I'm braced for the worst.
    I'll climb to the lookout tower and scan the
        horizon.
I'll wait to see what God says,
    how he'll answer my complaint.

FULL OF SELF, BUT SOUL-EMPTY
2.2-3 And then GOD answered: "Write this.
    Write what you see.
Write it out in big block letters
    so that it can be read on the run.
This vision-message is a witness
    pointing to what's coming.
It aches for the coming—it can hardly wait!
    And it doesn't lie.

NEW INTERNATIONAL VERSION

Though it linger, wait for it;
it [a] will certainly come and will not delay.

[4] "See, he is puffed up;
his desires are not upright—
but the righteous will live by his faith [b]—
[5] indeed, wine betrays him;
he is arrogant and never at rest.
Because he is as greedy as the grave [c]
and like death is never satisfied,
he gathers to himself all the nations
and takes captive all the peoples.

[6] "Will not all of them taunt him with ridicule
and scorn, saying,

" 'Woe to him who piles up stolen goods
and makes himself wealthy by extortion!
How long must this go on?'
[7] Will not your debtors [d] suddenly arise?
Will they not wake up and make you
tremble?
Then you will become their victim.
[8] Because you have plundered many nations,
the peoples who are left will plunder you.
For you have shed man's blood;
you have destroyed lands and cities and
everyone in them.

[9] "Woe to him who builds his realm by unjust
gain
to set his nest on high,
to escape the clutches of ruin!
[10] You have plotted the ruin of many peoples,
shaming your own house and forfeiting
your life.
[11] The stones of the wall will cry out,
and the beams of the woodwork will echo
it.

[12] "Woe to him who builds a city with
bloodshed
and establishes a town by crime!
[13] Has not the LORD Almighty determined
that the people's labor is only fuel for the
fire,

THE MESSAGE

If it seems slow in coming, wait.
It's on its way. It will come right on time.

✝

2.4 "Look at that man, bloated by
self-importance—
full of himself but soul-empty.
But the person in right standing before God
through loyal and steady believing
is fully alive, *really* alive.

2.5-6 "Note well: Money deceives.
The arrogant rich don't last.
They are more hungry for wealth
than the grave is for cadavers.
Like death, they always want more,
but the 'more' they get is dead bodies.
They are cemeteries filled with dead nations,
graveyards filled with corpses.
Don't give people like this a second thought.
Soon the whole world will be taunting
them:

2.6-8 " 'Who do you think you are—
getting rich by stealing and extortion?
How long do you think
you can get away with this?'
Indeed, how long before your victims wake
up,
stand up and make *you* the victim?
You've plundered nation after nation.
Now you'll get a taste of your own
medicine.
All the survivors are out to plunder you,
a payback for all your murders and
massacres.

2.9-11 "Who do you think you are—
recklessly grabbing and looting,
Living it up, acting like king of the mountain,
acting above it all, above trials and
troubles?
You've engineered the ruin of your own
house.
In ruining others you've ruined yourself.
You've undermined your foundations,
rotted out your own soul.
The bricks of your house will speak up and
accuse you.
The woodwork will step forward with
evidence.

2.12-14 "Who do you think you are—
building a town by murder, a city with
crime?
Don't you know that GOD-of-the-Angel-
Armies
makes sure nothing comes of that but
ashes,

---

[a] 3 Or *Though he linger, wait for him; / he*
[b] 4 Or *faithfulness*   [c] 5 Hebrew *Sheol*   [d] 7 Or *creditors*

NEW INTERNATIONAL VERSION	THE MESSAGE

NEW INTERNATIONAL VERSION

that the nations exhaust themselves for
    nothing?
[14] For the earth will be filled with the
    knowledge of the glory of the LORD,
    as the waters cover the sea.

[15] "Woe to him who gives drink to his
    neighbors,
    pouring it from the wineskin till they are
      drunk,
    so that he can gaze on their naked bodies.
[16] You will be filled with shame instead of
    glory.
    Now it is your turn! Drink and be
      exposed[a]!
The cup from the LORD's right hand is
    coming around to you,
    and disgrace will cover your glory.
[17] The violence you have done to Lebanon will
    overwhelm you,
    and your destruction of animals will
      terrify you.
For you have shed man's blood;
    you have destroyed lands and cities and
      everyone in them.

[18] "Of what value is an idol, since a man has
    carved it?
    Or an image that teaches lies?
For he who makes it trusts in his own
    creation;
    he makes idols that cannot speak.
[19] Woe to him who says to wood, 'Come to
    life!'
    Or to lifeless stone, 'Wake up!'
Can it give guidance?
    It is covered with gold and silver;
    there is no breath in it.
[20] But the LORD is in his holy temple;
    let all the earth be silent before him."

HABAKKUK'S PRAYER

3 A prayer of Habakkuk the prophet. On *shig-
ionoth.*[b]

[2] LORD, I have heard of your fame;
    I stand in awe of your deeds, O LORD.
Renew them in our day,
    in our time make them known;
    in wrath remember mercy.

THE MESSAGE

Makes sure the harder you work
    at that kind of thing, the less you are?
Meanwhile the earth fills up
    with awareness of GOD's glory
    as the waters cover the sea.

2.15-17 "Who do you think you are—
    inviting your neighbors to your drunken
      parties,
Giving them too much to drink,
    roping them into your sexual orgies?
You thought you were having the time of your
    life.
    Wrong! It's a time of disgrace.
All the time you were drinking,
    you were drinking from the cup of God's
      wrath.
You'll wake up holding your throbbing head,
    hung over—
    hung over from Lebanon violence,
Hung over from animal massacres,
    hung over from murder and mayhem,
From multiple violations
    of place and people.

2.18-19 "What's the use of a carved god
    so skillfully carved by its sculptor?
What good is a fancy cast god
    when all it tells is lies?
What sense does it make to be a pious god-
    maker
    who makes gods that can't even talk?
Who do you think you are—
    saying to a stick of wood, 'Wake up,'
Or to a dumb stone, 'Get up'?
    Can they teach you anything about
      anything?
There's nothing to them but surface.
    There's nothing on the inside.

2.20 "But oh! GOD is in his holy Temple!
    Quiet everyone—a holy silence. Listen!"

GOD RACING ON THE CREST OF THE WAVES

3 A prayer of the prophet Habakkuk, with
3.1-2   orchestra:

GOD, I've heard what our ancestors say about
    you,
    and I'm stopped in my tracks, down on my
      knees.
Do among us what you did among them.
    Work among us as you worked among
      them.
And as you bring judgment, as you surely
    must,
    remember mercy.

---

a 16 Masoretic Text; Dead Sea Scrolls, Aquila, Vulgate and
Syriac (see also Septuagint) *and stagger*   *b 1* Probably a
literary or musical term

✠

NEW INTERNATIONAL VERSION

³God came from Teman,
  the Holy One from Mount Paran. *Selah* [a]
His glory covered the heavens
  and his praise filled the earth.
⁴His splendor was like the sunrise;
  rays flashed from his hand,
  where his power was hidden.
⁵Plague went before him;
  pestilence followed his steps.
⁶He stood, and shook the earth;
  he looked, and made the nations tremble.
The ancient mountains crumbled
  and the age-old hills collapsed.
  His ways are eternal.
⁷I saw the tents of Cushan in distress,
  the dwellings of Midian in anguish.

⁸Were you angry with the rivers, O LORD?
  Was your wrath against the streams?
Did you rage against the sea
  when you rode with your horses
  and your victorious chariots?
⁹You uncovered your bow,
  you called for many arrows.   *Selah*
You split the earth with rivers;
¹⁰ the mountains saw you and writhed.
Torrents of water swept by;
  the deep roared
  and lifted its waves on high.

¹¹Sun and moon stood still in the heavens
  at the glint of your flying arrows,
  at the lightning of your flashing spear.
¹²In wrath you strode through the earth
  and in anger you threshed the nations.
¹³You came out to deliver your people,
  to save your anointed one.
You crushed the leader of the land of
    wickedness,
  you stripped him from head to foot.   *Selah*
¹⁴With his own spear you pierced his head
  when his warriors stormed out to scatter
    us,
  gloating as though about to devour
  the wretched who were in hiding.
¹⁵You trampled the sea with your horses,
  churning the great waters.

¹⁶I heard and my heart pounded,
  my lips quivered at the sound;
decay crept into my bones,
  and my legs trembled.

THE MESSAGE

3.3-7 God's on his way again,
  retracing the old salvation route,
Coming up from the south through Teman,
  the Holy One from Mount Paran.
Skies are blazing with his splendor,
  his praises sounding through the earth,
His cloud-brightness like dawn, exploding,
    spreading,
  forked-lightning shooting from his hand—
  what power hidden in that fist!
Plague marches before him,
  pestilence at his heels!
He stops. He shakes Earth.
  He looks around. Nations tremble.
The age-old mountains fall to pieces;
  ancient hills collapse like a spent balloon.
The paths God takes are older
  than the oldest mountains and hills.
I saw everyone worried, in a panic:
  Old wilderness adversaries,
Cushan and Midian, were terrified,
  hoping he wouldn't notice them.

☩

3.8-16 GOD, is it River you're mad at?
  Angry at old River?
Were you raging at Sea when you rode
  horse and chariot through to salvation?
You unfurled your bow
  and let loose a volley of arrows.
  You split Earth with rivers.
Mountains saw what was coming.
  They twisted in pain.
Flood Waters poured in.
  Ocean roared and reared huge waves.
Sun and Moon stopped in their tracks.
  Your flashing arrows stopped them,
  your lightning-strike spears impaled them.
Angry, you stomped through Earth.
  Furious, you crushed the godless nations.
You were out to save your people,
  to save your specially chosen people.
You beat the stuffing
  out of King Wicked,
Stripped him naked
  from head to toe,
Set his severed head on his own spear
  and blew away his army.
Scattered they were to the four winds—
  and ended up food for the sharks!
You galloped through the Sea on your horses,
  racing on the crest of the waves.
When I heard it, my stomach did flips.
  I stammered and stuttered.
My bones turned to water.
  I staggered and stumbled.

---

^a 3 A word of uncertain meaning; possibly a musical term;
also in verses 9 and 13

NEW INTERNATIONAL VERSION

Yet I will wait patiently for the day of
        calamity
    to come on the nation invading us.
¹⁷ Though the fig tree does not bud
    and there are no grapes on the vines,
though the olive crop fails
    and the fields produce no food,
though there are no sheep in the pen
    and no cattle in the stalls,
¹⁸ yet I will rejoice in the LORD,
    I will be joyful in God my Savior.

¹⁹ The Sovereign LORD is my strength;
    he makes my feet like the feet of a deer,
    he enables me to go on the heights.

For the director of music. On my stringed
        instruments.

THE MESSAGE

I sit back and wait for Doomsday
    to descend on our attackers.

3.17-19 Though the cherry trees don't blossom
    and the strawberries don't ripen,
Though the apples are worm-eaten
    and the wheat fields stunted,
Though the sheep pens are sheepless
    and the cattle barns empty,
I'm singing joyful praise to GOD.
    I'm turning cartwheels of joy to my Savior
        God.
Counting on GOD's Rule to prevail,
    I take heart and gain strength.
I run like a deer.
    I feel like I'm king of the mountain!

(For congregational use, with a full
        orchestra.)

ZEPHANIAH

1 The word of the LORD that came to Zephani-ah son of Cushi, the son of Gedaliah, the son of Amariah, the son of Hezekiah, during the reign of Josiah son of Amon king of Judah:

WARNING OF COMING DESTRUCTION

2 "I will sweep away everything
    from the face of the earth,"
                        declares the LORD.
3 "I will sweep away both men and animals;
    I will sweep away the birds of the air
    and the fish of the sea.
The wicked will have only heaps of rubble[a]
    when I cut off man from the face of the
        earth,"
                        declares the LORD.

AGAINST JUDAH

4 "I will stretch out my hand against Judah
    and against all who live in Jerusalem.
I will cut off from this place every remnant
        of Baal,
    the names of the pagan and the idolatrous
        priests—
5 those who bow down on the roofs
    to worship the starry host,
    those who bow down and swear by the LORD
    and who also swear by Molech,[b]
6 those who turn back from following the
        LORD
    and neither seek the LORD nor inquire of
        him.
7 Be silent before the Sovereign LORD,
    for the day of the LORD is near.
The LORD has prepared a sacrifice;
    he has consecrated those he has invited.
8 On the day of the LORD's sacrifice
    I will punish the princes
    and the king's sons
    and all those clad
        in foreign clothes.
9 On that day I will punish

ZEPHANIAH

NO LONGER GIVING GOD A THOUGHT OR A PRAYER

1.1 1 GOD's Message to Zephaniah son of Cushi, son of Gedaliah, son of Amariah, son of Hezekiah. It came during the reign of Josiah son of Amon, who was king of Judah:

1.2 "I'm going to make a clean sweep of the earth,
    a thorough housecleaning." GOD's Decree.

1.3 "Men and women and animals,
    including birds and fish—
Anything and everything that causes sin—
        will go,
    but especially people.

1.4-6 "I'll start with Judah
    and everybody who lives in Jerusalem.
I'll sweep the place clean of every trace
    of the sex-and-religion Baal shrines and
        their priests.
I'll get rid of the people who sneak up to their
        rooftops at night
    to worship the star gods and goddesses;
Also those who continue to worship GOD
    but cover their bases by worshiping other
        king-gods as well;
Not to mention those who've dumped GOD
        altogether,
    no longer giving him a thought or offering
        a prayer.

1.7-13 "Quiet now!
    Reverent silence before me, GOD, the
        Master!
Time's up. My Judgment Day is near:
    The Holy Day is all set, the invited guests
        made holy.
On the Holy Day, GOD's Judgment Day,
    I will punish the leaders and the royal sons;
I will punish those who dress up like foreign
        priests and priestesses,

---

a 3 The meaning of the Hebrew for this line is uncertain.
b 5 Hebrew *Malcam*, that is, Milcom

NEW INTERNATIONAL VERSION

all who avoid stepping on the threshold,[a]
who fill the temple of their gods
  with violence and deceit.

10 "On that day," declares the LORD,
  "a cry will go up from the Fish Gate,
  wailing from the New Quarter,
  and a loud crash from the hills.
11 Wail, you who live in the market district[b];
  all your merchants will be wiped out,
  all who trade with[c] silver will be ruined.
12 At that time I will search Jerusalem with
    lamps
  and punish those who are complacent,
  who are like wine left on its dregs,
who think, 'The LORD will do nothing,
  either good or bad.'
13 Their wealth will be plundered,
  their houses demolished.
They will build houses
  but not live in them;
they will plant vineyards
  but not drink the wine.

THE GREAT DAY OF THE LORD

14 "The great day of the LORD is near—
  near and coming quickly.
Listen! The cry on the day of the LORD will
    be bitter,
  the shouting of the warrior there.
15 That day will be a day of wrath,
  a day of distress and anguish,
  a day of trouble and ruin,
  a day of darkness and gloom,
  a day of clouds and blackness,
16 a day of trumpet and battle cry
  against the fortified cities
  and against the corner towers.
17 I will bring distress on the people
  and they will walk like blind men,
  because they have sinned against the
    LORD.
Their blood will be poured out like dust
  and their entrails like filth.
18 Neither their silver nor their gold
  will be able to save them
  on the day of the LORD's wrath.
In the fire of his jealousy
  the whole world will be consumed,
for he will make a sudden end
  of all who live in the earth."

THE MESSAGE

Who introduce pagan prayers and
    practices;
And I'll punish all who import pagan
    superstitions
  that turn holy places into hellholes.
Judgment Day!" GOD's Decree!
  "Cries of panic from the city's Fish Gate,
Cries of terror from the city's Second Quarter,
  sounds of great crashing from the hills!
Wail, you shopkeepers on Market Street!
  Moneymaking has had its day. The god
    Money is dead.
On Judgment Day,
  I'll search through every closet and alley in
    Jerusalem.
I'll find and punish those who are sitting it
    out, fat and lazy,
  amusing themselves and taking it easy,
Who think, 'GOD doesn't do anything, good or
    bad.
  He isn't involved, so neither are we.'
But just wait. They'll lose everything they
    have,
  money and house and land.
They'll build a house and never move in.
  They'll plant vineyards and never taste the
    wine.

A DAY OF DARKNESS AT NOON

1.14-18 "The Great Judgment Day of GOD is almost
    here.
  It's countdown time: . . . seven, six, five,
    four . . .
Bitter and noisy cries on my Judgment Day,
  even strong men screaming for help.
Judgment Day is payday—my anger paid out:
  a day of distress and anguish,
  a day of catastrophic doom,
  a day of darkness at noon,
  a day of black storm clouds,
  a day of bloodcurdling war cries,
  as forts are assaulted,
  as defenses are smashed.
I'll make things so bad they won't know what
    hit them.
  They'll walk around groping like the blind.
  They've sinned against GOD!
Their blood will be poured out like old
    dishwater,
  their guts shoveled into slop buckets.
Don't plan on buying your way out.
  Your money is worthless for this.
This is the Day of GOD's Judgment—my
    wrath!
  I *care* about sin with fiery passion—
A fire to burn up the corrupted world,
  a wildfire finish to the corrupting people."

---

a 9 See 1 Samuel 5:5.   b 11 Or *the Mortar*   c 11 Or *in*

NEW INTERNATIONAL VERSION

2 Gather together, gather together,
  O shameful nation,
2 before the appointed time arrives
  and that day sweeps on like chaff,
before the fierce anger of the LORD comes
  upon you,
  before the day of the LORD's wrath comes
  upon you.
3 Seek the LORD, all you humble of the land,
  you who do what he commands.
Seek righteousness, seek humility;
  perhaps you will be sheltered
  on the day of the LORD's anger.

AGAINST PHILISTIA

4 Gaza will be abandoned
  and Ashkelon left in ruins.
At midday Ashdod will be emptied
  and Ekron uprooted.
5 Woe to you who live by the sea,
  O Kerethite people;
the word of the LORD is against you,
  O Canaan, land of the Philistines.
"I will destroy you,
  and none will be left."
6 The land by the sea, where the Kerethites[a]
  dwell,
  will be a place for shepherds and sheep
  pens.
7 It will belong to the remnant of the house of
  Judah;
  there they will find pasture.
In the evening they will lie down
  in the houses of Ashkelon.
The LORD their God will care for them;
  he will restore their fortunes.[b]

AGAINST MOAB AND AMMON

8 "I have heard the insults of Moab
  and the taunts of the Ammonites,
who insulted my people
  and made threats against their land.
9 Therefore, as surely as I live,"
  declares the LORD Almighty, the God of
  Israel,
"surely Moab will become like Sodom,
  the Ammonites like Gomorrah—
a place of weeds and salt pits,
  a wasteland forever.
The remnant of my people will plunder
  them;
  the survivors of my nation will inherit
  their land."

---

a 6 The meaning of the Hebrew for this word is uncertain.
b 7 Or will bring back their captives

THE MESSAGE

SEEK GOD

2.1-2 **2** So get yourselves together. Shape up!
  You're a nation without a clue about what
  it wants.
Do it before you're blown away
  like leaves in a windstorm,
Before GOD's Judgment-anger
  sweeps down on you,
Before GOD's Judgment Day wrath
  descends with full force.

✝

2.3 Seek GOD, all you quietly disciplined people
  who live by GOD's justice.
Seek GOD's right ways. Seek a quiet and
  disciplined life.
Perhaps you'll be hidden on the Day of
  GOD's anger.

ALL EARTH-MADE GODS WILL BLOW AWAY

2.4-5 Gaza is scheduled for demolition,
  Ashdod will be cleaned out by high noon,
  Ekron pulled out by the roots.
Doom to the seaside people,
  the seafaring people from Crete!
The Word of GOD is bad news for you
  who settled Canaan, the Philistine country:
"You're slated for destruction—
  no survivors!"

✝

2.6-7 The lands of the seafarers
  will become pastureland,
A country for shepherds and sheep.
  What's left of the family of Judah will get it.
Day after day they'll pasture by the sea,
  and go home in the evening to Ashkelon to
  sleep.
Their very own GOD will look out for them.
  He'll make things as good as before.

✝

2.8-12 "I've heard the crude taunts of Moab,
  the mockeries flung by Ammon,
The cruel talk they've used to put down my
  people,
  their self-important strutting along Israel's
  borders.
Therefore, as sure as I am the living God,"
  says GOD-of-the-Angel-Armies,
  Israel's personal God,
"Moab will become a ruin like Sodom,
  Ammon a ghost town like Gomorrah,
One a field of rocks, the other a sterile salt flat,
  a moonscape forever.
What's left of my people will finish them off,
  will pick them clean and take over.

NEW INTERNATIONAL VERSION

[10] This is what they will get in return for their pride,
  for insulting and mocking the people of the LORD Almighty.
[11] The LORD will be awesome to them
  when he destroys all the gods of the land.
The nations on every shore will worship him,
  every one in its own land.

AGAINST CUSH

[12] "You too, O Cushites,[a]
  will be slain by my sword."

AGAINST ASSYRIA

[13] He will stretch out his hand against the north
  and destroy Assyria,
leaving Nineveh utterly desolate
  and dry as the desert.
[14] Flocks and herds will lie down there,
  creatures of every kind.
The desert owl and the screech owl
  will roost on her columns.
Their calls will echo through the windows,
  rubble will be in the doorways,
  the beams of cedar will be exposed.
[15] This is the carefree city
  that lived in safety.
She said to herself,
  "I am, and there is none besides me."
What a ruin she has become,
  a lair for wild beasts!
All who pass by her scoff
  and shake their fists.

THE FUTURE OF JERUSALEM

3 Woe to the city of oppressors,
  rebellious and defiled!
[2] She obeys no one,
  she accepts no correction.
She does not trust in the LORD,
  she does not draw near to her God.
[3] Her officials are roaring lions,
  her rulers are evening wolves,
  who leave nothing for the morning.
[4] Her prophets are arrogant;
  they are treacherous men.
Her priests profane the sanctuary
  and do violence to the law.
[5] The LORD within her is righteous;
  he does no wrong.
Morning by morning he dispenses his justice,
  and every new day he does not fail,

THE MESSAGE

This is what they get for their bloated pride,
  their taunts and mockeries of the people
  of GOD-of-the-Angel-Armies.
GOD will be seen as truly terrible—a Holy Terror.
  All earth-made gods will shrivel up and blow away;
And everyone, wherever they are, far or near,
  will fall to the ground and worship him.
Also you Ethiopians,
  you too will die—I'll see to it."

✛

2.13-15 Then GOD will reach into the north
  and destroy Assyria.
He will waste Nineveh,
  leave her dry and treeless as a desert.
The ghost town of a city,
  the haunt of wild animals,
Nineveh will be home to raccoons and coyotes—
  they'll bed down in its ruins.
Owls will hoot in the windows, ravens will croak in the doorways—
  all that fancy woodwork now a perch for birds.
Can this be the famous Fun City
  that had it made,
That boasted, "I'm the Number-One City!
  I'm King of the Mountain!"
So why is the place deserted,
  a lair for wild animals?
Passersby hardly give it a look;
  they dismiss it with a gesture.

SEWER CITY

3.1-5 **3** Doom to the rebellious city,
  the home of oppressors—Sewer City!
The city that wouldn't take advice,
  wouldn't accept correction,
Wouldn't trust GOD,
  wouldn't even get close to her own god!
Her very own leaders
  are rapacious lions,
Her judges are rapacious timber wolves
  out every morning prowling for a fresh kill.
Her prophets are out for what they can get.
  They're opportunists—you can't trust them.
Her priests desecrate the Sanctuary.
  They use God's law as a weapon to maim and kill souls.
Yet GOD remains righteous in her midst,
  untouched by the evil.
He stays at it, day after day, meting out justice.
  At evening he's still at it, strong as ever.

---

[a] 12 That is, people from the upper Nile region

NEW INTERNATIONAL VERSION

yet the unrighteous know no shame.

6 "I have cut off nations;
   their strongholds are demolished.
I have left their streets deserted,
   with no one passing through.
Their cities are destroyed;
   no one will be left—no one at all.
7 I said to the city,
   'Surely you will fear me
   and accept correction!'
Then her dwelling would not be cut off,
   nor all my punishments come upon her.
But they were still eager
   to act corruptly in all they did.
8 Therefore wait for me," declares the LORD,
   "for the day I will stand up to testify.ᵃ
I have decided to assemble the nations,
   to gather the kingdoms
and to pour out my wrath on them—
   all my fierce anger.
The whole world will be consumed
   by the fire of my jealous anger.

9 "Then will I purify the lips of the peoples,
   that all of them may call on the name of
      the LORD
   and serve him shoulder to shoulder.
10 From beyond the rivers of Cushᵇ
   my worshipers, my scattered people,
   will bring me offerings.
11 On that day you will not be put to shame
   for all the wrongs you have done to me,
because I will remove from this city
   those who rejoice in their pride.
Never again will you be haughty
   on my holy hill.
12 But I will leave within you
   the meek and humble,
   who trust in the name of the LORD.
13 The remnant of Israel will do no wrong;
   they will speak no lies,
   nor will deceit be found in their mouths.

THE MESSAGE

But evil men and women, without conscience
   and without shame, persist in evil.

✝

3.6 "So I cut off the godless nations.
   I knocked down their defense posts,
Filled her roads with rubble
   so no one could get through.
Her cities were bombed-out ruins,
   unlivable and unlived in.

3.7 "I thought, 'Surely she'll honor me now,
   accept my discipline and correction,
Find a way of escape from the trouble she's in,
   find relief from the punishment I'm
      bringing.'
But it didn't faze her. Bright and early
   she was up at it again, doing the same old
      things.

3.8 "Well, if that's what you want, stick around."
   GOD's Decree.
"Your day in court is coming,
   but remember I'll be there to bring
      evidence.
I'll bring all the nations to the courtroom,
   round up all the kingdoms,
And let them feel the brunt of my anger,
   my raging wrath.
My zeal is a fire
   that will purge and purify the earth.

GOD IS IN CHARGE AT THE CENTER

3.9-13 "In the end I will turn things around for the
      people.
   I'll give them a language undistorted,
      unpolluted,
Words to address GOD in worship
   and, united, to serve me with their
      shoulders to the wheel.
They'll come from beyond the Ethiopian
      rivers,
   they'll come praying—
All my scattered, exiled people
   will come home with offerings for worship.
You'll no longer have to be ashamed
   of all those acts of rebellion.
I'll have gotten rid of your arrogant leaders.
   No more pious strutting on my holy hill!
I'll leave a core of people among you
   who are poor in spirit—
What's left of Israel that's really Israel.
   They'll make their home in GOD.
This core holy people
   will not do wrong.
They won't lie,
   won't use words to flatter or seduce.

ᵃ 8 Septuagint and Syriac; Hebrew *will rise up to plunder*
ᵇ 10 That is, the upper Nile region

NEW INTERNATIONAL VERSION

They will eat and lie down
and no one will make them afraid."

¹⁴ Sing, O Daughter of Zion;
shout aloud, O Israel!
Be glad and rejoice with all your heart,
O Daughter of Jerusalem!
¹⁵ The LORD has taken away your punishment,
he has turned back your enemy.
The LORD, the King of Israel, is with you;
never again will you fear any harm.
¹⁶ On that day they will say to Jerusalem,
"Do not fear, O Zion;
do not let your hands hang limp.
¹⁷ The LORD your God is with you,
he is mighty to save.
He will take great delight in you,
he will quiet you with his love,
he will rejoice over you with singing."

¹⁸ "The sorrows for the appointed feasts
I will remove from you;
they are a burden and a reproach to you. ᵃ
¹⁹ At that time I will deal
with all who oppressed you;
I will rescue the lame
and gather those who have been scattered.
I will give them praise and honor
in every land where they were put to
shame.
²⁰ At that time I will gather you;
at that time I will bring you home.
I will give you honor and praise
among all the peoples of the earth
when I restore your fortunes ᵇ
before your very eyes,"
says the LORD.

THE MESSAGE

Content with who they are and where they
are,
unanxious, they'll live at peace."

3.14-15 So sing, Daughter Zion!
Raise the rafters, Israel!
Daughter Jerusalem,
be happy! celebrate!
GOD has reversed his judgments against you
and sent your enemies off chasing their
tails.
From now on, GOD is Israel's king,
in charge at the center.
There's nothing to fear from evil
ever again!

GOD IS PRESENT AMONG YOU

3.16-17 Jerusalem will be told:
"Don't be afraid.
Dear Zion,
don't despair.
Your GOD is present among you,
a strong Warrior there to save you.
Happy to have you back, he'll calm you with
his love
and delight you with his songs.

3.18-20 "The accumulated sorrows of your exile
will dissipate.
I, your God, will get rid of them for you.
You've carried those burdens long enough.
At the same time, I'll get rid of all those
who've made your life miserable.
I'll heal the maimed;
I'll bring home the homeless.
In the very countries where they were hated
they will be venerated.
On Judgment Day
I'll bring you back home—a great family
gathering!
You'll be famous and honored
all over the world.
You'll see it with your own eyes—
all those painful partings turned into
reunions!"
GOD's Promise.

ᵃ 18 Or "I will gather you who mourn for the appointed feasts;
/ your reproach is a burden to you   ᵇ 20 Or I bring back
your captives

HAGGAI

HAGGAI

A Call to Build the House of the Lord

1 In the second year of King Darius, on the first day of the sixth month, the word of the LORD came through the prophet Haggai to Zerubbabel son of Shealtiel, governor of Judah, and to Joshua*a* son of Jehozadak, the high priest: ²This is what the LORD Almighty says: "These people say, 'The time has not yet come for the LORD's house to be built.'"

³Then the word of the LORD came through the prophet Haggai: ⁴"Is it a time for you yourselves to be living in your paneled houses, while this house remains a ruin?"

⁵Now this is what the LORD Almighty says: "Give careful thought to your ways. ⁶You have planted much, but have harvested little. You eat, but never have enough. You drink, but never have your fill. You put on clothes, but are not warm. You earn wages, only to put them in a purse with holes in it."

⁷This is what the LORD Almighty says: "Give careful thought to your ways. ⁸Go up into the mountains and bring down timber and build the house, so that I may take pleasure in it and be honored," says the LORD. ⁹"You expected much, but see, it turned out to be little. What you

Caught Up with Taking Care of Your Own Houses

1 On the first day of the sixth month of the second year in the reign of King Darius of Persia, GOD's Message was delivered by the prophet Haggai to the governor of Judah, Zerubbabel son of Shealtiel, and to the high priest, Joshua son of Jehozadak:

1.2 A Message from GOD-of-the-Angel-Armies: "The people procrastinate. They say this isn't the right time to rebuild my Temple, the Temple of GOD."

1.3-4 Shortly after that, GOD said more and Haggai spoke it: "How is it that it's the 'right time' for you to live in your fine new homes while the Home, GOD's Temple, is in ruins?"

1.5-6 And then a little later, GOD-of-the-Angel-Armies spoke out again:

"Take a good, hard look at your life.
  Think it over.
You have spent a lot of money,
  but you haven't much to show for it.
You keep filling your plates,
  but you never get filled up.
You keep drinking and drinking and drinking,
  but you're always thirsty.
You put on layer after layer of clothes,
  but you can't get warm.
And the people who work for you,
  what are they getting out of it?
Not much—
  a leaky, rusted-out bucket, that's what.

1.7 That's why GOD-of-the-Angel-Armies said:

"Take a good, hard look at your life.
  Think it over."

1.8-9 Then GOD said:

"Here's what I want you to do:
  Climb into the hills and cut some timber.
Bring it down and rebuild the Temple.
  Do it just for me. Honor me.
You've had great ambitions for yourselves,
  but nothing has come of it.

NEW INTERNATIONAL VERSION

brought home, I blew away. Why?" declares the LORD Almighty. "Because of my house, which remains a ruin, while each of you is busy with his own house. [10]Therefore, because of you the heavens have withheld their dew and the earth its crops. [11]I called for a drought on the fields and the mountains, on the grain, the new wine, the oil and whatever the ground produces, on men and cattle, and on the labor of your hands."

[12]Then Zerubbabel son of Shealtiel, Joshua son of Jehozadak, the high priest, and the whole remnant of the people obeyed the voice of the LORD their God and the message of the prophet Haggai, because the LORD their God had sent him. And the people feared the LORD.

[13]Then Haggai, the LORD's messenger, gave this message of the LORD to the people: "I am with you," declares the LORD. [14]So the LORD stirred up the spirit of Zerubbabel son of Shealtiel, governor of Judah, and the spirit of Joshua son of Jehozadak, the high priest, and the spirit of the whole remnant of the people. They came and began to work on the house of the LORD Almighty, their God, [15]on the twenty-fourth day of the sixth month in the second year of King Darius.

THE PROMISED GLORY OF THE NEW HOUSE

2 On the twenty-first day of the seventh month, the word of the LORD came through the prophet Haggai: [2]"Speak to Zerubbabel son of Shealtiel, governor of Judah, to Joshua son of Jehozadak, the high priest, and to the remnant of the people. Ask them, [3]'Who of you is left who saw this house in its former glory? How does it look to you now? Does it not seem to you like nothing? [4]But now be strong, O Zerubbabel,' declares the LORD. 'Be strong, O Joshua son of Jehozadak, the high priest. Be strong, all you people of the land,' declares the LORD, 'and work. For I am with you,' declares the LORD Almighty. [5]'This is what I covenanted with you when you came out of Egypt. And my Spirit remains among you. Do not fear.'

[6]"This is what the LORD Almighty says: 'In a little while I will once more shake the heavens and the earth, the sea and the dry land. [7]I will shake all nations, and the desired of all nations

THE MESSAGE

The little you have brought to my Temple
I've blown away—there was nothing to it.

1.9-11 "And why?" (This is a Message from GOD-of-the-Angel-Armies, remember.) "Because while you've run around, caught up with taking care of your own houses, my Home is in ruins. That's why. Because of your stinginess. And so I've given you a dry summer and a skimpy crop. I've matched your tight-fisted stinginess by decreeing a season of drought, drying up fields and hills, withering gardens and orchards, stunting vegetables and fruit. Nothing—not man or woman, not animal or crop—is going to thrive."

✝

1.12 Then the governor, Zerubbabel son of Shealtiel, and the high priest, Joshua son of Jehozadak, and all the people with them listened, really listened, to the voice of their GOD. When GOD sent the prophet Haggai to them, they paid attention to him. In listening to Haggai, they honored GOD.

1.13 Then Haggai, GOD's messenger, preached GOD's Message to the people: "I am with you!" GOD's Word.

1.14-15 This is how GOD got Zerubbabel, Joshua, and all the people moving—got them working on the Temple of GOD-of-the-Angel-Armies. This happened on the twenty-fourth day of the sixth month in the second year of King Darius.

THIS TEMPLE WILL END UP BETTER THAN IT STARTED OUT

2.1-3 2 On the twenty-first day of the seventh month, the Word of GOD came through the prophet Haggai: "Tell Governor Zerubbabel son of Shealtiel and High Priest Joshua son of Jehozadak and all the people: 'Is there anyone here who saw the Temple the way it used to be, all glorious? And what do you see now? Not much, right?

2.4-5 "'So get to work, Zerubbabel!'—GOD is speaking.

"'Get to work, Joshua son of Jehozadak—high priest!'

"'Get to work, all you people!'—GOD is speaking.

"'Yes, get to work! For I am with you.' The GOD-of-the-Angel-Armies is speaking! 'Put into action the word I covenanted with you when you left Egypt. I'm living and breathing among you right now. Don't be timid. Don't hold back.'

2.6-7 "This is what GOD-of-the-Angel-Armies said: 'Before you know it, I will shake up sky and earth, ocean and fields. And I'll shake down all the godless nations. They'll bring bushels of

NEW INTERNATIONAL VERSION

will come, and I will fill this house with glory,'
says the LORD Almighty. 8'The silver is mine and
the gold is mine,' declares the LORD Almighty.
9'The glory of this present house will be greater
than the glory of the former house,' says the
LORD Almighty. 'And in this place I will grant
peace,' declares the LORD Almighty."

BLESSINGS FOR A DEFILED PEOPLE

10On the twenty-fourth day of the ninth
month, in the second year of Darius, the word of
the LORD came to the prophet Haggai: 11"This is
what the LORD Almighty says: 'Ask the priests
what the law says: 12If a person carries consecrated meat in the fold of his garment, and that
fold touches some bread or stew, some wine, oil
or other food, does it become consecrated?' "

The priests answered, "No."

13Then Haggai said, "If a person defiled by
contact with a dead body touches one of these
things, does it become defiled?"

"Yes," the priests replied, "it becomes defiled."

14Then Haggai said, " 'So it is with this people
and this nation in my sight,' declares the LORD.
'Whatever they do and whatever they offer there
is defiled.

15" 'Now give careful thought to this from this
day on[a]—consider how things were before one
stone was laid on another in the LORD's temple.
16When anyone came to a heap of twenty measures, there were only ten. When anyone went to
a wine vat to draw fifty measures, there were
only twenty. 17I struck all the work of your
hands with blight, mildew and hail, yet you did
not turn to me,' declares the LORD. 18'From this
day on, from this twenty-fourth day of the ninth
month, give careful thought to the day when the
foundation of the LORD's temple was laid. Give
careful thought: 19Is there yet any seed left in
the barn? Until now, the vine and the fig tree, the
pomegranate and the olive tree have not borne
fruit.

" 'From this day on I will bless you.' "

ZERUBBABEL THE LORD'S SIGNET RING

20The word of the LORD came to Haggai a second time on the twenty-fourth day of the month:

THE MESSAGE

wealth and I will fill this Temple with splendor.'
GOD-of-the-Angel-Armies says so.

2.8   'I own the silver,
       I own the gold.'
              Decree of GOD-of-the-Angel-Armies.

2.9   " 'This Temple is going to end up far better
than it started out, a glorious beginning but an
even more glorious finish: a place in which I
will hand out wholeness and holiness.' Decree
of GOD-of-the-Angel-Armies."

✣

2.10-12 On the twenty-fourth day of the ninth month
(again, this was in the second year of Darius),
GOD's Message came to Haggai: "GOD-of-the-
Angel-Armies speaks: Consult the priests for a
ruling. If someone carries a piece of sacred
meat in his pocket, meat that is set apart for
sacrifice on the altar, and the pocket touches a
loaf of bread, a dish of stew, a bottle of wine or
oil, or any other food, will these foods be made
holy by such contact?"

The priests said, "No."

2.13   Then Haggai said, "How about someone
who is contaminated by touching a corpse—if
that person touches one of these foods, will it
be contaminated?"

The priests said, "Yes, it will be contaminated."

2.14   Then Haggai said, " 'So, this people is contaminated. Their nation is contaminated. Everything they do is contaminated. Whatever
they do for me is contaminated.' GOD says so.

2.15-17   " 'Think back. Before you set out to lay the
first foundation stones for the rebuilding of my
Temple, how did it go with you? Isn't it true
that your foot-dragging, halfhearted efforts at
rebuilding the Temple of GOD were reflected in
a sluggish, halfway return on your crops—half
the grain you were used to getting, half the
wine? I hit you with drought and blight and
hail. Everything you were doing got hit. But it
didn't seem to faze you. You continued to ignore me.' GOD's Decree.

2.18-19   " 'Now think ahead from this same date—
this twenty-fourth day of the ninth month.
Think ahead from when the Temple rebuilding
was launched. Has anything in your fields—
vine, fig tree, pomegranate, olive tree—failed
to flourish? From now on you can count on a
blessing.' "

✣

2.20-21 GOD's Message came a second time to Haggai
on that most memorable day, the twenty-fourth

NEW INTERNATIONAL VERSION

²¹"Tell Zerubbabel governor of Judah that I will shake the heavens and the earth. ²²I will overturn royal thrones and shatter the power of the foreign kingdoms. I will overthrow chariots and their drivers; horses and their riders will fall, each by the sword of his brother.

²³" 'On that day,' declares the LORD Almighty, 'I will take you, my servant Zerubbabel son of Shealtiel,' declares the LORD, 'and I will make you like my signet ring, for I have chosen you,' declares the LORD Almighty."

THE MESSAGE

day of the ninth month: "Speak to Zerubbabel, the governor of Judah:

2.21-23   " 'I am about to shake up everything, to turn everything upside down and start over from top to bottom—overthrow governments, destroy foreign powers, dismantle the world of weapons and armaments, throw armies into confusion, so that they end up killing one another. And on that day' "—this is GOD's Message—" 'I will take you, O Zerubbabel son of Shealtiel, as my personal servant and I will set you as a signet ring, the sign of my sovereign presence and authority. I've looked over the field and chosen you for this work.' " The Message of GOD-of-the-Angel-Armies.

ZECHARIAH

ZECHARIAH

A CALL TO RETURN TO THE LORD

1 In the eighth month of the second year of Darius, the word of the LORD came to the prophet Zechariah son of Berekiah, the son of Iddo:

2 "The LORD was very angry with your forefathers. 3 Therefore tell the people: This is what the LORD Almighty says: 'Return to me,' declares the LORD Almighty, 'and I will return to you,' says the LORD Almighty. 4 Do not be like your forefathers, to whom the earlier prophets proclaimed: This is what the LORD Almighty says: 'Turn from your evil ways and your evil practices.' But they would not listen or pay attention to me, declares the LORD. 5 Where are your forefathers now? And the prophets, do they live forever? 6 But did not my words and my decrees, which I commanded my servants the prophets, overtake your forefathers?

"Then they repented and said, 'The LORD Almighty has done to us what our ways and practices deserve, just as he determined to do.' "

THE MAN AMONG THE MYRTLE TREES

7 On the twenty-fourth day of the eleventh month, the month of Shebat, in the second year of Darius, the word of the LORD came to the prophet Zechariah son of Berekiah, the son of Iddo.

8 During the night I had a vision—and there before me was a man riding a red horse! He was standing among the myrtle trees in a ravine. Behind him were red, brown and white horses.

9 I asked, "What are these, my lord?"

The angel who was talking with me answered, "I will show you what they are."

10 Then the man standing among the myrtle trees explained, "They are the ones the LORD has sent to go throughout the earth."

11 And they reported to the angel of the LORD, who was standing among the myrtle trees, "We have gone throughout the earth and found the whole world at rest and in peace."

12 Then the angel of the LORD said, "LORD Almighty, how long will you withhold mercy from Jerusalem and from the towns of Judah, which

1.1-4 1 In the eighth month of the second year in the reign of Darius, GOD's Message came to the prophet Zechariah son of Berechiah, son of Iddo: "GOD was very angry with your ancestors. So give to the people this Message from GOD-of-the-Angel-Armies: 'Come back to me and I'll come back to you. Don't be like your parents. The old-time prophets called out to them, "A Message from GOD-of-the-Angel-Armies: Leave your evil life. Quit your evil practices." But they ignored everything I said to them, stubbornly refused to listen.'

1.5-6 "And where are your ancestors now? Dead and buried. And the prophets who preached to them? Also dead and buried. But the Message that my servants the prophets spoke, that isn't dead and buried. That Message did its work on your ancestors, did it not? It woke them up and they came back, saying, 'He did what he said he would do, sure enough. We didn't get by with a thing.' "

FIRST VISION: FOUR RIDERS

1.7 On the twenty-fourth day of the eleventh month in the second year of the reign of Darius, the Message of GOD was given to the prophet Zechariah son of Berechiah, son of Iddo:

1.8 One night I looked out and saw a man astride a red horse. He was in the shadows in a grove of birches. Behind him were more horses—a red, a chestnut, and a white.

1.9 I said, "Sir, what are these horses doing here? What's the meaning of this?"

The Angel-Messenger said, "Let me show you."

1.10 Then the rider in the birch grove spoke up, "These are the riders that GOD sent to check things out on earth."

1.11 They reported their findings to the Angel of GOD in the birch grove: "We have looked over the whole earth and all is well. Everything's under control."

1.12 The Angel of GOD reported back, "O GOD-of-the-Angel-Armies, how long are you going to stay angry with Jerusalem and the cities of Ju-

NEW INTERNATIONAL VERSION

you have been angry with these seventy years?" ¹³So the LORD spoke kind and comforting words to the angel who talked with me.

¹⁴Then the angel who was speaking to me said, "Proclaim this word: This is what the LORD Almighty says: 'I am very jealous for Jerusalem and Zion, ¹⁵but I am very angry with the nations that feel secure. I was only a little angry, but they added to the calamity.'

¹⁶"Therefore, this is what the LORD says: 'I will return to Jerusalem with mercy, and there my house will be rebuilt. And the measuring line will be stretched out over Jerusalem,' declares the LORD Almighty.

¹⁷"Proclaim further: This is what the LORD Almighty says: 'My towns will again overflow with prosperity, and the LORD will again comfort Zion and choose Jerusalem.' "

FOUR HORNS AND FOUR CRAFTSMEN

¹⁸Then I looked up—and there before me were four horns! ¹⁹I asked the angel who was speaking to me, "What are these?"

He answered me, "These are the horns that scattered Judah, Israel and Jerusalem."

²⁰Then the LORD showed me four craftsmen. ²¹I asked, "What are these coming to do?"

He answered, "These are the horns that scattered Judah so that no one could raise his head, but the craftsmen have come to terrify them and throw down these horns of the nations who lifted up their horns against the land of Judah to scatter its people."

A MAN WITH A MEASURING LINE

2 Then I looked up—and there before me was a man with a measuring line in his hand! ²I asked, "Where are you going?"

He answered me, "To measure Jerusalem, to find out how wide and how long it is."

³Then the angel who was speaking to me left, and another angel came to meet him ⁴and said to him: "Run, tell that young man, 'Jerusalem will be a city without walls because of the great number of men and livestock in it. ⁵And I myself will

THE MESSAGE

dah? When are you going to let up? Isn't seventy years long enough?"

1.13-15   GOD reassured the Angel-Messenger—good words, comforting words—who then addressed me: "Tell them this. Tell them that GOD-of-the-Angel-Armies has spoken. This is GOD's Message: 'I care deeply for Jerusalem and Zion. I feel very possessive of them. But I'm thoroughly angry with the godless nations that act as if they own the whole world. I was only moderately angry earlier, but now they've gone too far. I'm going into action.

1.16-17   " 'I've come back to Jerusalem, but with
            compassion this time.'
         This is GOD speaking.
         'I'll see to it that my Temple is rebuilt.'
            A Decree of GOD-of-the-Angel-Armies!
         'The rebuilding operation is already staked
            out.'
         Say it again—a Decree of GOD-of-the-
            Angel-Armies:
         'My cities will prosper again,
            GOD will comfort Zion again,
            Jerusalem will be back in my favor again.' "

SECOND VISION: FOUR HORNS AND FOUR BLACKSMITHS

1.18   I looked up, and was surprised by another vision: four horns!

1.19   I asked the Messenger-Angel, "And what's the meaning of this?"

He said, "These are the powers that have scattered Judah, Israel, and Jerusalem abroad."

1.20   Then GOD expanded the vision to include four blacksmiths.

1.21   I asked, "And what are these all about?"

He said, "Since the 'horns' scattered Judah so badly that no one had any hope left, these blacksmiths have arrived to combat the horns. They'll dehorn the godless nations who used their horns to scatter Judah to the four winds."

THIRD VISION: THE MAN WITH THE TAPE MEASURE

2.1-5   **2** I looked up and was surprised to see a man holding a tape measure in his hand.

I said, "What are you up to?"
   "I'm on my way," he said, "to survey
         Jerusalem,
   to measure its width and length."
Just then the Messenger-Angel on his way out
   met another angel coming in and said,
"Run! Tell the Surveyor, 'Jerusalem will burst
   its walls—
   bursting with people, bursting with
      animals.

NEW INTERNATIONAL VERSION	THE MESSAGE

NEW INTERNATIONAL VERSION

be a wall of fire around it,' declares the Lord, 'and I will be its glory within.'

⁶"Come! Come! Flee from the land of the north," declares the Lord, "for I have scattered you to the four winds of heaven," declares the Lord.

⁷"Come, O Zion! Escape, you who live in the Daughter of Babylon!" ⁸For this is what the Lord Almighty says: "After he has honored me and has sent me against the nations that have plundered you—for whoever touches you touches the apple of his eye— ⁹I will surely raise my hand against them so that their slaves will plunder them.ª Then you will know that the Lord Almighty has sent me.

¹⁰"Shout and be glad, O Daughter of Zion. For I am coming, and I will live among you," declares the Lord. ¹¹"Many nations will be joined with the Lord in that day and will become my people. I will live among you and you will know that the Lord Almighty has sent me to you. ¹²The Lord will inherit Judah as his portion in the holy land and will again choose Jerusalem. ¹³Be still before the Lord, all mankind, because he has roused himself from his holy dwelling."

CLEAN GARMENTS FOR THE HIGH PRIEST

3 Then he showed me Joshuaᵇ the high priest standing before the angel of the Lord, and Satanᶜ standing at his right side to accuse him. ²The Lord said to Satan, "The Lord rebuke you, Satan! The Lord, who has chosen Jerusalem, rebuke you! Is not this man a burning stick snatched from the fire?"

³Now Joshua was dressed in filthy clothes as

ª 8,9 Or *says after . . . eye:* ⁹*"I . . . plunder them."*
ᵇ 1 A variant of *Jeshua;* here and elsewhere in Zechariah
ᶜ 1 *Satan* means *accuser.*

THE MESSAGE

And I'll be right there with her'—God's Decree—'a wall of fire around unwalled Jerusalem and a radiant presence within.' "

2.6-7 "Up on your feet! Get out of there—and now!" God says so.
"Return from your far exile.
I scattered you to the four winds." God's Decree.
"Escape from Babylon, Zion, and come home—now!"

2.8-9 God-of-the-Angel-Armies, the One of Glory who sent me on my mission, commenting on the godless nations who stripped you and left you homeless, said, "Anyone who hits you, hits me—bloodies my nose, blackens my eye. Yes, and at the right time I'll give the signal and they'll be stripped and thrown out by their own servants." Then you'll know for sure that God-of-the-Angel-Armies sent me on this mission.

2.10 "Shout and celebrate, Daughter of Zion!
I'm on my way. I'm moving into your neighborhood!"
God's Decree.

2.11-12 Many godless nations will be linked up with God at that time. ("They will become my family! I'll live in their homes!") And then you'll know for sure that God-of-the-Angel-Armies sent me on this mission. God will reclaim his Judah inheritance in the Holy Land. He'll again make clear that Jerusalem is his choice.

2.13 Quiet, everyone! Shh! Silence before God. Something's afoot in his holy house. He's on the move!

FOURTH VISION: JOSHUA'S NEW CLOTHES

3.1-2 **3** Next the Messenger-Angel showed me the high priest Joshua. He was standing before God's Angel where the Accuser showed up to accuse him. Then God said to the Accuser, "I, God, rebuke you, Accuser! I rebuke you and choose Jerusalem. Surprise! Everything is going up in flames, but I reach in and pull out Jerusalem!"

3.3-4 Joshua, standing before the angel, was dressed in dirty clothes. The angel spoke to his

NEW INTERNATIONAL VERSION

he stood before the angel. ⁴The angel said to those who were standing before him, "Take off his filthy clothes."

Then he said to Joshua, "See, I have taken away your sin, and I will put rich garments on you."

⁵Then I said, "Put a clean turban on his head." So they put a clean turban on his head and clothed him, while the angel of the LORD stood by.

⁶The angel of the LORD gave this charge to Joshua: ⁷"This is what the LORD Almighty says: 'If you will walk in my ways and keep my requirements, then you will govern my house and have charge of my courts, and I will give you a place among these standing here.

⁸" 'Listen, O high priest Joshua and your associates seated before you, who are men symbolic of things to come: I am going to bring my servant, the Branch. ⁹See, the stone I have set in front of Joshua! There are seven eyes[a] on that one stone, and I will engrave an inscription on it,' says the LORD Almighty, 'and I will remove the sin of this land in a single day.

¹⁰" 'In that day each of you will invite his neighbor to sit under his vine and fig tree,' declares the LORD Almighty."

THE GOLD LAMPSTAND AND THE TWO OLIVE TREES

4 Then the angel who talked with me returned and wakened me, as a man is wakened from his sleep. ²He asked me, "What do you see?"

I answered, "I see a solid gold lampstand with a bowl at the top and seven lights on it, with seven channels to the lights. ³Also there are two olive trees by it, one on the right of the bowl and the other on its left."

⁴I asked the angel who talked with me, "What are these, my lord?"

⁵He answered, "Do you not know what these are?"

"No, my lord," I replied.

⁶So he said to me, "This is the word of the LORD to Zerubbabel: 'Not by might nor by power, but by my Spirit,' says the LORD Almighty.

⁷"What[b] are you, O mighty mountain? Before Zerubbabel you will become level ground. Then he will bring out the capstone to shouts of 'God bless it! God bless it!' "

⁸Then the word of the LORD came to me: ⁹"The hands of Zerubbabel have laid the foundation of this temple; his hands will also complete it. Then you will know that the LORD Almighty has sent me to you.

THE MESSAGE

attendants, "Get him out of those filthy clothes," and then said to Joshua, "Look, I've stripped you of your sin and dressed you up in clean clothes."

3.5 I spoke up and said, "How about a clean new turban for his head also?" And they did it—put a clean new turban on his head. Then they finished dressing him, with GOD's Angel looking on.

3.6-7 GOD's Angel then charged Joshua, "Orders from GOD-of-the-Angel-Armies: 'If you live the way I tell you and remain obedient in my service, then you'll make the decisions around here and oversee my affairs. And all my attendants standing here will be at your service.

3.8-9 " 'Careful, High Priest Joshua—both you and your friends sitting here with you, for your friends are in on this, too! Here's what I'm doing next: I'm introducing my servant Branch. And note this: This stone that I'm placing before Joshua, a single stone with seven eyes'—Decree of GOD-of-the-Angel-Armies—'I'll engrave with these words: "I'll strip this land of its filthy sin, all at once, in a single day."

3.10 " 'At that time, everyone will get along with one another, with friendly visits across the fence, friendly visits on one another's porches.' "

FIFTH VISION: A LAMPSTAND AND TWO OLIVE TREES

4.1 **4** The Messenger-Angel again called me to attention. It was like being wakened out of deep sleep.

4.2-3 He said, "What do you see?"

I answered, "I see a lampstand of solid gold with a bowl on top. Seven lamps, each with seven spouts, are set on the bowl. And there are two olive trees, one on either side of the bowl."

4.4 Then I asked the Messenger-Angel, "What does this mean, sir?"

4.5-7 The Messenger-Angel said, "Can't you tell?"

"No, sir," I said.

Then he said, "This is GOD's Message to Zerubbabel: 'You can't force these things. They only come about through my Spirit,' says GOD-of-the-Angel-Armies. 'So, big mountain, who do you think you are? Next to Zerubbabel you're nothing but a molehill. He'll proceed to set the Cornerstone in place, accompanied by cheers: Yes! Yes! Do it!' "

4.8-10 After that, the Word of GOD came to me: "Zerubbabel started rebuilding this Temple and he will complete it. That will be your confirmation that GOD-of-the-Angel-Armies sent me

---

ᵃ 9 Or *facets*   ᵇ 7 Or *Who*

NEW INTERNATIONAL VERSION

¹⁰"Who despises the day of small things? Men will rejoice when they see the plumb line in the hand of Zerubbabel.

"(These seven are the eyes of the LORD, which range throughout the earth.)"

¹¹Then I asked the angel, "What are these two olive trees on the right and the left of the lampstand?"

¹²Again I asked him, "What are these two olive branches beside the two gold pipes that pour out golden oil?"

¹³He replied, "Do you not know what these are?"

"No, my lord," I said.

¹⁴So he said, "These are the two who are anointed to*ᵃ* serve the Lord of all the earth."

THE FLYING SCROLL

5 I looked again—and there before me was a flying scroll!

²He asked me, "What do you see?"

I answered, "I see a flying scroll, thirty feet long and fifteen feet wide.*ᵇ*"

³And he said to me, "This is the curse that is going out over the whole land; for according to what it says on one side, every thief will be banished, and according to what it says on the other, everyone who swears falsely will be banished. ⁴The LORD Almighty declares, 'I will send it out, and it will enter the house of the thief and the house of him who swears falsely by my name. It will remain in his house and destroy it, both its timbers and its stones.' "

THE WOMAN IN A BASKET

⁵Then the angel who was speaking to me came forward and said to me, "Look up and see what this is that is appearing."

⁶I asked, "What is it?"

He replied, "It is a measuring basket.*ᶜ*" And he added, "This is the iniquity*ᵈ* of the people throughout the land."

⁷Then the cover of lead was raised, and there in the basket sat a woman! ⁸He said, "This is wickedness," and he pushed her back into the basket and pushed the lead cover down over its mouth.

⁹Then I looked up—and there before me were two women, with the wind in their wings! They had wings like those of a stork, and they lifted up the basket between heaven and earth.

THE MESSAGE

to you. Does anyone dare despise this day of small beginnings? They'll change their tune when they see Zerubbabel setting the last stone in place!"

Going back to the vision, the Messenger-Angel said, "The seven lamps are the eyes of GOD probing the dark corners of the world like searchlights."

4:11-12 "And the two olive trees on either side of the lampstand?" I asked. "What's the meaning of them? And while you're at it, the two branches of the olive trees that feed oil to the lamps—what do they mean?"

4:13 He said, "You haven't figured that out?" I said, "No, sir."

4:14 He said, "These are the two who stand beside the Master of the whole earth and supply golden lamp oil worldwide."

SIXTH VISION: THE FLYING BOOK

5:1 5 I looked up again and saw—surprise!—a book on the wing! A book flying!

5:2 The Messenger-Angel said to me, "What do you see now?"

I said, "I see a book flying, a huge book—thirty feet long and fifteen feet wide!"

5:3-4 He told me, "This book is the verdict going out worldwide against thieves and liars. The first half of the book disposes of everyone who steals; the second half takes care of everyone who lies. I launched it"—Decree of GOD-of-the-Angel-Armies—"and so it will fly into the house of every thief and every liar. It will land in each house and tear it down, timbers and stones."

SEVENTH VISION: A WOMAN IN A BASKET

5:5 The Messenger-Angel appeared and said, "Look up. Tell me what you see."

5:6 I said, "What in the world is that?"

He said, "This is a bushel basket on a journey. It holds the sin of everyone, everywhere."

5:7 Then the lid made of lead was removed from the basket—and there was a woman sitting in it!

5:8 He said, "This is Miss Wicked." He pushed her back down into the basket and clamped the lead lid over her.

5:9 Then I looked up and to my surprise saw two women flying. On outstretched wings they airlifted the bushel basket into the sky.

ᵃ 14 Or *two who bring oil and*   *ᵇ* 2 Hebrew *twenty cubits long and ten cubits wide* (about 9 meters long and 4.5 meters wide)   *ᶜ* 6 Hebrew *an ephah*; also in verses 7-11
ᵈ 6 Or *appearance*

NEW INTERNATIONAL VERSION

¹⁰"Where are they taking the basket?" I asked the angel who was speaking to me.

¹¹He replied, "To the country of Babylonia*a* to build a house for it. When it is ready, the basket will be set there in its place."

FOUR CHARIOTS

6 I looked up again—and there before me were four chariots coming out from between two mountains—mountains of bronze! ²The first chariot had red horses, the second black, ³the third white, and the fourth dappled—all of them powerful. ⁴I asked the angel who was speaking to me, "What are these, my lord?"

⁵The angel answered me, "These are the four spirits*b* of heaven, going out from standing in the presence of the Lord of the whole world. ⁶The one with the black horses is going toward the north country, the one with the white horses toward the west,*c* and the one with the dappled horses toward the south."

⁷When the powerful horses went out, they were straining to go throughout the earth. And he said, "Go throughout the earth!" So they went throughout the earth.

⁸Then he called to me, "Look, those going toward the north country have given my Spirit*d* rest in the land of the north."

A CROWN FOR JOSHUA

⁹The word of the LORD came to me: ¹⁰"Take ₁silver and gold₁ from the exiles Heldai, Tobijah and Jedaiah, who have arrived from Babylon. Go the same day to the house of Josiah son of Zephaniah. ¹¹Take the silver and gold and make a crown, and set it on the head of the high priest, Joshua son of Jehozadak. ¹²Tell him this is what the LORD Almighty says: 'Here is the man whose name is the Branch, and he will branch out from his place and build the temple of the LORD. ¹³It is he who will build the temple of the LORD, and he will be clothed with majesty and will sit and rule on his throne. And he will be a priest on his throne. And there will be harmony between the two.' ¹⁴The crown will be given to Heldai,*e* Tobijah, Jedaiah and Hen*f* son of Zephaniah as a memorial in the temple of the LORD. ¹⁵Those who are far away will come and help to build the tem-

---

a 11 Hebrew Shinar   b 5 Or winds   c 6 Or horses after them   d 8 Or spirit   e 14 Syriac; Hebrew Helem   f 14 Or and the gracious one, the

THE MESSAGE

5.10   I said to the Messenger-Angel, "Where are they taking the bushel basket?"

5.11   He said, "East to the land of Shinar. They will build a garage to house it. When it's finished, the basket will be stored there."

EIGHTH VISION: FOUR CHARIOTS

6.1   6 Once again I looked up—another strange sight! Four chariots charging out from between two mountains. The mountains were bronze.

6.2-3   The first chariot was drawn by red horses, the second chariot by black horses, the third chariot by white horses, and the fourth chariot by dappled horses. All the horses were powerful.

6.4   I asked the Messenger-Angel, "Sir, what's the meaning here?"

6.5-7   The angel answered, "These are the four winds of heaven, which originate with the Master of the whole earth. The black horses are headed north with the white ones right after them. The dappled horses are headed south." The powerful horses galloped out, bursting with energy, eager to patrol through the earth. The Messenger-Angel commanded: "On your way! Survey the earth!" and they were off in every direction.

6.8   Then he called to me and said, "Look at them go! The ones going north are conveying a sense of my Spirit, serene and secure. No more trouble from that direction."

A MAN NAMED BRANCH

6.9-12   Then this Message from GOD came to me: "Take up a collection from the exiles. Target Heldai, Tobiah, and Jedaiah. They've just arrived from Babylon. You'll find them at the home of Josiah son of Zephaniah. Collect silver and gold from them and fashion crowns. Place one on the head of Joshua son of Jehozadak, the high priest, and give him this message:

6.12-13   " 'A Message from GOD-of-the-Angel-Armies. Be alert. We have a man here whose name is Branch. He will branch out from where he is and build the Temple of GOD. Yes, he's the one. He'll build the Temple of GOD. Then he'll assume the role of royalty, take his place on the throne and rule—a priest sitting on the throne!—showing that king and priest can co-exist in harmony.'

6.14   "The other crown will be in the Temple of GOD as a symbol of royalty, under the custodial care of Helem, Tobiah, Jedaiah, and Hen son of Zephaniah.

6.15   "People will come from faraway places to pitch in and rebuild the Temple of GOD. This

NEW INTERNATIONAL VERSION

ple of the LORD, and you will know that the LORD Almighty has sent me to you. This will happen if you diligently obey the LORD your God."

JUSTICE AND MERCY, NOT FASTING

7 In the fourth year of King Darius, the word of the LORD came to Zechariah on the fourth day of the ninth month, the month of Kislev. ²The people of Bethel had sent Sharezer and Regem-Melech, together with their men, to entreat the LORD ³by asking the priests of the house of the LORD Almighty and the prophets, "Should I mourn and fast in the fifth month, as I have done for so many years?"

⁴Then the word of the LORD Almighty came to me: ⁵"Ask all the people of the land and the priests, 'When you fasted and mourned in the fifth and seventh months for the past seventy years, was it really for me that you fasted? ⁶And when you were eating and drinking, were you not just feasting for yourselves? ⁷Are these not the words the LORD proclaimed through the earlier prophets when Jerusalem and its surrounding towns were at rest and prosperous, and the Negev and the western foothills were settled?' "

⁸And the word of the LORD came again to Zechariah: ⁹"This is what the LORD Almighty says: 'Administer true justice; show mercy and compassion to one another. ¹⁰Do not oppress the widow or the fatherless, the alien or the poor. In your hearts do not think evil of each other.'

¹¹"But they refused to pay attention; stubbornly they turned their backs and stopped up their ears. ¹²They made their hearts as hard as flint and would not listen to the law or to the words that the LORD Almighty had sent by his Spirit through the earlier prophets. So the LORD Almighty was very angry.

¹³" 'When I called, they did not listen; so when they called, I would not listen,' says the LORD Almighty. ¹⁴'I scattered them with a whirlwind among all the nations, where they were strangers. The land was left so desolate behind them that no one could come or go. This is how they made the pleasant land desolate.' "

THE MESSAGE

will confirm that GOD-of-the-Angel-Armies did, in fact, send me to you. All this follows as you put your minds to a life of responsive obedience to the voice of your GOD."

"YOU'RE INTERESTED IN RELIGION, I'M INTERESTED IN PEOPLE"

7.1 **7** On the fourth day of the ninth month, in the fourth year of the reign of King Darius, GOD's Message again came to Zechariah.

7.2-3 The town of Bethel had sent a delegation headed by Sarezer and Regem-Melech to pray for GOD's blessing and to confer with the priests of the Temple of GOD-of-the-Angel-Armies, and also with the prophets. They posed this question: "Should we plan for a day of mourning and abstinence next August, the seventieth anniversary of Jerusalem's fall, as we have been doing all these years?"

7.4-6 GOD-of-the-Angel-Armies gave me this Message for them, for all the people and for the priests: "When you held days of fasting every fifth and seventh month all these seventy years, were you doing it for me? And when you held feasts, was that for me? Hardly. You're interested in religion, I'm interested in people.

7.7-10 "There's nothing new to say on the subject. Don't you still have the message of the earlier prophets from the time when Jerusalem was still a thriving, bustling city and the outlying countryside, the Negev and Shephelah, was populated? [This is the message that GOD gave Zechariah.] Well, the message hasn't changed. GOD-of-the-Angel-Armies said then and says now:

" 'Treat one another justly.
Love your neighbors.
Be compassionate with each other.
Don't take advantage of widows, orphans,
       visitors, and the poor.
Don't plot and scheme against one
       another—that's evil.'

7.11-13 "But did your ancestors listen? No, they set their jaws in defiance. They shut their ears. They steeled themselves against GOD's revelation and the Spirit-filled sermons preached by the earlier prophets by order of GOD-of-the-Angel-Armies. And GOD became angry, really angry, because he told them everything plainly and they wouldn't listen to a word he said.

7.13-14 "So [this is what GOD-of-the-Angel-Armies said] if they won't listen to me, I won't listen to them. I scattered them to the four winds. They ended up strangers wherever they were. Their 'promised land' became a vacant lot—weeds and tin cans and thistles. Not a sign of life. They turned a dreamland into a wasteland."

NEW INTERNATIONAL VERSION

THE LORD PROMISES TO BLESS JERUSALEM

8 Again the word of the LORD Almighty came to me. ²This is what the LORD Almighty says: "I am very jealous for Zion; I am burning with jealousy for her."

³This is what the LORD says: "I will return to Zion and dwell in Jerusalem. Then Jerusalem will be called the City of Truth, and the mountain of the LORD Almighty will be called the Holy Mountain."

⁴This is what the LORD Almighty says: "Once again men and women of ripe old age will sit in the streets of Jerusalem, each with cane in hand because of his age. ⁵The city streets will be filled with boys and girls playing there."

⁶This is what the LORD Almighty says: "It may seem marvelous to the remnant of this people at that time, but will it seem marvelous to me?" declares the LORD Almighty.

⁷This is what the LORD Almighty says: "I will save my people from the countries of the east and the west. ⁸I will bring them back to live in Jerusalem; they will be my people, and I will be faithful and righteous to them as their God."

⁹This is what the LORD Almighty says: "You who now hear these words spoken by the prophets who were there when the foundation was laid for the house of the LORD Almighty, let your hands be strong so that the temple may be built. ¹⁰Before that time there were no wages for man or beast. No one could go about his business safely because of his enemy, for I had turned every man against his neighbor. ¹¹But now I will not deal with the remnant of this people as I did in the past," declares the LORD Almighty.

¹²"The seed will grow well, the vine will yield its fruit, the ground will produce its crops, and the heavens will drop their dew. I will give all

THE MESSAGE

REBUILDING THE TEMPLE

8 And then these Messages from GOD-of-the-Angel-Armies:

8.1-2

A Message from GOD-of-the-Angel-Armies:

"I am zealous for Zion—I *care!*
I'm angry about Zion—I'm *involved!*"

8.3 GOD's Message:

"I've come back to Zion,
I've moved back to Jerusalem.
Jerusalem's new names will be Truth City,
and Mountain of GOD-of-the-Angel-Armies,
and Mount Holiness."

8.4-5 A Message from GOD-of-the-Angel-Armies:

"Old men and old women will come back to Jerusalem, sit on benches on the streets and spin tales, move around safely with their canes—a good city to grow old in. And boys and girls will fill the public parks, laughing and playing—a good city to grow up in."

8.6 A Message from GOD-of-the-Angel-Armies:

"Do the problems of returning and rebuilding by just a few survivors seem too much? But is anything too much for me? Not if I have my say."

8.7-8 A Message from GOD-of-the-Angel-Armies:

"I'll collect my people from countries to the east and countries to the west. I'll bring them back and move them into Jerusalem. They'll be my people and I'll be their God. I'll stick with them and do right by them."

8.9-10 A Message from GOD-of-the-Angel-Armies:

"Get a grip on things. Hold tight, you who are listening to what I say through the preaching of the prophets. The Temple of GOD-of-the-Angel-Armies has been reestablished. The Temple is being rebuilt. We've come through a hard time: You worked for a pittance and were lucky to get that; the streets were dangerous; you could never let down your guard; I had turned the world into an armed camp.

8.11-12 "But things have changed. I'm taking the side of my core of surviving people:

Sowing and harvesting will resume,
Vines will grow grapes,
Gardens will flourish,
Dew and rain will make everything green.

NEW INTERNATIONAL VERSION

these things as an inheritance to the remnant of this people. [13]As you have been an object of cursing among the nations, O Judah and Israel, so will I save you, and you will be a blessing. Do not be afraid, but let your hands be strong."

[14]This is what the LORD Almighty says: "Just as I had determined to bring disaster upon you and showed no pity when your fathers angered me," says the LORD Almighty, [15]"so now I have determined to do good again to Jerusalem and Judah. Do not be afraid. [16]These are the things you are to do: Speak the truth to each other, and render true and sound judgment in your courts; [17]do not plot evil against your neighbor, and do not love to swear falsely. I hate all this," declares the LORD.

[18]Again the word of the LORD Almighty came to me. [19]This is what the LORD Almighty says: "The fasts of the fourth, fifth, seventh and tenth months will become joyful and glad occasions and happy festivals for Judah. Therefore love truth and peace."

[20]This is what the LORD Almighty says: "Many peoples and the inhabitants of many cities will yet come, [21]and the inhabitants of one city will go to another and say, 'Let us go at once to entreat the LORD and seek the LORD Almighty. I myself am going.' [22]And many peoples and powerful nations will come to Jerusalem to seek the LORD Almighty and to entreat him."

[23]This is what the LORD Almighty says: "In those days ten men from all languages and nations will take firm hold of one Jew by the hem of his robe and say, 'Let us go with you, because we have heard that God is with you.'"

JUDGMENT ON ISRAEL'S ENEMIES
An Oracle

9 The word of the LORD is against the land of Hadrach
and will rest upon Damascus—
for the eyes of men and all the tribes of Israel
are on the LORD—[a]

---

[a] 1 Or Damascus. / For the eye of the LORD is on all mankind, / as well as on the tribes of Israel,

THE MESSAGE

8.12-13 "My core survivors will get everything they need—and more. You've gotten a reputation as a bad-news people, you people of Judah and Israel, but I'm coming to save you. From now on, you're the good-news people. Don't be afraid. Keep a firm grip on what I'm doing."

KEEP YOUR LIVES SIMPLE AND HONEST

8.14-17 A Message from GOD-of-the-Angel-Armies:
"In the same way that I decided to punish you when your ancestors made me angry, and didn't pull my punches, at this time I've decided to bless Jerusalem and the country of Judah. Don't be afraid. And now here's what I want you to do: Tell the truth, the whole truth, when you speak. Do the right thing by one another, both personally and in your courts. Don't cook up plans to take unfair advantage of others. Don't do or say what isn't so. I hate all that stuff. Keep your lives simple and honest." Decree of GOD.

✝

8.18-19 Again I received a Message from GOD-of-the-Angel-Armies:
"The days of mourning set for the fourth, fifth, seventh, and tenth months will be turned into days of feasting for Judah—celebration and holiday. Embrace truth! Love peace!"

✝

8.20-21 A Message from GOD-of-the-Angel-Armies:
"People and their leaders will come from all over to see what's going on. The leaders will confer with one another: 'Shouldn't we try to get in on this? Get in on GOD's blessings? Pray to GOD-of-the-Angel-Armies? What's keeping us? Let's go!'

8.22 "Lots of people, powerful nations—they'll come to Jerusalem looking for what they can get from GOD-of-the-Angel-Armies, looking to get a blessing from GOD."

✝

8.23 A Message from GOD-of-the-Angel-Armies:
"At that time, ten men speaking a variety of languages will grab the sleeve of one Jew, hold tight, and say, 'Let us go with you. We've heard that God is with you.'"

THE WHOLE WORLD HAS ITS EYES ON GOD

9.1-6 **9** War Bulletin:

GOD's Message challenges the country of Hadrach.
It will settle on Damascus.
The whole world has its eyes on GOD.
Israel isn't the only one.

NEW INTERNATIONAL VERSION

² and upon Hamath too, which borders on it,
  and upon Tyre and Sidon, though they are
  very skillful.
³ Tyre has built herself a stronghold;
  she has heaped up silver like dust,
  and gold like the dirt of the streets.
⁴ But the Lord will take away her possessions
  and destroy her power on the sea,
  and she will be consumed by fire.
⁵ Ashkelon will see it and fear;
  Gaza will writhe in agony,
  and Ekron too, for her hope will wither.
  Gaza will lose her king
  and Ashkelon will be deserted.
⁶ Foreigners will occupy Ashdod,
  and I will cut off the pride of the
  Philistines.
⁷ I will take the blood from their mouths,
  the forbidden food from between their
  teeth.
  Those who are left will belong to our God
  and become leaders in Judah,
  and Ekron will be like the Jebusites.
⁸ But I will defend my house
  against marauding forces.
  Never again will an oppressor overrun my
  people,
  for now I am keeping watch.

THE COMING OF ZION'S KING

⁹ Rejoice greatly, O Daughter of Zion!
  Shout, Daughter of Jerusalem!
  See, your king*ᵃ* comes to you,
  righteous and having salvation,
  gentle and riding on a donkey,
  on a colt, the foal of a donkey.
¹⁰ I will take away the chariots from Ephraim
  and the war-horses from Jerusalem,
  and the battle bow will be broken.
  He will proclaim peace to the nations.
  His rule will extend from sea to sea
  and from the River*ᵇ* to the ends of the
  earth.*ᶜ*
¹¹ As for you, because of the blood of my
  covenant with you,
  I will free your prisoners from the
  waterless pit.
¹² Return to your fortress, O prisoners of hope;
  even now I announce that I will restore
  twice as much to you.
¹³ I will bend Judah as I bend my bow
  and fill it with Ephraim.
  I will rouse your sons, O Zion,

THE MESSAGE

That includes Hamath at the border,
  and Tyre and Sidon, clever as they think
  they are.
Tyre has put together quite a kingdom for
  herself;
  she has stacked up silver like cordwood,
  piled gold high as haystacks.
But God will certainly bankrupt her;
  he will dump all that wealth into the ocean
  and burn up what's left in a big fire.
Ashkelon will see it and panic,
  Gaza will wring its hands,
  Ekron will face a dead end.
Gaza's king will die.
  Ashkelon will be emptied out,
  And a villain will take over in Ashdod.

9.6-8 "I'll take proud Philistia down a peg:
  I'll make him spit out his bloody booty
  and abandon his vile ways."
What's left will be all God's—a core of
  survivors,
  a family brought together in Judah—
But enemies like Ekron will go the way of the
  Jebusites,
  into the dustbin of history.
"I will set up camp in my home country
  and defend it against invaders.
Nobody is going to hurt my people ever again.
  I'm keeping my eye on them.

A HUMBLE KING RIDING A DONKEY

9.9-10 "Shout and cheer, Daughter Zion!
  Raise the roof, Daughter Jerusalem!
Your king is coming!
  a good king who makes all things right,
  a humble king riding a donkey,
  a mere colt of a donkey.
  I've had it with war—no more chariots in
  Ephraim,
  no more war horses in Jerusalem,
  no more swords and spears, bows and
  arrows.
He will offer peace to the nations,
  a peaceful rule worldwide,
  from the four winds to the seven seas.

9.11-13 "And you, because of my blood covenant with
  you,
  I'll release your prisoners from their
  hopeless cells.
Come home, hope-filled prisoners!
  This very day I'm declaring a double
  bonus—
  everything you lost returned twice-over!
Judah is now my weapon, the bow I'll pull,
  setting Ephraim as an arrow to the string.
I'll wake up your sons, O Zion,

ᵃ 9 Or *King*   *ᵇ 10* That is, the Euphrates   *ᶜ 10* Or *the*
end of the land

NEW INTERNATIONAL VERSION	THE MESSAGE

NEW INTERNATIONAL VERSION

against your sons, O Greece,
  and make you like a warrior's sword.

THE LORD WILL APPEAR

¹⁴ Then the LORD will appear over them;
  his arrow will flash like lightning.
The Sovereign LORD will sound the trumpet;
  he will march in the storms of the south,
¹⁵ and the LORD Almighty will shield them.
They will destroy
  and overcome with slingstones.
They will drink and roar as with wine;
  they will be full like a bowl
  used for sprinkling*ᵃ* the corners of the
    altar.
¹⁶ The LORD their God will save them on that day
  as the flock of his people.
They will sparkle in his land
  like jewels in a crown.
¹⁷ How attractive and beautiful they will be!
  Grain will make the young men thrive,
  and new wine the young women.

THE LORD WILL CARE FOR JUDAH

10 Ask the LORD for rain in the springtime;
  it is the LORD who makes the storm
    clouds.
He gives showers of rain to men,
  and plants of the field to everyone.
² The idols speak deceit,
  diviners see visions that lie;
they tell dreams that are false,
  they give comfort in vain.
Therefore the people wander like sheep
  oppressed for lack of a shepherd.

³ "My anger burns against the shepherds,
  and I will punish the leaders;
for the LORD Almighty will care
  for his flock, the house of Judah,
  and make them like a proud horse in
    battle.
⁴ From Judah will come the cornerstone,
  from him the tent peg,
  from him the battle bow,
  from him every ruler.
⁵ Together theyᵇ will be like mighty men
  trampling the muddy streets in battle.
Because the LORD is with them,
  they will fight and overthrow the
    horsemen.

THE MESSAGE

to counter your sons, O Greece.
From now on
  people are my swords."

9.14-17 Then GOD will come into view,
  his arrows flashing like lightning!
Master GOD will blast his trumpet
  and set out in a whirlwind.
GOD-of-the-Angel-Armies will protect them—
  all-out war,
The war to end all wars,
  no holds barred.
Their GOD will save the day. He'll rescue them.
  They'll become like sheep, gentle and soft,
Or like gemstones in a crown,
  catching all the colors of the sun.
Then how they'll shine! shimmer! glow!
  the young men robust, the young women
    lovely!

GOD'S WORK OF REBUILDING

10.1 **10** Pray to GOD for rain—it's time for the
  spring rain—
to GOD, the rainmaker,
Spring thunderstorm maker,
  maker of grain and barley.

10.2-3 "Store-bought gods babble gibberish.
  Religious experts spout rubbish.
They pontificate hot air.
  Their prescriptions are nothing but smoke.
And so the people wander like lost sheep,
  poor lost sheep without a shepherd.
I'm furious with the so-called shepherds.
  They're worse than billy goats, and I'll treat
    them like goats."

10.3-5 GOD-of-the-Angel-Armies will step in
  and take care of his flock, the people of Judah.
He'll revive their spirits,
  make them proud to be on God's side.
God will use them in his work of rebuilding,
  use them as foundations and pillars,
Use them as tools and instruments,
  use them to oversee his work.
They'll be a workforce to be proud of,
  working as one,
  their heads held high, striding through
    swamps and mud,
Courageous and vigorous because GOD is with
  them,
  undeterred by the world's thugs.

✠

ᵃ 15 Or bowl, / like   ᵇ 4,5 Or ruler, all of them together. /
⁵They

NEW INTERNATIONAL VERSION

6 "I will strengthen the house of Judah
  and save the house of Joseph.
I will restore them
  because I have compassion on them.
They will be as though
  I had not rejected them,
for I am the LORD their God
  and I will answer them.
7 The Ephraimites will become like mighty
    men,
  and their hearts will be glad as with wine.
Their children will see it and be joyful;
  their hearts will rejoice in the LORD.
8 I will signal for them
  and gather them in.
Surely I will redeem them;
  they will be as numerous as before.
9 Though I scatter them among the peoples,
  yet in distant lands they will remember
    me.
They and their children will survive,
  and they will return.
10 I will bring them back from Egypt
  and gather them from Assyria.
I will bring them to Gilead and Lebanon,
  and there will not be room enough for
    them.
11 They will pass through the sea of trouble;
  the surging sea will be subdued
  and all the depths of the Nile will dry up.
Assyria's pride will be brought down
  and Egypt's scepter will pass away.
12 I will strengthen them in the LORD
  and in his name they will walk,"
                    declares the LORD.

11 Open your doors, O Lebanon,
   so that fire may devour your cedars!
2 Wail, O pine tree, for the cedar has fallen;
  the stately trees are ruined!
Wail, oaks of Bashan;
  the dense forest has been cut down!
3 Listen to the wail of the shepherds;
  their rich pastures are destroyed!
Listen to the roar of the lions;
  the lush thicket of the Jordan is ruined!

TWO SHEPHERDS

4 This is what the LORD my God says: "Pasture
the flock marked for slaughter. 5 Their buyers
slaughter them and go unpunished. Those who
sell them say, 'Praise the LORD, I am rich!' Their

THE MESSAGE

10.6-12 "I'll put muscle in the people of Judah;
  I'll save the people of Joseph.
I know their pain and will make them good as
    new.
  They'll get a fresh start, as if nothing had
    ever happened.
And why? Because I am their very own GOD,
  I'll do what needs to be done for them.
The people of Ephraim will be famous,
  their lives brimming with joy.
Their children will get in on it, too—
  oh, let them feel blessed by GOD!
I'll whistle and they'll all come running.
  I've set them free—oh, how they'll flourish!
Even though I scattered them to the far
    corners of earth,
  they'll remember me in the faraway places.
They'll keep the story alive in their children,
  and they will come back.
I'll bring them back from the Egyptian west
  and round them up from the Assyrian east.
I'll bring them back to sweet Gilead,
  back to leafy Lebanon.
Every square foot of land
  will be marked by homecoming.
They'll sail through troubled seas, brush aside
    brash ocean waves.
  Roaring rivers will turn to a trickle.
Gaudy Assyria will be stripped bare,
  bully Egypt exposed as a fraud.
But my people—oh, I'll make them strong,
    GOD-strong!
  and they'll live my way." GOD says so!

⊹

11.1-4 11 Open your borders to the immigrants,
       proud Lebanon!
  Your sentinel trees will burn.
Weep, great pine trees! Mourn, you sister
    cedars!
  Your towering trees are cordwood.
Weep Bashan oak trees!
  Your thick forest is now a field of stumps.
Do you hear the wailing of shepherds?
  They've lost everything they once owned.
Do you hear the outrage of the lions?
  The mighty jungle of the Jordan is wasted.
Make room for the returning exiles!

BREAKING THE BEAUTIFUL COVENANT

11.4-5 GOD commanded me, "Shepherd the sheep that
are soon to be slaughtered. The people who
buy them will butcher them for quick and easy
money. What's worse, they'll get away with it.
The people who sell them will say, 'Lucky me!

NEW INTERNATIONAL VERSION

own shepherds do not spare them. ⁶For I will no longer have pity on the people of the land," declares the LORD. "I will hand everyone over to his neighbor and his king. They will oppress the land, and I will not rescue them from their hands."

⁷So I pastured the flock marked for slaughter, particularly the oppressed of the flock. Then I took two staffs and called one Favor and the other Union, and I pastured the flock. ⁸In one month I got rid of the three shepherds.

The flock detested me, and I grew weary of them ⁹and said, "I will not be your shepherd. Let the dying die, and the perishing perish. Let those who are left eat one another's flesh."

¹⁰Then I took my staff called Favor and broke it, revoking the covenant I had made with all the nations. ¹¹It was revoked on that day, and so the afflicted of the flock who were watching me knew it was the word of the LORD.

¹²I told them, "If you think it best, give me my pay; but if not, keep it." So they paid me thirty pieces of silver.

¹³And the LORD said to me, "Throw it to the potter"—the handsome price at which they priced me! So I took the thirty pieces of silver and threw them into the house of the LORD to the potter.

¹⁴Then I broke my second staff called Union, breaking the brotherhood between Judah and Israel.

¹⁵Then the LORD said to me, "Take again the equipment of a foolish shepherd. ¹⁶For I am going to raise up a shepherd over the land who will not care for the lost, or seek the young, or heal the injured, or feed the healthy, but will eat the meat of the choice sheep, tearing off their hoofs.

¹⁷"Woe to the worthless shepherd,
    who deserts the flock!
May the sword strike his arm and his right
    eye!
May his arm be completely withered,
    his right eye totally blinded!"

JERUSALEM'S ENEMIES TO BE DESTROYED
An Oracle

12 This is the word of the LORD concerning Israel. The LORD, who stretches out the heavens, who lays the foundation of the earth,

THE MESSAGE

God's on my side; I've got it made!' They have shepherds who couldn't care less about them."

11.6   GOD's Decree: "I'm washing my hands of the people of this land. From now on they're all on their own. It's dog-eat-dog, survival of the fittest, and the devil take the hindmost. Don't look for help from me."

11.7-8   So I took over from the crass, money-grubbing owners, and shepherded the sheep marked for slaughter. I got myself two shepherd staffs. I named one Lovely and the other Harmony. Then I went to work shepherding the sheep. Within a month I got rid of the corrupt shepherds. I got tired of putting up with them—and they couldn't stand me.

11.9   And then I got tired of the sheep and said, "I've had it with you—no more shepherding from me. If you die, you die; if you're attacked, you're attacked. Whoever survives can eat what's left."

11.10-11   Then I took the staff named Lovely and broke it across my knee, breaking the beautiful covenant I had made with all the peoples. In one stroke, both staff and covenant were broken. The money-hungry owners saw me do it and knew GOD was behind it.

11.12   Then I addressed them: "Pay me what you think I'm worth." They paid me an insulting sum, counting out thirty silver coins.

11.13   GOD told me, "Throw it in the poor box." This stingy wage was all they thought of me and my work! So I took the thirty silver coins and threw them into the poor box in GOD's Temple.

11.14   Then I broke the other staff, Harmony, across my knee, breaking the concord between Judah and Israel.

11.15-16   GOD then said, "Dress up like a stupid shepherd. I'm going to install just such a shepherd in this land—a shepherd indifferent to victims, who ignores the lost, abandons the injured, and disdains decent citizens. He'll only be in it for what he can get out of it, using and abusing any and all.

11.17   "Doom to you, useless shepherd,
    walking off and leaving the sheep!
A curse on your arm!
    A curse on your right eye!
Your arm will hang limp and useless.
    Your right eye will go stone blind."

HOME AGAIN IN JERUSALEM
War Bulletin:

11.1-2 **12**   GOD's Message concerning Israel, GOD's Decree—the very GOD who threw the skies into space, set earth on a firm foundation, and

NEW INTERNATIONAL VERSION

and who forms the spirit of man within him, declares: ²"I am going to make Jerusalem a cup that sends all the surrounding peoples reeling. Judah will be besieged as well as Jerusalem. ³On that day, when all the nations of the earth are gathered against her, I will make Jerusalem an immovable rock for all the nations. All who try to move it will injure themselves. ⁴On that day I will strike every horse with panic and its rider with madness," declares the LORD. "I will keep a watchful eye over the house of Judah, but I will blind all the horses of the nations. ⁵Then the leaders of Judah will say in their hearts, 'The people of Jerusalem are strong, because the LORD Almighty is their God.'

⁶"On that day I will make the leaders of Judah like a firepot in a woodpile, like a flaming torch among sheaves. They will consume right and left all the surrounding peoples, but Jerusalem will remain intact in her place.

⁷"The LORD will save the dwellings of Judah first, so that the honor of the house of David and of Jerusalem's inhabitants may not be greater than that of Judah. ⁸On that day the LORD will shield those who live in Jerusalem, so that the feeblest among them will be like David, and the house of David will be like God, like the Angel of the LORD going before them. ⁹On that day I will set out to destroy all the nations that attack Jerusalem.

MOURNING FOR THE ONE THEY PIERCED

¹⁰"And I will pour out on the house of David and the inhabitants of Jerusalem a spirit*ᵃ* of grace and supplication. They will look on*ᵇ* me, the one they have pierced, and they will mourn for him as one mourns for an only child, and grieve bitterly for him as one grieves for a firstborn son. ¹¹On that day the weeping in Jerusalem will be great, like the weeping of Hadad Rimmon in the plain of Megiddo. ¹²The land will mourn, each clan by itself, with their wives by themselves: the clan of the house of David and their wives, the clan of the house of Nathan and their wives, ¹³the clan of the house of Levi and

THE MESSAGE

breathed his own life into men and women: "Watch for this: I'm about to turn Jerusalem into a cup of strong drink that will have the people who have set siege to Judah and Jerusalem staggering in a drunken stupor.

12.3   "On the Big Day, I'll turn Jerusalem into a huge stone blocking the way for everyone. All who try to lift it will rupture themselves. All the pagan nations will come together and try to get rid of it.

12.4-5   "On the Big Day"—this is GOD speaking— "I'll throw all the war horses into a crazed panic, and their riders along with them. But I'll keep my eye on Judah, watching out for her at the same time that I make the enemy horses go blind. The families of Judah will then realize, 'Why, our leaders are strong and able through GOD-of-the-Angel-Armies, their personal God.'

12.6   "On the Big Day, I'll turn the families of Judah into something like a burning match in a tinder-dry forest, like a fiercely flaming torch in a barn full of hay. They'll burn up everything and everyone in sight—people to the right, people to the left—while Jerusalem fills up with people moving in and making themselves at home—home again in Jerusalem.

12.7-8   "I, GOD, will begin by restoring the common households of Judah so that the glory of David's family and the leaders in Jerusalem won't overshadow the ordinary people in Judah. On the Big Day, I'll look after everyone who lives in Jerusalem so that the lowliest, weakest person will be as glorious as David and the family of David itself will be godlike, like the Angel of GOD leading the people.

12.9   "On the Big Day, I'll make a clean sweep of all the godless nations that fought against Jerusalem.

12.10-14   "Next I'll deal with the family of David and those who live in Jerusalem. I'll pour a spirit of grace and prayer over them. They'll then be able to recognize me as the One they so grievously wounded—that piercing spear-thrust! And they'll weep—oh, how they'll weep! Deep mourning as of a parent grieving the loss of the firstborn child. The lamentation in Jerusalem that day will be massive, as famous as the lamentation over Hadad-Rimmon on the fields of Megiddo:

> Everyone will weep and grieve,
>   the land and everyone in it:
> The family of David off by itself
>   and their women off by themselves;
> The family of Nathan off by itself
>   and their women off by themselves;
> The family of Levi off by itself

NEW INTERNATIONAL VERSION

their wives, the clan of Shimei and their wives, ¹⁴and all the rest of the clans and their wives.

CLEANSING FROM SIN

13 "On that day a fountain will be opened to the house of David and the inhabitants of Jerusalem, to cleanse them from sin and impurity.

²"On that day, I will banish the names of the idols from the land, and they will be remembered no more," declares the LORD Almighty. "I will remove both the prophets and the spirit of impurity from the land. ³And if anyone still prophesies, his father and mother, to whom he was born, will say to him, 'You must die, because you have told lies in the LORD's name.' When he prophesies, his own parents will stab him.

⁴"On that day every prophet will be ashamed of his prophetic vision. He will not put on a prophet's garment of hair in order to deceive. ⁵He will say, 'I am not a prophet. I am a farmer; the land has been my livelihood since my youth.^a' ⁶If someone asks him, 'What are these wounds on your body^b?' he will answer, 'The wounds I was given at the house of my friends.'

THE SHEPHERD STRUCK, THE SHEEP SCATTERED

⁷"Awake, O sword, against my shepherd,
   against the man who is close to me!"
   declares the LORD Almighty.
"Strike the shepherd,
   and the sheep will be scattered,
   and I will turn my hand against the little
      ones.
⁸In the whole land," declares the LORD,
   "two-thirds will be struck down and
      perish;
   yet one-third will be left in it.
⁹This third I will bring into the fire;
   I will refine them like silver
   and test them like gold.
They will call on my name
   and I will answer them;
I will say, 'They are my people,'
   and they will say, 'The LORD is our God.' "

THE MESSAGE

and their women off by themselves;
The family of Shimei off by itself
   and their women off by themselves;
And all the rest of the families off by
      themselves
   and their women off by themselves.

WASHING AWAY SINS

13.1 **13** "On the Big Day, a fountain will be opened for the family of David and all the leaders of Jerusalem for washing away their sins, for scrubbing their stained and soiled lives clean.

13.2-3 "On the Big Day"—this is GOD-of-the-Angel-Armies speaking—"I will wipe out the store-bought gods, erase their names from memory. People will forget they ever heard of them. And I'll get rid of the prophets who polluted the air with their diseased words. If anyone dares persist in spreading diseased, polluting words, his very own parents will step in and say, 'That's it! You're finished! Your lies about GOD put everyone in danger,' and then they'll stab him to death in the very act of prophesying lies about GOD—his own parents, mind you!

13.4-6 "On the Big Day, the lying prophets will be publicly exposed and humiliated. Then they'll wish they'd never swindled people with their 'visions.' No more masquerading in prophet clothes. But they'll deny they've even heard of such things: 'Me, a prophet? Not me. I'm a farmer—grew up on the farm.' And if someone says, 'And so where did you get that black eye?' they'll say, 'I ran into a door at a friend's house.'

✠

13.7-9 "Sword, get moving against my shepherd,
   against my close associate!"
      Decree of GOD-of-the-Angel-Armies.
"Kill the shepherd! Scatter the sheep!
   The back of my hand against even the
      lambs!
All across the country"—GOD's Decree—
   "two-thirds will be devastated
   and one-third survive.
I'll deliver the surviving third to the refinery
      fires.
   I'll refine them as silver is refined,
   test them for purity as gold is tested.
Then they'll pray to me by name
   and I'll answer them personally.
I'll say, 'That's my people.'
   They'll say, 'GOD—my God!' "

^a 5 Or farmer; a man sold me in my youth   ^b 6 Or wounds between your hands

NEW INTERNATIONAL VERSION

THE LORD COMES AND REIGNS

14 A day of the LORD is coming when your plunder will be divided among you.

²I will gather all the nations to Jerusalem to fight against it; the city will be captured, the houses ransacked, and the women raped. Half of the city will go into exile, but the rest of the people will not be taken from the city. ³Then the LORD will go out and fight against those nations, as he fights in the day of battle. ⁴On that day his feet will stand on the Mount of Olives, east of Jerusalem, and the Mount of Olives will be split in two from east to west, forming a great valley, with half of the mountain moving north and half moving south. ⁵You will flee by my mountain valley, for it will extend to Azel. You will flee as you fled from the earthquake*ᵃ* in the days of Uzziah king of Judah. Then the LORD my God will come, and all the holy ones with him.

⁶On that day there will be no light, no cold or frost. ⁷It will be a unique day, without daytime or nighttime—a day known to the LORD. When evening comes, there will be light.

⁸On that day living water will flow out from Jerusalem, half to the eastern sea*ᵇ* and half to the western sea,*ᶜ* in summer and in winter.

⁹The LORD will be king over the whole earth. On that day there will be one LORD, and his name the only name.

¹⁰The whole land, from Geba to Rimmon, south of Jerusalem, will become like the Arabah. But Jerusalem will be raised up and remain in its place, from the Benjamin Gate to the site of the First Gate, to the Corner Gate, and from the Tower of Hananel to the royal winepresses. ¹¹It will be inhabited; never again will it be destroyed. Jerusalem will be secure.

¹²This is the plague with which the LORD will strike all the nations that fought against Jerusalem: Their flesh will rot while they are still standing on their feet, their eyes will rot in their sockets, and their tongues will rot in their mouths. ¹³On that day men will be stricken by the LORD with great panic. Each man will seize the hand of another, and they will attack each other. ¹⁴Judah too will fight at Jerusalem. The

---

ᵃ 5 Or ⁵My mountain valley will be blocked and will extend to Azel. It will be blocked as it was blocked because of the earthquake *ᵇ 8 That is, the Dead Sea* *ᶜ 8 That is, the Mediterranean*

THE MESSAGE

THE DAY IS COMING

14.1-2 **14** Note well: GOD's Judgment Day is on the way:
"Plunder will be piled high and handed out.
I'm bringing all the godless nations to war against Jerusalem—
Houses plundered,
women raped,
Half the city taken into exile,
the other half left behind."

14.3-5 But then GOD will march out against the godless nations and fight—a great war! That's the Day he'll take his stand on the Mount of Olives, facing Jerusalem from the east. The Mount of Olives will be split right down the middle, from east to west, leaving a wide valley. Half the mountain will shift north, the other half south. Then you will run for your lives down the valley, your escape route that will take you all the way to Azal. You'll run for your lives, just as you ran on the day of the great earthquake in the days of Uzziah, king of Judah. Then my GOD will arrive and all the holy angels with him.

14.6-7 What a Day that will be! No more cold nights—in fact, no more nights! The Day is coming—the timing is GOD's—when it will be continuous day. Every evening will be a fresh morning.

14.8 What a Day that will be! Fresh flowing rivers out of Jerusalem, half to the eastern sea, half to the western sea, flowing year-round, summer and winter!

14.9 GOD will be king over all the earth, one GOD and only one. What a Day that will be!

✝

14.10-11 The land will stretch out spaciously around Jerusalem—to Geba in the north and Rimmon in the south, with Jerusalem towering at the center, and the commanding city gates—Gate of Benjamin to First Gate to Corner Gate to Hananel Tower to the Royal Winery—ringing the city full of people. Never again will Jerusalem be totally destroyed. From now on it will be a safe city.

14.12-14 But this is what will happen to all who fought against Jerusalem: GOD will visit them with a terrible plague. People's flesh will rot off their bones while they are walking around; their eyes will rot in their sockets and their tongues in their mouths; people will be dying on their feet! Mass hysteria when that happens—total panic! Fellow soldiers fighting and killing each other—holy terror! And then Judah will jump into the fray!

NEW INTERNATIONAL VERSION

wealth of all the surrounding nations will be collected—great quantities of gold and silver and clothing. 15A similar plague will strike the horses and mules, the camels and donkeys, and all the animals in those camps.

16Then the survivors from all the nations that have attacked Jerusalem will go up year after year to worship the King, the LORD Almighty, and to celebrate the Feast of Tabernacles. 17If any of the peoples of the earth do not go up to Jerusalem to worship the King, the LORD Almighty, they will have no rain. 18If the Egyptian people do not go up and take part, they will have no rain. The LORD*a* will bring on them the plague he inflicts on the nations that do not go up to celebrate the Feast of Tabernacles. 19This will be the punishment of Egypt and the punishment of all the nations that do not go up to celebrate the Feast of Tabernacles.

20On that day HOLY TO THE LORD will be inscribed on the bells of the horses, and the cooking pots in the LORD's house will be like the sacred bowls in front of the altar. 21Every pot in Jerusalem and Judah will be holy to the LORD Almighty, and all who come to sacrifice will take some of the pots and cook in them. And on that day there will no longer be a Canaanite*b* in the house of the LORD Almighty.

THE MESSAGE

14.14-15 Treasures from all the nations will be piled high—gold, silver, the latest fashions. The plague will also hit the animals—horses, mules, camels, donkeys. Everything alive in the military camps will be hit by the plague.

✝

14.16-19 All the survivors from the godless nations that fought against Jerusalem will travel to Jerusalem every year to worship the King, GOD-of-the-Angel-Armies, and celebrate the Feast of Booths. If any of these survivors fail to make the annual pilgrimage to Jerusalem to worship the King, GOD-of-the-Angel-Armies, there will be no rain. If the Egyptians don't make the pilgrimage and worship, there will be no rain for them. Every nation that does not go up to celebrate the Feast of Booths will be hit with the plague. Egypt and any other nation that does not make pilgrimage to celebrate the Feast of Booths gets punished.

14.20-21 On that Day, the Big Day, all the horses' harness bells will be inscribed "Holy to GOD." The cooking pots in the Temple of GOD will be as sacred as chalices and plates on the altar. In fact, all the pots and pans in all the kitchens of Jerusalem and Judah will be holy to GOD-of-the-Angel-Armies. People who come to worship, preparing meals and sacrifices, will use them. On that Big Day there will be no buying or selling in the Temple of GOD-of-the-Angel-Armies.

MALACHI

MALACHI

1 An oracle: The word of the LORD to Israel through Malachi.*a*

JACOB LOVED, ESAU HATED

2 "I have loved you," says the LORD.

"But you ask, 'How have you loved us?'

"Was not Esau Jacob's brother?" the LORD says. "Yet I have loved Jacob, 3 but Esau I have hated, and I have turned his mountains into a wasteland and left his inheritance to the desert jackals."

4 Edom may say, "Though we have been crushed, we will rebuild the ruins."

But this is what the LORD Almighty says: "They may build, but I will demolish. They will be called the Wicked Land, a people always under the wrath of the LORD. 5 You will see it with your own eyes and say, 'Great is the LORD—even beyond the borders of Israel!'

BLEMISHED SACRIFICES

6 "A son honors his father, and a servant his master. If I am a father, where is the honor due me? If I am a master, where is the respect due me?" says the LORD Almighty. "It is you, O priests, who show contempt for my name.

"But you ask, 'How have we shown contempt for your name?'

7 "You place defiled food on my altar.

"But you ask, 'How have we defiled you?'

"By saying that the LORD's table is contemptible. 8 When you bring blind animals for sacrifice, is that not wrong? When you sacrifice crippled or diseased animals, is that not wrong? Try offering them to your governor! Would he be pleased with you? Would he accept you?" says the LORD Almighty.

9 "Now implore God to be gracious to us. With such offerings from your hands, will he accept you?"—says the LORD Almighty.

NO MORE OF THIS SO-CALLED WORSHIP!

1.1 **1** A Message. GOD's Word to Israel through Malachi:

1.2-3　GOD said, "I love you."

You replied, "Really? How have you loved us?"

"Look at history" (this is GOD's answer). "Look at how differently I've treated you, Jacob, from Esau: I loved Jacob and hated Esau. I reduced pretentious Esau to a molehill, turned his whole country into a ghost town."

1.4　When Edom (Esau) said, "We've been knocked down, but we'll get up and start over, good as new," GOD-of-the-Angel-Armies said, "Just try it and see how far you get. When I knock you down, you stay down. People will take one look at you and say, 'Land of Evil!' and 'the GOD-cursed tribe!'

1.5　"Yes, take a good look. Then you'll see how faithfully I've loved you and you'll want even more, saying, 'May GOD be even greater, beyond the borders of Israel!'

✝

1.6　"Isn't it true that a son honors his father and a worker his master? So if I'm your Father, where's the honor? If I'm your Master, where's the respect?" GOD-of-the-Angel-Armies is calling you on the carpet: "You priests despise me!

"You say, 'Not so! How do we despise you?'

"By your shoddy, sloppy, defiling worship.

"You ask, 'What do you mean, "defiling"? What's defiling about it?'

1.7-8　"When you say, 'The altar of GOD is not important anymore; worship of GOD is no longer a priority,' that's defiling. And when you offer worthless animals for sacrifices in worship, animals that you're trying to get rid of—blind and sick and crippled animals—isn't that defiling? Try a trick like that with your banker or your senator—how far do you think it will get you?" GOD-of-the-Angel-Armies asks you.

1.9　"Get on your knees and pray that I will be gracious to you. You priests have gotten everyone in trouble. With this kind of conduct, do you think I'll pay attention to you?" GOD-of-the-Angel-Armies asks you.

---

a 1 *Malachi* means *my messenger.*

NEW INTERNATIONAL VERSION

¹⁰"Oh, that one of you would shut the temple doors, so that you would not light useless fires on my altar! I am not pleased with you," says the LORD Almighty, "and I will accept no offering from your hands. ¹¹My name will be great among the nations, from the rising to the setting of the sun. In every place incense and pure offerings will be brought to my name, because my name will be great among the nations," says the LORD Almighty.

¹²"But you profane it by saying of the Lord's table, 'It is defiled,' and of its food, 'It is contemptible.' ¹³And you say, 'What a burden!' and you sniff at it contemptuously," says the LORD Almighty.

"When you bring injured, crippled or diseased animals and offer them as sacrifices, should I accept them from your hands?" says the LORD. ¹⁴"Cursed is the cheat who has an acceptable male in his flock and vows to give it, but then sacrifices a blemished animal to the Lord. For I am a great king," says the LORD Almighty, "and my name is to be feared among the nations.

ADMONITION FOR THE PRIESTS

2 "And now this admonition is for you, O priests. ²If you do not listen, and if you do not set your heart to honor my name," says the LORD Almighty, "I will send a curse upon you, and I will curse your blessings. Yes, I have already cursed them, because you have not set your heart to honor me.

³"Because of you I will rebuke*a* your descendants*b*; I will spread on your faces the offal from your festival sacrifices, and you will be carried off with it. ⁴And you will know that I have sent you this admonition so that my covenant with Levi may continue," says the LORD Almighty. ⁵"My covenant was with him, a covenant of life and peace, and I gave them to him; this called for reverence and he revered me and stood in awe of my name. ⁶True instruction was in his mouth and nothing false was found on his lips. He walked with me in peace and uprightness, and turned many from sin.

⁷"For the lips of a priest ought to preserve

a 3 Or cut off (see Septuagint)   *b* 3 Or will blight your grain

THE MESSAGE

1.10   "Why doesn't one of you just shut the Temple doors and lock them? Then none of you can get in and play at religion with this silly, empty-headed worship. I am not pleased. The GOD-of-the-Angel-Armies is not pleased. And I don't want any more of this so-called worship!

OFFERING GOD SOMETHING HAND-ME-DOWN, BROKEN, OR USELESS

1.11   "I am honored all over the world. And there are people who know how to worship me all over the world, who honor me by bringing their best to me. They're saying it everywhere: 'God is greater, this GOD-of-the-Angel-Armies.'

1.12-13   "All except you. Instead of honoring me, you profane me. You profane me when you say, 'Worship is not important, and what we bring to worship is of no account,' and when you say, 'I'm bored—this doesn't do anything for me.' You act so superior, sticking your noses in the air—act superior to *me*, GOD-of-the-Angel-Armies! And when you do offer something to me, it's a hand-me-down, or broken, or useless. Do you think I'm going to accept it? This is GOD speaking to you!

1.14   "A curse on the person who makes a big show of doing something great for me—an expensive sacrifice, say—and then at the last minute brings in something puny and worthless! I'm a great king, GOD-of-the-Angel-Armies, honored far and wide, and I'll not put up with it!

DESECRATING THE HOLINESS OF GOD

2.1-3   2 "And now this indictment, you priests! If you refuse to obediently listen, and if you refuse to honor me, GOD-of-the-Angel-Armies, in worship, then I'll put you under a curse. I'll exchange all your blessings for curses. In fact, the curses are already at work because you're not serious about honoring me. Yes, and the curse will extend to your children. I'm going to plaster your faces with rotting garbage, garbage thrown out from your feasts. That's what you have to look forward to!

2.4-6   "Maybe that will wake you up. Maybe then you'll realize that I'm indicting you in order to put new life into my covenant with the priests of Levi, the covenant of GOD-of-the-Angel-Armies. My covenant with Levi was to give life and peace. I kept my covenant with him, and he honored me. He stood in reverent awe before me. He taught the truth and did not lie. He walked with me in peace and uprightness. He kept many out of the ditch, kept them on the road.

2.7-9   "It's the job of priests to teach the truth. Peo-

NEW INTERNATIONAL VERSION

knowledge, and from his mouth men should seek instruction—because he is the messenger of the LORD Almighty. ⁸But you have turned from the way and by your teaching have caused many to stumble; you have violated the covenant with Levi," says the LORD Almighty. ⁹"So I have caused you to be despised and humiliated before all the people, because you have not followed my ways but have shown partiality in matters of the law."

JUDAH UNFAITHFUL

¹⁰Have we not all one Father*ᵃ*? Did not one God create us? Why do we profane the covenant of our fathers by breaking faith with one another?

¹¹Judah has broken faith. A detestable thing has been committed in Israel and in Jerusalem: Judah has desecrated the sanctuary the LORD loves, by marrying the daughter of a foreign god. ¹²As for the man who does this, whoever he may be, may the LORD cut him off from the tents of Jacob*ᵇ*—even though he brings offerings to the LORD Almighty.

¹³Another thing you do: You flood the LORD's altar with tears. You weep and wail because he no longer pays attention to your offerings or accepts them with pleasure from your hands. ¹⁴You ask, "Why?" It is because the LORD is acting as the witness between you and the wife of your youth, because you have broken faith with her, though she is your partner, the wife of your marriage covenant.

¹⁵Has not ⌊the LORD⌋ made them one? In flesh and spirit they are his. And why one? Because he was seeking godly offspring.*ᶜ* So guard yourself in your spirit, and do not break faith with the wife of your youth.

¹⁶"I hate divorce," says the LORD God of Israel, "and I hate a man's covering himself*ᵈ* with violence as well as with his garment," says the LORD Almighty.

So guard yourself in your spirit, and do not break faith.

THE DAY OF JUDGMENT

¹⁷You have wearied the LORD with your words.

"How have we wearied him?" you ask.

By saying, "All who do evil are good in the eyes of the LORD, and he is pleased with them" or "Where is the God of justice?"

THE MESSAGE

ple are supposed to look to them for guidance. The priest is the messenger of GOD-of-the-Angel-Armies. But you priests have abandoned the way of priests. Your teaching has messed up many lives. You have corrupted the covenant of priest Levi. GOD-of-the-Angel-Armies says so. And so I am showing you up for who you are. Everyone will be disgusted with you and avoid you because you don't live the way I told you to live, and you don't teach my revelation truly and impartially."

2.10 Don't we all come from one Father? Aren't we all created by the same God? So why can't we get along? Why do we desecrate the covenant of our ancestors that binds us together?

2.11-12 Judah has cheated on GOD—a sickening violation of trust in Israel and Jerusalem: Judah has desecrated the holiness of GOD by falling in love and running off with foreign women, women who worship alien gods. GOD's curse on those who do this! Drive them out of house and home! They're no longer fit to be part of the community no matter how many offerings they bring to GOD-of-the-Angel-Armies.

2.13-15 And here's a second offense: You fill the place of worship with your whining and sniveling because you don't get what you want from GOD. Do you know why? Simple. Because GOD was there as a witness when you spoke your marriage vows to your young bride, and now you've broken those vows, broken the faith-bond with your vowed companion, your covenant wife. GOD, not you, made marriage. His Spirit inhabits even the smallest details of marriage. And what does he want from marriage? Children of God, that's what. So guard the spirit of marriage within you. Don't cheat on your spouse.

2.16 "I hate divorce," says the GOD of Israel. GOD-of-the-Angel-Armies says, "I hate the violent dismembering of the 'one flesh' of marriage." So watch yourselves. Don't let your guard down. Don't cheat.

2.17 You make GOD tired with all your talk.

"How do we tire him out?" you ask.

By saying, "GOD loves sinners and sin alike. GOD loves all." And also by saying, "Judgment? GOD's too nice to judge."

ᵃ 10 Or *father*   *ᵇ 12* Or *¹²May the* LORD *cut off from the tents of Jacob anyone who gives testimony in behalf of the man who does this*   *ᶜ 15* Or *¹⁵But the one* ⌊*who is our father*⌋ *did not do this, not as long as life remained in him. And what was he seeking? An offspring from God*   *ᵈ 16* Or *his wife*

NEW INTERNATIONAL VERSION

3 "See, I will send my messenger, who will prepare the way before me. Then suddenly the Lord you are seeking will come to his temple; the messenger of the covenant, whom you desire, will come," says the LORD Almighty.

²But who can endure the day of his coming? Who can stand when he appears? For he will be like a refiner's fire or a launderer's soap. ³He will sit as a refiner and purifier of silver; he will purify the Levites and refine them like gold and silver. Then the LORD will have men who will bring offerings in righteousness, ⁴and the offerings of Judah and Jerusalem will be acceptable to the LORD, as in days gone by, as in former years.

⁵"So I will come near to you for judgment. I will be quick to testify against sorcerers, adulterers and perjurers, against those who defraud laborers of their wages, who oppress the widows and the fatherless, and deprive aliens of justice, but do not fear me," says the LORD Almighty.

ROBBING GOD

⁶"I the LORD do not change. So you, O descendants of Jacob, are not destroyed. ⁷Ever since the time of your forefathers you have turned away from my decrees and have not kept them. Return to me, and I will return to you," says the LORD Almighty.

"But you ask, 'How are we to return?'

⁸"Will a man rob God? Yet you rob me.

"But you ask, 'How do we rob you?'

"In tithes and offerings. ⁹You are under a curse—the whole nation of you—because you are robbing me. ¹⁰Bring the whole tithe into the storehouse, that there may be food in my house. Test me in this," says the LORD Almighty, "and see if I will not throw open the floodgates of heaven and pour out so much blessing that you will not have room enough for it. ¹¹I will prevent pests from devouring your crops, and the vines in your fields will not cast their fruit," says the LORD Almighty. ¹²"Then all the nations will call you blessed, for yours will be a delightful land," says the LORD Almighty.

THE MESSAGE

THE MASTER YOU'VE BEEN LOOKING FOR

3.1 **3** "Look! I'm sending my messenger on ahead to clear the way for me. Suddenly, out of the blue, the Leader you've been looking for will enter his Temple—yes, the Messenger of the Covenant, the one you've been waiting for. Look! He's on his way!" A Message from the mouth of GOD-of-the-Angel-Armies.

3.2-4 But who will be able to stand up to that coming? Who can survive his appearance?

He'll be like white-hot fire from the smelter's furnace. He'll be like the strongest lye soap at the laundry. He'll take his place as a refiner of silver, as a cleanser of dirty clothes. He'll scrub the Levite priests clean, refine them like gold and silver, until they're fit for GOD, fit to present offerings of righteousness. Then, and only then, will Judah and Jerusalem be fit and pleasing to GOD, as they used to be in the years long ago.

✝

3.5 "Yes, I'm on my way to visit you with Judgment. I'll present compelling evidence against sorcerers, adulterers, liars, those who exploit workers, those who take advantage of widows and orphans, those who are inhospitable to the homeless—anyone and everyone who doesn't honor me." A Message from GOD-of-the-Angel-Armies.

✝

3.6-7 "I am GOD—yes, I AM. I haven't changed. And because I haven't changed, you, the descendants of Jacob, haven't been destroyed. You have a long history of ignoring my commands. You haven't done a thing I've told you. Return to me so I can return to you," says GOD-of-the-Angel-Armies.

"You ask, 'But how do we return?'

3.8-11 "Begin by being honest. Do honest people rob God? But you rob me day after day.

"You ask, 'How have we robbed you?'

"The tithe and the offering—that's how! And now you're under a curse—the whole lot of you—because you're robbing me. Bring your full tithe to the Temple treasury so there will be ample provisions in my Temple. Test me in this and see if I don't open up heaven itself to you and pour out blessings beyond your wildest dreams. For my part, I will defend you against marauders, protect your wheat fields and vegetable gardens against plunderers." The Message of GOD-of-the-Angel-Armies.

3.12 "You'll be voted 'Happiest Nation.' You'll experience what it's like to be a country of grace." GOD-of-the-Angel-Armies says so.

NEW INTERNATIONAL VERSION

13"You have said harsh things against me," says the Lord.

"Yet you ask, 'What have we said against you?'
14"You have said, 'It is futile to serve God. What did we gain by carrying out his requirements and going about like mourners before the Lord Almighty? 15But now we call the arrogant blessed. Certainly the evildoers prosper, and even those who challenge God escape.' "

16Then those who feared the Lord talked with each other, and the Lord listened and heard. A scroll of remembrance was written in his presence concerning those who feared the Lord and honored his name.

17"They will be mine," says the Lord Almighty, "in the day when I make up my treasured possession.*a* I will spare them, just as in compassion a man spares his son who serves him. 18And you will again see the distinction between the righteous and the wicked, between those who serve God and those who do not.

The Day of the Lord

4 "Surely the day is coming; it will burn like a furnace. All the arrogant and every evildoer will be stubble, and that day that is coming will set them on fire," says the Lord Almighty. "Not a root or a branch will be left to them. 2But for you who revere my name, the sun of righteousness will rise with healing in its wings. And you will go out and leap like calves released from the stall. 3Then you will trample down the wicked; they will be ashes under the soles of your feet on the day when I do these things," says the Lord Almighty.

4"Remember the law of my servant Moses, the decrees and laws I gave him at Horeb for all Israel.

5"See, I will send you the prophet Elijah before that great and dreadful day of the Lord comes. 6He will turn the hearts of the fathers to their children, and the hearts of the children to their fathers; or else I will come and strike the land with a curse."

THE MESSAGE

The Difference Between Serving God and Not Serving Him

3.13 God says, "You have spoken hard, rude words to me.

"You ask, 'When did we ever do that?'
3.14-15 "When you said, 'It doesn't pay to serve God. What do we ever get out of it? When we did what he said and went around with long faces, serious about God-of-the-Angel-Armies, what difference did it make? Those who take life into their own hands are the lucky ones. They break all the rules and get ahead anyway. They push God to the limit and get by with it.' "

3.16 Then those whose lives honored God got together and talked it over. God saw what they were doing and listened in. A book was opened in God's presence and minutes were taken of the meeting, with the names of the God-fearers written down, all the names of those who honored God's name.

3.17-18 God-of-the-Angel-Armies said, "They're mine, all mine. They'll get special treatment when I go into action. I treat them with the same consideration and kindness that parents give the child who honors them. Once more you'll see the difference it makes between being a person who does the right thing and one who doesn't, between serving God and not serving him.

The Sun of Righteousness Will Dawn

4.1-3 4 "Count on it: The day is coming, raging like a forest fire. All the arrogant people who do evil things will be burned up like stove wood, burned to a crisp, nothing left but scorched earth and ash—a black day. But for you, sunrise! The sun of righteousness will dawn on those who honor my name, healing radiating from its wings. You will be bursting with energy, like colts frisky and frolicking. And you'll tromp on the wicked. They'll be nothing but ashes under your feet on that Day." God-of-the-Angel-Armies says so.

4.4 "Remember and keep the revelation I gave through my servant Moses, the revelation I commanded at Horeb for all Israel, all the rules and procedures for right living.

4.5-6 "But also look ahead: I'm sending Elijah the prophet to clear the way for the Big Day of God—the decisive Judgment Day! He will convince parents to look after their children and children to look up to their parents. If they refuse, I'll come and put the land under a curse."

---

a 17 Or *Almighty, "my treasured possession, in the day when I act*

THE NEW TESTAMENT

MATTHEW

THE GENEALOGY OF JESUS

1 A record of the genealogy of Jesus Christ the son of David, the son of Abraham:

2 Abraham was the father of Isaac,
  Isaac the father of Jacob,
  Jacob the father of Judah and his brothers,
3 Judah the father of Perez and Zerah,
    whose mother was Tamar,
  Perez the father of Hezron,
  Hezron the father of Ram,
4 Ram the father of Amminadab,
  Amminadab the father of Nahshon,
  Nahshon the father of Salmon,
5 Salmon the father of Boaz, whose mother was Rahab,
  Boaz the father of Obed, whose mother was Ruth,
  Obed the father of Jesse,
6 and Jesse the father of King David.

David was the father of Solomon, whose mother had been Uriah's wife,
7 Solomon the father of Rehoboam,
  Rehoboam the father of Abijah,
  Abijah the father of Asa,
8 Asa the father of Jehoshaphat,
  Jehoshaphat the father of Jehoram,
  Jehoram the father of Uzziah,
9 Uzziah the father of Jotham,
  Jotham the father of Ahaz,
  Ahaz the father of Hezekiah,
10 Hezekiah the father of Manasseh,
  Manasseh the father of Amon,
  Amon the father of Josiah,
11 and Josiah the father of Jeconiah[a] and his brothers at the time of the exile to Babylon.

12 After the exile to Babylon:
  Jeconiah was the father of Shealtiel,
  Shealtiel the father of Zerubbabel,
13 Zerubbabel the father of Abiud,
  Abiud the father of Eliakim,
  Eliakim the father of Azor,

[a] 11 That is, Jehoiachin; also in verse 12

MATTHEW

1.1 1 The family tree of Jesus Christ, David's son, Abraham's son:

1.2-6 Abraham had Isaac,
  Isaac had Jacob,
  Jacob had Judah and his brothers,
  Judah had Perez and Zerah (the mother was Tamar),
  Perez had Hezron,
  Hezron had Aram,
  Aram had Amminadab,
  Amminadab had Nahshon,
  Nahshon had Salmon,
  Salmon had Boaz (his mother was Rahab),
  Boaz had Obed (Ruth was the mother),
  Obed had Jesse,
  Jesse had David,
    and David became king.

1.6-11 David had Solomon (Uriah's wife was the mother),
  Solomon had Rehoboam,
  Rehoboam had Abijah,
  Abijah had Asa,
  Asa had Jehoshaphat,
  Jehoshaphat had Joram,
  Joram had Uzziah,
  Uzziah had Jotham,
  Jotham had Ahaz,
  Ahaz had Hezekiah,
  Hezekiah had Manasseh,
  Manasseh had Amon,
  Amon had Josiah,
  Josiah had Jehoiachin and his brothers,
    and then the people were taken into the Babylonian exile.

1.12-16 When the Babylonian exile ended,
  Jehoiachin had Shealtiel,
  Shealtiel had Zerubbabel,
  Zerubbabel had Abiud,
  Abiud had Eliakim,
  Eliakim had Azor,

NEW INTERNATIONAL VERSION

14 Azor the father of Zadok,
Zadok the father of Akim,
Akim the father of Eliud,
15 Eliud the father of Eleazar,
Eleazar the father of Matthan,
Matthan the father of Jacob,
16 and Jacob the father of Joseph, the hus-
band of Mary, of whom was born
Jesus, who is called Christ.

17 Thus there were fourteen generations in all
from Abraham to David, fourteen from David to
the exile to Babylon, and fourteen from the exile
to the Christ. *a*

THE BIRTH OF JESUS CHRIST

18 This is how the birth of Jesus Christ came
about: His mother Mary was pledged to be married to Joseph, but before they came together,
she was found to be with child through the Holy
Spirit. 19 Because Joseph her husband was a righteous man and did not want to expose her to
public disgrace, he had in mind to divorce her
quietly.

20 But after he had considered this, an angel of
the Lord appeared to him in a dream and said,
"Joseph son of David, do not be afraid to take
Mary home as your wife, because what is conceived in her is from the Holy Spirit. 21 She will
give birth to a son, and you are to give him the
name Jesus, *b* because he will save his people
from their sins."

22 All this took place to fulfill what the Lord
had said through the prophet: 23 "The virgin will
be with child and will give birth to a son, and
they will call him Immanuel" *c*—which means,
"God with us."

24 When Joseph woke up, he did what the angel of the Lord had commanded him and took
Mary home as his wife. 25 But he had no union
with her until she gave birth to a son. And he
gave him the name Jesus.

THE VISIT OF THE MAGI

2 After Jesus was born in Bethlehem in Judea,
during the time of King Herod, Magi *d* from
the east came to Jerusalem 2 and asked, "Where
is the one who has been born king of the Jews?
We saw his star in the east *e* and have come to
worship him."

a 17 Or *Messiah.* "The Christ" (Greek) and "the Messiah"
(Hebrew) both mean "the Anointed One."   *b 21 Jesus* is
the Greek form of *Joshua,* which means *the LORD saves.*
c 23 Isaiah 7:14   *d 1* Traditionally *Wise Men*   *e 2* Or *star
when it rose*

THE MESSAGE

Azor had Zadok,
Zadok had Achim,
Achim had Eliud,
Eliud had Eleazar,
Eleazar had Matthan,
Matthan had Jacob,
Jacob had Joseph, Mary's husband,
the Mary who gave birth to Jesus,
the Jesus who was called Christ.

1.17   There were fourteen generations from Abraham
to David,
another fourteen from David to the
Babylonian exile,
and yet another fourteen from the
Babylonian exile to Christ.

THE BIRTH OF JESUS

1.18-19 The birth of Jesus took place like this. His mother, Mary, was engaged to be married to Joseph.
Before they came to the marriage bed, Joseph
discovered she was pregnant. (It was by the
Holy Spirit, but he didn't know that.) Joseph,
chagrined but noble, determined to take care of
things quietly so Mary would not be disgraced.

1.20-23   While he was trying to figure a way out, he
had a dream. God's angel spoke in the dream:
"Joseph, son of David, don't hesitate to get married. Mary's pregnancy is Spirit-conceived. God's
Holy Spirit has made her pregnant. She will
bring a son to birth, and when she does, you,
Joseph, will name him Jesus—'God saves'—because he will save his people from their sins."
This would bring the prophet's embryonic sermon to full term:

Watch for this—a virgin will get pregnant
and bear a son;
They will name him Emmanuel (Hebrew
for "God is with us").

1.24-25   Then Joseph woke up. He did exactly what
God's angel commanded in the dream: He married Mary. But he did not consummate the marriage until she had the baby. He named the
baby Jesus.

SCHOLARS FROM THE EAST

2.1-2 2 After Jesus was born in Bethlehem village,
Judah territory—this was during Herod's
kingship—a band of scholars arrived in Jerusalem from the East. They asked around, "Where
can we find and pay homage to the newborn
King of the Jews? We observed a star in the
eastern sky that signaled his birth. We're on
pilgrimage to worship him."

NEW INTERNATIONAL VERSION

³When King Herod heard this he was disturbed, and all Jerusalem with him. ⁴When he had called together all the people's chief priests and teachers of the law, he asked them where the Christ*ᵈ* was to be born. ⁵"In Bethlehem in Judea," they replied, "for this is what the prophet has written:

⁶" 'But you, Bethlehem, in the land of Judah,
　are by no means least among the rulers of
　　Judah;
for out of you will come a ruler
　who will be the shepherd of my people
　　Israel.'*ᵇ*"

⁷Then Herod called the Magi secretly and found out from them the exact time the star had appeared. ⁸He sent them to Bethlehem and said, "Go and make a careful search for the child. As soon as you find him, report to me, so that I too may go and worship him."

⁹After they had heard the king, they went on their way, and the star they had seen in the east*ᶜ* went ahead of them until it stopped over the place where the child was. ¹⁰When they saw the star, they were overjoyed. ¹¹On coming to the house, they saw the child with his mother Mary, and they bowed down and worshiped him. Then they opened their treasures and presented him with gifts of gold and of incense and of myrrh. ¹²And having been warned in a dream not to go back to Herod, they returned to their country by another route.

The Escape to Egypt

¹³When they had gone, an angel of the Lord appeared to Joseph in a dream. "Get up," he said, "take the child and his mother and escape to Egypt. Stay there until I tell you, for Herod is going to search for the child to kill him."

¹⁴So he got up, took the child and his mother during the night and left for Egypt, ¹⁵where he stayed until the death of Herod. And so was fulfilled what the Lord had said through the prophet: "Out of Egypt I called my son."*ᵈ*

¹⁶When Herod realized that he had been outwitted by the Magi, he was furious, and he gave orders to kill all the boys in Bethlehem and its vicinity who were two years old and under, in

THE MESSAGE

2.3-4　When word of their inquiry got to Herod, he was terrified—and not Herod alone, but most of Jerusalem as well. Herod lost no time. He gathered all the high priests and religion scholars in the city together and asked, "Where is the Messiah supposed to be born?"

2.5-6　They told him, "Bethlehem, Judah territory. The prophet Micah wrote it plainly:

It's you, Bethlehem, in Judah's land,
　no longer bringing up the rear.
From you will come the leader
　who will shepherd-rule my people, my
　　Israel."

2.7-8　Herod then arranged a secret meeting with the scholars from the East. Pretending to be as devout as they were, he got them to tell him exactly when the birth-announcement star appeared. Then he told them the prophecy about Bethlehem, and said, "Go find this child. Leave no stone unturned. As soon as you find him, send word and I'll join you at once in your worship."

2.9-10　Instructed by the king, they set off. Then the star appeared again, the same star they had seen in the eastern skies. It led them on until it hovered over the place of the child. They could hardly contain themselves: They were in the right place! They had arrived at the right time!

2.11　They entered the house and saw the child in the arms of Mary, his mother. Overcome, they kneeled and worshiped him. Then they opened their luggage and presented gifts: gold, frankincense, myrrh.

2.12　In a dream, they were warned not to report back to Herod. So they worked out another route, left the territory without being seen, and returned to their own country.

✝

2.13　After the scholars were gone, God's angel showed up again in Joseph's dream and commanded, "Get up. Take the child and his mother and flee to Egypt. Stay until further notice. Herod is on the hunt for this child, and wants to kill him."

2.14-15　Joseph obeyed. He got up, took the child and his mother under cover of darkness. They were out of town and well on their way by daylight. They lived in Egypt until Herod's death. This Egyptian exile fulfilled what Hosea had preached: "I called my son out of Egypt."

2.16-18　Herod, when he realized that the scholars had tricked him, flew into a rage. He commanded the murder of every little boy two years old and under who lived in Bethlehem and its surrounding hills. (He determined that age from

---

ᵃ 4 Or *Messiah*　　*ᵇ 6* Micah 5:2　　*ᶜ 9* Or *seen when it rose*
ᵈ 15 Hosea 11:1

NEW INTERNATIONAL VERSION

accordance with the time he had learned from the Magi. [17]Then what was said through the prophet Jeremiah was fulfilled:

[18]"A voice is heard in Ramah,
  weeping and great mourning,
Rachel weeping for her children
  and refusing to be comforted,
because they are no more."[a]

THE RETURN TO NAZARETH

[19]After Herod died, an angel of the Lord appeared in a dream to Joseph in Egypt [20]and said, "Get up, take the child and his mother and go to the land of Israel, for those who were trying to take the child's life are dead."

[21]So he got up, took the child and his mother and went to the land of Israel. [22]But when he heard that Archelaus was reigning in Judea in place of his father Herod, he was afraid to go there. Having been warned in a dream, he withdrew to the district of Galilee, [23]and he went and lived in a town called Nazareth. So was fulfilled what was said through the prophets: "He will be called a Nazarene."

JOHN THE BAPTIST PREPARES THE WAY

3 In those days John the Baptist came, preaching in the Desert of Judea [2]and saying, "Repent, for the kingdom of heaven is near." [3]This is he who was spoken of through the prophet Isaiah:

"A voice of one calling in the desert,
'Prepare the way for the Lord,
  make straight paths for him.' "[b]

[4]John's clothes were made of camel's hair, and he had a leather belt around his waist. His food was locusts and wild honey. [5]People went out to him from Jerusalem and all Judea and the whole region of the Jordan. [6]Confessing their sins, they were baptized by him in the Jordan River.

[7]But when he saw many of the Pharisees and Sadducees coming to where he was baptizing, he said to them: "You brood of vipers! Who warned you to flee from the coming wrath? [8]Produce fruit in keeping with repentance. [9]And do not think you can say to yourselves, 'We have Abraham as our father.' I tell you that out of these stones God can raise up children for Abra-

THE MESSAGE

information he'd gotten from the scholars.) That's when Jeremiah's sermon was fulfilled:

A sound was heard in Ramah,
  weeping and much lament.
Rachel weeping for her children,
  Rachel refusing all solace,
Her children gone,
  dead and buried.

2.19-20 Later, when Herod died, God's angel appeared in a dream to Joseph in Egypt: "Up, take the child and his mother and return to Israel. All those out to murder the child are dead."

2.21-23 Joseph obeyed. He got up, took the child and his mother, and reentered Israel. When he heard, though, that Archelaus had succeeded his father, Herod, as king in Judea, he was afraid to go there. But then Joseph was directed in a dream to go to the hills of Galilee. On arrival, he settled in the village of Nazareth. This move was a fulfillment of the prophetic words, "He shall be called a Nazarene."

THUNDER IN THE DESERT!

3.1-2 3 While Jesus was living in the Galilean hills, John, called "the Baptizer," was preaching in the desert country of Judea. His message was simple and austere, like his desert surroundings: "Change your life. God's kingdom is here."

3.3 John and his message were authorized by Isaiah's prophecy:

Thunder in the desert!
Prepare for God's arrival!
Make the road smooth and straight!

3.4-6 John dressed in a camel-hair habit tied at the waist by a leather strap. He lived on a diet of locusts and wild field honey. People poured out of Jerusalem, Judea, and the Jordanian countryside to hear and see him in action. There at the Jordan River those who came to confess their sins were baptized into a changed life.

3.7-10 When John realized that a lot of Pharisees and Sadducees were showing up for a baptismal experience because it was becoming the popular thing to do, he exploded: "Brood of snakes! What do you think you're doing slithering down here to the river? Do you think a little water on your snakeskins is going to make any difference? It's your life that must change, not your skin! And don't think you can pull rank by claiming Abraham as father. Being a descendant of Abraham is neither here nor there. Descendants of Abraham are a dime a

---

NEW INTERNATIONAL VERSION

ham. [10]The ax is already at the root of the trees, and every tree that does not produce good fruit will be cut down and thrown into the fire.

[11]"I baptize you with[a] water for repentance. But after me will come one who is more powerful than I, whose sandals I am not fit to carry. He will baptize you with the Holy Spirit and with fire. [12]His winnowing fork is in his hand, and he will clear his threshing floor, gathering his wheat into the barn and burning up the chaff with unquenchable fire."

THE BAPTISM OF JESUS

[13]Then Jesus came from Galilee to the Jordan to be baptized by John. [14]But John tried to deter him, saying, "I need to be baptized by you, and do you come to me?"

[15]Jesus replied, "Let it be so now; it is proper for us to do this to fulfill all righteousness." Then John consented.

[16]As soon as Jesus was baptized, he went up out of the water. At that moment heaven was opened, and he saw the Spirit of God descending like a dove and lighting on him. [17]And a voice from heaven said, "This is my Son, whom I love; with him I am well pleased."

THE TEMPTATION OF JESUS

4 Then Jesus was led by the Spirit into the desert to be tempted by the devil. [2]After fasting forty days and forty nights, he was hungry. [3]The tempter came to him and said, "If you are the Son of God, tell these stones to become bread."

[4]Jesus answered, "It is written: 'Man does not live on bread alone, but on every word that comes from the mouth of God.'[b]"

[5]Then the devil took him to the holy city and had him stand on the highest point of the temple. [6]"If you are the Son of God," he said, "throw yourself down. For it is written:

" 'He will command his angels concerning
        you,
    and they will lift you up in their hands,
so that you will not strike your foot against a
        stone.'[c]"

[7]Jesus answered him, "It is also written: 'Do not put the Lord your God to the test.'[d]"

[8]Again, the devil took him to a very high mountain and showed him all the kingdoms of the world and their splendor. [9]"All this I will

a 11 Or *in*   *b* 4 Deut. 8:3   *c* 6 Psalm 91:11,12
d 7 Deut. 6:16

THE MESSAGE

dozen. What counts is your life. Is it green and blossoming? Because if it's deadwood, it goes on the fire.

3.11-12   "I'm baptizing you here in the river, turning your old life in for a kingdom life. The real action comes next: The main character in this drama—compared to him I'm a mere stagehand—will ignite the kingdom life within you, a fire within you, the Holy Spirit within you, changing you from the inside out. He's going to clean house—make a clean sweep of your lives. He'll place everything true in its proper place before God; everything false he'll put out with the trash to be burned."

✝

3.13-14 Jesus then appeared, arriving at the Jordan River from Galilee. He wanted John to baptize him. John objected, "I'm the one who needs to be baptized, not *you!*"

3.15   But Jesus insisted. "Do it. God's work, putting things right all these centuries, is coming together right now in this baptism." So John did it.

3.16-17   The moment Jesus came up out of the baptismal waters, the skies opened up and he saw God's Spirit—it looked like a dove—descending and landing on him. And along with the Spirit, a voice: "This is my Son, chosen and marked by my love, delight of my life."

THE TEST

4.1-3 4 Next Jesus was taken into the wild by the Spirit for the Test. The Devil was ready to give it. Jesus prepared for the Test by fasting forty days and forty nights. That left him, of course, in a state of extreme hunger, which the Devil took advantage of in the first test: "Since you are God's Son, speak the word that will turn these stones into loaves of bread."

4.4   Jesus answered by quoting Deuteronomy: "It takes more than bread to stay alive. It takes a steady stream of words from God's mouth."

4.5-6   For the second test the Devil took him to the Holy City. He sat him on top of the Temple and said, "Since you are God's Son, jump." The Devil goaded him by quoting Psalm 91: "He has placed you in the care of angels. They will catch you so that you won't so much as stub your toe on a stone."

4.7   Jesus countered with another citation from Deuteronomy: "Don't you dare test the Lord your God."

4.8-9   For the third test, the Devil took him on the peak of a huge mountain. He gestured expansively, pointing out all the earth's kingdoms, how glorious they all were. Then he said,

NEW INTERNATIONAL VERSION

give you," he said, "if you will bow down and worship me."

¹⁰Jesus said to him, "Away from me, Satan! For it is written: 'Worship the Lord your God, and serve him only.'ᵃ"

¹¹Then the devil left him, and angels came and attended him.

JESUS BEGINS TO PREACH

¹²When Jesus heard that John had been put in prison, he returned to Galilee. ¹³Leaving Nazareth, he went and lived in Capernaum, which was by the lake in the area of Zebulun and Naphtali— ¹⁴to fulfill what was said through the prophet Isaiah:

¹⁵ "Land of Zebulun and land of Naphtali,
    the way to the sea, along the Jordan,
    Galilee of the Gentiles—
¹⁶ the people living in darkness
    have seen a great light;
 on those living in the land of the shadow of
        death
    a light has dawned."ᵇ

¹⁷From that time on Jesus began to preach, "Repent, for the kingdom of heaven is near."

THE CALLING OF THE FIRST DISCIPLES

¹⁸As Jesus was walking beside the Sea of Galilee, he saw two brothers, Simon called Peter and his brother Andrew. They were casting a net into the lake, for they were fishermen. ¹⁹"Come, follow me," Jesus said, "and I will make you fishers of men." ²⁰At once they left their nets and followed him.

²¹Going on from there, he saw two other brothers, James son of Zebedee and his brother John. They were in a boat with their father Zebedee, preparing their nets. Jesus called them, ²²and immediately they left the boat and their father and followed him.

JESUS HEALS THE SICK

²³Jesus went throughout Galilee, teaching in their synagogues, preaching the good news of the kingdom, and healing every disease and sickness among the people. ²⁴News about him spread all over Syria, and people brought to him

THE MESSAGE

"They're yours—lock, stock, and barrel. Just go down on your knees and worship me, and they're yours."

4.10   Jesus' refusal was curt: "Beat it, Satan!" He backed his rebuke with a third quotation from Deuteronomy: "Worship the Lord your God, and only him. Serve him with absolute single-heartedness."

4.11   The Test was over. The Devil left. And in his place, angels! Angels came and took care of Jesus' needs.

TEACHING AND HEALING

4.12-17 When Jesus got word that John had been arrested, he returned to Galilee. He moved from his hometown, Nazareth, to the lakeside village Capernaum, nestled at the base of the Zebulun and Naphtali hills. This move completed Isaiah's sermon:

    Land of Zebulun, land of Naphtali,
        road to the sea, over Jordan,
        Galilee, crossroads for the nations.
    People sitting out their lives in the dark
        saw a huge light;
    Sitting in that dark, dark country of death,
        they watched the sun come up.

This Isaiah-prophesied sermon came to life in Galilee the moment Jesus started preaching. He picked up where John left off: "Change your life. God's kingdom is here."

4.18-20 Walking along the beach of Lake Galilee, Jesus saw two brothers: Simon (later called Peter) and Andrew. They were fishing, throwing their nets into the lake. It was their regular work. Jesus said to them, "Come with me. I'll make a new kind of fisherman out of you. I'll show you how to catch men and women instead of perch and bass." They didn't ask questions, but simply dropped their nets and followed.

4.21-22 A short distance down the beach they came upon another pair of brothers, James and John, Zebedee's sons. These two were sitting in a boat with their father, Zebedee, mending their fishnets. Jesus made the same offer to them, and they were just as quick to follow, abandoning boat and father.

4.23-25 From there he went all over Galilee. He used synagogues for meeting places and taught people the truth of God. God's kingdom was his theme—that beginning right now they were under God's government, a good government! He also healed people of their diseases and of the bad effects of their bad lives. Word got around the entire Roman province of Syria. People brought anybody with an ailment, whether

ᵃ 10 Deut. 6:13   ᵇ 16 Isaiah 9:1,2

NEW INTERNATIONAL VERSION

all who were ill with various diseases, those suffering severe pain, the demon-possessed, those having seizures, and the paralyzed, and he healed them. ²⁵Large crowds from Galilee, the Decapolis,ᵃ Jerusalem, Judea and the region across the Jordan followed him.

THE BEATITUDES

5 Now when he saw the crowds, he went up on a mountainside and sat down. His disciples came to him, ²and he began to teach them, saying:

³ "Blessed are the poor in spirit,
　for theirs is the kingdom of heaven.
⁴ Blessed are those who mourn,
　for they will be comforted.
⁵ Blessed are the meek,
　for they will inherit the earth.
⁶ Blessed are those who hunger and thirst for
　　righteousness,
　for they will be filled.
⁷ Blessed are the merciful,
　for they will be shown mercy.
⁸ Blessed are the pure in heart,
　for they will see God.
⁹ Blessed are the peacemakers,
　for they will be called sons of God.
¹⁰ Blessed are those who are persecuted
　　because of righteousness,
　for theirs is the kingdom of heaven.

¹¹ "Blessed are you when people insult you, persecute you and falsely say all kinds of evil against you because of me. ¹²Rejoice and be glad, because great is your reward in heaven, for in the same way they persecuted the prophets who were before you.

SALT AND LIGHT

¹³ "You are the salt of the earth. But if the salt loses its saltiness, how can it be made salty again? It is no longer good for anything, except to be thrown out and trampled by men.

THE MESSAGE

mental, emotional, or physical. Jesus healed them, one and all. More and more people came, the momentum gathering. Besides those from Galilee, crowds came from the "Ten Towns" across the lake, others up from Jerusalem and Judea, still others from across the Jordan.

YOU'RE BLESSED

⁵·¹⁻² **5** When Jesus saw his ministry drawing huge crowds, he climbed a hillside. Those who were apprenticed to him, the committed, climbed with him. Arriving at a quiet place, he sat down and taught his climbing companions. This is what he said:

⁵·³ 　"You're blessed when you're at the end of your rope. With less of you there is more of God and his rule.

⁵·⁴ 　"You're blessed when you feel you've lost what is most dear to you. Only then can you be embraced by the One most dear to you.

⁵·⁵ 　"You're blessed when you're content with just who you are—no more, no less. That's the moment you find yourselves proud owners of everything that can't be bought.

⁵·⁶ 　"You're blessed when you've worked up a good appetite for God. He's food and drink in the best meal you'll ever eat.

⁵·⁷ 　"You're blessed when you care. At the moment of being 'care-full,' you find yourselves cared for.

⁵·⁸ 　"You're blessed when you get your inside world—your mind and heart—put right. Then you can see God in the outside world.

⁵·⁹ 　"You're blessed when you can show people how to cooperate instead of compete or fight. That's when you discover who you really are, and your place in God's family.

⁵·¹⁰ 　"You're blessed when your commitment to God provokes persecution. The persecution drives you even deeper into God's kingdom.

⁵·¹¹⁻¹² 　"Not only that—count yourselves blessed every time people put you down or throw you out or speak lies about you to discredit me. What it means is that the truth is too close for comfort and they are uncomfortable. You can be glad when that happens—give a cheer, even!—for though they don't like it, *I* do! And all heaven applauds. And know that you are in good company. My prophets and witnesses have always gotten into this kind of trouble.

SALT AND LIGHT

⁵·¹³ 　"Let me tell you why you are here. You're here to be salt-seasoning that brings out the God-flavors of this earth. If you lose your saltiness, how will people taste godliness? You've lost your usefulness and will end up in the garbage.

ᵃ 25 That is, the Ten Cities

NEW INTERNATIONAL VERSION

¹⁴"You are the light of the world. A city on a hill cannot be hidden. ¹⁵Neither do people light a lamp and put it under a bowl. Instead they put it on its stand, and it gives light to everyone in the house. ¹⁶In the same way, let your light shine before men, that they may see your good deeds and praise your Father in heaven.

THE FULFILLMENT OF THE LAW

¹⁷"Do not think that I have come to abolish the Law or the Prophets; I have not come to abolish them but to fulfill them. ¹⁸I tell you the truth, until heaven and earth disappear, not the smallest letter, not the least stroke of a pen, will by any means disappear from the Law until everything is accomplished. ¹⁹Anyone who breaks one of the least of these commandments and teaches others to do the same will be called least in the kingdom of heaven, but whoever practices and teaches these commands will be called great in the kingdom of heaven. ²⁰For I tell you that unless your righteousness surpasses that of the Pharisees and the teachers of the law, you will certainly not enter the kingdom of heaven.

MURDER

²¹"You have heard that it was said to the people long ago, 'Do not murder,ᵃ and anyone who murders will be subject to judgment.' ²²But I tell you that anyone who is angry with his brotherᵇ will be subject to judgment. Again, anyone who says to his brother, 'Raca,ᶜ' is answerable to the Sanhedrin. But anyone who says, 'You fool!' will be in danger of the fire of hell.

²³"Therefore, if you are offering your gift at the altar and there remember that your brother has something against you, ²⁴leave your gift there in front of the altar. First go and be reconciled to your brother; then come and offer your gift.

²⁵"Settle matters quickly with your adversary who is taking you to court. Do it while you are still with him on the way, or he may hand you over to the judge, and the judge may hand you over to the officer, and you may be thrown into prison. ²⁶I tell you the truth, you will not get out until you have paid the last penny.ᵈ

THE MESSAGE

5.14-16 "Here's another way to put it: You're here to be light, bringing out the God-colors in the world. God is not a secret to be kept. We're going public with this, as public as a city on a hill. If I make you light-bearers, you don't think I'm going to hide you under a bucket, do you? I'm putting you on a light stand. Now that I've put you there on a hilltop, on a light stand— shine! Keep open house; be generous with your lives. By opening up to others, you'll prompt people to open up with God, this generous Father in heaven.

COMPLETING GOD'S LAW

5.17-18 "Don't suppose for a minute that I have come to demolish the Scriptures—either God's Law or the Prophets. I'm not here to demolish but to complete. I am going to put it all together, pull it all together in a vast panorama. God's Law is more real and lasting than the stars in the sky and the ground at your feet. Long after stars burn out and earth wears out, God's Law will be alive and working.

5.19-20 "Trivialize even the smallest item in God's Law and you will only have trivialized yourself. But take it seriously, show the way for others, and you will find honor in the kingdom. Unless you do far better than the Pharisees in the matters of right living, you won't know the first thing about entering the kingdom.

MURDER

5.21-22 "You're familiar with the command to the ancients, 'Do not murder.' I'm telling you that anyone who is so much as angry with a brother or sister is guilty of murder. Carelessly call a brother 'idiot!' and you just might find yourself hauled into court. Thoughtlessly yell 'stupid!' at a sister and you are on the brink of hellfire. The simple moral fact is that words kill.

5.23-24 "This is how I want you to conduct yourself in these matters. If you enter your place of worship and, about to make an offering, you suddenly remember a grudge a friend has against you, abandon your offering, leave immediately, go to this friend and make things right. Then and only then, come back and work things out with God.

5.25-26 "Or say you're out on the street and an old enemy accosts you. Don't lose a minute. Make the first move; make things right with him. After all, if you leave the first move to him, knowing his track record, you're likely to end up in court, maybe even jail. If that happens, you won't get out without a stiff fine.

ᵃ 21 Exodus 20:13   ᵇ 22 Some manuscripts brother without cause   ᶜ 22 An Aramaic term of contempt
ᵈ 26 Greek kodrantes

NEW INTERNATIONAL VERSION

ADULTERY

27 "You have heard that it was said, 'Do not commit adultery.'[a] 28 But I tell you that anyone who looks at a woman lustfully has already committed adultery with her in his heart. 29 If your right eye causes you to sin, gouge it out and throw it away. It is better for you to lose one part of your body than for your whole body to be thrown into hell. 30 And if your right hand causes you to sin, cut it off and throw it away. It is better for you to lose one part of your body than for your whole body to go into hell.

DIVORCE

31 "It has been said, 'Anyone who divorces his wife must give her a certificate of divorce.'[b] 32 But I tell you that anyone who divorces his wife, except for marital unfaithfulness, causes her to become an adulteress, and anyone who marries the divorced woman commits adultery.

OATHS

33 "Again, you have heard that it was said to the people long ago, 'Do not break your oath, but keep the oaths you have made to the Lord.' 34 But I tell you, Do not swear at all: either by heaven, for it is God's throne; 35 or by the earth, for it is his footstool; or by Jerusalem, for it is the city of the Great King. 36 And do not swear by your head, for you cannot make even one hair white or black. 37 Simply let your 'Yes' be 'Yes,' and your 'No,' 'No'; anything beyond this comes from the evil one.

AN EYE FOR AN EYE

38 "You have heard that it was said, 'Eye for eye, and tooth for tooth.'[c] 39 But I tell you, Do not resist an evil person. If someone strikes you on the right cheek, turn to him the other also. 40 And if someone wants to sue you and take your tunic, let him have your cloak as well. 41 If someone forces you to go one mile, go with him two miles. 42 Give to the one who asks you, and do not turn away from the one who wants to borrow from you.

---

a 27 Exodus 20:14   *b 31* Deut. 24:1
c 38 Exodus 21:24; Lev. 24:20; Deut. 19:21

THE MESSAGE

ADULTERY AND DIVORCE

5.27-28 "You know the next commandment pretty well, too: 'Don't go to bed with another's spouse.' But don't think you've preserved your virtue simply by staying out of bed. Your *heart* can be corrupted by lust even quicker than your *body*. Those leering looks you think nobody notices—they also corrupt.

5.29-30   "Let's not pretend this is easier than it really is. If you want to live a morally pure life, here's what you have to do: You have to blind your right eye the moment you catch it in a lustful leer. You have to choose to live one-eyed or else be dumped on a moral trash pile. And you have to chop off your right hand the moment you notice it raised threateningly. Better a bloody stump than your entire being discarded for good in the dump.

5.31-32   "Remember the Scripture that says, 'Whoever divorces his wife, let him do it legally, giving her divorce papers and her legal rights'? Too many of you are using that as a cover for selfishness and whim, pretending to be righteous just because you are 'legal.' Please, no more pretending. If you divorce your wife, you're responsible for making her an adulteress (unless she has already made herself that by sexual promiscuity). And if you marry such a divorced adulteress, you're automatically an adulterer yourself. You can't use legal cover to mask a moral failure.

EMPTY PROMISES

5.33-37 "And don't say anything you don't mean. This counsel is embedded deep in our traditions. You only make things worse when you lay down a smoke screen of pious talk, saying, 'I'll pray for you,' and never doing it, or saying, 'God be with you,' and not meaning it. You don't make your words true by embellishing them with religious lace. In making your speech sound more religious, it becomes less true. Just say 'yes' and 'no.' When you manipulate words to get your own way, you go wrong.

LOVE YOUR ENEMIES

5.38-42 "Here's another old saying that deserves a second look: 'Eye for eye, tooth for tooth.' Is that going to get us anywhere? Here's what I propose: 'Don't hit back at all.' If someone strikes you, stand there and take it. If someone drags you into court and sues for the shirt off your back, giftwrap your best coat and make a present of it. And if someone takes unfair advantage of you, use the occasion to practice the servant life. No more tit-for-tat stuff. Live generously.

NEW INTERNATIONAL VERSION

LOVE FOR ENEMIES

43"You have heard that it was said, 'Love your neighbor[a] and hate your enemy.' 44But I tell you: Love your enemies[b] and pray for those who persecute you, 45that you may be sons of your Father in heaven. He causes his sun to rise on the evil and the good, and sends rain on the righteous and the unrighteous. 46If you love those who love you, what reward will you get? Are not even the tax collectors doing that? 47And if you greet only your brothers, what are you doing more than others? Do not even pagans do that? 48Be perfect, therefore, as your heavenly Father is perfect.

GIVING TO THE NEEDY

6 "Be careful not to do your 'acts of righteousness' before men, to be seen by them. If you do, you will have no reward from your Father in heaven.

2"So when you give to the needy, do not announce it with trumpets, as the hypocrites do in the synagogues and on the streets, to be honored by men. I tell you the truth, they have received their reward in full. 3But when you give to the needy, do not let your left hand know what your right hand is doing, 4so that your giving may be in secret. Then your Father, who sees what is done in secret, will reward you.

PRAYER

5"And when you pray, do not be like the hypocrites, for they love to pray standing in the synagogues and on the street corners to be seen by men. I tell you the truth, they have received their reward in full. 6But when you pray, go into your room, close the door and pray to your Father, who is unseen. Then your Father, who sees what is done in secret, will reward you. 7And when you pray, do not keep on babbling like pagans,

THE MESSAGE

5.43-47   "You're familiar with the old written law, 'Love your friend,' and its unwritten companion, 'Hate your enemy.' I'm challenging that. I'm telling you to love your enemies. Let them bring out the best in you, not the worst. When someone gives you a hard time, respond with the energies of prayer, for then you are working out of your true selves, your God-created selves. This is what God does. He gives his best—the sun to warm and the rain to nourish—to everyone, regardless: the good and bad, the nice and nasty. If all you do is love the lovable, do you expect a bonus? Anybody can do that. If you simply say hello to those who greet you, do you expect a medal? Any run-of-the-mill sinner does that.

5.48   "In a word, what I'm saying is, *Grow up*. You're kingdom subjects. Now live like it. Live out your God-created identity. Live generously and graciously toward others, the way God lives toward you.

THE WORLD IS NOT A STAGE

6.1   6 "Be especially careful when you are trying to be good so that you don't make a performance out of it. It might be good theater, but the God who made you won't be applauding.

6.2-4   "When you do something for someone else, don't call attention to yourself. You've seen them in action, I'm sure—'playactors' I call them—treating prayer meeting and street corner alike as a stage, acting compassionate as long as someone is watching, playing to the crowds. They get applause, true, but that's all they get. When you help someone out, don't think about how it looks. Just do it—quietly and unobtrusively. That is the way your God, who conceived you in love, working behind the scenes, helps you out.

PRAY WITH SIMPLICITY

6.5   "And when you come before God, don't turn that into a theatrical production either. All these people making a regular show out of their prayers, hoping for stardom! Do you think God sits in a box seat?

6.6   "Here's what I want you to do: Find a quiet, secluded place so you won't be tempted to role-play before God. Just be there as simply and honestly as you can manage. The focus will shift from you to God, and you will begin to sense his grace.

6.7-13   "The world is full of so-called prayer warriors who are prayer-ignorant. They're full of formulas and programs and advice, peddling

NEW INTERNATIONAL VERSION

for they think they will be heard because of their many words. ⁸Do not be like them, for your Father knows what you need before you ask him.

⁹"This, then, is how you should pray:

" 'Our Father in heaven,
hallowed be your name,
¹⁰your kingdom come,
your will be done
on earth as it is in heaven.
¹¹Give us today our daily bread.
¹²Forgive us our debts,
as we also have forgiven our debtors.
¹³And lead us not into temptation,
but deliver us from the evil one.ᵃ'

¹⁴For if you forgive men when they sin against you, your heavenly Father will also forgive you. ¹⁵But if you do not forgive men their sins, your Father will not forgive your sins.

FASTING

¹⁶"When you fast, do not look somber as the hypocrites do, for they disfigure their faces to show men they are fasting. I tell you the truth, they have received their reward in full. ¹⁷But when you fast, put oil on your head and wash your face, ¹⁸so that it will not be obvious to men that you are fasting, but only to your Father, who is unseen; and your Father, who sees what is done in secret, will reward you.

TREASURES IN HEAVEN

¹⁹"Do not store up for yourselves treasures on earth, where moth and rust destroy, and where thieves break in and steal. ²⁰But store up for yourselves treasures in heaven, where moth and rust do not destroy, and where thieves do not break in and steal. ²¹For where your treasure is, there your heart will be also.

²²"The eye is the lamp of the body. If your eyes are good, your whole body will be full of light. ²³But if your eyes are bad, your whole body will be full of darkness. If then the light within you is darkness, how great is that darkness!

²⁴"No one can serve two masters. Either he will hate the one and love the other, or he will be devoted to the one and despise the other. You cannot serve both God and Money.

DO NOT WORRY

²⁵"Therefore I tell you, do not worry about your life, what you will eat or drink; or about

---

THE MESSAGE

techniques for getting what you want from God. Don't fall for that nonsense. This is your Father you are dealing with, and he knows better than you what you need. With a God like this loving you, you can pray very simply. Like this:

Our Father in heaven,
Reveal who you are.
Set the world right;
Do what's best—
as above, so below.
Keep us alive with three square meals.
Keep us forgiven with you and forgiving others.
Keep us safe from ourselves and the Devil.
You're in charge!
You can do anything you want!
You're ablaze in beauty!
Yes. Yes. Yes.

6.14-15 "In prayer there is a connection between what God does and what you do. You can't get forgiveness from God, for instance, without also forgiving others. If you refuse to do your part, you cut yourself off from God's part.

6.16-18 "When you practice some appetite-denying discipline to better concentrate on God, don't make a production out of it. It might turn you into a small-time celebrity but it won't make you a saint. If you 'go into training' inwardly, act normal outwardly. Shampoo and comb your hair, brush your teeth, wash your face. God doesn't require attention-getting devices. He won't overlook what you are doing; he'll reward you well.

A LIFE OF GOD-WORSHIP

6.19-21 "Don't hoard treasure down here where it gets eaten by moths and corroded by rust or— worse!—stolen by burglars. Stockpile treasure in heaven, where it's safe from moth and rust and burglars. It's obvious, isn't it? The place where your treasure is, is the place you will most want to be, and end up being.

6.22-23 "Your eyes are windows into your body. If you open your eyes wide in wonder and belief, your body fills up with light. If you live squinty-eyed in greed and distrust, your body is a dank cellar. If you pull the blinds on your windows, what a dark life you will have!

6.24 "You can't worship two gods at once. Loving one god, you'll end up hating the other. Adoration of one feeds contempt for the other. You can't worship God and Money both.

6.25-26 "If you decide for God, living a life of God-worship, it follows that you don't fuss about what's on the table at mealtimes or whether the

---

ᵃ 13 Or *from evil*; some late manuscripts *one, / for yours is the kingdom and the power and the glory forever. Amen.*

NEW INTERNATIONAL VERSION

your body, what you will wear. Is not life more important than food, and the body more important than clothes? 26Look at the birds of the air; they do not sow or reap or store away in barns, and yet your heavenly Father feeds them. Are you not much more valuable than they? 27Who of you by worrying can add a single hour to his life *a*?

28"And why do you worry about clothes? See how the lilies of the field grow. They do not labor or spin. 29Yet I tell you that not even Solomon in all his splendor was dressed like one of these. 30If that is how God clothes the grass of the field, which is here today and tomorrow is thrown into the fire, will he not much more clothe you, O you of little faith? 31So do not worry, saying, 'What shall we eat?' or 'What shall we drink?' or 'What shall we wear?' 32For the pagans run after all these things, and your heavenly Father knows that you need them. 33But seek first his kingdom and his righteousness, and all these things will be given to you as well. 34Therefore do not worry about tomorrow, for tomorrow will worry about itself. Each day has enough trouble of its own.

JUDGING OTHERS

7 "Do not judge, or you too will be judged. 2For in the same way you judge others, you will be judged, and with the measure you use, it will be measured to you.

3"Why do you look at the speck of sawdust in your brother's eye and pay no attention to the plank in your own eye? 4How can you say to your brother, 'Let me take the speck out of your eye,' when all the time there is a plank in your own eye? 5You hypocrite, first take the plank out of your own eye, and then you will see clearly to remove the speck from your brother's eye.

6"Do not give dogs what is sacred; do not throw your pearls to pigs. If you do, they may trample them under their feet, and then turn and tear you to pieces.

ASK, SEEK, KNOCK

7"Ask and it will be given to you; seek and

a 27 Or *single cubit to his height*

THE MESSAGE

clothes in your closet are in fashion. There is far more to your life than the food you put in your stomach, more to your outer appearance than the clothes you hang on your body. Look at the birds, free and unfettered, not tied down to a job description, careless in the care of God. And you count far more to him than birds.

6.27-29 "Has anyone by fussing in front of the mirror ever gotten taller by so much as an inch? All this time and money wasted on fashion— do you think it makes that much difference? Instead of looking at the fashions, walk out into the fields and look at the wildflowers. They never primp or shop, but have you ever seen color and design quite like it? The ten best-dressed men and women in the country look shabby alongside them.

6.30-33 "If God gives such attention to the appearance of wildflowers—most of which are never even seen—don't you think he'll attend to you, take pride in you, do his best for you? What I'm trying to do here is to get you to relax, to not be so preoccupied with *getting*, so you can respond to God's *giving*. People who don't know God and the way he works fuss over these things, but you know both God and how he works. Steep your life in God-reality, God-initiative, God-provisions. Don't worry about missing out. You'll find all your everyday human concerns will be met.

6.34 "Give your entire attention to what God is doing right now, and don't get worked up about what may or may not happen tomorrow. God will help you deal with whatever hard things come up when the time comes.

A SIMPLE GUIDE FOR BEHAVIOR

7.1-5 **7** "Don't pick on people, jump on their failures, criticize their faults—unless, of course, you want the same treatment. That critical spirit has a way of boomeranging. It's easy to see a smudge on your neighbor's face and be oblivious to the ugly sneer on your own. Do you have the nerve to say, 'Let me wash your face for you,' when your own face is distorted by contempt? It's this whole traveling roadshow mentality all over again, playing a holier-than-thou part instead of just living your part. Wipe that ugly sneer off your own face, and you might be fit to offer a washcloth to your neighbor.

7.6 "Don't be flip with the sacred. Banter and silliness give no honor to God. Don't reduce holy mysteries to slogans. In trying to be relevant, you're only being cute and inviting sacrilege.

7.7-11 "Don't bargain with God. Be direct. Ask for

NEW INTERNATIONAL VERSION

you will find; knock and the door will be opened to you. ⁸For everyone who asks receives; he who seeks finds; and to him who knocks, the door will be opened.

⁹"Which of you, if his son asks for bread, will give him a stone? ¹⁰Or if he asks for a fish, will give him a snake? ¹¹If you, then, though you are evil, know how to give good gifts to your children, how much more will your Father in heaven give good gifts to those who ask him! ¹²So in everything, do to others what you would have them do to you, for this sums up the Law and the Prophets.

THE NARROW AND WIDE GATES

¹³"Enter through the narrow gate. For wide is the gate and broad is the road that leads to destruction, and many enter through it. ¹⁴But small is the gate and narrow the road that leads to life, and only a few find it.

A TREE AND ITS FRUIT

¹⁵"Watch out for false prophets. They come to you in sheep's clothing, but inwardly they are ferocious wolves. ¹⁶By their fruit you will recognize them. Do people pick grapes from thornbushes, or figs from thistles? ¹⁷Likewise every good tree bears good fruit, but a bad tree bears bad fruit. ¹⁸A good tree cannot bear bad fruit, and a bad tree cannot bear good fruit. ¹⁹Every tree that does not bear good fruit is cut down and thrown into the fire. ²⁰Thus, by their fruit you will recognize them.

²¹"Not everyone who says to me, 'Lord, Lord,' will enter the kingdom of heaven, but only he who does the will of my Father who is in heaven. ²²Many will say to me on that day, 'Lord, Lord, did we not prophesy in your name, and in your name drive out demons and perform many miracles?' ²³Then I will tell them plainly, 'I never knew you. Away from me, you evildoers!'

THE WISE AND FOOLISH BUILDERS

²⁴"Therefore everyone who hears these words of mine and puts them into practice is like a wise man who built his house on the rock. ²⁵The rain came down, the streams rose, and the winds blew and beat against that house; yet it did not fall, because it had its foundation on the rock. ²⁶But everyone who hears these words of mine and does not put them into practice is like a foolish man who built his house on sand. ²⁷The rain came down, the streams rose, and the winds blew and beat against that house, and it fell with a great crash."

THE MESSAGE

what you need. This isn't a cat-and-mouse, hide-and-seek game we're in. If your child asks for bread, do you trick him with sawdust? If he asks for fish, do you scare him with a live snake on his plate? As bad as you are, you wouldn't think of such a thing. You're at least decent to your own children. So don't you think the God who conceived you in love will be even better?

7.12 "Here is a simple, rule-of-thumb guide for behavior: Ask yourself what you want people to do for you, then grab the initiative and do it for *them*. Add up God's Law and Prophets and this is what you get.

BEING AND DOING

7.13-14 "Don't look for shortcuts to God. The market is flooded with surefire, easygoing formulas for a successful life that can be practiced in your spare time. Don't fall for that stuff, even though crowds of people do. The way to life—to God!—is vigorous and requires total attention.

7.15-20 "Be wary of false preachers who smile a lot, dripping with practiced sincerity. Chances are they are out to rip you off some way or other. Don't be impressed with charisma; look for character. Who preachers *are* is the main thing, not what they say. A genuine leader will never exploit your emotions or your pocketbook. These diseased trees with their bad apples are going to be chopped down and burned.

7.21-23 "Knowing the correct password—saying 'Master, Master,' for instance—isn't going to get you anywhere with me. What is required is serious obedience—*doing* what my Father wills. I can see it now—at the Final Judgment thousands strutting up to me and saying, 'Master, we preached the Message, we bashed the demons, our God-sponsored projects had everyone talking.' And do you know what I am going to say? 'You missed the boat. All you did was use me to make yourselves important. You don't impress me one bit. You're out of here.'

7.24-25 "These words I speak to you are not incidental additions to your life, homeowner improvements to your standard of living. They are foundational words, words to build a life on. If you work these words into your life, you are like a smart carpenter who built his house on solid rock. Rain poured down, the river flooded, a tornado hit—but nothing moved that house. It was fixed to the rock.

7.26-27 "But if you just use my words in Bible studies and don't work them into your life, you are like a stupid carpenter who built his house on the sandy beach. When a storm rolled in and the waves came up, it collapsed like a house of cards."

NEW INTERNATIONAL VERSION

28When Jesus had finished saying these things, the crowds were amazed at his teaching, 29because he taught as one who had authority, and not as their teachers of the law.

THE MAN WITH LEPROSY

8 When he came down from the mountainside, large crowds followed him. 2A man with leprosy*a* came and knelt before him and said, "Lord, if you are willing, you can make me clean."

3Jesus reached out his hand and touched the man. "I am willing," he said. "Be clean!" Immediately he was cured*b* of his leprosy. 4Then Jesus said to him, "See that you don't tell anyone. But go, show yourself to the priest and offer the gift Moses commanded, as a testimony to them."

THE FAITH OF THE CENTURION

5When Jesus had entered Capernaum, a centurion came to him, asking for help. 6"Lord," he said, "my servant lies at home paralyzed and in terrible suffering."

7Jesus said to him, "I will go and heal him."

8The centurion replied, "Lord, I do not deserve to have you come under my roof. But just say the word, and my servant will be healed. 9For I myself am a man under authority, with soldiers under me. I tell this one, 'Go,' and he goes; and that one, 'Come,' and he comes. I say to my servant, 'Do this,' and he does it."

10When Jesus heard this, he was astonished and said to those following him, "I tell you the truth, I have not found anyone in Israel with such great faith. 11I say to you that many will come from the east and the west, and will take their places at the feast with Abraham, Isaac and Jacob in the kingdom of heaven. 12But the subjects of the kingdom will be thrown outside, into the darkness, where there will be weeping and gnashing of teeth."

13Then Jesus said to the centurion, "Go! It will be done just as you believed it would." And his servant was healed at that very hour.

JESUS HEALS MANY

14When Jesus came into Peter's house, he saw Peter's mother-in-law lying in bed with a fever. 15He touched her hand and the fever left her, and she got up and began to wait on him.

16When evening came, many who were demon-possessed were brought to him, and he drove out the spirits with a word and healed all

THE MESSAGE

7.28-29   When Jesus concluded his address, the crowd burst into applause. They had never heard teaching like this. It was apparent that he was living everything he was saying—quite a contrast to their religion teachers! This was the best teaching they had ever heard.

HE CARRIED OUR DISEASES

8.1-2   **8** Jesus came down the mountain with the cheers of the crowd still ringing in his ears. Then a leper appeared and went to his knees before Jesus, praying, "Master, if you want to, you can heal my body."

8.3-4   Jesus reached out and touched him, saying, "I want to. Be clean." Then and there, all signs of the leprosy were gone. Jesus said, "Don't talk about this all over town. Just quietly present your healed body to the priest, along with the appropriate expressions of thanks to God. Your cleansed and grateful life, not your words, will bear witness to what I have done."

8.5-6   As Jesus entered the village of Capernaum, a Roman captain came up in a panic and said, "Master, my servant is sick. He can't walk. He's in terrible pain."

8.7   Jesus said, "I'll come and heal him."

8.8-9   "Oh, no," said the captain. "I don't want to put you to all that trouble. Just give the order and my servant will be fine. I'm a man who takes orders and gives orders. I tell one soldier, 'Go,' and he goes; to another, 'Come,' and he comes; to my slave, 'Do this,' and he does it."

8.10-12   Taken aback, Jesus said, "I've yet to come across this kind of simple trust in Israel, the very people who are supposed to know all about God and how he works. This man is the vanguard of many outsiders who will soon be coming from all directions—streaming in from the east, pouring in from the west, sitting down at God's kingdom banquet alongside Abraham, Isaac, and Jacob. Then those who grew up 'in the faith' but had no faith will find themselves out in the cold, outsiders to grace and wondering what happened."

8.13   Then Jesus turned to the captain and said, "Go. What you believed could happen has happened." At that moment his servant became well.

8.14-15   By this time they were in front of Peter's house. On entering, Jesus found Peter's mother-in-law sick in bed, burning up with fever. He touched her hand and the fever was gone. No sooner was she up on her feet than she was fixing dinner for him.

8.16-17   That evening a lot of demon-afflicted people were brought to him. He relieved the inwardly

---

a 2 The Greek word was used for various diseases affecting the skin—not necessarily leprosy.   *b* 3 Greek *made clean*

NEW INTERNATIONAL VERSION

the sick. ¹⁷This was to fulfill what was spoken through the prophet Isaiah:

> "He took up our infirmities
> and carried our diseases." ^a

The Cost of Following Jesus

¹⁸When Jesus saw the crowd around him, he gave orders to cross to the other side of the lake. ¹⁹Then a teacher of the law came to him and said, "Teacher, I will follow you wherever you go."

²⁰Jesus replied, "Foxes have holes and birds of the air have nests, but the Son of Man has no place to lay his head."

²¹Another disciple said to him, "Lord, first let me go and bury my father."

²²But Jesus told him, "Follow me, and let the dead bury their own dead."

Jesus Calms the Storm

²³Then he got into the boat and his disciples followed him. ²⁴Without warning, a furious storm came up on the lake, so that the waves swept over the boat. But Jesus was sleeping. ²⁵The disciples went and woke him, saying, "Lord, save us! We're going to drown!"

²⁶He replied, "You of little faith, why are you so afraid?" Then he got up and rebuked the winds and the waves, and it was completely calm.

²⁷The men were amazed and asked, "What kind of man is this? Even the winds and the waves obey him!"

The Healing of Two Demon-possessed Men

²⁸When he arrived at the other side in the region of the Gadarenes, ^b two demon-possessed men coming from the tombs met him. They were so violent that no one could pass that way. ²⁹"What do you want with us, Son of God?" they shouted. "Have you come here to torture us before the appointed time?"

³⁰Some distance from them a large herd of pigs was feeding. ³¹The demons begged Jesus, "If you drive us out, send us into the herd of pigs."

³²He said to them, "Go!" So they came out and went into the pigs, and the whole herd rushed down the steep bank into the lake and died in the water. ³³Those tending the pigs ran off, went into the town and reported all this, including what had happened to the demon-possessed men. ³⁴Then the whole town went out to meet Jesus. And when they saw him, they pleaded with him to leave their region.

^a 17 Isaiah 53:4   ^b 28 Some manuscripts *Gergesenes*; others *Gerasenes*

THE MESSAGE

tormented. He cured the bodily ill. He fulfilled Isaiah's well-known sermon:

> He took our illnesses,
> He carried our diseases.

Your Business Is Life, Not Death

8.18-19 When Jesus saw that a curious crowd was growing by the minute, he told his disciples to get him out of there to the other side of the lake. As they left, a religion scholar asked if he could go along. "I'll go with you, wherever," he said.

8.20   Jesus was curt: "Are you ready to rough it? We're not staying in the best inns, you know."

8.21   Another follower said, "Master, excuse me for a couple of days, please. I have my father's funeral to take care of."

8.22   Jesus refused. "First things first. Your business is life, not death. Follow me. Pursue life."

✠

8.23-25 Then he got in the boat, his disciples with him. The next thing they knew, they were in a severe storm. Waves were crashing into the boat—and he was sound asleep! They roused him, pleading, "Master, save us! We're going down!"

8.26   Jesus reprimanded them. "Why are you such cowards, such faint-hearts?" Then he stood up and told the wind to be silent, the sea to quiet down: "Silence!" The sea became smooth as glass.

8.27   The men rubbed their eyes, astonished. "What's going on here? Wind and sea come to heel at his command!"

The Madmen and the Pigs

8.28-31 They landed in the country of the Gadarenes and were met by two madmen, victims of demons, coming out of the cemetery. The men had terrorized the region for so long that no one considered it safe to walk down that stretch of road anymore. Seeing Jesus, the madmen screamed out, "What business do you have giving us a hard time? You're the Son of God! You weren't supposed to show up here yet!" Off in the distance a herd of pigs was browsing and rooting. The evil spirits begged Jesus, "If you kick us out of these men, let us live in the pigs."

8.32-34 Jesus said, "Go ahead, but get out of here!" Crazed, the pigs stampeded over a cliff into the sea and drowned. Scared to death, the swineherds bolted. They told everyone back in town what had happened to the madmen and the pigs. Those who heard about it were angry about the drowned pigs. A mob formed and demanded that Jesus get out and not come back.

NEW INTERNATIONAL VERSION

Jesus Heals a Paralytic

9 Jesus stepped into a boat, crossed over and came to his own town. ²Some men brought to him a paralytic, lying on a mat. When Jesus saw their faith, he said to the paralytic, "Take heart, son; your sins are forgiven."

³At this, some of the teachers of the law said to themselves, "This fellow is blaspheming!"

⁴Knowing their thoughts, Jesus said, "Why do you entertain evil thoughts in your hearts? ⁵Which is easier: to say, 'Your sins are forgiven,' or to say, 'Get up and walk'? ⁶But so that you may know that the Son of Man has authority on earth to forgive sins . . ." Then he said to the paralytic, "Get up, take your mat and go home." ⁷And the man got up and went home. ⁸When the crowd saw this, they were filled with awe; and they praised God, who had given such authority to men.

The Calling of Matthew

⁹As Jesus went on from there, he saw a man named Matthew sitting at the tax collector's booth. "Follow me," he told him, and Matthew got up and followed him.

¹⁰While Jesus was having dinner at Matthew's house, many tax collectors and "sinners" came and ate with him and his disciples. ¹¹When the Pharisees saw this, they asked his disciples, "Why does your teacher eat with tax collectors and 'sinners'?"

¹²On hearing this, Jesus said, "It is not the healthy who need a doctor, but the sick. ¹³But go and learn what this means: 'I desire mercy, not sacrifice.'ᵃ For I have not come to call the righteous, but sinners."

Jesus Questioned About Fasting

¹⁴Then John's disciples came and asked him, "How is it that we and the Pharisees fast, but your disciples do not fast?"

¹⁵Jesus answered, "How can the guests of the bridegroom mourn while he is with them? The time will come when the bridegroom will be taken from them; then they will fast.

¹⁶"No one sews a patch of unshrunk cloth on an old garment, for the patch will pull away from the garment, making the tear worse. ¹⁷Neither do men pour new wine into old wineskins. If they do, the skins will burst, the wine will run out and the wineskins will be ruined. No, they pour new wine into new wineskins, and both are preserved."

A Dead Girl and a Sick Woman

¹⁸While he was saying this, a ruler came and

ᵃ 13 Hosea 6:6

THE MESSAGE

Who Needs a Doctor?

9 9.1-3 Back in the boat, Jesus and the disciples recrossed the sea to Jesus' hometown. They were hardly out of the boat when some men carried a paraplegic on a stretcher and set him down in front of them. Jesus, impressed by their bold belief, said to the paraplegic, "Cheer up, son. I forgive your sins." Some religion scholars whispered, "Why, that's blasphemy!"

9.4-8 Jesus knew what they were thinking, and said, "Why this gossipy whispering? Which do you think is simpler: to say, 'I forgive your sins,' or, 'Get up and walk'? Well, just so it's clear that I'm the Son of Man and authorized to do either, or both. . . ." At this he turned to the paraplegic and said, "Get up. Take your bed and go home." And the man did it. The crowd was awestruck, amazed and pleased that God had authorized Jesus to work among them this way.

9.9 Passing along, Jesus saw a man at his work collecting taxes. His name was Matthew. Jesus said, "Come along with me." Matthew stood up and followed him.

9.10-11 Later when Jesus was eating supper at Matthew's house with his close followers, a lot of disreputable characters came and joined them. When the Pharisees saw him keeping this kind of company, they had a fit, and lit into Jesus' followers. "What kind of example is this from your Teacher, acting cozy with crooks and riffraff?"

9.12-13 Jesus, overhearing, shot back, "Who needs a doctor: the healthy or the sick? Go figure out what this Scripture means: 'I'm after mercy, not religion.' I'm here to invite outsiders, not coddle insiders."

Kingdom Come

9.14 A little later John's followers approached, asking, "Why is it that we and the Pharisees rigorously discipline body and spirit by fasting, but your followers don't?"

9.15 Jesus told them, "When you're celebrating a wedding, you don't skimp on the cake and wine. You feast. Later you may need to pull in your belt, but not now. No one throws cold water on a friendly bonfire. This is Kingdom Come!"

9.16-17 He went on, "No one cuts up a fine silk scarf to patch old work clothes; you want fabrics that match. And you don't put your wine in cracked bottles."

Just a Touch

9.18-19 As he finished saying this, a local official ap-

NEW INTERNATIONAL VERSION

knelt before him and said, "My daughter has just died. But come and put your hand on her, and she will live." ¹⁹Jesus got up and went with him, and so did his disciples.

²⁰Just then a woman who had been subject to bleeding for twelve years came up behind him and touched the edge of his cloak. ²¹She said to herself, "If I only touch his cloak, I will be healed."

²²Jesus turned and saw her. "Take heart, daughter," he said, "your faith has healed you." And the woman was healed from that moment.

²³When Jesus entered the ruler's house and saw the flute players and the noisy crowd, ²⁴he said, "Go away. The girl is not dead but asleep." But they laughed at him. ²⁵After the crowd had been put outside, he went in and took the girl by the hand, and she got up. ²⁶News of this spread through all that region.

JESUS HEALS THE BLIND AND MUTE

²⁷As Jesus went on from there, two blind men followed him, calling out, "Have mercy on us, Son of David!"

²⁸When he had gone indoors, the blind men came to him, and he asked them, "Do you believe that I am able to do this?"

"Yes, Lord," they replied.

²⁹Then he touched their eyes and said, "According to your faith will it be done to you"; ³⁰and their sight was restored. Jesus warned them sternly, "See that no one knows about this." ³¹But they went out and spread the news about him all over that region.

³²While they were going out, a man who was demon-possessed and could not talk was brought to Jesus. ³³And when the demon was driven out, the man who had been mute spoke. The crowd was amazed and said, "Nothing like this has ever been seen in Israel."

³⁴But the Pharisees said, "It is by the prince of demons that he drives out demons."

THE WORKERS ARE FEW

³⁵Jesus went through all the towns and villages, teaching in their synagogues, preaching the good news of the kingdom and healing every disease and sickness. ³⁶When he saw the crowds, he had compassion on them, because they were harassed and helpless, like sheep without a shepherd. ³⁷Then he said to his disciples, "The harvest is plentiful but the workers are few. ³⁸Ask the Lord of the harvest, therefore, to send out workers into his harvest field."

THE MESSAGE

peared, bowed politely, and said, "My daughter has just now died. If you come and touch her, she will live." Jesus got up and went with him, his disciples following along.

9.20-22 Just then a woman who had hemorrhaged for twelve years slipped in from behind and lightly touched his robe. She was thinking to herself, "If I can just put a finger on his robe, I'll get well." Jesus turned—caught her at it. Then he reassured her: "Courage, daughter. You took a risk of faith, and now you're well." The woman was well from then on.

9.23-26 By now they had arrived at the house of the town official, and pushed their way through the gossips looking for a story and the neighbors bringing in casseroles. Jesus was abrupt: "Clear out! This girl isn't dead. She's sleeping." They told him he didn't know what he was talking about. But when Jesus had gotten rid of the crowd, he went in, took the girl's hand, and pulled her to her feet—alive. The news was soon out, and traveled throughout the region.

BECOME WHAT YOU BELIEVE

9.27-28 As Jesus left the house, he was followed by two blind men crying out, "Mercy, Son of David! Mercy on us!" When Jesus got home, the blind men went in with him. Jesus said to them, "Do you really believe I can do this?" They said, "Why, yes, Master!"

9.29-31 He touched their eyes and said, "Become what you believe." It happened. They saw. Then Jesus became very stern. "Don't let a soul know how this happened." But they were hardly out the door before they started blabbing it to everyone they met.

9.32-33 Right after that, as the blind men were leaving, a man who had been struck speechless by an evil spirit was brought to Jesus. As soon as Jesus threw the evil tormenting spirit out, the man talked away just as if he'd been talking all his life. The people were up on their feet applauding: "There's never been anything like this in Israel!"

9.34 The Pharisees were left sputtering, "Hocus pocus. It's nothing but hocus pocus. He's probably made a pact with the Devil."

9.35-38 Then Jesus made a circuit of all the towns and villages. He taught in their meeting places, reported kingdom news, and healed their diseased bodies, healed their bruised and hurt lives. When he looked out over the crowds, his heart broke. So confused and aimless they were, like sheep with no shepherd. "What a huge harvest!" he said to his disciples. "How few workers! On your knees and pray for harvest hands!"

NEW INTERNATIONAL VERSION

Jesus Sends Out the Twelve

10 He called his twelve disciples to him and gave them authority to drive out evil[a] spirits and to heal every disease and sickness.

²These are the names of the twelve apostles: first, Simon (who is called Peter) and his brother Andrew; James son of Zebedee, and his brother John; ³Philip and Bartholomew; Thomas and Matthew the tax collector; James son of Alphaeus, and Thaddaeus; ⁴Simon the Zealot and Judas Iscariot, who betrayed him.

⁵These twelve Jesus sent out with the following instructions: "Do not go among the Gentiles or enter any town of the Samaritans. ⁶Go rather to the lost sheep of Israel. ⁷As you go, preach this message: 'The kingdom of heaven is near.' ⁸Heal the sick, raise the dead, cleanse those who have leprosy,[b] drive out demons. Freely you have received, freely give. ⁹Do not take along any gold or silver or copper in your belts; ¹⁰take no bag for the journey, or extra tunic, or sandals or a staff; for the worker is worth his keep.

¹¹"Whatever town or village you enter, search for some worthy person there and stay at his house until you leave. ¹²As you enter the home, give it your greeting. ¹³If the home is deserving, let your peace rest on it; if it is not, let your peace return to you. ¹⁴If anyone will not welcome you or listen to your words, shake the dust off your feet when you leave that home or town. ¹⁵I tell you the truth, it will be more bearable for Sodom and Gomorrah on the day of judgment than for that town. ¹⁶I am sending you out like sheep among wolves. Therefore be as shrewd as snakes and as innocent as doves.

¹⁷"Be on your guard against men; they will hand you over to the local councils and flog you in their synagogues. ¹⁸On my account you will

---

THE MESSAGE

The Twelve Harvest Hands

10 ¹⁰·¹⁻⁴ The prayer was no sooner prayed than it was answered. Jesus called twelve of his followers and sent them into the ripe fields. He gave them power to kick out the evil spirits and to tenderly care for the bruised and hurt lives. This is the list of the twelve he sent:

Simon (they called him Peter, or "Rock"),
Andrew, his brother,
James, Zebedee's son,
John, his brother,
Philip,
Bartholomew,
Thomas,
Matthew, the tax man,
James, son of Alphaeus,
Thaddaeus,
Simon, the Canaanite,
Judas Iscariot (who later turned on him).

¹⁰·⁵⁻⁸ Jesus sent his twelve harvest hands out with this charge:

"Don't begin by traveling to some far-off place to convert unbelievers. And don't try to be dramatic by tackling some public enemy. Go to the lost, confused people right here in the neighborhood. Tell them that the kingdom is here. Bring health to the sick. Raise the dead. Touch the untouchables. Kick out the demons. You have been treated generously, so live generously.

¹⁰·⁹⁻¹⁰ "Don't think you have to put on a fund-raising campaign before you start. You don't need a lot of equipment. *You* are the equipment, and all you need to keep that going is three meals a day. Travel light.

¹⁰·¹¹ "When you enter a town or village, don't insist on staying in a luxury inn. Get a modest place with some modest people, and be content there until you leave.

¹⁰·¹²⁻¹⁵ "When you knock on a door, be courteous in your greeting. If they welcome you, be gentle in your conversation. If they don't welcome you, quietly withdraw. Don't make a scene. Shrug your shoulders and be on your way. You can be sure that on Judgment Day they'll be mighty sorry—but it's no concern of yours now.

¹⁰·¹⁶ "Stay alert. This is hazardous work I'm assigning you. You're going to be like sheep running through a wolf pack, so don't call attention to yourselves. Be as cunning as a snake, inoffensive as a dove.

¹⁰·¹⁷⁻²⁰ "Don't be naive. Some people will impugn your motives, others will smear your reputation—just because you believe in me. Don't be upset when they haul you before the civil au-

---

ᵃ 1 Greek *unclean*   ᵇ 8 The Greek word was used for various diseases affecting the skin—not necessarily leprosy.

NEW INTERNATIONAL VERSION

be brought before governors and kings as witnesses to them and to the Gentiles. ¹⁹But when they arrest you, do not worry about what to say or how to say it. At that time you will be given what to say, ²⁰for it will not be you speaking, but the Spirit of your Father speaking through you.

²¹"Brother will betray brother to death, and a father his child; children will rebel against their parents and have them put to death. ²²All men will hate you because of me, but he who stands firm to the end will be saved. ²³When you are persecuted in one place, flee to another. I tell you the truth, you will not finish going through the cities of Israel before the Son of Man comes.

²⁴"A student is not above his teacher, nor a servant above his master. ²⁵It is enough for the student to be like his teacher, and the servant like his master. If the head of the house has been called Beelzebub,ᵃ how much more the members of his household!

²⁶"So do not be afraid of them. There is nothing concealed that will not be disclosed, or hidden that will not be made known. ²⁷What I tell you in the dark, speak in the daylight; what is whispered in your ear, proclaim from the roofs. ²⁸Do not be afraid of those who kill the body but cannot kill the soul. Rather, be afraid of the One who can destroy both soul and body in hell. ²⁹Are not two sparrows sold for a pennyᵇ? Yet not one of them will fall to the ground apart from the will of your Father. ³⁰And even the very hairs of your head are all numbered. ³¹So don't be afraid; you are worth more than many sparrows.

³²"Whoever acknowledges me before men, I will also acknowledge him before my Father in heaven. ³³But whoever disowns me before men, I will disown him before my Father in heaven.

³⁴"Do not suppose that I have come to bring peace to the earth. I did not come to bring peace, but a sword. ³⁵For I have come to turn

" 'a man against his father,
a daughter against her mother,
a daughter-in-law against her mother-in-law—
³⁶ a man's enemies will be the members of his own household.'ᶜ

³⁷"Anyone who loves his father or mother more than me is not worthy of me; anyone who loves his son or daughter more than me is not worthy of me; ³⁸and anyone who does not take

THE MESSAGE

thorities. Without knowing it, they've done you—and me—a favor, given you a platform for preaching the kingdom news! And don't worry about what you'll say or how you'll say it. The right words will be there; the Spirit of your Father will supply the words.

10.21-23 "When people realize it is the living God you are presenting and not some idol that makes them feel good, they are going to turn on you, even people in your own family. There is a great irony here: proclaiming so much love, experiencing so much hate! But don't quit. Don't cave in. It is all well worth it in the end. It is not success you are after in such times but survival. Be survivors! Before you've run out of options, the Son of Man will have arrived.

10.24-25 "A student doesn't get a better desk than her teacher. A laborer doesn't make more money than his boss. Be content—pleased, even—when you, my students, my harvest hands, get the same treatment I get. If they call me, the Master, 'Dungface,' what can the workers expect?

10.26-27 "Don't be intimidated. Eventually everything is going to be out in the open, and everyone will know how things really are. So don't hesitate to go public now.

10.28 "Don't be bluffed into silence by the threats of bullies. There's nothing they can do to your soul, your core being. Save your fear for God, who holds your entire life—body and soul—in his hands.

FORGET ABOUT YOURSELF

10.29-31 "What's the price of a pet canary? Some loose change, right? And God cares what happens to it even more than you do. He pays even greater attention to you, down to the last detail—even numbering the hairs on your head! So don't be intimidated by all this bully talk. You're worth more than a million canaries.

10.32-33 "Stand up for me against world opinion and I'll stand up for you before my Father in heaven. If you turn tail and run, do you think I'll cover for you?

10.34-37 "Don't think I've come to make life cozy. I've come to cut—make a sharp knife-cut between son and father, daughter and mother, bride and mother-in-law—cut through these cozy domestic arrangements and free you for God. Well-meaning family members can be your worst enemies. If you prefer father or mother over me, you don't deserve me. If you prefer son or daughter over me, you don't deserve me.

10.38-39 "If you don't go all the way with me, through thick and thin, you don't deserve me. If your first concern is to look after yourself,

ᵃ 25 Greek *Beezeboul* or *Beelzeboul*   ᵇ 29 Greek an *assarion*   ᶜ 36 Micah 7:6

NEW INTERNATIONAL VERSION

his cross and follow me is not worthy of me. ³⁹Whoever finds his life will lose it, and whoever loses his life for my sake will find it.

⁴⁰"He who receives you receives me, and he who receives me receives the one who sent me. ⁴¹Anyone who receives a prophet because he is a prophet will receive a prophet's reward, and anyone who receives a righteous man because he is a righteous man will receive a righteous man's reward. ⁴²And if anyone gives even a cup of cold water to one of these little ones because he is my disciple, I tell you the truth, he will certainly not lose his reward."

JESUS AND JOHN THE BAPTIST

11 After Jesus had finished instructing his twelve disciples, he went on from there to teach and preach in the towns of Galilee.^a

²When John heard in prison what Christ was doing, he sent his disciples ³to ask him, "Are you the one who was to come, or should we expect someone else?"

⁴Jesus replied, "Go back and report to John what you hear and see: ⁵The blind receive sight, the lame walk, those who have leprosy^b are cured, the deaf hear, the dead are raised, and the good news is preached to the poor. ⁶Blessed is the man who does not fall away on account of me."

⁷As John's disciples were leaving, Jesus began to speak to the crowd about John: "What did you go out into the desert to see? A reed swayed by the wind? ⁸If not, what did you go out to see? A man dressed in fine clothes? No, those who wear fine clothes are in kings' palaces. ⁹Then what did you go out to see? A prophet? Yes, I tell you, and more than a prophet. ¹⁰This is the one about whom it is written:

" 'I will send my messenger ahead of you,
who will prepare your way before you.'^c

¹¹I tell you the truth: Among those born of women there has not risen anyone greater than John the Baptist; yet he who is least in the kingdom of heaven is greater than he. ¹²From the days of John the Baptist until now, the kingdom of heaven has been forcefully advancing, and forceful men lay hold of it. ¹³For all the Prophets and the Law prophesied until John. ¹⁴And if you are

---

^a *1* Greek *in their towns*   ^b *5* The Greek word was used for various diseases affecting the skin—not necessarily leprosy.   ^c *10* Mal. 3:1

THE MESSAGE

you'll never find yourself. But if you forget about yourself and look to me, you'll find both yourself and me.

10.40-42   "We are intimately linked in this harvest work. Anyone who accepts what you do, accepts me, the One who sent you. Anyone who accepts what I do accepts my Father, who sent me. Accepting a messenger of God is as good as being God's messenger. Accepting someone's help is as good as giving someone help. This is a large work I've called you into, but don't be overwhelmed by it. It's best to start small. Give a cool cup of water to someone who is thirsty, for instance. The smallest act of giving or receiving makes you a true apprentice. You won't lose out on a thing."

JOHN THE BAPTIZER

11.1   **11** When Jesus finished placing this charge before his twelve disciples, he went on to teach and preach in their villages.

11.2-3   John, meanwhile, had been locked up in prison. When he got wind of what Jesus was doing, he sent his own disciples to ask, "Are you the One we've been expecting, or are we still waiting?"

11.4-6   Jesus told them, "Go back and tell John what's going on:

The blind see,
The lame walk,
Lepers are cleansed,
The deaf hear,
The dead are raised,
The wretched of the earth learn that God is
    on their side.

"Is this what you were expecting? Then count yourselves most blessed!"

11.7-10   When John's disciples left to report, Jesus started talking to the crowd about John. "What did you expect when you went out to see him in the wild? A weekend camper? Hardly. What then? A sheik in silk pajamas? Not in the wilderness, not by a long shot. What then? A prophet? That's right, a prophet! Probably the best prophet you'll ever hear. He is the prophet that Malachi announced when he wrote, 'I'm sending my prophet ahead of you, to make the road smooth for you.'

11.11-14   "Let me tell you what's going on here: No one in history surpasses John the Baptizer; but in the kingdom he prepared you for, the lowliest person is ahead of him. For a long time now people have tried to force themselves into God's kingdom. But if you read the books of the Prophets and God's Law closely, you will see them culminate in John, teaming up with

NEW INTERNATIONAL VERSION

willing to accept it, he is the Elijah who was to come. ¹⁵He who has ears, let him hear.

¹⁶"To what can I compare this generation? They are like children sitting in the marketplaces and calling out to others:

¹⁷" 'We played the flute for you,
    and you did not dance;
we sang a dirge,
    and you did not mourn.'

¹⁸For John came neither eating nor drinking, and they say, 'He has a demon.' ¹⁹The Son of Man came eating and drinking, and they say, 'Here is a glutton and a drunkard, a friend of tax collectors and "sinners." ' But wisdom is proved right by her actions."

WOE ON UNREPENTANT CITIES

²⁰Then Jesus began to denounce the cities in which most of his miracles had been performed, because they did not repent. ²¹"Woe to you, Korazin! Woe to you, Bethsaida! If the miracles that were performed in you had been performed in Tyre and Sidon, they would have repented long ago in sackcloth and ashes. ²²But I tell you, it will be more bearable for Tyre and Sidon on the day of judgment than for you. ²³And you, Capernaum, will you be lifted up to the skies? No, you will go down to the depths.ᵃ If the miracles that were performed in you had been performed in Sodom, it would have remained to this day. ²⁴But I tell you that it will be more bearable for Sodom on the day of judgment than for you."

REST FOR THE WEARY

²⁵At that time Jesus said, "I praise you, Father, Lord of heaven and earth, because you have hidden these things from the wise and learned, and revealed them to little children. ²⁶Yes, Father, for this was your good pleasure.

²⁷"All things have been committed to me by my Father. No one knows the Son except the Father, and no one knows the Father except the Son and those to whom the Son chooses to reveal him.

²⁸"Come to me, all you who are weary and burdened, and I will give you rest. ²⁹Take my yoke upon you and learn from me, for I am gentle and humble in heart, and you will find rest for your souls. ³⁰For my yoke is easy and my burden is light."

THE MESSAGE

him in preparing the way for the Messiah of the kingdom. Looked at in this way, John is the 'Elijah' you've all been expecting to arrive and introduce the Messiah.

11.15   "Are you listening to me? Really listening?

11.16-19   "How can I account for this generation? The people have been like spoiled children whining to their parents, 'We wanted to skip rope, and you were always too tired; we wanted to talk, but you were always too busy.' John came fasting and they called him crazy. I came feasting and they called me a lush, a friend of the riff-raff. Opinion polls don't count for much, do they? The proof of the pudding is in the eating."

THE UNFORCED RHYTHMS OF GRACE

11.20   Next Jesus let fly on the cities where he had worked the hardest but whose people had responded the least, shrugging their shoulders and going their own way.

11.21-24   "Doom to you, Chorazin! Doom, Bethsaida! If Tyre and Sidon had seen half of the powerful miracles you have seen, they would have been on their knees in a minute. At Judgment Day they'll get off easy compared to you. And Capernaum! With all your peacock strutting, you are going to end up in the abyss. If the people of Sodom had had your chances, the city would still be around. At Judgment Day they'll get off easy compared to you."

11.25-26   Abruptly Jesus broke into prayer: "Thank you, Father, Lord of heaven and earth. You've concealed your ways from sophisticates and know-it-alls, but spelled them out clearly to ordinary people. Yes, Father, that's the way you like to work."

11.27   Jesus resumed talking to the people, but now tenderly. "The Father has given me all these things to do and say. This is a unique Father-Son operation, coming out of Father and Son intimacies and knowledge. No one knows the Son the way the Father does, nor the Father the way the Son does. But I'm not keeping it to myself; I'm ready to go over it line by line with anyone willing to listen.

11.28-30   "Are you tired? Worn out? Burned out on religion? Come to me. Get away with me and you'll recover your life. I'll show you how to take a real rest. Walk with me and work with me—watch how I do it. Learn the unforced rhythms of grace. I won't lay anything heavy or ill-fitting on you. Keep company with me and you'll learn to live freely and lightly."

ᵃ 23 Greek *Hades*

NEW INTERNATIONAL VERSION

LORD OF THE SABBATH

12 At that time Jesus went through the grainfields on the Sabbath. His disciples were hungry and began to pick some heads of grain and eat them. ²When the Pharisees saw this, they said to him, "Look! Your disciples are doing what is unlawful on the Sabbath."

³He answered, "Haven't you read what David did when he and his companions were hungry? ⁴He entered the house of God, and he and his companions ate the consecrated bread—which was not lawful for them to do, but only for the priests. ⁵Or haven't you read in the Law that on the Sabbath the priests in the temple desecrate the day and yet are innocent? ⁶I tell you that one*ᵃ* greater than the temple is here. ⁷If you had known what these words mean, 'I desire mercy, not sacrifice,'*ᵇ* you would not have condemned the innocent. ⁸For the Son of Man is Lord of the Sabbath."

⁹Going on from that place, he went into their synagogue, ¹⁰and a man with a shriveled hand was there. Looking for a reason to accuse Jesus, they asked him, "Is it lawful to heal on the Sabbath?"

¹¹He said to them, "If any of you has a sheep and it falls into a pit on the Sabbath, will you not take hold of it and lift it out? ¹²How much more valuable is a man than a sheep! Therefore it is lawful to do good on the Sabbath."

¹³Then he said to the man, "Stretch out your hand." So he stretched it out and it was completely restored, just as sound as the other. ¹⁴But the Pharisees went out and plotted how they might kill Jesus.

GOD'S CHOSEN SERVANT

¹⁵Aware of this, Jesus withdrew from that place. Many followed him, and he healed all their sick, ¹⁶warning them not to tell who he was. ¹⁷This was to fulfill what was spoken through the prophet Isaiah:

¹⁸ "Here is my servant whom I have chosen,
    the one I love, in whom I delight;
I will put my Spirit on him,
    and he will proclaim justice to the
        nations.
¹⁹He will not quarrel or cry out;
    no one will hear his voice in the streets.
²⁰A bruised reed he will not break,
    and a smoldering wick he will not snuff
        out,
till he leads justice to victory.
²¹   In his name the nations will put their
        hope."*ᶜ*

THE MESSAGE

IN CHARGE OF THE SABBATH

12.1-2 **12** One Sabbath, Jesus was strolling with his disciples through a field of ripe grain. Hungry, the disciples were pulling off the heads of grain and munching on them. Some Pharisees reported them to Jesus: "Your disciples are breaking the Sabbath rules!"

12.3-5 Jesus said, "Really? Didn't you ever read what David and his companions did when they were hungry, how they entered the sanctuary and ate fresh bread off the altar, bread that no one but priests were allowed to eat? And didn't you ever read in God's Law that priests carrying out their Temple duties break Sabbath rules all the time and it's not held against them?

12.6-8 "There is far more at stake here than religion. If you had any idea what this Scripture meant—'I prefer a flexible heart to an inflexible ritual'—you wouldn't be nitpicking like this. The Son of Man is no lackey to the Sabbath; he's in charge."

12.9-10 When Jesus left the field, he entered their meeting place. There was a man there with a crippled hand. They said to Jesus, "Is it legal to heal on the Sabbath?" They were baiting him.

12.11-14 He replied, "Is there a person here who, finding one of your lambs fallen into a ravine, wouldn't, even though it was a Sabbath, pull it out? Surely kindness to people is as legal as kindness to animals!" Then he said to the man, "Hold out your hand." He held it out and it was healed. The Pharisees walked out furious, sputtering about how they were going to ruin Jesus.

IN CHARGE OF EVERYTHING

12.15-21 Jesus, knowing they were out to get him, moved on. A lot of people followed him, and he healed them all. He also cautioned them to keep it quiet, following guidelines set down by Isaiah:

Look well at my handpicked servant;
    I love him so much, take such delight in
        him.
I've placed my Spirit on him;
    he'll decree justice to the nations.
But he won't yell, won't raise his voice;
    there'll be no commotion in the streets.
He won't walk over anyone's feelings,
    won't push you into a corner.
Before you know it, his justice will
       triumph;
    the mere sound of his name will signal
       hope, even among far-off
       unbelievers.

ᵃ 6 Or *something*; also in verses 41 and 42   *ᵇ* 7 Hosea 6:6
ᶜ 21 Isaiah 42:1-4

NEW INTERNATIONAL VERSION

JESUS AND BEELZEBUB

22Then they brought him a demon-possessed man who was blind and mute, and Jesus healed him, so that he could both talk and see. 23All the people were astonished and said, "Could this be the Son of David?"

24But when the Pharisees heard this, they said, "It is only by Beelzebub,*a* the prince of demons, that this fellow drives out demons."

25Jesus knew their thoughts and said to them, "Every kingdom divided against itself will be ruined, and every city or household divided against itself will not stand. 26If Satan drives out Satan, he is divided against himself. How then can his kingdom stand? 27And if I drive out demons by Beelzebub, by whom do your people drive them out? So then, they will be your judges. 28But if I drive out demons by the Spirit of God, then the kingdom of God has come upon you.

29"Or again, how can anyone enter a strong man's house and carry off his possessions unless he first ties up the strong man? Then he can rob his house.

30"He who is not with me is against me, and he who does not gather with me scatters. 31And so I tell you, every sin and blasphemy will be forgiven men, but the blasphemy against the Spirit will not be forgiven. 32Anyone who speaks a word against the Son of Man will be forgiven, but anyone who speaks against the Holy Spirit will not be forgiven, either in this age or in the age to come.

33"Make a tree good and its fruit will be good, or make a tree bad and its fruit will be bad, for a tree is recognized by its fruit. 34You brood of vipers, how can you who are evil say anything good? For out of the overflow of the heart the mouth speaks. 35The good man brings good things out of the good stored up in him, and the evil man brings evil things out of the evil stored up in him. 36But I tell you that men will have to give account on the day of judgment for every careless word they have spoken. 37For by your words you will be acquitted, and by your words you will be condemned."

THE SIGN OF JONAH

38Then some of the Pharisees and teachers of

THE MESSAGE

NO NEUTRAL GROUND

12.22-23 Next a poor demon-afflicted wretch, both blind and deaf, was set down before him. Jesus healed him, gave him his sight and hearing. The people who saw it were impressed—"This has to be the Son of David!"

12.24 But the Pharisees, when they heard the report, were cynical. "Black magic," they said. "Some devil trick he's pulled from his sleeve."

12.25-27 Jesus confronted their slander. "A judge who gives opposite verdicts on the same person cancels himself out; a family that's in a constant squabble disintegrates; if Satan banishes Satan, is there any Satan left? If you're slinging devil mud at me, calling me a devil kicking out devils, doesn't the same mud stick to your own exorcists?

12.28-29 "But if it's by *God's* power that I am sending the evil spirits packing, then God's kingdom is here for sure. How in the world do you think it's possible in broad daylight to enter the house of an awake, able-bodied man and walk off with his possessions unless you tie him up first? Tie him up, though, and you can clean him out.

12.30 "This is war, and there is no neutral ground. If you're not on my side, you're the enemy; if you're not helping, you're making things worse.

12.31-32 "There's nothing done or said that can't be forgiven. But if you deliberately persist in your slanders against God's Spirit, you are repudiating the very One who forgives. If you reject the Son of Man out of some misunderstanding, the Holy Spirit can forgive you, but when you reject the Holy Spirit, you're sawing off the branch on which you're sitting, severing by your own perversity all connection with the One who forgives.

12.33 "If you grow a healthy tree, you'll pick healthy fruit. If you grow a diseased tree, you'll pick worm-eaten fruit. The fruit tells you about the tree.

12.34-37 "You have minds like a snake pit! How do you suppose what you say is worth anything when you are so foul-minded? It's your heart, not the dictionary, that gives meaning to your words. A good person produces good deeds and words season after season. An evil person is a blight on the orchard. Let me tell you something: Every one of these careless words is going to come back to haunt you. There will be a time of Reckoning. Words are powerful; take them seriously. Words can be your salvation. Words can also be your damnation."

JONAH-EVIDENCE

12.38 Later a few religion scholars and Pharisees got

---

a 24 Greek *Beezeboul* or *Beelzeboul*; also in verse 27

NEW INTERNATIONAL VERSION

the law said to him, "Teacher, we want to see a miraculous sign from you."

[39] He answered, "A wicked and adulterous generation asks for a miraculous sign! But none will be given it except the sign of the prophet Jonah. [40] For as Jonah was three days and three nights in the belly of a huge fish, so the Son of Man will be three days and three nights in the heart of the earth. [41] The men of Nineveh will stand up at the judgment with this generation and condemn it; for they repented at the preaching of Jonah, and now one[a] greater than Jonah is here. [42] The Queen of the South will rise at the judgment with this generation and condemn it; for she came from the ends of the earth to listen to Solomon's wisdom, and now one greater than Solomon is here.

[43] "When an evil[b] spirit comes out of a man, it goes through arid places seeking rest and does not find it. [44] Then it says, 'I will return to the house I left.' When it arrives, it finds the house unoccupied, swept clean and put in order. [45] Then it goes and takes with it seven other spirits more wicked than itself, and they go in and live there. And the final condition of that man is worse than the first. That is how it will be with this wicked generation."

JESUS' MOTHER AND BROTHERS

[46] While Jesus was still talking to the crowd, his mother and brothers stood outside, wanting to speak to him. [47] Someone told him, "Your mother and brothers are standing outside, wanting to speak to you."[c]

[48] He replied to him, "Who is my mother, and who are my brothers?" [49] Pointing to his disciples, he said, "Here are my mother and my brothers. [50] For whoever does the will of my Father in heaven is my brother and sister and mother."

THE MESSAGE

on him. "Teacher, we want to see your credentials. Give us some hard evidence that God is in this. How about a miracle?"

12.39-40   Jesus said, "You're looking for proof, but you're looking for the wrong kind. All you want is something to titillate your curiosity, satisfy your lust for miracles. The only proof you're going to get is what looks like the absence of proof: Jonah-evidence. Like Jonah, three days and nights in the fish's belly, the Son of Man will be gone three days and nights in a deep grave.

12.41-42   "On Judgment Day, the Ninevites will stand up and give evidence that will condemn this generation, because when Jonah preached to them they changed their lives. A far greater preacher than Jonah is here, and you squabble about 'proofs.' On Judgment Day, the Queen of Sheba will come forward and bring evidence that will condemn this generation, because she traveled from a far corner of the earth to listen to wise Solomon. Wisdom far greater than Solomon's is right in front of you, and you quibble over 'evidence.'

12.43-45   "When a defiling evil spirit is expelled from someone, it drifts along through the desert looking for an oasis, some unsuspecting soul it can bedevil. When it doesn't find anyone, it says, 'I'll go back to my old haunt.' On return it finds the person spotlessly clean, but vacant. It then runs out and rounds up seven other spirits more evil than itself and they all move in, whooping it up. That person ends up far worse off than if he'd never gotten cleaned up in the first place.

12.45   "That's what this generation is like: You may think you have cleaned out the junk from your lives and gotten ready for God, but you weren't hospitable to my kingdom message, and now all the devils are moving back in."

OBEDIENCE IS THICKER THAN BLOOD

12.46-47 While he was still talking to the crowd, his mother and brothers showed up. They were outside trying to get a message to him. Someone told Jesus, "Your mother and brothers are out here, wanting to speak with you."

12.48-50   Jesus didn't respond directly, but said, "Who do you think my mother and brothers are?" He then stretched out his hand toward his disciples. "Look closely. These are my mother and brothers. Obedience is thicker than blood. The person who obeys my heavenly Father's will is my brother and sister and mother."

---

[a] 41 Or *something*; also in verse 42   [b] 43 Greek *unclean*
[c] 47 Some manuscripts do not have verse 47.

NEW INTERNATIONAL VERSION

The Parable of the Sower

13 That same day Jesus went out of the house and sat by the lake. ²Such large crowds gathered around him that he got into a boat and sat in it, while all the people stood on the shore. ³Then he told them many things in parables, saying: "A farmer went out to sow his seed. ⁴As he was scattering the seed, some fell along the path, and the birds came and ate it up. ⁵Some fell on rocky places, where it did not have much soil. It sprang up quickly, because the soil was shallow. ⁶But when the sun came up, the plants were scorched, and they withered because they had no root. ⁷Other seed fell among thorns, which grew up and choked the plants. ⁸Still other seed fell on good soil, where it produced a crop—a hundred, sixty or thirty times what was sown. ⁹He who has ears, let him hear."

¹⁰The disciples came to him and asked, "Why do you speak to the people in parables?"

¹¹He replied, "The knowledge of the secrets of the kingdom of heaven has been given to you, but not to them. ¹²Whoever has will be given more, and he will have an abundance. Whoever does not have, even what he has will be taken from him. ¹³This is why I speak to them in parables:

"Though seeing, they do not see;
    though hearing, they do not hear or
        understand.

¹⁴In them is fulfilled the prophecy of Isaiah:

" 'You will be ever hearing but never
        understanding;
    you will be ever seeing but never
        perceiving.
¹⁵For this people's heart has become calloused;
    they hardly hear with their ears,
    and they have closed their eyes.
Otherwise they might see with their eyes,
    hear with their ears,
    understand with their hearts
and turn, and I would heal them.'ᵃ

¹⁶But blessed are your eyes because they see, and your ears because they hear. ¹⁷For I tell you the truth, many prophets and righteous men longed to see what you see but did not see it, and to hear what you hear but did not hear it.

¹⁸"Listen then to what the parable of the sower means: ¹⁹When anyone hears the message

ᵃ 15 Isaiah 6:9,10

THE MESSAGE

A Harvest Story

13.1-3 **13** At about that same time Jesus left the house and sat on the beach. In no time at all a crowd gathered along the shoreline, forcing him to get into a boat. Using the boat as a pulpit, he addressed his congregation, telling stories.

13.3-8 "What do you make of this? A farmer planted seed. As he scattered the seed, some of it fell on the road, and birds ate it. Some fell in the gravel; it sprouted quickly but didn't put down roots, so when the sun came up it withered just as quickly. Some fell in the weeds; as it came up, it was strangled by the weeds. Some fell on good earth, and produced a harvest beyond his wildest dreams.

13.9 "Are you listening to this? Really listening?"

Why Tell Stories?

13.10 The disciples came up and asked, "Why do you tell stories?"

13.11-15 He replied, "You've been given insight into God's kingdom. You know how it works. Not everybody has this gift, this insight; it hasn't been given to them. Whenever someone has a ready heart for this, the insights and understandings flow freely. But if there is no readiness, any trace of receptivity soon disappears. That's why I tell stories: to create readiness, to nudge the people toward receptive insight. In their present state they can stare till doomsday and not see it, listen till they're blue in the face and not get it. I don't want Isaiah's forecast repeated all over again:

Your ears are open but you don't hear a
        thing.
    Your eyes are awake but you don't see a
        thing.
The people are blockheads!
They stick their fingers in their ears
    so they won't have to listen;
They screw their eyes shut
    so they won't have to look,
    so they won't have to deal with me face-
        to-face
    and let me heal them.

13.16-17 "But you have God-blessed eyes—eyes that see! And God-blessed ears—ears that hear! A lot of people, prophets and humble believers among them, would have given anything to see what you are seeing, to hear what you are hearing, but never had the chance.

The Meaning of the Harvest Story

13.18-19 "Study this story of the farmer planting seed. When anyone hears news of the kingdom and

NEW INTERNATIONAL VERSION

about the kingdom and does not understand it, the evil one comes and snatches away what was sown in his heart. This is the seed sown along the path. 20The one who received the seed that fell on rocky places is the man who hears the word and at once receives it with joy. 21But since he has no root, he lasts only a short time. When trouble or persecution comes because of the word, he quickly falls away. 22The one who received the seed that fell among the thorns is the man who hears the word, but the worries of this life and the deceitfulness of wealth choke it, making it unfruitful. 23But the one who received the seed that fell on good soil is the man who hears the word and understands it. He produces a crop, yielding a hundred, sixty or thirty times what was sown."

THE PARABLE OF THE WEEDS

24Jesus told them another parable: "The kingdom of heaven is like a man who sowed good seed in his field. 25But while everyone was sleeping, his enemy came and sowed weeds among the wheat, and went away. 26When the wheat sprouted and formed heads, then the weeds also appeared.

27"The owner's servants came to him and said, 'Sir, didn't you sow good seed in your field? Where then did the weeds come from?'

28" 'An enemy did this,' he replied.

"The servants asked him, 'Do you want us to go and pull them up?'

29" 'No,' he answered, 'because while you are pulling the weeds, you may root up the wheat with them. 30Let both grow together until the harvest. At that time I will tell the harvesters: First collect the weeds and tie them in bundles to be burned; then gather the wheat and bring it into my barn.' "

THE PARABLES OF THE MUSTARD SEED
AND THE YEAST

31He told them another parable: "The kingdom of heaven is like a mustard seed, which a man took and planted in his field. 32Though it is the smallest of all your seeds, yet when it grows, it is the largest of garden plants and becomes a tree, so that the birds of the air come and perch in its branches."

33He told them still another parable: "The kingdom of heaven is like yeast that a woman took and mixed into a large amount*a* of flour until it worked all through the dough."

34Jesus spoke all these things to the crowd in parables; he did not say anything to them without using a parable. 35So was fulfilled what was spoken through the prophet:

a 33 Greek three satas (probably about 1/2 bushel or 22 liters)

THE MESSAGE

doesn't take it in, it just remains on the surface, and so the Evil One comes along and plucks it right out of that person's heart. This is the seed the farmer scatters on the road.

13.20-21 "The seed cast in the gravel—this is the person who hears and instantly responds with enthusiasm. But there is no soil of character, and so when the emotions wear off and some difficulty arrives, there is nothing to show for it.

13.22 "The seed cast in the weeds is the person who hears the kingdom news, but weeds of worry and illusions about getting more and wanting everything under the sun strangle what was heard, and nothing comes of it.

13.23 "The seed cast on good earth is the person who hears and takes in the News, and then produces a harvest beyond his wildest dreams."

✝

13.24-26 He told another story. "God's kingdom is like a farmer who planted good seed in his field. That night, while his hired men were asleep, his enemy sowed thistles all through the wheat and slipped away before dawn. When the first green shoots appeared and the grain began to form, the thistles showed up, too.

13.27 "The farmhands came to the farmer and said, 'Master, that was clean seed you planted, wasn't it? Where did these thistles come from?'

13.28 "He answered, 'Some enemy did this.'

"The farmhands asked, 'Should we weed out the thistles?'

13.29-30 "He said, 'No, if you weed the thistles, you'll pull up the wheat, too. Let them grow together until harvest time. Then I'll instruct the harvesters to pull up the thistles and tie them in bundles for the fire, then gather the wheat and put it in the barn.' "

13.31-32 Another story. "God's kingdom is like a pine nut that a farmer plants. It is quite small as seeds go, but in the course of years it grows into a huge pine tree, and eagles build nests in it."

13.33 Another story. "God's kingdom is like yeast that a woman works into the dough for dozens of loaves of barley bread—and waits while the dough rises."

13.34-35 All Jesus did that day was tell stories—a long storytelling afternoon. His storytelling fulfilled the prophecy:

NEW INTERNATIONAL VERSION

"I will open my mouth in parables,
  I will utter things hidden since the
    creation of the world." [a]

THE PARABLE OF THE WEEDS EXPLAINED

[36]Then he left the crowd and went into the house. His disciples came to him and said, "Explain to us the parable of the weeds in the field."

[37]He answered, "The one who sowed the good seed is the Son of Man. [38]The field is the world, and the good seed stands for the sons of the kingdom. The weeds are the sons of the evil one, [39]and the enemy who sows them is the devil. The harvest is the end of the age, and the harvesters are angels.

[40]"As the weeds are pulled up and burned in the fire, so it will be at the end of the age. [41]The Son of Man will send out his angels, and they will weed out of his kingdom everything that causes sin and all who do evil. [42]They will throw them into the fiery furnace, where there will be weeping and gnashing of teeth. [43]Then the righteous will shine like the sun in the kingdom of their Father. He who has ears, let him hear.

THE PARABLES OF THE HIDDEN TREASURE AND THE PEARL

[44]"The kingdom of heaven is like treasure hidden in a field. When a man found it, he hid it again, and then in his joy went and sold all he had and bought that field.

[45]"Again, the kingdom of heaven is like a merchant looking for fine pearls. [46]When he found one of great value, he went away and sold everything he had and bought it.

THE PARABLE OF THE NET

[47]"Once again, the kingdom of heaven is like a net that was let down into the lake and caught all kinds of fish. [48]When it was full, the fishermen pulled it up on the shore. Then they sat down and collected the good fish in baskets, but threw the bad away. [49]This is how it will be at the end of the age. The angels will come and separate the wicked from the righteous [50]and throw them into the fiery furnace, where there will be weeping and gnashing of teeth.

[51]"Have you understood all these things?" Jesus asked.

"Yes," they replied.

[52]He said to them, "Therefore every teacher of the law who has been instructed about the kingdom of heaven is like the owner of a house who brings out of his storeroom new treasures as well as old."

a 35 Psalm 78:2

THE MESSAGE

I will open my mouth and tell stories;
  I will bring out into the open
    things hidden since the world's first day.

THE CURTAIN OF HISTORY

13.36 Jesus dismissed the congregation and went into the house. His disciples came in and said, "Explain to us that story of the thistles in the field."

13.37-39 So he explained. "The farmer who sows the pure seed is the Son of Man. The field is the world, the pure seeds are subjects of the kingdom, the thistles are subjects of the Devil, and the enemy who sows them is the Devil. The harvest is the end of the age, the curtain of history. The harvest hands are angels.

13.40-43 "The picture of thistles pulled up and burned is a scene from the final act. The Son of Man will send his angels, weed out the thistles from his kingdom, pitch them in the trash, and be done with them. They are going to complain to high heaven, but nobody is going to listen. At the same time, ripe, holy lives will mature and adorn the kingdom of their Father.

"Are you listening to this? Really listening?

13.44 "God's kingdom is like a treasure hidden in a field for years and then accidently found by a trespasser. The finder is ecstatic—what a find!—and proceeds to sell everything he owns to raise money and buy that field.

13.45-46 "Or, God's kingdom is like a jewel merchant on the hunt for excellent pearls. Finding one that is flawless, he immediately sells everything and buys it.

13.47-50 "Or, God's kingdom is like a fishnet cast into the sea, catching all kinds of fish. When it is full, it is hauled onto the beach. The good fish are picked out and put in a tub; those unfit to eat are thrown away. That's how it will be when the curtain comes down on history. The angels will come and cull the bad fish and throw them in the garbage. There will be a lot of desperate complaining, but it won't do any good."

13.51 Jesus asked, "Are you starting to get a handle on all this?"

They answered, "Yes."

13.52 He said, "Then you see how every student well-trained in God's kingdom is like the owner of a general store who can put his hands on anything you need, old or new, exactly when you need it."

NEW INTERNATIONAL VERSION	THE MESSAGE

NEW INTERNATIONAL VERSION

A Prophet Without Honor

⁵³When Jesus had finished these parables, he moved on from there. ⁵⁴Coming to his hometown, he began teaching the people in their synagogue, and they were amazed. "Where did this man get this wisdom and these miraculous powers?" they asked. ⁵⁵"Isn't this the carpenter's son? Isn't his mother's name Mary, and aren't his brothers James, Joseph, Simon and Judas? ⁵⁶Aren't all his sisters with us? Where then did this man get all these things?" ⁵⁷And they took offense at him.

But Jesus said to them, "Only in his hometown and in his own house is a prophet without honor."

⁵⁸And he did not do many miracles there because of their lack of faith.

John the Baptist Beheaded

14 At that time Herod the tetrarch heard the reports about Jesus, ²and he said to his attendants, "This is John the Baptist; he has risen from the dead! That is why miraculous powers are at work in him."

³Now Herod had arrested John and bound him and put him in prison because of Herodias, his brother Philip's wife, ⁴for John had been saying to him: "It is not lawful for you to have her." ⁵Herod wanted to kill John, but he was afraid of the people, because they considered him a prophet.

⁶On Herod's birthday the daughter of Herodias danced for them and pleased Herod so much ⁷that he promised with an oath to give her whatever she asked. ⁸Prompted by her mother, she said, "Give me here on a platter the head of John the Baptist." ⁹The king was distressed, but because of his oaths and his dinner guests, he ordered that her request be granted ¹⁰and had John beheaded in the prison. ¹¹His head was brought in on a platter and given to the girl, who carried it to her mother. ¹²John's disciples came and took his body and buried it. Then they went and told Jesus.

Jesus Feeds the Five Thousand

¹³When Jesus heard what had happened, he withdrew by boat privately to a solitary place. Hearing of this, the crowds followed him on foot from the towns. ¹⁴When Jesus landed and saw a large crowd, he had compassion on them and healed their sick.

¹⁵As evening approached, the disciples came to him and said, "This is a remote place, and it's already getting late. Send the crowds away, so they can go to the villages and buy themselves some food."

THE MESSAGE

13.53-57 When Jesus finished telling these stories, he left there, returned to his hometown, and gave a lecture in the meetinghouse. He made a real hit, impressing everyone. "We had no idea he was this good!" they said. "How did he get so wise, get such ability?" But in the next breath they were cutting him down: "We've known him since he was a kid; he's the carpenter's son. We know his mother, Mary. We know his brothers James and Joseph, Simon and Judas. All his sisters live here. Who does he think he is?" They got their noses all out of joint.

13.58 But Jesus said, "A prophet is taken for granted in his hometown and his family." He didn't do many miracles there because of their hostile indifference.

The Death of John

14.1-2 **14** At about this time, Herod, the regional ruler, heard what was being said about Jesus. He said to his servants, "This has to be John the Baptizer come back from the dead. That's why he's able to work miracles!"

14.3-5 Herod had arrested John, put him in chains, and sent him to prison to placate Herodias, his brother Philip's wife. John had provoked Herod by naming his relationship with Herodias "adultery." Herod wanted to kill him, but was afraid because so many people revered John as a prophet of God.

14.6-12 But at his birthday celebration, he got his chance. Herodias's daughter provided the entertainment, dancing for the guests. She swept Herod away. In his drunken enthusiasm, he promised her on oath anything she wanted. Already coached by her mother, she was ready: "Give me, served up on a platter, the head of John the Baptizer." That sobered the king up fast. Unwilling to lose face with his guests, he did it—ordered John's head cut off and presented to the girl on a platter. She in turn gave it to her mother. Later, John's disciples got the body, gave it a reverent burial, and reported to Jesus.

Supper for Five Thousand

14.13-14 When Jesus got the news, he slipped away by boat to an out-of-the-way place by himself. But unsuccessfully—someone saw him and the word got around. Soon a lot of people from the nearby villages walked around the lake to where he was. When he saw them coming, he was overcome with pity and healed their sick.

14.15 Toward evening the disciples approached him. "We're out in the country and it's getting late. Dismiss the people so they can go to the villages and get some supper."

NEW INTERNATIONAL VERSION

¹⁶Jesus replied, "They do not need to go away. You give them something to eat."

¹⁷"We have here only five loaves of bread and two fish," they answered.

¹⁸"Bring them here to me," he said. ¹⁹And he directed the people to sit down on the grass. Taking the five loaves and the two fish and looking up to heaven, he gave thanks and broke the loaves. Then he gave them to the disciples, and the disciples gave them to the people. ²⁰They all ate and were satisfied, and the disciples picked up twelve basketfuls of broken pieces that were left over. ²¹The number of those who ate was about five thousand men, besides women and children.

JESUS WALKS ON THE WATER

²²Immediately Jesus made the disciples get into the boat and go on ahead of him to the other side, while he dismissed the crowd. ²³After he had dismissed them, he went up on a mountainside by himself to pray. When evening came, he was there alone, ²⁴but the boat was already a considerable distance^a from land, buffeted by the waves because the wind was against it.

²⁵During the fourth watch of the night Jesus went out to them, walking on the lake. ²⁶When the disciples saw him walking on the lake, they were terrified. "It's a ghost," they said, and cried out in fear.

²⁷But Jesus immediately said to them: "Take courage! It is I. Don't be afraid."

²⁸"Lord, if it's you," Peter replied, "tell me to come to you on the water."

²⁹"Come," he said.

Then Peter got down out of the boat, walked on the water and came toward Jesus. ³⁰But when he saw the wind, he was afraid and, beginning to sink, cried out, "Lord, save me!"

³¹Immediately Jesus reached out his hand and caught him. "You of little faith," he said, "why did you doubt?"

³²And when they climbed into the boat, the wind died down. ³³Then those who were in the boat worshiped him, saying, "Truly you are the Son of God."

³⁴When they had crossed over, they landed at Gennesaret. ³⁵And when the men of that place recognized Jesus, they sent word to all the surrounding country. People brought all their sick to him ³⁶and begged him to let the sick just touch the edge of his cloak, and all who touched him were healed.

^a 24 Greek *many stadia*

THE MESSAGE

14.16 But Jesus said, "There is no need to dismiss them. You give them supper."

14.17 "All we have are five loaves of bread and two fish," they said.

14.18-21 Jesus said, "Bring them here." Then he had the people sit on the grass. He took the five loaves and two fish, lifted his face to heaven in prayer, blessed, broke, and gave the bread to the disciples. The disciples then gave the food to the congregation. They all ate their fill. They gathered twelve baskets of leftovers. About five thousand were fed.

WALKING ON THE WATER

14.22-23 As soon as the meal was finished, he insisted that the disciples get in the boat and go on ahead to the other side while he dismissed the people. With the crowd dispersed, he climbed the mountain so he could be by himself and pray. He stayed there alone, late into the night.

14.24-26 Meanwhile, the boat was far out to sea when the wind came up against them and they were battered by the waves. At about four o'clock in the morning, Jesus came toward them walking on the water. They were scared out of their wits. "A ghost!" they said, crying out in terror.

14.27 But Jesus was quick to comfort them. "Courage, it's me. Don't be afraid."

14.28 Peter, suddenly bold, said, "Master, if it's really you, call me to come to you on the water."

14.29-30 He said, "Come ahead."

Jumping out of the boat, Peter walked on the water to Jesus. But when he looked down at the waves churning beneath his feet, he lost his nerve and started to sink. He cried, "Master, save me!"

14.31 Jesus didn't hesitate. He reached down and grabbed his hand. Then he said, "Faint-heart, what got into you?"

14.32-33 The two of them climbed into the boat, and the wind died down. The disciples in the boat, having watched the whole thing, worshiped Jesus, saying, "This is it! You are God's Son for sure!"

14.34-36 On return, they beached the boat at Gennesaret. When the people got wind that he was back, they sent out word through the neighborhood and rounded up all the sick, who asked for permission to touch the edge of his coat. And whoever touched him was healed.

NEW INTERNATIONAL VERSION

CLEAN AND UNCLEAN

15 Then some Pharisees and teachers of the law came to Jesus from Jerusalem and asked, ²"Why do your disciples break the tradition of the elders? They don't wash their hands before they eat!"

³Jesus replied, "And why do you break the command of God for the sake of your tradition? ⁴For God said, 'Honor your father and mother'ᵃ and 'Anyone who curses his father or mother must be put to death.'ᵇ ⁵But you say that if a man says to his father or mother, 'Whatever help you might otherwise have received from me is a gift devoted to God,' ⁶he is not to 'honor his father'ᶜ with it. Thus you nullify the word of God for the sake of your tradition. ⁷You hypocrites! Isaiah was right when he prophesied about you:

⁸ " 'These people honor me with their lips,
    but their hearts are far from me.
⁹They worship me in vain;
    their teachings are but rules taught by
        men.'ᵈ"

¹⁰Jesus called the crowd to him and said, "Listen and understand. ¹¹What goes into a man's mouth does not make him 'unclean,' but what comes out of his mouth, that is what makes him 'unclean.' "

¹²Then the disciples came to him and asked, "Do you know that the Pharisees were offended when they heard this?"

¹³He replied, "Every plant that my heavenly Father has not planted will be pulled up by the roots. ¹⁴Leave them; they are blind guides.ᵉ If a blind man leads a blind man, both will fall into a pit."

¹⁵Peter said, "Explain the parable to us."

¹⁶"Are you still so dull?" Jesus asked them. ¹⁷"Don't you see that whatever enters the mouth goes into the stomach and then out of the body? ¹⁸But the things that come out of the mouth come from the heart, and these make a man 'unclean.' ¹⁹For out of the heart come evil thoughts, murder, adultery, sexual immorality, theft, false testimony, slander. ²⁰These are what make a man 'unclean'; but eating with unwashed hands does not make him 'unclean.' "

THE FAITH OF THE CANAANITE WOMAN

²¹Leaving that place, Jesus withdrew to the region of Tyre and Sidon. ²²A Canaanite woman from that vicinity came to him, crying out, "Lord, Son of David, have mercy on me! My daughter is suffering terribly from demon-possession."

ᵃ 4 Exodus 20:12; Deut. 5:16   ᵇ 4 Exodus 21:17; Lev. 20:9
ᶜ 6 Some manuscripts *father or his mother*
ᵈ 9 Isaiah 29:13   ᵉ 14 Some manuscripts *guides of the blind*

THE MESSAGE

WHAT POLLUTES YOUR LIFE

15.1-2 **15** After that, Pharisees and religion scholars came to Jesus all the way from Jerusalem, criticizing, "Why do your disciples play fast and loose with the rules?"

15.3-9 But Jesus put it right back on them. "Why do you use your rules to play fast and loose with God's commands? God clearly says, 'Respect your father and mother,' and, 'Anyone denouncing father or mother should be killed.' But you weasel around that by saying, 'Whoever wants to, can say to father and mother, What I owed to you I've given to God.' That can hardly be called respecting a parent. You cancel God's command by your rules. Frauds! Isaiah's prophecy of you hit the bull's-eye:

These people make a big show of saying the
        right thing,
    but their heart isn't in it.
They act like they're worshiping me,
    but they don't mean it.
They just use me as a cover
    for teaching whatever suits their fancy."

15.10-11 He then called the crowd together and said, "Listen, and take this to heart. It's not what you swallow that pollutes your life, but what you vomit up."

15.12 Later his disciples came and told him, "Did you know how upset the Pharisees were when they heard what you said?"

15.13-14 Jesus shrugged it off. "Every tree that wasn't planted by my Father in heaven will be pulled up by its roots. Forget them. They are blind men leading blind men. When a blind man leads a blind man, they both end up in the ditch."

15.15 Peter said, "I don't get it. Put it in plain language."

15.16-20 Jesus replied, "You too? Are you being willfully stupid? Don't you know that anything that is swallowed works its way through the intestines and is finally defecated? But what comes out of the mouth gets its start in the heart. It's from the heart that we vomit up evil arguments, murders, adulteries, fornications, thefts, lies, and cussing. That's what pollutes. Eating or not eating certain foods, washing or not washing your hands—that's neither here nor there."

HEALING THE PEOPLE

15.21-22 From there Jesus took a trip to Tyre and Sidon. They had hardly arrived when a Canaanite woman came down from the hills and pleaded, "Mercy, Master, Son of David! My daughter is cruelly afflicted by an evil spirit."

NEW INTERNATIONAL VERSION

²³Jesus did not answer a word. So his disciples came to him and urged him, "Send her away, for she keeps crying out after us."

²⁴He answered, "I was sent only to the lost sheep of Israel."

²⁵The woman came and knelt before him. "Lord, help me!" she said.

²⁶He replied, "It is not right to take the children's bread and toss it to their dogs."

²⁷"Yes, Lord," she said, "but even the dogs eat the crumbs that fall from their masters' table."

²⁸Then Jesus answered, "Woman, you have great faith! Your request is granted." And her daughter was healed from that very hour.

JESUS FEEDS THE FOUR THOUSAND

²⁹Jesus left there and went along the Sea of Galilee. Then he went up on a mountainside and sat down. ³⁰Great crowds came to him, bringing the lame, the blind, the crippled, the mute and many others, and laid them at his feet; and he healed them. ³¹The people were amazed when they saw the mute speaking, the crippled made well, the lame walking and the blind seeing. And they praised the God of Israel.

³²Jesus called his disciples to him and said, "I have compassion for these people; they have already been with me three days and have nothing to eat. I do not want to send them away hungry, or they may collapse on the way."

³³His disciples answered, "Where could we get enough bread in this remote place to feed such a crowd?"

³⁴"How many loaves do you have?" Jesus asked.

"Seven," they replied, "and a few small fish."

³⁵He told the crowd to sit down on the ground. ³⁶Then he took the seven loaves and the fish, and when he had given thanks, he broke them and gave them to the disciples, and they in turn to the people. ³⁷They all ate and were satisfied. Afterward the disciples picked up seven basketfuls of broken pieces that were left over. ³⁸The number of those who ate was four thousand, besides women and children. ³⁹After Jesus had sent the crowd away, he got into the boat and went to the vicinity of Magadan.

THE DEMAND FOR A SIGN

16 The Pharisees and Sadducees came to Jesus and tested him by asking him to show them a sign from heaven.

THE MESSAGE

15.23 Jesus ignored her. The disciples came and complained, "Now she's bothering us. Would you please take care of her? She's driving us crazy."

15.24 Jesus refused, telling them, "I've got my hands full dealing with the lost sheep of Israel."

15.25 Then the woman came back to Jesus, went to her knees, and begged. "Master, help me."

15.26 He said, "It's not right to take bread out of children's mouths and throw it to dogs."

15.27 She was quick: "You're right, Master, but beggar dogs do get scraps from the master's table."

15.28 Jesus gave in. "Oh, woman, your faith is something else. What you want is what you get!" Right then her daughter became well.

15.29-31 After Jesus returned, he walked along Lake Galilee and then climbed a mountain and took his place, ready to receive visitors. They came, tons of them, bringing along the paraplegic, the blind, the maimed, the mute—all sorts of people in need—and more or less threw them down at Jesus' feet to see what he would do with them. He healed them. When the people saw the mutes speaking, the maimed healthy, the paraplegics walking around, the blind looking around, they were astonished and let everyone know that God was blazingly alive among them.

✝

15.32 But Jesus wasn't finished with them. He called his disciples and said, "I hurt for these people. For three days now they've been with me, and now they have nothing to eat. I can't send them away without a meal—they'd probably collapse on the road."

15.33 His disciples said, "But where in this deserted place are you going to dig up enough food for a meal?"

15.34-39 Jesus asked, "How much bread do you have?"

"Seven loaves," they said, "plus a few fish." At that, Jesus directed the people to sit down. He took the seven loaves and the fish. After giving thanks, he divided it up and gave it to the people. Everyone ate. They had all they wanted. It took seven large baskets to collect the leftovers. Over four thousand people ate their fill at that meal. After Jesus sent them away, he climbed in the boat and crossed over to the Magadan hills.

SOME BAD YEAST

16.1-4 **16** Some Pharisees and Sadducees were on him again, pressing him to prove himself to them. He told them, "You have a saying that

NEW INTERNATIONAL VERSION

[2]He replied,[a] "When evening comes, you say, 'It will be fair weather, for the sky is red,' [3]and in the morning, 'Today it will be stormy, for the sky is red and overcast.' You know how to interpret the appearance of the sky, but you cannot interpret the signs of the times. [4]A wicked and adulterous generation looks for a miraculous sign, but none will be given it except the sign of Jonah." Jesus then left them and went away.

THE YEAST OF THE PHARISEES AND SADDUCEES

[5]When they went across the lake, the disciples forgot to take bread. [6]"Be careful," Jesus said to them. "Be on your guard against the yeast of the Pharisees and Sadducees."

[7]They discussed this among themselves and said, "It is because we didn't bring any bread."

[8]Aware of their discussion, Jesus asked, "You of little faith, why are you talking among yourselves about having no bread? [9]Do you still not understand? Don't you remember the five loaves for the five thousand, and how many basketfuls you gathered? [10]Or the seven loaves for the four thousand, and how many basketfuls you gathered? [11]How is it you don't understand that I was not talking to you about bread? But be on your guard against the yeast of the Pharisees and Sadducees." [12]Then they understood that he was not telling them to guard against the yeast used in bread, but against the teaching of the Pharisees and Sadducees.

PETER'S CONFESSION OF CHRIST

[13]When Jesus came to the region of Caesarea Philippi, he asked his disciples, "Who do people say the Son of Man is?"

[14]They replied, "Some say John the Baptist; others say Elijah; and still others, Jeremiah or one of the prophets."

[15]"But what about you?" he asked. "Who do you say I am?"

[16]Simon Peter answered, "You are the Christ,[b] the Son of the living God."

[17]Jesus replied, "Blessed are you, Simon son of Jonah, for this was not revealed to you by man, but by my Father in heaven. [18]And I tell you that you are Peter,[c] and on this rock I will build my church, and the gates of Hades[d] will not overcome it.[e] [19]I will give you the keys of the kingdom of heaven; whatever you bind on earth will be[f] bound in heaven, and whatever you loose on earth will be[f] loosed in heaven." [20]Then he warned his disciples not to tell anyone that he was the Christ.

[a] 2 Some early manuscripts do not have the rest of verse 2 and all of verse 3.   [b] 16 Or Messiah; also in verse 20
[c] 18 Peter means rock.   [d] 18 Or hell   [e] 18 Or not prove stronger than it   [f] 19 Or have been

THE MESSAGE

goes, 'Red sky at night, sailor's delight; red sky at morning, sailors take warning.' You find it easy enough to forecast the weather—why can't you read the signs of the times? An evil and wanton generation is always wanting signs and wonders. The only sign you'll get is the Jonah sign." Then he turned on his heel and walked away.

16.5-6 On their way to the other side of the lake, the disciples discovered they had forgotten to bring along bread. In the meantime, Jesus said to them, "Keep a sharp eye out for Pharisee-Sadducee yeast."

16.7-12 Thinking he was scolding them for forgetting bread, they discussed in whispers what to do. Jesus knew what they were doing and said, "Why all these worried whispers about forgetting the bread? Runt believers! Haven't you caught on yet? Don't you remember the five loaves of bread and the five thousand people, and how many baskets of fragments you picked up? Or the seven loaves that fed four thousand, and how many baskets of leftovers you collected? Haven't you realized yet that bread isn't the problem? The problem is yeast, Pharisee-Sadducee yeast." Then they got it: that he wasn't concerned about eating, but teaching—the Pharisee-Sadducee kind of teaching.

SON OF MAN, SON OF GOD

16.13 When Jesus arrived in the villages of Caesarea Philippi, he asked his disciples, "What are people saying about who the Son of Man is?"

16.14 They replied, "Some think he is John the Baptizer, some say Elijah, some Jeremiah or one of the other prophets."

16.15 He pressed them, "And how about you? Who do you say I am?"

16.16 Simon Peter said, "You're the Christ, the Messiah, the Son of the living God."

16.17-18 Jesus came back, "God bless you, Simon, son of Jonah! You didn't get that answer out of books or from teachers. My Father in heaven, God himself, let you in on this secret of who I really am. And now I'm going to tell you who you are, really are. You are Peter, a rock. This is the rock on which I will put together my church, a church so expansive with energy that not even the gates of hell will be able to keep it out.

16.19 "And that's not all. You will have complete and free access to God's kingdom, keys to open any and every door: no more barriers between heaven and earth, earth and heaven. A yes on earth is yes in heaven. A no on earth is no in heaven."

16.20 He swore the disciples to secrecy. He made them promise they would tell no one that he was the Messiah.

NEW INTERNATIONAL VERSION

JESUS PREDICTS HIS DEATH

21From that time on Jesus began to explain to his disciples that he must go to Jerusalem and suffer many things at the hands of the elders, chief priests and teachers of the law, and that he must be killed and on the third day be raised to life.

22Peter took him aside and began to rebuke him. "Never, Lord!" he said. "This shall never happen to you!"

23Jesus turned and said to Peter, "Get behind me, Satan! You are a stumbling block to me; you do not have in mind the things of God, but the things of men."

24Then Jesus said to his disciples, "If anyone would come after me, he must deny himself and take up his cross and follow me. 25For whoever wants to save his life*a* will lose it, but whoever loses his life for me will find it. 26What good will it be for a man if he gains the whole world, yet forfeits his soul? Or what can a man give in exchange for his soul? 27For the Son of Man is going to come in his Father's glory with his angels, and then he will reward each person according to what he has done. 28I tell you the truth, some who are standing here will not taste death before they see the Son of Man coming in his kingdom."

THE TRANSFIGURATION

17 After six days Jesus took with him Peter, James and John the brother of James, and led them up a high mountain by themselves. 2There he was transfigured before them. His face shone like the sun, and his clothes became as white as the light. 3Just then there appeared before them Moses and Elijah, talking with Jesus.

4Peter said to Jesus, "Lord, it is good for us to be here. If you wish, I will put up three shelters—one for you, one for Moses and one for Elijah."

5While he was still speaking, a bright cloud enveloped them, and a voice from the cloud said, "This is my Son, whom I love; with him I am well pleased. Listen to him!"

6When the disciples heard this, they fell facedown to the ground, terrified. 7But Jesus came and touched them. "Get up," he said. "Don't be afraid." 8When they looked up, they saw no one except Jesus.

9As they were coming down the mountain, Jesus instructed them, "Don't tell anyone what you have seen, until the Son of Man has been raised from the dead."

a 25 The Greek word means either *life* or *soul*; also in verse 26.

THE MESSAGE

YOU'RE NOT IN THE DRIVER'S SEAT

16.21-22 Then Jesus made it clear to his disciples that it was now necessary for him to go to Jerusalem, submit to an ordeal of suffering at the hands of the religious leaders, be killed, and then on the third day be raised up alive. Peter took him in hand, protesting, "Impossible, Master! That can never be!"

16.23 But Jesus didn't swerve. "Peter, get out of my way. Satan, get lost. You have no idea how God works."

16.24-26 Then Jesus went to work on his disciples. "Anyone who intends to come with me has to let me lead. You're not in the driver's seat; *I* am. Don't run from suffering; embrace it. Follow me and I'll show you how. Self-help is no help at all. Self-sacrifice is the way, my way, to finding yourself, your true self. What kind of deal is it to get everything you want but lose yourself? What could you ever trade your soul for?

16.27-28 "Don't be in such a hurry to go into business for yourself. Before you know it the Son of Man will arrive with all the splendor of his Father, accompanied by an army of angels. You'll get everything you have coming to you, a personal gift. This isn't pie in the sky by and by. Some of you standing here are going to see it take place, see the Son of Man in kingdom glory."

SUNLIGHT POURED FROM HIS FACE

17.1-3 **17** Six days later, three of them saw that glory. Jesus took Peter and the brothers, James and John, and led them up a high mountain. His appearance changed from the inside out, right before their eyes. Sunlight poured from his face. His clothes were filled with light. Then they realized that Moses and Elijah were also there in deep conversation with him.

17.4 Peter broke in, "Master, this is a great moment! What would you think if I built three memorials here on the mountain—one for you, one for Moses, one for Elijah?"

17.5 While he was going on like this, babbling, a light-radiant cloud enveloped them, and sounding from deep in the cloud a voice: "This is my Son, marked by my love, focus of my delight. Listen to him."

17.6-8 When the disciples heard it, they fell flat on their faces, scared to death. But Jesus came over and touched them. "Don't be afraid." When they opened their eyes and looked around all they saw was Jesus, only Jesus.

17.9 Coming down the mountain, Jesus swore them to secrecy. "Don't breathe a word of what you've seen. After the Son of Man is raised from the dead, you are free to talk."

NEW INTERNATIONAL VERSION

¹⁰The disciples asked him, "Why then do the teachers of the law say that Elijah must come first?"

¹¹Jesus replied, "To be sure, Elijah comes and will restore all things. ¹²But I tell you, Elijah has already come, and they did not recognize him, but have done to him everything they wished. In the same way the Son of Man is going to suffer at their hands." ¹³Then the disciples understood that he was talking to them about John the Baptist.

THE HEALING OF A BOY WITH A DEMON

¹⁴When they came to the crowd, a man approached Jesus and knelt before him. ¹⁵"Lord, have mercy on my son," he said. "He has seizures and is suffering greatly. He often falls into the fire or into the water. ¹⁶I brought him to your disciples, but they could not heal him."

¹⁷"O unbelieving and perverse generation," Jesus replied, "how long shall I stay with you? How long shall I put up with you? Bring the boy here to me." ¹⁸Jesus rebuked the demon, and it came out of the boy, and he was healed from that moment.

¹⁹Then the disciples came to Jesus in private and asked, "Why couldn't we drive it out?"

²⁰He replied, "Because you have so little faith. I tell you the truth, if you have faith as small as a mustard seed, you can say to this mountain, 'Move from here to there' and it will move. Nothing will be impossible for you.ᵃ"

²²When they came together in Galilee, he said to them, "The Son of Man is going to be betrayed into the hands of men. ²³They will kill him, and on the third day he will be raised to life." And the disciples were filled with grief.

THE TEMPLE TAX

²⁴After Jesus and his disciples arrived in Capernaum, the collectors of the two-drachma tax came to Peter and asked, "Doesn't your teacher pay the temple taxᵇ?"

²⁵"Yes, he does," he replied.

When Peter came into the house, Jesus was the first to speak. "What do you think, Simon?" he asked. "From whom do the kings of the earth collect duty and taxes—from their own sons or from others?"

²⁶"From others," Peter answered.

"Then the sons are exempt," Jesus said to him. ²⁷"But so that we may not offend them, go

THE MESSAGE

17.10   The disciples, meanwhile, were asking questions. "Why do the religion scholars say that Elijah has to come first?"

17.11-13   Jesus answered, "Elijah does come and get everything ready. I'm telling you, Elijah has already come but they didn't know him when they saw him. They treated him like dirt, the same way they are about to treat the Son of Man." That's when the disciples realized that all along he had been talking about John the Baptizer.

WITH A MERE KERNEL OF FAITH

17.14-16   At the bottom of the mountain, they were met by a crowd of waiting people. As they approached, a man came out of the crowd and fell to his knees begging, "Master, have mercy on my son. He goes out of his mind and suffers terribly, falling into seizures. Frequently he is pitched into the fire, other times into the river. I brought him to your disciples, but they could do nothing for him."

17.17-18   Jesus said, "What a generation! No sense of God! No focus to your lives! How many times do I have to go over these things? How much longer do I have to put up with this? Bring the boy here." He ordered the afflicting demon out—and it was out, gone. From that moment on the boy was well.

17.19   When the disciples had Jesus off to themselves, they asked, "Why couldn't we throw it out?"

17.20   "Because you're not yet taking *God* seriously," said Jesus. "The simple truth is that if you had a mere kernel of faith, a poppy seed, say, you would tell this mountain, 'Move!' and it would move. There is nothing you wouldn't be able to tackle."

17.22-23   As they were regrouping in Galilee, Jesus told them, "The Son of Man is about to be betrayed to some people who want nothing to do with God. They will murder him—and three days later he will be raised alive." The disciples felt terrible.

✠

17.24   When they arrived at Capernaum, the tax men came to Peter and asked, "Does your teacher pay taxes?"

17.25   Peter said, "Of course."

But as soon as they were in the house, Jesus confronted him. "Simon, what do you think? When a king levies taxes, who pays—his children or his subjects?"

17.26-27   He answered, "His subjects."

Jesus said, "Then the children get off free, right? But so we don't upset them needlessly, go

---

ᵃ 20 Some manuscripts *you.* ²¹*But this kind does not go out except by prayer and fasting.*   ᵇ 24 Greek *the two drachmas*

NEW INTERNATIONAL VERSION

to the lake and throw out your line. Take the first fish you catch; open its mouth and you will find a four-drachma coin. Take it and give it to them for my tax and yours."

THE GREATEST IN THE KINGDOM OF HEAVEN

18 At that time the disciples came to Jesus and asked, "Who is the greatest in the kingdom of heaven?"

²He called a little child and had him stand among them. ³And he said: "I tell you the truth, unless you change and become like little children, you will never enter the kingdom of heaven. ⁴Therefore, whoever humbles himself like this child is the greatest in the kingdom of heaven.

⁵"And whoever welcomes a little child like this in my name welcomes me. ⁶But if anyone causes one of these little ones who believe in me to sin, it would be better for him to have a large millstone hung around his neck and to be drowned in the depths of the sea.

⁷"Woe to the world because of the things that cause people to sin! Such things must come, but woe to the man through whom they come! ⁸If your hand or your foot causes you to sin, cut it off and throw it away. It is better for you to enter life maimed or crippled than to have two hands or two feet and be thrown into eternal fire. ⁹And if your eye causes you to sin, gouge it out and throw it away. It is better for you to enter life with one eye than to have two eyes and be thrown into the fire of hell.

THE PARABLE OF THE LOST SHEEP

¹⁰"See that you do not look down on one of these little ones. For I tell you that their angels in heaven always see the face of my Father in heaven. *a*

¹²"What do you think? If a man owns a hundred sheep, and one of them wanders away, will he not leave the ninety-nine on the hills and go to look for the one that wandered off? ¹³And if he finds it, I tell you the truth, he is happier about that one sheep than about the ninety-nine that did not wander off. ¹⁴In the same way your Father in heaven is not willing that any of these little ones should be lost.

A BROTHER WHO SINS AGAINST YOU

¹⁵"If your brother sins against you, *b* go and show him his fault, just between the two of you. If he listens to you, you have won your brother over. ¹⁶But if he will not listen, take one or two others

---

THE MESSAGE

down to the lake, cast a hook, and pull in the first fish that bites. Open its mouth and you'll find a coin. Take it and give it to the tax men. It will be enough for both of us."

WHOEVER BECOMES SIMPLE AGAIN

18.1 **18** At about the same time, the disciples came to Jesus asking, "Who gets the highest rank in God's kingdom?"

18.2-5 For an answer Jesus called over a child, whom he stood in the middle of the room, and said, "I'm telling you, once and for all, that unless you return to square one and start over like children, you're not even going to get a look at the kingdom, let alone get in. Whoever becomes simple and elemental again, like this child, will rank high in God's kingdom. What's more, when you receive the childlike on my account, it's the same as receiving me.

18.6-7 "But if you give them a hard time, bullying or taking advantage of their simple trust, you'll soon wish you hadn't. You'd be better off dropped in the middle of the lake with a millstone around your neck. Doom to the world for giving these God-believing children a hard time! Hard times are inevitable, but you don't have to make it worse—and it's doomsday to you if you do.

18.8-9 "If your hand or your foot gets in the way of God, chop it off and throw it away. You're better off maimed or lame and alive than the proud owners of two hands and two feet, godless in a furnace of eternal fire. And if your eye distracts you from God, pull it out and throw it away. You're better off one-eyed and alive than exercising your twenty-twenty vision from inside the fire of hell.

18.10 "Watch that you don't treat a single one of these childlike believers arrogantly. You realize, don't you, that their personal angels are constantly in touch with my Father in heaven?

WORK IT OUT BETWEEN YOU

18.12-14 "Look at it this way. If someone has a hundred sheep and one of them wanders off, doesn't he leave the ninety-nine and go after the one? And if he finds it, doesn't he make far more over it than over the ninety-nine who stay put? Your Father in heaven feels the same way. He doesn't want to lose even one of these simple believers.

18.15-17 "If a fellow believer hurts you, go and tell him—work it out between the two of you. If he listens, you've made a friend. If he won't listen, take one or two others along so that the pres-

---

a 10 Some manuscripts *heaven. ¹¹The Son of Man came to save what was lost.*   *b 15* Some manuscripts do not have *against you.*

NEW INTERNATIONAL VERSION

along, so that 'every matter may be established by the testimony of two or three witnesses.'ᵃ ¹⁷If he refuses to listen to them, tell it to the church; and if he refuses to listen even to the church, treat him as you would a pagan or a tax collector.

¹⁸"I tell you the truth, whatever you bind on earth will beᵇ bound in heaven, and whatever you loose on earth will beᵇ loosed in heaven.

¹⁹"Again, I tell you that if two of you on earth agree about anything you ask for, it will be done for you by my Father in heaven. ²⁰For where two or three come together in my name, there am I with them."

THE PARABLE OF THE UNMERCIFUL SERVANT

²¹Then Peter came to Jesus and asked, "Lord, how many times shall I forgive my brother when he sins against me? Up to seven times?"

²²Jesus answered, "I tell you, not seven times, but seventy-seven times.ᶜ

²³"Therefore, the kingdom of heaven is like a king who wanted to settle accounts with his servants. ²⁴As he began the settlement, a man who owed him ten thousand talentsᵈ was brought to him. ²⁵Since he was not able to pay, the master ordered that he and his wife and his children and all that he had be sold to repay the debt.

²⁶"The servant fell on his knees before him. 'Be patient with me,' he begged, 'and I will pay back everything.' ²⁷The servant's master took pity on him, canceled the debt and let him go.

²⁸"But when that servant went out, he found one of his fellow servants who owed him a hundred denarii.ᵉ He grabbed him and began to choke him. 'Pay back what you owe me!' he demanded.

²⁹"His fellow servant fell to his knees and begged him, 'Be patient with me, and I will pay you back.'

³⁰"But he refused. Instead, he went off and had the man thrown into prison until he could pay the debt. ³¹When the other servants saw what had happened, they were greatly distressed and went and told their master everything that had happened.

³²"Then the master called the servant in. 'You wicked servant,' he said, 'I canceled all that debt of yours because you begged me to. ³³Shouldn't you have had mercy on your fellow servant just as I had on you?' ³⁴In anger his master turned him over to the jailers to be tortured, until he should pay back all he owed.

³⁵"This is how my heavenly Father will treat each of you unless you forgive your brother from your heart."

THE MESSAGE

ence of witnesses will keep things honest, and try again. If he still won't listen, tell the church. If he won't listen to the church, you'll have to start over from scratch, confront him with the need for repentance, and offer again God's forgiving love.

18.18-20   "Take this most seriously: A yes on earth is yes in heaven; a no on earth is no in heaven. What you say to one another is eternal. I mean this. When two of you get together on anything at all on earth and make a prayer of it, my Father in heaven goes into action. And when two or three of you are together because of me, you can be sure that I'll be there."

A STORY ABOUT FORGIVENESS

18.21   At that point Peter got up the nerve to ask, "Master, how many times do I forgive a brother or sister who hurts me? Seven?"

18.22   Jesus replied, "Seven! Hardly. Try seventy times seven.

18.23-25   "The kingdom of God is like a king who decided to square accounts with his servants. As he got under way, one servant was brought before him who had run up a debt of a hundred thousand dollars. He couldn't pay up, so the king ordered the man, along with his wife, children, and goods, to be auctioned off at the slave market.

18.26-27   "The poor wretch threw himself at the king's feet and begged, 'Give me a chance and I'll pay it all back.' Touched by his plea, the king let him off, erasing the debt.

18.28   "The servant was no sooner out of the room when he came upon one of his fellow servants who owed him ten dollars. He seized him by the throat and demanded, 'Pay up. Now!'

18.29-31   "The poor wretch threw himself down and begged, 'Give me a chance and I'll pay it all back.' But he wouldn't do it. He had him arrested and put in jail until the debt was paid. When the other servants saw this going on, they were outraged and brought a detailed report to the king.

18.32-35   "The king summoned the man and said, 'You evil servant! I forgave your entire debt when you begged me for mercy. Shouldn't you be compelled to be merciful to your fellow servant who asked for mercy?' The king was furious and put the screws to the man until he paid back his entire debt. And that's exactly what my Father in heaven is going to do to each one of you who doesn't forgive unconditionally anyone who asks for mercy."

ᵃ 16 Deut. 19:15   ᵇ 18 Or have been   ᶜ 22 Or seventy times seven   ᵈ 24 That is, millions of dollars   ᵉ 28 That is, a few dollars

NEW INTERNATIONAL VERSION	THE MESSAGE

DIVORCE

19 When Jesus had finished saying these things, he left Galilee and went into the region of Judea to the other side of the Jordan. ²Large crowds followed him, and he healed them there.

³Some Pharisees came to him to test him. They asked, "Is it lawful for a man to divorce his wife for any and every reason?"

⁴"Haven't you read," he replied, "that at the beginning the Creator 'made them male and female,'ᵃ ⁵and said, 'For this reason a man will leave his father and mother and be united to his wife, and the two will become one flesh'ᵇ? ⁶So they are no longer two, but one. Therefore what God has joined together, let man not separate."

⁷"Why then," they asked, "did Moses command that a man give his wife a certificate of divorce and send her away?"

⁸Jesus replied, "Moses permitted you to divorce your wives because your hearts were hard. But it was not this way from the beginning. ⁹I tell you that anyone who divorces his wife, except for marital unfaithfulness, and marries another woman commits adultery."

¹⁰The disciples said to him, "If this is the situation between a husband and wife, it is better not to marry."

¹¹Jesus replied, "Not everyone can accept this word, but only those to whom it has been given. ¹²For some are eunuchs because they were born that way; others were made that way by men; and others have renounced marriageᶜ because of the kingdom of heaven. The one who can accept this should accept it."

THE LITTLE CHILDREN AND JESUS

¹³Then little children were brought to Jesus for him to place his hands on them and pray for them. But the disciples rebuked those who brought them.

¹⁴Jesus said, "Let the little children come to me, and do not hinder them, for the kingdom of heaven belongs to such as these." ¹⁵When he had placed his hands on them, he went on from there.

THE RICH YOUNG MAN

¹⁶Now a man came up to Jesus and asked, "Teacher, what good thing must I do to get eternal life?"

¹⁷"Why do you ask me about what is good?" Jesus replied. "There is only One who is good. If you want to enter life, obey the commandments."

ᵃ 4 Gen. 1:27   ᵇ 5 Gen. 2:24   ᶜ 12 Or *have made themselves eunuchs*

DIVORCE

19 When Jesus had completed these teachings, he left Galilee and crossed the region of Judea on the other side of the Jordan. Great crowds followed him there, and he healed them.

19.1-2

19.3 One day the Pharisees were badgering him: "Is it legal for a man to divorce his wife for any reason?"

19.4-6 He answered, "Haven't you read in your Bible that the Creator originally made man and woman for each other, male and female? And because of this, a man leaves father and mother and is firmly bonded to his wife, becoming one flesh—no longer two bodies but one. Because God created this organic union of the two sexes, no one should desecrate his art by cutting them apart."

19.7 They shot back in rebuttal, "If that's so, why did Moses give instructions for divorce papers and divorce procedures?"

19.8-9 Jesus said, "Moses provided for divorce as a concession to your hardheartedness, but it is not part of God's original plan. I'm holding you to the original plan, and holding you liable for adultery if you divorce your faithful wife and then marry someone else. I make an exception in cases where the spouse has committed adultery."

19.10 Jesus' disciples objected, "If those are the terms of marriage, we're stuck. Why get married?"

19.11-12 But Jesus said, "Not everyone is mature enough to live a married life. It requires a certain aptitude and grace. Marriage isn't for everyone. Some, from birth seemingly, never give marriage a thought. Others never get asked—or accepted. And some decide not to get married for kingdom reasons. But if you're capable of growing into the largeness of marriage, do it."

TO ENTER GOD'S KINGDOM

19.13-15 One day children were brought to Jesus in the hope that he would lay hands on them and pray over them. The disciples shooed them off. But Jesus intervened: "Let the children alone, don't prevent them from coming to me. God's kingdom is made up of people like these." After laying hands on them, he left.

19.16 Another day, a man stopped Jesus and asked, "Teacher, what good thing must I do to get eternal life?"

19.17 Jesus said, "Why do you question me about what's good? *God* is the One who is good. If you want to enter the life of God, just do what he tells you."

NEW INTERNATIONAL VERSION

¹⁸"Which ones?" the man inquired.

Jesus replied, " 'Do not murder, do not commit adultery, do not steal, do not give false testimony, ¹⁹honor your father and mother,'ᵃ and 'love your neighbor as yourself.'ᵇ"

²⁰"All these I have kept," the young man said. "What do I still lack?"

²¹Jesus answered, "If you want to be perfect, go, sell your possessions and give to the poor, and you will have treasure in heaven. Then come, follow me."

²²When the young man heard this, he went away sad, because he had great wealth.

²³Then Jesus said to his disciples, "I tell you the truth, it is hard for a rich man to enter the kingdom of heaven. ²⁴Again I tell you, it is easier for a camel to go through the eye of a needle than for a rich man to enter the kingdom of God."

²⁵When the disciples heard this, they were greatly astonished and asked, "Who then can be saved?"

²⁶Jesus looked at them and said, "With man this is impossible, but with God all things are possible."

²⁷Peter answered him, "We have left everything to follow you! What then will there be for us?"

²⁸Jesus said to them, "I tell you the truth, at the renewal of all things, when the Son of Man sits on his glorious throne, you who have followed me will also sit on twelve thrones, judging the twelve tribes of Israel. ²⁹And everyone who has left houses or brothers or sisters or father or motherᶜ or children or fields for my sake will receive a hundred times as much and will inherit eternal life. ³⁰But many who are first will be last, and many who are last will be first.

THE PARABLE OF THE WORKERS IN THE VINEYARD

20 "For the kingdom of heaven is like a landowner who went out early in the morning to hire men to work in his vineyard. ²He agreed to pay them a denarius for the day and sent them into his vineyard.

³"About the third hour he went out and saw others standing in the marketplace doing nothing. ⁴He told them, 'You also go and work in my vineyard, and I will pay you whatever is right.' ⁵So they went.

"He went out again about the sixth hour and the ninth hour and did the same thing. ⁶About the eleventh hour he went out and found still

THE MESSAGE

19.18-19   The man asked, "What in particular?"

Jesus said, "Don't murder, don't commit adultery, don't steal, don't lie, honor your father and mother, and love your neighbor as you do yourself."

19.20   The young man said, "I've done all that. What's left?"

19.21   "If you want to give it all you've got," Jesus replied, "go sell your possessions; give everything to the poor. All your wealth will then be in heaven. Then come follow me."

19.22   That was the last thing the young man expected to hear. And so, crestfallen, he walked away. He was holding on tight to a lot of things, and he couldn't bear to let go.

19.23-24   As he watched him go, Jesus told his disciples, "Do you have any idea how difficult it is for the rich to enter God's kingdom? Let me tell you, it's easier to gallop a camel through a needle's eye than for the rich to enter God's kingdom."

19.25   The disciples were staggered. "Then who has any chance at all?"

19.26   Jesus looked hard at them and said, "No chance at all if you think you can pull it off yourself. Every chance in the world if you trust God to do it."

19.27   Then Peter chimed in, "We left everything and followed you. What do we get out of it?"

19.28-30   Jesus replied, "Yes, you have followed me. In the re-creation of the world, when the Son of Man will rule gloriously, you who have followed me will also rule, starting with the twelve tribes of Israel. And not only you, but anyone who sacrifices home, family, fields—whatever—because of me will get it all back a hundred times over, not to mention the considerable bonus of eternal life. This is the Great Reversal: many of the first ending up last, and the last first."

A STORY ABOUT WORKERS

20.1-2   **20** "God's kingdom is like an estate manager who went out early in the morning to hire workers for his vineyard. They agreed on a wage of a dollar a day, and went to work.

20.3-5   "Later, about nine o'clock, the manager saw some other men hanging around the town square unemployed. He told them to go to work in his vineyard and he would pay them a fair wage. They went.

20.5-6   "He did the same thing at noon, and again at three o'clock. At five o'clock he went back and

---

ᵃ 19 Exodus 20:12-16; Deut. 5:16-20   ᵇ 19 Lev. 19:18
ᶜ 29 Some manuscripts mother or wife

NEW INTERNATIONAL VERSION

others standing around. He asked them, 'Why have you been standing here all day long doing nothing?'

⁷ "'Because no one has hired us,' they answered.

"He said to them, 'You also go and work in my vineyard.'

⁸ "When evening came, the owner of the vineyard said to his foreman, 'Call the workers and pay them their wages, beginning with the last ones hired and going on to the first.'

⁹ "The workers who were hired about the eleventh hour came and each received a denarius. ¹⁰So when those came who were hired first, they expected to receive more. But each one of them also received a denarius. ¹¹When they received it, they began to grumble against the landowner. ¹²'These men who were hired last worked only one hour,' they said, 'and you have made them equal to us who have borne the burden of the work and the heat of the day.'

¹³ "But he answered one of them, 'Friend, I am not being unfair to you. Didn't you agree to work for a denarius? ¹⁴Take your pay and go. I want to give the man who was hired last the same as I gave you. ¹⁵Don't I have the right to do what I want with my own money? Or are you envious because I am generous?'

¹⁶ "So the last will be first, and the first will be last."

JESUS AGAIN PREDICTS HIS DEATH

¹⁷Now as Jesus was going up to Jerusalem, he took the twelve disciples aside and said to them, ¹⁸ "We are going up to Jerusalem, and the Son of Man will be betrayed to the chief priests and the teachers of the law. They will condemn him to death ¹⁹and will turn him over to the Gentiles to be mocked and flogged and crucified. On the third day he will be raised to life!"

A MOTHER'S REQUEST

²⁰Then the mother of Zebedee's sons came to Jesus with her sons and, kneeling down, asked a favor of him.

²¹ "What is it you want?" he asked.

She said, "Grant that one of these two sons of mine may sit at your right and the other at your left in your kingdom."

²² "You don't know what you are asking," Jesus said to them. "Can you drink the cup I am going to drink?"

"We can," they answered.

²³Jesus said to them, "You will indeed drink from my cup, but to sit at my right or left is not for me to grant. These places belong to those for whom they have been prepared by my Father."

THE MESSAGE

found still others standing around. He said, 'Why are you standing around all day doing nothing?'

20.7   "They said, 'Because no one hired us.'

"He told them to go to work in his vineyard.

20.8   "When the day's work was over, the owner of the vineyard instructed his foreman, 'Call the workers in and pay them their wages. Start with the last hired and go on to the first.'

20.9-12   "Those hired at five o'clock came up and were each given a dollar. When those who were hired first saw that, they assumed they would get far more. But they got the same, each of them one dollar. Taking the dollar, they groused angrily to the manager, 'These last workers put in only one easy hour, and you just made them equal to us, who slaved all day under a scorching sun.'

20.13-15   "He replied to the one speaking for the rest, 'Friend, I haven't been unfair. We agreed on the wage of a dollar, didn't we? So take it and go. I decided to give to the one who came last the same as you. Can't I do what I want with my own money? Are you going to get stingy because I am generous?'

20.16   "Here it is again, the Great Reversal: many of the first ending up last, and the last first."

TO DRINK FROM THE CUP

20.17-19 Jesus, now well on the way up to Jerusalem, took the Twelve off to the side of the road and said, "Listen to me carefully. We are on our way up to Jerusalem. When we get there, the Son of Man will be betrayed to the religious leaders and scholars. They will sentence him to death. They will then hand him over to the Romans for mockery and torture and crucifixion. On the third day he will be raised up alive."

20.20   It was about that time that the mother of the Zebedee brothers came with her two sons and knelt before Jesus with a request.

20.21   "What do you want?" Jesus asked.

She said, "Give your word that these two sons of mine will be awarded the highest places of honor in your kingdom, one at your right hand, one at your left hand."

20.22   Jesus responded, "You have no idea what you're asking." And he said to James and John, "Are you capable of drinking the cup that I'm about to drink?"

They said, "Sure, why not?"

20.23   Jesus said, "Come to think of it, you *are* going to drink my cup. But as to awarding places of honor, that's not my business. My Father is taking care of that."

NEW INTERNATIONAL VERSION

²⁴When the ten heard about this, they were indignant with the two brothers. ²⁵Jesus called them together and said, "You know that the rulers of the Gentiles lord it over them, and their high officials exercise authority over them. ²⁶Not so with you. Instead, whoever wants to become great among you must be your servant, ²⁷and whoever wants to be first must be your slave— ²⁸just as the Son of Man did not come to be served, but to serve, and to give his life as a ransom for many."

TWO BLIND MEN RECEIVE SIGHT

²⁹As Jesus and his disciples were leaving Jericho, a large crowd followed him. ³⁰Two blind men were sitting by the roadside, and when they heard that Jesus was going by, they shouted, "Lord, Son of David, have mercy on us!"

³¹The crowd rebuked them and told them to be quiet, but they shouted all the louder, "Lord, Son of David, have mercy on us!"

³²Jesus stopped and called them. "What do you want me to do for you?" he asked.

³³"Lord," they answered, "we want our sight."

³⁴Jesus had compassion on them and touched their eyes. Immediately they received their sight and followed him.

THE TRIUMPHAL ENTRY

21 As they approached Jerusalem and came to Bethphage on the Mount of Olives, Jesus sent two disciples, ²saying to them, "Go to the village ahead of you, and at once you will find a donkey tied there, with her colt by her. Untie them and bring them to me. ³If anyone says anything to you, tell him that the Lord needs them, and he will send them right away."

⁴This took place to fulfill what was spoken through the prophet:

⁵ "Say to the Daughter of Zion,
   'See, your king comes to you,
gentle and riding on a donkey,
   on a colt, the foal of a donkey.' "ᵃ

⁶The disciples went and did as Jesus had instructed them. ⁷They brought the donkey and the colt, placed their cloaks on them, and Jesus sat on them. ⁸A very large crowd spread their cloaks on the road, while others cut branches from the trees and spread them on the road. ⁹The crowds that went ahead of him and those that followed shouted,

ᵃ 5 Zech. 9:9

THE MESSAGE

20:24-28   When the ten others heard about this, they lost their tempers, thoroughly disgusted with the two brothers. So Jesus got them together to settle things down. He said, "You've observed how godless rulers throw their weight around, how quickly a little power goes to their heads. It's not going to be that way with you. Whoever wants to be great must become a servant. Whoever wants to be first among you must be your slave. That is what the Son of Man has done: He came to serve, not be served— and then to give away his life in exchange for the many who are held hostage."

✛

20:29-31 As they were leaving Jericho, a huge crowd followed. Suddenly they came upon two blind men sitting alongside the road. When they heard it was Jesus passing, they cried out, "Master, have mercy on us! Mercy, Son of David!" The crowd tried to hush them up, but they got all the louder, crying, "Master, have mercy on us! Mercy, Son of David!"

20:32   Jesus stopped and called over, "What do you want from me?"

20:33   They said, "Master, we want our eyes opened. We want to see!"

20:34   Deeply moved, Jesus touched their eyes. They had their sight back that very instant, and joined the procession.

THE ROYAL WELCOME

21:1-3 **21** When they neared Jerusalem, having arrived at Bethphage on Mount Olives, Jesus sent two disciples with these instructions: "Go over to the village across from you. You'll find a donkey tethered there, her colt with her. Untie her and bring them to me. If anyone asks what you're doing, say, 'The Master needs them!' He will send them with you."

21:4-5   This is the full story of what was sketched earlier by the prophet:

Tell Zion's daughter,
   "Look, your king's on his way,
      poised and ready, mounted
On a donkey, on a colt,
   foal of a pack animal."

21:6-9   The disciples went and did exactly what Jesus told them to do. They led the donkey and colt out, laid some of their clothes on them, and Jesus mounted. Nearly all the people in the crowd threw their garments down on the road, giving him a royal welcome. Others cut branches from the trees and threw them down as a welcome mat. Crowds went ahead and crowds followed, all of them calling out, "Ho-

NEW INTERNATIONAL VERSION

"Hosanna[a] to the Son of David!"

"Blessed is he who comes in the name of the Lord!"[b]

"Hosanna[a] in the highest!"

[10] When Jesus entered Jerusalem, the whole city was stirred and asked, "Who is this?" [11] The crowds answered, "This is Jesus, the prophet from Nazareth in Galilee."

JESUS AT THE TEMPLE

[12] Jesus entered the temple area and drove out all who were buying and selling there. He overturned the tables of the money changers and the benches of those selling doves. [13] "It is written," he said to them, " 'My house will be called a house of prayer,'[c] but you are making it a 'den of robbers.'[d]"

[14] The blind and the lame came to him at the temple, and he healed them. [15] But when the chief priests and the teachers of the law saw the wonderful things he did and the children shouting in the temple area, "Hosanna to the Son of David," they were indignant.

[16] "Do you hear what these children are saying?" they asked him.

"Yes," replied Jesus, "have you never read,

" 'From the lips of children and infants
    you have ordained praise'[e]?"

[17] And he left them and went out of the city to Bethany, where he spent the night.

THE FIG TREE WITHERS

[18] Early in the morning, as he was on his way back to the city, he was hungry. [19] Seeing a fig tree by the road, he went up to it but found nothing on it except leaves. Then he said to it, "May you never bear fruit again!" Immediately the tree withered.

[20] When the disciples saw this, they were amazed. "How did the fig tree wither so quickly?" they asked.

[21] Jesus replied, "I tell you the truth, if you have faith and do not doubt, not only can you do what was done to the fig tree, but also you can say to this mountain, 'Go, throw yourself into the sea,' and it will be done. [22] If you believe, you will receive whatever you ask for in prayer."

THE MESSAGE

sanna to David's son!" "Blessed is he who comes in God's name!" "Hosanna in highest heaven!"

[21.10] As he made his entrance into Jerusalem, the whole city was shaken. Unnerved, people were asking, "What's going on here? Who is this?"

[21.11] The parade crowd answered, "This is the prophet Jesus, the one from Nazareth in Galilee."

HE KICKED OVER THE TABLES

[21.12-14] Jesus went straight to the Temple and threw out everyone who had set up shop, buying and selling. He kicked over the tables of loan sharks and the stalls of dove merchants. He quoted this text:

My house was designated a house of
        prayer;
You have made it a hangout for thieves.

Now there was room for the blind and crippled to get in. They came to Jesus and he healed them.

[21.15-16] When the religious leaders saw the outrageous things he was doing, and heard all the children running and shouting through the Temple, "Hosanna to David's Son!" they were up in arms and took him to task. "Do you hear what these children are saying?"

Jesus said, "Yes, I hear them. And haven't you read in God's Word, 'From the mouths of children and babies I'll furnish a place of praise'?"

[21.17] Fed up, Jesus turned on his heel and left the city for Bethany, where he spent the night.

THE WITHERED FIG TREE

[21.18-20] Early the next morning Jesus was returning to the city. He was hungry. Seeing a lone fig tree alongside the road, he approached it anticipating a breakfast of figs. When he got to the tree, there was nothing but fig leaves. He said, "No more figs from this tree—ever!" The fig tree withered on the spot, a dry stick. The disciples saw it happen. They rubbed their eyes, saying, "Did we really see this? A leafy tree one minute, a dry stick the next?"

[21.21-22] But Jesus was matter-of-fact: "Yes—and if you embrace this kingdom life and don't doubt God, you'll not only do minor feats like I did to the fig tree, but also triumph over huge obstacles. This mountain, for instance, you'll tell, 'Go jump in the lake,' and it will jump. Absolutely everything, ranging from small to large, as you make it a part of your believing prayer, gets included as you lay hold of God."

---

[a] 9 A Hebrew expression meaning "Save!" which became an exclamation of praise; also in verse 15   [b] 9 Psalm 118:26
[c] 13 Isaiah 56:7   [d] 13 Jer. 7:11   [e] 16 Psalm 8:2

NEW INTERNATIONAL VERSION

THE AUTHORITY OF JESUS QUESTIONED

23Jesus entered the temple courts, and, while he was teaching, the chief priests and the elders of the people came to him. "By what authority are you doing these things?" they asked. "And who gave you this authority?"

24Jesus replied, "I will also ask you one question. If you answer me, I will tell you by what authority I am doing these things. 25John's baptism— where did it come from? Was it from heaven, or from men?"

They discussed it among themselves and said, "If we say, 'From heaven,' he will ask, 'Then why didn't you believe him?' 26But if we say, 'From men'—we are afraid of the people, for they all hold that John was a prophet."

27So they answered Jesus, "We don't know."

Then he said, "Neither will I tell you by what authority I am doing these things.

THE PARABLE OF THE TWO SONS

28"What do you think? There was a man who had two sons. He went to the first and said, 'Son, go and work today in the vineyard.'

29" 'I will not,' he answered, but later he changed his mind and went.

30"Then the father went to the other son and said the same thing. He answered, 'I will, sir,' but he did not go.

31"Which of the two did what his father wanted?"

"The first," they answered.

Jesus said to them, "I tell you the truth, the tax collectors and the prostitutes are entering the kingdom of God ahead of you. 32For John came to you to show you the way of righteousness, and you did not believe him, but the tax collectors and the prostitutes did. And even after you saw this, you did not repent and believe him.

THE PARABLE OF THE TENANTS

33"Listen to another parable: There was a landowner who planted a vineyard. He put a wall around it, dug a winepress in it and built a watchtower. Then he rented the vineyard to some farmers and went away on a journey. 34When the harvest time approached, he sent his servants to the tenants to collect his fruit.

35"The tenants seized his servants; they beat one, killed another, and stoned a third. 36Then he sent other servants to them, more than the first time, and the tenants treated them the same way. 37Last of all, he sent his son to them. 'They will respect my son,' he said.

THE MESSAGE

TRUE AUTHORITY

21.23 Then he was back in the Temple, teaching. The high priests and leaders of the people came up and demanded, "Show us your credentials. Who authorized you to teach here?"

21.24-25 Jesus responded, "First let me ask you a question. You answer my question and I'll answer yours. About the baptism of John—who authorized it: heaven or humans?"

21.25-27 They were on the spot and knew it. They pulled back into a huddle and whispered, "If we say 'heaven,' he'll ask us why we didn't believe him; if we say 'humans,' we're up against it with the people because they all hold John up as a prophet." They decided to concede that round to Jesus. "We don't know," they answered.

Jesus said, "Then neither will I answer your question.

THE STORY OF TWO SONS

21.28 "Tell me what you think of this story: A man had two sons. He went up to the first and said, 'Son, go out for the day and work in the vineyard.'

21.29 "The son answered, 'I don't want to.' Later on he thought better of it and went.

21.30 "The father gave the same command to the second son. He answered, 'Sure, glad to.' But he never went.

21.31-32 "Which of the two sons did what the father asked?"

They said, "The first."

Jesus said, "Yes, and I tell you that crooks and whores are going to precede you into God's kingdom. John came to you showing you the right road. You turned up your noses at him, but the crooks and whores believed him. Even when you saw their changed lives, you didn't care enough to change and believe him.

THE STORY OF THE GREEDY FARMHANDS

21.33-34 "Here's another story. Listen closely. There was once a man, a wealthy farmer, who planted a vineyard. He fenced it, dug a winepress, put up a watchtower, then turned it over to the farmhands and went off on a trip. When it was time to harvest the grapes, he sent his servants back to collect his profits.

21.35-37 "The farmhands grabbed the first servant and beat him up. The next one they murdered. They threw stones at the third but he got away. The owner tried again, sending more servants. They got the same treatment. The owner was at the end of his rope. He decided to send his son. 'Surely,' he thought, 'they will respect my son.'

NEW INTERNATIONAL VERSION

³⁸"But when the tenants saw the son, they said to each other, 'This is the heir. Come, let's kill him and take his inheritance.' ³⁹So they took him and threw him out of the vineyard and killed him.

⁴⁰"Therefore, when the owner of the vineyard comes, what will he do to those tenants?"

⁴¹"He will bring those wretches to a wretched end," they replied, "and he will rent the vineyard to other tenants, who will give him his share of the crop at harvest time."

⁴²Jesus said to them, "Have you never read in the Scriptures:

" 'The stone the builders rejected
        has become the capstone*ᵃ*;
    the Lord has done this,
        and it is marvelous in our eyes'*ᵇ*?

⁴³"Therefore I tell you that the kingdom of God will be taken away from you and given to a people who will produce its fruit. ⁴⁴He who falls on this stone will be broken to pieces, but he on whom it falls will be crushed."*ᶜ*

⁴⁵When the chief priests and the Pharisees heard Jesus' parables, they knew he was talking about them. ⁴⁶They looked for a way to arrest him, but they were afraid of the crowd because the people held that he was a prophet.

THE PARABLE OF THE WEDDING BANQUET

22 Jesus spoke to them again in parables, saying: ²"The kingdom of heaven is like a king who prepared a wedding banquet for his son. ³He sent his servants to those who had been invited to the banquet to tell them to come, but they refused to come.

⁴"Then he sent some more servants and said, 'Tell those who have been invited that I have prepared my dinner: My oxen and fattened cattle have been butchered, and everything is ready. Come to the wedding banquet.'

⁵"But they paid no attention and went off—one to his field, another to his business. ⁶The rest seized his servants, mistreated them and killed them. ⁷The king was enraged. He sent his army and destroyed those murderers and burned their city.

⁸"Then he said to his servants, 'The wedding banquet is ready, but those I invited did not deserve to come. ⁹Go to the street corners and invite to the banquet anyone you find.' ¹⁰So the servants went out into the streets and gathered all the people they could find, both good and bad, and the wedding hall was filled with guests.

ᵃ 42 Or *cornerstone*   *ᵇ 42* Psalm 118:22,23   *ᶜ 44* Some manuscripts do not have verse 44.

THE MESSAGE

21.38-39   "But when the farmhands saw the son arrive, they rubbed their hands in greed. 'This is the heir! Let's kill him and have it all for ourselves.' They grabbed him, threw him out, and killed him.

21.40   "Now, when the owner of the vineyard arrives home from his trip, what do you think he will do to the farmhands?"

21.41   "He'll kill them—a rotten bunch, and good riddance," they answered. "Then he'll assign the vineyard to farmhands who will hand over the profits when it's time."

21.42-44   Jesus said, "Right—and you can read it for yourselves in your Bibles:

The stone the masons threw out
    is now the cornerstone.
This is God's work;
    we rub our eyes, we can hardly believe it!

"This is the way it is with you. God's kingdom will be taken back from you and handed over to a people who will live out a kingdom life. Whoever stumbles on this Stone gets shattered; whoever the Stone falls on gets smashed."

21.45-46   When the religious leaders heard this story, they knew it was aimed at them. They wanted to arrest Jesus and put him in jail, but, intimidated by public opinion, they held back. Most people held him to be a prophet of God.

THE STORY OF THE WEDDING BANQUET

22.1-3   **22** Jesus responded by telling still more stories. "God's kingdom," he said, "is like a king who threw a wedding banquet for his son. He sent out servants to call in all the invited guests. And they wouldn't come!

22.4   "He sent out another round of servants, instructing them to tell the guests, 'Look, everything is on the table, the prime rib is ready for carving. Come to the feast!'

22.5-7   "They only shrugged their shoulders and went off, one to weed his garden, another to work in his shop. The rest, with nothing better to do, beat up on the messengers and then killed them. The king was outraged and sent his soldiers to destroy those thugs and level their city.

22.8-10   "Then he told his servants, 'We have a wedding banquet all prepared but no guests. The ones I invited weren't up to it. Go out into the busiest intersections in town and invite anyone you find to the banquet.' The servants went out on the streets and rounded up everyone they laid eyes on, good and bad, regardless. And so the banquet was on—every place filled.

NEW INTERNATIONAL VERSION

11"But when the king came in to see the guests, he noticed a man there who was not wearing wedding clothes. 12'Friend,' he asked, 'how did you get in here without wedding clothes?' The man was speechless.

13"Then the king told the attendants, 'Tie him hand and foot, and throw him outside, into the darkness, where there will be weeping and gnashing of teeth.'

14"For many are invited, but few are chosen."

PAYING TAXES TO CAESAR

15Then the Pharisees went out and laid plans to trap him in his words. 16They sent their disciples to him along with the Herodians. "Teacher," they said, "we know you are a man of integrity and that you teach the way of God in accordance with the truth. You aren't swayed by men, because you pay no attention to who they are. 17Tell us then, what is your opinion? Is it right to pay taxes to Caesar or not?"

18But Jesus, knowing their evil intent, said, "You hypocrites, why are you trying to trap me? 19Show me the coin used for paying the tax." They brought him a denarius, 20and he asked them, "Whose portrait is this? And whose inscription?"

21"Caesar's," they replied.

Then he said to them, "Give to Caesar what is Caesar's, and to God what is God's."

22When they heard this, they were amazed. So they left him and went away.

MARRIAGE AT THE RESURRECTION

23That same day the Sadducees, who say there is no resurrection, came to him with a question. 24"Teacher," they said, "Moses told us that if a man dies without having children, his brother must marry the widow and have children for him. 25Now there were seven brothers among us. The first one married and died, and since he had no children, he left his wife to his brother. 26The same thing happened to the second and third brother, right on down to the seventh. 27Finally, the woman died. 28Now then, at the resurrection, whose wife will she be of the seven, since all of them were married to her?"

29Jesus replied, "You are in error because you do not know the Scriptures or the power of God. 30At the resurrection people will neither marry nor be given in marriage; they will be like the angels in heaven. 31But about the resurrection of the dead—have you not read what God said to you, 32'I am the God of Abraham, the God of Isaac, and the God of Jacob'ᵃ? He is not the God of the dead but of the living."

ᵃ 32 Exodus 3:6

THE MESSAGE

22.11-13 "When the king entered and looked over the scene, he spotted a man who wasn't properly dressed. He said to him, 'Friend, how dare you come in here looking like that!' The man was speechless. Then the king told his servants, 'Get him out of here—fast. Tie him up and ship him to hell. And make sure he doesn't get back in.'

22.14 "That's what I mean when I say, 'Many get invited; only a few make it.' "

PAYING TAXES

22.15-17 That's when the Pharisees plotted a way to trap him into saying something damaging. They sent their disciples, with a few of Herod's followers mixed in, to ask, "Teacher, we know you have integrity, teach the way of God accurately, are indifferent to popular opinion, and don't pander to your students. So tell us honestly: Is it right to pay taxes to Caesar or not?"

22.18-19 Jesus knew they were up to no good. He said, "Why are you playing these games with me? Why are you trying to trap me? Do you have a coin? Let me see it." They handed him a silver piece.

22.20 "This engraving—who does it look like? And whose name is on it?"

22.21 They said, "Caesar."

"Then give Caesar what is his, and give God what is his."

22.22 The Pharisees were speechless. They went off shaking their heads.

MARRIAGE AND RESURRECTION

22.23-28 That same day, Sadducees approached him. This is the party that denies any possibility of resurrection. They asked, "Teacher, Moses said that if a man dies childless, his brother is obligated to marry his widow and get her with child. Here's a case where there were seven brothers. The first brother married and died, leaving no child, and his wife passed to his brother. The second brother also left her childless, then the third—and on and on, all seven. Eventually the wife died. Now here's our question: At the resurrection, whose wife is she? She was a wife to each of them."

22.29-33 Jesus answered, "You're off base on two counts: You don't know your Bibles, and you don't know how God works. At the resurrection we're beyond marriage. As with the angels, all our ecstasies and intimacies then will be with God. And regarding your speculation on whether the dead are raised or not, don't you read your Bibles? The grammar is clear: God says, 'I am—not was—the God of Abraham, the God of Isaac, the God of Jacob.' The living God defines himself not as the God of dead men,

NEW INTERNATIONAL VERSION

33When the crowds heard this, they were astonished at his teaching.

THE GREATEST COMMANDMENT

34Hearing that Jesus had silenced the Sadducees, the Pharisees got together. 35One of them, an expert in the law, tested him with this question: 36"Teacher, which is the greatest commandment in the Law?"

37Jesus replied: " 'Love the Lord your God with all your heart and with all your soul and with all your mind.'*a* 38This is the first and greatest commandment. 39And the second is like it: 'Love your neighbor as yourself.'*b* 40All the Law and the Prophets hang on these two commandments."

WHOSE SON IS THE CHRIST?

41While the Pharisees were gathered together, Jesus asked them, 42"What do you think about the Christ*c*? Whose son is he?"

"The son of David," they replied.

43He said to them, "How is it then that David, speaking by the Spirit, calls him 'Lord'? For he says,

44 " 'The Lord said to my Lord:
"Sit at my right hand
until I put your enemies
under your feet." '*d*

45If then David calls him 'Lord,' how can he be his son?" 46No one could say a word in reply, and from that day on no one dared to ask him any more questions.

SEVEN WOES

23 Then Jesus said to the crowds and to his disciples: 2"The teachers of the law and the Pharisees sit in Moses' seat. 3So you must obey them and do everything they tell you. But do not do what they do, for they do not practice what they preach. 4They tie up heavy loads and put them on men's shoulders, but they themselves are not willing to lift a finger to move them.

5"Everything they do is done for men to see: They make their phylacteries*e* wide and the tas-

a 37 Deut. 6:5   b 39 Lev. 19:18   c 42 Or *Messiah*
d 44 Psalm 110:1   e 5 That is, boxes containing Scripture verses, worn on forehead and arm

THE MESSAGE

but of the *living.*" Hearing this exchange the crowd was much impressed.

THE MOST IMPORTANT COMMAND

22.34-36 When the Pharisees heard how he had bested the Sadducees, they gathered their forces for an assault. One of their religion scholars spoke for them, posing a question they hoped would show him up: "Teacher, which command in God's Law is the most important?"

22.37-40 Jesus said, " 'Love the Lord your God with all your passion and prayer and intelligence.' This is the most important, the first on any list. But there is a second to set alongside it: 'Love others as well as you love yourself.' These two commands are pegs; everything in God's Law and the Prophets hangs from them."

DAVID'S SON AND MASTER

22.41-42 As the Pharisees were regrouping, Jesus caught them off balance with his own test question: "What do you think about the Christ? Whose son is he?" They said, "David's son."

22.43-45 Jesus replied, "Well, if the Christ is David's son, how do you explain that David, under inspiration, named Christ his 'Master'?

God said to my Master,
"Sit here at my right hand
until I make your enemies your
footstool."

"Now if David calls him 'Master,' how can he at the same time be his son?"

22.46 That stumped them, literalists that they were. Unwilling to risk losing face again in one of these public verbal exchanges, they quit asking questions for good.

RELIGIOUS FASHION SHOWS

23.1-3 **23** Now Jesus turned to address his disciples, along with the crowd that had gathered with them. "The religion scholars and Pharisees are competent teachers in God's Law. You won't go wrong in following their teachings on Moses. But be careful about following *them.* They talk a good line, but they don't live it. They don't take it into their hearts and live it out in their behavior. It's all spit-and-polish veneer.

23.4-7 "Instead of giving you God's Law as food and drink by which you can banquet on God, they package it in bundles of rules, loading you down like pack animals. They seem to take pleasure in watching you stagger under these loads, and wouldn't think of lifting a finger to help. Their lives are perpetual fashion shows, embroidered prayer shawls one day and flow-

NEW INTERNATIONAL VERSION

sels on their garments long; [6]they love the place of honor at banquets and the most important seats in the synagogues; [7]they love to be greeted in the marketplaces and to have men call them 'Rabbi.'

[8]"But you are not to be called 'Rabbi,' for you have only one Master and you are all brothers. [9]And do not call anyone on earth 'father,' for you have one Father, and he is in heaven. [10]Nor are you to be called 'teacher,' for you have one Teacher, the Christ.[a] [11]The greatest among you will be your servant. [12]For whoever exalts himself will be humbled, and whoever humbles himself will be exalted.

[13]"Woe to you, teachers of the law and Pharisees, you hypocrites! You shut the kingdom of heaven in men's faces. You yourselves do not enter, nor will you let those enter who are trying to.[b]

[15]"Woe to you, teachers of the law and Pharisees, you hypocrites! You travel over land and sea to win a single convert, and when he becomes one, you make him twice as much a son of hell as you are.

[16]"Woe to you, blind guides! You say, 'If anyone swears by the temple, it means nothing; but if anyone swears by the gold of the temple, he is bound by his oath.' [17]You blind fools! Which is greater: the gold, or the temple that makes the gold sacred? [18]You also say, 'If anyone swears by the altar, it means nothing; but if anyone swears by the gift on it, he is bound by his oath.' [19]You blind men! Which is greater: the gift, or the altar that makes the gift sacred? [20]Therefore, he who swears by the altar swears by it and by everything on it. [21]And he who swears by the temple swears by it and by the one who dwells in it. [22]And he who swears by heaven swears by God's throne and by the one who sits on it.

[23]"Woe to you, teachers of the law and Pharisees, you hypocrites! You give a tenth of your spices—mint, dill and cummin. But you have neglected the more important matters of the law—justice, mercy and faithfulness. You should

---

[a] 10 Or Messiah   [b] 13 Some manuscripts to. [14]Woe to you, teachers of the law and Pharisees, you hypocrites! You devour widows' houses and for a show make lengthy prayers. Therefore you will be punished more severely.

THE MESSAGE

ery prayers the next. They love to sit at the head table at church dinners, basking in the most prominent positions, preening in the radiance of public flattery, receiving honorary degrees, and getting called 'Doctor' and 'Reverend.'

23.8-10   "Don't let people do that to you, put you on a pedestal like that. You all have a single Teacher, and you are all classmates. Don't set people up as experts over your life, letting them tell you what to do. Save that authority for God; let him tell you what to do. No one else should carry the title of 'Father'; you have only one Father, and he's in heaven. And don't let people maneuver you into taking charge of them. There is only one Life-Leader for you and them—Christ.

23.11-12   "Do you want to stand out? Then step down. Be a servant. If you puff yourself up, you'll get the wind knocked out of you. But if you're content to simply be yourself, your life will count for plenty.

FRAUDS!

23.13   "I've had it with you! You're hopeless, you religion scholars, you Pharisees! Frauds! Your lives are roadblocks to God's kingdom. You refuse to enter, and won't let anyone else in either.

23.15   "You're hopeless, you religion scholars and Pharisees! Frauds! You go halfway around the world to make a convert, but once you get him you make him into a replica of yourselves, double-damned.

23.16-22   "You're hopeless! What arrogant stupidity! You say, 'If someone makes a promise with his fingers crossed, that's nothing; but if he swears with his hand on the Bible, that's serious.' What ignorance! Does the leather on the Bible carry more weight than the skin on your hands? And what about this piece of trivia: 'If you shake hands on a promise, that's nothing; but if you raise your hand that God is your witness, that's serious'? What ridiculous hairsplitting! What difference does it make whether you shake hands or raise hands? A promise is a promise. What difference does it make if you make your promise inside or outside a house of worship? A promise is a promise. God is present, watching and holding you to account regardless.

23.23-24   "You're hopeless, you religion scholars and Pharisees! Frauds! You keep meticulous account books, tithing on every nickel and dime you get, but on the meat of God's Law, things like fairness and compassion and commitment—the absolute basics!—you carelessly take it or leave it. Careful bookkeeping is com-

NEW INTERNATIONAL VERSION

have practiced the latter, without neglecting the former. ²⁴You blind guides! You strain out a gnat but swallow a camel.

²⁵"Woe to you, teachers of the law and Pharisees, you hypocrites! You clean the outside of the cup and dish, but inside they are full of greed and self-indulgence. ²⁶Blind Pharisee! First clean the inside of the cup and dish, and then the outside also will be clean.

²⁷"Woe to you, teachers of the law and Pharisees, you hypocrites! You are like whitewashed tombs, which look beautiful on the outside but on the inside are full of dead men's bones and everything unclean. ²⁸In the same way, on the outside you appear to people as righteous but on the inside you are full of hypocrisy and wickedness.

²⁹"Woe to you, teachers of the law and Pharisees, you hypocrites! You build tombs for the prophets and decorate the graves of the righteous. ³⁰And you say, 'If we had lived in the days of our forefathers, we would not have taken part with them in shedding the blood of the prophets.' ³¹So you testify against yourselves that you are the descendants of those who murdered the prophets. ³²Fill up, then, the measure of the sin of your forefathers!

³³"You snakes! You brood of vipers! How will you escape being condemned to hell? ³⁴Therefore I am sending you prophets and wise men and teachers. Some of them you will kill and crucify; others you will flog in your synagogues and pursue from town to town. ³⁵And so upon you will come all the righteous blood that has been shed on earth, from the blood of righteous Abel to the blood of Zechariah son of Berekiah, whom you murdered between the temple and the altar. ³⁶I tell you the truth, all this will come upon this generation.

³⁷"O Jerusalem, Jerusalem, you who kill the prophets and stone those sent to you, how often I have longed to gather your children together, as a hen gathers her chicks under her wings, but you were not willing. ³⁸Look, your house is left to you desolate. ³⁹For I tell you, you will not see me again until you say, 'Blessed is he who comes in the name of the Lord.'*^a*

SIGNS OF THE END OF THE AGE

24 Jesus left the temple and was walking away when his disciples came up to him to call his attention to its buildings. ²"Do you see all these things?" he asked. "I tell you the

a 39 Psalm 118:26

THE MESSAGE

mendable, but the basics are required. Do you have any idea how silly you look, writing a life story that's wrong from start to finish, nitpicking over commas and semicolons?

23.25-26 "You're hopeless, you religion scholars and Pharisees! Frauds! You burnish the surface of your cups and bowls so they sparkle in the sun, while the insides are maggoty with your greed and gluttony. Stupid Pharisee! Scour the insides, and then the gleaming surface will mean something.

23.27-28 "You're hopeless, you religion scholars and Pharisees! Frauds! You're like manicured grave plots, grass clipped and the flowers bright, but six feet down it's all rotting bones and worm-eaten flesh. People look at you and think you're saints, but beneath the skin you're total frauds.

23.29-32 "You're hopeless, you religion scholars and Pharisees! Frauds! You build granite tombs for your prophets and marble monuments for your saints. And you say that if you had lived in the days of your ancestors, no blood would have been on your hands. You protest too much! You're cut from the same cloth as those murderers, and daily add to the death count.

23.33-34 "Snakes! Reptilian sneaks! Do you think you can worm your way out of this? Never have to pay the piper? It's on account of people like you that I send prophets and wise guides and scholars generation after generation—and generation after generation you treat them like dirt, greeting them with lynch mobs, hounding them with abuse.

23.35-36 "You can't squirm out of this: Every drop of righteous blood ever spilled on this earth, beginning with the blood of that good man Abel right down to the blood of Zechariah, Barachiah's son, whom you murdered at his prayers, is on your head. All this, I'm telling you, is coming down on you, on your generation.

23.37-39 "Jerusalem! Jerusalem! Murderer of prophets! Killer of the ones who brought you God's news! How often I've ached to embrace your children, the way a hen gathers her chicks under her wings, and you wouldn't let me. And now you're so desolate, nothing but a ghost town. What is there left to say? Only this: I'm out of here soon. The next time you see me you'll say, 'Oh, God has blessed him! He's come, bringing God's rule!' "

ROUTINE HISTORY

24.1-2 **24** Jesus then left the Temple. As he walked away, his disciples pointed out how very impressive the Temple architecture was. Jesus said, "You're not impressed by all this sheer *size,* are you? The truth of the matter

NEW INTERNATIONAL VERSION

truth, not one stone here will be left on another; every one will be thrown down."

³As Jesus was sitting on the Mount of Olives, the disciples came to him privately. "Tell us," they said, "when will this happen, and what will be the sign of your coming and of the end of the age?"

⁴Jesus answered: "Watch out that no one deceives you. ⁵For many will come in my name, claiming, 'I am the Christ,'ᵃ and will deceive many. ⁶You will hear of wars and rumors of wars, but see to it that you are not alarmed. Such things must happen, but the end is still to come. ⁷Nation will rise against nation, and kingdom against kingdom. There will be famines and earthquakes in various places. ⁸All these are the beginning of birth pains.

⁹"Then you will be handed over to be persecuted and put to death, and you will be hated by all nations because of me. ¹⁰At that time many will turn away from the faith and will betray and hate each other, ¹¹and many false prophets will appear and deceive many people. ¹²Because of the increase of wickedness, the love of most will grow cold, ¹³but he who stands firm to the end will be saved. ¹⁴And this gospel of the kingdom will be preached in the whole world as a testimony to all nations, and then the end will come.

¹⁵"So when you see standing in the holy place 'the abomination that causes desolation,'ᵇ spoken of through the prophet Daniel—let the reader understand— ¹⁶then let those who are in Judea flee to the mountains. ¹⁷Let no one on the roof of his house go down to take anything out of the house. ¹⁸Let no one in the field go back to get his cloak. ¹⁹How dreadful it will be in those days for pregnant women and nursing mothers! ²⁰Pray that your flight will not take place in winter or on the Sabbath. ²¹For then there will be great distress, unequaled from the beginning of the world until now—and never to be equaled again. ²²If those days had not been cut short, no one would survive, but for the sake of the elect those days will be shortened. ²³At that time if

THE MESSAGE

is that there's not a stone in that building that is not going to end up in a pile of rubble."

24.3 Later as he was sitting on Mount Olives, his disciples approached and asked him, "Tell us, when are these things going to happen? What will be the sign of your coming, that the time's up?"

24.4-8 Jesus said, "Watch out for doomsday deceivers. Many leaders are going to show up with forged identities, claiming, 'I am Christ, the Messiah.' They will deceive a lot of people. When reports come in of wars and rumored wars, keep your head and don't panic. This is routine history; this is no sign of the end. Nation will fight nation and ruler fight ruler, over and over. Famines and earthquakes will occur in various places. This is nothing compared to what is coming.

24.9-10 "They are going to throw you to the wolves and kill you, everyone hating you because you carry my name. And then, going from bad to worse, it will be dog-eat-dog, everyone at each other's throat, everyone hating each other.

24.11-12 "In the confusion, lying preachers will come forward and deceive a lot of people. For many others, the overwhelming spread of evil will do them in—nothing left of their love but a mound of ashes.

24.13-14 "Staying with it—that's what God requires. Stay with it to the end. You won't be sorry, and you'll be saved. All during this time, the good news—the Message of the kingdom—will be preached all over the world, a witness staked out in every country. And then the end will come.

THE MONSTER OF DESECRATION

24.15-20 "But be ready to run for it when you see the monster of desecration set up in the Temple sanctuary. The prophet Daniel described this. If you've read Daniel, you'll know what I'm talking about. If you're living in Judea at the time, run for the hills; if you're working in the yard, don't return to the house to get anything; if you're out in the field, don't go back and get your coat. Pregnant and nursing mothers will have it especially hard. Hope and pray this won't happen during the winter or on a Sabbath.

24.21-22 "This is going to be trouble on a scale beyond what the world has ever seen, or will see again. If these days of trouble were left to run their course, nobody would make it. But on account of God's chosen people, the trouble will be cut short.

THE ARRIVAL OF THE SON OF MAN

24.23-25 "If anyone tries to flag you down, calling out,

ᵃ 5 Or Messiah; also in verse 23   ᵇ 15 Daniel 9:27; 11:31; 12:11

NEW INTERNATIONAL VERSION

anyone says to you, 'Look, here is the Christ!' or, 'There he is!' do not believe it. [24]For false Christs and false prophets will appear and perform great signs and miracles to deceive even the elect—if that were possible. [25]See, I have told you ahead of time.

[26]"So if anyone tells you, 'There he is, out in the desert,' do not go out; or, 'Here he is, in the inner rooms,' do not believe it. [27]For as lightning that comes from the east is visible even in the west, so will be the coming of the Son of Man. [28]Wherever there is a carcass, there the vultures will gather.

[29]"Immediately after the distress of those days

" 'the sun will be darkened,
   and the moon will not give its light;
the stars will fall from the sky,
   and the heavenly bodies will be shaken.'[a]

[30]"At that time the sign of the Son of Man will appear in the sky, and all the nations of the earth will mourn. They will see the Son of Man coming on the clouds of the sky, with power and great glory. [31]And he will send his angels with a loud trumpet call, and they will gather his elect from the four winds, from one end of the heavens to the other.

[32]"Now learn this lesson from the fig tree: As soon as its twigs get tender and its leaves come out, you know that summer is near. [33]Even so, when you see all these things, you know that it[b] is near, right at the door. [34]I tell you the truth, this generation[c] will certainly not pass away until all these things have happened. [35]Heaven and earth will pass away, but my words will never pass away.

THE DAY AND HOUR UNKNOWN

[36]"No one knows about that day or hour, not even the angels in heaven, nor the Son,[d] but only the Father. [37]As it was in the days of Noah, so it will be at the coming of the Son of Man. [38]For in the days before the flood, people were eating and drinking, marrying and giving in marriage, up to the day Noah entered the ark; [39]and they knew nothing about what would happen until the flood came and took them all away. That is how it will be at the coming of the Son of Man. [40]Two men will be in the field; one will be taken and the other left. [41]Two women will be grinding with a hand mill; one will be taken and the other left.

[42]"Therefore keep watch, because you do not know on what day your Lord will come. [43]But

THE MESSAGE

'Here's the Messiah!' or points, 'There he is!' don't fall for it. Fake Messiahs and lying preachers are going to pop up everywhere. Their impressive credentials and dazzling performances will pull the wool over the eyes of even those who ought to know better. But I've given you fair warning.

24.26-28 "So if they say, 'Run to the country and see him arrive!' or, 'Quick, get downtown, see him come!' don't give them the time of day. The Arrival of the Son of Man isn't something you go to see. He comes like swift lightning to you! Whenever you see crowds gathering, think of carrion vultures circling, moving in, hovering over a rotting carcass. You can be quite sure that it's not the living Son of Man pulling in those crowds.

24.29 "Following those hard times,

Sun will fade out,
   moon cloud over,
Stars fall out of the sky,
   cosmic powers tremble.

24.30-31 "Then, the Arrival of the Son of Man! It will fill the skies—no one will miss it. Unready people all over the world, outsiders to the splendor and power, will raise a huge lament as they watch the Son of Man blazing out of heaven. At that same moment, he'll dispatch his angels with a trumpet-blast summons, pulling in God's chosen from the four winds, from pole to pole.

24.32-35 "Take a lesson from the fig tree. From the moment you notice its buds form, the merest hint of green, you know summer's just around the corner. So it is with you: When you see all these things, you'll know he's at the door. Don't take this lightly. I'm not just saying this for some future generation, but for all of you. This age continues until all these things take place. Sky and earth will wear out; my words won't wear out.

24.36 "But the exact day and hour? No one knows that, not even heaven's angels, not even the Son. Only the Father knows.

24.37-39 "The Arrival of the Son of Man will take place in times like Noah's. Before the great flood everyone was carrying on as usual, having a good time right up to the day Noah boarded the ark. They knew nothing—until the flood hit and swept everything away.

24.39-44 "The Son of Man's Arrival will be like that: Two men will be working in the field—one will be taken, one left behind; two women will be grinding at the mill—one will be taken, one left behind. So stay awake, alert. You have no idea what day your Master will show up. But

---

[a] 29 Isaiah 13:10; 34:4   [b] 33 Or *he*   [c] 34 Or *race*
[d] 36 Some manuscripts do not have *nor the Son.*

NEW INTERNATIONAL VERSION

understand this: If the owner of the house had known at what time of night the thief was coming, he would have kept watch and would not have let his house be broken into. ⁴⁴So you also must be ready, because the Son of Man will come at an hour when you do not expect him.

⁴⁵"Who then is the faithful and wise servant, whom the master has put in charge of the servants in his household to give them their food at the proper time? ⁴⁶It will be good for that servant whose master finds him doing so when he returns. ⁴⁷I tell you the truth, he will put him in charge of all his possessions. ⁴⁸But suppose that servant is wicked and says to himself, 'My master is staying away a long time,' ⁴⁹and he then begins to beat his fellow servants and to eat and drink with drunkards. ⁵⁰The master of that servant will come on a day when he does not expect him and at an hour he is not aware of. ⁵¹He will cut him to pieces and assign him a place with the hypocrites, where there will be weeping and gnashing of teeth.

THE PARABLE OF THE TEN VIRGINS

25 "At that time the kingdom of heaven will be like ten virgins who took their lamps and went out to meet the bridegroom. ²Five of them were foolish and five were wise. ³The foolish ones took their lamps but did not take any oil with them. ⁴The wise, however, took oil in jars along with their lamps. ⁵The bridegroom was a long time in coming, and they all became drowsy and fell asleep.

⁶"At midnight the cry rang out: 'Here's the bridegroom! Come out to meet him!'

⁷"Then all the virgins woke up and trimmed their lamps. ⁸The foolish ones said to the wise, 'Give us some of your oil; our lamps are going out.'

⁹"'No,' they replied, 'there may not be enough for both us and you. Instead, go to those who sell oil and buy some for yourselves.'

¹⁰"But while they were on their way to buy the oil, the bridegroom arrived. The virgins who were ready went in with him to the wedding banquet. And the door was shut.

¹¹"Later the others also came. 'Sir! Sir!' they said. 'Open the door for us!'

¹²"But he replied, 'I tell you the truth, I don't know you.'

¹³"Therefore keep watch, because you do not know the day or the hour.

THE PARABLE OF THE TALENTS

¹⁴"Again, it will be like a man going on a journey, who called his servants and entrusted his

THE MESSAGE

you do know this: You know that if the homeowner had known what time of night the burglar would arrive, he would have been there with his dogs to prevent the break-in. Be vigilant just like that. You have no idea when the Son of Man is going to show up.

24.45-47 "Who here qualifies for the job of overseeing the kitchen? A person the Master can depend on to feed the workers on time each day. Someone the Master can drop in on unannounced and always find him doing his job. A God-blessed man or woman, I tell you. It won't be long before the Master will put this person in charge of the whole operation.

24.48-51 "But if that person only looks out for himself, and the minute the Master is away does what he pleases—abusing the help and throwing drunken parties for his friends—the Master is going to show up when he least expects it and make hash of him. He'll end up in the dump with the hypocrites, out in the cold shivering, teeth chattering.

THE STORY OF THE VIRGINS

25.1-5 **25** "God's kingdom is like ten young virgins who took oil lamps and went out to greet the bridegroom. Five were silly and five were smart. The silly virgins took lamps, but no extra oil. The smart virgins took jars of oil to feed their lamps. The bridegroom didn't show up when they expected him, and they all fell asleep.

25.6 "In the middle of the night someone yelled out, 'He's here! The bridegroom's here! Go out and greet him!'

25.7-8 "The ten virgins got up and got their lamps ready. The silly virgins said to the smart ones, 'Our lamps are going out; lend us some of your oil.'

25.9 "They answered, 'There might not be enough to go around; go buy your own.'

25.10 "They did, but while they were out buying oil, the bridegroom arrived. When everyone who was there to greet him had gone into the wedding feast, the door was locked.

25.11 "Much later, the other virgins, the silly ones, showed up and knocked on the door, saying, 'Master, we're here. Let us in.'

25.12 "He answered, 'Do I know you? I don't think I know you.'

25.13 "So stay alert. You have no idea when he might arrive.

THE STORY ABOUT INVESTMENT

25.14-18 "It's also like a man going off on an extended trip. He called his servants together and dele-

NEW INTERNATIONAL VERSION

property to them. [15]To one he gave five talents[a] of money, to another two talents, and to another one talent, each according to his ability. Then he went on his journey. [16]The man who had received the five talents went at once and put his money to work and gained five more. [17]So also, the one with the two talents gained two more. [18]But the man who had received the one talent went off, dug a hole in the ground and hid his master's money.

[19]"After a long time the master of those servants returned and settled accounts with them. [20]The man who had received the five talents brought the other five. 'Master,' he said, 'you entrusted me with five talents. See, I have gained five more.'

[21]"His master replied, 'Well done, good and faithful servant! You have been faithful with a few things; I will put you in charge of many things. Come and share your master's happiness!'

[22]"The man with the two talents also came. 'Master,' he said, 'you entrusted me with two talents; see, I have gained two more.'

[23]"His master replied, 'Well done, good and faithful servant! You have been faithful with a few things; I will put you in charge of many things. Come and share your master's happiness!'

[24]"Then the man who had received the one talent came. 'Master,' he said, 'I knew that you are a hard man, harvesting where you have not sown and gathering where you have not scattered seed. [25]So I was afraid and went out and hid your talent in the ground. See, here is what belongs to you.'

[26]"His master replied, 'You wicked, lazy servant! So you knew that I harvest where I have not sown and gather where I have not scattered seed? [27]Well then, you should have put my money on deposit with the bankers, so that when I returned I would have received it back with interest.

[28]"'Take the talent from him and give it to the one who has the ten talents. [29]For everyone who has will be given more, and he will have an abundance. Whoever does not have, even what he has will be taken from him. [30]And throw that worthless servant outside, into the darkness, where there will be weeping and gnashing of teeth.'

THE SHEEP AND THE GOATS

[31]"When the Son of Man comes in his glory, and all the angels with him, he will sit on his throne in heavenly glory. [32]All the nations will

---

[a] 15 A talent was worth more than a thousand dollars.

THE MESSAGE

gated responsibilities. To one he gave five thousand dollars, to another two thousand, to a third one thousand, depending on their abilities. Then he left. Right off, the first servant went to work and doubled his master's investment. The second did the same. But the man with the single thousand dug a hole and carefully buried his master's money.

25.19-21 "After a long absence, the master of those three servants came back and settled up with them. The one given five thousand dollars showed him how he had doubled his investment. His master commended him: 'Good work! You did your job well. From now on be my partner.'

25.22-23 "The servant with the two thousand showed how he also had doubled his master's investment. His master commended him: 'Good work! You did your job well. From now on be my partner.'

25.24-25 "The servant given one thousand said, 'Master, I know you have high standards and hate careless ways, that you demand the best and make no allowances for error. I was afraid I might disappoint you, so I found a good hiding place and secured your money. Here it is, safe and sound down to the last cent.'

25.26-27 "The master was furious. 'That's a terrible way to live! It's criminal to live cautiously like that! If you knew I was after the best, why did you do less than the least? The least you could have done would have been to invest the sum with the bankers, where at least I would have gotten a little interest.

25.28-30 "'Take the thousand and give it to the one who risked the most. And get rid of this "play-it-safe" who won't go out on a limb. Throw him out into utter darkness.'

THE SHEEP AND THE GOATS

25.31-33 "When he finally arrives, blazing in beauty and all his angels with him, the Son of Man will take his place on his glorious throne. Then all

NEW INTERNATIONAL VERSION

be gathered before him, and he will separate the people one from another as a shepherd separates the sheep from the goats. ³³He will put the sheep on his right and the goats on his left.

³⁴"Then the King will say to those on his right, 'Come, you who are blessed by my Father; take your inheritance, the kingdom prepared for you since the creation of the world. ³⁵For I was hungry and you gave me something to eat, I was thirsty and you gave me something to drink, I was a stranger and you invited me in, ³⁶I needed clothes and you clothed me, I was sick and you looked after me, I was in prison and you came to visit me.'

³⁷"Then the righteous will answer him, 'Lord, when did we see you hungry and feed you, or thirsty and give you something to drink? ³⁸When did we see you a stranger and invite you in, or needing clothes and clothe you? ³⁹When did we see you sick or in prison and go to visit you?'

⁴⁰"The King will reply, 'I tell you the truth, whatever you did for one of the least of these brothers of mine, you did for me.'

⁴¹"Then he will say to those on his left, 'Depart from me, you who are cursed, into the eternal fire prepared for the devil and his angels. ⁴²For I was hungry and you gave me nothing to eat, I was thirsty and you gave me nothing to drink, ⁴³I was a stranger and you did not invite me in, I needed clothes and you did not clothe me, I was sick and in prison and you did not look after me.'

⁴⁴"They also will answer, 'Lord, when did we see you hungry or thirsty or a stranger or needing clothes or sick or in prison, and did not help you?'

⁴⁵"He will reply, 'I tell you the truth, whatever you did not do for one of the least of these, you did not do for me.'

⁴⁶"Then they will go away to eternal punishment, but the righteous to eternal life."

THE PLOT AGAINST JESUS

26 When Jesus had finished saying all these things, he said to his disciples, ²"As you know, the Passover is two days away—and the Son of Man will be handed over to be crucified."

³Then the chief priests and the elders of the people assembled in the palace of the high

THE MESSAGE

the nations will be arranged before him and he will sort the people out, much as a shepherd sorts out sheep and goats, putting sheep to his right and goats to his left.

25.34-36 "Then the King will say to those on his right, 'Enter, you who are blessed by my Father! Take what's coming to you in this kingdom. It's been ready for you since the world's foundation. And here's why:

25.37-40
I was hungry and you fed me,
I was thirsty and you gave me a drink,
I was homeless and you gave me a room,
I was shivering and you gave me clothes,
I was sick and you stopped to visit,
I was in prison and you came to me.'

"Then those 'sheep' are going to say, 'Master, what are you talking about? When did we ever see you hungry and feed you, thirsty and give you a drink? And when did we ever see you sick or in prison and come to you?' Then the King will say, 'I'm telling the solemn truth: Whenever you did one of these things to someone overlooked or ignored, that was me—you did it to me.'

25.41-43 "Then he will turn to the 'goats,' the ones on his left, and say, 'Get out, worthless goats! You're good for nothing but the fires of hell. And why? Because—

I was hungry and you gave me no meal,
I was thirsty and you gave me no drink,
I was homeless and you gave me no bed,
I was shivering and you gave me no
         clothes,
Sick and in prison, and you never visited.'

25.44 "Then those 'goats' are going to say, 'Master, what are you talking about? When did we ever see you hungry or thirsty or homeless or shivering or sick or in prison and didn't help?'

25.45 "He will answer them, 'I'm telling the solemn truth: Whenever you failed to do one of these things to someone who was being overlooked or ignored, that was me—you failed to do it to me.'

25.46 "Then those 'goats' will be herded to their eternal doom, but the 'sheep' to their eternal reward."

ANOINTED FOR BURIAL

26.1-2 **26** When Jesus finished saying these things, he told his disciples, "You know that Passover comes in two days. That's when the Son of Man will be betrayed and handed over for crucifixion."

26.3-5 At that very moment, the party of high priests and religious leaders was meeting in the

NEW INTERNATIONAL VERSION

priest, whose name was Caiaphas, ⁴and they plotted to arrest Jesus in some sly way and kill him. ⁵"But not during the Feast," they said, "or there may be a riot among the people."

JESUS ANOINTED AT BETHANY

⁶While Jesus was in Bethany in the home of a man known as Simon the Leper, ⁷a woman came to him with an alabaster jar of very expensive perfume, which she poured on his head as he was reclining at the table.

⁸When the disciples saw this, they were indignant. "Why this waste?" they asked. ⁹"This perfume could have been sold at a high price and the money given to the poor."

¹⁰Aware of this, Jesus said to them, "Why are you bothering this woman? She has done a beautiful thing to me. ¹¹The poor you will always have with you, but you will not always have me. ¹²When she poured this perfume on my body, she did it to prepare me for burial. ¹³I tell you the truth, wherever this gospel is preached throughout the world, what she has done will also be told, in memory of her."

JUDAS AGREES TO BETRAY JESUS

¹⁴Then one of the Twelve—the one called Judas Iscariot—went to the chief priests ¹⁵and asked, "What are you willing to give me if I hand him over to you?" So they counted out for him thirty silver coins. ¹⁶From then on Judas watched for an opportunity to hand him over.

THE LORD'S SUPPER

¹⁷On the first day of the Feast of Unleavened Bread, the disciples came to Jesus and asked, "Where do you want us to make preparations for you to eat the Passover?"

¹⁸He replied, "Go into the city to a certain man and tell him, 'The Teacher says: My appointed time is near. I am going to celebrate the Passover with my disciples at your house.' " ¹⁹So the disciples did as Jesus had directed them and prepared the Passover.

²⁰When evening came, Jesus was reclining at the table with the Twelve. ²¹And while they were eating, he said, "I tell you the truth, one of you will betray me."

²²They were very sad and began to say to him one after the other, "Surely not I, Lord?"

²³Jesus replied, "The one who has dipped his hand into the bowl with me will betray me. ²⁴The Son of Man will go just as it is written about him. But woe to that man who betrays the Son of Man! It would be better for him if he had not been born."

THE MESSAGE

chambers of the Chief Priest named Caiaphas, conspiring to seize Jesus by stealth and kill him. They agreed that it should not be done during Passover Week. "We don't want a riot on our hands," they said.

26.6-9 When Jesus was at Bethany, a guest of Simon the Leper, a woman came up to him as he was eating dinner and anointed him with a bottle of very expensive perfume. When the disciples saw what was happening, they were furious. "That's criminal! This could have been sold for a lot and the money handed out to the poor."

26.10-13 When Jesus realized what was going on, he intervened. "Why are you giving this woman a hard time? She has just done something wonderfully significant for me. You will have the poor with you every day for the rest of your lives, but not me. When she poured this perfume on my body, what she really did was anoint me for burial. You can be sure that wherever in the whole world the Message is preached, what she has just done is going to be remembered and admired."

26.14-16 That is when one of the Twelve, the one named Judas Iscariot, went to the cabal of high priests and said, "What will you give me if I hand him over to you?" They settled on thirty silver pieces. He began looking for just the right moment to hand him over.

THE TRAITOR

26.17 On the first of the Days of Unleavened Bread, the disciples came to Jesus and said, "Where do you want us to prepare your Passover meal?"

26.18-19 He said, "Enter the city. Go up to a certain man and say, 'The Teacher says, My time is near. I and my disciples plan to celebrate the Passover meal at your house.' " The disciples followed Jesus' instructions to the letter, and prepared the Passover meal.

26.20-21 After sunset, he and the Twelve were sitting around the table. During the meal, he said, "I have something hard but important to say to you: One of you is going to hand me over to the conspirators."

26.22 They were stunned, and then began to ask, one after another, "It isn't me, is it, Master?"

26.23-24 Jesus answered, "The one who hands me over is someone I eat with daily, one who passes me food at the table. In one sense the Son of Man is entering into a way of treachery well-marked by the Scriptures—no surprises here. In another sense that man who turns him in, turns traitor to the Son of Man—better never to have been born than do this!"

NEW INTERNATIONAL VERSION

²⁵Then Judas, the one who would betray him, said, "Surely not I, Rabbi?"

Jesus answered, "Yes, it is you."^a

²⁶While they were eating, Jesus took bread, gave thanks and broke it, and gave it to his disciples, saying, "Take and eat; this is my body."

²⁷Then he took the cup, gave thanks and offered it to them, saying, "Drink from it, all of you. ²⁸This is my blood of the^b covenant, which is poured out for many for the forgiveness of sins. ²⁹I tell you, I will not drink of this fruit of the vine from now on until that day when I drink it anew with you in my Father's kingdom."

³⁰When they had sung a hymn, they went out to the Mount of Olives.

JESUS PREDICTS PETER'S DENIAL

³¹Then Jesus told them, "This very night you will all fall away on account of me, for it is written:

" 'I will strike the shepherd,
    and the sheep of the flock will be
        scattered.'^c

³²But after I have risen, I will go ahead of you into Galilee."

³³Peter replied, "Even if all fall away on account of you, I never will."

³⁴"I tell you the truth," Jesus answered, "this very night, before the rooster crows, you will disown me three times."

³⁵But Peter declared, "Even if I have to die with you, I will never disown you." And all the other disciples said the same.

GETHSEMANE

³⁶Then Jesus went with his disciples to a place called Gethsemane, and he said to them, "Sit here while I go over there and pray." ³⁷He took Peter and the two sons of Zebedee along with him, and he began to be sorrowful and troubled. ³⁸Then he said to them, "My soul is overwhelmed with sorrow to the point of death. Stay here and keep watch with me."

³⁹Going a little farther, he fell with his face to the ground and prayed, "My Father, if it is possible, may this cup be taken from me. Yet not as I will, but as you will."

⁴⁰Then he returned to his disciples and found them sleeping. "Could you men not keep watch with me for one hour?" he asked Peter. ⁴¹"Watch

THE MESSAGE

26.25 Then Judas, already turned traitor, said, "It isn't me, is it, Rabbi?"

Jesus said, "Don't play games with me, Judas."

THE BREAD AND THE CUP

26.26-29 During the meal, Jesus took and blessed the bread, broke it, and gave it to his disciples:

Take, eat.
This is my body.

Taking the cup and thanking God, he gave it to them:

Drink this, all of you.
This is my blood,
God's new covenant poured out for many
    people
    for the forgiveness of sins.

"I'll not be drinking wine from this cup again until that new day when I'll drink with you in the kingdom of my Father."

26.30 They sang a hymn and went directly to Mount Olives.

GETHSEMANE

26.31-32 Then Jesus told them, "Before the night's over, you're going to fall to pieces because of what happens to me. There is a Scripture that says,

I'll strike the shepherd;
helter-skelter the sheep will be scattered.

But after I am raised up, I, your Shepherd, will go ahead of you, leading the way to Galilee."

26.33 Peter broke in, "Even if everyone else falls to pieces on account of you, I won't."

26.34 "Don't be so sure," Jesus said. "This very night, before the rooster crows up the dawn, you will deny me three times."

26.35 Peter protested, "Even if I had to die with you, I would never deny you." All the others said the same thing.

26.36-38 Then Jesus went with them to a garden called Gethsemane and told his disciples, "Stay here while I go over there and pray." Taking along Peter and the two sons of Zebedee, he plunged into an agonizing sorrow. Then he said, "This sorrow is crushing my life out. Stay here and keep vigil with me."

26.39 Going a little ahead, he fell on his face, praying, "My Father, if there is any way, get me out of this. But please, not what I want. You, what do *you* want?"

26.40-41 When he came back to his disciples, he found them sound asleep. He said to Peter, "Can't you stick it out with me a single hour? Stay alert; be in prayer so you don't wander

---

^a 25 Or *"You yourself have said it"*   ^b 28 Some manuscripts *the new*   ^c 31 Zech. 13:7

NEW INTERNATIONAL VERSION

and pray so that you will not fall into temptation. The spirit is willing, but the body is weak."

⁴²He went away a second time and prayed, "My Father, if it is not possible for this cup to be taken away unless I drink it, may your will be done."

⁴³When he came back, he again found them sleeping, because their eyes were heavy. ⁴⁴So he left them and went away once more and prayed the third time, saying the same thing.

⁴⁵Then he returned to the disciples and said to them, "Are you still sleeping and resting? Look, the hour is near, and the Son of Man is betrayed into the hands of sinners. ⁴⁶Rise, let us go! Here comes my betrayer!"

JESUS ARRESTED

⁴⁷While he was still speaking, Judas, one of the Twelve, arrived. With him was a large crowd armed with swords and clubs, sent from the chief priests and the elders of the people. ⁴⁸Now the betrayer had arranged a signal with them: "The one I kiss is the man; arrest him." ⁴⁹Going at once to Jesus, Judas said, "Greetings, Rabbi!" and kissed him.

⁵⁰Jesus replied, "Friend, do what you came for." ᵃ

Then the men stepped forward, seized Jesus and arrested him. ⁵¹With that, one of Jesus' companions reached for his sword, drew it out and struck the servant of the high priest, cutting off his ear.

⁵²"Put your sword back in its place," Jesus said to him, "for all who draw the sword will die by the sword. ⁵³Do you think I cannot call on my Father, and he will at once put at my disposal more than twelve legions of angels? ⁵⁴But how then would the Scriptures be fulfilled that say it must happen in this way?"

⁵⁵At that time Jesus said to the crowd, "Am I leading a rebellion, that you have come out with swords and clubs to capture me? Every day I sat in the temple courts teaching, and you did not arrest me. ⁵⁶But this has all taken place that the writings of the prophets might be fulfilled." Then all the disciples deserted him and fled.

BEFORE THE SANHEDRIN

⁵⁷Those who had arrested Jesus took him to Caiaphas, the high priest, where the teachers of the law and the elders had assembled. ⁵⁸But Peter followed him at a distance, right up to the

THE MESSAGE

into temptation without even knowing you're in danger. There is a part of you that is eager, ready for anything in God. But there's another part that's as lazy as an old dog sleeping by the fire."

26.42 He then left them a second time. Again he prayed, "My Father, if there is no other way than this, drinking this cup to the dregs, I'm ready. Do it your way."

26.43-44 When he came back, he again found them sound asleep. They simply couldn't keep their eyes open. This time he let them sleep on, and went back a third time to pray, going over the same ground one last time.

26.45-46 When he came back the next time, he said, "Are you going to sleep on and make a night of it? My time is up, the Son of Man is about to be handed over to the hands of sinners. Get up! Let's get going! My betrayer is here."

WITH SWORDS AND CLUBS

26.47-49 The words were barely out of his mouth when Judas (the one from the Twelve) showed up, and with him a gang from the high priests and religious leaders brandishing swords and clubs. The betrayer had worked out a sign with them: "The one I kiss, that's the one—seize him." He went straight to Jesus, greeted him, "How are you, Rabbi?" and kissed him.

26.50-51 Jesus said, "Friend, why this charade?"

Then they came on him—grabbed him and roughed him up. One of those with Jesus pulled his sword and, taking a swing at the Chief Priest's servant, cut off his ear.

26.52-54 Jesus said, "Put your sword back where it belongs. All who use swords are destroyed by swords. Don't you realize that I am able right now to call to my Father, and twelve companies—more, if I want them—of fighting angels would be here, battle-ready? But if I did that, how would the Scriptures come true that say this is the way it has to be?"

26.55-56 Then Jesus addressed the mob: "What is this—coming out after me with swords and clubs as if I were a dangerous criminal? Day after day I have been sitting in the Temple teaching, and you never so much as lifted a hand against me. You've done it this way to confirm and fulfill the prophetic writings."

Then all the disciples cut and ran.

FALSE CHARGES

26.57-58 The gang that had seized Jesus led him before Caiaphas the Chief Priest, where the religion scholars and leaders had assembled. Peter followed at a safe distance until they got to the

---

ᵃ 50 Or *"Friend, why have you come?"*

NEW INTERNATIONAL VERSION

courtyard of the high priest. He entered and sat down with the guards to see the outcome.

⁵⁹The chief priests and the whole Sanhedrin were looking for false evidence against Jesus so that they could put him to death. ⁶⁰But they did not find any, though many false witnesses came forward.

Finally two came forward ⁶¹and declared, "This fellow said, 'I am able to destroy the temple of God and rebuild it in three days.' "

⁶²Then the high priest stood up and said to Jesus, "Are you not going to answer? What is this testimony that these men are bringing against you?" ⁶³But Jesus remained silent.

The high priest said to him, "I charge you under oath by the living God: Tell us if you are the Christ,ᵃ the Son of God."

⁶⁴"Yes, it is as you say," Jesus replied. "But I say to all of you: In the future you will see the Son of Man sitting at the right hand of the Mighty One and coming on the clouds of heaven."

⁶⁵Then the high priest tore his clothes and said, "He has spoken blasphemy! Why do we need any more witnesses? Look, now you have heard the blasphemy. ⁶⁶What do you think?"

"He is worthy of death," they answered.

⁶⁷Then they spit in his face and struck him with their fists. Others slapped him ⁶⁸and said, "Prophesy to us, Christ. Who hit you?"

Peter Disowns Jesus

⁶⁹Now Peter was sitting out in the courtyard, and a servant girl came to him. "You also were with Jesus of Galilee," she said.

⁷⁰But he denied it before them all. "I don't know what you're talking about," he said.

⁷¹Then he went out to the gateway, where another girl saw him and said to the people there, "This fellow was with Jesus of Nazareth."

⁷²He denied it again, with an oath: "I don't know the man!"

⁷³After a little while, those standing there went up to Peter and said, "Surely you are one of them, for your accent gives you away."

⁷⁴Then he began to call down curses on himself and he swore to them, "I don't know the man!"

Immediately a rooster crowed. ⁷⁵Then Peter remembered the word Jesus had spoken: "Before the rooster crows, you will disown me three times." And he went outside and wept bitterly.

ᵃ 63 Or *Messiah*; also in verse 68

THE MESSAGE

Chief Priest's courtyard. Then he slipped in and mingled with the servants, watching to see how things would turn out.

26.59-60 The high priests, conspiring with the Jewish Council, tried to cook up charges against Jesus in order to sentence him to death. But even though many stepped up, making up one false accusation after another, nothing was believable.

26.60-61 Finally two men came forward with this: "He said, 'I can tear down this Temple of God and after three days rebuild it.' "

26.62 The Chief Priest stood up and said, "What do you have to say to the accusation?"

26.63 Jesus kept silent.

Then the Chief Priest said, "I command you by the authority of the living God to say if you are the Messiah, the Son of God."

26.64 Jesus was curt: "You yourself said it. And that's not all. Soon you'll see it for yourself:

The Son of Man seated at the right hand of
the Mighty One,
Arriving on the clouds of heaven."

26.65-66 At that, the Chief Priest lost his temper, ripping his robes, yelling, "He blasphemed! Why do we need witnesses to accuse him? You all heard him blaspheme! Are you going to stand for such blasphemy?"

They all said, "Death! That seals his death sentence."

26.67-68 Then they were spitting in his face and banging him around. They jeered as they slapped him: "Prophesy, Messiah: Who hit you that time?"

Denial in the Courtyard

26.69 All this time, Peter was sitting out in the courtyard. One servant girl came up to him and said, "You were with Jesus the Galilean."

26.70 In front of everybody there, he denied it. "I don't know what you're talking about."

26.71 As he moved over toward the gate, someone else said to the people there, "This man was with Jesus the Nazarene."

26.72 Again he denied it, salting his denial with an oath: "I swear, I never laid eyes on the man."

26.73 Shortly after that, some bystanders approached Peter. "You've got to be one of them. Your accent gives you away."

26.74-75 Then he got really nervous and swore. "I don't know the man!"

Just then a rooster crowed. Peter remembered what Jesus had said: "Before the rooster crows, you will deny me three times." He went out and cried and cried and cried.

NEW INTERNATIONAL VERSION

JUDAS HANGS HIMSELF

27 Early in the morning, all the chief priests and the elders of the people came to the decision to put Jesus to death. ²They bound him, led him away and handed him over to Pilate, the governor.

³When Judas, who had betrayed him, saw that Jesus was condemned, he was seized with remorse and returned the thirty silver coins to the chief priests and the elders. ⁴"I have sinned," he said, "for I have betrayed innocent blood."

"What is that to us?" they replied. "That's your responsibility."

⁵So Judas threw the money into the temple and left. Then he went away and hanged himself.

⁶The chief priests picked up the coins and said, "It is against the law to put this into the treasury, since it is blood money." ⁷So they decided to use the money to buy the potter's field as a burial place for foreigners. ⁸That is why it has been called the Field of Blood to this day. ⁹Then what was spoken by Jeremiah the prophet was fulfilled: "They took the thirty silver coins, the price set on him by the people of Israel, ¹⁰and they used them to buy the potter's field, as the Lord commanded me." *a*

JESUS BEFORE PILATE

¹¹Meanwhile Jesus stood before the governor, and the governor asked him, "Are you the king of the Jews?"

"Yes, it is as you say," Jesus replied.

¹²When he was accused by the chief priests and the elders, he gave no answer. ¹³Then Pilate asked him, "Don't you hear the testimony they are bringing against you?" ¹⁴But Jesus made no reply, not even to a single charge—to the great amazement of the governor.

¹⁵Now it was the governor's custom at the Feast to release a prisoner chosen by the crowd. ¹⁶At that time they had a notorious prisoner, called Barabbas. ¹⁷So when the crowd had gathered, Pilate asked them, "Which one do you want me to release to you: Barabbas, or Jesus who is called Christ?" ¹⁸For he knew it was out of envy that they had handed Jesus over to him.

¹⁹While Pilate was sitting on the judge's seat, his wife sent him this message: "Don't have anything to do with that innocent man, for I have suffered a great deal today in a dream because of him."

a 10 See Zech. 11:12,13; Jer. 19:1-13; 32:6-9.

THE MESSAGE

THIRTY SILVER COINS

27 In the first light of dawn, all the high priests and religious leaders met and put the finishing touches on their plot to kill Jesus. Then they tied him up and paraded him to Pilate, the governor.

27.3-4 Judas, the one who betrayed him, realized that Jesus was doomed. Overcome with remorse, he gave back the thirty silver coins to the high priests, saying, "I've sinned. I've betrayed an innocent man."

They said, "What do we care? That's *your* problem!"

27.5 Judas threw the silver coins into the Temple and left. Then he went out and hung himself.

27.6-10 The high priests picked up the silver pieces, but then didn't know what to do with them. "It wouldn't be right to give this—a payment for murder!—as an offering in the Temple." They decided to get rid of it by buying the "Potter's Field" and use it as a burial place for the homeless. That's how the field got called "Murder Meadow," a name that has stuck to this day. Then Jeremiah's words became history:

They took the thirty silver pieces,
The price of the one priced by some sons of Israel,
And they purchased the potter's field.

And so they unwittingly followed the divine instructions to the letter.

PILATE

27.11 Jesus was placed before the governor, who questioned him: "Are you the 'King of the Jews'?"

Jesus said, "If you say so."

27.12-14 But when the accusations rained down hot and heavy from the high priests and religious leaders, he said nothing. Pilate asked him, "Do you hear that long list of accusations? Aren't you going to say something?" Jesus kept silence—not a word from his mouth. The governor was impressed, really impressed.

27.15-18 It was an old custom during the Feast for the governor to pardon a single prisoner named by the crowd. At the time, they had the infamous Jesus Barabbas in prison. With the crowd before him, Pilate said, "Which prisoner do you want me to pardon: Jesus Barabbas, or Jesus the so-called Christ?" He knew it was through sheer spite that they had turned Jesus over to him.

27.19 While court was still in session, Pilate's wife sent him a message: "Don't get mixed up in judging this noble man. I've just been through a long and troubled night because of a dream about him."

NEW INTERNATIONAL VERSION

²⁰But the chief priests and the elders persuaded the crowd to ask for Barabbas and to have Jesus executed.

²¹"Which of the two do you want me to release to you?" asked the governor.

"Barabbas," they answered.

²²"What shall I do, then, with Jesus who is called Christ?" Pilate asked.

They all answered, "Crucify him!"

²³"Why? What crime has he committed?" asked Pilate.

But they shouted all the louder, "Crucify him!"

²⁴When Pilate saw that he was getting nowhere, but that instead an uproar was starting, he took water and washed his hands in front of the crowd. "I am innocent of this man's blood," he said. "It is your responsibility!"

²⁵All the people answered, "Let his blood be on us and on our children!"

²⁶Then he released Barabbas to them. But he had Jesus flogged, and handed him over to be crucified.

THE SOLDIERS MOCK JESUS

²⁷Then the governor's soldiers took Jesus into the Praetorium and gathered the whole company of soldiers around him. ²⁸They stripped him and put a scarlet robe on him, ²⁹and then twisted together a crown of thorns and set it on his head. They put a staff in his right hand and knelt in front of him and mocked him. "Hail, king of the Jews!" they said. ³⁰They spit on him, and took the staff and struck him on the head again and again. ³¹After they had mocked him, they took off the robe and put his own clothes on him. Then they led him away to crucify him.

THE CRUCIFIXION

³²As they were going out, they met a man from Cyrene, named Simon, and they forced him to carry the cross. ³³They came to a place called Golgotha (which means The Place of the Skull). ³⁴There they offered Jesus wine to drink, mixed with gall; but after tasting it, he refused to drink it. ³⁵When they had crucified him, they divided up his clothes by casting lots.ᵃ ³⁶And sitting down, they kept watch over him there. ³⁷Above his head they placed the written charge against him: THIS IS JESUS, THE KING OF THE JEWS. ³⁸Two robbers were crucified with him, one on his right and one on his left. ³⁹Those who passed by hurled insults at him, shaking their heads ⁴⁰and saying, "You who are going to destroy the temple

ᵃ *35 A few late manuscripts lots that the word spoken by the prophet might be fulfilled: "They divided my garments among themselves and cast lots for my clothing" (Psalm 22:18)*

THE MESSAGE

27.20 Meanwhile, the high priests and religious leaders had talked the crowd into asking for the pardon of Barabbas and the execution of Jesus.

27.21 The governor asked, "Which of the two do you want me to pardon?"

They said, "Barabbas!"

27.22 "Then what do I do with Jesus, the so-called Christ?"

They all shouted, "Nail him to a cross!"

27.23 He objected, "But for what crime?"

But they yelled all the louder, "Nail him to a cross!"

27.24 When Pilate saw that he was getting nowhere and that a riot was imminent, he took a basin of water and washed his hands in full sight of the crowd, saying, "I'm washing my hands of responsibility for this man's death. From now on, it's in your hands. You're judge and jury."

27.25 The crowd answered, "We'll take the blame, we and our children after us."

27.26 Then he pardoned Barabbas. But he had Jesus whipped, and then handed over for crucifixion.

THE CRUCIFIXION

27.27-31 The soldiers assigned to the governor took Jesus into the governor's palace and got the entire brigade together for some fun. They stripped him and dressed him in a red toga. They plaited a crown from branches of a thorn bush and set it on his head. They put a stick in his right hand for a scepter. Then they knelt before him in mocking reverence: "Bravo, King of the Jews!" they said. "Bravo!" Then they spit on him and hit him on the head with the stick. When they had had their fun, they took off the toga and put his own clothes back on him. Then they proceeded out to the crucifixion.

27.32-34 Along the way they came on a man from Cyrene named Simon and made him carry Jesus' cross. Arriving at Golgotha, the place they call "Skull Hill," they offered him a mild painkiller (a mixture of wine and myrrh), but when he tasted it he wouldn't drink it.

27.35-40 After they had finished nailing him to the cross and were waiting for him to die, they whiled away the time by throwing dice for his clothes. Above his head they had posted the criminal charge against him: THIS IS JESUS, THE KING OF THE JEWS. Along with him, they also crucified two criminals, one to his right, the other to his left. People passing along the road jeered, shaking their heads in mock lament: "You bragged that you could tear down the Temple and then rebuild it in three days—so

NEW INTERNATIONAL VERSION

and build it in three days, save yourself! Come down from the cross, if you are the Son of God!"

⁴¹In the same way the chief priests, the teachers of the law and the elders mocked him. ⁴²"He saved others," they said, "but he can't save himself! He's the King of Israel! Let him come down now from the cross, and we will believe in him. ⁴³He trusts in God. Let God rescue him now if he wants him, for he said, 'I am the Son of God.' " ⁴⁴In the same way the robbers who were crucified with him also heaped insults on him.

THE DEATH OF JESUS

⁴⁵From the sixth hour until the ninth hour darkness came over all the land. ⁴⁶About the ninth hour Jesus cried out in a loud voice, *"Eloi, Eloi,ᵃ lama sabachthani?"*—which means, "My God, my God, why have you forsaken me?"ᵇ

⁴⁷When some of those standing there heard this, they said, "He's calling Elijah."

⁴⁸Immediately one of them ran and got a sponge. He filled it with wine vinegar, put it on a stick, and offered it to Jesus to drink. ⁴⁹The rest said, "Now leave him alone. Let's see if Elijah comes to save him."

⁵⁰And when Jesus had cried out again in a loud voice, he gave up his spirit.

⁵¹At that moment the curtain of the temple was torn in two from top to bottom. The earth shook and the rocks split. ⁵²The tombs broke open and the bodies of many holy people who had died were raised to life. ⁵³They came out of the tombs, and after Jesus' resurrection they went into the holy city and appeared to many people.

⁵⁴When the centurion and those with him who were guarding Jesus saw the earthquake and all that had happened, they were terrified, and exclaimed, "Surely he was the Sonᶜ of God!"

⁵⁵Many women were there, watching from a distance. They had followed Jesus from Galilee to care for his needs. ⁵⁶Among them were Mary Magdalene, Mary the mother of James and Joses, and the mother of Zebedee's sons.

THE BURIAL OF JESUS

⁵⁷As evening approached, there came a rich man from Arimathea, named Joseph, who had himself become a disciple of Jesus. ⁵⁸Going to Pilate, he asked for Jesus' body, and Pilate ordered that it be given to him. ⁵⁹Joseph took the body, wrapped it in a clean linen cloth, ⁶⁰and placed it in his own new tomb that he had cut out of the rock. He rolled a big stone in front of the entrance to the tomb and went away. ⁶¹Mary

---

ᵃ 46 Some manuscripts *Eli, Eli*   ᵇ 46 Psalm 22:1
ᶜ 54 Or *a son*

THE MESSAGE

show us your stuff! Save yourself! If you're really God's Son, come down from that cross!"

27.41-44 The high priests, along with the religion scholars and leaders, were right there mixing it up with the rest of them, having a great time poking fun at him: "He saved others—he can't save himself! King of Israel, is he? Then let him get down from that cross. We'll *all* become believers then! He was so sure of God—well, let him rescue his 'Son' now—if he wants him! He did claim to be God's Son, didn't he?" Even the two criminals crucified next to him joined in the mockery.

27.45-46 From noon to three, the whole earth was dark. Around mid-afternoon Jesus groaned out of the depths, crying loudly, *"Eli, Eli, lama sabachthani?"* which means, "My God, my God, why have you abandoned me?"

27.47-49 Some bystanders who heard him said, "He's calling for Elijah." One of them ran and got a sponge soaked in sour wine and lifted it on a stick so he could drink. The others joked, "Don't be in such a hurry. Let's see if Elijah comes and saves him."

27.50 But Jesus, again crying out loudly, breathed his last.

27.51-53 At that moment, the Temple curtain was ripped in two, top to bottom. There was an earthquake, and rocks were split in pieces. What's more, tombs were opened up, and many bodies of believers asleep in their graves were raised. (After Jesus' resurrection, they left the tombs, entered the holy city, and appeared to many.)

27.54 The captain of the guard and those with him, when they saw the earthquake and everything else that was happening, were scared to death. They said, "This has to be the Son of God!"

27.55-56 There were also quite a few women watching from a distance, women who had followed Jesus from Galilee in order to serve him. Among them were Mary Magdalene, Mary the mother of James and Joseph, and the mother of the Zebedee brothers.

THE TOMB

27.57-61 Late in the afternoon a wealthy man from Arimathea, a disciple of Jesus, arrived. His name was Joseph. He went to Pilate and asked for Jesus' body. Pilate granted his request. Joseph took the body and wrapped it in clean linens, put it in his own tomb, a new tomb only recently cut into the rock, and rolled a large stone across the entrance. Then he went off.

NEW INTERNATIONAL VERSION

Magdalene and the other Mary were sitting there opposite the tomb.

THE GUARD AT THE TOMB

⁶²The next day, the one after Preparation Day, the chief priests and the Pharisees went to Pilate. ⁶³"Sir," they said, "we remember that while he was still alive that deceiver said, 'After three days I will rise again.' ⁶⁴So give the order for the tomb to be made secure until the third day. Otherwise, his disciples may come and steal the body and tell the people that he has been raised from the dead. This last deception will be worse than the first."

⁶⁵"Take a guard," Pilate answered. "Go, make the tomb as secure as you know how." ⁶⁶So they went and made the tomb secure by putting a seal on the stone and posting the guard.

THE RESURRECTION

28 After the Sabbath, at dawn on the first day of the week, Mary Magdalene and the other Mary went to look at the tomb.

²There was a violent earthquake, for an angel of the Lord came down from heaven and, going to the tomb, rolled back the stone and sat on it. ³His appearance was like lightning, and his clothes were white as snow. ⁴The guards were so afraid of him that they shook and became like dead men.

⁵The angel said to the women, "Do not be afraid, for I know that you are looking for Jesus, who was crucified. ⁶He is not here; he has risen, just as he said. Come and see the place where he lay. ⁷Then go quickly and tell his disciples: 'He has risen from the dead and is going ahead of you into Galilee. There you will see him.' Now I have told you."

⁸So the women hurried away from the tomb, afraid yet filled with joy, and ran to tell his disciples. ⁹Suddenly Jesus met them. "Greetings," he said. They came to him, clasped his feet and worshiped him. ¹⁰Then Jesus said to them, "Do not be afraid. Go and tell my brothers to go to Galilee; there they will see me."

THE GUARDS' REPORT

¹¹While the women were on their way, some of the guards went into the city and reported to the chief priests everything that had happened. ¹²When the chief priests had met with the elders and devised a plan, they gave the soldiers a large sum of money, ¹³telling them, "You are to say, 'His disciples came during the night and stole him away while we were asleep.' ¹⁴If this

THE MESSAGE

But Mary Magdalene and the other Mary stayed, sitting in plain view of the tomb.

27.62-64 After sundown, the high priests and Pharisees arranged a meeting with Pilate. They said, "Sir, we just remembered that that liar announced while he was still alive, 'After three days I will be raised.' We've got to get that tomb sealed until the third day. There's a good chance his disciples will come and steal the corpse and then go around saying, 'He's risen from the dead.' Then we'll be worse off than before, the final deceit surpassing the first."

27.65-66 Pilate told them, "You will have a guard. Go ahead and secure it the best you can." So they went out and secured the tomb, sealing the stone and posting guards.

RISEN FROM THE DEAD

28.1-4 **28** After the Sabbath, as the first light of the new week dawned, Mary Magdalene and the other Mary came to keep vigil at the tomb. Suddenly the earth reeled and rocked under their feet as God's angel came down from heaven, came right up to where they were standing. He rolled back the stone and then sat on it. Shafts of lightning blazed from him. His garments shimmered snow-white. The guards at the tomb were scared to death. They were so frightened, they couldn't move.

28.5-6 The angel spoke to the women: "There is nothing to fear here. I know you're looking for Jesus, the One they nailed to the cross. He is not here. He was raised, just as he said. Come and look at the place where he was placed.

28.7 "Now, get on your way quickly and tell his disciples, 'He is risen from the dead. He is going on ahead of you to Galilee. You will see him there.' That's the message."

28.8-10 The women, deep in wonder and full of joy, lost no time in leaving the tomb. They ran to tell the disciples. Then Jesus met them, stopping them in their tracks. "Good morning!" he said. They fell to their knees, embraced his feet, and worshiped him. Jesus said, "You're holding on to me for dear life! Don't be frightened like that. Go tell my brothers that they are to go to Galilee, and that I'll meet them there."

28.11-15 Meanwhile, the guards had scattered, but a few of them went into the city and told the high priests everything that had happened. They called a meeting of the religious leaders and came up with a plan: They took a large sum of money and gave it to the soldiers, bribing them to say, "His disciples came in the night and stole the body while we were sleep-

NEW INTERNATIONAL VERSION

report gets to the governor, we will satisfy him and keep you out of trouble." ¹⁵So the soldiers took the money and did as they were instructed. And this story has been widely circulated among the Jews to this very day.

THE GREAT COMMISSION

¹⁶Then the eleven disciples went to Galilee, to the mountain where Jesus had told them to go. ¹⁷When they saw him, they worshiped him; but some doubted. ¹⁸Then Jesus came to them and said, "All authority in heaven and on earth has been given to me. ¹⁹Therefore go and make disciples of all nations, baptizing them in*ᵃ* the name of the Father and of the Son and of the Holy Spirit, ²⁰and teaching them to obey everything I have commanded you. And surely I am with you always, to the very end of the age."

THE MESSAGE

ing." They assured them, "If the governor hears about your sleeping on duty, we will make sure you don't get blamed." The soldiers took the bribe and did as they were told. That story, cooked up in the Jewish High Council, is still going around.

✝

28.16-17 Meanwhile, the eleven disciples were on their way to Galilee, headed for the mountain Jesus had set for their reunion. The moment they saw him they worshiped him. Some, though, held back, not sure about *worship*, about risking themselves totally.

28.18-20 Jesus, undeterred, went right ahead and gave his charge: "God authorized and commanded me to commission you: Go out and train everyone you meet, far and near, in this way of life, marking them by baptism in the threefold name: Father, Son, and Holy Spirit. Then instruct them in the practice of all I have commanded you. I'll be with you as you do this, day after day after day, right up to the end of the age."

ᵃ 19 Or *into*; see Acts 8:16; 19:5; Romans 6:3; 1 Cor. 1:13; 10:2 and Gal. 3:27.

MARK

MARK

JOHN THE BAPTIST PREPARES THE WAY

1 The beginning of the gospel about Jesus Christ, the Son of God. [a]

[2] It is written in Isaiah the prophet:

"I will send my messenger ahead of you,
    who will prepare your way" [b]—
[3] "a voice of one calling in the desert,
'Prepare the way for the Lord,
    make straight paths for him.' " [c]

[4] And so John came, baptizing in the desert region and preaching a baptism of repentance for the forgiveness of sins. [5] The whole Judean countryside and all the people of Jerusalem went out to him. Confessing their sins, they were baptized by him in the Jordan River. [6] John wore clothing made of camel's hair, with a leather belt around his waist, and he ate locusts and wild honey. [7] And this was his message: "After me will come one more powerful than I, the thongs of whose sandals I am not worthy to stoop down and untie. [8] I baptize you with [d] water, but he will baptize you with the Holy Spirit."

THE BAPTISM AND TEMPTATION OF JESUS

[9] At that time Jesus came from Nazareth in Galilee and was baptized by John in the Jordan. [10] As Jesus was coming up out of the water, he saw heaven being torn open and the Spirit descending on him like a dove. [11] And a voice came from heaven: "You are my Son, whom I love; with you I am well pleased."

[12] At once the Spirit sent him out into the desert, [13] and he was in the desert forty days, being tempted by Satan. He was with the wild animals, and angels attended him.

THE CALLING OF THE FIRST DISCIPLES

[14] After John was put in prison, Jesus went into Galilee, proclaiming the good news of God. [15] "The time has come," he said. "The kingdom of God is near. Repent and believe the good news!"

JOHN THE BAPTIZER

1.1-3 **1** The good news of Jesus Christ—the Message!—begins here, following to the letter the scroll of the prophet Isaiah.

Watch closely: I'm sending my preacher
        ahead of you;
He'll make the road smooth for you.
Thunder in the desert!
Prepare for God's arrival!
Make the road smooth and straight!

1.4-6   John the Baptizer appeared in the wild, preaching a baptism of life-change that leads to forgiveness of sins. People thronged to him from Judea and Jerusalem and, as they confessed their sins, were baptized by him in the Jordan River into a changed life. John wore a camel-hair habit, tied at the waist with a leather belt. He ate locusts and wild field honey.

1.7-8   As he preached he said, "The real action comes next: The star in this drama, to whom I'm a mere stagehand, will change your life. I'm baptizing you here in the river, turning your old life in for a kingdom life. His baptism—a holy baptism by the Holy Spirit—will change you from the inside out."

1.9-11   At this time, Jesus came from Nazareth in Galilee and was baptized by John in the Jordan. The moment he came out of the water, he saw the sky split open and God's Spirit, looking like a dove, come down on him. Along with the Spirit, a voice: "You are my Son, chosen and marked by my love, pride of my life."

GOD'S KINGDOM IS HERE

1.12-13 At once, this same Spirit pushed Jesus out into the wild. For forty wilderness days and nights he was tested by Satan. Wild animals were his companions, and angels took care of him.

1.14-15   After John was arrested, Jesus went to Galilee preaching the Message of God: "Time's up! God's kingdom is here. Change your life and believe the Message."

---

a 1 Some manuscripts do not have *the Son of God.*
b 2 Mal. 3:1   *c* 3 Isaiah 40:3   *d* 8 Or *in*

NEW INTERNATIONAL VERSION

¹⁶As Jesus walked beside the Sea of Galilee, he saw Simon and his brother Andrew casting a net into the lake, for they were fishermen. ¹⁷"Come, follow me," Jesus said, "and I will make you fishers of men." ¹⁸At once they left their nets and followed him.

¹⁹When he had gone a little farther, he saw James son of Zebedee and his brother John in a boat, preparing their nets. ²⁰Without delay he called them, and they left their father Zebedee in the boat with the hired men and followed him.

JESUS DRIVES OUT AN EVIL SPIRIT

²¹They went to Capernaum, and when the Sabbath came, Jesus went into the synagogue and began to teach. ²²The people were amazed at his teaching, because he taught them as one who had authority, not as the teachers of the law. ²³Just then a man in their synagogue who was possessed by an evil^a spirit cried out, ²⁴"What do you want with us, Jesus of Nazareth? Have you come to destroy us? I know who you are—the Holy One of God!"

²⁵"Be quiet!" said Jesus sternly. "Come out of him!" ²⁶The evil spirit shook the man violently and came out of him with a shriek.

²⁷The people were all so amazed that they asked each other, "What is this? A new teaching—and with authority! He even gives orders to evil spirits and they obey him." ²⁸News about him spread quickly over the whole region of Galilee.

JESUS HEALS MANY

²⁹As soon as they left the synagogue, they went with James and John to the home of Simon and Andrew. ³⁰Simon's mother-in-law was in bed with a fever, and they told Jesus about her. ³¹So he went to her, took her hand and helped her up. The fever left her and she began to wait on them.

³²That evening after sunset the people brought to Jesus all the sick and demon-possessed. ³³The whole town gathered at the door, ³⁴and Jesus healed many who had various diseases. He also drove out many demons, but he would not let the demons speak because they knew who he was.

JESUS PRAYS IN A SOLITARY PLACE

³⁵Very early in the morning, while it was still dark, Jesus got up, left the house and went off to a solitary place, where he prayed. ³⁶Simon and his companions went to look for him, ³⁷and when they found him, they exclaimed: "Everyone is looking for you!"

^a 23 Greek unclean; also in verses 26 and 27

THE MESSAGE

1.16-18 Passing along the beach of Lake Galilee, he saw Simon and his brother Andrew net-fishing. Fishing was their regular work. Jesus said to them, "Come with me. I'll make a new kind of fisherman out of you. I'll show you how to catch men and women instead of perch and bass." They didn't ask questions. They dropped their nets and followed.

1.19-20 A dozen yards or so down the beach, he saw the brothers James and John, Zebedee's sons. They were in the boat, mending their fishnets. Right off, he made the same offer. Immediately, they left their father Zebedee, the boat, and the hired hands, and followed.

CONFIDENT TEACHING

1.21-22 Then they entered Capernaum. When the Sabbath arrived, Jesus lost no time in getting to the meeting place. He spent the day there teaching. They were surprised at his teaching—so forthright, so confident—not quibbling and quoting like the religion scholars.

1.23-24 Suddenly, while still in the meeting place, he was interrupted by a man who was deeply disturbed and yelling out, "What business do you have here with us, Jesus? Nazarene! I know what you're up to! You're the Holy One of God, and you've come to destroy us!"

1.25-26 Jesus shut him up: "Quiet! Get out of him!" The afflicting spirit threw the man into spasms, protesting loudly—and got out.

1.27-28 Everyone there was incredulous, buzzing with curiosity. "What's going on here? A new teaching that does what it says? He shuts up defiling, demonic spirits and sends them packing!" News of this traveled fast and was soon all over Galilee.

1.29-31 Directly on leaving the meeting place, they came to Simon and Andrew's house, accompanied by James and John. Simon's mother-in-law was sick in bed, burning up with fever. They told Jesus. He went to her, took her hand, and raised her up. No sooner had the fever left than she was up fixing dinner for them.

1.32-34 That evening, after the sun was down, they brought sick and evil-afflicted people to him, the whole city lined up at his door! He cured their sick bodies and tormented spirits. Because the demons knew his true identity, he didn't let them say a word.

THE LEPER

1.35-37 While it was still night, way before dawn, he got up and went out to a secluded spot and prayed. Simon and those with him went looking for him. They found him and said, "Everybody's looking for you."

NEW INTERNATIONAL VERSION

³⁸Jesus replied, "Let us go somewhere else—to the nearby villages—so I can preach there also. That is why I have come." ³⁹So he traveled throughout Galilee, preaching in their synagogues and driving out demons.

A MAN WITH LEPROSY

⁴⁰A man with leprosy*a* came to him and begged him on his knees, "If you are willing, you can make me clean."

⁴¹Filled with compassion, Jesus reached out his hand and touched the man. "I am willing," he said. "Be clean!" ⁴²Immediately the leprosy left him and he was cured.

⁴³Jesus sent him away at once with a strong warning: ⁴⁴"See that you don't tell this to anyone. But go, show yourself to the priest and offer the sacrifices that Moses commanded for your cleansing, as a testimony to them." ⁴⁵Instead he went out and began to talk freely, spreading the news. As a result, Jesus could no longer enter a town openly but stayed outside in lonely places. Yet the people still came to him from everywhere.

JESUS HEALS A PARALYTIC

2 A few days later, when Jesus again entered Capernaum, the people heard that he had come home. ²So many gathered that there was no room left, not even outside the door, and he preached the word to them. ³Some men came, bringing to him a paralytic, carried by four of them. ⁴Since they could not get him to Jesus because of the crowd, they made an opening in the roof above Jesus and, after digging through it, lowered the mat the paralyzed man was lying on. ⁵When Jesus saw their faith, he said to the paralytic, "Son, your sins are forgiven."

⁶Now some teachers of the law were sitting there, thinking to themselves, ⁷"Why does this fellow talk like that? He's blaspheming! Who can forgive sins but God alone?"

⁸Immediately Jesus knew in his spirit that this was what they were thinking in their hearts, and he said to them, "Why are you thinking these things? ⁹Which is easier: to say to the paralytic, 'Your sins are forgiven,' or to say, 'Get up, take your mat and walk'? ¹⁰But that you may know that the Son of Man has authority on earth to forgive sins . . ." He said to the paralytic, ¹¹"I tell you, get up, take your mat and go home." ¹²He got up, took his mat and walked out in full view of them all. This amazed everyone and they praised God, saying, "We have never seen anything like this!"

a 40 The Greek word was used for various diseases affecting the skin—not necessarily leprosy.

THE MESSAGE

1.38-39 Jesus said, "Let's go to the rest of the villages so I can preach there also. This is why I've come." He went to their meeting places all through Galilee, preaching and throwing out the demons.

1.40 A leper came to him, begging on his knees, "If you want to, you can cleanse me."

1.41-45 Deeply moved, Jesus put out his hand, touched him, and said, "I want to. Be clean." Then and there the leprosy was gone, his skin smooth and healthy. Jesus dismissed him with strict orders: "Say nothing to anyone. Take the offering for cleansing that Moses prescribed and present yourself to the priest. This will validate your healing to the people." But as soon as the man was out of earshot, he told everyone he met what had happened, spreading the news all over town. So Jesus kept to out-of-the-way places, no longer able to move freely in and out of the city. But people found him, and came from all over.

A PARAPLEGIC

2.1-5 **2** After a few days, Jesus returned to Capernaum, and word got around that he was back home. A crowd gathered, jamming the entrance so no one could get in or out. He was teaching the Word. They brought a paraplegic to him, carried by four men. When they weren't able to get in because of the crowd, they removed part of the roof and lowered the paraplegic on his stretcher. Impressed by their bold belief, Jesus said to the paraplegic, "Son, I forgive your sins."

2.6-7 Some religion scholars sitting there started whispering among themselves, "He can't talk that way! That's blasphemy! God and only God can forgive sins."

2.8-12 Jesus knew right away what they were thinking, and said, "Why are you so skeptical? Which is simpler: to say to the paraplegic, 'I forgive your sins,' or say, 'Get up, take your stretcher, and start walking'? Well, just so it's clear that I'm the Son of Man and authorized to do either, or both . . ." (he looked now at the paraplegic), "Get up. Pick up your stretcher and go home." And the man did it—got up, grabbed his stretcher, and walked out, with everyone there watching him. They rubbed their eyes, incredulous—and then praised God, saying, "We've never seen anything like this!"

NEW INTERNATIONAL VERSION

THE CALLING OF LEVI

13Once again Jesus went out beside the lake. A large crowd came to him, and he began to teach them. 14As he walked along, he saw Levi son of Alphaeus sitting at the tax collector's booth. "Follow me," Jesus told him, and Levi got up and followed him.

15While Jesus was having dinner at Levi's house, many tax collectors and "sinners" were eating with him and his disciples, for there were many who followed him. 16When the teachers of the law who were Pharisees saw him eating with the "sinners" and tax collectors, they asked his disciples: "Why does he eat with tax collectors and 'sinners'?"

17On hearing this, Jesus said to them, "It is not the healthy who need a doctor, but the sick. I have not come to call the righteous, but sinners."

JESUS QUESTIONED ABOUT FASTING

18Now John's disciples and the Pharisees were fasting. Some people came and asked Jesus, "How is it that John's disciples and the disciples of the Pharisees are fasting, but yours are not?"

19Jesus answered, "How can the guests of the bridegroom fast while he is with them? They cannot, so long as they have him with them. 20But the time will come when the bridegroom will be taken from them, and on that day they will fast.

21"No one sews a patch of unshrunk cloth on an old garment. If he does, the new piece will pull away from the old, making the tear worse. 22And no one pours new wine into old wineskins. If he does, the wine will burst the skins, and both the wine and the wineskins will be ruined. No, he pours new wine into new wineskins."

LORD OF THE SABBATH

23One Sabbath Jesus was going through the grainfields, and as his disciples walked along, they began to pick some heads of grain. 24The Pharisees said to him, "Look, why are they doing what is unlawful on the Sabbath?"

25He answered, "Have you never read what David did when he and his companions were hungry and in need? 26In the days of Abiathar the high priest, he entered the house of God and ate the consecrated bread, which is lawful only for priests to eat. And he also gave some to his companions."

27Then he said to them, "The Sabbath was made for man, not man for the Sabbath. 28So the Son of Man is Lord even of the Sabbath."

THE MESSAGE

THE TAX COLLECTOR

2.13-14 Then Jesus went again to walk alongside the lake. Again a crowd came to him, and he taught them. Strolling along, he saw Levi, son of Alphaeus, at his work collecting taxes. Jesus said, "Come along with me." He came.

2.15-16 Later Jesus and his disciples were at home having supper with a collection of disreputable guests. Unlikely as it seems, more than a few of them had become followers. The religion scholars and Pharisees saw him keeping this kind of company and lit into his disciples: "What kind of example is this, acting cozy with the riff-raff?"

2.17 Jesus, overhearing, shot back, "Who needs a doctor: the healthy or the sick? I'm here inviting the sin-sick, not the spiritually-fit."

FEASTING OR FASTING?

2.18 The disciples of John and the disciples of the Pharisees made a practice of fasting. Some people confronted Jesus: "Why do the followers of John and the Pharisees take on the discipline of fasting, but your followers don't?"

2.19-20 Jesus said, "When you're celebrating a wedding, you don't skimp on the cake and wine. You feast. Later you may need to pull in your belt, but not now. As long as the bride and groom are with you, you have a good time. No one throws cold water on a friendly bonfire. This is Kingdom Come!"

2.21-22 He went on, "No one cuts up a fine silk scarf to patch old work clothes; you want fabrics that match. And you don't put your wine in cracked bottles."

2.23-24 One Sabbath day he was walking through a field of ripe grain. As his disciples made a path, they pulled off heads of grain. The Pharisees told on them to Jesus: "Look, your disciples are breaking Sabbath rules!"

2.25-28 Jesus said, "Really? Haven't you ever read what David did when he was hungry, along with those who were with him? How he entered the sanctuary and ate fresh bread off the altar, with the Chief Priest Abiathar right there watching—holy bread that no one but priests were allowed to eat—and handed it out to his companions?" Then Jesus said, "The Sabbath was made to serve us; we weren't made to serve the Sabbath. The Son of Man is no lackey to the Sabbath. He's in charge!"

NEW INTERNATIONAL VERSION

3 Another time he went into the synagogue, and a man with a shriveled hand was there. ²Some of them were looking for a reason to accuse Jesus, so they watched him closely to see if he would heal him on the Sabbath. ³Jesus said to the man with the shriveled hand, "Stand up in front of everyone."

⁴Then Jesus asked them, "Which is lawful on the Sabbath: to do good or to do evil, to save life or to kill?" But they remained silent. ⁵He looked around at them in anger and, deeply distressed at their stubborn hearts, said to the man, "Stretch out your hand." He stretched it out, and his hand was completely restored. ⁶Then the Pharisees went out and began to plot with the Herodians how they might kill Jesus.

CROWDS FOLLOW JESUS

⁷Jesus withdrew with his disciples to the lake, and a large crowd from Galilee followed. ⁸When they heard all he was doing, many people came to him from Judea, Jerusalem, Idumea, and the regions across the Jordan and around Tyre and Sidon. ⁹Because of the crowd he told his disciples to have a small boat ready for him, to keep the people from crowding him. ¹⁰For he had healed many, so that those with diseases were pushing forward to touch him. ¹¹Whenever the evil*a* spirits saw him, they fell down before him and cried out, "You are the Son of God." ¹²But he gave them strict orders not to tell who he was.

THE APPOINTING OF THE TWELVE APOSTLES

¹³Jesus went up on a mountainside and called to him those he wanted, and they came to him. ¹⁴He appointed twelve—designating them apostles*b*—that they might be with him and that he might send them out to preach ¹⁵and to have authority to drive out demons. ¹⁶These are the twelve he appointed: Simon (to whom he gave the name Peter); ¹⁷James son of Zebedee and his brother John (to them he gave the name Boanerges, which means Sons of Thunder); ¹⁸Andrew, Philip, Bartholomew, Matthew, Thomas, James son of Alphaeus, Thaddaeus, Simon the Zealot ¹⁹and Judas Iscariot, who betrayed him.

a 11 Greek unclean; also in verse 30   b 14 Some manuscripts do not have designating them apostles.

THE MESSAGE

DOING GOOD ON THE SABBATH

3.1-3 **3** Then he went back in the meeting place where he found a man with a crippled hand. The Pharisees had their eyes on Jesus to see if he would heal him, hoping to catch him in a Sabbath infraction. He said to the man with the crippled hand, "Stand here where we can see you."

3.4 Then he spoke to the people: "What kind of action suits the Sabbath best? Doing good or doing evil? Helping people or leaving them helpless?" No one said a word.

3.5-6 He looked them in the eye, one after another, angry now, furious at their hard-nosed religion. He said to the man, "Hold out your hand." He held it out—it was as good as new! The Pharisees got out as fast as they could, sputtering about how they would join forces with Herod's followers and ruin him.

THE TWELVE APOSTLES

3.7-10 Jesus went off with his disciples to the sea to get away. But a huge crowd from Galilee trailed after them—also from Judea, Jerusalem, Idumea, across the Jordan, and around Tyre and Sidon—swarms of people who had heard the reports and had come to see for themselves. He told his disciples to get a boat ready so he wouldn't be trampled by the crowd. He had healed many people, and now everyone who had something wrong was pushing and shoving to get near and touch him.

3.11-12 Evil spirits, when they recognized him, fell down and cried out, "You are the Son of God!" But Jesus would have none of it. He shut them up, forbidding them to identify him in public.

3.13-19 He climbed a mountain and invited those he wanted with him. They climbed together. He settled on twelve, and designated them apostles. The plan was that they would be with him, and he would send them out to proclaim the Word and give them authority to banish demons. These are the Twelve:

Simon (Jesus later named him Peter,
    meaning "Rock"),
James, son of Zebedee,
John, brother of James (Jesus nicknamed
    the Zebedee brothers Boanerges,
    meaning "Sons of Thunder"),
Andrew,
Philip,
Bartholomew,
Matthew,
Thomas,
James, son of Alphaeus,
Thaddaeus,
Simon the Canaanite,
Judas Iscariot (who betrayed him).

NEW INTERNATIONAL VERSION

JESUS AND BEELZEBUB

20Then Jesus entered a house, and again a crowd gathered, so that he and his disciples were not even able to eat. 21When his family heard about this, they went to take charge of him, for they said, "He is out of his mind."

22And the teachers of the law who came down from Jerusalem said, "He is possessed by Beelzebub*a*! By the prince of demons he is driving out demons."

23So Jesus called them and spoke to them in parables: "How can Satan drive out Satan? 24If a kingdom is divided against itself, that kingdom cannot stand. 25If a house is divided against itself, that house cannot stand. 26And if Satan opposes himself and is divided, he cannot stand; his end has come. 27In fact, no one can enter a strong man's house and carry off his possessions unless he first ties up the strong man. Then he can rob his house. 28I tell you the truth, all the sins and blasphemies of men will be forgiven them. 29But whoever blasphemes against the Holy Spirit will never be forgiven; he is guilty of an eternal sin."

30He said this because they were saying, "He has an evil spirit."

JESUS' MOTHER AND BROTHERS

31Then Jesus' mother and brothers arrived. Standing outside, they sent someone in to call him. 32A crowd was sitting around him, and they told him, "Your mother and brothers are outside looking for you."

33"Who are my mother and my brothers?" he asked.

34Then he looked at those seated in a circle around him and said, "Here are my mother and my brothers! 35Whoever does God's will is my brother and sister and mother."

THE PARABLE OF THE SOWER

4 Again Jesus began to teach by the lake. The crowd that gathered around him was so large that he got into a boat and sat in it out on the lake, while all the people were along the shore at the water's edge. 2He taught them many things by parables, and in his teaching said: 3"Listen! A farmer went out to sow his seed. 4As he was scattering the seed, some fell along the path, and

a 22 Greek Beezeboul or Beelzeboul

THE MESSAGE

SATAN FIGHTING SATAN?

3.20-21 Jesus came home and, as usual, a crowd gathered—so many making demands on him that there wasn't even time to eat. His friends heard what was going on and went to rescue him, by force if necessary. They suspected he was getting carried away with himself.

3.22-27 The religion scholars from Jerusalem came down spreading rumors that he was working black magic, using devil tricks to impress them with spiritual power. Jesus confronted their slander with a story: "Does it make sense to send a devil to catch a devil, to use Satan to get rid of Satan? A constantly squabbling family disintegrates. If Satan were fighting Satan, there soon wouldn't be any Satan left. Do you think it's possible in broad daylight to enter the house of an awake, able-bodied man, and walk off with his possessions unless you tie him up first? Tie him up, though, and you can clean him out."

3.28-30 "Listen to this carefully. I'm warning you. There's nothing done or said that can't be forgiven. But if you persist in your slanders against God's Holy Spirit, you are repudiating the very One who forgives, sawing off the branch on which you're sitting, severing by your own perversity all connection with the One who forgives." He gave this warning because they were accusing him of being in league with Evil.

JESUS' MOTHER AND BROTHERS

3.31-32 Just then his mother and brothers showed up. Standing outside, they relayed a message that they wanted a word with him. He was surrounded by the crowd when he was given the message, "Your mother and brothers and sisters are outside looking for you."

3.33-35 Jesus responded, "Who do you think are my mother and brothers?" Looking around, taking in everyone seated around him, he said, "Right here, right in front of you—my mother and my brothers. Obedience is thicker than blood. The person who obeys God's will is my brother and sister and mother."

THE STORY OF THE SCATTERED SEED

4.1-2 4 He went back to teaching by the sea. A crowd built up to such a great size that he had to get into an offshore boat, using the boat as a pulpit as the people pushed to the water's edge. He taught by using stories, many stories.

4.3-8 "Listen. What do you make of this? A farmer planted seed. As he scattered the seed, some of

NEW INTERNATIONAL VERSION

the birds came and ate it up. ⁵Some fell on rocky places, where it did not have much soil. It sprang up quickly, because the soil was shallow. ⁶But when the sun came up, the plants were scorched, and they withered because they had no root. ⁷Other seed fell among thorns, which grew up and choked the plants, so that they did not bear grain. ⁸Still other seed fell on good soil. It came up, grew and produced a crop, multiplying thirty, sixty, or even a hundred times."

⁹Then Jesus said, "He who has ears to hear, let him hear."

¹⁰When he was alone, the Twelve and the others around him asked him about the parables. ¹¹He told them, "The secret of the kingdom of God has been given to you. But to those on the outside everything is said in parables ¹²so that,

" 'they may be ever seeing but never
          perceiving,
     and ever hearing but never
          understanding;
otherwise they might turn and be
          forgiven!' ª"

¹³Then Jesus said to them, "Don't you understand this parable? How then will you understand any parable? ¹⁴The farmer sows the word. ¹⁵Some people are like seed along the path, where the word is sown. As soon as they hear it, Satan comes and takes away the word that was sown in them. ¹⁶Others, like seed sown on rocky places, hear the word and at once receive it with joy. ¹⁷But since they have no root, they last only a short time. When trouble or persecution comes because of the word, they quickly fall away. ¹⁸Still others, like seed sown among thorns, hear the word; ¹⁹but the worries of this life, the deceitfulness of wealth and the desires for other things come in and choke the word, making it unfruitful. ²⁰Others, like seed sown on good soil, hear the word, accept it, and produce a crop—thirty, sixty or even a hundred times what was sown."

A LAMP ON A STAND

²¹He said to them, "Do you bring in a lamp to put it under a bowl or a bed? Instead, don't you put it on its stand? ²²For whatever is hidden is meant to be disclosed, and whatever is concealed is meant to be brought out into the open. ²³If anyone has ears to hear, let him hear."

²⁴"Consider carefully what you hear," he continued. "With the measure you use, it will be measured to you—and even more. ²⁵Whoever

ª 12 Isaiah 6:9,10

THE MESSAGE

it fell on the road and birds ate it. Some fell in the gravel; it sprouted quickly but didn't put down roots, so when the sun came up it withered just as quickly. Some fell in the weeds; as it came up, it was strangled among the weeds and nothing came of it. Some fell on good earth and came up with a flourish, producing a harvest exceeding his wildest dreams."

4.9 "Are you listening to this? Really listening?"

4.10-12 When they were off by themselves, those who were close to him, along with the Twelve, asked about the stories. He told them, "You've been given insight into God's kingdom—you know how it works. But to those who can't see it yet, everything comes in stories, creating readiness, nudging them toward receptive insight. These are people—

Whose eyes are open but don't see a thing,
Whose ears are open but don't understand
          a word,
Who avoid making an about-face and
          getting forgiven."

4.13 He continued, "Do you see how this story works? All my stories work this way.

4.14-15 "The farmer plants the Word. Some people are like the seed that falls on the hardened soil of the road. No sooner do they hear the Word than Satan snatches away what has been planted in them.

4.16-17 "And some are like the seed that lands in the gravel. When they first hear the Word, they respond with great enthusiasm. But there is such shallow soil of character that when the emotions wear off and some difficulty arrives, there is nothing to show for it.

4.18-19 "The seed cast in the weeds represents the ones who hear the kingdom news but are overwhelmed with worries about all the things they have to do and all the things they want to get. The stress strangles what they heard, and nothing comes of it.

4.20 "But the seed planted in the good earth represents those who hear the Word, embrace it, and produce a harvest beyond their wildest dreams."

GIVING, NOT GETTING

4.21-22 Jesus went on: "Does anyone bring a lamp home and put it under a washtub or beneath the bed? Don't you put it up on a table or on the mantel? We're not keeping secrets, we're telling them; we're not hiding things, we're bringing them out into the open.

4.23 "Are you listening to this? Really listening?

4.24-25 "Listen carefully to what I am saying—and be wary of the shrewd advice that tells you how to get ahead in the world on your own. Giving,

NEW INTERNATIONAL VERSION	THE MESSAGE

has will be given more; whoever does not have, even what he has will be taken from him."

THE PARABLE OF THE GROWING SEED

26He also said, "This is what the kingdom of God is like. A man scatters seed on the ground. 27Night and day, whether he sleeps or gets up, the seed sprouts and grows, though he does not know how. 28All by itself the soil produces grain—first the stalk, then the head, then the full kernel in the head. 29As soon as the grain is ripe, he puts the sickle to it, because the harvest has come."

THE PARABLE OF THE MUSTARD SEED

30Again he said, "What shall we say the kingdom of God is like, or what parable shall we use to describe it? 31It is like a mustard seed, which is the smallest seed you plant in the ground. 32Yet when planted, it grows and becomes the largest of all garden plants, with such big branches that the birds of the air can perch in its shade."

33With many similar parables Jesus spoke the word to them, as much as they could understand. 34He did not say anything to them without using a parable. But when he was alone with his own disciples, he explained everything.

JESUS CALMS THE STORM

35That day when evening came, he said to his disciples, "Let us go over to the other side." 36Leaving the crowd behind, they took him along, just as he was, in the boat. There were also other boats with him. 37A furious squall came up, and the waves broke over the boat, so that it was nearly swamped. 38Jesus was in the stern, sleeping on a cushion. The disciples woke him and said to him, "Teacher, don't you care if we drown?"

39He got up, rebuked the wind and said to the waves, "Quiet! Be still!" Then the wind died down and it was completely calm.

40He said to his disciples, "Why are you so afraid? Do you still have no faith?"

41They were terrified and asked each other, "Who is this? Even the wind and the waves obey him!"

THE HEALING OF A DEMON-POSSESSED MAN

5 They went across the lake to the region of the Gerasenes.*a* 2When Jesus got out of the boat, a man with an evil*b* spirit came from the tombs to meet him. 3This man lived in the tombs, and no one could bind him any more, not even with a chain. 4For he had often been chained hand and foot, but he tore the chains apart and broke the irons on his feet. No one

---

not getting, is the way. Generosity begets generosity. Stinginess impoverishes."

NEVER WITHOUT A STORY

4.26-29 Then Jesus said, "God's kingdom is like seed thrown on a field by a man who then goes to bed and forgets about it. The seed sprouts and grows—he has no idea how it happens. The earth does it all without his help: first a green stem of grass, then a bud, then the ripened grain. When the grain is fully formed, he reaps—harvest time!

4.30-32 "How can we picture God's kingdom? What kind of story can we use? It's like a pine nut. When it lands on the ground it is quite small as seeds go, yet once it is planted it grows into a huge pine tree with thick branches. Eagles nest in it."

4.33-34 With many stories like these, he presented his message to them, fitting the stories to their experience and maturity. He was never without a story when he spoke. When he was alone with his disciples, he went over everything, sorting out the tangles, untying the knots.

THE WIND RAN OUT OF BREATH

4.35-38 Late that day he said to them, "Let's go across to the other side." They took him in the boat as he was. Other boats came along. A huge storm came up. Waves poured into the boat, threatening to sink it. And Jesus was in the stern, head on a pillow, sleeping! They roused him, saying, "Teacher, is it nothing to you that we're going down?"

4.39-40 Awake now, he told the wind to pipe down and said to the sea, "Quiet! Settle down!" The wind ran out of breath; the sea became smooth as glass. Jesus reprimanded the disciples: "Why are you such cowards? Don't you have any faith at all?"

4.41 They were in absolute awe, staggered. "Who is this, anyway?" they asked. "Wind and sea at his beck and call!"

THE MADMAN

5.1-5 5 They arrived on the other side of the sea in the country of the Gerasenes. As Jesus got out of the boat, a madman from the cemetery came up to him. He lived there among the tombs and graves. No one could restrain him— he couldn't be chained, couldn't be tied down. He had been tied up many times with chains and ropes, but he broke the chains, snapped the ropes. No one was strong enough to tame

---

a 1 Some manuscripts *Gadarenes*; other manuscripts *Gergesenes*   *b 2* Greek *unclean*; also in verses 8 and 13

NEW INTERNATIONAL VERSION

was strong enough to subdue him. ⁵Night and day among the tombs and in the hills he would cry out and cut himself with stones.

⁶When he saw Jesus from a distance, he ran and fell on his knees in front of him. ⁷He shouted at the top of his voice, "What do you want with me, Jesus, Son of the Most High God? Swear to God that you won't torture me!" ⁸For Jesus had said to him, "Come out of this man, you evil spirit!"

⁹Then Jesus asked him, "What is your name?"

"My name is Legion," he replied, "for we are many." ¹⁰And he begged Jesus again and again not to send them out of the area.

¹¹A large herd of pigs was feeding on the nearby hillside. ¹²The demons begged Jesus, "Send us among the pigs; allow us to go into them." ¹³He gave them permission, and the evil spirits came out and went into the pigs. The herd, about two thousand in number, rushed down the steep bank into the lake and were drowned.

¹⁴Those tending the pigs ran off and reported this in the town and countryside, and the people went out to see what had happened. ¹⁵When they came to Jesus, they saw the man who had been possessed by the legion of demons, sitting there, dressed and in his right mind; and they were afraid. ¹⁶Those who had seen it told the people what had happened to the demon-possessed man—and told about the pigs as well. ¹⁷Then the people began to plead with Jesus to leave their region.

¹⁸As Jesus was getting into the boat, the man who had been demon-possessed begged to go with him. ¹⁹Jesus did not let him, but said, "Go home to your family and tell them how much the Lord has done for you, and how he has had mercy on you." ²⁰So the man went away and began to tell in the Decapolis*a* how much Jesus had done for him. And all the people were amazed.

A DEAD GIRL AND A SICK WOMAN

²¹When Jesus had again crossed over by boat to the other side of the lake, a large crowd gathered around him while he was by the lake. ²²Then one of the synagogue rulers, named Jairus, came there. Seeing Jesus, he fell at his feet ²³and pleaded earnestly with him, "My little daughter is dying. Please come and put your hands on her so that she will be healed and live." ²⁴So Jesus went with him.

A large crowd followed and pressed around him. ²⁵And a woman was there who had been subject to bleeding for twelve years. ²⁶She had suffered a great deal under the care of many doc-

a 20 That is, the Ten Cities

THE MESSAGE

him. Night and day he roamed through the graves and the hills, screaming out and slashing himself with sharp stones.

5.6-8 When he saw Jesus a long way off, he ran and bowed in worship before him—then bellowed in protest, "What business do you have, Jesus, Son of the High God, messing with me? I swear to God, don't give me a hard time!" (Jesus had just commanded the tormenting evil spirit, "Out! Get out of the man!")

5.9-10 Jesus asked him, "Tell me your name."

He replied, "My name is Mob. I'm a rioting mob." Then he desperately begged Jesus not to banish them from the country.

5.11-13 A large herd of pigs was browsing and rooting on a nearby hill. The demons begged him, "Send us to the pigs so we can live in them." Jesus gave the order. But it was even worse for the pigs than for the man. Crazed, they stampeded over a cliff into the sea and drowned.

5.14-15 Those tending the pigs, scared to death, bolted and told their story in town and country. Everyone wanted to see what had happened. They came up to Jesus and saw the madman sitting there wearing decent clothes and making sense, no longer a walking madhouse of a man.

5.16-17 Those who had seen it told the others what had happened to the demon-possessed man and the pigs. At first they were in awe—and then they were upset, upset over the drowned pigs. They demanded that Jesus leave and not come back.

5.18-20 As Jesus was getting into the boat, the demon-delivered man begged to go along, but he wouldn't let him. Jesus said, "Go home to your own people. Tell them your story—what the Master did, how he had mercy on you." The man went back and began to preach in the Ten Towns area about what Jesus had done for him. He was the talk of the town.

A RISK OF FAITH

5.21-24 After Jesus crossed over by boat, a large crowd met him at the seaside. One of the meeting-place leaders named Jairus came. When he saw Jesus, he fell to his knees, beside himself as he begged, "My dear daughter is at death's door. Come and lay hands on her so she will get well and live." Jesus went with him, the whole crowd tagging along, pushing and jostling him.

5.25-29 A woman who had suffered a condition of hemorrhaging for twelve years—a long succession of physicians had treated her, and treated

NEW INTERNATIONAL VERSION

tors and had spent all she had, yet instead of getting better she grew worse. ²⁷When she heard about Jesus, she came up behind him in the crowd and touched his cloak, ²⁸because she thought, "If I just touch his clothes, I will be healed." ²⁹Immediately her bleeding stopped and she felt in her body that she was freed from her suffering.

³⁰At once Jesus realized that power had gone out from him. He turned around in the crowd and asked, "Who touched my clothes?"

³¹"You see the people crowding against you," his disciples answered, "and yet you can ask, 'Who touched me?' "

³²But Jesus kept looking around to see who had done it. ³³Then the woman, knowing what had happened to her, came and fell at his feet and, trembling with fear, told him the whole truth. ³⁴He said to her, "Daughter, your faith has healed you. Go in peace and be freed from your suffering."

³⁵While Jesus was still speaking, some men came from the house of Jairus, the synagogue ruler. "Your daughter is dead," they said. "Why bother the teacher any more?"

³⁶Ignoring what they said, Jesus told the synagogue ruler, "Don't be afraid; just believe."

³⁷He did not let anyone follow him except Peter, James and John the brother of James. ³⁸When they came to the home of the synagogue ruler, Jesus saw a commotion, with people crying and wailing loudly. ³⁹He went in and said to them, "Why all this commotion and wailing? The child is not dead but asleep." ⁴⁰But they laughed at him.

After he put them all out, he took the child's father and mother and the disciples who were with him, and went in where the child was. ⁴¹He took her by the hand and said to her, "*Talitha koum!*" (which means, "Little girl, I say to you, get up!"). ⁴²Immediately the girl stood up and walked around (she was twelve years old). At this they were completely astonished. ⁴³He gave strict orders not to let anyone know about this, and told them to give her something to eat.

A PROPHET WITHOUT HONOR

6 Jesus left there and went to his hometown, accompanied by his disciples. ²When the Sabbath came, he began to teach in the synagogue, and many who heard him were amazed.

THE MESSAGE

her badly, taking all her money and leaving her worse off than before—had heard about Jesus. She slipped in from behind and touched his robe. She was thinking to herself, "If I can put a finger on his robe, I can get well." The moment she did it, the flow of blood dried up. She could feel the change and knew her plague was over and done with.

5.30 At the same moment, Jesus felt energy discharging from him. He turned around to the crowd and asked, "Who touched my robe?"

5.31 His disciples said, "What are you talking about? With this crowd pushing and jostling you, you're asking, 'Who touched me?' Dozens have touched you!"

5.32-33 But he went on asking, looking around to see who had done it. The woman, knowing what had happened, knowing she was the one, stepped up in fear and trembling, knelt before him, and gave him the whole story.

5.34 Jesus said to her, "Daughter, you took a risk of faith, and now you're healed and whole. Live well, live blessed! Be healed of your plague."

✝

5.35 While he was still talking, some people came from the leader's house and told him, "Your daughter is dead. Why bother the Teacher any more?"

5.36 Jesus overheard what they were talking about and said to the leader, "Don't listen to them; just trust me."

5.37-40 He permitted no one to go in with him except Peter, James, and John. They entered the leader's house and pushed their way through the gossips looking for a story and neighbors bringing in casseroles. Jesus was abrupt: "Why all this busybody grief and gossip? This child isn't dead; she's sleeping." Provoked to sarcasm, they told him he didn't know what he was talking about.

5.40-43 But when he had sent them all out, he took the child's father and mother, along with his companions, and entered the child's room. He clasped the girl's hand and said, "*Talitha koum,*" which means, "Little girl, get up." At that, she was up and walking around! This girl was twelve years of age. They, of course, were all beside themselves with joy. He gave them strict orders that no one was to know what had taken place in that room. Then he said, "Give her something to eat."

JUST A CARPENTER

6.1-2 **6** He left there and returned to his hometown. His disciples came along. On the Sabbath, he gave a lecture in the meeting place. He made a real hit, impressing everyone. "We

NEW INTERNATIONAL VERSION

"Where did this man get these things?" they asked. "What's this wisdom that has been given him, that he even does miracles! ³Isn't this the carpenter? Isn't this Mary's son and the brother of James, Joseph,ᵃ Judas and Simon? Aren't his sisters here with us?" And they took offense at him.

⁴Jesus said to them, "Only in his hometown, among his relatives and in his own house is a prophet without honor." ⁵He could not do any miracles there, except lay his hands on a few sick people and heal them. ⁶And he was amazed at their lack of faith.

JESUS SENDS OUT THE TWELVE

Then Jesus went around teaching from village to village. ⁷Calling the Twelve to him, he sent them out two by two and gave them authority over evilᵇ spirits.

⁸These were his instructions: "Take nothing for the journey except a staff—no bread, no bag, no money in your belts. ⁹Wear sandals but not an extra tunic. ¹⁰Whenever you enter a house, stay there until you leave that town. ¹¹And if any place will not welcome you or listen to you, shake the dust off your feet when you leave, as a testimony against them."

¹²They went out and preached that people should repent. ¹³They drove out many demons and anointed many sick people with oil and healed them.

JOHN THE BAPTIST BEHEADED

¹⁴King Herod heard about this, for Jesus' name had become well known. Some were saying,ᶜ "John the Baptist has been raised from the dead, and that is why miraculous powers are at work in him."

¹⁵Others said, "He is Elijah."

And still others claimed, "He is a prophet, like one of the prophets of long ago."

¹⁶But when Herod heard this, he said, "John, the man I beheaded, has been raised from the dead!"

¹⁷For Herod himself had given orders to have John arrested, and he had him bound and put in prison. He did this because of Herodias, his brother Philip's wife, whom he had married. ¹⁸For John had been saying to Herod, "It is not lawful for you to have your brother's wife." ¹⁹So Herodias nursed a grudge against John and

THE MESSAGE

had no idea he was this good!" they said. "How did he get so wise all of a sudden, get such ability?"

6.3 But in the next breath they were cutting him down: "He's just a carpenter—Mary's boy. We've known him since he was a kid. We know his brothers, James, Justus, Jude, and Simon, and his sisters. Who does he think he is?" They tripped over what little they knew about him and fell, sprawling. And they never got any further.

6.4-6 Jesus told them, "A prophet has little honor in his hometown, among his relatives, on the streets he played in as a child." Jesus wasn't able to do much of anything there—he laid hands on a few sick people and healed them, that's all. He couldn't get over their stubbornness. He left and made a circuit of the other villages, teaching.

THE TWELVE

6.7-8 Jesus called the Twelve to him, and sent them out in pairs. He gave them authority and power to deal with the evil opposition. He sent them off with these instructions:

6.8-9 "Don't think you need a lot of extra equipment for this. *You* are the equipment. No special appeals for funds. Keep it simple.

6.10 "And no luxury inns. Get a modest place and be content there until you leave.

6.11 "If you're not welcomed, not listened to, quietly withdraw. Don't make a scene. Shrug your shoulders and be on your way."

6.12-13 Then they were on the road. They preached with joyful urgency that life can be radically different; right and left they sent the demons packing; they brought wellness to the sick, anointing their bodies, healing their spirits.

THE DEATH OF JOHN

6.14 King Herod heard of all this, for by this time the name of Jesus was on everyone's lips. He said, "This has to be John the Baptizer come back from the dead—that's why he's able to work miracles!"

6.15 Others said, "No, it's Elijah."

Others said, "He's a prophet, just like one of the old-time prophets."

6.16 But Herod wouldn't budge: "It's John, sure enough. I cut off his head, and now he's back, alive."

6.17-20 Herod was the one who had ordered the arrest of John, put him in chains, and sent him to prison at the nagging of Herodias, his brother Philip's wife. For John had provoked Herod by naming his relationship with Herodias "adultery." Herodias, smoldering with hate, wanted

---

ᵃ 3 Greek *Joses*, a variant of *Joseph*   ᵇ 7 Greek *unclean*
ᶜ 14 Some early manuscripts *He was saying*

NEW INTERNATIONAL VERSION

wanted to kill him. But she was not able to, [20]because Herod feared John and protected him, knowing him to be a righteous and holy man. When Herod heard John, he was greatly puzzled[a]; yet he liked to listen to him.

[21]Finally the opportune time came. On his birthday Herod gave a banquet for his high officials and military commanders and the leading men of Galilee. [22]When the daughter of Herodias came in and danced, she pleased Herod and his dinner guests.

The king said to the girl, "Ask me for anything you want, and I'll give it to you." [23]And he promised her with an oath, "Whatever you ask I will give you, up to half my kingdom."

[24]She went out and said to her mother, "What shall I ask for?"

"The head of John the Baptist," she answered.

[25]At once the girl hurried in to the king with the request: "I want you to give me right now the head of John the Baptist on a platter."

[26]The king was greatly distressed, but because of his oaths and his dinner guests, he did not want to refuse her. [27]So he immediately sent an executioner with orders to bring John's head. The man went, beheaded John in the prison, [28]and brought back his head on a platter. He presented it to the girl, and she gave it to her mother. [29]On hearing of this, John's disciples came and took his body and laid it in a tomb.

JESUS FEEDS THE FIVE THOUSAND

[30]The apostles gathered around Jesus and reported to him all they had done and taught. [31]Then, because so many people were coming and going that they did not even have a chance to eat, he said to them, "Come with me by yourselves to a quiet place and get some rest."

[32]So they went away by themselves in a boat to a solitary place. [33]But many who saw them leaving recognized them and ran on foot from all the towns and got there ahead of them. [34]When Jesus landed and saw a large crowd, he had compassion on them, because they were like sheep without a shepherd. So he began teaching them many things.

[35]By this time it was late in the day, so his disciples came to him. "This is a remote place," they said, "and it's already very late. [36]Send the people away so they can go to the surrounding countryside and villages and buy themselves something to eat."

[37]But he answered, "You give them something to eat."

They said to him, "That would take eight

THE MESSAGE

to kill him, but didn't dare because Herod was in awe of John. Convinced that he was a holy man, he gave him special treatment. Whenever he listened to him he was miserable with guilt—and yet he couldn't stay away. Something in John kept pulling him back.

6.21-22 But a portentous day arrived when Herod threw a birthday party, inviting all the brass and bluebloods in Galilee. Herodias's daughter entered the banquet hall and danced for the guests. She dazzled Herod and the guests.

6.22-23 The king said to the girl, "Ask me anything. I'll give you anything you want." Carried away, he kept on, "I swear, I'll split my kingdom with you if you say so!"

6.24 She went back to her mother and said, "What should I ask for?"

"Ask for the head of John the Baptizer."

6.25 Excited, she ran back to the king and said, "I want the head of John the Baptizer served up on a platter. And I want it now!"

6.26-29 That sobered the king up fast. But unwilling to lose face with his guests, he caved in and let her have her wish. The king sent the executioner off to the prison with orders to bring back John's head. He went, cut off John's head, brought it back on a platter, and presented it to the girl, who gave it to her mother. When John's disciples heard about this, they came and got the body and gave it a decent burial.

SUPPER FOR FIVE THOUSAND

6.30-31 The apostles then rendezvoused with Jesus and reported on all that they had done and taught. Jesus said, "Come off by yourselves; let's take a break and get a little rest." For there was constant coming and going. They didn't even have time to eat.

6.32-34 So they got in the boat and went off to a remote place by themselves. Someone saw them going and the word got around. From the surrounding towns people went out on foot, running, and got there ahead of them. When Jesus arrived, he saw this huge crowd. At the sight of them, his heart broke—like sheep with no shepherd they were. He went right to work teaching them.

6.35-36 When his disciples thought this had gone on long enough—it was now quite late in the day—they interrupted: "We are a long way out in the country, and it's very late. Pronounce a benediction and send these folks off so they can get some supper."

6.37 Jesus said, "You do it. Fix supper for them." They replied, "Are you serious? You want us

---

NEW INTERNATIONAL VERSION

months of a man's wages[a]! Are we to go and spend that much on bread and give it to them to eat?"

38"How many loaves do you have?" he asked. "Go and see."

When they found out, they said, "Five—and two fish."

39Then Jesus directed them to have all the people sit down in groups on the green grass. 40So they sat down in groups of hundreds and fifties. 41Taking the five loaves and the two fish and looking up to heaven, he gave thanks and broke the loaves. Then he gave them to his disciples to set before the people. He also divided the two fish among them all. 42They all ate and were satisfied, 43and the disciples picked up twelve basketfuls of broken pieces of bread and fish. 44The number of the men who had eaten was five thousand.

JESUS WALKS ON THE WATER

45Immediately Jesus made his disciples get into the boat and go on ahead of him to Bethsaida, while he dismissed the crowd. 46After leaving them, he went up on a mountainside to pray.

47When evening came, the boat was in the middle of the lake, and he was alone on land. 48He saw the disciples straining at the oars, because the wind was against them. About the fourth watch of the night he went out to them, walking on the lake. He was about to pass by them, 49but when they saw him walking on the lake, they thought he was a ghost. They cried out, 50because they all saw him and were terrified.

Immediately he spoke to them and said, "Take courage! It is I. Don't be afraid." 51Then he climbed into the boat with them, and the wind died down. They were completely amazed, 52for they had not understood about the loaves; their hearts were hardened.

53When they had crossed over, they landed at Gennesaret and anchored there. 54As soon as they got out of the boat, people recognized Jesus. 55They ran throughout that whole region and carried the sick on mats to wherever they heard he was. 56And wherever he went—into villages, towns or countryside—they placed the sick in the marketplaces. They begged him to let them touch even the edge of his cloak, and all who touched him were healed.

CLEAN AND UNCLEAN

7 The Pharisees and some of the teachers of the law who had come from Jerusalem gathered around Jesus and 2saw some of his disciples eating food with hands that were "unclean," that

THE MESSAGE

to go spend a fortune on food for their supper?"

6.38   But he was quite serious. "How many loaves of bread do you have? Take an inventory."

That didn't take long. "Five," they said, "plus two fish."

6.39-44   Jesus got them all to sit down in groups of fifty or a hundred—they looked like a patchwork quilt of wildflowers spread out on the green grass! He took the five loaves and two fish, lifted his face to heaven in prayer, blessed, broke, and gave the bread to the disciples, and the disciples in turn gave it to the people. He did the same with the fish. They all ate their fill. The disciples gathered twelve baskets of leftovers. More than five thousand were at the supper.

WALKING ON THE SEA

6.45-46 As soon as the meal was finished, Jesus insisted that the disciples get in the boat and go on ahead across to Bethsaida while he dismissed the congregation. After sending them off, he climbed a mountain to pray.

6.47-49   Late at night, the boat was far out at sea; Jesus was still by himself on land. He could see his men struggling with the oars, the wind having come up against them. At about four o'clock in the morning, Jesus came toward them, walking on the sea. He intended to go right by them. But when they saw him walking on the sea, they thought it was a ghost and screamed, scared out of their wits.

6.50-52   Jesus was quick to comfort them: "Courage! It's me. Don't be afraid." As soon as he climbed into the boat, the wind died down. They were stunned, shaking their heads, wondering what was going on. They didn't understand what he had done at the supper. None of this had yet penetrated their hearts.

6.53-56   They beached the boat at Gennesaret and tied up at the landing. As soon as they got out of the boat, word got around fast. People ran this way and that, bringing their sick on stretchers to where they heard he was. Wherever he went, village or town or country crossroads, they brought their sick to the marketplace and begged him to let them touch the edge of his coat—that's all. And whoever touched him became well.

THE SOURCE OF YOUR POLLUTION

7.1-4   7 The Pharisees, along with some religion scholars who had come from Jerusalem, gathered around him. They noticed that some of his disciples weren't being careful with ritual

---

a 37 Greek take two hundred denarii

NEW INTERNATIONAL VERSION

is, unwashed. ³(The Pharisees and all the Jews do not eat unless they give their hands a ceremonial washing, holding to the tradition of the elders. ⁴When they come from the marketplace they do not eat unless they wash. And they observe many other traditions, such as the washing of cups, pitchers and kettles.ᵃ)

⁵So the Pharisees and teachers of the law asked Jesus, "Why don't your disciples live according to the tradition of the elders instead of eating their food with 'unclean' hands?"

⁶He replied, "Isaiah was right when he prophesied about you hypocrites; as it is written:

" 'These people honor me with their lips,
   but their hearts are far from me.
⁷ They worship me in vain;
   their teachings are but rules taught by men.'ᵇ

⁸You have let go of the commands of God and are holding on to the traditions of men."

⁹And he said to them: "You have a fine way of setting aside the commands of God in order to observeᶜ your own traditions! ¹⁰For Moses said, 'Honor your father and your mother,'ᵈ and, 'Anyone who curses his father or mother must be put to death.'ᵉ ¹¹But you say that if a man says to his father or mother: 'Whatever help you might otherwise have received from me is Corban' (that is, a gift devoted to God), ¹²then you no longer let him do anything for his father or mother. ¹³Thus you nullify the word of God by your tradition that you have handed down. And you do many things like that."

¹⁴Again Jesus called the crowd to him and said, "Listen to me, everyone, and understand this. ¹⁵Nothing outside a man can make him 'unclean' by going into him. Rather, it is what comes out of a man that makes him 'unclean.'ᶠ"

¹⁷After he had left the crowd and entered the house, his disciples asked him about this parable. ¹⁸"Are you so dull?" he asked. "Don't you see that nothing that enters a man from the outside can make him 'unclean'? ¹⁹For it doesn't go into his heart but into his stomach, and then out of his body." (In saying this, Jesus declared all foods "clean.")

²⁰He went on: "What comes out of a man is what makes him 'unclean.' ²¹For from within, out of men's hearts, come evil thoughts, sexual immorality, theft, murder, adultery, ²²greed, malice, deceit, lewdness, envy, slander, arrogance and folly. ²³All these evils come from inside and make a man 'unclean.' "

ᵃ 4 Some early manuscripts *pitchers, kettles and dining couches* ᵇ 6,7 Isaiah 29:13 ᶜ 9 Some manuscripts *set up* ᵈ 10 Exodus 20:12; Deut. 5:16 ᵉ 10 Exodus 21:17; Lev. 20:9 ᶠ 15 Some early manuscripts *'unclean.' ¹⁶If anyone has ears to hear, let him hear.*

THE MESSAGE

washings before meals. The Pharisees—Jews in general, in fact—would never eat a meal without going through the motions of a ritual hand-washing, with an especially vigorous scrubbing if they had just come from the market (to say nothing of the scourings they'd give jugs and pots and pans).

7.5   The Pharisees and religion scholars asked, "Why do your disciples flout the rules, showing up at meals without washing their hands?"

7.6-8   Jesus answered, "Isaiah was right about frauds like you, hit the bull's-eye in fact:

These people make a big show of saying the
   right thing,
   but their heart isn't in it.
They act like they are worshiping me,
   but they don't mean it.
They just use me as a cover
   for teaching whatever suits their fancy,
Ditching God's command
   and taking up the latest fads."

7.9-13   He went on, "Well, good for you. You get rid of God's command so you won't be inconvenienced in following the religious fashions! Moses said, 'Respect your father and mother,' and, 'Anyone denouncing father or mother should be killed.' But you weasel out of that by saying that it's perfectly acceptable to say to father or mother, 'Gift! What I owed you I've given as a gift to God,' thus relieving yourselves of obligation to father or mother. You scratch out God's Word and scrawl a whim in its place. You do a lot of things like this."

7.14-15   Jesus called the crowd together again and said, "Listen now, all of you—take this to heart. It's not what you swallow that pollutes your life; it's what you vomit—that's the real pollution."

7.17   When he was back home after being with the crowd, his disciples said, "We don't get it. Put it in plain language."

7.18-19   Jesus said, "Are you being willfully stupid? Don't you see that what you swallow can't contaminate you? It doesn't enter your heart but your stomach, works its way through the intestines, and is finally flushed." (That took care of dietary quibbling; Jesus was saying that *all* foods are fit to eat.)

7.20-23   He went on: "It's what comes out of a person that pollutes: obscenities, lusts, thefts, murders, adulteries, greed, depravity, deceptive dealings, carousing, mean looks, slander, arrogance, foolishness—all these are vomit from the heart. *There* is the source of your pollution."

✝

NEW INTERNATIONAL VERSION

THE FAITH OF A SYROPHOENICIAN WOMAN

²⁴Jesus left that place and went to the vicinity of Tyre.ᵃ He entered a house and did not want anyone to know it; yet he could not keep his presence secret. ²⁵In fact, as soon as she heard about him, a woman whose little daughter was possessed by an evilᵇ spirit came and fell at his feet. ²⁶The woman was a Greek, born in Syrian Phoenicia. She begged Jesus to drive the demon out of her daughter.

²⁷"First let the children eat all they want," he told her, "for it is not right to take the children's bread and toss it to their dogs."

²⁸"Yes, Lord," she replied, "but even the dogs under the table eat the children's crumbs."

²⁹Then he told her, "For such a reply, you may go; the demon has left your daughter."

³⁰She went home and found her child lying on the bed, and the demon gone.

THE HEALING OF A DEAF AND MUTE MAN

³¹Then Jesus left the vicinity of Tyre and went through Sidon, down to the Sea of Galilee and into the region of the Decapolis.ᶜ ³²There some people brought to him a man who was deaf and could hardly talk, and they begged him to place his hand on the man.

³³After he took him aside, away from the crowd, Jesus put his fingers into the man's ears. Then he spit and touched the man's tongue. ³⁴He looked up to heaven and with a deep sigh said to him, *"Ephphatha!"* (which means, "Be opened!"). ³⁵At this, the man's ears were opened, his tongue was loosened and he began to speak plainly.

³⁶Jesus commanded them not to tell anyone. But the more he did so, the more they kept talking about it. ³⁷People were overwhelmed with amazement. "He has done everything well," they said. "He even makes the deaf hear and the mute speak."

JESUS FEEDS THE FOUR THOUSAND

8 During those days another large crowd gathered. Since they had nothing to eat, Jesus called his disciples to him and said, ²"I have compassion for these people; they have already been with me three days and have nothing to eat. ³If I send them home hungry, they will collapse on the way, because some of them have come a long distance."

⁴His disciples answered, "But where in this remote place can anyone get enough bread to feed them?"

⁵"How many loaves do you have?" Jesus asked.

THE MESSAGE

7.24-26 From there Jesus set out for the vicinity of Tyre. He entered a house there where he didn't think he would be found, but he couldn't escape notice. He was barely inside when a woman who had a disturbed daughter heard where he was. She came and knelt at his feet, begging for help. The woman was Greek, Syro-Phoenician by birth. She asked him to cure her daughter.

7.27 He said, "Stand in line and take your turn. The children get fed first. If there's any left over, the dogs get it."

7.28 She said, "Of course, Master. But don't dogs under the table get scraps dropped by the children?"

7.29-30 Jesus was impressed. "You're right! On your way! Your daughter is no longer disturbed. The demonic affliction is gone." She went home and found her daughter relaxed on the bed, the torment gone for good.

7.31-35 Then he left the region of Tyre, went through Sidon back to Galilee Lake and over to the district of the Ten Towns. Some people brought a man who could neither hear nor speak and asked Jesus to lay a healing hand on him. He took the man off by himself, put his fingers in the man's ears and some spit on the man's tongue. Then Jesus looked up in prayer, groaned mightily, and commanded, *"Ephphatha!*—Open up!" And it happened. The man's hearing was clear and his speech plain—just like that.

7.36-37 Jesus urged them to keep it quiet, but they talked it up all the more, beside themselves with excitement. "He's done it all and done it well. He gives hearing to the deaf, speech to the speechless."

A MEAL FOR FOUR THOUSAND

8.1-3 **8** At about this same time he again found himself with a hungry crowd on his hands. He called his disciples together and said, "This crowd is breaking my heart. They have stuck with me for three days, and now they have nothing to eat. If I send them home hungry, they'll faint along the way—some of them have come a long distance."

8.4 His disciples responded, "What do you expect us to do about it? Buy food out here in the desert?"

8.5 He asked, "How much bread do you have?"

ᵃ 24 Many early manuscripts *Tyre and Sidon*   ᵇ 25 Greek *unclean*   ᶜ 31 That is, the Ten Cities

NEW INTERNATIONAL VERSION

"Seven," they replied.

⁶He told the crowd to sit down on the ground. When he had taken the seven loaves and given thanks, he broke them and gave them to his disciples to set before the people, and they did so. ⁷They had a few small fish as well; he gave thanks for them also and told the disciples to distribute them. ⁸The people ate and were satisfied. Afterward the disciples picked up seven basketfuls of broken pieces that were left over. ⁹About four thousand men were present. And having sent them away, ¹⁰he got into the boat with his disciples and went to the region of Dalmanutha.

¹¹The Pharisees came and began to question Jesus. To test him, they asked him for a sign from heaven. ¹²He sighed deeply and said, "Why does this generation ask for a miraculous sign? I tell you the truth, no sign will be given to it." ¹³Then he left them, got back into the boat and crossed to the other side.

THE YEAST OF THE PHARISEES AND HEROD

¹⁴The disciples had forgotten to bring bread, except for one loaf they had with them in the boat. ¹⁵"Be careful," Jesus warned them. "Watch out for the yeast of the Pharisees and that of Herod."

¹⁶They discussed this with one another and said, "It is because we have no bread."

¹⁷Aware of their discussion, Jesus asked them: "Why are you talking about having no bread? Do you still not see or understand? Are your hearts hardened? ¹⁸Do you have eyes but fail to see, and ears but fail to hear? And don't you remember? ¹⁹When I broke the five loaves for the five thousand, how many basketfuls of pieces did you pick up?"

"Twelve," they replied.

²⁰"And when I broke the seven loaves for the four thousand, how many basketfuls of pieces did you pick up?"

They answered, "Seven."

²¹He said to them, "Do you still not understand?"

THE HEALING OF A BLIND MAN AT BETHSAIDA

²²They came to Bethsaida, and some people brought a blind man and begged Jesus to touch him. ²³He took the blind man by the hand and led him outside the village. When he had spit on the man's eyes and put his hands on him, Jesus asked, "Do you see anything?"

²⁴He looked up and said, "I see people; they look like trees walking around."

²⁵Once more Jesus put his hands on the man's eyes. Then his eyes were opened, his sight was

THE MESSAGE

"Seven loaves," they said.

8.6-10 So Jesus told the crowd to sit down on the ground. After giving thanks, he took the seven bread loaves, broke them into pieces, and gave them to his disciples so they could hand them out to the crowd. They also had a few fish. He pronounced a blessing over the fish and told his disciples to hand them out as well. The crowd ate its fill. Seven sacks of leftovers were collected. There were well over four thousand at the meal. Then he sent them home. He himself went straight to the boat with his disciples and set out for Dalmanoutha.

8.11-12 When they arrived, the Pharisees came out and started in on him, badgering him to prove himself, pushing him up against the wall. Provoked, he said, "Why does this generation clamor for miraculous guarantees? If I have anything to say about it, you'll not get so much as a hint of a guarantee."

CONTAMINATING YEAST

8.13-15 He then left them, got back in the boat, and headed for the other side. But the disciples forgot to pack a lunch. Except for a single loaf of bread, there wasn't a crumb in the boat. Jesus warned, "Be very careful. Keep a sharp eye out for the contaminating yeast of Pharisees and the followers of Herod."

8.16-19 Meanwhile, the disciples were finding fault with each other because they had forgotten to bring bread. Jesus overheard and said, "Why are you fussing because you forgot bread? Don't you see the point of all this? Don't you get it at all? Remember the five loaves I broke for the five thousand? How many baskets of leftovers did you pick up?"

They said, "Twelve."

8.20 "And the seven loaves for the four thousand—how many bags full of leftovers did you get?"

"Seven."

8.21 He said, "Do you still not get it?"

8.22-23 They arrived at Bethsaida. Some people brought a sightless man and begged Jesus to give him a healing touch. Taking him by the hand, he led him out of the village. He put spit in the man's eyes, laid hands on him, and asked, "Do you see anything?"

8.24-26 He looked up. "I see men. They look like walking trees." So Jesus laid hands on his eyes again. The man looked hard and realized that he had recovered perfect sight, saw everything

NEW INTERNATIONAL VERSION

restored, and he saw everything clearly. [26]Jesus sent him home, saying, "Don't go into the village. [a]"

PETER'S CONFESSION OF CHRIST

[27]Jesus and his disciples went on to the villages around Caesarea Philippi. On the way he asked them, "Who do people say I am?"

[28]They replied, "Some say John the Baptist; others say Elijah; and still others, one of the prophets."

[29]"But what about you?" he asked. "Who do you say I am?"

Peter answered, "You are the Christ. [b]"

[30]Jesus warned them not to tell anyone about him.

JESUS PREDICTS HIS DEATH

[31]He then began to teach them that the Son of Man must suffer many things and be rejected by the elders, chief priests and teachers of the law, and that he must be killed and after three days rise again. [32]He spoke plainly about this, and Peter took him aside and began to rebuke him.

[33]But when Jesus turned and looked at his disciples, he rebuked Peter. "Get behind me, Satan!" he said. "You do not have in mind the things of God, but the things of men."

[34]Then he called the crowd to him along with his disciples and said: "If anyone would come after me, he must deny himself and take up his cross and follow me. [35]For whoever wants to save his life [c] will lose it, but whoever loses his life for me and for the gospel will save it. [36]What good is it for a man to gain the whole world, yet forfeit his soul? [37]Or what can a man give in exchange for his soul? [38]If anyone is ashamed of me and my words in this adulterous and sinful generation, the Son of Man will be ashamed of him when he comes in his Father's glory with the holy angels."

9 And he said to them, "I tell you the truth, some who are standing here will not taste death before they see the kingdom of God come with power."

THE MESSAGE

in bright, twenty-twenty focus. Jesus sent him straight home, telling him, "Don't enter the village."

THE MESSIAH

8.27 Jesus and his disciples headed out for the villages around Caesarea Philippi. As they walked, he asked, "Who do the people say I am?"

8.28 "Some say 'John the Baptizer,'" they said. "Others say 'Elijah.' Still others say 'one of the prophets.'"

8.29 He then asked, "And you—what are you saying about me? Who am I?"

Peter gave the answer: "You are the Christ, the Messiah."

8.30-32 Jesus warned them to keep it quiet, not to breathe a word of it to anyone. He then began explaining things to them: "It is necessary that the Son of Man proceed to an ordeal of suffering, be tried and found guilty by the elders, high priests, and religion scholars, be killed, and after three days rise up alive." He said this simply and clearly so they couldn't miss it.

8.32-33 But Peter grabbed him in protest. Turning and seeing his disciples wavering, wondering what to believe, Jesus confronted Peter. "Peter, get out of my way! Satan, get lost! You have no idea how God works."

8.34-37 Calling the crowd to join his disciples, he said, "Anyone who intends to come with me has to let me lead. You're not in the driver's seat; I am. Don't run from suffering; embrace it. Follow me and I'll show you how. Self-help is no help at all. Self-sacrifice is the way, my way, to saving yourself, your true self. What good would it do to get everything you want and lose you, the real you? What could you ever trade your soul for?

8.38 "If any of you are embarrassed over me and the way I'm leading you when you get around your fickle and unfocused friends, know that you'll be an even greater embarrassment to the Son of Man when he arrives in all the splendor of God, his Father, with an army of the holy angels."

9.1 **9** Then he drove it home by saying, "This isn't pie in the sky by and by. Some of you who are standing here are going to see it happen, see the kingdom of God arrive in full force."

NEW INTERNATIONAL VERSION

THE TRANSFIGURATION

²After six days Jesus took Peter, James and John with him and led them up a high mountain, where they were all alone. There he was transfigured before them. ³His clothes became dazzling white, whiter than anyone in the world could bleach them. ⁴And there appeared before them Elijah and Moses, who were talking with Jesus.

⁵Peter said to Jesus, "Rabbi, it is good for us to be here. Let us put up three shelters—one for you, one for Moses and one for Elijah." ⁶(He did not know what to say, they were so frightened.)

⁷Then a cloud appeared and enveloped them, and a voice came from the cloud: "This is my Son, whom I love. Listen to him!"

⁸Suddenly, when they looked around, they no longer saw anyone with them except Jesus.

⁹As they were coming down the mountain, Jesus gave them orders not to tell anyone what they had seen until the Son of Man had risen from the dead. ¹⁰They kept the matter to themselves, discussing what "rising from the dead" meant.

¹¹And they asked him, "Why do the teachers of the law say that Elijah must come first?"

¹²Jesus replied, "To be sure, Elijah does come first, and restores all things. Why then is it written that the Son of Man must suffer much and be rejected? ¹³But I tell you, Elijah has come, and they have done to him everything they wished, just as it is written about him."

THE HEALING OF A BOY WITH AN EVIL SPIRIT

¹⁴When they came to the other disciples, they saw a large crowd around them and the teachers of the law arguing with them. ¹⁵As soon as all the people saw Jesus, they were overwhelmed with wonder and ran to greet him.

¹⁶"What are you arguing with them about?" he asked.

¹⁷A man in the crowd answered, "Teacher, I brought you my son, who is possessed by a spirit that has robbed him of speech. ¹⁸Whenever it seizes him, it throws him to the ground. He foams at the mouth, gnashes his teeth and becomes rigid. I asked your disciples to drive out the spirit, but they could not."

¹⁹"O unbelieving generation," Jesus replied, "how long shall I stay with you? How long shall I put up with you? Bring the boy to me."

²⁰So they brought him. When the spirit saw

THE MESSAGE

IN A LIGHT-RADIANT CLOUD

9.2-4 Six days later, three of them *did* see it. Jesus took Peter, James, and John and led them up a high mountain. His appearance changed from the inside out, right before their eyes. His clothes shimmered, glistening white, whiter than any bleach could make them. Elijah, along with Moses, came into view, in deep conversation with Jesus.

9.5-6 Peter interrupted, "Rabbi, this is a great moment! Let's build three memorials—one for you, one for Moses, one for Elijah." He blurted this out without thinking, stunned as they all were by what they were seeing.

9.7 Just then a light-radiant cloud enveloped them, and from deep in the cloud, a voice: "This is my Son, marked by my love. Listen to him."

9.8 The next minute the disciples were looking around, rubbing their eyes, seeing nothing but Jesus, only Jesus.

9.9-10 Coming down the mountain, Jesus swore them to secrecy. "Don't tell a soul what you saw. After the Son of Man rises from the dead, you're free to talk." They puzzled over that, wondering what on earth "rising from the dead" meant.

9.11 Meanwhile they were asking, "Why do the religion scholars say that Elijah has to come first?"

9.12-13 Jesus replied, "Elijah does come first and get everything ready for the coming of the Son of Man. They treated this Elijah like dirt, much like they will treat the Son of Man, who will, according to Scripture, suffer terribly and be kicked around contemptibly."

THERE ARE NO IFS

9.14-16 When they came back down the mountain to the other disciples, they saw a huge crowd around them, and the religion scholars cross-examining them. As soon as the people in the crowd saw Jesus, admiring excitement stirred them. They ran and greeted him. He asked, "What's going on? What's all the commotion?"

9.17-18 A man out of the crowd answered, "Teacher, I brought my mute son, made speechless by a demon, to you. Whenever it seizes him, it throws him to the ground. He foams at the mouth, grinds his teeth, and goes stiff as a board. I told your disciples, hoping they could deliver him, but they couldn't."

9.19-20 Jesus said, "What a generation! No sense of God! How many times do I have to go over these things? How much longer do I have to put up with this? Bring the boy here." They brought him. When the demon saw Jesus, it

NEW INTERNATIONAL VERSION

Jesus, it immediately threw the boy into a convulsion. He fell to the ground and rolled around, foaming at the mouth.

²¹Jesus asked the boy's father, "How long has he been like this?"

"From childhood," he answered. ²²"It has often thrown him into fire or water to kill him. But if you can do anything, take pity on us and help us."

²³"'If you can'?" said Jesus. "Everything is possible for him who believes."

²⁴Immediately the boy's father exclaimed, "I do believe; help me overcome my unbelief!"

²⁵When Jesus saw that a crowd was running to the scene, he rebuked the evil*ᵃ* spirit. "You deaf and mute spirit," he said, "I command you, come out of him and never enter him again."

²⁶The spirit shrieked, convulsed him violently and came out. The boy looked so much like a corpse that many said, "He's dead." ²⁷But Jesus took him by the hand and lifted him to his feet, and he stood up.

²⁸After Jesus had gone indoors, his disciples asked him privately, "Why couldn't we drive it out?"

²⁹He replied, "This kind can come out only by prayer.*ᵇ*"

³⁰They left that place and passed through Galilee. Jesus did not want anyone to know where they were, ³¹because he was teaching his disciples. He said to them, "The Son of Man is going to be betrayed into the hands of men. They will kill him, and after three days he will rise." ³²But they did not understand what he meant and were afraid to ask him about it.

WHO IS THE GREATEST?

³³They came to Capernaum. When he was in the house, he asked them, "What were you arguing about on the road?" ³⁴But they kept quiet because on the way they had argued about who was the greatest.

³⁵Sitting down, Jesus called the Twelve and said, "If anyone wants to be first, he must be the very last, and the servant of all."

³⁶He took a little child and had him stand among them. Taking him in his arms, he said to them, ³⁷"Whoever welcomes one of these little children in my name welcomes me; and whoever welcomes me does not welcome me but the one who sent me."

WHOEVER IS NOT AGAINST US IS FOR US

³⁸"Teacher," said John, "we saw a man driving out demons in your name and we told him to stop, because he was not one of us."

ᵃ 25 Greek *unclean*   *ᵇ 29* Some manuscripts *prayer and fasting*

THE MESSAGE

threw the boy into a seizure, causing him to writhe on the ground and foam at the mouth.

9.21-22 He asked the boy's father, "How long has this been going on?"

"Ever since he was a little boy. Many times it pitches him into fire or the river to do away with him. If you can do anything, do it. Have a heart and help us!"

9.23 Jesus said, "If? There are no 'ifs' among believers. Anything can happen."

9.24 No sooner were the words out of his mouth than the father cried, "Then I believe. Help me with my doubts!"

9.25-27 Seeing that the crowd was forming fast, Jesus gave the vile spirit its marching orders: "Dumb and deaf spirit, I command you—Out of him, and stay out!" Screaming, and with much thrashing about, it left. The boy was pale as a corpse, so people started saying, "He's dead." But Jesus, taking his hand, raised him. The boy stood up.

9.28 After arriving back home, his disciples cornered Jesus and asked, "Why couldn't we throw the demon out?"

9.29 He answered, "There is no way to get rid of this kind of demon except by prayer."

9.30-32 Leaving there, they went through Galilee. He didn't want anyone to know their whereabouts, for he wanted to teach his disciples. He told them, "The Son of Man is about to be betrayed to some people who want nothing to do with God. They will murder him. Three days after his murder, he will rise, alive." They didn't know what he was talking about, but were afraid to ask him about it.

SO YOU WANT FIRST PLACE?

9.33 They came to Capernaum. When he was safe at home, he asked them, "What were you discussing on the road?"

9.34 The silence was deafening—they had been arguing with one another over who among them was greatest.

9.35 He sat down and summoned the Twelve. "So you want first place? Then take the last place. Be the servant of all."

9.36-37 He put a child in the middle of the room. Then, cradling the little one in his arms, he said, "Whoever embraces one of these children as I do embraces me, and far more than me—God who sent me."

⊹

9.38 John spoke up, "Teacher, we saw a man using your name to expel demons and we stopped him because he wasn't in our group."

NEW INTERNATIONAL VERSION

³⁹"Do not stop him," Jesus said. "No one who does a miracle in my name can in the next moment say anything bad about me, ⁴⁰for whoever is not against us is for us. ⁴¹I tell you the truth, anyone who gives you a cup of water in my name because you belong to Christ will certainly not lose his reward.

CAUSING TO SIN

⁴²"And if anyone causes one of these little ones who believe in me to sin, it would be better for him to be thrown into the sea with a large millstone tied around his neck. ⁴³If your hand causes you to sin, cut it off. It is better for you to enter life maimed than with two hands to go into hell, where the fire never goes out. ^a ⁴⁵And if your foot causes you to sin, cut it off. It is better for you to enter life crippled than to have two feet and be thrown into hell. ^b ⁴⁷And if your eye causes you to sin, pluck it out. It is better for you to enter the kingdom of God with one eye than to have two eyes and be thrown into hell, ⁴⁸where

" 'their worm does not die,
and the fire is not quenched.' ^c

⁴⁹Everyone will be salted with fire.

⁵⁰"Salt is good, but if it loses its saltiness, how can you make it salty again? Have salt in yourselves, and be at peace with each other."

DIVORCE

10 Jesus then left that place and went into the region of Judea and across the Jordan. Again crowds of people came to him, and as was his custom, he taught them.

²Some Pharisees came and tested him by asking, "Is it lawful for a man to divorce his wife?"

³"What did Moses command you?" he replied.

⁴They said, "Moses permitted a man to write a certificate of divorce and send her away."

⁵"It was because your hearts were hard that Moses wrote you this law," Jesus replied. ⁶"But at the beginning of creation God 'made them male and female.' ^d ⁷For this reason a man will leave his father and mother and be united to his wife, ^e ⁸and the two will become one flesh.' ^f So they are no longer two, but one. ⁹Therefore what God has joined together, let man not separate."

¹⁰When they were in the house again, the dis-

THE MESSAGE

^{9.39-41} Jesus wasn't pleased. "Don't stop him. No one can use my name to do something good and powerful, and in the next breath cut me down. If he's not an enemy, he's an ally. Why, anyone by just giving you a cup of water in my name is on our side. Count on it that God will notice.

^{9.42} "On the other hand, if you give one of these simple, childlike believers a hard time, bullying or taking advantage of their simple trust, you'll soon wish you hadn't. You'd be better off dropped in the middle of the lake with a millstone around your neck.

^{9.43-48} "If your hand or your foot gets in God's way, chop it off and throw it away. You're better off maimed or lame and alive than the proud owner of two hands and two feet, godless in a furnace of eternal fire. And if your eye distracts you from God, pull it out and throw it away. You're better off one-eyed and alive than exercising your twenty-twenty vision from inside the fire of hell.

^{9.49-50} "Everyone's going through a refining fire sooner or later, but you'll be well-preserved, protected from the *eternal* flames. Be preservatives yourselves. Preserve the peace."

DIVORCE

10 From there he went to the area of Judea across the Jordan. A crowd of people, as was so often the case, went along, and he, as he so often did, taught them. Pharisees came up, intending to give him a hard time. They asked, "Is it legal for a man to divorce his wife?"

^{10.3} Jesus said, "What did Moses command?"

^{10.4} They answered, "Moses gave permission to fill out a certificate of dismissal and divorce her."

^{10.5-9} Jesus said, "Moses wrote this command only as a concession to your hardhearted ways. In the original creation, God made male and female to be together. Because of this, a man leaves father and mother, and in marriage he becomes one flesh with a woman—no longer two individuals, but forming a new unity. Because God created this organic union of the two sexes, no one should desecrate his art by cutting them apart."

^{10.10-12} When they were back home, the disciples

---

^a 43 Some manuscripts *out,* ⁴⁴*where* / " *'their worm does not die, / and the fire is not quenched.'* ^b 45 Some manuscripts *hell,* ⁴⁶*where* / " *'their worm does not die, / and the fire is not quenched.'* ^c 48 Isaiah 66:24 ^d 6 Gen. 1:27 ^e 7 Some early manuscripts do not have *and be united to his wife.* ^f 8 Gen. 2:24

NEW INTERNATIONAL VERSION

ciples asked Jesus about this. ¹¹He answered, "Anyone who divorces his wife and marries another woman commits adultery against her. ¹²And if she divorces her husband and marries another man, she commits adultery."

THE LITTLE CHILDREN AND JESUS

¹³People were bringing little children to Jesus to have him touch them, but the disciples rebuked them. ¹⁴When Jesus saw this, he was indignant. He said to them, "Let the little children come to me, and do not hinder them, for the kingdom of God belongs to such as these. ¹⁵I tell you the truth, anyone who will not receive the kingdom of God like a little child will never enter it." ¹⁶And he took the children in his arms, put his hands on them and blessed them.

THE RICH YOUNG MAN

¹⁷As Jesus started on his way, a man ran up to him and fell on his knees before him. "Good teacher," he asked, "what must I do to inherit eternal life?"

¹⁸"Why do you call me good?" Jesus answered. "No one is good—except God alone. ¹⁹You know the commandments: 'Do not murder, do not commit adultery, do not steal, do not give false testimony, do not defraud, honor your father and mother.'ᵃ"

²⁰"Teacher," he declared, "all these I have kept since I was a boy."

²¹Jesus looked at him and loved him. "One thing you lack," he said. "Go, sell everything you have and give to the poor, and you will have treasure in heaven. Then come, follow me."

²²At this the man's face fell. He went away sad, because he had great wealth.

²³Jesus looked around and said to his disciples, "How hard it is for the rich to enter the kingdom of God!"

²⁴The disciples were amazed at his words. But Jesus said again, "Children, how hard it isᵇ to enter the kingdom of God! ²⁵It is easier for a camel to go through the eye of a needle than for a rich man to enter the kingdom of God."

²⁶The disciples were even more amazed, and said to each other, "Who then can be saved?"

²⁷Jesus looked at them and said, "With man this is impossible, but not with God; all things are possible with God."

²⁸Peter said to him, "We have left everything to follow you!"

²⁹"I tell you the truth," Jesus replied, "no one who has left home or brothers or sisters or

THE MESSAGE

brought it up again. Jesus gave it to them straight: "A man who divorces his wife so he can marry someone else commits adultery against her. And a woman who divorces her husband so she can marry someone else commits adultery."

✝

10.13-16 The people brought children to Jesus, hoping he might touch them. The disciples shooed them off. But Jesus was irate and let them know it: "Don't push these children away. Don't ever get between them and me. These children are at the very center of life in the kingdom. Mark this: Unless you accept God's kingdom in the simplicity of a child, you'll never get in." Then, gathering the children up in his arms, he laid his hands of blessing on them.

TO ENTER GOD'S KINGDOM

10.17 As he went out into the street, a man came running up, greeted him with great reverence, and asked, "Good Teacher, what must I do to get eternal life?"

10.18-19 Jesus said, "Why are you calling me good? No one is good, only God. You know the commandments: Don't murder, don't commit adultery, don't steal, don't lie, don't cheat, honor your father and mother."

10.20 He said, "Teacher, I have—from my youth—kept them all!"

10.21 Jesus looked him hard in the eye—and loved him! He said, "There's one thing left: Go sell whatever you own and give it to the poor. All your wealth will then be heavenly wealth. And come follow me."

10.22 The man's face clouded over. This was the last thing he expected to hear, and he walked off with a heavy heart. He was holding on tight to a lot of things, and not about to let go.

10.23-25 Looking at his disciples, Jesus said, "Do you have any idea how difficult it is for people who 'have it all' to enter God's kingdom?" The disciples couldn't believe what they were hearing, but Jesus kept on: "You can't imagine how difficult. I'd say it's easier for a camel to go through a needle's eye than for the rich to get into God's kingdom."

10.26 *That* set the disciples back on their heels. "Then who has any chance at all?" they asked.

10.27 Jesus was blunt: "No chance at all if you think you can pull it off by yourself. Every chance in the world if you let God do it."

10.28 Peter tried another angle: "We left everything and followed you."

10.29-31 Jesus said, "Mark my words, no one who sacrifices house, brothers, sisters, mother, fa-

---

ᵃ 19 Exodus 20:12-16; Deut. 5:16-20   ᵇ 24 Some manuscripts *is for those who trust in riches*

NEW INTERNATIONAL VERSION

mother or father or children or fields for me and the gospel ³⁰will fail to receive a hundred times as much in this present age (homes, brothers, sisters, mothers, children and fields—and with them, persecutions) and in the age to come, eternal life. ³¹But many who are first will be last, and the last first."

JESUS AGAIN PREDICTS HIS DEATH

³²They were on their way up to Jerusalem, with Jesus leading the way, and the disciples were astonished, while those who followed were afraid. Again he took the Twelve aside and told them what was going to happen to him. ³³"We are going up to Jerusalem," he said, "and the Son of Man will be betrayed to the chief priests and teachers of the law. They will condemn him to death and will hand him over to the Gentiles, ³⁴who will mock him and spit on him, flog him and kill him. Three days later he will rise."

THE REQUEST OF JAMES AND JOHN

³⁵Then James and John, the sons of Zebedee, came to him. "Teacher," they said, "we want you to do for us whatever we ask."

³⁶"What do you want me to do for you?" he asked.

³⁷They replied, "Let one of us sit at your right and the other at your left in your glory."

³⁸"You don't know what you are asking," Jesus said. "Can you drink the cup I drink or be baptized with the baptism I am baptized with?"

³⁹"We can," they answered.

Jesus said to them, "You will drink the cup I drink and be baptized with the baptism I am baptized with, ⁴⁰but to sit at my right or left is not for me to grant. These places belong to those for whom they have been prepared."

⁴¹When the ten heard about this, they became indignant with James and John. ⁴²Jesus called them together and said, "You know that those who are regarded as rulers of the Gentiles lord it over them, and their high officials exercise authority over them. ⁴³Not so with you. Instead, whoever wants to become great among you must be your servant, ⁴⁴and whoever wants to be first must be slave of all. ⁴⁵For even the Son of Man did not come to be served, but to serve, and to give his life as a ransom for many."

BLIND BARTIMAEUS RECEIVES HIS SIGHT

⁴⁶Then they came to Jericho. As Jesus and his

THE MESSAGE

ther, children, land—whatever—because of me and the Message will lose out. They'll get it all back, but multiplied many times in homes, brothers, sisters, mothers, children, and land— but also in troubles. And then the bonus of eternal life! This is once again the Great Reversal: Many who are first will end up last, and the last first."

10.32-34 Back on the road, they set out for Jerusalem. Jesus had a head start on them, and they were following, puzzled and not just a little afraid. He took the Twelve and began again to go over what to expect next. "Listen to me carefully. We're on our way up to Jerusalem. When we get there, the Son of Man will be betrayed to the religious leaders and scholars. They will sentence him to death. Then they will hand him over to the Romans, who will mock and spit on him, give him the third degree, and kill him. After three days he will rise alive."

THE HIGHEST PLACES OF HONOR

10.35 James and John, Zebedee's sons, came up to him. "Teacher, we have something we want you to do for us."

10.36 "What is it? I'll see what I can do."

10.37 "Arrange it," they said, "so that we will be awarded the highest places of honor in your glory—one of us at your right, the other at your left."

10.38 Jesus said, "You have no idea what you're asking. Are you capable of drinking the cup I drink, of being baptized in the baptism I'm about to be plunged into?"

10.39-40 "Sure," they said. "Why not?"

Jesus said, "Come to think of it, you *will* drink the cup I drink, and be baptized in my baptism. But as to awarding places of honor, that's not my business. There are other arrangements for that."

10.41-45 When the other ten heard of this conversation, they lost their tempers with James and John. Jesus got them together to settle things down. "You've observed how godless rulers throw their weight around," he said, "and when people get a little power how quickly it goes to their heads. It's not going to be that way with you. Whoever wants to be great must become a servant. Whoever wants to be first among you must be your slave. That is what the Son of Man has done: He came to serve, not to be served— and then to give away his life in exchange for many who are held hostage."

✝

10.46-48 They spent some time in Jericho. As Jesus was

NEW INTERNATIONAL VERSION

disciples, together with a large crowd, were leaving the city, a blind man, Bartimaeus (that is, the Son of Timaeus), was sitting by the roadside begging. ⁴⁷When he heard that it was Jesus of Nazareth, he began to shout, "Jesus, Son of David, have mercy on me!"

⁴⁸Many rebuked him and told him to be quiet, but he shouted all the more, "Son of David, have mercy on me!"

⁴⁹Jesus stopped and said, "Call him."

So they called to the blind man, "Cheer up! On your feet! He's calling you." ⁵⁰Throwing his cloak aside, he jumped to his feet and came to Jesus.

⁵¹"What do you want me to do for you?" Jesus asked him.

The blind man said, "Rabbi, I want to see."

⁵²"Go," said Jesus, "your faith has healed you." Immediately he received his sight and followed Jesus along the road.

THE TRIUMPHAL ENTRY

11 As they approached Jerusalem and came to Bethphage and Bethany at the Mount of Olives, Jesus sent two of his disciples, ²saying to them, "Go to the village ahead of you, and just as you enter it, you will find a colt tied there, which no one has ever ridden. Untie it and bring it here. ³If anyone asks you, 'Why are you doing this?' tell him, 'The Lord needs it and will send it back here shortly.' "

⁴They went and found a colt outside in the street, tied at a doorway. As they untied it, ⁵some people standing there asked, "What are you doing, untying that colt?" ⁶They answered as Jesus had told them to, and the people let them go. ⁷When they brought the colt to Jesus and threw their cloaks over it, he sat on it. ⁸Many people spread their cloaks on the road, while others spread branches they had cut in the fields. ⁹Those who went ahead and those who followed shouted,

"Hosanna!ᵃ"

"Blessed is he who comes in the name of the Lord!"ᵇ

¹⁰"Blessed is the coming kingdom of our father David!"

"Hosanna in the highest!"

¹¹Jesus entered Jerusalem and went to the temple. He looked around at everything, but since it was already late, he went out to Bethany with the Twelve.

ᵃ 9 A Hebrew expression meaning "Save!" which became an exclamation of praise; also in verse 10
ᵇ 9 Psalm 118:25,26

THE MESSAGE

leaving town, trailed by his disciples and a parade of people, a blind beggar by the name of Bartimaeus, son of Timaeus, was sitting alongside the road. When he heard that Jesus the Nazarene was passing by, he began to cry out, "Son of David, Jesus! Mercy, have mercy on me!" Many tried to hush him up, but he yelled all the louder, "Son of David! Mercy, have mercy on me!"

10.49-50 Jesus stopped in his tracks. "Call him over." They called him. "It's your lucky day! Get up! He's calling you to come!" Throwing off his coat, he was on his feet at once and came to Jesus.

10.51 Jesus said, "What can I do for you?"
The blind man said, "Rabbi, I want to see."

10.52 "On your way," said Jesus. "Your faith has saved and healed you."

In that very instant he recovered his sight and followed Jesus down the road.

ENTERING JERUSALEM ON A COLT

11.1-3 **11** When they were nearing Jerusalem, at Bethphage and Bethany on Mount Olives, he sent off two of the disciples with instructions: "Go to the village across from you. As soon as you enter, you'll find a colt tethered, one that has never yet been ridden. Untie it and bring it. If anyone asks, 'What are you doing?' say, 'The Master needs him, and will return him right away.' "

11.4-7 They went and found a colt tied to a door at the street corner and untied it. Some of those standing there said, "What are you doing untying that colt?" The disciples replied exactly as Jesus had instructed them, and the people let them alone. They brought the colt to Jesus, spread their coats on it, and he mounted.

11.8-10 The people gave him a wonderful welcome, some throwing their coats on the street, others spreading out rushes they had cut in the fields. Running ahead and following after, they were calling out,

Hosanna!
Blessed is he who comes in God's name!
Blessed the coming kingdom of our father David!
Hosanna in highest heaven!

11.11 He entered Jerusalem, then entered the Temple. He looked around, taking it all in. But by now it was late, so he went back to Bethany with the Twelve.

NEW INTERNATIONAL VERSION

Jesus Clears the Temple

¹²The next day as they were leaving Bethany, Jesus was hungry. ¹³Seeing in the distance a fig tree in leaf, he went to find out if it had any fruit. When he reached it, he found nothing but leaves, because it was not the season for figs. ¹⁴Then he said to the tree, "May no one ever eat fruit from you again." And his disciples heard him say it.

¹⁵On reaching Jerusalem, Jesus entered the temple area and began driving out those who were buying and selling there. He overturned the tables of the money changers and the benches of those selling doves, ¹⁶and would not allow anyone to carry merchandise through the temple courts. ¹⁷And as he taught them, he said, "Is it not written:

" 'My house will be called
a house of prayer for all nations' *a*?

But you have made it 'a den of robbers.' *b*"

¹⁸The chief priests and the teachers of the law heard this and began looking for a way to kill him, for they feared him, because the whole crowd was amazed at his teaching.

¹⁹When evening came, they *c* went out of the city.

The Withered Fig Tree

²⁰In the morning, as they went along, they saw the fig tree withered from the roots. ²¹Peter remembered and said to Jesus, "Rabbi, look! The fig tree you cursed has withered!"

²²"Have *d* faith in God," Jesus answered. ²³"I tell you the truth, if anyone says to this mountain, 'Go, throw yourself into the sea,' and does not doubt in his heart but believes that what he says will happen, it will be done for him. ²⁴Therefore I tell you, whatever you ask for in prayer, believe that you have received it, and it will be yours. ²⁵And when you stand praying, if you hold anything against anyone, forgive him, so that your Father in heaven may forgive you your sins. *e*"

The Authority of Jesus Questioned

²⁷They arrived again in Jerusalem, and while Jesus was walking in the temple courts, the chief priests, the teachers of the law and the elders came to him. ²⁸"By what authority are you doing these things?" they asked. "And who gave you authority to do this?"

²⁹Jesus replied, "I will ask you one question.

a 17 Isaiah 56:7   *b 17* Jer. 7:11   *c 19* Some early manuscripts *he*   *d 22* Some early manuscripts *If you have*   *e 25* Some manuscripts *sins.* ²⁶*But if you do not forgive, neither will your Father who is in heaven forgive your sins.*

THE MESSAGE

The Cursed Fig Tree

11.12-14 As they left Bethany the next day, he was hungry. Off in the distance he saw a fig tree in full leaf. He came up to it expecting to find something for breakfast, but found nothing but fig leaves. (It wasn't yet the season for figs.) He addressed the tree: "No one is going to eat fruit from you again—ever!" And his disciples overheard him.

11.15-17 They arrived at Jerusalem. Immediately on entering the Temple Jesus started throwing out everyone who had set up shop there, buying and selling. He kicked over the tables of the bankers and the stalls of the pigeon merchants. He didn't let anyone even carry a basket through the Temple. And then he taught them, quoting this text:

My house was designated a house of prayer
for the nations;
You've turned it into a hangout for thieves.

11.18 The high priests and religion scholars heard what was going on and plotted how they might get rid of him. They panicked, for the entire crowd was carried away by his teaching.

11.19 At evening, Jesus and his disciples left the city.

11.20-21 In the morning, walking along the road, they saw the fig tree, shriveled to a dry stick. Peter, remembering what had happened the previous day, said to him, "Rabbi, look—the fig tree you cursed is shriveled up!"

11.22-25 Jesus was matter-of-fact: "Embrace this God-life. Really embrace it, and nothing will be too much for you. This mountain, for instance: Just say, 'Go jump in the lake'—no shuffling or shilly-shallying—and it's as good as done. That's why I urge you to pray for absolutely everything, ranging from small to large. Include everything as you embrace this God-life, and you'll get God's everything. And when you assume the posture of prayer, remember that it's not all *asking*. If you have anything against someone, *forgive*—only then will your heavenly Father be inclined to also wipe your slate clean of sins."

His Credentials

11.27-28 Then when they were back in Jerusalem once again, as they were walking through the Temple, the high priests, religion scholars, and leaders came up and demanded, "Show us your credentials. Who authorized you to speak and act like this?"

11.29-30 Jesus responded, "First let me ask you a

NEW INTERNATIONAL VERSION

Answer me, and I will tell you by what authority I am doing these things. ³⁰John's baptism—was it from heaven, or from men? Tell me!"

³¹They discussed it among themselves and said, "If we say, 'From heaven,' he will ask, 'Then why didn't you believe him?' ³²But if we say, 'From men' . . ." (They feared the people, for everyone held that John really was a prophet.)

³³So they answered Jesus, "We don't know."

Jesus said, "Neither will I tell you by what authority I am doing these things."

THE PARABLE OF THE TENANTS

12 He then began to speak to them in parables: "A man planted a vineyard. He put a wall around it, dug a pit for the winepress and built a watchtower. Then he rented the vineyard to some farmers and went away on a journey. ²At harvest time he sent a servant to the tenants to collect from them some of the fruit of the vineyard. ³But they seized him, beat him and sent him away empty-handed. ⁴Then he sent another servant to them; they struck this man on the head and treated him shamefully. ⁵He sent still another, and that one they killed. He sent many others; some of them they beat, others they killed.

⁶"He had one left to send, a son, whom he loved. He sent him last of all, saying, 'They will respect my son.'

⁷"But the tenants said to one another, 'This is the heir. Come, let's kill him, and the inheritance will be ours.' ⁸So they took him and killed him, and threw him out of the vineyard.

⁹"What then will the owner of the vineyard do? He will come and kill those tenants and give the vineyard to others. ¹⁰Haven't you read this scripture:

" 'The stone the builders rejected
    has become the capstone ᵃ;
¹¹ the Lord has done this,
    and it is marvelous in our eyes' ᵇ?"

¹²Then they looked for a way to arrest him because they knew he had spoken the parable against them. But they were afraid of the crowd; so they left him and went away.

PAYING TAXES TO CAESAR

¹³Later they sent some of the Pharisees and Herodians to Jesus to catch him in his words.

ᵃ *10* Or *cornerstone*   ᵇ *11* Psalm 118:22,23

THE MESSAGE

question. Answer my question and then I'll present my credentials. About the baptism of John—who authorized it: heaven or humans? Tell me."

11.31-33   They were on the spot, and knew it. They pulled back into a huddle and whispered, "If we say 'heaven,' he'll ask us why we didn't believe John; if we say 'humans,' we'll be up against it with the people because they all hold John up as a prophet." They decided to concede that round to Jesus. "We don't know," they said.

Jesus replied, "Then I won't answer your question either."

THE STORY ABOUT A VINEYARD

12.1-2   **12** Then Jesus started telling them stories. "A man planted a vineyard. He fenced it, dug a winepress, erected a watchtower, turned it over to the farmhands, and went off on a trip. At the time for harvest, he sent a servant back to the farmhands to collect his profits.

12.3-5   "They grabbed him, beat him up, and sent him off empty-handed. So he sent another servant. That one they tarred and feathered. He sent another and that one they killed. And on and on, many others. Some they beat up, some they killed.

12.6   "Finally there was only one left: a beloved son. In a last-ditch effort, he sent him, thinking, 'Surely they will respect my son.'

12.7-8   "But those farmhands saw their chance. They rubbed their hands together in greed and said, 'This is the heir! Let's kill him and have it all for ourselves.' They grabbed him, killed him, and threw him over the fence.

12.9-11   "What do you think the owner of the vineyard will do? Right. He'll come and clean house. Then he'll assign the care of the vineyard to others. Read it for yourselves in Scripture:

That stone the masons threw out
    is now the cornerstone!
This is God's work;
    we rub our eyes—we can hardly believe
        it!"

12.12   They wanted to lynch him then and there but, intimidated by public opinion, held back. They knew the story was about them. They got away from there as fast as they could.

PAYING TAXES TO CAESAR

12.13-14   They sent some Pharisees and followers of Herod to bait him, hoping to catch him saying something incriminating. They came up and

NEW INTERNATIONAL VERSION

[14] They came to him and said, "Teacher, we know you are a man of integrity. You aren't swayed by men, because you pay no attention to who they are; but you teach the way of God in accordance with the truth. Is it right to pay taxes to Caesar or not? [15] Should we pay or shouldn't we?"

But Jesus knew their hypocrisy. "Why are you trying to trap me?" he asked. "Bring me a denarius and let me look at it." [16] They brought the coin, and he asked them, "Whose portrait is this? And whose inscription?"

"Caesar's," they replied.

[17] Then Jesus said to them, "Give to Caesar what is Caesar's and to God what is God's."

And they were amazed at him.

Marriage at the Resurrection

[18] Then the Sadducees, who say there is no resurrection, came to him with a question. [19] "Teacher," they said, "Moses wrote for us that if a man's brother dies and leaves a wife but no children, the man must marry the widow and have children for his brother. [20] Now there were seven brothers. The first one married and died without leaving any children. [21] The second one married the widow, but he also died, leaving no child. It was the same with the third. [22] In fact, none of the seven left any children. Last of all, the woman died too. [23] At the resurrection[a] whose wife will she be, since the seven were married to her?"

[24] Jesus replied, "Are you not in error because you do not know the Scriptures or the power of God? [25] When the dead rise, they will neither marry nor be given in marriage; they will be like the angels in heaven. [26] Now about the dead rising—have you not read in the book of Moses, in the account of the bush, how God said to him, 'I am the God of Abraham, the God of Isaac, and the God of Jacob'[b]? [27] He is not the God of the dead, but of the living. You are badly mistaken!"

The Greatest Commandment

[28] One of the teachers of the law came and heard them debating. Noticing that Jesus had given them a good answer, he asked him, "Of all the commandments, which is the most important?"

[29] "The most important one," answered Jesus, "is this: 'Hear, O Israel, the Lord our God, the Lord is one.[c] [30] Love the Lord your God with all your heart and with all your soul and with all your mind and with all your strength.'[d] [31] The second is this: 'Love your neighbor as yourself.'[e] There is no commandment greater than these."

THE MESSAGE

said, "Teacher, we know you have integrity, that you are indifferent to public opinion, don't pander to your students, and teach the way of God accurately. Tell us: Is it lawful to pay taxes to Caesar or not?"

12.15-16 He knew it was a trick question, and said, "Why are you playing these games with me? Bring me a coin and let me look at it." They handed him one.

"This engraving—who does it look like? And whose name is on it?"

"Caesar," they said.

12.17 Jesus said, "Give Caesar what is his, and give God what is his."

Their mouths hung open, speechless.

Our Intimacies Will Be with God

12.18-23 Some Sadducees, the party that denies any possibility of resurrection, came up and asked, "Teacher, Moses wrote that if a man dies and leaves a wife but no child, his brother is obligated to marry the widow and have children. Well, there once were seven brothers. The first took a wife. He died childless. The second married her. He died, and still no child. The same with the third. All seven took their turn, but no child. Finally the wife died. When they are raised at the resurrection, whose wife is she? All seven were her husband."

12.24-27 Jesus said, "You're way off base, and here's why: One, you don't know your Bibles; two, you don't know how God works. After the dead are raised up, we're past the marriage business. As it is with angels now, all our ecstasies and intimacies then will be with God. And regarding the dead, whether or not they are raised, don't you ever read the Bible? How God at the bush said to Moses, 'I am—not *was*—the God of Abraham, the God of Isaac, and the God of Jacob'? The living God is God of the *living*, not the dead. You're way, way off base."

The Most Important Commandment

12.28 One of the religion scholars came up. Hearing the lively exchanges of question and answer and seeing how sharp Jesus was in his answers, he put in his question: "Which is most important of all the commandments?"

12.29-31 Jesus said, "The first in importance is, 'Listen, Israel: The Lord your God is one; so love the Lord God with all your passion and prayer and intelligence and energy.' And here is the second: 'Love others as well as you love yourself.' There is no other commandment that ranks with these."

---

[a] 23 Some manuscripts *resurrection, when men rise from the dead,* [b] 26 Exodus 3:6 [c] 29 Or *the Lord our God is one Lord* [d] 30 Deut. 6:4,5 [e] 31 Lev. 19:18

NEW INTERNATIONAL VERSION

³²"Well said, teacher," the man replied. "You are right in saying that God is one and there is no other but him. ³³To love him with all your heart, with all your understanding and with all your strength, and to love your neighbor as yourself is more important than all burnt offerings and sacrifices."

³⁴When Jesus saw that he had answered wisely, he said to him, "You are not far from the kingdom of God." And from then on no one dared ask him any more questions.

Whose Son Is the Christ?

³⁵While Jesus was teaching in the temple courts, he asked, "How is it that the teachers of the law say that the Christ[a] is the son of David? ³⁶David himself, speaking by the Holy Spirit, declared:

" 'The Lord said to my Lord:
  "Sit at my right hand
  until I put your enemies
    under your feet." '[b]

³⁷David himself calls him 'Lord.' How then can he be his son?"

The large crowd listened to him with delight.

³⁸As he taught, Jesus said, "Watch out for the teachers of the law. They like to walk around in flowing robes and be greeted in the marketplaces, ³⁹and have the most important seats in the synagogues and the places of honor at banquets. ⁴⁰They devour widows' houses and for a show make lengthy prayers. Such men will be punished most severely."

The Widow's Offering

⁴¹Jesus sat down opposite the place where the offerings were put and watched the crowd putting their money into the temple treasury. Many rich people threw in large amounts. ⁴²But a poor widow came and put in two very small copper coins,[c] worth only a fraction of a penny.[d]

⁴³Calling his disciples to him, Jesus said, "I tell you the truth, this poor widow has put more into the treasury than all the others. ⁴⁴They all gave out of their wealth; but she, out of her poverty, put in everything—all she had to live on."

Signs of the End of the Age

13 As he was leaving the temple, one of his disciples said to him, "Look, Teacher! What massive stones! What magnificent buildings!"

²"Do you see all these great buildings?" replied Jesus. "Not one stone here will be left on another; every one will be thrown down."

---

a 35 Or *Messiah*   b 36 Psalm 110:1   c 42 Greek *two lepta*   d 42 Greek *kodrantes*

THE MESSAGE

12.32-33   The religion scholar said, "A wonderful answer, Teacher! So lucid and accurate—that God is one and there is no other. And loving him with all passion and intelligence and energy, and loving others as well as you love yourself. Why, that's better than all offerings and sacrifices put together!"

12.34   When Jesus realized how insightful he was, he said, "You're almost there, right on the border of God's kingdom."

After that, no one else dared ask a question.

✠

12.35-37   While he was teaching in the Temple, Jesus asked, "How is it that the religion scholars say that the Messiah is David's 'son,' when we all know that David, inspired by the Holy Spirit, said,

God said to my Master,
  "Sit here at my right hand
  until I put your enemies under your
    feet."

"David here designates the Messiah 'my Master'—so how can the Messiah also be his 'son'?"

The large crowd was delighted with what they heard.

12.38-40   He continued teaching. "Watch out for the religion scholars. They love to walk around in academic gowns, preening in the radiance of public flattery, basking in prominent positions, sitting at the head table at every church function. And all the time they are exploiting the weak and helpless. The longer their prayers, the worse they get. But they'll pay for it in the end."

12.41-44   Sitting across from the offering box, he was observing how the crowd tossed money in for the collection. Many of the rich were making large contributions. One poor widow came up and put in two small coins—a measly two cents. Jesus called his disciples over and said, "The truth is that this poor widow gave more to the collection than all the others put together. All the others gave what they'll never miss; she gave extravagantly what she couldn't afford—she gave her all."

Doomsday Deceivers

13.1   **13** As he walked away from the Temple, one of his disciples said, "Teacher, look at that stonework! Those buildings!"

13.2   Jesus said, "You're impressed by this grandiose architecture? There's not a stone in the whole works that is not going to end up in a heap of rubble."

NEW INTERNATIONAL VERSION

³As Jesus was sitting on the Mount of Olives opposite the temple, Peter, James, John and Andrew asked him privately, ⁴"Tell us, when will these things happen? And what will be the sign that they are all about to be fulfilled?"

⁵Jesus said to them: "Watch out that no one deceives you. ⁶Many will come in my name, claiming, 'I am he,' and will deceive many. ⁷When you hear of wars and rumors of wars, do not be alarmed. Such things must happen, but the end is still to come. ⁸Nation will rise against nation, and kingdom against kingdom. There will be earthquakes in various places, and famines. These are the beginning of birth pains.

⁹"You must be on your guard. You will be handed over to the local councils and flogged in the synagogues. On account of me you will stand before governors and kings as witnesses to them. ¹⁰And the gospel must first be preached to all nations. ¹¹Whenever you are arrested and brought to trial, do not worry beforehand about what to say. Just say whatever is given you at the time, for it is not you speaking, but the Holy Spirit.

¹²"Brother will betray brother to death, and a father his child. Children will rebel against their parents and have them put to death. ¹³All men will hate you because of me, but he who stands firm to the end will be saved.

¹⁴"When you see 'the abomination that causes desolation'ᵃ standing where itᵇ does not belong—let the reader understand—then let those who are in Judea flee to the mountains. ¹⁵Let no one on the roof of his house go down or enter the house to take anything out. ¹⁶Let no one in the field go back to get his cloak. ¹⁷How dreadful it will be in those days for pregnant women and nursing mothers! ¹⁸Pray that this will not take place in winter, ¹⁹because those will be days of distress unequaled from the beginning, when God created the world, until now—and never to be equaled again. ²⁰If the Lord had not cut short those days, no one would survive. But for the sake of the elect, whom he has chosen, he has shortened them. ²¹At that time if anyone says to you, 'Look, here is the Christᶜ!' or, 'Look, there

THE MESSAGE

13.3-4   Later, as he was sitting on Mount Olives in full view of the Temple, Peter, James, John, and Andrew got him off by himself and asked, "Tell us, when is this going to happen? What sign will we get that things are coming to a head?"

13.5-8   Jesus began, "Watch out for doomsday deceivers. Many leaders are going to show up with forged identities claiming, 'I'm the One.' They will deceive a lot of people. When you hear of wars and rumored wars, keep your head and don't panic. This is routine history, and no sign of the end. Nation will fight nation and ruler fight ruler, over and over. Earthquakes will occur in various places. There will be famines. But these things are nothing compared to what's coming.

13.9-10   "And watch out! They're going to drag you into court. And then it will go from bad to worse, dog-eat-dog, everyone at your throat because you carry my name. You're placed there as sentinels to truth. The Message has to be preached all across the world.

13.11   "When they bring you, betrayed, into court, don't worry about what you'll say. When the time comes, say what's on your heart—the Holy Spirit will make his witness in and through you.

13.12-13   "It's going to be brother killing brother, father killing child, children killing parents. There's no telling who will hate you because of me.

"Stay with it—that's what is required. Stay with it to the end. You won't be sorry; you'll be saved.

RUN FOR THE HILLS

13.14-18   "But be ready to run for it when you see the monster of desecration set up where it should *never* be. You who can read, make sure you understand what I'm talking about. If you're living in Judea at the time, run for the hills; if you're working in the yard, don't go back to the house to get anything; if you're out in the field, don't go back to get your coat. Pregnant and nursing mothers will have it especially hard. Hope and pray this won't happen in the middle of winter.

13.19-20   "These are going to be hard days—nothing like it from the time God made the world right up to the present. And there'll be nothing like it again. If he let the days of trouble run their course, nobody would make it. But because of God's chosen people, those he personally chose, he has already intervened.

NO ONE KNOWS THE DAY OR HOUR

13.21-23   "If anyone tries to flag you down, calling out, 'Here's the Messiah!' or points, 'There he is!'

ᵃ 14 Daniel 9:27; 11:31; 12:11   ᵇ 14 Or *he*; also in verse 29   ᶜ 21 Or *Messiah*

NEW INTERNATIONAL VERSION

he is!' do not believe it. ²²For false Christs and false prophets will appear and perform signs and miracles to deceive the elect—if that were possible. ²³So be on your guard; I have told you everything ahead of time.

²⁴"But in those days, following that distress,

" 'the sun will be darkened,
  and the moon will not give its light;
²⁵the stars will fall from the sky,
  and the heavenly bodies will be shaken.'ᵃ

²⁶"At that time men will see the Son of Man coming in clouds with great power and glory. ²⁷And he will send his angels and gather his elect from the four winds, from the ends of the earth to the ends of the heavens.

²⁸"Now learn this lesson from the fig tree: As soon as its twigs get tender and its leaves come out, you know that summer is near. ²⁹Even so, when you see these things happening, you know that it is near, right at the door. ³⁰I tell you the truth, this generationᵇ will certainly not pass away until all these things have happened. ³¹Heaven and earth will pass away, but my words will never pass away.

THE DAY AND HOUR UNKNOWN

³²"No one knows about that day or hour, not even the angels in heaven, nor the Son, but only the Father. ³³Be on guard! Be alertᶜ! You do not know when that time will come. ³⁴It's like a man going away: He leaves his house and puts his servants in charge, each with his assigned task, and tells the one at the door to keep watch.

³⁵"Therefore keep watch because you do not know when the owner of the house will come back—whether in the evening, or at midnight, or when the rooster crows, or at dawn. ³⁶If he comes suddenly, do not let him find you sleeping. ³⁷What I say to you, I say to everyone: 'Watch!' "

JESUS ANOINTED AT BETHANY

14 Now the Passover and the Feast of Unleavened Bread were only two days away, and the chief priests and the teachers of the law were looking for some sly way to arrest Jesus and kill him. ²"But not during the Feast," they said, "or the people may riot."

³While he was in Bethany, reclining at the table in the home of a man known as Simon the Leper, a woman came with an alabaster jar of very expensive perfume, made of pure nard. She broke the jar and poured the perfume on his head.

THE MESSAGE

don't fall for it. Fake Messiahs and lying preachers are going to pop up everywhere. Their impressive credentials and dazzling performances will pull the wool over the eyes of even those who ought to know better. So watch out. I've given you fair warning.

13.24-25   "Following those hard times,

Sun will fade out,
  moon cloud over,
Stars fall out of the sky,
  cosmic powers tremble.

13.26-27   "And then they'll see the Son of Man enter in grand style, his Arrival filling the sky—no one will miss it! He'll dispatch the angels; they will pull in the chosen from the four winds, from pole to pole.

13.28-31   "Take a lesson from the fig tree. From the moment you notice its buds form, the merest hint of green, you know summer's just around the corner. And so it is with you. When you see all these things, you know he is at the door. Don't take this lightly. I'm not just saying this for some future generation, but for this one, too—these things will happen. Sky and earth will wear out; my words won't wear out.

13.32-37   "But the exact day and hour? No one knows that, not even heaven's angels, not even the Son. Only the Father. So keep a sharp lookout, for you don't know the timetable. It's like a man who takes a trip, leaving home and putting his servants in charge, each assigned a task, and commanding the gatekeeper to stand watch. So, stay at your post, watching. You have no idea when the homeowner is returning, whether evening, midnight, cockcrow, or morning. You don't want him showing up unannounced, with you asleep on the job. I say it to you, and I'm saying it to all: Stay at your post. Keep watch."

ANOINTING HIS HEAD

14.1-2   **14** In only two days the eight-day Festival of Passover and the Feast of Unleavened Bread would begin. The high priests and religion scholars were looking for a way they could seize Jesus by stealth and kill him. They agreed that it should not be done during Passover Week. "We don't want the crowds up in arms," they said.

14.3-5   Jesus was at Bethany, a guest of Simon the Leper. While he was eating dinner, a woman came up carrying a bottle of very expensive perfume. Opening the bottle, she poured it on

---

ᵃ 25 Isaiah 13:10; 34:4   ᵇ 30 Or race   ᶜ 33 Some manuscripts alert and pray

NEW INTERNATIONAL VERSION

⁴Some of those present were saying indignantly to one another, "Why this waste of perfume? ⁵It could have been sold for more than a year's wages*a* and the money given to the poor." And they rebuked her harshly.

⁶"Leave her alone," said Jesus. "Why are you bothering her? She has done a beautiful thing to me. ⁷The poor you will always have with you, and you can help them any time you want. But you will not always have me. ⁸She did what she could. She poured perfume on my body beforehand to prepare for my burial. ⁹I tell you the truth, wherever the gospel is preached throughout the world, what she has done will also be told, in memory of her."

¹⁰Then Judas Iscariot, one of the Twelve, went to the chief priests to betray Jesus to them. ¹¹They were delighted to hear this and promised to give him money. So he watched for an opportunity to hand him over.

THE LORD'S SUPPER

¹²On the first day of the Feast of Unleavened Bread, when it was customary to sacrifice the Passover lamb, Jesus' disciples asked him, "Where do you want us to go and make preparations for you to eat the Passover?"

¹³So he sent two of his disciples, telling them, "Go into the city, and a man carrying a jar of water will meet you. Follow him. ¹⁴Say to the owner of the house he enters, 'The Teacher asks: Where is my guest room, where I may eat the Passover with my disciples?' ¹⁵He will show you a large upper room, furnished and ready. Make preparations for us there."

¹⁶The disciples left, went into the city and found things just as Jesus had told them. So they prepared the Passover.

¹⁷When evening came, Jesus arrived with the Twelve. ¹⁸While they were reclining at the table eating, he said, "I tell you the truth, one of you will betray me—one who is eating with me."

¹⁹They were saddened, and one by one they said to him, "Surely not I?"

²⁰"It is one of the Twelve," he replied, "one who dips bread into the bowl with me. ²¹The Son of Man will go just as it is written about him. But woe to that man who betrays the Son of Man! It would be better for him if he had not been born."

---

a 5 Greek than three hundred denarii

THE MESSAGE

his head. Some of the guests became furious among themselves. "That's criminal! A sheer waste! This perfume could have been sold for well over a year's wages*a* and handed out to the poor." They swelled up in anger, nearly bursting with indignation over her.

14.6-9 But Jesus said, "Let her alone. Why are you giving her a hard time? She has just done something wonderfully significant for me. You will have the poor with you every day for the rest of your lives. Whenever you feel like it, you can do something for them. Not so with me. She did what she could when she could—she pre-anointed my body for burial. And you can be sure that wherever in the whole world the Message is preached, what she just did is going to be talked about admiringly."

14.10-11 Judas Iscariot, one of the Twelve, went to the cabal of high priests, determined to betray him. They couldn't believe their ears, and promised to pay him well. He started looking for just the right moment to hand him over.

TRAITOR TO THE SON OF MAN

14.12 On the first of the Days of Unleavened Bread, the day they prepare the Passover sacrifice, his disciples asked him, "Where do you want us to go and make preparations so you can eat the Passover meal?"

14.13-15 He directed two of his disciples, "Go into the city. A man carrying a water jug will meet you. Follow him. Ask the owner of whichever house he enters, 'The Teacher wants to know, Where is my guest room where I can eat the Passover meal with my disciples?' He will show you a spacious second-story room, swept and ready. Prepare for us there."

14.16 The disciples left, came to the city, found everything just as he had told them, and prepared the Passover meal.

14.17-18 After sunset he came with the Twelve. As they were at the supper table eating, Jesus said, "I have something hard but important to say to you: One of you is going to hand me over to the conspirators, one who at this moment is eating with me."

14.19 Stunned, they started asking, one after another, "It isn't me, is it?"

14.20-21 He said, "It's one of the Twelve, one who eats with me out of the same bowl. In one sense, it turns out that the Son of Man is entering into a way of treachery well-marked by the Scriptures—no surprises here. In another sense, the man who turns him in, turns traitor to the Son of Man—better never to have been born than do this!"

NEW INTERNATIONAL VERSION

²²While they were eating, Jesus took bread, gave thanks and broke it, and gave it to his disciples, saying, "Take it; this is my body."

²³Then he took the cup, gave thanks and offered it to them, and they all drank from it.

²⁴"This is my blood of the*ᵃ* covenant, which is poured out for many," he said to them. ²⁵"I tell you the truth, I will not drink again of the fruit of the vine until that day when I drink it anew in the kingdom of God."

²⁶When they had sung a hymn, they went out to the Mount of Olives.

JESUS PREDICTS PETER'S DENIAL

²⁷"You will all fall away," Jesus told them, "for it is written:

" 'I will strike the shepherd,
   and the sheep will be scattered.'*ᵇ*

²⁸But after I have risen, I will go ahead of you into Galilee."

²⁹Peter declared, "Even if all fall away, I will not."

³⁰"I tell you the truth," Jesus answered, "today—yes, tonight—before the rooster crows twice*ᶜ* you yourself will disown me three times."

³¹But Peter insisted emphatically, "Even if I have to die with you, I will never disown you." And all the others said the same.

GETHSEMANE

³²They went to a place called Gethsemane, and Jesus said to his disciples, "Sit here while I pray." ³³He took Peter, James and John along with him, and he began to be deeply distressed and troubled. ³⁴"My soul is overwhelmed with sorrow to the point of death," he said to them. "Stay here and keep watch."

³⁵Going a little farther, he fell to the ground and prayed that if possible the hour might pass from him. ³⁶"Abba,*ᵈ* Father," he said, "everything is possible for you. Take this cup from me. Yet not what I will, but what you will."

³⁷Then he returned to his disciples and found them sleeping. "Simon," he said to Peter, "are you asleep? Could you not keep watch for one hour? ³⁸Watch and pray so that you will not fall into temptation. The spirit is willing, but the body is weak."

³⁹Once more he went away and prayed the

THE MESSAGE

"THIS IS MY BODY"

14.22 In the course of their meal, having taken and blessed the bread, he broke it and gave it to them. Then he said,

Take, this is my body.

14.23-24 Taking the chalice, he gave it to them, thanking God, and they all drank from it. He said,

This is my blood,
God's new covenant,
Poured out for many people.

14.25 "I'll not be drinking wine again until the new day when I drink it in the kingdom of God."

14.26 They sang a hymn and then went directly to Mount Olives.

✠

14.27-28 Jesus told them, "You're all going to feel that your world is falling apart and that it's my fault. There's a Scripture that says,

I will strike the shepherd;
The sheep will go helter-skelter.

"But after I am raised up, I will go ahead of you, leading the way to Galilee."

14.29 Peter blurted out, "Even if everyone else is ashamed of you when things fall to pieces, I won't be."

14.30 Jesus said, "Don't be so sure. Today, this very night in fact, before the rooster crows twice, you will deny me three times."

14.31 He blustered in protest, "Even if I have to die with you, I will never deny you." All the others said the same thing.

GETHSEMANE

14.32-34 They came to an area called Gethsemane. Jesus told his disciples, "Sit here while I pray." He took Peter, James, and John with him. He plunged into a sinkhole of dreadful agony. He told them, "I feel bad enough right now to die. Stay here and keep vigil with me."

14.35-36 Going a little ahead, he fell to the ground and prayed for a way out: "Papa, Father, you can—can't you?—get me out of this. Take this cup away from me. But please, not what I want—what do *you* want?"

14.37-38 He came back and found them sound asleep. He said to Peter, "Simon, you went to sleep on me? Can't you stick it out with me a single hour? Stay alert, be in prayer, so you don't enter the danger zone without even knowing it. Don't be naive. Part of you is eager, ready for anything in God; but another part is as lazy as an old dog sleeping by the fire."

14.39-40 He then went back and prayed the same

ᵃ 24 Some manuscripts *the new*   *ᵇ 27* Zech. 13:7
ᶜ 30 Some early manuscripts do not have *twice.*
ᵈ 36 Aramaic for *Father*

NEW INTERNATIONAL VERSION

same thing. ⁴⁰When he came back, he again found them sleeping, because their eyes were heavy. They did not know what to say to him.

⁴¹Returning the third time, he said to them, "Are you still sleeping and resting? Enough! The hour has come. Look, the Son of Man is betrayed into the hands of sinners. ⁴²Rise! Let us go! Here comes my betrayer!"

JESUS ARRESTED

⁴³Just as he was speaking, Judas, one of the Twelve, appeared. With him was a crowd armed with swords and clubs, sent from the chief priests, the teachers of the law, and the elders. ⁴⁴Now the betrayer had arranged a signal with them: "The one I kiss is the man; arrest him and lead him away under guard." ⁴⁵Going at once to Jesus, Judas said, "Rabbi!" and kissed him. ⁴⁶The men seized Jesus and arrested him. ⁴⁷Then one of those standing near drew his sword and struck the servant of the high priest, cutting off his ear.

⁴⁸"Am I leading a rebellion," said Jesus, "that you have come out with swords and clubs to capture me? ⁴⁹Every day I was with you, teaching in the temple courts, and you did not arrest me. But the Scriptures must be fulfilled." ⁵⁰Then everyone deserted him and fled.

⁵¹A young man, wearing nothing but a linen garment, was following Jesus. When they seized him, ⁵²he fled naked, leaving his garment behind.

BEFORE THE SANHEDRIN

⁵³They took Jesus to the high priest, and all the chief priests, elders and teachers of the law came together. ⁵⁴Peter followed him at a distance, right into the courtyard of the high priest. There he sat with the guards and warmed himself at the fire.

⁵⁵The chief priests and the whole Sanhedrin were looking for evidence against Jesus so that they could put him to death, but they did not find any. ⁵⁶Many testified falsely against him, but their statements did not agree.

⁵⁷Then some stood up and gave this false testimony against him: ⁵⁸"We heard him say, 'I will destroy this man-made temple and in three days will build another, not made by man.' " ⁵⁹Yet even then their testimony did not agree.

⁶⁰Then the high priest stood up before them and asked Jesus, "Are you not going to answer? What is this testimony that these men are bringing against you?" ⁶¹But Jesus remained silent and gave no answer.

THE MESSAGE

prayer. Returning, he again found them sound asleep. They simply couldn't keep their eyes open, and they didn't have a plausible excuse.

14.41-42 He came back a third time and said, "Are you going to sleep all night? No—you've slept long enough. Time's up. The Son of Man is about to be betrayed into the hands of sinners. Get up. Let's get going. My betrayer has arrived."

A GANG OF RUFFIANS

14.43-47 No sooner were the words out of his mouth when Judas, the one out of the Twelve, showed up, and with him a gang of ruffians, sent by the high priests, religion scholars, and leaders, brandishing swords and clubs. The betrayer had worked out a signal with them: "The one I kiss, that's the one—seize him. Make sure he doesn't get away." He went straight to Jesus and said, "Rabbi!" and kissed him. The others then grabbed him and roughed him up. One of the men standing there unsheathed his sword, swung, and came down on the Chief Priest's servant, lopping off the man's ear.

14.48-50 Jesus said to them, "What is this, coming after me with swords and clubs as if I were a dangerous criminal? Day after day I've been sitting in the Temple teaching, and you never so much as lifted a hand against me. What you in fact have done is confirm the prophetic writings." All the disciples cut and ran.

14.51-52 A young man was following along. All he had on was a bedsheet. Some of the men grabbed him but he got away, running off naked, leaving them holding the sheet.

CONDEMNED TO DEATH

14.53-54 They led Jesus to the Chief Priest, where the high priests, religious leaders, and scholars had gathered together. Peter followed at a safe distance until they got to the Chief Priest's courtyard, where he mingled with the servants and warmed himself at the fire.

14.55-59 The high priests conspiring with the Jewish Council looked high and low for evidence against Jesus by which they could sentence him to death. They found nothing. Plenty of people were willing to bring in false charges, but nothing added up, and they ended up canceling each other out. Then a few of them stood up and lied: "We heard him say, 'I am going to tear down this Temple, built by hard labor, and in three days build another without lifting a hand.' " But even they couldn't agree exactly.

14.60-61 In the middle of this, the Chief Priest stood up and asked Jesus, "What do you have to say to the accusation?" Jesus was silent. He said nothing.

NEW INTERNATIONAL VERSION

Again the high priest asked him, "Are you the Christ,ᵃ the Son of the Blessed One?"

⁶²"I am," said Jesus. "And you will see the Son of Man sitting at the right hand of the Mighty One and coming on the clouds of heaven."

⁶³The high priest tore his clothes. "Why do we need any more witnesses?" he asked. ⁶⁴"You have heard the blasphemy. What do you think?"

They all condemned him as worthy of death. ⁶⁵Then some began to spit at him; they blindfolded him, struck him with their fists, and said, "Prophesy!" And the guards took him and beat him.

PETER DISOWNS JESUS

⁶⁶While Peter was below in the courtyard, one of the servant girls of the high priest came by. ⁶⁷When she saw Peter warming himself, she looked closely at him.

"You also were with that Nazarene, Jesus," she said.

⁶⁸But he denied it. "I don't know or understand what you're talking about," he said, and went out into the entryway.ᵇ

⁶⁹When the servant girl saw him there, she said again to those standing around, "This fellow is one of them." ⁷⁰Again he denied it.

After a little while, those standing near said to Peter, "Surely you are one of them, for you are a Galilean."

⁷¹He began to call down curses on himself, and he swore to them, "I don't know this man you're talking about."

⁷²Immediately the rooster crowed the second time.ᶜ Then Peter remembered the word Jesus had spoken to him: "Before the rooster crows twiceᵈ you will disown me three times." And he broke down and wept.

JESUS BEFORE PILATE

15 Very early in the morning, the chief priests, with the elders, the teachers of the law and the whole Sanhedrin, reached a decision. They bound Jesus, led him away and handed him over to Pilate.

²"Are you the king of the Jews?" asked Pilate.

"Yes, it is as you say," Jesus replied.

³The chief priests accused him of many things. ⁴So again Pilate asked him, "Aren't you going to answer? See how many things they are accusing you of."

THE MESSAGE

The Chief Priest tried again, this time asking, "Are you the Messiah, the Son of the Blessed?"

14.62 Jesus said, "Yes, I am, and you'll see it yourself:

The Son of Man seated
At the right hand of the Mighty One,
Arriving on the clouds of heaven."

14.63-64 The Chief Priest lost his temper. Ripping his clothes, he yelled, "Did you hear that? After that do we need witnesses? You heard the blasphemy. Are you going to stand for it?"

They condemned him, one and all. The sentence: death.

14.65 Some of them started spitting at him. They blindfolded his eyes, then hit him, saying, "Who hit you? Prophesy!" The guards, punching and slapping, took him away.

THE ROOSTER CROWED

14.66-67 While all this was going on, Peter was down in the courtyard. One of the Chief Priest's servant girls came in and, seeing Peter warming himself there, looked hard at him and said, "You were with the Nazarene, Jesus."

14.68 He denied it: "I don't know what you're talking about." He went out on the porch. A rooster crowed.

14.69-70 The girl spotted him and began telling the people standing around, "He's one of them." He denied it again.

After a little while, the bystanders brought it up again. "You've *got* to be one of them. You've got 'Galilean' written all over you."

14.71-72 Now Peter got really nervous and swore, "I never laid eyes on this man you're talking about." Just then the rooster crowed a second time. Peter remembered how Jesus had said, "Before a rooster crows twice, you'll deny me three times." He collapsed in tears.

STANDING BEFORE PILATE

15.1 **15** At dawn's first light, the high priests, with the religious leaders and scholars, arranged a conference with the entire Jewish Council. After tying Jesus securely, they took him out and presented him to Pilate.

15.2-3 Pilate asked him, "Are you the 'King of the Jews'?"

He answered, "If you say so." The high priests let loose a barrage of accusations.

15.4-5 Pilate asked again, "Aren't you going to answer anything? That's quite a list of accusations."

ᵃ 61 Or *Messiah*   ᵇ 68 Some early manuscripts *entryway and the rooster crowed*   ᶜ 72 Some early manuscripts do not have *the second time*.   ᵈ 72 Some early manuscripts do not have *twice*.

NEW INTERNATIONAL VERSION

⁵But Jesus still made no reply, and Pilate was amazed.

⁶Now it was the custom at the Feast to release a prisoner whom the people requested. ⁷A man called Barabbas was in prison with the insurrectionists who had committed murder in the uprising. ⁸The crowd came up and asked Pilate to do for them what he usually did.

⁹"Do you want me to release to you the king of the Jews?" asked Pilate, ¹⁰knowing it was out of envy that the chief priests had handed Jesus over to him. ¹¹But the chief priests stirred up the crowd to have Pilate release Barabbas instead.

¹²"What shall I do, then, with the one you call the king of the Jews?" Pilate asked them.

¹³"Crucify him!" they shouted.

¹⁴"Why? What crime has he committed?" asked Pilate.

But they shouted all the louder, "Crucify him!"

¹⁵Wanting to satisfy the crowd, Pilate released Barabbas to them. He had Jesus flogged, and handed him over to be crucified.

THE SOLDIERS MOCK JESUS

¹⁶The soldiers led Jesus away into the palace (that is, the Praetorium) and called together the whole company of soldiers. ¹⁷They put a purple robe on him, then twisted together a crown of thorns and set it on him. ¹⁸And they began to call out to him, "Hail, king of the Jews!" ¹⁹Again and again they struck him on the head with a staff and spit on him. Falling on their knees, they paid homage to him. ²⁰And when they had mocked him, they took off the purple robe and put his own clothes on him. Then they led him out to crucify him.

THE CRUCIFIXION

²¹A certain man from Cyrene, Simon, the father of Alexander and Rufus, was passing by on his way in from the country, and they forced him to carry the cross. ²²They brought Jesus to the place called Golgotha (which means The Place of the Skull). ²³Then they offered him wine mixed with myrrh, but he did not take it. ²⁴And they crucified him. Dividing up his clothes, they cast lots to see what each would get.

²⁵It was the third hour when they crucified him. ²⁶The written notice of the charge against him read: THE KING OF THE JEWS. ²⁷They crucified two robbers with him, one on his right and one on his left.[a] ²⁹Those who passed by hurled insults at him, shaking their heads and saying, "So! You who are going to destroy the temple

---

a 27 Some manuscripts *left,* ²⁸*and the scripture was fulfilled which says, "He was counted with the lawless ones"* (Isaiah 53:12)

THE MESSAGE

Still, he said nothing. Pilate was impressed, really impressed.

15.6-10 It was a custom at the Feast to release a prisoner, anyone the people asked for. There was one prisoner called Barabbas, locked up with the insurrectionists who had committed murder during the uprising against Rome. As the crowd came up and began to present its petition for him to release a prisoner, Pilate anticipated them: "Do you want me to release the King of the Jews to you?" Pilate knew by this time that it was through sheer spite that the high priests had turned Jesus over to him.

15.11-12 But the high priests by then had worked up the crowd to ask for the release of Barabbas. Pilate came back, "So what do I do with this man you call King of the Jews?"

15.13 They yelled, "Nail him to a cross!"

15.14 Pilate objected, "But for what crime?"

But they yelled all the louder, "Nail him to a cross!"

15.15 Pilate gave the crowd what it wanted, set Barabbas free and turned Jesus over for whipping and crucifixion.

15.16-20 The soldiers took Jesus into the palace (called Praetorium) and called together the entire brigade. They dressed him up in purple and put a crown plaited from a thorn bush on his head. Then they began their mockery: "Bravo, King of the Jews!" They banged on his head with a club, spit on him, and knelt down in mock worship. After they had had their fun, they took off the purple cape and put his own clothes back on him. Then they marched out to nail him to the cross.

THE CRUCIFIXION

15.21 There was a man walking by, coming from work, Simon from Cyrene, the father of Alexander and Rufus. They made him carry Jesus' cross.

15.22-24 The soldiers brought Jesus to Golgotha, meaning "Skull Hill." They offered him a mild painkiller (wine mixed with myrrh), but he wouldn't take it. And they nailed him to the cross. They divided up his clothes and threw dice to see who would get them.

15.25-30 They nailed him up at nine o'clock in the morning. The charge against him—THE KING OF THE JEWS—was printed on a poster. Along with him, they crucified two criminals, one to his right, the other to his left. People passing along the road jeered, shaking their heads in mock lament: "You bragged that you could tear down

NEW INTERNATIONAL VERSION

and build it in three days, ³⁰come down from the cross and save yourself!"

³¹In the same way the chief priests and the teachers of the law mocked him among themselves. "He saved others," they said, "but he can't save himself! ³²Let this Christ,^a this King of Israel, come down now from the cross, that we may see and believe." Those crucified with him also heaped insults on him.

The Death of Jesus

³³At the sixth hour darkness came over the whole land until the ninth hour. ³⁴And at the ninth hour Jesus cried out in a loud voice, *"Eloi, Eloi, lama sabachthani?"*—which means, "My God, my God, why have you forsaken me?"^b

³⁵When some of those standing near heard this, they said, "Listen, he's calling Elijah."

³⁶One man ran, filled a sponge with wine vinegar, put it on a stick, and offered it to Jesus to drink. "Now leave him alone. Let's see if Elijah comes to take him down," he said.

³⁷With a loud cry, Jesus breathed his last.

³⁸The curtain of the temple was torn in two from top to bottom. ³⁹And when the centurion, who stood there in front of Jesus, heard his cry and^c saw how he died, he said, "Surely this man was the Son^d of God!"

⁴⁰Some women were watching from a distance. Among them were Mary Magdalene, Mary the mother of James the younger and of Joses, and Salome. ⁴¹In Galilee these women had followed him and cared for his needs. Many other women who had come up with him to Jerusalem were also there.

The Burial of Jesus

⁴²It was Preparation Day (that is, the day before the Sabbath). So as evening approached, ⁴³Joseph of Arimathea, a prominent member of the Council, who was himself waiting for the kingdom of God, went boldly to Pilate and asked for Jesus' body. ⁴⁴Pilate was surprised to hear that he was already dead. Summoning the centurion, he asked him if Jesus had already died. ⁴⁵When he learned from the centurion that it was so, he gave the body to Joseph. ⁴⁶So Joseph bought some linen cloth, took down the body, wrapped it in the linen, and placed it in a tomb cut out of rock. Then he rolled a stone against the entrance of the tomb. ⁴⁷Mary Magdalene and Mary the mother of Joses saw where he was laid.

The Resurrection

16 When the Sabbath was over, Mary Magdalene, Mary the mother of James, and

THE MESSAGE

the Temple and then rebuild it in three days— so show us your stuff! Save yourself! If you're really God's Son, come down from that cross!"

15.31-32 The high priests, along with the religion scholars, were right there mixing it up with the rest of them, having a great time poking fun at him: "He saved others—but he can't save himself! Messiah, is he? King of Israel? Then let him climb down from that cross. We'll *all* become believers then!" Even the men crucified alongside him joined in the mockery.

15.33-34 At noon the sky became extremely dark. The darkness lasted three hours. At three o'clock, Jesus groaned out of the depths, crying loudly, *"Eloi, Eloi, lama sabachthani?"* which means, "My God, my God, why have you abandoned me?"

15.35-36 Some of the bystanders who heard him said, "Listen, he's calling for Elijah." Someone ran off, soaked a sponge in sour wine, put it on a stick, and gave it to him to drink, saying, "Let's see if Elijah comes to take him down."

15.37-39 But Jesus, with a loud cry, gave his last breath. At that moment the Temple curtain ripped right down the middle. When the Roman captain standing guard in front of him saw that he had quit breathing, he said, "This has to be the Son of God!"

Taken to a Tomb

15.40-41 There were women watching from a distance, among them Mary Magdalene, Mary the mother of the younger James and Joses, and Salome. When Jesus was in Galilee, these women followed and served him, and had come up with him to Jerusalem.

15.42-45 Late in the afternoon, since it was the Day of Preparation (that is, Sabbath eve), Joseph of Arimathea, a highly respected member of the Jewish Council, came. He was one who lived expectantly, on the lookout for the kingdom of God. Working up his courage, he went to Pilate and asked for Jesus' body. Pilate questioned whether he could be dead that soon and called for the captain to verify that he was really dead. Assured by the captain, he gave Joseph the corpse.

15.46-47 Having already purchased a linen shroud, Joseph took him down, wrapped him in the shroud, placed him in a tomb that had been cut into the rock, and rolled a large stone across the opening. Mary Magdalene and Mary, mother of Joses, watched the burial.

The Resurrection

16.1-3 **16** When the Sabbath was over, Mary Magdalene, Mary the mother of James, and

---

^a 32 Or *Messiah*   ^b 34 Psalm 22:1   ^c 39 Some manuscripts do not have *heard his cry and*   ^d 39 Or *a son*

NEW INTERNATIONAL VERSION

Salome bought spices so that they might go to anoint Jesus' body. ²Very early on the first day of the week, just after sunrise, they were on their way to the tomb ³and they asked each other, "Who will roll the stone away from the entrance of the tomb?"

⁴But when they looked up, they saw that the stone, which was very large, had been rolled away. ⁵As they entered the tomb, they saw a young man dressed in a white robe sitting on the right side, and they were alarmed.

⁶"Don't be alarmed," he said. "You are looking for Jesus the Nazarene, who was crucified. He has risen! He is not here. See the place where they laid him. ⁷But go, tell his disciples and Peter, 'He is going ahead of you into Galilee. There you will see him, just as he told you.'"

⁸Trembling and bewildered, the women went out and fled from the tomb. They said nothing to anyone, because they were afraid.

[The earliest manuscripts and some other ancient witnesses do not have Mark 16:9-20.]

⁹When Jesus rose early on the first day of the week, he appeared first to Mary Magdalene, out of whom he had driven seven demons. ¹⁰She went and told those who had been with him and who were mourning and weeping. ¹¹When they heard that Jesus was alive and that she had seen him, they did not believe it.

¹²Afterward Jesus appeared in a different form to two of them while they were walking in the country. ¹³These returned and reported it to the rest; but they did not believe them either.

¹⁴Later Jesus appeared to the Eleven as they were eating; he rebuked them for their lack of faith and their stubborn refusal to believe those who had seen him after he had risen.

¹⁵He said to them, "Go into all the world and preach the good news to all creation. ¹⁶Whoever believes and is baptized will be saved, but whoever does not believe will be condemned. ¹⁷And these signs will accompany those who believe: In my name they will drive out demons; they will speak in new tongues; ¹⁸they will pick up snakes with their hands; and when they drink deadly poison, it will not hurt them at all; they will place their hands on sick people, and they will get well."

¹⁹After the Lord Jesus had spoken to them, he was taken up into heaven and he sat at the right hand of God. ²⁰Then the disciples went out and preached everywhere, and the Lord worked with them and confirmed his word by the signs that accompanied it.

THE MESSAGE

Salome bought spices so they could embalm him. Very early on Sunday morning, as the sun rose, they went to the tomb. They worried out loud to each other, "Who will roll back the stone from the tomb for us?"

16.4-5 Then they looked up, saw that it had been rolled back—it was a huge stone—and walked right in. They saw a young man sitting on the right side, dressed all in white. They were completely taken aback, astonished.

16.6-7 He said, "Don't be afraid. I know you're looking for Jesus the Nazarene, the One they nailed on the cross. He's been raised up; he's here no longer. You can see for yourselves that the place is empty. Now—on your way. Tell his disciples and Peter that he is going on ahead of you to Galilee. You'll see him there, exactly as he said."

16.8 They got out as fast as they could, beside themselves, their heads swimming. Stunned, they said nothing to anyone.

16.9-11 [After rising from the dead, Jesus appeared early on Sunday morning to Mary Magdalene, whom he had delivered from seven demons. She went to his former companions, now weeping and carrying on, and told them. When they heard her report that she had seen him alive and well, they didn't believe her.

16.12-13 Later he appeared, but in a different form, to two of them out walking in the countryside. They went back and told the rest, but they weren't believed either.

16.14-16 Still later, as the Eleven were eating supper, he appeared and took them to task most severely for their stubborn unbelief, refusing to believe those who had seen him raised up. Then he said, "Go into the world. Go everywhere and announce the Message of God's good news to one and all. Whoever believes and is baptized is saved; whoever refuses to believe is damned.

16.17-18 "These are some of the signs that will accompany believers: They will throw out demons in my name, they will speak in new tongues, they will take snakes in their hands, they will drink poison and not be hurt, they will lay hands on the sick and make them well."

16.19-20 Then the Master Jesus, after briefing them, was taken up to heaven, and he sat down beside God in the place of honor. And the disciples went out everywhere preaching, the Master working right with them, validating the Message with indisputable evidence.]

Note: Mark 16:9-20 [the portion in brackets] is contained only in later manuscripts.

LUKE

LUKE

INTRODUCTION

1 Many have undertaken to draw up an account of the things that have been fulfilled[a] among us, [2]just as they were handed down to us by those who from the first were eyewitnesses and servants of the word. [3]Therefore, since I myself have carefully investigated everything from the beginning, it seemed good also to me to write an orderly account for you, most excellent Theophilus, [4]so that you may know the certainty of the things you have been taught.

THE BIRTH OF JOHN THE BAPTIST FORETOLD

[5]In the time of Herod king of Judea there was a priest named Zechariah, who belonged to the priestly division of Abijah; his wife Elizabeth was also a descendant of Aaron. [6]Both of them were upright in the sight of God, observing all the Lord's commandments and regulations blamelessly. [7]But they had no children, because Elizabeth was barren; and they were both well along in years.

[8]Once when Zechariah's division was on duty and he was serving as priest before God, [9]he was chosen by lot, according to the custom of the priesthood, to go into the temple of the Lord and burn incense. [10]And when the time for the burning of incense came, all the assembled worshipers were praying outside.

[11]Then an angel of the Lord appeared to him, standing at the right side of the altar of incense. [12]When Zechariah saw him, he was startled and was gripped with fear. [13]But the angel said to him: "Do not be afraid, Zechariah; your prayer has been heard. Your wife Elizabeth will bear you a son, and you are to give him the name John. [14]He will be a joy and delight to you, and many will rejoice because of his birth, [15]for he will be great in the sight of the Lord. He is never to take wine or other fermented drink, and he will be filled with the Holy Spirit even from birth.[b] [16]Many of the people of Israel will he bring back to the Lord their God. [17]And he will go on before the Lord, in the spirit and power of

---

1.1-4 **1** So many others have tried their hand at putting together a story of the wonderful harvest of Scripture and history that took place among us, using reports handed down by the original eyewitnesses who served this Word with their very lives. Since I have investigated all the reports in close detail, starting from the story's beginning, I decided to write it all out for you, most honorable Theophilus, so you can know beyond the shadow of a doubt the reliability of what you were taught.

A CHILDLESS COUPLE CONCEIVES

1.5-7 During the rule of Herod, King of Judea, there was a priest assigned service in the regiment of Abijah. His name was Zachariah. His wife was descended from the daughters of Aaron. Her name was Elizabeth. Together they lived honorably before God, careful in keeping to the ways of the commandments and enjoying a clear conscience before God. But they were childless because Elizabeth could never conceive, and now they were quite old.

1.8-12 It so happened that as Zachariah was carrying out his priestly duties before God, working the shift assigned to his regiment, it came his one turn in life to enter the sanctuary of God and burn incense. The congregation was gathered and praying outside the Temple at the hour of the incense offering. Unannounced, an angel of God appeared just to the right of the altar of incense. Zachariah was paralyzed in fear.

1.13-15 But the angel reassured him, "Don't fear, Zachariah. Your prayer has been heard. Elizabeth, your wife, will bear a son by you. You are to name him John. You're going to leap like a gazelle for joy, and not only you—many will delight in his birth. He'll achieve great stature with God.

1.15-17 "He'll drink neither wine nor beer. He'll be filled with the Holy Spirit from the moment he leaves his mother's womb. He will turn many sons and daughters of Israel back to their God. He will herald God's arrival in the style and

---

a 1 Or been surely believed   *b 15 Or from his mother's womb*

NEW INTERNATIONAL VERSION

Elijah, to turn the hearts of the fathers to their children and the disobedient to the wisdom of the righteous—to make ready a people prepared for the Lord."

¹⁸Zechariah asked the angel, "How can I be sure of this? I am an old man and my wife is well along in years."

¹⁹The angel answered, "I am Gabriel. I stand in the presence of God, and I have been sent to speak to you and to tell you this good news. ²⁰And now you will be silent and not able to speak until the day this happens, because you did not believe my words, which will come true at their proper time."

²¹Meanwhile, the people were waiting for Zechariah and wondering why he stayed so long in the temple. ²²When he came out, he could not speak to them. They realized he had seen a vision in the temple, for he kept making signs to them but remained unable to speak.

²³When his time of service was completed, he returned home. ²⁴After this his wife Elizabeth became pregnant and for five months remained in seclusion. ²⁵"The Lord has done this for me," she said. "In these days he has shown his favor and taken away my disgrace among the people."

THE BIRTH OF JESUS FORETOLD

²⁶In the sixth month, God sent the angel Gabriel to Nazareth, a town in Galilee, ²⁷to a virgin pledged to be married to a man named Joseph, a descendant of David. The virgin's name was Mary. ²⁸The angel went to her and said, "Greetings, you who are highly favored! The Lord is with you."

²⁹Mary was greatly troubled at his words and wondered what kind of greeting this might be. ³⁰But the angel said to her, "Do not be afraid, Mary, you have found favor with God. ³¹You will be with child and give birth to a son, and you are to give him the name Jesus. ³²He will be great and will be called the Son of the Most High. The Lord God will give him the throne of his father David, ³³and he will reign over the house of Jacob forever; his kingdom will never end."

³⁴"How will this be," Mary asked the angel, "since I am a virgin?"

³⁵The angel answered, "The Holy Spirit will come upon you, and the power of the Most High

THE MESSAGE

strength of Elijah, soften the hearts of parents to children, and kindle devout understanding among hardened skeptics—he'll get the people ready for God."

1.18 Zachariah said to the angel, "Do you expect me to believe this? I'm an old man and my wife is an old woman."

1.19-20 But the angel said, "I am Gabriel, the sentinel of God, sent especially to bring you this glad news. But because you won't believe me, you'll be unable to say a word until the day of your son's birth. Every word I've spoken to you will come true on time—*God's* time."

1.21-22 Meanwhile, the congregation waiting for Zachariah was getting restless, wondering what was keeping him so long in the sanctuary. When he came out and couldn't speak, they knew he had seen a vision. He continued speechless and had to use sign language with the people.

1.23-25 When the course of his priestly assignment was completed, he went back home. It wasn't long before his wife, Elizabeth, conceived. She went off by herself for five months, relishing her pregnancy. "So, this is how God acts to remedy my unfortunate condition!" she said.

A VIRGIN CONCEIVES

1.26-28 In the sixth month of Elizabeth's pregnancy, God sent the angel Gabriel to the Galilean village of Nazareth to a virgin engaged to be married to a man descended from David. His name was Joseph, and the virgin's name, Mary. Upon entering, Gabriel greeted her:

> Good morning!
> You're beautiful with God's beauty,
> Beautiful inside and out!
> God be with you.

1.29-33 She was thoroughly shaken, wondering what was behind a greeting like that. But the angel assured her, "Mary, you have nothing to fear. God has a surprise for you: You will become pregnant and give birth to a son and call his name Jesus.

> He will be great,
>   be called 'Son of the Highest.'
> The Lord God will give him
>   the throne of his father David;
> He will rule Jacob's house forever—
>   no end, ever, to his kingdom."

1.34 Mary said to the angel, "But how? I've never slept with a man."

1.35 The angel answered,

> The Holy Spirit will come upon you,
>   the power of the Highest hover over you;

NEW INTERNATIONAL VERSION

will overshadow you. So the holy one to be born will be called[a] the Son of God. 36Even Elizabeth your relative is going to have a child in her old age, and she who was said to be barren is in her sixth month. 37For nothing is impossible with God."

38"I am the Lord's servant," Mary answered. "May it be to me as you have said." Then the angel left her.

MARY VISITS ELIZABETH

39At that time Mary got ready and hurried to a town in the hill country of Judea, 40where she entered Zechariah's home and greeted Elizabeth. 41When Elizabeth heard Mary's greeting, the baby leaped in her womb, and Elizabeth was filled with the Holy Spirit. 42In a loud voice she exclaimed: "Blessed are you among women, and blessed is the child you will bear! 43But why am I so favored, that the mother of my Lord should come to me? 44As soon as the sound of your greeting reached my ears, the baby in my womb leaped for joy. 45Blessed is she who has believed that what the Lord has said to her will be accomplished!"

MARY'S SONG

46And Mary said:

"My soul glorifies the Lord
47   and my spirit rejoices in God my Savior,
48for he has been mindful
      of the humble state of his servant.
   From now on all generations will call me
      blessed,
49   for the Mighty One has done great things
      for me—
      holy is his name.
50His mercy extends to those who fear him,
      from generation to generation.
51He has performed mighty deeds with his
      arm;
      he has scattered those who are proud in
      their inmost thoughts.
52He has brought down rulers from their
      thrones
      but has lifted up the humble.
53He has filled the hungry with good things
      but has sent the rich away empty.
54He has helped his servant Israel,
      remembering to be merciful

THE MESSAGE

Therefore, the child you bring to birth
      will be called Holy, Son of God.

1.36-38   "And did you know that your cousin Elizabeth conceived a son, old as she is? Everyone called her barren, and here she is six months' pregnant! Nothing, you see, is impossible with God."

And Mary said,

Yes, I see it all now:
      I'm the Lord's maid, ready to serve.
Let it be with me
      just as you say.

Then the angel left her.

BLESSED AMONG WOMEN

1.39-45   Mary didn't waste a minute. She got up and traveled to a town in Judah in the hill country, straight to Zachariah's house, and greeted Elizabeth. When Elizabeth heard Mary's greeting, the baby in her womb leaped. She was filled with the Holy Spirit, and sang out exuberantly,

You're so blessed among women,
      and the babe in your womb, also
         blessed!
And why am I so blessed that
      the mother of my Lord visits me?
The moment the sound of your
      greeting entered my ears,
The babe in my womb
      skipped like a lamb for sheer joy.
Blessed woman, who believed what God
         said,
      believed every word would come true!

1.46-55   And Mary said,

I'm bursting with God-news;
      I'm dancing the song of my Savior God.
God took one good look at me, and look
         what happened—
      I'm the most fortunate woman on earth!
What God has done for me will never be
         forgotten,
      the God whose very name is holy, set
         apart from all others.
His mercy flows in wave after wave
      on those who are in awe before him.
He bared his arm and showed his strength,
      scattered the bluffing braggarts.
He knocked tyrants off their high horses,
      pulled victims out of the mud.
The starving poor sat down to a banquet;
      the callous rich were left out in the cold.
He embraced his chosen child, Israel;
      he remembered and piled on the
         mercies, piled them high.

---

a 35 Or So the child to be born will be called holy,

NEW INTERNATIONAL VERSION

⁵⁵ to Abraham and his descendants forever,
even as he said to our fathers."

⁵⁶ Mary stayed with Elizabeth for about three months and then returned home.

THE BIRTH OF JOHN THE BAPTIST

⁵⁷ When it was time for Elizabeth to have her baby, she gave birth to a son. ⁵⁸ Her neighbors and relatives heard that the Lord had shown her great mercy, and they shared her joy.

⁵⁹ On the eighth day they came to circumcise the child, and they were going to name him after his father Zechariah, ⁶⁰ but his mother spoke up and said, "No! He is to be called John."

⁶¹ They said to her, "There is no one among your relatives who has that name."

⁶² Then they made signs to his father, to find out what he would like to name the child. ⁶³ He asked for a writing tablet, and to everyone's astonishment he wrote, "His name is John." ⁶⁴ Immediately his mouth was opened and his tongue was loosed, and he began to speak, praising God. ⁶⁵ The neighbors were all filled with awe, and throughout the hill country of Judea people were talking about all these things. ⁶⁶ Everyone who heard this wondered about it, asking, "What then is this child going to be?" For the Lord's hand was with him.

ZECHARIAH'S SONG

⁶⁷ His father Zechariah was filled with the Holy Spirit and prophesied:

⁶⁸ "Praise be to the Lord, the God of Israel,
because he has come and has redeemed
his people.
⁶⁹ He has raised up a horn *a* of salvation for us
in the house of his servant David
⁷⁰ (as he said through his holy prophets of long
ago),
⁷¹ salvation from our enemies
and from the hand of all who hate us—
⁷² to show mercy to our fathers
and to remember his holy covenant,
⁷³ the oath he swore to our father Abraham:
⁷⁴ to rescue us from the hand of our enemies,
and to enable us to serve him without fear
⁷⁵ in holiness and righteousness before him
all our days.

⁷⁶ And you, my child, will be called a prophet
of the Most High;
for you will go on before the Lord to
prepare the way for him,
⁷⁷ to give his people the knowledge of salvation
through the forgiveness of their sins,

a 69 Horn here symbolizes strength.

THE MESSAGE

It's exactly what he promised,
beginning with Abraham and right up to
now.

1.56   Mary stayed with Elizabeth for three months and then went back to her own home.

THE BIRTH OF JOHN

1.57-58 When Elizabeth was full-term in her pregnancy, she bore a son. Her neighbors and relatives, seeing that God had overwhelmed her with mercy, celebrated with her.

1.59-60   On the eighth day, they came to circumcise the child and were calling him Zachariah after his father. But his mother intervened: "No. He is to be called John."

1.61-62   "But," they said, "no one in your family is named that." They used sign language to ask Zachariah what he wanted him named.

1.63-64   Asking for a tablet, Zachariah wrote, "His name is to be John." That took everyone by surprise. Surprise followed surprise—Zachariah's mouth was now open, his tongue loose, and he was talking, praising God!

1.65-66   A deep, reverential fear settled over the neighborhood, and in all that Judean hill country people talked about nothing else. Everyone who heard about it took it to heart, wondering, "What will become of this child? Clearly, God has his hand in this."

1.67-79   Then Zachariah was filled with the Holy Spirit and prophesied,

Blessed be the Lord, the God of Israel;
he came and set his people free.
He set the power of salvation in the center
of our lives,
and in the very house of David his
servant,
Just as he promised long ago
through the preaching of his holy
prophets:
Deliverance from our enemies
and every hateful hand;
Mercy to our fathers,
as he remembers to do what he said
he'd do,
What he swore to our father Abraham—
a clean rescue from the enemy camp,
So we can worship him without a care in
the world,
made holy before him as long as we live.

And you, my child, "Prophet of the
Highest,"
will go ahead of the Master to prepare
his ways,
Present the offer of salvation to his people,
the forgiveness of their sins.

NEW INTERNATIONAL VERSION

⁷⁸because of the tender mercy of our God,
   by which the rising sun will come to us
      from heaven
⁷⁹to shine on those living in darkness
   and in the shadow of death,
      to guide our feet into the path of peace."

⁸⁰And the child grew and became strong in spirit; and he lived in the desert until he appeared publicly to Israel.

THE BIRTH OF JESUS

2 In those days Caesar Augustus issued a decree that a census should be taken of the entire Roman world. ²(This was the first census that took place while Quirinius was governor of Syria.) ³And everyone went to his own town to register.

⁴So Joseph also went up from the town of Nazareth in Galilee to Judea, to Bethlehem the town of David, because he belonged to the house and line of David. ⁵He went there to register with Mary, who was pledged to be married to him and was expecting a child. ⁶While they were there, the time came for the baby to be born, ⁷and she gave birth to her firstborn, a son. She wrapped him in cloths and placed him in a manger, because there was no room for them in the inn.

THE SHEPHERDS AND THE ANGELS

⁸And there were shepherds living out in the fields nearby, keeping watch over their flocks at night. ⁹An angel of the Lord appeared to them, and the glory of the Lord shone around them, and they were terrified. ¹⁰But the angel said to them, "Do not be afraid. I bring you good news of great joy that will be for all the people. ¹¹Today in the town of David a Savior has been born to you; he is Christ^a the Lord. ¹²This will be a sign to you: You will find a baby wrapped in cloths and lying in a manger."

¹³Suddenly a great company of the heavenly host appeared with the angel, praising God and saying,

¹⁴"Glory to God in the highest,
   and on earth peace to men on whom his
      favor rests."

¹⁵When the angels had left them and gone into heaven, the shepherds said to one another, "Let's go to Bethlehem and see this thing that has happened, which the Lord has told us about."

¹⁶So they hurried off and found Mary and Jo-

^a 11 Or Messiah. "The Christ" (Greek) and "the Messiah" (Hebrew) both mean "the Anointed One"; also in verse 26.

THE MESSAGE

Through the heartfelt mercies of our God,
   God's Sunrise will break in upon us,
Shining on those in the darkness,
   those sitting in the shadow of death,
Then showing us the way, one foot at a
      time,
   down the path of peace.

1.80   The child grew up, healthy and spirited. He lived out in the desert until the day he made his prophetic debut in Israel.

THE BIRTH OF JESUS

2.1-5   **2** About that time Caesar Augustus ordered a census to be taken throughout the Empire. This was the first census when Quirinius was governor of Syria. Everyone had to travel to his own ancestral hometown to be accounted for. So Joseph went from the Galilean town of Nazareth up to Bethlehem in Judah, David's town, for the census. As a descendant of David, he had to go there. He went with Mary, his fiancée, who was pregnant.

2.6-7   While they were there, the time came for her to give birth. She gave birth to a son, her firstborn. She wrapped him in a blanket and laid him in a manger, because there was no room in the hostel.

AN EVENT FOR EVERYONE

2.8-12   There were sheepherders camping in the neighborhood. They had set night watches over their sheep. Suddenly, God's angel stood among them and God's glory blazed around them. They were terrified. The angel said, "Don't be afraid. I'm here to announce a great and joyful event that is meant for everybody, worldwide: A Savior has just been born in David's town, a Savior who is Messiah and Master. This is what you're to look for: a baby wrapped in a blanket and lying in a manger."

2.13-14   At once the angel was joined by a huge angelic choir singing God's praises:

Glory to God in the heavenly heights,
Peace to all men and women on earth who
   please him.

2.15-18   As the angel choir withdrew into heaven, the sheepherders talked it over. "Let's get over to Bethlehem as fast as we can and see for ourselves what God has revealed to us." They left, running, and found Mary and Joseph, and the

NEW INTERNATIONAL VERSION

seph, and the baby, who was lying in the manger. [17]When they had seen him, they spread the word concerning what had been told them about this child, [18]and all who heard it were amazed at what the shepherds said to them. [19]But Mary treasured up all these things and pondered them in her heart. [20]The shepherds returned, glorifying and praising God for all the things they had heard and seen, which were just as they had been told.

JESUS PRESENTED IN THE TEMPLE

[21]On the eighth day, when it was time to circumcise him, he was named Jesus, the name the angel had given him before he had been conceived.

[22]When the time of their purification according to the Law of Moses had been completed, Joseph and Mary took him to Jerusalem to present him to the Lord [23](as it is written in the Law of the Lord, "Every firstborn male is to be consecrated to the Lord"[a]), [24]and to offer a sacrifice in keeping with what is said in the Law of the Lord: "a pair of doves or two young pigeons."[b]

[25]Now there was a man in Jerusalem called Simeon, who was righteous and devout. He was waiting for the consolation of Israel, and the Holy Spirit was upon him. [26]It had been revealed to him by the Holy Spirit that he would not die before he had seen the Lord's Christ. [27]Moved by the Spirit, he went into the temple courts. When the parents brought in the child Jesus to do for him what the custom of the Law required, [28]Simeon took him in his arms and praised God, saying:

[29] "Sovereign Lord, as you have promised,
    you now dismiss[c] your servant in peace.
[30] For my eyes have seen your salvation,
[31]   which you have prepared in the sight of
       all people,
[32] a light for revelation to the Gentiles
    and for glory to your people Israel."

[33]The child's father and mother marveled at what was said about him. [34]Then Simeon blessed them and said to Mary, his mother: "This child is destined to cause the falling and rising of many in Israel, and to be a sign that will be spoken against, [35]so that the thoughts of many hearts will be revealed. And a sword will pierce your own soul too."

[36]There was also a prophetess, Anna, the daughter of Phanuel, of the tribe of Asher. She was very old; she had lived with her husband seven years after her marriage, [37]and then was a

---

THE MESSAGE

baby lying in the manger. Seeing was believing. They told everyone they met what the angels had said about this child. All who heard the sheepherders were impressed.

2.19-20 Mary kept all these things to herself, holding them dear, deep within herself. The sheepherders returned and let loose, glorifying and praising God for everything they had heard and seen. It turned out exactly the way they'd been told!

BLESSINGS

2.21 When the eighth day arrived, the day of circumcision, the child was named Jesus, the name given by the angel before he was conceived.

2.22-24 Then when the days stipulated by Moses for purification were complete, they took him up to Jerusalem to offer him to God as commanded in God's Law: "Every male who opens the womb shall be a holy offering to God," and also to sacrifice the "pair of doves or two young pigeons" prescribed in God's Law.

2.25-32 In Jerusalem at the time, there was a man, Simeon by name, a good man, a man who lived in the prayerful expectancy of help for Israel. And the Holy Spirit was on him. The Holy Spirit had shown him that he would see the Messiah of God before he died. Led by the Spirit, he entered the Temple. As the parents of the child Jesus brought him in to carry out the rituals of the Law, Simeon took him into his arms and blessed God:

God, you can now release your servant;
    release me in peace as you promised.
With my own eyes I've seen your salvation;
    it's now out in the open for everyone to
       see:
A God-revealing light to the non-Jewish
    nations,
    and of glory for your people Israel.

2.33-35 Jesus' father and mother were speechless with surprise at these words. Simeon went on to bless them, and said to Mary his mother,

This child marks both the failure and
    the recovery of many in Israel,
A figure misunderstood and contradicted—
    the pain of a sword-thrust through
       you—
But the rejection will force honesty,
    as God reveals who they really are.

2.36-38 Anna the prophetess was also there, a daughter of Phanuel from the tribe of Asher. She was by now a very old woman. She had been married seven years and a widow for

---

[a] 23 Exodus 13:2,12   [b] 24 Lev. 12:8   [c] 29 Or *promised,*
d now dismiss

NEW INTERNATIONAL VERSION

widow until she was eighty-four. *a* She never left the temple but worshiped night and day, fasting and praying. 38Coming up to them at that very moment, she gave thanks to God and spoke about the child to all who were looking forward to the redemption of Jerusalem.

39When Joseph and Mary had done everything required by the Law of the Lord, they returned to Galilee to their own town of Nazareth. 40And the child grew and became strong; he was filled with wisdom, and the grace of God was upon him.

THE BOY JESUS AT THE TEMPLE

41Every year his parents went to Jerusalem for the Feast of the Passover. 42When he was twelve years old, they went up to the Feast, according to the custom. 43After the Feast was over, while his parents were returning home, the boy Jesus stayed behind in Jerusalem, but they were unaware of it. 44Thinking he was in their company, they traveled on for a day. Then they began looking for him among their relatives and friends. 45When they did not find him, they went back to Jerusalem to look for him. 46After three days they found him in the temple courts, sitting among the teachers, listening to them and asking them questions. 47Everyone who heard him was amazed at his understanding and his answers. 48When his parents saw him, they were astonished. His mother said to him, "Son, why have you treated us like this? Your father and I have been anxiously searching for you."

49"Why were you searching for me?" he asked. "Didn't you know I had to be in my Father's house?" 50But they did not understand what he was saying to them.

51Then he went down to Nazareth with them and was obedient to them. But his mother treasured all these things in her heart. 52And Jesus grew in wisdom and stature, and in favor with God and men.

JOHN THE BAPTIST PREPARES THE WAY

3 In the fifteenth year of the reign of Tiberius Caesar—when Pontius Pilate was governor of Judea, Herod tetrarch of Galilee, his brother Philip tetrarch of Iturea and Traconitis, and Lysanias tetrarch of Abilene— 2during the high priesthood of Annas and Caiaphas, the word of God came to John son of Zechariah in the desert. 3He went into all the country around the Jordan, preaching a baptism of repentance for the forgiveness of sins. 4As is written in the book of the words of Isaiah the prophet:

a 37 Or widow for eighty-four years

THE MESSAGE

eighty-four. She never left the Temple area, worshiping night and day with her fastings and prayers. At the very time Simeon was praying, she showed up, broke into an anthem of praise to God, and talked about the child to all who were waiting expectantly for the freeing of Jerusalem.

2.39-40 When they finished everything required by God in the Law, they returned to Galilee and their own town, Nazareth. There the child grew strong in body and wise in spirit. And the grace of God was on him.

THEY FOUND HIM IN THE TEMPLE

2.41-45 Every year Jesus' parents traveled to Jerusalem for the Feast of Passover. When he was twelve years old, they went up as they always did for the Feast. When it was over and they left for home, the child Jesus stayed behind in Jerusalem, but his parents didn't know it. Thinking he was somewhere in the company of pilgrims, they journeyed for a whole day and then began looking for him among relatives and neighbors. When they didn't find him, they went back to Jerusalem looking for him.

2.46-48 The next day they found him in the Temple seated among the teachers, listening to them and asking questions. The teachers were all quite taken with him, impressed with the sharpness of his answers. But his parents were not impressed; they were upset and hurt.

His mother said, "Young man, why have you done this to us? Your father and I have been half out of our minds looking for you."

2.49-50 He said, "Why were you looking for me? Didn't you know that I had to be here, dealing with the things of my Father?" But they had no idea what he was talking about.

2.51-52 So he went back to Nazareth with them, and lived obediently with them. His mother held these things dearly, deep within herself. And Jesus matured, growing up in both body and spirit, blessed by both God and people.

A BAPTISM OF LIFE-CHANGE

3.1-6 **3** In the fifteenth year of the rule of Caesar Tiberius—it was while Pontius Pilate was governor of Judea; Herod, ruler of Galilee; his brother Philip, ruler of Iturea and Traconitis; Lysanias, ruler of Abilene; during the Chief-Priesthood of Annas and Caiaphas—John, Zachariah's son, out in the desert at the time, received a message from God. He went all through the country around the Jordan River preaching a baptism of life-change leading to forgiveness of sins, as described in the words of Isaiah the prophet:

NEW INTERNATIONAL VERSION

"A voice of one calling in the desert,
'Prepare the way for the Lord,
    make straight paths for him.
5 Every valley shall be filled in,
    every mountain and hill made low.
The crooked roads shall become straight,
    the rough ways smooth.
6 And all mankind will see God's salvation.' " *a*

7 John said to the crowds coming out to be baptized by him, "You brood of vipers! Who warned you to flee from the coming wrath? 8 Produce fruit in keeping with repentance. And do not begin to say to yourselves, 'We have Abraham as our father.' For I tell you that out of these stones God can raise up children for Abraham. 9 The ax is already at the root of the trees, and every tree that does not produce good fruit will be cut down and thrown into the fire."

10 "What should we do then?" the crowd asked.

11 John answered, "The man with two tunics should share with him who has none, and the one who has food should do the same."

12 Tax collectors also came to be baptized. "Teacher," they asked, "what should we do?"

13 "Don't collect any more than you are required to," he told them.

14 Then some soldiers asked him, "And what should we do?"

He replied, "Don't extort money and don't accuse people falsely—be content with your pay."

15 The people were waiting expectantly and were all wondering in their hearts if John might possibly be the Christ. *b* 16 John answered them all, "I baptize you with *c* water. But one more powerful than I will come, the thongs of whose sandals I am not worthy to untie. He will baptize you with the Holy Spirit and with fire. 17 His winnowing fork is in his hand to clear his threshing floor and to gather the wheat into his barn, but he will burn up the chaff with unquenchable fire." 18 And with many other words John exhorted the people and preached the good news to them.

19 But when John rebuked Herod the tetrarch because of Herodias, his brother's wife, and all the other evil things he had done, 20 Herod added this to them all: He locked John up in prison.

THE BAPTISM AND GENEALOGY OF JESUS

21 When all the people were being baptized, Jesus was baptized too. And as he was praying, heaven was opened 22 and the Holy Spirit de-

THE MESSAGE

Thunder in the desert!
"Prepare God's arrival!
Make the road smooth and straight!
Every ditch will be filled in,
Every bump smoothed out,
The detours straightened out,
All the ruts paved over.
Everyone will be there to see
The parade of God's salvation."

3.7-9 When crowds of people came out for baptism because it was the popular thing to do, John exploded: "Brood of snakes! What do you think you're doing slithering down here to the river? Do you think a little water on your snakeskins is going to deflect God's judgment? It's your *life* that must change, not your skin. And don't think you can pull rank by claiming Abraham as 'father.' Being a child of Abraham is neither here nor there—children of Abraham are a dime a dozen. God can make children from stones if he wants. What counts is your life. Is it green and blossoming? Because if it's deadwood, it goes on the fire."

3.10 The crowd asked him, "Then what are we supposed to do?"

3.11 "If you have two coats, give one away," he said. "Do the same with your food."

3.12 Tax men also came to be baptized and said, "Teacher, what should we do?"

3.13 He told them, "No more extortion—collect only what is required by law."

3.14 Soldiers asked him, "And what should we do?"

He told them, "No shakedowns, no blackmail—and be content with your rations."

3.15 The interest of the people by now was building. They were all beginning to wonder, "Could this John be the Messiah?"

3.16-17 But John intervened: "I'm baptizing you here in the river. The main character in this drama, to whom I'm a mere stagehand, will ignite the kingdom life, a fire, the Holy Spirit within you, changing you from the inside out. He's going to clean house—make a clean sweep of your lives. He'll place everything true in its proper place before God; everything false he'll put out with the trash to be burned."

3.18-20 There was a lot more of this—words that gave strength to the people, words that put heart in them. The Message! But Herod, the ruler, stung by John's rebuke in the matter of Herodias, his brother Philip's wife, capped his long string of evil deeds with this outrage: He put John in jail.

3.21-22 After all the people were baptized, Jesus was baptized. As he was praying, the sky opened up and the Holy Spirit, like a dove descending,

---

a 6 Isaiah 40:3-5   *b* 15 Or *Messiah*   *c* 16 Or *in*

NEW INTERNATIONAL VERSION

scended on him in bodily form like a dove. And a voice came from heaven: "You are my Son, whom I love; with you I am well pleased."

²³Now Jesus himself was about thirty years old when he began his ministry. He was the son, so it was thought, of Joseph,

the son of Heli, ²⁴the son of Matthat,
the son of Levi, the son of Melki,
the son of Jannai, the son of Joseph,
²⁵the son of Mattathias, the son of Amos,
the son of Nahum, the son of Esli,
the son of Naggai, ²⁶the son of Maath,
the son of Mattathias, the son of Semein,
the son of Josech, the son of Joda,
²⁷the son of Joanan, the son of Rhesa,
the son of Zerubbabel, the son of Shealtiel,
the son of Neri, ²⁸the son of Melki,
the son of Addi, the son of Cosam,
the son of Elmadam, the son of Er,
²⁹the son of Joshua, the son of Eliezer,
the son of Jorim, the son of Matthat,
the son of Levi, ³⁰the son of Simeon,
the son of Judah, the son of Joseph,
the son of Jonam, the son of Eliakim,
³¹the son of Melea, the son of Menna,
the son of Mattatha, the son of Nathan,
the son of David, ³²the son of Jesse,
the son of Obed, the son of Boaz,
the son of Salmon,ᵃ the son of Nahshon,
³³the son of Amminadab, the son of Ram,ᵇ

ᵃ 32 Some early manuscripts Sala   ᵇ 33 Some manuscripts Amminadab, the son of Admin, the son of Arni; other manuscripts vary widely.

THE MESSAGE

came down on him. And along with the Spirit, a voice: "You are my Son, chosen and marked by my love, pride of my life."

SON OF ADAM, SON OF GOD

3.23-38 When Jesus entered public life he was about thirty years old, the son (in public perception) of Joseph, who was—

son of Heli,
son of Matthat,
son of Levi,
son of Melchi,
son of Jannai,
son of Joseph,
son of Mattathias,
son of Amos,
son of Nahum,
son of Esli,
son of Naggai,
son of Maath,
son of Mattathias,
son of Semein,
son of Josech,
son of Joda,
son of Joanan,
son of Rhesa,
son of Zerubbabel,
son of Shealtiel,
son of Neri,
son of Melchi,
son of Addi,
son of Cosam,
son of Elmadam,
son of Er,
son of Joshua,
son of Eliezer,
son of Jorim,
son of Matthat,
son of Levi,
son of Simeon,
son of Judah,
son of Joseph,
son of Jonam,
son of Eliakim,
son of Melea,
son of Menna,
son of Mattatha,
son of Nathan,
son of David,
son of Jesse,
son of Obed,
son of Boaz,
son of Sala,
son of Nahshon,
son of Amminadab,
son of Admin,
son of Arni,

NEW INTERNATIONAL VERSION	THE MESSAGE

NEW INTERNATIONAL VERSION

the son of Hezron, the son of Perez,
the son of Judah, [34]the son of Jacob,
the son of Isaac, the son of Abraham,
the son of Terah, the son of Nahor,
[35]the son of Serug, the son of Reu,
the son of Peleg, the son of Eber,
the son of Shelah, [36]the son of Cainan,
the son of Arphaxad, the son of Shem,
the son of Noah, the son of Lamech,
[37]the son of Methuselah, the son of Enoch,
the son of Jared, the son of Mahalalel,
the son of Kenan, [38]the son of Enosh,
the son of Seth, the son of Adam,
the son of God.

THE TEMPTATION OF JESUS

4 Jesus, full of the Holy Spirit, returned from the Jordan and was led by the Spirit in the desert, [2]where for forty days he was tempted by the devil. He ate nothing during those days, and at the end of them he was hungry.

[3]The devil said to him, "If you are the Son of God, tell this stone to become bread."

[4]Jesus answered, "It is written: 'Man does not live on bread alone.'[a]"

[5]The devil led him up to a high place and showed him in an instant all the kingdoms of the world. [6]And he said to him, "I will give you all their authority and splendor, for it has been given to me, and I can give it to anyone I want to. [7]So if you worship me, it will all be yours."

[8]Jesus answered, "It is written: 'Worship the Lord your God and serve him only.'[b]"

[9]The devil led him to Jerusalem and had him stand on the highest point of the temple. "If you are the Son of God," he said, "throw yourself down from here. [10]For it is written:

" 'He will command his angels concerning you
to guard you carefully;
[11]they will lift you up in their hands,
so that you will not strike your foot
against a stone.'[c]"

THE MESSAGE

son of Hezron,
son of Perez,
son of Judah,
son of Jacob,
son of Isaac,
son of Abraham,
son of Terah,
son of Nahor,
son of Serug,
son of Reu,
son of Peleg,
son of Eber,
son of Shelah,
son of Cainan,
son of Arphaxad,
son of Shem,
son of Noah,
son of Lamech,
son of Methuselah,
son of Enoch,
son of Jared,
son of Mahalaleel,
son of Cainan,
son of Enos,
son of Seth,
son of Adam,
son of God.

TESTED BY THE DEVIL

[4.1-2] **4** Now Jesus, full of the Holy Spirit, left the Jordan and was led by the Spirit into the wild. For forty wilderness days and nights he was tested by the Devil. He ate nothing during those days, and when the time was up he was hungry.

[4.3] The Devil, playing on his hunger, gave the first test: "Since you're God's Son, command this stone to turn into a loaf of bread."

[4.4] Jesus answered by quoting Deuteronomy: "It takes more than bread to really live."

[4.5-7] For the second test he led him up and spread out all the kingdoms of the earth on display at once. Then the Devil said, "They're yours in all their splendor to serve your pleasure. I'm in charge of them all and can turn them over to whomever I wish. Worship me and they're yours, the whole works."

[4.8] Jesus refused, again backing his refusal with Deuteronomy: "Worship the Lord your God and only the Lord your God. Serve him with absolute single-heartedness."

[4.9-11] For the third test the Devil took him to Jerusalem and put him on top of the Temple. He said, "If you are God's Son, jump. It's written, isn't it, that 'he has placed you in the care of angels to protect you; they will catch you; you won't so much as stub your toe on a stone'?"

---

[a] 4 Deut. 8:3   [b] 8 Deut. 6:13   [c] 11 Psalm 91:11,12

NEW INTERNATIONAL VERSION

¹²Jesus answered, "It says: 'Do not put the Lord your God to the test.'ᵃ"

¹³When the devil had finished all this tempting, he left him until an opportune time.

JESUS REJECTED AT NAZARETH

¹⁴Jesus returned to Galilee in the power of the Spirit, and news about him spread through the whole countryside. ¹⁵He taught in their synagogues, and everyone praised him.

¹⁶He went to Nazareth, where he had been brought up, and on the Sabbath day he went into the synagogue, as was his custom. And he stood up to read. ¹⁷The scroll of the prophet Isaiah was handed to him. Unrolling it, he found the place where it is written:

¹⁸"The Spirit of the Lord is on me,
    because he has anointed me
    to preach good news to the poor.
He has sent me to proclaim freedom for the
        prisoners
    and recovery of sight for the blind,
to release the oppressed,
¹⁹   to proclaim the year of the Lord's favor."ᵇ

²⁰Then he rolled up the scroll, gave it back to the attendant and sat down. The eyes of everyone in the synagogue were fastened on him, ²¹and he began by saying to them, "Today this scripture is fulfilled in your hearing."

²²All spoke well of him and were amazed at the gracious words that came from his lips. "Isn't this Joseph's son?" they asked.

²³Jesus said to them, "Surely you will quote this proverb to me: 'Physician, heal yourself! Do here in your hometown what we have heard that you did in Capernaum.' "

²⁴"I tell you the truth," he continued, "no prophet is accepted in his hometown. ²⁵I assure you that there were many widows in Israel in Elijah's time, when the sky was shut for three and a half years and there was a severe famine throughout the land. ²⁶Yet Elijah was not sent to any of them, but to a widow in Zarephath in the region of Sidon. ²⁷And there were many in Israel with leprosyᶜ in the time of Elisha the prophet, yet not one of them was cleansed—only Naaman the Syrian."

²⁸All the people in the synagogue were furious when they heard this. ²⁹They got up, drove him out of the town, and took him to the brow of the hill on which the town was built, in order to throw him down the cliff. ³⁰But he walked right through the crowd and went on his way.

THE MESSAGE

4.12   "Yes," said Jesus, "and it's also written, 'Don't you dare tempt the Lord your God.' "

4.13   That completed the testing. The Devil retreated temporarily, lying in wait for another opportunity.

TO SET THE BURDENED FREE

4.14-15 Jesus returned to Galilee powerful in the Spirit. News that he was back spread through the countryside. He taught in their meeting places to everyone's acclaim and pleasure.

4.16-21 He came to Nazareth where he had been reared. As he always did on the Sabbath, he went to the meeting place. When he stood up to read, he was handed the scroll of the prophet Isaiah. Unrolling the scroll, he found the place where it was written,

God's Spirit is on me;
    he's chosen me to preach the Message of
        good news to the poor,
Sent me to announce pardon to prisoners
        and
    recovery of sight to the blind,
To set the burdened and battered free,
    to announce, "This is God's year to act!"

4.22   He rolled up the scroll, handed it back to the assistant, and sat down. Every eye in the place was on him, intent. Then he started in, "You've just heard Scripture make history. It came true just now in this place."

4.23-27 All who were there, watching and listening, were surprised at how well he spoke. But they also said, "Isn't this Joseph's son, the one we've known since he was a youngster?"

He answered, "I suppose you're going to quote the proverb, 'Doctor, go heal yourself. Do here in your hometown what we heard you did in Capernaum.' Well, let me tell you something: No prophet is ever welcomed in his hometown. Isn't it a fact that there were many widows in Israel at the time of Elijah during that three and a half years of drought when famine devastated the land, but the only widow to whom Elijah was sent was in Sarepta in Sidon? And there were many lepers in Israel at the time of the prophet Elisha but the only one cleansed was Naaman the Syrian."

4.28-30 That set everyone in the meeting place seething with anger. They threw him out, banishing him from the village, then took him to a mountain cliff at the edge of the village to throw him to his doom, but he gave them the slip and was on his way.

ᵃ 12 Deut. 6:16   ᵇ 19 Isaiah 61:1,2   ᶜ 27 The Greek word was used for various diseases affecting the skin—not necessarily leprosy.

NEW INTERNATIONAL VERSION

JESUS DRIVES OUT AN EVIL SPIRIT

³¹Then he went down to Capernaum, a town in Galilee, and on the Sabbath began to teach the people. ³²They were amazed at his teaching, because his message had authority.

³³In the synagogue there was a man possessed by a demon, an evil*a* spirit. He cried out at the top of his voice, ³⁴"Ha! What do you want with us, Jesus of Nazareth? Have you come to destroy us? I know who you are—the Holy One of God!"

³⁵"Be quiet!" Jesus said sternly. "Come out of him!" Then the demon threw the man down before them all and came out without injuring him.

³⁶All the people were amazed and said to each other, "What is this teaching? With authority and power he gives orders to evil spirits and they come out!" ³⁷And the news about him spread throughout the surrounding area.

JESUS HEALS MANY

³⁸Jesus left the synagogue and went to the home of Simon. Now Simon's mother-in-law was suffering from a high fever, and they asked Jesus to help her. ³⁹So he bent over her and rebuked the fever, and it left her. She got up at once and began to wait on them.

⁴⁰When the sun was setting, the people brought to Jesus all who had various kinds of sickness, and laying his hands on each one, he healed them. ⁴¹Moreover, demons came out of many people, shouting, "You are the Son of God!" But he rebuked them and would not allow them to speak, because they knew he was the Christ.*b*

⁴²At daybreak Jesus went out to a solitary place. The people were looking for him and when they came to where he was, they tried to keep him from leaving them. ⁴³But he said, "I must preach the good news of the kingdom of God to the other towns also, because that is why I was sent." ⁴⁴And he kept on preaching in the synagogues of Judea.*c*

THE CALLING OF THE FIRST DISCIPLES

5 One day as Jesus was standing by the Lake of Gennesaret,*d* with the people crowding around him and listening to the word of God, ²he saw at the water's edge two boats, left there by the fishermen, who were washing their nets. ³He got into one of the boats, the one belonging

THE MESSAGE

4.31-32 He went down to Capernaum, a village in Galilee. He was teaching the people on the Sabbath. They were surprised and impressed—his teaching was so forthright, so confident, so authoritative, not the quibbling and quoting they were used to.

4.33-34 In the meeting place that day there was a man demonically disturbed. He screamed, "Ho! What business do you have here with us, Jesus? Nazarene! I know what you're up to. You're the Holy One of God and you've come to destroy us!"

4.35 Jesus shut him up: "Quiet! Get out of him!" The demonic spirit threw the man down in front of them all and left. The demon didn't hurt him.

4.36-37 That set everyone back on their heels, whispering and wondering, "What's going on here? Someone whose words make things happen? Someone who orders demonic spirits to get out and they go?" Jesus was the talk of the town.

HE HEALED THEM ALL

4.38-39 He left the meeting place and went to Simon's house. Simon's mother-in-law was running a high fever and they asked him to do something for her. He stood over her, told the fever to leave—and it left. Before they knew it, she was up getting dinner for them.

4.40-41 When the sun went down, everyone who had anyone sick with some ailment or other brought them to him. One by one he placed his hands on them and healed them. Demons left in droves, screaming, "Son of God! You're the Son of God!" But he shut them up, refusing to let them speak because they knew too much, knew him to be the Messiah.

4.42-44 He left the next day for open country. But the crowds went looking and, when they found him, clung to him so he couldn't go on. He told them, "Don't you realize that there are yet other villages where I have to tell the Message of God's kingdom, that this is the work God sent me to do?" Meanwhile he continued preaching in the meeting places of Galilee.

PUSH OUT INTO DEEP WATER

5.1-3 **5** Once when he was standing on the shore of Lake Gennesaret, the crowd was pushing in on him to better hear the Word of God. He noticed two boats tied up. The fishermen had just left them and were out scrubbing their nets. He climbed into the boat that was Simon's

---

a 33 Greek *unclean;* also in verse 36   *b 41* Or *Messiah*
c 44 Or *the land of the Jews;* some manuscripts *Galilee*
d 1 That is, Sea of Galilee

NEW INTERNATIONAL VERSION

to Simon, and asked him to put out a little from shore. Then he sat down and taught the people from the boat.

⁴When he had finished speaking, he said to Simon, "Put out into deep water, and let down*ᵃ* the nets for a catch."

⁵Simon answered, "Master, we've worked hard all night and haven't caught anything. But because you say so, I will let down the nets."

⁶When they had done so, they caught such a large number of fish that their nets began to break. ⁷So they signaled their partners in the other boat to come and help them, and they came and filled both boats so full that they began to sink.

⁸When Simon Peter saw this, he fell at Jesus' knees and said, "Go away from me, Lord; I am a sinful man!" ⁹For he and all his companions were astonished at the catch of fish they had taken, ¹⁰and so were James and John, the sons of Zebedee, Simon's partners.

Then Jesus said to Simon, "Don't be afraid; from now on you will catch men." ¹¹So they pulled their boats up on shore, left everything and followed him.

THE MAN WITH LEPROSY

¹²While Jesus was in one of the towns, a man came along who was covered with leprosy.*ᵇ* When he saw Jesus, he fell with his face to the ground and begged him, "Lord, if you are willing, you can make me clean."

¹³Jesus reached out his hand and touched the man. "I am willing," he said. "Be clean!" And immediately the leprosy left him.

¹⁴Then Jesus ordered him, "Don't tell anyone, but go, show yourself to the priest and offer the sacrifices that Moses commanded for your cleansing, as a testimony to them."

¹⁵Yet the news about him spread all the more, so that crowds of people came to hear him and to be healed of their sicknesses. ¹⁶But Jesus often withdrew to lonely places and prayed.

JESUS HEALS A PARALYTIC

¹⁷One day as he was teaching, Pharisees and teachers of the law, who had come from every village of Galilee and from Judea and Jerusalem, were sitting there. And the power of the Lord was present for him to heal the sick. ¹⁸Some men came carrying a paralytic on a mat and tried to take him into the house to lay him before Jesus. ¹⁹When they could not find a way to do this because of the crowd, they went up on the roof

THE MESSAGE

and asked him to put out a little from the shore. Sitting there, using the boat for a pulpit, he taught the crowd.

5.4 When he finished teaching, he said to Simon, "Push out into deep water and let your nets out for a catch."

5.5-7 Simon said, "Master, we've been fishing hard all night and haven't caught even a minnow. But if you say so, I'll let out the nets." It was no sooner said than done—a huge haul of fish, straining the nets past capacity. They waved to their partners in the other boat to come help them. They filled both boats, nearly swamping them with the catch.

5.8-10 Simon Peter, when he saw it, fell to his knees before Jesus. "Master, leave. I'm a sinner and can't handle this holiness. Leave me to myself." When they pulled in that catch of fish, awe overwhelmed Simon and everyone with him. It was the same with James and John, Zebedee's sons, coworkers with Simon.

5.10-11 Jesus said to Simon, "There is nothing to fear. From now on you'll be fishing for men and women." They pulled their boats up on the beach, left them, nets and all, and followed him.

INVITATION TO A CHANGED LIFE

5.12 One day in one of the villages there was a man covered with leprosy. When he saw Jesus he fell down before him in prayer and said, "If you want to, you can cleanse me."

5.13 Jesus put out his hand, touched him, and said, "I want to. Be clean." Then and there his skin was smooth, the leprosy gone.

5.14-16 Jesus instructed him, "Don't talk about this all over town. Just quietly present your healed self to the priest, along with the offering ordered by Moses. Your cleansed and obedient life, not your words, will bear witness to what I have done." But the man couldn't keep it to himself, and the word got out. Soon a large crowd of people had gathered to listen and be healed of their ailments. As often as possible Jesus withdrew to out-of-the-way places for prayer.

5.17 One day as he was teaching, Pharisees and religion teachers were sitting around. They had come from nearly every village in Galilee and Judea, even as far away as Jerusalem, to be there. The healing power of God was on him.

5.18-20 Some men arrived carrying a paraplegic on a stretcher. They were looking for a way to get into the house and set him before Jesus. When they couldn't find a way in because of the crowd, they went up on the roof, removed

---

ᵃ 4 The Greek verb is plural. *ᵇ 12* The Greek word was used for various diseases affecting the skin—not necessarily leprosy.

NEW INTERNATIONAL VERSION

and lowered him on his mat through the tiles into the middle of the crowd, right in front of Jesus.

²⁰When Jesus saw their faith, he said, "Friend, your sins are forgiven."

²¹The Pharisees and the teachers of the law began thinking to themselves, "Who is this fellow who speaks blasphemy? Who can forgive sins but God alone?"

²²Jesus knew what they were thinking and asked, "Why are you thinking these things in your hearts? ²³Which is easier: to say, 'Your sins are forgiven,' or to say, 'Get up and walk'? ²⁴But that you may know that the Son of Man has authority on earth to forgive sins . . ." He said to the paralyzed man, "I tell you, get up, take your mat and go home." ²⁵Immediately he stood up in front of them, took what he had been lying on and went home praising God. ²⁶Everyone was amazed and gave praise to God. They were filled with awe and said, "We have seen remarkable things today."

The Calling of Levi

²⁷After this, Jesus went out and saw a tax collector by the name of Levi sitting at his tax booth. "Follow me," Jesus said to him, ²⁸and Levi got up, left everything and followed him.

²⁹Then Levi held a great banquet for Jesus at his house, and a large crowd of tax collectors and others were eating with them. ³⁰But the Pharisees and the teachers of the law who belonged to their sect complained to his disciples, "Why do you eat and drink with tax collectors and 'sinners'?"

³¹Jesus answered them, "It is not the healthy who need a doctor, but the sick. ³²I have not come to call the righteous, but sinners to repentance."

Jesus Questioned About Fasting

³³They said to him, "John's disciples often fast and pray, and so do the disciples of the Pharisees, but yours go on eating and drinking."

³⁴Jesus answered, "Can you make the guests of the bridegroom fast while he is with them? ³⁵But the time will come when the bridegroom will be taken from them; in those days they will fast."

³⁶He told them this parable: "No one tears a patch from a new garment and sews it on an old one. If he does, he will have torn the new garment, and the patch from the new will not match the old. ³⁷And no one pours new wine into old wineskins. If he does, the new wine will burst the skins, the wine will run out and the wineskins will be ruined. ³⁸No, new wine must

THE MESSAGE

some tiles, and let him down in the middle of everyone, right in front of Jesus. Impressed by their bold belief, he said, "Friend, I forgive your sins."

5.21 That set the religion scholars and Pharisees buzzing. "Who does he think he is? That's blasphemous talk! God and only God can forgive sins."

5.22-26 Jesus knew exactly what they were thinking and said, "Why all this gossipy whispering? Which is simpler: to say 'I forgive your sins,' or to say 'Get up and start walking'? Well, just so it's clear that I'm the Son of Man and authorized to do either, or both. . . ." He now spoke directly to the paraplegic: "Get up. Take your bedroll and go home." Without a moment's hesitation, he did it—got up, took his blanket, and left for home, giving glory to God all the way. The people rubbed their eyes, incredulous—and then also gave glory to God. Awestruck, they said, "We've never seen anything like that!"

5.27-28 After this he went out and saw a man named Levi at his work collecting taxes. Jesus said, "Come along with me." And he did—walked away from everything and went with him.

5.29-30 Levi gave a large dinner at his home for Jesus. Everybody was there, tax men and other disreputable characters as guests at the dinner. The Pharisees and their religion scholars came to his disciples greatly offended. "What is he doing eating and drinking with crooks and 'sinners'?"

5.31-32 Jesus heard about it and spoke up, "Who needs a doctor: the healthy or the sick? I'm here inviting outsiders, not insiders—an invitation to a changed life, changed inside and out."

5.33 They asked him, "John's disciples are well-known for keeping fasts and saying prayers. Also the Pharisees. But you seem to spend most of your time at parties. Why?"

5.34-35 Jesus said, "When you're celebrating a wedding, you don't skimp on the cake and wine. You feast. Later you may need to pull in your belt, but this isn't the time. As long as the bride and groom are with you, you have a good time. When the groom is gone, the fasting can begin. No one throws cold water on a friendly bonfire. This is Kingdom Come!

5.36-39 "No one cuts up a fine silk scarf to patch old work clothes; you want fabrics that match. And you don't put wine in old, cracked bottles;

NEW INTERNATIONAL VERSION	THE MESSAGE

be poured into new wineskins. ³⁹And no one after drinking old wine wants the new, for he says, 'The old is better.' "

you get strong, clean bottles for your fresh vintage wine. And no one who has ever tasted fine aged wine prefers unaged wine."

LORD OF THE SABBATH

6 One Sabbath Jesus was going through the grainfields, and his disciples began to pick some heads of grain, rub them in their hands and eat the kernels. ²Some of the Pharisees asked, "Why are you doing what is unlawful on the Sabbath?"

³Jesus answered them, "Have you never read what David did when he and his companions were hungry? ⁴He entered the house of God, and taking the consecrated bread, he ate what is lawful only for priests to eat. And he also gave some to his companions." ⁵Then Jesus said to them, "The Son of Man is Lord of the Sabbath."

⁶On another Sabbath he went into the synagogue and was teaching, and a man was there whose right hand was shriveled. ⁷The Pharisees and the teachers of the law were looking for a reason to accuse Jesus, so they watched him closely to see if he would heal on the Sabbath. ⁸But Jesus knew what they were thinking and said to the man with the shriveled hand, "Get up and stand in front of everyone." So he got up and stood there.

⁹Then Jesus said to them, "I ask you, which is lawful on the Sabbath: to do good or to do evil, to save life or to destroy it?"

¹⁰He looked around at them all, and then said to the man, "Stretch out your hand." He did so, and his hand was completely restored. ¹¹But they were furious and began to discuss with one another what they might do to Jesus.

THE TWELVE APOSTLES

¹²One of those days Jesus went out to a mountainside to pray, and spent the night praying to God. ¹³When morning came, he called his disciples to him and chose twelve of them, whom he also designated apostles: ¹⁴Simon (whom he named Peter), his brother Andrew, James, John, Philip, Bartholomew, ¹⁵Matthew, Thomas, James son of Alphaeus, Simon who was called the Zealot, ¹⁶Judas son of James, and Judas Iscariot, who became a traitor.

IN CHARGE OF THE SABBATH

6.1-2 **6** On a certain Sabbath Jesus was walking through a field of ripe grain. His disciples were pulling off heads of grain, rubbing them in their hands to get rid of the chaff, and eating them. Some Pharisees said, "Why are you doing that, breaking a Sabbath rule?"

6.3-4 But Jesus stood up for them. "Have you never read what David and those with him did when they were hungry? How he entered the sanctuary and ate fresh bread off the altar, bread that no one but priests were allowed to eat? He also handed it out to his companions."

6.5 Then he said, "The Son of Man is no slave to the Sabbath; he's in charge."

6.6-8 On another Sabbath he went to the meeting place and taught. There was a man there with a crippled right hand. The religion scholars and Pharisees had their eye on Jesus to see if he would heal the man, hoping to catch him in a Sabbath infraction. He knew what they were up to and spoke to the man with the crippled hand: "Get up and stand here before us." He did.

6.9 Then Jesus addressed them, "Let me ask you something: What kind of action suits the Sabbath best? Doing good or doing evil? Helping people or leaving them helpless?"

6.10-11 He looked around, looked each one in the eye. He said to the man, "Hold out your hand." He held it out—it was as good as new! They were beside themselves with anger, and started plotting how they might get even with him.

THE TWELVE APOSTLES

6.12-16 At about that same time he climbed a mountain to pray. He was there all night in prayer before God. The next day he summoned his disciples; from them he selected twelve he designated as apostles:

> Simon, whom he named Peter,
> Andrew, his brother,
> James,
> John,
> Philip,
> Bartholomew,
> Matthew,
> Thomas,
> James, son of Alphaeus,
> Simon, called the Zealot,
> Judas, son of James,
> Judas Iscariot, who betrayed him.

NEW INTERNATIONAL VERSION

BLESSINGS AND WOES

17He went down with them and stood on a level place. A large crowd of his disciples was there and a great number of people from all over Judea, from Jerusalem, and from the coast of Tyre and Sidon, 18who had come to hear him and to be healed of their diseases. Those troubled by evila spirits were cured, 19and the people all tried to touch him, because power was coming from him and healing them all.

20Looking at his disciples, he said:

"Blessed are you who are poor,
    for yours is the kingdom of God.
21Blessed are you who hunger now,
    for you will be satisfied.
Blessed are you who weep now,
    for you will laugh.
22Blessed are you when men hate you,
    when they exclude you and insult you
    and reject your name as evil,
        because of the Son of Man.

23"Rejoice in that day and leap for joy, because great is your reward in heaven. For that is how their fathers treated the prophets.

24"But woe to you who are rich,
    for you have already received your
        comfort.
25Woe to you who are well fed now,
    for you will go hungry.
Woe to you who laugh now,
    for you will mourn and weep.
26Woe to you when all men speak well of you,
    for that is how their fathers treated the
        false prophets.

LOVE FOR ENEMIES

27"But I tell you who hear me: Love your enemies, do good to those who hate you, 28bless those who curse you, pray for those who mistreat you. 29If someone strikes you on one cheek, turn to him the other also. If someone takes your

a 18 Greek unclean

THE MESSAGE

YOU'RE BLESSED

6.17-21 Coming down off the mountain with them, he stood on a plain surrounded by disciples, and was soon joined by a huge congregation from all over Judea and Jerusalem, even from the seaside towns of Tyre and Sidon. They had come both to hear him and to be cured of their ailments. Those disturbed by evil spirits were healed. Everyone was trying to touch him—so much energy surging from him, so many people healed! Then he spoke:

You're blessed when you've lost it all.
God's kingdom is there for the finding.

You're blessed when you're ravenously
    hungry.
Then you're ready for the Messianic meal.

You're blessed when the tears flow freely.
Joy comes with the morning.

6.22-23 "Count yourself blessed every time someone cuts you down or throws you out, every time someone smears or blackens your name to discredit me. What it means is that the truth is too close for comfort and that that person is uncomfortable. You can be glad when that happens—skip like a lamb, if you like!—for even though they don't like it, I do . . . and all heaven applauds. And know that you are in good company; my preachers and witnesses have always been treated like this.

GIVE AWAY YOUR LIFE

6.24 But it's trouble ahead if you think you have
    it made.
What you have is all you'll ever get.

6.25 And it's trouble ahead if you're satisfied
    with yourself.
Your self will not satisfy you for long.

And it's trouble ahead if you think life's all
    fun and games.
There's suffering to be met, and you're
    going to meet it.

6.26 "There's trouble ahead when you live only for the approval of others, saying what flatters them, doing what indulges them. Popularity contests are not truth contests—look how many scoundrel preachers were approved by your ancestors! Your task is to be true, not popular.

6.27-30 "To you who are ready for the truth, I say this: Love your enemies. Let them bring out the best in you, not the worst. When someone gives you a hard time, respond with the energies of prayer for that person. If someone slaps you in the face, stand there and take it. If some-

NEW INTERNATIONAL VERSION

cloak, do not stop him from taking your tunic. ³⁰Give to everyone who asks you, and if anyone takes what belongs to you, do not demand it back. ³¹Do to others as you would have them do to you.

³²"If you love those who love you, what credit is that to you? Even 'sinners' love those who love them. ³³And if you do good to those who are good to you, what credit is that to you? Even 'sinners' do that. ³⁴And if you lend to those from whom you expect repayment, what credit is that to you? Even 'sinners' lend to 'sinners,' expecting to be repaid in full. ³⁵But love your enemies, do good to them, and lend to them without expecting to get anything back. Then your reward will be great, and you will be sons of the Most High, because he is kind to the ungrateful and wicked. ³⁶Be merciful, just as your Father is merciful.

Judging Others

³⁷"Do not judge, and you will not be judged. Do not condemn, and you will not be condemned. Forgive, and you will be forgiven. ³⁸Give, and it will be given to you. A good measure, pressed down, shaken together and running over, will be poured into your lap. For with the measure you use, it will be measured to you."

³⁹He also told them this parable: "Can a blind man lead a blind man? Will they not both fall into a pit? ⁴⁰A student is not above his teacher, but everyone who is fully trained will be like his teacher.

⁴¹"Why do you look at the speck of sawdust in your brother's eye and pay no attention to the plank in your own eye? ⁴²How can you say to your brother, 'Brother, let me take the speck out of your eye,' when you yourself fail to see the plank in your own eye? You hypocrite, first take the plank out of your eye, and then you will see clearly to remove the speck from your brother's eye.

A Tree and Its Fruit

⁴³"No good tree bears bad fruit, nor does a bad tree bear good fruit. ⁴⁴Each tree is recognized by its own fruit. People do not pick figs from thornbushes, or grapes from briers. ⁴⁵The good man brings good things out of the good stored up in his heart, and the evil man brings evil things out of the evil stored up in his heart. For out of the overflow of his heart his mouth speaks.

The Wise and Foolish Builders

⁴⁶"Why do you call me, 'Lord, Lord,' and do not do what I say? ⁴⁷I will show you what he is

THE MESSAGE

one grabs your shirt, giftwrap your best coat and make a present of it. If someone takes unfair advantage of you, use the occasion to practice the servant life. No more tit-for-tat stuff. Live generously.

6.31-34   "Here is a simple rule of thumb for behavior: Ask yourself what you want people to do for you; then grab the initiative and do it for *them*! If you only love the lovable, do you expect a pat on the back? Run-of-the-mill sinners do that. If you only help those who help you, do you expect a medal? Garden-variety sinners do that. If you only give for what you hope to get out of it, do you think that's charity? The stingiest of pawnbrokers does that.

6.35-36   "I tell you, love your enemies. Help and give without expecting a return. You'll never—I promise—regret it. Live out this God-created identity the way our Father lives toward us, generously and graciously, even when we're at our worst. Our Father is kind; you be kind.

6.37-38   "Don't pick on people, jump on their failures, criticize their faults—unless, of course, you want the same treatment. Don't condemn those who are down; that hardness can boomerang. Be easy on people; you'll find life a lot easier. Give away your life; you'll find life given back, but not merely given back—given back with bonus and blessing. Giving, not getting, is the way. Generosity begets generosity."

6.39-40   He quoted a proverb: " 'Can a blind man guide a blind man?' Wouldn't they both end up in the ditch? An apprentice doesn't lecture the master. The point is to be careful who you follow as your teacher.

6.41-42   "It's easy to see a smudge on your neighbor's face and be oblivious to the ugly sneer on your own. Do you have the nerve to say, 'Let me wash your face for you,' when your own face is distorted by contempt? It's this I-know-better-than-you mentality again, playing a holier-than-thou part instead of just living your own part. Wipe that ugly sneer off your own face and you might be fit to offer a washcloth to your neighbor.

Work the Words into Your Life

6.43-45   "You don't get wormy apples off a healthy tree, nor good apples off a diseased tree. The health of the apple tells the health of the tree. You must begin with your own life-giving lives. It's who you are, not what you say and do, that counts. Your true being brims over into true words and deeds.

6.46-47   "Why are you so polite with me, always saying 'Yes, sir,' and 'That's right, sir,' but never doing a thing I tell you? These words I speak to

NEW INTERNATIONAL VERSION

like who comes to me and hears my words and puts them into practice. ⁴⁸He is like a man building a house, who dug down deep and laid the foundation on rock. When a flood came, the torrent struck that house but could not shake it, because it was well built. ⁴⁹But the one who hears my words and does not put them into practice is like a man who built a house on the ground without a foundation. The moment the torrent struck that house, it collapsed and its destruction was complete."

THE FAITH OF THE CENTURION

7 When Jesus had finished saying all this in the hearing of the people, he entered Capernaum. ²There a centurion's servant, whom his master valued highly, was sick and about to die. ³The centurion heard of Jesus and sent some elders of the Jews to him, asking him to come and heal his servant. ⁴When they came to Jesus, they pleaded earnestly with him, "This man deserves to have you do this, ⁵because he loves our nation and has built our synagogue." ⁶So Jesus went with them.

He was not far from the house when the centurion sent friends to say to him: "Lord, don't trouble yourself, for I do not deserve to have you come under my roof. ⁷That is why I did not even consider myself worthy to come to you. But say the word, and my servant will be healed. ⁸For I myself am a man under authority, with soldiers under me. I tell this one, 'Go,' and he goes; and that one, 'Come,' and he comes. I say to my servant, 'Do this,' and he does it."

⁹When Jesus heard this, he was amazed at him, and turning to the crowd following him, he said, "I tell you, I have not found such great faith even in Israel." ¹⁰Then the men who had been sent returned to the house and found the servant well.

JESUS RAISES A WIDOW'S SON

¹¹Soon afterward, Jesus went to a town called Nain, and his disciples and a large crowd went along with him. ¹²As he approached the town gate, a dead person was being carried out—the only son of his mother, and she was a widow. And a large crowd from the town was with her. ¹³When the Lord saw her, his heart went out to her and he said, "Don't cry."

¹⁴Then he went up and touched the coffin, and those carrying it stood still. He said, "Young man, I say to you, get up!" ¹⁵The dead man sat

THE MESSAGE

you are not mere additions to your life, homeowner improvements to your standard of living. They are foundation words, words to build a life on.

6.48-49 "If you work the words into your life, you are like a smart carpenter who dug deep and laid the foundation of his house on bedrock. When the river burst its banks and crashed against the house, nothing could shake it; it was built to last. But if you just use my words in Bible studies and don't work them into your life, you are like a dumb carpenter who built a house but skipped the foundation. When the swollen river came crashing in, it collapsed like a house of cards. It was a total loss."

A PLACE OF HOLY MYSTERY

7.1-5 7 When he finished speaking to the people, he entered Capernaum. A Roman captain there had a servant who was on his deathbed. He prized him highly and didn't want to lose him. When he heard Jesus was back, he sent leaders from the Jewish community asking him to come and heal his servant. They came to Jesus and urged him to do it, saying, "He deserves this. He loves our people. He even built our meeting place."

7.6-8 Jesus went with them. When he was still quite far from the house, the captain sent friends to tell him, "Master, you don't have to go to all this trouble. I'm not that good a person, you know. I'd be embarrassed for you to come to my house, even embarrassed to come to you in person. Just give the order and my servant will get well. I'm a man under orders; I also give orders. I tell one soldier, 'Go,' and he goes; another, 'Come,' and he comes; my slave, 'Do this,' and he does it."

7.9-10 Taken aback, Jesus addressed the accompanying crowd: "I've yet to come across this kind of simple trust anywhere in Israel, the very people who are supposed to know about God and how he works." When the messengers got back home, they found the servant up and well.

7.11-15 Not long after that, Jesus went to the village Nain. His disciples were with him, along with quite a large crowd. As they approached the village gate, they met a funeral procession—a woman's only son was being carried out for burial. And the mother was a widow. When Jesus saw her, his heart broke. He said to her, "Don't cry." Then he went over and touched the coffin. The pallbearers stopped. He said, "Young man, I tell you: Get up." The dead son

NEW INTERNATIONAL VERSION

up and began to talk, and Jesus gave him back to his mother.

¹⁶They were all filled with awe and praised God. "A great prophet has appeared among us," they said. "God has come to help his people." ¹⁷This news about Jesus spread throughout Judea^a and the surrounding country.

JESUS AND JOHN THE BAPTIST

¹⁸John's disciples told him about all these things. Calling two of them, ¹⁹he sent them to the Lord to ask, "Are you the one who was to come, or should we expect someone else?"

²⁰When the men came to Jesus, they said, "John the Baptist sent us to you to ask, 'Are you the one who was to come, or should we expect someone else?' "

²¹At that very time Jesus cured many who had diseases, sicknesses and evil spirits, and gave sight to many who were blind. ²²So he replied to the messengers, "Go back and report to John what you have seen and heard: The blind receive sight, the lame walk, those who have leprosy^b are cured, the deaf hear, the dead are raised, and the good news is preached to the poor. ²³Blessed is the man who does not fall away on account of me."

²⁴After John's messengers left, Jesus began to speak to the crowd about John: "What did you go out into the desert to see? A reed swayed by the wind? ²⁵If not, what did you go out to see? A man dressed in fine clothes? No, those who wear expensive clothes and indulge in luxury are in palaces. ²⁶But what did you go out to see? A prophet? Yes, I tell you, and more than a prophet. ²⁷This is the one about whom it is written:

" 'I will send my messenger ahead of you,
    who will prepare your way before you.'^c

²⁸I tell you, among those born of women there is no one greater than John; yet the one who is least in the kingdom of God is greater than he."

²⁹(All the people, even the tax collectors, when they heard Jesus' words, acknowledged that God's way was right, because they had been baptized by John. ³⁰But the Pharisees and experts in the law rejected God's purpose for them-

THE MESSAGE

sat up and began talking. Jesus presented him to his mother.

7.16-17 They all realized they were in a place of holy mystery, that God was at work among them. They were quietly worshipful—and then noisily grateful, calling out among themselves, "God is back, looking to the needs of his people!" The news of Jesus spread all through the country.

IS THIS WHAT YOU WERE EXPECTING?

7.18-19 John's disciples reported back to him the news of all these events taking place. He sent two of them to the Master to ask the question, "Are you the One we've been expecting, or are we still waiting?"

7.20 The men showed up before Jesus and said, "John the Baptizer sent us to ask you, 'Are you the One we've been expecting, or are we still waiting?' "

7.21-23 In the next two or three hours Jesus healed many from diseases, distress, and evil spirits. To many of the blind he gave the gift of sight. Then he gave his answer: "Go back and tell John what you have just seen and heard:

The blind see,
The lame walk,
Lepers are cleansed,
The deaf hear,
The dead are raised,
The wretched of the earth
    have God's salvation hospitality
        extended to them.

"Is this what you were expecting? Then count yourselves fortunate!"

7.24-27 After John's messengers left to make their report, Jesus said more about John to the crowd of people. "What did you expect when you went out to see him in the wild? A weekend camper? Hardly. What then? A sheik in silk pajamas? Not in the wilderness, not by a long shot. What then? A messenger from God? That's right, a messenger! Probably the greatest messenger you'll ever hear. He is the messenger Malachi announced when he wrote,

I'm sending my messenger on ahead
To make the road smooth for you.

7.28-30 "Let me lay it out for you as plainly as I can: No one in history surpasses John the Baptizer, but in the kingdom he prepared you for, the lowliest person is ahead of him. The ordinary and disreputable people who heard John, by being baptized by him into the kingdom, are the clearest evidence; the Pharisees and religious officials would have nothing to do with

^a 17 Or the land of the Jews ^b 22 The Greek word was used for various diseases affecting the skin—not necessarily leprosy. ^c 27 Mal. 3:1

NEW INTERNATIONAL VERSION

selves, because they had not been baptized by John.)

³¹"To what, then, can I compare the people of this generation? What are they like? ³²They are like children sitting in the marketplace and calling out to each other:

" 'We played the flute for you,
   and you did not dance;
we sang a dirge,
   and you did not cry.'

³³For John the Baptist came neither eating bread nor drinking wine, and you say, 'He has a demon.' ³⁴The Son of Man came eating and drinking, and you say, 'Here is a glutton and a drunkard, a friend of tax collectors and "sinners." ' ³⁵But wisdom is proved right by all her children."

JESUS ANOINTED BY A SINFUL WOMAN

³⁶Now one of the Pharisees invited Jesus to have dinner with him, so he went to the Pharisee's house and reclined at the table. ³⁷When a woman who had lived a sinful life in that town learned that Jesus was eating at the Pharisee's house, she brought an alabaster jar of perfume, ³⁸and as she stood behind him at his feet weeping, she began to wet his feet with her tears. Then she wiped them with her hair, kissed them and poured perfume on them.

³⁹When the Pharisee who had invited him saw this, he said to himself, "If this man were a prophet, he would know who is touching him and what kind of woman she is—that she is a sinner."

⁴⁰Jesus answered him, "Simon, I have something to tell you."

"Tell me, teacher," he said.

⁴¹"Two men owed money to a certain moneylender. One owed him five hundred denarii,ᵃ and the other fifty. ⁴²Neither of them had the money to pay him back, so he canceled the debts of both. Now which of them will love him more?"

⁴³Simon replied, "I suppose the one who had the bigger debt canceled."

"You have judged correctly," Jesus said.

⁴⁴Then he turned toward the woman and said to Simon, "Do you see this woman? I came into your house. You did not give me any water for my feet, but she wet my feet with her tears and wiped them with her hair. ⁴⁵You did not give me a kiss, but this woman, from the time I entered, has not stopped kissing my feet. ⁴⁶You did not put oil on my head, but she has poured perfume on my feet. ⁴⁷Therefore, I tell you, her many sins

---

ᵃ 41 A denarius was a coin worth about a day's wages.

THE MESSAGE

such a baptism, wouldn't think of giving up their place in line to their inferiors.

7.31-35 "How can I account for the people of this generation? They're like spoiled children complaining to their parents, 'We wanted to skip rope and you were always too tired; we wanted to talk but you were always too busy.' John the Baptizer came fasting and you called him crazy. The Son of Man came feasting and you called him a lush. Opinion polls don't count for much, do they? The proof of the pudding is in the eating."

ANOINTING HIS FEET

7.36-39 One of the Pharisees asked him over for a meal. He went to the Pharisee's house and sat down at the dinner table. Just then a woman of the village, the town harlot, having learned that Jesus was a guest in the home of the Pharisee, came with a bottle of very expensive perfume and stood at his feet, weeping, raining tears on his feet. Letting down her hair, she dried his feet, kissed them, and anointed them with the perfume. When the Pharisee who had invited him saw this, he said to himself, "If this man was the prophet I thought he was, he would have known what kind of woman this is who is falling all over him."

7.40 Jesus said to him, "Simon, I have something to tell you."

"Oh? Tell me."

7.41-42 "Two men were in debt to a banker. One owed five hundred silver pieces, the other fifty. Neither of them could pay up, and so the banker canceled both debts. Which of the two would be more grateful?"

7.43-47 Simon answered, "I suppose the one who was forgiven the most."

"That's right," said Jesus. Then turning to the woman, but speaking to Simon, he said, "Do you see this woman? I came to your home; you provided no water for my feet, but she rained tears on my feet and dried them with her hair. You gave me no greeting, but from the time I arrived she hasn't quit kissing my feet. You provided nothing for freshening up, but she has soothed my feet with perfume. Impressive, isn't it? She was forgiven many, many sins,

NEW INTERNATIONAL VERSION

have been forgiven—for she loved much. But he who has been forgiven little loves little."

⁴⁸Then Jesus said to her, "Your sins are forgiven."

⁴⁹The other guests began to say among themselves, "Who is this who even forgives sins?"

⁵⁰Jesus said to the woman, "Your faith has saved you; go in peace."

THE PARABLE OF THE SOWER

8 After this, Jesus traveled about from one town and village to another, proclaiming the good news of the kingdom of God. The Twelve were with him, ²and also some women who had been cured of evil spirits and diseases: Mary (called Magdalene) from whom seven demons had come out; ³Joanna the wife of Cuza, the manager of Herod's household; Susanna; and many others. These women were helping to support them out of their own means.

⁴While a large crowd was gathering and people were coming to Jesus from town after town, he told this parable: ⁵"A farmer went out to sow his seed. As he was scattering the seed, some fell along the path; it was trampled on, and the birds of the air ate it up. ⁶Some fell on rock, and when it came up, the plants withered because they had no moisture. ⁷Other seed fell among thorns, which grew up with it and choked the plants. ⁸Still other seed fell on good soil. It came up and yielded a crop, a hundred times more than was sown."

When he said this, he called out, "He who has ears to hear, let him hear."

⁹His disciples asked him what this parable meant. ¹⁰He said, "The knowledge of the secrets of the kingdom of God has been given to you, but to others I speak in parables, so that,

" 'though seeing, they may not see;
    though hearing, they may not
        understand.'^a

¹¹"This is the meaning of the parable: The seed is the word of God. ¹²Those along the path are the ones who hear, and then the devil comes and takes away the word from their hearts, so that they may not believe and be saved. ¹³Those on the rock are the ones who receive the word with joy when they hear it, but they have no root. They believe for a while, but in the time of testing they fall away. ¹⁴The seed that fell among thorns stands for those who hear, but as they go

THE MESSAGE

and so she is very, very grateful. If the forgiveness is minimal, the gratitude is minimal."

7.48   Then he spoke to her: "I forgive your sins."

7.49   That set the dinner guests talking behind his back: "Who does he think he is, forgiving sins!"

7.50   He ignored them and said to the woman, "Your faith has saved you. Go in peace."

8.1-3   8 He continued according to plan, traveled to town after town, village after village, preaching God's kingdom, spreading the Message. The Twelve were with him. There were also some women in their company who had been healed of various evil afflictions and illnesses: Mary, the one called Magdalene, from whom seven demons had gone out; Joanna, wife of Chuza, Herod's manager; and Susanna—along with many others who used their considerable means to provide for the company.

THE STORY OF THE SEEDS

8.4-8   As they went from town to town, a lot of people joined in and traveled along. He addressed them, using this story: "A farmer went out to sow his seed. Some of it fell on the road; it was tramped down and the birds ate it. Other seed fell in the gravel; it sprouted, but withered because it didn't have good roots. Other seed fell in the weeds; the weeds grew with it and strangled it. Other seed fell in rich earth and produced a bumper crop.

        "Are you listening to this? Really listening?"

8.9   His disciples asked, "Why did you tell this story?"

8.10   He said, "You've been given insight into God's kingdom—you know how it works. There are others who need stories. But even with stories some of them aren't going to get it:

        Their eyes are open but don't see a thing,
        Their ears are open but don't hear a thing.

8.11-12   "This story is about some of those people. The seed is the Word of God. The seeds on the road are those who hear the Word, but no sooner do they hear it than the Devil snatches it from them so they won't believe and be saved.

8.13   "The seeds in the gravel are those who hear with enthusiasm, but the enthusiasm doesn't go very deep. It's only another fad, and the moment there's trouble it's gone.

8.14   "And the seed that fell in the weeds—well, these are the ones who hear, but then the seed is crowded out and nothing comes of it as they

^a 10 Isaiah 6:9

NEW INTERNATIONAL VERSION

on their way they are choked by life's worries, riches and pleasures, and they do not mature. ¹⁵But the seed on good soil stands for those with a noble and good heart, who hear the word, retain it, and by persevering produce a crop.

A LAMP ON A STAND

¹⁶"No one lights a lamp and hides it in a jar or puts it under a bed. Instead, he puts it on a stand, so that those who come in can see the light. ¹⁷For there is nothing hidden that will not be disclosed, and nothing concealed that will not be known or brought out into the open. ¹⁸Therefore consider carefully how you listen. Whoever has will be given more; whoever does not have, even what he thinks he has will be taken from him."

JESUS' MOTHER AND BROTHERS

¹⁹Now Jesus' mother and brothers came to see him, but they were not able to get near him because of the crowd. ²⁰Someone told him, "Your mother and brothers are standing outside, wanting to see you."

²¹He replied, "My mother and brothers are those who hear God's word and put it into practice."

JESUS CALMS THE STORM

²²One day Jesus said to his disciples, "Let's go over to the other side of the lake." So they got into a boat and set out. ²³As they sailed, he fell asleep. A squall came down on the lake, so that the boat was being swamped, and they were in great danger.

²⁴The disciples went and woke him, saying, "Master, Master, we're going to drown!"

He got up and rebuked the wind and the raging waters; the storm subsided, and all was calm. ²⁵"Where is your faith?" he asked his disciples.

In fear and amazement they asked one another, "Who is this? He commands even the winds and the water, and they obey him."

THE HEALING OF A DEMON-POSSESSED MAN

²⁶They sailed to the region of the Gerasenes,ᵃ which is across the lake from Galilee. ²⁷When Jesus stepped ashore, he was met by a demon-possessed man from the town. For a long time this man had not worn clothes or lived in a house, but had lived in the tombs. ²⁸When he saw Jesus, he cried out and fell at his feet, shouting at the top of his voice, "What do you want with me, Jesus, Son of the Most High God? I beg you, don't torture me!" ²⁹For Jesus had commanded the

ᵃ 26 Some manuscripts *Gadarenes*; other manuscripts *Gergesenes*; also in verse 37

THE MESSAGE

go about their lives worrying about tomorrow, making money, and having fun.

8.15 "But the seed in the good earth—these are the good-hearts who seize the Word and hold on no matter what, sticking with it until there's a harvest.

MISERS OF WHAT YOU HEAR

8.16-18 "No one lights a lamp and then covers it with a washtub or shoves it under the bed. No, you set it up on a lamp stand so those who enter the room can see their way. We're not keeping secrets; we're telling them. We're not hiding things; we're bringing *everything* out into the open. So be careful that you don't become misers of what you hear. Generosity begets generosity. Stinginess impoverishes."

8.19-20 His mother and brothers showed up but couldn't get through to him because of the crowd. He was given the message, "Your mother and brothers are standing outside wanting to see you."

8.21 He replied, "My mother and brothers are the ones who hear and do God's Word. Obedience is thicker than blood."

8.22-24 One day he and his disciples got in a boat. "Let's cross the lake," he said. And off they went. It was smooth sailing, and he fell asleep. A terrific storm came up suddenly on the lake. Water poured in, and they were about to capsize. They woke Jesus: "Master, Master, we're going to drown!"

Getting to his feet, he told the wind, "Silence!" and the waves, "Quiet down!" They did it. The lake became smooth as glass.

8.25 Then he said to his disciples, "Why can't you trust me?"

They were in absolute awe, staggered and stammering, "Who is this, anyway? He calls out to the winds and sea, and they do what he tells them!"

THE MADMAN AND THE PIGS

8.26-29 They sailed on to the country of the Gerasenes, directly opposite Galilee. As he stepped out onto land, a madman from town met him; he was a victim of demons. He hadn't worn clothes for a long time, nor lived at home; he lived in the cemetery. When he saw Jesus he screamed, fell before him, and bellowed, "What business do you have messing with me? You're Jesus, Son of the High God, but don't give me a hard time!" (The man said this because Jesus

NEW INTERNATIONAL VERSION

evil*ᵃ* spirit to come out of the man. Many times it had seized him, and though he was chained hand and foot and kept under guard, he had broken his chains and had been driven by the demon into solitary places.

³⁰Jesus asked him, "What is your name?"

"Legion," he replied, because many demons had gone into him. ³¹And they begged him repeatedly not to order them to go into the Abyss.

³²A large herd of pigs was feeding there on the hillside. The demons begged Jesus to let them go into them, and he gave them permission. ³³When the demons came out of the man, they went into the pigs, and the herd rushed down the steep bank into the lake and was drowned.

³⁴When those tending the pigs saw what had happened, they ran off and reported this in the town and countryside, ³⁵and the people went out to see what had happened. When they came to Jesus, they found the man from whom the demons had gone out, sitting at Jesus' feet, dressed and in his right mind; and they were afraid. ³⁶Those who had seen it told the people how the demon-possessed man had been cured. ³⁷Then all the people of the region of the Gerasenes asked Jesus to leave them, because they were overcome with fear. So he got into the boat and left.

³⁸The man from whom the demons had gone out begged to go with him, but Jesus sent him away, saying, ³⁹"Return home and tell how much God has done for you." So the man went away and told all over town how much Jesus had done for him.

A Dead Girl and a Sick Woman

⁴⁰Now when Jesus returned, a crowd welcomed him, for they were all expecting him. ⁴¹Then a man named Jairus, a ruler of the synagogue, came and fell at Jesus' feet, pleading with him to come to his house ⁴²because his only daughter, a girl of about twelve, was dying.

As Jesus was on his way, the crowds almost crushed him. ⁴³And a woman was there who had been subject to bleeding for twelve years,*ᵇ* but no one could heal her. ⁴⁴She came up behind him and touched the edge of his cloak, and immediately her bleeding stopped.

⁴⁵"Who touched me?" Jesus asked.

When they all denied it, Peter said, "Master, the people are crowding and pressing against you."

ᵃ 29 Greek unclean   ᵇ 43 Many manuscripts years, and she had spent all she had on doctors

THE MESSAGE

had started to order the unclean spirit out of him.) Time after time the demon threw the man into convulsions. He had been placed under constant guard and tied with chains and shackles, but crazed and driven wild by the demon, he would shatter the bonds.

8.30-31   Jesus asked him, "What is your name?"

"Mob. My name is Mob," he said, because many demons afflicted him. And they begged Jesus desperately not to order them to the bottomless pit.

8.32-33   A large herd of pigs was browsing and rooting on a nearby hill. The demons begged Jesus to order them into the pigs. He gave the order. It was even worse for the pigs than for the man. Crazed, they stampeded over a cliff into the lake and drowned.

8.34-36   Those tending the pigs, scared to death, bolted and told their story in town and country. People went out to see what had happened. They came to Jesus and found the man from whom the demons had been sent, sitting there at Jesus' feet, wearing decent clothes and making sense. It was a holy moment, and for a short time they were more reverent than curious. Then those who had seen it happen told how the demoniac had been saved.

8.37-39   Later, a great many people from the Gerasene countryside got together and asked Jesus to leave—too much change, too fast, and they were scared. So Jesus got back in the boat and set off. The man whom he had delivered from the demons asked to go with him, but he sent him back, saying, "Go home and tell everything God did in you." So he went back and preached all over town everything Jesus had done in him.

His Touch

8.40-42 On his return, Jesus was welcomed by a crowd. They were all there expecting him. A man came up, Jairus by name. He was president of the meeting place. He fell at Jesus' feet and begged him to come to his home because his twelve-year-old daughter, his only child, was dying. Jesus went with him, making his way through the pushing, jostling crowd.

8.43-45   In the crowd that day there was a woman who for twelve years had been afflicted with hemorrhages. She had spent every penny she had on doctors but not one had been able to help her. She slipped in from behind and touched the edge of Jesus' robe. At that very moment her hemorrhaging stopped. Jesus said, "Who touched me?"

When no one stepped forward, Peter said, "But Master, we've got crowds of people on our hands. Dozens have touched you."

NEW INTERNATIONAL VERSION

⁴⁶But Jesus said, "Someone touched me; I know that power has gone out from me."

⁴⁷Then the woman, seeing that she could not go unnoticed, came trembling and fell at his feet. In the presence of all the people, she told why she had touched him and how she had been instantly healed. ⁴⁸Then he said to her, "Daughter, your faith has healed you. Go in peace."

⁴⁹While Jesus was still speaking, someone came from the house of Jairus, the synagogue ruler. "Your daughter is dead," he said. "Don't bother the teacher any more."

⁵⁰Hearing this, Jesus said to Jairus, "Don't be afraid; just believe, and she will be healed."

⁵¹When he arrived at the house of Jairus, he did not let anyone go in with him except Peter, John and James, and the child's father and mother. ⁵²Meanwhile, all the people were wailing and mourning for her. "Stop wailing," Jesus said. "She is not dead but asleep."

⁵³They laughed at him, knowing that she was dead. ⁵⁴But he took her by the hand and said, "My child, get up!" ⁵⁵Her spirit returned, and at once she stood up. Then Jesus told them to give her something to eat. ⁵⁶Her parents were astonished, but he ordered them not to tell anyone what had happened.

JESUS SENDS OUT THE TWELVE

9 When Jesus had called the Twelve together, he gave them power and authority to drive out all demons and to cure diseases, ²and he sent them out to preach the kingdom of God and to heal the sick. ³He told them: "Take nothing for the journey—no staff, no bag, no bread, no money, no extra tunic. ⁴Whatever house you enter, stay there until you leave that town. ⁵If people do not welcome you, shake the dust off your feet when you leave their town, as a testimony against them." ⁶So they set out and went from village to village, preaching the gospel and healing people everywhere.

⁷Now Herod the tetrarch heard about all that was going on. And he was perplexed, because some were saying that John had been raised from the dead, ⁸others that Elijah had appeared, and still others that one of the prophets of long ago had come back to life. ⁹But Herod said, "I beheaded John. Who, then, is this I hear such things about?" And he tried to see him.

JESUS FEEDS THE FIVE THOUSAND

¹⁰When the apostles returned, they reported to Jesus what they had done. Then he took them with him and they withdrew by themselves to a

THE MESSAGE

8.46 Jesus insisted, "Someone touched me. I felt power discharging from me."

8.47 When the woman realized that she couldn't remain hidden, she knelt trembling before him. In front of all the people, she blurted out her story—why she touched him and how at that same moment she was healed.

8.48 Jesus said, "Daughter, you took a risk trusting me, and now you're healed and whole. Live well, live blessed!"

8.49 While he was still talking, someone from the leader's house came up and told him, "Your daughter died. No need now to bother the Teacher."

8.50-51 Jesus overheard and said, "Don't be upset. Just trust me and everything will be all right." Going into the house, he wouldn't let anyone enter with him except Peter, John, James, and the child's parents.

8.52-53 Everyone was crying and carrying on over her. Jesus said, "Don't cry. She didn't die; she's sleeping." They laughed at him. They knew she was dead.

8.54-56 Then Jesus, gripping her hand, called, "My dear child, get up." She was up in an instant, up and breathing again! He told them to give her something to eat. Her parents were ecstatic, but Jesus warned them to keep quiet. "Don't tell a soul what happened in this room."

KEEP IT SIMPLE

9.1-5 **9** Jesus now called the Twelve and gave them authority and power to deal with all the demons and cure diseases. He commissioned them to preach the news of God's kingdom and heal the sick. He said, "Don't load yourselves up with equipment. Keep it simple; *you* are the equipment. And no luxury inns—get a modest place and be content there until you leave. If you're not welcomed, leave town. Don't make a scene. Shrug your shoulders and move on."

9.6 Commissioned, they left. They traveled from town to town telling the latest news of God, the Message, and curing people everywhere they went.

9.7-9 Herod, the ruler, heard of these goings on and didn't know what to think. There were people saying John had come back from the dead, others that Elijah had appeared, still others that some prophet of long ago had shown up. Herod said, "But I killed John—took off his head. So who is this that I keep hearing about?" Curious, he looked for a chance to see him in action.

9.10-11 The apostles returned and reported on what they had done. Jesus took them away, off by

NEW INTERNATIONAL VERSION

town called Bethsaida, [11]but the crowds learned about it and followed him. He welcomed them and spoke to them about the kingdom of God, and healed those who needed healing.

[12]Late in the afternoon the Twelve came to him and said, "Send the crowd away so they can go to the surrounding villages and countryside and find food and lodging, because we are in a remote place here."

[13]He replied, "You give them something to eat."

They answered, "We have only five loaves of bread and two fish—unless we go and buy food for all this crowd." [14](About five thousand men were there.)

But he said to his disciples, "Have them sit down in groups of about fifty each." [15]The disciples did so, and everybody sat down. [16]Taking the five loaves and the two fish and looking up to heaven, he gave thanks and broke them. Then he gave them to the disciples to set before the people. [17]They all ate and were satisfied, and the disciples picked up twelve basketfuls of broken pieces that were left over.

PETER'S CONFESSION OF CHRIST

[18]Once when Jesus was praying in private and his disciples were with him, he asked them, "Who do the crowds say I am?"

[19]They replied, "Some say John the Baptist; others say Elijah; and still others, that one of the prophets of long ago has come back to life."

[20]"But what about you?" he asked. "Who do you say I am?"

Peter answered, "The Christ[a] of God."

[21]Jesus strictly warned them not to tell this to anyone. [22]And he said, "The Son of Man must suffer many things and be rejected by the elders, chief priests and teachers of the law, and he must be killed and on the third day be raised to life."

[23]Then he said to them all: "If anyone would come after me, he must deny himself and take up his cross daily and follow me. [24]For whoever wants to save his life will lose it, but whoever loses his life for me will save it. [25]What good is it for a man to gain the whole world, and yet lose or forfeit his very self? [26]If anyone is ashamed of

THE MESSAGE

themselves, near the town called Bethsaida. But the crowds got wind of it and followed. Jesus graciously welcomed them and talked to them about the kingdom of God. Those who needed healing, he healed.

BREAD AND FISH FOR FIVE THOUSAND

9.12 As the day declined, the Twelve said, "Dismiss the crowd so they can go to the farms or villages around here and get a room for the night and a bite to eat. We're out in the middle of nowhere."

9.13-14 "You feed them," Jesus said.

They said, "We couldn't scrape up more than five loaves of bread and a couple of fish—unless, of course, you want us to go to town ourselves and buy food for everybody." (There were more than five thousand people in the crowd.)

9.14-17 But he went ahead and directed his disciples, "Sit them down in groups of about fifty." They did what he said, and soon had everyone seated. He took the five loaves and two fish, lifted his face to heaven in prayer, blessed, broke, and gave the bread and fish to the disciples to hand out to the crowd. After the people had all eaten their fill, twelve baskets of leftovers were gathered up.

DON'T RUN FROM SUFFERING

9.18 One time when Jesus was off praying by himself, his disciples nearby, he asked them, "What are the crowds saying about me, about who I am?"

9.19 They said, "John the Baptizer. Others say Elijah. Still others say that one of the prophets from long ago has come back."

9.20-21 He then asked, "And you—what are you saying about me? Who am I?"

Peter answered, "The Messiah of God." Jesus then warned them to keep it quiet. They were to tell no one what Peter had said.

9.22 He went on, "It is necessary that the Son of Man proceed to an ordeal of suffering, be tried and found guilty by the religious leaders, high priests, and religion scholars, be killed, and on the third day be raised up alive."

9.23-27 Then he told them what they could expect for themselves: "Anyone who intends to come with me has to let me lead. You're not in the driver's seat—I am. Don't run from suffering; embrace it. Follow me and I'll show you how. Self-help is no help at all. Self-sacrifice is the way, *my* way, to finding yourself, your true self. What good would it do to get everything you want and lose you, the real you? If any of you is embarrassed with me and the way I'm lead-

NEW INTERNATIONAL VERSION

me and my words, the Son of Man will be ashamed of him when he comes in his glory and in the glory of the Father and of the holy angels. ²⁷I tell you the truth, some who are standing here will not taste death before they see the kingdom of God."

THE TRANSFIGURATION

²⁸About eight days after Jesus said this, he took Peter, John and James with him and went up onto a mountain to pray. ²⁹As he was praying, the appearance of his face changed, and his clothes became as bright as a flash of lightning. ³⁰Two men, Moses and Elijah, ³¹appeared in glorious splendor, talking with Jesus. They spoke about his departure, which he was about to bring to fulfillment at Jerusalem. ³²Peter and his companions were very sleepy, but when they became fully awake, they saw his glory and the two men standing with him. ³³As the men were leaving Jesus, Peter said to him, "Master, it is good for us to be here. Let us put up three shelters—one for you, one for Moses and one for Elijah." (He did not know what he was saying.)

³⁴While he was speaking, a cloud appeared and enveloped them, and they were afraid as they entered the cloud. ³⁵A voice came from the cloud, saying, "This is my Son, whom I have chosen; listen to him." ³⁶When the voice had spoken, they found that Jesus was alone. The disciples kept this to themselves, and told no one at that time what they had seen.

THE HEALING OF A BOY WITH AN EVIL SPIRIT

³⁷The next day, when they came down from the mountain, a large crowd met him. ³⁸A man in the crowd called out, "Teacher, I beg you to look at my son, for he is my only child. ³⁹A spirit seizes him and he suddenly screams; it throws him into convulsions so that he foams at the mouth. It scarcely ever leaves him and is destroying him. ⁴⁰I begged your disciples to drive it out, but they could not."

⁴¹"O unbelieving and perverse generation," Jesus replied, "how long shall I stay with you and put up with you? Bring your son here."

⁴²Even while the boy was coming, the demon

THE MESSAGE

ing you, know that the Son of Man will be far more embarrassed with you when he arrives in all his splendor in company with the Father and the holy angels. This isn't, you realize, pie in the sky by and by. Some who have taken their stand right here are going to see it happen, see with their own eyes the kingdom of God."

JESUS IN HIS GLORY

9.28-31 About eight days after saying this, he climbed the mountain to pray, taking Peter, John, and James along. While he was in prayer, the appearance of his face changed and his clothes became blinding white. At once two men were there talking with him. They turned out to be Moses and Elijah—and what a glorious appearance they made! They talked over his exodus, the one Jesus was about to complete in Jerusalem.

9.32-33 Meanwhile, Peter and those with him were slumped over in sleep. When they came to, rubbing their eyes, they saw Jesus in his glory and the two men standing with him. When Moses and Elijah had left, Peter said to Jesus, "Master, this is a great moment! Let's build three memorials: one for you, one for Moses, and one for Elijah." He blurted this out without thinking.

9.34-35 While he was babbling on like this, a light-radiant cloud enveloped them. As they found themselves buried in the cloud, they became deeply aware of God. Then there was a voice out of the cloud: "This is my Son, the Chosen! Listen to him."

9.36 When the sound of the voice died away, they saw Jesus there alone. They were speechless. And they continued speechless, said not one thing to anyone during those days of what they had seen.

✠

9.37-40 When they came down off the mountain the next day, a big crowd was there to meet them. A man called from out of the crowd, "Please, please, Teacher, take a look at my son. He's my only child. Often a spirit seizes him. Suddenly he's screaming, thrown into convulsions, his mouth foaming. And then it beats him black and blue before it leaves. I asked your disciples to deliver him but they couldn't."

9.41 Jesus said, "What a generation! No sense of God! No focus to your lives! How many times do I have to go over these things? How much longer do I have to put up with this? Bring your son here."

9.42-43 While he was coming, the demon slammed

NEW INTERNATIONAL VERSION

threw him to the ground in a convulsion. But Jesus rebuked the evil[a] spirit, healed the boy and gave him back to his father. 43And they were all amazed at the greatness of God.

While everyone was marveling at all that Jesus did, he said to his disciples, 44"Listen carefully to what I am about to tell you: The Son of Man is going to be betrayed into the hands of men." 45But they did not understand what this meant. It was hidden from them, so that they did not grasp it, and they were afraid to ask him about it.

WHO WILL BE THE GREATEST?

46An argument started among the disciples as to which of them would be the greatest. 47Jesus, knowing their thoughts, took a little child and had him stand beside him. 48Then he said to them, "Whoever welcomes this little child in my name welcomes me; and whoever welcomes me welcomes the one who sent me. For he who is least among you all—he is the greatest."

49"Master," said John, "we saw a man driving out demons in your name and we tried to stop him, because he is not one of us."

50"Do not stop him," Jesus said, "for whoever is not against you is for you."

SAMARITAN OPPOSITION

51As the time approached for him to be taken up to heaven, Jesus resolutely set out for Jerusalem. 52And he sent messengers on ahead, who went into a Samaritan village to get things ready for him; 53but the people there did not welcome him, because he was heading for Jerusalem. 54When the disciples James and John saw this, they asked, "Lord, do you want us to call fire down from heaven to destroy them[b]?" 55But Jesus turned and rebuked them, 56and[c] they went to another village.

THE COST OF FOLLOWING JESUS

57As they were walking along the road, a man said to him, "I will follow you wherever you go." 58Jesus replied, "Foxes have holes and birds of the air have nests, but the Son of Man has no place to lay his head."

59He said to another man, "Follow me." But the man replied, "Lord, first let me go and bury my father."

60Jesus said to him, "Let the dead bury their own dead, but you go and proclaim the kingdom of God."

---

[a] 42 Greek unclean   [b] 54 Some manuscripts them, even as Elijah did   [c] 55,56 Some manuscripts them. And he said, "You do not know what kind of spirit you are of, for the Son of Man did not come to destroy men's lives, but to save them." 56And

THE MESSAGE

him to the ground and threw him into convulsions. Jesus stepped in, ordered the vile spirit gone, healed the boy, and handed him back to his father. They all shook their heads in wonder, astonished at God's greatness, God's majestic greatness.

YOUR BUSINESS IS LIFE

9.43-44 While they continued to stand around exclaiming over all the things he was doing, Jesus said to his disciples, "Treasure and ponder each of these next words: The Son of Man is about to be betrayed into human hands."

9.45 They didn't get what he was saying. It was like he was speaking a foreign language and they couldn't make heads or tails of it. But they were embarrassed to ask him what he meant.

9.46-48 They started arguing over which of them would be most famous. When Jesus realized how much this mattered to them, he brought a child to his side. "Whoever accepts this child as if the child were me, accepts me," he said. "And whoever accepts me, accepts the One who sent me. You become great by accepting, not asserting. Your spirit, not your size, makes the difference."

9.49 John spoke up, "Master, we saw a man using your name to expel demons and we stopped him because he wasn't of our group."

9.50 Jesus said, "Don't stop him. If he's not an enemy, he's an ally."

9.51-54 When it came close to the time for his Ascension, he gathered up his courage and steeled himself for the journey to Jerusalem. He sent messengers on ahead. They came to a Samaritan village to make arrangements for his hospitality. But when the Samaritans learned that his destination was Jerusalem, they refused hospitality. When the disciples James and John learned of it, they said, "Master, do you want us to call a bolt of lightning down out of the sky and incinerate them?"

9.55-56 Jesus turned on them: "Of course not!" And they traveled on to another village.

9.57 On the road someone asked if he could go along. "I'll go with you, wherever," he said.

9.58 Jesus was curt: "Are you ready to rough it? We're not staying in the best inns, you know."

Jesus said to another, "Follow me."

9.59 He said, "Certainly, but first excuse me for a couple of days, please. I have to make arrangements for my father's funeral."

9.60 Jesus refused. "First things first. Your business is life, not death. And life is urgent: Announce God's kingdom!"

NEW INTERNATIONAL VERSION

⁶¹Still another said, "I will follow you, Lord; but first let me go back and say good-by to my family."

⁶²Jesus replied, "No one who puts his hand to the plow and looks back is fit for service in the kingdom of God."

JESUS SENDS OUT THE SEVENTY-TWO

10 After this the Lord appointed seventy-two*ᵃ* others and sent them two by two ahead of him to every town and place where he was about to go. ²He told them, "The harvest is plentiful, but the workers are few. Ask the Lord of the harvest, therefore, to send out workers into his harvest field. ³Go! I am sending you out like lambs among wolves. ⁴Do not take a purse or bag or sandals; and do not greet anyone on the road.

⁵"When you enter a house, first say, 'Peace to this house.' ⁶If a man of peace is there, your peace will rest on him; if not, it will return to you. ⁷Stay in that house, eating and drinking whatever they give you, for the worker deserves his wages. Do not move around from house to house.

⁸"When you enter a town and are welcomed, eat what is set before you. ⁹Heal the sick who are there and tell them, 'The kingdom of God is near you.' ¹⁰But when you enter a town and are not welcomed, go into its streets and say, ¹¹'Even the dust of your town that sticks to our feet we wipe off against you. Yet be sure of this: The kingdom of God is near.' ¹²I tell you, it will be more bearable on that day for Sodom than for that town.

¹³"Woe to you, Korazin! Woe to you, Bethsaida! For if the miracles that were performed in you had been performed in Tyre and Sidon, they would have repented long ago, sitting in sackcloth and ashes. ¹⁴But it will be more bearable for Tyre and Sidon at the judgment than for you. ¹⁵And you, Capernaum, will you be lifted up to the skies? No, you will go down to the depths.*ᵇ*

¹⁶"He who listens to you listens to me; he who rejects you rejects me; but he who rejects me rejects him who sent me."

¹⁷The seventy-two returned with joy and said, "Lord, even the demons submit to us in your name."

¹⁸He replied, "I saw Satan fall like lightning from heaven. ¹⁹I have given you authority to

ᵃ 1 Some manuscripts *seventy*; also in verse 17
ᵇ 15 Greek *Hades*

THE MESSAGE

9.61 Then another said, "I'm ready to follow you, Master, but first excuse me while I get things straightened out at home."

9.62 Jesus said, "No procrastination. No backward looks. You can't put God's kingdom off till tomorrow. Seize the day."

LAMBS IN A WOLF PACK

10 Later the Master selected seventy and sent them ahead of him in pairs to every town and place where he intended to go. He gave them this charge:

"What a huge harvest! And how few the harvest hands. So on your knees; ask the God of the Harvest to send harvest hands.

10.3 "On your way! But be careful—this is hazardous work. You're like lambs in a wolf pack.

10.4 "Travel light. Comb and toothbrush and no extra luggage.

"Don't loiter and make small talk with everyone you meet along the way.

10.5-6 "When you enter a home, greet the family, 'Peace.' If your greeting is received, then it's a good place to stay. But if it's not received, take it back and get out. Don't impose yourself.

10.7 "Stay at one home, taking your meals there, for a worker deserves three square meals. Don't move from house to house, looking for the best cook in town.

10.8-9 "When you enter a town and are received, eat what they set before you, heal anyone who is sick, and tell them, 'God's kingdom is right on your doorstep!'

10.10-12 "When you enter a town and are not received, go out in the street and say, 'The only thing we got from you is the dirt on our feet, and we're giving it back. Did you have any idea that God's kingdom was right on your doorstep?' Sodom will have it better on Judgment Day than the town that rejects you.

10.13-14 "Doom, Chorazin! Doom, Bethsaida! If Tyre and Sidon had been given half the chances given you, they'd have been on their knees long ago, repenting and crying for mercy. Tyre and Sidon will have it easy on Judgment Day compared to you.

10.15 "And you, Capernaum! Do you think you're about to be promoted to heaven? Think again. You're on a mud slide to hell.

10.16 "The one who listens to you, listens to me. The one who rejects you, rejects me. And rejecting me is the same as rejecting God, who sent me."

10.17 The seventy came back triumphant. "Master, even the demons danced to your tune!"

10.18-20 Jesus said, "I know. I saw Satan fall, a bolt of lightning out of the sky. See what I've given

NEW INTERNATIONAL VERSION

trample on snakes and scorpions and to over-come all the power of the enemy; nothing will harm you. ²⁰However, do not rejoice that the spirits submit to you, but rejoice that your names are written in heaven."

²¹At that time Jesus, full of joy through the Holy Spirit, said, "I praise you, Father, Lord of heaven and earth, because you have hidden these things from the wise and learned, and revealed them to little children. Yes, Father, for this was your good pleasure.

²²"All things have been committed to me by my Father. No one knows who the Son is except the Father, and no one knows who the Father is except the Son and those to whom the Son chooses to reveal him."

²³Then he turned to his disciples and said privately, "Blessed are the eyes that see what you see. ²⁴For I tell you that many prophets and kings wanted to see what you see but did not see it, and to hear what you hear but did not hear it."

THE PARABLE OF THE GOOD SAMARITAN

²⁵On one occasion an expert in the law stood up to test Jesus. "Teacher," he asked, "what must I do to inherit eternal life?"

²⁶"What is written in the Law?" he replied. "How do you read it?"

²⁷He answered: " 'Love the Lord your God with all your heart and with all your soul and with all your strength and with all your mind'ᵃ; and, 'Love your neighbor as yourself.'ᵇ"

²⁸"You have answered correctly," Jesus replied. "Do this and you will live."

²⁹But he wanted to justify himself, so he asked Jesus, "And who is my neighbor?"

³⁰In reply Jesus said: "A man was going down from Jerusalem to Jericho, when he fell into the hands of robbers. They stripped him of his clothes, beat him and went away, leaving him half dead. ³¹A priest happened to be going down the same road, and when he saw the man, he passed by on the other side. ³²So too, a Levite, when he came to the place and saw him, passed by on the other side. ³³But a Samaritan, as he traveled, came where the man was; and when he saw him, he took pity on him. ³⁴He went to him and bandaged his wounds, pouring on oil and wine. Then he put the man on his own donkey, took him to an inn and took care of him. ³⁵The next day he took out two silver coinsᶜ and gave them to the innkeeper. 'Look after him,' he said,

THE MESSAGE

you? Safe passage as you walk on snakes and scorpions, and protection from every assault of the Enemy. No one can put a hand on you. All the same, the great triumph is not in your authority over evil, but in God's authority over you and presence with you. Not what you do for God but what God does for you—that's the agenda for rejoicing."

10.21 At that, Jesus rejoiced, exuberant in the Holy Spirit. "I thank you, Father, Master of heaven and earth, that you hid these things from the know-it-alls and showed them to these innocent newcomers. Yes, Father, it pleased you to do it this way.

10.22 "I've been given it all by my Father! Only the Father knows who the Son is and only the Son knows who the Father is. The Son can introduce the Father to anyone he wants to."

10.23-24 He then turned in a private aside to his disciples. "Fortunate the eyes that see what you're seeing! There are plenty of prophets and kings who would have given their right arm to see what you are seeing but never got so much as a glimpse, to hear what you are hearing but never got so much as a whisper."

DEFINING "NEIGHBOR"

10.25 Just then a religion scholar stood up with a question to test Jesus. "Teacher, what do I need to do to get eternal life?"

10.26 He answered, "What's written in God's Law? How do you interpret it?"

10.27 He said, "That you love the Lord your God with all your passion and prayer and muscle and intelligence—and that you love your neighbor as well as you do yourself."

10.28 "Good answer!" said Jesus. "Do it and you'll live."

10.29 Looking for a loophole, he asked, "And just how would you define 'neighbor'?"

10.30-32 Jesus answered by telling a story. "There was once a man traveling from Jerusalem to Jericho. On the way he was attacked by robbers. They took his clothes, beat him up, and went off leaving him half-dead. Luckily, a priest was on his way down the same road, but when he saw him he angled across to the other side. Then a Levite religious man showed up; he also avoided the injured man.

10.33-35 "A Samaritan traveling the road came on him. When he saw the man's condition, his heart went out to him. He gave him first aid, disinfecting and bandaging his wounds. Then he lifted him onto his donkey, led him to an inn, and made him comfortable. In the morning he took out two silver coins and gave them to the innkeeper, saying, 'Take good care of him. If it

---

ᵃ 27 Deut. 6:5   ᵇ 27 Lev. 19:18   ᶜ 35 Greek two denarii

NEW INTERNATIONAL VERSION

'and when I return, I will reimburse you for any extra expense you may have.'

³⁶"Which of these three do you think was a neighbor to the man who fell into the hands of robbers?"

³⁷The expert in the law replied, "The one who had mercy on him."

Jesus told him, "Go and do likewise."

AT THE HOME OF MARTHA AND MARY

³⁸As Jesus and his disciples were on their way, he came to a village where a woman named Martha opened her home to him. ³⁹She had a sister called Mary, who sat at the Lord's feet listening to what he said. ⁴⁰But Martha was distracted by all the preparations that had to be made. She came to him and asked, "Lord, don't you care that my sister has left me to do the work by myself? Tell her to help me!"

⁴¹"Martha, Martha," the Lord answered, "you are worried and upset about many things, ⁴²but only one thing is needed. ᵃ Mary has chosen what is better, and it will not be taken away from her."

JESUS' TEACHING ON PRAYER

11 One day Jesus was praying in a certain place. When he finished, one of his disciples said to him, "Lord, teach us to pray, just as John taught his disciples."

²He said to them, "When you pray, say:

" 'Father,ᵇ
hallowed be your name,
your kingdom come.ᶜ
³Give us each day our daily bread.
⁴Forgive us our sins,
for we also forgive everyone who sins
against us.ᵈ
And lead us not into temptation.ᵉ' "

⁵Then he said to them, "Suppose one of you has a friend, and he goes to him at midnight and says, 'Friend, lend me three loaves of bread, ⁶because a friend of mine on a journey has come to me, and I have nothing to set before him.'

⁷"Then the one inside answers, 'Don't bother me. The door is already locked, and my children are with me in bed. I can't get up and give you anything.' ⁸I tell you, though he will not get up and give him the bread because he is his friend, yet because of the man's boldnessᶠ he will get up and give him as much as he needs.

ᵃ 42 Some manuscripts *but few things are needed—or only one*   ᵇ 2 Some manuscripts *Our Father in heaven*
ᶜ 2 Some manuscripts *come. May your will be done on earth as it is in heaven.*   ᵈ 4 Greek *everyone who is indebted to us*
ᵉ 4 Some manuscripts *temptation but deliver us from the evil one*   ᶠ 8 Or *persistence*

THE MESSAGE

costs any more, put it on my bill—I'll pay you on my way back.'

10.36 "What do you think? Which of the three became a neighbor to the man attacked by robbers?"

10.37 "The one who treated him kindly," the religion scholar responded.

Jesus said, "Go and do the same."

MARY AND MARTHA

10.38-40 As they continued their travel, Jesus entered a village. A woman by the name of Martha welcomed him and made him feel quite at home. She had a sister, Mary, who sat before the Master, hanging on every word he said. But Martha was pulled away by all she had to do in the kitchen. Later, she stepped in, interrupting them. "Master, don't you care that my sister has abandoned the kitchen to me? Tell her to lend me a hand."

10.41-42 The Master said, "Martha, dear Martha, you're fussing far too much and getting yourself worked up over nothing. One thing only is essential, and Mary has chosen it—it's the main course, and won't be taken from her."

ASK FOR WHAT YOU NEED

11.1 **11** One day he was praying in a certain place. When he finished, one of his disciples said, "Master, teach us to pray just as John taught his disciples."

11.2-4 So he said, "When you pray, say,

Father,
Reveal who you are.
Set the world right.
Keep us alive with three square meals.
Keep us forgiven with you and forgiving
others.
Keep us safe from ourselves and the Devil."

11.5-6 Then he said, "Imagine what would happen if you went to a friend in the middle of the night and said, 'Friend, lend me three loaves of bread. An old friend traveling through just showed up, and I don't have a thing on hand.'

11.7 "The friend answers from his bed, 'Don't bother me. The door's locked; my children are all down for the night; I can't get up to give you anything.'

11.8 "But let me tell you, even if he won't get up because he's a friend, if you stand your ground, knocking and waking all the neighbors, he'll finally get up and get you whatever you need.

NEW INTERNATIONAL VERSION

⁹"So I say to you: Ask and it will be given to you; seek and you will find; knock and the door will be opened to you. ¹⁰For everyone who asks receives; he who seeks finds; and to him who knocks, the door will be opened.

¹¹"Which of you fathers, if your son asks for*ᵃ* a fish, will give him a snake instead? ¹²Or if he asks for an egg, will give him a scorpion? ¹³If you then, though you are evil, know how to give good gifts to your children, how much more will your Father in heaven give the Holy Spirit to those who ask him!"

JESUS AND BEELZEBUB

¹⁴Jesus was driving out a demon that was mute. When the demon left, the man who had been mute spoke, and the crowd was amazed. ¹⁵But some of them said, "By Beelzebub,*ᵇ* the prince of demons, he is driving out demons." ¹⁶Others tested him by asking for a sign from heaven.

¹⁷Jesus knew their thoughts and said to them: "Any kingdom divided against itself will be ruined, and a house divided against itself will fall. ¹⁸If Satan is divided against himself, how can his kingdom stand? I say this because you claim that I drive out demons by Beelzebub. ¹⁹Now if I drive out demons by Beelzebub, by whom do your followers drive them out? So then, they will be your judges. ²⁰But if I drive out demons by the finger of God, then the kingdom of God has come to you.

²¹"When a strong man, fully armed, guards his own house, his possessions are safe. ²²But when someone stronger attacks and overpowers him, he takes away the armor in which the man trusted and divides up the spoils.

²³"He who is not with me is against me, and he who does not gather with me, scatters.

²⁴"When an evil*ᶜ* spirit comes out of a man, it goes through arid places seeking rest and does not find it. Then it says, 'I will return to the house I left.' ²⁵When it arrives, it finds the house swept clean and put in order. ²⁶Then it goes and takes seven other spirits more wicked than itself, and they go in and live there. And the final condition of that man is worse than the first."

THE MESSAGE

11.9   "Here's what I'm saying:

Ask and you'll get;
Seek and you'll find;
Knock and the door will open.

11.10-13   "Don't bargain with God. Be direct. Ask for what you need. This is not a cat-and-mouse, hide-and-seek game we're in. If your little boy asks for a serving of fish, do you scare him with a live snake on his plate? If your little girl asks for an egg, do you trick her with a spider? As bad as you are, you wouldn't think of such a thing—you're at least decent to your own children. And don't you think the Father who conceived you in love will give the Holy Spirit when you ask him?"

NO NEUTRAL GROUND

11.14-16   Jesus delivered a man from a demon that had kept him speechless. The demon gone, the man started talking a blue streak, taking the crowd by complete surprise. But some from the crowd were cynical. "Black magic," they said. "Some devil trick he's pulled from his sleeve." Others were skeptical, waiting around for him to prove himself with a spectacular miracle.

11.17-20   Jesus knew what they were thinking and said, "Any country in civil war for very long is wasted. A constantly squabbling family falls to pieces. If Satan cancels Satan, is there any Satan left? You accuse me of ganging up with the Devil, the prince of demons, to cast out demons, but if you're slinging devil mud at me, calling me a devil who kicks out devils, doesn't the same mud stick to your own exorcists? But if it's *God's* finger I'm pointing that sends the demons on their way, then God's kingdom is here for sure.

11.21-22   "When a strong man, armed to the teeth, stands guard in his front yard, his property is safe and sound. But what if a stronger man comes along with superior weapons? Then he's beaten at his own game, the arsenal that gave him such confidence hauled off, and his precious possessions plundered.

11.23   "This is war, and there is no neutral ground. If you're not on my side, you're the enemy; if you're not helping, you're making things worse.

11.24-26   "When a corrupting spirit is expelled from someone, it drifts along through the desert looking for an oasis, some unsuspecting soul it can bedevil. When it doesn't find anyone, it says, 'I'll go back to my old haunt.' On return, it finds the person swept and dusted, but vacant. It then runs out and rounds up seven other spirits dirtier than itself and they all move in, whooping it up. That person ends up far worse than if he'd never gotten cleaned up in the first place."

ᵃ 11 Some manuscripts *for bread, will give him a stone; or if he asks for   ᵇ 15* Greek *Beezeboul* or *Beelzeboul*; also in verses 18 and 19   *ᶜ 24* Greek *unclean*

NEW INTERNATIONAL VERSION

27As Jesus was saying these things, a woman in the crowd called out, "Blessed is the mother who gave you birth and nursed you."

28He replied, "Blessed rather are those who hear the word of God and obey it."

THE SIGN OF JONAH

29As the crowds increased, Jesus said, "This is a wicked generation. It asks for a miraculous sign, but none will be given it except the sign of Jonah. 30For as Jonah was a sign to the Ninevites, so also will the Son of Man be to this generation. 31The Queen of the South will rise at the judgment with the men of this generation and condemn them; for she came from the ends of the earth to listen to Solomon's wisdom, and now one*a* greater than Solomon is here. 32The men of Nineveh will stand up at the judgment with this generation and condemn it; for they repented at the preaching of Jonah, and now one greater than Jonah is here.

THE LAMP OF THE BODY

33"No one lights a lamp and puts it in a place where it will be hidden, or under a bowl. Instead he puts it on its stand, so that those who come in may see the light. 34Your eye is the lamp of your body. When your eyes are good, your whole body also is full of light. But when they are bad, your body also is full of darkness. 35See to it, then, that the light within you is not darkness. 36Therefore, if your whole body is full of light, and no part of it dark, it will be completely lighted, as when the light of a lamp shines on you."

SIX WOES

37When Jesus had finished speaking, a Pharisee invited him to eat with him; so he went in and reclined at the table. 38But the Pharisee, noticing that Jesus did not first wash before the meal, was surprised.

39Then the Lord said to him, "Now then, you Pharisees clean the outside of the cup and dish, but inside you are full of greed and wickedness. 40You foolish people! Did not the one who made the outside make the inside also? 41But give what is inside ⌊the dish⌋*b* to the poor, and everything will be clean for you.

a 31 Or something; also in verse 32   *b 41 Or what you have*

THE MESSAGE

11.27   While he was saying these things, some woman lifted her voice above the murmur of the crowd: "Blessed the womb that carried you, and the breasts at which you nursed!"

11.28   Jesus commented, "Even more blessed are those who hear God's Word and guard it with their lives!"

KEEP YOUR EYES OPEN

11.29-30 As the crowd swelled, he took a fresh tack: "The mood of this age is all wrong. Everybody's looking for proof, but you're looking for the wrong kind. All you're looking for is something to titillate your curiosity, satisfy your lust for miracles. But the only proof you're going to get is the Jonah-proof given to the Ninevites, which looks like no proof at all. What Jonah was to Nineveh, the Son of Man is to this age.

11.32,31   "On Judgment Day the Ninevites will stand up and give evidence that will condemn this generation, because when Jonah preached to them they changed their lives. A far greater preacher than Jonah is here, and you squabble about 'proofs.' On Judgment Day the Queen of Sheba will come forward and bring evidence that condemns this generation, because she traveled from a far corner of the earth to listen to wise Solomon. Wisdom far greater than Solomon's is right in front of you, and you quibble over 'evidence.'

11.33-36   "No one lights a lamp, then hides it in a drawer. It's put on a lamp stand so those entering the room have light to see where they're going. Your eye is a lamp, lighting up your whole body. If you live wide-eyed in wonder and belief, your body fills up with light. If you live squinty-eyed in greed and distrust, your body is a dank cellar. Keep your eyes open, your lamp burning, so you don't get musty and murky. Keep your life as well-lighted as your best-lighted room."

FRAUDS!

11.37-41 When he finished that talk, a Pharisee asked him to dinner. He entered his house and sat right down at the table. The Pharisee was shocked and somewhat offended when he saw that Jesus didn't wash up before the meal. But the Master said to him, "I know you Pharisees burnish the surface of your cups and plates so they sparkle in the sun, but I also know your insides are maggoty with greed and secret evil. Stupid Pharisees! Didn't the One who made the outside also make the inside? Turn both your pockets and your hearts inside out and give generously to the poor; then your *lives* will be clean, not just your dishes and your hands.

NEW INTERNATIONAL VERSION

42"Woe to you Pharisees, because you give God a tenth of your mint, rue and all other kinds of garden herbs, but you neglect justice and the love of God. You should have practiced the latter without leaving the former undone.

43"Woe to you Pharisees, because you love the most important seats in the synagogues and greetings in the marketplaces.

44"Woe to you, because you are like unmarked graves, which men walk over without knowing it."

45One of the experts in the law answered him, "Teacher, when you say these things, you insult us also."

46Jesus replied, "And you experts in the law, woe to you, because you load people down with burdens they can hardly carry, and you yourselves will not lift one finger to help them.

47"Woe to you, because you build tombs for the prophets, and it was your forefathers who killed them. 48So you testify that you approve of what your forefathers did; they killed the prophets, and you build their tombs. 49Because of this, God in his wisdom said, 'I will send them prophets and apostles, some of whom they will kill and others they will persecute.' 50Therefore this generation will be held responsible for the blood of all the prophets that has been shed since the beginning of the world, 51from the blood of Abel to the blood of Zechariah, who was killed between the altar and the sanctuary. Yes, I tell you, this generation will be held responsible for it all.

52"Woe to you experts in the law, because you have taken away the key to knowledge. You yourselves have not entered, and you have hindered those who were entering."

53When Jesus left there, the Pharisees and the teachers of the law began to oppose him fiercely and to besiege him with questions, 54waiting to catch him in something he might say.

WARNINGS AND ENCOURAGEMENTS

12 Meanwhile, when a crowd of many thousands had gathered, so that they were trampling on one another, Jesus began to speak first to his disciples, saying: "Be on your guard against the yeast of the Pharisees, which is hypocrisy. 2There is nothing concealed that will not be disclosed, or hidden that will not be made known. 3What you have said in the dark will be

THE MESSAGE

11.42 "I've had it with you! You're hopeless, you Pharisees! Frauds! You keep meticulous account books, tithing on every nickel and dime you get, but manage to find loopholes for getting around basic matters of justice and God's love. Careful bookkeeping is commendable, but the basics are required.

11.43-44 "You're hopeless, you Pharisees! Frauds! You love sitting at the head table at church dinners, love preening yourselves in the radiance of public flattery. Frauds! You're just like unmarked graves: People walk over that nice, grassy surface, never suspecting the rot and corruption that is six feet under."

11.45 One of the religion scholars spoke up: "Teacher, do you realize that in saying these things you're insulting us?"

11.46 He said, "Yes, and I can be even more explicit. You're hopeless, you religion scholars! You load people down with rules and regulations, nearly breaking their backs, but never lift even a finger to help.

11.47-51 "You're hopeless! You build tombs for the prophets your ancestors killed. The tombs you build are monuments to your murdering ancestors more than to the murdered prophets. That accounts for God's Wisdom saying, 'I will send them prophets and apostles, but they'll kill them and run them off.' What it means is that every drop of righteous blood ever spilled from the time earth began until now, from the blood of Abel to the blood of Zechariah, who was struck down between altar and sanctuary, is on your heads. Yes, it's on the bill of this generation and this generation will pay.

11.52 "You're hopeless, you religion scholars! You took the key of knowledge, but instead of unlocking doors, you locked them. You won't go in yourself, and won't let anyone else in either."

11.53-54 As soon as Jesus left the table, the religion scholars and Pharisees went into a rage. They went over and over everything he said, plotting how they could trap him in something from his own mouth.

CAN'T HIDE BEHIND A RELIGIOUS MASK

12.1-3 **12** By this time the crowd, unwieldy and stepping on each other's toes, numbered into the thousands. But Jesus' primary concern was his disciples. He said to them, "Watch yourselves carefully so you don't get contaminated with Pharisee yeast, Pharisee phoniness. You can't keep your true self hidden forever; before long you'll be exposed. You can't hide behind a religious mask forever; sooner or later the mask will slip and your true face will be known. You can't whisper one thing in private

NEW INTERNATIONAL VERSION

heard in the daylight, and what you have whispered in the ear in the inner rooms will be proclaimed from the roofs.

4"I tell you, my friends, do not be afraid of those who kill the body and after that can do no more. 5But I will show you whom you should fear: Fear him who, after the killing of the body, has power to throw you into hell. Yes, I tell you, fear him. 6Are not five sparrows sold for two pennies*a*? Yet not one of them is forgotten by God. 7Indeed, the very hairs of your head are all numbered. Don't be afraid; you are worth more than many sparrows.

8"I tell you, whoever acknowledges me before men, the Son of Man will also acknowledge him before the angels of God. 9But he who disowns me before men will be disowned before the angels of God. 10And everyone who speaks a word against the Son of Man will be forgiven, but anyone who blasphemes against the Holy Spirit will not be forgiven.

11"When you are brought before synagogues, rulers and authorities, do not worry about how you will defend yourselves or what you will say, 12for the Holy Spirit will teach you at that time what you should say."

THE PARABLE OF THE RICH FOOL

13Someone in the crowd said to him, "Teacher, tell my brother to divide the inheritance with me."

14Jesus replied, "Man, who appointed me a judge or an arbiter between you?" 15Then he said to them, "Watch out! Be on your guard against all kinds of greed; a man's life does not consist in the abundance of his possessions."

16And he told them this parable: "The ground of a certain rich man produced a good crop. 17He thought to himself, 'What shall I do? I have no place to store my crops.'

18"Then he said, 'This is what I'll do. I will tear down my barns and build bigger ones, and there I will store all my grain and my goods. 19And I'll say to myself, "You have plenty of good things laid up for many years. Take life easy; eat, drink and be merry." '

20"But God said to him, 'You fool! This very night your life will be demanded from you. Then who will get what you have prepared for yourself?'

a 6 Greek *two assaria*

THE MESSAGE

and preach the opposite in public; the day's coming when those whispers will be repeated all over town.

12.4-5 "I'm speaking to you as dear friends. Don't be bluffed into silence or insincerity by the threats of religious bullies. True, they can kill you, but *then* what can they do? There's nothing they can do to your soul, your core being. Save your fear for God, who holds your entire life—body and soul—in his hands.

12.6-7 "What's the price of two or three pet canaries? Some loose change, right? But God never overlooks a single one. And he pays even greater attention to you, down to the last detail—even numbering the hairs on your head! So don't be intimidated by all this bully talk. You're worth more than a million canaries.

12.8-9 "Stand up for me among the people you meet and the Son of Man will stand up for you before all God's angels. But if you pretend you don't know me, do you think I'll defend you before God's angels?

12.10 "If you bad-mouth the Son of Man out of misunderstanding or ignorance, that can be overlooked. But if you're knowingly attacking God himself, taking aim at the Holy Spirit, that won't be overlooked.

12.11-12 "When they drag you into their meeting places, or into police courts and before judges, don't worry about defending yourselves—what you'll say or how you'll say it. The right words will be there. The Holy Spirit will give you the right words when the time comes."

THE STORY OF THE GREEDY FARMER

12.13 Someone out of the crowd said, "Teacher, order my brother to give me a fair share of the family inheritance."

12.14 He replied, "Mister, what makes you think it's any of my business to be a judge or mediator for you?"

12.15 Speaking to the people, he went on, "Take care! Protect yourself against the least bit of greed. Life is not defined by what you have, even when you have a lot."

12.16-19 Then he told them this story: "The farm of a certain rich man produced a terrific crop. He talked to himself: 'What can I do? My barn isn't big enough for this harvest.' Then he said, 'Here's what I'll do: I'll tear down my barns and build bigger ones. Then I'll gather in all my grain and goods, and I'll say to myself, Self, you've done well! You've got it made and can now retire. Take it easy and have the time of your life!'

12.20 "Just then God showed up and said, 'Fool! Tonight you die. And your barnful of goods—who gets it?'

NEW INTERNATIONAL VERSION

21"This is how it will be with anyone who stores up things for himself but is not rich toward God."

DO NOT WORRY

22Then Jesus said to his disciples: "Therefore I tell you, do not worry about your life, what you will eat; or about your body, what you will wear. 23Life is more than food, and the body more than clothes. 24Consider the ravens: They do not sow or reap, they have no storeroom or barn; yet God feeds them. And how much more valuable you are than birds! 25Who of you by worrying can add a single hour to his life*a*? 26Since you cannot do this very little thing, why do you worry about the rest?

27"Consider how the lilies grow. They do not labor or spin. Yet I tell you, not even Solomon in all his splendor was dressed like one of these. 28If that is how God clothes the grass of the field, which is here today, and tomorrow is thrown into the fire, how much more will he clothe you, O you of little faith! 29And do not set your heart on what you will eat or drink; do not worry about it. 30For the pagan world runs after all such things, and your Father knows that you need them. 31But seek his kingdom, and these things will be given to you as well.

32"Do not be afraid, little flock, for your Father has been pleased to give you the kingdom. 33Sell your possessions and give to the poor. Provide purses for yourselves that will not wear out, a treasure in heaven that will not be exhausted, where no thief comes near and no moth destroys. 34For where your treasure is, there your heart will be also.

WATCHFULNESS

35"Be dressed ready for service and keep your lamps burning, 36like men waiting for their master to return from a wedding banquet, so that when he comes and knocks they can immediately open the door for him. 37It will be good for those servants whose master finds them watching when he comes. I tell you the truth, he will dress himself to serve, will have them recline at the table and will come and wait on them. 38It will be good for those servants whose master finds them ready, even if he comes in the second or third watch of the night. 39But understand this: If the owner of the house had known at what hour the

a 25 Or single cubit to his height

THE MESSAGE

12.21   "That's what happens when you fill your barn with Self and not with God."

STEEP YOURSELF IN GOD-REALITY

12.22-24 He continued this subject with his disciples. "Don't fuss about what's on the table at mealtimes or if the clothes in your closet are in fashion. There is far more to your inner life than the food you put in your stomach, more to your outer appearance than the clothes you hang on your body. Look at the ravens, free and unfettered, not tied down to a job description, carefree in the care of God. And you count far more.

12.25-28   "Has anyone by fussing before the mirror ever gotten taller by so much as an inch? If fussing can't even do that, why fuss at all? Walk into the fields and look at the wildflowers. They don't fuss with their appearance—but have you ever seen color and design quite like it? The ten best-dressed men and women in the country look shabby alongside them. If God gives such attention to the wildflowers, most of them never even seen, don't you think he'll attend to you, take pride in you, do his best for you?

12.29-32   "What I'm trying to do here is get you to relax, not be so preoccupied with *getting* so you can respond to God's *giving*. People who don't know God and the way he works fuss over these things, but you know both God and how he works. Steep yourself in God-reality, God-initiative, God-provisions. You'll find all your everyday human concerns will be met. Don't be afraid of missing out. You're my dearest friends! The Father wants to give you the very kingdom itself.

12.33-34   "Be generous. Give to the poor. Get yourselves a bank that can't go bankrupt, a bank in heaven far from bankrobbers, safe from embezzlers, a bank you can bank on. It's obvious, isn't it? The place where your treasure is, is the place you will most want to be, and end up being.

WHEN THE MASTER SHOWS UP

12.35-38 "Keep your shirts on; keep the lights on! Be like house servants waiting for their master to come back from his honeymoon, awake and ready to open the door when he arrives and knocks. Lucky the servants whom the master finds on watch! He'll put on an apron, sit them at the table, and serve them a meal, sharing his wedding feast with them. It doesn't matter what time of the night he arrives; they're awake—and so blessed!

12.39-40   "You know that if the house owner had

NEW INTERNATIONAL VERSION

thief was coming, he would not have let his house be broken into. ⁴⁰You also must be ready, because the Son of Man will come at an hour when you do not expect him."

⁴¹Peter asked, "Lord, are you telling this parable to us, or to everyone?"

⁴²The Lord answered, "Who then is the faithful and wise manager, whom the master puts in charge of his servants to give them their food allowance at the proper time? ⁴³It will be good for that servant whom the master finds doing so when he returns. ⁴⁴I tell you the truth, he will put him in charge of all his possessions. ⁴⁵But suppose the servant says to himself, 'My master is taking a long time in coming,' and he then begins to beat the menservants and maidservants and to eat and drink and get drunk. ⁴⁶The master of that servant will come on a day when he does not expect him and at an hour he is not aware of. He will cut him to pieces and assign him a place with the unbelievers.

⁴⁷"That servant who knows his master's will and does not get ready or does not do what his master wants will be beaten with many blows. ⁴⁸But the one who does not know and does things deserving punishment will be beaten with few blows. From everyone who has been given much, much will be demanded; and from the one who has been entrusted with much, much more will be asked.

NOT PEACE BUT DIVISION

⁴⁹"I have come to bring fire on the earth, and how I wish it were already kindled! ⁵⁰But I have a baptism to undergo, and how distressed I am until it is completed! ⁵¹Do you think I came to bring peace on earth? No, I tell you, but division. ⁵²From now on there will be five in one family divided against each other, three against two and two against three. ⁵³They will be divided, father against son and son against father, mother against daughter and daughter against mother, mother-in-law against daughter-in-law and daughter-in-law against mother-in-law."

INTERPRETING THE TIMES

⁵⁴He said to the crowd: "When you see a cloud rising in the west, immediately you say, 'It's going to rain,' and it does. ⁵⁵And when the south wind blows, you say, 'It's going to be hot,' and it is. ⁵⁶Hypocrites! You know how to interpret the appearance of the earth and the sky. How is it that you don't know how to interpret this present time?

⁵⁷"Why don't you judge for yourselves what is right? ⁵⁸As you are going with your adversary to the magistrate, try hard to be reconciled to him on

THE MESSAGE

known what night the burglar was coming, he wouldn't have stayed out late and left the place unlocked. So don't you be slovenly and careless. Just when you don't expect him, the Son of Man will show up."

12.41   Peter said, "Master, are you telling this story just for us? Or is it for everybody?"

12.42-46   The Master said, "Let me ask you: Who is the dependable manager, full of common sense, that the master puts in charge of his staff to feed them well and on time? He is a blessed man if when the master shows up he's doing his job. But if he says to himself, 'The master is certainly taking his time,' begins maltreating the servants and maids, throws parties for his friends, and gets drunk, the master will walk in when he least expects it, give him the thrashing of his life, and put him back in the kitchen peeling potatoes.

12.47-48   "The servant who knows what his master wants and ignores it, or insolently does whatever he pleases, will be thoroughly thrashed. But if he does a poor job through ignorance, he'll get off with a slap on the hand. Great gifts mean great responsibilities; greater gifts, greater responsibilities!

TO START A FIRE

12.49-53   "I've come to start a fire on this earth—how I wish it were blazing right now! I've come to change everything, turn everything rightside up—how I long for it to be finished! Do you think I came to smooth things over and make everything nice? Not so. I've come to disrupt and confront! From now on, when you find five in a house, it will be—

Three against two,
     and two against three;
Father against son,
     and son against father;
Mother against daughter,
     and daughter against mother;
Mother-in-law against bride,
     and bride against mother-in-law."

12.54-56   Then he turned to the crowd: "When you see clouds coming in from the west, you say, 'Storm's coming'—and you're right. And when the wind comes out of the south, you say, 'This'll be a hot one'—and you're right. Frauds! You know how to tell a change in the weather, so don't tell me you can't tell a change in the season, the God-season we're in right now.

12.57-59   "You don't have to be a genius to understand these things. Just use your common sense, the kind you'd use if, while being taken to court, you decided to settle up with your accuser on

NEW INTERNATIONAL VERSION

the way, or he may drag you off to the judge, and the judge turn you over to the officer, and the officer throw you into prison. ⁵⁹I tell you, you will not get out until you have paid the last penny.ᵃ"

REPENT OR PERISH

13 Now there were some present at that time who told Jesus about the Galileans whose blood Pilate had mixed with their sacrifices. ²Jesus answered, "Do you think that these Galileans were worse sinners than all the other Galileans because they suffered this way? ³I tell you, no! But unless you repent, you too will all perish. ⁴Or those eighteen who died when the tower in Siloam fell on them—do you think they were more guilty than all the others living in Jerusalem? ⁵I tell you, no! But unless you repent, you too will all perish."

⁶Then he told this parable: "A man had a fig tree, planted in his vineyard, and he went to look for fruit on it, but did not find any. ⁷So he said to the man who took care of the vineyard, 'For three years now I've been coming to look for fruit on this fig tree and haven't found any. Cut it down! Why should it use up the soil?'

⁸" 'Sir,' the man replied, 'leave it alone for one more year, and I'll dig around it and fertilize it. ⁹If it bears fruit next year, fine! If not, then cut it down.' "

A CRIPPLED WOMAN HEALED ON THE SABBATH

¹⁰On a Sabbath Jesus was teaching in one of the synagogues, ¹¹and a woman was there who had been crippled by a spirit for eighteen years. She was bent over and could not straighten up at all. ¹²When Jesus saw her, he called her forward and said to her, "Woman, you are set free from your infirmity." ¹³Then he put his hands on her, and immediately she straightened up and praised God.

¹⁴Indignant because Jesus had healed on the Sabbath, the synagogue ruler said to the people, "There are six days for work. So come and be healed on those days, not on the Sabbath."

¹⁵The Lord answered him, "You hypocrites! Doesn't each of you on the Sabbath untie his ox or donkey from the stall and lead it out to give it water? ¹⁶Then should not this woman, a daughter of Abraham, whom Satan has kept bound for eighteen long years, be set free on the Sabbath day from what bound her?"

¹⁷When he said this, all his opponents were humiliated, but the people were delighted with all the wonderful things he was doing.

ᵃ 59 Greek lepton

THE MESSAGE

the way, knowing that if the case went to the judge you'd probably go to jail and pay every last penny of the fine. That's the kind of decision I'm asking you to make."

UNLESS YOU TURN TO GOD

13.1-5 **13** About that time some people came up and told him about the Galileans Pilate had killed while they were at worship, mixing their blood with the blood of the sacrifices on the altar. Jesus responded, "Do you think those murdered Galileans were worse sinners than all other Galileans? Not at all. Unless you turn to God, you too will die. And those eighteen in Jerusalem the other day, the ones crushed and killed when the Tower of Siloam collapsed and fell on them, do you think they were worse citizens than all other Jerusalemites? Not at all. Unless you turn to God, you too will die."

13.6-7 Then he told them a story: "A man had an apple tree planted in his front yard. He came to it expecting to find apples, but there weren't any. He said to his gardener, 'What's going on here? For three years now I've come to this tree expecting apples and not one apple have I found. Chop it down! Why waste good ground with it any longer?'

13.8-9 "The gardener said, 'Let's give it another year. I'll dig around it and fertilize, and maybe it will produce next year; if it doesn't, then chop it down.' "

HEALING ON THE SABBATH

13.10-13 He was teaching in one of the meeting places on the Sabbath. There was a woman present, so twisted and bent over with arthritis that she couldn't even look up. She had been afflicted with this for eighteen years. When Jesus saw her, he called her over. "Woman, you're free!" He laid hands on her and suddenly she was standing straight and tall, giving glory to God.

13.14 The meeting-place president, furious because Jesus had healed on the Sabbath, said to the congregation, "Six days have been defined as work days. Come on one of the six if you want to be healed, but not on the seventh, the Sabbath."

13.15-16 But Jesus shot back, "You frauds! Each Sabbath every one of you regularly unties your cow or donkey from its stall, leads it out for water, and thinks nothing of it. So why isn't it all right for me to untie this daughter of Abraham and lead her from the stall where Satan has had her tied these eighteen years?"

13.17 When he put it that way, his critics were left looking quite silly and red-faced. The congregation was delighted and cheered him on.

NEW INTERNATIONAL VERSION

THE PARABLES OF THE MUSTARD SEED AND THE YEAST

18Then Jesus asked, "What is the kingdom of God like? What shall I compare it to? **19**It is like a mustard seed, which a man took and planted in his garden. It grew and became a tree, and the birds of the air perched in its branches."

20Again he asked, "What shall I compare the kingdom of God to? **21**It is like yeast that a woman took and mixed into a large amount*ᵃ* of flour until it worked all through the dough."

THE NARROW DOOR

22Then Jesus went through the towns and villages, teaching as he made his way to Jerusalem. **23**Someone asked him, "Lord, are only a few people going to be saved?"

He said to them, **24**"Make every effort to enter through the narrow door, because many, I tell you, will try to enter and will not be able to. **25**Once the owner of the house gets up and closes the door, you will stand outside knocking and pleading, 'Sir, open the door for us.'

"But he will answer, 'I don't know you or where you come from.'

26"Then you will say, 'We ate and drank with you, and you taught in our streets.'

27"But he will reply, 'I don't know you or where you come from. Away from me, all you evildoers!'

28"There will be weeping there, and gnashing of teeth, when you see Abraham, Isaac and Jacob and all the prophets in the kingdom of God, but you yourselves thrown out. **29**People will come from east and west and north and south, and will take their places at the feast in the kingdom of God. **30**Indeed there are those who are last who will be first, and first who will be last."

JESUS' SORROW FOR JERUSALEM

31At that time some Pharisees came to Jesus and said to him, "Leave this place and go somewhere else. Herod wants to kill you."

32He replied, "Go tell that fox, 'I will drive out demons and heal people today and tomorrow, and on the third day I will reach my goal.' **33**In any case, I must keep going today and tomorrow and the next day—for surely no prophet can die outside Jerusalem!

34"O Jerusalem, Jerusalem, you who kill the prophets and stone those sent to you, how often I have longed to gather your children together,

ᵃ *21 Greek three satas (probably about 1/2 bushel or 22 liters)*

THE MESSAGE

THE WAY TO GOD

13.18-19 Then he said, "How can I picture God's kingdom for you? What kind of story can I use? It's like a pine nut that a man plants in his front yard. It grows into a huge pine tree with thick branches, and eagles build nests in it."

13.20-21 He tried again. "How can I picture God's kingdom? It's like yeast that a woman works into enough dough for three loaves of bread—and waits while the dough rises."

13.22 He went on teaching from town to village, village to town, but keeping on a steady course toward Jerusalem.

13.23-25 A bystander said, "Master, will only a few be saved?"

He said, "Whether few or many is none of your business. Put your mind on your life with God. The way to life—to God!—is vigorous and requires your total attention. A lot of you are going to assume that you'll sit down to God's salvation banquet just because you've been hanging around the neighborhood all your lives. Well, one day you're going to be banging on the door, wanting to get in, but you'll find the door locked and the Master saying, 'Sorry, you're not on my guest list.'

13.26-27 "You'll protest, 'But we've known you all our lives!' only to be interrupted with his abrupt, 'Your kind of knowing can hardly be called knowing. You don't know the first thing about me.'

13.28-30 "That's when you'll find yourselves out in the cold, strangers to grace. You'll watch Abraham, Isaac, Jacob, and all the prophets march into God's kingdom. You'll watch outsiders stream in from east, west, north, and south and sit down at the table of God's kingdom. And all the time you'll be outside looking in—and wondering what happened. This is the Great Reversal: the last in line put at the head of the line, and the so-called first ending up last.

✝

13.31 Just then some Pharisees came up and said, "Run for your life! Herod's on the hunt. He's out to kill you!"

13.32-35 Jesus said, "Tell that fox that I've no time for him right now. Today and tomorrow I'm busy clearing out the demons and healing the sick; the third day I'm wrapping things up. Besides, it's not proper for a prophet to come to a bad end outside Jerusalem.

Jerusalem, Jerusalem, killer of prophets,
abuser of the messengers of God!
How often I've longed to gather your
children,

NEW INTERNATIONAL VERSION

as a hen gathers her chicks under her wings, but you were not willing! ³⁵Look, your house is left to you desolate. I tell you, you will not see me again until you say, 'Blessed is he who comes in the name of the Lord.'ᵃ"

JESUS AT A PHARISEE'S HOUSE

14 One Sabbath, when Jesus went to eat in the house of a prominent Pharisee, he was being carefully watched. ²There in front of him was a man suffering from dropsy. ³Jesus asked the Pharisees and experts in the law, "Is it lawful to heal on the Sabbath or not?" ⁴But they remained silent. So taking hold of the man, he healed him and sent him away.

⁵Then he asked them, "If one of you has a sonᵇ or an ox that falls into a well on the Sabbath day, will you not immediately pull him out?" ⁶And they had nothing to say.

⁷When he noticed how the guests picked the places of honor at the table, he told them this parable: ⁸"When someone invites you to a wedding feast, do not take the place of honor, for a person more distinguished than you may have been invited. ⁹If so, the host who invited both of you will come and say to you, 'Give this man your seat.' Then, humiliated, you will have to take the least important place. ¹⁰But when you are invited, take the lowest place, so that when your host comes, he will say to you, 'Friend, move up to a better place.' Then you will be honored in the presence of all your fellow guests. ¹¹For everyone who exalts himself will be humbled, and he who humbles himself will be exalted."

¹²Then Jesus said to his host, "When you give a luncheon or dinner, do not invite your friends, your brothers or relatives, or your rich neighbors; if you do, they may invite you back and so you will be repaid. ¹³But when you give a banquet, invite the poor, the crippled, the lame, the blind, ¹⁴and you will be blessed. Although they cannot repay you, you will be repaid at the resurrection of the righteous."

THE MESSAGE

gather your children like a hen,
Her brood safe under her wings—
but you refused and turned away!
And now it's too late: You won't see me
again
until the day you say,
'Blessed is he
who comes in
the name of God.' "

14.1-3 **14** One time when Jesus went for a Sabbath meal with one of the top leaders of the Pharisees, all the guests had their eyes on him, watching his every move. Right before him there was a man hugely swollen in his joints. So Jesus asked the religion scholars and Pharisees present, "Is it permitted to heal on the Sabbath? Yes or no?"

14.4-6   They were silent. So he took the man, healed him, and sent him on his way. Then he said, "Is there anyone here who, if a child or animal fell down a well, wouldn't rush to pull him out immediately, not asking whether or not it was the Sabbath?" They were stumped. There was nothing they could say to that.

INVITE THE MISFITS

14.7-9   He went on to tell a story to the guests around the table. Noticing how each had tried to elbow into the place of honor, he said, "When someone invites you to dinner, don't take the place of honor. Somebody more important than you might have been invited by the host. Then he'll come and call out in front of everybody, 'You're in the wrong place. The place of honor belongs to this man.' Red-faced, you'll have to make your way to the very last table, the only place left.

14.10-11   "When you're invited to dinner, go and sit at the last place. Then when the host comes he may very well say, 'Friend, come up to the front.' That will give the dinner guests something to talk about! What I'm saying is, If you walk around with your nose in the air, you're going to end up flat on your face. But if you're content to be simply yourself, you will become more than yourself."

14.12-14   Then he turned to the host. "The next time you put on a dinner, don't just invite your friends and family and rich neighbors, the kind of people who will return the favor. Invite some people who never get invited out, the misfits from the wrong side of the tracks. You'll be—and experience—a blessing. They won't be able to return the favor, but the favor will be returned—oh, how it will be returned!—at the resurrection of God's people."

ᵃ 35 Psalm 118:26   ᵇ 5 Some manuscripts *donkey*

NEW INTERNATIONAL VERSION

THE PARABLE OF THE GREAT BANQUET

¹⁵When one of those at the table with him heard this, he said to Jesus, "Blessed is the man who will eat at the feast in the kingdom of God."

¹⁶Jesus replied: "A certain man was preparing a great banquet and invited many guests. ¹⁷At the time of the banquet he sent his servant to tell those who had been invited, 'Come, for everything is now ready.'

¹⁸"But they all alike began to make excuses. The first said, 'I have just bought a field, and I must go and see it. Please excuse me.'

¹⁹"Another said, 'I have just bought five yoke of oxen, and I'm on my way to try them out. Please excuse me.'

²⁰"Still another said, 'I just got married, so I can't come.'

²¹"The servant came back and reported this to his master. Then the owner of the house became angry and ordered his servant, 'Go out quickly into the streets and alleys of the town and bring in the poor, the crippled, the blind and the lame.'

²²" 'Sir,' the servant said, 'what you ordered has been done, but there is still room.'

²³"Then the master told his servant, 'Go out to the roads and country lanes and make them come in, so that my house will be full. ²⁴I tell you, not one of those men who were invited will get a taste of my banquet.' "

THE COST OF BEING A DISCIPLE

²⁵Large crowds were traveling with Jesus, and turning to them he said: ²⁶"If anyone comes to me and does not hate his father and mother, his wife and children, his brothers and sisters—yes, even his own life—he cannot be my disciple. ²⁷And anyone who does not carry his cross and follow me cannot be my disciple.

²⁸"Suppose one of you wants to build a tower. Will he not first sit down and estimate the cost to see if he has enough money to complete it? ²⁹For if he lays the foundation and is not able to finish it, everyone who sees it will ridicule him, ³⁰saying, 'This fellow began to build and was not able to finish.'

³¹"Or suppose a king is about to go to war against another king. Will he not first sit down and consider whether he is able with ten thousand men to oppose the one coming against him with twenty thousand? ³²If he is not able, he will send a delegation while the other is still a long way off and will ask for terms of peace. ³³In the same way, any of you who does not give up everything he has cannot be my disciple.

THE MESSAGE

THE STORY OF THE DINNER PARTY

14.15 That triggered a response from one of the guests: "How fortunate the one who gets to eat dinner in God's kingdom!"

14.16-17 Jesus followed up. "Yes. For there was once a man who threw a great dinner party and invited many. When it was time for dinner, he sent out his servant to the invited guests, saying, 'Come on in; the food's on the table.'

14.18 "Then they all began to beg off, one after another making excuses. The first said, 'I bought a piece of property and need to look it over. Send my regrets.'

14.19 "Another said, 'I just bought five teams of oxen, and I really need to check them out. Send my regrets.'

14.20 "And yet another said, 'I just got married and need to get home to my wife.'

14.21 "The servant went back and told the master what had happened. He was outraged and told the servant, 'Quickly, get out into the city streets and alleys. Collect all who look like they need a square meal, all the misfits and homeless and wretched you can lay your hands on, and bring them here.'

14.22 "The servant reported back, 'Master, I did what you commanded—and there's still room.'

14.23-24 "The master said, 'Then go to the country roads. Whoever you find, drag them in. I want my house full! Let me tell you, not one of those originally invited is going to get so much as a bite at my dinner party.' "

FIGURE THE COST

14.25-27 One day when large groups of people were walking along with him, Jesus turned and told them, "Anyone who comes to me but refuses to let go of father, mother, spouse, children, brothers, sisters—yes, even one's own self!—can't be my disciple. Anyone who won't shoulder his own cross and follow behind me can't be my disciple.

14.28-30 "Is there anyone here who, planning to build a new house, doesn't first sit down and figure the cost so you'll know if you can complete it? If you only get the foundation laid and then run out of money, you're going to look pretty foolish. Everyone passing by will poke fun at you: 'He started something he couldn't finish.'

14.31-32 "Or can you imagine a king going into battle against another king without first deciding whether it is possible with his ten thousand troops to face the twenty thousand troops of the other? And if he decides he can't, won't he send an emissary and work out a truce?

14.33 "Simply put, if you're not willing to take what is dearest to you, whether plans or people, and kiss it good-bye, you can't be my disciple.

NEW INTERNATIONAL VERSION

³⁴"Salt is good, but if it loses its saltiness, how can it be made salty again? ³⁵It is fit neither for the soil nor for the manure pile; it is thrown out.

"He who has ears to hear, let him hear."

THE PARABLE OF THE LOST SHEEP

15 Now the tax collectors and "sinners" were all gathering around to hear him. ²But the Pharisees and the teachers of the law muttered, "This man welcomes sinners and eats with them."

³Then Jesus told them this parable: ⁴"Suppose one of you has a hundred sheep and loses one of them. Does he not leave the ninety-nine in the open country and go after the lost sheep until he finds it? ⁵And when he finds it, he joyfully puts it on his shoulders ⁶and goes home. Then he calls his friends and neighbors together and says, 'Rejoice with me; I have found my lost sheep.' ⁷I tell you that in the same way there will be more rejoicing in heaven over one sinner who repents than over ninety-nine righteous persons who do not need to repent.

THE PARABLE OF THE LOST COIN

⁸"Or suppose a woman has ten silver coins*ᵃ* and loses one. Does she not light a lamp, sweep the house and search carefully until she finds it? ⁹And when she finds it, she calls her friends and neighbors together and says, 'Rejoice with me; I have found my lost coin.' ¹⁰In the same way, I tell you, there is rejoicing in the presence of the angels of God over one sinner who repents."

THE PARABLE OF THE LOST SON

¹¹Jesus continued: "There was a man who had two sons. ¹²The younger one said to his father, 'Father, give me my share of the estate.' So he divided his property between them.

¹³"Not long after that, the younger son got together all he had, set off for a distant country and there squandered his wealth in wild living. ¹⁴After he had spent everything, there was a severe famine in that whole country, and he began to be in need. ¹⁵So he went and hired himself out to a citizen of that country, who sent him to his fields to feed pigs. ¹⁶He longed to fill his stomach with the pods that the pigs were eating, but no one gave him anything.

¹⁷"When he came to his senses, he said, 'How many of my father's hired men have food to spare, and here I am starving to death! ¹⁸I will set out and go back to my father and say to him: Father, I have sinned against heaven and against you. ¹⁹I am no longer worthy to be called your

THE MESSAGE

14.34 "Salt is excellent. But if the salt goes flat, it's useless, good for nothing.

"Are you listening to this? Really listening?"

THE STORY OF THE LOST SHEEP

15.1-3 **15** By this time a lot of men and women of doubtful reputation were hanging around Jesus, listening intently. The Pharisees and religion scholars were not pleased, not at all pleased. They growled, "He takes in sinners and eats meals with them, treating them like old friends." Their grumbling triggered this story.

15.4-7 "Suppose one of you had a hundred sheep and lost one. Wouldn't you leave the ninety-nine in the wilderness and go after the lost one until you found it? When found, you can be sure you would put it across your shoulders, rejoicing, and when you got home call in your friends and neighbors, saying, 'Celebrate with me! I've found my lost sheep!' Count on it—there's more joy in heaven over one sinner's rescued life than over ninety-nine good people in no need of rescue.

THE STORY OF THE LOST COIN

15.8-10 "Or imagine a woman who has ten coins and loses one. Won't she light a lamp and scour the house, looking in every nook and cranny until she finds it? And when she finds it you can be sure she'll call her friends and neighbors: 'Celebrate with me! I found my lost coin!' Count on it—that's the kind of party God's angels throw every time one lost soul turns to God."

THE STORY OF THE LOST SON

15.11-12 Then he said, "There was once a man who had two sons. The younger said to his father, 'Father, I want right now what's coming to me.'

15.12-16 "So the father divided the property between them. It wasn't long before the younger son packed his bags and left for a distant country. There, undisciplined and dissipated, he wasted everything he had. After he had gone through all his money, there was a bad famine all through that country and he began to hurt. He signed on with a citizen there who assigned him to his fields to slop the pigs. He was so hungry he would have eaten the corncobs in the pig slop, but no one would give him any.

15.17-20 "That brought him to his senses. He said, 'All those farmhands working for my father sit down to three meals a day, and here I am starving to death. I'm going back to my father. I'll say to him, Father, I've sinned against God, I've sinned before you; I don't deserve to be called

---

ᵃ 8 Greek ten drachmas, each worth about a day's wages

NEW INTERNATIONAL VERSION

son; make me like one of your hired men.' ²⁰So he got up and went to his father.

"But while he was still a long way off, his father saw him and was filled with compassion for him; he ran to his son, threw his arms around him and kissed him.

²¹ "The son said to him, 'Father, I have sinned against heaven and against you. I am no longer worthy to be called your son.^{a'}

²² "But the father said to his servants, 'Quick! Bring the best robe and put it on him. Put a ring on his finger and sandals on his feet. ²³Bring the fattened calf and kill it. Let's have a feast and celebrate. ²⁴For this son of mine was dead and is alive again; he was lost and is found.' So they began to celebrate.

²⁵ "Meanwhile, the older son was in the field. When he came near the house, he heard music and dancing. ²⁶So he called one of the servants and asked him what was going on. ²⁷ 'Your brother has come,' he replied, 'and your father has killed the fattened calf because he has him back safe and sound.'

²⁸ "The older brother became angry and refused to go in. So his father went out and pleaded with him. ²⁹But he answered his father, 'Look! All these years I've been slaving for you and never disobeyed your orders. Yet you never gave me even a young goat so I could celebrate with my friends. ³⁰But when this son of yours who has squandered your property with prostitutes comes home, you kill the fattened calf for him!'

³¹ "'My son,' the father said, 'you are always with me, and everything I have is yours. ³²But we had to celebrate and be glad, because this brother of yours was dead and is alive again; he was lost and is found.' "

THE PARABLE OF THE SHREWD MANAGER

16 Jesus told his disciples: "There was a rich man whose manager was accused of wasting his possessions. ²So he called him in and asked him, 'What is this I hear about you? Give an account of your management, because you cannot be manager any longer.'

³ "The manager said to himself, 'What shall I do now? My master is taking away my job. I'm not strong enough to dig, and I'm ashamed to beg— ⁴I know what I'll do so that, when I lose my job here, people will welcome me into their houses.'

⁵ "So he called in each one of his master's debt-

THE MESSAGE

your son. Take me on as a hired hand.' He got right up and went home to his father.

15.20-21 "When he was still a long way off, his father saw him. His heart pounding, he ran out, embraced him, and kissed him. The son started his speech: 'Father, I've sinned against God, I've sinned before you; I don't deserve to be called your son ever again.'

15.22-24 "But the father wasn't listening. He was calling to the servants, 'Quick. Bring a clean set of clothes and dress him. Put the family ring on his finger and sandals on his feet. Then get a grain-fed heifer and roast it. We're going to feast! We're going to have a wonderful time! My son is here—given up for dead and now alive! Given up for lost and now found!' And they began to have a wonderful time.

15.25-27 "All this time his older son was out in the field. When the day's work was done he came in. As he approached the house, he heard the music and dancing. Calling over one of the houseboys, he asked what was going on. He told him, 'Your brother came home. Your father has ordered a feast—barbecued beef!—because he has him home safe and sound.'

15.28-30 "The older brother stalked off in an angry sulk and refused to join in. His father came out and tried to talk to him, but he wouldn't listen. The son said, 'Look how many years I've stayed here serving you, never giving you one moment of grief, but have you ever thrown a party for me and my friends? Then this son of yours who has thrown away your money on whores shows up and you go all out with a feast!'

15.31-32 "His father said, 'Son, you don't understand. You're with me all the time, and everything that is mine is yours—but this is a wonderful time, and we had to celebrate. This brother of yours was dead, and he's alive! He was lost, and he's found!' "

THE STORY OF THE CROOKED MANAGER

16.1-2 **16** Jesus said to his disciples, "There was once a rich man who had a manager. He got reports that the manager had been taking advantage of his position by running up huge personal expenses. So he called him in and said, 'What's this I hear about you? You're fired. And I want a complete audit of your books.'

16.3-4 "The manager said to himself, 'What am I going to do? I've lost my job as manager. I'm not strong enough for a laboring job, and I'm too proud to beg. . . . Ah, I've got a plan. Here's what I'll do . . . then when I'm turned out into the street, people will take me into their houses.'

16.5 "Then he went at it. One after another, he

NEW INTERNATIONAL VERSION

ors. He asked the first, 'How much do you owe my master?'

⁶ " 'Eight hundred gallons ͣ of olive oil,' he replied.

"The manager told him, 'Take your bill, sit down quickly, and make it four hundred.'

⁷ "Then he asked the second, 'And how much do you owe?'

" 'A thousand bushels ᵇ of wheat,' he replied.

"He told him, 'Take your bill and make it eight hundred.'

⁸ "The master commended the dishonest manager because he had acted shrewdly. For the people of this world are more shrewd in dealing with their own kind than are the people of the light. ⁹ I tell you, use worldly wealth to gain friends for yourselves, so that when it is gone, you will be welcomed into eternal dwellings.

¹⁰ "Whoever can be trusted with very little can also be trusted with much, and whoever is dishonest with very little will also be dishonest with much. ¹¹ So if you have not been trustworthy in handling worldly wealth, who will trust you with true riches? ¹² And if you have not been trustworthy with someone else's property, who will give you property of your own?

¹³ "No servant can serve two masters. Either he will hate the one and love the other, or he will be devoted to the one and despise the other. You cannot serve both God and Money."

¹⁴ The Pharisees, who loved money, heard all this and were sneering at Jesus. ¹⁵ He said to them, "You are the ones who justify yourselves in the eyes of men, but God knows your hearts. What is highly valued among men is detestable in God's sight.

ADDITIONAL TEACHINGS

¹⁶ "The Law and the Prophets were proclaimed until John. Since that time, the good news of the kingdom of God is being preached, and everyone is forcing his way into it. ¹⁷ It is easier for heaven and earth to disappear than for the least stroke of a pen to drop out of the Law.

¹⁸ "Anyone who divorces his wife and marries

ͣ 6 Greek one hundred batous (probably about 3 kiloliters)
ᵇ 7 Greek one hundred korous (probably about 35 kiloliters)

THE MESSAGE

called in the people who were in debt to his master. He said to the first, 'How much do you owe my master?'

16.6 "He replied, 'A hundred jugs of olive oil.'

"The manager said, 'Here, take your bill, sit down here—quick now—write "fifty."'

16.7 "To the next he said, 'And you, what do you owe?'

"He answered, 'A hundred sacks of wheat.'

"He said, 'Take your bill, write in eighty.'

16.8-9 "Now here's a surprise: The master praised the crooked manager! And why? Because he knew how to look after himself. Streetwise people are smarter in this regard than law-abiding citizens. They are on constant alert, looking for angles, surviving by their wits. I want you to be smart in the same way—but for what is *right*—using every adversity to stimulate you to creative survival, to concentrate your attention on the bare essentials, so you'll live, really live, and not complacently just get by on good behavior."

GOD SEES BEHIND APPEARANCES

16.10-13 Jesus went on to make these comments:

If you're honest in small things,
    you'll be honest in big things;
If you're a crook in small things,
    you'll be a crook in big things.
If you're not honest in small jobs,
    who will put you in charge of the store?
No worker can serve two bosses:
    He'll either hate the first and love the
        second
Or adore the first and despise the second.
    You can't serve both God and the Bank.

16.14-18 When the Pharisees, a money-obsessed bunch, heard him say these things, they rolled their eyes, dismissing him as hopelessly out of touch. So Jesus spoke to them: "You are masters at making yourselves look good in front of others, but God knows what's behind the appearance.

What society sees and calls monumental,
    God sees through and calls monstrous.
God's Law and the Prophets climaxed in
        John;
Now it's all kingdom of God—the glad
        news
    and compelling invitation to every man
        and woman.
The sky will disintegrate and the earth
        dissolve
    before a single letter of God's Law wears
        out.
Using the legalities of divorce

NEW INTERNATIONAL VERSION

another woman commits adultery, and the man who marries a divorced woman commits adultery.

THE RICH MAN AND LAZARUS

19"There was a rich man who was dressed in purple and fine linen and lived in luxury every day. 20At his gate was laid a beggar named Lazarus, covered with sores 21and longing to eat what fell from the rich man's table. Even the dogs came and licked his sores.

22"The time came when the beggar died and the angels carried him to Abraham's side. The rich man also died and was buried. 23In hell,ᵃ where he was in torment, he looked up and saw Abraham far away, with Lazarus by his side. 24So he called to him, 'Father Abraham, have pity on me and send Lazarus to dip the tip of his finger in water and cool my tongue, because I am in agony in this fire.'

25"But Abraham replied, 'Son, remember that in your lifetime you received your good things, while Lazarus received bad things, but now he is comforted here and you are in agony. 26And besides all this, between us and you a great chasm has been fixed, so that those who want to go from here to you cannot, nor can anyone cross over from there to us.'

27"He answered, 'Then I beg you, father, send Lazarus to my father's house, 28for I have five brothers. Let him warn them, so that they will not also come to this place of torment.'

29"Abraham replied, 'They have Moses and the Prophets; let them listen to them.'

30" 'No, father Abraham,' he said, 'but if someone from the dead goes to them, they will repent.'

31"He said to him, 'If they do not listen to Moses and the Prophets, they will not be convinced even if someone rises from the dead.' "

SIN, FAITH, DUTY

17 Jesus said to his disciples: "Things that cause people to sin are bound to come, but woe to that person through whom they come. 2It would be better for him to be thrown into the sea with a millstone tied around his neck than for him to cause one of these little ones to sin. 3So watch yourselves.

"If your brother sins, rebuke him, and if he repents, forgive him. 4If he sins against you seven

ᵃ 23 *Greek Hades*

THE MESSAGE

as a cover for lust is adultery;
Using the legalities of marriage
as a cover for lust is adultery.

THE RICH MAN AND LAZARUS

16.19-21 "There once was a rich man, expensively dressed in the latest fashions, wasting his days in conspicuous consumption. A poor man named Lazarus, covered with sores, had been dumped on his doorstep. All he lived for was to get a meal from scraps off the rich man's table. His best friends were the dogs who came and licked his sores.

16.22-24 "Then he died, this poor man, and was taken up by the angels to the lap of Abraham. The rich man also died and was buried. In hell and in torment, he looked up and saw Abraham in the distance and Lazarus in his lap. He called out, 'Father Abraham, mercy! Have mercy! Send Lazarus to dip his finger in water to cool my tongue. I'm in agony in this fire.'

16.25-26 "But Abraham said, 'Child, remember that in your lifetime you got the good things and Lazarus the bad things. It's not like that here. Here he's consoled and you're tormented. Besides, in all these matters there is a huge chasm set between us so that no one can go from us to you even if he wanted to, nor can anyone cross over from you to us.'

16.27-28 "The rich man said, 'Then let me ask you, Father: Send him to the house of my father where I have five brothers, so he can tell them the score and warn them so they won't end up here in this place of torment.'

16.29 "Abraham answered, 'They have Moses and the Prophets to tell them the score. Let them listen to them.'

16.30 " 'I know, Father Abraham,' he said, 'but they're not listening. If someone came back to them from the dead, they would change their ways.'

16.31 "Abraham replied, 'If they won't listen to Moses and the Prophets, they're not going to be convinced by someone who rises from the dead.' "

A KERNEL OF FAITH

17.1-2 **17** He said to his disciples, "Hard trials and temptations are bound to come, but too bad for whoever brings them on! Better to wear a millstone necklace and take a swim in the deep blue sea than give even one of these dear little ones a hard time!

17.3-4 "Be alert. If you see your friend going wrong, correct him. If he responds, forgive him. Even if it's personal against you and repeated seven

NEW INTERNATIONAL VERSION

times in a day, and seven times comes back to you and says, 'I repent,' forgive him."

⁵The apostles said to the Lord, "Increase our faith!"

⁶He replied, "If you have faith as small as a mustard seed, you can say to this mulberry tree, 'Be uprooted and planted in the sea,' and it will obey you.

⁷"Suppose one of you had a servant plowing or looking after the sheep. Would he say to the servant when he comes in from the field, 'Come along now and sit down to eat'? ⁸Would he not rather say, 'Prepare my supper, get yourself ready and wait on me while I eat and drink; after that you may eat and drink'? ⁹Would he thank the servant because he did what he was told to do? ¹⁰So you also, when you have done everything you were told to do, should say, 'We are unworthy servants; we have only done our duty.' "

TEN HEALED OF LEPROSY

¹¹Now on his way to Jerusalem, Jesus traveled along the border between Samaria and Galilee. ¹²As he was going into a village, ten men who had leprosy*a* met him. They stood at a distance ¹³and called out in a loud voice, "Jesus, Master, have pity on us!"

¹⁴When he saw them, he said, "Go, show yourselves to the priests." And as they went, they were cleansed.

¹⁵One of them, when he saw he was healed, came back, praising God in a loud voice. ¹⁶He threw himself at Jesus' feet and thanked him—and he was a Samaritan.

¹⁷Jesus asked, "Were not all ten cleansed? Where are the other nine? ¹⁸Was no one found to return and give praise to God except this foreigner?" ¹⁹Then he said to him, "Rise and go; your faith has made you well."

THE COMING OF THE KINGDOM OF GOD

²⁰Once, having been asked by the Pharisees when the kingdom of God would come, Jesus replied, "The kingdom of God does not come with your careful observation, ²¹nor will people say, 'Here it is,' or 'There it is,' because the kingdom of God is within*b* you."

²²Then he said to his disciples, "The time is coming when you will long to see one of the days of the Son of Man, but you will not see it. ²³Men will tell you, 'There he is!' or 'Here he is!' Do not go running off after them. ²⁴For the Son of Man in his day*c* will be like the lightning, which flash-

---

THE MESSAGE

times through the day, and seven times he says, 'I'm sorry, I won't do it again,' forgive him."

17.5 The apostles came up and said to the Master, "Give us more faith."

17.6 But the Master said, "You don't need *more* faith. There is no 'more' or 'less' in faith. If you have a bare kernel of faith, say the size of a poppy seed, you could say to this sycamore tree, 'Go jump in the lake,' and it would do it.

17.7-10 "Suppose one of you has a servant who comes in from plowing the field or tending the sheep. Would you take his coat, set the table, and say, 'Sit down and eat'? Wouldn't you be more likely to say, 'Prepare dinner; change your clothes and wait table for me until I've finished my coffee; then go to the kitchen and have your supper'? Does the servant get special thanks for doing what's expected of him? It's the same with you. When you've done everything expected of you, be matter-of-fact and say, 'The work is done. What we were told to do, we did.' "

17.11-13 It happened that as he made his way toward Jerusalem, he crossed over the border between Samaria and Galilee. As he entered a village, ten men, all lepers, met him. They kept their distance but raised their voices, calling out, "Jesus, Master, have mercy on us!"

17.14-16 Taking a good look at them, he said, "Go, show yourselves to the priests."

They went, and while still on their way, became clean. One of them, when he realized that he was healed, turned around and came back, shouting his gratitude, glorifying God. He kneeled at Jesus' feet, so grateful. He couldn't thank him enough—and he was a Samaritan.

17.17-19 Jesus said, "Were not ten healed? Where are the nine? Can none be found to come back and give glory to God except this outsider?" Then he said to him, "Get up. On your way. Your faith has healed and saved you."

WHEN THE SON OF MAN ARRIVES

17.20-21 Jesus, grilled by the Pharisees on when the kingdom of God would come, answered, "The kingdom of God doesn't come by counting the days on the calendar. Nor when someone says, 'Look here!' or, 'There it is!' And why? Because God's kingdom is already among you."

17.22-24 He went on to say to his disciples, "The days are coming when you are going to be desperately homesick for just a glimpse of one of the days of the Son of Man, and you won't see a thing. And they'll say to you, 'Look over there!' or, 'Look here!' Don't fall for any of that nonsense. The arrival of the Son of Man is not something you go out to see. He simply comes.

---

*a 12 The Greek word was used for various diseases affecting the skin—not necessarily leprosy.   b 21 Or among
c 24 Some manuscripts do not have in his day.*

NEW INTERNATIONAL VERSION

es and lights up the sky from one end to the other. 25But first he must suffer many things and be rejected by this generation.

26"Just as it was in the days of Noah, so also will it be in the days of the Son of Man. 27People were eating, drinking, marrying and being given in marriage up to the day Noah entered the ark. Then the flood came and destroyed them all.

28"It was the same in the days of Lot. People were eating and drinking, buying and selling, planting and building. 29But the day Lot left Sodom, fire and sulfur rained down from heaven and destroyed them all.

30"It will be just like this on the day the Son of Man is revealed. 31On that day no one who is on the roof of his house, with his goods inside, should go down to get them. Likewise, no one in the field should go back for anything. 32Remember Lot's wife! 33Whoever tries to keep his life will lose it, and whoever loses his life will preserve it. 34I tell you, on that night two people will be in one bed; one will be taken and the other left. 35Two women will be grinding grain together; one will be taken and the other left. *a*"

37"Where, Lord?" they asked.

He replied, "Where there is a dead body, there the vultures will gather."

THE PARABLE OF THE PERSISTENT WIDOW

18 Then Jesus told his disciples a parable to show them that they should always pray and not give up. 2He said: "In a certain town there was a judge who neither feared God nor cared about men. 3And there was a widow in that town who kept coming to him with the plea, 'Grant me justice against my adversary.'

4"For some time he refused. But finally he said to himself, 'Even though I don't fear God or care about men, 5yet because this widow keeps bothering me, I will see that she gets justice, so that she won't eventually wear me out with her coming!' "

6And the Lord said, "Listen to what the unjust judge says. 7And will not God bring about justice for his chosen ones, who cry out to him day and night? Will he keep putting them off? 8I tell you, he will see that they get justice, and quick-

---

THE MESSAGE

17.24-25 "You know how the whole sky lights up from a single flash of lightning? That's how it will be on the Day of the Son of Man. But first it's necessary that he suffer many things and be turned down by the people of today.

17.26-27 "The time of the Son of Man will be just like the time of Noah—everyone carrying on as usual, having a good time right up to the day Noah boarded the ship. They suspected nothing until the flood hit and swept everything away.

17.28-30 "It was the same in the time of Lot—the people carrying on, having a good time, business as usual right up to the day Lot walked out of Sodom and a firestorm swept down and burned everything to a crisp. That's how it will be—sudden, total—when the Son of Man is revealed.

17.31-33 "When the Day arrives and you're out working in the yard, don't run into the house to get anything. And if you're out in the field, don't go back and get your coat. Remember what happened to Lot's wife! If you grasp and cling to life on your terms, you'll lose it, but if you let that life go, you'll get life on God's terms.

17.34-35 "On that Day, two men will be in the same boat fishing—one taken, the other left. Two women will be working in the same kitchen—one taken, the other left."

17.37 Trying to take all this in, the disciples said, "Master, where?"

He told them, "Watch for the circling of the vultures. They'll spot the corpse first. The action will begin around my dead body."

THE STORY OF THE PERSISTENT WIDOW

18 Jesus told them a story showing that it was necessary for them to pray consistently and never quit. He said, "There was once a judge in some city who never gave God a thought and cared nothing for people. A widow in that city kept after him: 'My rights are being violated. Protect me!'

18.4-5 "He never gave her the time of day. But after this went on and on he said to himself, 'I care nothing what God thinks, even less what people think. But because this widow won't quit badgering me, I'd better do something and see that she gets justice—otherwise I'm going to end up beaten black and blue by her pounding.' "

18.6-8 Then the Master said, "Do you hear what that judge, corrupt as he is, is saying? So what makes you think God won't step in and work justice for his chosen people, who continue to cry out for help? Won't he stick up for them? I assure you, he will. He will not drag his feet. But how much of that kind of persistent faith

---

a 35 Some manuscripts left. 36Two men will be in the field; one will be taken and the other left.

NEW INTERNATIONAL VERSION

ly. However, when the Son of Man comes, will he find faith on the earth?"

THE PARABLE OF THE PHARISEE AND THE TAX COLLECTOR

⁹To some who were confident of their own righteousness and looked down on everybody else, Jesus told this parable: ¹⁰"Two men went up to the temple to pray, one a Pharisee and the other a tax collector. ¹¹The Pharisee stood up and prayed about*ᵃ* himself: 'God, I thank you that I am not like other men—robbers, evildoers, adulterers—or even like this tax collector. ¹²I fast twice a week and give a tenth of all I get.'

¹³"But the tax collector stood at a distance. He would not even look up to heaven, but beat his breast and said, 'God, have mercy on me, a sinner.'

¹⁴"I tell you that this man, rather than the other, went home justified before God. For everyone who exalts himself will be humbled, and he who humbles himself will be exalted."

THE LITTLE CHILDREN AND JESUS

¹⁵People were also bringing babies to Jesus to have him touch them. When the disciples saw this, they rebuked them. ¹⁶But Jesus called the children to him and said, "Let the little children come to me, and do not hinder them, for the kingdom of God belongs to such as these. ¹⁷I tell you the truth, anyone who will not receive the kingdom of God like a little child will never enter it."

THE RICH RULER

¹⁸A certain ruler asked him, "Good teacher, what must I do to inherit eternal life?"

¹⁹"Why do you call me good?" Jesus answered. "No one is good—except God alone. ²⁰You know the commandments: 'Do not commit adultery, do not murder, do not steal, do not give false testimony, honor your father and mother.'*ᵇ*"

²¹"All these I have kept since I was a boy," he said.

²²When Jesus heard this, he said to him, "You still lack one thing. Sell everything you have and give to the poor, and you will have treasure in heaven. Then come, follow me."

²³When he heard this, he became very sad, because he was a man of great wealth. ²⁴Jesus looked at him and said, "How hard it is for the

THE MESSAGE

will the Son of Man find on the earth when he returns?"

THE STORY OF THE TAX MAN AND THE PHARISEE

18.9-12 He told his next story to some who were complacently pleased with themselves over their moral performance and looked down their noses at the common people: "Two men went up to the Temple to pray, one a Pharisee, the other a tax man. The Pharisee posed and prayed like this: 'Oh, God, I thank you that I am not like other people—robbers, crooks, adulterers, or, heaven forbid, like this tax man. I fast twice a week and tithe on all my income.'

18.13 "Meanwhile the tax man, slumped in the shadows, his face in his hands, not daring to look up, said, 'God, give mercy. Forgive me, a sinner.'"

18.14 Jesus commented, "This tax man, not the other, went home made right with God. If you walk around with your nose in the air, you're going to end up flat on your face, but if you're content to be simply yourself, you will become more than yourself."

✝

18.15-17 People brought babies to Jesus, hoping he might touch them. When the disciples saw it, they shooed them off. Jesus called them back. "Let these children alone. Don't get between them and me. These children are the kingdom's pride and joy. Mark this: Unless you accept God's kingdom in the simplicity of a child, you'll never get in."

THE RICH OFFICIAL

18.18 One day one of the local officials asked him, "Good Teacher, what must I do to deserve eternal life?"

18.19-20 Jesus said, "Why are you calling me good? No one is good—only God. You know the commandments, don't you? No illicit sex, no killing, no stealing, no lying, honor your father and mother."

18.21 He said, "I've kept them all for as long as I can remember."

18.22 When Jesus heard that, he said, "Then there's only one thing left to do: Sell everything you own and give it away to the poor. You will have riches in heaven. Then come, follow me."

18.23 This was the last thing the official expected to hear. He was very rich and became terribly sad. He was holding on tight to a lot of things and not about to let them go.

18.24-25 Seeing his reaction, Jesus said, "Do you have any idea how difficult it is for people who have

---

ᵃ 11 Or *to* *ᵇ 20* Exodus 20:12-16; Deut. 5:16-20

NEW INTERNATIONAL VERSION	THE MESSAGE

NEW INTERNATIONAL VERSION

rich to enter the kingdom of God! ²⁵Indeed, it is easier for a camel to go through the eye of a needle than for a rich man to enter the kingdom of God."

²⁶Those who heard this asked, "Who then can be saved?"

²⁷Jesus replied, "What is impossible with men is possible with God."

²⁸Peter said to him, "We have left all we had to follow you!"

²⁹"I tell you the truth," Jesus said to them, "no one who has left home or wife or brothers or parents or children for the sake of the kingdom of God ³⁰will fail to receive many times as much in this age and, in the age to come, eternal life."

JESUS AGAIN PREDICTS HIS DEATH

³¹Jesus took the Twelve aside and told them, "We are going up to Jerusalem, and everything that is written by the prophets about the Son of Man will be fulfilled. ³²He will be handed over to the Gentiles. They will mock him, insult him, spit on him, flog him and kill him. ³³On the third day he will rise again."

³⁴The disciples did not understand any of this. Its meaning was hidden from them, and they did not know what he was talking about.

A BLIND BEGGAR RECEIVES HIS SIGHT

³⁵As Jesus approached Jericho, a blind man was sitting by the roadside begging. ³⁶When he heard the crowd going by, he asked what was happening. ³⁷They told him, "Jesus of Nazareth is passing by."

³⁸He called out, "Jesus, Son of David, have mercy on me!"

³⁹Those who led the way rebuked him and told him to be quiet, but he shouted all the more, "Son of David, have mercy on me!"

⁴⁰Jesus stopped and ordered the man to be brought to him. When he came near, Jesus asked him, ⁴¹"What do you want me to do for you?"

"Lord, I want to see," he replied.

⁴²Jesus said to him, "Receive your sight; your faith has healed you." ⁴³Immediately he received his sight and followed Jesus, praising God. When all the people saw it, they also praised God.

ZACCHAEUS THE TAX COLLECTOR

19 Jesus entered Jericho and was passing through. ²A man was there by the name of Zacchaeus; he was a chief tax collector and was wealthy. ³He wanted to see who Jesus was, but being a short man he could not, because of the crowd. ⁴So he ran ahead and climbed a syca-

THE MESSAGE

it all to enter God's kingdom? I'd say it's easier to thread a camel through a needle's eye than get a rich person into God's kingdom."

18.26 "Then who has any chance at all?" the others asked.

18.27 "No chance at all," Jesus said, "if you think you can pull it off by yourself. Every chance in the world if you trust God to do it."

18.28 Peter tried to regain some initiative: "We left everything we owned and followed you, didn't we?"

18.29-30 "Yes," said Jesus, "and you won't regret it. No one who has sacrificed home, spouse, brothers and sisters, parents, children—whatever—will lose out. It will all come back multiplied many times over in your lifetime. And then the bonus of eternal life!"

I WANT TO SEE AGAIN

18.31-34 Then Jesus took the Twelve off to the side and said, "Listen carefully. We're on our way up to Jerusalem. Everything written in the Prophets about the Son of Man will take place. He will be handed over to the Romans, jeered at, made sport of, and spit on. Then, after giving him the third degree, they will kill him. In three days he will rise, alive." But they didn't get it, could make neither heads nor tails of what he was talking about.

18.35-37 He came to the outskirts of Jericho. A blind man was sitting beside the road asking for handouts. When he heard the rustle of the crowd, he asked what was going on. They told him, "Jesus the Nazarene is going by."

18.38 He yelled, "Jesus! Son of David! Mercy, have mercy on me!"

18.39 Those ahead of Jesus told the man to shut up, but he only yelled all the louder, "Son of David! Mercy, have mercy on me!"

18.40 Jesus stopped and ordered him to be brought over. When he had come near, Jesus asked, "What do you want from me?"

18.41 He said, "Master, I want to see again."

18.42-43 Jesus said, "Go ahead—see again! Your faith has saved and healed you!" The healing was instant: He looked up, seeing—and then followed Jesus, glorifying God. Everyone in the street joined in, shouting praise to God.

ZACCHAEUS

19.1-4 **19** Then Jesus entered and walked through Jericho. There was a man there, his name Zacchaeus, the head tax man and quite rich. He wanted desperately to see Jesus, but the crowd was in his way—he was a short man and couldn't see over the crowd. So he ran on

NEW INTERNATIONAL VERSION

more-fig tree to see him, since Jesus was coming that way.

⁵When Jesus reached the spot, he looked up and said to him, "Zacchaeus, come down immediately. I must stay at your house today." ⁶So he came down at once and welcomed him gladly.

⁷All the people saw this and began to mutter, "He has gone to be the guest of a 'sinner.' "

⁸But Zacchaeus stood up and said to the Lord, "Look, Lord! Here and now I give half of my possessions to the poor, and if I have cheated anybody out of anything, I will pay back four times the amount."

⁹Jesus said to him, "Today salvation has come to this house, because this man, too, is a son of Abraham. ¹⁰For the Son of Man came to seek and to save what was lost."

THE PARABLE OF THE TEN MINAS

¹¹While they were listening to this, he went on to tell them a parable, because he was near Jerusalem and the people thought that the kingdom of God was going to appear at once. ¹²He said: "A man of noble birth went to a distant country to have himself appointed king and then to return. ¹³So he called ten of his servants and gave them ten minas.ᵃ 'Put this money to work,' he said, 'until I come back.'

¹⁴"But his subjects hated him and sent a delegation after him to say, 'We don't want this man to be our king.'

¹⁵"He was made king, however, and returned home. Then he sent for the servants to whom he had given the money, in order to find out what they had gained with it.

¹⁶"The first one came and said, 'Sir, your mina has earned ten more.'

¹⁷" 'Well done, my good servant!' his master replied. 'Because you have been trustworthy in a very small matter, take charge of ten cities.'

¹⁸"The second came and said, 'Sir, your mina has earned five more.'

¹⁹"His master answered, 'You take charge of five cities.'

²⁰"Then another servant came and said, 'Sir, here is your mina; I have kept it laid away in a piece of cloth. ²¹I was afraid of you, because you are a hard man. You take out what you did not put in and reap what you did not sow.'

²²"His master replied, 'I will judge you by your own words, you wicked servant! You knew, did you, that I am a hard man, taking out what I did not put in, and reaping what I did not sow? ²³Why then didn't you put my money on deposit, so that when I came back, I could have collected it with interest?'

ᵃ 13 A mina was about three months' wages.

THE MESSAGE

ahead and climbed up in a sycamore tree so he could see Jesus when he came by.

19.5-7   When Jesus got to the tree, he looked up and said, "Zacchaeus, hurry down. Today is my day to be a guest in your home." Zacchaeus scrambled out of the tree, hardly believing his good luck, delighted to take Jesus home with him. Everyone who saw the incident was indignant and grumped, "What business does he have getting cozy with this crook?"

19.8   Zacchaeus just stood there, a little stunned. He stammered apologetically, "Master, I give away half my income to the poor—and if I'm caught cheating, I pay four times the damages."

19.9-10   Jesus said, "Today is salvation day in this home! Here he is: Zacchaeus, son of Abraham! For the Son of Man came to find and restore the lost."

THE STORY ABOUT INVESTMENT

19.11   While he had their attention, and because they were getting close to Jerusalem by this time and expectation was building that God's kingdom would appear any minute, he told this story:

19.12-13   "There was once a man descended from a royal house who needed to make a long trip back to headquarters to get authorization for his rule and then return. But first he called ten servants together, gave them each a sum of money, and instructed them, 'Operate with this until I return.'

19.14   "But the citizens there hated him. So they sent a commission with a signed petition to oppose his rule: 'We don't want this man to rule us.'

19.15   "When he came back bringing the authorization of his rule, he called those ten servants to whom he had given the money to find out how they had done.

19.16   "The first said, 'Master, I doubled your money.'

19.17   "He said, 'Good servant! Great work! Because you've been trustworthy in this small job, I'm making you governor of ten towns.'

19.18   "The second said, 'Master, I made a fifty percent profit on your money.'

19.19   "He said, 'I'm putting you in charge of five towns.'

19.20-21   "The next servant said, 'Master, here's your money safe and sound. I kept it hidden in the cellar. To tell you the truth, I was a little afraid. I know you have high standards and hate sloppiness, and don't suffer fools gladly.'

19.22-23   "He said, 'You're right that I don't suffer fools gladly—and you've acted the fool! Why didn't you at least invest the money in securities so I would have gotten a little interest on it?'

NEW INTERNATIONAL VERSION

²⁴"Then he said to those standing by, 'Take his mina away from him and give it to the one who has ten minas.'

²⁵" 'Sir,' they said, 'he already has ten!'

²⁶"He replied, 'I tell you that to everyone who has, more will be given, but as for the one who has nothing, even what he has will be taken away. ²⁷But those enemies of mine who did not want me to be king over them—bring them here and kill them in front of me.' "

The Triumphal Entry

²⁸After Jesus had said this, he went on ahead, going up to Jerusalem. ²⁹As he approached Bethphage and Bethany at the hill called the Mount of Olives, he sent two of his disciples, saying to them, ³⁰"Go to the village ahead of you, and as you enter it, you will find a colt tied there, which no one has ever ridden. Untie it and bring it here. ³¹If anyone asks you, 'Why are you untying it?' tell him, 'The Lord needs it.' "

³²Those who were sent ahead went and found it just as he had told them. ³³As they were untying the colt, its owners asked them, "Why are you untying the colt?"

³⁴They replied, "The Lord needs it."

³⁵They brought it to Jesus, threw their cloaks on the colt and put Jesus on it. ³⁶As he went along, people spread their cloaks on the road.

³⁷When he came near the place where the road goes down the Mount of Olives, the whole crowd of disciples began joyfully to praise God in loud voices for all the miracles they had seen:

³⁸"Blessed is the king who comes in the name of the Lord!" ᵃ

"Peace in heaven and glory in the highest!"

³⁹Some of the Pharisees in the crowd said to Jesus, "Teacher, rebuke your disciples!"

⁴⁰"I tell you," he replied, "if they keep quiet, the stones will cry out."

⁴¹As he approached Jerusalem and saw the city, he wept over it ⁴²and said, "If you, even you, had only known on this day what would bring you peace—but now it is hidden from your eyes. ⁴³The days will come upon you when your enemies will build an embankment against you and encircle you and hem you in on every side. ⁴⁴They will dash you to the ground, you and the children within your walls. They will not leave one stone on another, because you did not recognize the time of God's coming to you."

Jesus at the Temple

⁴⁵Then he entered the temple area and began

THE MESSAGE

19.24 "Then he said to those standing there, 'Take the money from him and give it to the servant who doubled my stake.'

19.25 "They said, 'But Master, he already has double . . .'

19.26 "He said, 'That's what I mean: Risk your life and get more than you ever dreamed of. Play it safe and end up holding the bag.

19.27 " 'As for these enemies of mine who petitioned against my rule, clear them out of here. I don't want to see their faces around here again.' "

God's Personal Visit

19.28-31 After saying these things, Jesus headed straight up to Jerusalem. When he got near Bethphage and Bethany at the mountain called Olives, he sent off two of the disciples with instructions: "Go to the village across from you. As soon as you enter, you'll find a colt tethered, one that has never been ridden. Untie it and bring it. If anyone says anything, asks, 'What are you doing?' say, 'His Master needs him.' "

19.32-33 The two left and found it just as he said. As they were untying the colt, its owners said, "What are you doing untying the colt?"

19.34 They said, "His Master needs him."

19.35-36 They brought the colt to Jesus. Then, throwing their coats on its back, they helped Jesus get on. As he rode, the people gave him a grand welcome, throwing their coats on the street.

19.37-38 Right at the crest, where Mount Olives begins its descent, the whole crowd of disciples burst into enthusiastic praise over all the mighty works they had witnessed:

Blessed is he who comes,
    the king in God's name!
All's well in heaven!
    Glory in the high places!

19.39 Some Pharisees from the crowd told him, "Teacher, get your disciples under control!"

19.40 But he said, "If they kept quiet, the stones would do it for them, shouting praise."

19.41-44 When the city came into view, he wept over it. "If you had only recognized this day, and everything that was good for you! But now it's too late. In the days ahead your enemies are going to bring up their heavy artillery and surround you, pressing in from every side. They'll smash you and your babies on the pavement. Not one stone will be left intact. All this because you didn't recognize and welcome God's personal visit."

19.45-46 Going into the Temple he began to throw out

ᵃ *38* Psalm 118:26

NEW INTERNATIONAL VERSION

driving out those who were selling. 46"It is written," he said to them, " 'My house will be a house of prayer' *a*; but you have made it 'a den of robbers.' *b*"

47Every day he was teaching at the temple. But the chief priests, the teachers of the law and the leaders among the people were trying to kill him. 48Yet they could not find any way to do it, because all the people hung on his words.

THE AUTHORITY OF JESUS QUESTIONED

20 One day as he was teaching the people in the temple courts and preaching the gospel, the chief priests and the teachers of the law, together with the elders, came up to him. 2"Tell us by what authority you are doing these things," they said. "Who gave you this authority?"

3He replied, "I will also ask you a question. Tell me, 4John's baptism—was it from heaven, or from men?"

5They discussed it among themselves and said, "If we say, 'From heaven,' he will ask, 'Why didn't you believe him?' 6But if we say, 'From men,' all the people will stone us, because they are persuaded that John was a prophet."

7So they answered, "We don't know where it was from."

8Jesus said, "Neither will I tell you by what authority I am doing these things."

THE PARABLE OF THE TENANTS

9He went on to tell the people this parable: "A man planted a vineyard, rented it to some farmers and went away for a long time. 10At harvest time he sent a servant to the tenants so they would give him some of the fruit of the vineyard. But the tenants beat him and sent him away empty-handed. 11He sent another servant, but that one also they beat and treated shamefully and sent away empty-handed. 12He sent still a third, and they wounded him and threw him out.

13"Then the owner of the vineyard said, 'What shall I do? I will send my son, whom I love; perhaps they will respect him.'

14"But when the tenants saw him, they talked the matter over. 'This is the heir,' they said. 'Let's kill him, and the inheritance will be ours.' 15So they threw him out of the vineyard and killed him.

"What then will the owner of the vineyard do

THE MESSAGE

everyone who had set up shop, selling everything and anything. He said, "It's written in Scripture,

My house is a house of prayer;
You have turned it into a religious bazaar."

19.47-48   From then on he taught each day in the Temple. The high priests, religion scholars, and the leaders of the people were trying their best to find a way to get rid of him. But with the people hanging on every word he spoke, they couldn't come up with anything.

20 One day he was teaching the people in the Temple, proclaiming the Message. The high priests, religion scholars, and leaders confronted him and demanded, "Show us your credentials. Who authorized you to speak and act like this?"

20.3-4   Jesus answered, "First, let me ask you a question: About the baptism of John—who authorized it, heaven or humans?"

20.5-7   They were on the spot, and knew it. They pulled back into a huddle and whispered, "If we say 'heaven,' he'll ask us why we didn't believe him; if we say 'humans,' the people will tear us limb from limb, convinced as they are that John was God's prophet." They agreed to concede that round to Jesus and said they didn't know.

20.8   Jesus said, "Then neither will I answer your question."

THE STORY OF CORRUPT FARMHANDS

20.9-12 Jesus told another story to the people: "A man planted a vineyard. He handed it over to farmhands and went off on a trip. He was gone a long time. In time he sent a servant back to the farmhands to collect the profits, but they beat him up and sent him off empty-handed. He decided to try again and sent another servant. That one they beat black and blue, and sent him off empty-handed. He tried a third time. They worked that servant over from head to foot and dumped him in the street.

20.13   "Then the owner of the vineyard said, 'I know what I'll do: I'll send my beloved son. They're bound to respect my son.'

20.14-15   "But when the farmhands saw him coming, they quickly put their heads together. 'This is our chance—this is the heir! Let's kill him and have it all to ourselves.' They killed him and threw him over the fence.

20.15-16   "What do you think the owner of the vineyard

NEW INTERNATIONAL VERSION

to them? ¹⁶He will come and kill those tenants and give the vineyard to others."

When the people heard this, they said, "May this never be!"

¹⁷Jesus looked directly at them and asked, "Then what is the meaning of that which is written:

" 'The stone the builders rejected
has become the capstone*ᵃ*ᵇ*?

¹⁸Everyone who falls on that stone will be broken to pieces, but he on whom it falls will be crushed."

¹⁹The teachers of the law and the chief priests looked for a way to arrest him immediately, because they knew he had spoken this parable against them. But they were afraid of the people.

PAYING TAXES TO CAESAR

²⁰Keeping a close watch on him, they sent spies, who pretended to be honest. They hoped to catch Jesus in something he said so that they might hand him over to the power and authority of the governor. ²¹So the spies questioned him: "Teacher, we know that you speak and teach what is right, and that you do not show partiality but teach the way of God in accordance with the truth. ²²Is it right for us to pay taxes to Caesar or not?"

²³He saw through their duplicity and said to them, ²⁴"Show me a denarius. Whose portrait and inscription are on it?"

²⁵"Caesar's," they replied.

He said to them, "Then give to Caesar what is Caesar's, and to God what is God's."

²⁶They were unable to trap him in what he had said there in public. And astonished by his answer, they became silent.

THE RESURRECTION AND MARRIAGE

²⁷Some of the Sadducees, who say there is no resurrection, came to Jesus with a question. ²⁸"Teacher," they said, "Moses wrote for us that if a man's brother dies and leaves a wife but no children, the man must marry the widow and have children for his brother. ²⁹Now there were seven brothers. The first one married a woman and died childless. ³⁰The second ³¹and then the third married her, and in the same way the seven died, leaving no children. ³²Finally, the woman died too. ³³Now then, at the resurrection whose wife will she be, since the seven were married to her?"

³⁴Jesus replied, "The people of this age marry and are given in marriage. ³⁵But those who are considered worthy of taking part in that age and

---

THE MESSAGE

will do? Right. He'll come and clean house. Then he'll assign the care of the vineyard to others."

Those who were listening said, "Oh, no! He'd never do that!"

20.17-18 But Jesus didn't back down. "Why, then, do you think this was written:

That stone the masons threw out—
It's now the cornerstone!?

"Anyone falling over that stone will break every bone in his body; if the stone falls on anyone, it will be a total smashup."

20.19 The religion scholars and high priests wanted to lynch him on the spot, but they were intimidated by public opinion. They knew the story was about them.

PAYING TAXES

20.20-22 Watching for a chance to get him, they sent spies who posed as honest inquirers, hoping to trick him into saying something that would get him in trouble with the law. So they asked him, "Teacher, we know that you're honest and straightforward when you teach, that you don't pander to anyone but teach the way of God accurately. Tell us: Is it lawful to pay taxes to Caesar or not?"

20.23-24 He knew they were laying for him and said, "Show me a coin. Now, this engraving, who does it look like and what does it say?"

20.25 "Caesar," they said.

Jesus said, "Then give Caesar what is his and give God what is his."

20.26 Try as they might, they couldn't trap him into saying anything incriminating. His answer caught them off guard and left them speechless.

ALL INTIMACIES WILL BE WITH GOD

20.27-33 Some Sadducees came up. This is the Jewish party that denies any possibility of resurrection. They asked, "Teacher, Moses wrote us that if a man dies and leaves a wife but no child, his brother is obligated to take the widow to wife and get her with child. Well, there once were seven brothers. The first took a wife. He died childless. The second married her and died, then the third, and eventually all seven had their turn, but no child. After all that, the wife died. That wife, now—in the resurrection whose wife is she? All seven married her."

20.34-38 Jesus said, "Marriage is a major preoccupation here, but not there. Those who are includ-

---

ᵃ 17 Or *cornerstone*   *ᵇ* 17 Psalm 118:22

NEW INTERNATIONAL VERSION

in the resurrection from the dead will neither marry nor be given in marriage, ³⁶and they can no longer die; for they are like the angels. They are God's children, since they are children of the resurrection. ³⁷But in the account of the bush, even Moses showed that the dead rise, for he calls the Lord 'the God of Abraham, and the God of Isaac, and the God of Jacob.'ᵃ ³⁸He is not the God of the dead, but of the living, for to him all are alive."

³⁹Some of the teachers of the law responded, "Well said, teacher!" ⁴⁰And no one dared to ask him any more questions.

WHOSE SON IS THE CHRIST?

⁴¹Then Jesus said to them, "How is it that they say the Christᵇ is the Son of David? ⁴²David himself declares in the Book of Psalms:

" 'The Lord said to my Lord:
  "Sit at my right hand
⁴³until I make your enemies
  a footstool for your feet." 'ᶜ

⁴⁴David calls him 'Lord.' How then can he be his son?"

⁴⁵While all the people were listening, Jesus said to his disciples, ⁴⁶"Beware of the teachers of the law. They like to walk around in flowing robes and love to be greeted in the marketplaces and have the most important seats in the synagogues and the places of honor at banquets. ⁴⁷They devour widows' houses and for a show make lengthy prayers. Such men will be punished most severely."

THE WIDOW'S OFFERING

21 As he looked up, Jesus saw the rich putting their gifts into the temple treasury. ²He also saw a poor widow put in two very small copper coins.ᵈ ³"I tell you the truth," he said, "this poor widow has put in more than all the others. ⁴All these people gave their gifts out of their wealth; but she out of her poverty put in all she had to live on."

SIGNS OF THE END OF THE AGE

⁵Some of his disciples were remarking about how the temple was adorned with beautiful stones and with gifts dedicated to God. But Jesus said, ⁶"As for what you see here, the time will come when not one stone will be left on another; every one of them will be thrown down."

⁷"Teacher," they asked, "when will these things happen? And what will be the sign that they are about to take place?"

ᵃ 37 Exodus 3:6   ᵇ 41 Or Messiah   ᶜ 43 Psalm 110:1
ᵈ 2 Greek two lepta

THE MESSAGE

ed in the resurrection of the dead will no longer be concerned with marriage nor, of course, with death. They will have better things to think about, if you can believe it. All ecstasies and intimacies then will be with God. Even Moses exclaimed about resurrection at the burning bush, saying, 'God: God of Abraham, God of Isaac, God of Jacob!' God isn't the God of dead men, but of the living. To him all are alive."

20.39-40   Some of the religion scholars said, "Teacher, that's a great answer!" For a while, anyway, no one dared put questions to him.

✝

20.41-44   Then he put a question to them: "How is it that they say that the Messiah is David's son? In the Book of Psalms, David clearly says,

God said to my Master,
"Sit here at my right hand
  until I put your enemies under your
    feet."

"David here designates the Messiah as 'my Master'—so how can the Messiah also be his 'son'?"

20.45-47   With everybody listening, Jesus spoke to his disciples. "Watch out for the religion scholars. They love to walk around in academic gowns, preen in the radiance of public flattery, bask in prominent positions, sit at the head table at every church function. And all the time they are exploiting the weak and helpless. The longer their prayers, the worse they get. But they'll pay for it in the end."

20.1-4   **21** Just then he looked up and saw the rich people dropping offerings in the collection plate. Then he saw a poor widow put in two pennies. He said, "The plain truth is that this widow has given by far the largest offering today. All these others made offerings that they'll never miss; she gave extravagantly what she couldn't afford—she gave her all!"

WATCH OUT FOR DOOMSDAY DECEIVERS

21.5-6   One day people were standing around talking about the Temple, remarking how beautiful it was, the splendor of its stonework and memorial gifts. Jesus said, "All this you're admiring so much—the time is coming when every stone in that building will end up in a heap of rubble."

21.7   They asked him, "Teacher, when is this going to happen? What clue will we get that it's about to take place?"

NEW INTERNATIONAL VERSION

⁸He replied: "Watch out that you are not deceived. For many will come in my name, claiming, 'I am he,' and, 'The time is near.' Do not follow them. ⁹When you hear of wars and revolutions, do not be frightened. These things must happen first, but the end will not come right away."

¹⁰Then he said to them: "Nation will rise against nation, and kingdom against kingdom. ¹¹There will be great earthquakes, famines and pestilences in various places, and fearful events and great signs from heaven.

¹²"But before all this, they will lay hands on you and persecute you. They will deliver you to synagogues and prisons, and you will be brought before kings and governors, and all on account of my name. ¹³This will result in your being witnesses to them. ¹⁴But make up your mind not to worry beforehand how you will defend yourselves. ¹⁵For I will give you words and wisdom that none of your adversaries will be able to resist or contradict. ¹⁶You will be betrayed even by parents, brothers, relatives and friends, and they will put some of you to death. ¹⁷All men will hate you because of me. ¹⁸But not a hair of your head will perish. ¹⁹By standing firm you will gain life.

²⁰"When you see Jerusalem being surrounded by armies, you will know that its desolation is near. ²¹Then let those who are in Judea flee to the mountains, let those in the city get out, and let those in the country not enter the city. ²²For this is the time of punishment in fulfillment of all that has been written. ²³How dreadful it will be in those days for pregnant women and nursing mothers! There will be great distress in the land and wrath against this people. ²⁴They will fall by the sword and will be taken as prisoners to all the nations. Jerusalem will be trampled on by the Gentiles until the times of the Gentiles are fulfilled.

²⁵"There will be signs in the sun, moon and stars. On the earth, nations will be in anguish and perplexity at the roaring and tossing of the sea. ²⁶Men will faint from terror, apprehensive of what is coming on the world, for the heavenly bodies will be shaken. ²⁷At that time they will see the Son of Man coming in a cloud with power and great glory. ²⁸When these things begin to take place, stand up and lift up your heads, because your redemption is drawing near."

²⁹He told them this parable: "Look at the fig tree and all the trees. ³⁰When they sprout leaves, you can see for yourselves and know that sum-

THE MESSAGE

21.8-9 He said, "Watch out for the doomsday deceivers. Many leaders are going to show up with forged identities claiming, 'I'm the One,' or, 'The end is near.' Don't fall for any of that. When you hear of wars and uprisings, keep your head and don't panic. This is routine history and no sign of the end."

21.10-11 He went on, "Nation will fight nation and ruler fight ruler, over and over. Huge earthquakes will occur in various places. There will be famines. You'll think at times that the very sky is falling.

21.12-15 "But before any of this happens, they'll arrest you, hunt you down, and drag you to court and jail. It will go from bad to worse, dog-eat-dog, everyone at your throat because you carry my name. You'll end up on the witness stand, called to testify. Make up your mind right now not to worry about it. I'll give you the words and wisdom that will reduce all your accusers to stammers and stutters.

21.16-19 "You'll even be turned in by parents, brothers, relatives, and friends. Some of you will be killed. There's no telling who will hate you because of me. Even so, every detail of your body and soul—even the hairs of your head!—is in my care; nothing of you will be lost. Staying with it—that's what is required. Stay with it to the end. You won't be sorry; you'll be saved.

VENGEANCE DAY

21.20-24 "When you see soldiers camped all around Jerusalem, then you'll know that she is about to be devastated. If you're living in Judea at the time, run for the hills. If you're in the city, get out quickly. If you're out in the fields, don't go home to get your coat. This is Vengeance Day—everything written about it will come to a head. Pregnant and nursing mothers will have it especially hard. Incredible misery! Torrential rage! People dropping like flies; people dragged off to prisons; Jerusalem under the boot of barbarians until the nations finish what was given them to do.

21.25-26 "It will seem like all hell has broken loose—sun, moon, stars, earth, sea, in an uproar and everyone all over the world in a panic, the wind knocked out of them by the threat of doom, the powers-that-be quaking.

21.27-28 "And then—then!—they'll see the Son of Man welcomed in grand style—a glorious welcome! When all this starts to happen, up on your feet. Stand tall with your heads high. Help is on the way!"

21.29-33 He told them a story. "Look at a fig tree. Any tree for that matter. When the leaves begin to show, one look tells you that summer is right

NEW INTERNATIONAL VERSION

mer is near. ³¹Even so, when you see these things happening, you know that the kingdom of God is near.

³²"I tell you the truth, this generation^a will certainly not pass away until all these things have happened. ³³Heaven and earth will pass away, but my words will never pass away.

³⁴"Be careful, or your hearts will be weighed down with dissipation, drunkenness and the anxieties of life, and that day will close on you unexpectedly like a trap. ³⁵For it will come upon all those who live on the face of the whole earth. ³⁶Be always on the watch, and pray that you may be able to escape all that is about to happen, and that you may be able to stand before the Son of Man."

³⁷Each day Jesus was teaching at the temple, and each evening he went out to spend the night on the hill called the Mount of Olives, ³⁸and all the people came early in the morning to hear him at the temple.

JUDAS AGREES TO BETRAY JESUS

22 Now the Feast of Unleavened Bread, called the Passover, was approaching, ²and the chief priests and the teachers of the law were looking for some way to get rid of Jesus, for they were afraid of the people. ³Then Satan entered Judas, called Iscariot, one of the Twelve. ⁴And Judas went to the chief priests and the officers of the temple guard and discussed with them how he might betray Jesus. ⁵They were delighted and agreed to give him money. ⁶He consented, and watched for an opportunity to hand Jesus over to them when no crowd was present.

THE LAST SUPPER

⁷Then came the day of Unleavened Bread on which the Passover lamb had to be sacrificed. ⁸Jesus sent Peter and John, saying, "Go and make preparations for us to eat the Passover."

⁹"Where do you want us to prepare for it?" they asked.

¹⁰He replied, "As you enter the city, a man carrying a jar of water will meet you. Follow him to the house that he enters, ¹¹and say to the owner of the house, 'The Teacher asks: Where is the guest room, where I may eat the Passover with my disciples?' ¹²He will show you a large upper room, all furnished. Make preparations there."

¹³They left and found things just as Jesus had told them. So they prepared the Passover.

¹⁴When the hour came, Jesus and his apostles reclined at the table. ¹⁵And he said to them, "I

^a 32 Or race

THE MESSAGE

around the corner. The same here—when you see these things happen, you know God's kingdom is about here. Don't brush this off: I'm not just saying this for some future generation, but for this one, too—these things will happen. Sky and earth will wear out; my words won't wear out.

21.34-36   "But be on your guard. Don't let the sharp edge of your expectation get dulled by parties and drinking and shopping. Otherwise, that Day is going to take you by complete surprise, spring on you suddenly like a trap, for it's going to come on everyone, everywhere, at once. So, whatever you do, don't go to sleep at the switch. Pray constantly that you will have the strength and wits to make it through everything that's coming and end up on your feet before the Son of Man."

21.37-38   He spent his days in the Temple teaching, but his nights out on the mountain called Olives. All the people were up at the crack of dawn to come to the Temple and listen to him.

THE PASSOVER MEAL

22.1-2   **22** The Feast of Unleavened Bread, also called Passover, drew near. The high priests and religion scholars were looking for a way to do away with Jesus but, fearful of the people, they were also looking for a way to cover their tracks.

22.3-6   That's when Satan entered Judas, the one called Iscariot. He was one of the Twelve. Leaving the others, he conferred with the high priests and the Temple guards about how he might betray Jesus to them. They couldn't believe their good luck and agreed to pay him well. He gave them his word and started looking for a way to betray Jesus, but out of sight of the crowd.

22.7-8   The Day of Unleavened Bread came, the day the Passover lamb was butchered. Jesus sent Peter and John off, saying, "Go prepare the Passover for us so we can eat it together."

22.9   They said, "Where do you want us to do this?"

22.10-12   He said, "Keep your eyes open as you enter the city. A man carrying a water jug will meet you. Follow him home. Then speak with the owner of the house: The Teacher wants to know, 'Where is the guest room where I can eat the Passover meal with my disciples?' He will show you a spacious second-story room, swept and ready. Prepare the meal there."

22.13   They left, found everything just as he told them, and prepared the Passover meal.

22.14-16   When it was time, he sat down, all the apostles with him, and said, "You've no idea how

NEW INTERNATIONAL VERSION

have eagerly desired to eat this Passover with you before I suffer. ¹⁶For I tell you, I will not eat it again until it finds fulfillment in the kingdom of God."

¹⁷After taking the cup, he gave thanks and said, "Take this and divide it among you. ¹⁸For I tell you I will not drink again of the fruit of the vine until the kingdom of God comes."

¹⁹And he took bread, gave thanks and broke it, and gave it to them, saying, "This is my body given for you; do this in remembrance of me."

²⁰In the same way, after the supper he took the cup, saying, "This cup is the new covenant in my blood, which is poured out for you. ²¹But the hand of him who is going to betray me is with mine on the table. ²²The Son of Man will go as it has been decreed, but woe to that man who betrays him." ²³They began to question among themselves which of them it might be who would do this.

²⁴Also a dispute arose among them as to which of them was considered to be greatest. ²⁵Jesus said to them, "The kings of the Gentiles lord it over them; and those who exercise authority over them call themselves Benefactors. ²⁶But you are not to be like that. Instead, the greatest among you should be like the youngest, and the one who rules like the one who serves. ²⁷For who is greater, the one who is at the table or the one who serves? Is it not the one who is at the table? But I am among you as one who serves. ²⁸You are those who have stood by me in my trials. ²⁹And I confer on you a kingdom, just as my Father conferred one on me, ³⁰so that you may eat and drink at my table in my kingdom and sit on thrones, judging the twelve tribes of Israel.

³¹"Simon, Simon, Satan has asked to sift you*ᵃ* as wheat. ³²But I have prayed for you, Simon, that your faith may not fail. And when you have turned back, strengthen your brothers."

³³But he replied, "Lord, I am ready to go with you to prison and to death."

³⁴Jesus answered, "I tell you, Peter, before the rooster crows today, you will deny three times that you know me."

³⁵Then Jesus asked them, "When I sent you

THE MESSAGE

much I have looked forward to eating this Passover meal with you before I enter my time of suffering. It's the last one I'll eat until we all eat it together in the kingdom of God."

22.17-18 Taking the cup, he blessed it, then said, "Take this and pass it among you. As for me, I'll not drink wine again until the kingdom of God arrives."

22.19 Taking bread, he blessed it, broke it, and gave it to them, saying, "This is my body, given for you. Eat it in my memory."

22.20 He did the same with the cup after supper, saying, "This cup is the new covenant written in my blood, blood poured out for you.

22.21-22 "Do you realize that the hand of the one who is betraying me is at this moment on this table? It's true that the Son of Man is going down a path already marked out—no surprises there. But for the one who turns him in, turns traitor to the Son of Man, this is doomsday."

22.23 They immediately became suspicious of each other and began quizzing one another, wondering who might be about to do this.

GET READY FOR TROUBLE

22.24-26 Within minutes they were bickering over who of them would end up the greatest. But Jesus intervened: "Kings like to throw their weight around and people in authority like to give themselves fancy titles. It's not going to be that way with you. Let the senior among you become like the junior; let the leader act the part of the servant.

22.27-30 "Who would you rather be: the one who eats the dinner or the one who serves the dinner? You'd rather eat and be served, right? But I've taken my place among you as the one who serves. And you've stuck with me through thick and thin. Now I confer on you the royal authority my Father conferred on me so you can eat and drink at my table in my kingdom and be strengthened as you take up responsibilities among the congregations of God's people.

22.31-32 "Simon, stay on your toes. Satan has tried his best to separate all of you from me, like chaff from wheat. Simon, I've prayed for you in particular that you not give in or give out. When you have come through the time of testing, turn to your companions and give them a fresh start."

22.33 Peter said, "Master, I'm ready for anything with you. I'd go to jail for you. I'd *die* for you!"

22.34 Jesus said, "I'm sorry to have to tell you this, Peter, but before the rooster crows you will have three times denied that you know me."

22.35 Then Jesus said, "When I sent you out and

ᵃ 31 The Greek is plural.

| NEW INTERNATIONAL VERSION | THE MESSAGE |

without purse, bag or sandals, did you lack anything?"

"Nothing," they answered.

³⁶He said to them, "But now if you have a purse, take it, and also a bag; and if you don't have a sword, sell your cloak and buy one. ³⁷It is written: 'And he was numbered with the transgressors'ᵃ; and I tell you that this must be fulfilled in me. Yes, what is written about me is reaching its fulfillment."

³⁸The disciples said, "See, Lord, here are two swords."

"That is enough," he replied.

JESUS PRAYS ON THE MOUNT OF OLIVES

³⁹Jesus went out as usual to the Mount of Olives, and his disciples followed him. ⁴⁰On reaching the place, he said to them, "Pray that you will not fall into temptation." ⁴¹He withdrew about a stone's throw beyond them, knelt down and prayed, ⁴²"Father, if you are willing, take this cup from me; yet not my will, but yours be done." ⁴³An angel from heaven appeared to him and strengthened him. ⁴⁴And being in anguish, he prayed more earnestly, and his sweat was like drops of blood falling to the ground.ᵇ

⁴⁵When he rose from prayer and went back to the disciples, he found them asleep, exhausted from sorrow. ⁴⁶"Why are you sleeping?" he asked them. "Get up and pray so that you will not fall into temptation."

JESUS ARRESTED

⁴⁷While he was still speaking a crowd came up, and the man who was called Judas, one of the Twelve, was leading them. He approached Jesus to kiss him, ⁴⁸but Jesus asked him, "Judas, are you betraying the Son of Man with a kiss?"

⁴⁹When Jesus' followers saw what was going to happen, they said, "Lord, should we strike with our swords?" ⁵⁰And one of them struck the servant of the high priest, cutting off his right ear.

⁵¹But Jesus answered, "No more of this!" And he touched the man's ear and healed him.

⁵²Then Jesus said to the chief priests, the officers of the temple guard, and the elders, who had come for him, "Am I leading a rebellion, that you have come with swords and clubs? ⁵³Every day I was with you in the temple courts, and you did not lay a hand on me. But this is your hour—when darkness reigns."

PETER DISOWNS JESUS

⁵⁴Then seizing him, they led him away and

---

told you to travel light, to take only the bare necessities, did you get along all right?"

"Certainly," they said, "we got along just fine."

22.36-37 He said, "This is different. Get ready for trouble. Look to what you'll need; there are difficult times ahead. Pawn your coat and get a sword. What was written in Scripture, 'He was lumped in with the criminals,' gets its final meaning in me. Everything written about me is now coming to a conclusion."

22.38 They said, "Look, Master, two swords!"

But he said, "Enough of that; no more sword talk!"

A DARK NIGHT

22.39-40 Leaving there, he went, as he so often did, to Mount Olives. The disciples followed him. When they arrived at the place, he said, "Pray that you don't give in to temptation."

22.41-44 He pulled away from them about a stone's throw, knelt down, and prayed, "Father, remove this cup from me. But please, not what I want. What do *you* want?" At once an angel from heaven was at his side, strengthening him. He prayed on all the harder. Sweat, wrung from him like drops of blood, poured off his face.

22.45-46 He got up from prayer, went back to the disciples and found them asleep, drugged by grief. He said, "What business do you have sleeping? Get up. Pray so you won't give in to temptation."

22.47-48 No sooner were the words out of his mouth than a crowd showed up, Judas, the one from the Twelve, in the lead. He came right up to Jesus to kiss him. Jesus said, "Judas, you would betray the Son of Man with a kiss?"

22.49-50 When those with him saw what was happening, they said, "Master, shall we fight?" One of them took a swing at the Chief Priest's servant and cut off his right ear.

22.51 Jesus said, "Let them be. Even in this." Then, touching the servant's ear, he healed him.

22.52-53 Jesus spoke to those who had come—high priests, Temple police, religion leaders: "What is this, jumping me with swords and clubs as if I were a dangerous criminal? Day after day I've been with you in the Temple and you've not so much as lifted a hand against me. But do it your way—it's a dark night, a dark hour."

A ROOSTER CROWED

22.54-56 Arresting Jesus, they marched him off and took

ᵃ 37 Isaiah 53:12   ᵇ 44 Some early manuscripts do not have verses 43 and 44.

NEW INTERNATIONAL VERSION

took him into the house of the high priest. Peter followed at a distance. ⁵⁵But when they had kindled a fire in the middle of the courtyard and had sat down together, Peter sat down with them. ⁵⁶A servant girl saw him seated there in the firelight. She looked closely at him and said, "This man was with him."

⁵⁷But he denied it. "Woman, I don't know him," he said.

⁵⁸A little later someone else saw him and said, "You also are one of them."

"Man, I am not!" Peter replied.

⁵⁹About an hour later another asserted, "Certainly this fellow was with him, for he is a Galilean."

⁶⁰Peter replied, "Man, I don't know what you're talking about!" Just as he was speaking, the rooster crowed. ⁶¹The Lord turned and looked straight at Peter. Then Peter remembered the word the Lord had spoken to him: "Before the rooster crows today, you will disown me three times." ⁶²And he went outside and wept bitterly.

THE GUARDS MOCK JESUS

⁶³The men who were guarding Jesus began mocking and beating him. ⁶⁴They blindfolded him and demanded, "Prophesy! Who hit you?" ⁶⁵And they said many other insulting things to him.

JESUS BEFORE PILATE AND HEROD

⁶⁶At daybreak the council of the elders of the people, both the chief priests and teachers of the law, met together, and Jesus was led before them. ⁶⁷"If you are the Christ,ᵃ" they said, "tell us."

Jesus answered, "If I tell you, you will not believe me, ⁶⁸and if I asked you, you would not answer. ⁶⁹But from now on, the Son of Man will be seated at the right hand of the mighty God."

⁷⁰They all asked, "Are you then the Son of God?"

He replied, "You are right in saying I am."

⁷¹Then they said, "Why do we need any more testimony? We have heard it from his own lips."

23 Then the whole assembly rose and led him off to Pilate. ²And they began to accuse him, saying, "We have found this man subverting our nation. He opposes payment of taxes to Caesar and claims to be Christ,ᵇ a king."

THE MESSAGE

him into the house of the Chief Priest. Peter followed, but at a safe distance. In the middle of the courtyard some people had started a fire and were sitting around it, trying to keep warm. One of the serving maids sitting at the fire noticed him, then took a second look and said, "This man was with him!"

22.57 He denied it, "Woman, I don't even know him."

22.58 A short time later, someone else noticed him and said, "You're one of them."

But Peter denied it: "Man, I am not."

22.59 About an hour later, someone else spoke up, really adamant: "He's got to have been with him! He's got 'Galilean' written all over him."

22.60-62 Peter said, "Man, I don't know what you're talking about." At that very moment, the last word hardly off his lips, a rooster crowed. Just then, the Master turned and looked at Peter. Peter remembered what the Master had said to him: "Before the rooster crows, you will deny me three times." He went out and cried and cried and cried.

SLAPPING HIM AROUND

22.63-65 The men in charge of Jesus began poking fun at him, slapping him around. They put a blindfold on him and taunted, "Who hit you that time?" They were having a grand time with him.

22.66-67 When it was morning, the religious leaders of the people and the high priests and scholars all got together and brought him before their High Council. They said, "Are you the Messiah?"

22.67-69 He answered, "If I said yes, you wouldn't believe me. If I asked what you meant by your question, you wouldn't answer me. So here's what I have to say: From here on the Son of Man takes his place at God's right hand, the place of power."

22.70 They all said, "So you admit your claim to be the Son of God?"

"You're the ones who keep saying it," he said.

22.71 But they had made up their minds, "Why do we need any more evidence? We've all heard him as good as say it himself."

PILATE

23.1-2 **23** Then they all took Jesus to Pilate and began to bring up charges against him. They said, "We found this man undermining our law and order, forbidding taxes to be paid to Caesar, setting himself up as Messiah-King."

ᵃ 67 Or *Messiah*   ᵇ 2 Or *Messiah*; also in verses 35 and 39

NEW INTERNATIONAL VERSION

³So Pilate asked Jesus, "Are you the king of the Jews?"

"Yes, it is as you say," Jesus replied.

⁴Then Pilate announced to the chief priests and the crowd, "I find no basis for a charge against this man."

⁵But they insisted, "He stirs up the people all over Judea*a* by his teaching. He started in Galilee and has come all the way here."

⁶On hearing this, Pilate asked if the man was a Galilean. ⁷When he learned that Jesus was under Herod's jurisdiction, he sent him to Herod, who was also in Jerusalem at that time.

⁸When Herod saw Jesus, he was greatly pleased, because for a long time he had been wanting to see him. From what he had heard about him, he hoped to see him perform some miracle. ⁹He plied him with many questions, but Jesus gave him no answer. ¹⁰The chief priests and the teachers of the law were standing there, vehemently accusing him. ¹¹Then Herod and his soldiers ridiculed and mocked him. Dressing him in an elegant robe, they sent him back to Pilate. ¹²That day Herod and Pilate became friends—before this they had been enemies.

¹³Pilate called together the chief priests, the rulers and the people, ¹⁴and said to them, "You brought me this man as one who was inciting the people to rebellion. I have examined him in your presence and have found no basis for your charges against him. ¹⁵Neither has Herod, for he sent him back to us; as you can see, he has done nothing to deserve death. ¹⁶Therefore, I will punish him and then release him.*b*"

¹⁸With one voice they cried out, "Away with this man! Release Barabbas to us!" ¹⁹(Barabbas had been thrown into prison for an insurrection in the city, and for murder.)

²⁰Wanting to release Jesus, Pilate appealed to them again. ²¹But they kept shouting, "Crucify him! Crucify him!"

²²For the third time he spoke to them: "Why? What crime has this man committed? I have found in him no grounds for the death penalty. Therefore I will have him punished and then release him."

²³But with loud shouts they insistently demanded that he be crucified, and their shouts prevailed. ²⁴So Pilate decided to grant their demand. ²⁵He released the man who had been thrown into prison for insurrection and murder, the one they asked for, and surrendered Jesus to their will.

a 5 Or over the land of the Jews   b 16 Some manuscripts him." 17Now he was obliged to release one man to them at the Feast.

THE MESSAGE

23.3   Pilate asked him, "Is this true that you're 'King of the Jews'?"

"Those are your words, not mine," Jesus replied.

23.4   Pilate told the high priests and the accompanying crowd, "I find nothing wrong here. He seems harmless enough to me."

23.5   But they were vehement. "He's stirring up unrest among the people with his teaching, disturbing the peace everywhere, starting in Galilee and now all through Judea. He's a dangerous man, endangering the peace."

23.6-7   When Pilate heard that, he asked, "So, he's a Galilean?" Realizing that he properly came under Herod's jurisdiction, he passed the buck to Herod, who just happened to be in Jerusalem for a few days.

23.8-10   Herod was delighted when Jesus showed up. He had wanted for a long time to see him, he'd heard so much about him. He hoped to see him do something spectacular. He peppered him with questions. Jesus didn't answer—not one word. But the high priests and religion scholars were right there, saying their piece, strident and shrill in their accusations.

23.11-12   Mightily offended, Herod turned on Jesus. His soldiers joined in, taunting and jeering. Then they dressed him up in an elaborate king costume and sent him back to Pilate. That day Herod and Pilate became thick as thieves. Always before they had kept their distance.

23.13-16   Then Pilate called in the high priests, rulers, and the others and said, "You brought this man to me as a disturber of the peace. I examined him in front of all of you and found there was nothing to your charge. And neither did Herod, for he has sent him back here with a clean bill of health. It's clear that he's done nothing wrong, let alone anything deserving death. I'm going to warn him to watch his step and let him go."

23.18-20   At that, the crowd went wild: "Kill him! Give us Barabbas!" (Barabbas had been thrown in prison for starting a riot in the city and for murder.) Pilate still wanted to let Jesus go, and so spoke out again.

23.21   But they kept shouting back, "Crucify! Crucify him!"

23.22   He tried a third time. "But for what crime? I've found nothing in him deserving death. I'm going to warn him to watch his step and let him go."

23.23-25   But they kept at it, a shouting mob, demanding that he be crucified. And finally they shouted him down. Pilate caved in and gave them what they wanted. He released the man thrown in prison for rioting and murder, and gave them Jesus to do whatever they wanted.

NEW INTERNATIONAL VERSION

THE CRUCIFIXION

²⁶As they led him away, they seized Simon from Cyrene, who was on his way in from the country, and put the cross on him and made him carry it behind Jesus. ²⁷A large number of people followed him, including women who mourned and wailed for him. ²⁸Jesus turned and said to them, "Daughters of Jerusalem, do not weep for me; weep for yourselves and for your children. ²⁹For the time will come when you will say, 'Blessed are the barren women, the wombs that never bore and the breasts that never nursed!' ³⁰Then

" 'they will say to the mountains, "Fall on us!"
and to the hills, "Cover us!" ' ᵃ

³¹For if men do these things when the tree is green, what will happen when it is dry?"

³²Two other men, both criminals, were also led out with him to be executed. ³³When they came to the place called the Skull, there they crucified him, along with the criminals—one on his right, the other on his left. ³⁴Jesus said, "Father, forgive them, for they do not know what they are doing." ᵇ And they divided up his clothes by casting lots.

³⁵The people stood watching, and the rulers even sneered at him. They said, "He saved others; let him save himself if he is the Christ of God, the Chosen One."

³⁶The soldiers also came up and mocked him. They offered him wine vinegar ³⁷and said, "If you are the king of the Jews, save yourself."

³⁸There was a written notice above him, which read: THIS IS THE KING OF THE JEWS.

³⁹One of the criminals who hung there hurled insults at him: "Aren't you the Christ? Save yourself and us!"

⁴⁰But the other criminal rebuked him. "Don't you fear God," he said, "since you are under the same sentence? ⁴¹We are punished justly, for we are getting what our deeds deserve. But this man has done nothing wrong."

⁴²Then he said, "Jesus, remember me when you come into your kingdom. ᶜ "

⁴³Jesus answered him, "I tell you the truth, today you will be with me in paradise."

JESUS' DEATH

⁴⁴It was now about the sixth hour, and darkness came over the whole land until the ninth hour, ⁴⁵for the sun stopped shining. And the curtain of the temple was torn in two. ⁴⁶Jesus called

---

THE MESSAGE

SKULL HILL

23.26-31 As they led him off, they made Simon, a man from Cyrene who happened to be coming in from the countryside, carry the cross behind Jesus. A huge crowd of people followed, along with women weeping and carrying on. At one point Jesus turned to the women and said, "Daughters of Jerusalem, don't cry for me. Cry for yourselves and for your children. The time is coming when they'll say, 'Lucky the women who never conceived! Lucky the wombs that never gave birth! Lucky the breasts that never gave milk!' Then they'll start calling to the mountains, 'Fall down on us!' calling to the hills, 'Cover us up!' If people do these things to a live, green tree, can you imagine what they'll do with deadwood?"

23.32 Two others, both criminals, were taken along with him for execution.

23.33 When they got to the place called Skull Hill, they crucified him, along with the criminals, one on his right, the other on his left.

23.34-35 Jesus prayed, "Father, forgive them; they don't know what they're doing."

Dividing up his clothes, they threw dice for them. The people stood there staring at Jesus, and the ringleaders made faces, taunting, "He saved others. Let's see him save himself! The Messiah of God—ha! The Chosen—ha!"

23.36-37 The soldiers also came up and poked fun at him, making a game of it. They toasted him with sour wine: "So you're King of the Jews! Save yourself!"

23.38 Printed over him was a sign: THIS IS THE KING OF THE JEWS.

23.39 One of the criminals hanging alongside cursed him: "Some Messiah you are! Save yourself! Save us!"

23.40-41 But the other one made him shut up: "Have you no fear of God? You're getting the same as him. We deserve this, but not him—he did nothing to deserve this."

23.42 Then he said, "Jesus, remember me when you enter your kingdom."

23.43 He said, "Don't worry, I will. Today you will join me in paradise."

23.44-46 By now it was noon. The whole earth became dark, the darkness lasting three hours—a total blackout. The Temple curtain split right

---

ᵃ 30 Hosea 10:8   ᵇ 34 Some early manuscripts do not have this sentence.   ᶜ 42 Some manuscripts come with your kingly power

NEW INTERNATIONAL VERSION

out with a loud voice, "Father, into your hands I commit my spirit." When he had said this, he breathed his last.

⁴⁷The centurion, seeing what had happened, praised God and said, "Surely this was a righteous man." ⁴⁸When all the people who had gathered to witness this sight saw what took place, they beat their breasts and went away. ⁴⁹But all those who knew him, including the women who had followed him from Galilee, stood at a distance, watching these things.

JESUS' BURIAL

⁵⁰Now there was a man named Joseph, a member of the Council, a good and upright man, ⁵¹who had not consented to their decision and action. He came from the Judean town of Arimathea and he was waiting for the kingdom of God. ⁵²Going to Pilate, he asked for Jesus' body. ⁵³Then he took it down, wrapped it in linen cloth and placed it in a tomb cut in the rock, one in which no one had yet been laid. ⁵⁴It was Preparation Day, and the Sabbath was about to begin.

⁵⁵The women who had come with Jesus from Galilee followed Joseph and saw the tomb and how his body was laid in it. ⁵⁶Then they went home and prepared spices and perfumes. But they rested on the Sabbath in obedience to the commandment.

THE RESURRECTION

24 On the first day of the week, very early in the morning, the women took the spices they had prepared and went to the tomb. ²They found the stone rolled away from the tomb, ³but when they entered, they did not find the body of the Lord Jesus. ⁴While they were wondering about this, suddenly two men in clothes that gleamed like lightning stood beside them. ⁵In their fright the women bowed down with their faces to the ground, but the men said to them, "Why do you look for the living among the dead? ⁶He is not here; he has risen! Remember how he told you, while he was still with you in Galilee: ⁷'The Son of Man must be delivered into the hands of sinful men, be crucified and on the third day be raised again.' " ⁸Then they remembered his words.

⁹When they came back from the tomb, they told all these things to the Eleven and to all the others. ¹⁰It was Mary Magdalene, Joanna, Mary the mother of James, and the others with them who told this to the apostles. ¹¹But they did not believe the women, because their words seemed

THE MESSAGE

down the middle. Jesus called loudly, "Father, I place my life in your hands!" Then he breathed his last.

✠

23.47 When the captain there saw what happened, he honored God: "This man was innocent! A good man, and innocent!"

23.48-49 All who had come around as spectators to watch the show, when they saw what actually happened, were overcome with grief and headed home. Those who knew Jesus well, along with the women who had followed him from Galilee, stood at a respectful distance and kept vigil.

23.50-54 There was a man by the name of Joseph, a member of the Jewish High Council, a man of good heart and good character. He had not gone along with the plans and actions of the council. His hometown was the Jewish village of Arimathea. He lived in alert expectation of the kingdom of God. He went to Pilate and asked for the body of Jesus. Taking him down, he wrapped him in a linen shroud and placed him in a tomb chiseled into the rock, a tomb never yet used. It was the day before Sabbath, the Sabbath just about to begin.

23.55-56 The women who had been companions of Jesus from Galilee followed along. They saw the tomb where Jesus' body was placed. Then they went back to prepare burial spices and perfumes. They rested quietly on the Sabbath, as commanded.

LOOKING FOR THE LIVING ONE IN A CEMETERY

24.1-3 **24** At the crack of dawn on Sunday, the women came to the tomb carrying the burial spices they had prepared. They found the entrance stone rolled back from the tomb, so they walked in. But once inside, they couldn't find the body of the Master Jesus.

24.4-8 They were puzzled, wondering what to make of this. Then, out of nowhere it seemed, two men, light cascading over them, stood there. The women were awestruck and bowed down in worship. The men said, "Why are you looking for the Living One in a cemetery? He is not here, but raised up. Remember how he told you when you were still back in Galilee that he had to be handed over to sinners, be killed on a cross, and in three days rise up?" Then they remembered Jesus' words.

24.9-11 They left the tomb and broke the news of all this to the Eleven and the rest. Mary Magdalene, Joanna, Mary the mother of James, and the other women with them kept telling these things to the apostles, but the apostles didn't believe a word of it, thought they were making it all up.

NEW INTERNATIONAL VERSION

to them like nonsense. ¹²Peter, however, got up and ran to the tomb. Bending over, he saw the strips of linen lying by themselves, and he went away, wondering to himself what had happened.

ON THE ROAD TO EMMAUS

¹³Now that same day two of them were going to a village called Emmaus, about seven miles^a from Jerusalem. ¹⁴They were talking with each other about everything that had happened. ¹⁵As they talked and discussed these things with each other, Jesus himself came up and walked along with them; ¹⁶but they were kept from recognizing him.

¹⁷He asked them, "What are you discussing together as you walk along?"

They stood still, their faces downcast. ¹⁸One of them, named Cleopas, asked him, "Are you only a visitor to Jerusalem and do not know the things that have happened there in these days?"

¹⁹"What things?" he asked.

"About Jesus of Nazareth," they replied. "He was a prophet, powerful in word and deed before God and all the people. ²⁰The chief priests and our rulers handed him over to be sentenced to death, and they crucified him; ²¹but we had hoped that he was the one who was going to redeem Israel. And what is more, it is the third day since all this took place. ²²In addition, some of our women amazed us. They went to the tomb early this morning ²³but didn't find his body. They came and told us that they had seen a vision of angels, who said he was alive. ²⁴Then some of our companions went to the tomb and found it just as the women had said, but him they did not see."

²⁵He said to them, "How foolish you are, and how slow of heart to believe all that the prophets have spoken! ²⁶Did not the Christ^b have to suffer these things and then enter his glory?" ²⁷And beginning with Moses and all the Prophets, he explained to them what was said in all the Scriptures concerning himself.

²⁸As they approached the village to which they were going, Jesus acted as if he were going farther. ²⁹But they urged him strongly, "Stay with us, for it is nearly evening; the day is almost over." So he went in to stay with them.

³⁰When he was at the table with them, he took bread, gave thanks, broke it and began to give it to them. ³¹Then their eyes were opened and they recognized him, and he disappeared from their sight. ³²They asked each other, "Were

THE MESSAGE

²⁴·¹² But Peter jumped to his feet and ran to the tomb. He stooped to look in and saw a few grave clothes, that's all. He walked away puzzled, shaking his head.

THE ROAD TO EMMAUS

²⁴·¹³⁻¹⁶ That same day two of them were walking to the village Emmaus, about seven miles out of Jerusalem. They were deep in conversation, going over all these things that had happened. In the middle of their talk and questions, Jesus came up and walked along with them. But they were not able to recognize who he was.

²⁴·¹⁷⁻¹⁸ He asked, "What's this you're discussing so intently as you walk along?"

They just stood there, long-faced, like they had lost their best friend. Then one of them, his name was Cleopas, said, "Are you the only one in Jerusalem who hasn't heard what's happened during the last few days?"

²⁴·¹⁹ He said, "What has happened?"

²⁴·¹⁹⁻²⁴ They said, "The things that happened to Jesus the Nazarene. He was a man of God, a prophet, dynamic in work and word, blessed by both God and all the people. Then our high priests and leaders betrayed him, got him sentenced to death, and crucified him. And we had our hopes up that he was the One, the One about to deliver Israel. And it is now the third day since it happened. But now some of our women have completely confused us. Early this morning they were at the tomb and couldn't find his body. They came back with the story that they had seen a vision of angels who said he was alive. Some of our friends went off to the tomb to check and found it empty just as the women said, but they didn't see Jesus."

²⁴·²⁵⁻²⁷ Then he said to them, "So thick-headed! So slow-hearted! Why can't you simply believe all that the prophets said? Don't you see that these things had to happen, that the Messiah had to suffer and only then enter into his glory?" Then he started at the beginning, with the Books of Moses, and went on through all the Prophets, pointing out everything in the Scriptures that referred to him.

²⁴·²⁸⁻³¹ They came to the edge of the village where they were headed. He acted as if he were going on but they pressed him: "Stay and have supper with us. It's nearly evening; the day is done." So he went in with them. And here is what happened: He sat down at the table with them. Taking the bread, he blessed and broke and gave it to them. At that moment, open-eyed, wide-eyed, they recognized him. And then he disappeared.

²⁴·³² Back and forth they talked. "Didn't we feel

^a 13 Greek *sixty stadia* (about 11 kilometers)
^b 26 Or *Messiah*; also in verse 46

NEW INTERNATIONAL VERSION

not our hearts burning within us while he talked with us on the road and opened the Scriptures to us?"

33They got up and returned at once to Jerusalem. There they found the Eleven and those with them, assembled together 34and saying, "It is true! The Lord has risen and has appeared to Simon." 35Then the two told what had happened on the way, and how Jesus was recognized by them when he broke the bread.

JESUS APPEARS TO THE DISCIPLES

36While they were still talking about this, Jesus himself stood among them and said to them, "Peace be with you."

37They were startled and frightened, thinking they saw a ghost. 38He said to them, "Why are you troubled, and why do doubts rise in your minds? 39Look at my hands and my feet. It is I myself! Touch me and see; a ghost does not have flesh and bones, as you see I have."

40When he had said this, he showed them his hands and feet. 41And while they still did not believe it because of joy and amazement, he asked them, "Do you have anything here to eat?" 42They gave him a piece of broiled fish, 43and he took it and ate it in their presence.

44He said to them, "This is what I told you while I was still with you: Everything must be fulfilled that is written about me in the Law of Moses, the Prophets and the Psalms."

45Then he opened their minds so they could understand the Scriptures. 46He told them, "This is what is written: The Christ will suffer and rise from the dead on the third day, 47and repentance and forgiveness of sins will be preached in his name to all nations, beginning at Jerusalem. 48You are witnesses of these things. 49I am going to send you what my Father has promised; but stay in the city until you have been clothed with power from on high."

THE ASCENSION

50When he had led them out to the vicinity of Bethany, he lifted up his hands and blessed them. 51While he was blessing them, he left them and was taken up into heaven. 52Then they worshiped him and returned to Jerusalem with great joy. 53And they stayed continually at the temple, praising God.

THE MESSAGE

on fire as he conversed with us on the road, as he opened up the Scriptures for us?"

A GHOST DOESN'T HAVE MUSCLE AND BONE

24.33-34 They didn't waste a minute. They were up and on their way back to Jerusalem. They found the Eleven and their friends gathered together, talking away: "It's really happened! The Master has been raised up—Simon saw him!"

24.35   Then the two went over everything that happened on the road and how they recognized him when he broke the bread.

24.36-41   While they were saying all this, Jesus appeared to them and said, "Peace be with you." They thought they were seeing a ghost and were scared half to death. He continued with them, "Don't be upset, and don't let all these doubting questions take over. Look at my hands; look at my feet—it's really me. Touch me. Look me over from head to toe. A ghost doesn't have muscle and bone like this." As he said this, he showed them his hands and feet. They still couldn't believe what they were seeing. It was too much; it seemed too good to be true.

24.41-43   He asked, "Do you have any food here?" They gave him a piece of leftover fish they had cooked. He took it and ate it right before their eyes.

YOU'RE THE WITNESSES

24.44 Then he said, "Everything I told you while I was with you comes to this: All the things written about me in the Law of Moses, in the Prophets, and in the Psalms have to be fulfilled."

24.45-49   He went on to open their understanding of the Word of God, showing them how to read their Bibles this way. He said, "You can see now how it is written that the Messiah suffers, rises from the dead on the third day, and then a total life-change through the forgiveness of sins is proclaimed in his name to all nations—starting from here, from Jerusalem! You're the first to hear and see it. You're the witnesses. What comes next is very important: I am sending what my Father promised to you, so stay here in the city until he arrives, until you're equipped with power from on high."

24.50-51   He then led them out of the city over to Bethany. Raising his hands he blessed them, and while blessing them, took his leave, being carried up to heaven.

24.52-53   And they were on their knees, worshiping him. They returned to Jerusalem bursting with joy. They spent all their time in the Temple praising God. Yes.

JOHN

JOHN

THE WORD BECAME FLESH

1 In the beginning was the Word, and the Word was with God, and the Word was God. ²He was with God in the beginning.

³Through him all things were made; without him nothing was made that has been made. ⁴In him was life, and that life was the light of men. ⁵The light shines in the darkness, but the darkness has not understood[a] it.

⁶There came a man who was sent from God; his name was John. ⁷He came as a witness to testify concerning that light, so that through him all men might believe. ⁸He himself was not the light; he came only as a witness to the light. ⁹The true light that gives light to every man was coming into the world.[b]

¹⁰He was in the world, and though the world was made through him, the world did not recognize him. ¹¹He came to that which was his own, but his own did not receive him. ¹²Yet to all who received him, to those who believed in his name, he gave the right to become children of God— ¹³children born not of natural descent,[c] nor of human decision or a husband's will, but born of God.

¹⁴The Word became flesh and made his dwelling among us. We have seen his glory, the glory of the One and Only,[d] who came from the Father, full of grace and truth.

¹⁵John testifies concerning him. He cries out, saying, "This was he of whom I said, 'He who

THE LIFE-LIGHT

1 The Word was first,
    the Word present to God,
    God present to the Word.
The Word was God,
    in readiness for God from day one.

^{1.3-5} Everything was created through him;
    nothing—not one thing!—
    came into being without him.
What came into existence was Life,
    and the Life was Light to live by.
The Life-Light blazed out of the darkness;
    the darkness couldn't put it out.

^{1.6-8} There once was a man, his name John, sent
by God to point out the way to the Life-Light.
He came to show everyone where to look, who
to believe in. John was not himself the Light;
he was there to show the way to the Light.

^{1.9-13} The Life-Light was the real thing:
    Every person entering Life
    he brings into Light.
He was in the world,
    the world was there through him,
    and yet the world didn't even notice.
He came to his own people,
    but they didn't want him.
But whoever did want him,
    who believed he was who he claimed
    and would do what he said,
He made to be their true selves,
    their child-of-God selves.
These are the God-begotten,
    not blood-begotten,
    not flesh-begotten,
    not sex-begotten.

^{1.14} The Word became flesh and blood,
    and moved into the neighborhood.
We saw the glory with our own eyes,
    the one-of-a-kind glory,
    like Father, like Son,
Generous inside and out,
    true from start to finish.

^{1.15} John pointed him out and called, "This is the One! The One I told you was coming after me

---

[a] 5 Or *darkness, and the darkness has not overcome*
[b] 9 Or *This was the true light that gives light to every man who comes into the world*   [c] 13 Greek *of bloods*
[d] 14 Or *the Only Begotten*

NEW INTERNATIONAL VERSION

comes after me has surpassed me because he was before me.' " ¹⁶From the fullness of his grace we have all received one blessing after another. ¹⁷For the law was given through Moses; grace and truth came through Jesus Christ. ¹⁸No one has ever seen God, but God the One and Only,ᵃ,ᵇ who is at the Father's side, has made him known.

JOHN THE BAPTIST DENIES BEING THE CHRIST

¹⁹Now this was John's testimony when the Jews of Jerusalem sent priests and Levites to ask him who he was. ²⁰He did not fail to confess, but confessed freely, "I am not the Christ.ᶜ"

²¹They asked him, "Then who are you? Are you Elijah?"

He said, "I am not."

"Are you the Prophet?"

He answered, "No."

²²Finally they said, "Who are you? Give us an answer to take back to those who sent us. What do you say about yourself?"

²³John replied in the words of Isaiah the prophet, "I am the voice of one calling in the desert, 'Make straight the way for the Lord.' "ᵈ

²⁴Now some Pharisees who had been sent ²⁵questioned him, "Why then do you baptize if you are not the Christ, nor Elijah, nor the Prophet?"

²⁶"I baptize withᵉ water," John replied, "but among you stands one you do not know. ²⁷He is the one who comes after me, the thongs of whose sandals I am not worthy to untie."

²⁸This all happened at Bethany on the other side of the Jordan, where John was baptizing.

JESUS THE LAMB OF GOD

²⁹The next day John saw Jesus coming toward him and said, "Look, the Lamb of God, who takes away the sin of the world! ³⁰This is the one I meant when I said, 'A man who comes after me has surpassed me because he was before me.' ³¹I myself did not know him, but the reason I came baptizing with water was that he might be revealed to Israel."

ᵃ 18 Or the Only Begotten   ᵇ 18 Some manuscripts but the only (or only begotten) Son   ᶜ 20 Or Messiah. "The Christ" (Greek) and "the Messiah" (Hebrew) both mean "the Anointed One"; also in verse 25.   ᵈ 23 Isaiah 40:3   ᵉ 26 Or in; also in verses 31 and 33

THE MESSAGE

but in fact was ahead of me. He has always been ahead of me, has always had the first word."

1.16-18   We all live off his generous bounty,
            gift after gift after gift.
        We got the basics from Moses,
            and then this exuberant giving and
                receiving,
        This endless knowing and understanding—
            all this came through Jesus, the Messiah.
        No one has ever seen God,
            not so much as a glimpse.
        This one-of-a-kind God-Expression,
            who exists at the very heart of the
                Father,
        has made him plain as day.

THUNDER IN THE DESERT

1.19-20   When Jews from Jerusalem sent a group of priests and officials to ask John who he was, he was completely honest. He didn't evade the question. He told the plain truth: "I am not the Messiah."

1.21   They pressed him, "Who, then? Elijah?"
        "I am not."
        "The Prophet?"
        "No."

1.22   Exasperated, they said, "Who, then? We need an answer for those who sent us. Tell us something—anything!—about yourself."

1.23   "I'm thunder in the desert: 'Make the road straight for God!' I'm doing what the prophet Isaiah preached."

1.24-25   Those sent to question him were from the Pharisee party. Now they had a question of their own: "If you're neither the Messiah, nor Elijah, nor the Prophet, why do you baptize?"

1.26-27   John answered, "I only baptize using water. A person you don't recognize has taken his stand in your midst. He comes after me, but he is not in second place to me. I'm not even worthy to hold his coat for him."

1.28   These conversations took place in Bethany on the other side of the Jordan, where John was baptizing at the time.

THE GOD-REVEALER

1.29-31   The very next day John saw Jesus coming toward him and yelled out, "Here he is, God's Passover Lamb! He forgives the sins of the world! This is the man I've been talking about, 'the One who comes after me but is really ahead of me.' I knew nothing about who he was—only this: that my task has been to get Israel ready to recognize him as the God-Revealer. That is why I came here baptizing with water, giving you a good bath and scrubbing sins from your life so you can get a fresh start with God."

NEW INTERNATIONAL VERSION

³²Then John gave this testimony: "I saw the Spirit come down from heaven as a dove and remain on him. ³³I would not have known him, except that the one who sent me to baptize with water told me, 'The man on whom you see the Spirit come down and remain is he who will baptize with the Holy Spirit.' ³⁴I have seen and I testify that this is the Son of God."

JESUS' FIRST DISCIPLES

³⁵The next day John was there again with two of his disciples. ³⁶When he saw Jesus passing by, he said, "Look, the Lamb of God!"

³⁷When the two disciples heard him say this, they followed Jesus. ³⁸Turning around, Jesus saw them following and asked, "What do you want?"

They said, "Rabbi" (which means Teacher), "where are you staying?"

³⁹"Come," he replied, "and you will see."

So they went and saw where he was staying, and spent that day with him. It was about the tenth hour.

⁴⁰Andrew, Simon Peter's brother, was one of the two who heard what John had said and who had followed Jesus. ⁴¹The first thing Andrew did was to find his brother Simon and tell him, "We have found the Messiah" (that is, the Christ). ⁴²And he brought him to Jesus.

Jesus looked at him and said, "You are Simon son of John. You will be called Cephas" (which, when translated, is Peter*ᵃ*).

JESUS CALLS PHILIP AND NATHANAEL

⁴³The next day Jesus decided to leave for Galilee. Finding Philip, he said to him, "Follow me."

⁴⁴Philip, like Andrew and Peter, was from the town of Bethsaida. ⁴⁵Philip found Nathanael and told him, "We have found the one Moses wrote about in the Law, and about whom the prophets also wrote—Jesus of Nazareth, the son of Joseph."

⁴⁶"Nazareth! Can anything good come from there?" Nathanael asked.

"Come and see," said Philip.

⁴⁷When Jesus saw Nathanael approaching, he said of him, "Here is a true Israelite, in whom there is nothing false."

⁴⁸"How do you know me?" Nathanael asked.

Jesus answered, "I saw you while you were still under the fig tree before Philip called you."

⁴⁹Then Nathanael declared, "Rabbi, you are the Son of God; you are the King of Israel."

⁵⁰Jesus said, "You believeᵇ because I told you I saw you under the fig tree. You shall see greater

---

ᵃ 42 Both Cephas (Aramaic) and Peter (Greek) mean rock.
ᵇ 50 Or Do you believe . . . ?

THE MESSAGE

1.32-34 John clinched his witness with this: "I watched the Spirit, like a dove flying down out of the sky, making himself at home in him. I repeat, I know nothing about him except this: The One who authorized me to baptize with water told me, 'The One on whom you see the Spirit come down and stay, this One will baptize with the Holy Spirit.' That's exactly what I saw happen, and I'm telling you, there's no question about it: *This* is the Son of God."

COME, SEE FOR YOURSELF

1.35-36 The next day John was back at his post with two disciples, who were watching. He looked up, saw Jesus walking nearby, and said, "Here he is, God's Passover Lamb."

1.37-38 The two disciples heard him and went after Jesus. Jesus looked over his shoulder and said to them, "What are you after?"

They said, "Rabbi" (which means "Teacher"), "where are you staying?"

1.39 He replied, "Come along and see for yourself."

They came, saw where he was living, and ended up staying with him for the day. It was late afternoon when this happened.

1.40-42 Andrew, Simon Peter's brother, was one of the two who heard John's witness and followed Jesus. The first thing he did after finding where Jesus lived was find his own brother, Simon, telling him, "We've found the Messiah" (that is, "Christ"). He immediately led him to Jesus.

Jesus took one look up and said, "You're John's son, Simon? From now on your name is Cephas" (or Peter, which means "Rock").

1.43-44 The next day Jesus decided to go to Galilee. When he got there, he ran across Philip and said, "Come, follow me." (Philip's hometown was Bethsaida, the same as Andrew and Peter.)

1.45-46 Philip went and found Nathanael and told him, "We've found the One Moses wrote of in the Law, the One preached by the prophets. It's *Jesus*, Joseph's son, the one from Nazareth!" Nathanael said, "Nazareth? You've got to be kidding."

But Philip said, "Come, see for yourself."

1.47 When Jesus saw him coming he said, "There's a real Israelite, not a false bone in his body."

1.48 Nathanael said, "Where did you get that idea? You don't know me."

Jesus answered, "One day, long before Philip called you here, I saw you under the fig tree."

1.49 Nathanael exclaimed, "Rabbi! You are the Son of God, the King of Israel!"

1.50-51 Jesus said, "You've become a believer simply because I say I saw you one day sitting un-

NEW INTERNATIONAL VERSION

things than that." [51]He then added, "I tell you[a] the truth, you[a] shall see heaven open, and the angels of God ascending and descending on the Son of Man."

Jesus Changes Water to Wine

2 On the third day a wedding took place at Cana in Galilee. Jesus' mother was there, [2]and Jesus and his disciples had also been invited to the wedding. [3]When the wine was gone, Jesus' mother said to him, "They have no more wine."

[4]"Dear woman, why do you involve me?" Jesus replied. "My time has not yet come."

[5]His mother said to the servants, "Do whatever he tells you."

[6]Nearby stood six stone water jars, the kind used by the Jews for ceremonial washing, each holding from twenty to thirty gallons.[b]

[7]Jesus said to the servants, "Fill the jars with water"; so they filled them to the brim.

[8]Then he told them, "Now draw some out and take it to the master of the banquet."

They did so, [9]and the master of the banquet tasted the water that had been turned into wine. He did not realize where it had come from, though the servants who had drawn the water knew. Then he called the bridegroom aside [10]and said, "Everyone brings out the choice wine first and then the cheaper wine after the guests have had too much to drink; but you have saved the best till now."

[11]This, the first of his miraculous signs, Jesus performed at Cana in Galilee. He thus revealed his glory, and his disciples put their faith in him.

Jesus Clears the Temple

[12]After this he went down to Capernaum with his mother and brothers and his disciples. There they stayed for a few days.

[13]When it was almost time for the Jewish Passover, Jesus went up to Jerusalem. [14]In the temple courts he found men selling cattle, sheep and doves, and others sitting at tables exchanging money. [15]So he made a whip out of cords, and drove all from the temple area, both sheep and cattle; he scattered the coins of the money changers and overturned their tables. [16]To those who sold doves he said, "Get these out of here! How dare you turn my Father's house into a market!"

[17]His disciples remembered that it is written: "Zeal for your house will consume me."[c]

[18]Then the Jews demanded of him, "What miraculous sign can you show us to prove your authority to do all this?"

THE MESSAGE

der the fig tree? You haven't seen anything yet! Before this is over you're going to see heaven open and God's angels descending to the Son of Man and ascending again."

From Water to Wine

2.1-3 2 Three days later there was a wedding in the village of Cana in Galilee. Jesus' mother was there. Jesus and his disciples were guests also. When they started running low on wine at the wedding banquet, Jesus' mother told him, "They're just about out of wine."

2.4 Jesus said, "Is that any of our business, Mother—yours or mine? This isn't my time. Don't push me."

2.5 She went ahead anyway, telling the servants, "Whatever he tells you, do it."

2.6-7 Six stoneware water pots were there, used by the Jews for ritual washings. Each held twenty to thirty gallons. Jesus ordered the servants, "Fill the pots with water." And they filled them to the brim.

2.8 "Now fill your pitchers and take them to the host," Jesus said, and they did.

2.9-10 When the host tasted the water that had become wine (he didn't know what had just happened but the servants, of course, knew), he called out to the bridegroom, "Everybody I know begins with their finest wines and after the guests have had their fill brings in the cheap stuff. But you've saved the best till now!"

2.11 This act in Cana of Galilee was the first sign Jesus gave, the first glimpse of his glory. And his disciples believed in him.

2.12 After this he went down to Capernaum along with his mother, brothers, and disciples, and stayed several days.

Tear Down This Temple . . .

2.13-14 When the Passover Feast, celebrated each spring by the Jews, was about to take place, Jesus traveled up to Jerusalem. He found the Temple teeming with people selling cattle and sheep and doves. The loan sharks were also there in full strength.

2.15-17 Jesus put together a whip out of strips of leather and chased them out of the Temple, stampeding the sheep and cattle, upending the tables of the loan sharks, spilling coins left and right. He told the dove merchants, "Get your things out of here! Stop turning my Father's house into a shopping mall!" That's when his disciples remembered the Scripture, "Zeal for your house consumes me."

2.18-19 But the Jews were upset. They asked, "What credentials can you present to justify this?"

a 51 The Greek is plural.   b 6 Greek two to three metretes (probably about 75 to 115 liters)   c 17 Psalm 69:9

NEW INTERNATIONAL VERSION

¹⁹Jesus answered them, "Destroy this temple, and I will raise it again in three days."
²⁰The Jews replied, "It has taken forty-six years to build this temple, and you are going to raise it in three days?" ²¹But the temple he had spoken of was his body. ²²After he was raised from the dead, his disciples recalled what he had said. Then they believed the Scripture and the words that Jesus had spoken.

²³Now while he was in Jerusalem at the Passover Feast, many people saw the miraculous signs he was doing and believed in his name.ᵃ ²⁴But Jesus would not entrust himself to them, for he knew all men. ²⁵He did not need man's testimony about man, for he knew what was in a man.

JESUS TEACHES NICODEMUS

3 Now there was a man of the Pharisees named Nicodemus, a member of the Jewish ruling council. ²He came to Jesus at night and said, "Rabbi, we know you are a teacher who has come from God. For no one could perform the miraculous signs you are doing if God were not with him."

³In reply Jesus declared, "I tell you the truth, no one can see the kingdom of God unless he is born again.ᵇ"

⁴"How can a man be born when he is old?" Nicodemus asked. "Surely he cannot enter a second time into his mother's womb to be born!"

⁵Jesus answered, "I tell you the truth, no one can enter the kingdom of God unless he is born of water and the Spirit. ⁶Flesh gives birth to flesh, but the Spiritᶜ gives birth to spirit. ⁷You should not be surprised at my saying, 'Youᵈ must be born again.' ⁸The wind blows wherever it pleases. You hear its sound, but you cannot tell where it comes from or where it is going. So it is with everyone born of the Spirit."

⁹"How can this be?" Nicodemus asked.

THE MESSAGE

Jesus answered, "Tear down this Temple and in three days I'll put it back together."

2.20-22   They were indignant: "It took forty-six years to build this Temple, and you're going to rebuild it in three days?" But Jesus was talking about his body as the Temple. Later, after he was raised from the dead, his disciples remembered he had said this. They then put two and two together and believed both what was written in Scripture and what Jesus had said.

2.23-25   During the time he was in Jerusalem, those days of the Passover Feast, many people noticed the signs he was displaying and, seeing they pointed straight to God, entrusted their lives to him. But Jesus didn't entrust his life to them. He knew them inside and out, knew how untrustworthy they were. He didn't need any help in seeing right through them.

BORN FROM ABOVE

3.1-2   **3** There was a man of the Pharisee sect, Nicodemus, a prominent leader among the Jews. Late one night he visited Jesus and said, "Rabbi, we all know you're a teacher straight from God. No one could do all the God-pointing, God-revealing acts you do if God weren't in on it."

3.3   Jesus said, "You're absolutely right. Take it from me: Unless a person is born from above, it's not possible to see what I'm pointing to—to God's kingdom."

3.4   "How can anyone," said Nicodemus, "be born who has already been born and grown up? You can't re-enter your mother's womb and be born again. What are you saying with this 'born-from-above' talk?"

3.5-6   Jesus said, "You're not listening. Let me say it again. Unless a person submits to this original creation—the 'wind hovering over the water' creation, the invisible moving the visible, a baptism into a new life—it's not possible to enter God's kingdom. When you look at a baby, it's just that: a body you can look at and touch. But the person who takes shape within is formed by something you can't see and touch—the Spirit—and becomes a living spirit.

3.7-8   "So don't be so surprised when I tell you that you have to be 'born from above'—out of this world, so to speak. You know well enough how the wind blows this way and that. You hear it rustling through the trees, but you have no idea where it comes from or where it's headed next. That's the way it is with everyone 'born from above' by the wind of God, the Spirit of God."

3.9   Nicodemus asked, "What do you mean by this? How does this happen?"

ᵃ 23 Or and believed in him   ᵇ 3 Or born from above; also in verse 7   ᶜ 6 Or but spirit   ᵈ 7 The Greek is plural.

NEW INTERNATIONAL VERSION

¹⁰"You are Israel's teacher," said Jesus, "and do you not understand these things? ¹¹I tell you the truth, we speak of what we know, and we testify to what we have seen, but still you people do not accept our testimony. ¹²I have spoken to you of earthly things and you do not believe; how then will you believe if I speak of heavenly things? ¹³No one has ever gone into heaven except the one who came from heaven—the Son of Man. ª ¹⁴Just as Moses lifted up the snake in the desert, so the Son of Man must be lifted up, ¹⁵that everyone who believes in him may have eternal life. ᵇ

¹⁶"For God so loved the world that he gave his one and only Son, ᶜ that whoever believes in him shall not perish but have eternal life. ¹⁷For God did not send his Son into the world to condemn the world, but to save the world through him. ¹⁸Whoever believes in him is not condemned, but whoever does not believe stands condemned already because he has not believed in the name of God's one and only Son. ᵈ ¹⁹This is the verdict: Light has come into the world, but men loved darkness instead of light because their deeds were evil. ²⁰Everyone who does evil hates the light, and will not come into the light for fear that his deeds will be exposed. ²¹But whoever lives by the truth comes into the light, so that it may be seen plainly that what he has done has been done through God." ᵉ

JOHN THE BAPTIST'S TESTIMONY ABOUT JESUS

²²After this, Jesus and his disciples went out into the Judean countryside, where he spent some time with them, and baptized. ²³Now John also was baptizing at Aenon near Salim, because there was plenty of water, and people were constantly coming to be baptized. ²⁴(This was before John was put in prison.) ²⁵An argument developed between some of John's disciples and a certain Jew ᶠ over the matter of ceremonial washing. ²⁶They came to John and said to him, "Rabbi,

THE MESSAGE

3.10-12   Jesus said, "You're a respected teacher of Israel and you don't know these basics? Listen carefully. I'm speaking sober truth to you. I speak only of what I know by experience; I give witness only to what I have seen with my own eyes. There is nothing secondhand here, no hearsay. Yet instead of facing the evidence and accepting it, you procrastinate with questions. If I tell you things that are plain as the hand before your face and you don't believe me, what use is there in telling you of things you can't see, the things of God?

3.13-15   "No one has ever gone up into the presence of God except the One who came down from that Presence, the Son of Man. In the same way that Moses lifted the serpent in the desert so people could have something to see and then believe, it is necessary for the Son of Man to be lifted up—and everyone who looks up to him, trusting and expectant, will gain a real life, eternal life.

3.16-18   "This is how much God loved the world: He gave his Son, his one and only Son. And this is why: so that no one need be destroyed; by believing in him, anyone can have a whole and lasting life. God didn't go to all the trouble of sending his Son merely to point an accusing finger, telling the world how bad it was. He came to help, to put the world right again. Anyone who trusts in him is acquitted; anyone who refuses to trust him has long since been under the death sentence without knowing it. And why? Because of that person's failure to believe in the one-of-a-kind Son of God when introduced to him.

3.19-21   "This is the crisis we're in: God-light streamed into the world, but men and women everywhere ran for the darkness. They went for the darkness because they were not really interested in pleasing God. Everyone who makes a practice of doing evil, addicted to denial and illusion, hates God-light and won't come near it, fearing a painful exposure. But anyone working and living in truth and reality welcomes God-light so the work can be seen for the God-work it is."

THE BRIDEGROOM'S FRIEND

3.22-26   After this conversation, Jesus went on with his disciples into the Judean countryside and relaxed with them there. He was also baptizing. At the same time, John was baptizing over at Aenon near Salim, where water was abundant. This was before John was thrown into jail. John's disciples got into an argument with the establishment Jews over the nature of baptism. They came to John and said, "Rabbi, you know

---

ª 13 Some manuscripts *Man, who is in heaven*
ᵇ 15 Or *believes may have eternal life in him*   ᶜ 16 Or *his only begotten Son*   ᵈ 18 Or *God's only begotten Son*
ᵉ 21 Some interpreters end the quotation after verse 15.
ᶠ 25 Some manuscripts *and certain Jews*

NEW INTERNATIONAL VERSION

that man who was with you on the other side of the Jordan—the one you testified about—well, he is baptizing, and everyone is going to him."

27 To this John replied, "A man can receive only what is given him from heaven. 28 You yourselves can testify that I said, 'I am not the Christ*a* but am sent ahead of him.' 29 The bride belongs to the bridegroom. The friend who attends the bridegroom waits and listens for him, and is full of joy when he hears the bridegroom's voice. That joy is mine, and it is now complete. 30 He must become greater; I must become less.

31 "The one who comes from above is above all; the one who is from the earth belongs to the earth, and speaks as one from the earth. The one who comes from heaven is above all. 32 He testifies to what he has seen and heard, but no one accepts his testimony. 33 The man who has accepted it has certified that God is truthful. 34 For the one whom God has sent speaks the words of God, for God*b* gives the Spirit without limit. 35 The Father loves the Son and has placed everything in his hands. 36 Whoever believes in the Son has eternal life, but whoever rejects the Son will not see life, for God's wrath remains on him."*c*

JESUS TALKS WITH A SAMARITAN WOMAN

4 The Pharisees heard that Jesus was gaining and baptizing more disciples than John, 2 although in fact it was not Jesus who baptized, but his disciples. 3 When the Lord learned of this, he left Judea and went back once more to Galilee.

4 Now he had to go through Samaria. 5 So he came to a town in Samaria called Sychar, near the plot of ground Jacob had given to his son Joseph. 6 Jacob's well was there, and Jesus, tired as he was from the journey, sat down by the well. It was about the sixth hour.

7 When a Samaritan woman came to draw water, Jesus said to her, "Will you give me a drink?"

a 28 Or *Messiah*   *b* 34 Greek *he*   *c* 36 Some interpreters end the quotation after verse 30.

THE MESSAGE

the one who was with you on the other side of the Jordan? The one you authorized with your witness? Well, he's now competing with us. He's baptizing, too, and everyone's going to him instead of us."

3.27-29 John answered, "It's not possible for a person to succeed—I'm talking about *eternal* success—without heaven's help. You yourselves were there when I made it public that I was not the Messiah but simply the one sent ahead of him to get things ready. The one who gets the bride is, by definition, the bridegroom. And the bridegroom's friend, his 'best man'—that's me—in place at his side where he can hear every word, is genuinely happy. How could he be jealous when he knows that the wedding is finished and the marriage is off to a good start?

3.29-30 "That's why my cup is running over. This is the assigned moment for him to move into the center, while I slip off to the sidelines.

3.31-33 "The One who comes from above is head and shoulders over other messengers from God. The earthborn is earthbound and speaks earth language; the heavenborn is in a league of his own. He sets out the evidence of what he saw and heard in heaven. No one wants to deal with these facts. But anyone who examines this evidence will come to stake his life on this: that God himself is the truth.

3.34-36 "The One that God sent speaks God's words. And don't think he rations out the Spirit in bits and pieces. The Father loves the Son extravagantly. He turned everything over to him so he could give it away—a lavish distribution of gifts. That is why whoever accepts and trusts the Son gets in on everything, life complete and forever! And that is also why the person who avoids and distrusts the Son is in the dark and doesn't see life. All he experiences of God is darkness, and an angry darkness at that."

THE WOMAN AT THE WELL

4.1-3 4 Jesus realized that the Pharisees were keeping count of the baptisms that he and John performed (although his disciples, not Jesus, did the actual baptizing). They had posted the score that Jesus was ahead, turning him and John into rivals in the eyes of the people. So Jesus left the Judean countryside and went back to Galilee.

4.4-6 To get there, he had to pass through Samaria. He came into Sychar, a Samaritan village that bordered the field Jacob had given his son Joseph. Jacob's well was still there. Jesus, worn out by the trip, sat down at the well. It was noon.

4.7-8 A woman, a Samaritan, came to draw water. Jesus said, "Would you give me a drink of wa-

NEW INTERNATIONAL VERSION

8(His disciples had gone into the town to buy food.)

9The Samaritan woman said to him, "You are a Jew and I am a Samaritan woman. How can you ask me for a drink?" (For Jews do not associate with Samaritans.ᵃ)

10Jesus answered her, "If you knew the gift of God and who it is that asks you for a drink, you would have asked him and he would have given you living water."

11"Sir," the woman said, "you have nothing to draw with and the well is deep. Where can you get this living water? 12Are you greater than our father Jacob, who gave us the well and drank from it himself, as did also his sons and his flocks and herds?"

13Jesus answered, "Everyone who drinks this water will be thirsty again, 14but whoever drinks the water I give him will never thirst. Indeed, the water I give him will become in him a spring of water welling up to eternal life."

15The woman said to him, "Sir, give me this water so that I won't get thirsty and have to keep coming here to draw water."

16He told her, "Go, call your husband and come back."

17"I have no husband," she replied.

Jesus said to her, "You are right when you say you have no husband. 18The fact is, you have had five husbands, and the man you now have is not your husband. What you have just said is quite true."

19"Sir," the woman said, "I can see that you are a prophet. 20Our fathers worshiped on this mountain, but you Jews claim that the place where we must worship is in Jerusalem."

21Jesus declared, "Believe me, woman, a time is coming when you will worship the Father neither on this mountain nor in Jerusalem. 22You Samaritans worship what you do not know; we worship what we do know, for salvation is from the Jews. 23Yet a time is coming and has now come when the true worshipers will worship the Father in spirit and truth, for they are the kind of worshipers the Father seeks. 24God is spirit, and his worshipers must worship in spirit and in truth."

25The woman said, "I know that Messiah" (called Christ) "is coming. When he comes, he will explain everything to us."

26Then Jesus declared, "I who speak to you am he."

ᵃ 9 Or do not use dishes Samaritans have used

THE MESSAGE

ter?" (His disciples had gone to the village to buy food for lunch.)

4.9 The Samaritan woman, taken aback, asked, "How come you, a Jew, are asking me, a Samaritan woman, for a drink?" (Jews in those days wouldn't be caught dead talking to Samaritans.)

4.10 Jesus answered, "If you knew the generosity of God and who I am, you would be asking me for a drink, and I would give you fresh, living water."

4.11-12 The woman said, "Sir, you don't even have a bucket to draw with, and this well is deep. So how are you going to get this 'living water'? Are you a better man than our ancestor Jacob, who dug this well and drank from it, he and his sons and livestock, and passed it down to us?"

4.13-14 Jesus said, "Everyone who drinks this water will get thirsty again and again. Anyone who drinks the water I give will never thirst—not ever. The water I give will be an artesian spring within, gushing fountains of endless life."

4.15 The woman said, "Sir, give me this water so I won't ever get thirsty, won't ever have to come back to this well again!"

4.16 He said, "Go call your husband and then come back."

4.17-18 "I have no husband," she said.

"That's nicely put: 'I have no husband.' You've had five husbands, and the man you're living with now isn't even your husband. You spoke the truth there, sure enough."

4.19-20 "Oh, so you're a prophet! Well, tell me this: Our ancestors worshiped God at this mountain, but you Jews insist that Jerusalem is the only place for worship, right?"

4.21-23 "Believe me, woman, the time is coming when you Samaritans will worship the Father neither here at this mountain nor there in Jerusalem. You worship guessing in the dark; we Jews worship in the clear light of day. God's way of salvation is made available through the Jews. But the time is coming—it has, in fact, come—when what you're called will not matter and where you go to worship will not matter.

4.23-24 "It's who you are and the way you live that count before God. Your worship must engage your spirit in the pursuit of truth. That's the kind of people the Father is out looking for: those who are simply and honestly themselves before him in their worship. God is sheer being itself—Spirit. Those who worship him must do it out of their very being, their spirits, their true selves, in adoration."

4.25 The woman said, "I don't know about that. I do know that the Messiah is coming. When he arrives, we'll get the whole story."

4.26 "I am he," said Jesus. "You don't have to wait any longer or look any further."

NEW INTERNATIONAL VERSION

The Disciples Rejoin Jesus

27Just then his disciples returned and were surprised to find him talking with a woman. But no one asked, "What do you want?" or "Why are you talking with her?"

28Then, leaving her water jar, the woman went back to the town and said to the people, 29"Come, see a man who told me everything I ever did. Could this be the Christ*a*?" 30They came out of the town and made their way toward him.

31Meanwhile his disciples urged him, "Rabbi, eat something."

32But he said to them, "I have food to eat that you know nothing about."

33Then his disciples said to each other, "Could someone have brought him food?"

34"My food," said Jesus, "is to do the will of him who sent me and to finish his work. 35Do you not say, 'Four months more and then the harvest'? I tell you, open your eyes and look at the fields! They are ripe for harvest. 36Even now the reaper draws his wages, even now he harvests the crop for eternal life, so that the sower and the reaper may be glad together. 37Thus the saying 'One sows and another reaps' is true. 38I sent you to reap what you have not worked for. Others have done the hard work, and you have reaped the benefits of their labor."

Many Samaritans Believe

39Many of the Samaritans from that town believed in him because of the woman's testimony, "He told me everything I ever did." 40So when the Samaritans came to him, they urged him to stay with them, and he stayed two days. 41And because of his words many more became believers.

42They said to the woman, "We no longer believe just because of what you said; now we have heard for ourselves, and we know that this man really is the Savior of the world."

Jesus Heals the Official's Son

43After the two days he left for Galilee. 44(Now Jesus himself had pointed out that a prophet has no honor in his own country.) 45When he arrived in Galilee, the Galileans welcomed him. They had seen all that he had done in Jerusalem at the Passover Feast, for they also had been there.

a 29 Or Messiah

THE MESSAGE

4.27 Just then his disciples came back. They were shocked. They couldn't believe he was talking with that kind of a woman. No one said what they were all thinking, but their faces showed it.

4.28-30 The woman took the hint and left. In her confusion she left her water pot. Back in the village she told the people, "Come see a man who knew all about the things I did, who knows me inside and out. Do you think this could be the Messiah?" And they went out to see for themselves.

It's Harvest Time

4.31 In the meantime, the disciples pressed him, "Rabbi, eat. Aren't you going to eat?"

4.32 He told them, "I have food to eat you know nothing about."

4.33 The disciples were puzzled. "Who could have brought him food?"

4.34-35 Jesus said, "The food that keeps me going is that I do the will of the One who sent me, finishing the work he started. As you look around right now, wouldn't you say that in about four months it will be time to harvest? Well, I'm telling you to open your eyes and take a good look at what's right in front of you. These Samaritan fields are ripe. It's harvest time!

4.36-38 "The Harvester isn't waiting. He's taking his pay, gathering in this grain that's ripe for eternal life. Now the Sower is arm in arm with the Harvester, triumphant. That's the truth of the saying, 'This one sows, that one harvests.' I sent you to harvest a field you never worked. Without lifting a finger, you have walked in on a field worked long and hard by others."

4.39-42 Many of the Samaritans from that village committed themselves to him because of the woman's witness: "He knew all about the things I did. He knows me inside and out!" They asked him to stay on, so Jesus stayed two days. A lot more people entrusted their lives to him when they heard what he had to say. They said to the woman, "We're no longer taking this on your say-so. We've heard it for ourselves and know it for sure. He's the Savior of the world!"

✠

4.43-45 After the two days he left for Galilee. Now, Jesus knew well from experience that a prophet is not respected in the place where he grew up. So when he arrived in Galilee, the Galileans welcomed him, but only because they were impressed with what he had done in Jerusalem during the Passover Feast, not that they really had a clue about who he was or what he was up to.

NEW INTERNATIONAL VERSION

⁴⁶Once more he visited Cana in Galilee, where he had turned the water into wine. And there was a certain royal official whose son lay sick at Capernaum. ⁴⁷When this man heard that Jesus had arrived in Galilee from Judea, he went to him and begged him to come and heal his son, who was close to death.

⁴⁸"Unless you people see miraculous signs and wonders," Jesus told him, "you will never believe."

⁴⁹The royal official said, "Sir, come down before my child dies."

⁵⁰Jesus replied, "You may go. Your son will live."

The man took Jesus at his word and departed. ⁵¹While he was still on the way, his servants met him with the news that his boy was living. ⁵²When he inquired as to the time when his son got better, they said to him, "The fever left him yesterday at the seventh hour."

⁵³Then the father realized that this was the exact time at which Jesus had said to him, "Your son will live." So he and all his household believed.

⁵⁴This was the second miraculous sign that Jesus performed, having come from Judea to Galilee.

THE HEALING AT THE POOL

5 Some time later, Jesus went up to Jerusalem for a feast of the Jews. ²Now there is in Jerusalem near the Sheep Gate a pool, which in Aramaic is called Bethesda*a* and which is surrounded by five covered colonnades. ³Here a great number of disabled people used to lie—the blind, the lame, the paralyzed.*b* ⁵One who was there had been an invalid for thirty-eight years. ⁶When Jesus saw him lying there and learned that he had been in this condition for a long time, he asked him, "Do you want to get well?"

⁷"Sir," the invalid replied, "I have no one to help me into the pool when the water is stirred. While I am trying to get in, someone else goes down ahead of me."

⁸Then Jesus said to him, "Get up! Pick up your mat and walk." ⁹At once the man was cured; he picked up his mat and walked.

The day on which this took place was a Sabbath, ¹⁰and so the Jews said to the man who had been healed, "It is the Sabbath; the law forbids you to carry your mat."

¹¹But he replied, "The man who made me well said to me, 'Pick up your mat and walk.' "

a 2 Some manuscripts *Bethzatha;* other manuscripts *Bethsaida* *b 3* Some less important manuscripts *paralyzed—and they waited for the moving of the waters.* *⁴From time to time an angel of the Lord would come down and stir up the waters. The first one into the pool after each such disturbance would be cured of whatever disease he had.*

THE MESSAGE

4.46-48 Now he was back in Cana of Galilee, the place where he made the water into wine. Meanwhile in Capernaum, there was a certain official from the king's court whose son was sick. When he heard that Jesus had come from Judea to Galilee, he went and asked that he come down and heal his son, who was on the brink of death. Jesus put him off: "Unless you people are dazzled by a miracle, you refuse to believe."

4.49 But the court official wouldn't be put off. "Come down! It's life or death for my son."

4.50-51 Jesus simply replied, "Go home. Your son lives."

The man believed the bare word Jesus spoke and headed home. On his way back, his servants intercepted him and announced, "Your son lives!"

4.52-53 He asked them what time he began to get better. They said, "The fever broke yesterday afternoon at one o'clock." The father knew that that was the very moment Jesus had said, "Your son lives."

4.53-54 That clinched it. Not only he but his entire household believed. This was now the second sign Jesus gave after having come from Judea into Galilee.

EVEN ON THE SABBATH

5.1-6 5 Soon another Feast came around and Jesus was back in Jerusalem. Near the Sheep Gate in Jerusalem there was a pool, in Hebrew called *Bethesda,* with five alcoves. Hundreds of sick people—blind, crippled, paralyzed—were in these alcoves. One man had been an invalid there for thirty-eight years. When Jesus saw him stretched out by the pool and knew how long he had been there, he said, "Do you want to get well?"

5.7 The sick man said, "Sir, when the water is stirred, I don't have anybody to put me in the pool. By the time I get there, somebody else is already in."

5.8-9 Jesus said, "Get up, take your bedroll, start walking." The man was healed on the spot. He picked up his bedroll and walked off.

5.9-10 That day happened to be the Sabbath. The Jews stopped the healed man and said, "It's the Sabbath. You can't carry your bedroll around. It's against the rules."

5.11 But he told them, "The man who made me well told me to. He said, 'Take your bedroll and start walking.'"

NEW INTERNATIONAL VERSION

¹²So they asked him, "Who is this fellow who told you to pick it up and walk?"

¹³The man who was healed had no idea who it was, for Jesus had slipped away into the crowd that was there.

¹⁴Later Jesus found him at the temple and said to him, "See, you are well again. Stop sinning or something worse may happen to you." ¹⁵The man went away and told the Jews that it was Jesus who had made him well.

LIFE THROUGH THE SON

¹⁶So, because Jesus was doing these things on the Sabbath, the Jews persecuted him. ¹⁷Jesus said to them, "My Father is always at his work to this very day, and I, too, am working." ¹⁸For this reason the Jews tried all the harder to kill him; not only was he breaking the Sabbath, but he was even calling God his own Father, making himself equal with God.

¹⁹Jesus gave them this answer: "I tell you the truth, the Son can do nothing by himself; he can do only what he sees his Father doing, because whatever the Father does the Son also does. ²⁰For the Father loves the Son and shows him all he does. Yes, to your amazement he will show him even greater things than these. ²¹For just as the Father raises the dead and gives them life, even so the Son gives life to whom he is pleased to give it. ²²Moreover, the Father judges no one, but has entrusted all judgment to the Son, ²³that all may honor the Son just as they honor the Father. He who does not honor the Son does not honor the Father, who sent him.

²⁴"I tell you the truth, whoever hears my word and believes him who sent me has eternal life and will not be condemned; he has crossed over from death to life. ²⁵I tell you the truth, a time is coming and has now come when the dead will hear the voice of the Son of God and those who hear will live. ²⁶For as the Father has life in himself, so he has granted the Son to have life in himself. ²⁷And he has given him authority to judge because he is the Son of Man.

²⁸"Do not be amazed at this, for a time is coming when all who are in their graves will hear his voice ²⁹and come out—those who have

THE MESSAGE

5.12-13   They asked, "Who gave you the order to take it up and start walking?" But the healed man didn't know, for Jesus had slipped away into the crowd.

5.14   A little later Jesus found him in the Temple and said, "You look wonderful! You're well! Don't return to a sinning life or something worse might happen."

5.15-16   The man went back and told the Jews that it was Jesus who had made him well. That is why the Jews were out to get Jesus—because he did this kind of thing on the Sabbath.

5.17   But Jesus defended himself. "My Father is working straight through, even on the Sabbath. So am I."

5.18   That really set them off. The Jews were now not only out to expose him; they were out to *kill* him. Not only was he breaking the Sabbath, but he was calling God his own Father, putting himself on a level with God.

WHAT THE FATHER DOES, THE SON DOES

5.19-20   So Jesus explained himself at length. "I'm telling you this straight. The Son can't independently do a thing, only what he sees the Father doing. What the Father does, the Son does. The Father loves the Son and includes him in everything he is doing.

5.20-23   "But you haven't seen the half of it yet, for in the same way that the Father raises the dead and creates life, so does the Son. The Son gives life to anyone he chooses. Neither he nor the Father shuts anyone out. The Father handed all authority to judge over to the Son so that the Son will be honored equally with the Father. Anyone who dishonors the Son, dishonors the Father, for it was the Father's decision to put the Son in the place of honor.

5.24   "It's urgent that you listen carefully to this: Anyone here who believes what I am saying right now and aligns himself with the Father, who has in fact put me in charge, has at this very moment the real, lasting life and is no longer condemned to be an outsider. This person has taken a giant step from the world of the dead to the world of the living.

5.25-27   "It's urgent that you get this right: The time has arrived—I mean right now!—when dead men and women will hear the voice of the Son of God and, hearing, will come alive. Just as the Father has life in himself, he has conferred on the Son life in himself. And he has given him the authority, simply because he is the Son of Man, to decide and carry out matters of Judgment.

5.28-29   "Don't act so surprised at all this. The time is coming when everyone dead and buried will hear his voice. Those who have lived the right

NEW INTERNATIONAL VERSION

done good will rise to live, and those who have done evil will rise to be condemned. 30By myself I can do nothing; I judge only as I hear, and my judgment is just, for I seek not to please myself but him who sent me.

Testimonies About Jesus

31"If I testify about myself, my testimony is not valid. 32There is another who testifies in my favor, and I know that his testimony about me is valid.

33"You have sent to John and he has testified to the truth. 34Not that I accept human testimony; but I mention it that you may be saved. 35John was a lamp that burned and gave light, and you chose for a time to enjoy his light.

36"I have testimony weightier than that of John. For the very work that the Father has given me to finish, and which I am doing, testifies that the Father has sent me. 37And the Father who sent me has himself testified concerning me. You have never heard his voice nor seen his form, 38nor does his word dwell in you, for you do not believe the one he sent. 39You diligently study*a* the Scriptures because you think that by them you possess eternal life. These are the Scriptures that testify about me, 40yet you refuse to come to me to have life.

41"I do not accept praise from men, 42but I know you. I know that you do not have the love of God in your hearts. 43I have come in my Father's name, and you do not accept me; but if someone else comes in his own name, you will accept him. 44How can you believe if you accept praise from one another, yet make no effort to obtain the praise that comes from the only God*b*?

45"But do not think I will accuse you before the Father. Your accuser is Moses, on whom your hopes are set. 46If you believed Moses, you would believe me, for he wrote about me. 47But since you do not believe what he wrote, how are you going to believe what I say?"

THE MESSAGE

way will walk out into a resurrection Life; those who have lived the wrong way, into a resurrection Judgment.

5.30-33   "I can't do a solitary thing on my own: I listen, then I decide. You can trust my decision because I'm not out to get my own way but only to carry out orders. If I were simply speaking on my own account, it would be an empty, self-serving witness. But an independent witness confirms me, the most reliable Witness of all. Furthermore, you all saw and heard John, and he gave expert and reliable testimony about me, didn't he?

5.34-38   "But my purpose is not to get your vote, and not to appeal to mere human testimony. I'm speaking to you this way so that you will be saved. John was a torch, blazing and bright, and you were glad enough to dance for an hour or so in his bright light. But the witness that really confirms me far exceeds John's witness. It's the work the Father gave me to complete. These very tasks, as I go about completing them, confirm that the Father, in fact, sent me. The Father who sent me, confirmed me. And you missed it. You never heard his voice, you never saw his appearance. There is nothing left in your memory of his Message because you do not take his Messenger seriously.

✠

5.39-40   "You have your heads in your Bibles constantly because you think you'll find eternal life there. But you miss the forest for the trees. These Scriptures are all about *me*! And here I am, standing right before you, and you aren't willing to receive from me the life you say you want.

5.41-44   "I'm not interested in crowd approval. And do you know why? Because I know you and your crowds. I know that love, especially God's love, is not on your working agenda. I came with the authority of my Father, and you either dismiss me or avoid me. If another came, acting self-important, you would welcome him with open arms. How do you expect to get anywhere with God when you spend all your time jockeying for position with each other, ranking your rivals and ignoring God?

5.45-47   "But don't think I'm going to accuse you before my Father. Moses, in whom you put so much stock, is your accuser. If you believed, really believed, what Moses said, you would believe me. He wrote of me. If you won't take seriously what *he* wrote, how can I expect you to take seriously what *I* speak?"

---

a 39 Or Study diligently (the imperative)   *b 44 Some early* manuscripts *the Only One*

NEW INTERNATIONAL VERSION

Jesus Feeds the Five Thousand

6 Some time after this, Jesus crossed to the far shore of the Sea of Galilee (that is, the Sea of Tiberias), ²and a great crowd of people followed him because they saw the miraculous signs he had performed on the sick. ³Then Jesus went up on a mountainside and sat down with his disciples. ⁴The Jewish Passover Feast was near.

⁵When Jesus looked up and saw a great crowd coming toward him, he said to Philip, "Where shall we buy bread for these people to eat?" ⁶He asked this only to test him, for he already had in mind what he was going to do.

⁷Philip answered him, "Eight months' wages*ᵃ* would not buy enough bread for each one to have a bite!"

⁸Another of his disciples, Andrew, Simon Peter's brother, spoke up, ⁹"Here is a boy with five small barley loaves and two small fish, but how far will they go among so many?"

¹⁰Jesus said, "Have the people sit down." There was plenty of grass in that place, and the men sat down, about five thousand of them. ¹¹Jesus then took the loaves, gave thanks, and distributed to those who were seated as much as they wanted. He did the same with the fish.

¹²When they had all had enough to eat, he said to his disciples, "Gather the pieces that are left over. Let nothing be wasted." ¹³So they gathered them and filled twelve baskets with the pieces of the five barley loaves left over by those who had eaten.

¹⁴After the people saw the miraculous sign that Jesus did, they began to say, "Surely this is the Prophet who is to come into the world." ¹⁵Jesus, knowing that they intended to come and make him king by force, withdrew again to a mountain by himself.

Jesus Walks on the Water

¹⁶When evening came, his disciples went down to the lake, ¹⁷where they got into a boat and set off across the lake for Capernaum. By now it was dark, and Jesus had not yet joined them. ¹⁸A strong wind was blowing and the waters grew rough. ¹⁹When they had rowed three or three and a half miles,*ᵇ* they saw Jesus approaching the boat, walking on the water; and they were terrified. ²⁰But he said to them, "It is I; don't be afraid." ²¹Then they were willing to take him into the boat, and immediately the boat reached the shore where they were heading.

²²The next day the crowd that had stayed on the opposite shore of the lake realized that only one boat had been there, and that Jesus had not

THE MESSAGE

Bread and Fish for All

6 After this, Jesus went across the Sea of Galilee (some call it Tiberias). A huge crowd followed him, attracted by the miracles they had seen him do among the sick. When he got to the other side, he climbed a hill and sat down, surrounded by his disciples. It was nearly time for the Feast of Passover, kept annually by the Jews.

⁶·⁵⁻⁶ When Jesus looked out and saw that a large crowd had arrived, he said to Philip, "Where can we buy bread to feed these people?" He said this to stretch Philip's faith. He already knew what he was going to do.

⁶·⁷ Philip answered, "Two hundred silver pieces wouldn't be enough to buy bread for each person to get a piece."

⁶·⁸⁻⁹ One of the disciples—it was Andrew, brother to Simon Peter—said, "There's a little boy here who has five barley loaves and two fish. But that's a drop in the bucket for a crowd like this."

⁶·¹⁰⁻¹¹ Jesus said, "Make the people sit down." There was a nice carpet of green grass in this place. They sat down, about five thousand of them. Then Jesus took the bread and, having given thanks, gave it to those who were seated. He did the same with the fish. All ate as much as they wanted.

⁶·¹²⁻¹³ When the people had eaten their fill, he said to his disciples, "Gather the leftovers so nothing is wasted." They went to work and filled twelve large baskets with leftovers from the five barley loaves.

⁶·¹⁴⁻¹⁵ The people realized that God was at work among them in what Jesus had just done. They said, "This is the Prophet for sure, God's Prophet right here in Galilee!" Jesus saw that in their enthusiasm, they were about to grab him and make him king, so he slipped off and went back up the mountain to be by himself.

⁶·¹⁶⁻²¹ In the evening his disciples went down to the sea, got in the boat, and headed back across the water to Capernaum. It had grown quite dark and Jesus had not yet returned. A huge wind blew up, churning the sea. They were maybe three or four miles out when they saw Jesus walking on the sea, quite near the boat. They were scared senseless, but he reassured them, "It's me. It's all right. Don't be afraid." So they took him on board. In no time they reached land—the exact spot they were headed to.

⁶·²²⁻²⁴ The next day the crowd that was left behind realized that there had been only one boat, and that Jesus had not gotten into it with his disci-

ᵃ 7 Greek *two hundred denarii*   *ᵇ 19* Greek *rowed twenty-five or thirty stadia* (about 5 or 6 kilometers)

NEW INTERNATIONAL VERSION

entered it with his disciples, but that they had gone away alone. ²³Then some boats from Tiberias landed near the place where the people had eaten the bread after the Lord had given thanks. ²⁴Once the crowd realized that neither Jesus nor his disciples were there, they got into the boats and went to Capernaum in search of Jesus.

JESUS THE BREAD OF LIFE

²⁵When they found him on the other side of the lake, they asked him, "Rabbi, when did you get here?"

²⁶Jesus answered, "I tell you the truth, you are looking for me, not because you saw miraculous signs but because you ate the loaves and had your fill. ²⁷Do not work for food that spoils, but for food that endures to eternal life, which the Son of Man will give you. On him God the Father has placed his seal of approval."

²⁸Then they asked him, "What must we do to do the works God requires?"

²⁹Jesus answered, "The work of God is this: to believe in the one he has sent."

³⁰So they asked him, "What miraculous sign then will you give that we may see it and believe you? What will you do? ³¹Our forefathers ate the manna in the desert; as it is written: 'He gave them bread from heaven to eat.'ᵃ"

³²Jesus said to them, "I tell you the truth, it is not Moses who has given you the bread from heaven, but it is my Father who gives you the true bread from heaven. ³³For the bread of God is he who comes down from heaven and gives life to the world."

³⁴"Sir," they said, "from now on give us this bread."

³⁵Then Jesus declared, "I am the bread of life. He who comes to me will never go hungry, and he who believes in me will never be thirsty. ³⁶But as I told you, you have seen me and still you do not believe. ³⁷All that the Father gives me will come to me, and whoever comes to me I will never drive away. ³⁸For I have come down from heaven not to do my will but to do the will of him who sent me. ³⁹And this is the will of him who sent me, that I shall lose none of all that he has given me, but raise them up at the last day. ⁴⁰For my Father's will is that everyone who looks

THE MESSAGE

ples. They had seen them go off without him. By now boats from Tiberias had pulled up near where they had eaten the bread blessed by the Master. So when the crowd realized he was gone and wasn't coming back, they piled into the Tiberias boats and headed for Capernaum, looking for Jesus.

6.25 When they found him back across the sea, they said, "Rabbi, when did you get here?"

6.26 Jesus answered, "You've come looking for me not because you saw God in my actions but because I fed you, filled your stomachs—and for free.

THE BREAD OF LIFE

6.27 "Don't waste your energy striving for perishable food like that. Work for the food that sticks with you, food that nourishes your lasting life, food the Son of Man provides. He and what he does are guaranteed by God the Father to last."

6.28 To that they said, "Well, what do we do then to get in on God's works?"

6.29 Jesus said, "Throw your lot in with the One that God has sent. That kind of a commitment gets you in on God's works."

6.30-31 They waffled: "Why don't you give us a clue about who you are, just a hint of what's going on? When we see what's up, we'll commit ourselves. Show us what you can do. Moses fed our ancestors with bread in the desert. It says so in the Scriptures: 'He gave them bread from heaven to eat.' "

6.32-33 Jesus responded, "The real significance of that Scripture is not that Moses gave you bread from heaven but that my Father is right now offering you bread from heaven, the *real* bread. The Bread of God came down out of heaven and is giving life to the world."

6.34 They jumped at that: "Master, give us this bread, now and forever!"

6.35-38 Jesus said, "I am the Bread of Life. The person who aligns with me hungers no more and thirsts no more, ever. I have told you this explicitly because even though you have seen me in action, you don't really believe me. Every person the Father gives me eventually comes running to me. And once that person is with me, I hold on and don't let go. I came down from heaven not to follow my own whim but to accomplish the will of the One who sent me.

6.39-40 "This, in a nutshell, is that will: that everything handed over to me by the Father be completed—not a single detail missed—and at the wrap-up of time I have everything and everyone put together, upright and whole. This is what my Father wants: that anyone who sees

---

ᵃ 31 Exodus 16:4; Neh. 9:15; Psalm 78:24,25

NEW INTERNATIONAL VERSION

to the Son and believes in him shall have eternal life, and I will raise him up at the last day."

⁴¹At this the Jews began to grumble about him because he said, "I am the bread that came down from heaven." ⁴²They said, "Is this not Jesus, the son of Joseph, whose father and mother we know? How can he now say, 'I came down from heaven'?"

⁴³"Stop grumbling among yourselves," Jesus answered. ⁴⁴"No one can come to me unless the Father who sent me draws him, and I will raise him up at the last day. ⁴⁵It is written in the Prophets: 'They will all be taught by God.'ᵃ Everyone who listens to the Father and learns from him comes to me. ⁴⁶No one has seen the Father except the one who is from God; only he has seen the Father. ⁴⁷I tell you the truth, he who believes has everlasting life. ⁴⁸I am the bread of life. ⁴⁹Your forefathers ate the manna in the desert, yet they died. ⁵⁰But here is the bread that comes down from heaven, which a man may eat and not die. ⁵¹I am the living bread that came down from heaven. If anyone eats of this bread, he will live forever. This bread is my flesh, which I will give for the life of the world."

⁵²Then the Jews began to argue sharply among themselves, "How can this man give us his flesh to eat?"

⁵³Jesus said to them, "I tell you the truth, unless you eat the flesh of the Son of Man and drink his blood, you have no life in you. ⁵⁴Whoever eats my flesh and drinks my blood has eternal life, and I will raise him up at the last day. ⁵⁵For my flesh is real food and my blood is real drink. ⁵⁶Whoever eats my flesh and drinks my blood remains in me, and I in him. ⁵⁷Just as the living Father sent me and I live because of the Father, so the one who feeds on me will live because of me. ⁵⁸This is the bread that came down from heaven. Your forefathers ate manna and died, but he who feeds on this bread will live forever." ⁵⁹He said this while teaching in the synagogue in Capernaum.

THE MESSAGE

the Son and trusts who he is and what he does and then aligns with him will enter *real* life, *eternal* life. My part is to put them on their feet alive and whole at the completion of time."

6.41-42 At this, because he said, "I am the Bread that came down from heaven," the Jews started arguing over him: "Isn't this the son of Joseph? Don't we know his father? Don't we know his mother? How can he now say, 'I came down out of heaven' and expect anyone to believe him?"

6.43-46 Jesus said, "Don't bicker among yourselves over me. You're not in charge here. The Father who sent me is in charge. He draws people to me—that's the only way you'll ever come. Only then do I do my work, putting people together, setting them on their feet, ready for the End. This is what the prophets meant when they wrote, 'And then they will all be personally taught by God.' Anyone who has spent any time at all listening to the Father, really listening and therefore learning, comes to me to be taught personally—to see it with his own eyes, hear it with his own ears, from me, since I have it first-hand from the Father. No one has seen the Father except the One who has his Being alongside the Father—and you can see *me*.

6.47-51 "I'm telling you the most solemn and sober truth now: Whoever believes in me has real life, eternal life. I am the Bread of Life. Your ancestors ate the manna bread in the desert and died. But now here is Bread that truly comes down out of heaven. Anyone eating this Bread will not die, ever. I am the Bread—living Bread!—who came down out of heaven. Anyone who eats this Bread will live—and forever! The Bread that I present to the world so that it can eat and live is myself, this flesh-and-blood self."

6.52 At this, the Jews started fighting among themselves: "How can this man serve up his flesh for a meal?"

6.53-58 But Jesus didn't give an inch. "Only insofar as you eat and drink flesh and blood, the flesh and blood of the Son of Man, do you have life within you. The one who brings a hearty appetite to this eating and drinking has eternal life and will be fit and ready for the Final Day. My flesh is real food and my blood is real drink. By eating my flesh and drinking my blood you enter into me and I into you. In the same way that the fully alive Father sent me here and I live because of him, so the one who makes a meal of me lives because of me. This is the Bread from heaven. Your ancestors ate bread and later died. Whoever eats this Bread will live always."

6.59 He said these things while teaching in the meeting place in Capernaum.

ᵃ 45 Isaiah 54:13

NEW INTERNATIONAL VERSION

MANY DISCIPLES DESERT JESUS

⁶⁰On hearing it, many of his disciples said, "This is a hard teaching. Who can accept it?"

⁶¹Aware that his disciples were grumbling about this, Jesus said to them, "Does this offend you? ⁶²What if you see the Son of Man ascend to where he was before! ⁶³The Spirit gives life; the flesh counts for nothing. The words I have spoken to you are spirit*a* and they are life. ⁶⁴Yet there are some of you who do not believe." For Jesus had known from the beginning which of them did not believe and who would betray him. ⁶⁵He went on to say, "This is why I told you that no one can come to me unless the Father has enabled him."

⁶⁶From this time many of his disciples turned back and no longer followed him.

⁶⁷"You do not want to leave too, do you?" Jesus asked the Twelve.

⁶⁸Simon Peter answered him, "Lord, to whom shall we go? You have the words of eternal life. ⁶⁹We believe and know that you are the Holy One of God."

⁷⁰Then Jesus replied, "Have I not chosen you, the Twelve? Yet one of you is a devil!" ⁷¹(He meant Judas, the son of Simon Iscariot, who, though one of the Twelve, was later to betray him.)

JESUS GOES TO THE FEAST OF TABERNACLES

7 After this, Jesus went around in Galilee, purposely staying away from Judea because the Jews there were waiting to take his life. ²But when the Jewish Feast of Tabernacles was near, ³Jesus' brothers said to him, "You ought to leave here and go to Judea, so that your disciples may see the miracles you do. ⁴No one who wants to become a public figure acts in secret. Since you are doing these things, show yourself to the world." ⁵For even his own brothers did not believe in him.

⁶Therefore Jesus told them, "The right time for me has not yet come; for you any time is right. ⁷The world cannot hate you, but it hates me because I testify that what it does is evil. ⁸You go to the Feast. I am not yet*b* going up to this Feast, because for me the right time has not yet come." ⁹Having said this, he stayed in Galilee.

¹⁰However, after his brothers had left for the Feast, he went also, not publicly, but in se-

THE MESSAGE

TOO TOUGH TO SWALLOW

6.60 Many among his disciples heard this and said, "This is tough teaching, too tough to swallow."

6.61-65 Jesus sensed that his disciples were having a hard time with this and said, "Does this throw you completely? What would happen if you saw the Son of Man ascending to where he came from? The Spirit can make life. Sheer muscle and willpower don't make anything happen. Every word I've spoken to you is a Spirit-word, and so it is life-making. But some of you are resisting, refusing to have any part in this." (Jesus knew from the start that some weren't going to risk themselves with him. He knew also who would betray him.) He went on to say, "This is why I told you earlier that no one is capable of coming to me on his own. You get to me only as a gift from the Father."

6.66-67 After this a lot of his disciples left. They no longer wanted to be associated with him. Then Jesus gave the Twelve their chance: "Do you also want to leave?"

6.68-69 Peter replied, "Master, to whom would we go? You have the words of real life, eternal life. We've already committed ourselves, confident that you are the Holy One of God."

6.70-71 Jesus responded, "Haven't I handpicked you, the Twelve? Still, one of you is a devil!" He was referring to Judas, son of Simon Iscariot. This man—one from the Twelve!—was even then getting ready to betray him.

7.1-2 **7** Later Jesus was going about his business in Galilee. He didn't want to travel in Judea because the Jews there were looking for a chance to kill him. It was near the time of Tabernacles, a feast observed annually by the Jews.

7.3-5 His brothers said, "Why don't you leave here and go up to the Feast so your disciples can get a good look at the works you do? No one who intends to be publicly known does everything behind the scenes. If you're serious about what you are doing, come out in the open and show the world." His brothers were pushing him like this because they didn't believe in him either.

7.6-8 Jesus came back at them, "Don't crowd me. This isn't my time. It's your time—it's *always* your time; you have nothing to lose. The world has nothing against you, but it's up in arms against me. It's against me because I expose the evil behind its pretensions. You go ahead, go up to the Feast. Don't wait for me. I'm not ready. It's not the right time for me."

7.9-11 He said this and stayed on in Galilee. But later, after his family had gone up to the Feast, he also went. But he kept out of the way, care-

---

a 63 Or *Spirit*   *b* 8 Some early manuscripts do not have *yet.*

NEW INTERNATIONAL VERSION

cret. ¹¹Now at the Feast the Jews were watching for him and asking, "Where is that man?"

¹²Among the crowds there was widespread whispering about him. Some said, "He is a good man."

Others replied, "No, he deceives the people." ¹³But no one would say anything publicly about him for fear of the Jews.

JESUS TEACHES AT THE FEAST

¹⁴Not until halfway through the Feast did Jesus go up to the temple courts and begin to teach. ¹⁵The Jews were amazed and asked, "How did this man get such learning without having studied?"

¹⁶Jesus answered, "My teaching is not my own. It comes from him who sent me. ¹⁷If anyone chooses to do God's will, he will find out whether my teaching comes from God or whether I speak on my own. ¹⁸He who speaks on his own does so to gain honor for himself, but he who works for the honor of the one who sent him is a man of truth; there is nothing false about him. ¹⁹Has not Moses given you the law? Yet not one of you keeps the law. Why are you trying to kill me?"

²⁰"You are demon-possessed," the crowd answered. "Who is trying to kill you?"

²¹Jesus said to them, "I did one miracle, and you are all astonished. ²²Yet, because Moses gave you circumcision (though actually it did not come from Moses, but from the patriarchs), you circumcise a child on the Sabbath. ²³Now if a child can be circumcised on the Sabbath so that the law of Moses may not be broken, why are you angry with me for healing the whole man on the Sabbath? ²⁴Stop judging by mere appearances, and make a right judgment."

IS JESUS THE CHRIST?

²⁵At that point some of the people of Jerusalem began to ask, "Isn't this the man they are trying to kill? ²⁶Here he is, speaking publicly, and they are not saying a word to him. Have the authorities really concluded that he is the Christ*ᵃ*? ²⁷But we know where this man is from; when the Christ comes, no one will know where he is from."

²⁸Then Jesus, still teaching in the temple courts, cried out, "Yes, you know me, and you know where I am from. I am not here on my own, but he who sent me is true. You do not know him, ²⁹but I know him because I am from him and he sent me."

ᵃ 26 Or Messiah; also in verses 27, 31, 41 and 42

THE MESSAGE

ful not to draw attention to himself. The Jews were already out looking for him, asking around, "Where is that man?"

7.12-13 There was a lot of contentious talk about him circulating through the crowds. Some were saying, "He's a good man." But others said, "Not so. He's selling snake oil." This kind of talk went on in guarded whispers because of the intimidating Jewish leaders.

COULD IT BE THE MESSIAH?

7.14-15 With the Feast already half over, Jesus showed up in the Temple, teaching. The Jews were impressed, but puzzled: "How does he know so much without being schooled?"

7.16-19 Jesus said, "I didn't make this up. What I teach comes from the One who sent me. Anyone who wants to do his will can test this teaching and know whether it's from God or whether I'm making it up. A person making things up tries to make himself look good. But someone trying to honor the one who sent him sticks to the facts and doesn't tamper with reality. It was Moses, wasn't it, who gave you God's Law? But none of you are living it. So why are you trying to kill me?"

7.20 The crowd said, "You're crazy! Who's trying to kill you? You're demon-possessed."

7.21-24 Jesus said, "I did one miraculous thing a few months ago, and you're still standing around getting all upset, wondering what I'm up to. Moses prescribed circumcision—originally it came not from Moses but from his ancestors—and so you circumcise a man, dealing with one part of his body, even if it's the Sabbath. You do this in order to preserve one item in the Law of Moses. So why are you upset with me because I made a man's whole body well on the Sabbath? Don't be nitpickers; use your head—and heart!—to discern what is right, to test what is authentically right."

7.25-27 That's when some of the people of Jerusalem said, "Isn't this the one they were out to kill? And here he is out in the open, saying whatever he pleases, and no one is stopping him. Could it be that the rulers know that he is, in fact, the Messiah? And yet we know where this man came from. The Messiah is going to come out of nowhere. Nobody is going to know where he comes from."

7.28-29 That provoked Jesus, who was teaching in the Temple, to cry out, "Yes, you think you know me and where I'm from, but that's not where I'm from. I didn't set myself up in business. My true origin is in the One who sent me, and you don't know him at all. I come from him—that's how I know him. He sent me here."

NEW INTERNATIONAL VERSION

30At this they tried to seize him, but no one laid a hand on him, because his time had not yet come. 31Still, many in the crowd put their faith in him. They said, "When the Christ comes, will he do more miraculous signs than this man?"

32The Pharisees heard the crowd whispering such things about him. Then the chief priests and the Pharisees sent temple guards to arrest him.

33Jesus said, "I am with you for only a short time, and then I go to the one who sent me. 34You will look for me, but you will not find me; and where I am, you cannot come."

35The Jews said to one another, "Where does this man intend to go that we cannot find him? Will he go where our people live scattered among the Greeks, and teach the Greeks? 36What did he mean when he said, 'You will look for me, but you will not find me,' and 'Where I am, you cannot come'?"

37On the last and greatest day of the Feast, Jesus stood and said in a loud voice, "If anyone is thirsty, let him come to me and drink. 38Whoever believes in me, as a the Scripture has said, streams of living water will flow from within him." 39By this he meant the Spirit, whom those who believed in him were later to receive. Up to that time the Spirit had not been given, since Jesus had not yet been glorified.

40On hearing his words, some of the people said, "Surely this man is the Prophet."

41Others said, "He is the Christ."

Still others asked, "How can the Christ come from Galilee? 42Does not the Scripture say that the Christ will come from David's family b and from Bethlehem, the town where David lived?" 43Thus the people were divided because of Jesus. 44Some wanted to seize him, but no one laid a hand on him.

UNBELIEF OF THE JEWISH LEADERS

45Finally the temple guards went back to the chief priests and Pharisees, who asked them, "Why didn't you bring him in?"

46"No one ever spoke the way this man does," the guards declared.

47"You mean he has deceived you also?" the Pharisees retorted. 48"Has any of the rulers or of the Pharisees believed in him? 49No! But this mob that knows nothing of the law—there is a curse on them."

50Nicodemus, who had gone to Jesus earlier and who was one of their own number, asked, 51"Does our law condemn anyone without first hearing him to find out what he is doing?"

a 37,38 Or / If anyone is thirsty, let him come to me. / And let him drink, 38who believes in me. / As   b 42 Greek seed

THE MESSAGE

7.30-31   They were looking for a way to arrest him, but not a hand was laid on him because it wasn't yet God's time. Many from the crowd committed themselves in faith to him, saying, "Will the Messiah, when he comes, provide better or more convincing evidence than this?"

7.32-34   The Pharisees, alarmed at this seditious undertow going through the crowd, teamed up with the high priests and sent their police to arrest him. Jesus rebuffed them: "I am with you only a short time. Then I go on to the One who sent me. You will look for me, but you won't find me. Where I am, you can't come."

7.35-36   The Jews put their heads together. "Where do you think he is going that we won't be able to find him? Do you think he is about to travel to the Greek world to teach the Jews? What is he talking about, anyway: 'You will look for me, but you won't find me,' and 'Where I am, you can't come'?"

7.37-39   On the final and climactic day of the Feast, Jesus took his stand. He cried out, "If anyone thirsts, let him come to me and drink. Rivers of living water will brim and spill out of the depths of anyone who believes in me this way, just as the Scripture says." (He said this in regard to the Spirit, whom those who believed in him were about to receive. The Spirit had not yet been given because Jesus had not yet been glorified.)

7.40-44   Those in the crowd who heard these words were saying, "This has to be the Prophet." Others said, "He is the Messiah!" But others were saying, "The Messiah doesn't come from Galilee, does he? Don't the Scriptures tell us that the Messiah comes from David's line and from Bethlehem, David's village?" So there was a split in the crowd over him. Some went so far as wanting to arrest him, but no one laid a hand on him.

7.45   That's when the Temple police reported back to the high priests and Pharisees, who demanded, "Why didn't you bring him with you?"

7.46   The police answered, "Have you heard the way he talks? We've never heard anyone speak like this man."

7.47-49   The Pharisees said, "Are you carried away like the rest of the rabble? You don't see any of the leaders believing in him, do you? Or any from the Pharisees? It's only this crowd, ignorant of God's Law, that is taken in by him—and damned."

7.50-51   Nicodemus, the man who had come to Jesus earlier and was both a ruler and a Pharisee, spoke up. "Does our Law decide about a man's guilt without first listening to him and finding out what he is doing?"

NEW INTERNATIONAL VERSION

52They replied, "Are you from Galilee, too? Look into it, and you will find that a prophet*a* does not come out of Galilee."

[The earliest manuscripts and many other ancient witnesses do not have John 7:53–8:11.]

53Then each went to his own home.

8 But Jesus went to the Mount of Olives. 2At dawn he appeared again in the temple courts, where all the people gathered around him, and he sat down to teach them. 3The teachers of the law and the Pharisees brought in a woman caught in adultery. They made her stand before the group 4and said to Jesus, "Teacher, this woman was caught in the act of adultery. 5In the Law Moses commanded us to stone such women. Now what do you say?" 6They were using this question as a trap, in order to have a basis for accusing him.

But Jesus bent down and started to write on the ground with his finger. 7When they kept on questioning him, he straightened up and said to them, "If any one of you is without sin, let him be the first to throw a stone at her." 8Again he stooped down and wrote on the ground.

9At this, those who heard began to go away one at a time, the older ones first, until only Jesus was left, with the woman still standing there. 10Jesus straightened up and asked her, "Woman, where are they? Has no one condemned you?"

11"No one, sir," she said.

"Then neither do I condemn you," Jesus declared. "Go now and leave your life of sin."

THE VALIDITY OF JESUS' TESTIMONY

12When Jesus spoke again to the people, he said, "I am the light of the world. Whoever follows me will never walk in darkness, but will have the light of life."

13The Pharisees challenged him, "Here you are, appearing as your own witness; your testimony is not valid."

14Jesus answered, "Even if I testify on my own behalf, my testimony is valid, for I know where I came from and where I am going. But you have no idea where I come from or where I am going. 15You judge by human standards; I pass judgment on no one. 16But if I do judge, my deci-

a 52 Two early manuscripts *the Prophet*

THE MESSAGE

7.52-53 But they cut him off. "Are you also campaigning for the Galilean? Examine the evidence. See if any prophet ever comes from Galilee."

Then they all went home.

TO THROW THE STONE

8.1-2 8 Jesus went across to Mount Olives, but he was soon back in the Temple again. Swarms of people came to him. He sat down and taught them.

8.3-6 The religion scholars and Pharisees led in a woman who had been caught in an act of adultery. They stood her in plain sight of everyone and said, "Teacher, this woman was caught red-handed in the act of adultery. Moses, in the Law, gives orders to stone such persons. What do you say?" They were trying to trap him into saying something incriminating so they could bring charges against him.

8.6-8 Jesus bent down and wrote with his finger in the dirt. They kept at him, badgering him. He straightened up and said, "The sinless one among you, go first: Throw the stone." Bending down again, he wrote some more in the dirt.

8.9-10 Hearing that, they walked away, one after another, beginning with the oldest. The woman was left alone. Jesus stood up and spoke to her. "Woman, where are they? Does no one condemn you?"

8.11 "No one, Master."

8.11 "Neither do I," said Jesus. "Go on your way. From now on, don't sin."

YOU'RE MISSING GOD IN ALL THIS

8.12 Jesus once again addressed them: "I am the world's Light. No one who follows me stumbles around in the darkness. I provide plenty of light to live in."

8.13 The Pharisees objected, "All we have is your word on this. We need more than this to go on."

8.14-18 Jesus replied, "You're right that you only have my word. But you can depend on it being true. I know where I've come from and where I go next. You don't know where I'm from or where I'm headed. You decide according to what you can see and touch. I don't make judgments like that. But even if I did, my judgment would be true

NEW INTERNATIONAL VERSION

sions are right, because I am not alone. I stand with the Father, who sent me. ¹⁷In your own Law it is written that the testimony of two men is valid. ¹⁸I am one who testifies for myself; my other witness is the Father, who sent me."

¹⁹Then they asked him, "Where is your father?"

"You do not know me or my Father," Jesus replied. "If you knew me, you would know my Father also." ²⁰He spoke these words while teaching in the temple area near the place where the offerings were put. Yet no one seized him, because his time had not yet come.

²¹Once more Jesus said to them, "I am going away, and you will look for me, and you will die in your sin. Where I go, you cannot come."

²²This made the Jews ask, "Will he kill himself? Is that why he says, 'Where I go, you cannot come'?"

²³But he continued, "You are from below; I am from above. You are of this world; I am not of this world. ²⁴I told you that you would die in your sins; if you do not believe that I am ⌞the one I claim to be⌟,ᵃ you will indeed die in your sins."

²⁵"Who are you?" they asked.

"Just what I have been claiming all along," Jesus replied. ²⁶"I have much to say in judgment of you. But he who sent me is reliable, and what I have heard from him I tell the world."

²⁷They did not understand that he was telling them about his Father. ²⁸So Jesus said, "When you have lifted up the Son of Man, then you will know that I am ⌞the one I claim to be⌟ and that I do nothing on my own but speak just what the Father has taught me. ²⁹The one who sent me is with me; he has not left me alone, for I always do what pleases him." ³⁰Even as he spoke, many put their faith in him.

The Children of Abraham

³¹To the Jews who had believed him, Jesus said, "If you hold to my teaching, you are really my disciples. ³²Then you will know the truth, and the truth will set you free."

THE MESSAGE

because I wouldn't make it out of the narrowness of my experience but in the largeness of the One who sent me, the Father. That fulfills the conditions set down in God's Law: that you can count on the testimony of two witnesses. And that is what you have: You have my word and you have the word of the Father who sent me."

8.19   They said, "Where is this so-called Father of yours?"

Jesus said, "You're looking right at me and you don't see me. How do you expect to see the Father? If you knew me, you would at the same time know the Father."

8.20   He gave this speech in the Treasury while teaching in the Temple. No one arrested him because his time wasn't yet up.

8.21   Then he went over the same ground again. "I'm leaving and you are going to look for me, but you're missing God in this and are headed for a dead end. There is no way you can come with me."

8.22   The Jews said, "So, is he going to kill himself? Is that what he means by 'You can't come with me'?"

8.23-24   Jesus said, "You're tied down to the mundane; I'm in touch with what is beyond your horizons. You live in terms of what you see and touch. I'm living on other terms. I told you that you were missing God in all this. You're at a dead end. If you won't believe I am who I say I am, you're at the dead end of sins. You're missing God in your lives."

8.25-26   They said to him, "Just who are you anyway?"

Jesus said, "What I've said from the start. I have so many things to say that concern you, judgments to make that affect you, but if you don't accept the trustworthiness of the One who commanded my words and acts, none of it matters. That is who you are questioning—not me but the One who sent me."

8.27-29   They still didn't get it, didn't realize that he was referring to the Father. So Jesus tried again. "When you raise up the Son of Man, then you will know who I am—that I'm not making this up, but speaking only what the Father taught me. The One who sent me stays with me. He doesn't abandon me. He sees how much joy I take in pleasing him."

8.30   When he put it in these terms, many people decided to believe.

If the Son Sets You Free

8.31-32   Then Jesus turned to the Jews who had claimed to believe in him. "If you stick with this, living out what I tell you, you are my disciples for sure. Then you will experience for yourselves the truth, and the truth will free you."

ᵃ 24 Or *I am he*; also in verse 28

NEW INTERNATIONAL VERSION

³³They answered him, "We are Abraham's descendants[a] and have never been slaves of anyone. How can you say that we shall be set free?"

³⁴Jesus replied, "I tell you the truth, everyone who sins is a slave to sin. ³⁵Now a slave has no permanent place in the family, but a son belongs to it forever. ³⁶So if the Son sets you free, you will be free indeed. ³⁷I know you are Abraham's descendants. Yet you are ready to kill me, because you have no room for my word. ³⁸I am telling you what I have seen in the Father's presence, and you do what you have heard from your father.[b]"

³⁹"Abraham is our father," they answered.

"If you were Abraham's children," said Jesus, "then you would[c] do the things Abraham did. ⁴⁰As it is, you are determined to kill me, a man who has told you the truth that I heard from God. Abraham did not do such things. ⁴¹You are doing the things your own father does."

"We are not illegitimate children," they protested. "The only Father we have is God himself."

THE CHILDREN OF THE DEVIL

⁴²Jesus said to them, "If God were your Father, you would love me, for I came from God and now am here. I have not come on my own; but he sent me. ⁴³Why is my language not clear to you? Because you are unable to hear what I say. ⁴⁴You belong to your father, the devil, and you want to carry out your father's desire. He was a murderer from the beginning, not holding to the truth, for there is no truth in him. When he lies, he speaks his native language, for he is a liar and the father of lies. ⁴⁵Yet because I tell the truth, you do not believe me! ⁴⁶Can any of you prove me guilty of sin? If I am telling the truth, why don't you believe me? ⁴⁷He who belongs to God hears what God says. The reason you do not hear is that you do not belong to God."

THE CLAIMS OF JESUS ABOUT HIMSELF

⁴⁸The Jews answered him, "Aren't we right in saying that you are a Samaritan and demon-possessed?"

⁴⁹"I am not possessed by a demon," said Jesus, "but I honor my Father and you dishonor me. ⁵⁰I am not seeking glory for myself; but there is one who seeks it, and he is the judge. ⁵¹I tell you the truth, if anyone keeps my word, he will never see death."

a 33 Greek *seed*; also in verse 37   b 38 Or *presence. Therefore do what you have heard from the Father.*
c 39 Some early manuscripts *"If you are Abraham's children,"* said Jesus, *"then*

THE MESSAGE

8.33   Surprised, they said, "But we're descendants of Abraham. We've never been slaves to anyone. How can you say, 'The truth will free you'?"

8.34-38   Jesus said, "I tell you most solemnly that anyone who chooses a life of sin is trapped in a dead-end life and is, in fact, a slave. A slave is a transient, who can't come and go at will. The Son, though, has an established position, the run of the house. So if the Son sets you free, you are free through and through. I know you are Abraham's descendants. But I also know that you are trying to kill me because my message hasn't yet penetrated your thick skulls. I'm talking about things I have seen while keeping company with the Father, and you just go on doing what you have heard from your father."

8.39-41   They were indignant. "Our father is Abraham!"

Jesus said, "If you were Abraham's children, you would have been doing the things Abraham did. And yet here you are trying to kill me, a man who has spoken to you the truth he got straight from God! Abraham never did that sort of thing. You persist in repeating the works of your father."

They said, "We're not bastards. We have a legitimate father: the one and only God."

8.42-47   "If God was your father," said Jesus, "you would love me, for I came from God and arrived here. I didn't come on my own. He sent me. Why can't you understand one word I say? Here's why: You can't handle it. You're from your father, the Devil, and all you want to do is please him. He was a killer from the very start. He couldn't stand the truth because there wasn't a shred of truth in him. When the Liar speaks, he makes it up out of his lying nature and fills the world with lies. I arrive on the scene, tell you the plain truth, and you refuse to have a thing to do with me. Can any one of you convict me of a single misleading word, a single sinful act? But if I'm telling the truth, why don't you believe me? Anyone on God's side listens to God's words. This is why you're not listening—because you're not on God's side."

I AM WHO I AM

8.48   The Jews then said, "That clinches it. We were right all along when we called you a Samaritan and said you were crazy—demon-possessed!"

8.49-51   Jesus said, "I'm not crazy. I simply honor my Father, while you dishonor me. I am not trying to get anything for myself. God intends something gloriously grand here and is making the decisions that will bring it about. I say this with absolute confidence. If you practice what I'm telling you, you'll never have to look death in the face."

NEW INTERNATIONAL VERSION

⁵²At this the Jews exclaimed, "Now we know that you are demon-possessed! Abraham died and so did the prophets, yet you say that if anyone keeps your word, he will never taste death. ⁵³Are you greater than our father Abraham? He died, and so did the prophets. Who do you think you are?"

⁵⁴Jesus replied, "If I glorify myself, my glory means nothing. My Father, whom you claim as your God, is the one who glorifies me. ⁵⁵Though you do not know him, I know him. If I said I did not, I would be a liar like you, but I do know him and keep his word. ⁵⁶Your father Abraham rejoiced at the thought of seeing my day; he saw it and was glad."

⁵⁷"You are not yet fifty years old," the Jews said to him, "and you have seen Abraham!"

⁵⁸"I tell you the truth," Jesus answered, "before Abraham was born, I am!" ⁵⁹At this, they picked up stones to stone him, but Jesus hid himself, slipping away from the temple grounds.

JESUS HEALS A MAN BORN BLIND

9 As he went along, he saw a man blind from birth. ²His disciples asked him, "Rabbi, who sinned, this man or his parents, that he was born blind?"

³"Neither this man nor his parents sinned," said Jesus, "but this happened so that the work of God might be displayed in his life. ⁴As long as it is day, we must do the work of him who sent me. Night is coming, when no one can work. ⁵While I am in the world, I am the light of the world."

⁶Having said this, he spit on the ground, made some mud with the saliva, and put it on the man's eyes. ⁷"Go," he told him, "wash in the Pool of Siloam" (this word means Sent). So the man went and washed, and came home seeing.

⁸His neighbors and those who had formerly seen him begging asked, "Isn't this the same man who used to sit and beg?" ⁹Some claimed that he was.

Others said, "No, he only looks like him."

But he himself insisted, "I am the man."

¹⁰"How then were your eyes opened?" they demanded.

¹¹He replied, "The man they call Jesus made some mud and put it on my eyes. He told me to go to Siloam and wash. So I went and washed, and then I could see."

THE MESSAGE

8.52-53 At this point the Jews said, "Now we *know* you're crazy. Abraham died. The prophets died. And you show up saying, 'If you practice what I'm telling you, you'll never have to face death, not even a taste.' Are you greater than Abraham, who died? And the prophets died! Who do you think you are!"

8.54-56 Jesus said, "If I turned the spotlight on myself, it wouldn't amount to anything. But my Father, the same One you say is your Father, put me here at this time and place of splendor. You haven't recognized him in this. But I have. If I, in false modesty, said I didn't know what was going on, I would be as much of a liar as you are. But I do know, and I am doing what he says. Abraham—your 'father'—with jubilant faith looked down the corridors of history and saw my day coming. He saw it and cheered."

8.57 The Jews said, "You're not even fifty years old—and Abraham saw you?"

8.58 "Believe me," said Jesus, "*I am who I am* long before Abraham was anything."

8.59 That did it—pushed them over the edge. They picked up rocks to throw at him. But Jesus slipped away, getting out of the Temple.

TRUE BLINDNESS

9.1-2 **9** Walking down the street, Jesus saw a man blind from birth. His disciples asked, "Rabbi, who sinned: this man or his parents, causing him to be born blind?"

9.3-5 Jesus said, "You're asking the wrong question. You're looking for someone to blame. There is no such cause-effect here. Look instead for what God can do. We need to be energetically at work for the One who sent me here, working while the sun shines. When night falls, the workday is over. For as long as I am in the world, there is plenty of light. I am the world's Light."

9.6-7 He said this and then spit in the dust, made a clay paste with the saliva, rubbed the paste on the blind man's eyes, and said, "Go, wash at the Pool of Siloam" (Siloam means "Sent"). The man went and washed—and saw.

9.8 Soon the town was buzzing. His relatives and those who year after year had seen him as a blind man begging were saying, "Why, isn't this the man we knew, who sat here and begged?"

9.9 Others said, "It's him all right!"

But others objected, "It's not the same man at all. It just looks like him."

He said, "It's me, the very one."

9.10 They said, "How did your eyes get opened?"

9.11 "A man named Jesus made a paste and rubbed it on my eyes and told me, 'Go to Siloam and wash.' I did what he said. When I washed, I saw."

NEW INTERNATIONAL VERSION

¹²"Where is this man?" they asked him.

"I don't know," he said.

THE PHARISEES INVESTIGATE THE HEALING

¹³They brought to the Pharisees the man who had been blind. ¹⁴Now the day on which Jesus had made the mud and opened the man's eyes was a Sabbath. ¹⁵Therefore the Pharisees also asked him how he had received his sight. "He put mud on my eyes," the man replied, "and I washed, and now I see."

¹⁶Some of the Pharisees said, "This man is not from God, for he does not keep the Sabbath."

But others asked, "How can a sinner do such miraculous signs?" So they were divided.

¹⁷Finally they turned again to the blind man, "What have you to say about him? It was your eyes he opened."

The man replied, "He is a prophet."

¹⁸The Jews still did not believe that he had been blind and had received his sight until they sent for the man's parents. ¹⁹"Is this your son?" they asked. "Is this the one you say was born blind? How is it that now he can see?"

²⁰"We know he is our son," the parents answered, "and we know he was born blind. ²¹But how he can see now, or who opened his eyes, we don't know. Ask him. He is of age; he will speak for himself." ²²His parents said this because they were afraid of the Jews, for already the Jews had decided that anyone who acknowledged that Jesus was the Christ*a* would be put out of the synagogue. ²³That was why his parents said, "He is of age; ask him."

²⁴A second time they summoned the man who had been blind. "Give glory to God,*b*" they said. "We know this man is a sinner."

²⁵He replied, "Whether he is a sinner or not, I don't know. One thing I do know. I was blind but now I see!"

²⁶Then they asked him, "What did he do to you? How did he open your eyes?"

²⁷He answered, "I have told you already and you did not listen. Why do you want to hear it again? Do you want to become his disciples, too?"

²⁸Then they hurled insults at him and said, "You are this fellow's disciple! We are disciples of Moses! ²⁹We know that God spoke to Moses, but as for this fellow, we don't even know where he comes from."

³⁰The man answered, "Now that is remarkable! You don't know where he comes from, yet he opened my eyes. ³¹We know that God does not listen to sinners. He listens to the godly man

a 22 Or Messiah   *b 24 A solemn charge to tell the truth (see Joshua 7:19)*

THE MESSAGE

9.12   "So where is he?"

"I don't know."

9.13-15   They marched the man to the Pharisees. This day when Jesus made the paste and healed his blindness was the Sabbath. The Pharisees grilled him again on how he had come to see. He said, "He put a clay paste on my eyes, and I washed, and now I see."

9.16   Some of the Pharisees said, "Obviously, this man can't be from God. He doesn't keep the Sabbath."

Others countered, "How can a bad man do miraculous, God-revealing things like this?" There was a split in their ranks.

9.17   They came back at the blind man, "You're the expert. He opened *your* eyes. What do you say about him?"

He said, "He is a prophet."

9.18-19   The Jews didn't believe it, didn't believe the man was blind to begin with. So they called the parents of the man now bright-eyed with sight. They asked them, "Is this your son, the one you say was born blind? So how is it that he now sees?"

9.20-23   His parents said, "We know he is our son, and we know he was born blind. But we don't know how he came to see—haven't a clue about who opened his eyes. Why don't you ask him? He's a grown man and can speak for himself." (His parents were talking like this because they were intimidated by the Jewish leaders, who had already decided that anyone who took a stand that this was the Messiah would be kicked out of the meeting place. That's why his parents said, "Ask him. He's a grown man.")

9.24   They called the man back a second time—the man who had been blind—and told him, "Give credit to God. We know this man is an impostor."

9.25   He replied, "I know nothing about that one way or the other. But I know one thing for sure: I was blind . . . I now see."

9.26   They said, "What did he do to you? How did he open your eyes?"

9.27   "I've told you over and over and you haven't listened. Why do you want to hear it again? Are you so eager to become his disciples?"

9.28-29   With that they jumped all over him. "*You* might be a disciple of that man, but we're disciples of Moses. We know for sure that God spoke to Moses, but we have no idea where this man even comes from."

9.30-33   The man replied, "This is amazing! You claim to know nothing about him, but the fact is, he opened my eyes! It's well known that God isn't at the beck and call of sinners, but lis-

NEW INTERNATIONAL VERSION

who does his will. ³²Nobody has ever heard of opening the eyes of a man born blind. ³³If this man were not from God, he could do nothing."

³⁴To this they replied, "You were steeped in sin at birth; how dare you lecture us!" And they threw him out.

SPIRITUAL BLINDNESS

³⁵Jesus heard that they had thrown him out, and when he found him, he said, "Do you believe in the Son of Man?"

³⁶"Who is he, sir?" the man asked. "Tell me so that I may believe in him."

³⁷Jesus said, "You have now seen him; in fact, he is the one speaking with you."

³⁸Then the man said, "Lord, I believe," and he worshiped him.

³⁹Jesus said, "For judgment I have come into this world, so that the blind will see and those who see will become blind."

⁴⁰Some Pharisees who were with him heard him say this and asked, "What? Are we blind too?"

⁴¹Jesus said, "If you were blind, you would not be guilty of sin; but now that you claim you can see, your guilt remains.

THE SHEPHERD AND HIS FLOCK

10 "I tell you the truth, the man who does not enter the sheep pen by the gate, but climbs in by some other way, is a thief and a robber. ²The man who enters by the gate is the shepherd of his sheep. ³The watchman opens the gate for him, and the sheep listen to his voice. He calls his own sheep by name and leads them out. ⁴When he has brought out all his own, he goes on ahead of them, and his sheep follow him because they know his voice. ⁵But they will never follow a stranger; in fact, they will run away from him because they do not recognize a stranger's voice." ⁶Jesus used this figure of speech, but they did not understand what he was telling them.

⁷Therefore Jesus said again, "I tell you the truth, I am the gate for the sheep. ⁸All who ever came before me were thieves and robbers, but the sheep did not listen to them. ⁹I am the gate; whoever enters through me will be saved.ᵃ He will come in and go out, and find pasture. ¹⁰The thief comes only to steal and kill and destroy; I have come that they may have life, and have it to the full.

¹¹"I am the good shepherd. The good shepherd lays down his life for the sheep. ¹²The hired

ᵃ 9 Or kept safe

THE MESSAGE

tens carefully to anyone who lives in reverence and does his will. That someone opened the eyes of a man born blind has never been heard of—ever. If this man didn't come from God, he wouldn't be able to do anything."

9.34 They said, "You're nothing but dirt! How dare you take that tone with us!" Then they threw him out in the street.

9.35 Jesus heard that they had thrown him out, and went and found him. He asked him, "Do you believe in the Son of Man?"

9.36 The man said, "Point him out to me, sir, so that I can believe in him."

9.37 Jesus said, "You're looking right at him. Don't you recognize my voice?"

9.38 "Master, I believe," the man said, and worshiped him.

9.39 Jesus then said, "I came into the world to bring everything into the clear light of day, making all the distinctions clear, so that those who have never seen will see, and those who have made a great pretense of seeing will be exposed as blind."

9.40 Some Pharisees overheard him and said, "Does that mean you're calling us blind?"

9.41 Jesus said, "If you were really blind, you would be blameless, but since you claim to see everything so well, you're accountable for every fault and failure.

HE CALLS HIS SHEEP BY NAME

10.1-5 **10** "Let me set this before you as plainly as I can. If a person climbs over or through the fence of a sheep pen instead of going through the gate, you know he's up to no good—a sheep rustler! The shepherd walks right up to the gate. The gatekeeper opens the gate to him and the sheep recognize his voice. He calls his own sheep by name and leads them out. When he gets them all out, he leads them and they follow because they are familiar with his voice. They won't follow a stranger's voice but will scatter because they aren't used to the sound of it."

10.6-10 Jesus told this simple story, but they had no idea what he was talking about. So he tried again. "I'll be explicit, then. I am the Gate for the sheep. All those others are up to no good—sheep stealers, every one of them. But the sheep didn't listen to them. I am the Gate. Anyone who goes through me will be cared for—will freely go in and out, and find pasture. A thief is only there to steal and kill and destroy. I came so they can have real and eternal life, more and better life than they ever dreamed of.

10.11-13 "I am the Good Shepherd. The Good Shepherd puts the sheep before himself, sacrifices

NEW INTERNATIONAL VERSION

hand is not the shepherd who owns the sheep. So when he sees the wolf coming, he abandons the sheep and runs away. Then the wolf attacks the flock and scatters it. ¹³The man runs away because he is a hired hand and cares nothing for the sheep.

¹⁴"I am the good shepherd; I know my sheep and my sheep know me— ¹⁵just as the Father knows me and I know the Father—and I lay down my life for the sheep. ¹⁶I have other sheep that are not of this sheep pen. I must bring them also. They too will listen to my voice, and there shall be one flock and one shepherd. ¹⁷The reason my Father loves me is that I lay down my life—only to take it up again. ¹⁸No one takes it from me, but I lay it down of my own accord. I have authority to lay it down and authority to take it up again. This command I received from my Father."

¹⁹At these words the Jews were again divided. ²⁰Many of them said, "He is demon-possessed and raving mad. Why listen to him?"

²¹But others said, "These are not the sayings of a man possessed by a demon. Can a demon open the eyes of the blind?"

THE UNBELIEF OF THE JEWS

²²Then came the Feast of Dedication ᵃ at Jerusalem. It was winter, ²³and Jesus was in the temple area walking in Solomon's Colonnade. ²⁴The Jews gathered around him, saying, "How long will you keep us in suspense? If you are the Christ, ᵇ tell us plainly."

²⁵Jesus answered, "I did tell you, but you do not believe. The miracles I do in my Father's name speak for me, ²⁶but you do not believe because you are not my sheep. ²⁷My sheep listen to my voice; I know them, and they follow me. ²⁸I give them eternal life, and they shall never perish; no one can snatch them out of my hand. ²⁹My Father, who has given them to me, is greater than all ᶜ; no one can snatch them out of my Father's hand. ³⁰I and the Father are one."

³¹Again the Jews picked up stones to stone him, ³²but Jesus said to them, "I have shown you many great miracles from the Father. For which of these do you stone me?"

³³"We are not stoning you for any of these," replied the Jews, "but for blasphemy, because you, a mere man, claim to be God."

³⁴Jesus answered them, "Is it not written in your Law, 'I have said you are gods' ᵈ? ³⁵If he called them 'gods,' to whom the word of God

---

ᵃ 22 That is, Hanukkah   ᵇ 24 Or *Messiah*   ᶜ 29 Many early manuscripts *What my Father has given me is greater than all*   ᵈ 34 Psalm 82:6

THE MESSAGE

himself if necessary. A hired man is not a real shepherd. The sheep mean nothing to him. He sees a wolf come and runs for it, leaving the sheep to be ravaged and scattered by the wolf. He's only in it for the money. The sheep don't matter to him.

10.14-18 "I am the Good Shepherd. I know my own sheep and my own sheep know me. In the same way, the Father knows me and I know the Father. I put the sheep before myself, sacrificing myself if necessary. You need to know that I have other sheep in addition to those in this pen. I need to gather and bring them, too. They'll also recognize my voice. Then it will be one flock, one Shepherd. This is why the Father loves me: because I freely lay down my life. And so I am free to take it up again. No one takes it from me. I lay it down of my own free will. I have the right to lay it down; I also have the right to take it up again. I received this authority personally from my Father."

10.19-21 This kind of talk caused another split in the Jewish ranks. A lot of them were saying, "He's crazy, a maniac—out of his head completely. Why bother listening to him?" But others weren't so sure: "These aren't the words of a crazy man. Can a 'maniac' open blind eyes?"

10.22-24 They were celebrating Hanukkah just then in Jerusalem. It was winter. Jesus was strolling in the Temple across Solomon's Porch. The Jews, circling him, said, "How long are you going to keep us guessing? If you're the Messiah, tell us straight out."

10.25-30 Jesus answered, "I told you, but you don't believe. Everything I have done has been authorized by my Father, actions that speak louder than words. You don't believe because you're not my sheep. My sheep recognize my voice. I know them, and they follow me. I give them real and eternal life. They are protected from the Destroyer for good. No one can steal them from out of my hand. The Father who put them under my care is so much greater than the Destroyer and Thief. No one could ever get them away from him. I and the Father are one heart and mind."

10.31-32 Again the Jews picked up rocks to throw at him. Jesus said, "I have made a present to you from the Father of a great many good actions. For which of these acts do you stone me?"

10.33 The Jews said, "We're not stoning you for anything good you did, but for what you said— this blasphemy of calling yourself God."

10.34-38 Jesus said, "I'm only quoting your inspired Scriptures, where God said, 'I tell you—you are gods.' If God called your ancestors 'gods'—and

NEW INTERNATIONAL VERSION

came—and the Scripture cannot be broken—
³⁶what about the one whom the Father set apart
as his very own and sent into the world? Why
then do you accuse me of blasphemy because I
said, 'I am God's Son'? ³⁷Do not believe me unless I do what my Father does. ³⁸But if I do it,
even though you do not believe me, believe the
miracles, that you may know and understand
that the Father is in me, and I in the Father."
³⁹Again they tried to seize him, but he escaped
their grasp.

⁴⁰Then Jesus went back across the Jordan to
the place where John had been baptizing in the
early days. Here he stayed ⁴¹and many people
came to him. They said, "Though John never performed a miraculous sign, all that John said about
this man was true." ⁴²And in that place many believed in Jesus.

THE DEATH OF LAZARUS

11 Now a man named Lazarus was sick.
He was from Bethany, the village of Mary
and her sister Martha. ²This Mary, whose brother Lazarus now lay sick, was the same one who
poured perfume on the Lord and wiped his feet
with her hair. ³So the sisters sent word to Jesus,
"Lord, the one you love is sick."

⁴When he heard this, Jesus said, "This sickness will not end in death. No, it is for God's glory so that God's Son may be glorified through
it." ⁵Jesus loved Martha and her sister and Lazarus. ⁶Yet when he heard that Lazarus was sick,
he stayed where he was two more days.

⁷Then he said to his disciples, "Let us go back
to Judea."

⁸"But Rabbi," they said, "a short while ago the
Jews tried to stone you, and yet you are going
back there?"

⁹Jesus answered, "Are there not twelve hours
of daylight? A man who walks by day will not
stumble, for he sees by this world's light. ¹⁰It is
when he walks by night that he stumbles, for he
has no light."

¹¹After he had said this, he went on to tell
them, "Our friend Lazarus has fallen asleep; but
I am going there to wake him up."

¹²His disciples replied, "Lord, if he sleeps, he
will get better." ¹³Jesus had been speaking of his
death, but his disciples thought he meant natural
sleep.

¹⁴So then he told them plainly, "Lazarus is
dead, ¹⁵and for your sake I am glad I was not
there, so that you may believe. But let us go to
him."

THE MESSAGE

Scripture doesn't lie—why do you yell, 'Blasphemer! Blasphemer!' at the unique One the
Father consecrated and sent into the world,
just because I said, 'I am the Son of God'? If I
don't do the things my Father does, well and
good; don't believe me. But if I am doing them,
put aside for a moment what you hear me say
about myself and just take the evidence of the
actions that are right before your eyes. Then
perhaps things will come together for you, and
you'll see that not only are we doing the same
thing, we *are* the same—Father and Son. He is
in me; I am in him."

10.39-42   They tried yet again to arrest him, but he
slipped through their fingers. He went back
across the Jordan to the place where John first
baptized, and stayed there. A lot of people followed him over. They were saying, "John did
no miracles, but everything he said about this
man has come true." Many believed in him
then and there.

THE DEATH OF LAZARUS

11.1-3   **11** A man was sick, Lazarus of Bethany,
the town of Mary and her sister Martha.
This was the same Mary who massaged the
Lord's feet with aromatic oils and then wiped
them with her hair. It was her brother Lazarus
who was sick. So the sisters sent word to Jesus,
"Master, the one you love so very much is sick."

11.4   When Jesus got the message, he said, "This
sickness is not fatal. It will become an occasion
to show God's glory by glorifying God's Son."

11.5-7   Jesus loved Martha and her sister and Lazarus, but oddly, when he heard that Lazarus was
sick, he stayed on where he was for two more
days. After the two days, he said to his disciples, "Let's go back to Judea."

11.8   They said, "Rabbi, you can't do that. The Jews
are out to kill you, and you're going back?"

11.9-10   Jesus replied, "Are there not twelve hours of
daylight? Anyone who walks in daylight doesn't
stumble because there's plenty of light from the
sun. Walking at night, he might very well stumble because he can't see where he's going."

11.11   He said these things, and then announced,
"Our friend Lazarus has fallen asleep. I'm going
to wake him up."

11.12-13   The disciples said, "Master, if he's gone to
sleep, he'll get a good rest and wake up feeling
fine." Jesus was talking about death, while his
disciples thought he was talking about taking a
nap.

11.14-15   Then Jesus became explicit: "Lazarus died.
And I am glad for your sakes that I wasn't
there. You're about to be given new grounds for
believing. Now let's go to him."

NEW INTERNATIONAL VERSION

¹⁶Then Thomas (called Didymus) said to the rest of the disciples, "Let us also go, that we may die with him."

JESUS COMFORTS THE SISTERS

¹⁷On his arrival, Jesus found that Lazarus had already been in the tomb for four days. ¹⁸Bethany was less than two miles*ᵃ* from Jerusalem, ¹⁹and many Jews had come to Martha and Mary to comfort them in the loss of their brother. ²⁰When Martha heard that Jesus was coming, she went out to meet him, but Mary stayed at home.

²¹"Lord," Martha said to Jesus, "if you had been here, my brother would not have died. ²²But I know that even now God will give you whatever you ask."

²³Jesus said to her, "Your brother will rise again."

²⁴Martha answered, "I know he will rise again in the resurrection at the last day."

²⁵Jesus said to her, "I am the resurrection and the life. He who believes in me will live, even though he dies; ²⁶and whoever lives and believes in me will never die. Do you believe this?"

²⁷"Yes, Lord," she told him, "I believe that you are the Christ,*ᵇ* the Son of God, who was to come into the world."

²⁸And after she had said this, she went back and called her sister Mary aside. "The Teacher is here," she said, "and is asking for you." ²⁹When Mary heard this, she got up quickly and went to him. ³⁰Now Jesus had not yet entered the village, but was still at the place where Martha had met him. ³¹When the Jews who had been with Mary in the house, comforting her, noticed how quickly she got up and went out, they followed her, supposing she was going to the tomb to mourn there.

³²When Mary reached the place where Jesus was and saw him, she fell at his feet and said, "Lord, if you had been here, my brother would not have died."

³³When Jesus saw her weeping, and the Jews who had come along with her also weeping, he was deeply moved in spirit and troubled. ³⁴"Where have you laid him?" he asked.

"Come and see, Lord," they replied.

³⁵Jesus wept.

³⁶Then the Jews said, "See how he loved him!"

³⁷But some of them said, "Could not he who opened the eyes of the blind man have kept this man from dying?"

JESUS RAISES LAZARUS FROM THE DEAD

³⁸Jesus, once more deeply moved, came to the tomb. It was a cave with a stone laid across the entrance. ³⁹"Take away the stone," he said.

ᵃ 18 Greek *fifteen stadia* (about 3 kilometers)
ᵇ 27 Or *Messiah*

THE MESSAGE

11.16 That's when Thomas, the one called the Twin, said to his companions, "Come along. We might as well die with him."

11.17-20 When Jesus finally got there, he found Lazarus already four days dead. Bethany was near Jerusalem, only a couple of miles away, and many of the Jews were visiting Martha and Mary, sympathizing with them over their brother. Martha heard Jesus was coming and went out to meet him. Mary remained in the house.

11.21-22 Martha said, "Master, if you'd been here, my brother wouldn't have died. Even now, I know that whatever you ask God he will give you."

11.23 Jesus said, "Your brother will be raised up."

11.24 Martha replied, "I know that he will be raised up in the resurrection at the end of time."

11.25-26 "You don't have to wait for the End. I am, right now, Resurrection and Life. The one who believes in me, even though he or she dies, will live. And everyone who lives believing in me does not ultimately die at all. Do you believe this?"

11.27 "Yes, Master. All along I have believed that you are the Messiah, the Son of God who comes into the world."

11.28 After saying this, she went to her sister Mary and whispered in her ear, "The Teacher is here and is asking for you."

11.29-32 The moment she heard that, she jumped up and ran out to him. Jesus had not yet entered the town but was still at the place where Martha had met him. When her sympathizing Jewish friends saw Mary run off, they followed her, thinking she was on her way to the tomb to weep there. Mary came to where Jesus was waiting and fell at his feet, saying, "Master, if only you had been here, my brother would not have died."

11.33-34 When Jesus saw her sobbing and the Jews with her sobbing, a deep anger welled up within him. He said, "Where did you put him?"

11.34-35 "Master, come and see," they said. Now Jesus wept.

11.36 The Jews said, "Look how deeply he loved him."

11.37 Others among them said, "Well, if he loved him so much, why didn't he do something to keep him from dying? After all, he opened the eyes of a blind man."

11.38-39 Then Jesus, the anger again welling up within him, arrived at the tomb. It was a simple cave in the hillside with a slab of stone laid against it. Jesus said, "Remove the stone."

NEW INTERNATIONAL VERSION

"But, Lord," said Martha, the sister of the dead man, "by this time there is a bad odor, for he has been there four days."

⁴⁰Then Jesus said, "Did I not tell you that if you believed, you would see the glory of God?"

⁴¹So they took away the stone. Then Jesus looked up and said, "Father, I thank you that you have heard me. ⁴²I knew that you always hear me, but I said this for the benefit of the people standing here, that they may believe that you sent me."

⁴³When he had said this, Jesus called in a loud voice, "Lazarus, come out!" ⁴⁴The dead man came out, his hands and feet wrapped with strips of linen, and a cloth around his face.

Jesus said to them, "Take off the grave clothes and let him go."

The Plot to Kill Jesus

⁴⁵Therefore many of the Jews who had come to visit Mary, and had seen what Jesus did, put their faith in him. ⁴⁶But some of them went to the Pharisees and told them what Jesus had done. ⁴⁷Then the chief priests and the Pharisees called a meeting of the Sanhedrin.

"What are we accomplishing?" they asked. "Here is this man performing many miraculous signs. ⁴⁸If we let him go on like this, everyone will believe in him, and then the Romans will come and take away both our place *a* and our nation."

⁴⁹Then one of them, named Caiaphas, who was high priest that year, spoke up, "You know nothing at all! ⁵⁰You do not realize that it is better for you that one man die for the people than that the whole nation perish."

⁵¹He did not say this on his own, but as high priest that year he prophesied that Jesus would die for the Jewish nation, ⁵²and not only for that nation but also for the scattered children of God, to bring them together and make them one. ⁵³So from that day on they plotted to take his life.

⁵⁴Therefore Jesus no longer moved about publicly among the Jews. Instead he withdrew to a region near the desert, to a village called Ephraim, where he stayed with his disciples.

⁵⁵When it was almost time for the Jewish Passover, many went up from the country to Jerusalem for their ceremonial cleansing before the Passover. ⁵⁶They kept looking for Jesus, and as they stood in the temple area they asked one another, "What do you think? Isn't he coming to the Feast at all?" ⁵⁷But the chief priests and Pharisees had given orders that if anyone found

a 48 Or temple

THE MESSAGE

The sister of the dead man, Martha, said, "Master, by this time there's a stench. He's been dead four days!"

11.40 Jesus looked her in the eye. "Didn't I tell you that if you believed, you would see the glory of God?"

Then, to the others, "Go ahead, take away the stone."

11.41-42 They removed the stone. Jesus raised his eyes to heaven and prayed, "Father, I'm grateful that you have listened to me. I know you always do listen, but on account of this crowd standing here I've spoken so that they might believe that you sent me."

11.43-44 Then he shouted, "Lazarus, come out!" And he came out, a cadaver, wrapped from head to toe, and with a kerchief over his face.

Jesus told them, "Unwrap him and let him loose."

The Man Who Creates God-Signs

11.45-48 That was a turnaround for many of the Jews who were with Mary. They saw what Jesus did, and believed in him. But some went back to the Pharisees and told on Jesus. The high priests and Pharisees called a meeting of the Jewish ruling body. "What do we do now?" they asked. "This man keeps on doing things, creating God-signs. If we let him go on, pretty soon everyone will be believing in him and the Romans will come and remove what little power and privilege we still have."

11.49-52 Then one of them—it was Caiaphas, the designated Chief Priest that year—spoke up, "Don't you know anything? Can't you see that it's to our advantage that one man dies for the people rather than the whole nation be destroyed?" He didn't say this of his own accord, but as Chief Priest that year he unwittingly prophesied that Jesus was about to die sacrificially for the nation, and not only for the nation but so that all God's exile-scattered children might be gathered together into one people.

11.53-54 From that day on, they plotted to kill him. So Jesus no longer went out in public among the Jews. He withdrew into the country bordering the desert to a town called Ephraim and secluded himself there with his disciples.

11.55-56 The Jewish Passover was coming up. Crowds of people were making their way from the country up to Jerusalem to get themselves ready for the Feast. They were curious about Jesus. There was a lot of talk of him among those standing around in the Temple: "What do you think? Do you think he'll show up at the Feast or not?"

11.57 Meanwhile, the high priests and Pharisees gave out the word that anyone getting wind of

NEW INTERNATIONAL VERSION

out where Jesus was, he should report it so that they might arrest him.

JESUS ANOINTED AT BETHANY

12 Six days before the Passover, Jesus arrived at Bethany, where Lazarus lived, whom Jesus had raised from the dead. ²Here a dinner was given in Jesus' honor. Martha served, while Lazarus was among those reclining at the table with him. ³Then Mary took about a pint ͣ of pure nard, an expensive perfume; she poured it on Jesus' feet and wiped his feet with her hair. And the house was filled with the fragrance of the perfume.

⁴But one of his disciples, Judas Iscariot, who was later to betray him, objected, ⁵"Why wasn't this perfume sold and the money given to the poor? It was worth a year's wages. ᵇ" ⁶He did not say this because he cared about the poor but because he was a thief; as keeper of the money bag, he used to help himself to what was put into it.

⁷"Leave her alone," Jesus replied. "ᴸIt was intendedᴸ that she should save this perfume for the day of my burial. ⁸You will always have the poor among you, but you will not always have me."

⁹Meanwhile a large crowd of Jews found out that Jesus was there and came, not only because of him but also to see Lazarus, whom he had raised from the dead. ¹⁰So the chief priests made plans to kill Lazarus as well, ¹¹for on account of him many of the Jews were going over to Jesus and putting their faith in him.

THE TRIUMPHAL ENTRY

¹²The next day the great crowd that had come for the Feast heard that Jesus was on his way to Jerusalem. ¹³They took palm branches and went out to meet him, shouting,

"Hosanna! ͨ"

"Blessed is he who comes in the name of the Lord!" ͩ

"Blessed is the King of Israel!"

¹⁴Jesus found a young donkey and sat upon it, as it is written,

¹⁵"Do not be afraid, O Daughter of Zion;
  see, your king is coming,
    seated on a donkey's colt." ͤ

¹⁶At first his disciples did not understand all this. Only after Jesus was glorified did they realize that these things had been written about him and that they had done these things to him.

THE MESSAGE

him should inform them. They were all set to arrest him.

ANOINTING HIS FEET

12.1-3 **12** Six days before Passover, Jesus entered Bethany where Lazarus, so recently raised from the dead, was living. Lazarus and his sisters invited Jesus to dinner at their home. Martha served. Lazarus was one of those sitting at the table with them. Mary came in with a jar of very expensive aromatic oils, anointed and massaged Jesus' feet, and then wiped them with her hair. The fragrance of the oils filled the house.

12.4-6 Judas Iscariot, one of his disciples, even then getting ready to betray him, said, "Why wasn't this oil sold and the money given to the poor? It would have easily brought three hundred silver pieces." He said this not because he cared two cents about the poor but because he was a thief. He was in charge of their common funds, but also embezzled them.

12.7-8 Jesus said, "Let her alone. She's anticipating and honoring the day of my burial. You always have the poor with you. You don't always have me."

12.9-11 Word got out among the Jews that he was back in town. The people came to take a look, not only at Jesus but also at Lazarus, who had been raised from the dead. So the high priests plotted to kill Lazarus because so many of the Jews were going over and believing in Jesus on account of him.

SEE HOW YOUR KING COMES

12.12-15 The next day the huge crowd that had arrived for the Feast heard that Jesus was entering Jerusalem. They broke off palm branches and went out to meet him. And they cheered:

Hosanna!
Blessed is he who comes in God's name!
Yes! The King of Israel!

Jesus got a young donkey and rode it, just as the Scripture has it:

No fear, Daughter Zion:
  See how your king comes,
    riding a donkey's colt.

12.16 The disciples didn't notice the fulfillment of many Scriptures at the time, but after Jesus was glorified, they remembered that what was written about him matched what was done to him.

ͣ 3 Greek *a litra* (probably about 0.5 liter) ᵇ 5 Greek *three hundred denarii* ͨ 13 A Hebrew expression meaning "Save!" which became an exclamation of praise
ͩ 13 Psalm 118:25,26 ͤ 15 Zech. 9:9

NEW INTERNATIONAL VERSION	THE MESSAGE

NEW INTERNATIONAL VERSION

¹⁷Now the crowd that was with him when he called Lazarus from the tomb and raised him from the dead continued to spread the word. ¹⁸Many people, because they had heard that he had given this miraculous sign, went out to meet him. ¹⁹So the Pharisees said to one another, "See, this is getting us nowhere. Look how the whole world has gone after him!"

JESUS PREDICTS HIS DEATH

²⁰Now there were some Greeks among those who went up to worship at the Feast. ²¹They came to Philip, who was from Bethsaida in Galilee, with a request. "Sir," they said, "we would like to see Jesus." ²²Philip went to tell Andrew; Andrew and Philip in turn told Jesus.

²³Jesus replied, "The hour has come for the Son of Man to be glorified. ²⁴I tell you the truth, unless a kernel of wheat falls to the ground and dies, it remains only a single seed. But if it dies, it produces many seeds. ²⁵The man who loves his life will lose it, while the man who hates his life in this world will keep it for eternal life. ²⁶Whoever serves me must follow me; and where I am, my servant also will be. My Father will honor the one who serves me.

²⁷"Now my heart is troubled, and what shall I say? 'Father, save me from this hour'? No, it was for this very reason I came to this hour. ²⁸Father, glorify your name!"

Then a voice came from heaven, "I have glorified it, and will glorify it again." ²⁹The crowd that was there and heard it said it had thundered; others said an angel had spoken to him.

³⁰Jesus said, "This voice was for your benefit, not mine. ³¹Now is the time for judgment on this world; now the prince of this world will be driven out. ³²But I, when I am lifted up from the earth, will draw all men to myself." ³³He said this to show the kind of death he was going to die.

³⁴The crowd spoke up, "We have heard from the Law that the Christ[a] will remain forever, so how can you say, 'The Son of Man must be lifted up'? Who is this 'Son of Man'?"

³⁵Then Jesus told them, "You are going to have the light just a little while longer. Walk while you have the light, before darkness overtakes you. The man who walks in the dark does not know where he is going. ³⁶Put your trust in the light while you have it, so that you may become sons of light."

THE MESSAGE

12.17-19 The crowd that had been with him when he called Lazarus from the tomb, raising him from the dead, was there giving eyewitness accounts. It was because they had spread the word of this latest God-sign that the crowd swelled to a welcoming parade. The Pharisees took one look and threw up their hands: "It's out of control. The world's in a stampede after him."

A GRAIN OF WHEAT MUST DIE

12.20-21 There were some Greeks in town who had come up to worship at the Feast. They approached Philip, who was from Bethsaida in Galilee: "Sir, we want to see Jesus. Can you help us?"

12.22-23 Philip went and told Andrew. Andrew and Philip together told Jesus. Jesus answered, "Time's up. The time has come for the Son of Man to be glorified.

12.24-25 "Listen carefully: Unless a grain of wheat is buried in the ground, dead to the world, it is never any more than a grain of wheat. But if it is buried, it sprouts and reproduces itself many times over. In the same way, anyone who holds on to life just as it is destroys that life. But if you let it go, reckless in your love, you'll have it forever, real and eternal.

12.26 "If any of you wants to serve me, then follow me. Then you'll be where I am, ready to serve at a moment's notice. The Father will honor and reward anyone who serves me.

12.27-28 "Right now I am storm-tossed. And what am I going to say? 'Father, get me out of this'? No, this is why I came in the first place. I'll say, 'Father, put your glory on display.' "

A voice came out of the sky: "I have glorified it, and I'll glorify it again."

12.29 The listening crowd said, "Thunder!"

Others said, "An angel spoke to him!"

12.30-33 Jesus said, "The voice didn't come for me but for you. At this moment the world is in crisis. Now Satan, the ruler of this world, will be thrown out. And I, as I am lifted up from the earth, will attract everyone to me and gather them around me." He put it this way to show how he was going to be put to death.

12.34 Voices from the crowd answered, "We heard from God's Law that the Messiah lasts forever. How can it be necessary, as you put it, that the Son of Man 'be lifted up'? Who is this 'Son of Man'?"

12.35-36 Jesus said, "For a brief time still, the light is among you. Walk by the light you have so darkness doesn't destroy you. If you walk in darkness, you don't know where you're going. As you have the light, believe in the light. Then the light will be within you, and shining through your lives. You'll be children of light."

---

a 34 Or Messiah

NEW INTERNATIONAL VERSION

When he had finished speaking, Jesus left and hid himself from them.

THE JEWS CONTINUE IN THEIR UNBELIEF

37Even after Jesus had done all these miraculous signs in their presence, they still would not believe in him. 38This was to fulfill the word of Isaiah the prophet:

> "Lord, who has believed our message
>   and to whom has the arm of the Lord
>   been revealed?" *a*

39For this reason they could not believe, because, as Isaiah says elsewhere:

> 40 "He has blinded their eyes
>   and deadened their hearts,
> so they can neither see with their eyes,
>   nor understand with their hearts,
>   nor turn—and I would heal them." *b*

41Isaiah said this because he saw Jesus' glory and spoke about him.

42Yet at the same time many even among the leaders believed in him. But because of the Pharisees they would not confess their faith for fear they would be put out of the synagogue; 43for they loved praise from men more than praise from God.

44Then Jesus cried out, "When a man believes in me, he does not believe in me only, but in the one who sent me. 45When he looks at me, he sees the one who sent me. 46I have come into the world as a light, so that no one who believes in me should stay in darkness.

47"As for the person who hears my words but does not keep them, I do not judge him. For I did not come to judge the world, but to save it. 48There is a judge for the one who rejects me and does not accept my words; that very word which I spoke will condemn him at the last day. 49For I did not speak of my own accord, but the Father who sent me commanded me what to say and how to say it. 50I know that his command leads to eternal life. So whatever I say is just what the Father has told me to say."

JESUS WASHES HIS DISCIPLES' FEET

13 It was just before the Passover Feast. Jesus knew that the time had come for him to leave this world and go to the Father. Having loved his own who were in the world, he now showed them the full extent of his love. *c*

THE MESSAGE

THEIR EYES ARE BLINDED

12.36-40 Jesus said all this, and then went into hiding. All these God-signs he had given them and they still didn't get it, still wouldn't trust him. This proved that the prophet Isaiah was right:

> God, who believed what we preached?
> Who recognized God's arm, outstretched
>   and ready to act?

First they wouldn't believe, then they *couldn't*—again, just as Isaiah said:

> Their eyes are blinded,
>   their hearts are hardened,
> So that they wouldn't see with their eyes
>   and perceive with their hearts,
> And turn to me, God,
>   so I could heal them.

12.41 Isaiah said these things after he got a glimpse of God's cascading brightness that would pour through the Messiah.

12.42-43 On the other hand, a considerable number from the ranks of the leaders did believe. But because of the Pharisees, they didn't come out in the open with it. They were afraid of getting kicked out of the meeting place. When push came to shove they cared more for human approval than for God's glory.

12.44-46 Jesus summed it all up when he cried out, "Whoever believes in me, believes not just in me but in the One who sent me. Whoever looks at me is looking, in fact, at the One who sent me. I am Light that has come into the world so that all who believe in me won't have to stay any longer in the dark.

12.47-50 "If anyone hears what I am saying and doesn't take it seriously, I don't reject him. I didn't come to reject the world; I came to save the world. But you need to know that whoever puts me off, refusing to take in what I'm saying, is willfully choosing rejection. The Word, the Word-made-flesh that I have spoken and that I am, *that* Word and no other is the last word. I'm not making any of this up on my own. The Father who sent me gave me orders, told me what to say and how to say it. And I know exactly what his command produces: real and eternal life. That's all I have to say. What the Father told me, I tell you."

WASHING HIS DISCIPLES' FEET

13.1-2 **13** Just before the Passover Feast, Jesus knew that the time had come to leave this world to go to the Father. Having loved his dear companions, he continued to love

---

a 38 Isaiah 53:1   *b 40* Isaiah 6:10   *c 1* Or *he loved them to the last*

NEW INTERNATIONAL VERSION

²The evening meal was being served, and the devil had already prompted Judas Iscariot, son of Simon, to betray Jesus. ³Jesus knew that the Father had put all things under his power, and that he had come from God and was returning to God; ⁴so he got up from the meal, took off his outer clothing, and wrapped a towel around his waist. ⁵After that, he poured water into a basin and began to wash his disciples' feet, drying them with the towel that was wrapped around him.

⁶He came to Simon Peter, who said to him, "Lord, are you going to wash my feet?"

⁷Jesus replied, "You do not realize now what I am doing, but later you will understand."

⁸"No," said Peter, "you shall never wash my feet."

Jesus answered, "Unless I wash you, you have no part with me."

⁹"Then, Lord," Simon Peter replied, "not just my feet but my hands and my head as well!"

¹⁰Jesus answered, "A person who has had a bath needs only to wash his feet; his whole body is clean. And you are clean, though not every one of you." ¹¹For he knew who was going to betray him, and that was why he said not every one was clean.

¹²When he had finished washing their feet, he put on his clothes and returned to his place. "Do you understand what I have done for you?" he asked them. ¹³"You call me 'Teacher' and 'Lord,' and rightly so, for that is what I am. ¹⁴Now that I, your Lord and Teacher, have washed your feet, you also should wash one another's feet. ¹⁵I have set you an example that you should do as I have done for you. ¹⁶I tell you the truth, no servant is greater than his master, nor is a messenger greater than the one who sent him. ¹⁷Now that you know these things, you will be blessed if you do them.

JESUS PREDICTS HIS BETRAYAL

¹⁸"I am not referring to all of you; I know those I have chosen. But this is to fulfill the scripture: 'He who shares my bread has lifted up his heel against me.'ᵃ

¹⁹"I am telling you now before it happens, so that when it does happen you will believe that I am He. ²⁰I tell you the truth, whoever accepts anyone I send accepts me; and whoever accepts me accepts the one who sent me."

²¹After he had said this, Jesus was troubled in

THE MESSAGE

them right to the end. It was suppertime. The Devil by now had Judas, son of Simon the Iscariot, firmly in his grip, all set for the betrayal.

13.3-6 Jesus knew that the Father had put him in complete charge of everything, that he came from God and was on his way back to God. So he got up from the supper table, set aside his robe, and put on an apron. Then he poured water into a basin and began to wash the feet of the disciples, drying them with his apron. When he got to Simon Peter, Peter said, "Master, *you* wash *my* feet?"

13.7 Jesus answered, "You don't understand now what I'm doing, but it will be clear enough to you later."

13.8 Peter persisted, "You're not going to wash my feet—ever!"

Jesus said, "If I don't wash you, you can't be part of what I'm doing."

13.9 "Master!" said Peter. "Not only my feet, then. Wash my hands! Wash my head!"

13.10-12 Jesus said, "If you've had a bath in the morning, you only need your feet washed now and you're clean from head to toe. My concern, you understand, is holiness, not hygiene. So now you're clean. But not every one of you." (He knew who was betraying him. That's why he said, "Not every one of you.") After he had finished washing their feet, he took his robe, put it back on, and went back to his place at the table.

13.12-17 Then he said, "Do you understand what I have done to you? You address me as 'Teacher' and 'Master,' and rightly so. That is what I am. So if I, the Master and Teacher, washed your feet, you must now wash each other's feet. I've laid down a pattern for you. What I've done, you do. I'm only pointing out the obvious. A servant is not ranked above his master; an employee doesn't give orders to the employer. If you understand what I'm telling you, act like it—and live a blessed life.

THE ONE WHO ATE BREAD AT MY TABLE

13.18-20 "I'm not including all of you in this. I know precisely whom I've selected, so as not to interfere with the fulfillment of this Scripture:

The one who ate bread at my table
Turned on his heel against me.

"I'm telling you all this ahead of time so that when it happens you will believe that I am who I say I am. Make sure you get this right: Receiving someone I send is the same as receiving me, just as receiving me is the same as receiving the One who sent me."

13.21 After he said these things, Jesus became vis-

NEW INTERNATIONAL VERSION

spirit and testified, "I tell you the truth, one of you is going to betray me."

²²His disciples stared at one another, at a loss to know which of them he meant. ²³One of them, the disciple whom Jesus loved, was reclining next to him. ²⁴Simon Peter motioned to this disciple and said, "Ask him which one he means."

²⁵Leaning back against Jesus, he asked him, "Lord, who is it?"

²⁶Jesus answered, "It is the one to whom I will give this piece of bread when I have dipped it in the dish." Then, dipping the piece of bread, he gave it to Judas Iscariot, son of Simon. ²⁷As soon as Judas took the bread, Satan entered into him.

"What you are about to do, do quickly," Jesus told him, ²⁸but no one at the meal understood why Jesus said this to him. ²⁹Since Judas had charge of the money, some thought Jesus was telling him to buy what was needed for the Feast, or to give something to the poor. ³⁰As soon as Judas had taken the bread, he went out. And it was night.

JESUS PREDICTS PETER'S DENIAL

³¹When he was gone, Jesus said, "Now is the Son of Man glorified and God is glorified in him. ³²If God is glorified in him,ᵃ God will glorify the Son in himself, and will glorify him at once.

³³"My children, I will be with you only a little longer. You will look for me, and just as I told the Jews, so I tell you now: Where I am going, you cannot come.

³⁴"A new command I give you: Love one another. As I have loved you, so you must love one another. ³⁵By this all men will know that you are my disciples, if you love one another."

³⁶Simon Peter asked him, "Lord, where are you going?"

Jesus replied, "Where I am going, you cannot follow now, but you will follow later."

³⁷Peter asked, "Lord, why can't I follow you now? I will lay down my life for you."

³⁸Then Jesus answered, "Will you really lay down your life for me? I tell you the truth, before the rooster crows, you will disown me three times!

JESUS COMFORTS HIS DISCIPLES

14 "Do not let your hearts be troubled. Trust in God;ᵇ trust also in me. ²In my Father's house are many rooms; if it were not so, I would have told you. I am going there to prepare a

---

THE MESSAGE

ibly upset, and then he told them why. "One of you is going to betray me."

13.22-25 The disciples looked around at one another, wondering who on earth he was talking about. One of the disciples, the one Jesus loved dearly, was reclining against him, his head on his shoulder. Peter motioned to him to ask who Jesus might be talking about. So, being the closest, he said, "Master, who?"

13.26-27 Jesus said, "The one to whom I give this crust of bread after I've dipped it." Then he dipped the crust and gave it to Judas, son of Simon the Iscariot. As soon as the bread was in his hand, Satan entered him.

"What you must do," said Jesus, "do. Do it and get it over with."

13.28-29 No one around the supper table knew why he said this to him. Some thought that since Judas was their treasurer, Jesus was telling him to buy what they needed for the Feast, or that he should give something to the poor.

13.30 Judas, with the piece of bread, left. It was night.

A NEW COMMAND

13.31-32 When he had left, Jesus said, "Now the Son of Man is seen for who he is, and God seen for who he is in him. The moment God is seen in him, God's glory will be on display. In glorifying him, he himself is glorified—glory all around!

13.33 "Children, I am with you for only a short time longer. You are going to look high and low for me. But just as I told the Jews, I'm telling you: 'Where I go, you are not able to come.'

13.34-35 "Let me give you a new command: Love one another. In the same way I loved you, you love one another. This is how everyone will recognize that you are my disciples—when they see the love you have for each other."

13.36 Simon Peter asked, "Master, just where are you going?"

Jesus answered, "You can't now follow me where I'm going. You will follow later."

13.37 "Master," said Peter, "why can't I follow now? I'll lay down my life for you!"

13.38 "Really? You'll lay down your life for me? The truth is that before the rooster crows, you'll deny me three times."

THE ROAD

14.1-4 **14** "Don't let this throw you. You trust God, don't you? Trust me. There is plenty of room for you in my Father's home. If that weren't so, would I have told you that I'm on my way to get a room ready for you? And if I'm

---

ᵃ 32 Many early manuscripts do not have *If God is glorified in him.* ᵇ 1 Or *You trust in God*

NEW INTERNATIONAL VERSION

place for you. ³And if I go and prepare a place for you, I will come back and take you to be with me that you also may be where I am. ⁴You know the way to the place where I am going."

JESUS THE WAY TO THE FATHER

⁵Thomas said to him, "Lord, we don't know where you are going, so how can we know the way?"

⁶Jesus answered, "I am the way and the truth and the life. No one comes to the Father except through me. ⁷If you really knew me, you would know[a] my Father as well. From now on, you do know him and have seen him."

⁸Philip said, "Lord, show us the Father and that will be enough for us."

⁹Jesus answered: "Don't you know me, Philip, even after I have been among you such a long time? Anyone who has seen me has seen the Father. How can you say, 'Show us the Father'? ¹⁰Don't you believe that I am in the Father, and that the Father is in me? The words I say to you are not just my own. Rather, it is the Father, living in me, who is doing his work. ¹¹Believe me when I say that I am in the Father and the Father is in me; or at least believe on the evidence of the miracles themselves. ¹²I tell you the truth, anyone who has faith in me will do what I have been doing. He will do even greater things than these, because I am going to the Father. ¹³And I will do whatever you ask in my name, so that the Son may bring glory to the Father. ¹⁴You may ask me for anything in my name, and I will do it.

JESUS PROMISES THE HOLY SPIRIT

¹⁵"If you love me, you will obey what I command. ¹⁶And I will ask the Father, and he will give you another Counselor to be with you forever— ¹⁷the Spirit of truth. The world cannot accept him, because it neither sees him nor knows him. But you know him, for he lives with you and will be[b] in you. ¹⁸I will not leave you as orphans; I will come to you. ¹⁹Before long, the world will not see me anymore, but you will see me. Because I live, you also will live. ²⁰On that day you will realize that I am in my Father, and you are in me, and I am in you. ²¹Whoever has my commands and obeys them, he is the one who loves me. He who loves me will be loved by my Father, and I too will love him and show myself to him."

²²Then Judas (not Judas Iscariot) said, "But,

THE MESSAGE

on my way to get your room ready, I'll come back and get you so you can live where I live. And you already know the road I'm taking."

14.5 Thomas said, "Master, we have no idea where you're going. How do you expect us to know the road?"

14.6-7 Jesus said, "I am the Road, also the Truth, also the Life. No one gets to the Father apart from me. If you really knew me, you would know my Father as well. From now on, you do know him. You've even seen him!"

14.8 Philip said, "Master, show us the Father; then we'll be content."

14.9-10 "You've been with me all this time, Philip, and you still don't understand? To see me is to see the Father. So how can you ask, 'Where is the Father?' Don't you believe that I am in the Father and the Father is in me? The words that I speak to you aren't mere words. I don't just make them up on my own. The Father who resides in me crafts each word into a divine act.

14.11-14 "Believe me: I am in my Father and my Father is in me. If you can't believe that, believe what you see—these works. The person who trusts me will not only do what I'm doing but even greater things, because I, on my way to the Father, am giving you the same work to do that I've been doing. You can count on it. From now on, whatever you request along the lines of who I am and what I am doing, I'll do it. That's how the Father will be seen for who he is in the Son. I mean it. Whatever you request in this way, I'll do.

THE SPIRIT OF TRUTH

14.15-17 "If you love me, show it by doing what I've told you. I will talk to the Father, and he'll provide you another Friend so that you will always have someone with you. This Friend is the Spirit of Truth. The godless world can't take him in because it doesn't have eyes to see him, doesn't know what to look for. But you know him already because he has been staying with you, and will even be *in* you!

14.18-20 "I will not leave you orphaned. I'm coming back. In just a little while the world will no longer see me, but you're going to see me because I am alive and you're about to come alive. At that moment you will know absolutely that I'm in my Father, and you're in me, and I'm in you.

14.21 "The person who knows my commandments and keeps them, that's who loves me. And the person who loves me will be loved by my Father, and I will love him and make myself plain to him."

14.22 Judas (not Iscariot) said, "Master, why is it

---

a 7 Some early manuscripts *If you really have known me, you will know*   *b* 17 Some early manuscripts *and is*

NEW INTERNATIONAL VERSION

Lord, why do you intend to show yourself to us and not to the world?"

²³Jesus replied, "If anyone loves me, he will obey my teaching. My Father will love him, and we will come to him and make our home with him. ²⁴He who does not love me will not obey my teaching. These words you hear are not my own; they belong to the Father who sent me.

²⁵"All this I have spoken while still with you. ²⁶But the Counselor, the Holy Spirit, whom the Father will send in my name, will teach you all things and will remind you of everything I have said to you. ²⁷Peace I leave with you; my peace I give you. I do not give to you as the world gives. Do not let your hearts be troubled and do not be afraid.

²⁸"You heard me say, 'I am going away and I am coming back to you.' If you loved me, you would be glad that I am going to the Father, for the Father is greater than I. ²⁹I have told you now before it happens, so that when it does happen you will believe. ³⁰I will not speak with you much longer, for the prince of this world is coming. He has no hold on me, ³¹but the world must learn that I love the Father and that I do exactly what my Father has commanded me.

"Come now; let us leave.

THE VINE AND THE BRANCHES

15 "I am the true vine, and my Father is the gardener. ²He cuts off every branch in me that bears no fruit, while every branch that does bear fruit he prunes*a* so that it will be even more fruitful. ³You are already clean because of the word I have spoken to you. ⁴Remain in me, and I will remain in you. No branch can bear fruit by itself; it must remain in the vine. Neither can you bear fruit unless you remain in me.

⁵"I am the vine; you are the branches. If a man remains in me and I in him, he will bear much fruit; apart from me you can do nothing. ⁶If anyone does not remain in me, he is like a branch that is thrown away and withers; such branches are picked up, thrown into the fire and burned. ⁷If you remain in me and my words remain in you, ask whatever you wish, and it will be given you. ⁸This is to my Father's glory, that

a 2 The Greek for prunes also means cleans.

THE MESSAGE

that you are about to make yourself plain to us but not to the world?"

14.23-24 "Because a loveless world," said Jesus, "is a sightless world. If anyone loves me, he will carefully keep my word and my Father will love him—we'll move right into the neighborhood! Not loving me means not keeping my words. The message you are hearing isn't mine. It's the message of the Father who sent me.

14.25-27 "I'm telling you these things while I'm still living with you. The Friend, the Holy Spirit whom the Father will send at my request, will make everything plain to you. He will remind you of all the things I have told you. I'm leaving you well and whole. That's my parting gift to you. Peace. I don't leave you the way you're used to being left—feeling abandoned, bereft. So don't be upset. Don't be distraught.

14.28 "You've heard me tell you, 'I'm going away, and I'm coming back.' If you loved me, you would be glad that I'm on my way to the Father because the Father is the goal and purpose of my life.

14.29-31 "I've told you this ahead of time, before it happens, so that when it does happen, the confirmation will deepen your belief in me. I'll not be talking with you much more like this because the chief of this godless world is about to attack. But don't worry—he has nothing on me, no claim on me. But so the world might know how thoroughly I love the Father, I am carrying out my Father's instructions right down to the last detail.

"Get up. Let's go. It's time to leave here.

THE VINE AND THE BRANCHES

15.1-3 **15** "I am the Real Vine and my Father is the Farmer. He cuts off every branch of me that doesn't bear grapes. And every branch that is grape-bearing he prunes back so it will bear even more. You are already pruned back by the message I have spoken.

15.4 "Live in me. Make your home in me just as I do in you. In the same way that a branch can't bear grapes by itself but only by being joined to the vine, you can't bear fruit unless you are joined with me.

15.5-8 "I am the Vine, you are the branches. When you're joined with me and I with you, the relation intimate and organic, the harvest is sure to be abundant. Separated, you can't produce a thing. Anyone who separates from me is deadwood, gathered up and thrown on the bonfire. But if you make yourselves at home with me and my words are at home in you, you can be sure that whatever you ask will be listened to and acted upon. This is how my Father shows

NEW INTERNATIONAL VERSION

you bear much fruit, showing yourselves to be my disciples.

9 "As the Father has loved me, so have I loved you. Now remain in my love. 10 If you obey my commands, you will remain in my love, just as I have obeyed my Father's commands and remain in his love. 11 I have told you this so that my joy may be in you and that your joy may be complete. 12 My command is this: Love each other as I have loved you. 13 Greater love has no one than this, that he lay down his life for his friends. 14 You are my friends if you do what I command. 15 I no longer call you servants, because a servant does not know his master's business. Instead, I have called you friends, for everything that I learned from my Father I have made known to you. 16 You did not choose me, but I chose you and appointed you to go and bear fruit—fruit that will last. Then the Father will give you whatever you ask in my name. 17 This is my command: Love each other.

THE WORLD HATES THE DISCIPLES

18 "If the world hates you, keep in mind that it hated me first. 19 If you belonged to the world, it would love you as its own. As it is, you do not belong to the world, but I have chosen you out of the world. That is why the world hates you. 20 Remember the words I spoke to you: 'No servant is greater than his master.'[a] If they persecuted me, they will persecute you also. If they obeyed my teaching, they will obey yours also. 21 They will treat you this way because of my name, for they do not know the One who sent me. 22 If I had not come and spoken to them, they would not be guilty of sin. Now, however, they have no excuse for their sin. 23 He who hates me hates my Father as well. 24 If I had not done among them what no one else did, they would not be guilty of sin. But now they have seen these miracles, and yet they have hated both me and my Father. 25 But this is to fulfill what is written in their Law: 'They hated me without reason.'[b]

26 "When the Counselor comes, whom I will send to you from the Father, the Spirit of truth who goes out from the Father, he will testify about me. 27 And you also must testify, for you have been with me from the beginning.

a 20 John 13:16   b 25 Psalms 35:19; 69:4

THE MESSAGE

who he is—when you produce grapes, when you mature as my disciples.

15.9-10   "I've loved you the way my Father has loved me. Make yourselves at home in my love. If you keep my commands, you'll remain intimately at home in my love. That's what I've done—kept my Father's commands and made myself at home in his love.

15.11-15   "I've told you these things for a purpose: that my joy might be your joy, and your joy wholly mature. This is my command: Love one another the way I loved you. This is the very best way to love. Put your life on the line for your friends. You are my friends when you do the things I command you. I'm no longer calling you servants because servants don't understand what their master is thinking and planning. No, I've named you friends because I've let you in on everything I've heard from the Father.

15.16   "You didn't choose me, remember; I chose you, and put you in the world to bear fruit, fruit that won't spoil. As fruit bearers, whatever you ask the Father in relation to me, he gives you.

15.17   "But remember the root command: Love one another.

HATED BY THE WORLD

15.18-19   "If you find the godless world is hating you, remember it got its start hating me. If you lived on the world's terms, the world would love you as one of its own. But since I picked you to live on God's terms and no longer on the world's terms, the world is going to hate you.

15.20   "When that happens, remember this: Servants don't get better treatment than their masters. If they beat on me, they will certainly beat on you. If they did what I told them, they will do what you tell them.

15.21-25   "They are going to do all these things to you because of the way they treated me, because they don't know the One who sent me. If I hadn't come and told them all this in plain language, it wouldn't be so bad. As it is, they have no excuse. Hate me, hate my Father—it's all the same. If I hadn't done what I have done among them, works no one has *ever* done, they wouldn't be to blame. But they saw the God-signs and hated anyway, both me and my Father. Interesting—they have verified the truth of their own Scriptures where it is written, 'They hated me for no good reason.'

15.26-27   "When the Friend I plan to send you from the Father comes—the Spirit of Truth issuing from the Father—he will confirm everything about me. You, too, from your side must give your confirming evidence, since you are in this with me from the start.

NEW INTERNATIONAL VERSION

16 "All this I have told you so that you will not go astray. ²They will put you out of the synagogue; in fact, a time is coming when anyone who kills you will think he is offering a service to God. ³They will do such things because they have not known the Father or me. ⁴I have told you this, so that when the time comes you will remember that I warned you. I did not tell you this at first because I was with you.

THE WORK OF THE HOLY SPIRIT

⁵"Now I am going to him who sent me, yet none of you asks me, 'Where are you going?' ⁶Because I have said these things, you are filled with grief. ⁷But I tell you the truth: It is for your good that I am going away. Unless I go away, the Counselor will not come to you; but if I go, I will send him to you. ⁸When he comes, he will convict the world of guilt[a] in regard to sin and righteousness and judgment: ⁹in regard to sin, because men do not believe in me; ¹⁰in regard to righteousness, because I am going to the Father, where you can see me no longer; ¹¹and in regard to judgment, because the prince of this world now stands condemned.

¹²"I have much more to say to you, more than you can now bear. ¹³But when he, the Spirit of truth, comes, he will guide you into all truth. He will not speak on his own; he will speak only what he hears, and he will tell you what is yet to come. ¹⁴He will bring glory to me by taking from what is mine and making it known to you. ¹⁵All that belongs to the Father is mine. That is why I said the Spirit will take from what is mine and make it known to you.

¹⁶"In a little while you will see me no more, and then after a little while you will see me."

THE DISCIPLES' GRIEF WILL TURN TO JOY

¹⁷Some of his disciples said to one another, "What does he mean by saying, 'In a little while you will see me no more, and then after a little while you will see me,' and 'Because I am going to the Father'?" ¹⁸They kept asking, "What does he mean by 'a little while'? We don't understand what he is saying."

¹⁹Jesus saw that they wanted to ask him about this, so he said to them, "Are you asking one another what I meant when I said, 'In a little while you will see me no more, and then after a little while you will see me'? ²⁰I tell you the truth, you will weep and mourn while the world re-

THE MESSAGE

16 "I've told you these things to prepare you for rough times ahead. They are going to throw you out of the meeting places. There will even come a time when anyone who kills you will think he's doing God a favor. They will do these things because they never really understood the Father. I've told you these things so that when the time comes and they start in on you, you'll be well-warned and ready for them.

THE FRIEND WILL COME

16.4-7 "I didn't tell you this earlier because I was with you every day. But now I am on my way to the One who sent me. Not one of you has asked, 'Where are you going?' Instead, the longer I've talked, the sadder you've become. So let me say it again, this truth: It's better for you that I leave. If I don't leave, the Friend won't come. But if I go, I'll send him to you.

16.8-11 "When he comes, he'll expose the error of the godless world's view of sin, righteousness, and judgment: He'll show them that their refusal to believe in me is their basic sin; that righteousness comes from above, where I am with the Father, out of their sight and control; that judgment takes place as the ruler of this godless world is brought to trial and convicted.

16.12-15 "I still have many things to tell you, but you can't handle them now. But when the Friend comes, the Spirit of the Truth, he will take you by the hand and guide you into all the truth there is. He won't draw attention to himself, but will make sense out of what is about to happen and, indeed, out of all that I have done and said. He will honor me; he will take from me and deliver it to you. Everything the Father has is also mine. That is why I've said, 'He takes from me and delivers to you.'

16.16 "In a day or so you're not going to see me, but then in another day or so you will see me."

JOY LIKE A RIVER OVERFLOWING

16.17-18 That stirred up a hornet's nest of questions among the disciples: "What's he talking about: 'In a day or so you're not going to see me, but then in another day or so you will see me'? And, 'Because I'm on my way to the Father'? What is this 'day or so'? We don't know what he's talking about."

16.19-20 Jesus knew they were dying to ask him what he meant, so he said, "Are you trying to figure out among yourselves what I meant when I said, 'In a day or so you're not going to see me, but then in another day or so you will see me'? Then fix this firmly in your minds: You're going to be in deep mourning while the godless

---

a 8 Or *will expose the guilt of the world*

NEW INTERNATIONAL VERSION

joices. You will grieve, but your grief will turn to joy. ²¹A woman giving birth to a child has pain because her time has come; but when her baby is born she forgets the anguish because of her joy that a child is born into the world. ²²So with you: Now is your time of grief, but I will see you again and you will rejoice, and no one will take away your joy. ²³In that day you will no longer ask me anything. I tell you the truth, my Father will give you whatever you ask in my name. ²⁴Until now you have not asked for anything in my name. Ask and you will receive, and your joy will be complete.

²⁵"Though I have been speaking figuratively, a time is coming when I will no longer use this kind of language but will tell you plainly about my Father. ²⁶In that day you will ask in my name. I am not saying that I will ask the Father on your behalf. ²⁷No, the Father himself loves you because you have loved me and have believed that I came from God. ²⁸I came from the Father and entered the world; now I am leaving the world and going back to the Father."

²⁹Then Jesus' disciples said, "Now you are speaking clearly and without figures of speech. ³⁰Now we can see that you know all things and that you do not even need to have anyone ask you questions. This makes us believe that you came from God."

³¹"You believe at last!"ᵃ Jesus answered. ³²"But a time is coming, and has come, when you will be scattered, each to his own home. You will leave me all alone. Yet I am not alone, for my Father is with me.

³³"I have told you these things, so that in me you may have peace. In this world you will have trouble. But take heart! I have overcome the world."

JESUS PRAYS FOR HIMSELF

17 After Jesus said this, he looked toward heaven and prayed:

"Father, the time has come. Glorify your Son, that your Son may glorify you. ²For you granted him authority over all people that he might give eternal life to all those you have given him. ³Now this is eternal life: that they may know you, the only true

ᵃ 31 Or "Do you now believe?"

THE MESSAGE

world throws a party. You'll be sad, very sad, but your sadness will develop into gladness.

16.21-23 "When a woman gives birth, she has a hard time, there's no getting around it. But when the baby is born, there is joy in the birth. This new life in the world wipes out memory of the pain. The sadness you have right now is similar to that pain, but the coming joy is also similar. When I see you again, you'll be full of joy, and it will be a joy no one can rob from you. You'll no longer be so full of questions.

16.23-24 "This is what I want you to do: Ask the Father for whatever is in keeping with the things I've revealed to you. Ask in my name, according to my will, and he'll most certainly give it to you. Your joy will be a river overflowing its banks!

16.25-28 "I've used figures of speech in telling you these things. Soon I'll drop the figures and tell you about the Father in plain language. Then you can make your requests directly to him in relation to this life I've revealed to you. I won't continue making requests of the Father on your behalf. I won't need to. Because you've gone out on a limb, committed yourselves to love and trust in me, believing I came directly from the Father, the Father loves you directly. First, I left the Father and arrived in the world; now I leave the world and travel to the Father."

16.29-30 His disciples said, "Finally! You're giving it to us straight, in plain talk—no more figures of speech. Now we know that you know everything—it all comes together in you. You won't have to put up with our questions anymore. We're convinced you came from God."

16.31-33 Jesus answered them, "Do you finally believe? In fact, you're about to make a run for it—saving your own skins and abandoning me. But I'm not abandoned. The Father is with me. I've told you all this so that trusting me, you will be unshakable and assured, deeply at peace. In this godless world you will continue to experience difficulties. But take heart! I've conquered the world."

JESUS' PRAYER FOR HIS FOLLOWERS

17.1-5 **17** Jesus said these things. Then, raising his eyes in prayer, he said:

Father, it's time.
Display the bright splendor of your Son
So the Son in turn may show your bright
    splendor.
You put him in charge of everything human
So he might give real and eternal life to all
    in his charge.
And this is the real and eternal life:
That they know you,

NEW INTERNATIONAL VERSION

God, and Jesus Christ, whom you have sent. [4]I have brought you glory on earth by completing the work you gave me to do. [5]And now, Father, glorify me in your presence with the glory I had with you before the world began.

JESUS PRAYS FOR HIS DISCIPLES

[6]"I have revealed you[a] to those whom you gave me out of the world. They were yours; you gave them to me and they have obeyed your word. [7]Now they know that everything you have given me comes from you. [8]For I gave them the words you gave me and they accepted them. They knew with certainty that I came from you, and they believed that you sent me. [9]I pray for them. I am not praying for the world, but for those you have given me, for they are yours. [10]All I have is yours, and all you have is mine. And glory has come to me through them. [11]I will remain in the world no longer, but they are still in the world, and I am coming to you. Holy Father, protect them by the power of your name— the name you gave me—so that they may be one as we are one. [12]While I was with them, I protected them and kept them safe by that name you gave me. None has been lost except the one doomed to destruction so that Scripture would be fulfilled.

[13]"I am coming to you now, but I say these things while I am still in the world, so that they may have the full measure of my joy within them. [14]I have given them your word and the world has hated them,

THE MESSAGE

The one and only true God,
And Jesus Christ, whom you sent.
I glorified you on earth
By completing down to the last detail
What you assigned me to do.
And now, Father, glorify me with your very
    own splendor,
The very splendor I had in your presence
Before there was a world.

✝

17.6-12   I spelled out your character in detail
To the men and women you gave me.
They were yours in the first place;
Then you gave them to me,
And they have now done what you said.
They know now, beyond the shadow of a
    doubt,
That everything you gave me is firsthand
    from you,
For the message you gave me, I gave them;
And they took it, and were convinced
That I came from you.
They believed that you sent me.
I pray for them.
I'm not praying for the God-rejecting world
But for those you gave me,
For they are yours by right.
Everything mine is yours, and yours mine,
And my life is on display in them.
For I'm no longer going to be visible in the
    world;
They'll continue in the world
While I return to you.
Holy Father, guard them as they pursue
    this life
That you conferred as a gift through me,
So they can be one heart and mind
As we are one heart and mind.
As long as I was with them, I guarded them
In the pursuit of the life you gave
    through me;
I even posted a night watch.
And not one of them got away,
Except for the rebel bent on destruction
(the exception that proved the rule of
    Scripture).

✝

17.13-19   Now I'm returning to you.
I'm saying these things in the world's
    hearing
So my people can experience
My joy completed in them.
I gave them your word;
The godless world hated them because
    of it,

---

[a] 6 Greek *your name*; also in verse 26

NEW INTERNATIONAL VERSION

for they are not of the world any more than I am of the world. ¹⁵My prayer is not that you take them out of the world but that you protect them from the evil one. ¹⁶They are not of the world, even as I am not of it. ¹⁷Sanctify*ᵃ* them by the truth; your word is truth. ¹⁸As you sent me into the world, I have sent them into the world. ¹⁹For them I sanctify myself, that they too may be truly sanctified.

JESUS PRAYS FOR ALL BELIEVERS

²⁰"My prayer is not for them alone. I pray also for those who will believe in me through their message, ²¹that all of them may be one, Father, just as you are in me and I am in you. May they also be in us so that the world may believe that you have sent me. ²²I have given them the glory that you gave me, that they may be one as we are one: ²³I in them and you in me. May they be brought to complete unity to let the world know that you sent me and have loved them even as you have loved me.

²⁴"Father, I want those you have given me to be with me where I am, and to see my glory, the glory you have given me because you loved me before the creation of the world.

²⁵"Righteous Father, though the world does not know you, I know you, and they know that you have sent me. ²⁶I have made you known to them, and will continue to make you known in order that the love you have for me may be in them and that I myself may be in them."

THE MESSAGE

Because they didn't join the world's ways,
Just as I didn't join the world's ways.
I'm not asking that you take them out of
   the world
But that you guard them from the Evil One.
They are no more defined by the world
Than I am defined by the world.
Make them holy—consecrated—with the
   truth;
Your word is consecrating truth.
In the same way that you gave me a
   mission in the world,
I give them a mission in the world.
I'm consecrating myself for their sakes
So they'll be truth-consecrated in their
   mission.

✠

17.20-23   I'm praying not only for them
But also for those who will believe in me
Because of them and their witness about
   me.
The goal is for all of them to become one
   heart and mind—
Just as you, Father, are in me and I in you,
So they might be one heart and mind with
   us.
Then the world might believe that you, in
   fact, sent me.
The same glory you gave me, I gave them,
So they'll be as unified and together as we
   are—
I in them and you in me.
Then they'll be mature in this oneness,
And give the godless world evidence
That you've sent me and loved them
In the same way you've loved me.

✠

17.24-26   Father, I want those you gave me
To be with me, right where I am,
So they can see my glory, the splendor you
   gave me,
Having loved me
Long before there ever was a world.
Righteous Father, the world has never
   known you,
But I have known you, and these disciples
   know
That you sent me on this mission.
I have made your very being known to
   them—
Who you are and what you do—
And continue to make it known,
So that your love for me
Might be in them
Exactly as I am in them.

ᵃ 17 Greek hagiazo (set apart for sacred use or make holy); also in verse 19

NEW INTERNATIONAL VERSION

Jesus Arrested

18 When he had finished praying, Jesus left with his disciples and crossed the Kidron Valley. On the other side there was an olive grove, and he and his disciples went into it.

²Now Judas, who betrayed him, knew the place, because Jesus had often met there with his disciples. ³So Judas came to the grove, guiding a detachment of soldiers and some officials from the chief priests and Pharisees. They were carrying torches, lanterns and weapons.

⁴Jesus, knowing all that was going to happen to him, went out and asked them, "Who is it you want?"

⁵"Jesus of Nazareth," they replied.

"I am he," Jesus said. (And Judas the traitor was standing there with them.) ⁶When Jesus said, "I am he," they drew back and fell to the ground.

⁷Again he asked them, "Who is it you want?"

And they said, "Jesus of Nazareth."

⁸"I told you that I am he," Jesus answered. "If you are looking for me, then let these men go." ⁹This happened so that the words he had spoken would be fulfilled: "I have not lost one of those you gave me." ᵃ

¹⁰Then Simon Peter, who had a sword, drew it and struck the high priest's servant, cutting off his right ear. (The servant's name was Malchus.)

¹¹Jesus commanded Peter, "Put your sword away! Shall I not drink the cup the Father has given me?"

Jesus Taken to Annas

¹²Then the detachment of soldiers with its commander and the Jewish officials arrested Jesus. They bound him ¹³and brought him first to Annas, who was the father-in-law of Caiaphas, the high priest that year. ¹⁴Caiaphas was the one who had advised the Jews that it would be good if one man died for the people.

Peter's First Denial

¹⁵Simon Peter and another disciple were following Jesus. Because this disciple was known to the high priest, he went with Jesus into the high priest's courtyard, ¹⁶but Peter had to wait outside at the door. The other disciple, who was known to the high priest, came back, spoke to the girl on duty there and brought Peter in.

¹⁷"You are not one of his disciples, are you?" the girl at the door asked Peter.

He replied, "I am not."

¹⁸It was cold, and the servants and officials stood around a fire they had made to keep warm. Peter also was standing with them, warming himself.

ᵃ 9 John 6:39

THE MESSAGE

Seized in the Garden at Night

18.1 **18** Jesus, having prayed this prayer, left with his disciples and crossed over the brook Kidron at a place where there was a garden. He and his disciples entered it.

18.2-4 Judas, his betrayer, knew the place because Jesus and his disciples went there often. So Judas led the way to the garden, and the Roman soldiers and police sent by the high priests and Pharisees followed. They arrived there with lanterns and torches and swords. Jesus, knowing by now everything that was coming down on him, went out and met them. He said, "Who are you after?"

They answered, "Jesus the Nazarene."

18.5-6 He said, "That's me." The soldiers recoiled, totally taken aback. Judas, his betrayer, stood out like a sore thumb.

18.7 Jesus asked again, "Who are you after?"

They answered, "Jesus the Nazarene."

18.8-9 "I told you," said Jesus, "that's me. I'm the one. So if it's me you're after, let these others go." (This validated the words in his prayer, "I didn't lose one of those you gave.")

18.10 Just then Simon Peter, who was carrying a sword, pulled it from its sheath and struck the Chief Priest's servant, cutting off his right ear. Malchus was the servant's name.

18.11 Jesus ordered Peter, "Put back your sword. Do you think for a minute I'm not going to drink this cup the Father gave me?"

18.12-14 Then the Roman soldiers under their commander, joined by the Jewish police, seized Jesus and tied him up. They took him first to Annas, father-in-law of Caiaphas. Caiaphas was the Chief Priest that year. It was Caiaphas who had advised the Jews that it was to their advantage that one man die for the people.

18.15-16 Simon Peter and another disciple followed Jesus. That other disciple was known to the Chief Priest, and so he went in with Jesus to the Chief Priest's courtyard. Peter had to stay outside. Then the other disciple went out, spoke to the doorkeeper, and got Peter in.

18.17 The young woman who was the doorkeeper said to Peter, "Aren't you one of this man's disciples?"

He said, "No, I'm not."

18.18 The servants and police had made a fire because of the cold and were huddled there warming themselves. Peter stood with them, trying to get warm.

NEW INTERNATIONAL VERSION

THE HIGH PRIEST QUESTIONS JESUS

¹⁹Meanwhile, the high priest questioned Jesus about his disciples and his teaching.

²⁰"I have spoken openly to the world," Jesus replied. "I always taught in synagogues or at the temple, where all the Jews come together. I said nothing in secret. ²¹Why question me? Ask those who heard me. Surely they know what I said."

²²When Jesus said this, one of the officials nearby struck him in the face. "Is this the way you answer the high priest?" he demanded.

²³"If I said something wrong," Jesus replied, "testify as to what is wrong. But if I spoke the truth, why did you strike me?" ²⁴Then Annas sent him, still bound, to Caiaphas the high priest.ᵃ

PETER'S SECOND AND THIRD DENIALS

²⁵As Simon Peter stood warming himself, he was asked, "You are not one of his disciples, are you?"

He denied it, saying, "I am not."

²⁶One of the high priest's servants, a relative of the man whose ear Peter had cut off, challenged him, "Didn't I see you with him in the olive grove?" ²⁷Again Peter denied it, and at that moment a rooster began to crow.

JESUS BEFORE PILATE

²⁸Then the Jews led Jesus from Caiaphas to the palace of the Roman governor. By now it was early morning, and to avoid ceremonial uncleanness the Jews did not enter the palace; they wanted to be able to eat the Passover. ²⁹So Pilate came out to them and asked, "What charges are you bringing against this man?"

³⁰"If he were not a criminal," they replied, "we would not have handed him over to you."

³¹Pilate said, "Take him yourselves and judge him by your own law."

"But we have no right to execute anyone," the Jews objected. ³²This happened so that the words Jesus had spoken indicating the kind of death he was going to die would be fulfilled.

³³Pilate then went back inside the palace, summoned Jesus and asked him, "Are you the king of the Jews?"

³⁴"Is that your own idea," Jesus asked, "or did others talk to you about me?"

³⁵"Am I a Jew?" Pilate replied. "It was your people and your chief priests who handed you over to me. What is it you have done?"

³⁶Jesus said, "My kingdom is not of this world. If it were, my servants would fight to prevent my arrest by the Jews. But now my kingdom is from another place."

ᵃ 24 Or (Now Annas had sent him, still bound, to Caiaphas the high priest.)

THE MESSAGE

THE INTERROGATION

18:19-21 Annas interrogated Jesus regarding his disciples and his teaching. Jesus answered, "I've spoken openly in public. I've taught regularly in meeting places and the Temple, where the Jews all come together. Everything has been out in the open. I've said nothing in secret. So why are you treating me like a conspirator? Question those who have been listening to me. They know well what I have said. My teachings have all been aboveboard."

18:22 When he said this, one of the policemen standing there slapped Jesus across the face, saying, "How dare you speak to the Chief Priest like that!"

18:23 Jesus replied, "If I've said something wrong, prove it. But if I've spoken the plain truth, why this slapping around?"

18:24 Then Annas sent him, still tied up, to the Chief Priest Caiaphas.

18:25 Meanwhile, Simon Peter was back at the fire, still trying to get warm. The others there said to him, "Aren't you one of his disciples?"

He denied it, "Not me."

18:26 One of the Chief Priest's servants, a relative of the man whose ear Peter had cut off, said, "Didn't I see you in the garden with him?"

18:27 Again, Peter denied it. Just then a rooster crowed.

THE KING OF THE JEWS

18:28-29 They led Jesus then from Caiaphas to the Roman governor's palace. It was early morning. They themselves didn't enter the palace because they didn't want to be disqualified from eating the Passover. So Pilate came out to them and spoke. "What charge do you bring against this man?"

18:30 They said, "If he hadn't been doing something evil, do you think we'd be here bothering you?"

18:31-32 Pilate said, "You take him. Judge him by your law."

The Jews said, "We're not allowed to kill anyone." (This would confirm Jesus' word indicating the way he would die.)

18:33 Pilate went back into the palace and called for Jesus. He said, "Are you the 'King of the Jews'?"

18:34 Jesus answered, "Are you saying this on your own, or did others tell you this about me?"

18:35 Pilate said, "Do I look like a Jew? Your people and your high priests turned you over to me. What did you do?"

18:36 "My kingdom," said Jesus, "doesn't consist of what you see around you. If it did, my followers would fight so that I wouldn't be handed over to the Jews. But I'm not that kind of king, not the world's kind of king."

NEW INTERNATIONAL VERSION

³⁷"You are a king, then!" said Pilate.

Jesus answered, "You are right in saying I am a king. In fact, for this reason I was born, and for this I came into the world, to testify to the truth. Everyone on the side of truth listens to me."

³⁸"What is truth?" Pilate asked. With this he went out again to the Jews and said, "I find no basis for a charge against him. ³⁹But it is your custom for me to release to you one prisoner at the time of the Passover. Do you want me to release 'the king of the Jews'?"

⁴⁰They shouted back, "No, not him! Give us Barabbas!" Now Barabbas had taken part in a rebellion.

JESUS SENTENCED TO BE CRUCIFIED

19 Then Pilate took Jesus and had him flogged. ²The soldiers twisted together a crown of thorns and put it on his head. They clothed him in a purple robe ³and went up to him again and again, saying, "Hail, king of the Jews!" And they struck him in the face.

⁴Once more Pilate came out and said to the Jews, "Look, I am bringing him out to you to let you know that I find no basis for a charge against him." ⁵When Jesus came out wearing the crown of thorns and the purple robe, Pilate said to them, "Here is the man!"

⁶As soon as the chief priests and their officials saw him, they shouted, "Crucify! Crucify!"

But Pilate answered, "You take him and crucify him. As for me, I find no basis for a charge against him."

⁷The Jews insisted, "We have a law, and according to that law he must die, because he claimed to be the Son of God."

⁸When Pilate heard this, he was even more afraid, ⁹and he went back inside the palace. "Where do you come from?" he asked Jesus, but Jesus gave him no answer. ¹⁰"Do you refuse to speak to me?" Pilate said. "Don't you realize I have power either to free you or to crucify you?"

¹¹Jesus answered, "You would have no power over me if it were not given to you from above. Therefore the one who handed me over to you is guilty of a greater sin."

¹²From then on, Pilate tried to set Jesus free, but the Jews kept shouting, "If you let this man go, you are no friend of Caesar. Anyone who claims to be a king opposes Caesar."

¹³When Pilate heard this, he brought Jesus out and sat down on the judge's seat at a place known as the Stone Pavement (which in Aramaic is Gabbatha). ¹⁴It was the day of Preparation of Passover Week, about the sixth hour.

"Here is your king," Pilate said to the Jews.

THE MESSAGE

18.37 Then Pilate said, "So, are you a king or not?"

Jesus answered, "You tell me. Because I am King, I was born and entered the world so that I could witness to the truth. Everyone who cares for truth, who has any feeling for the truth, recognizes my voice."

18.38-39 Pilate said, "What is truth?"

Then he went back out to the Jews and told them, "I find nothing wrong in this man. It's your custom that I pardon one prisoner at Passover. Do you want me to pardon the 'King of the Jews'?"

18.40 They shouted back, "Not this one, but Barabbas!" Barabbas was a Jewish freedom fighter.

THE THORN CROWN OF THE KING

19.1-3 **19** So Pilate took Jesus and had him whipped. The soldiers, having braided a crown from thorns, set it on his head, threw a purple robe over him, and approached him with, "Hail, King of the Jews!" Then they greeted him with slaps in the face.

19.4-5 Pilate went back out again and said to them, "I present him to you, but I want you to know that I do not find him guilty of any crime." Just then Jesus came out wearing the thorn crown and purple robe.

19.6 Pilate announced, "Here he is: the Man."

When the high priests and police saw him, they shouted in a frenzy, "Crucify! Crucify!"

19.7 Pilate told them, "You take him. You crucify him. I find nothing wrong with him."

The Jews answered, "We have a law, and by that law he must die because he claimed to be the Son of God."

19.8-9 When Pilate heard this, he became even more scared. He went back into the palace and said to Jesus, "Where did you come from?"

Jesus gave no answer.

19.10 Pilate said, "You won't talk? Don't you know that I have the authority to pardon you, and the authority to—crucify you?"

19.11 Jesus said, "You haven't a shred of authority over me except what has been given you from heaven. That's why the one who betrayed me to you has committed a far greater fault."

19.12 At this, Pilate tried his best to pardon him, but the Jews shouted him down: "If you pardon this man, you're no friend of Caesar's. Anyone setting himself up as 'king' defies Caesar."

19.13-14 When Pilate heard those words, he led Jesus outside. He sat down at the judgment seat in the area designated Stone Court (in Hebrew, *Gabbatha*). It was the preparation day for Passover. The hour was noon. Pilate said to the Jews, "Here is your king."

NEW INTERNATIONAL VERSION

¹⁵But they shouted, "Take him away! Take him away! Crucify him!"

"Shall I crucify your king?" Pilate asked.

"We have no king but Caesar," the chief priests answered.

¹⁶Finally Pilate handed him over to them to be crucified.

THE CRUCIFIXION

So the soldiers took charge of Jesus. ¹⁷Carrying his own cross, he went out to the place of the Skull (which in Aramaic is called Golgotha). ¹⁸Here they crucified him, and with him two others—one on each side and Jesus in the middle.

¹⁹Pilate had a notice prepared and fastened to the cross. It read: JESUS OF NAZARETH, THE KING OF THE JEWS. ²⁰Many of the Jews read this sign, for the place where Jesus was crucified was near the city, and the sign was written in Aramaic, Latin and Greek. ²¹The chief priests of the Jews protested to Pilate, "Do not write 'The King of the Jews,' but that this man claimed to be king of the Jews."

²²Pilate answered, "What I have written, I have written."

²³When the soldiers crucified Jesus, they took his clothes, dividing them into four shares, one for each of them, with the undergarment remaining. This garment was seamless, woven in one piece from top to bottom.

²⁴"Let's not tear it," they said to one another. "Let's decide by lot who will get it."

This happened that the scripture might be fulfilled which said,

"They divided my garments among them
   and cast lots for my clothing." ᵃ

So this is what the soldiers did.

²⁵Near the cross of Jesus stood his mother, his mother's sister, Mary the wife of Clopas, and Mary Magdalene. ²⁶When Jesus saw his mother there, and the disciple whom he loved standing nearby, he said to his mother, "Dear woman, here is your son," ²⁷and to the disciple, "Here is your mother." From that time on, this disciple took her into his home.

THE DEATH OF JESUS

²⁸Later, knowing that all was now completed, and so that the Scripture would be fulfilled, Jesus said, "I am thirsty." ²⁹A jar of wine vinegar was there, so they soaked a sponge in it, put the sponge on a stalk of the hyssop plant, and lifted it to Jesus' lips. ³⁰When he had received the drink, Jesus said, "It is finished." With that, he bowed his head and gave up his spirit.

³¹Now it was the day of Preparation, and the

ᵃ 24 Psalm 22:18

THE MESSAGE

19.15   They shouted back, "Kill him! Kill him! Crucify him!"

Pilate said, "I am to crucify your king?"

The high priests answered, "We have no king except Caesar."

19.16-19   Pilate caved in to their demand. He turned him over to be crucified.

THE CRUCIFIXION

They took Jesus away. Carrying his cross, Jesus went out to the place called Skull Hill (the name in Hebrew is *Golgotha*), where they crucified him, and with him two others, one on each side, Jesus in the middle. Pilate wrote a sign and had it placed on the cross. It read:

JESUS THE NAZARENE
THE KING OF THE JEWS.

19.20-21   Many of the Jews read the sign because the place where Jesus was crucified was right next to the city. It was written in Hebrew, Latin, and Greek. The Jewish high priests objected. "Don't write," they said to Pilate, " 'The King of the Jews.' Make it, 'This man said, "I am the King of the Jews." ' "

19.22   Pilate said, "What I've written, I've written."

19.23-24   When they crucified him, the Roman soldiers took his clothes and divided them up four ways, to each soldier a fourth. But his robe was seamless, a single piece of weaving, so they said to each other, "Let's not tear it up. Let's throw dice to see who gets it." This confirmed the Scripture that said, "They divided up my clothes among them and threw dice for my coat." (The soldiers validated the Scriptures!)

19.24-27   While the soldiers were looking after themselves, Jesus' mother, his aunt, Mary the wife of Clopas, and Mary Magdalene stood at the foot of the cross. Jesus saw his mother and the disciple he loved standing near her. He said to his mother, "Woman, here is your son." Then to the disciple, "Here is your mother." From that moment the disciple accepted her as his own mother.

19.28   Jesus, seeing that everything had been completed so that the Scripture record might also be complete, then said, "I'm thirsty."

19.29-30   A jug of sour wine was standing by. Someone put a sponge soaked with the wine on a javelin and lifted it to his mouth. After he took the wine, Jesus said, "It's done . . . complete." Bowing his head, he offered up his spirit.

19.31-34   Then the Jews, since it was the day of Sabbath preparation, and so the bodies wouldn't

NEW INTERNATIONAL VERSION

next day was to be a special Sabbath. Because the Jews did not want the bodies left on the crosses during the Sabbath, they asked Pilate to have the legs broken and the bodies taken down. ³²The soldiers therefore came and broke the legs of the first man who had been crucified with Jesus, and then those of the other. ³³But when they came to Jesus and found that he was already dead, they did not break his legs. ³⁴Instead, one of the soldiers pierced Jesus' side with a spear, bringing a sudden flow of blood and water. ³⁵The man who saw it has given testimony, and his testimony is true. He knows that he tells the truth, and he testifies so that you also may believe. ³⁶These things happened so that the scripture would be fulfilled: "Not one of his bones will be broken," ᵃ ³⁷and, as another scripture says, "They will look on the one they have pierced." ᵇ

THE BURIAL OF JESUS

³⁸Later, Joseph of Arimathea asked Pilate for the body of Jesus. Now Joseph was a disciple of Jesus, but secretly because he feared the Jews. With Pilate's permission, he came and took the body away. ³⁹He was accompanied by Nicodemus, the man who earlier had visited Jesus at night. Nicodemus brought a mixture of myrrh and aloes, about seventy-five pounds.ᶜ ⁴⁰Taking Jesus' body, the two of them wrapped it, with the spices, in strips of linen. This was in accordance with Jewish burial customs. ⁴¹At the place where Jesus was crucified, there was a garden, and in the garden a new tomb, in which no one had ever been laid. ⁴²Because it was the Jewish day of Preparation and since the tomb was nearby, they laid Jesus there.

THE EMPTY TOMB

20 Early on the first day of the week, while it was still dark, Mary Magdalene went to the tomb and saw that the stone had been removed from the entrance. ²So she came running to Simon Peter and the other disciple, the one Jesus loved, and said, "They have taken the Lord out of the tomb, and we don't know where they have put him!"

³So Peter and the other disciple started for the tomb. ⁴Both were running, but the other disciple outran Peter and reached the tomb first. ⁵He bent over and looked in at the strips of linen lying there but did not go in. ⁶Then Simon Peter, who was behind him, arrived and went into the tomb. He saw the strips of linen lying there, ⁷as well as the burial cloth that had been around Jesus' head. The cloth was folded up by itself, separate from

THE MESSAGE

stay on the crosses over the Sabbath (it was a high holy day that year), petitioned Pilate that their legs be broken to speed death, and the bodies taken down. So the soldiers came and broke the legs of the first man crucified with Jesus, and then the other. When they got to Jesus, they saw that he was already dead, so they didn't break his legs. One of the soldiers stabbed him in the side with his spear. Blood and water gushed out.

19.35 The eyewitness to these things has presented an accurate report. He saw it himself and is telling the truth so that you, also, will believe.

19.36-37 These things that happened confirmed the Scripture, "Not a bone in his body was broken," and the other Scripture that reads, "They will stare at the one they pierced."

19.38 After all this, Joseph of Arimathea (he was a disciple of Jesus, but secretly, because he was intimidated by the Jews) petitioned Pilate to take the body of Jesus. Pilate gave permission. So Joseph came and took the body.

19.39-42 Nicodemus, who had first come to Jesus at night, came now in broad daylight carrying a mixture of myrrh and aloes, about seventy-five pounds. They took Jesus' body and, following the Jewish burial custom, wrapped it in linen with the spices. There was a garden near the place he was crucified, and in the garden a new tomb in which no one had yet been placed. So, because it was Sabbath preparation for the Jews and the tomb was convenient, they placed Jesus in it.

RESURRECTION!

20.1-2 **20** Early in the morning on the first day of the week, while it was still dark, Mary Magdalene came to the tomb and saw that the stone was moved away from the entrance. She ran at once to Simon Peter and the other disciple, the one Jesus loved, breathlessly panting, "They took the Master from the tomb. We don't know where they've put him."

20.3-10 Peter and the other disciple left immediately for the tomb. They ran, neck and neck. The other disciple got to the tomb first, outrunning Peter. Stooping to look in, he saw the pieces of linen cloth lying there, but he didn't go in. Simon Peter arrived after him, entered the tomb, observed the linen cloths lying there, and the kerchief used to cover his head not lying with the linen cloths but separate, neatly folded by

ᵃ 36 Exodus 12:46; Num. 9:12; Psalm 34:20
ᵇ 37 Zech. 12:10   ᶜ 39 Greek *a hundred litrai* (about 34 kilograms)

NEW INTERNATIONAL VERSION

the linen. [8]Finally the other disciple, who had reached the tomb first, also went inside. He saw and believed. [9](They still did not understand from Scripture that Jesus had to rise from the dead.)

JESUS APPEARS TO MARY MAGDALENE

[10]Then the disciples went back to their homes, [11]but Mary stood outside the tomb crying. As she wept, she bent over to look into the tomb [12]and saw two angels in white, seated where Jesus' body had been, one at the head and the other at the foot.

[13]They asked her, "Woman, why are you crying?"

"They have taken my Lord away," she said, "and I don't know where they have put him." [14]At this, she turned around and saw Jesus standing there, but she did not realize that it was Jesus.

[15]"Woman," he said, "why are you crying? Who is it you are looking for?"

Thinking he was the gardener, she said, "Sir, if you have carried him away, tell me where you have put him, and I will get him."

[16]Jesus said to her, "Mary."

She turned toward him and cried out in Aramaic, "Rabboni!" (which means Teacher).

[17]Jesus said, "Do not hold on to me, for I have not yet returned to the Father. Go instead to my brothers and tell them, 'I am returning to my Father and your Father, to my God and your God.' "

[18]Mary Magdalene went to the disciples with the news: "I have seen the Lord!" And she told them that he had said these things to her.

JESUS APPEARS TO HIS DISCIPLES

[19]On the evening of that first day of the week, when the disciples were together, with the doors locked for fear of the Jews, Jesus came and stood among them and said, "Peace be with you!" [20]After he said this, he showed them his hands and side. The disciples were overjoyed when they saw the Lord.

[21]Again Jesus said, "Peace be with you! As the Father has sent me, I am sending you." [22]And with that he breathed on them and said, "Receive the Holy Spirit. [23]If you forgive anyone his sins, they are forgiven; if you do not forgive them, they are not forgiven."

JESUS APPEARS TO THOMAS

[24]Now Thomas (called Didymus), one of the Twelve, was not with the disciples when Jesus came. [25]So the other disciples told him, "We have seen the Lord!"

But he said to them, "Unless I see the nail marks in his hands and put my finger where the nails were, and put my hand into his side, I will not believe it."

THE MESSAGE

itself. Then the other disciple, the one who had gotten there first, went into the tomb, took one look at the evidence, and believed. No one yet knew from the Scripture that he had to rise from the dead. The disciples then went back home.

20.11-13   But Mary stood outside the tomb weeping. As she wept, she knelt to look into the tomb and saw two angels sitting there, dressed in white, one at the head, the other at the foot of where Jesus' body had been laid. They said to her, "Woman, why do you weep?"

20.13-14   "They took my Master," she said, "and I don't know where they put him." After she said this, she turned away and saw Jesus standing there. But she didn't recognize him.

20.15   Jesus spoke to her, "Woman, why do you weep? Who are you looking for?"

She, thinking that he was the gardener, said, "Mister, if you took him, tell me where you put him so I can care for him."

20.16   Jesus said, "Mary."

Turning to face him, she said in Hebrew, "Rabboni!" meaning "Teacher!"

20.17   Jesus said, "Don't cling to me, for I have not yet ascended to the Father. Go to my brothers and tell them, 'I ascend to my Father and your Father, my God and your God.' "

20.18   Mary Magdalene went, telling the news to the disciples: "I saw the Master!" And she told them everything he said to her.

TO BELIEVE

20.19-20   Later on that day, the disciples had gathered together, but, fearful of the Jews, had locked all the doors in the house. Jesus entered, stood among them, and said, "Peace to you." Then he showed them his hands and side.

20.20-21   The disciples, seeing the Master with their own eyes, were exuberant. Jesus repeated his greeting: "Peace to you. Just as the Father sent me, I send you."

20.22-23   Then he took a deep breath and breathed into them. "Receive the Holy Spirit," he said. "If you forgive someone's sins, they're gone for good. If you don't forgive sins, what are you going to do with them?"

20.24-25   But Thomas, sometimes called the Twin, one of the Twelve, was not with them when Jesus came. The other disciples told him, "We saw the Master."

But he said, "Unless I see the nail holes in his hands, put my finger in the nail holes, and stick my hand in his side, I won't believe it."

NEW INTERNATIONAL VERSION

²⁶A week later his disciples were in the house again, and Thomas was with them. Though the doors were locked, Jesus came and stood among them and said, "Peace be with you!" ²⁷Then he said to Thomas, "Put your finger here; see my hands. Reach out your hand and put it into my side. Stop doubting and believe."

²⁸Thomas said to him, "My Lord and my God!"

²⁹Then Jesus told him, "Because you have seen me, you have believed; blessed are those who have not seen and yet have believed."

³⁰Jesus did many other miraculous signs in the presence of his disciples, which are not recorded in this book. ³¹But these are written that you may*ᵃ* believe that Jesus is the Christ, the Son of God, and that by believing you may have life in his name.

JESUS AND THE MIRACULOUS CATCH OF FISH

21 Afterward Jesus appeared again to his disciples, by the Sea of Tiberias.*ᵇ* It happened this way: ²Simon Peter, Thomas (called Didymus), Nathanael from Cana in Galilee, the sons of Zebedee, and two other disciples were together. ³"I'm going out to fish," Simon Peter told them, and they said, "We'll go with you." So they went out and got into the boat, but that night they caught nothing.

⁴Early in the morning, Jesus stood on the shore, but the disciples did not realize that it was Jesus.

⁵He called out to them, "Friends, haven't you any fish?"

"No," they answered.

⁶He said, "Throw your net on the right side of the boat and you will find some." When they did, they were unable to haul the net in because of the large number of fish.

⁷Then the disciple whom Jesus loved said to Peter, "It is the Lord!" As soon as Simon Peter heard him say, "It is the Lord," he wrapped his outer garment around him (for he had taken it off) and jumped into the water. ⁸The other disciples followed in the boat, towing the net full of fish, for they were not far from shore, about a hundred yards.*ᶜ* ⁹When they landed, they saw a fire of burning coals there with fish on it, and some bread.

¹⁰Jesus said to them, "Bring some of the fish you have just caught."

¹¹Simon Peter climbed aboard and dragged the net ashore. It was full of large fish, 153, but even with so many the net was not torn. ¹²Jesus

THE MESSAGE

20.26 Eight days later, his disciples were again in the room. This time Thomas was with them. Jesus came through the locked doors, stood among them, and said, "Peace to you."

20.27 Then he focused his attention on Thomas. "Take your finger and examine my hands. Take your hand and stick it in my side. Don't be unbelieving. Believe."

20.28 Thomas said, "My Master! My God!"

20.29 Jesus said, "So, you believe because you've seen with your own eyes. Even better blessings are in store for those who believe without seeing."

20.30-31 Jesus provided far more God-revealing signs than are written down in this book. These are written down so you will believe that Jesus is the Messiah, the Son of God, and in the act of believing, have real and eternal life in the way he personally revealed it.

FISHING

21 21.1-3 After this, Jesus appeared again to the disciples, this time at the Tiberias Sea (the Sea of Galilee). This is how he did it: Simon Peter, Thomas (nicknamed "Twin"), Nathanael from Cana in Galilee, the brothers Zebedee, and two other disciples were together. Simon Peter announced, "I'm going fishing."

21.3-4 The rest of them replied, "We're going with you." They went out and got in the boat. They caught nothing that night. When the sun came up, Jesus was standing on the beach, but they didn't recognize him.

21.5 Jesus spoke to them: "Good morning! Did you catch anything for breakfast?"

They answered, "No."

21.6 He said, "Throw the net off the right side of the boat and see what happens."

They did what he said. All of a sudden there were so many fish in it, they weren't strong enough to pull it in.

21.7-9 Then the disciple Jesus loved said to Peter, "It's the Master!"

When Simon Peter realized that it was the Master, he threw on some clothes, for he was stripped for work, and dove into the sea. The other disciples came in by boat for they weren't far from land, a hundred yards or so, pulling along the net full of fish. When they got out of the boat, they saw a fire laid, with fish and bread cooking on it.

21.10-11 Jesus said, "Bring some of the fish you've just caught." Simon Peter joined them and pulled the net to shore—153 big fish! And even with all those fish, the net didn't rip.

ᵃ 31 Some manuscripts *may continue to*   *ᵇ 1* That is, Sea of Galilee   *ᶜ 8* Greek *about two hundred cubits* (about 90 meters)

NEW INTERNATIONAL VERSION

said to them, "Come and have breakfast." None of the disciples dared ask him, "Who are you?" They knew it was the Lord. ¹³Jesus came, took the bread and gave it to them, and did the same with the fish. ¹⁴This was now the third time Jesus appeared to his disciples after he was raised from the dead.

JESUS REINSTATES PETER

¹⁵When they had finished eating, Jesus said to Simon Peter, "Simon son of John, do you truly love me more than these?"

"Yes, Lord," he said, "you know that I love you."

Jesus said, "Feed my lambs."

¹⁶Again Jesus said, "Simon son of John, do you truly love me?"

He answered, "Yes, Lord, you know that I love you."

Jesus said, "Take care of my sheep."

¹⁷The third time he said to him, "Simon son of John, do you love me?"

Peter was hurt because Jesus asked him the third time, "Do you love me?" He said, "Lord, you know all things; you know that I love you."

Jesus said, "Feed my sheep. ¹⁸I tell you the truth, when you were younger you dressed yourself and went where you wanted; but when you are old you will stretch out your hands, and someone else will dress you and lead you where you do not want to go." ¹⁹Jesus said this to indicate the kind of death by which Peter would glorify God. Then he said to him, "Follow me!"

²⁰Peter turned and saw that the disciple whom Jesus loved was following them. (This was the one who had leaned back against Jesus at the supper and had said, "Lord, who is going to betray you?") ²¹When Peter saw him, he asked, "Lord, what about him?"

²²Jesus answered, "If I want him to remain alive until I return, what is that to you? You must follow me." ²³Because of this, the rumor spread among the brothers that this disciple would not die. But Jesus did not say that he would not die; he only said, "If I want him to remain alive until I return, what is that to you?"

²⁴This is the disciple who testifies to these things and who wrote them down. We know that his testimony is true.

²⁵Jesus did many other things as well. If every one of them were written down, I suppose that even the whole world would not have room for the books that would be written.

THE MESSAGE

21.12 Jesus said, "Breakfast is ready." Not one of the disciples dared ask, "Who are you?" They knew it was the Master.

21.13-14 Jesus then took the bread and gave it to them. He did the same with the fish. This was now the third time Jesus had shown himself alive to the disciples since being raised from the dead.

DO YOU LOVE ME?

21.15 After breakfast, Jesus said to Simon Peter, "Simon, son of John, do you love me more than these?"

"Yes, Master, you know I love you."

Jesus said, "Feed my lambs."

21.16 He then asked a second time, "Simon, son of John, do you love me?"

"Yes, Master, you know I love you."

Jesus said, "Shepherd my sheep."

21.17-19 Then he said it a third time: "Simon, son of John, do you love me?"

Peter was upset that he asked for the third time, "Do you love me?" so he answered, "Master, you know everything there is to know. You've got to know that I love you."

Jesus said, "Feed my sheep. I'm telling you the very truth now: When you were young you dressed yourself and went wherever you wished, but when you get old you'll have to stretch out your hands while someone else dresses you and takes you where you don't want to go." He said this to hint at the kind of death by which Peter would glorify God. And then he commanded, "Follow me."

21.20-21 Turning his head, Peter noticed the disciple Jesus loved following right behind. When Peter noticed him, he asked Jesus, "Master, what's going to happen to *him*?"

21.22-23 Jesus said, "If I want him to live until I come again, what's that to you? You—follow me." That is how the rumor got out among the brothers that this disciple wouldn't die. But that is not what Jesus said. He simply said, "If I want him to live until I come again, what's that to you?"

21.24 This is the same disciple who was eyewitness to all these things and wrote them down. And we all know that his eyewitness account is reliable and accurate.

21.25 There are so many other things Jesus did. If they were all written down, each of them, one by one, I can't imagine a world big enough to hold such a library of books.

ACTS

ACTS

JESUS TAKEN UP INTO HEAVEN

1 In my former book, Theophilus, I wrote about all that Jesus began to do and to teach ²until the day he was taken up to heaven, after giving instructions through the Holy Spirit to the apostles he had chosen. ³After his suffering, he showed himself to these men and gave many convincing proofs that he was alive. He appeared to them over a period of forty days and spoke about the kingdom of God. ⁴On one occasion, while he was eating with them, he gave them this command: "Do not leave Jerusalem, but wait for the gift my Father promised, which you have heard me speak about. ⁵For John baptized with*ª* water, but in a few days you will be baptized with the Holy Spirit."

⁶So when they met together, they asked him, "Lord, are you at this time going to restore the kingdom to Israel?"

⁷He said to them: "It is not for you to know the times or dates the Father has set by his own authority. ⁸But you will receive power when the Holy Spirit comes on you; and you will be my witnesses in Jerusalem, and in all Judea and Samaria, and to the ends of the earth."

⁹After he said this, he was taken up before their very eyes, and a cloud hid him from their sight.

¹⁰They were looking intently up into the sky as he was going, when suddenly two men dressed in white stood beside them. ¹¹"Men of Galilee," they said, "why do you stand here looking into the sky? This same Jesus, who has been taken from you into heaven, will come back in the same way you have seen him go into heaven."

MATTHIAS CHOSEN TO REPLACE JUDAS

¹²Then they returned to Jerusalem from the hill called the Mount of Olives, a Sabbath day's walk*ᵇ* from the city. ¹³When they arrived, they went upstairs to the room where they were staying. Those present were Peter, John, James and Andrew; Philip and Thomas, Bartholomew and

---

ª 5 Or *in*   *ᵇ 12* That is, about 3/4 mile (about 1,100 meters)

TO THE ENDS OF THE WORLD

1.1-5 **1** Dear Theophilus, in the first volume of this book I wrote on everything that Jesus began to do and teach until the day he said good-bye to the apostles, the ones he had chosen through the Holy Spirit, and was taken up to heaven. After his death, he presented himself alive to them in many different settings over a period of forty days. In face-to-face meetings, he talked to them about things concerning the kingdom of God. As they met and ate meals together, he told them that they were on no account to leave Jerusalem but "must wait for what the Father promised: the promise you heard from me. John baptized in water; you will be baptized in the Holy Spirit. And soon."

1.6   When they were together for the last time they asked, "Master, are you going to restore the kingdom to Israel now? Is this the time?"

1.7-8   He told them, "You don't get to know the time. Timing is the Father's business. What you'll get is the Holy Spirit. And when the Holy Spirit comes on you, you will be able to be my witnesses in Jerusalem, all over Judea and Samaria, even to the ends of the world."

1.9-11   These were his last words. As they watched, he was taken up and disappeared in a cloud. They stood there, staring into the empty sky. Suddenly two men appeared—in white robes! They said, "You Galileans!—why do you stand here looking up at an empty sky? This very Jesus who was taken up from among you to heaven will come as certainly—and mysteriously—as he left."

RETURNING TO JERUSALEM

1.12-13 So they left the mountain called Olives and returned to Jerusalem. It was a little over half a mile. They went to the upper room they had been using as a meeting place:

Peter,
John,
James,
Andrew,
Philip,
Thomas,

NEW INTERNATIONAL VERSION

Matthew; James son of Alphaeus and Simon the Zealot, and Judas son of James. [14]They all joined together constantly in prayer, along with the women and Mary the mother of Jesus, and with his brothers.

[15]In those days Peter stood up among the believers[a] (a group numbering about a hundred and twenty) [16]and said, "Brothers, the Scripture had to be fulfilled which the Holy Spirit spoke long ago through the mouth of David concerning Judas, who served as guide for those who arrested Jesus— [17]he was one of our number and shared in this ministry."

[18](With the reward he got for his wickedness, Judas bought a field; there he fell headlong, his body burst open and all his intestines spilled out. [19]Everyone in Jerusalem heard about this, so they called that field in their language Akeldama, that is, Field of Blood.)

[20]"For," said Peter, "it is written in the book of Psalms,

" 'May his place be deserted;
    let there be no one to dwell in it,'[b]

and,

" 'May another take his place of leadership.'[c]

[21]Therefore it is necessary to choose one of the men who have been with us the whole time the Lord Jesus went in and out among us, [22]beginning from John's baptism to the time when Jesus was taken up from us. For one of these must become a witness with us of his resurrection."

[23]So they proposed two men: Joseph called Barsabbas (also known as Justus) and Matthias. [24]Then they prayed, "Lord, you know everyone's heart. Show us which of these two you have chosen [25]to take over this apostolic ministry, which Judas left to go where he belongs." [26]Then they cast lots, and the lot fell to Matthias; so he was added to the eleven apostles.

THE HOLY SPIRIT COMES AT PENTECOST

2 When the day of Pentecost came, they were all together in one place. [2]Suddenly a sound like the blowing of a violent wind came from heaven and filled the whole house where they were sitting. [3]They saw what seemed to be tongues of fire that separated and came to rest on each of them. [4]All of them were filled with the Holy Spirit and began to speak in other tongues[d] as the Spirit enabled them.

---

[a] 15 Greek brothers   [b] 20 Psalm 69:25
[c] 20 Psalm 109:8   [d] 4 Or languages; also in verse 11

THE MESSAGE

Bartholomew,
Matthew,
James, son of Alphaeus,
Simon the Zealot,
Judas, son of James.

1.14 They agreed they were in this for good, completely together in prayer, the women included. Also Jesus' mother, Mary, and his brothers.

REPLACING JUDAS

1.15-17 During this time, Peter stood up in the company—there were about one hundred twenty of them in the room at the time—and said, "Friends, long ago the Holy Spirit spoke through David regarding Judas, who became the guide to those who arrested Jesus. That Scripture had to be fulfilled, and now has been. Judas was one of us and had his assigned place in this ministry.

1.18-20 "As you know, he took the evil bribe money and bought a small farm. There he came to a bad end, rupturing his belly and spilling his guts. Everybody in Jerusalem knows this by now; they call the place Murder Meadow. It's exactly what we find written in the Psalms:

Let his farm become haunted
So no one can ever live there.

"And also what was written later:

Let someone else take over his post.

1.21-22 "Judas must now be replaced. The replacement must come from the company of men who stayed together with us from the time Jesus was baptized by John up to the day of his ascension, designated along with us as a witness to his resurrection."

1.23-26 They nominated two: Joseph Barsabbas, nicknamed Justus, and Matthias. Then they prayed, "You, O God, know every one of us inside and out. Make plain which of these two men you choose to take the place in this ministry and leadership that Judas threw away in order to go his own way." They then drew straws. Matthias won and was counted in with the eleven apostles.

A SOUND LIKE A STRONG WIND

2.1-4 2 When the Feast of Pentecost came, they were all together in one place. Without warning there was a sound like a strong wind, gale force—no one could tell where it came from. It filled the whole building. Then, like a wildfire, the Holy Spirit spread through their ranks, and they started speaking in a number of different languages as the Spirit prompted them.

NEW INTERNATIONAL VERSION

⁵Now there were staying in Jerusalem God-fearing Jews from every nation under heaven. ⁶When they heard this sound, a crowd came together in bewilderment, because each one heard them speaking in his own language. ⁷Utterly amazed, they asked: "Are not all these men who are speaking Galileans? ⁸Then how is it that each of us hears them in his own native language? ⁹Parthians, Medes and Elamites; residents of Mesopotamia, Judea and Cappadocia, Pontus and Asia, ¹⁰Phrygia and Pamphylia, Egypt and the parts of Libya near Cyrene; visitors from Rome ¹¹(both Jews and converts to Judaism); Cretans and Arabs—we hear them declaring the wonders of God in our own tongues!" ¹²Amazed and perplexed, they asked one another, "What does this mean?"

¹³Some, however, made fun of them and said, "They have had too much wine. ᵃ"

Peter Addresses the Crowd

¹⁴Then Peter stood up with the Eleven, raised his voice and addressed the crowd: "Fellow Jews and all of you who live in Jerusalem, let me explain this to you; listen carefully to what I say. ¹⁵These men are not drunk, as you suppose. It's only nine in the morning! ¹⁶No, this is what was spoken by the prophet Joel:

¹⁷ " 'In the last days, God says,
   I will pour out my Spirit on all people.
Your sons and daughters will prophesy,
   your young men will see visions,
   your old men will dream dreams.
¹⁸Even on my servants, both men and women,
   I will pour out my Spirit in those days,
   and they will prophesy.
¹⁹I will show wonders in the heaven above
   and signs on the earth below,
   blood and fire and billows of smoke.
²⁰The sun will be turned to darkness
   and the moon to blood
   before the coming of the great and
      glorious day of the Lord.
²¹And everyone who calls
   on the name of the Lord will be saved.' ᵇ

THE MESSAGE

2.5-11   There were many Jews staying in Jerusalem just then, devout pilgrims from all over the world. When they heard the sound, they came on the run. Then when they heard, one after another, their own mother tongues being spoken, they were thunderstruck. They couldn't for the life of them figure out what was going on, and kept saying, "Aren't these all Galileans? How come we're hearing them talk in our various mother tongues?

   Parthians, Medes, and Elamites;
   Visitors from Mesopotamia, Judea, and
         Cappadocia,
      Pontus and Asia, Phrygia and Pamphylia,
      Egypt and the parts of Libya belonging
         to Cyrene;
   Immigrants from Rome, both Jews and
         proselytes;
   Even Cretans and Arabs!

"They're speaking our languages, describing God's mighty works!"

2.12   Their heads were spinning; they couldn't make head or tail of any of it. They talked back and forth, confused: "What's going on here?"

2.13   Others joked, "They're drunk on cheap wine."

Peter Speaks Up

2.14-21 That's when Peter stood up and, backed by the other eleven, spoke out with bold urgency: "Fellow Jews, all of you who are visiting Jerusalem, listen carefully and get this story straight. These people aren't drunk as some of you suspect. They haven't had time to get drunk—it's only nine o'clock in the morning. This is what the prophet Joel announced would happen:

   "In the Last Days," God says,
   "I will pour out my Spirit
      on every kind of people:
   Your sons will prophesy,
      also your daughters;
   Your young men will see visions,
      your old men dream dreams.
   When the time comes,
      I'll pour out my Spirit
   On those who serve me, men and women
         both,
      and they'll prophesy.
   I'll set wonders in the sky above
      and signs on the earth below,
   Blood and fire and billowing smoke,
      the sun turning black and the moon
         blood-red,
   Before the Day of the Lord arrives,
      the Day tremendous and marvelous;
   And whoever calls out for help
      to me, God, will be saved."

ᵃ 13 Or *sweet wine*   ᵇ 21 Joel 2:28-32

NEW INTERNATIONAL VERSION

22"Men of Israel, listen to this: Jesus of Nazareth was a man accredited by God to you by miracles, wonders and signs, which God did among you through him, as you yourselves know. 23This man was handed over to you by God's set purpose and foreknowledge; and you, with the help of wicked men,ª put him to death by nailing him to the cross. 24But God raised him from the dead, freeing him from the agony of death, because it was impossible for death to keep its hold on him. 25David said about him:

" 'I saw the Lord always before me.
    Because he is at my right hand,
    I will not be shaken.
26Therefore my heart is glad and my tongue
        rejoices;
    my body also will live in hope,
27because you will not abandon me to the grave,
    nor will you let your Holy One see decay.
28You have made known to me the paths of life;
    you will fill me with joy in your presence.'b

29"Brothers, I can tell you confidently that the patriarch David died and was buried, and his tomb is here to this day. 30But he was a prophet and knew that God had promised him on oath that he would place one of his descendants on his throne. 31Seeing what was ahead, he spoke of the resurrection of the Christ,c that he was not abandoned to the grave, nor did his body see decay. 32God has raised this Jesus to life, and we are all witnesses of the fact. 33Exalted to the right hand of God, he has received from the Father the promised Holy Spirit and has poured out what you now see and hear. 34For David did not ascend to heaven, and yet he said,

" 'The Lord said to my Lord:
    "Sit at my right hand
35until I make your enemies
    a footstool for your feet." ' d

36"Therefore let all Israel be assured of this: God has made this Jesus, whom you crucified, both Lord and Christ."

37When the people heard this, they were cut to the heart and said to Peter and the other apostles, "Brothers, what shall we do?"

38Peter replied, "Repent and be baptized, every one of you, in the name of Jesus Christ for the forgiveness of your sins. And you will receive the gift of the Holy Spirit. 39The promise is for you and your children and for all who are far off—for all whom the Lord our God will call."

ª 23 Or of those not having the law (that is, Gentiles)
b 28 Psalm 16:8-11   c 31 Or Messiah. "The Christ"
(Greek) and "the Messiah" (Hebrew) both mean "the
Anointed One"; also in verse 36.   d 35 Psalm 110:1

THE MESSAGE

2.22-28   "Fellow Israelites, listen carefully to these words: Jesus the Nazarene, a man thoroughly accredited by God to you—the miracles and wonders and signs that God did through him are common knowledge—this Jesus, following the deliberate and well-thought-out plan of God, was betrayed by men who took the law into their own hands, and was handed over to you. And you pinned him to a cross and killed him. But God untied the death ropes and raised him up. Death was no match for him. David said it all:

I saw God before me for all time.
    Nothing can shake me; he's right by my
        side.
I'm glad from the inside out, ecstatic;
    I've pitched my tent in the land of hope.
I know you'll never dump me in Hades;
    I'll never even smell the stench of death.
You've got my feet on the life-path,
    with your face shining sun-joy all
        around.

2.29-36   "Dear friends, let me be completely frank with you. Our ancestor David is dead and buried—his tomb is in plain sight today. But being also a prophet and knowing that God had solemnly sworn that a descendant of his would rule his kingdom, seeing far ahead, he talked of the resurrection of the Messiah—'no trip to Hades, no stench of death.' This Jesus, God raised up. And every one of us here is a witness to it. Then, raised to the heights at the right hand of God and receiving the promise of the Holy Spirit from the Father, he poured out the Spirit he had just received. That is what you see and hear. For David himself did not ascend to heaven, but he did say,

God said to my Master, "Sit at my right
        hand
Until I make your enemies a stool for
        resting your feet."

"All Israel, then, know this: There's no longer room for doubt—God made him Master and Messiah, this Jesus whom you killed on a cross."

2.37   Cut to the quick, those who were there listening asked Peter and the other apostles, "Brothers! Brothers! So now what do we do?"

2.38-39   Peter said, "Change your life. Turn to God and be baptized, each of you, in the name of Jesus Christ, so your sins are forgiven. Receive the gift of the Holy Spirit. The promise is targeted to you and your children, but also to all who are far away—whomever, in fact, our Master God invites."

NEW INTERNATIONAL VERSION

40With many other words he warned them; and he pleaded with them, "Save yourselves from this corrupt generation." 41Those who accepted his message were baptized, and about three thousand were added to their number that day.

THE FELLOWSHIP OF THE BELIEVERS

42They devoted themselves to the apostles' teaching and to the fellowship, to the breaking of bread and to prayer. 43Everyone was filled with awe, and many wonders and miraculous signs were done by the apostles. 44All the believers were together and had everything in common. 45Selling their possessions and goods, they gave to anyone as he had need. 46Every day they continued to meet together in the temple courts. They broke bread in their homes and ate together with glad and sincere hearts, 47praising God and enjoying the favor of all the people. And the Lord added to their number daily those who were being saved.

PETER HEALS THE CRIPPLED BEGGAR

3 One day Peter and John were going up to the temple at the time of prayer—at three in the afternoon. 2Now a man crippled from birth was being carried to the temple gate called Beautiful, where he was put every day to beg from those going into the temple courts. 3When he saw Peter and John about to enter, he asked them for money. 4Peter looked straight at him, as did John. Then Peter said, "Look at us!" 5So the man gave them his attention, expecting to get something from them.

6Then Peter said, "Silver or gold I do not have, but what I have I give you. In the name of Jesus Christ of Nazareth, walk." 7Taking him by the right hand, he helped him up, and instantly the man's feet and ankles became strong. 8He jumped to his feet and began to walk. Then he went with them into the temple courts, walking and jumping, and praising God. 9When all the people saw him walking and praising God, 10they recognized him as the same man who used to sit begging at the temple gate called Beautiful, and they were filled with wonder and amazement at what had happened to him.

PETER SPEAKS TO THE ONLOOKERS

11While the beggar held on to Peter and John, all the people were astonished and came running to them in the place called Solomon's Colonnade. 12When Peter saw this, he said to them:

THE MESSAGE

2.40 He went on in this vein for a long time, urging them over and over, "Get out while you can; get out of this sick and stupid culture!"

2.41-42 That day about three thousand took him at his word, were baptized and were signed up. They committed themselves to the teaching of the apostles, the life together, the common meal, and the prayers.

✝

2.43-45 Everyone around was in awe—all those wonders and signs done through the apostles! And all the believers lived in a wonderful harmony, holding everything in common. They sold whatever they owned and pooled their resources so that each person's need was met.

2.46-47 They followed a daily discipline of worship in the Temple followed by meals at home, every meal a celebration, exuberant and joyful, as they praised God. People in general liked what they saw. Every day their number grew as God added those who were saved.

3.1-5 3 One day at three o'clock in the afternoon, Peter and John were on their way into the Temple for prayer meeting. At the same time there was a man crippled from birth being carried up. Every day he was set down at the Temple gate, the one named Beautiful, to beg from those going into the Temple. When he saw Peter and John about to enter the Temple, he asked for a handout. Peter, with John at his side, looked him straight in the eye and said, "Look here." He looked up, expecting to get something from them.

3.6-8 Peter said, "I don't have a nickel to my name, but what I do have, I give you: In the name of Jesus Christ of Nazareth, walk!" He grabbed him by the right hand and pulled him up. In an instant his feet and ankles became firm. He jumped to his feet and walked.

3.8-10 The man went into the Temple with them, walking back and forth, dancing and praising God. Everybody there saw him walking around and praising God. They recognized him as the one who sat begging at the Temple's Gate Beautiful and rubbed their eyes, astonished, scarcely believing what they were seeing.

3.11 The man threw his arms around Peter and John, ecstatic. All the people ran up to where they were at Solomon's Porch to see it for themselves.

TURN TO FACE GOD

3.12-16 When Peter saw he had a congregation, he addressed the people:

NEW INTERNATIONAL VERSION

"Men of Israel, why does this surprise you? Why do you stare at us as if by our own power or godliness we had made this man walk? ¹³The God of Abraham, Isaac and Jacob, the God of our fathers, has glorified his servant Jesus. You handed him over to be killed, and you disowned him before Pilate, though he had decided to let him go. ¹⁴You disowned the Holy and Righteous One and asked that a murderer be released to you. ¹⁵You killed the author of life, but God raised him from the dead. We are witnesses of this. ¹⁶By faith in the name of Jesus, this man whom you see and know was made strong. It is Jesus' name and the faith that comes through him that has given this complete healing to him, as you can all see.

¹⁷"Now, brothers, I know that you acted in ignorance, as did your leaders. ¹⁸But this is how God fulfilled what he had foretold through all the prophets, saying that his Christ ᵃ would suffer. ¹⁹Repent, then, and turn to God, so that your sins may be wiped out, that times of refreshing may come from the Lord, ²⁰and that he may send the Christ, who has been appointed for you—even Jesus. ²¹He must remain in heaven until the time comes for God to restore everything, as he promised long ago through his holy prophets. ²²For Moses said, 'The Lord your God will raise up for you a prophet like me from among your own people; you must listen to everything he tells you. ²³Anyone who does not listen to him will be completely cut off from among his people.' ᵇ

²⁴"Indeed, all the prophets from Samuel on, as many as have spoken, have foretold these days. ²⁵And you are heirs of the prophets and of the covenant God made with your fathers. He said to Abraham, 'Through your offspring all peoples on earth will be blessed.' ᶜ ²⁶When God raised up his servant, he sent him first to you to bless you by turning each of you from your wicked ways."

PETER AND JOHN BEFORE THE SANHEDRIN

4 The priests and the captain of the temple guard and the Sadducees came up to Peter and John while they were speaking to the people. ²They were greatly disturbed because the apostles were teaching the people and proclaiming in Jesus the resurrection of the dead. ³They seized Peter and John, and because it was evening, they put them in jail until the next day.

THE MESSAGE

"Oh, Israelites, why does this take you by such complete surprise, and why stare at us as if *our* power or piety made him walk? The God of Abraham and Isaac and Jacob, the God of our ancestors, has glorified his Son Jesus. The very One that Pilate called innocent, you repudiated. You repudiated the Holy One, the Just One, and asked for a murderer in his place. You no sooner killed the Author of Life than God raised him from the dead—and we're the witnesses. Faith in Jesus' name put this man, whose condition you know so well, on his feet—yes, faith and nothing but faith put this man healed and whole right before your eyes.

3.17-18   "And now, friends, I know you had no idea what you were doing when you killed Jesus, and neither did your leaders. But God, who through the preaching of all the prophets had said all along that his Messiah would be killed, knew exactly what you were doing and used it to fulfill his plans.

3.19-23   "Now it's time to change your ways! Turn to face God so he can wipe away your sins, pour out showers of blessing to refresh you, and send you the Messiah he prepared for you, namely, Jesus. For the time being he must remain out of sight in heaven until everything is restored to order again just the way God, through the preaching of his holy prophets of old, said it would be. Moses, for instance, said, 'Your God will raise up for you a prophet just like me from your family. Listen to every word he speaks to you. Every last living soul who refuses to listen to that prophet will be wiped out from the people.'

3.24-26   "All the prophets from Samuel on down said the same thing, said most emphatically that these days would come. These prophets, along with the covenant God made with your ancestors, are your family tree. God's covenant-word to Abraham provides the text: 'By your offspring all the families of the earth will be blessed.' But you are first in line: God, having raised up his Son, sent him to bless you as you turn, one by one, from your evil ways."

NOTHING TO HIDE

4.1-4   **4** While Peter and John were addressing the people, the priests, the chief of the Temple police, and some Sadducees came up, indignant that these upstart apostles were instructing the people and proclaiming that the resurrection from the dead had taken place in Jesus. They arrested them and threw them in jail until morning, for by now it was late in the

---

ᵃ 18 Or Messiah; also in verse 20   ᵇ 23 Deut. 18:15,18,19
ᶜ 25 Gen. 22:18; 26:4

NEW INTERNATIONAL VERSION

⁴But many who heard the message believed, and the number of men grew to about five thousand.

⁵The next day the rulers, elders and teachers of the law met in Jerusalem. ⁶Annas the high priest was there, and so were Caiaphas, John, Alexander and the other men of the high priest's family. ⁷They had Peter and John brought before them and began to question them: "By what power or what name did you do this?"

⁸Then Peter, filled with the Holy Spirit, said to them: "Rulers and elders of the people! ⁹If we are being called to account today for an act of kindness shown to a cripple and are asked how he was healed, ¹⁰then know this, you and all the people of Israel: It is by the name of Jesus Christ of Nazareth, whom you crucified but whom God raised from the dead, that this man stands before you healed. ¹¹He is

" 'the stone you builders rejected,
   which has become the capstone.ᵃ ᵇ

¹²Salvation is found in no one else, for there is no other name under heaven given to men by which we must be saved."

¹³When they saw the courage of Peter and John and realized that they were unschooled, ordinary men, they were astonished and they took note that these men had been with Jesus. ¹⁴But since they could see the man who had been healed standing there with them, there was nothing they could say. ¹⁵So they ordered them to withdraw from the Sanhedrin and then conferred together. ¹⁶"What are we going to do with these men?" they asked. "Everybody living in Jerusalem knows they have done an outstanding miracle, and we cannot deny it. ¹⁷But to stop this thing from spreading any further among the people, we must warn these men to speak no longer to anyone in this name."

¹⁸Then they called them in again and commanded them not to speak or teach at all in the name of Jesus. ¹⁹But Peter and John replied, "Judge for yourselves whether it is right in God's sight to obey you rather than God. ²⁰For we cannot help speaking about what we have seen and heard."

²¹After further threats they let them go. They could not decide how to punish them, because all the people were praising God for what had happened. ²²For the man who was miraculously healed was over forty years old.

THE MESSAGE

evening. But many of those who listened had already believed the Message—in round numbers about five thousand!

4.5-7 The next day a meeting was called in Jerusalem. The rulers, religious leaders, religion scholars, Annas the Chief Priest, Caiaphas, John, Alexander—everybody who was anybody was there. They stood Peter and John in the middle of the room and grilled them: "Who put you in charge here? What business do you have doing this?"

4.8-12 With that, Peter, full of the Holy Spirit, let loose: "Rulers and leaders of the people, if we have been brought to trial today for helping a sick man, put under investigation regarding this healing, I'll be completely frank with you—we have nothing to hide. By the name of Jesus Christ of Nazareth, the One you killed on a cross, the One God raised from the dead, by means of his name this man stands before you healthy and whole. Jesus is 'the stone you masons threw out, which is now the cornerstone.' Salvation comes no other way; no other name has been or will be given to us by which we can be saved, only this one."

4.13-14 They couldn't take their eyes off them—Peter and John standing there so confident, so sure of themselves! Their fascination deepened when they realized these two were laymen with no training in Scripture or formal education. They recognized them as companions of Jesus, but with the man right before them, seeing him standing there so upright—so healed!—what could they say against that?

4.15-17 They sent them out of the room so they could work out a plan. They talked it over: "What can we do with these men? By now it's known all over town that a miracle has occurred, and that they are behind it. There is no way we can refute that. But so that it doesn't go any further, let's silence them with threats so they won't dare to use Jesus' name ever again with anyone."

4.18-20 They called them back and warned them that they were on no account ever again to speak or teach in the name of Jesus. But Peter and John spoke right back, "Whether it's right in God's eyes to listen to you rather than to God, you decide. As for us, there's no question—we can't keep quiet about what we've seen and heard."

4.21-22 The religious leaders renewed their threats, but then released them. They couldn't come up with a charge that would stick, that would keep them in jail. The people wouldn't have stood for it—they were all praising God over what had happened. The man who had been miraculously healed was over forty years old.

ᵃ 11 Or cornerstone   ᵇ 11 Psalm 118:22

NEW INTERNATIONAL VERSION

THE BELIEVERS' PRAYER

²³On their release, Peter and John went back to their own people and reported all that the chief priests and elders had said to them. ²⁴When they heard this, they raised their voices together in prayer to God. "Sovereign Lord," they said, "you made the heaven and the earth and the sea, and everything in them. ²⁵You spoke by the Holy Spirit through the mouth of your servant, our father David:

" 'Why do the nations rage
    and the peoples plot in vain?
²⁶The kings of the earth take their stand
    and the rulers gather together
against the Lord
    and against his Anointed One.'ᵃ ᵇ

²⁷Indeed Herod and Pontius Pilate met together with the Gentiles and the peopleᶜ of Israel in this city to conspire against your holy servant Jesus, whom you anointed. ²⁸They did what your power and will had decided beforehand should happen. ²⁹Now, Lord, consider their threats and enable your servants to speak your word with great boldness. ³⁰Stretch out your hand to heal and perform miraculous signs and wonders through the name of your holy servant Jesus."

³¹After they prayed, the place where they were meeting was shaken. And they were all filled with the Holy Spirit and spoke the word of God boldly.

THE BELIEVERS SHARE THEIR POSSESSIONS

³²All the believers were one in heart and mind. No one claimed that any of his possessions was his own, but they shared everything they had. ³³With great power the apostles continued to testify to the resurrection of the Lord Jesus, and much grace was upon them all. ³⁴There were no needy persons among them. For from time to time those who owned lands or houses sold them, brought the money from the sales ³⁵and put it at the apostles' feet, and it was distributed to anyone as he had need.

³⁶Joseph, a Levite from Cyprus, whom the apostles called Barnabas (which means Son of Encouragement), ³⁷sold a field he owned and brought the money and put it at the apostles' feet.

ANANIAS AND SAPPHIRA

5 Now a man named Ananias, together with his wife Sapphira, also sold a piece of property. ²With his wife's full knowledge he kept

THE MESSAGE

ONE HEART, ONE MIND

4.23-26 As soon as Peter and John were let go, they went to their friends and told them what the high priests and religious leaders had said. Hearing the report, they lifted their voices in a wonderful harmony in prayer: "Strong God, you made heaven and earth and sea and everything in them. By the Holy Spirit you spoke through the mouth of your servant and our father, David:

Why the big noise, nations?
Why the mean plots, peoples?
Earth's leaders push for position,
Potentates meet for summit talks,
The God-deniers, the Messiah-defiers!

4.27-28 "For in fact they did meet—Herod and Pontius Pilate with nations and peoples, even Israel itself!—met in this very city to plot against your holy Son Jesus, the One you made Messiah, to carry out the plans you long ago set in motion.

4.29-30 "And now they're at it again! Take care of their threats and give your servants fearless confidence in preaching your Message, as you stretch out your hand to us in healings and miracles and wonders done in the name of your holy servant Jesus."

4.31 While they were praying, the place where they were meeting trembled and shook. They were all filled with the Holy Spirit and continued to speak God's Word with fearless confidence.

4.32-33 The whole congregation of believers was united as one—one heart, one mind! They didn't even claim ownership of their own possessions. No one said, "That's mine; you can't have it." They shared everything. The apostles gave powerful witness to the resurrection of the Master Jesus, and grace was on all of them.

4.34-35 And so it turned out that not a person among them was needy. Those who owned fields or houses sold them and brought the price of the sale to the apostles and made an offering of it. The apostles then distributed it according to each person's need.

4.36-37 Joseph, called by the apostles "Barnabas" (which means "Son of Comfort"), a Levite born in Cyprus, sold a field that he owned, brought the money, and made an offering of it to the apostles.

ANANIAS AND SAPPHIRA

5.1-2 **5** But a man named Ananias—his wife, Sapphira, conniving in this with him—sold a piece of land, secretly kept part of the price for

---

ᵃ 26 That is, Christ or Messiah   ᵇ 26 Psalm 2:1,2
ᶜ 27 The Greek is plural.

NEW INTERNATIONAL VERSION

back part of the money for himself, but brought the rest and put it at the apostles' feet.

³Then Peter said, "Ananias, how is it that Satan has so filled your heart that you have lied to the Holy Spirit and have kept for yourself some of the money you received for the land? ⁴Didn't it belong to you before it was sold? And after it was sold, wasn't the money at your disposal? What made you think of doing such a thing? You have not lied to men but to God."

⁵When Ananias heard this, he fell down and died. And great fear seized all who heard what had happened. ⁶Then the young men came forward, wrapped up his body, and carried him out and buried him.

⁷About three hours later his wife came in, not knowing what had happened. ⁸Peter asked her, "Tell me, is this the price you and Ananias got for the land?"

"Yes," she said, "that is the price."

⁹Peter said to her, "How could you agree to test the Spirit of the Lord? Look! The feet of the men who buried your husband are at the door, and they will carry you out also."

¹⁰At that moment she fell down at his feet and died. Then the young men came in and, finding her dead, carried her out and buried her beside her husband. ¹¹Great fear seized the whole church and all who heard about these events.

THE APOSTLES HEAL MANY

¹²The apostles performed many miraculous signs and wonders among the people. And all the believers used to meet together in Solomon's Colonnade. ¹³No one else dared join them, even though they were highly regarded by the people. ¹⁴Nevertheless, more and more men and women believed in the Lord and were added to their number. ¹⁵As a result, people brought the sick into the streets and laid them on beds and mats so that at least Peter's shadow might fall on some of them as he passed by. ¹⁶Crowds gathered also from the towns around Jerusalem, bringing their sick and those tormented by evil[a] spirits, and all of them were healed.

THE APOSTLES PERSECUTED

¹⁷Then the high priest and all his associates, who were members of the party of the Sadducees, were filled with jealousy. ¹⁸They arrested the apostles and put them in the public jail. ¹⁹But during the night an angel of the Lord opened the doors of the jail and brought them out. ²⁰"Go,

THE MESSAGE

himself, and then brought the rest to the apostles and made an offering of it.

5.3-4   Peter said, "Ananias, how did Satan get you to lie to the Holy Spirit and secretly keep back part of the price of the field? Before you sold it, it was all yours, and after you sold it, the money was yours to do with as you wished. So what got into you to pull a trick like this? You didn't lie to men but to God."

5.5-6   Ananias, when he heard those words, fell down dead. *That* put the fear of God into everyone who heard of it. The younger men went right to work and wrapped him up, then carried him out and buried him.

5.7-8   Not more than three hours later, his wife, knowing nothing of what had happened, came in. Peter said, "Tell me, were you given this price for your field?"

"Yes," she said, "that price."

5.9-10   Peter responded, "What's going on here that you connived to conspire against the Spirit of the Master? The men who buried your husband are at the door, and you're next." No sooner were the words out of his mouth than she also fell down, dead. When the young men returned they found her body. They carried her out and buried her beside her husband.

5.11   By this time the whole church and, in fact, everyone who heard of these things had a healthy respect for God. They knew God was not to be trifled with.

THEY ALL MET REGULARLY

5.12-16   Through the work of the apostles, many God-signs were set up among the people, many wonderful things done. They all met regularly and in remarkable harmony on the Temple porch named after Solomon. But even though people admired them a lot, outsiders were wary about joining them. On the other hand, those who put their trust in the Master were added right and left, men and women both. They even carried the sick out into the streets and laid them on stretchers and bedrolls, hoping they would be touched by Peter's shadow when he walked by. They came from the villages surrounding Jerusalem, throngs of them, bringing the sick and bedeviled. And they all were healed.

TO OBEY GOD RATHER THAN MEN

5.17-20   Provoked mightily by all this, the Chief Priest and those on his side, mainly the sect of Sadducees, went into action, arrested the apostles and put them in the town jail. But during the night an angel of God opened the jailhouse door and led them out. He said, "Go to the

---

[a] 16 Greek *unclean*

NEW INTERNATIONAL VERSION

stand in the temple courts," he said, "and tell the people the full message of this new life."

²¹At daybreak they entered the temple courts, as they had been told, and began to teach the people.

When the high priest and his associates arrived, they called together the Sanhedrin—the full assembly of the elders of Israel—and sent to the jail for the apostles. ²²But on arriving at the jail, the officers did not find them there. So they went back and reported, ²³"We found the jail securely locked, with the guards standing at the doors; but when we opened them, we found no one inside." ²⁴On hearing this report, the captain of the temple guard and the chief priests were puzzled, wondering what would come of this.

²⁵Then someone came and said, "Look! The men you put in jail are standing in the temple courts teaching the people." ²⁶At that, the captain went with his officers and brought the apostles. They did not use force, because they feared that the people would stone them.

²⁷Having brought the apostles, they made them appear before the Sanhedrin to be questioned by the high priest. ²⁸"We gave you strict orders not to teach in this name," he said. "Yet you have filled Jerusalem with your teaching and are determined to make us guilty of this man's blood."

²⁹Peter and the other apostles replied: "We must obey God rather than men! ³⁰The God of our fathers raised Jesus from the dead—whom you had killed by hanging him on a tree. ³¹God exalted him to his own right hand as Prince and Savior that he might give repentance and forgiveness of sins to Israel. ³²We are witnesses of these things, and so is the Holy Spirit, whom God has given to those who obey him."

³³When they heard this, they were furious and wanted to put them to death. ³⁴But a Pharisee named Gamaliel, a teacher of the law, who was honored by all the people, stood up in the Sanhedrin and ordered that the men be put outside for a little while. ³⁵Then he addressed them: "Men of Israel, consider carefully what you intend to do to these men. ³⁶Some time ago Theudas appeared, claiming to be somebody, and about four hundred men rallied to him. He was killed, all his followers were dispersed, and it all came to nothing. ³⁷After him, Judas the Galilean appeared in the days of the census and led a band of people in revolt. He too was killed, and all his followers were scattered. ³⁸Therefore, in the present case I advise you: Leave these men alone! Let them go! For if their purpose or activity is of human origin, it will fail. ³⁹But if it is from God, you will not be able to stop these men; you will only find yourselves fighting against God."

THE MESSAGE

Temple and take your stand. Tell the people everything there is to say about this Life."

Promptly obedient, they entered the Temple at daybreak and went on with their teaching.

5.21-23 Meanwhile, the Chief Priest and his cronies convened the High Council, Israel's senate, and sent to the jail to have the prisoners brought in. When the police got there, they couldn't find them anywhere in the jail. They went back and reported, "We found the jail locked tight as a drum and the guards posted at the doors, but when we went inside we didn't find a soul."

5.24 The chief of the Temple police and the high priests were puzzled. "What's going on here anyway?"

5.25-26 Just then someone showed up and said, "Did you know that the men you put in jail are back in the Temple teaching the people?" The chief and his police went and got them, but they handled them gently, fearful that the people would riot and turn on them.

5.27-28 Bringing them back, they stood them before the High Council. The Chief Priest said, "Didn't we give you strict orders not to teach in Jesus' name? And here you have filled Jerusalem with your teaching and are trying your best to blame us for the death of this man."

5.29-32 Peter and the apostles answered, "It's necessary to obey God rather than men. The God of our ancestors raised up Jesus, the One you killed by hanging him on a cross. God set him on high at his side, Prince and Savior, to give Israel the gift of a changed life and sins forgiven. And we are witnesses to these things. The Holy Spirit, whom God gives to those who obey him, corroborates every detail."

5.33-37 When they heard that, they were furious and wanted to kill them on the spot. But one of the council members stood up, a Pharisee by the name of Gamaliel, a teacher of God's Law who was honored by everyone. He ordered the men taken out of the room for a short time, then said, "Fellow Israelites, be careful what you do to these men. Not long ago Theudas made something of a splash, claiming to be somebody, and got about four hundred men to join him. He was killed, his followers dispersed, and nothing came of it. A little later, at the time of the census, Judas the Galilean appeared and acquired a following. He also fizzled out and the people following him were scattered to the four winds.

5.38-39 "So I am telling you: Hands off these men! Let them alone. If this program or this work is merely human, it will fall apart, but if it is of God, there is nothing you can do about it—and you better not be found fighting against God!"

NEW INTERNATIONAL VERSION

⁴⁰His speech persuaded them. They called the apostles in and had them flogged. Then they ordered them not to speak in the name of Jesus, and let them go.

⁴¹The apostles left the Sanhedrin, rejoicing because they had been counted worthy of suffering disgrace for the Name. ⁴²Day after day, in the temple courts and from house to house, they never stopped teaching and proclaiming the good news that Jesus is the Christ.ᵃ

The Choosing of the Seven

6 In those days when the number of disciples was increasing, the Grecian Jews among them complained against the Hebraic Jews because their widows were being overlooked in the daily distribution of food. ²So the Twelve gathered all the disciples together and said, "It would not be right for us to neglect the ministry of the word of God in order to wait on tables. ³Brothers, choose seven men from among you who are known to be full of the Spirit and wisdom. We will turn this responsibility over to them ⁴and will give our attention to prayer and the ministry of the word."

⁵This proposal pleased the whole group. They chose Stephen, a man full of faith and of the Holy Spirit; also Philip, Procorus, Nicanor, Timon, Parmenas, and Nicolas from Antioch, a convert to Judaism. ⁶They presented these men to the apostles, who prayed and laid their hands on them.

⁷So the word of God spread. The number of disciples in Jerusalem increased rapidly, and a large number of priests became obedient to the faith.

Stephen Seized

⁸Now Stephen, a man full of God's grace and power, did great wonders and miraculous signs among the people. ⁹Opposition arose, however, from members of the Synagogue of the Freedmen (as it was called)—Jews of Cyrene and Alexandria as well as the provinces of Cilicia and Asia. These men began to argue with Stephen, ¹⁰but they could not stand up against his wisdom or the Spirit by whom he spoke.

THE MESSAGE

5.40-42 That convinced them. They called the apostles back in. After giving them a thorough whipping, they warned them not to speak in Jesus' name and sent them off. The apostles went out of the High Council overjoyed because they had been given the honor of being dishonored on account of the Name. Every day they were in the Temple and homes, teaching and preaching Christ Jesus, not letting up for a minute.

The Word of God Prospered

6.1-4 6 During this time, as the disciples were increasing in numbers by leaps and bounds, hard feelings developed among the Greek-speaking believers—"Hellenists"—toward the Hebrew-speaking believers because their widows were being discriminated against in the daily food lines. So the Twelve called a meeting of the disciples. They said, "It wouldn't be right for us to abandon our responsibilities for preaching and teaching the Word of God to help with the care of the poor. So, friends, choose seven men from among you whom everyone trusts, men full of the Holy Spirit and good sense, and we'll assign them this task. Meanwhile, we'll stick to our assigned tasks of prayer and speaking God's Word."

6.5-6 The congregation thought this was a great idea. They went ahead and chose—

Stephen, a man full of faith and the Holy
    Spirit,
Philip,
Procorus,
Nicanor,
Timon,
Parmenas,
Nicolas, a convert from Antioch.

Then they presented them to the apostles. Praying, the apostles laid on hands and commissioned them for their task.

6.7 The Word of God prospered. The number of disciples in Jerusalem increased dramatically. Not least, a great many priests submitted themselves to the faith.

✠

6.8-10 Stephen, brimming with God's grace and energy, was doing wonderful things among the people, unmistakable signs that God was among them. But then some men from the meeting place whose membership was made up of freed slaves, Cyrenians, Alexandrians, and some others from Cilicia and Asia, went up against him trying to argue him down. But they were no match for his wisdom and spirit when he spoke.

ᵃ 42 Or Messiah

NEW INTERNATIONAL VERSION

¹¹Then they secretly persuaded some men to say, "We have heard Stephen speak words of blasphemy against Moses and against God."

¹²So they stirred up the people and the elders and the teachers of the law. They seized Stephen and brought him before the Sanhedrin. ¹³They produced false witnesses, who testified, "This fellow never stops speaking against this holy place and against the law. ¹⁴For we have heard him say that this Jesus of Nazareth will destroy this place and change the customs Moses handed down to us."

¹⁵All who were sitting in the Sanhedrin looked intently at Stephen, and they saw that his face was like the face of an angel.

STEPHEN'S SPEECH TO THE SANHEDRIN

7 Then the high priest asked him, "Are these charges true?"

²To this he replied: "Brothers and fathers, listen to me! The God of glory appeared to our father Abraham while he was still in Mesopotamia, before he lived in Haran. ³'Leave your country and your people,' God said, 'and go to the land I will show you.'*a*

⁴"So he left the land of the Chaldeans and settled in Haran. After the death of his father, God sent him to this land where you are now living. ⁵He gave him no inheritance here, not even a foot of ground. But God promised him that he and his descendants after him would possess the land, even though at that time Abraham had no child. ⁶God spoke to him in this way: 'Your descendants will be strangers in a country not their own, and they will be enslaved and mistreated four hundred years. ⁷But I will punish the nation they serve as slaves,' God said, 'and afterward they will come out of that country and worship me in this place.'*b* ⁸Then he gave Abraham the covenant of circumcision. And Abraham became the father of Isaac and circumcised him eight days after his birth. Later Isaac became the father of Jacob, and Jacob became the father of the twelve patriarchs.

⁹"Because the patriarchs were jealous of Joseph, they sold him as a slave into Egypt. But God was with him ¹⁰and rescued him from all his troubles. He gave Joseph wisdom and enabled him to gain the goodwill of Pharaoh king of Egypt; so he made him ruler over Egypt and all his palace.

¹¹"Then a famine struck all Egypt and Canaan, bringing great suffering, and our fathers could not find food. ¹²When Jacob heard that

THE MESSAGE

6.11   So in secret they bribed men to lie: "We heard him cursing Moses and God."

6.12-14   That stirred up the people, the religious leaders, and religion scholars. They grabbed Stephen and took him before the High Council. They put forward their bribed witnesses to testify: "This man talks nonstop against this Holy Place and God's Law. We even heard him say that Jesus of Nazareth would tear this place down and throw out all the customs Moses gave us."

6.15   As all those who sat on the High Council looked at Stephen, they found they couldn't take their eyes off him—his face was like the face of an angel!

STEPHEN, FULL OF THE HOLY SPIRIT

7.1   **7** Then the Chief Priest said, "What do you have to say for yourself?"

7.2-3   Stephen replied, "Friends, fathers, and brothers, the God of glory appeared to our father Abraham when he was still in Mesopotamia, before the move to Haran, and told him, 'Leave your country and family and go to the land I'll show you.'

7.4-7   "So he left the country of the Chaldees and moved to Haran. After the death of his father, he immigrated to this country where you now live, but God gave him nothing, not so much as a foothold. He did promise to give the country to him and his son later on, even though Abraham had no son at the time. God let him know that his offspring would move to an alien country where they would be enslaved and brutalized for four hundred years. 'But,' God said, 'I will step in and take care of those slaveholders and bring my people out so they can worship me in this place.'

7.8   "Then he made a covenant with him and signed it in Abraham's flesh by circumcision. When Abraham had his son Isaac, within eight days he reproduced the sign of circumcision in him. Isaac became father of Jacob, and Jacob father of twelve 'fathers,' each faithfully passing on the covenant sign.

7.9-10   "But then those 'fathers,' burning up with jealousy, sent Joseph off to Egypt as a slave. God was right there with him, though—he not only rescued him from all his troubles but brought him to the attention of Pharaoh, king of Egypt. He was so impressed with Joseph that he put him in charge of the whole country, including his own personal affairs.

7.11-15   "Later a famine descended on that entire region, stretching from Egypt to Canaan, bringing terrific hardship. Our hungry fathers looked high and low for food, but the cupboard

a 3 Gen. 12:1   *b 7* Gen. 15:13,14

NEW INTERNATIONAL VERSION

there was grain in Egypt, he sent our fathers on their first visit. ¹³On their second visit, Joseph told his brothers who he was, and Pharaoh learned about Joseph's family. ¹⁴After this, Joseph sent for his father Jacob and his whole family, seventy-five in all. ¹⁵Then Jacob went down to Egypt, where he and our fathers died. ¹⁶Their bodies were brought back to Shechem and placed in the tomb that Abraham had bought from the sons of Hamor at Shechem for a certain sum of money.

¹⁷"As the time drew near for God to fulfill his promise to Abraham, the number of our people in Egypt greatly increased. ¹⁸Then another king, who knew nothing about Joseph, became ruler of Egypt. ¹⁹He dealt treacherously with our people and oppressed our forefathers by forcing them to throw out their newborn babies so that they would die.

²⁰"At that time Moses was born, and he was no ordinary child.ᵃ For three months he was cared for in his father's house. ²¹When he was placed outside, Pharaoh's daughter took him and brought him up as her own son. ²²Moses was educated in all the wisdom of the Egyptians and was powerful in speech and action.

²³"When Moses was forty years old, he decided to visit his fellow Israelites. ²⁴He saw one of them being mistreated by an Egyptian, so he went to his defense and avenged him by killing the Egyptian. ²⁵Moses thought that his own people would realize that God was using him to rescue them, but they did not. ²⁶The next day Moses came upon two Israelites who were fighting. He tried to reconcile them by saying, 'Men, you are brothers; why do you want to hurt each other?'

²⁷"But the man who was mistreating the other pushed Moses aside and said, 'Who made you ruler and judge over us? ²⁸Do you want to kill me as you killed the Egyptian yesterday?'ᵇ ²⁹When Moses heard this, he fled to Midian, where he settled as a foreigner and had two sons.

³⁰"After forty years had passed, an angel appeared to Moses in the flames of a burning bush in the desert near Mount Sinai. ³¹When he saw this, he was amazed at the sight. As he went over to look more closely, he heard the Lord's voice: ³²'I am the God of your fathers, the God of Abraham, Isaac and Jacob.'ᶜ Moses trembled with fear and did not dare to look.

THE MESSAGE

was bare. Jacob heard there was food in Egypt and sent our fathers to scout it out. Having confirmed the report, they went back to Egypt a second time to get food. On that visit, Joseph revealed his true identity to his brothers and introduced the Jacob family to Pharaoh. Then Joseph sent for his father, Jacob, and everyone else in the family, seventy-five in all. That's how the Jacob family got to Egypt.

7.15-16 "Jacob died, and our fathers after him. They were taken to Shechem and buried in the tomb for which Abraham paid a good price to the sons of Hamor.

7.17-19 "When the four hundred years were nearly up, the time God promised Abraham for deliverance, the population of our people in Egypt had become very large. And there was now a king over Egypt who had never heard of Joseph. He exploited our race mercilessly. He went so far as forcing us to abandon our newborn infants, exposing them to the elements to die a cruel death.

7.20-22 "In just such a time Moses was born, a most beautiful baby. He was hidden at home for three months. When he could be hidden no longer, he was put outside—and immediately rescued by Pharaoh's daughter, who mothered him as her own son. Moses was educated in the best schools in Egypt. He was equally impressive as a thinker and an athlete.

7.23-26 "When he was forty years old, he wondered how everything was going with his Hebrew kin and went out to look things over. He saw an Egyptian abusing one of them and stepped in, avenging his underdog brother by knocking the Egyptian flat. He thought his brothers would be glad that he was on their side, and even see him as an instrument of God to deliver them. But they didn't see it that way. The next day two of them were fighting and he tried to break it up, told them to shake hands and get along with each other: 'Friends, you are brothers, why are you beating up on each other?'

7.27-29 "The one who had started the fight said, 'Who put you in charge of us? Are you going to kill me like you killed that Egyptian yesterday?' When Moses heard that, realizing that the word was out, he ran for his life and lived in exile over in Midian. During the years of exile, two sons were born to him.

7.30-32 "Forty years later, in the wilderness of Mount Sinai, an angel appeared to him in the guise of flames of a burning bush. Moses, not believing his eyes, went up to take a closer look. He heard God's voice: 'I am the God of your fathers, the God of Abraham, Isaac, and Jacob.' Frightened nearly out of his skin, Moses shut his eyes and turned away.

ᵃ 20 Or was fair in the sight of God   ᵇ 28 Exodus 2:14
ᶜ 32 Exodus 3:6

NEW INTERNATIONAL VERSION

33"Then the Lord said to him, 'Take off your sandals; the place where you are standing is holy ground. 34I have indeed seen the oppression of my people in Egypt. I have heard their groaning and have come down to set them free. Now come, I will send you back to Egypt.'*a*

35"This is the same Moses whom they had rejected with the words, 'Who made you ruler and judge?' He was sent to be their ruler and deliverer by God himself, through the angel who appeared to him in the bush. 36He led them out of Egypt and did wonders and miraculous signs in Egypt, at the Red Sea*b* and for forty years in the desert.

37"This is that Moses who told the Israelites, 'God will send you a prophet like me from your own people.'*c* 38He was in the assembly in the desert, with the angel who spoke to him on Mount Sinai, and with our fathers; and he received living words to pass on to us.

39"But our fathers refused to obey him. Instead, they rejected him and in their hearts turned back to Egypt. 40They told Aaron, 'Make us gods who will go before us. As for this fellow Moses who led us out of Egypt—we don't know what has happened to him!'*d* 41That was the time they made an idol in the form of a calf. They brought sacrifices to it and held a celebration in honor of what their hands had made. 42But God turned away and gave them over to the worship of the heavenly bodies. This agrees with what is written in the book of the prophets:

" 'Did you bring me sacrifices and offerings
    forty years in the desert, O house of Israel?
43You have lifted up the shrine of Molech
    and the star of your god Rephan,
      the idols you made to worship.
Therefore I will send you into exile'*e* beyond
    Babylon.

44"Our forefathers had the tabernacle of the Testimony with them in the desert. It had been made as God directed Moses, according to the pattern he had seen. 45Having received the tabernacle, our fathers under Joshua brought it with them when they took the land from the nations God drove out before them. It remained in the land until the time of David, 46who enjoyed God's favor and asked that he might provide a dwelling place for the God of Jacob.*f* 47But it was Solomon who built the house for him.

48"However, the Most High does not live in houses made by men. As the prophet says:

49" 'Heaven is my throne,
    and the earth is my footstool.

---

a 34 Exodus 3:5,7,8,10   b 36 That is, Sea of Reeds
c 37 Deut. 18:15   d 40 Exodus 32:1   e 43 Amos 5:25-27
f 46 Some early manuscripts the house of Jacob

THE MESSAGE

7.33-34   "God said, 'Kneel and pray. You are in a holy place, on holy ground. I've seen the agony of my people in Egypt. I've heard their groans. I've come to help them. So get yourself ready; I'm sending you back to Egypt.'

7.35-39   "This is the same Moses whom they earlier rejected, saying, 'Who put you in charge of us?' This is the Moses that God, using the angel flaming in the burning bush, sent back as ruler and redeemer. He led them out of their slavery. He did wonderful things, setting up God-signs all through Egypt, down at the Red Sea, and out in the wilderness for forty years. This is the Moses who said to his congregation, 'God will raise up a prophet just like me from your descendants.' This is the Moses who stood between the angel speaking at Sinai and your fathers assembled in the wilderness and took the life-giving words given to him and handed them over to us, words our fathers would have nothing to do with.

7.39-41   "They craved the old Egyptian ways, whining to Aaron, 'Make us gods we can see and follow. This Moses who got us out here miles from nowhere—who knows what's happened to him!' That was the time when they made a calf-idol, brought sacrifices to it, and congratulated each other on the wonderful religious program they had put together.

7.42-43   "God wasn't at all pleased; but he let them do it their way, worship every new god that came down the pike—and live with the consequences, consequences described by the prophet Amos:

    Did you bring me offerings of animals and
        grains
      those forty wilderness years, O Israel?
    Hardly. You were too busy building shrines
      to war gods, to sex goddesses,
    Worshiping them with all your might.
      That's why I put you in exile in Babylon.

7.44-47   "And all this time our ancestors had a tent shrine for true worship, made to the exact specifications God provided Moses. They had it with them as they followed Joshua, when God cleared the land of pagans, and still had it right down to the time of David. David asked God for a permanent place for worship. But Solomon built it.

7.48-50   "Yet that doesn't mean that Most High God lives in a building made by carpenters and masons. The prophet Isaiah put it well when he wrote,

    "Heaven is my throne room;
      I rest my feet on earth.

NEW INTERNATIONAL VERSION

What kind of house will you build for me?
says the Lord.
Or where will my resting place be?
[50] Has not my hand made all these things?'[a]

[51] "You stiff-necked people, with uncircumcised hearts and ears! You are just like your fathers: You always resist the Holy Spirit! [52] Was there ever a prophet your fathers did not persecute? They even killed those who predicted the coming of the Righteous One. And now you have betrayed and murdered him— [53] you who have received the law that was put into effect through angels but have not obeyed it."

THE STONING OF STEPHEN

[54] When they heard this, they were furious and gnashed their teeth at him. [55] But Stephen, full of the Holy Spirit, looked up to heaven and saw the glory of God, and Jesus standing at the right hand of God. [56] "Look," he said, "I see heaven open and the Son of Man standing at the right hand of God."

[57] At this they covered their ears and, yelling at the top of their voices, they all rushed at him, [58] dragged him out of the city and began to stone him. Meanwhile, the witnesses laid their clothes at the feet of a young man named Saul.

[59] While they were stoning him, Stephen prayed, "Lord Jesus, receive my spirit." [60] Then he fell on his knees and cried out, "Lord, do not hold this sin against them." When he had said this, he fell asleep.

8 And Saul was there, giving approval to his death.

THE CHURCH PERSECUTED AND SCATTERED

On that day a great persecution broke out against the church at Jerusalem, and all except the apostles were scattered throughout Judea and Samaria. [2] Godly men buried Stephen and mourned deeply for him. [3] But Saul began to destroy the church. Going from house to house, he dragged off men and women and put them in prison.

PHILIP IN SAMARIA

[4] Those who had been scattered preached the word wherever they went. [5] Philip went down to a city in Samaria and proclaimed the Christ[b] there. [6] When the crowds heard Philip and saw the miraculous signs he did, they all paid close attention to what he said. [7] With shrieks, evil[c] spirits came out of many, and many paralytics

---

THE MESSAGE

So what kind of house
will you build me?" says God.
"Where I can get away and relax?
It's already built, and I built it."

7.51-53   "And you continue, so bullheaded! Calluses on your hearts, flaps on your ears! Deliberately ignoring the Holy Spirit, you're just like your ancestors. Was there ever a prophet who didn't get the same treatment? Your ancestors killed anyone who dared talk about the coming of the Just One. And you've kept up the family tradition—traitors and murderers, all of you. You had God's Law handed to you by angels—giftwrapped!—and you squandered it!"

7.54-56   At that point they went wild, a rioting mob of catcalls and whistles and invective. But Stephen, full of the Holy Spirit, hardly noticed—he only had eyes for God, whom he saw in all his glory with Jesus standing at his side. He said, "Oh! I see heaven wide open and the Son of Man standing at God's side!"

7.57-58   Yelling and hissing, the mob drowned him out. Now in full stampede, they dragged him out of town and pelted him with rocks. The ringleaders took off their coats and asked a young man named Saul to watch them.

7.59-60   As the rocks rained down, Stephen prayed, "Master Jesus, take my life." Then he knelt down, praying loud enough for everyone to hear, "Master, don't blame them for this sin"— his last words. Then he died.

8.1   Saul was right there, congratulating the killers.

SIMON THE WIZARD

8.1-2   **8** That set off a terrific persecution of the church in Jerusalem. The believers were all scattered throughout Judea and Samaria. All, that is, but the apostles. Good and brave men buried Stephen, giving him a solemn funeral— not many dry eyes that day!

8.3-8   And Saul just went wild, devastating the church, entering house after house after house, dragging men and women off to jail. Forced to leave home base, the Christians all became missionaries. Wherever they were scattered, they preached the Message about Jesus. Going down to a Samaritan city, Philip proclaimed the Message of the Messiah. When the people heard what he had to say and saw the miracles, the clear signs of God's action, they hung on his every word. Many who could neither stand nor walk were healed that day. The evil spirits

---

a 50 Isaiah 66:1,2   *b 5 Or Messiah*   *c 7 Greek unclean*

NEW INTERNATIONAL VERSION

and cripples were healed. [8]So there was great joy in that city.

SIMON THE SORCERER

[9]Now for some time a man named Simon had practiced sorcery in the city and amazed all the people of Samaria. He boasted that he was someone great, [10]and all the people, both high and low, gave him their attention and exclaimed, "This man is the divine power known as the Great Power." [11]They followed him because he had amazed them for a long time with his magic. [12]But when they believed Philip as he preached the good news of the kingdom of God and the name of Jesus Christ, they were baptized, both men and women. [13]Simon himself believed and was baptized. And he followed Philip everywhere, astonished by the great signs and miracles he saw.

[14]When the apostles in Jerusalem heard that Samaria had accepted the word of God, they sent Peter and John to them. [15]When they arrived, they prayed for them that they might receive the Holy Spirit, [16]because the Holy Spirit had not yet come upon any of them; they had simply been baptized into[a] the name of the Lord Jesus. [17]Then Peter and John placed their hands on them, and they received the Holy Spirit.

[18]When Simon saw that the Spirit was given at the laying on of the apostles' hands, he offered them money [19]and said, "Give me also this ability so that everyone on whom I lay my hands may receive the Holy Spirit."

[20]Peter answered: "May your money perish with you, because you thought you could buy the gift of God with money! [21]You have no part or share in this ministry, because your heart is not right before God. [22]Repent of this wickedness and pray to the Lord. Perhaps he will forgive you for having such a thought in your heart. [23]For I see that you are full of bitterness and captive to sin."

[24]Then Simon answered, "Pray to the Lord for me so that nothing you have said may happen to me."

[25]When they had testified and proclaimed the word of the Lord, Peter and John returned to Jerusalem, preaching the gospel in many Samaritan villages.

PHILIP AND THE ETHIOPIAN

[26]Now an angel of the Lord said to Philip, "Go south to the road—the desert road—that goes down from Jerusalem to Gaza." [27]So he started out, and on his way he met an Ethiopian[b] eunuch, an important official in charge of all the treasury of Candace, queen of the Ethiopi-

---

[a] 16 Or in   [b] 27 That is, from the upper Nile region

THE MESSAGE

protested loudly as they were sent on their way. And what joy in the city!

8.9-11 Previous to Philip's arrival, a certain Simon had practiced magic in the city, posing as a famous man and dazzling all the Samaritans with his wizardry. He had them all, from little children to old men, eating out of his hand. They all thought he had supernatural powers, and called him "the Great Wizard." He had been around a long time and everyone was more or less in awe of him.

8.12-13 But when Philip came to town announcing the news of God's kingdom and proclaiming the name of Jesus Christ, they forgot Simon and were baptized, becoming believers right and left! Even Simon himself believed and was baptized. From that moment he was like Philip's shadow, so fascinated with all the God-signs and miracles that he wouldn't leave Philip's side.

8.14-17 When the apostles in Jerusalem received the report that Samaria had accepted God's Message, they sent Peter and John down to pray for them to receive the Holy Spirit. Up to this point they had only been baptized in the name of the Master Jesus; the Holy Spirit hadn't yet fallen on them. Then the apostles laid their hands on them and they did receive the Holy Spirit.

8.18-19 When Simon saw that the apostles by merely laying on hands conferred the Spirit, he pulled out his money, excited, and said, "Sell me your secret! Show me how you did that! How much do you want? Name your price!"

8.20-23 Peter said, "To hell with your money! And you along with it. Why, that's unthinkable—trying to buy God's gift! You'll never be part of what God is doing by striking bargains and offering bribes. Change your ways—and now! Ask the Master to forgive you for trying to use God to make money. I can see this is an old habit with you; you reek with money-lust."

8.24 "Oh!" said Simon, "pray for me! Pray to the Master that nothing like that will ever happen to me!"

8.25 And with that, the apostles were on their way, continuing to witness and spread the Message of God's salvation, preaching in every Samaritan town they passed through on their return to Jerusalem.

THE ETHIOPIAN EUNUCH

8.26-28 Later God's angel spoke to Philip: "At noon today I want you to walk over to that desolate road that goes from Jerusalem down to Gaza." He got up and went. He met an Ethiopian eunuch coming down the road. The eunuch had

NEW INTERNATIONAL VERSION

ans. This man had gone to Jerusalem to worship, ²⁸and on his way home was sitting in his chariot reading the book of Isaiah the prophet. ²⁹The Spirit told Philip, "Go to that chariot and stay near it."

³⁰Then Philip ran up to the chariot and heard the man reading Isaiah the prophet. "Do you understand what you are reading?" Philip asked.

³¹"How can I," he said, "unless someone explains it to me?" So he invited Philip to come up and sit with him.

³²The eunuch was reading this passage of Scripture:

"He was led like a sheep to the slaughter,
    and as a lamb before the shearer is silent,
    so he did not open his mouth.
³³In his humiliation he was deprived of justice.
    Who can speak of his descendants?
    For his life was taken from the earth." ^a

³⁴The eunuch asked Philip, "Tell me, please, who is the prophet talking about, himself or someone else?" ³⁵Then Philip began with that very passage of Scripture and told him the good news about Jesus.

³⁶As they traveled along the road, they came to some water and the eunuch said, "Look, here is water. Why shouldn't I be baptized?" ^b ³⁸And he gave orders to stop the chariot. Then both Philip and the eunuch went down into the water and Philip baptized him. ³⁹When they came up out of the water, the Spirit of the Lord suddenly took Philip away, and the eunuch did not see him again, but went on his way rejoicing. ⁴⁰Philip, however, appeared at Azotus and traveled about, preaching the gospel in all the towns until he reached Caesarea.

SAUL'S CONVERSION

9 Meanwhile, Saul was still breathing out murderous threats against the Lord's disciples. He went to the high priest ²and asked him for letters to the synagogues in Damascus, so that if he found any there who belonged to the Way, whether men or women, he might take them as prisoners to Jerusalem. ³As he neared Damascus on his journey, suddenly a light from heaven flashed around him. ⁴He fell to the ground and heard a voice say to him, "Saul, Saul, why do you persecute me?"

⁵"Who are you, Lord?" Saul asked.

"I am Jesus, whom you are persecuting," he replied. ⁶"Now get up and go into the city, and you will be told what you must do."

THE MESSAGE

been on a pilgrimage to Jerusalem and was returning to Ethiopia, where he was minister in charge of all the finances of Candace, queen of the Ethiopians. He was riding in a chariot and reading the prophet Isaiah.

8.29-30   The Spirit told Philip, "Climb into the chariot." Running up alongside, Philip heard the eunuch reading Isaiah and asked, "Do you understand what you're reading?"

8.31-33   He answered, "How can I without some help?" and invited Philip into the chariot with him. The passage he was reading was this:

As a sheep led to slaughter,
    and quiet as a lamb being sheared,
He was silent, saying nothing.
    He was mocked and put down, never got
        a fair trial.
But who now can count his kin
    since he's been taken from the earth?

8.34-35   The eunuch said, "Tell me, who is the prophet talking about: himself or some other?" Philip grabbed his chance. Using this passage as his text, he preached Jesus to him.

8.36-39   As they continued down the road, they came to a stream of water. The eunuch said, "Here's water. Why can't I be baptized?" He ordered the chariot to stop. They both went down to the water, and Philip baptized him on the spot. When they came up out of the water, the Spirit of God suddenly took Philip off, and that was the last the eunuch saw of him. But he didn't mind. He had what he'd come for and went on down the road as happy as he could be.

8.40   Philip showed up in Azotus and continued north, preaching the Message in all the villages along that route until he arrived at Caesarea.

THE BLINDING OF SAUL

9 All this time Saul was breathing down the necks of the Master's disciples, out for the kill. He went to the Chief Priest and got arrest warrants to take to the meeting places in Damascus so that if he found anyone there belonging to the Way, whether men or women, he could arrest them and bring them to Jerusalem.

9.3-4   He set off. When he got to the outskirts of Damascus, he was suddenly dazed by a blinding flash of light. As he fell to the ground, he heard a voice: "Saul, Saul, why are you out to get me?"

9.5-6   He said, "Who are you, Master?"

"I am Jesus, the One you're hunting down. I want you to get up and enter the city. In the city you'll be told what to do next."

---

^a 33 Isaiah 53:7,8   ^b 36 Some late manuscripts baptized?" ³⁷Philip said, "If you believe with all your heart, you may." The eunuch answered, "I believe that Jesus Christ is the Son of God."

NEW INTERNATIONAL VERSION

⁷The men traveling with Saul stood there speechless; they heard the sound but did not see anyone. ⁸Saul got up from the ground, but when he opened his eyes he could see nothing. So they led him by the hand into Damascus. ⁹For three days he was blind, and did not eat or drink anything.

¹⁰In Damascus there was a disciple named Ananias. The Lord called to him in a vision, "Ananias!"

"Yes, Lord," he answered.

¹¹The Lord told him, "Go to the house of Judas on Straight Street and ask for a man from Tarsus named Saul, for he is praying. ¹²In a vision he has seen a man named Ananias come and place his hands on him to restore his sight."

¹³"Lord," Ananias answered, "I have heard many reports about this man and all the harm he has done to your saints in Jerusalem. ¹⁴And he has come here with authority from the chief priests to arrest all who call on your name."

¹⁵But the Lord said to Ananias, "Go! This man is my chosen instrument to carry my name before the Gentiles and their kings and before the people of Israel. ¹⁶I will show him how much he must suffer for my name."

¹⁷Then Ananias went to the house and entered it. Placing his hands on Saul, he said, "Brother Saul, the Lord—Jesus, who appeared to you on the road as you were coming here—has sent me so that you may see again and be filled with the Holy Spirit." ¹⁸Immediately, something like scales fell from Saul's eyes, and he could see again. He got up and was baptized, ¹⁹and after taking some food, he regained his strength.

SAUL IN DAMASCUS AND JERUSALEM

Saul spent several days with the disciples in Damascus. ²⁰At once he began to preach in the synagogues that Jesus is the Son of God. ²¹All those who heard him were astonished and asked, "Isn't he the man who raised havoc in Jerusalem among those who call on this name? And hasn't he come here to take them as prisoners to the chief priests?" ²²Yet Saul grew more and more powerful and baffled the Jews living in Damascus by proving that Jesus is the Christ.ᵃ

²³After many days had gone by, the Jews conspired to kill him, ²⁴but Saul learned of their

ᵃ 22 Or Messiah

THE MESSAGE

9.7-9 His companions stood there dumbstruck—they could hear the sound, but couldn't see anyone—while Saul, picking himself up off the ground, found himself stone blind. They had to take him by the hand and lead him into Damascus. He continued blind for three days. He ate nothing, drank nothing.

9.10 There was a disciple in Damascus by the name of Ananias. The Master spoke to him in a vision: "Ananias."

"Yes, Master?" he answered.

9.11-12 "Get up and go over to Straight Avenue. Ask at the house of Judas for a man from Tarsus. His name is Saul. He's there praying. He has just had a dream in which he saw a man named Ananias enter the house and lay hands on him so he could see again."

9.13-14 Ananias protested, "Master, you can't be serious. Everybody's talking about this man and the terrible things he's been doing, his reign of terror against your people in Jerusalem! And now he's shown up here with papers from the Chief Priest that give him license to do the same to us."

9.15-16 But the Master said, "Don't argue. Go! I have picked him as my personal representative to Gentiles and kings and Jews. And now I'm about to show him what he's in for—the hard suffering that goes with this job."

9.17-19 So Ananias went and found the house, placed his hands on blind Saul, and said, "Brother Saul, the Master sent me, the same Jesus you saw on your way here. He sent me so you could see again and be filled with the Holy Spirit." No sooner were the words out of his mouth than something like scales fell from Saul's eyes—he could see again! He got to his feet, was baptized, and sat down with them to a hearty meal.

PLOTS AGAINST SAUL

9.19-21 Saul spent a few days getting acquainted with the Damascus disciples, but then went right to work, wasting no time, preaching in the meeting places that this Jesus was the Son of God. They were caught off guard by this and, not at all sure they could trust him, they kept saying, "Isn't this the man who wreaked havoc in Jerusalem among the believers? And didn't he come here to do the same thing—arrest us and drag us off to jail in Jerusalem for sentencing by the high priests?"

9.22 But their suspicions didn't slow Saul down for even a minute. His momentum was up now and he plowed straight into the opposition, disarming the Damascus Jews and trying to show them that this Jesus was the Messiah.

9.23-25 After this had gone on quite a long time, some Jews conspired to kill him, but Saul got

NEW INTERNATIONAL VERSION

plan. Day and night they kept close watch on the city gates in order to kill him. 25But his followers took him by night and lowered him in a basket through an opening in the wall.

26When he came to Jerusalem, he tried to join the disciples, but they were all afraid of him, not believing that he really was a disciple. 27But Barnabas took him and brought him to the apostles. He told them how Saul on his journey had seen the Lord and that the Lord had spoken to him, and how in Damascus he had preached fearlessly in the name of Jesus. 28So Saul stayed with them and moved about freely in Jerusalem, speaking boldly in the name of the Lord. 29He talked and debated with the Grecian Jews, but they tried to kill him. 30When the brothers learned of this, they took him down to Caesarea and sent him off to Tarsus.

31Then the church throughout Judea, Galilee and Samaria enjoyed a time of peace. It was strengthened; and encouraged by the Holy Spirit, it grew in numbers, living in the fear of the Lord.

AENEAS AND DORCAS

32As Peter traveled about the country, he went to visit the saints in Lydda. 33There he found a man named Aeneas, a paralytic who had been bedridden for eight years. 34"Aeneas," Peter said to him, "Jesus Christ heals you. Get up and take care of your mat." Immediately Aeneas got up. 35All those who lived in Lydda and Sharon saw him and turned to the Lord.

36In Joppa there was a disciple named Tabitha (which, when translated, is Dorcas[a]), who was always doing good and helping the poor. 37About that time she became sick and died, and her body was washed and placed in an upstairs room. 38Lydda was near Joppa; so when the disciples heard that Peter was in Lydda, they sent two men to him and urged him, "Please come at once!"

39Peter went with them, and when he arrived he was taken upstairs to the room. All the widows stood around him, crying and showing him the robes and other clothing that Dorcas had made while she was still with them.

[a] *36 Both* Tabitha *(Aramaic) and* Dorcas *(Greek) mean* gazelle.

THE MESSAGE

wind of it. They were watching the city gates around the clock so they could kill him. Then one night the disciples engineered his escape by lowering him over the wall in a basket.

9.26-27 Back in Jerusalem he tried to join the disciples, but they were all afraid of him. They didn't trust him one bit. Then Barnabas took him under his wing. He introduced him to the apostles and stood up for him, told them how Saul had seen and spoken to the Master on the Damascus Road and how in Damascus itself he had laid his life on the line with his bold preaching in Jesus' name.

9.28-30 After that he was accepted as one of them, going in and out of Jerusalem with no questions asked, uninhibited as he preached in the Master's name. But then he ran afoul of a group called Hellenists—he had been engaged in a running argument with them—who plotted his murder. When his friends learned of the plot, they got him out of town, took him to Caesarea, and then shipped him off to Tarsus.

9.31 Things calmed down after that and the church had smooth sailing for a while. All over the country—Judea, Samaria, Galilee—the church grew. They were permeated with a deep sense of reverence for God. The Holy Spirit was with them, strengthening them. They prospered wonderfully.

TABITHA

9.32-35 Peter went off on a mission to visit all the churches. In the course of his travels he arrived in Lydda and met with the believers there. He came across a man—his name was Aeneas—who had been in bed eight years paralyzed. Peter said, "Aeneas, Jesus Christ heals you. Get up and make your bed!" And he did it—jumped right out of bed. Everybody who lived in Lydda and Sharon saw him walking around and woke up to the fact that God was alive and active among them.

9.36-37 Down the road a way in Joppa there was a disciple named Tabitha, "Gazelle" in our language. She was well-known for doing good and helping out. During the time Peter was in the area she became sick and died. Her friends prepared her body for burial and put her in a cool room.

9.38-40 Some of the disciples had heard that Peter was visiting in nearby Lydda and sent two men to ask if he would be so kind as to come over. Peter got right up and went with them. They took him into the room where Tabitha's body was laid out. Her old friends, most of them widows, were in the room mourning. They showed Peter pieces of clothing the Gazelle had made while she was with them. Peter put the widows

NEW INTERNATIONAL VERSION

⁴⁰Peter sent them all out of the room; then he got down on his knees and prayed. Turning toward the dead woman, he said, "Tabitha, get up." She opened her eyes, and seeing Peter she sat up. ⁴¹He took her by the hand and helped her to her feet. Then he called the believers and the widows and presented her to them alive. ⁴²This became known all over Joppa, and many people believed in the Lord. ⁴³Peter stayed in Joppa for some time with a tanner named Simon.

CORNELIUS CALLS FOR PETER

10 At Caesarea there was a man named Cornelius, a centurion in what was known as the Italian Regiment. ²He and all his family were devout and God-fearing; he gave generously to those in need and prayed to God regularly. ³One day at about three in the afternoon he had a vision. He distinctly saw an angel of God, who came to him and said, "Cornelius!"

⁴Cornelius stared at him in fear. "What is it, Lord?" he asked.

The angel answered, "Your prayers and gifts to the poor have come up as a memorial offering before God. ⁵Now send men to Joppa to bring back a man named Simon who is called Peter. ⁶He is staying with Simon the tanner, whose house is by the sea."

⁷When the angel who spoke to him had gone, Cornelius called two of his servants and a devout soldier who was one of his attendants. ⁸He told them everything that had happened and sent them to Joppa.

PETER'S VISION

⁹About noon the following day as they were on their journey and approaching the city, Peter went up on the roof to pray. ¹⁰He became hungry and wanted something to eat, and while the meal was being prepared, he fell into a trance. ¹¹He saw heaven opened and something like a large sheet being let down to earth by its four corners. ¹²It contained all kinds of four-footed animals, as well as reptiles of the earth and birds of the air. ¹³Then a voice told him, "Get up, Peter. Kill and eat."

¹⁴"Surely not, Lord!" Peter replied. "I have never eaten anything impure or unclean."

¹⁵The voice spoke to him a second time, "Do not call anything impure that God has made clean."

¹⁶This happened three times, and immediately the sheet was taken back to heaven.

¹⁷While Peter was wondering about the meaning of the vision, the men sent by Cornelius found out where Simon's house was and stopped

THE MESSAGE

all out of the room. He knelt and prayed. Then he spoke directly to the body: "Tabitha, get up."

9.40-41 She opened her eyes. When she saw Peter, she sat up. He took her hand and helped her up. Then he called in the believers and widows, and presented her to them alive.

9.42-43 When this became known all over Joppa, many put their trust in the Master. Peter stayed on a long time in Joppa as a guest of Simon the Tanner.

PETER'S VISION

10.1-3 **10** There was a man named Cornelius who lived in Caesarea, captain of the Italian Guard stationed there. He was a thoroughly good man. He had led everyone in his house to live worshipfully before God, was always helping people in need, and had the habit of prayer. One day about three o'clock in the afternoon he had a vision. An angel of God, as real as his next-door neighbor, came in and said, "Cornelius."

10.4 Cornelius stared hard, wondering if he was seeing things. Then he said, "What do you want, sir?"

10.4-6 The angel said, "Your prayers and neighborly acts have brought you to God's attention. Here's what you are to do. Send men to Joppa to get Simon, the one everyone calls Peter. He is staying with Simon the Tanner, whose house is down by the sea."

10.7-8 As soon as the angel was gone, Cornelius called two servants and one particularly devout soldier from the guard. He went over with them in great detail everything that had just happened, and then sent them off to Joppa.

10.9-13 The next day as the three travelers were approaching the town, Peter went out on the balcony to pray. It was about noon. Peter got hungry and started thinking about lunch. While lunch was being prepared, he fell into a trance. He saw the skies open up. Something that looked like a huge blanket lowered by ropes at its four corners settled on the ground. Every kind of animal and reptile and bird you could think of was on it. Then a voice came: "Go to it, Peter—kill and eat."

10.14 Peter said, "Oh, no, Lord. I've never so much as tasted food that was not kosher."

10.15 The voice came a second time: "If God says it's okay, it's okay."

10.16 This happened three times, and then the blanket was pulled back up into the skies.

10.17-20 As Peter, puzzled, sat there trying to figure out what it all meant, the men sent by Cornelius showed up at Simon's front door. They called

NEW INTERNATIONAL VERSION

at the gate. ¹⁸They called out, asking if Simon who was known as Peter was staying there.

¹⁹While Peter was still thinking about the vision, the Spirit said to him, "Simon, three*ᵃ* men are looking for you. ²⁰So get up and go downstairs. Do not hesitate to go with them, for I have sent them."

²¹Peter went down and said to the men, "I'm the one you're looking for. Why have you come?"

²²The men replied, "We have come from Cornelius the centurion. He is a righteous and God-fearing man, who is respected by all the Jewish people. A holy angel told him to have you come to his house so that he could hear what you have to say." ²³Then Peter invited the men into the house to be his guests.

PETER AT CORNELIUS'S HOUSE

The next day Peter started out with them, and some of the brothers from Joppa went along. ²⁴The following day he arrived in Caesarea. Cornelius was expecting them and had called together his relatives and close friends. ²⁵As Peter entered the house, Cornelius met him and fell at his feet in reverence. ²⁶But Peter made him get up. "Stand up," he said, "I am only a man myself."

²⁷Talking with him, Peter went inside and found a large gathering of people. ²⁸He said to them: "You are well aware that it is against our law for a Jew to associate with a Gentile or visit him. But God has shown me that I should not call any man impure or unclean. ²⁹So when I was sent for, I came without raising any objection. May I ask why you sent for me?"

³⁰Cornelius answered: "Four days ago I was in my house praying at this hour, at three in the afternoon. Suddenly a man in shining clothes stood before me ³¹and said, 'Cornelius, God has heard your prayer and remembered your gifts to the poor. ³²Send to Joppa for Simon who is called Peter. He is a guest in the home of Simon the tanner, who lives by the sea.' ³³So I sent for you immediately, and it was good of you to come. Now we are all here in the presence of God to listen to everything the Lord has commanded you to tell us."

³⁴Then Peter began to speak: "I now realize how true it is that God does not show favoritism ³⁵but accepts men from every nation who fear him and do what is right. ³⁶You know the message God sent to the people of Israel, telling the

THE MESSAGE

in, asking if there was a Simon, also called Peter, staying there. Peter, lost in thought, didn't hear them, so the Spirit whispered to him, "Three men are knocking at the door looking for you. Get down there and go with them. Don't ask any questions. I sent them to get you."

10.21   Peter went down and said to the men, "I think I'm the man you're looking for. What's up?"

10.22-23   They said, "Captain Cornelius, a God-fearing man well-known for his fair play—ask any Jew in this part of the country—was commanded by a holy angel to get you and bring you to his house so he could hear what you had to say." Peter invited them in and made them feel at home.

GOD PLAYS NO FAVORITES

10.23-26   The next morning he got up and went with them. Some of his friends from Joppa went along. A day later they entered Caesarea. Cornelius was expecting them and had his relatives and close friends waiting with him. The minute Peter came through the door, Cornelius was up on his feet greeting him—and then down on his face worshiping him! Peter pulled him up and said, "None of that—I'm a man and only a man, no different from you."

10.27-29   Talking things over, they went on into the house, where Cornelius introduced Peter to everyone who had come. Peter addressed them, "You know, I'm sure that this is highly irregular. Jews just don't do this—visit and relax with people of another race. But God has just shown me that no race is better than any other. So the minute I was sent for, I came, no questions asked. But now I'd like to know why you sent for me."

10.30-32   Cornelius said, "Four days ago at about this time, midafternoon, I was home praying. Suddenly there was a man right in front of me, flooding the room with light. He said, 'Cornelius, your daily prayers and neighborly acts have brought you to God's attention. I want you to send to Joppa to get Simon, the one they call Peter. He's staying with Simon the Tanner down by the sea.'

10.33   "So I did it—I sent for you. And you've been good enough to come. And now we're all here in God's presence, ready to listen to whatever the Master put in your heart to tell us."

10.34-36   Peter fairly exploded with his good news: "It's God's own truth, nothing could be plainer: God plays no favorites! It makes no difference who you are or where you're from—if you want God and are ready to do as he says, the door is open. The Message he sent to the children of Israel—that through Jesus Christ everything is

---

ᵃ *19* One early manuscript *two*; other manuscripts do not have the number.

NEW INTERNATIONAL VERSION

good news of peace through Jesus Christ, who is Lord of all. ³⁷You know what has happened throughout Judea, beginning in Galilee after the baptism that John preached— ³⁸how God anointed Jesus of Nazareth with the Holy Spirit and power, and how he went around doing good and healing all who were under the power of the devil, because God was with him.

³⁹"We are witnesses of everything he did in the country of the Jews and in Jerusalem. They killed him by hanging him on a tree, ⁴⁰but God raised him from the dead on the third day and caused him to be seen. ⁴¹He was not seen by all the people, but by witnesses whom God had already chosen—by us who ate and drank with him after he rose from the dead. ⁴²He commanded us to preach to the people and to testify that he is the one whom God appointed as judge of the living and the dead. ⁴³All the prophets testify about him that everyone who believes in him receives forgiveness of sins through his name."

⁴⁴While Peter was still speaking these words, the Holy Spirit came on all who heard the message. ⁴⁵The circumcised believers who had come with Peter were astonished that the gift of the Holy Spirit had been poured out even on the Gentiles. ⁴⁶For they heard them speaking in tongues[a] and praising God.

Then Peter said, ⁴⁷"Can anyone keep these people from being baptized with water? They have received the Holy Spirit just as we have." ⁴⁸So he ordered that they be baptized in the name of Jesus Christ. Then they asked Peter to stay with them for a few days.

PETER EXPLAINS HIS ACTIONS

11 The apostles and the brothers throughout Judea heard that the Gentiles also had received the word of God. ²So when Peter went up to Jerusalem, the circumcised believers criticized him ³and said, "You went into the house of uncircumcised men and ate with them."

⁴Peter began and explained everything to them precisely as it had happened: ⁵"I was in the city of Joppa praying, and in a trance I saw a vision. I saw something like a large sheet being let down from heaven by its four corners, and it

THE MESSAGE

being put together again—well, he's doing it everywhere, among everyone.

10.37-38 "You know the story of what happened in Judea. It began in Galilee after John preached a total life-change. Then Jesus arrived from Nazareth, anointed by God with the Holy Spirit, ready for action. He went through the country helping people and healing everyone who was beaten down by the Devil. He was able to do all this because God was with him.

10.39-43 "And we saw it, saw it all, everything he did in the land of the Jews and in Jerusalem where they killed him, hung him from a cross. But in three days God had him up, alive, and out where he could be seen. Not everyone saw him—he wasn't put on public display. Witnesses had been carefully handpicked by God beforehand—us! We were the ones, there to eat and drink with him after he came back from the dead. He commissioned us to announce this in public, to bear solemn witness that he is in fact the One whom God destined as Judge of the living and dead. But we're not alone in this. Our witness that he is the means to forgiveness of sins is backed up by the witness of all the prophets."

10.44-46 No sooner were these words out of Peter's mouth than the Holy Spirit came on the listeners. The believing Jews who had come with Peter couldn't believe it, couldn't believe that the gift of the Holy Spirit was poured out on "outsider" Gentiles, but there it was—they heard them speaking in tongues, heard them praising God.

10.46-48 Then Peter said, "Do I hear any objections to baptizing these friends with water? They've received the Holy Spirit exactly as we did." Hearing no objections, he ordered that they be baptized in the name of Jesus Christ.

Then they asked Peter to stay on for a few days.

GOD HAS BROKEN THROUGH

11.1-3 **11** The news traveled fast and in no time the leaders and friends back in Jerusalem heard about it—heard that the non-Jewish "outsiders" were now "in." When Peter got back to Jerusalem, some of his old associates, concerned about circumcision, called him on the carpet: "What do you think you're doing rubbing shoulders with that crowd, eating what is prohibited and ruining our good name?"

11.4-6 So Peter, starting from the beginning, laid it out for them step-by-step: "Recently I was in the town of Joppa praying. I fell into a trance and saw a vision: Something like a huge blanket, lowered by ropes at its four corners, came down out of heaven and settled on the ground

NEW INTERNATIONAL VERSION

came down to where I was. ⁶I looked into it and saw four-footed animals of the earth, wild beasts, reptiles, and birds of the air. ⁷Then I heard a voice telling me, 'Get up, Peter. Kill and eat.'

⁸"I replied, 'Surely not, Lord! Nothing impure or unclean has ever entered my mouth.'

⁹"The voice spoke from heaven a second time, 'Do not call anything impure that God has made clean.' ¹⁰This happened three times, and then it was all pulled up to heaven again.

¹¹"Right then three men who had been sent to me from Caesarea stopped at the house where I was staying. ¹²The Spirit told me to have no hesitation about going with them. These six brothers also went with me, and we entered the man's house. ¹³He told us how he had seen an angel appear in his house and say, 'Send to Joppa for Simon who is called Peter. ¹⁴He will bring you a message through which you and all your household will be saved.'

¹⁵"As I began to speak, the Holy Spirit came on them as he had come on us at the beginning. ¹⁶Then I remembered what the Lord had said: 'John baptized with ᵃ water, but you will be baptized with the Holy Spirit.' ¹⁷So if God gave them the same gift as he gave us, who believed in the Lord Jesus Christ, who was I to think that I could oppose God?"

¹⁸When they heard this, they had no further objections and praised God, saying, "So then, God has granted even the Gentiles repentance unto life."

THE CHURCH IN ANTIOCH

¹⁹Now those who had been scattered by the persecution in connection with Stephen traveled as far as Phoenicia, Cyprus and Antioch, telling the message only to Jews. ²⁰Some of them, however, men from Cyprus and Cyrene, went to Antioch and began to speak to Greeks also, telling them the good news about the Lord Jesus. ²¹The Lord's hand was with them, and a great number of people believed and turned to the Lord.

²²News of this reached the ears of the church at Jerusalem, and they sent Barnabas to Antioch. ²³When he arrived and saw the evidence of the grace of God, he was glad and encouraged them all to remain true to the Lord with all their hearts. ²⁴He was a good man, full of the Holy Spirit and faith, and a great number of people were brought to the Lord.

²⁵Then Barnabas went to Tarsus to look for Saul, ²⁶and when he found him, he brought him

THE MESSAGE

in front of me. Milling around on the blanket were farm animals, wild animals, reptiles, birds—you name it, it was there. Fascinated, I took it all in.

11.7-10 "Then I heard a voice: 'Go to it, Peter—kill and eat.' I said, 'Oh, no, Master. I've never so much as tasted food that wasn't kosher.' The voice spoke again: 'If God says it's okay, it's okay.' This happened three times, and then the blanket was pulled back up into the sky.

11.11-14 "Just then three men showed up at the house where I was staying, sent from Caesarea to get me. The Spirit told me to go with them, no questions asked. So I went with them, I and six friends, to the man who had sent for me. He told us how he had seen an angel right in his own house, real as his next-door neighbor, saying, 'Send to Joppa and get Simon, the one they call Peter. He'll tell you something that will save your life—in fact, you and everyone you care for.'

11.15-17 "So I started in, talking. Before I'd spoken half a dozen sentences, the Holy Spirit fell on them just as he did on us the first time. I remembered Jesus' words: 'John baptized with water; you will be baptized with the Holy Spirit.' So I ask you: If God gave the same exact gift to them as to us when we believed in the Master Jesus Christ, how could I object to God?"

11.18 Hearing it all laid out like that, they quieted down. And then, as it sank in, they started praising God. "It's really happened! God has broken through to the other nations, opened them up to Life!"

11.19-21 Those who had been scattered by the persecution triggered by Stephen's death traveled as far as Phoenicia, Cyprus, and Antioch, but they were still only speaking and dealing with their fellow Jews. Then some of the men from Cyprus and Cyrene who had come to Antioch started talking to Greeks, giving them the Message of the Master Jesus. God was pleased with what they were doing and put his stamp of approval on it—quite a number of the Greeks believed and turned to the Master.

11.22-24 When the church in Jerusalem got wind of this, they sent Barnabas to Antioch to check on things. As soon as he arrived, he saw that God was behind and in it all. He threw himself in with them, got behind them, urging them to stay with it the rest of their lives. He was a good man that way, enthusiastic and confident in the Holy Spirit's ways. The community grew large and strong in the Master.

11.25-26 Then Barnabas went on to Tarsus to look for Saul. He found him and brought him back to

ᵃ 16 Or in

NEW INTERNATIONAL VERSION

to Antioch. So for a whole year Barnabas and Saul met with the church and taught great numbers of people. The disciples were called Christians first at Antioch.

27During this time some prophets came down from Jerusalem to Antioch. 28One of them, named Agabus, stood up and through the Spirit predicted that a severe famine would spread over the entire Roman world. (This happened during the reign of Claudius.) 29The disciples, each according to his ability, decided to provide help for the brothers living in Judea. 30This they did, sending their gift to the elders by Barnabas and Saul.

PETER'S MIRACULOUS ESCAPE FROM PRISON

12 It was about this time that King Herod arrested some who belonged to the church, intending to persecute them. 2He had James, the brother of John, put to death with the sword. 3When he saw that this pleased the Jews, he proceeded to seize Peter also. This happened during the Feast of Unleavened Bread. 4After arresting him, he put him in prison, handing him over to be guarded by four squads of four soldiers each. Herod intended to bring him out for public trial after the Passover.

5So Peter was kept in prison, but the church was earnestly praying to God for him.

6The night before Herod was to bring him to trial, Peter was sleeping between two soldiers, bound with two chains, and sentries stood guard at the entrance. 7Suddenly an angel of the Lord appeared and a light shone in the cell. He struck Peter on the side and woke him up. "Quick, get up!" he said, and the chains fell off Peter's wrists.

8Then the angel said to him, "Put on your clothes and sandals." And Peter did so. "Wrap your cloak around you and follow me," the angel told him. 9Peter followed him out of the prison, but he had no idea that what the angel was doing was really happening; he thought he was seeing a vision. 10They passed the first and second guards and came to the iron gate leading to the city. It opened for them by itself, and they went through it. When they had walked the length of one street, suddenly the angel left him.

11Then Peter came to himself and said, "Now I know without a doubt that the Lord sent his angel and rescued me from Herod's clutches and from everything the Jewish people were anticipating."

12When this had dawned on him, he went to the house of Mary the mother of John, also called Mark, where many people had gathered

THE MESSAGE

Antioch. They were there a whole year, meeting with the church and teaching a lot of people. It was in Antioch that the disciples were for the first time called Christians.

11.27-30 It was about this same time that some prophets came to Antioch from Jerusalem. One of them named Agabus stood up one day and, prompted by the Spirit, warned that a severe famine was about to devastate the country. (The famine eventually came during the rule of Claudius.) So the disciples decided that each of them would send whatever they could to their fellow Christians in Judea to help out. They sent Barnabas and Saul to deliver the collection to the leaders in Jerusalem.

PETER UNDER HEAVY GUARD

12.1-4 12 That's when King Herod got it into his head to go after some of the church members. He murdered James, John's brother. When he saw how much it raised his popularity ratings with the Jews, he arrested Peter—all this during Passover Week, mind you—and had him thrown in jail, putting four squads of four soldiers each to guard him. He was planning a public lynching after Passover.

12.5 All the time that Peter was under heavy guard in the jailhouse, the church prayed for him most strenuously.

12.6 Then the time came for Herod to bring him out for the kill. That night, even though shackled to two soldiers, one on either side, Peter slept like a baby. And there were guards at the door keeping their eyes on the place. Herod was taking no chances!

12.7-9 Suddenly there was an angel at his side and light flooding the room. The angel shook Peter and got him up: "Hurry!" The handcuffs fell off his wrists. The angel said, "Get dressed. Put on your shoes." Peter did it. Then, "Grab your coat and let's get out of here." Peter followed him, but didn't believe it was really an angel—he thought he was dreaming.

12.10-11 Past the first guard and then the second, they came to the iron gate that led into the city. It swung open before them on its own, and they were out on the street, free as the breeze. At the first intersection the angel left him, going his own way. That's when Peter realized it was no dream. "I can't believe it—this really happened! The Master sent his angel and rescued me from Herod's vicious little production and the spectacle the Jewish mob was looking forward to."

12.12-14 Still shaking his head, amazed, he went to Mary's house, the Mary who was John Mark's mother. The house was packed with praying

NEW INTERNATIONAL VERSION

and were praying. [13]Peter knocked at the outer entrance, and a servant girl named Rhoda came to answer the door. [14]When she recognized Peter's voice, she was so overjoyed she ran back without opening it and exclaimed, "Peter is at the door!"

[15]"You're out of your mind," they told her. When she kept insisting that it was so, they said, "It must be his angel."

[16]But Peter kept on knocking, and when they opened the door and saw him, they were astonished. [17]Peter motioned with his hand for them to be quiet and described how the Lord had brought him out of prison. "Tell James and the brothers about this," he said, and then he left for another place.

[18]In the morning, there was no small commotion among the soldiers as to what had become of Peter. [19]After Herod had a thorough search made for him and did not find him, he cross-examined the guards and ordered that they be executed.

HEROD'S DEATH

Then Herod went from Judea to Caesarea and stayed there a while. [20]He had been quarreling with the people of Tyre and Sidon; they now joined together and sought an audience with him. Having secured the support of Blastus, a trusted personal servant of the king, they asked for peace, because they depended on the king's country for their food supply.

[21]On the appointed day Herod, wearing his royal robes, sat on his throne and delivered a public address to the people. [22]They shouted, "This is the voice of a god, not of a man." [23]Immediately, because Herod did not give praise to God, an angel of the Lord struck him down, and he was eaten by worms and died.

[24]But the word of God continued to increase and spread.

[25]When Barnabas and Saul had finished their mission, they returned from[a] Jerusalem, taking with them John, also called Mark.

a 25 Some manuscripts to

THE MESSAGE

friends. When he knocked on the door to the courtyard, a young woman named Rhoda came to see who it was. But when she recognized his voice—Peter's voice!—she was so excited and eager to tell everyone Peter was there that she forgot to open the door and left him standing in the street.

12.15-16   But they wouldn't believe her, dismissing her, dismissing her report. "You're crazy," they said. She stuck by her story, insisting. They still wouldn't believe her and said, "It must be his angel." All this time poor Peter was standing out in the street, knocking away.

12.16-17   Finally they opened up and saw him—and went wild! Peter put his hands up and calmed them down. He described how the Master had gotten him out of jail, then said, "Tell James and the brothers what's happened." He left them and went off to another place.

12.18-19   At daybreak the jail was in an uproar. "Where is Peter? What's happened to Peter?" When Herod sent for him and they could neither produce him nor explain why not, he ordered their execution: "Off with their heads!" Fed up with Judea and Jews, he went for a vacation to Caesarea.

THE DEATH OF HEROD

12.20-22   But things went from bad to worse for Herod. Now people from Tyre and Sidon put him on the warpath. But they got Blastus, King Herod's right-hand man, to put in a good word for them and got a delegation together to iron things out. Because they were dependent on Judea for food supplies, they couldn't afford to let this go on too long. On the day set for their meeting, Herod, robed in pomposity, took his place on the throne and regaled them with a lot of hot air. The people played their part to the hilt and shouted flatteries: "The voice of God! The voice of God!"

12.23   That was the last straw. God had had enough of Herod's arrogance and sent an angel to strike him down. Herod had given God no credit for anything. Down he went. Rotten to the core, a maggoty old man if there ever was one, he died.

12.24   Meanwhile, the ministry of God's Word grew by leaps and bounds.

12.25   Barnabas and Saul, once they had delivered the relief offering to the church in Jerusalem, went back to Antioch. This time they took John with them, the one they called Mark.

NEW INTERNATIONAL VERSION

BARNABAS AND SAUL SENT OFF

13 In the church at Antioch there were prophets and teachers: Barnabas, Simeon called Niger, Lucius of Cyrene, Manaen (who had been brought up with Herod the tetrarch) and Saul. ²While they were worshiping the Lord and fasting, the Holy Spirit said, "Set apart for me Barnabas and Saul for the work to which I have called them." ³So after they had fasted and prayed, they placed their hands on them and sent them off.

ON CYPRUS

⁴The two of them, sent on their way by the Holy Spirit, went down to Seleucia and sailed from there to Cyprus. ⁵When they arrived at Salamis, they proclaimed the word of God in the Jewish synagogues. John was with them as their helper.

⁶They traveled through the whole island until they came to Paphos. There they met a Jewish sorcerer and false prophet named Bar-Jesus, ⁷who was an attendant of the proconsul, Sergius Paulus. The proconsul, an intelligent man, sent for Barnabas and Saul because he wanted to hear the word of God. ⁸But Elymas the sorcerer (for that is what his name means) opposed them and tried to turn the proconsul from the faith. ⁹Then Saul, who was also called Paul, filled with the Holy Spirit, looked straight at Elymas and said, ¹⁰"You are a child of the devil and an enemy of everything that is right! You are full of all kinds of deceit and trickery. Will you never stop perverting the right ways of the Lord? ¹¹Now the hand of the Lord is against you. You are going to be blind, and for a time you will be unable to see the light of the sun."

Immediately mist and darkness came over him, and he groped about, seeking someone to lead him by the hand. ¹²When the proconsul saw what had happened, he believed, for he was amazed at the teaching about the Lord.

IN PISIDIAN ANTIOCH

¹³From Paphos, Paul and his companions sailed to Perga in Pamphylia, where John left them to return to Jerusalem. ¹⁴From Perga they went on to Pisidian Antioch. On the Sabbath

THE MESSAGE

BARNABAS, SAUL, AND DOCTOR KNOW-IT-ALL

13 13.1-2 The congregation in Antioch was blessed with a number of prophet-preachers and teachers:

Barnabas,
Simon, nicknamed Niger,
Lucius the Cyrenian,
Manaen, an advisor to the ruler Herod,
Saul.

One day as they were worshiping God—they were also fasting as they waited for guidance—the Holy Spirit spoke: "Take Barnabas and Saul and commission them for the work I have called them to do."

13.3 So they commissioned them. In that circle of intensity and obedience, of fasting and praying, they laid hands on their heads and sent them off.

13.4-5 Sent off on their new assignment by the Holy Spirit, Barnabas and Saul went down to Seleucia and caught a ship for Cyprus. The first thing they did when they put in at Salamis was preach God's Word in the Jewish meeting places. They had John along to help out as needed.

13.6-7 They traveled the length of the island, and at Paphos came upon a Jewish wizard who had worked himself into the confidence of the governor, Sergius Paulus, an intelligent man not easily taken in by charlatans. The wizard's name was Bar-Jesus. He was as crooked as a corkscrew.

13.7-11 The governor invited Barnabas and Saul in, wanting to hear God's Word firsthand from them. But Dr. Know-It-All (that's the wizard's name in plain English) stirred up a ruckus, trying to divert the governor from becoming a believer. But Saul (or Paul), full of the Holy Spirit and looking him straight in the eye, said, "You bag of wind, you parody of a devil—why, you stay up nights inventing schemes to cheat people out of God. But now you've come up against God himself, and your game is up. You're about to go blind—no sunlight for you for a good long stretch." He was plunged immediately into a shadowy mist and stumbled around, begging people to take his hand and show him the way.

13.12 When the governor saw what happened, he became a believer, full of enthusiasm over what they were saying about the Master.

DON'T TAKE THIS LIGHTLY

13.13-14 From Paphos, Paul and company put out to sea, sailing on to Perga in Pamphylia. That's where John called it quits and went back to Jerusalem. From Perga the rest of them traveled on to Antioch in Pisidia.

NEW INTERNATIONAL VERSION

they entered the synagogue and sat down. ¹⁵After the reading from the Law and the Prophets, the synagogue rulers sent word to them, saying, "Brothers, if you have a message of encouragement for the people, please speak."

¹⁶Standing up, Paul motioned with his hand and said: "Men of Israel and you Gentiles who worship God, listen to me! ¹⁷The God of the people of Israel chose our fathers; he made the people prosper during their stay in Egypt, with mighty power he led them out of that country, ¹⁸he endured their conduct*a* for about forty years in the desert, ¹⁹he overthrew seven nations in Canaan and gave their land to his people as their inheritance. ²⁰All this took about 450 years.

"After this, God gave them judges until the time of Samuel the prophet. ²¹Then the people asked for a king, and he gave them Saul son of Kish, of the tribe of Benjamin, who ruled forty years. ²²After removing Saul, he made David their king. He testified concerning him: 'I have found David son of Jesse a man after my own heart; he will do everything I want him to do.'

²³"From this man's descendants God has brought to Israel the Savior Jesus, as he promised. ²⁴Before the coming of Jesus, John preached repentance and baptism to all the people of Israel. ²⁵As John was completing his work, he said: 'Who do you think I am? I am not that one. No, but he is coming after me, whose sandals I am not worthy to untie.'

²⁶"Brothers, children of Abraham, and you God-fearing Gentiles, it is to us that this message of salvation has been sent. ²⁷The people of Jerusalem and their rulers did not recognize Jesus, yet in condemning him they fulfilled the words of the prophets that are read every Sabbath. ²⁸Though they found no proper ground for a death sentence, they asked Pilate to have him executed. ²⁹When they had carried out all that was written about him, they took him down from the tree and laid him in a tomb. ³⁰But God raised him from the dead, ³¹and for many days he was seen by those who had traveled with him from Galilee to Jerusalem. They are now his witnesses to our people.

a 18 Some manuscripts and cared for them

THE MESSAGE

13.14-15   On the Sabbath they went to the meeting place and took their places. After the reading of the Scriptures—God's Law and the Prophets—the president of the meeting asked them, "Friends, do you have anything you want to say? A word of encouragement, perhaps?"

13.16-20   Paul stood up, paused and took a deep breath, then said, "Fellow Israelites and friends of God, listen. God took a special interest in our ancestors, pulled our people who were beaten down in Egyptian exile to their feet, and led them out of there in grand style. He took good care of them for nearly forty years in that godforsaken wilderness and then, having wiped out seven enemies who stood in the way, gave them the land of Canaan for their very own—a span in all of about four hundred fifty years.

13.20-22   "Up to the time of Samuel the prophet, God provided judges to lead them. But then they asked for a king, and God gave them Saul, son of Kish, out of the tribe of Benjamin. After Saul had ruled forty years, God removed him from office and put King David in his place, with this commendation: 'I've searched the land and found this David, son of Jesse. He's a man whose heart beats to my heart, a man who will do what I tell him.'

13.23-25   "From out of David's descendants God produced a Savior for Israel, Jesus, exactly as he promised—but only after John had thoroughly alerted the people to his arrival by preparing them for a total life-change. As John was finishing up his work, he said, 'Did you think I was the One? No, I'm not the One. But the One you've been waiting for all these years is just around the corner, about to appear. And I'm about to disappear.'

13.26-29   "Dear brothers and sisters, children of Abraham, and friends of God, this message of salvation has been precisely targeted to you. The citizens and rulers in Jerusalem didn't recognize who he was and condemned him to death. They couldn't find a good reason, but demanded that Pilate execute him anyway. They did just what the prophets said they would do, but had no idea they were following to the letter the script of the prophets, even though those same prophets are read every Sabbath in their meeting places.

13.29-31   "After they had done everything the prophets said they would do, they took him down from the cross and buried him. And then God raised him from death. There is no disputing that—he appeared over and over again many times and places to those who had known him well in the Galilean years, and these same people continue to give witness that he is alive.

NEW INTERNATIONAL VERSION

32 "We tell you the good news: What God promised our fathers 33 he has fulfilled for us, their children, by raising up Jesus. As it is written in the second Psalm:

" 'You are my Son;
  today I have become your Father.' *a* *b*

34 The fact that God raised him from the dead, never to decay, is stated in these words:

" 'I will give you the holy and sure blessings
  promised to David.' *c*

35 So it is stated elsewhere:

" 'You will not let your Holy One see decay.' *d*

36 "For when David had served God's purpose in his own generation, he fell asleep; he was buried with his fathers and his body decayed. 37 But the one whom God raised from the dead did not see decay.

38 "Therefore, my brothers, I want you to know that through Jesus the forgiveness of sins is proclaimed to you. 39 Through him everyone who believes is justified from everything you could not be justified from by the law of Moses. 40 Take care that what the prophets have said does not happen to you:

41 " 'Look, you scoffers,
    wonder and perish,
  for I am going to do something in your days
    that you would never believe,
    even if someone told you.' *e*"

42 As Paul and Barnabas were leaving the synagogue, the people invited them to speak further about these things on the next Sabbath. 43 When the congregation was dismissed, many of the Jews and devout converts to Judaism followed Paul and Barnabas, who talked with them and urged them to continue in the grace of God.

44 On the next Sabbath almost the whole city gathered to hear the word of the Lord. 45 When the Jews saw the crowds, they were filled with jealousy and talked abusively against what Paul was saying.

46 Then Paul and Barnabas answered them boldly: "We had to speak the word of God to you first. Since you reject it and do not consider yourselves worthy of eternal life, we now turn to the Gentiles. 47 For this is what the Lord has commanded us:

THE MESSAGE

13.32-35 "And we're here today bringing you good news: the Message that what God promised the fathers has come true for the children—for us! He raised Jesus, exactly as described in the second Psalm:

My Son! My very own Son!
Today I celebrate you!

"When he raised him from the dead, he did it for good—no going back to that rot and decay for him. That's why Isaiah said, 'I'll give to all of you David's guaranteed blessings.' So also the psalmist's prayer: 'You'll never let your Holy One see death's rot and decay.'

13.36-39 "David, of course, having completed the work God set out for him, has been in the grave, dust and ashes, a long time now. But the One God raised up—no dust and ashes for him! I want you to know, my very dear friends, that it is on account of this resurrected Jesus that the forgiveness of your sins can be promised. He accomplishes, in those who believe, everything that the Law of Moses could never make good on. But everyone who believes in this raised-up Jesus is declared good and right and whole before God.

13.40-41 "Don't take this lightly. You don't want the prophet's sermon to describe you:

Watch out, cynics;
Look hard—watch your world fall to
    pieces.
I'm doing something right before your eyes
That you won't believe, though it's staring
    you in the face."

13.42-43 When the service was over, Paul and Barnabas were invited back to preach again the next Sabbath. As the meeting broke up, a good many Jews and converts to Judaism went along with Paul and Barnabas, who urged them in long conversations to stick with what they'd started, this living in and by God's grace.

13.44-45 When the next Sabbath came around, practically the whole city showed up to hear the Word of God. Some of the Jews, seeing the crowds, went wild with jealousy and tore into Paul, contradicting everything he was saying, making an ugly scene.

13.46-47 But Paul and Barnabas didn't back down. Standing their ground they said, "It was required that God's Word be spoken first of all to you, the Jews. But seeing that you want no part of it—you've made it quite clear that you have no taste or inclination for eternal life—the door is open to all the outsiders. And we're on our way through it, following orders, doing what God commanded when he said,

---

a 33 Or *have begotten you*   *b* 33 Psalm 2:7
c 34 Isaiah 55:3   *d* 35 Psalm 16:10   *e* 41 Hab. 1:5

NEW INTERNATIONAL VERSION

" 'I have made you^a a light for the Gentiles,
that you^a may bring salvation to the ends
of the earth.'^b"

⁴⁸When the Gentiles heard this, they were glad and honored the word of the Lord; and all who were appointed for eternal life believed.

⁴⁹The word of the Lord spread through the whole region. ⁵⁰But the Jews incited the God-fearing women of high standing and the leading men of the city. They stirred up persecution against Paul and Barnabas, and expelled them from their region. ⁵¹So they shook the dust from their feet in protest against them and went to Iconium. ⁵²And the disciples were filled with joy and with the Holy Spirit.

IN ICONIUM

14 At Iconium Paul and Barnabas went as usual into the Jewish synagogue. There they spoke so effectively that a great number of Jews and Gentiles believed. ²But the Jews who refused to believe stirred up the Gentiles and poisoned their minds against the brothers. ³So Paul and Barnabas spent considerable time there, speaking boldly for the Lord, who confirmed the message of his grace by enabling them to do miraculous signs and wonders. ⁴The people of the city were divided; some sided with the Jews, others with the apostles. ⁵There was a plot afoot among the Gentiles and Jews, together with their leaders, to mistreat them and stone them. ⁶But they found out about it and fled to the Lycaonian cities of Lystra and Derbe and to the surrounding country, ⁷where they continued to preach the good news.

IN LYSTRA AND DERBE

⁸In Lystra there sat a man crippled in his feet, who was lame from birth and had never walked. ⁹He listened to Paul as he was speaking. Paul looked directly at him, saw that he had faith to be healed ¹⁰and called out, "Stand up on your feet!" At that, the man jumped up and began to walk.

¹¹When the crowd saw what Paul had done, they shouted in the Lycaonian language, "The gods have come down to us in human form!" ¹²Barnabas they called Zeus, and Paul they called Hermes because he was the chief speaker. ¹³The priest of Zeus, whose temple was just outside the city, brought bulls and wreaths to the city

THE MESSAGE

I've set you up
    as light to all nations.
You'll proclaim salvation
    to the four winds and seven seas!"

13.48-49   When the non-Jewish outsiders heard this, they could hardly believe their good fortune. All who were marked out for *real life* put their trust in God—they honored God's Word by receiving that life. And this Message of salvation spread like wildfire all through the region.

13.50-52   Some of the Jews convinced the most respected women and leading men of the town that their precious way of life was about to be destroyed. Alarmed, they turned on Paul and Barnabas and forced them to leave. Paul and Barnabas shrugged their shoulders and went on to the next town, Iconium, brimming with joy and the Holy Spirit, two happy disciples.

✝

14.1-3   **14** When they got to Iconium they went, as they always did, to the meeting place of the Jews and gave their message. The Message convinced both Jews and non-Jews—and not just a few, either. But the unbelieving Jews worked up a whispering campaign against Paul and Barnabas, sowing mistrust and suspicion in the minds of the people in the street. The two apostles were there a long time, speaking freely, openly, and confidently as they presented the clear evidence of God's gifts, God corroborating their work with miracles and wonders.

14.4-7   But then there was a split in public opinion, some siding with the Jews, some with the apostles. One day, learning that both the Jews and non-Jews had been organized by their leaders to beat them up, they escaped as best they could to the next towns—Lyconia, Lystra, Derbe, and that neighborhood—but then were right back at it again, getting out the Message.

GODS OR MEN?

14.8-10   There was a man in Lystra who couldn't walk. He sat there, crippled since the day of his birth. He heard Paul talking, and Paul, looking him in the eye, saw that he was ripe for God's work, ready to believe. So he said, loud enough for everyone to hear, "Up on your feet!" The man was up in a flash—jumped up and walked around as if he'd been walking all his life.

14.11-13   When the crowd saw what Paul had done, they went wild, calling out in their Lyconian dialect, "The gods have come down! These men are gods!" They called Barnabas "Zeus" and Paul "Hermes" (since Paul did most of the speaking). The priest of the local Zeus shrine got up a parade—bulls and banners and people

NEW INTERNATIONAL VERSION

gates because he and the crowd wanted to offer sacrifices to them.

¹⁴But when the apostles Barnabas and Paul heard of this, they tore their clothes and rushed out into the crowd, shouting: ¹⁵"Men, why are you doing this? We too are only men, human like you. We are bringing you good news, telling you to turn from these worthless things to the living God, who made heaven and earth and sea and everything in them. ¹⁶In the past, he let all nations go their own way. ¹⁷Yet he has not left himself without testimony: He has shown kindness by giving you rain from heaven and crops in their seasons; he provides you with plenty of food and fills your hearts with joy." ¹⁸Even with these words, they had difficulty keeping the crowd from sacrificing to them.

¹⁹Then some Jews came from Antioch and Iconium and won the crowd over. They stoned Paul and dragged him outside the city, thinking he was dead. ²⁰But after the disciples had gathered around him, he got up and went back into the city. The next day he and Barnabas left for Derbe.

THE RETURN TO ANTIOCH IN SYRIA

²¹They preached the good news in that city and won a large number of disciples. Then they returned to Lystra, Iconium and Antioch, ²²strengthening the disciples and encouraging them to remain true to the faith. "We must go through many hardships to enter the kingdom of God," they said. ²³Paul and Barnabas appointed elders[a] for them in each church and, with prayer and fasting, committed them to the Lord, in whom they had put their trust. ²⁴After going through Pisidia, they came into Pamphylia, ²⁵and when they had preached the word in Perga, they went down to Attalia.

²⁶From Attalia they sailed back to Antioch, where they had been committed to the grace of God for the work they had now completed. ²⁷On arriving there, they gathered the church together and reported all that God had done through them and how he had opened the door of faith to the Gentiles. ²⁸And they stayed there a long time with the disciples.

[a] 23 Or Barnabas ordained elders; or Barnabas had elders elected

THE MESSAGE

lined right up to the gates, ready for the ritual of sacrifice.

14.14-15 When Barnabas and Paul finally realized what was going on, they stopped them. Waving their arms, they interrupted the parade, calling out, "What do you think you're doing! We're not gods! We are men just like you, and we're here to bring you the Message, to persuade you to abandon these silly god-superstitions and embrace God himself, the living God. We don't make God; he makes us, and all of this—sky, earth, sea, and everything in them.

14.16-18 "In the generations before us, God let all the different nations go their own way. But even then he didn't leave them without a clue, for he made a good creation, poured down rain and gave bumper crops. When your bellies were full and your hearts happy, there was evidence of good beyond your doing." Talking fast and hard like this, they prevented them from carrying out the sacrifice that would have honored them as gods—but just barely.

14.19-20 Then some Jews from Antioch and Iconium caught up with them and turned the fickle crowd against them. They beat Paul unconscious, dragged him outside the town and left him for dead. But as the disciples gathered around him, he came to and got up. He went back into town and the next day left with Barnabas for Derbe.

PLENTY OF HARD TIMES

14.21-22 After proclaiming the Message in Derbe and establishing a strong core of disciples, they retraced their steps to Lystra, then Iconium, and then Antioch, putting muscle and sinew in the lives of the disciples, urging them to stick with what they had begun to believe and not quit, making it clear to them that it wouldn't be easy: "Anyone signing up for the kingdom of God has to go through plenty of hard times."

14.23-26 Paul and Barnabas handpicked leaders in each church. After praying—their prayers intensified by fasting—they presented these new leaders to the Master to whom they had entrusted their lives. Working their way back through Pisidia, they came to Pamphylia and preached in Perga. Finally, they made it to Attalia and caught a ship back to Antioch, where it had all started—launched by God's grace and now safely home by God's grace. A good piece of work.

14.27-28 On arrival, they got the church together and reported on their trip, telling in detail how God had used them to throw the door of faith wide open so people of all nations could come streaming in. Then they settled down for a long, leisurely visit with the disciples.

NEW INTERNATIONAL VERSION

THE COUNCIL AT JERUSALEM

15 Some men came down from Judea to Antioch and were teaching the brothers: "Unless you are circumcised, according to the custom taught by Moses, you cannot be saved." ²This brought Paul and Barnabas into sharp dispute and debate with them. So Paul and Barnabas were appointed, along with some other believers, to go up to Jerusalem to see the apostles and elders about this question. ³The church sent them on their way, and as they traveled through Phoenicia and Samaria, they told how the Gentiles had been converted. This news made all the brothers very glad. ⁴When they came to Jerusalem, they were welcomed by the church and the apostles and elders, to whom they reported everything God had done through them.

⁵Then some of the believers who belonged to the party of the Pharisees stood up and said, "The Gentiles must be circumcised and required to obey the law of Moses."

⁶The apostles and elders met to consider this question. ⁷After much discussion, Peter got up and addressed them: "Brothers, you know that some time ago God made a choice among you that the Gentiles might hear from my lips the message of the gospel and believe. ⁸God, who knows the heart, showed that he accepted them by giving the Holy Spirit to them, just as he did to us. ⁹He made no distinction between us and them, for he purified their hearts by faith. ¹⁰Now then, why do you try to test God by putting on the necks of the disciples a yoke that neither we nor our fathers have been able to bear? ¹¹No! We believe it is through the grace of our Lord Jesus that we are saved, just as they are."

¹²The whole assembly became silent as they listened to Barnabas and Paul telling about the miraculous signs and wonders God had done among the Gentiles through them. ¹³When they

THE MESSAGE

TO LET OUTSIDERS INSIDE

15 It wasn't long before some Jews showed up from Judea insisting that everyone be circumcised: "If you're not circumcised in the Mosaic fashion, you can't be saved." Paul and Barnabas were up on their feet at once in fierce protest. The church decided to resolve the matter by sending Paul, Barnabas, and a few others to put it before the apostles and leaders in Jerusalem.

15.3 After they were sent off and on their way, they told everyone they met as they traveled through Phoenicia and Samaria about the breakthrough to the Gentile outsiders. Everyone who heard the news cheered—it was terrific news!

15.4-5 When they got to Jerusalem, Paul and Barnabas were graciously received by the whole church, including the apostles and leaders. They reported on their recent journey and how God had used them to open things up to the outsiders. Some Pharisees stood up to say their piece. They had become believers, but continued to hold to the hard party line of the Pharisees. "You have to circumcise the pagan converts," they said. "You must make them keep the Law of Moses."

15.6-9 The apostles and leaders called a special meeting to consider the matter. The arguments went on and on, back and forth, getting more and more heated. Then Peter took the floor: "Friends, you well know that from early on God made it quite plain that he wanted the pagans to hear the Message of this good news and embrace it—and not in any secondhand or roundabout way, but firsthand, straight from my mouth. And God, who can't be fooled by any pretense on our part but always knows a person's thoughts, gave them the Holy Spirit exactly as he gave him to us. He treated the outsiders exactly as he treated us, beginning at the very center of who they were and working from that center outward, cleaning up their lives as they trusted and believed him.

15.10-11 "So why are you now trying to out-god God, loading these new believers down with rules that crushed our ancestors and crushed us, too? Don't we believe that we are saved because the Master Jesus amazingly and out of sheer generosity moved to save us just as he did those from beyond our nation? So what are we arguing about?"

15.12-13 There was dead silence. No one said a word. With the room quiet, Barnabas and Paul reported matter-of-factly on the miracles and wonders God had done among the other nations through their ministry. The silence deepened; you could hear a pin drop.

NEW INTERNATIONAL VERSION

finished, James spoke up: "Brothers, listen to me. [14]Simon[a] has described to us how God at first showed his concern by taking from the Gentiles a people for himself. [15]The words of the prophets are in agreement with this, as it is written:

[16]" 'After this I will return
  and rebuild David's fallen tent.
Its ruins I will rebuild,
  and I will restore it,
[17]that the remnant of men may seek the Lord,
  and all the Gentiles who bear my name,
says the Lord, who does these things'[b]
[18] that have been known for ages.[c]

[19]"It is my judgment, therefore, that we should not make it difficult for the Gentiles who are turning to God. [20]Instead we should write to them, telling them to abstain from food polluted by idols, from sexual immorality, from the meat of strangled animals and from blood. [21]For Moses has been preached in every city from the earliest times and is read in the synagogues on every Sabbath."

THE COUNCIL'S LETTER TO GENTILE BELIEVERS

[22]Then the apostles and elders, with the whole church, decided to choose some of their own men and send them to Antioch with Paul and Barnabas. They chose Judas (called Barsabbas) and Silas, two men who were leaders among the brothers. [23]With them they sent the following letter:

The apostles and elders, your brothers,

To the Gentile believers in Antioch, Syria and Cilicia:

Greetings.

[24]We have heard that some went out from us without our authorization and disturbed you, troubling your minds by what they said. [25]So we all agreed to choose some men and send them to you with our dear friends Barnabas and Paul— [26]men who have risked their lives for the name of our Lord Jesus Christ. [27]Therefore we are sending Judas and Silas to confirm by word of mouth what we are writing. [28]It seemed good to the Holy Spirit and to us not to burden you with anything beyond the following requirements: [29]You are to abstain from food sacrificed to idols, from blood,

---

[a] 14 Greek Simeon, a variant of Simon; that is, Peter
[b] 17 Amos 9:11,12   [c] 17,18 Some manuscripts things'— / [18]known to the Lord for ages is his work

THE MESSAGE

15.13-18 James broke the silence. "Friends, listen. Simeon has told us the story of how God at the very outset made sure that racial outsiders were included. This is in perfect agreement with the words of the prophets:

After this, I'm coming back;
  I'll rebuild David's ruined house;
I'll put all the pieces together again;
  I'll make it look like new
So outsiders who seek will find,
  so they'll have a place to come to,
All the pagan peoples
  included in what I'm doing.

"God said it and now he's doing it. It's no afterthought; he's always known he would do this.
15.19-21 "So here is my decision: We're not going to unnecessarily burden non-Jewish people who turn to the Master. We'll write them a letter and tell them, 'Be careful to not get involved in activities connected with idols, to guard the morality of sex and marriage, to not serve food offensive to Jewish Christians—blood, for instance.' This is basic wisdom from Moses, preached and honored for centuries now in city after city as we have met and kept the Sabbath."

15.22-23 Everyone agreed: apostles, leaders, all the people. They picked Judas (nicknamed Barsabbas) and Silas—they both carried considerable weight in the church—and sent them to Antioch with Paul and Barnabas with this letter:

From the apostles and leaders, your friends, to our friends in Antioch, Syria, and Cilicia:
  Hello!
15.24-27 We heard that some men from our church went to you and said things that confused and upset you. Mind you, they had no authority from us; we didn't send them. We have agreed unanimously to pick representatives and send them to you with our good friends Barnabas and Paul. We picked men we knew you could trust, Judas and Silas—they've looked death in the face time and again for the sake of our Master Jesus Christ. We've sent them to confirm in a face-to-face meeting with you what we've written.

15.28-29 It seemed to the Holy Spirit and to us that you should not be saddled with any crushing burden, but be responsible only for these bare necessities: Be careful not to get involved in activities connected with idols; avoid serving food offensive to Jewish Christians (blood, for instance);

NEW INTERNATIONAL VERSION

from the meat of strangled animals and from sexual immorality. You will do well to avoid these things.

Farewell.

³⁰The men were sent off and went down to Antioch, where they gathered the church together and delivered the letter. ³¹The people read it and were glad for its encouraging message. ³²Judas and Silas, who themselves were prophets, said much to encourage and strengthen the brothers. ³³After spending some time there, they were sent off by the brothers with the blessing of peace to return to those who had sent them. ᵃ ³⁵But Paul and Barnabas remained in Antioch, where they and many others taught and preached the word of the Lord.

DISAGREEMENT BETWEEN PAUL AND BARNABAS

³⁶Some time later Paul said to Barnabas, "Let us go back and visit the brothers in all the towns where we preached the word of the Lord and see how they are doing." ³⁷Barnabas wanted to take John, also called Mark, with them, ³⁸but Paul did not think it wise to take him, because he had deserted them in Pamphylia and had not continued with them in the work. ³⁹They had such a sharp disagreement that they parted company. Barnabas took Mark and sailed for Cyprus, ⁴⁰but Paul chose Silas and left, commended by the brothers to the grace of the Lord. ⁴¹He went through Syria and Cilicia, strengthening the churches.

TIMOTHY JOINS PAUL AND SILAS

16 He came to Derbe and then to Lystra, where a disciple named Timothy lived, whose mother was a Jewess and a believer, but whose father was a Greek. ²The brothers at Lystra and Iconium spoke well of him. ³Paul wanted to take him along on the journey, so he circumcised him because of the Jews who lived in that area, for they all knew that his father was a Greek. ⁴As they traveled from town to town, they delivered the decisions reached by the apostles and elders in Jerusalem for the people to obey. ⁵So the churches were strengthened in the faith and grew daily in numbers.

PAUL'S VISION OF THE MAN OF MACEDONIA

⁶Paul and his companions traveled throughout the region of Phrygia and Galatia, having been kept by the Holy Spirit from preaching the

---

THE MESSAGE

and guard the morality of sex and marriage.

These guidelines are sufficient to keep relations congenial between us. And God be with you!

BARNABAS AND PAUL GO THEIR SEPARATE WAYS

15.30-33 And so off they went to Antioch. On arrival, they gathered the church and read the letter. The people were greatly relieved and pleased. Judas and Silas, good preachers both of them, strengthened their new friends with many words of courage and hope. Then it was time to go home. They were sent off by their new friends with laughter and embraces all around to report back to those who had sent them.

15.35 Paul and Barnabas stayed on in Antioch, teaching and preaching the Word of God. But they weren't alone. There were a number of teachers and preachers at that time in Antioch.

15.36 After a few days of this, Paul said to Barnabas, "Let's go back and visit all our friends in each of the towns where we preached the Word of God. Let's see how they're doing."

15.37-41 Barnabas wanted to take John along, the John nicknamed Mark. But Paul wouldn't have him; he wasn't about to take along a quitter who, as soon as the going got tough, had jumped ship on them in Pamphylia. Tempers flared, and they ended up going their separate ways: Barnabas took Mark and sailed for Cyprus; Paul chose Silas and, offered up by their friends to the grace of the Master, went to Syria and Cilicia to build up muscle and sinew in those congregations.

A DREAM GAVE PAUL HIS MAP

16.1-3 **16** Paul came first to Derbe, then Lystra. He found a disciple there by the name of Timothy, son of a devout Jewish mother and Greek father. Friends in Lystra and Iconium all said what a fine young man he was. Paul wanted to recruit him for their mission, but first took him aside and circumcised him so he wouldn't offend the Jews who lived in those parts. They all knew that his father was Greek.

16.4-5 As they traveled from town to town, they presented the simple guidelines the Jerusalem apostles and leaders had come up with. That turned out to be most helpful. Day after day the congregations became stronger in faith and larger in size.

16.6-8 They went to Phrygia, and then on through the region of Galatia. Their plan was to turn west into Asia province, but the Holy Spirit

---

ᵃ 33 Some manuscripts *them, ³⁴but Silas decided to remain there*

NEW INTERNATIONAL VERSION

word in the province of Asia. ⁷When they came to the border of Mysia, they tried to enter Bithynia, but the Spirit of Jesus would not allow them to. ⁸So they passed by Mysia and went down to Troas. ⁹During the night Paul had a vision of a man of Macedonia standing and begging him, "Come over to Macedonia and help us." ¹⁰After Paul had seen the vision, we got ready at once to leave for Macedonia, concluding that God had called us to preach the gospel to them.

LYDIA'S CONVERSION IN PHILIPPI

¹¹From Troas we put out to sea and sailed straight for Samothrace, and the next day on to Neapolis. ¹²From there we traveled to Philippi, a Roman colony and the leading city of that district of Macedonia. And we stayed there several days.

¹³On the Sabbath we went outside the city gate to the river, where we expected to find a place of prayer. We sat down and began to speak to the women who had gathered there. ¹⁴One of those listening was a woman named Lydia, a dealer in purple cloth from the city of Thyatira, who was a worshiper of God. The Lord opened her heart to respond to Paul's message. ¹⁵When she and the members of her household were baptized, she invited us to her home. "If you consider me a believer in the Lord," she said, "come and stay at my house." And she persuaded us.

PAUL AND SILAS IN PRISON

¹⁶Once when we were going to the place of prayer, we were met by a slave girl who had a spirit by which she predicted the future. She earned a great deal of money for her owners by fortune-telling. ¹⁷This girl followed Paul and the rest of us, shouting, "These men are servants of the Most High God, who are telling you the way to be saved." ¹⁸She kept this up for many days. Finally Paul became so troubled that he turned around and said to the spirit, "In the name of Jesus Christ I command you to come out of her!" At that moment the spirit left her.

¹⁹When the owners of the slave girl realized that their hope of making money was gone, they seized Paul and Silas and dragged them into the marketplace to face the authorities. ²⁰They brought them before the magistrates and said, "These men are Jews, and are throwing our city into an uproar ²¹by advocating customs unlawful for us Romans to accept or practice."

THE MESSAGE

blocked that route. So they went to Mysia and tried to go north to Bithynia, but the Spirit of Jesus wouldn't let them go there either. Proceeding on through Mysia, they went down to the seaport Troas.

16.9-10 That night Paul had a dream: A Macedonian stood on the far shore and called across the sea, "Come over to Macedonia and help us!" The dream gave Paul his map. We went to work at once getting things ready to cross over to Macedonia. All the pieces had come together. We knew now for sure that God had called us to preach the good news to the Europeans.

16.11-12 Putting out from the harbor at Troas, we made a straight run for Samothrace. The next day we tied up at New City and walked from there to Philippi, the main city in that part of Macedonia and, even more importantly, a Roman colony. We lingered there several days.

16.13-14 On the Sabbath, we left the city and went down along the river where we had heard there was to be a prayer meeting. We took our place with the women who had gathered there and talked with them. One woman, Lydia, was from Thyatira and a dealer in expensive textiles, known to be a God-fearing woman. As she listened with intensity to what was being said, the Master gave her a trusting heart—and she believed!

16.15 After she was baptized, along with everyone in her household, she said in a surge of hospitality, "If you're confident that I'm in this with you and believe in the Master truly, come home with me and be my guests." We hesitated, but she wouldn't take no for an answer.

BEAT UP AND THROWN IN JAIL

16.16-18 One day, on our way to the place of prayer, a slave girl ran into us. She was a psychic and, with her fortunetelling, made a lot of money for the people who owned her. She started following Paul around, calling everyone's attention to us by yelling out, "These men are working for the Most High God. They're laying out the road of salvation for you!" She did this for a number of days until Paul, finally fed up with her, turned and commanded the spirit that possessed her, "Out! In the name of Jesus Christ, get out of her!" And it was gone, just like that.

16.19-22 When her owners saw that their lucrative little business was suddenly bankrupt, they went after Paul and Silas, roughed them up and dragged them into the market square. Then the police arrested them and pulled them into a court with the accusation, "These men are disturbing the peace—dangerous Jewish agitators subverting our Roman law and order." By this

NEW INTERNATIONAL VERSION

²²The crowd joined in the attack against Paul and Silas, and the magistrates ordered them to be stripped and beaten. ²³After they had been severely flogged, they were thrown into prison, and the jailer was commanded to guard them carefully. ²⁴Upon receiving such orders, he put them in the inner cell and fastened their feet in the stocks.

²⁵About midnight Paul and Silas were praying and singing hymns to God, and the other prisoners were listening to them. ²⁶Suddenly there was such a violent earthquake that the foundations of the prison were shaken. At once all the prison doors flew open, and everybody's chains came loose. ²⁷The jailer woke up, and when he saw the prison doors open, he drew his sword and was about to kill himself because he thought the prisoners had escaped. ²⁸But Paul shouted, "Don't harm yourself! We are all here!"

²⁹The jailer called for lights, rushed in and fell trembling before Paul and Silas. ³⁰He then brought them out and asked, "Sirs, what must I do to be saved?"

³¹They replied, "Believe in the Lord Jesus, and you will be saved—you and your household." ³²Then they spoke the word of the Lord to him and to all the others in his house. ³³At that hour of the night the jailer took them and washed their wounds; then immediately he and all his family were baptized. ³⁴The jailer brought them into his house and set a meal before them; he was filled with joy because he had come to believe in God—he and his whole family.

³⁵When it was daylight, the magistrates sent their officers to the jailer with the order: "Release those men." ³⁶The jailer told Paul, "The magistrates have ordered that you and Silas be released. Now you can leave. Go in peace."

³⁷But Paul said to the officers: "They beat us publicly without a trial, even though we are Roman citizens, and threw us into prison. And now do they want to get rid of us quietly? No! Let them come themselves and escort us out."

³⁸The officers reported this to the magistrates, and when they heard that Paul and Silas were Roman citizens, they were alarmed. ³⁹They came

THE MESSAGE

time the crowd had turned into a restless mob out for blood.

16.22-24 The judges went along with the mob, had Paul and Silas's clothes ripped off and ordered a public beating. After beating them black and blue, they threw them into jail, telling the jailkeeper to put them under heavy guard so there would be no chance of escape. He did just that—threw them into the maximum security cell in the jail and clamped leg irons on them.

16.25-26 Along about midnight, Paul and Silas were at prayer and singing a robust hymn to God. The other prisoners couldn't believe their ears. Then, without warning, a huge earthquake! The jailhouse tottered, every door flew open, all the prisoners were loose.

16.27-28 Startled from sleep, the jailer saw all the doors swinging loose on their hinges. Assuming that all the prisoners had escaped, he pulled out his sword and was about to do himself in, figuring he was as good as dead anyway, when Paul stopped him: "Don't do that! We're all still here! Nobody's run away!"

16.29-31 The jailer got a torch and ran inside. Badly shaken, he collapsed in front of Paul and Silas. He led them out of the jail and asked, "Sirs, what do I have to do to be saved, to really live?" They said, "Put your entire trust in the Master Jesus. Then you'll live as you were meant to live—and everyone in your house included!"

16.32-34 They went on to spell out in detail the story of the Master—the entire family got in on this part. They never did get to bed that night. The jailer made them feel at home, dressed their wounds, and then—he couldn't wait till morning!—was baptized, he and everyone in his family. There in his home, he had food set out for a festive meal. It was a night to remember: He and his entire family had put their trust in God; everyone in the house was in on the celebration.

16.35-36 At daybreak, the court judges sent officers with the instructions, "Release these men." The jailer gave Paul the message, "The judges sent word that you're free to go on your way. Congratulations! Go in peace!"

16.37 But Paul wouldn't budge. He told the officers, "They beat us up in public and threw us in jail, Roman citizens in good standing! And now they want to get us out of the way on the sly without anyone knowing? Nothing doing! If they want us out of here, let them come themselves and lead us out in broad daylight."

16.38-40 When the officers reported this, the judges panicked. They had no idea that Paul and Silas were Roman citizens. They hurried over and

NEW INTERNATIONAL VERSION

to appease them and escorted them from the prison, requesting them to leave the city. ⁴⁰After Paul and Silas came out of the prison, they went to Lydia's house, where they met with the brothers and encouraged them. Then they left.

IN THESSALONICA

17 When they had passed through Amphipolis and Apollonia, they came to Thessalonica, where there was a Jewish synagogue. ²As his custom was, Paul went into the synagogue, and on three Sabbath days he reasoned with them from the Scriptures, ³explaining and proving that the Christ*ᵃ* had to suffer and rise from the dead. "This Jesus I am proclaiming to you is the Christ,*ᵃ*" he said. ⁴Some of the Jews were persuaded and joined Paul and Silas, as did a large number of God-fearing Greeks and not a few prominent women.

⁵But the Jews were jealous; so they rounded up some bad characters from the marketplace, formed a mob and started a riot in the city. They rushed to Jason's house in search of Paul and Silas in order to bring them out to the crowd.*ᵇ* ⁶But when they did not find them, they dragged Jason and some other brothers before the city officials, shouting: "These men who have caused trouble all over the world have now come here, ⁷and Jason has welcomed them into his house. They are all defying Caesar's decrees, saying that there is another king, one called Jesus." ⁸When they heard this, the crowd and the city officials were thrown into turmoil. ⁹Then they made Jason and the others post bond and let them go.

IN BEREA

¹⁰As soon as it was night, the brothers sent Paul and Silas away to Berea. On arriving there, they went to the Jewish synagogue. ¹¹Now the Bereans were of more noble character than the Thessalonians, for they received the message with great eagerness and examined the Scriptures every day to see if what Paul said was true. ¹²Many of the Jews believed, as did also a number of prominent Greek women and many Greek men.

THE MESSAGE

apologized, personally escorted them from the jail, and then asked them if they wouldn't please leave the city. Walking out of the jail, Paul and Silas went straight to Lydia's house, saw their friends again, encouraged them in the faith, and only then went on their way.

THESSALONICA

17.1-3 **17** They took the road south through Amphipolis and Apollonia to Thessalonica, where there was a community of Jews. Paul went to their meeting place, as he usually did when he came to a town, and for three Sabbaths running he preached to them from the Scriptures. He opened up the texts so they understood what they'd been reading all their lives: that the Messiah absolutely *had* to be put to death and raised from the dead—there were no other options—and that "this Jesus I'm introducing you to is that Messiah."

17.4-5 Some of them were won over and joined ranks with Paul and Silas, among them a great many God-fearing Greeks and a considerable number of women from the aristocracy. But the hard-line Jews became furious over the conversions. Mad with jealousy, they rounded up a bunch of brawlers off the streets and soon had an ugly mob terrorizing the city as they hunted down Paul and Silas.

17.5-7 They broke into Jason's house, thinking that Paul and Silas were there. When they couldn't find them, they collared Jason and his friends instead and dragged them before the city fathers, yelling hysterically, "These people are out to destroy the world, and now they've shown up on our doorstep, attacking everything we hold dear! And Jason is hiding them, these traitors and turncoats who say Jesus is king and Caesar is nothing!"

17.8-9 The city fathers and the crowd of people were totally alarmed by what they heard. They made Jason and his friends post heavy bail and let them go while they investigated the charges.

BEREA

17.10-12 That night, under cover of darkness, their friends got Paul and Silas out of town as fast as they could. They sent them to Berea, where they again met with the Jewish community. They were treated a lot better there than in Thessalonica. The Jews received Paul's message with enthusiasm and met with him daily, examining the Scriptures to see if they supported what he said. A lot of them became believers, including many Greeks who were prominent in the community, women and men of influence.

ᵃ 3 Or *Messiah*   *ᵇ* 5 Or *the assembly of the people*

NEW INTERNATIONAL VERSION

¹³When the Jews in Thessalonica learned that Paul was preaching the word of God at Berea, they went there too, agitating the crowds and stirring them up. ¹⁴The brothers immediately sent Paul to the coast, but Silas and Timothy stayed at Berea. ¹⁵The men who escorted Paul brought him to Athens and then left with instructions for Silas and Timothy to join him as soon as possible.

IN ATHENS

¹⁶While Paul was waiting for them in Athens, he was greatly distressed to see that the city was full of idols. ¹⁷So he reasoned in the synagogue with the Jews and the God-fearing Greeks, as well as in the marketplace day by day with those who happened to be there. ¹⁸A group of Epicurean and Stoic philosophers began to dispute with him. Some of them asked, "What is this babbler trying to say?" Others remarked, "He seems to be advocating foreign gods." They said this because Paul was preaching the good news about Jesus and the resurrection. ¹⁹Then they took him and brought him to a meeting of the Areopagus, where they said to him, "May we know what this new teaching is that you are presenting? ²⁰You are bringing some strange ideas to our ears, and we want to know what they mean." ²¹(All the Athenians and the foreigners who lived there spent their time doing nothing but talking about and listening to the latest ideas.)

²²Paul then stood up in the meeting of the Areopagus and said: "Men of Athens! I see that in every way you are very religious. ²³For as I walked around and looked carefully at your objects of worship, I even found an altar with this inscription: TO AN UNKNOWN GOD. Now what you worship as something unknown I am going to proclaim to you.

²⁴"The God who made the world and everything in it is the Lord of heaven and earth and does not live in temples built by hands. ²⁵And he is not served by human hands, as if he needed anything, because he himself gives all men life and breath and everything else. ²⁶From one man he made every nation of men, that they should inhabit the whole earth; and he determined the times set for them and the exact places where they should live. ²⁷God did this so that men would seek him and perhaps reach out for him

THE MESSAGE

17.13-15 But it wasn't long before reports got back to the Thessalonian hard-line Jews that Paul was at it again, preaching the Word of God, this time in Berea. They lost no time responding, and created a mob scene there, too. With the help of his friends, Paul gave them the slip— caught a boat and put out to sea. Silas and Timothy stayed behind. The men who helped Paul escape got him as far as Athens and left him there. Paul sent word back with them to Silas and Timothy: "Come as quickly as you can!"

ATHENS

17.16 The longer Paul waited in Athens for Silas and Timothy, the angrier he got—all those idols! The city was a junkyard of idols.

17.17-18 He discussed it with the Jews and other like-minded people at their meeting place. And every day he went out on the streets and talked with anyone who happened along. He got to know some of the Epicurean and Stoic intellectuals pretty well through these conversations. Some of them dismissed him with sarcasm: "What an airhead!" But others, listening to him go on about Jesus and the resurrection, were intrigued: "That's a new slant on the gods. Tell us more."

17.19-21 These people got together and asked him to make a public presentation over at the Areopagus, where things were a little quieter. They said, "This is a new one on us. We've never heard anything quite like it. Where did you come up with this anyway? Explain it so we can understand." Downtown Athens was a great place for gossip. There were always people hanging around, natives and tourists alike, waiting for the latest tidbit on most anything.

17.22-23 So Paul took his stand in the open space at the Areopagus and laid it out for them. "It is plain to see that you Athenians take your religion seriously. When I arrived here the other day, I was fascinated with all the shrines I came across. And then I found one inscribed, TO THE GOD NOBODY KNOWS. I'm here to introduce you to this God so you can worship intelligently, know who you're dealing with.

17.24-29 "The God who made the world and everything in it, this Master of sky and land, doesn't live in custom-made shrines or need the human race to run errands for him, as if he couldn't take care of himself. He makes the creatures; the creatures don't make him. Starting from scratch, he made the entire human race and made the earth hospitable, with plenty of time and space for living so we could seek after God, and not just grope around in the dark but actually *find* him. He doesn't play

NEW INTERNATIONAL VERSION

and find him, though he is not far from each one of us. ²⁸'For in him we live and move and have our being.' As some of your own poets have said, 'We are his offspring.'

²⁹"Therefore since we are God's offspring, we should not think that the divine being is like gold or silver or stone—an image made by man's design and skill. ³⁰In the past God overlooked such ignorance, but now he commands all people everywhere to repent. ³¹For he has set a day when he will judge the world with justice by the man he has appointed. He has given proof of this to all men by raising him from the dead."

³²When they heard about the resurrection of the dead, some of them sneered, but others said, "We want to hear you again on this subject." ³³At that, Paul left the Council. ³⁴A few men became followers of Paul and believed. Among them was Dionysius, a member of the Areopagus, also a woman named Damaris, and a number of others.

In Corinth

18 After this, Paul left Athens and went to Corinth. ²There he met a Jew named Aquila, a native of Pontus, who had recently come from Italy with his wife Priscilla, because Claudius had ordered all the Jews to leave Rome. Paul went to see them, ³and because he was a tentmaker as they were, he stayed and worked with them. ⁴Every Sabbath he reasoned in the synagogue, trying to persuade Jews and Greeks.

⁵When Silas and Timothy came from Macedonia, Paul devoted himself exclusively to preaching, testifying to the Jews that Jesus was the Christ.ᵃ ⁶But when the Jews opposed Paul and became abusive, he shook out his clothes in protest and said to them, "Your blood be on your own heads! I am clear of my responsibility. From now on I will go to the Gentiles."

⁷Then Paul left the synagogue and went next door to the house of Titius Justus, a worshiper of God. ⁸Crispus, the synagogue ruler, and his entire household believed in the Lord; and many of the Corinthians who heard him believed and were baptized.

⁹One night the Lord spoke to Paul in a vision:

THE MESSAGE

hide-and-seek with us. He's not remote; he's *near*. We live and move in him, can't get away from him! One of your poets said it well: 'We're the God-created.' Well, if we are the God-created, it doesn't make a lot of sense to think we could hire a sculptor to chisel a god out of stone for *us*, does it?

17.30-31 "God overlooks it as long as you don't know any better—but that time is past. The unknown is now known, and he's calling for a radical life-change. He has set a day when the entire human race will be judged and everything set right. And he has already appointed the judge, confirming him before everyone by raising him from the dead."

17.32-34 At the phrase "raising him from the dead," the listeners split: Some laughed at him and walked off making jokes; others said, "Let's do this again. We want to hear more." But that was it for the day, and Paul left. There were still others, it turned out, who were convinced then and there, and stuck with Paul—among them Dionysius the Areopagite and a woman named Damaris.

Corinth

18.1-4 **18** After Athens, Paul went to Corinth. That is where he discovered Aquila, a Jew born in Pontus, and his wife, Priscilla. They had just arrived from Italy, part of the general expulsion of Jews from Rome ordered by Claudius. Paul moved in with them, and they worked together at their common trade of tentmaking. But every Sabbath he was at the meeting place, doing his best to convince both Jews and Greeks about Jesus.

18.5-6 When Silas and Timothy arrived from Macedonia, Paul was able to give all his time to preaching and teaching, doing everything he could to persuade the Jews that Jesus was in fact God's Messiah. But no such luck. All they did was argue contentiously and contradict him at every turn. Totally exasperated, Paul had finally had it with them and gave it up as a bad job. "Have it your way, then," he said. "You've made your bed; now lie in it. From now on I'm spending my time with the other nations."

18.7-8 He walked out and went to the home of Titius Justus, a God-fearing man who lived right next to the Jews' meeting place. But Paul's efforts with the Jews weren't a total loss, for Crispus, the meeting-place president, put his trust in the Master. His entire family believed with him.

18.8-11 In the course of listening to Paul, a great many Corinthians believed and were baptized. One night the Master spoke to Paul in a dream:

ᵃ 5 Or *Messiah*; also in verse 28

NEW INTERNATIONAL VERSION

"Do not be afraid; keep on speaking, do not be silent. [10]For I am with you, and no one is going to attack and harm you, because I have many people in this city." [11]So Paul stayed for a year and a half, teaching them the word of God.

[12]While Gallio was proconsul of Achaia, the Jews made a united attack on Paul and brought him into court. [13]"This man," they charged, "is persuading the people to worship God in ways contrary to the law."

[14]Just as Paul was about to speak, Gallio said to the Jews, "If you Jews were making a complaint about some misdemeanor or serious crime, it would be reasonable for me to listen to you. [15]But since it involves questions about words and names and your own law—settle the matter yourselves. I will not be a judge of such things." [16]So he had them ejected from the court. [17]Then they all turned on Sosthenes the synagogue ruler and beat him in front of the court. But Gallio showed no concern whatever.

PRISCILLA, AQUILA AND APOLLOS

[18]Paul stayed on in Corinth for some time. Then he left the brothers and sailed for Syria, accompanied by Priscilla and Aquila. Before he sailed, he had his hair cut off at Cenchrea because of a vow he had taken. [19]They arrived at Ephesus, where Paul left Priscilla and Aquila. He himself went into the synagogue and reasoned with the Jews. [20]When they asked him to spend more time with them, he declined. [21]But as he left, he promised, "I will come back if it is God's will." Then he set sail from Ephesus. [22]When he landed at Caesarea, he went up and greeted the church and then went down to Antioch.

[23]After spending some time in Antioch, Paul set out from there and traveled from place to place throughout the region of Galatia and Phrygia, strengthening all the disciples.

[24]Meanwhile a Jew named Apollos, a native of Alexandria, came to Ephesus. He was a learned man, with a thorough knowledge of the Scriptures. [25]He had been instructed in the way of the Lord, and he spoke with great fervor[a] and taught about Jesus accurately, though he knew only the baptism of John. [26]He began to speak boldly in

a 25 Or with fervor in the Spirit

THE MESSAGE

"Keep it up, and don't let anyone intimidate or silence you. No matter what happens, I'm with you and no one is going to be able to hurt you. You have no idea how many people I have on my side in this city." That was all he needed to stick it out. He stayed another year and a half, faithfully teaching the Word of God to the Corinthians.

18.12-13 But when Gallio was governor of Achaia province, the Jews got up a campaign against Paul, hauled him into court, and filed charges: "This man is seducing people into acts of worship that are illegal."

18.14-16 Just as Paul was about to defend himself, Gallio interrupted and said to the Jews, "If this was a matter of criminal conduct, I would gladly hear you out. But it sounds to me like one more Jewish squabble, another of your endless hairsplitting quarrels over religion. Take care of it on your own time. I can't be bothered with this nonsense," and he cleared them out of the courtroom.

18.17 Now the street rabble turned on Sosthenes, the new meeting-place president, and beat him up in plain sight of the court. Gallio didn't raise a finger. He could not have cared less.

EPHESUS

18.18 Paul stayed a while longer in Corinth, but then it was time to take leave of his friends. Saying his good-byes, he sailed for Syria, Priscilla and Aquila with him. Before boarding the ship in the harbor town of Cenchrea, he had his head shaved as part of a vow he had taken.

18.19-21 They landed in Ephesus, where Priscilla and Aquila got off and stayed. Paul left the ship briefly to go to the meeting place and preach to the Jews. They wanted him to stay longer, but he said he couldn't. But after saying good-bye, he promised, "I'll be back, God willing."

18.21-22 From Ephesus he sailed to Caesarea. He greeted the assembly of Christians there, and then went on to Antioch, completing the journey.

18.23 After spending a considerable time with the Antioch Christians, Paul set off again for Galatia and Phrygia, retracing his old tracks, one town after another, putting fresh heart into the disciples.

18.24-26 A man named Apollos came to Ephesus. He was a Jew, born in Alexandria, Egypt, and a terrific speaker, eloquent and powerful in his preaching of the Scriptures. He was well-educated in the way of the Master and fiery in his enthusiasm. Apollos was accurate in everything he taught about Jesus up to a point, but he only went as far as the baptism of John. He preached

NEW INTERNATIONAL VERSION

the synagogue. When Priscilla and Aquila heard him, they invited him to their home and explained to him the way of God more adequately. ²⁷When Apollos wanted to go to Achaia, the brothers encouraged him and wrote to the disciples there to welcome him. On arriving, he was a great help to those who by grace had believed. ²⁸For he vigorously refuted the Jews in public debate, proving from the Scriptures that Jesus was the Christ.

PAUL IN EPHESUS

19 While Apollos was at Corinth, Paul took the road through the interior and arrived at Ephesus. There he found some disciples ²and asked them, "Did you receive the Holy Spirit when^a you believed?"

They answered, "No, we have not even heard that there is a Holy Spirit."

³So Paul asked, "Then what baptism did you receive?"

"John's baptism," they replied.

⁴Paul said, "John's baptism was a baptism of repentance. He told the people to believe in the one coming after him, that is, in Jesus." ⁵On hearing this, they were baptized into^b the name of the Lord Jesus. ⁶When Paul placed his hands on them, the Holy Spirit came on them, and they spoke in tongues^c and prophesied. ⁷There were about twelve men in all.

⁸Paul entered the synagogue and spoke boldly there for three months, arguing persuasively about the kingdom of God. ⁹But some of them became obstinate; they refused to believe and publicly maligned the Way. So Paul left them. He took the disciples with him and had discussions daily in the lecture hall of Tyrannus. ¹⁰This went on for two years, so that all the Jews and Greeks who lived in the province of Asia heard the word of the Lord.

THE MESSAGE

with power in the meeting place. When Priscilla and Aquila heard him, they took him aside and told him the rest of the story.

_{18.27-28} When Apollos decided to go on to Achaia province, his Ephesian friends gave their blessing and wrote a letter of recommendation for him, urging the disciples there to welcome him with open arms. The welcome paid off: Apollos turned out to be a great help to those who had become believers through God's immense generosity. He was particularly effective in public debate with the Jews as he brought out proof after convincing proof from the Scriptures that Jesus was in fact God's Messiah.

_{19.1-2} **19** Now, it happened that while Apollos was away in Corinth, Paul made his way down through the mountains, came to Ephesus, and happened on some disciples there. The first thing he said was, "Did you receive the Holy Spirit when you believed? Did you take God into your mind only, or did you also embrace him with your heart? Did he get inside you?"

"We've never even heard of that—a Holy Spirit? God within us?"

_{19.3} "How were you baptized, then?" asked Paul. "In John's baptism."

_{19.4} "That explains it," said Paul. "John preached a baptism of radical life-change so that people would be ready to receive the One coming after him, who turned out to be Jesus. If you've been baptized in John's baptism, you're ready now for the real thing, for Jesus."

_{19.5-7} And they were. As soon as they heard of it, they were baptized in the name of the Master Jesus. Paul put his hands on their heads and the Holy Spirit entered them. From that moment on, they were praising God in tongues and talking about God's actions. Altogether there were about twelve people there that day.

_{19.8-10} Paul then went straight to the meeting place. He had the run of the place for three months, doing his best to make the things of the kingdom of God real and convincing to them. But then resistance began to form as some of them began spreading evil rumors through the congregation about the Christian way of life. So Paul left, taking the disciples with him, and set up shop in the school of Tyrannus, holding class there daily. He did this for two years, giving everyone in the province of Asia, Jews as well as Greeks, ample opportunity to hear the Message of the Master.

^a 2 Or after   ^b 5 Or in   ^c 6 Or other languages

NEW INTERNATIONAL VERSION

¹¹God did extraordinary miracles through Paul, ¹²so that even handkerchiefs and aprons that had touched him were taken to the sick, and their illnesses were cured and the evil spirits left them.

¹³Some Jews who went around driving out evil spirits tried to invoke the name of the Lord Jesus over those who were demon-possessed. They would say, "In the name of Jesus, whom Paul preaches, I command you to come out." ¹⁴Seven sons of Sceva, a Jewish chief priest, were doing this. ¹⁵One day the evil spirit answered them, "Jesus I know, and I know about Paul, but who are you?" ¹⁶Then the man who had the evil spirit jumped on them and overpowered them all. He gave them such a beating that they ran out of the house naked and bleeding.

¹⁷When this became known to the Jews and Greeks living in Ephesus, they were all seized with fear, and the name of the Lord Jesus was held in high honor. ¹⁸Many of those who believed now came and openly confessed their evil deeds. ¹⁹A number who had practiced sorcery brought their scrolls together and burned them publicly. When they calculated the value of the scrolls, the total came to fifty thousand drachmas.ᵃ ²⁰In this way the word of the Lord spread widely and grew in power.

²¹After all this had happened, Paul decided to go to Jerusalem, passing through Macedonia and Achaia. "After I have been there," he said, "I must visit Rome also." ²²He sent two of his helpers, Timothy and Erastus, to Macedonia, while he stayed in the province of Asia a little longer.

THE RIOT IN EPHESUS

²³About that time there arose a great disturbance about the Way. ²⁴A silversmith named Demetrius, who made silver shrines of Artemis, brought in no little business for the craftsmen. ²⁵He called them together, along with the workmen in related trades, and said: "Men, you know we receive a good income from this business. ²⁶And you see and hear how this fellow Paul has convinced and led astray large numbers of peo-

THE MESSAGE

WITCHES CAME OUT OF THE WOODWORK

19.11-12 God did powerful things through Paul, things quite out of the ordinary. The word got around and people started taking pieces of clothing—handkerchiefs and scarves and the like—that had touched Paul's skin and then touching the sick with them. The touch did it—they were healed and whole.

19.13-16 Some itinerant Jewish exorcists who happened to be in town at the time tried their hand at what they assumed to be Paul's "game." They pronounced the name of the Master Jesus over victims of evil spirits, saying, "I command you by the Jesus preached by Paul!" The seven sons of a certain Sceva, a Jewish high priest, were trying to do this on a man when the evil spirit talked back: "I know Jesus and I've heard of Paul, but who are you?" Then the possessed man went berserk—jumped the exorcists, beat them up, and tore off their clothes. Naked and bloody, they got away as best they could.

19.17-20 It was soon news all over Ephesus among both Jews and Greeks. The realization spread that God was in and behind this. Curiosity about Paul developed into reverence for the Master Jesus. Many of those who thus believed came out of the closet and made a clean break with their secret sorceries. All kinds of witches and warlocks came out of the woodwork with their books of spells and incantations and made a huge bonfire of them. Someone estimated their worth at fifty thousand silver coins. In such ways it became evident that the Word of the Master was now sovereign and prevailed in Ephesus.

THE GODDESS ARTEMIS

19.21-22 After all this had come to a head, Paul decided it was time to move on to Macedonia and Achaia provinces, and from there to Jerusalem. "Then," he said, "I'm off to Rome. I've got to see Rome!" He sent two of his assistants, Timothy and Erastus, on to Macedonia while he stayed for a while and wrapped things up in Asia.

19.23-26 But before he got away, a huge ruckus occurred over what was now being referred to as "the Way." A certain silversmith, Demetrius, conducted a brisk trade in the manufacture of shrines to the goddess Artemis, employing a number of artisans in his business. He rounded up his workers and others similarly employed and said, "Men, you well know that we have a good thing going here—and you've seen how Paul has barged in and discredited what we're doing by telling people that there's no such thing as a god made with hands. A lot of people

---

ᵃ 19 A drachma was a silver coin worth about a day's wages.

NEW INTERNATIONAL VERSION

ple here in Ephesus and in practically the whole province of Asia. He says that man-made gods are no gods at all. ²⁷There is danger not only that our trade will lose its good name, but also that the temple of the great goddess Artemis will be discredited, and the goddess herself, who is worshiped throughout the province of Asia and the world, will be robbed of her divine majesty."

²⁸When they heard this, they were furious and began shouting: "Great is Artemis of the Ephesians!" ²⁹Soon the whole city was in an uproar. The people seized Gaius and Aristarchus, Paul's traveling companions from Macedonia, and rushed as one man into the theater. ³⁰Paul wanted to appear before the crowd, but the disciples would not let him. ³¹Even some of the officials of the province, friends of Paul, sent him a message begging him not to venture into the theater.

³²The assembly was in confusion: Some were shouting one thing, some another. Most of the people did not even know why they were there. ³³The Jews pushed Alexander to the front, and some of the crowd shouted instructions to him. He motioned for silence in order to make a defense before the people. ³⁴But when they realized he was a Jew, they all shouted in unison for about two hours: "Great is Artemis of the Ephesians!"

³⁵The city clerk quieted the crowd and said: "Men of Ephesus, doesn't all the world know that the city of Ephesus is the guardian of the temple of the great Artemis and of her image, which fell from heaven? ³⁶Therefore, since these facts are undeniable, you ought to be quiet and not do anything rash. ³⁷You have brought these men here, though they have neither robbed temples nor blasphemed our goddess. ³⁸If, then, Demetrius and his fellow craftsmen have a grievance against anybody, the courts are open and there are proconsuls. They can press charges. ³⁹If there is anything further you want to bring up, it must be settled in a legal assembly. ⁴⁰As it is, we are in danger of being charged with rioting because of today's events. In that case we would not be able to account for this commotion, since there is no reason for it." ⁴¹After he had said this, he dismissed the assembly.

THROUGH MACEDONIA AND GREECE

20 When the uproar had ended, Paul sent for the disciples and, after encouraging them, said good-by and set out for Macedonia. ²He traveled through that area, speaking many

THE MESSAGE

are going along with him, not only here in Ephesus but all through Asia province.

19.27 "Not only is our little business in danger of falling apart, but the temple of our famous goddess Artemis will certainly end up a pile of rubble as her glorious reputation fades to nothing. And this is no mere local matter—the whole world worships our Artemis!"

19.28-31 That set them off in a frenzy. They ran into the street yelling, "Great Artemis of the Ephesians! Great Artemis of the Ephesians!" They put the whole city in an uproar, stampeding into the stadium, and grabbing two of Paul's associates on the way, the Macedonians Gaius and Aristarchus. Paul wanted to go in, too, but the disciples wouldn't let him. Prominent religious leaders in the city who had become friendly to Paul concurred: "By no means go near that mob!"

19.32-34 Some were yelling one thing, some another. Most of them had no idea what was going on or why they were there. As the Jews pushed Alexander to the front to try to gain control, different factions clamored to get him on their side. But he brushed them off and quieted the mob with an impressive sweep of his arms. But the moment he opened his mouth and they knew he was a Jew, they shouted him down: "Great Artemis of the Ephesians! Great Artemis of the Ephesians!"—on and on and on, for over two hours.

19.35-37 Finally, the town clerk got the mob quieted down and said, "Fellow citizens, is there anyone anywhere who doesn't know that our dear city Ephesus is protector of glorious Artemis and her sacred stone image that fell straight out of heaven? Since this is beyond contradiction, you had better get hold of yourselves. This is conduct unworthy of Artemis. These men you've dragged in here have done nothing to harm either our temple or our goddess.

19.38-41 "So if Demetrius and his guild of artisans have a complaint, they can take it to court and make all the accusations they want. If anything else is bothering you, bring it to the regularly scheduled town meeting and let it be settled there. There is no excuse for what's happened today. We're putting our city in serious danger. Rome, remember, does not look kindly on rioters." With that, he sent them home.

MACEDONIA AND GREECE

20.1-2 **20** With things back to normal, Paul called the disciples together and encouraged them to keep up the good work in Ephesus. Then, saying his good-byes, he left for Macedonia. Traveling through the country, passing

NEW INTERNATIONAL VERSION

words of encouragement to the people, and finally arrived in Greece, ³where he stayed three months. Because the Jews made a plot against him just as he was about to sail for Syria, he decided to go back through Macedonia. ⁴He was accompanied by Sopater son of Pyrrhus from Berea, Aristarchus and Secundus from Thessalonica, Gaius from Derbe, Timothy also, and Tychicus and Trophimus from the province of Asia. ⁵These men went on ahead and waited for us at Troas. ⁶But we sailed from Philippi after the Feast of Unleavened Bread, and five days later joined the others at Troas, where we stayed seven days.

EUTYCHUS RAISED FROM THE DEAD AT TROAS

⁷On the first day of the week we came together to break bread. Paul spoke to the people and, because he intended to leave the next day, kept on talking until midnight. ⁸There were many lamps in the upstairs room where we were meeting. ⁹Seated in a window was a young man named Eutychus, who was sinking into a deep sleep as Paul talked on and on. When he was sound asleep, he fell to the ground from the third story and was picked up dead. ¹⁰Paul went down, threw himself on the young man and put his arms around him. "Don't be alarmed," he said. "He's alive!" ¹¹Then he went upstairs again and broke bread and ate. After talking until daylight, he left. ¹²The people took the young man home alive and were greatly comforted.

PAUL'S FAREWELL TO THE EPHESIAN ELDERS

¹³We went on ahead to the ship and sailed for Assos, where we were going to take Paul aboard. He had made this arrangement because he was going there on foot. ¹⁴When he met us at Assos, we took him aboard and went on to Mitylene. ¹⁵The next day we set sail from there and arrived off Kios. The day after that we crossed over to Samos, and on the following day arrived at Miletus. ¹⁶Paul had decided to sail past Ephesus to avoid spending time in the province of Asia, for he was in a hurry to reach Jerusalem, if possible, by the day of Pentecost.

¹⁷From Miletus, Paul sent to Ephesus for the elders of the church. ¹⁸When they arrived, he said to them: "You know how I lived the whole time I was with you, from the first day I came into the province of Asia. ¹⁹I served the Lord with great humility and with tears, although I was severely tested by the plots of the Jews. ²⁰You know that I have not hesitated to preach

THE MESSAGE

from one gathering to another, he gave constant encouragement, lifting their spirits and charging them with fresh hope.

20.2-4   Then he came to Greece and stayed on for three months. Just as he was about to sail for Syria, the Jews cooked up a plot against him. So he went the other way, by land back through Macedonia, and gave them the slip. His companions for the journey were Sopater, son of Pyrrhus, from Berea; Aristarchus and Secundus, both Thessalonians; Gaius from Derbe; Timothy; and the two from western Asia, Tychicus and Trophimus.

20.5-6   They went on ahead and waited for us in Troas. Meanwhile, we stayed in Philippi for Passover Week, and then set sail. Within five days we were again in Troas and stayed a week.

20.7-9   We met on Sunday to worship and celebrate the Master's Supper. Paul addressed the congregation. Our plan was to leave first thing in the morning, but Paul talked on, way past midnight. We were meeting in a well-lighted upper room. A young man named Eutychus was sitting in an open window. As Paul went on and on, Eutychus fell sound asleep and toppled out the third-story window. When they picked him up, he was dead.

20.10-12   Paul went down, stretched himself on him, and hugged him hard. "No more crying," he said. "There's life in him yet." Then Paul got up and served the Master's Supper. And went on telling stories of the faith until dawn! On that note, they left—Paul going one way, the congregation another, leading the boy off alive, and full of life themselves.

20.13-16   In the meantime, the rest of us had gone on ahead to the ship and sailed for Assos, where we planned to pick up Paul. Paul wanted to walk there, and so had made these arrangements earlier. Things went according to plan: We met him in Assos, took him on board, and sailed to Mitylene. The next day we put in opposite Chios, Samos a day later, and then Miletus. Paul had decided to bypass Ephesus so that he wouldn't be held up in Asia province. He was in a hurry to get to Jerusalem in time for the Feast of Pentecost, if at all possible.

ON TO JERUSALEM

20.17-21   From Miletus he sent to Ephesus for the leaders of the congregation. When they arrived, he said, "You know that from day one of my arrival in Asia I was with you totally—laying my life on the line, serving the Master no matter what, putting up with no end of scheming by Jews who wanted to do me in. I didn't skimp or trim in any way. Every truth and encourage-

NEW INTERNATIONAL VERSION

anything that would be helpful to you but have taught you publicly and from house to house. ²¹I have declared to both Jews and Greeks that they must turn to God in repentance and have faith in our Lord Jesus.

²²"And now, compelled by the Spirit, I am going to Jerusalem, not knowing what will happen to me there. ²³I only know that in every city the Holy Spirit warns me that prison and hardships are facing me. ²⁴However, I consider my life worth nothing to me, if only I may finish the race and complete the task the Lord Jesus has given me—the task of testifying to the gospel of God's grace.

²⁵"Now I know that none of you among whom I have gone about preaching the kingdom will ever see me again. ²⁶Therefore, I declare to you today that I am innocent of the blood of all men. ²⁷For I have not hesitated to proclaim to you the whole will of God. ²⁸Keep watch over yourselves and all the flock of which the Holy Spirit has made you overseers.ᵃ Be shepherds of the church of God,ᵇ which he bought with his own blood. ²⁹I know that after I leave, savage wolves will come in among you and will not spare the flock. ³⁰Even from your own number men will arise and distort the truth in order to draw away disciples after them. ³¹So be on your guard! Remember that for three years I never stopped warning each of you night and day with tears.

³²"Now I commit you to God and to the word of his grace, which can build you up and give you an inheritance among all those who are sanctified. ³³I have not coveted anyone's silver or gold or clothing. ³⁴You yourselves know that these hands of mine have supplied my own needs and the needs of my companions. ³⁵In everything I did, I showed you that by this kind of hard work we must help the weak, remembering the words the Lord Jesus himself said: 'It is more blessed to give than to receive.' "

³⁶When he had said this, he knelt down with all of them and prayed. ³⁷They all wept as they embraced him and kissed him. ³⁸What grieved them most was his statement that they would never see his face again. Then they accompanied him to the ship.

ᵃ 28 Traditionally *bishops*   ᵇ 28 Many manuscripts *of the Lord*

THE MESSAGE

ment that could have made a difference to you, you got. I taught you out in public and I taught you in your homes, urging Jews and Greeks alike to a radical life-change before God and an equally radical trust in our Master Jesus.

20.22-24 "But there is another urgency before me now. I feel compelled to go to Jerusalem. I'm completely in the dark about what will happen when I get there. I do know that it won't be any picnic, for the Holy Spirit has let me know repeatedly and clearly that there are hard times and imprisonment ahead. But that matters little. What matters most to me is to finish what God started: the job the Master Jesus gave me of letting everyone I meet know all about this incredibly extravagant generosity of God.

20.25-27 "And so this is good-bye. You're not going to see me again, nor I you, you whom I have gone among for so long proclaiming the news of God's inaugurated kingdom. I've done my best for you, given you my all, held back nothing of God's will for you.

20.28 "Now it's up to you. Be on your toes—both for yourselves and your congregation of sheep. The Holy Spirit has put you in charge of these people—God's people they are—to guard and protect them. God himself thought they were worth dying for.

20.29-31 "I know that as soon as I'm gone, vicious wolves are going to show up and rip into this flock, men from your very own ranks twisting words so as to seduce disciples into following them instead of Jesus. So stay awake and keep up your guard. Remember those three years I kept at it with you, never letting up, pouring my heart out with you, one after another.

20.32 "Now I'm turning you over to God, our marvelous God whose gracious Word can make you into what he wants you to be and give you everything you could possibly need in this community of holy friends.

20.33-35 "I've never, as you so well know, had any taste for wealth or fashion. With these bare hands I took care of my own basic needs and those who worked with me. In everything I've done, I have demonstrated to you how necessary it is to work on behalf of the weak and not exploit them. You'll not likely go wrong here if you keep remembering that our Master said, 'You're far happier giving than getting.' "

20.36-38 Then Paul went down on his knees, all of them kneeling with him, and prayed. And then a river of tears. Much clinging to Paul, not wanting to let him go. They knew they would never see him again—he had told them quite plainly. The pain cut deep. Then, bravely, they walked him down to the ship.

NEW INTERNATIONAL VERSION

ON TO JERUSALEM

21 After we had torn ourselves away from them, we put out to sea and sailed straight to Cos. The next day we went to Rhodes and from there to Patara. ²We found a ship crossing over to Phoenicia, went on board and set sail. ³After sighting Cyprus and passing to the south of it, we sailed on to Syria. We landed at Tyre, where our ship was to unload its cargo. ⁴Finding the disciples there, we stayed with them seven days. Through the Spirit they urged Paul not to go on to Jerusalem. ⁵But when our time was up, we left and continued on our way. All the disciples and their wives and children accompanied us out of the city, and there on the beach we knelt to pray. ⁶After saying good-by to each other, we went aboard the ship, and they returned home.

⁷We continued our voyage from Tyre and landed at Ptolemais, where we greeted the brothers and stayed with them for a day. ⁸Leaving the next day, we reached Caesarea and stayed at the house of Philip the evangelist, one of the Seven. ⁹He had four unmarried daughters who prophesied.

¹⁰After we had been there a number of days, a prophet named Agabus came down from Judea. ¹¹Coming over to us, he took Paul's belt, tied his own hands and feet with it and said, "The Holy Spirit says, 'In this way the Jews of Jerusalem will bind the owner of this belt and will hand him over to the Gentiles.' "

¹²When we heard this, we and the people there pleaded with Paul not to go up to Jerusalem. ¹³Then Paul answered, "Why are you weeping and breaking my heart? I am ready not only to be bound, but also to die in Jerusalem for the name of the Lord Jesus." ¹⁴When he would not be dissuaded, we gave up and said, "The Lord's will be done."

¹⁵After this, we got ready and went up to Jerusalem. ¹⁶Some of the disciples from Caesarea accompanied us and brought us to the home of Mnason, where we were to stay. He was a man from Cyprus and one of the early disciples.

THE MESSAGE

TYRE AND CAESAREA

21 And so, with the tearful good-byes behind us, we were on our way. We made a straight run to Cos, the next day reached Rhodes, and then Patara. There we found a ship going direct to Phoenicia, got on board, and set sail. Cyprus came into view on our left, but was soon out of sight as we kept on course for Syria, and eventually docked in the port of Tyre. While the cargo was being unloaded, we looked up the local disciples and stayed with them seven days. Their message to Paul, from insight given by the Spirit, was "Don't go to Jerusalem."

21.5-6 When our time was up, they escorted us out of the city to the docks. Everyone came along—men, women, children. They made a farewell party of the occasion! We all kneeled together on the beach and prayed. Then, after another round of saying good-bye, we climbed on board the ship while they drifted back to their homes.

21.7-9 A short run from Tyre to Ptolemais completed the voyage. We greeted our Christian friends there and stayed with them a day. In the morning we went on to Caesarea and stayed with Philip the Evangelist, one of "the Seven." Philip had four virgin daughters who prophesied.

21.10-11 After several days of visiting, a prophet from Judea by the name of Agabus came down to see us. He went right up to Paul, took Paul's belt, and, in a dramatic gesture, tied himself up, hands and feet. He said, "This is what the Holy Spirit says: The Jews in Jerusalem are going to tie up the man who owns this belt just like this and hand him over to godless unbelievers."

21.12-13 When we heard that, we and everyone there that day begged Paul not to be stubborn and persist in going to Jerusalem. But Paul wouldn't budge: "Why all this hysteria? Why do you insist on making a scene and making it even harder for me? You're looking at this backwards. The issue in Jerusalem is not what they do to me, whether arrest or murder, but what the Master Jesus does through my obedience. Can't you see that?"

21.14 We saw that we weren't making even a dent in his resolve, and gave up. "It's in God's hands now," we said. "Master, you handle it."

21.15-16 It wasn't long before we had our luggage together and were on our way to Jerusalem. Some of the disciples from Caesarea went with us and took us to the home of Mnason, who received us warmly as his guests. A native of Cyprus, he had been among the earliest disciples.

NEW INTERNATIONAL VERSION

PAUL'S ARRIVAL AT JERUSALEM

¹⁷When we arrived at Jerusalem, the brothers received us warmly. ¹⁸The next day Paul and the rest of us went to see James, and all the elders were present. ¹⁹Paul greeted them and reported in detail what God had done among the Gentiles through his ministry.

²⁰When they heard this, they praised God. Then they said to Paul: "You see, brother, how many thousands of Jews have believed, and all of them are zealous for the law. ²¹They have been informed that you teach all the Jews who live among the Gentiles to turn away from Moses, telling them not to circumcise their children or live according to our customs. ²²What shall we do? They will certainly hear that you have come, ²³so do what we tell you. There are four men with us who have made a vow. ²⁴Take these men, join in their purification rites and pay their expenses, so that they can have their heads shaved. Then everybody will know there is no truth in these reports about you, but that you yourself are living in obedience to the law. ²⁵As for the Gentile believers, we have written to them our decision that they should abstain from food sacrificed to idols, from blood, from the meat of strangled animals and from sexual immorality."

²⁶The next day Paul took the men and purified himself along with them. Then he went to the temple to give notice of the date when the days of purification would end and the offering would be made for each of them.

PAUL ARRESTED

²⁷When the seven days were nearly over, some Jews from the province of Asia saw Paul at the temple. They stirred up the whole crowd and seized him, ²⁸shouting, "Men of Israel, help us! This is the man who teaches all men everywhere against our people and our law and this place. And besides, he has brought Greeks into the temple area and defiled this holy place." ²⁹(They

THE MESSAGE

JERUSALEM

21.17-19 In Jerusalem, our friends, glad to see us, received us with open arms. The first thing next morning, we took Paul to see James. All the church leaders were there. After a time of greeting and small talk, Paul told the story, detail by detail, of what God had done among the Gentiles through his ministry. They listened with delight and gave God the glory.

21.20-21 They had a story to tell, too: "And just look at what's been happening here—thousands upon thousands of God-fearing Jews have become believers in Jesus! But there's also a problem because they are more zealous than ever in observing the laws of Moses. They've been told that you advise believing Jews who live surrounded by Gentiles to go light on Moses, telling them that they don't need to circumcise their children or keep up the old traditions. This isn't sitting at all well with them.

21.22-24 "We're worried about what will happen when they discover you're in town. There's bound to be trouble. So here is what we want you to do: There are four men from our company who have taken a vow involving ritual purification, but have no money to pay the expenses. Join these men in their vows and pay their expenses. Then it will become obvious to everyone that there is nothing to the rumors going around about you and that you are in fact scrupulous in your reverence for the laws of Moses.

21.25 "In asking you to do this, we're not going back on our agreement regarding Gentiles who have become believers. We continue to hold fast to what we wrote in that letter, namely, to be careful not to get involved in activities connected with idols; to avoid serving food offensive to Jewish Christians; to guard the morality of sex and marriage."

21.26 So Paul did it—took the men, joined them in their vows, and paid their way. The next day he went to the Temple to make it official and stay there until the proper sacrifices had been offered and completed for each of them.

PAUL UNDER ARREST

21.27-29 When the seven days of their purification were nearly up, some Jews from around Ephesus spotted him in the Temple. At once they turned the place upside-down. They grabbed Paul and started yelling at the top of their lungs, "Help! You Israelites, help! This is the man who is going all over the world telling lies against us and our religion and this place. He's even brought Greeks in here and defiled this holy place." (What had happened was that they had seen

NEW INTERNATIONAL VERSION

had previously seen Trophimus the Ephesian in the city with Paul and assumed that Paul had brought him into the temple area.)

³⁰The whole city was aroused, and the people came running from all directions. Seizing Paul, they dragged him from the temple, and immediately the gates were shut. ³¹While they were trying to kill him, news reached the commander of the Roman troops that the whole city of Jerusalem was in an uproar. ³²He at once took some officers and soldiers and ran down to the crowd. When the rioters saw the commander and his soldiers, they stopped beating Paul.

³³The commander came up and arrested him and ordered him to be bound with two chains. Then he asked who he was and what he had done. ³⁴Some in the crowd shouted one thing and some another, and since the commander could not get at the truth because of the uproar, he ordered that Paul be taken into the barracks. ³⁵When Paul reached the steps, the violence of the mob was so great he had to be carried by the soldiers. ³⁶The crowd that followed kept shouting, "Away with him!"

PAUL SPEAKS TO THE CROWD

³⁷As the soldiers were about to take Paul into the barracks, he asked the commander, "May I say something to you?"

"Do you speak Greek?" he replied. ³⁸"Aren't you the Egyptian who started a revolt and led four thousand terrorists out into the desert some time ago?"

³⁹Paul answered, "I am a Jew, from Tarsus in Cilicia, a citizen of no ordinary city. Please let me speak to the people."

⁴⁰Having received the commander's permission, Paul stood on the steps and motioned to the crowd. When they were all silent, he said to them in Aramaic[a]:

22 ¹"Brothers and fathers, listen now to my defense."

²When they heard him speak to them in Aramaic, they became very quiet.

Then Paul said: ³"I am a Jew, born in Tarsus of Cilicia, but brought up in this city. Under Gamaliel I was thoroughly trained in the law of our fathers and was just as zealous for God as any of

[a] 40 Or possibly *Hebrew*; also in 22:2

THE MESSAGE

Paul and Trophimus, the Ephesian Greek, walking together in the city and had just assumed that he had also taken him to the Temple and shown him around.)

21.30 Soon the whole city was in an uproar, people running from everywhere to the Temple to get in on the action. They grabbed Paul, dragged him outside, and locked the Temple gates so he couldn't get back in and gain sanctuary.

21.31-32 As they were trying to kill him, word came to the captain of the guard, "A riot! The whole city's boiling over!" He acted swiftly. His soldiers and centurions ran to the scene at once. As soon as the mob saw the captain and his soldiers, they quit beating Paul.

21.33-36 The captain came up and put Paul under arrest. He first ordered him handcuffed, and then asked who he was and what he had done. All he got from the crowd were shouts, one yelling this, another that. It was impossible to tell one word from another in the mob hysteria, so the captain ordered Paul taken to the military barracks. But when they got to the Temple steps, the mob became so violent that the soldiers had to carry Paul. As they carried him away, the crowd followed, shouting, "Kill him! Kill him!"

21.37-38 When they got to the barracks and were about to go in, Paul said to the captain, "Can I say something to you?"

He answered, "Oh, I didn't know you spoke Greek. I thought you were the Egyptian who not long ago started a riot here, and then hid out in the desert with his four thousand thugs."

21.39 Paul said, "No, I'm a Jew, born in Tarsus. And I'm a citizen still of that influential city. I have a simple request: Let me speak to the crowd."

PAUL TELLS HIS STORY

21.40 Standing on the barracks steps, Paul turned and held his arms up. A hush fell over the crowd as Paul began to speak. He spoke in Hebrew.

22 ¹"My dear brothers and fathers, listen carefully to what I have to say before you jump to conclusions about me." When they heard him speaking Hebrew, they grew even quieter. No one wanted to miss a word of this.

22.1-2

22.2-3 He continued, "I am a good Jew, born in Tarsus in the province of Cilicia, but educated here in Jerusalem under the exacting eye of Rabbi Gamaliel, thoroughly instructed in our religious traditions. And I've always been passionately on God's side, just as you are right now.

NEW INTERNATIONAL VERSION

you are today. [4]I persecuted the followers of this Way to their death, arresting both men and women and throwing them into prison, [5]as also the high priest and all the Council can testify. I even obtained letters from them to their brothers in Damascus, and went there to bring these people as prisoners to Jerusalem to be punished.

[6]"About noon as I came near Damascus, suddenly a bright light from heaven flashed around me. [7]I fell to the ground and heard a voice say to me, 'Saul! Saul! Why do you persecute me?'

[8]"'Who are you, Lord?' I asked.

"'I am Jesus of Nazareth, whom you are persecuting,' he replied. [9]My companions saw the light, but they did not understand the voice of him who was speaking to me.

[10]"'What shall I do, Lord?' I asked.

"'Get up,' the Lord said, 'and go into Damascus. There you will be told all that you have been assigned to do.' [11]My companions led me by the hand into Damascus, because the brilliance of the light had blinded me.

[12]"A man named Ananias came to see me. He was a devout observer of the law and highly respected by all the Jews living there. [13]He stood beside me and said, 'Brother Saul, receive your sight!' And at that very moment I was able to see him.

[14]"Then he said: 'The God of our fathers has chosen you to know his will and to see the Righteous One and to hear words from his mouth. [15]You will be his witness to all men of what you have seen and heard. [16]And now what are you waiting for? Get up, be baptized and wash your sins away, calling on his name.'

[17]"When I returned to Jerusalem and was praying at the temple, I fell into a trance [18]and saw the Lord speaking. 'Quick!' he said to me. 'Leave Jerusalem immediately, because they will not accept your testimony about me.'

[19]"'Lord,' I replied, 'these men know that I went from one synagogue to another to imprison and beat those who believe in you. [20]And when the blood of your martyr[a] Stephen was shed, I stood there giving my approval and guarding the clothes of those who were killing him.'

[a] 20 Or witness

THE MESSAGE

22.4-5 "I went after anyone connected with this 'Way,' went at them hammer and tongs, ready to kill for God. I rounded up men and women right and left and had them thrown in prison. You can ask the Chief Priest or anyone in the High Council to verify this; they all knew me well. Then I went off to our brothers in Damascus, armed with official documents authorizing me to hunt down the Christians there, arrest them, and bring them back to Jerusalem for sentencing.

22.6-7 "As I arrived on the outskirts of Damascus about noon, a blinding light blazed out of the skies and I fell to the ground, dazed. I heard a voice: 'Saul, Saul, why are you out to get me?'

22.8-9 "'Who are you, Master?' I asked.

"He said, 'I am Jesus the Nazarene, the One you're hunting down.' My companions saw the light, but they didn't hear the conversation.

22.10 "Then I said, 'What do I do now, Master?'

22.10-11 "He said, 'Get to your feet and enter Damascus. There you'll be told everything that's been set out for you to do.' And so we entered Damascus, but nothing like the entrance I had planned—I was blind as a bat and my companions had to lead me in by the hand.

22.12-13 "And that's when I met Ananias, a man with a sterling reputation in observing our laws—the Jewish community in Damascus is unanimous on that score. He came and put his arm on my shoulder. 'Look up,' he said. I looked, and found myself looking right into his eyes—I could see again!

22.14-16 "Then he said, 'The God of our ancestors has handpicked you to be briefed on his plan of action. You've actually seen the Righteous Innocent and heard him speak. You are to be a key witness to everyone you meet of what you've seen and heard. So what are you waiting for? Get up and get yourself baptized, scrubbed clean of those sins and personally acquainted with God.'

22.17-18 "Well, it happened just as Ananias said. After I was back in Jerusalem and praying one day in the Temple, lost in the presence of God, I saw him, saw God's Righteous Innocent, and heard him say to me, 'Hurry up! Get out of here as quickly as you can. None of the Jews here in Jerusalem are going to accept what you say about me.'

22.19-20 "At first I objected: 'Who has better credentials? They all know how obsessed I was with hunting out those who believed in you, beating them up in the meeting places and throwing them in jail. And when your witness Stephen was murdered, I was right there, holding the coats of the murderers and cheering them on.

NEW INTERNATIONAL VERSION

21"Then the Lord said to me, 'Go; I will send you far away to the Gentiles.' "

PAUL THE ROMAN CITIZEN

22The crowd listened to Paul until he said this. Then they raised their voices and shouted, "Rid the earth of him! He's not fit to live!"

23As they were shouting and throwing off their cloaks and flinging dust into the air, 24the commander ordered Paul to be taken into the barracks. He directed that he be flogged and questioned in order to find out why the people were shouting at him like this. 25As they stretched him out to flog him, Paul said to the centurion standing there, "Is it legal for you to flog a Roman citizen who hasn't even been found guilty?"

26When the centurion heard this, he went to the commander and reported it. "What are you going to do?" he asked. "This man is a Roman citizen."

27The commander went to Paul and asked, "Tell me, are you a Roman citizen?"

"Yes, I am," he answered.

28Then the commander said, "I had to pay a big price for my citizenship."

"But I was born a citizen," Paul replied.

29Those who were about to question him withdrew immediately. The commander himself was alarmed when he realized that he had put Paul, a Roman citizen, in chains.

BEFORE THE SANHEDRIN

30The next day, since the commander wanted to find out exactly why Paul was being accused by the Jews, he released him and ordered the chief priests and all the Sanhedrin to assemble. Then he brought Paul and had him stand before them.

23 Paul looked straight at the Sanhedrin and said, "My brothers, I have fulfilled my duty to God in all good conscience to this day." 2At this the high priest Ananias ordered those standing near Paul to strike him on the mouth. 3Then Paul said to him, "God will strike you, you whitewashed wall! You sit there to judge me according to the law, yet you yourself violate the law by commanding that I be struck!"

4Those who were standing near Paul said, "You dare to insult God's high priest?"

THE MESSAGE

And now they see me totally converted. What better qualification could I have?'

22.21 "But he said, 'Don't argue. Go. I'm sending you on a long journey to outsider Gentiles.' "

A ROMAN CITIZEN

22.22-25 The people in the crowd had listened attentively up to this point, but now they broke loose, shouting out, "Kill him! He's an insect! Stomp on him!" They shook their fists. They filled the air with curses. That's when the captain intervened and ordered Paul taken into the barracks. By now the captain was thoroughly exasperated. He decided to interrogate Paul under torture in order to get to the bottom of this, to find out what he had done that provoked this outraged violence. As they spread-eagled him with thongs, getting him ready for the whip, Paul said to the centurion standing there, "Is this legal: torturing a Roman citizen without a fair trial?"

22.26 When the centurion heard that, he went directly to the captain. "Do you realize what you've done? This man is a Roman citizen!"

22.27 The captain came back and took charge. "Is what I hear right? You're a Roman citizen?"

Paul said, "I certainly am."

22.28 The captain was impressed. "I paid a huge sum for my citizenship. How much did it cost you?"

"Nothing," said Paul. "It cost me nothing. I was free from the day of my birth."

22.29 That put a stop to the interrogation. And it put the fear of God into the captain. He had put a Roman citizen in chains and come within a whisker of putting him under torture!

22.30 The next day, determined to get to the root of the trouble and know for sure what was behind the Jewish accusation, the captain released Paul and ordered a meeting of the high priests and the High Council to see what they could make of it. Paul was led in and took his place before them.

BEFORE THE HIGH COUNCIL

23.1-3 **23** Paul surveyed the members of the council with a steady gaze, and then said his piece: "Friends, I've lived with a clear conscience before God all my life, up to this very moment." That set the Chief Priest Ananias off. He ordered his aides to slap Paul in the face. Paul shot back, "God will slap you down! What a fake you are! You sit there and judge me by the Law and then break the Law by ordering me slapped around!"

23.4 The aides were scandalized: "How dare you talk to God's Chief Priest like that!"

NEW INTERNATIONAL VERSION

⁵Paul replied, "Brothers, I did not realize that he was the high priest; for it is written: 'Do not speak evil about the ruler of your people.'ᵃ"

⁶Then Paul, knowing that some of them were Sadducees and the others Pharisees, called out in the Sanhedrin, "My brothers, I am a Pharisee, the son of a Pharisee. I stand on trial because of my hope in the resurrection of the dead." ⁷When he said this, a dispute broke out between the Pharisees and the Sadducees, and the assembly was divided. ⁸(The Sadducees say that there is no resurrection, and that there are neither angels nor spirits, but the Pharisees acknowledge them all.)

⁹There was a great uproar, and some of the teachers of the law who were Pharisees stood up and argued vigorously. "We find nothing wrong with this man," they said. "What if a spirit or an angel has spoken to him?" ¹⁰The dispute became so violent that the commander was afraid Paul would be torn to pieces by them. He ordered the troops to go down and take him away from them by force and bring him into the barracks.

¹¹The following night the Lord stood near Paul and said, "Take courage! As you have testified about me in Jerusalem, so you must also testify in Rome."

THE PLOT TO KILL PAUL

¹²The next morning the Jews formed a conspiracy and bound themselves with an oath not to eat or drink until they had killed Paul. ¹³More than forty men were involved in this plot. ¹⁴They went to the chief priests and elders and said, "We have taken a solemn oath not to eat anything until we have killed Paul. ¹⁵Now then, you and the Sanhedrin petition the commander to bring him before you on the pretext of wanting more accurate information about his case. We are ready to kill him before he gets here."

¹⁶But when the son of Paul's sister heard of this plot, he went into the barracks and told Paul.

¹⁷Then Paul called one of the centurions and said, "Take this young man to the commander; he has something to tell him." ¹⁸So he took him to the commander.

ᵃ 5 Exodus 22:28

THE MESSAGE

23.5   Paul acted surprised. "How was I to know he was Chief Priest? He doesn't act like a Chief Priest. You're right, the Scripture does say, 'Don't speak abusively to a ruler of the people.' Sorry."

23.6   Paul, knowing some of the council was made up of Sadducees and others of Pharisees and how they hated each other, decided to exploit their antagonism: "Friends, I am a stalwart Pharisee from a long line of Pharisees. It's because of my Pharisee convictions—the hope and resurrection of the dead—that I've been hauled into this court."

23.7-9   The moment he said this, the council split right down the middle, Pharisees and Sadducees going at each other in heated argument. Sadducees have nothing to do with a resurrection or angels or even a spirit. If they can't see it, they don't believe it. Pharisees believe it all. And so a huge and noisy quarrel broke out. Then some of the religion scholars on the Pharisee side shouted down the others: "We don't find anything wrong with this man! And what if a spirit has spoken to him? Or maybe an angel? What if it turns out we're fighting against God?"

23.10   That was fuel on the fire. The quarrel flamed up and became so violent the captain was afraid they would tear Paul apart, limb from limb. He ordered the soldiers to get him out of there and escort him back to the safety of the barracks.

A PLOT AGAINST PAUL

23.11   That night the Master appeared to Paul: "It's going to be all right. Everything is going to turn out for the best. You've been a good witness for me here in Jerusalem. Now you're going to be my witness in Rome!"

23.12-15   Next day the Jews worked up a plot against Paul. They took a solemn oath that they would neither eat nor drink until they had killed him. Over forty of them ritually bound themselves to this murder pact and presented themselves to the high priests and religious leaders. "We've bound ourselves by a solemn oath to eat nothing until we have killed Paul. But we need your help. Send a request from the council to the captain to bring Paul back so that you can investigate the charges in more detail. We'll do the rest. Before he gets anywhere near you, we'll have killed him. You won't be involved."

23.16-17   Paul's nephew, his sister's son, overheard them plotting the ambush. He went immediately to the barracks and told Paul. Paul called over one of the centurions and said, "Take this young man to the captain. He has something important to tell him."

NEW INTERNATIONAL VERSION

The centurion said, "Paul, the prisoner, sent for me and asked me to bring this young man to you because he has something to tell you."

¹⁹The commander took the young man by the hand, drew him aside and asked, "What is it you want to tell me?"

²⁰He said: "The Jews have agreed to ask you to bring Paul before the Sanhedrin tomorrow on the pretext of wanting more accurate information about him. ²¹Don't give in to them, because more than forty of them are waiting in ambush for him. They have taken an oath not to eat or drink until they have killed him. They are ready now, waiting for your consent to their request."

²²The commander dismissed the young man and cautioned him, "Don't tell anyone that you have reported this to me."

PAUL TRANSFERRED TO CAESAREA

²³Then he called two of his centurions and ordered them, "Get ready a detachment of two hundred soldiers, seventy horsemen and two hundred spearmen*ᵃ* to go to Caesarea at nine tonight. ²⁴Provide mounts for Paul so that he may be taken safely to Governor Felix."

²⁵He wrote a letter as follows:

²⁶Claudius Lysias,

To His Excellency, Governor Felix:

Greetings.

²⁷This man was seized by the Jews and they were about to kill him, but I came with my troops and rescued him, for I had learned that he is a Roman citizen. ²⁸I wanted to know why they were accusing him, so I brought him to their Sanhedrin. ²⁹I found that the accusation had to do with questions about their law, but there was no charge against him that deserved death or imprisonment. ³⁰When I was informed of a plot to be carried out against the man, I sent him to you at once. I also ordered his accusers to present to you their case against him.

³¹So the soldiers, carrying out their orders, took Paul with them during the night and brought him as far as Antipatris. ³²The next day they let the cavalry go on with him, while they returned to the barracks. ³³When the cavalry ar-

THE MESSAGE

²³·¹⁸ The centurion brought him to the captain and said, "The prisoner Paul asked me to bring this young man to you. He said he has something urgent to tell you."

²³·¹⁹ The captain took him by the arm and led him aside privately. "What is it? What do you have to tell me?"

²³·²⁰⁻²¹ Paul's nephew said, "The Jews have worked up a plot against Paul. They're going to ask you to bring Paul to the council first thing in the morning on the pretext that they want to investigate the charges against him in more detail. But it's a trick to get him out of your safekeeping so they can murder him. Right now there are more than forty men lying in ambush for him. They've all taken a vow to neither eat nor drink until they've killed him. The ambush is set—all they're waiting for is for you to send him over."

²³·²² The captain dismissed the nephew with a warning: "Don't breathe a word of this to a soul."

²³·²³⁻²⁴ The captain called up two centurions. "Get two hundred soldiers ready to go immediately to Caesarea. Also seventy cavalry and two hundred light infantry. I want them ready to march by nine o'clock tonight. And you'll need a couple of mules for Paul and his gear. We're going to present this man safe and sound to Governor Felix."

²³·²⁵⁻³⁰ Then he wrote this letter:

From Claudius Lysias, to the Most Honorable Governor Felix:
Greetings!
I rescued this man from a Jewish mob. They had seized him and were about to kill him when I learned that he was a Roman citizen. So I sent in my soldiers. Wanting to know what he had done wrong, I had him brought before their council. It turned out to be a squabble turned vicious over some of their religious differences, but nothing remotely criminal.
The next thing I knew, they had cooked up a plot to murder him. I decided that for his own safety I'd better get him out of here in a hurry. So I'm sending him to you. I'm informing his accusers that he's now under your jurisdiction.

²³·³¹⁻³³ The soldiers, following orders, took Paul that same night to safety in Antipatris. In the morning the soldiers returned to their barracks in Jerusalem, sending Paul on to Caesarea under guard of the cavalry. The cavalry entered

---

ᵃ 23 The meaning of the Greek for this word is uncertain.

NEW INTERNATIONAL VERSION

rived in Caesarea, they delivered the letter to the governor and handed Paul over to him. [34]The governor read the letter and asked what province he was from. Learning that he was from Cilicia, [35]he said, "I will hear your case when your accusers get here." Then he ordered that Paul be kept under guard in Herod's palace.

THE TRIAL BEFORE FELIX

24 Five days later the high priest Ananias went down to Caesarea with some of the elders and a lawyer named Tertullus, and they brought their charges against Paul before the governor. [2]When Paul was called in, Tertullus presented his case before Felix: "We have enjoyed a long period of peace under you, and your foresight has brought about reforms in this nation. [3]Everywhere and in every way, most excellent Felix, we acknowledge this with profound gratitude. [4]But in order not to weary you further, I would request that you be kind enough to hear us briefly.

[5]"We have found this man to be a troublemaker, stirring up riots among the Jews all over the world. He is a ringleader of the Nazarene sect [6]and even tried to desecrate the temple; so we seized him. [8]By[a] examining him yourself you will be able to learn the truth about all these charges we are bringing against him."

[9]The Jews joined in the accusation, asserting that these things were true.

[10]When the governor motioned for him to speak, Paul replied: "I know that for a number of years you have been a judge over this nation; so I gladly make my defense. [11]You can easily verify that no more than twelve days ago I went up to Jerusalem to worship. [12]My accusers did not find me arguing with anyone at the temple, or stirring up a crowd in the synagogues or anywhere else in the city. [13]And they cannot prove to you the charges they are now making against me. [14]However, I admit that I worship the God of our fathers as a follower of the Way, which they call a sect. I believe everything that agrees with the Law and that is written in the Prophets, [15]and I have the same hope in God as these men, that there will be a resurrection of both the righ-

THE MESSAGE

Caesarea and handed Paul and the letter over to the governor.

23.34-35 After reading the letter, the governor asked Paul what province he came from and was told "Cilicia." Then he said, "I'll take up your case when your accusers show up." He ordered him locked up for the meantime in King Herod's official quarters.

PAUL STATES HIS DEFENSE

24.1-4 **24** Within five days, the Chief Priest Ananias arrived with a contingent of leaders, along with Tertullus, a trial lawyer. They presented the governor with their case against Paul. When Paul was called before the court, Tertullus spoke for the prosecution: "Most Honorable Felix, we are most grateful in all times and places for your wise and gentle rule. We are much aware that it is because of you and you alone that we enjoy all this peace and gain daily profit from your reforms. I'm not going to tire you out with a long speech. I beg your kind indulgence in listening to me. I'll be quite brief.

24.5-8 "We've found this man time and again disturbing the peace, stirring up riots against Jews all over the world, the ringleader of a seditious sect called Nazarenes. He's a real bad apple, I must say. We caught him trying to defile our holy Temple and arrested him. You'll be able to verify all these accusations when you examine him yourself."

24.9 The Jews joined in: "Hear, hear! That's right!"

24.10-13 The governor motioned to Paul that it was now his turn. Paul said, "I count myself fortunate to be defending myself before you, Governor, knowing how fair-minded you've been in judging us all these years. I've been back in the country only twelve days—you can check out these dates easily enough. I came with the express purpose of worshiping in Jerusalem on Pentecost, and I've been minding my own business the whole time. Nobody can say they saw me arguing in the Temple or working up a crowd in the streets. Not one of their charges can be backed up with evidence or witnesses.

24.14-15 "But I do freely admit this: In regard to the Way, which they malign as a dead-end street, I serve and worship the very same God served and worshiped by all our ancestors and embrace everything written in all our Scriptures. And I admit to living in hopeful anticipation that God will raise the dead, both the good and the bad. If that's my crime, my accusers are just as guilty as I am.

---

[a] 6-8 Some manuscripts *him and wanted to judge him according to our law.* [7]*But the commander, Lysias, came and with the use of much force snatched him from our hands* [8]*and ordered his accusers to come before you. By*

NEW INTERNATIONAL VERSION

teous and the wicked. ¹⁶So I strive always to keep my conscience clear before God and man.

¹⁷"After an absence of several years, I came to Jerusalem to bring my people gifts for the poor and to present offerings. ¹⁸I was ceremonially clean when they found me in the temple courts doing this. There was no crowd with me, nor was I involved in any disturbance. ¹⁹But there are some Jews from the province of Asia, who ought to be here before you and bring charges if they have anything against me. ²⁰Or these who are here should state what crime they found in me when I stood before the Sanhedrin— ²¹unless it was this one thing I shouted as I stood in their presence: 'It is concerning the resurrection of the dead that I am on trial before you today.' "

²²Then Felix, who was well acquainted with the Way, adjourned the proceedings. "When Lysias the commander comes," he said, "I will decide your case." ²³He ordered the centurion to keep Paul under guard but to give him some freedom and permit his friends to take care of his needs.

²⁴Several days later Felix came with his wife Drusilla, who was a Jewess. He sent for Paul and listened to him as he spoke about faith in Christ Jesus. ²⁵As Paul discoursed on righteousness, self-control and the judgment to come, Felix was afraid and said, "That's enough for now! You may leave. When I find it convenient, I will send for you." ²⁶At the same time he was hoping that Paul would offer him a bribe, so he sent for him frequently and talked with him.

²⁷When two years had passed, Felix was succeeded by Porcius Festus, but because Felix wanted to grant a favor to the Jews, he left Paul in prison.

THE TRIAL BEFORE FESTUS

25 Three days after arriving in the province, Festus went up from Caesarea to Jerusalem, ²where the chief priests and Jewish leaders appeared before him and presented the charges against Paul. ³They urgently requested Festus, as a favor to them, to have Paul transferred to Jerusalem, for they were preparing an ambush to

THE MESSAGE

24.16-19 "Believe me, I do my level best to keep a clear conscience before God and my neighbors in everything I do. I've been out of the country for a number of years and now I'm back. While I was away, I took up a collection for the poor and brought that with me, along with offerings for the Temple. It was while making those offerings that they found me quietly at my prayers in the Temple. There was no crowd, there was no disturbance. It was some Jews from around Ephesus who started all this trouble. And you'll notice they're not here today. They're cowards, too cowardly to accuse me in front of you.

24.20-21 "So ask these others what crime they've caught me in. Don't let them hide behind this smooth-talking Tertullus. The only thing they have on me is that one sentence I shouted out in the council: 'It's because I believe in the resurrection that I've been hauled into this court!' Does that sound to you like grounds for a criminal case?"

24.22-23 Felix shilly-shallied. He knew far more about the Way than he let on, and could have settled the case then and there. But uncertain of his best move politically, he played for time. "When Captain Lysias comes down, I'll decide your case." He gave orders to the centurion to keep Paul in custody, but to more or less give him the run of the place and not prevent his friends from helping him.

24.24-26 A few days later Felix and his wife, Drusilla, who was Jewish, sent for Paul and listened to him talk about a life of believing in Jesus Christ. As Paul continued to insist on right relations with God and his people, about a life of moral discipline and the coming Judgment, Felix felt things getting a little too close for comfort and dismissed him. "That's enough for today. I'll call you back when it's convenient." At the same time he was secretly hoping that Paul would offer him a substantial bribe. These conversations were repeated frequently.

24.27 After two years of this, Felix was replaced by Porcius Festus. Still playing up to the Jews and ignoring justice, Felix left Paul in prison.

AN APPEAL TO CAESAR

25.1-3 **25** Three days after Festus arrived in Caesarea to take up his duties as governor, he went up to Jerusalem. The high priests and top leaders renewed their vendetta against Paul. They asked Festus if he wouldn't please do them a favor by sending Paul to Jerusalem to respond to their charges. A lie, of course— they had revived their old plot to set an ambush and kill him along the way.

NEW INTERNATIONAL VERSION

kill him along the way. ⁴Festus answered, "Paul is being held at Caesarea, and I myself am going there soon. ⁵Let some of your leaders come with me and press charges against the man there, if he has done anything wrong."

⁶After spending eight or ten days with them, he went down to Caesarea, and the next day he convened the court and ordered that Paul be brought before him. ⁷When Paul appeared, the Jews who had come down from Jerusalem stood around him, bringing many serious charges against him, which they could not prove.

⁸Then Paul made his defense: "I have done nothing wrong against the law of the Jews or against the temple or against Caesar."

⁹Festus, wishing to do the Jews a favor, said to Paul, "Are you willing to go up to Jerusalem and stand trial before me there on these charges?"

¹⁰Paul answered: "I am now standing before Caesar's court, where I ought to be tried. I have not done any wrong to the Jews, as you yourself know very well. ¹¹If, however, I am guilty of doing anything deserving death, I do not refuse to die. But if the charges brought against me by these Jews are not true, no one has the right to hand me over to them. I appeal to Caesar!"

¹²After Festus had conferred with his council, he declared: "You have appealed to Caesar. To Caesar you will go!"

FESTUS CONSULTS KING AGRIPPA

¹³A few days later King Agrippa and Bernice arrived at Caesarea to pay their respects to Festus. ¹⁴Since they were spending many days there, Festus discussed Paul's case with the king. He said: "There is a man here whom Felix left as a prisoner. ¹⁵When I went to Jerusalem, the chief priests and elders of the Jews brought charges against him and asked that he be condemned.

¹⁶"I told them that it is not the Roman custom to hand over any man before he has faced his accusers and has had an opportunity to defend himself against their charges. ¹⁷When they came here with me, I did not delay the case, but convened the court the next day and ordered the man to be brought in. ¹⁸When his accusers got up to speak, they did not charge him with any of the crimes I had expected. ¹⁹Instead, they had some points of dispute with him about their own religion and about a dead man named Jesus who Paul claimed was alive. ²⁰I was at a loss how to

THE MESSAGE

25.4-5 Festus answered that Caesarea was the proper jurisdiction for Paul, and that he himself was going back there in a few days. "You're perfectly welcome," he said, "to go back with me then and accuse him of whatever you think he's done wrong."

25.6-7 About eight or ten days later, Festus returned to Caesarea. The next morning he took his place in the courtroom and had Paul brought in. The minute he walked in, the Jews who had come down from Jerusalem were all over him, hurling the most extreme accusations, none of which they could prove.

25.8 Then Paul took the stand and said simply, "I've done nothing wrong against the Jewish religion, or the Temple, or Caesar. Period."

25.9 Festus, though, wanted to get on the good side of the Jews and so said, "How would you like to go up to Jerusalem, and let me conduct your trial there?"

25.10-11 Paul answered, "I'm standing at this moment before Caesar's bar of justice, where I have a perfect right to stand. And I'm going to keep standing here. I've done nothing wrong to the Jews, and you know it as well as I do. If I've committed a crime and deserve death, name the day. I can face it. But if there's nothing to their accusations—and you know there isn't—nobody can force me to go along with their nonsense. We've fooled around here long enough. I appeal to Caesar."

25.12 Festus huddled with his advisors briefly and then gave his verdict: "You've appealed to Caesar; you'll go to Caesar!"

25.13-17 A few days later King Agrippa and his wife, Bernice, visited Caesarea to welcome Festus to his new post. After several days, Festus brought up Paul's case to the king. "I have a man on my hands here, a prisoner left by Felix. When I was in Jerusalem, the high priests and Jewish leaders brought a bunch of accusations against him and wanted me to sentence him to death. I told them that wasn't the way we Romans did things. Just because a man is accused, we don't throw him out to the dogs. We make sure the accused has a chance to face his accusers and defend himself of the charges. So when they came down here I got right on the case. I took my place in the courtroom and put the man on the stand.

25.18-21 "The accusers came at him from all sides, but their accusations turned out to be nothing more than arguments about their religion and a dead man named Jesus, who the prisoner claimed was alive. Since I'm a newcomer here

investigate such matters; so I asked if he would be willing to go to Jerusalem and stand trial there on these charges. ²¹When Paul made his appeal to be held over for the Emperor's decision, I ordered him held until I could send him to Caesar."

²²Then Agrippa said to Festus, "I would like to hear this man myself."

He replied, "Tomorrow you will hear him."

PAUL BEFORE AGRIPPA

²³The next day Agrippa and Bernice came with great pomp and entered the audience room with the high ranking officers and the leading men of the city. At the command of Festus, Paul was brought in. ²⁴Festus said: "King Agrippa, and all who are present with us, you see this man! The whole Jewish community has petitioned me about him in Jerusalem and here in Caesarea, shouting that he ought not to live any longer. ²⁵I found he had done nothing deserving of death, but because he made his appeal to the Emperor I decided to send him to Rome. ²⁶But I have nothing definite to write to His Majesty about him. Therefore I have brought him before all of you, and especially before you, King Agrippa, so that as a result of this investigation I may have something to write. ²⁷For I think it is unreasonable to send on a prisoner without specifying the charges against him."

26 Then Agrippa said to Paul, "You have permission to speak for yourself."

So Paul motioned with his hand and began his defense: ²"King Agrippa, I consider myself fortunate to stand before you today as I make my defense against all the accusations of the Jews, ³and especially so because you are well acquainted with all the Jewish customs and controversies. Therefore, I beg you to listen to me patiently.

⁴"The Jews all know the way I have lived ever since I was a child, from the beginning of my life in my own country, and also in Jerusalem. ⁵They have known me for a long time and can testify, if they are willing, that according to the strictest sect of our religion, I lived as a Pharisee. ⁶And now it is because of my hope in what God has promised our fathers that I am on trial today. ⁷This is the promise our twelve tribes are hoping

and don't understand everything involved in cases like this, I asked if he'd be willing to go to Jerusalem and be tried there. Paul refused and demanded a hearing before His Majesty in our highest court. So I ordered him returned to custody until I could send him to Caesar in Rome."

25.22   Agrippa said, "I'd like to see this man and hear his story."

"Good," said Festus. "We'll bring him in first thing in the morning and you'll hear it for yourself."

25.23   The next day everybody who was anybody in Caesarea found his way to the Great Hall, along with the top military brass. Agrippa and Bernice made a flourishing grand entrance and took their places. Festus then ordered Paul brought in.

25.24-26   Festus said, "King Agrippa and distinguished guests, take a good look at this man. A bunch of Jews petitioned me first in Jerusalem, and later here, to do away with him. They have been most vehement in demanding his execution. I looked into it and decided that he had committed no crime. He requested a trial before Caesar and I agreed to send him to Rome. But what am I going to write to my master, Caesar? All the charges made by the Jews were fabrications, and I've uncovered nothing else.

25.26-27   "That's why I've brought him before this company, and especially you, King Agrippa: so we can come up with something in the nature of a charge that will hold water. For it seems to me silly to send a prisoner all that way for a trial and not be able to document what he did wrong."

"I COULDN'T JUST WALK AWAY"

26.1-3   **26** Agrippa spoke directly to Paul: "Go ahead—tell us about yourself."

Paul took the stand and told his story. "I can't think of anyone, King Agrippa, before whom I'd rather be answering all these Jewish accusations than you, knowing how well you are acquainted with Jewish ways and all our family quarrels.

26.4-8   "From the time of my youth, my life has been lived among my own people in Jerusalem. Practically every Jew in town who watched me grow up—and if they were willing to stick their necks out they'd tell you in person—knows that I lived as a strict Pharisee, the most demanding branch of our religion. It's because I believed it and took it seriously, committed myself heart and soul to what God promised my ancestors—the identical hope, mind you, that the twelve tribes have lived for night and day

NEW INTERNATIONAL VERSION

to see fulfilled as they earnestly serve God day and night. O king, it is because of this hope that the Jews are accusing me. 8Why should any of you consider it incredible that God raises the dead?

9"I too was convinced that I ought to do all that was possible to oppose the name of Jesus of Nazareth. 10And that is just what I did in Jerusalem. On the authority of the chief priests I put many of the saints in prison, and when they were put to death, I cast my vote against them. 11Many a time I went from one synagogue to another to have them punished, and I tried to force them to blaspheme. In my obsession against them, I even went to foreign cities to persecute them.

12"On one of these journeys I was going to Damascus with the authority and commission of the chief priests. 13About noon, O king, as I was on the road, I saw a light from heaven, brighter than the sun, blazing around me and my companions. 14We all fell to the ground, and I heard a voice saying to me in Aramaic,ᵃ 'Saul, Saul, why do you persecute me? It is hard for you to kick against the goads.'

15"Then I asked, 'Who are you, Lord?'

" 'I am Jesus, whom you are persecuting,' the Lord replied. 16'Now get up and stand on your feet. I have appeared to you to appoint you as a servant and as a witness of what you have seen of me and what I will show you. 17I will rescue you from your own people and from the Gentiles. I am sending you to them 18to open their eyes and turn them from darkness to light, and from the power of Satan to God, so that they may receive forgiveness of sins and a place among those who are sanctified by faith in me.'

19"So then, King Agrippa, I was not disobedient to the vision from heaven. 20First to those in Damascus, then to those in Jerusalem and in all Judea, and to the Gentiles also, I preached that they should repent and turn to God and prove their repentance by their deeds. 21That is why the Jews seized me in the temple courts and tried to kill me. 22But I have had God's help to this very day, and so I stand here and testify to small

THE MESSAGE

all these centuries—it's because I have held on to this tested and tried hope that I'm being called on the carpet by the Jews. They should be the ones standing trial here, not me! For the life of me, I can't see why it's a criminal offense to believe that God raises the dead.

26.9-11 "I admit that I didn't always hold to this position. For a time I thought it was my duty to oppose this Jesus of Nazareth with all my might. Backed with the full authority of the high priests, I threw these believers—I had no idea they were God's people!—into the Jerusalem jail right and left, and whenever it came to a vote, I voted for their execution. I stormed through their meeting places, bullying them into cursing Jesus, a one-man terror obsessed with obliterating these people. And then I started on the towns outside Jerusalem.

26.12-14 "One day on my way to Damascus, armed as always with papers from the high priests authorizing my action, right in the middle of the day a blaze of light, light outshining the sun, poured out of the sky on me and my companions. Oh, King, it was so bright! We fell flat on our faces. Then I heard a voice in Hebrew: 'Saul, Saul, why are you out to get me? Why do you insist on going against the grain?'

26.15-16 "I said, 'Who are you, Master?'

"The voice answered, 'I am Jesus, the One you're hunting down like an animal. But now, up on your feet—I have a job for you. I've handpicked you to be a servant and witness to what's happened today, and to what I am going to show you.

26.17-18 " 'I'm sending you off to open the eyes of the outsiders so they can see the difference between dark and light, and choose light, see the difference between Satan and God, and choose God. I'm sending you off to present my offer of sins forgiven, and a place in the family, inviting them into the company of those who begin real living by believing in me.'

26.19-20 "What could I do, King Agrippa? I couldn't just walk away from a vision like that! I became an obedient believer on the spot. I started preaching this life-change—this radical turn to God and everything it meant in everyday life— right there in Damascus, went on to Jerusalem and the surrounding countryside, and from there to the whole world.

26.21-23 "It's because of this 'whole world' dimension that the Jews grabbed me in the Temple that day and tried to kill me. They want to keep God for themselves. But God has stood by me, just as he promised, and I'm standing here saying what I've been saying to anyone, whether king or child, who will listen. And everything

ᵃ 14 Or Hebrew

NEW INTERNATIONAL VERSION

and great alike. I am saying nothing beyond what the prophets and Moses said would happen— 23that the Christ[a] would suffer and, as the first to rise from the dead, would proclaim light to his own people and to the Gentiles."

24At this point Festus interrupted Paul's defense. "You are out of your mind, Paul!" he shouted. "Your great learning is driving you insane."

25"I am not insane, most excellent Festus," Paul replied. "What I am saying is true and reasonable. 26The king is familiar with these things, and I can speak freely to him. I am convinced that none of this has escaped his notice, because it was not done in a corner. 27King Agrippa, do you believe the prophets? I know you do."

28Then Agrippa said to Paul, "Do you think that in such a short time you can persuade me to be a Christian?"

29Paul replied, "Short time or long—I pray God that not only you but all who are listening to me today may become what I am, except for these chains."

30The king rose, and with him the governor and Bernice and those sitting with them. 31They left the room, and while talking with one another, they said, "This man is not doing anything that deserves death or imprisonment."

32Agrippa said to Festus, "This man could have been set free if he had not appealed to Caesar."

PAUL SAILS FOR ROME

27 When it was decided that we would sail for Italy, Paul and some other prisoners were handed over to a centurion named Julius, who belonged to the Imperial Regiment. 2We boarded a ship from Adramyttium about to sail for ports along the coast of the province of Asia, and we put out to sea. Aristarchus, a Macedonian from Thessalonica, was with us.

3The next day we landed at Sidon; and Julius, in kindness to Paul, allowed him to go to his friends so they might provide for his needs. 4From there we put out to sea again and passed to the lee of Cyprus because the winds were against us. 5When we had sailed across the open sea off the coast of Cilicia and Pamphylia, we landed at Myra in Lycia. 6There the centurion found an Alexandrian ship sailing for Italy and

THE MESSAGE

I'm saying is completely in line with what the prophets and Moses said would happen: One, the Messiah must die; two, raised from the dead, he would be the first rays of God's daylight shining on people far and near, people both godless and God-fearing."

26.24 That was too much for Festus. He interrupted with a shout: "Paul, you're crazy! You've read too many books, spent too much time staring off into space! Get a grip on yourself, get back in the real world!"

26.25-27 But Paul stood his ground. "With all respect, Festus, Your Honor, I'm not crazy. I'm both accurate and sane in what I'm saying. The King knows what I'm talking about. I'm sure that nothing of what I've said sounds crazy to him. He's known all about it for a long time. You must realize that this wasn't done behind the scenes. You believe the prophets, don't you, King Agrippa? Don't answer that—I know you believe."

26.28 But Agrippa did answer: "Keep this up much longer and you'll make a Christian out of me!"

26.29 Paul, still in chains, said, "That's what I'm praying for, whether now or later, and not only you but everyone listening today, to become like me—except, of course, for this prison jewelry!"

26.30-31 The king and the governor, along with Bernice and their advisors, got up and went into the next room to talk over what they had heard. They quickly agreed on Paul's innocence, saying, "There's nothing in this man deserving prison, let alone death."

26.32 Agrippa told Festus, "He could be set free right now if he hadn't requested the hearing before Caesar."

A STORM AT SEA

27 As soon as arrangements were complete for our sailing to Italy, Paul and a few other prisoners were placed under the supervision of a centurion named Julius, a member of an elite guard. We boarded a ship from Adramyttium that was bound for Ephesus and ports west. Aristarchus, a Macedonian from Thessalonica, went with us.

27.3 The next day we put in at Sidon. Julius treated Paul most decently—let him get off the ship and enjoy the hospitality of his friends there.

27.4-8 Out to sea again, we sailed north under the protection of the northeast shore of Cyprus because winds out of the west were against us, and then along the coast westward to the port of Myra. There the centurion found an Egyptian ship headed for Italy and transferred us on

NEW INTERNATIONAL VERSION

put us on board. ⁷We made slow headway for many days and had difficulty arriving off Cnidus. When the wind did not allow us to hold our course, we sailed to the lee of Crete, opposite Salmone. ⁸We moved along the coast with difficulty and came to a place called Fair Havens, near the town of Lasea.

⁹Much time had been lost, and sailing had already become dangerous because by now it was after the Fast.ᵃ So Paul warned them, ¹⁰"Men, I can see that our voyage is going to be disastrous and bring great loss to ship and cargo, and to our own lives also." ¹¹But the centurion, instead of listening to what Paul said, followed the advice of the pilot and of the owner of the ship. ¹²Since the harbor was unsuitable to winter in, the majority decided that we should sail on, hoping to reach Phoenix and winter there. This was a harbor in Crete, facing both southwest and northwest.

THE STORM

¹³When a gentle south wind began to blow, they thought they had obtained what they wanted; so they weighed anchor and sailed along the shore of Crete. ¹⁴Before very long, a wind of hurricane force, called the "northeaster," swept down from the island. ¹⁵The ship was caught by the storm and could not head into the wind; so we gave way to it and were driven along. ¹⁶As we passed to the lee of a small island called Cauda, we were hardly able to make the lifeboat secure. ¹⁷When the men had hoisted it aboard, they passed ropes under the ship itself to hold it together. Fearing that they would run aground on the sandbars of Syrtis, they lowered the sea anchor and let the ship be driven along. ¹⁸We took such a violent battering from the storm that the next day they began to throw the cargo overboard. ¹⁹On the third day, they threw the ship's tackle overboard with their own hands. ²⁰When neither sun nor stars appeared for many days and the storm continued raging, we finally gave up all hope of being saved.

²¹After the men had gone a long time without food, Paul stood up before them and said: "Men, you should have taken my advice not to sail from Crete; then you would have spared yourselves this damage and loss. ²²But now I urge you to keep up your courage, because not one of you will be lost; only the ship will be destroyed. ²³Last night an angel of the God whose I am and whom I serve stood beside me ²⁴and said, 'Do not be afraid, Paul. You must stand trial before Caesar; and God has graciously given you the lives of all who sail with you.' ²⁵So keep up your

ᵃ 9 That is, the Day of Atonement (Yom Kippur)

THE MESSAGE

board. We ran into bad weather and found it impossible to stay on course. After much difficulty, we finally made it to the southern coast of the island of Crete and docked at Good Harbor (appropriate name!).

27.9-10 By this time we had lost a lot of time. We had passed the autumn equinox, so it would be stormy weather from now on through the winter, too dangerous for sailing. Paul warned, "I see only disaster ahead for cargo and ship—to say nothing of our lives!—if we put out to sea now."

27.12,11 But it was not the best harbor for staying the winter. Phoenix, a few miles further on, was more suitable. The centurion set Paul's warning aside and let the ship captain and the shipowner talk him into trying for the next harbor.

27.13-15 When a gentle southerly breeze came up, they weighed anchor, thinking it would be smooth sailing. But they were no sooner out to sea than a gale-force wind, the infamous nor'easter, struck. They lost all control of the ship. It was a cork in the storm.

27.16-17 We came under the lee of the small island named Clauda, and managed to get a lifeboat ready and reef the sails. But rocky shoals prevented us from getting close. We only managed to avoid them by throwing out drift anchors.

27.18-20 Next day, out on the high seas again and badly damaged now by the storm, we dumped the cargo overboard. The third day the sailors lightened the ship further by throwing off all the tackle and provisions. It had been many days since we had seen either sun or stars. Wind and waves were battering us unmercifully, and we lost all hope of rescue.

27.21-22 With our appetite for both food and life long gone, Paul took his place in our midst and said, "Friends, you really should have listened to me back in Crete. We could have avoided all this trouble and trial. But there's no need to dwell on that now. From now on, things are looking up! I can assure you that there'll not be a single drowning among us, although I can't say as much for the ship—the ship itself is doomed.

27.23-26 "Last night God's angel stood at my side, an angel of this God I serve, saying to me, 'Don't give up, Paul. You're going to stand before Caesar yet—and everyone sailing with you is also going to make it.' So, dear friends, take heart. I

NEW INTERNATIONAL VERSION

courage, men, for I have faith in God that it will happen just as he told me. ²⁶Nevertheless, we must run aground on some island."

THE SHIPWRECK

²⁷On the fourteenth night we were still being driven across the Adriatic^a Sea, when about midnight the sailors sensed they were approaching land. ²⁸They took soundings and found that the water was a hundred and twenty feet^b deep. A short time later they took soundings again and found it was ninety feet^c deep. ²⁹Fearing that we would be dashed against the rocks, they dropped four anchors from the stern and prayed for daylight. ³⁰In an attempt to escape from the ship, the sailors let the lifeboat down into the sea, pretending they were going to lower some anchors from the bow. ³¹Then Paul said to the centurion and the soldiers, "Unless these men stay with the ship, you cannot be saved." ³²So the soldiers cut the ropes that held the lifeboat and let it fall away.

³³Just before dawn Paul urged them all to eat. "For the last fourteen days," he said, "you have been in constant suspense and have gone without food—you haven't eaten anything. ³⁴Now I urge you to take some food. You need it to survive. Not one of you will lose a single hair from his head." ³⁵After he said this, he took some bread and gave thanks to God in front of them all. Then he broke it and began to eat. ³⁶They were all encouraged and ate some food themselves. ³⁷Altogether there were 276 of us on board. ³⁸When they had eaten as much as they wanted, they lightened the ship by throwing the grain into the sea.

³⁹When daylight came, they did not recognize the land, but they saw a bay with a sandy beach, where they decided to run the ship aground if they could. ⁴⁰Cutting loose the anchors, they left them in the sea and at the same time untied the ropes that held the rudders. Then they hoisted the foresail to the wind and made for the beach. ⁴¹But the ship struck a sandbar and ran aground. The bow stuck fast and would not move, and the stern was broken to pieces by the pounding of the surf.

⁴²The soldiers planned to kill the prisoners to prevent any of them from swimming away and escaping. ⁴³But the centurion wanted to spare Paul's life and kept them from carrying out their plan. He ordered those who could swim to jump overboard first and get to land. ⁴⁴The rest were to get there on planks or on pieces of the ship. In this way everyone reached land in safety.

---

^a 27 In ancient times the name referred to an area extending well south of Italy.   ^b 28 Greek *twenty orguias* (about 37 meters)   ^c 28 Greek *fifteen orguias* (about 27 meters)

THE MESSAGE

believe God will do exactly what he told me. But we're going to shipwreck on some island or other."

27.27-29   On the fourteenth night, adrift somewhere on the Adriatic Sea, at about midnight the sailors sensed that we were approaching land. Sounding, they measured a depth of one hundred twenty feet, and shortly after that ninety feet. Afraid that we were about to run aground, they threw out four anchors and prayed for daylight.

27.30-32   Some of the sailors tried to jump ship. They let down the lifeboat, pretending they were going to set out more anchors from the bow. Paul saw through their guise and told the centurion and his soldiers, "If these sailors don't stay with the ship, we're all going down." So the soldiers cut the lines to the lifeboat and let it drift off.

27.33-34   With dawn about to break, Paul called everyone together and proposed breakfast: "This is the fourteenth day we've gone without food. None of us has felt like eating! But I urge you to eat something now. You'll need strength for the rescue ahead. You're going to come out of this without even a scratch!"

27.35-38   He broke the bread, gave thanks to God, passed it around, and they all ate heartily—two hundred seventy-six of us, all told! With the meal finished and everyone full, the ship was further lightened by dumping the grain overboard.

27.39-41   At daybreak, no one recognized the land—but then they did notice a bay with a nice beach. They decided to try to run the ship up on the beach. They cut the anchors, loosed the tiller, raised the sail, and ran before the wind toward the beach. But we didn't make it. Still far from shore, we hit a reef and the ship began to break up.

27.42-44   The soldiers decided to kill the prisoners so none could escape by swimming, but the centurion, determined to save Paul, stopped them. He gave orders for anyone who could swim to dive in and go for it, and for the rest to grab a plank. Everyone made it to shore safely.

☩

NEW INTERNATIONAL VERSION

Ashore on Malta

28 Once safely on shore, we found out that the island was called Malta. ²The islanders showed us unusual kindness. They built a fire and welcomed us all because it was raining and cold. ³Paul gathered a pile of brushwood and, as he put it on the fire, a viper, driven out by the heat, fastened itself on his hand. ⁴When the islanders saw the snake hanging from his hand, they said to each other, "This man must be a murderer; for though he escaped from the sea, Justice has not allowed him to live." ⁵But Paul shook the snake off into the fire and suffered no ill effects. ⁶The people expected him to swell up or suddenly fall dead, but after waiting a long time and seeing nothing unusual happen to him, they changed their minds and said he was a god.

⁷There was an estate nearby that belonged to Publius, the chief official of the island. He welcomed us to his home and for three days entertained us hospitably. ⁸His father was sick in bed, suffering from fever and dysentery. Paul went in to see him and, after prayer, placed his hands on him and healed him. ⁹When this had happened, the rest of the sick on the island came and were cured. ¹⁰They honored us in many ways and when we were ready to sail, they furnished us with the supplies we needed.

Arrival at Rome

¹¹After three months we put out to sea in a ship that had wintered in the island. It was an Alexandrian ship with the figurehead of the twin gods Castor and Pollux. ¹²We put in at Syracuse and stayed there three days. ¹³From there we set sail and arrived at Rhegium. The next day the south wind came up, and on the following day we reached Puteoli. ¹⁴There we found some brothers who invited us to spend a week with them. And so we came to Rome. ¹⁵The brothers there had heard that we were coming, and they traveled as far as the Forum of Appius and the Three Taverns to meet us. At the sight of these men Paul thanked God and was encouraged. ¹⁶When we got to Rome, Paul was allowed to live by himself, with a soldier to guard him.

Paul Preaches at Rome Under Guard

¹⁷Three days later he called together the leaders of the Jews. When they had assembled, Paul said to them: "My brothers, although I have

THE MESSAGE

28.1-2 **28** Once everyone was accounted for and we realized we had all made it, we learned that we were on the island of Malta. The natives went out of their way to be friendly to us. The day was rainy and cold and we were already soaked to the bone, but they built a huge bonfire and gathered us around it.

28.3-6 Paul pitched in and helped. He had gathered up a bundle of sticks, but when he put it on the fire, a venomous snake, roused from its torpor by the heat, struck his hand and held on. Seeing the snake hanging from Paul's hand like that, the natives jumped to the conclusion that he was a murderer getting his just deserts. Paul shook the snake off into the fire, none the worse for wear. They kept expecting him to drop dead, but when it was obvious he wasn't going to, they jumped to the conclusion that he was a god!

28.7-9 The head man in that part of the island was Publius. He took us into his home as his guests, drying us out and putting us up in fine style for the next three days. Publius's father was sick at the time, down with a high fever and dysentery. Paul went to the old man's room, and when he laid hands on him and prayed, the man was healed. Word of the healing got around fast, and soon everyone on the island who was sick came and got healed.

Rome

28.10-11 We spent a wonderful three months on Malta. They treated us royally, took care of all our needs and outfitted us for the rest of the journey. When an Egyptian ship that had wintered there in the harbor prepared to leave for Italy, we got on board. The ship had a carved Gemini for its figurehead: "the Heavenly Twins."

28.12-14 We put in at Syracuse for three days and then went up the coast to Rhegium. Two days later, with the wind out of the south, we sailed into the Bay of Naples. We found Christian friends there and stayed with them for a week.

28.14-16 And then we came to Rome. Friends in Rome heard we were on the way and came out to meet us. One group got as far as Appian Court; another group met us at Three Taverns—emotion-packed meetings, as you can well imagine. Paul, brimming over with praise, led us in prayers of thanksgiving. When we actually entered Rome, they let Paul live in his own private quarters with a soldier who had been assigned to guard him.

28.17-20 Three days later, Paul called the Jewish leaders together for a meeting at his house. He said, "The Jews in Jerusalem arrested me on trumped-up charges, and I was taken into cus-

NEW INTERNATIONAL VERSION

done nothing against our people or against the customs of our ancestors, I was arrested in Jerusalem and handed over to the Romans. [18]They examined me and wanted to release me, because I was not guilty of any crime deserving death. [19]But when the Jews objected, I was compelled to appeal to Caesar—not that I had any charge to bring against my own people. [20]For this reason I have asked to see you and talk with you. It is because of the hope of Israel that I am bound with this chain."

[21]They replied, "We have not received any letters from Judea concerning you, and none of the brothers who have come from there has reported or said anything bad about you. [22]But we want to hear what your views are, for we know that people everywhere are talking against this sect."

[23]They arranged to meet Paul on a certain day, and came in even larger numbers to the place where he was staying. From morning till evening he explained and declared to them the kingdom of God and tried to convince them about Jesus from the Law of Moses and from the Prophets. [24]Some were convinced by what he said, but others would not believe. [25]They disagreed among themselves and began to leave after Paul had made this final statement: "The Holy Spirit spoke the truth to your forefathers when he said through Isaiah the prophet:

[26]" 'Go to this people and say,
"You will be ever hearing but never
        understanding;
    you will be ever seeing but never
        perceiving."
[27]For this people's heart has become calloused;
    they hardly hear with their ears,
    and they have closed their eyes.
Otherwise they might see with their eyes,
    hear with their ears,
    understand with their hearts
and turn, and I would heal them.'[a]

[28]"Therefore I want you to know that God's salvation has been sent to the Gentiles, and they will listen!"[b]

[30]For two whole years Paul stayed there in his own rented house and welcomed all who came to see him. [31]Boldly and without hindrance he preached the kingdom of God and taught about the Lord Jesus Christ.

---

[a] 27 Isaiah 6:9,10   [b] 28 Some manuscripts *listen!" [29]After he said this, the Jews left, arguing vigorously among themselves.*

THE MESSAGE

tody by the Romans. I assure you that I did absolutely nothing against Jewish laws or Jewish customs. After the Romans investigated the charges and found there was nothing to them, they wanted to set me free, but the Jews objected so fiercely that I was forced to appeal to Caesar. I did this not to accuse them of any wrongdoing or to get our people in trouble with Rome. We've had enough trouble through the years that way. I did it *for* Israel. I asked you to come and listen to me today to make it clear that I'm on Israel's side, not against her. I'm a hostage here for hope, not doom."

28.21-22   They said, "Nobody wrote warning us about you. And no one has shown up saying anything bad about you. But we would like very much to hear more. The only thing we know about this Christian sect is that nobody seems to have anything good to say about it."

28.23   They agreed on a time. When the day arrived, they came back to his home with a number of their friends. Paul talked to them all day, from morning to evening, explaining everything involved in the kingdom of God, and trying to persuade them all about Jesus by pointing out what Moses and the prophets had written about him.

28.24-27   Some of them were persuaded by what he said, but others refused to believe a word of it. When the unbelievers got cantankerous and started bickering with each other, Paul interrupted: "I have just one more thing to say to you. The Holy Spirit sure knew what he was talking about when he addressed our ancestors through Isaiah the prophet:

Go to this people and tell them this:
"You're going to listen with your ears,
    but you won't hear a word;
You're going to stare with your eyes,
    but you won't see a thing.
These people are blockheads!
They stick their fingers in their ears
    so they won't have to listen;
They screw their eyes shut
    so they won't have to look,
    so they won't have to deal with me
        face-to-face
    and let me heal them."

28.28   "You've had your chance. The non-Jewish outsiders are next on the list. And believe me, they're going to receive it with open arms!"

28.30-31   Paul lived for two years in his rented house. He welcomed everyone who came to visit. He urgently presented all matters of the kingdom of God. He explained everything about Jesus Christ. His door was always open.

ROMANS

ROMANS

1 Paul, a servant of Christ Jesus, called to be an apostle and set apart for the gospel of God— ²the gospel he promised beforehand through his prophets in the Holy Scriptures ³regarding his Son, who as to his human nature was a descendant of David, ⁴and who through the Spirit*a* of holiness was declared with power to be the Son of God*b* by his resurrection from the dead: Jesus Christ our Lord. ⁵Through him and for his name's sake, we received grace and apostleship to call people from among all the Gentiles to the obedience that comes from faith. ⁶And you also are among those who are called to belong to Jesus Christ.

⁷To all in Rome who are loved by God and called to be saints:

Grace and peace to you from God our Father and from the Lord Jesus Christ.

PAUL'S LONGING TO VISIT ROME

⁸First, I thank my God through Jesus Christ for all of you, because your faith is being reported all over the world. ⁹God, whom I serve with my whole heart in preaching the gospel of his Son, is my witness how constantly I remember you ¹⁰in my prayers at all times; and I pray that now at last by God's will the way may be opened for me to come to you.

¹¹I long to see you so that I may impart to you some spiritual gift to make you strong— ¹²that is, that you and I may be mutually encouraged by each other's faith. ¹³I do not want you to be unaware, brothers, that I planned many times to come to you (but have been prevented from doing so until now) in order that I might have a harvest among you, just as I have had among the other Gentiles.

¹⁴I am obligated both to Greeks and non-Greeks, both to the wise and the foolish. ¹⁵That is why I am so eager to preach the gospel also to you who are at Rome.

¹⁶I am not ashamed of the gospel, because it is the power of God for the salvation of everyone

a 4 Or who as to his spirit   b 4 Or was appointed to be the Son of God with power

1.1 1 I, Paul, am a devoted slave of Jesus Christ on assignment, authorized as an apostle to proclaim God's words and acts. I write this letter to all the Christians in Rome, God's friends.

1.2-7 The sacred writings contain preliminary reports by the prophets on God's Son. His descent from David roots him in history; his unique identity as Son of God was shown by the Spirit when Jesus was raised from the dead, setting him apart as the Messiah, our Master. Through him we received both the generous gift of his life and the urgent task of passing it on to others who receive it by entering into obedient trust in Jesus. You are who you are through this gift and call of Jesus Christ! And I greet you now with all the generosity of God our Father and our Master Jesus, the Messiah.

1.8-12 I thank God through Jesus for every one of you. That's first. People everywhere keep telling me about your lives of faith, and every time I hear them, I thank him. And God, whom I so love to worship and serve by spreading the good news of his Son—the Message!—knows that every time I think of you in my prayers, which is practically all the time, I ask him to clear the way for me to come and see you. The longer this waiting goes on, the deeper the ache. I so want to be there to deliver God's gift in person and watch you grow stronger right before my eyes! But don't think I'm not expecting to get something out of this, too! You have as much to give me as I do to you.

1.13-15 Please don't misinterpret my failure to visit you, friends. You have no idea how many times I've made plans for Rome. I've been determined to get some personal enjoyment out of God's work among you, as I have in so many other non-Jewish towns and communities. But something has always come up and prevented it. Everyone I meet—it matters little whether they're mannered or rude, smart or simple—deepens my sense of interdependence and obligation. And that's why I can't wait to get to you in Rome, preaching this wonderful good news of God.

1.16-17 It's news I'm most proud to proclaim, this extraordinary Message of God's powerful plan

NEW INTERNATIONAL VERSION

who believes: first for the Jew, then for the Gentile. [17]For in the gospel a righteousness from God is revealed, a righteousness that is by faith from first to last,[a] just as it is written: "The righteous will live by faith."[b]

GOD'S WRATH AGAINST MANKIND

[18]The wrath of God is being revealed from heaven against all the godlessness and wickedness of men who suppress the truth by their wickedness, [19]since what may be known about God is plain to them, because God has made it plain to them. [20]For since the creation of the world God's invisible qualities—his eternal power and divine nature—have been clearly seen, being understood from what has been made, so that men are without excuse.

[21]For although they knew God, they neither glorified him as God nor gave thanks to him, but their thinking became futile and their foolish hearts were darkened. [22]Although they claimed to be wise, they became fools [23]and exchanged the glory of the immortal God for images made to look like mortal man and birds and animals and reptiles.

[24]Therefore God gave them over in the sinful desires of their hearts to sexual impurity for the degrading of their bodies with one another. [25]They exchanged the truth of God for a lie, and worshiped and served created things rather than the Creator—who is forever praised. Amen.

[26]Because of this, God gave them over to shameful lusts. Even their women exchanged natural relations for unnatural ones. [27]In the same way the men also abandoned natural relations with women and were inflamed with lust for one another. Men committed indecent acts with other men, and received in themselves the due penalty for their perversion.

[28]Furthermore, since they did not think it worthwhile to retain the knowledge of God, he gave them over to a depraved mind, to do what ought not to be done. [29]They have become filled with every kind of wickedness, evil, greed and depravity. They are full of envy, murder, strife, deceit and malice. They are gossips, [30]slanderers, God-haters, insolent, arrogant and boastful; they invent ways of doing evil; they disobey their parents; [31]they are senseless, faithless, heartless, ruthless. [32]Although they know God's righteous decree that those who do such

THE MESSAGE

to rescue everyone who trusts him, starting with Jews and then right on to everyone else! God's way of putting people right shows up in the acts of faith, confirming what Scripture has said all along: "The person in right standing before God by trusting him really lives."

IGNORING GOD LEADS TO A DOWNWARD SPIRAL

1.18-23 But God's angry displeasure erupts as acts of human mistrust and wrongdoing and lying accumulate, as people try to put a shroud over truth. But the basic reality of God is plain enough. Open your eyes and there it is! By taking a long and thoughtful look at what God has created, people have always been able to see what their eyes as such can't see: eternal power, for instance, and the mystery of his divine being. So nobody has a good excuse. What happened was this: People knew God perfectly well, but when they didn't treat him like God, refusing to worship him, they trivialized themselves into silliness and confusion so that there was neither sense nor direction left in their lives. They pretended to know it all, but were illiterate regarding life. They traded the glory of God who holds the whole world in his hands for cheap figurines you can buy at any roadside stand.

1.24-25 So God said, in effect, "If that's what you want, that's what you get." It wasn't long before they were living in a pigpen, smeared with filth, filthy inside and out. And all this because they traded the true God for a fake god, and worshiped the god they made instead of the God who made them—the God we bless, the God who blesses *us*. Oh, yes!

1.26-27 Worse followed. Refusing to know God, they soon didn't know how to be human either—women didn't know how to be women, men didn't know how to be men. Sexually confused, they abused and defiled one another, women with women, men with men—all lust, no love. And then they paid for it, oh, how they paid for it—emptied of God and love, godless and loveless wretches.

1.28-32 Since they didn't bother to acknowledge God, God quit bothering them and let them run loose. And then all hell broke loose: rampant evil, grabbing and grasping, vicious backstabbing. They made life hell on earth with their envy, wanton killing, bickering, and cheating. Look at them: mean-spirited, venomous, forktongued God-bashers. Bullies, swaggerers, insufferable windbags! They keep inventing new ways of wrecking lives. They ditch their parents when they get in the way. Stupid, slimy, cruel, cold-blooded. And it's not as if they don't know better. They know perfectly well they're spitting

---

[a] 17 Or *is from faith to faith*   [b] 17 Hab. 2:4

NEW INTERNATIONAL VERSION

things deserve death, they not only continue to do these very things but also approve of those who practice them.

GOD'S RIGHTEOUS JUDGMENT

2 You, therefore, have no excuse, you who pass judgment on someone else, for at whatever point you judge the other, you are condemning yourself, because you who pass judgment do the same things. ²Now we know that God's judgment against those who do such things is based on truth. ³So when you, a mere man, pass judgment on them and yet do the same things, do you think you will escape God's judgment? ⁴Or do you show contempt for the riches of his kindness, tolerance and patience, not realizing that God's kindness leads you toward repentance?

⁵But because of your stubbornness and your unrepentant heart, you are storing up wrath against yourself for the day of God's wrath, when his righteous judgment will be revealed. ⁶God "will give to each person according to what he has done." [a] ⁷To those who by persistence in doing good seek glory, honor and immortality, he will give eternal life. ⁸But for those who are self-seeking and who reject the truth and follow evil, there will be wrath and anger. ⁹There will be trouble and distress for every human being who does evil: first for the Jew, then for the Gentile; ¹⁰but glory, honor and peace for everyone who does good: first for the Jew, then for the Gentile. ¹¹For God does not show favoritism.

¹²All who sin apart from the law will also perish apart from the law, and all who sin under the law will be judged by the law. ¹³For it is not those who hear the law who are righteous in God's sight, but it is those who obey the law who will be declared righteous. ¹⁴(Indeed, when Gentiles, who do not have the law, do by nature things required by the law, they are a law for themselves, even though they do not have the law, ¹⁵since they show that the requirements of

THE MESSAGE

in God's face. And they don't care—worse, they hand out prizes to those who do the worst things best!

GOD IS KIND, BUT NOT SOFT

2.1-2 2 Those people are on a dark spiral downward. But if you think that leaves you on the high ground where you can point your finger at others, think again. Every time you criticize someone, you condemn yourself. It takes one to know one. Judgmental criticism of others is a well-known way of escaping detection in your own crimes and misdemeanors. But God isn't so easily diverted. He sees right through all such smoke screens and holds you to what *you've* done.

2.3-4 You didn't think, did you, that just by pointing your finger at others you would distract God from seeing all your misdoings and from coming down on you hard? Or did you think that because he's such a nice God, he'd let you off the hook? Better think this one through from the beginning. God is kind, but he's not soft. In kindness he takes us firmly by the hand and leads us into a radical life-change.

2.5-8 You're not getting by with anything. Every refusal and avoidance of God adds fuel to the fire. The day is coming when it's going to blaze hot and high, God's fiery and righteous judgment. Make no mistake: In the end you get what's coming to you—*Real Life* for those who work on God's side, but to those who insist on getting their own way and take the path of least resistance, *Fire!*

2.9-11 If you go against the grain, you get splinters, regardless of which neighborhood you're from, what your parents taught you, what schools you attended. But if you embrace the way God does things, there are wonderful payoffs, again without regard to where you are from or how you were brought up. Being a Jew won't give you an automatic stamp of approval. God pays no attention to what others say (or what you think) about you. He makes up his own mind.

2.12-13 If you sin without knowing what you're doing, God takes that into account. But if you sin knowing full well what you're doing, that's a different story entirely. Merely hearing God's law is a waste of your time if you don't do what he commands. Doing, not hearing, is what makes the difference with God.

2.14-16 When outsiders who have never heard of God's law follow it more or less by instinct, they confirm its truth by their obedience. They show that God's law is not something alien, imposed on us from without, but woven into the very fabric of our creation. There is something deep within them that echoes God's yes

[a] 6 Psalm 62:12; Prov. 24:12

NEW INTERNATIONAL VERSION

the law are written on their hearts, their consciences also bearing witness, and their thoughts now accusing, now even defending them.) [16]This will take place on the day when God will judge men's secrets through Jesus Christ, as my gospel declares.

THE JEWS AND THE LAW

[17]Now you, if you call yourself a Jew; if you rely on the law and brag about your relationship to God; [18]if you know his will and approve of what is superior because you are instructed by the law; [19]if you are convinced that you are a guide for the blind, a light for those who are in the dark, [20]an instructor of the foolish, a teacher of infants, because you have in the law the embodiment of knowledge and truth— [21]you, then, who teach others, do you not teach yourself? You who preach against stealing, do you steal? [22]You who say that people should not commit adultery, do you commit adultery? You who abhor idols, do you rob temples? [23]You who brag about the law, do you dishonor God by breaking the law? [24]As it is written: "God's name is blasphemed among the Gentiles because of you." [a]

[25]Circumcision has value if you observe the law, but if you break the law, you have become as though you had not been circumcised. [26]If those who are not circumcised keep the law's requirements, will they not be regarded as though they were circumcised? [27]The one who is not circumcised physically and yet obeys the law will condemn you who, even though you have the [b] written code and circumcision, are a lawbreaker.

[28]A man is not a Jew if he is only one outwardly, nor is circumcision merely outward and physical. [29]No, a man is a Jew if he is one inwardly; and circumcision is circumcision of the heart, by the Spirit, not by the written code. Such a man's praise is not from men, but from God.

GOD'S FAITHFULNESS

3 What advantage, then, is there in being a Jew, or what value is there in circumcision? [2]Much in every way! First of all, they have been entrusted with the very words of God.

[3]What if some did not have faith? Will their lack of faith nullify God's faithfulness? [4]Not at

THE MESSAGE

and no, right and wrong. Their response to God's yes and no will become public knowledge on the day God makes his final decision about every man and woman. The Message from God that I proclaim through Jesus Christ takes into account all these differences.

RELIGION CAN'T SAVE YOU

2.17-24 If you're brought up Jewish, don't assume that you can lean back in the arms of your religion and take it easy, feeling smug because you're an insider to God's revelation, a connoisseur of the best things of God, informed on the latest doctrines! I have a special word of caution for you who are sure that you have it all together yourselves and, because you know God's revealed Word inside and out, feel qualified to guide others through their blind alleys and dark nights and confused emotions to God. While you are guiding others, who is going to guide you? I'm quite serious. While preaching "Don't steal!" are you going to rob people blind? Who would suspect you? The same with adultery. The same with idolatry. You can get by with almost anything if you front it with eloquent talk about God and his law. The line from Scripture, "It's because of you Jews that the outsiders are down on God," shows it's an old problem that isn't going to go away.

2.25-29 Circumcision, the surgical ritual that marks you as a Jew, is great if you live in accord with God's law. But if you don't, it's worse than not being circumcised. The reverse is also true: The uncircumcised who keep God's ways are as good as the circumcised—in fact, better. Better to keep God's law uncircumcised than break it circumcised. Don't you see: It's not the cut of a knife that makes a Jew. You become a Jew by who you *are*. It's the mark of God on your heart, not of a knife on your skin, that makes a Jew. And recognition comes from God, not legalistic critics.

✝

3.1-2 **3** So what difference does it make who's a Jew and who isn't, who has been trained in God's ways and who hasn't? As it turns out, it makes a lot of difference—but not the difference so many have assumed.

3.2-6 First, there's the matter of being put in charge of writing down and caring for God's revelation, these Holy Scriptures. So, what if, in the course of doing that, some of those Jews abandoned their post? God didn't abandon them. Do you think their faithlessness cancels out his faithfulness? Not on your life! Depend on it: God keeps his word even when the whole

---

[a] 24 Isaiah 52:5; Ezek. 36:22   [b] 27 Or *who, by means of a*

NEW INTERNATIONAL VERSION

all! Let God be true, and every man a liar. As it is written:

"So that you may be proved right when you speak
and prevail when you judge." a

5But if our unrighteousness brings out God's righteousness more clearly, what shall we say? That God is unjust in bringing his wrath on us? (I am using a human argument.) 6Certainly not! If that were so, how could God judge the world? 7Someone might argue, "If my falsehood enhances God's truthfulness and so increases his glory, why am I still condemned as a sinner?" 8Why not say—as we are being slanderously reported as saying and as some claim that we say—"Let us do evil that good may result"? Their condemnation is deserved.

No One Is Righteous

9What shall we conclude then? Are we any better b? Not at all! We have already made the charge that Jews and Gentiles alike are all under sin. 10As it is written:

"There is no one righteous, not even one;
11   there is no one who understands,
     no one who seeks God.
12 All have turned away,
     they have together become worthless;
there is no one who does good,
     not even one." c
13 "Their throats are open graves;
     their tongues practice deceit." d
"The poison of vipers is on their lips." e
14   "Their mouths are full of cursing and
        bitterness." f
15 "Their feet are swift to shed blood;
16   ruin and misery mark their ways,
17 and the way of peace they do not know." g
18   "There is no fear of God before their
        eyes." h

19Now we know that whatever the law says, it says to those who are under the law, so that every mouth may be silenced and the whole world

THE MESSAGE

world is lying through its teeth. Scripture says the same:

Your words stand fast and true;
Rejection doesn't faze you.

But if our wrongdoing only underlines and confirms God's rightdoing, shouldn't we be commended for helping out? Since our bad words don't even make a dent in his good words, isn't it wrong of God to back us to the wall and hold us to our word? These questions come up. The answer to such questions is no, a most emphatic No! How else would things ever get straightened out if God didn't do the straightening?

3.7-8   It's simply perverse to say, "If my lies serve to show off God's truth all the more gloriously, why blame me? I'm doing God a favor." Some people are actually trying to put such words in our mouths, claiming that we go around saying, "The more evil we do, the more good God does, so let's just do it!" That's pure slander, as I'm sure you'll agree.

We're All in the Same Sinking Boat

3.9-20 So where does that put us? Do we Jews get a better break than the others? Not really. Basically, all of us, whether insiders or outsiders, start out in identical conditions, which is to say that we all start out as sinners. Scripture leaves no doubt about it:

There's nobody living right, not even one,
     nobody who knows the score, nobody
        alert for God.
They've all taken the wrong turn;
     they've all wandered down blind alleys.
No one's living right;
     I can't find a single one.
Their throats are gaping graves,
     their tongues slick as mud slides.
Every word they speak is tinged with
        poison.
They open their mouths and pollute the
        air.
They race for the honor of sinner-of-the-
        year,
     litter the land with heartbreak and ruin,
Don't know the first thing about living with
        others.
They never give God the time of day.

This makes it clear, doesn't it, that whatever is written in these Scriptures is not what God says about others but to us to whom these Scriptures were addressed in the first place! And it's clear enough, isn't it, that we're sinners, every one of us, in the same sinking boat with everybody

---

a 4 Psalm 51:4   b 9 Or worse   c 12 Psalms 14:1-3; 53:1-3; Eccles. 7:20   d 13 Psalm 5:9   e 13 Psalm 140:3   f 14 Psalm 10:7   g 17 Isaiah 59:7,8   h 18 Psalm 36:1

NEW INTERNATIONAL VERSION

held accountable to God. [20]Therefore no one will be declared righteous in his sight by observing the law; rather, through the law we become conscious of sin.

RIGHTEOUSNESS THROUGH FAITH

[21]But now a righteousness from God, apart from law, has been made known, to which the Law and the Prophets testify. [22]This righteousness from God comes through faith in Jesus Christ to all who believe. There is no difference, [23]for all have sinned and fall short of the glory of God, [24]and are justified freely by his grace through the redemption that came by Christ Jesus. [25]God presented him as a sacrifice of atonement,[a] through faith in his blood. He did this to demonstrate his justice, because in his forbearance he had left the sins committed beforehand unpunished— [26]he did it to demonstrate his justice at the present time, so as to be just and the one who justifies those who have faith in Jesus.

[27]Where, then, is boasting? It is excluded. On what principle? On that of observing the law? No, but on that of faith. [28]For we maintain that a man is justified by faith apart from observing the law. [29]Is God the God of Jews only? Is he not the God of Gentiles too? Yes, of Gentiles too, [30]since there is only one God, who will justify the circumcised by faith and the uncircumcised through that same faith. [31]Do we, then, nullify the law by this faith? Not at all! Rather, we uphold the law.

THE MESSAGE

else? Our involvement with God's revelation doesn't put us right with God. What it does is force us to face our complicity in everyone else's sin.

GOD HAS SET THINGS RIGHT

3.21-24 But in our time something new has been added. What Moses and the prophets witnessed to all those years has happened. The God-setting-things-right that we read about has become Jesus-setting-things-right for us. And not only for us, but for everyone who believes in him. For there is no difference between us and them in this. Since we've compiled this long and sorry record as sinners (both us and them) and proved that we are utterly incapable of living the glorious lives God wills for us, God did it for us. Out of sheer generosity he put us in right standing with himself. A pure gift. He got us out of the mess we're in and restored us to where he always wanted us to be. And he did it by means of Jesus Christ.

3.25-26 God sacrificed Jesus on the altar of the world to clear that world of sin. Having faith in him sets us in the clear. God decided on this course of action in full view of the public—to set the world in the clear with himself through the sacrifice of Jesus, finally taking care of the sins he had so patiently endured. This is not only clear, but it's *now*—this is current history! God sets things right. He also makes it possible for us to live in his rightness.

3.27-28 So where does that leave our proud Jewish insider claims and counterclaims? Canceled? Yes, canceled. What we've learned is this: God does not respond to what *we* do; we respond to what *God* does. We've finally figured it out. Our lives get in step with God and all others by letting him set the pace, not by proudly or anxiously trying to run the parade.

3.29-30 And where does that leave our proud Jewish claim of having a corner on God? Also canceled. God is the God of outsider non-Jews as well as insider Jews. How could it be otherwise since there is only one God? God sets right all who welcome his action and enter into it, both those who follow our religious system and those who have never heard of our religion.

3.31 But by shifting our focus from what *we* do to what *God* does, don't we cancel out all our careful keeping of the rules and ways God commanded? Not at all. What happens, in fact, is that by putting that entire way of life in its proper place, we confirm it.

---

[a] 25 Or *as the one who would turn aside his wrath, taking away sin*

NEW INTERNATIONAL VERSION

Abraham Justified by Faith

4 What then shall we say that Abraham, our forefather, discovered in this matter? [2]If, in fact, Abraham was justified by works, he had something to boast about—but not before God. [3]What does the Scripture say? "Abraham believed God, and it was credited to him as righteousness."[a]

[4]Now when a man works, his wages are not credited to him as a gift, but as an obligation. [5]However, to the man who does not work but trusts God who justifies the wicked, his faith is credited as righteousness. [6]David says the same thing when he speaks of the blessedness of the man to whom God credits righteousness apart from works:

[7]"Blessed are they
  whose transgressions are forgiven,
  whose sins are covered.
[8]Blessed is the man
  whose sin the Lord will never count
    against him."[b]

[9]Is this blessedness only for the circumcised, or also for the uncircumcised? We have been saying that Abraham's faith was credited to him as righteousness. [10]Under what circumstances was it credited? Was it after he was circumcised, or before? It was not after, but before! [11]And he received the sign of circumcision, a seal of the righteousness that he had by faith while he was still uncircumcised. So then, he is the father of all who believe but have not been circumcised, in order that righteousness might be credited to them. [12]And he is also the father of the circumcised who not only are circumcised but who also

THE MESSAGE

Trusting God

4.1-3 4 So how do we fit what we know of Abraham, our first father in the faith, into this new way of looking at things? If Abraham, by what he *did* for God, got God to approve him, he could certainly have taken credit for it. But the story we're given is a God-story, not an Abraham-story. What we read in Scripture is, "Abraham entered into what God was doing for him, and *that* was the turning point. He trusted God to set him right instead of trying to be right on his own."

4.4-5 If you're a hard worker and do a good job, you deserve your pay; we don't call your wages a gift. But if you see that the job is too big for you, that it's something only *God* can do, and you trust him to do it—you could never do it for yourself no matter how hard and long you worked—well, that trusting-him-to-do-it is what gets you set right with God, *by* God. Sheer gift.

4.6-9 David confirms this way of looking at it, saying that the one who trusts God to do the putting-everything-right without insisting on having a say in it is one fortunate man:

Fortunate those whose crimes are carted off,
  whose sins are wiped clean from the
    slate.
Fortunate the person against
  whom the Lord does not keep score.

Do you think for a minute that this blessing is only pronounced over those of us who keep our religious ways and are circumcised? Or do you think it possible that the blessing could be given to those who never even heard of our ways, who were never brought up in the disciplines of God? We all agree, don't we, that it was by embracing what God did for him that Abraham was declared fit before God?

4.10-11 Now *think*: Was that declaration made before or after he was marked by the covenant rite of circumcision? That's right, *before* he was marked. That means that he underwent circumcision as evidence and confirmation of what God had done long before to bring him into this acceptable standing with himself, an act of God he had embraced with his whole life.

4.12 And it means further that Abraham is father of *all* people who embrace what God does for them while they are still on the "outs" with God, as yet unidentified as God's, in an "uncircumcised" condition. It is precisely these people in this condition who are called "set right by God and with God"! Abraham is also, of course, father of those who have undergone the religious rite of circumcision *not* just because of the ritual but because they were willing to live

---

[a] 3 Gen. 15:6; also in verse 22   [b] 8 Psalm 32:1,2

NEW INTERNATIONAL VERSION

walk in the footsteps of the faith that our father Abraham had before he was circumcised.

¹³It was not through law that Abraham and his offspring received the promise that he would be heir of the world, but through the righteousness that comes by faith. ¹⁴For if those who live by law are heirs, faith has no value and the promise is worthless, ¹⁵because law brings wrath. And where there is no law there is no transgression.

¹⁶Therefore, the promise comes by faith, so that it may be by grace and may be guaranteed to all Abraham's offspring—not only to those who are of the law but also to those who are of the faith of Abraham. He is the father of us all. ¹⁷As it is written: "I have made you a father of many nations." ᵃ He is our father in the sight of God, in whom he believed—the God who gives life to the dead and calls things that are not as though they were.

¹⁸Against all hope, Abraham in hope believed and so became the father of many nations, just as it had been said to him, "So shall your offspring be." ᵇ ¹⁹Without weakening in his faith, he faced the fact that his body was as good as dead—since he was about a hundred years old—and that Sarah's womb was also dead. ²⁰Yet he did not waver through unbelief regarding the promise of God, but was strengthened in his faith and gave glory to God, ²¹being fully persuaded that God had power to do what he had promised. ²²This is why "it was credited to him as righteousness." ²³The words "it was credited to him" were written not for him alone, ²⁴but

THE MESSAGE

in the risky faith-embrace of God's action for them, the way Abraham lived long before he was marked by circumcision.

4.13-15 That famous promise God gave Abraham—that he and his children would possess the earth—was not given because of something Abraham did or would do. It was based on God's decision to put everything together for him, which Abraham then entered when he believed. If those who get what God gives them only get it by doing everything they are told to do and filling out all the right forms properly signed, that eliminates personal trust completely and turns the promise into an ironclad *contract*! That's not a holy promise; that's a business deal. A contract drawn up by a hard-nosed lawyer and with plenty of fine print only makes sure that you will never be able to collect. But if there is no contract in the first place, simply a *promise*—and God's promise at that—you can't break it.

4.16 This is why the fulfillment of God's promise depends entirely on trusting God and his way, and then simply embracing him and what he does. God's promise arrives as pure gift. That's the only way everyone can be sure to get in on it, those who keep the religious traditions *and* those who have never heard of them. For Abraham is father of us all. He is not our racial father—that's reading the story backwards. He is our *faith* father.

4.17-18 We call Abraham "father" not because he got God's attention by living like a saint, but because God made something out of Abraham when he was a nobody. Isn't that what we've always read in Scripture, God saying to Abraham, "I set you up as father of many peoples"? Abraham was first named "father" and then *became* a father because he dared to trust God to do what only God could do: raise the dead to life, with a word make something out of nothing. When everything was hopeless, Abraham believed anyway, deciding to live not on the basis of what he saw he *couldn't* do but on what God said he *would* do. And so he was made father of a multitude of peoples. God himself said to him, "You're going to have a big family, Abraham!"

4.19-25 Abraham didn't focus on his own impotence and say, "It's hopeless. This hundred-year-old body could never father a child." Nor did he survey Sarah's decades of infertility and give up. He didn't tiptoe around God's promise asking cautiously skeptical questions. He plunged into the promise and came up strong, ready for God, sure that God would make good on what he had said. That's why it is said, "Abraham was declared fit before God by trusting God to set him right." But it's not just Abraham; it's

ᵃ 17 Gen. 17:5   ᵇ 18 Gen. 15:5

NEW INTERNATIONAL VERSION

also for us, to whom God will credit righteousness—for us who believe in him who raised Jesus our Lord from the dead. [25]He was delivered over to death for our sins and was raised to life for our justification.

PEACE AND JOY

5 Therefore, since we have been justified through faith, we[a] have peace with God through our Lord Jesus Christ, [2]through whom we have gained access by faith into this grace in which we now stand. And we[a] rejoice in the hope of the glory of God. [3]Not only so, but we[a] also rejoice in our sufferings, because we know that suffering produces perseverance; [4]perseverance, character; and character, hope. [5]And hope does not disappoint us, because God has poured out his love into our hearts by the Holy Spirit, whom he has given us.

[6]You see, at just the right time, when we were still powerless, Christ died for the ungodly. [7]Very rarely will anyone die for a righteous man, though for a good man someone might possibly dare to die. [8]But God demonstrates his own love for us in this: While we were still sinners, Christ died for us.

[9]Since we have now been justified by his blood, how much more shall we be saved from God's wrath through him! [10]For if, when we were God's enemies, we were reconciled to him through the death of his Son, how much more, having been reconciled, shall we be saved through his life! [11]Not only is this so, but we also rejoice in God through our Lord Jesus Christ, through whom we have now received reconciliation.

THE MESSAGE

also us! The same thing gets said about us when we embrace and believe the One who brought Jesus to life when the conditions were equally hopeless. The sacrificed Jesus made us fit for God, set us *right with God.*

DEVELOPING PATIENCE

5.1-2 5 By entering through faith into what God has always wanted to do for us—set us right with him, make us fit for him—we have it all together with God because of our Master Jesus. And that's not all: We throw open our doors to God and discover at the same moment that he has already thrown open his door to us. We find ourselves standing where we always hoped we might stand—out in the wide open spaces of God's grace and glory, standing tall and shouting our praise.

5.3-5 There's more to come: We continue to shout our praise even when we're hemmed in with troubles, because we know how troubles can develop passionate patience in us, and how that patience in turn forges the tempered steel of virtue, keeping us alert for whatever God will do next. In alert expectancy such as this, we're never left feeling shortchanged. Quite the contrary—we can't round up enough containers to hold everything God generously pours into our lives through the Holy Spirit!

5.6-8 Christ arrives right on time to make this happen. He didn't, and doesn't, wait for us to get ready. He presented himself for this sacrificial death when we were far too weak and rebellious to do anything to get ourselves ready. And even if we hadn't been so weak, we wouldn't have known what to do anyway. We can understand someone dying for a person worth dying for, and we can understand how someone good and noble could inspire us to selfless sacrifice. But God put his love on the line for us by offering his Son in sacrificial death while we were of no use whatever to him.

5.9-11 Now that we are set right with God by means of this sacrificial death, the consummate blood sacrifice, there is no longer a question of being at odds with God in any way. If, when we were at our worst, we were put on friendly terms with God by the sacrificial death of his Son, now that we're at our best, just think of how our lives will expand and deepen by means of his resurrection life! Now that we have actually received this amazing friendship with God, we are no longer content to simply say it in plodding prose. We sing and shout our praises to God through Jesus, the Messiah!

a 1,2,3 Or *let us*

NEW INTERNATIONAL VERSION

Death Through Adam, Life Through Christ

12Therefore, just as sin entered the world through one man, and death through sin, and in this way death came to all men, because all sinned— 13for before the law was given, sin was in the world. But sin is not taken into account when there is no law. 14Nevertheless, death reigned from the time of Adam to the time of Moses, even over those who did not sin by breaking a command, as did Adam, who was a pattern of the one to come.

15But the gift is not like the trespass. For if the many died by the trespass of the one man, how much more did God's grace and the gift that came by the grace of the one man, Jesus Christ, overflow to the many! 16Again, the gift of God is not like the result of the one man's sin: The judgment followed one sin and brought condemnation, but the gift followed many trespasses and brought justification. 17For if, by the trespass of the one man, death reigned through that one man, how much more will those who receive God's abundant provision of grace and of the gift of righteousness reign in life through the one man, Jesus Christ.

18Consequently, just as the result of one trespass was condemnation for all men, so also the result of one act of righteousness was justification that brings life for all men. 19For just as through the disobedience of the one man the many were made sinners, so also through the obedience of the one man the many will be made righteous.

20The law was added so that the trespass might increase. But where sin increased, grace increased all the more, 21so that, just as sin reigned in death, so also grace might reign through righteousness to bring eternal life through Jesus Christ our Lord.

Dead to Sin, Alive in Christ

6 What shall we say, then? Shall we go on sinning so that grace may increase? 2By no means! We died to sin; how can we live in it any

THE MESSAGE

The Death-Dealing Sin, the Life-Giving Gift

5.12-14 You know the story of how Adam landed us in the dilemma we're in—first sin, then death, and no one exempt from either sin or death. That sin disturbed relations with God in everything and everyone, but the extent of the disturbance was not clear until God spelled it out in detail to Moses. So death, this huge abyss separating us from God, dominated the landscape from Adam to Moses. Even those who didn't sin precisely as Adam did by disobeying a specific command of God still had to experience this termination of life, this separation from God. But Adam, who got us into this, also points ahead to the One who will get us out of it.

5.15-17 Yet the rescuing gift is not exactly parallel to the death-dealing sin. If one man's sin put crowds of people at the dead-end abyss of separation from God, just think what God's gift poured through one man, Jesus Christ, will do! There's no comparison between that death-dealing sin and this generous, life-giving gift. The verdict on that one sin was the death sentence; the verdict on the many sins that followed was this wonderful life sentence. If death got the upper hand through one man's wrongdoing, can you imagine the breathtaking recovery life makes, sovereign life, in those who grasp with both hands this wildly extravagant life-gift, this grand setting-everything-right, that the one man Jesus Christ provides?

5.18-19 Here it is in a nutshell: Just as one person did it wrong and got us in all this trouble with sin and death, another person did it right and got us out of it. But more than just getting us out of trouble, he got us into life! One man said no to God and put many people in the wrong; one man said yes to God and put many in the right.

5.20-21 All that passing laws against sin did was produce more lawbreakers. But sin didn't, and doesn't, have a chance in competition with the aggressive forgiveness we call *grace*. When it's sin versus grace, grace wins hands down. All sin can do is threaten us with death, and that's the end of it. Grace, because God is putting everything together again through the Messiah, invites us into life—a life that goes on and on and on, world without end.

When Death Becomes Life

6.1-3 6 So what do we do? Keep on sinning so God can keep on forgiving? I should hope not! If we've left the country where sin is sovereign, how can we still live in our old house there? Or didn't you realize we packed up and left there

NEW INTERNATIONAL VERSION

longer? ³Or don't you know that all of us who were baptized into Christ Jesus were baptized into his death? ⁴We were therefore buried with him through baptism into death in order that, just as Christ was raised from the dead through the glory of the Father, we too may live a new life.

⁵If we have been united with him like this in his death, we will certainly also be united with him in his resurrection. ⁶For we know that our old self was crucified with him so that the body of sin might be done away with,ᵃ that we should no longer be slaves to sin— ⁷because anyone who has died has been freed from sin.

⁸Now if we died with Christ, we believe that we will also live with him. ⁹For we know that since Christ was raised from the dead, he cannot die again; death no longer has mastery over him. ¹⁰The death he died, he died to sin once for all; but the life he lives, he lives to God.

¹¹In the same way, count yourselves dead to sin but alive to God in Christ Jesus. ¹²Therefore do not let sin reign in your mortal body so that you obey its evil desires. ¹³Do not offer the parts of your body to sin, as instruments of wickedness, but rather offer yourselves to God, as those who have been brought from death to life; and offer the parts of your body to him as instruments of righteousness. ¹⁴For sin shall not be your master, because you are not under law, but under grace.

SLAVES TO RIGHTEOUSNESS

¹⁵What then? Shall we sin because we are not under law but under grace? By no means! ¹⁶Don't you know that when you offer yourselves to someone to obey him as slaves, you are slaves to the one whom you obey—whether you are slaves to sin, which leads to death, or to obedience, which leads to righteousness? ¹⁷But thanks be to God that, though you used to be slaves to sin, you wholeheartedly obeyed the form of teaching to which you were entrusted. ¹⁸You have been set free from sin and have become slaves to righteousness.

¹⁹I put this in human terms because you are weak in your natural selves. Just as you used to

ᵃ 6 Or be rendered powerless

THE MESSAGE

for good? That is what happened in baptism. When we went under the water, we left the old country of sin behind; when we came up out of the water, we entered into the new country of grace—a new life in a new land!

6.3-5 That's what baptism into the life of Jesus means. When we are lowered into the water, it is like the burial of Jesus; when we are raised up out of the water, it is like the resurrection of Jesus. Each of us is raised into a light-filled world by our Father so that we can see where we're going in our new grace-sovereign country.

6.6-11 Could it be any clearer? Our old way of life was nailed to the Cross with Christ, a decisive end to that sin-miserable life—no longer at sin's every beck and call! What we believe is this: If we get included in Christ's sin-conquering death, we also get included in his life-saving resurrection. We know that when Jesus was raised from the dead it was a signal of the end of death-as-the-end. Never again will death have the last word. When Jesus died, he took sin down with him, but alive he brings God down to us. From now on, think of it this way: Sin speaks a dead language that means nothing to you; God speaks your mother tongue, and you hang on every word. You are dead to sin and alive to God. That's what Jesus did.

6.12-14 That means you must not give sin a vote in the way you conduct your lives. Don't give it the time of day. Don't even run little errands that are connected with that old way of life. Throw yourselves wholeheartedly and fulltime—remember, you've been raised from the dead!—into God's way of doing things. Sin can't tell you how to live. After all, you're not living under that old tyranny any longer. You're living in the freedom of God.

WHAT IS TRUE FREEDOM?

6.15-18 So, since we're out from under the old tyranny, does that mean we can live any old way we want? Since we're free in the freedom of God, can we do anything that comes to mind? Hardly. You know well enough from your own experience that there are some acts of so-called freedom that destroy freedom. Offer yourselves to sin, for instance, and it's your last free act. But offer yourselves to the ways of God and the freedom never quits. All your lives you've let sin tell you what to do. But thank God you've started listening to a new master, one whose commands set you free to live openly in *his* freedom!

6.19 I'm using this freedom language because it's easy to picture. You can readily recall, can't you,

NEW INTERNATIONAL VERSION

offer the parts of your body in slavery to impurity and to ever-increasing wickedness, so now offer them in slavery to righteousness leading to holiness. ²⁰When you were slaves to sin, you were free from the control of righteousness. ²¹What benefit did you reap at that time from the things you are now ashamed of? Those things result in death! ²²But now that you have been set free from sin and have become slaves to God, the benefit you reap leads to holiness, and the result is eternal life. ²³For the wages of sin is death, but the gift of God is eternal life in*a* Christ Jesus our Lord.

AN ILLUSTRATION FROM MARRIAGE

7 Do you not know, brothers—for I am speaking to men who know the law—that the law has authority over a man only as long as he lives? ²For example, by law a married woman is bound to her husband as long as he is alive, but if her husband dies, she is released from the law of marriage. ³So then, if she marries another man while her husband is still alive, she is called an adulteress. But if her husband dies, she is released from that law and is not an adulteress, even though she marries another man.

⁴So, my brothers, you also died to the law through the body of Christ, that you might belong to another, to him who was raised from the dead, in order that we might bear fruit to God. ⁵For when we were controlled by the sinful nature,*b* the sinful passions aroused by the law were at work in our bodies, so that we bore fruit for death. ⁶But now, by dying to what once bound us, we have been released from the law so that we serve in the new way of the Spirit, and not in the old way of the written code.

STRUGGLING WITH SIN

⁷What shall we say, then? Is the law sin? Certainly not! Indeed I would not have known what sin was except through the law. For I would not have known what coveting really was if the law

THE MESSAGE

how at one time the more you did just what you felt like doing—not caring about others, not caring about God—the worse your life became and the less freedom you had? And how much different is it now as you live in God's freedom, your lives healed and expansive in holiness?

6.20-21 As long as you did what you felt like doing, ignoring God, you didn't have to bother with right thinking or right living, or right *anything* for that matter. But do you call that a free life? What did you get out of it? Nothing you're proud of now. Where did it get you? A dead end.

6.22-23 But now that you've found you don't have to listen to sin tell you what to do, and have discovered the delight of listening to God telling you, what a surprise! A whole, healed, put-together life right now, with more and more of life on the way! Work hard for sin your whole life and your pension is death. But God's gift is *real life*, eternal life, delivered by Jesus, our Master.

TORN BETWEEN ONE WAY AND ANOTHER

7.1-3 7 You shouldn't have any trouble understanding this, friends, for you know all the ins and outs of the law—how it works and how its power touches only the living. For instance, a wife is legally tied to her husband while he lives, but if he dies, she's free. If she lives with another man while her husband is living, she's obviously an adulteress. But if he dies, she is quite free to marry another man in good conscience, with no one's disapproval.

7.4-6 So, my friends, this is something like what has taken place with you. When Christ died he took that entire rule-dominated way of life down with him and left it in the tomb, leaving you free to "marry" a resurrection life and bear "offspring" of faith for God. For as long as we lived that old way of life, doing whatever we felt we could get away with, sin was calling most of the shots as the old law code hemmed us in. And this made us all the more rebellious. In the end, all we had to show for it was miscarriages and stillbirths. But now that we're no longer shackled to that domineering mate of sin, and out from under all those oppressive regulations and fine print, we're free to live a new life in the freedom of God.

7.7 But I can hear you say, "If the law code was as bad as all that, it's no better than sin itself." That's certainly not true. The law code had a perfectly legitimate function. Without its clear guidelines for right and wrong, moral behavior would be mostly guesswork. Apart from the succinct, surgical command, "You shall not covet," I could have dressed covetousness up to look like a virtue and ruined my life with it.

a 23 Or *through*   *b* 5 Or *the flesh*; also in verse 25

NEW INTERNATIONAL VERSION

had not said, "Do not covet." [a] 8But sin, seizing the opportunity afforded by the commandment, produced in me every kind of covetous desire. For apart from law, sin is dead. 9Once I was alive apart from law; but when the commandment came, sin sprang to life and I died. 10I found that the very commandment that was intended to bring life actually brought death. 11For sin, seizing the opportunity afforded by the commandment, deceived me, and through the commandment put me to death. 12So then, the law is holy, and the commandment is holy, righteous and good.

13Did that which is good, then, become death to me? By no means! But in order that sin might be recognized as sin, it produced death in me through what was good, so that through the commandment sin might become utterly sinful.

14We know that the law is spiritual; but I am unspiritual, sold as a slave to sin. 15I do not understand what I do. For what I want to do I do not do, but what I hate I do. 16And if I do what I do not want to do, I agree that the law is good. 17As it is, it is no longer I myself who do it, but it is sin living in me. 18I know that nothing good lives in me, that is, in my sinful nature. [b] For I have the desire to do what is good, but I cannot carry it out. 19For what I do is not the good I want to do; no, the evil I do not want to do—this I keep on doing. 20Now if I do what I do not want to do, it is no longer I who do it, but it is sin living in me that does it.

21So I find this law at work: When I want to do good, evil is right there with me. 22For in my inner being I delight in God's law; 23but I see another law at work in the members of my body, waging war against the law of my mind and making me a prisoner of the law of sin at work within my members. 24What a wretched man I am! Who will rescue me from this body of

THE MESSAGE

7.8-12 Don't you remember how it was? I do, perfectly well. The law code started out as an excellent piece of work. What happened, though, was that sin found a way to pervert the command into a temptation, making a piece of "forbidden fruit" out of it. The law code, instead of being used to guide me, was used to seduce me. Without all the paraphernalia of the law code, sin looked pretty dull and lifeless, and I went along without paying much attention to it. But once sin got its hands on the law code and decked itself out in all that finery, I was fooled, and fell for it. The very command that was supposed to guide me into life was cleverly used to trip me up, throwing me headlong. So sin was plenty alive, and I was stone dead. But the law code itself is God's good and common sense, each command sane and holy counsel.

7.13 I can already hear your next question: "Does that mean I can't even trust what is good [that is, the law]? Is good just as dangerous as evil?" No again! Sin simply did what sin is so famous for doing: using the good as a cover to tempt me to do what would finally destroy me. By hiding within God's good commandment, sin did far more mischief than it could ever have accomplished on its own.

7.14-16 I can anticipate the response that is coming: "I know that all God's commands are spiritual, but I'm not. Isn't this also your experience?" Yes. I'm full of myself—after all, I've spent a long time in sin's prison. What I don't understand about myself is that I decide one way, but then I act another, doing things I absolutely despise. So if I can't be trusted to figure out what is best for myself and then do it, it becomes obvious that God's command is necessary.

7.17-20 But I need something *more*! For if I know the law but still can't keep it, and if the power of sin within me keeps sabotaging my best intentions, I obviously need help! I realize that I don't have what it takes. I can will it, but I can't *do* it. I decide to do good, but I don't *really* do it; I decide not to do bad, but then I do it anyway. My decisions, such as they are, don't result in actions. Something has gone wrong deep within me and gets the better of me every time.

7.21-23 It happens so regularly that it's predictable. The moment I decide to do good, sin is there to trip me up. I truly delight in God's commands, but it's pretty obvious that not all of me joins in that delight. Parts of me covertly rebel, and just when I least expect it, they take charge.

7.24 I've tried everything and nothing helps. I'm at the end of my rope. Is there no one who can do anything for me? Isn't that the real question?

---

[a] 7 Exodus 20:17; Deut. 5:21   [b] 18 Or *my flesh*

NEW INTERNATIONAL VERSION	THE MESSAGE

death? ²⁵Thanks be to God—through Jesus Christ our Lord!

So then, I myself in my mind am a slave to God's law, but in the sinful nature a slave to the law of sin.

LIFE THROUGH THE SPIRIT

8 Therefore, there is now no condemnation for those who are in Christ Jesus,[a] ²because through Christ Jesus the law of the Spirit of life set me free from the law of sin and death. ³For what the law was powerless to do in that it was weakened by the sinful nature,[b] God did by sending his own Son in the likeness of sinful man to be a sin offering.[c] And so he condemned sin in sinful man,[d] ⁴in order that the righteous requirements of the law might be fully met in us, who do not live according to the sinful nature but according to the Spirit.

⁵Those who live according to the sinful nature have their minds set on what that nature desires; but those who live in accordance with the Spirit have their minds set on what the Spirit desires. ⁶The mind of sinful man[e] is death, but the mind controlled by the Spirit is life and peace; ⁷the sinful mind[f] is hostile to God. It does not submit to God's law, nor can it do so. ⁸Those controlled by the sinful nature cannot please God.

⁹You, however, are controlled not by the sinful nature but by the Spirit, if the Spirit of God lives in you. And if anyone does not have the Spirit of Christ, he does not belong to Christ. ¹⁰But if Christ is in you, your body is dead because of sin, yet your spirit is alive because of righteousness. ¹¹And if the Spirit of him who raised Jesus from the dead is living in you, he

---

^a 1 Some later manuscripts *Jesus, who do not live according to the sinful nature but according to the Spirit,* ^b 3 Or the flesh; also in verses 4, 5, 8, 9, 12 and 13 ^c 3 Or man, for sin ^d 3 Or in the flesh ^e 6 Or mind set on the flesh ^f 7 Or the mind set on the flesh

---

7.25   The answer, thank God, is that Jesus Christ can and does. He acted to set things right in this life of contradictions where I want to serve God with all my heart and mind, but am pulled by the influence of sin to do something totally different.

THE SOLUTION IS LIFE ON GOD'S TERMS

8.1-2   **8** With the arrival of Jesus, the Messiah, that fateful dilemma is resolved. Those who enter into Christ's being-here-for-us no longer have to live under a continuous, low-lying black cloud. A new power is in operation. The Spirit of life in Christ, like a strong wind, has magnificently cleared the air, freeing you from a fated lifetime of brutal tyranny at the hands of sin and death.

8.3-4   God went for the jugular when he sent his own Son. He didn't deal with the problem as something remote and unimportant. In his Son, Jesus, he personally took on the human condition, entered the disordered mess of struggling humanity in order to set it right once and for all. The law code, weakened as it always was by fractured human nature, could never have done that.

The law always ended up being used as a Band-Aid on sin instead of a deep healing of it. And now what the law code asked for but we couldn't deliver is accomplished as we, instead of redoubling our own efforts, simply embrace what the Spirit is doing in us.

8.5-8   Those who think they can do it on their own end up obsessed with measuring their own moral muscle but never get around to exercising it in real life. Those who trust God's action in them find that God's Spirit is in them—living and breathing God! Obsession with self in these matters is a dead end; attention to God leads us out into the open, into a spacious, free life. Focusing on the self is the opposite of focusing on God. Anyone completely absorbed in self ignores God, ends up thinking more about self than God. That person ignores who God is and what he is doing. And God isn't pleased at being ignored.

8.9-11   But if God himself has taken up residence in your life, you can hardly be thinking more of yourself than of him. Anyone, of course, who has not welcomed this invisible but clearly present God, the Spirit of Christ, won't know what we're talking about. But for you who welcome him, in whom he dwells—even though you still experience all the limitations of sin—you yourself experience life on God's terms. It stands to reason, doesn't it, that if the alive-and-present God who raised Jesus from the

NEW INTERNATIONAL VERSION

who raised Christ from the dead will also give life to your mortal bodies through his Spirit, who lives in you.

¹²Therefore, brothers, we have an obligation—but it is not to the sinful nature, to live according to it. ¹³For if you live according to the sinful nature, you will die; but if by the Spirit you put to death the misdeeds of the body, you will live, ¹⁴because those who are led by the Spirit of God are sons of God. ¹⁵For you did not receive a spirit that makes you a slave again to fear, but you received the Spirit of sonship.ᵃ And by him we cry, "*Abba*,ᵇ Father." ¹⁶The Spirit himself testifies with our spirit that we are God's children. ¹⁷Now if we are children, then we are heirs—heirs of God and co-heirs with Christ, if indeed we share in his sufferings in order that we may also share in his glory.

FUTURE GLORY

¹⁸I consider that our present sufferings are not worth comparing with the glory that will be revealed in us. ¹⁹The creation waits in eager expectation for the sons of God to be revealed. ²⁰For the creation was subjected to frustration, not by its own choice, but by the will of the one who subjected it, in hope ²¹thatᶜ the creation itself will be liberated from its bondage to decay and brought into the glorious freedom of the children of God.

²²We know that the whole creation has been groaning as in the pains of childbirth right up to the present time. ²³Not only so, but we ourselves, who have the firstfruits of the Spirit, groan inwardly as we wait eagerly for our adoption as sons, the redemption of our bodies. ²⁴For in this hope we were saved. But hope that is seen is no hope at all. Who hopes for what he already has? ²⁵But if we hope for what we do not yet have, we wait for it patiently.

²⁶In the same way, the Spirit helps us in our weakness. We do not know what we ought to pray for, but the Spirit himself intercedes for us with groans that words cannot express. ²⁷And he who searches our hearts knows the mind of the Spirit, because the Spirit intercedes for the saints in accordance with God's will.

MORE THAN CONQUERORS

²⁸And we know that in all things God works

ᵃ 15 Or *adoption*   ᵇ 15 Aramaic for *Father*
ᶜ 20,21 Or *subjected it in hope.* ²¹*For*

THE MESSAGE

dead moves into your life, he'll do the same thing in you that he did in Jesus, bringing you alive to himself? When God lives and breathes in you (and he does, as surely as he did in Jesus), you are delivered from that dead life. With his Spirit living in you, your body will be as alive as Christ's!

8.12-14   So don't you see that we don't owe this old do-it-yourself life one red cent. There's nothing in it for us, nothing at all. The best thing to do is give it a decent burial and get on with your new life. God's Spirit beckons. There are things to do and places to go!

8.15-17   This resurrection life you received from God is not a timid, grave-tending life. It's adventurously expectant, greeting God with a childlike "What's next, Papa?" God's Spirit touches our spirits and confirms who we really are. We know who he is, and we know who we are: Father and children. And we know we are going to get what's coming to us—an unbelievable inheritance! We go through exactly what Christ goes through. If we go through the hard times with him, then we're certainly going to go through the good times with him!

⊹

8.18-21   That's why I don't think there's any comparison between the present hard times and the coming good times. The created world itself can hardly wait for what's coming next. Everything in creation is being more or less held back. God reins it in until both creation and all the creatures are ready and can be released at the same moment into the glorious times ahead. Meanwhile, the joyful anticipation deepens.

8.22-25   All around us we observe a pregnant creation. The difficult times of pain throughout the world are simply birth pangs. But it's not only around us; it's *within* us. The Spirit of God is arousing us within. We're also feeling the birth pangs. These sterile and barren bodies of ours are yearning for full deliverance. That is why waiting does not diminish us, any more than waiting diminishes a pregnant mother. We are enlarged in the waiting. We, of course, don't see what is enlarging us. But the longer we wait, the larger we become, and the more joyful our expectancy.

8.26-28   Meanwhile, the moment we get tired in the waiting, God's Spirit is right alongside helping us along. If we don't know how or what to pray, it doesn't matter. He does our praying in and for us, making prayer out of our wordless sighs, our aching groans. He knows us far better than we know ourselves, knows our pregnant condition, and keeps us present before God. That's why we can be so sure that every detail in our

NEW INTERNATIONAL VERSION

for the good of those who love him,[a] who[b] have been called according to his purpose. 29For those God foreknew he also predestined to be conformed to the likeness of his Son, that he might be the firstborn among many brothers. 30And those he predestined, he also called; those he called, he also justified; those he justified, he also glorified.

31What, then, shall we say in response to this? If God is for us, who can be against us? 32He who did not spare his own Son, but gave him up for us all—how will he not also, along with him, graciously give us all things? 33Who will bring any charge against those whom God has chosen? It is God who justifies. 34Who is he that condemns? Christ Jesus, who died—more than that, who was raised to life—is at the right hand of God and is also interceding for us. 35Who shall separate us from the love of Christ? Shall trouble or hardship or persecution or famine or nakedness or danger or sword? 36As it is written:

"For your sake we face death all day long;
  we are considered as sheep to be
    slaughtered."[c]

37No, in all these things we are more than conquerors through him who loved us. 38For I am convinced that neither death nor life, neither angels nor demons,[d] neither the present nor the future, nor any powers, 39neither height nor depth, nor anything else in all creation, will be able to separate us from the love of God that is in Christ Jesus our Lord.

GOD'S SOVEREIGN CHOICE

9 I speak the truth in Christ—I am not lying, my conscience confirms it in the Holy Spirit— 2I have great sorrow and unceasing anguish in my heart. 3For I could wish that I myself were cursed and cut off from Christ for the sake of my brothers, those of my own race, 4the people

---

a 28 Some manuscripts And we know that all things work together for good to those who love God   b 28 Or works together with those who love him to bring about what is good—with those who   c 36 Psalm 44:22   d 38 Or nor heavenly rulers

THE MESSAGE

lives of love for God is worked into something good.

8.29-30   God knew what he was doing from the very beginning. He decided from the outset to shape the lives of those who love him along the same lines as the life of his Son. The Son stands first in the line of humanity he restored. We see the original and intended shape of our lives there in him. After God made that decision of what his children should be like, he followed it up by calling people by name. After he called them by name, he set them on a solid basis with himself. And then, after getting them established, he stayed with them to the end, gloriously completing what he had begun.

8.31-39   So, what do you think? With God on our side like this, how can we lose? If God didn't hesitate to put everything on the line for us, embracing our condition and exposing himself to the worst by sending his own Son, is there anything else he wouldn't gladly and freely do for us? And who would dare tangle with God by messing with one of God's chosen? Who would dare even to point a finger? The One who died for us—who was raised to life for us!—is in the presence of God at this very moment sticking up for us. Do you think anyone is going to be able to drive a wedge between us and Christ's love for us? There is no way! Not trouble, not hard times, not hatred, not hunger, not homelessness, not bullying threats, not backstabbing, not even the worst sins listed in Scripture:

They kill us in cold blood because they
    hate you.
We're sitting ducks; they pick us off one by
    one.

None of this fazes us because Jesus loves us. I'm absolutely convinced that nothing—nothing living or dead, angelic or demonic, today or tomorrow, high or low, thinkable or unthinkable—absolutely *nothing* can get between us and God's love because of the way that Jesus our Master has embraced us.

GOD IS CALLING HIS PEOPLE

9.1-5   **9** At the same time, you need to know that I carry with me at all times a huge sorrow. It's an enormous pain deep within me, and I'm never free of it. I'm not exaggerating—Christ and the Holy Spirit are my witnesses. It's the Israelites . . . If there were any way I could be cursed by the Messiah so they could be blessed by him, I'd do it in a minute. They're my fami-

NEW INTERNATIONAL VERSION

of Israel. Theirs is the adoption as sons; theirs the divine glory, the covenants, the receiving of the law, the temple worship and the promises. [5]Theirs are the patriarchs, and from them is traced the human ancestry of Christ, who is God over all, forever praised![a] Amen.

[6]It is not as though God's word had failed. For not all who are descended from Israel are Israel. [7]Nor because they are his descendants are they all Abraham's children. On the contrary, "It is through Isaac that your offspring will be reckoned."[b] [8]In other words, it is not the natural children who are God's children, but it is the children of the promise who are regarded as Abraham's offspring. [9]For this was how the promise was stated: "At the appointed time I will return, and Sarah will have a son."[c]

[10]Not only that, but Rebekah's children had one and the same father, our father Isaac. [11]Yet, before the twins were born or had done anything good or bad—in order that God's purpose in election might stand: [12]not by works but by him who calls—she was told, "The older will serve the younger."[d] [13]Just as it is written: "Jacob I loved, but Esau I hated."[e]

[14]What then shall we say? Is God unjust? Not at all! [15]For he says to Moses,

"I will have mercy on whom I have mercy,
and I will have compassion on whom I
have compassion."[f]

[16]It does not, therefore, depend on man's desire or effort, but on God's mercy. [17]For the Scripture says to Pharaoh: "I raised you up for this very purpose, that I might display my power in you and that my name might be proclaimed in all the earth."[g] [18]Therefore God has mercy on whom he wants to have mercy, and he hardens whom he wants to harden.

[19]One of you will say to me: "Then why does God still blame us? For who resists his will?" [20]But who are you, O man, to talk back to God? "Shall what is formed say to him who formed it, 'Why did you make me like this?' "[h] [21]Does not the potter have the right to make out of the same lump of clay some pottery for noble purposes and some for common use?

THE MESSAGE

ly. I grew up with them. They had everything going for them—family, glory, covenants, revelation, worship, promises, to say nothing of being the race that produced the Messiah, the Christ, who is God over everything, always. Oh, yes!

9.6-9 Don't suppose for a moment, though, that God's Word has malfunctioned in some way or other. The problem goes back a long way. From the outset, not all Israelites of the flesh were Israelites of the spirit. It wasn't Abraham's sperm that gave identity here, but God's *promise*. Remember how it was put: "Your family will be defined by Isaac"? That means that Israelite identity was never racially determined by sexual transmission, but it was *God*-determined by promise. Remember that promise, "When I come back next year at this time, Sarah will have a son"?

9.10-13 And that's not the only time. To Rebecca, also, a promise was made that took priority over genetics. When she became pregnant by our one-of-a-kind ancestor, Isaac, and her babies were still innocent in the womb—incapable of good or bad—she received a special assurance from God. What God did in this case made it perfectly plain that his purpose is not a hit-or-miss thing dependent on what we do or don't do, but a sure thing determined by his decision, flowing steadily from his initiative. God told Rebecca, "The firstborn of your twins will take second place." Later that was turned into a stark epigram: "I loved Jacob; I hated Esau."

9.14-18 Is that grounds for complaining that God is unfair? Not so fast, please. God told Moses, "I'm in charge of mercy. I'm in charge of compassion." Compassion doesn't originate in our bleeding hearts or moral sweat, but in God's mercy. The same point was made when God said to Pharaoh, "I picked you as a bit player in this drama of my salvation power." All we're saying is that God has the first word, initiating the action in which we play our part for good or ill.

9.19 Are you going to object, "So how can God blame us for anything since he's in charge of everything? If the big decisions are already made, what say do we have in it?"

9.20-33 Who in the world do you think you are to second-guess God? Do you for one moment suppose any of us knows enough to call God into question? Clay doesn't talk back to the fingers that mold it, saying, "Why did you shape me like this?" Isn't it obvious that a potter has a perfect right to shape one lump of clay into a vase for holding flowers and another into a pot

[a] 5 Or *Christ, who is over all. God be forever praised!* Or *Christ. God who is over all be forever praised!*
[b] 7 Gen. 21:12   [c] 9 Gen. 18:10,14   [d] 12 Gen. 25:23
[e] 13 Mal. 1:2,3   [f] 15 Exodus 33:19   [g] 17 Exodus 9:16
[h] 20 Isaiah 29:16; 45:9

NEW INTERNATIONAL VERSION

22What if God, choosing to show his wrath and make his power known, bore with great patience the objects of his wrath—prepared for destruction? 23What if he did this to make the riches of his glory known to the objects of his mercy, whom he prepared in advance for glory— 24even us, whom he also called, not only from the Jews but also from the Gentiles? 25As he says in Hosea:

"I will call them 'my people' who are not my
        people;
    and I will call her 'my loved one' who is
        not my loved one," [a]

26and,

"It will happen that in the very place where
        it was said to them,
    'You are not my people,'
they will be called 'sons of the living God.' " [b]

27Isaiah cries out concerning Israel:

"Though the number of the Israelites be like
        the sand by the sea,
    only the remnant will be saved.
28For the Lord will carry out
    his sentence on earth with speed and
        finality." [c]

29It is just as Isaiah said previously:

"Unless the Lord Almighty
    had left us descendants,
we would have become like Sodom,
    we would have been like Gomorrah." [d]

ISRAEL'S UNBELIEF

30What then shall we say? That the Gentiles, who did not pursue righteousness, have obtained it, a righteousness that is by faith; 31but Israel, who pursued a law of righteousness, has not attained it. 32Why not? Because they pursued it not by faith but as if it were by works. They stumbled over the "stumbling stone." 33As it is written:

"See, I lay in Zion a stone that causes men to
        stumble
    and a rock that makes them fall,
and the one who trusts in him will never be
        put to shame." [e]

THE MESSAGE

for cooking beans? If God needs one style of pottery especially designed to show his angry displeasure and another style carefully crafted to show his glorious goodness, isn't that all right? Either or both happens to Jews, but it also happens to the other people. Hosea put it well:

I'll call nobodies and make them
        somebodies;
I'll call the unloved and make them
        beloved.
In the place where they yelled out, "You're
        nobody!"
they're calling you "God's living
        children."

Isaiah maintained this same emphasis:
If each grain of sand on the seashore were
        numbered
    and the sum labeled "chosen of God,"
They'd be numbers still, not names;
    salvation comes by personal selection.
God doesn't count us; he calls us by name.
    Arithmetic is not his focus.

Isaiah had looked ahead and spoken the truth:
If our powerful God
    had not provided us a legacy of living
        children,
We would have ended up like ghost towns,
    like Sodom and Gomorrah.

How can we sum this up? All those people who didn't seem interested in what God was doing actually *embraced* what God was doing as he straightened out their lives. And Israel, who seemed so interested in reading and talking about what God was doing, missed it. How could they miss it? Because instead of trusting God, *they* took over. They were absorbed in what they themselves were doing. They were so absorbed in their "God projects" that they didn't notice God right in front of them, like a huge rock in the middle of the road. And so they stumbled into him and went sprawling. Isaiah (again!) gives us the metaphor for pulling this together:

Careful! I've put a huge stone on the road
        to Mount Zion,
    a stone you can't get around.
But the stone is me! If you're looking
        for me,
    you'll find me on the way, not in the way.

[a] 25 Hosea 2:23   [b] 26 Hosea 1:10   [c] 28 Isaiah 10:22,23
[d] 29 Isaiah 1:9   [e] 33 Isaiah 8:14; 28:16

NEW INTERNATIONAL VERSION

10 Brothers, my heart's desire and prayer to God for the Israelites is that they may be saved. ²For I can testify about them that they are zealous for God, but their zeal is not based on knowledge. ³Since they did not know the righteousness that comes from God and sought to establish their own, they did not submit to God's righteousness. ⁴Christ is the end of the law so that there may be righteousness for everyone who believes.

⁵Moses describes in this way the righteousness that is by the law: "The man who does these things will live by them." ᵃ ⁶But the righteousness that is by faith says: "Do not say in your heart, 'Who will ascend into heaven?' ᵇ" (that is, to bring Christ down) ⁷or 'Who will descend into the deep?' ᶜ" (that is, to bring Christ up from the dead). ⁸But what does it say? "The word is near you; it is in your mouth and in your heart," ᵈ that is, the word of faith we are proclaiming: ⁹That if you confess with your mouth, "Jesus is Lord," and believe in your heart that God raised him from the dead, you will be saved. ¹⁰For it is with your heart that you believe and are justified, and it is with your mouth that you confess and are saved. ¹¹As the Scripture says, "Anyone who trusts in him will never be put to shame." ᵉ ¹²For there is no difference between Jew and Gentile—the same Lord is Lord of all and richly blesses all who call on him, ¹³for, "Everyone who calls on the name of the Lord will be saved." ᶠ

¹⁴How, then, can they call on the one they have not believed in? And how can they believe in the one of whom they have not heard? And how can they hear without someone preaching to them? ¹⁵And how can they preach unless they

THE MESSAGE

ISRAEL REDUCED TO RELIGION

10.1-3 **10** Believe me, friends, all I want for Israel is what's best for Israel: salvation, nothing less. I want it with all my heart and pray to God for it all the time. I readily admit that the Jews are impressively energetic regarding God—but they are doing everything exactly backwards. They don't seem to realize that this comprehensive setting-things-right that is salvation is *God's* business, and a most flourishing business it is. Right across the street they set up their own salvation shops and noisily hawk their wares. After all these years of refusing to really deal with God on his terms, insisting instead on making their own deals, they have nothing to show for it.

10.4-10 The earlier revelation was intended simply to get us ready for the Messiah, who then puts everything right for those who trust him to do it. Moses wrote that anyone who insists on using the law code to live right before God soon discovers it's not so easy—every detail of life regulated by fine print! But trusting God to shape the right living in us is a different story—no precarious climb up to heaven to recruit the Messiah, no dangerous descent into hell to rescue the Messiah. So what exactly was Moses saying?

The word that saves is right here,
as near as the tongue in your mouth,
as close as the heart in your chest.

It's the word of faith that welcomes God to go to work and set things right for us. This is the core of our preaching. Say the welcoming word to God—"Jesus is my Master"—embracing, body and soul, God's work of doing in us what he did in raising Jesus from the dead. That's it. You're not "doing" anything; you're simply calling out to God, trusting him to do it for you. That's salvation. With your whole being you embrace God setting things right, and then you say it, right out loud: "God has set everything right between him and me!"

10.11-13 Scripture reassures us, "No one who trusts God like this—heart and soul—will ever regret it." It's exactly the same no matter what a person's religious background may be: the same God for all of us, acting the same incredibly generous way to everyone who calls out for help. "Everyone who calls, 'Help, God!' gets help."

10.14-17 But how can people call for help if they don't know who to trust? And how can they know who to trust if they haven't heard of the One who can be trusted? And how can they hear if nobody tells them? And how is anyone going to tell them, unless someone is sent to do it? That's why Scripture exclaims,

---

ᵃ5 Lev. 18:5   ᵇ6 Deut. 30:12   ᶜ7 Deut. 30:13
ᵈ8 Deut. 30:14   ᵉ11 Isaiah 28:16   ᶠ13 Joel 2:32

NEW INTERNATIONAL VERSION

are sent? As it is written, "How beautiful are the feet of those who bring good news!" [a]

¹⁶But not all the Israelites accepted the good news. For Isaiah says, "Lord, who has believed our message?" [b] ¹⁷Consequently, faith comes from hearing the message, and the message is heard through the word of Christ. ¹⁸But I ask: Did they not hear? Of course they did:

"Their voice has gone out into all the earth,
    their words to the ends of the world." [c]

¹⁹Again I ask: Did Israel not understand? First, Moses says,

"I will make you envious by those who are
        not a nation;
    I will make you angry by a nation that has
        no understanding." [d]

²⁰And Isaiah boldly says,

"I was found by those who did not seek me;
    I revealed myself to those who did not ask
        for me." [e]

²¹But concerning Israel he says,

"All day long I have held out my hands
    to a disobedient and obstinate people." [f]

THE REMNANT OF ISRAEL

11 I ask then: Did God reject his people? By no means! I am an Israelite myself, a descendant of Abraham, from the tribe of Benjamin. ²God did not reject his people, whom he foreknew. Don't you know what the Scripture says in the passage about Elijah—how he appealed to God against Israel: ³"Lord, they have killed your prophets and torn down your altars; I am the only one left, and they are trying to kill

THE MESSAGE

A sight to take your breath away!
Grand processions of people
    telling all the good things of God!

But not everybody is ready for this, ready to see and hear and act. Isaiah asked what we all ask at one time or another: "Does anyone care, God? Is anyone listening and believing a word of it?" The point is, Before you trust, you have to listen. But unless Christ's Word is preached, there's nothing to listen to.

10.18-21   But haven't there been plenty of opportunities for Israel to listen and understand what's going on? *Plenty*, I'd say.

Preachers' voices have gone 'round the world,
Their message to earth's seven seas.

So the big question is, Why didn't Israel understand that she had no corner on this message? Moses had it right when he predicted,

When you see God reach out to those
    you consider your inferiors—
        outsiders!—
    you'll become insanely jealous.
When you see God reach out to people
    you think are religiously stupid,
    you'll throw temper tantrums.

Isaiah dared to speak out these words of God:
People found and welcomed me
    who never so much as looked for me.
And I found and welcomed people
    who had never even asked about me.

Then he capped it with a damning indictment:
Day after day after day,
    I beckoned Israel with open arms,
And got nothing for my trouble
    but cold shoulders and icy stares.

THE LOYAL MINORITY

11.1-2   **11** Does this mean, then, that God is so fed up with Israel that he'll have nothing more to do with them? Hardly. Remember that I, the one writing these things, am an Israelite, a descendant of Abraham out of the tribe of Benjamin. You can't get much more Semitic than that! So we're not talking about repudiation. God has been too long involved with Israel, has too much invested, to simply wash his hands of them.

11.2-6   Do you remember that time Elijah was agonizing over this same Israel and cried out in prayer?

God, they murdered your prophets,
They trashed your altars;
I'm the only one left and now they're
        after me!

---

[a] 15 Isaiah 52:7   [b] 16 Isaiah 53:1   [c] 18 Psalm 19:4
[d] 19 Deut. 32:21   [e] 20 Isaiah 65:1   [f] 21 Isaiah 65:2

NEW INTERNATIONAL VERSION

me" [a]? [4]And what was God's answer to him? "I have reserved for myself seven thousand who have not bowed the knee to Baal." [b] [5]So too, at the present time there is a remnant chosen by grace. [6]And if by grace, then it is no longer by works; if it were, grace would no longer be grace. [c]

[7]What then? What Israel sought so earnestly it did not obtain, but the elect did. The others were hardened, [8]as it is written:

"God gave them a spirit of stupor,
    eyes so that they could not see
    and ears so that they could not hear,
to this very day." [d]

[9]And David says:

"May their table become a snare and a trap,
    a stumbling block and a retribution for
        them.
[10]May their eyes be darkened so they cannot
        see,
    and their backs be bent forever." [e]

INGRAFTED BRANCHES

[11]Again I ask: Did they stumble so as to fall beyond recovery? Not at all! Rather, because of their transgression, salvation has come to the Gentiles to make Israel envious. [12]But if their transgression means riches for the world, and their loss means riches for the Gentiles, how much greater riches will their fullness bring!

[13]I am talking to you Gentiles. Inasmuch as I am the apostle to the Gentiles, I make much of my ministry [14]in the hope that I may somehow arouse my own people to envy and save some of

THE MESSAGE

And do you remember God's answer?
    I still have seven thousand who haven't
        quit,
    Seven thousand who are loyal to the finish.

It's the same today. There's a fiercely loyal minority still—not many, perhaps, but probably more than you think. They're holding on, not because of what they think they're going to get out of it, but because they're convinced of God's grace and purpose in choosing them. If they were only thinking of their own immediate self-interest, they would have left long ago.

11:7-10 And then what happened? Well, when Israel tried to be right with God on her own, pursuing her own self-interest, she didn't succeed. The chosen ones of God were those who let God pursue his interest in them, and as a result received his stamp of legitimacy. The "self-interest Israel" became thick-skinned toward God. Moses and Isaiah both commented on this:

Fed up with their quarrelsome, self-
        centered ways,
    God blurred their eyes and dulled their
        ears,
Shut them in on themselves in a hall of
        mirrors,
    and they're there to this day.

David was upset about the same thing:
    I hope they get sick eating self-serving
        meals,
    break a leg walking their self-serving
        ways.
    I hope they go blind staring in their
        mirrors,
    get ulcers from playing at god.

PRUNING AND GRAFTING BRANCHES

11:11-12 The next question is, "Are they down for the count? Are they out of this for good?" And the answer is a clear-cut no. Ironically when they walked out, they left the door open and the outsiders walked in. But the next thing you know, the Jews were starting to wonder if perhaps they had walked out on a good thing. Now, if their leaving triggered this worldwide coming of non-Jewish outsiders to God's kingdom, just imagine the effect of their coming back! What a homecoming!

11:13-15 But I don't want to go on about them. It's you, the outsiders, that I'm concerned with now. Because my personal assignment is focused on the so-called outsiders, I make as much of this as I can when I'm among my Israelite kin, the so-called insiders, hoping they'll realize what they're missing and want to get in

---

[a] 3 1 Kings 19:10,14   [b] 4 1 Kings 19:18   [c] 6 Some manuscripts be grace. But if by works, then it is no longer grace; if it were, work would no longer be work.
[d] 8 Deut. 29:4; Isaiah 29:10   [e] 10 Psalm 69:22,23

NEW INTERNATIONAL VERSION

them. ¹⁵For if their rejection is the reconciliation of the world, what will their acceptance be but life from the dead? ¹⁶If the part of the dough offered as firstfruits is holy, then the whole batch is holy; if the root is holy, so are the branches.

¹⁷If some of the branches have been broken off, and you, though a wild olive shoot, have been grafted in among the others and now share in the nourishing sap from the olive root, ¹⁸do not boast over those branches. If you do, consider this: You do not support the root, but the root supports you. ¹⁹You will say then, "Branches were broken off so that I could be grafted in." ²⁰Granted. But they were broken off because of unbelief, and you stand by faith. Do not be arrogant, but be afraid. ²¹For if God did not spare the natural branches, he will not spare you either.

²²Consider therefore the kindness and sternness of God: sternness to those who fell, but kindness to you, provided that you continue in his kindness. Otherwise, you also will be cut off. ²³And if they do not persist in unbelief, they will be grafted in, for God is able to graft them in again. ²⁴After all, if you were cut out of an olive tree that is wild by nature, and contrary to nature were grafted into a cultivated olive tree, how much more readily will these, the natural branches, be grafted into their own olive tree!

ALL ISRAEL WILL BE SAVED

²⁵I do not want you to be ignorant of this mystery, brothers, so that you may not be conceited: Israel has experienced a hardening in part

THE MESSAGE

on what God is doing. If their falling out initiated this worldwide coming together, their recovery is going to set off something even better: mass homecoming! If the first thing the Jews did, even though it was wrong for them, turned out for your good, just think what's going to happen when they get it right!

11.16-18 Behind and underneath all this there is a holy, God-planted, God-tended root. If the primary root of the tree is holy, there's bound to be some holy fruit. Some of the tree's branches were pruned and you wild olive shoots were grafted in. Yet the fact that you are now fed by that rich and holy root gives you no cause to crow over the pruned branches. Remember, you aren't feeding the root; the root is feeding you.

11.19-20 It's certainly possible to say, "Other branches were pruned so that I could be grafted in!" Well and good. But they were pruned because they were deadwood, no longer connected by belief and commitment to the root. The only reason you're on the tree is because your graft "took" when you believed, and because you're connected to that belief-nurturing root. So don't get cocky and strut your branch. Be humbly mindful of the root that keeps you lithe and green.

11.21-22 If God didn't think twice about taking pruning shears to the natural branches, why would he hesitate over you? He wouldn't give it a second thought. Make sure you stay alert to these qualities of gentle kindness and ruthless severity that exist side by side in God—ruthless with the deadwood, gentle with the grafted shoot. But don't presume on this gentleness. The moment you become deadwood, you're out of there.

11.23-24 And don't get to feeling superior to those pruned branches down on the ground. If they don't persist in remaining deadwood, they could very well get grafted back in. God can do that. He can perform miracle grafts. Why, if he could graft *you*—branches cut from a tree out in the wild—into an orchard tree, he certainly isn't going to have any trouble grafting branches back into the tree they grew from in the first place. Just be glad you're in the tree, and hope for the best for the others.

A COMPLETE ISRAEL

11.25-29 I want to lay all this out on the table as clearly as I can, friends. This is complicated. It would be easy to misinterpret what's going on and arrogantly assume that you're royalty and they're just rabble, out on their ears for good. But that's not it at all. This hardness on the part of insid-

NEW INTERNATIONAL VERSION

until the full number of the Gentiles has come in. ²⁶And so all Israel will be saved, as it is written:

"The deliverer will come from Zion;
    he will turn godlessness away from Jacob.
²⁷And this is ᵃ my covenant with them
    when I take away their sins." ᵇ

²⁸As far as the gospel is concerned, they are enemies on your account; but as far as election is concerned, they are loved on account of the patriarchs, ²⁹for God's gifts and his call are irrevocable. ³⁰Just as you who were at one time disobedient to God have now received mercy as a result of their disobedience, ³¹so they too have now become disobedient in order that they too may now ᶜ receive mercy as a result of God's mercy to you. ³²For God has bound all men over to disobedience so that he may have mercy on them all.

DOXOLOGY

³³Oh, the depth of the riches of the wisdom
        and ᵈ knowledge of God!
    How unsearchable his judgments,
    and his paths beyond tracing out!
³⁴"Who has known the mind of the Lord?
    Or who has been his counselor?" ᵉ
³⁵"Who has ever given to God,
    that God should repay him?" ᶠ
³⁶For from him and through him and to him
    are all things.
    To him be the glory forever! Amen.

LIVING SACRIFICES

12 Therefore, I urge you, brothers, in view of God's mercy, to offer your bodies as living sacrifices, holy and pleasing to God—this is your spiritual ᵍ act of worship. ²Do not conform any longer to the pattern of this world, but be transformed by the renewing of your mind. Then you will be able to test and approve what God's will is—his good, pleasing and perfect will.

ᵃ 27 Or will be   ᵇ 27 Isaiah 59:20,21; 27:9; Jer. 31:33,34
ᶜ 31 Some manuscripts do not have now.   ᵈ 33 Or riches
and the wisdom and the   ᵉ 34 Isaiah 40:13
ᶠ 35 Job 41:11   ᵍ 1 Or reasonable

THE MESSAGE

er Israel toward God is temporary. Its effect is to open things up to all the outsiders so that we end up with a full house. Before it's all over, there will be a complete Israel. As it is written,

A champion will stride down from the
        mountain of Zion;
    he'll clean house in Jacob.
And this is my commitment to my people:
    removal of their sins.

From your point of view as you hear and embrace the good news of the Message, it looks like the Jews are God's enemies. But looked at from the long-range perspective of God's overall purpose, they remain God's oldest friends. God's gifts and God's call are under full warranty—never canceled, never rescinded.

11.30-32   There was a time not so long ago when you were on the outs with God. But then the Jews slammed the door on him and things opened up for you. Now *they* are on the outs. But with the door held wide open for you, they have a way back in. In one way or another, God makes sure that we all experience what it means to be outside so that he can personally open the door and welcome us back in.

11.33-36   Have you ever come on anything quite like this extravagant generosity of God, this deep, deep wisdom? It's way over our heads. We'll never figure it out.

Is there anyone around who can explain
        God?
Anyone smart enough to tell him what to do?
Anyone who has done him such a huge favor
    that God has to ask his advice?

Everything comes from him;
Everything happens through him;
Everything ends up in him.
Always glory! Always praise!
    Yes. Yes. Yes.

PLACE YOUR LIFE BEFORE GOD

12.1-2   **12** So here's what I want you to do, God helping you: Take your everyday, ordinary life—your sleeping, eating, going-to-work, and walking-around life—and place it before God as an offering. Embracing what God does for you is the best thing you can do for him. Don't become so well-adjusted to your culture that you fit into it without even thinking. Instead, fix your attention on God. You'll be changed from the inside out. Readily recognize what he wants from you, and quickly respond to it. Unlike the culture around you, always dragging you down to its level of immaturity, God brings the best out of you, develops well-formed maturity in you.

NEW INTERNATIONAL VERSION

³For by the grace given me I say to every one of you: Do not think of yourself more highly than you ought, but rather think of yourself with sober judgment, in accordance with the measure of faith God has given you. ⁴Just as each of us has one body with many members, and these members do not all have the same function, ⁵so in Christ we who are many form one body, and each member belongs to all the others. ⁶We have different gifts, according to the grace given us. If a man's gift is prophesying, let him use it in proportion to his*ᵃ* faith. ⁷If it is serving, let him serve; if it is teaching, let him teach; ⁸if it is encouraging, let him encourage; if it is contributing to the needs of others, let him give generously; if it is leadership, let him govern diligently; if it is showing mercy, let him do it cheerfully.

LOVE

⁹Love must be sincere. Hate what is evil; cling to what is good. ¹⁰Be devoted to one another in brotherly love. Honor one another above yourselves. ¹¹Never be lacking in zeal, but keep your spiritual fervor, serving the Lord. ¹²Be joyful in hope, patient in affliction, faithful in prayer. ¹³Share with God's people who are in need. Practice hospitality.

¹⁴Bless those who persecute you; bless and do not curse. ¹⁵Rejoice with those who rejoice; mourn with those who mourn. ¹⁶Live in harmony with one another. Do not be proud, but be willing to associate with people of low position.*ᵇ* Do not be conceited.

¹⁷Do not repay anyone evil for evil. Be careful to do what is right in the eyes of everybody. ¹⁸If it is possible, as far as it depends on you, live at peace with everyone. ¹⁹Do not take revenge, my friends, but leave room for God's wrath, for it is written: "It is mine to avenge; I will repay,"*ᶜ* says the Lord. ²⁰On the contrary:

ᵃ 6 Or in agreement with the   *ᵇ 16 Or willing to do menial*
work   *ᶜ 19 Deut. 32:35*

THE MESSAGE

12.3   I'm speaking to you out of deep gratitude for all that God has given me, and especially as I have responsibilities in relation to you. Living then, as every one of you does, in pure grace, it's important that you not misinterpret yourselves as people who are bringing this goodness to God. No, God brings it all to you. The only accurate way to understand ourselves is by what God is and by what he does for us, not by what we are and what we do for him.

12.4-6   In this way we are like the various parts of a human body. Each part gets its meaning from the body as a whole, not the other way around. The body we're talking about is Christ's body of chosen people. Each of us finds our meaning and function as a part of his body. But as a chopped-off finger or cut-off toe we wouldn't amount to much, would we? So since we find ourselves fashioned into all these excellently formed and marvelously functioning parts in Christ's body, let's just go ahead and be what we were made to be, without enviously or pridefully comparing ourselves with each other, or trying to be something we aren't.

12.6-8   If you preach, just preach God's Message, nothing else; if you help, just help, don't take over; if you teach, stick to your teaching; if you give encouraging guidance, be careful that you don't get bossy; if you're put in charge, don't manipulate; if you're called to give aid to people in distress, keep your eyes open and be quick to respond; if you work with the disadvantaged, don't let yourself get irritated with them or depressed by them. Keep a smile on your face.

⊹

12.9-10 Love from the center of who you are; don't fake it. Run for dear life from evil; hold on for dear life to good. Be good friends who love deeply; practice playing second fiddle.

12.11-13   Don't burn out; keep yourselves fueled and aflame. Be alert servants of the Master, cheerfully expectant. Don't quit in hard times; pray all the harder. Help needy Christians; be inventive in hospitality.

12.14-16   Bless your enemies; no cursing under your breath. Laugh with your happy friends when they're happy; share tears when they're down. Get along with each other; don't be stuck-up. Make friends with nobodies; don't be the great somebody.

12.17-19   Don't hit back; discover beauty in everyone. If you've got it in you, get along with everybody. Don't insist on getting even; that's not for you to do. "I'll do the judging," says God. "I'll take care of it."

NEW INTERNATIONAL VERSION

"If your enemy is hungry, feed him;
  if he is thirsty, give him something to
    drink.
In doing this, you will heap burning coals on
    his head." *a*

²¹Do not be overcome by evil, but overcome evil
with good.

SUBMISSION TO THE AUTHORITIES

13 Everyone must submit himself to the governing authorities, for there is no authority except that which God has established. The authorities that exist have been established by God. ²Consequently, he who rebels against the authority is rebelling against what God has instituted, and those who do so will bring judgment on themselves. ³For rulers hold no terror for those who do right, but for those who do wrong. Do you want to be free from fear of the one in authority? Then do what is right and he will commend you. ⁴For he is God's servant to do you good. But if you do wrong, be afraid, for he does not bear the sword for nothing. He is God's servant, an agent of wrath to bring punishment on the wrongdoer. ⁵Therefore, it is necessary to submit to the authorities, not only because of possible punishment but also because of conscience.

⁶This is also why you pay taxes, for the authorities are God's servants, who give their full time to governing. ⁷Give everyone what you owe him: If you owe taxes, pay taxes; if revenue, then revenue; if respect, then respect; if honor, then honor.

LOVE, FOR THE DAY IS NEAR

⁸Let no debt remain outstanding, except the continuing debt to love one another, for he who loves his fellowman has fulfilled the law. ⁹The commandments, "Do not commit adultery," "Do not murder," "Do not steal," "Do not covet," *b* and whatever other commandment there may be, are summed up in this one rule: "Love your neighbor as yourself." *c* ¹⁰Love does no harm to its neighbor. Therefore love is the fulfillment of the law.

¹¹And do this, understanding the present time. The hour has come for you to wake up from your slumber, because our salvation is nearer now than when we first believed. ¹²The night is nearly over; the day is almost here. So let us put aside the deeds of darkness and put on the armor of light. ¹³Let us behave decently, as in the daytime, not in orgies and drunkenness, not in sexual immorality and debauchery, not in dis-

a 20 Prov. 25:21,22   *b 9* Exodus 20:13-15,17; Deut. 5:17-19,21   *c 9* Lev. 19:18

THE MESSAGE

12.20-21   Our Scriptures tell us that if you see your enemy hungry, go buy that person lunch, or if he's thirsty, get him a drink. Your generosity will surprise him with goodness. Don't let evil get the best of you; get the best of evil by doing good.

TO BE A RESPONSIBLE CITIZEN

13.1-3   **13** Be a good citizen. All governments are under God. Insofar as there is peace and order, it's God's order. So live responsibly as a citizen. If you're irresponsible to the state, then you're irresponsible with God, and God will hold you responsible. Duly constituted authorities are only a threat if you're trying to get by with something. Decent citizens should have nothing to fear.

13.3-5   Do you want to be on good terms with the government? Be a responsible citizen and you'll get on just fine, the government working to your advantage. But if you're breaking the rules right and left, watch out. The police aren't there just to be admired in their uniforms. God also has an interest in keeping order, and he uses them to do it. That's why you must live responsibly—not just to avoid punishment but also because it's the right way to live.

13.6-7   That's also why you pay taxes—so that an orderly way of life can be maintained. Fulfill your obligations as a citizen. Pay your taxes, pay your bills, respect your leaders.

✝

13.8-10   Don't run up debts, except for the huge debt of love you owe each other. When you love others, you complete what the law has been after all along. The law code—don't sleep with another person's spouse, don't take someone's life, don't take what isn't yours, don't always be wanting what you don't have, and any other "don't" you can think of—finally adds up to this: Love other people as well as you do yourself. You can't go wrong when you love others. When you add up everything in the law code, the sum total is *love*.

13.11-14   But make sure that you don't get so absorbed and exhausted in taking care of all your day-by-day obligations that you lose track of the time and doze off, oblivious to God. The night is about over, dawn is about to break. Be up and awake to what God is doing! God is putting the finishing touches on the salvation work he began when we first believed. We can't afford to waste a minute, must not squander these precious daylight hours in frivolity and indulgence, in sleeping around and dissipation, in

NEW INTERNATIONAL VERSION

sension and jealousy. [14]Rather, clothe yourselves with the Lord Jesus Christ, and do not think about how to gratify the desires of the sinful nature. [a]

THE WEAK AND THE STRONG

14 Accept him whose faith is weak, without passing judgment on disputable matters. [2]One man's faith allows him to eat everything, but another man, whose faith is weak, eats only vegetables. [3]The man who eats everything must not look down on him who does not, and the man who does not eat everything must not condemn the man who does, for God has accepted him. [4]Who are you to judge someone else's servant? To his own master he stands or falls. And he will stand, for the Lord is able to make him stand.

[5]One man considers one day more sacred than another; another man considers every day alike. Each one should be fully convinced in his own mind. [6]He who regards one day as special, does so to the Lord. He who eats meat, eats to the Lord, for he gives thanks to God; and he who abstains, does so to the Lord and gives thanks to God. [7]For none of us lives to himself alone and none of us dies to himself alone. [8]If we live, we live to the Lord; and if we die, we die to the Lord. So, whether we live or die, we belong to the Lord.

[9]For this very reason, Christ died and returned to life so that he might be the Lord of both the dead and the living. [10]You, then, why do you judge your brother? Or why do you look down on your brother? For we will all stand before God's judgment seat. [11]It is written:

THE MESSAGE

bickering and grabbing everything in sight. Get out of bed and get dressed! Don't loiter and linger, waiting until the very last minute. Dress yourselves in Christ, and be up and about!

CULTIVATING GOOD RELATIONSHIPS

14.1 **14** Welcome with open arms fellow believers who don't see things the way you do. And don't jump all over them every time they do or say something you don't agree with—even when it seems that they are strong on opinions but weak in the faith department. Remember, they have their own history to deal with. Treat them gently.

14.2-4 For instance, a person who has been around for a while might well be convinced that he can eat anything on the table, while another, with a different background, might assume all Christians should be vegetarians and eat accordingly. But since both are guests at Christ's table, wouldn't it be terribly rude if they fell to criticizing what the other ate or didn't eat? God, after all, invited them both to the table. Do you have any business crossing people off the guest list or interfering with God's welcome? If there are corrections to be made or manners to be learned, God can handle that without your help.

14.5 Or, say, one person thinks that some days should be set aside as holy and another thinks that each day is pretty much like any other. There are good reasons either way. So, each person is free to follow the convictions of conscience.

14.6-9 What's important in all this is that if you keep a holy day, keep it for *God's* sake; if you eat meat, eat it to the glory of God and thank God for prime rib; if you're a vegetarian, eat vegetables to the glory of God and thank God for broccoli. None of us are permitted to insist on our own way in these matters. It's *God* we are answerable to—all the way from life to death and everything in between—not each other. That's why Jesus lived and died and then lived again: so that he could be our Master across the entire range of life and death, and free us from the petty tyrannies of each other.

14.10-12 So where does that leave you when you criticize a brother? And where does that leave you when you condescend to a sister? I'd say it leaves you looking pretty silly—or worse. Eventually, we're all going to end up kneeling side by side in the place of judgment, facing God. Your critical and condescending ways aren't going to improve your position there one bit. Read it for yourself in Scripture:

NEW INTERNATIONAL VERSION

" 'As surely as I live,' says the Lord,
  'every knee will bow before me;
    every tongue will confess to God.' " a

¹²So then, each of us will give an account of himself to God.

¹³Therefore let us stop passing judgment on one another. Instead, make up your mind not to put any stumbling block or obstacle in your brother's way. ¹⁴As one who is in the Lord Jesus, I am fully convinced that no food b is unclean in itself. But if anyone regards something as unclean, then for him it is unclean. ¹⁵If your brother is distressed because of what you eat, you are no longer acting in love. Do not by your eating destroy your brother for whom Christ died. ¹⁶Do not allow what you consider good to be spoken of as evil. ¹⁷For the kingdom of God is not a matter of eating and drinking, but of righteousness, peace and joy in the Holy Spirit, ¹⁸because anyone who serves Christ in this way is pleasing to God and approved by men.

¹⁹Let us therefore make every effort to do what leads to peace and to mutual edification. ²⁰Do not destroy the work of God for the sake of food. All food is clean, but it is wrong for a man to eat anything that causes someone else to stumble. ²¹It is better not to eat meat or drink wine or to do anything else that will cause your brother to fall.

²²So whatever you believe about these things keep between yourself and God. Blessed is the man who does not condemn himself by what he approves. ²³But the man who has doubts is condemned if he eats, because his eating is not from faith; and everything that does not come from faith is sin.

a 11 Isaiah 45:23   b 14 Or that nothing

THE MESSAGE

"As I live and breathe," God says,
  "every knee will bow before me;
  Every tongue will tell the honest truth
    that I and only I am God."

So tend to your knitting. You've got your hands full just taking care of your own life before God.

14.13-14   Forget about deciding what's right for each other. Here's what you need to be concerned about: that you don't get in the way of someone else, making life more difficult than it already is. I'm convinced—Jesus convinced me!—that everything as it is in itself is holy. We, of course, by the way we treat it or talk about it, can contaminate it.

14.15-16   If you confuse others by making a big issue over what they eat or don't eat, you're no longer a companion with them in love, are you? These, remember, are persons for whom Christ died. Would you risk sending them to hell over an item in their diet? Don't you dare let a piece of God-blessed food become an occasion of soul-poisoning!

14.17-18   God's kingdom isn't a matter of what you put in your stomach, for goodness' sake. It's what God does with your life as he sets it right, puts it together, and completes it with joy. Your task is to single-mindedly serve Christ. Do that and you'll kill two birds with one stone: pleasing the God above you and proving your worth to the people around you.

14.19-21   So let's agree to use all our energy in getting along with each other. Help others with encouraging words; don't drag them down by finding fault. You're certainly not going to permit an argument over what is served or not served at supper to wreck God's work among you, are you? I said it before and I'll say it again: All food is good, but it can turn bad if you use it badly, if you use it to trip others up and send them sprawling. When you sit down to a meal, your primary concern should not be to feed your own face but to share the life of Jesus. So be sensitive and courteous to the others who are eating. Don't eat or say or do things that might interfere with the free exchange of love.

14.22-23   Cultivate your own relationship with God, but don't impose it on others. You're fortunate if your behavior and your belief are coherent. But if you're not sure, if you notice that you are acting in ways inconsistent with what you believe—some days trying to impose your opinions on others, other days just trying to please them—then you know that you're out of line. If the way you live isn't consistent with what you believe, then it's wrong.

NEW INTERNATIONAL VERSION

15 We who are strong ought to bear with the failings of the weak and not to please ourselves. 2Each of us should please his neighbor for his good, to build him up. 3For even Christ did not please himself but, as it is written: "The insults of those who insult you have fallen on me."[a] 4For everything that was written in the past was written to teach us, so that through endurance and the encouragement of the Scriptures we might have hope.

5May the God who gives endurance and encouragement give you a spirit of unity among yourselves as you follow Christ Jesus, 6so that with one heart and mouth you may glorify the God and Father of our Lord Jesus Christ.

7Accept one another, then, just as Christ accepted you, in order to bring praise to God. 8For I tell you that Christ has become a servant of the Jews[b] on behalf of God's truth, to confirm the promises made to the patriarchs 9so that the Gentiles may glorify God for his mercy, as it is written:

"Therefore I will praise you among the
    Gentiles;
I will sing hymns to your name."[c]

10Again, it says,

"Rejoice, O Gentiles, with his people."[d]

11And again,

"Praise the Lord, all you Gentiles,
    and sing praises to him, all you peoples."[e]

12And again, Isaiah says,

"The Root of Jesse will spring up,
    one who will arise to rule over the
        nations;
the Gentiles will hope in him."[f]

13May the God of hope fill you with all joy and peace as you trust in him, so that you may overflow with hope by the power of the Holy Spirit.

PAUL THE MINISTER TO THE GENTILES

14I myself am convinced, my brothers, that you yourselves are full of goodness, complete in

a 3 Psalm 69:9   b 8 Greek circumcision
c 9 2 Samuel 22:50; Psalm 18:49   d 10 Deut. 32:43
e 11 Psalm 117:1   f 12 Isaiah 11:10

THE MESSAGE

15.1-2 **15** Those of us who are strong and able in the faith need to step in and lend a hand to those who falter, and not just do what is most convenient for us. Strength is for service, not status. Each one of us needs to look after the good of the people around us, asking ourselves, "How can I help?"

15.3-6 That's exactly what Jesus did. He didn't make it easy for himself by avoiding people's troubles, but waded right in and helped out. "I took on the troubles of the troubled," is the way Scripture puts it. Even if it was written in Scripture long ago, you can be sure it's written for us. God wants the combination of his steady, constant calling and warm, personal counsel in Scripture to come to characterize us, keeping us alert for whatever he will do next. May our dependably steady and warmly personal God develop maturity in you so that you get along with each other as well as Jesus gets along with us all. Then we'll be a choir—not our voices only, but our very lives singing in harmony in a stunning anthem to the God and Father of our Master Jesus!

15.7-13 So reach out and welcome one another to God's glory. Jesus did it; now you do it! Jesus, staying true to God's purposes, reached out in a special way to the Jewish insiders so that the old ancestral promises would come true for them. As a result, the non-Jewish outsiders have been able to experience mercy and to show appreciation to God. Just think of all the Scriptures that will come true in what we do! For instance:

Then I'll join outsiders in a hymn-sing;
I'll sing to your name!

And this one:
Outsiders and insiders, rejoice together!

And again:
People of all nations, celebrate God!
All colors and races, give hearty praise!

And Isaiah's word:
There's the root of our ancestor Jesse,
    breaking through the earth and growing
        tree tall,
Tall enough for everyone everywhere to see
    and take hope!

Oh! May the God of green hope fill you up with joy, fill you up with peace, so that your believing lives, filled with the life-giving energy of the Holy Spirit, will brim over with hope!

☩

15.14-16 Personally, I've been completely satisfied with who you are and what you are doing. You seem

NEW INTERNATIONAL VERSION

knowledge and competent to instruct one another. [15]I have written you quite boldly on some points, as if to remind you of them again, because of the grace God gave me [16]to be a minister of Christ Jesus to the Gentiles with the priestly duty of proclaiming the gospel of God, so that the Gentiles might become an offering acceptable to God, sanctified by the Holy Spirit.

[17]Therefore I glory in Christ Jesus in my service to God. [18]I will not venture to speak of anything except what Christ has accomplished through me in leading the Gentiles to obey God by what I have said and done— [19]by the power of signs and miracles, through the power of the Spirit. So from Jerusalem all the way around to Illyricum, I have fully proclaimed the gospel of Christ. [20]It has always been my ambition to preach the gospel where Christ was not known, so that I would not be building on someone else's foundation. [21]Rather, as it is written:

> "Those who were not told about him will
> see,
> and those who have not heard will
> understand." [a]

[22]This is why I have often been hindered from coming to you.

PAUL'S PLAN TO VISIT ROME

[23]But now that there is no more place for me to work in these regions, and since I have been longing for many years to see you, [24]I plan to do so when I go to Spain. I hope to visit you while passing through and to have you assist me on my journey there, after I have enjoyed your company for a while. [25]Now, however, I am on my way to Jerusalem in the service of the saints there. [26]For Macedonia and Achaia were pleased to make a contribution for the poor among the saints in Jerusalem. [27]They were pleased to do it, and indeed they owe it to them. For if the Gentiles have shared in the Jews' spiritual blessings, they owe it to the Jews to share with them their material blessings. [28]So after I have completed this task and have made sure that they have received this fruit, I will go to Spain and visit you on the way. [29]I know that when I come to you, I will come in the full measure of the blessing of Christ.

[a] 21 Isaiah 52:15

THE MESSAGE

to me to be well-motivated and well-instructed, quite capable of guiding and advising one another. So, my dear friends, don't take my rather bold and blunt language as criticism. It's not criticism. I'm simply underlining how very much I need your help in carrying out this highly focused assignment God gave me, this priestly and gospel work of serving the spiritual needs of the non-Jewish outsiders so they can be presented as an acceptable offering to God, made whole and holy by God's Holy Spirit.

15.17-21 Looking back over what has been accomplished and what I have observed, I must say I am most pleased—in the context of Jesus, I'd even say *proud*, but only in that context. I have no interest in giving you a chatty account of my adventures, only the wondrously powerful and transformingly present words and deeds of Christ in me that triggered a believing response among the outsiders. In such ways I have trailblazed a preaching of the Message of Jesus all the way from Jerusalem far into northwestern Greece. This has all been pioneer work, bringing the Message only into those places where Jesus was not yet known and worshiped. My text has been,

> Those who were never told of him—
> they'll see him!
> Those who've never heard of him—
> they'll get the message!

✝

15.22-24 And that's why it has taken me so long to finally get around to coming to you. But now that there is no more pioneering work to be done in these parts, and since I have looked forward to seeing you for many years, I'm planning my visit. I'm headed for Spain, and expect to stop off on the way to enjoy a good visit with you, and eventually have you send me off with God's blessing.

15.25-29 First, though, I'm going to Jerusalem to deliver a relief offering to the Christians there. The Greeks—all the way from the Macedonians in the north to the Achaians in the south—decided they wanted to take up a collection for the poor among the believers in Jerusalem. They were happy to do this, but it was also their duty. Seeing that they got in on all the spiritual gifts that flowed out of the Jerusalem community so generously, it is only right that they do what they can to relieve their poverty. As soon as I have done this—personally handed over this "fruit basket"—I'm off to Spain, with a stopover with you in Rome. My hope is that my visit with you is going to be one of Christ's more extravagant blessings.

NEW INTERNATIONAL VERSION

30I urge you, brothers, by our Lord Jesus Christ and by the love of the Spirit, to join me in my struggle by praying to God for me. 31Pray that I may be rescued from the unbelievers in Judea and that my service in Jerusalem may be acceptable to the saints there, 32so that by God's will I may come to you with joy and together with you be refreshed. 33The God of peace be with you all. Amen.

PERSONAL GREETINGS

16 I commend to you our sister Phoebe, a servant*a* of the church in Cenchrea. 2I ask you to receive her in the Lord in a way worthy of the saints and to give her any help she may need from you, for she has been a great help to many people, including me.

3Greet Priscilla*b* and Aquila, my fellow workers in Christ Jesus. 4They risked their lives for me. Not only I but all the churches of the Gentiles are grateful to them.
5Greet also the church that meets at their house.
Greet my dear friend Epenetus, who was the first convert to Christ in the province of Asia.
6Greet Mary, who worked very hard for you.
7Greet Andronicus and Junias, my relatives who have been in prison with me. They are outstanding among the apostles, and they were in Christ before I was.
8Greet Ampliatus, whom I love in the Lord.
9Greet Urbanus, our fellow worker in Christ, and my dear friend Stachys.
10Greet Apelles, tested and approved in Christ.
Greet those who belong to the household of Aristobulus.
11Greet Herodion, my relative.
Greet those in the household of Narcissus who are in the Lord.
12Greet Tryphena and Tryphosa, those women who work hard in the Lord.
Greet my dear friend Persis, another woman who has worked very hard in the Lord.
13Greet Rufus, chosen in the Lord, and his mother, who has been a mother to me, too.
14Greet Asyncritus, Phlegon, Hermes, Patrobas, Hermas and the brothers with them.

THE MESSAGE

15.30-33 I have one request, dear friends: Pray for me. Pray strenuously with and for me—to God the Father, through the power of our Master Jesus, through the love of the Spirit—that I will be delivered from the lions' den of unbelievers in Judea. Pray also that my relief offering to the Jerusalem Christians will be accepted in the spirit in which it is given. Then, God willing, I'll be on my way to you with a light and eager heart, looking forward to being refreshed by your company. God's peace be with all of you. Oh, yes!

✝

16.1-2 **16** Be sure to welcome our friend Phoebe in the way of the Master, with all the generous hospitality we Christians are famous for. I heartily endorse both her and her work. She's a key representative of the church at Cenchrea. Help her out in whatever she asks. She deserves anything you can do for her. She's helped many a person, including me.

16.3-5 Say hello to Priscilla and Aquila, who have worked hand in hand with me in serving Jesus. They once put their lives on the line for me. And I'm not the only one grateful to them. All the non-Jewish gatherings of believers also owe them plenty, to say nothing of the church that meets in their house.
Hello to my dear friend Epenetus. He was the very first Christian in the province of Asia.
16.6 Hello to Mary. What a worker she has turned out to be!
16.7 Hello to my cousins Andronicus and Junias. We once shared a jail cell. They were believers in Christ before I was. Both of them are outstanding leaders.
16.8 Hello to Ampliatus, my good friend in the family of God.
16.9 Hello to Urbanus, our companion in Christ's work, and my good friend Stachys.
16.10 Hello to Apelles, a tried-and-true veteran in following Christ.
Hello to the family of Aristobulus.
16.11 Hello to my cousin Herodion.
Hello to those Christians from the family of Narcissus.
16.12 Hello to Tryphena and Tryphosa—such diligent women in serving the Master.
Hello to Persis, a dear friend and hard worker in Christ.
16.13 Hello to Rufus—a good choice by the Master!—and his mother. She has also been a dear mother to me.
16.14 Hello to Asyncritus, Phlegon, Hermes, Patrobas, Hermas, and also to all of their families.

a 1 Or *deaconess*   *b* 3 Greek *Prisca*, a variant of *Priscilla*

NEW INTERNATIONAL VERSION

15 Greet Philologus, Julia, Nereus and his sister, and Olympas and all the saints with them. 16 Greet one another with a holy kiss.

All the churches of Christ send greetings.

17 I urge you, brothers, to watch out for those who cause divisions and put obstacles in your way that are contrary to the teaching you have learned. Keep away from them. 18 For such people are not serving our Lord Christ, but their own appetites. By smooth talk and flattery they deceive the minds of naive people. 19 Everyone has heard about your obedience, so I am full of joy over you; but I want you to be wise about what is good, and innocent about what is evil.

20 The God of peace will soon crush Satan under your feet.

The grace of our Lord Jesus be with you.

21 Timothy, my fellow worker, sends his greetings to you, as do Lucius, Jason and Sosipater, my relatives.

22 I, Tertius, who wrote down this letter, greet you in the Lord.

23 Gaius, whose hospitality I and the whole church here enjoy, sends you his greetings.

Erastus, who is the city's director of public works, and our brother Quartus send you their greetings. a

25 Now to him who is able to establish you by my gospel and the proclamation of Jesus Christ, according to the revelation of the mystery hidden for long ages past, 26 but now revealed and made known through the prophetic writings by the command of the eternal God, so that all nations might believe and obey him— 27 to the only wise God be glory forever through Jesus Christ! Amen.

THE MESSAGE

16.15   Hello to Philologus, Julia, Nereus and his sister, and Olympas—and all the Christians who live with them.

16.16   Holy embraces all around! All the churches of Christ send their warmest greetings!

16.17-18   One final word of counsel, friends. Keep a sharp eye out for those who take bits and pieces of the teaching that you learned and then use them to make trouble. Give these people a wide berth. They have no intention of living for our Master Christ. They're only in this for what they can get out of it, and aren't above using pious sweet talk to dupe unsuspecting innocents.

16.19-20   And so while there has never been any question about your honesty in these matters—I couldn't be more proud of you!—I want you also to be smart, making sure every "good" thing is the *real* thing. Don't be gullible in regard to smooth-talking evil. Stay alert like this, and before you know it the God of peace will come down on Satan with both feet, stomping him into the dirt. Enjoy the best of Jesus!

16.21   And here are some more greetings from our end. Timothy, my partner in this work, Lucius, and my cousins Jason and Sosipater all said to tell you hello.

16.22   I, Tertius, who wrote this letter at Paul's dictation, send you my personal greetings.

16.23   Gaius, who is host here to both me and the whole church, wants to be remembered to you.

Erastus, the city treasurer, and our good friend Quartus send their greetings.

16.25-26   All of our praise rises to the One who is strong enough to make *you* strong, exactly as preached in Jesus Christ, precisely as revealed in the mystery kept secret for so long but now an open book through the prophetic Scriptures. All the nations of the world can now know the truth and be brought into obedient belief, carrying out the orders of God, who got all this started, down to the very last letter.

16.27   All our praise is focused through Jesus on this incomparably wise God! Yes!

---

a 23 Some manuscripts *their greetings.* 24*May the grace of our Lord Jesus Christ be with all of you. Amen.*

1 CORINTHIANS

1 CORINTHIANS

1 Paul, called to be an apostle of Christ Jesus by the will of God, and our brother Sosthenes,

²To the church of God in Corinth, to those sanctified in Christ Jesus and called to be holy, together with all those everywhere who call on the name of our Lord Jesus Christ—their Lord and ours:

³Grace and peace to you from God our Father and the Lord Jesus Christ.

THANKSGIVING

⁴I always thank God for you because of his grace given you in Christ Jesus. ⁵For in him you have been enriched in every way—in all your speaking and in all your knowledge— ⁶because our testimony about Christ was confirmed in you. ⁷Therefore you do not lack any spiritual gift as you eagerly wait for our Lord Jesus Christ to be revealed. ⁸He will keep you strong to the end, so that you will be blameless on the day of our Lord Jesus Christ. ⁹God, who has called you into fellowship with his Son Jesus Christ our Lord, is faithful.

DIVISIONS IN THE CHURCH

¹⁰I appeal to you, brothers, in the name of our Lord Jesus Christ, that all of you agree with one another so that there may be no divisions among you and that you may be perfectly united in mind and thought. ¹¹My brothers, some from Chloe's household have informed me that there are quarrels among you. ¹²What I mean is this: One of you says, "I follow Paul"; another, "I follow Apollos"; another, "I follow Cephas*a*"; still another, "I follow Christ."

¹³Is Christ divided? Was Paul crucified for you? Were you baptized into*b* the name of Paul?

1 1.1-2 I, Paul, have been called and sent by Jesus, the Messiah, according to God's plan, along with my friend Sosthenes. I send this letter to you in God's church at Corinth, Christians cleaned up by Jesus and set apart for a God-filled life. I include in my greeting all who call out to Jesus, wherever they live. He's their Master as well as ours!

1.3 May all the gifts and benefits that come from God our Father, and the Master, Jesus Christ, be yours.

1.4-6 Every time I think of you—and I think of you often!—I thank God for your lives of free and open access to God, given by Jesus. There's no end to what has happened in you—it's beyond speech, beyond knowledge. The evidence of Christ has been clearly verified in your lives.

1.7-9 Just think—you don't need a thing, you've got it all! All God's gifts are right in front of you as you wait expectantly for our Master Jesus to arrive on the scene for the Finale. And not only that, but God himself is right alongside to keep you steady and on track until things are all wrapped up by Jesus. God, who got you started in this spiritual adventure, shares with us the life of his Son and our Master Jesus. He will never give up on you. Never forget that.

THE CROSS: THE IRONY OF GOD'S WISDOM

1.10 I have a serious concern to bring up with you, my friends, using the authority of Jesus, our Master. I'll put it as urgently as I can: You *must* get along with each other. You must learn to be considerate of one another, cultivating a life in common.

1.11-12 I bring this up because some from Chloe's family brought a most disturbing report to my attention—that you're fighting among yourselves! I'll tell you exactly what I was told: You're all picking sides, going around saying, "I'm on Paul's side," or "I'm for Apollos," or "Peter is my man," or "I'm in the Messiah group."

1.13-16 I ask you, "Has the Messiah been chopped up in little pieces so we can each have a relic all our own? Was Paul crucified for you? Was a single one of you baptized in Paul's name?" I was

---

a 12 That is, Peter   *b 13* Or *in;* also in verse 15

NEW INTERNATIONAL VERSION

[14]I am thankful that I did not baptize any of you except Crispus and Gaius, [15]so no one can say that you were baptized into my name. [16](Yes, I also baptized the household of Stephanas; beyond that, I don't remember if I baptized anyone else.) [17]For Christ did not send me to baptize, but to preach the gospel—not with words of human wisdom, lest the cross of Christ be emptied of its power.

CHRIST THE WISDOM AND POWER OF GOD

[18]For the message of the cross is foolishness to those who are perishing, but to us who are being saved it is the power of God. [19]For it is written:

"I will destroy the wisdom of the wise;
    the intelligence of the intelligent I will
        frustrate." [a]

[20]Where is the wise man? Where is the scholar? Where is the philosopher of this age? Has not God made foolish the wisdom of the world? [21]For since in the wisdom of God the world through its wisdom did not know him, God was pleased through the foolishness of what was preached to save those who believe. [22]Jews demand miraculous signs and Greeks look for wisdom, [23]but we preach Christ crucified: a stumbling block to Jews and foolishness to Gentiles, [24]but to those whom God has called, both Jews and Greeks, Christ the power of God and the wisdom of God. [25]For the foolishness of God is wiser than man's wisdom, and the weakness of God is stronger than man's strength.

[26]Brothers, think of what you were when you were called. Not many of you were wise by human standards; not many were influential; not many were of noble birth. [27]But God chose the foolish things of the world to shame the wise; God chose the weak things of the world to shame the strong. [28]He chose the lowly things of this world and the despised things—and the things that are not—to nullify the things that are, [29]so that no one may boast before him. [30]It is because of him that you are in Christ Jesus, who has become for us wisdom from God—that is, our righteousness, holiness and redemption. [31]Therefore, as it is written: "Let him who boasts boast in the Lord." [b]

[a] 19 Isaiah 29:14   [b] 31 Jer. 9:24

THE MESSAGE

not involved with any of your baptisms—except for Crispus and Gaius—and on getting this report, I'm sure glad I wasn't. At least no one can go around saying he was baptized in my name. (Come to think of it, I also baptized Stephanas's family, but as far as I can recall, that's it.)

1.17   God didn't send me out to collect a following for myself, but to preach the Message of what he has done, collecting a following for him. And he didn't send me to do it with a lot of fancy rhetoric of my own, lest the powerful action at the center—Christ on the Cross—be trivialized into mere words.

1.18-21   The Message that points to Christ on the Cross seems like sheer silliness to those hell-bent on destruction, but for those on the way of salvation it makes perfect sense. This is the way God works, and most powerfully as it turns out. It's written,

I'll turn conventional wisdom on its head,
I'll expose so-called experts as crackpots.

So where can you find someone truly wise, truly educated, truly intelligent in this day and age? Hasn't God exposed it all as pretentious nonsense? Since the world in all its fancy wisdom never had a clue when it came to knowing God, God in his wisdom took delight in using what the world considered dumb—*preaching*, of all things!—to bring those who trust him into the way of salvation.

1.22-25   While Jews clamor for miraculous demonstrations and Greeks go in for philosophical wisdom, we go right on proclaiming Christ, the Crucified. Jews treat this like an *anti*-miracle—and Greeks pass it off as absurd. But to us who are personally called by God himself—both Jews and Greeks—Christ is God's ultimate miracle and wisdom all wrapped up in one. Human wisdom is so tinny, so impotent, next to the seeming absurdity of God. Human strength can't begin to compete with God's "weakness."

1.26-31   Take a good look, friends, at who you were when you got called into this life. I don't see many of "the brightest and the best" among you, not many influential, not many from high-society families. Isn't it obvious that God deliberately chose men and women that the culture overlooks and exploits and abuses, chose these "nobodies" to expose the hollow pretensions of the "somebodies"? That makes it quite clear that none of you can get by with blowing your own horn before God. Everything that we have—right thinking and right living, a clean slate and a fresh start—comes from God by way of Jesus Christ. That's why we have the saying, "If you're going to blow a horn, blow a trumpet for God."

NEW INTERNATIONAL VERSION

2 When I came to you, brothers, I did not come with eloquence or superior wisdom as I proclaimed to you the testimony about God. [a] ²For I resolved to know nothing while I was with you except Jesus Christ and him crucified. ³I came to you in weakness and fear, and with much trembling. ⁴My message and my preaching were not with wise and persuasive words, but with a demonstration of the Spirit's power, ⁵so that your faith might not rest on men's wisdom, but on God's power.

WISDOM FROM THE SPIRIT

⁶We do, however, speak a message of wisdom among the mature, but not the wisdom of this age or of the rulers of this age, who are coming to nothing. ⁷No, we speak of God's secret wisdom, a wisdom that has been hidden and that God destined for our glory before time began. ⁸None of the rulers of this age understood it, for if they had, they would not have crucified the Lord of glory. ⁹However, as it is written:

"No eye has seen,
　no ear has heard,
no mind has conceived
　what God has prepared for those who love
　　him" [b]—

¹⁰but God has revealed it to us by his Spirit.

The Spirit searches all things, even the deep things of God. ¹¹For who among men knows the thoughts of a man except the man's spirit within him? In the same way no one knows the thoughts of God except the Spirit of God. ¹²We have not received the spirit of the world but the Spirit who is from God, that we may understand what God has freely given us. ¹³This is what we speak, not in words taught us by human wisdom but in words taught by the Spirit, expressing spiritual truths in spiritual words. [c] ¹⁴The man without the Spirit does not accept the things that come from the Spirit of God, for they are foolishness to him, and he cannot under-

THE MESSAGE

2.1-2　2 You'll remember, friends, that when I first came to you to let you in on God's master stroke, I didn't try to impress you with polished speeches and the latest philosophy. I deliberately kept it plain and simple: first Jesus and who he is; then Jesus and what he did—Jesus crucified.

2.3-5　I was unsure of how to go about this, and felt totally inadequate—I was scared to death, if you want the truth of it—and so nothing I said could have impressed you or anyone else. But the Message came through anyway. God's Spirit and God's power did it, which made it clear that your life of faith is a response to God's power, not to some fancy mental or emotional footwork by me or anyone else.

2.6-10　We, of course, have plenty of wisdom to pass on to you once you get your feet on firm spiritual ground, but it's not popular wisdom, the fashionable wisdom of high-priced experts that will be out-of-date in a year or so. God's wisdom is something mysterious that goes deep into the interior of his purposes. You don't find it lying around on the surface. It's not the latest message, but more like the oldest—what God determined as the way to bring out his best in us, long before we ever arrived on the scene. The experts of our day haven't a clue about what this eternal plan is. If they had, they wouldn't have killed the Master of the God-designed life on a cross. That's why we have this Scripture text:

No one's ever seen or heard anything like
　this,
Never so much as imagined anything quite
　like it—
What God has arranged for those who love
　him.

But *you've* seen and heard it because God by his Spirit has brought it all out into the open before you.

2.10-13　The Spirit, not content to flit around on the surface, dives into the depths of God, and brings out what God planned all along. Whoever knows what you're thinking and planning except you yourself? The same with God—except that he not only knows what he's thinking, but he lets *us* in on it. God offers a full report on the gifts of life and salvation that he is giving us. We don't have to rely on the world's guesses and opinions. We didn't learn this by reading books or going to school; we learned it from God, who taught us person-to-person through Jesus, and we're passing it on to you in the same firsthand, personal way.

2.14-16　The unspiritual self, just as it is by nature, can't receive the gifts of God's Spirit. There's no capacity for them. They seem like so much silli-

---

a 1 Some manuscripts *as I proclaimed to you God's mystery*
b 9 Isaiah 64:4　*c* 13 Or *Spirit, interpreting spiritual truths to spiritual men*

NEW INTERNATIONAL VERSION

stand them, because they are spiritually discerned. [15]The spiritual man makes judgments about all things, but he himself is not subject to any man's judgment:

[16]"For who has known the mind of the Lord
that he may instruct him?"[a]

But we have the mind of Christ.

ON DIVISIONS IN THE CHURCH

3 Brothers, I could not address you as spiritual but as worldly—mere infants in Christ. [2]I gave you milk, not solid food, for you were not yet ready for it. Indeed, you are still not ready. [3]You are still worldly. For since there is jealousy and quarreling among you, are you not worldly? Are you not acting like mere men? [4]For when one says, "I follow Paul," and another, "I follow Apollos," are you not mere men?

[5]What, after all, is Apollos? And what is Paul? Only servants, through whom you came to believe—as the Lord has assigned to each his task. [6]I planted the seed, Apollos watered it, but God made it grow. [7]So neither he who plants nor he who waters is anything, but only God, who makes things grow. [8]The man who plants and the man who waters have one purpose, and each will be rewarded according to his own labor. [9]For we are God's fellow workers; you are God's field, God's building.

[10]By the grace God has given me, I laid a foundation as an expert builder, and someone else is building on it. But each one should be careful how he builds. [11]For no one can lay any foundation other than the one already laid, which is Jesus Christ. [12]If any man builds on this foundation using gold, silver, costly stones, wood, hay or straw, [13]his work will be shown for what it is, because the Day will bring it to light. It will be revealed with fire, and the fire will test the quality of each man's work. [14]If what he has built survives, he will receive his reward. [15]If it is burned up, he will suffer loss; he himself will be saved, but only as one escaping through the flames.

[16]Don't you know that you yourselves are God's temple and that God's Spirit lives in you? [17]If anyone destroys God's temple, God will destroy him; for God's temple is sacred, and you are that temple.

a 16 Isaiah 40:13

THE MESSAGE

ness. Spirit can be known only by spirit—God's Spirit and our spirits in open communion. Spiritually alive, we have access to everything God's Spirit is doing, and can't be judged by unspiritual critics. Isaiah's question, "Is there anyone around who knows God's Spirit, anyone who knows what he is doing?" has been answered: Christ knows, and we have Christ's Spirit.

✝

3.1-4 **3** But for right now, friends, I'm completely frustrated by your unspiritual dealings with each other and with God. You're acting like infants in relation to Christ, capable of nothing much more than nursing at the breast. Well, then, I'll nurse you since you don't seem capable of anything more. As long as you grab for what makes you feel good or makes you look important, are you really much different than a babe at the breast, content only when everything's going your way? When one of you says, "I'm on Paul's side," and another says, "I'm for Apollos," aren't you being totally infantile?

3.5-9 Who do you think Paul is, anyway? Or Apollos, for that matter? Servants, both of us—servants who waited on you as you gradually learned to entrust your lives to our mutual Master. We each carried out our servant assignment. I planted the seed, Apollos watered the plants, but *God* made you grow. It's not the one who plants or the one who waters who is at the center of this process but God, who makes things grow. Planting and watering are menial servant jobs at minimum wages. What makes them worth doing is the God we are serving. You happen to be God's field in which we are working.

3.9-15 Or, to put it another way, you are God's house. Using the gift God gave me as a good architect, I designed blueprints; Apollos is putting up the walls. Let each carpenter who comes on the job take care to build on the foundation! Remember, there is only one foundation, the one already laid: Jesus Christ. Take particular care in picking out your building materials. Eventually there is going to be an inspection. If you use cheap or inferior materials, you'll be found out. The inspection will be thorough and rigorous. You won't get by with a thing. If your work passes inspection, fine; if it doesn't, your part of the building will be torn out and started over. But *you* won't be torn out; you'll survive—but just barely.

3.16-17 You realize, don't you, that you are the temple of God, and God himself is present in you? No one will get by with vandalizing God's temple, you can be sure of that. God's temple is sacred—and you, remember, *are* the temple.

NEW INTERNATIONAL VERSION

¹⁸Do not deceive yourselves. If any one of you thinks he is wise by the standards of this age, he should become a "fool" so that he may become wise. ¹⁹For the wisdom of this world is foolishness in God's sight. As it is written: "He catches the wise in their craftiness"ᵃ; ²⁰and again, "The Lord knows that the thoughts of the wise are futile."ᵇ ²¹So then, no more boasting about men! All things are yours, ²²whether Paul or Apollos or Cephasᶜ or the world or life or death or the present or the future—all are yours, ²³and you are of Christ, and Christ is of God.

APOSTLES OF CHRIST

4 So then, men ought to regard us as servants of Christ and as those entrusted with the secret things of God. ²Now it is required that those who have been given a trust must prove faithful. ³I care very little if I am judged by you or by any human court; indeed, I do not even judge myself. ⁴My conscience is clear, but that does not make me innocent. It is the Lord who judges me. ⁵Therefore judge nothing before the appointed time; wait till the Lord comes. He will bring to light what is hidden in darkness and will expose the motives of men's hearts. At that time each will receive his praise from God.

⁶Now, brothers, I have applied these things to myself and Apollos for your benefit, so that you may learn from us the meaning of the saying, "Do not go beyond what is written." Then you will not take pride in one man over against another. ⁷For who makes you different from anyone else? What do you have that you did not receive? And if you did receive it, why do you boast as though you did not?

⁸Already you have all you want! Already you have become rich! You have become kings—and that without us! How I wish that you really had become kings so that we might be kings with you! ⁹For it seems to me that God has put us

THE MESSAGE

3.18-20 Don't fool yourself. Don't think that you can be wise merely by being up-to-date with the times. Be God's fool—that's the path to true wisdom. What the world calls smart, God calls stupid. It's written in Scripture,

He exposes the chicanery of the chic.
The Master sees through the smoke screens of the know-it-alls.

3.21-23 I don't want to hear any of you bragging about yourself or anyone else. Everything is already yours as a gift—Paul, Apollos, Peter, the world, life, death, the present, the future—all of it is yours, and you are privileged to be in union with Christ, who is in union with God.

╬

4.1-4 Don't imagine us leaders to be something we aren't. We are servants of Christ, not his masters. We are guides into God's most sublime secrets, not security guards posted to protect them. The requirements for a good guide are reliability and accurate knowledge. It matters very little to me what you think of me, even less where I rank in popular opinion. I don't even rank myself. Comparisons in these matters are pointless. I'm not aware of anything that would disqualify me from being a good guide for you, but that doesn't mean much. The *Master* makes that judgment.

4.5 So don't get ahead of the Master and jump to conclusions with your judgments before all the evidence is in. When he comes, he will bring out in the open and place in evidence all kinds of things we never even dreamed of—inner motives and purposes and prayers. Only then will any one of us get to hear the "Well done!" of God.

4.6 All I'm doing right now, friends, is showing how these things pertain to Apollos and me so that you will learn restraint and not rush into making judgments without knowing all the facts. It's important to look at things from God's point of view. I would rather not see you inflating or deflating reputations based on mere hearsay.

4.7-8 For who do you know that really knows *you*, knows your heart? And even if they did, is there anything they would discover in you that you could take credit for? Isn't everything you *have* and everything you *are* sheer gifts from God? So what's the point of all this comparing and competing? You already have all you need. You already have more access to God than you can handle. Without bringing either Apollos or me into it, you're sitting on top of the world—at least God's world—and we're right there, sitting alongside you!

4.9-13 It seems to me that God has put us who bear

ᵃ 19 Job 5:13   ᵇ 20 Psalm 94:11   ᶜ 22 That is, Peter

NEW INTERNATIONAL VERSION

apostles on display at the end of the procession, like men condemned to die in the arena. We have been made a spectacle to the whole universe, to angels as well as to men. ¹⁰We are fools for Christ, but you are so wise in Christ! We are weak, but you are strong! You are honored, we are dishonored! ¹¹To this very hour we go hungry and thirsty, we are in rags, we are brutally treated, we are homeless. ¹²We work hard with our own hands. When we are cursed, we bless; when we are persecuted, we endure it; ¹³when we are slandered, we answer kindly. Up to this moment we have become the scum of the earth, the refuse of the world.

¹⁴I am not writing this to shame you, but to warn you, as my dear children. ¹⁵Even though you have ten thousand guardians in Christ, you do not have many fathers, for in Christ Jesus I became your father through the gospel. ¹⁶Therefore I urge you to imitate me. ¹⁷For this reason I am sending to you Timothy, my son whom I love, who is faithful in the Lord. He will remind you of my way of life in Christ Jesus, which agrees with what I teach everywhere in every church.

¹⁸Some of you have become arrogant, as if I were not coming to you. ¹⁹But I will come to you very soon, if the Lord is willing, and then I will find out not only how these arrogant people are talking, but what power they have. ²⁰For the kingdom of God is not a matter of talk but of power. ²¹What do you prefer? Shall I come to you with a whip, or in love and with a gentle spirit?

EXPEL THE IMMORAL BROTHER!

5 It is actually reported that there is sexual immorality among you, and of a kind that does not occur even among pagans: A man has his father's wife. ²And you are proud! Shouldn't you rather have been filled with grief and have put out of your fellowship the man who did this? ³Even though I am not physically present, I am

THE MESSAGE

his Message on stage in a theater in which no one wants to buy a ticket. We're something everyone stands around and stares at, like an accident in the street. We're the Messiah's misfits. You might be sure of yourselves, but we live in the midst of frailties and uncertainties. You might be well-thought-of by others, but we're mostly kicked around. Much of the time we don't have enough to eat, we wear patched and threadbare clothes, we get doors slammed in our faces, and we pick up odd jobs anywhere we can to eke out a living. When they call us names, we say, "God bless you." When they spread rumors about *us*, we put in a good word for *them*. We're treated like garbage, potato peelings from the culture's kitchen. And it's not getting any better.

4.14-16   I'm not writing all this as a neighborhood scold just to make you feel rotten. I'm writing as a father to you, my children. I love you and want you to grow up well, not spoiled. There are a lot of people around who can't wait to tell you what you've done wrong, but there aren't many fathers willing to take the time and effort to help you grow up. It was as Jesus helped me proclaim God's Message to you that I became your father. I'm not, you know, asking you to do anything I'm not already doing myself.

4.17   This is why I sent Timothy to you earlier. He is also my dear son, and true to the Master. He will refresh your memory on the instructions I regularly give all the churches on the way of Christ.

4.18-20   I know there are some among you who are so full of themselves they never listen to anyone, let alone me. They don't think I'll ever show up in person. But I'll be there sooner than you think, God willing, and then we'll see if they're full of anything but hot air. God's Way is not a matter of mere talk; it's an empowered life.

4.21   So how should I prepare to come to you? As a severe disciplinarian who makes you toe the mark? Or as a good friend and counselor who wants to share heart-to-heart with you? You decide.

THE MYSTERY OF SEX

5.1-2   **5** I also received a report of scandalous sex within your church family, a kind that wouldn't be tolerated even outside the church: One of your men is sleeping with his stepmother. And you're so above it all that it doesn't even faze you! Shouldn't this break your hearts? Shouldn't it bring you to your knees in tears? Shouldn't this person and his conduct be confronted and dealt with?

5.3-5   I'll tell you what I would do. Even though I'm not there in person, consider me right there with

NEW INTERNATIONAL VERSION

with you in spirit. And I have already passed judgment on the one who did this, just as if I were present. [4]When you are assembled in the name of our Lord Jesus and I am with you in spirit, and the power of our Lord Jesus is present, [5]hand this man over to Satan, so that the sinful nature[a] may be destroyed and his spirit saved on the day of the Lord.

[6]Your boasting is not good. Don't you know that a little yeast works through the whole batch of dough? [7]Get rid of the old yeast that you may be a new batch without yeast—as you really are. For Christ, our Passover lamb, has been sacrificed. [8]Therefore let us keep the Festival, not with the old yeast, the yeast of malice and wickedness, but with bread without yeast, the bread of sincerity and truth.

[9]I have written you in my letter not to associate with sexually immoral people— [10]not at all meaning the people of this world who are immoral, or the greedy and swindlers, or idolaters. In that case you would have to leave this world. [11]But now I am writing you that you must not associate with anyone who calls himself a brother but is sexually immoral or greedy, an idolater or a slanderer, a drunkard or a swindler. With such a man do not even eat.

[12]What business is it of mine to judge those outside the church? Are you not to judge those inside? [13]God will judge those outside. "Expel the wicked man from among you."[b]

LAWSUITS AMONG BELIEVERS

6 If any of you has a dispute with another, dare he take it before the ungodly for judgment instead of before the saints? [2]Do you not know that the saints will judge the world? And if you are to judge the world, are you not competent to

[a] 5 *Or that his body; or that the flesh*   [b] 13 Deut. 17:7; 19:19; 21:21; 22:21,24; 24:7

THE MESSAGE

you, because I can fully see what's going on. I'm telling you that this is wrong. You must not simply look the other way and hope it goes away on its own. Bring it out in the open and deal with it in the authority of Jesus our Master. Assemble the community—I'll be present in spirit with you and our Master Jesus will be present in power. Hold this man's conduct up to public scrutiny. Let him defend it if he can! But if he can't, then out with him! It will be totally devastating to him, of course, and embarrassing to you. But better devastation and embarrassment than damnation. You want him on his feet and forgiven before the Master on the Day of Judgment.

5.6-8   Your flip and callous arrogance in these things bothers me. You pass it off as a small thing, but it's anything but that. Yeast, too, is a "small thing," but it works its way through a whole batch of bread dough pretty fast. So get rid of this "yeast." Our true identity is flat and plain, not puffed up with the wrong kind of ingredient. The Messiah, our Passover Lamb, has already been sacrificed for the Passover meal, and we are the Unraised Bread part of the Feast. So let's live out our part in the Feast, not as raised bread swollen with the yeast of evil, but as flat bread—simple, genuine, unpretentious.

5.9-13   I wrote you in my earlier letter that you shouldn't make yourselves at home among the sexually promiscuous. I didn't mean that you should have nothing at all to do with outsiders of that sort. Or with crooks, whether blue- or white-collar. Or with spiritual phonies, for that matter. You'd have to leave the world entirely to do that! But I *am* saying that you shouldn't act as if everything is just fine when one of your Christian companions is promiscuous or crooked, is flip with God or rude to friends, gets drunk or becomes greedy and predatory. You can't just go along with this, treating it as acceptable behavior. I'm not responsible for what the *outsiders* do, but don't we have some responsibility for those within our community of believers? God decides on the outsiders, but we need to decide when our brothers and sisters are out of line and, if necessary, clean house.

6.1-4   **6** And how dare you take each other to court! When you think you have been wronged, does it make any sense to go before a court that knows nothing of God's ways instead of a family of Christians? The day is coming when the world is going to stand before a jury made up of Christians. If someday you are going to rule on the world's fate, wouldn't it be a good idea to practice on some of these smaller cases? Why,

NEW INTERNATIONAL VERSION

judge trivial cases? [3]Do you not know that we will judge angels? How much more the things of this life! [4]Therefore, if you have disputes about such matters, appoint as judges even men of little account in the church![a] [5]I say this to shame you. Is it possible that there is nobody among you wise enough to judge a dispute between believers? [6]But instead, one brother goes to law against another—and this in front of unbelievers!

[7]The very fact that you have lawsuits among you means you have been completely defeated already. Why not rather be wronged? Why not rather be cheated? [8]Instead, you yourselves cheat and do wrong, and you do this to your brothers.

[9]Do you not know that the wicked will not inherit the kingdom of God? Do not be deceived: Neither the sexually immoral nor idolaters nor adulterers nor male prostitutes nor homosexual offenders [10]nor thieves nor the greedy nor drunkards nor slanderers nor swindlers will inherit the kingdom of God. [11]And that is what some of you were. But you were washed, you were sanctified, you were justified in the name of the Lord Jesus Christ and by the Spirit of our God.

Sexual Immorality

[12]"Everything is permissible for me"—but not everything is beneficial. "Everything is permissible for me"—but I will not be mastered by anything. [13]"Food for the stomach and the stomach for food"—but God will destroy them both. The body is not meant for sexual immorality, but for the Lord, and the Lord for the body. [14]By his power God raised the Lord from the dead, and he will raise us also. [15]Do you not know that your bodies are members of Christ himself? Shall I then take the members of Christ and unite them with a prostitute? Never! [16]Do you not know that he who unites himself with a prostitute is one with her in body? For it is said, "The two will become one flesh."[b] [17]But he who unites himself with the Lord is one with him in spirit.

---

[a] 4 Or matters, do you appoint as judges men of little account in the church?   [b] 16 Gen. 2:24

THE MESSAGE

we're even going to judge angels! So why not these everyday affairs? As these disagreements and wrongs surface, why would you ever entrust them to the judgment of people you don't trust in any other way?

6.5-6 I say this as bluntly as I can to wake you up to the stupidity of what you're doing. Is it possible that there isn't one levelheaded person among you who can make fair decisions when disagreements and disputes come up? I don't believe it. And here you are taking each other to court before people who don't even believe in God! How can they render justice if they don't believe in the *God* of justice?

6.7-8 These court cases are an ugly blot on your community. Wouldn't it be far better to just take it, to let yourselves be wronged and forget it? All you're doing is providing fuel for more wrong, more injustice, bringing more hurt to the people of your own spiritual family.

6.9-11 Don't you realize that this is not the way to live? Unjust people who don't care about God will not be joining in his kingdom. Those who use and abuse each other, use and abuse sex, use and abuse the earth and everything in it, don't qualify as citizens in God's kingdom. A number of you know from experience what I'm talking about, for not so long ago you were on that list. Since then, you've been cleaned up and given a fresh start by Jesus, our Master, our Messiah, and by our God present in us, the Spirit.

6.12 Just because something is technically legal doesn't mean that it's spiritually appropriate. If I went around doing whatever I thought I could get by with, I'd be a slave to my whims.

6.13 You know the old saying, "First you eat to live, and then you live to eat"? Well, it may be true that the body is only a temporary thing, but that's no excuse for stuffing your body with food, or indulging it with sex. Since the Master honors you with a body, honor him with your body!

6.14-15 God honored the Master's body by raising it from the grave. He'll treat yours with the same resurrection power. Until that time, remember that your bodies are created with the same dignity as the Master's body. You wouldn't take the Master's body off to a whorehouse, would you? I should hope not.

6.16-20 There's more to sex than mere skin on skin. Sex is as much spiritual mystery as physical fact. As written in Scripture, "The two become one." Since we want to become spiritually one with the Master, we must not pursue the kind of sex that avoids commitment and intimacy, leaving us more lonely than ever—the kind of sex that can never "become one." There is a sense in which sexual sins are different from all others. In

NEW INTERNATIONAL VERSION

¹⁸Flee from sexual immorality. All other sins a man commits are outside his body, but he who sins sexually sins against his own body. ¹⁹Do you not know that your body is a temple of the Holy Spirit, who is in you, whom you have received from God? You are not your own; ²⁰you were bought at a price. Therefore honor God with your body.

MARRIAGE

7 Now for the matters you wrote about: It is good for a man not to marry.^a ²But since there is so much immorality, each man should have his own wife, and each woman her own husband. ³The husband should fulfill his marital duty to his wife, and likewise the wife to her husband. ⁴The wife's body does not belong to her alone but also to her husband. In the same way, the husband's body does not belong to him alone but also to his wife. ⁵Do not deprive each other except by mutual consent and for a time, so that you may devote yourselves to prayer. Then come together again so that Satan will not tempt you because of your lack of self-control. ⁶I say this as a concession, not as a command. ⁷I wish that all men were as I am. But each man has his own gift from God; one has this gift, another has that.

⁸Now to the unmarried and the widows I say: It is good for them to stay unmarried, as I am. ⁹But if they cannot control themselves, they should marry, for it is better to marry than to burn with passion.

¹⁰To the married I give this command (not I, but the Lord): A wife must not separate from her husband. ¹¹But if she does, she must remain unmarried or else be reconciled to her husband. And a husband must not divorce his wife.

¹²To the rest I say this (I, not the Lord): If any

---

^a *1 Or "It is good for a man not to have sexual relations with a woman."*

THE MESSAGE

sexual sin we violate the sacredness of our own bodies, these bodies that were made for God-given and God-modeled love, for "becoming one" with another. Or didn't you realize that your body is a sacred place, the place of the Holy Spirit? Don't you see that you can't live however you please, squandering what God paid such a high price for? The physical part of you is not some piece of property belonging to the spiritual part of you. God owns the whole works. So let people see God in and through your body.

TO BE MARRIED, TO BE SINGLE . . .

7.1 7 Now, getting down to the questions you asked in your letter to me. First, Is it a good thing to have sexual relations?

7.2-6   Certainly—but only within a certain context. It's good for a man to have a wife, and for a woman to have a husband. Sexual drives are strong, but marriage is strong enough to contain them and provide for a balanced and fulfilling sexual life in a world of sexual disorder. The marriage bed must be a place of mutuality—the husband seeking to satisfy his wife, the wife seeking to satisfy her husband. Marriage is not a place to "stand up for your rights." Marriage is a decision to serve the other, whether in bed or out. Abstaining from sex is permissible for a period of time if you both agree to it, and if it's for the purposes of prayer and fasting—but only for such times. Then come back together again. Satan has an ingenious way of tempting us when we least expect it. I'm not, understand, commanding these periods of abstinence—only providing my best counsel if you should choose them.

7.7   Sometimes I wish everyone were single like me—a simpler life in many ways! But celibacy is not for everyone any more than marriage is. God gives the gift of the single life to some, the gift of the married life to others.

7.8-9   I do, though, tell the unmarried and widows that singleness might well be the best thing for them, as it has been for me. But if they can't manage their desires and emotions, they should by all means go ahead and get married. The difficulties of marriage are preferable by far to a sexually tortured life as a single.

7.10-11   And if you are married, stay married. This is the Master's command, not mine. If a wife should leave her husband, she must either remain single or else come back and make things right with him. And a husband has no right to get rid of his wife.

7.12-14   For the rest of you who are in mixed marriages—Christian married to nonChristian—we have no explicit command from the Master. So

NEW INTERNATIONAL VERSION

brother has a wife who is not a believer and she is willing to live with him, he must not divorce her. [13]And if a woman has a husband who is not a believer and he is willing to live with her, she must not divorce him. [14]For the unbelieving husband has been sanctified through his wife, and the unbelieving wife has been sanctified through her believing husband. Otherwise your children would be unclean, but as it is, they are holy.

[15]But if the unbeliever leaves, let him do so. A believing man or woman is not bound in such circumstances; God has called us to live in peace. [16]How do you know, wife, whether you will save your husband? Or, how do you know, husband, whether you will save your wife?

[17]Nevertheless, each one should retain the place in life that the Lord assigned to him and to which God has called him. This is the rule I lay down in all the churches. [18]Was a man already circumcised when he was called? He should not become uncircumcised. Was a man uncircumcised when he was called? He should not be circumcised. [19]Circumcision is nothing and uncircumcision is nothing. Keeping God's commands is what counts. [20]Each one should remain in the situation which he was in when God called him. [21]Were you a slave when you were called? Don't let it trouble you—although if you can gain your freedom, do so. [22]For he who was a slave when he was called by the Lord is the Lord's freedman; similarly, he who was a free man when he was called is Christ's slave. [23]You were bought at a price; do not become slaves of men. [24]Brothers, each man, as responsible to God, should remain in the situation God called him to.

[25]Now about virgins: I have no command from the Lord, but I give a judgment as one who by the Lord's mercy is trustworthy. [26]Because of the present crisis, I think that it is good for you

THE MESSAGE

this is what you must do. If you are a man with a wife who is not a believer but who still wants to live with you, hold on to her. If you are a woman with a husband who is not a believer but he wants to live with you, hold on to him. The unbelieving husband shares to an extent in the holiness of his wife, and the unbelieving wife is likewise touched by the holiness of her husband. Otherwise, your children would be left out; as it is, they also are included in the spiritual purposes of God.

7.15-16 On the other hand, if the unbelieving spouse walks out, you've got to let him or her go. You don't have to hold on desperately. God has called us to make the best of it, as peacefully as we can. You never know, wife: The way you handle this might bring your husband not only back to you but to God. You never know, husband: The way you handle this might bring your wife not only back to you but to God.

7.17 And don't be wishing you were someplace else or with someone else. Where you are right now is God's place for you. Live and obey and love and believe right there. God, not your marital status, defines your life. Don't think I'm being harder on you than on the others. I give this same counsel in all the churches.

7.18-19 Were you Jewish at the time God called you? Don't try to remove the evidence. Were you non-Jewish at the time of your call? Don't become a Jew. Being Jewish isn't the point. The really important thing is obeying God's call, following his commands.

7.20-22 Stay where you were when God called your name. Were you a slave? Slavery is no roadblock to obeying and believing. I don't mean you're stuck and can't leave. If you have a chance at freedom, go ahead and take it. I'm simply trying to point out that under your new Master you're going to experience a marvelous freedom you would never have dreamed of. On the other hand, if you were free when Christ called you, you'll experience a delightful "enslavement to God" you would never have dreamed of.

7.23-24 All of you, slave and free both, were once held hostage in a sinful society. Then a huge sum was paid out for your ransom. So please don't, out of old habit, slip back into being or doing what everyone else tells you. Friends, stay where you were called to be. God is there. Hold the high ground with him at your side.

7.25-28 The Master did not give explicit direction regarding virgins, but as one much experienced in the mercy of the Master and loyal to him all the way, you can trust my counsel. Because of the current pressures on us from all sides, I think it would probably be best to stay just as you are.

NEW INTERNATIONAL VERSION

to remain as you are. [27]Are you married? Do not seek a divorce. Are you unmarried? Do not look for a wife. [28]But if you do marry, you have not sinned; and if a virgin marries, she has not sinned. But those who marry will face many troubles in this life, and I want to spare you this.

[29]What I mean, brothers, is that the time is short. From now on those who have wives should live as if they had none; [30]those who mourn, as if they did not; those who are happy, as if they were not; those who buy something, as if it were not theirs to keep; [31]those who use the things of the world, as if not engrossed in them. For this world in its present form is passing away.

[32]I would like you to be free from concern. An unmarried man is concerned about the Lord's affairs—how he can please the Lord. [33]But a married man is concerned about the affairs of this world—how he can please his wife— [34]and his interests are divided. An unmarried woman or virgin is concerned about the Lord's affairs: Her aim is to be devoted to the Lord in both body and spirit. But a married woman is concerned about the affairs of this world—how she can please her husband. [35]I am saying this for your own good, not to restrict you, but that you may live in a right way in undivided devotion to the Lord.

[36]If anyone thinks he is acting improperly toward the virgin he is engaged to, and if she is getting along in years and he feels he ought to marry, he should do as he wants. He is not sinning. They should get married. [37]But the man who has settled the matter in his own mind, who is under no compulsion but has control over his own will, and who has made up his mind not to marry the virgin—this man also does the right thing. [38]So then, he who marries the virgin does right, but he who does not marry her does even better. [a]

[39]A woman is bound to her husband as long as he lives. But if her husband dies, she is free to marry anyone she wishes, but he must belong to the Lord. [40]In my judgment, she is happier if she stays as she is—and I think that I too have the Spirit of God.

[a] 36-38 Or [36]If anyone thinks he is not treating his daughter properly, and if she is getting along in years, and he feels she ought to marry, he should do as he wants. He is not sinning. He should let her get married. [37]But the man who has settled the matter in his own mind, who is under no compulsion but has control over his own will, and who has made up his mind to keep the virgin unmarried—this man also does the right thing. [38]So then, he who gives his virgin in marriage does right, but he who does not give her in marriage does even better.

THE MESSAGE

Are you married? Stay married. Are you unmarried? Don't get married. But there's certainly no sin in getting married, whether you're a virgin or not. All I am saying is that when you marry, you take on additional stress in an already stressful time, and I want to spare you if possible.

7.29-31   I do want to point out, friends, that time is of the essence. There is no time to waste, so don't complicate your lives unnecessarily. Keep it simple—in marriage, grief, joy, whatever. Even in ordinary things—your daily routines of shopping, and so on. Deal as sparingly as possible with the things the world thrusts on you. This world as you see it is on its way out.

7.32-35   I want you to live as free of complications as possible. When you're unmarried, you're free to concentrate on simply pleasing the Master. Marriage involves you in all the nuts and bolts of domestic life and in wanting to please your spouse, leading to so many more demands on your attention. The time and energy that married people spend on caring for and nurturing each other, the unmarried can spend in becoming whole and holy instruments of God. I'm trying to be helpful and make it as easy as possible for you, not make things harder. All I want is for you to be able to develop a way of life in which you can spend plenty of time together with the Master without a lot of distractions.

7.36-38   If a man has a woman friend to whom he is loyal but never intended to marry, having decided to serve God as a "single," and then changes his mind, deciding he should marry her, he should go ahead and marry. It's no sin; it's not even a "step down" from celibacy, as some say. On the other hand, if a man is comfortable in his decision for a single life in service to God and it's entirely his own conviction and not imposed on him by others, he ought to stick with it. Marriage is spiritually and morally right and not inferior to singleness in any way, although as I indicated earlier, because of the times we live in, I do have pastoral reasons for encouraging singleness.

7.39-40   A wife must stay with her husband as long as he lives. If he dies, she is free to marry anyone she chooses. She will, of course, want to marry a believer and have the blessing of the Master. By now you know that I think she'll be better off staying single. The Master, in my opinion, thinks so, too.

NEW INTERNATIONAL VERSION

FOOD SACRIFICED TO IDOLS

8 Now about food sacrificed to idols: We know that we all possess knowledge.*a* Knowledge puffs up, but love builds up. ²The man who thinks he knows something does not yet know as he ought to know. ³But the man who loves God is known by God.

⁴So then, about eating food sacrificed to idols: We know that an idol is nothing at all in the world and that there is no God but one. ⁵For even if there are so-called gods, whether in heaven or on earth (as indeed there are many "gods" and many "lords"), ⁶yet for us there is but one God, the Father, from whom all things came and for whom we live; and there is but one Lord, Jesus Christ, through whom all things came and through whom we live.

⁷But not everyone knows this. Some people are still so accustomed to idols that when they eat such food they think of it as having been sacrificed to an idol, and since their conscience is weak, it is defiled. ⁸But food does not bring us near to God; we are no worse if we do not eat, and no better if we do.

⁹Be careful, however, that the exercise of your freedom does not become a stumbling block to the weak. ¹⁰For if anyone with a weak conscience sees you who have this knowledge eating in an idol's temple, won't he be emboldened to eat what has been sacrificed to idols? ¹¹So this weak brother, for whom Christ died, is destroyed

THE MESSAGE

FREEDOM WITH RESPONSIBILITY

8.1-3 **8** The question keeps coming up regarding meat that has been offered up to an idol: Should you attend meals where such meat is served, or not? We sometimes tend to think we know all we need to know to answer these kinds of questions—*but* sometimes our humble hearts can help us more than our proud minds. We never really know enough until we recognize that God alone knows it all.

8.4-6 Some people say, quite rightly, that idols have no actual existence, that there's nothing to them, that there is no God other than our one God, that no matter how many of these so-called gods are named and worshiped they still don't add up to anything but a tall story. They say—again, quite rightly—that there is only one God the Father, that everything comes from him, and that he wants us to live for him. Also, they say that there is only one Master—Jesus the Messiah—and that everything is for his sake, including us. Yes. It's true.

8.7 In strict logic, then, nothing happened to the meat when it was offered up to an idol. It's just like any other meat. I know that, and you know that. But knowing isn't everything. If it becomes everything, some people end up as know-it-alls who treat others as know-nothings. Real knowledge isn't that insensitive.

We need to be sensitive to the fact that we're not all at the same level of understanding in this. Some of you have spent your entire lives eating "idol meat," and are sure that there's something bad in the meat that then becomes something bad inside of you. An imagination and conscience shaped under those conditions isn't going to change overnight.

8.8-9 But fortunately God doesn't grade us on our diet. We're neither commended when we clean our plate nor reprimanded when we just can't stomach it. But God *does* care when you use your freedom carelessly in a way that leads a Christian still vulnerable to those old associations to be thrown off track.

8.10 For instance, say you flaunt your freedom by going to a banquet thrown in honor of idols, where the main course is meat sacrificed to idols. Isn't there great danger if someone still struggling over this issue, someone who looks up to you as knowledgeable and mature, sees you go into that banquet? The danger is that he will become terribly confused—maybe even to the point of getting mixed up himself in what his conscience tells him is wrong.

8.11-13 Christ gave up his life for that person. Wouldn't you at least be willing to give up going to dinner for him—because, as you say, it

---

a 1 Or "We all possess knowledge," as you say

NEW INTERNATIONAL VERSION

by your knowledge. ¹²When you sin against your brothers in this way and wound their weak conscience, you sin against Christ. ¹³Therefore, if what I eat causes my brother to fall into sin, I will never eat meat again, so that I will not cause him to fall.

THE RIGHTS OF AN APOSTLE

9 Am I not free? Am I not an apostle? Have I not seen Jesus our Lord? Are you not the result of my work in the Lord? ²Even though I may not be an apostle to others, surely I am to you! For you are the seal of my apostleship in the Lord.

³This is my defense to those who sit in judgment on me. ⁴Don't we have the right to food and drink? ⁵Don't we have the right to take a believing wife along with us, as do the other apostles and the Lord's brothers and Cephas*ᵃ*? ⁶Or is it only I and Barnabas who must work for a living?

⁷Who serves as a soldier at his own expense? Who plants a vineyard and does not eat of its grapes? Who tends a flock and does not drink of the milk? ⁸Do I say this merely from a human point of view? Doesn't the Law say the same thing? ⁹For it is written in the Law of Moses: "Do not muzzle an ox while it is treading out the grain."*ᵇ* Is it about oxen that God is concerned? ¹⁰Surely he says this for us, doesn't he? Yes, this was written for us, because when the plowman plows and the thresher threshes, they ought to do so in the hope of sharing in the harvest. ¹¹If we have sown spiritual seed among you, is it too much if we reap a material harvest from you? ¹²If others have this right of support from you, shouldn't we have it all the more?

But we did not use this right. On the contrary, we put up with anything rather than hinder the gospel of Christ. ¹³Don't you know that those who work in the temple get their food from the temple, and those who serve at the altar share in

THE MESSAGE

doesn't really make any difference? But it *does* make a difference if you hurt your friend terribly, risking his eternal ruin! When you hurt your friend, you hurt Christ. A free meal here and there isn't worth it at the cost of even one of these "weak ones." So, never go to these idol-tainted meals if there's any chance it will trip up one of your brothers or sisters.

✝

9.1-2 **9** And don't tell me that I have no authority to write like this. I'm perfectly free to do this—isn't that obvious? Haven't I been given a job to do? Wasn't I commissioned to this work in a face-to-face meeting with Jesus, our Master? Aren't you yourselves proof of the good work that I've done for the Master? Even if no one else admits the authority of my commission, *you* can't deny it. Why, my work with you is living proof of my authority!

9.3-7 I'm not shy in standing up to my critics. We who are on missionary assignments for God have a right to decent accommodations, and we have a right to support for us and our families. You don't seem to have raised questions with the other apostles and our Master's brothers and Peter in these matters. So, why me? Is it just Barnabas and I who have to go it alone and pay our own way? Are soldiers self-employed? Are gardeners forbidden to eat vegetables from their own gardens? Don't milkmaids get to drink their fill from the pail?

9.8-12 I'm not just sounding off because I'm irritated. This is all written in the scriptural law. Moses wrote, "Don't muzzle an ox to keep it from eating the grain when it's threshing." Do you think Moses' primary concern was the care of farm animals? Don't you think his concern extends to us? Of course. Farmers plow and thresh expecting something when the crop comes in. So if we have planted spiritual seed among you, is it out of line to expect a meal or two from you? Others demand plenty from you in these ways. Don't we who have never demanded deserve even more?

9.12-14 But we're not going to start demanding now what we've always had a perfect right to. Our decision all along has been to put up with anything rather than to get in the way or detract from the Message of Christ. All I'm concerned with right now is that you not use our decision to take advantage of others, depriving them of what is rightly theirs. You know, don't you, that it's always been taken for granted that those who work in the Temple live off the proceeds of the Temple, and that those who offer sacrifices at the altar eat their meals from what has been

---

ᵃ 5 That is, Peter   *ᵇ* 9 Deut. 25:4

NEW INTERNATIONAL VERSION

what is offered on the altar? ¹⁴In the same way, the Lord has commanded that those who preach the gospel should receive their living from the gospel.

¹⁵But I have not used any of these rights. And I am not writing this in the hope that you will do such things for me. I would rather die than have anyone deprive me of this boast. ¹⁶Yet when I preach the gospel, I cannot boast, for I am compelled to preach. Woe to me if I do not preach the gospel! ¹⁷If I preach voluntarily, I have a reward; if not voluntarily, I am simply discharging the trust committed to me. ¹⁸What then is my reward? Just this: that in preaching the gospel I may offer it free of charge, and so not make use of my rights in preaching it.

¹⁹Though I am free and belong to no man, I make myself a slave to everyone, to win as many as possible. ²⁰To the Jews I became like a Jew, to win the Jews. To those under the law I became like one under the law (though I myself am not under the law), so as to win those under the law. ²¹To those not having the law I became like one not having the law (though I am not free from God's law but am under Christ's law), so as to win those not having the law. ²²To the weak I became weak, to win the weak. I have become all things to all men so that by all possible means I might save some. ²³I do all this for the sake of the gospel, that I may share in its blessings.

²⁴Do you not know that in a race all the runners run, but only one gets the prize? Run in such a way as to get the prize. ²⁵Everyone who competes in the games goes into strict training. They do it to get a crown that will not last; but we do it to get a crown that will last forever. ²⁶Therefore I do not run like a man running aimlessly; I do not fight like a man beating the air. ²⁷No, I beat my body and make it my slave so that after I have preached to others, I myself will not be disqualified for the prize.

WARNINGS FROM ISRAEL'S HISTORY

10 For I do not want you to be ignorant of the fact, brothers, that our forefathers were all under the cloud and that they all passed through the sea. ²They were all baptized into Moses in the cloud and in the sea. ³They all ate the same spiritual food ⁴and drank the same spiritual drink; for they drank from the spiritual rock that accompanied them, and that rock was Christ. ⁵Nevertheless, God was not pleased with

THE MESSAGE

sacrificed? Along the same lines, the Master directed that those who spread the Message be supported by those who believe the Message.

9.15-18 Still, I want it made clear that I've never gotten anything out of this for myself, and that I'm not writing now to get something. I'd rather die than give anyone ammunition to discredit me or impugn my motives. If I proclaim the Message, it's not to get something out of it for myself. I'm *compelled* to do it, and doomed if I don't! If this was my own idea of just another way to make a living, I'd expect some pay. But since it's *not* my idea but something solemnly entrusted to me, why would I expect to get paid? So am I getting anything out of it? Yes, as a matter of fact: the pleasure of proclaiming the Message at no cost to you. You don't even have to pay my expenses!

9.19-23 Even though I am free of the demands and expectations of everyone, I have voluntarily become a servant to any and all in order to reach a wide range of people: religious, nonreligious, meticulous moralists, loose-living immoralists, the defeated, the demoralized—whoever. I didn't take on their way of life. I kept my bearings in Christ—but I entered their world and tried to experience things from their point of view. I've become just about every sort of servant there is in my attempts to lead those I meet into a God-saved life. I did all this because of the Message. I didn't just want to talk about it; I wanted to be *in* on it!

9.24-25 You've all been to the stadium and seen the athletes race. Everyone runs; one wins. Run to win. All good athletes train hard. They do it for a gold medal that tarnishes and fades. You're after one that's gold eternally.

9.26-27 I don't know about you, but I'm running hard for the finish line. I'm giving it everything I've got. No sloppy living for me! I'm staying alert and in top condition. I'm not going to get caught napping, telling everyone else all about it and then missing out myself.

✝

10.1-5 **10** Remember our history, friends, and be warned. All our ancestors were led by the providential Cloud and taken miraculously through the Sea. They went through the waters, in a baptism like ours, as Moses led them from enslaving death to salvation life. They all ate and drank identical food and drink, meals provided daily by God. They drank from the Rock, God's fountain for them that stayed with them wherever they were. And the Rock was Christ. But just experiencing God's wonder and grace didn't seem to mean much—most of them were

NEW INTERNATIONAL VERSION

most of them; their bodies were scattered over the desert.

⁶Now these things occurred as examples*ᵃ* to keep us from setting our hearts on evil things as they did. ⁷Do not be idolaters, as some of them were; as it is written: "The people sat down to eat and drink and got up to indulge in pagan revelry."*ᵇ* ⁸We should not commit sexual immorality, as some of them did—and in one day twenty-three thousand of them died. ⁹We should not test the Lord, as some of them did—and were killed by snakes. ¹⁰And do not grumble, as some of them did—and were killed by the destroying angel.

¹¹These things happened to them as examples and were written down as warnings for us, on whom the fulfillment of the ages has come. ¹²So, if you think you are standing firm, be careful that you don't fall! ¹³No temptation has seized you except what is common to man. And God is faithful; he will not let you be tempted beyond what you can bear. But when you are tempted, he will also provide a way out so that you can stand up under it.

Idol Feasts and the Lord's Supper

¹⁴Therefore, my dear friends, flee from idolatry. ¹⁵I speak to sensible people; judge for yourselves what I say. ¹⁶Is not the cup of thanksgiving for which we give thanks a participation in the blood of Christ? And is not the bread that we break a participation in the body of Christ? ¹⁷Because there is one loaf, we, who are many, are one body, for we all partake of the one loaf.

¹⁸Consider the people of Israel: Do not those who eat the sacrifices participate in the altar? ¹⁹Do I mean then that a sacrifice offered to an idol is anything, or that an idol is anything? ²⁰No, but the sacrifices of pagans are offered to demons, not to God, and I do not want you to be participants with demons. ²¹You cannot drink the cup of the Lord and the cup of demons too; you cannot have a part in both the Lord's table and the table of demons. ²²Are we trying to arouse the Lord's jealousy? Are we stronger than he?

THE MESSAGE

defeated by temptation during the hard times in the desert, and God was not pleased.

10.6-10 The same thing could happen to us. We must be on guard so that we never get caught up in wanting our own way as they did. And we must not turn our religion into a circus as they did— "First the people partied, then they threw a dance." We must not be sexually promiscuous— they paid for that, remember, with twenty-three thousand deaths in one day! We must never try to get Christ to serve us instead of us serving him; they tried it, and God launched an epidemic of poisonous snakes. We must be careful not to stir up discontent; discontent destroyed them.

10.11-12 These are all warning markers—DANGER!— in our history books, written down so that we don't repeat their mistakes. Our positions in the story are parallel—they at the beginning, we at the end—and we are just as capable of messing it up as they were. Don't be so naive and self-confident. You're not exempt. You could fall flat on your face as easily as anyone else. Forget about self-confidence; it's useless. Cultivate God-confidence.

10.13 No test or temptation that comes your way is beyond the course of what others have had to face. All you need to remember is that God will never let you down; he'll never let you be pushed past your limit; he'll always be there to help you come through it.

10.14 So, my very dear friends, when you see people reducing God to something they can use or control, get out of their company as fast as you can.

10.15-18 I assume I'm addressing believers now who are mature. Draw your own conclusions: When we drink the cup of blessing, aren't we taking into ourselves the blood, the very life, of Christ? And isn't it the same with the loaf of bread we break and eat? Don't we take into ourselves the body, the very life, of Christ? Because there is one loaf, our many-ness becomes one-ness— Christ doesn't become fragmented in us. Rather, we become unified in him. We don't reduce Christ to what we are; he raises us to what he is. That's basically what happened even in old Israel—those who ate the sacrifices offered on God's altar entered into God's action at the altar.

10.19-22 Do you see the difference? Sacrifices offered to idols are offered to nothing, for what's the idol but a nothing? Or worse than nothing, a minus, a demon! I don't want you to become part of something that reduces you to less than yourself. And you can't have it both ways, banqueting with the Master one day and slumming with demons the next. Besides, the Master won't put up with it. He wants *us*—all or nothing. Do you think you can get off with anything less?

ᵃ 6 Or *types*; also in verse 11   *ᵇ* 7 Exodus 32:6

NEW INTERNATIONAL VERSION

THE BELIEVER'S FREEDOM

23"Everything is permissible"—but not everything is beneficial. "Everything is permissible"—but not everything is constructive. 24Nobody should seek his own good, but the good of others.

25Eat anything sold in the meat market without raising questions of conscience, 26for, "The earth is the Lord's, and everything in it." *a*

27If some unbeliever invites you to a meal and you want to go, eat whatever is put before you without raising questions of conscience. 28But if anyone says to you, "This has been offered in sacrifice," then do not eat it, both for the sake of the man who told you and for conscience' sake *b*— 29the other man's conscience, I mean, not yours. For why should my freedom be judged by another's conscience? 30If I take part in the meal with thankfulness, why am I denounced because of something I thank God for?

31So whether you eat or drink or whatever you do, do it all for the glory of God. 32Do not cause anyone to stumble, whether Jews, Greeks or the church of God— 33even as I try to please everybody in every way. For I am not seeking my own good but the good of many, so that they may be saved.

11 1Follow my example, as I follow the example of Christ.

PROPRIETY IN WORSHIP

2I praise you for remembering me in everything and for holding to the teachings, *c* just as I passed them on to you.

---

a 26 Psalm 24:1   *b* 28 Some manuscripts *conscience' sake, for "the earth is the Lord's and everything in it"*
c 2 Or *traditions*

THE MESSAGE

10.23-24   Looking at it one way, you could say, "Anything goes. Because of God's immense generosity and grace, we don't have to dissect and scrutinize every action to see if it will pass muster." But the point is not to just get by. We want to live well, but our foremost efforts should be to help *others* live well.

10.25-28   With that as a base to work from, common sense can take you the rest of the way. Eat anything sold at the butcher shop, for instance; you don't have to run an "idolatry test" on every item. "The earth," after all, "is God's, and everything in it." That "everything" certainly includes the leg of lamb in the butcher shop. If a nonbeliever invites you to dinner and you feel like going, go ahead and enjoy yourself; eat everything placed before you. It would be both bad manners and bad spirituality to cross-examine your host on the ethical purity of each course as it is served. On the other hand, if he goes out of his way to tell you that this or that was sacrificed to god or goddess so-and-so, you should pass. Even though you may be indifferent as to where it came from, he isn't, and you don't want to send mixed messages to him about who *you* are worshiping.

10.29-30   But, except for these special cases, I'm not going to walk around on eggshells worrying about what small-minded people might say; I'm going to stride free and easy, knowing what our large-minded Master has already said. If I eat what is served to me, grateful to God for what is on the table, how can I worry about what someone will say? I thanked God for it and he blessed it!

10.31-33   So eat your meals heartily, not worrying about what others say about you—you're eating to God's glory, after all, not to please them. As a matter of fact, do everything that way, heartily and freely to God's glory. At the same time, don't be callous in your exercise of freedom, thoughtlessly stepping on the toes of those who aren't as free as you are. I try my best to be considerate of everyone's feelings in all these matters; I hope you will be, too.

TO HONOR GOD

11.1-2   11 It pleases me that you continue to remember and honor me by keeping up the traditions of the faith I taught you. All actual authority stems from Christ.

NEW INTERNATIONAL VERSION

³Now I want you to realize that the head of every man is Christ, and the head of the woman is man, and the head of Christ is God. ⁴Every man who prays or prophesies with his head covered dishonors his head. ⁵And every woman who prays or prophesies with her head uncovered dishonors her head—it is just as though her head were shaved. ⁶If a woman does not cover her head, she should have her hair cut off; and if it is a disgrace for a woman to have her hair cut or shaved off, she should cover her head. ⁷A man ought not to cover his head,ᵃ since he is the image and glory of God; but the woman is the glory of man. ⁸For man did not come from woman, but woman from man; ⁹neither was man created for woman, but woman for man. ¹⁰For this reason, and because of the angels, the woman ought to have a sign of authority on her head.

¹¹In the Lord, however, woman is not independent of man, nor is man independent of woman. ¹²For as woman came from man, so also man is born of woman. But everything comes from God. ¹³Judge for yourselves: Is it proper for a woman to pray to God with her head uncovered? ¹⁴Does not the very nature of things teach you that if a man has long hair, it is a disgrace to him, ¹⁵but that if a woman has long hair, it is her glory? For long hair is given to her as a covering. ¹⁶If anyone wants to be contentious about this, we have no other practice—nor do the churches of God.

THE LORD'S SUPPER

¹⁷In the following directives I have no praise for you, for your meetings do more harm than good. ¹⁸In the first place, I hear that when you come together as a church, there are divisions among you, and to some extent I believe it. ¹⁹No doubt there have to be differences among you to show which of you have God's approval. ²⁰When you come together, it is not the Lord's Supper you eat, ²¹for as you eat, each of you goes ahead without waiting for anybody else. One remains hungry, another gets drunk. ²²Don't you have homes to eat and drink in? Or do you despise the church of God and humiliate those who have nothing? What shall I say to you? Shall I praise you for this? Certainly not!

²³For I received from the Lord what I also

ᵃ 4-7 Or ⁴*Every man who prays or prophesies with long hair dishonors his head.* ⁵*And every woman who prays or prophesies with no covering of hair on her head dishonors her head—she is just like one of the "shorn women."* ⁶*If a woman has no covering, let her be for now with short hair, but since it is a disgrace for a woman to have her hair shorn or shaved, she should grow it again.* ⁷*A man ought not to have long hair*

THE MESSAGE

11.3-9　In a marriage relationship, there is authority from Christ to husband, and from husband to wife. The authority of Christ is the authority of God. Any man who speaks with God or about God in a way that shows a lack of respect for the authority of Christ, dishonors Christ. In the same way, a wife who speaks with God in a way that shows a lack of respect for the authority of her husband, dishonors her husband. Worse, she dishonors herself—an ugly sight, like a woman with her head shaved. This is basically the origin of these customs we have of women wearing head coverings in worship, while men take their hats off. By these symbolic acts, men and women, who far too often butt heads with each other, submit their "heads" to the Head: God.

11.10-12　Don't, by the way, read too much into the differences here between men and women. Neither man nor woman can go it alone or claim priority. Man was created first, as a beautiful shining reflection of God—that is true. But the head on a woman's body clearly outshines in beauty the head of her "head," her husband. The first woman came from man, true—but ever since then, every man comes from a woman! And since virtually everything comes from God anyway, let's quit going through these "who's first" routines.

11.13-16　Don't you agree there is something naturally powerful in the symbolism—a woman, her beautiful hair reminiscent of angels, praying in adoration; a man, his head bared in reverence, praying in submission? I hope you're not going to be argumentative about this. All God's churches see it this way; I don't want you standing out as an exception.

11.17-19　Regarding this next item, I'm not at all pleased. I am getting the picture that when you meet together it brings out your worst side instead of your best! First, I get this report on your divisiveness, competing with and criticizing each other. I'm reluctant to believe it, but there it is. The best that can be said for it is that the testing process will bring truth into the open and confirm it.

11.20-22　And then I find that you bring your divisions to worship—you come together, and instead of eating the Lord's Supper, you bring in a lot of food from the outside and make pigs of yourselves. Some are left out, and go home hungry. Others have to be carried out, too drunk to walk. I can't believe it! Don't you have your own homes to eat and drink in? Why would you stoop to desecrating God's church? Why would you actually shame God's poor? I never would have believed you would stoop to this. And I'm not going to stand by and say nothing.

11.23-26　Let me go over with you again exactly what

NEW INTERNATIONAL VERSION

passed on to you: The Lord Jesus, on the night he was betrayed, took bread, 24and when he had given thanks, he broke it and said, "This is my body, which is for you; do this in remembrance of me." 25In the same way, after supper he took the cup, saying, "This cup is the new covenant in my blood; do this, whenever you drink it, in remembrance of me." 26For whenever you eat this bread and drink this cup, you proclaim the Lord's death until he comes.

27Therefore, whoever eats the bread or drinks the cup of the Lord in an unworthy manner will be guilty of sinning against the body and blood of the Lord. 28A man ought to examine himself before he eats of the bread and drinks of the cup. 29For anyone who eats and drinks without recognizing the body of the Lord eats and drinks judgment on himself. 30That is why many among you are weak and sick, and a number of you have fallen asleep. 31But if we judged ourselves, we would not come under judgment. 32When we are judged by the Lord, we are being disciplined so that we will not be condemned with the world.

33So then, my brothers, when you come together to eat, wait for each other. 34If anyone is hungry, he should eat at home, so that when you meet together it may not result in judgment.

And when I come I will give further directions.

SPIRITUAL GIFTS

12 Now about spiritual gifts, brothers, I do not want you to be ignorant. 2You know that when you were pagans, somehow or other you were influenced and led astray to mute idols. 3Therefore I tell you that no one who is

THE MESSAGE

goes on in the Lord's Supper and why it is so centrally important. I received my instructions from the Master himself and passed them on to you. The Master, Jesus, on the night of his betrayal, took bread. Having given thanks, he broke it and said,

This is my body, broken for you.
Do this to remember me.

After supper, he did the same thing with the cup:
This cup is my blood, my new covenant
with you.
Each time you drink this cup, remember me.

What you must solemnly realize is that every time you eat this bread and every time you drink this cup, you reenact in your words and actions the death of the Master. You will be drawn back to this meal again and again until the Master returns. You must never let familiarity breed contempt.

11.27-28 Anyone who eats the bread or drinks the cup of the Master irreverently is like part of the crowd that jeered and spit on him at his death. Is that the kind of "remembrance" you want to be part of? Examine your motives, test your heart, come to this meal in holy awe.

11.29-32 If you give no thought (or worse, don't care) about the broken body of the Master when you eat and drink, you're running the risk of serious consequences. That's why so many of you even now are listless and sick, and others have gone to an early grave. If we get this straight now, we won't have to be straightened out later on. Better to be confronted by the Master now than to face a fiery confrontation later.

11.33-34 So, my friends, when you come together to the Lord's Table, be reverent and courteous with one another. If you're so hungry that you can't wait to be served, go home and get a sandwich. But by no means risk turning this Meal into an eating and drinking binge or a family squabble. It is a spiritual meal—a love feast.

The other things you asked about, I'll respond to in person when I make my next visit.

SPIRITUAL GIFTS

12.1-3 **12** What I want to talk about now is the various ways God's Spirit gets worked into our lives. This is complex and often misunderstood, but I want you to be informed and knowledgeable. Remember how you were when you didn't know God, led from one phony god to another, never knowing what you were doing, just doing it because everybody else did it? It's different in this life. God wants us to use our intelligence, to seek to understand as well as we can. For instance, by using your heads, you

NEW INTERNATIONAL VERSION

speaking by the Spirit of God says, "Jesus be cursed," and no one can say, "Jesus is Lord," except by the Holy Spirit.

⁴There are different kinds of gifts, but the same Spirit. ⁵There are different kinds of service, but the same Lord. ⁶There are different kinds of working, but the same God works all of them in all men.

⁷Now to each one the manifestation of the Spirit is given for the common good. ⁸To one there is given through the Spirit the message of wisdom, to another the message of knowledge by means of the same Spirit, ⁹to another faith by the same Spirit, to another gifts of healing by that one Spirit, ¹⁰to another miraculous powers, to another prophecy, to another distinguishing between spirits, to another speaking in different kinds of tongues,ᵃ and to still another the interpretation of tongues.ᵃ ¹¹All these are the work of one and the same Spirit, and he gives them to each one, just as he determines.

ONE BODY, MANY PARTS

¹²The body is a unit, though it is made up of many parts; and though all its parts are many, they form one body. So it is with Christ. ¹³For we were all baptized byᵇ one Spirit into one body—whether Jews or Greeks, slave or free—and we were all given the one Spirit to drink.

¹⁴Now the body is not made up of one part but of many. ¹⁵If the foot should say, "Because I am not a hand, I do not belong to the body," it would not for that reason cease to be part of the body. ¹⁶And if the ear should say, "Because I am not an eye, I do not belong to the body," it would not for that reason cease to be part of the body. ¹⁷If the whole body were an eye, where would

THE MESSAGE

know perfectly well that the Spirit of God would never prompt anyone to say "Jesus be damned!" Nor would anyone be inclined to say "Jesus is Master!" without the insight of the Holy Spirit.

12.4-11   God's various gifts are handed out everywhere; but they all originate in God's Spirit. God's various ministries are carried out everywhere; but they all originate in God's Spirit. God's various expressions of power are in action everywhere; but God himself is behind it all. Each person is given something to do that shows who God is: Everyone gets in on it, everyone benefits. All kinds of things are handed out by the Spirit, and to all kinds of people! The variety is wonderful:

> wise counsel
> clear understanding
> simple trust
> healing the sick
> miraculous acts
> proclamation
> distinguishing between spirits
> tongues
> interpretation of tongues.

All these gifts have a common origin, but are handed out one by one by the one Spirit of God. He decides who gets what, and when.

12.12-13   You can easily enough see how this kind of thing works by looking no further than your own body. Your body has many parts—limbs, organs, cells—but no matter how many parts you can name, you're still one body. It's exactly the same with Christ. By means of his one Spirit, we all said good-bye to our partial and piecemeal lives. We each used to independently call our own shots, but then we entered into a large and integrated life in which *he* has the final say in everything. (This is what we proclaimed in word and action when we were baptized.) Each of us is now a part of his resurrection body, refreshed and sustained at one fountain—his Spirit—where we all come to drink. The old labels we once used to identify ourselves—labels like Jew or Greek, slave or free—are no longer useful. We need something larger, more comprehensive.

12.14-18   I want you to think about how all this makes you more significant, not less. A body isn't just a single part blown up into something huge. It's all the different-but-similar parts arranged and functioning together. If Foot said, "I'm not elegant like Hand, embellished with rings; I guess I don't belong to this body," would that make it so? If Ear said, "I'm not beautiful like Eye, limpid and expressive; I don't deserve a place on the head," would you want to remove it from the body? If the body was all eye, how could it

---

ᵃ 10 Or *languages*; also in verse 28   ᵇ 13 Or *with; or in*

NEW INTERNATIONAL VERSION

the sense of hearing be? If the whole body were an ear, where would the sense of smell be? 18But in fact God has arranged the parts in the body, every one of them, just as he wanted them to be. 19If they were all one part, where would the body be? 20As it is, there are many parts, but one body.

21The eye cannot say to the hand, "I don't need you!" And the head cannot say to the feet, "I don't need you!" 22On the contrary, those parts of the body that seem to be weaker are indispensable, 23and the parts that we think are less honorable we treat with special honor. And the parts that are unpresentable are treated with special modesty, 24while our presentable parts need no special treatment. But God has combined the members of the body and has given greater honor to the parts that lacked it, 25so that there should be no division in the body, but that its parts should have equal concern for each other. 26If one part suffers, every part suffers with it; if one part is honored, every part rejoices with it.

27Now you are the body of Christ, and each one of you is a part of it. 28And in the church God has appointed first of all apostles, second prophets, third teachers, then workers of miracles, also those having gifts of healing, those able to help others, those with gifts of administration, and those speaking in different kinds of tongues. 29Are all apostles? Are all prophets? Are all teachers? Do all work miracles? 30Do all have gifts of healing? Do all speak in tongues*a*? Do all interpret? 31But eagerly desire*b* the greater gifts.

LOVE

And now I will show you the most excellent way.

THE MESSAGE

hear? If all ear, how could it smell? As it is, we see that God has carefully placed each part of the body right where he wanted it.

12.19-24 But I also want you to think about how this keeps your significance from getting blown up into self-importance. For no matter how significant you are, it is only because of what you are a *part* of. An enormous eye or a gigantic hand wouldn't be a body, but a monster. What we have is one body with many parts, each its proper size and in its proper place. No part is important on its own. Can you imagine Eye telling Hand, "Get lost; I don't need you"? Or, Head telling Foot, "You're fired; your job has been phased out"? As a matter of fact, in practice it works the other way—the "lower" the part, the more basic, and therefore necessary. You can live without an eye, for instance, but not without a stomach. When it's a part of your own body you are concerned with, it makes *no* difference whether the part is visible or clothed, higher or lower. You give it dignity and honor just as it is, without comparisons. If anything, you have more concern for the lower parts than the higher. If you had to choose, wouldn't you prefer good digestion to full-bodied hair?

12.25-26 The way God designed our bodies is a model for understanding our lives together as a church: every part dependent on every other part, the parts we mention and the parts we don't, the parts we see and the parts we don't. If one part hurts, every other part is involved in the hurt, and in the healing. If one part flourishes, every other part enters into the exuberance.

12.27-31 You are Christ's body—that's who you are! You must never forget this. Only as you accept your part of that body does your "part" mean anything. You're familiar with some of the parts that God has formed in his church, which is his "body":

apostles
prophets
teachers
miracle workers
healers
helpers
organizers
those who pray in tongues.

But it's obvious by now, isn't it, that Christ's church is a complete Body and not a gigantic, unidimensional Part? It's not all Apostle, not all Prophet, not all Miracle Worker, not all Healer, not all Prayer in Tongues, not all Interpreter of Tongues. And yet some of you keep competing for so-called "important" parts.

But now I want to lay out a far better way for you.

a 30 Or other languages *b 31 Or But you are eagerly desiring*

NEW INTERNATIONAL VERSION

13 If I speak in the tongues[a] of men and of angels, but have not love, I am only a resounding gong or a clanging cymbal. [2]If I have the gift of prophecy and can fathom all mysteries and all knowledge, and if I have a faith that can move mountains, but have not love, I am nothing. [3]If I give all I possess to the poor and surrender my body to the flames,[b] but have not love, I gain nothing.

[4]Love is patient, love is kind. It does not envy, it does not boast, it is not proud. [5]It is not rude, it is not self-seeking, it is not easily angered, it keeps no record of wrongs. [6]Love does not delight in evil but rejoices with the truth. [7]It always protects, always trusts, always hopes, always perseveres.

[8]Love never fails. But where there are prophecies, they will cease; where there are tongues, they will be stilled; where there is knowledge, it will pass away. [9]For we know in part and we prophesy in part, [10]but when perfection comes, the imperfect disappears. [11]When I was a child, I talked like a child, I thought like a child, I reasoned like a child. When I became a man, I put childish ways behind me. [12]Now we see but a poor reflection as in a mirror; then we shall see face to face. Now I know in part; then I shall know fully, even as I am fully known.

[13]And now these three remain: faith, hope and love. But the greatest of these is love.

GIFTS OF PROPHECY AND TONGUES

14 Follow the way of love and eagerly desire spiritual gifts, especially the gift of

---

THE MESSAGE

THE WAY OF LOVE

13 If I speak with human eloquence and angelic ecstasy but don't love, I'm nothing but the creaking of a rusty gate.

13.2   If I speak God's Word with power, revealing all his mysteries and making everything plain as day, and if I have faith that says to a mountain, "Jump," and it jumps, but I don't love, I'm nothing.

13.3-7   If I give everything I own to the poor and even go to the stake to be burned as a martyr, but I don't love, I've gotten nowhere. So, no matter what I say, what I believe, and what I do, I'm bankrupt without love.

    Love never gives up.
    Love cares more for others than for self.
    Love doesn't want what it doesn't have.
    Love doesn't strut,
    Doesn't have a swelled head,
    Doesn't force itself on others,
    Isn't always "me first,"
    Doesn't fly off the handle,
    Doesn't keep score of the sins of others,
    Doesn't revel when others grovel,
    Takes pleasure in the flowering of truth,
    Puts up with anything,
    Trusts God always,
    Always looks for the best,
    Never looks back,
    But keeps going to the end.

13.8-10   Love never dies. Inspired speech will be over some day; praying in tongues will end; understanding will reach its limit. We know only a portion of the truth, and what we say about God is always incomplete. But when the Complete arrives, our incompletes will be canceled.

13.11   When I was an infant at my mother's breast, I gurgled and cooed like any infant. When I grew up, I left those infant ways for good.

13.12   We don't yet see things clearly. We're squinting in a fog, peering through a mist. But it won't be long before the weather clears and the sun shines bright! We'll see it all then, see it all as clearly as God sees us, knowing him directly just as he knows us!

13.13   But for right now, until that completeness, we have three things to do to lead us toward that consummation: Trust steadily in God, hope unswervingly, love extravagantly. And the best of the three is love.

PRAYER LANGUAGE

14.1-3 **14** Go after a life of love as if your life depended on it—because it does. Give yourselves to the gifts God gives you. Most of

---

a 1 Or languages   b 3 Some early manuscripts body that I may boast

NEW INTERNATIONAL VERSION

prophecy. [2]For anyone who speaks in a tongue[a] does not speak to men but to God. Indeed, no one understands him; he utters mysteries with his spirit.[b] [3]But everyone who prophesies speaks to men for their strengthening, encouragement and comfort. [4]He who speaks in a tongue edifies himself, but he who prophesies edifies the church. [5]I would like every one of you to speak in tongues,[c] but I would rather have you prophesy. He who prophesies is greater than one who speaks in tongues,[c] unless he interprets, so that the church may be edified.

[6]Now, brothers, if I come to you and speak in tongues, what good will I be to you, unless I bring you some revelation or knowledge or prophecy or word of instruction? [7]Even in the case of lifeless things that make sounds, such as the flute or harp, how will anyone know what tune is being played unless there is a distinction in the notes? [8]Again, if the trumpet does not sound a clear call, who will get ready for battle? [9]So it is with you. Unless you speak intelligible words with your tongue, how will anyone know what you are saying? You will just be speaking into the air. [10]Undoubtedly there are all sorts of languages in the world, yet none of them is without meaning. [11]If then I do not grasp the meaning of what someone is saying, I am a foreigner to the speaker, and he is a foreigner to me. [12]So it is with you. Since you are eager to have spiritual gifts, try to excel in gifts that build up the church.

[13]For this reason anyone who speaks in a tongue should pray that he may interpret what he says. [14]For if I pray in a tongue, my spirit prays, but my mind is unfruitful. [15]So what shall I do? I will pray with my spirit, but I will also pray with my mind; I will sing with my spirit, but I will also sing with my mind. [16]If you are praising God with your spirit, how can one who finds himself among those who do not understand[d] say "Amen" to your thanksgiving, since

THE MESSAGE

all, try to proclaim his truth. If you praise him in the private language of tongues, God understands you but no one else does, for you are sharing intimacies just between you and him. But when you proclaim his truth in everyday speech, you're letting *others* in on the truth so that they can grow and be strong and experience his presence with you.

14.4-5 The one who prays using a private "prayer language" certainly gets a lot out of it, but proclaiming God's truth to the church in its common language brings the whole church into growth and strength. I want all of you to develop intimacies with God in prayer, but please don't stop with that. Go on and proclaim his clear truth to others. It's more important that everyone have access to the knowledge and love of God in language everyone understands than that you go off and cultivate God's presence in a mysterious prayer language—unless, of course, there is someone who can interpret what you are saying for the benefit of all.

14.6-8 Think, friends: If I come to you and all I do is pray privately to God in a way only he can understand, what are you going to get out of that? If I don't address you plainly with some insight or truth or proclamation or teaching, what help am I to you? If musical instruments—flutes, say, or harps—aren't played so that each note is distinct and in tune, how will anyone be able to catch the melody and enjoy the music? If the trumpet call can't be distinguished, will anyone show up for the battle?

14.9-12 So if you speak in a way no one can understand, what's the point of opening your mouth? There are many languages in the world and they all mean something to someone. But if *I* don't understand the language, it's not going to do me much good. It's no different with you. Since you're so eager to participate in what God is doing, why don't you concentrate on doing what helps everyone in the church?

14.13-17 So, when you pray in your private prayer language, don't hoard the experience for yourself. Pray for the insight and ability to bring others into that intimacy. If I pray in tongues, my spirit prays but my mind lies fallow, and all that intelligence is wasted. So what's the solution? The answer is simple enough. Do both. I should be spiritually free and expressive as I pray, but I should also be thoughtful and mindful as I pray. I should sing with my spirit, and sing with my mind. If you give a blessing using your private prayer language, which no one else understands, how can some outsider who has just shown up and has no idea what's going on know when to say "Amen"? Your

---

[a] 2 Or *another language*; also in verses 4, 13, 14, 19, 26 and 27   [b] 2 Or *by the Spirit*   [c] 5 Or *other languages*; also in verses 6, 18, 22, 23 and 39   [d] 16 Or *among the inquirers*

NEW INTERNATIONAL VERSION

he does not know what you are saying? ¹⁷You may be giving thanks well enough, but the other man is not edified.

¹⁸I thank God that I speak in tongues more than all of you. ¹⁹But in the church I would rather speak five intelligible words to instruct others than ten thousand words in a tongue.

²⁰Brothers, stop thinking like children. In regard to evil be infants, but in your thinking be adults. ²¹In the Law it is written:

"Through men of strange tongues
  and through the lips of foreigners
I will speak to this people,
  but even then they will not listen to me,"^a
      says the Lord.

²²Tongues, then, are a sign, not for believers but for unbelievers; prophecy, however, is for believers, not for unbelievers. ²³So if the whole church comes together and everyone speaks in tongues, and some who do not understand^b or some unbelievers come in, will they not say that you are out of your mind? ²⁴But if an unbeliever or someone who does not understand^c comes in while everybody is prophesying, he will be convinced by all that he is a sinner and will be judged by all, ²⁵and the secrets of his heart will be laid bare. So he will fall down and worship God, exclaiming, "God is really among you!"

ORDERLY WORSHIP

²⁶What then shall we say, brothers? When you come together, everyone has a hymn, or a word of instruction, a revelation, a tongue or an interpretation. All of these must be done for the strengthening of the church. ²⁷If anyone speaks in a tongue, two—or at the most three—should speak, one at a time, and someone must interpret. ²⁸If there is no interpreter, the speaker should keep quiet in the church and speak to himself and God.

²⁹Two or three prophets should speak, and the others should weigh carefully what is said. ³⁰And if a revelation comes to someone who is sitting down, the first speaker should stop. ³¹For you can all prophesy in turn so that everyone may be instructed and encouraged. ³²The spirits

^a 21 Isaiah 28:11,12   ^b 23 Or *some inquirers*   ^c 24 Or *or some inquirer*

THE MESSAGE

blessing might be beautiful, but you have very effectively cut that person out of it.

14.18-19 I'm grateful to God for the gift of praying in tongues that he gives us for praising him, which leads to wonderful intimacies we enjoy with him. I enter into this as much or more than any of you. But when I'm in a church assembled for worship, I'd rather say five words that everyone can understand and learn from than say ten thousand that sound to others like gibberish.

14.20-25 To be perfectly frank, I'm getting exasperated with your infantile thinking. How long before you grow up and use your head—your *adult* head? It's all right to have a childlike unfamiliarity with evil; a simple *no* is all that's needed there. But there's far more to saying *yes* to something. Only mature and well-exercised intelligence can save you from falling into gullibility. It's written in Scripture that God said,

In strange tongues
  and from the mouths of strangers
I will preach to this people,
  but they'll neither listen nor believe.

So where does it get you, all this speaking in tongues no one understands? It doesn't help believers, and it only gives unbelievers something to gawk at. Plain truth-speaking, on the other hand, goes straight to the heart of believers and doesn't get in the way of unbelievers. If you come together as a congregation and some unbelieving outsiders walk in on you as you're all praying in tongues, unintelligible to each other and to them, won't they assume you've taken leave of your senses and get out of there as fast as they can? But if some unbelieving outsiders walk in on a service where people are speaking out God's truth, the plain words will bring them up against the truth and probe their hearts. Before you know it, they're going to be on their faces before God, recognizing that God is among you.

14.26-33 So here's what I want you to do. When you gather for worship, each one of you be prepared with something that will be useful for all: Sing a hymn, teach a lesson, tell a story, lead a prayer, provide an insight. If prayers are offered in tongues, two or three's the limit, and then only if someone is present who can interpret what you're saying. Otherwise, keep it between God and yourself. And no more than two or three speakers at a meeting, with the rest of you listening and taking it to heart. Take your turn, no one person taking over. Then each speaker gets a chance to say something special from God, and you all learn from each other. If you choose to speak, you're also responsible for how and when you speak. When

NEW INTERNATIONAL VERSION

of prophets are subject to the control of prophets. ³³For God is not a God of disorder but of peace.

As in all the congregations of the saints, ³⁴women should remain silent in the churches. They are not allowed to speak, but must be in submission, as the Law says. ³⁵If they want to inquire about something, they should ask their own husbands at home; for it is disgraceful for a woman to speak in the church.

³⁶Did the word of God originate with you? Or are you the only people it has reached? ³⁷If anybody thinks he is a prophet or spiritually gifted, let him acknowledge that what I am writing to you is the Lord's command. ³⁸If he ignores this, he himself will be ignored. ᵃ

³⁹Therefore, my brothers, be eager to prophesy, and do not forbid speaking in tongues. ⁴⁰But everything should be done in a fitting and orderly way.

THE RESURRECTION OF CHRIST

15 Now, brothers, I want to remind you of the gospel I preached to you, which you received and on which you have taken your stand. ²By this gospel you are saved, if you hold firmly to the word I preached to you. Otherwise, you have believed in vain.

³For what I received I passed on to you as of first importance ᵇ: that Christ died for our sins according to the Scriptures, ⁴that he was buried, that he was raised on the third day according to the Scriptures, ⁵and that he appeared to Peter, ᶜ and then to the Twelve. ⁶After that, he appeared to more than five hundred of the brothers at the same time, most of whom are still living, though some have fallen asleep. ⁷Then he appeared to James, then to all the apostles, ⁸and last of all he appeared to me also, as to one abnormally born.

⁹For I am the least of the apostles and do not even deserve to be called an apostle, because I persecuted the church of God. ¹⁰But by the grace of God I am what I am, and his grace to me was not without effect. No, I worked harder than all

THE MESSAGE

we worship the right way, God doesn't stir us up into confusion; he brings us into harmony. This goes for all the churches—no exceptions.

14.34-36 Wives must not disrupt worship, talking when they should be listening, asking questions that could more appropriately be asked of their husbands at home. God's Book of the law guides our manners and customs here. Wives have no license to use the time of worship for unwarranted speaking. Do you—both women *and* men—imagine that you're a sacred oracle determining what's right and wrong? Do you think everything revolves around you?

14.37-38 If any one of you thinks God has something for you to say or has inspired you to do something, pay close attention to what I have written. This is the way the Master wants it. If you won't play by these rules, God can't use you. Sorry.

14.39-40 Three things, then, to sum this up: When you speak forth God's truth, speak your heart out. Don't tell people how they should or shouldn't pray when they're praying in tongues that you don't understand. Be courteous and considerate in everything.

RESURRECTION

15.1-2 **15** Friends, let me go over the Message with you one final time—this Message that I proclaimed and that you made your own; this Message on which you took your stand and by which your life has been saved. (I'm assuming, now, that your belief was the real thing and not a passing fancy, that you're in this for good and holding fast.)

15.3-9 The first thing I did was place before you what was placed so emphatically before me: that the Messiah died for our sins, exactly as Scripture tells it; that he was buried; that he was raised from death on the third day, again exactly as Scripture says; that he presented himself alive to Peter, then to his closest followers, and later to more than five hundred of his followers all at the same time, most of them still around (although a few have since died); that he then spent time with James and the rest of those he commissioned to represent him; and that he finally presented himself alive to *me*. It was fitting that I bring up the rear. I don't deserve to be included in that inner circle, as you well know, having spent all those early years trying my best to stamp God's church right out of existence.

15.10-11 But because God was so gracious, so very generous, here I am. And I'm not about to let his grace go to waste. Haven't I worked hard trying to do more than any of the others? Even then, my work didn't amount to all that much. It was

---

ᵃ 38 Some manuscripts *If he is ignorant of this, let him be ignorant*   ᵇ 3 Or *you at the first*   ᶜ 5 Greek *Cephas*

NEW INTERNATIONAL VERSION	THE MESSAGE

of them—yet not I, but the grace of God that was with me. [11]Whether, then, it was I or they, this is what we preach, and this is what you believed.

THE RESURRECTION OF THE DEAD

[12]But if it is preached that Christ has been raised from the dead, how can some of you say that there is no resurrection of the dead? [13]If there is no resurrection of the dead, then not even Christ has been raised. [14]And if Christ has not been raised, our preaching is useless and so is your faith. [15]More than that, we are then found to be false witnesses about God, for we have testified about God that he raised Christ from the dead. But he did not raise him if in fact the dead are not raised. [16]For if the dead are not raised, then Christ has not been raised either. [17]And if Christ has not been raised, your faith is futile; you are still in your sins. [18]Then those also who have fallen asleep in Christ are lost. [19]If only for this life we have hope in Christ, we are to be pitied more than all men.

[20]But Christ has indeed been raised from the dead, the firstfruits of those who have fallen asleep. [21]For since death came through a man, the resurrection of the dead comes also through a man. [22]For as in Adam all die, so in Christ all will be made alive. [23]But each in his own turn: Christ, the firstfruits; then, when he comes, those who belong to him. [24]Then the end will come, when he hands over the kingdom to God the Father after he has destroyed all dominion, authority and power. [25]For he must reign until he has put all his enemies under his feet. [26]The last enemy to be destroyed is death. [27]For he "has put everything under his feet." [a] Now when it says that "everything" has been put under him, it is clear that this does not include God himself, who put everything under Christ. [28]When he has done this, then the Son himself will be made subject to him who put everything under him, so that God may be all in all.

[29]Now if there is no resurrection, what will those do who are baptized for the dead? If the dead are not raised at all, why are people baptized for them? [30]And as for us, why do we endanger ourselves every hour? [31]I die every day—

God giving me the work to do, God giving me the energy to do it. So whether you heard it from me or from those others, it's all the same: We spoke God's truth and you entrusted your lives.

15.12-15   Now, let me ask you something profound yet troubling. If you became believers because you trusted the proclamation that Christ is alive, risen from the dead, how can you let people say that there is no such thing as a resurrection? If there's no resurrection, there's no living Christ. And face it—if there's no resurrection for Christ, everything we've told you is smoke and mirrors, and everything you've staked your life on is smoke and mirrors. Not only that, but we would be guilty of telling a string of barefaced lies about God, all these affidavits we passed on to you verifying that God raised up Christ—sheer fabrications, if there's no resurrection.

15.16-20   If corpses can't be raised, then Christ wasn't, because he was indeed dead. And if Christ wasn't raised, then all you're doing is wandering about in the dark, as lost as ever. It's even worse for those who died hoping in Christ and resurrection, because they're already in their graves. If all we get out of Christ is a little inspiration for a few short years, we're a pretty sorry lot. But the truth is that Christ *has* been raised up, the first in a long legacy of those who are going to leave the cemeteries.

15.21-28   There is a nice symmetry in this: Death initially came by a man, and resurrection from death came by a man. Everybody dies in Adam; everybody comes alive in Christ. But we have to wait our turn: Christ is first, then those with him at his Coming, the grand consummation when, after crushing the opposition, he hands over his kingdom to God the Father. He won't let up until the last enemy is down—and the very last enemy is death! As the psalmist said, "He laid them low, one and all; he walked all over them." When Scripture says that "he walked all over them," it's obvious that he couldn't at the same time be walked on. When everything and everyone is finally under God's rule, the Son will step down, taking his place with everyone else, showing that God's rule is absolutely comprehensive—a perfect ending!

15.29   Why do you think people offer themselves to be baptized for those already in the grave? If there's no chance of resurrection for a corpse, if God's power stops at the cemetery gates, why do we keep doing things that suggest he's going to clean the place out someday, pulling everyone up on their feet alive?

15.30-33   And why do you think I keep risking my neck in this dangerous work? I look death in the face practically every day I live. Do you

NEW INTERNATIONAL VERSION

I mean that, brothers—just as surely as I glory over you in Christ Jesus our Lord. [32]If I fought wild beasts in Ephesus for merely human reasons, what have I gained? If the dead are not raised,

"Let us eat and drink,
  for tomorrow we die." [a]

[33]Do not be misled: "Bad company corrupts good character." [34]Come back to your senses as you ought, and stop sinning; for there are some who are ignorant of God—I say this to your shame.

THE RESURRECTION BODY

[35]But someone may ask, "How are the dead raised? With what kind of body will they come?" [36]How foolish! What you sow does not come to life unless it dies. [37]When you sow, you do not plant the body that will be, but just a seed, perhaps of wheat or of something else. [38]But God gives it a body as he has determined, and to each kind of seed he gives its own body. [39]All flesh is not the same: Men have one kind of flesh, animals have another, birds another and fish another. [40]There are also heavenly bodies and there are earthly bodies; but the splendor of the heavenly bodies is one kind, and the splendor of the earthly bodies is another. [41]The sun has one kind of splendor, the moon another and the stars another; and star differs from star in splendor.

[42]So will it be with the resurrection of the dead. The body that is sown is perishable, it is raised imperishable; [43]it is sown in dishonor, it is raised in glory; it is sown in weakness, it is raised in power; [44]it is sown a natural body, it is raised a spiritual body.

If there is a natural body, there is also a spiri-

THE MESSAGE

think I'd do this if I wasn't convinced of your resurrection and mine as guaranteed by the resurrected Messiah Jesus? Do you think I was just trying to act heroic when I fought the wild beasts at Ephesus, hoping it wouldn't be the end of me? Not on your life! It's resurrection, resurrection, always resurrection, that undergirds what I do and say, the way I live. If there's no resurrection, "We eat, we drink, the next day we die," and that's all there is to it. But don't fool yourselves. Don't let yourselves be poisoned by this anti-resurrection loose talk. "Bad company ruins good manners."

15.34 Think straight. Awaken to the holiness of life. No more playing fast and loose with resurrection facts. Ignorance of God is a luxury you can't afford in times like these. Aren't you embarrassed that you've let this kind of thing go on as long as you have?

15.35-38 Some skeptic is sure to ask, "Show me how resurrection works. Give me a diagram; draw me a picture. What does this 'resurrection body' look like?" If you look at this question closely, you realize how absurd it is. There are no diagrams for this kind of thing. We do have a parallel experience in gardening. You plant a "dead" seed; soon there is a flourishing plant. There is no visual likeness between seed and plant. You could never guess what a tomato would look like by looking at a tomato seed. What we plant in the soil and what grows out of it don't look anything alike. The dead body that we bury in the ground and the resurrection body that comes from it will be dramatically different.

15.39-41 You will notice that the variety of bodies is stunning. Just as there are different kinds of seeds, there are different kinds of bodies—humans, animals, birds, fish—each unprecedented in its form. You get a hint at the diversity of resurrection glory by looking at the diversity of bodies not only on earth but in the skies—sun, moon, stars—all these varieties of beauty and brightness. And we're only looking at pre-resurrection "seeds"—who can imagine what the resurrection "plants" will be like!

15.42-44 This image of planting a dead seed and raising a live plant is a mere sketch at best, but perhaps it will help in approaching the mystery of the resurrection body—but only if you keep in mind that when we're raised, we're raised for *good*, alive forever! The corpse that's planted is no beauty, but when it's raised, it's glorious. Put in the ground weak, it comes up powerful. The seed sown is natural; the seed grown is supernatural—same seed, same body, but what a difference from when it goes down in physical mortality to when it is raised up in spiritual immortality!

NEW INTERNATIONAL VERSION

tual body. [45]So it is written: "The first man Adam became a living being"[a]; the last Adam, a life-giving spirit. [46]The spiritual did not come first, but the natural, and after that the spiritual. [47]The first man was of the dust of the earth, the second man from heaven. [48]As was the earthly man, so are those who are of the earth; and as is the man from heaven, so also are those who are of heaven. [49]And just as we have borne the likeness of the earthly man, so shall we[b] bear the likeness of the man from heaven.

[50]I declare to you, brothers, that flesh and blood cannot inherit the kingdom of God, nor does the perishable inherit the imperishable. [51]Listen, I tell you a mystery: We will not all sleep, but we will all be changed— [52]in a flash, in the twinkling of an eye, at the last trumpet. For the trumpet will sound, the dead will be raised imperishable, and we will be changed. [53]For the perishable must clothe itself with the imperishable, and the mortal with immortality. [54]When the perishable has been clothed with the imperishable, and the mortal with immortality, then the saying that is written will come true: "Death has been swallowed up in victory."[c]

[55] "Where, O death, is your victory?
Where, O death, is your sting?"[d]

[56]The sting of death is sin, and the power of sin is the law. [57]But thanks be to God! He gives us the victory through our Lord Jesus Christ.

[58]Therefore, my dear brothers, stand firm. Let nothing move you. Always give yourselves fully to the work of the Lord, because you know that your labor in the Lord is not in vain.

THE COLLECTION FOR GOD'S PEOPLE

16 Now about the collection for God's people: Do what I told the Galatian churches to do. [2]On the first day of every week, each one of you should set aside a sum of money in keeping with his income, saving it up, so that when I come no collections will have to be made. [3]Then, when I arrive, I will give letters of introduction to the men you approve and send them

---

THE MESSAGE

15.45-49   We follow this sequence in Scripture: The First Adam received life, the Last Adam is a life-giving Spirit. Physical life comes first, then spiritual—a firm base shaped from the earth, a final completion coming out of heaven. The First Man was made out of earth, and people since then are earthy; the Second Man was made out of heaven, and people now can be heavenly. In the same way that we've worked from our earthy origins, let's embrace our heavenly ends.

15.50   I need to emphasize, friends, that our natural, earthy lives don't in themselves lead us by their very nature into the kingdom of God. Their very "nature" is to die, so how could they "naturally" end up in the Life kingdom?

15.51-57   But let me tell you something wonderful, a mystery I'll probably never fully understand. We're not all going to die—*but* we are all going to be changed. You hear a blast to end all blasts from a trumpet, and in the time that you look up and blink your eyes—it's over. On signal from that trumpet from heaven, the dead will be up and out of their graves, beyond the reach of death, never to die again. At the same moment and in the same way, we'll all be changed. In the resurrection scheme of things, this has to happen: everything perishable taken off the shelves and replaced by the imperishable, this mortal replaced by the immortal. Then the saying will come true:

Death swallowed by triumphant Life!
Who got the last word, oh, Death?
Oh, Death, who's afraid of you now?

It was sin that made death so frightening and law-code guilt that gave sin its leverage, its destructive power. But now in a single victorious stroke of Life, all three—sin, guilt, death—are gone, the gift of our Master, Jesus Christ. Thank God!

15.58   With all this going for us, my dear, dear friends, stand your ground. And don't hold back. Throw yourselves into the work of the Master, confident that nothing you do for him is a waste of time or effort.

COMING TO SEE YOU

16.1-4   **16** Regarding the relief offering for poor Christians that is being collected, you get the same instructions I gave the churches in Galatia. Every Sunday each of you make an offering and put it in safekeeping. Be as generous as you can. When I get there you'll have it ready, and I won't have to make a special appeal. Then after I arrive, I'll write letters authorizing whomever you delegate, and send them off to Jerusalem to

NEW INTERNATIONAL VERSION

with your gift to Jerusalem. ⁴If it seems advisable for me to go also, they will accompany me.

PERSONAL REQUESTS

⁵After I go through Macedonia, I will come to you—for I will be going through Macedonia. ⁶Perhaps I will stay with you awhile, or even spend the winter, so that you can help me on my journey, wherever I go. ⁷I do not want to see you now and make only a passing visit; I hope to spend some time with you, if the Lord permits. ⁸But I will stay on at Ephesus until Pentecost, ⁹because a great door for effective work has opened to me, and there are many who oppose me.

¹⁰If Timothy comes, see to it that he has nothing to fear while he is with you, for he is carrying on the work of the Lord, just as I am. ¹¹No one, then, should refuse to accept him. Send him on his way in peace so that he may return to me. I am expecting him along with the brothers.

¹²Now about our brother Apollos: I strongly urged him to go to you with the brothers. He was quite unwilling to go now, but he will go when he has the opportunity.

¹³Be on your guard; stand firm in the faith; be men of courage; be strong. ¹⁴Do everything in love.

¹⁵You know that the household of Stephanas were the first converts in Achaia, and they have devoted themselves to the service of the saints. I urge you, brothers, ¹⁶to submit to such as these and to everyone who joins in the work, and labors at it. ¹⁷I was glad when Stephanas, Fortunatus and Achaicus arrived, because they have supplied what was lacking from you. ¹⁸For they refreshed my spirit and yours also. Such men deserve recognition.

FINAL GREETINGS

¹⁹The churches in the province of Asia send you greetings. Aquila and Priscilla[a] greet you warmly in the Lord, and so does the church that meets at their house. ²⁰All the brothers here send you greetings. Greet one another with a holy kiss.

²¹I, Paul, write this greeting in my own hand. ²²If anyone does not love the Lord—a curse be on him. Come, O Lord[b]! ²³The grace of the Lord Jesus be with you. ²⁴My love to all of you in Christ Jesus. Amen.[c]

---

a 19 Greek Prisca, a variant of Priscilla b 22 In Aramaic the expression Come, O Lord is Marana tha. c 24 Some manuscripts do not have Amen.

THE MESSAGE

deliver your gift. If you think it best that I go along, I'll be glad to travel with them.

16.5-9 I plan to visit you after passing through northern Greece. I won't be staying long there, but maybe I can stay awhile with you—maybe even spend the winter? Then you could give me a good send-off, wherever I may be headed next. I don't want to just drop by in between other "primary" destinations. I want a good, long, leisurely visit. If the Master agrees, we'll have it! For the present, I'm staying right here in Ephesus. A huge door of opportunity for good work has opened up here. (There is also mushrooming opposition.)

16.10-11 If Timothy shows up, take good care of him. Make him feel completely at home among you. He works so hard for the Master, just as I do. Don't let anyone disparage him. After a while, send him on to me with your blessing. Tell him I'm expecting him, and any friends he has with him.

16.12 About our friend Apollos, I've done my best to get him to pay you a visit, but haven't talked him into it yet. He doesn't think this is the right time. But there will be a "right time."

16.13-14 Keep your eyes open, hold tight to your convictions, give it all you've got, be resolute, and love without stopping.

16.15-16 Would you do me a favor, friends, and give special recognition to the family of Stephanas? You know, they were among the first converts in Greece, and they've put themselves out, serving Christians ever since then. I want you to honor and look up to people like that: companions and workers who show us how to do it, giving us something to aspire to.

16.17-18 I want you to know how delighted I am to have Stephanas, Fortunatus, and Achaicus here with me. They partially make up for your absence! They've refreshed me by keeping me in touch with you. Be proud that you have people like this among you.

16.19 The churches here in western Asia send greetings.

Aquila, Priscilla, and the church that meets in their house say hello.

16.20 All the friends here say hello.

Pass the greetings around with holy embraces!

16.21 And I, Paul—in my own handwriting!—send you my regards.

16.22 If anyone won't love the Master, throw him out. Make room for the Master!

16.23 Our Master Jesus has his arms wide open for you.

16.24 And I love all of you in the Messiah, in Jesus.

2 CORINTHIANS

2 CORINTHIANS

1 Paul, an apostle of Christ Jesus by the will of God, and Timothy our brother,

To the church of God in Corinth, together with all the saints throughout Achaia:

²Grace and peace to you from God our Father and the Lord Jesus Christ.

THE GOD OF ALL COMFORT

³Praise be to the God and Father of our Lord Jesus Christ, the Father of compassion and the God of all comfort, ⁴who comforts us in all our troubles, so that we can comfort those in any trouble with the comfort we ourselves have received from God. ⁵For just as the sufferings of Christ flow over into our lives, so also through Christ our comfort overflows. ⁶If we are distressed, it is for your comfort and salvation; if we are comforted, it is for your comfort, which produces in you patient endurance of the same sufferings we suffer. ⁷And our hope for you is firm, because we know that just as you share in our sufferings, so also you share in our comfort.

⁸We do not want you to be uninformed, brothers, about the hardships we suffered in the province of Asia. We were under great pressure, far beyond our ability to endure, so that we despaired even of life. ⁹Indeed, in our hearts we felt the sentence of death. But this happened that we might not rely on ourselves but on God, who raises the dead. ¹⁰He has delivered us from such a deadly peril, and he will deliver us. On him we have set our hope that he will continue to deliver us, ¹¹as you help us by your prayers. Then many will give thanks on our[a] behalf for the gra-

1.1-2 **1** I, Paul, have been sent on a special mission by the Messiah, Jesus, planned by God himself. I write this to God's congregation in Corinth, and to believers all over Achaia province. May all the gifts and benefits that come from God our Father and the Master, Jesus Christ, be yours! Timothy, someone you know and trust, joins me in this greeting.

THE RESCUE

1.3-5 All praise to the God and Father of our Master, Jesus the Messiah! Father of all mercy! God of all healing counsel! He comes alongside us when we go through hard times, and before you know it, he brings us alongside someone else who is going through hard times so that we can be there for that person just as God was there for us. We have plenty of hard times that come from following the Messiah, but no more so than the good times of his healing comfort—we get a full measure of that, too.

1.6-7 When we suffer for Jesus, it works out for your healing and salvation. If we are treated well, given a helping hand and encouraging word, that also works to your benefit, spurring you on, face forward, unflinching. Your hard times are also our hard times. When we see that you're just as willing to endure the hard times as to enjoy the good times, we know you're going to make it, no doubt about it.

1.8-11 We don't want you in the dark, friends, about how hard it was when all this came down on us in Asia province. It was so bad we didn't think we were going to make it. We felt like we'd been sent to death row, that it was all over for us. As it turned out, it was the best thing that could have happened. Instead of trusting in our own strength or wits to get out of it, we were forced to trust God totally—not a bad idea since he's the God who raises the dead! And he did it, rescued us from certain doom. *And* he'll do it again, rescuing us as many times as we need rescuing. You and your prayers are part of the rescue operation—I don't want you in the dark about that either. I can see your faces even now, lifted in praise for

NEW INTERNATIONAL VERSION

cious favor granted us in answer to the prayers of many.

PAUL'S CHANGE OF PLANS

¹²Now this is our boast: Our conscience testifies that we have conducted ourselves in the world, and especially in our relations with you, in the holiness and sincerity that are from God. We have done so not according to worldly wisdom but according to God's grace. ¹³For we do not write you anything you cannot read or understand. And I hope that, ¹⁴as you have understood us in part, you will come to understand fully that you can boast of us just as we will boast of you in the day of the Lord Jesus.

¹⁵Because I was confident of this, I planned to visit you first so that you might benefit twice. ¹⁶I planned to visit you on my way to Macedonia and to come back to you from Macedonia, and then to have you send me on my way to Judea. ¹⁷When I planned this, did I do it lightly? Or do I make my plans in a worldly manner so that in the same breath I say, "Yes, yes" and "No, no"?

¹⁸But as surely as God is faithful, our message to you is not "Yes" and "No." ¹⁹For the Son of God, Jesus Christ, who was preached among you by me and Silas[a] and Timothy, was not "Yes" and "No," but in him it has always been "Yes." ²⁰For no matter how many promises God has made, they are "Yes" in Christ. And so through him the "Amen" is spoken by us to the glory of God. ²¹Now it is God who makes both us and you stand firm in Christ. He anointed us, ²²set his seal of ownership on us, and put his Spirit in our hearts as a deposit, guaranteeing what is to come.

²³I call God as my witness that it was in order to spare you that I did not return to Corinth. ²⁴Not that we lord it over your faith, but we work with you for your joy, because it is by faith you stand firm.

2 ¹So I made up my mind that I would not make another painful visit to you. ²For if I grieve you, who is left to make me glad but you

THE MESSAGE

God's deliverance of us, a rescue in which your prayers played such a crucial part.

1.12-14 Now that the worst is over, we're pleased we can report that we've come out of this with conscience and faith intact, and can face the world—and even more importantly, face you with our heads held high. But it wasn't by any fancy footwork on our part. It was *God* who kept us focused on him, uncompromised. Don't try to read between the lines or look for hidden meanings in this letter. We're writing plain, unembellished truth, hoping that you'll now see the whole picture as well as you've seen some of the details. We want you to be as proud of us as we are of you when we stand together before our Master Jesus.

1.15-16 Confident of your welcome, I had originally planned two great visits with you—coming by on my way to Macedonia province, and then again on my return trip. Then we could have had a bon-voyage party as you sent me off to Judea. That was the plan.

1.17-19 Are you now going to accuse me of being flip with my promises because it didn't work out? Do you think I talk out of both sides of my mouth—a glib *yes* one moment, a glib *no* the next? Well, you're wrong. I try to be as true to my word as God is to his. Our word to you wasn't a careless yes canceled by an indifferent no. How could it be? When Silas and Timothy and I proclaimed the Son of God among you, did you pick up on any yes-and-no, on-again, off-again waffling? Wasn't it a clean, strong Yes?

1.20-22 Whatever God has promised gets stamped with the Yes of Jesus. In him, this is what we preach and pray, the great Amen, God's Yes and our Yes together, gloriously evident. God affirms us, making us a sure thing in Christ, putting his Yes within us. By his Spirit he has stamped us with his eternal pledge—a sure beginning of what he is destined to complete.

1.23 Now, are you ready for the real reason I didn't visit you in Corinth? As God is my witness, the only reason I didn't come was to spare you pain. I was being *considerate* of you, not indifferent, not manipulative.

1.24 We're not in charge of how you live out the faith, looking over your shoulders, suspiciously critical. We're partners, working alongside you, joyfully expectant. I know that you stand by your own faith, not by ours.

2.1-2 **2** That's why I decided not to make another visit that could only be painful to both of us. If by merely showing up I would put you in an embarrassingly painful position, how would you then be free to cheer and refresh me?

NEW INTERNATIONAL VERSION

whom I have grieved? ³I wrote as I did so that when I came I should not be distressed by those who ought to make me rejoice. I had confidence in all of you, that you would all share my joy. ⁴For I wrote you out of great distress and anguish of heart and with many tears, not to grieve you but to let you know the depth of my love for you.

FORGIVENESS FOR THE SINNER

⁵If anyone has caused grief, he has not so much grieved me as he has grieved all of you, to some extent—not to put it too severely. ⁶The punishment inflicted on him by the majority is sufficient for him. ⁷Now instead, you ought to forgive and comfort him, so that he will not be overwhelmed by excessive sorrow. ⁸I urge you, therefore, to reaffirm your love for him. ⁹The reason I wrote you was to see if you would stand the test and be obedient in everything. ¹⁰If you forgive anyone, I also forgive him. And what I have forgiven—if there was anything to forgive—I have forgiven in the sight of Christ for your sake, ¹¹in order that Satan might not outwit us. For we are not unaware of his schemes.

MINISTERS OF THE NEW COVENANT

¹²Now when I went to Troas to preach the gospel of Christ and found that the Lord had opened a door for me, ¹³I still had no peace of mind, because I did not find my brother Titus there. So I said good-by to them and went on to Macedonia.

¹⁴But thanks be to God, who always leads us in triumphal procession in Christ and through us spreads everywhere the fragrance of the knowledge of him. ¹⁵For we are to God the aroma of Christ among those who are being saved and those who are perishing. ¹⁶To the one we are the smell of death; to the other, the fragrance of life. And who is equal to such a task? ¹⁷Unlike so many, we do not peddle the word of God for

THE MESSAGE

2.3-4   That was my reason for writing a letter instead of coming—so I wouldn't have to spend a miserable time disappointing the very friends I had looked forward to cheering me up. I was convinced at the time I wrote it that what was best for me was also best for you. As it turned out, there was pain enough just in writing that letter, more tears than ink on the parchment. But I didn't write it to cause pain; I wrote it so you would know how much I care—oh, more than care—*love* you!

2.5-8   Now, regarding the one who started all this— the person in question who caused all this pain—I want you to know that I am not the one injured in this as much as, with a few exceptions, all of you. So I don't want to come down too hard. What the majority of you agreed to as punishment is punishment enough. Now is the time to forgive this man and help him back on his feet. If all you do is pour on the guilt, you could very well drown him in it. My counsel now is to pour on the love.

2.9-11   The focus of my letter wasn't on punishing the offender but on getting you to take responsibility for the health of the church. So if you forgive him, I forgive him. Don't think I'm carrying around a list of personal grudges. The fact is that I'm joining in with *your* forgiveness, as Christ is with us, guiding us. After all, we don't want to unwittingly give Satan an opening for yet more mischief—we're not oblivious to his sly ways!

AN OPEN DOOR

2.12-14   When I arrived in Troas to proclaim the Message of the Messiah, I found the place wide open: God had opened the door; all I had to do was walk through it. But when I didn't find Titus waiting for me with news of your condition, I couldn't relax. Worried about you, I left and came on to Macedonia province looking for Titus and a reassuring word on you. And I got it, thank God!

2.14-16   In the Messiah, in Christ, God leads us from place to place in one perpetual victory parade. Through us, he brings knowledge of Christ. Everywhere we go, people breathe in the exquisite fragrance. Because of Christ, we give off a sweet scent rising to God, which is recognized by those on the way of salvation—an aroma redolent with life. But those on the way to destruction treat us more like the stench from a rotting corpse.

2.16-17   This is a terrific responsibility. Is anyone competent to take it on? No—but at least we don't take God's Word, water it down, and then take it to the streets to sell it cheap. We stand

NEW INTERNATIONAL VERSION

profit. On the contrary, in Christ we speak before God with sincerity, like men sent from God.

3 Are we beginning to commend ourselves again? Or do we need, like some people, letters of recommendation to you or from you? ²You yourselves are our letter, written on our hearts, known and read by everybody. ³You show that you are a letter from Christ, the result of our ministry, written not with ink but with the Spirit of the living God, not on tablets of stone but on tablets of human hearts.

⁴Such confidence as this is ours through Christ before God. ⁵Not that we are competent in ourselves to claim anything for ourselves, but our competence comes from God. ⁶He has made us competent as ministers of a new covenant—not of the letter but of the Spirit; for the letter kills, but the Spirit gives life.

The Glory of the New Covenant

⁷Now if the ministry that brought death, which was engraved in letters on stone, came with glory, so that the Israelites could not look steadily at the face of Moses because of its glory, fading though it was, ⁸will not the ministry of the Spirit be even more glorious? ⁹If the ministry that condemns men is glorious, how much more glorious is the ministry that brings righteousness! ¹⁰For what was glorious has no glory now in comparison with the surpassing glory. ¹¹And if what was fading away came with glory, how much greater is the glory of that which lasts!

¹²Therefore, since we have such a hope, we are very bold. ¹³We are not like Moses, who would put a veil over his face to keep the Israelites from gazing at it while the radiance was fading away. ¹⁴But their minds were made dull, for to this day the same veil remains when the old covenant is read. It has not been removed, because only in Christ is it taken away. ¹⁵Even to this day when Moses is read, a veil covers their hearts. ¹⁶But whenever anyone turns to the Lord,

THE MESSAGE

in Christ's presence when we speak; God looks us in the face. We get what we say straight from God and say it as honestly as we can.

3.1-3 **3** Does it sound like we're patting ourselves on the back, insisting on our credentials, asserting our authority? Well, we're not. Neither do we need letters of endorsement, either to you or from you. You yourselves are all the endorsement we need. Your very lives are a letter that anyone can read by just looking at you. Christ himself wrote it—not with ink, but with God's living Spirit; not chiseled into stone, but carved into human lives—and we publish it.

3.4-6 We couldn't be more sure of ourselves in this—that *you*, written by Christ himself for God, are our letter of recommendation. We wouldn't think of writing this kind of letter about ourselves. Only God can write such a letter. His letter authorizes us to help carry out this new plan of action. The plan wasn't written out with ink on paper, with pages and pages of legal footnotes, killing your spirit. It's written with Spirit on spirit, his life on our lives!

Lifting the Veil

3.7-8 The Government of Death, its constitution chiseled on stone tablets, had a dazzling inaugural. Moses' face as he delivered the tablets was so bright that day (even though it would fade soon enough) that the people of Israel could no more look right at him than stare into the sun. How much more dazzling, then, the Government of Living Spirit?

3.9-11 If the Government of Condemnation was impressive, how about this Government of Affirmation? Bright as that old government was, it would look downright dull alongside this new one. If that makeshift arrangement impressed us, how much more this brightly shining government installed for eternity?

3.12-15 With that kind of hope to excite us, nothing holds us back. Unlike Moses, we have nothing to hide. Everything is out in the open with us. He wore a veil so the children of Israel wouldn't notice that the glory was fading away—and they *didn't* notice. They didn't notice it then and they don't notice it now, don't notice that there's nothing left behind that veil. Even today when the proclamations of that old, bankrupt government are read out, they can't see through it. Only Christ can get rid of the veil so they can see for themselves that there's nothing there.

3.16-18 Whenever, though, they turn to face God as Moses did, God removes the veil and there they

NEW INTERNATIONAL VERSION

the veil is taken away. [17]Now the Lord is the Spirit, and where the Spirit of the Lord is, there is freedom. [18]And we, who with unveiled faces all reflect[a] the Lord's glory, are being transformed into his likeness with ever-increasing glory, which comes from the Lord, who is the Spirit.

TREASURES IN JARS OF CLAY

4 Therefore, since through God's mercy we have this ministry, we do not lose heart. [2]Rather, we have renounced secret and shameful ways; we do not use deception, nor do we distort the word of God. On the contrary, by setting forth the truth plainly we commend ourselves to every man's conscience in the sight of God. [3]And even if our gospel is veiled, it is veiled to those who are perishing. [4]The god of this age has blinded the minds of unbelievers, so that they cannot see the light of the gospel of the glory of Christ, who is the image of God. [5]For we do not preach ourselves, but Jesus Christ as Lord, and ourselves as your servants for Jesus' sake. [6]For God, who said, "Let light shine out of darkness,"[b] made his light shine in our hearts to give us the light of the knowledge of the glory of God in the face of Christ.

[7]But we have this treasure in jars of clay to show that this all-surpassing power is from God and not from us. [8]We are hard pressed on every side, but not crushed; perplexed, but not in despair; [9]persecuted, but not abandoned; struck down, but not destroyed. [10]We always carry around in our body the death of Jesus, so that

THE MESSAGE

are—face to face! They suddenly recognize that God is a living, personal presence, not a piece of chiseled stone. And when God is personally present, a living Spirit, that old, constricting legislation is recognized as obsolete. We're free of it! All of us! Nothing between us and God, our faces shining with the brightness of his face. And so we are transfigured much like the Messiah, our lives gradually becoming brighter and more beautiful as God enters our lives and we become like him.

TRIAL AND TORTURE

4.1-2 4 Since God has so generously let us in on what he is doing, we're not about to throw up our hands and walk off the job just because we run into occasional hard times. We refuse to wear masks and play games. We don't maneuver and manipulate behind the scenes. And we don't twist God's Word to suit ourselves. Rather, we keep everything we do and say out in the open, the whole truth on display, so that those who want to can see and judge for themselves in the presence of God.

4.3-4   If our Message is obscure to anyone, it's not because we're holding back in any way. No, it's because these other people are looking or going the wrong way and refuse to give it serious attention. All they have eyes for is the fashionable god of darkness. They think he can give them what they want, and that they won't have to bother believing a Truth they can't see. They're stone-blind to the dayspring brightness of the Message that shines with Christ, who gives us the best picture of God we'll ever get.

4.5-6   Remember, our Message is not about ourselves; we're proclaiming Jesus Christ, the Master. All we are is messengers, errand runners from Jesus for you. It started when God said, "Light up the darkness!" and our lives filled up with light as we saw and understood God in the face of Christ, all bright and beautiful.

4.7-12   If you only look at us, you might well miss the brightness. We carry this precious Message around in the unadorned clay pots of our ordinary lives. That's to prevent anyone from confusing God's incomparable power with us. As it is, there's not much chance of that. You know for yourselves that we're not much to look at. We've been surrounded and battered by troubles, but we're not demoralized; we're not sure what to do, but we know that God knows what to do; we've been spiritually terrorized, but God hasn't left our side; we've been thrown down, but we haven't broken. What they did to Jesus, they do to us—trial and torture, mockery and murder; what Jesus did among them, he does in

NEW INTERNATIONAL VERSION

the life of Jesus may also be revealed in our body. ¹¹For we who are alive are always being given over to death for Jesus' sake, so that his life may be revealed in our mortal body. ¹²So then, death is at work in us, but life is at work in you.

¹³It is written: "I believed; therefore I have spoken." [a] With that same spirit of faith we also believe and therefore speak, ¹⁴because we know that the one who raised the Lord Jesus from the dead will also raise us with Jesus and present us with you in his presence. ¹⁵All this is for your benefit, so that the grace that is reaching more and more people may cause thanksgiving to overflow to the glory of God.

¹⁶Therefore we do not lose heart. Though outwardly we are wasting away, yet inwardly we are being renewed day by day. ¹⁷For our light and momentary troubles are achieving for us an eternal glory that far outweighs them all. ¹⁸So we fix our eyes not on what is seen, but on what is unseen. For what is seen is temporary, but what is unseen is eternal.

OUR HEAVENLY DWELLING

5 Now we know that if the earthly tent we live in is destroyed, we have a building from God, an eternal house in heaven, not built by human hands. ²Meanwhile we groan, longing to be clothed with our heavenly dwelling, ³because when we are clothed, we will not be found naked. ⁴For while we are in this tent, we groan and are burdened, because we do not wish to be unclothed but to be clothed with our heavenly dwelling, so that what is mortal may be swallowed up by life. ⁵Now it is God who has made us for this very purpose and has given us the Spirit as a deposit, guaranteeing what is to come.

⁶Therefore we are always confident and know that as long as we are at home in the body we are away from the Lord. ⁷We live by faith, not by sight. ⁸We are confident, I say, and would prefer to be away from the body and at home with the Lord. ⁹So we make it our goal to please him, whether we are at home in the body or away from it. ¹⁰For we must all appear before the judgment seat of Christ, that each one may receive what is due him for the things done while in the body, whether good or bad.

a 13 Psalm 116:10

THE MESSAGE

us—he lives! Our lives are at constant risk for Jesus' sake, which makes Jesus' life all the more evident in us. While we're going through the worst, you're getting in on the best!

4.13-15 We're not keeping this quiet, not on your life. Just like the psalmist who wrote, "I believed it, so I said it," we say what we believe. And what we believe is that the One who raised up the Master Jesus will just as certainly raise us up with you, alive. Every detail works to your advantage and to God's glory: more and more grace, more and more people, more and more praise!

4.16-18 So we're not giving up. How could we! Even though on the outside it often looks like things are falling apart on us, on the inside, where God is making new life, not a day goes by without his unfolding grace. These hard times are small potatoes compared to the coming good times, the lavish celebration prepared for us. There's far more here than meets the eye. The things we see now are here today, gone tomorrow. But the things we can't see now will last forever.

5.1-5 5 For instance, we know that when these bodies of ours are taken down like tents and folded away, they will be replaced by resurrection bodies in heaven—God-made, not handmade—and we'll never have to relocate our "tents" again. Sometimes we can hardly wait to move—and so we cry out in frustration. Compared to what's coming, living conditions around here seem like a stopover in an unfurnished shack, and we're tired of it! We've been given a glimpse of the real thing, our true home, our resurrection bodies! The Spirit of God whets our appetite by giving us a taste of what's ahead. He puts a little of heaven in our hearts so that we'll never settle for less.

5.6-8 That's why we live with such good cheer. You won't see us drooping our heads or dragging our feet! Cramped conditions here don't get us down. They only remind us of the spacious living conditions ahead. It's what we trust in but don't yet see that keeps us going. Do you suppose a few ruts in the road or rocks in the path are going to stop us? When the time comes, we'll be plenty ready to exchange exile for homecoming.

5.9-10 But neither exile nor homecoming is the main thing. Cheerfully pleasing God is the main thing, and that's what we aim to do, regardless of our conditions. Sooner or later we'll all have to face God, regardless of our conditions. We will appear before Christ and take what's coming to us as a result of our actions, either good or bad.

NEW INTERNATIONAL VERSION

THE MINISTRY OF RECONCILIATION

[11]Since, then, we know what it is to fear the Lord, we try to persuade men. What we are is plain to God, and I hope it is also plain to your conscience. [12]We are not trying to commend ourselves to you again, but are giving you an opportunity to take pride in us, so that you can answer those who take pride in what is seen rather than in what is in the heart. [13]If we are out of our mind, it is for the sake of God; if we are in our right mind, it is for you. [14]For Christ's love compels us, because we are convinced that one died for all, and therefore all died. [15]And he died for all, that those who live should no longer live for themselves but for him who died for them and was raised again.

[16]So from now on we regard no one from a worldly point of view. Though we once regarded Christ in this way, we do so no longer. [17]Therefore, if anyone is in Christ, he is a new creation; the old has gone, the new has come! [18]All this is from God, who reconciled us to himself through Christ and gave us the ministry of reconciliation: [19]that God was reconciling the world to himself in Christ, not counting men's sins against them. And he has committed to us the message of reconciliation. [20]We are therefore Christ's ambassadors, as though God were making his appeal through us. We implore you on Christ's behalf: Be reconciled to God. [21]God made him who had no sin to be sin[a] for us, so that in him we might become the righteousness of God.

6 As God's fellow workers we urge you not to receive God's grace in vain. [2]For he says,

> "In the time of my favor I heard you,
> and in the day of salvation I helped you."[b]

---

[a] 21 Or be a sin offering   [b] 2 Isaiah 49:8

THE MESSAGE

5.11-14   *That* keeps us vigilant, you can be sure. It's no light thing to know that we'll all one day stand in that place of Judgment. That's why we work urgently with everyone we meet to get them ready to face God. God alone knows how well we do this, but I hope you realize how much and deeply we care. We're not saying this to make ourselves look good to you. We just thought it would make you feel good, proud even, that we're on your side and not just nice to your face as so many people are. If I acted crazy, I did it for God; if I acted overly serious, I did it for you. Christ's love has moved me to such extremes. His love has the first and last word in everything we do.

A NEW LIFE

5.14-15   Our firm decision is to work from this focused center: One man died for everyone. That puts everyone in the same boat. He included everyone in his death so that everyone could also be included in his life, a resurrection life, a far better life than people ever lived on their own.

5.16-20   Because of this decision we don't evaluate people by what they have or how they look. We looked at the Messiah that way once and got it all wrong, as you know. We certainly don't look at him that way anymore. Now we look inside, and what we see is that anyone united with the Messiah gets a fresh start, is created new. The old life is gone; a new life burgeons! Look at it! All this comes from the God who settled the relationship between us and him, and then called us to settle our relationships with each other. God put the world square with himself through the Messiah, giving the world a fresh start by offering forgiveness of sins. God has given us the task of telling everyone what he is doing. We're Christ's representatives. God uses us to persuade men and women to drop their differences and enter into God's work of making things right between them. We're speaking for Christ himself now: Become friends with God; he's already a friend with you.

5.21   How? you say. In Christ. God put the wrong on him who never did anything wrong, so we could be put right with God.

STAYING AT OUR POST

6.1-10   **6** Companions as we are in this work with you, we beg you, please don't squander one bit of this marvelous life God has given us. God reminds us,

> I heard your call in the nick of time;
> The day you needed me, I was there to help.

NEW INTERNATIONAL VERSION

I tell you, now is the time of God's favor, now is the day of salvation.

PAUL'S HARDSHIPS

3We put no stumbling block in anyone's path, so that our ministry will not be discredited. 4Rather, as servants of God we commend ourselves in every way: in great endurance; in troubles, hardships and distresses; 5in beatings, imprisonments and riots; in hard work, sleepless nights and hunger; 6in purity, understanding, patience and kindness; in the Holy Spirit and in sincere love; 7in truthful speech and in the power of God; with weapons of righteousness in the right hand and in the left; 8through glory and dishonor, bad report and good report; genuine, yet regarded as impostors; 9known, yet regarded as unknown; dying, and yet we live on; beaten, and yet not killed; 10sorrowful, yet always rejoicing; poor, yet making many rich; having nothing, and yet possessing everything.

11We have spoken freely to you, Corinthians, and opened wide our hearts to you. 12We are not withholding our affection from you, but you are withholding yours from us. 13As a fair exchange— I speak as to my children—open wide your hearts also.

DO NOT BE YOKED WITH UNBELIEVERS

14Do not be yoked together with unbelievers. For what do righteousness and wickedness have in common? Or what fellowship can light have with darkness? 15What harmony is there between Christ and Belial*a*? What does a believer have in common with an unbeliever? 16What agreement is there between the temple of God and idols? For we are the temple of the living God. As God has said: "I will live with them and walk among them, and I will be their God, and they will be my people."*b*

17 "Therefore come out from them
　　and be separate,
　　　　　　　　　　　　says the Lord.
　　Touch no unclean thing,
　　　and I will receive you."*c*
18 "I will be a Father to you,
　　and you will be my sons and daughters,
　　　　　　　says the Lord Almighty."*d*

THE MESSAGE

Well, now is the right time to listen, the day to be helped. Don't put it off; don't frustrate God's work by showing up late, throwing a question mark over everything we're doing. Our work as God's servants gets validated—or not—in the details. People are watching us as we stay at our post, alertly, unswervingly . . . in hard times, tough times, bad times; when we're beaten up, jailed, and mobbed; working hard, working late, working without eating; with pure heart, clear head, steady hand; in gentleness, holiness, and honest love; when we're telling the truth, and when God's showing his power; when we're doing our best setting things right; when we're praised, and when we're blamed; slandered, and honored; true to our word, though distrusted; ignored by the world, but recognized by God; terrifically alive, though rumored to be dead; beaten within an inch of our lives, but refusing to die; immersed in tears, yet always filled with deep joy; living on handouts, yet enriching many; having nothing, having it all.

6.11-13　　Dear, dear Corinthians, I can't tell you how much I long for you to enter this wide-open, spacious life. We didn't fence you in. The smallness you feel comes from within you. Your lives aren't small, but you're living them in a small way. I'm speaking as plainly as I can and with great affection. Open up your lives. Live openly and expansively!

✠

6.14-18　Don't become partners with those who reject God. How can you make a partnership out of right and wrong? That's not partnership; that's war. Is light best friends with dark? Does Christ go strolling with the Devil? Do trust and mistrust hold hands? Who would think of setting up pagan idols in God's holy Temple? But that is exactly what we are, each of us a temple in whom God lives. God himself put it this way:

　　"I'll live in them, move into them;
　　　I'll be their God and they'll be my
　　　　　people.
　　So leave the corruption and compromise;
　　　leave it for good," says God.
　　"Don't link up with those who will pollute
　　　　you.
　　　I want you all for myself.
　　I'll be a Father to you;
　　　you'll be sons and daughters to me."
　　The Word of the Master, God.

---

a 15 Greek *Beliar,* a variant of *Belial*　　*b 16* Lev. 26:12;
Jer. 32:38; Ezek. 37:27　　*c 17* Isaiah 52:11; Ezek. 20:34,41
d 18 2 Samuel 7:14; 7:8

NEW INTERNATIONAL VERSION

7 Since we have these promises, dear friends, let us purify ourselves from everything that contaminates body and spirit, perfecting holiness out of reverence for God.

PAUL'S JOY

²Make room for us in your hearts. We have wronged no one, we have corrupted no one, we have exploited no one. ³I do not say this to condemn you; I have said before that you have such a place in our hearts that we would live or die with you. ⁴I have great confidence in you; I take great pride in you. I am greatly encouraged; in all our troubles my joy knows no bounds.

⁵For when we came into Macedonia, this body of ours had no rest, but we were harassed at every turn—conflicts on the outside, fears within. ⁶But God, who comforts the downcast, comforted us by the coming of Titus, ⁷and not only by his coming but also by the comfort you had given him. He told us about your longing for me, your deep sorrow, your ardent concern for me, so that my joy was greater than ever.

⁸Even if I caused you sorrow by my letter, I do not regret it. Though I did regret it—I see that my letter hurt you, but only for a little while—⁹yet now I am happy, not because you were made sorry, but because your sorrow led you to repentance. For you became sorrowful as God intended and so were not harmed in any way by us. ¹⁰Godly sorrow brings repentance that leads to salvation and leaves no regret, but worldly sorrow brings death. ¹¹See what this godly sorrow has produced in you: what earnestness, what eagerness to clear yourselves, what indignation, what alarm, what longing, what concern, what readiness to see justice done. At every point you have proved yourselves to be innocent in this matter. ¹²So even though I wrote to you, it was not on account of the one who did the wrong or of the injured party, but rather that before God you could see for yourselves how devoted to us you are. ¹³By all this we are encouraged.

THE MESSAGE

7 With promises like this to pull us on, dear friends, let's make a clean break with everything that defiles or distracts us, both within and without. Let's make our entire lives fit and holy temples for the worship of God.

MORE PASSIONATE, MORE RESPONSIBLE

7.2-4 Trust us. We've never hurt a soul, never exploited or taken advantage of anyone. Don't think I'm finding fault with you. I told you earlier that I'm with you all the way, no matter what. I have, in fact, the greatest confidence in you. If only you knew how proud I am of you! I am overwhelmed with joy despite all our troubles.

7.5-7 When we arrived in Macedonia province, we couldn't settle down. The fights in the church and the fears in our hearts kept us on pins and needles. We couldn't relax because we didn't know how it would turn out. Then the God who lifts up the downcast lifted our heads and our hearts with the arrival of Titus. We were glad just to see him, but the true reassurance came in what he told us about you: how much you cared, how much you grieved, how concerned you were for me. I went from worry to tranquility in no time!

7.8-9 I know I distressed you greatly with my letter. Although I felt awful at the time, I don't feel at all bad now that I see how it turned out. The letter upset you, but only for a while. Now I'm glad—not that you were upset, but that you were jarred into turning things around. You let the distress bring you to God, not drive you from him. The result was all gain, no loss.

7.10 Distress that drives us to God does that. It turns us around. It gets us back in the way of salvation. We never regret that kind of pain. But those who let distress drive them away from God are full of regrets, end up on a deathbed of regrets.

7.11-13 And now, isn't it wonderful all the ways in which this distress has goaded you closer to God? You're more alive, more concerned, more sensitive, more reverent, more human, more passionate, more responsible. Looked at from any angle, you've come out of this with purity of heart. And that is what I was hoping for in the first place when I wrote the letter. My primary concern was not for the one who did the wrong or even the one wronged, but for you—that you would realize and act upon the deep, deep ties between us before God. That's what happened—and we felt just great.

7.13-16 And then, when we saw how Titus felt—his exuberance over your response—our joy doubled. It was wonderful to see how revived and

NEW INTERNATIONAL VERSION

In addition to our own encouragement, we were especially delighted to see how happy Titus was, because his spirit has been refreshed by all of you. [14]I had boasted to him about you, and you have not embarrassed me. But just as everything we said to you was true, so our boasting about you to Titus has proved to be true as well. [15]And his affection for you is all the greater when he remembers that you were all obedient, receiving him with fear and trembling. [16]I am glad I can have complete confidence in you.

GENEROSITY ENCOURAGED

8 And now, brothers, we want you to know about the grace that God has given the Macedonian churches. [2]Out of the most severe trial, their overflowing joy and their extreme poverty welled up in rich generosity. [3]For I testify that they gave as much as they were able, and even beyond their ability. Entirely on their own, [4]they urgently pleaded with us for the privilege of sharing in this service to the saints. [5]And they did not do as we expected, but they gave themselves first to the Lord and then to us in keeping with God's will. [6]So we urged Titus, since he had earlier made a beginning, to bring also to completion this act of grace on your part. [7]But just as you excel in everything—in faith, in speech, in knowledge, in complete earnestness and in your love for us[a]—see that you also excel in this grace of giving.

[8]I am not commanding you, but I want to test the sincerity of your love by comparing it with the earnestness of others. [9]For you know the grace of our Lord Jesus Christ, that though he was rich, yet for your sakes he became poor, so that you through his poverty might become rich.

[10]And here is my advice about what is best for you in this matter: Last year you were the first not only to give but also to have the desire to do so. [11]Now finish the work, so that your eager willingness to do it may be matched by your completion of it, according to your means. [12]For if the willingness is there, the gift is acceptable according to what one has, not according to what he does not have.

[13]Our desire is not that others might be relieved while you are hard pressed, but that there might be equality. [14]At the present time your

THE MESSAGE

refreshed he was by everything you did. If I went out on a limb in telling Titus how great I thought you were, you didn't cut off that limb. As it turned out, I hadn't exaggerated one bit. Titus saw for himself that everything I had said about you was true. He can't quit talking about it, going over again and again the story of your prompt obedience, and the dignity and sensitivity of your hospitality. He was quite overwhelmed by it all! And I couldn't be more pleased—I'm so confident and proud of you.

THE OFFERING

8.1-4 **8** Now, friends, I want to report on the surprising and generous ways in which God is working in the churches in Macedonia province. Fierce troubles came down on the people of those churches, pushing them to the very limit. The trial exposed their true colors: They were incredibly happy, though desperately poor. The pressure triggered something totally unexpected: an outpouring of pure and generous gifts. I was there and saw it for myself. They gave offerings of whatever they could— far more than they could afford!—pleading for the privilege of helping out in the relief of poor Christians.

8.5-7 This was totally spontaneous, entirely their own idea, and caught us completely off guard. What explains it was that they had first given themselves unreservedly to God and to us. The other giving simply flowed out of the purposes of God working in their lives. That's what prompted us to ask Titus to bring the relief offering to your attention, so that what was so well begun could be finished up. You do so well in so many things—you trust God, you're articulate, you're insightful, you're passionate, you love us—now, do your best in this, too.

8.8-9 I'm not trying to order you around against your will. But by bringing in the Macedonians' enthusiasm as a stimulus to your love, I am hoping to bring the best out of you. You are familiar with the generosity of our Master, Jesus Christ. Rich as he was, he gave it all away for us—in one stroke he became poor and we became rich.

8.10-20 So here's what I think: The best thing you can do right now is to finish what you started last year and not let those good intentions grow stale. Your heart's been in the right place all along. You've got what it takes to finish it up, so go to it. Once the commitment is clear, you do what you can, not what you can't. The heart regulates the hands. This isn't so others can take it easy while you sweat it out. No, you're shoulder to shoulder with them all the way,

NEW INTERNATIONAL VERSION

plenty will supply what they need, so that in turn their plenty will supply what you need. Then there will be equality, [15]as it is written: "He who gathered much did not have too much, and he who gathered little did not have too little." [a]

TITUS SENT TO CORINTH

[16]I thank God, who put into the heart of Titus the same concern I have for you. [17]For Titus not only welcomed our appeal, but he is coming to you with much enthusiasm and on his own initiative. [18]And we are sending along with him the brother who is praised by all the churches for his service to the gospel. [19]What is more, he was chosen by the churches to accompany us as we carry the offering, which we administer in order to honor the Lord himself and to show our eagerness to help. [20]We want to avoid any criticism of the way we administer this liberal gift. [21]For we are taking pains to do what is right, not only in the eyes of the Lord but also in the eyes of men.

[22]In addition, we are sending with them our brother who has often proved to us in many ways that he is zealous, and now even more so because of his great confidence in you. [23]As for Titus, he is my partner and fellow worker among you; as for our brothers, they are representatives of the churches and an honor to Christ. [24]Therefore show these men the proof of your love and the reason for our pride in you, so that the churches can see it.

9 There is no need for me to write to you about this service to the saints. [2]For I know your eagerness to help, and I have been boasting about it to the Macedonians, telling them that since last year you in Achaia were ready to give; and your enthusiasm has stirred most of them to action. [3]But I am sending the brothers in order that our boasting about you in this matter should not prove hollow, but that you may be ready, as I said you would be. [4]For if any Macedonians come with me and find you unprepared, we—not to say anything about you—would be ashamed of having been so confident. [5]So I thought it necessary to urge the brothers to visit you in advance and finish the arrangements for

THE MESSAGE

your surplus matching their deficit, their surplus matching your deficit. In the end you come out even. As it is written,

> Nothing left over to the one with the most,
> Nothing lacking to the one with the least.

I thank God for giving Titus the same devoted concern for you that I have. He was most considerate of how we felt, but his eagerness to go to you and help out with this relief offering is his own idea. We're sending a companion along with him, someone very popular in the churches for his preaching of the Message. But there's far more to him than popularity. He's rock-solid trustworthy. The churches handpicked him to go with us as we travel about doing this work of sharing God's gifts to honor God as well as we can, taking every precaution against scandal.

8.20-22 We don't want anyone suspecting us of taking one penny of this money for ourselves. We're being as careful in our reputation with the public as in our reputation with God. That's why we're sending another trusted friend along. He's proved his dependability many times over, and carries on as energetically as the day he started. He's heard much about you, and liked what he's heard—so much so that he can't wait to get there.

8.23-24 I don't need to say anything further about Titus. We've been close associates in this work of serving you for a long time. The brothers who travel with him are delegates from churches, a real credit to Christ. Show them what you're made of, the love I've been talking up in the churches. Let them see it for themselves!

9.1-2 **9** If I wrote any more on this relief offering for the poor Christians, I'd be repeating myself. I know you're on board and ready to go. I've been bragging about you all through Macedonia province, telling them, "Achaia province has been ready to go on this since last year." Your enthusiasm by now has spread to most of them.

9.3-5 Now I'm sending the brothers to make sure you're ready, as I said you would be, so my bragging won't turn out to be just so much hot air. If some Macedonians and I happened to drop in on you and found you weren't prepared, we'd all be pretty red-faced—you and us—for acting so sure of ourselves. So to make sure there will be no slipup, I've recruited these brothers as an advance team to get you and your promised offering all ready before I get there. I want you to have all the time you need

NEW INTERNATIONAL VERSION

the generous gift you had promised. Then it will be ready as a generous gift, not as one grudgingly given.

SOWING GENEROUSLY

⁶Remember this: Whoever sows sparingly will also reap sparingly, and whoever sows generously will also reap generously. ⁷Each man should give what he has decided in his heart to give, not reluctantly or under compulsion, for God loves a cheerful giver. ⁸And God is able to make all grace abound to you, so that in all things at all times, having all that you need, you will abound in every good work. ⁹As it is written:

"He has scattered abroad his gifts to the
        poor;
    his righteousness endures forever." ᵃ

¹⁰Now he who supplies seed to the sower and bread for food will also supply and increase your store of seed and will enlarge the harvest of your righteousness. ¹¹You will be made rich in every way so that you can be generous on every occasion, and through us your generosity will result in thanksgiving to God.

¹²This service that you perform is not only supplying the needs of God's people but is also overflowing in many expressions of thanks to God. ¹³Because of the service by which you have proved yourselves, men will praise God for the obedience that accompanies your confession of the gospel of Christ, and for your generosity in sharing with them and with everyone else. ¹⁴And in their prayers for you their hearts will go out to you, because of the surpassing grace God has given you. ¹⁵Thanks be to God for his indescribable gift!

PAUL'S DEFENSE OF HIS MINISTRY

10By the meekness and gentleness of Christ, I appeal to you—I, Paul, who am "timid" when face to face with you, but "bold" when away! ²I beg you that when I come I may not have to be as bold as I expect to be toward some people who think that we live by the standards of this world. ³For though we live in the world, we do not wage war as the world does.

ᵃ 9 Psalm 112:9

THE MESSAGE

to make this offering in your own way. I don't want anything forced or hurried at the last minute.

9.6-7   Remember: A stingy planter gets a stingy crop; a lavish planter gets a lavish crop. I want each of you to take plenty of time to think it over, and make up your own mind what you will give. That will protect you against sob stories and arm-twisting. God loves it when the giver delights in the giving.

9.8-11   God can pour on the blessings in astonishing ways so that you're ready for anything and everything, more than just ready to do what needs to be done. As one psalmist puts it,

He throws caution to the winds,
    giving to the needy in reckless abandon.
His right-living, right-giving ways
    never run out, never wear out.

This most generous God who gives seed to the farmer that becomes bread for your meals is more than extravagant with you. He gives you something you can then give away, which grows into full-formed lives, robust in God, wealthy in every way, so that you can be generous in every way, producing with us great praise to God.

9.12-15   Carrying out this social relief work involves far more than helping meet the bare needs of poor Christians. It also produces abundant and bountiful thanksgivings to God. This relief offering is a prod to live at your very best, showing your gratitude to God by being openly obedient to the plain meaning of the Message of Christ. You show your gratitude through your generous offerings to your needy brothers and sisters, and really toward everyone. Meanwhile, moved by the extravagance of God in your lives, they'll respond by praying for you in passionate intercession for whatever you need. Thank God for this gift, his gift. No language can praise it enough!

TEARING DOWN BARRIERS

10.1-2   **10**And now a personal but most urgent matter; I write in the gentle but firm spirit of Christ. I hear that I'm being painted as cringing and wishy-washy when I'm with you, but harsh and demanding when at a safe distance writing letters. Please don't force me to take a hard line when I'm present with you. Don't think that I'll hesitate a single minute to stand up to those who say I'm an unprincipled opportunist. Then they'll have to eat their words.

10.3-6   The world is unprincipled. It's dog-eat-dog out there! The world doesn't fight fair. But we

NEW INTERNATIONAL VERSION

⁴The weapons we fight with are not the weapons of the world. On the contrary, they have divine power to demolish strongholds. ⁵We demolish arguments and every pretension that sets itself up against the knowledge of God, and we take captive every thought to make it obedient to Christ. ⁶And we will be ready to punish every act of disobedience, once your obedience is complete.

⁷You are looking only on the surface of things.ᵃ If anyone is confident that he belongs to Christ, he should consider again that we belong to Christ just as much as he. ⁸For even if I boast somewhat freely about the authority the Lord gave us for building you up rather than pulling you down, I will not be ashamed of it. ⁹I do not want to seem to be trying to frighten you with my letters. ¹⁰For some say, "His letters are weighty and forceful, but in person he is unimpressive and his speaking amounts to nothing." ¹¹Such people should realize that what we are in our letters when we are absent, we will be in our actions when we are present.

¹²We do not dare to classify or compare ourselves with some who commend themselves. When they measure themselves by themselves and compare themselves with themselves, they are not wise. ¹³We, however, will not boast beyond proper limits, but will confine our boasting to the field God has assigned to us, a field that reaches even to you. ¹⁴We are not going too far in our boasting, as would be the case if we had not come to you, for we did get as far as you with the gospel of Christ. ¹⁵Neither do we go beyond our limits by boasting of work done by others.ᵇ Our hope is that, as your faith continues to grow, our area of activity among you will greatly expand, ¹⁶so that we can preach the gospel in the regions beyond you. For we do not want to boast about work already done in another man's territory. ¹⁷But, "Let him who boasts boast in the Lord."ᶜ ¹⁸For it is not the one who commends himself who is approved, but the one whom the Lord commends.

ᵃ 7 Or *Look at the obvious facts*   ᵇ 13-15 Or *¹³We, however, will not boast about things that cannot be measured, but we will boast according to the standard of measurement that the God of measure has assigned us—a measurement that relates even to you. ¹⁴ . . . ¹⁵Neither do we boast about things that cannot be measured in regard to the work done by others.*
ᶜ 17 Jer. 9:24

THE MESSAGE

don't live or fight our battles that way—never have and never will. The tools of our trade aren't for marketing or manipulation, but they are for demolishing that entire massively corrupt culture. We use our powerful God-tools for smashing warped philosophies, tearing down barriers erected against the truth of God, fitting every loose thought and emotion and impulse into the structure of life shaped by Christ. Our tools are ready at hand for clearing the ground of every obstruction and building lives of obedience into maturity.

10.7-8   You stare and stare at the obvious, but you can't see the forest for the trees. If you're looking for a clear example of someone on Christ's side, why do you so quickly cut me out? Believe me, I am quite sure of my standing with Christ. You may think I overstate the authority he gave me, but I'm not backing off. Every bit of my commitment is for the purpose of building you up, after all, not tearing you down.

10.9-11   And what's this talk about me bullying you with my letters? "His letters are brawny and potent, but in person he's a weakling and mumbles when he talks." Such talk won't survive scrutiny. What we write when away, we do when present. We're the exact same people, absent or present, in letter or in person.

10.12   We're not, understand, putting ourselves in a league with those who boast that they're our superiors. We wouldn't dare do that. But in all this comparing and grading and competing, they quite miss the point.

10.13-14   We aren't making outrageous claims here. We're sticking to the limits of what God has set for us. But there can be no question that those limits reach to and include you. We're not moving into someone else's "territory." We were already there with you, weren't we? We were the first ones to get there with the Message of Christ, right? So how can there be any question of overstepping our bounds by writing or visiting you?

10.15-18   We're not barging in on the rightful work of others, interfering with their ministries, demanding a place in the sun with them. What we're hoping for is that as your lives grow in faith, you'll play a part within our expanding work. And we'll all still be within the limits God sets as we proclaim the Message in countries beyond Corinth. But we have no intention of moving in on what others have done and taking credit for it. "If you want to claim credit, claim it for God." What you say about yourself means nothing in God's work. It's what God says about you that makes the difference.

NEW INTERNATIONAL VERSION

PAUL AND THE FALSE APOSTLES

11 I hope you will put up with a little of my foolishness; but you are already doing that. ²I am jealous for you with a godly jealousy. I promised you to one husband, to Christ, so that I might present you as a pure virgin to him. ³But I am afraid that just as Eve was deceived by the serpent's cunning, your minds may somehow be led astray from your sincere and pure devotion to Christ. ⁴For if someone comes to you and preaches a Jesus other than the Jesus we preached, or if you receive a different spirit from the one you received, or a different gospel from the one you accepted, you put up with it easily enough. ⁵But I do not think I am in the least inferior to those "super-apostles." ⁶I may not be a trained speaker, but I do have knowledge. We have made this perfectly clear to you in every way.

⁷Was it a sin for me to lower myself in order to elevate you by preaching the gospel of God to you free of charge? ⁸I robbed other churches by receiving support from them so as to serve you. ⁹And when I was with you and needed something, I was not a burden to anyone, for the brothers who came from Macedonia supplied what I needed. I have kept myself from being a burden to you in any way, and will continue to do so. ¹⁰As surely as the truth of Christ is in me, nobody in the regions of Achaia will stop this boasting of mine. ¹¹Why? Because I do not love you? God knows I do! ¹²And I will keep on doing what I am doing in order to cut the ground from under those who want an opportunity to be considered equal with us in the things they boast about.

¹³For such men are false apostles, deceitful workmen, masquerading as apostles of Christ. ¹⁴And no wonder, for Satan himself masquerades as an angel of light. ¹⁵It is not surprising, then, if his servants masquerade as servants of righteousness. Their end will be what their actions deserve.

PAUL BOASTS ABOUT HIS SUFFERINGS

¹⁶I repeat: Let no one take me for a fool. But if you do, then receive me just as you would a fool,

THE MESSAGE

PSEUDO-SERVANTS OF GOD

11 ¹¹.¹⁻³ Will you put up with a little foolish aside from me? Please, just for a moment. The thing that has me so upset is that I care about you so much—this is the passion of God burning inside me! I promised your hand in marriage to Christ, presented you as a pure virgin to her husband. And now I'm afraid that exactly as the Snake seduced Eve with his smooth patter, you are being lured away from the simple purity of your love for Christ.

¹¹.⁴⁻⁶ It seems that if someone shows up preaching quite another Jesus than we preached—different spirit, different message—you put up with him quite nicely. But if you put up with these big-shot "apostles," why can't you put up with simple me? I'm as good as they are. It's true that I don't have their voice, haven't mastered that smooth eloquence that impresses you so much. But when I do open my mouth, I at least know what I'm talking about. We haven't kept anything back. We let you in on everything.

¹¹.⁷⁻¹² I wonder, did I make a bad mistake in proclaiming God's Message to you without asking for something in return, serving you free of charge so that you wouldn't be inconvenienced by me? It turns out that the other churches paid my way so that you could have a free ride. Not once during the time I lived among you did anyone have to lift a finger to help me out. My needs were always supplied by the Christians from Macedonia province. I was careful never to be a burden to you, and I never will be, you can count on it. With Christ as my witness, it's a point of honor with me, and I'm not going to keep it quiet just to protect you from what the neighbors will think. It's not that I don't love you; God knows I do. I'm just trying to keep things open and honest between us.

¹¹.¹²⁻¹⁵ And I'm not changing my position on this. I'd die before taking your money. I'm giving nobody grounds for lumping me in with those money-grubbing "preachers," vaunting themselves as something special. They're a sorry bunch—pseudo-apostles, lying preachers, crooked workers—posing as Christ's agents but sham to the core. And no wonder! Satan does it all the time, dressing up as a beautiful angel of light. So it shouldn't surprise us when his servants masquerade as servants of God. But they're not getting by with anything. They'll pay for it in the end.

MANY A LONG AND LONELY NIGHT

¹¹.¹⁶⁻²¹ Let me come back to where I started—and don't hold it against me if I continue to sound a little foolish. Or if you'd rather, just accept that

NEW INTERNATIONAL VERSION

so that I may do a little boasting. [17]In this self-confident boasting I am not talking as the Lord would, but as a fool. [18]Since many are boasting in the way the world does, I too will boast. [19]You gladly put up with fools since you are so wise! [20]In fact, you even put up with anyone who enslaves you or exploits you or takes advantage of you or pushes himself forward or slaps you in the face. [21]To my shame I admit that we were too weak for that!

What anyone else dares to boast about—I am speaking as a fool—I also dare to boast about. [22]Are they Hebrews? So am I. Are they Israelites? So am I. Are they Abraham's descendants? So am I. [23]Are they servants of Christ? (I am out of my mind to talk like this.) I am more. I have worked much harder, been in prison more frequently, been flogged more severely, and been exposed to death again and again. [24]Five times I received from the Jews the forty lashes minus one. [25]Three times I was beaten with rods, once I was stoned, three times I was shipwrecked, I spent a night and a day in the open sea, [26]I have been constantly on the move. I have been in danger from rivers, in danger from bandits, in danger from my own countrymen, in danger from Gentiles; in danger in the city, in danger in the country, in danger at sea; and in danger from false brothers. [27]I have labored and toiled and have often gone without sleep; I have known hunger and thirst and have often gone without food; I have been cold and naked. [28]Besides everything else, I face daily the pressure of my concern for all the churches. [29]Who is weak, and I do not feel weak? Who is led into sin, and I do not inwardly burn?

[30]If I must boast, I will boast of the things that show my weakness. [31]The God and Father of the Lord Jesus, who is to be praised forever, knows that I am not lying. [32]In Damascus the governor under King Aretas had the city of the Damascenes guarded in order to arrest me. [33]But I was lowered in a basket from a window in the wall and slipped through his hands.

THE MESSAGE

I am a fool and let me rant on a little. I didn't learn this kind of talk from Christ. Oh, no, it's a bad habit I picked up from the three-ring preachers that are so popular these days. Since you sit there in the judgment seat observing all these shenanigans, you can afford to humor an occasional fool who happens along. You have such admirable tolerance for impostors who rob your freedom, rip you off, steal you blind, put you down—even slap your face! I shouldn't admit it to you, but our stomachs aren't strong enough to tolerate that kind of stuff.

11.21-23   Since you admire the egomaniacs of the pulpit so much (remember, this is your old friend, the fool, talking), let me try my hand at it. Do they brag of being Hebrews, Israelites, the pure race of Abraham? I'm their match. Are they servants of Christ? I can go them one better. (I can't believe I'm saying these things. It's crazy to talk this way! But I started, and I'm going to finish.)

11.23-27   I've worked much harder, been jailed more often, beaten up more times than I can count, and at death's door time after time. I've been flogged five times with the Jews' thirty-nine lashes, beaten by Roman rods three times, pummeled with rocks once. I've been shipwrecked three times, and immersed in the open sea for a night and a day. In hard traveling year in and year out, I've had to ford rivers, fend off robbers, struggle with friends, struggle with foes. I've been at risk in the city, at risk in the country, endangered by desert sun and sea storm, and betrayed by those I thought were my brothers. I've known drudgery and hard labor, many a long and lonely night without sleep, many a missed meal, blasted by the cold, naked to the weather.

11.28-29   And that's not the half of it, when you throw in the daily pressures and anxieties of all the churches. When someone gets to the end of his rope, I feel the desperation in my bones. When someone is duped into sin, an angry fire burns in my gut.

11.30-33   If I have to "brag" about myself, I'll brag about the humiliations that make me like Jesus. The eternal and blessed God and Father of our Master Jesus knows I'm not lying. Remember the time I was in Damascus and the governor of King Aretas posted guards at the city gates to arrest me? I crawled through a window in the wall, was let down in a basket, and had to run for my life.

NEW INTERNATIONAL VERSION

PAUL'S VISION AND HIS THORN

12 I must go on boasting. Although there is nothing to be gained, I will go on to visions and revelations from the Lord. ²I know a man in Christ who fourteen years ago was caught up to the third heaven. Whether it was in the body or out of the body I do not know—God knows. ³And I know that this man—whether in the body or apart from the body I do not know, but God knows— ⁴was caught up to paradise. He heard inexpressible things, things that man is not permitted to tell. ⁵I will boast about a man like that, but I will not boast about myself, except about my weaknesses. ⁶Even if I should choose to boast, I would not be a fool, because I would be speaking the truth. But I refrain, so no one will think more of me than is warranted by what I do or say.

⁷To keep me from becoming conceited because of these surpassingly great revelations, there was given me a thorn in my flesh, a messenger of Satan, to torment me. ⁸Three times I pleaded with the Lord to take it away from me. ⁹But he said to me, "My grace is sufficient for you, for my power is made perfect in weakness." Therefore I will boast all the more gladly about my weaknesses, so that Christ's power may rest on me. ¹⁰That is why, for Christ's sake, I delight in weaknesses, in insults, in hardships, in persecutions, in difficulties. For when I am weak, then I am strong.

PAUL'S CONCERN FOR THE CORINTHIANS

¹¹I have made a fool of myself, but you drove me to it. I ought to have been commended by you, for I am not in the least inferior to the "super-apostles," even though I am nothing. ¹²The things that mark an apostle—signs, wonders and

THE MESSAGE

STRENGTH FROM WEAKNESS

12.1-5 **12** You've forced me to talk this way, and I do it against my better judgment. But now that we're at it, I may as well bring up the matter of visions and revelations that God gave me. For instance, I know a man who, fourteen years ago, was seized by Christ and swept in ecstasy to the heights of heaven. I really don't know if this took place in the body or out of it; only God knows. I also know that this man was hijacked into paradise—again, whether in or out of the body, I don't know; God knows. There he heard the unspeakable spoken, but was forbidden to tell what he heard. This is the man I want to talk about. But about myself, I'm not saying another word apart from the humiliations.

12.6 If I had a mind to brag a little, I could probably do it without looking ridiculous, and I'd still be speaking plain truth all the way. But I'll spare you. I don't want anyone imagining me as anything other than the fool you'd encounter if you saw me on the street or heard me talk.

12.7-10 Because of the extravagance of those revelations, and so I wouldn't get a big head, I was given the gift of a handicap to keep me in constant touch with my limitations. Satan's angel did his best to get me down; what he in fact did was push me to my knees. No danger then of walking around high and mighty! At first I didn't think of it as a gift, and begged God to remove it. Three times I did that, and then he told me,

My grace is enough; it's all you need.
My strength comes into its own in your
weakness.

Once I heard that, I was glad to let it happen. I quit focusing on the handicap and began appreciating the gift. It was a case of Christ's strength moving in on my weakness. Now I take limitations in stride, and with good cheer, these limitations that cut me down to size—abuse, accidents, opposition, bad breaks. I just let Christ take over! And so the weaker I get, the stronger I become.

✠

12.11-13 Well, now I've done it! I've made a complete fool of myself by going on like this. But it's not all my fault; you put me up to it. You should have been doing this for me, sticking up for me and commending me instead of making me do it for myself. You know from personal experience that even if I'm a nobody, a nothing, I wasn't second-rate compared to those big-shot apostles you're so taken with. All the signs that

NEW INTERNATIONAL VERSION

miracles—were done among you with great perseverance. [13]How were you inferior to the other churches, except that I was never a burden to you? Forgive me this wrong!

[14]Now I am ready to visit you for the third time, and I will not be a burden to you, because what I want is not your possessions but you. After all, children should not have to save up for their parents, but parents for their children. [15]So I will very gladly spend for you everything I have and expend myself as well. If I love you more, will you love me less? [16]Be that as it may, I have not been a burden to you. Yet, crafty fellow that I am, I caught you by trickery! [17]Did I exploit you through any of the men I sent you? [18]I urged Titus to go to you and I sent our brother with him. Titus did not exploit you, did he? Did we not act in the same spirit and follow the same course?

[19]Have you been thinking all along that we have been defending ourselves to you? We have been speaking in the sight of God as those in Christ; and everything we do, dear friends, is for your strengthening. [20]For I am afraid that when I come I may not find you as I want you to be, and you may not find me as you want me to be. I fear that there may be quarreling, jealousy, outbursts of anger, factions, slander, gossip, arrogance and disorder. [21]I am afraid that when I come again my God will humble me before you, and I will be grieved over many who have sinned earlier and have not repented of the impurity, sexual sin and debauchery in which they have indulged.

FINAL WARNINGS

13 This will be my third visit to you. "Every matter must be established by the testimony of two or three witnesses."[a] [2]I already gave you a warning when I was with you the second time. I now repeat it while absent: On my return

[a] 1 Deut. 19:15

THE MESSAGE

mark a true apostle were in evidence while I was with you through both good times and bad: signs of portent, signs of wonder, signs of power. Did you get less of me or of God than any of the other churches? The only thing you got less of was less responsibility for my upkeep. Well, I'm sorry. Forgive me for depriving you.

12.14-15 Everything is in readiness now for this, my third visit to you. But don't worry about it; you won't have to put yourselves out. I'll be no more of a bother to you this time than on the other visits. I have no interest in what you have—only in you. Children shouldn't have to look out for their parents; parents look out for the children. I'd be most happy to empty my pockets, even mortgage my life, for your good. So how does it happen that the more I love you, the less I'm loved?

12.16-18 And why is it that I keep coming across these whiffs of gossip about how my self-support was a front behind which I worked an elaborate scam? Where's the evidence? Did I cheat or trick you through anyone I sent? I asked Titus to visit, and sent some brothers along. Did they swindle you out of anything? And haven't we always been just as aboveboard, just as honest?

12.19 I hope you don't think that all along we've been making our defense before you, the jury. You're not the jury; God is the jury—God revealed in Christ—and we make our case before him. And we've gone to all the trouble of supporting ourselves so that we won't be in the way or get in the way of your growing up.

12.20-21 I do admit that I have fears that when I come you'll disappoint me and I'll disappoint you, and in frustration with each other everything will fall to pieces—quarrels, jealousy, flaring tempers, taking sides, angry words, vicious rumors, swelled heads, and general bedlam. I don't look forward to a second humiliation by God among you, compounded by hot tears over that crowd that keeps sinning over and over in the same old ways, who refuse to turn away from the pigsty of evil, sexual disorder, and indecency in which they wallow.

HE'S ALIVE NOW!

13.1-4 **13** Well, this is my third visit coming up. Remember the Scripture that says, "A matter becomes clear after two or three witnesses give evidence"? On my second visit I warned that bunch that keeps sinning over and over in the same old ways that when I came back I wouldn't go easy on them. Now, preparing for the third, I'm saying it again from a dis-

NEW INTERNATIONAL VERSION

I will not spare those who sinned earlier or any of the others, ³since you are demanding proof that Christ is speaking through me. He is not weak in dealing with you, but is powerful among you. ⁴For to be sure, he was crucified in weakness, yet he lives by God's power. Likewise, we are weak in him, yet by God's power we will live with him to serve you.

⁵Examine yourselves to see whether you are in the faith; test yourselves. Do you not realize that Christ Jesus is in you—unless, of course, you fail the test? ⁶And I trust that you will discover that we have not failed the test. ⁷Now we pray to God that you will not do anything wrong. Not that people will see that we have stood the test but that you will do what is right even though we may seem to have failed. ⁸For we cannot do anything against the truth, but only for the truth. ⁹We are glad whenever we are weak but you are strong; and our prayer is for your perfection. ¹⁰This is why I write these things when I am absent, that when I come I may not have to be harsh in my use of authority—the authority the Lord gave me for building you up, not for tearing you down.

FINAL GREETINGS

¹¹Finally, brothers, good-by. Aim for perfection, listen to my appeal, be of one mind, live in peace. And the God of love and peace will be with you.

¹²Greet one another with a holy kiss. ¹³All the saints send their greetings.

¹⁴May the grace of the Lord Jesus Christ, and the love of God, and the fellowship of the Holy Spirit be with you all.

THE MESSAGE

tance. If you haven't changed your ways by the time I get there, look out. You who have been demanding proof that Christ speaks through me will get more than you bargained for. You'll get the full force of Christ, don't think you won't. He was sheer weakness and humiliation when he was killed on the Cross, but oh, he's alive now—in the mighty power of God! We weren't much to look at, either, when we were humiliated among you, but when we deal with you this next time, we'll be alive in Christ, strengthened by God.

13.5-9 Test yourselves to make sure you are solid in the faith. Don't drift along taking everything for granted. Give yourselves regular checkups. You need firsthand evidence, not mere hearsay, that Jesus Christ is in you. Test it out. If you fail the test, do something about it. I hope the test won't show that we have failed. But if it comes to that, we'd rather the test showed our failure than yours. We're rooting for the truth to win out in you. We couldn't possibly do otherwise.

We don't just put up with our limitations; we celebrate them, and then go on to celebrate every strength, every triumph of the truth in you. We pray hard that it will all come together in your lives.

13.10 I'm writing this to you now so that when I come I won't have to say another word on the subject. The authority the Master gave me is for putting people together, not taking them apart. I want to get on with it, and not have to spend time on reprimands.

✝

13.11-13 And that's about it, friends. Be cheerful. Keep things in good repair. Keep your spirits up. Think in harmony. Be agreeable. Do all that, and the God of love and peace will be with you for sure. Greet one another with a holy embrace. All the brothers and sisters here say hello.

13.14 The amazing grace of the Master, Jesus Christ, the extravagant love of God, the intimate friendship of the Holy Spirit, be with all of you.

GALATIANS

GALATIANS

1 Paul, an apostle—sent not from men nor by man, but by Jesus Christ and God the Father, who raised him from the dead— ²and all the brothers with me,

To the churches in Galatia:

³Grace and peace to you from God our Father and the Lord Jesus Christ, ⁴who gave himself for our sins to rescue us from the present evil age, according to the will of our God and Father, ⁵to whom be glory for ever and ever. Amen.

No Other Gospel

⁶I am astonished that you are so quickly deserting the one who called you by the grace of Christ and are turning to a different gospel— ⁷which is really no gospel at all. Evidently some people are throwing you into confusion and are trying to pervert the gospel of Christ. ⁸But even if we or an angel from heaven should preach a gospel other than the one we preached to you, let him be eternally condemned! ⁹As we have already said, so now I say again: If anybody is preaching to you a gospel other than what you accepted, let him be eternally condemned!

¹⁰Am I now trying to win the approval of men, or of God? Or am I trying to please men? If I were still trying to please men, I would not be a servant of Christ.

Paul Called by God

¹¹I want you to know, brothers, that the gospel I preached is not something that man made up. ¹²I did not receive it from any man, nor was I taught it; rather, I received it by revelation from Jesus Christ.

¹³For you have heard of my previous way of life in Judaism, how intensely I persecuted the church of God and tried to destroy it. ¹⁴I was advancing in Judaism beyond many Jews of my

1.1-5 **1** I, Paul, and my companions in faith here, send greetings to the Galatian churches. My authority for writing to you does not come from any popular vote of the people, nor does it come through the appointment of some human higher-up. It comes directly from Jesus the Messiah and God the Father, who raised him from the dead. I'm God-commissioned. So I greet you with the great words, grace and peace! We know the meaning of those words because Jesus Christ rescued us from this evil world we're in by offering himself as a sacrifice for our sins. God's plan is that we all experience that rescue. Glory to God forever! Oh, yes!

The Message

1.6-9 I can't believe your fickleness—how easily you have turned traitor to him who called you by the grace of Christ by embracing a variant message! It is not a minor variation, you know; it is completely other, an alien message, a no-message, a lie about God. Those who are provoking this agitation among you are turning the Message of Christ on its head. Let me be blunt: If one of us—even if an angel from heaven!— were to preach something other than what we preached originally, let him be cursed. I said it once; I'll say it again: If anyone, regardless of reputation or credentials, preaches something other than what you received originally, let him be cursed.

1.10-12 Do you think I speak this strongly in order to manipulate crowds? Or curry favor with God? Or get popular applause? If my goal was popularity, I wouldn't bother being Christ's slave. Know this—I am most emphatic here, friends—this great Message I delivered to you is not mere human optimism. I didn't receive it through the traditions, and I wasn't taught it in some school. I got it straight from God, received the Message directly from Jesus Christ.

1.13-16 I'm sure that you've heard the story of my earlier life when I lived in the Jewish way. In those days I went all out in persecuting God's church. I was systematically destroying it. I was so enthusiastic about the traditions of my an-

NEW INTERNATIONAL VERSION

own age and was extremely zealous for the traditions of my fathers. [15]But when God, who set me apart from birth[a] and called me by his grace, was pleased [16]to reveal his Son in me so that I might preach him among the Gentiles, I did not consult any man, [17]nor did I go up to Jerusalem to see those who were apostles before I was, but I went immediately into Arabia and later returned to Damascus.

[18]Then after three years, I went up to Jerusalem to get acquainted with Peter[b] and stayed with him fifteen days. [19]I saw none of the other apostles—only James, the Lord's brother. [20]I assure you before God that what I am writing you is no lie. [21]Later I went to Syria and Cilicia. [22]I was personally unknown to the churches of Judea that are in Christ. [23]They only heard the report: "The man who formerly persecuted us is now preaching the faith he once tried to destroy." [24]And they praised God because of me.

PAUL ACCEPTED BY THE APOSTLES

2 Fourteen years later I went up again to Jerusalem, this time with Barnabas. I took Titus along also. [2]I went in response to a revelation and set before them the gospel that I preach among the Gentiles. But I did this privately to those who seemed to be leaders, for fear that I was running or had run my race in vain. [3]Yet not even Titus, who was with me, was compelled to be circumcised, even though he was a Greek. [4]This matter arose because some false brothers had infiltrated our ranks to spy on the freedom we have in Christ Jesus and to make us slaves. [5]We did not give in to them for a moment, so that the truth of the gospel might remain with you.

[6]As for those who seemed to be important— whatever they were makes no difference to me; God does not judge by external appearance— those men added nothing to my message. [7]On the contrary, they saw that I had been entrusted with the task of preaching the gospel to the Gentiles,[c] just as Peter had been to the Jews.[d] [8]For God, who was at work in the ministry of Peter as an apostle to the Jews, was also at work in my ministry as an apostle to the Gentiles. [9]James, Peter[e] and John, those reputed to be pillars, gave

a 15 Or from my mother's womb   b 18 Greek Cephas
c 7 Greek uncircumcised   d 7 Greek circumcised; also in verses 8 and 9   e 9 Greek Cephas; also in verses 11 and 14

THE MESSAGE

cestors that I advanced head and shoulders above my peers in my career. Even then God had designs on me. Why, when I was still in my mother's womb he chose and called me out of sheer generosity! Now he has intervened and revealed his Son to me so that I might joyfully tell non-Jews about him.

1.16-20   Immediately after my calling—without consulting anyone around me and without going up to Jerusalem to confer with those who were apostles long before I was—I got away to Arabia. Later I returned to Damascus, but it was three years before I went up to Jerusalem to compare stories with Peter. I was there only fifteen days—but what days they were! Except for our Master's brother James, I saw no other apostles. (I'm telling you the absolute truth in this.)

1.21-24   Then I began my ministry in the regions of Syria and Cilicia. After all that time and activity I was still unknown by face among the Christian churches in Judea. There was only this report: "That man who once persecuted us is now preaching the very message he used to try to destroy." Their response was to recognize and worship God because of me!

WHAT IS CENTRAL?

2.1-5   2 Fourteen years after that first visit, Barnabas and I went up to Jerusalem and took Titus with us. I went to clarify with them what had been revealed to me. At that time I placed before them exactly what I was preaching to the non-Jews. I did this in private with the leaders, those held in esteem by the church, so that our concern would not become a controversial public issue, marred by ethnic tensions, exposing my years of work to denigration and endangering my present ministry. Significantly, Titus, non-Jewish though he was, was not required to be circumcised. While we were in conference we were infiltrated by spies pretending to be Christians, who slipped in to find out just how free true Christians are. Their ulterior motive was to reduce us to their brand of servitude. We didn't give them the time of day. We were determined to preserve the truth of the Message for you.

2.6-10   As for those who were considered important in the church, their reputation doesn't concern me. God isn't impressed with mere appearances, and neither am I. And of course these leaders were able to add nothing to the message I had been preaching. It was soon evident that God had entrusted me with the same message to the non-Jews as Peter had been preaching to the Jews. Recognizing that my calling had been given by God, James, Peter, and John—the pillars of the church—shook hands with me and

NEW INTERNATIONAL VERSION

me and Barnabas the right hand of fellowship when they recognized the grace given to me. They agreed that we should go to the Gentiles, and they to the Jews. ¹⁰All they asked was that we should continue to remember the poor, the very thing I was eager to do.

PAUL OPPOSES PETER

¹¹When Peter came to Antioch, I opposed him to his face, because he was clearly in the wrong. ¹²Before certain men came from James, he used to eat with the Gentiles. But when they arrived, he began to draw back and separate himself from the Gentiles because he was afraid of those who belonged to the circumcision group. ¹³The other Jews joined him in his hypocrisy, so that by their hypocrisy even Barnabas was led astray.

¹⁴When I saw that they were not acting in line with the truth of the gospel, I said to Peter in front of them all, "You are a Jew, yet you live like a Gentile and not like a Jew. How is it, then, that you force Gentiles to follow Jewish customs?

¹⁵"We who are Jews by birth and not 'Gentile sinners' ¹⁶know that a man is not justified by observing the law, but by faith in Jesus Christ. So we, too, have put our faith in Christ Jesus that we may be justified by faith in Christ and not by observing the law, because by observing the law no one will be justified.

¹⁷"If, while we seek to be justified in Christ, it becomes evident that we ourselves are sinners, does that mean that Christ promotes sin? Absolutely not! ¹⁸If I rebuild what I destroyed, I prove that I am a lawbreaker. ¹⁹For through the law I died to the law so that I might live for God. ²⁰I

THE MESSAGE

Barnabas, assigning us to a ministry to the non-Jews, while they continued to be responsible for reaching out to the Jews. The only additional thing they asked was that we remember the poor, and I was already eager to do that.

2.11-13   Later, when Peter came to Antioch, I had a face-to-face confrontation with him because he was clearly out of line. Here's the situation. Earlier, before certain persons had come from James, Peter regularly ate with the non-Jews. But when that conservative group came from Jerusalem, he cautiously pulled back and put as much distance as he could manage between himself and his non-Jewish friends. That's how fearful he was of the conservative Jewish clique that's been pushing the old system of circumcision. Unfortunately, the rest of the Jews in the Antioch church joined in that hypocrisy so that even Barnabas was swept along in the charade.

2.14   But when I saw that they were not maintaining a steady, straight course according to the Message, I spoke up to Peter in front of them all: "If you, a Jew, live like a non-Jew when you're not being observed by the watchdogs from Jerusalem, what right do you have to require non-Jews to conform to Jewish customs just to make a favorable impression on your old Jerusalem cronies?"

2.15-16   We Jews know that we have no advantage of birth over "non-Jewish sinners." We know very well that we are not set right with God by rule-keeping but only through personal faith in Jesus Christ. How do we know? We tried it— and we had the best system of rules the world has ever seen! Convinced that no human being can please God by self-improvement, we believed in Jesus as the Messiah so that we might be set right before God by trusting in the Messiah, not by trying to be good.

2.17-18   Have some of you noticed that we are not yet perfect? (No great surprise, right?) And are you ready to make the accusation that since people like me, who go through Christ in order to get things right with God, aren't perfectly virtuous, Christ must therefore be an accessory to sin? The accusation is frivolous. If I was "trying to be good," I would be rebuilding the same old barn that I tore down. I would be acting as a charlatan.

2.19-21   What actually took place is this: I tried keeping rules and working my head off to please God, and it didn't work. So I quit being a "law man" so that I could be *God's* man. Christ's life showed me how, and enabled me to do it. I identified myself completely with him. Indeed, I have been crucified with Christ. My ego is no longer central. It is no longer important that I appear righteous before you or have your good

NEW INTERNATIONAL VERSION

have been crucified with Christ and I no longer live, but Christ lives in me. The life I live in the body, I live by faith in the Son of God, who loved me and gave himself for me. ²¹I do not set aside the grace of God, for if righteousness could be gained through the law, Christ died for nothing!" ᵃ

FAITH OR OBSERVANCE OF THE LAW

3 You foolish Galatians! Who has bewitched you? Before your very eyes Jesus Christ was clearly portrayed as crucified. ²I would like to learn just one thing from you: Did you receive the Spirit by observing the law, or by believing what you heard? ³Are you so foolish? After beginning with the Spirit, are you now trying to attain your goal by human effort? ⁴Have you suffered so much for nothing—if it really was for nothing? ⁵Does God give you his Spirit and work miracles among you because you observe the law, or because you believe what you heard?

⁶Consider Abraham: "He believed God, and it was credited to him as righteousness." ᵇ ⁷Understand, then, that those who believe are children of Abraham. ⁸The Scripture foresaw that God would justify the Gentiles by faith, and announced the gospel in advance to Abraham: "All nations will be blessed through you." ᶜ ⁹So those who have faith are blessed along with Abraham, the man of faith.

¹⁰All who rely on observing the law are under a curse, for it is written: "Cursed is everyone

ᵃ 21 Some interpreters end the quotation after verse 14.
ᵇ 6 Gen. 15:6   ᶜ 8 Gen. 12:3; 18:18; 22:18

THE MESSAGE

opinion, and I am no longer driven to impress God. Christ lives in me. The life you see me living is not "mine," but it is lived by faith in the Son of God, who loved me and gave himself for me. I am not going to go back on that.

Is it not clear to you that to go back to that old rule-keeping, peer-pleasing religion would be an abandonment of everything personal and free in my relationship with God? I refuse to do that, to repudiate God's grace. If a living relationship with God could come by rule-keeping, then Christ died unnecessarily.

TRUST IN CHRIST, NOT THE LAW

3.1 **3** You crazy Galatians! Did someone put a hex on you? Have you taken leave of your senses? Something crazy has happened, for it's obvious that you no longer have the crucified Jesus in clear focus in your lives. His sacrifice on the Cross was certainly set before you clearly enough.

3.2-4   Let me put this question to you: How did your new life begin? Was it by working your heads off to please God? Or was it by responding to God's Message to you? Are you going to continue this craziness? For only crazy people would think they could complete by their own efforts what was begun by God. If you weren't smart enough or strong enough to begin it, how do you suppose you could perfect it? Did you go through this whole painful learning process for nothing? It is not yet a total loss, but it certainly will be if you keep this up!

3.5-6   Answer this question: Does the God who lavishly provides you with his own presence, his Holy Spirit, working things in your lives you could never do for yourselves, does he do these things because of your strenuous moral striving *or* because you trust him to do them in you? Don't these things happen among you just as they happened with Abraham? He believed God, and that act of belief was turned into a life that was right with God.

3.7-8   Is it not obvious to you that persons who put their trust in Christ (not persons who put their trust in the law!) are like Abraham: children of faith? It was all laid out beforehand in Scripture that God would set things right with non-Jews by *faith*. Scripture anticipated this in the promise to Abraham: "All nations will be blessed in you."

3.9-10   So those now who live by faith are blessed along with Abraham, who lived by faith—this is no new doctrine! And that means that anyone who tries to live by his own effort, independent of God, is doomed to failure. Scripture backs this up: "Utterly cursed is every

NEW INTERNATIONAL VERSION

who does not continue to do everything written in the Book of the Law." [d] [11] Clearly no one is justified before God by the law, because, "The righteous will live by faith." [b] [12] The law is not based on faith; on the contrary, "The man who does these things will live by them." [c] [13] Christ redeemed us from the curse of the law by becoming a curse for us, for it is written: "Cursed is everyone who is hung on a tree." [d] [14] He redeemed us in order that the blessing given to Abraham might come to the Gentiles through Christ Jesus, so that by faith we might receive the promise of the Spirit.

THE LAW AND THE PROMISE

[15] Brothers, let me take an example from everyday life. Just as no one can set aside or add to a human covenant that has been duly established, so it is in this case. [16] The promises were spoken to Abraham and to his seed. The Scripture does not say "and to seeds," meaning many people, but "and to your seed," [e] meaning one person, who is Christ. [17] What I mean is this: The law, introduced 430 years later, does not set aside the covenant previously established by God and thus do away with the promise. [18] For if the inheritance depends on the law, then it no longer depends on a promise; but God in his grace gave it to Abraham through a promise.

[19] What, then, was the purpose of the law? It was added because of transgressions until the Seed to whom the promise referred had come. The law was put into effect through angels by a

THE MESSAGE

person who fails to carry out every detail written in the Book of the law."

3.11-12 The obvious impossibility of carrying out such a moral program should make it plain that no one can sustain a relationship with God that way. The person who lives in right relationship with God does it by embracing what God arranges for him. Doing things for God is the opposite of entering into what God does for you. Habakkuk had it right: "The person who believes God, is set right by God—and that's the real life." Rule-keeping does not naturally evolve into living by faith, but only perpetuates itself in more and more rule-keeping, a fact observed in Scripture: "The one who does these things [rule-keeping] continues to live by them."

3.13-14 Christ redeemed us from that self-defeating, cursed life by absorbing it completely into himself. Do you remember the Scripture that says, "Cursed is everyone who hangs on a tree"? That is what happened when Jesus was nailed to the Cross: He became a curse, and at the same time dissolved the curse. And now, because of that, the air is cleared and we can see that Abraham's blessing is present and available for non-Jews, too. We are *all* able to receive God's life, his Spirit, in and with us by believing—just the way Abraham received it.

✝

3.15-18 Friends, let me give you an example from everyday affairs of the free life I am talking about. Once a person's will has been ratified, no one else can annul it or add to it. Now, the promises were made to Abraham and to his descendant. You will observe that Scripture, in the careful language of a legal document, does not say "to descendants," referring to everybody in general, but "to your descendant" (the noun, note, is singular), referring to Christ. This is the way I interpret this: A will, earlier ratified by God, is not annulled by an addendum attached 430 years later, thereby negating the promise of the will. No, this addendum, with its instructions and regulations, has nothing to do with the promised inheritance in the will.

3.18-20 What is the point, then, of the law, the attached addendum? It was a thoughtful addition to the original covenant promises made to Abraham. The purpose of the law was to keep a sinful people in the way of salvation until Christ (the descendant) came, inheriting the promises and distributing them to us. Obviously this law was not a firsthand encounter with God. It was arranged by angelic messengers through a middleman, Moses. But if there is a middleman as there was at Sinai, then the

---

[a] *10* Deut. 27:26   [b] *11* Hab. 2:4   [c] *12* Lev. 18:5
[d] *13* Deut. 21:23   [e] *16* Gen. 12:7; 13:15; 24:7

NEW INTERNATIONAL VERSION

mediator. ²⁰A mediator, however, does not represent just one party; but God is one.

²¹Is the law, therefore, opposed to the promises of God? Absolutely not! For if a law had been given that could impart life, then righteousness would certainly have come by the law. ²²But the Scripture declares that the whole world is a prisoner of sin, so that what was promised, being given through faith in Jesus Christ, might be given to those who believe.

²³Before this faith came, we were held prisoners by the law, locked up until faith should be revealed. ²⁴So the law was put in charge to lead us to Christ*ᵃ* that we might be justified by faith. ²⁵Now that faith has come, we are no longer under the supervision of the law.

SONS OF GOD

²⁶You are all sons of God through faith in Christ Jesus, ²⁷for all of you who were baptized into Christ have clothed yourselves with Christ. ²⁸There is neither Jew nor Greek, slave nor free, male nor female, for you are all one in Christ Jesus. ²⁹If you belong to Christ, then you are Abraham's seed, and heirs according to the promise.

4 What I am saying is that as long as the heir is a child, he is no different from a slave, although he owns the whole estate. ²He is subject to guardians and trustees until the time set by his father. ³So also, when we were children, we were in slavery under the basic principles of the world. ⁴But when the time had fully come, God sent his Son, born of a woman, born under law, ⁵to redeem those under law, that we might re-

THE MESSAGE

people are not dealing directly with God, are they? But the original promise is the *direct* blessing of God, received by faith.

3.21-22   If such is the case, is the law, then, an anti-promise, a negation of God's will for us? Not at all. Its purpose was to make obvious to everyone that we are, in ourselves, out of right relationship with God, and therefore to show us the futility of devising some religious system for getting by our own efforts what we can only get by waiting in faith for God to complete his promise. For if any kind of rule-keeping had power to create life in us, we would certainly have gotten it by this time.

3.23-24   Until the time when we were mature enough to respond freely in faith to the living God, we were carefully surrounded and protected by the Mosaic law. The law was like those Greek tutors, with which you are familiar, who escort children to school and protect them from danger or distraction, making sure the children will really get to the place they set out for.

3.25-27   But now you have arrived at your destination: By faith in Christ you are in direct relationship with God. Your baptism in Christ was not just washing you up for a fresh start. It also involved dressing you in an adult faith wardrobe—Christ's life, the fulfillment of God's original promise.

IN CHRIST'S FAMILY

3.28-29   In Christ's family there can be no division into Jew and non-Jew, slave and free, male and female. Among us you are all equal. That is, we are all in a common relationship with Jesus Christ. Also, since you are Christ's family, then you are Abraham's famous "descendant," heirs according to the covenant promises.

4.1-3   **4** Let me show you the implications of this. As long as the heir is a minor, he has no advantage over the slave. Though legally he owns the entire inheritance, he is subject to tutors and administrators until whatever date the father has set for emancipation. That is the way it is with us: When we were minors, we were just like slaves ordered around by simple instructions (the tutors and administrators of this world), with no say in the conduct of our own lives.

4.4-7   But when the time arrived that was set by God the Father, God sent his Son, born among us of a woman, born under the conditions of the law so that he might redeem those of us who have been kidnapped by the law. Thus we have been set free to experience our rightful

NEW INTERNATIONAL VERSION

ceive the full rights of sons. [6]Because you are sons, God sent the Spirit of his Son into our hearts, the Spirit who calls out, "*Abba,[a] Father.*" [7]So you are no longer a slave, but a son; and since you are a son, God has made you also an heir.

PAUL'S CONCERN FOR THE GALATIANS

[8]Formerly, when you did not know God, you were slaves to those who by nature are not gods. [9]But now that you know God—or rather are known by God—how is it that you are turning back to those weak and miserable principles? Do you wish to be enslaved by them all over again? [10]You are observing special days and months and seasons and years! [11]I fear for you, that somehow I have wasted my efforts on you.

[12]I plead with you, brothers, become like me, for I became like you. You have done me no wrong. [13]As you know, it was because of an illness that I first preached the gospel to you. [14]Even though my illness was a trial to you, you did not treat me with contempt or scorn. Instead, you welcomed me as if I were an angel of God, as if I were Christ Jesus himself. [15]What has happened to all your joy? I can testify that, if you could have done so, you would have torn out your eyes and given them to me. [16]Have I now become your enemy by telling you the truth?

[17]Those people are zealous to win you over, but for no good. What they want is to alienate you ˌfrom usˌ, so that you may be zealous for them. [18]It is fine to be zealous, provided the purpose is good, and to be so always and not just when I am with you. [19]My dear children, for whom I am again in the pains of childbirth until Christ is formed in you, [20]how I wish I could be

THE MESSAGE

heritage. You can tell for sure that you are now fully adopted as his own children because God sent the Spirit of his Son into our lives crying out, "Papa! Father!" Doesn't that privilege of intimate conversation with God make it plain that you are not a slave, but a child? And if you are a child, you're also an heir, with complete access to the inheritance.

4.8-11   Earlier, before you knew God personally, you were enslaved to so-called gods that had nothing of the divine about them. But now that you know the real God—or rather since God knows you—how can you possibly subject yourselves again to those paper tigers? For that is exactly what you do when you are intimidated into scrupulously observing all the traditions, taboos, and superstitions associated with special days and seasons and years. I am afraid that all my hard work among you has gone up in a puff of smoke!

4.12-13   My dear friends, what I would really like you to do is try to put yourselves in my shoes to the same extent that I, when I was with you, put myself in yours. You were very sensitive and kind then. You did not come down on me personally. You were well aware that the reason I ended up preaching to you was that I was physically broken, and so, prevented from continuing my journey, I was forced to stop with you. That is how I came to preach to you.

4.14-16   And don't you remember that even though taking in a sick guest was most troublesome for you, you chose to treat me as well as you would have treated an angel of God—as well as you would have treated Jesus himself if he had visited you? What has happened to the satisfaction you felt at that time? There were some of you then who, if possible, would have given your very eyes to me—that is how deeply you cared! And now have I suddenly become your enemy simply by telling you the truth? I can't believe it.

4.17   Those heretical teachers go to great lengths to flatter you, but their motives are rotten. They want to shut you out of the free world of God's grace so that you will always depend on them for approval and direction, making them feel important.

✝

4.18-20 It is a good thing to be ardent in doing good, but not just when I am in your presence. Can't you continue the same concern for both my person and my message when I am away from you that you had when I was with you? Do you know how I feel right now, and will feel until Christ's life becomes visible in your lives? Like

NEW INTERNATIONAL VERSION

with you now and change my tone, because I am perplexed about you!

HAGAR AND SARAH

21Tell me, you who want to be under the law, are you not aware of what the law says? 22For it is written that Abraham had two sons, one by the slave woman and the other by the free woman. 23His son by the slave woman was born in the ordinary way; but his son by the free woman was born as the result of a promise.

24These things may be taken figuratively, for the women represent two covenants. One covenant is from Mount Sinai and bears children who are to be slaves: This is Hagar. 25Now Hagar stands for Mount Sinai in Arabia and corresponds to the present city of Jerusalem, because she is in slavery with her children. 26But the Jerusalem that is above is free, and she is our mother. 27For it is written:

"Be glad, O barren woman,
    who bears no children;
break forth and cry aloud,
    you who have no labor pains;
because more are the children of the desolate
        woman
    than of her who has a husband." [a]

28Now you, brothers, like Isaac, are children of promise. 29At that time the son born in the ordinary way persecuted the son born by the power of the Spirit. It is the same now. 30But what does the Scripture say? "Get rid of the slave woman and her son, for the slave woman's son will never share in the inheritance with the free woman's son." [b] 31Therefore, brothers, we are not children of the slave woman, but of the free woman.

FREEDOM IN CHRIST

5 It is for freedom that Christ has set us free. Stand firm, then, and do not let yourselves be burdened again by a yoke of slavery.

2Mark my words! I, Paul, tell you that if you let yourselves be circumcised, Christ will be of no value to you at all. 3Again I declare to every man who lets himself be circumcised that he is obligated to obey the whole law. 4You who are trying to be justified by law have been alienated

THE MESSAGE

a mother in the pain of childbirth. Oh, I keep wishing that I was with you. Then I wouldn't be reduced to this blunt, letter-writing language out of sheer frustration.

4.21-31 Tell me now, you who have become so enamored with the law: Have you paid close attention to that law? Abraham, remember, had *two* sons: one by the slave woman and one by the free woman. The son of the slave woman was born by human connivance; the son of the free woman was born by God's promise. This illustrates the very thing we are dealing with now. The two births represent two ways of being in relationship with God. One is from Mount Sinai in Arabia. It corresponds with what is now going on in Jerusalem—a slave life, producing slaves as offspring. This is the way of Hagar. In contrast to that, there is an invisible Jerusalem, a free Jerusalem, and she is our mother—this is the way of Sarah. Remember what Isaiah wrote:

Rejoice, barren woman who bears no
        children,
    shout and cry out, woman who has no
        birth pangs,
Because the children of the barren woman
    now surpass the children of the chosen
        woman.

Isn't it clear, friends, that you, like Isaac, are children of promise? In the days of Hagar and Sarah, the child who came from faithless connivance (Ishmael) harassed the child who came—empowered by the Spirit—from the faithful promise (Isaac). Isn't it clear that the harassment you are now experiencing from the Jerusalem heretics follows that old pattern? There is a Scripture that tells us what to do: "Expel the slave mother with her son, for the slave son will not inherit with the free son." Isn't that conclusive? We are not children of the slave woman, but of the free woman.

THE LIFE OF FREEDOM

5.1 5 Christ has set us free to live a free life. So take your stand! Never again let anyone put a harness of slavery on you.

5.2-3 I am emphatic about this. The moment any one of you submits to circumcision or any other rule-keeping system, at that same moment Christ's hard-won gift of freedom is squandered. I repeat my warning: The person who accepts the ways of circumcision trades all the advantages of the free life in Christ for the obligations of the slave life of the law.

5.4-6 I suspect you would never intend this, but this is what happens. When you attempt to live

NEW INTERNATIONAL VERSION

from Christ; you have fallen away from grace. [5]But by faith we eagerly await through the Spirit the righteousness for which we hope. [6]For in Christ Jesus neither circumcision nor uncircumcision has any value. The only thing that counts is faith expressing itself through love.

[7]You were running a good race. Who cut in on you and kept you from obeying the truth? [8]That kind of persuasion does not come from the one who calls you. [9]"A little yeast works through the whole batch of dough." [10]I am confident in the Lord that you will take no other view. The one who is throwing you into confusion will pay the penalty, whoever he may be. [11]Brothers, if I am still preaching circumcision, why am I still being persecuted? In that case the offense of the cross has been abolished. [12]As for those agitators, I wish they would go the whole way and emasculate themselves!

[13]You, my brothers, were called to be free. But do not use your freedom to indulge the sinful nature[a]; rather, serve one another in love. [14]The entire law is summed up in a single command: "Love your neighbor as yourself."[b] [15]If you keep on biting and devouring each other, watch out or you will be destroyed by each other.

LIFE BY THE SPIRIT

[16]So I say, live by the Spirit, and you will not gratify the desires of the sinful nature. [17]For the sinful nature desires what is contrary to the Spirit, and the Spirit what is contrary to the sinful nature. They are in conflict with each other, so that you do not do what you want. [18]But if you are led by the Spirit, you are not under law.

[19]The acts of the sinful nature are obvious:

THE MESSAGE

by your own religious plans and projects, you are cut off from Christ, you fall out of grace. Meanwhile we expectantly wait for a satisfying relationship with the Spirit. For in Christ, neither our most conscientious religion nor disregard of religion amounts to anything. What matters is something far more interior: faith expressed in love.

5.7-10 You were running superbly! Who cut in on you, deflecting you from the true course of obedience? This detour doesn't come from the One who called you into the race in the first place. And please don't toss this off as insignificant. It only takes a minute amount of yeast, you know, to permeate an entire loaf of bread. Deep down, the Master has given me confidence that you will not defect. But the one who is upsetting you, whoever he is, will bear the divine judgment.

5.11-12 As for the rumor that I continue to preach the ways of circumcision (as I did in those pre-Damascus Road days), that is absurd. Why would I still be persecuted, then? If I were preaching that old message, no one would be offended if I mentioned the Cross now and then—it would be so watered-down it wouldn't matter one way or the other. Why don't these agitators, obsessive as they are about circumcision, go all the way and castrate themselves!

5.13-15 It is absolutely clear that God has called you to a free life. Just make sure that you don't use this freedom as an excuse to do whatever you want to do and destroy your freedom. Rather, use your freedom to serve one another in love; that's how freedom grows. For everything we know about God's Word is summed up in a single sentence: Love others as you love yourself. That's an act of true freedom. If you bite and ravage each other, watch out—in no time at all you will be annihilating each other, and where will your precious freedom be then?

5.16-18 My counsel is this: Live freely, animated and motivated by God's Spirit. Then you won't feed the compulsions of selfishness. For there is a root of sinful self-interest in us that is at odds with a free spirit, just as the free spirit is incompatible with selfishness. These two ways of life are antithetical, so that you cannot live at times one way and at times another way according to how you feel on any given day. Why don't you choose to be led by the Spirit and so escape the erratic compulsions of a law-dominated existence?

5.19-21 It is obvious what kind of life develops out of trying to get your own way all the time: repeti-

---

[a] 13 Or *the flesh*; also in verses 16, 17, 19 and 24
[b] 14 Lev. 19:18

NEW INTERNATIONAL VERSION

sexual immorality, impurity and debauchery; ²⁰idolatry and witchcraft; hatred, discord, jealousy, fits of rage, selfish ambition, dissensions, factions ²¹and envy; drunkenness, orgies, and the like. I warn you, as I did before, that those who live like this will not inherit the kingdom of God.

²²But the fruit of the Spirit is love, joy, peace, patience, kindness, goodness, faithfulness, ²³gentleness and self-control. Against such things there is no law. ²⁴Those who belong to Christ Jesus have crucified the sinful nature with its passions and desires. ²⁵Since we live by the Spirit, let us keep in step with the Spirit. ²⁶Let us not become conceited, provoking and envying each other.

DOING GOOD TO ALL

6 Brothers, if someone is caught in a sin, you who are spiritual should restore him gently. But watch yourself, or you also may be tempted. ²Carry each other's burdens, and in this way you will fulfill the law of Christ. ³If anyone thinks he is something when he is nothing, he deceives himself. ⁴Each one should test his own actions. Then he can take pride in himself, without comparing himself to somebody else, ⁵for each one should carry his own load.

THE MESSAGE

tive, loveless, cheap sex; a stinking accumulation of mental and emotional garbage; frenzied and joyless grabs for happiness; trinket gods; magic-show religion; paranoid loneliness; cutthroat competition; all-consuming-yet-never-satisfied wants; a brutal temper; an impotence to love or be loved; divided homes and divided lives; small-minded and lopsided pursuits; the vicious habit of depersonalizing everyone into a rival; uncontrolled and uncontrollable addictions; ugly parodies of community. I could go on.

This isn't the first time I have warned you, you know. If you use your freedom this way, you will not inherit God's kingdom.

5.22-23   But what happens when we live God's way? He brings gifts into our lives, much the same way that fruit appears in an orchard—things like affection for others, exuberance about life, serenity. We develop a willingness to stick with things, a sense of compassion in the heart, and a conviction that a basic holiness permeates things and people. We find ourselves involved in loyal commitments, not needing to force our way in life, able to marshal and direct our energies wisely.

5.23-24   Legalism is helpless in bringing this about; it only gets in the way. Among those who belong to Christ, everything connected with getting our own way and mindlessly responding to what everyone else calls necessities is killed off for good—crucified.

5.25-26   Since this is the kind of life we have chosen, the life of the Spirit, let us make sure that we do not just hold it as an idea in our heads or a sentiment in our hearts, but work out its implications in every detail of our lives. That means we will not compare ourselves with each other as if one of us were better and another worse. We have far more interesting things to do with our lives. Each of us is an original.

NOTHING BUT THE CROSS

6.1-3   **6** Live creatively, friends. If someone falls into sin, forgivingly restore him, saving your critical comments for yourself. You might be needing forgiveness before the day's out. Stoop down and reach out to those who are oppressed. Share their burdens, and so complete Christ's law. If you think you are too good for that, you are badly deceived.

6.4-5   Make a careful exploration of who you are and the work you have been given, and then sink yourself into that. Don't be impressed with yourself. Don't compare yourself with others. Each of you must take responsibility for doing the creative best you can with your own life.

NEW INTERNATIONAL VERSION

⁶Anyone who receives instruction in the word must share all good things with his instructor.

⁷Do not be deceived: God cannot be mocked. A man reaps what he sows. ⁸The one who sows to please his sinful nature, from that nature*ª* will reap destruction; the one who sows to please the Spirit, from the Spirit will reap eternal life. ⁹Let us not become weary in doing good, for at the proper time we will reap a harvest if we do not give up. ¹⁰Therefore, as we have opportunity, let us do good to all people, especially to those who belong to the family of believers.

NOT CIRCUMCISION BUT A NEW CREATION

¹¹See what large letters I use as I write to you with my own hand!

¹²Those who want to make a good impression outwardly are trying to compel you to be circumcised. The only reason they do this is to avoid being persecuted for the cross of Christ. ¹³Not even those who are circumcised obey the law, yet they want you to be circumcised that they may boast about your flesh. ¹⁴May I never boast except in the cross of our Lord Jesus Christ, through which*ᵇ* the world has been crucified to me, and I to the world. ¹⁵Neither circumcision nor uncircumcision means anything; what counts is a new creation. ¹⁶Peace and mercy to all who follow this rule, even to the Israel of God.

¹⁷Finally, let no one cause me trouble, for I bear on my body the marks of Jesus.

¹⁸The grace of our Lord Jesus Christ be with your spirit, brothers. Amen.

THE MESSAGE

6.6 Be very sure now, you who have been trained to a self-sufficient maturity, that you enter into a generous common life with those who have trained you, sharing all the good things that you have and experience.

6.7-8 Don't be misled: No one makes a fool of God. What a person plants, he will harvest. The person who plants selfishness, ignoring the needs of others—ignoring God!—harvests a crop of weeds. All he'll have to show for his life is weeds! But the one who plants in response to God, letting God's Spirit do the growth work in him, harvests a crop of real life, eternal life.

6.9-10 So let's not allow ourselves to get fatigued doing good. At the right time we will harvest a good crop if we don't give up, or quit. Right now, therefore, every time we get the chance, let us work for the benefit of all, starting with the people closest to us in the community of faith.

6.11-13 Now, in these last sentences, I want to emphasize in the bold scrawls of my personal handwriting the immense importance of what I have written to you. These people who are attempting to force the ways of circumcision on you have only one motive: They want an easy way to look good before others, lacking the courage to live by a faith that shares Christ's suffering and death. All their talk about the law is gas. They *themselves* don't keep the law! And they are highly selective in the laws they *do* observe. They only want you to be circumcised so they can boast of their success in recruiting you to their side. That is contemptible!

6.14-16 For my part, I am going to boast about nothing but the Cross of our Master, Jesus Christ. Because of that Cross, I have been crucified in relation to the world, set free from the stifling atmosphere of pleasing others and fitting into the little patterns that they dictate. Can't you see the central issue in all this? It is not what you and I do—submit to circumcision, reject circumcision. It is what *God* is doing, and he is creating something totally new, a free life! All who walk by this standard are the true Israel of God—his chosen people. Peace and mercy on them!

6.17 Quite frankly, I don't want to be bothered anymore by these disputes. I have far more important things to do—the serious living of this faith. I bear in my body scars from my service to Jesus.

6.18 May what our Master Jesus Christ gives freely be deeply and personally yours, my friends. Oh, yes!

ª 8 Or his flesh, from the flesh   *ᵇ 14 Or whom*

EPHESIANS

EPHESIANS

1 Paul, an apostle of Christ Jesus by the will of God,

To the saints in Ephesus,[a] the faithful[b] in Christ Jesus:

²Grace and peace to you from God our Father and the Lord Jesus Christ.

SPIRITUAL BLESSINGS IN CHRIST

³Praise be to the God and Father of our Lord Jesus Christ, who has blessed us in the heavenly realms with every spiritual blessing in Christ. ⁴For he chose us in him before the creation of the world to be holy and blameless in his sight. In love ⁵he[c] predestined us to be adopted as his sons through Jesus Christ, in accordance with his pleasure and will— ⁶to the praise of his glorious grace, which he has freely given us in the One he loves. ⁷In him we have redemption through his blood, the forgiveness of sins, in accordance with the riches of God's grace ⁸that he lavished on us with all wisdom and understanding. ⁹And he[d] made known to us the mystery of his will according to his good pleasure, which he purposed in Christ, ¹⁰to be put into effect when the times will have reached their fulfillment—to bring all things in heaven and on earth together under one head, even Christ.

¹¹In him we were also chosen,[e] having been predestined according to the plan of him who works out everything in conformity with the purpose of his will, ¹²in order that we, who were the first to hope in Christ, might be for the praise of his glory. ¹³And you also were included in Christ when you heard the word of truth, the gospel of your salvation. Having believed, you were marked in him with a seal, the promised Holy Spirit, ¹⁴who is a deposit guaranteeing our inheritance until the redemption of those who are God's possession—to the praise of his glory.

1.1-2 **1** I, Paul, am under God's plan as an apostle, a special agent of Christ Jesus, writing to you faithful Christians in Ephesus. I greet you with the grace and peace poured into our lives by God our Father and our Master, Jesus Christ.

THE GOD OF GLORY

1.3-6 How blessed is God! And what a blessing he is! He's the Father of our Master, Jesus Christ, and takes us to the high places of blessing in him. Long before he laid down earth's foundations, he had us in mind, had settled on us as the focus of his love, to be made whole and holy by his love. Long, long ago he decided to adopt us into his family through Jesus Christ. (What pleasure he took in planning this!) He wanted us to enter into the celebration of his lavish gift-giving by the hand of his beloved Son.

1.7-10 Because of the sacrifice of the Messiah, his blood poured out on the altar of the Cross, we're a free people—free of penalties and punishments chalked up by all our misdeeds. And not just barely free, either. *Abundantly* free! He thought of everything, provided for everything we could possibly need, letting us in on the plans he took such delight in making. He set it all out before us in Christ, a long-range plan in which everything would be brought together and summed up in him, everything in deepest heaven, everything on planet earth.

1.11-12 It's in Christ that we find out who we are and what we are living for. Long before we first heard of Christ and got our hopes up, he had his eye on us, had designs on us for glorious living, part of the overall purpose he is working out in everything and everyone.

1.13-14 It's in Christ that you, once you heard the truth and believed it (this Message of your salvation), found yourselves home free—signed, sealed, and delivered by the Holy Spirit. This signet from God is the first installment on what's coming, a reminder that we'll get everything God has planned for us, a praising and glorious life.

---

a 1 Some early manuscripts do not have *in Ephesus*.
b 1 Or *believers who are*   *c* 4,5 Or *sight in love.* ⁵*He*
d 8,9 Or *us. With all wisdom and understanding,* ⁹*he*
e 11 Or *were made heirs*

NEW INTERNATIONAL VERSION

THANKSGIVING AND PRAYER

[15]For this reason, ever since I heard about your faith in the Lord Jesus and your love for all the saints, [16]I have not stopped giving thanks for you, remembering you in my prayers. [17]I keep asking that the God of our Lord Jesus Christ, the glorious Father, may give you the Spirit[a] of wisdom and revelation, so that you may know him better. [18]I pray also that the eyes of your heart may be enlightened in order that you may know the hope to which he has called you, the riches of his glorious inheritance in the saints, [19]and his incomparably great power for us who believe. That power is like the working of his mighty strength, [20]which he exerted in Christ when he raised him from the dead and seated him at his right hand in the heavenly realms, [21]far above all rule and authority, power and dominion, and every title that can be given, not only in the present age but also in the one to come. [22]And God placed all things under his feet and appointed him to be head over everything for the church, [23]which is his body, the fullness of him who fills everything in every way.

MADE ALIVE IN CHRIST

2 As for you, you were dead in your transgressions and sins, [2]in which you used to live when you followed the ways of this world and of the ruler of the kingdom of the air, the spirit who is now at work in those who are disobedient. [3]All of us also lived among them at one time, gratifying the cravings of our sinful nature[b] and following its desires and thoughts. Like the rest, we were by nature objects of wrath. [4]But because of his great love for us, God, who is rich in mercy, [5]made us alive with Christ even when we were dead in transgressions—it is by grace you have been saved. [6]And God raised us up with Christ and seated us with him in the heavenly realms in Christ Jesus, [7]in order that in the coming ages he might show the incomparable riches of his grace, expressed in his kindness to us in Christ Jesus. [8]For it is by grace you have been saved, through faith—and this not from yourselves, it is the gift of God— [9]not by works, so that no one can boast. [10]For we are God's workmanship, created

[a] 17 Or *a spirit*   [b] 3 Or *our flesh*

THE MESSAGE

1.15-19   That's why, when I heard of the solid trust you have in the Master Jesus and your outpouring of love to all the Christians, I couldn't stop thanking God for you—every time I prayed, I'd think of you and give thanks. But I do more than thank. I ask—ask the God of our Master, Jesus Christ, the God of glory—to make you intelligent and discerning in knowing him personally, your eyes focused and clear, so that you can see exactly what it is he is calling you to do, grasp the immensity of this glorious way of life he has for Christians, oh, the utter extravagance of his work in us who trust him—endless energy, boundless strength!

1.20-23   All this energy issues from Christ: God raised him from death and set him on a throne in deep heaven, in charge of running the universe, everything from galaxies to governments, no name and no power exempt from his rule. And not just for the time being, but *forever*. He is in charge of it all, has the final word on everything. At the center of all this, Christ rules the church. The church, you see, is not peripheral to the world; the world is peripheral to the church. The church is Christ's body, in which he speaks and acts, by which he fills everything with his presence.

HE TORE DOWN THE WALL

2.1-6   **2** It wasn't so long ago that you were mired in that old stagnant life of sin. You let the world, which doesn't know the first thing about living, tell you how to live. You filled your lungs with polluted unbelief, and then exhaled disobedience. We all did it, all of us doing what we felt like doing, when we felt like doing it, all of us in the same boat. It's a wonder God didn't lose his temper and do away with the whole lot of us. Instead, immense in mercy and with an incredible love, he embraced us. He took our sin-dead lives and made us alive in Christ. He did all this on his own, with no help from us! Then he picked us up and set us down in highest heaven in company with Jesus, our Messiah.

2.7-10   Now God has us where he wants us, with all the time in this world and the next to shower grace and kindness upon us in Christ Jesus. Saving is all his idea, and all his work. All we do is trust him enough to let him do it. It's God's gift from start to finish! We don't play the major role. If we did, we'd probably go around bragging that we'd done the whole thing! No, we neither make nor save ourselves. God does both the making and saving. He creates each of us by Christ Jesus to join him in the work he does,

NEW INTERNATIONAL VERSION

in Christ Jesus to do good works, which God prepared in advance for us to do.

ONE IN CHRIST

[11]Therefore, remember that formerly you who are Gentiles by birth and called "uncircumcised" by those who call themselves "the circumcision" (that done in the body by the hands of men)—[12]remember that at that time you were separate from Christ, excluded from citizenship in Israel and foreigners to the covenants of the promise, without hope and without God in the world. [13]But now in Christ Jesus you who once were far away have been brought near through the blood of Christ.

[14]For he himself is our peace, who has made the two one and has destroyed the barrier, the dividing wall of hostility, [15]by abolishing in his flesh the law with its commandments and regulations. His purpose was to create in himself one new man out of the two, thus making peace, [16]and in this one body to reconcile both of them to God through the cross, by which he put to death their hostility. [17]He came and preached peace to you who were far away and peace to those who were near. [18]For through him we both have access to the Father by one Spirit.

[19]Consequently, you are no longer foreigners and aliens, but fellow citizens with God's people and members of God's household, [20]built on the foundation of the apostles and prophets, with Christ Jesus himself as the chief cornerstone. [21]In him the whole building is joined together and rises to become a holy temple in the Lord. [22]And in him you too are being built together to become a dwelling in which God lives by his Spirit.

PAUL THE PREACHER TO THE GENTILES

3 For this reason I, Paul, the prisoner of Christ Jesus for the sake of you Gentiles—

[2]Surely you have heard about the administration of God's grace that was given to me for you, [3]that is, the mystery made known to me by revelation, as I have already written briefly. [4]In reading this, then, you will be able to understand my

THE MESSAGE

the good work he has gotten ready for us to do, work we had better be doing.

2.11-13   But don't take any of this for granted. It was only yesterday that you outsiders to God's ways had no idea of any of this, didn't know the first thing about the way God works, hadn't the faintest idea of Christ. You knew nothing of that rich history of God's covenants and promises in Israel, hadn't a clue about what God was doing in the world at large. Now because of Christ— dying that death, shedding that blood—you who were once out of it altogether are in on everything.

2.14-15   The Messiah has made things up between us so that we're now together on this, both non-Jewish outsiders and Jewish insiders. He tore down the wall we used to keep each other at a distance. He repealed the law code that had become so clogged with fine print and footnotes that it hindered more than it helped. Then he started over. Instead of continuing with two groups of people separated by centuries of animosity and suspicion, he created a new kind of human being, a fresh start for everybody.

2.16-18   Christ brought us together through his death on the Cross. The Cross got us to embrace, and that was the end of the hostility. Christ came and preached peace to you outsiders and peace to us insiders. He treated us as equals, and so made us equals. Through him we both share the same Spirit and have equal access to the Father.

2.19-22   That's plain enough, isn't it? You're no longer wandering exiles. This kingdom of faith is now your home country. You're no longer strangers or outsiders. You *belong* here, with as much right to the name Christian as anyone. God is building a home. He's using us all—irrespective of how we got here—in what he is building. He used the apostles and prophets for the foundation. Now he's using you, fitting you in brick by brick, stone by stone, with Christ Jesus as the cornerstone that holds all the parts together. We see it taking shape day after day— a holy temple built by God, all of us built into it, a temple in which God is quite at home.

THE SECRET PLAN OF GOD

3.1-3   **3** This is why I, Paul, am in jail for Christ, having taken up the cause of you outsiders, so-called. I take it that you're familiar with the part I was given in God's plan for including everybody. I got the inside story on this from God himself, as I just wrote you in brief.

3.4-6   As you read over what I have written to you, you'll be able to see for yourselves into the

NEW INTERNATIONAL VERSION

insight into the mystery of Christ, [5]which was not made known to men in other generations as it has now been revealed by the Spirit to God's holy apostles and prophets. [6]This mystery is that through the gospel the Gentiles are heirs together with Israel, members together of one body, and sharers together in the promise in Christ Jesus.

[7]I became a servant of this gospel by the gift of God's grace given me through the working of his power. [8]Although I am less than the least of all God's people, this grace was given me: to preach to the Gentiles the unsearchable riches of Christ, [9]and to make plain to everyone the administration of this mystery, which for ages past was kept hidden in God, who created all things. [10]His intent was that now, through the church, the manifold wisdom of God should be made known to the rulers and authorities in the heavenly realms, [11]according to his eternal purpose which he accomplished in Christ Jesus our Lord. [12]In him and through faith in him we may approach God with freedom and confidence. [13]I ask you, therefore, not to be discouraged because of my sufferings for you, which are your glory.

A PRAYER FOR THE EPHESIANS

[14]For this reason I kneel before the Father, [15]from whom his whole family[a] in heaven and on earth derives its name. [16]I pray that out of his glorious riches he may strengthen you with power through his Spirit in your inner being, [17]so that Christ may dwell in your hearts through faith. And I pray that you, being rooted and established in love, [18]may have power, together with all the saints, to grasp how wide and long and high and deep is the love of Christ, [19]and to know this love that surpasses knowledge—that you may be filled to the measure of all the fullness of God.

[20]Now to him who is able to do immeasurably more than all we ask or imagine, according to his power that is at work within us, [21]to him be

---

[a] 15 Or whom all fatherhood

THE MESSAGE

mystery of Christ. None of our ancestors understood this. Only in our time has it been made clear by God's Spirit through his holy apostles and prophets of this new order. The mystery is that people who have never heard of God and those who have heard of him all their lives (what I've been calling outsiders and insiders) stand on the same ground before God. They get the same offer, same help, same promises in Christ Jesus. The Message is accessible and welcoming to everyone, across the board.

3.7-8 This is my life work: helping people understand and respond to this Message. It came as a sheer gift to me, a real surprise, God handling all the details. When it came to presenting the Message to people who had no background in God's way, I was the least qualified of any of the available Christians. God saw to it that I was equipped, but you can be sure that it had nothing to do with my natural abilities.

3.8-10 And so here I am, preaching and writing about things that are way over my head, the inexhaustible riches and generosity of Christ. My task is to bring out in the open and make plain what God, who created all this in the first place, has been doing in secret and behind the scenes all along. Through Christians like yourselves gathered in churches, this extraordinary plan of God is becoming known and talked about even among the angels!

3.11-13 All this is proceeding along lines planned all along by God and then executed in Christ Jesus. When we trust in him, we're free to say whatever needs to be said, bold to go wherever we need to go. So don't let my present trouble on your behalf get you down. Be proud!

✛

3.14-19 My response is to get down on my knees before the Father, this magnificent Father who parcels out all heaven and earth. I ask him to strengthen you by his Spirit—not a brute strength but a glorious inner strength—that Christ will live in you as you open the door and invite him in. And I ask him that with both feet planted firmly on love, you'll be able to take in with all Christians the extravagant dimensions of Christ's love. Reach out and experience the breadth! Test its length! Plumb the depths! Rise to the heights! Live full lives, full in the fullness of God.

3.20-21 God can do anything, you know—far more than you could ever imagine or guess or request in your wildest dreams! He does it not by pushing us around but by working within us, his Spirit deeply and gently within us.

NEW INTERNATIONAL VERSION

glory in the church and in Christ Jesus throughout all generations, for ever and ever! Amen.

UNITY IN THE BODY OF CHRIST

4 As a prisoner for the Lord, then, I urge you to live a life worthy of the calling you have received. ²Be completely humble and gentle; be patient, bearing with one another in love. ³Make every effort to keep the unity of the Spirit through the bond of peace. ⁴There is one body and one Spirit—just as you were called to one hope when you were called— ⁵one Lord, one faith, one baptism; ⁶one God and Father of all, who is over all and through all and in all.

⁷But to each one of us grace has been given as Christ apportioned it. ⁸This is why it*a* says:

"When he ascended on high,
  he led captives in his train
  and gave gifts to men."*b*

⁹(What does "he ascended" mean except that he also descended to the lower, earthly regions*c*? ¹⁰He who descended is the very one who ascended higher than all the heavens, in order to fill the whole universe.) ¹¹It was he who gave some to be apostles, some to be prophets, some to be evangelists, and some to be pastors and teachers, ¹²to prepare God's people for works of service, so that the body of Christ may be built up ¹³until we all reach unity in the faith and in the knowledge of the Son of God and become mature, attaining to the whole measure of the fullness of Christ.

¹⁴Then we will no longer be infants, tossed back and forth by the waves, and blown here and there by every wind of teaching and by the cunning and craftiness of men in their deceitful scheming. ¹⁵Instead, speaking the truth in love, we will in all things grow up into him who is the Head, that is, Christ. ¹⁶From him the whole body, joined and held together by every supporting ligament, grows and builds itself up in love, as each part does its work.

a 8 Or God   *b* 8 Psalm 68:18   *c* 9 Or the depths of the earth

THE MESSAGE

Glory to God in the church!
Glory to God in the Messiah, in Jesus!
Glory down all the generations!
Glory through all millennia! Oh, yes!

TO BE MATURE

4.1-3 **4** In light of all this, here's what I want you to do. While I'm locked up here, a prisoner for the Master, I want you to get out there and walk—better yet, run!—on the road God called you to travel. I don't want any of you sitting around on your hands. I don't want anyone strolling off, down some path that goes nowhere. And mark that you do this with humility and discipline—not in fits and starts, but steadily, pouring yourselves out for each other in acts of love, alert at noticing differences and quick at mending fences.

4.4-6 You were all called to travel on the same road and in the same direction, so stay together, both outwardly and inwardly. You have one Master, one faith, one baptism, one God and Father of all, who rules over all, works through all, and is present in all. Everything you are and think and do is permeated with Oneness.

4.7-13 But that doesn't mean you should all look and speak and act the same. Out of the generosity of Christ, each of us is given his own gift. The text for this is,

He climbed the high mountain,
He captured the enemy and seized the booty,
He handed it all out in gifts to the people.

It's true, is it not, that the One who climbed up also climbed down, down to the valley of earth? And the One who climbed down is the One who climbed back up, up to highest heaven. He handed out gifts above and below, filled heaven with his gifts, filled earth with his gifts. He handed out gifts of apostle, prophet, evangelist, and pastor-teacher to train Christians in skilled servant work, working within Christ's body, the church, until we're all moving rhythmically and easily with each other, efficient and graceful in response to God's Son, fully mature adults, fully developed within and without, fully alive like Christ.

4.14-16 No prolonged infancies among us, please. We'll not tolerate babes in the woods, small children who are an easy mark for impostors. God wants us to grow up, to know the whole truth and tell it in love—like Christ in everything. We take our lead from Christ, who is the source of everything we do. He keeps us in step with each other. His very breath and blood flow through us, nourishing us so that we will grow up healthy in God, robust in love.

NEW INTERNATIONAL VERSION

LIVING AS CHILDREN OF LIGHT

¹⁷So I tell you this, and insist on it in the Lord, that you must no longer live as the Gentiles do, in the futility of their thinking. ¹⁸They are darkened in their understanding and separated from the life of God because of the ignorance that is in them due to the hardening of their hearts. ¹⁹Having lost all sensitivity, they have given themselves over to sensuality so as to indulge in every kind of impurity, with a continual lust for more.

²⁰You, however, did not come to know Christ that way. ²¹Surely you heard of him and were taught in him in accordance with the truth that is in Jesus. ²²You were taught, with regard to your former way of life, to put off your old self, which is being corrupted by its deceitful desires; ²³to be made new in the attitude of your minds; ²⁴and to put on the new self, created to be like God in true righteousness and holiness.

²⁵Therefore each of you must put off falsehood and speak truthfully to his neighbor, for we are all members of one body. ²⁶"In your anger do not sin"ᵃ: Do not let the sun go down while you are still angry, ²⁷and do not give the devil a foothold. ²⁸He who has been stealing must steal no longer, but must work, doing something useful with his own hands, that he may have something to share with those in need.

²⁹Do not let any unwholesome talk come out of your mouths, but only what is helpful for building others up according to their needs, that it may benefit those who listen. ³⁰And do not grieve the Holy Spirit of God, with whom you were sealed for the day of redemption. ³¹Get rid of all bitterness, rage and anger, brawling and slander, along with every form of malice. ³²Be kind and compassionate to one another, forgiving each other, just as in Christ God forgave you.

5 Be imitators of God, therefore, as dearly loved children ²and live a life of love, just as Christ loved us and gave himself up for us as a fragrant offering and sacrifice to God.

ᵃ 26 Psalm 4:4

THE MESSAGE

THE OLD WAY HAS TO GO

4.17-19 And so I insist—and God backs me up on this—that there be no going along with the crowd, the empty-headed, mindless crowd. They've refused for so long to deal with God that they've lost touch not only with God but with reality itself. They can't think straight anymore. Feeling no pain, they let themselves go in sexual obsession, addicted to every sort of perversion.

4.20-24 But that's no life for you. You learned Christ! My assumption is that you have paid careful attention to him, been well instructed in the truth precisely as we have it in Jesus. Since, then, we do not have the excuse of ignorance, everything—and I do mean everything—connected with that old way of life has to go. It's rotten through and through. Get rid of it! And then take on an entirely new way of life—a God-fashioned life, a life renewed from the inside and working itself into your conduct as God accurately reproduces his character in you.

4.25 What this adds up to, then, is this: no more lies, no more pretense. Tell your neighbor the truth. In Christ's body we're all connected to each other, after all. When you lie to others, you end up lying to yourself.

4.26-27 Go ahead and be angry. You do well to be angry—but don't use your anger as fuel for revenge. And don't stay angry. Don't go to bed angry. Don't give the Devil that kind of foothold in your life.

4.28 Did you used to make ends meet by stealing? Well, no more! Get an honest job so that you can help others who can't work.

4.29 Watch the way you talk. Let nothing foul or dirty come out of your mouth. Say only what helps, each word a gift.

4.30 Don't grieve God. Don't break his heart. His Holy Spirit, moving and breathing in you, is the most intimate part of your life, making you fit for himself. Don't take such a gift for granted.

4.31-32 Make a clean break with all cutting, backbiting, profane talk. Be gentle with one another, sensitive. Forgive one another as quickly and thoroughly as God in Christ forgave you.

WAKE UP FROM YOUR SLEEP

5.1-2 **5** Watch what God does, and then you do it, like children who learn proper behavior from their parents. Mostly what God does is love you. Keep company with him and learn a life of love. Observe how Christ loved us. His love was not cautious but extravagant. He didn't love in order to get something from us but to give everything of himself to us. Love like that.

NEW INTERNATIONAL VERSION

³But among you there must not be even a hint of sexual immorality, or of any kind of impurity, or of greed, because these are improper for God's holy people. ⁴Nor should there be obscenity, foolish talk or coarse joking, which are out of place, but rather thanksgiving. ⁵For of this you can be sure: No immoral, impure or greedy person—such a man is an idolater—has any inheritance in the kingdom of Christ and of God.*a* ⁶Let no one deceive you with empty words, for because of such things God's wrath comes on those who are disobedient. ⁷Therefore do not be partners with them.

⁸For you were once darkness, but now you are light in the Lord. Live as children of light ⁹(for the fruit of the light consists in all goodness, righteousness and truth) ¹⁰and find out what pleases the Lord. ¹¹Have nothing to do with the fruitless deeds of darkness, but rather expose them. ¹²For it is shameful even to mention what the disobedient do in secret. ¹³But everything exposed by the light becomes visible, ¹⁴for it is light that makes everything visible. This is why it is said:

> "Wake up, O sleeper,
>   rise from the dead,
> and Christ will shine on you."

¹⁵Be very careful, then, how you live—not as unwise but as wise, ¹⁶making the most of every opportunity, because the days are evil. ¹⁷Therefore do not be foolish, but understand what the Lord's will is. ¹⁸Do not get drunk on wine, which leads to debauchery. Instead, be filled with the Spirit. ¹⁹Speak to one another with psalms, hymns and spiritual songs. Sing and make music in your heart to the Lord, ²⁰always giving thanks to God the Father for everything, in the name of our Lord Jesus Christ.

²¹Submit to one another out of reverence for Christ.

WIVES AND HUSBANDS

²²Wives, submit to your husbands as to the Lord. ²³For the husband is the head of the wife as Christ is the head of the church, his body, of which he is the Savior. ²⁴Now as the church sub-

---

a 5 Or kingdom of the Christ and God

THE MESSAGE

5.3-4   Don't allow love to turn into lust, setting off a downhill slide into sexual promiscuity, filthy practices, or bullying greed. Though some tongues just love the taste of gossip, Christians have better uses for language than that. Don't talk dirty or silly. That kind of talk doesn't fit our style. Thanksgiving is our dialect.

5.5   You can be sure that using people or religion or things just for what you can get out of them—the usual variations on idolatry—will get you nowhere, and certainly nowhere near the kingdom of Christ, the kingdom of God.

5.6-7   Don't let yourselves get taken in by religious smooth talk. God gets furious with people who are full of religious sales talk but want nothing to do with him. Don't even hang around people like that.

5.8-10   You groped your way through that murk once, but no longer. You're out in the open now. The bright light of Christ makes your way plain. So no more stumbling around. Get on with it! The good, the right, the true—these are the actions appropriate for daylight hours. Figure out what will please Christ, and then do it.

5.11-16   Don't waste your time on useless work, mere busywork, the barren pursuits of darkness. Expose these things for the sham they are. It's a scandal when people waste their lives on things they must do in the darkness where no one will see. Rip the cover off those frauds and see how attractive they look in the light of Christ.

> Wake up from your sleep,
>   Climb out of your coffins;
> Christ will show you the light!

So watch your step. Use your head. Make the most of every chance you get. These are desperate times!

5.17   Don't live carelessly, unthinkingly. Make sure you understand what the Master wants.

5.18-20   Don't drink too much wine. That cheapens your life. Drink the Spirit of God, huge draughts of him. Sing hymns instead of drinking songs! Sing songs from your heart to Christ. Sing praises over everything, any excuse for a song to God the Father in the name of our Master, Jesus Christ.

RELATIONSHIPS

5.21   Out of respect for Christ, be courteously reverent to one another.

5.22-24   Wives, understand and support your husbands in ways that show your support for Christ. The husband provides leadership to his wife the way Christ does to his church, not by domineering but by cherishing. So just as the

NEW INTERNATIONAL VERSION

mits to Christ, so also wives should submit to their husbands in everything.

[25]Husbands, love your wives, just as Christ loved the church and gave himself up for her [26]to make her holy, cleansing[a] her by the washing with water through the word, [27]and to present her to himself as a radiant church, without stain or wrinkle or any other blemish, but holy and blameless. [28]In this same way, husbands ought to love their wives as their own bodies. He who loves his wife loves himself. [29]After all, no one ever hated his own body, but he feeds and cares for it, just as Christ does the church— [30]for we are members of his body. [31]"For this reason a man will leave his father and mother and be united to his wife, and the two will become one flesh."[b] [32]This is a profound mystery—but I am talking about Christ and the church. [33]However, each one of you also must love his wife as he loves himself, and the wife must respect her husband.

CHILDREN AND PARENTS

6 Children, obey your parents in the Lord, for this is right. [2]"Honor your father and mother"—which is the first commandment with a promise— [3]"that it may go well with you and that you may enjoy long life on the earth."[c]

[4]Fathers, do not exasperate your children; instead, bring them up in the training and instruction of the Lord.

SLAVES AND MASTERS

[5]Slaves, obey your earthly masters with respect and fear, and with sincerity of heart, just as you would obey Christ. [6]Obey them not only to win their favor when their eye is on you, but like slaves of Christ, doing the will of God from your heart. [7]Serve wholeheartedly, as if you were serving the Lord, not men, [8]because you know that the Lord will reward everyone for whatever good he does, whether he is slave or free.

[9]And masters, treat your slaves in the same way. Do not threaten them, since you know that he who is both their Master and yours is in heaven, and there is no favoritism with him.

THE ARMOR OF GOD

[10]Finally, be strong in the Lord and in his mighty power. [11]Put on the full armor of God so that you can take your stand against the devil's schemes. [12]For our struggle is not against flesh

a 26 Or *having cleansed*   *b* 31 Gen. 2:24   *c* 3 Deut. 5:16

THE MESSAGE

church submits to Christ as he exercises such leadership, wives should likewise submit to their husbands.

5.25-28 Husbands, go all out in your love for your wives, exactly as Christ did for the church—a love marked by giving, not getting. Christ's love makes the church whole. His words evoke her beauty. Everything he does and says is designed to bring the best out of her, dressing her in dazzling white silk, radiant with holiness. And that is how husbands ought to love their wives. They're really doing themselves a favor—since they're already "one" in marriage.

5.29-33 No one abuses his own body, does he? No, he feeds and pampers it. That's how Christ treats us, the church, since we are part of his body. And this is why a man leaves father and mother and cherishes his wife. No longer two, they become "one flesh." This is a huge mystery, and I don't pretend to understand it all. What is clearest to me is the way Christ treats the church. And this provides a good picture of how each husband is to treat his wife, loving himself in loving her, and how each wife is to honor her husband.

6.1-3 6 Children, do what your parents tell you. This is only right. "Honor your father and mother" is the first commandment that has a promise attached to it, namely, "so you will live well and have a long life."

6.4 Fathers, don't exasperate your children by coming down hard on them. Take them by the hand and lead them in the way of the Master.

6.5-8 Servants, respectfully obey your earthly masters but always with an eye to obeying the *real* master, Christ. Don't just do what you have to do to get by, but work heartily, as Christ's servants doing what God wants you to do. And work with a smile on your face, always keeping in mind that no matter who happens to be giving the orders, you're really serving God. Good work will get you good pay from the Master, regardless of whether you are slave or free.

6.9 Masters, it's the same with you. No abuse, please, and no threats. You and your servants are both under the same Master in heaven. He makes no distinction between you and them.

A FIGHT TO THE FINISH

6.10-12 And that about wraps it up. God is strong, and he wants you strong. So take everything the Master has set out for you, well-made weapons of the best materials. And put them to use so you will be able to stand up to everything the Devil throws your way. This is no afternoon

NEW INTERNATIONAL VERSION

and blood, but against the rulers, against the authorities, against the powers of this dark world and against the spiritual forces of evil in the heavenly realms. [13]Therefore put on the full armor of God, so that when the day of evil comes, you may be able to stand your ground, and after you have done everything, to stand. [14]Stand firm then, with the belt of truth buckled around your waist, with the breastplate of righteousness in place, [15]and with your feet fitted with the readiness that comes from the gospel of peace. [16]In addition to all this, take up the shield of faith, with which you can extinguish all the flaming arrows of the evil one. [17]Take the helmet of salvation and the sword of the Spirit, which is the word of God. [18]And pray in the Spirit on all occasions with all kinds of prayers and requests. With this in mind, be alert and always keep on praying for all the saints.

[19]Pray also for me, that whenever I open my mouth, words may be given me so that I will fearlessly make known the mystery of the gospel, [20]for which I am an ambassador in chains. Pray that I may declare it fearlessly, as I should.

FINAL GREETINGS

[21]Tychicus, the dear brother and faithful servant in the Lord, will tell you everything, so that you also may know how I am and what I am doing. [22]I am sending him to you for this very purpose, that you may know how we are, and that he may encourage you.

[23]Peace to the brothers, and love with faith from God the Father and the Lord Jesus Christ. [24]Grace to all who love our Lord Jesus Christ with an undying love.

THE MESSAGE

athletic contest that we'll walk away from and forget about in a couple of hours. This is for keeps, a life-or-death fight to the finish against the Devil and all his angels.

6.13-18 Be prepared. You're up against far more than you can handle on your own. Take all the help you can get, every weapon God has issued, so that when it's all over but the shouting you'll still be on your feet. Truth, righteousness, peace, faith, and salvation are more than words. Learn how to apply them. You'll need them throughout your life. God's Word is an *indispensable* weapon. In the same way, prayer is essential in this ongoing warfare. Pray hard and long. Pray for your brothers and sisters. Keep your eyes open. Keep each other's spirits up so that no one falls behind or drops out.

6.19-20 And don't forget to pray for me. Pray that I'll know what to say and have the courage to say it at the right time, telling the mystery to one and all, the Message that I, jailbird preacher that I am, am responsible for getting out.

6.21-22 Tychicus, my good friend here, will tell you what I'm doing and how things are going with me. He is certainly a dependable servant of the Master! I've sent him not only to tell you about us but to cheer you on in your faith.

6.23-24 Good-bye, friends. Love mixed with faith be yours from God the Father and from the Master, Jesus Christ. Pure grace and nothing but grace be with all who love our Master, Jesus Christ.

PHILIPPIANS

PHILIPPIANS

1 Paul and Timothy, servants of Christ Jesus,

To all the saints in Christ Jesus at Philippi, together with the overseers*a* and deacons:

²Grace and peace to you from God our Father and the Lord Jesus Christ.

THANKSGIVING AND PRAYER

³I thank my God every time I remember you. ⁴In all my prayers for all of you, I always pray with joy ⁵because of your partnership in the gospel from the first day until now, ⁶being confident of this, that he who began a good work in you will carry it on to completion until the day of Christ Jesus.

⁷It is right for me to feel this way about all of you, since I have you in my heart; for whether I am in chains or defending and confirming the gospel, all of you share in God's grace with me. ⁸God can testify how I long for all of you with the affection of Christ Jesus.

⁹And this is my prayer: that your love may abound more and more in knowledge and depth of insight, ¹⁰so that you may be able to discern what is best and may be pure and blameless until the day of Christ, ¹¹filled with the fruit of righteousness that comes through Jesus Christ— to the glory and praise of God.

PAUL'S CHAINS ADVANCE THE GOSPEL

¹²Now I want you to know, brothers, that what has happened to me has really served to advance the gospel. ¹³As a result, it has become clear throughout the whole palace guard*b* and to

1 Paul and Timothy, both of us committed servants of Christ Jesus, write this letter to all the Christians in Philippi, pastors and ministers included. We greet you with the grace and peace that comes from God our Father and our Master, Jesus Christ.

A LOVE THAT WILL GROW

1.3-6 Every time you cross my mind, I break out in exclamations of thanks to God. Each exclamation is a trigger to prayer. I find myself praying for you with a glad heart. I am so pleased that you have continued on in this with us, believing and proclaiming God's Message, from the day you heard it right up to the present. There has never been the slightest doubt in my mind that the God who started this great work in you would keep at it and bring it to a flourishing finish on the very day Christ Jesus appears.

1.7-8 It's not at all fanciful for me to think this way about you. My prayers and hopes have deep roots in reality. You have, after all, stuck with me all the way from the time I was thrown in jail, put on trial, and came out of it in one piece. All along you have experienced with me the most generous help from God. He knows how much I love and miss you these days. Sometimes I think I feel as strongly about you as Christ does!

1.9-11 So this is my prayer: that your love will flourish and that you will not only love much but well. Learn to love appropriately. You need to use your head and test your feelings so that your love is sincere and intelligent, not sentimental gush. Live a lover's life, circumspect and exemplary, a life Jesus will be proud of: bountiful in fruits from the soul, making Jesus Christ attractive to all, getting everyone involved in the glory and praise of God.

THEY CAN'T IMPRISON THE MESSAGE

1.12-14 I want to report to you, friends, that my imprisonment here has had the opposite of its intended effect. Instead of being squelched, the Message has actually prospered. All the soldiers here, and everyone else too, found out that I'm

a 1 Traditionally *bishops*   *b* 13 Or *whole palace*

NEW INTERNATIONAL VERSION

everyone else that I am in chains for Christ.
¹⁴Because of my chains, most of the brothers in
the Lord have been encouraged to speak the
word of God more courageously and fearlessly.

¹⁵It is true that some preach Christ out of
envy and rivalry, but others out of goodwill.
¹⁶The latter do so in love, knowing that I am put
here for the defense of the gospel. ¹⁷The former
preach Christ out of selfish ambition, not sincerely, supposing that they can stir up trouble
for me while I am in chains.ᵃ ¹⁸But what does it
matter? The important thing is that in every way,
whether from false motives or true, Christ is
preached. And because of this I rejoice.

Yes, and I will continue to rejoice, ¹⁹for I
know that through your prayers and the help
given by the Spirit of Jesus Christ, what has happened to me will turn out for my deliverance.ᵇ
²⁰I eagerly expect and hope that I will in no way
be ashamed, but will have sufficient courage so
that now as always Christ will be exalted in my
body, whether by life or by death. ²¹For to me, to
live is Christ and to die is gain. ²²If I am to go on
living in the body, this will mean fruitful labor
for me. Yet what shall I choose? I do not know!
²³I am torn between the two: I desire to depart
and be with Christ, which is better by far; ²⁴but
it is more necessary for you that I remain in the
body. ²⁵Convinced of this, I know that I will remain, and I will continue with all of you for your
progress and joy in the faith, ²⁶so that through
my being with you again your joy in Christ Jesus
will overflow on account of me.

²⁷Whatever happens, conduct yourselves in a
manner worthy of the gospel of Christ. Then,
whether I come and see you or only hear about
you in my absence, I will know that you stand
firm in one spirit, contending as one man for the
faith of the gospel ²⁸without being frightened in

THE MESSAGE

in jail because of this Messiah. That piqued
their curiosity, and now they've learned all
about him. Not only that, but most of the
Christians here have become far more sure of
themselves in the faith than ever, speaking out
fearlessly about God, about the Messiah.

1.15-17 It's true that some here preach Christ because with me out of the way, they think they'll
step right into the spotlight. But the others do
it with the best heart in the world. One group
is motivated by pure love, knowing that I am
here defending the Message, wanting to help.
The others, now that I'm out of the picture, are
merely greedy, hoping to get something out of
it for themselves. Their motives are bad. They
see me as their competition, and so the worse it
goes for me, the better—they think—for them.

1.18-21 So how am I to respond? I've decided that I
really don't care about their motives, whether
mixed, bad, or indifferent. Every time one of
them opens his mouth, Christ is proclaimed,
so I just cheer them on!

And I'm going to keep that celebration going
because I know how it's going to turn out.
Through your faithful prayers and the generous
response of the Spirit of Jesus Christ, everything he wants to do in and through me will be
done. I can hardly wait to continue on my
course. I don't expect to be embarrassed in the
least. On the contrary, everything happening to
me in this jail only serves to make Christ more
accurately known, regardless of whether I live
or die. They didn't shut me up; they gave me a
pulpit! Alive, I'm Christ's messenger; dead, I'm
his bounty. Life versus even more life! I can't
lose.

1.22-26 As long as I'm alive in this body, there is
good work for me to do. If I had to choose
right now, I hardly know which I'd choose.
Hard choice! The desire to break camp here
and be with Christ is powerful. Some days I
can think of nothing better. But most days, because of what you are going through, I am sure
that it's better for me to stick it out here. So I
plan to be around awhile, companion to you as
your growth and joy in this life of trusting God
continues. You can start looking forward to a
great reunion when I come visit you again.
We'll be praising Christ, enjoying each other.

1.27-30 Meanwhile, live in such a way that you are a
credit to the Message of Christ. Let nothing in
your conduct hang on whether I come or not.
Your conduct must be the same whether I show
up to see things for myself or hear of it from a
distance. Stand united, singular in vision, contending for people's trust in the Message, the
good news, not flinching or dodging in the

NEW INTERNATIONAL VERSION

any way by those who oppose you. This is a sign to them that they will be destroyed, but that you will be saved—and that by God. ²⁹For it has been granted to you on behalf of Christ not only to believe on him, but also to suffer for him, ³⁰since you are going through the same struggle you saw I had, and now hear that I still have.

IMITATING CHRIST'S HUMILITY

2 If you have any encouragement from being united with Christ, if any comfort from his love, if any fellowship with the Spirit, if any tenderness and compassion, ²then make my joy complete by being like-minded, having the same love, being one in spirit and purpose. ³Do nothing out of selfish ambition or vain conceit, but in humility consider others better than yourselves. ⁴Each of you should look not only to your own interests, but also to the interests of others.

⁵Your attitude should be the same as that of Christ Jesus:

⁶Who, being in very nature*ᵃ* God,
   did not consider equality with God
      something to be grasped,
⁷but made himself nothing,
   taking the very nature*ᵇ* of a servant,
   being made in human likeness.
⁸And being found in appearance as a man,
   he humbled himself
   and became obedient to death—
      even death on a cross!
⁹Therefore God exalted him to the highest
   place
   and gave him the name that is above every
   name,
¹⁰that at the name of Jesus every knee should
   bow,
   in heaven and on earth and under the
   earth,
¹¹and every tongue confess that Jesus Christ is
   Lord,
   to the glory of God the Father.

SHINING AS STARS

¹²Therefore, my dear friends, as you have always obeyed—not only in my presence, but now much more in my absence—continue to work out your salvation with fear and trembling, ¹³for it is God who works in you to will and to act according to his good purpose.

ᵃ 6 Or in the form of   *ᵇ 7 Or the form*

THE MESSAGE

slightest before the opposition. Your courage and unity will show them what they're up against: defeat for them, victory for you—and both because of God. There's far more to this life than trusting in Christ. There's also suffering for him. And the suffering is as much a gift as the trusting. You're involved in the same kind of struggle you saw me go through, on which you are now getting an updated report in this letter.

HE TOOK ON THE STATUS OF A SLAVE

2.1-4   2 If you've gotten anything at all out of following Christ, if his love has made any difference in your life, if being in a community of the Spirit means anything to you, if you have a heart, if you *care*—then do me a favor: Agree with each other, love each other, be deep-spirited friends. Don't push your way to the front; don't sweet-talk your way to the top. Put yourself aside, and help others get ahead. Don't be obsessed with getting your own advantage. Forget yourselves long enough to lend a helping hand.

2.5-8   Think of yourselves the way Christ Jesus thought of himself. He had equal status with God but didn't think so much of himself that he had to cling to the advantages of that status no matter what. Not at all. When the time came, he set aside the privileges of deity and took on the status of a slave, became *human*! Having become human, he stayed human. It was an incredibly humbling process. He didn't claim special privileges. Instead, he lived a selfless, obedient life and then died a selfless, obedient death—and the worst kind of death at that: a crucifixion.

2.9-11   Because of that obedience, God lifted him high and honored him far beyond anyone or anything, ever, so that all created beings in heaven and on earth—even those long ago dead and buried—will bow in worship before this Jesus Christ, and call out in praise that he is the Master of all, to the glorious honor of God the Father.

REJOICING TOGETHER

2.12-13   What I'm getting at, friends, is that you should simply keep on doing what you've done from the beginning. When I was living among you, you lived in responsive obedience. Now that I'm separated from you, keep it up. Better yet, redouble your efforts. Be energetic in your life of salvation, reverent and sensitive before God. That energy is *God's* energy, an energy deep within you, God himself willing and working at what will give him the most pleasure.

NEW INTERNATIONAL VERSION

¹⁴Do everything without complaining or arguing, ¹⁵so that you may become blameless and pure, children of God without fault in a crooked and depraved generation, in which you shine like stars in the universe ¹⁶as you hold out*a* the word of life—in order that I may boast on the day of Christ that I did not run or labor for nothing. ¹⁷But even if I am being poured out like a drink offering on the sacrifice and service coming from your faith, I am glad and rejoice with all of you. ¹⁸So you too should be glad and rejoice with me.

TIMOTHY AND EPAPHRODITUS

¹⁹I hope in the Lord Jesus to send Timothy to you soon, that I also may be cheered when I receive news about you. ²⁰I have no one else like him, who takes a genuine interest in your welfare. ²¹For everyone looks out for his own interests, not those of Jesus Christ. ²²But you know that Timothy has proved himself, because as a son with his father he has served with me in the work of the gospel. ²³I hope, therefore, to send him as soon as I see how things go with me. ²⁴And I am confident in the Lord that I myself will come soon.

²⁵But I think it is necessary to send back to you Epaphroditus, my brother, fellow worker and fellow soldier, who is also your messenger, whom you sent to take care of my needs. ²⁶For he longs for all of you and is distressed because you heard he was ill. ²⁷Indeed he was ill, and almost died. But God had mercy on him, and not on him only but also on me, to spare me sorrow upon sorrow. ²⁸Therefore I am all the more eager to send him, so that when you see him again you may be glad and I may have less anxiety. ²⁹Welcome him in the Lord with great joy, and honor men like him, ³⁰because he almost died for the work of Christ, risking his life to make up for the help you could not give me.

NO CONFIDENCE IN THE FLESH

3 Finally, my brothers, rejoice in the Lord! It is no trouble for me to write the same things to you again, and it is a safeguard for you.

a 16 Or hold on to

THE MESSAGE

2.14-16 Do everything readily and cheerfully—no bickering, no second-guessing allowed! Go out into the world uncorrupted, a breath of fresh air in this squalid and polluted society. Provide people with a glimpse of good living and of the living God. Carry the light-giving Message into the night so I'll have good cause to be proud of you on the day that Christ returns. You'll be living proof that I didn't go to all this work for nothing.

2.17-18 Even if I am executed here and now, I'll rejoice in being an element in the offering of your faith that you make on Christ's altar, a part of your rejoicing. But turnabout's fair play—you must join me in *my* rejoicing. Whatever you do, don't feel sorry for me.

2.19-24 I plan (according to Jesus' plan) to send Timothy to you very soon so he can bring back all the news of you he can gather. Oh, how that will do my heart good! I have no one quite like Timothy. He is loyal, and genuinely concerned for you. Most people around here are looking out for themselves, with little concern for the things of Jesus. But you know yourselves that Timothy's the real thing. He's been a devoted son to me as together we've delivered the Message. As soon as I see how things are going to fall out for me here, I plan to send him off. And then I'm hoping and praying to be right on his heels.

2.25-27 But for right now, I'm dispatching Epaphroditus, my good friend and companion in my work. You sent him to help me out; now I'm sending him to help you out. He has been wanting in the worst way to get back with you. Especially since recovering from the illness you heard about, he's been wanting to get back and reassure you that he is just fine. He nearly died, as you know, but God had mercy on him. And not only on him—he had mercy on me, too. His death would have been one huge grief piled on top of all the others.

2.28-30 So you can see why I'm so delighted to send him on to you. When you see him again, hale and hearty, how you'll rejoice and how relieved I'll be. Give him a grand welcome, a joyful embrace! People like him deserve the best you can give. Remember the ministry to me that you started but weren't able to complete? Well, in the process of finishing up that work, he put his life on the line and nearly died doing it.

TO KNOW HIM PERSONALLY

3.1 **3** And that's about it, friends. Be glad in God! I don't mind repeating what I have written in earlier letters, and I hope you don't mind hearing it again. Better safe than sorry—so here goes.

NEW INTERNATIONAL VERSION

²Watch out for those dogs, those men who do evil, those mutilators of the flesh. ³For it is we who are the circumcision, we who worship by the Spirit of God, who glory in Christ Jesus, and who put no confidence in the flesh— ⁴though I myself have reasons for such confidence.

If anyone else thinks he has reasons to put confidence in the flesh, I have more: ⁵circumcised on the eighth day, of the people of Israel, of the tribe of Benjamin, a Hebrew of Hebrews; in regard to the law, a Pharisee; ⁶as for zeal, persecuting the church; as for legalistic righteousness, faultless.

⁷But whatever was to my profit I now consider loss for the sake of Christ. ⁸What is more, I consider everything a loss compared to the surpassing greatness of knowing Christ Jesus my Lord, for whose sake I have lost all things. I consider them rubbish, that I may gain Christ ⁹and be found in him, not having a righteousness of my own that comes from the law, but that which is through faith in Christ—the righteousness that comes from God and is by faith. ¹⁰I want to know Christ and the power of his resurrection and the fellowship of sharing in his sufferings, becoming like him in his death, ¹¹and so, somehow, to attain to the resurrection from the dead.

PRESSING ON TOWARD THE GOAL

¹²Not that I have already obtained all this, or have already been made perfect, but I press on to take hold of that for which Christ Jesus took hold of me. ¹³Brothers, I do not consider myself yet to have taken hold of it. But one thing I do: Forgetting what is behind and straining toward what is ahead, ¹⁴I press on toward the goal to win the prize for which God has called me heavenward in Christ Jesus.

¹⁵All of us who are mature should take such a view of things. And if on some point you think differently, that too God will make clear to you. ¹⁶Only let us live up to what we have already attained.

THE MESSAGE

3.2-6   Steer clear of the barking dogs, those religious busybodies, all bark and no bite. All they're interested in is appearances—knife-happy circumcisers, I call them. The *real* believers are the ones the Spirit of God leads to work away at this ministry, filling the air with Christ's praise as we do it. We couldn't carry this off by our own efforts, and we know it— even though we can list what many might think are impressive credentials. You know my pedigree: a legitimate birth, circumcised on the eighth day; an Israelite from the elite tribe of Benjamin; a strict and devout adherent to God's law; a fiery defender of the purity of my religion, even to the point of persecuting Christians; a meticulous observer of everything set down in God's law Book.

3.7-9   The very credentials these people are waving around as something special, I'm tearing up and throwing out with the trash—along with everything else I used to take credit for. And why? Because of Christ. Yes, all the things I once thought were so important are gone from my life. Compared to the high privilege of knowing Christ Jesus as my Master, firsthand, everything I once thought I had going for me is insignificant—dog dung. I've dumped it all in the trash so that I could embrace Christ and be embraced by him. I didn't want some petty, inferior brand of righteousness that comes from keeping a list of rules when I could get the robust kind that comes from trusting Christ—*God's* righteousness.

3.10-11   I gave up all that inferior stuff so I could know Christ personally, experience his resurrection power, be a partner in his suffering, and go all the way with him to death itself. If there was any way to get in on the resurrection from the dead, I wanted to do it.

FOCUSED ON THE GOAL

3.12-14 I'm not saying that I have this all together, that I have it made. But I am well on my way, reaching out for Christ, who has so wondrously reached out for me. Friends, don't get me wrong: By no means do I count myself an expert in all of this, but I've got my eye on the goal, where God is beckoning us onward—to Jesus. I'm off and running, and I'm not turning back.

3.15-16   So let's keep focused on that goal, those of us who want everything God has for us. If any of you have something else in mind, something less than total commitment, God will clear your blurred vision—you'll see it yet! Now that we're on the right track, let's stay on it.

NEW INTERNATIONAL VERSION

¹⁷Join with others in following my example, brothers, and take note of those who live according to the pattern we gave you. ¹⁸For, as I have often told you before and now say again even with tears, many live as enemies of the cross of Christ. ¹⁹Their destiny is destruction, their god is their stomach, and their glory is in their shame. Their mind is on earthly things. ²⁰But our citizenship is in heaven. And we eagerly await a Savior from there, the Lord Jesus Christ, ²¹who, by the power that enables him to bring everything under his control, will transform our lowly bodies so that they will be like his glorious body.

4 Therefore, my brothers, you whom I love and long for, my joy and crown, that is how you should stand firm in the Lord, dear friends!

EXHORTATIONS

²I plead with Euodia and I plead with Syntyche to agree with each other in the Lord. ³Yes, and I ask you, loyal yokefellow,ᵃ help these women who have contended at my side in the cause of the gospel, along with Clement and the rest of my fellow workers, whose names are in the book of life.

⁴Rejoice in the Lord always. I will say it again: Rejoice! ⁵Let your gentleness be evident to all. The Lord is near. ⁶Do not be anxious about anything, but in everything, by prayer and petition, with thanksgiving, present your requests to God. ⁷And the peace of God, which transcends all understanding, will guard your hearts and your minds in Christ Jesus.

⁸Finally, brothers, whatever is true, whatever is noble, whatever is right, whatever is pure, whatever is lovely, whatever is admirable—if anything is excellent or praiseworthy—think about such things. ⁹Whatever you have learned

THE MESSAGE

3.17-19 Stick with me, friends. Keep track of those you see running this same course, headed for this same goal. There are many out there taking other paths, choosing other goals, and trying to get you to go along with them. I've warned you of them many times; sadly, I'm having to do it again. All they want is easy street. They hate Christ's Cross. But easy street is a dead-end street. Those who live there make their bellies their gods; belches are their praise; all they can think of is their appetites.

3.20-21 But there's far more to life for us. We're citizens of high heaven! We're waiting the arrival of the Savior, the Master, Jesus Christ, who will transform our earthy bodies into glorious bodies like his own. He'll make us beautiful and whole with the same powerful skill by which he is putting everything as it should be, under and around him.

4.1 **4** My dear, dear friends! I love you so much. I do want the very best for you. You make me feel such joy, fill me with such pride. Don't waver. Stay on track, steady in God.

PRAY ABOUT EVERYTHING

4.2 I urge Euodia and Syntyche to iron out their differences and make up. God doesn't want his children holding grudges.

4.3 And, oh, yes, Syzygus, since you're right there to help them work things out, do your best with them. These women worked for the Message hand in hand with Clement and me, and with the other veterans—worked as hard as any of us. Remember, their names are also in the book of life.

4.4-5 Celebrate God all day, every day. I mean, *revel* in him! Make it as clear as you can to all you meet that you're on their side, working with them and not against them. Help them see that the Master is about to arrive. He could show up any minute!

4.6-7 Don't fret or worry. Instead of worrying, pray. Let petitions and praises shape your worries into prayers, letting God know your concerns. Before you know it, a sense of God's wholeness, everything coming together for good, will come and settle you down. It's wonderful what happens when Christ displaces worry at the center of your life.

4.8-9 Summing it all up, friends, I'd say you'll do best by filling your minds and meditating on things true, noble, reputable, authentic, compelling, gracious—the best, not the worst; the beautiful, not the ugly; things to praise, not things to curse. Put into practice what you

---

ᵃ 3 Or loyal *Syzygus*

NEW INTERNATIONAL VERSION

or received or heard from me, or seen in me—put it into practice. And the God of peace will be with you.

THANKS FOR THEIR GIFTS

[10]I rejoice greatly in the Lord that at last you have renewed your concern for me. Indeed, you have been concerned, but you had no opportunity to show it. [11]I am not saying this because I am in need, for I have learned to be content whatever the circumstances. [12]I know what it is to be in need, and I know what it is to have plenty. I have learned the secret of being content in any and every situation, whether well fed or hungry, whether living in plenty or in want. [13]I can do everything through him who gives me strength.

[14]Yet it was good of you to share in my troubles. [15]Moreover, as you Philippians know, in the early days of your acquaintance with the gospel, when I set out from Macedonia, not one church shared with me in the matter of giving and receiving, except you only; [16]for even when I was in Thessalonica, you sent me aid again and again when I was in need. [17]Not that I am looking for a gift, but I am looking for what may be credited to your account. [18]I have received full payment and even more; I am amply supplied, now that I have received from Epaphroditus the gifts you sent. They are a fragrant offering, an acceptable sacrifice, pleasing to God. [19]And my God will meet all your needs according to his glorious riches in Christ Jesus.

[20]To our God and Father be glory for ever and ever. Amen.

FINAL GREETINGS

[21]Greet all the saints in Christ Jesus. The brothers who are with me send greetings. [22]All the saints send you greetings, especially those who belong to Caesar's household.

[23]The grace of the Lord Jesus Christ be with your spirit. Amen. [a]

THE MESSAGE

learned from me, what you heard and saw and realized. Do that, and God, who makes everything work together, will work you into his most excellent harmonies.

CONTENT WHATEVER THE CIRCUMSTANCES

4.10-14 I'm glad in God, far happier than you would ever guess—happy that you're again showing such strong concern for me. Not that you ever quit praying and thinking about me. You just had no chance to show it. Actually, I don't have a sense of needing anything personally. I've learned by now to be quite content whatever my circumstances. I'm just as happy with little as with much, with much as with little. I've found the recipe for being happy whether full or hungry, hands full or hands empty. Whatever I have, wherever I am, I can make it through anything in the One who makes me who I am. I don't mean that your help didn't mean a lot to me—it did. It was a beautiful thing that you came alongside me in my troubles.

4.15-17 You Philippians well know, and you can be sure I'll never forget it, that when I first left Macedonia province, venturing out with the Message, not one church helped out in the give-and-take of this work except you. You were the only one. Even while I was in Thessalonica, you helped out—and not only once, but twice. Not that I'm looking for handouts, but I do want you to experience the blessing that issues from generosity.

4.18-20 And now I have it all—and keep getting more! The gifts you sent with Epaphroditus were more than enough, like a sweet-smelling sacrifice roasting on the altar, filling the air with fragrance, pleasing God no end. You can be sure that God will take care of everything you need, his generosity exceeding even yours in the glory that pours from Jesus. Our God and Father abounds in glory that just pours out into eternity. Yes.

4.21-22 Give our regards to every Christian you meet. Our friends here say hello. All the Christians here, especially the believers who work in the palace of Caesar, want to be remembered to you.

4.23 Receive and experience the amazing grace of the Master, Jesus Christ, deep, deep within yourselves.

---

[a] 23 Some manuscripts do not have *Amen*.

COLOSSIANS

COLOSSIANS

1 Paul, an apostle of Christ Jesus by the will of God, and Timothy our brother,

²To the holy and faithful*ᵃ* brothers in Christ at Colosse:

Grace and peace to you from God our Father.*ᵇ*

THANKSGIVING AND PRAYER

³We always thank God, the Father of our Lord Jesus Christ, when we pray for you, ⁴because we have heard of your faith in Christ Jesus and of the love you have for all the saints— ⁵the faith and love that spring from the hope that is stored up for you in heaven and that you have already heard about in the word of truth, the gospel ⁶that has come to you. All over the world this gospel is bearing fruit and growing, just as it has been doing among you since the day you heard it and understood God's grace in all its truth. ⁷You learned it from Epaphras, our dear fellow servant, who is a faithful minister of Christ on our*ᶜ* behalf, ⁸and who also told us of your love in the Spirit.

⁹For this reason, since the day we heard about you, we have not stopped praying for you and asking God to fill you with the knowledge of his will through all spiritual wisdom and understanding. ¹⁰And we pray this in order that you may live a life worthy of the Lord and may please him in every way: bearing fruit in every good work, growing in the knowledge of God, ¹¹being strengthened with all power according to his glorious might so that you may have great endurance and patience, and joyfully ¹²giving thanks to the Father, who has qualified you*ᵈ* to share in the inheritance of the saints in the king-

1.1-2 **1** I, Paul, have been sent on special assignment by Christ as part of God's master plan. Together with my friend Timothy, I greet the Christians and stalwart followers of Christ who live in Colosse. May everything good from God our Father be yours!

WORKING IN HIS ORCHARD

1.3-5 Our prayers for you are always spilling over into thanksgivings. We can't quit thanking God our Father and Jesus our Messiah for you! We keep getting reports on your steady faith in Christ, our Jesus, and the love you continuously extend to all Christians. The lines of purpose in your lives never grow slack, tightly tied as they are to your future in heaven, kept taut by hope.

1.5-8 The Message is as true among you today as when you first heard it. It doesn't diminish or weaken over time. It's the same all over the world. The Message bears fruit and gets larger and stronger, just as it has in you. From the very first day you heard and recognized the truth of what God is doing, you've been hungry for more. It's as vigorous in you now as when you learned it from our friend and close associate Epaphras. He is one reliable worker for Christ! I could always depend on him. He's the one who told us how thoroughly love had been worked into your lives by the Spirit.

1.9-12 Be assured that from the first day we heard of you, we haven't stopped praying for you, asking God to give you wise minds and spirits attuned to his will, and so acquire a thorough understanding of the ways in which God works. We pray that you'll live well for the Master, making him proud of you as you work hard in his orchard. As you learn more and more how God works, you will learn how to do *your* work. We pray that you'll have the strength to stick it out over the long haul—not the grim strength of gritting your teeth but the glory-strength God gives. It is strength that endures the unendurable and spills over into joy, thanking the Father who makes us strong enough to take part in everything bright and beautiful that he has for us.

ᵃ 2 Or *believing*   *ᵇ 2* Some manuscripts *Father and the Lord Jesus Christ*   *ᶜ 7* Some manuscripts *your*
ᵈ 12 Some manuscripts *us*

NEW INTERNATIONAL VERSION

dom of light. ¹³For he has rescued us from the dominion of darkness and brought us into the kingdom of the Son he loves, ¹⁴in whom we have redemption,ᵃ the forgiveness of sins.

THE SUPREMACY OF CHRIST

¹⁵He is the image of the invisible God, the firstborn over all creation. ¹⁶For by him all things were created: things in heaven and on earth, visible and invisible, whether thrones or powers or rulers or authorities; all things were created by him and for him. ¹⁷He is before all things, and in him all things hold together. ¹⁸And he is the head of the body, the church; he is the beginning and the firstborn from among the dead, so that in everything he might have the supremacy. ¹⁹For God was pleased to have all his fullness dwell in him, ²⁰and through him to reconcile to himself all things, whether things on earth or things in heaven, by making peace through his blood, shed on the cross.

²¹Once you were alienated from God and were enemies in your minds because ofᵇ your evil behavior. ²²But now he has reconciled you by Christ's physical body through death to present you holy in his sight, without blemish and free from accusation— ²³if you continue in your faith, established and firm, not moved from the hope held out in the gospel. This is the gospel that you heard and that has been proclaimed to every creature under heaven, and of which I, Paul, have become a servant.

PAUL'S LABOR FOR THE CHURCH

²⁴Now I rejoice in what was suffered for you, and I fill up in my flesh what is still lacking in regard to Christ's afflictions, for the sake of his body, which is the church. ²⁵I have become its servant by the commission God gave me to present to you the word of God in its fullness—

THE MESSAGE

1.13-14   God rescued us from dead-end alleys and dark dungeons. He's set us up in the kingdom of the Son he loves so much, the Son who got us out of the pit we were in, got rid of the sins we were doomed to keep repeating.

CHRIST HOLDS IT ALL TOGETHER

1.15-18 We look at this Son and see the God who cannot be seen. We look at this Son and see God's original purpose in everything created. For everything, absolutely everything, above and below, visible and invisible, rank after rank after rank of angels—*everything* got started in him and finds its purpose in him. He was there before any of it came into existence and holds it all together right up to this moment. And when it comes to the church, he organizes and holds it together, like a head does a body.

1.18-20   He was supreme in the beginning and—leading the resurrection parade—he is supreme in the end. From beginning to end he's there, towering far above everything, everyone. So spacious is he, so roomy, that everything of God finds its proper place in him without crowding. Not only that, but all the broken and dislocated pieces of the universe—people and things, animals and atoms—get properly fixed and fit together in vibrant harmonies, all because of his death, his blood that poured down from the Cross.

1.21-23   You yourselves are a case study of what he does. At one time you all had your backs turned to God, thinking rebellious thoughts of him, giving him trouble every chance you got. But now, by giving himself completely at the Cross, actually *dying* for you, Christ brought you over to God's side and put your lives together, whole and holy in his presence. You don't walk away from a gift like that! You stay grounded and steady in that bond of trust, constantly tuned in to the Message, careful not to be distracted or diverted. There is no other Message—just this one. Every creature under heaven gets this same Message. I, Paul, am a messenger of this Message.

☩

1.24-25 I want you to know how glad I am that it's me sitting here in this jail and not you. There's a lot of suffering to be entered into in this world—the kind of suffering Christ takes on. I welcome the chance to take my share in the church's part of that suffering. When I became a servant in this church, I experienced this suffering as a sheer gift, God's way of helping me serve you, laying out the whole truth.

ᵃ 14 A few late manuscripts *redemption through his blood*
ᵇ 21 Or *minds, as shown by*

NEW INTERNATIONAL VERSION

²⁶the mystery that has been kept hidden for ages and generations, but is now disclosed to the saints. ²⁷To them God has chosen to make known among the Gentiles the glorious riches of this mystery, which is Christ in you, the hope of glory.

²⁸We proclaim him, admonishing and teaching everyone with all wisdom, so that we may present everyone perfect in Christ. ²⁹To this end I labor, struggling with all his energy, which so powerfully works in me.

2 I want you to know how much I am struggling for you and for those at Laodicea, and for all who have not met me personally. ²My purpose is that they may be encouraged in heart and united in love, so that they may have the full riches of complete understanding, in order that they may know the mystery of God, namely, Christ, ³in whom are hidden all the treasures of wisdom and knowledge. ⁴I tell you this so that no one may deceive you by fine-sounding arguments. ⁵For though I am absent from you in body, I am present with you in spirit and delight to see how orderly you are and how firm your faith in Christ is.

FREEDOM FROM HUMAN REGULATIONS THROUGH LIFE WITH CHRIST

⁶So then, just as you received Christ Jesus as Lord, continue to live in him, ⁷rooted and built up in him, strengthened in the faith as you were taught, and overflowing with thankfulness.

⁸See to it that no one takes you captive through hollow and deceptive philosophy, which

THE MESSAGE

1.26-29   This mystery has been kept in the dark for a long time, but now it's out in the open. God wanted everyone, not just Jews, to know this rich and glorious secret inside and out, regardless of their background, regardless of their religious standing. The mystery in a nutshell is just this: Christ is in you, therefore you can look forward to sharing in God's glory. It's that simple. That is the substance of our Message. We preach *Christ*, warning people not to add to the Message. We teach in a spirit of profound common sense so that we can bring each person to maturity. To be mature is to be basic. Christ! No more, no less. That's what I'm working so hard at day after day, year after year, doing my best with the energy God so generously gives me.

2.1   2 I want you to realize that I continue to work as hard as I know how for you, and also for the Christians over at Laodicea. Not many of you have met me face-to-face, but that doesn't make any difference. Know that I'm on your side, right alongside you. You're not in this alone.

2.2-4   I want you woven into a tapestry of love, in touch with everything there is to know of God. Then you will have minds confident and at rest, focused on Christ, God's great mystery. All the richest treasures of wisdom and knowledge are embedded in that mystery and nowhere else. And we've been shown the mystery! I'm telling you this because I don't want anyone leading you off on some wild-goose chase, after other so-called mysteries, or "the Secret."

2.5   I'm a long way off, true, and you may never lay eyes on me, but believe me, I'm on your side, right beside you. I am delighted to hear of the careful and orderly ways you conduct your affairs, and impressed with the solid substance of your faith in Christ.

FROM THE SHADOWS TO THE SUBSTANCE

2.6-7   My counsel for you is simple and straightforward: Just go ahead with what you've been given. You received Christ Jesus, the Master; now *live* him. You're deeply rooted in him. You're well constructed upon him. You know your way around the faith. Now do what you've been taught. School's out; quit studying the subject and start *living* it! And let your living spill over into thanksgiving.

2.8-10   Watch out for people who try to dazzle you with big words and intellectual double-talk. They want to drag you off into endless arguments that never amount to anything. They

NEW INTERNATIONAL VERSION

depends on human tradition and the basic principles of this world rather than on Christ.

⁹For in Christ all the fullness of the Deity lives in bodily form, ¹⁰and you have been given fullness in Christ, who is the head over every power and authority. ¹¹In him you were also circumcised, in the putting off of the sinful nature,ᵃ not with a circumcision done by the hands of men but with the circumcision done by Christ, ¹²having been buried with him in baptism and raised with him through your faith in the power of God, who raised him from the dead.

¹³When you were dead in your sins and in the uncircumcision of your sinful nature,ᵇ God made youᶜ alive with Christ. He forgave us all our sins, ¹⁴having canceled the written code, with its regulations, that was against us and that stood opposed to us; he took it away, nailing it to the cross. ¹⁵And having disarmed the powers and authorities, he made a public spectacle of them, triumphing over them by the cross.ᵈ

¹⁶Therefore do not let anyone judge you by what you eat or drink, or with regard to a religious festival, a New Moon celebration or a Sabbath day. ¹⁷These are a shadow of the things that were to come; the reality, however, is found in Christ. ¹⁸Do not let anyone who delights in false humility and the worship of angels disqualify you for the prize. Such a person goes into great detail about what he has seen, and his unspiritual mind puffs him up with idle notions. ¹⁹He has lost connection with the Head, from whom the whole body, supported and held together by its ligaments and sinews, grows as God causes it to grow.

²⁰Since you died with Christ to the basic principles of this world, why, as though you still belonged to it, do you submit to its rules: ²¹"Do not handle! Do not taste! Do not touch!"? ²²These are all destined to perish with use, because they are based on human commands and teachings. ²³Such regulations indeed have an appearance of wisdom, with their self-imposed worship, their false humility and their harsh treatment of the body, but they lack any value in restraining sensual indulgence.

THE MESSAGE

spread their ideas through the empty traditions of human beings and the empty superstitions of spirit beings. But that's not the way of Christ. Everything of God gets expressed in him, so you can see and hear him clearly. You don't need a telescope, a microscope, or a horoscope to realize the fullness of Christ, and the emptiness of the universe without him. When you come to him, that fullness comes together for you, too. His power extends over everything.

2.11-15 Entering into this fullness is not something you figure out or achieve. It's not a matter of being circumcised or keeping a long list of laws. No, you're already *in*—insiders—not through some secretive initiation rite but rather through what Christ has already gone through for you, destroying the power of sin. If it's an initiation ritual you're after, you've already been through it by submitting to baptism. Going under the water was a burial of your old life; coming up out of it was a resurrection, God raising you from the dead as he did Christ. When you were stuck in your old sin-dead life, you were incapable of responding to God. God brought you alive—right along with Christ! Think of it! All sins forgiven, the slate wiped clean, that old arrest warrant canceled and nailed to Christ's Cross. He stripped all the spiritual tyrants in the universe of their sham authority at the Cross and marched them naked through the streets.

2.16-17 So don't put up with anyone pressuring you in details of diet, worship services, or holy days. All those things are mere shadows cast before what was to come; the substance is Christ.

2.18-19 Don't tolerate people who try to run your life, ordering you to bow and scrape, insisting that you join their obsession with angels and that you seek out visions. They're a lot of hot air, that's all they are. They're completely out of touch with the source of life, Christ, who puts us together in one piece, whose very breath and blood flow through us. He is the Head and we are the body. We can grow up healthy in God only as he nourishes us.

2.20-23 So, then, if with Christ you've put all that pretentious and infantile religion behind you, why do you let yourselves be bullied by it? "Don't touch this! Don't taste that! Don't go near this!" Do you think things that are here today and gone tomorrow are worth that kind of attention? Such things sound impressive if said in a deep enough voice. They even give the illusion of being pious and humble and ascetic. But they're just another way of showing off, making yourselves look important.

ᵃ 11 Or *the flesh*   ᵇ 13 Or *your flesh*   ᶜ 13 Some manuscripts *us*   ᵈ 15 Or *them in him*

NEW INTERNATIONAL VERSION

Rules for Holy Living

3 Since, then, you have been raised with Christ, set your hearts on things above, where Christ is seated at the right hand of God. ²Set your minds on things above, not on earthly things. ³For you died, and your life is now hidden with Christ in God. ⁴When Christ, who is your[a] life, appears, then you also will appear with him in glory.

⁵Put to death, therefore, whatever belongs to your earthly nature: sexual immorality, impurity, lust, evil desires and greed, which is idolatry. ⁶Because of these, the wrath of God is coming.[b] ⁷You used to walk in these ways, in the life you once lived. ⁸But now you must rid yourselves of all such things as these: anger, rage, malice, slander, and filthy language from your lips. ⁹Do not lie to each other, since you have taken off your old self with its practices ¹⁰and have put on the new self, which is being renewed in knowledge in the image of its Creator. ¹¹Here there is no Greek or Jew, circumcised or uncircumcised, barbarian, Scythian, slave or free, but Christ is all, and is in all.

¹²Therefore, as God's chosen people, holy and dearly loved, clothe yourselves with compassion, kindness, humility, gentleness and patience. ¹³Bear with each other and forgive whatever grievances you may have against one another. Forgive as the Lord forgave you. ¹⁴And over all these virtues put on love, which binds them all together in perfect unity.

¹⁵Let the peace of Christ rule in your hearts, since as members of one body you were called to peace. And be thankful. ¹⁶Let the word of Christ dwell in you richly as you teach and admonish one another with all wisdom, and as you sing psalms, hymns and spiritual songs with grati-

---

THE MESSAGE

He Is Your Life

3.1-2 **3** So if you're serious about living this new resurrection life with Christ, *act* like it. Pursue the things over which Christ presides. Don't shuffle along, eyes to the ground, absorbed with the things right in front of you. Look up, and be alert to what is going on around Christ—that's where the action is. See things from *his* perspective.

3.3-4 Your old life is dead. Your new life, which is your *real* life—even though invisible to spectators—is with Christ in God. *He* is your life. When Christ (your real life, remember) shows up again on this earth, you'll show up, too—the real you, the glorious you. Meanwhile, be content with obscurity, like Christ.

3.5-8 And that means killing off everything connected with that way of death: sexual promiscuity, impurity, lust, doing whatever you feel like whenever you feel like it, and grabbing whatever attracts your fancy. That's a life shaped by things and feelings instead of by God. It's because of this kind of thing that God is about to explode in anger. It wasn't long ago that you were doing all that stuff and not knowing any better. But you know better now, so make sure it's all gone for good: bad temper, irritability, meanness, profanity, dirty talk.

3.9-11 Don't lie to one another. You're done with that old life. It's like a filthy set of ill-fitting clothes you've stripped off and put in the fire. Now you're dressed in a new wardrobe. Every item of your new way of life is custom-made by the Creator, with his label on it. All the old fashions are now obsolete. Words like Jewish and non-Jewish, religious and irreligious, insider and outsider, uncivilized and uncouth, slave and free, mean nothing. From now on everyone is defined by Christ, everyone is included in Christ.

3.12-14 So, chosen by God for this new life of love, dress in the wardrobe God picked out for you: compassion, kindness, humility, quiet strength, discipline. Be even-tempered, content with second place, quick to forgive an offense. Forgive as quickly and completely as the Master forgave you. And regardless of what else you put on, wear love. It's your basic, all-purpose garment. Never be without it.

3.15-17 Let the peace of Christ keep you in tune with each other, in step with each other. None of this going off and doing your own thing. And cultivate thankfulness. Let the Word of Christ—the Message—have the run of the house. Give it plenty of room in your lives. Instruct and direct one another using good common sense. And sing, sing your hearts out to

---

a 4 Some manuscripts *our*   *b 6* Some early manuscripts *coming on those who are disobedient*

NEW INTERNATIONAL VERSION

tude in your hearts to God. [17]And whatever you do, whether in word or deed, do it all in the name of the Lord Jesus, giving thanks to God the Father through him.

RULES FOR CHRISTIAN HOUSEHOLDS

[18]Wives, submit to your husbands, as is fitting in the Lord.

[19]Husbands, love your wives and do not be harsh with them.

[20]Children, obey your parents in everything, for this pleases the Lord.

[21]Fathers, do not embitter your children, or they will become discouraged.

[22]Slaves, obey your earthly masters in everything; and do it, not only when their eye is on you and to win their favor, but with sincerity of heart and reverence for the Lord. [23]Whatever you do, work at it with all your heart, as working for the Lord, not for men, [24]since you know that you will receive an inheritance from the Lord as a reward. It is the Lord Christ you are serving. [25]Anyone who does wrong will be repaid for his wrong, and there is no favoritism.

4 Masters, provide your slaves with what is right and fair, because you know that you also have a Master in heaven.

FURTHER INSTRUCTIONS

[2]Devote yourselves to prayer, being watchful and thankful. [3]And pray for us, too, that God may open a door for our message, so that we may proclaim the mystery of Christ, for which I am in chains. [4]Pray that I may proclaim it clearly, as I should. [5]Be wise in the way you act toward outsiders; make the most of every opportunity. [6]Let your conversation be always full of grace, seasoned with salt, so that you may know how to answer everyone.

FINAL GREETINGS

[7]Tychicus will tell you all the news about me. He is a dear brother, a faithful minister and fellow servant in the Lord. [8]I am sending him to you for the express purpose that you may know about our[a] circumstances and that he may encourage your hearts. [9]He is coming with Onesimus, our faithful and dear brother, who is one of you. They will tell you everything that is happening here.

[10]My fellow prisoner Aristarchus sends you his greetings, as does Mark, the cousin of Barna-

THE MESSAGE

God! Let every detail in your lives—words, actions, whatever—be done in the name of the Master, Jesus, thanking God the Father every step of the way.

✠

3.18 Wives, understand and support your husbands by submitting to them in ways that honor the Master.

3.19 Husbands, go all out in love for your wives. Don't take advantage of them.

3.20 Children, do what your parents tell you. This delights the Master no end.

3.21 Parents, don't come down too hard on your children or you'll crush their spirits.

3.22-25 Servants, do what you're told by your earthly masters. And don't just do the minimum that will get you by. Do your best. Work from the heart for your real Master, for God, confident that you'll get paid in full when you come into your inheritance. Keep in mind always that the ultimate Master you're serving is Christ. The sullen servant who does shoddy work will be held responsible. Being Christian doesn't cover up bad work.

4.1 4 And masters, treat your servants considerately. Be fair with them. Don't forget for a minute that you, too, serve a Master—God in heaven.

PRAY FOR OPEN DOORS

4.2-4 Pray diligently. Stay alert, with your eyes wide open in gratitude. Don't forget to pray for us, that God will open doors for telling the mystery of Christ, even while I'm locked up in this jail. Pray that every time I open my mouth I'll be able to make Christ plain as day to them.

4.5-6 Use your heads as you live and work among outsiders. Don't miss a trick. Make the most of every opportunity. Be gracious in your speech. The goal is to bring out the best in others in a conversation, not put them down, not cut them out.

4.7-9 My good friend Tychicus will tell you all about me. He's a trusted minister and companion in the service of the Master. I've sent him to you so that you would know how things are with us, and so he could encourage you in your faith. And I've sent Onesimus with him. Onesimus is one of you, and has become such a trusted and dear brother! Together they'll bring you up-to-date on everything that has been going on here.

4.10-11 Aristarchus, who is in jail here with me, sends greetings; also Mark, cousin of Barnabas

NEW INTERNATIONAL VERSION

bas. (You have received instructions about him; if he comes to you, welcome him.) ¹¹Jesus, who is called Justus, also sends greetings. These are the only Jews among my fellow workers for the kingdom of God, and they have proved a comfort to me. ¹²Epaphras, who is one of you and a servant of Christ Jesus, sends greetings. He is always wrestling in prayer for you, that you may stand firm in all the will of God, mature and fully assured. ¹³I vouch for him that he is working hard for you and for those at Laodicea and Hierapolis. ¹⁴Our dear friend Luke, the doctor, and Demas send greetings. ¹⁵Give my greetings to the brothers at Laodicea, and to Nympha and the church in her house.

¹⁶After this letter has been read to you, see that it is also read in the church of the Laodiceans and that you in turn read the letter from Laodicea.

¹⁷Tell Archippus: "See to it that you complete the work you have received in the Lord."

¹⁸I, Paul, write this greeting in my own hand. Remember my chains. Grace be with you.

THE MESSAGE

(you received a letter regarding him; if he shows up, welcome him); and also Jesus, the one they call Justus. These are the only ones left from the old crowd who have stuck with me in working for God's kingdom. Don't think they haven't been a big help!

4.12-13 Epaphras, who is one of you, says hello. What a trooper he has been! He's been tireless in his prayers for you, praying that you'll stand firm, mature and confident in everything God wants you to do. I've watched him closely, and can report on how hard he has worked for you and for those in Laodicea and Hierapolis.

4.14 Luke, good friend and physician, and Demas both send greetings.

4.15 Say hello to our friends in Laodicea; also to Nympha and the church that meets in her house.

4.16 After this letter has been read to you, make sure it gets read also in Laodicea. And get the letter that went to Laodicea and have it read to you.

4.17 And, oh, yes, tell Archippus, "Do your best in the job you received from the Master. Do your very best."

4.18 I'm signing off in my own handwriting— Paul. Remember to pray for me in this jail. Grace be with you.

1 THESSALONIANS

1 THESSALONIANS

1 Paul, Silas[a] and Timothy,

To the church of the Thessalonians in God the Father and the Lord Jesus Christ:

Grace and peace to you.[b]

THANKSGIVING FOR THE THESSALONIANS' FAITH

[2]We always thank God for all of you, mentioning you in our prayers. [3]We continually remember before our God and Father your work produced by faith, your labor prompted by love, and your endurance inspired by hope in our Lord Jesus Christ.

[4]For we know, brothers loved by God, that he has chosen you, [5]because our gospel came to you not simply with words, but also with power, with the Holy Spirit and with deep conviction. You know how we lived among you for your sake. [6]You became imitators of us and of the Lord; in spite of severe suffering, you welcomed the message with the joy given by the Holy Spirit. [7]And so you became a model to all the believers in Macedonia and Achaia. [8]The Lord's message rang out from you not only in Macedonia and Achaia—your faith in God has become known everywhere. Therefore we do not need to say anything about it, [9]for they themselves report what kind of reception you gave us. They tell how you turned to God from idols to serve the living and true God, [10]and to wait for his Son from heaven, whom he raised from the dead—Jesus, who rescues us from the coming wrath.

PAUL'S MINISTRY IN THESSALONICA

2 You know, brothers, that our visit to you was not a failure. [2]We had previously suffered

1 1.1 I, Paul, together here with Silas and Timothy, send greetings to the church at Thessalonica, Christians assembled by God the Father and by the Master, Jesus Christ. God's amazing grace be with you! God's robust peace!

CONVICTIONS OF STEEL

1.2-5 Every time we think of you, we thank God for you. Day and night you're in our prayers as we call to mind your work of faith, your labor of love, and your patience of hope in following our Master, Jesus Christ, before God our Father. It is clear to us, friends, that God not only loves you very much but also has put his hand on you for something special. When the Message we preached came to you, it wasn't just words. Something happened in you. The Holy Spirit put steel in your convictions.

1.5-6 You paid careful attention to the way we lived among you, and determined to live that way yourselves. In imitating us, you imitated the Master. Although great trouble accompanied the Word, you were able to take great joy from the Holy Spirit!—taking the trouble with the joy, the joy with the trouble.

1.7-10 Do you know that all over the provinces of both Macedonia and Achaia believers look up to you? The word has gotten around. Your lives are echoing the Master's Word, not only in the provinces but all over the place. The news of your faith in God is out. We don't even have to say anything anymore—*you're* the message! People come up and tell us how you received us with open arms, how you deserted the dead idols of your old life so you could embrace and serve God, the true God. They marvel at how expectantly you await the arrival of his Son, whom he raised from the dead—Jesus, who rescued us from certain doom.

2 2.1-2 So, friends, it's obvious that our visit to you was no waste of time. We had just been giv-

NEW INTERNATIONAL VERSION

and been insulted in Philippi, as you know, but with the help of our God we dared to tell you his gospel in spite of strong opposition. ³For the appeal we make does not spring from error or impure motives, nor are we trying to trick you. ⁴On the contrary, we speak as men approved by God to be entrusted with the gospel. We are not trying to please men but God, who tests our hearts. ⁵You know we never used flattery, nor did we put on a mask to cover up greed—God is our witness. ⁶We were not looking for praise from men, not from you or anyone else.

As apostles of Christ we could have been a burden to you, ⁷but we were gentle among you, like a mother caring for her little children. ⁸We loved you so much that we were delighted to share with you not only the gospel of God but our lives as well, because you had become so dear to us. ⁹Surely you remember, brothers, our toil and hardship; we worked night and day in order not to be a burden to anyone while we preached the gospel of God to you.

¹⁰You are witnesses, and so is God, of how holy, righteous and blameless we were among you who believed. ¹¹For you know that we dealt with each of you as a father deals with his own children, ¹²encouraging, comforting and urging you to live lives worthy of God, who calls you into his kingdom and glory.

¹³And we also thank God continually because, when you received the word of God, which you heard from us, you accepted it not as the word of men, but as it actually is, the word of God, which is at work in you who believe. ¹⁴For you, brothers, became imitators of God's churches in Judea, which are in Christ Jesus: You suffered from your own countrymen the same things those churches suffered from the Jews, ¹⁵who killed the Lord Jesus and the prophets and

THE MESSAGE

en rough treatment in Philippi, as you know, but that didn't slow us down. We were sure of ourselves in God, and went right ahead and said our piece, presenting God's Message to you, defiant of the opposition.

No Hidden Agendas

2.3-5 God tested us thoroughly to make sure we were qualified to be trusted with this Message. Be assured that when we speak to you we're not after crowd approval—only God approval. Since we've been put through that battery of tests, you're guaranteed that both we and the Message are free of error, mixed motives, or hidden agendas. We never used words to butter you up. No one knows that better than you. And God knows we never used words as a smoke screen to take advantage of you.

2.6-8 Even though we had some standing as Christ's apostles, we never threw our weight around or tried to come across as important, with you or anyone else. We weren't aloof with you. We took you just as you were. We were never patronizing, never condescending, but we cared for you the way a mother cares for her children. We loved you dearly. Not content to just pass on the Message, we wanted to give you our hearts. And we *did*.

2.9-12 You remember us in those days, friends, working our fingers to the bone, up half the night, moonlighting so you wouldn't have the burden of supporting us while we proclaimed God's Message to you. You saw with your own eyes how discreet and courteous we were among you, with keen sensitivity to you as fellow believers. And God knows we weren't freeloaders! You experienced it all firsthand. With each of you we were like a father with his child, holding your hand, whispering encouragement, showing you step-by-step how to live well before God, who called us into his own kingdom, into this delightful life.

2.13 And now we look back on all this and thank God, an artesian well of thanks! When you got the Message of God we preached, you didn't pass it off as just one more human opinion, but you took it to heart as God's true word to you, which it is, God himself at work in you believers!

2.14-16 Friends, do you realize that you followed in the exact footsteps of the churches of God in Judea, those who were the first to follow in the footsteps of Jesus Christ? You got the same bad treatment from your countrymen as they did from theirs, the Jews who killed the Master Jesus (to say nothing of the prophets) and followed it up by running us out of town. They

NEW INTERNATIONAL VERSION

also drove us out. They displease God and are hostile to all men ¹⁶in their effort to keep us from speaking to the Gentiles so that they may be saved. In this way they always heap up their sins to the limit. The wrath of God has come upon them at last. ᵃ

PAUL'S LONGING TO SEE THE THESSALONIANS

¹⁷But, brothers, when we were torn away from you for a short time (in person, not in thought), out of our intense longing we made every effort to see you. ¹⁸For we wanted to come to you—certainly I, Paul, did, again and again—but Satan stopped us. ¹⁹For what is our hope, our joy, or the crown in which we will glory in the presence of our Lord Jesus when he comes? Is it not you? ²⁰Indeed, you are our glory and joy.

3 So when we could stand it no longer, we thought it best to be left by ourselves in Athens. ²We sent Timothy, who is our brother and God's fellow worker ᵇ in spreading the gospel of Christ, to strengthen and encourage you in your faith, ³so that no one would be unsettled by these trials. You know quite well that we were destined for them. ⁴In fact, when we were with you, we kept telling you that we would be persecuted. And it turned out that way, as you well know. ⁵For this reason, when I could stand it no longer, I sent to find out about your faith. I was afraid that in some way the tempter might have tempted you and our efforts might have been useless.

TIMOTHY'S ENCOURAGING REPORT

⁶But Timothy has just now come to us from you and has brought good news about your faith and love. He has told us that you always have pleasant memories of us and that you long to see us, just as we also long to see you. ⁷Therefore, brothers, in all our distress and persecution we were encouraged about you because of your faith. ⁸For now we really live, since you are standing firm in the Lord. ⁹How can we thank God enough for you in return for all the joy we have in the presence of our God because of you? ¹⁰Night and day we pray most earnestly that we may see you again and supply what is lacking in your faith.

¹¹Now may our God and Father himself and our Lord Jesus clear the way for us to come to

THE MESSAGE

make themselves offensive to God and everyone else by trying to keep us from telling people who've never heard of our God how to be saved. They've made a career of opposing God, and have gotten mighty good at it. But God is fed up, ready to put an end to it.

2.17-20 Do you have any idea how very homesick we became for you, dear friends? Even though it hadn't been that long and it was only our bodies that were separated from you, not our hearts, we tried our very best to get back to see you. You can't imagine how much we missed you! I, Paul, tried over and over to get back, but Satan stymied us each time. Who do you think we're going to be proud of when our Master Jesus appears if it's not you? You're our pride and joy!

3.1-2 **3** So when we couldn't stand being separated from you any longer and could find no way to visit you ourselves, we stayed in Athens and sent Timothy to get you up and about, cheering you on so you wouldn't be discouraged by these hard times. He's a brother and companion in the faith, God's man in spreading the Message, preaching Christ.

3.3-5 Not that the troubles should come as any surprise to you. You've always known that we're in for this kind of thing. It's part of our calling. When we were with you, we made it quite clear that there was trouble ahead. And now that it's happened, you know what it's like. That's why I couldn't quit worrying; I had to know for myself how you were doing in the faith. I didn't want the Tempter getting to you and tearing down everything we had built up together.

3.6-8 But now that Timothy is back, bringing this terrific report on your faith and love, we feel a lot better. It's especially gratifying to know that you continue to think well of us, and that you want to see us as much as we want to see you! In the middle of our trouble and hard times here, just knowing how you're doing keeps us going. Knowing that your faith is alive keeps us alive.

3.9-10 What would be an adequate thanksgiving to offer God for all the joy we experience before him because of you? We do what we can, praying away, night and day, asking for the bonus of seeing your faces again and doing what we can to help when your faith falters.

3.11-13 May God our Father himself and our Master Jesus clear the road to you! And may the Mas-

NEW INTERNATIONAL VERSION

you. ¹²May the Lord make your love increase and overflow for each other and for everyone else, just as ours does for you. ¹³May he strengthen your hearts so that you will be blameless and holy in the presence of our God and Father when our Lord Jesus comes with all his holy ones.

LIVING TO PLEASE GOD

4 Finally, brothers, we instructed you how to live in order to please God, as in fact you are living. Now we ask you and urge you in the Lord Jesus to do this more and more. ²For you know what instructions we gave you by the authority of the Lord Jesus.

³It is God's will that you should be sanctified: that you should avoid sexual immorality; ⁴that each of you should learn to control his own body^a in a way that is holy and honorable, ⁵not in passionate lust like the heathen, who do not know God; ⁶and that in this matter no one should wrong his brother or take advantage of him. The Lord will punish men for all such sins, as we have already told you and warned you. ⁷For God did not call us to be impure, but to live a holy life. ⁸Therefore, he who rejects this instruction does not reject man but God, who gives you his Holy Spirit.

⁹Now about brotherly love we do not need to write to you, for you yourselves have been taught by God to love each other. ¹⁰And in fact, you do love all the brothers throughout Macedonia. Yet we urge you, brothers, to do so more and more.

¹¹Make it your ambition to lead a quiet life, to mind your own business and to work with your hands, just as we told you, ¹²so that your daily life may win the respect of outsiders and so that you will not be dependent on anybody.

THE COMING OF THE LORD

¹³Brothers, we do not want you to be ignorant about those who fall asleep, or to grieve like the rest of men, who have no hope. ¹⁴We believe that Jesus died and rose again and so we believe that God will bring with Jesus those who have fallen asleep in him. ¹⁵According to the Lord's own word, we tell you that we who are still alive, who are left till the coming of the Lord, will cer-

^a 4 Or learn to live with his own wife; or learn to acquire a wife

THE MESSAGE

ter pour on the love so it fills your lives and splashes over on everyone around you, just as it does from us to you. May you be infused with strength and purity, filled with confidence in the presence of God our Father when our Master Jesus arrives with all his followers.

YOU'RE GOD-TAUGHT

4.1-3 4 One final word, friends. We ask you—urge is more like it—that you keep on doing what we told you to do to please God, not in a dogged religious plod, but in a living, spirited dance. You know the guidelines we laid out for you from the Master Jesus. God wants you to live a pure life.

Keep yourselves from sexual promiscuity.

4.4-5 Learn to appreciate and give dignity to your body, not abusing it, as is so common among those who know nothing of God.

4.6-7 Don't run roughshod over the concerns of your brothers and sisters. Their concerns are God's concerns, and *he* will take care of them. We've warned you about this before. God hasn't invited us into a disorderly, unkempt life but into something holy and beautiful—as beautiful on the inside as the outside.

4.8 If you disregard this advice, you're not offending your neighbors; you're rejecting God, who is making you a gift of his Holy Spirit.

4.9-10 Regarding life together and getting along with each other, you don't need me to tell you what to do. You're *God*-taught in these matters. Just love one another! You're already good at it; your friends all over the province of Macedonia are the evidence. Keep it up; get better and better at it.

4.11-12 Stay calm; mind your own business; do your own job. You've heard all this from us before, but a reminder never hurts. We want you living in a way that will command the respect of outsiders, not lying around sponging off your friends.

THE MASTER'S COMING

4.13-14 And regarding the question, friends, that has come up about what happens to those already dead and buried, we don't want you in the dark any longer. First off, you must not carry on over them like people who have nothing to look forward to, as if the grave were the last word. Since Jesus died and broke loose from the grave, God will most certainly bring back to life those who died in Jesus.

4.15-18 And then this: We can tell you with complete confidence—we have the Master's word on it—that when the Master comes again to get

NEW INTERNATIONAL VERSION

tainly not precede those who have fallen asleep. ¹⁶For the Lord himself will come down from heaven, with a loud command, with the voice of the archangel and with the trumpet call of God, and the dead in Christ will rise first. ¹⁷After that, we who are still alive and are left will be caught up together with them in the clouds to meet the Lord in the air. And so we will be with the Lord forever. ¹⁸Therefore encourage each other with these words.

5 Now, brothers, about times and dates we do not need to write to you, ²for you know very well that the day of the Lord will come like a thief in the night. ³While people are saying, "Peace and safety," destruction will come on them suddenly, as labor pains on a pregnant woman, and they will not escape.

⁴But you, brothers, are not in darkness so that this day should surprise you like a thief. ⁵You are all sons of the light and sons of the day. We do not belong to the night or to the darkness. ⁶So then, let us not be like others, who are asleep, but let us be alert and self-controlled. ⁷For those who sleep, sleep at night, and those who get drunk, get drunk at night. ⁸But since we belong to the day, let us be self-controlled, putting on faith and love as a breastplate, and the hope of salvation as a helmet. ⁹For God did not appoint us to suffer wrath but to receive salvation through our Lord Jesus Christ. ¹⁰He died for us so that, whether we are awake or asleep, we may live together with him. ¹¹Therefore encourage one another and build each other up, just as in fact you are doing.

FINAL INSTRUCTIONS

¹²Now we ask you, brothers, to respect those who work hard among you, who are over you in the Lord and who admonish you. ¹³Hold them in the highest regard in love because of their work. Live in peace with each other. ¹⁴And we urge you, brothers, warn those who are idle, encour-

THE MESSAGE

us, those of us who are still alive will not get a jump on the dead and leave them behind. In actual fact, they'll be ahead of us. The Master himself will give the command. Archangel thunder! God's trumpet blast! He'll come down from heaven and the dead in Christ will rise— they'll go first. Then the rest of us who are still alive at the time will be caught up with them into the clouds to meet the Master. Oh, we'll be walking on air! And then there will be one huge family reunion with the Master. So reassure one another with these words.

5.1-3 5 I don't think, friends, that I need to deal with the question of when all this is going to happen. You know as well as I that the day of the Master's coming can't be posted on our calendars. He won't call ahead and make an appointment any more than a burglar would. About the time everybody's walking around complacently, congratulating each other— "We've sure got it made! Now we can take it easy!"—suddenly everything will fall apart. It's going to come as suddenly and inescapably as birth pangs to a pregnant woman.

5.4-8 But friends, you're not in the dark, so how could you be taken off guard by any of this? You're sons of Light, daughters of Day. We live under wide open skies and know where we stand. So let's not sleepwalk through life like those others. Let's keep our eyes open and be smart. People sleep at night and get drunk at night. But not us! Since we're creatures of Day, let's act like it. Walk out into the daylight sober, dressed up in faith, love, and the hope of salvation.

5.9-11 God didn't set us up for an angry rejection but for salvation by our Master, Jesus Christ. He died for us, a death that triggered life. Whether we're awake with the living or asleep with the dead, we're *alive* with him! So speak encouraging words to one another. Build up hope so you'll all be together in this, no one left out, no one left behind. I know you're already doing this; just keep on doing it.

THE WAY HE WANTS YOU TO LIVE

5.12-13 And now, friends, we ask you to honor those leaders who work so hard for you, who have been given the responsibility of urging and guiding you along in your obedience. Overwhelm them with appreciation and love!

5.13-15 Get along among yourselves, each of you doing your part. Our counsel is that you warn the freeloaders to get a move on. Gently encourage the stragglers, and reach out for the

NEW INTERNATIONAL VERSION

age the timid, help the weak, be patient with everyone. 15Make sure that nobody pays back wrong for wrong, but always try to be kind to each other and to everyone else.

16Be joyful always; 17pray continually; 18give thanks in all circumstances, for this is God's will for you in Christ Jesus.

19Do not put out the Spirit's fire; 20do not treat prophecies with contempt. 21Test everything. Hold on to the good. 22Avoid every kind of evil.

23May God himself, the God of peace, sanctify you through and through. May your whole spirit, soul and body be kept blameless at the coming of our Lord Jesus Christ. 24The one who calls you is faithful and he will do it.

25Brothers, pray for us. 26Greet all the brothers with a holy kiss. 27I charge you before the Lord to have this letter read to all the brothers.

28The grace of our Lord Jesus Christ be with you.

THE MESSAGE

exhausted, pulling them to their feet. Be patient with each person, attentive to individual needs. And be careful that when you get on each other's nerves you don't snap at each other. Look for the best in each other, and always do your best to bring it out.

5.16-18   Be cheerful no matter what; pray all the time; thank God no matter what happens. This is the way God wants you who belong to Christ Jesus to live.

5.19-22   Don't suppress the Spirit, and don't stifle those who have a word from the Master. On the other hand, don't be gullible. Check out everything, and keep only what's good. Throw out anything tainted with evil.

5.23-24   May God himself, the God who makes everything holy and whole, make you holy and whole, put you together—spirit, soul, and body—and keep you fit for the coming of our Master, Jesus Christ. The One who called you is completely dependable. If he said it, he'll do it!

5.25-27   Friends, keep up your prayers for us. Greet all the Christians there with a holy embrace. And make sure this letter gets read to all the brothers and sisters. Don't leave anyone out.

5.28   The amazing grace of Jesus Christ be with you!

2 THESSALONIANS

2 THESSALONIANS

1 Paul, Silas[a] and Timothy,

To the church of the Thessalonians in God our Father and the Lord Jesus Christ:

²Grace and peace to you from God the Father and the Lord Jesus Christ.

THANKSGIVING AND PRAYER

³We ought always to thank God for you, brothers, and rightly so, because your faith is growing more and more, and the love every one of you has for each other is increasing. ⁴Therefore, among God's churches we boast about your perseverance and faith in all the persecutions and trials you are enduring.

⁵All this is evidence that God's judgment is right, and as a result you will be counted worthy of the kingdom of God, for which you are suffering. ⁶God is just: He will pay back trouble to those who trouble you ⁷and give relief to you who are troubled, and to us as well. This will happen when the Lord Jesus is revealed from heaven in blazing fire with his powerful angels. ⁸He will punish those who do not know God and do not obey the gospel of our Lord Jesus. ⁹They will be punished with everlasting destruction and shut out from the presence of the Lord and from the majesty of his power ¹⁰on the day he comes to be glorified in his holy people and to be marveled at among all those who have believed. This includes you, because you believed our testimony to you.

¹¹With this in mind, we constantly pray for you, that our God may count you worthy of his calling, and that by his power he may fulfill every good purpose of yours and every act prompted by your faith. ¹²We pray this so that the name of our Lord Jesus may be glorified in you, and you in him, according to the grace of our God and the Lord Jesus Christ.[b]

1 1.1-2 I, Paul, together with Silas and Timothy, greet the church of the Thessalonian Christians in the name of God our Father and our Master, Jesus Christ. Our God gives you everything you need, makes you everything you're to be.

JUSTICE IS ON THE WAY

1.3-4 You need to know, friends, that thanking God over and over for you is not only a pleasure; it's a must. We *have* to do it. Your faith is growing phenomenally; your love for each other is developing wonderfully. Why, it's only right that we give thanks. We're so proud of you; you're so steady and determined in your faith despite all the hard times that have come down on you. We tell everyone we meet in the churches all about you.

1.5-10 All this trouble is a clear sign that God has decided to make you fit for the kingdom. You're suffering now, but justice is on the way. When the Master Jesus appears out of heaven in a blaze of fire with his strong angels, he'll even up the score by settling accounts with those who gave you such a bad time. His coming will be the break we've been waiting for. Those who refuse to know God and refuse to obey the Message will pay for what they've done. Eternal exile from the presence of the Master and his splendid power is their sentence. But on that very same day when he comes, he will be exalted by his followers and celebrated by all who believe—and all because you believed what we told you.

1.11-12 Because we know that this extraordinary day is just ahead, we pray for you all the time—pray that our God will make you fit for what he's called you to be, pray that he'll fill your good ideas and acts of faith with his own energy so that it all amounts to something. If your life honors the name of Jesus, he will honor you. Grace is behind and through all of this, our God giving himself freely, the Master, Jesus Christ, giving himself freely.

NEW INTERNATIONAL VERSION

THE MAN OF LAWLESSNESS

2 Concerning the coming of our Lord Jesus Christ and our being gathered to him, we ask you, brothers, ²not to become easily unsettled or alarmed by some prophecy, report or letter supposed to have come from us, saying that the day of the Lord has already come. ³Don't let anyone deceive you in any way, for ⌐that day will not come⌐ until the rebellion occurs and the man of lawlessness*ᵃ* is revealed, the man doomed to destruction. ⁴He will oppose and will exalt himself over everything that is called God or is worshiped, so that he sets himself up in God's temple, proclaiming himself to be God.

⁵Don't you remember that when I was with you I used to tell you these things? ⁶And now you know what is holding him back, so that he may be revealed at the proper time. ⁷For the secret power of lawlessness is already at work; but the one who now holds it back will continue to do so till he is taken out of the way. ⁸And then the lawless one will be revealed, whom the Lord Jesus will overthrow with the breath of his mouth and destroy by the splendor of his coming. ⁹The coming of the lawless one will be in accordance with the work of Satan displayed in all kinds of counterfeit miracles, signs and wonders, ¹⁰and in every sort of evil that deceives those who are perishing. They perish because they refused to love the truth and so be saved. ¹¹For this reason God sends them a powerful delusion so that they will believe the lie ¹²and so that all will be condemned who have not believed the truth but have delighted in wickedness.

STAND FIRM

¹³But we ought always to thank God for you, brothers loved by the Lord, because from the beginning God chose you*ᵇ* to be saved through the sanctifying work of the Spirit and through belief in the truth. ¹⁴He called you to this through our gospel, that you might share in the glory of our Lord Jesus Christ. ¹⁵So then, brothers, stand firm and hold to the teachings*ᶜ* we passed on to you, whether by word of mouth or by letter.

¹⁶May our Lord Jesus Christ himself and God our Father, who loved us and by his grace gave us eternal encouragement and good hope, ¹⁷encourage your hearts and strengthen you in every good deed and word.

THE MESSAGE

THE ANARCHIST

2.1-3 2 Now, friends, read these next words carefully. Slow down and don't go jumping to conclusions regarding the day when our Master, Jesus Christ, will come back and we assemble to welcome him. Don't let anyone shake you up or get you excited over some breathless report or rumored letter from me that the day of the Master's arrival has come and gone. Don't fall for any line like that.

2.3-5 Before that day comes, a couple of things have to happen. First, the Apostasy. Second, the debut of the Anarchist, a real dog of Satan. He'll defy and then take over every so-called god or altar. Having cleared away the opposition, he'll then set himself up in God's Temple as "God Almighty." Don't you remember me going over all this in detail when I was with you? Are your memories that short?

2.6-8 You'll also remember that I told you the Anarchist is being held back until just the right time. That doesn't mean that the spirit of anarchy is not now at work. It is, secretly and underground. But the time will come when the Anarchist will no longer be held back, but will be let loose. But don't worry. The Master Jesus will be right on his heels and blow him away. The Master appears and—puff!—the Anarchist is out of there.

2.9-12 The Anarchist's coming is all Satan's work. All his power and signs and miracles are fake, evil sleight of hand that plays to the gallery of those who hate the truth that could save them. And since they're so obsessed with evil, God rubs their noses in it—gives them what they want. Since they refuse to trust truth, they're banished to their chosen world of lies and illusions.

2.13-14 Meanwhile, we've got our hands full continually thanking God for you, our good friends—so loved by God! God picked you out as his from the very start. Think of it: included in God's original plan of salvation by the bond of faith in the living truth. This is the life of the Spirit he invited you to through the Message we delivered, in which you get in on the glory of our Master, Jesus Christ.

2.15-17 So, friends, take a firm stand, feet on the ground and head high. Keep a tight grip on what you were taught, whether in personal conversation or by our letter. May Jesus himself and God our Father, who reached out in love and surprised you with gifts of unending help and confidence, put a fresh heart in you, invigorate your work, enliven your speech.

ᵃ 3 Some manuscripts *sin*   *ᵇ 13* Some manuscripts *because God chose you as his firstfruits*   *ᶜ 15* Or *traditions*

NEW INTERNATIONAL VERSION

REQUEST FOR PRAYER

3 Finally, brothers, pray for us that the message of the Lord may spread rapidly and be honored, just as it was with you. ²And pray that we may be delivered from wicked and evil men, for not everyone has faith. ³But the Lord is faithful, and he will strengthen and protect you from the evil one. ⁴We have confidence in the Lord that you are doing and will continue to do the things we command. ⁵May the Lord direct your hearts into God's love and Christ's perseverance.

WARNING AGAINST IDLENESS

⁶In the name of the Lord Jesus Christ, we command you, brothers, to keep away from every brother who is idle and does not live according to the teaching*ª* you received from us. ⁷For you yourselves know how you ought to follow our example. We were not idle when we were with you, ⁸nor did we eat anyone's food without paying for it. On the contrary, we worked night and day, laboring and toiling so that we would not be a burden to any of you. ⁹We did this, not because we do not have the right to such help, but in order to make ourselves a model for you to follow. ¹⁰For even when we were with you, we gave you this rule: "If a man will not work, he shall not eat."

¹¹We hear that some among you are idle. They are not busy; they are busybodies. ¹²Such people we command and urge in the Lord Jesus Christ to settle down and earn the bread they eat. ¹³And as for you, brothers, never tire of doing what is right.

¹⁴If anyone does not obey our instruction in this letter, take special note of him. Do not associate with him, in order that he may feel ashamed. ¹⁵Yet do not regard him as an enemy, but warn him as a brother.

FINAL GREETINGS

¹⁶Now may the Lord of peace himself give you peace at all times and in every way. The Lord be with all of you.

¹⁷I, Paul, write this greeting in my own hand, which is the distinguishing mark in all my letters. This is how I write.

¹⁸The grace of our Lord Jesus Christ be with you all.

ª 6 Or tradition

THE MESSAGE

THOSE WHO ARE LAZY

3.1-3 **3** One more thing, friends: Pray for us. Pray that the Master's Word will simply take off and race through the country to a groundswell of response, just as it did among you. And pray that we'll be rescued from these scoundrels who are trying to do us in. I'm finding that not all "believers" are believers. But the Master never lets us down. He'll stick by you and protect you from evil.

3.4-5 Because of the *Master*, we have great confidence in *you*. We know you're doing everything we told you and will continue doing it. May the Master take you by the hand and lead you along the path of God's love and Christ's endurance.

3.6-9 Our orders—backed up by the Master, Jesus—are to refuse to have anything to do with those among you who are lazy and refuse to work the way we taught you. Don't permit them to freeload on the rest. We showed you how to pull your weight when we were with you, so get on with it. We didn't sit around on our hands expecting others to take care of us. In fact, we worked our fingers to the bone, up half the night moonlighting so you wouldn't be burdened with taking care of us. And it wasn't because we didn't have a right to your support; we did. We simply wanted to provide an example of diligence, hoping it would prove contagious.

3.10-13 Don't you remember the rule we had when we lived with you? "If you don't work, you don't eat." And now we're getting reports that a bunch of lazy good-for-nothings are taking advantage of you. This must not be tolerated. We command them to get to work immediately—no excuses, no arguments—and earn their own keep. Friends, don't slack off in doing your duty.

3.14-15 If anyone refuses to obey our clear command written in this letter, don't let him get by with it. Point out such a person and refuse to subsidize his freeloading. Maybe then he'll think twice. But don't treat him as an enemy. Sit him down and talk about the problem as someone who cares.

3.16 May the Master of Peace himself give you the gift of getting along with each other at all times, in all ways. May the Master be truly among you!

3.17 I, Paul, bid you good-bye in my own handwriting. I do this in all my letters, so examine my signature as proof that the letter is genuine.

3.18 The incredible grace of our Master, Jesus Christ, be with all of you!

1 TIMOTHY

1 TIMOTHY

1 Paul, an apostle of Christ Jesus by the command of God our Savior and of Christ Jesus our hope,

²To Timothy my true son in the faith:

Grace, mercy and peace from God the Father and Christ Jesus our Lord.

WARNING AGAINST FALSE TEACHERS OF THE LAW

³As I urged you when I went into Macedonia, stay there in Ephesus so that you may command certain men not to teach false doctrines any longer ⁴nor to devote themselves to myths and endless genealogies. These promote controversies rather than God's work—which is by faith. ⁵The goal of this command is love, which comes from a pure heart and a good conscience and a sincere faith. ⁶Some have wandered away from these and turned to meaningless talk. ⁷They want to be teachers of the law, but they do not know what they are talking about or what they so confidently affirm.

⁸We know that the law is good if one uses it properly. ⁹We also know that law*ᵃ* is made not for the righteous but for lawbreakers and rebels, the ungodly and sinful, the unholy and irreligious; for those who kill their fathers or mothers, for murderers, ¹⁰for adulterers and perverts, for slave traders and liars and perjurers—and for whatever else is contrary to the sound doctrine ¹¹that conforms to the glorious gospel of the blessed God, which he entrusted to me.

THE LORD'S GRACE TO PAUL

¹²I thank Christ Jesus our Lord, who has given me strength, that he considered me faithful, appointing me to his service. ¹³Even though I was once a blasphemer and a persecutor and a violent man, I was shown mercy because I acted in ignorance and unbelief. ¹⁴The grace of our Lord was poured out on me abundantly, along with the faith and love that are in Christ Jesus.

1.1-2 **1** I, Paul, am an apostle on special assignment for Christ, our living hope. Under God our Savior's command, I'm writing this to you, Timothy, my son in the faith. All the best from our God and Christ be yours!

SELF-APPOINTED EXPERTS ON LIFE

1.3-4 On my way to the province of Macedonia, I advised you to stay in Ephesus. Well, I haven't changed my mind. Stay right there on top of things so that the teaching stays on track. Apparently some people have been introducing fantasy stories and fanciful family trees that digress into silliness instead of pulling the people back into the center, deepening faith and obedience.

1.5-7 The whole point of what we're urging is simply *love*—love uncontaminated by self-interest and counterfeit faith, a life open to God. Those who fail to keep to this point soon wander off into cul-de-sacs of gossip. They set themselves up as experts on religious issues, but haven't the remotest idea of what they're holding forth with such imposing eloquence.

1.8-11 It's true that moral guidance and counsel need to be given, but the way you say it and to whom you say it are as important as what you say. It's obvious, isn't it, that the law code isn't primarily for people who live responsibly, but for the irresponsible, who defy all authority, riding roughshod over God, life, sex, truth, whatever! They are contemptuous of this great Message I've been put in charge of by this great God.

✝

1.12-14 I'm so grateful to Christ Jesus for making me adequate to do this work. He went out on a limb, you know, in trusting me with this ministry. The only credentials I brought to it were invective and witch hunts and arrogance. But I was treated mercifully because I didn't know what I was doing—didn't know Who I was doing it against! Grace mixed with faith and love poured over me and into me. And all because of Jesus.

ᵃ 9 Or that the law

NEW INTERNATIONAL VERSION

¹⁵Here is a trustworthy saying that deserves full acceptance: Christ Jesus came into the world to save sinners—of whom I am the worst. ¹⁶But for that very reason I was shown mercy so that in me, the worst of sinners, Christ Jesus might display his unlimited patience as an example for those who would believe on him and receive eternal life. ¹⁷Now to the King eternal, immortal, invisible, the only God, be honor and glory for ever and ever. Amen.

¹⁸Timothy, my son, I give you this instruction in keeping with the prophecies once made about you, so that by following them you may fight the good fight, ¹⁹holding on to faith and a good conscience. Some have rejected these and so have shipwrecked their faith. ²⁰Among them are Hymenaeus and Alexander, whom I have handed over to Satan to be taught not to blaspheme.

INSTRUCTIONS ON WORSHIP

2 I urge, then, first of all, that requests, prayers, intercession and thanksgiving be made for everyone— ²for kings and all those in authority, that we may live peaceful and quiet lives in all godliness and holiness. ³This is good, and pleases God our Savior, ⁴who wants all men to be saved and to come to a knowledge of the truth. ⁵For there is one God and one mediator between God and men, the man Christ Jesus, ⁶who gave himself as a ransom for all men—the testimony given in its proper time. ⁷And for this purpose I was appointed a herald and an apostle—I am telling the truth, I am not lying—and a teacher of the true faith to the Gentiles.

⁸I want men everywhere to lift up holy hands in prayer, without anger or disputing.

⁹I also want women to dress modestly, with decency and propriety, not with braided hair or gold or pearls or expensive clothes, ¹⁰but with good deeds, appropriate for women who profess to worship God.

¹¹A woman should learn in quietness and full submission. ¹²I do not permit a woman to teach or to have authority over a man; she must be si-

THE MESSAGE

1.15-19 Here's a word you can take to heart and depend on: Jesus Christ came into the world to save sinners. I'm proof—Public Sinner Number One—of someone who could never have made it apart from sheer mercy. And now he shows me off—evidence of his endless patience—to those who are right on the edge of trusting him forever.

Deep honor and bright glory
  to the King of All Time—
One God, Immortal, Invisible,
  ever and always. Oh, yes!

I'm passing this work on to you, my son Timothy. The prophetic word that was directed to you prepared us for this. All those prayers are coming together now so you will do this well, fearless in your struggle, keeping a firm grip on your faith and on yourself. After all, this is a fight we're in.

1.19-20 There are some, you know, who by relaxing their grip and thinking anything goes have made a thorough mess of their faith. Hymenaeus and Alexander are two of them. I let them wander off to Satan to be taught a lesson or two about not blaspheming.

SIMPLE FAITH AND PLAIN TRUTH

2.1-3 **2** The first thing I want you to do is pray. Pray every way you know how, for everyone you know. Pray especially for rulers and their governments to rule well so we can be quietly about our business of living simply, in humble contemplation. This is the way our Savior God wants us to live.

2.4-7 He wants not only us but *everyone* saved, you know, everyone to get to know the truth *we've* learned: that there's one God and only one, and one Priest-Mediator between God and us—Jesus, who offered himself in exchange for everyone held captive by sin, to set them all free. Eventually the news is going to get out. This and this only has been my appointed work: getting this news to those who have never heard of God, and explaining how it works by simple faith and plain truth.

2.8-10 Since prayer is at the bottom of all this, what I want mostly is for men to pray—not shaking angry fists at enemies but raising holy hands to God. And I want women to get in there with the men in humility before God, not primping before a mirror or chasing the latest fashions but doing something beautiful for God and becoming beautiful doing it.

2.11-15 I don't let women take over and tell the men what to do. They should study to be quiet and obedient along with everyone else. Adam was

NEW INTERNATIONAL VERSION

lent. ¹³For Adam was formed first, then Eve.
¹⁴And Adam was not the one deceived; it was
the woman who was deceived and became a sinner. ¹⁵But women[a] will be saved[b] through childbearing—if they continue in faith, love and holiness with propriety.

OVERSEERS AND DEACONS

3 Here is a trustworthy saying: If anyone sets
his heart on being an overseer,[c] he desires a
noble task. ²Now the overseer must be above reproach, the husband of but one wife, temperate,
self-controlled, respectable, hospitable, able to
teach, ³not given to drunkenness, not violent but
gentle, not quarrelsome, not a lover of money.
⁴He must manage his own family well and see
that his children obey him with proper respect.
⁵(If anyone does not know how to manage his
own family, how can he take care of God's
church?) ⁶He must not be a recent convert, or he
may become conceited and fall under the same
judgment as the devil. ⁷He must also have a
good reputation with outsiders, so that he will
not fall into disgrace and into the devil's trap.

⁸Deacons, likewise, are to be men worthy of
respect, sincere, not indulging in much wine,
and not pursuing dishonest gain. ⁹They must
keep hold of the deep truths of the faith with a
clear conscience. ¹⁰They must first be tested; and
then if there is nothing against them, let them
serve as deacons.

¹¹In the same way, their wives[d] are to be
women worthy of respect, not malicious talkers
but temperate and trustworthy in everything.

¹²A deacon must be the husband of but one
wife and must manage his children and his
household well. ¹³Those who have served well
gain an excellent standing and great assurance in
their faith in Christ Jesus.

¹⁴Although I hope to come to you soon, I am
writing you these instructions so that, ¹⁵if I am
delayed, you will know how people ought to
conduct themselves in God's household, which
is the church of the living God, the pillar and
foundation of the truth. ¹⁶Beyond all question,
the mystery of godliness is great:

He[e] appeared in a body,[f]
 was vindicated by the Spirit,
was seen by angels,
 was preached among the nations,
was believed on in the world,
 was taken up in glory.

THE MESSAGE

made first, then Eve; woman was deceived
first—our pioneer in sin!—with Adam right on
her heels. On the other hand, her childbearing
brought about salvation, reversing Eve. But this
salvation only comes to those who continue in
faith, love, and holiness, gathering it all into
maturity. You can depend on this.

LEADERSHIP IN THE CHURCH

3.1-7 **3** If anyone wants to provide leadership in
the church, good! But there are precondi-
tions: A leader must be well-thought-of, committed to his wife, cool and collected, accessible, and hospitable. He must know what he's
talking about, not be overfond of wine, not
pushy but gentle, not thin-skinned, not money-
hungry. He must handle his own affairs well,
attentive to his own children and having their
respect. For if someone is unable to handle his
own affairs, how can he take care of God's
church? He must not be a new believer, lest the
position go to his head and the Devil trip him
up. Outsiders must think well of him, or else
the Devil will figure out a way to lure him into
his trap.

3.8-13 The same goes for those who want to be servants in the church: serious, not deceitful, not
too free with the bottle, not in it for what they
can get out of it. They must be reverent before
the mystery of the faith, not using their position to try to run things. Let them prove themselves first. If they show they can do it, take
them on. No exceptions are to be made for
women—same qualifications: serious, dependable, not sharp-tongued, not overfond of wine.
Servants in the church are to be committed to
their spouses, attentive to their own children,
and diligent in looking after their own affairs.
Those who do this servant work will come to
be highly respected, a real credit to this Jesus-
faith.

3.14-16 I hope to visit you soon, but just in case I'm
delayed, I'm writing this letter so you'll know
how things ought to go in God's household,
this God-alive church, bastion of truth. This
Christian life is a great mystery, far exceeding
our understanding, but some things are clear
enough:

He appeared in a human body,
 was proved right by the invisible Spirit,
  was seen by angels.
He was proclaimed among all kinds of
  peoples,
 believed in all over the world,
  taken up into heavenly glory.

---

a 15 Greek *she*   b 15 Or *restored*   c 1 Traditionally
bishop; also in verse 2   d 11 Or *way, deaconesses*
e 16 Some manuscripts *God*   f 16 Or *in the flesh*

NEW INTERNATIONAL VERSION

INSTRUCTIONS TO TIMOTHY

4 The Spirit clearly says that in later times some will abandon the faith and follow deceiving spirits and things taught by demons. ²Such teachings come through hypocritical liars, whose consciences have been seared as with a hot iron. ³They forbid people to marry and order them to abstain from certain foods, which God created to be received with thanksgiving by those who believe and who know the truth. ⁴For everything God created is good, and nothing is to be rejected if it is received with thanksgiving, ⁵because it is consecrated by the word of God and prayer.

⁶If you point these things out to the brothers, you will be a good minister of Christ Jesus, brought up in the truths of the faith and of the good teaching that you have followed. ⁷Have nothing to do with godless myths and old wives' tales; rather, train yourself to be godly. ⁸For physical training is of some value, but godliness has value for all things, holding promise for both the present life and the life to come.

⁹This is a trustworthy saying that deserves full acceptance ¹⁰(and for this we labor and strive), that we have put our hope in the living God, who is the Savior of all men, and especially of those who believe.

¹¹Command and teach these things. ¹²Don't let anyone look down on you because you are young, but set an example for the believers in speech, in life, in love, in faith and in purity. ¹³Until I come, devote yourself to the public reading of Scripture, to preaching and to teaching. ¹⁴Do not neglect your gift, which was given you through a prophetic message when the body of elders laid their hands on you.

¹⁵Be diligent in these matters; give yourself wholly to them, so that everyone may see your progress. ¹⁶Watch your life and doctrine closely. Persevere in them, because if you do, you will save both yourself and your hearers.

ADVICE ABOUT WIDOWS, ELDERS AND SLAVES

5 Do not rebuke an older man harshly, but exhort him as if he were your father. Treat younger men as brothers, ²older women as mothers, and younger women as sisters, with absolute purity.

³Give proper recognition to those widows who are really in need. ⁴But if a widow has children or grandchildren, these should learn first of all to put their religion into practice by caring for their own family and so repaying their parents and grandparents, for this is pleasing to God. ⁵The widow who is really in need and left all

THE MESSAGE

TEACH WITH YOUR LIFE

4 4.1-5 The Spirit makes it clear that as time goes on, some are going to give up on the faith and chase after demonic illusions put forth by professional liars. These liars have lied so well and for so long that they've lost their capacity for truth. They will tell you not to get married. They'll tell you not to eat this or that food—perfectly good food God created to be eaten heartily and with thanksgiving by Christians! Everything God created is good, and to be received with thanks. Nothing is to be sneered at and thrown out. God's Word and our prayers make every item in creation holy.

4.6-10 You've been raised on the Message of the faith and have followed sound teaching. Now pass on this counsel to the Christians there, and you'll be a good servant of Jesus. Stay clear of silly stories that get dressed up as religion. Exercise daily in God—no spiritual flabbiness, please! Workouts in the gymnasium are useful, but a disciplined life in God is far more so, making you fit both today and forever. You can count on this. Take it to heart. This is why we've thrown ourselves into this venture so totally. We're banking on the living God, Savior of all men and women, especially believers.

4.11-14 Get the word out. Teach all these things. And don't let anyone put you down because you're young. Teach believers with your life: by word, by demeanor, by love, by faith, by integrity. Stay at your post reading Scripture, giving counsel, teaching. And that special gift of ministry you were given when the leaders of the church laid hands on you and prayed—keep that dusted off and in use.

4.15-16 Cultivate these things. Immerse yourself in them. The people will all see you mature right before their eyes! Keep a firm grasp on both your character and your teaching. Don't be diverted. Just keep at it. Both you and those who hear you will experience salvation.

THE FAMILY OF FAITH

5 5.1-2 Don't be harsh or impatient with an older man. Talk to him as you would your own father, and to the younger men as your brothers. Reverently honor an older woman as you would your mother, and the younger women as sisters.

5.3-8 Take care of widows who are destitute. If a widow has family members to take care of her, let them learn that religion begins at their own doorstep and that they should pay back with gratitude some of what they have received. This pleases God immensely. You can tell a legitimate widow by the way she has put all her

NEW INTERNATIONAL VERSION

alone puts her hope in God and continues night and day to pray and to ask God for help. ⁶But the widow who lives for pleasure is dead even while she lives. ⁷Give the people these instructions, too, so that no one may be open to blame. ⁸If anyone does not provide for his relatives, and especially for his immediate family, he has denied the faith and is worse than an unbeliever.

⁹No widow may be put on the list of widows unless she is over sixty, has been faithful to her husband, *ᵃ* ¹⁰and is well known for her good deeds, such as bringing up children, showing hospitality, washing the feet of the saints, helping those in trouble and devoting herself to all kinds of good deeds.

¹¹As for younger widows, do not put them on such a list. For when their sensual desires overcome their dedication to Christ, they want to marry. ¹²Thus they bring judgment on themselves, because they have broken their first pledge. ¹³Besides, they get into the habit of being idle and going about from house to house. And not only do they become idlers, but also gossips and busybodies, saying things they ought not to. ¹⁴So I counsel younger widows to marry, to have children, to manage their homes and to give the enemy no opportunity for slander. ¹⁵Some have in fact already turned away to follow Satan.

¹⁶If any woman who is a believer has widows in her family, she should help them and not let the church be burdened with them, so that the church can help those widows who are really in need.

¹⁷The elders who direct the affairs of the church well are worthy of double honor, especially those whose work is preaching and teaching. ¹⁸For the Scripture says, "Do not muzzle the ox while it is treading out the grain," *ᵇ* and "The worker deserves his wages." *ᶜ* ¹⁹Do not entertain an accusation against an elder unless it is brought by two or three witnesses. ²⁰Those who sin are to be rebuked publicly, so that the others may take warning.

²¹I charge you, in the sight of God and Christ Jesus and the elect angels, to keep these instructions without partiality, and to do nothing out of favoritism.

²²Do not be hasty in the laying on of hands, and do not share in the sins of others. Keep yourself pure.

²³Stop drinking only water, and use a little wine because of your stomach and your frequent illnesses.

²⁴The sins of some men are obvious, reaching

THE MESSAGE

hope in God, praying to him constantly for the needs of others as well as her own. But a widow who exploits people's emotions and pocketbooks—well, there's nothing to her. Tell these things to the people so that they will do the right thing in their extended family. Anyone who neglects to care for family members in need repudiates the faith. That's worse than refusing to believe in the first place.

5.9-10 Sign some widows up for the special ministry of offering assistance. They will in turn receive support from the church. They must be over sixty, married only once, and have a reputation for helping out with children, strangers, tired Christians, the hurt and troubled.

5.11-15 Don't put young widows on this list. No sooner will they get on than they'll want to get off, obsessed with wanting to get a husband rather than serving Christ in this way. By breaking their word, they're liable to go from bad to worse, frittering away their days on empty talk, gossip, and trivialities. No, I'd rather the young widows go ahead and get married in the first place, have children, manage their homes, and not give critics any foothold for finding fault. Some of them have already left and gone after Satan.

5.16 Any Christian woman who has widows in her family is responsible for them. They shouldn't be dumped on the church. The church has its hands full already with widows who need help.

⊹

5.17-18 Give a bonus to leaders who do a good job, especially the ones who work hard at preaching and teaching. Scripture tells us, "Don't muzzle a working ox," and, "A worker deserves his pay."

5.19 Don't listen to a complaint against a leader that isn't backed up by two or three responsible witnesses.

5.20 If anyone falls into sin, call that person on the carpet. Those who are inclined that way will know right off they can't get by with it.

5.21-23 God and Jesus and angels all back me up in these instructions. Carry them out without favoritism, without taking sides. Don't appoint people to church leadership positions too hastily. If a person is involved in some serious sins, you don't want to become an unwitting accomplice. In any event, keep a close check on yourself. And don't worry too much about what the critics will say. Go ahead and drink a little wine, for instance; it's good for your digestion, good medicine for what ails you.

5.24-25 The sins of some people are blatant and

ᵃ 9 Or has had but one husband   *ᵇ 18 Deut. 25:4*
ᶜ 18 Luke 10:7

NEW INTERNATIONAL VERSION

the place of judgment ahead of them; the sins of others trail behind them. ²⁵In the same way, good deeds are obvious, and even those that are not cannot be hidden.

6 All who are under the yoke of slavery should consider their masters worthy of full respect, so that God's name and our teaching may not be slandered. ²Those who have believing masters are not to show less respect for them because they are brothers. Instead, they are to serve them even better, because those who benefit from their service are believers, and dear to them. These are the things you are to teach and urge on them.

LOVE OF MONEY

³If anyone teaches false doctrines and does not agree to the sound instruction of our Lord Jesus Christ and to godly teaching, ⁴he is conceited and understands nothing. He has an unhealthy interest in controversies and quarrels about words that result in envy, strife, malicious talk, evil suspicions ⁵and constant friction between men of corrupt mind, who have been robbed of the truth and who think that godliness is a means to financial gain.

⁶But godliness with contentment is great gain. ⁷For we brought nothing into the world, and we can take nothing out of it. ⁸But if we have food and clothing, we will be content with that. ⁹People who want to get rich fall into temptation and a trap and into many foolish and harmful desires that plunge men into ruin and destruction. ¹⁰For the love of money is a root of all kinds of evil. Some people, eager for money, have wandered from the faith and pierced themselves with many griefs.

PAUL'S CHARGE TO TIMOTHY

¹¹But you, man of God, flee from all this, and pursue righteousness, godliness, faith, love, endurance and gentleness. ¹²Fight the good fight of the faith. Take hold of the eternal life to which you were called when you made your good confession in the presence of many witnesses. ¹³In the sight of God, who gives life to everything, and of Christ Jesus, who while testifying before Pontius Pilate made the good confession, I charge you ¹⁴to keep this command without spot or blame until the appearing of our Lord Jesus Christ, ¹⁵which God will bring about in his own time—God, the blessed and only Ruler, the King of kings and Lord of lords, ¹⁶who alone is immortal and who lives in unapproachable light, whom no one has seen or can see. To him be honor and might forever. Amen.

THE MESSAGE

march them right into court. The sins of others don't show up until much later. The same with good deeds. Some you see right off, but none are hidden forever.

6.1-2 **6** Whoever is a slave must make the best of it, giving respect to his master so that outsiders don't blame God and our teaching for his behavior. Slaves with Christian masters all the more so—their masters are really their beloved brothers!

THE LUST FOR MONEY

6.2-5 These are the things I want you to teach and preach. If you have leaders there who teach otherwise, who refuse the solid words of our Master Jesus and this godly instruction, tag them for what they are: ignorant windbags who infect the air with germs of envy, controversy, bad-mouthing, suspicious rumors. Eventually there's an epidemic of backstabbing, and truth is but a distant memory. They think religion is a way to make a fast buck.

6.6-8 A devout life does bring wealth, but it's the rich simplicity of being yourself before God. Since we entered the world penniless and will leave it penniless, if we have bread on the table and shoes on our feet, that's enough.

6.9-10 But if it's only money these leaders are after, they'll self-destruct in no time. Lust for money brings trouble and nothing but trouble. Going down that path, some lose their footing in the faith completely and live to regret it bitterly ever after.

RUNNING HARD

6.11-12 But you, Timothy, man of God: Run for your life from all this. Pursue a righteous life—a life of wonder, faith, love, steadiness, courtesy. Run hard and fast in the faith. Seize the eternal life, the life you were called to, the life you so fervently embraced in the presence of so many witnesses.

6.13-16 I'm charging you before the life-giving God and before Christ, who took his stand before Pontius Pilate and didn't give an inch: Keep this command to the letter, and don't slack off. Our Master, Jesus Christ, is on his way. He'll show up right on time, his arrival guaranteed by the Blessed and Undisputed Ruler, High King, High God. He's the only one death can't touch, his light so bright no one can get close. He's never been seen by human eyes—human eyes can't take him in! Honor to him, and eternal rule! Oh, yes.

NEW INTERNATIONAL VERSION

¹⁷Command those who are rich in this present world not to be arrogant nor to put their hope in wealth, which is so uncertain, but to put their hope in God, who richly provides us with everything for our enjoyment. ¹⁸Command them to do good, to be rich in good deeds, and to be generous and willing to share. ¹⁹In this way they will lay up treasure for themselves as a firm foundation for the coming age, so that they may take hold of the life that is truly life.

²⁰Timothy, guard what has been entrusted to your care. Turn away from godless chatter and the opposing ideas of what is falsely called knowledge, ²¹which some have professed and in so doing have wandered from the faith.

Grace be with you.

THE MESSAGE

6.17-19 Tell those rich in this world's wealth to quit being so full of themselves and so obsessed with money, which is here today and gone tomorrow. Tell them to go after God, who piles on all the riches we could ever manage—to do good, to be rich in helping others, to be extravagantly generous. If they do that, they'll build a treasury that will last, gaining life that is truly life.

6.20-21 And oh, my dear Timothy, guard the treasure you were given! Guard it with your life. Avoid the talk-show religion and the practiced confusion of the so-called experts. People caught up in a lot of talk can miss the whole point of faith.

Overwhelming grace keep you!

2 TIMOTHY

2 TIMOTHY

1 Paul, an apostle of Christ Jesus by the will of God, according to the promise of life that is in Christ Jesus,

²To Timothy, my dear son:

Grace, mercy and peace from God the Father and Christ Jesus our Lord.

ENCOURAGEMENT TO BE FAITHFUL

³I thank God, whom I serve, as my forefathers did, with a clear conscience, as night and day I constantly remember you in my prayers. ⁴Recalling your tears, I long to see you, so that I may be filled with joy. ⁵I have been reminded of your sincere faith, which first lived in your grandmother Lois and in your mother Eunice and, I am persuaded, now lives in you also. ⁶For this reason I remind you to fan into flame the gift of God, which is in you through the laying on of my hands. ⁷For God did not give us a spirit of timidity, but a spirit of power, of love and of self-discipline.

⁸So do not be ashamed to testify about our Lord, or ashamed of me his prisoner. But join with me in suffering for the gospel, by the power of God, ⁹who has saved us and called us to a holy life—not because of anything we have done but because of his own purpose and grace. This grace was given us in Christ Jesus before the beginning of time, ¹⁰but it has now been revealed through the appearing of our Savior, Christ Jesus, who has destroyed death and has brought life and immortality to light through the gospel. ¹¹And of this gospel I was appointed a herald and an apostle and a teacher. ¹²That is why I am suffering as I am. Yet I am not ashamed, because I know whom I have believed, and am convinced that he is able to guard what I have entrusted to him for that day.

¹³What you heard from me, keep as the pattern of sound teaching, with faith and love in Christ Jesus. ¹⁴Guard the good deposit that was entrusted to you—guard it with the help of the Holy Spirit who lives in us.

1 1.1-2 I, Paul, am on special assignment for Christ, carrying out God's plan laid out in the Message of Life by Jesus. I write this to you, Timothy, the son I love so much. All the best from our God and Christ be yours!

TO BE BOLD WITH GOD'S GIFTS

1.3-4 Every time I say your name in prayer—which is practically all the time—I thank God for you, the God I worship with my whole life in the tradition of my ancestors. I miss you a lot, especially when I remember that last tearful good-bye, and I look forward to a joy-packed reunion.

1.5-7 That precious memory triggers another: your honest faith—and what a rich faith it is, handed down from your grandmother Lois to your mother Eunice, and now to you! And the special gift of ministry you received when I laid hands on you and prayed—keep that ablaze! God doesn't want us to be shy with his gifts, but bold and loving and sensible.

1.8-10 So don't be embarrassed to speak up for our Master or for me, his prisoner. Take your share of suffering for the Message along with the rest of us. We can only keep on going, after all, by the power of God, who first saved us and then called us to this holy work. We had nothing to do with it. It was all *his* idea, a gift prepared for us in Jesus long before we knew anything about it. But we know it now. Since the appearance of our Savior, nothing could be plainer: death defeated, life vindicated in a steady blaze of light, all through the work of Jesus.

1.11-12 This is the Message I've been set apart to proclaim as preacher, emissary, and teacher. It's also the cause of all this trouble I'm in. But I have no regrets. I couldn't be more sure of my ground—the One I've trusted in can take care of what he's trusted me to do right to the end.

1.13-14 So keep at your work, this faith and love rooted in Christ, exactly as I set it out for you. It's as sound as the day you first heard it from me. Guard this precious thing placed in your custody by the Holy Spirit who works in us.

NEW INTERNATIONAL VERSION

¹⁵You know that everyone in the province of Asia has deserted me, including Phygelus and Hermogenes.

¹⁶May the Lord show mercy to the household of Onesiphorus, because he often refreshed me and was not ashamed of my chains. ¹⁷On the contrary, when he was in Rome, he searched hard for me until he found me. ¹⁸May the Lord grant that he will find mercy from the Lord on that day! You know very well in how many ways he helped me in Ephesus.

2 You then, my son, be strong in the grace that is in Christ Jesus. ²And the things you have heard me say in the presence of many witnesses entrust to reliable men who will also be qualified to teach others. ³Endure hardship with us like a good soldier of Christ Jesus. ⁴No one serving as a soldier gets involved in civilian affairs—he wants to please his commanding officer. ⁵Similarly, if anyone competes as an athlete, he does not receive the victor's crown unless he competes according to the rules. ⁶The hardworking farmer should be the first to receive a share of the crops. ⁷Reflect on what I am saying, for the Lord will give you insight into all this.

⁸Remember Jesus Christ, raised from the dead, descended from David. This is my gospel, ⁹for which I am suffering even to the point of being chained like a criminal. But God's word is not chained. ¹⁰Therefore I endure everything for the sake of the elect, that they too may obtain the salvation that is in Christ Jesus, with eternal glory.

¹¹Here is a trustworthy saying:

If we died with him,
  we will also live with him;
¹²if we endure,
  we will also reign with him.
If we disown him,
  he will also disown us;
¹³if we are faithless,
  he will remain faithful,
  for he cannot disown himself.

A WORKMAN APPROVED BY GOD

¹⁴Keep reminding them of these things. Warn them before God against quarreling about words; it is of no value, and only ruins those who listen. ¹⁵Do your best to present yourself to God as one approved, a workman who does not need to be ashamed and who correctly handles the word of truth. ¹⁶Avoid godless chatter, because those who indulge in it will become more and more ungodly. ¹⁷Their teaching will spread like gangrene. Among them are Hymenaeus and Phile-

THE MESSAGE

1.15-18 I'm sure you know by now that everyone in the province of Asia deserted me, even Phygelus and Hermogenes. But God bless Onesiphorus and his family! Many's the time I've been refreshed in that house. And he wasn't embarrassed a bit that I was in jail. The first thing he did when he got to Rome was look me up. May God on the Last Day treat him as well as he treated me. And then there was all the help he provided in Ephesus—but you know that better than I.

DOING YOUR BEST FOR GOD

2.1-7 **2** So, my son, throw yourself into this work for Christ. Pass on what you heard from me—the whole congregation saying Amen!—to reliable leaders who are competent to teach others. When the going gets rough, take it on the chin with the rest of us, the way Jesus did. A soldier on duty doesn't get caught up in making deals at the marketplace. He concentrates on carrying out orders. An athlete who refuses to play by the rules will never get anywhere. It's the diligent farmer who gets the produce. Think it over. God will make it all plain.

2.8-13 Fix this picture firmly in your mind: Jesus, descended from the line of David, raised from the dead. It's what you've heard from me all along. It's what I'm sitting in jail for right now—but God's Word isn't in jail! That's why I stick it out here—so that everyone God calls will get in on the salvation of Christ in all its glory. This is a sure thing:

If we die with him, we'll live with him;
If we stick it out with him, we'll rule with
  him;
If we turn our backs on him, he'll turn his
  back on us;
If we give up on him, he does not give
  up—
  for there's no way he can be false to
  himself.

2.14-18 Repeat these basic essentials over and over to God's people. Warn them before God against pious nitpicking, which chips away at the faith. It just wears everyone out. Concentrate on doing your best for God, work you won't be ashamed of, laying out the truth plain and simple. Stay clear of pious talk that is only talk. Words are not mere words, you know. If they're not backed by a godly life, they accumulate as poison in the soul. Hymenaeus and Philetus

NEW INTERNATIONAL VERSION

tus, [18]who have wandered away from the truth. They say that the resurrection has already taken place, and they destroy the faith of some. [19]Nevertheless, God's solid foundation stands firm, sealed with this inscription: "The Lord knows those who are his," [a] and, "Everyone who confesses the name of the Lord must turn away from wickedness."

[20]In a large house there are articles not only of gold and silver, but also of wood and clay; some are for noble purposes and some for ignoble. [21]If a man cleanses himself from the latter, he will be an instrument for noble purposes, made holy, useful to the Master and prepared to do any good work.

[22]Flee the evil desires of youth, and pursue righteousness, faith, love and peace, along with those who call on the Lord out of a pure heart. [23]Don't have anything to do with foolish and stupid arguments, because you know they produce quarrels. [24]And the Lord's servant must not quarrel; instead, he must be kind to everyone, able to teach, not resentful. [25]Those who oppose him he must gently instruct, in the hope that God will grant them repentance leading them to a knowledge of the truth, [26]and that they will come to their senses and escape from the trap of the devil, who has taken them captive to do his will.

GODLESSNESS IN THE LAST DAYS

3 But mark this: There will be terrible times in the last days. [2]People will be lovers of themselves, lovers of money, boastful, proud, abusive, disobedient to their parents, ungrateful, unholy, [3]without love, unforgiving, slanderous, without self-control, brutal, not lovers of the good, [4]treacherous, rash, conceited, lovers of pleasure rather than lovers of God— [5]having a form of godliness but denying its power. Have nothing to do with them.

[6]They are the kind who worm their way into homes and gain control over weak-willed women, who are loaded down with sins and are swayed by all kinds of evil desires, [7]always learning but never able to acknowledge the truth. [8]Just as Jannes and Jambres opposed Moses, so also these men oppose the truth—men of depraved minds, who, as far as the faith is concerned, are rejected. [9]But they will not get very far because, as in the case of those men, their folly will be clear to everyone.

THE MESSAGE

are examples, throwing believers off stride and missing the truth by a mile by saying the resurrection is over and done with.

2.19 Meanwhile, God's firm foundation is as firm as ever, these sentences engraved on the stones:

> GOD KNOWS WHO BELONGS TO HIM.
> SPURN EVIL, ALL YOU WHO NAME GOD AS GOD.

2.20-21 In a well-furnished kitchen there are not only crystal goblets and silver platters, but waste cans and compost buckets—some containers used to serve fine meals, others to take out the garbage. Become the kind of container God can use to present any and every kind of gift to his guests for their blessing.

2.22-26 Run away from infantile indulgence. Run after mature righteousness—faith, love, peace—joining those who are in honest and serious prayer before God. Refuse to get involved in inane discussions; they always end up in fights. God's servant must not be argumentative, but a gentle listener and a teacher who keeps cool, working firmly but patiently with those who refuse to obey. You never know how or when God might sober them up with a change of heart and a turning to the truth, enabling them to escape the Devil's trap, where they are caught and held captive, forced to run his errands.

DIFFICULT TIMES AHEAD

3.1-5 **3** Don't be naive. There are difficult times ahead. As the end approaches, people are going to be self-absorbed, money-hungry, self-promoting, stuck-up, profane, contemptuous of parents, crude, coarse, dog-eat-dog, unbending, slanderers, impulsively wild, savage, cynical, treacherous, ruthless, bloated windbags, addicted to lust, and allergic to God. They'll make a show of religion, but behind the scenes they're animals. Stay clear of these people.

3.6-9 These are the kind of people who smooth-talk themselves into the homes of unstable and needy women and take advantage of them; women who, depressed by their sinfulness, take up with every new religious fad that calls itself "truth." They get exploited every time and never really learn. These men are like those old Egyptian frauds Jannes and Jambres, who challenged Moses. They were rejects from the faith, twisted in their thinking, defying truth itself. But nothing will come of these latest impostors. Everyone will see through them, just as people saw through that Egyptian hoax.

---

[a] 19 Num. 16:5 (see Septuagint)

NEW INTERNATIONAL VERSION

PAUL'S CHARGE TO TIMOTHY

¹⁰You, however, know all about my teaching, my way of life, my purpose, faith, patience, love, endurance, ¹¹persecutions, sufferings—what kinds of things happened to me in Antioch, Iconium and Lystra, the persecutions I endured. Yet the Lord rescued me from all of them. ¹²In fact, everyone who wants to live a godly life in Christ Jesus will be persecuted, ¹³while evil men and impostors will go from bad to worse, deceiving and being deceived. ¹⁴But as for you, continue in what you have learned and have become convinced of, because you know those from whom you learned it, ¹⁵and how from infancy you have known the holy Scriptures, which are able to make you wise for salvation through faith in Christ Jesus. ¹⁶All Scripture is God-breathed and is useful for teaching, rebuking, correcting and training in righteousness, ¹⁷so that the man of God may be thoroughly equipped for every good work.

4 In the presence of God and of Christ Jesus, who will judge the living and the dead, and in view of his appearing and his kingdom, I give you this charge: ²Preach the Word; be prepared in season and out of season; correct, rebuke and encourage—with great patience and careful instruction. ³For the time will come when men will not put up with sound doctrine. Instead, to suit their own desires, they will gather around them a great number of teachers to say what their itching ears want to hear. ⁴They will turn their ears away from the truth and turn aside to myths. ⁵But you, keep your head in all situations, endure hardship, do the work of an evangelist, discharge all the duties of your ministry.

⁶For I am already being poured out like a drink offering, and the time has come for my departure. ⁷I have fought the good fight, I have finished the race, I have kept the faith. ⁸Now there is in store for me the crown of righteousness, which the Lord, the righteous Judge, will award to me on that day—and not only to me, but also to all who have longed for his appearing.

PERSONAL REMARKS

⁹Do your best to come to me quickly, ¹⁰for Demas, because he loved this world, has deserted me and has gone to Thessalonica. Crescens has gone to Galatia, and Titus to Dalmatia. ¹¹Only Luke is with me. Get Mark and bring him with

THE MESSAGE

KEEP THE MESSAGE ALIVE

3.10-13 You've been a good apprentice to me, a part of my teaching, my manner of life, direction, faith, steadiness, love, patience, troubles, sufferings—suffering along with me in all the grief I had to put up with in Antioch, Iconium, and Lystra. And you also well know that God rescued me! Anyone who wants to live all out for Christ is in for a lot of trouble; there's no getting around it. Unscrupulous con men will continue to exploit the faith. They're as deceived as the people they lead astray. As long as they are out there, things can only get worse.

3.14-17 But don't let it faze you. Stick with what you learned and believed, sure of the integrity of your teachers—why, you took in the sacred Scriptures with your mother's milk! There's nothing like the written Word of God for showing you the way to salvation through faith in Christ Jesus. Every part of Scripture is God-breathed and useful one way or another—showing us truth, exposing our rebellion, correcting our mistakes, training us to live God's way. Through the Word we are put together and shaped up for the tasks God has for us.

4.1-2 4 I can't impress this on you too strongly. God is looking over your shoulder. Christ himself is the Judge, with the final say on everyone, living and dead. He is about to break into the open with his rule, so proclaim the Message with intensity; keep on your watch. Challenge, warn, and urge your people. Don't ever quit. Just keep it simple.

4.3-5 You're going to find that there will be times when people will have no stomach for solid teaching, but will fill up on spiritual junk food—catchy opinions that tickle their fancy. They'll turn their backs on truth and chase mirages. But you—keep your eye on what you're doing; accept the hard times along with the good; keep the Message alive; do a thorough job as God's servant.

4.6-8 You take over. I'm about to die, my life an offering on God's altar. This is the only race worth running. I've run hard right to the finish, believed all the way. All that's left now is the shouting—God's applause! Depend on it, he's an honest judge. He'll do right not only by me, but by everyone eager for his coming.

✝

4.9-13 Get here as fast as you can. Demas, chasing fads, went off to Thessalonica and left me here. Crescens is in Galatia province, Titus in Dalmatia. Luke is the only one here with me. Bring Mark

NEW INTERNATIONAL VERSION

you, because he is helpful to me in my ministry. [12]I sent Tychicus to Ephesus. [13]When you come, bring the cloak that I left with Carpus at Troas, and my scrolls, especially the parchments.

[14]Alexander the metalworker did me a great deal of harm. The Lord will repay him for what he has done. [15]You too should be on your guard against him, because he strongly opposed our message.

[16]At my first defense, no one came to my support, but everyone deserted me. May it not be held against them. [17]But the Lord stood at my side and gave me strength, so that through me the message might be fully proclaimed and all the Gentiles might hear it. And I was delivered from the lion's mouth. [18]The Lord will rescue me from every evil attack and will bring me safely to his heavenly kingdom. To him be glory for ever and ever. Amen.

FINAL GREETINGS

[19]Greet Priscilla[a] and Aquila and the household of Onesiphorus. [20]Erastus stayed in Corinth, and I left Trophimus sick in Miletus. [21]Do your best to get here before winter. Eubulus greets you, and so do Pudens, Linus, Claudia and all the brothers.

[22]The Lord be with your spirit. Grace be with you.

THE MESSAGE

with you; he'll be my right-hand man since I'm sending Tychicus to Ephesus. Bring the winter coat I left in Troas with Carpus; also the books and parchment notebooks.

4.14-15 Watch out for Alexander the coppersmith. Fiercely opposed to our Message, he caused no end of trouble. God will give him what he's got coming.

4.16-18 At my preliminary hearing no one stood by me. They all ran like scared rabbits. But it doesn't matter—the Master stood by me and helped me spread the Message loud and clear to those who had never heard it. I was snatched from the jaws of the lion! God's looking after me, keeping me safe in the kingdom of heaven. All praise to him, praise forever! Oh, yes!

4.19-20 Say hello to Priscilla and Aquila; also, the family of Onesiphorus. Erastus stayed behind in Corinth. I had to leave Trophimus sick in Miletus.

4.21 Try hard to get here before winter.

Eubulus, Pudens, Linus, Claudia, and all your friends here send greetings.

4.22 God be with you. Grace be with you.

---

[a] 19 Greek *Prisca*, a variant of *Priscilla*

TITUS

TITUS

1 Paul, a servant of God and an apostle of Jesus Christ for the faith of God's elect and the knowledge of the truth that leads to godliness— ²a faith and knowledge resting on the hope of eternal life, which God, who does not lie, promised before the beginning of time, ³and at his appointed season he brought his word to light through the preaching entrusted to me by the command of God our Savior,

⁴To Titus, my true son in our common faith:

Grace and peace from God the Father and Christ Jesus our Savior.

TITUS'S TASK ON CRETE

⁵The reason I left you in Crete was that you might straighten out what was left unfinished and appoint*a* elders in every town, as I directed you. ⁶An elder must be blameless, the husband of but one wife, a man whose children believe and are not open to the charge of being wild and disobedient. ⁷Since an overseer*b* is entrusted with God's work, he must be blameless—not overbearing, not quick-tempered, not given to drunkenness, not violent, not pursuing dishonest gain. ⁸Rather he must be hospitable, one who loves what is good, who is self-controlled, upright, holy and disciplined. ⁹He must hold firmly to the trustworthy message as it has been taught, so that he can encourage others by sound doctrine and refute those who oppose it.

¹⁰For there are many rebellious people, mere talkers and deceivers, especially those of the circumcision group. ¹¹They must be silenced, because they are ruining whole households by teaching things they ought not to teach—and that for the sake of dishonest gain. ¹²Even one of their own prophets has said, "Cretans are always liars, evil brutes, lazy gluttons." ¹³This testimony is true. Therefore, rebuke them sharply, so that they will be sound in the faith ¹⁴and will pay no attention to Jewish myths or to the commands of those who reject the truth. ¹⁵To the pure, all things are pure, but to those who are corrupted and do not believe, nothing is pure. In fact, both

1.1-4 **1** I, Paul, am God's slave and Christ's agent for promoting the faith among God's chosen people, getting out the accurate word on God and how to respond rightly to it. My aim is to raise hopes by pointing the way to life without end. This is the life God promised long ago—and he doesn't break promises! And then when the time was ripe, he went public with his truth. I've been entrusted to proclaim this Message by order of our Savior, God himself. Dear Titus, legitimate son in the faith: Receive everything God our Father and Jesus our Savior give you!

A GOOD GRIP ON THE MESSAGE

1.5-9 I left you in charge in Crete so you could complete what I left half-done. Appoint leaders in every town according to my instructions. As you select them, ask, "Is this man well-thought-of? Are his children believers? Do they respect him and stay out of trouble?" It's important that a church leader, responsible for the affairs in God's house, be looked up to—not pushy, not short-tempered, not a drunk, not a bully, not money-hungry. He must welcome people, be helpful, wise, fair, reverent, have a good grip on himself, and have a good grip on the Message, knowing how to use the truth to either spur people on in knowledge or stop them in their tracks if they oppose it.

1.10-16 For there are a lot of rebels out there, full of loose, confusing, and deceiving talk. Those who were brought up religious and ought to know better are the worst. They've got to be shut up. They're disrupting entire families with their teaching, and all for the sake of a fast buck. One of their own prophets said it best:

The Cretans are liars from the womb,
barking dogs, lazy bellies.

He certainly spoke the truth. Get on them right away. Stop that diseased talk of Jewish make-believe and made-up rules so they can recover a robust faith. Everything is clean to the clean-minded; nothing is clean to dirty-minded unbelievers. They leave their dirty fingerprints on

---

a 5 Or *ordain*   *b* 7 Traditionally *bishop*

NEW INTERNATIONAL VERSION

their minds and consciences are corrupted. [16]They claim to know God, but by their actions they deny him. They are detestable, disobedient and unfit for doing anything good.

WHAT MUST BE TAUGHT TO VARIOUS GROUPS

2 You must teach what is in accord with sound doctrine. [2]Teach the older men to be temperate, worthy of respect, self-controlled, and sound in faith, in love and in endurance.

[3]Likewise, teach the older women to be reverent in the way they live, not to be slanderers or addicted to much wine, but to teach what is good. [4]Then they can train the younger women to love their husbands and children, [5]to be self-controlled and pure, to be busy at home, to be kind, and to be subject to their husbands, so that no one will malign the word of God.

[6]Similarly, encourage the young men to be self-controlled. [7]In everything set them an example by doing what is good. In your teaching show integrity, seriousness [8]and soundness of speech that cannot be condemned, so that those who oppose you may be ashamed because they have nothing bad to say about us.

[9]Teach slaves to be subject to their masters in everything, to try to please them, not to talk back to them, [10]and not to steal from them, but to show that they can be fully trusted, so that in every way they will make the teaching about God our Savior attractive.

[11]For the grace of God that brings salvation has appeared to all men. [12]It teaches us to say "No" to ungodliness and worldly passions, and to live self-controlled, upright and godly lives in this present age, [13]while we wait for the blessed hope—the glorious appearing of our great God and Savior, Jesus Christ, [14]who gave himself for us to redeem us from all wickedness and to purify for himself a people that are his very own, eager to do what is good.

[15]These, then, are the things you should teach. Encourage and rebuke with all authority. Do not let anyone despise you.

DOING WHAT IS GOOD

3 Remind the people to be subject to rulers and authorities, to be obedient, to be ready to do whatever is good, [2]to slander no one, to be peaceable and considerate, and to show true humility toward all men.

[3]At one time we too were foolish, disobedient, deceived and enslaved by all kinds of passions and pleasures. We lived in malice and envy, being hated and hating one another. [4]But when the kindness and love of God our Savior appeared,

THE MESSAGE

every thought and act. They say they know God, but their actions speak louder than their words. They're real creeps, disobedient good-for-nothings.

A GOD-FILLED LIFE

2 2.1-6 Your job is to speak out on the things that make for solid doctrine. Guide older men into lives of temperance, dignity, and wisdom, into healthy faith, love, and endurance. Guide older women into lives of reverence so they end up as neither gossips nor drunks, but models of goodness. By looking at them, the younger women will know how to love their husbands and children, be virtuous and pure, keep a good house, be good wives. We don't want anyone looking down on God's Message because of their behavior. Also, guide the young men to live disciplined lives.

2.7-8 But mostly, show them all this by doing it yourself, incorruptible in your teaching, your words solid and sane. Then anyone who is dead set against us, when he finds nothing weird or misguided, might eventually come around.

2.9-10 Guide slaves into being loyal workers, a bonus to their masters—no back talk, no petty thievery. Then their good character will shine through their actions, adding luster to the teaching of our Savior God.

2.11-14 God's readiness to give and forgive is now public. Salvation's available for everyone! We're being shown how to turn our backs on a godless, indulgent life, and how to take on a God-filled, God-honoring life. This new life is starting right now, and is whetting our appetites for the glorious day when our great God and Savior, Jesus Christ, appears. He offered himself as a sacrifice to free us from a dark, rebellious life into this good, pure life, making us a people he can be proud of, energetic in goodness.

2.15 Tell them all this. Build up their courage, and discipline them if they get out of line. You're in charge. Don't let anyone put you down.

HE PUT OUR LIVES TOGETHER

3 3.1-2 Remind the people to respect the government and be law-abiding, always ready to lend a helping hand. No insults, no fights. God's people should be bighearted and courteous.

3.3-8 It wasn't so long ago that we ourselves were stupid and stubborn, dupes of sin, ordered every which way by our glands, going around with a chip on our shoulder, hated and hating back. But when God, our kind and loving Sav-

NEW INTERNATIONAL VERSION

⁵he saved us, not because of righteous things we had done, but because of his mercy. He saved us through the washing of rebirth and renewal by the Holy Spirit, ⁶whom he poured out on us generously through Jesus Christ our Savior, ⁷so that, having been justified by his grace, we might become heirs having the hope of eternal life. ⁸This is a trustworthy saying. And I want you to stress these things, so that those who have trusted in God may be careful to devote themselves to doing what is good. These things are excellent and profitable for everyone.

⁹But avoid foolish controversies and genealogies and arguments and quarrels about the law, because these are unprofitable and useless. ¹⁰Warn a divisive person once, and then warn him a second time. After that, have nothing to do with him. ¹¹You may be sure that such a man is warped and sinful; he is self-condemned.

FINAL REMARKS

¹²As soon as I send Artemas or Tychicus to you, do your best to come to me at Nicopolis, because I have decided to winter there. ¹³Do everything you can to help Zenas the lawyer and Apollos on their way and see that they have everything they need. ¹⁴Our people must learn to devote themselves to doing what is good, in order that they may provide for daily necessities and not live unproductive lives.

¹⁵Everyone with me sends you greetings. Greet those who love us in the faith.

Grace be with you all.

THE MESSAGE

ior God, stepped in, he saved us from all that. It was all his doing; we had nothing to do with it. He gave us a good bath, and we came out of it new people, washed inside and out by the Holy Spirit. Our Savior Jesus poured out new life so generously. God's gift has restored our relationship with him and given us back our lives. And there's more life to come—an eternity of life! You can count on this.

3.8-11 I want you to put your foot down. Take a firm stand on these matters so that those who have put their trust in God will concentrate on the essentials that are good for everyone. Stay away from mindless, pointless quarreling over genealogies and fine print in the law code. That gets you nowhere. Warn a quarrelsome person once or twice, but then be done with him. It's obvious that such a person is out of line, rebellious against God. By persisting in divisiveness he cuts himself off.

☩

3.12-13 As soon as I send either Artemas or Tychicus to you, come immediately and meet me in Nicopolis. I've decided to spend the winter there. Give Zenas the lawyer and Apollos a hearty send-off. Take good care of them.

3.14 Our people have to learn to be diligent in their work so that all necessities are met (especially among the needy) and they don't end up with nothing to show for their lives.

3.15 All here want to be remembered to you. Say hello to our friends in the faith. Grace to all of you.

PHILEMON

PHILEMON

¹Paul, a prisoner of Christ Jesus, and Timothy our brother,

To Philemon our dear friend and fellow worker, ²to Apphia our sister, to Archippus our fellow soldier and to the church that meets in your home:

³Grace to you and peace from God our Father and the Lord Jesus Christ.

THANKSGIVING AND PRAYER

⁴I always thank my God as I remember you in my prayers, ⁵because I hear about your faith in the Lord Jesus and your love for all the saints. ⁶I pray that you may be active in sharing your faith, so that you will have a full understanding of every good thing we have in Christ. ⁷Your love has given me great joy and encouragement, because you, brother, have refreshed the hearts of the saints.

PAUL'S PLEA FOR ONESIMUS

⁸Therefore, although in Christ I could be bold and order you to do what you ought to do, ⁹yet I appeal to you on the basis of love. I then, as Paul—an old man and now also a prisoner of Christ Jesus— ¹⁰I appeal to you for my son Onesimus,ᵃ who became my son while I was in chains. ¹¹Formerly he was useless to you, but now he has become useful both to you and to me.

¹²I am sending him—who is my very heart—back to you. ¹³I would have liked to keep him with me so that he could take your place in helping me while I am in chains for the gospel. ¹⁴But I did not want to do anything without your consent, so that any favor you do will be spontaneous and not forced. ¹⁵Perhaps the reason he was separated from you for a little while was that you might have him back for good— ¹⁶no longer as a slave, but better than a slave, as a dear brother. He is very dear to me but even dearer to you, both as a man and as a brother in the Lord.

¹⁷So if you consider me a partner, welcome him as you would welcome me. ¹⁸If he has done

1-3 I, Paul, am a prisoner for the sake of Christ, here with my brother Timothy. I write this letter to you, Philemon, my good friend and companion in this work—also to our sister Apphia, to Archippus, a real trooper, and to the church that meets in your house. God's best to you! Christ's blessings on you!

4-7 Every time your name comes up in my prayers, I say, "Oh, thank you, God!" I keep hearing of the love and faith you have for the Master Jesus, which brims over to other Christians. And I keep praying that this faith we hold in common keeps showing up in the good things we do, and that people recognize Christ in all of it. Friend, you have no idea how good your love makes me feel, doubly so when I see your hospitality to fellow believers.

TO CALL THE SLAVE YOUR FRIEND

8-9 In line with all this I have a favor to ask of you. As Christ's ambassador and now a prisoner for him, I wouldn't hesitate to command this if I thought it necessary, but I'd rather make it a personal request.

10-14 While here in jail, I've fathered a child, so to speak. And here he is, hand-carrying this letter—Onesimus! He was useless to you before; now he's useful to both of us. I'm sending him back to you, but it feels like I'm cutting off my right arm in doing so. I wanted in the worst way to keep him here as your stand-in to help out while I'm in jail for the Message. But I didn't want to do anything behind your back, make you do a good deed that you hadn't willingly agreed to.

15-16 Maybe it's all for the best that you lost him for a while. You're getting him back now for good—and no mere slave this time, but a true Christian brother! That's what he was to me—he'll be even more than that to you.

17-20 So if you still consider me a comrade-in-arms, welcome him back as you would me. If

---

ᵃ 10 *Onesimus* means *useful*.

NEW INTERNATIONAL VERSION

you any wrong or owes you anything, charge it to me. [19]I, Paul, am writing this with my own hand. I will pay it back—not to mention that you owe me your very self. [20]I do wish, brother, that I may have some benefit from you in the Lord; refresh my heart in Christ. [21]Confident of your obedience, I write to you, knowing that you will do even more than I ask.

[22]And one thing more: Prepare a guest room for me, because I hope to be restored to you in answer to your prayers.

[23]Epaphras, my fellow prisoner in Christ Jesus, sends you greetings. [24]And so do Mark, Aristarchus, Demas and Luke, my fellow workers.

[25]The grace of the Lord Jesus Christ be with your spirit.

THE MESSAGE

he damaged anything or owes you anything, chalk it up to my account. This is my personal signature—Paul—and I stand behind it. (I don't need to remind you, do I, that you owe your very life to me?) Do me this big favor, friend. You'll be doing it for Christ, but it will also do my heart good.

[21-22] I know you well enough to know you will. You'll probably go far beyond what I've written. And by the way, get a room ready for me. Because of your prayers, I fully expect to be your guest again.

[23-25] Epaphras, my cellmate in the cause of Christ, says hello. Also my coworkers Mark, Aristarchus, Demas, and Luke. All the best to you from the Master, Jesus Christ!

HEBREWS

HEBREWS

THE SON SUPERIOR TO ANGELS

1 In the past God spoke to our forefathers through the prophets at many times and in various ways, [2] but in these last days he has spoken to us by his Son, whom he appointed heir of all things, and through whom he made the universe. [3] The Son is the radiance of God's glory and the exact representation of his being, sustaining all things by his powerful word. After he had provided purification for sins, he sat down at the right hand of the Majesty in heaven. [4] So he became as much superior to the angels as the name he has inherited is superior to theirs.

[5] For to which of the angels did God ever say,

"You are my Son;
　today I have become your Father[a]"[b]?

Or again,

"I will be his Father,
　and he will be my Son"[c]?

[6] And again, when God brings his firstborn into the world, he says,

"Let all God's angels worship him."[d]

[7] In speaking of the angels he says,

"He makes his angels winds,
　his servants flames of fire."[e]

[8] But about the Son he says,

"Your throne, O God, will last for ever and ever,
　and righteousness will be the scepter of
　　your kingdom.
[9] You have loved righteousness and hated
　　wickedness;
　therefore God, your God, has set you
　　above your companions
　by anointing you with the oil of joy."[f]

[10] He also says,

"In the beginning, O Lord, you laid the
　foundations of the earth,

1.1-3 **1** Going through a long line of prophets, God has been addressing our ancestors in different ways for centuries. Recently he spoke to us directly through his Son. By his Son, God created the world in the beginning, and it will all belong to the Son at the end. This Son perfectly mirrors God, and is stamped with God's nature. He holds everything together by what he says—powerful words!

THE SON IS HIGHER THAN ANGELS

1.3-6 After he finished the sacrifice for sins, the Son took his honored place high in the heavens right alongside God, far higher than any angel in rank and rule. Did God ever say to an angel, "You're my Son; today I celebrate you"? Or, "I'm his Father, he's my Son"? When he presents his honored Son to the world, he says, "All angels must worship him."

1.7 Regarding angels he says,

The messengers are winds,
　the servants are tongues of fire.

1.8-9 But he says to the Son,
You're God, and on the throne for good;
　your rule makes everything right.
You love it when things are right;
　you hate it when things are wrong.
That is why God, your God,
　poured fragrant oil on your head,
Marking you out as king,
　far above your dear companions.

1.10-12 And again to the Son,
You, Master, started it all, laid earth's
　　foundations,

---

[a] 5 Or *have begotten you*　[b] 5 Psalm 2:7
[c] 5 2 Samuel 7:14; 1 Chron. 17:13　[d] 6 Deut. 32:43 (see
Dead Sea Scrolls and Septuagint)　[e] 7 Psalm 104:4
[f] 9 Psalm 45:6,7

NEW INTERNATIONAL VERSION

and the heavens are the work of your
hands.
¹¹They will perish, but you remain;
they will all wear out like a garment.
¹²You will roll them up like a robe,
like a garment they will be changed.
But you remain the same,
and your years will never end." ᵃ

¹³To which of the angels did God ever say,

"Sit at my right hand
until I make your enemies
a footstool for your feet" ᵇ?

¹⁴Are not all angels ministering spirits sent to
serve those who will inherit salvation?

WARNING TO PAY ATTENTION

2 We must pay more careful attention, therefore, to what we have heard, so that we do
not drift away. ²For if the message spoken by angels was binding, and every violation and disobedience received its just punishment, ³how
shall we escape if we ignore such a great salvation? This salvation, which was first announced
by the Lord, was confirmed to us by those who
heard him. ⁴God also testified to it by signs,
wonders and various miracles, and gifts of the
Holy Spirit distributed according to his will.

JESUS MADE LIKE HIS BROTHERS

⁵It is not to angels that he has subjected the
world to come, about which we are speaking.
⁶But there is a place where someone has testified:

"What is man that you are mindful of him,
the son of man that you care for him?
⁷You made him a little ᶜ lower than the angels;
you crowned him with glory and honor
⁸ and put everything under his feet." ᵈ

In putting everything under him, God left nothing that is not subject to him. Yet at present we
do not see everything subject to him. ⁹But we
see Jesus, who was made a little lower than the
angels, now crowned with glory and honor because he suffered death, so that by the grace of
God he might taste death for everyone.

¹⁰In bringing many sons to glory, it was fitting
that God, for whom and through whom everything exists, should make the author of their salvation perfect through suffering. ¹¹Both the one
who makes men holy and those who are made

THE MESSAGE

then crafted the stars in the sky.
Earth and sky will wear out, but not you;
they become threadbare like an old coat;
You'll fold them up like a worn-out cloak,
and lay them away on the shelf.
But you'll stay the same, year after year;
you'll never fade, you'll never wear out.

1.13 And did he ever say anything like this to an
angel?

Sit alongside me here on my throne
Until I make your enemies a stool for your
feet.

1.14 Isn't it obvious that all angels are sent to
help out with those lined up to receive salvation?

2 2.1-4 It's crucial that we keep a firm grip on what
we've heard so that we don't drift off. If the
old message delivered by the angels was valid
and nobody got away with anything, do you
think we can risk neglecting this latest message, this magnificent salvation? First of all, it
was delivered in person by the Master, then accurately passed on to us by those who heard it
from him. All the while God was validating it
with gifts through the Holy Spirit, all sorts of
signs and miracles, as he saw fit.

THE SALVATION PIONEER

2.5-9 God didn't put angels in charge of this business of salvation that we're dealing with here. It
says in Scripture,

What is man and woman that you bother
with them;
why take a second look their way?
You made them not quite as high as angels,
bright with Eden's dawn light;
Then you put them in charge
of your entire handcrafted world.

When God put them in charge of everything,
nothing was excluded. But we don't see it yet,
don't see everything under human jurisdiction.
What we do see is Jesus, made "not quite as
high as angels," and then, through the experience of death, crowned so much higher than
any angel, with a glory "bright with Eden's
dawn light." In that death, by God's grace, he
fully experienced death in every person's place.

2.10-13 It makes good sense that the God who got
everything started and keeps everything going
now completes the work by making the Salvation Pioneer perfect through suffering as he
leads all these people to glory. Since the One
who saves and those who are saved have a

ᵃ 12 Psalm 102:25-27   ᵇ 13 Psalm 110:1   ᶜ 7 Or *him for
a little while*; also in verse 9   ᵈ 8 Psalm 8:4-6

NEW INTERNATIONAL VERSION

holy are of the same family. So Jesus is not ashamed to call them brothers. 12He says,

> "I will declare your name to my brothers;
>   in the presence of the congregation I will
>   sing your praises." *a*

13And again,

> "I will put my trust in him." *b*

And again he says,

> "Here am I, and the children God has given
>   me." *c*

14Since the children have flesh and blood, he too shared in their humanity so that by his death he might destroy him who holds the power of death—that is, the devil— 15and free those who all their lives were held in slavery by their fear of death. 16For surely it is not angels he helps, but Abraham's descendants. 17For this reason he had to be made like his brothers in every way, in order that he might become a merciful and faithful high priest in service to God, and that he might make atonement for *d* the sins of the people. 18Because he himself suffered when he was tempted, he is able to help those who are being tempted.

JESUS GREATER THAN MOSES

3 Therefore, holy brothers, who share in the heavenly calling, fix your thoughts on Jesus, the apostle and high priest whom we confess. 2He was faithful to the one who appointed him, just as Moses was faithful in all God's house. 3Jesus has been found worthy of greater honor than Moses, just as the builder of a house has greater honor than the house itself. 4For every house is built by someone, but God is the builder of everything. 5Moses was faithful as a servant in all God's house, testifying to what would be said in the future. 6But Christ is faithful as a son over God's house. And we are his house, if we hold on to our courage and the hope of which we boast.

WARNING AGAINST UNBELIEF

7So, as the Holy Spirit says:

> "Today, if you hear his voice,
> 8   do not harden your hearts
>   as you did in the rebellion,
>   during the time of testing in the desert,
> 9where your fathers tested and tried me
>   and for forty years saw what I did.

THE MESSAGE

common origin, Jesus doesn't hesitate to treat them as family, saying,

> I'll tell my good friends, my brothers and
>   sisters, all I know about you;
> I'll join them in worship and praise to you.

Again, he puts himself in the same family circle when he says,

> Even *I* live by placing my trust in God.

And yet again,

> I'm here with the children God gave me.

2.14-15 Since the children are made of flesh and blood, it's logical that the Savior took on flesh and blood in order to rescue them by his death. By embracing death, taking it into himself, he destroyed the Devil's hold on death and freed all who cower through life, scared to death of death.

2.16-18 It's obvious, of course, that he didn't go to all this trouble for angels. It was for people like us, children of Abraham. That's why he had to enter into every detail of human life. Then, when he came before God as high priest to get rid of the people's sins, he would have already experienced it all himself—all the pain, all the testing—and would be able to help where help was needed.

THE CENTERPIECE OF ALL WE BELIEVE

3.1-6 **3** So, my dear Christian friends, companions in following this call to the heights, take a good hard look at Jesus. He's the centerpiece of everything we believe, faithful in everything God gave him to do. Moses was also faithful, but Jesus gets far more honor. A builder is more valuable than a building any day. Every house has a builder, but the Builder behind them all is God. Moses did a good job in God's house, but it was all servant work, getting things ready for what was to come. Christ as Son is in charge of the house.

3.6-11 Now, if we can only keep a firm grip on this bold confidence, we're the house! That's why the Holy Spirit says,

> Today, please listen;
>   don't turn a deaf ear as in "the bitter
>   uprising,"
>   that time of wilderness testing!
> Even though they watched me at work for
>   forty years,
>   your ancestors refused to let me do it my
>   way;
>   over and over they tried my patience.

NEW INTERNATIONAL VERSION

¹⁰That is why I was angry with that
    generation,
  and I said, 'Their hearts are always going
    astray,
  and they have not known my ways.'
¹¹So I declared on oath in my anger,
  'They shall never enter my rest.' " ᵃ

¹²See to it, brothers, that none of you has a sinful, unbelieving heart that turns away from the living God. ¹³But encourage one another daily, as long as it is called Today, so that none of you may be hardened by sin's deceitfulness. ¹⁴We have come to share in Christ if we hold firmly till the end the confidence we had at first. ¹⁵As has just been said:

  "Today, if you hear his voice,
    do not harden your hearts
    as you did in the rebellion." ᵇ

¹⁶Who were they who heard and rebelled? Were they not all those Moses led out of Egypt? ¹⁷And with whom was he angry for forty years? Was it not with those who sinned, whose bodies fell in the desert? ¹⁸And to whom did God swear that they would never enter his rest if not to those who disobeyed ᶜ? ¹⁹So we see that they were not able to enter, because of their unbelief.

A SABBATH-REST FOR THE PEOPLE OF GOD

4 Therefore, since the promise of entering his rest still stands, let us be careful that none of you be found to have fallen short of it. ²For we also have had the gospel preached to us, just as they did; but the message they heard was of no value to them, because those who heard did not combine it with faith. ᵈ ³Now we who have believed enter that rest, just as God has said,

  "So I declared on oath in my anger,
    'They shall never enter my rest.' " ᵉ

And yet his work has been finished since the creation of the world. ⁴For somewhere he has spoken about the seventh day in these words: "And on the seventh day God rested from all his work." ᶠ ⁵And again in the passage above he says, "They shall never enter my rest."

⁶It still remains that some will enter that rest, and those who formerly had the gospel preached to them did not go in, because of their disobedience. ⁷Therefore God again set a certain day, call-

ᵃ 11 Psalm 95:7-11   ᵇ 15 Psalm 95:7,8
ᶜ 18 Or disbelieved   ᵈ 2 Many manuscripts because they
did not share in the faith of those who obeyed
ᵉ 3 Psalm 95:11; also in verse 5   ᶠ 4 Gen. 2:2

THE MESSAGE

  And I was provoked, oh, so provoked!
    I said, "They'll never keep their minds
      on God;
    they refuse to walk down my road."
  Exasperated, I vowed,
    "They'll never get where they're going,
    never be able to sit down and rest."

3.12-14   So watch your step, friends. Make sure there's no evil unbelief lying around that will trip you up and throw you off course, diverting you from the living God. For as long as it's still God's Today, keep each other on your toes so sin doesn't slow down your reflexes. If we can only keep our grip on the sure thing we started out with, we're in this with Christ for the long haul.

These words keep ringing in our ears:

  Today, please listen;
    don't turn a deaf ear as in the bitter
      uprising.

3.15-19   For who were the people who turned a deaf ear? Weren't they the very ones Moses led out of Egypt? And who was God provoked with for forty years? Wasn't it those who turned a deaf ear and ended up corpses in the wilderness? And when he swore that they'd never get where they were going, wasn't he talking to the ones who turned a deaf ear? They never got there because they never listened, never believed.

WHEN THE PROMISES ARE MIXED WITH FAITH

4.1-3   4 For as long, then, as that promise of resting in him pulls us on to God's goal for us, we need to be careful that we're not disqualified. We received the same promises as those people in the wilderness, but the promises didn't do them a bit of good because they didn't receive the promises with faith. If we believe, though, we'll experience that state of resting. But not if we don't have faith. Remember that God said,

  Exasperated, I vowed,
    "They'll never get where they're going,
    never be able to sit down and rest."

4.3-7   God made that vow, even though he'd finished his part before the foundation of the world. Somewhere it's written, "God rested the seventh day, having completed his work," but in this other text he says, "They'll never be able to sit down and rest." So this promise has not yet been fulfilled. Those earlier ones never did get to the place of rest because they were disobedient. God keeps renewing the promise and setting the date

NEW INTERNATIONAL VERSION

ing it Today, when a long time later he spoke through David, as was said before:

> "Today, if you hear his voice,
> do not harden your hearts." [a]

[8]For if Joshua had given them rest, God would not have spoken later about another day. [9]There remains, then, a Sabbath-rest for the people of God; [10]for anyone who enters God's rest also rests from his own work, just as God did from his. [11]Let us, therefore, make every effort to enter that rest, so that no one will fall by following their example of disobedience.

[12]For the word of God is living and active. Sharper than any double-edged sword, it penetrates even to dividing soul and spirit, joints and marrow; it judges the thoughts and attitudes of the heart. [13]Nothing in all creation is hidden from God's sight. Everything is uncovered and laid bare before the eyes of him to whom we must give account.

JESUS THE GREAT HIGH PRIEST

[14]Therefore, since we have a great high priest who has gone through the heavens,[b] Jesus the Son of God, let us hold firmly to the faith we profess. [15]For we do not have a high priest who is unable to sympathize with our weaknesses, but we have one who has been tempted in every way, just as we are—yet was without sin. [16]Let us then approach the throne of grace with confidence, so that we may receive mercy and find grace to help us in our time of need.

[5] Every high priest is selected from among men and is appointed to represent them in matters related to God, to offer gifts and sacrifices for sins. [2]He is able to deal gently with those who are ignorant and are going astray, since he himself is subject to weakness. [3]This is why he has to offer sacrifices for his own sins, as well as for the sins of the people.

[4]No one takes this honor upon himself; he must be called by God, just as Aaron was. [5]So Christ also did not take upon himself the glory of becoming a high priest. But God said to him,

> "You are my Son;
> today I have become your Father." [c] [d]

[6]And he says in another place,

> "You are a priest forever,
> in the order of Melchizedek." [e]

THE MESSAGE

as *today*, just as he did in David's psalm, centuries later than the original invitation:

> Today, please listen,
> don't turn a deaf ear . . .

4.8-11 And so this is still a live promise. It wasn't canceled at the time of Joshua; otherwise, God wouldn't keep renewing the appointment for "today." The promise of "arrival" and "rest" is still there for God's people. God himself is at rest. And at the end of the journey we'll surely rest with God. So let's keep at it and eventually arrive at the place of rest, not drop out through some sort of disobedience.

4.12-13 God means what he says. What he says goes. His powerful Word is sharp as a surgeon's scalpel, cutting through everything, whether doubt or defense, laying us open to listen and obey. Nothing and no one is impervious to God's Word. We can't get away from it—no matter what.

THE HIGH PRIEST WHO CRIED OUT IN PAIN

4.14-16 Now that we know what we have—Jesus, this great High Priest with ready access to God—let's not let it slip through our fingers. We don't have a priest who is out of touch with our reality. He's been through weakness and testing, experienced it all—all but the sin. So let's walk right up to him and get what he is so ready to give. Take the mercy, accept the help.

5.1-3 [5] Every high priest selected to represent men and women before God and offer sacrifices for their sins should be able to deal gently with their failings, since he knows what it's like from his own experience. But that also means that he has to offer sacrifices for his own sins as well as the people's.

5.4-6 No one elects himself to this honored position. He's called to it by God, as Aaron was. Neither did Christ presume to set himself up as high priest, but was set apart by the One who said to him, "You're my Son; today I celebrate you!" In another place God declares, "You're a priest forever in the royal order of Melchizedek."

---

[a] 7 Psalm 95:7,8   [b] 14 Or gone into heaven   [c] 5 Or have begotten you   [d] 5 Psalm 2:7   [e] 6 Psalm 110:4

NEW INTERNATIONAL VERSION

⁷During the days of Jesus' life on earth, he offered up prayers and petitions with loud cries and tears to the one who could save him from death, and he was heard because of his reverent submission. ⁸Although he was a son, he learned obedience from what he suffered ⁹and, once made perfect, he became the source of eternal salvation for all who obey him ¹⁰and was designated by God to be high priest in the order of Melchizedek.

WARNING AGAINST FALLING AWAY

¹¹We have much to say about this, but it is hard to explain because you are slow to learn. ¹²In fact, though by this time you ought to be teachers, you need someone to teach you the elementary truths of God's word all over again. You need milk, not solid food! ¹³Anyone who lives on milk, being still an infant, is not acquainted with the teaching about righteousness. ¹⁴But solid food is for the mature, who by constant use have trained themselves to distinguish good from evil.

6 Therefore let us leave the elementary teachings about Christ and go on to maturity, not laying again the foundation of repentance from acts that lead to death,ᵃ and of faith in God, ²instruction about baptisms, the laying on of hands, the resurrection of the dead, and eternal judgment. ³And God permitting, we will do so.

⁴It is impossible for those who have once been enlightened, who have tasted the heavenly gift, who have shared in the Holy Spirit, ⁵who have tasted the goodness of the word of God and the powers of the coming age, ⁶if they fall away, to be brought back to repentance, becauseᵇ to their loss they are crucifying the Son of God all over again and subjecting him to public disgrace.

⁷Land that drinks in the rain often falling on it and that produces a crop useful to those for whom it is farmed receives the blessing of God. ⁸But land that produces thorns and thistles is worthless and is in danger of being cursed. In the end it will be burned.

⁹Even though we speak like this, dear friends, we are confident of better things in your case—things that accompany salvation. ¹⁰God is not unjust; he will not forget your work and the love you have shown him as you have helped his people and continue to help them. ¹¹We want each

THE MESSAGE

5.7-10 While he lived on earth, anticipating death, Jesus cried out in pain and wept in sorrow as he offered up priestly prayers to God. Because he honored God, God answered him. Though he was God's Son, he learned trusting-obedience by what he suffered, just as we do. Then, having arrived at the full stature of his maturity and having been announced by God as high priest in the order of Melchizedek, he became the source of eternal salvation to all who believingly obey him.

RE-CRUCIFYING JESUS

5.11-14 I have a lot more to say about this, but it is hard to get it across to you since you've picked up this bad habit of not listening. By this time you ought to be teachers yourselves, yet here I find you need someone to sit down with you and go over the basics on God again, starting from square one—baby's milk, when you should have been on solid food long ago! Milk is for beginners, inexperienced in God's ways; solid food is for the mature, who have some practice in telling right from wrong.

6.1-3 6 So come on, let's leave the preschool fingerpainting exercises on Christ and get on with the grand work of art. Grow up in Christ. The basic foundational truths are in place: turning your back on "salvation by self-help" and turning in trust toward God; baptismal instructions; laying on of hands; resurrection of the dead; eternal judgment. God helping us, we'll stay true to all that. But there's so much more. Let's get on with it!

6.4-8 Once people have seen the light, gotten a taste of heaven and been part of the work of the Holy Spirit, once they've personally experienced the sheer goodness of God's Word and the powers breaking in on us—if then they turn their backs on it, washing their hands of the whole thing, well, they can't start over as if nothing happened. That's impossible. Why, they've re-crucified Jesus! They've repudiated him in public! Parched ground that soaks up the rain and then produces an abundance of carrots and corn for its gardener gets God's "Well done!" But if it produces weeds and thistles, it's more likely to get cussed out. Fields like that are burned, not harvested.

6.9-12 I'm sure that won't happen to you, friends. I have better things in mind for you—salvation things! God doesn't miss anything. He knows perfectly well all the love you've shown him by helping needy Christians, and that you keep at it. And now I want each of you to extend that

---

ᵃ 1 Or from useless rituals   ᵇ 6 Or repentance while

NEW INTERNATIONAL VERSION

of you to show this same diligence to the very end, in order to make your hope sure. ¹²We do not want you to become lazy, but to imitate those who through faith and patience inherit what has been promised.

THE CERTAINTY OF GOD'S PROMISE

¹³When God made his promise to Abraham, since there was no one greater for him to swear by, he swore by himself, ¹⁴saying, "I will surely bless you and give you many descendants."ᵃ ¹⁵And so after waiting patiently, Abraham received what was promised.

¹⁶Men swear by someone greater than themselves, and the oath confirms what is said and puts an end to all argument. ¹⁷Because God wanted to make the unchanging nature of his purpose very clear to the heirs of what was promised, he confirmed it with an oath. ¹⁸God did this so that, by two unchangeable things in which it is impossible for God to lie, we who have fled to take hold of the hope offered to us may be greatly encouraged. ¹⁹We have this hope as an anchor for the soul, firm and secure. It enters the inner sanctuary behind the curtain, ²⁰where Jesus, who went before us, has entered on our behalf. He has become a high priest forever, in the order of Melchizedek.

MELCHIZEDEK THE PRIEST

7 This Melchizedek was king of Salem and priest of God Most High. He met Abraham returning from the defeat of the kings and blessed him, ²and Abraham gave him a tenth of everything. First, his name means "king of righteousness"; then also, "king of Salem" means "king of peace." ³Without father or mother, without genealogy, without beginning of days or end of life, like the Son of God he remains a priest forever.

⁴Just think how great he was: Even the patriarch Abraham gave him a tenth of the plunder! ⁵Now the law requires the descendants of Levi who become priests to collect a tenth from the people—that is, their brothers—even though their brothers are descended from Abraham. ⁶This man, however, did not trace his descent from Levi, yet he collected a tenth from Abraham and blessed him who had the promises. ⁷And without doubt the lesser person is blessed by the greater. ⁸In the one case, the tenth is collected by men who die; but in the other case, by

THE MESSAGE

same intensity toward a full-bodied hope, and keep at it till the finish. Don't drag your feet. Be like those who stay the course with committed faith and then get everything promised to them.

GOD GAVE HIS WORD

6.13-18 When God made his promise to Abraham, he backed it to the hilt, putting his own reputation on the line. He said, "I promise that I'll bless you with everything I have—bless and bless and bless!" Abraham stuck it out and got everything that had been promised to him. When people make promises, they guarantee them by appeal to some authority above them so that if there is any question that they'll make good on the promise, the authority will back them up. When God wanted to guarantee his promises, he gave his word, a rock-solid guarantee—God *can't* break his word. And because his word cannot change, the promise is likewise unchangeable.

6.18-20 We who have run for our very lives to God have every reason to grab the promised hope with both hands and never let go. It's an unbreakable spiritual lifeline, reaching past all appearances right to the very presence of God where Jesus, running on ahead of us, has taken up his permanent post as high priest for us, in the order of Melchizedek.

MELCHIZEDEK, PRIEST OF GOD

7.1-3 **7** Melchizedek was king of Salem and priest of the Highest God. He met Abraham, who was returning from "the royal massacre," and gave him his blessing. Abraham in turn gave him a tenth of the spoils. "Melchizedek" means "King of Righteousness." "Salem" means "Peace." So, he is also "King of Peace." Melchizedek towers out of the past—without record of family ties, no account of beginning or end. In this way he is like the Son of God, one huge priestly presence dominating the landscape always.

7.4-7 You realize just how great Melchizedek is when you see that Father Abraham gave him a tenth of the captured treasure. Priests descended from Levi are commanded by law to collect tithes from the people, even though they are all more or less equals, priests and people, having a common father in Abraham. But this man, a complete outsider, collected tithes from Abraham and blessed him, the one to whom the promises had been given. In acts of blessing, the lesser is blessed by the greater.

7.8-10 Or look at it this way: We pay our tithes to priests who die, but Abraham paid tithes to a

NEW INTERNATIONAL VERSION

him who is declared to be living. ⁹One might even say that Levi, who collects the tenth, paid the tenth through Abraham, ¹⁰because when Melchizedek met Abraham, Levi was still in the body of his ancestor.

Jesus Like Melchizedek

¹¹If perfection could have been attained through the Levitical priesthood (for on the basis of it the law was given to the people), why was there still need for another priest to come— one in the order of Melchizedek, not in the order of Aaron? ¹²For when there is a change of the priesthood, there must also be a change of the law. ¹³He of whom these things are said belonged to a different tribe, and no one from that tribe has ever served at the altar. ¹⁴For it is clear that our Lord descended from Judah, and in regard to that tribe Moses said nothing about priests. ¹⁵And what we have said is even more clear if another priest like Melchizedek appears, ¹⁶one who has become a priest not on the basis of a regulation as to his ancestry but on the basis of the power of an indestructible life. ¹⁷For it is declared:

"You are a priest forever,
  in the order of Melchizedek." ᵃ

¹⁸The former regulation is set aside because it was weak and useless ¹⁹(for the law made nothing perfect), and a better hope is introduced, by which we draw near to God.

²⁰And it was not without an oath! Others became priests without any oath, ²¹but he became a priest with an oath when God said to him:

"The Lord has sworn
  and will not change his mind:
'You are a priest forever.' " ᵃ

²²Because of this oath, Jesus has become the guarantee of a better covenant.

²³Now there have been many of those priests, since death prevented them from continuing in office; ²⁴but because Jesus lives forever, he has a permanent priesthood. ²⁵Therefore he is able to save completely ᵇ those who come to God through him, because he always lives to intercede for them.

²⁶Such a high priest meets our need—one who is holy, blameless, pure, set apart from sinners, exalted above the heavens. ²⁷Unlike the other high priests, he does not need to offer sacrifices day after day, first for his own sins, and then for the sins of the people. He sacrificed for their sins once for all when he offered himself. ²⁸For the law appoints as high priests men who

THE MESSAGE

priest who, the Scripture says, "lives." Ultimately you could even say that since Levi descended from Abraham, who paid tithes to Melchizedek, when we pay tithes to the priestly tribe of Levi they end up with Melchizedek.

A Permanent Priesthood

7.11-14 If the priesthood of Levi and Aaron, which provided the framework for the giving of the law, could really make people perfect, there wouldn't have been need for a new priesthood like that of Melchizedek. But since it didn't get the job done, there was a change of priesthood, which brought with it a radical new kind of law. There is no way of understanding this in terms of the old Levitical priesthood, which is why there is nothing in Jesus' family tree connecting him with that priestly line.

7.15-19 But the Melchizedek story provides a perfect analogy: Jesus, a priest like Melchizedek, not by genealogical descent but by the sheer force of resurrection life—he lives!—"priest forever in the royal order of Melchizedek." The former way of doing things, a system of commandments that never worked out the way it was supposed to, was set aside; the law brought nothing to maturity. Another way—Jesus!—a way that *does* work, that brings us right into the presence of God, is put in its place.

7.20-22 The old priesthood of Aaron perpetuated itself automatically, father to son, without explicit confirmation by God. But then God intervened and called this new, permanent priesthood into being with an added promise:

God gave his word;
  he won't take it back:
"You're the permanent priest."

This makes Jesus the guarantee of a far better way between us and God—one that really works! A new covenant.

7.23-25 Earlier there were a lot of priests, for they died and had to be replaced. But Jesus' priesthood is permanent. He's there from now to eternity to save everyone who comes to God through him, always on the job to speak up for them.

7.26-28 So now we have a high priest who perfectly fits our needs: completely holy, uncompromised by sin, with authority extending as high as God's presence in heaven itself. Unlike the other high priests, he doesn't have to offer sacrifices for his own sins every day before he can get around to us and our sins. He's done it, once and for all: offered up *himself* as the sacrifice. The law appoints as high priests men who

---

ᵃ 17,21 Psalm 110:4 ᵇ 25 Or *forever*

NEW INTERNATIONAL VERSION

are weak; but the oath, which came after the law, appointed the Son, who has been made perfect forever.

THE HIGH PRIEST OF A NEW COVENANT

8 The point of what we are saying is this: We do have such a high priest, who sat down at the right hand of the throne of the Majesty in heaven, ²and who serves in the sanctuary, the true tabernacle set up by the Lord, not by man.

³Every high priest is appointed to offer both gifts and sacrifices, and so it was necessary for this one also to have something to offer. ⁴If he were on earth, he would not be a priest, for there are already men who offer the gifts prescribed by the law. ⁵They serve at a sanctuary that is a copy and shadow of what is in heaven. This is why Moses was warned when he was about to build the tabernacle: "See to it that you make everything according to the pattern shown you on the mountain." *a* ⁶But the ministry Jesus has received is as superior to theirs as the covenant of which he is mediator is superior to the old one, and it is founded on better promises.

⁷For if there had been nothing wrong with that first covenant, no place would have been sought for another. ⁸But God found fault with the people and said *b*:

"The time is coming, declares the Lord,
    when I will make a new covenant
with the house of Israel
    and with the house of Judah.
⁹It will not be like the covenant
    I made with their forefathers
when I took them by the hand
    to lead them out of Egypt,
because they did not remain faithful to my
        covenant,
    and I turned away from them,
            declares the Lord.
¹⁰This is the covenant I will make with the
        house of Israel
    after that time, declares the Lord.
I will put my laws in their minds
    and write them on their hearts.
I will be their God,
    and they will be my people.
¹¹No longer will a man teach his neighbor,
    or a man his brother, saying, 'Know the
        Lord,'
because they will all know me,
    from the least of them to the greatest.
¹²For I will forgive their wickedness
    and will remember their sins no more." *c*

a 5 Exodus 25:40   *b* 8 Some manuscripts may be translated *fault and said to the people.*   *c* 12 Jer. 31:31-34

THE MESSAGE

are never able to get the job done right. But this intervening command of God, which came later, appoints the Son, who is absolutely, eternally perfect.

A NEW PLAN WITH ISRAEL

8.1-2 **8** In essence, we have just such a high priest: authoritative right alongside God, conducting worship in the one true sanctuary built by God.

8.3-5 The assigned task of a high priest is to offer both gifts and sacrifices, and it's no different with the priesthood of Jesus. If he were limited to earth, he wouldn't even be a priest. We wouldn't need him since there are plenty of priests who offer the gifts designated in the law. These priests provide only a hint of what goes on in the true sanctuary of heaven, which Moses caught a glimpse of as he was about to set up the tent-shrine. It was then that God said, "Be careful to do it exactly as you saw it on the Mountain."

8.6-13 But Jesus' priestly work far surpasses what these other priests do, since he's working from a far better plan. If the first plan—the old covenant—had worked out, a second wouldn't have been needed. But we know the first was found wanting, because God said,

Heads up! The days are coming
    when I'll set up a new plan
        for dealing with Israel and Judah.
I'll throw out the old plan
    I set up with their ancestors
        when I led them by the hand out of
            Egypt.
They didn't keep their part of the bargain,
    so I looked away and let it go.
This new plan I'm making with Israel
    isn't going to be written on paper,
    isn't going to be chiseled in stone;
This time I'm writing out the plan *in* them,
    carving it on the lining of their hearts.
I'll be their God,
    they'll be my people.
They won't go to school to learn about me,
    or buy a book called *God in Five Easy
        Lessons.*
They'll all get to know me firsthand,
    the little and the big, the small and the
        great.
They'll get to know me by being kindly
        forgiven,
    with the slate of their sins forever wiped
        clean.

NEW INTERNATIONAL VERSION

¹³By calling this covenant "new," he has made the first one obsolete; and what is obsolete and aging will soon disappear.

WORSHIP IN THE EARTHLY TABERNACLE

9 Now the first covenant had regulations for worship and also an earthly sanctuary. ²A tabernacle was set up. In its first room were the lampstand, the table and the consecrated bread; this was called the Holy Place. ³Behind the second curtain was a room called the Most Holy Place, ⁴which had the golden altar of incense and the gold-covered ark of the covenant. This ark contained the gold jar of manna, Aaron's staff that had budded, and the stone tablets of the covenant. ⁵Above the ark were the cherubim of the Glory, overshadowing the atonement cover.ᵃ But we cannot discuss these things in detail now. ⁶When everything had been arranged like this, the priests entered regularly into the outer room to carry on their ministry. ⁷But only the high priest entered the inner room, and that only once a year, and never without blood, which he offered for himself and for the sins the people had committed in ignorance. ⁸The Holy Spirit was showing by this that the way into the Most Holy Place had not yet been disclosed as long as the first tabernacle was still standing. ⁹This is an illustration for the present time, indicating that the gifts and sacrifices being offered were not able to clear the conscience of the worshiper. ¹⁰They are only a matter of food and drink and various ceremonial washings—external regulations applying until the time of the new order.

THE BLOOD OF CHRIST

¹¹When Christ came as high priest of the good things that are already here,ᵇ he went through the greater and more perfect tabernacle that is not man-made, that is to say, not a part of this creation. ¹²He did not enter by means of the blood of goats and calves; but he entered the Most Holy Place once for all by his own blood, having obtained eternal redemption. ¹³The blood of goats and bulls and the ashes of a heifer sprinkled on those who are ceremonially unclean sanctify them so that they are outwardly clean. ¹⁴How much more, then, will the blood of Christ, who through the eternal Spirit offered himself unblemished to God, cleanse our consciences from acts that lead to death,ᶜ so that we may serve the living God! ¹⁵For this reason Christ is the mediator of a new covenant, that those who are called may re-

THE MESSAGE

By coming up with a new plan, a new covenant between God and his people, God put the old plan on the shelf. And there it stays, gathering dust.

A VISIBLE PARABLE

9.1-5 **9** That first plan contained directions for worship, and a specially designed place of worship. A large outer tent was set up. The lampstand, the table, and "the bread of presence" were placed in it. This was called "the Holy Place." Then a curtain was stretched, and behind it a smaller, inside tent set up. This was called "the Holy of Holies." In it were placed the gold incense altar and the gold-covered ark of the covenant containing the gold urn of manna, Aaron's rod that budded, the covenant tablets, and the angel-wing-shadowed mercy seat. But we don't have time to comment on these now.

9.6-10 After this was set up, the priests went about their duties in the large tent. Only the high priest entered the smaller, inside tent, and then only once a year, offering a blood sacrifice for his own sins and the people's accumulated sins. This was the Holy Spirit's way of showing with a visible parable that as long as the large tent stands, people can't just walk in on God. Under this system, the gifts and sacrifices can't really get to the heart of the matter, can't assuage the conscience of the people, but are limited to matters of ritual and behavior. It's essentially a temporary arrangement until a complete overhaul could be made.

POINTING TO THE REALITIES OF HEAVEN

9.11-15 But when the Messiah arrived, high priest of the superior things of this new covenant, he bypassed the old tent and its trappings in this created world and went straight into heaven's "tent"—the true Holy Place—once and for all. He also bypassed the sacrifices consisting of goat and calf blood, instead using his own blood as the price to set us free once and for all. If that animal blood and the other rituals of purification were effective in cleaning up certain matters of our religion and behavior, think how much more the blood of Christ cleans up our whole lives, inside and out. Through the Spirit, Christ offered himself as an unblemished sacri-

ᵃ 5 Traditionally *the mercy seat*   ᵇ 11 Some early manuscripts *are to come*   ᶜ 14 Or *from useless rituals*

NEW INTERNATIONAL VERSION

ceive the promised eternal inheritance—now that he has died as a ransom to set them free from the sins committed under the first covenant.

16In the case of a will,[a] it is necessary to prove the death of the one who made it, 17because a will is in force only when somebody has died; it never takes effect while the one who made it is living. 18This is why even the first covenant was not put into effect without blood. 19When Moses had proclaimed every commandment of the law to all the people, he took the blood of calves, together with water, scarlet wool and branches of hyssop, and sprinkled the scroll and all the people. 20He said, "This is the blood of the covenant, which God has commanded you to keep."[b] 21In the same way, he sprinkled with the blood both the tabernacle and everything used in its ceremonies. 22In fact, the law requires that nearly everything be cleansed with blood, and without the shedding of blood there is no forgiveness.

23It was necessary, then, for the copies of the heavenly things to be purified with these sacrifices, but the heavenly things themselves with better sacrifices than these. 24For Christ did not enter a man-made sanctuary that was only a copy of the true one; he entered heaven itself, now to appear for us in God's presence. 25Nor did he enter heaven to offer himself again and again, the way the high priest enters the Most Holy Place every year with blood that is not his own. 26Then Christ would have had to suffer many times since the creation of the world. But now he has appeared once for all at the end of the ages to do away with sin by the sacrifice of himself. 27Just as man is destined to die once, and after that to face judgment, 28so Christ was sacrificed once to take away the sins of many people; and he will appear a second time, not to bear sin, but to bring salvation to those who are waiting for him.

CHRIST'S SACRIFICE ONCE FOR ALL

10 The law is only a shadow of the good things that are coming—not the realities themselves. For this reason it can never, by the same sacrifices repeated endlessly year after year,

---

a 16 Same Greek word as *covenant*; also in verse 17
b 20 Exodus 24:8

THE MESSAGE

fice, freeing us from all those dead-end efforts to make ourselves respectable, so that we can live all out for God.

9.16-17 Like a will that takes effect when someone dies, the new covenant was put into action at Jesus' death. His death marked the transition from the old plan to the new one, canceling the old obligations and accompanying sins, and summoning the heirs to receive the eternal inheritance that was promised them. He brought together God and his people in this new way.

9.18-22 Even the first plan required a death to set it in motion. After Moses had read out all the terms of the plan of the law—God's "will"—he took the blood of sacrificed animals and, in a solemn ritual, sprinkled the document and the people who were its beneficiaries. And then he attested its validity with the words, "This is the blood of the covenant commanded by God." He did the same thing with the place of worship and its furniture. Moses said to the people, "This is the blood of the covenant God has established with you." Practically everything in a will hinges on a death. That's why blood, the evidence of death, is used so much in our tradition, especially regarding forgiveness of sins.

9.23-26 That accounts for the prominence of blood and death in all these secondary practices that point to the realities of heaven. It also accounts for why, when the real thing takes place, these animal sacrifices aren't needed anymore, having served their purpose. For Christ didn't enter the earthly version of the Holy Place; he entered the Place Itself, and offered himself to God as the sacrifice for our sins. He doesn't do this every year as the high priests did under the old plan with blood that was not their own; if that had been the case, he would have to sacrifice himself repeatedly throughout the course of history. But instead he sacrificed himself once and for all, summing up all the other sacrifices in this sacrifice of himself, the final solution of sin.

9.27-28 Everyone has to die once, then face the consequences. Christ's death was also a one-time event, but it was a sacrifice that took care of sins forever. And so, when he next appears, the outcome for those eager to greet him is, precisely, *salvation*.

THE SACRIFICE OF JESUS

10.1-10 **10** The old plan was only a hint of the good things in the new plan. Since that old "law plan" wasn't complete in itself, it couldn't complete those who followed it. No matter how many sacrifices were offered year

NEW INTERNATIONAL VERSION

make perfect those who draw near to worship. [2]If it could, would they not have stopped being offered? For the worshipers would have been cleansed once for all, and would no longer have felt guilty for their sins. [3]But those sacrifices are an annual reminder of sins, [4]because it is impossible for the blood of bulls and goats to take away sins.

[5]Therefore, when Christ came into the world, he said:

"Sacrifice and offering you did not desire,
  but a body you prepared for me;
[6]with burnt offerings and sin offerings
  you were not pleased.
[7]Then I said, 'Here I am—it is written about
  me in the scroll—
I have come to do your will, O God.' " [a]

[8]First he said, "Sacrifices and offerings, burnt offerings and sin offerings you did not desire, nor were you pleased with them" (although the law required them to be made). [9]Then he said, "Here I am, I have come to do your will." He sets aside the first to establish the second. [10]And by that will, we have been made holy through the sacrifice of the body of Jesus Christ once for all.

[11]Day after day every priest stands and performs his religious duties; again and again he offers the same sacrifices, which can never take away sins. [12]But when this priest had offered for all time one sacrifice for sins, he sat down at the right hand of God. [13]Since that time he waits for his enemies to be made his footstool, [14]because by one sacrifice he has made perfect forever those who are being made holy.

[15]The Holy Spirit also testifies to us about this. First he says:

[16]"This is the covenant I will make with them
    after that time, says the Lord.
I will put my laws in their hearts,
    and I will write them on their minds." [b]

[17]Then he adds:

"Their sins and lawless acts
    I will remember no more." [c]

[18]And where these have been forgiven, there is no longer any sacrifice for sin.

A CALL TO PERSEVERE

[19]Therefore, brothers, since we have confidence to enter the Most Holy Place by the blood of Jesus, [20]by a new and living way opened for us through the curtain, that is, his body, [21]and since we have a great priest over the house of God,

[a] 7 Psalm 40:6-8 (see Septuagint) [b] 16 Jer. 31:33
[c] 17 Jer. 31:34

THE MESSAGE

after year, they never added up to a complete solution. If they had, the worshipers would have gone merrily on their way, no longer dragged down by their sins. But instead of removing awareness of sin, when those animal sacrifices were repeated over and over they actually heightened awareness and guilt. The plain fact is that bull and goat blood can't get rid of sin. That is what is meant by this prophecy, put in the mouth of Christ:

You don't want sacrifices and offerings year
    after year;
  you've prepared a body for me for a
    sacrifice.
It's not fragrance and smoke from the altar
    that whet your appetite.
So I said, "I'm here to do it your way,
    O God,
  the way it's described in your Book."

When he said, "You don't want sacrifices and offerings," he was referring to practices according to the old plan. When he added, "I'm here to do it your way," he set aside the first in order to enact the new plan—*God's* way—by which we are made fit for God by the once-for-all sacrifice of Jesus.

10.11-18 Every priest goes to work at the altar each day, offers the same old sacrifices year in, year out, and never makes a dent in the sin problem. As a priest, Christ made a single sacrifice for sins, and that was it! Then he sat down right beside God and waited for his enemies to cave in. It was a perfect sacrifice by a perfect person to perfect some very imperfect people. By that single offering, he did everything that needed to be done for everyone who takes part in the purifying process. The Holy Spirit confirms this:

This new plan I'm making with Israel
    isn't going to be written on paper,
    isn't going to be chiseled in stone;
This time "I'm writing out the plan *in*
    them,
    carving it on the lining of their hearts."

He concludes,
    I'll forever wipe the slate clean of their sins.

Once sins are taken care of for good, there's no longer any need to offer sacrifices for them.

DON'T THROW IT ALL AWAY

10.19-21 So, friends, we can now—without hesitation—walk right up to God, into "the Holy Place." Jesus has cleared the way by the blood of his sacrifice, acting as our priest before God. The "curtain" into God's presence is his body.

NEW INTERNATIONAL VERSION

²²let us draw near to God with a sincere heart in full assurance of faith, having our hearts sprinkled to cleanse us from a guilty conscience and having our bodies washed with pure water. ²³Let us hold unswervingly to the hope we profess, for he who promised is faithful. ²⁴And let us consider how we may spur one another on toward love and good deeds. ²⁵Let us not give up meeting together, as some are in the habit of doing, but let us encourage one another—and all the more as you see the Day approaching.

²⁶If we deliberately keep on sinning after we have received the knowledge of the truth, no sacrifice for sins is left, ²⁷but only a fearful expectation of judgment and of raging fire that will consume the enemies of God. ²⁸Anyone who rejected the law of Moses died without mercy on the testimony of two or three witnesses. ²⁹How much more severely do you think a man deserves to be punished who has trampled the Son of God under foot, who has treated as an unholy thing the blood of the covenant that sanctified him, and who has insulted the Spirit of grace? ³⁰For we know him who said, "It is mine to avenge; I will repay,"ᵃ and again, "The Lord will judge his people."ᵇ ³¹It is a dreadful thing to fall into the hands of the living God.

³²Remember those earlier days after you had received the light, when you stood your ground in a great contest in the face of suffering. ³³Sometimes you were publicly exposed to insult and persecution; at other times you stood side by side with those who were so treated. ³⁴You sympathized with those in prison and joyfully accepted the confiscation of your property, because you knew that you yourselves had better and lasting possessions.

³⁵So do not throw away your confidence; it will be richly rewarded. ³⁶You need to persevere so that when you have done the will of God, you will receive what he has promised. ³⁷For in just a very little while,

"He who is coming will come and will not delay.
³⁸ But my righteous oneᶜ will live by faith.
And if he shrinks back,
 I will not be pleased with him."ᵈ

³⁹But we are not of those who shrink back and are destroyed, but of those who believe and are saved.

THE MESSAGE

10.22-25 So let's *do* it—full of belief, confident that we're presentable inside and out. Let's keep a firm grip on the promises that keep us going. He always keeps his word. Let's see how inventive we can be in encouraging love and helping out, not avoiding worshiping together as some do but spurring each other on, especially as we see the big Day approaching.

10.26-31 If we give up and turn our backs on all we've learned, all we've been given, all the truth we now know, we repudiate Christ's sacrifice and are left on our own to face the Judgment—and a mighty fierce judgment it will be! If the penalty for breaking the law of Moses is physical death, what do you think will happen if you turn on God's Son, spit on the sacrifice that made you whole, and insult this most gracious Spirit? This is no light matter. God has warned us that he'll hold us to account and make us pay. He was quite explicit: "Vengeance is mine, and I won't overlook a thing," and, "God will judge his people." Nobody's getting by with anything, believe me.

10.32-39 Remember those early days after you first saw the light? Those were the hard times! Kicked around in public, targets of every kind of abuse—some days it was you, other days your friends. If some friends went to prison, you stuck by them. If some enemies broke in and seized your goods, you let them go with a smile, knowing they couldn't touch your real treasure. Nothing they did bothered you, nothing set you back. So don't throw it all away now. You were sure of yourselves then. It's *still* a sure thing! But you need to stick it out, staying with God's plan so you'll be there for the promised completion.

It won't be long now, he's on the way;
 he'll show up most any minute.
But anyone who is right with me thrives on
 loyal trust;
 if he cuts and runs, I won't be very
 happy.

But we're not quitters who lose out. Oh, no! We'll stay with it and survive, trusting all the way.

ᵃ 30 Deut. 32:35 ᵇ 30 Deut. 32:36; Psalm 135:14
ᶜ 38 One early manuscript *But the righteous* ᵈ 38 Hab. 2:3,4

NEW INTERNATIONAL VERSION

By Faith

11 Now faith is being sure of what we hope for and certain of what we do not see. ²This is what the ancients were commended for.

³By faith we understand that the universe was formed at God's command, so that what is seen was not made out of what was visible.

⁴By faith Abel offered God a better sacrifice than Cain did. By faith he was commended as a righteous man, when God spoke well of his offerings. And by faith he still speaks, even though he is dead.

⁵By faith Enoch was taken from this life, so that he did not experience death; he could not be found, because God had taken him away. For before he was taken, he was commended as one who pleased God. ⁶And without faith it is impossible to please God, because anyone who comes to him must believe that he exists and that he rewards those who earnestly seek him.

⁷By faith Noah, when warned about things not yet seen, in holy fear built an ark to save his family. By his faith he condemned the world and became heir of the righteousness that comes by faith.

⁸By faith Abraham, when called to go to a place he would later receive as his inheritance, obeyed and went, even though he did not know where he was going. ⁹By faith he made his home in the promised land like a stranger in a foreign country; he lived in tents, as did Isaac and Jacob, who were heirs with him of the same promise. ¹⁰For he was looking forward to the city with foundations, whose architect and builder is God.

¹¹By faith Abraham, even though he was past age—and Sarah herself was barren—was enabled to become a father because he ᵃ considered him faithful who had made the promise. ¹²And so from this one man, and he as good as dead, came descendants as numerous as the stars in the sky and as countless as the sand on the seashore.

¹³All these people were still living by faith when they died. They did not receive the things promised; they only saw them and welcomed them from a distance. And they admitted that

ᵃ *11 Or By faith even Sarah, who was past age, was enabled to bear children because she*

THE MESSAGE

Faith in What We Don't See

11.1-2 **11** The fundamental fact of existence is that this trust in God, this faith, is the firm foundation under everything that makes life worth living. It's our handle on what we can't see. The act of faith is what distinguished our ancestors, set them above the crowd.

11.3 By faith, we see the world called into existence by God's word, what we see created by what we don't see.

11.4 By an act of faith, Abel brought a better sacrifice to God than Cain. It was what he *believed*, not what he *brought*, that made the difference. That's what God noticed and approved as righteous. After all these centuries, that belief continues to catch our notice.

11.5-6 By an act of faith, Enoch skipped death completely. "They looked all over and couldn't find him because God had taken him." We know on the basis of reliable testimony that before he was taken "he pleased God." It's impossible to please God apart from faith. And why? Because anyone who wants to approach God must believe both that he exists *and* that he cares enough to respond to those who seek him.

11.7 By faith, Noah built a ship in the middle of dry land. He was warned about something he couldn't see, and acted on what he was told. The result? His family was saved. His act of faith drew a sharp line between the evil of the unbelieving world and the rightness of the believing world. As a result, Noah became intimate with God.

11.8-10 By an act of faith, Abraham said yes to God's call to travel to an unknown place that would become his home. When he left he had no idea where he was going. By an act of faith he lived in the country promised him, lived as a stranger camping in tents. Isaac and Jacob did the same, living under the same promise. Abraham did it by keeping his eye on an unseen city with real, eternal foundations—the City designed and built by God.

11.11-12 By faith, barren Sarah was able to become pregnant, old woman as she was at the time, because she believed the One who made a promise would do what he said. That's how it happened that from one man's dead and shriveled loins there are now people numbering into the millions.

✝

11.13-16 Each one of these people of faith died not yet having in hand what was promised, but still believing. How did they do it? They saw it way off in the distance, waved their greeting, and

NEW INTERNATIONAL VERSION

they were aliens and strangers on earth. ¹⁴People who say such things show that they are looking for a country of their own. ¹⁵If they had been thinking of the country they had left, they would have had opportunity to return. ¹⁶Instead, they were longing for a better country—a heavenly one. Therefore God is not ashamed to be called their God, for he has prepared a city for them.

¹⁷By faith Abraham, when God tested him, offered Isaac as a sacrifice. He who had received the promises was about to sacrifice his one and only son, ¹⁸even though God had said to him, "It is through Isaac that your offspring*ᵃ* will be reckoned." *ᵇ* ¹⁹Abraham reasoned that God could raise the dead, and figuratively speaking, he did receive Isaac back from death.

²⁰By faith Isaac blessed Jacob and Esau in regard to their future.

²¹By faith Jacob, when he was dying, blessed each of Joseph's sons, and worshiped as he leaned on the top of his staff.

²²By faith Joseph, when his end was near, spoke about the exodus of the Israelites from Egypt and gave instructions about his bones.

²³By faith Moses' parents hid him for three months after he was born, because they saw he was no ordinary child, and they were not afraid of the king's edict.

²⁴By faith Moses, when he had grown up, refused to be known as the son of Pharaoh's daughter. ²⁵He chose to be mistreated along with the people of God rather than to enjoy the pleasures of sin for a short time. ²⁶He regarded disgrace for the sake of Christ as of greater value than the treasures of Egypt, because he was looking ahead to his reward. ²⁷By faith he left Egypt, not fearing the king's anger; he persevered because he saw him who is invisible. ²⁸By faith he kept the Passover and the sprinkling of blood, so that the destroyer of the firstborn would not touch the firstborn of Israel.

²⁹By faith the people passed through the Red Sea*ᶜ* as on dry land; but when the Egyptians tried to do so, they were drowned.

³⁰By faith the walls of Jericho fell, after the people had marched around them for seven days.

³¹By faith the prostitute Rahab, because she welcomed the spies, was not killed with those who were disobedient.*ᵈ*

THE MESSAGE

accepted the fact that they were transients in this world. People who live this way make it plain that they are looking for their true home. If they were homesick for the old country, they could have gone back any time they wanted. But they were after a far better country than that—*heaven* country. You can see why God is so proud of them, and has a City waiting for them.

11.17-19   By faith, Abraham, at the time of testing, offered Isaac back to God. Acting in faith, he was as ready to return the promised son, his only son, as he had been to receive him—and this after he had already been told, "Your descendants shall come from Isaac." Abraham figured that if God wanted to, he could raise the dead. In a sense, that's what happened when he received Isaac back, alive from off the altar.

11.20   By an act of faith, Isaac reached into the future as he blessed Jacob and Esau.

11.21   By an act of faith, Jacob on his deathbed blessed each of Joseph's sons in turn, blessing them with God's blessing, not his own—as he bowed worshipfully upon his staff.

11.22   By an act of faith, Joseph, while dying, prophesied the exodus of Israel, and made arrangements for his own burial.

11.23   By an act of faith, Moses' parents hid him away for three months after his birth. They saw the child's beauty, and they braved the king's decree.

11.24-28   By faith, Moses, when grown, refused the privileges of the Egyptian royal house. He chose a hard life with God's people rather than an opportunistic soft life of sin with the oppressors. He valued suffering in the Messiah's camp far greater than Egyptian wealth because he was looking ahead, anticipating the payoff. By an act of faith, he turned his heel on Egypt, indifferent to the king's blind rage. He had his eye on the One no eye can see, and kept right on going. By an act of faith, he kept the Passover Feast and sprinkled Passover blood on each house so that the destroyer of the firstborn wouldn't touch them.

11.29   By an act of faith, Israel walked through the Red Sea on dry ground. The Egyptians tried it and drowned.

11.30   By faith, the Israelites marched around the walls of Jericho for seven days, and the walls fell flat.

11.31   By an act of faith, Rahab, the Jericho harlot, welcomed the spies and escaped the destruction that came on those who refused to trust God.

⊹

ᵃ 18 Greek *seed*   *ᵇ* 18 Gen. 21:12   *ᶜ* 29 That is, Sea of Reeds   *ᵈ* 31 Or *unbelieving*

NEW INTERNATIONAL VERSION

³²And what more shall I say? I do not have time to tell about Gideon, Barak, Samson, Jephthah, David, Samuel and the prophets, ³³who through faith conquered kingdoms, administered justice, and gained what was promised; who shut the mouths of lions, ³⁴quenched the fury of the flames, and escaped the edge of the sword; whose weakness was turned to strength; and who became powerful in battle and routed foreign armies. ³⁵Women received back their dead, raised to life again. Others were tortured and refused to be released, so that they might gain a better resurrection. ³⁶Some faced jeers and flogging, while still others were chained and put in prison. ³⁷They were stoned ª; they were sawed in two; they were put to death by the sword. They went about in sheepskins and goatskins, destitute, persecuted and mistreated— ³⁸the world was not worthy of them. They wandered in deserts and mountains, and in caves and holes in the ground.

³⁹These were all commended for their faith, yet none of them received what had been promised. ⁴⁰God had planned something better for us so that only together with us would they be made perfect.

GOD DISCIPLINES HIS SONS

12 Therefore, since we are surrounded by such a great cloud of witnesses, let us throw off everything that hinders and the sin that so easily entangles, and let us run with perseverance the race marked out for us. ²Let us fix our eyes on Jesus, the author and perfecter of our faith, who for the joy set before him endured the cross, scorning its shame, and sat down at the right hand of the throne of God. ³Consider him who endured such opposition from sinful men, so that you will not grow weary and lose heart.

⁴In your struggle against sin, you have not yet resisted to the point of shedding your blood. ⁵And you have forgotten that word of encouragement that addresses you as sons:

"My son, do not make light of the Lord's discipline,
and do not lose heart when he rebukes you,
⁶because the Lord disciplines those he loves,
and he punishes everyone he accepts as a son." ᵇ

THE MESSAGE

11:32-38 I could go on and on, but I've run out of time. There are so many more—Gideon, Barak, Samson, Jephthah, David, Samuel, the prophets. . . . Through acts of faith, they toppled kingdoms, made justice work, took the promises for themselves. They were protected from lions, fires, and sword thrusts, turned disadvantage to advantage, won battles, routed alien armies. Women received their loved ones back from the dead. There were those who, under torture, refused to give in and go free, preferring something better: resurrection. Others braved abuse and whips, and, yes, chains and dungeons. We have stories of those who were stoned, sawed in two, murdered in cold blood; stories of vagrants wandering the earth in animal skins, homeless, friendless, powerless—the world didn't deserve them!—making their way as best they could on the cruel edges of the world.

11:39-40 Not one of these people, even though their lives of faith were exemplary, got their hands on what was promised. God had a better plan for us: that their faith and our faith would come together to make one completed whole, their lives of faith not complete apart from ours.

DISCIPLINE IN A LONG-DISTANCE RACE

12:1-3 **12** Do you see what this means—all these pioneers who blazed the way, all these veterans cheering us on? It means we'd better get on with it. Strip down, start running—and never quit! No extra spiritual fat, no parasitic sins. Keep your eyes on *Jesus*, who both began and finished this race we're in. Study how he did it. Because he never lost sight of where he was headed—that exhilarating finish in and with God—he could put up with anything along the way: cross, shame, whatever. And now he's *there*, in the place of honor, right alongside God. When you find yourselves flagging in your faith, go over that story again, item by item, that long litany of hostility he plowed through. *That* will shoot adrenaline into your souls!

12:4-11 In this all-out match against sin, others have suffered far worse than you, to say nothing of what Jesus went through—all that bloodshed! So don't feel sorry for yourselves. Or have you forgotten how good parents treat children, and that God regards you as *his* children?

My dear child, don't shrug off God's discipline,
but don't be crushed by it either.
It's the child he loves that he disciplines;
the child he embraces, he also corrects.

ª 37 Some early manuscripts *stoned; they were put to the test;*
ᵇ 6 Prov. 3:11,12

NEW INTERNATIONAL VERSION

[7]Endure hardship as discipline; God is treating you as sons. For what son is not disciplined by his father? [8]If you are not disciplined (and everyone undergoes discipline), then you are illegitimate children and not true sons. [9]Moreover, we have all had human fathers who disciplined us and we respected them for it. How much more should we submit to the Father of our spirits and live! [10]Our fathers disciplined us for a little while as they thought best; but God disciplines us for our good, that we may share in his holiness. [11]No discipline seems pleasant at the time, but painful. Later on, however, it produces a harvest of righteousness and peace for those who have been trained by it.

[12]Therefore, strengthen your feeble arms and weak knees. [13]"Make level paths for your feet," [a] so that the lame may not be disabled, but rather healed.

WARNING AGAINST REFUSING GOD

[14]Make every effort to live in peace with all men and to be holy; without holiness no one will see the Lord. [15]See to it that no one misses the grace of God and that no bitter root grows up to cause trouble and defile many. [16]See that no one is sexually immoral, or is godless like Esau, who for a single meal sold his inheritance rights as the oldest son. [17]Afterward, as you know, when he wanted to inherit this blessing, he was rejected. He could bring about no change of mind, though he sought the blessing with tears.

[18]You have not come to a mountain that can be touched and that is burning with fire; to darkness, gloom and storm; [19]to a trumpet blast or to such a voice speaking words that those who heard it begged that no further word be spoken to them, [20]because they could not bear what was commanded: "If even an animal touches the mountain, it must be stoned." [b] [21]The sight was so terrifying that Moses said, "I am trembling with fear." [c]

[22]But you have come to Mount Zion, to the heavenly Jerusalem, the city of the living God. You have come to thousands upon thousands of angels in joyful assembly, [23]to the church of the firstborn, whose names are written in heaven. You have come to God, the judge of all men, to the spirits of righteous men made perfect, [24]to Jesus the mediator of a new covenant, and to the sprinkled blood that speaks a better word than the blood of Abel.

[25]See to it that you do not refuse him who speaks. If they did not escape when they refused him who warned them on earth, how much less

THE MESSAGE

God is educating you; that's why you must never drop out. He's treating you as dear children. This trouble you're in isn't punishment; it's *training*, the normal experience of children. Only irresponsible parents leave children to fend for themselves. Would you prefer an irresponsible God? We respect our own parents for training and not spoiling us, so why not embrace God's training so we can truly *live*? While we were children, our parents did what *seemed* best to them. But God is doing what *is* best for us, training us to live God's holy best. At the time, discipline isn't much fun. It always feels like it's going against the grain. Later, of course, it pays off handsomely, for it's the well-trained who find themselves mature in their relationship with God.

12.12-13 So don't sit around on your hands! No more dragging your feet! Clear the path for long-distance runners so no one will trip and fall, so no one will step in a hole and sprain an ankle. Help each other out. And run for it!

12.14-17 Work at getting along with each other and with God. Otherwise you'll never get so much as a glimpse of God. Make sure no one gets left out of God's generosity. Keep a sharp eye out for weeds of bitter discontent. A thistle or two gone to seed can ruin a whole garden in no time. Watch out for the Esau syndrome: trading away God's lifelong gift in order to satisfy a short-term appetite. You well know how Esau later regretted that impulsive act and wanted God's blessing—but by then it was too late, tears or no tears.

AN UNSHAKABLE KINGDOM

12.18-21 Unlike your ancestors, you didn't come to Mount Sinai—all that volcanic blaze and earthshaking rumble—to hear God speak. The earsplitting words and soul-shaking message terrified them and they begged him to stop. When they heard the words—"If an animal touches the Mountain, it's as good as dead"—they were afraid to move. Even Moses was terrified.

12.22-24 No, that's not *your* experience at all. You've come to Mount Zion, the city where the living God resides. The invisible Jerusalem is populated by throngs of festive angels and Christian citizens. It is the city where God is Judge, with judgments that make us just. You've come to Jesus, who presents us with a new covenant, a fresh charter from God. He is the Mediator of this covenant. The murder of Jesus, unlike Abel's—a homicide that cried out for vengeance—became a proclamation of grace.

12.25-27 So don't turn a deaf ear to these gracious words. If those who ignored earthly warnings didn't get away with it, what will happen to us

NEW INTERNATIONAL VERSION

will we, if we turn away from him who warns us from heaven? 26At that time his voice shook the earth, but now he has promised, "Once more I will shake not only the earth but also the heavens." *a* 27The words "once more" indicate the removing of what can be shaken—that is, created things—so that what cannot be shaken may remain.

28Therefore, since we are receiving a kingdom that cannot be shaken, let us be thankful, and so worship God acceptably with reverence and awe, 29for our "God is a consuming fire." *b*

CONCLUDING EXHORTATIONS

13 Keep on loving each other as brothers. 2Do not forget to entertain strangers, for by so doing some people have entertained angels without knowing it. 3Remember those in prison as if you were their fellow prisoners, and those who are mistreated as if you yourselves were suffering.

4Marriage should be honored by all, and the marriage bed kept pure, for God will judge the adulterer and all the sexually immoral. 5Keep your lives free from the love of money and be content with what you have, because God has said,

"Never will I leave you;
    never will I forsake you." *c*

6So we say with confidence,

"The Lord is my helper; I will not be afraid.
    What can man do to me?" *d*

7Remember your leaders, who spoke the word of God to you. Consider the outcome of their way of life and imitate their faith. 8Jesus Christ is the same yesterday and today and forever.

9Do not be carried away by all kinds of strange teachings. It is good for our hearts to be strengthened by grace, not by ceremonial foods, which are of no value to those who eat them. 10We have an altar from which those who minister at the tabernacle have no right to eat. 11The high priest carries the blood of animals into the Most Holy Place as a sin offering, but the bodies are burned outside the camp. 12And so Jesus also suffered outside the city gate to

a 26 Haggai 2:6   b 29 Deut. 4:24   c 5 Deut. 31:6
d 6 Psalm 118:6,7

THE MESSAGE

if we turn our backs on heavenly warnings? His voice that time shook the earth to its foundations; this time—he's told us this quite plainly—he'll also rock the heavens: "One last shaking, from top to bottom, stem to stern." The phrase "one last shaking" means a thorough housecleaning, getting rid of all the historical and religious junk so that the unshakable essentials stand clear and uncluttered.

12.28-29 Do you see what we've got? An unshakable kingdom! And do you see how thankful we must be? Not only thankful, but brimming with worship, deeply reverent before God. For God is not an indifferent bystander. He's actively cleaning house, torching all that needs to burn, and he won't quit until it's all cleansed. God himself is Fire!

JESUS DOESN'T CHANGE

13.1-4 **13** Stay on good terms with each other, held together by love. Be ready with a meal or a bed when it's needed. Why, some have extended hospitality to angels without ever knowing it! Regard prisoners as if you were in prison with them. Look on victims of abuse as if what happened to them had happened to you. Honor marriage, and guard the sacredness of sexual intimacy between wife and husband. God draws a firm line against casual and illicit sex.

13.5-6 Don't be obsessed with getting more material things. Be relaxed with what you have. Since God assured us, "I'll never let you down, never walk off and leave you," we can boldly quote,

God is there, ready to help;
I'm fearless no matter what.
Who or what can get to me?

13.7-8 Appreciate your pastoral leaders who gave you the Word of God. Take a good look at the way they live, and let their faithfulness instruct you, as well as their truthfulness. There should be a consistency that runs through us all. For Jesus doesn't change—yesterday, today, tomorrow, he's always totally himself.

13.9 Don't be lured away from him by the latest speculations about him. The grace of Christ is the only good ground for life. Products named after Christ don't seem to do much for those who buy them.

13.10-12 The altar from which God gives us the gift of himself is not for exploitation by insiders who grab and loot. In the old system, the animals are killed and the bodies disposed of outside the camp. The blood is then brought inside to the altar as a sacrifice for sin. It's the same with Jesus. He was crucified outside the city gates—

NEW INTERNATIONAL VERSION

make the people holy through his own blood. ¹³Let us, then, go to him outside the camp, bearing the disgrace he bore. ¹⁴For here we do not have an enduring city, but we are looking for the city that is to come.

¹⁵Through Jesus, therefore, let us continually offer to God a sacrifice of praise—the fruit of lips that confess his name. ¹⁶And do not forget to do good and to share with others, for with such sacrifices God is pleased.

¹⁷Obey your leaders and submit to their authority. They keep watch over you as men who must give an account. Obey them so that their work will be a joy, not a burden, for that would be of no advantage to you.

¹⁸Pray for us. We are sure that we have a clear conscience and desire to live honorably in every way. ¹⁹I particularly urge you to pray so that I may be restored to you soon.

²⁰May the God of peace, who through the blood of the eternal covenant brought back from the dead our Lord Jesus, that great Shepherd of the sheep, ²¹equip you with everything good for doing his will, and may he work in us what is pleasing to him, through Jesus Christ, to whom be glory for ever and ever. Amen.

²²Brothers, I urge you to bear with my word of exhortation, for I have written you only a short letter.

²³I want you to know that our brother Timothy has been released. If he arrives soon, I will come with him to see you.

²⁴Greet all your leaders and all God's people. Those from Italy send you their greetings.

²⁵Grace be with you all.

THE MESSAGE

that is where he poured out the sacrificial blood that was brought to God's altar to cleanse his people.

13.13-15   So let's go outside, where Jesus is, where the action is—not trying to be privileged insiders, but taking our share in the abuse of Jesus. This "insider world" is not our home. We have our eyes peeled for the City about to come. Let's take our place outside with Jesus, no longer pouring out the sacrificial blood of animals but pouring out sacrificial praises from our lips to God in Jesus' name.

✝

13.16   Make sure you don't take things for granted and go slack in working for the common good; share what you have with others. God takes particular pleasure in acts of worship—a different kind of "sacrifice"—that take place in kitchen and workplace and on the streets.

13.17   Be responsive to your pastoral leaders. Listen to their counsel. They are alert to the condition of your lives and work under the strict supervision of God. Contribute to the joy of their leadership, not its drudgery. Why would you want to make things harder for them?

13.18-21   Pray for us. We have no doubts about what we're doing or why, but it's hard going and we need your prayers. All we care about is living well before God. Pray that we may be together soon.

May God, who puts all things together,
 makes all things whole,
Who made a lasting mark through the
  sacrifice of Jesus,
 the sacrifice of blood that sealed the
  eternal covenant,
Who led Jesus, our Great Shepherd,
 up and alive from the dead,
Now put you together, provide you
 with everything you need to please him,
Make us into what gives him most pleasure,
 by means of the sacrifice of Jesus, the
  Messiah.
All glory to Jesus forever and always!
 Oh, yes, yes, yes.

13.22-23   Friends, please take what I've written most seriously. I've kept this as brief as possible; I haven't piled on a lot of extras. You'll be glad to know that Timothy has been let out of prison. If he leaves soon, I'll come with him and get to see you myself.

13.24   Say hello to your pastoral leaders and all the congregations. Everyone here in Italy wants to be remembered to you.

13.25   Grace be with you, every one.

JAMES

JAMES

1 James, a servant of God and of the Lord Jesus Christ,

To the twelve tribes scattered among the nations:

Greetings.

TRIALS AND TEMPTATIONS

² Consider it pure joy, my brothers, whenever you face trials of many kinds, ³ because you know that the testing of your faith develops perseverance. ⁴ Perseverance must finish its work so that you may be mature and complete, not lacking anything. ⁵ If any of you lacks wisdom, he should ask God, who gives generously to all without finding fault, and it will be given to him. ⁶ But when he asks, he must believe and not doubt, because he who doubts is like a wave of the sea, blown and tossed by the wind. ⁷ That man should not think he will receive anything from the Lord; ⁸ he is a double-minded man, unstable in all he does.

⁹ The brother in humble circumstances ought to take pride in his high position. ¹⁰ But the one who is rich should take pride in his low position, because he will pass away like a wild flower. ¹¹ For the sun rises with scorching heat and withers the plant; its blossom falls and its beauty is destroyed. In the same way, the rich man will fade away even while he goes about his business.

¹² Blessed is the man who perseveres under trial, because when he has stood the test, he will receive the crown of life that God has promised to those who love him.

¹³ When tempted, no one should say, "God is tempting me." For God cannot be tempted by evil, nor does he tempt anyone; ¹⁴ but each one is tempted when, by his own evil desire, he is dragged away and enticed. ¹⁵ Then, after desire has conceived, it gives birth to sin; and sin, when it is full-grown, gives birth to death.

¹⁶ Don't be deceived, my dear brothers. ¹⁷ Every good and perfect gift is from above, coming

1 1.1 I, James, am a slave of God and the Master Jesus, writing to the twelve tribes scattered to Kingdom Come: Hello!

FAITH UNDER PRESSURE

1.2-4 Consider it a sheer gift, friends, when tests and challenges come at you from all sides. You know that under pressure, your faith-life is forced into the open and shows its true colors. So don't try to get out of anything prematurely. Let it do its work so you become mature and well-developed, not deficient in any way.

1.5-8 If you don't know what you're doing, pray to the Father. He loves to help. You'll get his help, and won't be condescended to when you ask for it. Ask boldly, believingly, without a second thought. People who "worry their prayers" are like wind-whipped waves. Don't think you're going to get anything from the Master that way, adrift at sea, keeping all your options open.

1.9-11 When down-and-outers get a break, cheer! And when the arrogant rich are brought down to size, cheer! Prosperity is as short-lived as a wildflower, so don't ever count on it. You know that as soon as the sun rises, pouring down its scorching heat, the flower withers. Its petals wilt and, before you know it, that beautiful face is a barren stem. Well, that's a picture of the "prosperous life." At the very moment everyone is looking on in admiration, it fades away to nothing.

1.12 Anyone who meets a testing challenge head-on and manages to stick it out is mighty fortunate. For such persons loyally in love with God, the reward is life and more life.

1.13-15 Don't let anyone under pressure to give in to evil say, "God is trying to trip me up." God is impervious to evil, and puts evil in no one's way. The temptation to give in to evil comes from us and only us. We have no one to blame but the leering, seducing flare-up of our own lust. Lust gets pregnant, and has a baby: sin! Sin grows up to adulthood, and becomes a real killer.

1.16-18 So, my very dear friends, don't get thrown off course. Every desirable and beneficial gift

NEW INTERNATIONAL VERSION

down from the Father of the heavenly lights, who does not change like shifting shadows. ¹⁸He chose to give us birth through the word of truth, that we might be a kind of firstfruits of all he created.

LISTENING AND DOING

¹⁹My dear brothers, take note of this: Everyone should be quick to listen, slow to speak and slow to become angry, ²⁰for man's anger does not bring about the righteous life that God desires. ²¹Therefore, get rid of all moral filth and the evil that is so prevalent and humbly accept the word planted in you, which can save you.

²²Do not merely listen to the word, and so deceive yourselves. Do what it says. ²³Anyone who listens to the word but does not do what it says is like a man who looks at his face in a mirror ²⁴and, after looking at himself, goes away and immediately forgets what he looks like. ²⁵But the man who looks intently into the perfect law that gives freedom, and continues to do this, not forgetting what he has heard, but doing it—he will be blessed in what he does.

²⁶If anyone considers himself religious and yet does not keep a tight rein on his tongue, he deceives himself and his religion is worthless. ²⁷Religion that God our Father accepts as pure and faultless is this: to look after orphans and widows in their distress and to keep oneself from being polluted by the world.

FAVORITISM FORBIDDEN

2 My brothers, as believers in our glorious Lord Jesus Christ, don't show favoritism. ²Suppose a man comes into your meeting wearing a gold ring and fine clothes, and a poor man in shabby clothes also comes in. ³If you show special attention to the man wearing fine clothes and say, "Here's a good seat for you," but say to the poor man, "You stand there" or "Sit on the floor by my feet," ⁴have you not discriminated among yourselves and become judges with evil thoughts?

⁵Listen, my dear brothers: Has not God chosen those who are poor in the eyes of the world to be rich in faith and to inherit the kingdom he promised those who love him? ⁶But you have insulted the poor. Is it not the rich who are exploiting you? Are they not the ones who are dragging you into court? ⁷Are they not the ones

THE MESSAGE

comes out of heaven. The gifts are rivers of light cascading down from the Father of Light. There is nothing deceitful in God, nothing two-faced, nothing fickle. He brought us to life using the true Word, showing us off as the crown of all his creatures.

ACT ON WHAT YOU HEAR

1.19-21 Post this at all the intersections, dear friends: Lead with your ears, follow up with your tongue, and let anger straggle along in the rear. God's righteousness doesn't grow from human anger. So throw all spoiled virtue and cancerous evil in the garbage. In simple humility, let our gardener, God, landscape you with the Word, making a salvation-garden of your life.

1.22-24 Don't fool yourself into thinking that you are a listener when you are anything but, letting the Word go in one ear and out the other. *Act* on what you hear! Those who hear and don't act are like those who glance in the mirror, walk away, and two minutes later have no idea who they are, what they look like.

1.25 But whoever catches a glimpse of the revealed counsel of God—the free life!—even out of the corner of his eye, and sticks with it, is no distracted scatterbrain but a man or woman of action. That person will find delight and affirmation in the action.

1.26-27 Anyone who sets himself up as "religious" by talking a good game is self-deceived. This kind of religion is hot air and only hot air. Real religion, the kind that passes muster before God the Father, is this: Reach out to the homeless and loveless in their plight, and guard against corruption from the godless world.

THE ROYAL RULE OF LOVE

2.1-4 2 My dear friends, don't let public opinion influence how you live out our glorious, Christ-originated faith. If a man enters your church wearing an expensive suit, and a street person wearing rags comes in right after him, and you say to the man in the suit, "Sit here, sir; this is the best seat in the house!" and either ignore the street person or say, "Better sit here in the back row," haven't you segregated God's children and proved that you are judges who can't be trusted?

2.5-7 Listen, dear friends. Isn't it clear by now that God operates quite differently? He chose the world's down-and-out as the kingdom's first citizens, with full rights and privileges. This kingdom is promised to anyone who loves God. And here you are abusing these same citizens! Isn't it the high and mighty who exploit you, who use the courts to rob you blind? Aren't

NEW INTERNATIONAL VERSION

who are slandering the noble name of him to whom you belong?

⁸If you really keep the royal law found in Scripture, "Love your neighbor as yourself,"ᵃ you are doing right. ⁹But if you show favoritism, you sin and are convicted by the law as lawbreakers. ¹⁰For whoever keeps the whole law and yet stumbles at just one point is guilty of breaking all of it. ¹¹For he who said, "Do not commit adultery,"ᵇ also said, "Do not murder."ᶜ If you do not commit adultery but do commit murder, you have become a lawbreaker.

¹²Speak and act as those who are going to be judged by the law that gives freedom, ¹³because judgment without mercy will be shown to anyone who has not been merciful. Mercy triumphs over judgment!

FAITH AND DEEDS

¹⁴What good is it, my brothers, if a man claims to have faith but has no deeds? Can such faith save him? ¹⁵Suppose a brother or sister is without clothes and daily food. ¹⁶If one of you says to him, "Go, I wish you well; keep warm and well fed," but does nothing about his physical needs, what good is it? ¹⁷In the same way, faith by itself, if it is not accompanied by action, is dead.

¹⁸But someone will say, "You have faith; I have deeds."

Show me your faith without deeds, and I will show you my faith by what I do. ¹⁹You believe that there is one God. Good! Even the demons believe that—and shudder.

²⁰You foolish man, do you want evidence that faith without deeds is uselessᵈ? ²¹Was not our ancestor Abraham considered righteous for what he did when he offered his son Isaac on the altar? ²²You see that his faith and his actions were working together, and his faith was made complete by what he did. ²³And the scripture was fulfilled that says, "Abraham believed God, and it was credited to him as righteousness,"ᵉ and

---

THE MESSAGE

they the ones who scorn the new name— "Christian"—used in your baptisms?

2.8-11 You do well when you complete the Royal Rule of the Scriptures: "Love others as you love yourself." But if you play up to these so-called important people, you go against the Rule and stand convicted by it. You can't pick and choose in these things, specializing in keeping one or two things in God's law and ignoring others. The same God who said, "Don't commit adultery," also said, "Don't murder." If you don't commit adultery but go ahead and murder, do you think your non-adultery will cancel out your murder? No, you're a murderer, period.

2.12-13 Talk and act like a person expecting to be judged by the Rule that sets us free. For if you refuse to act kindly, you can hardly expect to be treated kindly. Kind mercy wins over harsh judgment every time.

FAITH IN ACTION

2.14-17 Dear friends, do you think you'll get anywhere in this if you learn all the right words but never do anything? Does merely talking about faith indicate that a person really has it? For instance, you come upon an old friend dressed in rags and half-starved and say, "Good morning, friend! Be clothed in Christ! Be filled with the Holy Spirit!" and walk off without providing so much as a coat or a cup of soup—where does that get you? Isn't it obvious that God-talk without God-acts is outrageous nonsense?

2.18 I can already hear one of you agreeing by saying, "Sounds good. You take care of the faith department, I'll handle the works department." Not so fast. You can no more show me your works apart from your faith than I can show you my faith apart from my works. Faith and works, works and faith, fit together hand in glove.

2.19-20 Do I hear you professing to believe in the one and only God, but then observe you complacently sitting back as if you had done something wonderful? That's just great. Demons do that, but what good does it do them? Use your heads! Do you suppose for a minute that you can cut faith and works in two and not end up with a corpse on your hands?

2.21-24 Wasn't our ancestor Abraham "made right with God by works" when he placed his son Isaac on the sacrificial altar? Isn't it obvious that faith and works are yoked partners, that faith expresses itself in works? That the works are "works of faith"? The full meaning of "believe" in the Scripture sentence, "Abraham believed God and was set right with God," in-

---

ᵃ 8 Lev. 19:18   ᵇ 11 Exodus 20:14; Deut. 5:18
ᶜ 11 Exodus 20:13; Deut. 5:17   ᵈ 20 Some early
manuscripts *dead*   ᵉ 23 Gen. 15:6

NEW INTERNATIONAL VERSION

he was called God's friend. 24You see that a person is justified by what he does and not by faith alone.

25In the same way, was not even Rahab the prostitute considered righteous for what she did when she gave lodging to the spies and sent them off in a different direction? 26As the body without the spirit is dead, so faith without deeds is dead.

TAMING THE TONGUE

3 Not many of you should presume to be teachers, my brothers, because you know that we who teach will be judged more strictly. 2We all stumble in many ways. If anyone is never at fault in what he says, he is a perfect man, able to keep his whole body in check.

3When we put bits into the mouths of horses to make them obey us, we can turn the whole animal. 4Or take ships as an example. Although they are so large and are driven by strong winds, they are steered by a very small rudder wherever the pilot wants to go. 5Likewise the tongue is a small part of the body, but it makes great boasts. Consider what a great forest is set on fire by a small spark. 6The tongue also is a fire, a world of evil among the parts of the body. It corrupts the whole person, sets the whole course of his life on fire, and is itself set on fire by hell.

7All kinds of animals, birds, reptiles and creatures of the sea are being tamed and have been tamed by man, 8but no man can tame the tongue. It is a restless evil, full of deadly poison.

9With the tongue we praise our Lord and Father, and with it we curse men, who have been made in God's likeness. 10Out of the same mouth come praise and cursing. My brothers, this should not be. 11Can both fresh water and salt*a* water flow from the same spring? 12My brothers, can a fig tree bear olives, or a grapevine bear figs? Neither can a salt spring produce fresh water.

TWO KINDS OF WISDOM

13Who is wise and understanding among you? Let him show it by his good life, by deeds done in the humility that comes from wisdom. 14But if you harbor bitter envy and selfish ambition in your hearts, do not boast about it or deny the truth. 15Such "wisdom" does not come down

a 11 Greek bitter (see also verse 14)

THE MESSAGE

cludes his action. It's that mesh of believing and acting that got Abraham named "God's friend." Is it not evident that a person is made right with God not by a barren faith but by faith fruitful in works?

2.25-26 The same with Rahab, the Jericho harlot. Wasn't her action in hiding God's spies and helping them escape—that seamless unity of *believing* and *doing*—what counted with God? The very moment you separate body and spirit, you end up with a corpse. Separate faith and works and you get the same thing: a corpse.

WHEN YOU OPEN YOUR MOUTH

3.1-2 3 Don't be in any rush to become a teacher, my friends. Teaching is highly responsible work. Teachers are held to the strictest standards. And none of us is perfectly qualified. We get it wrong nearly every time we open our mouths. If you could find someone whose speech was perfectly true, you'd have a perfect person, in perfect control of life.

3.3-5 A bit in the mouth of a horse controls the whole horse. A small rudder on a huge ship in the hands of a skilled captain sets a course in the face of the strongest winds. A word out of your mouth may seem of no account, but it can accomplish nearly anything—or destroy it!

3.5-6 It only takes a spark, remember, to set off a forest fire. A careless or wrongly placed word out of your mouth can do that. By our speech we can ruin the world, turn harmony to chaos, throw mud on a reputation, send the whole world up in smoke and go up in smoke with it, smoke right from the pit of hell.

3.7-10 This is scary: You can tame a tiger, but you can't tame a tongue—it's never been done. The tongue runs wild, a wanton killer. With our tongues we bless God our Father; with the same tongues we curse the very men and women he made in his image. Curses and blessings out of the same mouth!

3.10-12 My friends, this can't go on. A spring doesn't gush fresh water one day and brackish the next, does it? Apple trees don't bear strawberries, do they? Raspberry bushes don't bear apples, do they? You're not going to dip into a polluted mud hole and get a cup of clear, cool water, are you?

LIVE WELL, LIVE WISELY

3.13-16 Do you want to be counted wise, to build a reputation for wisdom? Here's what you do: Live well, live wisely, live humbly. It's the way you live, not the way you talk, that counts. Mean-spirited ambition isn't wisdom. Boasting that you are wise isn't wisdom. Twisting the truth to

NEW INTERNATIONAL VERSION

from heaven but is earthly, unspiritual, of the devil. ¹⁶For where you have envy and selfish ambition, there you find disorder and every evil practice.

¹⁷But the wisdom that comes from heaven is first of all pure; then peace-loving, considerate, submissive, full of mercy and good fruit, impartial and sincere. ¹⁸Peacemakers who sow in peace raise a harvest of righteousness.

Submit Yourselves to God

4 What causes fights and quarrels among you? Don't they come from your desires that battle within you? ²You want something but don't get it. You kill and covet, but you cannot have what you want. You quarrel and fight. You do not have, because you do not ask God. ³When you ask, you do not receive, because you ask with wrong motives, that you may spend what you get on your pleasures.

⁴You adulterous people, don't you know that friendship with the world is hatred toward God? Anyone who chooses to be a friend of the world becomes an enemy of God. ⁵Or do you think Scripture says without reason that the spirit he caused to live in us envies intensely?ᵃ ⁶But he gives us more grace. That is why Scripture says:

"God opposes the proud
but gives grace to the humble."ᵇ

⁷Submit yourselves, then, to God. Resist the devil, and he will flee from you. ⁸Come near to God and he will come near to you. Wash your hands, you sinners, and purify your hearts, you double-minded. ⁹Grieve, mourn and wail. Change your laughter to mourning and your joy to gloom. ¹⁰Humble yourselves before the Lord, and he will lift you up.

¹¹Brothers, do not slander one another. Anyone who speaks against his brother or judges him speaks against the law and judges it. When you judge the law, you are not keeping it, but sitting in judgment on it. ¹²There is only one Lawgiver and Judge, the one who is able to save and destroy. But you—who are you to judge your neighbor?

ᵃ 5 Or that God jealously longs for the spirit that he made to live in us; or that the Spirit he caused to live in us longs jealously   ᵇ 6 Prov. 3:34

THE MESSAGE

make yourselves sound wise isn't wisdom. It's the furthest thing from wisdom—it's animal cunning, devilish conniving. Whenever you're trying to look better than others or get the better of others, things fall apart and everyone ends up at the others' throats.

3.17-18 Real wisdom, God's wisdom, begins with a holy life and is characterized by getting along with others. It is gentle and reasonable, overflowing with mercy and blessings, not hot one day and cold the next, not two-faced. You can develop a healthy, robust community that lives right with God and enjoy its results *only* if you do the hard work of getting along with each other, treating each other with dignity and honor.

Get Serious

4.1-2 4 Where do you think all these appalling wars and quarrels come from? Do you think they just happen? Think again. They come about because you want your own way, and fight for it deep inside yourselves. You lust for what you don't have and are willing to kill to get it. You want what isn't yours and will risk violence to get your hands on it.

4.2-3 You wouldn't think of just asking God for it, would you? And why not? Because you know you'd be asking for what you have no right to. You're spoiled children, each wanting your own way.

4.4-6 You're cheating on God. If all you want is your own way, flirting with the world every chance you get, you end up enemies of God and his way. And do you suppose God doesn't care? The proverb has it that "he's a fiercely jealous lover." And what he gives in love is far better than anything else you'll find. It's common knowledge that "God goes against the willful proud; God gives grace to the willing humble."

4.7-10 So let God work his will in you. Yell a loud *no* to the Devil and watch him scamper. Say a quiet *yes* to God and he'll be there in no time. Quit dabbling in sin. Purify your inner life. Quit playing the field. Hit bottom, and cry your eyes out. The fun and games are over. Get serious, really serious. Get down on your knees before the Master; it's the only way you'll get on your feet.

4.11-12 Don't bad-mouth each other, friends. It's God's Word, his Message, his Royal Rule, that takes a beating in that kind of talk. You're supposed to be honoring the Message, not writing graffiti all over it. God is in charge of deciding human destiny. Who do you think you are to meddle in the destiny of others?

NEW INTERNATIONAL VERSION

BOASTING ABOUT TOMORROW

13Now listen, you who say, "Today or tomorrow we will go to this or that city, spend a year there, carry on business and make money." 14Why, you do not even know what will happen tomorrow. What is your life? You are a mist that appears for a little while and then vanishes. 15Instead, you ought to say, "If it is the Lord's will, we will live and do this or that." 16As it is, you boast and brag. All such boasting is evil. 17Anyone, then, who knows the good he ought to do and doesn't do it, sins.

WARNING TO RICH OPPRESSORS

5 Now listen, you rich people, weep and wail because of the misery that is coming upon you. 2Your wealth has rotted, and moths have eaten your clothes. 3Your gold and silver are corroded. Their corrosion will testify against you and eat your flesh like fire. You have hoarded wealth in the last days. 4Look! The wages you failed to pay the workmen who mowed your fields are crying out against you. The cries of the harvesters have reached the ears of the Lord Almighty. 5You have lived on earth in luxury and self-indulgence. You have fattened yourselves in the day of slaughter.*a* 6You have condemned and murdered innocent men, who were not opposing you.

PATIENCE IN SUFFERING

7Be patient, then, brothers, until the Lord's coming. See how the farmer waits for the land to yield its valuable crop and how patient he is for the autumn and spring rains. 8You too, be patient and stand firm, because the Lord's coming is near. 9Don't grumble against each other, brothers, or you will be judged. The Judge is standing at the door!

10Brothers, as an example of patience in the face of suffering, take the prophets who spoke in the name of the Lord. 11As you know, we consider blessed those who have persevered. You have heard of Job's perseverance and have seen what the Lord finally brought about. The Lord is full of compassion and mercy.

12Above all, my brothers, do not swear—not

THE MESSAGE

NOTHING BUT A WISP OF FOG

4.13-15 And now I have a word for you who brashly announce, "Today—at the latest, tomorrow—we're off to such and such a city for the year. We're going to start a business and make a lot of money." You don't know the first thing about tomorrow. You're nothing but a wisp of fog, catching a brief bit of sun before disappearing. Instead, make it a habit to say, "If the Master wills it and we're still alive, we'll do this or that."

4.16-17 As it is, you are full of your grandiose selves. All such vaunting self-importance is evil. In fact, if you know the right thing to do and don't do it, that, for you, is evil.

DESTROYING YOUR LIFE FROM WITHIN

5.1-3 And a final word to you arrogant rich: Take some lessons in lament. You'll need buckets for the tears when the crash comes upon you. Your money is corrupt and your fine clothes stink. Your greedy luxuries are a cancer in your gut, destroying your life from within. You thought you were piling up wealth. What you've piled up is judgment.

5.4-6 All the workers you've exploited and cheated cry out for judgment. The groans of the workers you used and abused are a roar in the ears of the Master Avenger. You've looted the earth and lived it up. But all you'll have to show for it is a fatter than usual corpse. In fact, what you've done is condemn and murder perfectly good persons, who stand there and take it.

✠

5.7-8 Meanwhile, friends, wait patiently for the Master's Arrival. You see farmers do this all the time, waiting for their valuable crops to mature, patiently letting the rain do its slow but sure work. Be patient like that. Stay steady and strong. The Master could arrive at any time.

5.9 Friends, don't complain about each other. A far greater complaint could be lodged against you, you know. The Judge is standing just around the corner.

5.10-11 Take the old prophets as your mentors. They put up with anything, went through everything, and never once quit, all the time honoring God. What a gift life is to those who stay the course! You've heard, of course, of Job's staying power, and you know how God brought it all together for him at the end. That's because God cares, cares right down to the last detail.

5.12 And since you know that he cares, let your language show it. Don't add words like "I swear

---

a 5 Or yourselves as in a day of feasting

NEW INTERNATIONAL VERSION

by heaven or by earth or by anything else. Let your "Yes" be yes, and your "No," no, or you will be condemned.

THE PRAYER OF FAITH

¹³Is any one of you in trouble? He should pray. Is anyone happy? Let him sing songs of praise. ¹⁴Is any one of you sick? He should call the elders of the church to pray over him and anoint him with oil in the name of the Lord. ¹⁵And the prayer offered in faith will make the sick person well; the Lord will raise him up. If he has sinned, he will be forgiven. ¹⁶Therefore confess your sins to each other and pray for each other so that you may be healed. The prayer of a righteous man is powerful and effective.

¹⁷Elijah was a man just like us. He prayed earnestly that it would not rain, and it did not rain on the land for three and a half years. ¹⁸Again he prayed, and the heavens gave rain, and the earth produced its crops.

¹⁹My brothers, if one of you should wander from the truth and someone should bring him back, ²⁰remember this: Whoever turns a sinner from the error of his way will save him from death and cover over a multitude of sins.

THE MESSAGE

to God" to your own words. Don't show your impatience by concocting oaths to hurry up God. Just say yes or no. Just say what is true. That way, your language can't be used against you.

PRAYER TO BE RECKONED WITH

5.13-15 Are you hurting? Pray. Do you feel great? Sing. Are you sick? Call the church leaders together to pray and anoint you with oil in the name of the Master. Believing-prayer will heal you, and Jesus will put you on your feet. And if you've sinned, you'll be forgiven—healed inside and out.

5.16-18 Make this your common practice: Confess your sins to each other and pray for each other so that you can live together whole and healed. The prayer of a person living right with God is something powerful to be reckoned with. Elijah, for instance, human just like us, prayed hard that it wouldn't rain, and it didn't—not a drop for three and a half years. Then he prayed that it would rain, and it did. The showers came and everything started growing again.

5.19-20 My dear friends, if you know people who have wandered off from God's truth, don't write them off. Go after them. Get them back and you will have rescued precious lives from destruction and prevented an epidemic of wandering away from God.

1 PETER

1 PETER

1 Peter, an apostle of Jesus Christ,

To God's elect, strangers in the world, scattered throughout Pontus, Galatia, Cappadocia, Asia and Bithynia, ²who have been chosen according to the foreknowledge of God the Father, through the sanctifying work of the Spirit, for obedience to Jesus Christ and sprinkling by his blood:

Grace and peace be yours in abundance.

PRAISE TO GOD FOR A LIVING HOPE

³Praise be to the God and Father of our Lord Jesus Christ! In his great mercy he has given us new birth into a living hope through the resurrection of Jesus Christ from the dead, ⁴and into an inheritance that can never perish, spoil or fade—kept in heaven for you, ⁵who through faith are shielded by God's power until the coming of the salvation that is ready to be revealed in the last time. ⁶In this you greatly rejoice, though now for a little while you may have had to suffer grief in all kinds of trials. ⁷These have come so that your faith—of greater worth than gold, which perishes even though refined by fire—may be proved genuine and may result in praise, glory and honor when Jesus Christ is revealed. ⁸Though you have not seen him, you love him; and even though you do not see him now, you believe in him and are filled with an inexpressible and glorious joy, ⁹for you are receiving the goal of your faith, the salvation of your souls.

¹⁰Concerning this salvation, the prophets, who spoke of the grace that was to come to you, searched intently and with the greatest care, ¹¹trying to find out the time and circumstances to which the Spirit of Christ in them was pointing when he predicted the sufferings of Christ and the glories that would follow. ¹²It was revealed to them that they were not serving themselves but you, when they spoke of the things that have now been told you by those who have preached the gospel to you by the Holy Spirit sent from heaven. Even angels long to look into these things.

1.1-2 1 I, Peter, am an apostle on assignment by Jesus, the Messiah, writing to exiles scattered to the four winds. Not one is missing, not one forgotten. God the Father has his eye on each of you, and has determined by the work of the Spirit to keep you obedient through the sacrifice of Jesus. May everything good from God be yours!

A NEW LIFE

1.3-5 What a God we have! And how fortunate we are to have him, this Father of our Master Jesus! Because Jesus was raised from the dead, we've been given a brand-new life and have everything to live for, including a future in heaven—and the future starts now! God is keeping careful watch over us and the future. The Day is coming when you'll have it all—life healed and whole.

1.6-7 I know how great this makes you feel, even though you have to put up with every kind of aggravation in the meantime. Pure gold put in the fire comes out of it *proved* pure; genuine faith put through this suffering comes out *proved* genuine. When Jesus wraps this all up, it's your faith, not your gold, that God will have on display as evidence of his victory.

1.8-9 You never saw him, yet you love him. You still don't see him, yet you trust him—with laughter and singing. Because you kept on believing, you'll get what you're looking forward to: total salvation.

1.10-12 The prophets who told us this was coming asked a lot of questions about this gift of life God was preparing. The Messiah's Spirit let them in on some of it—that the Messiah would experience suffering, followed by glory. They clamored to know who and when. All they were told was that they were serving you, you who by orders from heaven have now heard for yourselves—through the Holy Spirit—the Message of those prophecies fulfilled. Do you realize how fortunate you are? Angels would have given anything to be in on this!

NEW INTERNATIONAL VERSION

BE HOLY

[13]Therefore, prepare your minds for action; be self-controlled; set your hope fully on the grace to be given you when Jesus Christ is revealed. [14]As obedient children, do not conform to the evil desires you had when you lived in ignorance. [15]But just as he who called you is holy, so be holy in all you do; [16]for it is written: "Be holy, because I am holy." [a]

[17]Since you call on a Father who judges each man's work impartially, live your lives as strangers here in reverent fear. [18]For you know that it was not with perishable things such as silver or gold that you were redeemed from the empty way of life handed down to you from your forefathers, [19]but with the precious blood of Christ, a lamb without blemish or defect. [20]He was chosen before the creation of the world, but was revealed in these last times for your sake. [21]Through him you believe in God, who raised him from the dead and glorified him, and so your faith and hope are in God.

[22]Now that you have purified yourselves by obeying the truth so that you have sincere love for your brothers, love one another deeply, from the heart. [b] [23]For you have been born again, not of perishable seed, but of imperishable, through the living and enduring word of God. [24]For,

"All men are like grass,
and all their glory is like the flowers of
the field;
the grass withers and the flowers fall,
[25]   but the word of the Lord stands forever." [c]

And this is the word that was preached to you.

2 Therefore, rid yourselves of all malice and all deceit, hypocrisy, envy, and slander of every kind. [2]Like newborn babies, crave pure spiritual milk, so that by it you may grow up in your salvation, [3]now that you have tasted that the Lord is good.

THE LIVING STONE AND A CHOSEN PEOPLE

[4]As you come to him, the living Stone—rejected by men but chosen by God and precious to him— [5]you also, like living stones, are being built into a spiritual house to be a holy priest-

THE MESSAGE

A FUTURE IN GOD

1.13-16 So roll up your sleeves, put your mind in gear, be totally ready to receive the gift that's coming when Jesus arrives. Don't lazily slip back into those old grooves of evil, doing just what you feel like doing. You didn't know any better then; you do now. As obedient children, let yourselves be pulled into a way of life shaped by God's life, a life energetic and blazing with holiness. God said, "I am holy; you be holy."

1.17   You call out to God for help and he helps—he's a good Father that way. But don't forget, he's also a responsible Father, and won't let you get by with sloppy living.

1.18-21   Your life is a journey you must travel with a deep consciousness of God. It cost God plenty to get you out of that dead-end, empty-headed life you grew up in. He paid with Christ's sacred blood, you know. He died like an unblemished, sacrificial lamb. And this was no afterthought. Even though it has only lately—at the end of the ages—become public knowledge, God always knew he was going to do this for you. It's because of this sacrificed Messiah, whom God then raised from the dead and glorified, that you trust God, that you know you have a future in God.

1.22-25   Now that you've cleaned up your lives by following the truth, love one another as if your lives depended on it. Your new life is not like your old life. Your old birth came from mortal sperm; your new birth comes from God's living Word. Just think: a life conceived by God himself! That's why the prophet said,

The old life is a grass life,
its beauty as short-lived as wildflowers;
Grass dries up, flowers droop,
God's Word goes on and on forever.

This is the Word that conceived the new life in you.

2 So clean house! Make a clean sweep of malice and pretense, envy and hurtful talk. You've had a taste of God. Now, like infants at the breast, drink deep of God's pure kindness. Then you'll grow up mature and whole in God.

THE STONE

2.4-8 Welcome to the living Stone, the source of life. The workmen took one look and threw it out; God set it in the place of honor. Present yourselves as building stones for the construction of a sanctuary vibrant with life, in which you'll

[a] 16 Lev. 11:44,45; 19:2   [b] 22 Some early manuscripts from a pure heart   [c] 25 Isaiah 40:6-8

NEW INTERNATIONAL VERSION

hood, offering spiritual sacrifices acceptable to God through Jesus Christ. ⁶For in Scripture it says:

> "See, I lay a stone in Zion,
> a chosen and precious cornerstone,
> and the one who trusts in him
> will never be put to shame." ᵃ

⁷Now to you who believe, this stone is precious. But to those who do not believe,

> "The stone the builders rejected
> has become the capstone," ᵇ ᶜ

⁸and,

> "A stone that causes men to stumble
> and a rock that makes them fall." ᵈ

They stumble because they disobey the message—which is also what they were destined for.
⁹But you are a chosen people, a royal priesthood, a holy nation, a people belonging to God, that you may declare the praises of him who called you out of darkness into his wonderful light. ¹⁰Once you were not a people, but now you are the people of God; once you had not received mercy, but now you have received mercy.
¹¹Dear friends, I urge you, as aliens and strangers in the world, to abstain from sinful desires, which war against your soul. ¹²Live such good lives among the pagans that, though they accuse you of doing wrong, they may see your good deeds and glorify God on the day he visits us.

SUBMISSION TO RULERS AND MASTERS

¹³Submit yourselves for the Lord's sake to every authority instituted among men: whether to the king, as the supreme authority, ¹⁴or to governors, who are sent by him to punish those who do wrong and to commend those who do right. ¹⁵For it is God's will that by doing good you should silence the ignorant talk of foolish men. ¹⁶Live as free men, but do not use your freedom as a cover-up for evil; live as servants of God. ¹⁷Show proper respect to everyone: Love the brotherhood of believers, fear God, honor the king.
¹⁸Slaves, submit yourselves to your masters with all respect, not only to those who are good and considerate, but also to those who are harsh. ¹⁹For it is commendable if a man bears up under the pain of unjust suffering because he is conscious of God. ²⁰But how is it to your credit if you receive a beating for doing wrong and endure it? But if you suffer for doing good and you endure it, this is commendable before God. ²¹To

ᵃ 6 Isaiah 28:16   ᵇ 7 Or *cornerstone*   ᶜ 7 Psalm 118:22
ᵈ 8 Isaiah 8:14

THE MESSAGE

serve as holy priests offering Christ-approved lives up to God. The Scriptures provide precedent:

> Look! I'm setting a stone in Zion,
> a cornerstone in the place of honor.
> Whoever trusts in this stone as a
> foundation
> will never have cause to regret it.

To you who trust him, he's a Stone to be proud of, but to those who refuse to trust him,

> The stone the workmen threw out
> is now the chief foundation stone.

For the untrusting it's

> . . . a stone to trip over,
> a boulder blocking the way.

They trip and fall because they refuse to obey, just as predicted.
2.9-10   But you are the ones chosen by God, chosen for the high calling of priestly work, chosen to be a holy people, God's instruments to do his work and speak out for him, to tell others of the night-and-day difference he made for you—from nothing to something, from rejected to accepted.

✝

2.11-12 Friends, this world is not your home, so don't make yourselves cozy in it. Don't indulge your ego at the expense of your soul. Live an exemplary life among the natives so that your actions will refute their prejudices. Then they'll be won over to God's side and be there to join in the celebration when he arrives.
2.13-17   Make the Master proud of you by being good citizens. Respect the authorities, whatever their level; they are God's emissaries for keeping order. It is God's will that by doing good, you might cure the ignorance of the fools who think you're a danger to society. Exercise your freedom by serving God, not by breaking the rules. Treat everyone you meet with dignity. Love your spiritual family. Revere God. Respect the government.

THE KIND OF LIFE HE LIVED

2.18-20 You who are servants, be good servants to your masters—not just to good masters, but also to bad ones. What counts is that you put up with it for God's sake when you're treated badly for no good reason. There's no particular virtue in accepting punishment that you well deserve. But if you're treated badly for good behavior and continue in spite of it to be a good servant, that is what counts with God.

NEW INTERNATIONAL VERSION

this you were called, because Christ suffered for you, leaving you an example, that you should follow in his steps.

²²"He committed no sin,
    and no deceit was found in his mouth." [a]

²³When they hurled their insults at him, he did not retaliate; when he suffered, he made no threats. Instead, he entrusted himself to him who judges justly. ²⁴He himself bore our sins in his body on the tree, so that we might die to sins and live for righteousness; by his wounds you have been healed. ²⁵For you were like sheep going astray, but now you have returned to the Shepherd and Overseer of your souls.

WIVES AND HUSBANDS

3 Wives, in the same way be submissive to your husbands so that, if any of them do not believe the word, they may be won over without words by the behavior of their wives, ²when they see the purity and reverence of your lives. ³Your beauty should not come from outward adornment, such as braided hair and the wearing of gold jewelry and fine clothes. ⁴Instead, it should be that of your inner self, the unfading beauty of a gentle and quiet spirit, which is of great worth in God's sight. ⁵For this is the way the holy women of the past who put their hope in God used to make themselves beautiful. They were submissive to their own husbands, ⁶like Sarah, who obeyed Abraham and called him her master. You are her daughters if you do what is right and do not give way to fear.

⁷Husbands, in the same way be considerate as you live with your wives, and treat them with respect as the weaker partner and as heirs with you of the gracious gift of life, so that nothing will hinder your prayers.

SUFFERING FOR DOING GOOD

⁸Finally, all of you, live in harmony with one another; be sympathetic, love as brothers, be compassionate and humble. ⁹Do not repay evil with evil or insult with insult, but with blessing, because to this you were called so that you may inherit a blessing. ¹⁰For,

"Whoever would love life
    and see good days
must keep his tongue from evil
    and his lips from deceitful speech.
¹¹He must turn from evil and do good;
    he must seek peace and pursue it.

THE MESSAGE

2.21-25   This is the kind of life you've been invited into, the kind of life Christ lived. He suffered everything that came his way so you would know that it could be done, and also know how to do it, step-by-step.

He never did one thing wrong,
    Not once said anything amiss.

They called him every name in the book and he said nothing back. He suffered in silence, content to let God set things right. He used his servant body to carry our sins to the Cross so we could be rid of sin, free to live the right way. His wounds became your healing. You were lost sheep with no idea who you were or where you were going. Now you're named and kept for good by the Shepherd of your souls.

CULTIVATE INNER BEAUTY

3.1-4 3 The same goes for you wives: Be good wives to your husbands, responsive to their needs. There are husbands who, indifferent as they are to any words about God, will be captivated by your life of holy beauty. What matters is not your outer appearance—the styling of your hair, the jewelry you wear, the cut of your clothes—but your inner disposition.

3.4-6   Cultivate inner beauty, the gentle, gracious kind that God delights in. The holy women of old were beautiful before God that way, and were good, loyal wives to their husbands. Sarah, for instance, taking care of Abraham, would address him as "my dear husband." You'll be true daughters of Sarah if you do the same, unanxious and unintimidated.

3.7   The same goes for you husbands: Be good husbands to your wives. Honor them, delight in them. As women they lack some of your advantages. But in the new life of God's grace, you're equals. Treat your wives, then, as equals so your prayers don't run aground.

SUFFERING FOR DOING GOOD

3.8-12 Summing up: Be agreeable, be sympathetic, be loving, be compassionate, be humble. That goes for all of you, no exceptions. No retaliation. No sharp-tongued sarcasm. Instead, bless—that's your job, to bless. You'll be a blessing and also get a blessing.

Whoever wants to embrace life
    and see the day fill up with good,
Here's what you do:
    Say nothing evil or hurtful;
Snub evil and cultivate good;
    run after peace for all you're worth.

[a] 22 Isaiah 53:9

NEW INTERNATIONAL VERSION

¹²For the eyes of the Lord are on the righteous
   and his ears are attentive to their prayer,
but the face of the Lord is against those who
   do evil."ᵃ

¹³Who is going to harm you if you are eager
to do good? ¹⁴But even if you should suffer for
what is right, you are blessed. "Do not fear what
they fearᵇ; do not be frightened."ᶜ ¹⁵But in your
hearts set apart Christ as Lord. Always be prepared to give an answer to everyone who asks
you to give the reason for the hope that you
have. But do this with gentleness and respect,
¹⁶keeping a clear conscience, so that those who
speak maliciously against your good behavior in
Christ may be ashamed of their slander. ¹⁷It is
better, if it is God's will, to suffer for doing good
than for doing evil. ¹⁸For Christ died for sins
once for all, the righteous for the unrighteous, to
bring you to God. He was put to death in the
body but made alive by the Spirit, ¹⁹through
whomᵈ also he went and preached to the spirits
in prison ²⁰who disobeyed long ago when God
waited patiently in the days of Noah while the
ark was being built. In it only a few people, eight
in all, were saved through water, ²¹and this water
symbolizes baptism that now saves you also—
not the removal of dirt from the body but the
pledgeᵉ of a good conscience toward God. It
saves you by the resurrection of Jesus Christ,
²²who has gone into heaven and is at God's right
hand—with angels, authorities and powers in
submission to him.

LIVING FOR GOD

4 Therefore, since Christ suffered in his body,
arm yourselves also with the same attitude,
because he who has suffered in his body is done
with sin. ²As a result, he does not live the rest of
his earthly life for evil human desires, but rather
for the will of God. ³For you have spent enough
time in the past doing what pagans choose to
do—living in debauchery, lust, drunkenness, orgies, carousing and detestable idolatry. ⁴They
think it strange that you do not plunge with
them into the same flood of dissipation, and they
heap abuse on you. ⁵But they will have to give
account to him who is ready to judge the living
and the dead. ⁶For this is the reason the gospel
was preached even to those who are now dead,
so that they might be judged according to men

ᵃ 12 Psalm 34:12-16   ᵇ 14 Or *not fear their threats*
ᶜ 14 Isaiah 8:12   ᵈ 18,19 Or *alive in the spirit,* ¹⁹*through
which*   ᵉ 21 Or *response*

THE MESSAGE

God looks on all this with approval,
   listening and responding well to what
   he's asked;
But he turns his back
   on those who do evil things.

3.13-18   If with heart and soul you're doing good, do
you think you can be stopped? Even if you suffer for it, you're still better off. Don't give the
opposition a second thought. Through thick and
thin, keep your hearts at attention, in adoration
before Christ, your Master. Be ready to speak up
and tell anyone who asks why you're living the
way you are, and always with the utmost courtesy. Keep a clear conscience before God so that
when people throw mud at you, none of it will
stick. They'll end up realizing that *they're* the
ones who need a bath. It's better to suffer for doing good, if that's what God wants, than to be
punished for doing bad. That's what Christ did
definitively: suffered because of others' sins, the
Righteous One for the unrighteous ones. He
went through it all—was put to death and then
made alive—to bring us to God.

3.19-22   He went and proclaimed God's salvation to
earlier generations who ended up in the prison
of judgment because they wouldn't listen. You
know, even though God waited patiently all the
days that Noah built his ship, only a few were
saved then, eight to be exact—saved *from* the
water *by* the water. The waters of baptism do
that for you, not by washing away dirt from
your skin but by presenting you through Jesus'
resurrection before God with a clear conscience.
Jesus has the last word on everything and everyone, from angels to armies. He's standing right
alongside God, and what he says goes.

LEARN TO THINK LIKE HIM

4.1-2   **4** Since Jesus went through everything you're
going through and more, learn to think like
him. Think of your sufferings as a weaning
from that old sinful habit of always expecting
to get your own way. Then you'll be able to live
out your days free to pursue what God wants
instead of being tyrannized by what you want.

4.3-5   You've already put in your time in that God-
ignorant way of life, partying night after night,
a drunken and profligate life. Now it's time to
be done with it for good. Of course, your old
friends don't understand why you don't join in
with the old gang anymore. But you don't have
to give an account to them. They're the ones
who will be called on the carpet—and before
God himself.

4.6   Listen to the Message. It was preached to
those believers who are now dead, and yet even
though they died (just as all people must), they

NEW INTERNATIONAL VERSION

in regard to the body, but live according to God in regard to the spirit.

⁷The end of all things is near. Therefore be clear minded and self-controlled so that you can pray. ⁸Above all, love each other deeply, because love covers over a multitude of sins. ⁹Offer hospitality to one another without grumbling. ¹⁰Each one should use whatever gift he has received to serve others, faithfully administering God's grace in its various forms. ¹¹If anyone speaks, he should do it as one speaking the very words of God. If anyone serves, he should do it with the strength God provides, so that in all things God may be praised through Jesus Christ. To him be the glory and the power for ever and ever. Amen.

SUFFERING FOR BEING A CHRISTIAN

¹²Dear friends, do not be surprised at the painful trial you are suffering, as though something strange were happening to you. ¹³But rejoice that you participate in the sufferings of Christ, so that you may be overjoyed when his glory is revealed. ¹⁴If you are insulted because of the name of Christ, you are blessed, for the Spirit of glory and of God rests on you. ¹⁵If you suffer, it should not be as a murderer or thief or any other kind of criminal, or even as a meddler. ¹⁶However, if you suffer as a Christian, do not be ashamed, but praise God that you bear that name. ¹⁷For it is time for judgment to begin with the family of God; and if it begins with us, what will the outcome be for those who do not obey the gospel of God? ¹⁸And,

"If it is hard for the righteous to be saved,
    what will become of the ungodly and the
        sinner?" *a*

¹⁹So then, those who suffer according to God's will should commit themselves to their faithful Creator and continue to do good.

TO ELDERS AND YOUNG MEN

5 To the elders among you, I appeal as a fellow elder, a witness of Christ's sufferings and one who also will share in the glory to be revealed: ²Be shepherds of God's flock that is under your care, serving as overseers—not because you must, but because you are willing, as God wants you to be; not greedy for money, but eager to serve; ³not lording it over those entrusted to you, but being examples to the flock. ⁴And when the Chief Shepherd appears, you will receive the crown of glory that will never fade away.

THE MESSAGE

will still get in on the *life* that God has given in Jesus.

4.7-11 Everything in the world is about to be wrapped up, so take nothing for granted. Stay wide-awake in prayer. Most of all, love each other as if your life depended on it. Love makes up for practically anything. Be quick to give a meal to the hungry, a bed to the homeless—cheerfully. Be generous with the different things God gave you, passing them around so all get in on it: if words, let it be God's words; if help, let it be God's hearty help. That way, God's bright presence will be evident in everything through Jesus, and *he'll* get all the credit as the One mighty in everything—encores to the end of time. Oh, yes!

GLORY JUST AROUND THE CORNER

4.12-13 Friends, when life gets really difficult, don't jump to the conclusion that God isn't on the job. Instead, be glad that you are in the very thick of what Christ experienced. This is a spiritual refining process, with glory just around the corner.

4.14-16 If you're abused because of Christ, count yourself fortunate. It's the Spirit of God and his glory in you that brought you to the notice of others. If they're on you because you broke the law or disturbed the peace, that's a different matter. But if it's because you're a Christian, don't give it a second thought. Be proud of the distinguished status reflected in that name!

4.17-19 It's judgment time for Christians. We're first in line. If it starts with us, think what it's going to be like for those who refuse God's Message!

If good people barely make it,
What's in store for the bad?

So if you find life difficult because you're doing what God said, take it in stride. Trust him. He knows what he's doing, and he'll keep on doing it.

HE'LL PROMOTE YOU AT THE RIGHT TIME

5.1-3 **5** I have a special concern for you church leaders. I know what it's like to be a leader, in on Christ's sufferings as well as the coming glory. Here's my concern: that you care for God's flock with all the diligence of a shepherd. Not because you have to, but because you want to please God. Not calculating what you can get out of it, but acting spontaneously. Not bossily telling others what to do, but tenderly showing them the way.

5.4-5 When God, who is the best shepherd of all, comes out in the open with his rule, he'll see that you've done it right and commend you lav-

NEW INTERNATIONAL VERSION

⁵Young men, in the same way be submissive to those who are older. All of you, clothe yourselves with humility toward one another, because,

"God opposes the proud
but gives grace to the humble." ᵃ

⁶Humble yourselves, therefore, under God's mighty hand, that he may lift you up in due time. ⁷Cast all your anxiety on him because he cares for you.

⁸Be self-controlled and alert. Your enemy the devil prowls around like a roaring lion looking for someone to devour. ⁹Resist him, standing firm in the faith, because you know that your brothers throughout the world are undergoing the same kind of sufferings.

¹⁰And the God of all grace, who called you to his eternal glory in Christ, after you have suffered a little while, will himself restore you and make you strong, firm and steadfast. ¹¹To him be the power for ever and ever. Amen.

FINAL GREETINGS

¹²With the help of Silas, ᵇ whom I regard as a faithful brother, I have written to you briefly, encouraging you and testifying that this is the true grace of God. Stand fast in it.

¹³She who is in Babylon, chosen together with you, sends you her greetings, and so does my son Mark. ¹⁴Greet one another with a kiss of love.

Peace to all of you who are in Christ.

THE MESSAGE

ishly. And you who are younger must follow your leaders. But all of you, leaders and followers alike, are to be down to earth with each other, for—

God has had it with the proud,
But takes delight in just plain people.

5.6-7 So be content with who you are, and don't put on airs. God's strong hand is on you; he'll promote you at the right time. Live carefree before God; he is most careful with you.

HE GETS THE LAST WORD

5.8-11 Keep a cool head. Stay alert. The Devil is poised to pounce, and would like nothing better than to catch you napping. Keep your guard up. You're not the only ones plunged into these hard times. It's the same with Christians all over the world. So keep a firm grip on the faith. The suffering won't last forever. It won't be long before this generous God who has great plans for us in Christ—eternal and glorious plans they are!—will have you put together and on your feet for good. He gets the last word; yes, he does.

5.12 I'm sending this brief letter to you by Silas, a most dependable brother. I have the highest regard for him.

I've written as urgently and accurately as I know how. This is God's generous truth; embrace it with both arms!

5.13-14 The church in exile here with me—but not for a moment forgotten by God—wants to be remembered to you. Mark, who is like a son to me, says hello. Give holy embraces all around! Peace to you—to all who walk in Christ's ways.

ᵃ 5 Prov. 3:34   ᵇ 12 Greek Silvanus, a variant of Silas

2 PETER

2 PETER

¹ Simon Peter, a servant and apostle of Jesus Christ,

To those who through the righteousness of our God and Savior Jesus Christ have received a faith as precious as ours:

²Grace and peace be yours in abundance through the knowledge of God and of Jesus our Lord.

MAKING ONE'S CALLING AND ELECTION SURE

³His divine power has given us everything we need for life and godliness through our knowledge of him who called us by his own glory and goodness. ⁴Through these he has given us his very great and precious promises, so that through them you may participate in the divine nature and escape the corruption in the world caused by evil desires.

⁵For this very reason, make every effort to add to your faith goodness; and to goodness, knowledge; ⁶and to knowledge, self-control; and to self-control, perseverance; and to perseverance, godliness; ⁷and to godliness, brotherly kindness; and to brotherly kindness, love. ⁸For if you possess these qualities in increasing measure, they will keep you from being ineffective and unproductive in your knowledge of our Lord Jesus Christ. ⁹But if anyone does not have them, he is nearsighted and blind, and has forgotten that he has been cleansed from his past sins.

¹⁰Therefore, my brothers, be all the more eager to make your calling and election sure. For if you do these things, you will never fall, ¹¹and you will receive a rich welcome into the eternal kingdom of our Lord and Savior Jesus Christ.

PROPHECY OF SCRIPTURE

¹²So I will always remind you of these things, even though you know them and are firmly established in the truth you now have. ¹³I think it is right to refresh your memory as long as I live in the tent of this body, ¹⁴because I know that I

1.1-2 ¹ I, Simon Peter, am a servant and apostle of Jesus Christ. I write this to you whose experience with God is as life-changing as ours, all due to our God's straight dealing and the intervention of our God and Savior, Jesus Christ. Grace and peace to you many times over as you deepen in your experience with God and Jesus, our Master.

DON'T PUT IT OFF

1.3-4 Everything that goes into a life of pleasing God has been miraculously given to us by getting to know, personally and intimately, the One who invited us to God. The best invitation we ever received! We were also given absolutely terrific promises to pass on to you—your tickets to participation in the life of God after you turned your back on a world corrupted by lust.

1.5-9 So don't lose a minute in building on what you've been given, complementing your basic faith with good character, spiritual understanding, alert discipline, passionate patience, reverent wonder, warm friendliness, and generous love, each dimension fitting into and developing the others. With these qualities active and growing in your lives, no grass will grow under your feet, no day will pass without its reward as you mature in your experience of our Master Jesus. Without these qualities you can't see what's right before you, oblivious that your old sinful life has been wiped off the books.

1.10-11 So, friends, confirm God's invitation to you, his choice of you. Don't put it off; do it now. Do this, and you'll have your life on a firm footing, the streets paved and the way wide open into the eternal kingdom of our Master and Savior, Jesus Christ.

THE ONE LIGHT IN A DARK TIME

1.12-15 Because the stakes are so high, even though you're up-to-date on all this truth and practice it inside and out, I'm not going to let up for a minute in calling you to attention before it. This is the post to which I've been assigned—keeping you alert with frequent reminders—and I'm sticking to it as long as I live. I know

NEW INTERNATIONAL VERSION

will soon put it aside, as our Lord Jesus Christ has made clear to me. [15]And I will make every effort to see that after my departure you will always be able to remember these things.

[16]We did not follow cleverly invented stories when we told you about the power and coming of our Lord Jesus Christ, but we were eyewitnesses of his majesty. [17]For he received honor and glory from God the Father when the voice came to him from the Majestic Glory, saying, "This is my Son, whom I love; with him I am well pleased."[a] [18]We ourselves heard this voice that came from heaven when we were with him on the sacred mountain.

[19]And we have the word of the prophets made more certain, and you will do well to pay attention to it, as to a light shining in a dark place, until the day dawns and the morning star rises in your hearts. [20]Above all, you must understand that no prophecy of Scripture came about by the prophet's own interpretation. [21]For prophecy never had its origin in the will of man, but men spoke from God as they were carried along by the Holy Spirit.

FALSE TEACHERS AND THEIR DESTRUCTION

2 But there were also false prophets among the people, just as there will be false teachers among you. They will secretly introduce destructive heresies, even denying the sovereign Lord who bought them—bringing swift destruction on themselves. [2]Many will follow their shameful ways and will bring the way of truth into disrepute. [3]In their greed these teachers will exploit you with stories they have made up. Their condemnation has long been hanging over them, and their destruction has not been sleeping.

[4]For if God did not spare angels when they sinned, but sent them to hell,[b] putting them into gloomy dungeons[c] to be held for judgment; [5]if he did not spare the ancient world when he brought the flood on its ungodly people, but protected Noah, a preacher of righteousness, and seven others; [6]if he condemned the cities of Sodom and Gomorrah by burning them to ashes, and made them an example of what is going to happen to the ungodly; [7]and if he rescued Lot, a righteous man, who was distressed by the filthy

THE MESSAGE

that I'm to die soon; the Master has made that quite clear to me. And so I am especially eager that you have all this down in black and white so that after I die, you'll have it for ready reference.

1.16-18   We weren't, you know, just wishing on a star when we laid the facts out before you regarding the powerful return of our Master, Jesus Christ. We were there for the preview! We saw it with our own eyes: Jesus resplendent with light from God the Father as the voice of Majestic Glory spoke: "This is my Son, marked by my love, focus of all my delight." We were there on the holy mountain with him. We heard the voice out of heaven with our very own ears.

1.19-21   We couldn't be more sure of what we saw and heard—God's glory, God's voice. The prophetic Word was confirmed to us. You'll do well to keep focusing on it. It's the one light you have in a dark time as you wait for daybreak and the rising of the Morning Star in your hearts. The main thing to keep in mind here is that no prophecy of Scripture is a matter of private opinion. And why? Because it's not something concocted in the human heart. Prophecy resulted when the Holy Spirit prompted men and women to speak God's Word.

LYING RELIGIOUS LEADERS

2.1-2   2 But there were also lying prophets among the people then, just as there will be lying religious teachers among you. They'll smuggle in destructive divisions, pitting you against each other—biting the hand of the One who gave them a chance to have their lives back! They've put themselves on a fast downhill slide to destruction, but not before they recruit a crowd of mixed-up followers who can't tell right from wrong.

2.2-3   They give the way of truth a bad name. They're only out for themselves. They'll say anything, anything, that sounds good to exploit you. They won't, of course, get by with it. They'll come to a bad end, for God has never just stood by and let that kind of thing go on.

2.4-5   God didn't let the rebel angels off the hook, but jailed them in hell till Judgment Day. Neither did he let the ancient ungodly world off. He wiped it out with a flood, rescuing only eight people—Noah, the sole voice of righteousness, was one of them.

2.6-8   God decreed destruction for the cities of Sodom and Gomorrah. A mound of ashes was all that was left—grim warning to anyone bent on an ungodly life. But that good man Lot, driven nearly out of his mind by the sexual

---

[a] 17 Matt. 17:5; Mark 9:7; Luke 9:35   [b] 4 Greek Tartarus
[c] 4 Some manuscripts into chains of darkness

NEW INTERNATIONAL VERSION

lives of lawless men [8](for that righteous man, living among them day after day, was tormented in his righteous soul by the lawless deeds he saw and heard)— [9]if this is so, then the Lord knows how to rescue godly men from trials and to hold the unrighteous for the day of judgment, while continuing their punishment.[a] [10]This is especially true of those who follow the corrupt desire of the sinful nature[b] and despise authority.

Bold and arrogant, these men are not afraid to slander celestial beings; [11]yet even angels, although they are stronger and more powerful, do not bring slanderous accusations against such beings in the presence of the Lord. [12]But these men blaspheme in matters they do not understand. They are like brute beasts, creatures of instinct, born only to be caught and destroyed, and like beasts they too will perish.

[13]They will be paid back with harm for the harm they have done. Their idea of pleasure is to carouse in broad daylight. They are blots and blemishes, reveling in their pleasures while they feast with you.[c] [14]With eyes full of adultery, they never stop sinning; they seduce the unstable; they are experts in greed—an accursed brood! [15]They have left the straight way and wandered off to follow the way of Balaam son of Beor, who loved the wages of wickedness. [16]But he was rebuked for his wrongdoing by a donkey—a beast without speech—who spoke with a man's voice and restrained the prophet's madness.

[17]These men are springs without water and mists driven by a storm. Blackest darkness is reserved for them. [18]For they mouth empty, boastful words and, by appealing to the lustful desires of sinful human nature, they entice people who are just escaping from those who live in error. [19]They promise them freedom, while they themselves are slaves of depravity—for a man is a slave to whatever has mastered him. [20]If they have escaped the corruption of the world by knowing our Lord and Savior Jesus Christ and are again entangled in it and overcome, they are worse off at the end than they were at the beginning. [21]It would have been better for them not to have known the way of righteousness, than to have known it and then to turn their backs on the sacred command that was passed on to them. [22]Of them the proverbs are true: "A dog returns to its vomit,"[d] and, "A sow that is washed goes back to her wallowing in the mud."

[a] 9 Or unrighteous for punishment until the day of judgment
[b] 10 Or the flesh   [c] 13 Some manuscripts in their love feasts   [d] 22 Prov. 26:11

THE MESSAGE

filth and perversity, was rescued. Surrounded by moral rot day after day after day, that righteous man was in constant torment.

2.9   So God knows how to rescue the godly from evil trials. And he knows how to hold the feet of the wicked to the fire until Judgment Day.

PREDATORS ON THE PROWL

2.10-11 God is especially incensed against these "teachers" who live by lust, addicted to a filthy existence. They despise interference from true authority, preferring to indulge in self-rule. Insolent egotists, they don't hesitate to speak evil against the most splendid of creatures. Even angels, their superiors in every way, wouldn't think of throwing their weight around like that, trying to slander others before God.

2.12-14   These people are nothing but brute beasts, born in the wild, predators on the prowl. In the very act of bringing down others with their ignorant blasphemies, they themselves will be brought down, losers in the end. Their evil will boomerang on them. They're so despicable and addicted to pleasure that they indulge in wild parties, carousing in broad daylight. They're obsessed with adultery, compulsive in sin, seducing every vulnerable soul they come upon. Their specialty is greed, and they're experts at it. Dead souls!

2.15-16   They've left the main road and are directionless, having taken the way of Balaam, son of Beor, the prophet who turned profiteer, a connoisseur of evil. But Balaam was stopped in his wayward tracks: A dumb animal spoke in a human voice and prevented the prophet's craziness.

2.17-19   There's nothing to these people—they're dried-up fountains, storm-scattered clouds, headed for a black hole in hell. They are loudmouths, full of hot air, but still they're dangerous. Men and women who have recently escaped from a deviant life are most susceptible to their brand of seduction. They promise these newcomers freedom, but they themselves are slaves of corruption, for if they're addicted to corruption—and they are—they're *enslaved*.

2.20-22   If they've escaped from the slum of sin by experiencing our Master and Savior, Jesus Christ, and then slid back into that same old life again, they're worse than if they had never left. Better not to have started out on the straight road to God than to start out and then turn back, repudiating the experience and the holy command. They prove the point of the proverbs, "A dog goes back to its own vomit," and, "A scrubbed-up pig heads for the mud."

NEW INTERNATIONAL VERSION

THE DAY OF THE LORD

3 Dear friends, this is now my second letter to you. I have written both of them as reminders to stimulate you to wholesome thinking. ²I want you to recall the words spoken in the past by the holy prophets and the command given by our Lord and Savior through your apostles.

³First of all, you must understand that in the last days scoffers will come, scoffing and following their own evil desires. ⁴They will say, "Where is this 'coming' he promised? Ever since our fathers died, everything goes on as it has since the beginning of creation." ⁵But they deliberately forget that long ago by God's word the heavens existed and the earth was formed out of water and by water. ⁶By these waters also the world of that time was deluged and destroyed. ⁷By the same word the present heavens and earth are reserved for fire, being kept for the day of judgment and destruction of ungodly men.

⁸But do not forget this one thing, dear friends: With the Lord a day is like a thousand years, and a thousand years are like a day. ⁹The Lord is not slow in keeping his promise, as some understand slowness. He is patient with you, not wanting anyone to perish, but everyone to come to repentance.

¹⁰But the day of the Lord will come like a thief. The heavens will disappear with a roar; the elements will be destroyed by fire, and the earth and everything in it will be laid bare.*ᵃ*

¹¹Since everything will be destroyed in this way, what kind of people ought you to be? You ought to live holy and godly lives ¹²as you look forward to the day of God and speed its coming.*ᵇ* That day will bring about the destruction of the heavens by fire, and the elements will melt in the heat. ¹³But in keeping with his promise we are looking forward to a new heaven and a new earth, the home of righteousness.

¹⁴So then, dear friends, since you are looking forward to this, make every effort to be found spotless, blameless and at peace with him. ¹⁵Bear in mind that our Lord's patience means salvation, just as our dear brother Paul also wrote you with the wisdom that God gave him. ¹⁶He writes

---

ᵃ 10 Some manuscripts be burned up   *ᵇ 12 Or as you wait eagerly for the day of God to come*

THE MESSAGE

IN THE LAST DAYS

3.1-2 **3** My dear friends, this is now the second time I've written to you, both letters reminders to hold your minds in a state of undistracted attention. Keep in mind what the holy prophets said, and the command of our Master and Savior that was passed on by your apostles.

3.3-4 First off, you need to know that in the last days, mockers are going to have a heyday. Reducing everything to the level of their puny feelings, they'll mock, "So what's happened to the promise of his Coming? Our ancestors are dead and buried, and everything's going on just as it has from the first day of creation. Nothing's changed."

3.5-7 They conveniently forget that long ago all the galaxies and this very planet were brought into existence out of watery chaos by God's word. Then God's word brought the chaos back in a flood that destroyed the world. The current galaxies and earth are fuel for the final fire. God is poised, ready to speak his word again, ready to give the signal for the judgment and destruction of the desecrating skeptics.

THE DAY THE SKY WILL COLLAPSE

3.8-9 Don't overlook the obvious here, friends. With God, one day is as good as a thousand years, a thousand years as a day. God isn't late with his promise as some measure lateness. He is restraining himself on account of you, holding back the End because he doesn't want anyone lost. He's giving everyone space and time to change.

3.10 But when the Day of God's Judgment does come, it will be unannounced, like a thief. The sky will collapse with a thunderous bang, everything disintegrating in a huge conflagration, earth and all its works exposed to the scrutiny of Judgment.

3.11-13 Since everything here today might well be gone tomorrow, do you see how essential it is to live a holy life? Daily expect the Day of God, eager for its arrival. The galaxies will burn up and the elements melt down that day—but *we'll* hardly notice. We'll be looking the other way, ready for the promised new heavens and the promised new earth, all landscaped with righteousness.

✛

3.14-16 So, my dear friends, since this is what you have to look forward to, do your very best to be found living at your best, in purity and peace. Interpret our Master's patient restraint for what it is: salvation. Our good brother Paul, who was given much wisdom in these matters, refers to

NEW INTERNATIONAL VERSION

the same way in all his letters, speaking in them of these matters. His letters contain some things that are hard to understand, which ignorant and unstable people distort, as they do the other Scriptures, to their own destruction.

¹⁷Therefore, dear friends, since you already know this, be on your guard so that you may not be carried away by the error of lawless men and fall from your secure position. ¹⁸But grow in the grace and knowledge of our Lord and Savior Jesus Christ. To him be glory both now and forever! Amen.

THE MESSAGE

this in all his letters, and has written you essentially the same thing. Some things Paul writes are difficult to understand. Irresponsible people who don't know what they are talking about twist them every which way. They do it to the rest of the Scriptures, too, destroying themselves as they do it.

3.17-18   But you, friends, are well-warned. Be on guard lest you lose your footing and get swept off your feet by these lawless and loose-talking teachers. Grow in grace and understanding of our Master and Savior, Jesus Christ.

Glory to the Master, now and forever! Yes!

1 JOHN

1 JOHN

THE WORD OF LIFE

1 That which was from the beginning, which we have heard, which we have seen with our eyes, which we have looked at and our hands have touched—this we proclaim concerning the Word of life. ²The life appeared; we have seen it and testify to it, and we proclaim to you the eternal life, which was with the Father and has appeared to us. ³We proclaim to you what we have seen and heard, so that you also may have fellowship with us. And our fellowship is with the Father and with his Son, Jesus Christ. ⁴We write this to make our*a* joy complete.

WALKING IN THE LIGHT

⁵This is the message we have heard from him and declare to you: God is light; in him there is no darkness at all. ⁶If we claim to have fellowship with him yet walk in the darkness, we lie and do not live by the truth. ⁷But if we walk in the light, as he is in the light, we have fellowship with one another, and the blood of Jesus, his Son, purifies us from all*b* sin.

⁸If we claim to be without sin, we deceive ourselves and the truth is not in us. ⁹If we confess our sins, he is faithful and just and will forgive us our sins and purify us from all unrighteousness. ¹⁰If we claim we have not sinned, we make him out to be a liar and his word has no place in our lives.

2 My dear children, I write this to you so that you will not sin. But if anybody does sin, we have one who speaks to the Father in our defense—Jesus Christ, the Righteous One. ²He is the atoning sacrifice for our sins, and not only

1.1-2 **1** From the very first day, we were there, taking it all in—we heard it with our own ears, saw it with our own eyes, verified it with our own hands. The Word of Life appeared right before our eyes; we saw it happen! And now we're telling you in most sober prose that what we witnessed was, incredibly, this: The infinite Life of God himself took shape before us.

1.3-4 We saw it, we heard it, and now we're telling you so you can experience it along with us, this experience of communion with the Father and his Son, Jesus Christ. Our motive for writing is simply this: We want you to enjoy this, too. Your joy will double our joy!

WALK IN THE LIGHT

1.5 This, in essence, is the message we heard from Christ and are passing on to you: God is light, pure light; there's not a trace of darkness in him.

1.6-7 If we claim that we experience a shared life with him and continue to stumble around in the dark, we're obviously lying through our teeth—we're not *living* what we claim. But if we walk in the light, God himself being the light, we also experience a shared life with one another, as the sacrificed blood of Jesus, God's Son, purges all our sin.

1.8-10 If we claim that we're free of sin, we're only fooling ourselves. A claim like that is errant nonsense. On the other hand, if we admit our sins—make a clean breast of them—he won't let us down; he'll be true to himself. He'll forgive our sins and purge us of all wrongdoing. If we claim that we've never sinned, we out-and-out contradict God—make a liar out of him. A claim like that only shows off our ignorance of God.

2.1-2 **2** I write this, dear children, to guide you out of sin. But if anyone does sin, we have a Priest-Friend in the presence of the Father: Jesus Christ, righteous Jesus. When he served as a sacrifice for our sins, he solved the sin

---

*a 4 Some manuscripts *your*   *b 7 Or *every*

NEW INTERNATIONAL VERSION

for ours but also for[a] the sins of the whole world.

[3]We know that we have come to know him if we obey his commands. [4]The man who says, "I know him," but does not do what he commands is a liar, and the truth is not in him. [5]But if anyone obeys his word, God's love[b] is truly made complete in him. This is how we know we are in him: [6]Whoever claims to live in him must walk as Jesus did.

[7]Dear friends, I am not writing you a new command but an old one, which you have had since the beginning. This old command is the message you have heard. [8]Yet I am writing you a new command; its truth is seen in him and you, because the darkness is passing and the true light is already shining.

[9]Anyone who claims to be in the light but hates his brother is still in the darkness. [10]Whoever loves his brother lives in the light, and there is nothing in him[c] to make him stumble. [11]But whoever hates his brother is in the darkness and walks around in the darkness; he does not know where he is going, because the darkness has blinded him.

[12]I write to you, dear children,
    because your sins have been forgiven on
        account of his name.
[13]I write to you, fathers,
    because you have known him who is from
        the beginning.
I write to you, young men,
    because you have overcome the evil one.
I write to you, dear children,
    because you have known the Father.
[14]I write to you, fathers,
    because you have known him who is from
        the beginning.
I write to you, young men,
    because you are strong,
    and the word of God lives in you,
    and you have overcome the evil one.

DO NOT LOVE THE WORLD

[15]Do not love the world or anything in the world. If anyone loves the world, the love of the Father is not in him. [16]For everything in the world—the cravings of sinful man, the lust of his eyes and the boasting of what he has and does—comes not from the Father but from the world. [17]The world and its desires pass away, but the man who does the will of God lives forever.

WARNING AGAINST ANTICHRISTS

[18]Dear children, this is the last hour; and as you have heard that the antichrist is coming,

a 2 Or He is the one who turns aside God's wrath, taking away our sins, and not only ours but also   b 5 Or word, love for God   c 10 Or it

THE MESSAGE

problem for good—not only ours, but the whole world's.

THE ONLY WAY TO KNOW WE'RE IN HIM

2.3 Here's how we can be sure that we know God in the right way: Keep his commandments.

2.4-6 If someone claims, "I know him well!" but doesn't keep his commandments, he's obviously a liar. His life doesn't match his words. But the one who keeps God's word is the person in whom we see God's mature love. This is the only way to be sure we're in God. Anyone who claims to be intimate with God ought to live the same kind of life Jesus lived.

2.7-8 My dear friends, I'm not writing anything new. This is the oldest commandment in the book, and you've known it from day one. It's always been implicit in the Message you've heard. On the other hand, perhaps it is new, freshly minted as it is in both Christ and you—the darkness on its way out and the True Light already blazing!

2.9-11 Anyone who claims to live in God's light and hates a brother or sister is still in the dark. It's the person who loves brother and sister who dwells in God's light and doesn't block the light from others. But whoever hates is still in the dark, stumbles around in the dark, doesn't know which end is up, blinded by the darkness.

LOVING THE WORLD

2.12-13 I remind you, my dear children: Your sins are forgiven in Jesus' name. You veterans were in on the ground floor, and know the One who started all this; you newcomers have won a big victory over the Evil One.

2.13-14 And a second reminder, dear children: You know the Father from personal experience. You veterans know the One who started it all; and you newcomers—such vitality and strength! God's word is so steady in you. Your fellowship with God enables you to gain a victory over the Evil One.

2.15-17 Don't love the world's ways. Don't love the world's goods. Love of the world squeezes out love for the Father. Practically everything that goes on in the world—wanting your own way, wanting everything for yourself, wanting to appear important—has nothing to do with the Father. It just isolates you from him. The world and all its wanting, wanting, wanting is on the way out—but whoever does what God wants is set for eternity.

ANTICHRISTS EVERYWHERE YOU LOOK

2.18 Children, time is just about up. You heard that Antichrist is coming. Well, they're all over the

NEW INTERNATIONAL VERSION

even now many antichrists have come. This is how we know it is the last hour. [19]They went out from us, but they did not really belong to us. For if they had belonged to us, they would have remained with us; but their going showed that none of them belonged to us.

[20]But you have an anointing from the Holy One, and all of you know the truth.[a] [21]I do not write to you because you do not know the truth, but because you do know it and because no lie comes from the truth. [22]Who is the liar? It is the man who denies that Jesus is the Christ. Such a man is the antichrist—he denies the Father and the Son. [23]No one who denies the Son has the Father; whoever acknowledges the Son has the Father also.

[24]See that what you have heard from the beginning remains in you. If it does, you also will remain in the Son and in the Father. [25]And this is what he promised us—even eternal life.

[26]I am writing these things to you about those who are trying to lead you astray. [27]As for you, the anointing you received from him remains in you, and you do not need anyone to teach you. But as his anointing teaches you about all things and as that anointing is real, not counterfeit—just as it has taught you, remain in him.

CHILDREN OF GOD

[28]And now, dear children, continue in him, so that when he appears we may be confident and unashamed before him at his coming.

[29]If you know that he is righteous, you know that everyone who does what is right has been born of him.

3 How great is the love the Father has lavished on us, that we should be called children of God! And that is what we are! The reason the world does not know us is that it did not know him. [2]Dear friends, now we are children of God, and what we will be has not yet been made known. But we know that when he appears,[b] we shall be like him, for we shall see him as he is. [3]Everyone who has this hope in him purifies himself, just as he is pure.

THE MESSAGE

place, antichrists everywhere you look. That's how we know that we're close to the end.

2.19 They left us, but they were never really with us. If they had been, they would have stuck it out with us, loyal to the end. In leaving, they showed their true colors, showed they never did belong.

2.20-21 But you belong. The Holy One anointed you, and you all know it. I haven't been writing this to tell you something you don't know, but to confirm the truth you do know, and to remind you that the truth doesn't breed lies.

2.22-23 So who is lying here? It's the person who denies that Jesus is the Divine Christ, that's who. This is what makes an antichrist: denying the Father, denying the Son. No one who denies the Son has any part with the Father, but affirming the Son is an embrace of the Father as well.

2.24-25 Stay with what you heard from the beginning, the original message. Let it sink into your life. If what you heard from the beginning lives deeply in you, you will live deeply in both Son and Father. This is exactly what Christ promised: eternal life, real life!

2.26-27 I've written to warn you about those who are trying to deceive you. But they're no match for what is embedded deeply within you—Christ's anointing, no less! You don't need any of their so-called teaching. Christ's anointing teaches you the truth on everything you need to know about yourself and him, uncontaminated by a single lie. Live deeply in what you were taught.

LIVE DEEPLY IN CHRIST

2.28 And now, children, stay with Christ. Live deeply in Christ. Then we'll be ready for him when he appears, ready to receive him with open arms, with no cause for red-faced guilt or lame excuses when he arrives.

2.29 Once you're convinced that he is right and righteous, you'll recognize that all who practice righteousness are God's true children.

3.1 **3** What marvelous love the Father has extended to us! Just look at it—we're called children of God! That's who we really are. But that's also why the world doesn't recognize us or take us seriously, because it has no idea who he is or what he's up to.

3.2-3 But friends, that's exactly who we are: children of God. And that's only the beginning. Who knows how we'll end up! What we know is that when Christ is openly revealed, we'll see him—and in seeing him, become like him. All of us who look forward to his Coming stay ready, with the glistening purity of Jesus' life as a model for our own.

NEW INTERNATIONAL VERSION

⁴Everyone who sins breaks the law; in fact, sin is lawlessness. ⁵But you know that he appeared so that he might take away our sins. And in him is no sin. ⁶No one who lives in him keeps on sinning. No one who continues to sin has either seen him or known him.

⁷Dear children, do not let anyone lead you astray. He who does what is right is righteous, just as he is righteous. ⁸He who does what is sinful is of the devil, because the devil has been sinning from the beginning. The reason the Son of God appeared was to destroy the devil's work. ⁹No one who is born of God will continue to sin, because God's seed remains in him; he cannot go on sinning, because he has been born of God. ¹⁰This is how we know who the children of God are and who the children of the devil are: Anyone who does not do what is right is not a child of God; nor is anyone who does not love his brother.

LOVE ONE ANOTHER

¹¹This is the message you heard from the beginning: We should love one another. ¹²Do not be like Cain, who belonged to the evil one and murdered his brother. And why did he murder him? Because his own actions were evil and his brother's were righteous. ¹³Do not be surprised, my brothers, if the world hates you. ¹⁴We know that we have passed from death to life, because we love our brothers. Anyone who does not love remains in death. ¹⁵Anyone who hates his brother is a murderer, and you know that no murderer has eternal life in him.

¹⁶This is how we know what love is: Jesus Christ laid down his life for us. And we ought to lay down our lives for our brothers. ¹⁷If anyone has material possessions and sees his brother in need but has no pity on him, how can the love of God be in him? ¹⁸Dear children, let us not love with words or tongue but with actions and in truth. ¹⁹This then is how we know that we belong to the truth, and how we set our hearts at

THE MESSAGE

3.4-6 All who indulge in a sinful life are dangerously lawless, for sin is a major disruption of God's order. Surely you know that Christ showed up in order to get rid of sin. There is no sin in him, and sin is not part of his program. No one who lives deeply in Christ makes a practice of sin. None of those who do practice sin have taken a good look at Christ. They've got him all backwards.

3.7-8 So, my dear children, don't let anyone divert you from the truth. It's the person who *acts* right who *is* right, just as we see it lived out in our righteous Messiah. Those who make a practice of sin are straight from the Devil, the pioneer in the practice of sin. The Son of God entered the scene to abolish the Devil's ways.

3.9-10 People conceived and brought into life by God don't make a practice of sin. How could they? God's seed is deep within them, making them who they are. It's not in the nature of the God-begotten to practice and parade sin. Here's how you tell the difference between God's children and the Devil's children: The one who won't practice righteous ways isn't from God, nor is the one who won't love brother or sister. A simple test.

3.11 For this is the original message we heard: We should love each other.

3.12-13 We must not be like Cain, who joined the Evil One and then killed his brother. And why did he kill him? Because he was deep in the practice of evil, while the acts of his brother were righteous. So don't be surprised, friends, when the world hates you. This has been going on a long time.

3.14-15 The way we know we've been transferred from death to life is that we love our brothers and sisters. Anyone who doesn't love is as good as dead. Anyone who hates a brother or sister is a murderer, and you know very well that eternal life and murder don't go together.

3.16-17 This is how we've come to understand and experience love: Christ sacrificed his life for us. This is why we ought to live sacrificially for our fellow believers, and not just be out for ourselves. If you see some brother or sister in need and have the means to do something about it but turn a cold shoulder and do nothing, what happens to God's love? It disappears. And you made it disappear.

WHEN WE PRACTICE REAL LOVE

3.18-20 My dear children, let's not just talk about love; let's practice real love. This is the only way we'll know we're living truly, living in God's reality. It's also the way to shut down debilitating self-

NEW INTERNATIONAL VERSION

rest in his presence [20]whenever our hearts condemn us. For God is greater than our hearts, and he knows everything.

[21]Dear friends, if our hearts do not condemn us, we have confidence before God [22]and receive from him anything we ask, because we obey his commands and do what pleases him. [23]And this is his command: to believe in the name of his Son, Jesus Christ, and to love one another as he commanded us. [24]Those who obey his commands live in him, and he in them. And this is how we know that he lives in us: We know it by the Spirit he gave us.

TEST THE SPIRITS

4 Dear friends, do not believe every spirit, but test the spirits to see whether they are from God, because many false prophets have gone out into the world. [2]This is how you can recognize the Spirit of God: Every spirit that acknowledges that Jesus Christ has come in the flesh is from God, [3]but every spirit that does not acknowledge Jesus is not from God. This is the spirit of the antichrist, which you have heard is coming and even now is already in the world.

[4]You, dear children, are from God and have overcome them, because the one who is in you is greater than the one who is in the world. [5]They are from the world and therefore speak from the viewpoint of the world, and the world listens to them. [6]We are from God, and whoever knows God listens to us; but whoever is not from God does not listen to us. This is how we recognize the Spirit[a] of truth and the spirit of falsehood.

GOD'S LOVE AND OURS

[7]Dear friends, let us love one another, for love comes from God. Everyone who loves has been born of God and knows God. [8]Whoever does not love does not know God, because God is love. [9]This is how God showed his love among us: He sent his one and only Son[b] into the world that we might live through him. [10]This is love: not that we loved God, but that he loved us and

THE MESSAGE

criticism, even when there is something to it. For God is greater than our worried hearts and knows more about us than we do ourselves.

3.21-24 And friends, once that's taken care of and we're no longer accusing or condemning ourselves, we're bold and free before God! We're able to stretch our hands out and receive what we asked for because we're doing what he said, doing what pleases him. Again, this is God's command: to believe in his personally named Son, Jesus Christ. He told us to love each other, in line with the original command. As we keep his commands, we live deeply and surely in him, and he lives in us. And this is how we experience his deep and abiding presence in us: by the Spirit he gave us.

DON'T BELIEVE EVERYTHING YOU HEAR

4.1 **4** My dear friends, don't believe everything you hear. Carefully weigh and examine what people tell you. Not everyone who talks about God comes from God. There are a lot of lying preachers loose in the world.

4.2-3 Here's how you test for the genuine Spirit of God. Everyone who confesses openly his faith in Jesus Christ—the Son of God, who came as an actual flesh-and-blood person—comes from God and belongs to God. And everyone who refuses to confess faith in Jesus has nothing in common with God. This is the spirit of antichrist that you heard was coming. Well, here it is, sooner than we thought!

4.4-6 My dear children, you come from God and belong to God. You have already won a big victory over those false teachers, for the Spirit in you is far stronger than anything in the world. These people belong to the Christ-denying world. They talk the world's language and the world eats it up. But we come from God and belong to God. Anyone who knows God understands us and listens. The person who has nothing to do with God will, of course, not listen to us. This is another test for telling the Spirit of Truth from the spirit of deception.

GOD IS LOVE

4.7-10 My beloved friends, let us continue to love each other since love comes from God. Everyone who loves is born of God and experiences a relationship with God. The person who refuses to love doesn't know the first thing about God, because God is love—so you can't know him if you don't love. This is how God showed his love for us: God sent his only Son into the world so we might live through him. This is the kind of love we are talking about—not that we once upon a time loved God, but that he

NEW INTERNATIONAL VERSION

sent his Son as an atoning sacrifice for[a] our sins. [11]Dear friends, since God so loved us, we also ought to love one another. [12]No one has ever seen God; but if we love one another, God lives in us and his love is made complete in us.

[13]We know that we live in him and he in us, because he has given us of his Spirit. [14]And we have seen and testify that the Father has sent his Son to be the Savior of the world. [15]If anyone acknowledges that Jesus is the Son of God, God lives in him and he in God. [16]And so we know and rely on the love God has for us.

God is love. Whoever lives in love lives in God, and God in him. [17]In this way, love is made complete among us so that we will have confidence on the day of judgment, because in this world we are like him. [18]There is no fear in love. But perfect love drives out fear, because fear has to do with punishment. The one who fears is not made perfect in love.

[19]We love because he first loved us. [20]If anyone says, "I love God," yet hates his brother, he is a liar. For anyone who does not love his brother, whom he has seen, cannot love God, whom he has not seen. [21]And he has given us this command: Whoever loves God must also love his brother.

FAITH IN THE SON OF GOD

5 Everyone who believes that Jesus is the Christ is born of God, and everyone who loves the father loves his child as well. [2]This is how we know that we love the children of God: by loving God and carrying out his commands. [3]This is love for God: to obey his commands. And his commands are not burdensome, [4]for everyone born of God overcomes the world. This is the victory that has overcome the world, even

---

[a] 10 Or as the one who would turn aside his wrath, taking away

THE MESSAGE

loved us and sent his Son as a sacrifice to clear away our sins and the damage they've done to our relationship with God.

4.11-12   My dear, dear friends, if God loved us like this, we certainly ought to love each other. No one has seen God, ever. But if we love one another, God dwells deeply within us, and his love becomes complete in us—perfect love!

4.13-16   This is how we know we're living steadily and deeply in him, and he in us: He's given us life from his life, from his very own Spirit. Also, we've seen for ourselves and continue to state openly that the Father sent his Son as Savior of the world. Everyone who confesses that Jesus is God's Son participates continuously in an intimate relationship with God. We know it so well, we've embraced it heart and soul, this love that comes from God.

TO LOVE, TO BE LOVED

4.17-18   God is love. When we take up permanent residence in a life of love, we live in God and God lives in us. This way, love has the run of the house, becomes at home and mature in us, so that we're free of worry on Judgment Day—our standing in the world is identical with Christ's. There is no room in love for fear. Well-formed love banishes fear. Since fear is crippling, a fearful life—fear of death, fear of judgment—is one not yet fully formed in love.

4.19   We, though, are going to love—love and be loved. First we were loved, now we love. He loved us first.

4.20-21   If anyone boasts, "I love God," and goes right on hating his brother or sister, thinking nothing of it, he is a liar. If he won't love the person he can see, how can he love the God he can't see? The command we have from Christ is blunt: Loving God includes loving people. You've got to love both.

THE POWER THAT BRINGS THE WORLD TO ITS KNEES

5.1-3   **5** Every person who believes that Jesus is, in fact, the Messiah, is God-begotten. If we love the One who conceives the child, we'll surely love the child who was conceived. The reality test on whether or not we love God's children is this: Do we love God? Do we keep his commands? The proof that we love God comes when we keep his commandments and they are not at all troublesome.

THE POWER THAT BRINGS THE WORLD TO ITS KNEES

5.4-5   Every God-begotten person conquers the world's ways. The conquering power that brings the world to its knees is our faith. The person who

NEW INTERNATIONAL VERSION

our faith. ⁵Who is it that overcomes the world? Only he who believes that Jesus is the Son of God.

⁶This is the one who came by water and blood—Jesus Christ. He did not come by water only, but by water and blood. And it is the Spirit who testifies, because the Spirit is the truth. ⁷For there are three that testify: ⁸the*a* Spirit, the water and the blood; and the three are in agreement. ⁹We accept man's testimony, but God's testimony is greater because it is the testimony of God, which he has given about his Son. ¹⁰Anyone who believes in the Son of God has this testimony in his heart. Anyone who does not believe God has made him out to be a liar, because he has not believed the testimony God has given about his Son. ¹¹And this is the testimony: God has given us eternal life, and this life is in his Son. ¹²He who has the Son has life; he who does not have the Son of God does not have life.

Concluding Remarks

¹³I write these things to you who believe in the name of the Son of God so that you may know that you have eternal life. ¹⁴This is the confidence we have in approaching God: that if we ask anything according to his will, he hears us. ¹⁵And if we know that he hears us—whatever we ask—we know that we have what we asked of him.

¹⁶If anyone sees his brother commit a sin that does not lead to death, he should pray and God will give him life. I refer to those whose sin does not lead to death. There is a sin that leads to death. I am not saying that he should pray about that. ¹⁷All wrongdoing is sin, and there is sin that does not lead to death.

¹⁸We know that anyone born of God does not continue to sin; the one who was born of God keeps him safe, and the evil one cannot harm him. ¹⁹We know that we are children of God, and that the whole world is under the control of the evil one. ²⁰We know also that the Son of God has come and has given us understanding, so that we may know him who is true. And we are in him who is true—even in his Son Jesus Christ. He is the true God and eternal life.

²¹Dear children, keep yourselves from idols.

---

a 7,8 Late manuscripts of the Vulgate *testify in heaven: the Father, the Word and the Holy Spirit, and these three are one.* ⁸*And there are three that testify on earth: the* (not found in any Greek manuscript before the fourteenth century)

THE MESSAGE

wins out over the world's ways is simply the one who believes Jesus is the Son of God.

5.6-8   Jesus—the Divine Christ! He experienced a life-giving birth and a death-killing death. Not only birth from the womb, but baptismal birth of his ministry and sacrificial death. And all the while the Spirit is confirming the truth, the reality of God's presence at Jesus' baptism and crucifixion, bringing those occasions alive for us. A triple testimony: the Spirit, the Baptism, the Crucifixion. And the three in perfect agreement.

5.9-10   If we take human testimony at face value, how much more should we be reassured when God gives testimony as he does here, testifying concerning his Son. Whoever believes in the Son of God inwardly confirms God's testimony. Whoever refuses to believe in effect calls God a liar, refusing to believe God's own testimony regarding his Son.

5.11-12   This is the testimony in essence: God gave us eternal life; the life is in his Son. So, whoever has the Son, has life; whoever rejects the Son, rejects life.

The Reality, Not the Illusion

5.13-15   My purpose in writing is simply this: that you who believe in God's Son will know beyond the shadow of a doubt that you have eternal life, the reality and not the illusion. And how bold and free we then become in his presence, freely asking according to his will, sure that he's listening. And if we're confident that he's listening, we know that what we've asked for is as good as ours.

5.16-17   For instance, if we see a Christian believer sinning (clearly I'm not talking about those who make a practice of sin in a way that is "fatal," leading to eternal death), we ask for God's help and he gladly gives it, gives life to the sinner whose sin is not fatal. There is such a thing as a fatal sin, and I'm not urging you to pray about that. Everything we do wrong is sin, but not all sin is fatal.

5.18-21   We know that none of the God-begotten makes a practice of sin—fatal sin. The God-begotten are also the God-protected. The Evil One can't lay a hand on them. We know that we are held firm by God; it's only the people of the world who continue in the grip of the Evil One. And we know that the Son of God came so we could recognize and understand the truth of God—what a gift!—and we are living in the Truth itself, in God's Son, Jesus Christ. This Jesus is both True God and Real Life. Dear children, be on guard against all clever facsimiles.

2 JOHN

2 JOHN

¹The elder,

To the chosen lady and her children, whom I love in the truth—and not I only, but also all who know the truth— ²because of the truth, which lives in us and will be with us forever:

³Grace, mercy and peace from God the Father and from Jesus Christ, the Father's Son, will be with us in truth and love.

⁴It has given me great joy to find some of your children walking in the truth, just as the Father commanded us. ⁵And now, dear lady, I am not writing you a new command but one we have had from the beginning. I ask that we love one another. ⁶And this is love: that we walk in obedience to his commands. As you have heard from the beginning, his command is that you walk in love.

⁷Many deceivers, who do not acknowledge Jesus Christ as coming in the flesh, have gone out into the world. Any such person is the deceiver and the antichrist. ⁸Watch out that you do not lose what you have worked for, but that you may be rewarded fully. ⁹Anyone who runs ahead and does not continue in the teaching of Christ does not have God; whoever continues in the teaching has both the Father and the Son. ¹⁰If anyone comes to you and does not bring this teaching, do not take him into your house or welcome him. ¹¹Anyone who welcomes him shares in his wicked work.

¹²I have much to write to you, but I do not want to use paper and ink. Instead, I hope to visit you and talk with you face to face, so that our joy may be complete.

¹³The children of your chosen sister send their greetings.

1-2 My dear congregation, I, your pastor, love you in very truth. And I'm not alone—everyone who knows the Truth that has taken up permanent residence in us loves you.

3 Let grace, mercy, and peace be with us in truth and love from God the Father and from Jesus Christ, Son of the Father!

4-6 I can't tell you how happy I am to learn that many members of your congregation are diligent in living out the Truth, exactly as commanded by the Father. But permit me a reminder, friends, and this is not a new commandment but simply a repetition of our original and basic charter: that we love each other. Love means following his commandments, and his unifying commandment is that you conduct your lives in love. This is the first thing you heard, and nothing has changed.

DON'T WALK OUT ON GOD

7 There are a lot of smooth-talking charlatans loose in the world who refuse to believe that Jesus Christ was truly human, a flesh-and-blood human being. Give them their true title: Deceiver! Antichrist!

8-9 And be very careful around them so you don't lose out on what we've worked so diligently in together; I want you to get every reward you have coming to you. Anyone who gets so progressive in his thinking that he walks out on the teaching of Christ, walks out on God. But whoever stays with the teaching, stays faithful to both the Father and the Son.

10-11 If anyone shows up who doesn't hold to this teaching, don't invite him in and give him the run of the place. That would just give him a platform to perpetuate his evil ways, making you his partner.

12-13 I have a lot more things to tell you, but I'd rather not use paper and ink. I hope to be there soon in person and have a heart-to-heart talk. That will be far more satisfying to both you and me. Everyone here in your sister congregation sends greetings.

3 JOHN

3 JOHN

¹The elder,

To my dear friend Gaius, whom I love in the truth.

²Dear friend, I pray that you may enjoy good health and that all may go well with you, even as your soul is getting along well. ³It gave me great joy to have some brothers come and tell about your faithfulness to the truth and how you continue to walk in the truth. ⁴I have no greater joy than to hear that my children are walking in the truth.

⁵Dear friend, you are faithful in what you are doing for the brothers, even though they are strangers to you. ⁶They have told the church about your love. You will do well to send them on their way in a manner worthy of God. ⁷It was for the sake of the Name that they went out, receiving no help from the pagans. ⁸We ought therefore to show hospitality to such men so that we may work together for the truth.

⁹I wrote to the church, but Diotrephes, who loves to be first, will have nothing to do with us. ¹⁰So if I come, I will call attention to what he is doing, gossiping maliciously about us. Not satisfied with that, he refuses to welcome the brothers. He also stops those who want to do so and puts them out of the church.

¹¹Dear friend, do not imitate what is evil but what is good. Anyone who does what is good is from God. Anyone who does what is evil has not seen God. ¹²Demetrius is well spoken of by everyone—and even by the truth itself. We also speak well of him, and you know that our testimony is true.

¹³I have much to write you, but I do not want to do so with pen and ink. ¹⁴I hope to see you soon, and we will talk face to face.

Peace to you. The friends here send their greetings. Greet the friends there by name.

1-4 The Pastor, to my good friend Gaius: How truly I love you! We're the best of friends, and I pray for good fortune in everything you do, and for your good health—that your everyday affairs prosper, as well as your soul! I was most happy when some friends arrived and brought the news that you persist in following the way of Truth. Nothing could make me happier than getting reports that my children continue diligently in the way of Truth!

MODEL THE GOOD

5-8 Dear friend, when you extend hospitality to Christian brothers and sisters, even when they are strangers, you make the faith visible. They've made a full report back to the church here, a message about your love. It's good work you're doing, helping these travelers on their way, hospitality worthy of God himself! They set out under the banner of the Name, and get no help from unbelievers. So they deserve any support we can give them. In providing meals and a bed, we become their companions in spreading the Truth.

9-10 Earlier I wrote something along this line to the church, but Diotrephes, who loves being in charge, denigrates my counsel. If I come, you can be sure I'll hold him to account for spreading vicious rumors about us.

As if that weren't bad enough, he not only refuses hospitality to traveling Christians but tries to stop others from welcoming them. Worse yet, instead of inviting them in he throws them out.

11 Friend, don't go along with evil. Model the good. The person who does good does God's work. The person who does evil falsifies God, doesn't know the first thing about God.

12 Everyone has a good word for Demetrius—the Truth itself stands up for Demetrius! We concur, and you know we don't hand out endorsements lightly.

13-14 I have a lot more things to tell you, but I'd rather not use pen and ink. I hope to be there soon in person and have a heart-to-heart talk.

Peace to you. The friends here say hello. Greet our friends there by name.

JUDE

JUDE

¹Jude, a servant of Jesus Christ and a brother of James,

To those who have been called, who are loved by God the Father and kept by*a* Jesus Christ:

²Mercy, peace and love be yours in abundance.

THE SIN AND DOOM OF GODLESS MEN

³Dear friends, although I was very eager to write to you about the salvation we share, I felt I had to write and urge you to contend for the faith that was once for all entrusted to the saints. ⁴For certain men whose condemnation was written about*b* long ago have secretly slipped in among you. They are godless men, who change the grace of our God into a license for immorality and deny Jesus Christ our only Sovereign and Lord.

⁵Though you already know all this, I want to remind you that the Lord*c* delivered his people out of Egypt, but later destroyed those who did not believe. ⁶And the angels who did not keep their positions of authority but abandoned their own home—these he has kept in darkness, bound with everlasting chains for judgment on the great Day. ⁷In a similar way, Sodom and Gomorrah and the surrounding towns gave themselves up to sexual immorality and perversion. They serve as an example of those who suffer the punishment of eternal fire.

⁸In the very same way, these dreamers pollute their own bodies, reject authority and slander celestial beings. ⁹But even the archangel Michael, when he was disputing with the devil about the body of Moses, did not dare to bring a slanderous accusation against him, but said, "The Lord rebuke you!" ¹⁰Yet these men speak abusively against whatever they do not understand; and

1-2 I, Jude, am a slave to Jesus Christ and brother to James, writing to those loved by God the Father, called and kept safe by Jesus Christ. Relax, everything's going to be all right; rest, everything's coming together; open your hearts, love is on the way!

FIGHT WITH ALL YOU HAVE IN YOU

3-4 Dear friends, I've dropped everything to write you about this life of salvation that we have in common. I have to write insisting—begging!— that you fight with everything you have in you for this faith entrusted to us as a gift to guard and cherish. What has happened is that some people have infiltrated our ranks (our Scriptures warned us this would happen), who beneath their pious skin are shameless scoundrels. Their design is to replace the sheer grace of our God with sheer license—which means doing away with Jesus Christ, our one and only Master.

LOST STARS IN OUTER SPACE

5-7 I'm laying this out as clearly as I can, even though you once knew all this well enough and shouldn't need reminding. Here it is in brief: The Master saved a people out of the land of Egypt. Later he destroyed those who defected. And you know the story of the angels who didn't stick to their post, abandoning it for other, darker missions. But they are now chained and jailed in a black hole until the great Judgment Day. Sodom and Gomorrah, which went to sexual rack and ruin along with the surrounding cities that acted just like them, are another example. Burning and burning and never burning up, they serve still as a stock warning.

8 This is exactly the same program of these latest infiltrators: dirty sex, rule and rulers thrown out, glory dragged in the mud.

9-11 The Archangel Michael, who went to the mat with the Devil as they fought over the body of Moses, wouldn't have dared level him with a blasphemous curse, but said simply, "No you don't. *God* will take care of you!" But these people sneer at anything they can't understand,

---

a 1 Or *for;* or *in*   *b* 4 Or *men who were marked out for condemnation*   *c* 5 Some early manuscripts *Jesus*

NEW INTERNATIONAL VERSION

what things they do understand by instinct, like unreasoning animals—these are the very things that destroy them.

¹¹Woe to them! They have taken the way of Cain; they have rushed for profit into Balaam's error; they have been destroyed in Korah's rebellion.

¹²These men are blemishes at your love feasts, eating with you without the slightest qualm—shepherds who feed only themselves. They are clouds without rain, blown along by the wind; autumn trees, without fruit and uprooted—twice dead. ¹³They are wild waves of the sea, foaming up their shame; wandering stars, for whom blackest darkness has been reserved forever.

¹⁴Enoch, the seventh from Adam, prophesied about these men: "See, the Lord is coming with thousands upon thousands of his holy ones ¹⁵to judge everyone, and to convict all the ungodly of all the ungodly acts they have done in the ungodly way, and of all the harsh words ungodly sinners have spoken against him." ¹⁶These men are grumblers and faultfinders; they follow their own evil desires; they boast about themselves and flatter others for their own advantage.

A CALL TO PERSEVERE

¹⁷But, dear friends, remember what the apostles of our Lord Jesus Christ foretold. ¹⁸They said to you, "In the last times there will be scoffers who will follow their own ungodly desires." ¹⁹These are the men who divide you, who follow mere natural instincts and do not have the Spirit.

²⁰But you, dear friends, build yourselves up in your most holy faith and pray in the Holy Spirit. ²¹Keep yourselves in God's love as you wait for the mercy of our Lord Jesus Christ to bring you to eternal life.

²²Be merciful to those who doubt; ²³snatch others from the fire and save them; to others show mercy, mixed with fear—hating even the clothing stained by corrupted flesh.

DOXOLOGY

²⁴To him who is able to keep you from falling and to present you before his glorious presence without fault and with great joy— ²⁵to the only God our Savior be glory, majesty, power and authority, through Jesus Christ our Lord, before all ages, now and forevermore! Amen.

THE MESSAGE

and by doing whatever they feel like doing—living by animal instinct only—they participate in their own destruction. I'm fed up with them! They've gone down Cain's road; they've been sucked into Balaam's error by greed; they're canceled out in Korah's rebellion.

12-13 These people are warts on your love feasts as you worship and eat together. They're giving you a black eye—carousing shamelessly, grabbing anything that isn't nailed down. They're—

Puffs of smoke pushed by gusts of wind;
   late autumn trees stripped clean of leaf
      and fruit,
Doubly dead, pulled up by the roots;
   wild ocean waves leaving nothing on the
      beach
   but the foam of their shame;
Lost stars in outer space
   on their way to the black hole.

14-16 Enoch, the seventh after Adam, prophesied of them: "Look! The Master comes with thousands of holy angels to bring judgment against them all, convicting each person of every defiling act of shameless sacrilege, of every dirty word they have spewed of their pious filth." These are the "grumpers," the bellyachers, grabbing for the biggest piece of the pie, talking big, saying anything they think will get them ahead.

17-19 But remember, dear friends, that the apostles of our Master, Jesus Christ, told us this would happen: "In the last days there will be people who don't take these things seriously anymore. They'll treat them like a joke, and make a religion of their own whims and lusts." These are the ones who split churches, thinking only of themselves. There's nothing to them, no sign of the Spirit!

✠

20-21 But you, dear friends, carefully build yourselves up in this most holy faith by praying in the Holy Spirit, staying right at the center of God's love, keeping your arms open and outstretched, ready for the mercy of our Master, Jesus Christ. This is the unending life, the *real* life!

22-23 Go easy on those who hesitate in the faith. Go after those who take the wrong way. Be tender with sinners, but not soft on sin. The sin itself stinks to high heaven.

24-25 And now to him who can keep you on your feet, standing tall in his bright presence, fresh and celebrating—to our one God, our only Savior, through Jesus Christ, our Master, be glory, majesty, strength, and rule before all time, and now, and to the end of all time. Yes.

REVELATION

REVELATION

PROLOGUE

1 The revelation of Jesus Christ, which God gave him to show his servants what must soon take place. He made it known by sending his angel to his servant John, ²who testifies to everything he saw—that is, the word of God and the testimony of Jesus Christ. ³Blessed is the one who reads the words of this prophecy, and blessed are those who hear it and take to heart what is written in it, because the time is near.

GREETINGS AND DOXOLOGY

⁴John,

To the seven churches in the province of Asia:

Grace and peace to you from him who is, and who was, and who is to come, and from the seven spirits *a* before his throne, ⁵and from Jesus Christ, who is the faithful witness, the firstborn from the dead, and the ruler of the kings of the earth.

To him who loves us and has freed us from our sins by his blood, ⁶and has made us to be a kingdom and priests to serve his God and Father—to him be glory and power for ever and ever! Amen.

⁷Look, he is coming with the clouds,
 and every eye will see him,
even those who pierced him;
 and all the peoples of the earth will
 mourn because of him.
 So shall it be! Amen.

⁸"I am the Alpha and the Omega," says the Lord God, "who is, and who was, and who is to come, the Almighty."

ONE LIKE A SON OF MAN

⁹I, John, your brother and companion in the suffering and kingdom and patient endurance that are ours in Jesus, was on the island of Patmos because of the word of God and the testimony of Jesus. ¹⁰On the Lord's Day I was in the Spirit, and I heard behind me a loud voice like a trumpet, ¹¹which said: "Write on a scroll what you see and send it to the seven churches: to

1 A revealing of Jesus, the Messiah. God gave it to make plain to his servants what is about to happen. He published and delivered it by Angel to his servant John. And John told everything he saw: God's Word—the witness of Jesus Christ!

1.3 How blessed the reader! How blessed the hearers and keepers of these oracle words, all the words written in this book!

Time is just about up.

HIS EYES POURING FIRE-BLAZE

1.4-7 I, John, am writing this to the seven churches in Asia province: All the best to you from THE GOD WHO IS, THE GOD WHO WAS, AND THE GOD ABOUT TO ARRIVE, and from the Seven Spirits assembled before his throne, and from Jesus Christ—Loyal Witness, Firstborn from the dead, Ruler of all earthly kings.

Glory and strength to Christ, who loves us,
 who blood-washed our sins from our
 lives,
Who made us a Kingdom, Priests for his
 Father,
 forever—and yes, he's on his way!
Riding the clouds, he'll be seen by every
 eye,
 those who mocked and killed him will
 see him,
People from all nations and all times
 will tear their clothes in lament.
 Oh, Yes.

1.8 The Master declares, "I'm A to Z. I'm THE GOD WHO IS, THE GOD WHO WAS, AND THE GOD ABOUT TO ARRIVE. I'm the Sovereign-Strong."

1.9-17 I, John, with you all the way in the trial and the Kingdom and the passion of patience in Jesus, was on the island called Patmos because of God's Word, the witness of Jesus. It was Sunday and I was in the Spirit, praying. I heard a loud voice behind me, trumpet-clear and piercing: "Write what you see into a book. Send it to the seven churches: to Ephesus,

NEW INTERNATIONAL VERSION

Ephesus, Smyrna, Pergamum, Thyatira, Sardis, Philadelphia and Laodicea."

¹²I turned around to see the voice that was speaking to me. And when I turned I saw seven golden lampstands, ¹³and among the lampstands was someone "like a son of man," *ᵃ* dressed in a robe reaching down to his feet and with a golden sash around his chest. ¹⁴His head and hair were white like wool, as white as snow, and his eyes were like blazing fire. ¹⁵His feet were like bronze glowing in a furnace, and his voice was like the sound of rushing waters. ¹⁶In his right hand he held seven stars, and out of his mouth came a sharp double-edged sword. His face was like the sun shining in all its brilliance.

¹⁷When I saw him, I fell at his feet as though dead. Then he placed his right hand on me and said: "Do not be afraid. I am the First and the Last. ¹⁸I am the Living One; I was dead, and behold I am alive for ever and ever! And I hold the keys of death and Hades.

¹⁹"Write, therefore, what you have seen, what is now and what will take place later. ²⁰The mystery of the seven stars that you saw in my right hand and of the seven golden lampstands is this: The seven stars are the angels*ᵇ* of the seven churches, and the seven lampstands are the seven churches.

To the Church in Ephesus

2 "To the angel*ᶜ* of the church in Ephesus write:

These are the words of him who holds the seven stars in his right hand and walks among the seven golden lampstands: ²I know your deeds, your hard work and your perseverance. I know that you cannot tolerate wicked men, that you have tested those who claim to be apostles but are not, and have found them false. ³You have persevered and have endured hardships for my name, and have not grown weary.

⁴Yet I hold this against you: You have forsaken your first love. ⁵Remember the height from which you have fallen! Repent and do the things you did at first. If you do not repent, I will come to you and remove your lampstand from its place. ⁶But you have this in your favor: You hate the practices of the Nicolaitans, which I also hate.

⁷He who has an ear, let him hear what the Spirit says to the churches. To him who overcomes, I will give the right to eat from the tree of life, which is in the paradise of God.

ᵃ 13 Daniel 7:13   *ᵇ 20* Or *messengers*   *ᶜ 1* Or *messenger*; also in verses 8, 12 and 18

THE MESSAGE

Smyrna, Pergamum, Thyatira, Sardis, Philadelphia, Laodicea." I turned and saw the voice.

I saw a gold menorah
  with seven branches,
And in the center, the Son of Man,
  in a robe and gold breastplate,
  hair a blizzard of white,
Eyes pouring fire-blaze,
  both feet furnace-fired bronze,
His voice a cataract,
  right hand holding the Seven Stars,
His mouth a sharp-biting sword,
  his face a perigee sun.

¹·¹⁷⁻²⁰ I saw this and fainted dead at his feet. His right hand pulled me upright, his voice reassured me: "Don't fear: I am First, I am Last, I'm Alive. I died, but I came to life, and my life is now forever. See these keys in my hand? They open and lock Death's doors, they open and lock Hell's gates. Now write down everything you see: things that are, things about to be. The Seven Stars you saw in my right hand and the seven-branched gold menorah—do you want to know what's behind them? The Seven Stars are the Angels of the seven churches; the menorah's seven branches are the seven churches."

To Ephesus

2 ²·¹ Write this to Ephesus, to the Angel of the church. The One with Seven Stars in his right-fist grip, striding through the golden seven-lights' circle, speaks:

²·²⁻³ "I see what you've done, your hard, hard work, your refusal to quit. I know you can't stomach evil, that you weed out apostolic pretenders. I know your persistence, your courage in my cause, that you never wear out.

²·⁴⁻⁵ "But you walked away from your first love—why? What's going on with you, anyway? Do you have any idea how far you've fallen? A Lucifer fall!

"Turn back! Recover your dear early love. No time to waste, for I'm well on my way to removing your light from the golden circle.

²·⁶ "You do have this to your credit: You hate the Nicolaitan business. I hate it, too.

²·⁷ "Are your ears awake? Listen. Listen to the Wind Words, the Spirit blowing through the churches. I'm about to call each conqueror to dinner. I'm spreading a banquet of Tree-of-Life fruit, a supper plucked from God's orchard."

NEW INTERNATIONAL VERSION

TO THE CHURCH IN SMYRNA

8 "To the angel of the church in Smyrna write:

These are the words of him who is the First and the Last, who died and came to life again. 9 I know your afflictions and your poverty—yet you are rich! I know the slander of those who say they are Jews and are not, but are a synagogue of Satan. 10 Do not be afraid of what you are about to suffer. I tell you, the devil will put some of you in prison to test you, and you will suffer persecution for ten days. Be faithful, even to the point of death, and I will give you the crown of life.

11 He who has an ear, let him hear what the Spirit says to the churches. He who overcomes will not be hurt at all by the second death.

TO THE CHURCH IN PERGAMUM

12 "To the angel of the church in Pergamum write:

These are the words of him who has the sharp, double-edged sword. 13 I know where you live—where Satan has his throne. Yet you remain true to my name. You did not renounce your faith in me, even in the days of Antipas, my faithful witness, who was put to death in your city—where Satan lives.

14 Nevertheless, I have a few things against you: You have people there who hold to the teaching of Balaam, who taught Balak to entice the Israelites to sin by eating food sacrificed to idols and by committing sexual immorality. 15 Likewise you also have those who hold to the teaching of the Nicolaitans. 16 Repent therefore! Otherwise, I will soon come to you and will fight against them with the sword of my mouth.

17 He who has an ear, let him hear what the Spirit says to the churches. To him who overcomes, I will give some of the hidden manna. I will also give him a white stone with a new name written on it, known only to him who receives it.

TO THE CHURCH IN THYATIRA

18 "To the angel of the church in Thyatira write:

These are the words of the Son of God, whose eyes are like blazing fire and whose feet are like burnished bronze. 19 I know your deeds, your love and faith, your service and perseverance, and that you are now doing more than you did at first.

THE MESSAGE

TO SMYRNA

2.8 Write this to Smyrna, to the Angel of the church. The Beginning and Ending, the First and Final One, the Once Dead and Then Come Alive, speaks:

2.9 "I can see your pain and poverty—constant pain, dire poverty—but I also see your wealth. And I hear the lie in the claims of those who pretend to be good Jews, who in fact belong to Satan's crowd.

2.10 "Fear nothing in the things you're about to suffer—but stay on guard! Fear nothing! The Devil is about to throw you in jail for a time of testing—ten days. It won't last forever.

"Don't quit, even if it costs you your life. Stay there believing. I have a Life-Crown sized and ready for you.

2.11 "Are your ears awake? Listen. Listen to the Wind Words, the Spirit blowing through the churches. Christ-conquerors are safe from Devil-death."

TO PERGAMUM

2.12 Write this to Pergamum, to the Angel of the church. The One with the sharp-biting sword draws from the sheath of his mouth—out come the sword words:

2.13 "I see where you live, right under the shadow of Satan's throne. But you continue boldly in my Name; you never once denied my Name, even when the pressure was worst, when they martyred Antipas, my witness who stayed faithful to me on Satan's turf.

2.14-15 "But why do you indulge that Balaam crowd? Don't you remember that Balaam was an enemy agent, seducing Balak and sabotaging Israel's holy pilgrimage by throwing unholy parties? And why do you put up with the Nicolaitans, who do the same thing?

2.16 "Enough! Don't give in to them; I'll be with you soon. I'm fed up and about to cut them to pieces with my sword-sharp words.

2.17 "Are your ears awake? Listen. Listen to the Wind Words, the Spirit blowing through the churches. I'll give the sacred manna to every conqueror; I'll also give a clear, smooth stone inscribed with your new name, your secret new name."

TO THYATIRA

2.18 Write this to Thyatira, to the Angel of the church. God's Son, eyes pouring fire-blaze, standing on feet of furnace-fired bronze, says this:

2.19 "I see everything you're doing for me. Impressive! The love and the faith, the service and persistence. Yes, very impressive! You get better at it every day.

NEW INTERNATIONAL VERSION

20Nevertheless, I have this against you: You tolerate that woman Jezebel, who calls herself a prophetess. By her teaching she misleads my servants into sexual immorality and the eating of food sacrificed to idols. 21I have given her time to repent of her immorality, but she is unwilling. 22So I will cast her on a bed of suffering, and I will make those who commit adultery with her suffer intensely, unless they repent of her ways. 23I will strike her children dead. Then all the churches will know that I am he who searches hearts and minds, and I will repay each of you according to your deeds. 24Now I say to the rest of you in Thyatira, to you who do not hold to her teaching and have not learned Satan's so-called deep secrets (I will not impose any other burden on you): 25Only hold on to what you have until I come.

26To him who overcomes and does my will to the end, I will give authority over the nations—

27 'He will rule them with an iron scepter;
    he will dash them to pieces like
        pottery' *a*—

just as I have received authority from my Father. 28I will also give him the morning star. 29He who has an ear, let him hear what the Spirit says to the churches.

To the Church in Sardis

3 "To the angel*b* of the church in Sardis write:

These are the words of him who holds the seven spirits*c* of God and the seven stars. I know your deeds; you have a reputation of being alive, but you are dead. 2Wake up! Strengthen what remains and is about to die, for I have not found your deeds complete in the sight of my God. 3Remember, therefore, what you have received and heard; obey it, and repent. But if you do not wake up, I will come like a thief, and you will not know at what time I will come to you.

4Yet you have a few people in Sardis who have not soiled their clothes. They will walk with me, dressed in white, for they are worthy. 5He who overcomes will, like them, be dressed in white. I will never blot out his name from the book of life, but

---

a 27 Psalm 2:9   *b* 1 Or *messenger*; also in verses 7 and 14
c 1 Or *the sevenfold Spirit*

THE MESSAGE

2.20-23 "But why do you let that Jezebel who calls herself a prophet mislead my dear servants into Cross-denying, self-indulging religion? I gave her a chance to change her ways, but she has no intention of giving up a career in the god-business. I'm about to lay her low, along with her partners, as they play their sex-and-religion games. The bastard offspring of their idol-whoring I'll kill. Then every church will know that appearances don't impress me. I x-ray every motive and make sure you get what's coming to you.

2.24-25 "The rest of you Thyatirans, who have nothing to do with this outrage, who scorn this playing around with the Devil that gets paraded as profundity, be assured I'll not make life any harder for you than it already is. Hold on to the truth you have until I get there.

2.26-28 "Here's the reward I have for every conqueror, everyone who keeps at it, refusing to give up: You'll rule the nations, your Shepherd-King rule as firm as an iron staff, their resistance fragile as clay pots. This was the gift my Father gave me; I pass it along to you—and with it, the Morning Star!

2.29 "Are your ears awake? Listen. Listen to the Wind Words, the Spirit blowing through the churches."

To Sardis

3.1 **3** Write this to Sardis, to the Angel of the church. The One holding the Seven Spirits of God in one hand, a firm grip on the Seven Stars with the other, speaks:

"I see right through your work. You have a reputation for vigor and zest, but you're dead, stone dead.

3.2-3 "Up on your feet! Take a deep breath! Maybe there's life in you yet. But I wouldn't know it by looking at your busywork; nothing of *God's* work has been completed. Your condition is desperate. Think of the gift you once had in your hands, the Message you heard with your ears—grasp it again and turn back to God.

"If you pull the covers back over your head and sleep on, oblivious to God, I'll return when you least expect it, break into your life like a thief in the night.

3.4 "You still have a few Christians in Sardis who haven't ruined themselves wallowing in the muck of the world's ways. They'll walk with me on parade! They've proved their worth!

3.5 "Conquerors will march in the victory parade, their names indelible in the Book of Life.

NEW INTERNATIONAL VERSION

will acknowledge his name before my Father and his angels. [6]He who has an ear, let him hear what the Spirit says to the churches.

TO THE CHURCH IN PHILADELPHIA

[7]"To the angel of the church in Philadelphia write:

These are the words of him who is holy and true, who holds the key of David. What he opens no one can shut, and what he shuts no one can open. [8]I know your deeds. See, I have placed before you an open door that no one can shut. I know that you have little strength, yet you have kept my word and have not denied my name. [9]I will make those who are of the synagogue of Satan, who claim to be Jews though they are not, but are liars—I will make them come and fall down at your feet and acknowledge that I have loved you. [10]Since you have kept my command to endure patiently, I will also keep you from the hour of trial that is going to come upon the whole world to test those who live on the earth.

[11]I am coming soon. Hold on to what you have, so that no one will take your crown. [12]Him who overcomes I will make a pillar in the temple of my God. Never again will he leave it. I will write on him the name of my God and the name of the city of my God, the new Jerusalem, which is coming down out of heaven from my God; and I will also write on him my new name. [13]He who has an ear, let him hear what the Spirit says to the churches.

TO THE CHURCH IN LAODICEA

[14]"To the angel of the church in Laodicea write:

These are the words of the Amen, the faithful and true witness, the ruler of God's creation. [15]I know your deeds, that you are neither cold nor hot. I wish you were either one or the other! [16]So, because you are lukewarm—neither hot nor cold—I am about to spit you out of my mouth. [17]You say, 'I am rich; I have acquired wealth and do not need a thing.' But you do not realize that you are wretched, pitiful, poor, blind and naked. [18]I counsel you to buy from me gold refined in the fire, so you can become rich; and white clothes to wear, so you can cover your shameful nakedness; and salve to put on your eyes, so you can see.

THE MESSAGE

I'll lead them up and present them by name to my Father and his Angels.

3.6 "Are your ears awake? Listen. Listen to the Wind Words, the Spirit blowing through the churches."

TO PHILADELPHIA

3.7 Write this to Philadelphia, to the Angel of the church. The Holy, the True—David's key in his hand, opening doors no one can lock, locking doors no one can open—speaks:

3.8 "I see what you've done. Now see what I've done. I've opened a door before you that no one can slam shut. You don't have much strength, I know that; you used what you had to keep my Word. You didn't deny me when times were rough.

3.9 "And watch as I take those who call themselves true believers but are nothing of the kind, pretenders whose true membership is in the club of Satan—watch as I strip off their pretensions and they're forced to acknowledge it's you that I've loved.

3.10 "Because you kept my Word in passionate patience, I'll keep you safe in the time of testing that will be here soon, and all over the earth, every man, woman, and child put to the test.

3.11 "I'm on my way; I'll be there soon. Keep a tight grip on what you have so no one distracts you and steals your crown.

3.12 "I'll make each conqueror a pillar in the sanctuary of my God, a permanent position of honor. Then I'll write names on you, the pillars: the Name of my God, the Name of God's City—the new Jerusalem coming down out of Heaven—and my new Name.

3.13 "Are your ears awake? Listen. Listen to the Wind Words, the Spirit blowing through the churches."

TO LAODICEA

3.14 Write to Laodicea, to the Angel of the church. God's Yes, the Faithful and Accurate Witness, the First of God's creation, says:

3.15-17 "I know you inside and out, and find little to my liking. You're not cold, you're not hot—far better to be either cold or hot! You're stale. You're stagnant. You make me want to vomit. You brag, 'I'm rich, I've got it made, I need nothing from anyone,' oblivious that in fact you're a pitiful, blind beggar, threadbare and homeless.

3.18 "Here's what I want you to do: Buy your gold from me, gold that's been through the refiner's fire. Then you'll be rich. Buy your clothes from me, clothes designed in Heaven. You've gone around half-naked long enough. And buy medicine for your eyes from me so you can see, *really* see.

NEW INTERNATIONAL VERSION

¹⁹Those whom I love I rebuke and discipline. So be earnest, and repent. ²⁰Here I am! I stand at the door and knock. If anyone hears my voice and opens the door, I will come in and eat with him, and he with me.

²¹To him who overcomes, I will give the right to sit with me on my throne, just as I overcame and sat down with my Father on his throne. ²²He who has an ear, let him hear what the Spirit says to the churches."

THE THRONE IN HEAVEN

4 After this I looked, and there before me was a door standing open in heaven. And the voice I had first heard speaking to me like a trumpet said, "Come up here, and I will show you what must take place after this." ²At once I was in the Spirit, and there before me was a throne in heaven with someone sitting on it. ³And the one who sat there had the appearance of jasper and carnelian. A rainbow, resembling an emerald, encircled the throne. ⁴Surrounding the throne were twenty-four other thrones, and seated on them were twenty-four elders. They were dressed in white and had crowns of gold on their heads. ⁵From the throne came flashes of lightning, rumblings and peals of thunder. Before the throne, seven lamps were blazing. These are the seven spirits*a* of God. ⁶Also before the throne there was what looked like a sea of glass, clear as crystal.

In the center, around the throne, were four living creatures, and they were covered with eyes, in front and in back. ⁷The first living creature was like a lion, the second was like an ox, the third had a face like a man, the fourth was like a flying eagle. ⁸Each of the four living creatures had six wings and was covered with eyes all around, even under his wings. Day and night they never stop saying:

> "Holy, holy, holy
> is the Lord God Almighty,
> who was, and is, and is to come."

⁹Whenever the living creatures give glory, honor and thanks to him who sits on the throne and who lives for ever and ever, ¹⁰the twenty-four elders fall down before him who sits on the throne, and worship him who lives for ever and ever. They lay their crowns before the throne and say:

a 5 Or *the sevenfold Spirit*

THE MESSAGE

3.19 "The people I love, I call to account—prod and correct and guide so that they'll live at their best. Up on your feet, then! About face! Run after God!

3.20-21 "Look at me. I stand at the door. I knock. If you hear me call and open the door, I'll come right in and sit down to supper with you. Conquerors will sit alongside me at the head table, just as I, having conquered, took the place of honor at the side of my Father. That's my gift to the conquerors!

3.22 "Are your ears awake? Listen. Listen to the Wind Words, the Spirit blowing through the churches."

A DOOR INTO HEAVEN

4.1 4 Then I looked, and, oh!—a door open into Heaven. The trumpet-voice, the first voice in my vision, called out, "Ascend and enter. I'll show you what happens next."

4.2-6 I was caught up at once in deep worship and, oh!—a Throne set in Heaven with One Seated on the Throne, suffused in gem hues of amber and flame with a nimbus of emerald. Twenty-four thrones circled the Throne, with Twenty-four Elders seated, white-robed, gold-crowned. Lightning flash and thunder crash pulsed from the Throne. Seven fire-blazing torches fronted the Throne (these are the Sevenfold Spirit of God). Before the Throne it was like a clear crystal sea.

4.6-8 Prowling around the Throne were Four Animals, all eyes. Eyes to look ahead, eyes to look behind. The first Animal like a lion, the second like an ox, the third with a human face, the fourth like an eagle in flight. The Four Animals were winged, each with six wings. They were all eyes, seeing around and within. And they chanted night and day, never taking a break:

> Holy, holy, holy
> Is God our Master, Sovereign-Strong,
> THE WAS, THE IS, THE COMING.

4.9-11 Every time the Animals gave glory and honor and thanks to the One Seated on the Throne—the age-after-age Living One—the Twenty-four Elders would fall prostrate before the One Seated on the Throne. They worshiped the age-after-age Living One. They threw their crowns at the foot of the Throne, chanting,

NEW INTERNATIONAL VERSION

¹¹ "You are worthy, our Lord and God,
 to receive glory and honor and power,
 for you created all things,
  and by your will they were created
  and have their being."

THE SCROLL AND THE LAMB

5 Then I saw in the right hand of him who sat on the throne a scroll with writing on both sides and sealed with seven seals. ²And I saw a mighty angel proclaiming in a loud voice, "Who is worthy to break the seals and open the scroll?" ³But no one in heaven or on earth or under the earth could open the scroll or even look inside it. ⁴I wept and wept because no one was found who was worthy to open the scroll or look inside. ⁵Then one of the elders said to me, "Do not weep! See, the Lion of the tribe of Judah, the Root of David, has triumphed. He is able to open the scroll and its seven seals."

⁶Then I saw a Lamb, looking as if it had been slain, standing in the center of the throne, encircled by the four living creatures and the elders. He had seven horns and seven eyes, which are the seven spirits* of God sent out into all the earth. ⁷He came and took the scroll from the right hand of him who sat on the throne. ⁸And when he had taken it, the four living creatures and the twenty-four elders fell down before the Lamb. Each one had a harp and they were holding golden bowls full of incense, which are the prayers of the saints. ⁹And they sang a new song:

 "You are worthy to take the scroll
  and to open its seals,
 because you were slain,
  and with your blood you purchased men
   for God
  from every tribe and language and people
   and nation.
¹⁰ You have made them to be a kingdom and
   priests to serve our God,
  and they will reign on the earth."

¹¹Then I looked and heard the voice of many angels, numbering thousands upon thousands, and ten thousand times ten thousand. They encircled the throne and the living creatures and the elders. ¹²In a loud voice they sang:

 "Worthy is the Lamb, who was slain,
  to receive power and wealth and wisdom and
   strength
  and honor and glory and praise!"

¹³Then I heard every creature in heaven and on earth and under the earth and on the sea, and all that is in them, singing:

ᵃ 6 Or *the sevenfold Spirit*

THE MESSAGE

 Worthy, O Master! Yes, our God!
 Take the glory! the honor! the power!
 You created it all;
 It was created because you wanted it.

THE LION IS A LAMB

5.1-2 **5** I saw a scroll in the right hand of the One Seated on the Throne. It was written on both sides, fastened with seven seals. I also saw a powerful Angel, calling out in a voice like thunder, "Is there anyone who can open the scroll, who can break its seals?"

5.3 There was no one—no one in Heaven, no one on earth, no one from the underworld—able to break open the scroll and read it.

5.4-5 I wept and wept and wept that no one was found able to open the scroll, able to read it. One of the Elders said, "Don't weep. Look—the Lion from Tribe Judah, the Root of David's Tree, has conquered. He can open the scroll, can rip through the seven seals."

5.6-10 So I looked, and there, surrounded by Throne, Animals, and Elders, was a Lamb, slaughtered but standing tall. Seven horns he had, and seven eyes, the Seven Spirits of God sent into all the earth. He came to the One Seated on the Throne and took the scroll from his right hand. The moment he took the scroll, the Four Animals and Twenty-four Elders fell down and worshiped the Lamb. Each had a harp and each had a bowl, a gold bowl filled with incense, the prayers of God's holy people. And they sang a new song:

 Worthy! Take the scroll, open its seals.
 Slain! Paying in blood, you bought men
   and women,
 Bought them back from all over the earth,
 Bought them back for God.
 Then you made them a Kingdom, Priests
   for our God,
 Priest-kings to rule over the earth.

5.11-14 I looked again. I heard a company of Angels around the Throne, the Animals, and the Elders—ten thousand times ten thousand their number, thousand after thousand after thousand in full song:

 The slain Lamb is worthy!
 Take the power, the wealth, the wisdom,
   the strength!
 Take the honor, the glory, the blessing!

Then I heard every creature in Heaven and earth, in underworld and sea, join in, all voices in all places, singing:

NEW INTERNATIONAL VERSION

"To him who sits on the throne and to the Lamb
be praise and honor and glory and power,
for ever and ever!"

¹⁴The four living creatures said, "Amen," and the elders fell down and worshiped.

The Seals

6 I watched as the Lamb opened the first of the seven seals. Then I heard one of the four living creatures say in a voice like thunder, "Come!" ²I looked, and there before me was a white horse! Its rider held a bow, and he was given a crown, and he rode out as a conqueror bent on conquest.

³When the Lamb opened the second seal, I heard the second living creature say, "Come!" ⁴Then another horse came out, a fiery red one. Its rider was given power to take peace from the earth and to make men slay each other. To him was given a large sword.

⁵When the Lamb opened the third seal, I heard the third living creature say, "Come!" I looked, and there before me was a black horse! Its rider was holding a pair of scales in his hand. ⁶Then I heard what sounded like a voice among the four living creatures, saying, "A quart*ᵃ* of wheat for a day's wages,*ᵇ* and three quarts of barley for a day's wages,*ᵇ* and do not damage the oil and the wine!"

⁷When the Lamb opened the fourth seal, I heard the voice of the fourth living creature say, "Come!" ⁸I looked, and there before me was a pale horse! Its rider was named Death, and Hades was following close behind him. They were given power over a fourth of the earth to kill by sword, famine and plague, and by the wild beasts of the earth.

⁹When he opened the fifth seal, I saw under the altar the souls of those who had been slain because of the word of God and the testimony they had maintained. ¹⁰They called out in a loud voice, "How long, Sovereign Lord, holy and true, until you judge the inhabitants of the earth and avenge our blood?" ¹¹Then each of them was given a white robe, and they were told to wait a little longer, until the number of their fellow servants and brothers who were to be killed as they had been was completed.

¹²I watched as he opened the sixth seal. There was a great earthquake. The sun turned black like sackcloth made of goat hair, the whole moon turned blood red, ¹³and the stars in the sky fell to earth, as late figs drop from a fig tree

---

THE MESSAGE

To the One on the Throne! To the Lamb!
The blessing, the honor, the glory, the strength,
For age after age after age.

The Four Animals called out, "Oh, Yes!" The Elders fell to their knees and worshiped.

Unsealing the Scroll

6.1-2 **6** I watched while the Lamb ripped off the first of the seven seals. I heard one of the Animals roar, "Come out!" I looked—I saw a white horse. Its rider carried a bow and was given a victory garland. He rode off victorious, conquering right and left.

6.3-4 When the Lamb ripped off the second seal, I heard the second Animal cry, "Come out!" Another horse appeared, this one red. Its rider was off to take peace from the earth, setting people at each other's throats, killing one another. He was given a huge sword.

6.5-6 When he ripped off the third seal, I heard the third Animal cry, "Come out!" I looked. A black horse this time. Its rider carried a set of scales in his hand. I heard a message (it seemed to issue from the Four Animals): "A quart of wheat for a day's wages, or three quarts of barley, but all the oil and wine you want."

6.7-8 When he ripped off the fourth seal, I heard the fourth Animal cry, "Come out!" I looked. A colorless horse, sickly pale. Its rider was Death, and Hell was close on its heels. They were given power to destroy a fourth of the earth by war, famine, disease, and wild beasts.

6.9-11 When he ripped off the fifth seal, I saw the souls of those killed because they had held firm in their witness to the Word of God. They were gathered under the Altar, and cried out in loud prayers, "How long, Strong God, Holy and True? How long before you step in and avenge our murders?" Then each martyr was given a white robe and told to sit back and wait until the full number of martyrs was filled from among their servant companions and friends in the faith.

6.12-17 I watched while he ripped off the sixth seal: a bone-jarring earthquake, sun turned black as ink, moon all bloody, stars falling out of the sky like figs shaken from a tree in a high wind, sky

---

ᵃ 6 Greek *a choinix* (probably about a liter)   *ᵇ 6* Greek *a denarius*

NEW INTERNATIONAL VERSION

when shaken by a strong wind. ¹⁴The sky receded like a scroll, rolling up, and every mountain and island was removed from its place.

¹⁵Then the kings of the earth, the princes, the generals, the rich, the mighty, and every slave and every free man hid in caves and among the rocks of the mountains. ¹⁶They called to the mountains and the rocks, "Fall on us and hide us from the face of him who sits on the throne and from the wrath of the Lamb! ¹⁷For the great day of their wrath has come, and who can stand?"

144,000 SEALED

7 After this I saw four angels standing at the four corners of the earth, holding back the four winds of the earth to prevent any wind from blowing on the land or on the sea or on any tree. ²Then I saw another angel coming up from the east, having the seal of the living God. He called out in a loud voice to the four angels who had been given power to harm the land and the sea: ³"Do not harm the land or the sea or the trees until we put a seal on the foreheads of the servants of our God." ⁴Then I heard the number of those who were sealed: 144,000 from all the tribes of Israel.

⁵From the tribe of Judah 12,000 were sealed,
 from the tribe of Reuben 12,000,
 from the tribe of Gad 12,000,
 ⁶from the tribe of Asher 12,000,
 from the tribe of Naphtali 12,000,
 from the tribe of Manasseh 12,000,
 ⁷from the tribe of Simeon 12,000,
 from the tribe of Levi 12,000,
 from the tribe of Issachar 12,000,
 ⁸from the tribe of Zebulun 12,000,
 from the tribe of Joseph 12,000,
 from the tribe of Benjamin 12,000.

THE GREAT MULTITUDE IN WHITE ROBES

⁹After this I looked and there before me was a great multitude that no one could count, from every nation, tribe, people and language, standing before the throne and in front of the Lamb. They were wearing white robes and were holding palm branches in their hands. ¹⁰And they cried out in a loud voice:

"Salvation belongs to our God,
 who sits on the throne,
 and to the Lamb."

¹¹All the angels were standing around the throne and around the elders and the four living creatures. They fell down on their faces before the throne and worshiped God, ¹²saying:

"Amen!
Praise and glory

THE MESSAGE

snapped shut like a book, islands and mountains sliding this way and that. And then pandemonium, everyone and his dog running for cover—kings, princes, generals, rich and strong, along with every commoner, slave or free. They hid in mountain caves and rocky dens, calling out to mountains and rocks, "Refuge! Hide us from the One Seated on the Throne and the wrath of the Lamb! The great Day of their wrath has come—who can stand it?"

THE SERVANTS OF GOD

7.1 7 Immediately I saw Four Angels standing at the four corners of earth, standing steady with a firm grip on the four winds so no wind would blow on earth or sea, not even rustle a tree.

7.2-3 Then I saw another Angel rising from where the sun rose, carrying the seal of the Living God. He thundered to the Four Angels assigned the task of hurting earth and sea, "Don't hurt the earth! Don't hurt the sea! Don't so much as hurt a tree until I've sealed the servants of our God on their foreheads!"

7.4-8 I heard the count of those who were sealed: 144,000! They were sealed out of every Tribe of Israel: 12,000 sealed from Judah, 12,000 from Reuben, 12,000 from Gad, 12,000 from Asher, 12,000 from Naphtali, 12,000 from Manasseh, 12,000 from Simeon, 12,000 from Levi, 12,000 from Issachar, 12,000 from Zebulun, 12,000 from Joseph, 12,000 sealed from Benjamin.

✝

7.9-12 I looked again. I saw a huge crowd, too huge to count. Everyone was there—all nations and tribes, all races and languages. And they were *standing*, dressed in white robes and waving palm branches, standing before the Throne and the Lamb and heartily singing:

Salvation to our God on his Throne!
Salvation to the Lamb!

All who were standing around the Throne—Angels, Elders, Animals—fell on their faces before the Throne and worshiped God, singing:

Oh, Yes!
The blessing and glory and wisdom and
  thanksgiving,

NEW INTERNATIONAL VERSION

and wisdom and thanks and honor
and power and strength
be to our God for ever and ever.
Amen!"

¹³Then one of the elders asked me, "These in white robes—who are they, and where did they come from?"

¹⁴I answered, "Sir, you know."

And he said, "These are they who have come out of the great tribulation; they have washed their robes and made them white in the blood of the Lamb. ¹⁵Therefore,

"they are before the throne of God
    and serve him day and night in his temple;
and he who sits on the throne will spread his
        tent over them.
¹⁶Never again will they hunger;
    never again will they thirst.
The sun will not beat upon them,
    nor any scorching heat.
¹⁷For the Lamb at the center of the throne will
        be their shepherd;
    he will lead them to springs of living water.
And God will wipe away every tear from
        their eyes."

The Seventh Seal and the Golden Censer

8 When he opened the seventh seal, there was silence in heaven for about half an hour.

²And I saw the seven angels who stand before God, and to them were given seven trumpets.

³Another angel, who had a golden censer, came and stood at the altar. He was given much incense to offer, with the prayers of all the saints, on the golden altar before the throne. ⁴The smoke of the incense, together with the prayers of the saints, went up before God from the angel's hand. ⁵Then the angel took the censer, filled it with fire from the altar, and hurled it on the earth; and there came peals of thunder, rumblings, flashes of lightning and an earthquake.

The Trumpets

⁶Then the seven angels who had the seven trumpets prepared to sound them.

⁷The first angel sounded his trumpet, and there came hail and fire mixed with blood, and it was hurled down upon the earth. A third of the earth was burned up, a third of the trees were burned up, and all the green grass was burned up.

⁸The second angel sounded his trumpet, and something like a huge mountain, all ablaze, was thrown into the sea. A third of the sea turned

THE MESSAGE

The honor and power and strength,
To our God forever and ever and ever!
Oh, Yes!

7.13-14 Just then one of the Elders addressed me: "Who are these dressed in white robes, and where did they come from?" Taken aback, I said, "O Sir, I have no idea—but you must know."

7.14-17 Then he told me, "These are those who come from the great tribulation, and they've washed their robes, scrubbed them clean in the blood of the Lamb. That's why they're standing before God's Throne. They serve him day and night in his Temple. The One on the Throne will pitch his tent there for them: no more hunger, no more thirst, no more scorching heat. The Lamb on the Throne will shepherd them, will lead them to spring waters of Life. And God will wipe every last tear from their eyes."

8.1 **8** When the Lamb ripped off the seventh seal, Heaven fell quiet—complete silence for about half an hour.

Blowing the Trumpets

8.2-4 I saw the Seven Angels who are always in readiness before God handed seven trumpets. Then another Angel, carrying a gold censer, came and stood at the Altar. He was given a great quantity of incense so that he could offer up the prayers of all the holy people of God on the Golden Altar before the Throne. Smoke billowed up from the incense-laced prayers of the holy ones, rose before God from the hand of the Angel.

8.5 Then the Angel filled the censer with fire from the Altar and heaved it to earth. It set off thunders, voices, lightnings, and an earthquake.

8.6-7 The Seven Angels with the trumpets got ready to blow them. At the first trumpet blast, hail and fire mixed with blood were dumped on earth. A third of the earth was scorched, a third of the trees, and every blade of green grass—burned to a crisp.

8.8-9 The second Angel trumpeted. Something like a huge mountain blazing with fire was flung into the sea. A third of the sea turned to

NEW INTERNATIONAL VERSION

into blood, ⁹a third of the living creatures in the sea died, and a third of the ships were destroyed.

¹⁰The third angel sounded his trumpet, and a great star, blazing like a torch, fell from the sky on a third of the rivers and on the springs of water— ¹¹the name of the star is Wormwood.ᵃ A third of the waters turned bitter, and many people died from the waters that had become bitter.

¹²The fourth angel sounded his trumpet, and a third of the sun was struck, a third of the moon, and a third of the stars, so that a third of them turned dark. A third of the day was without light, and also a third of the night.

¹³As I watched, I heard an eagle that was flying in midair call out in a loud voice: "Woe! Woe! Woe to the inhabitants of the earth, because of the trumpet blasts about to be sounded by the other three angels!"

9 The fifth angel sounded his trumpet, and I saw a star that had fallen from the sky to the earth. The star was given the key to the shaft of the Abyss. ²When he opened the Abyss, smoke rose from it like the smoke from a gigantic furnace. The sun and sky were darkened by the smoke from the Abyss. ³And out of the smoke locusts came down upon the earth and were given power like that of scorpions of the earth. ⁴They were told not to harm the grass of the earth or any plant or tree, but only those people who did not have the seal of God on their foreheads. ⁵They were not given power to kill them, but only to torture them for five months. And the agony they suffered was like that of the sting of a scorpion when it strikes a man. ⁶During those days men will seek death, but will not find it; they will long to die, but death will elude them.

⁷The locusts looked like horses prepared for battle. On their heads they wore something like crowns of gold, and their faces resembled human faces. ⁸Their hair was like women's hair, and their teeth were like lions' teeth. ⁹They had breastplates like breastplates of iron, and the sound of their wings was like the thundering of many horses and chariots rushing into battle. ¹⁰They had tails and stings like scorpions, and in their tails they had power to torment people for five months. ¹¹They had as king over them the angel of the Abyss, whose name in Hebrew is Abaddon, and in Greek, Apollyon.ᵇ

¹²The first woe is past; two other woes are yet to come.

¹³The sixth angel sounded his trumpet, and I heard a voice coming from the hornsᶜ of the

THE MESSAGE

blood, a third of the living sea creatures died, and a third of the ships sank.

8.10-11   The third Angel trumpeted. A huge Star, blazing like a torch, fell from Heaven, wiping out a third of the rivers and a third of the springs. The Star's name was Wormwood. A third of the water turned bitter, and many people died from the poisoned water.

8.12   The fourth Angel trumpeted. A third of the sun, a third of the moon, and a third of the stars were hit, blacked out by a third, both day and night in one-third blackout.

8.13   I looked hard; I heard a lone eagle, flying through Middle-Heaven, crying out ominously, "Doom! Doom! Doom to everyone left on earth! There are three more Angels about to blow their trumpets. Doom is on its way!"

✝

9.1-2   **9** The fifth Angel trumpeted. I saw a Star plummet from Heaven to earth. The Star was handed a key to the Well of the Abyss. He unlocked the Well of the Abyss—smoke poured out of the Well, billows and billows of smoke, sun and air in blackout from smoke pouring out of the Well.

9.3-6   Then out of the smoke crawled locusts with the venom of scorpions. They were given their orders: "Don't hurt the grass, don't hurt anything green, don't hurt a single tree—only men and women, and then only those who lack the seal of God on their foreheads." They were ordered to torture but not kill, torture them for five months, the pain like a scorpion sting. When this happens, people are going to prefer death to torture, look for ways to kill themselves. But they won't find a way—death will have gone into hiding.

9.7-11   The locusts looked like horses ready for war. They had gold crowns, human faces, women's hair, the teeth of lions, and iron breastplates. The sound of their wings was the sound of horse-drawn chariots charging into battle. Their tails were equipped with stings, like scorpion tails. With those tails they were ordered to torture the human race for five months. They had a king over them, the Angel of the Abyss. His name in Hebrew is *Abaddon*, in Greek, *Apollyon*—"Destroyer."

9.12   The first doom is past. Two dooms yet to come.

9.13-14   The sixth Angel trumpeted. I heard a voice speaking to the sixth Angel from the horns of

---

ᵃ 11 That is, Bitterness   ᵇ 11 *Abaddon* and *Apollyon* mean *Destroyer.*   ᶜ 13 That is, projections

NEW INTERNATIONAL VERSION

golden altar that is before God. ¹⁴It said to the sixth angel who had the trumpet, "Release the four angels who are bound at the great river Euphrates." ¹⁵And the four angels who had been kept ready for this very hour and day and month and year were released to kill a third of mankind. ¹⁶The number of the mounted troops was two hundred million. I heard their number.

¹⁷The horses and riders I saw in my vision looked like this: Their breastplates were fiery red, dark blue, and yellow as sulfur. The heads of the horses resembled the heads of lions, and out of their mouths came fire, smoke and sulfur. ¹⁸A third of mankind was killed by the three plagues of fire, smoke and sulfur that came out of their mouths. ¹⁹The power of the horses was in their mouths and in their tails; for their tails were like snakes, having heads with which they inflict injury.

²⁰The rest of mankind that were not killed by these plagues still did not repent of the work of their hands; they did not stop worshiping demons, and idols of gold, silver, bronze, stone and wood—idols that cannot see or hear or walk. ²¹Nor did they repent of their murders, their magic arts, their sexual immorality or their thefts.

THE ANGEL AND THE LITTLE SCROLL

10 Then I saw another mighty angel coming down from heaven. He was robed in a cloud, with a rainbow above his head; his face was like the sun, and his legs were like fiery pillars. ²He was holding a little scroll, which lay open in his hand. He planted his right foot on the sea and his left foot on the land, ³and he gave a loud shout like the roar of a lion. When he shouted, the voices of the seven thunders spoke. ⁴And when the seven thunders spoke, I was about to write; but I heard a voice from heaven say, "Seal up what the seven thunders have said and do not write it down."

⁵Then the angel I had seen standing on the sea and on the land raised his right hand to heaven. ⁶And he swore by him who lives for ever and ever, who created the heavens and all that is in them, the earth and all that is in it, and the sea and all that is in it, and said, "There will be no more delay! ⁷But in the days when the seventh angel is about to sound his trumpet, the mystery of God will be accomplished, just as he announced to his servants the prophets."

⁸Then the voice that I had heard from heaven spoke to me once more: "Go, take the scroll that lies open in the hand of the angel who is standing on the sea and on the land."

⁹So I went to the angel and asked him to give me the little scroll. He said to me, "Take it and

THE MESSAGE

the Golden Altar before God: "Let the Four Angels loose, the Angels confined at the great River Euphrates."

9.15-19 The Four Angels were untied and let loose, Four Angels all prepared for the exact year, month, day, and even hour when they were to kill a third of the human race. The number of the army of horsemen was twice ten thousand times ten thousand. I heard the count and saw both horses and riders in my vision: fiery breastplates on the riders, lion heads on the horses breathing out fire and smoke and brimstone. With these three weapons—fire and smoke and brimstone—they killed a third of the human race. The horses killed with their mouths and tails; their serpentlike tails also had heads that wreaked havoc.

9.20-21 The remaining men and women who weren't killed by these weapons went on their merry way—didn't change their way of life, didn't quit worshiping demons, didn't quit centering their lives around lumps of gold and silver and brass, hunks of stone and wood that couldn't see or hear or move. There wasn't a sign of a change of heart. They plunged right on in their murderous, occult, promiscuous, and thieving ways.

✝

10.1-4 **10** I saw another powerful Angel coming down out of Heaven wrapped in a cloud. There was a rainbow over his head, his face was sun-radiant, his legs pillars of fire. He had a small book open in his hand. He placed his right foot on the sea and his left foot on land, then called out thunderously, a lion roar. When he called out, the Seven Thunders called back. When the Seven Thunders spoke, I started to write it all down, but a voice out of Heaven stopped me, saying, "Seal with silence the Seven Thunders; don't write a word."

10.5-7 Then the Angel I saw astride sea and land lifted his right hand to Heaven and swore by the One Living Forever and Ever, who created Heaven and everything in it, earth and everything in it, sea and everything in it, that time was up—that when the seventh Angel blew his trumpet, which he was about to do, the Mystery of God, all the plans he had revealed to his servants, the prophets, would be completed.

10.8-11 The voice out of Heaven spoke to me again: "Go, take the book held open in the hand of the Angel astride sea and earth." I went up to the Angel and said, "Give me the little book." He said, "Take it, then eat it. It will taste sweet

NEW INTERNATIONAL VERSION

eat it. It will turn your stomach sour, but in your mouth it will be as sweet as honey." 10I took the little scroll from the angel's hand and ate it. It tasted as sweet as honey in my mouth, but when I had eaten it, my stomach turned sour. 11Then I was told, "You must prophesy again about many peoples, nations, languages and kings."

THE TWO WITNESSES

11 I was given a reed like a measuring rod and was told, "Go and measure the temple of God and the altar, and count the worshipers there. 2But exclude the outer court; do not measure it, because it has been given to the Gentiles. They will trample on the holy city for 42 months. 3And I will give power to my two witnesses, and they will prophesy for 1,260 days, clothed in sackcloth." 4These are the two olive trees and the two lampstands that stand before the Lord of the earth. 5If anyone tries to harm them, fire comes from their mouths and devours their enemies. This is how anyone who wants to harm them must die. 6These men have power to shut up the sky so that it will not rain during the time they are prophesying; and they have power to turn the waters into blood and to strike the earth with every kind of plague as often as they want.

7Now when they have finished their testimony, the beast that comes up from the Abyss will attack them, and overpower and kill them. 8Their bodies will lie in the street of the great city, which is figuratively called Sodom and Egypt, where also their Lord was crucified. 9For three and a half days men from every people, tribe, language and nation will gaze on their bodies and refuse them burial. 10The inhabitants of the earth will gloat over them and will celebrate by sending each other gifts, because these two prophets had tormented those who live on the earth.

11But after the three and a half days a breath of life from God entered them, and they stood on their feet, and terror struck those who saw them. 12Then they heard a loud voice from heaven saying to them, "Come up here." And they went up to heaven in a cloud, while their enemies looked on.

13At that very hour there was a severe earthquake and a tenth of the city collapsed. Seven thousand people were killed in the earthquake, and the survivors were terrified and gave glory to the God of heaven.

14The second woe has passed; the third woe is coming soon.

THE MESSAGE

like honey, but turn sour in your stomach." I took the little book from the Angel's hand and it was sweet honey in my mouth, but when I swallowed, my stomach curdled. Then I was told, "You must go back and prophesy again over many peoples and nations and languages and kings."

THE TWO WITNESSES

11.1-2 **11** I was given a stick for a measuring rod and told, "Get up and measure God's Temple and Altar and everyone worshiping in it. Exclude the outside court; don't measure it. It's been handed over to non-Jewish outsiders. They'll desecrate the Holy City for forty-two months.

11.3-6 "Meanwhile, I'll provide my two Witnesses. Dressed in sackcloth, they'll prophesy for one thousand two hundred sixty days. These are the two Olive Trees, the two Lampstands, standing at attention before God on earth. If anyone tries to hurt them, a blast of fire from their mouths will incinerate them—burn them to a crisp just like that. They'll have power to seal the sky so that it doesn't rain for the time of their prophesying, power to turn rivers and springs to blood, power to hit earth with any and every disaster as often as they want.

11.7-10 "When they've completed their witness, the Beast from the Abyss will emerge and fight them, conquer and kill them, leaving their corpses exposed on the street of the Great City spiritually called Sodom and Egypt, the same City where their Master was crucified. For three and a half days they'll be there—exposed, prevented from getting a decent burial, stared at by the curious from all over the world. Those people will cheer at the spectacle, shouting 'Good riddance!' and calling for a celebration, for these two prophets pricked the conscience of all the people on earth, made it impossible for them to enjoy their sins.

11.11 "Then, after three and a half days, the Living Spirit of God will enter them—they're on their feet!—and all those gloating spectators will be scared to death."

11.12-13 I heard a strong voice out of Heaven calling, "Come up here!" and up they went to Heaven, wrapped in a cloud, their enemies watching it all. At that moment there was a gigantic earthquake—a tenth of the city fell to ruin, seven thousand perished in the earthquake, the rest frightened to the core of their being, frightened into giving honor to the God of Heaven.

11.14 The second doom is past, the third doom coming right on its heels.

NEW INTERNATIONAL VERSION

THE SEVENTH TRUMPET

[15]The seventh angel sounded his trumpet, and there were loud voices in heaven, which said:

"The kingdom of the world has become the
      kingdom of our Lord and of his
      Christ,
   and he will reign for ever and ever."

[16]And the twenty-four elders, who were seated on their thrones before God, fell on their faces and worshiped God, [17]saying:

"We give thanks to you, Lord God Almighty,
   the One who is and who was,
because you have taken your great power
   and have begun to reign.
[18]The nations were angry;
   and your wrath has come.
The time has come for judging the dead,
   and for rewarding your servants the
      prophets
and your saints and those who reverence
      your name,
   both small and great—
and for destroying those who destroy the
      earth."

[19]Then God's temple in heaven was opened, and within his temple was seen the ark of his covenant. And there came flashes of lightning, rumblings, peals of thunder, an earthquake and a great hailstorm.

THE WOMAN AND THE DRAGON

12 A great and wondrous sign appeared in heaven: a woman clothed with the sun, with the moon under her feet and a crown of twelve stars on her head. [2]She was pregnant and cried out in pain as she was about to give birth. [3]Then another sign appeared in heaven: an enormous red dragon with seven heads and ten horns and seven crowns on his heads. [4]His tail swept a third of the stars out of the sky and flung them to the earth. The dragon stood in front of the woman who was about to give birth, so that he might devour her child the moment it was born. [5]She gave birth to a son, a male child, who will rule all the nations with an iron scepter. And her child was snatched up to God and to his throne. [6]The woman fled into the desert to a place prepared for her by God, where she might be taken care of for 1,260 days.

[7]And there was war in heaven. Michael and his angels fought against the dragon, and the dragon and his angels fought back. [8]But he was not strong enough, and they lost their place in

THE MESSAGE

THE LAST TRUMPET SOUNDS

11.15-18 The seventh Angel trumpeted. A crescendo of voices in Heaven sang out,

The kingdom of the world is now
   the Kingdom of our God and his
      Messiah!
He will rule forever and ever!

The Twenty-four Elders seated before God on their thrones fell to their knees, worshiped, and sang,

We thank you, O God, Sovereign-Strong,
   WHO IS AND WHO WAS.
You took your great power
   and took over—reigned!
The angry nations now
   get a taste of *your* anger.
The time has come to judge the dead,
   to reward your servants, all prophets and
      saints,
Reward small and great who fear your
      Name,
   and destroy the destroyers of earth.

11.19 The doors of God's Temple in Heaven flew open, and the Ark of his Covenant was clearly seen surrounded by flashes of lightning, loud shouts, peals of thunder, an earthquake, and a fierce hailstorm.

THE WOMAN, HER SON, AND THE DRAGON

12.1-2 **12** A great Sign appeared in Heaven: a Woman dressed all in sunlight, standing on the moon, and crowned with Twelve Stars. She was giving birth to a Child and cried out in the pain of childbirth.

12.3-4 And then another Sign alongside the first: a huge and fiery Dragon! It had seven heads and ten horns, a crown on each of the seven heads. With one flick of its tail it knocked a third of the Stars from the sky and dumped them on earth. The Dragon crouched before the Woman in childbirth, poised to eat up the Child when it came.

12.5-6 The Woman gave birth to a Son who will shepherd all nations with an iron rod. Her Son was seized and placed safely before God on his Throne. The Woman herself escaped to the desert to a place of safety prepared by God, all comforts provided her for one thousand two hundred and sixty days.

12.7-12 War broke out in Heaven. Michael and his Angels fought the Dragon. The Dragon and his Angels fought back, but were no match for Michael. They were cleared out of Heaven, not a

NEW INTERNATIONAL VERSION

heaven. 9The great dragon was hurled down—that ancient serpent called the devil, or Satan, who leads the whole world astray. He was hurled to the earth, and his angels with him.

10Then I heard a loud voice in heaven say:

"Now have come the salvation and the
            power and the kingdom of our God,
      and the authority of his Christ.
For the accuser of our brothers,
      who accuses them before our God day
            and night,
      has been hurled down.
11They overcame him
      by the blood of the Lamb
      and by the word of their testimony;
they did not love their lives so much
      as to shrink from death.
12Therefore rejoice, you heavens
      and you who dwell in them!
But woe to the earth and the sea,
      because the devil has gone down to you!
He is filled with fury,
      because he knows that his time is short."

13When the dragon saw that he had been hurled to the earth, he pursued the woman who had given birth to the male child. 14The woman was given the two wings of a great eagle, so that she might fly to the place prepared for her in the desert, where she would be taken care of for a time, times and half a time, out of the serpent's reach. 15Then from his mouth the serpent spewed water like a river, to overtake the woman and sweep her away with the torrent. 16But the earth helped the woman by opening its mouth and swallowing the river that the dragon had spewed out of his mouth. 17Then the dragon was enraged at the woman and went off to make war against the rest of her offspring—those who obey God's commandments and hold to the testimony of Jesus.

13

1And the dragon*a* stood on the shore of the sea.

THE BEAST OUT OF THE SEA

And I saw a beast coming out of the sea. He had ten horns and seven heads, with ten crowns on his horns, and on each head a blasphemous name. 2The beast I saw resembled a leopard, but had feet like those of a bear and a mouth like that of a lion. The dragon gave the beast his power and his throne and great authority. 3One of the heads of the beast seemed to have had a fatal wound, but the fatal wound had been

a 1 Some late manuscripts *And I*

THE MESSAGE

sign of them left. The great Dragon—ancient Serpent, the one called Devil and Satan, the one who led the whole earth astray—thrown out, and all his Angels thrown out with him, thrown down to earth. Then I heard a strong voice out of Heaven saying,

Salvation and power are established!
      Kingdom of our God, authority of his
            Messiah!
The Accuser of our brothers and sisters
            thrown out,
      who accused them day and night before
            God.
They defeated him through the blood of the
            Lamb
      and the bold word of their witness.
They weren't in love with themselves;
      they were willing to die for Christ.
So rejoice, O Heavens, and all who live there,
      but doom to earth and sea,
For the Devil's come down on you with
            both feet;
      he's had a great fall;
He's wild and raging with anger;
      he hasn't much time and he knows it.

12.13-17   When the Dragon saw he'd been thrown to earth, he went after the Woman who had given birth to the Man-Child. The Woman was given wings of a great eagle to fly to a place in the desert to be kept in safety and comfort for a time and times and half a time, safe and sound from the Serpent. The Serpent vomited a river of water to swamp and drown her, but earth came to her help, swallowing the water the Dragon spewed from its mouth. Helpless with rage, the Dragon raged at the Woman, then went off to make war with the rest of her children, the children who keep God's commands and hold firm to the witness of Jesus. And the Dragon stood on the shore of the sea.

THE BEAST FROM THE SEA

13.1-2   I saw a Beast rising from the sea. It had ten horns and seven heads—on each horn a crown, and each head inscribed with a blasphemous name. The Beast I saw looked like a leopard with bear paws and a lion's mouth. The Dragon turned over its power to it, its throne and great authority.

13.3-4   One of the Beast's heads looked as if it had been struck a deathblow, and then healed. The

NEW INTERNATIONAL VERSION

healed. The whole world was astonished and followed the beast. [4]Men worshiped the dragon because he had given authority to the beast, and they also worshiped the beast and asked, "Who is like the beast? Who can make war against him?"

[5]The beast was given a mouth to utter proud words and blasphemies and to exercise his authority for forty-two months. [6]He opened his mouth to blaspheme God, and to slander his name and his dwelling place and those who live in heaven. [7]He was given power to make war against the saints and to conquer them. And he was given authority over every tribe, people, language and nation. [8]All inhabitants of the earth will worship the beast—all whose names have not been written in the book of life belonging to the Lamb that was slain from the creation of the world. [a]

[9]He who has an ear, let him hear.

[10]If anyone is to go into captivity,
    into captivity he will go.
If anyone is to be killed [b] with the sword,
    with the sword he will be killed.

This calls for patient endurance and faithfulness on the part of the saints.

THE BEAST OUT OF THE EARTH

[11]Then I saw another beast, coming out of the earth. He had two horns like a lamb, but he spoke like a dragon. [12]He exercised all the authority of the first beast on his behalf, and made the earth and its inhabitants worship the first beast, whose fatal wound had been healed. [13]And he performed great and miraculous signs, even causing fire to come down from heaven to earth in full view of men. [14]Because of the signs he was given power to do on behalf of the first beast, he deceived the inhabitants of the earth. He ordered them to set up an image in honor of the beast who was wounded by the sword and yet lived. [15]He was given power to give breath to the image of the first beast, so that it could speak and cause all who refused to worship the image to be killed. [16]He also forced everyone, small and great, rich and poor, free and slave, to receive a mark on his right hand or on his forehead, [17]so that no one could buy or sell unless he had the mark, which is the name of the beast or the number of his name.

[18]This calls for wisdom. If anyone has insight, let him calculate the number of the beast, for it is man's number. His number is 666.

[a] 8 Or written from the creation of the world in the book of life belonging to the Lamb that was slain   [b] 10 Some manuscripts anyone kills

THE MESSAGE

whole earth was agog, gaping at the Beast. They worshiped the Dragon who gave the Beast authority, and they worshiped the Beast, exclaiming, "There's never been anything like the Beast! No one would dare go to war with the Beast!"

13.5-8   The Beast had a loud mouth, boastful and blasphemous. It could do anything it wanted for forty-two months. It yelled blasphemies against God, blasphemed his Name, blasphemed his Church, especially those already dwelling with God in Heaven. It was permitted to make war on God's holy people and conquer them. It held absolute sway over all tribes and peoples, tongues and races. Everyone on earth whose name was not written from the world's foundation in the slaughtered Lamb's Book of Life will worship the Beast.

13.9-10   Are you listening to this? They've made their bed; now they must lie in it. Anyone marked for prison goes straight to prison; anyone pulling a sword goes down by the sword. Meanwhile, God's holy people passionately and faithfully stand their ground.

THE BEAST FROM UNDER THE GROUND

13.11-12 I saw another Beast rising out of the ground. It had two horns like a lamb but sounded like a dragon when it spoke. It was a puppet of the first Beast, made earth and everyone in it worship the first Beast, which had been healed of its deathblow.

13.13-17   This second Beast worked magical signs, dazzling people by making fire come down from Heaven. It used the magic it got from the Beast to dupe earth dwellers, getting them to make an image of the Beast that received the deathblow and lived. It was able to animate the image of the Beast so that it talked, and then arrange that anyone not worshiping the Beast would be killed. It forced all people, small and great, rich and poor, free and slave, to have a mark on the right hand or forehead. Without the mark of the name of the Beast or the number of its name, it was impossible to buy or sell anything.

13.18   Solve a riddle: Put your heads together and figure out the meaning of the number of the Beast. It's a human number: six hundred sixty-six.

NEW INTERNATIONAL VERSION

THE LAMB AND THE 144,000

14 Then I looked, and there before me was the Lamb, standing on Mount Zion, and with him 144,000 who had his name and his Father's name written on their foreheads. ²And I heard a sound from heaven like the roar of rushing waters and like a loud peal of thunder. The sound I heard was like that of harpists playing their harps. ³And they sang a new song before the throne and before the four living creatures and the elders. No one could learn the song except the 144,000 who had been redeemed from the earth. ⁴These are those who did not defile themselves with women, for they kept themselves pure. They follow the Lamb wherever he goes. They were purchased from among men and offered as firstfruits to God and the Lamb. ⁵No lie was found in their mouths; they are blameless.

THE THREE ANGELS

⁶Then I saw another angel flying in midair, and he had the eternal gospel to proclaim to those who live on the earth—to every nation, tribe, language and people. ⁷He said in a loud voice, "Fear God and give him glory, because the hour of his judgment has come. Worship him who made the heavens, the earth, the sea and the springs of water."

⁸A second angel followed and said, "Fallen! Fallen is Babylon the Great, which made all the nations drink the maddening wine of her adulteries."

⁹A third angel followed them and said in a loud voice: "If anyone worships the beast and his image and receives his mark on the forehead or on the hand, ¹⁰he, too, will drink of the wine of God's fury, which has been poured full strength into the cup of his wrath. He will be tormented with burning sulfur in the presence of the holy angels and of the Lamb. ¹¹And the smoke of their torment rises for ever and ever. There is no rest day or night for those who worship the beast and his image, or for anyone who receives the mark of his name." ¹²This calls for patient endurance on the part of the saints who obey God's commandments and remain faithful to Jesus.

¹³Then I heard a voice from heaven say, "Write: Blessed are the dead who die in the Lord from now on."

"Yes," says the Spirit, "they will rest from their labor, for their deeds will follow them."

THE HARVEST OF THE EARTH

¹⁴I looked, and there before me was a white cloud, and seated on the cloud was one "like a son of man"ᵃ with a crown of gold on his head

ᵃ *14* Daniel 7:13

THE MESSAGE

A PERFECT OFFERING

14.1-2 **14** I saw—it took my breath away!—the Lamb standing on Mount Zion, One Hundred and Forty-four Thousand standing there with him, his Name and the Name of his Father inscribed on their foreheads. And I heard a voice out of Heaven, the sound like a cataract, like the crash of thunder.

14.2-5 And then I heard music, harp music and the harpists singing a new song before the Throne and the Four Animals and the Elders. Only the Hundred and Forty-four Thousand could learn to sing the song. They were bought from earth, lived without compromise, virgin-fresh before God. Wherever the Lamb went, they followed. They were bought from humankind, firstfruits of the harvest for God and the Lamb. Not a false word in their mouths. A perfect offering.

VOICES FROM HEAVEN

14.6-7 I saw another Angel soaring in Middle-Heaven. He had an Eternal Message to preach to all who were still on earth, every nation and tribe, every tongue and people. He preached in a loud voice, "Fear God and give him glory! His hour of judgment has come! Worship the Maker of Heaven and earth, salt sea and fresh water!"

14.8 A second Angel followed, calling out, "Ruined, ruined, Great Babylon ruined! She made all the nations drunk on the wine of her whoring!"

14.9-11 A third Angel followed, shouting, warning, "If anyone worships the Beast and its image and takes the mark on forehead or hand, that person will drink the wine of God's wrath, prepared unmixed in his chalice of anger, and suffer torment from fire and brimstone in the presence of Holy Angels, in the presence of the Lamb. Smoke from their torment will rise age after age. No respite for those who worship the Beast and its image, who take the mark of its name."

14.12 Meanwhile, the saints stand passionately patient, keeping God's commands, staying faithful to Jesus.

14.13 I heard a voice out of Heaven, "Write this: Blessed are those who die in the Master from now on; how blessed to die that way!"

"Yes," says the Spirit, "and blessed rest from their hard, hard work. None of what they've done is wasted; God blesses them for it all in the end."

HARVEST TIME

14.14-16 I looked up, I caught my breath!—a white cloud and one like the Son of Man sitting on it. He wore a gold crown and held a sharp sickle.

NEW INTERNATIONAL VERSION

and a sharp sickle in his hand. ¹⁵Then another angel came out of the temple and called in a loud voice to him who was sitting on the cloud, "Take your sickle and reap, because the time to reap has come, for the harvest of the earth is ripe." ¹⁶So he who was seated on the cloud swung his sickle over the earth, and the earth was harvested.

¹⁷Another angel came out of the temple in heaven, and he too had a sharp sickle. ¹⁸Still another angel, who had charge of the fire, came from the altar and called in a loud voice to him who had the sharp sickle, "Take your sharp sickle and gather the clusters of grapes from the earth's vine, because its grapes are ripe." ¹⁹The angel swung his sickle on the earth, gathered its grapes and threw them into the great winepress of God's wrath. ²⁰They were trampled in the winepress outside the city, and blood flowed out of the press, rising as high as the horses' bridles for a distance of 1,600 stadia.ᵃ

SEVEN ANGELS WITH SEVEN PLAGUES

15 I saw in heaven another great and marvelous sign: seven angels with the seven last plagues—last, because with them God's wrath is completed. ²And I saw what looked like a sea of glass mixed with fire and, standing beside the sea, those who had been victorious over the beast and his image and over the number of his name. They held harps given them by God ³and sang the song of Moses the servant of God and the song of the Lamb:

"Great and marvelous are your deeds,
　Lord God Almighty.
Just and true are your ways,
　King of the ages.
⁴Who will not fear you, O Lord,
　and bring glory to your name?
For you alone are holy.
All nations will come
　and worship before you,
for your righteous acts have been revealed."

⁵After this I looked and in heaven the temple, that is, the tabernacle of the Testimony, was opened. ⁶Out of the temple came the seven angels with the seven plagues. They were dressed in clean, shining linen and wore golden sashes around their chests. ⁷Then one of the four living creatures gave to the seven angels seven golden bowls filled with the wrath of God, who lives for ever and ever. ⁸And the temple was filled with smoke from the glory of God and from his power, and no one could enter the temple until the seven plagues of the seven angels were completed.

ᵃ 20 That is, about 180 miles (about 300 kilometers)

THE MESSAGE

Another Angel came out of the Temple, shouting to the Cloud-Enthroned, "Swing your sickle and reap. It's harvest time. Earth's harvest is ripe for reaping." The Cloud-Enthroned gave a mighty sweep of his sickle, began harvesting earth in a stroke.

14.17-18　Then another Angel came out of the Temple in Heaven. He also had a sharp sickle. Yet another Angel, the one in charge of tending the fire, came from the Altar. He thundered to the Angel who held the sharp sickle, "Swing your sharp sickle. Harvest earth's vineyard. The grapes are bursting with ripeness."

14.19-20　The Angel swung his sickle, harvested earth's vintage, and heaved it into the winepress, the giant winepress of God's wrath. The winepress was outside the City. As the vintage was trodden, blood poured from the winepress as high as a horse's bridle, a river of blood for two hundred miles.

THE SONG OF MOSES, THE SONG OF THE LAMB

15.1　**15** I saw another Sign in Heaven, huge and breathtaking: seven Angels with seven disasters. These are the final disasters, the wrap-up of God's wrath.

15.2-4　I saw something like a sea made of glass, the glass all shot through with fire. Carrying harps of God, triumphant over the Beast, its image, and the number of its name, the saved ones stood on the sea of glass. They sang the Song of Moses, servant of God; they sang the Song of the Lamb:

Mighty your acts and marvelous,
　O God, the Sovereign-Strong!
Righteous your ways and true,
　King of the nations!
Who can fail to fear you, God,
　give glory to your Name?
Because you and you only are holy,
　all nations will come and worship you,
　because they see your judgments are
　　right.

15.5-8　Then I saw the doors of the Temple, the Tent of Witness in Heaven, open wide. The Seven Angels carrying the seven disasters came out of the Temple. They were dressed in clean, bright linen and wore gold vests. One of the Four Animals handed the Seven Angels seven gold bowls, brimming with the wrath of God, who lives forever and ever. Smoke from God's glory and power poured out of the Temple. No one was permitted to enter the Temple until the seven disasters of the Seven Angels were finished.

NEW INTERNATIONAL VERSION

THE SEVEN BOWLS OF GOD'S WRATH

16 Then I heard a loud voice from the temple saying to the seven angels, "Go, pour out the seven bowls of God's wrath on the earth."

²The first angel went and poured out his bowl on the land, and ugly and painful sores broke out on the people who had the mark of the beast and worshiped his image.

³The second angel poured out his bowl on the sea, and it turned into blood like that of a dead man, and every living thing in the sea died.

⁴The third angel poured out his bowl on the rivers and springs of water, and they became blood. ⁵Then I heard the angel in charge of the waters say:

"You are just in these judgments,
    you who are and who were, the Holy One,
    because you have so judged;
⁶for they have shed the blood of your saints
        and prophets,
    and you have given them blood to drink
        as they deserve."

⁷And I heard the altar respond:

"Yes, Lord God Almighty,
    true and just are your judgments."

⁸The fourth angel poured out his bowl on the sun, and the sun was given power to scorch people with fire. ⁹They were seared by the intense heat and they cursed the name of God, who had control over these plagues, but they refused to repent and glorify him.

¹⁰The fifth angel poured out his bowl on the throne of the beast, and his kingdom was plunged into darkness. Men gnawed their tongues in agony ¹¹and cursed the God of heaven because of their pains and their sores, but they refused to repent of what they had done.

¹²The sixth angel poured out his bowl on the great river Euphrates, and its water was dried up to prepare the way for the kings from the East. ¹³Then I saw three evilª spirits that looked like frogs; they came out of the mouth of the dragon, out of the mouth of the beast and out of the mouth of the false prophet. ¹⁴They are spirits of demons performing miraculous signs, and they go out to the kings of the whole world, to gather them for the battle on the great day of God Almighty.

¹⁵"Behold, I come like a thief! Blessed is he who stays awake and keeps his clothes with him, so that he may not go naked and be shamefully exposed."

¹⁶Then they gathered the kings together to the place that in Hebrew is called Armageddon.

ª *13 Greek unclean*

THE MESSAGE

POURING OUT THE SEVEN DISASTERS

16.1 **16** I heard a shout of command from the Temple to the Seven Angels: "Begin! Pour out the seven bowls of God's wrath on earth!"

16.2 The first Angel stepped up and poured his bowl out on earth: Loathsome, stinking sores erupted on all who had taken the mark of the Beast and worshiped its image.

16.3 The second Angel poured his bowl on the sea: The sea coagulated into blood, and everything in it died.

16.4-7 The third Angel poured his bowl on rivers and springs: The waters turned to blood. I heard the Angel of Waters say,

Righteous you are, and your judgments are
        righteous,
    THE IS, THE WAS, THE HOLY.
They poured out the blood of saints and
        prophets
    so you've given them blood to drink—
    they've gotten what they deserve!

Just then I heard the Altar chime in,

Yes, O God, the Sovereign-Strong!
    Your judgments are true and just!

16.8-9 The fourth Angel poured his bowl on the sun: Fire blazed from the sun and scorched men and women. Burned and blistered, they cursed God's Name, the God behind these disasters. They refused to repent, refused to honor God.

16.10-11 The fifth Angel poured his bowl on the throne of the Beast: Its kingdom fell into sudden eclipse. Mad with pain, men and women bit and chewed their tongues, cursed the God of Heaven for their torment and sores, and refused to repent and change their ways.

16.12-14 The sixth Angel poured his bowl on the great Euphrates River: It dried up to nothing. The dry riverbed became a fine roadbed for the kings from the East. From the mouths of the Dragon, the Beast, and the False Prophet I saw three foul demons crawl out—they looked like frogs. These are demon spirits performing signs. They're after the kings of the whole world to get them gathered for battle on the Great Day of God, the Sovereign-Strong.

16.15 "Keep watch! I come unannounced, like a thief. You're blessed if, awake and dressed, you're ready for me. Too bad if you're found running through the streets, naked and ashamed."

16.16 The frog-demons gathered the kings together at the place called in Hebrew *Armageddon*.

NEW INTERNATIONAL VERSION

¹⁷The seventh angel poured out his bowl into the air, and out of the temple came a loud voice from the throne, saying, "It is done!" ¹⁸Then there came flashes of lightning, rumblings, peals of thunder and a severe earthquake. No earthquake like it has ever occurred since man has been on earth, so tremendous was the quake. ¹⁹The great city split into three parts, and the cities of the nations collapsed. God remembered Babylon the Great and gave her the cup filled with the wine of the fury of his wrath. ²⁰Every island fled away and the mountains could not be found. ²¹From the sky huge hailstones of about a hundred pounds each fell upon men. And they cursed God on account of the plague of hail, because the plague was so terrible.

THE WOMAN ON THE BEAST

17 One of the seven angels who had the seven bowls came and said to me, "Come, I will show you the punishment of the great prostitute, who sits on many waters. ²With her the kings of the earth committed adultery and the inhabitants of the earth were intoxicated with the wine of her adulteries."

³Then the angel carried me away in the Spirit into a desert. There I saw a woman sitting on a scarlet beast that was covered with blasphemous names and had seven heads and ten horns. ⁴The woman was dressed in purple and scarlet, and was glittering with gold, precious stones and pearls. She held a golden cup in her hand, filled with abominable things and the filth of her adulteries. ⁵This title was written on her forehead:

MYSTERY
BABYLON THE GREAT
THE MOTHER OF PROSTITUTES
AND OF THE ABOMINATIONS OF THE EARTH.

⁶I saw that the woman was drunk with the blood of the saints, the blood of those who bore testimony to Jesus.

When I saw her, I was greatly astonished. ⁷Then the angel said to me: "Why are you astonished? I will explain to you the mystery of the woman and of the beast she rides, which has the seven heads and ten horns. ⁸The beast, which you saw, once was, now is not, and will come up out of the Abyss and go to his destruction. The inhabitants of the earth whose names have not been written in the book of life from the creation of the world will be astonished when they see the beast, because he once was, now is not, and yet will come.

⁹"This calls for a mind with wisdom. The seven heads are seven hills on which the woman sits. ¹⁰They are also seven kings. Five have fall-

THE MESSAGE

16.17-21   The seventh Angel poured his bowl into the air: From the Throne in the Temple came a shout, "Done!" followed by lightning flashes and shouts, thunder crashes and a colossal earthquake—a huge and devastating earthquake, never an earthquake like it since time began. The Great City split three ways, the cities of the nations toppled to ruin. Great Babylon had to drink the wine of God's raging anger—God remembered to give her the cup! Every island fled and not a mountain was to be found. Hailstones weighing a ton plummeted, crushing and smashing men and women as they cursed God for the hail, the epic disaster of hail.

GREAT BABYLON, MOTHER OF WHORES

17.1-2   **17** One of the Seven Angels who carried the seven bowls came and invited me, "Come, I'll show you the judgment of the great Whore who sits enthroned over many waters, the Whore with whom the kings of the earth have gone whoring, show you the judgment on earth dwellers drunk on her whorish lust."

17.3-6   In the Spirit he carried me out in the desert. I saw a woman mounted on a Scarlet Beast. Stuffed with blasphemies, the Beast had seven heads and ten horns. The woman was dressed in purple and scarlet, festooned with gold and gems and pearls. She held a gold chalice in her hand, brimming with defiling obscenities, her foul fornications. A riddle-name was branded on her forehead: GREAT BABYLON, MOTHER OF WHORES AND ABOMINATIONS OF THE EARTH. I could see that the woman was drunk, drunk on the blood of God's holy people, drunk on the blood of the martyrs of Jesus.

17.6-8   Astonished, I rubbed my eyes. I shook my head in wonder. The Angel said, "Does this surprise you? Let me tell you the riddle of the woman and the Beast she rides, the Beast with seven heads and ten horns. The Beast you saw once was, is no longer, and is about to ascend from the Abyss and head straight for Hell. Earth dwellers whose names weren't written in the Book of Life from the foundation of the world will be dazzled when they see the Beast that once was, is no longer, and is to come.

17.9-11   "But don't drop your guard. Use your head. The seven heads are seven hills; they are where the woman sits. They are also seven kings: five

NEW INTERNATIONAL VERSION

en, one is, the other has not yet come; but when he does come, he must remain for a little while. ¹¹The beast who once was, and now is not, is an eighth king. He belongs to the seven and is going to his destruction.

¹²"The ten horns you saw are ten kings who have not yet received a kingdom, but who for one hour will receive authority as kings along with the beast. ¹³They have one purpose and will give their power and authority to the beast. ¹⁴They will make war against the Lamb, but the Lamb will overcome them because he is Lord of lords and King of kings—and with him will be his called, chosen and faithful followers."

¹⁵Then the angel said to me, "The waters you saw, where the prostitute sits, are peoples, multitudes, nations and languages. ¹⁶The beast and the ten horns you saw will hate the prostitute. They will bring her to ruin and leave her naked; they will eat her flesh and burn her with fire. ¹⁷For God has put it into their hearts to accomplish his purpose by agreeing to give the beast their power to rule, until God's words are fulfilled. ¹⁸The woman you saw is the great city that rules over the kings of the earth."

THE FALL OF BABYLON

18 After this I saw another angel coming down from heaven. He had great authority, and the earth was illuminated by his splendor. ²With a mighty voice he shouted:

"Fallen! Fallen is Babylon the Great!
  She has become a home for demons
and a haunt for every evil*ᵃ* spirit,
  a haunt for every unclean and detestable
    bird.
³For all the nations have drunk
  the maddening wine of her adulteries.
The kings of the earth committed adultery
    with her,
  and the merchants of the earth grew rich
    from her excessive luxuries."

⁴Then I heard another voice from heaven say:

"Come out of her, my people,
  so that you will not share in her sins,
  so that you will not receive any of her
    plagues;
⁵for her sins are piled up to heaven,
  and God has remembered her crimes.
⁶Give back to her as she has given;
  pay her back double for what she has done.
  Mix her a double portion from her own
    cup.
⁷Give her as much torture and grief

ᵃ 2 Greek unclean

THE MESSAGE

dead, one living, the other not yet here—and when he does come his time will be brief. The Beast that once was and is no longer is both an eighth and one of the seven—and headed for Hell.

17.12-14 "The ten horns you saw are ten kings, but they're not yet in power. They will come to power with the Scarlet Beast, but won't last long—a *very* brief reign. These kings will agree to turn over their power and authority to the Beast. They will go to war against the Lamb but the Lamb will defeat them, proof that he is Lord over all lords, King over all kings, and those with him will be the called, chosen, and faithful."

17.15-18 The Angel continued, "The waters you saw on which the Whore was enthroned are peoples and crowds, nations and languages. And the ten horns you saw, together with the Beast, will turn on the Whore—they'll hate her, violate her, strip her naked, rip her apart with their teeth, then set fire to her. It was God who put the idea in their heads to turn over their rule to the Beast until the words of God are completed. The woman you saw is the great city, tyrannizing the kings of the earth."

DOOM TO THE CITY OF DARKNESS

18.1-8 **18** Following this I saw another Angel descend from Heaven. His authority was immense, his glory flooded earth with brightness, his voice thunderous:

Ruined, ruined, Great Babylon, ruined!
  A ghost town for demons is all that's left!
A garrison of carrion spirits,
  garrison of loathsome, carrion birds.
All nations drank the wild wine of her
    whoring;
  kings of the earth went whoring with
    her;
  entrepreneurs made millions exploiting
    her.

Just then I heard another shout out of Heaven:

Get out, my people, as fast as you can,
  so you don't get mixed up in her sins,
  so you don't get caught in her doom.
Her sins stink to high Heaven;
  God has remembered every evil she's
    done.
Give her back what she's given,
  double what she's doubled in her works,
  double the recipe in the cup she mixed;
Bring her flaunting and wild ways

NEW INTERNATIONAL VERSION

as the glory and luxury she gave herself.
In her heart she boasts,
'I sit as queen; I am not a widow,
and I will never mourn.'
⁸ Therefore in one day her plagues will
overtake her:
death, mourning and famine.
She will be consumed by fire,
for mighty is the Lord God who judges her.

⁹ "When the kings of the earth who committed adultery with her and shared her luxury see the smoke of her burning, they will weep and mourn over her. ¹⁰ Terrified at her torment, they will stand far off and cry:

" 'Woe! Woe, O great city,
O Babylon, city of power!
In one hour your doom has come!'

¹¹ "The merchants of the earth will weep and mourn over her because no one buys their cargoes any more— ¹² cargoes of gold, silver, precious stones and pearls; fine linen, purple, silk and scarlet cloth; every sort of citron wood, and articles of every kind made of ivory, costly wood, bronze, iron and marble; ¹³ cargoes of cinnamon and spice, of incense, myrrh and frankincense, of wine and olive oil, of fine flour and wheat; cattle and sheep; horses and carriages; and bodies and souls of men.
¹⁴ "They will say, 'The fruit you longed for is gone from you. All your riches and splendor have vanished, never to be recovered.' ¹⁵ The merchants who sold these things and gained their wealth from her will stand far off, terrified at her torment. They will weep and mourn ¹⁶ and cry out:

" 'Woe! Woe, O great city,
dressed in fine linen, purple and scarlet,
and glittering with gold, precious stones
and pearls!
¹⁷ In one hour such great wealth has been
brought to ruin!'

"Every sea captain, and all who travel by ship, the sailors, and all who earn their living from the sea, will stand far off. ¹⁸ When they see the smoke of her burning, they will exclaim, 'Was there ever a city like this great city?' ¹⁹ They will throw dust on their heads, and with weeping and mourning cry out:

" 'Woe! Woe, O great city,
where all who had ships on the sea
became rich through her wealth!
In one hour she has been brought to ruin!
²⁰ Rejoice over her, O heaven!
Rejoice, saints and apostles and prophets!
God has judged her for the way she treated
you.' "

THE MESSAGE

to torment and tears.
Because she gloated, "I'm queen over all,
and no widow, never a tear on my face,"
In one day, disasters will crush her—
death, heartbreak, and famine—
Then she'll be burned by fire, because God,
the Strong God who judges her,
has had enough.

18.9-10 "The kings of the earth will see the smoke of her burning, and they'll cry and carry on, the kings who went night after night to her brothel. They'll keep their distance for fear they'll get burned, and they'll cry their lament:

Doom, doom, the great city doomed!
City of Babylon, strong city!
In one hour it's over, your judgment come!

18.11-17 "The traders will cry and carry on because the bottom dropped out of business, no more market for their goods: gold, silver, precious gems, pearls; fabrics of fine linen, purple, silk, scarlet; perfumed wood and vessels of ivory, precious woods, bronze, iron, and marble; cinnamon and spice, incense, myrrh, and frankincense; wine and oil, flour and wheat; cattle, sheep, horses, and chariots. And slaves—their terrible traffic in human lives.

Everything you've lived for, gone!
All delicate and delectable luxury, lost!
Not a scrap, not a thread to be found!

"The traders who made millions off her kept their distance for fear of getting burned, and cried and carried on all the more:

Doom, doom, the great city doomed!
Dressed in the latest fashions,
adorned with the finest jewels,
in one hour such wealth wiped out!

18.17-19 "All the ship captains and travelers by sea, sailors and toilers of the sea, stood off at a distance and cried their lament when they saw the smoke from her burning: 'Oh, what a city! There was never a city like her!' They threw dust on their heads and cried as if the world had come to an end:

Doom, doom, the great city doomed!
All who owned ships or did business by
sea
Got rich on her getting and spending.
And now it's over—wiped out in one
hour!

18.20 "O Heaven, celebrate! And join in, saints, apostles, and prophets! God has judged her; every wrong you suffered from her has been judged."

NEW INTERNATIONAL VERSION

²¹Then a mighty angel picked up a boulder the size of a large millstone and threw it into the sea, and said:

"With such violence
    the great city of Babylon will be thrown
        down,
    never to be found again.
²²The music of harpists and musicians, flute
        players and trumpeters,
    will never be heard in you again.
No workman of any trade
    will ever be found in you again.
The sound of a millstone
    will never be heard in you again.
²³The light of a lamp
    will never shine in you again.
The voice of bridegroom and bride
    will never be heard in you again.
Your merchants were the world's great men.
    By your magic spell all the nations were
        led astray.
²⁴In her was found the blood of prophets and
        of the saints,
    and of all who have been killed on the
        earth."

HALLELUJAH!

19 After this I heard what sounded like the roar of a great multitude in heaven shouting:

"Hallelujah!
Salvation and glory and power belong to our
    God,
²   for true and just are his judgments.
He has condemned the great prostitute
    who corrupted the earth by her adulteries.
He has avenged on her the blood of his
    servants."

³And again they shouted:

"Hallelujah!
The smoke from her goes up for ever and
    ever."

⁴The twenty-four elders and the four living creatures fell down and worshiped God, who was seated on the throne. And they cried:

"Amen, Hallelujah!"

⁵Then a voice came from the throne, saying:

"Praise our God,
    all you his servants,
you who fear him,
    both small and great!"

THE MESSAGE

18.21-24   A strong Angel reached for a boulder—huge, like a millstone—and heaved it into the sea, saying,

Heaved and sunk, the great city Babylon,
    sunk in the sea, not a sign of her ever
        again.
Silent the music of harpists and singers—
    you'll never hear flutes and trumpets
        again.
Artisans of every kind—gone;
    you'll never see their likes again.
The voice of a millstone grinding falls
        dumb;
    you'll never hear that sound again.
The light from lamps, never again;
    never again laughter of bride and groom.
Her traders robbed the whole earth blind,
    and by black-magic arts deceived the
        nations.
The only thing left of Babylon is blood—
    the blood of saints and prophets,
    the murdered and the martyred.

THE SOUND OF HALLELUJAHS

19.1-3   **19** I heard a sound like massed choirs in Heaven singing,

Hallelujah!
The salvation and glory and power are
        God's—
    his judgments true, his judgments just.
He judged the great Whore
    who corrupted the earth with her lust.
He avenged on her the blood of his
        servants.

Then, more singing:
Hallelujah!
The smoke from her burning billows up
    to high Heaven forever and ever and
        ever.

19.4   The Twenty-four Elders and the Four Animals fell to their knees and worshiped God on his Throne, praising,

Amen! Yes! Hallelujah!

19.5   From the Throne came a shout, a command:

Praise our God, all you his servants,
All you who fear him, small and great!

NEW INTERNATIONAL VERSION

⁶Then I heard what sounded like a great multitude, like the roar of rushing waters and like loud peals of thunder, shouting:

"Hallelujah!
      For our Lord God Almighty reigns.
⁷Let us rejoice and be glad
      and give him glory!
For the wedding of the Lamb has come,
      and his bride has made herself ready.
⁸Fine linen, bright and clean,
      was given her to wear."
(Fine linen stands for the righteous acts of the
      saints.)

⁹Then the angel said to me, "Write: 'Blessed are those who are invited to the wedding supper of the Lamb!' " And he added, "These are the true words of God."

¹⁰At this I fell at his feet to worship him. But he said to me, "Do not do it! I am a fellow servant with you and with your brothers who hold to the testimony of Jesus. Worship God! For the testimony of Jesus is the spirit of prophecy."

THE RIDER ON THE WHITE HORSE

¹¹I saw heaven standing open and there before me was a white horse, whose rider is called Faithful and True. With justice he judges and makes war. ¹²His eyes are like blazing fire, and on his head are many crowns. He has a name written on him that no one knows but he himself. ¹³He is dressed in a robe dipped in blood, and his name is the Word of God. ¹⁴The armies of heaven were following him, riding on white horses and dressed in fine linen, white and clean. ¹⁵Out of his mouth comes a sharp sword with which to strike down the nations. "He will rule them with an iron scepter." ᵃ He treads the winepress of the fury of the wrath of God Almighty. ¹⁶On his robe and on his thigh he has this name written:

KING OF KINGS AND LORD OF LORDS.

¹⁷And I saw an angel standing in the sun, who cried in a loud voice to all the birds flying in midair, "Come, gather together for the great supper of God, ¹⁸so that you may eat the flesh of kings, generals, and mighty men, of horses and their riders, and the flesh of all people, free and slave, small and great."

¹⁹Then I saw the beast and the kings of the earth and their armies gathered together to make war against the rider on the horse and his army. ²⁰But the beast was captured, and with him the false prophet who had performed the miraculous signs on his behalf. With these signs he had deluded those who had received the mark of the

ᵃ 15 Psalm 2:9

THE MESSAGE

19.6-8 Then I heard the sound of massed choirs, the sound of a mighty cataract, the sound of strong thunder:

Hallelujah!
The Master reigns,
      our God, the Sovereign-Strong!
Let us celebrate, let us rejoice,
      let us give him the glory!
The Marriage of the Lamb has come;
      his Wife has made herself ready.
She was given a bridal gown
      of bright and shining linen.

The linen is the righteousness of the saints.

19.9 The Angel said to me, "Write this: 'Blessed are those invited to the Wedding Supper of the Lamb.' " He added, "These are the true words of God!"

19.10 I fell at his feet to worship him, but he wouldn't let me. "Don't do that," he said. "I'm a servant just like you, and like your brothers and sisters who hold to the witness of Jesus. The witness of Jesus is the spirit of prophecy."

A WHITE HORSE AND ITS RIDER

19.11-16 Then I saw Heaven open wide—and oh! a white horse and its Rider. The Rider, named Faithful and True, judges and makes war in pure righteousness. His eyes are a blaze of fire, on his head many crowns. He has a Name inscribed that's known only to himself. He is dressed in a robe soaked with blood, and he is addressed as "Word of God." The armies of Heaven, mounted on white horses and dressed in dazzling white linen, follow him. A sharp sword comes out of his mouth so he can subdue the nations, then rule them with a rod of iron. He treads the winepress of the raging wrath of God, the Sovereign-Strong. On his robe and thigh is written, KING OF KINGS, LORD OF LORDS.

19.17-18 I saw an Angel standing in the sun, shouting to all flying birds in Middle-Heaven, "Come to the Great Supper of God! Feast on the flesh of kings and captains and champions, horses and their riders. Eat your fill of them all—free and slave, small and great!"

19.19-21 I saw the Beast and, assembled with him, earth's kings and their armies, ready to make war against the One on the horse and his army. The Beast was taken, and with him, his puppet, the False Prophet, who used signs to dazzle and deceive those who had taken the mark of

NEW INTERNATIONAL VERSION

beast and worshiped his image. The two of them were thrown alive into the fiery lake of burning sulfur. ²¹The rest of them were killed with the sword that came out of the mouth of the rider on the horse, and all the birds gorged themselves on their flesh.

THE THOUSAND YEARS

20 And I saw an angel coming down out of heaven, having the key to the Abyss and holding in his hand a great chain. ²He seized the dragon, that ancient serpent, who is the devil, or Satan, and bound him for a thousand years. ³He threw him into the Abyss, and locked and sealed it over him, to keep him from deceiving the nations anymore until the thousand years were ended. After that, he must be set free for a short time.

⁴I saw thrones on which were seated those who had been given authority to judge. And I saw the souls of those who had been beheaded because of their testimony for Jesus and because of the word of God. They had not worshiped the beast or his image and had not received his mark on their foreheads or their hands. They came to life and reigned with Christ a thousand years. ⁵(The rest of the dead did not come to life until the thousand years were ended.) This is the first resurrection. ⁶Blessed and holy are those who have part in the first resurrection. The second death has no power over them, but they will be priests of God and of Christ and will reign with him for a thousand years.

SATAN'S DOOM

⁷When the thousand years are over, Satan will be released from his prison ⁸and will go out to deceive the nations in the four corners of the earth—Gog and Magog—to gather them for battle. In number they are like the sand on the seashore. ⁹They marched across the breadth of the earth and surrounded the camp of God's people, the city he loves. But fire came down from heaven and devoured them. ¹⁰And the devil, who deceived them, was thrown into the lake of burning sulfur, where the beast and the false prophet had been thrown. They will be tormented day and night for ever and ever.

THE DEAD ARE JUDGED

¹¹Then I saw a great white throne and him who was seated on it. Earth and sky fled from his presence, and there was no place for them. ¹²And I saw the dead, great and small, standing before the throne, and books were opened. Another book was opened, which is the book of life. The dead were judged according to what they had done as recorded in the books. ¹³The

THE MESSAGE

the Beast and worshiped his image. They were thrown alive, those two, into Lake Fire and Brimstone. The rest were killed by the sword of the One on the horse, the sword that comes from his mouth. All the birds held a feast on their flesh.

A THOUSAND YEARS

20.1-3 **20** I saw an Angel descending out of Heaven. He carried the key to the Abyss and a chain—a huge chain. He grabbed the Dragon, that old Snake—the very Devil, Satan himself!—chained him up for a thousand years, dumped him into the Abyss, slammed it shut and sealed it tight. No more trouble out of him, deceiving the nations—until the thousand years are up. After that he has to be let loose briefly.

20.4-6 I saw thrones. Those put in charge of judgment sat on the thrones. I also saw the souls of those beheaded because of their witness to Jesus and the Word of God, who refused to worship either the Beast or his image, refused to take his mark on forehead or hand—they lived and reigned with Christ for a thousand years! The rest of the dead did not live until the thousand years were up. This is the first resurrection—and those involved most blessed, most holy. No second death for them! They're priests of God and Christ; they'll reign with him a thousand years.

20.7-10 When the thousand years are up, Satan will be let loose from his cell, and will launch again his old work of deceiving the nations, searching out victims in every nook and cranny of earth, even Gog and Magog! He'll talk them into going to war and will gather a huge army, millions strong. They'll stream across the earth, surround and lay siege to the camp of God's holy people, the Beloved City. They'll no sooner get there than fire will pour out of Heaven and burn them up. The Devil who deceived them will be hurled into Lake Fire and Brimstone, joining the Beast and False Prophet, the three in torment around the clock for ages without end.

JUDGMENT

20.11-15 I saw a Great White Throne and the One Enthroned. Nothing could stand before or against the Presence, nothing in Heaven, nothing on earth. And then I saw all the dead, great and small, standing there—before the Throne! And books were opened. Then another book was opened: the Book of Life. The dead were judged by what was written in the books, by the way

NEW INTERNATIONAL VERSION

sea gave up the dead that were in it, and death and Hades gave up the dead that were in them, and each person was judged according to what he had done. ¹⁴Then death and Hades were thrown into the lake of fire. The lake of fire is the second death. ¹⁵If anyone's name was not found written in the book of life, he was thrown into the lake of fire.

THE NEW JERUSALEM

21 Then I saw a new heaven and a new earth, for the first heaven and the first earth had passed away, and there was no longer any sea. ²I saw the Holy City, the new Jerusalem, coming down out of heaven from God, prepared as a bride beautifully dressed for her husband. ³And I heard a loud voice from the throne saying, "Now the dwelling of God is with men, and he will live with them. They will be his people, and God himself will be with them and be their God. ⁴He will wipe every tear from their eyes. There will be no more death or mourning or crying or pain, for the old order of things has passed away."

⁵He who was seated on the throne said, "I am making everything new!" Then he said, "Write this down, for these words are trustworthy and true."

⁶He said to me: "It is done. I am the Alpha and the Omega, the Beginning and the End. To him who is thirsty I will give to drink without cost from the spring of the water of life. ⁷He who overcomes will inherit all this, and I will be his God and he will be my son. ⁸But the cowardly, the unbelieving, the vile, the murderers, the sexually immoral, those who practice magic arts, the idolaters and all liars—their place will be in the fiery lake of burning sulfur. This is the second death."

⁹One of the seven angels who had the seven bowls full of the seven last plagues came and said to me, "Come, I will show you the bride, the wife of the Lamb." ¹⁰And he carried me away in the Spirit to a mountain great and high, and showed me the Holy City, Jerusalem, coming down out of heaven from God. ¹¹It shone with the glory of God, and its brilliance was like that of a very precious jewel, like a jasper, clear as crystal. ¹²It had a great, high wall with twelve gates, and with twelve angels at the gates. On the gates were written the names of the twelve tribes of Israel. ¹³There were three gates on the east, three on the north, three on the south and three on the west. ¹⁴The wall of the city had twelve foundations, and on them were the names of the twelve apostles of the Lamb.

¹⁵The angel who talked with me had a measuring rod of gold to measure the city, its gates

THE MESSAGE

they had lived. Sea released its dead, Death and Hell turned in their dead. Each man and woman was judged by the way he or she had lived. Then Death and Hell were hurled into Lake Fire. This is the second death—Lake Fire. Anyone whose name was not found inscribed in the Book of Life was hurled into Lake Fire.

EVERYTHING NEW

21.1 **21** I saw Heaven and earth new-created. Gone the first Heaven, gone the first earth, gone the sea.

21.2 I saw Holy Jerusalem, new-created, descending resplendent out of Heaven, as ready for God as a bride for her husband.

21.3-5 I heard a voice thunder from the Throne: "Look! Look! God has moved into the neighborhood, making his home with men and women! They're his people, he's their God. He'll wipe every tear from their eyes. Death is gone for good—tears gone, crying gone, pain gone—all the first order of things gone." The Enthroned continued, "Look! I'm making everything new. Write it all down—each word dependable and accurate."

21.6-8 Then he said, "It's happened. I'm A to Z. I'm the Beginning, I'm the Conclusion. From Water-of-Life Well I give freely to the thirsty. Conquerors inherit all this, they'll be sons and daughters to me. But for the rest—the feckless and faithless, degenerates and murderers, sex peddlers and sorcerers, idolaters and all liars—for them it's Lake Fire and Brimstone. Second death!"

THE CITY OF LIGHT

21.9-12 One of the Seven Angels who had carried the bowls filled with the seven final disasters spoke to me: "Come here. I'll show you the Bride, the Wife of the Lamb." He took me away in the Spirit to an enormous, high mountain and showed me Holy Jerusalem descending out of Heaven from God, resplendent in the bright glory of God.

21.12-14 The City shimmered like a precious gem, light-filled, pulsing light. She had a wall majestic and high with twelve gates. At each gate stood an Angel, and on the gates were inscribed the names of the Twelve Tribes of the sons of Israel: three gates on the east, three gates on the north, three gates on the south, three gates on the west. The wall was set on twelve foundations, the names of the Twelve Apostles of the Lamb inscribed on them.

21.15-21 The Angel speaking with me had a gold measuring stick to measure the City, its gates,

NEW INTERNATIONAL VERSION

and its walls. [16]The city was laid out like a square, as long as it was wide. He measured the city with the rod and found it to be 12,000 stadia[a] in length, and as wide and high as it is long. [17]He measured its wall and it was 144 cubits[b] thick,[c] by man's measurement, which the angel was using. [18]The wall was made of jasper, and the city of pure gold, as pure as glass. [19]The foundations of the city walls were decorated with every kind of precious stone. The first foundation was jasper, the second sapphire, the third chalcedony, the fourth emerald, [20]the fifth sardonyx, the sixth carnelian, the seventh chrysolite, the eighth beryl, the ninth topaz, the tenth chrysoprase, the eleventh jacinth, and the twelfth amethyst.[d] [21]The twelve gates were twelve pearls, each gate made of a single pearl. The great street of the city was of pure gold, like transparent glass.

[22]I did not see a temple in the city, because the Lord God Almighty and the Lamb are its temple. [23]The city does not need the sun or the moon to shine on it, for the glory of God gives it light, and the Lamb is its lamp. [24]The nations will walk by its light, and the kings of the earth will bring their splendor into it. [25]On no day will its gates ever be shut, for there will be no night there. [26]The glory and honor of the nations will be brought into it. [27]Nothing impure will ever enter it, nor will anyone who does what is shameful or deceitful, but only those whose names are written in the Lamb's book of life.

THE RIVER OF LIFE

22 Then the angel showed me the river of the water of life, as clear as crystal, flowing from the throne of God and of the Lamb [2]down the middle of the great street of the city. On each side of the river stood the tree of life, bearing twelve crops of fruit, yielding its fruit every month. And the leaves of the tree are for the healing of the nations. [3]No longer will there be any curse. The throne of God and of the Lamb will be in the city, and his servants will serve him. [4]They will see his face, and his name will be on their foreheads. [5]There will be no more night. They will not need the light of a lamp or the light of the sun, for the Lord God will give them light. And they will reign for ever and ever.

[6]The angel said to me, "These words are trustworthy and true. The Lord, the God of the spirits

THE MESSAGE

and its wall. The City was laid out in a perfect square. He measured the City with the measuring stick: twelve thousand stadia, its length, width, and height all equal. Using the standard measure, the Angel measured the thickness of its wall: 144 cubits. The wall was jasper, the color of Glory, and the City was pure gold, translucent as glass. The foundations of the City walls were garnished with every precious gem imaginable: the first foundation jasper, the second sapphire, the third agate, the fourth emerald, the fifth onyx, the sixth carnelian, the seventh chrysolite, the eighth beryl, the ninth topaz, the tenth chrysoprase, the eleventh jacinth, the twelfth amethyst. The twelve gates were twelve pearls, each gate a single pearl.

21.21-27 The main street of the City was pure gold, translucent as glass. But there was no sign of a Temple, for the Lord God—the Sovereign-Strong—and the Lamb are the Temple. The City doesn't need sun or moon for light. God's Glory is its light, the Lamb its lamp! The nations will walk in its light and earth's kings bring in their splendor. Its gates will never be shut by day, and there won't be any night. They'll bring the glory and honor of the nations into the City. Nothing dirty or defiled will get into the City, and no one who defiles or deceives. Only those whose names are written in the Lamb's Book of Life will get in.

✝

22.1-5 **22** Then the Angel showed me Water-of-Life River, crystal bright. It flowed from the Throne of God and the Lamb, right down the middle of the street. The Tree of Life was planted on each side of the River, producing twelve kinds of fruit, a ripe fruit each month. The leaves of the Tree are for healing the nations. Never again will anything be cursed. The Throne of God and of the Lamb is at the center. His servants will offer God service—worshiping, they'll look on his face, their foreheads mirroring God. Never again will there be any night. No one will need lamplight or sunlight. The shining of God, the Master, is all the light anyone needs. And they will rule with him age after age after age.

DON'T PUT IT AWAY ON THE SHELF

22.6-7 The Angel said to me, "These are dependable and accurate words, every one. The God and Master of the spirits of the prophets sent his

---

[a] 16 That is, about 1,400 miles (about 2,200 kilometers)
[b] 17 That is, about 200 feet (about 65 meters)
[c] 17 Or high   [d] 20 The precise identification of some of these precious stones is uncertain.

NEW INTERNATIONAL VERSION

of the prophets, sent his angel to show his servants the things that must soon take place."

Jesus Is Coming

7 "Behold, I am coming soon! Blessed is he who keeps the words of the prophecy in this book."

8 I, John, am the one who heard and saw these things. And when I had heard and seen them, I fell down to worship at the feet of the angel who had been showing them to me. 9 But he said to me, "Do not do it! I am a fellow servant with you and with your brothers the prophets and of all who keep the words of this book. Worship God!"

10 Then he told me, "Do not seal up the words of the prophecy of this book, because the time is near. 11 Let him who does wrong continue to do wrong; let him who is vile continue to be vile; let him who does right continue to do right; and let him who is holy continue to be holy."

12 "Behold, I am coming soon! My reward is with me, and I will give to everyone according to what he has done. 13 I am the Alpha and the Omega, the First and the Last, the Beginning and the End.

14 "Blessed are those who wash their robes, that they may have the right to the tree of life and may go through the gates into the city. 15 Outside are the dogs, those who practice magic arts, the sexually immoral, the murderers, the idolaters and everyone who loves and practices falsehood.

16 "I, Jesus, have sent my angel to give you*a* this testimony for the churches. I am the Root and the Offspring of David, and the bright Morning Star."

17 The Spirit and the bride say, "Come!" And let him who hears say, "Come!" Whoever is thirsty, let him come; and whoever wishes, let him take the free gift of the water of life.

18 I warn everyone who hears the words of the prophecy of this book: If anyone adds anything to them, God will add to him the plagues described in this book. 19 And if anyone takes words away from this book of prophecy, God will take away from him his share in the tree of life and in the holy city, which are described in this book.

20 He who testifies to these things says, "Yes, I am coming soon."

Amen. Come, Lord Jesus.

21 The grace of the Lord Jesus be with God's people. Amen.

a 16 The Greek is plural.

THE MESSAGE

Angel to show his servants what must take place, and soon. And tell them, 'Yes, I'm on my way!' Blessed be the one who keeps the words of the prophecy of this book."

22.8-9 I, John, saw all these things with my own eyes, heard them with my ears. Immediately when I heard and saw, I fell on my face to worship at the feet of the Angel who laid it all out before me. He objected, "No you don't! I'm a servant just like you and your companions, the prophets, and all who keep the words of this book. Worship God!"

22.10-11 The Angel continued, "Don't seal the words of the prophecy of this book; don't put it away on the shelf. Time is just about up. Let evildoers do their worst and the dirty-minded go all out in pollution, but let the righteous maintain a straight course and the holy continue on in holiness."

✛

22.12-13 "Yes, I'm on my way! I'll be there soon! I'm bringing my payroll with me. I'll pay all people in full for their life's work. I'm A to Z, the First and the Final, Beginning and Conclusion.

22.14-15 "How blessed are those who wash their robes! The Tree of Life is theirs for good, and they'll walk through the gates to the City. But outside for good are the filthy curs: sorcerers, fornicators, murderers, idolaters—all who love and live lies.

22.16 "I, Jesus, sent my Angel to testify to these things for the churches. I'm the Root and Branch of David, the Bright Morning Star."

22.17 "Come!" say the Spirit and the Bride.
Whoever hears, echo, "Come!"
Is anyone thirsty? Come!
All who will, come and drink,
Drink freely of the Water of Life!

22.18-19 I give fair warning to all who hear the words of the prophecy of this book: If you add to the words of this prophecy, God will add to your life the disasters written in this book; if you subtract from the words of the book of this prophecy, God will subtract your part from the Tree of Life and the Holy City that are written in this book.

22.20 He who testifies to all these things says it again: "I'm on my way! I'll be there soon!"

Yes! Come, Master Jesus!

22.21 The grace of the Master Jesus be with all of you. Oh, Yes!

TABLE OF WEIGHTS AND MEASURES

BIBLICAL UNIT	APPROXIMATE AMERICAN EQUIVALENT	APPROXIMATE METRIC EQUIVALENT
WEIGHTS		
talent (60 minas)	75 pounds	34 kilograms
mina (50 shekels)	1¹/₄ pounds	0.6 kilogram
shekel (2 bekas)	²/₅ ounce	11.5 grams
pim (²/₃ shekel)	¹/₃ ounce	7.6 grams
beka (10 gerahs)	¹/₅ ounce	5.5 grams
gerah	¹/₅₀ ounce	0.6 gram
LENGTH		
cubit	18 inches	0.5 meter
span	9 inches	23 centimeters
handbreadth	3 inches	8 centimeters
CAPACITY		
Dry Measure		
cor [homer] (10 ephahs)	6 bushels	220 liters
lethek (5 ephahs)	3 bushels	110 liters
ephah (10 omers)	³/₅ bushel	22 liters
seah (¹/₃ ephah)	7 quarts	7.3 liters
omer (¹/₁₀ ephah)	2 quarts	2 liters
cab (¹/₁₈ ephah)	1 quart	1 liter
Liquid Measure		
bath (1 ephah)	6 gallons	22 liters
hin (¹/₆ bath)	4 quarts	4 liters
log (¹/₇₂ bath)	¹/₃ quart	0.3 liter

The figures of the table are calculated on the basis of a shekel equaling 11.5 grams, a cubit equaling 18 inches and an ephah equaling 22 liters. The quart referred to is either a dry quart (slightly larger than a liter) or a liquid quart (slightly smaller than a liter), whichever is applicable. The ton referred to in the footnotes is the American ton of 2,000 pounds.

This table is based upon the best available information, but it is not intended to be mathematically precise; like the measurement equivalents in the footnotes, it merely gives approximate amounts and distances. Weights and measures differed somewhat at various times and places in the ancient world. There is uncertainty particularly about the ephah and the bath; further discoveries may shed more light on these units of capacity.